SUBJECT GUIDE TO BOOKS IN PRINT 1981-1982

This edition of SUBJECT GUIDE TO BOOKS IN PRINT was
prepared by the R. R. Bowker Company's Department of
Bibliography in collaboration with the
Publication Systems Department.

Senior staff of the Department of Bibliography includes:
Peter Simon and Brenda Sutton, Senior Database Production Managers;
Dean Hollister, Project Manager;
Tyrone Elliott, Editorial Coordinator;
Vincent Parrillo and John Rush, Assistant Editors.

Michael B. Howell, Manager, Systems Development.

Andrew H. Uszak, Vice President, Data Services/Systems.
Gertrude Jennings, Manager, Product Research and Development, Data Services Division.

SUBJECT GUIDE TO BOOKS IN PRINT

1981-1982

Volume 2
F-O

R.R. BOWKER COMPANY
New York & London

Published by R. R. Bowker Co. (a Xerox Publishing Company)
1180 Avenue of the Americas, New York, N.Y. 10036

International Standard Book Numbers: Set 0-8352-1383-8,
Vol. 1 0-8352-1410-9; Vol. 2 0-8352-1411-7; Vol. 3 0-8352-1412-5
International Standard Serial Number 0000-0159
Library of Congress Catalog Card Number 4-12648
Printed and bound in the
United States of America

SUBJECT GUIDE TO BOOKS IN PRINT 1981-1982

Volume 2

F-O

F

F CENTERS
see Color Centers

F-EIGHTY-SIX PLANES
see also sabre (jet fighter planes)

Allward, Maurice. F-Eighty Six Sabre. (Illus.). 1978. 9.95 (ISBN 0-684-15883-3, ScribT). Scribner.

F-FIFTY-ONE (FIGHTER PLANES)
see Mustang (Fighter Planes)

F-ONE-ELEVEN (FIGHTER PLANES)

Coulam, Robert F. Illusions of Choice: Robert McNamara, the F-111 & the Problem of Weapons Acquisition Reform. LC 76-24292. 1977. text ed. 31.50 (ISBN 0-691-07583-2). Princeton U Pr.

Gunston, Bill. F-One Eleven. (Illus.). 1978. 9.95 (ISBN 0-684-15753-5, ScribT). Scribner.

Kinzey, Bert. F-One-Eleven & FB-One-Eleven in Detail & Scale. (Detail & Scale Ser.). (Illus.). 72p. (Orig.). 1982. pap. 6.95 (ISBN 0-8168-5014-3). Aero.

Miller, Jay. General Dynamics F-111. (Aero Ser.: Vol. 29). (Illus.). 104p. (Orig.). 1981. pap. 7.95 (ISBN 0-8168-0606-3, 200). Aero.

F-ONE-O-FIVE REPUBLIC

Archer, Robert D. Republic F-105 Thunderchief. LC 71-102870. (Illus., Orig.). 1969. pap. 6.95 (ISBN 0-8168-1500-3). Aero.

FABERGE, KARL GUSTAVOVICH, 1846-1920

Forbes, Christopher. Faberge Eggs: Imperial Russian Fantasies. (Illus., Orig.). 1980. pap. 12.50 (ISBN 0-8109-2227-4). Abrams.

Hawley, Henry. Faberge & His Contemporaries: The India Early Minshall Collection of the Cleveland Museum of Art. LC 67-28951. (Illus.). 148p. 1967. 10.00x (ISBN 0-910386-10-2, Pub. by Cleveland Mus Art). Ind U Pr.

Lesley, Parker. Faberge: A Catalogue of the Lillian Thomas Pratt Collection of Russian Imperial Jewels. LC 76-16557. (Illus.). 160p. 1979. Repr. of 1976 ed. 22.50x (ISBN 0-917046-00-5). VA Mus Fine Arts.

Snowman, A. Kenneth. Carl Faberge. (Illus.). 1979. 35.00 (ISBN 0-670-20486-2, Debrett's Peerage, Ltd.). Viking Pr.

Von Hapsburg, Geza & Von Solodkoff, Alexander. Faberge: Court Jeweler to the Tsars. LC 79-64335. (Illus.). 1979. 35.00 (ISBN 0-8478-0244-2). Rizzoli Intl.

FABIAN SOCIETY, LONDON

Bosanquet, N. Labour & Equality. 1980. text ed. 35.00x (ISBN 0-435-83105-4). Heinemann Ed.

Cole, George D. Fabian Socialism. 164p. 1971. Repr. of 1943 ed. 24.00x (ISBN 0-7146-1553-6, F Cass Co). Biblio Dist.

Cole, Margaret. The Story of Fabian Socialism. LC 61-16949. (Illus.). 1961. 15.00x (ISBN 0-8047-0091-5); pap. 4.50 (ISBN 0-8047-0092-3, SP105). Stanford U Pr.

Crane, Philip M. Democrat's Dilemma: How the Liberal Left Captured the Democratic Party. LC 64-14592. 1964. pap. 0.75 (ISBN 0-911956-08-5). Constructive Action.

McBriar, A. M. Fabian Socialism & English Politics, Eighteen Eighty-Four - Nineteen Eighteen. 1962. pap. 14.95x (ISBN 0-521-09351-1). Cambridge U Pr.

Pease, E. History of Fabian Society. 3rd ed. (Illus.). 306p. 1962. 28.50x (ISBN 0-7146-1569-2, F Cass Co). Biblio Dist.

Wolfe, Willard. From Radicalism to Socialism: Men & Ideas in the Formation of Fabian Socialist Doctrines, 1881-1889. LC 74-14371. 352p. 1975. 25.00x (ISBN 0-300-01303-5). Yale U Pr.

FABLES
see also Animals, Legends and Stories Of; Bestiaries; Folk-Lore; Gesta Romanorum; Parables; Romances

Aesop. Aesop's Fables. Winder, Blanche, ed. (Classics Ser). (Illus.). (gr. 4 up). pap. 1.25 (ISBN 0-8049-0081-7, CL-81). Airmont.

--Aesop's Fables. (Illus.). (gr. 4-6). 1947-63. Illustrated Junior Library. illus. jr. lib. o.p. 5.95 (ISBN 0-448-05803-0); deluxe ed. 7.95 (ISBN 0-448-06003-5); Companion Library. companion lib. 2.95 (ISBN 0-448-05453-1); pap. ed (IJL) 4.95 (ISBN 0-686-76870-1). G&D.

--Aesop's Fables. White, Anne T., ed. (Illus.). (gr. 2-5). 1964. PLB 6.99 (ISBN 0-394-90895-3, BYR). Random.

--The Book of the Subtyl Historyes & Fables of Esope. LC 76-177403. (English Experience Ser.: No. 439). 288p. Repr. of 1484 ed. 49.00 (ISBN 90-221-0439-7). Walter J Johnson.

--Fables of Aesop. Handford, S. A., tr. (Classics Ser.). (Orig.). 1964. pap. 3.50 (ISBN 0-14-044043-7). Penguin.

--The Fables of Aesop: With Designs on Wood by Thomas Bewick. new ed. LC 75-11176. (Masterpieces of the Illustrated Bk). (Illus.). 383p. (Orig.). 1975. pap. 6.95 (ISBN 0-448-23325-8). Paddington.

--Fables of Aesop: With Fifty Drawings by Alexander Calder. LC 67-14002. 1967. lib. bdg. 9.50 (ISBN 0-88307-655-1). Gannon.

--The Morall Fabillis of Esope in Scottis Meter Be Maister Henrisone. LC 79-25964. (English Experience Ser.: No. 282). 104p. 1970. Repr. of 1570 ed. 14.00 (ISBN 90-221-0282-3). Walter J Johnson.

Aesop & Calder, Alexander. Fables of Aesop According to Sir Roger L'Estrange. (Illus.). (gr. k-6). pap. 2.25 (ISBN 0-486-21780-9). Dover.

Aesop & Holder, Heidi, illus. Aesop's Fables. (Illus.). 1981. 10.95 (ISBN 0-670-10643-7). Viking Pr.

Aesopus. The Book of Subtyl Histories & Fables of Esope. Bd. with The Siege of Rhodes. Caoursin, Guillaume. LC 76-14086. 1975. Repr. of 1484 ed. 34.00x (ISBN 0-8201-1154-6). Schol Facsimilies.

Althaus, Hans P. Die Cambridger Loewenfabel von 1382: Untersuchung und Edition eines defektiven Textes. (Quellen und Forschungen Zur Sprach-und Kulturgeschichte der Germanischen Voelker Ser.). (Illus.). 238p. 1971. 48.25x (ISBN 3-11-003939-7). De Gruyter.

Babrius, Valerius. Aesop's Fables. Hull, Denison B., tr. from Gr. LC 60-14237. 112p. 1974. pap. 2.95 (ISBN 0-226-03384-8, P577, Phoen). U of Chicago Pr.

Bassey, Linus A. African Fables. (Illus.). 53p. pap. text ed. write for info. African Policy.

Bennett, Charles H., tr. Bennett's Fables from Aesop & Others. (Illus.). 1978. 8.95 (ISBN 0-670-15807-0, Studio). Viking Pr.

Bierce, Ambrose. Fantastic Fables. LC 73-92026. lib. bdg. 9.50x (ISBN 0-88307-018-9). Gannon.

Clark, Glenn. God's Voice in the Folklore. 3.50 (ISBN 0-910924-06-6). Macalester.

Croxall, Samuel & L'Estrange, Roger, trs. Aesop's Fables. 1969. gift ed. 4.95 (ISBN 0-915720-10-8). Brownlow Pub Co.

De La Fontaine, Jean. Fables, 2 tomes. Incl. Tome I, Livre I-VI; Tome II, Livres VII-XII. (Fr.). 1962. Set. pap. 9.90 (ISBN 0-685-36015-6). French & Eur.

--Fables choisies, 2 Vols. (Documentation thematique). (Illus., Fr.). pap. 2.95 (ISBN 0-685-13914-X). Larousse.

Dodsley, Robert. Select Fables of Esop & Other Fabulists. new ed. LC 70-161796. Repr. of 1781 ed. 27.50 (ISBN 0-404-54101-1). AMS Pr.

Dolch, Edward W. & Dolch, M. P. Aesop's Stories. (Pleasure Reading Ser). (Illus.). (gr. 3-12). 1951. PLB 6.57 (ISBN 0-8116-2602-4). Garrard.

Dorizas, H. Workbook for Aesop's Fables Reader. 1976. 2.20 (ISBN 0-685-73008-5). Divry.

Fenn, Ellenor F. Fables in Monosyllables. LC 21-2685. (Early Children's Bks). 1970. Repr. of 1783 ed. 12.50 (ISBN 0-384-15470-0). Johnson Repr.

Fox, Michael. Dr. Fox's Fables: Lessons from Nature. (Illus.). 1980. 9.95 (ISBN 0-87491-291-1); pap. 4.95 (ISBN 0-87491-516-3). Acropolis.

Fujikawa, Gyo, illus. Fairy Tales & Fables. (Illus.). (gr. k-3). 1970. 5.95 (ISBN 0-448-02814-X). G&D.

Gaer, Joseph. The Fables of India. (Illus.). (gr. 7 up). 1955. 6.95 (ISBN 0-316-30153-1). Little.

Godwin, William. Fables, Ancient & Modern: Adapted for the Use of Children, 2 vols. in 1. LC 75-32153. (Classics of Children's Literature, 1621-1932: Vol. 19). 1976. Repr. of 1805 ed. PLB 38.00 (ISBN 0-8240-2267-X). Garland Pub.

Grandville, J. J. Public & Private Life of Animals. LC 77-5708. (Masterpieces of the Illustrated Book Ser.). (Illus.). 1977. pap. 6.95 (ISBN 0-448-22362-7). Paddington.

Grozny, Yvonne. The Fables of Phonecius. LC 78-68416. 1978. 10.00 (ISBN 0-932364-00-4). Ann Arbor Bk.

Hervieux, A. Leopold. Les Fabulistes Latins Depuis le Siecle d'Auguste Jusqu'a la Fin Du Moyen Age, 5 Vols. 1964. Set. 210.00 (ISBN 0-8337-1685-9). B Franklin.

Holder, Heidi. Aesop's Fables. LC 80-26265. (Illus.). 1981. 12.95 (ISBN 0-670-10643-7). Viking Pr.

Huckaby, Gerald. Huckaby's Fables: The Virtuous Piglet & Other Likely Stones. 80p. 1981. 4.95 (ISBN 0-89524-141-2). Cherry Lane.

Jacobs, Joseph, ed. The Fables of Aesop. LC 66-24908. (Illus.). (gr. k up). 1966. 6.00x (ISBN 0-8052-3068-8); pap. 3.95 (ISBN 0-8052-0138-6). Schocken.

--Fables of Aesop. (Facsimile Classics Ser.). (Illus.). 1979. 5.95 (ISBN 0-8317-3115-X, Mayflower Bks). Smith Pubs.

Kavanaugh, James. A Fable. (Illus.). 64p. 1980. 8.95 (ISBN 0-525-93154-6). Dutton.

Kottmeyer, William, et al. Fables & Folktales, Level A. (Plus Ten Vocabulary Booster Ser.). (Illus.). 256p. (gr. 4). 1972. text ed. 6.08 (ISBN 0-07-033974-0, W). McGraw.

Krylov, Ivan A. Krylov's Fables. Pares, Bernard, tr. from Rus. LC 76-23880. (Classics of Russian Literature). 1977. 11.95 (ISBN 0-88355-489-5); pap. 3.95 (ISBN 0-88355-490-9). Hyperion Conn.

Krylov, Ivan H. Kriloff & His Fables. Coxwell, C. Fillingham, tr. from Rus. LC 79-108502. 1970. Repr. of 1869 ed. 19.00 (ISBN 0-403-00368-7). Scholarly.

Leekley, Thomas B. Riddle of the Black Knight & Other Stories from the Middle Ages Based on the Gesta Romanorum. LC 57-12262. (Illus.). (gr. 3-7). 1957. 6.95 (ISBN 0-8149-0347-9). Vanguard.

Leonard, William E. Aesop & Hyssop. 158p. 1921. 12.95 (ISBN 0-87548-252-X); pap. 3.95 (ISBN 0-87548-253-8). Open Court.

Levine, David, ed. & illus. The Fables of Aesop. LC 72-96878. (Illus.). (gr. 5 up). 1975. 9.95 (ISBN 0-87645-074-5). Gambit.

McKendry, John J. Aesop: Five Centuries of Illustrated Fables. LC 64-2049. (Illus.). (gr. 4-6). 1964. 6.95 (ISBN 0-87099-029-2, Pub. by Metro Mus Art). NYGS.

Marzuban-Nama. Tales of Marzuban. Levy, Reuben, tr. LC 68-8337. (Illus.). 1968. Repr. of 1959 ed. lib. bdg. 15.00 (ISBN 0-8371-0162-X, MATM). Greenwood.

Mills, Barriss. Domestic Fables. 1971. 8.00 (ISBN 0-685-01006-6, Pub. by Elizabeth Pr). SBD.
Newbigging, Thomas. Fables & Fabulists, Ancient & Modern. LC 70-78212. 1971. Repr. of 1895 ed. 22.00 (ISBN 0-8103-3770-3). Gale.
Raffel, B., intro. by. Sir Gawain & the Green Knight. (Orig.). 1970. pap. 1.75 (ISBN 0-451-61848-3, ME1848, Ment). NAL.
Reed, A. W. Aboriginal Fables. (Illus.). 144p. 1979. pap. 5.95 (ISBN 0-589-07000-2, Pub. by Reed Books Australia). C E Tuttle.
Rice, Eve. Once in a Wood: Ten Tales from Aesop. LC 78-16294. (Greenwillow Read-Alone Bks). (Illus.). (gr. 1-3). 1979. 5.95 (ISBN 0-688-80191-9); PLB 5.71 (ISBN 0-688-84191-0). Greenwillow.
Rice, Stanley P. Ancient Indian Fables & Stories. LC 74-12477. 1974. Repr. of 1924 ed. lib. bdg. 17.50 (ISBN 0-8414-7329-3). Folcroft.
Roche, Paul. New Tales from Aesop: For Reading Aloud. Date not set. price not set. U of Notre Dame Pr.
Skeat, Walter. Fables & Folk-Tales from an Eastern Forest. (Folklore Ser). 7.50 (ISBN 0-88305-635-6). Norwood Edns.
Smith, Edward, compiled by. The Frogs Who Wanted a King & Other Songs from La Fontaine. LC 77-5819. (Illus.). 64p. (gr. 1 up). 1977. 11.95 (ISBN 0-590-17294-8, Four Winds). Schol Bk Serv.
Snow, Helen F. Fables & Parables. LC 70-166603. 1952. 21.00 (ISBN 0-403-08988-3). Scholarly.
Spriggs, Ruth, ed. The Fables of Aesop. LC 75-41965. (Illus.). 120p. (gr. 4 up). 1976. 7.95 (ISBN 0-528-82070-2). Rand.
Steuer, Aron. Aesop in the Courts, Vol. 2. 1978. write for info (ISBN 0-88238-061-3). Law Arts.
Swisher, Robert K. The Weaver: A Collection of Fables. 1975. pap. 1.95 (ISBN 0-912852-05-4). Echo Pubs.
Thomas, Vernon. Aesop's Fables. (Illus.). 135p. (gr. 1-7). 1981. 6.25 (ISBN 0-89744-231-8, Pub. by Hemkunt India). Auromere.
Thurber, James. Further Fables for Our Time. (Illus.). 1978. pap. 2.95 (ISBN 0-671-24218-0, Fireside). S&S.
Wright, Freire & Foreman, Michael. Borrowed Feathers & Other Fables. LC 77-79844. (ps-3). 1978. 3.95 (ISBN 0-394-83730-4, BYR); PLB 4.99 (ISBN 0-394-93730-9). Random.

FABLES–HISTORY AND CRITICISM

Aesopus. Fables Fo Aesop, Vol. One: History of the Aesopic Fable. Jacobs, Joseph, ed. 1970. Repr. of 1889 ed. text ed. 24.50 (ISBN 0-8337-1818-5). B Franklin.
Bulfinch, Thomas. Age of Fable. 1969. 9.95x (ISBN 0-460-00472-7, Evman). Biblio Dist.
--Poetry of the Age of Fable. 59.95 (ISBN 0-8490-0864-6). Gordon Pr.
Lall, Rama Rani. Satiric Fable in English. 1980. text ed. 12.00x (ISBN 0-391-01732-2). Humanities.
Newbigging, Thomas. Fables & Fabulists: Ancient & Modern. facsimile ed. LC 76-37799. (Essay Index Reprint Ser). Repr. of 1895 ed. 15.00 (ISBN 0-8369-2615-3). Arno.
Noel, Thomas. Theories of the Fable in the Eighteenth Century. LC 74-23251. 175p. 1975. 17.50x (ISBN 0-231-03858-5). Columbia U Pr.
Plessow, Max. Geschichte der Fabeldichtung in England Bis Zu John Gay (1762) Repr. of 1906 ed. 44.50 (ISBN 0-384-46821-7); pap. 41.50 (ISBN 0-384-46820-9). Johnson Repr.

FABRE, EMILE, 1870-1955

Santa Vicca, Edmund F. Four French Dramatists: A Bibliography of Criticism of the Works of Eugene Brieux, Francois De Curel, Emile Fabre, Paul Hervieu. LC 74-7495. (Author Bibliographies Ser.: No. 17). 1974. 10.00 (ISBN 0-8108-0755-6). Scarecrow.

FABRE, JEAN HENRI CASIMIR, 1823-1915

Doorly, Eleanor. Insect Man. (New Windmill Ser). (Illus.). (gr. 6-8). 1936-1964. 4.25 (ISBN 0-435-12011-5). Dufour.

FABRI, FELIX, 1441-1502

Prescott, Hilda F. Friar Felix at Large: A Fifteenth Century Pilgrimage to the Holy Land. Repr. of 1950 ed. lib. bdg. 15.00x (ISBN 0-8371-3016-6, PRFF). Greenwood.
--Once to Sinai. LC 78-63358. (The Crusades & Military Orders: Second Ser.). Repr. of 1957 ed. 27.00 (ISBN 0-404-17028-5). AMS Pr.

FABRIC PICTURES

Appell, Madeleine. One-Stitch Stitchery. LC 78-51063. (Little Craft Book). (Illus.). 1978. 5.95 (ISBN 0-8069-5384-5); lib. bdg. 6.69 (ISBN 0-8069-5385-3). Sterling.
Clouzot, Henri & Morris, Frances. Painted & Printed Fabrics: the History of the Manufactory at Jouy & Other Ateliers in France, 1760-1815 by Henri Clouzot: Notes on the History of Cotton Printing Especially in England & America by Frances Morris. LC 70-168418. (Metropolitan Museum of Art Publications in Reprint). (Illus.). 222p. 1972. Repr. of 1927 ed. 28.00 (ISBN 0-405-02256-5). Arno.
Crommelin, Jennyfer. Fabric Crafts. LC 79-20121. (Pegasus Books: No. 26). 1970. 10.50x (ISBN 0-234-77275-1). Intl Pubns Serv.
Fiberarts Magazine, ed. The Fiberarts Design Book. (Illus.). 176p. 1980. 24.95 (ISBN 0-8038-2394-0, Visual Communications); pap. 15.95 (ISBN 0-8038-2395-9). Hastings.
Newland, Mary & Walklin, Carol. Printing & Embroidery. 1977. 19.95 (ISBN 0-7134-0136-2, Pub. by Batsford England). David & Charles.
Waller, Irene. Design Sources for the Fiber Artist. Horn, George & Rainey, Sarita, eds. LC 78-51290. (Illus.). 1979. 12.95 (ISBN 0-87192-098-0). Davis Mass.

FABRICS

see Textile Fabrics

FABRICS, CREASE-RESISTANT

see Crease-Resistant Fabrics

FABRICS, NONWOVEN

see Nonwoven Fabrics

FABRICS, SYNTHETIC

see Synthetic Fabrics

FACADES

see also Architecture–Details

Hoffmann, Kurt, et al. Designing Architectural Facades: An Ideas File for Architects. (Illus.). 168p. 1975. 35.00x (ISBN 0-7114-3408-5). Intl Ideas.

FACE

see also Beauty, Personal; Chin; Mouth; Nose; Physiognomy

Alling, Charles C., III & Mahan, Parker E., eds. Facial Pain. 2nd ed. LC 76-52405. (Illus.). 286p. 1977. text ed. 22.00 (ISBN 0-8121-0577-X). Lea & Febiger.
Andrew, R. J. & Huber, Ernst. Evolution of Facial Expression: Two Accounts. Incl. The Origin & Evolution of the Calls & Facial Expressions of the Primates. 1963; Evolution of Facial Musculature & Facial Expression. 1931. LC 72-344. (Body Movement Ser.: Perspectives in Research). 312p. 1972. Repr. of 1972 ed. 17.00 (ISBN 0-405-03143-2). Arno.
Bales, William J. Facial Rejuvenation by Applied Pressure. 3rd & rev. ed. (Illus.). 1978. pap. text ed. write for info. (ISBN 0-686-10618-0). Bales.
Bell, Welden E. Orofacial Pain: Differential Diagnosis. 2nd ed. (Illus.). 1979. 39.50 (ISBN 0-8151-0655-6). Year Bk Med.
Brand, Richard W. & Isselhard, Donald E. Anatomy of Orofacial Structures. LC 77-14586. 1977. pap. text ed. 19.95 (ISBN 0-8016-0740-X). Mosby.
Bridgman, George B. Heads, Features, & Faces. LC 74-78681. (Illus.). 64p. 1974. pap. 2.00 (ISBN 0-486-22708-1). Dover.
Buck, Margaret W. The Face: What It Means. LC 78-56844. 1980. 7.95 (ISBN 0-87212-138-0); pap. 4.95 (ISBN 0-87212-106-2). Libra.
Clark, Linda. Face Improvement Through Exercise & Nutrition. LC 72-97919. (Pivot Original Health Bk.). (Illus.). 96p. 1973. pap. 2.25 (ISBN 0-87983-034-4). Keats.
Craig, Marjorie. Miss Craig's Face-Saving Exercises. 1970. 12.95 (ISBN 0-394-42412-3). Random.
Davies, David. The Influence of Teeth, Diet & Habits on the Human Face. 1972. 16.00x (ISBN 0-8448-0743-5). Crane-Russak Co.
Davis, Martha, ed. Recognition of Facial Expression: An Original Anthology. LC 74-9160. (Body Movement Perspectives in Research Ser). 252p. 1975. Repr. 26.00x (ISBN 0-405-06198-6). Arno.
Dubner, Ronald & Kawamura, Yojiro, eds. Oral-Facial Sensory & Motor Mechanisms. LC 75-135617. 384p. 1971. 32.50 (ISBN 0-306-50018-3, Plenum Pr). Plenum Pub.
Ekman, P. & Friesen, W. Unmasking the Face. 1975. 12.95 (ISBN 0-13-938183-X, Spec); pap. 4.25 (ISBN 0-13-938175-9, Spec). P-H.
Enlow, Donald H. A Handbook of Facial Growth. LC 75-293. (Illus.). 423p. 1975. 22.00 (ISBN 0-7216-3385-4). Saunders.
Facial Expression in Children: Three Surveys. Incl. A Study of the Smiling & Laughing of Infants in the First Year of Life. Washburn, Ruth W; The Smiling Response. Spitz, Rene A. & Wolf, K. M.; Expression of the Emotions in a Blind-Deaf Child. Goodenough, Florence L. LC 72-345. (Body Movement Ser.: Perspectives in Research). 226p. 1972. Repr. of 1972 ed. 15.00 (ISBN 0-405-03144-0). Arno.
Fried, Lawerence A. Anatomy of the Head, Neck, Face, & Jaws. 2nd ed. LC 80-16800. (Illus.). 299p. 1980. text ed. 17.50 (ISBN 0-8121-0717-9). Lea & Febiger.
Gerlock, Amil J. & Sinn, Douglas P. Clinical & Radiographic Interpretation of Facial Fractures. 1981. text ed. price not set (ISBN 0-316-30836-6). Little.
Hewitt, James. New Faces. 1978. pap. 3.95 (ISBN 0-85454-034-2). Newcastle Pub.
--New Faces. rev. ed. (Illus.). 1978. pap. 2.95 (ISBN 0-89437-041-3). Baronet.
Jody, Ruth & Lindner, Vicki. Face Lift Without Surgery: A Four Point Program to Maintain a Youthful Face. LC 78-21474. 1979. 9.95 (ISBN 0-397-01313-2). Har-Row.
Krane, Jessica. How to Use Your Hands to Save Your Face. 156p. 1976. pap. 1.95 (ISBN 0-346-12209-0). Cornerstone.
Lane, Nancy. How to Keep Your Face Looking Young. 224p. (Orig.). 1980. pap. 2.25 (ISBN 0-523-40926-5). Pinnacle Bks.
Liggett, John. Human Face. LC 74-83442. 1974. 35.00x (ISBN 0-8128-1754-0). Stein & Day.
Mar, Timothy T. Face Reading. 1975. pap. 1.50 (ISBN 0-451-06539-5, W6539, Sig). NAL.
Patterson, Clara E. How to Get Rid of Wrinkles. rev ed. LC 79-27184. (Illus.). 1980. 7.95 (ISBN 0-688-06546-5, Quill); pap. 2.95 (ISBN 0-688-03673-2, Quill). Morrow.
Penry, Jacques. Looking at Faces & Remembering Them. 1971. pap. 9.95 (ISBN 0-236-17664-1, Pub. by Paul Elek). Merrimack Bk Serv.
Ranly, Don M., illus. Synopsis of Craniofacial Growth. (Illus.). 188p. 1979. 13.50 (ISBN 0-8385-8779-8). ACC.
Remnick, Herbert S. Embryology of the Face & Oral Cavity. LC 79-76842. (Illus.). 98p. 1970. 10.00 (ISBN 0-8386-7346-5). Fairleigh Dickinson.
Runge, Senta M. Face Lifting by Exercise. 9th ed. LC 56-6321. (Illus.). 1977. Repr. of 1961 ed. 16.00 (ISBN 0-9601042-1-6). Allegro Pub.
Seiler, R. Gesichtsmuskeln. Hofer, H., et al, eds. (Primatologia: Vol. 4, Lieferung 6). 290p. 1976. 92.25 (ISBN 3-8055-2324-6). S Karger.

FACE–ABNORMITIES AND DEFORMITIES

Aita, John. Congenital Facial Anomalies with Neurologic Defects: A Clinical Atlas. (Illus.). 352p. 1969. ed. spiral bdg. 29.75photocopy (ISBN 0-398-00021-2). C C Thomas.
Bell, William H., et al. Surgical Correction of Dentofacial Deformities. LC 76-27050. 1979. text ed. 150.00 (ISBN 0-7216-1671-2); Vol. 1. 70.00 (ISBN 0-7216-1675-5); Vol. 2. 80.00 (ISBN 0-7216-1707-7). Saunders.
Bergsma, Daniel, ed. Morphogenesis & Malformation of Face & Brain. LC 75-24570. (Alan R. Liss, Inc. Ser.: Vol. 11, No. 7). 1976. 30.00 (ISBN 0-686-14575-5). March of Dimes.
Garliner, Daniel. Myofunctional Therapy. LC 75-14781. (Illus.). 450p. 1976. text ed. 39.00 (ISBN 0-7216-4055-9). Saunders.
Goodman, Richard M. & Gorlin, Robert J. Atlas of the Face in Genetic Disorders. 2nd ed. LC 76-40327. (Illus.). 1977. 69.50 (ISBN 0-8016-1895-9). Mosby.
Graham, Malcolm & House, William F., eds. Disorders of the Facial Nerve: Anatomy, Diagnosis & Management. 535p. 1981. text ed. 53.00 (ISBN 0-89004-624-7). Raven.
Melnick, Michael, ed. Clinical Dysmorphology of Oral-Facial Structures. Shields, Edward D. & Burzynski, Norbert J. (Post Graduate Dental Handbook Ser.: Vol. 12). 1981. 85.00 (ISBN 0-88416-169-2). Wright-PSG.
Melnick, Michael & Jorgenson, Ronald, eds. Developmental Aspects of Craniofacial Dysmorphology. LC 79-2487. (Alan R. Liss Ser.: Vol. 15, No. 8). 1979. 16.00 (ISBN 0-8451-1033-0). March of Dimes.
Moldaver, J. & Conley, J. The Facial Palsies. (Illus.). 272p. 1980. 35.75 (ISBN 0-398-03988-7). C C Thomas.
Pruzansky, Samuel. Congenital Anomalies of the Face & Associated Structures: Proceedings of an International Symposium. (Illus.). 416p. 1961. photocopy ed. spiral 41.75 (ISBN 0-398-04396-5). C C Thomas.
Saffon, M. J. The Fifteen Minute-a-Day Natural Face Lift. LC 78-26282. 1979. 7.95 (ISBN 0-13-314401-1). P-H.

FACE–SURGERY

Beder, Oscar E. Surgical & Maxillofacial Prosthesis. rev. ed. LC 49-50002. (Illus.). 94p. 1959. pap. 10.00 spiral bdg. (ISBN 0-295-74090-6). U of Wash Pr.
Browning, Norman L. Face Lifts: Everything You Always Wanted to Know. LC 80-2404. 240p. 1981. 12.95 (ISBN 0-385-04425-9). Doubleday.
Conley, John. Face-Lift Operation. (Illus.). 1968. pap. 24.75 photocopy ed. spiral (ISBN 0-398-00340-8). C C Thomas.
Dingman, Reed O. & Natvig, Paul. Surgery of Facial Fractures. LC 63-14507. (Illus.). 1964. 30.00 (ISBN 0-7216-3085-5). Saunders.
Goulian, Dicran & Courtiss, Eugene H., eds. Symposium of Surgery of the Aging Face, Vol. 19. LC 78-12298. (Symposia of the Educational Foundation of the American Society of Plastic & Reconstructive Surgeons Inc. Ser.). 1978. text ed. 47.50 (ISBN 0-8016-1941-6). Mosby.
Jackson, Ian T., et al. Atlas of Cranio-Maxillo-Facial Surgery. (Illus.). 600p. 1981. text ed. 82.50 (ISBN 0-8016-4295-7). Mosby.
Longacre, J. J. Rehabilitation of the Facially Disfigured. (Illus.). 144p. 1973. 21.50 (ISBN 0-398-02597-5). C C Thomas.
Miehlke, Adolf. Surgery of the Facial Nerve. 2nd ed. Michaelis, L. S., tr. LC 72-85770. (Illus.). 255p. 1973. text ed. 35.00 (ISBN 0-7216-6318-4). Saunders.
Pirruccello, Frank W. Plastic & Reconstructive Surgery of the Face: Cosmetic Surgery. (Illus.). 104p. 1981. 26.00 (ISBN 0-686-77751-4, 6891-1). Williams & Wilkins.
Sisson, George A. & Tardy, Eugene M., eds. Plastic & Reconstructive Surgery of the Face & Neck: Proceedings of the Second International Symposium. Repr. of 1977 ed. 131.75 set (ISBN 0-686-76868-X); Vol. I. 63.50 (ISBN 0-8089-0941-X); Vol. II. 78.00 (ISBN 0-8089-0956-8). Grune.

FACE–WOUNDS AND INJURIES

Bernstein, Norman. Emotional Care of the Facially Burned & Disfigured. 1976. pap. 15.95 (ISBN 0-316-09193-6). Little.
Longacre, J. J. Rehabilitation of the Facially Disfigured. (Illus.). 144p. 1973. 21.50 (ISBN 0-398-02597-5). C C Thomas.
Schultz, Richard C. Facial Injuries. 2nd ed. (Illus.). 1977. 59.50 (ISBN 0-8151-7579-5). Year Bk Med.
Zook, Elvin G., ed. The Primary Care of Facial Injuries. LC 79-16117. (Illus.). 186p. 1980. text ed. 24.00 (ISBN 0-88416-205-2). Wright-PSG.

FACE IN ART

Ames, Lee J. Draw Fifty Famous Faces. LC 77-15878. (gr. 1 up). 1978. 7.95a (ISBN 0-385-13217-4); PLB (ISBN 0-385-13218-2). Doubleday.
Bridgeman, George B. Heads, Features & Faces. LC 74-78681. 1974. lib. bdg. 9.50x (ISBN 0-88307-602-0). Gannon.
Emberley, Ed. Ed Emberley's Drawing Book of Faces. (Illus.). 32p. (gr. k-3). 1975. 5.95g (ISBN 0-316-23609-8). Little.
Emerson, Ellen R. Masks, Heads, & Faces with Some Considerations Respecting the Rise & Development of Art. (Illus.). 1979. Repr. of 1891 ed. lib. bdg. 45.00 (ISBN 0-8495-1324-3). Arden Lib.
Laidman, Hugh. Figures-Faces: A Sketcher's Handbook. (Illus.). 1979. 12.95 (ISBN 0-670-31319-X, Studio). Viking Pr.
Selleck, Jack. Faces. Brommer, Gerald F., ed. LC 76-50511. (Insights to Art Ser.). (Illus.). 1977. 10.50 (ISBN 0-87192-088-3). Davis Mass.
Zaidenberg, Arthur. How to Draw Heads & Faces. LC 66-10314. (How to Draw Ser). (Illus.). (gr. 5-10). 1966. PLB 8.79 (ISBN 0-200-71813-4, B37801, AbS-J). Har-Row.

FACETIAE

see Wit and Humor;

see American Wit and Humor, English Wit and Humor, and similar headings subdivided by subject, e.g. American Wit and Humor–Sports

FACIAL BONES

Enlow, Donald H. A Handbook of Facial Growth. LC 75-293. (Illus.). 423p. 1975. 22.00 (ISBN 0-7216-3385-4). Saunders.
Killey, H. C. Fractures of the Middle Third of the Facial Skeleton. 1977. 10.95 (ISBN 0-8151-5042-3). Year Bk Med.
Moore, W. J. & Lavelle, C. L. Growth of the Facial Skeleton in the Hominoidea. 1975. 38.00 (ISBN 0-12-505650-8). Acad Pr.

FACIAL MANIFESTATIONS OF GENERAL DISEASES

Graham, Malcolm & House, William F., eds. Disorders of the Facial Nerve: Anatomy, Diagnosis & Management. 535p. 1981. text ed. 53.00 (ISBN 0-89004-624-7). Raven.
Irby, William B. Facial Trauma & Concomitant Problems: Evaluation & Treatment. 2nd ed. LC 79-15473. 1979. text ed. 39.50 (ISBN 0-8016-2349-9). Mosby.
Kay, L. W. & Haskell, R. Color Atlas of Oro-Facial Diseases. (Year Book Color Atlas Ser.). (Illus.). 1972. 32.50 (ISBN 0-8151-5000-8). Year Bk Med.
Little, Samuel C. Abnormal Movements of the Face: With Special Consideration of Abnormal Facial Movements Occurring in Paroxysmal Disorders. LC 54-10881. 70p. 1954. pap. 2.25 (ISBN 0-8173-2000-8). U of Ala Pr.
Moldaver, J. & Conley, J. The Facial Palsies. (Illus.). 272p. 1980. 35.75 (ISBN 0-398-03988-7). C C Thomas.
Stewart & Prescott. Oral Facial Genetics. LC 76-21322. (Illus.). 1976. 49.50 (ISBN 0-8016-4810-6). Mosby.

FACILITATORY TRACT

see Reticular Formation

FACSIMILE TRANSMISSION

Costigan, Daniel M. Electronic Delivery of Documents & Graphics. 1978. text ed. 24.95x (ISBN 0-442-80036-3). Van Nos Reinhold.

FACSIMILES

see Reproduction of Money, Documents, etc.

FACTOR ANALYSIS

see also Factorial Experiment Designs; Psychology–Mathematical Models

Adelman, Irma & Morris, Cynthia Taft. Society, Politics, & Economic Development: A Quantitative Approach. 336p. 1967. 21.50x (ISBN 0-8018-0006-4); pap. 6.50x (ISBN 0-8018-1301-8). Johns Hopkins.
Anastasia, Salvatore & Willig, Paul M. Structure of Factors. new ed. LC 72-78469. 1974. 30.00x (ISBN 0-917448-04-9). Algorithmics.
Cattell, Raymond B. Factor Analysis. LC 72-10689. 462p. 1973. Repr. of 1952 ed. lib. bdg. 28.75x (ISBN 0-8371-6615-2, CAFA). Greenwood.
Cattell, Raymond B., ed. The Scientific Use of Factor Analysis: In Behavioral & Life Sciences. LC 77-10695. (Illus.). 640p. 1978. 32.50 (ISBN 0-306-30939-4, Plenum Pr). Plenum Pub.
Harman, Harry H. Modern Factor Analysis. 3rd, rev ed. LC 75-22267. (Illus.). 512p. 1976. 27.50x (ISBN 0-226-31652-1). U of Chicago Pr.
Hinman, Suki & Bolton, Brian. Factor Analytic Studies, 1971-1975. LC 78-69873. 1978. 27.50x (ISBN 0-87875-165-3). Whitston Pub.
Hinman, Sukit & Bolton, Brian. Factor Analytic Studies: 1941-1975, 5 vols. Set. 32.50x (ISBN 0-686-64136-1). Whitston Pub.
Jackson, David J. & Borgatta, Edgar F., eds. Factor Analysis & Measurement in Sociological Research: A Multi-Dimensional Perspective. LC 80-40746. (Sage Studies in International Sociology: Vol. 21). 316p. 1981. pap. 9.95 (ISBN 0-8039-9815-5). Sage.
Jarett, Irwin M. & Brady, Patricia A., eds. A Conference on Key Factor Analysis: A Logic Leading to Social Accountability. LC 76-20624. 450p. 1976. 10.00x (ISBN 0-8093-0793-6); pap. 4.95x (ISBN 0-8093-0795-2). S Ill U Pr.
Jonassen, Christen T. & Peres, Sherwood H. Interrelationships of Dimensions of Community Systems: A Factor Analysis of Eighty-Two Variables. LC 60-15700. (Orig.). 1960. pap. 1.75 (ISBN 0-8142-0068-0). Ohio St U Pr.
Joreskog, Karl G. & Sorbom, Dag. EFAP Two: Exploratory Factor Analysis Program. pap. 3.50 (ISBN 0-89498-007-6). Natl Ed Res.
Rummel, R. J. The Dimensions of Nations, Vol. 1. LC 72-84054. 416p. 1972. 25.00x (ISBN 0-8039-0170-4). Sage.
Rummel, Rudolph J. Applied Factor Analysis. 1970. 20.95x (ISBN 0-8101-0254-4). Northwestern U Pr.
Vincent, Jack E. Factor Analysis in International Relations: Interpretation, Problem Areas, & an Application. LC 71-137854. (U of Fla. Social Sciences Monographs: No. 43). 1971. pap. 3.50 (ISBN 0-8130-0315-6). U Presses Fla.

FACTORIAL EXPERIMENT DESIGNS

Box, George E. & Draper, Norman R. Evolutionary Operation: A Statistical Method for Process Improvement. LC 68-56159. (Applied Probability & Mathematical Statistics Ser). 1969. 28.95 (ISBN 0-471-09305-X, Pub. by Wiley-Interscience). Wiley.
Keppel, Geoffrey. Design & Analysis: A Researcher's Handbook. LC 72-6434. (Illus.). 640p. 1973. ref. ed. 22.95 (ISBN 0-13-200030-X). P-H.

FACTORIES

see also Chemical Plants; Mills and Mill-Work; Plant Shutdowns;
also headings beginning with the word Factory
Althea. A Visit to the Factory. (Illus.). 24p. 1980. pap. 1.45 ea.; pap. in 5 pk. avail. (ISBN 0-85122-192-0, Pub. by Dinosaur Pubns). Merrimack Bk Serv.
Balzer, Richard. Clockwork: Life in & Outside an American Factory. LC 75-21209. 352p. 1976. 10.00 (ISBN 0-385-11036-7). Doubleday.
Bender, Richard. & Wilson, Forrest. Crack in the Rear View Mirror. 1973. 19.95x (ISBN 0-442-20686-0). Van Nos Reinhold.
Elonka, S & Robinson, J. F. Standard Plant Operator's Questions & Answers, 2 vols. 2nd ed. 1981. Set. 36.50 (ISBN 0-07-019238-3); Vol. 1. 19.50 (ISBN 0-07-019315-0); Vol. 2. 19.50 (ISBN 0-07-019316-9). McGraw.
Fielden, John. Curse of the Factory System. 2nd rev. ed. 74p. 1969. 25.00x (ISBN 0-7146-1394-0, F Cass Co). Biblio Dist.
Fisher, Leonard E. The Factories. LC 79-2092. (Nineteenth Century America Bk.). (Illus.). 64p. (gr. 4-6). 1979. PLB 7.95 (ISBN 0-8234-0367-X). Holiday.
Hennessey, Robert. Factories. (Past into Present Ser.). (Illus.). 15.00x (ISBN 0-392-02822-0, LTB). Sportshelf.
Hong, Alfred, ed. Marketing Economics Key Plants, 1973: The Guide to Industrial Purchasing Power (National Edition) new ed. LC 73-642154. 600p. 1973. 90.00 (ISBN 0-914078-00-3). Marketing Econ.
Lewis, J. Slater. The Commercial Organization of Factories. LC 76-10639. (Management History Ser.: No. 10). 578p. Repr. of 1896 ed. 45.00 (ISBN 0-87960-018-7). Hive Pub.
Magison, E. C. Electrical Instruments in Hazardous Locations. 3rd ed. LC 70-184225. 1978. text ed. 35.00 (ISBN 0-87664-376-4). Instru Soc.
Marsh, Robert M. & Mannari, Hiroshi. Modernization & the Japanese Factory. LC 75-3466. 560p. 1976. 35.00 (ISBN 0-691-09365-2); pap. 12.50 ltd. ed. (ISBN 0-691-10037-3). Princeton U Pr.
Price, George M. Modern Factory: Safety, Sanitation & Welfare. LC 74-89758. (American Labor, from Conspiracy to Collective Bargaining, Ser. 1). 574p. 1969. Repr. of 1914 ed. 35.00 (ISBN 0-405-02144-5). Arno.
Rudman, Jack. Factory Inspector. (Career Examination Ser.: C-283). (Cloth bdg. avail. on request). pap. 8.00 (ISBN 0-8373-0283-8). Natl Learning.
Scherer, F. M., et al. The Economics of Multi-Plant Operation. LC 74-33697. (Harvard Economic Studies: NO. 145). 448p. 1975. text ed. 20.00x (ISBN 0-674-23340-9). Harvard U Pr.
Warner, William L. & Low, J. O. The Social System of the Modern Factory. LC 75-31426. (Yankee City Series: Vol. 4). 245p. 1976. Repr. lib. bdg. 17.50x (ISBN 0-8371-8503-3, WAMF). Greenwood.

FACTORIES–ACCOUNTING

Elbourne, Edward T. Factory Administration & Accounts. Chandler, Alfred D., ed. LC 79-7543. (History of Management Thought & Practice Ser.). 1980. Repr. of 1919 ed. lib. bdg. 48.00x (ISBN 0-405-12327-2). Arno.
Garcke, Emile & Fells, John M. Factory Accounts, Their Principles & Practice. 4th ed. LC 75-18470. (History of Accounting Ser.). 1976. 19.00x (ISBN 0-405-07553-7). Arno.
Lewis, J. Slater. The Commercial Organization of Factories: A Handbook. Brief, Richard P., ed. LC 77-87274. (Development of Contemporary Accounting Thought Ser). 1978. Repr. of 1896 ed. lib. bdg. 42.00 (ISBN 0-405-10902-4). Arno.
Matheson, Ewing. The Depreciation of Factories, Mines & Industrial Undertakings & Their Valuation. 2nd ed. LC 75-18476. (History of Accounting Ser.). (Illus.). 1976. Repr. 14.00x (ISBN 0-405-07558-8). Arno.

FACTORIES–CLEAN ROOMS

see Clean Rooms

FACTORIES–DESIGN AND CONSTRUCTION

Apple, J. M. Plant Layout & Materials Handling. 3rd ed. LC 77-75127. (Illus.). 600p. 1977. 24.95 (ISBN 0-8260-0501-2). Wiley.
Butt, L. T. & Wright, D. C. Use of Polymers in Plant Construction. (Illus.). 156p. 1980. text ed. 28.00 (ISBN 0-85334-914-2, Pub. by Applied Sci England). J K Burgess.
Drury, Jolyon. Factories: Planning & Design. (Illus.). 260p. 1981. 68.50 (ISBN 0-89397-113-8). Nichols Pub.
Kharbanda, O. P. Process Plant & Equipment Cost Estimation. LC 79-21139. 1979. pap. 19.00 (ISBN 0-910460-68-X). Craftsman.
Moore, James M. Plant Layout & Design. (Illus.). 1962. 22.95 (ISBN 0-02-383180-4). Macmillan.
Muther, Richard. Practical Plant Layout. 1956. text ed. 21.00 (ISBN 0-07-044156-1, C). McGraw.
--Systematic Layout Planning. 2nd ed. LC 72-91983. 1973. 27.50 (ISBN 0-8436-0814-5). CBI Pub.
Peters, Max S. & Timmerhaus, Klaus. Plant Design & Economics for Chemical Engineers. 3rd ed. (Chemical Engineering Ser.). (Illus.). 1980. text ed. 31.50 (ISBN 0-07-049582-3); solution manual 7.95 (ISBN 0-07-049583-1). McGraw.

FACTORIES–ELECTRIC EQUIPMENT

see also Industrial Electronics
Institute of Electrical & Electronics Engineers, Inc. Recommended Practice for Electric Power Distribution for Industrial Plants. 388p. 1976. 19.95 (ISBN 0-471-02686-7). Wiley.
Moore, Arthur H. & Elonka, Stephen M. Electrical Systems & Equipment for Industry. LC 77-5640. (Illus.). 368p. 1977. Repr. of 1971 ed. lib. bdg. 19.50 (ISBN 0-88275-561-7). Krieger.
Twitchell, Paul. Eckankar: Compiled Writings. 196p. 1975. 5.95 (ISBN 0-914766-26-0). IWP Pub.

FACTORIES–LAW AND LEGISLATION

see Factory Laws and Legislation

FACTORIES–LOCATION

see also Industries, Location of
Halbritter, Gunter. Multidimensionale Optimierung bei der Standortwahl von Grosstechnischen Anlagen. (Interdisciplinary Systems Research: No. 62). (Illus.). 178p. (Ger.). 1979. pap. 22.80 (ISBN 3-7643-1055-3). Birkhauser.
Hunker, Henry L. & Wright, Alfred J. Factors of Industrial Location in Ohio. 1964. 5.00x (ISBN 0-87776-119-1, R-119); pap. 3.50x (ISBN 0-685-19028-5, R-119P). Ohio St U Admin Sci.
Rowe, James E. Industrial Plant Location. (Public Administation Ser.: Bibliography P-575). 52p. 1980. pap. 5.50 (ISBN 0-686-29055-0). Vance Biblios.
Weber, Alfred. Theory of the Location of Industries. Friedrich, Carl J., tr. LC 77-102554. (Illus.). 1971. Repr. of 1929 ed. 13.50 (ISBN 0-8462-1521-7). Russell.
White, John A. & Francis, Richard L. Facility Layout & Location: An Analytical Approach. LC 73-18455. (Int'l. Series in Industrial & Systems Engineering). (Illus.). 448p. 1974. ref. ed. 22.95x (ISBN 0-13-299149-7). P-H.

FACTORIES–MAINTENANCE AND REPAIR

see Plant Maintenance

FACTORIES–MANAGEMENT

see Factory Management

FACTORIES–NOISE

see Industrial Noise

FACTORIES–PROTECTION

see also Industry-Security Measures
Factory Mutual System. Handbook of Industrial Loss Prevention. 2nd ed. (Insurance Ser). 1967. 41.95 (ISBN 0-07-019888-8, P&RB). McGraw.
Momboisse, Raymond M. Industrial Security for Strikes, Riots & Disasters. 516p. 1977. 24.75 (ISBN 0-398-01325-X). C C Thomas.
Vervalin, Charles H., ed. Fire Protection Manual for Hydrocarbon Processing Plants, Vol. 1. 2nd ed. (Illus.). 498p. 1973. 45.50x (ISBN 0-87201-286-7). Gulf Pub.

FACTORIES–SAFETY APPLIANCES

see also Employers' Liability
Heinrich, Herbert W. Industrial Accident Prevention. 4th ed. 1959. text ed. 22.00 (ISBN 0-07-028058-4, C). McGraw.

FACTORS

see Commission Merchants

FACTORY AND TRADE WASTE

see also Agricultural Wastes; Petroleum Waste; Pollution; Refuse and Refuse Disposal
Alter & Dunn. Solid Waste Conversion to Energy. (Pollution Engineering & Technology Ser.: Vol. 11). 184p. 1980. 24.75 (ISBN 0-8247-6917-1). Dekker.
Azad, Hardam S. Industrial Wastewater Management Handbook. 1976. 35.75 (ISBN 0-07-002661-0, P&RB). McGraw.
Basta, Daniel J., et al. Analysis for Residuals-Environmental Quality Management: A Case Study of the Ljubljana Area of Yugoslavia. (Resources for the Future Ser.). 1978. pap. text ed. 8.50 (ISBN 0-8018-2088-X). Johns Hopkins.
Bell, John M., ed. Proceedings: 30th Industrial Waste Conference (Purdue Univ.) LC 77-70293. 1977. 59.95 (ISBN 0-250-40163-0). Ann Arbor Science.
--Proceedings: 31st Industrial Waste Conference (Purdue Univ.) LC 77-84415. 1977. 59.95 (ISBN 0-250-40164-9). Ann Arbor Science.
Berkowitz, Joan B., et al, eds. Unit Operations for Treatment of Hazardous Industrial Wastes. LC 78-62520. (Pollution Technology Review: No. 47). (Illus.). 1979. 42.00 (ISBN 0-8155-0717-8). Noyes.
Besselievre, Edmond & Schwartz, Max. The Treatment of Industrial Waste. 2nd ed. 1976. 25.95 (ISBN 0-07-005047-3, P&RB). McGraw.
Brown, Michael. Laying Waste: The Poisoning of America by Toxic Chemicals. 1981. pap. 3.50 (ISBN 0-671-42263-4). WSP.
Brown, William H. How to Stop the Corporate Polluters. (Illus.). 1972. pap. 1.50 (ISBN 0-88388-020-2). Bellerophon Bks.
Calleley, A. & Forster, C. Treatment of Industrial Effluents. LC 76-54909. 1977. 30.95 (ISBN 0-470-98934-3). Halsted Pr.
CEP & Boothe, Norris. Cleaning up: The Cost of Refinery Pollution Control. Haley, Mary J., ed. LC 75-10535. 1975. pap. 75.00 (ISBN 0-87871-002-7). CEP.
Chemical Engineering, compiled By. Industrial Waste Water & Solid Waste Engineering. LC 80-12608. 376p. 1980. pap. 23.50 (ISBN 0-07-010694-0, Chem Eng). McGraw.
Chemical Engineering Magazine, compiled By. Industrial Air Pollution Engineering. LC 80-12609. 304p. 1980. pap. 24.50 (ISBN 0-07-606664-9, Chem Eng). McGraw.
Cheremisinoff, Nicholas P. & Cheremisinoff, Paul N. Industrial & Hazardous Wastes Impoundment. LC 78-71428. 1979. 37.50 (ISBN 0-250-40280-7). Ann Arbor Science.
Commission on Natural Resources, National Research Council. The Shallow Land Burial of Low-Level Radioactively Contaminated Solid Waste. LC 76-56928. 1976. pap. 7.00 (ISBN 0-309-02535-4). Natl Acad Pr.
Connon, James. A Clear View - Guide to Industrial Pollution Control. LC 75-15321. 1975. pap. 4.00 (ISBN 0-686-70491-6). Inform.
Conway, Richard A. & Ross, Richard D. Handbook of Industrial Waste Disposal. 576p. 1980. text ed. 36.50 (ISBN 0-442-27053-4). Van Nos Reinhold.
Cross, Frank L., Jr. Management Primer on Water Pollution Control. LC 74-76523. 150p. 1974. pap. 25.00 (ISBN 0-87762-136-5). Technomic.
Curi, K. Treatment & Disposal of Liquid & Solid Industrial Wastes: Proceedings of the Third Turkish-German Environmental Engineering Symposium, Istanbul, July 1979. LC 80-40993. (Illus.). 515p. 1980. 81.00 (ISBN 0-08-023999-4). Pergamon.
De Renzo, D. J., ed. Biodegradation Techniques for Industrial Organic Wastes. LC 80-12834. (Pollution Technology Review Ser. 65; Chemical Technology Review Ser. 158). (Illus.). 358p. 1980. 28.00 (ISBN 0-8155-0800-X). Noyes.
Disposal of Industrial Wastes by Combustion, Present State-of-the-Art, Vol. 3. 62p. 1977. pap. text ed. 15.00 (ISBN 0-685-86859-1, H00092). ASME.
Dyer, Jon C. Handbook of Industrial Wastes Pretreatment. LC 79-25702. 300p. 1981. lib. bdg. 32.50 (ISBN 0-8240-7066-6). Garland Pub.
Eckenfelder, William W. Industrial Water Pollution Control. (Sanitary & Water Resources Engineering Ser.). 1966. text ed. 24.50 (ISBN 0-07-018900-5, C). McGraw.
Gelb, Bernard A. & Myers, John G. Measuring the Cost of Industrial Water Pollution Control. LC 76-45533. (Report: No. 700). (Illus., Orig.). 1976. pap. 30.00 (ISBN 0-8237-0134-4). Conference Bd.
Goodman, G. T. & Chadwick, M. H., eds. Environmental Management of Mineral Wastes. 382p. 1978. 42.50x (ISBN 9-0286-0054-X). Sijthoff & Noordhoff.
Green, John H. & Kramer, Amihud. Food Processing Waste Management. (Illus.). 1979. text ed. 46.00 (ISBN 0-87055-331-3). AVI.
Hackman, E. E. Toxic Organic Chemicals Destruction & Waste Treatment. LC 78-54001. (Polution Technology Review No. 40; Chemical Technology Review No. 107). 1978. 42.00 (ISBN 0-8155-0700-3). Noyes.
Handling of Tritium-Bearing Wastes. (Technical Reports Ser.: No. 203). 137p. 1981. pap. 21.75 (ISBN 92-0-125081-9, IDC 203, IAEA). Unipub.
Hooper, G. V., ed. Offshore Ship & Platform Incineration of Hazardous Wastes. LC 81-38372. (Pollution Tech. Rev. 79). (Illus.). 468p. 1981. 42.00 (ISBN 0-8155-0854-9). Noyes.
Huang, C. P. Thirteenth Mid-Atlantic Industrial Waste Conference. LC 81-65971. 650p. 1981. text ed. 39.95 (ISBN 0-250-40473-7). Ann Arbor Science.
Imhoff, Karl & Fair, Gordon. Sewage Treatment. 2nd ed. LC 56-11025. 1956. 31.00 (ISBN 0-471-42669-5, Pub. by Wiley-Interscience). Wiley.
Industrial Waste Conference, 1977, 32nd, Purdue University. Proceedings. Bell, John M., ed. LC 77-84415. 1978. 49.95 (ISBN 0-250-40165-7). Ann Arbor Science.
Industrial Waste Symposia, 1980. Proceedings. 40.00 (ISBN 0-686-30995-2, T00053). Water Pollution.
Jones, Jerry L. & Radding, Shirley B., eds. Thermal Conversion of Solid Waste & Biomass. LC 80-14754. (ACS Symposium Ser.: No. 130). 1980. 57.50 (ISBN 0-8412-0565-5). Am Chemical.
Jorgensen, S. E., ed. Industrial Waste Water Management. (Studies in Environmental Science: Vol. 5). 388p. 1979. 46.50 (ISBN 0-686-62655-9). Elsevier.
Ketchum, Bostwick H., et al, eds. Ocean Dumping of Industrial Wastes. (Marine Science Ser.: Vol. 12). 525p. 1981. 59.50 (ISBN 0-306-40653-5, Plenum Pr). Plenum Pub.
Khoury, D. L., ed. Flue Gas Cleaning Wastes Disposal & Utilization. LC 81-1631. (Pollution Technology, Review: No. 77, Energy Technology Review: No. 65). (Illus.). 1981. 45.00 (ISBN 0-8155-0847-6). Noyes.
Lund, H. F. Industrial Pollution Control Handbook. 1971. 46.50 (ISBN 0-07-039095-9, P&RB). McGraw.
Management & Disposal of Residues from the Treatment of Industrial Wastewaters. (Illus.). 1975. softcover 25.00 (ISBN 0-686-26014-7, 1WW5). Info Transfer.
Management of Alpha-Contaminated Wastes. 714p. 1981. pap. 95.50 (ISBN 92-0-020081-8, ISP 562, IAEA). Unipub.
Managing Industrial & Agricultural Wastes: Some Experiences. 137p. 1980. pap. 13.25 (ISBN 92-833-1460-3, APO 89, APO). Unipub.
Mantell, Charles L. Solid Wastes: Origin, Collection, Processing & Disposal. LC 74-26930. 1152p. 1975. 80.00 (ISBN 0-471-56777-9, Pub by Wiley-Interscience). Wiley.

Martin, Louis F. Industrial Water Purification. LC 74-84302. (Pollution Technology Review Ser: No. 16). (Illus.). 300p. 1975. 36.00 (ISBN 0-8155-0554-X). Noyes.
Mid-Atlantic Industrial Waste Conference Proceedings, Ninth. (Illus.). 1977. softcover 17.50 (ISBN 0-686-25731-6, 91W7). Info Transfer.
Mid-Atlantic Industrial Waste Conference Proceedings, Tenth. (Illus.). 1978. softcover 15.00 (ISBN 0-686-25730-8, 101W8). Info Transfer.
Miller, Stanton S., ed. Solid Wastes - II. LC 73-87146. 1973. 8.50 (ISBN 0-8412-0184-6); pap. 5.50 (ISBN 0-8412-0238-9). Am Chemical.
Minor, Paul S. The Industry - EPA Confrontation: Living with the Water Pollution Control Act Amendments of 1972 Today. LC 76-14470. 1976. pap. 195.00 (ISBN 0-07-042401-2, P&RB). McGraw.
Moore, Ralph L. Neutralization of Waste Water by pH Control. LC 77-94491. 160p. 1978. text ed. 18.00 (ISBN 0-87664-383-7). Instru Soc.
OECD Staff. Used Types in Solid Waste Management. (Illus., Orig.). 1981. pap. text ed. 6.00x (ISBN 92-64-12131-5, 97-80-07-1). OECD.
Overcash, Michael R. & Pal, Dhiraj. Design of Land Treatment Systems for Industrial Wastes: Theory & Practice. LC 79-88908. 1979. 39.95 (ISBN 0-250-40291-2). Ann Arbor Science.
Purdue University Industrial Waste Conference, 34th, 1979. Proceedings. Bell, John M., ed. LC 77-84415. 1980. 59.95 (ISBN 0-250-40348-X). Ann Arbor Science.
Purdue University Industrial Waste Conference, 35th. Proceedings. Bell, John M., ed. 994p. 1981. text ed. 69.95 (ISBN 0-250-40363-3). Ann Arbor Science.
Purdue University Industrial Waste Conference, 33rd, 1978. Proceedings. Bell, John M., ed. LC 77-84415. 1979. 59.95 (ISBN 0-250-40276-9). Ann Arbor Science.
Residue Utilization: Management of Agricultural & Agro-Industrial Wastes. 1978. pap. 7.50 (ISBN 92-5-100320-3, F1265, FAO). Unipub.
Sax, N. Irving. Industrial Pollution. 1974. text ed. 37.50 (ISBN 0-442-27366-5). Van Nos Reinhold.
Shinskey, F. G. PH & P Ion: Control in Process & Waste Streams. LC 73-7853. (Environmental Science & Technology Ser.). 288p. 1973. 29.95 (ISBN 0-471-78640-3, Pub. by Wiley-Interscience). Wiley.
Sittig, M. Pollution Control in the Asbestos, Cement, Glass & Allied Mineral Industries. LC 75-10353. (Pollution Technology Review Ser.: No. 19). (Illus.). 333p. 1975. 36.00 (ISBN 0-8155-0578-7). Noyes.
--Pollution Control in the Plastics & Rubber Industry. LC 75-2940. (Pollution Technology Review Ser: No. 18). (Illus.). 306p. 1975. 36.00 (ISBN 0-8155-0572-8). Noyes.
State of California. Health Aspects of Wastewater Recharge: A State-of-the-Art Review. LC 78-69808. (Illus.). 1978. Repr. 22.00 (ISBN 0-912394-18-8). Water Info.
Survey of Industrial Wastes & by-Products in Australia. 58p. 1978. pap. 6.00 (ISBN 0-686-71847-X, CO 41, CSIRO). Unipub.
Tearle, Keith, ed. Industrial Pollution Control. 1973. 22.00x (ISBN 0-8464-0510-5). Beekman Pubs.
Theodore, Louis & Buonicore, Anthony. Industrial Air Pollution Control Equipment for Particulates. LC 76-25095. (Uniscience Ser.). 288p. 1976. 59.95 (ISBN 0-8493-5132-4). CRC Pr.
Treatment & Disposal of Industrial Wastewaters & Residues. (Illus.). 1978. softcover 25.00 (ISBN 0-686-26017-1, 1WW8). Info Transfer.
Treatment & Disposal of Industrial Wastewaters & Residues. (Illus.). 1977. 30.00 (ISBN 0-686-26018-X, 1WW7); softcover 25.00 (ISBN 0-686-26019-8). Info Transfer.
Walters, J. K. & Wint, A., eds. Industrial Effluent Treatment, Vol. 1. (Water & Solid Wastes). (Illus.). 351p. 1981. text ed. 44.00 (ISBN 0-85334-891-X, Pub. by Applied Sci England). J K Burgess.
Water Pollution Control Federation. Industrial Wastes Symposia: Proceedings. Date not set. pap. 20.00 (ISBN 0-686-30423-3). Water Pollution.
Williams, Roy E. Waste Production & Disposal in Mining, Milling & Metallurgical Industries. LC 74-20167. (A World Mining Book). (Illus.). 489p. 1975. 45.00 (ISBN 0-87930-035-3). Miller Freeman.
Yehaskel, Albert. Industrial Wastewater Cleanup: Recent Developments. LC 79-12395. (Pollution Technology Review Ser.: No. 57). (Illus.). 1979. 39.00 (ISBN 0-8155-0758-5). Noyes.

FACTORY BUILDINGS
see Factories

FACTORY COSTS
see Manufactures-Costs

FACTORY DESIGN
see Factories-Design and Construction

FACTORY HOUSEKEEPING
see Industrial Housekeeping

FACTORY LAWS AND LEGISLATION
see also Employers' Liability; Industrial Accidents; Labor Laws and Legislation

Hutchins, Elizabeth L. & Harrison, A. A History of Factory Legislation. LC 74-22746. Repr. of 1926 ed. 19.50 (ISBN 0-404-58498-5). AMS Pr.
Hutchins, Elizabeth L. & Harrison, Amy. History of Factory Legislation. 298p. 1966. Repr. 25.00x (ISBN 0-7146-1324-X, F Cass Co). Biblio Dist.
LaDou. Occupational Health Law: A Guide for Industry. (Occupational Safety & Health Ser.: Vol. 7). 232p. 1981. 24.50 (ISBN 0-8247-1329-X). Dekker.
Thomas, Maurice W. Early Factory Legislation. Repr. of 1948 ed. lib. bdg. 19.75x (ISBN 0-8371-3432-3, THFL). Greenwood.
Whitin, Ernest S. Factory Legislation in Maine. LC 78-76681. (Columbia University. Studies in the Social Sciences: No. 86). Repr. of 1908 ed. 15.00 (ISBN 0-404-51086-8). AMS Pr.

FACTORY LAWS AND LEGISLATION–GREAT BRITAIN

The Factory Act of Eighteen Nineteen: 1818-1819. LC 72-2524. (British Labour Struggles Before 1850 Ser). (6 pamphlets). 1972. Repr. 14.00 (ISBN 0-405-04417-8). Arno.
The Factory Act of Eighteen Thirty Three. LC 72-2525. (British Labour Struggles Before 1850 Ser). (8 pamphlets). 1972. Repr. 12.00 (ISBN 0-405-04418-6). Arno.
The Factory Education Bill of Eighteen Forty Three. LC 72-2526. (British Labour Struggles Before 1850 Ser.). (6 pamphlets). 10.00 (ISBN 0-405-04419-4). Arno.
Hutchins, Elizabeth L. & Harrison, A. History of Factory Legislation. LC 74-121219. (Research & Source Works Ser.: No. 612). 1971. Repr. lib. bdg. 20.50 (ISBN 0-8337-3348-6). B Franklin.
Prelude to Victory of the Ten Hour Movement: 1844. LC 72-2536. (British Labour Struggles Before 1850 Ser). (4 pamphlets). 1972. 10.00 (ISBN 0-405-04429-1). Arno.
Thomas, Maurice W. Early Factory Legislation. Repr. of 1948 ed. lib. bdg. 19.75x (ISBN 0-8371-3432-3, THFL). Greenwood.

FACTORY LAYOUT
see Factories-Design and Construction

FACTORY MANAGEMENT
see also Assembly-Line Methods; Industrial Engineering; Office Management; Personnel Management; Plant Engineering; Production Control; Production Engineering; Quality Control; Supervisors, Industrial

Amrine, Harold & Ritchey, John A. Manufacturing Organization & Management. 4th ed. (Illus.). 576p. 1982. 19.95 (ISBN 0-13-555748-8). P-H.
Baron, Stephen L. Manual of Energy Saving in Existing Buildings & Plants, Vol. I. (Illus.). 1978. 29.95 (ISBN 0-13-553578-6, Busn). P-H.
Cannons, H. G. Bibliography of Industrial Efficiency & Factory Management. LC 72-9506. (Management History Ser.: No. 18). 175p. 1973. Repr. of 1920 ed. 17.50 (ISBN 0-87960-021-7). Hive Pub.
Casson, Herbert N. Factory Efficiency: How to Increase Output, Wages, Dividends & Good-Will. Chandler, Alfred D., ed. LC 79-7537. (History of Management Thought & Practice Ser.). 1980. Repr. of 1917 ed. lib. bdg. 15.00x (ISBN 0-405-12322-1). Arno.
Chandler, Alfred, ed. Pioneers in Modern Factory Management: An Original Anthology. LC 79-7526. (History of Management Thought & Practice Ser.). 1980. lib. bdg. 16.00x (ISBN 0-405-12310-8). Arno.
Diemer, Hugo. Factory Organization & Administration, 2 vols. in 1. Chandler, Alfred D., ed. LC 79-7542. (History of Management Thought & Practice Ser.). 1980. Repr. of 1935 ed. lib. bdg. 58.00x (ISBN 0-405-12326-4). Arno.
Drury, Horace B. Scientific Management. 2nd rev. ed. LC 68-56654. (Columbia University. Studies in the Social Sciences: No. 157). 1922. 21.00 (ISBN 0-404-51157-0). AMS Pr.
Elbourne, Edward T. Factory Administration & Accounts. Chandler, Alfred D., ed. LC 79-7543. (History of Management Thought & Practice Ser.). 1980. Repr. of 1919 ed. lib. bdg. 48.00x (ISBN 0-405-12327-2). Arno.
Gedye, G. R. Scientific Method in Production Management. (Illus.). 1965. 8.50x (ISBN 0-19-859802-5). Oxford U Pr.
Guide to Operation "F". 95p. 1973. 5.00 (ISBN 0-686-70975-6, APO23, APO). Unipub.
Haber, Samuel. Efficiency & Uplift: Scientific Management in the Progressive Era, 1890-1920. (Midway Reprint Ser). 1973. Repr. of 1964 ed. pap. 6.50x (ISBN 0-226-31172-4). U of Chicago Pr.
Heyel, Carl. Foreman's Handbook. 4th ed. 1967. 25.50 (ISBN 0-07-028627-2, P&RB). McGraw.
Hoxie, Robert F. Scientific Management & Labor. LC 66-21677. Repr. of 1915 ed. 15.00x (ISBN 0-678-00169-3). Kelley.
Kratfel, Edward R. & Drake, George R. Modern Shop Procedures. LC 73-19644. (Illus.). 368p. 1974. pap. text ed. 8.95 (ISBN 0-87909-505-9). Reston.
Lockyer, K. G. Factory & Production Management. 3rd ed. 1974. 14.95x (ISBN 0-8464-0398-6). Beekman Pubs.
Ritchey, John A. & Hulley, O. S. Manufacturing Organization & Management. 3rd ed. (Int'l. Series in Industrial & Systems Engineering). (Illus.). 608p. 1975. 19.95 (ISBN 0-13-555854-9). P-H.
Ronken, Harriet O. & Lawrence, Paul R. Administering Changes: A Case Study of Human Relations in a Factory. LC 72-5458. 324p. 1972. Repr. of 1952 ed. lib. bdg. 15.75x (ISBN 0-8371-6437-0, ROAD). Greenwood.
Rudman, Jack. Superintendent of Plant Operations. (Career Examination Ser.: C-2478). (Cloth bdg. avail. on request). pap. 12.00 (ISBN 0-8373-2478-5). Natl Learning.
Saunders, N. F. Factory Organization & Management. 5th ed. 1973. 14.95x (ISBN 0-8464-0399-4). Beekman Pubs.
Shepard, George H. The Application of Efficiency Principles. LC 73-10363. (Management History Ser.: No. 59). 378p. Repr. of 1917 ed. 22.50 (ISBN 0-87960-061-6). Hive Pub.
Taylor, Frederick W. Scientific Management, Comprising Shop Management, the Principles of Scientific Management, & Testimony Before the Special House Committee, 3 vols. in 1. LC 77-138133. (Illus.). Repr. of 1947 ed. lib. bdg. 33.50x (ISBN 0-8371-5706-4, TASM). Greenwood.
Thumann, Albert. Plant Engineers & Managers Guide to Energy Conservation. 1977. text ed. 22.50 (ISBN 0-442-28510-8). Van Nos Reinhold.

FACTORY NOISE
see Industrial Noise

FACTORY PROTECTION
see Factories-Protection

FACTORY SANITATION
see also Industrial Housekeeping

FACTORY SCHOOLS
see Evening and Continuation Schools

FACTORY SYSTEM
see also Children-Employment; Factories; Factory Laws and Legislation

Anderson, Sherwood. Perhaps Women. LC 76-105301. 1970. Repr. of 1931 ed. 8.95 (ISBN 0-911858-05-9). Appel.
Chenery, William L. Industry & Human Welfare. Stein, Leon, ed. LC 77-70487. (Work Ser.). 1977. Repr. of 1922 ed. lib. bdg. 15.00x (ISBN 0-405-10159-7). Arno.
Dodd, George. Days at the Factories: Manufacturing in the Nineteenth Century. (Illus.). 408p. 1975. Repr. of 1843 ed. 16.95x (ISBN 0-8464-0313-7). Beekman Pubs.
Dubreuil, Hyacinth. Robots or Men: French Workman's Experience in American Industry. Stein, Leon, ed. LC 77-70491. (Work Ser.). 1977. Repr. of 1930 ed. lib. bdg. 18.00x (ISBN 0-405-10163-5). Arno.
Fielden, John. Curse of the Factory System. 2nd rev. ed. 74p. 1969. 25.00x (ISBN 0-7146-1394-0, F Cass Co). Biblio Dist.
Foner, Philip S., ed. The Factory Girls: A Collection of Writings on Life & Struggles in the New England Factories of the 1840s. LC 77-22410. 1977. 17.50 (ISBN 0-252-00422-1). U of Ill Pr.
Goldmann, Robert B. A Work Experiment: Six Americans in a Swedish Plant. LC 75-45049. 48p. 1976. pap. 3.50 (ISBN 0-916584-00-3). Ford Found.
Hayek, Friedrich A., ed. Capitalism & the Historians. 1954. 9.00x (ISBN 0-226-32071-5). U of Chicago Pr.
--Capitalism & the Historians. 1963. pap. 3.95 (ISBN 0-226-32072-3, P120, Phoen). U of Chicago Pr.
Kolaja, Jiri. A Polish Factory. LC 73-10736. 157p. 1973. Repr. of 1960 ed. lib. bdg. 15.00x (ISBN 0-8371-7026-5, KOPF). Greenwood.
Kydd, Samuel. History of the Factory Movement from the Year Eighteen Hundred Two to the Enactment of the Ten Hours Bill in Eighteen Forty Seven, 2 vols. in 1. 1965. Repr. of 1857 ed. 30.50 (ISBN 0-8337-1967-X). B Franklin.
Kydd, Samuel A. History of the Factory Movement, 2 Vols. in 1. LC 66-18320. Repr. of 1857 ed. 25.00x (ISBN 0-678-00163-4). Kelley.
Nelson, Daniel. Managers & Workers: Origins of the New Factory System in the United States, 1880-1920. 1975. 20.00x (ISBN 0-299-06900-1). U of Wis Pr.
--Managers & Workers: Origins of the New Factory System in the United States, 1880-1920. 1975. pap. 6.95 (ISBN 0-299-06904-4). U of Wis Pr.
Scoresby, William. American Factories & Their Female Operatives: With an Appeal on Behalf of the British Factory Population & Suggestions for the Improvement of Their Condition. (Research & Source Works Ser.: No. 184). 1967. Repr. of 1845 ed. 19.00 (ISBN 0-8337-3206-4). B Franklin.
Stein, Leon, ed. Work or Labor: Original Anthology. LC 77-70551. (Work Ser.). (Illus.). 1977. lib. bdg. 28.00x (ISBN 0-405-10205-4). Arno.
Ure, Andrew. Philosophy of Manufactures. 3rd ed. 1969. 29.50 (ISBN 0-8337-3599-3). B Franklin.
Wing, Charles, compiled by. Evils of the Factory System Demonstrated by Parliamentary Evidence. LC 67-19730. Repr. of 1837 ed. 27.50x (ISBN 0-678-05096-1). Kelley.

FACTORY SYSTEM–GREAT BRITAIN

The Battle for the Ten Hour Day Continues: 1837-1843. LC 72-2519. (British Labour Struggles Before 1850 Ser). 1972. Repr. 12.00 (ISBN 0-405-04412-7). Arno.
Conditions of Work & Living: The Reawakening of the English Conscience, 1838-1844. LC 72-2520. (British Labour Struggles Before 1850 Ser). (5 pamphlets). 1972. Repr. 11.00 (ISBN 0-405-04413-5). Arno.
Dodd, William. Factory System Illustrated. LC 67-28260. (Illus.). Repr. of 1842 ed. 24.00x (ISBN 0-678-05043-0). Kelley.
--Factory System Illustrated. 3rd ed. 319p. 1968. Repr. of 1842 ed. 30.00x (ISBN 0-7146-1389-4, F Cass Co.). Biblio Dist.
--Labouring Classes of England. LC 68-55703. Repr. of 1847 ed. 13.50x (ISBN 0-678-00961-9). Kelley.
Fang, Hsien-T'Ing. The Triumph of the Factory System in England. LC 78-15111. (Perspectives in European History Ser.: No. 17). (Illus.). 310p. Repr. of 1930 ed. lib. bdg. 22.50x (ISBN 0-87991-624-9). Porcupine Pr.
Fielden, John. Curse of the Factory System. LC 68-23399. Repr. of 1836 ed. 15.00x (ISBN 0-678-05010-4). Kelley.
Fitton, R. S. & Wadsworth, A. P. Strutts & the Arkwrights, 1758-1830. LC 72-375. Repr. of 1958 ed. 17.50x (ISBN 0-678-06758-9). Kelley.
Gaskell, Peter. Artisans & Machinery. LC 68-28259. Repr. of 1836 ed. 30.00x (ISBN 0-678-05047-3). Kelley.
--The Manufacturing Population of England. LC 73-38266. (The Evolution of Capitalism Ser.). 374p. 1972. Repr. of 1833 ed. 19.00 (ISBN 0-405-04120-9). Arno.
Prelude to Victory of the Ten Hour Movement: 1844. LC 72-2536. (British Labour Struggles Before 1850 Ser). (4 pamphlets). 1972. 10.00 (ISBN 0-405-04429-1). Arno.
Richard Oastler: King of Factory Children, 1835-61. LC 72-2541. (British Labour Struggles Before 1850 Ser). 1972. 14.00 (ISBN 0-405-04433-X). Arno.
Taylor, William C. Notes of a Tour in the Manufacturing Districts of Lancashire. LC 67-131562. Repr. of 1842 ed. 17.50x (ISBN 0-678-05088-0). Kelley.
The Ten Hours Movement in 1831 & 1832. LC 72-2548. (British Labour Struggles Before 1850 Ser). (7 pamphlets). 1972. 12.00 (ISBN 0-405-04439-9). Arno.
Wing, C. Evils of the Factory System Demonstrated by Parliamentary Evidence. 498p. 1967. 35.00x (ISBN 0-7146-1049-6, F Cass Co). Biblio Dist.

FACTORY WASTE
see Factory and Trade Waste

FACULTY (EDUCATION)
see College Teachers; Educators; Teachers; Universities and Colleges-Faculty

FACULTY-PRINCIPAL RELATIONSHIPS
see Teacher-Principal Relationships

FAGAN, MARK, G. 1869

Steffens, Lincoln. Upbuilders. LC 68-19419. (Americana Library Ser: No. 6). (Illus.). 373p. 1968. pap. 2.95 (ISBN 0-295-95036-6). U of Wash Pr.

FAIENCE
see Pottery

FAILURE IN BUSINESS
see also Business Mortality

Banta, Martha. Failure & Success in America: A Literary Debate. LC 78-51156. 1978. text ed. 30.00 (ISBN 0-691-06366-4); pap. 12.50 (ISBN 0-691-10070-5). Princeton U Pr.
Van Frederikslust, R. A. I. Predictability of Corporate Failure. 1978. lib. bdg. 26.00 (ISBN 90-207-0736-1, Pub. by Martinus Nijhoff Netherlands). Kluwer Boston.

FAILURE (PSYCHOLOGY)

Fitzgerald, Ernest A. How to Be a Successful Failure. LC 77-13463. 1978. 6.95 (ISBN 0-689-10842-7). Atheneum.
Ginter, Joe. I Wanted to Be Famous. (Illus.). 1981. pap. 5.00 (ISBN 0-682-49806-8). Exposition.
Hobbs, John. The Failure. 1979. 7.95 (ISBN 0-533-03700-X). Vantage.

Lewis, Robert T. Taking Chances: The Psychology of Losing & How to Profit from It. 1979. 7.95 (ISBN 0-395-27606-3). HM.
Morris, Ivan. The Nobility of Failure. 1976. pap. 4.95 (ISBN 0-452-00447-0, F447, Mer). NAL.
Raudsepp, Eugene. Success & Failure. (Best Thoughts Ser.). (Illus.). 80p. (Orig.). 1981. pap. 2.50 (ISBN 0-8431-0390-6). Price Stern.
Steele, Bill. The Need to Fail. 72p. 1974. pap. text ed. 3.50x (ISBN 0-89039-060-6). Ann Arbor Pubs.

FAILURE OF METALS
see Metals–Fracture

FAILURE OF SOLIDS
see Fracture Mechanics

FAILURE TO ASSIST IN EMERGENCIES
see Assistance in Emergencies

FAINTING
see Syncope (Pathology)

FAIR BUILDINGS
see Exhibition Buildings

FAIR EMPLOYMENT PRACTICE
see Discrimination in Employment; United States–Committee on Fair Employment Practice

FAIR HOUSING
see Discrimination in Housing

FAIR TRADE
see Competition, Unfair; Price Maintenance

FAIR TRADE (TARIFF)
see Free Trade and Protection; Reciprocity

FAIR USE (COPYRIGHT)
see also Copyright and Electronic Data Processing

Association for Educational Communications & Technology & Association of Media Producers. Copyright & Educational Media: A Guide to Fair Use & Permissions Procedures. 1977. pap. 3.95 (ISBN 0-89240-004-8). Assn Ed Comm Tech.
Henry, Nicholas L., ed. Copyright, Congress & Technology: The Public Record, 5 vols. Incl. The Formative Years, 1958-1966. (Vol. I). 1979. 22.50 (ISBN 0-912700-29-7); The Political Years, 1967-1973. (Vol. II). 1979. 22.50 (ISBN 0-912700-30-0); The Future of Copyright, 1973-1977. (Vol. III). 1980. 22.50 (ISBN 0-912700-31-9); The Future of Information Technology. (Vol. IV). 1980. 22.50 (ISBN 0-912700-32-7); Vol. V. Contu's Report & Recommendations. 1980. 22.50 (ISBN 0-912700-74-2). LC 78-2347. Set. 95.00x (ISBN 0-912700-13-0). Oryx Pr.
Lawrence, John S. & Timberg, Bernard, eds. Fair Use & Free Inquiry: Copyright Law & the New Media. (Communication & Information Science Ser.). 1980. 32.50 (ISBN 0-89391-028-7). Ablex Pub.
The New Copyright Law: Questions Teachers & Librarians Ask. 76p. 1977. pap. 2.00 (ISBN 0-686-63694-5, 1394-8-06). NEA.
Seltzer, Leon E. Exemptions & Fair Use in Copyright: The Exclusive Rights Tensions in the 1976 Copyright Act. LC 77-13676. 1978. 17.50x (ISBN 0-674-27335-4). Harvard U Pr.
Spoor, J. H., et al. Copies in Copyright. Jehoram, Herman C., ed. LC 80-50456. (Monographs on Industrial Property & Copyright Law: Vol. IV). 187p. 1980. 37.50x (ISBN 90-286-0350-6). Sijthoff & Noordhoff.

FAIRBAIRN, WILLIAM, SIR, 1789-1874
Pole, William, ed. The Life of Sir William Fairbairn, (1877) 552p. 1970. 8.95 (ISBN 0-7153-4890-6). David & Charles.

FAIRBANKS, DOUGLAS, SR., 1883-1939
Herndon, Booton. Mary Pickford & Douglas Fairbanks: The Most Popular Couple the World Has Known. (Illus.). 1977. 9.95 (ISBN 0-393-07508-7). Norton.

FAIRBANKS, ALASKA
Dixon, Mim. What Happened to Fairbanks? The Effects of the Trans-Alaska Oil Pipeline on the Community of Fairbanks, Alaska. (Social Impact Assessment Ser.: No. 1). (Illus.). 337p. 1980. pap. text ed. 9.50x (ISBN 0-89158-961-9). Westview.
Fears, Jerry. Boom, Cash, & Balderdash: A Different Look at Fairbanks During Pipeline Construction. LC 77-87430. (Illus.). 1978. 8.95 (ISBN 0-918270-02-2). That New Pub.
Naske, Claus M. & Rowinski, Ludwig J. Fairbanks: A Pictorial History. Friedman, Donna R., ed. LC 80-27429. (Illus.). 208p. 1981. pap. 12.95 (ISBN 0-89865-108-5). Donning Co.
Sessions, Frank Q. Fairbanks Community Survey: A Profile of Poverty. (Institute of Social, Economic & Government Research: No. 16). (Illus.). 75p. 1967. pap. 5.00 (ISBN 0-295-95113-3). U of Wash Pr.

FAIRFAX, THOMAS FAIRFAX, 6TH BARON, 1692-1782
Brown, Stuart E. Virginia Baron: The Story of Thomas, Sixth Lord of Fairfax. LC 65-19262. (Illus.). 245p. 1965. 12.50 (ISBN 0-685-65062-6). Va Bk.
Morrison, Charles. The Fairfax Line: A Profile in History & Geography. (Illus.). 1970. pap. 1.75 (ISBN 0-87012-085-9). McClain.

FAIRFAX COUNTY, VIRGINIA–HISTORY
Dawson, Grace. No Little Plans: Fairfax County's PLUS Program with Managing Growth. 168p. 1977. pap. 3.95 (ISBN 0-87766-185-5, 17100). Urban Inst.
Fairfax County Historical Highlights. LC 67-16331. (Illus.). 1967. pap. 2.00 (ISBN 0-87714-027-8). Denlingers.
Netherton, Nan, et al. Fairfax County, Virginia: A History. LC 77-95356. (Illus.). 1978. 15.00 (ISBN 0-686-24339-0). Fairfax County.

FAIRIES
Arrowsmith, Nancy & Moorse, George. A Field Guide to the Little People. 1978. pap. 3.95 (ISBN 0-671-79036-6, Wallaby). PB.
Barker, Cicely M., illus. ABC of Flower Fairies. (Illus.). 1980. pap. 3.95 (ISBN 0-216-90720-9, Pub. by Blackie England). Hippocrene Bks.
--Flower Fairies Birthday Book. (Illus.). 157p. 1980. 5.95 (ISBN 0-216-90814-0, Pub. by Blackie England). Hippocrene Bks.
Briggs, Katharine M. Abbey Lubbers, Banshees & Boggarts: An Illustrated Encyclopedia of Fairies. LC 79-1897. 1979. 10.00 (ISBN 0-394-50806-8). Pantheon.
--An Encyclopedia of Fairies: Hobgoblins, Brownies, Bogies, & Other Supernatural Creatures. LC 76-12939. (Illus.). (gr. 4 up). 1978. pap. 4.95 (ISBN 0-394-73467-X). Pantheon.
--Fairies in Tradition & Literature. 1977. pap. 7.95 (ISBN 0-7100-8687-3). Routledge & Kegan.
--Personnel of Fairyland: A Short Account of the Fairy People of Great Britain for Those Who Tell Stories to Children. LC 70-147084. (Illus.). 1971. Repr. of 1953 ed. 19.00 (ISBN 0-8103-3372-4). Gale.
--The Vanishing People: Fairy Lore & Legends. LC 78-53523. (Illus.). 1978. 8.95 (ISBN 0-394-50248-5). Pantheon.
Briggs, Katherine M. The Anatomy of Puck: An Examination of Fairy Beliefs Among Shakespeare's Contemporaries & Successors. Dorson, Richard M., ed. LC 77-70581. (International Folklore Ser.). 1977. Repr. of 1959 ed. lib. bdg. 18.00x (ISBN 0-405-10082-5). Arno.
Cohen, Daniel. The Magic of the Little People. LC 73-19236. (Illus.). 96p. (gr. 3 up). 1974. PLB 6.64 (ISBN 0-671-32638-4). Messner.
Froud, Brian & Lee, Alan L., illus. The Faeries Pop-up Book. (Illus.). (ps-3). 1980. 7.95 (ISBN 0-8109-0910-3). Abrams.
Gardner, E. L. Fairies. 11.95 (ISBN 0-8356-5090-1). Theos Pub Hse.
Haining, Peter. The Leprechaun's Kingdom: The Irish World of Banshees, Fairies, Demons, Giants, Monsters, Mermaids, Phoukas, Vampires, Werewolves, Witches & Many Others. (Illus.). 128p. 1980. 12.95 (ISBN 0-517-54079-7, Harmony); pap. 5.95 (ISBN 0-517-54080-0). Crown.
Halliwell-Phillipps, James O. Illustrations of the Fairy Mythology of a Midsummer Night's Dream. LC 78-127903. Repr. of 1845 ed. 25.00 (ISBN 0-404-03058-0). AMS Pr.
Huygen, Wil. Gnomes. LC 77-82805. (Illus.). 1977. 17.50 (ISBN 0-8109-0965-0). Abrams.
Keightley. The Fairy Mythology. LC 74-16410. 1975. Repr. of 1870 ed. 30.00 (ISBN 0-8103-3466-6). Gale.
Lang, Andrew. The Blue Fairy Book. 7.50 (ISBN 0-8446-5495-7). Peter Smith.
--The Brown Fairy Book. 7.50 (ISBN 0-8446-5496-5). Peter Smith.
Lang, Andrew, ed. The Green Fairy Book. (Illus.). 7.50 (ISBN 0-8446-5056-0). Peter Smith.
Larkin, David, ed. Faeries. (Illus.). 1979. pap. 9.95 (ISBN 0-553-01159-6, M01159-6). Bantam.
--Faeries. (Illus.). 1978. 17.50 (ISBN 0-8109-0901-4). Abrams.
Latham, Minor W. The Elizabethan Fairies: The Fairies of Folklore & the Fairies of Shakespeare. LC 71-39032. 1972. Repr. of 1930 ed. lib. bdg. 17.50x (ISBN 0-374-94811-9). Octagon.
MacManus, Diarmuid. Irish Earth Folk. (Illus.). 1959. 6.95 (ISBN 0-8159-5814-5). Devin.
Macritchie, David. Fians, Fairies & Picts. LC 75-44195. 1976. Repr. of 1893 ed. lib. bdg. 12.50 (ISBN 0-8414-6147-3). Folcroft.
O'Brien, John. Elves, Gnomes & Other Little People: A Coloring Book. (Illus.). 48p. 1980. pap. 2.00 (ISBN 0-486-24049-5). Dover.
Paton, Lucy A. Studies in the Fairy Mythology of Arthurian Romance. 2nd enl. ed. Loomis, Roger S., ed. 1963. 22.50 (ISBN 0-8337-2683-8). B Franklin.
Phillpotts, Beatrice. The Book of Fairies. (Illus.). 1979. 15.00 (ISBN 0-345-28091-1). Ballantine.
Poorvliet, Rien & Huygen, Wil. Gnomes. 1979. pap. 9.95 (ISBN 0-553-01141-3). Bantam.
Rathborne, Isabel E. Meaning of Spenser's Fairyland. LC 64-66398. 1965. Repr. of 1937 ed. 8.50 (ISBN 0-8462-0569-6). Russell.
Stewart, W. Grant. The Popular Superstitions & Festive Amusements of the Highlanders of Scotland. 1978. Repr. of 1851 ed. lib. bdg. 25.00 (ISBN 0-8492-8007-9). R West.
Van Gelder, Dora. The Real World of Fairies. LC 77-5250. (Illus., Orig.). 1977. pap. 3.25 (ISBN 0-8356-0497-7, Quest). Theos Pub Hse.
White, Carolyn. History of Irish Fairies. 1976. pap. 3.95 (ISBN 0-85342-455-1). Irish Bk Ctr.

FAIRLEIGH DICKINSON UNIVERSITY
Barron's Profile of Fairleigh Dickinson University: Teaneck. (College Profiles Ser.). 1978. pap. text ed. 2.50 (ISBN 0-8120-1229-1). Barron.
Barron's Profile of Fairleigh Dickinson University: Madison. (College Profiles Ser.). 1978. pap. text ed. 2.50 (ISBN 0-8120-1230-5). Barron.
Barron's Profile of Fairleigh Dickinson University: Rutherford. (College Profiles Ser.). 1978. pap. text ed. 2.50 (ISBN 0-8120-1040-X). Barron.
Sammartino, Peter. Of Castles & Colleges: Notes toward an Autobiography. LC 72-167771. (Illus.). 300p. 1972. 8.50 (ISBN 0-498-01026-0). A S Barnes.

FAIRNESS
see also Justice
Braithwaite, Richard B. Theory of Games As a Tool for the Moral Philosopher. 1955. 15.50 (ISBN 0-521-04307-7). Cambridge U Pr.

FAIRS
see also Exhibitions; Markets
Albert, Maurice. Theatres de la foire, 1660-1789. LC 78-135169. (Drama Ser). 1971. Repr. of 1900 ed. 21.00 (ISBN 0-8337-0030-8). B Franklin.
Augur, Helen. The Book of Fairs. LC 75-159875. (Tower Bks). (Illus.). xviii, 308p. 1972. Repr. of 1939 ed. 24.00 (ISBN 0-8103-3927-7). Gale.
Better Homes & Gardens Books Editors. Easy Bazaar Crafts. (Illus.). 96p. 1981. 5.95 (ISBN 0-696-00665-0). Meredith Corp.
Birk, Dorothy D. The World Came to St. Louis: A Visit to the 1904 World's Fair. (Illus.). 1979. 10.95 (ISBN 0-8272-4213-1). Bethany Pr.
Dexter, Kerry. Bazaars, Fairs & Festivals: A How-to Book. 1978. pap. 4.50 (ISBN 0-8192-1238-5). Morehouse.
Distad, Audree. Come to the Fair. LC 77-3812. (Illus.). (gr. 3-7). 1977. 5.95 (ISBN 0-06-021686-7, HarpJ); PLB 6.49 (ISBN 0-06-021687-5). Har-Row.
Gale, Janice & Gale, Stephen. Guide to Fairs, Festivals & Fun Events. (Illus.). 190p. 1981. pap. 6.95 (ISBN 0-937928-00-3). Sightseer.
Hilton, Suzanne. Here Today & Gone Tomorrow: The Story of World Fairs & Expositions. 1978. 8.95 (ISBN 0-664-32633-1). Westminster.
Konikow, Robert. How to Participate Profitably in Trade Shows. 1977. 65.50 (ISBN 0-85013-074-3). Dartnell Corp.
Life in America: A Special Loan, Exhibition of Paintings Held During the Period of the New York World's Fair, April 24 to October 29 (1939) LC 70-168423. (Metropolitan Museum of Art Publications in Reprint). (Illus.). 262p. 1972. Repr. of 1939 ed. 19.00 (ISBN 0-405-02261-1). Arno.
Linsley, Leslie. The Great Bazaar. (Illus.). 1981. 17.95 (ISBN 0-440-03077-3). Delacorte.
Neely, Wayne C. Agricultural Fair. LC 73-181962. Repr. of 1935 ed. 17.50 (ISBN 0-404-04669-X). AMS Pr.
Perl, Lila. America Goes to the Fair: All About State & County Fairs in the U. S. A. LC 74-5938. 128p. (gr. 5-9). 1974. 7.25 (ISBN 0-688-21830-X); PLB 6.96 (ISBN 0-688-31830-4). Morrow.
Pierce, Jack. The State Fair Book. LC 79-91308. (Illus.). (ps-3). 1980. PLB 6.95g (ISBN 0-87614-124-6). Carolrhoda Bks.
Quertermous, Steve. Flea Market Trader. 3rd, rev. ed. (Illus.). 1980. pap. 7.95 (ISBN 0-89145-147-1). Collector Bks.
Sunrise Publishing Company Editors, ed. The Greatest of Expositions: St. Louis World's Fair, 1904. rev. ed. 1981. pap. 8.95 (ISBN 0-86629-029-X). Sunrise MO.
Tudor, Tasha. Corgiville Fair. LC 72-154042. (Illus.). (ps-3). 1971. 8.95 (ISBN 0-690-21791-9, TYC-J). Har-Row.
Walford, Cornelius. Fairs, Past & Present: A Chapter in the History of Commerce. 1967. Repr. of 1883 ed. 20.50 (ISBN 0-8337-3668-X). B Franklin.
--Fairs, Past & Present: A Chapter in the History of Commerce. LC 68-16699. Repr. of 1883 ed. 17.50x (ISBN 0-678-00367-X). Kelley.
Ware, Michael E. Historic Fairground Scenes. 96p. 1980. 21.00x (ISBN 0-903485-33-8, Pub. by Moorland England). State Mutual Bk.
White, Paul. Fairs & Circuses. (Junior Reference Ser.). (Illus.). 64p. (gr. 7 up). 1972. 7.95 (ISBN 0-7136-1323-8). Dufour.

FAIRS IN ART
Harkonen, Helen B. Circuses & Fairs in Art. LC 64-8205. (Fine Art Books). (Illus.). (gr. 5-11). 1965. PLB 4.95 (ISBN 0-8225-0156-2). Lerner Pubns.

FAIRY TALES
see also Folk-Lore; Legends; Tales
Afanas'Ev, Aleksandr, ed. Russian Fairy Tales. Guterman, Norbert, tr. from Rus. LC 45-37884. (Illus.). 664p. 1975. Repr. of 1945 ed. 14.95 (ISBN 0-394-49914-X). Pantheon.
Alice in Wonderland. (Illustrated Junior Library). (Illus.). 304p. 1981. pap. 4.95 (ISBN 0-448-11004-0). G&D.
Andersen, Hans. Stories from Hans Andersen. LC 79-50552. (Illus.). 1979. 35.00 (ISBN 0-913870-79-X). Abaris Bks.
Andersen, Hans C. Andersen's Fairy Tales. (Illus.). (gr. 4-6). 1945. companion lib. 2.95 (ISBN 0-448-05455-8); Illus. Junior Lib. pap. 4.95 (ISBN 0-448-11005-9); deluxe ed. 8.95 (ISBN 0-448-06005-1). G&D.
--Hans Andersen's Fairy Tales. Lewis, Naomi, ed. (Puffin Story Bk.). (Illus.). 176p. 1981. pap. 2.95 (ISBN 0-14-030333-2). Penguin.
--Hans Christian Andersen's Fairy Tales. (Classics Ser). (gr. 3 up). pap. 1.25 (ISBN 0-8049-0169-4, CL-169). Airmont.
--The Princess & the Pea. LC 77-12707. (Illus.). (ps-2). 1978. 8.95 (ISBN 0-395-28807-X, Clarion). HM.
--Tales & Stories by Hans Christian Andersen. Conroy, Patricia & Rossel, Sven H., trs. LC 80-50867. (Illus.). 316p. 1980. 17.50 (ISBN 0-295-95769-7). U of Wash Pr.
Andersen, Hans Christian. Hans Andersen's Fairy Tales. LC 79-20407. (Illus.). 96p. 1980. 9.95 (ISBN 0-8052-3732-1). Schocken.
--The Wild Swans. (Illus.). 32p. (gr. k-2). 1981. PLB 5.79 (ISBN 0-89375-480-3); pap. text ed. 1.50 (ISBN 0-89375-481-1). Troll Assocs.
Andersen's Fairy Tales. (Illustrated Junior Library). (Illus.). 352p. 1981. pap. 4.95 (ISBN 0-448-11022-9). G&D.
Anderson, Hans C. Fairy Tales of Hans Christian Anderson. (Illus.). 156p. 1981. 14.95 (ISBN 0-670-30557-X, Studio). Viking Pr.
Anglund, Joan W. Nibble Nibble Mousekin: A Tale of Hansel & Gretel. LC 62-14422. (Illus.). (gr. k-3). 1977. pap. 1.95 (ISBN 0-15-257404-2, VoyB). HarBraceJ.
Asbjornsen, Peter C. Tales from the Fjeld. Dasent, George W., tr. LC 69-13232. (Illus.). 1969. Repr. of 1896 ed. 20.00 (ISBN 0-405-08217-7). Arno.
Aurelio, John R. Story Sunday: Christian Fairy Tales for Children, Parents & Educators. LC 78-51587. 1978. pap. 3.50 (ISBN 0-8091-2115-8). Paulist Pr.
Bain, R. Nisbet, ed. Cossack Fairy Tales & Folk-Tales. LC 76-9882. (Children's Literature Reprint Ser). (Illus.). (gr. 4-6). 1976. 18.75x (ISBN 0-8486-0200-5). Core Collection.
Bain, Robert N., ed. & tr. Cossack Fairy Tales & Folk-Tales. LC 11-132. Repr. of 1894 ed. 14.00 (ISBN 0-527-04404-0). Kraus Repr.
Baldwin, James. Horse Fair. LC 76-9890. (Children's Literature Reprint Ser). (Illus.). (gr. 5-6). 1976. 19.75x (ISBN 0-8486-0201-3). Core Collection.
Baring-Gould, William S. & Baring-Gould, Ceil, eds. The Annotated Mother Goose. (Illus.). 350p. 1962. 10.00 (ISBN 0-517-02959-6). Crown.
Barker, Cicely M., illus. Flower Fairies Address Book. (Illus.). (gr. 1-8). 1980. 5.95 (ISBN 0-216-91027-7, Pub. by Blackie England). Hippocrene Bks.
--Flower Fairies Gift Pack. 1981. 11.95 (ISBN 0-216-91056-0, Pub. by Blackie England). Hippocrene Bks.
Basile, Giambattista. Petrosinella. (Illus.). 11.95 (ISBN 0-7232-6196-2); until 12/31/1981 10.95 (ISBN 0-686-77419-1). Warne.
Baum, L. Frank. American Fairy Tales. (Illus.). 6.75 (ISBN 0-8446-5731-X). Peter Smith.
--Dorothy & the Wicked Witch. Naden, C. J., ed. LC 79-84149. (Illus.). 32p. (gr. 2-5). 1980. PLB 6.89 (ISBN 0-89375-195-2); pap. 2.50 (ISBN 0-89375-191-X). Troll Assocs.
--Dorothy & the Wizard. Naden, C. J., ed. LC 79-84150. (Illus.). 32p. (gr. 2-5). 1980. PLB 6.89 (ISBN 0-89375-196-0); pap. 2.50 (ISBN 0-89375-192-8). Troll Assocs.
Bonville, W. J. Footnotes to a Fairytale: A Study in the Nature of Expression in the Arts. 192p. 1979. 15.00 (ISBN 0-87527-192-8). Green.
Book of Classic Fairy Tales. (Brimax Bks). 1978. 6.95 (ISBN 0-686-64103-5). Borden.
Bourhill, E. J. & Drake, J. B. Fairy Tales from South Africa. LC 78-67690. (The Folktale). (Illus.). Repr. of 1908 ed. 25.50 (ISBN 0-404-16058-1). AMS Pr.
Brenner, Barbara. Little One Inch. (Illus.). 32p. (ps-3). 1977. 6.95 (ISBN 0-698-20408-5). Coward.
Breznau. The Real Happily Ever After Book. (Illus.). (gr. k-3). 1980. pap. 6.95 (ISBN 0-913916-66-8, IP 66-8). Incentive Pubns.

Briggs, Raymond, illus. The Mother Goose Treasury. (Illus.). 224p. Date not set. 13.95 (ISBN 0-698-20094-2). Coward.
Brocket, E. Old European Fairy Tales. (gr. 1-4). 1971. 8.50 (ISBN 0-584-62385-2). Transatlantic.
Brothers Grimm. The Bremen Town Musicians. LC 79-16944. (Illus.). 32p. (gr. k-3). 1980. 7.95 (ISBN 0-688-80233-8); PLB 7.63 (ISBN 0-688-84233-X). Greenwillow.
--Cinderella. LC 80-15394. (Illus.). 32p. (gr. k-3). 1981. 7.95 (ISBN 0-688-80299-0); PLB 7.63 (ISBN 0-688-84299-2). Greenwillow.
--The Elves & the Shoemaker. (Illus.). 32p. (gr. k-2). 1981. PLB 5.79 (ISBN 0-89375-472-2); pap. text ed. 1.50 (ISBN 0-89375-473-0). Troll Assocs.
--Fairy Tales of the Brothers Grimm. (Illus.). 1979. 12.95 (ISBN 0-670-30565-0, Studio). Viking Pr.
--The Fisherman & His Wife. Shub, Elizabeth, tr. from Ger. LC 78-8133. (Illus.). (gr. k-3). 1979. 9.50 (ISBN 0-688-86003-6). Greenwillow.
--The Golden Goose. (Illus.). 32p. (gr. k-2). 1981. PLB 5.79 (ISBN 0-89375-476-5); pap. 1.50 (ISBN 0-89375-477-3). Troll Assocs.
--Little Red Riding Hood. (Illus.). 32p. (gr. k-2). 1981. PLB 5.79 (ISBN 0-89375-488-9); pap. 1.50 (ISBN 0-89375-489-7). Troll Assocs.
--The Seven Ravens. LC 77-14252. (Illus.). (gr. k-3). 1979. 6.95 (ISBN 0-670-63557-X). Viking Pr.
Brown, Beth, compiled by. Fairy Tales of Birds & Beasts, Vol. 1. (Illus.). 128p. (gr. 3-7). 1981. PLB 8.95 (ISBN 0-87460-375-7). Lion Bks.
Buj, Moira, illus. Mother Goose, Fourth Book. (Mother Goose Ser.). (Illus.). 12p. 1977. text ed. 1.75 (ISBN 0-85953-080-9, Pub. by Child's Play England). Playspaces.
Caraway, Caren. Cinderella. (A Stemmer House Story-to-Color Bk.). (Illus.). 32p. (Orig.). (ps-4). 1981. pap. 2.95 (ISBN 0-916144-85-2). Stemmer Hse.
--Snow White & the Seven Dwarfs. (Stemmer House Story-to-Color Bks). (Illus.). 32p. (ps up). 1980. pap. 2.95 (ISBN 0-916144-57-7). Stemmer Hse.
Carle, Eric. Seven Stories by Hans Christian Andersen. LC 78-2302. (Illus.). (gr. k-3). 1978. 7.90 (ISBN 0-531-02919-0); PLB 5.95 s&l (ISBN 0-531-02493-8). Watts.
Carroll, Lewis. Alice in Wonderland. (Pop-up Classics: No. 3). (Illus.). (ps up). 1968. 3.95 (ISBN 0-394-80898-3). Random.
Carruth, Jane, ed. Enchanted Tales. LC 78-7085. (Illus.). (gr. 1 up). 1978. 6.95 (ISBN 0-528-82206-3). Rand.
Chodzko, A. B. Fairy Tales of the Slav Peasants & Herdsmen. Repr. of 1896 ed. 20.00 (ISBN 0-527-16900-5). Kraus Repr.
Cinderella. Date not set. 1.75 (ISBN 0-394-84382-7). Random.
Cinderella. (Puppet Story Bks.). (ps-3). 1970. 2.95 (ISBN 0-448-09747-8). G&D.
Clouston, William A. Popular Tales & Fictions, Their Migrations & Transformations, 2 Vols. LC 67-23920. 1968. Repr. of 1887 ed. Set. 63.00 (ISBN 0-8103-3460-7). Gale.
Cohen, Barbara, retold by. Lovely Vassilisa. LC 80-12494. (Illus.). 48p. (ps-4). 1980. 9.95 (ISBN 0-689-30773-X). Atheneum.
Corrin, Stephen, tr. Ardizzone's Hans Andersen: Fourteen Classic Tales. LC 78-18908. (Illus.). (gr. 3 up). 1979. 10.95 (ISBN 0-689-50128-5, McElderry Bks). Atheneum.
The Cossack Chief. (Classics Illus. Ser.). (Illus.). pap. 0.59 (ISBN 0-685-74107-9, 164). Guild Bks.
Cuentos de Andersen. (Span.). 7.95 (ISBN 84-241-5629-3). E Torres & Sons.
Curtin, Jeremiah. Tales of the Fairies & the Ghost-World. LC 75-152760. Repr. of 1895 ed. 14.00 (ISBN 0-405-08416-1, Blom Pubns). Arno.
Daniels, Patricia. Aladdin & the Magic Lamp. LC 79-27304. (Raintree Fairy Tales). (Illus.). 24p. (gr. k-3). 1980. PLB 9.85 (ISBN 0-8393-0257-6). Raintree Child.
--Ali Baba & the Forty Thieves. LC 79-27042. (Raintree Fairy Tales). (Illus.). 24p. (gr. k-3). 1980. PLB 9.85 (ISBN 0-8393-0255-X). Raintree Child.
--Beauty & the Beast. LC 79-28433. (Raintree Fairy Tales). (Illus.). 24p. (gr. k-3). 1980. PLB 9.85 (ISBN 0-8393-0258-4). Raintree Child.
--Cinderella. LC 79-28526. (Raintree Fairy Tales). (Illus.). 24p. (gr. k-3). 1980. PLB 9.85 (ISBN 0-8393-0253-3). Raintree Child.
--Rumpelstiltskin. LC 79-27140. (Raintree Fairy Tales). (Illus.). 24p. (gr. k-3). 1980. PLB 9.85 (ISBN 0-8393-0252-5). Raintree Child.
--Sinbad the Sailor. LC 79-28588. (Raintree Fairy Tales). (Illus.). 24p. (gr. k-3). 1980. PLB 9.85 (ISBN 0-8393-0256-8). Raintree Child.
--Sleeping Beauty. LC 79-26974. (Raintree Fairy Tales). (Illus.). 24p. (gr. k-3). 1980. PLB 9.85 (ISBN 0-8393-0254-1). Raintree Child.
Dasent, George W. East O' the Sun & West O' the Moon. LC 70-97214. (gr. 1 up). 1970. pap. 4.50 (ISBN 0-486-22521-6). Dover.
D'Aulnoy, Marie C. White Cat & Other Old French Fairy Tales. Field, Rachel, tr. (Illus.). (gr. 1-6). 1967. 8.95 (ISBN 0-02-726250-2). Macmillan.
De Angeli, Marguerite. The Goose Girl. (ps-3). 4.95 (ISBN 0-385-05148-4). Doubleday.
Deans Book of Fairy Tales. (Illus.). 176p. 1981. 6.95 (ISBN 0-686-31196-5, 2200). Playmore & Prestige.
De Regniers, Beatrice. Red Riding Hood. (Illus.). 1977. pap. 1.95 (ISBN 0-689-70435-6, Aladdin). Atheneum.
Desparmet, J. Contes populaires sur les ogres, recueillis a Bilda, 2 vols. LC 78-20144. (Collection de contes et de chansons populaires: Vols. 35-36). Repr. of 1910 ed. Set. 43.00 (ISBN 0-404-60385-8). AMS Pr.
De Valera, Sinead. Irish Fairy Tales. (Illus.). 128p. 1973. pap. 1.95 (ISBN 0-330-23504-4, Pub. by Pan Bks England). Irish Bk Ctr.
--More Irish Fairy Tales. (Illus.). 123p. 1979. pap. 2.50 (ISBN 0-330-25669-6, Pub. by Pan Bks England). Irish Bk Ctr.
Diamond, Donna, adapted by. & illus. The Bremen Town Musicians: A Grimms' Fairytale. LC 80-36838. (Illus.). 32p. (gr. k-2). 1981. 8.95 (ISBN 0-440-00826-3); PLB 8.44 (ISBN 0-440-00827-1). Delacorte.
Disney, Walt. Cinderella. (Walt Disney Square Bks.). (Illus.). (gr. k-3). 1978. PLB 5.38 (ISBN 0-307-66087-7, Golden Pr). Western Pub.
Dolch, Edward W. & Dolch, M. P. Andersen Stories. (Pleasure Reading Ser.). (Illus.). (gr. 3-12). 1956. PLB 6.57 (ISBN 0-8116-2601-6). Garrard.
--Fairy Stories. (Pleasure Reading Ser). (gr. 3-12). 1950. PLB 6.57 (ISBN 0-8116-2600-8). Garrard.
Douglas, George B. & Dorson, Richard M., eds. Scottish Fairy & Folk Tales. LC 77-70591. (International Folklore Ser.). (Illus.). 1977. Repr. of 1901 ed. lib. bdg. 19.00x (ISBN 0-405-10092-2). Arno.
Dutfoy, Serge, illus. Cinderella. LC 79-18772. (Goodnight Bks). (Illus.). 24p. (gr. 1). 1980. 1.75 (ISBN 0-394-84382-7). Knopf.
Eberhard, Wolfram. Chinese Authors: Fairy Tales & Folk Tales. 1978. Repr. of 1937 ed. lib. bdg. 30.00 (ISBN 0-8492-0763-0). R West.
Eells, E. S., ed. Fairy Tales from Brazil. LC 17-25892. Repr. of 1917 ed. 16.00 (ISBN 0-527-26500-4). Kraus Repr.
Fillmore, Parker H. Czechoslovak Fairy Tales. LC 78-67709. (The Folktale). (Illus.). 1980. Repr. of 1919 ed. 23.50 (ISBN 0-404-16086-7). AMS Pr.
Francis, Joseph H. The Diamond Ring & Other Stories. 1979. 4.50 (ISBN 0-533-03748-4). Vantage.
Freeman, Cynthia. Fairytales. LC 76-50340. 1977. 8.95 (ISBN 0-87795-163-2). Arbor Hse.
Fujikawa, Gyo, illus. Fairy Tales. (Pandaback Ser.). (Illus.). 24p. (ps-3). 1980. PLB 7.65 (ISBN 0-448-13144-7); pap. 1.25 (ISBN 0-448-49615-1). Platt.
--Fairy Tales & Fables. (Illus.). (gr. k-3). 1970. 5.95 (ISBN 0-448-02814-X). G&D.
Gag, Wanda. More Tales from Grimm. (Illus.). (gr. 3-5). 1947. 6.95 (ISBN 0-698-20093-4). Coward.
--Tales from Grimm. (Illus.). (gr. 3-5). 1936. 7.95 (ISBN 0-698-20139-6). Coward.
Galdone, Paul. Cinderella. (Illus.). (gr. k-3). 1978. 7.95 (ISBN 0-07-022684-9, GB). McGraw.
Galdone, Paul, retold by. & illus. Hans in Luck. LC 79-16154. (Illus.). 48p. (ps-3). 1980. 4.95 (ISBN 0-8193-1011-5); PLB 5.95 (ISBN 0-8193-1012-3). Parents.
Gallico, Paul. The Snow Goose & Other Legends. (gr. 6-9). pap. 3.95 (ISBN 0-671-79055-2, Wallaby). PB.
Garcia, David. Fairy Tales of Puerto Rico. (Children's Bks: No. 166). (Illus.). 50p. (gr. 1-5). 1981. 8.95 (ISBN 0-934642-02-8). Puerto Rico Almanacs.
Giant Three-D Fairy Tales, 4 bks. (Illus.). 30p. 1981. write for info. (1430). Playmore & Prestige.
Gift Book of Fairy Tales. (Illus.). 124p. 1981. 6.95 (ISBN 0-686-31195-7, 2120). Playmore & Prestige.
Gift Book of Fairyland Tales. (Illus.). 124p. 1981. 6.95 (ISBN 0-686-31194-9, 2110). Playmore & Prestige.
Gilbert, W. S. Foggerty's Fairy, & Other Tales. 1980. Repr. of 1890 ed. lib. bdg. 35.00 (ISBN 0-89341-441-0). Longwood Pr.
Gorsline, Douglas, illus. Nursery Rhymes. LC 76-24168. (Picturebacks Ser). (Illus.). (ps-2). 1977. pap. 1.25 (ISBN 0-394-83550-6, BYR). Random.
Green, Roger L. Old Greek Fairy Tales. (Illus.). 1979. 8.95 (ISBN 0-7135-1849-9). Transatlantic.
Grimm. Household Stories by the Brothers Grimm. (Illus.). 7.25 (ISBN 0-8446-2167-6). Peter Smith.
Grimm & Grimm. Cinderella. Date not set. 14.95 (ISBN 0-85440-332-9). Dawne-Leigh.
Grimm Brothers. Grimms' Fairy Tales. (Classics Ser). (gr. 3 up). pap. 1.25 (ISBN 0-8049-0168-6, CL-168). Airmont.
--Grimms' Fairy Tales. (Illus.). (gr. 4-9). pap. 4.95 (ISBN 0-448-11009-1); companion lib. ed. 2.95 (ISBN 0-448-05460-4); deluxe ed. 8.95 (ISBN 0-448-06009-4). G&D.
--Grimms' Fairy Tales. Morel, Eve, ed. (Grow-up Books Ser.). (Illus.). (gr. k-3). 1962. 1.95 (ISBN 0-448-02251-6). G&D.
--The Musicians of Bremen. LC 74-78599. (Illus.). 6.95 (ISBN 0-88332-060-6). Larousse.
Grimm, Jacob & Grimm, Wilhelm. The Brothers Grimm: Popular Folk Tales. LC 77-17748. (gr. 3-8). 1978. 9.95 (ISBN 0-385-14356-7). Doubleday.
Grimm, Jakob. Grimm's Household Tales. 59.95 (ISBN 0-87968-214-0). Gordon Pr.
Grimm, Jakob L. Grimm's Household Tales, 2 Vols. Hunt, Margaret, tr. LC 68-31090. 1968. Repr. of 1884 ed. 44.00 (ISBN 0-8103-3463-1). Gale.
Grimm, Wilhelm K. & Grimm, Jacob. Household Stories of the Brothers Grimm. Crane, Lucy, tr. (Illus.). (gr. 3-9). 1886. pap. 3.50 (ISBN 0-486-21080-4). Dover.
Grimm Brothers. The Complete Grimm's Fairy Tales. Stern, James, ed. LC 44-40373. (gr. 6 up). 1976. pap. 5.95 (ISBN 0-394-70930-6). Pantheon.
--Grimm's Fairy Tales. Dobbs, Rose, ed. (Illus.). (gr. k-3). 1955. PLB 3.50 (ISBN 0-394-80657-3, BYR); PLB 4.39 (ISBN 0-394-90657-8). Random.
--Grimm's Fairy Tales. (Span. & Fr.). Span. ed. 3.95 (ISBN 0-685-23350-2); fr. ed 5.50 (ISBN 0-685-23351-0). French & Eur.
Grimms' Fairy Tales. (Illustrated Junior Library). (Illus.). 384p. 1981. pap. 4.95 (ISBN 0-448-11009-1). G&D.
Grosset Treasury of Fairy Tales. (gr. k-6). 1971. 4.95 (ISBN 0-448-12986-8). G&D.
Grundtvig, Svendt. Danish Fairy Tales. Cramer, J. Grant, tr. from Danish. (Illus.). 136p. (gr. k-5). 1972. pap. 3.50 (ISBN 0-486-22891-6). Dover.
Hans Andersen's Thumbelina. (Children's Library of Picture Bks.). (Illus.). 10p. (ps). 1979. 1.95 (ISBN 0-89346-135-0, TA38, Pub. by Froebel-Kan Japan). Heian Intl.
Hartland, Edwin S. Science of Fairy Tales: An Inquiry into Fairy Mythology. LC 68-31149. 1968. Repr. of 1891 ed. 26.00 (ISBN 0-8103-3464-X). Gale.
Haviland, Virginia. The Fairy Tale Treasury. (Illus.). 192p. Date not set. 12.95 (ISBN 0-698-20184-1). Coward.
--The Fairy Tale Treasury. (Illus.). 192p. (gr. k-4). 1972. PLB 8.49 (ISBN 0-698-30438-1). Coward.
--Favorite Fairy Tales Told in Czechoslovakia. (gr. 3 up). 1966. 7.95 (ISBN 0-316-35083-4). Little.
--Favorite Fairy Tales Told in India. LC 71-117019. (Illus.). 96p. (gr. k-3). 1973. 6.95g (ISBN 0-316-35055-9). Little.
--Favorite Fairy Tales Told in Ireland. (Illus.). (gr. 2-6). 1961. 7.95g (ISBN 0-316-35051-6). Little.
--Favorite Fairy Tales Told in Italy. (Illus.). (gr. 3 up). 1965. 6.95g (ISBN 0-316-35076-1). Little.
--Favorite Fairy Tales Told in Japan. (Illus.). (gr. 1-3). 1967. 7.95 (ISBN 0-316-35091-5); PLB (ISBN 0-316-35074-5). Little.
--Favorite Fairy Tales Told in Norway. (Illus.). (gr. 2-6). 1961. 7.95 (ISBN 0-316-35053-2). Little.
--Favorite Fairy Tales Told in Scotland. (Illus.). (gr. 3 up). 1963. 6.95 (ISBN 0-316-35043-5). Little.
--Favorite Fairy Tales Told in Spain. (Illus.). (gr. 3 up). 1963. 6.95 (ISBN 0-316-35047-8). Little.
--Favorite Fairy Tales Told in Sweden. (Illus.). (gr. 2-6). 1966. 6.95g (ISBN 0-316-35052-4). Little.
Hazen, Barbara. Wonderful Wizard of Oz. (Kids Paperbacks). (Illus.). (ps-4). 1977. PLB 7.62 (ISBN 0-307-62361-0, Golden Pr); pap. 1.95 (ISBN 0-307-12361-8). Western Pub.
Hearn, Lafcadio, et al. Japanese Fairy Tales. LC 78-74515. (Children's Literature Reprint Ser). (gr. 4-6). 1979. Repr. of 1918 ed. 16.75x (ISBN 0-8486-0218-8). Core Collection.
Heidi. (Illustrated Junior Library). (Illus.). 336p. 1981. pap. 4.95 (ISBN 0-448-11012-1). G&D.
In Freedom's Cause. (Classics Illus. Ser.). (Illus.). pap. 0.59 (ISBN 0-685-74104-4, 168). Guild Bks.
Irving, Washington. Spanish Papers. Irving, Pierre, ed. LC 78-74516. (Children's Literature Reprint Ser.). (gr. 7 up). 1979. Repr. of 1868 ed. 42.50x (ISBN 0-8486-0219-6). Core Collection.
Iwaya, Sazanami. Japanese Fairy Tales. (Illus.). 1938. pap. 6.95 (ISBN 0-89346-030-3, Pub. by Hokuseido Pr). Heian Intl.
Izawa, T. & Hijkata, S., illus. Hansel & Gretel. (Puppet Storybooks). (Illus.). 18p. (gr. k-2). 1981. 3.50 (ISBN 0-448-09754-0). G&D.
--Snow White & the Seven Dwarfs. (Puppet Storybooks). (Illus.). 18p. (gr. k-2). 1981. 3.50 (ISBN 0-448-09757-5). G&D.
Jacobs, J. Celtic Fairy Tales. (Illus.). 7.50 (ISBN 0-8446-2302-4). Peter Smith.
--English Fairy Tales. (Illus.). 6.75 (ISBN 0-8446-2303-2). Peter Smith.
Jacobs, Joseph. Celtic Fairy Tales. LC 67-24223. (Illus.). (ps-6). 1968. pap. 3.50 (ISBN 0-486-21826-0). Dover.
--English Fairy Tales. (Illus.). (gr. 3-6). 1898. pap. 3.00 (ISBN 0-486-21818-X). Dover.
--Indian Fairy Tales. (Illus.). (ps-4). 1969. pap. 3.50 (ISBN 0-486-21828-7). Dover.
--More Celtic Fairy Tales. LC 67-24224. (ps-6). 1968. pap. 3.00 (ISBN 0-486-21827-9). Dover.
Jacobs, Joseph, ed. Indian Fairy Tales. LC 76-9897. (Children's Literature Reprint Ser). (Illus.). (gr. 4-6). 1976. 17.00x (ISBN 0-8486-0205-6). Core Collection.
Japrisot, Sebastien. Trap for Cinderella. (Crime Monthly Ser). 1979. pap. 2.50 (ISBN 0-14-005364-6). Penguin.
Johnson, William D. Jack & the Beanstalk. (gr. 1-3). 1976. 6.95 (ISBN 0-316-46941-6). Little.
Keary, Annie & Keary, Eliza. Heroes of Asgard: Tales from Scandinavian Mythology. LC 76-9898. (Children's Literature Reprint Ser). (Illus.). (gr. 4-6). 1976. Repr. of 1870 ed. 16.00x (ISBN 0-8486-0206-4). Core Collection.
Keightley, T. Fairy Mythology. LC 68-26357. (Studies in Shakespeare, No. 24). 1969. Repr. of 1850 ed. lib. bdg. 39.95 (ISBN 0-8383-0281-5). Haskell.
Keightley, Thomas. Fairy Mythology. LC 68-55794. (Bohn's Antiquarian Library Ser). Repr. of 1850 ed. 17.50 (ISBN 0-404-50019-6). AMS Pr.
--Fairy Mythology. rev. ed. (Folklore & Society Ser). 1969. Repr. of 1860 ed. 23.00 (ISBN 0-384-29010-8). Johnson Repr.
Kingsley, Charles. The Heroes; or, Greek Fairy Tales. Repr. of 1882 ed. 20.00 (ISBN 0-686-20097-7). Quality Lib.
Kohen, Apy. Beauty & the Beast. (Illus.). 1980. pap. 15.95 (ISBN 0-914676-47-4). Star & Elephant.
Laboulaye, Edouard. Fairy Book: Fairy Tales of All Nations. Booth, Mary L., tr. LC 76-9899. (Children's Literature Reprint Ser). (Illus.). (gr. 4-6). 1976. Repr. of 1870 ed. 19.00x (ISBN 0-8486-0207-2). Core Collection.
--Last Fairy Tales. Booth, Mary L, tr. LC 76-9900. (Children's Literature Reprint Ser). (Illus.). (gr. 4-6). 1976. Repr. of 1866 ed. 19.50x (ISBN 0-8486-0208-0). Core Collection.
La Motte-Foque, Friedrich H. Undine. Gosse, Edmund, tr. from Ger. LC 76-48431. (Library of World Literature Ser.). 1978. Repr. of 1912 ed. 16.50 (ISBN 0-88355-558-1). Hyperion Conn.
Lang, A., ed. Grey Fairy Book. (Illus.). 7.50 (ISBN 0-8446-2424-1). Peter Smith.
Lang, Andrew. Aladdin & the Wonderful Lamp. LC 81-4861. (Illus.). (gr. 1 up). 1981. 10.95 (ISBN 0-670-11146-5). Viking Pr.
--Blue Fairy Book. Alderson, Brian, ed. LC 77-28343. (Illus.). 1978. 14.95 (ISBN 0-670-17481-5). Viking Pr.
--Favorite Andrew Dang Fairy Tale Books in Many Colors: Red, Green & Blue Fairy Tale Books. (Illus.). 1979. pap. 14.95 boxed set (ISBN 0-486-23407-X). Dover.
--Green Fairy Book. (Classics Ser). (Illus.). (gr. 4 up). 1969. pap. 0.75 (ISBN 0-8049-0197-X, CL-197). Airmont.
--Pink Fairy Book. (Illus.). (gr. 4-6). 1966. pap. 3.00 (ISBN 0-486-21792-2). Dover.
--Red Fairy Book. Alderson, Brian, ed. LC 77-28770. (Illus.). (gr. 4-6). 1978. 14.95 (ISBN 0-670-59110-6, Co-Pub by Kestrel Bks). Viking Pr.
--The Twelve Dancing Princesses. LC 66-10104. (Illus.). 48p. (gr. 1-3). 1980. pap. 2.95 (ISBN 0-03-057493-5). HR&W.
--Yellow Fairy Book. Alderson, Brian, ed. LC 79-4118. (The Colour Fairy Ser.). 1980. 14.95 (ISBN 0-670-79385-X). Viking Pr.
Lang, Andrew, ed. Blue Fairy Book. (Classics Ser). (Illus.). (gr. 4 up). 1969. pap. 1.25 (ISBN 0-8049-0196-1, CL-196). Airmont.
--Blue Fairy Book. (Illus.). (gr. 1-6). 1965. pap. 3.95 (ISBN 0-486-21437-0). Dover.
--Brown Fairy Book. (Illus.). (gr. 1-6). pap. 4.00 (ISBN 0-486-21438-9). Dover.
--Crimson Fairy Book. (Illus.). (gr. 4-6). 1966. pap. 4.00 (ISBN 0-486-21799-X). Dover.
--Green Fairy Book. (gr. 4-6). 1965. pap. 4.00 (ISBN 0-486-21439-7). Dover.
--Grey Fairy Book. (Illus.). (gr. 4-6). 1900. pap. 4.00 (ISBN 0-486-21791-4). Dover.
--Lilac Fairy Book. (Illus.). (ps-4). 1968. pap. 4.00 (ISBN 0-486-21907-0). Dover.
--Olive Fairy Book. (Illus.). (gr. 4-6). 1966. pap. 3.50 (ISBN 0-486-21908-9). Dover.
--Orange Fairy Book. (Illus.). (gr. 1-6). 1968. pap. 4.00 (ISBN 0-486-21909-7). Dover.

--Red Fairy Book. (Illus.). (gr. 4-6). pap. 3.50 (ISBN 0-486-21673-X). Dover.
--Violet Fairy Book. (Illus.). (gr. 4-6). pap. 3.50 (ISBN 0-486-21675-6). Dover.
--Yellow Fairy Book. (Illus.). (gr. 4-6). pap. 4.00 (ISBN 0-486-21674-8). Dover.
Leamy, Edmund. Fairy Minstrel of Glenmalure & Other Stories for Children. LC 76-9901. (Children's Literature Reprint Ser). (Illus.). (gr. 4-6). 1976. Repr. of 1913 ed. 15.00x (ISBN 0-8486-0210-2). Core Collection.
--Golden Spears & Other Fairy Tales. LC 76-9902. (Children's Literature Reprint Ser). (Illus.). (gr. 4-6). 1976. Repr. of 1928 ed. 15.00x (ISBN 0-8486-0211-0). Core Collection.
Lear, Edward. The Owl & the Pussycat. (Illus.). 1969. 6.95 (ISBN 0-316-51840-9, Pub. by Atlantic-Little Brown). Little.
Little Red Riding Hood. (Puppet Story Bks). 2.95 (ISBN 0-448-09749-4). G&D.
The Little Savage. (Classics Illus. Ser.). (Illus.). pap. 0.59 (ISBN 0-685-74106-0, 137). Guild Bks.
Lux, P. Fairy Tales from the Barbary Coast. (gr. 1-4). 1971. 7.95 (ISBN 0-584-62366-6). Transatlantic.
Macdonald, George. The Golden Key & Other Stories. (Macdonald Fairy Tales Ser.). 1979. pap. 1.95 (ISBN 0-89191-166-9). Cook.
--Macdonald Fairy Tales Gift Set. (Macdonald Fairy Tales Ser.). 1979. boxed gift set 6.95 (ISBN 0-89191-172-3). Cook.
Mace, Jean. Home Fairy Tales. Booth, Mary L., tr. from Fr. LC 78-74517. (Children's Literature Reprint Ser.). (Illus.). (gr. 4-5). 1979. Repr. of 1867 ed. 24.75x (ISBN 0-8486-0220-X). Core Collection.
McKinley, Robin. The Door in the Hedge. LC 80-21903. 224p. (gr. 7 up). 1981. 8.95 (ISBN 0-688-00312-5). Greenwillow.
McLenighan, Valjean. What You See Is What You Get. (Illus.). 32p. 1980. PLB 4.39 (ISBN 0-695-41370-8); pap. 1.50 (ISBN 0-695-31370-3). Follett.
MacManus, Seumas, ed. Donegal Fairy Stories. (Illus.). (gr. 4-6). 1968. pap. 3.50 (ISBN 0-486-21971-2). Dover.
Macourek, Milos. Curious Tales. 96p. (gr. 4 up). 1980. 11.95 (ISBN 0-19-271427-9). Oxford U Pr.
Manheim, Ralph, tr. Grimm's Tales for Young & Old: The Complete Stories. LC 76-56318. 1977. 14.95 (ISBN 0-385-11005-7). Doubleday.
--Rare Treasures from Grimm: Fifteen Little Known Tales. (Illus.). 112p. 1981. 12.95 (ISBN 0-385-14548-9); PLB (ISBN 0-385-14549-7). Doubleday.
Mehdevi, Anne S. Persian Folk & Fairy Tales. (Illus.). (gr. 5 up). 1965. PLB 5.99 (ISBN 0-394-91496-1). Knopf.
Miller, A. G., adapted by. Aladdin & the Wonderful Lamp. (Pop-Up Classics: No. 7). (Illus.). (ps up). 1970. 3.95 (ISBN 0-394-81105-4). Random.
Mozley, Charles, illus. Oscar Wilde Fairy Tales. (Illus.). 190p. (gr. 4-8). 1980. 7.95 (ISBN 0-370-01042-6, Pub. by Chatto Bodley Jonathan). Merrimack Bk Serv.
Onassis, Jacqueline, ed. The Firebird & Other Russian Fairy Tales. (Illus.). 1978. 12.95 (ISBN 0-670-31544-3, Studio). Viking Pr.
Opie, Iona & Opie, Peter. The Classic Fairy Tales. (Illus.). 352p. 1974. pap. 7.95 (ISBN 0-19-520219-8). Oxford U Pr.
--The Classic Fairy Tales. (Illus.). 1974. 22.50x (ISBN 0-19-211559-6). Oxford U Pr.
Otto, Svend S., illus. Tom Thumb. (Grimm's Fairy Tales). (Illus.). (gr. 2). 1976. PLB 4.95 (ISBN 0-88332-043-6, 8077). Larousse.
Ozaki, Yei Theodora, compiled by. The Japanese Fairy Book. LC 70-109415. (Illus.). 320p. (gr. 3-8). 1970. pap. 5.95 (ISBN 0-8048-0885-6). C E Tuttle.
Percy, Graham, illus. Sleeping Beauty. LC 79-18233. (Goodnight Bks). (Illus.). 24p. (gr. 1). 1980. 1.75 (ISBN 0-394-84384-3). Knopf.
Perrault, Charles. Cinderella. LC 72-93811. (Illus.). 32p. (gr. k-3). 1973. 6.95 (ISBN 0-87888-056-9). Bradbury Pr.
--Perrault's Fairy Tales. LC 72-79522. (Illus.). lib. bdg. 11.50x (ISBN 0-88307-606-3). Gannon.
--Perrault's Fairy Tales. LC 72-79522. (Illus.). (gr. 4-6). 1969. pap. 3.50 (ISBN 0-486-22311-6). Dover.
--The Sleeping Beauty. Walker, David, tr. & illus. LC 76-22697. (Illus.). (gr. k-5). 1977. PLB 8.79 (ISBN 0-690-01279-9, TYC-J). Har-Row.
Piper, Watty, ed. Stories That Never Grow Old. (Illus.). (ps-3). 4.95 (ISBN 0-448-42004-X). Platt.
Pyle, Howard. Pepper & Salt: Or Seasoning for Young Folks. LC 24-712. (Illus.). (gr. 1-5). PLB 9.89 (ISBN 0-06-024811-4, HarpJ). Har-Row.
--Wonder Clock. (Illus.). 8.50 (ISBN 0-8446-2767-4). Peter Smith.
--The Wonder Clock or, Four & Twenty Marvelous Tales, Being One for Each Hour of the Day. (Illus.). (gr. 3-6). pap. 4.50 (ISBN 0-486-21446-X). Dover.
Quiller-Couch, Arthur. Sleeping Beauty & Other Stories from the Old French. (Fairy Tale Ser.). (Illus.). 176p. 1980. 35.00 (ISBN 0-913870-98-6). Abaris Bks.
Rackham, Arthur. Arthur Rackham Fairy Book. (Illus.). (gr. 4-6). 1950. 10.00 (ISBN 0-397-30218-5, JBL-J). Har-Row.
Reeves, James. English Fables & Fairy Stories. (Oxford Myths & Legends). (Illus.). (gr. 6-12). 1978. Repr. of 1954 ed. 10.95 (ISBN 0-19-274101-2). Oxford U Pr.
Rhys, Ernest, ed. Fairy Gold: A Book of Old English Fairy Tales. facsimile ed. LC 77-114912. (Select Bibliographies Reprint Ser). 1907. 17.00 (ISBN 0-8369-5317-7). Arno.
Ritson, Joseph. Fairy Tales, Legends & Romances, Illustrating Shakespeare & Other Early English Writers. LC 70-174323. Repr. of 1875 ed. 29.00 (ISBN 0-404-05339-4). AMS Pr.
Roberts, Moss, ed. Chinese Fairy Tales & Fantasies. (Pantheon Fairy Tale & Folklore Library). (Illus.). 1980. pap. 4.95 (ISBN 0-394-73994-9). Pantheon.
Roberts, Moss, ed. & tr. Chinese Fairy Tales & Fantasies. LC 79-1894. 1979. 11.95 (ISBN 0-394-42039-X). Pantheon.
Rockwell, Anne. Up a Tall Tree. LC 79-7695. (Reading-on-My-Own Bks.). (Illus.). 64p. (gr. 2). 1981. 4.95a (ISBN 0-385-15556-5); PLB (ISBN 0-385-15557-3). Doubleday.
Rojankovsky, Feodor. Tall Book of Nursery Tales. LC 44-3881. (Tall Book Ser.). (Illus.). (ps-1). 1944. 5.95 (ISBN 0-06-025065-8, HarpJ); PLB 6.89 (ISBN 0-06-025066-6). Har-Row.
Roll-Hansen, Joan, ed. Time for Trolls: Fairy Tales from Norway. 3rd ed. (Norwegian Guides Ser). (Illus., Orig.). 1964. pap. 7.50x (ISBN 0-8002-2087-0). Intl Pubns Serv.
Ross, Tony. Jack & the Beanstalk. LC 80-67493. (Illus.). 32p. (gr. k-3). 1981. 8.95 (ISBN 0-440-04168-6); PLB 8.44 (ISBN 0-440-04174-0). Delacorte.
Ruskin, John. King of the Golden River. (Illus.). 1974. 5.00 (ISBN 0-87482-056-1). Wake-Brook.
Saunders, Susan. Wale's Tale. LC 79-21985. (Illus.). (gr. k-3). 1980. 8.95 (ISBN 0-670-74870-6). Viking Pr.
Segal, Lore. The Juniper Tree & Other Tales from Grimm. (Illus.). (gr. k-6). 1981. pap. 6.95 (ISBN 0-440-44331-8, YB). Dell.
Segovia, Gertrudis. The Spanish Fairy Book. Quinn, Elizabeth V., tr. LC 78-74519. (Children's Literature Reprint Ser.). (gr. 5-7). 1979. Repr. of 1918 ed. 22.50x (ISBN 0-8486-0222-6). Core Collection.
Shannon, George W. Humpty Dumpty. (Illus., Orig.). 1980. pap. 5.95 (ISBN 0-914676-37-7). Star & Elephant.
Sheldon, Aure. Of Cobblers & Kings. LC 77-24725. (Illus.). 40p. (ps-3). 1978. lib. bdg. 6.95 (ISBN 0-590-07728-7, Four Winds). Schol Bk Serv.
Slator, Lana. Giants & Gnomes Coloring Album. (Illus.). 32p. 1978. pap. 3.50 (ISBN 0-912300-94-9, 94-9). Troubador Pr.
Sologub, Fiodor K. Sweet-Scented Name & Other Fairy Tales & Stories. Graham, S., ed. LC 76-23900. (Classics of Russian Literature). 1977. 11.95 (ISBN 0-88355-519-0); pap. 3.95 (ISBN 0-88355-520-4). Hyperion Conn.
Spock, Marjorie. Fairy Worlds & Workers: A Natural History of the Middle Kingdom. (Illus.). 1980. pap. 5.95 (ISBN 0-916786-46-3). St George Bk Serv.
Stang, Judy, illus. Mother Goose. (Read-Aloud Bks.). (gr. k-3). 0.79 (ISBN 0-448-02003-3). Wonder.
Stephens, James. Irish Fairy Tales. LC 20-21207. (Illus.). (gr. 4 up). 1968. Repr. of 1920 ed. 9.95g (ISBN 0-02-788000-1). Macmillan.
--Irish Fairy Tales. LC 78-53630. (Illus.). 1978. 35.00 (ISBN 0-913870-77-3). Abaris Bks.
Story of Hansel & Gretel. (Children's Library of Picture Bks.). (Illus.). 10p. (ps). 1979. 1.95 (ISBN 0-89346-124-5, TA13, Pub. by Froebel-Kan Japan). Heian Intl.
Story of the Ugly Duckling. (Children's Library of Picture Bks.). (Illus.). 10p. 1971. 1.95 (ISBN 0-89346-126-1, TA35, Pub. by Froebel-Kan Japan). Heian Intl.
Tenggren, Gustav. The Tenggren Tell-It-Again Book. (Illus.). (gr. 1-3). 1942. 6.95 (ISBN 0-316-83724-5). Little.
Thomas, Vernon, ed. Fairy Tales from India. (Illus.). (gr. 1-9). 1979. 6.25 (ISBN 0-89744-137-0). Auromere.
Tolstoy, Leo. Fables & Fairy Tales. 1972. pap. 3.95 (ISBN 0-452-25302-0, Z5302, Plume). NAL.
Tudor, Tasha. Tasha Tudor Book of Fairy Tales. (Illus.). (ps-2). 1961. 4.95 (ISBN 0-448-44200-0). Platt.
Underhill, Zoe D., ed. The Dwarf's Tailor, & Other Fairy Tales. LC 78-74521. (Children's Literature Reprint Ser.). (gr. 4-5). 1979. Repr. of 1896 ed. 21.75x (ISBN 0-8486-0224-2). Core Collection.
Vetalapanchavimsati. Jambhaladatta's Version of the Vetalapancavinsati, Sanskrit & Eng. Emeneau, M. B., tr. 1934. pap. 12.00 (ISBN 0-527-02678-6). Kraus Repr.
Von Franz, M-L. Shadow & Evil in Fairytales. Hillman, James, ed. (Seminar Ser., No. 9). 250p. 1973. pap. 12.50 (ISBN 0-88214-109-0). Spring Pubns.
Wade, Mary H. Indian Fairy Tales As Told to the Little Children of the Wigwam. LC 78-74523. (Children's Literature Reprint Ser.). (Illus.). (gr. 4-8). 1979. Repr. of 1906 ed. 21.75x (ISBN 0-8486-0225-0). Core Collection.
Wilde, Oscar. The Happy Prince. (Illus.). (gr. 2-5). 1981. 12.95 (ISBN 0-686-76774-8). Oxford U Pr.
--The Happy Prince & Other Tales. LC 79-3512. (Illus.). 1980. pap. 6.95 (ISBN 0-394-73881-0). Shambhala Pubns.
Williams, Jay. The Water of Life. LC 79-19438. (Illus.). 40p. (gr. k-3). 1980. 8.95 (ISBN 0-590-07530-6, Four Winds). Schol Bk Serv.
Wizard of Oz. (Illustrated Junior Library). (Illus.). 224p. 1981. pap. 4.95 (ISBN 0-448-11026-1). G&D.
Yearsley, Macleod. Folklore of Fairy-Tale. LC 68-31517. 1968. Repr. of 1924 ed. 22.00 (ISBN 0-8103-3457-7). Gale.
Yolen, Jane. The Hundreth Dove & Other Tales. LC 77-1591. (Illus.). (gr. 3-7). 1977. 8.95 (ISBN 0-690-01366-3, TYC-J). Har-Row.
Zuromskis, Diane, illus. Farmer in the Dell. (Illus.). (gr. 1-3). 1978. 6.95 (ISBN 0-686-63889-1). Little.

FAIRY TALES–CLASSIFICATION

see also Literature, Comparative–Themes, Motives; Plots (Drama, Novel, etc.)

Andersen, Hans C. Michael Hague's Favorite Hans Christian Andersen Fairy Tales. LC 81-47455. (Illus.). 176p. (gr. 4 up). 1981. 16.95 (ISBN 0-03-059528-2). HR&W.
Bergsten, Staffan. Mary Poppins & Myth. (Illus.). 1978. text ed. 14.25x (ISBN 91-22-00127-1). Humanities.
Briggs, Raymond. The Fairy Tale Treasury. Haviland, Virginia, ed. (gr. k-6). 1980. pap. 6.95 (ISBN 0-440-42556-5, YB). Dell.
Groome, Francis H. Gypsy Folk-Tales. Dorson, Richard M., ed. LC 77-70599. (International Folklore Ser.). 1977. Repr. of 1899 ed. lib. bdg. 21.00x (ISBN 0-405-10098-1). Arno.
Propp, V. Morphology of the Folktale. 2nd ed. Wagner, Louis A., ed. Scott, Laurence, tr. (American Folklore Society Bibliographical & Special Ser.: No. 9). 184p. 1968. pap. 4.95x (ISBN 0-292-78376-0). U of Tex Pr.
Waelti-Walters, Jennifer. Fairy Tales & the Female Imagination. 225p. 1981. write for info. (ISBN 0-920792-07-3). EPWP.

FAIRY TALES–HISTORY AND CRITICISM

Bergsten, Staffan. Mary Poppins & Myth. (Illus.). 1978. text ed. 14.25x (ISBN 91-22-00127-1). Humanities.
Bettelheim, Bruno. The Uses of Enchantment: The Meaning & Importance of Fairy Tales. 1976. 15.00 (ISBN 0-394-49771-6). Knopf.
--The Uses of Enchantment: The Meaning & Importance of Fairy Tales. 1977. pap. 3.95 (ISBN 0-394-72265-5, Vin). Random.
Duffy, Maureen. The Erotic World of Faery. 1980. pap. 3.50 (ISBN 0-380-48108-1, 48108, Discus). Avon.
Favat, F. Andre. Child & Tale: The Origins of Interest. LC 77-6698. (Orig.). 1977. pap. 7.00 (ISBN 0-8141-0595-5). NCTE.
Hartland, E. S. The Science of Fairy Tales. 59.95 (ISBN 0-8490-1001-2). Gordon Pr.
Kidder. Fairy Mythology As a Contributor to Human Happiness. 59.95 (ISBN 0-8490-0148-X). Gordon Pr.
Luthi, Max. Once Upon a Time: On the Nature of Fairy Tales. Chadeayne, Lee & Gottwald, Paul, trs. from Ger. LC 79-118870. 1970. 10.50 (ISBN 0-8044-2565-5). Ungar.
--Once Upon a Time: On the Nature of Fairy Tales. Chadeayne, Lee & Gottwald, Paul, trs. from Ger. LC 76-6992. (Midland Bks.: No. 203). 192p. 1976. pap. 3.95x (ISBN 0-253-20203-5). Ind U Pr.
Mitchell, Jane T. A Thematic Analysis of Mme. D'Aulnoy's "Contes De Fees". LC 78-6947. (Romance Monographs: No. 30). 1978. 16.00x (ISBN 84-399-8448-0). Romance.
Ricklin, Franz. Wish Fulfillment & Symbolism in Fairy Tales. White, William A., tr. (Nervous & Mental Disease Monographs: No. 21). Repr. of 1915 ed. 15.50 (ISBN 0-384-50820-0). Johnson Repr.
Thalmann, Marianne. The Literary Sign Language of German Romanticism. Basilius, Harold A., tr. from Ger. LC 77-184484. 144p. 1972. 9.95x (ISBN 0-8143-1468-6). Wayne St U Pr.
Tolkien, J. R. Tree & Leaf. 1965. 7.95 (ISBN 0-395-08253-6). HM.
Von Franz, Marie-Louise. Individuation in Fairytales. 1976. pap. 9.00 (ISBN 0-88214-112-0). Spring Pubns.
--An Introduction to the Interpretation of Fairy Tales. Hillman, James, ed. (Seminar Ser.). 159p. 1978. pap. text ed. 7.50 (ISBN 0-88214-101-5). Spring Pubns.
Von Franz, Mary-Louise. Problems of the Feminine in Fairytales. Hillman, James, ed. (Seminar Ser). 1979. pap. text ed. 8.50 (ISBN 0-88214-105-8). Spring Pubns.
Zipes, Jack. Breaking the Magic Spell: Radical Theories of Folk & Fairy Tales. LC 79-87883. 1979. text ed. 13.95 (ISBN 0-292-70725-8). U of Tex Pr.

FAIRY TALES–INDEXES

Eastman, Mary H. Index to Fairy Tales, Myths & Legends. 2nd rev. enl. ed. (The Useful Reference Ser. of Library Bks: Vol. 28). 1926. lib. bdg. 14.00x (ISBN 0-87305-028-2). Faxon.
--Index to Fairy Tales, Myths & Legends, Suppl. 1. (The Useful Reference Ser. of Library Bks: Vol. 61). 1937. lib. bdg. 12.00x (ISBN 0-87305-061-4). Faxon.
--Index to Fairy Tales, Myths & Legends, Suppl. 2. (The Useful Reference Ser. of Library Bks: Vol. 82). 1952. lib. bdg. 11.00x (ISBN 0-87305-082-7). Faxon.
Ireland Index to Fairy Tales, Nineteen Seventy-Three to Nineteen Seventy-Seven, Including Folklore, Legends & Myths in Collections: Fourth Supplement. (Useful Reference Ser. of Library Bks.: Vol. III). 1979. lib. bdg. 20.00 (ISBN 0-87305-111-4). Faxon.
Ireland, Norma O. Index to Fairy Tales, 1949-1972, Including Folklore, Legends & Myths in Collections. LC 26-11491. (The Useful Reference Ser. of Library Bks: Vol. 101). 1973. lib. bdg. 18.00x (ISBN 0-87305-101-7). Faxon.
Jankuhn, Herbert. Einfuhrung in die Siedlungasarchaologie: De Gruyter Studienbuch, Vol.1. 1977. 24.00x (ISBN 3-11-004752-7). De Gruyter.

FAIRY TALES–THEMES, MOTIVES

see Fairy Tales–Classification

FAISAL, KING OF SAUDI ARABIA, 1906-1975

Beling, Willard A., ed. King Faisal & the Modernisation of Saudi Arabia. LC 79-5134. 1979. lib. bdg. 31.25x (ISBN 0-89158-693-8). Westview.

FAITH

see also Apostasy; Atheism; Evidence; Faith and Reason; Hope; Salvation; Sanctification; Skepticism; Trust in God; Truth

Abrecht, Paul, ed. Faith, Science, & the Future. LC 79-7035. 240p. 1979. pap. 3.95 (ISBN 0-8006-1365-1, 1-1365). Fortress.
Alberione, James. A Time for Faith. 1978. 4.00 (ISBN 0-8198-0371-5); pap. 3.00 (ISBN 0-8198-0372-3). Dghtrs St Paul.
Al-Ghazzali. Foundations of the Articles of Faith. 1969. 6.50x (ISBN 0-87902-058-X). Orientalia.
Andrew, Dick. Even YOU Can Share Your Faith. 45p. (gr. 5-8). 1981. tchrs'. ed. 2.00 (ISBN 0-914936-47-6); 1.50 (ISBN 0-914936-48-4). Bible Pr.
Ansari, F. R. Foundations of Faith. pap. 0.95 (ISBN 0-686-18472-6). Kazi Pubns.
Armstrong, Anne, tr. Viendo Lo Invisible. (Spanish Bks.). (Span.). 1979. 1.90 (ISBN 0-8297-0670-4). Life Pubs Intl.
Baillie, John. Invitation to Pilgrimage. (Minister's Paperback Library). pap. 2.95 (ISBN 0-8010-0654-6). Baker Bk.
Baker, Albert E. Prophets for a Day of Judgment. facsimile ed. LC 72-90605. (Essay Index Reprint Ser). 1944. 15.00 (ISBN 0-8369-1390-6). Arno.
Barbotin, Edmond. Faith for Today. O'Connell, Matthew J., tr. from Fr. LC 73-85155. Orig. Title: Croire. (Illus.). 160p. 1974. 3.95x (ISBN 0-88344-125-X). Orbis Bks.
Barney, Kenneth. Mas Vale Creerlo. (Span.). Date not set. 1.75 (ISBN 0-686-76320-3). Life Pubs Intl.
Barney, Kenneth D. Mais Croyez Donc! Date not set. 1.75 (ISBN 0-686-76405-6). Life Pubs Intl.
Barnidge, Thomas & Grow, Douglas. The Jim Hart Story. (Illus.). 1977. 6.95 (ISBN 0-8272-1705-6); pap. 4.95 (ISBN 0-8272-1704-8). Bethany Pr.
Barrington, George. God Will Not Let Me Go. LC 77-4191. 1977. pap. 5.00 (ISBN 0-8309-0185-X). Herald Hse.
Bartlett, David L. Fact & Faith. LC 74-22517. 144p. (Orig.). 1975. pap. 3.95 (ISBN 0-8170-0654-0). Judson.
Bauman, Edward W. God's Presence in My Life. (Journeys in Faith Ser.). 144p. 1981. 7.95 (ISBN 0-687-15444-8). Abingdon.
Beard, Charles A. Written History As an Act of Faith. pap. 3.00 (ISBN 0-685-64640-8). Tex Western.
Beck, Frederick O. The Faith for All Seasons. LC 71-149652. 214p. 1971. 5.25 (ISBN 0-88263-400-3). St Charles Hse.

Benton, John. Sherri. 192p. 1980. pap. 2.50 (ISBN 0-8007-8390-5, New Hope). Revell.
Bin-Nun, Aaron. The Language of Faith. LC 78-65723. 1979. 8.95 (ISBN 0-88400-061-3). Shengold.
Birmingham, Jean. I Still Believe in Tomorrow. 62p. (Orig.). 1980. pap. 1.95 (ISBN 0-88347-120-5). Thomas More.
Bloesch, Donald G. Faith & Its Counterfeits. LC 81-3704. 108p. (Orig.). 1981. pap. 3.95 (ISBN 0-87784-822-X). Inter Varsity.
Boros, Ladislaus. The Closeness of God. 1978. pap. 3.95 (ISBN 0-8245-0210-8). Crossroad NY.
Bothwell, Sr. Mary D. We Believe. (Christ Our Life Ser.). (Illus.). (gr. 4). 1981. pap. text ed. 3.80 (ISBN 0-8294-0367-1); tchr's ed. 6.95 (ISBN 0-8294-0368-X). Loyola.
Bright, Bill. How to Love by Faith. (Transferable Concepts Ser.). 64p. 1981. pap. 1.25 (ISBN 0-918956-95-1). Campus Crusade.
Brokhoff, Barbara & Brokhoff, John. Faith Alive! 1978. 4.35 (ISBN 0-89536-342-9). CSS Pub.
Brown, Robert M. Is Faith Obsolete? LC 74-13420. 1979. pap. 3.95 (ISBN 0-664-24230-8). Westminster.
Brown, Willis M. How I Got Faith. 199p. 2.00 (ISBN 0-686-29117-4). Faith Pub Hse.
Brunner, Emil. The Christian Doctrine of the Church Faith & the Consummation, Vol. 3. (Dogmatic Ser.). 1978. softcover 8.95 (ISBN 0-664-24218-9). Westminster.
Bulle, Florence. Lord of the Valleys: Overcoming Suffering by Faith. LC 72-85630. 240p. 1972. pap. 3.95 (ISBN 0-912106-01-8). Logos.
Bunson, Maggie. Faith in Paradise. 1977. 8.00 (ISBN 0-8198-0414-2). Dghtrs St Paul.
--Founding of Faith. 1977. 6.00 (ISBN 0-8198-0412-6); pap. 5.00 (ISBN 0-8198-0413-4). Dghtrs St Paul.
Burgess, Andrew J. Passion, Knowing How, & Understanding: An Essay on the Concept of Faith. LC 75-31550. (American Academy of Religion. Dissertation Ser.). 1975. pap. 7.50 (ISBN 0-89130-044-9, 010109). Scholars Pr Ca.
Burke, George. Faith Speaks. 1975. pap. 2.50x (ISBN 0-932104-00-2). St George Pr.
Burrell, Jill & Burrell, Maurice. Arctic Mission. 1976. 1.55 (ISBN 0-08-017621-6). Pergamon.
Cabestrero, Teofilo, ed. Faith: Conversations with Contemporary Theologians. Walsh, Donald D., tr. LC 80-1431. 192p. 1980. pap. 7.95 (ISBN 0-88344-126-8). Orbis Bks.
Capps, Charles. Can Your Faith Fail? 1978. pap. 1.50 (ISBN 0-89274-105-8). Harrison Hse.
Casselman, Robert C. Continuum: How Science, Psychology & Mysticism Point to a Life Beyond...& to an Extraordinary Kind of God. LC 78-7670. 1978. 9.95 (ISBN 0-399-90017-9). Marek.
Catherine, Renee. The King & Queen...a Fairy Tale. (Illus.). 1979. 5.00 (ISBN 0-682-49393-7). Exposition.
Chirban, John T. Human Growth & Faith: Intrinsic & Extrinsic Motivation in Human Development. LC 81-40175. (Illus.). 221p. (Orig.). 1981. lib. bdg. 20.25 (ISBN 0-8191-1784-6); pap. text ed. 10.25 (ISBN 0-8191-1785-4). U Pr of Amer.
Cho, Paul Y. Solucion Para los Problemas De la Vida. Marosi, Esteban & Whidden, Angela, eds. Julio, C. & Orozco, O., trs. from Chinese. 155p. (Span.). 1980. pap. 1.35 (ISBN 0-8297-0999-1). Life Pubs Intl.
Colson, Charles. Born Again. (Illus.). 1976. 6.95 (ISBN 0-912376-35-X). Chosen Bks Pub.
Cook, Michael L. The Jesus of Faith: A Study in Christology. LC 80-84510. 192p. (Orig.). pap. 6.95 (ISBN 0-8091-2349-5). Paulist Pr.
Cooke, Bernard. Formation of Faith. LC 65-27619. (Pastoral Ser). 1965. pap. 2.00 (ISBN 0-8294-0014-1). Loyola.
--Rethinking Your Faith. (Illus.). 1977. pap. 1.95 (ISBN 0-89570-073-5). Claretian Pubns.
Cookson, Catherine. The Glass Virgin. 352p. 1981. pap. 2.50 (ISBN 0-553-13937-1). Bantam.
Cornwall, Judson. Unfeigned Faith. 192p. (Orig.). 1981. pap. 4.95 (ISBN 0-8007-5057-8, Power Bks). Revell.
Corrigan, John T. Archives: The Light of Faith. (Catholic Library Association Studies in Librarianship: No. 4). 1980. 4.00 (ISBN 0-87507-008-6). Cath Lib Assn.
Cowan, Charles. Refusing Doubt. 32p. 1977. pap. 1.00 (ISBN 0-89274-062-0). Harrison Hse.
Crowley, Mary. A Pocketful of Hope. 1981. 9.50 (ISBN 0-8007-1272-2). Revell.
D'Arcy, Martin C. The Nature of Belief. facsimile ed. (Select Bibliographies Reprint Ser). Repr. of 1931 ed. 19.00 (ISBN 0-8369-5930-2). Arno.
Daugherty, Billy Joe. More Faith Power to You. 1978. pap. 2.50 (ISBN 0-89274-100-7). Harrison Hse.
Daughters of St. Paul. Everyman's Challenge. LC 73-89938. 1974. 5.00 (ISBN 0-8198-0294-8). Dghtrs St Paul.
--Faces of Courage. (Illus.). 1974. 5.00 (ISBN 0-8198-0292-1); pap. 4.00 (ISBN 0-8198-0293-X). Dghtrs St Paul.
--Faith We Live By. LC 68-59044. (Divine Master Ser., Vol. 3). (Illus.). 1969. 7.00 (ISBN 0-8198-0039-2); pap. 6.00 (ISBN 0-8198-0040-6); discussion & project manual 0.60 (ISBN 0-8198-0041-4). Dghtrs St Paul.
Daujat, Jean. The Faith Applied. 1963. 5.95 (ISBN 0-933932-22-7). Scepter Pubs.
Davis, Stephen. Faith, Skepticism & Evidence. 233p. 1978. 13.50 (ISBN 0-8387-2039-0). Bucknell U Pr.
Deal, William S. Faith, Facts & Feelings. 3rd ed. 1978. pap. 0.95 (ISBN 0-686-05527-6). Deal Pubns.
Dean, Robert. How Can We Believe? LC 77-87248. 1978. 6.50 (ISBN 0-8054-8135-4). Broadman.
De Benedittis, Suzanne M. Education in Faith & Morals. 200p. (Orig.). 1981. pap. 4.95 (ISBN 0-86683-621-7). Winston Pr.
DeGidio, Sandra. Sharing Faith in the Family. (Illus.). 154p. 1980. pap. 12.95 (ISBN 0-89622-119-9). Twenty-Third.
De Vries, James E. You Can Live with a Heartache: Hope for Long-Term Heartaches. (Christian Counseling Aids Ser.). 1977. pap. 0.75 (ISBN 0-8010-2876-0). Baker Bk.
DeWitt, John R. What Is the Reformed Faith. (Orig.). 1981. pap. text ed. 1.45 (ISBN 0-85151-326-3). Banner of Truth.
DiGiacomo, James, ed. Faith. (Conscience & Concern Ser.: No. 4). 1969. text ed. 1.95 (ISBN 0-03-083016-8, 206). Winston Pr.
Digiacomo, James, et al. The Longest Step: Searching for God. (The Encounter Ser.). (Illus.). 1977. pap. text ed. 3.85 (ISBN 0-03-021276-6, 315); resource manual 1.95 (ISBN 0-03-021871-3, 316). Winston Pr.
--Meet the Lord: Encounters with Jesus. (The Encounter Ser.). 1977. pap. 3.85 (ISBN 0-03-021281-2, 317); resource manual 1.95 (ISBN 0-03-021866-7, 318). Winston Pr.
Dixon, John W., Jr. The Physiology of Faith: A Theory of Theological Relativity. LC 79-1782. 1979. 15.00 (ISBN 0-06-061926-0, HarpR). Har-Row.
Douglass, Herbert. Faith-Saying Yes to God. (Waymark Ser.). 1978. pap. 4.50 (ISBN 0-8127-0173-9). Review & Herald.
Eareckson, Joni & Musser, Joe. Joni. (Illus.). 256p. 1980. pap. 2.95 (ISBN 0-310-23982-6). Zondervan.
Ebeling, Gerhard. The Nature of Faith. Smith, Ronald G., tr. from Ger. LC 62-7194. 192p. 1967. pap. 5.95 (ISBN 0-8006-1914-5, 1-1914). Fortress.
Elbert, John A. Newman's Concept of Faith. 59.95 (ISBN 0-8490-0729-1). Gordon Pr.
Elliot, Elisabeth. The Liberty of Obedience. LC 68-31110. 1976. pap. 1.25 (ISBN 0-87680-831-3, 91018, Key-Word Bks). Word Bks.
Engstrom, Barbie. Faith to See: Reflections & Photographs. LC 74-25540. (Illus.). 64p. 1979. pap. 3.00 (ISBN 0-932210-00-7). Kurios Found.
Evans, Donald. Faith, Authenticity, & Morality. 1980. 25.00x (ISBN 0-8020-5424-2). U of Toronto Pr.
The Faith Builder. 2.95 (ISBN 0-686-12914-8). Schmul Pub Co.
Faris, N. A. Foundation of Articles of Faith. 4.50 (ISBN 0-686-18607-9). Kazi Pubns.
Ferguson, Franklin C. A Pilgrimage in Faith: An Introduction to the Episcopal Church. rev. ed. LC 75-5220. 180p. (Orig.). 1979. pap. 5.95 (ISBN 0-8192-1277-6). Morehouse.
Ferre, Nels F. The Finality of Faith, & Christianity Among the World Religions. LC 78-11979. 1979. Repr. of 1963 ed. lib. bdg. 15.00x (ISBN 0-313-21182-5, FEFF). Greenwood.
Ferries, George. The Growth of Christian Faith. 385p. Repr. of 1905 ed. text ed. 4.50 (ISBN 0-567-02106-8). Attic Pr.
Fichte, Johann G. The Vocation of Man. Smith, William, tr. LC 56-44104. 1956. pap. 3.95 (ISBN 0-672-60220-2, LLA50). Bobbs.
--Vocation of Man. Smith, William, tr. from Ger. xii, 178p. 1965. 12.95 (ISBN 0-87548-074-8); pap. 4.95 (ISBN 0-87548-075-6). Open Court.
Fisher, Eugene. Faith Without Prejudice. LC 77-83550. 196p. 1977. pap. 2.95 (ISBN 0-8091-2064-X). Paulist Pr.
Fisher, Wallace E. Stand Fast in Faith: Finding Freedom Through Discipline in the Ten Commandments. LC 77-13284. 1978. pap. 4.95 (ISBN 0-687-39271-3). Abingdon.
Flesseman-Van Leer, E. A Faith for Today. Steely, John E., tr. LC 79-56514. (Special Studies Ser.: No. 7). 1980. 6.95 (ISBN 0-932180-06-X). Assn Baptist Profs.
Ford, Leighton. Good News Is for Sharing. 208p. pap. 3.95 (ISBN 0-89191-083-2, 52969). Cook.
Forliti, John. Faith Without Anger. (Infinity Ser.: No. 2). 1972. text ed. 2.50 (ISBN 0-03-004021-3, 229); tchr's guide 1.15 (ISBN 0-03-004026-4, 230). Winston Pr.
Fowler, Jim & Keen, Sam. Life Maps: Conversations on the Journey to Faith. Berryman, Jerome, ed. 164p. 1980. pap. 5.95 (ISBN 0-8499-2848-6). Winston Pr.
Franzblau, Abraham N. Religious Belief & Character Among Jewish Adolescents. LC 78-176783. (Columbia University. Teachers College. Contributions to Education: No. 634). Repr. of 1934 ed. 17.50 (ISBN 0-404-55634-5). AMS Pr.
Garrotto, Alfred J. Christ in Our Lives. (Orig.). 1980. pap. text ed. 3.95 (ISBN 0-03-056979-6). Winston Pr.
Genszler, G. William. Don't Fall Flat on Your Faith. 1973. pap. 3.40 (ISBN 0-89536-054-3). CSS Pub.
Gordis, Robert. Faith for Moderns. 2nd rev. ed. LC 76-136424. 1971. pap. 6.95x (ISBN 0-8197-0001-0, 10001). Bloch.
Gordon, Ernest. Me, Myself & Who? 1980. pap. 4.95 (ISBN 0-88270-418-4). Logos.
Gordon, S. D. Quiet Talks on Following the Christ. (S. D. Gordon Library). (Orig.). 1980. pap. 2.95 (ISBN 0-8010-3751-4). Baker Bk.
Goudge, Elizabeth. A Book of Faith. 336p. 1980. pap. 2.50 (ISBN 0-553-11052-7). Bantam.
--A Book of Faith. LC 76-35977. 288p. 1976. 8.95 (ISBN 0-698-10705-5). Coward.
Gowan, Donald E. The Triumph of Faith in Habakkuk. LC 75-32943. (The Bible Speaks to Us Today Ser.). 1976. 5.95 (ISBN 0-8042-0195-1). John Knox.
Graham, James W. Let Us Affirm Our Faith. 1979. pap. 3.40 (ISBN 0-89536-369-0). CSS Pub.
Grant, Edward F. The Kingdom Within You. 1977. 6.50 (ISBN 0-682-48874-7). Exposition.
Griffith, Gwilym O. Interpreters of Reality: Lao-Tse, Heraclitus & the Christian Faith. 1977. lib. bdg. 59.95 (ISBN 0-8490-2065-4). Gordon Pr.
Groenhoff, Edwin L. It's Your Choice. 1975. pap. 1.75 (ISBN 0-911802-38-X). Free Church Pubns.
Grubb, Norman P. Law of Faith. 1969. pap. 2.75 (ISBN 0-87508-223-8). Chr Lit.
Hagin, Kenneth E. Faith Food for Autumn. (Illus.). 1978. pap. text ed. 1.95 (ISBN 0-89276-040-0). Hagin Ministries.
--Faith Food for Spring. (Illus.). 1978. pap. text ed. 1.95 (ISBN 0-89276-042-7). Hagin Ministries.
--Faith Food for Summer. (Illus.). 1978. pap. text ed. 1.95 (ISBN 0-89276-043-5). Hagin Ministries.
--Faith Food for Winter. (Illus.). 1977. pap. text ed. 1.95 (ISBN 0-89276-041-9). Hagin Ministries.
Hagin, Kenneth, Jr. Blueprint for Building Strong Faith. 1980. pap. 0.50 (ISBN 0-89276-704-9). Hagin Ministry.
--Faith Worketh by Love. 1979. minibk. 0.50 (ISBN 0-89276-703-0). Hagin Ministries.
Hallesby, O. Why I Am a Christian. LC 77-73797. 1977. pap. 1.95 (ISBN 0-8066-1571-0, 10-7156). Augsburg.
Hanks, Geoffrey. Children of Naples. 1976. 1.55 (ISBN 0-08-017619-4). Pergamon.
Happold, F. C. Religious Faith & Twentieth Century Man. 192p. 1981. 6.95 (ISBN 0-8245-0046-6). Crossroad NY.
Harbuck, Don B. Dynamics of Belief. LC 75-84502. (Orig.). 1969. pap. 1.95 (ISBN 0-8054-1909-8). Broadman.
Hatch, W. H. Pauline Idea of Faith in Its Relation to Jewish & Hellenistic Religion. 1917. pap. 7.00 (ISBN 0-527-01002-2). Kraus Repr.
Hatfield, Mark O. Between a Rock & a Hard Place. LC 75-42906. 1977. pap. 1.75 (ISBN 0-8499-4101-6, 4101-6). Word Bks.
Haughey, John C. The Faith That Does Justice. LC 77-74578. 312p. (Orig.). 1977. pap. 5.95 (ISBN 0-8091-2026-7). Paulist Pr.
Hayes, Norvel. God's Medicine of Faith. 1978. pap. 2.25 (ISBN 0-917726-20-0). Hunter Bks.
--How to Protect Your Faith. 1978. pap. 2.25 (ISBN 0-917726-19-7). Hunter Bks.
Heinecken, Martin J. We Believe & Teach. Rast, Harold W., ed. LC 80-16363. (A Lead Book). 128p. (Orig.). 1980. pap. 3.25 (ISBN 0-8006-1387-2, 1-1387). Fortress.
Helm, Paul. The Varieties of Belief. (Muirhead Library of Philosophy). 170p. 1973. text ed. 12.00x (ISBN 0-04-121017-4). Humanities.
Hermission, Hans-Jurgen & Lohse, Eduard. Faith. Stott, Douglas, tr. LC 80-22542. (Biblical Encounter Ser.). 176p. 1981. pap. 6.95 (ISBN 0-687-12520-0). Abingdon.
Herrmann, Wilhelm. Communion of the Christian with God. Voelkel, Robert T. & Keck, Leander E., eds. Stanyon, J. Sandys, tr. from Ger. LC 78-154491. (Lives of Jesus Ser). 440p. 1971. pap. 6.95 (ISBN 0-8006-1270-1, 1-1270). Fortress.
Hick, John. Faith & Knowledge. (Fount Religious Paperbacks Ser). 1976. pap. 3.95 (ISBN 0-00-643639-0, FA3639). Collins Pubs.
Hickman, Martha W. The Growing Season. LC 80-68983. 128p. (Orig.). 1980. pap. 4.50x (ISBN 0-8358-0411-9). Upper Room.
Hicks, Roy H. Use It or Lose It: The Word of Faith. (Orig.). 1976. pap. 1.95 (ISBN 0-89274-002-7). Harrison Hse.
Hinson, E. Glenn. Seekers After Mature Faith. LC 76-48577. 1977. pap. 3.95 (ISBN 0-8054-6531-6). Broadman.
Holmer, Paul L. The Grammar of Faith. LC 78-3351. 1978. 10.00 (ISBN 0-06-064003-0, HarpR). Har-Row.
Holmes, Marjorie. How Can I Find You, God? LC 74-25107. 1975. 2.95 (ISBN 0-385-04437-2). Doubleday.
--I've Got to Talk to Somebody, God. 1971. pap. 1.95 (ISBN 0-8007-8080-9, Spire Bks). Revell.
Hoover, Arlie J. Fallacies of Unbelief. LC 75-36313. (Way of Life Ser: No. 128). 94p. 1976. pap. 2.95 (ISBN 0-89112-128-5). Bibl Res Pr.
Hubbard, Howard. Always God's People. 96p. (Orig.). 1980. pap. 1.75 (ISBN 0-912228-68-7). St Anthony Mess Pr.
Hulme, William E. Am I Losing My Faith? LC 71-133035. (Pocket Counsel Bks.). 56p. (Orig.). 1971. pap. 1.75 (ISBN 0-8006-0154-8, 1-154). Fortress.
Hunter, John. Faith That Works. 1972. pap. 1.25 (ISBN 0-87508-245-9). Chr Lit.
Hutton, Richard Holt. Essays on Some of the Modern Guides to English Thought in Matters of Faith. LC 72-8580. (Essay Index Reprint Ser.). 1972. Repr. of 1887 ed. 21.00 (ISBN 0-8369-7319-4). Arno.
Inge, William R. Faith & Its Psychology. (Studies in Theology Ser.: No. 12). 1909. text ed. 6.00x (ISBN 0-8401-6012-7). Allenson-Breckinridge.
Jackson, W. Barbara. Faith & Freedom: A Study of Western Society. LC 72-8239. 308p. 1974. Repr. of 1954 ed. lib. bdg. 15.00x (ISBN 0-8371-6542-3, JAFF). Greenwood.
James, William. Essays on Faith & Morals. 8.50 (ISBN 0-8446-5841-3). Peter Smith.
Jenkins, Daniel. Believing in God. (Layman's Theological Library). 1965. pap. 1.45 (ISBN 0-664-24004-6). Westminster.
Job, John. Job Speaks to Us Today. LC 79-19632. (Bible Speaks to Us Today Ser.). 128p. 1980. pap. 4.25 (ISBN 0-8042-0132-3). John Knox.
Johnson, Luke T. Sharing Possessions: Mandate & Symbol of Faith, No. 9. Brueggemann, Walter & Donahue, John R., eds. LC 80-2390. (Overtures to Biblical Theology Ser.). 176p. (Orig.). 1981. pap. 8.95 (ISBN 0-8006-1534-4, 1-1534). Fortress.
Keidel, Levi. Caught in the Crossfire. LC 79-10910. 1979. pap. 5.95 (ISBN 0-8361-1888-X). Herald Pr.
Kelly, Douglas, et al. The Westminster Confession of Faith: A New Edition. 102p. 1981. pap. 5.95 (ISBN 0-87921-065-6). Attic Pr.
Kemp, Raymond. A Journey in Faith. Date not set. pap. 5.95 (ISBN 0-8215-9329-3). Sadlier.
Kendall, R. T. Who by Faith. 224p. 1981. pap. price not set (ISBN 0-310-38321-8). Zondervan.
Kennedy, D. James. Why I Believe. 1980. 6.95 (ISBN 0-8499-0194-4). Word Bks.
Kennedy, Eugene C., M.M. Believing. LC 73-79681. 1977. pap. 2.45 (ISBN 0-385-12614-X, Im). Doubleday.
Knox, Lloyd H., ed. A Faith to Grow by. 1977. pap. 2.95 (ISBN 0-89367-009-X). Light & Life.
Kochman, Max. Shall We Believe in God & the Meaning of Life? 1980. 6.95 (ISBN 0-533-04559-2). Vantage.
Kroner, Richard. The Primacy of Faith. LC 77-27184. (Gifford Lectures: 1939-40). Repr. of 1943 ed. 21.00 (ISBN 0-404-60497-8). AMS Pr.
Kuasten, J. & Plumpe, J., eds. St. Augustine, Faith, Hope & Charity. Arand, Louis A., tr. LC 78-62450. (Ancient Christian Writers Ser.: No. 3). 165p. 1947. 8.95 (ISBN 0-8091-0045-2). Paulist Pr.
Kuhn, Margaret E. Get Out There & Do Something About Injustice. 128p. 1972. pap. 1.95 (ISBN 0-377-02121-0). Friend Pr.
Laidlaw, Robert A. The Reason Why. 48p. 1975. pap. 0.95 (ISBN 0-310-27112-6). Zondervan.
Larson, Christian D. Leave It to God. pap. 0.75 (ISBN 0-87516-191-X). De Vorss.
Lauxstermann, E. M. The Believer's Delight. 1975. pap. 2.95 (ISBN 0-87552-317-X). Presby & Reformed.
Lehmann, Jerry. We Walked to Moscow. (Illus.). 1966. pap. 3.00 (ISBN 0-934676-07-0). Greenlf Bks.
Le Roy, Douglas. We Believe. 56p. 1975. pap. 3.50 (ISBN 0-87148-906-6). Pathway Pr.
Lewis, Gordon R. Judge for Yourself: A Workbook on Contemporary Challenges to Christian Faith. LC 73-81575. 128p. 1974. pap. 2.95 (ISBN 0-87784-637-5). Inter-Varsity.
Lewis, Margie M. & Lewis, Gregg. The Hurting Parent. 160p. (Orig.). 1980. pap. 3.95 (ISBN 0-310-41731-7). Zondervan.
Lings, Martin. Ancient Beliefs & Modern Superstitions. (Unwin Paperbacks Ser.). 1980. pap. 4.50 (ISBN 0-04-200034-3). Allen Unwin.

Linton, Irwin H. A Lawyer Examines the Bible: A Defense of the Faith. 1977. pap. 4.50 (ISBN 0-8010-5565-2). Baker Bk.
Little, Paul E. Paul Little's Why & What Book. 240p. 1980. text ed. 8.95 (ISBN 0-88207-814-3). Victor Bks.
Lovett, C. S. The Thrill of Faith. 1960. pap. 2.25 (ISBN 0-938148-21-4). Personal Christianity.
Lovette, Roger. A Faith of Our Own. LC 75-27086. 144p. 1976. 6.95 (ISBN 0-8298-0299-1). Pilgrim NY.
Lown, Albert J. Portraits of Faith. 155p. (Orig.). 1981. pap. 3.95 (ISBN 0-8341-0695-7). Beacon Hill.
Luebering, Carol, ed. Brokenness: The Stories of Six Women Whose Faith Grew in Crises. 104p. (Orig.). 1980. pap. 1.95 (ISBN 0-912228-72-5). St Anthony Mess Pr.
McDonald, H. D. Salvation. (Foundations for Faith). 1981. pap. 7.95 (ISBN 0-89107-229-2, Cornerstone Bks.). Good News.
McDowell, Mildred. With an Open Heart. 1978. pap. 2.45 (ISBN 0-8091-2075-5). Paulist Pr.
Machen, J. Gresham. What Is Faith? 1962. pap. 4.95 (ISBN 0-8028-1122-1). Eerdmans.
McHugh, Gerald A. Christian Faith & Criminal Justice: Toward a Christian Response to Crime & Punishment. LC 78-58956. 244p. 1978. pap. 5.95 (ISBN 0-8091-2105-0). Paulist Pr.
McIntire, Russell. Live Your Faith! LC 78-25579. 167p. 1979. 6.95 (ISBN 0-88289-217-7). Pelican.
McKenna, Megan & Ducote, Darryl. Old Testament Journeys in Faith. LC 78-71528. (Followers of the Way Ser.: Vol. 1). (gr. 9-12). 1979. 22.50 (ISBN 0-8091-9542-9); 7.50 (ISBN 0-8091-7666-1). Paulist Pr.
Mackey, James P. The Problems of Religious Faith. 344p. 1975. 12.95 (ISBN 0-8199-0454-6). Franciscan Herald.
McMillan, Robert M. Faith Without Fantasy. LC 80-66541. 1981. 3.25 (ISBN 0-8054-5285-0). Broadman.
McPherson, J. The Westminster Confession of Faith. (Handbooks for Bible Classes). 175p. 1977. pap. text ed. 7.95 (ISBN 0-567-28143-4). Attic Pr.
MacRae, George W. Faith in the Word: The Fourth Gospel. (Biblical Booklets Ser). 1975. pap. 0.95 (ISBN 0-8199-0515-1). Franciscan Herald.
Madauss, Martyria. The Shield of Faith. 1974. gift edition 0.50 (ISBN 3-872-09659-1). Evang Sisterhood Mary.
Magno, Joseph A. & LaMotte, Victor S. The Christian, the Atheist, & Freedom. LC 74-165170. 99p. 1975. 5.50 (ISBN 0-913750-08-5). Precedent Pub.
Makarim, Sami N. Druze Faith. LC 73-19819. 1974. 18.00x (ISBN 0-88206-003-1). Caravan Bks.
Marcel, Gabriel. Being & Having: An Existentialist Diary. 7.00 (ISBN 0-8446-2528-0). Peter Smith.
--The Mystery of Being, 2 vols. Incl. Vol. 1. Reflections & Mystery. 288p. pap. 4.25 (ISBN 0-89526-929-5); Vol. 2. Faith & Reality. 222p. pap. 3.95x (ISBN 0-89526-930-9). 1960. Repr. Regnery-Gateway.
Marie, Patricia. Night Cries. 1981. 4.75 (ISBN 0-8062-1794-4). Carlton.
Marty, Martin E. Our Faiths. 1976. pap. 1.75 (ISBN 0-89129-113-X). Jove Pubns.
Mathews, W. R. Our Faith in God. 1936. 5.00 (ISBN 0-8414-6457-X). Folcroft.
Maxwell, L. E. Crowded to Christ. 256p. (Orig.). 1976. pap. 3.95 (ISBN 0-8024-1666-7). Moody.
Melanchthon, Philipp. The Justification of Man by Faith Only. Lesse, Nicholas, tr. LC 79-84123. (English Experience Ser.: No. 942). 204p. 1979. Repr. of 1548 ed. lib. bdg. 15.00 (ISBN 90-221-0942-9). Walter J Johnson.
Metz, Johann B. Faith in History & Society: Toward a Practical Fundamental Theology. 1979. 12.95 (ISBN 0-8245-0305-8). Crossroad NY.
Miller, Lew A. You Can Beat Those Spiritual Blahs. LC 78-72866. 1979. pap. 2.95 (ISBN 0-89636-015-6). Accent Bks.
Mitchell, Basil. The Justification of Religious Belief. 188p. (Orig.). 1981. pap. 4.95x (ISBN 0-19-520124-8). Oxford U Pr.
Mitchell, Hubert. Putting Your Faith on the Line. (Orig.). 1981. pap. 4.95 (ISBN 0-89840-027-9). Heres Life.
Mitchell, Joan. Me, Believing. (Infinity Ser.: No. 8). 1972. text ed. 2.25 (ISBN 0-03-004061-2, 241). Winston Pr.
Mohler, James A. Dimensions of Faith. LC 69-13120. (Orig.). 1969. pap. 2.80 (ISBN 0-8294-0100-8). Loyola.
Mollenkott, Virginia R. Speech, Silence, Action! The Cycle of Faith. LC 80-15812. (Journey in Faith Ser.). 144p. 1980. 7.95 (ISBN 0-687-39169-5). Abingdon.
Mooney, Christopher F., ed. Presence & Absence of God. LC 68-8748. 1969. 15.00 (ISBN 0-8232-0810-9). Fordham.
Moreno, Francisco Jose. Between Faith & Reason: An Approach to Individual & Social Psychology. LC 76-56926. 1977. 12.50x (ISBN 0-8147-5416-3). NYU Pr.
Morgan, G. Campbell. This Was His Faith: The Expository Letters of G. Campbell Morgan. Morgan, Jill, ed. (Morgan Library). 1977. pap. 3.95 (ISBN 0-8010-5969-0). Baker Bk.
Morse, Charles & Morse, Ann. Whobody There? 1977. pap. 3.95x (ISBN 0-8358-0350-3). Upper Room.
Mueller, J. J. Faith & Appreciative Awareness: The Culture Theology of Bernard E. Meland. LC 80-5969. 166p. 1981. lib. bdg. 17.75 (ISBN 0-8191-1560-6); pap. text ed. 8.75 (ISBN 0-8191-1561-4). U Pr of Amer.
Mueller, Virginia. What Is Faith? Sparks, Judith, ed. (A Happy Day Book). (Illus.). 24p. (gr. k-2). 1980. 0.98 (ISBN 0-87239-411-5, 3643). Standard Pub.
Mullino, Shirley B. The Rambling Life. 1981. 7.95 (ISBN 0-533-04810-9). Vantage.
Murdoch, Elmer H. Shattering Religious Boredom. pap. 1.75 (ISBN 0-87509-129-6). Chr Pubns.
Murphy, Chuck. Fundamentals of the Faith. LC 75-30505. 1976. pap. 2.95 (ISBN 0-687-13699-7). Abingdon.
Murphy, Joseph. Magic of Faith. pap. 1.50 (ISBN 0-87516-291-6). De Vorss.
Murray, Andrew. Secret of the Faith Life. (Secret Ser.). (Orig.). 1979. pap. 1.25 (ISBN 0-87508-387-0). Chr Lit.
--Why Do You Not Believe? (Summit Bks.). 1979. pap. 2.95 (ISBN 0-8010-6090-7). Baker Bk.
Muschalek, Georg. Certainty of Life & Certainty of Faith. LC 80-81020. 71p. 1980. pap. text ed. 2.50 (ISBN 0-935780-00-9). Herbert Pubs.
Nason, Michael & Nason, Donna. Tara. (Illus.). 192p. 1981. pap. 1.95 (ISBN 0-8007-8400-6, Spire Bks). Revell.
Nelson, C. Ellis. Don't Let Your Conscience Be Your Guide. LC 77-94430. 120p. 1978. pap. 2.45 (ISBN 0-8091-2099-2). Paulist Pr.
--Where Faith Begins. 1968. pap. 6.95 (ISBN 0-8042-1471-9). John Knox.
Neville. Your Faith Is Your Fortune. pap. 4.95 (ISBN 0-87516-078-6). De Vorss.
Newman, John H. The Theological Papers of John Henry Newman: On Faith & Certainty, Vol. 1. Holmes, Derek, ed. 1976. 19.95x (ISBN 0-19-920071-8). Oxford U Pr.
Nida, Eugene. Message & Mission: The Communication of the Christian Faith. LC 60-11785. (Applied Cultural Anthropology Ser.). 256p. 1975. pap. text ed. 3.95x (ISBN 0-87808-711-7). William Carey Lib.
Nordtvedt, Matilda. Defeating Despair & Depression. 128p. 1976. pap. 1.25 (ISBN 0-8024-2083-4). Moody.
Norgren, William A. Forum: Religious Faith Speaks to American Issues. (Orig.). 1975. pap. 2.95 (ISBN 0-377-00044-2). Friend Pr.
Nuzum, C. The Life of Faith. 1928. pap. 1.00 (ISBN 0-88243-539-6, 02-0539). Gospel Pub.
Ogden, R. James, ed. Going Public with One's Faith. LC 74-31462. 128p. (Orig.). 1975. pap. 2.50 (ISBN 0-8170-0673-7). Judson.
Ogden, Schubert M. Faith & Freedom: Toward a Theology of Liberation. LC 78-12898. 1979. pap. 3.95 (ISBN 0-687-12590-1). Abingdon.
Olson, Mildred. Diamondola. 1980. pap. 3.25 (ISBN 0-8280-0046-8, 04305-9). Review & Herald.
O'Malley, William J. The Roots of Unbelief: In Defense of Everything. 1976. pap. 1.95 (ISBN 0-8091-1915-3). Paulist Pr.
Owen, R. J. Trial of Faith. 1.55 (ISBN 0-08-017609-7). Pergamon.
Peachment, Brian. An Aeroplane or a Grave. 1976. pap. 1.55 (ISBN 0-08-017841-3). Pergamon.
--Devil's Island. 1976. pap. 1.55 (ISBN 0-08-017613-5). Pergamon.
--Down Among the Dead Men. 1976. pap. 1.55 (ISBN 0-08-017615-1). Pergamon.
Perl, Susan. Faith, Hope & Charity. (Illus.). 7.95 (ISBN 0-915696-46-0). Determined Prods.
The Pilgrim's Staff or Daily Steps Heavenward by the Pathway of Faith. 1979. Repr. of 1897 ed. lib. bdg. 20.00 (ISBN 0-8495-4332-0). Arden Lib.
Pink, A. W. Studies on Saving Faith. 5.95 (ISBN 0-685-41832-4). Reiner.
Pink, Arthur W. Beatitudes & the Lord's Prayer. 1979. 5.95 (ISBN 0-8010-7043-0). Baker Bk.
Price, Charles. La Fe Real. (Span.). Date not set. 1.75 (ISBN 0-686-76288-6). Life Pubs Intl.
Price, Charles S. Real Faith: One of the Classic Faith-Builders. 1972. pap. 2.95 (ISBN 0-912106-82-4). Logos.
Price, Frederick. How Faith Works. (Orig.). 1976. pap. 3.95 (ISBN 0-89274-001-9). Harrison Hse.
Price, Frederick K. How to Obtain Strong Faith: Six Principles. pap. 3.50 (ISBN 0-89274-042-6). Harrison Hse.
Prince, Derek. Faith to Live By. 1977. pap. 3.50 (ISBN 0-89283-042-5). Servant.
--Foundation for Faith. (Foundation Ser.: Bk. I). 1965-66. pap. 1.75 (ISBN 0-934920-00-1, B-10). Derek Prince.
Radhakrishnan, Sarvepalli. Recovery of Faith. Repr. of 1955 ed. lib. bdg. 15.00x (ISBN 0-8371-0197-2, RARF). Greenwood.
Ratzinger, Joseph. Faith & the Future. Walls, Ronald, tr. 1971. 4.95 (ISBN 0-8199-0427-9). Franciscan Herald.
Reeve, Pamela. Faith Is. 1970. pap. 3.95 (ISBN 0-930014-05-7). Multnomah.
Ridder, H. Faith Makes Sense. pap. 1.65 (ISBN 0-686-14198-9). Rose Pub MI.
Rideman, Peter. Confession of Faith. LC 74-115840. 1970. 9.95 (ISBN 0-87486-202-7). Plough.
Ripley, Francis J. This Is the Faith. 317p. 1973. pap. 4.95 (ISBN 0-903348-02-0). Lumen Christi.
Robinson, Wayne. Questions Are the Answer. LC 80-36780. 110p. 1980. pap. 5.95 (ISBN 0-8298-0409-9). Pilgrim NY.
Romaine, William. The Life of Faith. (Summit Bks.). 178p. 1981. pap. 2.25 (ISBN 0-8010-7704-4). Baker Bk.
Routley, Erik. Church Music & the Christian & Faith. LC 78-110219. 1979. 8.95 (ISBN 0-916642-11-9, Agape). Hope Pub.
Roy, Paul S. Building Christian Communities for Justice: The Faith Experience Book. LC 81-80050. 188p. (Orig.). 1981. pap. 8.95 (ISBN 0-8091-2380-0). Paulist Pr.
Russell, Robert A. God Works Through Faith. 1957. pap. 2.50 (ISBN 0-87516-325-4). De Vorss.
Rusthoi, Mrs. Ralph W. Discovering Your Faith: A Workbook for New Converts. pap. 1.50 (ISBN 0-685-58451-8). Rusthoi.
Samuel, Leith. Share Your Faith. (Contemporary Discussion Ser.). 104p. 1981. pap. 2.95 (ISBN 0-8010-8187-4). Baker Bk.
Sanders, J. Oswald. Mighty Faith. 1980. pap. 0.90 (ISBN 0-85363-030-5). OMF Bks.
--Mighty Faith. 1975. pap. 2.95 (ISBN 0-8024-5371-6). Moody.
Sanford, Agnes. Let's Believe. LC 54-5854. 1976. pap. 4.95 (ISBN 0-06-067051-7, RD 190, HarpR). Har-Row.
Schleiermacher, Friedrich. The Christian Faith. Mackintosh, H. R. & Stewart, J. S., eds. LC 76-53313. 772p. 1977. 16.50x (ISBN 0-8006-0487-3, 1-487). Fortress.
Schmidt, Herman & Power, David, eds. The Liturgical Experience of Faith. (Concilium Ser.: Religion in the Seventies: Vol. 82). 156p. 1973. pap. 4.95 (ISBN 0-8245-0241-8). Crossroad NY.
Sheldon, Charles. In His Steps. pap. 3.95 (ISBN 0-8007-5011-X, Power Bks); pap. 1.75 (ISBN 0-8007-8022-1, Spire Bks). Revell.
Short, Robert L. Something to Believe in. LC 75-36754. (Illus.). 1977. pap. 5.95 (ISBN 0-06-067381-8, RD 169, HarpR). Har-Row.
Simpson, A. B. In the School of Faith. pap. 2.25 (ISBN 0-87509-022-2). Chr Pubns.
Smart, James D. The Cultural Subversion of the Biblical Faith. 1977. pap. 4.95 (ISBN 0-664-24148-4). Westminster.
Smith, Chuck. The Gospel According to Grace. 176p. 1981. pap. 3.95 (ISBN 0-936728-12-4). Word for Today.
Smith, Hannah W. Christian's Secret of a Happy Life. 1968. 7.95 (ISBN 0-8007-0044-9); large-print ed. 10.95 (ISBN 0-8007-0045-7); pap. 3.95 (ISBN 0-8007-5004-7, Power Bks); pap. 1.95 (ISBN 0-8007-8007-8, Spire Bks). Revell.
Smith, Wilfred C. Belief & History. LC 75-50587. 1977. 12.95x (ISBN 0-8139-0670-9). U Pr of Va.
--Faith & Belief. LC 78-63601. 1979. 22.50 (ISBN 0-691-07232-9). Princeton U Pr.
Sobosan, Jeffrey. The Ascent to God. 1981. 8.95 (ISBN 0-88347-128-0). Thomas More.
Spencer, Bonnell. God Who Dares to Be Man: Theology of Prayer & Suffering. 128p. Date not set. 12.95 (ISBN 0-8164-0478-X). Seabury.
Spurgeon, C. H. Sin of Unbelief. 1977. pap. 0.50 (ISBN 0-686-23224-0). Pilgrim Pubns.
Spurgeon, Charles H. Faith's Checkbook. pap. 2.50 (ISBN 0-8024-0014-0, 35-14). Moody.
Stanley, Walter E. Keeping the Home Fires Burning. 52p. 1979. 3.95 (ISBN 0-8059-2598-8). Dorrance.
Steckley, Anna M. A Song in the Night. 126p. (Orig.). 1981. pap. 2.50 (ISBN 0-87178-806-3). Brethren.
Stewart, James S. Faith to Proclaim. (James S. Stewart Library). 2.95 (ISBN 0-8010-7977-2). Baker Bk.
Stewart, Ken. Do's & Don'ts for an Overnight Stay in the Lion's Den. 31p. 1977. pap. 1.00 (ISBN 0-89274-043-4). Harrison Hse.
--Doubt: The Enemy of Faith. 32p. (Orig.). 1976. pap. 1.00 (ISBN 0-89274-034-5). Harrison Hse.
Stroud, Matthew D. Celos Aun Del Aire Matan. LC 80-54543. 1981. 12.00 (ISBN 0-911536-90-6). Trinity U Pr.
Surath, Sri. To God Through Faith: From Christ to Sri Ramakrishna. 1978. pap. 3.00 (ISBN 0-685-58452-6). Ranney Pubns.
Sweeting, George. Como Iniciar la Vida Cristiana. new ed. Clifford, Alec, tr. from Eng. (Editorial Moody - Spanish Publications Ser.). 1977. pap. 2.50 (ISBN 0-8024-1615-2). Moody.
Talmage, James E. Articles of Faith. 1970. pocket brown leather ed. 11.00 (ISBN 0-87747-374-9); pocket black leather ed. 11.00 (ISBN 0-87747-320-X); pocket blue fab. leather ed. o.s.i. 5.50 (ISBN 0-87747-457-5); black leather ed. 14.50 (ISBN 0-87747-319-6); brown leather ed. 14.50 (ISBN 0-87747-373-0); missionary ed. 6.95 (ISBN 0-87747-317-X); lib. bdg. 5.50 (ISBN 0-87747-318-8). Deseret Bk.
Tengbom, Mildred. Sometimes I Hurt. 192p. 1980. pap. 7.95 (ISBN 0-8407-5727-1). Nelson.
Theissen, Gerd. A Critical Faith: A Case for Religion. Bowden, John, tr. from Ger. LC 79-7393. 112p. 1979. pap. 4.95 (ISBN 0-8006-1373-2, 1-1373). Fortress.
Thielicke, Helmut. The Faith Letters. 1978. 7.95 (ISBN 0-8499-0039-5, 0039-5). Word Bks.
Thompson, William M. Christ & Consciousness: Exploring Christ's Contribution to Human Consciousness. LC 77-83557. 206p. 1977. pap. 5.95 (ISBN 0-8091-2066-6). Paulist Pr.
Thurman, Howard, intro. by. Why I Believe There Is a God. 121p. 3.95 (ISBN 0-87485-015-0). Johnson Chi.
Tillich, Paul. Dynamics of Faith. pap. 2.95 (ISBN 0-06-090488-7, CN488, CN). Har-Row.
Troki, Isaac. Faith Strengthened. Mocatta, Moses, tr. from Hebrew. LC 74-136768. 320p. 1975. pap. 7.50 (ISBN 0-87203-022-9). Hermon.
Upton, Charles B. Lectures on the Bases of Religious Belief. 2nd ed. LC 77-27161. (Hibbert Lectures: 1893). Repr. of 1897 ed. 31.50 (ISBN 0-404-60411-0). AMS Pr.
Vander Kolk, Justin. To Set Things Right: The Bible Speaks on Faith & Justice. 48p. 1971. pap. 1.25 (ISBN 0-377-02001-X). Friend Pr.
Van Til, C. Why I Believe in God. pap. 0.30 (ISBN 0-87552-496-6). Presby & Reformed.
Van Til, Cornelius. Defense of Faith. pap. 5.00 (ISBN 0-8010-9272-8). Baker Bk.
Verdery, John D. It's Better to Believe. LC 64-20780. 224p. 1964. 7.95 (ISBN 0-87131-009-0). M Evans.
Verhalen, Philip A. Faith in a Secularized World. LC 75-46067. 180p. 1976. pap. 3.95 (ISBN 0-8091-1937-4). Paulist Pr.
Warfield, B. B. Faith & Life. 1974. pap. 5.45 (ISBN 0-85151-188-0). Banner of Truth.
Watts, Alan W. Does It Matter. LC 72-89988. 1971. pap. 2.45 (ISBN 0-394-71665-5, Vin). Random.
Weyland, Jack. First Day Forever & the Other Stories for LDS Youth. LC 80-82455. 120p. 1980. 6.95 (ISBN 0-88290-136-2, 2037). Horizon Utah.
Wieman, Henry N. Seeking a Faith for a New Age. Hepler, Cedric L., ed. LC 74-34052. 1975. 15.00 (ISBN 0-8108-0795-5). Scarecrow.
Wigglesworth, Smith. Ever Increasing Faith. rev. ed. 1971. pap. 1.95 (ISBN 0-88243-494-2, 02-0494). Gospel Pub.
--Faith That Prevails. 1938. pap. 1.25 (ISBN 0-88243-711-9, 02-0711). Gospel Pub.
William Of St Thierry. The Mirror of Faith. Elder, E. Rozanne, ed. Davis, Thomas X., tr. from Lat. LC 78-12897. (Cistercian Fathers Ser.). 1979. 12.95 (ISBN 0-87907-315-2). Cistercian Pubns.
Williams, Herbert L. No Room for Doubt. LC 75-39574. 168p. 1976. pap. 2.95 (ISBN 0-8054-5236-2). Broadman.
Williams, Paul L., ed. Christian Faith in a Neo-Pagan Society: Proceedings of the Fellowship of Catholic Scholara. LC 81-80229. 128p. (Orig.). 1981. pap. 5.95 (ISBN 0-937374-02-4); pap. text ed. 4.50 (ISBN 0-937374-03-2). NE Bks.
Winley, Jesse. Fe Incommovible. 218p. (Span.). 1980. pap. 2.25 (ISBN 0-8297-0979-7). Life Pubs Intl.
Wintz, Jack, ed. Has Change Shattered Our Faith? A Hopeful Look at the Church Today, Vol. 2. (Catholic Update Ser). (Illus.). 111p. 1976. pap. 1.95 (ISBN 0-912228-22-9). St Anthony Mess Pr.
--Our Journey in Faith. (Catholic Update Book Ser.). 124p. (Orig.). 1980. pap. 2.25 (ISBN 0-912228-65-2). St Anthony Mess Pr.
Wirt, Sherwood E. Faith's Heroes. LC 78-71943. 1979. pap. 2.95 (ISBN 0-89107-162-8, Cornerstone Bks). Good News.
Wise, Karen. Confessions of a Totaled Woman. 160p. 1980. 6.95 (ISBN 0-8407-5725-5). Nelson.
Wolff, Robert L. Gains & Losses. (Victorian Fiction Ser). Orig. Title: Faith & Doubt in Victorian England. 1975. lib. bdg. 66.00 (ISBN 0-8240-1617-3). Garland Pub.
Woodward, Mary A. Be Still & Know: Devotional Readings. rev. ed. 1976. pap. 1.95 (ISBN 0-87604-019-9). ARE Pr.

Wurmbrand, Richard. Victorious Faith. 1979. pap. 3.95 (ISBN 0-88264-120-4). Diane Bks.
Youngblood, Ronald F. Faith of Our Fathers. LC 75-23514. 1976. pap. 1.85 (ISBN 0-8307-0370-5, S302-1-01). Regal.

FAITH, CONFESSIONS OF

see Creeds

FAITH AND JUSTIFICATION

see Justification

FAITH AND REASON

see also Philosophy and Religion; Religion and Science

Ashbrook, James B. & Walaskay, Paul W. Christianity for Pious Skeptics. LC 77-911. 1977. pap. 4.95 (ISBN 0-687-07646-3). Abingdon.
Beardsmore, R. W. Moral Reasoning. LC 75-77605. 1969. 7.00x (ISBN 0-8052-3166-8). Schocken.
Bewkes, Eugene G. & Keene, J. Calvin. Western Heritage of Faith & Reason. LC 63-9052. 1963. 13.95 (ISBN 0-9603084-0-7). J Calvin Keene.
Blanshard, Brand. Reason & Belief. LC 74-13253. 600p. 1975. 37.00x (ISBN 0-300-01825-8). Yale U Pr.
Crowley, Mary C. You Can Too. (Power Bks.). 128p. 1980. pap. 3.95 (ISBN 0-8007-5028-4). Revell.
Farah, Charles, Jr. From the Pinnacle of the Temple: Faith or Presumption. 1979. pap. 4.95 (ISBN 0-88270-462-1). Logos.
Ferre, Nels F. Faith & Reason. facsimile ed. LC 78-142626. (Essay Index Reprints - Reason & the Christian Faith Ser.: Vol. 1). Repr. of 1946 ed. 17.00 (ISBN 0-8369-2392-8). Arno.
Flewelling, Ralph T. The Reason in Faith. LC 75-3148. Repr. of 1924 ed. 17.00 (ISBN 0-404-59155-8). AMS Pr.
Hegel. Glauben und Wissen (Faith & Knowledge) Cerf, Walter & Harris, H. S., eds. Cerf, Walter & Harris, H. S., trs. from Ger. LC 76-10250. 1977. 19.00 (ISBN 0-87395-338-X); microfiche o.p. 17.00 (ISBN 0-87395-339-8). State U NY Pr.
Holmes, Arthur F. All Truth Is God's Truth. LC 77-3567. 1977. pap. 3.95 (ISBN 0-8028-1701-7). Eerdmans.
LeNoir, C. P. Dictionnaire des Droits et de la Raison. Migne, J. P., ed. (Troisieme et Derniere Encyclopedie Theologique Ser.: Vol. 57). 952p. (Fr.). Date not set. Repr. of 1860 ed. lib. bdg. 120.00x (ISBN 0-89241-323-9). Caratzas Bros.
--Dictionnaire des Harmonies de la Raison et de la Foi. Migne, J. P., ed. (Troisieme et Derniere Encyclopedie Theologique Ser.: Vol. 19). 876p. (Fr.). Date not set. Repr. of 1856 ed. lib. bdg. 110.50x (ISBN 0-89241-302-6). Caratzas Bros.
Martin, Maurice. Identity & Faith. (Focal Pamphlet Ser.: No. 31). 112p. (Orig.). 1981. pap. 3.95 (ISBN 0-8361-1979-7). Human Serv Dev.
Moltmann, Jurgen. Experiences of God. Kohl, Margaret, tr. from Ger. LC 80-8046. 96p. 1980. pap. 3.95 (ISBN 0-8006-1406-2, 1-1406). Fortress.
Moreno, Francisco J. Between Faith & Reason. 1977. pap. 2.95 (ISBN 0-06-090593-X, CN 593, CN). Har-Row.
Parker, Francis H. Reason & Faith Revisited. (Aquinas Lecture 1971). 6.95 (ISBN 0-87462-136-4). Marquette.
Pieper, Josef. Belief & Faith: A Philosophical Tract. Winston, Richard & Winston, Clara, trs. from German. LC 75-31841. 106p. 1976. Repr. of 1963 ed. lib. bdg. 15.00x (ISBN 0-8371-8490-8, PIBF). Greenwood.
Ramm, Bernard L. A Christian Appeal to Reason. LC 70-188071. Orig. Title: The God Who Makes a Difference. 1977. pap. 3.95 (ISBN 0-8499-2812-5, 2812-5). Word Bks.
Redwood, John. Reason, Ridicule & Religion. 1976. 12.00x (ISBN 0-674-74953-7). Harvard U Pr.
Roberts, James D. Faith & Reason: A Comparative Study of Pascal, Bergson & James. 1962. 4.50 (ISBN 0-8158-0176-9). Chris Mass.
Sandberg, Karl C. At the Crossroads of Faith & Reason: An Essay on Pierre Bayle. LC 66-18531. 1966. 2.00 (ISBN 0-8165-0011-8). U of Ariz Pr.
Stott, John R. Your Mind Matters. LC 72-94672. 64p. 1973. pap. 1.75 (ISBN 0-87784-441-0). Inter-Varsity.
White, Ellen G. Selected Messages, Vol. III. 1980. Christian Home Library Ed. 5.95 (ISBN 0-8280-0055-7, 19275-7); Shield Ser. Ed. 4.50 (ISBN 0-8280-0056-5, 19276-5); Special Ed. pap. 2.95 (ISBN 0-8280-0057-3, 19277-3). Review & Herald.
--Selected Messages, 3 vols. 1980. Set. pap. 7.95 (ISBN 0-8280-0059-X, 19269-0). Review & Herald.

FAITH-CURE

see also Christian Science; Medicine, Magic, Mystic, and Spagiric; Mental Healing; Miracles; Therapeutics, Suggestive

Anthony, C. & Anthony, R. Heal Yourself. 1950. 7.95 (ISBN 0-910140-00-6). Anthony.
Bailey, Keith M. The Children's Bread. LC 77-83941. 1977. 5.95 (ISBN 0-87509-063-X). Chr Pubns.
Baker, Robert J. God Healed Me. LC 74-17801. (Pivot Family Reader Ser). 176p. (Orig.). 1974. pap. 1.75 (ISBN 0-87983-101-4). Keats.
Bales, James D. Miracles or Mirages. 1956. 3.00 (ISBN 0-686-21487-0). Firm Foun Pub.
Bartow, Donald W. The Adventures of Healing: How to Use New Testament Practices & Receive New Testament Results. rev. ed. 371p. 1981. pap. 5.95 (ISBN 0-938736-02-7). Life Enrich.
Baxter, J. Sidlow. Divine Healing of the Body. 1979. 7.95 (ISBN 0-310-20720-7). Zondervan.
Beierie, Herbert L. How to Give a Healing Treatment. 1979. 1.00 (ISBN 0-686-23900-8). U of Healing.
Beierle, Herbert L. Proclaim Your God. 1.00 (ISBN 0-686-23899-0). U of Healing.
--Quiet Healing Zone. 1980. 10.00 (ISBN 0-686-23897-4). U of Healing.
--School for Masters. 1979. 1.00 (ISBN 0-686-23901-6). U of Healing.
--Why I Can Say I Am God. 1978. 1.00 (ISBN 0-686-23898-2). U of Healing.
Bittner, Vernon J. Make Your Illness Count: A Hospital Chaplain Shows How God's Healing Power Can Be Released in Your Life. LC 76-3862. 128p. (Orig.). 1976. pap. 3.50 (ISBN 0-8066-1532-X, 10-4260). Augsburg.
--You Can Help with Your Healing: A Guide for Recovering Wholeness in Body, Mind, & Spirit. LC 78-66946. 1979. pap. 3.95 (ISBN 0-8066-1698-9, 10-7411). Augsburg.
Bloch, Marc. The Royal Touch: Sacred Monarchy & Scrofula in England & France. Anderson, J. E., tr. (Illus.). 496p. 1973. 20.00x (ISBN 0-7735-0071-5). McGill-Queens U Pr.
Bosworth, F. F. Christ the Healer. pap. 3.95 (ISBN 0-8007-0647-1). Revell.
Brennan, R. O. & Hosier, Helen K. Coronary? Cancer? God's Answer: Prevent It. LC 79-84719. 1979. pap. 3.95 (ISBN 0-89081-181-4, 1814). Harvest Hse.
Campbell, Roger. Weight! A Better Way to Lose. 128p. 1976. pap. 3.50 (ISBN 0-88207-735-X). Victor Bks.
Carter, Craig. How to Use the Power of Mind in Everyday Life. 96p. 1976. pap. 3.50 (ISBN 0-911336-65-6). Sci of Mind.
A Century of Christian Science Healing. LC 66-15060. 1966. 6.00 (ISBN 0-87510-001-5); pap. 2.75 (ISBN 0-87510-067-8). Chr Science.
Cerutti, Edwina. Mystic with the Healing Hands: The Life of Olga Worrall. LC 75-9317. 1977. pap. 5.95 (ISBN 0-06-061357-2, RD 244, HarpR). Har-Row.
--Olga Worrall: Mystic with the Healing Hands. LC 75-9317. 192p. 1975. 7.95 (ISBN 0-06-061358-0, HarpR). Har-Row.
Clark, Glenn. How to Find Health Through Prayer. LC 77-7830. 1977. pap. 2.95 (ISBN 0-06-061391-2, RD 242, HarpR). Har-Row.
Cohen, Daniel E. The Far Side of Consciousness. LC 74-11747. (Illus.). 234p. 1974. 6.95 (ISBN 0-396-07002-7). Dodd.
Daneel, M. L. Zionism & Faith-Healing in Rhodesia: Aspects of African Independent Churches. V. A. February Communications, tr. from Dutch. (Illus.). 1970. pap. 8.35x (ISBN 90-2796-278-2). Mouton.
Day, Wilbur V. Through Hell to Heaven. 1978. 5.95 (ISBN 0-533-03543-0). Vantage.
Dearing, Trevor. Supernatural Healing Today. 1979. pap. 3.95 (ISBN 0-88270-340-4). Logos.
Divine Physical Healing, Past & Present. 272p. pap. 2.50 (ISBN 0-686-29107-7). Faith Pub Hse.
Eddy, Mary B. Science & Health with Key to the Scriptures. standard ed. 9.00 (ISBN 0-686-01047-7); new type ed. 17.50 (ISBN 0-686-01048-5); new type lea. bdg. 53.00 (ISBN 0-686-01049-3); readers ed. 30.00 (ISBN 0-686-01050-7); lea. bdg. 75.00 (ISBN 0-686-01051-5); brown lea. bdg 32.50 (ISBN 0-686-01052-3); pap. 3.50 (ISBN 0-686-01053-1); new type bonded lea. ed. 35.00 (ISBN 0-686-01054-X). First Church.
--Science & Health with Key to the Scriptures. Incl. Vol. 1. Danish Ed. 20.00 (ISBN 0-686-24384-6); Vol. 2. Dutch Ed. 20.00 (ISBN 0-686-24385-4); Vol. 3. French Ed. 20.00 (ISBN 0-686-24386-2); Vol. 4. German Ed. 20.00 (ISBN 0-686-24387-0); Vol. 5. Norwegian Ed. 20.00 (ISBN 0-686-24388-9); Vol. 6. Swedish Ed. 20.00 (ISBN 0-686-24389-7); Vol. 7. Russian Ed. 20.00 (ISBN 0-686-24390-0); Vol. 8. Greek Ed. 15.00 (ISBN 0-686-24391-9); Vol. 9. Italian Ed. 15.00 (ISBN 0-686-24392-7); Vol. 10. Spanish Ed. 12.00 (ISBN 0-686-24393-5). First Church.
Fillmore, Charles. Jesus Christ Heals. 1939. 2.95 (ISBN 0-87159-070-0). Unity Bks.
Fisk, Samuel. Divine Healing Under the Searchlight. LC 78-15083. 1978. pap. 2.25 (ISBN 0-87227-057-2). Reg Baptist.
Glennon, Canon J. Your Healing Is Within You. 1980. pap. 4.95 (ISBN 0-88270-457-5). Logos.
Goldsmith, Joel S. Realization of Oneness: The Practice of Spiritual Healing. 200p. 1974. pap. 4.95 (ISBN 0-8065-0453-6). Citadel Pr.
Gordon, Adoniram J. Ministry of Healing. 3.95 (ISBN 0-87509-106-7); pap. 2.75 (ISBN 0-87509-107-5). Chr Pubns.
Hagin, Kenneth E. Seven Things You Should Know About Divine Healing. 1979. pap. 1.95 (ISBN 0-89276-400-7). Hagin Ministries.
Hagin, Kenneth, Jr. Seven Hindrances to Healing. 1980. pap. 0.50 (ISBN 0-89276-705-7). Hagin Ministry.
Harrell, David E., Jr. All Things Are Possible: The Healing & Charismatic Revivals in Modern America. LC 75-1937. (Midland Bks.: No. 221). (Illus.). 320p. 1976. 15.00x (ISBN 0-253-10090-9); pap. 7.95x (ISBN 0-253-20221-3). Ind U Pr.
Harwood, Alan. Rx: Spiritist As Needed; a Study of a Puerto Rican Community Mental Health Resource. LC 76-54841. (Contemporary Religious Movements). 1977. 28.95 (ISBN 0-471-35828-2, Pub. by Wiley-Interscience). Wiley.
Heline, Corinne. Healing & Regeneration Through Color. 17th ed. 65p. 1980. pap. 2.25 (ISBN 0-87516-430-7). De Vorss.
--Healing & Regeneration Through Music. 19th ed. 1980. pap. 1.95 (ISBN 0-87516-431-5). De Vorss.
Jeter, Hugh P. By His Stripes: The Doctrine of Divine Healing. LC 76-20893. 1977. pap. 3.95 (ISBN 0-88243-521-3, 02-0521). Gospel Pub.
Johnson, Margaret. Beyond Heartache. 1980. 6.95 (ISBN 0-310-26690-4). Zondervan.
Judd, Wayne. Healing: Faith or Fraud. (Uplook Ser.). 1978. pap. 0.75 (ISBN 0-8163-0199-9, 08303-0). Pacific Pr Pub Assn.
Kelsey, Morton. Healing & Christianity. LC 72-78065. 1976. pap. 6.95 (ISBN 0-06-064381-1, RD 161, HarpR). Har-Row.
Kinnear, Willis. Spiritual Healing. 110p. (Orig.). 1973. pap. 3.95 (ISBN 0-911336-50-8). Sci of Mind.
Koch, Kurt E. Between Christ & Satan. LC 79-160690. 1972. pap. 2.95 (ISBN 0-8254-3003-8). Kregel.
Kuhlman, Kathryn. I Believe in Miracles. 1969. pap. 1.95 (ISBN 0-8007-8051-5, Spire Bks). Revell.
--Ten Thousand Miles for a Miracle. LC 74-4851. (Kathryn Kuhlman Ser). 96p. 1974. pap. 0.95 (ISBN 0-87123-536-6, 200536). Bethany Hse.
Lawson, Jo. Curado Do Cancer. (Port.). Date not set. pap. 1.20 (ISBN 0-686-75290-2). Life Pubs Intl.
Lightner, Robert P. Speaking in Tongues & Divine Healing. LC 65-5805. 1978. pap. 1.95 (ISBN 0-87227-059-9). Reg Baptist.
Lindsay, Gordon. The Real Reason Why Christians Are Sick. (Divine Healing & Health Ser.). 1.50 (ISBN 0-89985-029-4). Christ Nations.
--Twenty-Five Objections to Divine Healing & the Bible Answers. (Divine Healing & Health Ser.). 0.95 (ISBN 0-89985-030-8). Christ Nations.
Linn, Matthew L. & Linn, D. Healing of Memories: Prayers & Confession-Steps to Inner Healing. LC 74-17697. 112p. (Orig.). 1974. pap. 2.50 (ISBN 0-8091-1854-8). Paulist Pr.
Loomis, Evarts G. & Paulson, Sig. Healing for Everyone. 2nd, rev. ed. LC 74-345. (Illus., Orig.). 1979. pap. 5.95 (ISBN 0-87516-377-7). De Vorss.
Mackes, Shy. Seven Steps to God's Healing Power. pap. 0.50 (ISBN 0-910924-28-7). Macalester.
Maclachlan, Lewis. How to Pray for Healing. 112p. 1977. pap. 3.50 (ISBN 0-227-67486-3). Attic Pr.
MacNutt, Francis. Healing. LC 74-81446. (Illus.). 336p. 1974. pap. 3.50 (ISBN 0-87793-074-0). Ave Maria.
--Healing. 1977. pap. 2.50 (ISBN 0-553-13792-1, C13792-1). Bantam.
--The Prayer That Heals. LC 80-69770. 120p. (Orig.). 1981. pap. 2.95 (ISBN 0-87793-219-0). Ave Maria.
Marsingill, Leroy. I Have Seen Visions of God. 1978. 6.95 (ISBN 0-533-03636-4). Vantage.
Medhaug, Eleanore. Joy in the Valley. 1978. 7.95 (ISBN 0-533-03418-3). Vantage.
Miner, Malcolm. Healing Is for Real. pap. 3.95 (ISBN 0-8192-1132-X). Morehouse.
Morningland Publications, Inc., ed. Healing: As It Is, 2 vols. (Illus.). 320p. (Orig.). 1981. Set. pap. 10.00 (ISBN 0-935146-59-8). Morningland.
Murphy, Joseph. Amazing Laws of Cosmic Mind Power. 1965. pap. 3.95 (ISBN 0-13-023804-X, Reward). P-H.
--How to Use Your Healing Power. 158p. 1973. pap. 3.00 (ISBN 0-87516-186-3). De Vorss.
--Infinite Power for Richer Living. 1969. 8.95 (ISBN 0-13-464396-8, Reward); pap. 3.95 (ISBN 0-685-93566-3). P-H.
Murray, Andrew. Divine Healing. 1962. pap. 1.75 (ISBN 0-87508-375-7). Chr Lit.
Neal, Emily G. The Healing Power of Christ. 1972. pap. 4.50 (ISBN 0-8015-3348-1, Hawthorn). Dutton.
--Reporter Finds God Through Spiritual Healing. (Orig.). 1965. pap. 4.50 (ISBN 0-8192-1057-9). Morehouse.
Noonan, Richard H. Cancer! The Mind As a Factor in Healing. LC 77-71456. (Illus.). 1977. pap. 5.00 (ISBN 0-89506-000-0). Foun Better.
Paramananda, Swami. Healing Meditations. 3rd ed. 1980. 1.00 (ISBN 0-911564-28-4). Vedanta Ctr.
Parker, Faye W. Mental, Physical, Spiritual Health. LC 79-56170. 80p. 1980. pap. 2.95 (ISBN 0-87516-397-1). De Vorss.
Parkhurst, Genevieve. Healing & Wholeness. 5.95 (ISBN 0-910924-90-2). Macalester.
Peterman, Mary E. Healing: A Spiritual Adventure. LC 74-80416. 104p. 1974. pap. 3.25 (ISBN 0-8006-1086-5, 1-1086). Fortress.
Peterson, John H. Healing Touch. LC 81-80629. (Illus.). 112p. (Orig.). 1981. pap. 4.95 (ISBN 0-8192-1291-1). Morehouse.
Podmore, Frank. From Mesmer to Christian Science: A Short History of Mental Healing. 10.00 (ISBN 0-8216-0034-6). Univ Bks.
Popejoy, Bill. The Case for Divine Healing. 1976. pap. 0.95 (ISBN 0-88243-478-0, 02-0478). Gospel Pub.
Price, Frederick K. Is Healing for All? (Orig.). 1976. pap. 2.95 (ISBN 0-89274-005-1). Harrison Hse.
Prince, Derek. Laying on of Hands. (Foundation Ser.: Bk. V). 1965-66. pap. 1.50 (ISBN 0-934920-04-4, B-14). Derek Prince.
Puryear, Meredith. Healing Through Meditation & Prayer. rev. ed. 1978. pap. 2.95 (ISBN 0-87604-104-7). ARE Pr.
Reed, William S. Healing the Whole Man. (Power Bks.). 128p. 1980. pap. 3.95 (ISBN 0-8007-5025-X). Revell.
Sanford, Agnes. Healing Gifts of the Spirit. 1976. pap. 1.75 (ISBN 0-89129-188-1). Jove Pubns.
--Healing Light. 4.95 (ISBN 0-910924-36-8); pap. 3.25 (ISBN 0-910924-37-6); pocketsize 2.50 (ISBN 0-910924-52-X). Macalester.
--Healing Power of the Bible. 1976. pap. 1.75 (ISBN 0-89129-192-X). Jove Pubns.
Scanlan, Michael. Inner Healing. LC 74-81901. 96p. (Orig.). 1974. pap. 2.95 (ISBN 0-8091-1846-7). Paulist Pr.
Schuller, Robert H. & Schuller, Arvella. The Courage of Carol: Pearls from Tears. LC 78-65619. 1978. pap. 1.75 (ISBN 0-89081-182-2, 1822). Harvest Hse.
Scott-Whiting, John. Return to God & His Gift of Healing. 1980. 9.50 (ISBN 0-682-49545-X). Exposition.
Shlemon, Barbara Leahy. Healing Prayer. LC 75-36056. 88p. 1975. pap. 1.75 (ISBN 0-87793-108-9). Ave Maria.
Simpson, Albert B. Gospel of Healing. pap. 2.95 (ISBN 0-87509-012-5). Chr Pubns.
Spiritual Healing Techniques: Methods of Diagnosis. 2.45 (ISBN 0-686-23673-4). Lotus Ashram.
Stapleton, Ruth C. Experiencing Inner Healing. 1977. 7.95 (ISBN 0-87680-507-1). Word Bks.
Steinke, Frank F. Greater Works Shall Ye Do. 101p. (Orig.). 1980. pap. 2.25 (ISBN 0-686-73996-5). Impact Bks Mo.
Tyrrell, Bernard J. Christotheraphy: Healing Through Enlightment. 1981. pap. 5.95 (ISBN 0-8164-2304-0). Seabury.
Weatherhead, Leslie D. Psychology, Religion & Healing. LC 54-6986. (Series D). 1959. pap. 6.95 (ISBN 0-687-34885-4, Apex). Abingdon.
Wolf, William. Healers, Gurus, Spiritual Guide. LC 76-2180. 1969. pap. 6.50 (ISBN 0-933900-07-4). Foun Human Under.
Woodward, Mary A., compiled by. That Ye May Heal: A Manual for Individual & Group Study of Meditation for Healing, from the Edgar Cayce Records. rev. ed. 53p. 1970. pap. 2.50 (ISBN 0-87604-075-X). ARE Pr.
Worrall, A. & Worrall, O. The Gift of Healing. LC 65-26006. 1976. pap. 4.95 (ISBN 0-06-069687-7, RD 154, HarpR). Har-Row.
Yeomans, Lilian B. The Great Physician. 1933. pap. 1.00 (ISBN 0-88243-729-1, 02-0729). Gospel Pub.
--Healing from Heaven. 1926. pap. 1.25 (ISBN 0-88243-730-5, 02-0730). Gospel Pub.
--Health & Healing. 1938. pap. 1.00 (ISBN 0-88243-732-1, 02-0732). Gospel Pub.
Yoder, Jonathan G. Healing: Prayer or Pills? LC 74-30988. 56p. 1975. pap. 0.95 (ISBN 0-8361-1763-8). Herald Pr.

FAITH HEALING

see Faith-Cure

FALAISE GAP, BATTLE OF, 1944

Lucas, James S. & Barker, James. The Battle of Normandy: Falaise Gap. LC 78-17771. 1978. text ed. 18.50x (ISBN 0-8419-0418-9). Holmes & Meier.

FALANGE ESPANOLA TRADICIONALISTA Y DE LAS JUNTAS OFENSIVAS NACIONAL-SINDICALISTAS

Chase, Allen. Falange: The Axis Secret Army in the Americas. LC 78-63659. (Studies in Fascism: Ideology & Practice). Repr. of 1943 ed. 26.00 (ISBN 0-404-16919-8). AMS Pr.

FALASHAS

Leslau, Wolf, tr. Falasha Anthology. (Judaica Ser.: No. 6). (Illus.). 1951. 20.00x (ISBN 0-300-00681-0). Yale U Pr.

FALCONER, WILLIAM, 1732-1769

Friedrich, Johann. William Falconer's the Shipwreck. pap. 10.00 (ISBN 0-384-16940-6). Johnson Repr.

FALCONRY

see also Fowling

Allen, Mark. Falconry in Arabia. (Illus.). 143p. Date not set. 40.00 (ISBN 0-89182-034-5). Charles River Bks.

Ap Evans, Humphrey. Falconry. LC 73-80791. (Illus.). 160p. 1974. 15.00 (ISBN 0-668-03339-8). Arco.

Beebe, F. L. Hawks Falcons & Falconry. (Illus.). 1976. 25.00x (ISBN 0-919654-40-1, Pub. by Hancock Hse). Universe.

Beebe, Frank L. & Webster, Harold M., eds. North American Falconry & Hunting Hawks. 4th ed. (Illus.). 330p. 1976. 30.00x (ISBN 0-685-66290-X). North Am Fal Hunt.

Berners, Juliana. The Boke of Saint Albans Containing Treatises on Hawking, Hunting & Cote Armour. 1976. Repr. of 1881 ed. 25.00 (ISBN 0-403-06683-2, Regency). Scholarly.

--The Book of Hawking, Hunting & Blasing of Arms. LC 74-25849. (English Experience Ser.: No. 151). 180p. 1969. Repr. of 1486 ed. 42.00 (ISBN 90-221-0151-7). Walter J Johnson.

Bert, Edmund. An Approved Treatise of Hawkes & Hawking Divided into Three Bookes. LC 68-54618. (English Experience Ser.: No. 23). 110p. 1968. Repr. of 1619 ed. 16.00 (ISBN 90-221-0023-5). Walter J Johnson.

Burton, Richard F. Falconry in the Valley of the Indus. 1971. 13.50 (ISBN 0-914802-02-X). Falcon Head Pr.

Danielsson, Bror, ed. Middle English Falconry Treatises, Pt. 1. (Mediaeval English Hunt, Cynegetica Anglica: Vol. 2). 1980. pap. text ed. write for info. (ISBN 0-391-01141-3). Humanities.

Falconer's Club of American Journals: 1941-1961. 1974. 32.50 (ISBN 0-914802-01-1). Falcon Head Pr.

Fisher, Charles H. Falconry Reminiscences. 1972. 15.00 (ISBN 0-914802-03-8); deluxe ed. 25.00, limited (ISBN 0-914802-04-6). Falcon Head Pr.

Frederick II Of Hohenstaufen. The Art of Falconry. Wood, Casey A. & Fyfe, F. Marjorie, eds. (Illus.). 1943. 39.50 (ISBN 0-8047-0374-4). Stanford U Pr.

Freeman, Gage E. & Salvin, Francis H. Falconry: Its Claims, History & Practice. 1972. 12.50 (ISBN 0-914802-05-4); deluxe ed. 25.00, limited (ISBN 0-914802-06-2). Falcon Head Pr.

Glasier. Falconry & Hawking. 53.00 (ISBN 0-7134-0232-6). David & Charles.

Glasier, Phillip. Falconry & Hawking. (Illus.). 312p. 1979. 15.50 (ISBN 0-8231-2020-1). Branford.

Gryndall, William. Hawking, Hunting, Fouling & Fishing; Newly Corrected by W. Gryndall Faulkener. LC 70-38194. (English Experience Ser.: No. 463). 88p. 1972. Repr. of 1596 ed. 13.00 (ISBN 90-221-0463-X). Walter J Johnson.

Hands, Rachel, ed. English Hawking & Hunting in the Boke of St. Albans. facsimile ed. (Oxford English Monographs). (Illus.). 264p. 1975. 55.00x (ISBN 0-19-811715-9). Oxford U Pr.

Harting, James E. Bibliotheca Accipitraria, a Catalogue of Books Ancient & Modern Relating to Falconry: With Notes, Glossary & Vocabulary. xxviii, 289p. 1977. Repr. of 1963 ed. 45.00 (ISBN 0-900470-82-8). Oak Knoll.

Jameson, E. W., Jr. The Hawking of Japan, the History & Development of Japanese Falconry. (Illus.). 94p. Repr. of 1962 ed. 24.50 (ISBN 0-686-15629-3). E W Jameson Jr.

Jameson, E. W., Jr. & Peeters, Hans J. Introduction to Hawking. 2nd ed. (Illus.). 1977. pap. 8.95 (ISBN 0-686-15630-7). E W Jameson Jr.

Lascelles, Gerald. Art of Falconry. 10.50 (ISBN 0-8231-2015-5). Branford.

Latham, Simon. Lathams Falconry, 2 pts. LC 76-57395. (English Experience Ser.: No. 812). 1977. Repr. of 1615 ed. Set. lib. bdg. 32.50 (ISBN 90-221-0812-0). Walter J Johnson.

McElroy, Harry. Desert Hawking II. LC 78-300502. (Illus.). 1977. 17.00 (ISBN 0-686-14434-1). H C McElroy.

Madden, D. H. Chapter of Mediaeval History. LC 74-91048. 1969. Repr. of 1924 ed. 15.00 (ISBN 0-8046-0658-7). Kennikat.

Mellor, J. E. Falconry Notes by Mellor. 1972. 8.50 (ISBN 0-914802-07-0). Falcon Head Pr.

Phillott, D. C. & Harcourt, E. S., trs. from Persian, Urdu. Falconry - Two Treatises. 1968. text ed. 30.00 (ISBN 0-685-57148-3). Falcon Head Pr.

Saiga Editors, ed. Falconry. 1981. 10.00x (ISBN 0-86230-031-2, Pub. by Saiga Pub). State Mutual Bk.

Salvin, Francis H. & Broderick, William. Falconry in the British Isles. 1970. Repr. of 1855 ed. 22.50x (ISBN 0-901951-18-8). North Am Fal Hunt.

Schlegel, H. & Verster De Wulverhorst, J. A. The World of Falconry. Chilvers, Timothy, tr. LC 80-51189. Orig. Title: La Chasse Au Vol. (Illus.). 184p. (Fr.). 1980. 60.00 (ISBN 0-86565-004-7). Vendome.

Schlegel, H. & Wulverhorst, A. H. Traite De Fauconnerie: Treatise of Falconry. Hanlon, Thomas, tr. (Illus.). 1973. 32.50 (ISBN 0-913930-01-6). Chasse Pubns.

FALCONRY–JUVENILE LITERATURE

Kaufmann, John & Meng, Heinz. Falcons Return: Restoring an Endangered Species. (Illus.). 128p. (gr. 7 up). 1975. PLB 7.92 (ISBN 0-688-32027-9). Morrow.

FALCONS

see also Peregrine Falcon

Beebe, F. L. Hawks Falcons & Falconry. (Illus.). 1976. 25.00x (ISBN 0-919654-40-1, Pub. by Hancock Hse). Universe.

FALKLAND, LUCIUS CARY, 2ND VISCOUNT, 1610-1643

Weber, Kurt. Lucius Cary. LC 41-2183. Repr. of 1940 ed. 17.50 (ISBN 0-404-06887-1). AMS Pr.

FALKLAND ISLANDS

Barnard, Charles H. Marooned: Being a Narrative of the Sufferings & Adventures of Captain Charles H. Barnard, Embracing an Account of the Seizure of His Vessel at the Falkland Islands, 1812-1816. Dodge, Bertha S., ed. LC 78-24058. (Illus.). 1979. 14.95 (ISBN 0-8195-5031-0, Pub. by Wesleyan U Pr). Columbia U Pr.

Goebel, Julius, Jr. Struggle for the Falkland Islands. LC 75-130330. (Latin-American History & Culture Ser). 1971. Repr. of 1927 ed. 22.50 (ISBN 0-8046-1390-7). Kennikat.

Strange, Ian. The Falkland Islands. LC 80-85509. (Illus.). 256p. 1981. 22.50 (ISBN 0-7153-8133-4). David & Charles.

FALL, ALBERT BACON, 1861-1944

Werner, Morris R. & Starr, John. Teapot Dome. LC 70-122057. (Illus.). Repr. of 1959 ed. 15.00x (ISBN 0-678-03179-7). Kelley.

FALL

see Autumn

FALL OF MAN

see also Good and Evil; Paradise; Sin; Sin, Original

Bonhoeffer, Dietrich. Creation & Fall. Bd. with Temptation. 1965. pap. 1.95 (ISBN 0-02-083890-5, 08389). Macmillan.

Gurteen, S. Humphreys. Epic of the Fall of Man. LC 65-15879. (Studies in Comparative Literature, No. 35). 1969. Repr. of 1896 ed. lib. bdg. 49.95 (ISBN 0-8383-0561-X). Haskell.

Sharpless, F. Parvin. The Myth of the Fall: Literature of Innocence & Experience. (Humanities Ser). 256p. (gr. 9-12). 1974. pap. text ed. 5.94x (ISBN 0-8104-5072-0). Hayden.

Williams, Norman P. The Ideas of the Fall & of Original Sin: A Historical & Critical Study. LC 79-8125. Repr. of 1927 ed. 49.00 (ISBN 0-404-18439-1). AMS Pr.

Woodhull, Marianna. Epic of Paradise Lost. LC 72-194899. 1907. lib. bdg. 8.00 (ISBN 0-8414-9501-7). Folcroft.

--Epic of Paradise Lost: Twelve Essays. LC 68-57833. 1968. Repr. of 1907 ed. 8.50 (ISBN 0-87752-124-7). Gordian.

FALL RIVER LINE

McAdam, Roger W. Commonwealth: Giantess of the Sound. LC 59-11668. (Illus.). 1959. 12.50 (ISBN 0-8044-1613-3, Pub. by Stephen Daye Pr). Ungar.

--Floating Palaces: New England to New York on the Old River Line. LC 72-85203. (Illus.). 1972. 20.00 (ISBN 0-917218-03-5). Mowbray Co.

FALLA, MANUEL DE, 1876-1946

Pahissa, Jaime. Manuel De Falla, His Life & Works. Wagstaff, Jean, tr. LC 78-66917. (Encore Music Editions Ser.). 1979. Repr. of 1954 ed. 17.50 (ISBN 0-88355-756-8). Hyperion Conn.

FALLACIES (LOGIC)

Buridan, John. Sophisms on Meaning & Truth. Scott, Theodore K., ed. LC 66-26800. (Orig.). 1966. pap. text ed. 6.95x (ISBN 0-89197-418-0). Irvington.

Capaldi, Nicholas. The Art of Deception. 2nd ed. LC 75-21077. 200p. 1979. pap. text ed. 5.95 (ISBN 0-87975-058-8). Prometheus Bks.

De Rijk, Lambertus M. Logica Modernorum, Vol. 2. (Philos. Texts & Studies: Vol. 16). 1967. text ed. 116.50x (ISBN 90-232-0440-9). Humanities.

Engel, S. Analyzing Informal Fallacies. 1980. pap. 7.95 (ISBN 0-13-032854-5). P-H.

Engel, S. Morris. With Good Reason: An Introduction to Informal Fallacies. LC 75-33579. 224p. 1976. 14.95 (ISBN 0-312-88480-X); pap. text ed. 4.95 (ISBN 0-312-88515-6). St Martin.

Jouffroy, A. Dictionnaire des Erreurs Sociales. Migne, J. P., ed. (Nouvelle Encyclopedie Theologique Ser.: Vol. 19). 664p. (Fr.). Date not set. Repr. of 1852 ed. lib. bdg. 84.50x (ISBN 0-89241-266-6). Caratzas Bros.

Kahane, Howard. Logic & Contemporary Rhetoric. 3rd ed. 288p. 1980. pap. text ed. 10.95x (ISBN 0-534-00850-X). Wadsworth Pub.

Michalos, A. Improving Your Reasoning. 1970. pap. 7.50 (ISBN 0-13-453456-5). P-H.

Schwanauer, Francis. Those Fallacies by Slight of Reason. 1978. pap. text ed. 7.50 (ISBN 0-8191-0619-4). U Pr of Amer.

Smith, H. B. How the Mind Falls into Error. 93p. 1980. Repr. of 1923 ed. lib. bdg. 20.00 (ISBN 0-89987-757-5). Darby Bks.

FALLIBILITY

see also Errors, Popular

Lowe, Walter J. Mystery & the Unconscious: A Study in the Thought of Paul Ricoeur. LC 76-44865. (ATLA Monograph: No. 9). 1977. 10.00 (ISBN 0-8108-0989-3). Scarecrow.

FALLING-STARS

see Meteors

FALLOPIAN TUBES

Reyniak, J. Victor & Lauersen, Niels H., eds. Principles of Microsurgical Techniques in Infertility. LC 81-3045. 225p. 1981. text ed. price not set (ISBN 0-306-40781-7, Plenum Med Bk). Plenum Pub.

Woodruff, J. Donald & Pauerstein, Carl J. The Fallopian Tube. 370p. 1969. 18.50 (ISBN 0-683-09239-1, Pub. by Williams & Wilkins). Krieger.

FALLOUT, RADIOACTIVE

see Radioactive Fallout

FALLOUT SHELTERS

see Atomic Bomb Shelters

FALLOWING

see also Shifting Cultivation

Broderick, Carlfred B. Marriage & the Family. (Illus.). 1979. text ed. 18.95 (ISBN 0-13-559112-0). P-H.

FALSE SWEARING

see Perjury

FALSEHOOD

see Truthfulness and Falsehood

FAMILIES OF MILITARY PERSONNEL

see Air Force Wives; Army Wives; Navy Wives

FAMILIES OF ROYAL DESCENT

see Royal Descent, Families of

FAMILIES, AFRO-AMERICAN

see Afro-American Families

FAMILY

see also Birth Order; Brothers and Sisters; Children; Church Work with Families; Clans and Clan System; Divorce; Domestic Education; Domestic Relations; Eugenics; Family Life Education; Family Life Surveys; Family Size; Fathers; Foster Home Care; Grandparents; Heredity, Human; Home; Kinship; Marriage; Master and Servant; Matriarchy; Mothers; Parent and Child; Single-Parent Family; Tribes and Tribal System; Twins; Unmarried Couples; Widows

Abrams, Ray H., ed. The American Family in World War Two. LC 79-169365. (Family in America Ser). 196p. 1972. Repr. of 1943 ed. 14.00 (ISBN 0-405-03842-9). Arno.

Ackerman, Nathan W. Psychodynamics of Family Life: Diagnosis & Treatment of Family Relationships. LC 58-13043. 1958. pap. 5.95x (ISBN 0-465-09503-8, TB5004). Basic.

Ackerman, Nathan W., ed. Family Process. LC 75-135562. 1970. text ed. 12.50x (ISBN 0-465-02357-6). Basic.

Adams, Bert N. The Family: A Sociological Interpretation. 3rd ed. LC 81-80805. 530p. 1980. text ed. 16.95x (ISBN 0-395-30555-1); instr. manual free (ISBN 0-528-68112-5). HM.

Aginsky, Bernard W. Kinship Systems & the Forms of Marriage. LC 36-6759. 1935. pap. 7.00 (ISBN 0-527-00544-4). Kraus Repr.

Ainsworth, Charles H., ed. Selected Readings for Marriage & the Family. LC 72-11042. 1973. 34.50x (ISBN 0-8422-5123-5). Irvington.

Albin, Mel & Cavallo, Dominick. Family Life in America. (Illus.). 350p. 1980. 8.95 (ISBN 0-686-64847-1). Revisionary.

Aldous, Joan. Family Careers: Developmental Change in Families. LC 77-15043. 358p. 1978. text ed. 19.95 (ISBN 0-471-02046-X). Wiley.

Aldous, Joan, et al, eds. Politics & Programs of Family Policy: United States & European Perspectives. LC 80-50270. 224p. (Orig.). 1980. pap. text ed. 8.95 (ISBN 0-268-01539-2). U of Notre Dame Pr.

American Sociological Society. The Family. LC 78-169370. (Family in America Ser). 226p. 1972. Repr. of 1909 ed. 16.00 (ISBN 0-405-03846-1). Arno.

Amneus, Daniel. Back to Patriarchy! 1979. 9.95 (ISBN 0-87000-436-0). Arlington Hse.

Anderson, Betty A., et al. The Childbearing Family, Vol. 1: Pregnancy & Family Health. 2nd ed. (Illus.). 1979. pap. text ed. 10.95 (ISBN 0-07-001683-6, HP). Macgraw.

--The Childbearing Family, Vol. 2: Interruptions in Family Health During Pregnancy. 2nd ed. (Illus.). 1979. pap. text ed. 10.95 (ISBN 0-07-001684-4, HP). McGraw.

Andrews, Ernest E. The Emotionally Disturbed Family. LC 73-17734. 256p. 1974. 22.50x (ISBN 0-87668-112-7). Aronson.

Angell, Robert C. The Family Encounters the Depression. 1936. 7.50 (ISBN 0-8446-1030-5). Peter Smith.

Anthony, E. James & Koupernik, Cyrille, eds. The Child in His Family: The International Yearbook for Child Psychiatry & Allied Disciplines, Vol. 1. LC 78-31654. 525p. 1979. Repr. of 1970 ed. lib. bdg. 23.00 (ISBN 0-88275-863-2). Krieger.

Anway, Carol. Family Enrichment Book. 1979. pap. 8.00 (ISBN 0-8309-0247-3). Herald Hse.

Babcock, Dorothy E. Introduction to Growth, Development & Family Life. 3rd ed. 192p. 1972. pap. text ed. 6.00 (ISBN 0-8036-0541-2). Davis Co.

Ball, Gerry. Circle of Warmth: Family Program. 1980. 34.95 (ISBN 0-86584-040-7). Human Dev Train.

--Grounds for Growth: Comprehensive Theory Manual. 1980. 14.95 (ISBN 0-86584-009-1). Human Dev Train.

Bane, Mary J. Here to Stay: American Families in the 20th Century. LC 76-44877. 1978. pap. 4.95x (ISBN 0-465-09726-X, CN-5026). Basic.

Bane, Mary Jo. Here to Stay: American Families in the Twentieth Century. LC 76-7674. (Illus.). 1976. 13.50x (ISBN 0-465-02927-2). Basic.

Barbeau, C., ed. Future of the Family. 1971. pap. 2.95 (ISBN 0-685-07635-0, 80009). Glencoe.

Beck, Dorothy F. Marriage & the Family Under Challenge. 2nd ed. LC 76-26307. 1976. pap. 4.00 (ISBN 0-87304-145-3). Family Serv.

Bell, Norman W. & Vogel, Ezra F., eds. Modern Introduction to the Family. rev. ed. LC 68-12830. 1968. text ed. 15.95 (ISBN 0-02-902330-0). Free Pr.

Bell, Robert R. Marriage & Family Interaction. 5th ed. 1979. text ed. 19.50x (ISBN 0-256-02110-4); pap. study guide 6.50x (ISBN 0-256-02243-7). Dorsey.

Belnap, W. Dean. Raising Families in Our Permissive Society. (Orig.). 1978. pap. 5.95 (ISBN 0-89036-108-8). Hawkes Pub Inc.

Benz, Margaret G. Family Counseling Service in a University Community. LC 70-176556. (Columbia University. Teachers College. Contributions to Education: No. 800). Repr. of 1940 ed. 17.50 (ISBN 0-404-55800-3). AMS Pr.

Berman, Eleanor. The New-Fashioned Parent: How to Make Your Family Style Work. LC 79-25728. 1980. 8.95 (ISBN 0-13-613406-8). P-H.

Bernard, Jessie. American Family Behavior. LC 72-84978. (Illus.). 564p. (With a new intro.). 1973. Repr. of 1942 ed. 27.00 (ISBN 0-8462-1690-6). Russell.

Bernard, Jessie, commentary by. Self-Portrait of a Family: Letters by Jessie, Dorothy Lee, Claude, & David Bernard. LC 77-88361. (Illus.). 1978. pap. 6.95 (ISBN 0-8070-3799-0, BP597). Beacon Pr.

Blankenship, Judy. Scenes from Life: Views of Family, Marriage & Intimacy. 1976. pap. 12.95 (ISBN 0-316-09945-7). Little.

Blitsten, Dorothy. The World of the Family: A Comparative Study of Family Organization in Their Social & Cultural Settings. 1963. text ed. 6.95x (ISBN 0-685-77219-5, 0-394-30072). Phila Bk Co.

Blood, Robert O., Jr. The Family. LC 71-161235. 1972. text ed. 15.95 (ISBN 0-02-904150-3). Free Pr.

Blood, Robert O., Jr. & Wolfe, D. M. Husbands & Wives: The Dynamics of Married Living. LC 59-6824. 1965. pap. text ed. 5.95 (ISBN 0-02-904070-1). Free Pr.

Borland, Marie, ed. Violence in the Family. 1976. text ed. 19.50x (ISBN 0-391-00610-X). Humanities.

Bosanquet, Helen. The Family. 1906. 20.00 (ISBN 0-686-17692-8). Quality Lib.

Bossard, James & Boll, Eleanor. Ritual in Family Living. LC 75-45454. 228p. 1976. Repr. of 1950 ed. lib. bdg. 17.75x (ISBN 0-8371-8678-1, BORF). Greenwood.

Bossard, James H. & Boll, Eleanor S. Family Situations: An Introduction to the Study of Child Behavior. LC 69-10071. 1969. Repr. of 1943 ed. lib. bdg. 14.00x (ISBN 0-8371-0024-0, BOCB). Greenwood.

--The Large Family System. LC 74-25536. 325p. 1975. Repr. of 1956 ed. lib. bdg. 17.50x (ISBN 0-8371-7871-1, BOLF). Greenwood.

Bott, Elizabeth. Family & Social Network: Roles, Norms & External Relationships. 2nd ed. LC 71-161235. (Illus.). 1972. pap. text ed. 5.95 (ISBN 0-02-904510-X). Free Pr.

Boy Scouts of America. Family Living Skill Book. (Illus.). 32p. (gr. 3-4). 1974. pap. 0.50x (ISBN 0-8395-6587-9, 6587). BSA.

Brayer, Herbert O. & Cleary, Zella W. Valuing in the Family: A Workshop Guide for Parents. LC 72-93445. 171p. 1972. 4.95 (ISBN 0-913458-11-2). Pennant Pr.

Breckinridge, Sophonisba P. The Family & the State: Select Documents. LC 76-169375. (Family in America Ser). 584p. 1972. Repr. of 1934 ed. 26.00 (ISBN 0-405-03851-8). Arno.

Bremner, Marjorie. Dependency & the Family: A Psychological Study in Preferences Between Family & Official Decision Making. (Institute of Economic Affairs, Research Monographs: No. 16). (Illus., Orig.). 1969. pap. 2.50 (ISBN 0-255-69628-0). Transatlantic.

Brenton, Myron. The Runaways: Children, Husbands, Wives, & Parents. (Modern Medicine). 1978. 8.95 (ISBN 0-316-10773-5). Little.

Broderick, Carlfred B. Marriage & the Family. (Illus.). 1979. text ed. 18.95 (ISBN 0-13-559112-0). P-H.

Buhler, Charlotte M., et al. The Child & His Family. LC 72-156177. 187p. 1972. Repr. of 1939 ed. lib. bdg. 15.00x (ISBN 0-8371-6120-7, BUCF). Greenwood.

Bullinger, Heinrich. The Christian State of Matrimonye. Coverdale, Myles, tr. LC 74-80167. (English Experience Ser.: No. 646). 168p. 1974. Repr. of 1541 ed. 11.50 (ISBN 90-221-0646-2). Walter J Johnson.

Burgess, Ernest W. Ernest W. Burgess on Community, Family & Delinquency. Cottrell, Leonard S., Jr., et al, eds. LC 73-83572. (Illus.). 1977. pap. 4.45 (ISBN 0-226-08058-7, P715, Phoen). U of Chicago Pr.

--On Community, Family & Delinquency. Cottrell, Leonard S., Jr., et al, eds. (Heritage of Sociology Ser). 1974. 15.00x (ISBN 0-226-08057-9). U of Chicago Pr.

Burgess, Ernest W., et al. The Family: From Traditional to Companionship. 4th ed. 1971. 12.95x (ISBN 0-442-20893-6); instructor's manual 1.50x (ISBN 0-442-20894-4). D Van Nostrand.

Burghard, August. America's First Family: The Savages of Virginia. LC 74-80943. 60p. 1974. 4.00 (ISBN 0-8059-2038-2). Dorrance.

Burr, Wesley R., et al, eds. Contemporary Theories About the Family, Vol. I. LC 77-81430. (Illus.). 1979. 29.95 (ISBN 0-02-904940-7). Free Pr.

--Contemporary Theories About the Family: General Theories & Theoretical Orientations, Vol. II. LC 77-81430. (Illus.). 1979. 16.95 (ISBN 0-02-904950-4). Free Pr.

Byington, Margaret. Homestead: The Households of a Milltown. (Illus.). 1974. text ed. 9.95x (ISBN 0-916002-13-6, Pub. by U Ctr Intl St); pap. text ed. 3.95x (ISBN 0-916002-05-5). U of Pittsburgh Pr.

Calverton, V. F. & Schmalhausen, Samuel D., eds. New Generation: The Intimate Problems of Modern Parents & Children. LC 70-165712. (American Education, Ser. 2). (Illus.). 1971. Repr. of 1930 ed. 35.00 (ISBN 0-405-03701-5). Arno.

Campion, Michael A. Especially for Wives. (When Was the Last Time Ser.). 1979. pap. 5.95 (ISBN 0-87123-138-7, 210138). Bethany Hse.

Carr, Gwen B., ed. Marriage & Family in a Decade of Change: A Humanistic Reader. 1972. pap. text ed. 6.50 (ISBN 0-201-00899-8). A-W.

Carter, Elizabeth A. & Orfanidis, Monica M., eds. The Family Life Cycle. LC 79-17131. 1980. 25.00x (ISBN 0-470-26782-8). Halsted Pr.

Castle, David. Toward Caring: People Building in the Family. 1973. pap. 1.00 (ISBN 0-913408-09-3). Friends United.

Cavan, Ruth S. & Ranck, Katherine H. Family & the Depression: A Study of One Hundred Chicago Families. LC 79-137158. (Poverty U.S.A. Historical Record Ser). 1971. Repr. of 1938 ed. 14.00 (ISBN 0-405-03096-7). Arno.

--Family & the Depression: A Study of One Hundred Chicago Families. facsimile ed. LC 79-102229. (Select Bibliographies Reprint Ser). 1938. 20.00 (ISBN 0-8369-5114-X). Arno.

Chester, R. & Peel, J., eds. Equalities & Inequalities in Family Life. 1978. 24.50 (ISBN 0-12-171650-3). Acad Pr.

Child Study Association Of America Conference - 43rd. Children of Poverty - Children of Affluence: Proceedings. LC 66-17843. (Orig.). 1967. pap. 2.45 (ISBN 0-87183-325-5, 737). Child Study.

Child Study Association Of America Conference - 1963. Future of the American Family: Proceedings. 1963. pap. 1.00 (ISBN 0-87183-300-X). Child Study.

Child Study Association of America Conference, 1969. Where We Are: A Hard Look at Family & Society: Proceedings. 45th ed. LC 66-17843. (Orig.). 1970. pap. 3.50 (ISBN 0-87183-331-X). Child Study.

Christenson, Larry. The Christian Family: Tenth Anniversary Edition. 224p. 1980. pap. 2.95 (ISBN 0-87123-088-7, 210114); 6.95 (ISBN 0-87123-062-3); study guide 1.50 (ISBN 0-87123-071-2). Bethany Hse.

Clayton, Richard R. Family Marriage & Social Change. 2nd ed. 1979. text ed. 17.95x (ISBN 0-669-01957-7); instr's manual 1.95 (ISBN 0-669-01956-9). Heath.

Coale, Ansley J., et al, eds. Aspects of the Analysis of Family Structure. 1965. 18.50 (ISBN 0-691-09306-7). Princeton U Pr.

Cohen, Sherry S. Tough Gazoobies on That. Young, Billie, ed. LC 73-83476. 1974. 8.95 (ISBN 0-87949-016-0). Ashley Bks.

College of Home Economics, Iowa State University. Families of the Future. facsimile ed. 1972. pap. 6.65x (ISBN 0-8138-2370-6). Iowa St U Pr.

Commander, Lydia K. The American Idea. LC 77-169378. (Family in America Ser). 352p. 1972. Repr. of 1907 ed. 15.00 (ISBN 0-405-03855-0). Arno.

Community Service Society of New York. Family in a Democratic Society. facsimile ed. LC 77-167330. (Essay Index Reprint Ser). Repr. of 1949 ed. 18.00 (ISBN 0-8369-2491-6). Arno.

Congressional Quarterly Editorial Research Reports Staff. Editorial Research Reports on the Changing American Family. (Editorial Research Reports Ser.). 1979. pap. text ed. 6.95 (ISBN 0-87187-149-1). Congr Quarterly.

Cook, et al. Family Mediation Workbook. Polk, Donice, ed. 90p. (Orig.). 1980. pap. 10.00 (ISBN 0-686-29084-4). D Polk.

Cooper, Wyatt. Families: A Memoir & a Celebration. LC 75-9347. (Illus.). 224p. 1975. 11.95 (ISBN 0-06-010857-6, HarpT). Har-Row.

Corwin, Sheila. Marriage & the Family & Child-Rearing Practices. Zak, Therese A., ed. (Lifeworks Ser.). (Illus.). 160p. 1981. text ed. 4.56 (ISBN 0-07-013198-8). McGraw.

Coser, Rose L. The Family: Its Structure & Functions. 2nd ed. 600p. 1974. 16.95 (ISBN 0-312-28105-6); pap. text ed. 8.95 (ISBN 0-312-28140-4). St Martin.

Coward, Raymond T. & Smith, William M., eds. The Family in Rural Society. (Special Studies in Contemporary Social Issues). 280p. 1981. lib. bdg. 26.25x (ISBN 0-86531-121-8). Westview.

Cox, Frank D. Human Intimacy: Marriage, the Family & Its Meaning. 2nd ed. (Illus.). 560p. 1981. 19.50 (ISBN 0-8299-0367-4). West Pub.

--Human Intimacy: Marriage, the Family & Its Meaning. (Illus.). 1978. text ed. 16.95 (ISBN 0-8299-0152-3); instrs.' manual avail. (ISBN 0-8299-0473-5). West Pub.

Cromwell, R. & Olson, D. E., eds. Power in Families. LC 75-17648. 264p. 1975. 17.95 (ISBN 0-470-18846-4); pap. 9.95 (ISBN 0-470-18847-2). Halsted Pr.

Cushman, Nancy. We're a Family, Aren't We? 1979. 8.50 (ISBN 0-686-24268-8). T Weatherby.

Deacon, Ruth E. & Firebaugh, Francille M. Family Resource Management: Principles & Applications. 280p. 1980. text ed. 18.95 (ISBN 0-205-06994-0, 4569946); tchr's. manual free (ISBN 0-205-07000-0). Allyn.

Decisions About Self & Family. (Adoptions Builds Families Ser.: Unit II). (Illus.). (gr. 9-12). 1980. multimedia teaching kit 44.95 (ISBN 0-89994-257-1). Soc Sci Ed.

Delliquadri, Fred, ed. Helping the Family in Urban Society. LC 63-9804. (National Conference on Social Welfare Ser.). 184p. 1963. 17.50x (ISBN 0-231-02620-X). Columbia U Pr.

DeLora, Jack & DeLora, JoAnn. Intimate Life Styles: Marriage & Its Alternatives. 2nd ed. LC 74-10231. 448p. 1975. pap. text ed. 10.95 (ISBN 0-87620-462-0). Goodyear.

Demos, John. Little Commonwealth: Family Life in Plymouth Colony. (Illus.). 1971. pap. 4.95 (ISBN 0-19-501355-7, 344, GB). Oxford U Pr.

Dempsey, John J. The Family & Public Policy: The Issue of the 1980s. LC 81-1740. (Illus.). 182p. 1981. text ed. 16.95 (ISBN 0-933716-15-X). P H Brookes.

Ditzion, Sidney. Marriage, Morals & Sex in America: A History of Ideas. LC 72-96179. 1970. Repr. of 1953 ed. lib. bdg. 22.50x (ISBN 0-374-92204-7). Octagon.

Dobos, David E., et al. Family Portrait: A Study of Contemporary Life Styles. 2nd alt. ed. 192p. 1980. pap. text ed. 8.95x (ISBN 0-534-00876-3). Wadsworth Pub.

--Family Portrait: A Study of Contemporary Life Styles. 2nd ed. 264p. 1980. pap. text ed. 6.95x (ISBN 0-534-00874-7). Wadsworth Pub.

Drescher, John M. If I Were Starting My Family Again. 1981. pap. 1.50 (ISBN 0-687-18674-9). Aberigdow.

Duberman, Lucile. Reconstituted Family: A Study of Remarried Couples & Their Children. LC 75-8840. 185p. 1975. 16.95x (ISBN 0-88229-168-8). Nelson-Hall.

Dubrin, Andrew J. The New Husbands & How to Become One. LC 76-15359. 1976. 14.95 (ISBN 0-88229-358-3). Nelson-Hall.

Duvall, Evelyn M. Marriage & Family Development. 5th ed. LC 76-30744. 1977. text ed. 19.50 scp (ISBN 0-397-47362-1, HarpC). Har-Row.

Dyer, Everett D. The American Family: Variety & Change. (Illus.). 1979. text ed. 14.95 (ISBN 0-07-018540-9, C); instructor's manual 2.95 (ISBN 0-07-018541-7). McGraw.

Dyer, William G. Creating Closer Families: Principles of Positive Family Interaction. LC 75-20169. (Illus.). 144p. 1975. pap. 6.95 (ISBN 0-8425-0726-4). Brigham.

Dylong, John. Living History: Nineteen Twenty-Five to Nineteen Fifty. 144p. 1979. pap. 10.00 (ISBN 0-8294-0289-6). Loyola.

Edwards. Family & Change. pap. text ed. 5.95x (ISBN 0-685-69590-5). Phila Bk Co.

Elder, Glen H., Jr. Children of the Great Depression: Social Charge in Life Experience. LC 73-87301. (Illus.). 1977. pap. 6.95 (ISBN 0-226-20263-1, P713, Phoen). U of Chicago Pr.

--Family Structure & Socialization. Zuckerman, Harriet & Merton, Robert K., eds. LC 79-8995. (Dissertations on Sociology Ser.). 1980. lib. bdg. 42.00x (ISBN 0-405-12966-1). Arno.

Elshtain, Jean B., ed. The Family in Political Thought. LC 81-11435. 352p. 1982. lib. bdg. 22.50x (ISBN 0-87023-341-6); pap. text ed. 10.00x (ISBN 0-87023-342-4). U of Mass Pr.

Eshleman, J. Ross. The Family: An Introduction. 3rd ed. 640p. 1981. text ed. 19.90 (ISBN 0-205-07241-0, 817241-2); tchrs'. ed. free (ISBN 0-205-07242-9). Allyn.

Fairfield, James G. T. When You Don't Agree. LC 77-3133. 1977. pap. text ed. 3.95 (ISBN 0-8361-1819-7). Herald Pr.

Family Development. (Adoption Builds Families Ser.: Unit I). (Illus.). 1980. multimedia teaching kit 34.95 (ISBN 0-89994-256-3). Soc Sci Ed.

Farber, B. Effects of a Severely Mentally Retarded Child on Family Integration. 1959. pap. 6.00 (ISBN 0-527-01578-4). Kraus Repr.

--Family Organization and Crisis: Maintenance of Integration in Families with a Severely Mentally Retarded Child. 1960. pap. 5.00 (ISBN 0-527-01583-0). Kraus Repr.

Farber, Bernard. Family & Kinship in Modern Society. 250p. 1973. pap. 5.95x (ISBN 0-673-05963-4). Scott F.

Feldman, Frances L. The Family in Today's Money World. 2nd ed. 1976. 12.95 (ISBN 0-87304-130-5); pap. 7.00 (ISBN 0-87304-131-3). Family Serv.

Ferriss, Abbott L. Indicators of Change in the American Family. LC 76-102385. 1970. pap. 5.50 (ISBN 0-87154-250-1). Russell Sage.

Flugel, John C. Psychoanalytic Study of the Family. 1960. text ed. 10.00x (ISBN 0-7012-0103-7). Humanities.

Fogarty, Michael P., et al. Sex, Career & Family. LC 70-158823. 581p. 1970. pap. 12.50 (ISBN 0-8039-0348-0). Sage.

Foote, Nelson N. & Cottrell, Leonard S., Jr. Identity & Interpersonal Competence: A New Direction in Family Research. LC 56-11957. 1955. pap. 14.00x (ISBN 0-226-25685-5). U of Chicago Pr.

Ford, Lee E., ed. Women of the Eighties: Vol. 1: the Family Woman. 100p. (Orig.). 1981. pap. 12.00 (ISBN 0-88017-103-0). Ford Assocs.

Franciscan Ideals & Family Problems. (Franciscan Educational Conferences Ser). 1960. pap. 4.50 (ISBN 0-685-77535-6). Franciscan Herald.

Francoeur, Robert T. Eve's New Rib. 1973. pap. 2.65 (ISBN 0-440-52340-0, Delta). Dell.

--Eve's New Rib: Twenty Faces of Sex, Marriage, & Family. LC 78-182328. 256p. 1972. 6.50 (ISBN 0-15-129384-8). HarBraceJ.

Freedman, Hy. Sex Link: The Three-Billion-Year-Old Urge & What the Animals Do About It. LC 77-8546. 224p. 1977. 8.95 (ISBN 0-87131-242-5). M Evans.

Gagnon, John H. & Greenblat, Cathy S. Life Designs: Individuals, Marriages, & Families. 1978. text ed. 16.95x (ISBN 0-673-07911-2). Scott F.

Gap Committee on the Family. Divorce, Child Custody & the Family, Vol. 10. LC 80-25935. (Publications Ser.: No. 106). 1980. pap. 12.95 (ISBN 0-910958-10-6, 106, Mental Health Materials Center). Mental Health.

--Integration & Conflict in Family Behavior, Vol. 6. (Report No. 27A). 1968. pap. 2.00 (ISBN 0-87318-096-8, Pub. by Adv Psychiatry). Mental Health.

Gardner, Annell. Family Reunion Profile. 1979. 4.50 (ISBN 0-8062-1366-3). Carlton.

Gay, Kathlyn. Family Is for Living. LC 74-122772. (Illus.). (gr. 4-6). 1972. 4.95 (ISBN 0-440-02596-6); PLB 4.58 (ISBN 0-440-02597-4). Delacorte.

Geismar, Ludwig L. Five Hundred Fifty Five Families: A Social Psychological Study of Young Families in Transition. LC 72-82196. 1973. 14.95 (ISBN 0-87855-044-5). Transaction Bks.

Geismar, Ludwig L. & Geismar, Shirley. Families in an Urban Mold: Policy Implications of an Australian-U.S. Comparison. (Pergamon Policy Studies). 1979. 27.00 (ISBN 0-08-023379-1). Pergamon.

Gelles, Richard J. Family Violence. LC 79-14813. (Sage Library of Social Research: Vol. 84). (Illus.). 219p. 1979. 20.00x (ISBN 0-8039-1234-X); pap. 9.95x (ISBN 0-8039-1235-8). Sage.

Gerhardt, Sidney & McKay, Elizabeth. There Is a Better Way of Living! A Sensible Approach to Personal & Family Growth. LC 75-14443. 128p. 1975. 5.95 (ISBN 0-8164-9268-9). Continuum.

Glick, Paul C. American Families. LC 73-84751. (Census Monograph). (Illus.). xiv, 240p. 1976. Repr. of 1957 ed. 18.00 (ISBN 0-8462-1743-0). Russell.

God, Family, Country. 1974. 8.95 (ISBN 0-87747-541-5). Deseret Bk.

Golanty, Eric & Kephart, William M. Marriage & the Family. LC 81-82013. (Illus.). 480p. 1981. text ed. 15.95 (ISBN 0-686-73126-3); write for info. HM.

Goldberg, Stella & Deutsch, Francine. Life-Span Individual & Family Development. LC 77-23485. 1977. text ed. 17.95 (ISBN 0-8185-0241-X); wkbk. 5.95 (ISBN 0-8185-0242-8). Brooks-Cole.

Goode, Ruth. A Book for Grandmothers. (Paperbacks Ser.). 1977. pap. 3.95 (ISBN 0-07-023740-9, SP). McGraw.

Goode, W. The Family. 1964. pap. 6.95 (ISBN 0-13-301812-1). P-H.

Goode, William J. World Revolution & Family Patterns. LC 63-13538. 1970. pap. text ed. 9.95 (ISBN 0-02-912460-3). Free Pr.

Goode, William J., et al. Social Systems & Family Patterns: A Propositional Inventory. LC 75-158851. 1971. 44.50x (ISBN 0-672-61151-1). Irvington.

Goodman, Jane G. Aging Parents: Whose Responsibility? LC 80-14945. (Workshop Models for Family Life Education Ser.). 168p. 1980. plastic bdg. 10.95 (ISBN 0-87304-175-5). Family Serv.

Goody, Jack. Developmental Cycle in Domestic Groups. LC 78-160087. (Papers in Social Anthropology: No. 1). (Illus.). 1972. 19.95 (ISBN 0-521-05116-9); pap. 9.95x (ISBN 0-521-09660-X). Cambridge U Pr.

Gordon, Michael. The American Family in Social-Historical Perspective. 2nd ed. LC 77-86000. 1978. text ed. 16.95 (ISBN 0-312-02311-1); pap. text ed. 9.95 (ISBN 0-312-02312-X). St Martin.

--The American Family: Past, Present, & Future. 1977. text ed. 16.95 (ISBN 0-394-31722-X). Random.

Green, Ernest J. Marriage & Family. LC 76-30848. (McGraw-Hill Basic Self-Instructional Guide Ser.). 1977. pap. text ed. 7.95 (ISBN 0-07-024261-5, C); instructor's guide 2.95 (ISBN 0-07-024262-3). McGraw.

Grey, Alan L., ed. Man, Woman, & Marriage: Studies of Small Group Process in the Family. LC 72-105607. (Controversy Ser). 225p. 1970. text ed. 9.95x (ISBN 0-202-25057-1). Lieber-Atherton.

Gross, Irman H., et al. Management for Modern Families. 4th ed. (Illus.). 1980. text ed. 16.95 (ISBN 0-13-549477-X). P-H.

Grossman, Frances K. Brothers & Sisters of Retarded Children: An Exploratory Study. LC 73-170664. (Special Education & Rehabilitation Monograph: No. 9). 1972. text ed. 9.50x (ISBN 0-8156-2154-X). Syracuse U Pr.

Groves, Ernest R. & Ogburn, William F. American Marriage & Family Relationships. LC 75-38129. (Demography Ser.). (Illus.). 1976. Repr. of 1928 ed. 30.00x (ISBN 0-405-07983-4). Arno.

Haley, Jay, ed. Changing Families: A Family Therapy Reader. LC 72-118654. 353p. 1971. 22.50 (ISBN 0-8089-0681-X). Grune.

Hall, Manly P. Basic Principles of Domestic Psychology. pap. 1.75 (ISBN 0-89314-305-7). Philos Res.

Handel, Gerald, ed. Psychosocial Interior of the Family: A Sourcebook for the Study of Whole Families. 2nd ed. 1972. 26.95x (ISBN 0-202-25104-7). Aldine Pub.

Harrington, Paul V. Parent & Child. (Illus., Orig.). 1965. 1.50 (ISBN 0-8198-0113-5). Dghtrs St Paul.

Harris, C. C. The Family. (Studies in Sociology Ser.). 1971. pap. text ed. 7.50x (ISBN 0-04-301020-2). Allen Unwin.

--Readings in Kinship in Urban Society. 1970. 23.00 (ISBN 0-08-016039-5); pap. 12.75 (ISBN 0-08-016038-7). Pergamon.

Haughton, Rosemary. Problems of Christian Marriage. (Orig.). 1968. pap. 1.45 (ISBN 0-8091-1665-0). Paulist Pr.
Hayworth, Don. It's the Family That Counts. 1976. 6.95 (ISBN 0-912598-14-X). Florham.
Hellfach. Future of the Family. (Future Studies Ser.). 1977. 5.76 (ISBN 0-13-345546-7). P-H.
Henry, Jules. Pathways to Madness. 512p. 1973. pap. 4.95 (ISBN 0-394-71882-8, Vin). Random.
Henslin, James M., ed. Marriage & Family in a Changing Society. LC 79-7853. (Illus.). 1980. pap. text ed. 10.95 (ISBN 0-02-914580-5). Free Pr.
Hess, Robert D. & Handel, Gerald. Family Worlds. LC 59-5773. 306p. 1974. pap. 4.45 (ISBN 0-226-33035-4, P581, Phoen). U of Chicago Pr.
--Family Worlds: A Psychosocial Approach to Family Life. LC 59-5773. 1959. 12.50x (ISBN 0-226-33034-6). U of Chicago Pr.
Hiesberger, Jean M., ed. Healing Family Hurts. LC 79-90991. (Paths of Life Ser.). 128p. (Orig.). 1979. pap. 2.45 (ISBN 0-8091-2266-9). Paulist Pr.
Hill, Reuben. Families Under Stress: Adjustment to the Crises of War Separation & Reunion. LC 73-90529. (Illus.). 1971. Repr. of 1949 ed. lib. bdg. 24.25 (ISBN 0-8371-3108-1, HIFU). Greenwood.
--Family Development in Three Generations. (gr. 10-12). 1971. text ed. 16.25 (ISBN 0-87073-088-6). Schenkman.
Hill, Reuben & Konig, Rene, eds. Families in East & West: Socialization Process & Kinship Ties. (Illus.). 1970. text ed. 61.50x (ISBN 90-2796-429-7). Mouton.
Hof, Larry & Miller, William. Marriage Enrichment: Philosophy Process & Program. (Illus.). 192p. 1980. text ed. 14.95 (ISBN 0-87619-717-9). R J Brady.
Hofling, Charles K. & Lewis, Jerry M., eds. The Family: Evaluation & Treatment. LC 79-21933. (American College of Psychiatrists Ser.). 1980. 20.00 (ISBN 0-87630-223-1). Brunner-Mazel.
Horowitz, June A. & Hughes, Cynthia B. Parenting Reassessed: A Nursing Perspective. (Illus.). 416p. 1982. 15.95 (ISBN 0-13-650085-4). P-H.
Howard, Jane. Families. 1980. pap. 2.75 (ISBN 0-425-04486-6). Berkley Pub.
--Families. 1978. 9.95 (ISBN 0-671-22536-7). S&S.
Howe, Florence & Rothermich, John A., eds. Household & Kin: Families in Flux. (Women's Lives - Women's Work Ser.). 208p. (Orig.). Date not set. pap. text ed. 4.71 (ISBN 0-07-020427-6). Webster-McGraw.
Howell, Mary. Helping Ourselves: Families & the Human Network. LC 75-5291. 1975. pap. 4.95 (ISBN 0-8070-2759-6, BP551). Beacon Pr.
Hubbard, David A. Is the Family Here to Stay? LC 74-170912. 1971. pap. 0.95 (ISBN 0-87680-928-X, 90028). Word Bks.
Hulme, William E. Building a Christian Marriage. LC 65-22192. 1968. pap. 2.95 (ISBN 0-8066-0813-7, 10-0940). Augsburg.
Hunt, Richard A. & Rydman, Edward J. Creative Marriage. 2nd ed. LC 78-32004. 1979. pap. text ed. 13.95 (ISBN 0-205-06597-X); tchr's man. avail. (ISBN 0-205-06605-4). Allyn.
Hymovich, Debra & Barnard, Martha. Family Health Care, Vol. I. (Illus.). 1979. pap. text ed. 8.95 (ISBN 0-07-031675-9, HP). McGraw.
James, D. & Kennedy. Healing for Your Family Ills. LC 77-78461. (Lifeline Ser.). 1977. pap. 0.95 (ISBN 0-88419-139-7). Creation Hse.
Jenkins, Shirley & Norman, Elaine. Beyond Placement: Mothers View Foster Care. LC 75-15916. (Social Work & Social Issues Ser.). 149p. 1975. 13.50x (ISBN 0-231-03812-7). Columbia U Pr.
Kamerman, Sheila B. & Kahn, Alfred J., eds. Family Policy: Government & Families in Fourteen Countries. LC 78-18015. 522p. 1978. 27.50x (ISBN 0-231-04464-X); pap. 12.50x (ISBN 0-231-04465-8). Columbia U Pr.
Kammeyer, Kenneth. Confronting the Issues: Sex Roles, Marriage & the Family. 2nd ed. 372p. 1980. pap. text ed. 10.95 (ISBN 0-205-06996-7, 816996-9). Allyn.
Kantor, David & Lehr, William. Inside the Family. 1976. pap. 4.95 (ISBN 0-06-090481-X, CN481, CN). Har-Row.
--Inside the Family: Toward a Theory of Family Process. LC 74-27910. (Social & Behavioral Science Ser.). 288p. 1975. 15.95x (ISBN 0-87589-250-7). Jossey-Bass.
Kanwar, M. A., ed. Sociology of Family: An Interdisciplinary Approach. 1971. pap. 13.50 (ISBN 0-208-01232-X, Linnet). Shoe String.
Kaplan, Benjamin. Jew & His Family. LC 67-21376. 1967. 15.00x (ISBN 0-8071-0545-7). La State U Pr.
Kaplan, Berton H. & Cassel, John C. Family & Health: An Epidemiological Approach. LC 75-38720. (Life Styles-Health Ser: No. 1). 1975. pap. text ed. 5.00 (ISBN 0-89143-075-X). U NC Inst Res Soc Sci.
Kasper, Walter. Theology of Christian Marriage. 112p. 1980. 7.95 (ISBN 0-8245-0395-3). Crossroad NY.
Kearney, Michael J. & Von Kaenel, Lisa. Midwest Families. LC 79-83599. 1979. 25.00 (ISBN 0-686-24786-8). Kearney.
Keesing, R. M. Kin Groups & Social Structure. LC 74-16008. 1975. pap. text ed. 5.95 (ISBN 0-03-012846-3, HoltC). HR&W.
Keniston, Kenneth & Carnegie Council on Children. All Our Children: The American Family Under Pressure. LC 77-74800. (Illus.). 1977. 10.95 (ISBN 0-15-104611-5). HarBraceJ.
Kenkel, William F. The Family in Perspective. 4th ed. LC 76-21491. 1977. text ed. 17.95 (ISBN 0-87620-291-1); test bank by Hart free (ISBN 0-87620-292-X). Goodyear.
Kephart, William M. The Family, Society, & the Individual. 5th ed. LC 80-81847. (Illus.). 624p. 1981. text ed. 16.95 (ISBN 0-395-29760-5); instr's. manual 0.75 (ISBN 0-395-29761-3). HM.
--The Family, Society, & the Individual. 4th ed. LC 76-13094. (Illus.). 1977. text ed. 16.95 (ISBN 0-395-24247-9); inst. manual 1.00 (ISBN 0-395-24246-0). HM.
Kirkendall, Lester A. & Adams, Wesley J. Student's Guide to Marriage-Family Life Literature: An Aid to Individualized Study & Instruction. 8th ed. 200p. 1980. pap. text ed. write for info. (ISBN 0-697-07559-1). Wm C Brown.
Knafl, Kathleen A. & Grace, Helen K. Families Across the Life Cycle. 1978. pap. text ed. 8.95 (ISBN 0-316-49897-1). Little.
Knowles, Edmond. Dynamics of the Family Unit. LC 76-18593. (Illus.). 1976. 4.00 (ISBN 0-917954-01-7); pap. 3.00 (ISBN 0-917954-02-5). E & E Enterprise.
Koller, Marvin. Families: A Multigenerational Approach. (Illus.). 320p. 1974. pap. text ed. 10.95 (ISBN 0-07-035331-X, C). McGraw.
Komarovsky, Mirra. Unemployed Man & His Family. LC 73-120637. 1970. Repr. lib. bdg. 15.00x (ISBN 0-374-94621-3). Octagon.
--Unemployed Man & His Family: The Effect of Unemployment Upon the Status of the Man in Fifty-Nine Families. LC 79-137174. (Poverty U.S.A. Historical Record Ser). 1971. Repr. of 1940 ed. 10.00 (ISBN 0-405-03113-0). Arno.
Konopka, Coles, et al. Function of Rebellion: Is Youth Creating New Family Values? LC 66-17843. 1968. pap. 2.45 (ISBN 0-686-25738-3). Jewish Bd Family.
Kurian, George, ed. Cross-Cultural Perspectives of Mate-Selection & Marriage. LC 78-19306. (Contributions in Family Studies: No. 3). 1979. lib. bdg. 25.00 (ISBN 0-313-20624-4, KCC/). Greenwood.
L'Abate, Luciano. Understanding & Helping the Individual in the Family. LC 76-42234. (Illus.). 272p. 1976. 31.75 (ISBN 0-8089-0969-X). Grune.
Laing, R. D. The Politics of the Family & Other Essays. 1972. pap. 1.95 (ISBN 0-394-71809-7, Vin). Random.
Laing, R. D. & Esterson, A. Sanity, Madness & the Family. 1970. pap. 2.95 (ISBN 0-14-021157-8, Pelican). Penguin.
Landau, Elliott D. Family Within Your Walls. LC 78-52116. 1978. 6.95 (ISBN 0-88290-095-1). Horizon Utah.
Landis, Judson T., et al. Personal Adjustment, Marriage & Family Living. 6th ed. 1975. text ed. 15.96 (ISBN 0-13-657338-X). P-H.
Landis, Paul H. Your Marriage & Family Living. 3rd ed. (American Home & Family Ser.). 1969. text ed. 14.00 (ISBN 0-07-036185-1, W); tchrs' manual 1.32 (ISBN 0-07-036186-X). McGraw.
--Your Marriage & Family Living. 4th ed. (Illus.). (gr. 10-12). 1976. text ed. 14.00 (ISBN 0-07-036187-8, W). McGraw.
Larsen, Larry & Seifert, Kenneth. Parents & Families. 1977. pap. 3.95 (ISBN 0-532-39100-4). Woodhill.
Laslett, P. & Wall, R., eds. Household & Family in Past Time. LC 77-190420. 608p. 1972. 49.95 (ISBN 0-521-08473-3); pap. 15.95x (ISBN 0-521-09901-3). Cambridge U Pr.
Lasswell, Thomas E. & Lasswell, Marcia E. Love - Marriage - Family: A Developmental Approach. 544p. 1973. pap. 8.95x (ISBN 0-673-07523-0). Scott F.
Lasswell, Thomas E. & Lasswell, Marcia. Marriage & the Family. 544p. 1982. text ed. 16.95 (ISBN 0-669-04373-7). Heath.
Laucks, Eulah C. The Meaning of Children: Attitudes & Opinions of a Selected Group of U.S. University Graduates. (Special Studies in Contemporary Social Issues). 225p. 1981. lib. bdg. 20.00x (ISBN 0-89158-881-7). Westview.
Lawrence, Margaret. Young Inner City Families: Development of Ego Strength Under Stress. LC 74-8153. 144p. 1975. text ed. 16.95 (ISBN 0-87705-156-9). Human Sci Pr.
Leichter, Hope J., ed. The Family As Educator. LC 75-16252. 1975. 8.75x (ISBN 0-8077-2497-1); pap. 6.00x (ISBN 0-8077-2496-3). Tchrs Coll.
Lenero-Otero, Luis, ed. Beyond the Nuclear Family Model: Cross-Cultural Perspectives. LC 76-22901. (Sage Studies in International Sociology: Vol. 7). 226p. 1977. 22.50 (ISBN 0-8039-9985-2); pap. 9.95 (ISBN 0-8039-9986-0). Sage.
Leslie, Gerald R. The Family in Social Context. 4th ed. (Illus.). 1979. text ed. 16.95x (ISBN 0-19-502423-0). Oxford U Pr.
Lesy, Michael. Time Frames: The Meaning of Family Pictures. (Illus.). 1980. 20.00 (ISBN 0-394-42456-5); pap. 8.95 (ISBN 0-394-73958-2). Pantheon.
Levine, D., ed. Family Formation in an Age of Nascent Capitalism. 1977. 22.00 (ISBN 0-12-445050-4). Acad Pr.
Levitan, Sar A. & Belous, Richard S. What's Happening to the American Family. LC 81-47592. (Illus.). 1981. text ed. 16.50x (ISBN 0-8018-2690-X); pap. 5.95 (ISBN 0-8018-2691-8). Johns Hopkins.
Lewis, J. M., et al. No Single Thread: Psychological Health in Family Systems. LC 75-25777. 1976. 17.50 (ISBN 0-87630-111-1). Brunner-Mazel.
Lewis, Jerry M. How's Your Family? LC 78-11820. 1979. 13.50 (ISBN 0-87630-181-2). Brunner-Mazel.
Li, Fei-Kan. The Family. Pa, Chin, ed. 1976. lib. bdg. 59.95 (ISBN 0-8490-1800-5). Gordon Pr.
Lidz, Theodore. The Family & Human Adaptation. LC 63-20457. 126p. 1963. text ed. 15.00 (ISBN 0-8236-1880-3); pap. text ed. 4.95x (ISBN 0-8236-8051-7, 021880). Intl Univs Pr.
Lidz, Theodore, et al. Schizophrenia & the Family. LC 65-23613. (Monograph Ser. on Schizophrenia: No. 7). 1967. text ed. 25.00 (ISBN 0-8236-6000-1). Intl Univs Pr.
Lindsey, Karen. Friends As Family. LC 80-70360. 204p. 1981. 12.95 (ISBN 0-8070-3242-5). Beacon Pr.
Lipetz, Marcia. Studying Life Designs. 1978. pap. 4.95x (ISBN 0-673-15121-2). Scott F.
Liu, William T., ed. Family & Fertility. (Charts). 1967. 9.95x (ISBN 0-268-00095-6). U of Notre Dame Pr.
Lueth, Shirley. I Didn't Plan to Be a Witch. 240p. 1981. pap. 2.50 (ISBN 0-380-77875-0, 77875). Avon.
Lundberg, David W. Government by the People: What You Can Do for America. LC 79-65905. 1979. 8.95 (ISBN 0-934762-00-7); pap. 5.95 (ISBN 0-934762-01-5). Voice of Liberty.
Luthman, Shirley & Kirschenbaum, Martin. The Dynamic Family. LC 74-84560. 1975. 7.95 (ISBN 0-8314-0037-4). Sci & Behavior.
Malinowski, Bronislaw. Father in Primitive Psychology. 1966. pap. 2.95 (ISBN 0-393-00332-9, Norton Lib). Norton.
--Sex & Repression in Savage Society. (International Library of Psycological Philosophy & Scientific Mathematics). 1953. text ed. 22.50x (ISBN 0-7100-3046-0). Humanities.
Manocchio, Tony & Petitt, William. Families Under Stress: A Psychological Interpretation. 1975. 18.00 (ISBN 0-7100-8176-6). Routledge & Kegan.
Masnick, George & Bane, Mary Jo. The Nation's Families: 1960-1990. LC 80-20531. (Illus.). 200p. (Orig.). 1980. 17.95 (ISBN 0-86569-050-2); pap. 10.00 (ISBN 0-86569-051-0). Auburn Hse.
Melson, Gail F. Family & Environment: An Ecosystem Perspective. LC 79-56585. 1980. 16.95 (ISBN 0-8087-1395-7). Burgess.
Melville, Keith. Marriage & Family Today. 2nd ed. 491p. 1980. text ed. 18.95 (ISBN 0-394-32346-7). Random.
Melville, Keith & Melville, Charles. Exploring Marriage & Family Today. (Illus.). 280p. 1980. pap. text ed. 5.95 (ISBN 0-394-32183-9). Random.
Merriam, Eve. Family Circle. LC 78-144750. (No. 44). Repr. of 1946 ed. 11.00 (ISBN 0-404-53844-4). AMS Pr.
Michel, Andree. La Sociologie De la Famille: Recueil De Textes Presentes et Commentes. (Textes De Sciences Sociales: No. 11). 1971. pap. 17.75x (ISBN 0-686-21815-9). Mouton.
Miller, Sherod, ed. Marriage & Families: Enrichment Through Communication. LC 75-27012. (Sage Contemporary Social Science Issues Ser.: Vol. 20). 125p. 1975. 5.95 (ISBN 0-8039-0569-6). Sage.
Mindel, Charles H. & Habenstein, Robert W., eds. Ethnic Families in America: Patterns & Variations. LC 75-40654. 456p. 1976. text ed. 15.95 (ISBN 0-444-99022-4); pap. text ed. 9.50 (ISBN 0-444-99025-9). Elsevier.
Minuchin, Salvador. Families & Family Therapy. LC 73-89710. 320p. 1974. 10.00x (ISBN 0-674-29236-7). Harvard U Pr.
Minuchin, Salvador, et al. Families of the Slums: An Exploration of Their Structure Treatment. LC 67-28507. (Illus.). 1967. 15.00x (ISBN 0-465-02330-4). Basic.
Monfalcone, Wesley R. Coping with Abuse in the Family. LC 80-15125. (Christian Care Books). 1980. pap. 5.95 (ISBN 0-664-24326-6). Westminster.
Monroe, Day. Chicago Families: A Study of Unpublished Census Data. LC 70-169395. (Family in America Ser). 370p. 1972. Repr. of 1932 ed. 16.00 (ISBN 0-405-03872-0). Arno.
Moorhead, Ted B., Jr. How to Be a Family & Survive. LC 76-2863. 1976. 5.95 (ISBN 0-87680-466-0, 80466). Word Bks.
Morgan, D. H. Social Theory & the Family. (International Library of Sociology). 320p. 1975. 22.50x (ISBN 0-7100-8179-0); pap. 10.00 (ISBN 0-7100-8180-4). Routledge & Kegan.
Morgan, James N. & Duncan, Greg J. Five Thousand American Families: Patterns of Economic Progress, 8 vols. Incl. Vol. 1. An Analyses of the First Five Years of the Panel Study of Income Dynamics; Vol. 2. Special Studies of the First Five Years of the Panel Study of Income Dynamics. 376p. 1974. Set Vols. 1 & 2. 15.00 (ISBN 0-87944-154-2); Set Vols. 1 & 2. pap. 9.50 (ISBN 0-87944-153-4); Vol. 3. Analyses of the First Six Years of the Panel Study of Income Dynamics. 490p. 1975. 12.50 (ISBN 0-87944-176-3); pap. 7.50 (ISBN 0-87944-175-5); Vol. 4. Family Composition Change & Other Analyses of the First Seven Years of the Panel Study of Income Dynamics. 520p. 1976. 12.50 (ISBN 0-87944-197-6); pap. 7.50 (ISBN 0-87944-196-8); Vol. 5. Components of Change in Family Well-Being & Other Analyses of the First Eight Years of the Panel Study of Income Dynamics. 536p. 1977. 12.50 (ISBN 0-87944-212-3); pap. 7.50 (ISBN 0-87944-211-5); Vol. 6. Accounting for Race & Sex Differences in Earnings & Other Analyses of the First Nine Years of the Panel Study of Income Dynamics. 392p. 1978. 16.00 (ISBN 0-87944-223-9); Vol. 7, Analyses Of The First Ten Years Of The Panel Study Of Income Dynamics, 1979. 16.00 (ISBN 0-87944-234-4). Set. 74.00 (ISBN 0-87944-249-2). Inst Soc. Res.
Morris, Edward & Gregory, Freida. TV: The Family School. LC 76-27102. (Illus.). 1976. pap. 3.00x (ISBN 0-914790-53-6). Avatar Pr.
Mowrer, Ernest R. Family Disorganization: An Introduction to a Sociological Analysis. LC 74-169396. (Family in America Ser). 322p. 1972. Repr. of 1927 ed. 16.00 (ISBN 0-405-03873-9). Arno.
Mueller-Lyer, Franz C. The Evolution of Modern Marriage: A Sociology of Sexual Relations. LC 72-11292. Repr. of 1930 ed. 20.50 (ISBN 0-404-57484-X). AMS Pr.
Murdock, George P. Social Structure. 1965. pap. text ed. 8.95 (ISBN 0-02-922290-7). Free Pr.
Myers, D'Alton B. & Myers, Dorice M. None's Been Fun. LC 79-50705. 312p. 1979. 8.95 (ISBN 0-8059-2625-9). Dorrance.
Myers, Theodore R. Intra - Family Relationships & Pupil Adjustment: The Relation Between Certain Selected Factors of the Home Environment of Junior-Senoir High School Pupils & the Adjustment & Behavior of These Pupils in School. LC 71-177103. (Columbia University. Teachers College. Contributions to Education: No. 651). Repr. of 1935 ed. 17.50 (ISBN 0-404-55651-5). AMS Pr.
Narain, Dhirendra, ed. Explorations in the Family & Other Essays: In Memory of K. M. Kapadia. 1974. text ed. 27.50x (ISBN 0-391-00403-4). Humanities.
Narramore, Clyde M. Discipline in the Christian Home. (Christian Psychology Ser). 1961. pap. 0.95 (ISBN 0-310-30072-X). Zondervan.
--How to Succeed in Family Living. LC 67-31425. (Orig.). 1968. pap. 1.95 (ISBN 0-8307-0531-7, 5015901). Regal.
Nass, Gilbert D. Marriage & the Family. (Illus.). 1978. text ed. 16.95 (ISBN 0-201-02500-0); instr's man 3.00 (ISBN 0-201-02502-7); study guide 4.95 (ISBN 0-201-02501-9); tests 2.00 (ISBN 0-201-02503-5). A-W.
Neuhaus, Robert & Neuhaus, Ruby. Family Crises. LC 73-85104. 1974. pap. 14.95 (ISBN 0-675-08890-9). Merrill.
Nickell, Paulena, et al. Management in Family Living. 5th ed. LC 75-41398. 475p. 1976. text ed. 23.95 (ISBN 0-471-63721-1). Wiley.
Nye, F. Ivan. Family Relationships & Delinquent Behavior. LC 73-8562. 168p. 1973. Repr. of 1958 ed. lib. bdg. 14.50x (ISBN 0-8371-6967-4, NYFR). Greenwood.
--Role Structure & Analysis of the Family. LC 75-40424. (Sage Library of Social Research: Vol. 24). 224p. 1976. 20.00 (ISBN 0-8039-0663-3); pap. 9.95 (ISBN 0-8039-0664-1). Sage.
Nye, F. Ivan & Berardo, Felix M. The Family: Its Structure & Interaction. Scott, Kenneth J., ed. (Illus.). 658p. 1973. text ed. 18.95 (ISBN 0-02-388740-0). Macmillan.

O'Connor, Andrea B., ed. Nursing: The Child Bearing Family. LC 79-140956. (Contemporary Nursing Ser.). 252p. 1979. pap. text ed. 7.95 (ISBN 0-937126-23-3). Am Journal Nurse.
Ogburn, William F. & Nimkoff, Meyer. Technology & the Changing Family. LC 76-44366. 1976. Repr. of 1955 ed. lib. bdg. 22.50 (ISBN 0-8371-9311-7, OGTC). Greenwood.
Oliver, Bernard J., Jr. Marriage & You. 1964. 7.00 (ISBN 0-8084-0211-0); pap. 3.45 (ISBN 0-8084-0212-9, B48). Coll & U Pr.
Oppenheim. Living Today. (gr. 9-12). 1981. text ed. 11.92 (ISBN 0-87002-343-8). Bennett IL.
Otto, Herbert A., ed. Family in Search of a Future: Alternate Models for Moderns. LC 75-111879. 1970. pap. text ed. 9.95 (ISBN 0-13-302869-0). P-H.
Papajohn, John & Spiegel, John. Transactions in Families: A Modern Approach for Resolving Cultural & Generational Conflicts. LC 74-6740. (Social & Behavioral Science Ser.). 336p. 1974. 16.95x (ISBN 0-87589-237-X). Jossey-Bass.
Peaslee, Ann. Supermom! The Positive Approach to Family Living. rev. ed. Fleming, Gerry & Green, Pat, eds. LC 79-91623. (Illus.). 187p. 1980. pap. 6.95 (ISBN 0-934126-03-8). Randall Pubs.
Peristiany, J. G., ed. Mediterranean Family Structure. LC 75-20833. (Cambridge Studies in Social Anthropology: No. 13). (Illus.). 434p. 1976. 39.95 (ISBN 0-521-20964-1). Cambridge U Pr.
Perlman, John. Notes Toward a Family. 1975. pap. 8.00 (ISBN 0-685-56236-0, Pub. by Elizabeth Pr). SBD.
Perlman, Robert & Warren, Roland L. Families in the Energy Crisis: Impacts & Implications for Theory & Policy. LC 77-24314. 1977. 17.50 (ISBN 0-88410-068-5). Ballinger Pub.
Perry, John & Perry, Erna. Pairing & Parenthood. (Illus.). 1976. text ed. 18.95 scp (ISBN 0-06-386751-6, HarpC); tchrs ed. free (ISBN 0-06-375931-4). Har-Row.
Phelan, Gladys K. Family Relationships. 1979. pap. 11.95x (ISBN 0-8087-1656-5). Burgess.
Pincus, Lily & Dare, Christopher. Secrets in the Family. LC 77-88763. 1980. pap. 3.95 (ISBN 0-06-090669-3, CN 669, CN). Har-Row.
Piotrkowski, Chaya S. Work & the Family System: A Naturalistic Study of Working-Class & Lower-Middle-Class Families. LC 79-7478. (Illus.). 1979. 14.95 (ISBN 0-02-925340-3). Free Pr.
Pogrebin, Letty C. Growing up Free. 656p. 1981. pap. 8.95 (ISBN 0-553-01340-8). Bantam.
Pollak, Otto. Invitation to a Dialogue: Union & Separation in Family Life. LC 79-19154. 1979. text ed. 11.95 (ISBN 0-89335-081-8). Spectrum Pub.
Pomeroy, Claire. Fight It Out, Work It Out, Love It Out. 1979. pap. 2.25 (ISBN 0-451-08703-8, E8703, Sig). NAL.
Poster, Mark. Critical Theory of the Family. LC 77-28487. 1978. 14.95 (ISBN 0-8164-9343-X); pap. 7.95 (ISBN 0-8164-9226-3). Continuum.
Powers, Edward A. & Lees, Mary W. Encounter with Family Realities. (Illus.). 1977. pap. 9.95 (ISBN 0-8299-0051-9). West Pub.
Pratt, Lois. Family Structure & Effective Health Behavior: The Energized Family. LC 75-29817. (Illus.). 256p. 1976. pap. text ed. 10.50 (ISBN 0-395-18702-8). HM.
Prescod, Suzanne. Current Research on Marriage, Families, & Divorce. 1979. looseleaf bdg. 25.50 (ISBN 0-915260-09-3). Atcom.
Queen, Stuart A. & Habenstein, Robert W. The Family in Various Cultures. 4th ed. LC 73-21517. 1974. pap. text ed. 8.50 scp (ISBN 0-397-47297-8, HarpC). Har-Row.
Rapoport, Rhona & Rapoport, Robert. Dual-Career Families Re-Examined. rev. ed. 1977. pap. 4.95 (ISBN 0-06-090521-2, CN 521, CN). Har-Row.
Rapoport, Rhona, et al. Fathers, Mothers & Society: Toward New Alliances. LC 76-43474. 1977. 15.00x (ISBN 0-465-02366-5). Basic.
Rayner, Claire. Related to Sex: Understanding Sexual Tensions in Your Family. LC 78-26728. 1979. pap. 8.95 (ISBN 0-448-22918-8). Paddington.
Readings in Marriage & Family 77-78. new ed. LC 74-84596. (Annual Editions Ser). (Illus., Orig.). 1977. write for info. (ISBN 0-87967-174-2). Dushkin Pub.
Reiss, David. The Family's Construction of Reality. LC 81-2703. (Illus.). 448p. 1981. text ed. 26.00 (ISBN 0-674-29415-7). Harvard U Pr.
Reiss, David & Hoffman, Howard, eds. The American Family: Dying or Developing? LC 78-24447. 264p. 1979. 21.95 (ISBN 0-306-40117-7, Plenum Pr). Plenum Pub.
Reiss, Ira L. Family Systems in America. 3rd ed. LC 80-10168. 544p. 1980. text ed. 16.95 (ISBN 0-03-047246-6, HoltC); instrs'. manual avail. (ISBN 0-03-047251-2). HR&W.
Renvoizie, Jean. Web of Violence: A Study of Violence in the Family. 1978. 18.00 (ISBN 0-7100-8804-3). Routledge & Kegan.
Resnick, Jane, compiled by. For You, a Very Special Aunt. 1979. pap. 2.50 (ISBN 0-8378-5029-0). Gibson.
Reynolds, William. The American Father: Himself, His Woman, His Child. LC 78-8951. 1978. 8.95 (ISBN 0-448-22917-X). Paddington.
Rice, Robert M. American Family Policy: Content & Context. LC 77-15664. 1977. pap. 6.95 (ISBN 0-87304-160-7). Family Serv.
Rickerson, Wayne. Family Fun & Togetherness. 1979. pap. 3.95 (ISBN 0-88207-641-8). Victor Bks.
Robison, James. Attack on the Family. pap. 2.25 (ISBN 0-686-73855-1). Tyndale.
Rodman, Hyman, ed. Marriage, Family & Society: A Reader. 1965. pap. text ed. 4.95x (ISBN 0-685-69597-2). Phila Bk Co.
Roosevelt, Ruth. Living in Step. (Paperbacks Ser.). 1977. Repr. of 1976 ed. pap. 4.95 (ISBN 0-07-053596-5, SP). McGraw.
Rosenberg, Charles E., ed. The Family in History. LC 75-14962. (Haney Foundation Ser.). 1975. 12.95 (ISBN 0-8122-7702-3); pap. 5.95 (ISBN 0-8122-1100-6). U of Pa Pr.
Rosenthal, Gilbert S., ed. The Jewish Family in a Changing World. LC 72-114612. 1970. 8.95 (ISBN 0-498-07679-2, Yoseloff). A S Barnes.
Rossi, Alice S., et al, eds. The Family. 1978. 10.95 (ISBN 0-393-01167-4); pap. 6.95x (ISBN 0-393-09064-7). Norton.
Rothman, David J. & Rothman, Sheila M., eds. Family in America, 44 bks. 1972. Set. 779.00 (ISBN 0-405-03840-2). Arno.
Rowatt, G. Wade, Jr. & Rowatt, Mary Jo. The Two-Career Marriage. LC 79-28408. (Christian Care Books). 1980. pap. 5.95 (ISBN 0-664-24298-7). Westminster.
Rubin, Lillian. Worlds of Pain: Life in the Working Class Family. LC 76-21648. 1977. pap. 4.95x (ISBN 0-465-09724-3, CN-5024). Basic.
Rubin, Lillian B. Worlds of Pain: Life in the Working Class Family. LC 76-7677. 1976. 12.95x (ISBN 0-465-09245-4). Basic.
Runck, Bette, et al. Families Today: A Research Sampler on Families & Children, 2 vols. LC 79-66976. (Science Monographs: No. 1). (Illus., Orig.). 1980. Vol. 1. pap. 8.50 (ISBN 0-686-27076-2); Vol. 2. pap. 8.00 (ISBN 0-686-27077-0). Gov Printing Office.
St. Andre, Lucien. The American Matriarchy: A Study of Married Life in 1997 A.D. 2nd ed. 1970. 5.95 (ISBN 0-912598-01-8). Florham.
Saltykov-Shchedrin. The Golovyov Family. Cioran, Samuel, tr. from Rus. (Eng.). 1976. 17.50 (ISBN 0-88233-209-0); pap. 4.50 (ISBN 0-88233-210-4). Ardis Pubs.
Sanders, Ed. The Family. 1972. pap. 1.95 (ISBN 0-380-00771-1, 24802). Avon.
Sapone, Edith. To You Mom. (Illus.). 1961. 3.00 (ISBN 0-8198-0162-3); pap. 2.00 (ISBN 0-8198-0163-1). Dghtrs St Paul.
Saturday Evening Post Editors. The Saturday Evening Post Family Album. LC 80-67059. (Illus.). 144p. 1980. padded leatherette with 4-color onlay 15.95 (ISBN 0-89387-047-1). Curtis Pub Co.
Savells, J. & Cross, L. The Changing Family: Making Way for Tomorrow. LC 77-51079. 1978. pap. 10.95 (ISBN 0-03-036411-6, HoltC). HR&W.
Saxton, Lloyd. Individual, Marriage & the Family. 4th ed. 672p. 1980. text ed. 18.95x (ISBN 0-534-00799-6); study guide 6.95x (ISBN 0-534-00800-3). Wadsworth Pub.
Scanzoni, John H. Sex Roles, Life Styles & Childbearing: Changing Patterns in Marriage & the Family. LC 74-28939. (Illus.). 1975. 17.95 (ISBN 0-02-927720-5). Free Pr.
Schaeffer, Edith. What Is a Family. 1975. 9.95 (ISBN 0-8007-0757-5). Revell.
Schafly, Phyllis. Power Ideas for a Happy Family. (Orig.). pap. 1.75 (ISBN 0-515-05104-7). Jove Pubns.
Schatzman, Morton. Soul Murder: Persecution in the Family. 1976. pap. 1.75 (ISBN 0-451-61499-2, ME1499, Ment). NAL.
Schneider, David M. & Cottrell, Calvert B. The American Kin Universe: A Genealogical Study. LC 75-37961. (Univ. of Chicago Studies in Anthropology Ser. in Social, Cultural, & Linguistic Anthropology Ser: No. 3). 109p. 1975. pap. 5.00 (ISBN 0-916256-02-2). U Chi Dept Anthro.
Schultz, David A. & Rodgers, Stanley F. Marriage, Family & Personal Fulfillment. (Illus.). 432p. 1975. text ed. 19.95 (ISBN 0-13-559377-8). P-H.
Schultz, Theodore W., ed. Economics of the Family: Marriage, Children, & Human Capital. LC 73-81484. x, 584p. 1975. text ed. 16.00x (ISBN 0-226-74085-4). U of Chicago Pr.
Schulz, David A. The Changing Family: Its Function & Future. 3rd ed. (Illus.). 368p. 1982. reference 19.95 (ISBN 0-13-127910-6). P-H.
--The Changing Family: Its Function & Future. 2nd ed. (Illus.). 432p. 1976. 18.95 (ISBN 0-13-127977-7). P-H.
Schulz, David A. & Rogers, Stanley F. Marriage, the Family & Personal Fulfillment. 2nd ed. (P-H Ser. in Sociology). (Illus.). 1980. text ed. 19.95 (ISBN 0-13-559385-9). P-H.
Senn, Milton & Hartford, Claire, eds. Firstborn: Experiences of Eight American Families. LC 68-25619. (Commonwealth Fund Publications Ser). 1968. 25.00x (ISBN 0-674-30300-8). Harvard U Pr.
Sennett, Richard. Families Against the City: Middle Class Homes of Industrial Chicago, 1872-1890. LC 73-115190. (Joint Center for Urban Studies Publications Ser). (Illus.). 1970. 14.00x (ISBN 0-674-29225-1). Harvard U Pr.
Seton, Cynthia P. Mother of the Graduate. LC 70-116111. 1970. 4.95 (ISBN 0-393-08612-7). Norton.
Shapiro, David S. & Shapiro, Elaine S. The Search for Love & Achievement: Marriage & the Family in a Changing World. 2nd ed. 1980. pap. text ed. 10.95x (ISBN 0-917974-48-4). Waveland Pr.
Shedd, Charlie W. Is Your Family Turned on? Coping with the Drug Culture. LC 71-165959. (Illus.). 1971. pap. 1.25 (ISBN 0-87680-929-8, 90029). Word Bks.
Shorter, Edward. The Making of the Modern Family. LC 75-7266. (Illus.). 1975. 16.50x (ISBN 0-465-04327-5); pap. 5.95x (ISBN 0-465-09722-7, CN-5022). Basic.
Shoulson, Abraham B., ed. Marriage & Family Life: A Jewish View. 7.50 (ISBN 0-8084-0378-8). Coll & U Pr.
Silverstone, Barbara & Hyman, Helen K. You & Your Aging Parent: The Modern Family's Guide to Emotional, Physical & Financial Problems. 1982. 15.95 (ISBN 0-394-52169-2); pap. 8.95 (ISBN 0-394-74948-0). Pantheon.
Simon, Norma. All Kinds of Families. Rubin, Caroline, ed. LC 75-42283. (Concept Bks). (Illus.). 40p. (gr. k-2). 1975. 7.50 (ISBN 0-8075-0282-0). A Whitman.
Simon, Sidney. Caring, Feeling, Touching. LC 76-17446. (Illus.). 1976. pap. 2.25 (ISBN 0-913592-67-6). Argus Comm.
Simpson. The American Family: A History in Photographs. Date not set. 3.98 (ISBN 0-517-29695-0). Bonanza.
Skolnick, Arlene. The Intimate Environment: Exploring Marriage & Family. 2nd ed. 1978. 17.95 (ISBN 0-316-79700-6); instructor's manual free, by dale harrentsian (ISBN 0-316-79701-4). Little.
Skolnick, Arlene & Skolnick, Jerome H. Family in Transition: Rethinking Marriage, Sexuality, Child Rearing, & Family Organization. 3rd ed. 579p. 1980. pap. text ed. 10.95 (ISBN 0-316-79722-7); test bank free (ISBN 0-316-79704-9). Little.
--Intimacy, Family, & Society. 1974. pap. 10.95 (ISBN 0-316-79719-7); examination questions by Marie Jones free (ISBN 0-316-79716-2). Little.
Slater, Philip. Footholds: Understanding the Shifting Family & Sexual Tensions in Our Culture. LC 77-12124. 1978. 9.95 (ISBN 0-8070-4160-2). Beacon Pr.
Sloan, Bernard. The Best Friend You'll Ever Have. 224p. 1980. 9.95 (ISBN 0-517-54003-7). Crown.
Sluzki, Carlos E. & Ransom, Donald C., eds. Double Bind: The Foundation of the Communicational Approach to the Family. LC 76-19112. 384p. 1976. 34.00 (ISBN 0-8089-0950-9). Grune.
Smart, Laura S & Smart, Mollie S. Families: Developing Realtionships. 2nd ed. (Illus.). 1980. text ed. 18.95 (ISBN 0-02-411930-X). Macmillan.
Smith, Malcolm L. Working with People, Bugs & Apples: An Old Fashioned Family, L. M. & Grace Smith, Parents of Ten. LC 78-73543. (Illus.). 1979. 11.50 (ISBN 0-686-28585-9). M L Smith.
Smith, Rebecca M. Klemer's Marriage & Family Relationships. 2nd ed. 424p. 1975. text ed. 20.95 scp (ISBN 0-06-046311-2, HarpC); instructor's manual free (ISBN 0-06-366303-1). Har-Row.
Snyder, David P., ed. The Family in Post-Industrial America: Some Fundamental Perceptions for Public Policy Development. (AAAS Selected Symposium: No. 32). 1979. lib. bdg. 15.00 (ISBN 0-89158-482-X). Westview.
Spanier, Graham B. Human Sexuality in a Changing Society. LC 78-68400. 1979. pap. 10.95x (ISBN 0-8087-4577-8). Burgess.
Spencer, Anna G. The Family & Its Members. LC 74-33956. (Pioneers of the Woman's Movement: an International Perspective Ser.). (Illus.). 322p. 1976. Repr. of 1923 ed. 21.50 (ISBN 0-88355-275-2). Hyperion Conn.
Stein, Peter J., et al. The Family: Functions, Conflicts & Symbols. (Sociology Ser.). 1977. pap. text ed. 12.95 (ISBN 0-201-07362-5). A-W.
Steiner, Gilbert Y. The Futility of Family Policy. 250p. 1981. 15.95 (ISBN 0-8157-8124-5); pap. 5.95 (ISBN 0-8157-8123-7). Brookings.
Steinmetz, Suzanne K. & Straus, Murray A., eds. Violence in the Family. LC 73-11991. 337p. (Orig.). 1974. pap. text ed. 11.50 scp (ISBN 0-06-046419-4, HarpC). Har-Row.
Stinnett, Nick & Birdsong, Craig W. The Family & Alternate Life-Styles. LC 77-16593. 1978. text ed. 16.95x (ISBN 0-88229-208-0). Nelson-Hall.
Stinnett, Nick & Walters, James. Relationships in Marriage & Family. 1977. 13.95 (ISBN 0-02-417530-7). Macmillan.
Stinnett, Nick, et al, eds. Building Family Strengths: Blueprints for Action. LC 79-51329. 1979. 19.50x (ISBN 0-8032-4114-3); pap. 9.95x (ISBN 0-8032-9113-2). U of Nebr Pr.
Stolz, Lois M. Influences on Parent Behavior. 1967. 15.00x (ISBN 0-8047-0232-2). Stanford U Pr.
Strauss, Murray & Gelles, Richard J. Behind Closed Doors: Violence in the American Family. LC 78-22741. (Illus.). 1980. 11.95 (ISBN 0-385-14259-5, Anchor Pr). Doubleday.
Streib, Gordon F., ed. The Changing Family: Adaptation & Diversity. LC 72-11076. 1973. pap. text ed. 5.50 (ISBN 0-201-07320-X). A-W.
Strong, F. Bryan, et al. The Marriage & Family Experience: A Text with Readings. (Illus.). 1979. pap. text ed. 17.95 (ISBN 0-8299-0278-3); instrs.' manual avail. (ISBN 0-8299-0577-4). West Pub.
Sussman, Marvin B. Marriage & the Family: Current Critical Issues. LC 79-53232. (Collected Essay Ser.). 1979. pap. 6.95 (ISBN 0-917724-08-9). Haworth Pr.
Sussman, Marvin B., ed. Sourcebook in Marriage & the Family. 4th ed. 432p. 1974. pap. text ed. 11.50 (ISBN 0-395-17538-0). HM.
Talmon, Yonina. Family & Community in the Kibbutz. LC 72-76561. (Illus.). 540p. 1972. 15.00x (ISBN 0-674-29275-8); pap. 5.95x (ISBN 0-674-29276-6). Harvard U Pr.
Tansey, Anne. Where to Get Help for Your Family. rev. ed. LC 77-10443. 1977. pap. 3.95 (ISBN 0-87029-131-9, 20153). Abbey.
Thacker, Chadley A. Family Facts at Your Fingertips. (Pertinent Events, Dates, & Places Ser.). 144p. pap. write for info. (ISBN 0-89036-157-6). Hawkes Pub Inc.
Thompson, David A. A Premarital Guide for Couples & Their Counselors. 1979. pap. 3.95 (ISBN 0-87123-465-3, 210465). Bethany Hse.
Thorman, George. Family Violence. 196p. 1980. text ed. 16.50 (ISBN 0-398-03953-4). C C Thomas.
Thorne, Yalom. Rethinking the Family: Some Feminist Questions. 1981. pap. text ed. 9.95x tent. (ISBN 0-582-28265-9). Longman.
--Rethinking the Family: Some Feminist Questions. 1981. pap. text ed. 9.95x (ISBN 0-582-28265-9). Longman.
Touliatos, John & Lindholm, Byron W., eds. The Family & Child Mental Health: Selected Readings. 1973. pap. text ed. 8.95x (ISBN 0-8422-0306-0); 24.50x (ISBN 0-8422-5096-4). Irvington.
Travis, Georgia. Chronic Illness in Children: Its Impact on Child & Family. LC 75-185. xiv, 546p. 1976. 19.50x (ISBN 0-8047-0893-2). Stanford U Pr.
Troll, Lillian E., et al. Families in Later Life. 1979. pap. 8.95x (ISBN 0-534-00613-2). Wadsworth Pub.
Tufte, Virginia & Myerhoff, Barbara, eds. Changing Images of the Family. LC 79-537. 1979. 25.00 (ISBN 0-300-02361-8). Yale U Pr.
--Changing Images of the Family. LC 79-537. (Illus.). 413p. 1981. pap. 6.95 (ISBN 0-300-02671-4). Yale U Pr.
Turner, Ralph H. Family Interaction. LC 71-118627. (Illus.). 505p. 1970. 24.95 (ISBN 0-471-89300-5). Wiley.
Umana, Roseann, et al. Crisis in the Family: Three Approaches. LC 78-14945. 1980. 21.95x (ISBN 0-470-26506-X). Halsted Pr.
Understanding Adoption: Resources & Activities for Teaching Adults About Adoption. (Adoption Builds Families Ser.). (Orig.). 1980. pap. 14.95 (ISBN 0-89994-258-X). Soc Sci Ed.
Valentine, Steven R. Each Time a Man: Family Roots & a Young Life in Politics. LC 78-62664. 1978. pap. text ed. 4.95 (ISBN 0-913408-43-3). Friends United.
Vaughan, James & Vaughan, Peggy. Beyond Affairs. 224p. 1981. pap. 2.95 (ISBN 0-553-20208-1). Bantam.
Vaughan, Victor C. The Family: Can It Be Saved? (Illus.). 1976. 20.00 (ISBN 0-8151-9025-5). Year Bk Med.
Victor, Joan Berg & Sander, Joelle. The Family. LC 77-15450. (Illus.). (gr. 6 up). 1978. 7.95 (ISBN 0-672-52343-4). Bobbs.
Voydanoff, Patricia. Implications of Work-Family Relationships for Productivity, Vol. 13. (Studies in Productivity-Highlights of the Literature). (Orig.). 1980. pap. 25.00 (ISBN 0-89361-020-8). Work in Amer.

Wakefield Washington Associates, Inc. Family Research: A Source Book, Analysis & Guide to Federal Funding, 2 vols. LC 79-7732. (Illus.). 1979. Set. lib. bdg. 95.00 (ISBN 0-313-21139-6, WFR/). Greenwood.
Wallace, Arthur & Bousfield, Shirley. Successful Family Organizations, Record Keeping, & Genealogy in Family Activities. 3rd ed. (Illus.). 189p. 1978. pap. 3.95 (ISBN 0-937892-02-5). LL Co.
Watzlawick, Paul & Weakland, John H., eds. The Interactional View: Studies at the Mental Research Institute, Palo Alto, 1965-1974. 1977. 19.95x (ISBN 0-393-01131-3). Norton.
Weil, Mildred W. Marriage, the Family, & Society: Toward a Sociology of Marriage & the Family. 2nd ed. LC 76-50685. 1977. pap. 6.95x (ISBN 0-8134-1897-6, 1897). Interstate.
Weil, Mildred W., ed. Sociological Perspectives in Marriage & the Family. 2nd ed. LC 78-54230. 1979. pap. text ed. 8.95x (ISBN 0-8134-2033-4, 2033). Interstate.
Weinheimer, Janice M. Families Are Forever...If I Can Just Get Through Today! LC 79-17807. 1979. 6.95 (ISBN 0-87747-782-5). Deseret Bk.
Welter, Paul. Family Problems & Predicaments. 1977. pap. 4.95 (ISBN 0-8423-0853-9). Tyndale.
Wernick, Robert. The Family. (Human Behavior Ser.). 1974. 9.95 (ISBN 0-8094-1908-4); lib. bdg. avail. (ISBN 0-685-50862-5). Time-Life.
Westoff, Charles F., et al. Family Growth in Metropolitan America. (Office of Population Research Ser.). 1961. 28.00x (ISBN 0-691-09316-4). Princeton U Pr.
--Third Child: A Study in the Prediction of Fertility. (Office of Population Research Ser). 1963. 22.00x (ISBN 0-691-09339-3). Princeton U Pr.
White House Conference on Child Health & Protection. The Adolescent in the Family: A Study of Personality Development in the Home Environment. LC 79-169401. (Family in America Ser). 478p. 1972. Repr. of 1934 ed. 23.00 (ISBN 0-405-03878-X). Arno.
Williamson, Robert C. Marriage & Family Relations. 2nd ed. LC 70-37027. 1972. text ed. 19.95 (ISBN 0-471-94905-1). Wiley.
Wilson, Carl. Our Dance Has Turned to Death. 1981. 3.95 (ISBN 0-8423-4782-8). Tyndale.
Winch, Robert F., et al. Familial Organization. LC 77-2434. (Illus.). 1978. 17.95 (ISBN 0-02-935340-8). Free Pr.
Wingfield, Marshall. Pioneer Families of Franklin County, Virginia. 373p. 1964. 18.50 (ISBN 0-685-65092-8). Va Bk.
Winnicott, Donald W. Family & Individual Development. (Orig.). 1968. pap. 11.95x (ISBN 0-422-72370-3, Pub by Tavistock England). Methuen Inc.
Wishy, Bernard & Scott, Donald, eds. America's Families: A Documentary History. LC 79-3402. (Illus.). 560p. 1981. 19.95 (ISBN 0-06-014048-8, HarpT). Har-Row.
Wright, H. Norman. How to Be a Better-Than-Average In-Law. 1981. pap. 3.95 (ISBN 0-88207-342-7). Victor Bks.
Wright, Norman. Answer to Family Communication. LC 76-52832. (Answer Ser.). 1977. pap. 1.25 (ISBN 0-89081-031-1, 0311). Harvest Hse.
Yorburg, Betty G. The Changing Family: A Sociological Perspective. LC 72-7284. 1973. 17.50x (ISBN 0-231-03461-X); pap. 6.00x (ISBN 0-231-08317-3). Columbia U Pr.
Young, Donald, ed. The Modern American Family. LC 72-169402. (Family in America Ser). 232p. 1972. Repr. of 1932 ed. 14.00 (ISBN 0-405-03879-8). Arno.
Young, Michael & Willmott, Peter. The Symmetrical Family. 1977. pap. 2.95 (ISBN 0-14-021908-0, Pelican). Penguin.
Your Family & You. (Benziger Family Life Program Ser.). (gr. 2). 1978. 2.00 (ISBN 0-02-651550-4); tchrs. ed. 4.00 (ISBN 0-02-651560-1); family handbook 1.00 (ISBN 0-02-651590-3). Benziger Pub Co.
Zanzucchi, Anne M. Family Portrait, from a Mother's Diary. Szczesniak, Lenny, tr. from It. LC 81-80031. Orig. Title: Giorno per Giorno. 100p. 1981. pap. 2.95 (ISBN 0-911782-19-2). New City.
Zaretsky, Eli. Capitalism, the Family & Personal Life. 1976. pap. 3.95 (ISBN 0-06-090538-7, CN538, CN). Har-Row.
Zinkiewicz, Crystal. The Anytime Book for Busy Families. LC 79-67098. 1979. spiral bdg. 4.95x (ISBN 0-8358-0378-3). Upper Room.
Zouras, Nicholas L. & Zouras, Mary A. America, Who Shall We Be? (Illus.). 1979. 8.37 (ISBN 0-934176-00-0). Family World Pub Hse.

FAMILY-BIBLICAL TEACHING

Balch, David. Let Wives Be Submissive: The Domestic Code in 1 Peter. Crenshaw, Tannehill, ed. LC 80-21203. (Society of Biblical Literature Monograph Ser.). 1981. pap. 25.00 (ISBN 0-89130-428-2, 060026); pap. 21.00 (ISBN 0-89130-429-0). Scholars Pr CA.
Brian L. Famous Couples of the Bible. LC 78-60053. 1979. pap. 3.50 (ISBN 0-8054-5630-9). Broadman.
Lewis, Margie M. & Lewis, Gregg. The Hurting Parent. 160p. (Orig.). 1980. pap. 3.95 (ISBN 0-310-41731-7). Zondervan.
Mack, Wayne. Homework Manual for Biblical Counseling: Family & Marital Problems, Vol. 2. pap. 3.50 (ISBN 0-87552-357-9). Presby & Reformed.
Robison, James. Attack on the Family. pap. 2.25 (ISBN 0-686-73855-1). Tyndale.
Soergel, Mary. Sing a Gentle Breeze. 1977. pap. 4.95 (ISBN 0-8423-5889-7). Tyndale.

FAMILY-BIBLIOGRAPHY

Croce, Camille, compiled by. Directory of Member Agencies, 1980. rev. ed. LC 21-3975. 87p. 1980. pap. 8.00 (ISBN 0-87304-177-1). Family Serv.
Milden, James W. The Family in Past Time: A Guide to the Literature. LC 76-24767. (Reference Library of Social Science Ser.: Vol. 32). 1977. lib. bdg. 21.00 (ISBN 0-8240-9910-9). Garland Pub.
Olson, David H., ed. Inventory of Marriage & Family Literature, Vol. 5. LC 67-63014. 485p. 1979. 60.00x (ISBN 0-8039-1232-3); pap. 29.95 (ISBN 0-8039-1233-1). Sage.
Women & Family: In Rural Development. (Special Index: No. 31). 1978. pap. 7.50 (ISBN 0-685-09222-4, F1329, FAO). Unipub.

FAMILY-HISTORY

Cobb, John E., Jr. The Complete Book for Doing the Family History. LC 80-70108. (Illus., Orig.). 1981. pap. 10.00 (ISBN 0-9606128-3-1). Durant Pub.
Costner, Herbert L. The Changing Folkways of Parenthood: A Content Analysis. Zuckerman, Harriet & Merton, Robert K., eds. LC 79-8987. (Dissertations on Sociology Ser.). 1980. lib. bdg. 31.00x (ISBN 0-405-12960-2). Arno.
Degler, Carl N. At Odds: Women & the Family in America, from the Revolution to the Present. 1980. 25.00 (ISBN 0-19-502657-8). Oxford U Pr.
Demos, John & Boocock, Sarane, eds. Turning Points: Historical & Sociological Essays on the Family. 1978. lib. bdg. 20.00x (ISBN 0-685-87016-2, 14284-1); pap. 10.00 (ISBN 0-685-87017-0, 14286-8). U of Chicago Pr.
Engles, Frederick. Origin of the Family: Private Property & the State. LC 72-85711. 1972. pap. 3.45 (ISBN 0-87348-261-1). Path Pr NY.
Forster, Robert & Ranum, Orest, eds. Family & Society: Selections from the Annales: Economies, Societes,Civilisations, Vol. 2. Ranum, Patricia, tr. from Fr. LC 76-17299. (Illus.). 288p. 1976. text ed. 16.50x (ISBN 0-8018-1780-3); pap. 4.95 (ISBN 0-8018-1781-1). Johns Hopkins.
Fox, Vivian C. & Quitt, Martin H. Loving, Parenting, & Dying: The Family Cycle in England & America, Past & Present. 488p. 1981. 38.50 (ISBN 0-914434-14-4); pap. 11.95 (ISBN 0-914434-15-2). Psychohistory Pr.
Glazer Malbin, Nona. Old Family-New Family. 1975. pap. text ed. 5.50x (ISBN 0-442-24976-4). D Van Nostrand.
Hareven, Tamara K., ed. Themes in the History of the Family. LC 78-53938. 1978. pap. 6.50 (ISBN 0-912296-15-1, Dist. by U Pr of Va). Am Antiquarian.
--Transitions: The Family & the Life Course in Historical Perspectives. (Studies in Social Discontinuity Ser.). 1978. 28.00 (ISBN 0-12-325150-8). Acad Pr.
Howard, Ronald L. A Social History of American Family Sociology, 1865-1940. Mogey, John H. & Van Leeuwen, Louis Th., eds. LC 80-1790. (Contributions in Family Studies Ser.: No. 4). xiii, 150p. 1981. lib. bdg. 22.50 (ISBN 0-313-22767-5, MOA/). Greenwood.
Laslett, Peter. Family Life & Illicit Love in Earlier Generations. 1977. 47.50 (ISBN 0-521-21408-4); pap. 12.95x (ISBN 0-521-29221-2). Cambridge U Pr.
Miller, Betty A. & Miller, Oscar R. Cornelius Jansen Family History, 1822-1973. (Illus.). 73p. 1974. pap. 4.50 (ISBN 0-685-64818-4). O R Miller.
Miller Family History: Descendants of Daniel D. Miller & Lydia B. Troyer 1847-1974. 90p. 1974. 4.50 (ISBN 0-685-64819-2). O R Miller.
Oliver, Egbert S. The Shaping of a Family. (Illus.). 1979. pap. 9.95 (ISBN 0-913244-19-8). Hapi Pr.
Phillips, Roderick. Family Breakdown in Late Eighteenth Century France: Divorces in Rouen 1792-1803. (Illus.). 288p. 1981. 55.00x (ISBN 0-19-822572-5). Oxford U Pr.
Posey, Joanna W. Ties That Bind. LC 81-90120. (Illus.). 1981. looseleaf 24.95 (ISBN 0-940348-00-4); pap. 12.95 (ISBN 0-940348-01-2). Posey Pubns.
Powell, James W. Edgewood: The Story of a Family & Their House. LC 78-50671. (Illus.). 1978. 10.95 (ISBN 0-9601518-1-8). J W Powell.
Rabb, Theodore K. & Rotberg, Robert I. Family in History: Interdisciplinary Essays. LC 73-12978. 256p. (Orig.). 1973. pap. 3.95x (ISBN 0-06-131757-8, TB1757, Torch). Har-Row.
--The Family in History: Interdisciplinary Essays. 240p. 1976. Repr. of 1973 ed. lib. bdg. 13.50x (ISBN 0-374-96705-9). Octagon.
Rothman, David J. & Rothman, Sheila M., eds. The Family. LC 88-19594. (Great Contemporary Issues Ser.). 1979. lib. bdg. 35.00 (ISBN 0-405-11197-5). Arno.
Seward, Rudy R., ed. The American Family: A Demographic History. LC 78-19609. (Sage Library of Social Research: Vol. 70). 223p. 1978. 20.00x (ISBN 0-8039-1112-2); pap. 9.95x (ISBN 0-8039-1113-0). Sage.
Soliday, Gerald L., ed. History of the Family & Kinship: A Select International Bibliography. LC 80-11782. 1980. lib. bdg. 50.00 (ISBN 0-527-84451-9). Kraus Intl.
Starcke, Carl N. The Primitive Family in Its Origin & Development. Needham, Rodney, ed. LC 75-12232. 336p. pap. 14.00x (ISBN 0-226-77133-4, Midway). U of Chicago Pr.
Swerdlow, Amy, et al. Household & Kin: Families in Flux. (Women's Lives - Women's Work Ser.). (Illus.). 208p. (Orig.). (gr. 11 up). 1981. 14.95 (ISBN 0-912670-91-6); pap. 5.95 (ISBN 0-912670-68-1). Feminist Pr.
Thiry, Joan, et al. You Must Tell Your Children. Thiry, Joan, ed. (Illus.). 64p. 1981. pap. 6.00 (ISBN 0-935046-01-1); oral history cassettes 9.95 (ISBN 0-935046-00-3). Chateau Thiry.
Thwing, Charles F. & Thwing, Carrie F. The Family: An Historical & Social Study. 258p. 1980. Repr. of 1913 ed. lib. bdg. 40.00 (ISBN 0-8495-5157-9). Arden Lib.
Tilly, Louise & Scott, Joan. Women, Work, & Family. LC 74-19821. 1978. 10.95 (ISBN 0-03-033326-1, HoltC); pap. text ed. 8.95 (ISBN 0-03-038181-9, HoltC). HR&W.
Van Den Berghe, P. L. Human Family Systems: An Evolutionary View. 1979. pap. 8.95 (ISBN 0-444-99064-X); pap. 8.95 (ISBN 0-444-99064-X). Elsevier.
Wandersee, Winifred D. Women's Work & Family Values, Nineteen Twenty to Nineteen Forty. LC 80-21100. 192p. 1981. text ed. 18.50x (ISBN 0-674-95535-8). Harvard U Pr.
Wrangham, Elizabeth, et al. The Family. Yapp, Malcolm, et al, eds. (World History Ser.). (Illus.). 32p. (gr. 10). 1980. lib. bdg. 5.95 (ISBN 0-89908-148-7); pap. text ed. 1.95 (ISBN 0-89908-123-1). Greenhaven.

FAMILY-JUVENILE LITERATURE

Abels, Harriette S. Future Family. Schroeder, Howard, ed. LC 80-16400. (Our Future World Ser.). (Illus.). 48p. (gr. 6-9). 1980. PLB 6.95 (ISBN 0-89686-085-X); pap. text ed. 3.25 (ISBN 0-89686-094-9). Crestwood Hse.
Booher, Dianna D. Coping-When Your Family Falls Apart. LC 79-17342. 192p. (gr. 7 up). 1979. PLB 8.29 (ISBN 0-671-33083-7). Messner.
Carbo, Marie L. & Carbo, Nicholas A. La Historia De Mi Familia: My Family History. (Illus.). (gr. 2-6). 1977. wkbk. in Span. 4.50x (ISBN 0-930804-02-3); wkbk. in Eng. 4.50x (ISBN 0-930804-01-5). World Rec Pubns.
Charlip, Remy & Moore, Lilian. Hooray for Me! LC 80-15285. (Illus.). 40p. (ps-3). 1980. Repr. of 1975 ed. 8.95 (ISBN 0-590-07768-6, Four Winds). Schol Bk Serv.
Drescher, Joan. Your Family, My Family. (Illus.). 32p. (gr. 2-5). 1980. 7.95 (ISBN 0-8027-6382-0); PLB 8.85 (ISBN 0-8027-6383-9). Walker & Co.
Fideler, Ruth E., ed. Families. (Illus.). (gr. k-1). 1979. PLB 39.50 (ISBN 0-88296-001-6); tchrs' guide incl. (ISBN 0-88296-316-3). Fideler.
Goodman, Walter & Goodman, Elaine. The Family: Yesterday, Today, Tomorrow. LC 74-32069. 128p. (gr. 7 up). 1975. 7.95 (ISBN 0-374-32260-0). FS&G.
Keane, Bil. Smile! (Family Circus Ser.). (Illus.). 1979. pap. 1.50 (ISBN 0-449-14172-1, GM). Fawcett.
Lee, Essie E. Marriage & Families. LC 77-26962. 224p. (gr. 7 up). 1978. PLB 7.79 (ISBN 0-671-32854-9). Messner.
Lessin, Roy. Families Are God's Idea. (God's Idea Books Ser.). (Illus.). 32p. (ps-4). 1981. pap. 1.50 (ISBN 0-87123-177-8, 210177). Bethany Hse.
--Kids Are God's Idea. (God's Idea Books Ser.). (Illus.). 32p. (ps-4). 1981. pap. 1.50 (ISBN 0-87123-178-6, 210178). Bethany Hse.
Naylor, Phyllis R. Getting Along in Your Family. LC 75-44295. (Illus.). 112p. (gr. 4-7). 1976. PLB 5.50 (ISBN 0-687-14120-6). Abingdon.
Rossel, Seymour. Family. (gr. 4 up). 1980. PLB 6.90 (ISBN 0-531-04102-6). Watts.
Schlein, Miriam. My House. LC 79-165820. (Illus.). (ps-2). 1971. 5.50g (ISBN 0-8075-5357-3). A Whitman.
Smith, Marion H. & Prescott, Carol S. Families Around the World. rev. ed. LC 76-17687. (Fideler Social Studies Ser.). (Illus.). 96p. (gr. 1-2). 1979. text ed. 6.20 ea. 1-4 copies (ISBN 0-88296-007-5); text ed. 4.96 ea. 5 or more copies; tchrs' ed 4.96 (ISBN 0-88296-322-8). Fideler.
Stein, Sarah B. That New Baby. LC 73-15271. (Open Family Ser). (Illus.). 48p. (gr. 1 up). 1974. 7.95 (ISBN 0-8027-6175-5). Walker & Co.
Twinn, Michael, illus. My Baby Brother. (Nursery Ser.). (Illus.). 8p. 1977. text ed. 1.75 (ISBN 0-85953-068-X, Pub. by Child's Play England). Playspaces.

FAMILY-LAW

see Domestic Relations

FAMILY-PRAYER-BOOKS AND DEVOTIONS

Aaseng, Rolf E. Come, Lord Jesus. LC 74-77675. (Illus.). 144p. 1974. pap. 3.95 (ISBN 0-8066-1423-4, 10-1550). Augsburg.
Anderson, Margaret J. Happy Moments with God. (Illus.). 192p. 1969. pap. 3.95 (ISBN 0-87123-212-X, 210212). Bethany Hse.
Brandt, Leslie & Brandt, Edith. Growing Together: Prayers for Married People. LC 75-2830. 96p. (Orig.). 1975. pap. 2.95 (ISBN 0-8066-1476-5, 10-2903). Augsburg.
Brusius, Ron & Noettl, Margaret. Family Evening Activity Devotions. (gr. k-7). pap. 3.95 (ISBN 0-570-03803-0, 12-2912). Concordia.
Bryant, Al. Love Songs: Daily Meditations for Married Couples. 1978. 7.95 (ISBN 0-8499-0080-8). Word Bks.
Carr, Jo. Living on Tiptoe. (Orig.). 1972. pap. 1.95x (ISBN 0-8358-0269-8). Upper Room.
Gesch, Roy G. A Husband Prays. Bd. with A Wife Prays. LC 68-22574. 1968. 10.95 (ISBN 0-570-03066-8, 6-1126). Concordia.
Henshaw, Paul & Weemhoff, H. Family Worship. 84p. 1981. pap. 2.25x (ISBN 0-8358-0421-6). Upper Room.
Howard, Barbara. Be Swift to Love. LC 74-82423. 1974. 8.00 (ISBN 0-8309-0128-0). Herald Hse.
Huxhold, Harry N. Family Altar. rev. ed. 1964. 0.95 (ISBN 0-570-03071-4, 6-1085). Concordia.
Jahsmann, Allan H. & Simon, Martin P. Little Visits with God. (gr. k-3). 1957. 6.95 (ISBN 0-570-03016-1, 6-1055); pap. 4.95 (ISBN 0-570-03032-3, 6-1158). Concordia.
--More Little Visits with God. 1961. 6.95 (ISBN 0-570-03017-X, 6-1080); pap. 4.95 (ISBN 0-570-03033-1, 6-1159). Concordia.
Jasper, Tony. The Illustrated Family Prayer Book. 1981. 18.95 (ISBN 0-8164-0480-1); pap. 10.95 (ISBN 0-8164-2292-3). Seabury.
Johnson, Ruth I. Devotions for the Family, 3 Vols. pap. 1.95 ea. Vol. 1 (ISBN 0-8024-2191-1). Vol. 2 (ISBN 0-8024-2192-X). Vol. 3 (ISBN 0-8024-2193-8). Moody.
Jurries, Ginger & Mulder, Karen. Fun Ideas for Family Devotions (with Activity Pages) LC 81-50347. (Illus.). 176p. (Orig.). 1981. pap. 6.50 (ISBN 0-87239-415-8, 2968). Standard Pub.
LeBar, Lois E. Family Devotions with School-Age Children. (Power Bks.). 256p. 1980. pap. 5.95 (ISBN 0-8007-5033-0). Revell.
Martin, Paul. Family Fare. 1976. pap. 1.25 (ISBN 0-8341-0403-2). Beacon Hill.
May, Edward. Family Worship Idea Book. LC 65-27694. 1965. 2.95 (ISBN 0-570-03022-6, 6-1097). Concordia.
Priester, Gertrude A. Let's Talk About God: Devotions for Families with Young Children. (Illus.). 1967. 3.95 (ISBN 0-664-20750-2). Westminster.
Reilly, Terry & Reilly, Mimi. Family Nights: Advent-Christmas. 1977. pap. 1.45 (ISBN 0-87029-135-1, 20161). Abbey.
--Family Nights: Lent - Easter. 1977. pap. 1.45 (ISBN 0-87029-130-0, 20158). Abbey.
--Family Nights: Summer - Vacation. 1977. pap. 1.45 (ISBN 0-87029-134-3, 20160). Abbey.
Seifert, Lois. Our Family Night In: Workbook of Covenant Living. LC 80-54803. 200p. (Orig.). pap. 4.95x (ISBN 0-8358-0420-8). Upper Room.
Toelke, Otto W. In the Presence of God. rev. ed. LC 61-18225. 1962. 3.75 (ISBN 0-570-03019-6, 6-1152). Concordia.
Vogel, Lois. God & Your Family. (Orig.). 1963. pap. 3.50 (ISBN 0-570-03128-1, 12-2219). Concordia.
Webb, Barbara O. Devotions for Families: Building Blocks of Christian Life. LC 75-22162. 48p. 1976. pap. 1.95 (ISBN 0-8170-0680-X). Judson.
--Devotions for Families: Fruit of the Family. LC 74-7516. (Illus.). 48p. (Orig.). 1974. pap. 1.95 (ISBN 0-8170-0640-0). Judson.

FAMILY-RECREATION

see Family Recreation

FAMILY-RELIGIOUS LIFE

see also Religious Education-Home Training

Archdiocesan Office of Religious Education, Dubuque, Iowa. Home Program: Resources for Family Sharing. LC 77-14800. (Illus.). 66p. 1978. pap. 4.95 (ISBN 0-8091-2079-8). Paulist Pr.

Atkinson, David. To Have & to Hold: The/Marriage Covenant & the Discipline of Divorce. 208p. (Orig.). 1981. pap. 6.95 (ISBN 0-8028-1889-7). Eerdmans.

Baer, Mervin. The Christian Home. 1976. 1.50 (ISBN 0-686-11147-8). Rod & Staff.

Banks, J. A. Victorian Values: Secularism & the Smaller Family. 288p. 1981. price not set (ISBN 0-7100-0807-4). Routledge & Kegan.

Bell, George L. Making It Together: Dates Before & After Marriage. (Orig.). 1974. pap. 4.70 (ISBN 0-89536-150-7). CSS Pub.

Bock, Lois & Working, Miji. Happiness Is a Family Time Together. (Illus.). 1975. pap. 6.95 (ISBN 0-8007-0761-3). Revell.

--Happiness Is a Family Walk with God. 1977. pap. 4.95 (ISBN 0-8007-0850-4). Revell.

Bomgren, Marilyn J. Godparents, Why? 1981. 1.35 (ISBN 0-89536-473-5). CSS Pub.

Boone, Pat. Pat Boone Devotional Book. 7.95 (ISBN 0-89728-050-4, 678753). Omega Pubns OR.

Bradley, Ruth O. Great Themes from the Book of Mormon. LC 73-19257. 1974. 7.95 (ISBN 0-8309-0115-9). Herald Hse.

Brandt, Henry & Landrum, Phil. I Want to Enjoy My Children. 160p. 1975. 5.95 (ISBN 0-310-21630-3); pap. 4.95 (ISBN 0-310-21631-1). Zondervan.

Breig, James & Knopp, Patricia. A Guide for Family Bible Reading. (Illus.). 40p. 1977. pap. 1.50 (ISBN 0-89570-100-6). Claretian Pubns.

Brestin, Steve & Brestin, Dee. Building Your House on the Lord. rev. ed. (Fisherman Bible Studyguides). 78p. 1980. saddle stitch 2.25 (ISBN 0-87788-099-9). Shaw Pubs.

Brock, Raymond T. The Christ-Centered Family. (Radiant Life Ser.). 1977. pap. 1.95 (ISBN 0-88243-903-0, 02-0903); teacher's ed 2.50 (ISBN 0-88243-173-0, 32-0173). Gospel Pub.

Buder, et al. Where We Are: A Hard Look at Family & Society. 1970. pap. 3.50 (ISBN 0-87183-331-X). Jewish Bd Family.

Chafin, Kenneth. Is There a Family in the House? A Realistic & Hopeful Look at Marriage & the Family. 1978. 6.95 (ISBN 0-8499-0109-X); pap. 3.95 (ISBN 0-8499-2839-7). Word Bks.

Clark, Glenn. Beatitudes of Married Life. pap. 0.20 (ISBN 0-910924-02-3). Macalester.

Compton, Al. Armonia Familiar. 1980. pap. 0.95 (ISBN 0-311-46078-X). Casa Bautista.

Daughters of St. Paul. Teenagers Today. 1981. 4.00 (ISBN 0-8198-7303-9); pap. 3.00 (ISBN 0-8198-7304-7). Dghtrs St Paul.

Demarest, Gary. Christian Alternatives Within Marriage. LC 77-83322. 1977. 5.95 (ISBN 0-8499-0021-2). Word Bks.

Dickey, Esther. Skills for Survival. LC 78-52124. (Illus.). 1978. 9.95 (ISBN 0-88290-093-5). Horizon Utah.

Drescher, John M. If I Were Starting My Family Again. LC 78-13278. (Illus.). 1979. 5.95 (ISBN 0-687-18675-7). Abingdon.

Dufresne, Edward R. Partnership: Marriage & the Committed Life. LC 74-27423. 141p. 1975. pap. 5.95 (ISBN 0-8091-1866-1). Paulist Pr.

Durka, Gloria & Smith, Joanmarie. Family Ministry. 216p. (Orig.). 1980. pap. 7.95 (ISBN 0-03-057844-2). Winston Pr.

Elders of Bible Temple & Iverson, Dick. Priniciples of Family Life. 2nd ed. (Illus.). 195p. 1981. pap. 7.75 (ISBN 0-914936-35-2). Bible Pr.

Evans, David. Living Together in Marriage. (Christian Living Ser). 16p. 1976. pap. 0.30 (ISBN 0-8170-0731-8). Judson.

Fairchild, Roy W. Christians in Families. (Orig.). 1964. pap. 3.95 (ISBN 0-8042-9612-X). John Knox.

The Family in the Pastoral Activity of the Church. pap. 0.75 (ISBN 0-686-15368-5, V-588). US Catholic.

Fisher, Robert. The Family & the Church. LC 77-99163. 1978. 4.75 (ISBN 0-87148-334-3); pap. 3.75 (ISBN 0-87148-335-1). Pathway Pr.

Galloway, Dale E. We're Making Our Home a Happy Place. 1976. pap. 2.95 (ISBN 0-8423-7860-X). Tyndale.

Gangel, Kenneth & Gangel, Elizabeth. Between Christian Parent & Child. (Contemporary Discussion Ser.). (Orig.). 1974. pap. 1.45 (ISBN 0-8010-3680-1). Baker Bk.

Gaulke, Earl H. You Can Have a Family Where Everybody Wins. LC 75-23574. 104p. 1975. pap. 2.50 (ISBN 0-570-03723-9, 12-2625). Concordia.

Geromel, Gene, Jr. How You Can Help Your Engaged Child Prepare for Christian Marriage. (Illus.). 40p. 1981. pap. 1.95 (ISBN 0-89570-203-7). Claretian Pubns.

Getting Your Family Together: Study Guide. 48p. 1978. pap. 1.39 (ISBN 0-8307-0563-5, 61-009-02). Regal.

Getz, Gene A. Measure of a Family. LC 76-46872. (Orig.). 1977. pap. 2.95 (ISBN 0-8307-0445-0, 50-150-06). Regal.

Godard, James M. Blue Light. (Orig.). 1964. pap. 1.95 (ISBN 0-8042-9614-6). John Knox.

Greeley, Andrew. Young Catholic Family. (Illus.). 1980. pap. 12.95 (ISBN 0-88347-122-1). Thomas More.

Hall, Ruthann. That's Life. 1974. pap. 1.95 (ISBN 0-89265-020-6). Randall Hse.

Hanks, Darla & Bascom, Arlene. To Parents, with Love: Practical Pointers for Family Success. 1978. 8.95 (ISBN 0-88290-090-0). Horizon Utah.

Hendricks, Howard G. Heaven Help the Home! LC 73-78689. 1974. pap. 3.95 (ISBN 0-88207-240-4). Victor Bks.

Hendrix, Lelia. Extended Family: Combining Ages in Church Experiences. LC 78-659278. 1979. pap. 3.95 (ISBN 0-8054-3426-7). Broadman.

Herr, Ethel. Growing up Is a Family Affair. 1978. pap. 6.95 (ISBN 0-8024-3357-X). Moody.

Heynen, Ralph. Christian Home. (Contemporary Discussion Ser.). (Orig.). 1974. pap. 1.25 (ISBN 0-8010-4109-0). Baker Bk.

Hiesberger, Jean M., ed. Family Enrichment Manual. (Path of Life Ser.). 1980. 1.95 (ISBN 0-8091-9190-3). Paulist Pr.

--Family Healing Manual. (Path of Life Ser.). 1980. 9.95 (ISBN 0-8091-9189-X). Paulist Pr.

--Our Family Scripture: Family Book. (Paths of Life Ser.). 1980. 5.95 (ISBN 0-8091-2272-3). Paulist Pr.

--Our Family Scripture: Leader's Manual. (Paths of Life Ser.). 1980. 4.95 (ISBN 0-8091-2271-5). Paulist Pr.

Hinshaw, Edwin & Hinshaw, Dorothy. Toward Caring: Couple Enrichment. (Illus.). 1977. pap. 1.50 (ISBN 0-913408-36-0). Friends United.

Hopkins, Mary. Celebrating: Family Prayer Services. LC 75-30486. 164p. 1975. pap. 7.95 (ISBN 0-8091-1893-9). Paulist Pr.

Howell, John C. Equality & Submission in Marriage. LC 78-67292. 1979. 6.50 (ISBN 0-8054-5632-5). Broadman.

Hoyer, George W. The Lord Be with You. LC 77-85172. (Child of God Ser.: Vol. 1). 1977. pap. text ed. 2.95 (ISBN 0-915644-11-8). Clayton Pub Hse.

Hubbard, David A. Is the Family Here to Stay? LC 74-170912. 1971. pap. 0.95 (ISBN 0-87680-928-X, 90028). Word Bks.

Huffman, John A., Jr. Becoming a Whole Family. LC 75-10093. 160p. 1975. 5.95 (ISBN 0-87680-418-0). Word Bks.

Hulme, William E. The Pastoral Care of Families. LC 61-11784. 1974. pap. 3.50 (ISBN 0-687-30291-9). Abingdon.

Hunter, Christine. Anna's Family. 1975. pap. 1.95 (ISBN 0-87508-639-X). Chr Lit.

Iatesta, Robert. Fathers: A Fresh Start for the Christian Family. 238p. (Orig.). 1980. pap. 4.95 (ISBN 0-89283-083-2). Servant.

Kaye, Evelyn. Crosscurrents: Children, Families, & Religion. 256p. 1980. 11.95 (ISBN 0-517-53292-1). Potter.

Kotre, John. Simple Gifts: The Lives of Pat & Patty Crowley. 1979. 10.00 (ISBN 0-8362-3900-8). Andrews & McMeel.

LaHaye, Tim. The Battle for the Family. 256p. 1981. 9.95 (ISBN 0-8007-1277-3). Revell.

LaHaye, Tim & LaHaye, Beverly. Spirit Controlled Family Living. 1978. 7.95 (ISBN 0-8007-0950-0); pap. 4.95 (ISBN 0-8007-5026-8, Power Bks). Revell.

Larson, Bruce. No Longer Strangers. LC 74-146675. 1976. pap. 2.50 (ISBN 0-87680-827-5, 91021, Key-Word Bks). Word Bks.

Larson, Roland & Larson, Doris. Values & Faith: Value Clarifying Exercises for Family & Church Groups. (Illus.). 260p. 1976. pap. 5.95 (ISBN 0-03-018046-5). Winston Pr.

Lasch, Christopher. Haven in a Heartless World: The Family Besieged. LC 77-75246. 1979. 12.95x (ISBN 0-465-02883-7, CN-5035); pap. 4.95 (ISBN 0-465-02884-5). Basic.

Lee, Mark W. Time Bombs in Marriage. LC 81-65727. 192p. 1981. pap. 5.95 (ISBN 0-915684-92-6). Christian Herald.

Lockerbie, Bruce D. Who Educates Your Child: A Book for Parents. LC 79-7500. 1980. 8.95 (ISBN 0-385-14826-7, Galilee). Doubleday.

Lovett, C. S. Unequally Yoked Wives. 1968. pap. 4.45 (ISBN 0-938148-22-2). Personal Christianity.

Mace, David & Mace, Vera. Men, Women, & God. 1976. pap. 4.50 (ISBN 0-8042-8076-2). John Knox.

McGinnis, Alan L. La Amistad Factor Decisivo. Orig. Title: The Friendship Factor. 176p. (Span.). Date not set. pap. price not set (ISBN 0-311-46093-3, Edit Mundo). Casa Bautista.

McGinnis, Kathleen & McGinnis, James. Parenting for Peace & Justice. LC 81-3917. 160p. (Orig.). 1981. pap. 4.95 (ISBN 0-88344-376-7). Orbis Bks.

Mains, David. God, Help Us with the Kids. (Chapel Talks Ser.). 1.75 (ISBN 0-89191-259-2, 52597). Cook.

Mains, Karen. Open Heart, Open Home Study Guide. 32p. pap. 1.95 (ISBN 0-89191-142-1, 22954). Cook.

Martin, Dorothy. Creative Family Worship. 1976. pap. 1.25 (ISBN 0-8024-1641-1). Moody.

Martin, Ralph. Husbands, Wives, Parents, Children. 1978. pap. 4.95 (ISBN 0-89283-050-6). Servant.

Mason, Rosalie. Beginners Guide to Family Preparedness. LC 77-79750. (Illus.). 1977. pap. 5.95 (ISBN 0-88290-082-X). Horizon Utah.

Meet the Holy Family. 7.50 (ISBN 0-686-76789-6, 101-24). Prow Bks-Franciscan.

Meier, Paul & Meier, Richard. Family Foundations. 96p. (Orig.). Date not set. 8.95 (ISBN 0-8010-6117-2); pap. 4.95 (ISBN 0-8010-6122-9). Baker Bk.

Miller, John F. The Art of Parenting in a Changing Society. 1979. 8.95 (ISBN 0-8199-0761-8). Franciscan Herald.

National Conference of Catholic Bishops, United States Catholic Conference. The Plan of Pastoral Action for Family Ministry: A Vision & Strategy. (Illus., Orig.). 1978. pap. 1.75 (ISBN 0-686-23714-5). US Catholic.

Nichols, Francis W. What Puzzled Parents Can Do About Kids & Confession. 48p. 1981. pap. 1.95 (ISBN 0-686-73394-0). Claretian Pubns.

O'Brien, Joachim. Parish Family Life & Social Action. LC 77-3573. 1977. pap. 1.50 (ISBN 0-8199-0673-5). Franciscan Herald.

Orso, Kathryn W. Parenthood: A Commitment in Faith. LC 75-5219. 64p. (Orig.). 1975. pap. text ed. 2.95 (ISBN 0-8192-1198-2); tchr's ed. 3.75 (ISBN 0-8192-1204-0); wkbk. 3.95 (ISBN 0-8192-1199-0). Morehouse.

Pappas, Michael G. Prime Time for Families. (Illus.). 120p. (Orig.). 1980. pap. 5.95 (ISBN 0-03-056672-X). Winston Pr.

Perkins, Richard F. Image of a Christian Family. 1964. pap. 1.95 (ISBN 0-8042-9610-3). John Knox.

Petersen, Evelyn & Petersen, J. Allan. For Women Only. 1975. 6.95 (ISBN 0-8423-0895-4); pap. 4.95 (ISBN 0-8423-0896-2). Tyndale.

Petersen, J. Allan. For Men Only. 1973. pap. 3.95 (ISBN 0-8423-0891-1). Tyndale.

Phillips, Mike. A Christian Family in Action. LC 77-1887. 1977. pap. 3.95 (ISBN 0-87123-085-2, 210085). Bethany Hse.

Puccio, Carolyn. Touched by God's Promise: A Family Remembrance Book. 1979. 9.95 (ISBN 0-03-041971-9). Winston Pr.

Quesnell, John G. Holy Terrors & Holy Parents. 228p. 1976. 7.95 (ISBN 0-8199-0561-5). Franciscan Herald.

Rickerson, Wayne E. Getting Your Family Together. LC 77-78848. 1977. pap. 3.25 (ISBN 0-8307-0426-4, 54-035-02). Regal.

Scheuring, Tom & Scheuring, Lyn. God Longs for Family: Family Evangelization. LC 79-92535. 149p. (Orig.). 1980. pap. 2.95 (ISBN 0-87973-533-3, 533). Our Sunday Visitor.

Schroeder, L. Celebrate-While We Wait. (Illus.). 1977. pap. 3.75 (ISBN 0-570-03052-8, 6-1177). Concordia.

Schrum, David. Creating Love & Warmth for Our Children. LC 77-78473. 1977. 4.50 (ISBN 0-8054-5623-6). Broadman.

Schuller, Robert. Power Ideas for a Happy Family. 1976. pap. 1.75 (ISBN 0-515-05104-7). Jove Pubns.

Sell, Charles M. Family Ministry: Family Life Through the Church. 272p. 11.95 (ISBN 0-310-42580-8). Zondervan.

Showalter, Carol. Three-D. LC 77-90947. 144p. 1980. pap. 4.95 (ISBN 0-932260-04-7). Rock Harbor.

Sloane, Valerie. Creative Family Activities: Loving Learning & Living Together. LC 75-45208. 1976. 4.95 (ISBN 0-687-09828-9). Abingdon.

Sparks, Merla J. Creative Christian Home. pap. 1.95 (ISBN 0-8010-8050-9). Baker Bk.

Stephens, John F. Spirit Filled Family, No. 11. 48p. (Orig.). 1980. pap. 1.50 (ISBN 0-89841-008-8). Zoe Pubns.

Stewart, Charles W. The Minister As Family Counselor. LC 79-10854. 1979. 8.95 (ISBN 0-687-26955-5). Abingdon.

Stine, Alan. Love Power: New Dimensions for Building Strong Families. LC 78-70360. 1978. 6.95 (ISBN 0-88290-105-2). Horizon Utah.

Strauss, Richard L. Confident Children & How They Grow. 1975. 5.95 (ISBN 0-8423-0433-9); pap. 3.95 (ISBN 0-8423-0431-2). Tyndale.

Sweeting, George. Special Sermons on the Family. (Special Sermon Ser.). 144p. 1981. pap. 2.95 (ISBN 0-8024-8208-2). Moody.

Swindoll, Charles. You & Your Child. LC 77-1692. 1977. pap. 3.95 (ISBN 0-8407-5616-X). Nelson.

Taylor, Florence M. As for Me & My Family. LC 76-48532. 1977. 5.95 (ISBN 0-87680-512-8, 80512). Word Bks.

Taylor, Robert R., Jr. Christ in the Home. pap. 4.95 (ISBN 0-8010-8811-9). Baker Bk.

Thomas, David. Family Life & the Church. LC 79-90004. (Paths of Life Family Life Programs). 128p. 1979. pap. 4.95 (ISBN 0-8091-2255-3). Paulist Pr.

Thomas, David M. When God Is at Home with Your Family. LC 78-73019. (When Bks). (Illus.). 1979. pap. 2.45 (ISBN 0-87029-146-7, 20231). Abbey.

Thomas, David M., ed. Family Life Ministry. LC 79-53513. (Marriage & Family Living in Depth: Vol. VII). (Orig.). 1979. pap. 2.45 (ISBN 0-87029-157-2, 20243). Abbey.

--God, Religion, & Family Life. LC 79-53512. (Marriage & Family Living in Depth: Vol. VI). (Orig.). 1979. pap. 2.45 (ISBN 0-87029-156-4, 20242). Abbey.

Thomas, John L. The American Catholic Family. LC 80-15221. (Illus.). xii, 471p. 1980. Repr. of 1956 ed. lib. bdg. 33.50x (ISBN 0-313-22473-0, THAC). Greenwood.

Thompson, James. Our Life Together. LC 77-79338. (Journey Bks.). 1977. pap. 2.95 (ISBN 0-8344-0095-2). Sweet.

Thresh, Arline C. Little Things That Keep Families Together. LC 76-24116. 1977. pap. 2.75 (ISBN 0-8054-5617-1). Broadman.

Tietjen, Mary L. Summer Savory: A Family Resource Book. LC 77-78961. 1977. pap. 3.95 (ISBN 0-8091-2034-8). Paulist Pr.

Turnage, Mac N. & Turnage, Anne S. People, Families, & God. 1981. pap. 5.95 (ISBN 0-8042-8077-0). John Knox.

Vaught, Laud O. Focus on the Christian Family. 1976. pap. 3.50 (ISBN 0-87148-332-7). Pathway Pr.

Wakefield, Norman. You Can Have a Happier Family. LC 76-24320. 1977. pap. 3.25 (ISBN 0-8307-0403-5, 54-025-06); study guide 1.39 (ISBN 0-686-17336-8). Regal.

Webb, Barbara O. Families Sharing God. 48p. 1981. pap. 3.50 (ISBN 0-8170-0900-0). Judson.

Wilczak, Paul F., ed. Healing in the Family. LC 79-53515. (Marriage & Family Living in Depth: Vol. VIII). (Orig.). 1979. pap. 2.45 (ISBN 0-87029-158-0, 20244). Abbey.

Zanzucchi, Annamaria. My Child & God: Religious Education in the Family. Hartman, Thomas, ed. Sczesniak, Lenny, tr. LC 78-52599. 1978. pap. 2.25 (ISBN 0-911782-31-1). New City.

Zuck, Roy B. & Getz, Gene A. Adult Education in the Church. LC 79-123154. 1970. 11.95 (ISBN 0-8024-0155-4). Moody.

FAMILY-AFRICA

Bernard, Guy. Ville Africaine, Famille Urbaine: Les Enseignants De Kinshasa. (Recherches Africaines: No. 6). 1968. pap. 23.50x (ISBN 90-2797-543-4). Mouton.

Gray, Robert F. & Gulliver, P. H., eds. The Family Estate in Africa: Studies in the Role of Property in Family Structure & Lineage Continuity. LC 64-19442. 1964. 9.50x, USA (ISBN 0-8147-0169-8). NYU Pr.

Marris, Peter. Family & Social Change in an African City: A Study of Rehousing in Lagos. (African Studies Ser.: No. 8). (Illus.). 1962. 9.95x (ISBN 0-8101-0156-4). Northwestern U Pr.

Nwogugu, E. I. Family Law in Nigeria. 1977. pap. text ed. 50.00x (ISBN 0-435-89601-6). Heinemann Ed.

FAMILY-ASIA

Das, Man S. & Bardis, Panos D., eds. The Family in Asia. 1979. text ed. 35.00x (ISBN 0-04-301097-0). Allen Unwin.

FAMILY-BARBADOS

Greenfield, Sidney M. English Rustics in Black Skin: A Study of Modern Family Forms in a Pre-Industrialized Society. 1966. 5.00x (ISBN 0-8084-0121-1); pap. 1.95 (ISBN 0-8084-0122-X, B40). Coll & U Pr.

FAMILY-BRITISH GUIANA

Smith, Raymond T. Negro Family in British Guiana: Family Structure & Social Status in the Villages. (International Library of Sociology & Social Reconstruction Ser.). 1971. Repr. of 1956 ed. text ed. 15.50x (ISBN 0-7100-3355-9). Humanities.

FAMILY-CARIBBEAN AREA

Conference on the Family in the Caribbean, 2nd, Aruba, Netherlands Antilles, Dec. 1-5, 1969. The Family in the Caribbean: Proceedings. Gerber, Standford N., ed. 167p. 1973. pap. 10.50x (ISBN 0-8002-1415-3). Intl Pubns Serv.

Roberts, George W. & Sinclair, Sonja A. Women in Jamaica: Patterns of Reproduction & Family. LC 76-56911. (Caribbean Monographs). 1978. 25.00 (ISBN 0-527-75870-1). Kraus Intl.

FAMILY-CHINA

Baker, Hugh D. A Chinese Lineage Village: Sheung-Shui. (Illus.). 1968. 22.50x (ISBN 0-8047-0670-0). Stanford U Pr.

Che, Wai-Kin. The Modern Chinese Family. LC 77-91415. 1979. perfect bdg. 9.00 (ISBN 0-88247-554-1). R & E Res Assoc.

Freedman, Maurice. Chinese Family & Marriage in Singapore. (Colonial Research Studies). pap. 23.00 (ISBN 0-384-16760-8). Johnson Repr.

Freedman, Maurice, ed. Family & Kinship in Chinese Society. (Studies in Chinese Society). 350p. 1970. 12.50x (ISBN 0-8047-0713-8). Stanford U Pr.
Greenblatt, Sidney L., ed. People of Taihang: An Anthology of Family Histories. LC 74-15389. (The China Book Project Ser.). 1976. 22.50 (ISBN 0-87332-059-X). M E Sharpe.
Kao Ta-Kuan. Changes in Family & Society. (National Peking University & Chinese Assn. for Folklore, Folklore & Folkliterature Ser.: No. 124). (Chinese.). 6.00 (ISBN 0-89986-199-7). E Langstaff.
Kingston, Maxine H. China Men. LC 79-3469. 1980. 10.95 (ISBN 0-394-42463-8). Knopf.
Levy, Marion J., Jr. Family Revolution in Modern China. 1963. lib. bdg. 24.00x (ISBN 0-374-94960-3). Octagon.
Liu Fei-Yen, ed. The Women & Children. (National Peking University& Chinese Assn. for Folklore, Folklore & Folkliterature Ser.: No. 58). (Chinese.). 6.00 (ISBN 0-89986-149-0). E Langstaff.
Mai Hui-T'ing. Problems of Change of the Chinese Family. (National Peking University & Chinese Assn. for Folklore, Folklore & Folkliterature Ser.: No. 82 & 83). (Chinese.). 14.00 (ISBN 0-89986-166-0). E Langstaff.
Mitchell, Robert E. Family Life in Urban Hong Kong, 2 vols, Nos. 24-25. (Asian Folklore & Social Life Monograph). 1972. 9.20 (ISBN 0-89986-026-5). E Langstaff.
Orleans, Leo A. Chinese Approaches to Family Planning. LC 79-64372. 1979. 22.50 (ISBN 0-87332-139-1). M E Sharpe.
Pa Chin. Family. 7.95 (ISBN 0-8351-0589-X). China Bks.
P'an Kuang-Tan. Problems of the Chinese Family. (National Peking University & Chinese Assn. for Folklore, Folklore & Folkliterature Ser.: No. 123). (Chinese.). 9.00 (ISBN 0-89986-198-9). E Langstaff.
Parish, William L. & Whyte, Martin K. Village & Family in Contemporary China. LC 78-3411. (Illus.). 1978. lib. bdg. 25.00x (ISBN 0-226-64590-8). U of Chicago Pr.
Wilkinson, Hiran P. Family in Classical China. (Studies in Chinese History & Civilization). 239p. 1977. Repr. of 1926 ed. 19.50 (ISBN 0-89093-085-6). U Pubns Amer.
Wolf, Margery. Women & the Family in Rural Taiwan. LC 70-183895. (Illus.). 1972. 15.00x (ISBN 0-8047-0808-8); pap. 3.95 (ISBN 0-8047-0849-5, SP132). Stanford U Pr.
Wolfe. House of Lim: Study of a Chinese Farm Family. 1960. pap. text ed. 6.95 (ISBN 0-13-394973-7). P-H.
Yang, C. K. Chinese Communist Society: The Family & the Village. 1965. pap. 4.95 (ISBN 0-262-74001-X). MIT Pr.

FAMILY-FLORENCE

Alberti, Leon B. Family in Renaissance Florence: A Translation of I Libri Della Famiglia. Watkins, Renee Neu, tr. LC 75-79129. 1969. 14.95x (ISBN 0-87249-152-8). U of SC Pr.

FAMILY-FRANCE

Aries, Philippe. Centuries of Childhood: A Social History of Family Life. 1965. pap. 4.95 (ISBN 0-394-70286-7, V286, Vin). Random.
Flandrin, J. L. Families in Former Times. LC 78-18095. (Themes in the Social Sciences Ser.). (Illus.). 1979. 39.50 (ISBN 0-521-22323-7); pap. 9.95x (ISBN 0-521-29449-5). Cambridge U Pr.
Phillips, Roderick. Family Breakdown in Late Eighteenth Century France: Divorces in Rouen 1792-1803. (Illus.). 288p. 1981. 55.00x (ISBN 0-19-822572-5). Oxford U Pr.
Traer, James F. Marriage & the Family in Eighteenth-Century France. LC 80-11121. 240p. 1980. 17.50x (ISBN 0-8014-1298-6). Cornell U Pr.
Wheaton, Robert & Hareven, Tamara K., eds. Family & Sexuality in French History. LC 79-5255. 288p. 1980. 22.50 (ISBN 0-8122-7775-9). U of Pa Pr.

FAMILY-GREAT BRITAIN

Anderson, Michael. Family Structure in Nineteenth Century Lancashire. LC 79-164448. (Cambridge Studies in Sociology: No. 5). (Illus.). 1971. 29.50 (ISBN 0-521-08237-4). Cambridge U Pr.
Crabtree, Tom. Tom Crabtree on Teenagers. 160p. 1980. pap. 14.95 (ISBN 0-241-10398-3, Pub. by Hamish Hamilton England). David & Charles.
Firth, Raymond, et al. Families & Their Relatives, Kinship in a Middle-Class Sector of London: An Anthropological Study. (International Library of Sociology & Social Reconstruction). 1970. text ed. 16.25x (ISBN 0-7100-6431-4). Humanities.
Gavron, Hannah. Captive Wife. (International Library of Sociology & Social Reconstruction Ser.). 1966. text ed. 17.00x (ISBN 0-7100-3457-1). Humanities.
Greve, John. London's Homeless. 76p. 1964. pap. text ed. 3.75x (ISBN 0-686-70849-0, Pub. by Bedford England). Renouf.
Harris, Chris, et al, eds. The Sociology of the Family: New Directions for Britain. (Sociological Review Monograph: No. 28). 240p. 1979. 30.00x (ISBN 0-8476-3265-2); pap. 18.50x (ISBN 0-8476-3258-X). Rowman.
Land, Hilarly. Large Families in London. 154p. 1969. pap. text ed. 6.25x (ISBN 0-7135-1577-5, Pub. by Bedford England). Renouf.
Moroney, R. M. The Family & the State: Considerations for Social Policy. LC 75-45230. (Illus.). 1976. pap. text ed. 9.50x (ISBN 0-582-48493-6). Longman.
Rapoport, Rhona & Rapoport, Robert N. Dual-Career Families Re-Examined: New Integrations of Work & Family. 2nd ed. 382p. 1976. o. p. 25.50x (ISBN 0-85520-125-8, Pub. by Martin Robertson England); pap. 10.95x (ISBN 0-85520-124-X). Biblio Dist.
Toson, Shimazaki. The Family. 1979. pap. 9.95 (ISBN 0-86008-254-7, Pub. by U of Tokyo Pr). Intl Schol Bk Serv.
Turner, Christopher. Family & Kinship in Modern Britain. (Students Library of Sociology). 1969. pap. text ed. 1.50x (ISBN 0-7100-6347-4). Humanities.
Wohl, A. Victorian Family. LC 77-9234. 1978. 17.95x (ISBN 0-312-84276-7). St Martin.
Young, Michael & Willmott, Peter. Family & Kinship in East London. 7.50 (ISBN 0-8446-5103-6). Peter Smith.
--Family & Kinship in East London. 1957. text ed. 12.00x (ISBN 0-7100-3911-5). Humanities.

FAMILY-GREECE

Glotz, Gustave. La Solidarite de la Famille Dan le Droit Criminel en Grece. LC 72-7891. (Greek History Ser.). (Fr.). Repr. of 1904 ed. 32.00 (ISBN 0-405-04787-8). Arno.

FAMILY-INDIA

Bebarta, Prafulla C. Family Type & Fertility in India. LC 76-4268. (Illus.). 224p. 1977. 8.95 (ISBN 0-8158-0339-7). Chris Mass.
Kurian. The Family in India: A Regional View. (Studies in the Social Sciences: No. 12). 1974. pap. 61.50x (ISBN 90-2793-312-X). Mouton.
Lannoy, Richard. Speaking Tree: A Study of Indian Culture & Society. 1971. 25.00 (ISBN 0-19-501469-3). Oxford U Pr.
--The Speaking Tree: A Study of Indian Culture & Society. LC 74-158205. (Illus.). 528p. 1974. pap. 5.95 (ISBN 0-19-519754-2, GB). Oxford U Pr.
Mukherjee, Ramkrishna. West Bengal Family Structures, 1946-1966. LC 76-904812. 1976. 12.50x (ISBN 0-8364-0478-5). South Asia Bks.
Puthenkalam, J. Marriage & Family in Kerala. 1981. 16.00x (ISBN 0-8364-0687-7, Pub. by U Calgary India). South Asia Bks.
Shah, A. M. The Household Dimension of the Family in India. LC 71-126757. 1974. 25.00x (ISBN 0-520-01790-0). U of Cal Pr.

FAMILY-JAMAICA

Blake, Judith, et al. Family Structure in Jamaica: The Social Context of Reproduction. LC 80-12362. (Illus.). x, 262p. 1980. Repr. of 1961 ed. lib. bdg. 21.25x (ISBN 0-313-22448-X, BLFS). Greenwood.
Clark, Edith. My Mother Who Fathered Me: A Study of the Family in the Selected Communities in Jamaica. 1976. pap. text ed. 8.95x (ISBN 0-04-573010-5). Allen Unwin.
Henriques, Fernando. Family & Colour in Jamaica. 2nd ed. 1968. text ed. 9.00x (ISBN 0-261-62000-2). Humanities.

FAMILY-JAPAN

Sano, Chie. Changing Values of the Japanese Family. LC 73-8257. 142p. 1973. Repr. of 1958 ed. lib. bdg. 15.00x (ISBN 0-8371-6974-7, SACV). Greenwood.

FAMILY-LATIN AMERICA

Das, Man S. & Jesser, Clinton J., eds. The Family in Latin America. 1980. text ed. 40.00x (ISBN 0-7069-0800-7, Pub. by Vikas India). Advent NY.
Hill, Rueben, et al. The Family & Population Control. pap. 4.50 (ISBN 0-8084-0130-0, B24). Coll & U Pr.
Lewis, Oscar, et al. Four Men-Living the Revolution: An Oral History of Contemporary Cuba. LC 76-54878. 1976. 22.50 (ISBN 0-252-00628-3). U of Ill Pr.

FAMILY-MEXICO

Lewis, Oscar. Children of Sanchez. 1961. 19.95 (ISBN 0-394-41922-7). Random.
--Children of Sanchez. 1966. pap. 4.95 (ISBN 0-394-70280-8, Vin). Random.
--Death in the Sanchez Family. 1969. 7.95 (ISBN 0-394-42160-4). Random.
--Five Families: Mexican Case Studies in the Culture of Poverty. LC 59-10644. 1959. 12.00x (ISBN 0-465-02466-1); pap. 4.95x (ISBN 0-465-09705-7, CN-5005). Basic.

FAMILY-RUSSIA

Elnett, Elaine. Historic Origin & Social Development of Family Life in Russia. LC 72-153317. Repr. of 1926 ed. 16.00 (ISBN 0-404-02322-3). AMS Pr.
Geiger, H. Kent. Family in Soviet Russia. LC 68-15637. (Russian Research Center Studies: No. 56). (Illus.). 1968. 17.50x (ISBN 0-674-29300-2). Harvard U Pr.
Luzbetak, Louis J. Marriage & the Family in Caucasia. Repr. of 1951 ed. 38.50 (ISBN 0-384-34300-7). Johnson Repr.
Makarenko, A. S. Collective Family: A Handbook for Russian Parents. Orig. Title: Book for Parents. 7.50 (ISBN 0-8446-2515-9). Peter Smith.
Ransel, David L., ed. The Family in Imperial Russia: New Lines of Historical Research. LC 78-17579. 1978. 16.50 (ISBN 0-252-00701-8); pap. 6.95 (ISBN 0-252-00777-8). U of Ill Pr.
VonFrank, April A. Family Policy in the USSR Since 1944. LC 77-1123. 1979. perfect bdg. 10.00 (ISBN 0-88247-552-5). R & E Res Assoc.

FAMILY-TAIWAN

Che, Wai-Kin. The Modern Chinese Family. LC 77-91415. 1979. perfect bdg. 9.00 (ISBN 0-88247-554-1). R & E Res Assoc.
Cohen, Myron L. House United, House Divided: A Chinese Family in Taiwan. LC 75-28473. (Studies of the East Asian Institute). (Illus.). 272p. 1975. 15.00x (ISBN 0-231-03849-6). Columbia U Pr.
Pasternak, Burton. Kinship & Community in Two Chinese Villages. LC 72-78870. (Illus.). 208p. 1972. 10.00x (ISBN 0-8047-0823-1). Stanford U Pr.

FAMILY-WEST INDIES

Matthews, Basil. Crisis of the West Indian Family, a Sample Study. LC 75-98782. 1971. Repr. of 1953 ed. lib. bdg. 15.00 (ISBN 0-8371-3127-8, MAIF). Greenwood.

FAMILY-YUGOSLAVIA

St. Ehrlich, Vera. Family in Transition: A Study of 300 Yugoslav Villages. 1966. 30.00x (ISBN 0-691-09317-2). Princeton U Pr.

FAMILY ALLOWANCES

Children's Allowance Conference, 1967. Children's Allowance & the Economic Welfare of Children: The Report of a Conference. facsimile ed. Burns, Eveline M., ed. LC 74-1695. (Children & Youth Ser.). 208p. 1974. Repr. of 1968 ed. 15.00x (ISBN 0-405-05971-X). Arno.

FAMILY BUDGETS

see Home Economics-Accounting

FAMILY CASE WORK

see Family Social Work

FAMILY COURTS

see Domestic Relations Courts; Juvenile Courts

FAMILY ENDOWMENT

see Family Allowances

FAMILY FARMS

Kada, Ryohei. Part-Time Family Farming. 264p. 1980. 26.00x (ISBN 0-89955-222-6, Pub. by Japan Sci Sol Pr Japan). Intl Schol Bk Serv.
Lahiri, R. K. Family Farming in a Developing Economy. 1979. pap. text ed. 8.00x (ISBN 0-391-01851-5). Humanities.
Lee, Hollis. Crops on a Few Acres. (Country Home & Small Farm Guides). 96p. 1981. 5.95 (ISBN 0-442-27224-3); pap. 2.95 (ISBN 0-442-27223-5). Van Nos Reinhold.
Ruck, Ruth J. Hill Farm Story. (Illus.). 240p. 1977. 5.95 (ISBN 0-571-11081-9, Pub. by Faber & Faber). Merrimack Bk Serv.
Sublett, Michael W. Farmers on the Road. LC 75-8522. (Research Papers Ser.: No. 168). (Illus.). 1975. pap. 8.00 (ISBN 0-89065-075-6). U Chicago Dept Geog.
Vivian, John. The Manual of Practical Homesteading. LC 75-6853. 352p. 1975. 12.95 (ISBN 0-87857-092-6). Rodale Pr Inc.
Wolfe. House of Lim: Study of a Chinese Farm Family. 1960. pap. text ed. 6.95 (ISBN 0-13-394973-7). P-H.

FAMILY FUN

see Family Recreation

FAMILY GROUP THERAPY

see Family Psychotherapy

FAMILY HISTORIES

see subdivision genealogy under countries, e.g., United States-Genealogy; and individual families, e.g. Lee Family

FAMILY IN LITERATURE

Armens, Sven. Archetypes of the Family in Literature. LC 66-19562. 278p. 1966. 10.50 (ISBN 0-295-74038-8). U of Wash Pr.
Ellis, Anne W. Nineteen Sixties. 1970. 7.50 (ISBN 0-208-00881-0, Archon). Shoe String.
Mickelson, Anne Z. Thomas Hardy's Women & Men: The Defeat of Nature. LC 76-28366. 1976. 10.00 (ISBN 0-8108-0985-0). Scarecrow.
Olson, David H. Inventory of Marriage & Family Literature. (Inventory of Family & Marriage Literature Ser.: Vol. 7). 520p. 1981. 75.00 (ISBN 0-8039-1661-2); pap. 35.00 (ISBN 0-8039-1662-0). Sage.
Somerville, Rose M., ed. Intimate Relationships: Marriage, Family & Lifestyles Through Literature. (Family & Consumer Science Ser.). (Illus.). 480p. 1975. ref. ed. o.p. 16.95 (ISBN 0-13-476861-2); pap. 11.95 (ISBN 0-13-476879-5). P-H.
Sundquist, Eric J. Home As Found: Authority & Genealogy in Nineteenth Century American Literature. LC 79-4949. 1979. text ed. 15.00 (ISBN 0-8018-2241-6). Johns Hopkins.
Tavuchis, Nicholas & Goode, William J. The Family Through Literature. LC 74-8935. (Sociology Ser.). 448p. 1974. pap. text ed. 9.95 (ISBN 0-07-062919-6, C). McGraw.

FAMILY LAW

see Domestic Relations

FAMILY LIFE EDUCATION

see also Counseling; Finance, Personal; Home Economics; Interpersonal Relations; Marriage Counseling; Sex Instruction

Acus, Leah K. Quarreling Kids: Stop the Fighting & Develop Loving Relationship Within the Family. (Illus.). 192p. 1981. 12.95 (ISBN 0-13-748012-1, Spec); pap. 5.95 (ISBN 0-13-748004-0). P-H.
Anson, Elva & Liden, Kathie. The Compleat Family Book. (Illus.). 1979. text ed. 7.95 (ISBN 0-8024-1594-6). Moody.
Bahr, Stephen J., ed. Economics & the Family. LC 79-47985. 208p. 1980. 19.95x (ISBN 0-669-03623-4). Lexington Bks.
Ball, Gerry. Circle of Warmth: Card Pack, Family Program. 1980. 12.00 (ISBN 0-86584-039-3). Human Dev Train.
--Circle of Warmth: Guided Journal, Family Program. 1980. 8.00 (ISBN 0-86584-038-5). Human Dev Train.
--Circle of Warmth: Sourcebook, Family Program. 1980. 14.95 (ISBN 0-86584-037-7). Human Dev Train.
Benson, Jeanette & Hilyard, Jack. Becoming Family. LC 78-62677. 1978. 9.95 (ISBN 0-88489-107-0). St Mary's.
Benson, Leonard. The Family Bond: Marriage, Love & Sex in America. 1971. pap. text ed. 9.95x (ISBN 0-685-77204-7). Phila Bk Co.
Bignell, Steven, ed. Family Life Education: Curriculum Guide. rev. ed. 1980. 18.00 (ISBN 0-686-29693-1). Planned Parent Santa Cruz.
Bittman, Sam & Zalk, Sue. Expectant Fathers. LC 78-54666. 1979. 12.95 (ISBN 0-8015-2444-X, Hawthorn). Dutton.
Book Review Committee. Family Life & Child Development. 48p. 1976. pap. 1.00 (ISBN 0-87183-187-2). Jewish Bd Family.
Brayer, Herbert O. & Cleary, Zella W. Valuing in the Family: A Workshop Guide for Parents. LC 72-93445. 171p. 1972. 4.95 (ISBN 0-913458-11-2). Pennant Pr.
Brenton, Myron. How to Survive Your Child's Rebellious Teens: New Solutions for Troubled Parents. 1979. 9.95 (ISBN 0-397-01340-X). Har-Row.
Brinkley. A Family Is... (gr. 9-12). 1981. text ed. 7.92 (ISBN 0-87002-320-9). Bennett IL.
Campbell, Philip. Future Family. LC 80-84365. 1981. pap. 4.95 (ISBN 0-933350-39-2). Morse Pr.
Chadwick, Janet. How to Live on Almost Nothing & Have Plenty. LC 79-2246. (Illus.). 1979. 12.95 (ISBN 0-394-42811-0); pap. 6.95 (ISBN 0-394-73753-9). Knopf.
Chalmers, Edlen. Making the Most of Family Living. LC 79-84303. 1979. pap. 5.95 (ISBN 0-8163-0244-8). Pacific Pr Pub Assn.
Child Study Association Of America. Recruiting Low-Income Families for Family Life Education Programs. 1965. pap. 0.60 (ISBN 0-87183-200-3). Child Study.
Christenson, Larry. Which Way the Family? 1973. pap. 0.75 (ISBN 0-87123-643-5, 260643). Bethany Hse.
Com. on Sex Ed. Dio. of Rochester. Education in Love: Handbook for Parents. 1971. pap. 0.75 (ISBN 0-8091-1554-9); Grades 1-8. teacher's guide 3.25 (ISBN 0-8091-1555-7); Grades 9-12. teacher's guide 2.50 (ISBN 0-8091-1556-5). Paulist Pr.
Compton, Al. Armonia Familiar. 1980. pap. 0.95 (ISBN 0-311-46078-X). Casa Bautista.
Cooper, Darien B. You Can Be the Wife of a Happy Husband. LC 74-77450. 156p. 1974. pap. 3.95 (ISBN 0-88207-711-2). Victor Bks.
Craig. Thresholds to Adult Living. rev. ed. (gr. 9-12). 1982. text ed. 21.16 (ISBN 0-87002-338-1). Bennett IL.
Csillag. The Augustan Laws of Family Relations. 1976. 18.50 (ISBN 0-9960006-2-3, Pub. by Kaido Hungary). Heyden.
Deal, William S. Picking a Partner. (Orig.). 1972. pap. 2.95 (ISBN 0-87123-456-4, 200456). Bethany Hse.
DeSpelder, Lynne & Strickland, Albert. Family Life Education: Parent Involvement Handbook. 1981. 12.00 (ISBN 0-686-30462-4). Planned Parent Santa Cruz.
--Family Life Education: Resources for the Elementary Classroom. 1981. 20.00 (ISBN 0-686-30463-2). Planned Parent Santa Cruz.
DeSpelder, Lynne A. & Prettyman, Nathalie. A Guidebook for Teaching Family Living. 280p. 1980. text ed. 17.95 (ISBN 0-205-06977-0). Allyn.
Donzelot, Jacques. The Policing of Families. LC 79-1888. 1980. 10.00 (ISBN 0-394-50338-4); pap. 4.95 (ISBN 0-394-73752-0). Pantheon.

Drummond, Laura W. Youth & Instruction in Marriage & Family Living. LC 74-176731. (Columbia University. Teachers College. Contributions to Education: No. 856). Repr. of 1942 ed. 17.50 (ISBN 0-404-55856-9). AMS Pr.

Duffey, Eliza B. What Women Should Know: Information for Wives & Mothers. LC 73-20620. (Sex, Marriage & Society Ser.). 324p. 1974. Repr. of 1873 ed. 18.00x (ISBN 0-405-05825-X). Arno.

Ehrenreich, Barbara & English, Deirdre. For Her Own Good. LC 77-76234. (Illus.). 1978. 10.00 (ISBN 0-385-12650-6, Anchor Pr). Doubleday.

Elwood, J. Murray. Growing Together in Marriage. LC 76-51468. 176p. 1977. pap. 2.95 (ISBN 0-87793-128-3). Ave Maria.

Entwisle, Doris B. & Doering, Susan G. The First Birth: A Family Turning Point. LC 80-22741. (Illus.). 304p. 1981. text ed. 25.00x (ISBN 0-8018-2408-7). Johns Hopkins.

Expert Consultation on the Development of a Cooperative "Planning for Better Family Living" Programme. 132p. 1975. pap. 9.50 (ISBN 0-685-54183-5, FAO). Unipub.

Family Factbook. 2nd ed. 670p. 1981. cancelled (ISBN 0-8379-4602-6). Marquis.

Family Life & Child Development: Annotated Bibliography 1972. LC 67-14888. 1974. 0.75 (ISBN 0-87183-185-6). Child Study.

Family Life & Child Development: Annotated Bibliography 1975. LC 67-1488. 1976. 2.50 (ISBN 0-87183-187-2). Child Study.

Farrell, Kathy & Sweeney, Mary. What Can We Do Today, Mommy. (Illus.). 127p. (Orig.). 1980. 6.95 (ISBN 0-9604118-0-1). Growing Together.

Force, Elizabeth S. Teaching Family Life Education. LC 62-12325. 1962. pap. 2.25 (ISBN 0-8077-1359-7). Tchrs Coll.

Functional Education for Family Life Planning: No. 3, Program Evalution. LC 75-33573. 1975. 4.00 (ISBN 0-914262-03-3). World Educ.

Galvin, Kathleen M. & Brommel, Bernard J. Family Communication: Cohesion & Change. 1981. pap. text ed. 8.95x (ISBN 0-673-15380-0). Scott F.

Garland, Diana R. Couples Communication & Negotiation Skills. LC 77-26981. (Workshop Models for Family Life Education Ser.). 1978. plastic 7.95 (ISBN 0-87304-158-5). Family Serv.

Gaulke, Earle. You Can Have a Family Where Everybody Wins: Christian Perspectives on Parent Effectiveness Training. 1977. pap. 2.95 (ISBN 0-452-25164-8, Z5164, Plume). NAL.

Getty, Cathleen & Humphreys, Winnifred. Understanding the Family: Stress & Change in American Fammily Life. (Illus.). 608p. 1981. pap. 12.95 (ISBN 0-8385-9265-1). ACC.

Grams, Betty J. Families Can Be Happy. LC 81-82420. 128p. (Orig.). 1981. pap. price not set (ISBN 0-88243-759-3, 02-0759). Gospel Pub.

Green, Ernest J. Personal Relationships: An Approach to Marriage & Family. (Illus.). 1978. text ed. 15.95 (ISBN 0-07-024270-4, C); instructor's manual with test bank 3.95 (ISBN 0-07-024271-2). McGraw.

--Personal Relationships: An Approach to Marriage & Family. (Illus.). 1978. text ed. 15.95 (ISBN 0-07-024270-4, C); instructor's manual with test bank 3.95 (ISBN 0-07-024271-2). McGraw.

Green, K. Family Life Education: Focus on Student Involvement. LC 75-4098. 1975. pap. 4.00 (ISBN 0-686-14989-0, 261-08420). Home Econ Educ.

Greenberg, Kenneth R. A Tiger by the Tail: Parenting in a Troubled Society. LC 73-93103. 1974. 15.95x (ISBN 0-911012-77-X). Nelson-Hall.

Hannon, Robert J. & Slattery, Anastasia S. Marriage & Family: A Complete Course. 172p. (Orig.). 1978. tchrs. ed. 30.00 (ISBN 0-9606040-0-6). Patio Pubns.

Harris, Oliver & Janzen, Curtis, eds. Family Treatment in Social Work Practice. LC 79-91098. 300p. 1980. pap. text ed. 8.50 (ISBN 0-87581-254-6). Peacock Pubs.

Hill, Reuben. Families Under Stress: Adjustment to the Crises of War Separation & Reunion. LC 73-90529. (Illus.). 1971. Repr. of 1949 ed. lib. bdg. 24.25 (ISBN 0-8371-3108-1, HIFU). Greenwood.

Holm, Lewis N. The American Home: A Guide for Parents. 1979. 7.95 (ISBN 0-533-04062-0). Vantage.

Holmes, Monica, et al. The Language of Trust: Dialogue of the Generations. LC 76-172939. 1972. 17.50x (ISBN 0-87668-049-X). Aronson.

Holstrom, Linda L. The Two Career Family. LC 70-189095. 204p. 1972. text ed. 13.95 (ISBN 0-87073-092-4); pap. text ed. 8.95 (ISBN 0-87073-093-2). Schenkman.

Hottois, James W. & Milner, Neal. The Sex-Education Controversy. LC 72-469. (Politics of Education Ser.). 1975. 18.95 (ISBN 0-669-83634-6). Lexington Bks.

Hover, Margot. A Happier Family: (Facing 10 Common Causes of Family Failure) (Illus., Orig.). 1978. pap. 2.95 (ISBN 0-89622-074-5). Twenty-Third.

Hutter, Mark. The Family & Social Change: Changing Family. LC 80-28829. 551p. 1981. text ed. 16.95 (ISBN 0-471-08394-1). Wiley.

Johnson, Rex. Communication: Key to Your Parents. LC 78-61874. 1978. pap. 2.95 (ISBN 0-89081-157-1, 1571). Harvest Hse.

Kelley, Robert K. Courtship, Marriage, & the Family. 3rd ed. 650p. 1979. text ed. 17.95 (ISBN 0-15-515338-2, HC); student guidebk. 5.95 (ISBN 0-15-516120-2); instructor's manual avail. (ISBN 0-15-516121-0). HarBraceJ.

Kelly & Landers. Today's Teen. (YA) 1977. cancelled (ISBN 0-87002-192-3); tchr's guide 6.60 (ISBN 0-87002-264-4); student guide 3.96 (ISBN 0-87002-268-7). Bennett IL.

Kesler, Jay. I Want a Home with No Problems. LC 77-83339. 1977. 5.95 (ISBN 0-8499-0038-7). Word Bks.

Keyes, Ken, Jr. A Conscious Person's Guide to Relationships. LC 78-71456. 1979. pap. 3.95 (ISBN 0-915972-00-X). Living Love.

Khan, Alfred & Kamerman, Sheila. Helping America's Families. 1981. 20.00 (ISBN 0-87722-212-6); pap. 9.95 (ISBN 0-87722-213-4). Temple U Pr.

Klemer, Richard H. & Smith, Rebecca M. Teaching About Family Relationships. LC 74-20040. 450p. 1975. pap. text ed. 11.95x (ISBN 0-8087-1991-2). Burgess.

Koller, Marvin. Families: A Multigenerational Approach. (Illus.). 320p. 1974. pap. text ed. 10.95 (ISBN 0-07-035331-X, C). McGraw.

L'Abate, Luciano & Rupp, Gary. Enrichment: Skills Training for Family Life. LC 81-40156. 229p. 1981. lib. bdg. 18.50 (ISBN 0-8191-1592-4); pap. text ed. 9.75 (ISBN 0-8191-1593-2). U Pr of Amer.

Landis. Building a Successful Marriage. 7th ed. 1977. 18.95 (ISBN 0-13-087007-2). P-H.

Lecker, Sidney. Family Ties: How to Love the Bonds & Leave the Bondage. LC 79-4875. 1979. 9.95 (ISBN 0-87223-552-1, Dist. by Har-Row). Wyden.

Lewis, Helen C. All About Families: The Second Time Around. Reynolds, Amy, ed. LC 79-26694. (Illus.). 1980. 7.95 (ISBN 0-931948-06-1). Peachtree Pubs.

Loomis, Mildred J. Go Ahead & Live. LC 65-10659. 1965. 4.00 (ISBN 0-8022-0996-3). Philos Lib.

Lowry, Lois. Anastasia Again! (Illus.). (gr. 3-6). 1981. 7.95 (ISBN 0-395-31147-0). HM.

Lynne, Cooper. Family Life & Sex Education: A Summary of Facts & Findings. 1979. 2.50 (ISBN 0-686-29696-6). Planned Parent Santa Cruz.

Mace, David & Mace, Vera. Men, Women, & God. 1976. pap. 4.50 (ISBN 0-8042-8076-2). John Knox.

McKinney, Eleanor & Baechtold, Marquerite. Libraries & Family Development. (Orig.). 1981. price not set (ISBN 0-208-01856-5, Lib Prof Pubns); pap. price not set (ISBN 0-208-01855-7). Shoe String.

Marney, Carlyle. Achieving Family Togetherness. (Festival Bks.). 1980. pap. 1.50 (ISBN 0-687-00691-0). Abingdon.

Marston, V. Paul. The Biblical Family. LC 80-68332. 208p. 1980. pap. 4.95 (ISBN 0-89107-192-X, Cornerstone Bks.). Good News.

Meister, Robert. Fathers: Daughters, Sons, Fathers Reveal Their Deepest Feelings. 224p. 1981. 11.95 (ISBN 0-399-90107-8). Marek.

Miller, Levi, ed. Family in Today's Society. LC 79-170198. 1972. pap. 1.75 (ISBN 0-8361-1659-3). Herald Pr.

Montgomery, Jason. Family Crisis As Process: Persistence & Change. LC 81-40566. (Illus.). 144p. (Orig.). 1981. lib. bdg. 17.75 (ISBN 0-8191-1788-9); pap. text ed. 7.75 (ISBN 0-8191-1789-7). U Pr of Amer.

Napier, Augustus Y. & Whitaker, Carl A. The Family Crucible. 320p. 1980. pap. 3.95 (ISBN 0-553-13576-7). Bantam.

National Information Center for Special Education Materials (NICSEM) NICSEM Mini-Index to Special Education Materials: Family Life & Sex Education. LC 80-82540. 1980. pap. 16.00 (ISBN 0-89320-043-3). Univ SC Natl Info.

Olson, David H., ed. Inventory of Marriage & Family Literature, Vol. 6. LC 67-63014. (Illus.). 390p. 60.00 (ISBN 0-8039-1474-1); pap. 29.95 (ISBN 0-8039-1475-X). Sage.

Paolucci, Beatrice, et al. Family Decision Making: An Ecosystem Approach. LC 76-39953. 1977. text ed. 8.95 (ISBN 0-471-65838-3). Wiley.

Patterson, Gerald R. Families: Applications of Social Learning to Family Life. rev. ed. (Illus., Orig.). 1975. pap. text ed. 6.95 (ISBN 0-87822-156-5). Res Press.

--Professional Guide for Families & Living with Children. (Illus., Orig.). 1975. pap. text ed. 2.95 (ISBN 0-87822-160-3). Res Press.

--Social Learning Approach to Family Intervention: Coercive Family Process, Vol. 3. 1981. pap. write for info. Castalia Pub.

Perez, Joseph F. Family Counciling. 1979. trade ed. o.p. 15.95 (ISBN 0-442-26536-0); college ed. 13.95 (ISBN 0-442-26537-9). Van Nos Reinhold.

Petersen, J. Allan. Conquering Family Stress. 1978. pap. 3.95 (ISBN 0-88207-632-9). Victor Bks.

Petersen, J. Allan, compiled by. The Marriage Affair. pap. 5.95 (ISBN 0-8423-4171-4). Tyndale.

Prevo, Helen R. Family Life: Book One. 1967. pap. 2.75x (ISBN 0-88323-010-0, 110); wkbk. 2.50x (ISBN 0-88323-011-9, 111). Richards Pub.

--Family Life: Book Two. 1969. pap. 2.75x (ISBN 0-88323-012-7, 112); wkbk. 2.50x (ISBN 0-88323-013-5, 113). Richards Pub.

Ravi Dass & Aparna, eds. The Marriage & Family Book: A Spiritual Guide. LC 77-87862. (Illus., Orig.). 1978. pap. 5.95 (ISBN 0-8052-0582-9). Schocken.

Readings in Marriage & Family 76-77. rev. ed. LC 74-84596. (Annual Editions Ser.). (Illus.). 224p. (Orig.). 1976. pap. text ed. 4.95 (ISBN 0-87967-140-8). Dushkin Pub.

Reflections on Relationships. (gr. 11-12). 1978. wkbk. 6.00 (ISBN 0-13-770081-4). P-H.

Reilly, Terry & Reilly, Mimi. Family Nights Throughout the Year. LC 80-68028. (Series II). 64p. 1980. pap. 2.95 (ISBN 0-87029-168-8). Abbey.

Rich, Dorothy & Jones, Cynthia. A Family Affair: Education. 1980. pap. text ed. write for info. (ISBN 0-8302-2890-X). Goodyear.

Riker, Audrey, et al. Married Life. rev. ed. (gr. 10-12). 1976. text ed. 15.60 (ISBN 0-87002-071-4); student guide 3.08 (ISBN 0-87002-208-3). tchr's guide free. Bennett IL.

Ripple, Paula. The Pain & the Possibility. LC 78-67745. 144p. 1978. pap. 2.95 (ISBN 0-87793-162-3). Ave Maria.

Roman, Mel & Raley, Patricia E. The Indelible Family. LC 78-64812. 288p. 1980. 12.95 (ISBN 0-89256-093-2). Rawson Wade.

Rosenfeld, Jeffrey P. Relationships: The Marriage & Family Reader. 1981. pap. text ed. 8.95x (ISBN 0-673-15267-7). Scott F.

Rucki, Alexander. Fascinating (Australian) Family Life Collection. 1981. 6.95 (ISBN 0-533-04979-2). Vantage.

Ryder, Verdene. Contemporary Living. (Illus.). 352p. 1981. text ed. 13.20 (ISBN 0-87006-319-7). Goodheart.

--Contemporary Living. LC 78-23516. (Illus.). 1979. text ed. 13.20 (ISBN 0-87006-266-2); wkbk. 3.20 (ISBN 0-87006-280-8). Goodheart.

Sandford, John & Sandford, Paula. Restoring the Christian Family. 1979. 6.95 (ISBN 0-88270-347-1). Logos.

Saxton, Lloyd. Individual, Marriage & the Family. 4th ed. 672p. 1980. text ed. 18.95x (ISBN 0-534-00799-6); study guide 6.95x (ISBN 0-534-00800-3). Wadsworth Pub.

Scanzoni, John. Sex Roles, Women's Work, & Marital Conflict. LC 78-58981. (Illus.). 1978. 17.95 (ISBN 0-669-02400-7). Lexington Bks.

Scanzoni, John & Szinovacz, Maximiliane. Family Decision-Making: Sex Roles & Change Over the Life Cycle. LC 80-18243. (Sage Library of Social Research: Vol. 111). (Illus.). 310p. 1980. 20.00 (ISBN 0-8039-1533-0); pap. 9.95 (ISBN 0-8039-1534-9). Sage.

Schneid, Hayyim, ed. The Family. LC 73-11760. (Popular Judaica Library). (Illus.). 1974. pap. 3.95 (ISBN 0-8276-0029-1, 341). Jewish Pubn.

Silverstone, Barbara & Hyman, Helen K. You & Your Aging Parent: The Modern Family's Guide to Emotional, Physical & Financial Problems. LC 76-9608. 1977. pap. 5.95 (ISBN 0-394-73406-8). Pantheon.

Somerville, Rose M. Introduction to Family Life & Sex Education. (Family & Consumer Sciences Ser). 432p. 1972. ref. ed. 16.95 (ISBN 0-13-483149-7); pap. text ed. 12.95 (ISBN 0-13-483131-4). P-H.

Srinivasan, Lyra. Ideas Para Seminarios De Capacitacion De Educadores En: Planificacion Familiar, Desarrollo Agricola, Nutricion, Salud, y Desarrollo Comunitario. LC 79-65003. Orig. Title: Workshop Ideas for Family Planning Education. (Span.). 1979. 7.00 (ISBN 0-914262-18-1). World Educ.

Stewart, Maxwell S., ed. Problems of Family Life. LC 70-132094. (Essay & General Literature Index Reprint Ser). 1971. Repr. of 1956 ed. 12.00 (ISBN 0-8046-1422-9). Kennikat.

Stinnett, Nick, et al, eds. Family Strengths: Positive Models for Family Life. LC 80-50917. x, 518p. 1980. 21.50x (ISBN 0-8032-4125-9); pap. 9.95x (ISBN 0-8032-9122-1). U of Nebr Pr.

--Family Strengths Three: Roots of Well-Being. LC 81-50712. x, 395p. 21.50x (ISBN 0-8032-4128-3); pap. 10.95 (ISBN 0-8032-9124-8). U of Nebr Pr.

Stoop, Dave. A Parent's Cry for Help. rev. ed. LC 78-62916. 144p. 1981. pap. 2.50 (ISBN 0-89081-270-5). Harvest Hse.

Thodes, Sonya & Wilson, Josleen. Surviving Family Life: The Seven Crises of Living Together. 300p. 1981. 13.95 (ISBN 0-399-12507-8). Putnam.

Tittle, Carol K. Careers & Family: Sex Roles & Adolescent Life Plans. LC 81-2015. (Sage Library of Social Research: Vol. 121). (Illus.). 319p. 1981. pap. 9.95 (ISBN 0-8039-1353-2). Sage.

Touliatos, John, ed. Family & Human Development. LC 72-6350. 197p. 1972. 24.50x (ISBN 0-8422-5050-6); pap. text ed. 9.75x (ISBN 0-8422-0245-5). Irvington.

Trachtenberg, Inge. My Daughter, My Son. LC 78-16962. 1978. 10.00 (ISBN 0-671-40043-6). Summit Bks.

Trobisch, Walter. I Loved a Girl. LC 75-12281. (Jubilee Bks.). 128p. 1975. pap. 3.95 (ISBN 0-06-068443-7, RD 352, HarpR). Har-Row.

--I Loved a Girl. LC 75-12281. 1965. pap. 2.25 (ISBN 0-06-068445-3, CB 12, HarpR). Har-Row.

Trojan, Judith. American Family Life Films. LC 80-14748. 508p. 1981. 25.00 (ISBN 0-8108-1313-0). Scarecrow.

Turner, Ralph H. Family Interaction. LC 71-118627. (Illus.). 505p. 1970. 24.95 (ISBN 0-471-89300-5). Wiley.

Understanding Us: Family Development 1. 8.95 (ISBN 0-917340-10-8). Interpersonal Comm.

Vincent, John P., ed. Advances in Family Intervention Assessment & Theory, Vol. 2. 300p. 1981. 32.50 (ISBN 0-89232-192-X). Jai Pr.

Wagman, Ellen & Cooper, Lynne. Family Life Education Teacher Training Manual. 1981. 25.00 (ISBN 0-686-29695-8). Planned Parent Santa Cruz.

Wahlroos, Sven. Family Communication. 1976. pap. 1.95 (ISBN 0-451-07067-4, J7067, Sig). NAL.

Wells, J. Gipson. Current Issues in Marriage & the Family. 2nd ed. 1979. pap. text ed. 9.95 (ISBN 0-02-425440-1). Macmillan.

Wessel, Helen. Under the Apple Tree: Marrying - Birthing - Parenting. LC 79-52050. 325p. (Orig.). 1981. pap. 5.95 (ISBN 0-933082-02-9). Bookmates Intl.

Whitfield, Richard C. Education for Family Life: Some New Policies for Child Care. 161p. 1980. pap. text ed. 10.00 (ISBN 0-340-25524-2). Verry.

WHO Study Group, Geneva, 1970. Health Education in Health Aspects of Family Planning: Report. (Technical Report Ser.: No. 483). (Also avail. in French & spanish). 1971. pap. 2.40 (ISBN 92-4-120483-4). World Health.

Wiseman, Jacqueline P. People As Partners. 2nd ed. (Orig.). 1977. pap. text ed. 10.50 scp (ISBN 0-06-389425-4, HarpC). Har-Row.

Wright, H. Norman & Johnson, Rex. Characteristics of a Caring Home. LC 78-68704. 1979. pap. 3.95 (ISBN 0-88449-038-6). Vision Hse.

Wright, Norman. An Answer to in-Law Relationships. (Orig.). pap. 1.25 (ISBN 0-89081-076-1). Harvest Hse.

--An Answer to Parent-Teen Relationships. (Orig.). pap. 1.25 (ISBN 0-89081-075-3). Harvest Hse.

--An Answer to Submission & Decision Making. pap. 1.25 (ISBN 0-89081-078-8). Harvest Hse.

Wright, Norman & Inmon, Marvin. Guidebook to Dating, Waiting & Choosing a Mate. LC 78-26913. 1978. pap. 3.95 (ISBN 0-89081-150-4, 1504). Harvest Hse.

Wright, Norman & Johnson, Rex. Communication: Key to Your Teens. LC 78-61872. 1978. pap. 2.95 (ISBN 0-89081-158-X, 158X). Harvest Hse.

FAMILY LIFE SURVEYS

American Family Styles: Current Guide to the Literature. (Spcialized Bibliography Ser.: No. 4). 1981. 8.95 (ISBN 0-915574-11-X). Soc Sci & Soc Res.

Berk, Richard A., et al. Labor & Leisure at Home: Content & Organization of the Household Day. LC 79-13644. (Sage Library of Social Research: No. 87). (Illus.). 280p. 1979. 20.00x (ISBN 0-8039-1101-7); pap. 9.95x (ISBN 0-8039-1102-5). Sage.

Kanter, Rosabeth M. Work & Family in the United States: A Critical Review & Agenda for Research & Policy. LC 76-46870. (Social Science Frontiers Ser.). 1977. pap. 4.00 (ISBN 0-87154-433-4). Russell Sage.

Niemi, Richard G. How Family Members Perceive Each Other: Political & Social Attitudes in Two Generations. LC 73-86913. (Illus.). 248p. 1974. 16.50x (ISBN 0-300-01698-0). Yale U Pr.

Nye, F. Ivan & Berardo, Felix M., eds. Emerging Conceptual Frameworks in Family Analyses. 356p. 1981. 13.95 (ISBN 0-03-057043-3). Praeger.

Peterson, Samiha S., et al. The Two-Career Family: Issues & Alternatives. LC 78-66418. 1978. pap. text ed. 10.25 (ISBN 0-8191-0020-X). U Pr of Amer.
United States Inter-Agency Committtee on Background Materials for the National Conference on Family Life. The American Family: A Factual Background Report. LC 78-12193. (Illus.). 1978. Repr. of 1948 ed. lib. bdg. 37.00x (ISBN 0-313-20682-1, NCAF). Greenwood.
Wallach, Harold C. Making of Child & Family Policy. Chambers, Lyn, ed. (AAAS Selected Symposium Ser.: No. 56). 160p. 1980. lib. bdg. 20.00x (ISBN 0-89158-956-2). Westview.

FAMILY MEDICINE

American National Red Cross. Family Health & Home Nursing. (Illus.). 1979. pap. 3.95 (ISBN 0-385-15281-7). Doubleday.
Anderson, Kenneth N. The Newsweek Encyclopedia of Family Health & Fitness. Wagman, Richard J., ed. LC 79-3539. (Illus.). 1980. 18.95 (ISBN 0-88225-292-5). Newsweek.
Annarino, Anthony A. & Kahms, Frederick W. First Aid, Safety, & Family Health Emergencies: Study Guide. 2nd ed. 1979. pap. text ed. 6.95x (ISBN 0-8087-0063-4). Burgess.
Barber, J. H. & Boddy, F. A., eds. General Practice Medicine. (Illus.). 364p. 1975. text ed. 19.00 (ISBN 0-443-01143-5). Churchill.
Baumslag, Naomi, ed. Family Care. 392p. 1973. 13.50 (ISBN 0-683-00412-3, Pub. by W & W). Krieger.
Bhardwaj, Vidya B. & Yen, Ernest Y. Specialty Board Review: Family Practice. LC 75-39895. 1977. pap. text ed. 12.00 (ISBN 0-668-03943-4, 3943). Arco.
Bishop, Carol. Book of Home Remedies & Herbal Cures. (Octopus Bk.). (Illus.). 1979. 12.50 (ISBN 0-7064-1069-6, Mayfower Bks); pap. 6.95 (ISBN 0-7064-1088-2). Smith Pubs.
Bowling, Ann. Delegation in General Practice: A Study of Doctors & Nurses. 1981. 26.00x (ISBN 0-422-77490-1, Pub. by Tavistock). Methuen Inc.
Bryce, Marvin & Lloyd, June C. Treating Families in the Home: An Alternative to Placement. (Illus.). 352p. 1981. text ed. 24.75 (ISBN 0-398-04085-0). C C Thomas.
Cartwright, Ann & Anderson, Robert. General Practice Revisted: A Second Study of Patients & Their Doctors. 1981. 28.95x (ISBN 0-422-77360-3, Pub. by Tavistock). Methuen Inc.
Clemen & Eigsti. Comprehensive Family & Community Health Nursing. (Illus.). 544p. 1981. text ed. 19.95 (ISBN 0-07-011324-6, HP). McGraw.
Congress of Psychosomatic Obstetrics & Gynecology 4th, Israel, 1974. The Family: Proceeding. Hirsh, H., et al, eds. 600p. 1975. 105.50 (ISBN 3-8055-2206-1). S Karger.
Cornacchia, Harold J. & Barrett, Stephen. Consumer Health: A Guide to Intelligent Decisions. 2nd ed. LC 80-11515. (Illus.). 1980. pap. text ed. 12.95 (ISBN 0-8016-1037-0). Mosby.
Cozzetto, Frank J. & Brettell, H. R., eds. Topics in Family Practice. LC 76-18331. (Illus.). 1976. text ed. 33.95 (ISBN 0-8151-1874-0, Pub. by Symposia Special). Year Bk Med.
Davis, R. Harvard. General Practice for Students of Medicine. (Monographs for Students of Medicine Ser.). 1975. 16.50 (ISBN 0-12-328850-9). Acad Pr.
Deaton, John G. & Pascoe, Elizabeth J. Book of Family Medical Questions. Alper, Philip R., ed. LC 79-4804. 1979. 15.95 (ISBN 0-394-41468-3). Random.
Diagram Group. The Body Manual: A Complete Family Guide. LC 79-21673. (Illus.). 1980. 16.95 (ISBN 0-448-22214-0). Paddington.
Drury, M. & Hull, Robin. Introduction to General Practice: Concise Medical Textbook. (Illus.). 1979. pap. text ed. 13.95 (ISBN 0-02-857610-1). Macmillan.
Eisenberg, Howard & Eisenberg, Arlene. Alive & Well: Decisions in Health. 1979. text ed. 15.95 (ISBN 0-07-019113-1, C); instructor's manual 5.95 (ISBN 0-07-019114-X); study guide 6.95 (ISBN 0-07-019136-0); test bank 3.95 (ISBN 0-07-019137-9). McGraw.
Freeman, Arthur, et al. Psychiatry for the Primary Care Physician. (Illus.). 1979. pap. 23.00 (ISBN 0-683-03376-X). Williams & Wilkins.
Fry, John, et al. Scientific Foundations of Family Medicine. (Illus.). 1979. 72.50 (ISBN 0-8151-3275-1). Year Bk Med.
Galton, Lawrence. The Complete Book of Symptoms. 1980. pap. 6.95 (ISBN 0-671-25457-X, 25457, Fireside). S&S.
Geyman. Family Practice: Foundation of Changing Health Care. LC 79-18290. (Illus.). 543p. 1979. 32.50 (ISBN 0-8385-2537-7). ACC.
Geyman, John P. Archives of Family Practice 1981. 448p. 1981. 34.50 (ISBN 0-8385-0325-X). ACC.
--Content of Family Practice. (Illus.). 68p. 1979. pap. 10.00 (ISBN 0-8385-7901-9). ACC.
Geyman, John P., ed. Archives of Family Practice 1980. (Illus.). 413p. 1980. 34.50x (ISBN 0-8385-0324-1). ACC.
--Profile of the Residency-Trained Family Physician in the United States 1970-1979. 72p. 1980. pap. 12.00 (ISBN 0-8385-7961-2). ACC.
Haessler, Herbert & Harris, Raymond. Bodyworkbook. 1980. pap. 6.95 (ISBN 0-380-75309-X, 75309). Avon.
Hoole, Axalla J., et al. Patient Care Guidelines for Family Nurse Practitioners. 1976. pap. 11.95 (ISBN 0-316-37221-8). Little.
Hymovich, Debra & Barnard, Martha. Family Health Care, Vol. I. (Illus.). 1979. pap. text ed. 8.95 (ISBN 0-07-031675-9, HP). McGraw.
Kandzari, Judith H. & Howard, Joan R. The Well Family: A Developmental Approach to Assessment. pap. text ed. write for info. (ISBN 0-316-48269-2). Little.
Kaplan, Berton H. & Ibrahim, Michel A., eds. Family Medicine & Supportive Interventions: An Epidemiological Approach. LC 80-39948. (Life Styles-Health Ser.). vi, 71p. (Orig.). 1981. pap. text ed. 4.00 (ISBN 0-89143-076-8). U NC Inst Res Soc Sci.
Kozloff, Martin A. Reaching the Autistic Child: A Parent Training Program. 200p. 1973. pap. 9.95 (ISBN 0-87822-023-2). Res Press.
MacKichan, N. D. The GP & the Primary Health Care Team. (Illus.). 1976. text ed. 22.00x (ISBN 0-685-83074-8). State Mutual Bk.
McWhinney, Ian R. An Introduction to Family Medicine. (Illus.). 240p. 1981. text ed. 16.95x (ISBN 0-19-502807-4); pap. text ed. 9.95 (ISBN 0-19-502808-2). Oxford U Pr.
Medalie, Jack H., ed. Family Medicine: Principles & Applications. (Illus.). 400p. 1978. 16.95 (ISBN 0-683-05902-5). Williams & Wilkins.
Medley, E. Scott. Common Health Problems in Medical Practice. (Illus.). 410p. 1981. lib. bdg. 25.00 (ISBN 0-683-05903-3). Williams & Wilkins.
Miller, Jean R. & Janosik, Ellen. Family Focused Care. (Illus.). 1979. text ed. 13.95 (ISBN 0-07-042060-2, HP). McGraw.
Miller, Sally & Winstead-Fry, Patricia. Family Systems Theory & Nursing Practice. 176p. 1982. text ed. 13.95 (ISBN 0-686-76719-5); pap. text ed. 10.95 (ISBN 0-8359-1849-1). Reston.
Noble, John, ed. Primary Care & the Practice of Medicine. LC 75-41569. 1976. text ed. 19.95 (ISBN 0-316-61148-4). Little.
Pieroni, Robert E. Family Practice Review, Vol. 2. LC 79-91973. 1980. pap. 14.50 (ISBN 0-87488-181-1). Med Exam.
Pieroni, Robert E. & Scutchfield, F. Family Practice Review. 1978. spiral bdg. 16.50 (ISBN 0-87488-134-X). Med Exam.
PreTest Service Inc. Family Practice: PreTest Self-Assessment & Review. Catlin, Robin J., ed. (Illus.). 250p. (Orig.). 1981. pap. 27.50 (ISBN 0-07-051652-9). McGraw.
Pritchard, Peter. Manual of Primary Health Care: Its Nature & Organization. (Illus.). 1979. pap. text ed. 10.95x (ISBN 0-19-264228-6). Oxford U Pr.
Prudden, Bonnie. How to Keep Your Family Fit & Healthy. (Illus.). 1975. 10.95 (ISBN 0-88349-041-2). Aquarian Pr.
Rakel, Robert E. Principles of Family Medicine. LC 76-41541. (Illus.). 1977. text ed. 19.95 (ISBN 0-7216-7449-6). Saunders.
Rakel, Robert E., ed. Year Book of Family Practice Nineteen Eighty-One. 1981. 36.75 (ISBN 0-8151-7022-X). Year Bk Med.
--Year Book of Family Practice 1980. (Illus.). 530p. 1980. 35.95 (ISBN 0-8151-7021-1). Year Bk Med.
Rakel, Robert E., et al, eds. Year Book of Family Practice, 1979. (Illus.). 1979. 31.50 (ISBN 0-8151-7020-3). Year Bk Med.
Rosen. Psychological Approaches to Family Practice. 1979. 9.95 (ISBN 0-8391-1327-7). Univ Park.
Rosen, Gerald M., et al, eds. Behavioral Science in Family Practice. (Illus.). 300p. 1980. 22.00x (ISBN 0-8385-0638-0). ACC.
Salk, Lee. Dear Dr. Salk: Answers to Your Questions About Your Family. LC 78-69629. 1979. 8.95 (ISBN 0-06-013768-1, HarpT). Har-Row.
Shires, David B. & Hennen, Brian. Family Medicine: A Guidebook for Practitioners of the Art. (Illus.). 1980. pap. text ed. 15.95 (ISBN 0-07-056920-7). McGraw.
Stephen, W. J. An Analysis of Primary Medical Care. LC 77-83999. (Illus.). 1979. 37.50 (ISBN 0-521-21860-8). Cambridge U Pr.
Stettner, Allison P. & Cowen, Anita P. Health Aspects of Family Planning Review: A Guide to Resources in the United States. LC 81-1651. 1981. 19.95 (ISBN 0-89885-005-3). Human Sci Pr.
Stewart, Jane E. Home Health Care. LC 78-31116. (Illus.). 1979. pap. text ed. 11.50 (ISBN 0-8016-4801-7). Mosby.
Summers, Anthony. Conspiracy. (McGraw-Hill Paperbacks Ser.). (Illus.). 656p. 1981. pap. 7.95 (ISBN 0-07-062400-3). McGraw.
Taylor, R. B., et al, eds. Family Medicine: Principles & Practice. LC 78-817. (Illus.). 1978. 48.30 (ISBN 0-387-90303-8). Springer-Verlag.
Thurmond, Nancy M. Mother's Medicine. LC 78-12552. (Illus.). 1979. 9.95 (ISBN 0-688-03384-9). Morrow.
Tubesing, Donald A. Wholistic Health: A Whole Person Approach to Primary Health Care. LC 78-3466. 1978. 22.95 (ISBN 0-87705-370-7). Human Sci Pr.
Vanes, J. C., ed. General Practice & University. 1979. pap. 13.00 (ISBN 90-313-0358-5, Pub. by Martinus Nijhoff Netherlands). Kluwer Boston.
Walker, Ingram J. Clinical Psychiatry in Primary Care. 1981. 28.95 (ISBN 0-201-08220-9, Med-Nurse). A-W.
Wilder, Charles S. Family Out-of-Pocket Health Expenses, United States, 1975. Shipp, Audrey, ed. (Ser. 10: No. 127). 1978. pap. text ed. 1.75 (ISBN 0-8406-0149-2). Natl Ctr Health Stats.
Wood, Clive, ed. Health & the Family. 239p. 1979. 31.00 (ISBN 0-8089-1185-6). Grune.
Yen, Ernest Y. Review & Assessment in Family Practice. 184p. 1980. pap. 12.95 (ISBN 0-8385-8423-3). ACC.

FAMILY PLANNING

see Birth Control

FAMILY PLANNING SERVICES

see Birth Control Clinics

FAMILY PRACTICE (MEDICINE)

see Family Medicine

FAMILY PSYCHOTHERAPY

Ackerman, Nathan W. Treating the Troubled Family. LC 66-27943. 1966. text ed. 12.00x (ISBN 0-465-08749-3); pap. 4.95x (ISBN 0-465-09522-4, TB5023). Basic.
Alexander, James & Parsons, Bruce V. Functional Family Therapy. (Counseling Ser.). 233p. 1982. text ed. 8.95 (ISBN 0-8185-0485-4). Brooks-Cole.
Andolfi, Maurizio. Family Therapy: An Interactional Approach. LC 78-27741. 186p. 1979. 19.95 (ISBN 0-306-40200-9, Plenum Pr). Plenum Pub.
Andolfi, Maurizio, ed. Dimensions of Family Therapy. Zwerling, Israel. 280p. 1980. text ed. 20.00 (ISBN 0-89862-602-1). Guilford Pr.
Arnold, Eugene L., ed. Helping Parents Help Their Children. LC 77-24520. 1978. 20.00 (ISBN 0-87630-146-4). Brunner-Mazel.
Bagarozzi, Dennis & Jackson, Robert W. Marital & Family Therapy: New Perspectives in Theory, Research & Practice. 1982. in prep. (ISBN 0-89885-069-X). Human Sci Pr.
Barker, Philip. Basic Family Therapy. 224p. (Orig.). 1981. pap. write for info. (ISBN 0-8391-1673-X). Univ Park.
Barnard, Charles P. & Corrales, Ramon G. The Theory & Technique of Family Therapy. (Illus.). 352p. 1979. text ed. 16.75 (ISBN 0-398-03859-7). C C Thomas.
Beavers, W. Robert. Psychotherapy & Growth: A Family Systems Perspective. LC 77-2639. 1977. 20.00 (ISBN 0-87630-143-X). Brunner-Mazel.
Beck, Dorothy F. New Treatment Modalities: An Outline of Some Options & Source Materials. (Orig.). 1978. pap. 5.00 (ISBN 0-87304-166-6). Family Serv.
Bell, John E. Family Therapy. LC 73-17736. 700p. 1974. 30.00x (ISBN 0-87668-114-3). Aronson.
Bloch, Donald A., ed. Techniques of Family Psychotherapy: A Primer. LC 73-6655. 136p. 1973. 22.50 (ISBN 0-8089-0818-9). Grune.
Boszormenyi-Nagy, Ivan & Framo, James L. Intensive Family Therapy. 1965. pap. 18.00x (ISBN 0-06-140522-1, Harper Medical). Har-Row.
Boszormenyi-Nagy, Ivan & Spark, Geraldine. Invisible Loyalties. 1973. 22.00x (ISBN 0-06-140521-3, Harper Medical). Har-Row.
Bowen, Murray. Family Therapy in Clinical Practice. LC 77-94096. 1978. 30.00x (ISBN 0-87668-334-0). Aronson.
Box, Sally, et al, eds. Psychotherapy with Families: An Analytic Approach. 160p. (Orig.). 1981. pap. price not set (ISBN 0-7100-0854-6). Routledge & Kegan.
Brown, Judith R. Back to the Beanstalk: Enchantment & Reality for Couples. LC 79-89476. 1980. 8.95 (ISBN 0-930626-03-6); pap. 3.95 (ISBN 0-930626-04-4). Psych & Consul Assocs.
Brown, William D. Families Under Stress. 154p. 1977. pap. text ed. 7.95 (ISBN 0-87619-844-2). R J Brady.
Cowley, Au-Deane S. Family Integration & Mental Health. LC 78-62234. 1978. soft cover 9.00 (ISBN 0-88247-539-8). R & E Res Assoc.
Don, Marvin, et al, eds. Self-Assessment of Current Knowledge in Family Practice. 2nd ed. 1976. pap. 14.50 (ISBN 0-87488-261-3). Med Exam.
Erickson, Gerald D. & Hogan, Terrance P. Family Therapy: An Introduction to Theory & Technique. LC 70-181720. 384p. (Orig.). 1972. pap. text ed. 12.95 (ISBN 0-8185-0039-5). Brooks-Cole.
Erickson, Gerald D. & Hogan, Terrence P. Family Therapy: An Introduction to Theory & Technique. 2nd ed. 448p. (Orig.). 1980. pap. text ed. 14.95 (ISBN 0-8185-0437-4). Brooks-Cole.
Ferber, Andrew, et al. The Book of Family Therapy. 1973. pap. 10.95 (ISBN 0-395-17227-6, 77, SenEd). HM.
Flomenhaft, Kalman & Christ, Adolf E., eds. The Challenge of Family Therapy: A Dialogue for Child Psychiatric Educators. (Downstate Series of Research in Psychiatry & Psychology: Vol. 3). 225p. 1980. 22.50 (ISBN 0-306-40553-9, Plenum Pr). Plenum Pub.
Foley, Vincent D. An Introduction to Family Therapy. 244p. 1974. 19.50 (ISBN 0-8089-0846-4). Grune.
Framo, James L. Explorations in Marital & Family Therapy: Selected Papers of James L. Framo. Date not set. price not set (ISBN 0-8261-3400-9). Springer Pub.
Framo, James L., et al. Family Interaction: A Dialogue Between Family Researchers & Family Therapists. LC 77-188704. 1972. text ed. 12.95 (ISBN 0-8261-1211-0). Springer Pub.
Freeman, David S. Techniques of Family Therapy. LC 80-69669. 350p. 1981. 25.00 (ISBN 0-87668-431-2). Aronson.
French, Alfred. Disturbed Children & Their Families: Innovations in Evaluation & Treatment. LC 75-11003. 1977. text ed. 29.95 (ISBN 0-87705-263-8); pap. 12.95 (ISBN 0-87705-439-8). Human Sci Pr.
Friedman, Alfred S., et al. Psychotherapy for the Whole Family. LC 65-25762. 1965. text ed. 12.95 (ISBN 0-8261-0791-5). Springer Pub.
Gerald, Berenson & White, Harvey M. Annual Review of Family Therapy, Vol. I. 494p. 1981. 29.95 (ISBN 0-87705-508-4). Human Sci Pr.
Gerald, Zuk. Family Therapy: A Triadic Based Approach. rev. ed. LC 80-24708. 352p. 1981. 24.95 (ISBN 0-87705-430-4); pap. 13.95 (ISBN 0-87705-955-1). Human Sci Pr.
Geyman, John P., ed. Research in Family Practice. 112p. 1978. pap. 10.00 (ISBN 0-8385-8402-0). ACC.
Glick, Ira D. & Haley, Jay. Family Therapy & Research: An Annotated Bibliography of Articles & Books, 1950-1970. LC 72-153577. 280p. 1971. 31.50 (ISBN 0-8089-0688-7). Grune.
Glick, Ira D. & Kessler, David, eds. Marital & Family Therapy: An Introductory Text. 2nd ed. 352p. 1980. 23.50 (ISBN 0-8089-1232-1). Grune.
Goldenberg, Irene & Goldenberg, Herbert. Family Therapy: An Overview. LC 79-9403. 1980. text ed. 14.95 (ISBN 0-8185-0361-0). Brooks-Cole.
--A Family Therapy Workbook. 1980. pap. text ed. 4.95 (ISBN 0-8185-0412-9). Brooks-Cole.
Green, Robert J. & Framo, James L., eds. Family Therapy: The Major Contributions. 620p. 1981. text ed. 30.00 (ISBN 0-8236-1885-4). Intl Univs Pr.
Gurman, Alan S. & Kniskern, David P. Handbook of Family Therapy. LC 80-20357. 800p. 1981. 39.95 (ISBN 0-87630-242-8). Brunner Mazel.
Gurman, Alan S., ed. Questions & Answers in the Practice of Family Therapy. LC 80-22460. 544p. 1981. 25.00 (ISBN 0-87630-246-0). Brunner-Mazel.
Haley, Jay. Leaving Home: The Therapy of Disturbed Young People. 1980. 16.95 (ISBN 0-07-025570-9). McGraw.
--Problem-Solving Therapy: New Strategies for Effective Family Therapy. LC 76-11889. (Social & Behavioral Science Ser.). 1976. 15.95x (ISBN 0-87589-300-7). Jossey-Bass.
--Uncommon Therapy: The Psychiatric Techniques of Milton H. Erickson, M. D. 1977. Repr. of 1973 ed. 10.00x (ISBN 0-393-01100-3, Norton Lib); pap. 3.95 (ISBN 0-393-00846-0). Norton.
Haley, Jay & Hoffman, Lynn. Techniques of Family Therapy. LC 75-78460. 1968. pap. 4.95x (ISBN 0-465-09512-7, TB5013). Basic.
Haley, Jay, ed. Changing Families: A Family Therapy Reader. LC 72-118654. 353p. 1971. 22.50 (ISBN 0-8089-0681-X). Grune.
Hall, C. Margaret. The Bowen Family Theory & Its Uses. LC 79-64456. 1981. 25.00 (ISBN 0-87668-373-1). Aronson.
Hansen, James & L'Abate, Lucinano. Approaches to Family Therapy. 1982. text ed. 15.95 (ISBN 0-686-75015-2). Macmillan.
Hansen, James C. & Rosenthal, David. Strategies & Techniques in Family Therapy. (Illus.). 464p. 1981. 28.50 (ISBN 0-398-04435-X); pap. 19.75 (ISBN 0-398-04154-7). C C Thomas.
Harrisson, Sheila P. Families in Stress. 124p. 1978. text ed. 6.25 (ISBN 0-443-01885-5). Churchill.

Headley, Lee. Adults & Their Parents in Family Therapy. 193p. 1977. 14.95 (ISBN 0-306-31087-2, Plenum Pr). Plenum Pub.

Helfer, Ray E. & Kempe, C. Henry, eds. Child Abuse & Neglect: The Family & the Community. LC 76-8891. 1976. 25.00 (ISBN 0-88410-217-3); pap. text ed. 11.50 (ISBN 0-88410-240-8). Ballinger Pub.

Hiesberger, Jean M., ed. Healing Family Hurts. LC 79-90991. (Paths of Life Ser.). 128p. (Orig.). 1979. pap. 2.45 (ISBN 0-8091-2266-9). Paulist Pr.

Hoffman, Lynn. Foundations of Family Therapy: A Conceptual Framework for System Change. LC 80-68956. 416p. 1981. 20.00x (ISBN 0-465-02498-X). Basic.

Hoover, Helene M. & Hoover, Kenneth H. Concepts & Methodologies in the Family: An Instructor's Resource Handbook. 1978. pap. text ed. 17.95 (ISBN 0-205-06159-1). Allyn.

Horewitz, James. Transactional Analysis & Family Therapy. LC 79-51923. 1979. 25.00x (ISBN 0-87668-381-2). Aronson.

Howells, John G. Advances in Family Psychiatry, Vol. 2. LC 101. 1980. text ed. 29.95 (ISBN 0-8236-0101-3). Intl Univs Pr.

--Principles of Family Psychiatry. LC 73-90298. 1975. 30.00 (ISBN 0-87630-089-1). Brunner-Mazel.

Howells, John G. & Guirguis, Wahuih. The Family & Schizophrenia. 1982. text ed. price not set (ISBN 0-8236-1850-1). Intl Univs Pr.

Howells, John G., ed. Advances in Family Psychiatry, Vol. 1. 1980. text ed. 29.95 (ISBN 0-8236-0097-1). Intl Univs Pr.

--Advances in Family Psychiatry, Vol. 3. 1981. pap. text ed. write for info. (ISBN 0-8236-0102-1). Intl Univs Pr.

Jackson, Don D., ed. Communication, Family & Marriage. LC 68-21576. (The Human Communication Ser.: Vol. 1). (Orig.). 1968. pap. 5.95x (ISBN 0-8314-0015-3). Sci & Behavior.

--Therapy, Communication & Change. LC 68-21577. (The Human Communication Ser: Vol. 2). 1968. pap. 5.95x (ISBN 0-8314-0016-1). Sci & Behavior.

Jones, Susan L. Family Therapy: A Comparison of Approaches. new ed. LC 80-10161. (Illus.). 1980. text ed. 15.95 (ISBN 0-87619-625-3). R J Brady.

--Family Therapy: A Comparison of Approaches. new ed. LC 80-10161. (Illus.). 1980. text ed. 15.95 (ISBN 0-87619-625-3). R J Brady.

Justice, Rita & Justice, Blair. The Abusing Family. LC 76-6478. 1976. text ed. 19.95 (ISBN 0-87705-294-8); pap. 8.95 (ISBN 0-87705-315-4). Human Sci Pr.

Kaufman, Edward & Kaufmann, Pauline. Family Therapy of Drug & Alcohol Abusers. 1979. 24.95 (ISBN 0-470-26385-7). Halsted Pr.

Kempler, Walter. Experiential Psychotherapy Within Families. 320p. 1981. 20.00 (ISBN 0-87630-267-3). Brunner-Mazel.

Kramer, Charles H. Becoming a Family Therapist: Developing an Integrated Approach to Working with Families. LC 80-11322. 256p. 1980. text ed. 22.95 (ISBN 0-87705-470-3). Human Sci Pr.

Kroth, Jerome A. Child Sexual Abuse: Analysis of a Family Therapy Approach. (Illus.). 216p. 1979. text ed. 19.25 (ISBN 0-398-03906-2). C C Thomas.

Kwiatkowska, Hanna Y. Family Therapy & Evaluation Through Art. (Illus.). 304p. 1978. 26.75 (ISBN 0-398-03729-9). C C Thomas.

L'Abate, Luciano. Understanding & Helping the Individual in the Family. LC 76-42234. (Illus.). 272p. 1976. 31.75 (ISBN 0-8089-0969-X). Grune.

Langsley, Donald G. & Kaplan, David M. The Treatment of Families in Crisis. LC 68-29400. 208p. 1968. 25.50 (ISBN 0-8089-0251-2). Grune.

Lansky, Melvin. Family Therapy & Major Psychopathology. (Seminars in Psychiatry Ser.). (Illus.). 448p. 1981. 27.50 (ISBN 0-8089-1360-3, 792441). Grune.

Lantz, James E. Family & Marital Therapy: A Transactional Approach. (Illus.). 224p. 1978. pap. 13.50 (ISBN 0-8385-2521-0). ACC.

Lewis, J. M., et al. No Single Thread: Psychological Health in Family Systems. LC 75-25777. 1976. 17.50 (ISBN 0-87630-111-1). Brunner-Mazel.

Lieberman, Stuart. Transgenerational Family Therapy. 240p. 1980. 39.00x (ISBN 0-85664-776-4, Pub. by Croom Helm England). State Mutual Bk.

--Transgenerational Family Therapy. (Illus.). 234p. 1979. 35.00x (ISBN 0-85664-776-4, Pub. by Croom Helm Ltd England). Biblio Dist.

Madanes, Cloe. Strategic Family Therapy. LC 80-26286. (Social & Behavioral Science Ser.). 1981. text ed. 15.95x (ISBN 0-87589-487-9). Jossey-Bass.

Miller, Sally & Winstead-Fry, Patricia. Family Systems Theory & Nursing Practice. 176p. 1982. text ed. 13.95 (ISBN 0-686-76719-5); pap. text ed. 10.95 (ISBN 0-8359-1849-1). Reston.

Minuchin, Salvador. Families & Family Therapy. LC 73-89710. 320p. 1974. 10.00x (ISBN 0-674-29236-7). Harvard U Pr.

Minuchin, Salvador & Fishman, H. Charles. Family Therapy Techniques. LC 80-25392. (Illus.). 352p. 1981. 15.00 (ISBN 0-674-29410-6). Harvard U Pr.

Minuchin, Salvador, et al. Families of the Slums: An Exploration of Their Structure Treatment. LC 67-28507. (Illus.). 1967. 15.00x (ISBN 0-465-02330-4). Basic.

Mitchison, Naomi. Family at Ditlabeng. LC 71-125149. 136p. (gr. 4 up). 1970. 3.95 (ISBN 0-374-32265-1). FS&G.

Mostwin, Danuta. Social Dimension of Family Treatment. LC 79-92201. (Illus.). 245p. 1980. pap. 12.50x (ISBN 0-87101-083-6, CBF-083-C). Natl Assn Soc Wkrs.

Napier, Augustus Y. & Whitaker, Carl. The Family Crucible. LC 74-1872. 1978. 14.95 (ISBN 0-06-014568-4, HarpT). Har-Row.

North American Symposium on Family Practice. The Many Dimensions of Family Practice: Proceedings. LC 80-14847. 340p. 1980. pap. 14.95 (ISBN 0-87304-179-8). Family Serv.

Okpaku, S. Family Planning & Preventive Psychiatry. 1981. 20.00 (ISBN 0-89388-003-5). Okpaku Communications.

Okun, Barbara F. & Rappaport, Louis J. Working with Families: An Introduction to Family Therapy. (Illus.). 1980. text ed. 12.95 (ISBN 0-87872-234-3); wkbk avail. (ISBN 0-87872-242-4). Duxbury Pr.

Patterson, G. R., et al. A Social Learning Approach to Family Intervention, Vol. 1: Families with Aggressive Children. LC 75-27000. 179p. 1975. pap. 10.95 (ISBN 0-916154-00-9). Castalia Pub.

Pearce, John & Friedman, Leonard, eds. Family Therapy: Combining Psychodynamic & Family Systems Approaches. 192p. 1980. 14.00 (ISBN 0-8089-1245-3). Grune.

Peck, Bruce B. A Family Therapy Notebook. LC 74-83895. 1975. 11.50 (ISBN 0-87212-042-2). Libra.

Raymond, Margaret, et al. The Healing Alliance: A New View of the Family's Role in the Treatment of Emotional Problems. 1977. pap. 3.95x (ISBN 0-393-00807-X, Norton Lib). Norton.

Rueveni, Uri. Networking Families in Crisis. LC 78-8024. 1979. 19.95 (ISBN 0-87705-374-X). Human Sci Pr.

Sager, Clifford J. & Kaplan, Helen S. Progress in Group & Family Therapy. LC 72-153376. 960p. 1972. 35.00 (ISBN 0-87630-048-4); pap. 15.95 (ISBN 0-87630-073-5). Brunner-Mazel.

Sander, Fred. Individual & Family Therapy. LC 79-91901. 242p. 1979. 20.00 (ISBN 0-87668-400-2). Aronson.

Satir, Virginia, et al. Changing with Families. LC 76-15450. 1976. 9.95x (ISBN 0-8314-0051-X). Sci & Behavior.

--Helping Families to Change. LC 75-29697. 296p. 1976. 20.00x (ISBN 0-87668-238-7). Aronson.

Satir, Virginia M. Conjoint Family Therapy. rev ed. LC 67-27269. 1967. pap. 6.95 (ISBN 0-8314-0013-7). Sci & Behavior.

Sauer, Arlene R. Procedures for Operating a Service Delivery Information System: Daily Reporting Model. LC 78-53910. (Orig.). 1978. pap. 8.00 (ISBN 0-87304-152-6). Family Serv.

Sedgwick, Rae. Family Mental Health: Theory & Practice. LC 80-20160. (Illus.). 296p. 1980. pap. text ed. 10.45 (ISBN 0-8016-4447-X). Mosby.

Sholevar, G. Pirooz. Changing Sexual Values & the Family. (Illus.). 192p. 1977. 16.50 (ISBN 0-398-03519-9). C C Thomas.

Skynner, A. C. Systems of Family & Marital Psychotherapy. LC 76-2577. 1976. 20.00 (ISBN 0-87630-117-0). Brunner-Mazel.

Smith, Gerald W. & Phillips, Alice I. Couple Therapy. 160p. 1973. pap. 1.95 (ISBN 0-02-078000-1, Collier). Macmillan.

Solomon, Neil. Family Therapy & Social Change. 1981. text ed. 24.50x (ISBN 0-8290-0088-7); audio cassette incl. Irvington.

Speers, Rex W. & Lansing, Cornelius. Group Therapy in Childhood Psychosis. (Illus.). 1965. 12.50x (ISBN 0-8078-0945-4). U of NC Pr.

Stewart, Charles W. The Minister As Family Counselor. LC 79-10854. 1979. 8.95 (ISBN 0-687-26955-5). Abingdon.

Stierlin, Helm. Psychoanalysis Family Therapy. LC 76-45568. 1977. 25.00x (ISBN 0-87668-257-3, 25734). Aronson.

Stierlin, Helm & Rucker-Embden, Ingeborg. The First Interview with the Family. Tooze, Sarah, tr. LC 79-27830. 1980. 20.00 (ISBN 0-87630-225-8). Brunner-Mazel.

Straus, Murray A. & Brown, Bruce W. Family Measurement Techniques: Abstracts of Published Instruments, 1935-1975. 1978. 28.50x (ISBN 0-8166-0799-0). U of Minn Pr.

Tymchuk, Alexander J. Parent & Family Therapy: An Integrative Approach to Family Interventions. new ed. LC 79-1085. 1979. text ed. 14.95 (ISBN 0-89335-080-X). Spectrum Pub.

Visher, Emily B. & Visher, John S. Stepfamilies: A Guide to Working with Stepparents & Stepchildren. LC 78-25857. 1979. 17.50 (ISBN 0-87630-190-1). Brunner-Mazel.

Walrond-Skinner, Sue, ed. Developments in Family Therapy: Theories & Applications Since 1948. 248p. (Orig.). 1981. pap. 8.95 (ISBN 0-7100-8705-5). Routledge & Kegan.

--Family & Marital Psychotherapy. (Orig.). 1979. pap. 11.50 (ISBN 0-7100-8981-3). Routledge & Kegan.

Walsh, W. M. A Primer in Family Therapy. (Illus.). 152p. 1980. 13.50 (ISBN 0-398-03992-5). C C Thomas.

Watzlawick, Paul & Weakland, John H., eds. The Interactional View: Studies at the Mental Research Institute, Palo Alto, 1965-1974. 1977. 19.95x (ISBN 0-393-01131-3). Norton.

Wegscheider, Don. If Only My Family Understood Me: A Family Can Find New Balance Through Stress. LC 79-53160. (Illus., Orig.). 1979. pap. 4.95 (ISBN 0-89638-038-6). Compcare.

Wile, B. Couples Therapy: A Nontraditional Approach. LC 81-4958. 240p. 1981. 22.50 (ISBN 0-471-07811-5, Pub. by Wiley Interscience). Wiley.

Wolberg, Lewis R. & Aronson, Marvin L., eds. Group & Family Therapy: 1980. LC 72-10881. 432p. 1980. 25.00 (ISBN 0-87630-238-X). Brunner-Mazel.

--Group & Family Therapy 1981. LC 72-10881. 350p. 1981. price not set (ISBN 0-87630-275-4). Brunner-Mazel.

Woody, R. H. & Woody, J. D. Sexual, Marital, & Familial Relations. (Illus.). 312p. 1973. 16.50 (ISBN 0-398-02803-6). C C Thomas.

Zuk, Gerald H. Family Therapy: A Triadic-Based Approach. LC 72-174269. (Clinical Service Ser.). (Illus.). 288p. 1972. text ed. 19.95 (ISBN 0-87705-069-4). Human Sci Pr.

--Process & Practice in Family Therapy. 123p. 1975. pap. 6.50 (ISBN 0-686-17203-5). Psychiatry & Behavioral.

FAMILY RECREATION

Bellew, Frank. The Art of Amusing. LC 74-15725. (Popular Culture in America Ser.). (Illus.). 328p. 1975. Repr. of 1866 ed. 19.00x (ISBN 0-405-06362-8). Arno.

Beram, Sandy. Back Before Bedtime. LC 77-88727. 1978. pap. 7.95 (ISBN 0-8256-3093-2, Quick Fox). Music Sales.

Bright, James L. Outdoor Recreation Projects. LC 77-28410. 1978. 13.95 (ISBN 0-912336-62-5); pap. 6.95 (ISBN 0-912336-63-3). Structures Pub.

Coletti, Mina S. & Giesea, Roberta K. The Family Idea Book. LC 80-10921. 210p. 1980. pap. 5.95 (ISBN 0-87747-813-9). Deseret Bk.

Edgren, Harry D. Fun for the Family. (Game & Party Books). 144p. 1975. pap. 2.50 (ISBN 0-8010-3321-7). Baker Bk.

Hudgins, Barbara. Trips & Treks: A Guide to Family Outings in the New Jersey Area. (Illus.). 121p. (Orig.). 1980. pap. text ed. 3.95 (ISBN 0-686-31589-8). Woodmont Pr.

Kramer, Jack. Backyard Games: A Handbook for Homeowners & Gardners. 1977. pap. 3.95 (ISBN 0-425-03401-1, Windhover). Berkley Pub.

Orlick, Terry. The Cooperative Sports & Games Book: Challenge Without Competition. LC 77-88771. 1978. 10.00 (ISBN 0-394-42215-5); pap. 5.95 (ISBN 0-394-73494-7). Pantheon.

Pappas, Michael G. Prime Time for Families. (Illus.). 120p. (Orig.). 1980. pap. 5.95 (ISBN 0-03-056672-X). Winston Pr.

Rapoport, Rhona & Rapoport, Robert N. Leisure & the Family Life Cycle. 1975. 32.00x (ISBN 0-7100-8134-0). Routledge & Kegan.

FAMILY SERVICE ASSOCIATION OF AMERICA

Fisk, Helen I. & McCurdy, William B., eds. Statistical Procedures Recommended for FSAA Member Agencies: System D. 1965. pap. 2.00 (ISBN 0-87304-071-6). Family Serv.

--Statistical Procedures Recommended for FSAA Member Agencies: System C. 1965. pap. 3.00 (ISBN 0-87304-070-8). Family Serv.

Manser, Gordon & Cass, Rosemary H. Voluntarism at the Crossroads. LC 75-27967. 1976. 12.95 (ISBN 0-87304-140-2). Family Serv.

FAMILY SIZE

see also Birth Control; Eugenics

Askham, Janet. Fertility & Deprivation. LC 75-2718. (Papers in Sociology Ser.: No. 5). (Illus.). 192p. 1975. 24.95 (ISBN 0-521-20795-9). Cambridge U Pr.

Bianchi, Suzanne M. Household Composition & Racial Inequality. 192p. 1981. 16.00 (ISBN 0-8135-0913-0). Rutgers U Pr.

Busfield, Joan & Paddon, M. Thinking About Children. LC 76-22986. (Illus.). 1977. 29.95 (ISBN 0-521-21402-5). Cambridge U Pr.

Cartwright, Ann. How Many Children? (Direct Editions Ser.). (Orig.). 1976. pap. 16.50x (ISBN 0-7100-8341-6). Routledge & Kegan.

Carvajal, M. J. & Geithman, David T. Family Planning & Family Size Determination: The Evidence from Seven Latin American Cities. LC 75-27700. (Latin American Monographs: Ser. 2, No. 18). (Illus.). 1976. 7.50 (ISBN 0-8130-0526-4). U Presses Fla.

Epstein, T. Scarlett & Jackson, Darrell, eds. The Feasibility of Fertility Planning: Micro Perspectives. 1977. text ed. 37.00 (ISBN 0-08-021452-5); pap. text ed. 12.25 (ISBN 0-08-021837-7). Pergamon.

Espenshade, Thomas J. The Cost of Children in Urban United States. LC 76-4798. (Population Monograph Ser.: No. 14). 1976. Repr. of 1973 ed. lib. bdg. 15.00x (ISBN 0-8371-8835-0, ESCC). Greenwood.

French, Dwight K. National Survey of Family Growth, Cycle I: Sample Design, Estimation Procedures & Variance Estimation. Stevenson, Taloria, ed. (Series 2: No. 76). 1977. pap. text ed. 1.75 (ISBN 0-8406-0116-6). Natl Ctr Health Stats.

Hawke, Sharryl & Knox, David. One Child by Choice. 1977. 9.95 (ISBN 0-13-634618-9, Spec); pap. 3.95 (ISBN 0-13-634600-6, Spec). P-H.

Keyfitz, Nathan. Urban Influence on Farm Family Size. Zuckerman, Harriet & Merton, Robert K., eds. LC 79-9009. (Dissertations on Sociology Ser.). 1980. lib. bdg. 11.00x (ISBN 0-405-12977-7). Arno.

Lindert, Peter H. Fertility & Scarcity in America. LC 77-71991. 1978. text ed. 28.50 (ISBN 0-691-04217-9). Princeton U Pr.

Measuring the Effect of Family Planning Programs on Fertility. 1979. pap. 45.00 (ISBN 0-685-90711-2, ORD 5, ORDINA). Unipub.

Poffenberger, Thomas & Sebaly, Kim. The Socialization of Family Size Values: Youth & Family Planning in an Indian Village. LC 76-53996. (Michigan Papers on South and Southeast Asia: No. 12). (Illus.). 150p. 1976. pap. 5.00x (ISBN 0-89148-012-9). Ctr S&SE Asian.

Rosenberg, Charles E. & Rosenberg, Carroll-Smith. Fertility Controlled: The British Argument for Family Limitation. LC 73-20644. (Sex, Marriage & Society Ser.). 137p. 1974. Repr. 11.00x (ISBN 0-405-05799-7). Arno.

Ruprecht, Theodore K. & Jewett, Frank I. The Micro-Economics of Demographic Change: Family Planning & Economic Wellbeing. LC 75-57. (Illus.). 176p. 1975. text ed. 25.00 (ISBN 0-275-05530-2). Praeger.

Ryder, Norman B. & Westoff, Charles F. Reproduction in the United States: 1965. LC 78-120760. (Office of Population Research Ser.). 1971. 28.00x (ISBN 0-691-09318-0). Princeton U Pr.

Scanzoni, John H. Sex Roles, Life Styles & Childbearing: Changing Patterns in Marriage & the Family. LC 74-28939. (Illus.). 1975. 17.95 (ISBN 0-02-927720-5). Free Pr.

Seminar on Family Planning, Chicago, 1971. Proceedings. Isenman, Albert W., et al, eds. LC 73-153179. (Illus.). 101p. 1974. 5.00 (ISBN 0-686-05692-2). Am Coll Obstetric.

Turchi, Boone A. The Demand for Children: The Economics of Fertility in the United States. LC 75-22111. 256p. 1975. 18.50 (ISBN 0-88410-353-6). Ballinger Pub.

Udry, J. Richard & Huyck, Earl E., eds. Demographic Evaluation of Domestic Family Planning Programs. LC 75-4661. 128p. 1975. text ed. 16.00 (ISBN 0-88410-355-2). Ballinger Pub.

Westoff, Charles F. & Bumpass, Larry L. Later Years of Childbearing. LC 74-120751. (Population Research Office). 1970. 16.50x (ISBN 0-691-09303-2). Princeton U Pr.

Westoff, Charles F., et al. Family Growth in Metropolitan America. (Office of Population Research Ser.). 1961. 28.00x (ISBN 0-691-09316-4). Princeton U Pr.

--College Women & Fertility Values. (Office of Population Research Ser.). 1967. 18.50x (ISBN 0-691-09311-3). Princeton U Pr.

WHO Scientific Group, Geneva, 1969. Health Aspects of Family Planning: A Report. (Technical Report Ser: No. 442). 50p. 1970. pap. 2.00 (ISBN 92-4-120442-7, 612). World Health.

FAMILY SOCIAL WORK

see also Family Life Education; Marriage Counseling

Assembly of Behavioral and Social Sciences, National Research Council. Toward a National Policy for Children & Families. LC 76-56640. 1976. pap. 6.25 (ISBN 0-309-02533-8). Natl Acad Pr.

Beck, Dorothy F. & Jones, Mary Ann. How to Conduct a Client Follow-up Study. LC 73-94027. 1974. pap. 10.95 with 1979 suplement (ISBN 0-87304-181-X). Family Serv.
Bradshaw, Barbara R., et al. Counseling on Family Planning & Human Sexuality. LC 75-27961. (Illus.). 1977. 12.95 (ISBN 0-87304-142-9); pap. 7.95 (ISBN 0-87304-129-1). Family Serv.
Duncan, Cora, et al. Guide for Board Members of Voluntary Family Service Agencies. 1975. pap. 3.25 (ISBN 0-87304-136-4). Family Serv.
Elbow, Margaret. Patterns in Family Violence. 160p. 1980. pap. 9.95 (ISBN 0-87304-185-2). Family Serv.
Elshtain, Jean B., ed. The Family in Political Thought. LC 81-11435. 352p. 1982. lib. bdg. 22.50x (ISBN 0-87023-341-6); pap. text ed. 10.00x (ISBN 0-87023-342-4). U of Mass Pr.
The Family Service Executive: Selection & Performance Appraisal. rev. ed. 1974. pap. 4.00 (ISBN 0-87304-033-3). Family Serv.
Feldman, Frances L. & Scherz, Frances H. Family Social Welfare: Helping Troubled Families. LC 67-18276. 1967. 22.95x (ISBN 0-202-36001-6). Aldine Pub.
Fullmer, Daniel W. & Bernard, Harold W. Family Consultation. (Guidance Monograph Ser). 1968. pap. 2.40 (ISBN 0-395-09921-8). HM.
Geismar, Ludwig L. Family & Community Functioning: A Manual of Measurement for Social-Work Practice & Policy. 2nd, rev. ed. LC 80-17785. 317p. 1980. 15.00 (ISBN 0-8108-1332-7); pap. 9.75 (ISBN 0-8108-1341-6). Scarecrow.
Geismar, Ludwig L., et al. Early Supports for Family Life: A Social Work Experiment. LC 70-188665. 1972. 10.00 (ISBN 0-8108-0476-X). Scarecrow.
Heywood, J. S. & Allen, B. K. Financial Help in Social Work: A Study of Preventive Work with Families Under the Children & Young Persons Act, 1963. 102p. 1971. 21.00x (ISBN 0-7190-0487-X, Pub. by Manchester U Pr England). State Mutual Bk.
Hill, William G., et al. Family Service Agencies & Mental Health Clinics: A Comparative Study. LC 76-151628. 1971. pap. 2.95 (ISBN 0-87304-095-3). Family Serv.
Human Resources Corporation. Models, Theories & Concepts of Family Counseling: Annotated Bibliography of the Literature, 1975-1980. 208p. 1981. text ed. 22.50 (ISBN 0-89946-094-1). Oelgeschlager.
Jones, Mary Ann, et al. A Second Chance for Families. LC 76-1518. (Orig.). 1976. pap. text ed. 7.20 (ISBN 0-87868-158-2). Child Welfare.
Karpf, Maurice J. The Scientific Basis of Social Work. 424p. 1981. Repr. of 1931 ed. lib. bdg. 35.00 (ISBN 0-8495-3049-0). Arden Lib.
Keith-Lucas, Alan & Sanford, Clifford W. Group Child Care As a Family Service. LC 76-40411. 1977. 17.00x (ISBN 0-8078-1303-6). U of NC Pr.
Leissner, Aryeh. Family Advice Services. 1967. pap. text ed. 3.00x (ISBN 0-582-32408-4). Humanities.
McMurrain, T. Thomas. Developing Skills for Helping Families: A Primer for Family Service Workers. 1976. 6.00 (ISBN 0-685-65138-X, 205). Humanics Ltd.
Manser, Ellen P., ed. Family Advocacy: A Manual for Action. LC 72-94392. 1973. pap. 6.00 (ISBN 0-87304-101-1). Family Serv.
Mnookin, Robert. Child, Family & State, Cases & Materials on Children & the Law. 857p. (Orig.). 1978. text ed. 23.25 (ISBN 0-316-57650-6). Little.
Munson, Carlton E. Social Work with Families: Theory & Practice. LC 79-7851. 1980. 17.50 (ISBN 0-02-922300-8); pap. text ed. 9.95 (ISBN 0-02-922310-5). Free Pr.
NSPCC. At Risk: An Account of the Work of the Battered Child Research Department. (Routledge Direct Editions). (Orig.). 1976. pap. 12.50 (ISBN 0-7100-8313-0). Routledge & Kegan.
Parizeau, Alice. Parenting & Delinquent Youth. LC 79-47982. 208p. 1980. 22.95x (ISBN 0-669-03620-X). Lexington Bks.
Polansky, Norman A., et al. Child Neglect: Understanding & Reaching the Parent. LC 72-83496. 1972. pap. 5.45 (ISBN 0-87868-097-7). Child Welfare.
Reid, William J. & Epstein, Laura. Task-Centered Practice. LC 76-28177. 1977. 13.00x (ISBN 0-231-04072-5). Columbia U Pr.
Rich, William. Smaller Families Through Social & Economic Progress. LC 72-97989. (Monographs: No. 7). 74p. 1973. 2.00 (ISBN 0-686-28688-X). Overseas Dev Council.
Sainsbury, Eric. Social Work with Families. (Library of Social Work). 1975. 15.00x (ISBN 0-7100-8039-5); pap. 7.45 (ISBN 0-7100-8040-9). Routledge & Kegan.
Social Work Practice in a Family Agency. 1959. pap. 2.00 (ISBN 0-87304-040-6). Family Serv.
Tolson, Eleanor R. & Reid, William J., eds. Models of Family Treatment. (Illus.). 302p. 1981. 18.50x (ISBN 0-231-04950-1). Columbia U Pr.
Weissman, Harold H. Integrating Services for Troubled Families: Dilemmas of Program Design & Implementation. LC 78-62563. (Social & Behavioral Science Ser.). (Illus.). 1978. text ed. 14.95x (ISBN 0-87589-385-6). Jossey-Bass.

FAMILY THERAPY
see Family Psychotherapy

FAMILY WAGES
see Family Allowances

FAMILY WORSHIP
see Family-Prayer-Books and Devotions; Family-Religious Life

FAMINES
Alamgir, Mohiuddin. Famine in South Asia: Political Economy of Mass Starvation. LC 80-13708. 448p. 1980. text ed. 30.00 (ISBN 0-89946-042-9). Oelgeschlager.
Appleby, Andrew B. Famine in Tudor & Stuart England. LC 77-76151. 1978. 14.50x (ISBN 0-8047-0956-4). Stanford U Pr.
Blumberg, Rhoda. Famine. LC 78-6837. (Impact Bks.). (Illus.). (gr. 9 up). 1978. PLB 7.45 s&l (ISBN 0-531-02201-3). Watts.
Bolton, G. C. Fine Country to Starve in. LC 72-86808. 1972. 18.00 (ISBN 0-85564-061-8, Pub. by U of W Austral Pr). Intl Schol Bk Serv.
Brown, Walter R. & Anderson, Norman D. Historical Catastrophes: Famines. LC 75-22297. (Historical Catastrophes Ser). (Illus.). 192p. (gr. 5 up). 1976. PLB 7.95 (ISBN 0-201-00827-0, 0827, A-W Childrens). A-W.
Dando, William A. The Geography of Famine. LC 80-11145. (Scripta Series in Geography). 365p. 1980. 30.95x (ISBN 0-470-26956-1). Halsted Pr.
Garcia, Rolando V. & Escudero, Jose. Drought of Man the Nineteen Seventy-Two Case History: Vol. 2, The Constant Catastrophe-Malnutrition, Famines & Drought. (IFIAS Publications: Vol. 2). (Illus.). 304p. 1981. 56.00 (ISBN 0-08-025824-7). Pergamon.
Johnson, D. Gale, ed. Famine in India: An Original Anthology. LC 75-29759. (World Food Supply Ser). 1976. 14.00x (ISBN 0-405-07774-2). Arno.
Lateef, Noel V. Crisis in the Sahel. (Westview Special Studies in Social, Political, & Economic Development). (Illus.). 285p. 1980. lib. bdg. 26.25x (ISBN 0-89158-991-0). Westview.
Lucas, George R., Jr. & Ogletree, Thomas W., eds. Lifeboat Ethics: The Moral Dilemma of World Hunger. LC 76-10002. 192p. 1976. 8.95 (ISBN 0-06-065308-6, HarpR); pap. 4.95x (ISBN 0-06-065309-4, RD170, HarpR). Har-Row.
Minear, Larry. New Hope for the Hungry? The Challenge of the World Food Crisis. (Orig.). 1975. pap. 1.95 (ISBN 0-377-00043-4). Friend Pr.
Newman, James L., ed. Drought, Famine & Population Movements in Africa. LC 74-25877. (Foreign & Comparative Studies-Eastern African Ser.: No. 17). 144p. 1975. pap. 4.50x (ISBN 0-915984-14-8). Syracuse U Foreign Comp.
Read, Bernard E. Famine Foods List in the Chiu Huang Pen Ts'ao. 1977. 4.50 (ISBN 0-89986-318-3). E Langstaff.
Robson, J. R. Famine: Its Causes Effects & Management. (Food & Nutrition in History & Anthropology Ser.). 180p. 1981. 27.50 (ISBN 0-677-16180-8). Gordon.
Sen, Amartya. Poverty & Famines: An Essay on Entitlement & Deprivation. 256p. 1981. 15.00x (ISBN 0-19-828426-8). Oxford U Pr.
Vandier, Jacques. Le Famine dans l'Egypte Ancienne. Finley, Moses, ed. LC 79-5011. (Ancient Economic History Ser.). (Fr.). 1980. Repr. of 1936 ed. lib. bdg. 14.00x (ISBN 0-405-12399-X). Arno.
Walford, Cornelius. Famines of the World: Past & Present. LC 74-131414. (Research & Source Works Ser: No. 556). 1970. Repr. of 1879 ed. lib. bdg. 22.50 (ISBN 0-8337-3669-8). B Franklin.

FAMOUS PROBLEMS (IN GEOMETRY)
see Geometry-Problems, Famous

FAN (AFRICAN PEOPLE)
Fernandez, J. W. Fang Architectonics. LC 76-53553. (Working Papers in the Traditional Arts Ser: No.1). (Illus.). 48p. 1977. pap. text ed. 2.95x (ISBN 0-915980-65-7). Inst Study Human.
Tessmann, Gunter. Die Pangwe: Volkerkundliche Monographie Eines Westafrikanischen Negerstammes, 2 vols. in 1. (Ger). Repr. of 1913 ed. 54.00 (ISBN 0-384-59860-9). Johnson Repr.

FAN-IN-WING AIRCRAFT
see also Short Take-Off and Landing Aircraft; Vertically Rising Aircraft

FANATICISM
see also Asceticism; Enthusiasm
Ahmed, K. Fanaticism, Intolerance & Islam. pap. 1.00 (ISBN 0-686-18491-2). Kazi Pubns.
Enroth, Ronald M. Youth, Brainwashing & the Extremist Cults. 1977. pap. 5.95 (ISBN 0-310-44041-6). Zondervan.
Hoffer, Eric. True Believer. LC 51-1405. 1951. 9.95 (ISBN 0-06-011920-9, HarpT). Har-Row.
--True Believer. 1966. pap. 2.95 (ISBN 0-06-080071-2, P71, PL). Har-Row.
Matthews, Ronald. English Messiahs: Studies of Six English Religious Pretenders, 1656-1927. LC 76-172553. Repr. of 1936 ed. 12.75 (ISBN 0-405-08783-7, Pub. by Blom). Arno.
Rudin, Josef. Fanaticism. LC 69-14813. (Ger). 1969. Repr. of 1965 ed. 7.95x (ISBN 0-268-00318-1). U of Notre Dame Pr.
Strachey, Ray, ed. Religious Fanaticism (Extracts from the Papers of Hannah Whitall Smith) 1978. Repr. of 1928 ed. lib. bdg. 35.00 (ISBN 0-89760-801-1, Telegraph). Dynamic Learn Corp.

FANCY DRESS
see Costume

FANCY WORK
see also Hooking; Pressed Flower Pictures
Aldrich, Dot & Aldrich, Genevieve. Creating with Cattails, Cones & Pods. LC 68-8521. (Illus.). 1971. 6.95 (ISBN 0-686-76844-2). Hearthside.
Biasiny, Nan. Beautiful Baby Clothes: To Knit, Crochet & Embroider. LC 76-51753. 1977. 12.50 (ISBN 0-671-22467-0). S&S.
Grainger, Stuart E. Creative Ropecraft. (Illus.). 1977. 10.95 (ISBN 0-393-08746-8). Norton.
Snook, Barbara. Needlework Stitches. (Illus.). 1963. 3.50 (ISBN 0-517-02516-7); pap. 1.95 (ISBN 0-517-50079-5). Crown.

FANG (AFRICAN PEOPLE)
see Fan (African People)

FANNING DAVID, 1756?-1825
Fanning, David. The Narrative of Colonel David Fanning (a Tory in the Revolutionary War with Great Britain) LC 73-2736. 112p. 1973. Repr. of 1865 ed. 10.50 (ISBN 0-87152-132-6). Reprint.

FANNING, TALBERT, 1810-1874
Wilburn, James R. The Hazard of the Die: Tolbert Fanning & the Restoration Movement. LC 74-77235. 1980. 9.95 (ISBN 0-932612-04-0). Pepperdine U Pr.

FANON, FRANTZ, 1925-1961
Frantz Fanon. 200p. 1976. pap. text ed. 4.95x (ISBN 0-8277-4839-6). British Bk Ctr.
Hansen, Emmanuel. Frantz Fanon: Social & Political Thought. LC 76-2619. (Illus.). 1977. 15.00 (ISBN 0-8142-0243-8). Ohio St U Pr.
Woddis, Jack. New Theories of Revolution: A Commentary on the Views of Frantz Fanon, Regis Debray & Herbert Marcuse. LC 75-85923. 415p. 1972. 10.00 (ISBN 0-7178-0350-3); pap. 4.00 (ISBN 0-7178-0366-X). Intl Pub Co.

FANS
Armstrong, Nancy. The Book of Fans. (Illus.). 1979. 12.95 (ISBN 0-8317-0952-9, Mayflower Bks). Smith Pubs.
Bennett, Anna G. & Berson, Ruth. Fans in Fashion. LC 81-65612. (Illus.). 128p. 1981. pap. 15.00x (ISBN 0-88401-037-6). Fine Arts Mus.
--Fans in Fashion. LC 81-65612. (Illus.). 128p. (Orig.). 1981. pap. 15.00 (ISBN 0-88401-037-6, Pub by Fine Arts Mus). C E Tuttle.
Chiba, Reiko. Painted Fans of Japan: Fifteen Noh Drama Masterpieces. LC 62-20775. (Illus., Fr., Or Eng). 1962. 15.50 (ISBN 0-8048-0468-0). C E Tuttle.
Flory, M. A. A Book About Fans: The History of Fans & Fan-Painting. LC 72-174940. (Illus.). xiv, 141p. 1975. Repr. of 1895 ed. 24.00 (ISBN 0-8103-4049-6). Gale.
Flory, M. A. & Jones, Mary C. A Book About Fans: The History of Fans & Fan-Painting. LC 77-23572. 1977. Repr. of 1895 ed. lib. bdg. 25.00 (ISBN 0-89341-204-X). Longwood Pr.
Green, Bertha D. Fans Over the Ages. LC 77-74118. (Illus.). 1979. 25.00 (ISBN 0-498-02097-5). A S Barnes.
Mayor, Susan. Collecting Fans. (The Christies International Collectors Ser.). (Illus.). 128p. 1980. 14.95 (ISBN 0-8317-3199-0, Mayflower Bks). Smith Pubs.
Mourey, Gabriel, et al. Art Nouveau Jewelry & Fans. (Illus.). 150p. 1973. pap. 5.00 (ISBN 0-486-22961-0). Dover.

FANS (MACHINERY)
Daly, B. B. Woods Practical Guide to Fan Engineering. 3rd ed. (Illus.). 376p. 1978. 27.50x (ISBN 0-8002-2238-5). Intl Pubns Serv.
Eck, B. Fans: Design & Operation of Centrifugal, Axial Flow & Cross Flow Fans. LC 72-137613. 612p. 1974. 105.00 (ISBN 0-08-015872-2). Pergamon.
Osborne, W. C. Fans. 1977. text ed. 26.00 (ISBN 0-08-021725-7); pap. text ed. 14.00 (ISBN 0-08-021726-5). Pergamon.

FANTASTIC FICTION
see also Ghost Stories; Science Fiction (Collections); Supernatural in Literature
Aquino, John. Fantasy in Literature. 64p. 1977. pap. 3.50 (ISBN 0-686-63667-8, 1817-6-06). NEA.
Ashley, Mike. Who's Who in Horror & Fantasy Fiction. LC 77-4608. 1978. pap. 4.95 (ISBN 0-8008-8278-4). Taplinger.
Boyer, Robert & Zahorski, Kenneth, eds. The Phoenix Tree: An Anthology of Myth Fantasy. 272p. 1980. pap. 2.50 (ISBN 0-380-76380-X, 76380). Avon.
Boyer, Robert H. & Zahorski, Kenneth J., eds. The Fantastic Imagination, Vol. II. 1978. pap. 2.50 (ISBN 0-380-41533-X, 41533). Avon.
Carew, Henry. The Vampires of the Andes. Reginald, R. & Menville, Douglas, eds. LC 77-84206. (Lost Race & Adult Fantasy Ser.). 1978. Repr. of 1925 ed. lib. bdg. 20.00x (ISBN 0-405-10962-8). Arno.
Carr & Greenberg. Treasury of Modern Fantasy. 1981. pap. 8.95 (ISBN 0-380-77115-2, 77115). Avon.
Cowl, R. P. An Anthology of Imaginative Prose. 1977. 15.00 (ISBN 0-89984-171-6). Century Bookbindery.
De Camp, L. Sprague. Literary Swordsmen & Sorcerers: The Makers of Heroic Fantasy. (Illus.). 1976. 10.00 (ISBN 0-87054-076-9). Arkham.
Disch, Thomas M. & Naylor, Charles, eds. Strangeness. 1978. pap. 2.50 (ISBN 0-380-41434-1, 41434). Avon.
Hoke, Helen, ed. Ghostly, Grim & Gruesome. LC 76-54258. (gr. 6 up). 1977. 7.95 (ISBN 0-525-66545-5). Elsevier-Nelson.
Le Fanu, Joseph S. A Stable for Nightmares or Weird Tales: Anthology. LC 75-46286. (Supernatural & Occult Fiction Ser.). (Illus.). 1976. Repr. of 1896 ed. lib. bdg. 15.00x (ISBN 0-405-08147-2). Arno.
McCaffrey, Anne. Get off the Unicorn. LC 77-1709. 1977. pap. 2.25 (ISBN 0-345-28508-5). Ballantine.
Manley, Seon & Lewis, Gogo, eds. Ladies of Horror: Two Centuries of Supernatural Stories by the Gentle Sex. LC 77-148485. (Illus.). (gr. 7 up). 1971. PLB 7.92 (ISBN 0-688-51358-1). Lothrop.
Parry, Michel, ed. Savage Heroes: Tales of Magical Fantasy. LC 79-66645. (Illus.). 190p. 1980. 9.95 (ISBN 0-8008-6996-6). Taplinger.
Rabkin, Eric S., ed. Fantastic Worlds: Myths, Tales, & Stories. 1979. 17.95 (ISBN 0-19-502542-3, GB 572); pap. 7.95 (ISBN 0-19-502541-5). Oxford U Pr.
Reginald, R., ed. The Spectre Bridegroom & Other Horrors: Original Anthology. LC 75-46305. (Supernatural & Occult Fiction Ser.). (Illus.). 1976. lib. bdg. 17.00x (ISBN 0-405-08165-0). Arno.
Reginald, R. & Melville, Douglas, eds. Dreamers of Dreams: An Anthology of Fantasy. new ed. LC 77-84280. (Lost Race & Adult Fantasy Ser.). (Illus.). 1978. lib. bdg. 30.00x (ISBN 0-405-11017-0). Arno.
Reginald, R. & Menville, Douglas, eds. Ancient Haunting: An Orginal Anthology. LC 75-46269. (Supernatural & Occult Fiction Ser.). (Illus.). 1976. lib. bdg. 26.00x (ISBN 0-405-08163-4). Arno.
--RIP: Five Stories of the Supernatural. original anthology ed. LC 75-1539. (Supernatural & Occult Fiction Ser.). (Illus.). 1976. lib. bdg. 18.00x (ISBN 0-405-08425-0). Arno.
--Supernatural & Occult Fiction Series, 63 bks. 1976. lib. bdg. 1120.00 set (ISBN 0-405-08107-3). Arno.
Rothman, Joel. I Can Be Anything You Can Be. LC 72-90694. (Illus.). 32p. (gr. k-4). 1973. 4.75 (ISBN 0-87592-024-1). Scroll Pr.
Tymn, Marshall, ed. American Fantasy & Science Fiction. LC 76-55151. 1979. 6.95 (ISBN 0-913960-15-2). Fax Collect.
Tymn, Marshall B. & Schlobin, Roger C., eds. The Year's Scholarship in Science Fiction & Fantasy, 1976 to 1979. 1982. price not set (ISBN 0-87338-257-9). Kent St U Pr.
Whaley, Stephen & Cook, Stanley. Man Unwept: Visions from the Inner Eye. (Illus.). 384p. 1974. pap. text ed. 8.95 (ISBN 0-07-069481-8, C). McGraw.
Wiggin, Kate D. & Smith, Nora A. Tales of Wonder. Repr. of 1909 ed. 20.00 (ISBN 0-89987-113-5). Darby Bks.

FANTASTIC FICTION–BIBLIOGRAPHY
Ashley, Michael. Fantasy Readers Guide, No. 1: The John Spencer Fantasy Publications. 54p. 1980. Repr. of 1979 ed. lib. bdg. 8.95 cancelled (ISBN 0-89370-099-1). Borgo Pr.
--Fantasy Readers Guide to Ramsey Campbell. 64p. 1980. Repr. lib. bdg. 8.95x (ISBN 0-89370-098-3). Borgo Pr.
Bishop, Gerald. New British Science Fiction & Fantasy Books Published During 1970 & 1971. LC 80-20579. 1980. Repr. of 1972 ed. lib. bdg. 9.95x (ISBN 0-89370-057-6). Borgo Pr.
Cockcroft, T. G. Index to the Weird Fiction Magazines, 2 vols. in 1. LC 74-15955. (Science Fiction Ser). (Illus.). 101p. 1975. 8.00x (ISBN 0-405-06322-9). Arno.

Currey, L. W. & Reginald, R. Science Fiction & Fantasy Reference Guide: An Annotated History of Critical & Biographical Works. LC 80-22715. (Borgo Reference Library: Vol. 4). 64p. (Orig.). 1981. lib. bdg. 8.95x (ISBN 0-89370-145-9); pap. text ed. 2.95x (ISBN 0-89370-245-5). Borgo Pr.

Day, Bradford M., ed. The Checklist of Fantastic Literature in Paperbound Books. LC 74-15961. (Science Fiction Ser). 128p. 1975. Repr. 10.00x (ISBN 0-405-06326-1). Arno.

--The Supplemental Checklist of Fantastic Literature. LC 74-15962. (Science Fiction Ser). 160p. 1975. Repr. 9.00x (ISBN 0-405-06327-X). Arno.

Day, Bradford M., et al, eds. Bibliography of Adventure: Mundy, Burroughs, Rohmer, Haggard. rev. ed. LC 77-84282. (Lost Race & Adult Fantasy Ser.). 1978. lib. bdg. 12.00x (ISBN 0-405-11019-7). Arno.

Lynn, Ruth N. Fantasy for Children: An Annotated Checklist. LC 79-21401. 288p. 1979. 14.95 (ISBN 0-8352-1232-7). Bowker.

Schlobin, Roger C. The Literature of Fantasy: An Annotated Bibliography of Modern Fantasy Fiction. LC 78-68287. (Garland Reference Library of the Humanities: No. 176). 1979. lib. bdg. 30.00 (ISBN 0-8240-9757-2). Garland Pub.

Sellin, B. The Life & Works of David Lindsay. 320p. Date not set. 39.50 (ISBN 0-521-22768-2). Cambridge U Pr.

Tymn, Marshall. American Fantasy & Science Fiction. LC 80-19217. 224p. 1980. Repr. of 1979 ed. lib. bdg. 12.95x (ISBN 0-89370-029-0). Borgo Pr.

Tymn, Marshall, et al, eds. Fantasy Literature: A Core Collection & Reference Guide. LC 79-1533. 1979. 14.95 (ISBN 0-8352-1153-3). Bowker.

FANTASTIC FICTION–HISTORY AND CRITICISM

Barnes, Myra J. Linguistics & Languages in Science Fiction-Fantasy. new ed. LC 74-17864. (Science Fiction Ser). 208p. 1975. Repr. of 1974 ed. 11.00x (ISBN 0-405-06319-9). Arno.

Jackson, Rosemary. Fantasy: The Literature of Subversion. 1981. 14.95x (ISBN 0-416-71170-7); pap. 6.95x (ISBN 0-416-71180-4). Methuen Inc.

Le Guin, Ursula K. The Language of the Night: Essays on Fantasy & Science Fiction. Wood, Susan, ed. (Orig.). 1982. pap. 2.75 (ISBN 0-425-05205-2). Berkley Pub.

Leguin, Ursula K. The Language of the Night: Essays on Fantasy & Science Fiction. Wood, Susan, intro. by. 1979. 9.95 (ISBN 0-399-12325-3). Berkley Pub.

Little, T. E. The Fantasts: Studies of J. R. R. Tolkien, Lewis Carroll, Mervyn Peake, Nikolay Gogol & Kenneth Grahame. 1981. 50.00x (ISBN 0-86127-212-9, Pub. by Avebury Pub England). State Mutual Bk.

Lochead, Marion. Renaissance of Wonder: The Fantasy Worlds of J. R. Tolkein, C. S. Lewis, George MacDonald, E. Nesbit, & Others. LC 80-7753. 192p. 1980. 8.95 (ISBN 0-06-250520-3, HarpR). Har-Row.

Manlove, C. N. Modern Fantasy: Five Studies. LC 74-31798. 320p. 1975. 42.00 (ISBN 0-521-20746-0); pap. 9.95x (ISBN 0-521-29386-3). Cambridge U Pr.

Prickett, Stephen. Victorian Fantasy. LC 78-21751. (Illus.). 276p. 1979. 17.50x (ISBN 0-253-17461-9). Ind U Pr.

Rabkin, Eric S. The Fantastic in Literature. LC 75-30201. 1976. 17.00 (ISBN 0-691-06301-X); pap. 6.95 (ISBN 0-691-01340-3). Princeton U Pr.

Reginald, Robert, ed. Science Fiction & Fantasy Literature: A Checklist from 1700 to 1974...with Contemporary Science Fiction Authors II, 2 vols. LC 76-46130. 1979. 110.00 set (ISBN 0-8103-1051-1). Gale.

Sammons, Martha C. A Guide Through Narnia. LC 78-26476. (Wheaton Literary Ser.). 1979. pap. 3.95 (ISBN 0-87788-325-4). Shaw Pubs.

Sellin, B. The Life & Works of David Lindsay. 320p. Date not set. 39.50 (ISBN 0-521-22768-2). Cambridge U Pr.

Todorov, Tzvetan. The Fantastic: A Structural Approach to a Literary Genre. Howard, Richard, tr. from Fr. LC 74-10407. (Illus.). 192p. 1975. pap. 4.95 (ISBN 0-8014-9146-0). Cornell U Pr.

Urang, Gunnar. Shadows of Heaven: Religion & Fantasy in the Writing of C. S. Lewis, Charles Williams & J. R. R. Tolkien. LC 73-153998. 208p. 1971. 7.95 (ISBN 0-8298-0197-9). Pilgrim NY.

FANTASY

Ahsen, Akhter. Psycheye. new ed. 288p. 1977. 12.95 (ISBN 0-913412-47-3). Brandon Hse.

Alter, Judy. Stewart Edward White. LC 75-7011. (Western Writers Ser.: No. 18). (Illus., Orig.). 1975. pap. text ed. 2.00 (ISBN 0-88430-017-X). Boise St Univ.

Carroll, Lewis & Tenniel, Sir John. Alice's Adventures in Wonderland. LC 77-77324. (Illus.). (gr. 5 up). 1977. 7.95 (ISBN 0-312-01821-5). St Martin.

Cazet, Denys. The Non-Coloring Book: A Drawing Book for Mind Stretching & Fantasy Building. 64p. 1973. pap. 3.50 (ISBN 0-88316-501-5). Chandler & Sharp.

Cooper, Susan. Silver on the Tree. LC 77-5361. 256p. (gr. 5-9). 1977. 9.95 (ISBN 0-689-50088-2, McElderry Bk). Atheneum.

Cox, Harvey. Feast of Fools: A Theological Essay on Festivity & Fantasy. LC 75-75914. (William Belden Noble Lectures Ser). 1969. 10.00x (ISBN 0-674-29525-0). Harvard U Pr.

Dally, Peter. The Fantasy Game: How Men's & Women's Sexual Fantasies Affect Our Lives. LC 74-31112. 252p. 1975. 25.00 (ISBN 0-8128-1790-7). Stein & Day.

Davidson, Audrey & Fay, Judith. Phantasy in Childhood. LC 77-38129. 188p. 1972. Repr. of 1952 ed. lib. bdg. 15.00x (ISBN 0-8371-6327-7, DAPH). Greenwood.

Featherman, Buzz. The Fun & Fantasy Book. LC 80-54612. (Illus.). 144p. (Orig.). 1981. pap. text ed. 5.95 (ISBN 0-932238-04-1). Word Shop.

--The Fun & Fantasy Book. new ed. (Illus.). cancelled (ISBN 0-932238-03-3). Word Shop.

Ferman, Edward L., ed. Fantasy & Science Fiction, April Nineteen Sixty-Five. (Alternatives Ser.). (Illus.). 160p. 1981. 16.95 (ISBN 0-8093-1007-4). S Ill U Pr.

Fisher, Paul. Mont Cant Gold. LC 80-23851. 264p. (gr. 5-9). 1981. PLB 10.95 (ISBN 0-689-30808-6, Argo). Atheneum.

Hook, R. H., ed. Fantasy & Symbol: Studies in Anthropological Interpretation. LC 78-67899. (Studies in Anthropology). 1980. 31.50 (ISBN 0-12-355480-2). Acad Pr.

Irwin, W. R. The Game of the Impossible: A Rhetoric of Fantasy. LC 76-13459. 220p. 1976. 14.95 (ISBN 0-252-00587-2). U of Ill Pr.

Johnson, David. Waterworks. LC 79-90852. (The Works). (Illus.). 48p. (Orig.). 1980. pap. 7.95 (ISBN 0-935342-00-1). Jalapeno Pr.

Jones, Diana W. Power of Three. LC 77-3028. (gr. 5-9). 1977. 8.25 (ISBN 0-688-80106-4); PLB 7.92 (ISBN 0-688-84106-6). Greenwillow.

Kolisko, Eugen. Memory & Phantasy. 1977. pap. 1.95x (ISBN 0-906492-07-6, Pub. by Kolisko Archives). St George Bk Serv.

Lanyon, Ellen. Transformations I: 1973-74. new ed. pap. 10.00 (ISBN 0-89439-005-8). Printed Matter.

Lee, Tanith. Companions on the Road. LC 76-62780. 1977. 8.95 (ISBN 0-312-15312-0). St Martin.

Leeming, David A. Flights: Readings in Magic, Mysticism, Fantasy & Myth. 384p. (Orig.). 1974. pap. text ed. 8.95 (ISBN 0-15-527556-9, HC). HarBraceJ.

Post, J. B. An Atlas of Fantasy. (Illus.). 1979. pap. 8.95 (ISBN 0-345-27399-0). Ballantine.

Rose, Alan H. Demonic Vision: Racial Fantasy & Southern Fiction. 1976. 17.50 (ISBN 0-208-01582-5, Archon). Shoe String.

Rottensteiner, Franz. The Fantasy Book: An Illustrated History from Dracula to Tolkien. 1978. pap. 7.95 (ISBN 0-02-053560-0, Collier). Macmillan.

Schlobin, Roger, ed. The Aesthetics of Fantasy Literature. LC 81-40446. 288p. 1982. text ed. 19.95 (ISBN 0-268-00598-2); pap. text ed. 7.95 (ISBN 0-268-00600-8). U of Notre Dame Pr.

Segal, Bernard, et al. Drugs, Daydreaming, & Personality: A Study of College Youth. LC 80-10094. 256p. 1980. 19.95x (ISBN 0-89859-042-6). L Erlbaum Assocs.

Sheikh, A. A. & Shaffer, John T. The Potential of Fantasy & Imagination. LC 79-88092. 1979. lib. bdg. 15.00 (ISBN 0-913412-31-7). Brandon Hse.

Silvestri, Richard. CT: The Astounding New Confrontation Therapy. LC 78-7302. 1978. 7.95 (ISBN 0-688-03352-0). Morrow.

Sime, Sidney & Holbrooke, Josef. Bogey Beasts. (Illus.). 1975. pap. 5.00 (ISBN 0-9603300-0-3). Purple Mouth.

Singer, Jerome. The Inner World of Daydreaming. 1976. pap. 3.45 (ISBN 0-06-090519-0, CN519, CN). Har-Row.

Singer, Jerome L. & Switzer, Ellen. Mind Play: The Creative Uses of Fantasy. 1980. 13.95 (ISBN 0-13-198069-6, Spec); pap. 4.95 (ISBN 0-13-198051-3, Spec). P-H.

Snyder, Zilpha K. Until the Celebration. LC 76-40984. (Illus.). (gr. 5-8). 1977. 7.95 (ISBN 0-689-30572-9). Atheneum.

Waggoner, Diane. The Hills of Faraway: A Guide to Fantasy. LC 76-900. 1978. 16.95 (ISBN 0-689-10846-X). Atheneum.

Watkins, Mary M. Waking Dreams. 1977. pap. 3.45 (ISBN 0-06-090586-7, CN586, CN). Har-Row.

--Waking Dreams. new ed. (Psychic Studies Ser.). 188p. 1976. 24.25x (ISBN 0-677-05100-X). Gordon.

Wheeler, Thomas G. Loose Chippings. LC 69-11990. (Illus.). (YA) 1969. 9.95 (ISBN 0-87599-152-1). S G Phillips.

Williams, Thomas. Tsuga's Children. 1977. 7.95 (ISBN 0-394-49731-7). Random.

Yolen, Jane. The Acorn Quest. LC 80-2755. (Illus.). 64p. (gr. 3-6). 1981. 8.95 (ISBN 0-690-04106-3, TYC-J); PLB 8.89 (ISBN 0-690-04107-1). Har-Row.

FANTI LANGUAGE

Welmers, William E. Descriptive Grammar of Fanti. 1946. pap. 6.00 (ISBN 0-527-00785-4). Kraus Repr.

FANTI LAW

see Law, Fanti

FANTIN-LATOUR, IGNACE HENRI JEAN THEODORE, 1836-1904

Fantin-Latour, Victoria. Catalogue De L'oeuve Comblet De Fantin Latour. (Graphic Art Ser.). 320p. (Fr.). 1970. Repr. of 1911 ed. 47.50 (ISBN 0-306-71924-X). Da Capo.

Verrier, Michelle. Fantin-Latour. (Illus.). 1978. pap. 6.95 (ISBN 0-517-53414-2, Harmony). Crown.

FANTIS

see also Akans (African People)

Kwame, Arhin, ed. The Papers of George Ekem Ferguson: A Fanti Official of the Government of the Gold Coast, 1890-1897. LC 75-321109. (African Social Research Documents: Vol. 7). 1974. pap. 13.50x (ISBN 0-8002-1780-2). Intl Pubns Serv.

FANTSI LANGUAGE

see also Fanti Language

FAO

see Food and Agriculture Organization of the United Nations

FAR EAST

see East (Far East)

FAR EASTERN QUESTION

see Eastern Question (Far East)

FARADAY, MICHAEL, 1791-1867

Agassi, Joseph. Faraday As a Natural Philosopher. LC 73-151130. 1972. 16.50x (ISBN 0-226-01046-5). U of Chicago Pr.

Jeffreys, Alan E. Michael Faraday: A List of His Lectures & Published Writings. 1961. 28.50 (ISBN 0-12-383050-8). Acad Pr.

Lipscomb, F. W. The Wise Men of the Wires: The History of Faraday House. (Illus.). 1973. text ed. 9.25x (ISBN 0-09-117060-5). Humanities.

Ludwig, Charles. Michael Faraday, Father of Electronics. LC 78-15028. 1978. 6.95 (ISBN 0-8361-1864-2). Herald Pr.

Morgan, B. Men & Discoveries in Electricity. (Illus.). (gr. 9 up). 6.95 (ISBN 0-7195-0943-2). Transatlantic.

Ronan, Colin. Faraday & Electricity. (Jackdaw Ser: No. S5). (Illus.). 1968. 6.95 (ISBN 0-670-30732-7, Grossman). Viking Pr.

Thompson, Silvanus P. Michael Faraday: His Life & Work. 2nd ed. Date not set. 12.95 (ISBN 0-8284-0311-2). Chelsea Pub.

--Michael Faraday: His Life & Work. LC 73-84764. (Illus.). ix, 308p. Date not set. Repr. of 1901 ed. cancelled (ISBN 0-8462-1748-1). Russell.

Tricker, R. A. Contributions of Faraday & Maxwell to Electrical Science. 1966. 23.00 (ISBN 0-08-011977-8); pap. 11.25 (ISBN 0-08-011976-X). Pergamon.

Veglahn, Nancy. Coils, Magnets & Rings: Michael Faraday's World. LC 76-14385. (Science Discovery Book). (Illus.). (gr. 2-6). 1976. 5.95 (ISBN 0-698-20384-4). Coward.

FARCE

see also Commedia Dell'Arte; Comedy Films

Davis, Jessica M. Farce. (The Critical Idiom Ser.). 1978. 12.95x (ISBN 0-416-81580-4); pap. 5.50 (ISBN 0-416-81590-1). Methuen Inc.

Hughes, Leo. A Century of English Farce. LC 79-13278. 1980. Repr. of 1956 ed. lib. bdg. 25.00x (ISBN 0-313-21993-1, HUCEF). Greenwood.

Rubsamen, Walter H., ed. Farce, Broad or Satirical. (The Ballad Opera Ser.). 1974. lib. bdg. 50.00 (ISBN 0-8240-0910-X). Garland Pub.

FARCES

see also french farces and similar headings

Inchbald, Elizabeth, ed. Collection of Farces & Other Afterpieces, 7 Vols. in 4. LC 67-13344. 1969. Repr. of 1809 ed. 100.00 (ISBN 0-405-08646-6, Pub. by Blom). Arno.

Zobel, K. Deutsche Schwanke. LC 75-140666. 1971. pap. text ed. 9.95 (ISBN 0-03-085565-9, HoltC). HR&W.

FARE, BILLS OF

see Menus

FARGUE, LEON PAUL, 1878-1947

Beucler, Andre. Last of the Bohemians: Twenty Years with Leon-Paul Fargue. Sainsbury, Geoffrey, tr. LC 79-108841. Repr. of 1954 ed. lib. bdg. 12.25x (ISBN 0-8371-3729-2, BEBO). Greenwood.

FARINACEOUS PRODUCTS

see Starch

FARM ANIMALS

see Domestic Animals

FARM BUILDINGS

see also Agricultural Engineering; Architecture, Domestic; Barns; Cottages; Livestock–Housing; Silos; Stables

Beyer, Glenn H. & Rose, J. Hugh. Farm Housing. LC 73-86719. (Census Monograph). (Illus.). xii, 194p. Date not set. Repr. of 1957 ed. cancelled (ISBN 0-8462-1762-7). Russell.

Boyd, James S. Practical Farm Buildings: A Text & Handbook. 2nd ed. LC 78-179872. 1979. 10.60 (ISBN 0-8134-2054-7, 2054). Interstate.

Cook, G. C. & Phipps, Lloyd J. Six Hundred More Things to Make for the Farm & Home. (Illus.). (gr. 9-12). 1952. 16.65 (ISBN 0-8134-0198-4). Interstate.

Cook, Glenn C. Five Hundred More Things to Make for Farm & Home. (Illus.). (gr. 9-12). 1944. 16.65 (ISBN 0-8134-0038-4). Interstate.

Halsted, Byron D., ed. Barns, Sheds & Outbuildings. LC 76-50020. (Illus.). 1977. Repr. of 1881 ed. 7.95 (ISBN 0-8289-0293-3). Greene.

Leavy, Herbert T. Successful Small Farms: Building Plans & Methods. LC 78-7987. 1978. 14.00 (ISBN 0-912336-67-6); pap. 7.95 (ISBN 0-912336-68-4). Structures Pub.

Lytle, R. J., et al. Farm Builders Handbook. 3rd rev. ed. LC 78-73354. (Illus.). 288p. 1978. 24.95 (ISBN 0-912336-75-7). Structures Pub.

Midwest Plan Service. Professional Design Supplement to the MWPS Structures & Environment Handbook. 5th ed. LC 77-24229. (Illus.). 1978. pap. text ed. 11.50 (ISBN 0-89373-037-8, MWPS-17). Midwest Plan Serv.

Orem, Howard & Snyder, Suzen. Country Land & Its Uses. LC 74-22154. (Illus.). 310p. 1975. 10.95 (ISBN 0-87961-031-X); pap. 6.95 (ISBN 0-87961-030-1). Naturegraph.

Peters, J. E. The Development of Farm Buildings. 298p. 1969. 35.00x (ISBN 0-7190-0386-5). State Mutual Bk.

Phillips, Richard E. Farm Buildings: From Planning to Completion. (Illus.). 350p. (Orig.). 1981. pap. 16.95 (ISBN 0-932250-12-2). Doane Agricultural.

Promersberger, William J., et al. Modern Farm Power. 2nd ed. 1971. text ed. 18.00 (ISBN 0-13-594630-1). P-H.

Radford, William. Practical Plans for Barns, Carriage, Stables, & Other Farm Buildings. LC 78-60318. 1978. pap. 8.95 (ISBN 0-912944-50-1). Berkshire Traveller.

Sloane, Eric. Age of Barns. LC 66-26946. (Funk & W Bk.). (Illus.). 1966. 16.95 (ISBN 0-308-70052-X). T Y Crowell.

Weller, John B. Farm Buildings: Foundations & Floors, Vol. 2. (Illus.). 200p. 1972. text ed. 18.95x (ISBN 0-8464-0402-8). Beekman Pubs.

Whitaker. Agricultural Buildings & Structures. (Illus.). 1979. text ed. 18.95 (ISBN 0-8359-0176-9); instrs'. manual avail. (ISBN 0-8359-0177-7). Reston.

FARM CORPORATIONS

see also Agricultural Laws and Legislation; Corporation Law; Corporations; Farm Management

Browning, Frank. The Vanishing Land: The Corporate Theft of America. 8.00 (ISBN 0-8446-5166-4). Peter Smith.

FARM CROPS

see Field Crops

FARM EQUIPMENT

see also Agricultural Engineering; Agricultural Implements; Agricultural Machinery

Cook, G. C. & Phipps, Lloyd J. Six Hundred More Things to Make for the Farm & Home. (Illus.). (gr. 9-12). 1952. 16.65 (ISBN 0-8134-0198-4). Interstate.

Cook, Glenn C. Five Hundred More Things to Make for Farm & Home. (Illus.). (gr. 9-12). 1944. 16.65 (ISBN 0-8134-0038-4). Interstate.

Field & Equipment Record Book. new ed. 1979. pap. 9.45 (ISBN 0-932250-07-6); ringed binder 15.95 (ISBN 0-686-77231-8). Doane Agricultural.

Jenkins, J. Geraint. The English Farm Wagon: Origins & Structure. (Illus.). 264p. 1981. 25.00 (ISBN 0-7153-8119-9). David & Charles.

Martin, George A., ed. Farm Equipment & Hand Tools: Yesterday's Devices for Today's Homesteader. LC 79-27074. (Illus.). 1980. 7.95 (ISBN 0-8289-0356-5). Greene.

Sloane, Eric. Diary of an Early American Boy. LC 62-18313. 1977. pap. 4.95 (ISBN 0-345-29451-3). Ballantine.

Society of Automotive Engineers. Historical Perspective of Farm Machinery. 1980. 12.50 (ISBN 0-89883-241-1). SAE.

FARM FORESTRY

see Wood-Lots

FARM IMPLEMENTS

see Agricultural Implements

FARM INCOME

see also Agricultural Prices

Ankli, Robert E. Gross Farm Revenue in Pre-Civil War Illinois. Bruchley, Stuart, ed. LC 76-39820. (Nineteen Seventy-Seven Dissertations Ser.). (Illus.). 1977. lib. bdg. 26.00x (ISBN 0-405-09901-0). Arno.

Brake, J. R., ed. Farm & Personal Finance. LC 68-13437. (gr. 9-12). 1968. pap. 3.50 (ISBN 0-8134-0115-1, 115). Interstate.
De Crevecoeur, St. John. Sketches of Eighteenth Century America. Boudin, H. L., et al, eds. LC 72-83505. Repr. of 1925 ed. 15.00 (ISBN 0-405-08406-4). Arno.
Hirsch, Eva. Poverty & Plenty on the Turkish Farm: An Economic Study of Turkish Agriculture in the 1950's. LC 75-136744. (Modern Middle East Ser.). 1970. pap. 15.00x (ISBN 0-231-03442-3). Columbia U Pr.
Johnson, D. Gale. Farm Commodity Programs: an Opportunity for Change. 1973. pap. 5.25 (ISBN 0-8447-3101-3). Am Enterprise.
Lang, Edith M. The Effects of Net Interregional Migration on Agricultural Income Growth: The United States, 1850-1860. LC 75-2585. (Dissertations in American Economic History). (Illus.). 1975. 15.00x (ISBN 0-405-07205-8). Arno.
O'Byrne, John C. Farm Income Tax Manual: 1980 Supplement for Use in 1981. 1980. 20.25 (ISBN 0-686-60284-6). A Smith Co.
Penson, John B., et al. Farm Investment & Financial Analysis. (Illus.). 336p. 1982. 24.95 (ISBN 0-13-305037-8). P-H.
Purcal, J. D. Rice Economy: Employment & Income in Malaysia. (Illus.). 1972. text ed. 10.00x (ISBN 0-8248-0103-2, Eastwest Ctr). U Pr of Hawaii.
U. S. National Commission on Food Marketing. Food from Farmer to Consumer. LC 75-39286. (Getting & Spending: the Consumer's Dilemma). (Illus.). 1976. Repr. of 1966 ed. 15.00x (ISBN 0-405-08052-2). Arno.

FARM LABORERS

see Agricultural Laborers

FARM LAW

see also Agricultural Laws and Legislation

Farm Policy Proposals: Legislative Analysis. 3.75 (ISBN 0-8447-0188-2). Am Enterprise.

FARM LIFE

see also Country Life; Farm Life in Literature; Rural Conditions; Rural Youth; Sociology, Rural

Barnes, Margaret A. The Buzzard Is My Best Friend. LC 81-8170. 356p. 1981. 11.95 (ISBN 0-02-507260-9). Macmillan.
Bennet, John W. Of Time & Enterprise: North American Family Farm Management in a Context of Resource Marginality. (Illus.). 384p. 1981. 32.50x (ISBN 0-8166-1051-7). U of Minn Pr.
Berry, Romeyn. Stoneposts in the Sunset. 1950. 6.00 (ISBN 0-87282-011-4). Century Hse.
Bohlen, James. The New Pioneer's Handbook: Gettting Back to the Land in an Energy-Scarce World. LC 75-7767. (Illus.). 256p. 1975. 8.95x (ISBN 0-8052-3591-4); pap. 4.95 (ISBN 0-8052-0581-0). Schocken.
Brown, Margaret D. Shepherdess of Elk River Valley. 2nd ed. (Illus.). 1967. 4.75 (ISBN 0-87315-037-6). Golden Bell.
Bruyere, Christain & Inwood, Robert. In Harmony with Nature. LC 74-22581. (Illus.). 200p. 1979. pap. 7.95 (ISBN 0-8069-8432-5). Sterling.
Caffey, David L. The Old Home Place: Farming on the West Texas Frontier. (Illus.). 224p. 1981. 11.95 (ISBN 0-89015-283-7). Eakin Pubns.
Caldwell, Erskine & Bourke-White, Margaret. You Have Seen Their Faces. facsimile ed. McCurry, Dan C. & Rubenstein, Richard E., eds. LC 74-30622. (American Farmers & the Rise of Agribusiness Ser.). (Illus., With a new introductory note by Erskine Caldwell). 1975. Repr. of 1937 ed. 15.00x (ISBN 0-405-06769-0). Arno.
Clift, William. Tim Bunker Papers Or, Yankee Farming. facs. ed. LC 72-137727. (American Fiction Reprint Ser). 1868. 18.00 (ISBN 0-8369-7026-8). Arno.
Commission on Country Life. Report of the Commission on Country Life. facsimile ed. McCurry, Dan C. & Rubenstein, Richard E., eds. LC 74-30625. (American Farmers & the Rise of Agribusiness Ser.). 1975. Repr. of 1911 ed. 12.00x (ISBN 0-405-06787-9). Arno.
Conrat, Maisie & Conrat, Richard. The American Farm: A Photographic History. (Illus.). 1977. 17.50 (ISBN 0-395-25105-2); pap. 9.95 (ISBN 0-395-25359-4). HM.
Cook, G. C. & Phipps, Lloyd J. Six Hundred More Things to Make for the Farm & Home. (Illus.). (gr. 9-12). 1952. 16.65 (ISBN 0-8134-0198-4). Interstate.
Creaton, David. The Beasts of My Fields. 1978. pap. 1.95 (ISBN 0-380-38497-3, 38497). Avon.
Crow, Martha F. The American Country Girl. LC 74-3936. (Women in America Ser). (Illus.). 398p. 1974. Repr. of 1915 ed. 23.00x (ISBN 0-405-06083-1). Arno.
Davis, John C. The Furrows of Freedom. LC 61-11032. pap. 3.25 (ISBN 0-912806-14-1). Long Hse.
Edgerton, Wanda M. Our Home Place. (Illus.). 1977. softcover 5.50 (ISBN 0-686-22841-3). Pine Hill Pr.
Farm Journal Editors & Larson, Kathryn, eds. Listen to the Land: A Farm Journal Treasury. 1978. lib. bdg. 13.50 (ISBN 0-8161-6574-2, Large Print Bks). G K Hall.
Flaten, Essye Price. Our Farm Years. 1981. 5.00 (ISBN 0-682-49737-1). Exposition.
Follett, Muriel. New England Year: A Journal of Vermont Farm Life. LC 73-145711. 1971. Repr. of 1939 ed. 19.00 (ISBN 0-8103-3393-7). Gale.
Forpe, Will. The Best of the Old Farmer's Almanac. (Illus.). 1977. 12.95 (ISBN 0-8246-0209-9). Jonathan David.
Hall, Donald. String Too Short to Be Saved. 1980. lib. bdg. 11.95 (ISBN 0-8161-3086-8, Large Print Bks). G K Hall.
Hewes, Leslie. The Suitcase Farming Frontier: A Study in the Historical Geography of the Central Great Plains. LC 72-85031. xviii, 281p. 1973. 17.95x (ISBN 0-8032-0825-1). U of Nebr Pr.
Janney, John J. John Jay Janney's Virginia: An American Farm Lad's Life in the Early 19th Century. Janney, Asa M. & Janney, Werner L., eds. LC 78-23319. (Illus.). 1978. pap. 5.95 (ISBN 0-914440-25-X). EPM Pubns.
Johnson, Jerry M. Country Scrapbook. 1978. 16.95 (ISBN 0-671-22848-X); pap. 5.95 (ISBN 0-671-22895-1). S&S.
Johnson, Mary E., ed. Times Down Home. LC 78-59619. (Illus.). 1978. 17.95 (ISBN 0-8487-0491-6). Oxmoor Hse.
Ketchum, Richard M. Second Cutting: Letters from the Country. LC 81-50516. (Illus.). 192p. 1981. 11.95 (ISBN 0-670-42588-5). Viking Pr.
Kirkpatrick, Ellis L. Farmer's Standard of Living. LC 75-137173. (Poverty U.S.A. Historical Record Ser). 1971. Repr. of 1929 ed. 19.00 (ISBN 0-405-03112-2). Arno.
Lange, Dorothea & Taylor, Paul S. An American Exodus: A Record of Human Erosion. facsimile ed. LC 74-30641. (American Farmers & the Rise of Agribusiness Ser.). (Illus.). 1975. Repr. of 1939 ed. 15.00x (ISBN 0-405-06811-5). Arno.
Leatherbarrow, Margaret. Gold in the Grass. Bargyla & Rateaver, Gylver, eds. LC 75-23179. (Conservation Gardening & Farming Ser: Ser. C). 1975. pap. 10.00 (ISBN 0-9600698-8-7). Rateavers.
Leimbach, Patricia. A Thread of Blue Denim. LC 73-22451. (Illus.). 240p. 1974. 10.95 (ISBN 0-13-920280-3). P-H.
Leimbach, Patricia P. All My Meadows. LC 77-24352. (Illus.). 1977. 9.95 (ISBN 0-13-022525-8). P-H.
Logan, Ben. The Land Remembers. 1976. pap. 1.75 (ISBN 0-380-00663-4, 27714). Avon.
--The Land Remembers: The Story of a Farm & Its People. LC 74-6565. 320p. 1975. 8.95 (ISBN 0-670-41761-0). Viking Pr.
Logsdon, Gene. Two Acre Eden. (Illus.). 1980. 8.95 (ISBN 0-87857-290-2); pap. 5.95 (ISBN 0-87857-308-9). Rodale Pr Inc.
Longwell, Maude, ed. This Way of Life. LC 72-97091. 1977. pap. 4.95x (ISBN 0-89795-002-X). Farm Journal.
McCurry, Dan C. & Rubenstein, Richard E., eds. American Farmers & the Rise of Agribusiness: Seeds of Struggle, 46 bks. 1975. Set. 1200.00 (ISBN 0-405-06760-7). Arno.
MacDonald, Betty. Egg & I. LC 45-336. 1963. 10.95 (ISBN 0-397-00279-3). Har-Row.
McKenzie, Scotty & Goode, Ruth. My Love Affair with the State of Maine. 1977. pap. 4.95 (ISBN 0-685-80278-7). Durrell.
McMillen, Wheeler. Ohio Farm. LC 74-12216. (Illus.). 1974. 11.00 (ISBN 0-8142-0217-9). Ohio St U Pr.
Mungo, Raymond. Total Loss Farm: A Year in the Life. LC 73-125905. 1977. pap. 5.95 (ISBN 0-914842-16-1). Madrona Pubs.
Pearson, Jeffrey & Pearson, Jessica. No Time but Place. (Illus.). 256p. 1980. 16.95 (ISBN 0-07-049030-9). McGraw.
Perrin, Noel. First Person Rural: Essays of a Sometime Farmer. (Illus.). 1980. pap. 3.95 (ISBN 0-14-005561-4). Penguin.
--Second Person Rural: More. 1981. pap. 3.95 (ISBN 0-14-005920-2). Penguin.
Poortvliet, Rien. The Farm Book. (Illus.). 240p. 1980. 18.50 (ISBN 0-686-62683-4, 0817-4) (ISBN 0-686-62684-2). Abrams.
Rebarchek, Ray. Memoirs of an Alaskan Farmer. LC 79-56330. 1981. 8.95 (ISBN 0-533-04526-6). Vantage.
Redfield, Malissa. Scenes from Country Life. LC 78-31856. 1979. 8.95 (ISBN 0-13-791632-9). P-H.
Rhoads, Bert. Bickie's Cow College. 1980. pap. 2.95 (ISBN 0-8280-0042-5). Review & Herald.
Seim, Richard K. The American Farmer. LC 74-13903. (Illus.). 192p. 1974. pap. 5.95 (ISBN 0-528-88169-8). Rand.
Seymour, John. The Fat of the Land. (Illus.). 176p. (Orig.). 1974. pap. 5.95 (ISBN 0-571-10532-7, Pub. by Faber & Faber). Merrimack Bk Serv.
Seymour, John & Seymour, Sally. Farming for Self-Sufficiency: Independence on a Five-Acre Farm. LC 73-81834. (Illus.). 256p. 1976. pap. 5.50 (ISBN 0-8052-0510-1). Schocken.
Sifford, Darrell. A Love of the Land. LC 80-18379. (Illus.). 288p. 1980. 11.95 (ISBN 0-89795-010-0). Farm Journal.
Simons, A. M. The American Farmer. facsimile ed. LC 74-30652. (American Farmers & the Rise of Agribusiness Ser.). 1975. Repr. of 1903 ed. 14.00x (ISBN 0-405-06828-X). Arno.
Slaughter, Steven S. History of a Missouri Farm Family: The O. V. Slaughters, 1700-1944. LC 78-9549. (Illus.). 1978. 15.00 (ISBN 0-916346-27-7). Harbor Hill Bks.
Sloane, Eric. Diary of an Early American Boy. LC 62-18313. 1977. pap. 4.95 (ISBN 0-345-29451-3). Ballantine.
--Seasons of America Past. LC 58-11350. (Funk & W Bk.). (gr. 9-12). text ed. 10.95 (ISBN 0-308-70049-X). T Y Crowell.
Sneller, Anne G. Vanished World. LC 64-16923. (Illus.). 1964. 6.00 (ISBN 0-8156-0037-2). Syracuse U Pr.
Starr, Fred. Of These Hills and Us. 1958. 3.95 (ISBN 0-8158-0284-6). Chris Mass.
Taylor, Henry C. Tarpleywick: A Century of Iowa Farming. LC 70-103840. (Illus.). 1970. 4.95 (ISBN 0-8138-1690-4). Iowa St U Pr.
Thomas, Sherry. We Didn't Have Much but We Sure Had Plenty: Stories of Rural Women. LC 80-956. (Illus.). 208p. 1981. pap. 7.95 (ISBN 0-385-14951-4, Anch). Doubleday.
U.S. Department of Agriculture. Yearbook of Agriculture, 1940: Farmers in a Changing World. LC 75-26320. (Illus.). 1976. Repr. of 1940 ed. 70.00x (ISBN 0-405-07796-3). Arno.
Walker, Diana. The Hundred Thousand Dollar Farm. LC 76-44320. (gr. 5 up). 1977. 7.95 (ISBN 0-200-00170-1, AbS-J). Har-Row.
Williams, James M. Expansion of Rural Life. LC 72-1292. (Select Bibliographies Reprints Ser.). 1972. Repr. of 1926 ed. 20.00 (ISBN 0-8369-6841-7). Arno.
Woofter, Thomas Jackson & Winston, Ellen E. Seven Lean Years. LC 79-39479. (FDR & the Era of the New Deal Ser). 1972. Repr. of 1939 ed. lib. bdg. 20.00 (ISBN 0-306-70463-3). Da Capo.

FARM LIFE–JUVENILE LITERATURE

Battaglia, Aurelius, illus. A Farm. LC 77-83860. (A Pandaback Book). (Illus.). (gr. 1-3). 1978. pap. 0.95 (ISBN 0-448-49605-4). Platt.
Behrens, June & Brower, Pauline. Colonial Farm. LC 75-28292. (Living Heritage Ser.). (Illus.). 32p. (gr. 1-4). 1976. PLB 9.25 (ISBN 0-516-08718-5, Golden Gate). Childrens.
Demuth, Patricia. Joel: Growing up on Farm Man. (Illus.). 96p. (gr. 4-7). 1981. PLB 8.95 (ISBN 0-396-07997-0). Dodd.
Evans, George E. The Farm & the Village. (Illus.). 182p. (gr. 5 up). 1969. (Pub. by Faber & Faber); pap. 4.95 (ISBN 0-571-10551-3). Merrimack Bk Serv.
Humphrey, Henry. The Farm. LC 76-23768. (gr. 1-3). 1978. 6.95a (ISBN 0-385-01388-4); PLB (ISBN 0-385-03447-4). Doubleday.
Ingle, Annie. The Big Farm Book. (Illus.). 72p. (gr. k-2). 1976. 4.95 (ISBN 0-448-47617-7). Platt.
Pfloog, Jan. The Farm Book. (ps-1). 1964. PLB 5.38 (ISBN 0-307-68905-0, Golden Pr). Western Pub.
Rudstrom, Lennart & Larsson, Carl. A Farm. LC 76-2130. (Illus.). (gr. 3 up). 1976. 7.95 (ISBN 0-399-20541-1). Putnam.

FARM LIFE–AFRICA

Loudon, J. B. White Farmers, Black Labourers. 136p. (Orig.). 1970. pap. 8.50x (ISBN 90-701-1001-6). Intl Pubns Serv.

FARM LIFE–ENGLAND

Coleman, Roger. Downland: A Farm & a Village. Larkin, David, ed. LC 81-50433. (Illus.). 144p. 1981. 19.95 (ISBN 0-670-28116-6, Studio). Viking Pr.
Fussell, G. E. & Fussell, K. R. The English Country Woman: A Farmhouse Social History A.D. 1500-1900. LC 73-174864. (Illus.). Repr. of 1953 ed. 22.00 (ISBN 0-405-08543-5, Blom Pubns). Arno.
Lacey, Roy. Cowpasture: The Every Day Life of an English Allotment. LC 79-56041. (Illus.). 1980. 17.95 (ISBN 0-7153-7916-X). David & Charles.

FARM LIFE–RUSSIA

Kataev, Valentin. The Small Farm in the Steppe. Bostock, Anna, tr. from Russ. LC 74-10362. 1976. Repr. of 1958 ed. lib. bdg. 17.75x (ISBN 0-8371-7674-3, KASF). Greenwood.

FARM LIFE–THAILAND

Anuman, Rajadhon Phraya. Life & Ritual in Old Siam: Three Studies of Thai Life & Customs. Gedney, William J., ed. LC 78-23833. (Illus.). 1979. Repr. of 1961 ed. lib. bdg. 18.75x (ISBN 0-313-21193-0, ARLF). Greenwood.

FARM LIFE CLUBS

see Agricultural Societies

FARM LIFE IN ART

Harkonen, Helen B. Farms & Farmers in Art. LC 64-8204. (Fine Art Books). (Illus.). (gr. 5-11). 1965. PLB 4.95 (ISBN 0-8225-0152-X). Lerner Pubns.
McManigal, J. W. & Heilman, Grant. Farm Town: A Memoir of the Nineteen Thirties. LC 73-86031. (Illus.). 100p. 1974 (ISBN 0-8289-0205-4). pap. 7.95 (ISBN 0-8289-0204-6). Greene.
Wyeth, Betsy J. Wyeth at Kuerners. 1976. 75.00 (ISBN 0-395-21990-6). HM.

FARM LIFE IN LITERATURE

Williams, Merryn. Thomas Hardy & Rural England. LC 72-318. 1972. 17.50x (ISBN 0-231-03674-4). Columbia U Pr.

FARM MACHINERY

see Agricultural Machinery

FARM MANAGEMENT

see also Agriculture–Safety Measures; Farm Corporations; Farm Mechanization

Adams, R. L. Farm Manegement Crop Manual. 1981. 25.00x (ISBN 0-686-76636-9, Pub. by Oxford & IBH India). State Mutual Bk.
Allaby, Michael. Making & Managing a Small Holding. LC 79-51103. (Making & Managing Ser.). (Illus.). 1980. 17.95 (ISBN 0-7153-7803-1). David & Charles.
Angier, Bradford. One Acre & Security: How to Live off the Earth Without Ruining It. 1973. pap. 3.95 (ISBN 0-394-71963-8, Vin). Random.
Barnard, C. S. & Nix, J. S. Farm Planning & Control. 2nd ed. LC 79-10572. 1980. 72.50 (ISBN 0-521-22658-9); pap. 23.95x (ISBN 0-521-29604-8). Cambridge U Pr.
Beneke, Raymond R. & Winterboer, Ronald D. Linear Programming Applications to Agriculture. LC 72-2298. (Illus.). 251p. 1973. text ed. 12.95 (ISBN 0-8138-1035-3). Iowa St U Pr.
Bennet, John W. Of Time & Enterprise: North American Family Farm Management in a Context of Resource Marginality. (Illus.). 384p. 1981. 32.50x (ISBN 0-8166-1051-7). U of Minn Pr.
Boy Scouts of America. Farm & Ranch Management. (Illus.). 32p. (gr. 6-12). 1980. pap. 0.70x (ISBN 0-8395-3348-9, 3348). BSA.
Buckett, M. Introduction to Farm Organization & Managements. (Illus.). 280p. Date not set. 50.00 (ISBN 0-08-024433-5); pap. 21.00 (ISBN 0-08-024432-7). Pergamon.
Castle, Emory N. & Becker, Manning H. Farm Business Management: The Decision-Making Process. 2nd ed. (Illus.). 320p. 1972. text ed. 19.95 (ISBN 0-02-320250-5, 32025). Macmillan.
Chessmore, Roy A. Profitable Pasture Management. LC 78-70056. 1979. 13.95 (ISBN 0-8134-2056-3, 2056). Interstate.
Christian, Portia, ed. Agricultural Enterprises Management in an Urban-Industrial Society: A Guide to Information Sources. LC 76-27856. (Management Information Guide: No. 34). 1978. 30.00 (ISBN 0-8103-0834-7). Gale.
Connor, Larry J., et al. Managing Farm Business. (Illus.). 384p. 1981. text ed. 18.95 (ISBN 0-13-550376-0). P-H.
Country Magazine Eds., ed. How to Save Money on the Farm. Date not set. pap. 7.50x (ISBN 0-392-08166-0, ABC). Sportshelf.
Crawford, Patricia. Homesteading. 224p. 1976. pap. 3.95 (ISBN 0-02-064820-0, Collier). Macmillan.
Davis, John C. The Furrows of Freedom. LC 61-11032. pap. 3.25 (ISBN 0-912806-14-1). Long Hse.
Do It Right the First Time: A Guide to Successful Farm Business & Arrangements. (Illus.). 1978. pap. 7.95 (ISBN 0-932250-03-3). Doane Agricultural.
Farm Level Water Management in Selected Asian Countries. 159p. 1980. pap. 13.25 (ISBN 92-833-1461-1, APO 88, APO). Unipub.
Farm Management by Banks. 48p. 1971. 3.50 (ISBN 0-89982-038-7, 044000). Am Bankers.
Farm Management Data Collection & Analysis. (FAO Agriculture Services Bulletin Ser.: No. 34). 1978. pap. 7.00 (ISBN 92-5-100464-1, F1366, FAO). Unipub.
Farm Management Research for Small Farmer Development. (FAO Agricultural Services Bulletin: No. 41). 145p. 1981. pap. 10.00 (ISBN 92-5-100822-1, F2119, FAO). Unipub.
Farm Planning in the Early Stages of Development. (Agricultural Services Bulletin: No. 1). 106p. 1968. pap. 6.00 (ISBN 0-686-70622-6, F1971, FAO). Unipub.
Farmers Weekly, ed. Farm Workshop & Maintenance. (Illus.). 192p. 1972. text ed. 15.95x (ISBN 0-8464-0404-4). Beekman Pubs.
Forster, D. Lynn & Erven, Bernard L. Foundations for Managing the Farm Business. LC 80-20832. (Agricultural Economics Ser.). 320p. 1981. text ed. 23.00 (ISBN 0-88244-230-9). Grid Pub.

Giles, Tony & Stansfield, Malcolm. The Farmer As Manager. (Illus., Orig.). 1980. text ed. 22.50x (ISBN 0-04-658228-2); pap. text ed. 10.50x (ISBN 0-04-658229-0). Allen Unwin.

Herbst, John. Farm Management: Principles, Plan. Budgets. 1980. pap. text ed. 9.80x (ISBN 0-87563-182-7). Stipes.

Howell, H. B. Better Farm Accounting. 4th ed. 1981. pap. 1.20 (ISBN 0-8138-0180-X); depreciation schedules 0.30 ea. (ISBN 0-8138-0181-8). Iowa St U Pr.

Hunt, Robert L. Farm Management in the South. (Illus.). (gr. 9-12). 1953. 6.75 (ISBN 0-8134-0028-7). Interstate.

James, Sydney C., ed. Midwest Farm Planning Manual. 4th ed. (Illus.). 1979. pap. text ed. 16.95 (ISBN 0-8138-1101-5). Iowa St U Pr.

Kains, M. G. Five Acres & Independence. (Illus.). 401p. 1973. pap. 3.95 (ISBN 0-486-20974-1). Dover.

--Five Acres & Independence: A Practical Guide to the Selection & Management of the Small Farm. rev. & enl. ed. (Illus.). 8.00 (ISBN 0-8446-4761-6). Peter Smith.

Kay, Ronald D. Farm & Ranch Management. Vastyan, James E., ed. (Agricultural Sciences Publications). (Illus.). 384p. Date not set. text ed. 15.95 (ISBN 0-07-033462-5, C). McGraw.

Levitt, Paul & Guralnick, Elissa. The ABC's of Farm Estate Planning. 112p. (Orig.). 1981. pap. write for info. (ISBN 0-932250-14-9). Doane Agricultural.

Luening, R. A. & Mortenson, W. P. Farm Management Handbook. 6th ed. (Illus.). (gr. 9-12). 1979. 18.00 (ISBN 0-8134-2082-2, 2082). Interstate.

Management Training for Agricultural & Food Marketing. 1978. pap. 7.50 (ISBN 92-5-100546-X, F1375, FAO). Unipub.

Methods of Farm Management Investigations. 258p. 1965. pap. 27.75 (ISBN 92-5-101016-1, F2154, FAO). Unipub.

Minneman, Paul G. Large Land Holdings in Ohio & Their Operation. Bruchey, Stuart, ed. LC 78-56664. (Management of Public Lands in the U. S. Ser.). 1979. lib. bdg. 13.00x (ISBN 0-405-11344-7). Arno.

Nash, M. J. Crop Conservation & Storage. LC 77-30345. 1978. text ed. 75.00 (ISBN 0-08-021137-2); pap. text ed. 19.75 (ISBN 0-08-023762-2). Pergamon.

Osburn, Donald O. & Schneeberger, Kenneth C. Modern Agriculture Management. 1978. 17.95 (ISBN 0-87909-495-8); instrs'. manual avail. Reston.

Rae, Allan N. Crop Management Economics. LC 76-55129. 1977. 17.95 (ISBN 0-312-17657-0). St Martin.

Ruthenberg, Hans. Farming Systems in the Tropics. 3rd ed. 400p. 1980. 89.00x (ISBN 0-19-859481-X). Oxford U Pr.

Scarborough, William K. Overseer: Plantation Management in the Old South. LC 66-17216. (Illus.). 1966. 17.50x (ISBN 0-8071-0732-8). La State U Pr.

Schneeberger, Kenneth C. & Osburn, Donald D. Farm Management Manual: A Guide for Classroom & Contest Training. 1978. pap. 4.95x (ISBN 0-8134-1967-0, 1967). Interstate.

Smith, Irving D., ed. Doane's Farm Management Guide. 14th ed. LC 79-56892. (Illus.). 1980. pap. 8.95 (ISBN 0-932250-09-2). Doane Agricultural.

Sublett, Michael W. Farmers on the Road. LC 75-8522. (Research Papers Ser.: No. 168). (Illus.). 1975. pap. 8.00 (ISBN 0-89065-075-6). U Chicago Dept Geog.

Upton, Martin. Farm Management in Africa: The Principles of Production & Planning. 1973. 47.50x (ISBN 0-19-215646-2). Oxford U Pr.

Van Elderen, E. Heuristic Strategy for Job Scheduling of Farm Operations. (Simulation Monographs). 1977. pap. 18.00 (ISBN 90-220-0612-3, Pub. by PUDOC). Unipub.

Welsch, Delane E., et al. The Account Book: For Farm & Ranch Management. 5th ed. 1978. spiral bdg. 6.95x (ISBN 0-8087-2368-5). Burgess.

FARM MANAGEMENT–MATHEMATICAL MODELS

Dillon, John L. The Analysis of Response in Crop & Livestock Production. 2nd ed. 1977. text ed. 26.00 (ISBN 0-08-021118-6); pap. text ed. 12.75 (ISBN 0-08-021115-1). Pergamon.

Heady, Earl O. & Dillon, John. Agricultural Production Functions. fasc. ed. 1961. pap. text ed. 22.00x (ISBN 0-8138-2250-5). Iowa St U Pr.

FARM MANAGEMENT–STUDY AND TEACHING

Population Concepts in Farm Management Courses. 32p. 1978. pap. 7.50 (ISBN 92-5-100471-4, F1333, FAO). Unipub.

FARM MANAGEMENT RESEARCH

Agrawal, R. C. & Heady, Earl O. Operations Research Methods for Agricultural Decisions. (Illus.). 1972. 10.95x (ISBN 0-8138-1200-3). Iowa St U Pr.

Social Science Research Council, et al. Farm Management Research, Nineteen Forty-Nineteen Forty One. LC 44-4129. 1943. pap. 2.00 (ISBN 0-527-03281-6). Kraus Repr.

FARM MECHANICS

see Agricultural Engineering

FARM MECHANIZATION

see also Agricultural Machinery; Electricity in Agriculture; Machine-Tractor Stations

Berry, Wendell. The Unsettling of America. 1978. pap. 5.95 (ISBN 0-380-40147-9, 50922). Avon.

Clements, Harold M., Sr. Mechanization of Agriculture in Brazil: A Sociological Study of Minas Gerais. LC 76-93194. (Latin American Monographs: Ser. 2, No. 7). (Illus.). 1969. 7.50 (ISBN 0-8130-0281-8). U Presses Fla.

Culpin, Claude. Profitable Farm Mechanization. 3rd ed. (Illus.). 336p. 1975. text ed. 24.95x (ISBN 0-8464-0037-5). Beekman Pubs.

Mechanisation & Employment in Agriculture: Case Studies from Four Continents. 2nd ed. 1974. 8.55 (ISBN 92-2-101009-0). Intl Labour Office.

Meij, J. L. Mechanization in Agriculture. 1960. 47.50x (ISBN 0-686-50048-2). Elliots Bks.

Street, James H. New Revolution in the Cotton Economy: Mechanization & Its Consequences. LC 57-2545. Repr. of 1957 ed. 24.00 (ISBN 0-384-58640-6). Johnson Repr.

FARM PRODUCE

see also Field Crops; Food Industry and Trade; Produce Trade; Surplus Agricultural Commodities

Agricultural Commodities: Projections for 1970. (Suppl. to FAO Commodity Review, 1962). 1963. pap. 9.25 (ISBN 0-685-36268-X, F 6, FAO). Unipub.

Benedict, M. R. The Agricultural Commodity Programs, Two Decades of Experience. (Twentieth Century Fund Ser.). Repr. of 1956 ed. 6.00 (ISBN 0-527-02815-0). Kraus Repr.

Boone, L. V., et al, eds. Producing Farm Crops. 3rd ed. 1980. 16.65 (ISBN 0-8134-2151-9). Interstate.

FAO Agricultural Commodity Projections, 1975-1985. (FAO Economic & Social Development Ser.: No. 16). 128p. 1980. pap. 12.25 (ISBN 92-5-100778-0, F1836, FAO). Unipub.

Farm Policy Proposals: Legislative Analysis. 3.75 (ISBN 0-8447-0188-2). Am Enterprise.

Food Legumes: Distribution, Adaptability & Biology of Yield. (FAO Plant Production & Protection Paper: No. 3). 1977. pap. 8.50 (ISBN 92-5-100186-3, F1067, FAO). Unipub.

Heat & Mass Transfer During Cooling & Storage of Agricultural Products As Influenced by Natural Convection. 158p. 1980. pap. 32.50 (ISBN 90-220-0728-6, PDC 208, Pudoc). Unipub.

McFall, Jane B., ed. Agricultural Commodities Index: Ready-Reference Index to USDA Statistical Ser. LC 78-59614. 1978. lib. bdg. 95.00x (ISBN 0-912700-09-2). Oryx Pr.

Nash, M. J. Crop Conservation & Storage. LC 77-30345. 1978. text ed. 75.00 (ISBN 0-08-021137-2); pap. text ed. 19.75 (ISBN 0-08-023762-2). Pergamon.

OECD. The Instability of Agricultural Commodity Markets. (Agricultural Products & Markets Ser.). (Illus.). 237p. 1980. pap. text ed. 9.50x (ISBN 92-64-12041-6, 51-80-03-1). OECD.

Post-Harvest Food Crop Conservation: Association of Consulting Scientists Symposium on Post-Harvest Food Crop Conservaion, Harrogate, 13-15 November, 1979. (Progress in Food & Nutrition Ser.: Vol. 4). (Illus.). 138p. 1980. 40.00 (ISBN 0-08-025907-3). Pergamon.

Youtz, H. & Carlson, A. Judging Livestock, Dairy Cattle, Poultry & Crops. 2nd ed. 1970. text ed. 21.04 (ISBN 0-13-511717-8). P-H.

FARM PRODUCE–MARKETING

Here are entered works on the marketing of farm produce from the point of view of the farmer.

see also Field Crops; Food Industry and Trade; Produce Trade; Roadside Marketing; Surplus Agricultural Commodities;

also subdivision Marketing under specific commodities, e.g. Eggs–Marketing

Abbott, J. C. & Creupelandt, H. C. Agricultural Marketing Boards: Their Establishment & Operation. (FAO Marketing Guides: No. 5). 1969. pap. 14.25 (ISBN 0-685-02459-8, F 14, FAO). Unipub.

Adams, Arthur B. Marketing Perishable Farm Products. LC 70-76718. (Columbia University Studies in the Social Sciences: No. 170). Repr. of 1916 ed. 17.50 (ISBN 0-404-51170-8). AMS Pr.

Agricultural Cooperative Marketing. (FAO Economic & Social Development Ser: No. 8). 1955. pap. 7.25 (ISBN 92-5-100477-3, F1460, FAO). Unipub.

Assessment & Collection of Data on Post-Harvest Foodgrain Losses. (FAO Economic & Social Development Paper: No. 13). 71p. 1981. pap. 7.50 (ISBN 92-5-100934-1, F2072, FAO). Unipub.

Beals, Ralph L. The Peasant Marketing System of Oaxaca, Mexico. LC 73-76098. 1975. 34.50x (ISBN 0-520-02435-4). U of Cal Pr.

Bibliography of Food & Agricultural Marketing. (Second Ser: No. 3). 1978. pap. 8.25 (ISBN 92-5-100248-7, F726, FAO). Unipub.

Bolsen, Barbara & Petty, Roy. The Chicagoland Bounty Book. 1978. pap. 5.95 (ISBN 0-8092-7505-8). Contemp Bks.

Breimyer, Harold F. Economics of the Product Markets of Agriculture. (Illus.). 280p. 1976. text ed. 12.95x (ISBN 0-8138-1840-0). Iowa St U Pr.

Deupree, Robert G. The Wholesale Marketing of Fruits & Vegetables in Baltimore. LC 78-64175. (Johns Hopkins University. Studies in the Social Sciences. Fifty-Seventh Ser. 1939: 2). Repr. of 1939 ed. 16.00 (ISBN 0-404-61284-9). AMS Pr.

Dubov, Irving, ed. Contemporary Agricultural Marketing. LC 67-29414. 1968. 13.50x (ISBN 0-87049-082-6). U of Tenn Pr.

FAO Commodity Review & Outlook, 1975-1976. (Illus.). 1976. pap. 18.00 (ISBN 92-5-100054-9, FAO). Unipub.

Farm Sales & Pick Your Own. 1981. 15.00x (ISBN 0-686-75412-3, Pub. by Grower Bks). State Mutual Bk.

Farm Sales & Pick Your Own. 91p. 1980. pap. 9.95 (ISBN 0-901361-28-3, Pub. by Grower Bks England). Intl Schol Bk Serv.

Farmers Markets of America: A Renaissance. Sommer, Robert. (Illus.). 96p. 1980. pap. 6.95 (ISBN 0-88496-150-8). Capra Pr.

Farmers Weekly. Farmhouse Fare. pap. 5.95x (ISBN 0-392-06210-0, LTB). Sportshelf.

Farris, Paul L., ed. Market Structure Research. facs. ed. 1964. pap. 11.00x (ISBN 0-8138-2270-X). Iowa St U Pr.

Finney, Essex E., Jr., ed. Handbook of Transportation & Marketing in Agriculture, Vol. II: Field Crops. (CRC Ser. in Agriculture). 416p. 1981. 59.95 (ISBN 0-8493-3852-2). CRC Pr.

--Handbook of Transportation & Marketing in Agriculture: Volume 1: Food Commodities. 384p. 1981. 59.95 (ISBN 0-8493-3851-4). CRC Pr.

Hallett, Graham & James, Gwyn. Farming for Consumers. (Institute of Economic Affairs, Hobart Papers Ser.: No. 22). (Illus., Orig.). 1969. pap. 2.50 (ISBN 0-685-20583-5). Transatlantic.

International Conference on Marketing Systems for Developing Countries. Agricultural Marketing for Developing Countries: Proceedings, Vol. 2. Izaeli, D. N. & Messner, F., eds. 1977. 43.95 (ISBN 0-470-15095-5). Halsted Pr.

--Marketing Systems for Developing Countries: Proceedings, Vol. 1. Izraeli, D. N. & Messner, F., eds. LC 76-8243. 1977. 38.95 (ISBN 0-470-15094-7). Halsted Pr.

Kohls, Richard L. & Uhl, Joseph N. The Marketing of Agriculture Products. 5th ed. (Illus.). 1980. text ed. 22.95 (ISBN 0-02-365640-9). Macmillan.

Management Training for Agricultural & Food Marketing. 1978. pap. 7.50 (ISBN 92-5-100546-X, F1375, FAO). Unipub.

OECD. The Instability of Agricultural Commodity Markets. (Agricultural Products & Markets Ser.). (Illus.). 237p. 1980. pap. text ed. 9.50x (ISBN 92-64-12041-6, 51-80-03-1). OECD.

Organization for Economic Cooperation & Development. Standardization of Fruit & Vegetables: Technical & Economic Aspects. 94p. 1970. 3.50x (ISBN 0-686-14711-1). OECD.

Oster, Merrill J. Commodity Futures for Profit. LC 77-92119. 1979. 24.95 (ISBN 0-914230-04-2). Investor Pubns.

Report on the FAO-RED Workshop on the Effective Use of Marketing for the Development of Small Farmers in Asia, Held in Bangkok, Thailand, 3-7 May 1976. 86p. 1976. pap. 9.75 (ISBN 92-5-100083-2, F1135, FAO). Unipub.

Report on the Training in Agricultural & Food Marketing at University Level in Africa. 74p. 1976. pap. 8.50 (ISBN 92-5-100044-1, F1142, FAO). Unipub.

Rhodes, James. The Agricultural Marketing System. LC 77-95339. (Agricultural Economics Ser.). 1978. text ed. 24.00 (ISBN 0-88244-170-1). Grid Pub.

Roy, Ewell P. Contract Farming & Economic Integration. LC 70-134471. (Illus.). 661p. 1972. pap. 11.95 (ISBN 0-8134-1425-3, 1425). Interstate.

Shepherd, Geoffrey, et al. Marketing Farm Products: Economic Analysis. 6th ed. (Illus.). 1976. text ed. 19.95x (ISBN 0-8138-1080-9). Iowa St U Pr.

Upton, M. Agricultural Production Economics & Resource-Use. (Illus.). 1976. 45.00x (ISBN 0-19-859452-6). Oxford U Pr.

Warley, Thorald K., ed. Agricultural Producers & Their Markets. LC 67-6960. 1967. 17.50x (ISBN 0-678-06263-3). Kelley.

Watts, Gilbert S. The Complete Guide for the Everyday Use of Gardeners, Fruit Growers, Poultrymen & Farmers on the Maketing of Their Products Directly to the Consumer. (Illus.). 156p. Date not set. Repr. of 1926 ed. deluxe ed. 49.85 (ISBN 0-89901-013-X). Found Class Reprints.

FARM PRODUCE–TRANSPORTATION

see also Plant Quarantine

Finney, Essex E., Jr., ed. Handbook of Transportation & Marketing in Agriculture, Vol. II: Field Crops. (CRC Ser. in Agriculture). 416p. 1981. 59.95 (ISBN 0-8493-3852-2). CRC Pr.

--Handbook of Transportation & Marketing in Agriculture: Volume 1: Food Commodities. 384p. 1981. 59.95 (ISBN 0-8493-3851-4). CRC Pr.

Krzyminski, James. Agricultural Transportation: The National Policy Issues. (Agriculture Committee Ser.). 32p. (Orig.). 1981. pap. 2.00 (ISBN 0-89068-046-9). Natl Planning.

Physiology, Quality & Transportation of Bananas. 1962. pap. 9.00 (ISBN 0-685-99160-1, IIR30, IIR). Unipub.

FARM SHOPS

see Agricultural Machinery

FARM SUPPLIES

see Farm Equipment

FARM SURPLUSES

see Surplus Agricultural Commodities

FARM TENANCY

see also Landlord and Tenant; Share-Cropping

Abensour, E. S., et al. Principles of Land Tenancy Legislation: A Comparative Study. rev. ed. (FAO Legislative Ser.: No. 6). (Orig.). 1966. pap. 4.75 (ISBN 0-685-09401-4, F332, FAO). Unipub.

Brooks, Robert P. The Agrarian Revolution in Georgia, 1865-1912. LC 72-181919. Repr. of 1914 ed. 15.00 (ISBN 0-404-00007-X). AMS Pr.

Cogswell, Seddie. Tenure, Nativity & Age As Factors in Iowa Agriculture,1850-1880. (Replica Ser). (Illus.). 170p. 1975. pap. text ed. 5.00x (ISBN 0-8138-1685-8). Iowa St U Pr.

Diller, Robert. Farm Ownership, Tenancy, & Land Use in the Nebraska Community. Bruchey, Stuart, ed. LC 78-56629. (Management of Public Lands in the U. S. Ser.). 1979. Repr. of 1932 ed. lib. bdg. 15.00x (ISBN 0-405-11339-0). Arno.

Farm Tenancy: Black & White, Two Reports. LC 79-137166. (Poverty U.S.A. Historical Record Ser). 1971. Repr. of 1935 ed. 12.00 (ISBN 0-405-03134-3). Arno.

Holland, Ruth. Forgotten Minority: America's Tenant Farmers & Migrant Workers. LC 75-119144. (Illus.). (gr. 5-8). 1970. 8.95 (ISBN 0-02-744390-6, CCPr). Macmillan.

Johnson, Charles S. & Embree, Edwin R. Collapse of Cotton Tenancy. (Select Bibliographies Reprint Ser.). 1972. Repr. of 1935 ed. 12.00 (ISBN 0-8369-6830-1). Arno.

Maris, Paul V. Land Is Mine: From Tenancy to Family Farm Ownership. Repr. of 1950 ed. lib. bdg. 24.50x (ISBN 0-8371-1871-9, MALM). Greenwood.

Winters, Donald L. Farmers Without Farms: Agricultural Tenancy in Nineteenth-Century Iowa. LC 78-4021. (Contributions in American History Ser.: No. 79). (Illus.). 1978. lib. bdg. 17.50 (ISBN 0-313-20408-X, WFL/). Greenwood.

Woofter, T. J., Jr. Landlord & Tenant on the Cotton Plantation. LC 77-165691. (FDR & the Era of the New Deal Ser.). 1971. Repr. of 1936 ed. lib. bdg. 27.50 (ISBN 0-306-70337-8). Da Capo.

FARM TENANCY–FORMOSA

Cheung, Steven N. Theory of Share Tenancy. LC 70-80862. 1969. 9.50x (ISBN 0-226-10358-7). U of Chicago Pr.

FARM TOOLS

see Agricultural Implements

FARM WOODLOTS

see Wood-Lots

FARMER-LABOR PARTY

Dobbs, Farrell. Teamster Politics. LC 75-17324. (Illus.). 256p. 1975. 17.00 (ISBN 0-913460-38-9); pap. 4.95 (ISBN 0-913460-39-7). Monad Pr.

McCurry, Dan C. & Rubenstein, Richard E., eds. The Farmer-Labor Party-History, Platform & Programs: An Original Press Anthology. facsimile ed. LC 74-30628. (American Farmers & the Rise of Agribusiness Ser.). 1975. 12.00x (ISBN 0-405-06790-9). Arno.

Rice, Stuart A. Farmers & Workers in American Politics. LC 78-82242. (Columbia University. Studies in the Social Sciences: No. 253). Repr. of 1924 ed. 20.00 (ISBN 0-404-51253-4). AMS Pr.

FARMERS

see also Agricultural Laborers; Agriculture–Vocational Guidance; Farm Life; Farm Management; Peasantry

Davis, John C. The Furrows of Freedom. LC 61-11032. pap. 3.25 (ISBN 0-912806-14-1). Long Hse.
De Crevecoeur, J. Hector. Letters from an American Farmer. Repr. of 1782 ed. 8.50 (ISBN 0-8446-1139-5). Peter Smith.
Foust, James D. The Yeoman Farmer & Westward Expansion of U. S. Cotton Production. facsimile ed. LC 75-2581. (Dissertations in American Economic History). (Illus.). 1975. 19.00x (ISBN 0-405-07201-5). Arno.
Grant, H. Roger & Purcell, L. Edward, eds. Years of Struggle: The Farm Diary of Elmer G. Powers, 1931-1936. (Illus.). 162p. 1976. 7.50 (ISBN 0-8138-0600-3). Iowa St U Pr.
Hayter, Earl W. Troubled Farmer: Rural Adjustment to Industrialism, 1850-1900. LC 67-26267. 349p. pap. 6.00 (ISBN 0-87580-515-9). N Ill U Pr.
Holley, Donald. Uncle Sam's Farmers: The New Deal Communities in the Lower Mississippi Valley. LC 75-20091. 1975. 19.95 (ISBN 0-252-00510-4). U of Ill Pr.
Leonard, Jonathan N. The First Farmers. (Emergence of Man Ser.). (Illus.). 1973. 9.95 (ISBN 0-8094-1304-3); lib. bdg. avail. (ISBN 0-685-41616-X). Time-Life.
Looney, J. W. Estate Planning for Farmers. 3rd ed. LC 79-52023. (Illus.). 1979. pap. 8.25 (ISBN 0-932250-06-8). Doane Agricultural.
Lord, Russell. Men of Earth. facsimile ed. McCurry, Dan C. & Rubenstein, Richard E., eds. LC 74-30642. (American Farmers & the Rise of Agribusiness Ser.). 1975. Repr. of 1931 ed. 22.00x (ISBN 0-405-06812-3). Arno.
McMillen, Wheeler. Farmer. LC 66-14227. (U.S.A. Survey Ser.). (Illus.). 126p. 1966. 3.75 (ISBN 0-87107-004-9). Potomac.
Nichols, Mark. Young Farmers: Their Problems, Activities & Educational Program. (Illus.). 1952. text ed. 7.50x (ISBN 0-8134-0234-4, 234). Interstate.
Periam, Jonathan. The Groundswell: A History of the Origins, Aims, & Progress of the Farmers' Movement Embracing an Authoritative Account of the Farmers' Clubs Granges Etc. LC 72-89080. (Rural America Ser.). 1973. Repr. of 1874 ed. 27.00 (ISBN 0-8420-1493-4). Scholarly Res Inc.
Perrin, Noel. First Person Rural: Essays of a Sometime Farmer. (Illus.). 1980. pap. 3.95 (ISBN 0-14-005561-4). Penguin.
Redman, Charles L. The Rise of Civilization: From Early Farmers to Urban Society in the Ancient Near East. LC 78-1493. (Illus.). 1978. text ed. 24.95x (ISBN 0-7167-0056-5); pap. text ed. 14.95x (ISBN 0-7167-0055-7). W H Freeman.
Richards, Bartlett, Jr. & Van Ackeren, Ruth. Bartlett Richards: Nebraska Sandhills Cattleman. (Illus.). 289p. (Orig.). 1980. 12.00 (ISBN 0-686-31143-4). Nebraska Hist.
Saarinen, Thomas F. Perception of the Drought Hazard on the Great Plains. LC 66-22754. (Research Papers Ser.: No. 106). 183p. 1966. pap. 8.00 (ISBN 0-89065-015-2). U Chicago Dept Geog.
Schmidt, Carl T. American Farmers in the World Crisis. LC 79-1591. 1981. Repr. of 1941 ed. 23.50 (ISBN 0-88355-896-3). Hyperion Conn.
Seim, Richard K. The American Farmer. LC 74-13903. (Illus.). 192p. 1974. pap. 5.95 (ISBN 0-528-88169-8). Rand.
Socolofsky, Homer E. Landlord William Scully. LC 78-31477. (Illus.). 1979. 15.00x (ISBN 0-7006-0189-9). Regents Pr KS.
Sublett, Michael W. Farmers on the Road. LC 75-8522. (Research Papers Ser.: No. 168). (Illus.). 1975. pap. 8.00 (ISBN 0-89065-075-6). U Chicago Dept Geog.
Thane, Elswyth. Strength of the Hills. write for info. (ISBN 0-88411-961-0). Amereon Ltd.

FARMERS–INDIA

Nair, Kusum. In Defense of the Irrational Peasant: Indian Agriculture After the Green Revolution. LC 78-26707. 1979. lib. bdg. 17.00x (ISBN 0-226-56798-2). U of Chicago Pr.
Sampath, R. K. & Ganesan, Jayalakshmi. Economics of Dry Farming in Tamil Nadu. 128p. 1974. 4.50 (ISBN 0-88253-431-9). Ind-US Inc.

FARMERS, AFRO-AMERICAN

see Afro-American Farmers

FARMERS' ALLIANCE

Dunning, N. A. & McCurry, Dan C., eds. The Farmers' Alliance History & Agricultural Digest. facsimile ed. LC 74-30629. (American Farmers & the Rise of Agribusiness Ser.). (Illus.). 1975. Repr. of 1891 ed. 54.00x (ISBN 0-405-06798-4). Arno.
Hicks, John D. Populist Revolt: A History of the Farmers' Alliance & the People's Party. LC 61-7237. 1961. pap. 2.75x (ISBN 0-8032-5085-1, BB 111, Bison). U of Nebr Pr.

FARMERS BROTHER, SENECA CHIEF

Stone, William L. Life & Times of Red Jacket or Sa-Go-Ye-Wat-Ha. LC 71-108543. (American Indian History Sers). 1970. Repr. of 1841 ed. 25.00 (ISBN 0-403-00227-3). Scholarly.

FARMERS' COOPERATIVES

see Agriculture, Cooperative

FARMERS' ORGANIZATIONS

see Agricultural Societies

FARMING

see Agriculture

FARMS

see also Family Farms; Farm Management; Plantations

American Society of Appraisers. Appraisal of Farmland: Use-Value Assessment Laws & Property Taxation, No. 8. new ed. LC 78-74140. (Monograph). 1979. pap. 5.00 (ISBN 0-937828-17-3). Am Soc Appraisers.
Berry, Albert R. & Cline, William R. Agrarian Structure & Productivity in Developing Countries. LC 78-20524. 1979. text ed. 17.50x (ISBN 0-8018-2190-8). Johns Hopkins.
Conrat, Maisie & Conrat, Richard. The American Farm. 1977. (Co-Pub. by HM); pap. 9.95 (ISBN 0-395-25359-4). Calif Hist.
The Farm Book. (Illus.). 1980. pap. 10.00 (ISBN 0-913990-09-4). Book Pub Co.
Hamil, Harold. Farmland, USA. LC 75-18756. (Illus.). 112p. 1975. 25.00 (ISBN 0-913504-24-6); deluxe ed. 100.00 (ISBN 0-913504-61-0). Lowell Pr.
Johnson, A. H. The Disappearance of the Small Landowner. LC 79-14625. (Illus.). 1979. Repr. of 1909 ed. lib. bdg. 13.50 (ISBN 0-678-08077-1). Kelly.
Kaiser, Ann, ed. Farm Visits. LC 80-54411. 160p. (Orig.). 1981. pap. 9.95 (ISBN 0-89821-036-4). Reiman Assocs.
Khan, Mahmood H. The Economics of the Green Revolution in Pakistan. LC 75-19796. (Special Studies). (Illus.). 320p. 1975. text ed. 26.95 (ISBN 0-275-55680-8). Praeger.
Laycock, George. How to Buy & Enjoy a Small Farm: Your Comprehensive Guide to the Country Life. (Illus.). 1978. pap. 5.95 (ISBN 0-679-50865-1). McKay.
McBride, George M. Chile: Land & Society. LC 71-154618. 1971. Repr. of 1936 ed. lib. bdg. 25.00x (ISBN 0-374-95429-1). Octagon.
Midwest Plan Service Personnel. Farmstead Planning Handbook. (Illus.). 44p. 1974. pap. 4.00 (ISBN 0-89373-001-7, MWPS-2). Midwest Plan Serv.
Minneman, Paul G. Large Land Holdings in Ohio & Their Operation. Bruchey, Stuart, ed. LC 78-56664. (Management of Public Lands in the U. S. Ser.). 1979. lib. bdg. 13.00x (ISBN 0-405-11344-7). Arno.
Olson, Michael K. The Mini-Farm. Date not set. 8.95 (ISBN 0-916172-08-2). Janus Pr.
Schreiner, Olive. The Story of an African Farm: Intro. by. 7.00 (ISBN 0-8446-0247-7). Peter Smith.
Throckmorton, Verdi. The Small Farm: A Practical Approach to Survival Still Obtainable in 1971. 317p. (Orig.). 1979. pap. 16.95 (ISBN 0-935812-01-6). Original Pr.
Trullinger, Robert W. & Warren, George M. Clean Water & Sewage Disposal on the Farm. facs. ed. Repr. of 1914 ed. pap. 4.95 (ISBN 0-8466-6036-9, SJU36). Shorey.
Weller, John. History of the Farmstead: The Development of Energy Sources. (Illus.). 272p. 1981. 32.00 (ISBN 0-571-11804-6, Pub. by Faber & Faber); pap. 15.95 (ISBN 0-571-11805-4, Pub. by Faber & Faber). Merrimack Bk Serv.
Woodruff, Archibald M., ed. The Farm & the City: Rivals or Allies? (American Assembly Ser.). (Illus.). 208p. 1980. 12.95 (ISBN 0-13-304980-9, Spec); pap. 5.95 (ISBN 0-13-304972-8). P-H.
Woofter, T. J., Jr. Landlord & Tenant on the Cotton Plantation. LC 77-165691. (FDR & the Era of the New Deal Ser.). 1971. Repr. of 1936 ed. lib. bdg. 27.50 (ISBN 0-306-70337-8). Da Capo.
Woofter, Thomas J. Landlord & Tenant on the Cotton Plantation. LC 74-75537. (Illus.). Repr. of 1936 ed. 14.25x (ISBN 0-8371-1035-1, Pub. by Negro U Pr). Greenwood.

FARMS–ACCOUNTING

see Agriculture–Accounting

FARMS–VALUATION

Cook, Charles C., pref. by. Land Valuation Methods, Rural & Transitionary Land. (Lincoln Institute Monograph: No. 80-2). 1980. pap. text ed. 10.00 (ISBN 0-686-27944-1). Lincoln Inst Land.
Jundt, Dwight W. Buying & Selling Farmland: A Guide to Profitable Investment. LC 80-67887. (Illus.). 309p. 1980. 14.95 (ISBN 0-686-77523-6); pap. text ed. 9.95 (ISBN 0-932250-10-6). Doane Agricultural.
Kolesar, John & Scholl, Jaye. Saving Farmland. 1975. 3.50 (ISBN 0-686-23336-0). Ctr Analysis Public Issues.
Murray, William G. Farm Appraisal & Valuation. 5th ed. LC 61-11034. (Illus.). 1969. 12.50x (ISBN 0-8138-0570-8). Iowa St U Pr.
Roberts, Neal A., ed. Property Tax Preferences for Agricultural Land. LC 79-52473. (Illus.). 140p. 1980. text ed. 18.00 (ISBN 0-916672-32-8). Allanheld.

FARNSWORTH, PHILO TAYLOR, 1906-

Everson, George. The Story of Television: The Life of Philo T. Farnsworth. LC 74-4677. (Illus.). 270p. 1974. Repr. of 1949 ed. 18.00x (ISBN 0-405-06042-4). Arno.

FAROE

Annandale, Nelson. The Faroes & Iceland: Studies in Island Life. LC 77-87701. (Illus.). Repr. of 1905 ed. 27.50 (ISBN 0-404-16495-1). AMS Pr.
Landt, Jorgen. A Description of the Feroe Islands. LC 77-87703. Repr. of 1810 ed. 32.50 (ISBN 0-404-16497-8). AMS Pr.
Leikur & Torshavn. Islands & People. 150p. 1980. 27.50 (ISBN 0-906191-22-X, Pub. by Thule Pr England). Intl Schol Bk Serv.

FAROESE BALLADS AND SONGS

Wylie, Jonathan & Margolin, David. The Ring of Dancers: Images of Faroese Culture. (Symbol & Culture Ser.). 1980. text ed. 19.95x (ISBN 0-8122-7783-X). U of Pa Pr.

FARQUHAR, GEORGE, 1677-1707

Connely, Willard. Young George Farquhar. 333p. 1980. Repr. of 1949 ed. lib. bdg. 25.00 (ISBN 0-8495-0787-1). Arden Lib.
Farquhar, George. The Beaux' Strategem. Cordner, Michael, ed. (New Mermaids Ser.). pap. 2.95x (ISBN 0-393-90007-X). Norton.
--The Recruiting Officer. Ross, John, ed. (New Mermaids Ser.). 1977. pap. 4.95x (ISBN 0-393-90039-8). Norton.
Rothstein, Eric. George Farquhar. (English Authors Ser.: No. 58). 10.95 (ISBN 0-8057-1188-0). Twayne.
Schmid, David. George Farquhar: Sein Leben und Seine Original-Dramen. Repr. of 1904 ed. pap. 21.00 (ISBN 0-384-54040-6). Johnson Repr.

FARRAGUT, DAVID GLASGOW, 1801-1870

David G. Farragut. 1978. Repr. of 1899 ed. lib. bdg. 17.50 (ISBN 0-8492-3557-X). R West.
Latham, Jean L. Anchor's Aweigh: The Story of David Glasgow Farragut. LC 68-24319. (Illus.). (gr. 5-9). 1968. PLB 8.79 (ISBN 0-06-023703-1, HarpJ). Har-Row.
Lewis, Charles L. David Glasgow Farragut. LC 79-6115. (Navies & Men Ser.). (Illus.). 1980. Vol. Repr. Of 1941 Ed. lib. bdg. 35.00x (ISBN 0-405-13043-0); Vol. 2, Repr, Of 1943 Ed. lib. bdg. 40.00x (ISBN 0-405-13044-9). Arno.
Mahan, A. T. Admiral Farragut. LC 68-26360. (American Biography Ser., No. 32). 1969. Repr. of 1895 ed. lib. bdg. 32.95 (ISBN 0-8383-0268-8). Haskell.
Mahan, Alfred T. Admiral Farragut. LC 69-10126. 1969. Repr. of 1895 ed. lib. bdg. 15.00 (ISBN 0-8371-0553-6, MAAF). Greenwood.
--Admiral Farragut. LC 74-108509. 1970. Repr. of 1892 ed. 10.00 (ISBN 0-403-00217-6). Scholarly.

FARRELL, JAMES THOMAS, 1904-

Branch, Edgar M. James T. Farrell. (Pamphlets on American Writers Ser: No. 29). (Orig.). 1963. pap. 1.25x (ISBN 0-8166-0303-0, MPAW29). U of Minn Pr.
Rao, B. Ramachandra. The American Fictional Hero: An Analysis of the Works of Fitzgerald, Wolfe, Farrell, Dos Passos & Steinbeck. (English Language & Literature Ser.: No. 4). 1979. text ed. 8.95x (ISBN 0-210-40620-8, Pub. by Bahri India). Asia.
Wald, Alan M. James T. Farrell: The Revolutionary Socialist Years. LC 77-84156. 1978. 18.50x (ISBN 0-8147-9179-4); pap. 9.00x (ISBN 0-8147-9180-8). NYU Pr.

FARRELL, JEFF

Henning, Jean M. Six Days to Swim - Jeff Farrell: A Story of Olympic Courage. LC 71-103031. (Illus.). (gr. 6-12). 1970. 2.00 (ISBN 0-911822-02-X). Swimming.

FARRIER, DENIS, 1921-

Farrier, Denis. Country Vet. LC 72-6615. 1973. 6.95 (ISBN 0-8008-1950-0). Taplinger.

FARRIERY

see Horses; Horseshoeing; Veterinary Medicine; Veterinary Surgery

FARTHINGALE

see Crinoline

FASCISM

see also National Socialism; Totalitarianism

Aronowitz, Stanley. Honor America: The Nature of Fascism, Historic Struggles Against It & a Strategy for Today. (Orig.). 1971. pap. 0.75 (ISBN 0-87810-011-3). Times Change.
Baraveli, G. G. The Policy of Public Works Under the Fascist Regime. 1976. lib. bdg. 59.95 (ISBN 0-8490-2450-1). Gordon Pr.
Barnes, J. S. Fascism. LC 72-7055. (Select Bibliographies Reprint Ser.). 1972. Repr. of 1931 ed. 18.00 (ISBN 0-8369-6922-7). Arno.
--Fascism. 1979. Repr. of 1931 ed. lib. bdg. 17.50 (ISBN 0-8495-0545-3). Arden Lib.
Basch, Ernst. The Fascist: His State & His Mind. LC 72-180386. (Studies in Fascism, Ideology & Practice). Repr. of 1937 ed. 24.50 (ISBN 0-404-56101-2). AMS Pr.
Bell, Leland V. In Hitler's Shadow: The Anatomy of American Nazism. LC 72-89991. 1973. 9.95 (ISBN 0-8046-9029-4, Natl U). Kennikat.
Billig, Michael. Fascists: A Second Psychological View of the National Front. 1979. 48.50 (ISBN 0-12-097940-3). Acad Pr.
Borgese, Guiseppe A. Goliath: The March of Fascism. LC 78-14102. 1979. Repr. of 1938 ed. 32.50 (ISBN 0-88355-776-2). Hyperion Conn.
Borkenau, Franz. The Totalitarian Enemy. LC 78-63654. (Studies in Fascism: Ideology & Practice). Repr. of 1940 ed. 22.50 (ISBN 0-404-16914-7). AMS Pr.
Bramstedt, Ernest K. Dictatorship & Political Police: The Technique of Control by Fear. LC 75-41034. Repr. of 1945 ed. 17.50 (ISBN 0-404-14510-8). AMS Pr.
Cassels, Alan. Fascism. LC 73-13716. (Illus.). 1975. pap. 10.95x (ISBN 0-88295-718-X). Harlan Davidson.
Cohen, Carl. Communism, Fascism, & Democracy. 2nd ed. 620p. 1972. pap. text ed. 10.95x (ISBN 0-394-31319-4, RanC). Random.
Davis, Frances P. A Fearful Innocence. LC 81-11793. (Illus.). 1981. 14.95 (ISBN 0-87338-260-9). Kent St U Pr.
De Felice, Renzo. Interpretations of Facism. Everett, Brenda H., tr. 1977. 15.00x (ISBN 0-674-45962-8). Harvard U Pr.
Dennis, Lawrence. Coming American Fascism. LC 73-180397. Repr. of 1936 ed. 21.50 (ISBN 0-404-56118-7). AMS Pr.
Dimitrov, Georgi. The Working Class Against Fascism. LC 78-63662. (Studies in Fascism: Ideology & Practice). Repr. of 1935 ed. 17.00 (ISBN 0-404-16925-2). AMS Pr.
Dutt, R. Palme. Facism & Social Revolution. 2nd ed. 318p. 1974. pap. 4.95 (ISBN 0-89380-014-7). Proletarian Pubs.
Ebenstein, William. Fascism at Work. LC 75-180384. (Studies in Fascism, Ideology & Practice). Repr. of 1934 ed. 24.50 (ISBN 0-404-56120-9). AMS Pr.
Einzig, Paul. The Economic Foundation of Fascism. LC 78-63666. (Studies in Fascism: Ideology & Practice). Repr. of 1934 ed. 18.00 (ISBN 0-404-16929-5). AMS Pr.
Entwistle, Harold. Antonio Gramsci: Conservative Schooling for Radical Politics. (Routledge Education Bks.). 1979. 21.00 (ISBN 0-7100-0333-1); pap. 9.50 (ISBN 0-7100-0334-X). Routledge & Kegan.
Evola, Niccolo D. Origini e dottrina del fascismo. LC 79-180385. Repr. of 1935 ed. 18.00 (ISBN 0-404-56121-7). AMS Pr.
Florinsky, Michael T. Fascism & National Socialism: A Study of the Economic & Social Policies of the Totalitarian State. LC 78-63667. (Studies in Fascism: Ideology & Practice). Repr. of 1936 ed. 24.50 (ISBN 0-404-16934-1). AMS Pr.
Flynn, John T. As We Go Marching. LC 79-172212. (Right Wing Individualist Tradition in America Ser). 1972. Repr. of 1944 ed. 15.00 (ISBN 0-405-00421-4). Arno.
--As We Go Marching. LC 73-88237. 292p. 1973. pap. 3.45 (ISBN 0-914156-00-4). Free Life.
Forman, James. Fascism. 1976. pap. 1.25 (ISBN 0-440-94707-3, LFL). Dell.
Formann, J. D. Fascism: The Meaning & Experience of Reactionary Revolution. LC 73-11480. (gr. 7 up). 1974. pap. 3.95 (ISBN 0-686-77028-5). Watts.
Germani, Gino. Authoritarianism, Fascism & National Populism. LC 77-80871. 1978. 17.95 (ISBN 0-87855-241-3); pap. 5.95 (ISBN 0-87855-642-7). Transaction Bks.
Greene, Nathanael, ed. Fascism: An Anthology. LC 67-30582. (Orig.). 1968. pap. 8.95x (ISBN 0-88295-736-8). Harlan Davidson.
Gregor, A. James. The Fascist Persuasion in Radical Politics, LC 73-2463. 424p. 1974. 26.50 (ISBN 0-691-07556-5). Princeton U Pr.
Guerin, Daniel. Fascism & Big Business. rev. 2nd ed. Merrill, Francis, et al, trs. from Fr. LC 73-80854. 352p. 1973. 17.00 (ISBN 0-913460-24-9, Dist. by Path Pr NY); pap. 5.95 (ISBN 0-913460-25-7). Monad Pr.
Haider, Carmen. Do We Want Fascism? LC 78-63676. (Studies in Fascism: Ideology & Practice). Repr. of 1934 ed. 24.50 (ISBN 0-404-16938-4). AMS Pr.
Hayes, Paul. Fascism. LC 73-13448. 1973. 7.95 (ISBN 0-02-914320-9). Free Pr.
Heimann, Eduard. Communism, Fascism or Democracy? LC 78-67622. (Studies in Fascism: Ideology & Practice). Repr. of 1938 ed. 24.00 (ISBN 0-404-16945-7). AMS Pr.
Hills, C. A. The Fascist Dictatorships. 1979. 16.95 (ISBN 0-7134-0979-7, Pub. by Batsford England). David & Charles.

Joes, Anthony J. Fascism in the Contemporary World: Ideology, Evolution, Resurgence. LC 77-14141. (A Westview Special Study Ser.). 1978. pap. text ed. 9.50x (ISBN 0-89158-159-6). Westview.
Kirkpatrick, Jeane. Leader & Vanguard: A Study of Peronist Argentina. 1971. 20.00x (ISBN 0-262-11041-5). MIT Pr.
Laclau, Ernesto. Politics & Ideology in Marxist Theory: Capitalism - Fascism - Populism. 1979. 12.50x (ISBN 0-902308-74-2); pap. 5.75 (ISBN 0-86091-714-2, Pub. by NLB). Schocken.
Laqueur, Walter, ed. Fascism-a Readers' Guide: Analysis, Interpretations, Bibliography. LC 75-13158. 1977. 34.50x (ISBN 0-520-03033-8); pap. 6.95 (ISBN 0-520-03642-5). U of Cal Pr.
Larsen, Stein U., ed. Who Were the Fascists? Social Roots of European Fascism. 800p. 1981. 48.00x (ISBN 8-20005-331-8). Universitet.
Lloyd, Roger B. Revolutionary Religion: Christianity, Fascism, & Communism. LC 78-63686. (Studies in Fascism: Ideology & Practice). Repr. of 1938 ed. 18.50 (ISBN 0-404-16903-1). AMS Pr.
Mandle, W. F. Fascism. (History Monographs). 1969. pap. text ed. 4.50x (ISBN 0-435-31270-7). Heinemann Ed.
Matthews, Herbert L. The Fruits of Fascism. LC 78-63694. (Studies in Fascism: Ideology & Practice). Repr. of 1943 ed. 28.00 (ISBN 0-404-16955-4). AMS Pr.
Mitchell, Otis C. Fascism: An Introductory Perspective. LC 78-59115. 1978. pap. 5.50 (ISBN 0-87716-091-0, Pub. by Moore Pub Co). F Apple.
Mosse, George L., ed. International Fascism: New Thoughts & New Approaches. LC 78-63148. (Sage Readers in Twentieth Century History: Vol. 3). (Illus.). 386p. 1979. 24.00x (ISBN 0-8039-9842-2); pap. 12.50 (ISBN 0-8039-9843-0). Sage.
Mussolini, Benito. The Corporate State. 1976. lib. bdg. 59.95 (ISBN 0-8490-1675-4). Gordon Pr.
--The Political & Social Doctrine of Fascism. 59.95 (ISBN 0-87968-434-8). Gordon Pr.
Neumann, Sigmund. Permanent Revolution: The Total State in a World at War. LC 78-63700. (Studies in Fascism: Ideology & Practice). Repr. of 1942 ed. 32.00 (ISBN 0-404-16969-4). AMS Pr.
Nitti, Francesco S. Bolshevism, Fascism, & Democracy. Green, Margaret M., tr. LC 78-63701. (Studies in Fascism: Ideology & Practice). Repr. of 1927 ed. 21.00 (ISBN 0-404-16973-2). AMS Pr.
Nolte, Ernst. Three Faces of Fascism. 1969. pap. 2.95 (ISBN 0-451-61835-1, ME1835, Ment). NAL.
Osborne, Harrison. In Defense of Fascism: A New Critical Evaluation of the Fascist Experience in Modern History. (Science of Man Library Bk.). 1978. 51.75 (ISBN 0-89266-128-3). Am Classical Coll Pr.
Pareto, Vilfredo. The Mind & Society, 4 vols. Livingston, Arthur, ed. Bongiorno, Andrew, tr. LC 78-63704. (Studies in Fascism: Ideology & Practice). Repr. of 1935 ed. 37.50 ea.; 145.00 set (ISBN 0-404-16990-2). AMS Pr.
Payne, S. G. Fascism: A Comparative Approach Toward a Definition. LC 79-5413. 240p. 1980. 16.75 (ISBN 0-299-08060-9). U of Wis Pr.
Poulantzas, Nicos. Fascism & Dictatorship. 1974. 18.50x (ISBN 0-902308-85-8, Pub by NLB). Schocken.
Prezzolini, Giuseppe. Fascism. Macmillan, Kathleen, tr. LC 78-63707. (Studies in Fascism: Ideology & Practice). 1977. Repr. of 1927 ed. 19.00 (ISBN 0-404-16977-5). AMS Pr.
Reich, Wilhelm. The Mass Psychology of Fascism. Carfagno, Vincent R., tr. 1980. pap. write for info. (ISBN 0-374-50884-4). FS&G.
--The Mass Psychology of Fascism. 1974. pap. 3.95 (ISBN 0-671-21790-9, Touchstone Bks). S&S.
--Die Massenpsychologie Des Fashismus. 421p. 1969. 35.00 (ISBN 0-374-13977-6). FS&G.
Salvemini, Gaetano. Italian Fascist Activities in the United States. Cannistraro, Philip V., intro. by. LC 76-44920. 1977. lib. bdg. 15.00x (ISBN 0-913256-23-4, Dist. by Ozer). Ctr Migration.
--Under the Axe of Fascism. 1971. pap. 3.95 (ISBN 0-8065-0240-1). Citadel Pr.
Seldes, G. You Can't Do That. LC 70-37287. (Civil Liberties in American History Ser). 308p. 1972. Repr. of 1938 ed. lib. bdg. 27.50 (ISBN 0-306-70201-0). Da Capo.
Sergio, L. From Intervention to Empire: A Book of Fascist Dates. 1979. lib. bdg. 46.95 (ISBN 0-685-96395-0). Revisionist Pr.
Simpson, Kemper. Big Business, Efficiency & Fascism. LC 78-63717. (Studies in Fascism: Ideology & Practice). Repr. of 1941 ed. 21.50 (ISBN 0-404-16529-X). AMS Pr.
Soucy, Robert. Fascist Intellectual: Drieu la Rochelle. 1979. 32.75x (ISBN 0-520-03463-5). U of Cal Pr.
Studies in Fascism: Ideology & Practice, 126 titles in 142 vols. (AMS Press Reprint Ser.). Repr. of 1955 ed. Set. write for info. (ISBN 0-404-56100-4). AMS Pr.
Swing, Raymond G. Forerunners of American Fascism. facs. ed. LC 69-18938. (Essay Index Reprint Ser). 1935. 15.00 (ISBN 0-8369-0055-3). Arno.
Thomas, Norman N. Choice Before Us: Mankind at the Crossroads. LC 76-120217. Repr. of 1934 ed. 17.50 (ISBN 0-404-06389-6). AMS Pr.
Togliatti, Palmiro. Lectures on Fascism. LC 74-30435. 1976. 6.95 (ISBN 0-7178-0429-1); pap. 2.95 (ISBN 0-7178-0430-5). Intl Pub Co.
Trotsky, Leon. Fascism, What It Is & How to Fight It. (Orig.). pap. 0.60 (ISBN 0-87348-106-2). Path Pr NY.
Tucker, William R. The Fascist Ego: A Political Biography of Robert Brasillach. 1975. 36.50x (ISBN 0-520-02710-8). U of Cal Pr.
Turner, Henry A., Jr., ed. Reappraisals of Fascism. (Modern Scholarship on European History Ser). 288p. 1975. text ed. 12.50 (ISBN 0-531-05372-5); pap. text ed. 5.95 (ISBN 0-531-05579-5). Watts.
University Of Colorado Department Of Philosophy. Readings on Fascism & National Socialism. 112p. (Orig.). 1952. pap. 4.95x (ISBN 0-8040-0259-2). Swallow.
Vajda, Mihaly. Fascism As a Mass Movement. LC 76-19160. 1976. 14.95 (ISBN 0-312-28350-4). St Martin.
Weber, Eugene. Varieties of Fascism: Doctrines of Revolution in the Twentieth Century. (Orig.). 1964. pap. 5.95x (ISBN 0-442-00073-1, 73, Anv). Van Nos Reinhold.
Webster, Richard A. The Cross & the Fasces: Christian Democracy and Fascism in Italy. 1960. 12.50x (ISBN 0-8047-0043-5). Stanford U Pr.
Weiss, John. The Fascist Tradition: Radical Right-Wing Extremism in Modern Europe. (Orig.). 1967. pap. text ed. 9.95 scp (ISBN 0-06-046995-1, HarpC). Har-Row.
Wilkinson, Ellen C. & Conze, Edward. Why Fascism? LC 78-177843. Repr. of 1934 ed. 18.00 (ISBN 0-404-56169-1). AMS Pr.
Wittke, Carl F. Democracy Is Different. LC 78-63729. (Studies in Fascism: Ideology & Practice). Repr. of 1941 ed. 19.50 (ISBN 0-404-16525-7). AMS Pr.

FASCISM–EUROPE

Carsten, F. L. The Rise of Fascism. LC 67-21223. 1967. pap. 6.95x (ISBN 0-520-01447-2, CAL176). U of Cal Pr.
Carsten, Francis L. Fascist Movements in Austria: From Schonerer to Hitler. LC 76-22935. (Sage Studies in Twentieth Century History: Vol. 7). 356p. 1977. pap. 12.50 (ISBN 0-8039-9857-0). Sage.
Kedward, H. R. Fascism in Western Europe Nineteen Hundred to Nineteen Forty-Five. LC 78-135658. 1971. 14.50x (ISBN 0-8147-4551-2). NYU Pr.
Mosse, George L. Masses & Man: Nationalist & Fascist Perceptions of Reality. LC 80-15399. xi, 362p. 1980. 25.00 (ISBN 0-86527-334-0). Fertig.
Von Starhemberg, Ernst R. Between Hitler & Mussolini: Memoirs of Ernst Rudiger Prince Starhemberg. LC 78-63720. (Studies in Fascism: Ideology & Practice). Repr. of 1942 ed. 26.00 (ISBN 0-404-16989-9). AMS Pr.
Weiss, John. The Fascist Tradition: Radical Right-Wing Extremism in Modern Europe. (Orig.). 1967. pap. text ed. 9.95 scp (ISBN 0-06-046995-1, HarpC). Har-Row.

FASCISM–GERMANY

Angolia, John R. For Fuhrer & Fatherland: Civil Awards of the Third Reich. 1978. 19.00 (ISBN 0-912138-16-5). Quaker.
Brady, Robert A. Spirit & Structure of German Fascism. 1971. pap. 3.95 (ISBN 0-8065-0239-8). Citadel Pr.
--The Spirit & Structure of German Fascism. LC 68-9629. 1970. Repr. of 1937 ed. 25.00 (ISBN 0-86527-189-5). Fertig.
--The Spirit & Structure of German Fascism. 1978. Repr. of 1937 ed. lib. bdg. 25.00 (ISBN 0-89760-031-2, Telegraph). Dynamic Learn Corp.
Hedin, Sven. German Diary. 1977. lib. bdg. 59.95 (ISBN 0-8490-1883-8). Gordon Pr.
Katz, William L. An Album of Nazism. LC 78-12723. (Picture Album Ser.). (Illus.). (gr. 5 up). 1979. PLB 8.40 s&l (ISBN 0-531-01500-9). Watts.
Poulantzas, Nicos. Fascism & Dictatorship. 1980. pap. 7.95. (ISBN 0-86091-716-9, Pub. by Verso). Schocken.
Sohn-Rethel, Alfred. Economy & Class Structure of German Fascism. 1978. text ed. 15.50x (ISBN 0-906336-00-7, Trans. by M. Sohn-Rethel); pap. text ed. 7.75x (ISBN 0-906336-01-5). Humanities.
Trotsky, Leon. The Struggle Against Fascism in Germany. Breitman, George & Maisel, Merry, eds. LC 73-119532. 1970. 25.00 (ISBN 0-87348-135-6); pap. 6.95 (ISBN 0-87348-136-4). Path Pr NY.
Von Salomon, Ernst. Answers of Ernst Von Salomon to the One Hundred Thirty-One Questions in the Allied Military Government "Fragebogen". Fitzgibbon, Constantine, tr. LC 78-63711. (Studies in Fascism: Ideology & Practice). Repr. of 1954 ed. 37.50 (ISBN 0-404-16984-8). AMS Pr.

FASCISM–GREAT BRITAIN

Drennan, James. Oswald Mosley & British Fascism. 1976. lib. bdg. 69.95 (ISBN 0-8490-2388-2). Gordon Pr.
Lunn, Kenneth & Thurlow, Richard C., eds. British Fascism: Essays on the Radical Right in Inter-War Britain. LC 79-21249. 1980. write for info. (ISBN 0-312-10130-9). St Martin.

FASCISM–HUNGARY

Nagy-Talavera, Nicholas M. Green Shirts & the Others: A History of Fascism in Hungary & Rumania. LC 74-98136. (Publications Ser.: No. 85). 1970. 12.95 (ISBN 0-8179-1851-5). Hoover Inst Pr.

FASCISM–ITALY

Borgese, Giuseppe A. Goliath: The March of Fascism. LC 78-63653. (Studies in Fascism: Ideology & Practice). Repr. of 1937 ed. 37.50 (ISBN 0-404-16909-0). AMS Pr.
Cassels, Alan. Fascist Italy. LC 68-9740. (AHM Europe Since 1500 Ser.). (Illus.). 1968. pap. 5.95x (ISBN 0-88295-719-8). Harlan Davidson.
Corner, Paul. Fascism in Ferrara Nineteen Fifteen to Nineteen Twenty-Five. (Oxford Historical Monographs). 312p. 1975. 36.00x (ISBN 0-19-821857-5). Oxford U Pr.
De Grand, Alexander J. The Italian Nationalist Association & the Rise of Fascism in Italy. LC 77-24633. 1978. 16.50x (ISBN 0-8032-0949-5). U of Nebr Pr.
Ebenstein, William. Fascist Italy. LC 72-84985. (Illus.). 310p. 1973. Repr. of 1939 ed. 18.00 (ISBN 0-8462-1672-8). Russell.
Evola, Niccolo D. Origini e dottrina del fascismo. LC 79-180385. Repr. of 1935 ed. 18.00 (ISBN 0-404-56121-7). AMS Pr.
Ferrero, G. Four Years of Fascism. Dickes, E. W., tr. LC 77-180398. Repr. of 1924 ed. 16.00 (ISBN 0-404-56122-5). AMS Pr.
Field, G. Lowell. Syndical & Corporative Institutions of Italian Fascism. (Columbia University. Studies in the Social Sciences: No. 443). Repr. of 1938 ed. 14.00 (ISBN 0-404-51433-2). AMS Pr.
Flynn, John T. As We Go Marching. LC 79-172212. (Right Wing Individualist Tradition in America Ser). 1972. Repr. of 1944 ed. 15.00 (ISBN 0-405-00421-4). Arno.
Fordriner, Gustav H. Italian Fascism & American New Deal. (Illus.). 134p. 1981. 66.75 (ISBN 0-930008-92-8). Inst Econ Pol.
Gentile, Giovanni. The Reform of Education. Bigongiari, Dino, tr. LC 78-63672. (Studies in Fascism: Ideology & Practice). Repr. of 1922 ed. 22.50 (ISBN 0-404-16935-X). AMS Pr.
Gorgolini, Pietro. The Fascist Movement in Italian Life. Petre, M. D., ed. LC 78-63674. (Studies in Fascism: Ideology & Practice). Repr. of 1923 ed. 22.00 (ISBN 0-404-16936-8). AMS Pr.
Haider, Carmen. Capital & Labor Under Fascism. LC 68-58586. (Columbia University. Studies in the Social Sciences: No. 318). Repr. of 1930 ed. 25.00 (ISBN 0-404-51318-2). AMS Pr.
Histoire Du Fascisme Italien: 1919-1937. Repr. of 1938 ed. 21.75 (ISBN 0-404-56131-4). AMS Pr.
Keene, Frances. Neither Liberty nor Bread. LC 76-86029. 1969. Repr. of 1940 ed. 15.00 (ISBN 0-8046-0618-8). Kennikat.
Lussu, Emilio. Enter Mussolini: Observations & Adventures of an Anti-Fascist. Rawson, Marion, tr. from Ital. LC 78-63690. (Studies in Fascism: Ideology & Practice). Repr. of 1936 ed. 24.00 (ISBN 0-404-16952-X). AMS Pr.
Matteotti, Giacomo. The Fascisti Exposed: A Year of Fascist Domination. LC 68-9637. 1969. Repr. of 1924 ed. 14.75 (ISBN 0-86527-064-3). Fertig.
Minio-Paluello, Lorenzo. Education in Fascist Italy. LC 78-63697. (Studies in Fascism: Ideology & Practice). Repr. of 1946 ed. 19.00 (ISBN 0-404-16958-9). AMS Pr.
Molony, John N. The Emergence of Political Catholicism in Italy: Partito Popolare 1919-1926. 225p. 1977. 17.50x (ISBN 0-87471-943-7). Rowman.
Roberts, David D. The Syndicalist Tradition & Italian Fascism. LC 78-23347. 1979. 24.50x (ISBN 0-8078-1351-6). U of NC Pr.
Salvemini, Gaetano. The Fascist Dictatorship in Italy. 1967. 27.50 (ISBN 0-86527-063-5). Fertig.
--Under the Axe of Fascism. LC 68-9589. 1970. Repr. of 1936 ed. 25.00 (ISBN 0-86527-201-8). Fertig.
Schmidt, Carl T. The Corporate State in Action: Italy Under Fascism. LC 72-85008. 173p. 1973. Repr. of 1939 ed. 12.00 (ISBN 0-8462-1676-0). Russell.
--Plough & the Sword. LC 38-3030. Repr. of 1938 ed. 16.50 (ISBN 0-404-05608-3). AMS Pr.
Schneider, Herbert W. The Fascist Government of Italy. LC 75-16856. 173p. 1975. Repr. of 1936 ed. lib. bdg. 15.00x (ISBN 0-8371-8273-5, SCFG). Greenwood.
--Making the Fascist State. LC 67-24597. 1968. Repr. 24.50 (ISBN 0-86527-121-6). Fertig.
Treves, Paolo. What Mussolini Did to Us. Isolani, Casimiro T., tr. LC 77-180434. Repr. of 1940 ed. 24.50 (ISBN 0-404-56167-5). AMS Pr.
Villari, Luigi. The Fascist Experiment. LC 74-180436. Repr. of 1926 ed. 16.50 (ISBN 0-404-56168-3). AMS Pr.
Welk, William G. Fascist Economic Policy. LC 68-10954. (Illus.). 1968. Repr. of 1938 ed. 11.00 (ISBN 0-8462-1056-8). Russell.
Wiskemann, Elizabeth. Fascism in Italy: Its Development & Influence. 2nd ed. (Making of the Twentieth Century Ser). 1970. pap. 4.95 (ISBN 0-312-28385-7). St Martin.

FASCISM–RUMANIA

Nagy-Talavera, Nicholas M. Green Shirts & the Others: A History of Fascism in Hungary & Rumania. LC 74-98136. (Publications Ser.: No. 85). 1970. 12.95 (ISBN 0-8179-1851-5). Hoover Inst Pr.

FASCISM–SPAIN

Acier, Marcel. From Spanish Trenches. LC 78-63648. (Studies in Fascism: Ideology & Practice). Repr. of 1937 ed. 19.00 (ISBN 0-404-16898-1). AMS Pr.
Payne, Stanley G. Falange: A History of Spanish Fascism. 1961. 15.00x (ISBN 0-8047-0058-3); pap. 5.95x (ISBN 0-8047-0059-1). Stanford U Pr.

FASHION

see also Clothing and Dress; Costume; Costume Design; Dressmaking; Men's Clothing; Tailoring

Adler, France-Michele. Sportsfashion. 192p. 1980. pap. 7.95 (ISBN 0-380-76075-4, 76075). Avon.
Aulson, Pam, ed. Timeless Fashions. (Illus.). 72p. (Orig.). 1981. pap. 2.00 (ISBN 0-918178-25-8). Simplicity.
Bennett-England, Rodney. Dress Optional, the Revolution in Menswear. LC 68-29951. (Illus.). 1968. 10.25 (ISBN 0-8023-1177-6). Dufour.
Bernard, Barbara. Fashion in the Sixties. LC 78-60788. (Illus.). 1978. pap. 4.95 (ISBN 0-312-28460-8). St Martin.
Bigelow, Marybelle S. Fashion in History: Western Dress, Prehistoric to Present. 2nd ed. LC 78-62539. 1979. text ed. 22.95x (ISBN 0-8087-2800-8). Burgess.
Blum, Stella. Everyday Fashions of the Twenties As Pictured in Sears & Other Catalogs. (Illus.). 160p. 1981. pap. price not set (ISBN 0-486-24134-3). Dover.
Boehn, Max Von. Modes & Manners: From the Middle Ages to the End of the Eighteenth Century, 4 vols. in 2. LC 68-56493. (Illus.). Repr. of 1932 ed. 50.00 (ISBN 0-405-08280-0, Blom Pubns). Arno.
Bond, David. Twentieth Century Fashion. (A Guiness Superlatives Guide Ser.). (Illus.). 224p. 1981. 24.95 (ISBN 0-8069-9258-1, Pub. by Guinness Superlatives England). Sterling.
Calasibetta, Charlotte M. Fairchild's Dictionary of Fashion. Davis, Lorraine & Goble, Ermina S., eds. LC 74-84805. (Illus.). 700p. 1975. 50.00 (ISBN 0-87005-133-4). Fairchild.
Caldwell, Doreen. And All Was Revealed. (Illus.). 144p. 1981. 8.95 (ISBN 0-312-03613-2). St Martin.
Carlsen, Peter & Wilson, William. Manstyle: The GQ Guide to Fashion, Fitness, & Grooming. (Illus.). 1977. 14.95 (ISBN 0-517-53076-7); pap. 8.95 (ISBN 0-517-53077-5). Potter.
Cordwell, Miriam & Rudoy, Marion. Hair Design & Fashion: Principles & Relationships. 6th & rev. ed. (Illus.). 1977. 14.95 (ISBN 0-517-53121-6). Crown.
Cremers van der Does, Eline. The Agony of Fashion. (Illus.). 128p. 1980. 17.50 (ISBN 0-7137-1058-6, Pub. by Blandford Pr England). Sterling.
DePaula, H. & Mueller, C. Marketing Today's Fashion. 1980. 15.95 (ISBN 0-13-558155-9). P-H.
Epstein, Beryl. Fashion Is Our Business. facs. ed. LC 72-117787. (Essay Index Reprint Ser). 1945. 18.00 (ISBN 0-8369-1920-3). Arno.
Erte. Things I Remember. LC 75-8286. (Illus.). 1975. 13.50 (ISBN 0-8129-0575-X). Times Bks.
Evans, Susan & Brown, Kirsten. Fashionsmarts. LC 80-82156. 256p. (Orig.). 1980. pap. 2.50 (ISBN 0-87216-723-2). Playboy Pbks.
Fairchild Market Research Division. The Customer Speaks. (Fairchild Fact File Ser.). 1979. pap. 20.00 (ISBN 0-87005-317-5). Fairchild.

--Fashion Accessories. (Fact File Ser). (Orig.). 1979. pap. 10.00 (ISBN 0-87005-319-1). Fairchild.
Fashion Buying. 1968. pap. 7.60 (ISBN 0-672-96044-3). Bobbs.
Fashion Merchandising Internship. 1968. pap. 15.15 wkbk. (ISBN 0-672-96060-5). Bobbs.
The Fashion Survival Manual. 256p. 15.95 (ISBN 0-686-73641-9); pap. 11.95 (ISBN 0-686-73642-7). Everest Hse.
Fashion Vocabulary & Dictation. 1969. pap. 8.50 (ISBN 0-672-96058-3). Bobbs.
Fraser, Kennedy. The Fashionable Mind: Essays on Fashion, 1970-1981. LC 81-47479. 256p. 1981. 13.95 (ISBN 0-686-72801-7). Knopf.
Frings, Virginia S. Fashion: From Concept to Consumer. (Illus.). 320p. 1982. 22.95 (ISBN 0-13-306605-3). P-H.
Gioello & Berke. Fashion Production Terms. LC 78-62289. (The Languages of Fashion Ser.). (Illus.). 1979. lib. bdg. 22.50 (ISBN 0-87005-200-4). Fairchild.
Gold, Annalee. How to Sell Fashion. 2nd ed. LC 78-51903. (Illus.). 1978. 12.50 (ISBN 0-87005-201-2). Fairchild.
Goldsworth, Maureen. New Fashion from Old. 1978. pap. 8.95 (ISBN 0-7134-0913-4, Pub. by Batsford England). David & Charles.
Gorsline, Douglas. What People Wore. (Illus.). 266p. 1974. pap. 5.95 (ISBN 0-517-14321-6). Crown.
Goschie, Susan. Fashion Direction & Coordination. 2nd ed. 1980. pap. 9.90 (ISBN 0-672-97266-2); tchr's manual 3.33 (ISBN 0-672-97267-0). Bobbs.
Grace, Evelyn. Introduction to Fashion Merchandising. LC 78-1318. (Illus.). 1978. ref. ed. 16.95 (ISBN 0-13-483206-X). P-H.
Green, Robert L. Robert L. Green's Live with Style. LC 78-9457. 1978. 10.95 (ISBN 0-698-10920-1). Coward.
Greenwood, Kathryn M. & Murphy, Mary F. Fashion Innovation & Marketing. (Illus.). 1978. 18.95 (ISBN 0-02-346950-1). Macmillan.
Groeg, Otto J., ed. Who's Who in Fashion, 3 vols. (Who's Who Ser.). 1980. Set. 228.00x (ISBN 3-921220-09-2, Pub. by Who's Who Germany). Standing Orders.
Hix, Charles & Burdine, Brian. Dressing Right. LC 78-3972. (Illus.). 1978. 17.50 (ISBN 0-312-21968-7). St Martin.
Hurlock, Elizabeth B. The Psychology of Dress: An Analysis of Fashion & Its Motive. LC 72-176089. (Illus.). Repr. of 1929 ed. 17.00 (ISBN 0-405-08644-X, Blom Pubns). Arno.
Jabenis, Elaine. The Fashion Director: What She Does & How to Be One. LC 72-768. 300p. 1972. pap. text ed. 16.50 (ISBN 0-471-43126-5). Wiley.
Jarnow, J. A. & Judelle, B. Inside the Fashion Business: Text & Readings. 1965. 19.95 (ISBN 0-87245-154-2). Textile Bk.
Jarnow, Jeannette A. Inside the Fashion Business: Text & Readings. 3rd ed. LC 80-25000. 427p. 1981. text ed. 18.95 (ISBN 0-471-06038-0). Wiley.
Judelle, Beatrice. The Fashion Buyer's Job. (Illus.). 1971. 14.50, member 9.70 (ISBN 0-685-24671-X, M46470). Natl Ret Merch.
Keenan, Bridgett. Dior in Vogue. 192p. 1981. 25.00 (ISBN 0-517-54448-2, Harmony). Crown.
Kushel, Lillian. Fashion Textiles & Laboratory Workbook. 2nd ed. 1971. pap. 15.15 (ISBN 0-672-96046-X); wkbk & kit 28.75 (ISBN 0-672-96049-4); textile kit 15.50 (ISBN 0-672-96048-6). Bobbs.
Lambert, Eleanor. Quips & Quotes About Fashion. LC 77-18242. 1978. pap. 2.95 (ISBN 0-87576-065-1). Pilot Bks.
Lenz, Bernie. The Complete Book of Fashion Modeling. (Illus.). 320p. 1969. 8.95 (ISBN 0-517-50193-7). Crown.
Leopold, Allison K. & Cloutier, Anne Marie. Short Chic: An Everything-You-Need-to-Know Fashion Guide for Every Woman Under 5'4". (Illus.). 1981. 12.95 (ISBN 0-89256-173-4). Rawson Wade.
Lepape, Georges, et al. French Fashion Plates in Full Color from the Gazette Du Bon Ton (1912-1925) 58 Illustrations of Styles by Paul Poiret, Worth, Paquin & Others. LC 79-50347. (Illus.). 1979. pap. 6.00 (ISBN 0-486-23805-9). Dover.
Lewis, Diehl & Loh, May. Patternless Fashions: How to Design & Make Your Own Fashions. (Illus.). 1980. 14.95 (ISBN 0-87491-416-7); pap. 8.95 (ISBN 0-87491-413-2). Acropolis.
McJimsey, Harriet T. Art & Fashion in Clothing Selection. 2nd ed. 295p. 1973. 12.50 (ISBN 0-8138-0150-8). Iowa St U Pr.
Mademoiselle Magazine Editors. Make It with Mademoiselle. 1977. pap. 5.95 (ISBN 0-517-52865-7, Harmony). Crown.
Madison Avenue Handbook. 300p. 1979. 13.00 (ISBN 0-686-62466-1). B Klein Pubns.
Milinaire, Caterine & Troy, Carol. Cheap Chic. (Illus.). 250p. (YA) 1976. pap. 5.95 (ISBN 0-517-52368-X, Harmony). Crown.
O'Connor, K. The Anthropology of Fashion. Date not set. price not set (ISBN 0-07-047528-8, GB). McGraw.
Old, Leila S. & Csizinsky, A. Vimlati. Personalized Apparel Design. LC 76-56466. 1977. 11.50 (ISBN 0-89301-040-5). U Pr of Idaho.
Packard & Axelrod. Instructor's Guide to Concepts & Cases in Fashion Buying & Merchandising. 1977. 2.50 (ISBN 0-87005-197-0). Fairchild.
--Instructor's Guide to Fashion Buying & Merchandising. 1978. 2.50 (ISBN 0-87005-287-X). Fairchild.
Packard, et al. Fashion Buying & Merchandising. LC 76-13571. (Illus.). 384p. 1976. 13.95 (ISBN 0-87005-142-3). Fairchild.
Packard, Sidney & Axelrod, Nathan. Concepts & Cases in Fashion Buying & Merchandising. LC 76-50439. 1977. text ed. 10.00 (ISBN 0-87005-182-2). Fairchild.
Packard, Sidney & Raine, Abraham A. Consumer Behavior & Fashion Marketing. 2nd ed. 315p. 1979. pap. text ed. write for info. (ISBN 0-697-08027-7); instr's manual avail. (ISBN 0-685-91860-2). Wm C Brown.
Peltz, Leslie R. Fashion, Color, Line, & Design. 2nd ed. 1980. 9.90 (ISBN 0-672-97277-8); tchr's manual 3.33 (ISBN 0-672-97278-6). Bobbs.
Probert, Christina. Shoes in Vogue Since Nineteen Ten. Benjamin, Phyllis, ed. (Accessories in Vogue Ser.). (Illus.). 96p. 1981. pap. 9.95 (ISBN 0-89659-241-3). Abbeville Pr.
Revson, Lyn. Lyn Revson's World of Style: How to Join It & Live It. LC 77-14945. (Illus.). 224p. 1980. pap. 7.95 (ISBN 0-87223-572-6, Dist. by Har-Row). Wideview Bks.
Robb. Lifestyle: The Autobiography of Robb. (Illus.). 1979. 19.95 (ISBN 0-241-10169-7, Pub. by Hamish Hamilton England). David & Charles.
Robinson, Julian. Fashions in the Forties. 88p. 1977. pap. 5.95 (ISBN 0-312-28456-X). St Martin.
Rubin, Leonard G. The World of Fashion: An Introduction. 1976. text ed. 20.95 scp (ISBN 0-06-453500-2, HarpC); tchr's ed o.p. free (ISBN 0-06-453501-0). Har-Row.
Sirkis, Susan B. Fashions Eighteen Seventy-One to Eighteen Seventy-Five. (The Wish Bklets: Vol. 3). 47p. 1967. pap. 5.50x (ISBN 0-913786-03-9). Wish Bklets.
--First Ladies Fashions, 1789-1865. (The Wish Bklets: Vol. 4). (Illus.). 48p. 1968. pap. 5.50x (ISBN 0-913786-04-7). Wish Bklets.
--First Ladies Fashions, 1865-1969. (The Wish Bklets: Vol. 5). (Illus.). 50p. (Orig.). 1969. pap. 5.50x (ISBN 0-913786-05-5). Wish Bklets.
--Miniature Fashions, 1848-1880-1896. (The Wish Bklets: Vol. 8). (Illus.). 48p. (Orig.). 1971. pap. 5.50x (ISBN 0-913786-08-X). Wish Bklets.
--Nineteenth Century Children's Fashions, Vol.9. (The Wish Booklets). 48p. 1972. pap. 5.50x (ISBN 0-913786-09-8). Wish Bklets.
--La Petite Bebe Eighteen Eighty Three to Eighteen Eighty-Seven, Vol. 11. (The Wish Booklets). 48p. 1973. pap. 5.50x (ISBN 0-913786-11-X). Wish Bklets.
Smith, Jane S. & Vreeland, Diana. Elsie De Wolfe: A Life in the High Style. LC 81-66447. 1982. 14.95 (ISBN 0-686-75367-4). Atheneum.
Spencer, Charles. Erte. (Illus.). 192p. 1970. 25.00 (ISBN 0-517-54564-0). Potter.
Sproles, George B. Fashion: Consumer Behavior Toward Dress. 1979. pap. 13.95x (ISBN 0-8087-3535-7). Burgess.
--Perspectives of Fashion. 160p. (Orig.). 1981. pap. text ed. write for info. (ISBN 0-8087-4510-7, Feffer & Simons). Burgess.
Stegemeyer, Ann. Who's Who in Fashion. (Illus.). 1980. text ed. 13.50 (ISBN 0-87005-257-8). Fairchild.
Thelen, Marilyn. Sew Big: A Fashion Guide for the Fuller Figure. rev. ed. (Illus.). 128p. 1981. pap. 5.95 (ISBN 0-935278-06-0). Palmer-Pletsch.
Tolman, Ruth. Fashion Marketing & Merchandising, Vol. 2. 1974. soft cover 13.25 (ISBN 0-87350-254-X). Milady.
--Guide to Fashion Merchandise Knowledge, Vol. 1. 1973. soft cover 13.25 (ISBN 0-87350-253-1). Milady.
Troxell, Mary D. Fashion Merchandising. 2nd ed. 1976. text ed. 16.50 (ISBN 0-07-065278-3, G); instructor's manual & key 3.50 (ISBN 0-07-065279-1). McGraw.
Troxell, Mary D. & Stone, Elaine. Fashion Merchandising. 3rd ed. LC 80-25077. (Gregg McGraw-Hill Marketing Ser.). (Illus.). 480p. 1981. 16.95 (ISBN 0-07-065280-5); instr's manual & key 4.00 (ISBN 0-07-065281-3). McGraw.
Wills, Gordon & Midgley, David. Fashion Marketing: An Anthology of Viewpoints & Perspectives. 1973. text ed. 35.00x (ISBN 0-04-380017-3). Allen Unwin.
Winters & Goodman. Fashion Advertising & Promotion. 1978. text ed. 13.50 (ISBN 0-87005-211-X). Fairchild.
Winters, Arthur A. & Goodman, Stanley. Fashion Sales Promotion Handbook. 3rd ed. 1967. pap. text ed. 8.95 (ISBN 0-672-96040-0); tchr's manual 5.00 (ISBN 0-672-96041-9). Bobbs.

FASHION–HISTORY

Ackermann. Ackermann's Costume Plates: Women's Fashions in England, 1818-1828. Blum, Stella, ed. 10.00 (ISBN 0-8446-5727-1). Peter Smith.
Baines, Barbara. Fashion Revivals. (Illus.). 200p. 1981. text ed. 13.95x (ISBN 0-7134-1929-6, Pub. by Batsford England). Drama Bk.
Batterberry, Michael & Batterberry, Ariane R. Mirror, Mirror: A Social History of Fashion. LC 77-71372. (Illus.). 1977. 29.95 (ISBN 0-03-021016-X). HR&W.
Black, J. Anderson & Garland, Madge. A History of Fashion. rev. ed. LC 80-82797. (Illus.). 304p. 1980. 35.00 (ISBN 0-688-03742-9). Morrow.
Boehn, Max Von. Ornaments--Lace, Fans, Gloves, Walking-Sticks, Parasols, Jewelry & Trinkets: Modes & Manners Supplement. LC 70-148467. (Illus.). Repr. of 1929 ed. 20.00 (ISBN 0-405-08286-X, Blom Pubns). Arno.
DeGraw, Imelda G. Twenty Five Years, Twenty Five Couturiers. LC 75-21427. (Illus.). 116p. (Orig.). 1975. pap. 2.95 (ISBN 0-914738-10-0). Denver Art Mus.
De Marley, Diana. The History of Haute Couture. LC 79-22987. (Illus.). 1980. Repr. text ed. 38.00 (ISBN 0-8419-0586-X). Holmes & Meier.
Ebbett, Eve. In True Colonial Fashion: A Lively Look at What Victorian New Zealanders Wore. 1977. 7.50 (ISBN 0-589-01037-9, Pub. by Reed Books Australia). C E Tuttle.
Ewing, Elizabeth. History of Twentieth-Century Fashion. LC 74-22731. 1975. 14.95 (ISBN 0-684-14190-6, ScribT). Scribner.
Gernsheim, Alison. Victorian & Edwardian Fashion: A Photographic Survey. Orig. Title: Fashion & Reality, 1840-1914. (Illus.). 240p. 1981. pap. price not set (ISBN 0-486-24205-6). Dover.
Gold, Annalee. Seventy-Five Years of Fashion. LC 74-24531. (Illus.). 1975. 8.95 (ISBN 0-87005-144-X). Fairchild.
Hill, Hamilton & Bucknell. Evolution of Fashion: Pattern & Cut from 1066-1930. 25.00x (ISBN 0-89676-064-2). Drama Bk.
Horn, Marilyn J. The Second Skin. 2nd ed. 1975. text ed. 19.50 (ISBN 0-395-18552-1); instructor's manual pap. 2.00 (ISBN 0-395-18780-X). HM.
Howell, Georgina. In Vogue. (Large Format Ser.). (Illus.). 1979. pap. 14.95 (ISBN 0-14-004955-X). Penguin.
Jachimowicz, Elizabeth. Eight Chicago Women & Their Fashions, 1860-1929. LC 78-53885. (Illus.). 1978. pap. 8.95 (ISBN 0-913820-09-1). Chicago Hist.
Laver, James. Concise History of Costume & Fashion. LC 73-18802. (Illus.). 1974. pap. 8.95 (ISBN 0-684-13522-1, SL477, ScribT). Scribner.
La Vine, Paul. In a Glamorous Fashion. (Illus.). 224p. 1980. 25.00 (ISBN 0-684-16610-0, ScribT). Scribner.
Lepape, Georges & Barbier, George. French Fashion Plates in Full Color from the Gazette Due Bon Ton(1912-1925) 12.50 (ISBN 0-8446-5785-9). Peter Smith.
Lotz, Arthur. Bibliographie der Modelbuecher: Beschreibendes Verzeichnis der Stick- und Spitzenmusterbuecher Des 16 und 17 Jahrhunderts. 2nd ed. (Illus.). 1963. Repr. of 1933 ed. 33.50 (ISBN 0-8337-5470-X). B Franklin.
Metropolitan Museum of Art. The Imperial Style: Fashions of the Hapsburg Era. (Illus.). 1980. 40.00 (ISBN 0-8478-5322-5). Rizzoli Intl.
Mills, Betty J. Flashes of Fashion: 1830-1972. Webber, Gale, ed. (Illus.). 192p. 1973. 10.00 (ISBN 0-911618-02-3). West Tex Mus.
Newton, Stella M. Fashion in the Age of the Black Prince: A Study of the Years 1340-1365. (Illus.). 151p. 1980. 37.50x (ISBN 0-8476-6939-4). Rowman.
Nuzzi, Christina. Parisian Fashions: From the "Journal Des Dames et Des Modes". LC 79-88270. (Illus.). 124p. 1980. Vol. 2. pap. 12.50 (ISBN 0-8478-0307-4). Rizzoli Intl.
--Parisian Fashions: From the "Journal des dames et des modes". LC 79-88270. (Illus., Orig.). 1979. pap. 12.50 (ISBN 0-8478-0253-1). Rizzoli Intl.
Peacock, John. Fashion Sketchbook Nineteen Twenty to Nineteen Sixty. (Illus.). 1977. pap. 4.95 (ISBN 0-380-01654-0, 33670). Avon.
Penn, Irving & Vreeland, Diana. Inventive Paris Clothes 1909-1939: A Photographic Essay. (Illus.). 1978. 18.95 (ISBN 0-670-40067-X, Studio). Viking Pr.
Rawlings, Eleanor, ed. Godey Costume Plates in Color for Decoupage & Framing. (Illus.). 1980. pap. 3.95 (ISBN 0-486-23879-2). Dover.
Robinson, Julian. Fashion in the Forties. LC 76-17338. (Illus.). 1976. pap. 7.95 (ISBN 0-312-28455-1). St Martin.
--Fashion in the 'Thirties. 1981. 27.00x (ISBN 0-905368-44-4, Pub. by Jupiter England). State Mutual Bk.
--Fashion in the Thirties. (Oresko Art Bks). (Illus.). 1978. 15.95 (ISBN 0-8467-0426-9, Pub. by Two Continents); pap. 9.95 (ISBN 0-8467-0427-7). Hippocrene Bks.
Sirkis, Susan B. Fashions Eighteen Eighty-Five. (The Wish Bklets: Vol. 13). (Illus.). 48p. 1974. pap. 5.50x (ISBN 0-913786-13-6). Wish Bklets.
--Fashions, Eighteen Hundred Six to Eighteen Ten. (The Wish Bklets: Vol. 15). (Illus.). 48p. 1975. pap. 5.50x (ISBN 0-913786-15-2). Wish Bklets.
--Men's Fashions: 1776-1850. (Wish Booklets Ser.: Vol. 20). (Illus.). 60p. 1977. pap. 5.50x (ISBN 0-913786-20-9). Wish Bklets.
--Men's Fashions: 1860-1970. (Wish Booklets Ser: Vol. 21). (Illus.). 52p. 1978. pap. 5.50x (ISBN 0-913786-21-7). Wish Bklets.
Wilson, Eunice. History of Shoe Fashion. LC 75-89994. (Illus.). pap. 10.95 (ISBN 0-87830-548-3). Theatre Arts.
Women's Wear Daily. Two Hundred Years of American Fashion. (Illus.). 1976. 9.50 (ISBN 0-87005-180-6); pap. 5.00 (ISBN 0-87005-181-4). Fairchild.

FASHION–VOCATIONAL GUIDANCE

Cassiday, Doris & Cassiday, Bruce. Fashion Industry Careers. (Career Concise Guides Ser.). (gr. 7 up). 6.90 (ISBN 0-531-01303-0). Watts.
Guerin, Polly. Fashion Writing. 1972. pap. text ed. 15.10 (ISBN 0-672-96033-8); tchr's manual 6.67 (ISBN 0-672-96034-6). Bobbs.
Hamburger, Estelle. The Fashion Business: It's All Yours. 1976. text ed. 15.95 scp (ISBN 0-06-453503-7, HarpC); pap. text ed. 12.50 scp (ISBN 0-06-453502-9). Har-Row.
LeVathes, Christine, ed. Your Future in the New World of American Fashion. (Careers in Depth Ser.). (gr. 7-12). 1979. PLB 5.97 (ISBN 0-8239-0458-X). Rosen Pr.
Lulow, JoAnn. Your Career in the Fashion Industry. LC 78-12724. (Arco Career Guidance Ser.). 1979. pap. 3.95 (ISBN 0-668-04613-9); pap. 3.50 (ISBN 0-668-04620-1). Arco.
McDermott, Irene E. & Norris, Jeanne L. Opportunities in Clothing. rev. ed. (Illus.). (gr. 9-12). 1972. text ed. 16.52 (ISBN 0-87002-140-0). Bennett IL.
Packard, Sidney & Guerreiro, Miriam. The Buying Game: Fashion Buying & Merchandising. (Illus.). 1979. ring-binder, wkbk. 15.50 (ISBN 0-87005-315-9). Fairchild.
Servian, Martha S. Fashion & Textile Careers. (Home Economics Careers Ser.). (gr. 10-12). 1977. 5.96 (ISBN 0-13-392779-2); pap. 3.96 (ISBN 0-13-392761-X). P-H.
Westerman, Maxine. Elementary Fashion Design & Trade Sketching. (Illus.). 128p. 1975. 10.00 (ISBN 0-87005-103-2). Fairchild.

FASHION DESIGN

see Costume Design

FASHION DRAWING

Erte. Designs by Erte: Fashion Drawings & Illustrations from Harper's Bazaar. Blum, S., ed. (Illus.). 13.50 (ISBN 0-8446-5571-6). Peter Smith.
Gioello, Debbie A. Fairchild's Designer: Stylist Handbook, 2 vols. (Illus.). 1979. Vol. 1. (ISBN 0-87005-332-9); Vol. 2. (ISBN 0-87005-333-7); Set. 35.00 (ISBN 0-686-76815-9); tracing pad 7.95 (ISBN 0-87005-334-5). Fairchild.
Ireland, Patrick J. Drawing & Designing Menswear. LC 76-22674. 1976. 12.95 (ISBN 0-470-98897-5). Halsted Pr.
Ridley, Pauline, intro. by. Fashion Illustration. LC 79-64758. (Illus.). 1980. pap. 8.50 (ISBN 0-8478-0248-5). Rizzoli Intl.
Rowe, P. L. Shorthand Fashion Sketching. 15.95 (ISBN 0-87245-286-7). Textile Bk.
Rowe, Patricia L. Shorthand Fashion Sketching. 4th ed. LC 60-6848. 1964. 13.50 (ISBN 0-87005-068-0). Fairchild.
Shackell, Dora & Masters, W. Stuart. Modern Fashion Drawing. 1978. lib. bdg. 69.95 (ISBN 0-8490-2266-5). Gordon Pr.
Sloane, Eunice M. Illustrating Fashion. rev. ed. LC 76-26254. (Illus.). 1977. 29.95 (ISBN 0-06-013893-9, HarpT). Har-Row.
Stephenson, Ann. Introduction to Fashion Illustrating. (Illus.). 140p. 1981. text ed. 14.50 (ISBN 0-87005-369-8). Fairchild.
Westerman, Maxine. Elementary Fashion Design & Trade Sketching. (Illus.). 128p. 1975. 10.00 (ISBN 0-87005-103-2). Fairchild.

FASHION MODELS

see Models, Fashion

FASHION PHOTOGRAPHY

Busselle, Michael. The Complete Book of Nude & Glamour Photography. (Illus.). 1981. 24.95 (ISBN 0-671-43445-4). S&S.

Devlin, Polly. The Vogue Book of Fashion Photography. 1979. 35.00 (ISBN 0-671-24371-3). S&S.
Duncan, Nancy H. The History of Fashion Photography. (Alpine Fine Arts Collection). (Illus.). 1979. 35.00 (ISBN 0-933516-00-2). Alpine Bk Co.
Farber, Robert. The Fashion Photographer. (Illus.). 192p. 1981. 24.95 (ISBN 0-8174-3850-5). Watson-Guptill.
--Professional Fashion Photography. (Illus.). 1978. 19.95 (ISBN 0-8174-2440-7). Amphoto.
Kelly, John. Successful Glamour Photography. (Illus.). 176p. 1981. 25.00 (ISBN 0-87165-117-3, ZD Bks). Ziff-Davis Pub.
O'Flaherty, Michael & David, Karen. Workshop in Glamour Photography. LC 78-24677. (Workshops in Photography Ser.). (Illus.). 1979. pap. 9.95 (ISBN 0-918696-13-5). Camera Graphic.
Tosches, Nick. Rear View. (Illus.). 96p. (Orig.). 1981. pap. 8.95 (ISBN 0-933328-06-0). Delilah Comm.
White, Nancy & Esten, John. Style in Motion: Munkacski Photographs of the Twenties, Thirties & Forties. (Illus.). 1979. 25.00 (ISBN 0-517-53858-X). Potter.

FASHION SHOWS

Corinth, K. Fashion Showmanship: Everything You Need to Know to Give a Fashion Show. 20.95 (ISBN 0-87245-061-9). Textile Bk.
Corinth, Kay. Fashion Showmanship: Everything You Need to Know to Give a Fashion Show. LC 76-109430. (Illus.). 1970. 20.95 (ISBN 0-471-17480-7). Wiley.
Diehl, Mary Ellen. How to Produce a Fashion Show. LC 76-20221. (Illus.). 160p. 1976. 10.00 (ISBN 0-87005-159-8). Fairchild.
Shirley, Thelma H. Success Guide to Exciting Fashion Shows. LC 78-75210. (Illus., Orig.). 1978. pap. 12.50 (ISBN 0-686-52691-0). Fashion Imprints.

FASHIONABLE SOCIETY

see Upper Classes

FASSBINDER, RAINER WERNER

McCormick, Ruth, tr. from Ger. Fassbinder. (Illus.). 224p. 1981. 15.95 (ISBN 0-686-72839-4); pap. 7.95 (ISBN 0-934378-18-5). Tanam Pr.
Rayns, Tony, ed. Fassbinder. 2nd, rev. ed. (BFI Ser.). (Illus.). 1980. 18.25 (ISBN 0-85170-095-0); pap. 9.95 (ISBN 0-85170-096-9). NY Zoetrope.

FAST DAYS

see Fasts and Feasts

FAST PULSE REACTORS

see Pulsed Reactors

FAST-RESPONSE DATA PROCESSING

see Real-Time Data Processing

FASTENERS

see also Buttons; Locks and Keys; Sealing (Technology)

Crouse, William H. & Anglin, Donald L. Automotive Tools, Fasteners, and Measurements: A Text-Workbook. (Automotive Technology Series). (Illus.). (gr. 9-12). 1977. pap. text ed. 6.95 (ISBN 0-07-014630-6, G). McGraw.
Design News, ed. Design News Fastening Directory. (Design News Directories Ser.). 175p. 1981. pap. 12.00x (ISBN 0-686-73566-8, DNF). Herman Pub.
Din Standards: Fasteners, Dimensional Standards for Screws, Nuts & Accessories. 1100.00 (ISBN 0-686-28165-9, 10049-5/10). Heyden.
Din Standards, Fasteners: Standards for Accessories for Bolted Connections. 312.00 (ISBN 0-686-28195-0, 11200-4/140). Heyden.
Din Standards for Clamping Devices. 429.00 (ISBN 0-686-28167-5, 10050-4/14). Heyden.
Dinstandards Fastners: Basic Standards, Quality Standards & Technical Conditions of Delivery for Screws, Bolts, Nuts & Accessories. 224.00 (ISBN 0-686-28190-X, 10794-5/55). Heyden.
Fasteners: Bolts & Pins, Studes, Rivets, Keys, Adjusting Rings, Retaining Rings. 487.00 (ISBN 0-686-28182-9, 10407-5/43). Heyden.
Industrial Fasteners. (Industrial Equipment & Supplies Ser.). 160p. 1981. 350.00 (ISBN 0-686-31537-5). Busn Trend.
Institute for Power System. Handbook of Industrial Fasteners. 700p. 1979. 99.00x (ISBN 0-85461-062-6). State Mutual Bks.
Metric Mechanical Fasteners. 1975. pap. 12.00 (ISBN 0-686-52060-2, 04-587000-34). ASTM.
Morgan-Grampian Books, ed. Fastenings Locator, 1980. 114p. 1980. 35.00x (ISBN 0-686-75512-X, Pub. by Morgan-Grampian Bk). State Mutual Bk.
Standards on Fasteners. 1978. 17.50 (ISBN 0-686-52102-1, 03-601600-01). ASTM.
Trade & Technical Press Editors. Handbook of Industrial Fasteners. 700p. 1975. 108.00 (ISBN 0-85461-062-6, Pub by Trade & Tech England). Renouf.
Transactions of Technical Conference on Metric Mechanical Fasteners. 122p. 1975. pap. text ed. 12.00 (ISBN 0-685-62576-1, E00092). ASME.

FASTER READING

see Rapid Reading

FASTING

see also Fasts and Feasts

Airola, Paavo. How to Keep Slim, Healthy & Young with Juice Fasting. 1971. 3.95 (ISBN 0-932090-02-8). Health Plus.
Anderson, Andy. Fasting Changed My Life. LC 77-82404. 1977. pap. 2.94 (ISBN 0-8054-5259-1). Broadman.
Beall, James L. The Adventure of Fasting. 96p. 1974. pap. 2.95 (ISBN 0-8007-0683-8); pap. 1.95 (ISBN 0-8007-8397-2, Spire Bks). Revell.
Bragg, Paul C. & Bragg, Patricia. Miracle of Fasting. 30th ed. LC 66-18775. pap. 4.95 (ISBN 0-87790-002-7). Health Sci.
Brianchaninov, Ignatius. Fasting. pap. 0.25 (ISBN 0-686-05642-6). Eastern Orthodox.
Cott, Allan, et al. Fasting: A Way of Life. 1977. pap. 2.25 (ISBN 0-553-14484-7). Bantam.
Ehret, Arnold. Instructions for Fasting & Dieting. 1980. pap. 2.95 (ISBN 0-87904-003-3). Lust.
--Rational Fasting. 168p. 1971. pap. 2.25 (ISBN 0-87904-005-X). Lust.
Faris, N. A. The Mysteries of Fasting. pap. 2.75 (ISBN 0-686-18615-X). Kazi Pubns.
Fulton, Alvenia M. The Fasting Primer. 2nd & rev. ed. Williams, James C., ed. LC 78-60661. 1978. pap. 4.95 (ISBN 0-931564-04-2). BCA Pub.
Goldstein, Jack. Triumph Over Disease - by Fasting & Natural Diet. LC 76-44863. 1977. 5.95. (ISBN 0-668-04138-2). Arco.
Hazzard, Linda B. About Scientific Fasting. 1980. pap. 1.95 (ISBN 0-87904-044-0). Lust.
Hills, Christopher. Rejuvenating the Body Through Fasting with Spirulina Plankton. 2nd ed. (Illus.). 64p. 1980. pap. text ed. 2.50 (ISBN 0-916438-35-X). Univ of Trees.
Johnson, Charles W., Jr. Fasting, Longevity, & Immortality. (Illus.). 213p. (Orig.). pap. 3.00 (ISBN 0-686-27081-9). Survival CT.
Kirban, Salem. How to Keep Healthy & Happy by Fasting. (Illus.). 1976. 6.95 (ISBN 0-912582-23-5); pap. 2.95 (ISBN 0-912582-23-5). Kirban.
Lindsay, Gordon. Prayer & Fasting. (School of Prayer Ser.). 1.50 (ISBN 0-89985-076-6). Christ Nations.
--Prayer That Moves Mountains. (School of Prayer Ser.). 1.95 (ISBN 0-89985-078-2). Christ Nations.
Linn, Robert & Stuart, Sandra L. The Last Chance Diet. 1976. 10.00 (ISBN 0-8184-0239-3). Lyle Stuart.
MacFadden, Bernarr. Fasting for Health. LC 77-14957. (Classic of Health & Nutrition Ser.). 1978. pap. 1.65 (ISBN 0-668-04492-6, 4492). Arco.
Palmer, W. Robert. What the Bible Says About Faith & Opinion. LC 79-57088. (What the Bible Says Ser.). 1980. 13.50 (ISBN 0-89900-076-2). College Pr Pub.
Partee, Phillip E. The Layman's Guide to Fasting & Losing Weight: Introduced by Dick Gregory. Levy, H. M., Jr., ed. LC 78-64863. (Illus., Orig.). (gr. 10-12). 1979. pap. text ed. 3.95 (ISBN 0-685-94383-6). Sprout Pubns.
Perry, Paul. Fasting Safely. LC 78-68564. 128p. (Orig.). 1981. pap. 4.95 (ISBN 0-89037-217-9). Anderson World.
Prince, Derek. How to Fast Successfully. 1976. pap. 1.50 (ISBN 0-934920-19-2, B-28). Derek Prince.
--Restoration Through Fasting. 1970. pap. 0.75 (ISBN 0-934920-12-5, B-21). Derek Prince.
--Shaping History Through Prayer & Fasting. 192p. 1973. 4.95 (ISBN 0-8007-0616-1). Revell.
--Shaping History Through Prayer & Fasting. 1975. pap. 1.95 (ISBN 0-8007-8180-5, Spire Bks). Revell.
Ryan, Thomas. Fasting Rediscovered: A Guide to Health & Wholeness for Your Body-Spirit. LC 80-81581. 160p. (Orig.). 1981. pap. 5.95 (ISBN 0-8091-2323-1). Paulist Pr.
Shelton, Herbert M. Fasting Can Save Your Life. 2nd ed. LC 78-70060. (Illus.). 1978. pap. 2.25 (ISBN 0-914532-23-5). Natural Hygiene.
--Fasting for Renewal of Life. LC 74-82368. 316p. (Orig.). 1974. pap. 3.25 (ISBN 0-914532-09-X). Natural Hygiene.
--The Science & Fine Art of Fasting. rev. ed. LC 77-99219. 1978. pap. 7.25 (ISBN 0-914532-21-9). Natural Hygiene.
Smith, D. Fasting. 1973. 1.95 (ISBN 0-87508-516-4); pap. 1.50 (ISBN 0-87508-515-6). Chr Lit.
Smith, J. Harold. Fast Your Way to Health. LC 79-1437. 1979. pap. 3.95 (ISBN 0-8407-5676-3). Nelson.
Wade, Carlson. Natural Way to Health Through Controlled Fasting. LC 68-14769. 1970. pap. 1.95 (ISBN 0-668-02132-2). Arco.
Wallis, Arthur. God's Chosen Fast. 1970. pap. 1.50 (ISBN 0-87508-555-5). Chr Lit.
Wimmer, Joseph F. Fasting in the New Testament. 160p. (Orig.). 1982. pap. 7.95 (ISBN 0-8091-2420-3). Paulist Pr.

FASTS AND FEASTS

Here are entered works on religious fasts and feasts in general and on Christian fasts and feasts.
see also Agape; Christmas; Chronology; Church Year; Easter; Epiphany; Festivals; Good Friday; Holidays; Lent; Pentecost Festival; Sacred Meals; Thanksgiving Day

Bludau, August. Die Pilgerreise der Aetheria. pap. 18.50 (ISBN 0-384-04760-2). Johnson Repr.
Chambers, Robert, ed. Book of Days: A Miscellany of Popular Antiquities in Connection with the Calendar, Including Anecdote, Biography & History, Curiosities of Literature, & Oddities of Human Life & Character, 2 Vols. LC 67-13009. (Illus.). 1967. Repr. of 1862 ed. 74.00 (ISBN 0-8103-3002-4). Gale.
Courtney, Margaret A. Cornish Feasts & Folk-Lore. LC 77-8082. 1977. lib. bdg. 25.00 (ISBN 0-8414-1829-2). Folcroft.
Cronin, Gaynell & Cronin, Jim. Celebrations. 1980. pap. 7.55 (ISBN 0-88479-031-2). Arena Lettres.
Deems, Edward M., ed. Holy-Days & Holidays: A Treasury of Historical Material, Sermons in Full & in Brief, Suggestive Thoughts & Poetry, Relating to Holy Days & Holidays. LC 68-17940. 1968. Repr. of 1902 ed. 40.00 (ISBN 0-8103-3352-X). Gale.
Duddington, John W. Festal Christianity: A Theology of the Mighty Acts. 1977. 10.00 (ISBN 0-533-02802-7). Vantage.
Falwell, Jerry. Fasting. 1981. pap. 2.50 (ISBN 0-8423-0849-0). Tyndale.
Gaster, Theodor H. Festivals of the Jewish Year: A Modern Interpretation & Guide. 1961. pap. 4.95 (ISBN 0-688-06008-0). Morrow.
Hackwood, Frederick W. Good Cheer: The Romance of Food & Feasting. LC 68-9571. 1968. Repr. of 1911 ed. 22.00 (ISBN 0-8103-3508-5). Gale.
Hatch, Jane M., ed. American Book of Days. 1212p. 1978. 50.00 (ISBN 0-8242-0593-6). Wilson.
Hazlitt, William C. Faiths & Folklore of the British Isles, 2 Vols. LC 64-18758. 1905. Set. 40.00 (ISBN 0-405-08604-0, Blom Pubns); 20.00 ea. Vol. 1 (ISBN 0-405-08605-9). Vol. 2 (ISBN 0-405-08606-7). Arno.
Huck, Gabe. Major Feasts & Seasons: November, Christmas, Lent, Easter, & Summer, 5 vols. 1976. pap. 8.95 ea. (ISBN 0-686-51450-5). Liturgical Conf.
Long, George. Folklore Calendar. LC 76-78191. 1970. Repr. of 1930 ed. 21.00 (ISBN 0-8103-3367-8). Gale.
Nieting, Lorenz. Lesser Festivals 4: Saints' Days & Special Occasions. Achtemeier, Elizabeth, et al, eds. LC 79-7377. (Proclamation Two Ser.: Aids for Interpreting the Lessons of the Church Year). 64p. (Orig.). 1981. pap. 2.50 (ISBN 0-8006-1396-1, 1-1396). Fortress.
Reid, Richard & Crum, Milton, Jr. Lesser Festivals 3: Saints' Days & Special Occasions. Achtemeier, Elizabeth, et al, eds. LC 79-7377. (Proclamation 2: Aids for Interpreting the Lessons of the Church Year). 64p. (Orig.). 1981. pap. 2.50 (ISBN 0-8006-1395-3, 1-1395). Fortress.
Ritchie, John. Feasts of Jehovah. 80p. 1981. pap. 2.95 (ISBN 0-8254-3613-3). Kregel.
Rogers, E. N. Fasting: The Phenomenon of Self-Denial. LC 76-143. 160p. (gr. 8 up). 1976. 6.95 (ISBN 0-525-66462-9). Elsevier-Nelson.
Smith, Fredrick W. Journal of a Fast. LC 75-36493. 1976. 7.95 (ISBN 0-8052-3609-0). Schocken.
Smith, Waldemar R. Fiesta System & Economic Change. LC 77-390. 1977. 16.00x (ISBN 0-231-04180-2). Columbia U Pr.
Zimmerman, Martha. Celebrate the Feasts: Of the Old Testament in Your Own Home or Church. 186p. 1981. pap. 4.95 (ISBN 0-87123-228-6). Bethany Hse.

FASTS AND FEASTS–CATHOLIC CHURCH

De Balaguer, J. Escriva. Christ Is Passing by. LC 74-78783. (Illus.). 276p. (Foreign language editions avail). 1977. pap. write for info. (ISBN 0-933932-04-9). Scepter Pubs.

FASTS AND FEASTS–JUDAISM

see also names of individual fasts and feast, e.g. sukkoth

Abramson, Lillian S. & Leiderman, Lillian T. Jewish Holiday Party Book: A Practical Guide to Parties Planned for Children Ages 5-12. 2nd ed. LC 54-11436. 1966. 3.50 (ISBN 0-8197-0051-7). Bloch.
Adler, David A. A Picture Book of Jewish Holidays. (Illus.). 32p. (gr. k-3). 1981. reinforced bdg 8.95 (ISBN 0-8234-0433-1). Holiday.
Agnon, Shmuel Y. Days of Awe: A Treasury of Tradition, Legends & Learned Commentaries Concerning Rosh Hashanah, Yom Kippur & the Days Between. LC 48-8316. 1965. 7.50x (ISBN 0-8052-3049-1); pap. 5.95 (ISBN 0-8052-0100-9). Schocken.
Batist, Bessie, ed. A Treasure for My Daughter. pap. 3.95 (ISBN 0-8015-7939-2, Hawthorn). Dutton.
Bloch, A. P. The Biblical & Historical Background of the Jewish Holy Days. 20.00x (ISBN 0-87068-338-1). Ktav.
Brinn, Ruth E. Lets Celebrate: Fifty-Seven Jewish Holiday Crafts for Young Children. (Illus.). (ps-4). 1977. pap. 3.95 (ISBN 0-930494-02-4). Kar Ben.
Brinn, Ruth E. & Saypol, Judyth R. Let's Have a Party: 101 Mix & Match a Party Ideas for the Jewish Holidays. (Illus.). 80p. 1981. pap. 4.95 (ISBN 0-930494-10-5). Kar Ben.
Cashman, Greer F. Jewish Days & Holidays. (Illus.). 64p. 1979. Repr. of 1976 ed. 8.95 (ISBN 0-89961-000-5). SBS Pub.
Chaikin, Miriam. The Seventh Day: The Story of the Jewish Sabbath. (Illus.). (gr. k-3). 1981. lib. bdg. 7.35 (ISBN 0-385-14920-4). Doubleday.
Challenge Your Child to Pesach. Date not set. pap. 0.79 (ISBN 0-686-76487-0). Feldheim.
Chanover, Hyman & Zusman, Evelyn. A Book of Prayer for Junior Congregations: Sabbath & Festivals. 256p. (Eng. & Heb.). (gr. 4-7). 4.50x (ISBN 0-8381-0174-7, 10-174). United Syn Bk.
Cycle of the Jewish Year. Date not set. 6.00 (ISBN 0-686-76502-8). Feldheim.
Drucker, Malka. Rosh Hashanah & Yom Kippur: Sweet Beginnings. (Illus.). 96p. (gr. 5 up). 1981. reinforced bdg 8.95 (ISBN 0-8234-0427-7). Holiday.
Edidin, Ben M. Jewish Holidays & Festivals. 226p. 1941. 4.95 (ISBN 0-88482-428-4). Hebrew Pub.
Eisenberg, Azriel & Robinson, Jessie B. My Jewish Holidays. 208p. (gr. 5-6). 3.95x (ISBN 0-8381-0176-3, 10-176). United Syn Bk.
Elias, Joseph. The Haggadah. (The Art Scroll Mesorah Ser.). 224p. 1977. 8.95 (ISBN 0-89906-150-8); pap. 5.95 (ISBN 0-89906-151-6). Mesorah Pubns.
Epstein, Morris. Pictorial Treasury of Jewish Holidays. (Illus.). (gr. 7 up). 1959. pap. 9.95x (ISBN 0-87068-360-8). Ktav.
Gaster, Theodor H. Festivals of the Jewish Year. 1962. 8.50 (ISBN 0-8446-2113-7). Peter Smith.
Gilbert, Arthur & Tarcov, Oscar. Your Neighbor Celebrates. 38p. 0.75 (ISBN 0-686-74967-7). ADL.
Goldman, Alex J. A Handbook for the Jewish Family: Understanding & Enjoying the Sabbath & Other Holidays. LC 58-12938. (Illus.). 1977. pap. 6.95 (ISBN 0-8197-0085-1). Bloch.
The Gospel in the Feasts of Israel. 1954. pap. 1.95 (ISBN 0-915540-00-2). Friends Israel-Spearhead Pr.
Jewish Holiday Fun Book. Date not set. pap. 1.95 (ISBN 0-686-76520-6). Feldheim.
Kanter, Shamai. Rabban Gamaliel II: The Legal Traditions. LC 80-12229. (Brown Judaic Studies: No. 8). 15.00x (ISBN 0-89130-403-7, 14 00 08); pap. 10.50x (ISBN 0-89130-404-5). Scholars Pr CA.
Kaplan, Aryeh. The Story of Tisha B'Av. 160p. (Orig.). 1981. pap. 2.95 (ISBN 0-940118-32-7). Maznaim.
Kripke, Dorothy K. Let's Talk About the Jewish Holidays. LC 75-104328. (Illus.). (gr. k-4). 1970. 5.95 (ISBN 0-8246-0106-8). Jonathan David.
Machzorim-Rosh Hashana & Yom Kippur. Date not set. 9.00 (ISBN 0-686-76540-0). Feldheim.
Margolis, Isidor & Markowitz, Sidney L. Jewish Holidays & Festivals. (Orig.). 1962. pap. 2.95 (ISBN 0-8065-0285-1). Citadel Pr.
Orovitz, Norma A. & Tabachnikoff, Barry. Time to Rhyme: Jewish Holiday Book. LC 76-19970. (Illus.). 32p. 1976. pap. 2.50 (ISBN 0-88400-046-X). Shengold.
Passover Holiday Fun Book. Date not set. pap. 1.95 (ISBN 0-686-76245-2). Feldheim.
Roth, Cecil. Soncino Haggadah. 9.75x (ISBN 0-685-01039-2). Bloch.
Saypol, Judyth R. & Wikler, Madeline. My Very Own Haggadah. (Illus.). (ps-4). 1974. pap. 1.95 (ISBN 0-930494-00-8). Kar Ben.
--My Very Own Megillah. (Illus.). (ps-4). 1977. pap. 1.95 (ISBN 0-930494-01-6). Kar Ben.
--My Very Own Sukkot Book. (Illus.). 40p. (Orig.). (gr. k-6). 1980. pap. 2.95 (ISBN 0-930494-09-1). Kar Ben.
Schauss, Hayyim. Jewish Festivals: From Their Beginnings to Our Own Day. rev. ed. (Illus.). (YA) 1969. 8.00 (ISBN 0-8074-0095-5, 383202); course syll. 1.25 (ISBN 0-686-66555-4, 247330). UAHC.
--The Jewish Festivals: History & Observance. LC 62-13140. 1973. pap. 5.95 (ISBN 0-8052-0413-X). Schocken.
Scherman, Nossen, tr. The Family Haggadah. (Artscroll Mesorah Ser.). 96p. (Orig.). 1981. pap. 1.95 (ISBN 0-89906-178-8). Mesorah Pubns.
Scherman, Nosson. The Haggadah Treasury. (The Art Scroll Mesorah Ser.). 200p. 1978. 8.95 (ISBN 0-89906-200-8); pap. 5.95 (ISBN 0-89906-201-6). Mesorah Pubns.

Seidman, Hillel. The Glory of the Jewish Holidays. 2nd ed. LC 68-58504. (Illus.). 1980. 13.95 (ISBN 0-88400-065-6). Shengold.

Shepherd, Coulson. Jewish Holy Days: Their Prophetic & Christian Significance. LC 61-16660. 1961. pap. 2.50 (ISBN 0-87213-780-5). Loizeaux.

Silverman, Morris, ed. Passover Haggadah. 4.95x (ISBN 0-686-02385-4); pap. 1.95x (ISBN 0-686-02386-2). Hartmore.

Simon, Norma. Tu Bishvat. (Festival Series of Picture Story Books). (Illus.). (ps-k). 1961. plastic cover 3.95 (ISBN 0-8381-0709-5). United Syn Bk.

Sperling, Abraham I. Reasons for Jewish Customs & Traditions. Matts, Abraham, tr. LC 68-31711. 1975. 10.00x (ISBN 0-8197-0184-X); pap. 6.95x (ISBN 0-8197-0008-8). Bloch.

Stern, Chaim, ed. Gates of Repentance. 1978. 10.00 (ISBN 0-916694-38-0); pulpit ed. 20.00 (ISBN 0-916694-40-2); Hebrew ed. 10.00 (ISBN 0-916694-39-9); hebrew pulpit ed. 20.00 (ISBN 0-686-77334-9). Central Conf.

The Weekday Seder. Date not set. 12.50 (ISBN 0-686-76276-2). Feldheim.

Zevin, Shlomo Y. The Festivals in Halachah, Vol. II. Kaploon, Uri, ed. Fox-Ashrei, Meir, tr. from Hebrew. (Artscroll Judica Classics Ser.). 336p. 1981. 13.95 (ISBN 0-89906-908-8); pap. 10.95 (ISBN 0-89906-909-6). Mesorah Pubns.

FASTS AND FEASTS–JUDAISM–DRAMA

Rosenberg, David. Chosen Days: Celebrating Jewish Festivals in Poetry & Art. LC 79-7906. (Illus.). 224p. 1980. 14.95 (ISBN 0-385-14365-6). Doubleday.

FASTS AND FEASTS–JUDAISM–JUVENILE LITERATURE

Bates, Barbara. Bible Festivals & Holy Days. LC 68-22254. (Illus.). (gr. 4 up). 1968. 4.25 (ISBN 0-8054-4406-8). Broadman.

Becker, Joyce. Jewish Holiday Crafts. (Illus.). (gr. 1 up). 1977. 9.95 (ISBN 0-88482-757-7, Bonim Bks); pap. 6.95 (ISBN 0-88482-755-0, Bonim Bks). Hebrew Pub.

Cuyler, Margery. Jewish Holidays. LC 77-10801. (Illus.). (gr. 2-5). 1978. 5.95 (ISBN 0-03-039936-X). HR&W.

Englander, Lois, et al. The Jewish Holiday Do-Book. new ed. 1977. 9.95 (ISBN 0-685-76976-3); pap. 6.95 (ISBN 0-8197-0451-2). Bloch.

Epstein, Morris. All About Jewish Holidays & Customs. rev. ed. (gr. 5-6). 1969. pap. 5.95x (ISBN 0-87068-500-7). Ktav.

--My Holiday Story Book. rev. ed. (gr. 4-5). 1958. 5.00x (ISBN 0-87068-368-3). Ktav.

Fine, Helen. G'Dee. (Illus.). (gr. 4-5). 1958. text ed. 4.50 (ISBN 0-8074-0137-4, 123702). UAHC.

Garvey, Robert. First Book of Jewish Holidays. (Illus.). (gr. 1-2). 1954. 4.00x (ISBN 0-87068-362-4). Ktav.

--Holidays Are Nice. (Illus.). (gr. 4-5). 1960. 6.95x (ISBN 0-87068-363-2). Ktav.

Gersh, Harry. When a Jew Celebrates. LC 70-116678. (Jewish Values Ser). (Illus.). 256p. (gr. 5-6). 1971. pap. text ed. 6.95x (ISBN 0-87441-091-6). Behrman.

Grand, Tamar. Holiday-Craft Kit for the Jewish Child. (Illus.). (ps). 1976. pap. text ed. 5.00 (ISBN 0-8074-0138-2, 103901). UAHC.

Greenfeld, Howard. Rosh Hashanah & Yom Kippur. LC 79-4818. (Illus.). (gr. k-4). 1979. 5.95 (ISBN 0-03-044756-9). HR&W.

Jaffe, Leonard. The Pitzel Holiday Book. (Illus.). (gr. 5-8). 1962. 5.95x (ISBN 0-87068-359-4). Ktav.

Kozodoy, Ruth. The Book of Jewish Holidays. Rossel, Seymour, ed. (Illus.). 192p. (Orig.). (gr. 4-5). 1981. pap. text ed. 5.95x (ISBN 0-87441-334-6). Behrman.

Lazar, Wendy Phillips. Jewish Holiday Book. LC 76-42342. (gr. 6-12). 1977. 8.95a (ISBN 0-385-11426-5); PLB (ISBN 0-385-11427-3). Doubleday.

FAT

Here is entered material on fat in its relation to the animal organism. Works on the technological aspects of fats in general are entered under the heading Oils and Fats.

see also Fat Metabolism; Low-Fat Diet

Fat Emulsions in Parenteral Nutrition. pap. 7.00 (ISBN 0-89970-042-X, OP-140). AMA.

Hausman, Patricia. Jack Sprat's Legacy: The Science & Politics of Fat & Cholesterol. 320p. 1981. 12.95 (ISBN 0-399-90111-6). Marek.

Holman, Ralph T., et al, eds. Progress in the Chemistry of Fats & Other Lipids, Vols. 5-14. Incl. Vol. 5. Advances in Technology. 1958. 50.00 (ISBN 0-08-009098-2); Vol. 6. 1963. 50.00 (ISBN 0-08-009863-0); Vol. 7. Pt. 1, 1964. pap. 15.50 (ISBN 0-08-010087-2); Vol. 8. 1965. Vol. 8, Pt. 2. pap. 15.50 (ISBN 0-686-57466-4); Vol. 9, Pt. 1. Polyunsaturated Acids. 1966. pap. 15.50 (ISBN 0-08-011797-X); Vol. 9, Pts. 2-5. pap. 20.00 ea.; Pt. 2, 1968. pap. (ISBN 0-08-012632-4); Pt. 3. 1967. pap. (ISBN 0-08-013239-1); Pt. 4. 1968. pap. (ISBN 0-08-015971-0); Pt. 5, 1970. pap. (ISBN 0-08-016111-1); Vol. 9, Complete, 1971 Cloth. 62.50 (ISBN 0-08-016041-7); Complete, 1970. Cloth. 50.00 (ISBN 0-08-016040-9); Vol. 10, 1-4. pap. 15.50 ea.; Pt. 1, 1967. pap. (ISBN 0-08-012292-2); Pt. 2, 1969. pap. (ISBN 0-08-012996-X); Pt. 3, 1969. pap. (ISBN 0-08-012997-8); Pt. 4, 1969. 62.50 (ISBN 0-08-013990-6); Complete, 1972. Cloth. 50.00 (ISBN 0-08-016795-0); Vol. 11, Pts. 1-3. pap. 15.50 ea.; Pt. 1, 1970. pap. (ISBN 0-08-015847-1); Pt. 2, 1970. pap. (ISBN 0-08-016150-2); Pt. 3, 1971. pap. (ISBN 0-08-016571-0); Vol. 12. 1972. 50.00 (ISBN 0-08-016758-6); Complete. Cloth. 50.00 (ISBN 0-08-017146-X); Vol. 13, Pts. 1-4. pap. 15.50 ea.; Pt. 1. pap. (ISBN 0-08-016942-2); Pt. 2. pap. (ISBN 0-08-017043-9); Pt. 3. pap. (ISBN 0-08-017176-1); Pt. 4. 62.50 (ISBN 0-08-017129-X); Vol. 14, Pt. 1. pap. 15.50 (ISBN 0-08-017130-3); Vol. 14, Pt. 2. Lipids of Fungi. pap. 15.50 (ISBN 0-08-017880-4); Vol. 14, Pt. 3. Infrared Absorption Spectroscopy of Normal & Substituted Long-Chain Fatty Acids & Esters in Solid State. Fischmeister. pap. 15.00 (ISBN 0-08-018073-6); Vol. 14, Pt. 4. Lipid Metabolism Membrane Functions of the Mammary Gland. Patton, S. & Jensen, R. G. pap. 15.50 (ISBN 0-08-018222-4); Vol. 14, Complete. 1975. 50.00 (ISBN 0-08-017808-1). LC 53-22998. Pergamon.

Parizkova, Jana. Body Fat & Physical Fitness. Osancova, K., tr. from Czech. (Illus.). 280p. 1977. 32.50 (ISBN 90-247-1925-9, Pub. by Nijhoff). Wright-PSG.

FAT METABOLISM

Sherbet, G. V., ed. Neoplasia & Cell Differentiation. (Illus.). 1974. 84.00 (ISBN 3-8055-1581-2). S Karger.

Soling, H. D. & Seufert, C. D., eds. Biochemical & Clinical Aspects of Ketone Body Metabolism. LC 76-52978. (Illus.). 280p. 1978. 34.50 (ISBN 0-88416-144-7). Wright-PSG.

FATE AND FATALISM

see also Free Will and Determinism; Necessity (Philosophy); Predestination

Bryans, J. Lonsdale. The Curve of Fate: From Man-Ape to the Man-God. 1977. lib. bdg. 59.95 (ISBN 0-8490-1696-7). Gordon Pr.

Cather, Willa. Obscure Destinies. LC 74-5323. 1974. pap. 1.95 (ISBN 0-394-71179-3, V-179, Vin). Random.

Curtiss, H. A. & Curtiss, F. H. The Key of Destiny. 372p. 1981. pap. 12.00 (ISBN 0-89540-070-7, SB-070). Sun Pub.

--The Key to the Universe. 391p. 1981. pap. 13.50 (ISBN 0-89540-069-3, SB-069). Sun Pub.

Deacon, Richard. Napoleon's Book of Fate. Orig. Title: The Book of Fate: Its Origins & Uses. 1977. 10.00 (ISBN 0-8065-0564-8); pap. 4.95 (ISBN 0-8065-0577-X). Citadel Pr.

Eberhard, Engelbert. Das Schicksal Als Poetische Idee Bei Homer. 1923. pap. 6.00 (ISBN 0-384-13785-7). Johnson Repr.

Elliott, Albert P. Fatalism in the Works of Thomas Hardy. LC 74-10791. 1972. lib. bdg. 8.75 (ISBN 0-8414-3950-8). Folcroft.

--Fatalism in the Works of Thomas Hardy. LC 66-11360. 1966. Repr. of 1935 ed. 9.00 (ISBN 0-8462-0663-3). Russell.

Fortes, Meyer. Oedipus & Job in West African Religion. 1980. Repr. of 1959 ed. lib. bdg. 13.50x (ISBN 0-374-92820-7). Octagon.

Guardini, Romano. Freedom, Grace, & Destiny. Murray, John, tr. from Ger. LC 75-8786. 384p. 1975. Repr. of 1961 ed. lib. bdg. 14.50x (ISBN 0-8371-8111-9, GUFG). Greenwood.

Haich, Elisabeth & Yesudian, Selvarajan. Yoga & Destiny. LC 74-83157. 1974. 4.95 (ISBN 0-88231-008-9). ASI Pubs Inc.

Hughes, Albert E. Your Fate in Your Handwriting. 160p. 20.00x (ISBN 0-85435-334-8, Pub. by Spearman England). State Mutual Bk.

Ledbetter, Ferman. The Power of Warnings. 1978. 4.95 (ISBN 0-533-03571-6). Vantage.

May, Rollo. Freedom & Destiny. 1981. 14.95 (ISBN 0-393-01477-0). Norton.

Percival, Harold W. Thinking & Destiny. LC 47-1811. 1978. 15.95 (ISBN 0-911650-01-6); deluxe ed. 18.95 in 2 vols. (ISBN 0-911650-02-4); pap. 8.95 (ISBN 0-911650-06-7). Word Foun.

Turner, Bryan S. For Weber: Essays in the Sociology of Fate. 360p. 1981. 30.00 (ISBN 0-7100-0780-9). Routledge & Kegan.

FATEHPUR, SIKRI

Rizvi, Saiyid A. Fatehpur-Sikri. LC 75-906456. (Illus.). 210p. 1975. 27.50x (ISBN 0-8002-1416-1). Intl Pubns Serv.

FATHER AND CHILD

Brower, Kenneth. The Starship & the Canoe. LC 77-15200. 1978. 8.95 (ISBN 0-03-039196-2). HR&W.

Burton, Jerome & Rosen, Milt. The Fatherhood Formula. LC 75-20812. 176p. 1976. pap. 1.50 (ISBN 0-89041-064-X, 3064). Major Bks.

Crook, Roger H., ed. Affectionately, Dad. LC 80-67461. 1981. 5.95 (ISBN 0-8054-5641-4). Broadman.

Daley, Eliot A. Father Feelings. LC 77-22820. 1978. 7.95 (ISBN 0-688-03251-6). Morrow.

Dodson, Fitzhugh. How to Father. 1975. pap. 3.50 (ISBN 0-451-08416-0, E9002, Sig). NAL.

Gatley, Richard & Koulack, David. Single Father's Handbook. LC 78-1204. 1979. pap. 4.95 (ISBN 0-385-13653-6, Anch). Doubleday.

Green, Maureen. Life Without Fathering. LC 75-26874. (Paperbacks Ser.). 1977. pap. text ed. 3.50 (ISBN 0-07-024291-7, SP). McGraw.

Gresh, Sean. Becoming a Father: A Handbook for Expectant Fathers. Leedham, L., ed. 160p. 1980. 12.95 (ISBN 0-8329-0187-3). New Century.

Hale, Nathan C. The Birth of a Family: The New Role of the Father in Childbirth. LC 78-68340. 1979. pap. 7.95 (ISBN 0-385-14162-9, Anch). Doubleday.

Hamilton, Marshall L. Father's Influence on Children. LC 76-41799. 1977. 15.95x (ISBN 0-88229-142-4); pap. 8.95 (ISBN 0-88229-503-9). Nelson-Hall.

Hammer, Signe. Passionate Attachments: Fathers & Daughters in America Today. 1982. 12.95 (ISBN 0-89256-182-3). Rawson Wade.

Heiderbrecht, Paul & Rohrbach, Jerry. Fathering a Son. 1979. pap. 4.95 (ISBN 0-8024-3356-1). Moody.

Kahan, Stuart. Expectant Father's Survival Kit. LC 77-17919. 1979. 8.95 (ISBN 0-671-18371-0); pap. 3.95 (ISBN 0-671-18345-1). Sovereign Bks.

Lamb, Michael E. The Role of the Father in Child Development. LC 76-21778. (Personality Processes Ser.). 407p. 1976. 25.95 (ISBN 0-471-51172-2, Pub. by Wiley-Interscience). Wiley.

Lederer, Wolfgang. Dragons, Delinquents & Destiny: An Essay on Positive Superego Functions. LC 64-23955. (Psychological Issues Monograph: No. 15, Vol. 4, No. 3). (Orig.). 1964. text ed. 11.00 (ISBN 0-8236-1420-4). Intl Univs Pr.

Leenhouts, Keith. A Father...a Son...& a Three-Mile Run. 1977. pap. 1.95 (ISBN 0-310-27512-1). Zondervan.

Lockerbie, D. Bruce. Fatherlove: Learning to Give the Best You've Got. LC 80-711. 240p. 1981. 10.95 (ISBN 0-385-15865-3, Galilee). Doubleday.

MacDonald, Gordon. Action Guide for the Effective Father. 1979. 3.95 (ISBN 0-8423-0688-9). Tyndale.

Parke, Ross D. Fathers. LC 80-29079. (Developing Child Ser.). (Illus.). 128p. 1981. text ed. 8.95 (ISBN 0-674-29515-3); pap. 3.95 (ISBN 0-674-29516-1). Harvard U Pr.

Pedersen, Frank A., ed. The Father-Infant Relationship: Observational Studies in Family Settings. LC 79-20514. (Praeger Special Studies Ser.). 196p. 1980. 22.95 (ISBN 0-03-049506-7). Praeger.

Raynor, Dorka. This Is My Father & Me. LC 73-7320. (Concept Bks.). (Illus.). 40p. (ps up). 1973. 7.50g (ISBN 0-8075-7883-5). A Whitman.

Rue, James & Shanahan, Louise. Daddy's Girl, Mama's Boy. 1979. pap. 2.25 (ISBN 0-451-08822-0, E8822, Sig). NAL.

Schoenstein, Ralph. Yes, My Darling Daughters: Adventures in Fathering. 1976. 6.95 (ISBN 0-374-29360-0). FS&G.

Shedd, Charlie. The Best Dad Is a Good Lover. 1977. 5.95 (ISBN 0-8362-0660-6). Andrews & McMeel.

--Smart Dads I Know. 4.95 (ISBN 0-686-31412-3). NACAC.

--Smart Dads I Know. 128p. 1975. 4.95 (ISBN 0-8362-0612-6). Andrews & McMeel.

Shedd, Charlie W. Smart Dads I Know. 1978. pap. 1.75 (ISBN 0-380-39388-3, 39388). Avon.

Shepard, Morris A. & Goldman, Gerald. Divorced Dads: Their Kids, Ex-Wives & New Lives. LC 78-14637. 1979. 7.95 (ISBN 0-8019-6755-4). Chilton.

Stein, Edward V., ed. Fathering: Fact or Fable? LC 76-56840. 1977. 6.95 (ISBN 0-687-12864-1). Abingdon.

Steinberg, David. Fatherjournal: Five Years of Awakening to Fatherhood. LC 77-5908. (Illus., Orig.). 1977. pap. 3.00 (ISBN 0-87810-034-2). Times Change.

Stolz, Lois H., et al. Father Relations of War-Born Children: The Effect of Postwar Adjustment of Fathers on the Behavior & Personality of First Children Born While Fathers Were at War. LC 69-10160. 1969. Repr. of 1954 ed. lib. bdg. 18.50x (ISBN 0-8371-0672-9, STWC). Greenwood.

Swinnerton, Frank A. Galaxy of Fathers. LC 77-117851. (Essay Index Reprint Ser). 1966. 17.00 (ISBN 0-8369-1725-1). Arno.

FATHER DIVINE

see also Baker, George Pierce, 1866-1935

Hoshor, John. God in a Rolls Royce. facsimile ed. LC 70-170698. (Black Heritage Library Collection). Repr. of 1936 ed. 15.00 (ISBN 0-8369-8888-4). Arno.

FATHERS

see also Adolescent Parents; Grandparents; Stepfathers

Allon, Yigal. My Father's House. Ben-Yosef, Reuven, tr. from Hebrew. (Illus.). 1976. 7.95 (ISBN 0-393-07498-6). Norton.

Appleton, William. Fathers & Daughters. LC 80-1649. 224p. 1981. 12.95 (ISBN 0-385-15511-5). Doubleday.

Atkin, Edith & Rubin, Estelle. Part-Time Father. LC 75-25146. 1976. 8.95 (ISBN 0-8149-0766-0). Vanguard.

Atkins, Edith & Rubin, Estelle. Part-Time Father: A Guide for the Divorced Father. 1977. pap. 1.75 (ISBN 0-451-07461-0, E7461, Sig). NAL.

Biller, Henry B. Paternal Deprivation: Family, School, Sexuality & Society. LC 74-928. 1974. pap. 9.95 (ISBN 0-669-02517-8). Lexington Bks.

Bottomly, Heath. Prodigal Father. LC 75-14884. 1976. pap. 3.95 (ISBN 0-8307-0431-0, 54-038-04). Regal.

Bugg, Ralph. A Father Shares: How to Enrich Family Life. 1980. pap. 4.95 (ISBN 0-8010-0776-3). Baker Bk.

Cammarata, Jerry & Leighton, Frances S. The Fun Book of Fatherhood. 1979. pap. 2.50 (ISBN 0-523-40603-7). Pinnacle Bks.

Cammarata, Jerry & Leighton, Francis S. The Fun Book of Fatherhood. (Illus.). 1978. 9.95 (ISBN 0-89474-012-1). Corwin.

Carton, Lonnie. Daddies. (Illus.). (ps). 1963. PLB 4.99 (ISBN 0-394-90724-8, BYR). Random.

Coleman, Sheila S. Robert Schuller, My Father & My Friend. (Illus.). 1980. 8.95 (ISBN 0-89542-026-0). Ideals.

Colman, Arthur & Colman, Libby. Earth Sky-Sky Father: The Changing Concept of Fathering. (Illus.). 224p. 1981. 12.95 (ISBN 0-13-223032-1, Spec); pap. 5.95 (ISBN 0-13-223024-0). P-H.

Crippa, Erminio. Father. 1957. 2.00 (ISBN 0-8198-0042-2); pap. 1.00 (ISBN 0-8198-0043-0). Dghtrs St Paul.

Daley, Eliot A. Father Feelings. 1979. pap. 2.25 (ISBN 0-671-82271-3). PB.

--Father Feelings. LC 77-22820. 1978. 7.95 (ISBN 0-688-03251-6). Morrow.

Dubrin, Andrew J. The New Husbands & How to Become One. LC 76-15359. 1976. 14.95 (ISBN 0-88229-358-3). Nelson-Hall.

Green, Maureen. Life Without Fathering. LC 75-26874. 1976. 7.95 (ISBN 0-07-024290-9, GB). McGraw.

--Life Without Fathering. LC 75-26874. (Paperbacks Ser.). 1977. pap. text ed. 3.50 (ISBN 0-07-024291-7, SP). McGraw.

Hamilton, Marshall L. Father's Influence on Children. LC 76-41799. 1977. 15.95x (ISBN 0-88229-142-4); pap. 8.95 (ISBN 0-88229-503-9). Nelson-Hall.

Hazen, Barbara S., compiled by. To the World's Greatest Dad. 1979. pap. 4.50 (ISBN 0-8378-5017-7). Gibson.

Hurwitz, Johanna. Baseball Fever. (Junior Bks). (Illus.). (gr. 8-12). 1981. 7.95 (ISBN 0-686-76691-1); lib. bdg. 7.63 (ISBN 0-686-76692-X). Morrow.

Kahan, Stuart. Expectant Father's Survival Kit. LC 77-17919. 1979. 8.95 (ISBN 0-671-18371-0); pap. 3.95 (ISBN 0-671-18345-1). Sovereign Bks.

--The Expectant Father's Survival Kit. 1978. pap. 3.95 (ISBN 0-671-18345-1, Monarch). Monarch Pr.

--For Divorced Fathers Only. LC 77-17836. 1979. 8.95 (ISBN 0-671-18372-9); pap. 3.95 (ISBN 0-671-18338-9). Sovereign Bks.

Kenney, Stanley & Cruise, James. To You Dad. (Illus.). 1962. 2.25 (ISBN 0-8198-0159-3); pap. 1.25 (ISBN 0-8198-0160-7). Dghtrs St Paul.

Kitzinger, Sheila. Giving Birth: The Parents' Emotions in Childbirth. LC 77-2518. (Orig.). 1978. pap. 4.95 (ISBN 0-8052-0573-X). Schocken.

Lamb, Michael R. The Role of the Father in Child Development. 2nd ed. (Wiley Series on Personality Process). 450p. 1981. 25.00 (ISBN 0-471-07739-9, Pub. by Wiley-Interscience). Wiley.

Lessin, Roy. Dads Are God's Idea. (God's Idea Books Ser.). (Illus.). 32p. (ps-4). 1981. pap. 1.50 (ISBN 0-87123-176-X, 210176). Bethany Hse.

Lucarini, Spartaco. The Difficult Role of a Father. Moran, Hugh, tr. from It. LC 79-84940. (Education in the Family Ser.). 1979. pap. 2.25 (ISBN 0-911782-32-X). New City.
Lyle, Katie. Dark but Full of Diamonds. (gr. 12 up). Date not set. 9.95 (ISBN 0-686-76711-X). Coward.
MacDonald, Gordon. The Effective Father. 1977. pap. 4.95 (ISBN 0-8423-0680-3). Tyndale.
Mayle, Peter. How to Be a Pregnant Father? 1977. 10.00 (ISBN 0-8184-0245-8). Lyle Stuart.
Parke, Ross D. Fathers. LC 80-29079. (Developing Child Ser.). (Illus.). 128p. 1981. text ed. 8.95 (ISBN 0-674-29515-3); pap. 3.95 (ISBN 0-674-29516-1). Harvard U Pr.
Phillips, Celeste R. & Anzalone, Joseph T. Fathering: Participation in Labor & Birth. LC 77-13224. (Illus.). 1978. pap. 9.50 (ISBN 0-8016-3919-0). Mosby.
Pinegar, Ed J., ed. Fatherhood. 1976. 5.95 (ISBN 0-87747-593-8). Deseret Bk.
Preston, William H., ed. Fathers Are Special. LC 76-39715. (Illus.). 1977. 5.95 (ISBN 0-8054-5622-8, 4256-22). Broadman.
Reynolds, William. The American Father: Himself, His Woman, His Child. LC 78-8951. 1978. 8.95 (ISBN 0-448-22917-X). Paddington.
Robinson, James & Cox, Jimmie. In Search of a Father. 1979. pap. write for info. (ISBN 0-8423-1634-5). Tyndale.
Schwantes, David. I'm Jenny's Dad. (Better Living Ser.). 1977. pap. 0.95 (ISBN 0-8127-0152-6). Review & Herald.
Shedd, Charlie. The Best Dad Is a Good Lover. 1978. pap. 1.75 (ISBN 0-380-01931-0, 37804). Avon.
--A Dad Is for Spending Time with. 1978. 5.95 (ISBN 0-8362-2802-2). Andrews & McMeel.
Stanley, Charles F. A Man's Touch. 1977. pap. 3.50 (ISBN 0-88207-753-8). Victor Bks.
Stein, Shifra, compiled by. Dear Dad. 1977. boxed 4.95 (ISBN 0-8378-1736-6). Gibson.
Steinberg, David. Father Journal: Five Years of Awakening to Fatherhood. 96p. pap. 3.00 (ISBN 0-87810-034-2). Crossing Pr.
--Fatherjournal: Five Years of Awakening to Fatherhood. LC 77-5908. (Illus., Orig.). 1977. pap. 3.00 (ISBN 0-87810-034-2). Times Change.
Sullivan, S. Adams. The Fathers Almanac. LC 78-22650. (Illus.). 384p. 1980. pap. 7.95 (ISBN 0-385-13626-9, Dolp). Doubleday.
Taber, Gladys. Especially Father. LC 79-84304. 1979. Repr. of 1948 ed. 11.95 (ISBN 0-915224-04-6). Pine St Pr.
Valentine, Alan C., ed. Fathers to Sons: Advice Without Consent. 1963. 12.95x (ISBN 0-8061-0586-0). U of Okla Pr.
Weiss, Robert R. & Pexton, Myron R. Dr. Pexton's Guide for the Expectant Father. 1970. 5.95 (ISBN 0-8158-0230-7). Chris Mass.

FATHERS, APOSTOLIC
see Apostolic Fathers

FATHERS, UNMARRIED
see Unmarried Fathers

FATHERS OF THE CHURCH
Here are entered works on the life and thought of the Fathers of the Church, a term that embraces the leaders of the early church to the time of Gregory the Great in the West and John of Damascus in the east. Works on their writing are entered under the heading Christian Literature, Early.
see also Apostolic Fathers; Persecution

Bettenson, Henry, ed. & tr. The Later Christian Fathers: A Selection from the Writings of the Fathers from St. Cyril of Jerusalem to St. Leo the Great. (OPB No. 293). 1972. pap. 5.95x (ISBN 0-19-283012-0). Oxford U Pr.
Campbell, James. Greek Fathers. LC 63-10279. (Our Debt to Greece & Rome Ser). 167p. 1963. Repr. of 1930 ed. 16.50x (ISBN 0-8154-0046-2). Cooper Sq.
Cruttwell, Charles T. Literary History of Early Christianity, 2 Vols. LC 76-129369. Repr. of 1893 ed. 42.50 (ISBN 0-404-01877-7). AMS Pr.
Cyprian, St. Life & Works of St. Cyprian of Carthage, 4 vols. Vols. 1, 2, & 4. pap. 1.50 ea.; Vol. 3. pap. 2.95 (ISBN 0-686-05649-3); pap. 6.95 set (ISBN 0-686-05650-7). Eastern Orthodox.
Giordani, Igino. Social Message of the Early Church Fathers. 1977. 3.95 (ISBN 0-8198-0469-X); pap. 2.95 (ISBN 0-8198-0470-3). Dghtrs St Paul.
Gregorius, Saint Les Livres Des Miracles et Autres Opuscules, 4 Vols. 1863. Set. 126.00 (ISBN 0-384-19888-0); 31.50 ea.; pap. 27.00 ea.; Set. pap. 108.00 (ISBN 0-384-19889-9). Johnson Repr.
Heine, Ronald E. Perfection in the Virtuous Life. LC 75-17086. (Patristic Monograph Ser.: No. 2). 247p. 1975. pap. 6.50 (ISBN 0-915646-01-3). Phila Patristic.
Leigh-Bennett, Ernest. Handbook of the Early Church Fathers. 1980. lib. bdg. 75.00 (ISBN 0-8490-3107-9). Gordon Pr.
Mackay, Henry F. Followers in the Way. LC 71-93359. (Essay Index Reprint Ser). 1934. 15.00 (ISBN 0-8369-1304-3). Arno.
Matsagouras, E. The Early Church Fathers As Educators. 1977. pap. 3.95 (ISBN 0-937032-10-7). Light & Life Pub Co MN.
Meijering, Eginhard P. God Being History: Studies in Patristic Philosophy. 1975. pap. 29.50 (ISBN 0-444-10803-3, North-Holland). Elsevier.
Patrick, John, tr. Lenten Readings from the Writings of the Fathers of the Church. pap. 1.50 (ISBN 0-686-05647-7). Eastern Orthodox.
Patterson, Lloyd G. God & History in Early Christian Thought: A Study of Themes from Justin Martyr to Gregory the Great. (Studies in Patristic Thought: No. 2). 1967. text ed. 10.00x (ISBN 0-8401-1828-7). Allenson-Breckinridge.
Pelikan, Jaroslav J. The Shape of Death: Life, Death, & Immortality in the Early Fathers. LC 78-6030. 1978. Repr. of 1961 ed. lib. bdg. 16.75x (ISBN 0-313-20458-6, PESD). Greenwood.
Plott, John C. Global History of Philosophy: The Patristic-Sutra Period, Vol. 3. 1980. 27.00 (ISBN 0-8426-1680-2). Verry.
Plummer, Alfred. The Church of the Early Fathers. 1892. 15.00 (ISBN 0-8414-9261-1). Folcroft.
Smith, William & Wace, Henry, eds. Dictionary of Christian Biography, Literature, Sects & Doctrines, 4 Vols. LC 12-3122. Repr. of 1887 ed. Set. 178.00 (ISBN 0-404-06140-0). AMS Pr.
Stinger, Charles L. Humanism & the Church Fathers: Ambrogio Traversari (1386-1439) & the Revival of Patristic Theology in the Early Italian Renaissance. LC 76-21699. 1977. 36.00 (ISBN 0-87395-311-8). State U NY Pr.
Von Campenhausen, Hans. The Fathers of the Latin Church. Hoffmann, Manfred, tr. LC 76-75260. 1964. 18.50x (ISBN 0-8047-0685-9). Stanford U Pr.

FATHERS OF THE CHURCH–BIOBLIOGRAPHY

Gregory, St. Life of St. Macrina. 1974. pap. 1.50 (ISBN 0-686-10202-9). Eastern Orthodox.
Hamell, Patrick J. Handbook of Patrology. 1968. pap. 3.95 (ISBN 0-8189-0057-1). Alba.
Schneemelcher, Wilhelm, ed. Bibliographia Patristica: Internationale Patristische Bibliographie. Incl. Vol. 1. Erscheinungen des Jahres 1956. xxviii, 103p. 1959. 21.75x (ISBN 3-11-001248-0); Vol. 2. Erscheinungen des Jahres 1957. xxx, 115p. 1959. 19.30 (ISBN 3-11-001249-9); Vol. 3. Erscheinungen des Jahres 1958. xxxi, 119p. 1960. 21.75x (ISBN 3-11-001250-2); Vol. 4. Erscheinungen des Jahres 1959. xxxiii, 126p. 1961. 14.50x (ISBN 3-11-001251-0); Vol. 5. Erscheinungen des Jahres 1960. xxxiii, 114p. 1962. 14.50x (ISBN 3-11-001252-9); Vol. 6. Erscheinungen des Jahres 1961. xxxiii, 98p. 1963. 14.50x (ISBN 3-11-001253-7); Vol. 7. Erscheinungen des Jahres 1962. xxxiv, 108p. 1964. 14.50x (ISBN 3-11-001254-5); Vol. 8. Erscheinungen des Jahres 1963. xxxiv, 120p. 1966. 18.75x (ISBN 3-11-001255-3); Vol. 9. Erscheinungen des Jahres 1964. xxxiv, 157p. 1967. 18.75x (ISBN 3-11-001256-1); Vol. 10. Erscheinungen Des Jahres 1965. xxxiv, 127p. 1969. 18.75x (ISBN 3-11-001257-X); Vol. 11. Erscheinungen Des Jahres 1966. 1971. 37.50x (ISBN 3-11-003531-6); Erscheinungen Des Jahres 1967-68. 1975. 45.00x (ISBN 3-11-004631-8). De Gruyter.

FATHERS OF THE CHURCH–BIBLIOGRAPHY

Krueger, Gustav. History of Early Christian Literature in the First Three Centuries. Gillet, Charles R., tr. from Ger. 1969. 26.00 (ISBN 0-8337-1963-7). B Franklin.

FATHERS OF THE CHURCH–DICTIONARIES

Goodspeed, Edgar J. Index Patristicus, Sive Clavis Patrum Apostolicorum Operum. 1960. 12.50x (ISBN 0-8401-0863-X). Allenson-Breckinridge.
Hebert, Peter E., ed. Selections from the Latin Fathers. (College Classical Ser.). xvii, 186p. (gr. 11-12). Date not set. pap. text ed. 12.50x (ISBN 0-89241-110-4). Caratzas Bros.
Smith, William & Wace, Henry, eds. Dictionary of Christian Biography, Literature, Sects & Doctrines, 4 Vols. LC 12-3122. Repr. of 1887 ed. Set. 178.00 (ISBN 0-404-06140-0). AMS Pr.
--Dictionary of Christian Biography, Literature, Sects & Doctrines: Being a Continuation of the Dictionary of the Bible, 4 Vols. LC 12-3122. 1968. Repr. of 1877 ed. Set. 180.00 (ISBN 0-527-84200-1). Kraus Repr.

FATIGUE
see also Rest

Bartley, S. Howard. Fatigue: Mechanism & Management. (American Lecture Living Chemistry). 112p. 1965. photocopy spiral ed. 14.75 (ISBN 0-398-00099-9). C C Thomas.
Bullen, Adelaide K. New Answers to the Fatigue Problem. LC 56-12857. 1956. 4.50 (ISBN 0-8130-0031-9). U Presses Fla.
Florence, Philip S. Use of Factory Statistics in the Investigation of Industrial Fatigue. LC 76-76627. (Columbia University. Studies in the Social Sciences: No. 190). Repr. of 1918 ed. 16.50 (ISBN 0-404-51190-2). AMS Pr.
Floyd, W. F. & Welford, A. T., eds. Symposium on Fatigue & Symposium on Human Factors in Equipment Design, 2 vols. in one. LC 77-70494. (Work Ser.). (Illus.). 1977. Repr. of 1954 ed. lib. bdg. 25.00x (ISBN 0-405-10165-1). Arno.
Gilbreth, Frank B. & Gilbreth, Lillian M. Fatigue Study. LC 73-1155. (Management History Ser.: No. 29). (Illus.). viii, 159p. 1973. Repr. of 1916 ed. 17.50 (ISBN 0-87960-028-4). Hive Pub.
Goldmark, Josephine & Hopkins, Mary D. Comparison of an Eight-Hour Plant & a Ten-Hour Plant: U.S. Public Health Bulletin, No. 106. Stein, Leon, ed. LC 77-70495. (Work Ser.). 1977. Repr. of 1920 ed. lib. bdg. 15.00x (ISBN 0-405-10168-6). Arno.
Graham, M. F. Inner Energy: How to Overcome Fatigue. LC 78-7089. 1978. 9.95 (ISBN 0-8069-8440-6); PLB 8.29 (ISBN 0-8069-8441-4). Sterling.
Hashimoto, K., et al, eds. Methodology in Human Fatigue Assessment. (Illus.). 200p. 1971. 22.50x (ISBN 0-85066-049-1). Intl Pubns Serv.
--Methodology in Human Fatigue Assessment. 1971. 19.95x (ISBN 0-85066-049-1). Intl Ideas.
Myers, Charles S. Industrial Psychology. Stein, Leon, ed. LC 77-70519. (Work Ser.). (Illus.). 1977. Repr. of 1925 ed. lib. bdg. 12.00x (ISBN 0-405-10188-0). Arno.
Pembrook, Linda. How to Beat Fatigue. 1975. pap. 1.75 (ISBN 0-380-00671-5, 29371). Avon.
Rathbone, Josephine L. Relaxation. LC 70-85845. 171p. 1969. text ed. 5.95 (ISBN 0-8121-0266-5). Lea & Febiger.
Simonson, Ernst. Physiology of Work Capacity & Fatigue. (Illus.). 592p. 1971. photocopy ed. spiral 58.75 (ISBN 0-398-01750-6). C C Thomas.
Simonson, Ernst & Weiser, Philip C. Psychological Aspects & Physiological Correlates of Work & Fatigue. (Illus.). 472p. 1976. 49.00 (ISBN 0-398-03430-3). C C Thomas.
Tournier, Paul, ed. Fatigue in Modern Society. LC 65-19582. 1965. pap. 2.45 (ISBN 0-8042-3395-0). John Knox.
Vernon, Horace M. Industrial Fatigue & Efficiency. Stein, Leon, ed. LC 77-70543. (Work Ser.). (Illus.). 1977. Repr. of 1921 ed. lib. bdg. 18.00x (ISBN 0-405-10212-7). Arno.
Wunderlich, Ray C., Jr. Fatigue: What Causes It, What It Does to You, What You Can Do About It. new ed. (Illus.). 59p. 1976. pap. 2.10 (ISBN 0-910812-18-7). Johnny Reads.

FATIGUE, MENTAL
see also Boredom; Inefficiency, Intellectual

Arai, Tsuru. Mental Fatigue. LC 70-176521. (Columbia University. Teachers College. Contributions to Education: No. 54). Repr. of 1912 ed. 17.50 (ISBN 0-404-55054-1). AMS Pr.
Carlson, Dwight L. How to Win Over Fatigue. (Power Bks.). 224p. 1980. pap. 4.95 (ISBN 0-8007-5027-6). Revell.
Marmorstein, Jerome & Marmorstein, Nanette. The Psychometabolic Blues: Practical Solutions for Anxiety, Depression, Fatigue, Hypoglycemia & Related Stressful Problems. LC 79-4271. 1979. 8.95 (ISBN 0-912800-58-5); pap. 4.95 (ISBN 0-912800-59-3). Woodbridge Pr.
Mitchell, S. Weir. Wear & Tear; or, Hints for the Overworked. 5th ed. LC 73-2407. (Mental Illness & Social Policy; the American Experience Ser.). Repr. of 1887 ed. 9.50 (ISBN 0-405-05217-0). Arno.
Schuller, Robert H. Discover How to Turn Activity into Energy. (Orig.). 1978. pap. 1.25 (ISBN 0-89081-135-0). Harvest Hse.
Thorndike, Edward L., et al. Ventilation in Relation to Mental Work. LC 71-177714. (Columbia University. Teachers College. Contributions to Education: No. 78). Repr. of 1916 ed. 17.50 (ISBN 0-404-55078-9). AMS Pr.

FATIGUE OF MATERIALS
see Materials–Fatigue

FATIGUE OF METALS
see Metals–Fatigue

FATIMA, NOSSA SENHORA DA

Dacruz, J. More About Fatima. De Oca, V. Montes, tr. from Port. 1979. pap. 1.00 (ISBN 0-913382-16-7, 102-95). Prow Bks-Franciscan.
Walsh, William Thomas. Our Lady of Fatima. pap. 3.50 (ISBN 0-385-02869-5, D1, Im). Doubleday.

FATIMA, PORTUGAL (SHRINE)

Alonso, Joaquin M. The Secret of Fatima Fact & Legend. Dominican Nuns of the Perpetual Rosary, tr. from Span. LC 79-13182. (Illus.). 1979. 8.95 (ISBN 0-911218-14-9); pap. 3.95 (ISBN 0-911218-15-7). Ravengate Pr.
Cappa, Alphonse. Fatima: Cove of Wonders. 1980. 4.50 (ISBN 0-8198-0569-6); pap. 3.25 (ISBN 0-8198-0570-X). Dghtrs St Paul.
Culligan, Emmett. Fatima Secret. 1975. pap. 1.50 (ISBN 0-89555-052-0, 300). TAN Bks Pubs.
Di Marchi, John. Fatima from the Beginning. (Illus.). 1980. pap. 5.95 (ISBN 0-911218-16-5). Ravengate Pr.
Johnston, Francis. Fatima: The Great Sign. 1980. Repr. of 1979 ed. write for info. Tan Bks Pubs.
--Fatima: The Great Sign. 1980. 3.50 (ISBN 0-911988-37-8). AMI Pr.
Oliveira, Joseph De. Jacinta, Flower of Fatima. 192p. 1972. 4.75 (ISBN 0-911988-16-5). AMI Pr.

FATIMITES

Lewis, Bernard. The Origins of Isma'ilism: A Study of the Historical Background of the Fatimid Caliphate. LC 74-180357. Repr. of 1940 ed. 14.50 (ISBN 0-404-56289-2). AMS Pr.

FATNESS
see Obesity

FATS
see Fat; Oils and Fats

FATTY ACID METABOLISM

Dietary Fats & Oils in Human Nutrition. (FAO Food & Nutrition Paper Ser.: No. 3). 1978. pap. 7.50 (ISBN 92-5-100467-6, F1422, FAO). Unipub.
Florkin, M. & Stotz, E. H., eds. Comprehensive Biochemistry: Pyruvates & Fatty Acid Metabolism, Vol. 18s. LC 62-10359. (Illus.). 125p. 1971. 27.00 (ISBN 0-444-40950-5, North Holland). Elsevier.
Gran, F. C. & Gran, F. C., eds. Cellular Compartmentalization & Control of Fatty Acid Metabolism. LC 68-31571. (Illus.). 1968. 21.50 (ISBN 0-12-295050-X). Acad Pr.
Holmes, W. L. & Bortz, W. M., eds. Biochemistry & Pharmacology of Free Fatty Acids. (Progress in Biochemical Pharmacology: Vol. 6). 1971. 58.25 (ISBN 3-8055-1211-2). S Karger.

FATTY ACIDS
see Acids, Fatty

FATTY TISSUE
see Adipose Tissues

FAULKNER, WILLIAM, 1897-1962

Adams, Richard P. Faulkner: Myth & Motion. 1968. 19.00 (ISBN 0-691-06141-6). Princeton U Pr.
Barger, James. William Faulkner, Modern American Novelist & Nobel Prize Winner. Rahmas, D. Steve, ed. (Outstanding Personalities Ser.: No. 63). 32p. (Orig.). (gr. 7-12). 1973. lib. bdg. 2.95 incl. catalog cards (ISBN 0-87157-063-7); pap. 1.50 vinyl laminated covers (ISBN 0-686-05484-9). SamHar Pr.
Bassett, John, ed. William Faulkner: The Critical Heritage. (The Critical Heritage Ser.). 1975. 36.00 (ISBN 0-7100-8124-3). Routledge & Kegan.
Beck, Warren. Faulkner: Essays by Warren Beck. LC 72-7982. 672p. 1976. 17.50x (ISBN 0-299-06500-6, 650). U of Wis Pr.
--Man in Motion: Faulkner's Trilogy. (Orig.). 1961. pap. 4.25x (ISBN 0-299-02414-8). U of Wis Pr.
Bedell, George C. Kierkegaard & Faulkner: Modalities of Existence. LC 71-181356. 262p. 1972. 20.00 (ISBN 0-8071-0043-9). La State U Pr.
Bezzerides, A. I. William Faulkner: A Life on Paper. LC 79-15371. (Illus.). 1980. 10.00x (ISBN 0-87805-098-1); pap. text ed. 5.00x (ISBN 0-87805-085-X). U Pr of Miss.
Bleikasten, Andre. The Most Splendid Failure: Faulkner's the Sound & the Fury. Bleikasten, Andre, tr. from French. LC 75-22638. 288p. 1976. 12.50x (ISBN 0-253-33877-8). Ind U Pr.
Blotner, Joseph. Faulkner: A Biography, 2 vols. (Illus.). 1974. Boxed Set. 30.00 (ISBN 0-394-47452-X). Random.
Blotner, Joseph, ed. Selected Letters of William Faulkner. 1977. 15.00 (ISBN 0-394-49485-7). Random.
--Selected Letters of William Faulkner. 1978. pap. 4.95 (ISBN 0-394-72505-0, Vin). Random.
Boozer, William. William Faulkner's First Book: The Marble Faun Fifty Years Later. LC 75-6916. (Illus.). 1975. 7.50 (ISBN 0-686-12125-2). Pigeon Roost Pr.
Brooks, Cleanth. William Faulkner: The Yoknapatawpha Country. LC 63-17023. (Illus.). 1963. 35.00x (ISBN 0-300-00329-3); pap. 7.95x (ISBN 0-300-00028-6, Y170). Yale U Pr.

--William Faulkner: Toward Yoknapatawpha & Beyond. LC 77-10898. 1980. 25.00x (ISBN 0-300-02204-2); pap. 9.95 (ISBN 0-300-02493-2). Yale U Pr.

Broughton, Panthea R. William Faulkner: The Abstract & the Actual. LC 74-77324. 222p. 1974. 15.00 (ISBN 0-8071-0083-8). La State U Pr.

Campbell, Harry M. & Foster, Ruel E. William Faulkner: A Critical Appraisal. LC 70-135270. 1971. Repr. of 1951 ed. lib. bdg. 11.50x (ISBN 0-8154-0363-1). Cooper Sq.

Capps, Jack L., ed. As I Lay Dying: A Concordance to the Novel. LC 77-298. (Faulkner Concordances: No. 1). 1977. 37.25 (ISBN 0-8357-0254-5, IS-00019, Pub. by Faulkner Concordance Advisory Board). Univ Microfilms.

Carey, Glenn O. Faulkner: the Unappeased Imagination: A Collection of Critical Essays. 290p. 1980. 18.50x (ISBN 0-87875-181-5, 57440). Whitston Pub.

Carnegie Institute of Technology & Hayes, Ann L. Studies in Faulkner. LC 72-1325. (Essay Index Reprint Ser.). Repr. of 1961 ed. 12.00 (ISBN 0-8369-2839-3). Arno.

Cofield, Jack. William Faulkner, the Cofield Collection. Wells, Lawrence, ed. LC 78-54859. (Illus.). 1978. 24.95 (ISBN 0-916242-02-1). Yoknapatawpha.

Coindreau, Maurice E., et al. Time of William Faulkner: A French View of Modern American Fiction. Reeves, George M., ed. Reeves, George M., tr. LC 74-144804. 1971. 14.95x (ISBN 0-87249-212-5). U of SC Pr.

Coughlan, Robert. The Private World of William Faulkner. LC 72-78474. 1972. Repr. of 1954 ed. lib. bdg. 7.50x (ISBN 0-8154-0424-7). Cooper Sq.

Cowley, Malcolm. The Faulkner-Cowley File: Letters & Memories, 1944-1962. 1978. pap. 2.50 (ISBN 0-14-004684-4). Penguin.

Creighton, Joanne V. William Faulkner's Craft of Revision: The Snopes Trilogy, the Unvanquished & Go Down Moses. LC 76-51441. 1977. text ed. 12.95x (ISBN 0-685-76208-4). Wayne St U Pr.

Cullen, John B. & Watkins, Floyd C. Old Times in the Faulkner Country. LC 61-1874. 132p. 1975. 9.95 (ISBN 0-8071-0099-4). La State U Pr.

Early, James. The Making of Go Down, Moses. LC 72-80404. 148p. 1972. 5.95 (ISBN 0-87074-003-2). SMU Press.

Everett, Walter K. Faulkner's Art & Characters. LC 68-31478. (Orig.). (gr. 9 up). 1969. pap. text ed. 3.50 (ISBN 0-8120-0392-6). Barron.

Fadiman, Regina K. Faulkner's Light in August: A Description & Interpretation of the Revisions. LC 74-8242. 1975. 12.50 (ISBN 0-8139-0584-2, Bibliographical Society, University of Virginia). U Pr of Va.

Falkner, Murry C. Falkners of Mississippi: A Memoir. LC 67-24417. (Illus.). 1967. 11.95 (ISBN 0-8071-0446-9). La State U Pr.

Faulker, John. My Brother Bill. LC 63-13769. 1975. Repr. of 1963 ed. 12.50 (ISBN 0-686-77300-4). Yoknapatawpha.

Ford, Margaret P. & Kincaid, Suzanne. Who's Who in Faulkner. LC 63-19233. 1963. pap. text ed. 3.95x (ISBN 0-8071-0107-9). La State U Pr.

Fowler, Doreen & Abadie, Ann J., eds. Fifty Years of Yoknapatawpha: Faulkner & Yoknapatawpha, 1979. LC 80-12255. 1980. 15.95x (ISBN 0-87805-121-X); pap. 7.95x (ISBN 0-87805-122-8). U Pr of Miss.

Fried, Barbara. The Spider in the Cup: Yoknapatawpha County's Fall into the Unknowable. 1978. 3.75x (ISBN 0-674-83205-1). Harvard U Pr.

Gold, Joseph. William Faulkner: A Study in Humanism, from Metaphor to Discourse. 1967. Repr. of 1966 ed. 9.95x (ISBN 0-8061-0706-5). U of Okla Pr.

Guerard, Albert J. The Triumph of the Novel: Dickens, Dostoevsky & Faulkner. LC 75-46357. 1976. 17.50 (ISBN 0-19-502066-9). Oxford U Pr.

Gwynn, Frederick L. & Blotner, Joseph L., eds. Faulkner in the University: Class Conferences at the University of Virginia, 1957-1958. LC 59-13713. (Illus.). 1977. Repr. of 1959 ed. 13.95x (ISBN 0-8139-0843-4). U Pr of Va.

Hamblin, Robert W. & Brodsky, Louis D. Selections from the William Faulkner Collection of Louis Daniel Brodsky: A Descriptive Catalogue. LC 79-375. 1980. 17.50x (ISBN 0-8139-0830-2). U Pr of Va.

Harrington, Evans & Abadie, Ann J., eds. Faulkner, Modernism, & Film: Faulkner & Yoknapatawpha, 1978. LC 79-11298. 1979. text ed. 12.50x (ISBN 0-87805-102-3); pap. text ed. 6.95x (ISBN 0-87805-103-1). U Pr of Miss.

--The Maker & the Myth: Faulkner & Yoknapatawpha, 1977. LC 78-60158. 1978. 9.95x (ISBN 0-87805-049-3); pap. 4.95x (ISBN 0-87805-075-2). U Pr of Miss.

--The South & Faulkner's Yoknapatawpha: The Actual & the Apocryphal. LC 77-8741. 1977. 10.95x (ISBN 0-87805-035-3); pap. 5.95x (ISBN 0-87805-037-X). U Pr of Miss.

Hoffman, Frederick J. William Faulkner. (Twayne's United States Authors Ser). 1966. pap. 3.45 (ISBN 0-8084-0326-5, T1, Twayne). Coll & U Pr.

--William Faulkner. (U. S. Authors Ser.: No. 1). lib. bdg. 9.95 (ISBN 0-8057-0244-X). Twayne.

Holman, C. Hugh. Three Modes of Modern Southern Fiction: Ellen Glasgow, William Faulkner, Thomas Wolfe. LC 66-19490. (Mercer University Lamar Lecture Ser: No. 9). 95p. 1966. 7.00x (ISBN 0-8203-0185-X). U of Ga Pr.

Howe, Irving. William Faulkner: A Critical Study. 3rd ed. 320p. 1975. pap. 4.95 (ISBN 0-226-35484-9, P650, Phoen). U of Chicago Pr.

Irwin, John T. Doubling & Incest - Repetition & Revenge: A Speculative Reading of Faulkner. LC 75-11341. 192p. 1981. pap. 4.95 (ISBN 0-8018-2564-4). Johns Hopkins.

--Doubling and Incest Repetition and Revenge: A Speculative Reading of Faulkner. LC 75-11341. 192p. 1975. 12.50x (ISBN 0-8018-1722-6); pap. text ed. 4.95 (ISBN 0-8018-2564-4). Johns Hopkins.

Jehlen, Myra. Class & Character in Faulkner's South. LC 76-3519. 181p. 1976. 12.50x (ISBN 0-231-04011-3). Columbia U Pr.

Jelliffe, Robert A. Faulkner at Nagano. LC 73-9952. 1956. Repr. lib. bdg. 25.00 (ISBN 0-8414-2189-7). Folcroft.

Juhasz, Leslie A. Monarch Notes on Faulkner's As I Lay Dying. (Orig.). pap. 1.95 (ISBN 0-671-00665-7). Monarch Pr.

--Monarch Notes on Faulkner's Light in August. (Orig.). pap. 1.95 (ISBN 0-671-00666-5). Monarch Pr.

Kaluza, Irena. Functioning of Sentence Structure in the Stream of Consciousness Technique of William Faulkner's the Sound and the Fury. 1967. lib. bdg. 10.00 (ISBN 0-8414-5550-3). Folcroft.

Kartiganer, Donald M. The Fragile Thread: The Meaning of Form in Faulkner's Novels. LC 78-19693. 1979. 15.00x (ISBN 0-87023-268-1). U of Mass Pr.

Kawin, Bruce F. Faulkner & Film. LC 77-2519. (Ungar Fil Library). (Illus.). 1977. 11.00 (ISBN 0-8044-2454-3); pap. 4.95 (ISBN 0-8044-6347-6). Ungar.

Kerr, Elizabeth M. William Faulkner's Gothic Domain. (National University Pubns., Literary Criticism Ser.). 1979. 15.00 (ISBN 0-8046-9228-9). Kennikat.

--Yoknapatawpha: Faulkner's Little Postage Stamp of Native Soil. 2nd ed. LC 68-8747. (Illus.). 1976. pap. 8.00 (ISBN 0-8232-0816-8). Fordham.

Kinney, Arthur F. Faulkner's Narrative Poetics: Style As Vision. LC 77-90731. 1978. 15.00x (ISBN 0-87023-144-8). U of Mass Pr.

Leary, Lewis. William Faulkner of Yoknapatawpha County. LC 72-7551. (Twentieth-Century American Writers Ser). (gr. 7 up). 1973. 6.50 (ISBN 0-690-89173-3, TYC-J). Har-Row.

Longley, John Lewis, Jr. The Tragic Mask: A Study of Faulkner's Heroes. LC 63-22806. 252p. 1967. pap. 5.00x (ISBN 0-8078-4005-X). U of NC Pr.

McHaney, Thomas L. William Faulkner's "The Wild Palms". A Study. LC 75-3648. 209p. 1975. 3.00x (ISBN 0-87805-070-1). U Pr of Miss.

Malin, Irving. William Faulkner: An Interpretation. LC 76-165664. 1972. Repr. of 1957 ed. 7.50 (ISBN 0-87752-154-9). Gordian.

Meriwether, James B. Literary Career of William Faulkner: A Bibliographical Study. LC 79-149488. 1971. 14.95x (ISBN 0-87249-213-3). U of SC Pr.

--Studies in The Sound & the Fury. LC 70-126048. 1970. pap. text ed. 2.95x (ISBN 0-675-09300-7). Merrill.

Meriwether, James B. & Millgate, Michael, eds. Lion in the Garden: Interviews with William Faulkner, 1926-1962. LC 80-17080. xvi, 299p. 1980. 17.50x (ISBN 0-8032-3068-0); pap. 5.95 (ISBN 0-8032-8108-0, BB 749, Bison). U of Nebr Pr.

Millgate, Michael. The Achievement of William Faulkner. LC 78-16318. 1978. 15.00x (ISBN 0-8032-3054-0); pap. 4.95 (ISBN 0-8032-8102-1, BB 680, Bison). U of Nebr Pr.

Miner, Ward. World of William Faulkner. LC 59-8274. Repr. of 1952 ed. 8.50x (ISBN 0-8154-0153-1). Cooper Sq.

Minter, David. William Faulkner: His Life & Work. LC 80-13089. 325p. 1980. text ed. 16.95x (ISBN 0-8018-2347-1). Johns Hopkins.

Monarch Notes on Faulkner's Sound & the Fury. pap. 2.25 (ISBN 0-671-00613-4). Monarch Pr.

Oberhelman, Harley D. The Presence of Faulkner in the Writings of Garcia Marquez. (Graduate Studies, Texas Tech Univ.: No. 22). (Illus.). 1980. pap. 7.00 (ISBN 0-89672-080-2). Tex Tech Pr.

O'Connor, William V. William Faulkner. rev. ed. (Pamphlets on American Writers Ser: No. 3). (Orig.). 1964. pap. 1.25x (ISBN 0-8166-0193-3, MPAW3). U of Minn Pr.

O'Connor, William Van. Tangled Fire of William Faulkner. LC 68-22386. 1968. Repr. of 1953 ed. 8.50 (ISBN 0-87752-078-X). Gordian.

Peavy, Charles D. Go Slow Now: Faulkner & the Race Question. LC 72-185291. 1972. 6.50 (ISBN 0-87114-056-X). U of Oreg Bks.

Petersen. On the Track of the Dixie Limited. (Illus.). 64p. 8.50 (ISBN 0-936610-00-X). Colophon.

Phillips, Elizabeth C. Monarch Notes on Faulkner's Absalom, Absalom. (Orig.). pap. 1.95 (ISBN 0-671-00664-9). Monarch Pr.

Pilkington, John. The Heart of Yoknapatawpha. LC 80-29686. 336p. 1981. 24.95x (ISBN 0-87805-135-X). U Pr of Miss.

Polk, Noel. Faulkner's Requiem for a Nun: A Critical Study. LC 80-8099. (Illus.). 288p. 1981. 17.50x (ISBN 0-253-13302-5). Ind U Pr.

Powers, Lyall H. Faulkner's Yoknapatawpha Comedy. 296p. 1980. 18.50x (ISBN 0-472-08727-4). U of Mich Pr.

Roberts, James L. Absalom, Absalom Notes. rev. ed. (Orig.). 1970. pap. 1.95 (ISBN 0-8220-0110-1). Cliffs.

--As I Lay Dying Notes. 3rd ed. (Orig.). 1969. pap. 2.25 (ISBN 0-8220-0210-8). Cliffs.

--Light in August Notes. rev. ed. (Orig.). 1968. pap. 2.25 (ISBN 0-8220-0744-4). Cliffs.

--Sound & the Fury Notes. (Orig.). pap. 2.25 (ISBN 0-8220-1219-7). Cliffs.

Sachs, Viola, ed. Le Blanc et le Noir chez Melville et Faulkner. 291p. (French.). 1975. pap. text ed. 34.50x (ISBN 90-2797-961-8). Mouton.

Samway, Patrick H. Faulkner's Intruder in the Dust: A Critical Study of the Typescripts. LC 79-57439. 408p. 1980. 28.50x (ISBN 0-87875-186-6). Whitston Pub.

Schoenberg, Estella. Old Tales & Talking: Quentin Compson in William Faulkner's "Absalom, Absalom!" & Related Works. LC 76-58514. 1977. 9.95x (ISBN 0-87805-030-2). U Pr of Miss.

Scott, Evelyn. On William Faulkner's the Sound & the Fury. LC 73-7508. Repr. of 1929 ed. lib. bdg. 6.00 (ISBN 0-8414-7553-9). Folcroft.

Seyppel, Joachim. William Faulkner. LC 74-134826. (Modern Literature Ser.). 120p. pap. 4.95 (ISBN 0-8044-6858-3). Ungar.

Slatoff, Walter J. Quest for Failure: A Study of William Faulkner. LC 72-4084. 275p. 1972. Repr. of 1960 ed. lib. bdg. 16.00x (ISBN 0-8371-6432-X, SLQF). Greenwood.

Stonum, Gary L. Faulkner's Career: An Internal Literary History. LC 78-23503. 1979. 17.50x (ISBN 0-8014-1196-3). Cornell U Pr.

Strandberg, Victor. A Faulkner Overview: Six Perspectives. (Literary Criticism Ser.). 130p. 1981. 13.50 (ISBN 0-8046-9289-0). Kennikat.

Turner, Dixie M. A Jungian Psychoanalytic Interpretation of William Faulkner's "As I Lay Dying". LC 80-5582. 107p. 1981. lib. bdg. 16.50 (ISBN 0-8191-1451-0); pap. text ed. 7.50 (ISBN 0-8191-1452-9). U Pr of Amer.

Vickery, Olga W. Novels of William Faulkner: A Critical Interpretation. rev. ed. LC 64-23150. 1964. 20.00x (ISBN 0-8071-0817-0). La State U Pr.

Volpe, Edmond. Reader's Guide to William Faulkner. 427p. (Orig.). 1964. pap. 8.95 (ISBN 0-374-50336-2, N255). FS&G.

Volpe, Edmond L. A Reader's Guide to William Faulkner. 427p. 1975. Repr. of 1964 ed. lib. bdg. 20.00x (ISBN 0-374-98086-1). Octagon.

Wagner, Linda W. Hemingway & Faulkner: Inventors-Masters. LC 75-23367. 1975. 13.50 (ISBN 0-8108-0862-5). Scarecrow.

Wagner, Linda W., ed. William Faulkner; Four Decades of Criticism. 374p. 1973. 10.00 (ISBN 0-87013-176-1). Mich St U Pr.

Watkins, Floyd C. Flesh & the Word: Eliot, Hemingway, Faulkner. LC 75-157740. 1971. 8.95 (ISBN 0-8265-1169-4). Vanderbilt U Pr.

Watson, James G. Snopes Dilemma: Faulkner's Trilogy. LC 72-102699. 1968. 12.95x (ISBN 0-87024-150-8). U of Miami Pr.

Webb, James W. & Green, A. Wigfall, eds. William Faulkner of Oxford. LC 65-23763. (Illus.). 1965. pap. 6.95x (ISBN 0-8071-0143-5). La State U Pr.

Weisgerber, Jean. Faulkner & Dostoevsky: Influence & Confluence. McWilliams, Dean, tr. from Fr. LC 72-85537. xxii, 383p. 1974. 18.00x (ISBN 0-8214-0149-1). Ohio U Pr.

Williams, David. Faulkner's Women: The Myth & the Muse. 1977. 16.00x (ISBN 0-7735-0257-2). McGill-Queens U Pr.

Wittenberg, Judith B. Faulkner: The Transfiguration of Biography. LC 79-9230. 1979. 17.50x (ISBN 0-8032-4707-9). U of Nebr Pr.

Wolfe, George H., ed. Faulkner; Fifty Years After "The Marble Faun". LC 75-40380. 192p. 1976. 12.95x (ISBN 0-8173-7609-7). U of Ala Pr.

FAULKNER, WILLIAM, 1897-1962–BIBLIOGRAPHY

Bosha, Francis J., ed. William Faulkner's Soldier's Pay: A Bibliographical Study. LC 80-54205. 542p. 1982. 38.50x (ISBN 0-87875-211-0). Whitston Pub.

Faulkner, William. Each in Its Ordered Place: a Faulkner Collector's Notebook: A Comprehensive International Bibliography of Faulkner & Faulkneriana, 1924-1974. Peterson, Carl, compiled by. 256p. 1975. 20.00 (ISBN 0-88233-096-9). Ardis Pubs.

Harmon, Robert B. The First Editions of William Faulkner. LC 77-26499. (First Edition Pocket Guides Ser.). 1978. pap. 3.95 (ISBN 0-910720-09-6). Hermes.

McHaney, Thomas. William Faulkner: A Reference Guide. (Reference Bks.). 1976. lib. bdg. 30.00 (ISBN 0-8161-1132-4). G K Hall.

Massey, Linton R. William Faulkner - Man Working, 1919-1962: A Catalogue of the William Faulkner Collections at the University of Virginia. LC 68-19477. (Illus.). 288p. 1968. 25.00x (ISBN 0-8139-0174-X, Bibliographic Society, University of Virginia). U Pr of Va.

FAULKNER, WILLIAM, 1897-1962–DICTIONARIES, INDEXES, ETC.

Bonner, Thomas, Jr. & Falcon, Guillermo N. William Faulkner, the William B. Wisdom Collection: A Descriptive Catalog. LC 79-26556. (Illus.). 1980. pap. 13.00 (ISBN 0-9603212-2-5). Tulane Univ.

Brown, Calvin S. A Glossary of Faulkner's South. LC 75-43308. (Illus.). 1976. 20.00x (ISBN 0-300-01944-0). Yale U Pr.

Capps, Jack L., ed. Go Down Moses: A Concordance to the Novel, 2 vols. LC 77-15831. (The Faulkner Concordances: No. 2). 1977. 60.00 set (ISBN 0-8357-0279-0, IS-00039, Pub. by Faulkner Concordance Advisory Board). Univ Microfilms.

Dasher, Thomas E. An Index to the Characters in the Published & Unpublished Fiction of William Faulkner. 1981. lib. bdg. 50.00 (ISBN 0-8240-9305-4). Garland Pub.

Everett, Walter K. Faulkner's Art & Characters. LC 68-31478. (Orig.). (gr. 9 up). 1969. pap. text ed. 3.50 (ISBN 0-8120-0392-6). Barron.

Polk, Noel & Privratsky, Kenneth. A Fable: A Concordance to the Novel, 2 vols. LC 81-3369. (The Faulkner Concordances Ser.: No. 6). 1981. Set. 90.00 (ISBN 0-8357-0587-0, IS-00136, Pub. by Faulkner Concordance). Vol. 1, A-Meal (ISBN 0-8357-0589-7). Vol. 2, Mean-z (ISBN 0-8357-0590-0). Univ Microfilms.

Polk, Noel & Privratsky, Kenneth L. The Sound & the Fury: A Concordance to the Novel. LC 80-12310. (The Faulkner Concordances Ser.: No. 5). 412p. 1980. Set. 62.00 (ISBN 0-8357-0513-7, IS-00108, Pub. by Faulkner Concordance). A-L (ISBN 0-8357-0558-7). M-Z (ISBN 0-8357-0559-5). Univ Microfilms.

Polk, Noel, ed. Requiem for a Nun: A Concordance to the Novel. LC 78-31191. (The Faulkner Concordances: No. 3). 1979. 35.00 (ISBN 0-8357-0370-3, IS-00072, The Faulkner Concordance Advisory Board). Univ Microfilms.

Runyon, Harry. Faulkner Glossary. 1966. pap. 2.25 (ISBN 0-8065-0152-9, 228). Citadel Pr.

FAULTS (GEOLOGY)

Anderson, E. M. The Dynamics of Faulting. 2nd rev ed. LC 72-188368. (Illus.). 1972. Repr. of 1952 ed. 13.75 (ISBN 0-02-840310-X). Hafner.

Hubbert, M. King, et al. Role of Fluid Pressure in Mechanics of Overthrust Faulting, Discussion & Reply. (Illus.). 1959. 5.00x (ISBN 0-685-11733-2). Geol Soc.

Neumann, Else-Ragnhild & Ramberg, Ivar B., eds. Petrology & Geochemistry of Continental Rifts. (Nato Advanced Study Institute Ser. C: No. 36). 1978. lib. bdg. 42.00 (ISBN 90-277-0866-5, Pub. by Reidel Holland). Kluwer Boston.

Ramberg, Ivar B. & Neumann, Else-Ragnhild, eds. Tectonics & Geophysics of Continental Rifts. (NATO Advanced Study Institute Ser.: No. 37). 1978. lib. bdg. 42.00 (ISBN 90-277-0867-3, Pub. by Reidel Holland). Kluwer Boston.

Silberling, N. J. Age Relationships of the Golconda Thrust Fault, Sonoma Range, North-Central Nevada. LC 74-31780. (Special Paper: No. 163). (Illus.). 1975. pap. 9.00x (ISBN 0-8137-2163-6). Geol Soc.

Voight, Barry, ed. Mechanics of Thrust Faults & Decollement. (Benchmark Papers in Geology: Vol. 32). 1977. 50.00 (ISBN 0-12-787680-4). Acad Pr.

FAUNA

see Animals; Fresh-Water Biology; Zoology

FAUNA, PREHISTORIC

see Paleontology

FAUQUIER COUNTY, VIRGINIA–HISTORY

Groome, Harry C. Fauquier During the Proprietorship: A Chronicle of a Northern Neck County, Virginia. LC 77-88164. (Illus.). 1969. Repr. of 1927 ed. 15.00 (ISBN 0-8063-7959-6). Regional.

Reese, George, ed. The Official Papers of Francis Fauquier, Lieutenant Governor of Virginia, Seventeen Fifty-Eight to Seventeen Sixty-Eight, Vol. 1. LC 80-19866. (Virginia Historical Society Documents Ser.: Vol. 14). 1981. 37.50x (ISBN 0-8139-0856-6). U Pr of Va.

FAURE GABRIEL, 1845-1924

Koechlin, Charles L. Gabriel Faure, 1845-1924. LC 75-41167. Repr. of 1945 ed. 12.45 (ISBN 0-404-14679-1). AMS Pr.

Long, Marguerite. At the Piano with Faure. LC 79-63623. (Illus.). 1981. 11.95 (ISBN 0-8008-0505-4, Crescendo). Taplinger.

Suckling, Norman. Faure. LC 78-13797. (Encore Music Editions Ser.). (Illus.). 1979. Repr. of 1951 ed. 22.00 (ISBN 0-88355-745-2). Hyperion Conn.

--Faure. LC 78-23842. (Illus.). 1979. Repr. of 1951 ed. lib. bdg. 19.75x (ISBN 0-313-20667-8, SUFA). Greenwood.

FAUST, FREDERICK, 1892-1944

Easton, Robert. Max Brand the Big "Westerner". LC 68-16732. (Illus.). 1970. 17.90 (ISBN 0-8061-0870-3); pap. 9.95 (ISBN 0-8061-1233-6). U of Okla Pr.

FAUST

Butler, E. M. The Fortunes of Faust. 1979. 42.00 (ISBN 0-521-22562-0); pap. 10.95 (ISBN 0-521-29552-1). Cambridge U Pr.

Butler, Eliza M. The Fortunes of Faust. LC 78-14109. (Illus.). 1979. Repr. of 1952 ed. 26.50 (ISBN 0-88355-780-0). Hyperion Conn.

Enright, D. J. A Faust Book. 1980. pap. 9.95 (ISBN 0-19-211895-1). Oxford U Pr.

Faust - Bibliographie, 3 vols. Incl. Vol. 1; Vol. 2, Pt. 1. Goethes Faust, Ausgaben und Uebersetzungen. 242p. 1968. 12.50x (ISBN 0-8002-1575-3); Vol. 2, Pt. 2. Goethes Faust, Sekundaer Literatur. 647p. 1970. 30.00x (ISBN 0-8002-2209-1); Vol. 3. (Ger.). Intl Pubns Serv.

Faustus, Johann. The Historie of Damnable Live & Deserved Death of Doctor John Faustus. Gent, P. F., tr. LC 74-26934. (English Experience Ser.: No. 173). 80p. 1969. Repr. of 1592 ed. 14.00 (ISBN 90-221-0173-8). Walter J Johnson.

Kelly, James W. The Faust Legend in Music. LC 74-75893. (Detroit Reprints in Music). 1976. 10.00 (ISBN 0-911772-81-2). Info Coord.

Palmer, Philip M. & More, Robert P. Sources of the Faust Tradition. LC 65-29231. (Studies in Comparative Literature, No. 35). 1969. Repr. of 1936 ed. lib. bdg. 33.95 (ISBN 0-8383-0608-X). Haskell.

--Sources of the Faust Tradition. 1966. lib. bdg. 15.00x (ISBN 0-374-96194-8). Octagon.

Soldati, Joseph A. Configurations of Faust: Three Studies in the Gothic (1798-1820) Varma, Devendra P., ed. LC 79-8482. (Gothic Studies & Dissertations Ser.). 1980. lib. bdg. 17.00x (ISBN 0-405-12662-X). Arno.

Weinberg, Kurt. The Figure of Faust in Valery & Goethe. LC 75-30211. (Princeton Essays in Literature Ser.). 1976. 19.50 (ISBN 0-691-06304-4). Princeton U Pr.

FAUST-DRAMA

Goethe, Johann W. Von. Faust: Pt. I. MacIntyre, C. F., tr. LC 51-1865. 1957. pap. 2.95 (ISBN 0-8112-0056-6, NDP70). New Directions.

FAUVISM

Denvir, B. Fauvism & Expressionism. LC 77-80181. (Modern Movements in Art Ser.). 1978. pap. 1.95 (ISBN 0-8120-0878-2). Barron.

Elderfield, John. The Wild Beasts: Fauvism & Its Affinities. LC 76-9230. (Illus.). 1976. 15.00 (ISBN 0-19-519889-1); pap. 9.95 (ISBN 0-19-519890-5). Oxford U Pr.

Movement in Modern Art: Cubism, Expressionism & Fauvism, 3 bks. 0.95 ea. Bk. 1 (ISBN 0-517-02522-1). Bk. 2 (ISBN 0-517-02523-X). Bk. 3 (ISBN 0-517-02524-8). Crown.

Oppler, Ellen C. Fauvism Reexamined. LC 75-23805. (Outstanding Dissertations in the Fine Arts - 20th Century). (Illus.). 1976. lib. bdg. 45.00 (ISBN 0-8240-1999-7). Garland Pub.

FAVER, MILTON

Corning, Leavitt, Jr. Baronial Forts of the Big Bend. (Illus.). 1969. 4.00 (ISBN 0-911536-08-6). Trinity U Pr.

FAVORITES, ROYAL

see also Fools and Jesters; Courts and Courtiers

FAYETTE, CONTY, KENTUCKY

Perrin, W. H. History of Fayette County, Kentucky, with an Outline Sketch of the Bluegrass Region. 905p. 1979. 40.00 (ISBN 0-89308-163-9). Southern Hist Pr.

FBI

see United States-Federal Bureau of Investigation

FEAR

see also Agoraphobia; Anxiety; Courage; Hysteria (Social Psychology); Panic; Peace of Mind; Phobias; School Phobia

Angell, James W. Learning to Manage Our Fears. LC 81-1878. 128p. 1981. 6.95 (ISBN 0-687-21329-0). Abingdon.

Bamber, J. H. The Fears of Adolescents. 1979. 34.00 (ISBN 0-12-077550-6). Acad Pr.

Belina, Tom. Flight to Fear: Pacesetters. (gr. 4 up). 1978. 8.65 (ISBN 0-516-02155-9). Childrens.

Berkey, Velma & Berkey, Barry. Robbers, Bones & Mean Dogs. LC 77-10727. (Illus.). 1978. PLB 5.95 (ISBN 0-201-00570-0, A-W Childrens). A-W.

Buckley, Michael. Why Are You Afraid. pap. 5.95 (ISBN 0-87061-060-0). Chr Classics.

Burton, Wilma. Living Without Fear. LC 81-65473. 1981. pap. 3.95 (ISBN 0-89107-184-9). Good News.

Cayce, Hugh L. Faces of Fear. LC 80-7748. 192p. 1980. 9.95 (ISBN 0-06-061352-1, HarpR). Har-Row.

Coles, Robert. Children of Crisis. 1968. pap. 3.95 (ISBN 0-440-51235-2, Delta). Dell.

--Children of Crisis, Vol. 1: A Study of Courage & Fear. (Children of Crisis Ser.). (Illus.). 1967. 16.95 (ISBN 0-316-15159-9, Pub. by Atlantic Monthly Pr); pap. 6.95 (ISBN 0-316-15154-8). Little.

Conaway, Judith. Sometimes It Scares Me. LC 76-46342. (Moods & Emotions Ser.). (Illus.). (gr. k-3). 1977. PLB 10.25 (ISBN 0-8172-0060-6). Raintree Pubs.

Dollard, John. Fear in Battle. LC 75-41076. Repr. of 1944 ed. 9.50 (ISBN 0-404-14714-3). AMS Pr.

Dollard, John & Horton, Donald. Fear in Battle. LC 77-2970. 1977. Repr. of 1944 ed. lib. bdg. 15.00x (ISBN 0-8371-9579-9, DOFB). Greenwood.

Dyer, Wayne W. Your Erroneous Zones. LC 75-35621. (Funk & W Bk.). 256p. 1976. 10.95 (ISBN 0-308-10228-2). T Y Crowell.

--Your Erroneous Zones. 1981. pap. 2.75 (ISBN 0-380-01669-9, 51706). Avon.

Fensterheim, H. & Baer, J. Stop Running Scared. 1978. pap. 2.25 (ISBN 0-440-17734-0). Dell.

Forgione, Albert G., et al. Fear: Learning to Cope. 1978. 11.95 (ISBN 0-442-26388-0). Van Nos Reinhold.

Friedman, Martha. Overcoming the Fear of Success: Why & How We Defeat Ourselves & What to Do About It. LC 79-3628. 256p. 1980. 10.95 (ISBN 0-87223-594-7, Dist. by Har-Row). Seaview Bks.

Gossett, Don. How to Conquer Fear. Orig. Title: How You Can Rise Above Fear. 160p. 1981. pap. 2.95 (ISBN 0-88368-092-0). Whitaker Hse.

Gray, Jeffrey. Psychology of Fear & Stress. LC 70-104742. (Illus., Orig.). 1971. pap. 3.95 (ISBN 0-07-024225-9, SP). McGraw.

Gross, Alan. Sometimes I Worry. LC 78-8019. (Illus.). (gr. k-3). 1978. PLB 8.65 (ISBN 0-516-03670-X). Childrens.

Hall, Manly P. Basic Fears. pap. 1.75 (ISBN 0-89314-304-9). Philos Res.

Hauck, Paul A. Overcoming Worry & Fear. LC 74-20629. 1975. pap. 4.95 (ISBN 0-664-24811-X). Westminster.

Hubbard, David A. How to Face Your Fears. LC 72-5670. 1972. 3.95 (ISBN 0-87981-013-0). Holman.

Hyde, Margaret O. Fears & Phobias. (gr. 9-12). 1977. PLB 10.95 (ISBN 0-07-031648-1, GB). McGraw.

Kahn, Samuel. Anxieties, Phobias & Fears. LC 76-14497. 1977. 10.00 (ISBN 0-8022-2187-4). Philos Lib.

Leahy, Michael P. How to Overcome Your Fears. pap. 3.00 (ISBN 0-87980-062-3). Wilshire.

Lederer, Wolfgang. Fear of Women. LC 68-16305. (Illus.). 1970. pap. 4.95 (ISBN 0-15-630419-8, HB184, Harv). HarBraceJ.

--The Fear of Women. LC 68-16305. (Illus.). 368p. 1968. 40.25 (ISBN 0-8089-0260-1). Grune.

Lembo, John M. How to Cope with Your Fears & Frustrations. LC 76-52139. 1977. 6.95 (ISBN 0-87212-091-0). Libra.

Living Beyond Worry & Anger. LC 79-83659. 1979. 7.95 (ISBN 0-89081-194-6). Harvest Hse.

Lowen, Alexander. Fear of Life. 274p. 1981. pap. 3.95 (ISBN 0-02-077330-7). Macmillan.

Mann, Stella T. How to Analyze & Overcome Your Fears. 2nd ed. 179p. 1972. pap. 3.95 (ISBN 0-87516-175-8). De Vorss.

Marks, Isaac M. Living with Fear: You As a Therapist. 1978. 10.95 (ISBN 0-07-040395-3, P&RB). McGraw.

Meerloo, Abraham M. Patterns of Panic. LC 73-9371. 120p. 1974. Repr. of 1950 ed. lib. bdg. 15.00 (ISBN 0-8371-7009-5, MEPP). Greenwood.

Moore, William. The Thin Yellow Line. LC 74-21799. 1975. 8.95 (ISBN 0-312-80010-X). St Martin.

Murphy, Joseph. Supreme Mastery of Fear. pap. 0.75 (ISBN 0-87516-340-8). De Vorss.

Odier, Charles. Anxiety & Magic Thinking: The Psychogenetic Analysis of Phobia & the Neurosis of Abandonment. Schoelly, Marie-Louise & Sherfey, Mary J., trs. LC 56-9335. 1956. text ed. 17.50 (ISBN 0-8236-0400-4). Intl Univs Pr.

Olshan, Neal & Wang, Julie. Phobia Free & Flying High. LC 78-52970. 1978. pap. 2.25 (ISBN 0-89516-031-5). Condor Pub Co.

Olshan, Neil & Dreyer, Julie. Fears & Phobias. (gr. 7 up). 1980. PLB 7.90 (ISBN 0-531-02865-8, B08). Watts.

Osborne, Cecil G. Release from Fear & Anxiety. LC 75-19908. 1976. pap. 1.79 (ISBN 0-87680-998-0, 98050). Word Bks.

Rachman, Stanley J. Fear & Courage. LC 78-464. (Psychology Ser.). (Illus.). 1978. text ed. 17.95x (ISBN 0-7167-0089-1); pap. text ed. 8.95x (ISBN 0-7167-0087-5). W H Freeman.

Reed, Jonathan. Do Armadillos Come in Houses? LC 81-2526. (Illus.). 80p. (gr. 2-5). 1981. price not set (ISBN 0-689-30858-2). Atheneum.

Riley, Sue. Afraid. LC 77-15627. (What Does It Mean Ser.). (Illus.). (gr. k-2). 1978. PLB 5.50 (ISBN 0-89565-011-8). Childs World.

Russell, Robert. Victory Over Fear & Worry. 132p. 1981. pap. 3.50 (ISBN 0-87516-439-0). De Vorss.

Saliba, David R. A Psychology of Fear: The Nightmare Formula of Edgar Allan Poe. LC 80-8267. 277p. 1980. lib. bdg. 18.50 (ISBN 0-8191-1269-0); pap. text ed. 10.25 (ISBN 0-8191-1270-4). U Pr of Amer.

Samaan, Sadek H. & Samaan, Anne J. Fears & Worries of Nigerian Igbo Secondary School Students: An Empirical Psychocultural Study. LC 76-620061. (Papers in International Studies: Africa: No. 30). (Illus.). 1976. pap. 6.00 (ISBN 0-89680-062-8). Ohio U Ctr Intl.

Seabury, David. Stop Being Afraid. 1965. pap. 3.95 (ISBN 0-911336-19-2). Sci of Mind.

Sluckin, W. Fear in Animals & Man. 330p. 1979. text ed. 22.50 (ISBN 0-442-30164-2). Van Nos Reinhold.

Tolle, James M. Living Without Fear. 1977. 4.95 (ISBN 0-915378-13-2). Tolle Pubns.

Tracy, Ann B. Patterns of Fear in the Gothic Novel, 1790 to 1830. Varma, Devendra P., ed. LC 79-8487. (Gothic Studies & Dissertations Ser.). 1980. lib. bdg. 35.00x (ISBN 0-405-12682-4). Arno.

Tuan, Yi-Fu. Landscapes of Fear. LC 79-1890. 272p. 1981. pap. 8.95 (ISBN 0-8166-1021-5). U of Minn Pr.

--Landscapes of Fear. LC 79-1890. 1980. 11.95 (ISBN 0-394-42035-7). Pantheon.

Welford, E. H. Fear & Common Sense. 1956. pap. 1.00 (ISBN 0-685-06555-3). Assoc Bk.

Wier, John S. The Tyranny of Fear. LC 79-63153. 1979. 6.95 (ISBN 0-533-04247-X). Vantage.

Wilkins, W. R., ed. Nitty-Gritty: Fear, Vol. 2, No. 1. pap. 4.00 (ISBN 0-916402-05-3). Goldermood Rainbow.

Williams, Tom A. Dreads & Besetting Fears. Repr. of 1923 ed. 30.00 (ISBN 0-89987-089-9). Darby Bks.

Wolpe, Joseph & Wolpe, David. Our Useless Fears. 1981. 10.00 (ISBN 0-395-31334-1). HM.

Wood, John T. What Are You Afraid of? A Guide to Dealing with Your Fears. 192p. 1975 (ISBN 0-13-951889-4, Spec). pap. 2.95 (ISBN 0-13-951871-1). P-H.

Writers Collective, tr. from Ital. It's Scary Sometimes. LC 77-17641. (gr. 4-8). 1978. 9.95 (ISBN 0-87705-366-9). Human Sci Pr.

FEAR OF FLYING

Ellis, Albert. How to Master Your Fear of Flying. LC 77-182928. 1977. pap. 1.95 (ISBN 0-917476-10-7). Rational Living.

Griest, John H. & Griest, Georgia L. Fearless Flying: A Passenger Guide to Modern Airline Travel. 160p. 1981. 14.95 (ISBN 0-88229-710-4). Nelson-Hall.

FEAR OF GOD

Bunyan, John. Fear of God. pap. 3.95 (ISBN 0-685-19828-6). Reiner.

FEAST OF DEDICATION

see Hanukkah (Feast of Lights)

FEAST OF ESTHER

see Purim (Feast of Esther)

FEAST OF LIGHTS

see Hanukkah (Feast of Lights)

FEAST OF REJOICING OVER THE LAW

see Simhat Torah

FEAST OF TABERNACLES

see Sukkoth

FEAST OF THE MACCABEES

see Hanukkah (Feast of Lights)

FEAST OF WEEKS

see Shavu'oth (Feast of Weeks)

FEASTS

see Fasts and Feasts

FEATHER-WORK-MEXICO

Nuttall, Zelia. Standard or Head-Dress? 1888. pap. 8.00 (ISBN 0-527-01183-5). Kraus Repr.

FEATHERS

Doughty, Robin W. Feather Fashions & Bird Preservation: A Study in Nature Protection. LC 72-619678. 1975. 19.50x (ISBN 0-520-02588-1). U of Cal Pr.

Lerner, Marguerite R. Fur, Feathers, Hair. LC 62-16851. (Medical Books for Children). (Illus.). (gr. 3-9). 1962. PLB 3.95 (ISBN 0-8225-0014-0). Lerner Pubns.

Rabineau, Phyllis. Feather Arts: Beauty, Wealth & Spirit from Five Continents. LC 78-74595. (Illus., Orig.). 1979. pap. 7.95 (ISBN 0-914868-04-7). Field Mus.

Voitkevick, A. A. Feather & Plumage of Birds. 1966. 9.75 (ISBN 0-8079-0050-8). October.

Welker, Robert H. Birds & Men: American Birds in Science, Art, Literature, & Conservation, 1800-1900. LC 55-11608. (Illus.). 1966. pap. 2.45 (ISBN 0-689-70202-7, 82). Atheneum.

FEBOLDSON, FEBOLD

Beath, Paul R., compiled by. Febold Feboldson: Tall Tales from the Great Plains. LC 62-8725. (Illus.). 1962. pap. 4.25 (ISBN 0-8032-5012-6, BB 161, Bison). U of Nebr Pr.

FECHTER, CHARLES ALBERT, 1824-1879

Field, Kate. Charles Albert Fechter. LC 70-82827. 1882. 12.00 (ISBN 0-405-08502-8, Blom Pubns). Arno.

FECUNDITY

see Fertility

FEDERAL AID TO EDUCATION

see also Educational Equalization

Ashline, Nelson F., et al, eds. Education, Inequality & National Policy. LC 75-21833. 224p. 1976. 18.95 (ISBN 0-669-00053-1). Lexington Bks.

Bailey, Stephen K. & Mosher, Edith K. ESEA: The Office of Education Administers a Law. LC 68-27692. 1968. text ed. 11.95x (ISBN 0-8156-2121-3). Syracuse U Pr.

Blum, Virgil C. Freedom of Choice in Education. LC 77-8086. 1977. Repr. of 1958 ed. lib. bdg. 17.50x (ISBN 0-8371-9677-9, BLFC). Greenwood.

Education & the Public Good. Incl. The Federal Role in Education. Green, Edith. (The Burton Lectures Ser: 1963); The Challenge to Education in a Changing World. Reuther, Walter P. (Inglis Lectures Ser: 1964). LC 64-25934. 67p. 1964. 4.50x (ISBN 0-674-23875-3). Harvard U Pr.

Federal Aid for Industrial Arts. 1966. 4.75 (ISBN 0-686-16548-9); pap. 3.75 (ISBN 0-686-16549-7). Am Indus Arts.

Finn, Chester E., Jr. Education & the Presidency. LC 75-32871. (Politics of Education Ser.). 1977. 18.95 (ISBN 0-669-00365-4). Lexington Bks.

Garms, Walter I., et al. School Finance: The Economics & Politics of Public Education. (Illus.). 1978. text ed. 18.95 (ISBN 0-13-793315-0). P-H.

Goltz, Diane & Behrmann, Michael. Getting the Buck to Stop Here: A Guide to Federal Resources for Special Needs. LC 79-92681. 225p. (Orig.). 1979. pap. 19.95 (ISBN 0-86586-098-X). Coun Exc Child.

Heer, C. Federal Aid & the Tax Problem. LC 77-74943. (American Federalism-the Urban Dimension). (Illus.). 1978. Repr. of 1939 ed. lib. bdg. 12.00x (ISBN 0-405-10491-X). Arno.

Hughes, John F. & Hughes, Anne O. Equal Education: A New National Strategy. LC 72-75635. 256p. 1973. 10.00x (ISBN 0-253-12350-X). Ind U Pr.

Johns, Roe L. Full State Funding of Education: Evolution & Implications. LC 72-91863. (Horace Mann Lecture Ser.). 1973. 4.95x (ISBN 0-8229-3258-X). U of Pittsburgh Pr.

Kaiser, O'Neil. Impact of Federal Funding on Small School Districts. (Bulletin 20). 1976. 4.00 (ISBN 0-685-05658-9); member 3.00 (ISBN 0-685-05659-7). Assn Sch Busn.

Keith, J. A. & Bagley, W. C. The Nation & the Schools. LC 77-74944. (American Federalism-the Urban Dimension). (Illus.). 1978. Repr. of 1920 ed. lib. bdg. 22.00x (ISBN 0-405-10492-8). Arno.

Landers, Thomas J. & Myers, Judith. Essentials of School Management. LC 76-41539. (Illus.). 1977. text ed. 15.95 (ISBN 0-7216-5619-6). HR&W.

League of Women Voters Education Fund. Campaigning for Fair School Finance: Cases in Point. 1978. pap. 3.00 (ISBN 0-89959-101-9, 353). LWV US.

Lee, Gordon C. The Struggle for Federal Aid, First Phase: A History of the Attempts to Obtain Federal Aid for the Common Schools. LC 79-176979. (Columbia University. Teachers College. Contributions to Education: No. 957). Repr. of 1949 ed. 17.50 (ISBN 0-404-55957-3). AMS Pr.

Long, Kate. Johnny's Such a Bright Boy, What a Shame He's Retarded. 1977. 10.00 (ISBN 0-395-25346-2); pap. 4.95 (ISBN 0-395-27164-9). HM.

Meranto, Philip. Politics of Federal Aid to Education in 1965: A Study in Political Innovation. LC 67-16846. (Orig.). (gr. 9-12). pap. 4.95x (ISBN 0-8156-2107-8). Syracuse U Pr.

Milstein, Mike M. Impact & Response: Federal Education Programs & State Agencies. LC 76-14887. 1976. text ed. 13.95 (ISBN 0-8077-2502-1); pap. 8.25x (ISBN 0-8077-2501-3). Tchrs Coll.

O'Neil, Robert M. The Courts, Government, & Higher Education. LC 72-90171. 40p. 1972. pap. 1.00 (ISBN 0-87186-237-9). Comm Econ Dev.

Smart, Don. Federal Aid to Australian Schools. (Illus.). 1979. 20.00x (ISBN 0-7022-1237-7). U of Queensland Pr.

Vanecko, James J., et al, eds. Who Benefits from Federal Education Dollars? The Development of ESEA Title I Allocation Policy. LC 79-55777. (Illus.). 1980. text ed. 27.00 (ISBN 0-89011-541-9). Abt Assoc.

FEDERAL AID TO HIGHER EDUCATION

Agria, John J. College Housing: A Critique of the Federal College Housing Loan Program. 1972. pap. 5.25 (ISBN 0-8447-3074-2). Am Enterprise.

Belknap, Robert L. & Kuhns, Richard. Tradition & Innovation: General Education & the Reintegration of the University, a Columbia Report. LC 77-3315. 130p. 1977. 12.00x (ISBN 0-231-04322-8); pap. 4.00x (ISBN 0-231-04323-6). Columbia U Pr.

Carnegie Council on Policy Studies in Higher Education. The Federal Role in Postsecondary Education: Unfinished Business, 1975-1980. LC 75-4482. (Carnegie Council Ser). (Illus.). 112p. 1975. 10.95x (ISBN 0-87589-259-0). Jossey-Bass.

--Low or No Tuition: The Feasibility of a National Policy for the First Two Years of College. LC 75-4276. (Carnegie Council Ser). (Illus.). 96p. 1975. 10.95x (ISBN 0-87589-257-4). Jossey-Bass.

Chronicle Guidance Research Staff. Chronicle Student Aid Annual. rev. ed. 420p. 1981. pap. 12.50 (ISBN 0-912578-04-1). Chron Guide.

Finn, Chester E., Jr. Scholars, Dollars, & Bureaucrats. LC 78-13363. (Studies in Higher Education Policy). 1978. 14.95 (ISBN 0-8157-2828-X); pap. 5.95 (ISBN 0-8157-2827-1). Brookings.

Kaysen, Carl. Higher Learning, the Universities & the Public. 1969. 12.00 (ISBN 0-691-09343-1); pap. 4.95 (ISBN 0-691-02810-9). Princeton U Pr.

Keeslar, Oreon. Financial Aids for Higher Education 1981-1982. 10th ed. 1000p. 1981. pap. text ed. price not set (ISBN 0-697-06129-9). Wm C Brown.

Leider, Robert. Your Own Financial Aid Factory: The Guide to Locating College Money. 2nd rev. ed. LC 80-11185. 184p. 1981. pap. 5.95 (ISBN 0-917760-22-0). Octameron Assocs.

Pray, Francis C., ed. Handbook for Educational Fund Raising: A Guide to Successful Principles & Practices for Colleges, Universities & Schools. LC 81-81964. (Higher Education Ser.). 1981. text ed. price not set (ISBN 0-87589-501-8). Jossey-Bass.

Rainsford, George N. Congress & Higher Education in the Nineteenth Century. LC 72-83343. 1972. 10.50x (ISBN 0-87049-140-7). U of Tenn Pr.

Simmons, Ronald. Managing Special Programs in Higher Education. 260p. 1980. 16.50x (ISBN 0-87073-064-9); pap. text ed. 8.95x (ISBN 0-87073-585-3). Schenkman.

Tuckman, Howard P. & Whalen, Edward L., eds. Subsidies to Higher Education: The Issues. 320p. 1980. 27.95 (ISBN 0-03-055791-7). Praeger.

FEDERAL AID TO THE ARTS

Dace, Wallace. A Proposal for a National Theater. (YA) 1978. PLB 7.97 (ISBN 0-8239-0422-9). Rosen Pr.

--Subsidies for the Theatre. 1972. pap. 7.95 (ISBN 0-686-00366-7). AG Pr.

--Subsidies for the Theatre: A Study of the Central European System of Financing Drama, Opera & Ballet. LC 72-84841. 188p. 1973. pap. 7.95 (ISBN 0-686-05610-8). AG Pr.

McKinzie, R. The New Deal for Artists. 1972. 27.50 (ISBN 0-691-04613-1); pap. 8.95 (ISBN 0-691-00584-2). Princeton U Pr.

Mangione, Jerre. The Dream & the Deal: The Federal Writers Project 1935-1943. LC 75-187787. (Illus.). 1972. 12.50 (ISBN 0-916224-22-8). Banyan Bks.

Moser, Lida. Grants in Photography: How to Get Them. (Illus.). 1978. 12.50 (ISBN 0-8174-2445-8). Amphoto.

Netzer, D. The Subsidized Muse. LC 77-25441. (Illus.). 1978. 24.95 (ISBN 0-521-21966-3). Cambridge U Pr.

FEDERAL ART PROJECT

Berman, Greta. The Lost Years: Mural Painting in New York City Under the Works Progress Administration's Federal Art Project 1935-1943. LC 77-94687. (Outstanding Dissertations in the Fine Arts Ser.). 1978. lib. bdg. 45.00 (ISBN 0-8240-3216-0). Garland Pub.

McKinzie, R. The New Deal for Artists. 1972. 27.50 (ISBN 0-691-04613-1); pap. 8.95 (ISBN 0-691-00584-2). Princeton U Pr.

Meltzer, Milton. Violins & Shovels: The WPA Arts Project. LC 75-32916. (Illus.). (YA) (gr. 7 up). 1976. 6.95 (ISBN 0-440-09316-3). Delacorte.

O'Connor, Francis V., ed. The New Deal Art Projects: An Anthology of Memoirs. LC 72-181525. (Illus.). 339p. 1972. 19.95 (ISBN 0-87474-113-0). Smithsonian.

FEDERAL BUREAU OF INVESTIGATION

see United States–Federal Bureau of Investigation

FEDERAL-CITY RELATIONS

Betters, P. V. & Williams, J. Kerwin. Cities & the 1936 Congress & Recent Federal-City Relations. LC 77-74929. (American Federalism-the Urban Dimension). 1978. Repr. of 1936 ed. lib. bdg. 12.00x (ISBN 0-405-10478-2). Arno.

Betters, Paul V. Federal Services to Municipal Governments. LC 77-749330. (American Federalism-the Urban Dimension). 1977. Repr. of 1931 ed. lib. bdg. 12.00x (ISBN 0-405-10479-0). Arno.

Bingham, Richard D. Public Housing & Urban Renewal: An Analysis of Federal-Local Relations. LC 74-19822. (Illus.). 282p. 1975. text ed. 27.95 (ISBN 0-275-05810-7). Praeger.

Committee for Economic Development. An Approach to Federal Urban Policy. LC 77-27893. 1977. lib. bdg. 4.00 (ISBN 0-87186-765-6); pap. 2.50 (ISBN 0-87186-065-1). Comm Econ Dev.

Fogelson, Robert M., et al, eds. Federal Aid to the Cities: An Original Anthology. LC 77-74925. (American Federalism-the Urban Dimension). (Illus.). 1978. lib. bdg. 34.00x (ISBN 0-405-10481-2). Arno.

--Federal-City Relations in the Nineteen Thirties: An Original Anthology. LC 77-74963. (American Federalism-the Urban Dimension). 1978. lib. bdg. 15.00x (ISBN 0-405-10506-1). Arno.

Frieden, Bernard J. & Kaplan, Marshall. The Politics of Neglect: Urban Aid from Model Cities to Revenue Sharing. LC 75-6792. (MIT-Harvard Joint Center for Urban Studies). 386p. 1975. 17.50 (ISBN 0-262-06061-2); pap. 5.95 (ISBN 0-262-56016-X). MIT Pr.

Gelfand, Mark I. A Nation of Cities: The Federal Government & Urban America 1933-1965. (Urban Life in America Ser). 432p. 1975. 19.95 (ISBN 0-19-501941-5). Oxford U Pr.

Glickman, Norman J., ed. Urban Impacts of Federal Policies. LC 79-2368. 1979. 16.50x (ISBN 0-8018-2292-0); pap. 5.95x (ISBN 0-8018-2299-8). Johns Hopkins.

Martin, R. C. The Cities & the Federal System. LC 77-74949. (American Federalism-the Urban Dimension). 1978. Repr. of 1965 ed. lib. bdg. 15.00x (ISBN 0-405-10495-2). Arno.

Mathews, R. L., ed. Urban Federalism: Urban Studies in a Federal Context. LC 81-65732. 169p. 1981. pap. text ed. 14.95 (ISBN 0-908160-85-2, 0103, Pub. by ANUP Australia). Bks Australia.

President's Commission for a National Agenda: Panel on Policies & Prospects for Metropolitan & Nonmetropolitan America. Urban America in the Eighties: Perspectives & Prospects. 127p. 1981. pap. 6.95 (ISBN 0-87855-883-7). Transaction Bks.

Pressman, Jeffrey L. Federal Programs & City Politics: The Dynamics of the Aid Process in Oakland. (Oakland Project Ser). 1975. 22.50x (ISBN 0-520-02749-3); pap. 5.95x (ISBN 0-520-03508-9). U of Cal Pr.

Urban Government: Supplementary Report of the Urbanism Committee to the National Resources Committee, Vol. 1. LC 77-74951. (American Federalism-the Urban Dimension). (Illus.). 1978. Repr. of 1939 ed. lib. bdg. 18.00x (ISBN 0-405-10509-6). Arno.

Yin, Robert K., et al. Tinkering with the System: Technological Innovations in State & Local Services. LC 76-57903. (Illus.). 1977. 16.00 (ISBN 0-669-01360-9). Lexington Bks.

FEDERAL CORPORATION TAX

see Corporations–Taxation

FEDERAL GOVERNMENT

see also Confederation of States; Decentralization in Government; Democracy; European Federation; Grants-In-Aid; Imperial Federation; Intergovernmental Fiscal Relations; Intergovernmental Tax Relations; Interstate Controversies; Legislative Power; State Governments; State Rights; also subdivision Constitution and subdivision Politics and Government under names of federal states, e.g. United States–Constitution; France–Politics and Government

Anderson, William. Intergovernmental Relations in Review. LC 73-16639. (Intergovernmental Realtions in the U.S. Research Monograph: No. 10). 178p. 1974. Repr. of 1960 ed. lib. bdg. 20.00x (ISBN 0-8371-7208-X, ANIG). Greenwood.

--The Nation & the States, Rivals or Partners? LC 73-16640. 263p. 1974. Repr. of 1955 ed. lib. bdg. 15.00 (ISBN 0-8371-7210-1, ANNS). Greenwood.

Ashford, Douglas E. National Resources & Urban Policy. LC 77-94185. (Illus.). 320p. 1980. text ed. 27.50 (ISBN 0-416-60181-2). Methuen Inc.

Bennett, Walter H. American Theories of Federalism. LC 63-17399. 1964. 18.95x (ISBN 0-8173-4710-0). U of Ala Pr.

Benson, G. C. The New Centralization: A Study of Intergovernmental Relationships in the U.S. LC 77-74928. (American Federalism-the Urban Dimension). 1978. Repr. of 1941 ed. lib. bdg. 12.00x (ISBN 0-405-10477-4). Arno.

Bent, Alan E. Escape from Anarchy: A Strategy for Urban Survival. LC 72-80172. 204p. 1972. 8.95x (ISBN 0-87870-010-2). Memphis St Univ.

Bernier, Ivan. International Legal Aspects of Federalism. xiv, 296p. (Orig.). 1973. 19.50 (ISBN 0-208-01384-9, Archon). Shoe String.

Boogman, J. C. & Van Der Plaat, G. N., eds. Federalism: History & Current Significance of a Form of Government. (Illus.). 307p. 1980. pap. 17.00 (ISBN 90-247-9003-4, Pub. by Martinus Nijhoff Netherlands). Kluwer Boston.

Breton, Albert & Scott, Anthony. The Economic Constitution of Federal States. LC 77-18526. 1978. 15.00x (ISBN 0-8020-5410-2). U of Toronto Pr.

Burrows, Bernard, et al, eds. Federal Solutions to European Issues. LC 78-8066. 1978. 21.95x (ISBN 0-312-28546-9). St Martin.

Colean, M. L. Housing for Defense: A Review of the Role of Housing in Relation to America's Defense & a Program for Actions. LC 77-74932. (American Federalism-the Urban Dimension). (Illus.). 1978. Repr. of 1940 ed. lib. bdg. 15.00x (ISBN 0-405-10480-4). Arno.

Committee for Economic Development. Fiscal Issues in the Future of Federalism. LC 68-26846. 288p. 1968. pap. 3.00 (ISBN 0-87186-223-9). Comm Econ Dev.

Coordination of State & Federal Apprenticeship Administration, Vol. II. 81p. 1980. 4.95 (ISBN 0-89940-804-4). LBJ Sch Public Affairs.

Council of State Governments. Federal-State Relations. LC 77-74938. (American Federalism-the Urban Dimension). (Illus.). 1978. Repr. of 1949 ed. lib. bdg. 20.00x (ISBN 0-405-10485-5). Arno.

Danielson, Michael N., et al. One Nation, So Many Governments: A Ford Foundation Report. LC 76-53868. 1977. 16.95 (ISBN 0-669-01293-9). Lexington Bks.

Davis, S. Rufus. The Federal Principle: A Journey Through Time in Quest of Meaning. LC 75-32673. 1978. 19.50x (ISBN 0-520-03146-6). U of Cal Pr.

Derthick, Martha. New Towns in-Town: Why a Federal Program Failed. 102p. 1972. pap. 4.00 (ISBN 0-87766-022-0, 70006). Urban Inst.

Di Marzo, Luigi. Component Units of Federal States & International Agreement. LC 80-83265. 272p. 1981. 45.00x (ISBN 90-286-0330-1). Sijthoff & Noordhoff.

Elazar, Daniel J. American Federalism: A View from the States. 2nd ed. 1972. pap. text ed. 9.50 scp (ISBN 0-690-06683-X, HarpC). Harrow.

--American Partnership: Intergovernmental Cooperation in Nineteenth Century United States. LC 62-17132. 1962. 15.00x (ISBN 0-226-20236-4). U of Chicago Pr.

--Federalism & Political Integration. LC 79-120599. 1979. 15.00x (ISBN 965-20-0013-2, Pub. by Turtledove Pub Ltd Israel). Intl Schol Bk Serv.

Federal Monster. LC 76-26409. 1976. 1.50 (ISBN 0-686-18638-9). Ind American.

Fogelson, Robert M., et al, eds. American Federalism Series: The Urban Dimension, 37 vols. 1978. lib. bdg. 812.00 set (ISBN 0-405-10474-X). Arno.

Franck, Thomas M., ed. Why Federations Fail: An Inquiry into the Requisites for Successful Federalism. LC 68-29426. (Studies in Peaceful Change: Vol. 1). 1968. 10.00x (ISBN 0-8147-0152-3). NYU Pr.

Gilbreth, Terry J. Governing Geothermal Steam: Intergovernmental Relations & Energy Policy. Bruchey, Stuart, ed. LC 78-22685. (Energy in the American Economy Ser.). 1979. lib. bdg. 22.00x (ISBN 0-405-11988-7). Arno.

Graves, W. B., ed. Intergovernmental Relations in the United States. (American Federalism-the Urban Dimension). (Illus.). 1978. Repr. of 1940 ed. lib. bdg. 15.00x (ISBN 0-405-10490-1). Arno.

Grewal, B. S., et al, eds. The Economics of Federalism. LC 79-54070. 432p. 1981. text ed. 27.95 (ISBN 0-7081-1301-X, 0457, Pub. by ANUP Australia). Bks Australia.

Haider, Donald H. When Governments Come to Washington: Governors, Mayors, & Intergovernmental Lobbying. LC 73-17643. (Illus.). 1974. 15.95 (ISBN 0-02-913370-X). Free Pr.

Hallman, Howard W. Emergency Employment: A Study in Federalism. LC 75-20323. 208p. 1977. 13.95x (ISBN 0-8173-4832-8). U of Ala Pr.

Hendry, James M. Treaties & Federal Constitutions. LC 75-1361. 186p. 1975. Repr. of 1955 ed. lib. bdg. 15.00 (ISBN 0-8371-8010-4, HETF). Greenwood.

Hicks, Ursula K. Federalism: Failure & Success: A Comparative Study. 1979. 19.50x (ISBN 0-19-520105-1). Oxford U Pr.

Hill, C. William, Jr. The Political Theory of John Taylor of Caroline. LC 75-39115. 343p. 1977. 18.50 (ISBN 0-8386-1902-9). Fairleigh Dickinson.

Holloway, William V. Intergovernmental Relations in the United States. LC 72-7472. 182p. 1972. 29.50x (ISBN 0-8422-5054-9); pap. text ed. 6.95x (ISBN 0-8422-0257-9). Irvington.

Johnston, Richard E. Effect of Judicial Review on Federal-State Relations in Australia, Canada, & the United States. LC 70-80045. 1969. 22.50x (ISBN 0-8071-0901-0). La State U Pr.

Kaufman, Herbert. The Administrative Behavior of Federal Bureau Chiefs. 220p. 1981. 22.95 (ISBN 0-8157-4844-2); pap. 8.95 (ISBN 0-8157-4843-4). Brookings.

League of Women Voters Education Fund. Our "Compound Republic". Perspectives on American Federalism. (The Federalist Papers Reexamined: No. 6). 28p. 1977. pap. 1.00 (ISBN 0-89959-042-X, 333). LWV US.

Livingston, William S. Federalism & Constitutional Change. LC 74-9226. 380p. 1974. Repr. of 1956 ed. lib. bdg. 29.00x (ISBN 0-8371-7623-9, LIFC). Greenwood.

Martin, R. C. The Cities & the Federal System. LC 77-74949. (American Federalism-the Urban Dimension). 1978. Repr. of 1965 ed. lib. bdg. 15.00x (ISBN 0-405-10495-2). Arno.

Martin, Roscoe C., ed. Federalism in Ferment. (Controversy Ser.). Date not set. 9.95x (ISBN 0-88311-017-2); pap. 3.95 (ISBN 0-88311-018-0). Lieber-Atherton.

Mason, Alpheus T. The States Rights Debate: Antifederalism & the Constitution. 2nd ed. 224p. 1972. pap. text ed. 3.95x (ISBN 0-19-501553-3). Oxford U Pr.

Maxwell, James A. Fiscal Impact of Federalism in the U. S. LC 79-83861. 1970. Repr. of 1946 ed. 15.00 (ISBN 0-8462-1413-X). Russell.

Musolf, Lloyd D. Federal Examiners & the Conflict of Law & Administration. LC 78-64217. (Johns Hopkins University. Studies in the Social Sciences. Seventieth Ser. 1952: 1). Repr. of 1953 ed. 19.50 (ISBN 0-404-61321-7). AMS Pr.

Nagel, Paul C. One Nation Indivisible: The Union in American Thought, 1776 to 1861. vii, 328p. 1980. Repr. of 1964 ed. lib. bdg. 25.00x (ISBN 0-313-22656-3, NAON). Greenwood.

Patterson, James T. The New Deal & the States: Federalism in Transition. LC 80-29606. viii, 226p. 1981. Repr. of 1969 ed. lib. bdg. 25.00x (ISBN 0-313-22841-8, PAND). Greenwood.

Pound, Roscoe, et al. Federalism As a Democratic Process. LC 78-23818. Repr. of 1942 ed. 8.50 (ISBN 0-685-57096-7). Zenger Pub.

Powell, Thomas R. Vagaries & Varieties in Constitutional Interpretation. LC 74-181973. Repr. of 1956 ed. write for info. (ISBN 0-404-05118-9). AMS Pr.

Pritchett, G. Herman. The Federal System in Constitutional Law. (Illus.). 1978. pap. 11.95 ref. ed. (ISBN 0-13-308460-4). P-H.

Proudhon, P-J. The Principle of Federation. Vernon, Richard, tr. from Fr. LC 79-4192. 1979. 10.00x (ISBN 0-8020-5458-7); pap. 4.50 (ISBN 0-8020-6365-9). U of Toronto Pr.

Ridgeway, Marian E. Interstate Compacts: A Question of Federalism. LC 75-132481. 398p. 1971. 12.50x (ISBN 0-8093-0492-9). S Ill U Pr.

Rockefeller, Nelson A. Future of Federalism. LC 62-17224. 1963. pap. 1.95 (ISBN 0-689-70165-9, 46). Atheneum.

--Future of Federalism. LC 62-17224. (Godkin Lectures Ser: 1962). 1962. 5.95x (ISBN 0-674-33800-6). Harvard U Pr.

Rostow, W. W., et al. Big Government; Myth or Might. Sparer, Phineas J., ed. LC 78-3729. (ML Seidman Memorial Town Hall Lecture Ser.). 1978. 5.00 (ISBN 0-87870-041-2). Memphis St Univ.

Rottschaefer, Henry. The Constitution & Socio-Economic Change. LC 77-173667. (American Constitutional & Legal History Ser.). 253p. 1971. Repr. of 1948 ed. lib. bdg. 29.50 (ISBN 0-306-70410-2). Da Capo.

Ruttenberg, Stanley H. & Gutchess, Jocelyn. The Federal-State Employment Service: A Critique. LC 79-128824. (Policy Studies in Employment & Welfare: No. 5). (Illus.). 105p. 1970. 7.50x (ISBN 0-8018-1229-1); pap. 2.95x (ISBN 0-8018-1228-3). Johns Hopkins.

Schaevitz, Robert C. & Van, Elizabeth A. Handbook of Federal Assistance: Financing, Grants, Technical Aids. 48.50 (ISBN 0-88262-373-7, 80-50774). Warren.

Schlesinger, Rudolf. Federalism in Central & Eastern Europe. Repr. of 1945 ed. lib. bdg. 21.00x (ISBN 0-8371-3402-1, SCFE). Greenwood.

Schmidhauser, John R. The Supreme Court As Final Arbiter in Federal-State Relations, 1789-1957. LC 73-7676. 241p. 1973. Repr. of 1958 ed. lib. bdg. 15.00x (ISBN 0-8371-6945-3, SCFA). Greenwood.

Schultz, Richard J. Federalism & the Regulatory Process. 91p. 1979. pap. text ed. 1.50x (ISBN 0-686-68857-0, Pub. by Inst Res Pub Canada). Renouf.

Shuman, Samuel I., ed. The Future of Federalism. LC 68-64032. 1968. 7.95x (ISBN 0-8143-1357-4). Wayne St U Pr.

Sundquist, James L. Making Federalism Work: A Study of Program Coordination at the Community Level. 1969. 14.95 (ISBN 0-8157-8218-7); pap. 5.95 (ISBN 0-8157-8217-9). Brookings.

Taylor, John. Construction Construed & Constitutions Vindicated. LC 77-117311. (American Constitutional & Legal History Ser). 1970. Repr. of 1820 ed. lib. bdg. 35.00 (ISBN 0-306-71983-5). Da Capo.

Thompson, W. Federal Centralization: A Study & Criticism of the Expanding Scope of Congressional Legislation. LC 77-74960. (American Federalism-the Urban Dimension). 1978. Repr. of 1923 ed. lib. bdg. 23.00x (ISBN 0-405-10504-5). Arno.

Upshur, A. P. A Brief Enquiry into the True Nature & Character of Our Federal Government. LC 71-169643. (American Constitutional & Legal History Ser.). 128p. 1971. Repr. of 1840 ed. lib. bdg. 12.50 (ISBN 0-306-70363-7). Da Capo.

U.S. Commission on Intergovernmental Relations. A Report to the President for Transmittal to the Congress. LC 77-74962. (American Federalism-the Urban Dimension). (Illus.). 1978. Repr. of 1955 ed. lib. bdg. 20.00x (ISBN 0-405-10505-3). Arno.

U.S. House Committee on Government Operations. Federal-State-Local Relations: Federal Grants-in Aid State & Local Officials, 2 vols. in 1. LC 77-74935. (American Federalism-the Urban Dimension). 1978. lib. bdg. 32.00 (ISBN 0-405-10482-0). Arno.

Wagner, Francis. Toward a New Central Europe: A Symposium. (Illus.). 394p. 1970. 8.50 (ISBN 0-87934-002-9). Danubian.

Wallace, S. C. Federal Departmentalization: A Critique of Theories of Organization. LC 79-152615. 251p. 1972. Repr. of 1941 ed. lib. bdg. 15.00 (ISBN 0-8371-6050-2, WAFE). Greenwood.

Weidner, Edward W. Intergovernmental Relations As Seen by Public Officials. LC 73-16645. (Intergovernmental Relations in the U.S., Research Monograph: No. 9). 162p. 1974. Repr. of 1960 ed. lib. bdg. 16.75x (ISBN 0-8371-7209-8, WEIR). Greenwood.

Wheare, Kenneth C. Federal Government. 4th ed. LC 80-19305. 266p. 1980. Repr. of 1963 ed. lib. bdg. 23.50x (ISBN 0-313-22702-0, WHFG). Greenwood.

White, Leonard D. The States & the Nation. LC 53-13242. Repr. of 1953 ed. 15.50 (ISBN 0-384-68033-X). Johnson Repr.

FEDERAL GOVERNMENT-AFRICA, SUB-SAHARAN

Franck, Thomas M., ed. Why Federations Fail: An Inquiry into the Requisites for Successful Federalism. LC 68-29426. (Studies in Peaceful Change: Vol. 1). 1968. 10.00x (ISBN 0-8147-0152-3). NYU Pr.

FEDERAL GOVERNMENT-AUSTRALIA

Deakin, Alfred. Federated Australia. LaNauze, T. A., ed. 1968. 18.50x (ISBN 0-522-83842-1, Pub. by Melbourne U Pr). Intl Schol Bk Serv.

Hodgins, Bruce W., et al, eds. Federalism in Canada & Australia: The Early Years. 318p. 1978. text ed. 13.75 (ISBN 0-88920-061-0, Pub. by Laurier U Pr Canada). Humanities.

Johnston, Richard E. Effect of Judicial Review on Federal-State Relations in Australia, Canada, & the United States. LC 70-80045. 1969. 22.50x (ISBN 0-8071-0901-0). La State U Pr.

Joyner, Conrad. Holman Versus Hughes: Extension of Australian Commonwealth Powers. LC 61-63516. (U of Fla. Social Science Monographs: No. 10). 1961. pap. 3.00 (ISBN 0-8130-0123-4). U Presses Fla.

Menzies, Robert. Central Power in the Australian Commonwealth: An Examination of the Growth of Commonwealth Power in the Australian Federation. LC 67-28061. (Virginia Legal Studies Ser). 1967. 8.50x (ISBN 0-8139-0177-4). U Pr of Va.

Sawer, Geoffrey. Australian Federalism in the Courts. 1967. 16.50x (ISBN 0-522-83836-7, Pub. by Melbourne U Pr). Intl Schol Bk Serv.

FEDERAL GOVERNMENT-CANADA

Black, Edwin R. Divided Loyalties: Canadian Concepts of Federalism. 264p. 1975. 13.00x (ISBN 0-7735-0230-0); pap. 6.00 (ISBN 0-7735-0238-6). McGill-Queens U Pr.

Eggleston, Wilfrid. The Road to Nationhood: A Chronicle of Dominion-Provincial Relations. LC 70-147218. 337p. 1972. Repr. of 1946 ed. lib. bdg. 16.00x (ISBN 0-8371-5983-0, EGRN). Greenwood.

Johnston, Richard E. Effect of Judicial Review on Federal-State Relations in Australia, Canada, & the United States. LC 70-80045. 1969. 22.50x (ISBN 0-8071-0901-0). La State U Pr.

Lower, Arthur R., et al. Evolving Canadian Federalism. LC 58-11382. (Commonwealth Studies Center: No. 9). 1958. 9.75 (ISBN 0-8223-0111-3). Duke.

FEDERAL GOVERNMENT-GERMANY

Brecht, Arnold. Federalism & Regionalism in Germany: The Division of Prussia. LC 77-151541. (Illus.). xvi, 202p. 1971. Repr. of 1945 ed. 12.00 (ISBN 0-8462-1592-6). Russell.

Hodgins, Bruce W., et al, eds. Federalism in Canada & Australia: The Early Years. 318p. 1978. text ed. 13.75 (ISBN 0-88920-061-0, Pub. by Laurier U Pr Canada). Humanities.

Johnson, Nevil. Government in the Federal Republic of Germany: The Executive at Work. LC 73-12759. 232p. 1974. text ed. 16.50 (ISBN 0-08-017699-2). Pergamon.

Wells, Roger H. The States in West German Federalism. 1961. 6.00x (ISBN 0-8084-0282-X); pap. 1.65x (ISBN 0-8084-0283-8, B10). Coll & U Pr.

FEDERAL GOVERNMENT-GREECE

Francotte, Henri. Le Polis Greccue. pap. 15.50 (ISBN 0-384-16710-1). Johnson Repr.

FEDERAL GOVERNMENT-INDIA

Bombwall, K. R. Foundations of Indian Federalism. 1967. 10.00x (ISBN 0-210-22721-4). Asia.

Haqqi, S. A., ed. Union-State Relations in India. 1967. 6.50x (ISBN 0-8426-1294-7). Verry.

FEDERAL GOVERNMENT-MALAYSIA

Franck, Thomas M., ed. Why Federations Fail: An Inquiry into the Requisites for Successful Federalism. LC 68-29426. (Studies in Peaceful Change: Vol. 1). 1968. 10.00x (ISBN 0-8147-0152-3). NYU Pr.

Ongkili, James P. Modernization in East Malaysia 1960-1970. (Oxford in Asia Current Affairs Ser.). (Illus.). 134p. 1972. pap. text ed. 6.25x (ISBN 0-19-519672-4). Oxford U Pr.

FEDERAL GOVERNMENT-WEST INDIES, BRITISH

Franck, Thomas M., ed. Why Federations Fail: An Inquiry into the Requisites for Successful Federalism. LC 68-29426. (Studies in Peaceful Change: Vol. 1). 1968. 10.00x (ISBN 0-8147-0152-3). NYU Pr.

FEDERAL GOVERNMENT-YUGOSLAVIA

Shoup, Paul. Communism & the Yugoslav National Question. LC 68-19759. (East Central European Studies). 1968. 20.00x (ISBN 0-231-03125-4). Columbia U Pr.

FEDERAL GRANTS FOR EDUCATION

see Federal Aid to Education

FEDERAL GRANTS FOR THE ARTS

see Federal Aid to the Arts

FEDERAL LOYALTY-SECURITY PROGRAM, 1947-

see Loyalty-Security Program, 1947-

FEDERAL PARTY

Adams, Henry, ed. Documents Relating to New England Federalism, 1800-1815. 1964. Repr. of 1905 ed. 24.50 (ISBN 0-8337-0012-X). B Franklin.

Broussard, James H. Southern Federalists, 1800-1816. LC 78-2374. 1978. 30.00x (ISBN 0-8071-0288-1). La State U Pr.

Cox, Joseph W. Champion of Southern Federalism: Robert Goodloe Harper of South Carolina. LC 78-189554. 1972. 15.00 (ISBN 0-8046-9025-1, Natl U). Kennikat.

Dauer, Manning J. The Adams Federalists. LC 53-11171. 408p. 1953. pap. 5.95x (ISBN 0-8018-0152-4). Johns Hopkins.

Fairfield, Roy P., ed. The Federalist Papers. 2nd ed. LC 80-8862. 368p. 1981. pap. text ed. 5.95x (ISBN 0-8018-2607-1). Johns Hopkins.

Fay, Bernard. Two Franklins. LC 70-93277. Repr. of 1933 ed. 18.50 (ISBN 0-404-02372-X). AMS Pr.

Hamilton, Alexander, et al. Federalist or the New Constitution. 1961. 8.95x (ISBN 0-460-00519-7, Evman). Biblio Dist.

Miller, John C. Federalist Era, Seventeen Eighty-Nine to Eighteen-One. LC 60-15321. (New American Nation Ser.). (Illus.). 1960. 17.50x (ISBN 0-06-012980-8, HarpT). Har-Row.

Pasler, Rudolph J. & Pasler, Margaret C. The New Jersey Federalists. LC 73-22570. 256p. 1975. 16.50 (ISBN 0-8386-1525-2). Fairleigh Dickinson.

Renzulli, L. Marx. Maryland: The Federalist Years. LC 70-149405. 354p. 1972. 18.00 (ISBN 0-8386-7903-X). Fairleigh Dickinson.

Simpson, Lewis P., ed. Federalist Literary Mind: Selections from the Monthly Anthology & Boston Review, 1803-1811. LC 61-13013. (Illus.). 1962. pap. 7.95x (ISBN 0-8071-0207-5). La State U Pr.

FEDERAL RESERVE BANKS

Adams, Silas W. The Federal Reserve System. 1979. lib. bdg. 59.95 (ISBN 0-8490-2915-5). Gordon Pr.

Ahearn, Daniel S. Federal Reserve Policy Reappraised, 1951-1959. LC 63-10522. 376p. 1963. 18.00x (ISBN 0-231-02575-0). Columbia U Pr.

Clark, S. H. & Campbell, W. The Federal Reserve Monster. 1979. lib. bdg. 59.95 (ISBN 0-8490-2914-7). Gordon Pr.

Clifford, A. Jerome. Independence of the Federal Reserve System. LC 63-7862. 1965. 20.00x (ISBN 0-8122-7388-5). U of Pa Pr.

Currie, Lauchlin. Supply & Control of Money in the U. S: Containing the 1934 Proposed Revision of the Monetary System of the U. S. 3rd ed. LC 67-18291. (Illus.). 199p. (With a prefatory paper by Karl Brunner). 1968. Repr. of 1934 ed. 17.50 (ISBN 0-8462-1060-6). Russell.

DeRosa, Paul & Stern, Gary H. In the Name of Money: A Professional's Guide to the Federal Reserve, Interest Rates & Money. (Illus.). 192p. 1980. 16.95 (ISBN 0-07-016521-1, P&RB). McGraw.

Eccles, Marriner S. Economic Balance & a Balanced Budget. LC 72-2367. (FDR & the Era of the New Deal Ser). 328p. 1973. Repr. of 1940 ed. lib. bdg. 35.00 (ISBN 0-306-70479-X). Da Capo.

Erb, Richard D., ed. Federal Reserve Policies & Public Disclosure. 1978. 12.25 (ISBN 0-8447-2118-2); pap. 5.25 (ISBN 0-8447-2117-4). Am Enterprise.

Federal Reserve Audit Bill. 13p. 1973. pap. 3.75 (ISBN 0-8447-0159-9). Am Enterprise.

The Federal Reserve Audit Proposal. (Legislative Analyses). (Orig.). 1975. pap. 3.75 (ISBN 0-8447-0170-X). Am Enterprise.

Federal Reserve System. 1972. 11.00 (ISBN 0-89982-148-0, 054400). Am Bankers.

Glass, Carter. An Adventure in Constructive Finance. facsimile ed. LC 75-2635. (Wall Street & the Security Markets Ser.). 1975. Repr. of 1927 ed. 26.00x (ISBN 0-405-06960-X). Arno.

Groseclose, Elgin. America's Money Machine: The Story of the Federal Reserve. 320p. 1980. 14.95 (ISBN 0-87000-477-8). Arlington Hse.

Harding, William P. Formative Period of the Federal Reserve System During the World Crisis. LC 71-120221. Repr. of 1925 ed. 24.50 (ISBN 0-404-03107-2). AMS Pr.

Hepburn, A. Barton. History of Currency in the United States. rev. ed. LC 67-27411. Repr. of 1924 ed. 19.50x (ISBN 0-678-00311-4). Kelley.

Josephson, Emanuel M. The Federal Reserve Conspiracy. (Blacked-Out History Ser.). 1979. 12.00 (ISBN 0-685-91967-6); pap. 5.00 (ISBN 0-685-91968-4). Chedney.

--Federal Reserve Conspiracy & Rockefeller. 1979. write for info. (ISBN 0-685-96461-2). Revisionist Pr.

--The Federal Reserve Conspiracy & Rockefeller: Their Gold Corner. 384p. 1976. 12.50 (ISBN 0-685-66415-5); pap. 10.00 (ISBN 0-685-66416-3). Chedney.

Kemmerer, Edwin W. ABC of the Federal Reserve System. 12th ed. LC 70-138118. (Illus.). 1971. Repr. of 1950 ed. lib. bdg. 15.00x (ISBN 0-8371-5694-7, KEFR). Greenwood.

Labadie, Laurance. The Federal Reserve System: An Essay. (Men & Movements in the History & Philosophy of Anarchism Ser.). 1979. lib. bdg. 59.95 (ISBN 0-685-96414-0). Revisionist Pr.

Larson, Martin A. The Federal Reserve & Our Manipulated Dollar. LC 75-13346. 192p. (Orig.). 1975. pap. 5.95 (ISBN 0-8159-5514-6). Devin.

McFadden, Louis T. Federal Reserve Corporation. 59.95 (ISBN 0-8490-0157-9). Gordon Pr.

Miller, Randall J. Regional Impact of Monetary Policy in the United States. LC 78-59750. (Illus.). 1978. 19.95 (ISBN 0-669-02373-6). Lexington Bks.

National Bureau Committee for Economic Research. Role of Direct & Indirect Taxes in the Federal Reserve System - a Conference: National Bureau of Economic Research Publications. (Special Conference Series by the Universities). 1964. 15.00x (ISBN 0-691-04173-3). Princeton U Pr.

Prochnow, Herbert V. Federal Reserve System. LC 60-6767. (Illus.). 1960. 10.95x (ISBN 0-06-035070-9, HarpT). Har-Row.

Russell, Etta M. Basic Principles of Constitutional Money: A Textbook for High Schools and the General Public on the Federal Reserve Conspiracy. 1980. lib. bdg. 59.95 (ISBN 0-8490-3096-X). Gordon Pr.

Shoemaker, Frank H. The Greatest Swindle in American History: The Federal Reserve Hoax. 1980. lib. bdg. 75.00 (ISBN 0-8490-3086-2). Gordon Pr.

U. S. Board of Governors of the Federal Reserve System. The Federal Reserve System: Its Purposes & Functions. LC 75-41279. Repr. of 1939 ed. 15.00 (ISBN 0-404-14744-5). AMS Pr.

Warburg, Paul M. The Federal Reserve System: Its Origin & Growth-Reflections & Recollections, 2 vols. facsimile ed. LC 75-2680. (Wall Street & the Security Markets Ser.). 1975. Repr. of 1930 ed. Set. 100.00x (ISBN 0-405-07242-2). Arno.

West, Robert C. Banking Reform & Federal Reserve, 1863-1923. LC 76-28028. (Illus.). 1977. 22.50x (ISBN 0-8014-1035-5). Cornell U Pr.

Weyforth, William O. The Federal Reserve Board: A Study of Federal Reserve Structure & Credit Control. LC 78-64289. (Johns Hopkins University. Studies in the Social Sciences. Extra Volumes.: 19). Repr. of 1933 ed. 20.50 (ISBN 0-404-61389-6). AMS Pr.

Whitney, Caroline. Experiments in Credit Control. LC 68-58639. (Columbia University. Studies in the Social Sciences: No. 400). Repr. of 1934 ed. 20.00 (ISBN 0-404-51400-6). AMS Pr.

Willis, Henry P. The Federal Reserve System: Legislation, Organization & Operation. facsimile ed. LC 75-2685. (Wall Street & the Security Markets Ser.). 1975. Repr. of 1923 ed. 100.00x (ISBN 0-405-07246-5). Arno.

Wood, Elmer. Monetary Control. 1963. 10.00 (ISBN 0-8262-0021-4). U of Mo Pr.

Wright, Ivan. Bank Credit & Agriculture. Bruchey, Stuart, ed. LC 80-1174. (The Rise of Commercial Banking Ser.). (Illus.). 1981. Repr. of 1922 ed. lib. bdg. 29.00x (ISBN 0-405-13685-4). Arno.

FEDERAL REVENUE SHARING

see Intergovernmental Fiscal Relations; Intergovernmental Tax Relations

FEDERAL-STATE FISCAL RELATIONS

see Intergovernmental Fiscal Relations

FEDERAL-STATE RELATIONS

see Federal Government

FEDERAL-STATE TAX RELATIONS

see Intergovernmental Tax Relations

FEDERAL THEATER PROJECT

Flanagan, Hallie. Arena: The History of the Federal Theatre. LC 65-23693. (Illus.). Repr. of 1940 ed. 29.00 (ISBN 0-405-08521-4, Blom Pubns). Arno.

Whitman, Willson. Bread & Circuses: A Study of Federal Theatre. facsimile ed. LC 74-37919. (Select Bibliographies Reprint Ser). Repr. of 1937 ed. 15.00 (ISBN 0-8369-6756-9). Arno.

FEDERAL THEOLOGY

see Covenants (Theology)

FEDERALISM

see Federal Government

FEDERALIST

Alexander, Holmes. How to Read the Federalist. 1961. pap. 1.00 (ISBN 0-88279-124-9). Western Islands.

Bassett, John S., ed. Selections from the Federalist. 1979. Repr. of 1921 ed. lib. bdg. 25.00 (ISBN 0-8495-0541-0). Arden Lib.

Borden, Morton, ed. The Antifederalist Papers. xv, 260p. 1967. 6.50 (ISBN 0-87013-093-5). Mich St U Pr.

Dietze, Gottfried. The Federalist: A Classic of Federalism & Free Government. LC 76-57682. 1977. Repr. of 1960 ed. lib. bdg. 22.25x (ISBN 0-8371-9466-0, DIFED). Greenwood.

--The Federalist: A Classic on Federalism & Free Government. 388p. 1960. pap. 5.95x (ISBN 0-8018-0169-9). Johns Hopkins.

Engeman, Thomas S., et al, eds. The Federalist Concordance. LC 80-10406. 630p. 1980. 48.75 (ISBN 0-8195-5045-0, IS-00106, Pub. by Wesleyan U Pr). Univ Microfilm.

Hacker, Andrew, ed. Federalist Papers. 1971. pap. 1.95 (ISBN 0-671-48814-7). WSP.

Livermore, Shaw, Jr. Twilight of Federalism: The Disintegration of the Federalist Party - 1815-1830. LC 73-150413. 1972. Repr. of 1962 ed. text ed. 10.00 (ISBN 0-87752-137-9). Gordian.

Mace, George. Locke, Hobbes, & the Federalist Papers: An Essay on the Genesis of the American Political Heritage. LC 78-22091. 176p. 1979. 12.50x (ISBN 0-8093-0890-8). S Ill U Pr.

Stearns, Jean. The Federalist Without Tears. 178p. 1977. pap. text ed. 5.75 (ISBN 0-8191-0106-0). U Pr of Amer.

Storing, Herbert J. The Complete Anti-Federalist: Vol. 1, What the Anti-Federalists Were For. 1981. price not set (ISBN 0-226-77574-7, Phoen). U of Chicago Pr.
Wills, Garry. Explaining America: The Federalist. LC 79-6542. 336p. 1981. 14.95 (ISBN 0-385-14689-2). Doubleday.

FEDERALISTS (U. S.)
see Federal Party

FEDERATION, INTERNATIONAL
see International Organization

FEDERATION DE L'EDUCATION NATIONALE
Clark, James M. Teachers & Politics in France: A Pressure Group Study of the Federation de l'Education Nationale. LC 67-13494. 1967. 12.00x (ISBN 0-8156-2103-5). Syracuse U Pr.

FEDERATION OF AMERICAN SCIENTISTS
Smith, Alice K. Peril & a Hope: The Scientists' Movement in America, 1945-47. rev. ed. 1971. pap. 4.95 (ISBN 0-262-69026-8). MIT Pr.

FEDERATION OF EUROPE
see European Federation

FEDERATIONS, FINANCIAL (SOCIAL SERVICE)
Hieb, Elizabeth, ed. Fund Advisors Institute, July 1980, Williamsburg, Va. Proceedings. 80p. (Orig.). 1980. pap. 8.00 (ISBN 0-89154-137-3). Intl Found Employ.
Lawe, Theodore M. How to Secure & Manage Foundation & Federal Funds in the 1980's. LC 80-81753. 185p. (Orig.). 1980. pap. text ed. 12.95 (ISBN 0-9604706-0-3, 92142). MRDC Educ Inst.
McCallum, Tara, ed. Swipe File III. LC 81-50258. 180p. (Orig.). 1981. pap. 9.95 (ISBN 0-914756-45-1). Taft Corp.
Ritterbush, Philip C. Federal Programs for Popular Education in the Sciences. 143p. 1980. pap. 24.00x (ISBN 0-89062-118-7). Inst Cult Prog.

FEDERATIONS FOR CHARITY AND PHILANTHROPY
see Federations, Financial (Social Service)

FEE SYSTEM (TAXATION)
see Costs (Law); Taxation

FEEBLE MINDED
see Mental Deficiency; Mentally Handicapped

FEED
see Feeds

FEED INDUSTRY AND TRADE
see Flour and Feed Trade

FEED MECHANISMS
see also Conveying Machinery

FEED-WATER
Flanagan, G. T. Feed Water Systems & Treatment. (Marine Engineering Ser.). 144p. 1978. pap. 9.50x (ISBN 0-540-07343-1). Sheridan.
McCoy, James W. Chemical Treatment of Boiler Water. (Illus.). 1981. 40.00 (ISBN 0-8206-0284-1). Chem Pub.
National Research Council, Committee on Animal Nutrition. Nutrients & Toxic Substances in Water for Livestock & Poultry. LC 74-2836. (Illus.). v, 93p. 1974. pap. 4.75 (ISBN 0-309-02312-2). Natl Acad Pr.
Pincus, Leo I. Practical Boiler Water Treatment: Including Air-Conditioning Systems. 284p. 1981. Repr. of 1962 ed. lib. bdg. 19.50 (ISBN 0-89874-255-2). Krieger.
--Practical Boiler Water Treatment: Including Air Conditioning Systems. 1962. 26.00 (ISBN 0-07-050027-4, P&RB). McGraw.

FEEDBACK (ELECTRONICS)
Desoer, C. A. & Vidyasagar, M. Feedback Systems: Input-Output Properties. (Electrical Science Ser.). 1975. 50.00 (ISBN 0-12-212050-7). Acad Pr.
Horowitz, Isaac M. Synthesis of Feedback Systems. 1963. text ed. 24.95 (ISBN 0-12-355950-2). Acad Pr.
Klapper, Jacob & Frankle, John T. Phase Lock & Frequency Feedback Systems: Principles & Techniques. (Electrical Science Ser.). 1972. 60.00 (ISBN 0-12-410850-4). Acad Pr.
Waldhauer, Fred D. Feedback. 896p. 1981. 47.50 (ISBN 0-471-05319-8, Pub. by Wiley Interscience). Wiley.

FEEDBACK (PSYCHOLOGY)
see also Biofeedback Training
Barber, Theodore X., et al, eds. Biofeedback & Self-Control: An Aldine Reader on the Regulation of Bodily Processes & Consciousness. LC 71-167858. 1971. 39.95x (ISBN 0-202-25048-2). Aldine Pub.
Formative Exercise, T-TE-15a: Instant Feedback, Specific Prescription Version. 2.00 (ISBN 0-685-40630-X). Brolet.
Formative Exercise, T-TE-15b: Response-Contingent Corrective Feedbakc. 2.00 (ISBN 0-685-40631-8). Brolet.
Ray, W. J., et al. Evaluation of Clinical Biofeedback. LC 79-370. 342p. 1979. 25.00 (ISBN 0-306-40206-8, Plenum Pr). Plenum Pub.
Shapiro, David, et al, eds. Biofeedback & Self-Control, 1972: An Aldine Annual on the Regulation of Bodily Processes & Consciousness. LC 73-75702. 513p. 1973. 39.95x (ISBN 0-202-25107-1). Aldine Pub.
Stoyva, Johann, et al, eds. Biofeedback & Self-Control, 1971: An Aldine Annual on the Regulation of Bodily Processes & Consciousness. LC 74-151109. 350p. 1972. 39.95x (ISBN 0-202-25085-7). Aldine Pub.
Thompson, Richard F. Introduction to Biopsychology. (Illus.). pap. 4.95 (ISBN 0-87843-610-3). Albion.

FEEDBACK CONTROL SYSTEMS
see also Adaptive Control Systems; Biological Control Systems; Feedback (Electronics); Servomechanisms
AIP Conference, Princeton, 1970. Feedback & Dynamic Control of Plasmas: Proceedings, No. 1. Chu, T. K. & Hendel, H. W., eds. LC 70-141596. 364p. 1970. 14.00 (ISBN 0-88318-100-2). Am Inst Physics.
Atkinson, P. Feedback Control Systems for Engineers. LC 68-31674. 425p. 1968. 45.00 (ISBN 0-306-30363-9, Plenum Pr). Plenum Pub.
Automated Education Center. On the Feedback Complexity of Automata. LC 75-120080. 19.00 (ISBN 0-686-02004-9). Mgmt Info Serv.
Bishop, Albert B. Introduction to Discrete-Linear Controls: Theory & Applications. (Operations Research & Industrial Engineering Ser). 1975. 48.50 (ISBN 0-12-101650-1). Acad Pr.
Corduneanu, Constantin. Integral Equations & Stability of Feedback Systems. (Mathematics in Science & Engineering Ser.). 1973. 43.00 (ISBN 0-12-188350-7). Acad Pr.
Davis, Sidney. Feedback & Control Systems. pap. 4.95 (ISBN 0-671-18903-4). Monarch Pr.
D'Azzo, John J. & Houpis, Constantine. Feedback Control System Analysis & Synthesis. 2nd ed. (Electronic & Electrical Engineering Ser.). 1966. text ed. 27.50 (ISBN 0-07-016175-5, C); instructor's guide & solutions manual 5.95 (ISBN 0-07-016177-1). McGraw.
DeRusso, P. M., et al. State Variables for Engineers. LC 65-21443. 1965. 42.95 (ISBN 0-471-20380-7). Wiley.
DiStefano, J. J., et al. Feedback & Control Systems. (Schaum's Outline Ser). (Orig.). 1967. pap. 6.95 (ISBN 0-07-017045-2, SP). McGraw.
Horowitz, Isaac M. Synthesis of Feedback Systems. 1963. text ed. 24.95 (ISBN 0-12-355950-2). Acad Pr.
Jones, Richard W. Principles of Biological Regulation: An Introduction to Feedback Systems. 1973. 38.00 (ISBN 0-12-389950-8). Acad Pr.
Jury, Eliahu I. Sampled-Data Control Systems. LC 76-57949. 476p. 1977. Repr. of 1958 ed. 23.50 (ISBN 0-88275-529-3). Krieger.
McDonald, A. C. & Lowe, H. Feedback & Control Systems. 1981. text ed. 22.95 (ISBN 0-8359-1898-X). Reston.
Mayr, Otto. Origins of Feedback Control. 1970. pap. 3.95 (ISBN 0-262-63056-7). MIT Pr.
Mees, A. I. Dynamics of Feedback Systems. LC 80-40501. 214p. 1981. 39.50 (ISBN 0-471-27822-X, Pub. by Wiley-Interscience). Wiley.
Nadler, David A. Feedback & Organization Development: Using Data-Based Methods. (Illus.). 1977. pap. text ed. 7.50 (ISBN 0-201-05006-4). A-W.
Pervozvansky, A. A. Random Processes in Nonlinear Control Systems. (Mathematics in Science & Engineering Ser.: Vol. 15). 1965. 56.00 (ISBN 0-12-551650-9). Acad Pr.
Smith, Harold W. Approximate Analysis of Randomly Excited Non-Linear Controls. (Press Research Monographs: No. 34). 1966. 13.00x (ISBN 0-262-19027-3). MIT Pr.
Thaler, George J. Design of Feedback Systems. LC 72-93614. (Illus.). 350p. 1973. text ed. 36.50 (ISBN 0-12-787531-X). Acad Pr.

FEEDBACK CONTROL SYSTEMS–MATHEMATICAL MODELS
Bellman, Richard E. Adaptive Control Processes: A Guided Tour. (Rand Corporation Research Studies). 1961. 17.00 (ISBN 0-691-07901-3). Princeton U Pr.

FEEDING
see Animal Nutrition

FEEDING, ARTIFICIAL
see Artificial Feeding

FEEDING BEHAVIOR
see Animals, Food Habits of

FEEDS
see also Animal Nutrition; Forage Plants
also subdivision Feeding and Feeds under names of animals and groups of animals, e.g. Poultry–Feeding and Feeds
CAN Task Force, National Research Council. Feeding Value of Ethanol Production by-Products. 1981. pap. text ed. 6.50 (ISBN 0-309-03136-2). Natl Acad Pr.
Committee to the Human Health Effects of Subtherapeutic Antibiotic Use in Animal Feeds. The Effects on Human Health of Subtherapeutic Use of Antimicrobials in Animal Feeds. LC 80-81486. 1980. pap. text ed. 10.25 (ISBN 0-309-03044-7). Natl Acad Pr.
Crampton, E. W. & Harris, L. E. Applied Animal Nutrition: The Use of Feedstuffs in the Formulation of Livestock Rations. 2nd ed. LC 68-10996. (Animal Science Ser.). (Illus.). 1969. text ed. 26.95x (ISBN 0-7167-0814-0). W H Freeman.
Cullison, Arthur E. Feeds & Feeding. 3rd ed. 600p. 1981. text ed. 18.95 (ISBN 0-8359-1905-6); tchr's manual free (ISBN 0-8359-1906-4). Reston.
Decontamination of Animal Feeds by Irridation. 1979. pap. 20.50 (ISBN 92-0-111079-0, ISP508, IAEA). Unipub.
Dyer, Irwin A. & O'Mary, Clayton C., eds. The Feedlot. 2nd ed. LC 75-40180. (Illus.). 297p. 1977. text ed. 18.50 (ISBN 0-8121-0553-2). Lea & Febiger.
Feed Formulation Manual. 2nd ed. 1976. pap. text ed. 2.75x (ISBN 0-8134-1813-5, 1813); ans. bk. 0.50 (ISBN 0-8134-2202-7). Interstate.
Feed from Animal Wastes: State of Knowledge. (FAO Animal Production & Health Paper Ser.: No. 18). 201p. 1981. pap. 13.00 (ISBN 92-5-100946-5, F2100, FAO). Unipub.
Gillies, M. T. Animal Feeds from Waste Materials. LC 77-94236. (Food Technology Review Ser.: No. 46). (Illus.). 1978. 39.00 (ISBN 0-8155-0699-6). Noyes.
Keith, T. B. & Baker, John P. Feed Formulation Manual. 3rd ed. xi, 93p. 1981. pap. text ed. 2.75 (ISBN 0-8134-2201-9); Answer Bk. pap. text ed. 0.50 (ISBN 0-8134-2202-7). Interstate.
Krobloch, E. & Cerna-Heyrovska, J. Fodder Biofactors. LC 78-25777. 318p. 1980. 63.00 (ISBN 0-444-99783-0). Elsevier.
Matsushima, J. K. Feeding Beef Cattle. (Advanced Ser. in Agricultural Sciences: Vol. 7). (Illus.). 1979. 27.70 (ISBN 0-387-09198-X). Springer-Verlag.
New Feed Resources. (Animal Production & Health Paper: No. 4). 1978. pap. 20.25 (ISBN 92-5-000431-1, F1312, FAO). Unipub.
Perry, T. W., ed. Feed Formulations. 3rd ed. 1981. 12.35 (ISBN 0-8134-2174-8). Interstate.
Pirie, N. W. Leaf Protein & Other Aspects of Fodder Fractionation. LC 77-87387. (Illus.). 1978. 32.50 (ISBN 0-521-21920-5). Cambridge U Pr.
Sauchelli, Vincent. Trace Elements in Agriculture. 228p. 1969. 16.50 (ISBN 0-442-15633-2, Pub. by Van Nos Reinhold). Krieger.
Sodano, C. S. Animal Feeds & Pet Foods: Recent Developments. LC 78-70746. (Food Technology Review Ser.: No. 50). 1979. 36.00 (ISBN 0-8155-0737-2). Noyes.
Symposium On Energy Metabolism - 3rd - Troon Scotland - 1964. Energy Metabolism: Proceedings, No. 11. Blaxter, K. L., ed. 1965. 72.00 (ISBN 0-12-105550-7). Acad Pr.
Treating Straw for Animal Feeding: An Assessment of Its Technological & Economic Feasibility. (FAO Animal Production & Health Paper Ser.: No. 10). 1978. pap. 7.50 (ISBN 92-5-100584-2, F1480, FAO). Unipub.

FEELING
see Perception; Touch

FEELINGS
see Emotions

FEES (LAW)
see Costs (Law)

FEES, ECCLESIASTICAL
see also Tithes

FEES, LEGAL
see Costs (Law); Lawyers–Fees

FEES, MEDICAL
see Medical Fees

FEET
see Foot

FEIGL, HERBERT
Cohen, Robert S., ed. Herbert Feigl: Inquiries & Provocations, Selected Writings. 1929 to 1974. (Vienna Circle Collection: No. 14). 450p. 1980. lib. bdg. 50.00 (ISBN 90-277-1101-1, Pub. by Reidel Holland); pap. 23.50 (ISBN 90-277-1102-X). Kluwer Boston.
Feyerabend, Paul & Maxwell, Grover, eds. Mind, Matter & Method: Essays in Philosophy & Science in Honor of Herbert Feigl. LC 66-13467. 1966. 17.50x (ISBN 0-8166-0379-0). U of Minn Pr.

FEIJOO Y MONTENEGRO BENITO JERONIMO, FRAY, 1676-1764
McClelland, I. L. Benito Jeronimo Feijoo. LC 68-17230. (World Authors Ser.). 1969. lib. bdg. 12.95x (ISBN 0-8057-2308-0). Irvington.

FEININGER, ANDREAS
Feininger, Andreas. Andreas Feininger: Experimental Work. (Illus.). 1978. pap. 9.95 (ISBN 0-8174-2116-5). Amphoto.

FEININGER, LYONEL CHARLES ADRIAN, 1871-1956
Prasse, Leona E. Lyonel Feininger: A Definitive Catalogue of His Graphic Work: Etchings, Lithographs, Woodcuts. LC 74-108899. (Illus.). 304p. 1972. 35.00x (ISBN 0-910386-18-8, Pub. by Cleveland Mus Art). Ind U Pr.
Schardt, Alois J., et al. Feininger-Hartley. LC 66-26122. (Museum of Modern Art Publications in Reprint Ser.). Repr. of 1944 ed. 14.00 (ISBN 0-405-01511-9). Arno.
Scheyer, Ernst. Lyonel Feininger: Caricature & Fantasy. LC 64-15880. (Illus.). 1964. 17.50x (ISBN 0-8143-1202-0). Wayne St U Pr.

FEKE, ROBERT, 1705-1750
Foote, Henry W. Robert Feke, Colonial Portrait Painter. LC 72-75357. (Library of American Art Ser). 1969. Repr. of 1950 ed. lib. bdg. 29.50 (ISBN 0-306-71319-5). Da Capo.

FELASHAS
see Falashas

FELATA
see Fulahs

FELDSPAR
see also Rocks, Crystalline and Metamorphic
Mackenzie, W. S., ed. The Feldspars. LC 73-87831. 717p. 1974. 59.50x (ISBN 0-8448-0251-4). Crane-Russak Co.
Smith, J. V. Feldspar Minerals, Vol. 1: Physical Properties. LC 73-14236. (Illus.). 600p. 1974. 58.20 (ISBN 0-387-06490-7). Springer-Verlag.
--Feldspar Minerals, Vol. 2: Chemical & Textural Properties. LC 73-15294. (Illus.). 690p. 1974. 61.50 (ISBN 0-387-06516-4). Springer-Verlag.
Van Der Plas, Leendert. Identification of Detrital Feldspars. (Developments in Sedimentology: Vol. 6). 1966. 63.50 (ISBN 0-444-40597-6). Elsevier.

FELIBRIGE
Roche, Alphonse V. Provencal Regionalism. LC 74-128942. (Northwestern University Humanities Ser.: No. 30). Repr. of 1954 ed. 21.50 (ISBN 0-404-50730-1). AMS Pr.

FELIDAE
Fichter, George S. Cats. (Golden Guide Ser.). 160p. 1973. PLB 10.58 (ISBN 0-307-64356-5, Golden Pr). Western Pub.
Ricciuti, Edward R. The Wild Cats. LC 78-24725. (Illus.). 1979. 24.95 (ISBN 0-88225-270-4). Newsweek.

FELIDAE–JUVENILE LITERATURE
Wildlife Education, Ltd. Big Cats. (Zoobooks). (Illus.). 20p. (Orig.). 1981. pap. 1.50 (ISBN 0-937934-04-6). Wildlife Educ.

FELIPE 2ND, KING OF SPAIN, 1527-1598
Cadoux, Cecil J. Philip of Spain & the Netherlands: An Essay on Moral Judgments in History. 1969. Repr. of 1947 ed. 17.50 (ISBN 0-208-00735-0, Archon). Shoe String.
Elder, John. The Copie of a Letter Sent in to Scotlande, or the Arivall of Prynce of Spaine. LC 72-193. (English Experience Ser.: No. 308). 96p. 1971. Repr. of 1555 ed. 9.50 (ISBN 90-221-0308-0). Walter J Johnson.
Hume, Martin. Philip Second of Spain. LC 68-25245. (World History Ser., No. 48). (Illus.). 1968. Repr. of 1903 ed. lib. bdg. 49.95 (ISBN 0-8383-0206-8). Haskell.
Hume, Martin A. Philip Second of Spain. Ketcham, Henry, ed. Repr. of 1903 ed. lib. bdg. 15.00x (ISBN 0-8371-4091-9, HUPH). Greenwood.
Parker, Geoffery. Philip Second. LC 78-17122. (Library of World Biography). 1978. 9.95 (ISBN 0-316-69080-5). Little.
Pierson, Peter. Philip Second of Spain. (Men in Office Ser.). (Illus.). 1977. 16.95 (ISBN 0-500-87003-9). Thames Hudson.
Walsh, W. T. Philip Second. 1972. lib. bdg. 59.95 (ISBN 0-8490-0823-9). Gordon Pr.

FELIPE 4TH, KING OF SPAIN, 1605-1665
Von Barghahn, Barbara. Philip IV of Spain: His Art Collections at the Buen Retiro Palace, a Hapsburg "Versailles". LC 80-67180. (Illus.). 701p. 1980. lib. bdg. 29.50 (ISBN 0-8191-1208-9). U Pr of Amer.

FELIS PARDALIS
see also Ocelots

FELIX, ELISA RACHEL, 1821-1858
Agate, James. Rachel. LC 72-84504. 1928. 9.00 (ISBN 0-405-08192-8, Pub. by Blom). Arno.
Falk, Bernard. Rachel the Immortal. LC 70-91900. 1935. 15.00 (ISBN 0-405-08495-1, Blom Pubns). Arno.

FELL, JESSE W.
Morehouse, Frances M. Life of Jesse W. Fell. Repr. of 1916 ed. 9.50 (ISBN 0-384-40125-2). Johnson Repr.

FELLANS
see also Fulahs

FELLINI, FEDERICO
Benderson, Albert E. Critical Approaches to Federico Fellini's Eight & Half, Vol. 4. LC 74-2078. (Dissertations on Film Ser.). 239p. 1974. 12.00 (ISBN 0-405-04877-7). Arno.
Betti, Liliana. Fellini: An Intimate Portrait. LC 79-12360. 1979. 9.95 (ISBN 0-316-09230-4). Little.

Bondanella, Peter, ed. Federico Fellini: Essays in Criticism. (Illus.). 1978. pap. 5.95 (ISBN 0-19-502274-2, GB515, GB). Oxford U Pr.

Bondanella, Peter E., ed. Federico Fellini: Essays in Criticism. (Illus.). 1978. text ed. 12.95x (ISBN 0-19-502273-4). Oxford U Pr.

Fellini, Frederico. Fellini on Fellini. 1977. pap. 2.95 (ISBN 0-440-52531-4, Delta). Dell.

Murray, Edward. Fellini the Artist. LC 75-25423. (Illus.). 1976. 12.95 (ISBN 0-8044-2648-1). Ungar.

Price, Barbara A. & Price, Theodore. Federico Fellini: An Annotated International Bibliography. LC 77-26310. 1978. 13.50 (ISBN 0-8108-1104-9). Scarecrow.

Rosenthal, Stuart. The Cinema of Federico Fellini. LC 73-13193. (Illus.). 192p. 1976. 9.95 (ISBN 0-498-01450-9). A S Barnes.

Stubbs, John C., et al, eds. Federico Fellini: A Guide to References & Resources. (Reference & Resource Guide Ser.). 1978. lib. bdg. 30.00 (ISBN 0-8161-7885-2). G K Hall.

FELLOWSHIPS
see Scholarships

FELONY
see Criminal Law

FELT (IN RELIGION, FOLK-LORE, ETC.)

Olschki, Leonardo. The Myth of Felt. 1949. 15.00x (ISBN 0-520-00974-6). U of Cal Pr.

FELT WORK

Deems, Betty. Easy-to-Make Felt Ornaments for Christmas and Other Occasions. (Dover Needlework Ser). (Illus., Orig.). 1976. pap. 3.00 (ISBN 0-486-23389-8). Dover.

Gordon, Beverly. Feltmaking: Traditions, Techniques & Contemporary Explorations. (Illus.). 1980. 17.50 (ISBN 0-8230-1647-1). Watson-Guptill.

Lammer, Jutta. Fun with Felt. 1970. 14.95 (ISBN 0-7134-2459-1, Pub. by Batsford England). David & Charles.

Newsome, Arden J. Make It with Felt: An Art & Craft Book. LC 77-181892. (Illus.). 96p. (gr. 3-12). 1972. PLB 6.96 (ISBN 0-688-50984-3). Lothrop.

FELTWORK
see Felt Work

FEMALE
see Women

FEMALE IMPERSONATORS
see Impersonators, Female

FEMALE OFFENDERS
see also Reformatories for Women

Adler, F. Sisters in Crime: The Rise of the New Female Criminal. 1975. 9.95 (ISBN 0-07-000415-3, GB). McGraw.

--Sisters in Crime: The Rise of the New Female Criminal. LC 76-23387. (McGraw-Hill Paperbacks). 1976. pap. 3.95 (ISBN 0-07-000416-1, SP). McGraw.

Adler, Freda. The Incidence of Female Criminality in the Contemporary World. 352p. 1981. text ed. 30.00x (ISBN 0-8147-0576-6). NYU Pr.

Adler, Freda & Simon, Rita J. The Criminology of Deviant Women. LC 78-69555. (Illus.). 1979. pap. text ed. 8.95 (ISBN 0-395-26719-6). HM.

Bowker, Lee H. Women & Crime in America. 1981. pap. text ed. 9.95x (ISBN 0-02-476830-8). Macmillan.

--Women, Crime, & the Criminal Justice System. LC 78-57180. (Illus.). 1978. 23.95 (ISBN 0-669-02374-4). Lexington Bks.

Brodsky, Annette M., ed. The Female Offender. LC 75-27014. (Sage Contemporary Social Science Issues: Vol. 19). 108p. 1975. 5.95 (ISBN 0-8039-0568-8). Sage.

Bronner, Augusta F. A Comparative Study of the Intelligence of Delinquent Girls. LC 72-176594. (Columbia University. Teachers College. Contributions to Education: No. 68). Repr. of 1914 ed. 17.50 (ISBN 0-404-55068-1). AMS Pr.

Chapman, Jane R. Economic Realities & Female Crime: Program Choices & Economic Rehabilitation. LC 79-3785. 240p. 1980. 21.95x (ISBN 0-669-03515-7). Lexington Bks.

Crites, Laura, ed. The Female Offender: A Total Look at Women in the Criminal Justice System. 1977. 21.50 (ISBN 0-669-00635-1). Lexington Bks.

Datesman, Susan K., ed. Women, Crime & Justice. Scarpitti, Frank R. (Illus., Orig.). 1980. pap. text ed. 6.95x (ISBN 0-19-502676-4). Oxford U Pr.

Deming, Richard. Women: The New Criminals. LC 76-40209. (gr. 8 up). 1977. 7.95 (ISBN 0-525-66513-7). Elsevier-Nelson.

Earnest, Marion R. Criminal Self-Conceptions in the Penal Community of Female Offenders: An Empirical Study. LC 77-90378. 1978. pap. 9.00 perfect bdg. (ISBN 0-88247-511-8). R & E Res Assoc.

Feinman, Clarice. Women in the Criminal Justice System. LC 80-12539. (Illus.). 1980. 19.95 (ISBN 0-03-052561-6); pap. 8.95 (ISBN 0-03-052566-7). Praeger.

Fernald, Mabel R., et al. Study of Women Delinquents in New York State. LC 68-55770. (Criminology, Law Enforcement, & Social Problems Ser.: No. 23). 1968. Repr. of 1920 ed. 20.00 (ISBN 0-87585-023-5). Patterson Smith.

Ford, Lee E., ed. Women of the Eighties: Vol. 7: the Woman Criminal. 100p. (Orig.). 1981. pap. 12.00 (ISBN 0-88017-108-1). Ford Assocs.

Freedman, Estelle B. Their Sister's Keepers: Women's Prison Reform in America, 1830-1930. LC 80-24918. (Women & Culture Ser.). 272p. 1981. text ed. 18.50x (ISBN 0-472-10008-4). U of Mich Pr.

Gabel, Katherine & Bartleson, Henrietta. Legal Rights for Women Prisoners. LC 74-27509. Date not set. price not set (ISBN 0-669-97675-X). Lexington Bks.

Giallombardo, Rose. The Social World of Imprisoned Girls. 328p. 1981. Repr. text ed. 22.50 (ISBN 0-89874-285-4). Krieger.

Glueck, S. & Glueck, Eleanor. Five Hundred Delinquent Women. Repr. of 1934 ed. 24.00 (ISBN 0-527-34080-4). Kraus Repr.

Hartman, Mary S. Victorian Murderesses: A True History of Thirteen Respectable French & English Women Accused of Unspeakable Crimes. LC 75-34877. (Illus.). 1979. pap. 6.95 (ISBN 0-8052-0627-2). Schocken.

Jenkins, Elizabeth. Six Criminal Women. facs. ed. LC 76-148222. (Biography Index Reprint Ser.). 1949. 18.00 (ISBN 0-8369-8069-7). Arno.

Jones, Ann. Women Who Kill. 448p. 1981. 7.95 (ISBN 0-449-90058-4). Fawcett.

--Women Who Kill. LC 80-12329. 420p. 1980. 15.95 (ISBN 0-03-040711-7). HR&W.

Jurjevich, Ratibor-Ray M. No Water in My Cup. LC 68-9415. 1968. 5.00 (ISBN 0-87212-010-4). Libra.

Konopka, Gisela. Young Girls: A Portrait of Adolescence. 8.95 (ISBN 0-13-977215-4, Spec); pap. 3.45 (ISBN 0-13-977207-3, Spec). P-H.

Lampman, Henry P. The Wire Womb: Life in a Girls' Penal Institution. LC 72-90555. 1973. 13.95x (ISBN 0-911012-23-0). Nelson-Hall.

Leonard, Eileen B. Women, Crime & Society: A Critique of Theoretical Criminology. LC 81-8148. (Illus.). 256p. (Orig.). 1981. text ed. 18.00x (ISBN 0-582-28288-8); pap. text ed. 9.95x (ISBN 0-582-28289-6). Longman.

Lombroso, Cesar & Ferrero, William. The Female Offender. (Illus.). xxvi, 313p. 1980. Repr. of 1895 ed. lib. bdg. 32.50x (ISBN 0-8377-0807-9). Rothman.

Lombroso, Cesare. Basic Characteristics Typical of Women Criminals. (The Library of Scientific Psychology). (Illus.). 1981. 74.95 (ISBN 0-89901-032-6). Found Class Reprints.

Lytton, Constance. Prisons & Prisoners: Experiences of a Suffragette. 1977. Repr. of 1914 ed. 25.00x (ISBN 0-7158-1154-1). Charles River Bks.

McCarthy, Belinda R. Easy Time: The Experiences of Female Inmates on Temporary Release. LC 78-13819. 1979. 22.50 (ISBN 0-669-02669-7). Lexington Bks.

MacClure, Victor. She Stands Accused: Being a Series of Accounts of the Lives & Deeds of Notorious Women Murderesses. LC 74-10429. (Classics of Crime & Criminology Ser). (Illus.). 239p. 1975. Repr. of 1935 ed. 14.00 (ISBN 0-88355-196-9). Hyperion Conn.

Mc Nulty, Faith. The Burning Bed: The True Story of a Wife Who Killed. LC 79-2764. 320p. 1980. 12.95 (ISBN 0-15-114981-X). HarBraceJ.

Pollak, Otto. The Criminality of Women. 1961. pap. 3.95 (ISBN 0-498-04056-9, Prpta). A S Barnes.

--The Criminality of Women. LC 77-13959. 1978. Repr. of 1950 ed. lib. bdg. 20.00x (ISBN 0-8371-9869-0, POCW). Greenwood.

Simon, Rita J. Women & Crime. 1978. pap. text ed. 6.95x (ISBN 0-669-01646-2). Heath.

Smart, Carol. Women, Crime & Criminology: A Feminist Critique. 1976. 15.00 (ISBN 0-7100-8449-8). Routledge & Kegan.

--Women, Crime & Criminology: A Feminist Critique. 1978. pap. 7.95 (ISBN 0-7100-8833-7). Routledge & Kegan.

Spaulding, Edith R. Experimental Study of Psychopathic Delinquent Women. LC 69-14947. (Criminology, Law Enforcement, & Social Problems Ser.: No. 60). (Illus.). 1969. Repr. of 1923 ed. 17.00 (ISBN 0-87585-060-X). Patterson Smith.

Stanton, Ann M. When Mothers Go to Jail. LC 79-3522. 224p. 1980. 22.95 (ISBN 0-669-03461-4). Lexington Bks.

Sturgeon, S. & Rans, L. The Woman Offender: A Bibiliographic Sourcebook. vi, 63p. 1975. pap. 5.00 (ISBN 0-686-28749-5). Entropy Ltd.

Sullivan, Katharine. Girls on Parole. LC 73-9259. 243p. 1973. Repr. of 1956 ed. lib. bdg. 15.00x (ISBN 0-8371-6994-1, SUGP). Greenwood.

Tappan, Paul W. Delinquent Girls in Court: A Study of the Wayward Minor Court of New York. LC 69-14950. (Criminology, Law Enforcement, & Social Problems Ser.: No. 67). 1969. Repr. of 1947 ed. 15.00- (ISBN 0-87585-067-7). Patterson Smith.

Thomas, William I. Unadjusted Girl, with Cases & Standpoint for Behavior Analysis. LC 69-14951. (Criminology, Law Enforcement, & Social Problems Ser.: No. 26). 1969. Repr. of 1923 ed. 12.00 (ISBN 0-87585-026-X). Patterson Smith.

Totman, Jane. The Murderess: A Psychosocial Study of Criminal Homicide. LC 77-90373. 1978. pap. 10.00 perfect bdg. (ISBN 0-88247-525-8). R & E Res Assoc.

Vedder, Clyde B. & Somerville, Dora B. The Delinquent Girl. 2nd ed. 192p. 1975. 18.50 (ISBN 0-398-03260-2). C C Thomas.

FEMALE SEX HORMONE
see Hormones, Sex

FEMALE STERILIZATION
see Sterilization of Women

FEMALE STUDIES
see Women'S Studies

FEMININITY (PSYCHOLOGY)
see also Sex (Psychology)

Andelin, Helen B. The Fascinating Girl. LC 71-106916. 10.95 (ISBN 0-911094-01-6). Pacific Santa Barbara.

--Fascinating Womanhood. 10.95 (ISBN 0-911094-00-8). Pacific Santa Barbara.

--La Mujer Encantadora. (Span.). 6.95 (ISBN 0-911094-02-4). Pacific Santa Barbara.

Appignanesi, Lisa. Femininity & the Creative Imagination: A Study of Henry James, Robert Musil & Marcel Proust. 1973. 12.95x (ISBN 0-8464-0407-9). Beekman Pubs.

Breen, Dana. The Birth of a First Child: Towards an Understanding of Femininity. (Illus.). 1975. pap. 11.95 (ISBN 0-422-74340-2, Pub. by Tavistock England). Methuen Inc.

Brown, Richard, ed. Knowledge, Education, & Cultural Change. 1979. pap. 14.50x (ISBN 0-422-75750-0, Pub. by Tavistock England). Methuen Inc.

Burnham, Sue. Fascinating Women. (Orig.). 1975. pap. 1.50 (ISBN 0-8024-2530-5). Moody.

Colegrave, Sukie. Spirit of the Valley: Harmonizing the Masculine & Feminine in the Human Spirit. 264p. 1981. 10.95 (ISBN 0-87477-188-9); pap. 5.95 (ISBN 0-686-72110-1). J P Tarcher.

Daly, Bruce. The Psychological Theory of the Voluptuous Woman. (Illus.). 1978. deluxe ed. 49.75 (ISBN 0-930582-18-7). Gloucester Art.

D'Avenant, David. What the Sophisticated Man of the World Ought to Know About Women. (Illus.). 1980. 41.45 (ISBN 0-89266-213-1). Am Classical Coll Pr.

Douglas, Ann. The Feminization of American Culture. 1978. pap. 3.95 (ISBN 0-380-01968-X, 51870, Discus). Avon.

Foreman, Ann. Feminity As Alienation. 176p. 1980. text ed. 12.00 (ISBN 0-904383-63-6); pap. 5.95 (ISBN 0-904383-62-8). Pluto Pr.

Hartlett, Oonagh, ed. Sex Role Stereotyping. (Tavistock Women's Studies). 1979. 19.95x (ISBN 0-422-76770-0, Pub. by Tavistock England); pap. 7.95x (ISBN 0-422-76780-8). Methuen Inc.

Henry, George W. Masculinity & Femininity. Orig. Title: All the Sexes. 320p. 1973. pap. 1.95 (ISBN 0-02-076840-0, Collier). Macmillan.

Lasky, Ella, ed. Humanness: An Exploration into the Mythologies About Men & Women. 543p. 1975. 39.50x (ISBN 0-8422-5221-5); pap. text ed. 18.75x (ISBN 0-685-55478-3). Irvington.

Miller, Benjamin F., et al. Masculinity & Femininity. LC 75-134861. (Illus.). 120p. (gr. 7 up). 1971. pap. text ed. 4.23 (ISBN 0-395-03243-1, 2-37390); instructor's manual 1.17 (ISBN 0-395-11210-9). HM.

Morgan, Marabel. The Total Woman. 1976. pap. 2.50 (ISBN 0-671-41664-2). PB.

Rush, Anne K. Moon, Moon. LC 76-16003. 1976. 15.00 (ISBN 0-685-78827-X); pap. 7.95 (ISBN 0-685-78828-8). Moon Bks.

Spence, Janet T. & Helmreich, Robert L. Masculinity & Femininity: Their Psychological Dimensions, Correlates, & Antecedents. (Illus.). 309p. 1979. pap. text ed. 8.95x (ISBN 0-292-75052-8). U of Tex Pr.

Terman, Lewis M. & Miles, Catherine C. Sex & Personality. 600p. 1980. Repr. of 1936 ed. lib. bdg. 50.00 (ISBN 0-89987-811-3). Darby Bks.

Trobisch, Ingrid. The Joy of Being a Woman. LC 75-9324. 144p. 1975. pap. 3.95 (ISBN 0-06-068453-4, RD 353, HarpR). Har-Row.

Ulanov, Ann B. Feminine. 1971. 19.95x (ISBN 0-8101-0351-6); pap. 8.95 (ISBN 0-8101-0608-6). Northwestern U Pr.

Zolla, Elemire. The Androgyne: The Creative Tension of Male & Female. Purce, Jill, ed. LC 81-67701. (The Illustrated Library of Sacred Imagination Ser.). (Illus.). 96p. 1981. 19.95 (ISBN 0-8245-0060-1); pap. 9.95 (ISBN 0-8245-0065-2). Crossroad NY.

FEMINISM
see also Sex Discrimination; Women-History; Women-Legal Status, Laws, etc.; Women's Rights; Women-Social Conditions

Abbott & Love, eds. Sappho Was a Right-on Woman. 1978. pap. 1.95 (ISBN 0-8128-7006-9). Stein & Day.

Adam, Ruth. Woman's Place 1910-1975. (Illus.). 1977. 8.95 (ISBN 0-393-05622-8). Norton.

Adams, Elsie & Briscoe, Mary L. Up Against the Wall, Mother: On Women's Liberation. 1971. 8.95 (ISBN 0-02-470200-5, 47020). Macmillan.

Adelstein, Michael E. & Pival, Jean G., eds. Women's Liberation. (Perspectives Ser). 128p. 1972. pap. text ed. 4.95 (ISBN 0-312-88760-4); tchrs. manual avail. (ISBN 0-685-02757-0). St Martin.

Allen, Pamela. Free Space: A Perspective on the Small Group in Women's Liberation. (Illus., Orig.). 1971. pap. 2.00 (ISBN 0-87810-006-7). Times Change.

Altbach, Edith H., ed. From Feminism to Liberation. LC 70-137492. 328p. 1980. text ed. 15.95x (ISBN 0-87073-822-4); pap. text ed. 8.95x (ISBN 0-686-63316-4). Schenkman.

Anticaglia, Elizabeth. A Housewife's Guide to Women's Liberation. LC 72-85889. 1972. 14.95 (ISBN 0-911012-69-9). Nelson-Hall.

Atkinson, Ti-Grace. Amazon Odyssey: The First Collection of Writings by the Political Pioneer of the Women's Movement. LC 73-80394. (Illus.). 1974. 15.00 (ISBN 0-8256-3023-1, Quick Fox); pap. 5.95 (ISBN 0-8256-3016-9, Links Bks). Music Sales.

Bardon, Edward J. The Sexual Arena & Women's Liberation. LC 77-23937. 1978. 17.95x (ISBN 0-88229-219-6); pap. 8.95x (ISBN 0-88229-558-6). Nelson-Hall.

Barrett, Michele. Women's Oppression Today: Problems in Marxist Feminist Analysis. 280p. 1981. 19.50x (ISBN 0-8052-7091-4, Pub. by NLB England); pap. 8.50 (ISBN 0-8052-7090-6). Schocken.

Beard, Mary R. Mary Ritter Beard: A Sourcebook. Lane, Anne J., ed. LC 77-3135. (Studies in the Life of Women). 1977. lib. bdg. 15.00x (ISBN 0-8052-3668-6); pap. 6.95 (ISBN 0-8052-0576-4). Schocken.

Berg, Barbara. The Remembered Gate: Origins of American Feminism - the Woman & the City 1800-1860. (Urban Life in America Ser.). 1978. 16.95x (ISBN 0-19-502280-7). Oxford U Pr.

Berg, Barbara J. The Remembered Gate: Origins of American Feminism - the Woman & the City, 1800-1860. (Illus.). 1980. pap. 5.95 (ISBN 0-19-502704-3, GB 595, GB). Oxford U Pr.

Bergman, Arlene E. Women of Vietnam. LC 74-13544. 1975. pap. 3.95 (ISBN 0-914750-02-X). Peoples Pr.

Bernard, Jessie. Women & the Public Interest: An Essay on Policy & Protest. LC 79-140005. 1971. 24.95x (ISBN 0-202-25024-5). Aldine Pub.

Birkby, Phyllis, et al, eds. Amazon Expedition: A Lesbian-Feminist Anthology. LC 73-79902. (Illus.). 96p. (Orig.). 1973. 6.50 (ISBN 0-87810-526-3); pap. 3.00 (ISBN 0-87810-026-1). Times Change.

Bishop, Sharon & Weinzweig, Marjorie. Philosophy & Women. 1979. pap. text ed. 13.95x (ISBN 0-534-00609-4). Wadsworth Pub.

Blair, Karen. The Club Woman As Feminist: True Womanhood Redefined, 1868 to 1914. LC 79-26390. 1980. text ed. 29.50x (ISBN 0-8419-0538-X). Holmes & Meier.

Bloom, L. Z., et al. The New Assertive Woman. 1976. pap. 2.95 (ISBN 0-440-16393-5, LE). Dell.

Bornstein, Diane, ed. Feminist Controversy of the Renaissance, 3 vols. in 1. LC 80-14701. 1980. 25.00x (ISBN 0-8201-1343-3). Schol Facsimiles.

Borun, Minda, et al. Women's Liberation: An Anthropological View. 1971. pap. 1.75 (ISBN 0-912786-19-1). Know Inc.

Boxer, M. J. & Quataert, J. H., eds. Socialist Women: European Feminism in the Nineteenth & Early Twentieth Centuries. 1978. pap. 9.95 (ISBN 0-444-99042-9); pap. 9.95 (ISBN 0-444-99050-X). Elsevier.

Brin, Ruth F. Contributions of Women: Social Reform. LC 77-9585. (Contributions of Women Ser.). (Illus.). (gr. 6 up). 1977. PLB 8.95 (ISBN 0-87518-145-7). Dillon.

Brown, Cheryl L. & Olson, Karen, eds. Feminist Criticism: Essays on Theory, Poetry & Prose. LC 78-8473. 1978. 18.00 (ISBN 0-8108-1143-X). Scarecrow.

Broyelle, Claudie. Women's Liberation in China. Cohen, Michele & Herman, Gary, trs. from Fr. LC 76-4524. (Marxist Theory & Contemporary Capitalism Ser.). 1977. text ed. 22.50x (ISBN 0-391-00587-1). Humanities.

Bunch, Charlotte & Myron, Nancy, eds. Class & Feminism. 92p. pap. 3.50 (ISBN 0-88447-004-0). Crossing Pr.

--Class & Feminism. (Illus.). 1974. pap. 3.50 (ISBN 0-88447-004-0). Diana Pr.

Burton, Gabrielle. I'm Running Away from Home, but I'm Not Allowed to Cross the Street: A Primer on Women's Liberation. 208p. 1972. 5.00 (ISBN 0-912786-00-0). Know Inc.

Butler, Francelia & Bakker, Jan. Marxism, Feminism & Free Love: The Story of the Ruskin Commonwealth. (Illus.). 140p. 1981. Repr. lib. bdg. 12.95x (ISBN 0-87991-034-8). Porcupine Pr.

Cahones, Carolyn. Women's Lip. (Illus.). 160p. (Orig.). 1973. pap. 4.95 (ISBN 0-685-28251-1). Omen Pr.

Carden, Maren L. Feminism in the Mid 1970s: The Non-Establishment, the Establishment, & the Future. LC 77-4367. 1977. pap. 3.95 (ISBN 0-916584-04-6, Pub. by Ford Found). Pub Ctr Cult Res.

--The New Feminist Movement. LC 73-83889. 252p. 1974. 9.95 (ISBN 0-87154-196-3). Russell Sage.

Carter, Angela. The Sadeian Woman: And the Ideology of Pornography. LC 78-20412. 1979. 7.95 (ISBN 0-394-50575-1). Pantheon.

Carter, John M. All the Lovely Ladies. 1981. 13.95 (ISBN 0-698-11073-0). Coward.

Cassell, Joan. A Group Called Women: Sisterhood & Symbolism in the Feminist Movement. LC 76-58837. 1977. pap. 7.95x (ISBN 0-679-30331-6). Longman.

Chabrol, Claude. Le Recit Feminin: Contribution a L'Analyse Semiologique Du Courrier Du Coeur et Des Entreveuves Ou Enquetes Sur La Femme Dans La Presse Feminine Actuelle. (Approaches to Semiotics Ser.: No. 15). (Fr.). 1971. text ed. 24.50x (ISBN 90-2791-787-6). Mouton.

Chafe, William H. Women & Equality: Changing Patterns in American Culture. LC 76-42639. 1977. 12.95 (ISBN 0-19-502158-4). Oxford U Pr.

Clemens, Lois G. Woman Liberated. LC 79-141830. 176p. 1975. pap. 1.75 (ISBN 0-87983-111-1). Keats.

Congressional Quarterly Editorial Research Reports Staff. Editorial Research Reports on the Women's Movement. 2nd ed. LC 77-9245. 1977. pap. 6.95 (ISBN 0-87187-115-7). Congr Quarterly.

Courtney, Janet E. Adventurous Thirties: A Chapter in the Women's Movement. facs. ed. LC 67-26728. (Essay Index Reprint Ser). 1933. 16.00 (ISBN 0-8369-0341-2). Arno.

Croll, Elisabeth. Feminism & Socialism in China. LC 80-13164. 376p. 1980. pap. 8.95 (ISBN 0-8052-0657-4). Schocken.

Daly, Mary. Beyond God the Father: Toward a Philosophy of Women's Liberation. LC 73-6245. 256p. 1973. pap. 5.95 (ISBN 0-8070-4165-3, BP488). Beacon Pr.

--Gyn-Ecology: The Metaethics of Radical Feminism. LC 78-53790. 1979. pap. 7.95 (ISBN 0-8070-1511-3, BP601). Beacon Pr.

Davaney, Sheila G., ed. Feminism & Process Thought: The Harvard Divinity School-Claremont Center for Process Studies Symposium Papers. (Symposium Ser.: Vol. 6). 1980. soft cover 9.95x (ISBN 0-88946-903-2). E Mellen.

Davison, Jaquie. I Am a Housewife. LC 72-91284. (Illus.). iv, 108p. (Orig.). 1972. pap. 1.95 (ISBN 0-685-30126-5). Guild Bks.

De Armas, F. A. The Invisible Mistress: Aspects of Feminism & Fantasy in the Golden Age. (Biblioteca Siglo De Oro Ser.). 1976. pap. 7.50 (ISBN 84-399-5958-3). Biblio Siglo.

DeCrow, Karen. The Young Woman's Guide to Liberation: Alternatives to a Half-Life While the Choice Is Still Yours. LC 72-141377. 1971. pap. 7.50 (ISBN 0-672-63615-8). Pegasus.

Delacoste, Frederique & Newman, Felice, eds. Fight Back: Feminist Resistance to Male Violence. (Illus., Orig.). 1981. pap. price not set (ISBN 0-939416-01-8). Cleis Pr.

Dell, Floyd. Women As World Builders: Studies in Modern Feminism. LC 75-21810. (Pioneers of the Woman's Movement: an International Perspective Ser.). 104p. 1976. Repr. of 1913 ed. 13.00 (ISBN 0-88355-258-2). Hyperion-Conn.

Deming, Barbara. Remembering Who We Are. LC 80-66371. 224p. (Orig.). 1980. pap. cancelled (ISBN 0-9603628-1-9). Frog in Well.

De Noyelles, Diana A. & Smith, Joan D. Women in California: A Guide to Organizations & Resources. LC 76-4327. (California Information Guides Ser.). 1977. pap. 16.75x (ISBN 0-912102-26-8). Cal Inst Public.

Donovan, Josephine, ed. Feminist Literary Criticism: Explorations in Theory. LC 75-12081. 96p. 1975. pap. 5.00x (ISBN 0-8131-1334-2). U Pr of Ky.

DuBois, Ellen C. Feminism & Suffrage: The Emergence of an Independent Women's Movement in America Eighteen Forty-Eight to Eighteen Sixty-Nine. 1978. 17.50 (ISBN 0-8014-1043-6); pap. 4.95 1980 ed. (ISBN 0-8014-9182-7). Cornell U Pr.

Dworkin, Andrea. Woman Hating: A Radical Look at Sexuality. 217p. 1976. pap. 4.95 (ISBN 0-525-47423-4). Dutton.

Dye, Nancy S. As Equals & As Sisters: Feminism, the Labor Movement, & the Women's Trade Union League of New York. LC 80-16751. 208p. 1981. text ed. 17.50x (ISBN 0-8262-0318-3). U of Mo Pr.

Dyhouse, Carol. Girls Growing up in Late Victorian & Edwardian England. (Studies in Social History). 224p. 1981. price not set (ISBN 0-7100-0821-X). Routledge & Kegan.

Eichler, Margrit. The Double Standard: A Feminist Critique of the Social Sciences. 1979. write for info. (ISBN 0-312-21823-0). St Martin.

Eisenstein, Zillah R. The Radical Future of Liberal Feminism. (Feminist Theory Ser.). (Illus.). 400p. 1980. text ed. 17.95x (ISBN 0-582-28205-5); pap. text ed. 10.95x (ISBN 0-582-28206-3). Longman.

Ellsworth, Edward W. Liberators of the Female Mind: The Shirreff Sisters, Educational Reform, & the Women's Movement. LC 78-67910. (Contributions in Women's Studies: No. 7). (Illus.). 1979. lib. bdg. 25.00 (ISBN 0-313-20644-9, ELL/). Greenwood.

English, Jane. Sex Equality. LC 76-53000. (Illus.). 256p. 1977. text ed. 14.95 (ISBN 0-13-807594-8); pap. text ed. 11.95 (ISBN 0-13-807586-7). P-H.

Ephron, Nora. Crazy Salad: Some Things About Women. 224p. 1976. pap. 2.50 (ISBN 0-553-14312-3). Bantam.

Evans, Richard J. The Feminists: Women's Emancipation Movements in Europe, America & Australasia 1840-1920. LC 77-77490. 1977. text ed. 22.50x (ISBN 0-06-492037-2); pap. text ed. 8.50x (ISBN 0-06-492044-5). B&N.

Ferguson, Kathy E. Self, Society, & Womankind: The Dialectic of Liberation. LC 79-6831. (Contributions in Women's Studies: No. 17). xii, 200p. 1980. lib. bdg. 22.95 (ISBN 0-313-22245-2, FSS/). Greenwood.

Fibush, Esther & Morgan, Martha. Forgive Me No Longer: The Liberation of Martha. LC 75-27965. 1977. 14.95 (ISBN 0-87304-148-8). Family Serv.

Firestone, Shulamith. The Dialectic of Sex. LC 70-123149. 288p. 1974. pap. 4.95 (ISBN 0-688-06454-X). Morrow.

Follis, Anne B. I'm Not a Women's Libber, but... LC 81-1241. 128p. 1981. 7.95 (ISBN 0-687-18687-0). Abingdon.

Fordham, Jim & Fordham, Andrea. The Assault on the Sexes. (Illus.). 1977. 9.95 (ISBN 0-87000-377-1). Arlington Hse.

Friedan, Betty. The Feminine Mystique. 2nd ed. 430p. 1974. 10.00 (ISBN 0-393-08685-2). Norton.

--It Changed My Life: Writings on the Women's Movement. 1976. Random.

--The Second Stage. 320p. 1981. 12.95 (ISBN 0-671-41034-2). Summit Bks.

Fritz, Leah. Dreamers & Dealers: An Intimate Appraisal of the Women's Movement. LC 78-73852. 350p. 1980. pap. 5.95 (ISBN 0-8070-3793-1, BP-604). Beacon Pr.

Fulenwider, Claire K. Feminism in American Politics: A Study of Ideological Influence. LC 79-25131. 182p. 1980. 20.95 (ISBN 0-03-053461-5). Praeger.

Gilbert, Sandra M. & Gubar, Susan, eds. Shakespeare's Sisters: Feminist Essays on Women Poets. LC 78-9510. 368p. 1979. 19.50x (ISBN 0-253-11258-3). Ind U Pr.

Gisborne, Thomas. An Enquiry into the Duties of the Female Sex. Luria, Gina, ed. LC 74-8236. (The Feminist Controversy in England, 1788-1810 Ser.). 1974. lib. bdg. 50.00 (ISBN 0-8240-0860-X). Garland Pub.

Gittelson, Natalie. Dominus: A Woman Looks at Men's Lives. LC 78-23725. 1979. pap. 3.95 (ISBN 0-15-626118-9, Harv). HarBraceJ.

Glennon, Lynda M. Women & Dualism. 1979. pap. text ed. 9.95x (ISBN 0-582-28076-1). Longman.

Gluck, Sherna, ed. From Parlor to Prison: Five American Suffragists Talk About Their Lives. 1976. pap. 3.95 (ISBN 0-394-71642-6, Vin). Random.

Goldman, Emma. Traffic in Women & Other Essays on Feminism. Shulman, Alix K., ed. (Illus., Orig.). 1971. pap. 3.00 (ISBN 0-87810-001-6). Times Change.

Goldsmith, Margaret. Seven Women Against the World. LC 75-21989. (Pioneers of the Woman's Movement Ser.). (Illus.). ix, 236p. 1976. Repr. of 1894 ed. 19.00 (ISBN 0-88355-316-3). Hyperion-Conn.

Goodman, Florence J. The A B C's of Feminine Happiness. 88p. 1980. 8.95x (ISBN 0-917232-09-7). Gee Tee Bee.

Gould, E. American Woman Today: Free or Frustrated. 2nd ed. 1977. text ed. 8.84 (ISBN 0-13-032367-5); pap. text ed. 5.28 (ISBN 0-13-032359-4). P-H.

Grahn, Judy. Edward the Dyke. 66p. pap. 3.00 (ISBN 0-686-74710-0). Crossing Pr.

--Edward the Dyke. (Illus.). 1971. 2.50 (ISBN 0-88447-018-0). Diana Pr.

Greer, Germaine. The Female Eunuch. (McGraw-Hill Paperback Ser.). 360p. 1980. pap. 5.95 (ISBN 0-07-024375-1). McGraw.

--The Female Eunuch. 384p. 1972. pap. 2.50 (ISBN 0-553-12195-2, 12195-2). Bantam.

Griffiths, N. E. Penelope's Web: Some Perceptions of Women in European & Canadian Society. (Illus.). 1976. pap. 5.95x (ISBN 0-19-540268-5). Oxford U Pr.

Gurko, Miriam. The Ladies of Seneca Falls: The Birth of the Woman's Rights Movement. LC 76-9144. (Studies in the Life of Women). (Illus.). 1976. pap. 5.95 (ISBN 0-8052-0545-4). Schocken.

Hahn, Emily. Once Upon a Pedestal. (RL 9). 1975. pap. 2.25 (ISBN 0-451-61415-1, ME1415, Ment). NAL.

--Once Upon a Pedestal: An Informal History of Women's Lib. 224p. 1974. 6.95 (ISBN 0-690-00507-5). T Y Crowell.

Hall, C. M. Woman Unliberated: Difficulties & Limitations in Changing Self. new ed. LC 78-21874. 1979. pap. text ed. 14.95 (ISBN 0-89116-097-3). Hemisphere Pub.

Hartman, Mary S. & Banner, Lois W. Consciousness Raised: New Perspectives on the History of Women. 253p. 1976. Repr. lib. bdg. 12.00x (ISBN 0-374-93712-5). Octagon.

Hartsock, Nancy. Money, Sex & Power: An Essay on Domination & Community. (Feminist Theory Ser.). 1981. text ed. 22.50x (ISBN 0-582-28279-9); pap. text ed. 12.50x (ISBN 0-582-28280-2). Longman.

Havice, Doris. Roadmap for a Rebel. 1980. 7.95 (ISBN 0-8062-1532-1). Carlton.

Hericourt, Jenny P. A Woman's Philosophy of Woman: Or, Woman Affranchised. an Answer to Michelet, Proudhon, Girardin, Legouve, Comte, & Other Modern Innovators. LC 79-2940. 317p. 1981. Repr. of 1864 ed. 23.50 (ISBN 0-8305-0105-3). Hyperion Conn.

Hersh, Blanch G. The Slavery of Sex: Feminist-Abolitionists in America. LC 78-14591. 1978. 17.95 (ISBN 0-252-00695-X). U of Ill Pr.

Hill, Mary A. Charlotte Perkins Gilman: The Making of a Radical Feminist, 1860-1896. (Illus.). 250p. 1981. pap. 8.95 (ISBN 0-87722-225-8). Temple U Pr.

Hill-Peters, Mary. Charlotte Perkins Gilman: The Making of a Radical Feminist, 1860-1896. Davis, Allen F., ed. (American Civilization Ser.). (Illus.). 1979. 19.95x (ISBN 0-87722-160-X). Temple U Pr.

Hole, Judith & Levine, Ellen. Rebirth of Feminism. LC 70-162808. 500p. 1973. 10.00 (ISBN 0-8129-0227-0); pap. 4.50 (ISBN 0-8129-6211-7). Times Bks.

Hooks, Bell. Ain't I a Woman: Black Women & Feminism. 220p. 1981. 17.50 (ISBN 0-89608-130-3); pap. 7.00 (ISBN 0-89608-129-X). South End Pr.

Insdorf, Cecile. Montaigne & Feminism. (Studies in the Romance Languages & Literatures). (Orig.). 1978. pap. 7.00x (ISBN 0-8078-9194-0). U of NC Pr.

Jacoby, Susan. The Possible She. 208p. 1979. 8.95 (ISBN 0-374-23645-3). FS&G.

Jessup, Josephine L. Faith of Our Feminists. LC 65-23482. 1950. 9.00x (ISBN 0-8196-0158-6). Biblo.

Joseph, Gloria & Lewis, Jill. Common Differences. LC 79-6885. 240p. 1981. pap. 8.95 (ISBN 0-385-14271-4, Anch). Doubleday.

Joseph, Gloria I. & Lewis, Jill. Common Differences: Conflicts in Black & White Feminist Perspectives. 1981. 7.95 (ISBN 0-385-14271-4, Anchor Pr). Doubleday.

Kanowitz, Leo. Equal Rights: The Male Stake. 168p. 1981. 19.95 (ISBN 0-8263-0594-6); pap. 9.95 (ISBN 0-8263-0595-4). U of NM Pr.

Kaplan, Marion. The Jewish Feminist Movement in Germany: The Campaigns of the Judischer Frauenbund, 1904-1938. LC 78-67567. (Contributions in Women's Studies: No. 8). (Illus.). lib. bdg. 17.50 (ISBN 0-313-20736-4, KGJ/). Greenwood.

Kimball, Gayle, ed. Women's Culture: The Women's Renaissance of the Seventies. LC 81-9004. 302p. 1981. 16.00 (ISBN 0-8108-1455-2); pap. 8.50 (ISBN 0-686-73579-X). Scarecrow.

Koedt, Anne, et al, eds. Radical Feminism. LC 72-91380. 424p. 1973. 10.00 (ISBN 0-8129-0316-1); pap. 4.95 (ISBN 0-8129-6220-6). Times Bks.

Koen, Susan & Swaim, Nina. A Handbook for Women on the Nuclear Mentality. 74p. pap. 3.50 (ISBN 0-686-74728-3). Crossing Pr.

Kraditor, Aileen. Up from the Pedestal: Selected Writings in the History of American Feminism. LC 68-26443. 1972. 8.95 (ISBN 0-8129-0062-6); pap. 4.50 (ISBN 0-8129-6127-7). Times Bks.

Kreig, Nita, ed. Women's Liberation & the Socialist Revolution. LC 78-65347. 1979. lib. bdg. 8.00 (ISBN 0-87348-568-8); pap. 2.25 (ISBN 0-87348-569-6). Path Pr NY.

Krichmar, Albert, et al. The Women's Movement in the Seventies: An International English-Language Bibliography. LC 77-21416. 1977. 35.00 (ISBN 0-8108-1063-8). Scarecrow.

Kuhn, Annette & Wolpe, Annmarie, eds. Feminism & Materialism. 1978. 22.50x (ISBN 0-7100-0072-3); pap. 9.00 (ISBN 0-7100-0074-X). Routledge & Kegan.

Lagemann, Ellen C. A Generation of Women: Education in the Lives of Progressive Reformers. LC 79-13528. (Illus.). 1979. 12.50x (ISBN 0-674-34471-5). Harvard U Pr.

Leach, William. True Love & Perfect Union: The Feminist Reform of Sex & Society. LC 80-50557. 320p. 1980. 17.50 (ISBN 0-465-08752-3). Basic.

Lemons, J. Stanley. The Woman Citizen: Social Feminism in the 1920s. LC 72-75488. 288p. 1973. 12.50 (ISBN 0-252-00267-9). U of Ill Pr.

Lipshitz, Susan, ed. Tearing the Veil: Essays on Femininity. (Orig.). 1978. pap. 7.95 (ISBN 0-7100-8721-7). Routledge & Kegan.

Lloyd, Cynthia B., ed. Sex, Discrimination, & the Division of Labor. LC 74-32175. 431p. 1975. 25.00x (ISBN 0-231-03750-3); pap. 10.00x (ISBN 0-231-03751-1). Columbia U Pr.

Ludovici, A. M. Lysistrata: Woman's Future or Future Woman. 59.95 (ISBN 0-8490-0569-8). Gordon Pr.

McBride, Angela B. Living with Contradictions: A Married Feminist. 1977. pap. 4.95 (ISBN 0-06-090556-5, CN 556, CN). Har-Row.

McCracken, Robert D. The Fallacies of Women's Liberation. LC 72-89863. (Illus.). 150p. 1972. pap. 3.95 (ISBN 0-88310-000-2). Publishers Consult.

MacLean, Ian. Woman Triumphant: Feminism in French Literature 1610-1652. (Illus.). 1977. 54.00x (ISBN 0-19-815741-X). Oxford U Pr.

McPhee, Carol & FitzGerald, Ann, eds. Feminist Quotations: Voices of Rebels, Reformers & Visionaries. LC 78-3308. 1979. 12.95 (ISBN 0-690-01770-7). T Y Crowell.

McRobbie, Angela & McCabe, Trisha, eds. Feminism for Girls: An Adventure Story. (Illus.). 256p. (Orig.). 1981. pap. price not set (ISBN 0-7100-0961-5). Routledge & Kegan.

Mander, Anica V. & Rush, Anne K. Feminism As Therapy. LC 74-8097. (Illus.). 1975. pap. 4.95 (ISBN 0-394-70937-3). Random.

--Feminism As Therapy. 2.45 (ISBN 0-685-78832-6). Moon Bks.

Marks, Elaine & De Courtivron, Isabelle, eds. New French Feminisms. (Women's Studies Ser.). 320p. 1981. pap. 8.95 (ISBN 0-8052-0681-7). Schocken.

--New French Feminisms. LC 79-4698. 1979. 13.95x (ISBN 0-87023-280-0). U of Mass Pr.

Martin, Wendy, ed. American Sisterhood: Writings of the Feminist Movement from Colonial Times to the Present. (Illus.). 1972. pap. text ed. 11.50 scp (ISBN 0-06-044234-4, HarpC). Har-Row.

Mayreder, Rosa. A Survey of the Woman Problem. Herman, Scheffauer, tr. from Ger. LC 79-2944. 275p. 1981. Repr. of 1913 ed. 21.50 (ISBN 0-8305-0108-8). Hyperion Conn.

Mickelson, Anne Z. Reaching Out: Sensitivity & Order in Recent American Fiction by Women. LC 78-26164. 1979. lib. bdg. 12.00 (ISBN 0-8108-1194-4). Scarecrow.

Miles, Barbara, ed. Rainbow Snake: An Anthology of Women Poets Ranging from Those Not So Well Known, Who Are a Joy to Discover, to Those More Families Including Diane Wakoski, Alta, & Anne Sexton. (Illus.). 64p. 1971. pap. 2.25 (ISBN 0-9600856-1-0, B&H Bks). CWSS Pr.

Miller, Casey & Swift, Kate. Words & Women. 200p. 1977. 7.95 (ISBN 0-385-04857-2, Anchor Pr); pap. 2.95 (ISBN 0-385-04858-0). Doubleday.

Miller, Sally M., ed. Flawed Liberation: Socialism & Feminism. LC 80-1050. (Contributions to Women's Studies Ser.: No. 19). 240p. 1981. lib. bdg. 27.50 (ISBN 0-313-21401-8, MFL/). Greenwood.

Millett, Kate. Sita. 1978. pap. 2.25 (ISBN 0-345-27362-1). Ballantine.

Mitchell, Juliet. Woman's Estate. 192p. 1973. pap. 2.95 (ISBN 0-394-71905-0, Vin). Random.

Moltmann-Wendel, Elisabeth. Liberty, Equality, Sisterhood: On the Emancipation of Women in Church & Society. Gritsch, Ruth C., tr. from Ger. LC 77-15240. 96p. 1978. pap. 3.50 (ISBN 0-8006-1325-2, 1-1325). Fortress.

Moraga, Cherrie & Anzaldua, Gloria, eds. This Bridge Called My Back: Writings by Radical Women of Color. (Orig.). 1981. pap. 8.95 (ISBN 0-930436-10-5). Persephone.
Moran, Miriam G., ed. What You Should Know About Women's Lib. LC 74-75980. 128p. 1974. pap. 1.50 (ISBN 0-87983-084-0). Keats.
Morgan, Helen L. Maria Mitchell, First Lady of American Astronomy. LC 77-5871. (gr. 7-10). 1977. 7.95 (ISBN 0-664-32614-5). Westminster.
Morgan, Robin, ed. Sisterhood Is Powerful: An Anthology of Writings from the Women's Liberation Movement. 1970. 12.95 (ISBN 0-394-45240-2). Random.
--Sisterhood Is Powerful: An Anthology of Writings from the Women's Liberation Movement. 1970. pap. 4.95 (ISBN 0-394-70539-4, Vin). Random.
Myron, Nancy & Bunch, Charlotte, eds. Lesbianism & the Women's Movement. (Illus.). 1976. pap. 3.50 (ISBN 0-88447-006-7). Diana Pr.
National Association for Women Deans, Administratos & Counselors. Two Symposia: Ethnic Minority Feminism & Two Sides of the Coin. 1978. pap. 3.00 (ISBN 0-686-23415-4). Natl Assn Women.
Negrin, Sue. Begin at Start: Some Thoughts on Personal Liberation & World Change. 176p. pap. 3.25 (ISBN 0-87810-020-2). Crossing Pr.
Novack, George. Revolutionary Dynamics of Women's Liberation. 1970. pap. 0.25 (ISBN 0-87348-120-8). Path Pr NY.
Oakley, Ann. The Sociology of Housework. LC 75-4668. 264p. 1975. pap. 3.95 (ISBN 0-394-73088-7). Pantheon.
O'Neill, William L. Everyone Was Brave: A History of Feminism in America. LC 71-78313. 384p. 1972. 7.95 (ISBN 0-8129-0103-7); pap. 4.95 (ISBN 0-8129-6192-7, QP88). Times Bks.
Papachristou, Judith. Women Together: A History in Documents of the Women's Movement in the United States. 1976. 15.00 (ISBN 0-394-49429-6); pap. 8.95 (ISBN 0-394-73102-6). Knopf.
Paulsen, Kathryn & Kuhn, Ryan A., eds. Woman's Almanac: Twelve How to Handbooks in One. LC 76-2055. (Illus.). 1976. pap. 8.95 (ISBN 0-397-01138-5). Har-Row.
Redstockings. Feminist Revolution. 1978. 12.95 (ISBN 0-394-40821-7); pap. 5.95 (ISBN 0-394-73240-5). Random.
Reed, Evelyn. Problems of Women's Liberation: A Marxist Approach. new & rev. ed. LC 78-143808. (Orig.). 1971. 8.00 (ISBN 0-87348-166-6); pap. 2.45 (ISBN 0-87348-167-4). Path Pr NY.
Reeves, Joyce A. Motherless Victim. 1981. 5.95 (ISBN 0-8062-1576-3). Carlton.
Reilly, Sue. What Do Women Want? (Illus.). 1972. pap. 2.50 (ISBN 0-912518-03-0). Druid Bks.
Rennie, Susan & Grimstad, Kirsten, eds. The New Woman's Survival Sourcebook. 1975. pap. 6.95 (ISBN 0-394-73035-6). Knopf.
Rich, Adrienne. Of Woman Born: Motherhood As Experience & Institution. 1976. 12.95 (ISBN 0-393-08750-6). Norton.
Richards, Janet R. The Sceptical Feminist: A Philosophical Enquiry. 320p. 1980. 32.00 (ISBN 0-7100-0673-X). Routledge & Kegan.
Riegel, Robert E. American Feminists. LC 80-13163. (Illus.). 223p. 1980. Repr. of 1963 ed. lib. bdg. 20.25x (ISBN 0-313-22434-X, RIAF). Greenwood.
--A High Point of American Feminism. (Cotton Memorial Papers). pap. 3.00 (ISBN 0-685-64636-X). Tex Western.
Roberts, Helen, ed. Doing Feminist Research. 224p. (Orig.). 1981. pap. 9.50 (ISBN 0-7100-0772-8). Routledge & Kegan.
Robins, Elizabeth. Ancilla's Share: An Indictment of Sex Antagonism. LC 75-21815. (Pioneers of the Woman's Movement Ser.). 1976. Repr. of 1924 ed. 21.50 (ISBN 0-88355-272-8). Hyperion-Conn.
Rossi, Alice S., ed. The Feminist Papers: From Adams to Beauvoir. 736p. (gr. 9 up). 1974. pap. 3.50 (ISBN 0-553-14190-2). Bantam.
--The Feminist Papers: From Adams to De Beauvoir. 600p. 1973. 22.50x (ISBN 0-231-03795-3). Columbia U Pr.
Rover, Constance. Love, Morals & the Feminists. (Illus.). 1970. 9.75 (ISBN 0-7100-6693-7). Routledge & Kegan.
Rowbotham, Sheila. New World for Women: Stella Browne, Socialist Feminist. 128p. 1980. text ed. 10.00 (ISBN 0-904383-55-5); pap. 4.50 (ISBN 0-904383-54-7). Pluto Pr.
--Woman's Consciousness, Man's World. 1974. pap. 1.95 (ISBN 0-14-021717-7, Pelican). Penguin.
Rowbotham, Sheila, et al. Beyond the Fragments: Feminism & the Making of Socialism. 270p. (Orig.). 1981. pap. 6.95 (ISBN 0-932870-11-2). Alyson Pubns.
Rush, Anne K. Getting Clear. 1973. pap. 5.95 (ISBN 0-394-70970-5). Random.
Russell, Diana E. & Van de Ven, Nicole, eds. Crimes Against Women. LC 76-25356. 1977. 6.95 (ISBN 0-89087-921-4). Les Femmes Pub.
Russell, Dora. The Tamarisk Tree. pap. cancelled (ISBN 0-86068-001-0). Academy Chi Ltd.
Ruth, Sheila. Issues in Feminism. LC 79-88795. (Illus.). 1980. text ed. 10.95 (ISBN 0-395-28691-3). HM.
Safilios-Rothschild, Constantina. Women & Social Policy. (P-H Series in Social Policy). 224p. 1974. pap. 8.95 ref. ed. (ISBN 0-13-961680-2). P-H.
Sanger, Margaret & Baskin, Alex, eds. Woman Rebel. LC 75-3728. 1976. 18.75 (ISBN 0-914924-02-8). Archives Soc Hist.
Scanzoni, Letha & Hardesty, Nancy. All We're Meant to Be: A Biblical Approach to Women's Liberation. LC 74-78041. 1975. pap. 5.95 (ISBN 0-87680-897-6, 98053). Word Bks.
Schlafly, Phyllis. The Power of the Positive Woman. 1977. 9.95 (ISBN 0-87000-373-9). Arlington Hse.
Schmalhausen, Samuel D. & Calverton, Victor F. Woman's Coming-of-Age: A Symposium. 1976. Repr. of 1931 ed. lib. bdg. 30.00x (ISBN 0-374-97118-8). Octagon.
Schneir, Miriam, ed. Feminism. 1971. pap. 3.95 (ISBN 0-394-71738-4, Vin). Random.
Schramm, Sarah S. Plow Women Rather Than Reapers: An Intellectual History of Feminism in the United States. LC 78-10907. 1979. lib. bdg. 19.00 (ISBN 0-8108-1183-9). Scarecrow.
Shaffer, Gail. Women's Fight for Liberation. (Topics of Our Times Ser.: No. 11). 32p. lib. bdg. 2.95 incl. catalog cards (ISBN 0-686-07242-1); pap. 1.50 vinyl laminated covers (ISBN 0-686-07243-X). SamHar Pr.
Shull, Valdaree W. Today's Women. 1978. 4.95 (ISBN 0-533-03434-5). Vantage.
Smart, Carol & Smart, Barry. Women, Sexuality & Social Control. (Orig.). 1978. pap. 6.95 (ISBN 0-7100-8723-3). Routledge & Kegan.
Smith, Barbara. Toward a Black Feminist Criticism. (Out & Out Pamphlet Ser). pap. 1.00 (ISBN 0-918314-14-3). Out & Out.
Smith, Elizabeth Oakes & Diaz, Abby M. Liberating the Home, 2 bks. in 1. Incl. Woman & Her Needs. Smith, Elizabeth Oakes. Repr. of 1851 ed; A Domestic Problem: Work & Culture in the Household. Diaz, Abby M. Repr. of 1875 ed. LC 74-3988. (Women in America Series). 1974. 13.00 (ISBN 0-405-06107-2). Arno.
Sochen, June. The New Woman: Feminism in Greenwich Village, Nineteen-Ten to Nineteen-Twenty. LC 70-190125. 256p. 1972. 6.95 (ISBN 0-8129-0257-2); pap. 3.50 (ISBN 0-8129-6261-3). Times Bks.
Sparkman, R. B. Is Feminism Really a Positive Advance for You? (Illus.). 102p. (Orig.). 1979. pap. 2.45 (ISBN 0-935658-00-9). Cope Allied Pub.
Spretnak, Charlene. Politics of Women's Spirituality: Essays on the Rise of Spiritualist Power Within the Feminist Movement. LC 80-2876. 552p. 1981. pap. 9.95 (ISBN 0-385-17241-9, Anch). Doubleday.
Stannard, Una. Mrs Man. LC 76-58834. (Illus.). 1977. 14.00 (ISBN 0-914142-02-X). Germainbooks.
Stites, Richard. The Women's Liberation Movement in Russia: Feminism, Nihilism, & Bolshevism, 1860-1930. LC 77-72137. (Illus.). 1978. text ed. 40.00 (ISBN 0-691-05254-9); pap. 12.50 (ISBN 0-691-10058-6). Princeton U Pr.
Thibert, Marguerite. Le Feminisme Dans le Socialisme Francais De Eighteen Thirty a Eighteen Fifty. (Perspectives in European History: No. 30). (Fr.). Repr. of 1926 ed. lib. bdg. 25.00x (ISBN 0-87991-822-5). Porcupine Pr.
Thompson, Mary L., ed. Voices of the New Feminism. LC 76-119679. 1970. pap. 3.95x (ISBN 0-8070-4175-0, BP411). Beacon Pr.
Thorne, Yalom. Rethinking the Family: Some Feminist Questions. 1981. pap. text ed. 9.95x (ISBN 0-582-28265-9). Longman.
Tingley, Elizabeth & Tingley, Donald F., eds. Women & Feminism in American History: A Guide to Information Sources. LC 80-19793. (American Government & History Information Guide Ser.: Vol. 12). 289p. 1981. 36.00 (ISBN 0-8103-1492-4). Gale.
Tripp, Maggie, ed. Woman in the Year Two Thousand. 352p. 1976. pap. 2.25 (ISBN 0-440-39709-X, LE). Dell.
Twin, Stephanie, ed. Out of the Bleachers. (Women's Lives-Women's Work Ser). (Illus.). 1979. pap. 5.95 (ISBN 0-912670-59-2, Co-Pub. by McGraw). Feminist Pr.
Vetterling-Braggin, Mary, et al, eds. Feminism & Philosophy. (Quality Paperback Ser: No. 335). 1977. pap. 7.95 (ISBN 0-8226-0335-7). Littlefield.
Vicinus, Martha, ed. A Widening Sphere: Changing Roles of Victorian Women. LC 76-26433. 352p. 1977. 15.95x (ISBN 0-253-36540-6). Ind U Pr.
Von Hippel, Theodor G. On Improving the Status of Women. Sellner, Timothy F., tr. from Ger. LC 78-23302. 1979. 16.95x (ISBN 0-8143-1622-0). Wayne St U Pr.
Wagner, Geoffrey. Five for Freedom: A Study of Feminism in Fiction. LC 73-8284. 234p. 1973. 14.50 (ISBN 0-8386-1423-X). Fairleigh Dickinson.
Wakefield, Priscilla. Reflections on the Present Condition of the Female Sex: With Suggestions for Its Improvement. Luria, Gina, ed. (The Feminist Controversy in England, 1788-1810 Ser.). 1974. lib. bdg. 50.00 (ISBN 0-8240-0882-0). Garland Pub.
Warren, Mary A. The Nature of Woman: An Encyclopedia. LC 79-55299. 736p. 1980. 20.00 (ISBN 0-918528-07-0); pap. 16.00 (ISBN 0-918528-06-2). Edgepress.
Waters, Mary-Alice. Feminism & the Marxist Movement. 1972. pap. 0.60 (ISBN 0-87348-241-7). Path Pr NY.
Watt, Robert. This Insults Women, No. I. 1973. pap. 2.00 (ISBN 0-912518-05-7). Druid Bks.
--This Insults Women, No. II. 1973. pap. 2.00 (ISBN 0-912518-04-9). Druid Bks.
Welter, Barbara. Dimity Convictions: The American Woman in the Nineteenth Century. LC 76-8305. 230p. 1976. 14.95x (ISBN 0-8214-0352-4); pap. 6.95x (ISBN 0-8214-0358-3). Ohio U Pr.
Wheeler, Kenneth W. & Lussier, Virginia L., eds. Women, the Arts, & the Nineteen Twenties in Paris & New York. 250p. (Orig.). 1982. pap. 5.95 (ISBN 0-87855-782-2). Transaction Bks.
Williams, Elizabeth F. Notes of a Feminist Therapist. 1977. pap. 1.50 (ISBN 0-440-36427-2, LE). Dell.
Wilson, John. Love, Sex, Feminism. LC 79-24902. 1980. 18.95 (ISBN 0-03-056103-5). Praeger.
Wollstonecraft, Mary. Thoughts on the Education of Daughters: With Reflections on Female Conduct, in the More Important Duties of Life. Luria, Gina, ed. (The Feminist Controversy in England, 1788-1810 Ser.). 1974. lib. bdg. 50.00 (ISBN 0-8240-0890-1). Garland Pub.
Women's Studies Group Centre for Contemporary Cultural Studies. Women Take Issue: Aspects of Women's Subordination. (Illus.). 1979. text ed. 17.00x (ISBN 0-09-133600-7, Hutchinson U Lib); pap. text ed. 8.50x (ISBN 0-09-133601-5, Hutchinson U Lib). Humanities.
Wortis, H. & Rabinowitz, C., eds. The Women's Movement: Social & Psychological Perspectives. LC 72-6125. 151p. 1972. pap. 5.95 (ISBN 0-470-96165-1). Halsted Pr.
Wortis, Helen & Rabinowitz, Clara, eds. The Women's Movement: Social & Psychological Perspectives. LC 72-6125. (AMS Studies in Modern Society: Political & Social Issues: No. 2). 1972. 16.50 (ISBN 0-404-10520-3). AMS Pr.
Wright, F. A. Feminism in Greek Literature from Homer to Aristotle. 69.95 (ISBN 0-8490-0159-5). Gordon Pr.
Wright, Henry C. The Empire of the Mother. (Pioneers of Womens Liberation Ser.). 1978. lib. bdg. 69.95 (ISBN 0-685-06645-2). Revisionist Pr.
Yates, Gayle G. What Women Want: The Ideologies of the Movement. 224p. 1975. 12.50x (ISBN 0-674-95077-1); pap. 3.95 (ISBN 0-674-95079-8). Harvard U Pr.

FEMINISM AND LITERATURE

Brown, Janet. Feminist Drama: Definition & Critical Analysis. LC 79-22382. 167p. 1979. 10.00 (ISBN 0-8108-1267-3). Scarecrow.
Fell, Alison, ed. Hard Feelings: Fiction & Poetry from Spare Rib. 4.95 (ISBN 0-7043-3838-6, Pub. by Quartet England). Charles River Bks.

FEMINIST STUDIES

see Women'S Studies

FEMUR

Kulowski, Jacob. Accident Injuries of the Conjoined Femur: Clinical & Paraclinical Aspects of Automotive & Comparable Injuries of the Hip, Femur & Knee. (Illus.). 312p. 1964. photocopy ed. spiral 29.75 (ISBN 0-398-01063-3). C C Thomas.
McArdle, J. Functional Morphology of the Hip & Thigh of the Lorisiformes. (Contributions to Primatology Ser.: Vol. 17). (Illus.). 148p. 1981. pap. 19.25 (ISBN 3-8055-1767-X). S Karger.
Zinn, W. M., ed. Idiopathic Ischemic Necrosis of the Femoral Head in Adults. (Illus.). 250p. 1971. 49.50 (ISBN 0-8391-0582-7). Univ Park.

FENCES

see also Gates; Hedges

Brann, Donald R. How to Build Outdoor Furniture. LC 76-14045. 1978. pap. 5.95 (ISBN 0-87733-754-3). Easi-Bild.
Martin, George A. Fences, Gates & Bridges. Date not set. 6.95 (ISBN 0-686-26689-7). Dairy Goat.
Russell, James E. Walks, Walls & Fences. Auer, Marilyn M., ed. LC 81-65752. (Illus., Orig.). 1981. 17.95 (ISBN 0-932944-35-3); pap. 6.95 (ISBN 0-932944-36-1). Creative Homeowner.
Schuler, Stanley. How to Build Fences, Gates & Walls. (Illus.). 256p. 1976. 13.50 (ISBN 0-02-607370-6). Macmillan.
--How to Build Fences, Gates & Walls. (Illus.). 256p. 1976. 13.50 (ISBN 0-02-607370-6). Macmillan.
Sunset Editors. Fences & Gates. 4th ed. LC 81-81379. (Illus.). 96p. 1981. pap. 4.95 (ISBN 0-376-01105-X, Sunset Bks.). Sunset-Lane.
--Fences & Gates. 4th ed. LC 81-81379. (Illus.). 96p. 1981. pap. 4.95 (ISBN 0-376-01105-X, Sunset Bks). Sunset-Lane.

FENCES–LAW

see also Boundaries (Estates)

FENCING

see also Dueling; Kendo; Stage Fencing

Alaux, Michel. Modern Fencing. 1981. pap. 8.95 (ISBN 0-684-16945-2, ScribT). Scribner.
Anderson, Bob. All About Fencing. LC 72-142252. (Illus.). 1970. 3.00 (ISBN 0-668-02432-1). Arco.
--Better Fencing: Foil. LC 73-168478. (Better Sports Ser.). (Illus.). 1973. 8.50x (ISBN 0-7182-0491-3). Intl Pubns Serv.
--Tackle Fencing: An Introduction to the Foil. (Illus.). 1979. 6.95 (ISBN 0-09-131220-5, Pub. by Hutchinson); pap. 4.50 (ISBN 0-09-131221-3). Merrimack Bk Serv.
Archery-Fencing Guide 1978-80. 1978. pap. 2.50 (ISBN 0-685-29028-X, 243-26178). AAHPERD.
Blakeslee, Fred G. Sword Play for Actors. 1976. Repr. of 1905 ed. 25.00 (ISBN 0-685-71165-X, Regency). Scholarly.
Bower, Muriel. Foil Fencing. 4th ed. (Physical Education Ser.). 112p. 1980. pap. text ed. write for info. (ISBN 0-697-07097-2). Wm C Brown.
Bowling-Golf Guide: 1979-81. 1977. pap. 2.50x (ISBN 0-685-77225-X, 243-26362). AAHPERD.
Castello, Hugo & Castello, James. Fencing. LC 62-17868. 116p. 1962. 9.95 (ISBN 0-471-07135-8). Krieger.
Crosnier, Roger. Fencing with a Foil: Instruction & Technique. 2nd ed. (Illus.). 208p. 1969. 10.95 (ISBN 0-571-04594-4, Pub. by Faber & Faber). Merrimack Bk Serv.
De Beaumont, C. L. Fencing: Ancient Art & Modern Sport. Anderson, R., ed. LC 78-59827. (Illus.). 1979. 13.50 (ISBN 0-498-02332-X). A S Barnes.
Diagram Group. Enjoying Combat Sports. LC 77-5024. (Enjoying Sports Ser.). (Illus.). 1977. pap. 3.95 (ISBN 0-448-22189-6). Paddington.
Fencing. 1976. pap. 2.50 (ISBN 0-8277-4818-3). British Bk Ctr.
Fencing: A Know the Game Handbook. Date not set. pap. 3.00x (ISBN 0-7158-0112-0, SpS). Sportshelf.
Garret, Maxwell R. & Poulson, Mary H. Foil Fencing: Skills, Safety, Operations, & Responsibilities for the 1980s. LC 80-18426. (Illus.). 160p. 1981. text ed. 9.75x (ISBN 0-271-00273-5). Pa St U Pr.
Jackson, James L., ed. Three Elizabethan Fencing Manuals, 3 vols. in one. Incl. True Arte of Defence. Di Grassi, Giacomo. Repr. of 1594 ed; His Practice. Saviolo, Vincentio. Repr. of 1595 ed; Paradoxes of Defence. Silver, George. Repr. of 1599 ed. LC 72-6321. 640p. 1972. Repr. 59.00x (ISBN 0-8201-1107-4). Schol Facsimiles.
Lownds, Camille & August, Tony. Foil Around & Stay Fit: Exercise Secrets of a Fencer. LC 76-54896. (Illus.). 1977. pap. 5.95 (ISBN 0-15-132228-7, Harv). HarBraceJ.
Lukovich, I. Electric Foil Fencing. (Illus.). 1978. 13.00 (ISBN 0-912728-95-7). Newbury Bks.
Lukovich, Istvan. Electric Foil Fencing. Coutts, Charles, tr. from Hungarian. (Illus.). 290p. (YA) 1971. 7.50x (ISBN 0-686-74256-7). Intl Pubns Serv.
--Electric Foil Fencing. (Illus.). 1971. 16.50x (ISBN 0-392-05526-0, SpS). Sportshelf.
Nelson, Marvin & Reiff, Rick. Winning Fencing. LC 75-13235. (Illus.). 144p. 1975. pap. 5.95 (ISBN 0-8092-8334-4). Contemp Bks.
Shaff, Jo. Fencing for All. LC 81-66031. 1981. 9.95 (ISBN 0-689-11182-7). Atheneum.
Silver, George. Paradoxes of Defence, Wherein Is Proved the True Grounds of Fight to Be in the Short Auncient Weapons. LC 68-27484. (English Experience Ser.: No. 8). 72p. 1968. Repr. of 1599 ed. 8.00 (ISBN 90-221-0008-1). Walter J Johnson.
Simonian, Charles. Basic Foil Fencing. (Orig.). 1979. pap. text ed. 3.95 (ISBN 0-8403-1430-2). Kendall-Hunt.
Thimm, Carl A. Complete Bibliography of Fencing & Duelling. LC 68-17152. (Illus.). 1968. Repr. of 1846 ed. 23.00 (ISBN 0-405-09028-5). Arno.
Vass, I. Epee Fencing. (Illus.). 1976. 10.00x (ISBN 963-13-3703-0, H-377). Vanous.
--Fencing. (Illus.). 1977. 13.00 (ISBN 0-912728-95-7). Newbury Bks.
Vass, Imre. Epee Fencing. Coutts, Charles, tr. from Hungarian. (Illus.). 392p. (YA) 1976. 10.00x (ISBN 0-686-74257-5). Intl Pubns Serv.

FENELON, FRANCOIS DE SALIGNAC DE LA MOTHE, ABP., 1651-1715
Barnard, H. C. Fenelon on Education. (Cambridge Texts & Studies in the History of Education: No. 1). 1966. 24.50 (ISBN 0-521-04107-4). Cambridge U Pr.
Davis, James H., Jr. Fenelon. (World Authors Ser.: France: No. 542). 1979. lib. bdg. 14.95 (ISBN 0-8057-6384-8). Twayne.
De Fenelon, Marquis. Adventures of Telemachus. Wight, O. W., ed. Hawkesworth, tr. 1977. Repr. of 1882 ed. lib. bdg. 50.00 (ISBN 0-8495-1610-2). Arden Lib.
Duclaux, Agnes M. French Ideal. facs. ed. LC 67-23209. (Essay Index Reprint Ser). 1911. 16.00 (ISBN 0-8369-0393-5). Arno.
Janet, Paul. Fenelon: His Life & Works. LC 78-113315. 1970. Repr. of 1914 ed. 13.50 (ISBN 0-8046-0997-7). Kennikat.
St. Cyres, Viscount. Francois De Fenelon. LC 72-113319. 1970. Repr. of 1901 ed. 13.50 (ISBN 0-8046-0998-5). Kennikat.

FENG, YU-HSIANG, 1882-1948
Sheridan, James E. Chinese Warlord: The Career of Feng Yu-hsiang. LC 65-18978. (Illus.). 1966. 18.50x (ISBN 0-8047-0145-8); pap. 4.95 (ISBN 0-8047-0146-6, SP111). Stanford U Pr.

FENIANS
see also Irish Question
Armstrong, Kenneth & Crawford, Michael. Fenians. (Canadian Jackdaw Ser: No. C21). (Illus.). 1970. 6.95 (ISBN 0-670-31163-4, Grossman). Viking Pr.
Comerford, Anthony. Easter Rising: Dublin 1916. (Jackdaw Ser: No. 61). (Illus.). 1969. 6.95 (ISBN 0-670-28732-6, Grossman). Viking Pr.
D'Arcy, William. Fenian Movement in the U. S. 1858-1886. LC 70-151542. 1971. Repr. of 1947 ed. 18.00 (ISBN 0-8462 1534-9). Russell
Harmon, Maurice, ed. Fenians & Fenianism. LC 79-103321. 101p. 1970. pap. 1.95 (ISBN 0-295-95074-9). U of Wash Pr.
Jenkins, Brian. Fenians & Anglo-American Relations During Reconstruction. LC 79-81595. 1969. 22.50x (ISBN 0-8014-0500-9). Cornell U Pr.
Neidhardt, W. S. Fenianism in North America. LC 74-31392. 216p. 1975. 12.95 (ISBN 0-271-01188-2). Pa St U Pr.
O'Broin, Leon. Fenian Fever: An Anglo-American Dilemma. LC 79-169251. 1971. 10.00 (ISBN 0-8147-6151-8). NYU Pr.
O'Leary, John. Recollections of Fenians & Fenianism, 2 vols. in 1. 248p. 1968. Repr. of 1896 ed. 20.00x (ISBN 0-7165-0054-X, Pub. by Irish Academic Pr Ireland). Biblio Dist.
Walker, Mabel G. Fenian Movement. LC 70-85337. 1969. 5.95 (ISBN 0-87926-004-1); pap. 2.95 (ISBN 0-87926-005-X). R Myles.

FENJAS
see Falashas

FENOLLOSA, ERNEST, 1853-1908
Chisolm, Lawrence W. Fenollossa: The Far East & American Culture. LC 76-22680. (Yale Publications in American Studies Ser: No. 8). (Illus.). 297p. 1976. Repr. of 1963 ed. lib. bdg. 24.75x (ISBN 0-8371-8975-6, CHFE). Greenwood.

FENS
see also Marshes; Moors and Heaths; Reclamation of Land
Davis, Hubert J. Great Dismal Swamp: Its Science, History & Folklore. (Illus.). 1971. 7.50 (ISBN 0-930230-11-6). Johnson NC.
Godwin, H. Fenland: Its Ancient Past & Uncertain Future. LC 77-8824. (Illus.). 1978. 32.50 (ISBN 0-521-21768-7). Cambridge U Pr.
Schueler, Don. Preserving the Pascagoula. LC 80-15931. (Illus.). 1980. 12.50x (ISBN 0-87805-123-6). U Pr of Miss.

FEPC
see United States-Committee on Fair Employment Practice

FERAL CHILDREN
see Wolf Children

FERBERITE
see also Tungsten

FERDINAND 5TH, KING OF SPAIN
see Fernando 5th, el Catolico, King of Spain, 1452-1516

FERGUSON, ADAM, 1723-1816
Kettler, David. Social & Political Thought of Adam Ferguson. LC 65-18736. 1965. 6.50 (ISBN 0-8142-0074-5). Ohio St U Pr.
Lehmann, William C. Adam Ferguson & the Beginnings of Modern Sociology. 1972. lib. bdg. 16.00x (ISBN 0-374-94894-1). Octagon.

FERGUSON, HARRY, 1884-1960
Fraser, Colin. Tractor Pioneer: The Life of Harry Ferguson. LC 73-85451. (Illus.). vi, 294p. 1973. 15.00x (ISBN 0-8214-0134-3). Ohio U Pr.

FERGUSON, JOHN T.
Olsen, Otto, ed. Thin Disguise: Turning Point in Negro History-Plessy Vs. Ferguson-a Documentary Presentation, 1864-1896. 1967. text ed. 6.00x (ISBN 0-391-00460-3). Humanities.

FERGUSON, SAMUEL, SIR, 1810-1886
Brown, Malcom. Sir Samuel Ferguson. (Irish Writers Ser.). 101p. 1973. 4.50 (ISBN 0-8387-1083-2); pap. 1.95 (ISBN 0-8387-1208-8). Bucknell U Pr.
Ferguson, Samuel. Poems of Samuel Ferguson. 1963. 2.50 (ISBN 0-900372-67-2). Irish Bk Ctr.

FERGUSSON, ROBERT, 1750-1774
Holmes, D. T. French Essays on British Poets: Robert Fergusson, Pope, Wordsworth. 1979. Repr. of 1902 ed. lib. bdg. 25.00 (ISBN 0-8495-2329-X). Arden Lib.
MacLaine, Allan H. Robert Fergusson. LC 65-18225. (English Authors Ser.). 1965. lib. bdg. 12.95x (ISBN 0-8057-1192-9). Irvington.

FERLINGHETTI, LAWRENCE, 1919-
Morgan, Bill. Lawrence Ferlinghetti: A Comprehensive Bibliography. 1981. lib. bdg. 40.00 (ISBN 0-8240-9362-3). Garland Pub.

FERMAT, PIERRE DE, 1601-1665
Vekerdi, Laszlo. Letters on Probability. Renyi, Alfred, tr. from Hung. LC 74-179559. (Waynebooks Ser: No. 33). 112p. (Eng.). 1973. pap. 3.95x (ISBN 0-8143-1465-1). Wayne St U Pr.

FERMAT'S THEOREM
Klein, Felix. Famous Problems of Elementary Geometry & Other Monographs, 4 vols. in 1. Incl. From Determinant to Tensor. Sheppard, William F; Introduction to Combinatory Analysis. MacMahon, Percy A; Fermat's Last Theorem. Mordell, Louis J; Famous Problems of Elementary Geometry. Klein, Felix. (gr. 9 up). 1956. 9.95 (ISBN 0-8284-0108-X). Chelsea Pub.
Munk, Max M. Congruence Surds & Fermat's Last Theorem. 1977. 7.00 (ISBN 0-533-02824-8). Vantage.
Ribenboim, P. Thirteen Lectures on Fermant's Last Theorem. 1980. 25.20 (ISBN 0-387-90432-8). Springer-Verlag.

FERMENTATION
see also Bacteriology; Brewing; Enzymes; Sugars; Wine and Wine Making;
also particular groups of organisms involved in fermentation, e.g. Bacteria, Molds (Botany)
Armiger, William B., ed. Computer Applications in Fermentation Technology, No. 9. (Biotechnology & Bioengineering Symposium). 398p. 1980. pap. 30.95 (ISBN 0-471-05746-0, Pub. by Wiley-Interscience). Wiley.
Blakebrough, N., ed. Biochemical & Biological Engineering Science, 2 Vols. Vol. 1. 1967. o. p. 32.00 (ISBN 0-12-103601-4); Vol. 2. 1969. 48.50 (ISBN 0-12-103602-2). Acad Pr.
Business Communications, ed. Fermentation Products: Processes & New Developments, C-018. 1980. 800.00 (ISBN 0-89336-222-0). BCC.
Carr, J. G. Biological Principles in Fermentation. 1968. pap. text ed. 3.50x (ISBN 0-435-61152-6). Heinemann Ed.
Gastineau, Clifford F., et al, eds. Fermented Food Beverages in Nutrition. (Nutrition Foundation Ser.). 1979. 48.00 (ISBN 0-12-277050-1). Acad Pr.
Gray, William D. The Use of Fungi As Food & in Food Processing, Pt. 1. (Monotopic Reprint Ser.). 1971. 11.95 (ISBN 0-87819-104-6). CRC Pr.
Hollaender, A., et al, eds. Trends in the Biology of Fermentations for Fuels & Chemicals. (Basic Life Sciences Ser.). 580p. 1981. 65.00 (ISBN 0-306-40752-3, Plenum Pr). Plenum Pub.
Hunderfund, Richard. Wines, Spirits & Fermentations. (Illus.). 192p. (Orig.). 1981. price not set. Star Pub CA.
Jefferis, R. R. Workshop Computer Applications in Fermentation Technology, Nineteen Seventy-Six. (Illus.). 1977. pap. 38.30 (ISBN 3-527-25719-5). Verlag Chemie.
Malek, Ivan & Fencl, Zdenek, eds. Continuous Cultivation of Microorganisms: Proceedings. 1970. 63.00 (ISBN 0-12-466260-9). Acad Pr.
Pasteur, Louis. Studies on Fermentation. (Illus.). 1879. 22.00 (ISBN 0-527-69930-6). Kraus Repr.
Pederson, Carl S. Microbiology of Food Fermentations. 2nd ed. (Illus.). 1979. text ed. 32.00 (ISBN 0-87055-277-5). AVI.
Peppler, Henry J., ed. Microbial Technology. LC 77-796. (Illus.). 464p. 1977. Repr. of 1967 ed. lib. bdg. 21.00 (ISBN 0-88275-538-2). Krieger.
Peppler, Henry J. & Perlman, David, eds. Microbial Technology, Vol. 2: Fermentation Technology. 2nd ed. 1979. 47.00 (ISBN 0-12-551502-2); 85.50 set (ISBN 0-686-77091-9). Acad Pr.
Perlman. Fermentation: 1977: Annual Reports. 1977. 34.00 (ISBN 0-12-040301-3). Acad Pr.
Perlman, D., ed. Fermentation Advances. 1969. 56.00 (ISBN 0-12-550850-6). Acad Pr.
Perlman, D. & Tsao, G. T., eds. Annual Reports on Fermentation Processes. 1978. 28.00 (ISBN 0-12-040302-1). Acad Pr.
--Annual Reports on Fermentation Processes, Vol. 3. (Serial Publication). 1979. 28.50 (ISBN 0-12-040303-X). Acad Pr.
Solomons, G. L. Materials & Methods in Fermentation. 1970. 50.50 (ISBN 0-12-654450-6). Acad Pr.
Wang, Daniel I., et al. Fermentation & Enzyme Technology. LC 78-7596. (Techniques in Pure & Applied Microbiology Ser.). 1979. 33.50 (ISBN 0-471-91945-4, Pub. by Wiley-Interscience). Wiley.
Whitaker, John R., ed. Food Related Enzymes. LC 74-20861. (Advances in Chemistry Ser: No. 136). 1974. 30.00 (ISBN 0-8412-0209-5). Am Chemical.
Wiseman, Alan, ed. Topics in Enzyme & Fermentation Biotechnology, Vol. 2. LC 76-25441. 1978. 41.95 (ISBN 0-470-99318-9). Vol. 2. Halsted Pr.
--Topics in Enzyme & Fermentation Biotechnology, Vol. 4. (Topics in Enzyme & Fermentation Biotechnology Ser.). 242p. 1980. 76.95x (ISBN 0-470-26922-7). Halsted Pr.
Wright, Barbara, ed. Control Mechanisms in Respiration & Fermentation. LC 63-9257. 366p. 1963. 16.00 (ISBN 0-685-91064-4, Pub. by Wiley). Krieger.

FERMENTATION GUM
see Dextran

FERMENTS
see Enzymes

FERMI, ENRICO, 1901-1954
Lichello, Robert. Enrico Fermi: Father of the Atomic Bomb. Rahmas, D. Steve, ed. LC 70-185667. (Outstanding Personalities Ser.: No. 11). 32p. (Orig.). (gr. 7-12). 1972. lib. bdg. 2.95 incl. catalog cards (ISBN 0-87157-511-6); pap. 1.50 vinyl laminated covers (ISBN 0-87157-011-4). SamHar Pr.
Segre, Emilio. Enrico Fermi, Physicist. LC 71-107424. (Illus.). 1970. 12.50x (ISBN 0-226-74472-8). U of Chicago Pr.
--Enrico Fermi, Physicist. LC 71-107424. 288p. 1972. pap. 2.95 (ISBN 0-226-74473-6, P468, Phoen). U of Chicago Pr.

FERMI SURFACES
Bogolyubov, N. N. A Method for Studying-Model Hamiltonians. 180p. 1972. text ed. 37.00 (ISBN 0-08-016742-X). Pergamon.
Cracknell, A. P. & Wong, K. C. Fermi Surface: Its Concept, Determination & Use in the Physics of Metals. (Monographs on the Physics & Chemistry of Materials). (Illus.). 558p. 1973. 89.00x (ISBN 0-19-851330-5). Oxford U Pr.

FERMIONS
Fries & Wess, eds. New Phenomena in Lepton-Hadron Physics. (NATO Advanced Study Institutes, Ser. B, Physics: Vol. 49). 1979. 49.50 (ISBN 0-306-40301-3, Plenum Pr). Plenum Pub.
Iachello, F., ed. Interacting Bose-Fermi Systems in Nuclei. LC 80-24447. (Ettore Majorana International Science (Physical Sciences) Ser.: Vol. 10). 412p. 1981. text ed. 49.50 (ISBN 0-306-40733-7, Plenum Pr). Plenum Pub.

FERN ALLIES
see Pteridophyta

FERNALD, ALVIN
Hicks, Clifford B. Alvin Fernald: Foreign Trader. (gr. 4-6). 1972. pap. 1.50 (ISBN 0-671-29941-7). Archway.

FERNANDO 5TH, EL CATOLICO, KING OF SPAIN, 1452-1516
Fernandez-Armesto, Felipe. Ferdinand & Isabella. LC 73-14366. (Illus.). 232p. 1975. 15.00 (ISBN 0-8008-2621-3). Taplinger.
McKendrick, Melveena. Ferdinand & Isabella. LC 68-14974. (Horizon Caravel Bks.). 1544p. (YA) (gr. 7 up). 1968. PLB 12.89 (ISBN 0-06-024165-9, HarpJ). Har-Row.

FERNANDO, INFANTE OF SPAIN, 1609-1641
Rubens, Peter P. Pompa Introitus: Ferdinandi Austriaci Cum Antiverpiam Adventu Suo Bearet, 15 Kal. Maii Anno 1665. LC 68-21225. (Illus., Lat). 1969. 60.00 (ISBN 0-405-08902-3). Arno.

FERNEL, JEAN, 1497-1558
Sherrington, Charles S. Man on His Nature. 1951. 39.95 (ISBN 0-521-06436-8); pap. 11.95x (ISBN 0-521-09203-5). Cambridge U Pr.

FERNS
see also Cryptogams
Ayrey, Betty. Ferns: Facts & Fantasy. (Illus.). 1979. 6.95x (ISBN 0-85091-062-5, Pub. by Lothian); pap. 4.95x (ISBN 0-85091-063-3). Intl Schol Bk Serv.
Beddome, R. H. Ferns of Southern India. 1969. Repr. of 1873 ed. 45.00 (ISBN 0-934454-31-0). Lubrecht & Cramer.
--Handbook to the Ferns of British India Ceylon & Malay Peninsula. 1969. Repr. of 1883 ed. 16.00 (ISBN 0-934454-47-7). Lubrecht & Cramer.
Billington, Cecil. Ferns of Michigan. LC 52-12080. (Bulletin Ser.: No. 32). (Illus.). 240p. 1952. text ed. 9.00x (ISBN 0-87737-012-5). Cranbrook.
Birdseye, Clarence & Birdseye, Eleanor. Growing Woodland Plants. (Illus.). 1972. pap. 3.00 (ISBN 0-486-20661-0). Dover.
Blatter, E. Ferns of Bombay. 1979. 15.00x (ISBN 0-89955-261-7, Pub. by Intl Bk Dist). Intl Schol Bk Serv.
Brown, D. F. A Monographic Study of Thr Fern Genus Woodsia. (Illus.). 1964. 30.00 (ISBN 3-7682-5416-X). Lubrecht & Cramer.
Brownlie, G. The Pteridophyte Flora of Fiji. (Beihefte Zur Nova Hedwigia 55). 1977. lib. bdg. 100.00x (ISBN 3-7682-5455-0). Lubrecht & Cramer.
Clarke, Charles B. A Review of the Ferns of Northern India: With an Index of the Species & 36 Plates. (Illus.). 1978. Repr. of 1880 ed. 28.00x (ISBN 0-89955-303-6, Pub. by Intl Bk Dist). Intl Schol Bk Serv.
Clifford, H. T. & Constantine, J. Ferns, Fern Allies & Conifers of Australia. (Illus.). 150p. 1980. text ed. 29.95x (ISBN 0-7022-1447-7). U of Queensland Pr.
Cobb, Boughton. A Field Guide to the Ferns & Their Related Families. (Peterson Field Guide Ser.). 1977. 10.95 (ISBN 0-395-07560-2); pap. 6.95 (ISBN 0-395-19431-8). HM.
Crittenden, Mabel. The Fern Book. LC 77-90021. (Illus.). 1978. pap. 4.95 (ISBN 0-89087-227-9). Celestial Arts.
Davenport, Elaine. Ferns for Modern Living. Wilson, Helen V., ed. (Modern Living Ser.). (Illus.). 80p. (Orig.). 1977. pap. 2.95 (ISBN 0-89484-004-5, 10105). Merchants Pub Co.
Dean, Blanche E. Ferns. (Southern Regional Nature Ser). (Illus.). 1969. pap. 8.95 (ISBN 0-87651-019-5). Southern U Pr.
Dhir, K. K. Ferns of the Northwestern Himalayas. (Bibliotheca Pteridologica 1). (Illus.). 1979. pap. text ed. 20.00x (ISBN 3-7682-1222-X). Lubrecht & Cramer.
Dhir, K. K. & Sood, A. Fern Flora of Mussoorie Hills. (Bibliotheca Pteridologica 2). (Illus.). 1981. pap. text ed. 20.00x (ISBN 3-7682-1232-7). Lubrecht & Cramer.
Dyer, A. F., ed. The Experimental Biology of Ferns. (Experimental Biology Ser.). 1979. 99.50 (ISBN 0-12-226350-2). Acad Pr.
Fee, A. L. Memoires sur la Famille des Fougeres: 1844-66, 11parts in 1 vol. (Illus.). 1966. 350.00 (ISBN 3-7682-0447-2). Lubrecht & Cramer.
Ferns. 1.95 (ISBN 0-686-21153-7). Bklyn Botanic.
Foster, F. Gordon. Ferns to Know & Grow. rev. ed. 1976. pap. 6.95 (ISBN 0-8015-2600-0, Hawthorn). Dutton.
Frankel, Edward. Ferns: A Natural History. (Illus.). 256p. 1981. 17.50 (ISBN 0-8289-0429-4). Greene.
Hires, Clara S. Spores, Ferns, Microscopic Illusions Analyzed, Vol. 1. LC 65-19563. 1965. 22.50 (ISBN 0-686-21423-4). Mistaire.
--Spores. Ferns. Microscopic Illusions Analyzed, Vol 2. LC 65-19563. (Illus.). 1978. 50.00 (ISBN 0-686-23109-0). Mistaire.
Hooker, W. J. Species Filicum, 5 vols. 1970. Repr. of 1864 ed. 250.00 (ISBN 3-7682-0690-4). Lubrecht & Cramer.
Hope, C. W. The Ferns of North Western India. (Illus.). 1978. Repr. 21.50x (ISBN 0-89955-262-5, Pub. by Intl Bk Dist). Intl Schol Bk Serv.
Hoshizaki, Barbara J. Fern Growers Manual. 1975. 15.95 (ISBN 0-394-49687-6). Knopf.
--Fern Growers Manual. LC 75-8220. (Illus.). 1979. 15.95 (ISBN 0-394-49687-6); pap. 7.95 (ISBN 0-394-73774-1). Knopf.
Jones, David L. & Clemesha, Stephen C. Australian Ferns & Fern Allies. rev. ed. (Illus.). 232p. (YA) 1981. 33.50 (ISBN 0-589-50265-4, Pub. by Reed Books Australia). C E Tuttle.
Kepler, Angela K. Common Ferns of Luquillo Forest. Zebrowski, John, ed. LC 72-91603. (Illus.). 125p. 1975. 15.00 (ISBN 0-913480-06-1); spanish ed. 15.00 (ISBN 0-913480-07-X); pap. 5.00 (ISBN 0-913480-08-8); pap. 5.00 Spanish ed. (ISBN 0-913480-09-6). Inter Am U Pr.
Lakela, Olga & Long, Robert W. Ferns of Florida. LC 76-18950. (Illus.). 1976. 10.00 (ISBN 0-916224-03-1). Banyan Bks.
McVaugh, Rogers & Pyron, Joseph H. Ferns of Georgia. LC 52-882. (Illus.). 195p. 1951. 12.00 (ISBN 0-8203-0209-0). U of Ga Pr.
Mickel, John & Fiore, Evelyn. The Home Gardener's Book of Ferns. LC 78-14418. (Illus.). 1979. 12.95 (ISBN 0-03-045736-X); pap. 7.95 (ISBN 0-03-045741-6). HR&W.
Mickel, John T. How to Know the Ferns & Fern Allies. 250p. 1979. write for info. wire coil (ISBN 0-697-04770-9); wire coil 6.95x (ISBN 0-697-04771-7). Wm C Brown.
Mohlenbrock, Robert H. Ferns. LC 65-16533. (Illustrated Flora of Illinois Ser). (Illus.). 207p. 1967. 15.00x (ISBN 0-8093-0251-9). S Ill U Pr.
Parsons, Frances T. How to Know the Ferns. (Illus.). 7.00 (ISBN 0-8446-2707-0). Peter Smith.
--How to Know the Ferns: A Guide to the Names, Haunts, & Habits of Our Common Ferns. 2nd ed. (Illus.). 1899. pap. 2.75 (ISBN 0-486-20740-4). Dover.
Perl, P. Ferns. (Encyclopedia of Gardening Ser.). (gr. 6 up). 1977. PLB 11.97 (ISBN 0-8094-2559-9). Silver.

Perl, Philip. Ferns. (Encyclopedia of Gardening). 1977. 12.95 (ISBN 0-8094-2558-0). Time-Life.
Petrik-Ott, A. J. The Pteridophytes of Kansas, Nebraska, South Dakota & North Dakota, USA Nova Hedwigia Beiheft, No. 61. 1979. lib. bdg. 50.00 (ISBN 3-7682-5461-5). Lubrecht & Cramer.
Piggott, Audrey. Heinemann Guide to Common Epiphytic Ferns 0f Malaysia & Singapore. (Orig.). 1979. pap. text ed. 8.95 (ISBN 0-686-74446-2). Heinemann Ed.
Shaver, Jesse M. Ferns of Eastern Central States. Orig. Title: Ferns of Tennessee. (Illus.). 1970. pap. 4.00 (ISBN 0-486-22541-0). Dover.
--Ferns of the East Central States: With Special Reference to Tennessee. (Illus.). 7.50 (ISBN 0-8446-0908-0). Peter Smith.
Small, John K. Ferns of the Southeastern States. (Illus.). 1964. Repr. of 1938 ed. 16.25 (ISBN 0-02-852400-4). Hafner.
--Ferns of the Vicinity of New York. (Illus.). 288p. 1975. pap. 4.50 (ISBN 0-486-23118-6). Dover.
--Ferns of the Vicinity of New York. (Illus.). 6.00 (ISBN 0-8446-5244-X). Peter Smith.
Tilton, George H. The Fern Lover's Companion: Guide for the Northeastern States & Canada. 1978. Repr. of 1923 ed. lib. bdg. 30.00 (ISBN 0-8495-5118-8). Arden Lib.
Tryon, Rolla M., Jr. The Ferns of Minnesota. rev. ed. LC 80-10368. (Illus.). 1980. 15.00x (ISBN 0-8166-0932-2); pap. 6.95 (ISBN 0-8166-0935-7). U of Minn Pr.
Wharton, Mary E. & Barbour, Roger W. A Guide to the Wildflowers & Ferns of Kentucky. LC 79-132833. (Illus.). 352p. 1971. 16.00 (ISBN 0-8131-1234-6). U Pr of Ky.
Wiley, Farida A. Ferns of Northeastern United States. (Illus.). 4.00 (ISBN 0-8446-4840-X). Peter Smith.
--Ferns of the Northeastern United States. (Illus.). 108p. 1973. pap. 1.75 (ISBN 0-486-22946-7). Dover.

FERRARA-HISTORY

Corner, Paul. Fascism in Ferrara Nineteen Fifteen to Nineteen Twenty-Five. (Oxford Historical Monographs). 312p. 1975. 36.00x (ISBN 0-19-821857-5). Oxford U Pr.
Gardner, Edmund G. Dukes & Poets in Ferrara: A Study in the Poetry, Religion & Politics of the 15th & Early 16th Centuries. LC 68-25235. (Studies in Italian Literature, No. 46). 1969. Repr. of 1904 ed. lib. bdg. 64.95 (ISBN 0-8383-0943-7). Haskell.
--Dukes & Poets of Ferrara: A Story in the Poetry, Religion & Politics of Fifteenth & Early Sixteenth Centuries. LC 78-145033. xiv, 578p. 1972. Repr. of 1904 ed. 32.00 (ISBN 0-403-00776-3). Scholarly.
Gundersheimer, Werner L. Ferrara: The Style of a Renaissance Despotism. LC 72-6518. 368p. 1973. 22.00 (ISBN 0-691-05210-7). Princeton U Pr.

FERRARA-FLORENCE, COUNCIL OF, 1438-1439

Halecki, Oscar. From Florence to Brest, 1439-1596. 2nd ed. 1968. 22.50 (ISBN 0-208-00702-4, Archon). Shoe String.
Ostroumoff, Ivan N. The History of the Council of Florence. 189p. 1972. pap. 6.00 (ISBN 0-913026-03-4). St Nectarios.

FERRARI, ENZO, 1898-

Lauda, Niki. My Years with Ferrari. LC 78-7559. (Illus.). 1978. 13.95 (ISBN 0-87938-059-4). Motorbooks Intl.

FERRARI (AUTOMOBILE)

see Automobiles, Foreign-Types-Ferrari

FERRATES

see Ferrites (Magnetic Materials)

FERRER GUARDIA, FRANCISCO, 1859-1909

Archer, William. Life, Trial & Death of Francisco Ferrer. 59.95 (ISBN 0-8490-0540-X). Gordon Pr.

FERRETS

see also Weasels

Brodie, Iain. Ferrets & Ferreting. (Illus.). 1979. 9.95 (ISBN 0-7137-0903-0, Pub. by Blandford Pr England). Sterling.
Harding, A. R. Ferret Facts & Fancies. (Illus.). 214p. pap. 3.00 (ISBN 0-936622-04-0). A R Harding Pub.
Marchington, John. Pugs & Drummers: Ferrets & Rabbits in Britain. (Illus.). 224p. 1978. 15.95 (ISBN 0-571-11204-8, Pub. by Faber & Faber). Merrimack Bk Serv.
Roberts, Mervin F. All About Ferrets. (Illus.). 1977. pap. 2.95 (ISBN 0-87666-914-3, PS-754). TFH Pubns.
Taylor, Joan & Treon, Ray. Success with Ferrets. Van de John, Richard, ed. (Mini Pet Reference Ser.: No. 2). (Illus.). 1977. pap. 2.95 (ISBN 0-915096-05-6). Palmetto Pub.
Wellstead, Graham. Ferrets & Ferreting. LC 80-68900. (Illus.). 160p. 1981. 19.95 (ISBN 0-7153-8013-3). David & Charles.
Winsted, Wendy. Ferrets. (Illus.). 96p. 1981. 2.95 (ISBN 0-87666-930-5, KW-074). TFH Pubns.

FERRIER, SUSAN EDMONSTONE, 1782-1854

Grant, Aline. Susan Ferrier of Edinburgh: A Biography. 174p. 1957. 4.95 (ISBN 0-8040-0286-X). Swallow.

FERRIES

Downs, Art. Paddlewheels on the Frontier. (Illus.). 160p. 11.95 (ISBN 0-686-74128-5). Superior Pub.
Graves, Al, et al. Narrow-Gauge to the Redwoods: The Story of the North Pacific Coast Railroad & San Francisco Bay Paddle-Wheel Ferries. 2nd rev. ed. 15.00 (ISBN 0-87046-010-2). Trans-Anglo.
Hilton, George W. The Great Lakes Car Ferries. LC 62-17073. (Illus.). 1962. 9.95 (ISBN 0-8310-7030-7). Howell-North.
Huntley, James L. Ferryboats in Idaho. LC 77-78212. (Illus.). 1979. pap. 7.95 (ISBN 0-87004-263-7). Caxton.
McNeill, Donald B. Irish Passenger Steamship Services Vol. 1: North of Ireland. LC 69-10861. (Illus.). 1969. 11.95x (ISBN 0-678-05610-2). Kelley.
Martin, Nancy. River Ferries. 144p. 1981. 30.00x (ISBN 0-900963-99-9, Pub. by Terence Dalton England). State Mutual Bk.
Narrow Gauge to the Redwoods. 15.00 (ISBN 0-685-83361-5). Chatham Pub CA.
Phillips, G. A. Thames Crossings: Bridges, Tunnels & Ferries. LC 81-65954. (Illus.). 288p. 1981. 36.00 (ISBN 0-7153-8202-0). David & Charles.
Ruby, Robert H. & Brown, John A. Ferryboats on the Columbia River. LC 74-75658. (Illus.). 1974. 17.95 (ISBN 0-87564-616-6). Superior Pub.
Rudman, Jack. Ferry Terminal Supervisor. (Career Examination Ser.: C-2142). (Cloth bdg. avail. on request). 1977. pap. 8.00 (ISBN 0-8373-2142-5). Natl Learning.

FERRIMAGNETISM

Brown, William F., Jr. Micromagnetics. LC 78-2342. 152p. 1978. Repr. of 1963 ed. lib. bdg. 11.50 (ISBN 0-88275-665-6). Krieger.

FERRISS, HUGH

Leich, Jean F. & Goldberger, Paul. Architectural Visions: The Drawing of Hugh Ferriss. (Illus.). 1980. 19.95 (ISBN 0-8230-7054-9, Whitney Lib). Watson-Guptill.

FERRITE

see also Ferrites (Magnetic Materials)

FERRITES (MAGNETIC MATERIALS)

Hoshino, Y., et al, eds. Ferrites. (Illus.). 1971. 65.00 (ISBN 0-8391-0623-8). Univ Park.
Standley, K. J. Oxide Magnetic Materials. 2nd ed. (Monographs on the Physics & Chemistry of Materials). (Illus.). 265p. 1972. 55.00x (ISBN 0-19-851327-5). Oxford U Pr.
Toughness of Ferritic Stainless Steels. (Special Technical Publications Ser.). 348p. 1980. 32.50x (ISBN 0-686-76090-5, 706, 04-706000-02). ASTM.
Von Aulock, Wilhelm H., ed. Handbook of Microwave Ferrite Materials. (Illus.). 1965. 51.00 (ISBN 0-12-723350-4). Acad Pr.
Waldron, R. A. Ferrites: An Introduction for Microwave Engineers. 265p. 1961. 12.00 (ISBN 0-442-09267-9, Pub. by Van Nos Reinhold). Krieger.

FERROCEMENT

see Reinforced Concrete

FERROCEMENT BOATS

see Concrete Boats

FERROELECTRIC CRYSTALS

Fridkin, V. M. Photoferroelectrics. (Ser. in Solid-State Sciences: Vol. 9). (Illus.). 1979. 34.10 (ISBN 0-387-09418-0). Springer-Verlag.
Gurevich, Y. M. Electrical Conductivity of Ferroelectrics. 368p. 1971. 35.00x (ISBN 0-7065-1172-7, Pub. by IPST). Intl Schol Bk Serv.
Lines, M. E. & Glass, A. M. Principles & Applications of Ferroelectrics & Related Materials. (Illus.). 1977. pap. 29.95x (ISBN 0-19-852003-4). Oxford U Pr.

FERROELECTRICITY

see also Domain Structure

Blinc, R. & Zeks, B. Soft Modes in Ferroelectrics & Antiferroelectrics. LC 73-88156. (Selected Topics in Solid State Physics: Vol. 13). 317p. 1975. 44.00 (ISBN 0-444-10582-4, North-Holland). Elsevier.
Burfoot, J. C. Ferroelectrics: An Introduction to the Physical Principles. 1967. 10.95x (ISBN 0-442-31161-3). Van Nos Reinhold.
Grindlay, J. An Introduction to the Phenomenological Theory of Ferroelectricity. LC 72-90455. 1970. 36.00 (ISBN 0-08-006362-4). Pergamon.
Hellwege, K. H., ed. Landolt-Boernstein Numerical Data & Functional Relationships in Science & Technology, New Series, Group 3: Crystal & Solid State Physics, Vols. 1-6. Incl. Vol. 1. Elastic, Piezoelectric, Piezooptic & Electrooptic Constants of Crystals. Bechman, R. & Hearmon, R. F. x, 160p. 1966. 64.90 (ISBN 0-387-03594-X); Vol. 2. Elastic, Piezoelectric, Piezooptic, Electrooptic Constants, & Non-Linear Dielectric Susceptibilities of Crystals. Bechman, R., et al. (Illus.). ix, 232p. 1969. 121.00 (ISBN 0-387-04594-5); Vol. 3. Ferro- & Antiferroelectric Substances. Mitsui, T., et al. (Illus.). viii, 584p. 1969. 268.50 (ISBN 0-387-04595-3); Vol. 4, Pt. A. Magnetic & Other Properties of Oxides & Related Compounds. Goodenough, J. B., et al. (Illus.). xv, 367p. 1970. 182.90 (ISBN 0-387-04898-7); Vol. 4, Pt. B: Magnetic & Other Properties of Oxides & Related Compounds. Bonnenberg, F., et al. (Illus.). xvi, 666p. 1970. 330.40 (ISBN 0-387-05176-7); Vol. 5. Structure Data of Organic Crystals, 2 vols. Schudt, E. & Weitz, G. (Illus.). 1971. Set. 601.80 (ISBN 0-387-05177-5); Vol. 6. Structure Data of Elements & Intermetallic Phases. Eckerlin, P. & Kandler, H. 1971. 486.80 (ISBN 0-387-05500-2). LC 62-53136. Springer-Verlag.
Kanzig, Werner. Ferroelectrics & Antiferroelectrics. (Solid State Reprints Ser). 1964. 14.00 (ISBN 0-12-608462-9). Acad Pr.
Lefkowitz, I. & Taylor, G., eds. Proceedings of the Nineteen Seventy-Five Ieee Symposium on Applications of Ferroelectrics (Albuquerque) 1976. 252.50x (ISBN 0-677-40195-7). Gordon.
--Proceedings of the Third European Meeting on Ferroelectrics (Zurich, 1975) 1976. 420.75x (ISBN 0-677-40205-8). Gordon.
--Proceedings of the Third International Meeting on Ferroelectrics, Edingurgh, 1973. 1974. 252.50 (ISBN 0-677-40215-5). Gordon.
Lines, Malcom E. & Glass, Alastair M. Principles & Applications of Ferreolectrics & Related Materials. (International Series of Monographs on Physics). (Illus.). 1977. 98.00x (ISBN 0-19-851286-4). Oxford U Pr.
Mitsui, T. An Introduction to the Physics of Ferroelectrics. (Ferroelectricity & Related Phenomena Ser.). 1976. 68.75 (ISBN 0-677-30600-8). Gordon.
Mitsui, T., et al. Ferro & Antiferroelectric Substances. Hellwege, K. H. & Hellwege, A. M., eds. LC 62-53136. (Landolt-Bornstein Ser.: Group 3, Vol. 9). (Illus.). vii, 496p. 1975. 298.00 (ISBN 0-387-06580-6). Springer-Verlag.
Novakovic, L. The Pseudo-Spin Method in Magnetism & Ferroelectricity. 200p. 1976. text ed. 34.00 (ISBN 0-08-018060-4). Pergamon.

FERROELECTRICS

see Ferroelectric Crystals

FERROMAGNETIC DOMAIN

see Domain Structure

FERROMAGNETISM

see also Domain Structure

DeMaw, M. Ferromagnetic-Core Design & Application Handbook. 1980. 19.95 (ISBN 0-13-314088-1). P-H.
McCoy, Barry & Wu, Tai T. The Two-Dimensional Ising Model. LC 72-188972. (Illus.). 1973. 25.00x (ISBN 0-674-91440-6). Harvard U Pr.
Novakovic, L. The Pseudo-Spin Method in Magnetism & Ferroelectricity. 200p. 1976. text ed. 34.00 (ISBN 0-08-018060-4). Pergamon.
Odel, T. H. Ferromagnetodynamics: The Dynamics of Magnetic Bubbles Domains & Domain Walls. LC 80-25331. 232p. 1981. 54.95 (ISBN 0-470-27084-5). Halsted Pr.
Sodha, M. S. & Srivastava, N. C. Microwave Propagation in Ferrimagnetics. 350p. 1981. text ed. 45.00 (ISBN 0-306-40716-7, Plenum Pr). Plenum Pub.
Turov, E. A. & Petrov, M. P. Nuclear Magnetic Resonance in Ferro & Antiferromagnetics. 206p. 1972. 54.95 (ISBN 0-470-89323-0). Halsted Pr.
Vonsovskii, S. V., ed. Ferromagnetic Resonance. 1966. 34.00 (ISBN 0-08-011027-4); pap. 21.00 (ISBN 0-08-013670-2). Pergamon.

FERROUS METAL INDUSTRIES

see Iron Industry and Trade; Steel Industry and Trade

FERRY, JULES FRANCOIS CAMILLE, 1832-1893

Power, Thomas F., Jr. Jules Ferry & the Renaissance of French Imperialism. 1966. lib. bdg. 15.00x (ISBN 0-374-96555-2). Octagon.

FERTILITY

see also Heterosis

Bollack, C. G. & Clavert, A., eds. Epididymis & Fertility: Biology & Pathology. (Progress in Reproductive Biology Ser.: Vol. 8). (Illus.). viii, 192p. 1981. 58.75 (ISBN 3-8055-2157-X). S Karger.
Chowdhury, R. H. Social Aspects of Fertility. 200p. 1981. text ed. 22.50x (ISBN 0-7069-1211-X, Pub by Vikas India). Advent NY.
Cochrane, Susan H. Fertility & Education: What Do We Really Know? LC 78-26070. (World Bank Staff Occasional Paper Ser: No. 26). (Orig.). 1978. pap. text ed. 6.95x (ISBN 0-8018-2140-1). Johns Hopkins.
Cunningham, G. R., et al, eds. Regulation of Male Fertility. (Clinics in Andrology Ser.: No. 5). (Illus.). 245p. 1981. PLB 68.50 (ISBN 90-247-2373-6, Pub. by Martinus Nijhoff Netherlands). Kluwer Boston.
Food & Nutrition Board. Nutrition and Fertility Interrelationships. 1975. pap. 4.50 (ISBN 0-309-02341-6). Natl Acad Pr.
Freedman, Ronald & Coombs, Lolagene C. Cross-Cultural Comparisons: Data on Two Factors in Fertility Behavior. LC 74-80928. 1974. pap. text ed. 3.95 (ISBN 0-87834-022-X). Population Coun.
Hawthorn, G. Sociology of Fertility. 1969. pap. text ed. 2.45x (ISBN 0-02-974030-4). Macmillan.
Ingelman-Sundberg, Axel & Lunell, Nils-Olov, eds. Current Problems in Fertility. LC 76-145405. 244p. 1971. 29.50 (ISBN 0-306-30522-4, Plenum Pr). Plenum Pub.
International Planned Parenthood Federation. Handbook of Infertility. Kleinman, Ronald L. & Senayake, Pramilla, eds. (Illus.). 58p. (Orig.). 1979. pap. 6.50x (ISBN 0-86089-034-1). Intl Pubns Serv.
Laing, J. A., ed. Fertility & Infertility in Domestic Animals. 33rd ed. (Illus.). 262p. 1979. pap. text ed. 28.50 (ISBN 0-8121-0723-3). Lea & Febiger.
Mishell, Daniel R., Jr., ed. Advances in Fertility Research, Vol. 1. 225p. 1981. text ed. 24.50 (ISBN 0-89004-577-1). Raven.
Newton, J. R., et al. Workshop on Fertility Control. (Royal Society of Medicine International Congress & Symposium Ser.: No. 31). 80p. 1980. pap. 17.00 (ISBN 0-8089-1297-6). Grune.
Potts, Malcolm & Selman, Peter. Society & Fertility. 384p. 1979. 35.00x (ISBN 0-686-75500-6, Pub. by Macdonald & Evans). State Mutual Bk.
--Society & Fertility. (Illus.). 384p. 1979. 27.50x (ISBN 0-7121-1960-4, Pub. by Macdonald & Evans England). Intl Ideas.
Roberts, D. F. & Chester, R., eds. Changing Patterns of Conception & Fertility. 1981. price not set (ISBN 0-12-589640-9). Acad Pr.
Robertson, W. B. The Endometrium. (Postgraduate Pathology Ser.). 1981. text ed. 59.95 (ISBN 0-407-00171-9). Butterworth.
Rothberg, R. I. & Rabb, T. K. Marriage & Fertility. (Studies in Interdisciplinary History Ser.). 1980. 20.00 (ISBN 0-691-05319-7); pap. 5.95 (ISBN 0-691-00781-0). Princeton U Pr.
Shain, Rochelle & Pauerstein, Carl J., eds. Fertility Control: Biologic & Behavioral Aspects. (Illus.). 500p. 1980. 35.00 (ISBN 0-06-142376-9, Harper Medical). Har-Row.
Sivin, Irving. Contraception & Fertility Change in the International Postpartum Program. LC 74-75361. 1974. pap. text ed. 3.95 (ISBN 0-87834-020-3). Population Coun.
Speroff, Leon, et al. Clinical Gynecologic Endocrinology & Infertility. 2nd ed. (Illus.). 444p. 1978. 35.00 (ISBN 0-683-07894-1). Williams & Wilkins.
Taymor, Melvin L. Infertility. LC 77-18735. 224p. 1978. 29.50 (ISBN 0-8089-1075-2). Grune.
Wrong, Dennis H. Class Fertility Trends in Western Nations. Zuckerman, Harriet & Merton, Robert K., eds. LC 79-9039. (Dissertations on Sociology Ser.). 1980. lib. bdg. 23.00x (ISBN 0-405-13006-6). Arno.
Zondek & Zondek, eds. Sixth World Congress on Fertility & Sterility: Proceedings. 1970. 80.25x (ISBN 0-677-62100-0). Gordon.

FERTILITY, EFFECT OF DRUGS ON

see also Oral Contraceptives

FERTILITY, HUMAN

see also subdivision Population under names of countries

Aitken-Swan, Jean. Fertility Control & the Medical Profession. 238p. 1977. 30.00x (ISBN 0-85664-463-3, Pub by Croom Helm Ltd England). Biblio Dist.
Arriaga, Eduardo E. Mortality Decline & Its Demographic Effects in Latin America. LC 76-4852. (Population Monograph Ser.: No. 6). (Illus.). 1976. Repr. of 1970 ed. lib. bdg. 34.75x (ISBN 0-8371-8827-X, ARLT). Greenwood.
Barker, Graham H. Your Search for Fertility: A Sympathetic Guide to Achieving Pregnancy for Childless Couples. LC 80-81515. (Illus.). 208p. 1981. 9.95 (ISBN 0-688-00184-X). Morrow.
Bebarta, Prafulla C. Family Type & Fertility in India. LC 76-4268. (Illus.). 224p. 1977. 8.95 (ISBN 0-8158-0339-7). Chris Mass.
Behrman, S. J. & Kistner, Robert W., eds. Progress in Infertility. 2nd ed. 1975. 67.50 (ISBN 0-316-08769-6). Little.

Benagiano, Giuseppe. Fertility Control. (Comprehensive Endocrinology Ser.). 1981. write for info. (ISBN 0-89004-464-3, 409). Raven.
Benagiano, Giuseppe & Diczfalusy, Egon, eds. Endocrine Mechanisms in Fertility Regulation. (Comprehensive Endocrinology Ser.). 1981. text ed. price not set (ISBN 0-89004-464-3). Raven.
Bouvier, Leon & Rao, Sethu. Socioreligious Factors in Fertility Decline. LC 75-26602. 192p. 1975. text ed. 17.50 (ISBN 0-88410-352-8). Ballinger Pub.
Carr-Saunders, A. M. The Population Problem: A Study in Human Evolution. LC 73-14150. (Perspectives in Social Inquiry Ser.). 520p. 1974. Repr. 27.00x (ISBN 0-405-05496-3). Arno.
Chamie, Joseph. Religion & Fertility: Arab Christian-Muslim Differentials. LC 80-19787. (ASA Rose Monograph Ser.). (Illus.). 176p. 1981. 19.95 (ISBN 0-521-23677-0); pap. 6.95 (ISBN 0-521-28147-4). Cambridge U Pr.
Cho, Lee-Jay & Kobayashi, Kazumasa, eds. Fertility Transition of East Asian Populations. (Monographs of the Center for Southeast Asian Studies, Kyoto University). 1979. text ed. 20.00x (ISBN 0-8248-0648-4); pap. text ed. 13.00x (ISBN 0-8248-0649-2). U Pr of Hawaii.
Cicourel, Aaron V. Theory & Method in a Study of Argentine Fertility. 212p. 1974. lib. bdg. 16.00 (ISBN 0-471-15793-7). Krieger.
Coale, Ansley J. & Anderson, Barbara. Human Fertility in Russia Since the Nineteenth Century. LC 78-70284. (Publications of the Office of Population Research). (Illus.). 1979. 20.00 (ISBN 0-691-03122-3). Princeton U Pr.
Cohen, Wilbur J. & Westoff, Charles F. Demographic Dynamics in America. LC 77-80227. 1977. 12.95 (ISBN 0-02-905780-9). Free Pr.
Cook, Robert C. Human Fertility: The Modern Dilemma. LC 72-156185. 1971. Repr. of 1951 ed. lib. bdg. 17.00x (ISBN 0-8371-6128-2, COHU). Greenwood.
Cortes-Prieto, J. & De Paz, A. Campos. Research on Fertility & Sterility. 352p. 1981. text ed. 39.50 (ISBN 0-8391-1684-5). Univ Park.
Cutright, Phillips & Jaffe, Fredericks S. Impact of Family Planning Programs on Fertility: The U. S. Experience. LC 76-12847. 1977. text ed. 22.95 (ISBN 0-275-23350-2). Praeger.
Diczfalusy, E. & Borell, U. Control of Human Fertility. 354p. 1971. 29.95 (ISBN 0-471-21300-4). Halsted Pr.
Driver, Edwin D. Differential Fertility in Central India. 1963. 13.00x (ISBN 0-691-09314-8). Princeton U Pr.
Duncan, Gordon W., et al, eds. Fertility Control Methods. 1973. 23.00 (ISBN 0-12-224060-X). Acad Pr.
Easterlin, Richard A. Population, Labor Force & Long Swings in Economic Growth: The American Experience. (General Ser: No. 86). (Illus.). 1968. 15.00x (ISBN 0-87014-474-X, Dist. by Columbia U Pr). Natl Bur Econ Res.
Eberstadt, Nick, ed. Fertility Decline in the Less Developed Countries. 250p. 1981. 34.95 (ISBN 0-03-055271-0). Praeger.
Elder, M. G. & Hawkins, D. F. Human Fertility Control: The Theory & Practice. 1979. text ed. 61.95 (ISBN 0-407-00127-1). Butterworth.
Epstein, T. Scarlett & Jackson, Darrell, eds. The Feasibility of Fertility Planning: Micro Perspectives. 1977. text ed. 37.00 (ISBN 0-08-021452-5); pap. text ed. 12.25 (ISBN 0-08-021837-7). Pergamon.
Estimation of Recent Trends in Fertility & Mortality in the Republic of Korea. 1980. 3.75 (ISBN 0-309-02890-6). Natl Acad Pr.
Eversley, David. Social Theories of Fertility & the Malthusian Debate. LC 74-9219. 313p. 1975. Repr. of 1959 ed. lib. bdg. 16.50x (ISBN 0-8371-7628-X, EVST). Greenwood.
Fawcett, James T., ed. Psychological Perspectives on Population. LC 72-76920. 608p. 1973. text ed. 15.00x (ISBN 0-465-06673-9). Basic.
Fenton, Judith A. & Lifchez, Aaron S. The Fertility Handbook. (Orig.). 1980. 12.95 (ISBN 0-517-53991-8); pap. 5.95 (ISBN 0-517-54125-4). Potter.
Fertility Analysis Through Extension of Stable Population Concepts. LC 76-5439. (Population Monograph Ser.: No.2). (Illus.). 1976. Repr. lib. bdg. 18.50x (ISBN 0-8371-8826-1, REFA). Greenwood.
Fertility & Mortality Changes in Thailand, 1950-1975. 1980. 3.50 (ISBN 0-309-02943-0). Natl Acad Pr.
Freedman, Ronald. The Sociology of Human Fertility: An Annotated Bibliography. LC 73-12272. 283p. 1975. 14.95 (ISBN 0-470-27732-7, Pub. by Wiley). Krieger.
--The Sociology of Human Fertility: An Annotated Bibliography. LC 73-12272. (Population & Demography Ser.). 283p. 1975. 14.95 (ISBN 0-470-27732-7). Halsted Pr.
Garcia, Celso-Ramon & Rosenfeld, David L. Human Fertility: The Regulation of Reproduction. LC 76-15411. (Illus.). 163p. 1977. pap. text ed. 15.00 (ISBN 0-8036-3910-4). Davis Co.
Guentert, Kenneth. What's Ahead for Childless Couples? 1977. 0.25 (ISBN 0-89570-110-3). Claretian Pubns.
Gwatkin, Ralph B. Fertilization Mechanisms in Man & Mammals. LC 77-1189. (Illus.). 161p. 1977. 22.50 (ISBN 0-306-31009-0, Plenum Pr). Plenum Pub.
Haines, Michael. Fertility & Occupation: Population Patterns in Industrialization. LC 79-6936. (Studies in Social Discontinuity Ser.). 1979. 23.00 (ISBN 0-12-315550-9). Acad Pr.
Harrison, R. G. & DeBoer, C. H. Sex & Infertility. 1977. 16.50 (ISBN 0-12-327850-3). Acad Pr.
Hendershot, Gerry E. Predicting Fertility. Placek, Paul J., ed. LC 79-9686. 352p. 1981. 23.95x (ISBN 0-669-03618-8). Lexington Bks.
Henry, Louis. On the Measurement of Human Fertility. LC 72-76712. 1972. 16.50 (ISBN 0-444-41029-5). Elsevier.
Heuser, Robert L. Fertility Tables for Birth Cohorts by Color: U. S. 1917-73. LC 75-619342. 54p. 1976. pap. text ed. 1.25 (ISBN 0-8406-0059-3). Natl Ctr Health Stats.
International Symposium on Neuroendocrine Regulation of Fertility. Neuroendocrine Regulation of Fertility: Proceedings. Anand Kumar, T. C., ed. (Illus.). 1976. 91.75 (ISBN 3-8055-2199-5). S Karger.
Kaplan, Bernice, ed. Anthropological Studies of Human Fertility. LC 76-2663. 1976. 8.95 (ISBN 0-8143-1558-5). Wayne St U Pr.
Kiser, Clyde V., et al. Trends & Variations in Fertility in the United States. LC 68-25613. (Vital & Health Statistics Monographs, American Public Health Association). (Illus.). 1968. 16.50x (ISBN 0-674-90780-9). Harvard U Pr.
Kleinman, David S. Human Adaptation & Population Growth: A Non-Malthusian Perspective. LC 78-59176. 296p. 1980. text ed. 23.50 (ISBN 0-916672-18-2). Allanheld.
Knaus, Hermann. Human Procreation & Its Natural Regulation. (Illus.). 1965. 5.95 (ISBN 0-8392-1138-4). Astor-Honor.
Kuczynski, P. The Measurement of Population Growth, Methods & Result. (Demographic Monographs Ser.). 1969. 39.00x (ISBN 0-677-02220-4). Gordon.
Kupinsky, Stanley, ed. The Fertility of Working Women: A Synthesis of International Research. LC 76-12861. (Praeger Special Studies). 1977. text ed. 37.50 (ISBN 0-275-23100-3). Praeger.
Law & Fertility in Europe, 2 vols. 1979. Set. pap. 45.00 (ISBN 0-685-90710-4, ORD 3, ORDINA). Unipub.
Leridon, Henri. Human Fertility: The Basic Components. Helzner, Judith F., tr. from Fr. LC 77-1913. 1977. lib. bdg. 21.00x (ISBN 0-226-47297-3). U of Chicago Pr.
Lesthaeghe, Ron J. The Decline of Belgian Fertility: 1890-1970. LC 77-71991. 1978. text ed. 19.50 (ISBN 0-691-05253-0). Princeton U Pr.
Lewis, C. J. & Lewis, J. Norman. Natality & Fecundity: A Contribution to National Demography. LC 75-38135. (Demography Ser.). 1976. Repr. of 1906 ed. 13.00x (ISBN 0-405-07988-5). Arno.
Lindert, Peter H. Fertility & Scarcity in America. LC 77-71991. 1978. text ed. 28.50 (ISBN 0-691-04217-9). Princeton U Pr.
Liu, William T., ed. Family & Fertility. (Charts). 1967. 9.95x (ISBN 0-268-00095-6). U of Notre Dame Pr.
Livi Bacci, Massimo. Century of Portuguese Fertility. LC 70-120758. (Office of Population Research). 1971. 16.00 (ISBN 0-691-09307-5). Princeton U Pr.
Livi-Bacci, Massimo. A History of Italian Fertility During the Last Two Centuries. LC 76-3271. (Office of Population Research). 1977. text ed. 24.00 (ISBN 0-691-09369-5). Princeton U Pr.
Lorimer, Frank. Culture & Human Fertility: A Study of the Relation of Cultural Conditions to Fertility in Non-Industrial & Transitional Societies. Repr. of 1954 ed. lib. bdg. 24.25 (ISBN 0-8371-2152-3, LOHF). Greenwood.
Ludwig, H. & Tauber, P. F., eds. Human Fertilization. LC 77-99146. (Illus.). 300p. 1978. 36.00 (ISBN 0-88416-245-1). Wright-PSG.
Macandrew, Rennie. Wanted a Child. 1958. 2.00 (ISBN 0-685-06613-4). Assoc Bk.
Mahadevan, K. Sociology of Fertility: Determinants of Fertility Differentials in South India. 1978. 11.00x (ISBN 0-8364-0293-6). South Asia Bks.
Mancini, R. E. & Martini, L. Male Fertility & Sterility. 1975. 84.50 (ISBN 0-12-467250-7). Acad Pr.
Moghissi, Kamran S. & Evans, Tommy N., eds. Regulation of Human Fertility. LC 75-29482. 320p. 1976. 22.00 (ISBN 0-8143-1551-8). Wayne St U Pr.
Nag, Moni. Factors Affecting Human Fertility in Nonindustrial Societies: A Cross-Cultural Study. LC 68-22204. (Yale University Publications in Anthropology Reprints Ser: No. 66). 227p. 1968. pap. 8.00x (ISBN 0-87536-514-0). HRAFP.
NCHS. Statistics Needed for National Policies Related to Fertility. (Ser. 4). 1976. pap. 1.95 (ISBN 0-8406-0080-1). Natl Ctr Health Stats.
Nikolowski, W., et al. Kohabitations-und Fertilitaets-Stoerungen: Ein Leitfaden fuer die aerztliche Praxis. (Illus.). 1977. 14.50 (ISBN 3-8055-2682-2). S Karger.
Niphuis-Nell, M., ed. Demographic Aspects of the Changing Status of Women in Europe. (Publications of the Netherlands Inter-University Demographic Institute & the Population & Family Study Centre: Vol. 7). 1978. pap. text ed. 18.50 (ISBN 90-207-0714-0, Pub. by Martinus Nijhoff Netherlands). Kluwer Boston.
Philipp, Elliot. Overcoming Childlessness: Its Causes & What to Do About Them. LC 75-8201. (Illus.). 192p. 1975. 8.50 (ISBN 0-8008-6161-2). Taplinger.
Pincus, Gregory, ed. Control of Fertility. 1965. 38.00 (ISBN 0-12-557056-2). Acad Pr.
Prabhu, John C. Social & Cultural Determinants of Fertility in India. LC 75-901184. 1974. 10.50x (ISBN 0-8002-0313-5). Intl Pubns Serv.
Preston, Samuel H., ed. The Effects of Infant & Child Mortality on Fertility. 1977. 27.00 (ISBN 0-12-564440-X). Acad Pr.
Ridker, Ronald G. Population and Development: The Search for Selective Interventions. LC 76-16806. (Resources for the Future Ser). (Illus.). 488p. 1977. 27.50x (ISBN 0-8018-1884-2). Johns Hopkins.
Roberts, George W. & Sinclair, Sonja A. Women in Jamaica: Patterns of Reproduction & Family. LC 76-56911. (Caribbean Monographs). 1978. 25.00 (ISBN 0-527-75870-1). Kraus Intl.
Rosemberg, Eugenia, ed. Gonadotropin Therapy in Female Infertility. (International Congress Ser.: No. 266). 300p. 1973. 55.25 (ISBN 0-444-15028-5, Excerpta Medica). Elsevier.
Ryder, Norman B. & Westoff, Charles F. Reproduction in the United States: 1965. LC 78-120760. (Office of Population Research Ser.). 1971. 28.00x (ISBN 0-691-09318-0). Princeton U Pr.
Santow, Gigi. A Simulation Approach to the Study of Human Fertility. (Publications of the Netherlands Inter-University Demographic Institute & the Population & Family Study Centre: Vol. 5). 1978. pap. 25.50 (ISBN 90-207-0765-5, Pub. by Martinus Nijhoff Netherlands). Kluwer Boston.
Saunders, J. V. Differential Fertility in Brazil. LC 58-13205. (Illus.). 1958. 4.95 (ISBN 0-8130-0201-X). U Presses Fla.
Sciarra, John J., et al. Control of Male Fertility. (Illus.). 1975. 12.50x (ISBN 0-06-142365-3, Harper Medical). Har-Row.
Sciarra, John J., et al, eds. Risks, Benefits, & Controversies in Fertility Control. (Illus.). 1978. text ed. 27.50x (ISBN 0-06-142372-6, Harper Medical). Har-Row.
Seventh World Congress of Fertility & Sterility, Tokyo, & Kyoto, Japan, Oct., 1971. Fertility & Sterility: Proceedings. Hasegawa, et al, eds. (International Congress Ser.: No. 278). 900p. 1974. 99.50 (ISBN 0-444-15035-8, Excerpta Medica). Elsevier.
Simon, Julian L. The Economics of Population Growth. LC 75-15278. 1977. 40.00 (ISBN 0-691-04212-8); pap. 15.00 (ISBN 0-691-10053-5). Princeton U Pr.
Spengler, Joseph J. France Faces Depopulation. LC 69-10158. (Illus.). 1968. Repr. of 1938 ed. lib. bdg. 16.75x (ISBN 0-8371-0235-9, SPFD). Greenwood.
Spillane, William & Ryser, Paul E. Fertility Knowledge, Attitudes, & Practices of Married Men. LC 74-22251. 212p. 1975. text ed. 16.50 (ISBN 0-88410-354-4). Ballinger Pub.
Spratley, Ernell. Birth & Fertility Rates for States & Metropolitan Areas: United States. Stevenson, Taloria, ed. (Series 21, No. 27). pap. text ed. 1.25 (ISBN 0-8406-0101-8). Natl Ctr Health Stats.
Stangel, John J. Fertility & Conception: An Essential Guide for Childless Couples. 223p. 1978. 12.95 (ISBN 0-87196-319-1). Facts on File.
--Fertility & Conception: An Essential Guide for Childless Couples. 1980. pap. 4.95 (ISBN 0-452-25232-6, Z5232, Plume). NAL.
--Fertility & Conception: An Essential Guide for Childless Couples. LC 78-21642. (Illus.). 1979. 8.95 (ISBN 0-448-22979-X). Paddington.
Stevens, Barbara C. Marriage & Fertility of Women Suffering from Schizophrenia or Affective Disorders. (Maudsley Monographs). 1969. 9.75x (ISBN 0-19-712141-1). Oxford U Pr.
Stevenson, Taloria, ed. Trends in Fertility in the United States. (Ser. 21, No. 28). 1977. pap. text ed. 1.95 (ISBN 0-8406-0108-5). Natl Ctr Health Stats.
Stycos, J. Mayone. Family & Fertility in Puerto Rico: A Study of the Lower Income Group. LC 73-5273. (Illus.). 332p. 1973. Repr. of 1955 ed. lib. bdg. 15.75x (ISBN 0-8371-6886-4, STFF). Greenwood.
Symposium, New Delhi, October 1978. Recent Advances in Reproduction & Regulation of Fertility: Proceedings. Talwar, G. P., ed. 1979. 73.25 (ISBN 0-444-80123-5, North Holland). Elsevier.
Tien, H. Y. Social Mobility & Controlled Fertility. 1965. 6.00x (ISBN 0-8084-0280-3). Coll & U Pr.
Tilly, Charles, ed. Historical Studies of Changing Fertility. LC 77-85569. (Quantitative Studies in History). (Illus.). 1978. text ed. 32.50 (ISBN 0-691-07595-6); pap. 12.50 (ISBN 0-691-10066-7). Princeton U Pr.
Turchi, Boone A. The Demand for Children: The Economics of Fertility in the United States. LC 75-22111. 256p. 1975. 18.50 (ISBN 0-88410-353-6). Ballinger Pub.
Van De Walle, Etienne. The Female Population of France in the Nineteenth Century: A Reconstruction of 82 Departments. (Office of Population Research, Princeton University). 512p. 1974. text ed. 35.00x (ISBN 0-691-09360-1). Princeton U Pr.
Wallach, Edward, ed. American Fertility Society: Modern Trends in Infertility & Conception Control. 1979. 23.50 (ISBN 0-683-08706-1). Williams & Wilkins.
Westoff, Charles F. & Bumpass, Larry L. Later Years of Childbearing. LC 74-120751. (Population Research Office). 1970. 16.50x (ISBN 0-691-09303-2). Princeton U Pr.
Westoff, Charles F., et al. Family Growth in Metropolitan America. (Office of Population Research Ser.). 1961. 28.00x (ISBN 0-691-09316-4). Princeton U Pr.
--Third Child: A Study in the Prediction of Fertility. (Office of Population Research Ser). 1963. 22.00x (ISBN 0-691-09339-3). Princeton U Pr.
--College Women & Fertility Values. (Office of Population Research Ser.). 1967. 18.50x (ISBN 0-691-09311-3). Princeton U Pr.
Whelpton, Pascal K. Cohort Fertility. LC 78-159108. 520p. 1973. Repr. of 1954 ed. 25.00x (ISBN 0-8046-1752-X). Kennikat.
WHO Scientific Group. Methods of Fertility Regulation - Advances in Research & Clinical Experience: A Report. (Technical Report Ser: No. 473). 48p. 1971. pap. 2.00 (ISBN 92-4-120473-7, 613). World Health.
WHO Scientific Group. Geneva, 1968. Developments in Fertility Control: Report. (Technical Report Ser.: No. 424). (Also avail. in French, Russian & Spanish). 1969. pap. 2.00 (ISBN 92-4-120424-9). World Health.
WHO Scientific Group. Geneva, 1972. Agents Stimulating Gonadal Function in the Human: Report. (Technical Report Ser.: No. 514). (Also avail. in French & Spanish). 1973. pap. 1.60 (ISBN 92-4-120514-8). World Health.
Yaukey, David. Fertility Differences in a Modernizing Country. LC 71-159109. 1971. Repr. of 1961 ed. 12.50 (ISBN 0-8046-1652-3). Kennikat.
Yu, Elena S. & Liu, W. T. Fertility & Kinship in the Philippines: An Ethnography Study. 310p. 1981. 20.00 (ISBN 0-268-00949-X). U of Notre Dame Pr.
Zatuchni, Gerald I., et al. Research Frontiers in Fertility Regulation. (Illus.). 416p. 1981. text ed. 25.00 (ISBN 0-06-142902-3, Harper Medical). Har-Row.

FERTILITY CULTS

see also Cultus; Mysteries, Religious

Runeberg, Anne. Witches, Demons & Fertility Magic. 273p. 1980. Repr. of 1947 ed. lib. bdg. 30.00 (ISBN 0-8414-7399-4). Folcroft.

FERTILIZATION (BIOLOGY)

Afzelius, B., ed. The Functional Anatomy of the Spermatazoan. 1975. text ed. 79.00 (ISBN 0-08-018006-X). Pergamon.
Austin, C. R. & Short, R. V., eds. Germ Cells & Fertilization. LC 73-174261. (Reproduction in Mammals Ser.: Bk. 1). (Illus.). 1972. 24.50 (ISBN 0-521-08408-3); pap. 6.50x (ISBN 0-521-09690-1). Cambridge U Pr.
Edwards, Robert & Steptoe, Patrick. A Matter of Life. LC 80-17293. (Illus.). 208p. 1980. Repr. 9.95 (ISBN 0-688-03698-8). Morrow.
Forest Fertilization. LC 72-92357. (Bibliographic Ser.: No. 258, Supplement 1). 1975. pap. 25.00 (ISBN 0-87010-042-4). Inst Paper Chem.
Gwatkin, Ralph B. Fertilization Mechanisms in Man & Mammals. LC 77-1189. (Illus.). 161p. 1977. 22.50 (ISBN 0-306-31009-0, Plenum Pr). Plenum Pub.

Hadek, Robert. Mammalian Fertilization: An Atlas of Ultrastructure. 1969. 37.50 (ISBN 0-12-312950-8). Acad Pr.
International Seminar on Reproductive Physiology & Sexual Endocrinology, 5th, Brussels, May, 1975. Sperm Action: Proceedings. Hubinont, P. O., ed. 1976. 58.25 (ISBN 3-8055-2244-4). S Karger.
Isotope Studies on Wheat Fertilization. (Illus.). 99p. (Orig.). 1975. pap. 10.25 (ISBN 92-0-115074-1, IDC157, IAEA). Unipub.
Ludwig, H. & Tauber, P. F., eds. Human Fertilization. LC 77-99146. (Illus.). 300p. 1978. 36.00 (ISBN 0-88416-245-1). Wright-PSG.
Metz, Charles B. & Monroy, Alberto, eds. Fertilization: Comparative Morphology, Biochemistry & Immunology, 2 vols. Incl. Vol. 1. 1967. 63.50 (ISBN 0-12-492650-9); Vol. 2. 1969. 72.50 (ISBN 0-12-492651-7). Acad Pr.
Moghissi, Kamran S. & Hafez, E. S., eds. Biology of Mammalian Fertilization & Implantation. (Illus.). 520p. 1972. 42.50 (ISBN 0-398-02362-X). C C Thomas.

FERTILIZATION IN VITRO, HUMAN

Edwards, R. G. Test-Tube Babies. Head, J. J., ed. LC 79-50741. (Carolina Biology Readers Ser.). 16p. (gr. 11 up). 1981. pap. 1.65 (ISBN 0-89278-289-7, 45-9689). Carolina Biological.
Grobstein, C. From Chance to Purpose: An Appraisal of External Human Fertilization. 1981. pap. 17.50 (ISBN 0-201-04585-0). A-W.
Mastroianni, Luigi, et al, eds. Fertilization & Embryonic Development in Vitro. 350p. 1981. text ed. price not set (ISBN 0-306-40783-3, Plenum Pr). Plenum Pub.

FERTILIZATION OF PLANTS

Darwin, Charles R. The Effects of Cross & Self Fertilisation in the Vegetable Kingdom. 1889. 40.00 (ISBN 0-8274-2230-X). R West.
Frankel, R. & Galun, E. Pollination Mechanisms, Reproduction & Plant Breeding. (Monographs on Theoretical & Applied Genetics: Vol. 2). 1977. 33.70 (ISBN 0-387-07934-3). Springer-Verlag.
Free, John B. Insect Pollination of Crops. 1971. 84.00 (ISBN 0-12-266650-X). Acad Pr.
Grant, Karen A. & Grant, Verne. Flower Pollination in the Phlox Family. LC 65-19809. 180p. 1965. 17.50x (ISBN 0-231-02843-1). Columbia U Pr.
--Hummingbirds & Their Flowers. LC 68-23462. (Illus.). 1968. 20.00x (ISBN 0-231-03126-2). Columbia U Pr.
Kennedy, Helen. Systematics & Pollination of the "Closed Flowered" Species of Calathea (Mar-Antaceae) (Publications in Botany: No. 71). 1978. pap. 9.50x (ISBN 0-520-09572-3). U of Cal Pr.
Mulik, J. D. & Sawicki, E. Ion Chromatographic Analysis of Environmental Pollutants, Vol. 2. LC 77-92589. 1979. 37.50 (ISBN 0-250-40322-6). Ann Arbor Science.
Muller, Hermann. The Fertilisation of Flowers. Egerton, Frank N., 3rd, ed. Thompson, D'Arcy W., tr. LC 77-74241. (History of Ecology Ser.). (Illus.). 1978. Repr. of 1883 ed. lib. bdg. 39.00x (ISBN 0-405-10410-3). Arno.
Nye, W. P. Nectar & Pollen Plants of Utah. 81p. (Orig.). 1971. pap. 3.00 (ISBN 0-87421-040-2). Utah St U Pr.
Percival, M. Floral Biology. 1965. 10.50 (ISBN 0-08-010610-2); pap. 7.00 (ISBN 0-08-010609-9). Pergamon.
Physiochemical Properties of Submerged Soils in Relationship to Fertility. (IRRI Research Paper Ser.: No. 5). 32p. 1977. pap. 5.00 (ISBN 0-686-70589-0, R045, IRRI). Unipub.
Proctor, Michael & Yeo, Peter. The Pollination of Flowers. LC 70-185876. (The New Naturalist Ser). (Illus.). 416p. 1973. 14.95x (ISBN 0-8008-6408-5). Taplinger.
Rahn, Joan E. How Plants Are Pollinated. LC 75-9526. 160p. (gr. 3-7). 1975. 8.95 (ISBN 0-689-30482-X). Atheneum.
Richard, A. J., ed. The Pollination of Flowers by Insects. (Linnean Society Symposium Ser.). 1979. 37.50 (ISBN 0-12-587460-X). Acad Pr.
Sprengel, Christian K. Das Entdectke Geheimnis der Natur Im Bau & der Befruchtung der Blumen. 1973. Repr. of 1793 ed. 50.00 (ISBN 3-7682-0828-1). Lubrecht & Cramer.

FERTILIZER INDUSTRY

Annual Fertilizer Review, 1971. annual 191p. (Orig.). 1973. pap. 16.25 (ISBN 0-685-30141-9, FAO). Unipub.
British Sulphur Corp. Ltd. World Directory of Fertilizer Manufacturers. 4th ed. Wahba, C., ed. LC 76-356341. 1977. 210.00x (ISBN 0-902777-28-9). Intl Pubns Serv.
Choksi, Armeane, et al. The Planning of Investment Programs in the Fertilizer Industry. LC 78-8436. (World Bank Ser: No. 2). 1978. text ed. 19.50x (ISBN 0-8018-2138-X); pap. text ed. 8.95x (ISBN 0-8018-2153-3). Johns Hopkins.
Fertilizer Distribution in Selected Asian Countries. 1979. pap. 9.00 (ISBN 92-833-1453-0, APO75, APO). Unipub.
Fertilizers: An Annual Review of World Production, Consumption & Trade. (Orig.). pap. 6.75 1960 (ISBN 0-685-38528-0, F39, FAO); pap. 6.75 1964 (ISBN 0-685-38529-9, F41); pap. 13.24 1966 (ISBN 0-685-38530-2, F42); pap. 11.50 1967 (ISBN 0-685-38531-0, F43); pap. 13.25 1968 (ISBN 0-685-38532-9, F44); pap. 15.75 1969 (ISBN 0-685-38533-7, F45). Unipub.
Lamer, Mirko. The World Fertilizer Economy. 1957. 20.00x (ISBN 0-8047-0474-0). Stanford U Pr.
Liu, Jung Chao. China's Fertilizer Economy. LC 74-123587. (Committee on the Economy of China Monographs). 1970. text ed. 6.95x (ISBN 0-202-31004-3). Beresford Bk Serv.
Markham, Jesse W. Fertilizer Industry: Study of an Imperfect Market. Repr. of 1958 ed. lib. bdg. 15.00 (ISBN 0-8371-2324-0, MAFI). Greenwood.
Moldovan, I. The Technology of Mineral Fertilizers. 800p. 1970. 32.50x (ISBN 0-902777-03-3). Intl Pubns Serv.
Olson, R. A., ed. Fertilizer Technology & Use. (Illus.). 1971. 10.00 (ISBN 0-89118-752-9). Soil Sci Soc Am.
World Fertilizer Legislation & Tariff's Manual. 4th ed. 175p. 1974. 35.00x (ISBN 0-902777-09-2). Intl Pubns Serv.

FERTILIZER INDUSTRY–INDIA

Kapoor, A. International Business Negotiations: A Study in India. LC 70-114622. 361p. 1973. 12.00 (ISBN 0-87850-016-2); pap. 6.00x (ISBN 0-87850-017-0). Darwin Pr.

FERTILIZERS AND MANURES

see also Agricultural Chemistry; Compost; Deficiency Diseases in Plants; Garden Fertilizers; Humus; Lime; Nitrogen Fertilizers; Nitrates; Peat; Phosphates; Salt; Soil Fertility

Annual Fertilizer Review, 1970. annual 176p. (Orig.). 1972. pap. 12.00 (ISBN 0-685-23606-4, FAO). Unipub.
Annual Fertilizer Review, 1971. annual 191p. (Orig.). 1973. pap. 16.25 (ISBN 0-685-30141-9, FAO). Unipub.
Annual Fertilizer Review, 1972. annual 190p. (Orig.). 1974. pap. 13.25 (ISBN 0-685-40957-0, FAO). Unipub.
Annual Fertilizer Review 1973. 194p. 1975. pap. 20.00 (ISBN 0-685-54034-0, FAO). Unipub.
Annual Fertilizer Review, 1974. 205p. 1976. pap. 20.50 (ISBN 0-685-66328-0, FAO). Unipub.
Annual Fertilizer Review, 1975. (Illus.). 205p. 1977. pap. 30.00 (ISBN 92-5-000069-3, FAO). Unipub.
Annual Fertilizer Review, 1976. (Statistical Ser.: No. 9). 1978. pap. 17.00 (ISBN 92-5-000335-8, F1226, FAO). Unipub.
Annual Fertilizer Review, 1977. 1979. pap. 17.00 (ISBN 92-5-000605-5, F 1488, FAO). Unipub.
Bould, C., et al, eds. Plant Analysis & Fertilizer Problems, Vol. 4. 1964. 7.50 (ISBN 0-934454-68-X). Lubrecht & Cramer.
Brinton, William F., Jr., ed. Effects of Organic & Inorganic Fertilizers on Soils & Crops. LC 79-55519. (Illus., Orig.). 1979. pap. 6.50 (ISBN 0-9603554-0-5). W F Brinton.
California Fertilizer Association. Western Fertilizer Handbook. 6th ed. 252p. 1980. pap. text ed. 5.50 (ISBN 0-8134-2122-5). Interstate.
Cooke, G. W. Fertilizing for Maximum Yield. 297p. 1975. 17.95x (ISBN 0-8464-1094-X). Beekman Pubs.
Cornell Waste Management Conference, 9th. Food, Fertilizer & Agricultural Residues: Proceedings. Loehr, Raymond C., ed. LC 77-85092. 1977. 37.50 (ISBN 0-250-40190-8). Ann Arbor Science.
Deichmann, William B. Safe Farming & Gardening. 1972. pap. 3.00 (ISBN 0-89970-077-2, OP-389). AMA.
Development of a Programme Promoting the Use of Organic Materials As Fertilizers. 1976. pap. 7.50 (ISBN 92-5-100008-5, F749, FAO). Unipub.
FAO Fertilizer Yearbook, 1978. (FAO Statistical Ser.: No. 23). 115p. 1979. 18.50 (ISBN 92-5-000783-3, F1634, FAO). Unipub.
FAO Fertilizer Yearbook 1979, Vol. 29. 143p. 1981. 23.00 (ISBN 92-5-000942-9, F2122, FAO). Unipub.
The Fertilization Technology Described in Historical Japanese Farm Manuals & That Utilized by Modern Farm Households. 65p. 1981. pap. 5.00 (ISBN 92-808-0259-3, TUNU143, UNU). Unipub.
Fertilizer Distribution & Credit Schemes for Small-Sclae Farmers. (FAO Fertilizer Bulletin Ser.: No. 1). 47p. 1980. pap. 9.00 (ISBN 92-5-100837-X, F 1900, FAO). Unipub.
Fertilizer Management Practices for Maize: Results of Experiments with Isotopes. (Technical Reports Ser.: No. 121). (Orig.). 1971. pap. 8.75 (ISBN 92-0-115770-3, IDC121, IAEA). Unipub.
Fertilizers & Their Use. 51p. 1978. 8.50 (ISBN 0-686-74015-7, F 2026, FAO). Unipub.
Fowler, Clifford W. Urea & Urea Phosphate Fertilizers. LC 75-32118. (Chemical Technology Review Ser.: No. 59). (Illus.). 265p. 1976. 32.00 (ISBN 0-8155-0604-X). Noyes.
Gaerity, Jack. Bread & Roses from Stone. facs. ed. pap. 9.95 (ISBN 0-8466-0126-5, SJS126). Shorey.
Hendrie, Robert A. Granulated Fertilizers. LC 75-32116. (Chemical Technology Review: No. 58). (Illus.). 339p. 1976. 36.00 (ISBN 0-8155-0602-3). Noyes.
Hernando Fernandez, V. Fertilizers, Crop Quality & Economy. 1400p. 1975. 109.75 (ISBN 0-444-41277-8). Elsevier.
Jacob, Kenneth D., ed. Fertilizer Technology & Resources in the United States. (Agronomy Ser.: Vol. 3). 1953. 39.50 (ISBN 0-12-379750-0). Acad Pr.
Jones, Ulysses. Fertilizers & Soil Fertility. 2nd ed. 464p. 1982. text ed. 17.95 (ISBN 0-8359-1962-5); instr's. manual free (ISBN 0-8359-1963-3). Reston.
Jones, Ulysses S. Fertilizers & Soil Fertility. (Illus.). 1979. text ed. 17.95 (ISBN 0-8359-1960-9); instrs'. manual avail. (ISBN 0-8359-1961-7). Reston.
McVickar, Malcolm H. & Walker, William. Using Commercial Fertilizers. 4th ed. LC 76-53095. (Illus.). (gr. 9-12). 1978. 18.00 (ISBN 0-8134-1894-1). Interstate.
Mariakulandai, A. & Manickam, T. S. Chemistry of Fertilizers & Manures: A Textbook for Students of Agriculture. 400p. 1976. pap. text ed. 10.95x (ISBN 0-210-22249-2). Asia.
Markham, Gervase. The Inrichment of the Weald of Kent: Or, a Direction to the Husbandman. LC 73-6151. (English Experience Ser.: No. 614). 24p. 1973. Repr. of 1625 ed. 3.50 (ISBN 90-221-0614-4). Walter J Johnson.
Maximizing the Efficiency of Fertilizer Use by Grain Crops. (FAO Fertilizer Bulletin Ser.: No. 3). 30p. 1980. pap. 7.50 (ISBN 92-5-100954-6, F2131, FAO). Unipub.
Mays, D. A., ed. Forage Fertilization. (Illus.). 1973. 12.50 (ISBN 0-686-51659-1). Am Soc Agron.
Nelson, L. B., ed. Changing Patterns in Fertilizer Use. (Illus.). 1968. 7.50 (ISBN 0-686-51666-4). Soil Sci Soc Am.
Organic Materials As Fertilizers. (Soils Bulletin: No. 27). (Illus.). 394p. 1975. pap. 40.50 (ISBN 0-685-62846-9, F1170, FAO). Unipub.
Papers Presented at the FAO-SIDA Workshop on the Use of Organic Materials As Fertilizers in Africa: Organic Recycling in Africa. 308p. 1981. pap. 20.00 (ISBN 92-5-100945-7, F2096, FAO). Unipub.
Planning & Organization of Fertilizer Use Development in Africa. (Soils Bulletin: No. 26). (Illus.). 184p. 1975. pap. 12.75 (ISBN 0-685-57607-8, F1168, FAO). Unipub.
Ranney, M. W. Fertilizer Additives & Soil Conditioners. LC 78-62514. (Chemical Technology Review: No. 116). (Illus.). 1979. 39.00 (ISBN 0-8155-0721-6). Noyes.
Report of the FAO-NORAD Seminar on Fertilizer Use Development in Zambia. (Illus.). 1978. pap. 11.50 (ISBN 92-5-100378-5, F1255, FAO). Unipub.
Rollett, R., et al. Fertilizers & Soil Amendments. 1981. 24.95 (ISBN 0-13-314336-8). P-H.
Ruffin, Edmund. Essay on Calcareous Manures. Sitterson, J. Carlyle, ed. LC 61-6352. (The John Harvard Library). (Illus.). 1961. 10.00x (ISBN 0-674-26201-8). Harvard U Pr.
Sauchelli, Vincent. Trace Elements in Agriculture. 228p. 1969. 16.50 (ISBN 0-442-15633-2, Pub. by Van Nos Reinhold). Krieger.
Sittig, M. Fertilizer Industry: Processes, Pollution Control & Energy Conservation. LC 78-70743. (Chem. Tech. Rev. 123; Pollution Tech. Rev. 55; Energy Tech. Rev, 36). (Illus.). 1979. 32.00 (ISBN 0-8155-0734-8). Noyes.
Soil & Plant Testing As a Basis of Fertilizer Recommendations. (FAO Soils Bulletin Ser.: No. 38-2). 122p. 1980. pap. 8.00 (ISBN 92-5-100956-2, F 2034, FAO). Unipub.
Stafford, D. A., et al. Methane Production from Waste Organic Matter. LC 78-31274. 1980. 79.95 (ISBN 0-8493-5223-1). CRC Pr.
Statistics of Crop Responses to Fertilizers. (Orig.). 1966. pap. 6.75 (ISBN 0-685-09408-1, F449, FAO). Unipub.
Tisdale, Samuel & Nelson, Werner. Soil Fertility & Fertilizers. 3rd ed. (Illus.). 752p. 1974. text ed. 24.95 (ISBN 0-02-420860-4). Macmillan.
Usherwood, N. R. & Doll, E. C., eds. International & National Outlook: The Necessity for Efficient Nutrient Utilization. (Illus.). 1975. pap. 3.75 (ISBN 0-89118-041-9). Am Soc Agron.
Western Fertilizer Handbook. 6th ed. perfect bdg. 9.00 (ISBN 0-8134-2122-5). Thomson Pub CA.
Wise, Donald L., ed. Fuel Gas Production from Biomass, 2 vols. 1981. Vol. I, 288 Pgs. 76.95 (ISBN 0-8493-5990-2); Vol. II, 272 Pgs. 74.95 (ISBN 0-8493-5991-0). CRC Pr.
World Directory of Fertilizer Products. 4th ed. 80p. 1974. 75.00x (ISBN 0-902777-35-1). Intl Pubns Serv.
World Fertilizer Atlas. 5th ed. LC 72-654375. (Illus.). 1976. 140.00x (ISBN 0-902777-23-8). Intl Pubns Serv.
World Guide to Fertilizer Processes & Constructors. 5th ed. LC 71-856081. 170p. 1974. 45.00x (ISBN 0-902777-31-9). Intl Pubns Serv.

FERTILIZERS AND MANURES–MATHEMATICAL MODELS

Dillon, John L. The Analysis of Response in Crop & Livestock Production. 2nd ed. 1977. text ed. 26.00 (ISBN 0-08-021118-6); pap. text ed. 12.75 (ISBN 0-08-021115-1). Pergamon.
Statistics of Crop Responses to Fertilizers. (Orig.). 1966. pap. 6.75 (ISBN 0-685-09408-1, F449, FAO). Unipub.

FESSENDEN, WILLIAM PITT, 1806-1869

Fessenden, William P. Life & Public Services of William Pitt Fessenden, 2 Vols. Fessenden, Francis, ed. LC 70-87532. (American Public Figures Ser). (Illus.). 1970. Repr. of 1907 ed. lib. bdg. 69.50 (ISBN 0-306-71446-9). Da Capo.
Jellison, Charles A. Fessenden of Maine, Civil War Senator. LC 62-10726. (Illus.). 1962. 12.95x (ISBN 0-8156-0023-2). Syracuse U Pr.

FESSENDEN FAMILY

Ridlon, G. T. Fessenden Family. LC 73-94954. (Saco Valley Settlements Ser). 1970. pap. 2.75 (ISBN 0-8048-0764-7). C E Tuttle.

FESTIVAL OF HANUKKAH

see Hanukkah (Feast of Lights)

FESTIVALS

see also Anniversaries; Fasts and Feasts; Holidays; Music Festivals; Pageants; Processions; Tournaments
also names of particular festivals, e.g. Christmas; Hanukkah (Feast of Lights)

Akin, Ronald E. & Fingerhut, Bruce M., eds. The Book of Festivals in the Midwest, 1980 & 1981. (Illus.). 1980. pap. 6.95 (ISBN 0-89651-052-2). Icarus.
Alford, Violet. Pyrenean Festivals: Calendar Customs, Music & Magic, Drama & Dance. LC 77-87730. 1977. Repr. of 1937 ed. 25.00 (ISBN 0-404-16577-X). AMS Pr.
Alternative Celebrations Catalogue. 4th ed. LC 78-60409. 1978. 5.00 (ISBN 0-914966-04-9). Alternatives.
Asian Cultural Centre for Unesco, compiled by. Festivals in Asia. LC 75-30415. (Illus.). 68p. (gr. 9-12). 1975. 7.95 (ISBN 0-87011-265-1). Kodansha.
--More Festivals in Asia. LC 75-34740. (Illus.). 68p. (gr. 9-12). 1975. 7.95 (ISBN 0-87011-273-2). Kodansha.
Bodde, D. Festivals in Classical China: New Year & Other Annual Observances During the Han Dynasty-206 B.C.-A.D. 220. 1975. 32.00 (ISBN 0-691-03098-7). Princeton U Pr.
Bredon, Juliet & Mitrophanow, Igor. Moon Year. (Illus.). 1966. 22.00 (ISBN 0-8188-0011-9). Paragon.
Brumfield, Allaire C. The Attic Festivals of Demeter & Their Relation to the Agricultural Year. Connor, W. R., ed. LC 80-2643. (Monographs in Classical Studies). 1981. lib. bdg. 29.00 (ISBN 0-405-14031-2). Arno.
Burland, C. A. Echoes of Magic: A Study of Seasonal Festivals Through the Ages. (Illus.). 234p. 1972. 13.50x (ISBN 0-87471-087-1). Rowman.
Capel, Evelyn. Festivals in North & South. 1979. pap. 2.50 (ISBN 0-903540-21-5, Pub. by Floris Books). St George Bk Serv.
Chittenden, Margaret. Merrymaking in Great Britain. LC 73-12822. (Around the World Holidays Ser). (Illus.). 96p. (gr. 4-7). 1974. PLB 6.48 (ISBN 0-8116-4952-0). Garrard.
Cosman, Madeleine P. Medieval Holidays & Festivals. (Illus.). 128p. (gr. 7 up). 1981. 11.95 (ISBN 0-684-17172-4, ScribJ). Scribner.
Cox, Harvey. Feast of Fools: A Theological Essay on Festivity & Fantasy. LC 75-75914. (William Belden Noble Lectures Ser). 1969. 10.00x (ISBN 0-674-29525-0). Harvard U Pr.
De Cervantes, Miguel, ed. Fesstival De Flor y Canto. (Span.). 1976. pap. text ed. 4.95 (ISBN 0-88474-031-5). U of S Cal Pr.
DeFrancis, John. Things Japanese in Hawaii. (Illus.). 224p. 1973. pap. 8.50 (ISBN 0-8248-0233-0). U Pr of Hawaii.
Eaton, Allen H. Immigrant Gifts to American Life: Some Experiments in Appreciation of the Contributions of Our Foreign Born. LC 73-129395. (American Immigration Collection, Ser. 2). (Illus.). 1970. Repr. of 1932 ed. 12.00 (ISBN 0-405-00576-8). Arno.
Eberhard, Wolfram. Chinese Festivals, No. 38. (Asian Folklore & Social Life Monograph). 1972. 4.60 (ISBN 0-89986-038-9). E Langstaff.
Epstein, Sam & Epstein, Beryl. A Year of Japanese Festivals. LC 73-22045. (Around the World Holidays Ser). (Illus.). 96p. (gr. 4-7). 1974. PLB 6.48 (ISBN 0-8116-4954-7). Garrard.

Epton, Nina. Spanish Fiestas. LC 69-10781. (Illus.). 1969. 9.95 (ISBN 0-498-06986-9). A S Barnes.
Gale, Janice & Gale, Stephen. Guide to Fairs, Festivals and Fun Events. 190p. 1981. pap. 6.95 (ISBN 0-686-75092-6, S-007). Banyan Bks.
--Guide to Fairs, Festivals & Fun Events. (Illus.). 190p. 1981. pap. 6.95 (ISBN 0-937928-00-3). Sightseer.
Golomb, Morris. Know Your Festivals & Enjoy Them. 2nd ed. LC 72-90771. (Illus.). 189p. (gr. 3-6). 1973. 7.95 (ISBN 0-88400-035-4). Shengold.
Green, Victor. Festivals & Saints Day: A Calendar of Festivals for School & Home. (Illus.). 1978. 7.95 (ISBN 0-7137-0889-1, Pub. by Blandford Pr England). Sterling.
Handbook of Special Events. 12.95 (ISBN 0-686-31267-8). New Century.
Hart, Thomas R. Gil Vicente: Farces & Festival Plays. LC 73-115231. 1972. 8.00 (ISBN 0-87114-055-1). U of Oreg Bks.
Hatch, Jane M., ed. American Book of Days. 1212p. 1978. 50.00 (ISBN 0-8242-0593-6). Wilson.
Hodous, Lewis. Folkways in China. LC 73-38073. Repr. of 1929 ed. 21.50 (ISBN 0-404-56935-8). AMS Pr.
Hole, Christina. British Folk Customs. (Illus.). 1977. 14.95x (ISBN 0-09-127340-4, Pub. by Hutchinson Pub. Group Ltd). Standing Orders.
Huang Suih. History of the Tuan-Wu Festival Customs. (National Peking University & Chinese Assn. for Folklore, Folklore & Folkliterature Ser.: No. 102). (Chinese.). 6.00 (ISBN 0-89986-180-6). E Langstaff.
Huxford, Sharon & Huxford, Bob. Collector's Encyclopedia of Fiesta. 4th rev. ed. (Illus.). 1981. pap. 9.95 (ISBN 0-89145-168-4). Collector Bks.
Jitsupenshva. The Traditional Japanese Annual Brothel Festival. (Asian Folklore & Social Life Monographs: Vol. 99). 1977. 4.50 (ISBN 0-89986-329-9). E Langstaff.
Joy, Margaret. Highdays & Holidays. (Illus.). 128p. (gr. 3 up). 1981. 11.95 (ISBN 0-571-11771-6, Pub. by Faber & Faber). Merrimack Bk Serv.
Kaufmann, Thomas D. Variations on the Imperial Theme: Studies in Ceremonial Art & Collecting in the Age of Maximilian II & Rudolf II. LC 77-94699. (Outstanding Dissertations in the Fine Arts Ser.). 1978. lib. bdg. 24.00x (ISBN 0-8240-3231-4). Garland Pub.
Klee, Theophil. Zur Geschichte der Gymnischen Agone an Griechischen Festen. 136p. 1980. 12.50 (ISBN 0-89005-336-7). Ares.
Ku Lu. Annual Festivals of Su-Chou, 1821-1850. (Nationalpeking University & Chinese Assn. for Folklore, Folklore & Folkliterature Ser.: No. 128). (Chinese.). 7.00 (ISBN 0-89986-202-0). E Langstaff.
LaChapelle, Dolores & Bourque, Janet. Earth Festivals: Seasonal Celebrations for Everyone, Young & Old. LC 76-15321. (Illus.). 196p. (Orig.). 1976. pap. 12.50 (ISBN 0-917270-00-2). Finn Hill.
Laurie, Roma. Festivals & Adjudication: The Organization of Music & Drama Festivals. 160p. 1975. 14.95x (ISBN 0-8464-0408-7). Beekman Pubs.
Marcus, Rebecca B. & Marcus, Judith. Fiesta Time in Mexico. LC 73-12834. (Around the World Holidays Ser). (Illus.). 96p. (gr. 4-7). 1974. PLB 6.48 (ISBN 0-8116-4953-9). Garrard.
Myers, Robert J. & Hallmark Cards Editors. Celebrations: The Complete Book of American Holidays. LC 77-163086. 288p. 1972. 10.95 (ISBN 0-385-07677-0). Doubleday.
Pallis, Svend A. The Babylonian Akitu Festival. LC 78-72756. (Ancient Mesopotamian Texts & Studies). Repr. of 1926 ed. 42.50 (ISBN 0-404-18203-8). AMS Pr.
Parke, H. W. Festivals of the Athenians. LC 76-12819. (Aspects of Greek & Roman Life). (Illus.). 1977. 22.50x (ISBN 0-8014-1054-1). Cornell U Pr.
Pieper, Josef. In Tune with the World. 1978. pap. 4.50 (ISBN 0-8199-0464-3). Franciscan Herald.
Seabough, Ed & Hendrix, John. The Festival of Night & Light. new ed. 16p. 1975. 1.50 (ISBN 0-8054-9722-6). Broadman.
Sorensen, Alice J. Springtime in Sweden. LC 58-10484. (Illus.). 1958. pap. 4.00 (ISBN 0-295-73939-8). U of Wash Pr.
Spangler, David. Festivals in the New Age. 92p. 1981. pap. 4.95 (ISBN 0-905249-12-7, Pub. by Findhorn-Thule Scotland). Hydra Bk.
Spicer, Dorothy G. Book of Festivals. LC 75-92667. 1969. Repr. of 1937 ed. 28.00 (ISBN 0-8103-3143-8). Gale.
--Folk Festivals & the Foreign Community. LC 70-167201. 1976. Repr. of 1923 ed. 22.00 (ISBN 0-8103-4301-0). Gale.
--Yearbook of English Festivals. LC 74-162632. (Illus.). 298p. 1954. Repr. lib. bdg. 16.50x (ISBN 0-8371-6132-0, SPEF). Greenwood.
Spicer, Dorothy G., ed. Festivals of Western Europe. 1958. 8.00 (ISBN 0-8242-0016-0). Wilson.
Stewart, W. Grant. The Popular Superstitions & Festive Amusements of the Highlanders of Scotland. 1978. Repr. of 1851 ed. lib. bdg. 25.00 (ISBN 0-8492-8007-9). R West.
Truck, Fred, ed. The Des Moines Festival of the Avant-Garde Invites You to a Show Without Really Being There. (Orig.). pap. text ed. 7.50 (ISBN 0-938236-02-4). Cookie Pr.
Urlin, Ethel L. Festivals, Holy Days & Saints Days. LC 70-89301. (Illus.). 1971. Repr. of 1915 ed. 26.00 (ISBN 0-8103-3745-2). Gale.
Wasserman, Paul & Herman, Esther, eds. Festivals Sourcebook: A Reference Guide to Fairs, Festivals, & Celebrations. 1st ed. LC 76-48852. 1977. 74.00 (ISBN 0-8103-0311-6). Gale.
Watson, Jane W. Parade of Soviet Holidays. LC 73-12785. (Around the World Holidays Ser). (Illus.). 96p. (gr. 4-7). 1974. PLB 6.48 (ISBN 0-8116-4951-2). Garrard.
Weilerstein, Sadie R. What the Moon Brought. (Illus.). (gr. 1-3). 1942. 4.50 (ISBN 0-8276-0166-2, 261). Jewish Pubn.
Wilson, Joseph T. Presenting Folk Culture: A Handbook on Folk Festival Organization & Management. Udall, Lee, ed. Date not set. write for info. (ISBN 0-87049-300-0). U of Tenn Pr.
Yamamoto, Yoshiko. The Namahage: A Festival in the Northeast of Japan. LC 78-1500. (Illus.). 1978. text ed. 16.00x (ISBN 0-915980-66-5). Inst Study Human.

FESTIVALS–JEWS
see Fasts and Feasts–Judaism

FESTSCHRIFTEN–BIBLIOGRAPHY
Danton, J. Periam & Pulis, Jane F., eds. Index to Festschriften in Librarianship, 1967-1975. 1979. 52.95 (ISBN 3-7940-7034-8, Verlag Dokumentation). Bowker.
Feinberg, Gerald, et al, eds. A Festschrift for Maurice Goldhaber. new ed. LC 80-20599. (Transaction Ser.: Vol. 40). 293p. 1980. 25.00x (ISBN 0-89766-086-2). NY Acad Sci.
Golden, H. H. & Simches, S. O. Modern French Literature & Language. Repr. of 1953 ed. 9.00 (ISBN 0-527-34300-5). Kraus Repr.
Marcus, J. R. & Bilgray, A., eds. Index to Jewish Festschriften. Repr. of 1937 ed. 18.00 (ISBN 0-527-61300-2). Kraus Repr.
Neighbour, O. W., ed. Music & Bibliography: A Festschrift for Alec Hyatt King. 1980. text ed. 30.00 (ISBN 0-85157-296-0). K G Saur.
New York Public Library & the Library of Congress. Guide to Festschriften. (Festschriften Collection of the New York Public Library). 1977. lib. bdg. 120.00 (ISBN 0-8161-0069-1). G K Hall.
Sayre, John L. & Hamburger, Roberta, eds. An Index of Festschriften in Religion in the Graduate Seminary Library of Phillips University: New Titles, 1971-1973. 136p. 1973. pap. 6.50x (ISBN 0-912832-05-3). Seminary Pr.

FESTUCA
Aman, Reinhold, ed. G. Legman Festschrift. LC 78-69966. (Maledicta: International Journal of Verbal Aggression: Vol. 1 No. 2). 1978. pap. 10.00 (ISBN 0-916500-51-9). Maledicta.
Hackel, Eduard. Monographia Festucarum Europaearum. 15.50 (ISBN 0-384-20660-3). Johnson Repr.

FET, AFANASY
see Shenshin, Afanasii Afanasevich, 1820-1892

FETAL ERYTHROBLASTOSIS
see Erythroblastosis Fetalis

FETICIDE
see Abortion

FETISHISM
see also Animism; Idols and Images; Nature Worship; Voodooism
Doutreloux, Albert D. Ombre Des Fetiches, Societe et Culture Yombe. (Fr). 1967. pap. 7.50x (ISBN 2-7637-6191-7, Pub. by Laval). Intl Schol Bk Serv.
Farrow, Stephen S. Faith, Fancies & Fetish or Yoruba Paganism. LC 76-98718. (Illus.). Repr. of 1926 ed. 12.25x (ISBN 0-8371-2759-9, Pub. by Negro U Pr). Greenwood.
Milligan, Robert H. Fetish Folk of West Africa. LC 73-116017. Repr. of 1912 ed. 24.75 (ISBN 0-404-00200-5). AMS Pr.
Nassau, Robert H. Fetichism in West Africa: Fourty Years' Observation of Native Customs & Superstitions. LC 69-18995. (Illus.). Repr. of 1904 ed. 20.50x (ISBN 0-8371-0977-9, Pub. by Negro U Pr). Greenwood.

FETUS
see also Maternal-Fetal Exchange; Obstetrics
Austin, C. R. & Short, R. V., eds. Embryonic & Fetal Development. (Reproduction in Mammals Ser.: Bk. 2). (Illus.). 1972. 24.50 (ISBN 0-521-08373-7); pap. 6.50x (ISBN 0-521-09682-0). Cambridge U Pr.
Babson, S. Gorham, et al. Diagnosis & Management of the Fetus & Neonate at Risk: A Guide for Team Care. 4th ed. LC 79-16957. (Illus.). 1979. text ed. 27.50 (ISBN 0-8016-0415-X). Mosby.
Barnes, Allan C. & Seeds, A. Elmore. The Water Metabolism of the Fetus. (Illus.). 184p. 1972. ed. spiral bdg. 18.75photocopy (ISBN 0-398-02224-0). C C Thomas.
Beard, R. W. & Nathanielsz, P. W. Fetal Physiology & Medicine. LC 76-20126. (Illus.). 1976. text ed. 32.00 (ISBN 0-7216-1600-3). Saunders.
Bloom, Arthur D. & James, L. S., eds. The Fetus & the Newborn. (Alan R. Less, Inc. Ser.: Vol. 17, No.1). 1981. 36.00 (ISBN 0-8451-1041-1). March of Dimes.
Cibils, Luis A. Electronic Fetal-Material Monitoring: Antepartum-Intrapartum. (Illus.). 416p. 1981. text ed. 56.00 (ISBN 0-88416-192-7). Wright-PSG.
Cross, K. W., et al, eds. Foetal & Neonatal Physiology: Proceedings. LC 72-93673. (Illus.). 600p. 1973. 95.00 (ISBN 0-521-20178-0). Cambridge U Pr.
Curran, J. T. Fetal Heart Monitoring. 1975. 21.95 (ISBN 0-407-00014-3). Butterworth.
Dito, William R., et al. Clinical Pathologic Correlations in Amniotic Fluid. (Illus.). 1975. 12.00 (ISBN 0-89189-010-6, 45-9-005-00). Am Soc Clinical.
Fazekas, Gy & Kosa, F. Forensic Fetal Osteology. (Illus.). 1978. 42.50x (ISBN 963-05-1491-5). Intl Pubns Serv.
Fazekas, I. & Kosa, F. Forensic Fetal Osteology. 1978. 41.50 (ISBN 0-9960011-9-0, Pub. by Kiado Hungary). Heyden.
Flanagan, Geraldine. First Nine Months of Life. 1962. 11.95 (ISBN 0-671-26105-3). S&S.
Freeman, Roger & Garite, Thomas. Fetal Monitoring. (Illus.). 187p. 1981. lib. bdg. 27.00 (ISBN 0-683-03378-6). Williams & Wilkins.
Goodlin, Robert C. Care of the Fetus. LC 78-62542. (Illus.). 580p. 1979. 43.50x (ISBN 0-89352-021-7). Masson Pub.
Goodwin, J. W., et al. Perinatal Medicine. (Illus.). 642p. 1976. 59.95 (ISBN 0-683-03649-1). Williams & Wilkins.
Hafez, E. S. The Mammalian Fetus: Comparative Biology & Methodology. (Illus.). 368p. 1976. 37.75 (ISBN 0-398-03285-8). C C Thomas.
Hawker, Ross W. Notebook of Medical Physiology - Endocrinology. LC 77-4459. (Illus.). 1978. pap. text ed. 10.75 (ISBN 0-443-01516-3). Churchill.
Hodari, A. Alberto & Mariona, Federico. Physiological Biochemistry of the Fetus: Proceedings of the International Symposium. (Illus.). 392p. 1972. photocopy ed. spiral 34.75 (ISBN 0-398-02316-6). C C Thomas.
Kaback, M. M. & Valenti, C. Intrauterine Fetal Visualization. (International Congress Ser.: No. 371). 1976. 50.25 (ISBN 0-444-15196-6, Excerpta Medica). Elsevier.
Kerpel-Fronius, E., ed. Perinatal Medicine, 2 vols. (Illus.). 1449p. 1978. Set. 125.00x (ISBN 963-05-1413-3). Intl Pubns Serv.
Klingberg, M. A., et al, eds. Drugs & Fetal Development. LC 72-86141. (Advances in Experimental Medicine & Biology Ser.: Vol. 27). 559p. 1972. 49.50 (ISBN 0-306-39027-2, Plenum Pr). Plenum Pub.
Lauersen, Neils H. & Hochberg, Howard. Clinical Perinatal Biochemical Monitoring. 320p. 1981. 30.00 (ISBN 0-686-77745-X, 1901-1). Williams & Wilkins.
McClung, Jean. Effects of High Altitude on Human Birth: Observations on Mothers, Placentas, & the Newborn in Two Peruvian Populations. LC 72-91629. 1969. 8.50x (ISBN 0-674-24065-0). Harvard U Pr.
Miller, Herbert C. & Merritt, T. Allen. Fetal Growth in Humans. (Illus.). 1979. pap. 13.95 (ISBN 0-8151-5907-2). Year Bk Med.
Moore, Keith L. The Developing Human. 2nd ed. LC 76-20098. (Illus.). 1977. text ed. 17.50 (ISBN 0-7216-6471-7). Saunders.
Nathanielsz, Peter W., ed. Fetal Endocrinology: An Experimental Approach. LC 76-22194. 1976. 41.50 (ISBN 0-7204-0582-3, North-Holland). Elsevier.
Nitzan, Menachem, ed. The Influence of Maternal Hormones on the Fetus & Newborn. (Pediatric & Adolescent Endocrinology: Vol. 5). (Illus.). 1979. pap. 59.50 (ISBN 3-8055-2902-3). S Karger.
Norgaard-Pederson. Human Alpha Feto-Protein. 1976. 6.95 (ISBN 0-8391-0987-3). Univ Park.
Notake, Y. & Suzuki, S. Biological & Clinical Aspects of the Fetus. (Illus.). 1977. 65.00 (ISBN 0-8391-0986-5). Univ Park.
Parke, Wesley. Photographic Atlas of Fetal Anatomy. (Illus.). 1975. 44.50 (ISBN 0-8391-0644-0). Univ Park.
Patterson, William B. Fetal Adrenal Hyperplasia: Its Relationship to Late Toxemia. LC 73-90025. (Illus.). 81p. 1973. 6.00 (ISBN 0-686-05608-6). W B Patterson.
Rementeria, Jose L., ed. Drug Abuse in Pregnancy & Neonatal Effects. LC 77-3541. (Illus.). 1977. text ed. 23.50 (ISBN 0-8016-4108-X). Mosby.
Roberts, D. F. & Thomson, A. M. The Biology of Human Fetal Growth. LC 75-28154. (Study of Human Biology Ser: Vol. 15). 1976. 32.95 (ISBN 0-470-72584-2). Halsted Pr.
Russell, J. G. Radiology in Obstetrics & Antenatal Paediatrics. Trapnell, David H., ed. (Radiology in Clinical Diagnosis Ser.: Vol. 8). (Illus.). 1973. 18.95 (ISBN 0-407-38410-3). Butterworth.
Sandler. Amnotic Fluid & Its Clinical Significance. (Reproductive Medicine Ser.: Vol. 2). 328p. 1981. 35.00 (ISBN 0-8247-1346-X). Dekker.
Schardein, James L. Drugs As Teratogens. LC 76-22749. (Uniscience Ser.). 304p. 1976. 59.95 (ISBN 0-8493-5171-5). CRC Pr.
Solomon, J. B. Foetal & Neonatal Immunology. 1971. 38.00 (ISBN 0-444-10066-0, North-Holland). Elsevier.
Sontag, Lester W. Fetal Heart Rate As a Behavioral Indicator. 1938. pap. 5.00 (ISBN 0-527-01504-0). Kraus Repr.
Stave, Uwe. Perinatal Physiology. LC 77-12596. (Illus.). 875p. 1978. 59.50 (ISBN 0-306-30999-8, Plenum Pr). Plenum Pub.
Stein, Zena, et al. Famine & Human Development: The Dutch Hunger Winter 1944-1945. (Illus.). 425p. 1974. text ed. 14.95x (ISBN 0-19-501811-7). Oxford U Pr.
Taylor, Stewart, ed. Beck's Obstetrical Practice & Fetal Medicine. 10th ed. (Illus.). 650p. 1976. 38.50 (ISBN 0-683-08123-3). Williams & Wilkins.
Walsh, S. Zoe, et al. The Human Fetal & Neonatal Circulation: Function & Structure. (American Lectures in Cerebral Palsy Ser.). (Illus.). 368p. 1974. 21.75 (ISBN 0-398-02662-9). C C Thomas.
WHO Scientific Group. Geneva, 1973. Maturation of Fetal Body Systems: Report. (Technical Report Ser.: No. 540). (Also avail. in French & Spanish). 1974. pap. 2.00 (ISBN 92-4-120540-7). World Health.
Windle, William F. Physiology of the Fetus: Relation to Brain Damage in the Perinatal Period. (Illus.). 176p. 1971. text ed. 13.50 (ISBN 0-398-02438-3). C C Thomas.
Winick, Myron, ed. Nutrition & Fetal Development. LC 73-19663. 200p. 1974. 26.50 (ISBN 0-471-95435-7). Krieger.
Wirsen, Claes, et al. Child Is Born: The Drama of Life Before Birth. 1969. pap. 6.95 (ISBN 0-440-51214-X, Dell Trade Pbks). Dell.

FETUS–ABNORMALITIES AND DEFORMITIES
Athey, Patricia A. & Hadlock, Frank P. Ultrasound in Obstetrics & Gynecology. LC 81-4646. (Illus.). 283p. 1981. text ed. 44.50 (ISBN 0-8016-0374-9). Mosby.
Bergsma, Daniel, ed. Cytogenetics, Environmental Malformation Syndromes. LC 76-20510. (Alan R. Liss., Inc. Ser.: Vol 12, No. 5). 1976. 30.00 (ISBN 0-686-18079-8). March of Dimes.
Bloom, Arthur D. & James, L. Stanley, eds. The Fetus & the Newborn. LC 81-3745. (Birth Defects: Original Article Ser.: Vol. XVII, No. 1). 280p. 1981. 36.00 (ISBN 0-8451-1041-1). A R Liss.
Moghissi, Kamran S. Birth Defects & Fetal Development: Endocrine & Metabolic Factors. (Illus.). 352p. 1974. text ed. 32.75 (ISBN 0-398-02784-6). C C Thomas.
Naftolin, Frederick, ed. Abnormal Fetal Growth: Biological Bases & Consequences, LSRR 10. (Dahlem Workshop Reports Ser.: No. 10). 1978. pap. 30.60 (ISBN 0-89573-094-4). Verlag Chemie.
Torpin, Richard. Fetal Malformations: Caused by Amnion Rupture During Gestation. (Illus.). 180p. 1968. pap. 18.50 (ISBN 0-398-01933-9). C C Thomas.

FETUS–DISEASES
see also Erythroblastosis Fetalis
Abel, Ernest L. Fetal Alcohol Syndrome, Vol. I: An Annotated & Comprehensive Bibliography. 208p. 1981. 64.95 (ISBN 0-8493-6192-3). CRC Pr.
Aladjem, Silvio, et al. Clinical Perinatology. 2nd ed. LC 79-24340. (Illus.). 1979. text ed. 52.50 (ISBN 0-8016-0103-7). Mosby.
Barson. Laboratory Investigation of Fetal Disease. 1981. 50.00 (ISBN 0-8151-0416-2). Year Bk Med.
Beard, R. W. & Nathanielsz, P. W. Fetal Physiology & Medicine. LC 76-20126. (Illus.). 1976. text ed. 32.00 (ISBN 0-7216-1600-3). Saunders.
Bolognese, Ronald J. Perinatal Medicine: Clinical Management of the High Risk Fetus & Neonate. 332p. 1977. 33.00 (ISBN 0-683-00907-9). Williams & Wilkins.
Crosignani, Pier G. & Pardi, Giorgio, eds. Fetal Evaluation During Pregnancy & Labor: Experimental & Clinical Aspects. 307p. 1972. 49.50 (ISBN 0-12-198350-1). Acad Pr.

Evans, Hugh E. & Glass, Leonard. Perinatal Medicine. (Illus.). 1976. 44.00x (ISBN 0-06-140791-7, Harper Medical). Har-Row.
Lambert, H. P. & Wood, C. B., eds. Immunological Aspects of Infection in the Fetus & New Born. (Beecham Colloquia Ser.). 1981. 39.50 (ISBN 0-12-434660-X). Acad Pr.
Lubchenco, Lula O. The High Risk Infant. LC 76-1229. (Major Problems in Clinical Pediatrics: Vol. 14). (Illus.). 1976. 19.50 (ISBN 0-7216-5800-8). Saunders.
Milunsky, Aubrey. The Prenatal Diagnosis of Hereditary Disorders. (Illus.). 276p. 1973. text ed. 16.75 (ISBN 0-398-02747-1). C C Thomas.
Milunsky, Aubrey, et al, eds. Advances in Perinatal Medicine, Vol. 1. 450p. 1981. 35.00 (ISBN 0-306-40482-6, Plenum Pr). Plenum Pub.
Persaud, T. V. Prenatal Pathology: Fetal Medicine. (Illus.). 212p. 1979. 25.25 (ISBN 0-398-03756-6). C C Thomas.
Potter, Edith L. Pathology of the Fetus & the Infant. 3rd ed. (Illus.). 1975. 77.50 (ISBN 0-8151-6760-1). Year Bk Med.
Remington, Jack S. & Klein, Jerome O., eds. Infectious Diseases of the Fetus & Newborn Infant. LC 74-9438. (Illus.). 500p. 1976. text ed. 55.00 (ISBN 0-7216-7547-6). Saunders.
Schwarz, Richard A. & Yaffe, Sumner J., eds. Drug & Chemical Risks to the Fetus & Newborn. LC 79-26191. (Progress in Clinical & Biological Research Ser.: Vol. 36). 166p. 1980. 20.00 (ISBN 0-8451-0036-X). A R Liss.
Symposium by the New York University Medical Center & the National Foundation-March of Dimes, New York City, Mar. 1975. Infections of the Fetus & the Newborn Infant: Proceedings. Krugman, Saul & Gershon, Anne A., eds. LC 75-13856. (Progress in Clinical & Biological Research: Vol. 3). 204p. 1975. 23.00x (ISBN 0-8451-0003-3). A R Liss.
Tucker, Susan M. & Bryant, Sandra. Fetal Monitoring & Fetal Assesment in High Risk Pregnancy. LC 77-19098. 1978. pap. text ed. 11.95 (ISBN 0-8016-5121-2). Mosby.

FETUS, DEATH OF

see also Abortion

Bierschwal, C. J. & DeBois, C. H. The Technique of Fetotomy in Large Animals. (Illus.). 1972. soft bdg. 8.75 (ISBN 0-935078-05-3, VM 16). Veterinary Med.
Porter, Ian H. & Hook, Ernest B., eds. Human Embryonic & Fetal Death. LC 80-19011. (Birth Defects Institute Symposium X Ser.). 1980. 27.00 (ISBN 0-12-562860-9). Acad Pr.
WHO Expert Committee, Geneva, 1970. Prevention of Perinatal Mortality & Morbidity: A Report. (Technical Report Ser: No. 457). 60p. 1970. pap. 2.40 (ISBN 92-4-120457-5, 664). World Health.
WHO Seminar, Tours, 1969. Prevention of Perinatal Mortality & Morbidity: A Report. (Public Health Papers Ser: No. 42). 97p. 1972. pap. 2.80 (ISBN 92-4-130042-6, 668). World Health.

FEUCHTWANGER, LION, 1884-1958

Kahn, Lothar. Insight & Action: The Life & Work of Lion Feuchtwanger. LC 73-2897. (Illus.). 380p. 1976. 18.00 (ISBN 0-8386-1314-4). Fairleigh Dickinson.
Spalek, John M., ed. Lion Feuchtwanger: The Man, His Ideas & His Work. LC 75-188985. (University of Southern California Studies in Comparative Literature Ser: No. 3). 12.95x (ISBN 0-912158-16-6). Hennessey.

FEUDAL CASTLES

see Castles

FEUDAL LAW

Jacoby, David. La Feodalite En Grece Medievale: Les "Assises De Romanie", Sources, Application et Diffusion. (Documents et Recheroches Sur L'economie Des Pays Byzantins, Islamiques et Slaves et Leurs Relations Commerciales Au Moyen Age: No. 10). (Illus.). 1971. pap. 38.50x (ISBN 90-2796-876-4). Mouton.
Lyon, Bryce D. From Fief to Indenture: The Transition from Feudal to Non-Feudal Contract in Western Europe. 1971. lib. bdg. 17.50x (ISBN 0-374-95211-6). Octagon.

FEUDALISM

see also Chivalry; Clans and Clan System; Land Tenure; Middle Ages; Peasantry

Anderson, Perry. Passages from Antiquity to Feudalism. 1978. pap. 7.75 (ISBN 0-86091-709-6, Pub. by NLB). Schocken.
Bartha, Antal. Hungarian Society in the Ninth & Tenth Centuries. 147p. 1975. 12.50x (ISBN 963-05-0308-5). Intl Pubns Serv.
Bellette, Emile. La Succession Aux Fiefs Dans les Coutumes Flamandes. LC 80-1997. Repr. of 1926 ed. 23.50 (ISBN 0-404-18553-3). AMS Pr.
Bloch, Marc. Feudal Society, 2 Vols. Manyon, L. A., tr. LC 61-4322. 1961. Vol. 1. pap. 3.45 (ISBN 0-226-05978-2, P156, Phoen); Vol. 2. pap. 3.95 (ISBN 0-226-05979-0, P157, Phoen). U of Chicago Pr.
Borkenau, Franz. Der Ubergang Vom Feudalen Zum Burgerlichen Weltbild. LC 74-25740. (European Sociology Ser.). 574p. 1974. Repr. 32.00x (ISBN 0-405-06496-9). Arno.
Cahen, Claude. La Regime Feodal De l'Italie Normande. LC 80-1995. Repr. of 1923 ed. 22.00 (ISBN 0-404-18555-X). AMS Pr.
Calmette, Joseph L. La Societe Feodale. LC 80-1994. Repr. of 1923 ed. 26.50 (ISBN 0-404-18556-8). AMS Pr.
Cheetham, Nicholas. The Feudal Age of Greece. 288p. cancelled. Yale U Pr.
Clouscard, Michel. L' Etre & le Code: Le Proces De Production D'un Ensemble Precapitaliste. 1972. pap. 38.50x (ISBN 90-2797-010-6). Mouton.
Coulborn, Rushton, ed. Feudalism in History. 1965. Repr. of 1956 ed. 22.50 (ISBN 0-208-00274-X, Archon). Shoe String.
Critchley, John. Feudalism. 1977. text ed. 18.95x (ISBN 0-04-909009-7); pap. text ed. 8.95x (ISBN 0-04-909010-0). Allen Unwin.
Dobb, Maurice, et al. The Transition from Feudalism to Capitalism. 1978. (Pub by NLB); pap. 6.25 (ISBN 0-86091-701-0). Schocken.
Duby, Georges. The Three Orders: Feudal Society Imagined. Goldhammer, Arthur, tr. LC 80-13158. 432p. 1980. lib. bdg. 25.00x (ISBN 0-226-16771-2). U of Chicago Pr.
English, Barbara. The Lord of Holderness, Ten Eighty-Six to Twelve Sixty: A Study in Feudal Society. (Illus.). 288p. 1979. 49.50x (ISBN 0-19-713437-8). Oxford U Pr.
Fourquin, Guy. Lordship & Feudalism in the Middle Ages. LC 75-11141. 1976. 12.50x (ISBN 0-87663-718-7, Pica). Universe.
Ganshof, Francois L. Feudalism. Grierson, Philip, tr. pap. 3.95x (ISBN 0-06-131058-1, TB1058, Torch). Har-Row.
Green, Dennis H. Carolingian Lord. 1965. 90.00 (ISBN 0-521-05138-X). Cambridge U Pr.
Herlihy, David, ed. History of Feudalism. 1979. pap. text ed. 6.95x (ISBN 0-391-00901-X). Humanities.
Jenks, Edward. Law & Politics in the Middle Ages with a Synoptic Table of Sources. LC 76-114814. (Research & Source Works: No. 429). 1970. Repr. of 1913 ed. text ed. 22.50 (ISBN 0-8337-1839-8). B Franklin.
Kamenka, E. & Neale, R. S. Feudalism Capitalism & Beyond. LC 75-32936. 1976. 16.95x (ISBN 0-312-28805-0). St Martin.
Kula, Witold. An Economic Theory of the Feudal System. (Illus.). 1976. 14.50 (ISBN 0-902308-19-X, Pub. by NLB). Schocken.
Lyon, Bryce D. From Fief to Indenture: The Transition from Feudal to Non-Feudal Contract in Western Europe. 1971. lib. bdg. 17.50x (ISBN 0-374-95211-6). Octagon.
Mor, Carlo G. L' Eta Feudale, 2 vols. LC 80-2016. Repr. of 1952 ed. Set. 110.00 (ISBN 0-404-18609-2). AMS Pr.
Perrin, Charles E. La Societe Feodale Allemande et Ses Institutions Du Xe Au XIIe Siecle. LC 80-2013. Repr. of 1956 ed. 34.50 (ISBN 0-404-18583-5). AMS Pr.
Poliak, Abraham N. Feudalism in Egypt, Syria, Palestine & Lebanon 1250-1900: With Two Additional Articles. LC 77-10729. (Studies in Islamic History: No. 13). 125p. Repr. of 1939 ed. lib. bdg. 12.50x (ISBN 0-87991-462-9). Porcupine Pr.
Rader, Trout. The Economics of Feudalism. Lieberman, Bernhardt, ed. LC 77-132148. (Monographs & Texts in Behavioural Sciences). (Illus.). 146p. 1971. 22.50x (ISBN 0-677-03280-3). Gordon.
Sanchez-Albornoz y Menduina, Claudio. En Torno a los Origenes del Feudalismo, 3 vols. LC 80-2004. Repr. of 1942 ed. Set. 110.00 (ISBN 0-404-18590-8). Vol. 1 (ISBN 0-404-18591-6). Vol. 2 (ISBN 0-404-18592-4). Vol. 3 (ISBN 0-404-18593-2). AMS Pr.
Seignobos, Charles. The Feudal Regime. 1902. Repr. 10.00 (ISBN 0-685-43297-1). Norwood Edns.
Stephenson, Carl. Mediaeval Feudalism. (Illus.). 116p. (YA) (gr. 9-12). 1967. 14.50x (ISBN 0-8014-0410-X); pap. 2.95 (ISBN 0-8014-9013-8, CP13). Cornell U Pr.
Strayer, Joseph R. Feudalism. LC 78-24523. (Anvil Ser.). 192p. 1979. pap. text ed. 4.95 (ISBN 0-88275-810-1). Krieger.
Stubbs, W. Historical Introductions to the Rolls Series. LC 68-25267. (British History Ser., No. 30). 1969. Repr. of 1902 ed. lib. bdg. 45.95 (ISBN 0-8383-0243-2). Haskell.
Therborn, Goran. What Does the Ruling Class Do When It Rules? 290p. 1980. pap. 8.75 (ISBN 0-86091-725-8, Pub. by NLB). Schocken.
Thompson, James W. Feudal Germany. LC 80-2001. Repr. of 1928 ed. 67.50 (ISBN 0-404-18601-7). AMS Pr.
Tierney, Brian, et al. Feudalism. 1968. pap. text ed. 1.95 (ISBN 0-394-32052-2, RanC). Random.
Tierney, Brian, et al, eds. Feudalism: Cause or Cure of Anarchy? 3rd ed. (Historical Pamphlets). 1977. pap. text ed. 1.95x (ISBN 0-394-32052-2). Random.

FEUDALISM–JUVENILE LITERATURE

Buehr, Walter. Knights, Castles & Feudal Life. (Illus.). (gr. 4-6). 1957. PLB 5.29 (ISBN 0-399-60341-7). Putnam.

FEUDALISM–CANADA

Harris, Richard C. Seigneurial System in Early Canada. (Illus.). 264p. 1966. 20.00x (ISBN 0-299-03980-3). U of Wis Pr.
Munro, William B., ed. Documents Relating to the Seigniorial Tenure in Canada, 1598-1854. LC 68-28598. 1968. Repr. of 1908 ed. lib. bdg. 30.50x (ISBN 0-8371-5042-6, MUDS). Greenwood.

FEUDALISM–EGYPT

Hardy, Edward R., Jr. Large Estates of Byzantine Egypt. LC 68-58589. (Columbia University Studies in the Social Sciences: No. 354). 16.50 (ISBN 0-404-51354-9). AMS Pr.
Poliak, A. N. Feudalism in Egypt, 1250-1900. 1978. lib. bdg. 49.95 (ISBN 0-685-62293-2). Revisionist Pr.

FEUDALISM–FRANCE

Bloch, Marc. French Rural History: An Essay on Its Basic Characteristics. Sondheimer, Janet, tr. LC 66-15483. (Illus.). 1966. 25.00x (ISBN 0-520-00127-3); pap. 7.95x (ISBN 0-520-01660-2, CAMPUS28). U of Cal Pr.
Boncerf, Pierre-Francois. Les Inconveniens Des Droits Feodaux. Repr. of 1776 ed. 18.50 (ISBN 0-8287-0105-9). Clearwater Pub.
Evergates, Theodore. Feudal Society in the Bailliage of Troyes under the Counts of Champagne, 1152-1284. LC 75-11346. (Illus.). 228p. 1976. 18.00x (ISBN 0-8018-1663-7). Johns Hopkins.
Flach, Jacques. Origines De L'ancienne France, 4 Vols. LC 69-18612. (Research & Source Works: No. 391). (Fr). 1970. Repr. of 1917 ed. Set. text ed. 135.00 (ISBN 0-8337-1148-2). B Franklin.
Fundenberg, George B. Feudal France in the French Epic. LC 65-27108. 1966. Repr. of 1918 ed. 10.00 (ISBN 0-8046-0161-5). Kennikat.
Lagouelle, Henri. Essai Sur la Conception Juridique De la Propriete Fonciere Dans le Tres Anciendroit Normand: Premiere Partie, la Conception Feodale. LC 80-2020. Repr. of 1902 ed. 31.50 (ISBN 0-404-18574-6). AMS Pr.
Odegaard, Charles E. Vassi & Fideles in the Carolingian Empire. 1971. lib. bdg. 12.00x (ISBN 0-374-96135-2). Octagon.
Petit-Dutaillis, Charles E. The Feudal Monarchy in France & England from the Tenth to the Thirteenth Century. LC 80-2011. Repr. of 1936 ed. 44.50 (ISBN 0-404-18585-1). AMS Pr.

FEUDALISM–GREAT BRITAIN

Barlow, Frank. The Feudal Kingdom of England: 1042-1216. 3rd ed. (Illus.). 1972. pap. text ed. 11.95x (ISBN 0-582-48237-2). Longman.
Berkowitz, David S. & Thorne, Samuel E., eds. George Meriton. Sir Henry Spelman. Anon. Charles Fearne. (English Legal History Ser.: Vol. 137). 370p. 1979. lib. bdg. 55.00 (ISBN 0-8240-3174-1). Garland Pub.
Milsom, S. F. The Legal Framework of English Feudalism. LC 75-23531. (Cambridge Studies in English Legal History). 1976. 33.95 (ISBN 0-521-20947-1). Cambridge U Pr.
Painter, Sidney. Studies in the History of the English Feudal Barony. 1980. Repr. 14.00x (ISBN 0-374-96177-8). Octagon.
--Studies in the History of the English Feudal Barony. LC 78-64191. (Johns Hopkins University. Studies in the Social Sciences. Sixty-First Ser. 1943: 3). Repr. of 1943 ed. 20.00 (ISBN 0-404-61298-9). AMS Pr.
Petit-Dutaillis, Charles E. The Feudal Monarchy in France & England from the Tenth to the Thirteenth Century. LC 80-2011. Repr. of 1936 ed. 44.50 (ISBN 0-404-18585-1). AMS Pr.
Stenton, Frank M. The First Century of English Feudalism, 1066-1166. 2nd ed. LC 78-26688. 1979. Repr. of 1961 ed. lib. bdg. 22.50x (ISBN 0-313-20915-4, STFR). Greenwood.

FEUDALISM–JAPAN

Duus, Peter. Feudalism in Japan. (Studies in World Civilization). (Orig.). 1969. pap. text ed. 4.95x (ISBN 0-394-31076-4, KnopfC). Knopf.
Tsukahira, Toshio G. Feudal Control in Tokugawa Japan: The Sankin Kotai System. LC 67-3532. (East Asian Monographs Ser: No. 20). 1966. pap. 9.00x (ISBN 0-674-29900-0). Harvard U Pr.

FEUDALISM–JERUSALEM (LATIN KINGDOM, 1099-1244)

LaMonte, J. L. Feudal Monarchy in the Latin Kingdom of Jerusalem, 1100-1291. 1932. 18.00 (ISBN 0-527-01685-3). Kraus Repr.
Riley-Smith, Jonathan. Feudal Nobility & the Kingdom of Jerusalem, 1174-1277. xiv, 340p. 1973. 19.50 (ISBN 0-208-01348-2, Archon). Shoe String.
Topping, Peter W., tr. Feudal Institutions As Revealed in the Assizes of Romania. LC 80-13052. (The Crusades & Military Orders: Second Ser.). Repr. of 1949 ed. 23.50 (ISBN 0-404-17023-4). AMS Pr.

FEUDALISM–RUSSIA

Eck, Alexandre. Moyen Age Russe. LC 74-149685. Repr. of 1933 ed. 22.00 (ISBN 0-404-02243-X). AMS Pr.

FEUDS

see Vendetta

FEUERBACH, LUDWIG ANDREAS, 1804-1872

Engels, Frederick. Ludwig Feuerbach. 1976. 3.50 (ISBN 0-8351-0141-X); pap. 1.95 (ISBN 0-8351-0142-8). China Bks.
--Ludwig Feuerbach & the Outcome of Classical German Philosophy. 1941. pap. 1.25 (ISBN 0-7178-0120-9). Intl Pub Co.
Engels, Friedrich. Ludwig Feuerbach & the End of Classical German Philosophy. 61p. 1969. pap. 0.50 (ISBN 0-8285-0032-0, Pub. by Progress Pubs Russia). Imported Pubns.
--Ludwig Feuerbach & the Outcome of Classical German Philosophy. LC 76-42701. Repr. of 1934 ed. 18.00 (ISBN 0-404-15369-0). AMS Pr.
--Ludwig Feuerbach y el Fin De la Filosofia Clasica Alemana. 67p. (Span.). 1978. pap. 0.90 (ISBN 0-8285-1672-3, Pub. by Progress Pubs Russia). Imported Pubns.
Marx, Karl & Engels, Frederick. Feuerbach: Opposition of the Materialistic & Idealistic Outlooks. 128p. 1970. 9.95x (ISBN 0-8464-0409-5). Beekman Pubs.
Marx, Karl & Engels, Friedrich. Feuerbach, Opposition of Materialistic & Idealistic Outlook. 140p. 1976. pap. 0.50 (ISBN 0-8285-0026-6, Pub. by Progress Pubs Russia). Imported Pubns.
--Feuerbach, Opposition of Materialistic & Idealistic Outlook. 140p. 1976. pap. 0.50 (ISBN 0-8285-0026-6, Pub. by Progress Pubs Russia). Imported Pubns.
Wartofsky, Marx W. Feuerbach. LC 76-9180. 1977. 47.50 (ISBN 0-521-21257-X). Cambridge U Pr.

FEVER

see also Body Temperature; Malaria

Brazier, Mary A. & Coceani, Flavio. Brain Dysfunction in Infantile Febrile Convulsions. LC 75-14564. (International Brain Research Organization Monograph: Vol. 2). 384p. 1976. 37.50 (ISBN 0-89004-068-0). Raven.
Gilbert, Miriam. Karen Gets a Fever. LC 61-13576. (Medical Bks for Children). (Illus.). (gr. k-7). 1961. PLB 3.95 (ISBN 0-8225-0011-6). Lerner Pubns.
Hale, Enoch, Jr. History & Description of an Epidemic Fever. LC 78-165170. 1971. Repr. of 1818 ed. lib. bdg. 25.00 (ISBN 0-87821-038-5). Milford Hse.
Kluger, Matthew J. Fever: Its Biology, Evolution & Function. LC 79-83998. (Illus.). 1979. 20.00 (ISBN 0-691-08234-0). Princeton U Pr.
Lawson, J. H. A Synopsis of Fevers & Their Treatment. 12th ed. 1977. pap. 13.95 (ISBN 0-8151-5335-X). Year Bk Med.
Lennox-Buchthal, M. A. Febrile Convulsions, Vol. 32. LC 72-83208. 152p. 1973. 36.75 (ISBN 0-444-41026-0). Elsevier.
Lipton, James M., ed. Fever. 275p. 1980. text ed. 34.50 (ISBN 0-89004-451-1). Raven.
Lomax & Schonbaum. Body Temperature: Regulation, Drug Effects, & Theraputic Implications. (Modern Pharmacology-Toxicology Ser.: Vol. 16). 1979. 65.00 (ISBN 0-8247-6655-5). Dekker.
Mosquito-Borne Haemorrhagic Fevers of South-East Asia & the Western Pacific. (Bulletin of WHO: Vol. 35, No. 1). 104p. (Eng. & Fr.). 1966. pap. 3.60 (ISBN 0-686-09224-4). World Health.
Rosenkrantz, Barbara G., ed. Animalcular & Cryptogamic Theories on the Origins of Fevers: An Original Anthology. LC 76-40658. (Public Health in America Ser.). 1977. Repr. of 1977 ed. 15.00x (ISBN 0-405-09839-1). Arno.
Villaverde, Manuel M. & MacMillan, C. Wright. Fever: From Symptom to Treatment. 1978. text ed. 26.50x (ISBN 0-442-29026-8). Van Nos Reinhold.

FEVER–JUVENILE LITERATURE

Berry, James. Why You Feel Hot, Why You Feel Cold: Your Body's Temperature. (Illus.). 64p. (gr. 1-3). 1973. 6.95 (ISBN 0-316-09211-8, 092118R). Little.

FEVER, ENTERIC

see Typhoid Fever

FEVER, PUERPERAL

see Puerperal Septicemia

FEYDEAU, GEORGES LEON JULES MARIE, 1862-1921

Pronko, Leonard C. Georges Feydeau. LC 74-16788. (World Dramatists Ser.). (Illus.). 218p. 1975. 10.95 (ISBN 0-8044-2700-3). Ungar.

FEZ

Le Tourneau, Roger. Fes avant le Protectorat: Etude economique et sociale d'une fille de l'occident musulman. LC 74-15063. (Illus.). Repr. of 1949 ed. 49.50 (ISBN 0-404-12104-7). AMS Pr.

--Fez in the Age of the Marinides. Clement, Besse A., tr. LC 61-6496. (Centers of Civilization Ser: Vol. 4). 1961. 7.95x (ISBN 0-8061-0482-1); pap. 4.95x (ISBN 0-8061-1198-4). U of Okla Pr.

FEZZAN-DESCRIPTION AND TRAVEL

Nachtigal, Gustav. Sahara & Sudan, Vol. IV: Wadai & Darfur. 1971. 43.75x (ISBN 0-520-01789-7). U of Cal Pr.

FIAT (AUTOMOBILE)

see Automobiles, Foreign-Types-Fiat

FIAT MONEY

see Currency Question; Paper Money

FIBER BUNDLES (MATHEMATICS)

Borel, A. Topics in the Homology Theory of Fibre Bundles. (Lecture Notes in Mathematics: Vol. 36). 1967. pap. 10.70 (ISBN 0-387-03907-4). Springer-Verlag.

Drechsler, W. & Mayer, M. E. Fiber Bundle Techniques in Gauge Theory: Lectures in Mathematical Physics at the University of Texas at Austin. Boehm, A. & Dollard, J. D., eds. LC 77-25936. (Lecture Notes in Physics: Vol. 67). 1977. pap. text ed. 16.80 (ISBN 0-387-08350-2). Springer-Verlag.

Gunning, Robert C. Lectures on Vector Bundles Over Riemann Surfaces. (Mathematical Notes Ser.: No. 6). (Orig.). 1967. pap. 14.00 (ISBN 0-691-07998-6). Princeton U Pr.

Hirschowitz, A., ed. Vector Bundles & Differential Equations. 255p. 1980. pap. text ed. 16.00 (ISBN 3-7643-3022-8). Birkhauser.

Husemoller, D. Fibre Bundles. 2nd ed. LC 74-23157. (Graduate Texts in Mathematics: Vol. 20). (Illus.). 340p. 1975. Repr. of 1966 ed. 26.00 (ISBN 0-387-90103-5). Springer-Verlag.

Kamber, F. & Tondeur, P. Flat Manifolds. LC 68-55623. (Lecture Notes in Mathematics: Vol. 67). 1968. pap. 10.70 (ISBN 0-387-04237-7). Springer-Verlag.

Kamber, F. W. & Tondeur, P. Foliated Bundle & Characteristic Classes. (Lecture Notes in Mathematics: Vol. 493). xiii, 208p. 1976. pap. 12.70 (ISBN 0-387-07420-1). Springer-Verlag.

Karras, U., et al. Cutting and Pasting of Manifolds: SK-Groups. LC 73-76374. (Mathematics Lecture Ser: No. 1). 70p. 1973. pap. 3.00 (ISBN 0-914098-10-1). Publish or Perish.

Koschorke, U. Vector Fields & Other Vector Bundle Morphisms: A Singularity Approach. (Lecture Notes in Mathematics Ser.: Vol. 847). 304p. 1981. pap. 18.00 (ISBN 0-387-10572-7). Springer-Verlag.

Orlik, P. Seifert Manifolds. LC 72-90184. (Lecture Notes in Mathematics: Vol. 291). 155p. 1972. pap. 6.30 (ISBN 0-387-06014-6). Springer-Verlag.

Porter, Richard D. Introduction to Fibre Bundles. (Lecture Notes in Pure & Applied Math: Vol. 31). 1977. 24.50 (ISBN 0-8247-6626-1). Dekker.

Schwartz, Jacob T. Differential Geometry & Topology. (Notes on Mathematics & Its Applications Ser). 1968. 37.50- (ISBN 0-677-01510-0). Gordon.

Stone, D. A. Stratified Polyhedra. LC 77-187427. (Lecture Notes in Mathematics: Vol. 252). 193p. 1972. pap. 7.00 (ISBN 0-387-05726-9). Springer-Verlag.

FIBER IN THE DIET

see High-Fiber Diet

FIBER OPTICS

Allan, W. B. Fibre Optics: Theory & Practice. LC 72-95066. (Optical Physics & Engineering Ser). 247p. 1973. 35.00 (ISBN 0-306-30735-9, Plenum Pr). Plenum Pub.

Arnaud, J. A. Beam & Fiber Optics. (Quantum Electronics Ser.). 1976. 55.50 (ISBN 0-12-063250-0). Acad Pr.

Barnoski, M. K., ed. Fundamentals of Fiber Optic Communications. 1976. 22.00 (ISBN 0-12-079150-1). Acad Pr.

BCC Staff. Fiber Optics: G-044. 1978. 850.00 (ISBN 0-89336-116-X). BCC.

Bendow & Mitra, eds. Fiber Optics: Advances in Research and Development. 1979. 59.50 (ISBN 0-306-40167-3, Plenum Pr). Plenum Pub.

Bendow, Bernard & Mitra, Shashanka S., eds. Physics of Fiber Optics, Vol. II. (Advances in Ceramics Ser.). (Illus.). 1981. pap. text ed. 50.00 (ISBN 0-916094-42-1). Am Ceramic.

Bodson, Dennis, ed. & frwd. by. Fiberoptics & Lightwave Communications Vocabulary. LC 80-26168. 156p. (Orig.). 1981. pap. text ed. 12.95 (ISBN 0-07-606706-8, R-030). McGraw.

Centro Studi e Laboratori Telecomunicazioni. Optical Fibre Communication. (Illus.). 928p. 1981. 39.50 (ISBN 0-07-014882-1, P&RB). McGraw.

Clarricoats, P. J., ed. Progress in Optical Communication. 1980. Repr. soft cover 40.50 (ISBN 0-906048-32-X). Inst Elect Eng.

Elion, G. & Elion, H. Fiber Optics in Communications Systems. (Electro-Optics Ser.: Vol. 2). 1978. 21.50 (ISBN 0-8247-6742-X). Dekker.

Fiber Optics Patent Directory, 1881-1979. LC 79-93150. 161p. 1980. 74.00 (ISBN 0-935714-01-4). Patent Data.

Gloge, Detlef. Optical Fiber Technology. LC 75-23777. 1976. 28.95 (ISBN 0-87942-061-8). Inst Electrical.

Happey, F., ed. Recent Advances in Fibre Science. 1977. Vol. 1. 99.00 (ISBN 0-12-323701-7). Acad Pr.

Hewlett-Packard. Optoelectronics-Fiber-Optics Applications Manual. 2nd ed. (Illus.). 448p. 1981. 27.50 (ISBN 0-07-028606-X, P&RB). McGraw.

Hill, D. A. Fibre Optics. 176p. 1977. text ed. 29.50x (ISBN 0-220-66333-5, Pub. by Busn Bks England). Renouf.

Howes, M. J. & Morgan, D. V. Optical Fibre Communications: Devices, Circuits & Systems. LC 79-40512. (Wiley Series in Solid State Devices & Circuits). 1980. 51.50 (ISBN 0-471-27611-1, Pub. by Wiley-Interscience). Wiley.

Kao, C. K. Optical Fiber Systems: Technology, Design & Applications. 1982. price not set (ISBN 0-07-033277-0). McGraw.

--Optical Fiber Technology, Vol. 2 Ed. LC 80-25665. 1981. 29.95 (ISBN 0-87942-143-6). Inst Electrical.

--Optical Fiber Technology II. LC 80-25665. 343p. 1981. 29.95 (ISBN 0-471-09169-3, Pub. by Wiley-Interscience); pap. 19.50 (ISBN 0-471-09171-5, Pub. by Wiley-Interscience). Wiley.

Keucken, John A. Fiberoptics. (Illus.). 363p. 1980. 14.95 (ISBN 0-8306-9709-8); pap. 9.95 (ISBN 0-8306-1236-X). TAB Bks.

Lacy, Edward A. Fiber Optics. (Illus.). 256p. 1982. 20.95 (ISBN 0-13-314278-7). P-H.

Marcuse, Dietrich. Theory of Dielectric Optical Waveguides. (Quantum Electronics Ser.). 1974. 43.00 (ISBN 0-12-470950-8). Acad Pr.

Miller, Stewart E. & Chynoweth, Alan G., eds. Optical Fiber Telecommunications. LC 78-20046. 1979. 55.50 (ISBN 0-12-497350-7). Acad Pr.

Okoshi, Takanori. Optical Fibers. Butler, J. K., ed. 1982. price not set (ISBN 0-12-525260-9). Acad Pr.

Sandbank, C. P. Optical Fibre Communications. LC 79-40822. 1980. 53.95 (ISBN 0-471-27667-7, Pub. by Wiley-Interscience). Wiley.

Sharma, A. B., et al. Optical Fiber Systems & Their Components. (Springer Ser. in Optical Sciences: Vol. 24). (Illus.). 250p. 1981. 38.35 (ISBN 0-387-10437-2). Springer-Verlag.

Society of Photo-Optical Instrumentation Engineers, Seminar. Fiber Optics Comes of Age: Proceedings, Vol. 31. 11.00 (ISBN 0-89252-042-6). Photo-Optical.

Tiedeken, R. Fibre Optics & Its Applications. (Focal Library Ser.). 1972. 29.95 (ISBN 0-240-50732-0). Focal Pr.

Two Thousand Five Hundred Fiber Optics Patent Abstracts: 1881-1979. LC 79-93149. (Illus.). 382p. 1980. 167.50 (ISBN 0-935714-00-6). Patent Data.

Unger, H. G. Planar Optical Waveguides & Fibres. (Oxford Engineering Science Ser.). (Illus.). 1978. 89.00x (ISBN 0-19-856133-4). Oxford U Pr.

Weik, Martin H. Fiber Optics & Lightwave Communications Standard Dictionary. 320p. 1980. text ed. 18.50 (ISBN 0-442-25658-2). Van Nos Reinhold.

Wolf, Helmut F. Handbook of Fiber Optics: Theory & Applications. LC 78-31977. 560p. 1980. lib. bdg. 47.50 (ISBN 0-8240-7054-2). Garland Pub.

FIBER PLANTS

see Fibers

FIBER SCULPTURE

see Tapestry

FIBER SPACES (MATHEMATICS)

see also Fiber Bundles (Mathematics)

Jaco, W. H. & Shalen, P. B. Seifert Fibered Spaces in Three-Manifolds. (Memoirs Ser.: No. 220). 1979. 10.00 (ISBN 0-8218-2220-9). Am Math.

Massey, William S. & Peterson, F. P. Mod Two Cohomology Structure of Certain Fibre Spaces. LC 52-42839. (Memoirs: No. 74). 1967. pap. 7.20 (ISBN 0-8218-1274-2, MEMO-74). Am Math.

May, J. Peter. Classifying Spaces & Fibrations. (Memoirs: No. 155). 98p. 1980. pap. 10.00 (ISBN 0-8218-1855-4, MEMO-155). Am Math.

Seminar on Fiber Spaces, 1964-65. Proceedings. Thomas, E., ed. (Lecture Notes in Mathematics: Vol. 13). 1966. pap. 10.70 (ISBN 0-387-03596-6). Springer-Verlag.

FIBERBOARD

see Hardboard; Particle Board

FIBERGLASS

see Glass Fibers

FIBERGLASS BOATS

Collins, Michael. From a Fiberglass Hull. (Illus.). 1980. 10.95 (ISBN 0-229-11616-7, ScribT). Scribner.

Duplessis, Hugo. Fiberglass Boats, Fitting Out, Maintenance & Repair. rev. ed. LC 72-94973. 1973. 18.50 (ISBN 0-8286-0064-3). De Graff.

Edmunds, Arthur. Fiberglass Boat Survey Manual. 1979. 15.00 (ISBN 0-8286-0083-X). De Graff.

Figg, Keith & Hayward, John. G R P Boat Construction. (Questions & Answers Ser.). (Illus.). 86p. (Orig.). 1979. pap. 7.50 (ISBN 0-408-00317-0). Transatlantic.

Hankinson, Ken. How to Fiberglass Boats. LC 74-27715. (Illus.). pap. 7.95 (ISBN 0-686-09424-7). Glen-L Marine.

Jones, Charles. Glass Fibre Yachts: Improvement & Repair. 128p. 1980. 12.00x (ISBN 0-686-69884-3, Pub. by Nautical England). State Mutual Bk.

Petrick, Paul J. Fiberglass Repairs. LC 76-17811. (Illus.). 1976. spiral bdg. 6.00 (ISBN 0-87033-222-8). Cornell Maritime.

Vaitses, Allan H. Covering Wooden Boats with Fiberglass. LC 81-80581. (Illus.). 192p. 1981. 15.95 (ISBN 0-87742-137-4). Intl Marine.

Wiley, Jack. Modifying Fiberglass Boats. LC 74-25164. (Illus.). 200p. 1975. 12.50 (ISBN 0-87742-048-3). Intl Marine.

Willis, Melvin D. Boatbuilding & Repairing with Fiberglass. LC 74-176120. (Illus.). 1972. 12.50 (ISBN 0-87742-018-1). Intl Marine.

FIBERGLASS REINFORCED PLASTICS

see Glass Reinforced Plastics

FIBERS

see also Cotton; Fibrous Composites; Jute; Linen; Paper; Silk; Textile Fibers; Wool

Agarwal, B. D. & Broutman, Lawrence J. Analysis & Performance of Fiber Composites. (Society of Plastics Engineers Monograph). 1980. 28.50 (ISBN 0-471-05928-5, Pub. by Wiley-Interscience). Wiley.

Appel, Ellen. The Fibercraft Sampler. LC 78-7144. 1978. 13.95 (ISBN 0-8019-6643-4); pap. 7.95 (ISBN 0-8019-6644-2). Chilton.

Battista, Orlando A., ed. Synthetic Fibers in Papermaking. 340p. 1964. text ed. 18.75 (ISBN 0-470-05894-3, Pub. by Wiley). Krieger.

Bird, John & Catherall, Ed. Fibres & Fabrics. LC 77-82983. (Teaching Primary Science Ser.). (Illus.). 1977. pap. text ed. 6.95 (ISBN 0-356-05076-9). Raintree Child.

Bockholt, A. J. World Food & Fiber Crops. 1975. coil bdg. 4.95 (ISBN 0-88252-037-7). Paladin Hse.

Building Research Establishment, ed. Fibre Reinforced Materials. (Building Research Ser.: Vol. 2). (Illus.). 1978. text ed. 35.00x (ISBN 0-904406-38-5, Construction Pr). Longman.

Catling, D. M. & Graywon, J. Identification of Vegetable Fibers. 1981. 35.00x (ISBN 0-412-22300-7, Pub. by Chapman & Hall). Methuen Inc.

Chapman, C. B. Fibres. 1974. 5.95 (ISBN 0-87245-508-4). Textile Bk.

Fiber: A Bibliography (Knotting, Stitchery & Surface Design) 1979. 5.70 (ISBN 0-88321-039-8). Am Craft.

Fiber Conservation & Utilization Seminar, Chicago, May 1974. Fiber Conservation & Utilization: Proceedings. Van Derveer, Paul D. & Lowe, Kenneth E., eds. LC 74-20163. (A Pulp & Paper Book). (Illus.). 288p. 1975. 27.50 (ISBN 0-87930-032-9). Miller Freeman.

Fibres & Fibre Products. (Terminology Bulletin: No. 29). 121p. (Eng, Fr, Span.). 1977. pap. 14.00 (ISBN 92-5-000055-3, F1193, FAO). Unipub.

French, Alfred D. & Gardner, KennCorwin H., eds. Fiber Diffraction Methods. LC 80-21566. (ACS Symposium Ser.: No. 141). 1980. 34.50 (ISBN 0-8412-0589-2). Am Chemical.

Galasso, F. S. High Modulus Fibers & Composites. 1970. 34.75 (ISBN 0-677-02550-5). Gordon.

Hannant, D. J. Fibre Cements & Fibre Concretes. 219p. 1978. 43.75 (ISBN 0-471-99620-3, Pub. by Wiley-Interscience). Wiley.

Happey, F., ed. Applied Fibre Science, Vol. 3. LC 77-75367. 1980. 87.00 (ISBN 0-12-323703-3). Acad Pr.

Hearle, J. W., ed. Mechanics of Flexible Fiber Assemblies. (NATO-Advanced Study Institute Ser.). 700p. 1980. 72.50x (ISBN 9-0286-0720-X). Sijthoff & Noordhoff.

Houck, Carter. Warm As Wool, Cool As Cotton: The Story of Natural Fibers & Fabrics & How to Work with Them. LC 74-18089. (Illus.). 96p. (gr. 3-6). 1975. 6.95 (ISBN 0-395-28861-4, Clarion). HM.

Impact of Synthetics on Jute & Allied Fibers. (Commodity Bulletin Ser.: No. 46). (Orig.). 1969. pap. 10.00 (ISBN 0-685-09390-5, F239, FAO). Unipub.

Intergovernmental Group on Hard Fibres, 11th Session. Report. (Illus.). 10p. 1976. pap. 7.50 (ISBN 92-5-100074-3, F1118, FAO). Unipub.

Intergovernmental Group on Hard Fibres, 12th Session. Report. 13p. 1977. pap. 7.50 (ISBN 92-5-100302-5, F1125, FAO). Unipub.

Intergovernmental Group on Jute, Kenaf & Allied Fibres, 12th Session. Report. 17p. 1977. pap. 7.50 (ISBN 92-5-100125-1, F1121, FAO). Unipub.

Jaques, H. E. Plants We Eat & Wear. (Illus.). 5.00 (ISBN 0-8446-5207-5). Peter Smith.

Levitt, Albert P. Whisker Technology. LC 75-114917. 492p. 1970. 38.00 (ISBN 0-471-53150-2). Krieger.

Lewin, M., ed. Fiber Science: JAPS Symposium, No. 31. 1977. 26.50 (ISBN 0-471-04563-2, Pub. by Wiley-Interscience). Wiley.

Lyth, Mike. Man-Made Fibres. (Science in Action Ser.). 1977. 9.95x (ISBN 0-8448-1087-8). Crane-Russak Co.

McCreight, L. R., et al. Ceramic & Graphic Fibers & Whiskers: A Survey of Technology. (Refractory Materials Ser., Vol. 1). 1965. 47.00 (ISBN 0-12-482950-3). Acad Pr.

McGregor, R. Diffusion & Sorption in the Fibers & Films: An Introduction with Particular Reference to Dyes, Vol. 1. 1974. 42.50 (ISBN 0-12-484101-5). Acad Pr.

Mark, H. F., et al. Man-Made Fibers: Science & Technology, Vols. 2 & 3. LC 67-13954. 1968. Vol. 2, 504pp. 42.50 (ISBN 0-686-74185-4); Vol. 3, 718 Pp. 62.50 (ISBN 0-686-74186-2). Krieger.

Moncrieff, R. W. Man-Made Fibres. 6th ed. LC 74-10686. 1094p. 1975. 90.95x (ISBN 0-470-61318-1). Halsted Pr.

Per Capita Fibre Consumption 1973-1974: Cotton, Wool & Man-Made Fibres. 1977. pap. 8.25 (ISBN 92-5-000102-9, F1190, FAO). Unipub.

Per Caput Fibre Consumption 1971-1973: Cotton, Wool, Flax, Silk, & Man Made Fibre. 188p. 1975. pap. 16.25 (ISBN 0-685-61022-5, F1189, FAO). Unipub.

Philippoff, Diane M. Fiber Arts: Crochet, Wrapping, Coiling, Weaving. LC 78-7143. 1978. 13.95 (ISBN 0-8019-6659-0); pap. 7.95 (ISBN 0-8019-6660-4). Chilton.

Preston, J. & Economy, J., eds. High-Temperature & Flame-Resistant Fibers. 232p. (Orig.). 1973. 21.50 (ISBN 0-686-74168-4). Krieger.

Reilly, Richard W. & Kirsner, Joseph B., eds. Fiber Deficiency & Colonic Disorders. LC 75-12756. 184p. 1975. 25.00 (ISBN 0-306-30854-1, Plenum Pr). Plenum Pub.

Report of the Fifteenth Session of the Intergovernmental Group on Hard Fibres to the Committee on Commodity Problems. 1980. pap. 7.50 (ISBN 92-5-100905-8, F1951, FAO). Unipub.

Report of the Fourteenth Session of the Intergovernmental Group on Jute, Kenaf, & Allied Fibres. 1979. pap. 7.50 (ISBN 92-5-100669-5, F1533, FAO). Unipub.

Report of the Sixteenth Session of the Intergovernmental Group on Hard Fibres to the Committee on Commodity Problems. 11p. 1981. pap. 7.50 (ISBN 92-5-101072-2, F2111, FAO). Unipub.

Sadov, P., et al. Chemical Technology of Fibrous Materials. 668p. 1978. 13.00 (ISBN 0-8285-0673-6, Pub. by Mir Pubs Russia). Imported Pubns.

Schick, Martin, ed. Surface Characteristics of Fibers & Textiles, Pt. 2. (Fiber Science Ser.: Vol. 7). 1977. 45.00 (ISBN 0-8247-6531-1). Dekker.

Schnick. Surface Characteristics of Fibers & Textiles. (Fiber Science Ser.: Vol. 7, Pt. 1). 59.00 (ISBN 0-8247-6316-5). Dekker.

Tewary, V. K. Mechanics of Fibre Composites. LC 77-29117. 1978. 16.95x (ISBN 0-470-99240-9). Halsted Pr.

Thomas, Gerald W., et al. Food & Fiber for a Changing World: Third-Century Challenge to American Agriculture. xiv, 225p. 1976. 7.95 (ISBN 0-8134-1817-8). Interstate.

Tisdell, C. A. & McDonald, P. W. Economics of Fibre Markets: Interdependence Between Man-Made Fibres, Wool, & Cotton. 1979. text ed. 45.00 (ISBN 0-08-022468-7). Pergamon.

Usenko, V. Processing of Man Made Fibers. 428p. 1979. 9.00 (ISBN 0-8285-1544-1, Pub. by Mir Pubs Russia). Imported Pubns.

Watt, W., et al. New Fibres & Their Composites. (Royal Society Ser.). (Illus.). 189p. 1980. text ed. 66.00x (ISBN 0-85403-130-8, Pub. by Royal Society London). Scholium Intl.

FIBERS, CERAMIC

see Ceramic Fibers

FIBERS, GLASS

see Glass Fibers

FIBONACCI NUMBERS

Fibonacci, Leonardo. The Fibonacci Rhythm Theory As It Applies to Life, History, & the Course of the Stock Market, 2 vols. in one. new exp. ed. Flumiani, C. M., ed. (The Most Meaningful Classics in World Culture Ser.). (Illus.). 1979. Set. 81.75 (ISBN 0-89266-192-5). Am Classical Coll Pr.

Fibonacci, Leonardo & Flumiani, Carlo M. The Fibonacci Rhythm Theory As It Applies to Life, History, & the Future of the Stock Market. (Illus.). 1976. 87.50 (ISBN 0-89266-041-4). Am Classical Coll Pr.
Leclerque, James R. Nature & the Fibonacci's Conception of the Universe. (Illus.). 180p. 1980. deluxe ed. 69.85 (ISBN 0-89266-263-8). Am Classical Coll Pr.
Manning, George. The Metaphysics of Figures & Symbols in Fibonacci's Conception of the Universe. (Illus.). 1978. 77.50 (ISBN 0-89266-132-1). Am Classical Coll Pr.
Steiner, Ludwig, ed. Fibonacci's Secret Discoveries into the Occult Power of Numbers. (Illus.). 1979. 77.85 (ISBN 0-89266-150-X). Am Classical Coll Pr.

FIBRE SPACES (MATHEMATICS)
see Fiber Spaces (Mathematics)

FIBRINOLYSIS
Davidson, John F., ed. Progress in Chemical Fibrinolysis & Thrombolysis, Vol. 2. LC 75-14335. 212p. 1976. 19.00 (ISBN 0-89004-136-9). Raven.
--Progress in Chemical Fibrinolysis & Thrombolysis, Vol. 4. (Illus.). 1981. text ed. 65.00 (ISBN 0-443-01972-X). Churchill.
Davidson, John F., et al, eds. Progress in Chemical Fibrinolysis & Thrombolysis, Vol. 1. LC 75-14335. 425p. 1975. 36.00 (ISBN 0-89004-036-2). Raven.
Gaffney, P. J. Fibrinolysis: Current Fundamental & Clinical Concepts. Balkuv-Ulutin, S., ed. 1978. 40.00 (ISBN 0-12-273050-X). Acad Pr.
Kline, Daniel L. & Reddy, K. N. Fibrinolysis. 256p. 1980. 69.95 (ISBN 0-8493-5425-0). CRC Pr.
Marsh, Neville. Fibrinolysis. LC 80-42309. 272p. 1981. 49.50 (ISBN 0-471-28029-1, Pub. by Wiley-Interscience). Wiley.
Protides of the Biological Fluids, Colloquium 28: Proceedings of the 28th Colloquium on Protides of the Biological Fluids, Brussels, 5-8 May 1980. LC 58-5908. (Illus.). 600p. 1980. 120.00 (ISBN 0-08-026370-4). Pergamon.
Volkmar, Tilsner & Lenau, H., eds. Fibronolysis & Urokinase. LC 80-41295. (Serono Symposia Ser.: No. 31). 1981. 63.00 (ISBN 0-12-691150-9). Acad Pr.
--Fibronolysis & Urokinase. LC 80-41295. (Serono Symposia Ser.: No. 31). 1981. 63.00 (ISBN 0-12-691150-9). Acad Pr.
Wiman, B., et al. The Physiological Inhibitors of Blood Coagulation & Fibrinolysis. 1979. 44.00 (ISBN 0-444-80092-1, Biomedical Pr). Elsevier.
Zoological Society of London - 27th Symposium. Haemostatic Mechanism in Man & Other Animals. MacFarlane, R. G., ed. 39.00 (ISBN 0-12-613327-1). Acad Pr.

FIBRINOLYTIC AGENTS
Chazov. Anticoagulants & Fibrinolytics. 1980. 34.50 (ISBN 0-8151-1649-7). Year Bk Med.
Davidson, John F., ed. Progress in Chemical Fibrinolysis & Thrombolysis, Vol. 2. LC 75-14335. 212p. 1976. 19.00 (ISBN 0-89004-136-9). Raven.
Forster, Werner, et al. Prostaglandins & Thromboxins: Proceedings of the Third International Symposium on Prostaglandins & Thromboxanes in the Cardiovascular System, Hale-Salle, GDR, 5-7 May 1980. LC 80-41802. (Illus.). 500p. 1981. 80.00 (ISBN 0-08-027369-6). Pergamon.
Lundblad, R. L., et al, eds. Chemistry & Biology of Thrombin. LC 77-76907. 1977. 39.95 (ISBN 0-250-40160-6). Ann Arbor Science.
Markwardt, F., ed. Fibrinolytics & Antifibrinolytics. (Handbook of Experimental Pharmacology: Vol. 46). (Illus.). 1978. 184.80 (ISBN 0-387-08608-0). Springer-Verlag.
Samuelsson, Bengt, et al, eds. Advances in Prostaglandin & Thromboxane Research, Vols. 6-8. 1980. Set. text ed. 173.00 (ISBN 0-89004-452-X); text ed. 59.50 ea. Vol. 6 (ISBN 0-89004-452-X). Vol. 7 (ISBN 0-89004-513-5). Vol. 8 (ISBN 0-89004-514-3). Raven.
Von Kaulla, K. N. & Davidson, J. F., eds. Synthetic Fibrinolytic Thrombolytic Agents: Chemical, Biochemical, Pharmacological & Clinical Aspects. (Illus.). 528p. 1975. text ed. 46.75 (ISBN 0-398-02927-X). C C Thomas.

FIBROBLASTS
Baheri, Antti, et al, eds. Fibroblast Surface Protein. (Annals of the New York Academy of Sciences: Vol. 312). 456p. 1978. pap. 52.00x (ISBN 0-89072-068-1). NY Acad Sci.
Kulonen, E. & Kulonen, E., eds. Biology of Fibroblast. 1974. 111.00 (ISBN 0-12-428950-9). Acad Pr.

FIBROCYSTIC DISEASE OF PANCREAS
see Cystic Fibrosis

FIBROCYTES
see Fibroblasts

FIBROSIS, CYSTIC
see Cystic Fibrosis

FIBROUS COMPOSITES
see also Reinforced Plastics
Analysis of the Test Methods for High Modulus Fibers & Composites. 1973. 30.75 (ISBN 0-8031-0080-9, 04-521000-33). ASTM.
Fatigue of Filamentary Composite Materials. 1977. 26.50 (ISBN 0-686-51999-X, 04-636000-33). ASTM.
Galasso, F. S. High Modulus Fibers & Composites. 1970. 34.75 (ISBN 0-677-02550-5). Gordon.
Gill, R. M. Carbon Fibres in Composite Materials. (Illus.). 207p. 1972. 22.50x (ISBN 0-8448-0642-0). Crane-Russak Co.
Lenoe, Edward M., et al, eds. Fibrous Composites in Structural Design. 900p. 1980. 85.00 (ISBN 0-306-40354-4). Plenum Pub.
Levitt, Albert P. Whisker Technology. LC 75-114917. 492p. 1970. 38.00 (ISBN 0-471-53150-2). Krieger.
McCullough, R. L. Concepts of Fiber - Resin Composites. (Monographs & Textbks in Material Science Ser.: Vol. 2). 1971. 24.75 (ISBN 0-8247-1460-1). Dekker.
Rauch, H. W., et al. Ceramic Fibers & Fibrous Composite Materials. (Refractory Materials Ser: Vol. 3). 1968. 52.50 (ISBN 0-12-582850-0). Acad Pr.
Schwartz, R. T. & Schwartz, H. S. Fundamental Aspects of Fiber Reinforced Plastic Composites. 284p. 1968. 18.50 (ISBN 0-470-76603-4, Pub. by Wiley). Krieger.
Symposium on Advanced Fibrous Reinforced Composites, San Diego, Ca. Nov. 9-11, 1966. Proceedings. (Science of Advanced Materials & Process Engineering Ser., Vol. 10). 8.00 (ISBN 0-938994-10-7). Soc Adv Material.

FICHTE, JOHANN GOTTLIEB, 1762-1814
Adamson, Robert. Fichte: Philosophical Classics for English Readers. facsimile ed. LC 76-94262. (Select Bibliographies Reprint Ser). 1903. 17.00 (ISBN 0-8369-5036-4). Arno.
Engelbrecht, Helmuth C. Johann Gottlieb Fichte: A Study of His Political Writings with Special Reference to His Nationalism. LC 68-54262. (Columbia University Studies in the Social Sciences: No. 383). 1971. Repr. of 1926 ed. 14.50 (ISBN 0-404-51383-2). AMS Pr.
Fichte, Johann G. Nachgelassene Werke, 3 Vols. Fichte, Immanuel H., ed. (Ger). 1962. Repr. of 1834 ed. 84.00x (ISBN 3-11-005101-X). De Gruyter.
Gladden, Washington. Witnesses of the Light. facs. ed. LC 77-84307. (Essay Index Reprint Ser). 1903. 15.75 (ISBN 0-8369-1081-8). Arno.
Hegel. Differenz (Difference Between Fichte's & Schelling's System of Philosophy) Cerf, Walter & Harris, H. S., eds. Cerf, Walter & Harris, H. S., trs. LC 76-9821. 1977. 19.00 (ISBN 0-87395-336-3); microfiche 17.00 (ISBN 0-686-67361-1). State U NY Pr.
Hegel, G. W. The Difference Between the Fichtean & Schellingian Systems of Philosophy. Surber, Jere P., tr. from Ger. 1978. pap. text ed. 6.50x (ISBN 0-917930-12-6); lib. bdg. 21.00 (ISBN 0-917930-32-0). Ridgeview.
Janke, Wolfgang. Fichte: Sein und Reflexion Grundlagen der Kritischen Vernunft. (Ger). 1970. 48.75x (ISBN 3-11-006436-7). De Gruyter.
Sandorvan, Lee W. A Negative Critique of the Philosophy of Johann Gottlieb Fichte. (Essential Library of the Great Philosophers). (Illus.). 141p. 1980. deluxe ed. 49.85 (ISBN 0-89266-268-9). Am Classical Coll Pr.
Storrs, Margaret. Relations of Carlyle to Kant & Fichte. LC 77-9971. 1929. lib. bdg. 12.50 (ISBN 0-8414-7562-8). Folcroft.

FICINO, MARSILIO, 1433-1499
Allen, Michael J., ed. Marsilio Ficino: The Philebus Commentary. 1979. 36.50x (ISBN 0-520-03977-7). U of Cal Pr.
Ficino, Marsilio. The Letters, 2 vols. 1975. Vol. 1. 18.50 (ISBN 0-85683-010-0); Vol. 2. 16.50 (ISBN 0-85683-036-4). Attic Pr.
--The Letters of Marsilio Ficino, Vol. 3, Bk. 4. 160p. 1980. 39.00x (ISBN 0-85683-045-3, Pub. by Shepheard-Walwyn England). State Mutual Bk.
Jayne, Sears R. John Colet & Marsilio Ficino. LC 80-17262. (Illus.). 172p. 1980. Repr. of 1963 ed. lib. bdg. 18.75x (ISBN 0-313-22606-7, JACF). Greenwood.
Kristeller, Paul O. The Philosophy of Marsilio Ficino. 8.75 (ISBN 0-8446-1273-1). Peter Smith.

FICTION
see also Baseball Stories; Children's Stories; Detective and Mystery Stories; Fables; Fairy Tales; Fantastic Fiction; Fishing Stories; Folk-Lore; Ghost Stories; Historical Fiction; Horror Tales; Hunting Stories; Legends; Musical Fiction; Nature Stories; Picaresque Literature; Radio Stories; Railroad Stories; Romances; Romanticism; Science Fiction (Collections); Sea Stories; Short Stories; Sports Stories; Spy Stories; Tales; Western Stories
also American Fiction, English Fiction, French Fiction, and similar headings; and subdivision Fiction under historical events and characters, etc. e.g. Gettysburg, Battle of, 1863–Fiction; Napolean 1st, Emperor of the French, 1769-1821–Fiction; World War, 1939-1945–Fiction
Allen, Walter. Reading a Novel. rev ed. 1975. pap. text ed. 3.00x (ISBN 0-391-00529-4). Humanities.
Ames, Van M. Aesthetics of the Novel. LC 66-29460. 1966. Repr. of 1928 ed. 6.50 (ISBN 0-87752-003-8). Gordian.
Auchincloss, Louis. Reflections of a Jacobite. LC 74-156968. Repr. of 1961 ed. lib. bdg. 12.50x (ISBN 0-678-03571-7). Kelley.
Beaty, Jerome, ed. The Norton Introduction to Fiction. 2nd ed. 640p. 1981. pap. text ed. 8.95x (ISBN 0-393-95156-1); classroom guide avail. (ISBN 0-393-95159-6). Norton.
Beckford, William. Modern Novel Writing, 4 vols. in 1. Incl. Azemia. Repr. of 1797 ed. LC 74-81366. 264p. 1970. Repr. of 1796 ed. 35.00x (ISBN 0-8201-1063-9). Schol Facsimiles.
Bellamy, Joe D. The New Fiction: Interviews with Innovative American Writers. LC 74-14841. 225p. 1974. 10.00 (ISBN 0-252-00430-2); pap. 4.50 (ISBN 0-252-00555-4). U of Ill Pr.
Bishop, Morris, ed. Renaissance Storybook. LC 79-129332. (Illus.). 1971. 14.50 (ISBN 0-8014-0592-0). Cornell U Pr.
Bluestone, George. Novels into Film: The Metamorphosis of Fiction into Cinema. 1957. pap. 3.95 (ISBN 0-520-00130-3, CAL41). U of Cal Pr.
Brace, Gerald W. The Stuff of Fiction. LC 71-77391. 1969 4.50 (ISBN 0-393-04312-6, Norton Lib); pap. 1.95 1972 (ISBN 0-393-00648-4). Norton.
Burton, Richard. Forces in Fiction & Other Essays. facs. ed. LC 70-76896. (Essay Index Reprint Ser). 1902. 12.25 (ISBN 0-8369-0008-1). Arno.
Cornillon, Susan K., ed. Images of Women in Fiction. 1972. casebound 15.95 (ISBN 0-87972-048-4); pap. 7.95 (ISBN 0-87972-049-2). Bowling Green Univ.
Crawford, F. Marion. Novel, What It Is. facs. ed. LC 79-75506. (Select Bibliographies Reprint Ser). 1893. 12.50 (ISBN 0-8369-5003-8). Arno.
Crawford, Francis M. Novel: What It Is. LC 73-98831. Repr. of 1893 ed. lib. bdg. 15.00x (ISBN 0-8371-2924-9, CRTN). Greenwood.
--The Novel: What It Is. LC 76-104434. Repr. of 1893 ed. lib. bdg. 12.75x (ISBN 0-8398-0280-3); pap. text ed. 6.25x (ISBN 0-89197-869-0). Irvington.
Dolan, Paul J. Modes of Fiction. LC 79-77318. 1970. pap. text ed. 7.95 (ISBN 0-02-907450-9). Free Pr.
Eaglestone, Arthur A., pseud. Plain Man & the Novel. LC 78-105776. 1970. Repr. of 1940 ed. 11.00 (ISBN 0-8046-0946-2). Kennikat.
Epp, Margaret. Great Frederick & Other Stories. 128p. (gr. 7 up). 1971. pap. 1.50 (ISBN 0-8024-1325-0). Moody.
Forster, E. M. Aspects of the Novel. LC 27-23181. 1956. pap. 2.50 (ISBN 0-15-609180-1, HB19, Harv). HarBraceJ.
Foster-Harris, William. Basic Patterns of Plot. 1969. Repr. of 1959 ed. 6.95 (ISBN 0-8061-0435-X). U of Okla Pr.
Freedman, Richard. The Novel. LC 74-84890. (World of Culture Ser.). (Illus.). 192p. 1975. 12.95 (ISBN 0-88225-115-5). Newsweek.
George, W. L. Novelist on Novels. LC 70-105790. 1970. Repr. of 1918 ed. 12.50 (ISBN 0-8046-0955-1). Kennikat.
Gerould, Gordon H. How to Read Fiction. LC 73-75463. 1969. Repr. of 1937 ed. 8.00 (ISBN 0-8462-1336-2). Russell.
Goldknopf, David. The Life of the Novel. LC 72-75512. 256p. 1972. 12.50x (ISBN 0-226-30142-7). U of Chicago Pr.
--The Life of the Novel. LC 72-75512. x, 218p. 1974. pap. 2.95 (ISBN 0-226-30143-5, P591, Phoen). U of Chicago Pr.
Hemingway, Ernest. Islands in the Stream. LC 71-123834. 1970. Hudson River Edition. 20.00x (ISBN 0-684-16499-X); pap. 4.95 (ISBN 0-684-14642-8, ScribT). Scribner.
James, Henry. Theory of Fiction: Henry James. Miller, James E., Jr., ed. LC 78-147168. 1972. pap. 6.50x (ISBN 0-8032-5747-3, BB 542, Bison). U of Nebr Pr.
Jhabvala, Ruth P. Heat & Dust. 1977. pap. 1.95 (ISBN 0-06-080431-9, P431, PL). Har-Row.
--Travelers. 1977. pap. 2.25 (ISBN 0-06-080432-7, P432, PL). Har-Row.
Kennedy, X. J. An Introduction to Fiction. 2nd ed. 1979. pap. text ed. 9.95 (ISBN 0-316-48865-8); instr's manual free (ISBN 0-316-48866-6). Little.
Kumar, Raj. The New Concept of the Novel. LC 73-18192. 1959. Repr. lib. bdg. 6.00 (ISBN 0-8414-5481-7). Folcroft.
Lathrop, Henry B. Art of the Novelist. LC 73-15737. 1921. Repr. lib. bdg. 20.00 (ISBN 0-8414-5689-5). Folcroft.
Leavis, Q. D. Fiction & the Reading Public. LC 73-3445. 1932. lib. bdg. 35.00 (ISBN 0-8414-2265-6). Folcroft.
Lewald, H. Ernest, ed. The Cry of Home: Cultural Nationalism & the Modern Writer. LC 76-173656. 412p. 1972. 15.50x (ISBN 0-87049-135-0). U of Tenn Pr.
Liddell, Robert. Robert Liddell on the Novel. LC 78-76204. 1969. pap. 3.50 (ISBN 0-226-48042-9). U of Chicago Pr.
Medina, Angel. Reflection, Time & the Novel. (International Library of Phenomenology & Moral Sciences). 1979. 20.00x (ISBN 0-7100-0273-4). Routledge & Kegan.
Meyer, Herman. Poetics of Quotation in the European Novel. Ziolkowski, Y. & Ziolkowski, T., trs. LC 65-17152. 1968. 20.00 (ISBN 0-691-06094-0). Princeton U Pr.
Miller, James E., Jr., ed. Myth & Method: Modern Theories of Fiction. LC 60-12941. 1960. pap. 2.45x (ISBN 0-8032-5134-3, BB 105, Bison). U of Nebr Pr.
Monarch Notes on Black Short Fiction. pap. 1.50 (ISBN 0-671-00969-9). Monarch Pr.
Murray, H. Morality of Fiction: or an Inquiry into the Tendency of Fictitious Narrative. LC 72-6240. 1972. Repr. of 1805 ed. lib. bdg. 10.00 (ISBN 0-8414-0116-0). Folcroft.
Nelson, William. Fact or Fiction: The Dilemma of the Renaissance Storyteller. LC 73-77990. 128p. 1974. text ed. 7.95x (ISBN 0-674-29065-8). Harvard U Pr.
Nemerov, Howard. Poetry & Fiction: Essays. 1963. 22.00 (ISBN 0-8135-0438-4). Rutgers U Pr.
Newton, Alfred E. Format of the English Novel. LC 78-153025. (Essays in Literature & Criticism Ser: No. 168). (Illus.). 52p. 1972. Repr. of 1928 ed. lib. bdg. 18.50 (ISBN 0-8337-2522-X). B Franklin.
Norris, Frank. Responsibilities of the Novelist, & Other Literary Essays. Repr. of 1903 ed. lib. bdg. 15.00 (ISBN 0-8371-0591-9, NONE). Greenwood.
Olmstead, John. The Design of the Narrative. new ed. Buell, Lawrence, ed. LC 73-75456. 74p. (gr. 7-12). 1973. pap. text ed. 1.45 (ISBN 0-88301-079-8). Pendulum Pr.
Ortega Y Gasset, Jose. Meditations on Quixote. 1963. pap. 3.95 (ISBN 0-393-00125-3, Norton Lib). Norton.
Rehder, Jessie. The Nature of Fiction. 1978. Repr. of 1948 ed. lib. bdg. 8.50 (ISBN 0-8482-5850-9). Norwood Edns.
Robbe-Grillet, Alain. For a New Novel. LC 72-128301. (Essay Index Reprint Ser). 1965. 15.00 (ISBN 0-8369-1844-4). Arno.
Rosenheim, Edward W., Jr. What Happens in Literature: A Student's Guide to Poetry, Drama & Fiction. LC 60-15458. 1962. pap. 2.95 (ISBN 0-226-72793-9, P77, Phoen). U of Chicago Pr.
Ruiz, Juan. Libro de Buen Amor. LC 77-181876. 536p. 1972. 40.00x (ISBN 0-691-06086-X). Princeton U Pr.
Scholes, Robert. Fabulation & Metafiction. LC 78-10776. 1979. 15.00 (ISBN 0-252-00704-2); pap. 5.95 (ISBN 0-252-00761-1). U of Ill Pr.
Selby, Thomas G. Theology of Modern Fiction. LC 73-3430. 1897. lib. bdg. 20.00 (ISBN 0-8414-2649-X). Folcroft.
Spilka, Mark, ed. Towards a Poetics of Fiction. LC 76-48550. 352p. 1977. 15.00x (ISBN 0-253-37500-2). Ind U Pr.
Stein, Gertrude. Ida, a Novel. LC 77-147315. 1971. Repr. of 1941 ed. 8.50x (ISBN 0-8154-0378-X). Cooper Sq.
Stevick, Philip, ed. Theory of the Novel. LC 67-25335. 1967. pap. text ed. 10.95 (ISBN 0-02-931490-9). Free Pr.
Trilling, Diana. Reviewing the Forties. LC 78-5182. 1978. 9.95 (ISBN 0-15-177084-0). HarBraceJ.
Walpole, Hugh. Letter to a Modern Novelist. LC 77-22268. 1932. lib. bdg. 8.50 (ISBN 0-8414-9392-8). Folcroft.
Ward, Wilfrid P. Last Lectures. facs. ed. LC 67-26793. (Essay Index Reprint Ser). 1918. 17.50 (ISBN 0-8369-0976-3). Arno.

FICTION (COLLECTIONS)
Ahern, Tom, et al. The Treacle Story Series, Vol. 1, Nos. 1-4. LC 76-43558. (Illus.). 1976. 10.00 (ISBN 0-914232-14-2). Treacle.
Ardizzone, Tony, ed. Intro Eleven. LC 80-65855. (Intro Ser.). 264p. 1980. pap. 6.95 (ISBN 0-936266-00-7). Assoc Writing Progs.
Bahr, Jerome. Five Novellas. LC 76-53357. 220p. 1977. 8.95 (ISBN 0-685-59469-6). Trempealeau.
Beaty, Jerome, ed. The Norton Introduction to the Short Novel. (gr. 12). 1981. pap. text ed. price not set (ISBN 0-393-95187-1); price not set classroom guide (ISBN 0-393-95190-1). Norton.
Bennett, John, et al. The Vagabond Anthology. LC 77-90626. 1978. pap. 4.95 (ISBN 0-912824-45-X). Vagabond Pr.
Blackburn, William. Duke Miscellany. LC 74-142290. 1970. 12.75 (ISBN 0-8223-0242-X). Duke.

Bleiler, E. F., ed. Eight Dime Novels. (Illus.). 6.50 (ISBN 0-8446-5114-1). Peter Smith.
Bonazza, Blaze O. & Roy, Emil. Studies in Fiction. enl. 3rd ed. 1056p. 1981. pap. text ed. price not set (ISBN 0-06-040832-4, HarpC). Har-Row.
Bonazzi, Robert, ed. Extreme Unctions & Other Last Rites. (New Departures in Fiction Ser: Vol. 1). 1974. 6.00 (ISBN 0-685-46805-4, Pub. by Latitudes Pr); pap. 3.00 (ISBN 0-685-46806-2). SBD.
Braziller, Michael & Braziller, Karen, eds. Persea I: An International Review. 1977. pap. 3.95 (ISBN 0-89255-020-1). Persea Bks.
--Persea Two: An International Review. 1978. pap. 3.95 (ISBN 0-89255-028-7). Persea Bks.
Bulkin, Elly, ed. Lesbian Fiction: An Anthology. 336p. (Orig.). 1981. pap. price not set (ISBN 0-930436-11-3). Persephone.
Cassill, R. V., ed. The Norton Anthology of Short Fiction. 1977. Pgs. 1472. complete ed. 9.95 (ISBN 0-393-09072-8); Pgs. 752. shrter ed. 6.95 (ISBN 0-393-09075-2); instr's. handbook 1.95 (ISBN 0-393-09050-7). Orton.
--The Norton Anthology of Short Fiction. 2nd. ed. (gr. 12). 1981. pap. text ed. price not set regular ed. (ISBN 0-393-95178-2); pap. text ed. price not set shorter ed. (ISBN 0-393-95182-0); price not set instr.'s handbook (ISBN 0-393-95186-3). Norton.
Clay, Albert T. Hebrew Deluge Story. (Yale Oriental Researches Ser.: No. V, Pt. III). 1922. 19.50x (ISBN 0-685-69802-5). Elliots Bks.
Clerc, Charles & Leiter, Louis H. Seven Contemporary Short Novels. 1969. pap. 9.95x (ISBN 0-673-05676-7). Scott F.
Custodio, Maurice M., ed. Contemporary Fiction: Today's Ouststanding Writers. LC 76-28714. (Illus.). 1976. 10.00x (ISBN 0-914024-26-4); pap. 4.00 (ISBN 0-914024-27-2). SF Arts & Letters.
Cutlip, Ralph. Stories That Live. (gr. 7-12). 1973. 4.58 (ISBN 0-87720-352-0). AMSCO Sch.
Gunnell, Bryn. The Cashew-Nut Girl & Other Stories of India. 1974. 9.95 (ISBN 0-236-17623-4, Pub. by Paul Elek). Merrimack Bk Serv.
Hamalian, Leo & Volpe, Edmond L., eds. Eleven Modern Short Novels. 1971. pap. 5.45 (ISBN 0-399-30004-X). Putnam.
--Seven Short Novel Masterpieces. Incl. Daughters of the Vicar. Lawrence, D. H; Metamorphosis. Kafka, Franz; Candide. Voltaire; Lesson of the Master. James, Henry; First Love. Turgenev, Ivan; Benito Cereno. Melville, Herman; Master & Man. Tolstoy, Leo. (YA) (gr. 7up). pap. 2.50 (ISBN 0-445-08504-5). Popular Lib.
Hite, Mary E. My Rappahannock Story Book. LC 50-13328. (Illus.). 232p. 1950. Repr. of 1950 ed. 15.00 (ISBN 0-685-65069-3). Va Bk.
Howe, Irving, ed. Classics of Modern Fiction: Ten Short Novels. 3rd ed. 690p. 1980. pap. text ed. 11.95 (ISBN 0-686-64975-3, HC). HarBraceJ.
Kraus, Richard & Wiegand, William. Students Choice. LC 75-112876. 1970. pap. text ed. 3.95x (ISBN 0-675-09342-2). Merrill.
Laughlin, James, et al, eds. New Directions in Prose & Poetry 32. LC 37-1751. 192p. 1976. 8.95 (ISBN 0-8112-0602-5); pap. 2.95 (ISBN 0-8112-0603-3, NDP412). New Directions.
Leif, Norway & Bayes, Ronald. Sister City & Other Tales. (Illus.). 22p. (Orig.). 1971. pap. 1.95 (ISBN 0-932264-18-2). Trask Hse Bks.
MacArthur, Mary, ed. Carry Me Back. (Orig.). 1978. pap. 4.95 (ISBN 0-916300-13-7). Gallimaufry.
Marcus, Steven, ed. World of Modern Fiction, 2 Vols. 1966. Set. 17.50 (ISBN 0-671-82956-4). S&S.
Moloney, B., ed. Novelle del novecento. 170p. 1966. 9.00 (ISBN 0-7190-0200-1, Pub. by Manchester U Pr England). State Mutual Bk.
Penner, Dick. Fiction of the Absurd: Pratfalls in the Void. (Orig.). 1980. pap. 3.50 (ISBN 0-451-61904-8, ME1904, Ment). NAL.
Pirandello, L. Novelle per un anno: An Anthology. McCormick, C. A., ed. 240p. (It.). 1972. 9.00x (ISBN 0-7190-0469-1, Pub. by Manchester U Pr England). State Mutual Bk.
Schmidt, Stanley, ed. Analog's Golden Anniversary Anthology. 384p. 1980. 10.95 (ISBN 0-8037-0217-5). Davis Pubns.
Scholes, Robert, ed. Elements of Fiction: An Anthology. 1008p. 1981. pap. text ed. 10.95x (ISBN 0-19-502881-3). Oxford U Pr.
Six Great Modern Short Novels. Incl. Dead. Joyce, James; Billy Budd, Foretopman. Melville, Herman; Noon Wine. Porter, Katherine A; Overcoat. Gogol, Nikolai; Pilgrim Hawks. Wescott, Glenway; Bear. Faulkner, William. pap. 2.25 (ISBN 0-440-37996-2, LE). Dell.
The Smith - Twenty-Two. LC 64-9367. 200p. 1980. pap. 3.00 (ISBN 0-912292-63-6). The Smith.
Smith, Raymond J. & Oates, Joyce C., eds. Ontario Review, No. 15. 120p. (Orig.). Date not set. price not set. Ontario Rev NJ.
Stoker, Bram. Dracula. Schick, Alice & Schick, Joel, eds. LC 80-13619. (Illus.). 48p. (gr. 3 up). 1980. PLB 8.44 (ISBN 0-440-01349-6); pap. 4.95 (ISBN 0-440-01348-8). Delacorte.
We Read More Stories. pap. 9.00 set (ISBN 0-917186-11-7); tchrs guide 2.24 (ISBN 0-917186-12-5). McQueen.

FICTION–AUTHORSHIP

Block, Lawrence. Writing the Novel: From Plot to Print. LC 79-10677. 197p. 1979. 10.95x (ISBN 0-911654-67-4). Writers Digest.
Braine, John. Writing a Novel. 224p. 1975. pap. 4.95 (ISBN 0-07-007112-8, SP). McGraw.
Burnett, Hallie & Burnett, Whit. Fiction Writer's Handbook. LC 74-1797. 1979. pap. 4.50 (ISBN 0-06-463492-2, EH 492, EH). Har-Row.
--Fiction Writer's Handbook. LC 74-1797. 224p. 1975. 11.95 (ISBN 0-06-010574-7, HarpT). Har-Row.
D'Orsay, Laurence R. Stories You Can Sell. LC 79-101280. (Short Story Index Reprint Ser.). 1935. 16.00 (ISBN 0-8369-3217-X). Arno.
Gadney, Alan. How to Enter & Win Fiction Writing Contests. 1981. 12.95 (ISBN 0-87196-519-4); pap. 5.95 (ISBN 0-87196-552-6). Facts on File.
Hale, Nancy. The Realities of Fiction: A Book About Writing. LC 76-53839. 1977. Repr. of 1962 ed. lib. bdg. 17.00x (ISBN 0-8371-9351-6, HARE). Greenwood.
Knight, Damon. Creating Short Fiction. 215p. 1981. 11.95 (ISBN 0-89879-042-5). Writers Digest.
Koontz, Dean R. How to Write Best Selling Fiction. 312p. 1981. 13.95 (ISBN 0-89879-045-X). Writers Digest.
Macnichol, Kenneth. Twelve Lectures on the Technique of Fiction Writing. 385p. 1980. lib. bdg. 40.00 (ISBN 0-89760-545-4). Telegraph Bks.
Peck, Robert N. Secrets of Successful Fiction. LC 80-14049. 119p. 1980. 8.95 (ISBN 0-89879-023-9). Writers Digest.
Sloane, William. The Craft of Writing. Sloane, Julia, ed. LC 78-24551. 1979. 10.95 (ISBN 0-393-04471-8). Norton.
Tooker, Dan & Hofheins, Roger. Fiction! Interviews with Northern California Novelists. LC 76-28744. (Illus.). 196p. 1976. 8.95 (ISBN 0-913232-18-1, Co-Pub. by HarBraceJ); pap. 3.95 (ISBN 0-913232-19-X). W Kaufmann.

FICTION–BIBLIOGRAPHY

Baym, Nina. Woman's Fiction: A Guide to Novels by & About Women in America, 1820-1870. 1980. 18.50x (ISBN 0-8014-1128-9); pap. 4.95 (ISBN 0-8014-9184-3). Cornell U Pr.
Black, Frank. Epistolary Novel in the Late Eighteenth Century. LC 74-6155. 1940. lib. bdg. 15.00 (ISBN 0-8414-3151-5). Folcroft.
Bracken, Jeanne, et al. Books for Today's Young Readers: An Annotated Bibliography of Recommended Fiction. 64p. (Orig.). (gr. 4-7). 1981. 4.95 (ISBN 0-935312-03-X). Feminist Pr.
Brown, Stephen J., ed. Ireland in Fiction: A Guide to Irish Novels, Tales, Romances, & Folk-Lore. LC 76-113998. (Bibliography & Reference Ser.: No. 311). 1970. Repr. of 1919 ed. text ed. 18.50 (ISBN 0-8337-0388-9). B Franklin.
Fiction Catalog. 10th ed. (With four annual supplements). 1980. 70.00 (ISBN 0-8242-0660-6). Wilson.
Gerstenberger, Donna & Hendrick, George. The American Novel, 1789 to 1959, 2 vols. LC 61-9356. 333p. 1961. Vol. I. pap. 10.95x (ISBN 0-8040-0006-9). Swallow.
Griswold, William H. Descriptive Lists of American, International, Romantic & British Novels, 2 Vols. (Bibliography & Reference Ser.: No. 134). 1968. Repr. of 1964 ed. 48.00 (ISBN 0-8337-1463-5). B Franklin.
Kerr, Elizabeth M. Bibliography of the Sequence Novel. 1971. lib. bdg. 13.50x (ISBN 0-374-94568-3). Octagon.
Lingenfelter, Mary R. Vocations in Fiction: An Annotated Bibliography. LC 74-3102. (Studies in Fiction, No. 34). 1974. lib. bdg. 39.95 (ISBN 0-8383-2052-X). Haskell.
Messerli, Douglas & Fox, Howard N., eds. Index to Periodical Fiction in English, 1965-69. LC 76-42288. 1977. 35.00 (ISBN 0-8108-0952-4). Scarecrow.
Moore, Ernest R. Bibliografia De Novelistas De la Revolucion Mexicana. LC 72-82322. 189p. 1973. Repr. of 1941 ed. 18.50 (ISBN 0-8337-4661-8). B Franklin.
Nield, J. A Guide to the Best Historical Novels & Tales. 59.95 (ISBN 0-8490-0270-2). Gordon Pr.

FICTION–DICTIONARIES

Brewer, E. Cobham. Reader's Handbook: Famous Names in Fiction, Allusions, References, Proverbs, Plots, Stories, & Poems, 3 vols. LC 71-134907. 1966. Repr. of 1899 ed. Set. 78.00 (ISBN 0-8103-0153-9). Gale.
Dixson, Zella. Comprehensive Subject Index to Universal Prose Fiction. LC 72-13508. 1897. lib. bdg. 30.00 (ISBN 0-8414-1203-0). Folcroft.
Frey, Albert R. Sobriquets & Nicknames. LC 66-22671. 1966. Repr. of 1888 ed. 22.00 (ISBN 0-8103-3003-2). Gale.
Spence, L. A Dictionary of Medieval Romance & Romance Writers. 35.00 (ISBN 0-8490-0039-4). Gordon Pr.
Wheeler, William A. Explanatory & Pronouncing Dictionary of the Noted Names of Fictions. LC 66-25811. 1966. Repr. of 1889 ed. 22.00 (ISBN 0-8103-0165-2). Gale.

FICTION–HISTORY AND CRITICISM

see also Psychological Fiction;
also subdivision History and Criticism under fiction of various nationalities, e.g. English Fiction–History and Criticism

Abcarian, Richard & Klotz, Marvin, eds. The Experience of Fiction. LC 74-23048. (Illus.). 500p. 1975. pap. text ed. 6.95 (ISBN 0-312-27615-X). St Martin.
Adelman, Irving & Dworkin, Rita. The Contemporary Novel: A Checklist of Critical Literature on the British & American Novel Since 1945. LC 72-4451. 1972. 20.50 (ISBN 0-8108-0517-0). Scarecrow.
Allen, Walter. Reading a Novel. rev ed. 1975. pap. text ed. 3.00x (ISBN 0-391-00529-4). Humanities.
--Reading a Novel. LC 72-194361. 1949. 5.00 (ISBN 0-8414-2924-3). Folcroft.
Allen, Walter E. Reading a Novel. 1978. Repr. of 1956 ed. lib. bdg. 8.50 (ISBN 0-8495-0109-1). Arden Lib.
Ashley, Robert, et al. Victorian Fiction: A Guide to Research. Stevenson, Lionel, ed. LC 64-21246. (Reviews of Research). 1980. Repr. of 1964 ed. 20.00x (ISBN 0-87352-258-3). Modern Lang.
Bennett, Arnold. Fame & Fiction. 59.95 (ISBN 0-8490-0150-1). Gordon Pr.
Berman, Neil D. Playful Fictions & Fictional Players: Game, Sport & Survival in Contemporary American Fiction. (National University Publications, Literary Criticism Ser.). 125p. 1981. 13.50 (ISBN 0-8046-9265-3). Kennikat.
Black, Frank. Epistolary Novel in the Late Eighteenth Century. LC 74-6155. 1940. lib. bdg. 15.00 (ISBN 0-8414-3151-5). Folcroft.
Blotner, Joseph L. The Political Novel. LC 78-9868. 1979. Repr. of 1955 ed. lib. bdg. 14.75x (ISBN 0-313-21228-7, BLPN). Greenwood.
Bluestone, George. Novels into Film: The Metamorphosis of Fiction into Cinema. 1957. pap. 3.95 (ISBN 0-520-00130-3, CAL41). U of Cal Pr.
Bonazza, Blaze O. & Roy, Emil. Studies in Fiction. enl. 3rd ed. 1056p. 1981. pap. text ed. price not set (ISBN 0-06-040832-4, HarpC). Har-Row.
Booth, Wayne C. Rhetoric of Fiction. LC 61-14947. 1961. 17.50x (ISBN 0-226-06577-4). U of Chicago Pr.
--Rhetoric of Fiction. LC 61-14947. 1961. pap. 4.95 (ISBN 0-226-06578-2, P267, Phoen). U of Chicago Pr.
Bowen, James K., ed. Classic Short Fiction: An International Collection. Van Der Beets, Richard. LC 70-183111. 1972. pap. 6.95 (ISBN 0-672-61240-2). Bobbs.
Bradbury, Malcolm. Possibilities: Essays on the State of the Novel. (Oxford Paperbacks Ser). 288p. 1973. pap. 4.95x (ISBN 0-19-281126-6). Oxford U Pr.
Brewster, Dorothy & Burrell, Angus. Adventure or Experience: Four Essays on Certain Writers & Readers of Novels. facs. ed. LC 67-23185. (Essay Index Reprint Ser). 1967. Repr. of 1930 ed. 15.00 (ISBN 0-8369-0252-1). Arno.
--Dead Reckonings in Fiction. facsimile ed. LC 76-90614. (Essay Index Reprint Ser). 1924. 14.50 (ISBN 0-8369-1248-9). Arno.
--Modern Fiction. facs. ed. LC 75-86732. (Essay Index Reprint Ser). 1934. 21.25 (ISBN 0-8369-1123-7). Arno.
Brooks, Cleanth & Warren, Robert P. Scope of Fiction. 1960. text ed. 11.95 (ISBN 0-13-796656-3). P-H.
Brown, E. K. Rhythm in the Novel. LC 77-14165. 1978. 9.95x (ISBN 0-8032-1150-3); pap. 3.25x (ISBN 0-8032-6050-4, BB 667, Bison). U of Nebr Pr.
Buckley, Jerome H. Season of Youth: The Bildungsroman from Dickens to Golding. LC 73-85887. 352p. 1974. 17.50x (ISBN 0-674-79640-3). Harvard U Pr.
Carnegie Institute of Technology Department of English, ed. Six Novelists: Stendhal, Dostoevski, Tolstoy, Hardy, Dreiser & Proust. LC 72-1311. (Essay Index Reprint Ser.). Repr. of 1959 ed. 13.00 (ISBN 0-8369-2837-7). Arno.
Cawelti, John G. Adventure, Mystery, & Romance: Formula Stories As Art & Popular Culture. LC 75-5077. (Phoenix Ser.). 1977. pap. 5.95 (ISBN 0-226-09867-2, P732). U of Chicago Pr.
Chandler, Frank W. Romances of Roguery: An Episode in the History of the Novel. 1961. Repr. of 1899 ed. 29.00 (ISBN 0-8337-0527-X). B Franklin.
Christensen, Inger. The Meaning of Metafiction. 200p. 1981. pap. 20.00 (ISBN 0-8200-5697-9). Universitet.
Cockshut, A. O., intro. by. The Novel to Nineteen Hundred. 320p. 1981. pap. 7.95 (ISBN 0-312-57965-9). St Martin.
Cohn, Dorritt. Transparent Minds: Narrative Modes for Presenting Consciousness in Fiction. LC 78-51161. 1978. 20.00 (ISBN 0-691-06369-9). Princeton U Pr.
Conger, Syndy M. & Welsch, Janice R., eds. Narrative Strategies: Original Essays in Film & Prose Fiction. LC 80-53296. (Essays in Literature Ser.: Bk. 4). 140p. (Orig.). 1981. pap. 8.00x (ISBN 0-934312-03-6). Western Ill Univ.
Conrad, Joseph. Joseph Conrad on Fiction. Wright, Walter F., ed. LC 64-11355. (Regents Critics Ser). 1964. 15.95x (ISBN 0-8032-0452-3); pap. 3.45x (ISBN 0-8032-5452-0, BB 400, Bison). U of Nebr Pr.
Dunlop, John C. History of Prose Fiction, 2 Vols. Wilson, Henry, ed. LC 71-95396. 1969. Repr. of 1906 ed. Set. 32.50 (ISBN 0-404-02218-9); 17.00 ea. Vol. 1 (ISBN 0-404-02219-7). Vol. 2 (ISBN 0-404-02220-0). AMS Pr.
Dunlop, John C., ed. History of Prose Fiction, 2 Vols. new ed. 1970. text ed. 34.50 (ISBN 0-8337-0967-4). B Franklin.
Edgar, Pelham. Art of the Novel from 1700 to the Present Time. LC 66-13168. 1965. Repr. of 1933 ed. 16.00 (ISBN 0-8462-0710-9). Russell.
Esterhill, Francis J. Monarch Notes on Roman Literature. (Orig.). pap. 1.95 (ISBN 0-671-00865-X). Monarch Pr.
Federman, Raymond, ed. Surfiction: Fiction Now & Tomorrow. 2nd ed. LC 80-54657. viii, 316p. 1981. pap. 8.95x (ISBN 0-8040-0652-0). Swallow.
--Surfiction: Fiction Now & Tomorrow. LC 73-13215. 294p. 1973. 18.00x (ISBN 0-8040-0651-2). Swallow.
Flannagan, Roy C. Paradise Lost Notes. 1970. pap. 1.95 (ISBN 0-8220-0977-3). Cliffs.
Fletcher, John. Novel & Reader. 196p. 1980. 16.00 (ISBN 0-7145-2620-7, Pub. by M Boyars). Merrimack Bk Serv.
Frakes, James R. & Traschen, Isadore. Short Fiction: A Critical Collection. 2nd ed. LC 69-11382. 1968. pap. text ed. 10.95 (ISBN 0-13-809178-1). P-H.
Friedman, Norman. Form & Meaning in Fiction. LC 73-90843. 431p. 1975. 20.00x (ISBN 0-8203-0357-7). U of Ga Pr.
Gardner, John C. On Moral Fiction. LC 77-20409. 1978. 10.95 (ISBN 0-465-05225-8); pap. 4.95 (ISBN 0-465-05226-6, CN-5048). Basic.
Gaus, Helmut. The Function of Fiction. 1979. text ed. 17.25x (ISBN 90-6439-156-4). Humanities.
Gilman, Stephen. Galdos & the Art of the European Novel, Eighteen Sixty-Seven to Eighteen Eighty-Seven. LC 80-8550. 416p. 1981. 30.00x (ISBN 0-691-06456-3). Princeton U Pr.
Girard, Rene. Deceit, Desire & the Novel: Self & Other in Literary Structure. Freccero, Yvonne, tr. from Fr. LC 65-28582. 305p. 1966. pap. 5.95 (ISBN 0-8018-1830-3). Johns Hopkins.
Gissing, George. George Gissing on Fiction. Korg, Jacob, ed. (Gissing Ser.: No. 9). 1978. 10.00 (ISBN 0-685-99425-2, Pub. by Enitharmon Pr). SBD.
Goldmann, Lucien. Toward a Sociology of the Novel. 1975. pap. 10.95x (ISBN 0-422-76350-0, Pub. by Tavistock). Methuen Inc.
Gordon, Raoul, ed. The Puerto Rican Novel & Short Story. 1976. lib. bdg. 59.95 (ISBN 0-8490-0919-7). Gordon Pr.
Gove, Philip B. The Imaginary Voyage in Prose Fiction. LC 74-15972. (Science Fiction Ser). 459p. 1975. Repr. of 1941 ed. 25.00x (ISBN 0-405-06328-8). Arno.
Greene, Suzanne E. Books for Pleasure: Popular Fiction 1914-1945. LC 74-17776. 208p. 1974. 10.95 (ISBN 0-87972-073-5); pap. 7.95 (ISBN 0-87972-072-7). Bowling Green Univ.
Grivel, Charles. Production E l'interet Romanesque: Un Etat Du Texte (1870-1880), un Essai De Constitution De Sa Theorie. (Approaches to Semiotics: No. 34). 1973. 72.00x (ISBN 90-2792-413-9). Mouton.
Grossvogel, David I. Limits of the Novel: Evolutions of a Form from Chaucer to Robbe-Grillet. 357p. 1968. 17.50x (ISBN 0-8014-0162-3); pap. 4.95 (ISBN 0-8014-9115-0, CP-115). Cornell U Pr.
Guetti, James L. Word-Music: The Aesthetic Aspect of Narrative Fiction. 1980. 14.75 (ISBN 0-8135-0883-5). Rutgers U Pr.
Halperin, John, ed. The Theory of the Novel: New Essays. 416p. 1975. pap. text ed. 6.95x (ISBN 0-19-501701-3). Oxford U Pr.

Hart, Francis R. The Scottish Novel: From Smollett to Spark. LC 77-20680. 1978. 25.00x (ISBN 0-674-79584-9). Harvard U Pr.
Hayman, David & Rabkin, Eric S. Form in Fiction. 400p. (Orig.). 1974. pap. text ed. 7.95 (ISBN 0-312-29925-7). St Martin.
Henkle, Roger B. Reading the Novel: An Introduction to the Technique of Interpreting Fiction. 1977. pap. text ed. 8.95 scp (ISBN 0-06-042785-X, HarpC). Har-Row.
Hoare, Dorothy. Some Studies in the Modern Novel. LC 72-3668. (Studies in Fiction, No. 34). 1972. Repr. of 1938 ed. lib. bdg. 31.95 (ISBN 0-8383-1544-5). Haskell.
Holman, C. Hugh. Windows on the World: Essays on American Social Fiction. LC 78-13241. 1979. 13.50x (ISBN 0-87049-264-0). U of Tenn Pr.
Howe, Irving. Politics & the Novel. LC 74-117810. (Essay Index Reprint Ser). 1957. 18.00 (ISBN 0-8369-1710-3). Arno.
--Politics & the Novel. 1977. pap. 5.95 (ISBN 0-8180-1170-X). Horizon.
Howells, William D. Criticism & Fiction, & Other Essays. Kirk, Clara M. & Kirk, Rudolf, eds. LC 76-57973. 1977. Repr. of 1959 ed. lib. bdg. 28.25x (ISBN 0-8371-9460-1, HOCF). Greenwood.
Hurtik, Emil & Yarber, Robert, eds. Introduction to Short Fiction & Criticism. LC 73-138096. (Orig.). 1971. pap. text ed. 13.50 (ISBN 0-471-00273-9). Wiley.
James, Henry. Art of the Novel. 1934. lib. rep. ed. 6.95x (ISBN 0-684-15531-1, ScribC); (ScribC). Scribner.
--Notes on Novelists, with Some Other Notes. LC 68-56451. 1969. Repr. of 1914 ed. 16.00x (ISBN 0-8196-0233-7). Biblo.
Jefferson, Ann. The Nouveau Roman & the Poetics of Fiction. LC 79-41507. 225p. 1980. 29.50 (ISBN 0-521-22239-7). Cambridge U Pr.
Johnson, R. Brimley. Novelists on Novels. LC 73-3429. Repr. of 1928 ed. lib. bdg. 20.00 (ISBN 0-8414-2159-5). Folcroft.
Josipovici, Gabriel. World & the Book: A Study of Modern Fiction. LC 79-170983. 1971. 10.00x (ISBN 0-8047-0797-9). Stanford U Pr.
Kahler, Erich. The Inward Turn of Narrative. Winston, Richard & Winston, Clara, trs. from Ger. LC 72-4036. (The Bollingen Ser.: Vol. 83). 240p. 1973. 15.00 (ISBN 0-691-09891-3). Princeton U Pr.
Kany, Charles E. The Beginnings of the Epistolatory Novel in France, Italy, & Spain. (Studies in Comparative Literature: No. 6). (Illus.). 158p. Repr. of 1937 ed. lib. bdg. 15.00x (ISBN 0-87991-505-6). Porcupine Pr.
Kaplan, Harold. The Passive Voice: An Approach to Modern Fiction. LC 66-11300. xi, 239p. 1966. 12.00x (ISBN 0-8214-0017-7). Ohio U Pr.
Keating, P. J. The Working Classes in Victorian Fiction. (Illus.). 1979. pap. 8.95 (ISBN 0-7100-0196-7). Routledge & Kegan.
Kellogg, Gene. The Vital Tradition: The Catholic Novel in a Period of Convergence. LC 74-108375. 1970. 8.35 (ISBN 0-8294-0192-X). Loyola.
Kennedy, Margaret. Outlaws on Parnassus. LC 73-121484. (Essay Index Reprint Ser). 1960. 16.00 (ISBN 0-8369-1968-8). Arno.
Kennerley, Mitchell. Frank Harris to Arnold Bennett: Fifty Eight Letters, 1908-1910. LC 73-4394. 1936. lib. bdg. 6.50 (ISBN 0-8414-2209-5). Folcroft.
Kenney, William. How to Analyze Fiction. (Orig.). 1976. pap. 1.95 (ISBN 0-671-18746-5). Monarch Pr.
Kestner, Joseph A. The Spatiality of the Novel. LC 78-14377. 1979. 15.95x (ISBN 0-8143-1612-3). Wayne St U Pr.
Klein, Holger, ed. The First World War in Fiction: A Collection of Critical Essays. LC 76-28822. 1978. text ed. 23.50x (ISBN 0-06-493792-5). B&N.
Kloesel, Christion J. & Smitten, Jeffrey R. English Novel Explication: Supplement II, Through 1979. (Novel Explication Ser.). vi, 326p. 1981. 27.50 (ISBN 0-208-01709-7). Shoe String.
Knight, Everett. A Theory of the Classical Novel. 1970. 8.95 (ISBN 0-7100-6773-9). Routledge & Kegan.
Kunar, Raj. The New Concept of the Novel. 49p. 1980. Repr. of 1959 ed. lib. bdg. 7.50 (ISBN 0-8482-1446-3). Norwood Edns.
Lawlor, P. A. The Mystery of Maata: A Katherine Mansfield Novel. LC 73-541. 1972. Repr. of 1946 ed. lib. bdg. 12.50 (ISBN 0-8414-1459-9). Folcroft.
Lea, Sydney L. Gothic to Fantastic: Readings in Supernatural Fiction. Varma, Devendra P., ed. LC 79-8463. (Gothic Studies & Dissertations Ser.). 1980. lib. bdg. 22.00x (ISBN 0-405-12653-0). Arno.
Leibowitz, Judith. Narrative Purpose in the Novella. (De Proprietatibus Litterarum, Ser. Minor: No. 10). 139p. 1974. pap. text ed. 18.25x (ISBN 90-2793-007-4). Mouton.
Lewis, Wyndham. Satire & Fiction. LC 74-34424. 1927. lib. bdg. 10.00 (ISBN 0-8414-5713-1). Folcroft.
Liebman, Arthur. Thirteen Classic Detective Stories. LC 73-84994. (Masterworks of Mystery Ser.). 192p. (gr. 7-12). 1974. PLB 7.97 (ISBN 0-8239-0290-0); tchrs' manual 1.50 (ISBN 0-686-66890-1). Rosen Pr.
Liljegren, S. B. Studies on the Origin & Early Tradition of English Utopian Fiction. LC 73-5537. 1973. lib. bdg. 20.00 (ISBN 0-8414-2278-8). Folcroft.
Lindenberger, Herbert. Saul's Fall: A Critical Fiction. LC 78-22003. 1979. 14.95x (ISBN 0-8018-2176-2). Johns Hopkins.
Lodge, David. Novelist at the Crossroads & Other Essays on Fiction & Criticism. LC 77-163130. 308p. 1971. 17.50x (ISBN 0-8014-0674-9). Cornell U Pr.
Loomis, Edward. On Fiction: Critical Essays & Notes. LC 66-30425. 71p. 1966. 3.25 (ISBN 0-8040-0231-2). Swallow.
Lovett, Robert M. The History of the Novel in England. LC 73-15772. 1932. Repr. lib. bdg. 35.00 (ISBN 0-8414-5695-X). Folcroft.
--Preface to Fiction. LC 72-191229. 1931. Repr. lib. bdg. 6.95 (ISBN 0-8414-5891-X). Folcroft.
Lukacs, Georg. Theory of the Novel. Bostock, Anna, tr. from Ger. 1971. pap. 4.95 (ISBN 0-262-62027-8). MIT Pr.
Lukacs, George. Historical Novel. 1978. Repr. of 1962 ed. text ed. 12.50x (ISBN 0-85036-068-4). Humanities.
McCleary, George F. On Detective Fiction & Other Things. 161p. 1980. Repr. of 1960 ed. lib. bdg. 20.00 (ISBN 0-8492-6501-0, 0-8492-6600-9). R West.
MacCulloch, John A. Childhood of Fiction. LC 74-78208. 1971. Repr. of 1905 ed. 32.00 (ISBN 0-8103-3628-6). Gale.
McElrath, Joseph. Walden Notes. (Orig.). 1971. pap. 1.95 (ISBN 0-8220-1358-4). Cliffs.
McMahon, Helen. Criticism of Fiction: A Study of Trends in the Atlantic Monthly. LC 74-148278. Repr. of 1952 ed. 18.00 (ISBN 0-404-04144-2). AMS Pr.
McMaster, Juliet & McMaster, Rowland. The Novel from Sterne to James: Essays on the Relation of Literature to Life. (Illus.). 228p. 1981. 26.50x (ISBN 0-389-20193-6). B&N.
Magill, Frank N. Critical Survey of Short Fiction, 7 vols. LC 81-51697. 3000p. 1981. 275.00 (ISBN 0-89356-210-6). Salem Pr.
Maugham, W. Somerset. The Art of Fiction: An Introduction to Ten Novels & Their Authors. LC 75-25371. (Works of W. Somerset Maugham Ser.). 1977. Repr. of 1955 ed. 15.00x (ISBN 0-405-07825-0). Arno.
--Points of View: Five Essays. LC 75-25374. (Works of W. Somerset Maugham Ser.). 1977. Repr. of 1959 ed. 15.00x (ISBN 0-405-07827-7). Arno.
Mauriac, Francois. Le Roman. LC 75-41191. (Fr.). Repr. of 1928 ed. 12.75 (ISBN 0-404-14766-6). AMS Pr.
Maurice, A. B. The Paris of the Novelists. 59.95 (ISBN 0-8490-0801-8). Gordon Pr.
Maurice, Arthur B. The Paris of the Novelists. LC 74-153276. (Illus.). 299p. 1973. Repr. of 1919 ed. 16.00 (ISBN 0-8046-1736-8). Kennikat.
Mellard, James M. The Exploded Form: The Modernist Novel in America. LC 79-25993. 224p. 1980. 15.00 (ISBN 0-252-00801-4). U of Ill Pr.
Meyer, Herman. Poetics of Quotation in the European Novel. Ziolkowski, Y. & Ziolkowski, T., trs. LC 65-17152. 1968. 20.00 (ISBN 0-691-06094-0). Princeton U Pr.
Miller, D. A. Narrative & Its Discontents: Problems of Closure in the Traditional Novel. LC 80-8565. 320p. 1981. 18.50 (ISBN 0-691-06459-8). Princeton U Pr.
Miller, Lucien. Masks of Fiction in Dream of the Red Chamber: Myth, Mimesis, & Persona. LC 75-23643. (Association for Asian Studies Monographs: No. 28). 7.95x (ISBN 0-8165-0543-8); pap. 3.95x (ISBN 0-8165-0479-2). U of Ariz Pr.
Millgate, Jane, ed. Editing Nineteenth-Century Fiction, Vol. 13. LC 78-3393. (Conference on Editorial Problems Ser.). 1978. lib. bdg. 16.50 (ISBN 0-8240-2428-1). Garland Pub.
Monarch Notes on Paton's Cry the Beloved Country, Too Late the Phalarope. (Orig.). pap. 1.50 (ISBN 0-671-00720-3). Monarch Pr.
Morris, Robert K. Continuance & Change: Contemporary British Novel Sequence. LC 74-175951. (Crosscurrents-Modern Critiques Ser.). 185p. 1972. 7.95 (ISBN 0-8093-0544-5). S Ill U Pr.
Mowshowitz, Abbe. Inside Information: Computers in Fiction. 345p. 1977. pap. text ed. 9.95 (ISBN 0-201-04929-5). A-W.
Muir, E. Structure of the Novel. 2nd ed. 1963. text ed. 4.25x (ISBN 0-7012-0174-6). Humanities.
Murray, H. Morality of Fiction: or an Inquiry into the Tendency of Fictitious Narrative. LC 72-6240. 1972. Repr. of 1805 ed. lib. bdg. 10.00 (ISBN 0-8414-0116-0). Folcroft.
Newby, Percy H. The Novel, Nineteen Forty-Five to Nineteen Fifty. LC 74-23504. 1974. Repr. of 1951 ed. lib. bdg. 6.00 (ISBN 0-8414-6265-8). Folcroft.
Norris, F. Responsibilities of the Novelist & Other Literary Essays. LC 68-26364. (Studies in Fiction, No. 34). 1969. Repr. of 1903 ed. lib. bdg. 32.95 (ISBN 0-8383-0269-6). Haskell.
O'Connor, Frank. Mirror in the Roadway. facs. ed. LC 77-117886. (Select Bibliographies Reprint Ser). 1956. 22.00 (ISBN 0-8369-5339-8). Arno.
Palmer, Jerry. Thrillers: Genesis & Structure of a Popular Genre. 1979. 22.50x (ISBN 0-312-80347-8). St Martin.
Paris, Bernard J. A Psychological Approach to Fiction: Studies in Thackeray, Stendhal, George Eliot, Dostoevsky, & Conrad. LC 73-15239. 320p. 1974. 12.50x (ISBN 0-253-34650-9). Ind U Pr.
Pearce, Richard. Stages of the Clown: Perspectives on Modern Fiction from Dostoyevsky to Beckett. LC 74-86188. (Crosscurrents-Modern Critiques Ser.). 181p. 1970. 6.95 (ISBN 0-8093-0449-X). S Ill U Pr.
Phelan, James. Worlds from Words: A Theory of Language in Fiction. LC 80-25844. (Chicago Originals Ser.). 256p. 1981. lib. bdg. 19.00x (ISBN 0-226-66690-5). U of Chicago Pr.
Politi, Jina. The Novel & Its Presuppositions: Changes in the Conceptual Structure of Novels in the 18th & 19th Centuries. 1979. text ed. 16.00x (ISBN 0-391-02018-8). Humanities.
Pratt, Annis. Archetypal Patterns in Women's Fiction. LC 81-47167. 256p. 1981. 22.50x (ISBN 0-253-10252-9); pap. 6.95x (ISBN 0-253-20272-8). Ind U Pr.
Priestley, L. A. Feminine in Fiction. LC 74-7185. 1918. lib. bdg. 15.00 (ISBN 0-8414-6770-6). Folcroft.
Pritchett, V. S. The Living Novel & Later Appreciations. 1964. 10.00 (ISBN 0-686-72088-1). Random.
Ransom, Ellene. Utopus Discovers America or Critical Realism in American Utopian Fiction 1798-1900. LC 76-12358. 1947. lib. bdg. 5.50 (ISBN 0-8414-7356-0). Folcroft.
Reed, Walter L. An Exemplary History of the Novel: The Quixotic Versus the Picaresque. LC 80-17908. 336p. 1981. lib. bdg. 22.00x (ISBN 0-226-70683-4). U of Chicago Pr.
Riggan, William. Picaros, Madmen, Naifs, & Clowns: The Unreliable First-Person Narrator. LC 81-2791. 240p. 1981. 14.95x (ISBN 0-8061-1714-1). U of Okla Pr.
Robert, Marthe. Origins of the Novel. Rabinovitch, Sacha, tr. from Fr. LC 80-7970. 224p. 1981. 19.95x (ISBN 0-253-18824-5). Ind U Pr.
Roberts, James L. Notes from Underground Notes. (Orig.). 1970. pap. 1.95 (ISBN 0-8220-0900-5). Cliffs.
Romantic Times. 24p. tabloid 1.95 (ISBN 0-940338-00-9). Romantic Times.
Ross, Stephen D. Literature & Philosophy: An Analysis of the Philosophical Novel. LC 69-11284. (Century Philosophy Ser.). (Orig.). 1969. pap. text ed. 6.95x (ISBN 0-89197-278-1). Irvington.
Scholes, Robert. Elements of Fiction. 1968. pap. 2.50x (ISBN 0-19-501046-9). Oxford U Pr.
--Fabulation & Metafiction. LC 78-10776. 1979. 15.00 (ISBN 0-252-00704-2); pap. 5.95 (ISBN 0-252-00761-1). U of Ill Pr.
Scholes, Robert & Kellogg, Robert. Nature of Narrative. 1968. pap. 5.95 (ISBN 0-19-500773-5, GB). Oxford U Pr.
Seltzer, Alvin J. Chaos in the Novel - The Novel in Chaos. LC 73-91347. 384p. 1974. 17.50x (ISBN 0-8052-3543-4). Schocken.
Singer, Godfrey F. Epistolary Novel: Its Origin, Development, Decline & Residuary Influence. LC 63-9508. 1963. Repr. of 1933 ed. 10.00 (ISBN 0-8462-0396-0). Russell.
Skene Melvin, David & Skene Melvin, Ann. Crime, Detective, Espionage, Mystery, & Thriller Fiction & Film: A Comprehensive Bibliography of Critical Writing Through 1979. LC 80-1194. xx, 367p. 1980. lib. bdg. 29.95 (ISBN 0-313-22062-X, MCD/). Greenwood.
Slochower, Harry. Three Ways of Modern Man. LC 37-17328. 1968. Repr. of 1937 ed. 12.00 (ISBN 0-527-83656-7). Kraus Repr.
Smith, Seymour. Novels & Novelists. (Illus.). 288p. 1980. 19.95 (ISBN 0-312-57966-7). St Martin.
Somer, John & Klinkowitz, Jerome, eds. Innovative Fiction. 256p. (Orig.). 1972. pap. 1.50 (ISBN 0-440-34011-X, LE). Dell.
Spiegel, Alan. Fiction & the Camera Eye: Visual Consciousness in Film & the Modern Novel. LC 75-22353. 1976. 12.95x (ISBN 0-8139-0598-2). U Pr of Va.
Spivey, Ted R. The Journey Beyond Tragedy: A Study of Myth & Modern Fiction. LC 80-18348. xi, 190p. 1981. 20.00 (ISBN 0-8130-0681-3). U Presses Fla.
Stone, Irving, et al. Three Views of the Novel. LC 77-7608. 1957. lib. bdg. 8.50 (ISBN 0-8414-7692-6). Folcroft.
Stratford, Philip. Faith & Fiction: Creative Process in Greene & Mauriac. 1964. pap. 2.95x (ISBN 0-268-00379-3). U of Notre Dame Pr.
Thompson, Henry D. Masters of Mystery: A Study of the Detective Story. 59.95 (ISBN 0-8490-0592-2). Gordon Pr.
Thomson, H. Douglas. Masters of Mystery: A Study of the Detective Story. LC 73-786. Repr. of 1931 ed. lib. bdg. 20.00 (ISBN 0-8414-1600-1). Folcroft.
Tieje, Arthur J. The Theory of Characterization in Prose Fiction Prior to 1040. LC 74-12383. 1975. lib. bdg. 17.50 (ISBN 0-8414-8595-X). Folcroft.
Toliver, Harold. Animate Illusions: Explorations of Narrative Structure. LC 72-97975. x, 412p. 1974. 19.95x (ISBN 0-8032-0831-6). U of Nebr Pr.
Tracy, Ann B. The Gothic Novel, Seventeen Ninety to Eighteen Thirty: Plot Summaries & Index to Motifs. LC 79-4013. 224p. 1981. 14.00x (ISBN 0-8131-1397-0). U Pr of Ky.
Tytler, Graeme. Physiognomy in the European Novel: Faces & Fortunes. LC 81-47160. (Illus.). 384p. 1981. 25.00x (ISBN 0-691-06491-1). Princeton U Pr.
Wagner, Geoffrey. Five for Freedom: A Study of Feminism in Fiction. LC 73-8284. 234p. 1973. 14.50 (ISBN 0-8386-1423-X). Fairleigh Dickinson.
Wake, Clive. The Novels of Pierre Loti. LC 73-80224. (De Proprietatibus Litterarum, Ser. Practica: No. 82). 1974. pap. text ed. 21.25x (ISBN 90-2792-660-3). Mouton.
Wallace, Irving. The Fabulous Originals: Lives of Extraordinary People Who Inspired Memorable Characters in Fiction. Repr. of 1955 ed. 30.00 (ISBN 0-527-94160-3). Kraus Repr.
Walpole, Hugh. Tendencies of the Modern Novel. LC 76-23121. 1934. lib. bdg. 10.50 (ISBN 0-8414-9528-9). Folcroft.
Walpole, Hugh, et al. Tendencies of the Modern Novel. facs. ed. LC 67-23272. (Essay Index Reprint Ser). 1934. 15.00 (ISBN 0-8369-0929-1). Arno.
Warren, Frederick M. History of the Novel Previous to the 17th Century. LC 76-23108. 1895. lib. bdg. 25.00 (ISBN 0-8414-9532-7). Folcroft.
--A History of the Novel Previous to the Seventeenth Century. 361p. 1980. Repr. of 1895 ed. lib. bdg. 45.00 (ISBN 0-8492-8806-1). R West.
Watson, George. The Story of the Novel. LC 79-13093. 1979. text ed. 23.50x (ISBN 0-06-497493-6); pap. 9.95x (ISBN 0-06-497494-4). B&N.
Weinstein, Arnold L. Vision & Response in Modern Fiction. LC 73-20793. 288p. 1974. 22.50x (ISBN 0-8014-0833-4). Cornell U Pr.
What's Novel in the Novel. (YFS Ser.: No. 8). 1951. pap. 6.00 (ISBN 0-527-01716-7). Kraus Repr.
Wicker, Brian. The Story-Shaped World: Fiction & Metaphysics: Some Variations on a Theme. LC 74-27889. 238p. 1976. text ed. 12.95x (ISBN 0-268-01669-0); pap. 3.95x (ISBN 0-268-01671-2). U of Notre Dame Pr.
Williams, D. Z., ed. The Monster in the Mirror: Studies in Nineteenth-Century Realism. 1978. 34.50x (ISBN 0-19-713433-5). Oxford U Pr.
Williams, Ioan. The Idea of the Novel in Europe, Sixteen Hundred to Eighteen Hundred. LC 78-78112. (The Gotham Library). 1979. usa 22.50x (ISBN 0-8147-9187-5); pap. 11.50x usa (ISBN 0-8147-9188-3). NYU Pr.
--Novel & Romance, 1700-1800: A Documentary Record. 1970. 40.00x (ISBN 0-7100-6595-7). Routledge & Kegan.
Williams, M. A. Our Early Female Novelists & Other Essays. 1904. lib. bdg. 15.00 (ISBN 0-8414-9737-0). Folcroft.
Wilson, Angus. The Wild Garden or Speaking of Writing. 1963. 14.95x (ISBN 0-520-01346-8); pap. 1.25 (ISBN 0-520-01347-6, CAL112). U of Cal Pr.
Woods, John. The Logic of Fiction. LC 73-92089. (De Proprietatibus Litterarum, Ser. Minor: No. 16). 152p. 1974. pap. text ed. 21.25x (ISBN 90-2793-113-5). Mouton.
Woolf, Virginia. Granite & Rainbow. LC 75-6782. 240p. 1975. pap. 3.45 (ISBN 0-15-636475-1, HB318, Harv). HarBraceJ.
Zatlin, Linda G. Nineteenth Century Anglo-Jewish Novel. (English Authors Ser.: No. 295). 13.95 (ISBN 0-8057-6787-8). Twayne.

FICTION–HISTORY AND CRITICISM–20TH CENTURY

Adams, Robert M. After Joyce: Studies in Fiction After Ulysses. 1977. 12.95 (ISBN 0-19-502168-1). Oxford U Pr.

Aronson, Alex. Music & the Novel: A Study in Twentieth Century Fiction. 267p. 1980. 22.50x (ISBN 0-8476-6170-9). Rowman.
Bradbury, Malcolm, ed. The Novel Today: Contemporary Writers on Modern Fiction. 256p. 1977. 15.00x (ISBN 0-87471-964-X). Rowman.
Brewster, Dorothy & Burrell, John A. Modern World Fiction. (Quality Paperback: No. 18). 220p. (Orig.). 1963. pap. 2.95 (ISBN 0-8226-0018-8). Littlefield.
Carnegie Institute of Technology Department of English, ed. Six Novelists: Stendhal, Dostoevski, Tolstoy, Hardy, Dreiser & Proust. LC 72-1311. (Essay Index Reprint Ser.). Repr. of 1959 ed. 13.00 (ISBN 0-8369-2837-7). Arno.
Chattopadhyaya, Sissir. Technique of the Modern English Novel. 1959. lib. bdg. 20.00 (ISBN 0-8414-3604-5). Folcroft.
Cohen. Film & Fiction. LC 79-64073. 1979. 14.50x (ISBN 0-300-02366-9). Yale U Pr.
Comfort, Alex. Novel & Our Time. LC 76-57724. 1948. lib. bdg. 8.50 (ISBN 0-8414-3415-8). Folcroft.
Davies, Hugh S. Browning & the Modern Novel. LC 76-43278. 1976. Repr. of 1962 ed. lib. bdg. 6.00 (ISBN 0-8414-3793-9). Folcroft.
Devlin, Laura K. Looking Inward: Studies in James Joyce, E.M. Forster, & the Twentieth Century Novel. 1980. lib. bdg. 59.95 (ISBN 0-87700-269-X). Revisionist Pr.
Friedman, Melvin J., ed. Vision Obscured: Perceptions of Some Twentieth-Century Catholic Novelists. LC 72-126130. 1970. 20.00 (ISBN 0-8232-0890-7). Fordham.
Garvin, Harry R., ed. Makers of the Twentieth-Century Novel. LC 74-4975. 322p. 1976. 18.00 (ISBN 0-8387-1522-2). Bucknell U Pr.
Hartt, Julian N. Lost Image of Man. LC 63-19232. (Rockwell Lectures). 1963. 10.00x (ISBN 0-8071-0526-0). La State U Pr.
Henderson, Philip. Novel Today. LC 73-12887. 1936. lib. bdg. 20.00 (ISBN 0-8414-4750-0). Folcroft.
Hicks, Granville. Literary Horizons: A Quarter Century of American Fiction. LC 72-133011. 1970. 15.00x (ISBN 0-8147-3354-9). NYU Pr.
Hoare, Dorothy. Some Studies in the Modern Novel. LC 72-3668. (Studies in Fiction, No. 34). 1972. Repr. of 1938 ed. lib. bdg. 31.95 (ISBN 0-8383-1544-5). Haskell.
Hoare, Dorothy M. Some Studies in the Modern Novel. LC 78-58260. (Essay Index in Reprint Ser.). Repr. 17.50x (ISBN 0-8486-3022-X). Core Collection.
Humphrey, Robert. Stream of Consciousness in the Modern Novel. LC 54-6673. (Perspectives in Criticism: No. 3). 1954. pap. 2.95 (ISBN 0-520-00585-6, CAL14). U of Cal Pr.
Ingram, Forrest L. Representative Short Story Cycles of the Twentieth Century: Studies in a Literary Genre. LC 75-159465. (De Proprietatibus Litterarum, Ser. Major: No. 15). 234p. 1971. text ed. 37.50x (ISBN 90-2791-848-1). Mouton.
Kennedy, Alan. The Protean Self: Dramatic Action in Contemporary Fiction. LC 74-9792. 304p. 1974. 17.50 (ISBN 0-231-03922-0). Columbia U Pr.
Larson, Charles R. The Novel in the Third World. 305p. 1976. 16.50 (ISBN 0-87953-402-8). Inscape Corp.
Lewald, H. Ernest, ed. The Cry of Home: Cultural Nationalism & the Modern Writer. LC 76-173656. 412p. 1972. 15.50x (ISBN 0-87049-135-0). U of Tenn Pr.
Lovett, Robert M. Preface to Fiction: A Discussion of Great Modern Novels. facs. ed. LC 68-16948. (Essay Index Reprint Ser). 1931. 12.00 (ISBN 0-8369-0625-X). Arno.
McKenzie, Barbara, ed. Process of Fiction: Contemporary Stories & Criticism. 2nd ed. 1974. pap. text ed. 11.95 (ISBN 0-15-571986-6, HC). HarBraceJ.
Mandel, Siegfried, ed. Contemporary European Novelists. LC 68-21416. (Crosscurrents-Modern Critiques Ser.). 192p. 1968. 7.95 (ISBN 0-8093-0314-0). S Ill U Pr.
Meyer, Roy W. The Middle Western Farm Novel in the Twentieth Century. LC 64-17221. viii, 265p. 1974. pap. 3.45x (ISBN 0-8032-5798-8, BB 587, Bison). U of Nebr Pr.
Miles, Rosalind. The Fiction of Sex: Themes & Functions of Sex Difference in the Modern Novel. (Critical Studies). 208p. 1974. 18.50x (ISBN 0-06-494822-6). B&N.
Mooney, Harry J., Jr. & Staley, Thomas F., eds. The Shapeless God: Essays on Modern Fiction. LC 68-21630. 1968. 10.95 (ISBN 0-8229-3161-3). U of Pittsburgh Pr.
Robbe-Grillet, Alain. For a New Novel: Essays on Fiction. Howard, Richard, tr. from Fr. 1966. pap. 2.25 (ISBN 0-394-17107-1, B112, BC). Grove.
Ross, Stephen D. Literature & Philosophy: An Analysis of the Philosophical Novel. LC 69-11284. (Century Philosophy Ser.). (Orig.). 1969. pap. text ed. 6.95x (ISBN 0-89197-278-1). Irvington.
Ruotolo, Lucio P. Six Existential Heroes: The Politics of Faith. LC 72-86386. 192p. 1973. 10.00x (ISBN 0-674-81025-2). Harvard U Pr.
Sarraute, Nathalie. Age of Suspicion: Essays on the Novel. 5.00 (ISBN 0-8076-0209-4). Braziller.
--Ere De Soupcon: Essais sur le roman. 1964. pap. 6.50 (ISBN 0-685-11165-2). French & Eur.
--L' Ere du Soupcon. 192p. 1970. 3.95 (ISBN 0-686-54964-3). French & Eur.
Schulz, Max F. Black Humor Fiction of the Sixties: A Pluralistic Definition of Man & His World. LC 72-85538. 156p. 1980. pap. 5.95x (ISBN 0-8214-0574-8). Ohio U Pr.
Spencer, Sharon. Space, Time & Structure in the Modern Novel. 1971. 12.00x (ISBN 0-8147-7751-1). NYU Pr.
Spivey, Ted R. The Journey Beyond Tragedy: A Study of Myth & Modern Fiction. LC 80-18348. xi, 190p. 1981. 20.00 (ISBN 0-8130-0681-3). U Presses Fla.
Springer, Mary D. Forms of the Modern Novella. LC 75-9055. x, 198p. 1976. lib. bdg. 14.00x (ISBN 0-226-76986-0). U of Chicago Pr.
Stevick, Philip. Alternative Pleasures: Post-Realist Fiction & the Tradition. LC 80-25900. 140p. 1981. 13.95 (ISBN 0-252-00877-4). U of Ill Pr.
White, John J. Mythology in the Modern Novel: A Study of Prefigurative Techniques. LC 71-155004. 1972. 18.00x (ISBN 0-691-06210-2). Princeton U Pr.

FICTION–STORIES, PLOTS, ETC.
see Plots (Drama, Novel, etc.)

FICTION–STUDY AND TEACHING
Altenbernd, Lynn & Lewis, Leslie L. Handbook for the Study of Fiction. rev. ed. (Orig.). 1966. pap. text ed. 5.25 (ISBN 0-02-301950-6, 30195). Macmillan.
Cassill, R. V. Writing Fiction. 2nd ed. 192p. 1975. pap. 3.45 (ISBN 0-13-970103-6, Spec). P-H.
Casty, Alan H. The Shape of Fiction. 2nd ed. 448p. 1975. pap. text ed. 10.95x (ISBN 0-669-91066-X); instr's manual 1.95 (ISBN 0-669-91074-0). Heath.
Chandler, G. How to Find Out About the Novel. 4th ed. 1974. write for info. (ISBN 0-685-25212-4). Pergamon.
Field, C. & Hamley, D. C. Fiction in the Middle School. 144p. 1975. 14.95 (ISBN 0-7134-2922-4). David & Charles.
James, Henry & Edel, Leon. The House of Fiction: Essays on the Novel. LC 73-10849. 286p. 1973. Repr. of 1957 ed. lib. bdg. 15.00x (ISBN 0-8371-7039-7, JAHF). Greenwood.
Mphahlele, Ezekiel. Wanderers. McPherson, Malcolm, ed. 1971. 6.95 (ISBN 0-02-587900-6). Macmillan.

FICTION–TECHNIQUE
see also Detective and Mystery Stories–Technique; Plots (Drama, Novel, etc.); Psychological Fiction
Aldridge, John W., ed. Critiques & Essays on Modern Fiction, 1920-1951: Representing the Achievement of Modern American & British Critics. LC 52-6180. 610p. 1952. 15.95 (ISBN 0-8260-0275-7). Wiley.
Banfield, Ann. Unspeakable Sentences: Narration & Representation in the Language of Fiction. 304p. 1982. price not set (ISBN 0-7100-0905-4). Routledge & Kegan.
Block, Lawrence. Telling Lies for Fun & Profit: A Manual for Fiction Writers. LC 81-66965. 240p. 1981. 13.95 (ISBN 0-87795-334-1). Arbor Hse.
Blumenthal, Margarete. Technik Des Englischen Gegenwartsromanes. pap. 6.00 (ISBN 0-384-04775-0). Johnson Repr.
Boulton, Marjorie. Anatomy of the Novel. 1975. pap. 7.95 (ISBN 0-7100-8136-7). Routledge & Kegan.
Brewer, Derek. Symbolic Stories: Traditional Narratives of the Family Drama in English Literature. 190p. 1980. 31.50x (ISBN 0-8476-6900-9). Rowman.
Brophy, Jere, et al. Student Characteristics & Teaching. (Professional Ser.). 224p. 1981. text ed. 22.50x (ISBN 0-582-28152-0). Longman.
Bryant, Dorothy. Writing a Novel. LC 78-69766. 1978. pap. 5.00 (ISBN 0-931688-02-7). Ata Bks.
Burack, A. S., ed. Techniques of Novel Writing. 1973. 9.95 (ISBN 0-87116-000-5). Writer.
Burns, Alan & Sugnet, Charles. The Imagination on Trial: Conversations with the British & American Novelists. 192p. 1981. 16.95x (ISBN 0-8052-8084-7); pap. 7.95 (ISBN 0-8052-8083-9). Schocken.
Cowley, Malcolm, ed. Writers at Work: The Paris Review Interviews, First Series. 1977. pap. 4.95 (ISBN 0-14-004540-6). Penguin.
Cross, Wilbur L. Development of the English Novel. LC 78-90494. Repr. of 1899 ed. lib. bdg. 15.00x (ISBN 0-8371-2204-X, CREN). Greenwood.
Derleth, August W. Writing Fiction. LC 72-141413. 1971. Repr. of 1946 ed. lib. bdg. 15.00x (ISBN 0-8371-4694-1, DEWF). Greenwood.
Doubtfire, Dianne. The Craft of Novel Writing. 1981. pap. 5.95 (ISBN 0-8052-8087-1, Pub. by Allison & Busby England). Schocken.
Enholm, Eric. Basic Story Structure: The Structural Method for English Composition. 3rd ed. 1968. 7.50 (ISBN 0-685-06810-2); pap. 6.00 (ISBN 0-685-06811-0). Bayside.
Ford, Ford M. Critical Writings of Ford Madox Ford. MacShane, Frank, ed. LC 64-11356. (Regents Critics Ser). 1964. 12.95x (ISBN 0-8032-0455-8); pap. 2.65x (ISBN 0-8032-5454-7, BB 401, Bison). U of Nebr Pr.
Foster-Harris, William. Basic Formulas of Fiction. rev. ed. 1977. Repr. of 1960 ed. 7.95x (ISBN 0-8061-0135-0). U of Okla Pr.
Friedman, Norman. Form & Meaning in Fiction. LC 73-90843. 431p. 1975. 20.00x (ISBN 0-8203-0357-7). U of Ga Pr.
Glasgow, Ellen A. Certain Measure: An Interpretation of Prose Fiction. 1943. 14.00 (ISBN 0-527-34000-6). Kraus Repr.
Glicksberg, Charles I. Creative Writing. 604p. 1961. 5.00 (ISBN 0-87532-168-2); pap. 3.95 (ISBN 0-87532-169-0). Hendricks House.
Grabo, Carl H. Technique of the Novel. LC 64-8178. 1964. Repr. of 1928 ed. 7.50 (ISBN 0-87752-046-1). Gordian.
Hamilton, Clayton. A Manual of the Art of Fiction. Repr. of 1924 ed. 20.00 (ISBN 0-8492-9998-5). R West.
Hellmann, John. Fables of Fact: The New Journalism As New Fiction. LC 80-23881. 175p. 1981. 12.95 (ISBN 0-252-00847-2). U of Ill Pr.
Hubert, Karen M. Teaching & Writing Popular Fiction: Horror, Adventure, Mystery & Romance in the American Classroom. new ed. 1976. pap. 4.00 (ISBN 0-915924-04-8). Tchrs & Writers Coll.
Humphrey, Robert. Stream of Consciousness in the Modern Novel. LC 54-6673. (Perspectives in Criticism: No. 3). 1954. pap. 2.95 (ISBN 0-520-00585-6, CAL14). U of Cal Pr.
James, Henry & Wells, H. G. Henry James & H. G. Wells: A Record of Their Friendship, Their Debate on the Art of Fiction, & Their Quarrel. Edel, Leon & Ray, Gordon N., eds. LC 78-25756. 1979. Repr. of 1958 ed. lib. bdg. 22.50x (ISBN 0-313-20810-7, JAHJ). Greenwood.
Kaplan, Harold. The Passive Voice: An Approach to Modern Fiction. LC 66-11300. xi, 239p. 1979. pap. 4.95x (ISBN 0-8214-0434-2). Ohio U Pr.
Kennedy, Margaret. The Outlaws on Parnassus. 1979. Repr. of 1958 ed. lib. bdg. 20.00 (ISBN 0-8495-3032-6). Arden Lib.
Lanser, Susan L. The Narrative Act: Point of View in Prose Fiction. LC 81-47141. 320p. 1981. 21.00x (ISBN 0-691-06486-5). Princeton U Pr.
Lewis, Wyndham. Satire & Fiction. 63p. 1980. Repr. of 1927 ed. lib. bdg. 15.00 (ISBN 0-8495-3328-7). Arden Lib.
Linn, J. W. & Taylor, H. W. A Foreword to Fiction. 1935. 30.00 (ISBN 0-8274-2353-5). R West.
McCarthy, Mary. Ideas & the Novel. 7.95 (ISBN 0-15-143682-7). HarBraceJ.
McHugh, Vincent. Primer of the Novel. xv, 308p. 1975. Repr. of 1950 ed. lib. bdg. 15.00x (ISBN 0-374-95515-8). Octagon.
Madden, David. A Primer of the Novel: For Readers & Writers. LC 79-21881. 466p. 1980. lib. bdg. 17.50 (ISBN 0-8108-1265-7). Scarecrow.
Marston, Doris. A Guide to Writing History. 1975. 8.50 (ISBN 0-911654-34-8). Writers Digest.
Meredith, Scott. Writing to Sell. rev. ed. LC 74-1837. 256p. (YA) 1974. 11.95 (ISBN 0-06-012929-8, HarpT). Har-Row.
O'Hara, John. An Artist Is His Own Fault: John O'Hara on Writers & Writing. Bruccoli, Matthew J., intro. by. LC 76-43279. 242p. 1977. 8.95 (ISBN 0-8093-0796-0). S Ill U Pr.
Owen, Jean Z. Professional Fiction Writing. 1974. 8.95 (ISBN 0-87116-015-3). Writer.
Peeples, Edwin A. Professional Storywriter's Handbook. LC 60-6901. 1960. 6.50 (ISBN 0-9600080-0-4). Peeples.
Perry, F. M. The Art of Story-Writing. LC 73-4411. 1973. lib. bdg. 15.00 (ISBN 0-8414-2468-3). Folcroft.
Rehder, Jessie, ed. Young Writer at Work. LC 62-11938. 1962. 8.95 (ISBN 0-672-63148-2). Odyssey Pr.
Rockwell, F. A. Modern Fiction Techniques. 1969. text ed. 12.00 (ISBN 0-87116-047-1). Writer.
Romberg, Bertil. Studies in the Narrative Technique of the First-Person Novel. LC 73-11327. 1962. Repr. lib. bdg. 30.00 (ISBN 0-8414-2589-2). Folcroft.
Surmelian, Leon. Techniques of Fiction Writing: Measure & Madness. LC 66-24323. 1969. pap. 2.95 (ISBN 0-385-06391-1, A549, Anch). Doubleday.
Tieje, Arthur J. The Theory of Characterization in Prose Fiction Prior to 1040. LC 74-12383. 1975. lib. bdg. 17.50 (ISBN 0-8414-8595-X). Folcroft.
Ulrich, P. Gustav Freytags Romantechnik. Repr. of 1907 ed. pap. 7.00 (ISBN 0-384-62640-8). Johnson Repr.
Walcutt, Charles C. Man's Changing Mask: Modes & Methods of Characterization in Fiction. LC 66-24088. 1966. pap. 2.95x (ISBN 0-8166-0468-1, MP15). U of Minn Pr.
Weston, Harold. Form in Literature: A Theory of Technique & Construction. LC 74-31015. 1973. Repr. of 1932 ed. lib. bdg. 15.00 (ISBN 0-8414-9580-7). Folcroft.
Wharton, Edith. Writing of Fiction. LC 66-28379. 1967. Repr. lib. bdg. 14.00x (ISBN 0-374-98398-4). Octagon.

FICTION, HISTORICAL
see Historical Fiction

FICTION IN LIBRARIES
see also Children's Literature (Collections); also subdivisions under Children's Literature
Atkinson, Frank. Fiction Librarianship. (Outlines of Modern Librarianship Ser.). 1980. text ed. 12.00 (ISBN 0-85157-293-6). K G Saur.
IFLA Council Meeting, 44th, Strbske, Pleso, et al. IFLA Annual 1978: Proceedings. Koops, Willem R. & Harvard-Williams, Peter, eds. 197p. Date not set. text ed. 30.00 (ISBN 0-89664-112-0). K G Saur.
Rankin, Marie. Children's Interests in Library Books of Fiction. LC 70-177178. (Columbia University. Teachers College. Contributions to Education: No. 906). Repr. of 1944 ed. 17.50 (ISBN 0-404-55906-9). AMS Pr.

FICTIONS (LAW)
Fuller, Lon L. Legal Fictions. 1967. 10.00x (ISBN 0-8047-0327-2); pap. 2.25 (ISBN 0-8047-0328-0, SP70). Stanford U Pr.
Polak, Alfred S. More Legal Fictions: A Series of Cases from Shakespeare. LC 73-153344. Repr. of 1946 ed. 14.00 (ISBN 0-404-05068-9). AMS Pr.

FICTIONS, THEORY OF
Ogden, Charles K. Bentham's Theory of Fictions. (Quality Paperback: No. 202). 1959. pap. 2.95 (ISBN 0-8226-0202-4). Littlefield.

FICTITIOUS ANIMALS
see Animals, Mythical

FICTITIOUS NAMES
see Anonyms and Pseudonyms

FICTITIOUS PLACES
see Geographical Myths

FICUS
Condit, Ira J. Ficus: The Exotic Species. 1969. pap. 4.00x (ISBN 0-931876-10-9, 4025). Ag Sci Pubns.
King, G. The Species of Ficus of the Indo-Malayan & Chinese Countries. (Illus.). 1969. Repr. 250.00 (ISBN 3-7682-0609-2). Lubrecht & Cramer.

FIDDLE
see Violin

FIDUCIA
see Trusts and Trustees

FIEDLER, ARTHUR, 1894-1979
Holland, James. Mr. Pops. (Illus.). 96p. 1979. pap. 4.95 (ISBN 0-517-51738-8). Barre.
Moore, Robin. Fiedler. (Music Reprint Ser.). 1980. Repr. of 1968 ed. cancelled (ISBN 0-306-76008-8). Da Capo.
--Fiedler: The Colorful Mr. Pops. (Music Reprint Ser.). (Illus.). 1980. Repr. of 1968 ed. lib. bdg. 27.50 (ISBN 0-306-76008-8). Da Capo.

FIEFS
see Feudalism; Land Tenure

FIELD, CYRUS WEST, 1819-1892
Judson, Isabella F., ed. Cyrus W. Field: His Life & Work, 1819-1892. 1972. Repr. of 1896 ed. 26.00x (ISBN 0-8422-8085-5). Irvington.

FIELD, DAVID DUDLEY, 1802-1894
Hicks, Frederick C., ed. High Finance in the Sixties. LC 65-27118. 1966. Repr. of 1929 ed. 15.00 (ISBN 0-8046-0205-0). Kennikat.
Reppy, Alison, ed. David Dudley Field: Centenary Essays Celebrating 100 Years of Legal Reform. 1949. 25.00 (ISBN 0-379-00145-4). Oceana.

FIELD, EUGENE, 1850-1895
Below, Ida C. Eugene Field in His Home. 1978. Repr. of 1898 ed. lib. bdg. 20.00 (ISBN 0-8414-0268-X). Folcroft.
Burt, Mary E. & Cable, Mary B. Eugene Field Book. facsimile ed. LC 76-86794. (Granger Index Reprint Ser). 1898. 12.00 (ISBN 0-8369-6071-8). Arno.
Conrow, Robert. Field Days: The Life, Times & Reputation of Eugene Field. LC 73-19358. (Illus.). 244p. 1974. 17.50 (ISBN 0-684-13780-1). Ultramarine Pub.
Dennis, Charles H. Eugene Field's Creative Years. LC 72-144971. 339p. 1924. Repr. 19.00 (ISBN 0-403-00939-1). Scholarly.
--Eugene Field's Creative Years. 1924. 25.00 (ISBN 0-8274-2318-7). R West.
Fisher, Henry. Abroad with Mark Twain & Eugene Field. 1922. 20.00 (ISBN 0-8274-1814-0). R West.

Thompson, Slason. Eugene Field: A Study in Heredity & Contradictions, 2 vols. (American Newspapermen 1790-1933 Ser.). (Illus.). 629p. 1973. Repr. of 1901 ed. Set. 37.50x (ISBN 0-8464-0005-7). Beekman Pubs.
--Life of Eugene Field: The Poet of Childhood. 1927. 40.00 (ISBN 0-8274-2926-6). R West.
Wilson, Francis. The Eugene Field I Knew. 1898. 25.00 (ISBN 0-8274-2317-9). R West.

FIELD, JOHN, 1782-1837

Branson, David. John Field & Chopin. LC 70-171229. (Illus.). 240p. 1972. 8.95 (ISBN 0-312-44345-5, J60500). St Martin.
Nikolayev, Aleksandr A. John Field. Doscher, David, ed. LC 73-79275. 1973. pap. 10.00x (ISBN 0-913000-99-X). Musical Scope.
Piggott, Patrick. The Life & Music of John Field, 1782-1837: Creator of the Nocturne. (Illus.). 1974. 45.00x (ISBN 0-520-02412-5). U of Cal Pr.

FIELD, NATHAN, 1587-1620?

Brinkley, Roberta F. Nathan Field, the Actor-Playwright. (Yale Studies in English Ser.: No. 77). 153p. 1973. Repr. of 1928 ed. 15.00 (ISBN 0-208-01124-2, Archon). Shoe String.

FIELD, STEPHEN JOHNSON, 1816-1899

Swisher, Carl B. Stephen J. Field: Craftsman of the Law. (Court & the Constitution Ser). 1969. pap. 2.95 (ISBN 0-226-78747-8, P345, Phoen). U of Chicago Pr.
--Stephen J. Field: Craftsman of the Law. (Brookings Institution Reprint Ser). (Illus.). lib. bdg. 14.00x (ISBN 0-697-00171-7); pap. 2.50x (ISBN 0-89197-948-4). Irvington.

FIELD ATHLETICS

see Track-Athletics

FIELD BIOLOGY

see Biology-Field Work

FIELD CAMERAS

see View Cameras

FIELD CROPS

see also Forage Plants; Grain; Horticulture; Irrigation Farming; Tropical Crops
also names of specific crops, e.g. Cotton, Hay

Analysis of an FAO Survey of Post-Harvest Crop Losses in Developing Countries. (Illus.). 1978. pap. 13.00 (ISBN 0-685-86537-1, F-719, FAO). Unipub.
Babakina, V. S., ed. Grain & Pulse Crops. 255p. 1981. 60.00x (ISBN 0-686-76641-5, Pub. by Oxford & IBH India). State Mutual Bk.
Bishop, Douglas D. Working in Plant Science. Amberson, Max L. & Chapman, Stephen, eds. (Illus.). (gr. 9-10). 1978. pap. text ed. 6.96 (ISBN 0-07-000835-3, G). McGraw.
Brickbauer, Elwood A. & Mortenson, William P. Approved Practices in Crop Production. LC 77-89853. (Illus.). (gr. 9-12). 1978. 14.00 (ISBN 0-8134-1975-1, 1975). Interstate.
Burger, A. W. Laboratory Exercises in Field Crop Science. 1977. spiral bdg. 6.80x (ISBN 0-87563-031-6). Stipes.
Carter, Jack, ed. Sunflower Science & Technology. 1978. write for info. Am Soc Agron.
Chapman, Stephen R. & Carter, Lark P. Crop Production: Principles & Practices. LC 75-40318. (Illus.). 1976. text ed. 23.95x (ISBN 0-7167-0581-8). W H Freeman.
Checklist of Economic Plants in Australia. 214p. 1980. pap. 9.00 (ISBN 0-643-02551-0, CO04, CSIRO). Unipub.
China: Multiple Cropping & Related Crop Production Technology. (FAO Plant Protection Paper Ser.: No. 22). 66p. 1981. pap. 7.50 (ISBN 92-5-100977-5, F2108, FAO). Unipub.
Commonwealth Secretariat. Plantation Crops. 318p. 1974. pap. 15.00x (ISBN 0-85092-063-9). Intl Pubns Serv.
Crop Calendars. (Plant Production & Protection Papers: No. 12). 1979. pap. 8.50 (ISBN 92-5-000684-5, F1579, FAO). Unipub.
Crop Farming. (Better Farming Ser: No. 7). 29p. 1977. pap. 4.50 (ISBN 92-5-100146-4, F65, FAO). Unipub.
Delorit, Richard, et al. Crop Production. 4th ed. 1973. text ed. 24.96 (ISBN 0-13-194761-3). P-H.
Dickson, James G. Diseases of Field Crops. 2nd ed. (Agricultural Sciences Ser). (Illus.). 1956. text ed. 18.95 (ISBN 0-07-016804-0, C). McGraw.
Eastin, J. D., ed. Physiological Aspects of Crop Yield. (Illus.). 1969. 10.00 (ISBN 0-89118-004-4). Am Soc Agron.
Ennes, W. B., Jr., ed. Introduction to Crop Protection. (Illus.). 1979. 20.00 (ISBN 0-89118-033-8). Am Soc Agron.
Free, John B. Insect Pollination of Crops. 1971. 84.00 (ISBN 0-12-266650-X). Acad Pr.
Harlan, Jack R. Crops & Man. (Foundations for Modern Crop Science Ser.: Vol. 1). (Illus.). 1975. 11.25 (ISBN 0-89118-032-X). Am Soc Agron.
Hoveland, C. S., ed. Crop Quality, Storage & Utilization. (Illus.). 1980. 15.00 (ISBN 0-89118-035-4). Am Soc Agron.
Hughes, Harold & Metcalfe, Darrel. Crop Production. 3rd ed. (Illus.). 640p. 1972. text ed. 17.95x (ISBN 0-685-26664-8). Macmillan.
Janick, Jules, et al. Plant Science: An Introduction to World Crops. 3rd ed. LC 81-4897. (Illus.). 1981. text ed. 23.95x (ISBN 0-7167-1261-X). W H Freeman.
Jung, Gerald A., ed. Crop Tolerance to Suboptimal Land Conditions. 11.00 (ISBN 0-89118-051-6). Am Soc Agron.
Kipps, M. S. Production of Field Crops. 6th ed. (Agricultural Science Ser.). 1970. text ed. 22.95 (ISBN 0-07-034783-2, C). McGraw.
Langer, R. H. & Hill, G. D. Agricultural Plants. LC 80-41536. (Illus.). 300p. Date not set. price not set (ISBN 0-521-22450-0); pap. price not set (ISBN 0-521-29506-8). Cambridge U Pr.
Lockhart, J. A. & Wiseman, A. J. Introduction to Crop Husbandry. 4th ed. 1978. text ed. 45.00 (ISBN 0-08-022653-1); pap. text ed. 14.00 (ISBN 0-08-022652-3). Pergamon.
Martin, John H., et al. Principles of Field Crop Production. 3rd ed. (Illus.). 1056p. 1976. text ed. 25.95 (ISBN 0-02-376720-0). Macmillan.
Nyvall, Robert F. Field Crop Disease Handbook. (Illus.). 1979. lib. bdg. 47.50 (ISBN 0-87055-336-4); pap. text ed. 25.00 (ISBN 0-87055-344-5). AVI.
Oschwald, W. R., ed. Crop Residue Management Systems. 1978. 9.00 (ISBN 0-89118-050-8). Am Soc Agron.
Papendick, R. I., et al, eds. Multiple Cropping. (Illus.). 1977. 9.00 (ISBN 0-89118-045-1). Am Soc Agron.
Pillai, K. M. Crop Nutrition. 1968. pap. 4.00x (ISBN 0-210-22717-6). Asia.
Poehlam, J. M. & Borthakur, D. N. Breeding Asian Field Crops 2r. 504p. 1981. 30.00x (ISBN 0-686-76626-1, Pub by Oxford & IBH India). State Mutual Bk.
Poehlman, John M. Breeding Field Crops. 2nd ed. (Illus.). 1979. text ed. 29.50 (ISBN 0-87055-328-3). AVI.
Prately, J. E. Principles of Field Crop Production. 1979. 25.00x (ISBN 0-424-00057-1, Pub. by Sydney U Pr); pap. 20.00 (ISBN 0-424-00058-X, Pub. by Sydney U Pr). Intl Schol Bk Serv.
Rechcigl, Miloslav, Jr. CRC Handbook of Agricultural Productivity, Vol. I: Plant Productivity. 464p. 1981. 72.95 (ISBN 0-8493-3961-8). CRC Pr.
Simmonds, N. W. Principles of Crop Improvement. LC 78-40726. (Illus.). 1979. text ed. 32.00x (ISBN 0-582-45586-3); pap. text ed. 19.95x (ISBN 0-582-44630-9). Longman.
Simmonds, N. W., ed. Evolution of Crop Plants. LC 75-32563. (Illus.). 360p. 1976. text ed. 45.00x (ISBN 0-582-46678-4); pap. text ed. 19.95x (ISBN 0-582-44496-9). Longman.
Wilson, Harold K. & Larson, Alvin H. Identification & Judging Crops, Weeds, Diseases. (Illus.). 1940. text ed. 2.75x spiral bdg. (ISBN 0-8134-0045-7, 45). Interstate.

FIELD EFFECT TRANSISTORS

Craig, George B. & Sesnic, Steve S. Investigations of Field Effect Transistors at Cryogenic Temperatures. LC 75-139809. 85p. 1970. 17.50 (ISBN 0-686-01936-9). Mgmt Info Serv.
Crawford, Robert H. Mosfet in Circuit Design. (Texas Instruments Electronics Ser). (Illus.). 1967. 29.50 (ISBN 0-07-013475-8, P&RB). McGraw.
Lenk, John D. Handbook of Electronic Components & Circuits. LC 73-11038. (Illus.). 224p. 1973. ref. ed. 18.95x (ISBN 0-13-377283-7). P-H.
Richman, Paul. Characteristics & Operations. 1967. 24.50 (ISBN 0-07-052340-1, P&RB). McGraw.
--MOS Field-Effect Transistors & Integrated Circuits. LC 73-9892. 259p. 1973. pap. text ed. 30.50 (ISBN 0-471-72030-5, Pub. by Wiley-Interscience). Wiley.
Sessions, Kenneth W. & Tuite, Donald. New IC FET Principles & Projects. LC 72-86692. (Illus.). 160p. 1972. pap. 4.95 (ISBN 0-8306-1613-6, 613). TAB Bks.
Sevin, Leonce J. Field-Effect Transistors. (Illus.). 1965. 22.50 (ISBN 0-07-056355-1, P&RB). McGraw.
Texas Instruments Inc. M O S, Special-Purpose Bipolar Integrated-Circuits & R-F Power Transistor Circuit Design. (Illus.). 1976. 21.50 (ISBN 0-07-063751-2, P&RB). McGraw.
Towers, T. D. Tower's International FET Selector. 1978. leatherette 7.95 (ISBN 0-8306-9988-0); pap. 4.95 (ISBN 0-8306-1016-2, 1016). TAB Bks.
Turner, Rufus P. FET Circuits. 2nd ed. LC 77-72611. (Illus.). 1977. pap. 4.95 (ISBN 0-672-21439-3). Sams.

FIELD EMISSION

see also Field-Ion Microscope

Cutler, P. H. & Tsong, T. T. Field Emission & Related Topics. 1978. 92.75 (ISBN 0-444-85131-3, North-Holland). Elsevier.

FIELD FAMILY

Ridlon, G. T. Field Family. LC 77-94955. (Saco Valley Settlements Ser). 1970. pap. 2.00 (ISBN 0-8048-0765-5). C E Tuttle.

FIELD GEOLOGY

see also Geology-Field Work

Anderson, J. G. C. & Owen, T. R. Field Geology in Britain. Date not set. 40.01 (ISBN 0-08-022054-1); pap. 19.21 (ISBN 0-08-022055-X). Pergamon.

FIELD GLASSES

Magowan, Robin. Looking for Binoculars. 50p. 1976. pap. 2.00 (ISBN 0-87711-062-X). Kayak.
Paul, Henry. Binoculars & All Purpose Telescopes. (Illus.). 96p. 1980. 10.95 (ISBN 0-8174-3558-1); pap. 5.95 (ISBN 0-8174-3559-X). Amphoto.

FIELD HOCKEY

American Alliance for Health, Physical Education & Recreation. Field Hockey Guide 1978-80. 1978. pap. 2.50 (ISBN 0-685-29038-7, 243-26186). AAHPERD.
American Alliance for Health, Physical Education, & Recreation. Field Hockey-Lacrosse Selected Articles. 1974. pap. 0.60x (ISBN 0-685-05087-4, 243-25538). AAHPERD.
Barnes, Mildred J. & Kentwell, Richard G. Field Hockey: The Coach & the Player. 2nd ed. 1978. text ed. 19.95 (ISBN 0-205-06512-0). Allyn.
Bryant, Carol A. Hockey for Schools. (Illus.). 1969. 8.75x (ISBN 0-7207-0872-9). Intl Pubns Serv.
Cadman, John. Hockey Rules Illustrated. (Illus.). 112p. 1980. 18.00 (ISBN 0-7207-1112-6). Transatlantic.
Carr, Gerry. Tackle Hockey. (Tackle Ser). (Illus.). 1977. pap. text ed. 5.95x (ISBN 0-09-127551-2, SpS). Sportshelf.
Delano, Anne. Field Hockey. (Physical Education Activities Ser.). 80p. 1968. pap. text ed. write for info. (ISBN 0-697-07010-7); tchrs.' manual avail. (ISBN 0-686-66579-1). Wm C Brown.
Dillahunt, et al. Field Hockey for Teachers. 1976. 8.95 (ISBN 0-686-17810-6). Sauk.
Flint, Rachael H. Field Hockey. 1978. pap. 4.95 (ISBN 0-8120-5158-0). Barron.
Gros, Vonnie. Inside Field Hockey for Women. LC 79-50977. (Illus.). 1979. o. p. 12.95 (ISBN 0-8092-7216-4); pap. 5.95 (ISBN 0-8092-7215-6). Contemp Bks.
Gujral, Sunil. Indian Hockey. 1979. 9.00x (ISBN 0-7069-0716-7, Pub. by Vikas India). Advent NY.
Hockey Association. Hockey. (Teach Yourself Ser.). 1973. pap. 2.95 (ISBN 0-679-10431-3). McKay.
John, Jenny. Field Hockey Handbook. (Physical Education Ser.). (Illus.). 72p. (Orig.). 1980. pap. text ed. 6.95 (ISBN 0-87663-616-4, Pub. by Hancock Hse). Universe.
Kentwell, Richard. Field Hockey Techniques & Tactics. 1976. 8.95 (ISBN 0-686-17811-4). Sauk.
Lacrosse Guide Nineteen Eighty-One to Eighty Three. 1981. 3.50 (ISBN 0-685-67030-9, 243-81681). AAHPERD.
Reed, Brenda & Walker, Freda. Advanced Hockey for Women. (Illus.). 182p. 1976. 18.50 (ISBN 0-571-09881-9). Transatlantic.
Sullivan, George. Better Field Hockey for Girls. (Better Sports Ser.). (Illus.). 64p. (gr. 5 up). 1981. PLB 6.95 (ISBN 0-396-07970-9). Dodd.
Wein, Horst. The Advanced Science of Field Hockey. Copus, Martin, tr. (Illus.). 240p. 1980. cancelled (ISBN 0-7207-1171-1). Transatlantic.
Williams, Lee Ann. Basic Field Hockey Strategy. LC 77-80921. (gr. 4-7). 1978. 7.95 (ISBN 0-385-12727-8). Doubleday.

FIELD HOSPITALS

see Medicine, Military; Red Cross

FIELD-ION MICROSCOPE

Beckey, H. D. Field Ionization & Field Desorption Mass Spectroscopy. 1978. text ed. 53.00 (ISBN 0-08-020612-3). Pergamon.
Hren, John J. & Ranganathan, S., eds. Field-Ion Microscopy. LC 68-14853. 244p. 1968. 32.50 (ISBN 0-306-30323-X, Plenum Pr). Plenum Pub.

FIELD MARSHALS

see Marshals

FIELD MUSEUM ANTHROPOLOGICAL EXPEDITION TO THE NEAR EAST, 1934

Field, Henry. Anthropology of Iraq Pt. 1, Pt. 1. (Illus.). 1940. pap. 28.00 (ISBN 0-527-01890-2). Kraus Repr.
--Contributions to the Anthropology of Iran. (Illus.). 1939. pap. 35.00 (ISBN 0-527-01889-9). Kraus Repr.

FIELD OF VISION, MEASUREMENT OF

see Perimetry

FIELD SPORTS

see Hunting; Sports

FIELD THEORIES, UNIFIED

see Unified Field Theories

FIELD THEORY (PHYSICS)

see also Continuum Mechanics; Electromagnetic Fields; Electromagnetic Theory; Gravitation; Magnetic Fields; Quantum Field Theory; Unified Field Theories

Agarwal, B. K. Quantum Mechanics and Field Theory. 1977. text ed. 30.00x (ISBN 0-210-26945-6). Asia.
AIP Conference, Rochester 1971. Particles & Fields 1971: Proceedings, No. 2. Melissinos, A. C. & Slattery, P. S., eds. LC 71-184662. 323p. 1971. 13.00x (ISBN 0-88318-101-0). Am Inst Physics.
Alonso, M. & Finn, E. J. Fundamental University Physics, Vol. 2: Fields & Waves. 2nd ed. 1981. write for info. (ISBN 0-201-00077-6). A-W.
Aly, H. H. Lectures on Particles & Fields. 390p. 1970. 67.25x (ISBN 0-677-13740-0). Gordon.
Amit, Daniel A. Field Theory: The Renormalization Group & Critical Phenomena. (International Series in Pure & Applied Physics). (Illus.). 1978. text ed. 24.50x (ISBN 0-07-001575-9, C). McGraw.
Arnowitt, Richard & Nath, Pran, eds. Gauge Theories & Modern Field Theory. LC 76-5836. 423p. 1976. text ed. 23.00x (ISBN 0-262-01046-1). MIT Pr.
Baden-Fuller, A. J. Engineering Field Theory. 272p. 1973. text ed. 32.00 (ISBN 0-08-017033-1); pap. text ed. 16.25 (ISBN 0-08-017034-X). Pergamon.
Balian, Roger, et al. Methods in Field Theory. LC 76-3651. 1977. 49.00 (ISBN 0-7204-0433-9, North-Holland). Elsevier.
Bolton, W. Fields, Bk. 5. LC 80-41166. (Study Topics in Physics Ser.). 96p. 1981. pap. text ed. 4.50 (ISBN 0-408-10656-5). Butterworth.
Coulter, C. A. & Shatas, R. A., eds. Topics in Fields & Solids. 1968. 45.75 (ISBN 0-677-12740-5). Gordon.
Croxton, C. A. Introductory Eigenphysics: An Approach to the Theory of Fields. LC 74-13153. 275p. 1974. text ed. 41.25 (ISBN 0-471-18929-4, Pub. by Wiley-Interscience); pap. text ed. 20.95 (ISBN 0-471-18930-8, Pub. by Wiley-Interscience). Wiley.
Dittrich, W. Recent Developments in Particle & Field Theory. 1978. casebound 47.50 (ISBN 0-9940012-0-7, Pub. by Vieweg & Sohn Germany). Heyden.
Gombas, Szondy T. Solutions of the Simplified Self-Consistent Field. 282p. 1971. 17.50x (ISBN 0-8448-0130-5). Crane-Russak Co.
Hilbers, C. W. & MacLean, C. N M R of Molecules Oriented in Electric Fields. Bd. with N M R & Relaxation of Molecules Absorbed on Solids. Pfeifer, H. (N M R Basic Principles & Progress, Vol. 7). (Illus.). 1972. 31.90 (ISBN 0-387-05687-4). Springer-Verlag.
International Conference on Nuclear Self-Consistent Fields. Proceedings. Ripka, G. & Porneuf, M., eds. LC 75-23198. 1975. 44.00 (ISBN 0-444-10962-5, North-Holland). Elsevier.
Kemmer, N. Vector Analysis. LC 75-36025. (Illus.). 230p. 1977. 49.50 (ISBN 0-521-21158-1); pap. 15.95x (ISBN 0-521-29064-3). Cambridge U Pr.
Kijowski, J. & Tulczyjew, W. M. A Symplectic Framework for Field Theories. (Lecture Notes in Physics: Vol. 107). 1979. pap. 15.00 (ISBN 0-387-09538-1). Springer-Verlag.
Klein, L. Dispersion Relations & the Abstract Approach to Field Theory. (International Science Review Ser.). 1961. pap. 43.00 (ISBN 0-677-00420-6). Gordon.
Lannutti, J. E. & Williams, P. K., eds. Current Trends in the Theory of Fields: Tallahassee, 1979. (AIP Conference Proceedings: No. 48). (Illus.). 1978. lib. bdg. 16.25 (ISBN 0-88318-147-9). Am Inst Physics.
Lee, T. D., ed. Particle Physics & Introduction to Field Theory. (Concepts in Contemporary Physics Ser.: Vol. 1). 750p. 1981. 55.00 (ISBN 3-7186-0032-3); pap. 19.50 (ISBN 0-686-65735-7). Harwood Academic.
Lodge, Arthur S. Body Tensor Fields in Continuum Mechanics. 1975. 55.00 (ISBN 0-12-454950-0). Acad Pr.
Lopes, J. Leite. Gauge Field Theories: An Introduction. (Illus.). 450p. 1981. 40.00 (ISBN 0-08-026501-4). Pergamon.
Moon, P. & Spencer, D. E. Field Theory Handbook: Including Coordinate Systems, Differential Equations & Their Solutions. 2nd ed. LC 77-178288. (Illus.). viii, 236p. 1971. 57.90 (ISBN 0-387-02732-7). Springer-Verlag.
Nishijima, K. Fields & Particles: Field Theory & Dispersion Relations. 4th ed. 1981. 19.50 (ISBN 0-8053-7397-7). A-W.
--Fields & Particles: Field Theory & Dispersion Relations. (Lecture Notes & Supplements in Physics: No. 11). 1969. pap. text ed. 14.50 (ISBN 0-8053-7397-7, Adv Bk Prog). Benjamin-Cummings.
Ramond, P. Field Theory: A Modern Primer. 1981. 16.50 (ISBN 0-8053-7892-8); pap. 14.50 (ISBN 0-8053-7893-6). A-W.

Rummel, R. J. Field Theory Evolving. LC 76-6313. (Dimensions of Nations Ser.: Vol. 2). (Illus.). 531p. 1977. 29.95 (ISBN 0-8039-0391-X). Sage.
Rzewuski, Jan. Field Theory, 2 vols. Incl. Part 1. Classical Theory. 1964. Repr. of 1958 ed. 14.25 (ISBN 0-02-851270-7); Part 2. Functional Formulation of S-Matrix Theory. 1969. 15.25 (ISBN 0-02-851280-4). Hafner.
Sachs, Mendel. The Field Concept in Contemporary Science. (Amer. Lec. in Philosophy Ser.). 132p. 1973. 12.50 (ISBN 0-398-02607-6). C C Thomas.
Schwinger, Julian. Particles, Sources & Fields, Vol. 1. LC 73-119670. (Physics Ser). 1970. text ed. 28.50 (ISBN 0-201-06782-X, Adv Bk Prog). A-W.
--Particles, Sources, & Fields, Vol. 2. (Physics Ser.). 1973. 28.50 (ISBN 0-201-06783-8, Adv Bk Prog). A-W.
Sen, Dipak K. Fields & or Particles. LC 67-30767. 1968. 23.00 (ISBN 0-12-636750-7). Acad Pr.
Sen, R. N. & Weil, C., eds. Statistical Mechanics & Field Theory. LC 72-4108. 333p. 1972. 35.95 (ISBN 0-470-77595-5). Krieger.
--Statistical Mechanics & Field Theory. LC 72-4108. 1972. 49.95 (ISBN 0-470-77595-5). Halsted Pr.
Society for Industrial & Applied Mathematics-American Mathematical Society Symposia-N.C.-April, 1968. Numerical Solution of Field Problems in Continuum Physics: Proceedings, Vol. 2. Birkhoff, G. & Varga, R. S., eds. LC 75-92659. 1970. 24.40 (ISBN 0-8218-1321-8, SIAMS-2). Am Math.
Soper, Davison E. Classical Field Theory. LC 75-37659. 300p. 1976. text ed. 35.50 (ISBN 0-471-81368-0, Pub. by Wiley-Interscience). Wiley.
Steinmann, O. Perturbation Expansions in Axiomatic Field Theory. LC 72-183483. (Lecture Notes in Physics: Vol. 11). iii, 126p. 1971. pap. 10.70 (ISBN 0-387-05698-X). Springer-Verlag.
Turchi, Peter J., ed. Megagauss Physics & Technology. 678p. 1980. 69.50 (ISBN 0-306-40461-3, Plenum Pr). Plenum Pub.
Urban, P., ed. Field Theory & Strong Interactions: Proceedings. (Acta Physica Austriaca Supplementum Ser.: No. 22). (Illus.). 815p. 1981. 98.00 (ISBN 0-387-81615-1). Springer-Verlag.
White, Carol. Energy Potential: Toward a New Electromagnetic Field Theory. Cleary, James, tr. 305p. 1978. pap. 7.95 (ISBN 0-918388-04-X, QC665.E4W45, Univ Edns). New Benjamin.
Williams, L. Pearce. The Origins of Field Theory. LC 80-5710. 160p. 1980. lib. bdg. 15.50 (ISBN 0-8191-1175-9); pap. text ed. 7.50 (ISBN 0-8191-1176-7). U Pr of Amer.

FIELD THEORY, QUANTIZED
see Quantum Field Theory

FIELD WORK (BIOLOGY)
see Biology–Field Work

FIELD WORK (EDUCATIONAL METHOD)
see also Education, Cooperative; Project Method in Teaching; School Excursions

Dodgshon, Robert A. The Origin of British Field Systems: An Interpretation. LC 80-49987. 1980. 25.00 (ISBN 0-12-219260-5). Acad Pr.
Maxwell, Lawrence. Pathfinder Field Guide. rev. ed. 1980. 6.95 (ISBN 0-8280-0053-0, 16070-5); pap. 4.95 (ISBN 0-686-62242-1, 16071-3). Review & Herald.

FIELD WORK (GEOLOGY)
see Geology–Field Work

FIELD WORK (SOCIAL SERVICE)
see Social Service–Field Work

FIELDING, HENRY, 1707-1754

Allen, Walter. Six Great Novelists. LC 73-5556. 1955. lib. bdg. 17.50 (ISBN 0-8414-1737-7). Folcroft.
Allen, Walter E. Six Great Novelists. 1978. Repr. of 1955 ed. lib. bdg. 15.00 (ISBN 0-8495-0106-7). Arden Lib.
Banerji, Hiran K. Henry Fielding: Playwright, Journalist & Master of the Art of Fiction, His Life & Works. LC 62-13825. 1962. Repr. of 1929 ed. 9.50 (ISBN 0-8462-0116-X). Russell.
Battestin, Martin C. Moral Basis of Fielding's Art: A Study of Joseph Andrews. LC 59-10177. 1959. 15.00x (ISBN 0-8195-3007-7, Pub. by Wesleyan U Pr); pap. 6.00x (ISBN 0-8195-6038-3). Columbia U Pr.
Bingham, Chas. W. Wise Sayings & Favorite Passages from the Works of Henry Fielding, Including His Essay on Conversation. LC 74-12102. 1974. Repr. of 1909 ed. lib. bdg. 10.00 (ISBN 0-8414-3211-2). Folcroft.
Bispham, G. T. Fielding's Jonathan Wild in Eighteenth Century Literary: An Oxford Miscellany. 1909. 12.50 (ISBN 0-8274-2343-8). R West.
Bissell, Frederick O. Fielding's Theory of the Novel. LC 68-57713. Repr. of 1933 ed. 8.50x (ISBN 0-8154-0302-X). Cooper Sq.
Blanchard, Frederic T. Fielding the Novelist: A Study in Historical Criticism. LC 66-24669. (Illus.). 1966. Repr. of 1926 ed. 12.50 (ISBN 0-8462-0776-1). Russell.
Cronin, Grover. Monarch Notes on Fielding's Tom Jones. (Orig.). pap. 1.95 (ISBN 0-671-00614-2). Monarch Pr.
Cross, Wilbur L. History of Henry Fielding, 3 Vols. LC 64-10385. (Illus.). 1963. Repr. of 1918 ed. Set. 60.00 (ISBN 0-8462-0403-7). Russell.
De Voogd, Peter. Henry Fielding & William Hogarth: The Correspondence of the Arts. 195p. 1981. pap. text ed. 23.00x (ISBN 90-6203-543-4, Pub. by Rodopi Holland). Humanities.
Digeon, Aurelien. Novels of Fielding. LC 62-20320. (Illus.). 1962. Repr. of 1925 ed. 14.00 (ISBN 0-8462-0168-2). Russell.
Dobson, Austin. Fielding. 210p. 1980. Repr. of 1902 ed. lib. bdg. 15.00 (ISBN 0-89987-153-4). Darby Bks.
--Fielding. Morley, John, ed. LC 73-100820. (English Men of Letters). Repr. of 1889 ed. 12.50 (ISBN 0-404-51708-0). AMS Pr.
--Fielding. 1889. lib. bdg. 15.00 (ISBN 0-8482-9951-5). Norwood Edns.
Elliott, Robert C., ed. Twentieth Century Interpretations of Moll Flanders. (Twentieth Century Interpretations Ser). 1970. pap. 1.25 (ISBN 0-13-322230-6, Spec). P-H.
Evans, James C., ed. Tom Jones Notes. (Orig.). pap. 2.25 (ISBN 0-8220-1293-6). Cliffs.
Fielding, Henry. Fielding: Selections with Essays by Hazlitt, Scott, Thackeray. 1923. 20.00 (ISBN 0-8274-2342-X). R West.
Godden, G. M. Henry Fielding: A Memoir. LC 74-3417. 1978. Repr. of 1909 ed. lib. bdg. 50.00 (ISBN 0-8414-4500-1). Folcroft.
Godden, Gertrude M. Henry Fielding: A Memoior. 326p. 1980. Repr. of 1909 ed. lib. bdg. 40.00 (ISBN 0-8495-2125-4). Arden Lib.
Goldberg, Homer. Art of Joseph Andrews. LC 69-14826. 1969. 10.50x (ISBN 0-226-30090-0). U of Chicago Pr.
Golden, Morris. Fielding's Moral Psychology. LC 66-28115. 1966. 10.50x (ISBN 0-87023-022-0). U of Mass Pr.
Grennen, Joseph. Monarch Notes on Fielding's Joseph Andrews. (Orig.). pap. 1.75 (ISBN 0-671-00711-4). Monarch Pr.
Hahn, H. George. Henry Fielding: An Annotated Bibliography. LC 79-4498. (Author Bibliographies Ser.: No. 41). 1979. 11.00 (ISBN 0-8108-1212-6). Scarecrow.
Harper, Howard. Genius of Henry Fielding. LC 72-6572. 1919. lib. bdg. 25.00 (ISBN 0-8414-0170-5). Folcroft.
Harrison, Bernard. Henry Fielding's Tom Jones: The Novelist As Moral Philosopher. (Text & Context Ser.). 1975. text ed. 6.25x (ISBN 0-85621-044-7). Humanities.
Hassall, A. J. Fielding's Tom Jones. (Sydney Studies in Literature: No. 8). 1979. 7.50x (ISBN 0-424-00054-7, Pub. by Sydney U Pr). Intl Schol Bk Serv.
Hatfield, Glenn W. Henry Fielding & the Language of Irony. LC 68-16693. 1968. 12.00x (ISBN 0-226-31921-0). U of Chicago Pr.
Hunter, J. Paul. Occasional Form: Henry Fielding & the Chains of Circumstance. LC 75-11337. 248p. 1976. 16.50 (ISBN 0-8018-1672-6). Johns Hopkins.
Jenkins, Elizabeth. Henry Fielding. LC 74-8471. 1948. Repr. lib. bdg. 10.00 (ISBN 0-8414-5295-4). Folcroft.
Joesten, Maria. De Philosophie Fieldings. 1932. pap. 7.00 (ISBN 0-384-27580-X). Johnson Repr.
Jones, B. M. Henry Fielding, Novelist & Magistrate. 1978. lib. bdg. 30.00 (ISBN 0-8492-1265-0). R West.
Kalpakgian, Mitchell. The Marvellous in Fielding's Novels. LC 80-1411. 243p. 1981. lib. bdg. 18.75 (ISBN 0-8191-1505-3); pap. text ed. 9.75 (ISBN 0-8191-1506-1). U Pr of Amer.
Kay, Donald, ed. A Provision of Human Nature: Essays on Fielding & Others in Honor of Miriam Austin Locke. LC 76-40469. xiii, 207p. 1977. 8.50x (ISBN 0-8173-7425-6). U of Ala Pr.
Keightley, Thomas. The Life & Writings of Henry Fielding, Esq. LC 75-26962. 1975. lib. bdg. 27.50 (ISBN 0-8414-5497-3). Folcroft.
Lawrence, Frederick. The Life of Henry Fielding. LC 76-9795. 1976. Repr. of 1855 ed. lib. bdg. 40.00 (ISBN 0-8414-5744-1). Folcroft.
McCrea, Brian. Henry Fielding & the Politics of Mid-Eighteenth-Century England. LC 80-14711. (South Atlantic Modern Language Association Award Study, 1979). 272p. 1981. 20.00x (ISBN 0-8203-0531-6). U of Ga Pr.
Mavor, Michael B. Joseph Andrews Notes. (Orig.). pap. 2.25 (ISBN 0-8220-0682-0). Cliffs.
Morrissey, Leroy J. Henry Fielding: A Reference Guide. (Reference Bks.). 1980. lib. bdg. 35.00 (ISBN 0-8161-8139-X). G K Hall.
Murphy, Arthur. Lives of Henry Fielding & Samuel Johnson, with Essays from Gray's Inn Journal, 1752-1792. LC 68-24212. 1968. 49.00x (ISBN 0-8201-1035-3). Schol Facsimiles.
Newton, A...abel. Wordsworth in Early American Criticism. LC 74-23675. 1974. Repr. lib. bdg. 25.00 (ISBN 0-8414-6281-X). Folcroft.
Rawson, C. J. Henry Fielding & the Augustan Ideal Under Stress: Nature's Dance of Death & Other Studies. 280p. 1972. 18.00x (ISBN 0-7100-7454-9). Routledge & Kegan.
Rice-Oxley, Leonard, intro. by. Fielding: Selections, with Essays by Hazlitt, Scott, Thackeray. 1979. Repr. of 1924 ed. lib. bdg. 20.00 (ISBN 0-8414-7404-4). Folcroft.
Rogers, Pat. Henry Fielding. (Illus.). 1979. 15.95 (ISBN 0-684-16264-4, ScribT). Scribner.
Ronte, Heinz. Richardson Und Fielding. Repr. of 1935 ed. pap. 13.50 (ISBN 0-384-51910-5). Johnson Repr.
Sacks, Sheldon. Fiction & the Shape of Belief: A Study of Henry Fielding - with Glances at Swift, Johnson, & Richardson. LC 79-24436. 1980. pap. 5.95 (ISBN 0-226-73337-8, P877, Phoen). U of Chicago Pr.
Shesgreen, Sean. Literary Portraits in the Novels of Henry Fielding. LC 72-1389. 206p. 1972. 10.00 (ISBN 0-87580-029-7). N Ill U Pr.
Stoler, John A. & Fulton, Richard. An Annotated Bibliography of Fielding Criticism. LC 78-68276. (Garland Reference Library of the Humanities: No. 147). 1980. lib. bdg. 30.00 (ISBN 0-8240-9796-3). Garland Pub.
Thornbury, Ethel M. Henry Fielding's Theory of the Comic Prose Epic. LC 78-3747. Repr. of 1931 ed. lib. bdg. 12.50 (ISBN 0-8414-8417-1). Folcroft.
Van Der Voorde, F. R. Henry Fielding: Critic & Satirist. LC 68-755. (Studies in Fiction, No. 34). 1969. Repr. of 1931 ed. lib. bdg. 33.95 (ISBN 0-8383-0639-X). Haskell.
Vitale, Philip H. Barron's Simplified Approach to Fielding's Tom Jones. LC 67-24536. (Orig.). 1967. pap. 1.50 (ISBN 0-8120-0262-8). Barron.
Watt, Ian. The Rise of the Novel: Studies in Defoe, Richardson & Fielding. 1957. pap. 3.95 (ISBN 0-520-01318-2). U of Cal Pr.
Willcocks, M. P. A True-Born Englishman: Being the Life of Henry Fielding. LC 74-8472. 1947. lib. bdg. 20.00 (ISBN 0-8414-9529-7). Folcroft.
Williams, Ioan. The Criticism of Henry Fielding. 1970. 30.00 (ISBN 0-7100-6596-5). Routledge & Kegan.
Wright, Andrew. Henry Fielding: Mask & Feast. 1965. pap. 1.50 (ISBN 0-520-01367-0, CAL128). U of Cal Pr.

FIELDING, JOHN, SIR, 1721-1780

Williams, Murial B. Marriage: Fielding's Mirror of Morality. LC 73-56. (Studies in the Humanities Ser.: No. 1). 160p. 1973. pap. 2.95 (ISBN 0-8173-7312-8). U of Ala Pr.

FIELDS, ALGEBRAIC
see also Algebra, Differential; Algebraic Number Theory; Ideals (Algebra); Modular Fields; Numbers, Theory of; Quaternions; Rings (Algebra)

Abhyankar, S. Ramification Theoretic Methods in Algebraic Geometry. (Annals of Mathematics Studies Ser.: No. 43). (Orig.). 1959. 10.00 (ISBN 0-691-08023-2, AM43). Princeton U Pr.
Bhattacharya, P. B. & Jain, S. K. First Course in Rings, Fields & Vector Spaces. 1977. 12.95 (ISBN 0-470-99047-3, 76-55303). Halsted Pr.
Cohn, P. M. Skew Field Constructions. LC 76-46854. (London Mathematical Society Lecture Note Series: No. 27). (Illus.). 1977. limp bdg. 26.95x (ISBN 0-521-21497-1). Cambridge U Pr.
Curtis, Charles W. & Reiner, Irving. Representation Theory of Finite Groups & Associative Algebras. LC 62-16994. (Pure & Applied Mathematics Ser). 1962. 53.00 (ISBN 0-470-18975-4, Pub. by Wiley-Interscience). Wiley.
Deuring, M. Lectures on the Theory of Algebraic Functions of One Variable. LC 72-97679. (Lecture Notes in Mathematics: Vol. 314). 151p. 1973. pap. 8.80 (ISBN 0-387-06152-5). Springer-Verlag.
Endler, O. Valuation Theory. LC 72-92285. (Universitext). xii, 243p. 1972. pap. 13.10 (ISBN 0-387-06070-7). Springer-Verlag.
Frohlich, A., ed. Algebraic Number Field: L Functions & Galois Properties. 1977. 88.50 (ISBN 0-12-268960-7). Acad Pr.
Gerritzen, L. & Van Der Put, M. Schottky Groups & Mumford Curves. (Lecture Notes in Mathematics: Vol. 817). 317p. 1980. pap. 19.50 (ISBN 0-387-10229-9). Springer-Verlag.
Hecke, Erich. Algebraische Zahlen. 2nd ed. LC 50-3732. (Ger). 1970. 11.95 (ISBN 0-8284-0046-6). Chelsea Pub.
Hsu, D. F. Cyclic Neofields & Combinatorial Designs. (Lecture Notes in Mathematics Ser.: Vol. 824). (Illus.). 230p. 1981. pap. 14.00 (ISBN 0-387-10243-4). Springer-Verlag.
Kaplansky, Irving. Fields & Rings. rev. 2nd ed. LC 72-78251. (Chicago Lectures in Mathematics Ser). 224p. 1972. text ed. 10.00x (ISBN 0-226-42450-2); pap. text ed. 8.00x (ISBN 0-226-42451-0). U of Chicago Pr.
Lam, T. Y. The Algebraic Theory of Quadratic Forms. LC 72-11103. (Math Lecture Notes Ser.: No. 54). 350p. 1973. text ed. 15.00 (ISBN 0-8053-5664-9, Adv Bk Prog); pap. text ed. 12.50 (ISBN 0-8053-5665-7, Adv Bk Prog). Benjamin-Cummings.
Landau, Edmund. Algebraische Zahlen. 2nd ed. (Ger). 8.95 (ISBN 0-8284-0062-8). Chelsea Pub.
Langlands, R. Base Change for GL (2) LC 79-28820. (Annals of Mathematics Studies: No. 96). 225p. 1980. 17.50x (ISBN 0-691-08263-4); pap. 7.00x (ISBN 0-691-08272-3). Princeton U Pr.
Lightstone, A. H. & Robinson, A. Nonarchimedean Fields & Asymptotic Expansions. (Mathematical Library: Vol. 13). 204p. 1975. 36.75 (ISBN 0-444-10731-2, North-Holland). Elsevier.
Linnik, Yu V. Ergodic Properties of Algebraic Fields. (Ergebnisse der Mathematik und Ihrer Grenzgebiete: Vol. 45). 1968. 28.10 (ISBN 0-387-04101-X). Springer-Verlag.
McCarthy, Paul J. Algebraic Extensions of Fields. 2nd ed. LC 75-41499. ix, 166p. 1976. 9.50 (ISBN 0-8284-1284-7). Chelsea Pub.
Marcus, D. A. Number Fields (Universitext) LC 77-21467. 1977. text ed. 16.30 (ISBN 0-387-90279-1). Springer-Verlag.
Meyer, R. M. Essential Mathematics for Applied Fields. (Universitets). (Illus.). 555p. 1980. pap. 17.60 (ISBN 0-387-90450-6). Springer-Verlag.
Nagata, Masayoshi. Field Theory, Vol. 40. (Monographs & Textbooks in Pure & Applied Mathematics). 1977. 27.75 (ISBN 0-8247-6466-8). Dekker.
Reid, Legh Wilber. The Elements of the Theory of Algebraic Numbers. 3rd ed. 464p. 1946. 28.00x (ISBN 0-8018-0547-3). Johns Hopkins.
Reiner, I. Maximal Orders. (London Mathematical Society Monographs). 1975. 61.00 (ISBN 0-12-586650-X). Acad Pr.
Room, Thomas G. & Kirkpatrick, P. B. Miniquaternion Geometry. LC 79-123347. (Tracts in Mathematics: No. 60). 1971. 28.95 (ISBN 0-521-07926-8). Cambridge U Pr.
Rucker, I., et al. Field Mathematics Program Series. Incl. Program K. pap. text ed. 3.40 (ISBN 0-13-314880-7); Program 1. pap. text ed. 4.68 (ISBN 0-13-314906-4); achievement tests 0.92 (ISBN 0-685-47414-3); Program 2. pap. text ed. 4.68 (ISBN 0-13-314948-X); 0.92 (ISBN 0-685-47415-1); Program 3. text ed. 7.00 (ISBN 0-13-314997-8); pap. text ed. 5.64 (ISBN 0-13-314989-7); wkbk. for hardcover ed. 2.44 (ISBN 0-685-47416-X); achievement tests 0.92 (ISBN 0-685-47417-8); Program 4. text ed. 7.44 (ISBN 0-13-315077-1); wkbk. 2.44 (ISBN 0-685-47418-6); achievement tests 0.92 (ISBN 0-685-47419-4); Program 5. text ed. 7.44 (ISBN 0-13-315135-2); wkbk. 2.44 (ISBN 0-685-47420-8); achievement tests 0.92 (ISBN 0-685-47421-6); Program 6. text ed. 7.44 (ISBN 0-13-315192-1); wkbk. 2.44 (ISBN 0-685-47422-4); achievement tests 0.92 (ISBN 0-685-47423-2); Program 7. McNabb, W., et al. text ed. 8.92 (ISBN 0-13-315267-7); wkbk. 2.80 (ISBN 0-685-47424-0); achievement tests 0.92 (ISBN 0-685-47425-9); Program 8. McNabb, W., et al. text ed. 8.92 (ISBN 0-13-315473-4); wkbk. 2.80 (ISBN 0-685-47426-7); achievement tests 0.92 (ISBN 0-685-47427-5). (gr. k-8). 1974. P-H.
Schilling, O. F. Theory of Valuations. 3rd ed. LC 50-12178. (Mathematical Surveys Ser.: No. 4). 1978. Repr. of 1950 ed. 30.40 (ISBN 0-8218-1504-0, SURV-4). Am Math.
Stolarsky, Kenneth B. Algebraic Numbers & Diophantine Approximation. (Pure & Applied Mathematics Ser.: Vol. 26). 320p. 1974. 32.25 (ISBN 0-8247-6102-2). Dekker.
Taibleson, M. H. Fourier Analysis on Local Fields. LC 74-32047. (Mathematical Notes Ser.: No. 15). 308p. 1977. 16.00x (ISBN 0-691-08165-4). Princeton U Pr.
Weil, A. Dirichlet Series & Automorphic Forms. LC 72-151320. (Lecture Notes in Mathematics: Vol. 189). 1971. pap. 11.80 (ISBN 0-387-05382-4). Springer-Verlag.
Winter, D. J. The Structure of Fields. LC 73-21824. (Graduate Texts in Mathematics Ser.: Vol. 16). (Illus.). 320p. 1974. 20.80 (ISBN 0-387-90074-8). Springer-Verlag.

FIELDS, JAMES THOMAS, 1817-1881

Bonner, William H. De Quincey at Work. LC 73-9715. 1936. lib. bdg. 15.00 (ISBN 0-8414-3162-0). Folcroft.
Fields, Annie, ed. James T. Fields: Biographical Notes & Personal Sketches with Unpublished Fragments & Tributes from Men & Women of Letters. LC 73-157501. 1971. Repr. of 1881 ed. 24.00 (ISBN 0-8103-3724-X). Gale.

Fields, Annie A. James T. Fields: Biographical Notes & Personal Sketches. LC 75-122653. 1971. Repr. of 1882 ed. 13.75 (ISBN 0-8046-1301-X). Kennikat.

FIELDS, WILLIAM C., 1880-1946

Anobile, Richard J., ed. A Flask of Fields. 1975. pap. 3.95 (ISBN 0-380-01189-1, 17533). Avon.
--Godfrey Daniels. (Illus.). 224p. 1975. 8.95 (ISBN 0-517-52034-6). Crown.
Deschner, Donald. Films of W. C. Fields. (Illus.). 12.00 (ISBN 0-8065-0374-2); pap. 6.95 (ISBN 0-8065-0143-X). Citadel Pr.
Fields, R., ed. Himself by W.C. Fields: His Hitherto Unpublished Letters, Articles, & Scripts for Stage, Screen & Radio. 1973. 7.95 (ISBN 0-13-109876-4). P-H.
Fields, Ronald J., ed. W. C. Fields by Himself. (Illus.). 592p. 1974. pap. 1.95 (ISBN 0-446-79470-8). Warner Bks.
Fields, W. C. Drat! Anobile, Richard J., ed. (Illus.). 152p. 1973. pap. 1.25 (ISBN 0-451-06887-4, Y6887, Sig). NAL.
Finke, Blythe F. W. C. Fields: Renowned Comedian of the Early Modern Picture Industry. Rahmas, D. Steve, ed. (Outstanding Personalities Ser.: No. 48). 32p. (Orig.). (gr. 7-12). 1972. lib. bdg. 2.95 incl. catalog cards (ISBN 0-87157-552-3); pap. 1.50 vinyl laminated covers (ISBN 0-87157-052-1). SamHar Pr.
Taylor, Robert L. W. C. Fields: His Follies & Fortunes. (Illus.). 1967. pap. 1.25 (ISBN 0-685-17283-X, CY653, Sig Classics). NAL.
W. C. Fields Speaks. 80p. 1981. pap. 2.75 (ISBN 0-8431-0392-2). Price Stern.

FIELDS, ELECTROMAGNETIC

see Electromagnetic Fields

FIESOLE, GIOVANNI DA

see Fra Angelico (Giovanni Da Fiesole), 1387-1455

FIFTEENTH CENTURY

Foster, Genevieve. Year of Columbus, 1492. LC 77-85268. (Illus.). (gr. 2-6). 1969. write for info. (ISBN 0-684-12695-8, ScribJ). Scribner.
Johnson, Jerah & Percy, William A. Age of Recovery: The Fifteenth Century. Fox, Edward, ed. LC 76-10816. (Development of Western Civilization Ser). (Illus.). 1970. pap. text ed. 3.45x (ISBN 0-8014-9858-9). Cornell U Pr.
Mermier, Guy R. & DuBruck, Edelgard E., eds. Fifteenth Century Studies, Vol. 2. LC 79-640105. 1979. pap. 17.25 (ISBN 0-8357-0392-4, SS-00085). Univ Microfilms.
--Fifteenth-Century Studies, Vol. 3. LC 79-640105. (Fifteenth-Century Studies Ser.). (Illus.). 252p. (Orig.). 1980. pap. 17.25 (ISBN 0-8357-0505-6, SS-00129). Univ Microfilms.

FIFTH COLUMN

see Subversive Activities; World War, 1939-1945-Collaborationists

FIFTH MONARCHY MEN

Brown, Louise F. Political Activities of the Baptists & the Fifth Monarchy Men in England During the Interregnum. 1964. Repr. of 1911 ed. 20.50 (ISBN 0-8337-0399-4). B Franklin.

FIGGIS, JOHN NEVILLE, 1866-1919

Magid, Henry M. English Political Pluralism: The Problem of Freedom & Organization. LC 41-15264. Repr. of 1941 ed. 12.45 (ISBN 0-404-04149-3). AMS Pr.

FIGHTER-BOMBER SABRES

see Sabre (Jet Fighter Planes)

FIGHTER PLANES

see also Corsair (Fighter Planes); Focke-Wulf One Ninety (Fighter Planes); Heinkel (Fighter Planes); Hellcat (Fighter Planes); Hurricane (Fighter Planes); Mustang (Fighter Planes); P-Forty (Fighter Planes); Pfeil (Fighter Planes); Skyraider (Fighter Planes); Spitfire (Fighter Planes); Thunderbolt (Fighter Planes)

Abrams, Richard. F Four-U Corsair at War. (Illus.). 160p. 1981. pap. 10.95 (ISBN 0-684-17013-2, ScribT). Scribner.
--F-Four-U Corsair at War. LC 78-311995. (Illus.). 1977. 17.50x (ISBN 0-7110-0766-7). Intl Pubns Serv.
Aeronautical Staff of Aero Publishers, et al. Boeing P12, F4B. LC 66-17554. (Aero Ser.: Vol. 5). 1966. pap. 3.00 (ISBN 0-8168-0516-4). Aero.
Aeronautical Staff of Aero Publishers. Nakajima KI-84. LC 65-24308. (Aero Ser: Vol. 2). (Illus.). 1965. pap. 3.00 (ISBN 0-8168-0504-0). Aero.
Allward, Maurice. F-Eighty Six Sabre. (Illus.). 1978. 9.95 (ISBN 0-684-15883-3, ScribT). Scribner.
Archer, Robert D. Republic F-105 Thunderchief. LC 71-102870. (Illus., Orig.). 1969. pap. 6.95 (ISBN 0-8168-1500-3). Aero.
Arnold, Rhodes. The Republic F-Eighty-Four: From "Lead Sled" to "Super Hawg". (Illus.). 128p. 1981. pap. 12.95 (ISBN 0-89404-054-5). Aztex.
Bowers, Peter M. Forgotten Fighters & Experimental Aircraft of the U. S. Army, 1918-1941. LC 70-124505. (Illus.). 80p. (Orig.). 1971. pap. 3.95 (ISBN 0-668-02403-8). Arco.
Bowyer, Chaz. Mosquito at War. (Illus.). 1978. 14.95 (ISBN 0-684-15699-7, ScribT). Scribner.
Bowyer, Michael J. F. Aircraft for the Royal Air Force. (Illus.). 160p. 1980. 27.00 (ISBN 0-571-11515-2, Pub. by Faber & Faber). Merrimack Bk Serv.
Brown, David. Carrier Fighters. 1981. 8.95 (ISBN 0-356-08095-1, Pub. by MacDonald & Jane's England). Hippocrene Bks.
Cain, Charles W. Fighters of World War Two. (Illus.). 128p. 1979. 16.50x (ISBN 0-85383-414-8). Intl Pubns Serv.
Colby, C. B. Fighter Parade: Headliners in Fighter Plane History. (Illus.). (gr. 4-7). 1960. PLB 5.29 (ISBN 0-698-30076-9). Coward.
Davis, Maggie. Eagles. LC 80-14471. 384p. 1980. 13.95 (ISBN 0-688-03727-5). Morrow.
Drendel, Lou. And Kill MIGs. pap. 6.95 (ISBN 0-89747-056-7). Squad Sig Pubns.
Ethell, Jeffrey & Christy, Joe. P-Thirty Eight Lightning at War. (Illus.). 1978. 20.00 (ISBN 0-684-15740-3, ScribT). Scribner.
F-Four-U Corsair in Action. pap. 4.95 (ISBN 0-89747-028-1). Squad Sig Pubns.
Green, William. Famous Fighters of the Second World War. rev. ed. 1976. 10.95 (ISBN 0-385-12395-7). Doubleday.
Green, William & Swanborough, Gordon. Japanese Army Airforce Fighters. (World War II Aircraft Fact Files Ser.). (Illus.). 1977. pap. 4.95 (ISBN 0-668-04119-6). Arco.
--Japanese Army Fighters, Pt. 2. LC 76-29071. (World War 2 Fact Files Ser.). (Illus.). 1978. pap. 4.95 (ISBN 0-668-04427-6, 4427). Arco.
--Soviet Airforce Fighters: Part 1. LC 77-3200. (World War II Aircraft Fact Files Ser.). (Illus.). 1977. 6.95 (ISBN 0-668-04167-6); pap. 4.95 (ISBN 0-668-04170-6). Arco.
--U. S. Army Airforce Fighters: Part 1. (World War II Aircraft Fact Files Ser.). (Illus.). 1977. 6.95 (ISBN 0-668-04169-2); pap. 4.95 (ISBN 0-668-04166-8). Arco.
Groh, Richard. Fifty Famous Fighter Aircraft. LC 68-22395. (Illus., Orig.). 1968. pap. 2.95 (ISBN 0-668-01751-1). Arco.
Gunston, Bill. Early Supersonic Fighters of the West. LC 75-15313. 1976. 10.95 (ISBN 0-684-14491-3, ScribT). Scribner.
--An Illustrated Guide to Allied Fighters of World War II. LC 80-70976. (Illustrated Military Guides Ser.). (Illus.). 160p. 1981. 8.95 (ISBN 0-668-05228-7, 5228). Arco.
--The Illustrated Guide to German, Italian & Japanese Fighters of World War II. LC 80-67627. (Illustrated Military Guides). (Illus.). 160p. 1981. 7.95 (ISBN 0-668-05093-4, 5093). Arco.
--The Illustrated Guide to Modern Fighters & Attack Aircraft. LC 80-65164. (Illustrated Military Guides Ser.). (Illus.). 160p. 1980. 7.95 (ISBN 0-668-04964-2, 4964-2). Arco.
--Nightfighters: A Development & Combat History. LC 76-24140. (Illus.). 1977. 8.95 (ISBN 0-684-14842-0, ScribT). Scribner.
Higham, Robin & Siddall, Abigail, eds. Flying Combat Aircraft of the USAAF-USAF, Vol. 1. (Illus.). 1975. 11.95 (ISBN 0-8138-0325-X). Iowa St U Pr.
Holder, William G. Convair F-106 Delta Dart. LC 75-15272. (Aero Ser.: Vol. 27). 104p. 1977. pap. 7.95 (ISBN 0-8168-0600-4). Aero.
Holder, William G. & Siuru, William D., Jr. General Dynamics F-16. LC 75-25245. (Aero Ser.: Vol. 26). 104p. 1976. pap. 7.95 (ISBN 0-8168-0596-2). Aero.
Horikoshi, Jiro. Eagles of Mitsubishi: The Story of the Zero Fighter. Shindo, Shojiro & Wantiez, Harald N., trs. from Japanese. (Illus.). 184p. 1981. 18.95 (ISBN 0-295-95826-X). U of Wash Pr.
Jones, Lloyd. U. S. Fighters. LC 75-25246. (Illus.). 1975. 15.95 (ISBN 0-8168-9200-8). Aero.
--U. S. Naval Fighters. LC 77-20693. (Illus.). 1977. 15.95 (ISBN 0-8168-9254-7). Aero.
Kinzey, Bert. F-Sixteen in Detail & Scale. (Detail & Scale Ser.). (Illus.). 72p. (Orig.). 1982. pap. 6.95 (ISBN 0-8168-5013-5). Aero.
--USAF F-4 in Detail & Scale, Pt. 1: Fd-4c, F-4c, F-4c, F-4c, F-4d. (Detail & Scale Ser.). (Illus.). 72p. 1981. pap. 6.95 (ISBN 0-8168-5011-9). Aero.
Koku-Fan, ed. Kawasaki Ki-61, Tony Fighter. (Illus.). 1967. pap. 3.95 (ISBN 0-913076-08-2). Beachcomber Bks.
Lewis, Peter. British Fighter Since 1912: LC 65-19381. (Illus.). 1965. 12.95 (ISBN 0-370-00063-3). Aero.
Luukkanen, Eino. Fighter Over Finland: The Memorirs of a Fighter Pilot. Gilbert, James & Green, William, eds. Salo, Mauno A., tr. LC 79-7282. (Flight: Its First Seventy-Five Years Ser.). (Illus.). 1979. Repr. of 1963 ed. lib. bdg. 20.00x (ISBN 0-405-12191-1). Arno.
Maloney, Edward T. Zero Sen: Japanese Fighter. (Illus.). 1978. pap. 3.00 (ISBN 0-686-70936-5, Pub. by WW II). Aviation.
Matt, Paul R. U. S. Navy & Marine Corps Fighters, 1918-1962. Robertson, Bruce, ed. LC 62-19914. (Harleyford Ser). (Illus.). 1962. 18.95 (ISBN 0-8168-6390-3). Aero.
Mikesh, Robert C. B-Fifty-Seven Canberra at War: Nineteen Sixty-Four to Nineteen Seventy-Two. (Illus.). 160p. 1980. 17.95 (ISBN 0-684-16726-3, ScribT). Scribner.
--Zero Fighter, Bk. 6. (Crown's World War II Fighter Planes Ser.). 1981. 15.95 (ISBN 0-517-54260-9). Crown.
Morgan, T. L. Fighter Aircraft of the United States. LC 66-19792. (Illus.). 1966. pap. 2.95 (ISBN 0-668-01554-3). Arco.
Munson, Kenneth. Fighters: Attack & Training Aircraft, 1914-1919. (Illus.). 1968. 8.95 (ISBN 0-02-588070-5). Macmillan.
--Fighters in Service: Attack & Training Aircraft Since 1960. rev. ed. LC 75-12742. (Illus.). 168p. 1975. 8.95 (ISBN 0-02-587960-X, 58796). Macmillan.
--Fighters, Nineteen Thirty-Nine to Nineteen Forty-Five: World War Two. (Illus.). 1969. 8.95 (ISBN 0-02-588010-1). Macmillan.
P-Four Phantom in Action. pap. 4.95 (ISBN 0-686-31769-6). Squad Sig Pubns.
P-Thirty-Nine, P-Sixty-Three in Action. 1980. pap. 4.95 (ISBN 0-89747-102-4). Squad Sig Pubns.
Philpott, Bryan. Fighters Defending the Reich. (World War Two Photo Album: No. 4). (Illus.). 96p. 1981. pap. 5.95 (ISBN 0-89404-044-8). Aztex.
--Fighters Over the Mediterranean. (World War Two Photo Album: No. 6). (Illus.). 96p. 1981. pap. 6.95 (ISBN 0-89404-048-0). Aztex.
--German Fighters Over England. (World War Two Photo Album). (Illus.). 96p. 1981. pap. 5.95 (ISBN 0-89404-056-1). Aztex.
--German Fighters Over Russia. (World War Two Photo Album: No. 16). (Illus.). 96p. 1980. pap. 5.95 (ISBN 0-89404-040-5). Aztex.
Price, Alfred. Focke Wulf One-Ninety at War. LC 77-8704. (Illus.). 1977. 17.50x (ISBN 0-7110-0768-3). Intl Pubns Serv.
Reed, Arthur. F-Fourteen Tomcat. (Illus.). 1978. 12.50 (ISBN 0-684-15881-7, ScribT). Scribner.
--F-One Hundred & Four Starfighter at War. 1981. 17.50 (ISBN 0-684-16989-4, ScribT). Scribner.
Rice, Michael S., ed. Pilot's Flight Operating Instructions for P-39 Airacobra. (Illus.). 48p. 1973. pap. 4.50 (ISBN 0-87994-024-7). Aviation.
--Pilots Manual for Northrop P-61 Black Widow Airplane. (Illus.). 72p. 1973. pap. 5.95 (ISBN 0-87994-025-5, Pub. by AvPubns). Aviation.
Scutts, Jerry. F-One Hundred & Five Thunderchief at War. 1981. 16.95 (ISBN 0-684-16983-5, ScribT). Scribner.
Tillman, Barrett. MIG Master: The Story of the F-8 Crusader. LC 80-83019. (Illus.). 260p. 1980. 17.95 (ISBN 0-933852-17-7). Nautical & Aviation.
Ward, Richard. Sharkmouth, Vol. 1. LC 79-111766. (Arco-Aircam Aviation Ser. 21). 1970. pap. 2.95 (ISBN 0-668-02225-6). Arco.
Wooldridge, E. T., Jr. The P-Eighty Shooting Star: Evolution of a Jet Fighter. LC 79-17648. (Famous Aircraft of the National Air & Space Museum Ser.: Bk. 3). (Illus.). 110p. 1979. pap. 6.95 (ISBN 0-87474-965-4). Smithsonian.

FIGHTING

see Battles; Boxing; Bull-Fights; Cock-Fighting; Dueling; Karate; Military Art and Science; Naval Art and Science; Tournaments; War

FIGHTING (PSYCHOLOGY)

see also Aggressiveness (Psychology)

Bach, George R. & Wyden, Peter. Intimate Enemy: How to Fight Fair in Love & Marriage. LC 69-14232. 1969. 12.95 (ISBN 0-688-01884-X). Morrow.
Badayum, T. B. A Short Handbook of Fiqh. pap. 2.95 (ISBN 0-686-63895-6). Kazi Pubns.

FIGHTING, HAND-TO-HAND

see Hand-To-Hand Fighting

FIGURATION

see Figurative Art

FIGURATIVE ART

Hills, Patricia & Tarbell, Roberta K. The Figurative Tradition & the Whitney Museum of American Art: Paintings & Sculpture from the Permanent Collection. LC 80-12650. 192p. 1980. 25.00 (ISBN 0-87413-184-7). U Delaware Pr.

FIGURE DRAWING

see also Children in Art; Face; Hand in Art; Head in Art; Human Figure in Art

Berry, William A. Drawing the Human Form. (Illus.). 1977. 16.95 (ISBN 0-442-20718-2); pap. 12.95 (ISBN 0-442-20717-4). Van Nos Reinhold.
Blake, Wendon. Figure Drawing. (The Artist's Painting Library). (Illus.). 80p. 1981. pap. 5.95 (ISBN 0-8230-1696-X). Watson-Guptill.
Caligor, Leopold. A New Approach to Figure Drawing: Based Upon an Interrelated Series of Drawings. (American Lecture Psychology). (Illus.). 160p. 1957. ed. spiral bdg. 14.75photocopy (ISBN 0-398-04226-8). C C Thomas.
Carter, Stanley N. Practical Instruction in Figure Drawing. (A Promotion of the Arts Library Book). (Illus.). 103p. 1981. 47.25 (ISBN 0-86650-002-2). Gloucester Art.
Glenn, Constance W. Jim Dine Figure Drawings, Nineteen Seventy Five-Nineteen Seventy Nine. LC 79-3060. (Icon Edns.). (Illus.). 1980. pap. 12.95 (ISBN 0-06-430102-8, HarpT). Har-Row.
Goldstein, N. Figure Drawing: Structure, Anatomy & Expressive Design of Human Form. 1976. 18.95 (ISBN 0-13-314765-7). P-H.
Goldstein, Nathan. Figure Drawing: The Structure, Anatomy, & Expressive Design of Human Form. (Illus.). 330p. 1981. text ed. 21.95 (ISBN 0-13-314518-2); pap. text ed. 18.95 (ISBN 0-13-314435-6). P-H.
Graves, Douglas R. Life Drawing in Charcoal. (Illus.). 1979. pap. 9.95 (ISBN 0-8230-2766-X). Watson-Guptill.
Hale, Robert B. Drawing Lessons from the Great Masters. (Illus.). 1964. 17.95 (ISBN 0-8230-1400-2). Watson-Guptill.
Hamm, Jack. Cartooning the Head & Figure. (Illus., Orig.). (gr. 9 up). 1967. pap. 4.95 (ISBN 0-448-01541-2). G&D.
Hatton, Richard G. Figure Drawing. (Illus., Orig). pap. 4.00 (ISBN 0-486-21377-3). Dover.
Hogarth, Burne. Dynamic Figure Drawing. LC 73-87324. (Illus.). 1970. 14.95 (ISBN 0-8230-1575-0). Watson-Guptill.
Klavins, Uldis. Figure Drawings. (Illus.). 1981. price not set (ISBN 0-8230-1696-X). Watson-Guptill.
Kramer, Jack. Human Anatomy & Figure Drawing: The Integration of Structure & Form. 1972. pap. 10.95 (ISBN 0-442-20822-7). Van Nos Reinhold.
Loomis, Andrew. Figure Drawing for All It's Worth. (Illus.). (YA) (gr. 9 up). 1943. 16.95 (ISBN 0-670-31255-X). Viking Pr.
Mills, J. W. Head & Figure Modelling. 1977. 24.00 (ISBN 0-7134-3258-6, Pub. by Batsford England). David & Charles.
Munce, Howard. Drawing the Nude. (Illus.). 1980. 17.50 (ISBN 0-8230-1411-8). Watson-Guptill.
Perard, Victor. Figure Drawing. (Grosset Art Instruction Ser.: Vol. 20). pap. 2.95 (ISBN 0-448-00529-8). G&D.
Reed, Walt, ed. The Figure: An Artist's Approach to Drawing & Construction. (Illus.). 144p. 1976. 16.00 (ISBN 0-8230-1695-1). Watson-Guptill.
Sheppard, Joseph. Drawing the Female Figure. (Illus.). 160p. 1975. 16.50 (ISBN 0-8230-1370-7). Watson-Guptill.
Shimer. Drawing Children. (Grosset Art Introduction Ser.: Vol. 9). pap. 2.95 (ISBN 0-448-00518-2). G&D.
Szabo, Marc. Drawing File for Architects, Illustrators, & Designers. (Illus.). 256p. 1976. pap. 14.95 (ISBN 0-442-27878-0). Van Nos Reinhold.
Vanderpoel, John H. Human Figure. 1935. pap. 3.00 (ISBN 0-486-20432-4). Dover.

FIGURE PAINTING

see also Genre Painting; Human Figure in Art; Portrait Painting

American Artist Magazine Staff. Twenty Figure Painters & How They Work. Meyer, Susan E., ed. (Illus.). 1979. 21.95 (ISBN 0-8230-5489-6). Watson-Guptill.
Blake, Wendon. The Portrait & Figure Painting Book. (Illus.). 1980. 25.00 (ISBN 0-8230-4095-X); prepub. 22.50 pre-pub (ISBN 0-686-65963-5). Watson-Guptill.
Graves, Douglas R. Figure Painting in Oil. (Illus.). 1979. pap. 9.95 (ISBN 0-8230-1703-6). Watson-Guptill.
Kinstler, Everett R. Painting Faces, Figures & Landscapes. 144p. 1981. 22.50 (ISBN 0-8230-3625-1). Watson-Guptill.
Schmid, Richard. Richard Schmid Paints the Figure: Advanced Techniques in Oil. LC 73-5549. (Illus.). 144p. 1973. 18.50 (ISBN 0-8230-4865-9). Watson-Guptill.
Schwarz, Hans. Figure Painting. LC 79-84662. (Start to Paint Ser.). (Illus.). 1979. pap. 3.95 (ISBN 0-8008-2717-1, Pentalic). Taplinger.
Singer, Joe. How to Paint Figures in Pastel. (Illus.). 168p. 1976. 19.95 (ISBN 0-8230-2460-1). Watson-Guptill.
Van Rensselaer, Mariana G. Book of American Figure Painters. Weinberg, H. Barbara, ed. LC 75-28875. (Art Experience in Late 19th Century America Ser.: Vol. 11). (Illus.). 1976. Repr. of 1886 ed. lib. bdg. 72.50 (ISBN 0-8240-2235-1). Garland Pub.

FIGURE SKATING

see Skating

FIGURED BASS

see Thorough Bass

FIGUREHEADS OF SHIPS

Brewington, M. V. Shipcarvers of North America. LC 79-187020. (Illus.). 190p. 1972. pap. 4.00 (ISBN 0-486-22168-7). Dover.

Norton, Peter. Ships' Figureheads. (Illus.). 1976. 10.00 (ISBN 0-517-52561-5). Crown.

FIGURES OF SPEECH

see also particular figures of speech, e.g. Metaphor, Simile

Banks, Theodore H. Milton's Imagery. LC 69-19874. (BCL Ser. II). Repr. of 1950 ed. 17.00 (ISBN 0-404-00498-9). AMS Pr.

Beach, Joseph W. Obsessive Images. O'Connor, William V., ed. LC 73-11620. 396p. 1973. Repr. of 1960 ed. lib. bdg. 29.75 (ISBN 0-8371-7079-6, BEOI). Greenwood.

Butter, Peter. Shelley's Idols of the Cave. LC 68-24118. (Studies in Shelley, No. 25). 1969. Repr. of 1954 ed. lib. bdg. 33.95 (ISBN 0-8383-0781-7). Haskell.

Carpenter, Frederic I. Metaphor & Simile in Minor Elizabethan Drama. LC 67-30900. 1967. Repr. of 1901 ed. 6.00 (ISBN 0-87753-007-6). Phaeton.

Carpenter, Frederick I. Metaphor & Simile in the Minor Elizabethan Drama. LC 77-136372. (Chicago. University. English Studies: No. 4). Repr. of 1895 ed. 19.00 (ISBN 0-404-50264-4). AMS Pr.

De Man. Allegories of Reading. LC 79-64075. 1979. 19.50x (ISBN 0-300-02322-7). Yale U Pr.

Dowden, Wilfred S. Joseph Conrad: The Imaged Style. LC 74-112936. 1970. 7.50 (ISBN 0-8265-1153-8). Vanderbilt U Pr.

English Language Services. Key to English Figurative Expressions. (Key to English Ser.). pap. 1.60 (ISBN 0-02-971740-X). Macmillan.

Hankins, John E. Shakespeare's Derived Imagery. 1967. Repr. lib. bdg. 16.50x (ISBN 0-374-93629-3). Octagon.

Hiatt, Mary P. Artful Balance: The Parallel Structures of Style. LC 75-11673. 192p. 1975. text ed. 13.60x (ISBN 0-8077-2487-4); pap. text ed. 7.50x (ISBN 0-8077-2486-6). Tchrs Coll.

Holder-Barell, Alexander. Development of Imagery & Its Functional Significance in Henry James's Novels. LC 68-1739. (Studies in Henry James, No. 17). 1969. Repr. of 1959 ed. lib. bdg. 29.95 (ISBN 0-8383-0665-9). Haskell.

Lanham, Richard A. A Handlist of Rhetorical Terms: A Guide for Students of English Literature. LC 68-31636. 1968. pap. 5.95x (ISBN 0-520-01414-6). U of Cal Pr.

Linder, Cynthia A. Romantic Imagery in the Novels of Charlotte Bronte. LC 78-2903. 1978. text ed. 23.50x (ISBN 0-06-494280-5). B&N.

Matsuura, Kaichi. Study of Donne's Imagery: A Revelation of His Outlook on the World & His Vision of a Christian Monarchy. LC 72-7223. Repr. of 1953 ed. lib. bdg. 20.00 (ISBN 0-8414-0270-1). Folcroft.

Partridge, Edward B. The Broken Compass: A Study of the Major Comedies of Ben Jonson. LC 75-38386. 254p. 1976. Repr. of 1958 ed. lib. bdg. 15.25x (ISBN 0-8371-8662-5, PABC). Greenwood.

Pollio, H. R., et al. Psychology & the Poetics of Growth: Figurative Language in Psychology, Psychotherapy, & Education. LC 77-9880. 1977. 16.50 (ISBN 0-470-99158-5). Halsted Pr.

Rushton, William L. Shakespeare & the Arte of English Poesie. LC 70-174792. Repr. of 1909 ed. 7.50 (ISBN 0-404-05458-7). AMS Pr.

Schleiner, Winfried. Imagery of John Donne's Sermons. LC 70-91655. 264p. 1970. text ed. 12.50x (ISBN 0-87057-116-8, Pub. by Brown U Pr). U Pr of New Eng.

Sherry, Richard. A Treatise of Schemes & Tropes. LC 61-5030. 1977. Repr. of 1550 ed. 26.00x (ISBN 0-8201-1258-5). Schol Facsimiles.

Smith, C. Willard. Browning's Star-Imagery. 1965. lib. bdg. 14.50x (ISBN 0-374-97505-1). Octagon.

Spurgeon, Caroline. Leading Motives in the Imagery of Shakespeare's Tragedies. LC 73-95446. (Studies in Shakespeare, No. 24). 1970. Repr. of 1930 ed. lib. bdg. 22.95 (ISBN 0-8383-1203-9). Haskell.

--Shakespeare's Imagery. 1952. 54.00 (ISBN 0-521-06538-0); pap. 9.95x (ISBN 0-521-09258-2). Cambridge U Pr.

Spurgeon, Caroline F. Leading Motives in the Imagery of Shakespeare's Tragedies. LC 73-914. 1930. lib. bdg. 8.50 (ISBN 0-8414-2609-0). Folcroft.

--Shakespeare's Iterative Imagery. LC 73-978. 1931. lib. bdg. 8.50 (ISBN 0-8414-2606-6). Folcroft.

Stacy, R. H. Defamiliarization in Language & Literature. 1977. 14.00x (ISBN 0-8156-2184-1). Syracuse U Pr.

Svartengren, Torsten H. Intensifying Similes in English. LC 79-176463. Repr. of 1918 ed. 41.50 (ISBN 0-404-06307-1). AMS Pr.

Syatt, Dick. Country Talk. 1980. 8.95 (ISBN 0-8065-0684-9). Citadel Pr.

Tuve, Rosemond. Elizabethan & Metaphysical Imagery. LC 47-4244. 1961. pap. 7.50x (ISBN 0-226-81819-5, P68, Phoen). U of Chicago Pr.

FIGURINES

see Bronzes; Dolls; Dummy Board Figures; Ivories; Jade

FIJI ISLANDS

Baxter, M. W. Food in Fiji: The Produce & Processed Foods Distribution Systems. (Development Studies Centre-Monographs: No. 22). 282p. 1980. pap. text ed. 13.95 (ISBN 0-909150-03-6, 0064, Pub. by ANUP Australia). Bks Australia.

Belshaw, Cyril S. Under the Ivi Tree: Society & Economic Growth in Rural Fiji. 1964. 21.50x (ISBN 0-520-00106-0). U of Cal Pr.

Brewster, Adolph B. Hill Tribes of Fiji. (Illus.). Repr. of 1922 ed. 23.00 (ISBN 0-384-05690-3). Johnson Repr.

Bromilow, William E. Twenty Years Among Primitive Papuans. LC 75-32800. Repr. of 1929 ed. 26.00 (ISBN 0-404-14103-X). AMS Pr.

Brown, Stanley. Men from Under the Sky: The Arrival of Westerners in Fiji. LC 72-96774. (Illus.). 1973. 10.00 (ISBN 0-8048-1103-2). C E Tuttle.

Carter, John, ed. Fiji Handbook & Travel Guide. 304p. 1980. pap. 13.95 (ISBN 0-85807-046-4, 3012, Pub. by Pacific Pubns Australia). Bks Australia.

Coulter, John W. Drama of Fiji: A Contemporary History. LC 67-14279. 1967. 3.50 (ISBN 0-8048-0146-0). C E Tuttle.

Fiji I Love You Fullspeed. 144p. 1980. 11.50 (ISBN 0-85467-015-7, Pub. by Viking Sevenseas New Zealand). Intl Schol Bk Serv.

Fischer, Edward. Fiji Revisited: A Columban Father's Memories of Twenty-Eight Years in the Islands. LC 81-5365. (Illus.). 1981. pap. 5.95 (ISBN 0-8245-0097-0). Crossroad NY.

Frost, Everett L. Archaeological Excavations of Fortified Sites on Taveuni, Fiji. (Social Science & Linguistics Institute Special Publications). (Illus.). 1974. pap. 5.00x (ISBN 0-8248-0266-7). U Pr of Hawaii.

Green, Mason S. The Maps of Fiji: A Selective & Annotated Cartobibliography. LC 78-24066. (Western Association of Map Libraries: Occasional Paper; No. 5). (Illus.). 90p. (Orig.). 1978. pap. 4.00x (ISBN 0-686-29712-1). Western Assn Map.

Hocart, A. M. Lau Islands, Fiji. (BMB Ser.: No. 62). Repr. of 1929 ed. pap. 21.00 (ISBN 0-527-02168-7). Kraus Repr.

Knox-Mawer, June. Gift of Islands: Living in Figi. 8.75 (ISBN 0-7195-0780-4). Transatlantic.

Legge, John D. Britain in Fiji 1858-1880. 1958. 5.50x (ISBN 0-8426-1351-X). Verry.

Lipton, Sheree. Fiji, I Love You, Full Speed. LC 74-176941. (Illus.). 144p. 1972. 13.50x (ISBN 0-85467-015-7). Intl Pubns Serv.

Mamak, Alexander F. Colour, Culture & Conflict: A Study of Pluralism in Fiji. (Illus.). 1979. 29.00 (ISBN 0-08-023354-6); pap. 13.25 (ISBN 0-08-023353-8). Pergamon.

Mayer, Adrian C. Peasants in the Pacific: A Study of Fiji Indian Rural Society. 2nd, rev. ed. LC 72-91618. (Illus.). 1973. 20.00x (ISBN 0-520-02333-1). U of Cal Pr.

Meller, Norman & Anthony, James M. Fiji Goes to the Polls: The Crucial Legislative Council Elections of 1963. LC 68-20260. (Illus.). 1969. 9.00x (ISBN 0-8248-0080-X, Eastwest Ctr). U Pr of Hawaii.

Nation, John. Customs of Respect: The Traditional Basis of Fijian Communal Politics. LC 78-74980. (Development Studies Centre Monograph: No. 14). 1979. pap. text ed. 11.95 (ISBN 0-7081-0494-0, Pub. by ANUP Australia). Bks Australia.

Nayacakalou, R. R. Leadership in Fiji. 1976. 22.00x (ISBN 0-19-550462-3). Oxford U Pr.

Norton, Robert. Race & Politics in Figi. LC 77-78122. (Illus.). 1978. 18.95x (ISBN 0-312-66138-X). St Martin.

Population Environment Relations in Tropical Islands: The Case of Eastern Fiji. (MAB Technical Notes Ser.: No. 13). 233p. 1981. pap. 18.00 (ISBN 92-3-101821-3, U1054, UNESCO). Unipub.

Rural Energy in Fiji. 1981. pap. 13.00 (ISBN 0-88936-256-4, IDRC 157, IDRC). Unipub.

Seemann, Berthold. Flora Vitiensis. (Historiae Naturalis Classica: Tomas 103). (Illus.). 1978. 160.00 (ISBN 3-7682-1144-4, Pub. by J Cramer). Intl Schol Bk Serv.

Snow, Philip A. Bibliography of Fiji, Tonga, & Rotuma. LC 69-16193. 1969. pap. 19.95x (ISBN 0-87024-109-5). U of Miami Pr.

Stanner, W. E. The South Seas in Transition: A Study of Post-War Rehabilitation & Reconstruction in Three British Pacific Dependencies. LC 75-30084. (Institute of Pacific Relations). Repr. of 1953 ed. 34.50 (ISBN 0-404-59562-6). AMS Pr.

Thompson, Laura. Fijian Frontier. LC 70-120671. xxx, 153p. 1970. Repr. lib. bdg. 12.50x (ISBN 0-374-97863-8). Octagon.

Wallis, Mary D. Life in Feejee: Or Five Years Among the Cannibals. 422p. 1967. Repr. of 1851 ed. 20.00 (ISBN 0-8398-2150-6). Parnassus Imprints.

Waterhouse, Joseph. The King & the People of Fiji, Containing a Life of Thakombau. LC 75-35162. Repr. of 1866 ed. 36.00 (ISBN 0-404-14176-5). AMS Pr.

Williams, Thomas & Calvert, James. Fiji & the Fijians, 2 vols. Rowe, George S., ed. LC 75-35167. Repr. of 1858 ed. Set. 48.50 (ISBN 0-404-14190-0). AMS Pr.

FIJIAN LANGUAGE

see also Melanesian Languages

Hazlewood, David. A Fijian & English & an English & Fijian Dictionary. 2nd ed. LC 75-35119. Repr. of 1872 ed. 28.00 (ISBN 0-404-14136-6). AMS Pr.

Schutz, Albert J. Nguna Grammar. (Oceanic Linguistics Special Publication: No. 5). (Orig., Nguna & Eng). 1969. pap. text ed. 3.00x (ISBN 0-87022-744-0). U Pr of Hawaii.

Schutz, Albert J. & Komaitai, Rusiate T. Spoken Fijian. LC 76-157881. 304p. 1971. pap. text ed. 7.00x (ISBN 0-87022-746-7). U Pr of Hawaii.

FIJIAN TALES

see Tales, Fijian

FIJIANS

Deane, Wallace. Fijian Society: Or, The Sociology & Psychology of the Fijians. LC 75-32813. Repr. of 1921 ed. 24.50 (ISBN 0-404-14117-X). AMS Pr.

Mishra, Vijay. Rama's Banishment: A Centenary Tribute to the Fiji Indians. 1980. 13.50x (ISBN 0-86863-407-7, Pub. by Heinemann New Zealand). South Asia Bks.

Nair, Shashikant. Rural-Born Fijians & Indo-Fijians in Suva: A Study of Movements & Linkages. (Development Studies Centre-Monographs: No. 24). 97p. 1981. pap. text ed. 12.95 (ISBN 0-909150-13-3, 0067, Pub. by ANUP Australia). Bks Australia.

Subramani, ed. The Indo-Fijian Experience. (Asian & Pacific Writing Series). 207p. 1980. 14.95x (ISBN 0-7022-1386-1); pap. 8.50x (ISBN 0-7022-1387-X). U of Queensland Pr.

Thompson, Laura. Fijian Frontier. LC 70-120671. xxx, 153p. 1970. Repr. lib. bdg. 12.50x (ISBN 0-374-97863-8). Octagon.

Tippet, Alan R. Fijian Material Culture: A Study of Cultural Context, Function, & Change. LC 68-22460. (Bulletin Ser: No. 232). (Illus.). 189p. 1968. 8.00 (ISBN 0-910240-02-7). Bishop Mus.

FILAMENT REINFORCED COMPOSITES

see Fibrous Composites

FILARIA AND FILARIASIS

see also Onchoceriasis

Sasa, M., ed. Human Filariasis: A Global Study. 1976. 49.50 (ISBN 0-8391-0957-1). Univ Park.

Sasa, Manabu, ed. Recent Advances in Researches on Filariasis & Schistosomiasis in Japan. (Illus.). 1970. 39.50 (ISBN 0-8391-0032-9). Univ Park.

Soni, M. D. Filariata of Animals & Man & Diseases Caused by Them: Part One - Aproctoidea. Theodor, O., ed. Lavoot, R., tr. from Rus. (Essentials of Nematodology Ser.: No. 17). (Illus.). 372p. 1975. 32.50x (ISBN 0-7065-1490-4, Pub. by IPST). Intl Schol Bk Serv.

WHO Expert Committee. Athens, 1973, 3rd. WHO Expert Committee on Filariasis: Report. (Technical Report Ser.: No. 542). (Also avail. in French & Spanish). 1974. pap. 2.00 (ISBN 92-4-120542-3). World Health.

WHO Expert Committee on Filariasis, Geneva, 1961. Report. (Technical Report Ser: No. 233). 49p. (Eng, Fr, Rus, & Span.). 1962. pap. 1.20 (ISBN 92-4-120233-5). World Health.

Yokogawa, M. Research in Filariasis & Schistosomiasis, Vol. 2. 1972. 39.50 (ISBN 0-8391-0743-9). Univ Park.

FILES AND FILING (DOCUMENTS)

see also Alphabeting; Data Tapes; Indexing; Vertical Files (Libraries)

Bassett, Ernest D., et al. Business Filing & Records Control. 3rd ed. (gr. 9-12). 1964. text ed. 5.96 (ISBN 0-538-11970-5). SW Pub.

--Business Filing & Records Control. 4th ed. 1974. text ed. 5.96 (ISBN 0-538-11100-3, K10); 4.96, practice set (ISBN 0-538-11105-4); final exam 0.48 (ISBN 0-538-11103-8). SW Pub.

Beil, Donald. File Processing with Cobol. (Illus.). 1981. text ed. 19.95 (ISBN 0-8359-1985-4); pap. text ed. 13.95 (ISBN 0-8359-1984-6). Reston.

Fahrner & Gibbs. Basic Rules of Alphabetic Filing. (Prog. Bk., Combined ed. text & wkbk.). (gr. 9-12). 1965. pap. text ed. 2.64 (ISBN 0-538-11570-X). SW Pub.

Gericke, Paul. Minister's Filing System. 1978. pap. 1.95 (ISBN 0-8010-3721-2). Baker Bk.

Heicher, Merlo W. Minister's Simplified Filing System. 96p. 1976. 3.95 (ISBN 0-8010-4142-2). Baker Bk.

Kahn, Gilbert, et al. Filing Systems & Records Management. 2nd ed. 1971. text ed. 10.95 (ISBN 0-07-033231-2, G); tests 2.56 (ISBN 0-07-033238-X); practice materials 7.95 (ISBN 0-07-033232-0); instructors guide & key 6.70 (ISBN 0-07-033241-X). McGraw.

--Progressive Filing. 8th ed. 1968. text ed. 9.04 (ISBN 0-07-033225-8, G); tchr's manual 5.35 (ISBN 0-07-033227-4); tests 1.36 (ISBN 0-07-033226-6); supplies pad 2.96 (ISBN 0-07-033220-7). McGraw.

--Progressive Filing. 7th ed. 1961. text ed. 9.04 (ISBN 0-07-033210-X, G); tchr's. manual & key 5.35 (ISBN 0-07-033211-8). McGraw.

Miller, Shirley. The Vertical File & Its Satellites: A Handbook of Acquisition, Processing, & Organization. 2nd ed. LC 79-13773. (Library Science Text Ser.). 1979. lib. bdg. 17.50x (ISBN 0-87287-164-9). Libs Unl.

Piper, Joanne. Filing: Syllabus. 2nd ed. 1979. pap. text ed. 6.95 (ISBN 0-89420-037-2, 327007); cassette recordings 104.25 (ISBN 0-89420-146-8, 106000). Natl Book.

Place, Irene, et al. Fundamental Filing Practice. (Office Occupations Ser). (Illus.). 256p. 1973. pap. text ed. 9.95x (ISBN 0-13-332742-6). P-H.

Place, Irene M. & Popham, E. L. Filing & Records Management. 1966. text ed. 12.95x (ISBN 0-13-314625-1). P-H.

Rudman, Jack. Principal File Clerk. (Career Examination Ser.: C-659). (Cloth bdg. avail. on request). pap. 10.00 (ISBN 0-8373-0659-0). Natl Learning.

Sherster, Joyce. OJT File Clerk Resource Materials. 2nd ed. (Gregg Office Job Training Program). (Illus.). 104p. (gr. 11-12). soft-cover 4.80 (ISBN 0-07-056640-2, G). McGraw.

Sherster, Joyce A. OJT File Clerk Training Manual. 2nd ed. (Gregg Office Job Training Program Ser.). (Illus.). 80p. (gr. 11-12). Date not set. pap. text ed. 3.56 (ISBN 0-07-056641-0, G). McGraw.

Stewart, Jeffrey R., et al. Progressive Filing. 9th ed. Pezzuti, Ella, ed. LC 79-26178. (Illus.). 160p. (gr. 9-12). 1980. text ed. 9.04 (ISBN 0-07-061445-8, G); practice set 8.48 (ISBN 0-07-061446-6). McGraw.

Stewart, Jeffrey R., Jr. & Kahn, Gilbert. Gregg Quick Filing Practice. 2nd ed. (Illus.). 1979. pap. text ed. 5.76 (ISBN 0-07-061430-X); tchr's manual & visual key 5.45 (ISBN 0-07-061431-8). McGraw.

Stewart, Jeffrey R., Jr., et al. Filing Systems & Records Management. 3rd ed. LC 80-21605. (Illus.). 240p. 1981. text ed. 10.95 (ISBN 0-07-061471-7, G); instr's. manual & kety 7.35 (ISBN 0-07-061473-3); practice materials 8.70 (ISBN 0-07-061472-5). McGraw.

Turner, David R. File Clerk. 6th ed. LC 77-22297. (Orig.). 1977. pap. 6.00 (ISBN 0-668-04377-6). Arco.

--File Clerk. 6th ed. LC 77-22297. (Orig.). 1977. pap. 6.00 (ISBN 0-668-04377-6). Arco.

Wood, Merle W. Number Filing on the Job. 1972. pap. text ed. 3.44 (ISBN 0-538-11810-5, K81). SW Pub.

Workbook Exercises in Alphabetic Filing. 3rd. rev. ed. 48p. 1980. pap. text ed. 3.68 (ISBN 0-07-061451-2). McGraw.

FILIBUSTERS

Brown, Charles H. Agents of Manifest Destiny: The Lives & Times of the Filibusters. LC 79-383. 1980. 25.00x (ISBN 0-8078-1361-3). U of NC Pr.

Scroggs, William O. Filibusters & Financiers: The Story of William Walker & His Associates. LC 72-83846. (Illus.). 1969. Repr. of 1916 ed. 13.00 (ISBN 0-8462-1419-9). Russell.

Stout, Joseph A., Jr. The Liberators. (Great West & Indian Ser: Vol. 41). 9.50 (ISBN 0-87026-029-4). Westernlore.

Warren, Harris G. Sword Was Their Passport. LC 77-15077. 1971. Repr. of 1943 ed. 14.50 (ISBN 0-8046-1676-0). Kennikat.

FILIBUSTERS (WEST INDIAN BUCCANEERS)

see Buccaneers

FILICINEAE

see Ferns

FILIGRAINS

see Water-Marks

FILING SYSTEMS

see Files and Filing (Documents)

FILIPINO FOLK-LORE

see Folk-Lore, Filipino

FILIPINO MAGIC

see Magic, Filipino

FILIPINOS IN HAWAII

Alcantara, Ruben R. Sakada: Filipino Adaptation in Hawaii. LC 80-5858. 202p. (Orig.). 1981. lib. bdg. 18.75 (ISBN 0-8191-1578-9); pap. text ed. 9.25 (ISBN 0-8191-1579-7). U Pr of Amer.

Alcantara, Ruben R. & Alconcel, Nancy S. The Filipinos in Hawaii: An Annotated Bibliography. LC 77-84531. (Hawaii Bibliographies Ser: No. 6). 1977. pap. text ed. 5.00x (ISBN 0-8248-0612-3). U Pr of Hawaii.
Dorita, Mary. Filipino Immigration to Hawaii. LC 75-5373. 1975. Repr. of 1954 ed. soft bdg. 9.00 (ISBN 0-88247-354-9). R & E Res Assoc.
Lasker, Bruno. Filipino Immigration to the Continental United States & to Hawaii. LC 69-18783. (American Immigration Collection Ser., No. 1). (Illus.). 1969. Repr. of 1931 ed. 18.00 (ISBN 0-405-00531-8). Arno.
Teodoro, Luis V., ed. Out of This Struggle: The Filipinos in Hawaii. LC 81-714. (Illus.). 168p. 1981. 10.95 (ISBN 0-8248-0747-2). U Pr of Hawaii.
Wentworth, Edna L. Filipino Plantation Workers in Hawaii: A Study of Incomes, Expenditures, & Living Standards of Filipino Families on an Hawaiian Sugar Plantation. LC 75-30121. (International Research Series of the Institute of Pacific Relations). Repr. of 1941 ed. 21.00 (ISBN 0-404-59569-3). AMS Pr.
--Living Standards of Filipino Families on an Hawaiian Sugar Plantation: Summarizing a Detailed Study. LC 75-30088. (Institute of Pacific Relations). Repr. of 1936 ed. 9.50 (ISBN 0-404-59570-7). AMS Pr.

FILIPINOS IN THE UNITED STATES

Aquino, Valentin R. The Filipino Community in Los Angeles: Thesis. LC 74-76502. 1974. Repr. of 1952 ed. soft bdg. 7.00 (ISBN 0-88247-272-0). R & E Res Assoc.
Ave, Mario P. Characteristics of Filipino Organizations in Los Angeles: Thesis. LC 74-76500. 1974. soft bdg. 8.00 (ISBN 0-88247-248-8). R & E Res Assoc.
California Dept. of Industrial Relations, ed. Facts About Filipino Immigration into California. LC 73-146901. 1972. Repr. of 1930 ed. lib. bdg. 6.00 (ISBN 0-88247-165-1). R & E Res Assoc.
Catapusan, Benicio. The Filipino Occupational & Recreational Activities in Los Angeles. LC 74-83364. 1975. Repr. of 1934 ed. soft bdg. 8.00 (ISBN 0-88247-350-6). R & E Res Assoc.
Coloma, Casiano P. A Study of the Filipino Repatriation Movement: Thesis. LC 74-76750. 1974. soft bdg. 8.00 (ISBN 0-88247-256-9). R & E Res Assoc.
Corpus, Severino F. An Analysis of the Racial Adjustment Activities & Problems of the Filipino-American Christian Fellowship in Los Angeles. 1975. soft bdg. 8.00 (ISBN 0-685-59168-9). R & E Res Assoc.
Espiritu, Socorro C. A Study of the Treatment of the Philippines in Selected Social Studies Textbooks Published in the U. S. for Use in Elementary & Secondary Schools. LC 74-76469. 1974. Repr. of 1954 ed. soft bdg. 9.00 (ISBN 0-88247-234-8). R & E Res Assoc.
Kim, Hyung-Chan & Cuison, Mejia C. The Filipinos in America: A Chronology & Fact Book. LC 75-73949. (Ethnic Chronology Ser.). 160p. 1976. lib. bdg. 8.50 (ISBN 0-379-00521-2). Oceana.
Lasker, Bruno. Filipino Immigration to the Continental United States & to Hawaii. LC 69-18783. (American Immigration Collection Ser., No. 1). (Illus.). 1969. Repr. of 1931 ed. 18.00 (ISBN 0-405-00531-8). Arno.
Mariano, Honorante. The Filipino Immigrants in the U. S. LC 75-166066. 1972. pap. 7.00 (ISBN 0-88247-160-0). R & E Res Assoc.
Melendy, H. Brett. Asians in America: Filipinos, Koreans, & East Indians. (Immigrant Heritage of America Ser.). 1977. lib. bdg. 10.95 (ISBN 0-8057-8414-4). Twayne.
Norell, Irene P. Literature of the Filipino-American in the United States: A Selective & Annotated Bibliography. LC 75-41666. 1976. perfect bdg. softcover 8.00 (ISBN 0-88247-388-3). R & E Res Assoc.
Obando, Aquino B. A Study of the Problems of Filipino Students in the United States: Thesis. LC 74-76667. 1974. soft bdg. 8.00 (ISBN 0-88247-263-1). R & E Res Assoc.
Peterson, Roberta. The Elder Pilipino. LC 77-83488. (Elder Minority Ser). 1978. pap. 3.50x (ISBN 0-916304-37-X). Campanile.
Provido, Generoso P. Oriental Immigration from an American Dependence (Philippines) Thesis. LC 74-76665. 1974. soft bdg. 7.00 (ISBN 0-88247-264-X). R & E Res Assoc.
Sikat, Dorian. Filipino Immigrant. 1981. 7.50 (ISBN 0-682-49405-4). Exposition.
Vallangca, Roberto V. Pinoy: The First Wave. LC 76-47180. (Illus., Orig.). 1977. pap. 6.95 (ISBN 0-89407-000-2). Strawberry Hill.
Wallovits, Sonia. Filipinos in California. LC 71-168532. 1972. pap. 7.00 (ISBN 0-88247-173-2). R & E Res Assoc.

FILLING STATIONS

see Automobiles–Service Stations

FILLMORE, CHARLES, 1854-1948

Freeman, James D. The Story of Unity. rev ed. (Illus.). 1978. 3.95 (ISBN 0-87159-145-6). Unity Bks.

FILLMORE, MILLARD, PRES. U. S., 1800-1874

Barre, W. L. Life & Public Services of Millard Fillmore. LC 70-170962. (American Classics in History & Social Science Ser.: No. 203). 1971. Repr. of 1856 ed. 25.50 (ISBN 0-8337-4634-0). B Franklin.
--Life & Public Services of Millard Fillmore. LC 70-170962. (American Classics in History & Social Science Ser.: No. 203). 1971. Repr. of 1856 ed. 25.50 (ISBN 0-8337-4634-0). B Franklin.
Farrell, J. J. Zachary Taylor, 1784-1850 & Millard Fillmore, 1800-1874; Chronology, Documents, Bibliographical Aids. LC 78-116061. (Presidental Chronology Ser). 1971. 8.00 (ISBN 0-379-12078-X). Oceana.
Grayson, Benson L. The Unknown President: The Administration of President Millard Fillmore. LC 80-5962. 179p. 1981. lib. bdg. 17.75 (ISBN 0-8191-1456-1); pap. text ed. 8.75 (ISBN 0-8191-1457-X). U Pr of Amer.
Rayback, Robert J. Millard Fillmore: Biography of a President. LC 58-14009. 1972. 15.00 (ISBN 0-685-20410-3). Stewart.

FILLMORE, MYRTLE (PAGE), d. 1931

Witherspoon, Thomas E. Myrtle Fillmore: Mother of Unity. LC 77-78221. (Illus.). 1977. 5.95 (ISBN 0-87159-102-2). Unity Bks.

FILLS (EARTHWORK)

American Society of Civil Engineers, compiled by. Sanitary Landfill, Manual 39. (ASCE Manual & Report on Engineering Practice Ser.: No. 39). 92p. looseleaf binder 27.50 (ISBN 0-87262-215-0). Am Soc Civil Eng.

FILM, TELEVISION

see Television Film

FILM ACTORS

see Moving-Picture Actors and Actresses

FILM ADAPTATIONS

Bluestone, George. Novels into Film: The Metamorphosis of Fiction into Cinema. 1957. pap. 3.95 (ISBN 0-520-00130-3, CAL41). U of Cal Pr.
Brosnan, John. James Bond in the Cinema. LC 71-38993. (Illus.). 224p. 1972. 7.95 (ISBN 0-498-01173-9). A S Barnes.
Harwell, Richard B. GWTW: The Screenplay. (Illus.). 1980. pap. 10.95 (ISBN 0-02-012410-4, Collier). Macmillan.
Haydock, Ron. Deerstalker! Holmes & Watson on the Screen. LC 77-24465. 1978. 15.00 (ISBN 0-8108-1061-1). Scarecrow.
Horton, Andrew S. & Magretta, Joan, eds. Modern European Filmmakers & the Art of Adaption. LC 79-48073. (Ungar Film Library). (Illus.). 400p. 1981. 14.95 (ISBN 0-8044-2403-9); pap. 6.95 (ISBN 0-8044-6277-1). Ungar.
Kittredge, William & Krauzer, Steven M., eds. Stories into Film. LC 78-73542. (Illus., Orig.). 1979. pap. 5.95 (ISBN 0-06-090638-3, CN 638, CN). Har-Row.
Laurence, Frank M. Hemingway & the Movies. LC 79-1437. 336p. 1980. 20.00x (ISBN 0-87805-115-5). U Pr of Miss.
Maddux, Rachel, et al. Fiction into Film: A Walk in the Spring Rain. LC 72-111050. (Illus.). 1970. 14.50x (ISBN 0-87049-112-1). U of Tenn Pr.
Mann, Heinrich & Von Sternberg, Josef. The Blue Angel. LC 78-20934. (Ungar Film Library). 1979. 12.50 (ISBN 0-8044-2591-4); pap. 5.95 (ISBN 0-8044-6468-5). Ungar.
Manvell, Roger. Theatre & Film. LC 78-57405. (Illus.). 304p. 1979. 18.00 (ISBN 0-8386-2077-9). Fairleigh Dickinson.
Marcus, Fred H. Short Story-Short Film. (Illus.). 1977. pap. text ed. 11.95 (ISBN 0-13-809558-2). P-H.
Miller, Gabriel. Screening the Novel: Rediscovered American Fiction in Film. LC 79-48071. (Ungar Film Library). (Illus.). 250p. 1981. pap. 5.95 (ISBN 0-8044-6504-5). Ungar.
Osborne, John. Tom Jones: A Film Script. 142p. 1964. 4.95 (ISBN 0-571-05723-3, Pub. by Faber & Faber). Merrimack Bk Serv.
Peary, Gerald & Shatzkin, Roger, eds. The Modern American Novel & the Movies. LC 78-4373. (Ungar Film Library). (Illus.). 1978. 15.95 (ISBN 0-8044-2682-1); pap. 6.95 (ISBN 0-8044-6649-1). Ungar.
Phillips, Gene D. Graham Greene: The Films of His Fiction. LC 73-85252. 1974. pap. 7.95 (ISBN 0-8077-2376-2). Tchrs Coll.
Williams, Tennessee. A Streetcar Named Desire: A Screen Adaptation Directed by Elia Kazan. Garrett, George P., et al, eds. LC 71-135273. (Film Scripts Ser.). 1971. pap. text ed. 8.95x (ISBN 0-89197-954-9). Irvington.
Zambrano, A. L. Dickens & Film. 1976. lib. bdg. 75.00 (ISBN 0-87968-456-9). Gordon Pr.

FILM ADAPTATIONS–BIBLIOGRAPHY

Enser, A. G. Filmed Books & Plays: 1928-1974. rev. ed. 1975. 43.00 (ISBN 0-12-785201-8). Acad Pr.
Parlato, Salvatore J. Films Ex Libris: Literature in Sixteen mm & Video. LC 80-10181. (Illus.). 283p. 1980. lib. bdg. 16.95x (ISBN 0-89950-006-4). McFarland & Co.

FILM AUTHORSHIP

see Moving-Picture Authorship

FILM CATALOGS

see Moving-Pictures–Catalogs

FILM COLLECTIONS

see Moving-Picture Film Collections

FILM DOSIMETRY

see Photographic Dosimetry

FILM EDITING (CINEMATOGRAPHY)

see Moving-Pictures–Editing

FILM MUSIC

see Moving-Picture Music

FILM STARS

see Moving-Picture Actors and Actresses

FILM STRIPS

see Filmstrips

FILMER, ROBERT, SIR, d. 1653. PATRIARCHA

Daly, James. Sir Robert Filmer & English Political Thought. LC 78-25913. 1979. 25.00x (ISBN 0-8020-5433-1). U of Toronto Pr.
Locke, John. Of Civil Government, 2nd Essay. 1960. pap. 2.95 (ISBN 0-89526-921-X). Regnery-Gateway.
--Two Treatises of Government. Laslett, Peter, ed. 1960. 39.95 (ISBN 0-521-06903-3). Cambridge U Pr.

FILMS

see Filmstrips; Microfilms; Moving-Pictures; Photography–Films

FILMS, METALLIC

see Metallic Films

FILMS, THIN

see Thin Films

FILMS FROM BOOKS

see Film Adaptations

FILMS ON ART

see Art in Moving-Pictures

FILMSTRIPS

see also Slides (Photography)

Beatty, LaMond F. Filmstrips. Duane, James E., ed. LC 80-21338. (The Instructional Media Library: Vol. 4). (Illus.). 104p. 1981. 13.95 (ISBN 0-87778-164-8). Educ Tech Pubns.
Carroll, Walter J., ed. Olympic's Film Finder: Nineteen Eighty-One Business Edition. 1981. 24.00x (ISBN 0-88367-601-X). Olympic Media.
Diffor, John C., ed. Educators Guide to Free Filmstrips. 32st rev. ed. LC 50-11650. 1980. pap. 13.00 (ISBN 0-87708-102-6). Ed Prog.
Duncalf, Brian. The Focalguide to Slide Tape. (Focalguide Ser.). (Illus.). 1978. pap. 7.95 (ISBN 0-240-51006-2). Focal Pr.
Gill, Suzanne L. File Management & Information Retrieval Systems: A Manual for Managers & Technicians. LC 80-22785. (Illus.). 193p. 1981. lib. bdg. 18.50x (ISBN 0-87287-229-7). Libs Unl.
Library of Congress. National Union Catalog: A Cumulative Author List, 1958-1962. Incl. Vol. 51. Music & Phonorecords - Authors List, Pt. 1 (ISBN 0-87471-731-0); Vol. 52. Music & Phonorecords - Subject Index, Pt. 2 (ISBN 0-87471-732-9); Vol. 53. Motion Pictures & Film Strips, Titles, Pt. 1 (ISBN 0-87471-733-7); Vol. 54. Motion Pictures & Film Strips, Pt. 2 - Subject Index (ISBN 0-87471-734-5). 40.00x ea. Rowman.
--National Union Catalog, a Cumulative Author List, 1953-57, 28 Vols. Set. 395.00x (ISBN 0-87471-728-0); vol. 27 music & phonorecords 40.00x (ISBN 0-87471-729-9); vol. 28 motion pictures & film strips 40.00 (ISBN 0-87471-730-2). Rowman.
May, Jill P. Films & Filmstrips for Language Arts: An Annotated Bibliography. 1981. pap. price not set (ISBN 0-8141-1726-0, 17260). NCTE.
Mental Health Materials Center, ed. Current Audiovisuals for Mental Health Education. 2nd ed. LC 78-71134. 1979. pap. 8.50 (ISBN 0-8379-5201-8). Marquis.
Otto, W. & Chester, R. D. Guide to Three Filmstrips. 1.25 (ISBN 0-201-19370-1). A-W.
Romberg, T. A. Guide for Filmstrips. 1.50 (ISBN 0-201-19470-8). A-W.
Rothwell, Helene F. de. Canadian Selection: Filmstrips. 516p. 1980. 35.00 (ISBN 0-8020-4586-3). U of Toronto Pr.
Selected List of Catalogues for Short Films & Filmstrips. (Orig.). 1964. pap. 2.25 (ISBN 92-3-100586-3, UNESCO). Unipub.
Shaffer, Dale E. The Filmstrip Collection: Complete Instructions on How to Process & Organize. 1972. pap. 2.00 (ISBN 0-915060-02-7). D E Shaffer.
Sunier, John. Slide, Sound, & Film Strip Production. (Illus.). 220p. 1981. 15.95 (ISBN 0-240-51074-7). Focal Pr.
Wilson, LaVisa C. Caregiver Training for Child Care: A Multimedia Program. (Elementary Education Ser.). 1977. pap. text ed. 7.95 (ISBN 0-675-08482-2); instr's manual 3.95 (ISBN 0-686-67613-0). Merrill.
Wynar, Lubomyr R. & Buttlar, Lois. Ethnic Film & Filmstrip Guide for Libraries & Media Centers: A Selective Filmography. LC 80-18056. 277p. 1980. lib. bdg. 25.00x (ISBN 0-87287-233-5). Libs Unl.

FILTERS, DIGITAL (MATHEMATICS)

see Digital Filters (Mathematics)

FILTERS, LIGHT

see Light Filters

FILTERS AND FILTRATION

see also Chemistry–Manipulation; Dialysis; Separators (Machines); Ultrafiltration

Anderson, Brian & Moore, John B. Optimal Filtering. 1979. 29.95 (ISBN 0-13-638122-7). P-H.
Berlin, Howard M. Design of Active Filters, with Experiments. LC 78-56612. 1978. pap. 8.95 (ISBN 0-672-21539-X). Sams.
Comfort, W. W. & Negreponts, S. The Theory of Ultra Filters. (Die Grundlehren der Mathematischen Wissenschaften Ser.: Vol. 211). 480p. 1974. 52.30 (ISBN 0-387-06604-7). Springer-Verlag.
Daniels, Richard W. Approximation Methods for Electronic Filter Design: With Applications to Passive, Active & Digital Networks. (Illus.). 448p. 1974. 33.50 (ISBN 0-07-015308-6, P&RB). McGraw.
Driscoll, H. T. Filter Aids & Materials-Technology & Applications. LC 77-71926. (Chemical Technology Review Ser.: No. 86). (Illus.). 1977. 39.00 (ISBN 0-8155-0658-9). Noyes.
First World Filtration Congress, May 14-17, 1974. Papers Presented at the First World Filtration Congress, Paris. 1974. 50.95 (ISBN 0-470-25965-5). Halsted Pr.
Ghausi, M. & Laker, K. Modern Filter Design: Active RC & Switched Capacitor. 1982. 36.00 (ISBN 0-13-594663-8). P-H.
Huisman, L. & Wood, W. E. Slow Sand Filtration. (Also avail. in French). 1974. 6.40 (ISBN 92-4-154037-0). World Health.
Ives, K. J., ed. The Scientific Basis of Filtration, No. 2. (NATO Advanced Study, Applied Science Ser.). 450p. 1975. 45.00x (ISBN 90-286-0523-1). Sijthoff & Noordhoff.
Johnson, D. E. & Hilburn, J. L. Rapid Practical Designs of Active Filters. LC 75-14074. 264p. 1975. 29.00 (ISBN 0-471-44304-2, Pub. by Wiley-Interscience). Wiley.
Johnson, David E. Introduction to Filter Theory. (Illus.). 336p. 1976. 26.95 (ISBN 0-13-483776-2). P-H.
Johnson, David E., et al. A Handbook of Active Filters. (Illus.). 1980. text ed. 22.95 (ISBN 0-13-372409-3). P-H.
Liddell, Heather. Computer-Aided Techniques for the Design of Multilayer Filters. 1981. 49.00 (ISBN 0-9960020-2-2, Pub. by A Hilger England). Heyden.
Mitra, Sanjit K., ed. Active Inductorless Filters. LC 70-179914. 1971. 17.95 (ISBN 0-87942-003-0). Inst Electrical.
Orr, Clyde. Filtration, Pt. 2. (Chemical Processing & Engineering; an International Ser.: Vol. 10). 1979. 46.75 (ISBN 0-8247-6763-2). Dekker.
--Filtration: Principles & Practices, Pt. 1. (Chemical Processing & Engineering Ser.: Vol. 10). 1977. 54.50 (ISBN 0-8247-6283-5). Dekker.
Sarner, Erik. Plastic-Packed Trickling Filters. new ed. 1980. text ed. 12.50 (ISBN 0-250-40371-4). Ann Arbor Science.
Schaumann. Modern Active Filter Design. 430p. 1981. 34.00 (ISBN 0-471-09734-9, Pub. by Wiley-Interscience); pap. 20.00 (ISBN 0-471-09733-0, Pub. by Wiley-Interscience). Wiley.
Schaumann, R., et al, eds. Modern Active Filter Design. Laker, R. R. LC 81-2368. 1981. 30.95 (ISBN 0-87942-147-9). Inst Electrical.
Sheahan, Desmond & Johnson, Robert, eds. Modern Crystal & Mechanical Filters. LC 76-57822. 1977. 33.95 (ISBN 0-87942-095-2). Inst Electrical.
Wakeman, R. Filtration Post-Treatment Processes. LC 75-31613. 149p. 1975. 34.25 (ISBN 0-444-41391-X). Elsevier.
Wakeman, R. J., ed. Progress in Filtration & Separation. (Progress in Filtration & Separation: Vol. 1). 1979. 53.75 (ISBN 0-444-41819-9). Elsevier.
Warring, R. H. Filters & Filtration. 250p. 1969. 33.00x (ISBN 0-85461-025-1, Pub by Trade & Tech England). Renouf.
--Filters & Filtration. (Illus.). 1969. 35.00x (ISBN 0-85461-025-1). Intl Ideas.

FINAL CAUSE

see Causation; Teleology

FINAL UTILITY

see Marginal Utility

FINANCE

see also Bankruptcy; Banks and Banking; Bonds; Budget in Business; Business Losses; Business Mathematics; Capital; Capitalists and Financiers; Church Finance; Commerce; Controllership; Credit; Currency Question; Finance, Personal; Finance, Public; Foreign Exchange; Income; Inflation (Finance); Insurance; Interest and Usury; International Finance; Investments; Liquidity (Economics); Loans; Money; Prices; Profit; Saving and Investment; Securities; Sinking-Funds; Speculation; Stock-Exchange; Syndicates (Finance); Wealth;

also subdivision Finance under special subjects, e.g. Corporations–Finance; Railroads–Finance

Abbott, Charles C. The New York Bond Market, Nineteen Twenty to Nineteen Thirty. facsimile ed. LC 75-2618. (Wall Street & the Security Market Ser.). 1975. Repr. of 1937 ed. 18.00x (ISBN 0-405-06945-6). Arno.

Abrams, Don. The Profit-Taker: The Proven Rapid Money-Maker in Good & Bad Markets. LC 79-22695. 124p. 1980. 9.95 (ISBN 0-471-06228-6, Pub. by Wiley-Interscience). Wiley.

Aby, Carroll, Jr. & Vaughn, Donald E. Financial Management Classics. LC 79-10710. (Illus.). 1979. pap. text ed. 14.95 (ISBN 0-87620-288-1). Goodyear.

Altman, Edward I. Financial Handbook. 5th ed. 1736p. 1981. 42.50 (ISBN 0-471-07727-5, Pub. by Ronald Pr). Wiley.

Altman, Edward I. & Sametz, Arnold W. Financial Crises: Institutions & Markets in a Fragile Environment. LC 77-2308. 336p. 1977. 29.95 (ISBN 0-471-02685-9). Ronald Pr.

Angell, James W. Financial Foreign Policy of the United States. LC 65-18785. 1965. Repr. of 1933 ed. 7.50 (ISBN 0-8462-0625-0). Russell.

Apilado, Vincent P., et al. Cases in Financial Management. 1977. pap. text ed. 10.95 (ISBN 0-8299-0120-5); instrs.' manual avail. (ISBN 0-8299-0456-5). West Pub.

Archer, S. H., et al. Financial Management: An Introduction. 724p. 1979. 26.50 (ISBN 0-471-02987-4); study guide 9.95 (ISBN 0-471-02988-2). Wiley.

Archer, Stephen H. & D'Ambrosie, Charles A. Theory of Business Finance: A Book of Readings. 2nd ed. (Illus.). 1976. text ed. 21.95 (ISBN 0-02-303820-9). Macmillan.

Auden, C. How to Finance Your Company. 1977. 18.00x (ISBN 0-8464-0491-5). Beekman Pubs.

Aydon, Cyril. How to Finance Your Company. 206p. 1976. text ed. 19.50x (ISBN 0-220-66309-2, Pub. by Busn Bks England). Renouf.

Ayre, Peter, ed. Finance in Developing Countries. 174p. 1977. 25.00x (ISBN 0-7146-3077-2, F Cass Co). Biblio Dist.

Beckhart, Benjamin H., ed. New York Money Market, 4 Vols. LC 79-155152. Repr. of 1932 ed. Set. 115.00 (ISBN 0-404-04550-2). Vol. 1 (ISBN 0-404-04551-0). Vol. 2 (ISBN 0-404-04552-9). Vol. 3 (ISBN 0-404-04553-7). Vol. 4 (ISBN 0-404-04554-5). AMS Pr.

Beehler, Paul J. Contemporary Cash Management: Principles, Practices, Perspectives. LC 77-18998. (Systems & Controls for Financial Management Ser.). 1978. 29.95 (ISBN 0-471-06172-7). Ronald Pr.

Bhattacharyya, D. K. Demand for Financial Assets. 200p. 1978. text ed. 30.25x (ISBN 0-566-00228-0, Pub. by Gower Pub Co England). Renouf.

Bicksler, J. L., ed. Handbook of Financial Economics. 470p. 1980. 80.50 (ISBN 0-444-85224-7, North Holland). Elsevier.

Bierman, Harold, Jr. Strategic Financial Planning: A Manager's Guide to Improving Profit Performance. LC 80-1058. (Illus.). 1980. 15.95 (ISBN 0-02-903560-0). Free Pr.

Bierman, Harold, Jr. & Haas, Jerome. An Introduction to Managerial Finance. 1973. text ed. 12.95x (ISBN 0-393-09353-0). Norton.

Bladen, Ashby. How to Cope with Developing Financial Crisis. 1979. 8.95 (ISBN 0-07-005547-5). McGraw.

Block, Stanley B. & Hirt, Geoffrey A. Foundations of Financial Management. rev. ed. 1981. 20.95x (ISBN 0-256-02498-7). Irwin.

--Introduction to Finance. 1980. write for info. (CPCU 8). IIA.

Bogen, J. I. & Shipman, S. S. Financial Handbook. 4th ed. 1208p. 1968. 44.50 (ISBN 0-471-06556-0). Wiley.

Bolten, Steven E. & Conn, Robert L. Essentials of Managerial Finance: Principles & Practice. LC 80-80961. (Illus.). 800p. 1981. text ed. 21.95 (ISBN 0-395-29639-0); instr's manual 2.00 (ISBN 0-395-20461-5); test-bank 1.50 (ISBN 0-395-30359-1); study guide 8.50 (ISBN 0-395-30089-4). HM.

Book Research Staff. Electronic News Financial Fact Book & Directory: 1980. (Illus.). 640p. 1980. pap. text ed. 90.00 (ISBN 0-87005-360-4). Fairchild.

Brandeis, Louis D. Other People's Money & How the Bankers Use It. 2nd ed. LC 79-156937. Repr. of 1932 ed. lib. bdg. 15.00x (ISBN 0-678-00856-6). Kelley.

--Other People's Money & How the Bankers Use It. 1977. Repr. of 1932 ed. lib. bdg. 20.00 (ISBN 0-8482-3382-4). Norwood Edns.

Brealey, Richard & Myers, Stewart C. Principles of Corporate Finance. (Finance Ser.). (Illus.). 1980. text ed. 19.95x (ISBN 0-07-007380-5, C); study guide 8.95 (ISBN 0-07-007381-3); instructor's manual 20.00 (ISBN 0-07-007382-1). McGraw.

Brigham, E. F., et al. Decisions in Financial Management: Cases. 2nd ed. LC 75-21320. (Dryden Press). 1976. pap. text ed. 7.95 (ISBN 0-03-016801-5, HoltC). HR&W.

Brigham, Eugene & Pappas, James. Liberalized Depreciation & the Cost of Capital. LC 77-631430. 1970. 6.00 (ISBN 0-87744-087-5). Mich St U Busn.

Bryce, James R. Basic Finance: An Introduction to Financial Theory, Practices & Institutions. 158p. 1980. pap. text ed. 5.95x (ISBN 0-89641-038-2). American Pr.

Business Financial Management, 5 vols. 1974. Set. 14.00 (ISBN 0-89982-093-X, 050200). Am Bankers.

Butterfield, William H. Letters That Build Bank Business. 1953. text ed. 2.75x (ISBN 0-8134-0306-5, 306). Interstate.

Butters, J. Keith, et al. Case Problems in Finance. 8th ed. 1981. 20.95x (ISBN 0-256-02500-2). Irwin.

Carey, Henry C. Miscellaneous Works of Henry C. Carey, 2 vols. 1966. Repr. of 1883 ed. Set. 60.50 (ISBN 0-8337-0473-7). B Franklin.

Carter, H. & Partington, I. Applied Economics in Banking & Finance. 1979. 37.50x (ISBN 0-19-877108-8). Oxford U Pr.

Cavin, Ruth. A Matter of Money: What Do You Do with a Dollar? LC 78-1723. (Illus.). (gr. 3-7). 1978. 8.95 (ISBN 0-87599-223-4). S G Phillips.

Chandler, Lester V. The Monetary-Financial System. 1979. text ed. 20.95 scp (ISBN 0-06-041219-4, HarpC). Har-Row.

Childs, J. Encyclopedia of Long Term Financing & Capital Management. 1976. 34.95 (ISBN 0-13-276113-0). P-H.

Christy, George A. & Roden, Peyton F. Finance: Environment & Decisions. 3rd ed. 512p. 1981. text ed. 20.50 scp (ISBN 0-06-041302-6, HarpC). Har-Row.

Clapp, John M., ed. Innovations & New Directions in the U. S. Financial System: Implications for Real Estate Markets & Investments. (Real Estate Chair Lecture Ser). (Illus.). 1977. pap. 5.00 (ISBN 0-911798-18-8). UCLA Mgmt.

Clark, John J., et al. Financial Management: A Capital Market Approach. 1976. text ed. 21.95 (ISBN 0-205-05445-5, 105445-7); instructor's manual free (ISBN 0-205-05447-1, 105447-3). Allyn.

Clarkson, G. P. & Elliott, B. J. Managing Money & Finance. 2nd ed. 272p. 1973. 21.95x (ISBN 0-8464-0596-2). Beekman Pubs.

Clews, Henry. Wall Street Point of View. LC 68-28620. (Illus.). 1968. Repr. of 1900 ed. lib. bdg. 15.00x (ISBN 0-8371-0048-8, CLWS). Greenwood.

Clugston, Donald L. All That Money & No Cash. (Illus.). 128p. 1981. 7.50 (ISBN 0-682-49678-2). Exposition.

Cohen, Bernard. Compendium of Finance. LC 68-55511. Repr. of 1822 ed. 25.00x (ISBN 0-678-01042-0). Kelley.

Cohen, J. Special Bibliography in Monetary Economics & Finance. 1976. 54.00x (ISBN 0-677-00690-X). Gordon.

Colm, G. & Lehmann, F. Economic Consequences of Recent American Tax Policy. (Social Reasearch Supplement: No. 1). 1938. pap. 4.00 (ISBN 0-527-00861-3). Kraus Repr.

Committee for Economic Development. Financing a Better Election System. LC 68-59440. 84p. 1968. lib. bdg. 2.00 (ISBN 0-87186-731-1); pap. 1.00 (ISBN 0-87186-031-7). Comm Econ Dev.

Consulting Practice Development Workplan. 1977. 29.95 (ISBN 0-934752-00-1). Eckman Ctr.

Cooper, S. K. & Fraser, D. R. The Financial Marketplace. 1982. price not set (ISBN 0-201-00196-9). A-W.

Cowan, T. K. Financial Analysis: Data for Decisions. 382p. 1972. 26.00x (ISBN 0-457-01310-9). Intl Pubns Serv.

Cowperthwait, John H. Money, Silver & Finance. LC 69-19666. Repr. of 1892 ed. lib. bdg. 14.00x (ISBN 0-8371-0363-0, COMS). Greenwood.

Coyle, David C. Irrepressible Conflict: Business Vs. Finance. facsimile ed. LC 73-103648. (Select Bibliographies Reprint Ser). 1933. 12.00 (ISBN 0-8369-5148-4). Arno.

Crawford, Ann. This Is No Place for a Nervous Person. (Illus., Orig.). 1981. pap. 5.00x (ISBN 0-915494-12-4). Fibonacci Corp.

Crawford, Lucy & Lynch, Richard. Finance & Credit. (Career Competencies in Marketing). (Illus.). (gr. 11-12). 1978. pap. text ed. 5.36 (ISBN 0-07-013481-2, G); teacher's manual & key 3.00 (ISBN 0-07-013482-0). McGraw.

Crum, Lawrence L. Electronic Funds Transference in Texas: The Stage of Its Development & Outlook for the 1980's. (Research Monograph Ser.: 1979-2). 45p. (Orig.). 1980. pap. 5.00x (ISBN 0-87755-240-1). U of Tex Busn Res.

Dauten, Carl A. & Welshans, Merle. Principles of Finance. 4th ed. 1975. text ed. 11.95 (ISBN 0-538-06130-8). SW Pub.

Davidson, Paul. Money & the Real World. 2nd ed. 1978. pap. text ed. 16.95 (ISBN 0-470-99217-4). Halsted Pr.

Dearden, John & Shank, John. Financial Accounting & Reporting: A Contemporary Emphasis. (Illus.). 544p. 1975. ref. ed. 19.95 (ISBN 0-13-314757-6). P-H.

De Felice, Frank, ed. A Primer on Business Finance. LC 73-20489. 1974. 29.75 (ISBN 0-8422-5132-4); pap. text ed. 12.50x (ISBN 0-686-77022-6). Irvington.

Dell, Sidney. The Inter-American Development Bank: A Study in Development Financing. LC 70-185778. (Special Studies in International Economics & Development). 1972. 26.75x (ISBN 0-275-28606-1). Irvington.

Derkinderen, Frans G. & Crum, Roy L. Project Set Strategies. (Nijenrode Studies in Business: Vol. 4). 1979. lib. bdg. 20.75 (ISBN 0-89838-014-6, Pub. by Martinus Nijhoff Netherlands). Kluwer Boston.

--Risk, Capital Costs & Project Financing Decisions. (Nijenrode Studies in Business: Vol. 6). 288p. 1980. lib. bdg. 22.00 (ISBN 0-89838-046-4, Pub. by Martinus Nijhoff Netherlands). Kluwer Boston.

Deshmukh, C. D. Reflections on Finance, Education & Society. 1972. 6.95 (ISBN 0-8426-0416-2). Orient Bk Dist.

Dickmeyer, Nathan & Hughes, K. Scott. Financial Self-Assessment: A Workbook for Colleges. 72p. 1980. pap. text ed. 15.00 (ISBN 0-915164-11-6). Natl Assn Coll.

Dobyns, L. R. Money: It Comes in Many Packages. LC 73-6710. (Illus.). 92p. Date not set. 7.95 (ISBN 0-913842-03-6); pap. 5.95 (ISBN 0-913842-07-9). Correlan Pubns.

Donaldson, Gordon. Strategy for Financial Mobility. LC 73-94406. 1969. 16.50x (ISBN 0-87584-078-7). Harvard Busn.

Dorrance, G. S. National Monetary & Financial Analysis. LC 77-82744. (Illus.). 1978. 19.95 (ISBN 0-312-55946-1). St Martin.

Drake, Peter J. Money, Finance & Development. 244p. 1980. 30.95x (ISBN 0-470-26992-8). Halsted Pr.

Droms, William G. Finance & Accounting for Non-Financial Managers. LC 78-73368. 1979. pap. text ed. 7.95 (ISBN 0-201-01392-4). A-W.

Duesenberry, James. Money & Credit: Impact & Control. 3rd ed. LC 70-173310. (Foundations of Modern Economics Ser). (Illus.). 160p. 1972. pap. 9.95 ref. ed. (ISBN 0-13-600304-4). P-H.

Edwards, William E. Action Guide to Big Money Selling. 1972. 49.50 (ISBN 0-13-918698-0). Exec Reports.

Emery, Sarah E. Seven Financial Conspiracies Which Have Enslaved the American People. LC 75-112. (The Radical Tradition in America Ser). 112p. 1975. Repr. of 1891 ed. 13.50 (ISBN 0-88355-216-7). Hyperion Conn.

Executive Checklist for Finance & Administration. 70.00 (ISBN 0-686-51437-8). Auerbach.

Ferris, Paul. The City. (Jackdaw Ser: No. 134). (gr. 7 up). 1974. 6.95 (ISBN 0-670-22445-6). Viking Pr.

Financial Management Handbook. (Illus.). 400p. 1972. 24.00x (ISBN 0-8464-0410-9). Beekman Pubs.

Financial Net Lease Tables No. 78. 27.50 (ISBN 0-685-32724-8). Finan Pub.

Financial Publishing Co. Bond Yield Tables, Four Percent to Fourteen Percent Nos. 154, 254, 2 vols. 6.00 ea. Finan Pub.

--Financial Compound Interest & Annuity Tables No. 376. 6th ed. 40.00 (ISBN 0-685-02543-8). Finan Pub.

--Financial Constant Percent Amortization Table No. 287. 5.00 (ISBN 0-685-02544-6). Finan Pub.

--Financial Monthly Refun Table, 78's Method No. 227. 20.00 (ISBN 0-685-02545-4). Finan Pub.

--Financial Simple Interest Table, 360 Day Basis, No. 243: 4 Percent to 10 Percent by One-Fourth Percent. 3rd ed. 35.00 (ISBN 0-685-02547-0). Finan Pub.

Financing American Enterprise. 1963. 3.50 (ISBN 0-89982-109-X, 291200). Am Bankers.

Flink, Salomon J. & Grunewald, Donald. Managerial Finance. LC 68-8714. 639p. 1969. 20.25 (ISBN 0-471-26420-2, Pub. by Wiley). Krieger.

Flumiani, C. M. The Financial Education of Children & Teenagers. (Idea Books Ser.). (Illus.). 1978. 28.45 (ISBN 0-89266-127-5). Am Classical Coll Pr.

--The Teenager's Life Extension Financial Test. (The Seminar for Human Development Books). (Illus.). 1978. plastic spiral bdg. 12.00 (ISBN 0-89266-124-0). Am Classical Coll Pr.

Focus on Managing Money, Bk. 2. (Handy Math Ser.). 1981. 6.25 (ISBN 0-88488-211-X, 10618). Creative Pubns.

Ford, John K. A Framework for Financial Analysis. 176p. 1981. pap. text ed. 9.95 (ISBN 0-13-330241-5). P-H.

Francis, Clark & Archer, Stephen H. Portfolio Analysis. 2nd ed. (Foundations of Finance Ser.). (Illus.). 1979. text ed. 21.00 (ISBN 0-13-686675-1). P-H.

Frankel, Tamar. The Regulation of Money Managers, 4 vols. 1980. Vol. 1. (ISBN 0-316-29191-9); Vol. 2. text ed. (ISBN 0-316-29192-7); text ed. write for info. (ISBN 0-316-29193-5); Vol. 4. text ed. 50.00 ea. (ISBN 0-316-29194-3); 195.00 set (ISBN 0-316-29190-0). Little.

Friend, Irwin & Bicksler, James L., eds. Risk & Return in Finance, 2 vols. LC 76-44240. 1977. Set. text ed. 50.00 (ISBN 0-88410-264-5); Vol. 1. 25.00 (ISBN 0-88410-653-5); Vol. 2. 25.00 (ISBN 0-88410-652-7). Ballinger Pub.

Fruhan, William E., Jr. Financial Strategy. 1979. 17.95 (ISBN 0-256-02228-3). Irwin.

Furness, E. L. Introduction to Financial Economics. 1972. pap. 13.95x (ISBN 0-434-90596-8). Intl Ideas.

Gibbons, James S. Public Debt of the United States. LC 78-129033. (Research & Source Works Ser.: No. 525). 1970. Repr. of 1867 ed. lib. bdg. 19.00 (ISBN 0-8337-1328-0). B Franklin.

Gitman, Lawrence J. Fundamentos De Administracion Financiera. Herrera, Jesus V. & Mei Mei Alicia Chu Polido, eds. Restrepo, Carlos S., tr. from Eng. (Span.). 1978. text ed. 15.50 (ISBN 0-06-313160-9, Pub. HarLA Mexico). Har-Row.

Goff, Walter S. Finance for Managers. LC 76-35239. (Practical Management Ser.). 1975. pap. 8.50x (ISBN 0-7121-0620-0). Intl Pubns Serv.

Grawoig, Dennis E. & Hubbard, Charles L. Strategic Financial Planning with Simulation. (Illus.). 1981. 35.00 (ISBN 0-89433-115-9). Petrocelli.

Greenlaw, Paul S., et al. Finansim: A Financial Management Simulation. 2nd ed. 1979. pap. text ed. 13.95 (ISBN 0-8299-0248-1); instrs.' maual avail. (ISBN 0-8299-0613-4). West Pub.

Gross, Harry. Current Techniques in Financing. 1975. pap. 2.00 (ISBN 0-87576-012-0). Pilot Bks.

Guide for a Review of a Financial Forecast. 1980. pap. 6.00 (ISBN 0-686-70231-X). Am Inst CPA.

Gup, Benton. Guide to Strategic Planning. (McGraw-Hill Series in Finance). (Illus.). 1980. text ed. 15.95 (ISBN 0-07-025210-6); pap. text ed. 9.95 (ISBN 0-07-025211-4). McGraw.

Gup, Benton E. Financial Intermediaries: An Introduction. 2nd ed. LC 79-87858. 1979. text ed. 19.50 (ISBN 0-395-28138-5); instrs' manual 1.50 (ISBN 0-395-28157-1). HM.

Gurley, John G. & Shaw, Edward S. Money in a Theory of Finance. 1960. 18.95 (ISBN 0-8157-3322-4). Brookings.

Haines, Walter W. Money, Prices & Policy. 2nd ed. 1966. text ed. 16.00 (ISBN 0-07-025525-3, C). McGraw.

Halverson, Richard P. Financial Freedom: The New Guide to Economic Security & Success. 384p. 1981. 12.95 (ISBN 0-936602-21-X). Harbor Pub CA.

Hamilton, Alexander. Works of Alexander Hamilton, 12 Vols. Lodge, Henry C., ed. LC 68-24980. (American History & Americana Ser., No. 47). 1969. Repr. of 1904 ed. lib. bdg. 450.00 (ISBN 0-8383-0160-6). Haskell.

Hampton, J. Handbook for Financial Decision Makers. 1978. 29.95 (ISBN 0-87909-353-6). Reston.

Hanrahan, J. & Dipchand, C. Fundamentals of Financial Management. 3rd ed. 1977. 23.50 (ISBN 0-13-339374-7). P-H.

Hartley, W. C. Cash: Planning, Forecasting & Control. 210p. 1976. text ed. 24.50x (ISBN 0-220-66288-6, Pub. by Busn Bks England). Renouf.

Hartley, W. C. & Meltzer, Yale L. Cash Management: Planning, Forecasting, Control. (Illus.). 1979. 12.95 (ISBN 0-13-120295-2, Spec); pap. text ed. 6.95 (ISBN 0-13-120287-1). P-H.

Hastings, Paul G. The Management of Business Finance. 544p. 1966. 14.00 (ISBN 0-442-03185-8, Pub by Van Nos Reinhold). Krieger.

Helfert, Erich A., ed. Techniques of Financial Analysis. 4th ed. 1977. pap. text ed. 11.95x (ISBN 0-256-01916-9). Irwin.

Hemingway, G. S. Introduction to Business Finance. 1975. 19.95x (ISBN 0-434-90730-8); pap. 12.95x (ISBN 0-434-90731-6). Intl Ideas.

Henning, Charles, et al. Financial Markets & the Economy. 2nd ed. (Illus.). 1978. ref. 19.95 (ISBN 0-13-316083-1). P-H.

Herrick, Tracy G. Bank Analysts Handbook. LC 78-987. 1978. 39.95 (ISBN 0-471-02025-7, Pub. by Wiley-Interscience). Wiley.

Hicks, Tyler G. & Beach, Sean C. Tyler Hicks Encyclopedia of Wealth-Building Secrets. 1980. 12.95 (ISBN 0-13-935254-6, Parker). P-H.

Hieb, Elizabeth, ed. Institute for Fund Advisors, Tahoe, Nevada, June 24-27, 1979: Proceedings. 97p. (Orig.). 1980. pap. text ed. 10.50 (ISBN 0-89154-115-2). Intl Found Employ.

Holzer, Henry M. The Gold Clause. LC 79-55801. 1980. 19.95 (ISBN 0-916728-26-9). Bks in Focus.

Horgen, Gregory C. Playing the Funding Game. Terry, Sharon, ed. LC 80-85069. (Illus.). 350p. (Orig.). 1981. pap. 24.95 (ISBN 0-938850-00-8). Human Serv Dev.

Horvitz, P. Monetary Policy & the Financial System. 4th ed. 1979. 19.95 (ISBN 0-13-599944-8). P-H.

Hosek, William R. & Zahn, Frank. Monetary Theory, Policy & Financial Markets. (Illus.). 1977. text ed. 18.95 (ISBN 0-07-030436-X, C); instructor's manual 4.95 (ISBN 0-07-030437-8). McGraw.

How to Analyze & Interpret Financial Information. pap. 10.00 (ISBN 0-686-02522-9). Preston.

Humphrey, Thomas J. Basic Programming for the Financial Executive. LC 78-5670. 1978. 32.95 (ISBN 0-471-03020-1, Pub. by Wiley-Interscience). Wiley.

Hunt, Pearson, et al. Basic Business Finance: Text & Cases. 4th ed. 1971. 20.95x (ISBN 0-256-00209-6). Irwin.

--Basic Business Finance: Text. 1974. text ed. 18.95x (ISBN 0-256-01553-8). Irwin.

IBP Research & Editorial Staff. How to Raise Money to Make Money. LC 80-26568. (Illus.). 432p. 1980. 39.50 (ISBN 0-87624-214-X). Inst Busn Plan.

Indexation of Financial Assets: Further Material on Problems & Experiences. 1976. 5.50x (ISBN 92-64-11417-3). OECD.

Institute of C. F. A. Readings in Financial Analysis. 5th ed. 1981. pap. 9.00 (ISBN 0-256-02583-5). Irwin.

International Seminar on Systems & Planning in Banking & Finance, 1974. Proceedings. 1975. 30.00x (ISBN 0-8002-1868-X). Intl Pubns Serv.

J. K. Lasser Tax Institute. Financial Planning for Your Family. 1979. 10.95 (ISBN 0-671-96099-7); pap. 3.95 (ISBN 0-346-12410-7). Cornerstone.

Jackendoff, Nathaniel. Money, Flow of Funds, & Economic Policy. LC 68-30892. (Illus.). 523p. 1968. 23.50 (ISBN 0-471-06632-X). Wiley.

Jevons, William S. Investigations in Currency & Finance. Foxwell, H. S., ed. LC 64-22238. (Illus.). Repr. of 1884 ed. 19.50x (ISBN 0-678-00060-3). Kelley.

Johnson, Alexander B. An Inquiry into the Nature of Value & of Capital. Bd. with The Advanced Value of Gold (1862; Our Monetary Condition (1864. LC 67-30859. Repr. of 1813 ed. 13.50x (ISBN 0-678-00375-0). Kelley.

Johnson, Robert W. Financial Management. 4th ed. 1971. text ed. 20.95x (ISBN 0-205-03231-1, 1032313); tchrs. manual o.p. 2.00 (ISBN 0-685-00328-0). Allyn.

Jones, Frank J. Macrofinance: The Financial System & the Economy. 1978. pap. text ed. 9.95 (ISBN 0-87626-543-3). Winthrop.

Jones, G. L. Financial Measurement for Managers. 1976. pap. text ed. 13.95x (ISBN 0-7131-3367-8). Intl Ideas.

Jones, J. William. Budget - Finance Campaigns. 1977. pap. 9.50 (ISBN 0-87545-010-5). Natl Sch Pr.

Jones, Ray G. & Dudley, Dean. Essentials of Finance. (Illus.). 1978. 19.95 (ISBN 0-13-286088-0). P-H.

Jorgenson, W. L. & Jorgenson, B. J. Corporate Profiles for Executives & Investors. 1977. pap. 9.95 (ISBN 0-685-76961-5). J Lloyd Corp.

Joy, O. Maurice. Introduction to Financial Management. rev. ed. 1980. 20.95x (ISBN 0-256-02340-9). Irwin.

Kaplan, Robert S. Financial Crisis in the Social Security System. LC 76-21170. 1976. pap. 2.25 (ISBN 0-8447-3214-1). Am Enterprise.

Kaufman, G. U. S. Financial Systems: The Money Markets & Institutions. 1980. 19.95 (ISBN 0-13-938084-1). P-H.

Kelley, William D. Speeches, Addresses & Letters on Industrial & Financial Questions. Repr. of 1872 ed. lib. bdg. 21.00x (ISBN 0-8371-1383-0, KESL). Greenwood.

Kelso, Louis O. & Adler, Mortimer J. The New Capitalists. LC 75-14801. 109p. 1975. Repr. of 1961 ed. lib. bdg. 15.00x (ISBN 0-8371-8211-5, KENC). Greenwood.

Kidwell, David S. & Peterson, Richard L. Financial Institutions & Markets. LC 80-65804. 640p. 1981. text ed. 21.95 (ISBN 0-03-046066-2). Dryden Pr.

Kim, Suk H. & Guithues, Henry J. Capital Expenditure Analysis. LC 80-6070. 338p. 1981. 20.00 (ISBN 0-8191-1462-6); pap. 11.25 (ISBN 0-8191-1463-4). U Pr of Amer.

King, George. The Theory of Finance: Being a Short Treatise on the Doctrine of Interest & Annuities-Certain. Brief, Richard P., ed. LC 80-1506. (Dimensions of Accounting Theory & Practice Ser.). 1981. Repr. of 1882 ed. lib. bdg. 12.00x (ISBN 0-405-13531-9). Arno.

Klimley, April. Here Is Your Career: Banking, Money & Finance. LC 77-28281. (Here Is Your Career Ser.). (Illus.). (gr. 6 up). 1978. 7.95 (ISBN 0-399-20628-0). Putnam.

Kroncke, Charles, et al. Managerial Finance: Essentials. 2nd ed. (Illus.). 1978. text ed. 20.95 (ISBN 0-8299-0159-0); study guide 6.95 (ISBN 0-8299-0161-2); instrs.' manual avail. (ISBN 0-8299-0550-2). West Pub.

Lavely, Joe & Ruckman, Paul. Simultaneous Compounding & Discounting Tables & Uses. 1979. 59.95 (ISBN 0-669-02810-X). Lexington Bks.

LBJ School of Public Affairs & Schmandt, Jurgen. Financing & Control of Academic Research. (Working Paper Ser.: No. 6). 1977. 2.50 (ISBN 0-686-10610-5). LBJ Sch Public Affairs.

Levine, Summer N., ed. Financial Analyst's Handbook. Incl. Vol. 1. Portfolio Management. 1492p. 37.50 (ISBN 0-87094-082-1); Vol. 2. Analysis by Industry. 1032p. LC 74-81386. 1975. Dow Jones-Irwin.

Levy, H. & Sarnat, M. Capital Investment & Financial Decisions. 1978. 22.95 (ISBN 0-13-113423-X). P-H.

Levy, Haim, ed. Research in Finance, Vol. 2. 250p. (Orig.). 1980. lib. bdg. 34.50 (ISBN 0-89232-043-5). Jai Pr.

Levy, Louis E. Business, Money & Credit. 1979. lib. bdg. 49.95 (ISBN 0-685-96458-2). Revisionist Pr.

Light, J. O. & White, William L. The Financial System. 1979. 20.95x (ISBN 0-256-02120-1). Irwin.

Lindholm, Richard W. Money Management & Institutions. 1978. pap. 7.95 (ISBN 0-8226-0334-9). Littlefield.

Linker, Joseph R. & Hill, M. A. Mathematics of Finance. LC 48-2598. 1948. text ed. 4.00x (ISBN 0-911090-14-2). Pacific Bk Supply.

Lohmann, Roger A. Breaking Even: Financial Management in Human Service Organizations. 316p. 1981. pap. text ed. 12.95 (ISBN 0-87722-247-9). Temple U Pr.

London Business School, September 25-27, 1975 & Brealey, Richard. European Finance Association, 1975: Proceedings. Rankine, Graeme, ed. 1976. 41.50 (ISBN 0-7204-0527-0, North-Holland). Elsevier.

Lumb, Fred A. What Every Woman Should Know About Finances. 1979. pap. 2.25 (ISBN 0-425-04132-8). Berkley Pub.

McAnally, Stanley R. Educational Fund Raising Manual: Major Gift Societies. 1970. pap. 5.00 (ISBN 0-89964-021-4). CASE.

McKinnon, Ronald I. Money & Capital in Economic Development. 1973. 11.95 (ISBN 0-8157-5614-3); pap. 4.95 (ISBN 0-8157-5613-5). Brookings.

McKinnon, Ronald I., ed. Money & Finance in Economic Growth & Development. (Business Economics & Finance Ser.: Vol. 8). 1976. 43.75 (ISBN 0-8247-6366-1). Dekker.

McKitrick, M. Money Management. (Contemporary Consumer Ser.). 1974. text ed. 4.24 (ISBN 0-07-045318-7, G); tchr's. manual & key 4.95 (ISBN 0-07-045319-5). McGraw.

Martin, John D., et al. Basic Financial Management. (Illus.). 1979. ref. 21.95 (ISBN 0-13-060541-7); study guide 8.95 (ISBN 0-13-060558-1). P-H.

Martin, Thomas J. Financing the Growing Business. LC 80-18955. 1980. 15.95 (ISBN 0-686-71702-3). HR&W.

Mathewson, Kent & Neenan, William B., eds. Financing the Metropolis. 352p. 1980. 29.95 (ISBN 0-03-056886-2). Praeger.

Mathur, Iqbal. Introduction to Financial Management. (Illus.). 1979. text ed. 20.95x (ISBN 0-02-377250-6); student study guide avail.; intrs'. manual avail. Macmillan.

Mathur, Iqbal & Scherr, Frederick C. Cases in Financial Management. 1979. pap. text ed. 6.95 (ISBN 0-02-377260-3); instrs'. manual avail. Macmillan.

Mathur, Iqbal & Snodgrass, Coral. Introductory to Financial Management: Study Guide. 1979. pap. text ed. 5.95 (ISBN 0-02-377280-8). Macmillan.

Matsushita, Shutaro. Economic Effects of Public Debts. LC 73-78012. (Columbia University. Studies in the Social Sciences: No. 309). Repr. of 1929 ed. 17.50 (ISBN 0-404-51309-3). AMS Pr.

Maxwell, James A. Fiscal Impact of Federalism in the U. S. LC 79-83861. 1970. Repr. of 1946 ed. 15.00 (ISBN 0-8462-1413-X). Russell.

Mayes, Herbert R. The Magazine Maze: A Prejudiced Perspective. LC 79-8028. 384p. 1980. 14.95 (ISBN 0-385-15322-8). Doubleday.

Mayo. Basic Finance. 1978. 20.95 (ISBN 0-7216-6209-9). Dryden Pr.

Mayo, Herbert B. Basic Finance: An Introduction to Money & Financial Management. (Illus.). 1978. text ed. 16.95 (ISBN 0-7216-6209-9). HR&W.

Milford, Richard. Financial Consultant's Advisory Report. 1980. pap. 10.00 (ISBN 0-936292-00-8). R Milford.

Miller, Jama. Theory of Finance. 1972. 21.95 (ISBN 0-03-086732-0). Dryden Pr.

Miller, James. A Key to Financial Survival: The Secret Investment Diary of a Portfolio Manager. LC 77-1071. 1977. pap. 2.95 (ISBN 0-87576-060-0). Pilot Bks.

Mises, Ludwig Von. The Theory of Money & Credit. 493p. 1971. 6.00 (ISBN 0-910614-34-2). Foun Econ Ed.

Moffat, Donald W. Concise Desk Book of Business Finance. 1975. 27.95 (ISBN 0-13-166454-9, Busn). P-H.

Moore, Basil J. Introduction to the Theory of Finance: Asset Holder Behaviour Under Uncertainty. LC 68-12033. (Orig.). 1968. pap. text ed. 7.95 (ISBN 0-02-921950-7). Free Pr.

Mosburg, Lewis G., Jr., ed. Financing Coal Ventures. 45.00 (ISBN 0-89419-003-2). Inst Energy.

--Financing Oil & Gas Ventures: 1977 Update. 1977. 37.00 (ISBN 0-89419-011-3). Inst Energy.

Moscato, Donald R. Building Financial Decision-Making Models: An Introduction to Principles & Procedures. 144p. 1980. 12.95 (ISBN 0-8144-5609-X). Am Mgmt.

Moulton, Harold G. Financial Organization & the Economic System. facsimile ed. LC 75-2652. (Wall Street & the Security Markets Ser.). 1975. Repr. of 1938 ed. 32.00x (ISBN 0-405-06977-4). Arno.

--The Financial Organization of Society. facsimile ed. LC 75-2653. (Wall Street & the Security Markets Ser.). 1975. Repr. of 1930 ed. 46.00x (ISBN 0-405-06978-2). Arno.

OECD. Published Offical Sources of Financial Statistics. (Illus.). 132p. (Orig.). 1980. pap. 11.00x (ISBN 92-64-02095-0). OECD.

Ornstien, Edwin J. Marketing of Money. 1972. 21.00x (ISBN 0-8464-0610-1). Beekman Pubs.

Osteryoung, Jerome S. & McCarty, Daniel E. Analytical Techniques for Financial Management. LC 79-17196. (Finance Ser.). 1980. pap. text ed. 12.95 (ISBN 0-88244-196-5). Grid Pub.

Palyi, Melchior. The Chicago Credit Market: Organization & Institutional Structure. facsimile ed. LC 75-2659. (Wall Street & the Security Markets Ser.). 1975. Repr. of 1937 ed. 27.00x (ISBN 0-405-06983-9). Arno.

Persen, William & Lessig, Van. Evaluating the Financial Performance of Overseas Operations. LC 78-74235. 1980. 3.75 (ISBN 0-910586-30-6). Finan Exec.

Personal Finance Record Book. 50p. 1980. 3.95 (ISBN 0-686-73972-8). Alexandria Hse.

Philippatos, George C. & Nast, Donald A. Case Studies in Basic Finance. LC 77-11351. 1978. pap. text ed. 7.95 (ISBN 0-7216-7214-0). HR&W.

Poindexter, J. C. & Jones, Charles P. Money, Financial Markets & the Economy. 1979. text ed. 21.95 (ISBN 0-8299-0225-2); cancelled (ISBN 0-8299-0270-8). West Pub.

Polakoff, Murray E., et al. Financial Institutions & Markets. 1970. text ed. 21.95 (ISBN 0-395-05062-6). HM.

Pollard, A. H. An Introduction to the Mathematics of Finance. rev. ed. 1978. pap. 7.00 (ISBN 0-08-021796-6). Pergamon.

Popp, Edward E. The Great Cookie Jar: Taking the Mysteries Out of the Money System. LC 78-62961. 1978. pap. 1.95 (ISBN 0-9600358-2-6). Wis Ed Fund.

Pratt, Stanley E. Guide to Venture Capital Sources. 5th ed. 1981. 62.50 (ISBN 0-914470-12-4). Capital Pub Corp.

Pring, Martin J. How to Forecast Interest Rates: A Guide to Profits for Consumers, Managers & Investors. 192p. 1981. 14.95 (ISBN 0-07-050865-8, P&RB). McGraw.

Prochnow, Herbert V. American Financial Institutions. facs. ed. LC 76-128290. (Essay Index Reprint Ser). 1951. 39.00 (ISBN 0-8369-2017-1). Arno.

Prodham, B. The Board & Financial Management. 175p. 1979. text ed. 24.50 (ISBN 0-220-66354-8, Pub. by Business Books England). Renouf.

The Pros & Cons in Financial Management for Professionals. LC 71-166924. (Illus.). 5.95 (ISBN 0-686-20664-9). Financial Pr.

Pulvino, Charles J. & Lee, James L. Financial Counseling: Interviewing Skills. 1979. pap. text ed. 8.95 (ISBN 0-8403-2046-9, 40204602). Kendall-Hunt.

Purcell, W. R., Jr. Understanding a Company's Finances: A Graphic Approach. (Illus.). 160p. 1981. 10.95 (ISBN 0-395-30540-3). HM.

--Visualizing Business Finance. Date not set. 25.00 (ISBN 0-8436-0760-2). CBI Pub.

Randle, Paul A. & Swensen, Philip R. Personal Financial Planning for Exec Tives. (Finance Ser.). (Illus.). 300p. 1981. text ed. 15.95 (ISBN 0-686-69771-5). Lifetime Learn.

Ranlett, John G. Money & Banking: An Introduction to Analysis & Policy. 3rd ed. LC 77-23251. 1977. text ed. 26.50 (ISBN 0-471-70815-1). Wiley.

Ray & Scott. Finance. (Illus.). 1979. pap. 9.95 (ISBN 0-87626-266-3). Winthrop.

Riefler, Winfield W. Money Rates & Money Markets in the U. S. (Illus.). Repr. of 1930 ed. lib. bdg. 15.00x (ISBN 0-678-01242-3). Kelley.

Ritter, Lawrence S. & Silber, William L. Principles of Money, Banking, & Financial Markets. 3rd, rev. ed. LC 79-3139. 1980. text ed. 14.95x (ISBN 0-465-06339-X); tchrs' ed. free (ISBN 0-465-06340-3); student manual 6.95x (ISBN 0-465-06341-1). Basic.

--Principles of Money Banking & Financial Markets. 2nd rev. ed. LC 76-43477. 1977. text ed. 13.95x (ISBN 0-465-06337-3); instrs' manual avail. (ISBN 0-465-06338-1). Basic.

Robichek, Alexander, et al. Management of Financial Institutions. 2nd ed. LC 75-21449. 1976. text ed. 22.95 (ISBN 0-03-089912-5). Dryden Pr.

Robinson, Roland & Wrightman, Dwayne. Financial Markets: The Accumulation & Allocation of Wealth. 2nd ed. (Illus.). 1980. text ed. 19.95 (ISBN 0-07-053274-5); instrs'. manual 5.95 (ISBN 0-07-053275-3). McGraw.

Rockley, L. E. Finance for the Non-Accountant. 3rd ed. 337p. 1979. pap. 12.25x (ISBN 0-220-67022-6, Pub. by Busn Bks England). Renouf.

--Finance for the Purchasing Executive. 191p. 1978. text ed. 24.50x (ISBN 0-220-66362-9, Pub. by Busn Bks England). Renouf.

Roll, Eric. The Uses & Abuses of Economics. 304p. 1979. 23.95 (ISBN 0-571-11228-5, Pub. by Faber & Faber). Merrimack Bk Serv.

Rudman, Jack. Finance, Level 1. (ACT Proficiency Examination Program: PEP-15). (Cloth bdg. avail. on request). pap. 9.95 (ISBN 0-8373-5565-6); pap. 9.95 (ISBN 0-8373-5515-X). Natl Learning.

--Finance, Level 2. (ACT Proficiency Examination Program: PEP-16). (Cloth bdg. avail. on request). pap. 9.95 (ISBN 0-8373-5566-4). Natl Learning.

--Finance, Level 3. (ACT Proficiency Examination Program: PEP-17). (Cloth bdg. avail. on request). pap. 9.95 (ISBN 0-8373-5517-6). Natl Learning.

--Finance One. (Regents External Degree Ser.: REDP-4). (Cloth bdg. avail. on request). pap. 9.95 (ISBN 0-8373-5654-7). Natl Learning.

--Finance Three. (Regents External Degree Ser.: REDP-6). (Cloth bdg. avail. on request). pap. 9.95 (ISBN 0-8373-5606-7). Natl Learning.

--Finance Two. (Regents External Degree Ser.: REDP-5). (Cloth bdg. avail. on request). pap. 9.95 (ISBN 0-8373-5605-9). Natl Learning.

Rutters, J. Keith, et al. Case Problems in Finance. 8th ed. 1981. 20.95x (ISBN 0-256-02500-2). Irwin.

Sahner, Ron. Finanical Analysis for Information Professionals. 1981. pap. 39.95 (ISBN 0-936648-06-6). Telecom Lib.

Sanderson, Fred & Cleveland, Harold. Finance & Trade. LC 74-78422. (The Washington Papers: No. 14). 1974. 4.00x (ISBN 0-8039-0443-6). Sage.

Saulnier, Raymond J., et al. Financial Policies in Transition: A Critique of Selected Issues. Depperschmidt, Thomas O., ed. LC 38-66603. (M. L. Seidman Town Hall Lecture Ser.). 1967. 5.00 (ISBN 0-87870-000-5). Memphis St Univ.

Savage, Donald T. Money & Banking. LC 76-56134. 1977. text ed. 26.50x (ISBN 0-471-75519-2); tchrs. manual avail. (ISBN 0-471-02578-X). Wiley.

Schall, Lawrence D. & Haley, Charles W. Introduction to Financial Management. 2nd ed. (Finance Ser.). (Illus.). 1980. text ed. 19.95 (ISBN 0-07-055100-6); instr's manual 12.00x (ISBN 0-07-055101-4); study guide 7.50 (ISBN 0-07-055102-2). McGraw.

Schiller, Marvin, et al. Development of Financial Managers. LC 70-118262. 1970. 6.95 (ISBN 0-910586-40-3). Finan Exec.

Schultze, Charles L. & Lynn, James T. The Federal Budget: What Are the Nation's Priorities? LC 76-16471. 1976. pap. 4.25 (ISBN 0-8447-2085-2). Am Enterprise.

Seltz, David D. MESBIC: An Exciting New Financial Concept with Great Growth Potential for Business. 1981. 15.00 (ISBN 0-87863-197-6). Farnswth Pub.

Serraino, William J., et al. Frontiers of Financial Management. 1971. pap. text ed. 6.95 (ISBN 0-538-06250-9). SW Pub.

Seybert, Adam. Statistical Annals. LC 68-18229. Repr. of 1818 ed. 37.50x (ISBN 0-678-00553-2). Kelley.

--Statistical Annals, of the United States: 1789-1818. LC 68-56774. (Research & Source Works Ser: No. 260). 1968. Repr. of 1818 ed. 39.00 (ISBN 0-8337-3238-2). B Franklin.

Shank, John, et al. Assessing the Economic Impact of FASB No. 8. LC 79-329. 1979. 3.95 (ISBN 0-910586-31-4). Finan Exec.
Shapiro, Eli & Wolf, Charles R. The Role of Private Placements in Corporate Finance. LC 72-87769. (Illus.). 200p. 1972. 12.50x (ISBN 0-87584-099-X). Harvard Busn.
Sharpe, W. F. Portfolio Theory & Capital Markets. (Foundations of American Government & Political Science). 1970. 17.95 (ISBN 0-07-056487-6, C). McGraw.
Shuckett, D. H., et al. Financing for Growth. LC 75-118285. 1971. 21.00 (ISBN 0-8144-5218-3). Am Mgmt.
Simmons, James G. How to Obtain Financing & Make Your Best Deal with Any Bank, Finance or Leasing Company. (Illus.). 380p. (Orig.). 1980. pap. 19.95 (ISBN 0-937700-00-2). Cambrian.
Simon, Matthew. Cyclical Fluctuations & International Capital Movements of the U. S. 1865-1897. Wilkins, Mira, ed. LC 78-3949. (International Finance Ser.). 1978. lib. bdg. 46.00x (ISBN 0-405-11249-1). Arno.
Simons, Leon. The Basic Arts of Financial Management. 2nd ed. 249p. 1978. text ed. 25.75x (ISBN 0-220-66370-X, Pub. by Busn Bks England). Renouf.
--Basic Arts of Financial Management. 228p. 1975. 21.00x (ISBN 0-8464-0169-X). Beekman Pubs.
Sinn, Gerald R. Cash Operations Management: Profit from Within. 1980. 19.00 (ISBN 0-89433-116-7). Petrocelli.
Skousen, K. Fred, et al. Financial Accounting. 1981. text ed. 18.95x (ISBN 0-87901-156-4); study guide 6.95x (ISBN 0-87901-157-2); practice set, transaction analysis 4.95x (ISBN 0-87901-159-9); practice set, financial statement analysis 3.95 (ISBN 0-87901-160-2); working papers 6.95 (ISBN 0-87901-158-0). H S Worth.
Skousen, Mark A. Mark Skousen's Complete Guide to Financial Privacy. 237p. 1980. 14.95 (ISBN 0-686-73973-6). Alexandria Hse.
Smith, Paul F. Money & Financial Intermediation: The Theory & Structure of Financial Systems. LC 77-21636. (Illus.). 1978. 19.95 (ISBN 0-13-600288-9). P-H.
Solomon, Ezra. Theory of Financial Management. LC 63-8405. (Illus.). 1963. 12.50x (ISBN 0-231-02604-8). Columbia U Pr.
Solomon, Ezra & Pringle, John J. An Introduction to Financial Management. 2nd ed. 1980. text ed. 18.95 (ISBN 0-87620-475-2); inst. manual by john j. pringle free (ISBN 0-8302-4753-X); study guide by john a. holloran & howard p. lanser 7.95 (ISBN 0-8302-4754-8). Goodyear.
Solomon, Morton B., et al. Main Hurdman & Cranston Guide to Preparing Financial Reports, 1981. LC 81-2454. 290p. 1981. 75.00 (ISBN 0-471-09104-9, Pub. by Wiley-Interscience). Wiley.
Spiro, Herbert T. Finance for the Nonfinancial Manager. LC 76-56371. 1977. 19.95 (ISBN 0-471-01788-4, Pub. by Wiley-Interscience). Wiley.
--Finance for the Nonfinancial Manager, Student Edition. LC 76-56371. 1978. 19.95x (ISBN 0-471-04803-8, Pub. by Wiley-Interscience). Wiley.
Spronk, Jaap. Interactive Multiple Goal Programming: Applications to Financial Planning. (Management Science-Operations Research International Ser.). 272p. 1981. lib. bdg. 20.00 (ISBN 0-89838-064-2). Kluwer Boston.
Stabler, C. Norman. How to Read the Financial News. 10th ed. 239p. 1972. pap. 3.50 (ISBN 0-06-463327-6, EH 327, EH). Har-Row.
Standard & Poor's Research Dept. Standard & Poor's Rating Guide. Incl. Corporate Bonds; Commercial Paper; Municipal Bonds; International Securities. (Illus.). 1979. 19.95 (ISBN 0-07-051883-1). McGraw.
Stevenson, Richard. Fundamentals of Finance. (McGraw-Hill Ser. in Finance). (Illus.). 1979. text ed. 16.95x (ISBN 0-07-061275-7); study guide 5.95x (ISBN 0-07-061277-3); instrs.' manual 7.50 (ISBN 0-07-061276-5). McGraw.
Stigum, Marcia. Money Market Calculations. LC 80-66022. 1981. 27.50 (ISBN 0-87094-192-5). Dow Jones-Irwin.
Stillman, Richard. Guide to Personal Finance: A Lifetime Program of Money Management. 3rd ed. 1979. text ed. 19.95 (ISBN 0-13-370486-6). P-H.
Sweezy, Paul M. & Magdoff, Harry. The Dynamics of U.S. Capitalism: Corporate Structure, Inflation, Credit, Gold & the Dollar. LC 79-179962. (Illus.). 240p. 1972. pap. 3.95 (ISBN 0-85345-225-3, PB-2253). Monthly Rev.
Symonds, Curtis W. Basic Financial Management. rev. ed. (Illus.). 1978. 13.95 (ISBN 0-8144-5481-X). Am Mgmt.
Tamari, M. Financial Ratios: Analysis & Prediction. 1979. 22.50 (ISBN 0-236-40133-5, Pub. by Paul Elek). Merrimack Bk Serv.
Thomas, Arthur L. The Allocation Problem: Part Two, Vol. 9. (Studies in Accounting Research). 194p. 1974. 6.00 (ISBN 0-686-31102-7). Am Accounting.
Thomson, James W. An Introduction to the Fundamentals of Financial Analysis for Business Students. LC 79-8512. 1979. pap. text ed. 12.25 (ISBN 0-8191-0872-3). U Pr of Amer.
Tobias, Andrew P. Funny Money Game. LC 74-167612. 1972. pap. 1.95 (ISBN 0-87216-452-7). Playboy Pbks.
Trotter, Alexander. Observations on the Financial Position & Credit of Such of the States of the North American Union As Have Contracted Public Debts. LC 67-21885. Repr. of 1839 ed. 19.50x (ISBN 0-678-00378-5). Kelley.
Tyran, Michael. Computerized Financial System Standardization. (Illus.). 1978. 34.95 (ISBN 0-13-166215-5, Busn). P-H.
Ullyot, James R. Moneymaking in the Twin Cities Local Over-the-Counter Marketplace. LC 72-9654. (Illus.). 166p. (Orig.). 1972. pap. 4.95 (ISBN 0-913514-01-2). Am Natl Pub.
U. S. Congress - House Committee On Banking And Currency. Money Trust Investigation of Financial & Monetary Conditions in the United States. Repr. of 1913 ed. lib. bdg. 86.50x (ISBN 0-8371-3181-2, MTIN). Greenwood.
Valentine, Jerome L. & Mennis, Edmund A. Quantitative Techniques for Financial Analysis. rev. ed. 1980. pap. 7.50x (ISBN 0-256-02268-2). Irwin.
Vancil, Richard F. Decentralization: Managerial Ambiguity by Design. LC 79-51782. 1979. 22.50 (ISBN 0-910586-32-2). Finan Exec.
Van Dam, Cees. Trends in Financial Decision Making: Planning & Capital Investment Decisions. (Nijenrode Studies in Business: Vol. 2). 1978. lib. bdg. 27.00 (ISBN 90-207-0692-6, Martinus Nijhoff Pubs). Kluwer Boston.
Van Horne, James C. Function & Analysis of Capital Market Rates. LC 73-99453. 1970. pap. 10.95 ref. ed. (ISBN 0-13-331934-2). P-H.
--Fundamentals of Financial Management. 4th ed. (Illus.). 1980. text ed. 21.95 (ISBN 0-13-339408-5); study guide 8.95 (ISBN 0-13-339424-7). P-H.
Viscione, Jerry & Aragon, George. Cases in Financial Management. LC 79-87854. 1979. text ed. 18.50 (ISBN 0-395-26715-3); instructor's manual 3.00 (ISBN 0-395-26716-1). HM.
Waterman, Marvin, et al. Essays on Business Finance. 4th ed. LC 57-1744. 1952. 10.00 (ISBN 0-685-73275-4). Masterco Pr.
Webster, Pelatiah. Political Essays on the Nature & Operation of Money, Public Finances & Other Subjects, 2 vols. in 1. LC 78-77603. (Research & Source Works Ser.: No. 354). (American Classics in History & Social Science Ser, No. 82). 1969. Repr. of 1791 ed. 29.00 (ISBN 0-8337-3712-0). B Franklin.
Weston. Plaid for Financial Management. rev ed. 1981. write for info. (ISBN 0-256-02135-X, 06-0848-02). Learning Syst.
--Plaid for Financial Management. 1975. pap. 5.50 (ISBN 0-256-01285-7, 06-0848-00). Learning Syst.
Wilczynski, J. Comparative Monetary Economics: Capatalist & Socialist Monetary Systems & Their Interrelations in the Changing International Scene. (Illus.). 1978. 23.00 (ISBN 0-19-520032-2). Oxford U Pr.
Williams, Edward E. & Findlay, M. Chapman. Integrated Analysis for Managerial Finance. 1970. pap. text ed. 9.95 (ISBN 0-13-469072-9). P-H.
Wilson, J. P. Inflation, Deflation, Reflation: Managemnent & Accounting in Economic Uncertainty. 345p. 1980. text ed. 36.75x (ISBN 0-220-67015-3, Pub. by Busn Bks England). Renouf.
Winger, Bernard J. Cases in Financial Management. LC 80-11532. (Finance Ser.). 211p. 1981. pap. 8.95 (ISBN 0-88244-224-4). Grid Pub.
Wippern, Ronald F. Cases in Modern Financial Management: Public & Private Sector Perspectives. 1980. 18.95x (ISBN 0-256-02363-8). Irwin.
Wiseman, Brian L. Basic Financial Control. 186p. 1979. 25.00x (ISBN 0-85042-020-2, Pub. by Plunkett Found England). State Mutual Bk.
Wood, E. G. Costing Matters for Managers. 199p. 1974. text ed. 24.50x (ISBN 0-686-70287-5, Pub. by Busn Bks England). Renouf.
Wood, Frederick A. Finances of Vermont. LC 70-127452. (Columbia University Social Science Studies Ser.: No. 130). Repr. of 1913 ed. 16.50 (ISBN 0-404-51130-9). AMS Pr.
Ziemba, W. T. Stochastic Optimization Models in Finance. 1975. 47.50 (ISBN 0-12-780850-7). Acad Pr.

FINANCE–BIBLIOGRAPHY

Aggarwal, Raj. International Business Finance. 1981. 19.95 (ISBN 0-03-047191-5). Praeger.
Joint Bank-Fund Library, Washington, D.C. Economics & Finance: Index to Periodical Articles, Nineteen Forty-Seven to Nineteen Seventy-One. Second Supplement. (Library Catalogs-Bib. Guides). 1979. lib. bdg. 95.00 (ISBN 0-8161-0302-X). G K Hall.
Joint Bank-Fund Library, Washington, D. C. Economics & Finance: Index to Periodical Articles, 1947-1971, 4 vols. 1972. Set. lib. bdg. 485.00 (ISBN 0-8161-0977-X). G K Hall.
Joint Bank-Fund Library (Washington, D. C.) Economics, Finance & Development: Subject Headings Used in the Main Catalog of the Joint Bank-Fund Library. 1979. lib. bdg. 88.00 (ISBN 0-8161-0276-7). G K Hall.
Ladley, Barbara. Money & Finance: Sources of Print & Nonprint Materials. (Neal-Schuman Sourcebook Ser.). 208p. 1980. 19.95x (ISBN 0-918212-23-5). Neal-Schuman.
Masui, Mitsuzo, ed. Bibliography of Finance, 3 Vols. LC 68-56724. (Bibliography & Reference Ser.: No. 221). 1969. Repr. of 1935 ed. 99.50 (ISBN 0-8337-2296-4). B Franklin.
Soetbeer, Adolf. Liraturnachweis Ueber Geld-und Muenzwesen Insbesondere Weber der Waehrungsstreit, 1871-1891. LC 72-85106. iv, 322p. 1972. Repr. of 1892 ed. lib. bdg. 32.50 (ISBN 0-8337-3304-4). B Franklin.

FINANCE–DICTIONARIES

Bellisco Hernandez, Manuel. Diccionario de Banca y Bolsa, Tomo I: Ingles-Espanol. 170p. (Eng.-Span.). 1977. pap. 15.75 (ISBN 84-85198-02-6, S-50120). French & Eur.
Bernard, Yves & Colli, Jean-Claude. Vocabulaire Economique et Financier: Coll. Points Economie. 384p. (Fr.). 1976. pap. 7.95 (ISBN 0-686-56915-6, M-6031). French & Eur.
Bernard, Yves, et al. Dictionnaire Economique et Financier. Lewandowski, Dominique, ed. 1200p. (Fr.). 1975. 95.00 (ISBN 0-686-57297-1, M-4643). French & Eur.
Blanes Prieto, Joaquin. Diccionario de Terminos Contables. 2nd ed. 388p. (Eng.-Span.). 1972. pap. 21.95 (ISBN 0-686-57342-0, S-28549). French & Eur.
Brownstone, David M., et al. The VNR Dictionary of Business & Finance. 320p. 1980. text ed. 18.95 (ISBN 0-442-20949-5). Van Nos Reinhold.
Clark, Donald T. & Gottfried, Bert A., eds. University Dictionary of Business & Finance. (Apollo Eds.). pap. 4.95 (ISBN 0-8152-0143-5, A143). T Y Crowell.
Conso, P. La Gestion Financiee De L'entreprise, 2 vols. 5th ed. 768p. (Fr.). 1979. Set. 39.95 (ISBN 0-686-56962-8, M-6085). French & Eur.
Davids, Lewis E. Dictionary of Banking & Finance. 229p. 1980. Repr. of 1978 ed. 15.00x (ISBN 0-8476-6132-6). Rowman.
--Dictionary of Banking & Finance. (Littlefield, Adams Quality Paperback: No. 336). 1979. pap. 7.95 (ISBN 0-8226-0336-5). Littlefield.
Diccionario Bursatil. 195p. (Espn.). 1977. pap. 17.50 (ISBN 84-85307-01-1, S-50126). French & Eur.
Freshman, Samuel K. Real Estate Finance & Syndication Glossary. 3rd., rev. ed. LC 79-2801. 109p. 1979. 5.95 (ISBN 0-9600708-3-4). Law & Cap Dynamics.
Garmendia Miangolarra, J. Ignacio de. Diccionario De Bolsa. 208p. (Espn.). 1977. leatherette 14.95 (ISBN 84-368-0057-5, S-50182). French & Eur.
Glossaire De la Finance. 284p. (Fr & Eng.). 1976. 22.50 (ISBN 0-686-57009-X, M-6350). French & Eur.
Gunston, C. A. Glossaries of Financial & Economic Terms: German-English. 1288p. 1980. 99.00x (ISBN 0-7121-5508-2, Pub. by Macdonald & Evans). State Mutual Bk.
Gunston, C. A. & Corner, C. M. German-English Glossary of Financial & Commercial Terms. new ed. (Ger. & Eng.). 1977. 57.50 (ISBN 3-7819-2008-9). Adler.
Herbst, Robert. Dictionary of Commerce, Finance & Law. (Eng. -Ger.). 1975. 92.00 (ISBN 3-85942-003-8, M-7118). French & Eur.
--Woerterbuch der Handels, Finanz und Rechtssprache. 2nd ed. (Ger., Eng. & Fr., Dictionary of Commercial, Fininancial & Legal Terms). 1975. 92.00 (ISBN 3-85942-001-1, M-7002). French & Eur.
Kafitz, Franz. Lexikon des Wirtschaftsrechnens. 2nd ed. (Ger.). 1976. 15.00 (ISBN 3-470-71192-5, M-7210). French & Eur.
Kettridge, J. O. French-English & English-French Dictionary of Commercial & Financial Terms, Phrases & Practice. 2nd ed. 1969. Repr. of 1968 ed. 30.00 (ISBN 0-7100-1671-9). Routledge & Kegan.
--French-English & English-French Dictionary of Financial & Mercantile Terms Phrases & Practice. 1971. Repr. of 1934 ed. 20.00 (ISBN 0-7100-1667-0). Routledge & Kegan.
Kettridge, Julius O. Financial & Mercantile Dictionary. (Fr. & Eng.). 13.95 (ISBN 0-685-11187-3). French & Eur.
Martinez Cerezo, Antonio. Diccionario De Banca. 3rd ed. 208p. (Espn.). 1976. leatherette 13.95 (ISBN 84-368-0028-1, S-50179). French & Eur.
Munn, Glenn G. Encyclopedia of Banking & Finance. 7th, rev. ed. Garcia, Ferdinand L., ed. LC 73-83395. (Illus.). 953p. 1973. 49.75x (ISBN 0-87267-019-8). Bankers.
Rosenberg, Jerry M. Dictionary of Banking & Finance. 540p. 1982. 24.95 (ISBN 0-471-08096-9, Pub. by Wiley-Interscience). Wiley.
Thomik, Rudolf. Fachwoerterbuch Fur Wirtschaft, Handel und Finanzen. 685p. (Fr. & Ger.). 1977. 59.95 (ISBN 3-452-18138-3, 7400, Pub. by Carl Heymanns Verlag KG). French & Eur.
Thomson, F. J. Elsevier's Dictionary of Financial Terms. LC 79-11810. 496p. (Eng., Ger., Span., Fr., Ital., Dutch.). 1979. 122.00 (ISBN 0-686-62653-2). Elsevier.
Zahn, Hans E. English-German Glossary of Financial & Economic Terms. 1977. 56.00x (ISBN 3-7819-2013-5). Intl Pubns Serv.

FINANCE–HISTORY

Allen, Frederick L. Lords of Creation. 1966. pap. 3.45 (ISBN 0-8129-6033-5, QP35). Times Bks.
Blyn, Martin R. & Krooss, Herman E. History of Financial Intermediaries. 1971. text ed. 7.95x (ISBN 0-685-47982-X). Phila Bk Co.
Bogart, Ernest L. Financial History of Ohio. (Illus.). Repr. of 1912 ed. 25.50 (ISBN 0-384-04950-8). Johnson Repr.
Bolles, Albert S. Financial History of the United States, 3 vols. Incl. Vol. 1. From 1774 to 1789. 4th ed. Repr. of 1896 ed (ISBN 0-678-04033-8); Vol. 2. From 1789 to 1860. 4th ed. Repr. of 1894 ed (ISBN 0-678-04034-6); Vol. 3. From 1861-1885. 2nd ed. LC 68-22311. Repr. of 1894 ed (ISBN 0-678-04035-4). LC 68-22371. Set. 57.50x (ISBN 0-678-00465-X); 22.50 ea. Kelley.
Bouchard, Leon. Systeme financier de l'ancienne monarchie. 1971. Repr. of 1891 ed. lib. bdg. 29.00 (ISBN 0-8337-0341-2). B Franklin.
Bourne, Edward G. History of the Surplus Revenue of Eighteen Thirty-Seven. LC 68-58463. (Research & Source Ser.: No. 327). 1969. Repr. of 1885 ed. 16.50 (ISBN 0-8337-0342-0). B Franklin.
Corey, Lewis. House of Morgan. LC 78-94469. Repr. of 1930 ed. 32.50 (ISBN 0-404-01728-2). AMS Pr.
Davis, Andrew M., ed. Colonial Currency Reprints Sixteen Niney-Two-Seventeen Fifty-One, 4 vols. (Prince Society Ser.: Nos. 32-35). Repr. of 1910 ed. 81.00 (ISBN 0-8337-0789-2). B Franklin.
--Colonial Currency Reprints 1682-1751, 4 Vols. LC 64-14707. Repr. of 1910 ed. 75.00x (ISBN 0-678-00041-7). Kelley.
Dewey, Davis R. Financial History of the United States. 12th ed. LC 67-30857. Repr. of 1934 ed. 25.00x (ISBN 0-678-00463-3). Kelley.
Dies, Edward J. Behind the Wall Street Curtain. facs. ed. LC 73-86745. (Essay Index Reprint Ser). 1952. 15.00 (ISBN 0-8369-1178-4). Arno.
Ducrocq, Theophile G. Etudes D'histoire Financiere et Monetaire. LC 75-132536. (Research & Source Works: No. 559). (Fr). 1970. Repr. of 1887 ed. lib. bdg. 23.50 (ISBN 0-8337-0939-9). B Franklin.
Edwards, George W. Evolution of Finance Capitalism. LC 66-22622. Repr. of 1938 ed. 19.50x (ISBN 0-678-00290-8). Kelley.
Felt, Joseph B. Historical Account of Massachusetts Currency. LC 68-57905. (Research & Source Works Ser.: No. 223). (Illus.). 1967. Repr. of 1839 ed. 21.00 (ISBN 0-8337-1106-7). B Franklin.
Fetter, Frank W. Development of British Monetary Orthodoxy 1797-1875. LC 76-30912. Repr. of 1965 ed. lib. bdg. 17.50x (ISBN 0-678-01386-1). Kelley.
Findley, William. Review of the Revenue System Adopted by the First Congress. Repr. of 1794 ed. 13.50x (ISBN 0-678-01068-4). Kelley.
Goodhart, Charles A. New York Money Market & the Finance of Trade, 1900-1913. LC 69-12723. (Economic Studies: No. 132). 1969. 8.50x (ISBN 0-674-61950-1). Harvard U Pr.
Gouge, William M. Fiscal History of Texas: An Account of Its Revenues, Debts, & Currency from the Commencement of the Revolution in 1834 to 1851-52 with Remarks on American Debts. 1969. Repr. of 1852 ed. 20.00 (ISBN 0-8337-1397-3). B Franklin.
Grayson, Theodore J. Leaders & Periods of American Finance. facs. ed. LC 68-29211. (Essay Index Reprint Ser). 1932. 32.00 (ISBN 0-8369-1240-3). Arno.
Kindleberger, Charles. Manias, Panics, & Crashes: A History of Financial Crises. LC 77-20242. 271p. 1980. pap. 5.95 (ISBN 0-465-04402-6). Basic.
McGrane, Reginald C. Panic of Eighteen Thirty Seven: Some Financial Problems of the Jacksonian Era. 1965. pap. 1.95 (ISBN 0-226-55858-4, P202, Phoen). U of Chicago Pr.

Madox, Thomas. History & Antiquities of the Exchequer of the Kings of England, 2 Vols. 2nd ed. LC 68-57386. Repr. of 1769 ed. Set. 60.00x (ISBN 0-678-04500-3). Kelley.
--History & Antiquities of the Exchequer, 2 Vols. 2nd ed. LC 68-57386. 1969. Repr. of 1769 ed. Set. 60.00x (ISBN 0-8377-2426-0). Rothman.
Mirrors of Wall Street. facsimile ed. LC 77-152198. (Essay Index Reprint Ser). Repr. of 1933 ed. 14.00 (ISBN 0-8369-2247-6). Arno.
Mueller, Reinhold C. The Procuratori Di San Marco & the Ventian Credit Market: A Study of the Development of Credit & Banking in the Trecento. Bruchey, Stuart, ed. LC 77-77181. (Dissertations in European Economic History Ser.). 1977. lib. bdg. 27.00 (ISBN 0-405-10794-3). Arno.
Myers, Margaret G. A Financial History of the United States. LC 70-104900. 1970. 22.50x (ISBN 0-231-02442-8); pap. 7.50x (ISBN 0-231-08309-2). Columbia U Pr.
Noyes, Alexander D. Market Place: Reminiscences of a Financial Editor. Repr. of 1938 ed. lib. bdg. 17.75x (ISBN 0-8371-0592-7, NOMP). Greenwood.
--Thirty Years of American Finance. Repr. of 1900 ed. lib. bdg. 16.00x (ISBN 0-8371-1084-X, NOTY). Greenwood.
Otenasek, Mildred B. Alexander Hamilton's Financial Policies. Bruchey, Stuart, ed. LC 76-39837. (Nineteen Seventy-Seven Dissertations Ser.). 1977. lib. bdg. 15.00x (ISBN 0-405-09917-7). Arno.
Postan, M. M. Medieval Trade & Finance. (Illus.). 350p. 1973. 41.95 (ISBN 0-521-08745-7). Cambridge U Pr.
Ratner, Sidney, ed. The New American State Papers: Public Finance Subject Set, 32 vols. LC 72-95580. 1973. Set. lib. bdg. 1525.00 (ISBN 0-8420-1610-4). Scholarly Res Inc.
Ripley, William Z. Financial History of Virginia 1609-1776. 1893. 20.50 (ISBN 0-8337-2997-7). B Franklin.
Smith, Walter B. Economic Aspects of the Second Bank of the United States. Repr. of 1953 ed. lib. bdg. 15.00 (ISBN 0-8371-2329-1, SMSB). Greenwood.
Sobel, Robert. Great Bull Market: Wall Street in the 1920's. LC 68-19795. (Essays in American History). 1968. pap. 5.95x (ISBN 0-393-09817-6, NortonC). Norton.
Sumner, William G. Financier & the Finances of the American Revolution, 2 Vols. 1891. Set. 38.00 (ISBN 0-8337-3460-1). B Franklin.
--Financier & the Finances of the American Revolution, 2 Vols. LC 68-18224. Repr. of 1891 ed. Set. 35.00x (ISBN 0-678-00435-8). Kelley.
Sylla, Richard E. The American Capital Market, Eighteen Forty-Six to Nineteen Fourteen: A Study of the Effects of Public Policy on Economic Development. facsimile ed. LC 75-2599. (Dissertations in American Economic History). (Illus.). 1975. 27.00x (ISBN 0-405-07220-1). Arno.
U. S. Treasury Department. The National Loans of the United States, from July 4, 1776 to June 30, 1880. 2nd ed. Bayley, Rafael, ed. LC 74-96856. (Research & Source Works Ser: No. 554). 1970. Repr. of 1882 ed. lib. bdg. 26.50 (ISBN 0-8337-0195-9). B Franklin.
Wildman, Murray S. Money Inflation in the United States: A Study in Social Pathology. Repr. lib. bdg. 14.50x (ISBN 0-8371-1408-X, WIMI). Greenwood.

FINANCE–MATHEMATICAL MODELS

Elliott, R. N. & Massey, James G. The Decisive Speculative Signifigance of the Elliott Wave Theory. (Illus.). 158p. 1980. deluxe ed. 47.55 (ISBN 0-89266-239-5). Am Classical Coll Pr.
Hummel & Seebeck. Mathematics of Finance. 3rd ed. 1970. text ed. 16.50 (ISBN 0-07-031161-7, C). McGraw.
Hunt, Lacy H. Dynamics of Forecasting Financial Cycles: Theory, Technique & Implementation, Vol. 1. Altman, Edward I. & Walter, Ingo, eds. LC 76-5756. (Contemporary Studies in Economic & Financial Analysis). 300p. 1976. lib. bdg. 30.00 (ISBN 0-89232-002-8). Jai Pr.
Mao, J. C. Quantitative Analysis of Financial Decisions. 1969. text ed. 22.95 (ISBN 0-02-375820-1). Macmillan.
Thore, Sten. Programming the Network of Financial Intermediation. 224p. 1983. pap. text ed. 14.00x (ISBN 82-00-05379-2). Universitet.
Van Horne, James C. Financial Market Rates & Flows. (Illus.). 1978. pap. text ed. 10.95 (ISBN 0-13-316190-0). P-H.

FINANCE–RESEARCH

see Financial Research

FINANCE–STUDY AND TEACHING

Fama, E. & Miller, M. Theory of Finance. LC 74-168400. (Dryden Press). 1972. text ed. 19.95 (ISBN 0-03-086732-0, HoltC). HR&W.
Frame, Robert & Curry, Dudley. Financial Management. LC 73-89292. (Business Ser.). 576p. 1974. text ed. 18.95 (ISBN 0-675-08852-6); media: audiocassettes & filmstrips 450.00, 2-7 sets, 380.00 ea., 8-15 sets, 340.00 ea., 16 or more sets, 275.00 ea. (ISBN 0-675-08807-0); instructor's manual 3.95 (ISBN 0-686-66911-8). Merrill.
Krohn, Edward & Mayo, Herbert. Basic Finance: Study Guide & Workbook. 1978. pap. text ed. 6.95 (ISBN 0-7216-5519-X). HR&W.
Robinson, Roland I. & Johnson, Robert W. Self-Correcting Problems in Finance. 3rd ed. 272p. 1976. pap. text ed. 12.95 (ISBN 0-205-05444-7, 0854441). Allyn.
Teacher's Guide to Financial Education. LC 68-20395. 1967. pap. 1.00 (ISBN 0-686-00796-4, 261-08398). Home Econ Educ.

FINANCE–AFRICA

Okigbo, P. N. Nigeria's Financial System. (Illus.). 320p. 1981. text ed. 25.00x (ISBN 0-582-59733-1). Longman.
Pim, Alan. Financial & Economic History of the African Tropical Territories. 1970. Repr. of 1940 ed. 15.00 (ISBN 0-87266-046-X). Argosy.

FINANCE–ARGENTINE REPUBLIC

Williams, John H. Argentine International Trade Under Incontrovertible Paper Money 1880-1900. Repr. of 1920 ed. lib. bdg. 14.75x (ISBN 0-8371-1050-5, WIAT). Greenwood.
--Argentine International Trade Under Inconvertible Paper Money 1880-1900. LC 75-178302. Repr. of 1920 ed. 12.50 (ISBN 0-404-06979-7). AMS Pr.

FINANCE–ASIA

Financial Leaders of Pacific Asia. 1977. 50.00x (ISBN 0-686-19006-8, Pub. by Busn Comm). Intl Schol Bk Serv.
Rosen, C. Some Aspects of Industrial Finance in India. LC 62-11761. 1962. 6.00 (ISBN 0-02-926910-5). Free Pr.

FINANCE–ATHENS

Calhoun, George M. Business Life of Ancient Athens. LC 68-18490. 175p. 1968. Repr. of 1926 ed. 8.50x (ISBN 0-8154-0043-8). Cooper Sq.

FINANCE–AUSTRALIA

Copland, Douglas B. Australia in the World Crisis, 1929-1933. LC 74-111474. (BCL Ser. I). Repr. of 1934 ed. 19.00 (ISBN 0-404-01718-5). AMS Pr.
Wood, Gordon. Borrowing & Business in Australia: A Study of the Correlation Between Imports of Capital & Changes in National Prosperity. Wilkins, Mira, ed. LC 76-29986. (European Business Ser.). (Illus.). 1977. Repr. of 1930 ed. lib. bdg. 17.00x (ISBN 0-405-09718-2). Arno.

FINANCE–BOLIVIA

Marsh, Margaret C. Bankers in Bolivia: A Study in American Foreign Investment. LC 76-99250. Repr. of 1928 ed. 19.75 (ISBN 0-404-04190-6). AMS Pr.

FINANCE–BRAZIL

Normano, Joao F. Brazil: A Study of Economic Types. LC 67-29551. 1935. 12.00x (ISBN 0-8196-0208-6). Biblo.
Wileman, J. P. Brazilian Exchange: The Study of an Inconvertible Currency. Repr. of 1896 ed. lib. bdg. 16.75x (ISBN 0-8371-1082-3, WIBE). Greenwood.

FINANCE–CANADA

Neufeld, E. P. The Financial System of Canada. LC 70-178200. 635p. 1972. 27.50 (ISBN 0-312-28980-4). St Martin.
Viner, Jacob. Canada's Balance of International Indebtedness: 1900-1913. Wilkins, Mira, ed. LC 78-3953. (International Finance Ser.). (Illus.). 1978. Repr. of 1924 ed. lib. bdg. 22.00x (ISBN 0-405-11254-8). Arno.

FINANCE–CHINA

Miyashita, Tadao. The Currency & Financial System of Mainland China. (China in the 20th Century Ser.). 1976. Repr. of 1966 ed. lib. bdg. 22.50 (ISBN 0-306-70758-6). Da Capo.
Overlach, Theodore W. Foreign Financial Control in China. Bruchey, Stuart & Bruchey, Eleanor, eds. LC 76-5027. (American Business Abroad Ser.). 1976. Repr. of 1919 ed. 20.00x (ISBN 0-405-09293-8). Arno.
Shaw, Kinn W. Democracy & Finance in China. LC 73-127445. (Columbia University Studies in the Social Sciences: No. 282). Repr. of 1926 ed. 18.50 (ISBN 0-404-51282-8). AMS Pr.
Stanley, John C. Late Ch'ing Finance: Hu Kuang-Yung As an Innovator. LC 62-1254. (East Asian Monographs Ser: No. 12). 1961. pap. text ed. 9.00x (ISBN 0-674-51165-4). Harvard U Pr.

FINANCE–CONFEDERATE STATES OF AMERICA

Schwab, John C. The Confederate States of America 1861-65: A Financial & Industrial History of the South During the Civil War. LC 68-65680. (Research & Source Works Ser.: No. 294). 1968. Repr. of 1901 ed. 22.50 (ISBN 0-8337-3178-5). B Franklin.
Thian, Raphael P. Register of the Confederate Debt (1880) LC 70-189169. (Illus.). 212p. 1972. Repr. of 1880 ed. 35.00x (ISBN 0-88000-002-3). Quarterman.

FINANCE–EUROPE

Donovan, Michael. Official Grants & Financial Aids to Business in Western Europe. 400p. 1977. 40.00x (ISBN 0-86010-057-X, Pub. by Graham & Trotman England). State Mutual Bk.
--Official Grants & Finanial Aids to Business in Western Europe: Basic Volume with the First Two Updating Supplements (1978 & 1979) 400p. 1979. 66.00x (ISBN 0-686-64024-1, Pub. by Graham & Trotman England). State Mutual Bk.
Ferris, Paul. Money-Men of Europe. LC 69-11177. Orig. Title: Man & Money. 1969. 6.95 (ISBN 0-02-537400-1). Macmillan.
Garland, John S. Financing Foreign Trade in Eastern Europe: Problems of Bilateralism & Currency Inconvertibility. LC 76-24351. 1977. text ed. 23.95 (ISBN 0-275-23800-8). Praeger.
Jacquillat. European Finance Association: 1974 Proceedings. 402p. 1975. 49.00 (ISBN 0-444-11004-6, North-Holland). Elsevier.
Van Brabant, Jozef M. East European Cooperation: The Role of Money & Finance. LC 76-2911. (Illus.). 1976. text ed. 34.50 (ISBN 0-275-56650-1). Praeger.
Wilczynski, J. Comparative Monetary Economics: Capatalist & Socialist Monetary Systems & Their Interrelations in the Changing International Scene. (Illus.). 1978. 23.00 (ISBN 0-19-520032-2). Oxford U Pr.

FINANCE–FRANCE

Beik, Paul H. Judgment of the Old Regime. LC 44-2365. (Columbia University Studies in the Social Sciences: No. 509). Repr. of 1944 ed. 18.50 (ISBN 0-404-51509-6). AMS Pr.
Bouchard, Leon. Systeme financier de l'ancienne monarchie. 1971. Repr. of 1891 ed. lib. bdg. 29.00 (ISBN 0-8337-0341-2). B Franklin.
Ducrocq, Theophile G. Etudes D'histoire Financiere et Monetaire. LC 75-132536. (Research & Source Works: No. 559). (Fr). 1970. Repr. of 1887 ed. lib. bdg. 23.50 (ISBN 0-8337-0939-9). B Franklin.
John Crerar Library. Catalogue of French Economic Documents from the Sixteenth, Seventeenth & Eighteenth Centuries. (Bibliography & Reference Ser.: No. 222). (Fr). 1969. Repr. of 1918 ed. 18.50 (ISBN 0-8337-0734-5). B Franklin.
Marion, Marcel. Histoire Financiere De la France Depuis 1715, 6 Vols. (Research & Source Works: No. 196). 1968. Repr. of 1927 ed. Set. 209.00 (ISBN 0-8337-2223-9). B Franklin.
Miskimin, Harry A. Money, Prices, & Foreign Exchange in Fourteenth Century France. LC 63-7942. 1970. Repr. of 1963 ed. 15.00 (ISBN 0-08-022307-9). Pergamon.
Parker, William. Paris Bourse & French Finance with Reference to Organized Speculation in New York. LC 20-18734. (Columbia University Studies in the Social Sciences: No. 204). Repr. of 1920 ed. 14.50 (ISBN 0-404-51204-6). AMS Pr.
Stourm, Rene. Bibliographie Historique Des Finances De la France Au Dix-Huitieme Siecle. LC 68-56590. (Bibliography & Reference Ser.: No. 114). (Fr). 1969. Repr. of 1895 ed. 32.50 (ISBN 0-8337-3426-1). B Franklin.
--Finances de l'Ancient Regime et de la Revolution, 2 Vols. LC 68-56718. (Research & Source Works Ser.: No. 203). (Fr). 1968. Repr. of 1885 ed. Set. 55.50 (ISBN 0-8337-3429-6). B Franklin.

FINANCE–GERMANY

Engberg, Holger L. Mixed Banking & Economic Growth in Germany, 1850-1931. Bruchey, Stuart, ed. LC 80-2806. (Dissertations in European Economic History II). (Illus.). 1981. lib. bdg. 24.00x (ISBN 0-405-13990-X). Arno.
Herring, R. J. & Marston, R. C. National Monetary Policies & International Financial Markets. (Contributions to Economic Analysis: Vol. 104). 1977. 39.00 (ISBN 0-7204-0519-X, North-Holland). Elsevier.
Heyn, Udo. Private Banking & Industrialization: The Case of Frankfurt Am Main, 1825-1875. Bruchey, Stuart, ed. LC 80-2810. (Dissertations in European Economic History II). (Illus.). 1981. lib. bdg. 38.00x (ISBN 0-405-13994-2). Arno.
Roll, Erich. Spotlight on Germany. LC 70-180424. Repr. of 1933 ed. 18.50 (ISBN 0-404-56158-6). AMS Pr.
Schacht, Hjalmar H. Confessions of the Old Wizard. LC 74-15559. (Illus.). 484p. 1975. Repr. of 1956 ed. lib. bdg. 27.50x (ISBN 0-8371-7827-4, SCOW). Greenwood.

FINANCE–GREAT BRITAIN

Adams, Charles F., Jr. & Adams, Henry. Chapters of Erie, & Other Essays. LC 66-22613. (Library of Early American Business & Industry: No. VIII). Repr. of 1871 ed. 17.50x (ISBN 0-678-00788-8). Kelley.
Andreades, Andreas M. History of the Bank of England, 1640 to 1903. 4th ed. Meredith, C., tr. LC 66-31537. Repr. of 1909 ed. 27.50x (ISBN 0-678-05023-6). Kelley.
Bagehot, Walter. Lombard Street. Wilkins, Mira, ed. LC 78-3895. (International Finance Ser.). 1978. Repr. of 1917 ed. lib. bdg. 22.00x (ISBN 0-405-11201-7). Arno.
Buxton, Sydney C. Finance & Politics: An Historical Study, 1783-1885 2 Vols. LC 66-21367. Repr. of 1888 ed. Set. 35.00x (ISBN 0-678-00164-2). Kelley.
Colquhoun, Patrick. A Treatise on the Wealth, Power & Resources of the British Empire. 2nd ed. 1815. 54.00 (ISBN 0-384-09710-3). Johnson Repr.
Congleton, Henry B. On Financial Reform. 3rd ed. LC 68-56560. Repr. of 1831 ed. 19.50x (ISBN 0-678-00452-8). Kelley.
Doubleday, Thomas. Financial, Monetary & Statistical History of England, from the Revolution of 1688 to the Present Time. LC 68-28626. 1968. Repr. of 1847 ed. lib. bdg. 21.00x (ISBN 0-8371-0388-6, DOFM). Greenwood.
Financial Times, London. Guide to FT Statistics. (Illus.). 32p. 1973. 7.50x (ISBN 0-900671-14-9). Intl Pubns Serv.
Guy, Henry. Moneys Received & Paid for Secret Services of Charles II & James II. 15.50 (ISBN 0-384-20490-2). Johnson Repr.
Hollis, Christopher. The Two Nations. 69.95 (ISBN 0-87968-230-2). Gordon Pr.
Lavington, Frederick. English Capital Market. LC 67-30469. Repr. of 1921 ed. 15.00x (ISBN 0-678-00345-9). Kelley.
Lyon, Bryce & Verhulst, A. E. Medieval Finance: A Comparison of Financial Institutions in Northwestern Europe. LC 67-19657. 100p. 1968. Repr. of 1967 ed. text ed. 8.00x (ISBN 0-87057-102-8, Pub. by Brown U Pr). U Pr of New Eng.
Mason, Sandra. The Flow of Funds in Britain: An Introduction to Financial Markets. 245p. 1976. 19.50x (ISBN 0-87471-828-7). Rowman.
Morton, Walter A. British Finance: Nineteen Thirty - Nineteen Forty. Wilkins, Mira, ed. LC 78-3942. (International Finance Ser.). (Illus.). 1978. Repr. of 1943 ed. lib. bdg. 24.00x (ISBN 0-405-11242-4). Arno.
Nishimura, Shizuya. Decline of Inland Bills of Exchange in the London Money Market, 1855-1913. LC 70-134613. (Illus.). 1971. 41.00 (ISBN 0-521-08055-X). Cambridge U Pr.
Paterson, William. Writings of William Paterson, 3 Vols. 2nd ed. Bannister, Saxe, ed. LC 68-54311. Repr. of 1859 ed. 57.50x (ISBN 0-678-00427-7). Kelley.
Postlethwayt, Malachy. Great Britain's True System. LC 67-18579. Repr. of 1757 ed. 25.00x (ISBN 0-678-00250-9). Kelley.
Powell, Ellis T. Evolution of the Money Market, 1385-1915. LC 66-8146. Repr. of 1915 ed. 35.00x (ISBN 0-678-05080-5). Kelley.
Sinclair, John. History of the Public Revenue of the British Empire, 3 Vols. 3rd ed. LC 66-22636. Repr. of 1803 ed. 67.50x (ISBN 0-678-00194-4). Kelley.
Unwin, George, ed. Finance & Trade Under Edward III. Repr. of 1918 ed. 27.50x (ISBN 0-678-05199-2). Kelley.
Wallace, Robert. Characteristics of the Present Political State of Great Britain. 2nd ed. LC 69-19551. Repr. of 1758 ed. 15.00x (ISBN 0-678-00496-X). Kelley.
Wilson, Charles Henry. Anglo-Dutch Commerce & Finance in the Eighteenth Century. Wilkins, Mira, ed. LC 76-29980. (European Business Ser.). (Illus.). 1977. Repr. of 1941 ed. lib. bdg. 16.00x (ISBN 0-405-09746-8). Arno.

FINANCE–INDIA

Deshmukh, C. D. Reflections on Finance, Education & Society (India) 1973. text ed. 11.50x (ISBN 0-8426-0416-2). Verry.
Gupta, L. C. Readings in Industrial Finance, India. 1976. 14.00x (ISBN 0-333-90136-3). South Asia Bks.

FINANCE–JAPAN

Adams, T. F. M. & Hoshii, Iwao. A Financial History of the New Japan. LC 75-185642. (Illus.). 547p. 1972. 22.50x (ISBN 0-87011-157-4). Kodansha.
Furuya, Seikow Y. Japan's Foreign Exchange & Her Balance of International Payments, with Special Reference to Recent Theories of Foreign Exchange. LC 68-58576. (Columbia University. Studies in the Social Sciences: No. 299). 18.50 (ISBN 0-404-51299-2). AMS Pr.
Moulton, Harold G. & Ko, Junichi. Japan: An Economic & Financial Appraisal. LC 77-97886. Repr. of 1931 ed. 38.45 (ISBN 0-404-04507-3). AMS Pr.
Pressnell, S. L., ed. Money & Banking in Japan. LC 72-93885. 450p. 1974. 25.00 (ISBN 0-312-54460-X). St Martin.

FINANCE–MEXICO

Brothers, Dwight S. & Solis, M. Leopoldo. Mexican Financial Development. 252p. 1965. 12.95x (ISBN 0-292-73304-6). U of Tex Pr.

FINANCE–NETHERLANDS

Barbour, Violet. Capitalism in Amsterdam in the 17th Century. 1963. pap. 3.95 (ISBN 0-472-06074-0, 74, AA). U of Mich Pr.

Wilson, Charles Henry. Anglo-Dutch Commerce & Finance in the Eighteenth Century. Wilkins, Mira, ed. LC 76-29980. (European Business Ser.). (Illus.). 1977. Repr. of 1941 ed. lib. bdg. 16.00x (ISBN 0-405-09746-8). Arno.

FINANCE–RUSSIA

Miller, Margaret S. Economic Development of Russia, 1905-1914. 2nd ed. LC 67-3033. Repr. of 1926 ed. 24.00x (ISBN 0-678-05074-0). Kelley.

FINANCE–SWITZERLAND

Jacob, Johann J. Financing in Switzerland-Geld aus der Schweiz. 1978. 17.95 (ISBN 0-89532-008-8). United Seabears.

FINANCE–TURKEY

Blaisdell, Donald C. European Financial Control in the Ottoman Empire. LC 29-15742. Repr. of 1929 ed. 10.00 (ISBN 0-404-00895-X). AMS Pr.

FINANCE–YUGOSLAVIA

Dimitrijevic, Dimitrije & Macesich, George. Money & Finance in Contemporary Yugoslavia. LC 72-92889. (Special Studies in International Economics & Development). 1973. 29.50x (ISBN 0-275-28725-4); pap. text ed. 18.50x (ISBN 0-89197-857-7). Irvington.

FINANCE, CHURCH

see Church Finance

FINANCE, INTERNATIONAL

see International Finance

FINANCE, LOCAL

see Local Finance

FINANCE, MUNICIPAL

see Municipal Finance

FINANCE, PERSONAL

see also Consumer Credit; Estate Planning; Home Economics–Accounting; Insurance; Investments; Saving and Thrift

Aabert, Geoffry F. After the Crash: How to Survive & Prosper During the Depression of the 1980's. 1980. pap. 2.50 (ISBN 0-451-09119-1, E9119, Sig). NAL.

Ackerman, Diane L. Getting Rich: The Smart Woman's Guide to Successful Money Management. 288p. 1981. 11.95 (ISBN 0-89479-063-3). A & W Pubs.

Advice About Insurance, Credit, Budgeting. (Home Adviser Ser.). 80p. (Orig.). 1981. pap. 1.95 (ISBN 0-8326-2407-1, 7051). Delair.

Aherne, Dee Dee & Bliss, Betsy. The Economics of Being a Woman. 1977. pap. 3.95 (ISBN 0-07-000650-4, SP). McGraw.

Albin, Francis M. Consumer Economics & Personal Money Management. (Illus.). 496p. 1982. 18.95 (ISBN 0-13-169490-1). P-H.

Allentuck, Andrew J. & Bivens, Gordon E. Consumer Choice: The Economics of Personal Living. 1977. text ed. 15.95 (ISBN 0-15-513456-6, HC); instructor's guide incl. (ISBN 0-15-513457-4); wkbk. 5.95 (ISBN 0-15-513458-2). HarBraceJ.

Amazing Life Games. Good Cents. (Illus.). 1974. pap. 3.95 (ISBN 0-395-19501-2, Sandpiper). HM.

Andereggen, Anton. Blueprint for Crisis Preparedness. 200p. (Orig.). 1981. write for info. (ISBN 0-938942-01-8); pap. write for info. (ISBN 0-938942-00-X). Pacific Gallery.

Anderson, Jim. How to Live Rent Free in the 1980's: It's Not Too Late, Vol. 2. 376p. 1980. luxury hardcover 25.00 (ISBN 0-932574-02-5); pap. 15.00 (ISBN 0-932574-03-3). Brun Pr.

Apilado, Vincent P. & Morehart, Thomas B. Personal Financial Management. (Illus.). 650p. 1980. text ed. 19.50 (ISBN 0-8299-0327-5); instrs.' manual avail. (ISBN 0-8299-0457-3); study guide 6.95 (ISBN 0-8299-0308-9). West Pub.

Appleman, John A. How to Increase Your Money-Making Power in the '80s. 4th rev. ed. LC 81-66409. 320p. 1981. 12.95 (ISBN 0-8119-0433-4). Fell.

Ashton, Marvin J. One for the Money. LC 75-14995. 21p. 1975. 1.95 (ISBN 0-87747-555-5). Deseret Bk.

Aspaklaria, Shelley & Geltner, Gerson. What You Should Know About Your Husband's Money... Before the Divorce. LC 80-52403. Orig. Title: Everything You Want to Know About Your Husband's Money... & Need to Know Before the Divorce. 256p. 1981. pap. 6.95 (ISBN 0-87223-646-3). Wideview Bks.

Bagby, Martha C. Consumer Economics & Personal Finance: Syllabus. 1974. pap. text ed. 6.95 (ISBN 0-89420-063-1, 100030); cassette recordings 223.75 (ISBN 0-89420-136-0, 100000). Natl Book.

Bailard, Thomas E., et al. Personal Money Management. 3rd ed. 1979. text ed. 17.95 (ISBN 0-574-19395-2, 13-2395); instr's guide avail. (ISBN 0-574-19396-0, 13-2396); study guide 6.95 (ISBN 0-574-19397-9, 13-2397). SRA.

Baker, C. R. & Hayes, R. S. Lease Financing: Alternative to Buying. LC 8-1576. 200p. 1981. 19.95 (ISBN 0-471-06040-2, Pub. by Wiley Interscience). Wiley.

Barnes, John. How to Have More Money. LC 73-21960. 288p. 1974. 8.95 (ISBN 0-688-00255-2). Morrow.

Barnes, Leo & Feldman, Stephen. Handbook of Wealth Management. (Illus.). 1977. 42.50 (ISBN 0-07-003765-5, P&RB). McGraw.

Barngrover, Charles L., et al. Personal Finance. 2nd ed. LC 80-18010. (Finance Ser.). 505p. 1981. text ed. 22.95 (ISBN 0-88244-216-3). Grid Pub.

Barry, Jim. Financial Freedom: A Positive Strategy for Putting Your Money to Work. 1981. text ed. 12.95 (ISBN 0-8359-2018-6). Reston.

Bart, Joe. The Ten Dollar Book That Can Make You Rich. 1976. 10.00 (ISBN 0-8184-0232-6); lib. bdg. 10.00 (ISBN 0-685-69538-7). Lyle Stuart.

Becker, Dennis & Becker, Nancy. How to Succeed with Your Money: Leader's Guide. (Leader's Guide Ser.). (Illus.). 1978. text ed. 3.25 (ISBN 0-8024-3661-7). Moody.

Bennett, Paul. Up Your Accountability: How to up Your Serviceability & Funding Credibility by Upping Your Accounting Ability. LC 73-89364. (Nonprofit-Ability Ser.). (Illus.). 1973. pap. 9.95 (ISBN 0-914756-02-8). Taft Corp.

Bennett, Vivo & Clagett, Cricket. One Thousand & One Ways to Stretch a Dollar. 1977. 10.00 (ISBN 0-13-636688-0); pap. 5.95 (ISBN 0-13-636670-8). P-H.

Benning, Lee Edwards. How to Bring up a Child Without Spending a Fortune. LC 75-25436. 320p. 1976. pap. 2.95 (ISBN 0-385-11513-X, Dolp). Doubleday.

Bladen, Ashby. How to Cope with the Developing Financial Crisis. 192p. 1981. pap. 4.95 (ISBN 0-07-005549-1, GB). McGraw.

Blessman, Lyle. The Blessman Approach. LC 78-64483. 1978. 9.95 (ISBN 0-87863-175-5). Farnswth Pub.

Blodgett, Richard. New York Times Book of Money. LC 72-88117. (Illus.). 1976. 9.95 (ISBN 0-8129-0273-4). Times Bks.

Blotnick, Srully. Getting Rich Your Own Way. LC 79-6657. 1980. 10.95 (ISBN 0-385-15702-9). Doubleday.

Bohn, Robert F. Budget Book & Much More: Your Money, Goals, Time, Assets, Vital Records. 2nd ed. 128p. pap. text ed. 5.95 (ISBN 0-8403-2185-6). Kendall-Hunt.

Bowman, George M. How to Succeed with Your Money. pap. 1.95 (ISBN 0-8024-3656-0). Moody.

Brake, J. R., ed. Farm & Personal Finance. LC 68-13437. (gr. 9-12). 1968. pap. 3.50 (ISBN 0-8134-0115-1, 115). Interstate.

Browne, Harry. New Profits from the Monetary Crisis. 1979. pap. 3.50 (ISBN 0-446-91351-0). Warner Bks.

Brownlow, Leroy. God's Plan for Financial Success. 1979. pap. 2.95 (ISBN 0-915720-49-3). Brownlow Pub Co.

Brownstone, David M. & Sartisky, Jacques. Financial Planning Guide for the 1980's & Beyond: Taking Your Future into Your Own Hands. LC 81-1796. 496p. 1981. 17.95 (ISBN 0-471-05588-3, Pub. by Wiley-Interscience). Wiley.

Broy, Anthony. Managing Your Money: How to Make the Most of Your Income & Have a Financially Secure Future. 1979. 8.95 (ISBN 0-531-09906-7). Watts.

Burton, Robert H. & Petrello, George J. Personal Finance. (Illus.). 1978. text ed. 19.95 (ISBN 0-02-317350-5). Macmillan.

Canario, Jack. Be Ad-Wise. (Money Matters). (Illus.). 64p. (gr. 7-12). 1981. pap. 3.10 (ISBN 0-915510-54-5). Janus Bks.

Cantelon, Willard. New Money or None. 1979. pap. 2.95 pocketsize (ISBN 0-88270-388-9). Logos.

Carrol, Frieda. How to Get Something for Almost Nothing & More. LC 78-59909. 52p. (Orig.). 1981. pap. text ed. 5.00 (ISBN 0-9605246-0-6). Biblio Pr GA.

--Prescriptions for Survival. LC 78-72312. 148p. 1981. pap. text ed. 14.95 (ISBN 0-9605246-1-4). Biblio Pr GA.

Casey, Douglas R. The International Man. rev. ed. LC 78-60333. 144p. 1981. 19.95 (ISBN 0-932496-09-1). Alexandria Hse.

Chan, Janis F. Pay by Check. (Money Matters). (Illus.). 64p. (gr. 7-12). 1981. pap. 3.10 (ISBN 0-915510-52-9). Janus Bks.

Changing Times Education Service Editors. Money Management. rev. ed. LC 81-7859. (Illus.). 1981. pap. text ed. 3.95 (ISBN 0-88436-810-6, CEA995051). EMC.

--Saving & Investing. rev. ed. LC 81-7860. (Illus.). 1981. pap. text ed. 4.45 (ISBN 0-88436-807-6, CEA994051). EMC.

Charell, Ralph. Great New Way to Make Money. 1979. 10.00 (ISBN 0-8128-1826-1); pap. 1.95 (ISBN 0-8128-7009-3). Stein & Day.

Cheeks, James. How Proper Planning Can Reduce Your Income Taxes. LC 73-16036. 1971. 2.00 (ISBN 0-87576-034-1). Pilot Bks.

Christenson, Larry. Larry Christenson's Financial Record System for Families & Individuals. 160p. (Orig.). 1980. spiral bdg. 4.95 (ISBN 0-87123-344-4, 210344). Bethany Hse.

Clark, Doug. How to Survive the Money Crash. LC 78-71426. 1979. pap. 1.95 (ISBN 0-89081-188-1). Harvest Hse.

Cobb, C. G. The Bad Times Primer: A Complete Guide to Survival on a Budget. LC 81-52089. (Illus.). 336p. (Orig.). 1981. pap. 14.95 (ISBN 0-9606608-0-1). Times Pr.

Cohen. Plaid for Personal Finance. 3rd ed. 1981. write for info. (ISBN 0-256-02126-0, 06-0117-03). Learning Syst.

Cohen, Jerome B. Personal Finance. 6th ed. 1979. 18.95x (ISBN 0-256-02154-6). Irwin.

Cohen, Jerome B. & Bingham, Harry H. Plaid for Personal Finance. 1975. pap. 4.95 (ISBN 0-256-01257-1, 06-0117-00). Learning Syst.

Coleman, B. D. Money: How to Save It, Spend It, & Make It. 1969. 22.00 (ISBN 0-08-012936-6); pap. text ed. 10.75 (ISBN 0-08-012935-8). Pergamon.

Crary, David T., et al. Personal Finance. 7th ed. LC 79-27578. 1980. text ed. 23.50 (ISBN 0-471-05639-1). study guide (ISBN 0-471-07919-7). Wiley.

Dann, D. Forms in Your Life. 1977. pap. 2.50 (ISBN 0-671-18771-6). Monarch Pr.

Davis, Ken & Taylor, Tom. Inflation, Taxes & Other Economic Mysteries. LC 79-25124. (Illus., Orig.). (gr. 6-10). 1980. pap. write for info. (ISBN 0-916392-46-5). Oak Tree Pubns.

De Flumiani, Carlo M. The Eternal Principles of Managerial Excellence for the Benefit of Businessmen: Corporate Executives, Junior Clerks, Housewives, Students, Politicians, Statesmen & Anyone Genuinely Interested in Improving His Station in Life. (Illus.). 1977. 39.75 (ISBN 0-89266-061-9). Am Classical Coll Pr.

Del Bueno, Dorothy. A Financial Guide for Nurses: Investing in Yourself & Others. (Illus.). 240p. 1981. text ed. 15.00 (ISBN 0-86542-007-6). Blackwell Sci.

De Salvo, Louis J. Consumer Finance. LC 76-46450. 1977. pap. text ed. 17.95 (ISBN 0-471-04391-5); tchr's manual avail. (ISBN 0-471-02418-X). Wiley.

Dorfman, John. Family Investment Guide. LC 81-66020. 1981. 10.95 (ISBN 0-689-11208-4). Atheneum.

Dunn, Thomas F. Financially Surviving the 1980's. (Illus.). 100p. spiral bdg. 14.95 (ISBN 0-686-31584-7). R&D Pubs.

Edelhart, Mike. Living on a Shoestring. LC 79-6535. (Illus.). 216p. 1980. pap. 5.95 (ISBN 0-385-15580-8, Anch). Doubleday.

Edmunds, Charles P. Essentials of Personal Finance. LC 78-26740. (Illus.). 1979. text ed. 16.95 (ISBN 0-87620-234-2); inst. manual avail. (ISBN 0-87620-237-7); study guide 8.50 (ISBN 0-87620-235-0). Goodyear.

Eiteman, Wilford J. Personal Finance & Investment. 1952. 3.25 (ISBN 0-685-79083-5). Masterco Pr.

Faulkner. More Money in Your Pocket. 2.50 (ISBN 0-448-06980-6). G&D.

Feldman, Frances L. The Family in Today's Money World. 2nd ed. 1976. 12.95 (ISBN 0-87304-130-5); pap. 7.00 (ISBN 0-87304-131-3). Family Serv.

Felix, Joseph. It's Easier for a Rich Man to Enter Heaven Than for a Poor Man to Remain on Earth. 1981. pap. 4.95 (ISBN 0-8407-5766-2). Nelson.

Finley, Lewis M. The Complete Guide to Getting Yourself Out of Debt. LC 75-12716. 1975. 9.95 (ISBN 0-8119-0251-X). Fell.

Flumiani, C. M. The Method. (Illus.). 1977. 37.75 (ISBN 0-89266-083-X). Am Classical Coll Pr.

Fooshee, George, Jr. You Can Be Financially Free. 1976. 5.95 (ISBN 0-8007-0790-7). Revell.

Freeman, M. Herbert & Graf, David K. Money Management: A Consumer's Guide to Savings, Spending, & Investing. 1980. pap. 14.95 (ISBN 0-672-97181-X); tchrs. manual 3.33 (ISBN 0-672-97182-8). Bobbs.

Frisch, Nathan. Your Income Tax Organizer. 1976. pap. 4.95 (ISBN 0-517-52748-0). Crown.

Gitman, Lawrence J. Personal Finance. 2nd ed. LC 80-65798. 672p. 1981. text ed. 20.95 (ISBN 0-03-058094-3). Dryden Pr.

Goldsmith, W. B., Jr. BASIC Programs for Home Financial Management. 250p. 1981. 17.95 (ISBN 0-13-066522-3); pap. 12.95 (ISBN 0-13-066514-2). P-H.

Greenwald, Carol S. Banks Are Dangerous to Your Wealth. LC 80-18176. 372p. 1980. 12.95 (ISBN 0-13-055806-0). P-H.

Greer, Rebecca. How to Live Rich When You're Not. 1977. pap. 1.75 (ISBN 0-345-25204-7). Ballantine.

Guide to Money, Power, & Politics. 1981. 8.00 (ISBN 0-686-31341-0). Common Cause.

Hadley, Ray G. Financial & Property Records for Your Successors. 1978. spiral bdg. 2.37 (ISBN 0-9600988-2-8). R G Hadley.

Hallman, G. V. & Rosenbloom, J. S. Personal Financial Planning: How to Plan for Your Financial Freedom. 2nd ed. (McGraw-Hill Paperback Ser.). 1981. pap. price not set (ISBN 0-07-025644-6). McGraw.

Hallman, G. Victor & Rosenbloom, Jerry. Personal Financial Planning. 2nd ed. (Illus.). 1978. 14.95 (ISBN 0-07-025641-1, P&RB). McGraw.

Harden, Linda B. & Harden, Gerald. The LTR Money Book: The Personal Finance Guide for Every Kind of Living Together Relationship. 1978. 9.95 (ISBN 0-89696-011-0). Everest Hse.

Hardy, C. Colburn. Your Money & Your Life: How to Plan Your Long-Range Financial Security. (Illus.). 1979. 15.95 (ISBN 0-8144-5529-8). Am Mgmt.

Hastings, Paul G. & Mietus, Norbert J. Personal Finance. 2nd ed. (Finance Ser.). 1977. text ed. 16.95 (ISBN 0-07-027013-9, C); instructor's manual 4.95 (ISBN 0-07-027014-7). McGraw.

Hefferling, Jonathan. Making Inflation Pay. (Illus.). 224p. 1980. 9.95 (ISBN 0-937554-00-6). Regency Pubs CA.

Heil, Paula. Financial Fitness. 128p. (Orig.). 1981. pap. 4.95 (ISBN 0-346-12543-X). Cornerstone.

Hembree, Ron. You & Your Money: A Guide from God's Word. (Orig.). 1981. pap. 4.95 (ISBN 0-8010-4252-6). Baker Bk.

Hempel, Marvin W. Record Keeping for Personal Finance: Syllabus. 1976. pap. text ed. 7.95 (ISBN 0-89420-005-4, 358080); cassette recordings 123.25 (ISBN 0-89420-181-6, 358000). Natl Book.

Holtje, Herbert & Stockwell, John. How to Borrow Everything You Need to Build a Great Personal Fortune. 1974. 9.95 (ISBN 0-13-396614-3). P-H.

Hover, Craig R. Beyond the Valley of the Dollar. (Illus.). 224p. Date not set. 10.95 (ISBN 0-89913-004-6). Entity Pub Co.

How to Manage Your Money. 80p. 1975. pap. 0.50 (ISBN 0-89982-044-1, 245700). Am Bankers.

Hudson, Margaret W. & Weaver, Ann A. Getting Ready for Pay Day, 3 bks. Incl. Bk. 1. Checking Accounts (ISBN 0-88323-028-3, 126); Bk. 2. Savings Accounts (ISBN 0-88323-029-1, 127); Bk. 3. Planning Ahead (ISBN 0-88323-030-5, 128). 1963. pap. 2.50x ea. Richards Pub.

Hurley, Gale E. Personal Money Management. 2nd ed. (Illus.). 528p. 1981. text ed. 18.95 (ISBN 0-13-657544-7). P-H.

Hutka, Ed F. Boom or Busted: Family Dollars & Sense. 1979. 2.95 (ISBN 0-88270-452-4). Logos.

Irving, Hancock. Money Begets Money: A Guide to Personal Finance. LC 75-28508. 1975. pap. 5.00 (ISBN 0-916202-02-X). Zimmerman.

Ivener, Martin H. & Rosefsky, Robert S. Telecourse Study Guide for Personal Finance & Money Management. 1978. pap. text ed. 10.50 (ISBN 0-471-03797-4); Set. 26.95 (ISBN 0-471-03796-6). Wiley.

James, Elizabeth & Barkin, Carol. Managing Your Money. LC 76-48287. (Money Ser.). (Illus.). (gr. 4-6). 1977. PLB 9.85 (ISBN 0-8172-0279-X). Raintree Pubs.

Janeway, Eliot. Money Sense. Date not set. cancelled (ISBN 0-671-24702-6). S&S.

Jenkins, Emyl. Why You're Richer Than You Think. (Illus.). 1981. 12.95 (ISBN 0-89256-186-6). Rawson Wade.

Johnstad, Jack & Johnstad, Lois. Attaining Financial Peace of Mind: A Practical Guide for the Thinking Person. LC 80-67104. (Illus.). 320p. 1980. pap. 8.95 (ISBN 0-937346-00-4). Bright Spirit.

Judd, Stanley H. Think Rich. 1980. pap. 2.50 (ISBN 0-440-18653-6). Dell.

Juroe, David J. Money: How to Spend Less & Have More. 1981. pap. 4.95 (ISBN 0-8007-5056-X). Revell.

Kaufman, Daniel. How to Get Out of Debt. 208p. (Orig.). 1981. pap. 7.95 (ISBN 0-523-74014-X). Pinnacle Bks.

--How to Get Out of Debt. LC 77-92522. 1978. pap. 7.95 (ISBN 0-89474-014-8). Corwin.

Kelly, Joan & Chamberlain, Valerie. Survival: A Guide to Living on Your Own. (Illus.). 1980. text ed. 12.36 (ISBN 0-07-033870-1, G); tchrs. ed. 3.64 (ISBN 0-07-033871-X). McGraw.

Kelsey & Gundlach. More for Your Money. (Money Matters). (Illus.). 64p. (gr. 7-12). 1981. pap. 3.10 (ISBN 0-915510-53-7). Janus Bks.

Kelsey, Lorne, et al. Eye to the Future. LC 72-96333. (Illus.). 1973. pap. 4.50x (ISBN 0-87076-317-2); tchr's. manual 2.50x (ISBN 0-87076-319-9). Stanwix.

Kennaway, James. The Cost of Living Like This. 200p. 1981. 30.00x (ISBN 0-906391-08-3, Pub. by Mainstream). State Mutual Bk.

Kimbrell, Grady & Vineyard, Ben S. Succeeding in the World of Work. rev. ed. (gr. 10-12). 1981. text ed. 15.32 (ISBN 0-87345-536-3); filmstrip set 330.00 (ISBN 0-686-31670-3). McKnight.

Klein, David & Klein, Marymae. More for Your Money: A Young Person's Guide to Earning, Saving & Spending. (Handbook Ser.). 1979. pap. 2.95 (ISBN 0-14-046400-X). Penguin.

Koertge, Ronald. How to Live on Five Dollars a Week. 1977. 5.50 (ISBN 0-912664-06-1); pap. 2.50 (ISBN 0-912664-07-X). VPC Pr.

Koller, Roland H., 2nd. The Nature of the Game. LC 79-56602. 128p. (Orig.). 1980. pap. 3.95 (ISBN 0-9603756-1-9). Aspen Pubns.

Lang, Larry. Strategy for Personal Finance. 2nd ed. 1981. text ed. 18.95 (ISBN 0-07-036281-5, C); instr's manual 20.00 (ISBN 0-07-036283-1); wkbk. 7.95 (ISBN 0-07-036282-3). McGraw.

Lang, Larry & Gillespie, Thomas. Strategy for Personal Finance. (Illus.). 1976. text ed. 16.00 (ISBN 0-07-036247-5, C); instructor's manual 5.95 (ISBN 0-07-036249-1); wkbk. 6.50 (ISBN 0-07-036248-3); transparency masters 4.95 (ISBN 0-07-074713-X). McGraw.

Lankford, Francis G., Jr. Consumer Mathematics. (gr. 9-12). 1981. text ed. 13.32 (ISBN 0-205-07190-2, 567906); tchr's guide 14.00 (ISBN 0-205-07191-0); wkbk. 5.12 (ISBN 0-205-07192-9). Allyn.

Lassen, Richard. Currency Management. 168p. 1980. 40.00x (ISBN 0-85941-154-0, Pub. by Woodhead-Faulkner England). State Mutual Bk.

Lee, Kaiman & Yang, Rita. Encyclopedia of Financial & Personal Survival: Six Hundred Fifty Coping Strategies. LC 80-130472. 1980. 210.00 (ISBN 0-915250-34-9). Environ Design.

Lee, Steven J. & Hassay, Karen A. Women's Handbook of Independent Financial Management. 1979. 12.95 (ISBN 0-442-26154-3). Van Nos Reinhold.

Levin, Martin. You May Be Losing Your Inheritance: A Guide to Legal Financial & Psychological Hazards & What You Can Do About Them Now. 1979. 9.95 (ISBN 0-686-65929-5). Times Bks.

Little, Royal. How to Lose One Hundred Million Dollars & Other Valuable Advice. LC 79-11628. (Illus.). 1979. 12.50 (ISBN 0-316-52786-6). Little.

Lumb, Fred A. What Every Woman Should Know About Finances. LC 77-93504. 1978. 8.95 (ISBN 0-87863-148-8). Farnswth Pub.

MacGregor, Malcolm. Financial Planning Guide for Your Money Matters. (Illus.). 240p. 1981. pap. 5.95 (ISBN 0-87123-166-2). Bethany Hse.

--Financial Planning Guide for Your Money Matters. LC 78-55443. (Illus.). 1978. spiral wkbk 5.95 (ISBN 0-87123-154-9, 210154). Bethany Hse.

MacGregor, Malcolm & Baldwin, Stanley C. Your Money Matters. LC 75-56123. 1977. pap. 3.95 (ISBN 0-87123-662-1, 210662). Bethany Hse.

Mackevich, Gene. The Woman's Money Book. 224p. 1981. pap. 2.95 (ISBN 0-553-14711-0). Bantam.

--The Woman's Money Book: A Simple, Successful Formula to Help You Profit from Investments, Increase Your Assets, Beat Inflation, Avoid Unnecessary Taxes. (Illus.). 1979. 14.95 (ISBN 0-87491-279-2); pap. 7.95 (ISBN 0-87491-284-9). Acropolis.

McKitrick, M. Financial Security. (Contemporary Consumer Ser.). 1974. text ed. 4.24 (ISBN 0-07-045315-2, G); tchr's. manual & key 4.95 (ISBN 0-07-045316-0). McGraw.

McLaughlin, Terence & McLaughlin, Eve. Cost-Effective Self-Sufficiency: Middle Class Peasant. 1978. 17.95 (ISBN 0-7153-7474-5). David & Charles.

McNeil, Edward A. Out of the Money Trap. LC 76-56539. 1977. pap. 9.95 (ISBN 0-918324-00-9). Allison Ent.

Mathies, F. The Ultimate Inflation Shelter. 1980. 25.00 (ISBN 0-686-58614-X). Windsor.

Meyer, Martin J. Don't Bank on It. 240p. pap. 2.50 (ISBN 0-671-41606-5). PB.

Meyer, Martin J. & Hunter, Mark. How to Turn Plastic into Gold. LC 74-76493. 1974. 6.95 (ISBN 0-87863-076-7). Farnswth Pub.

Meyers, Jerome I. Wipe Out Your Debts & Make a Fresh Start. pap. 3.95 (ISBN 0-440-19067-3, 9067-01, Delta). Dell.

Miller, Roger L. Personal Finance Today. (Illus.). 1979. text ed. 19.50 (ISBN 0-8299-0233-3); pap. study guide & wkbk. by Grant J. Wells 7.95 (ISBN 0-8299-0256-2); instrs.' manual avail. (ISBN 0-8299-0561-8). West Pub.

Milliron, Robert R. How to Do Your Own Accounting for a Small Business. LC 79-53800. 200p. 1980. 9.95 (ISBN 0-913864-34-X); with practice man. 14.95 (ISBN 0-686-65977-5). Enterprise Del.

Milton, Arthur. You Are Worth a Fortune. 1977. 6.95 (ISBN 0-8065-0589-3). Citadel Pr.

Minkow, Rosalie. Money Management for Women. LC 80-84373. 256p. (Orig.). 1981. pap. 2.50 (ISBN 0-87216-816-6). Playboy Pbks.

Money Made Mysterious. 3.00 (ISBN 0-686-24166-5). Liberty Lobby.

Mooney, Thomas. The Getting Along Series of Skills, 5 vols. Incl. Vol. I. After School Is Out. 1963 (ISBN 0-88323-021-6, 121); Vol. II. Al Looks for a Job. 1964 (ISBN 0-88323-022-4, 122); Vol. III. A Job at Last. 1964 (ISBN 0-88323-023-2, 123); Vol. IV. Money in the Pocket. 1965 (ISBN 0-88323-024-0, 124); Vol. V. From Tires to Teeth. 1965 (ISBN 0-88323-025-9, 125). wkbk. 2.50x ea. Richards Pub.

Mumford, Amy R. It Only Hurts Between Paydays. 2nd ed. 160p. 1981. pap. 2.25 (ISBN 0-89636-067-9). Accent Bks.

Neave, Edwin H. & Wiginton, John C. Financial Management: Theory & Strategies. (Illus.). 416p. 1981. text ed. 21.95 (ISBN 0-13-316109-9). P-H.

Neilson, Stefan F. Color Me Rich, Color Me Wealthy. Wigington, Ralph, tr. (Illus.). 168p. (Orig.). (YA) (gr. 10). 1981. pap. text ed. 10.00 (ISBN 0-9606110-0-2). AEON-Hierophant.

Nelson, Paula. The Joy of Money. 1977. pap. 2.95 (ISBN 0-553-20451-3). Bantam.

--The Joy of Money: A Contemporary Woman's Guide to Financial Freedom. LC 75-9847. 248p. 1975. 7.95 (ISBN 0-8128-1816-4). Stein & Day.

Nelson, Roger H. Personal Money Management: An Objectives & Systems Approach. LC 77-190163. 1973. text ed. 16.95 (ISBN 0-201-05255-5). A-W.

Newcomb, Duane. The Poor Man's Road to Riches. 1976. 9.95 (ISBN 0-13-686717-0). P-H.

Newcomb, Duane G. Spare-Time Fortune Guide. 1976. pap. 9.95 (ISBN 0-13-824185-6, Reward). P-H.

Nicholas, Ted. Income Portfolio. new, rev. ed. 1981. 9.95 (ISBN 0-913864-25-0). Enterprise Del.

--Increase Your Take-Home Pay up to Forty Percent: How to Turn Your Job into Your Own Corporation. LC 79-57023. Orig. Title: Income Portfolio. 1980. pap. 4.95 (ISBN 0-913864-44-7). Enterprise Del.

Officer's Manual of Personal Finance & Insurance. rev 3rd ed. LC 79-140746. (Illus.). 320p. 1979. pap. 11.95 (ISBN 0-8117-1154-4). Stackpole.

Oppenheim, Irene. Consumer Skills. 1977. 13.28 (ISBN 0-87002-184-2); tchr's guide 5.00 (ISBN 0-87002-186-9); student guide 4.40 (ISBN 0-87002-267-9). Bennett IL.

Otte, Elmer. Inherit Your Own Money. LC 78-13201. 169p. 1979. 9.95 (ISBN 0-679-51100-8); pap. 6.95 (ISBN 0-679-51101-6). Retirement Res.

Pasadena Art Alliance. To Talk of Many Things. 1977. pap. 4.95 (ISBN 0-937042-01-3). Pasadena Art.

Penson, John B., Jr., et al. Personal Finance. (Illus.). 480p. 1982. 18.95 (ISBN 0-13-657320-7). P-H.

Perkins, Gail & Rhoades, Judith. Women's Financial Survival Handbook. (Orig.). 1980. pap. 5.95 (ISBN 0-452-25231-8, Z5231, Plume). NAL.

Personal Financial Statements. (Industry Audit Guides). 1968. pap. 4.00 (ISBN 0-685-58484-4). Am Inst CPA.

Phalon, Richard. Your Money. (Illus.). 320p. 1981. 5.95 (ISBN 0-312-89823-1). St Martin.

--Your Money How to Make It Work Harder for You. LC 78-21363. 1979. 8.95 (ISBN 0-312-89822-3). St Martin.

Phillips, E. B. & Lane, S. Personal Finance: Text & Case Problems. 4th ed. 620p. 1980. 23.95 (ISBN 0-471-02580-1). Wiley.

Phillips, E. Bryant & Lane, Sylvia, eds. How to Manage Your Personal Finances: A Short Course for Professionals. (Professional Development Programs Ser.). 1978. text ed. 24.95 (ISBN 0-471-02316-7). Wiley.

Piltch, Benjamin & Smergut, Peter. Money Matters. 64p. (gr. 7-12). 1981. wkbk. 4.00 (ISBN 0-934618-03-8). SkyView Pub.

Porter, Sylvia. Sylvia Porter's New Money Book. LC 76-20275. 1979. 24.95 (ISBN 0-385-12612-3). Doubleday.

--Sylvia Porter's New Money Book for the 80's. 1328p. 1980. pap. 9.95 (ISBN 0-380-51060-X, 51060). Avon.

Prosser, David R. The Romance of Money: How to Make It, How to Invest It, How to Accumulate It. (Illus.). 1979. deluxe ed. 33.45 (ISBN 0-918968-27-5). Inst Econ Finan.

Pulvino, Charles J. & Lee, James L. Financial Counseling: Interviewing Skills. 1979. pap. text ed. 8.95 (ISBN 0-8403-2046-9, 40204602). Kendall-Hunt.

Purgraski, Carolyn B., et al. Sorting Out Money Values & Student Packet of Ready-to-Be-Duplicated Worksheets. rev. ed. LC 59-4503. (Sorting Life Out Ser.). 292p. 1981. tchr's. ed. 25.00 (ISBN 0-930004-02-7); student packet, 68p. free. C E M Comp.

Quinn, Jane B. Everyone's Money Book. 1980. pap. 9.95 (ISBN 0-440-55725-9, Dell Trade Pbks). Dell.

--Everyone's Money Book. 1979. 14.95 (ISBN 0-440-05725-6). Delacorte.

Quirin, G. David & Wiginton, John C. Analyzing Capital Expenditures: Private & Public Perspectives. 1981. 22.00x (ISBN 0-256-00460-9). Irwin.

Rachlin, Robert. Return on Investment: Strategies for Profit. LC 75-44668. 1976. 14.95 (ISBN 0-938712-00-4). Marr Pubns.

Rathbone, David. How to Keep the Money You Owe: One Hundred One Legal Ways to Confound Your Creditors. (Illus.). 70p. (Orig.). 1981. pap. 10.00 (ISBN 0-686-29043-7). Phoenix Laguna.

Reynolds, Bruford S. Becoming Self Sufficient with Dollars & Sense. new ed. 1977. pap. 3.95 (ISBN 0-89036-070-7). Hawkes Pub Inc.

Rhodabarger. Personal Money Management for Physicians. rev. ed. (Medical Economics Books). 1973. 16.50 (ISBN 0-442-84016-0). Van Nos Reinhold.

Rifenbark, Richard K. How to Beat the Salary Trap. 1979. pap. 2.50 (ISBN 0-380-43737-6, 43737). Avon.

Rifenbark, Richard K. & Johnson, D. How to Beat the Salary Trap: Eight Steps to Financial Independence. 1978. 9.95 (ISBN 0-07-052810-1, GB). McGraw.

Rinaldi, John F. The Art & Science of Wall Street Scalping for the Gaining of Superlative Profits. 1980. 45.50 (ISBN 0-918968-50-X). Inst Econ Finan.

Rogers, Mary & Joyce, Nancy. Women & Money. 1979. pap. 2.25 (ISBN 0-380-46003-3, 46003). Avon.

--Women & Money. (Illus.). 1978. 8.95 (ISBN 0-07-053495-0, GB). McGraw.

Rosefsky, Robert S. Personal Finance & Money Management. LC 77-20283. 1978. text ed. 17.95 (ISBN 0-471-01740-X); study guide by M. H. Ivener avail. Wiley.

Rosenberg, R. Robert & Naples, Ralph V. Outline of Personal Finance. (Schaum's Outline Ser.). (Orig.). 1976. pap. 3.95 (ISBN 0-07-053834-4, SP). McGraw.

Ruff, Howard J. How to Prosper During the Coming Bad Years. rev. ed. 1981. pap. 3.50 (ISBN 0-446-96952-4). Warner Bks.

--How to Prosper During the Coming Bad Years. LC 78-13919. 1979. 8.95 (ISBN 0-8129-0804-X). Times Bks.

Ruthberg, Sidney. Playboy's Investment & Financial Planning Guide for Singles. LC 81-80402. 288p. 1981. 12.95 (ISBN 0-87223-701-X). Seaview Bks.

Salisbury, David F. Money Matters: Personal Financial Decision-Making with a Pocket Calculator. 288p. 1981. 13.95 (ISBN 0-13-600528-4); pap. 6.95 (ISBN 0-13-600510-1). P-H.

Schultz, Harry D. Panics & Crashes: How You Can Make Money from Them. rev. ed. 256p. 1980. 12.95 (ISBN 0-87000-491-3). Arlington Hse.

Scott, Carole E. Your Financial Plan: A Consumer's Guide. 1979. text ed. 20.95 scp (ISBN 0-06-045844-5, HarpC); inst. manual avail. (ISBN 0-06-365968-9). Har-Row.

Sheagren, John N. Financial Advice for Physicians. 132p. 1972. text ed. 11.75 (ISBN 0-398-02409-X). C C Thomas.

Simons, Gustave & Simons, Alice. Money & Women. 1979. pap. 2.75 (ISBN 0-445-04394-6). Popular Lib.

Skousen, Mark. High Finance on a Low Budget. 1981. pap. 2.95 (ISBN 0-686-73197-2). Bantam.

--Mark Skousen's Complete Guide to Financial Privacy. rev. ed. 233p. 1980. 19.95 (ISBN 0-932496-07-5). Alexandria Hse.

Smith, Adam. Supermoney. 288p. 1973. pap. 2.95 (ISBN 0-445-08236-4). Popular Lib.

Smith, Thurman L. The Lazy Investor's Way to Beat Inflation. (Illus.). 1979. pap. 5.95 (ISBN 0-934410-00-3). Explorer Pub Co.

Spiro, Herbert T. Financial Planning for the Independent Professional. LC 78-18179. 1978. 27.95 (ISBN 0-471-03111-9, Pub. by Wiley-Interscience). Wiley.

Stark, Richard, ed. How to Be Rich & Grow Richer. (Illus.). 120p. 1974. 39.15 (ISBN 0-913314-41-2). Am Classical Coll Pr.

Sterne, George & Oesterie, John. Dynamics of Personal Money Management. Von Hoelscher, Russ, ed. 216p. 1981. 19.95 (ISBN 0-940398-03-6). Profit Ideas.

Stillman, Richard. Personal Finance Guide & Workbook: A Managerial Approach to Successful Household Record Keeping. LC 76-51767. 1977. pap. 8.95x (ISBN 0-88289-148-0). Pelican.

Stillman, Richard J. More for Your Money! Personal Finance Techniques to Cope with Inflation & the Energy Shortage. (Illus.). 288p. 1980. 13.95 (ISBN 0-13-601005-9, Spec); pap. 6.95 (ISBN 0-13-600999-9). P-H.

--Your Personal Financial Planner. (Illus.). 176p. 1980. 15.95 (ISBN 0-13-980516-8, Spec); pap. 7.95 (ISBN 0-13-980508-7). P-H.

Summers, D. B. Personal Management in Banking. 1981. 39.95 (ISBN 0-07-062558-1). McGraw.

Sutton, Robert M. What You Should Know to Make Money from Your Investments. 1979. 10.00 (ISBN 0-682-49206-X, Banner). Exposition.

Swaton, J. Norman. Personal Finance: Getting Along & Getting Ahead. 1980. text ed. 15.95 (ISBN 0-442-28116-1); instr's. manual 3.95 (ISBN 0-442-26236-1). D Van Nostrand.

Taggart, Leo J. Your Personal Financial I.Q. Test. (Essential Knowledge Library). 1979. spiral bdg. 8.00 (ISBN 0-89266-171-2). Am Classical Coll Pr.

Teague, Burton W. Financial Planning for Executives. (Report Ser: No. 608). 36p. (Orig.). 1973. pap. 5.00 (ISBN 0-8237-0023-2). Conference Bd.

--Financial Planning for Executives. (Report Ser: No. 608). 36p. (Orig.). 1973. pap. 5.00 (ISBN 0-8237-0023-2). Conference Bd.

Thal, Helen M. Your Family & Its Money. (gr. 9-12). 1973. text ed. 13.28 (ISBN 0-395-14225-3). HM.

Thomason, James C. Common Sense About Your Family Dollars. 1979. pap. 3.95 (ISBN 0-88207-636-1). Victor Bks.

Thypin, Marilyn & Glasner, Lynne. Checking & Balancing (Banking) LC 79-9527. (Consumer Education Ser.: No. 2). (Orig.). (gr. 9-12). 1980. pap. text ed. 3.50 (ISBN 0-88436-511-5). EMC.

Tobias, Andrew. Getting by on One Hundred Thousand a Year. 1981. pap. 3.50 (ISBN 0-671-43351-2). WSP.

--Getting by on One Hundred Thousand Dollars a Year & Other Sad Tales. 1980. 10.95 (ISBN 0-671-25518-5). S&S.

Troelstrup, Archibald & Hall, E. Carl. The Consumer in American Society: Personal & Family Finance. 6th ed. (Illus.). 1978. text ed. 17.50 (ISBN 0-07-065215-5, C); instructor's manual 4.95 (ISBN 0-07-065216-3); study guide 6.50 (ISBN 0-07-065219-8). McGraw.

Trubo, Richard. The Consumer Book of Hints & Tips. LC 76-26125. (Illus.). 1978. 12.50 (ISBN 0-8246-0212-9). Jonathan David.

Tuccille, Jerome. The Optimist's Guide to Making Money in the 1980's. LC 78-14771. 1978. 7.95 (ISBN 0-688-03387-3); pap. 4.95 (ISBN 0-688-08387-0). Morrow.

Tucker, Gilbert M. Your Money & What to Do With It. 1960. 4.50 (ISBN 0-8159-7401-9). Devin.

Twenty-Five Ways to Make & Save Money. 1980. 2.00 (ISBN 0-686-30853-0). Deal Pubns.

Ulbrich, Holley H. & Yandle, Bruce. Managing Personal Finance. 1979. 15.50x (ISBN 0-256-02208-9). Business Pubns.

Ungaro, Susan. The H & R Block Family Budget Workbook. (H & R Block Ser.). 160p. 1980. pap. 4.95 (ISBN 0-02-007320-8, Collier). Macmillan.

United Business Services, ed. Successful Investing. 1979. 14.95 (ISBN 0-671-24604-6). S&S.

University Of California Heller Committee For Research In Social Economics. Cost of Living Studies, No. 5, How Mexicans Earn & Live. 1933. pap. 6.00 (ISBN 0-685-13463-6). Johnson Repr.

Volkerling, Michael. Food for Flatters: Or How to Close the Edibility Gap. LC 72-93096. 112p. 1973. pap. 3.75 (ISBN 0-589-00755-6, Pub. by Reed Books Australia). C E Tuttle.

Vreeland, R. Become Financially Independent: An Investment Plan That Really Works. 1979. 11.95 (ISBN 0-13-073635-X, Spec); pap. 4.95 (ISBN 0-13-073627-9, Spec). P-H.

Watkins, Art. Dollars & Sense: A Guide to Mastering Your Money. LC 72-90468. 288p. 1973. 7.95 (ISBN 0-8129-0335-8). Times Bks.

Watson, Walter A. Master Plan for Financial Security. 1966. pap. 3.95 deluxe ed. (ISBN 0-685-21860-0). Watson Pub.

Weinstein, Grace W. Money of Your Own. (gr. 5-9). 1977. 7.50 (ISBN 0-525-35145-0). Dutton.

Weiss, Martin D. The Great Money Panic: A Guide for Survival & Action. (Illus.). 256p. 1981. 15.95 (ISBN 0-87000-502-2). Arlington Hse.

West, David & Wood, Glenn. Personal Financial Management. LC 75-172124. 80p. (Orig.). 1972. text ed. 18.95 (ISBN 0-395-12428-X, 3-59690); tchr's. manual. pap. 1.75 (ISBN 0-395-13495-1, 3-59691). HM.

Williams, Larry R. How to Prosper in the Coming Good Times. 1981. 10.95 (ISBN 0-89526-667-9). Regnery Gateway.

Wilson, Rachel. Master Your Money. (Money Matters). (Illus.). 64p. (gr. 7-12). 1981. pap. 3.10 (ISBN 0-915510-51-0). Janus Bks.

Wingert, Norman A. To Have Is to Owe. 185p. (YA) pap. 4.95 (ISBN 0-937594-00-8). Bunkhouse.
Winston, R. Working Your Way Through College. 1979. pap. 7.95 (ISBN 0-930204-04-2). Lord Pub.
Wolf, Harold. Personal Finance. 6th ed. 700p. 1981. 20.95 (ISBN 0-205-07298-4, 1072986); tchr's ed. free (ISBN 0-205-07299-2, 1072994). Allyn.
Yohn, Rick. God's Answers to Financial Problems: A Study Manual. LC 77-94132. 1978. pap. 2.95 (ISBN 0-89081-129-6, 1296). Harvest Hse.
Zimmerman, Gary. Managing Your Own Money: A Self-Teaching Guide. LC 80-12294. (Wiley Self-Teaching Guide Ser.). 224p. 1980. pap. text ed. 7.95 (ISBN 0-471-05226-4). Wiley.
Zwart, David L. Dollar Sense for Todays Woman. (224). 1976. pap. 3.95 (ISBN 0-917904-00-1). DaCa Pub.

FINANCE, PRIMITIVE
see Economics, Primitive

FINANCE, PUBLIC
see also Bonds; Budget; Claims; Currency Question; Customs Administration; Debts, Public; Deficit Financing; Expenditures, Public; Fiscal Policy; Government Lending; Government Spending Policy; Grants-In-Aid; Intergovernmental Fiscal Relations; Loans; Local Finance; Metropolitan Finance; Money; Municipal Finance; Paper Money; Repudiation; Revenue; Sinking-Funds; Tariff; Taxation; Taxation, State; also subdivision Finance under special subjects, e.g. Education–Finance; World War, 1939-1945–Finance
Adams, Henry C. Public Debts: An Essay in the Science of Finance. facsimile ed. LC 75-2619. (Wall Street & the Security Market Ser.). 1975. Repr. of 1898 ed. 25.00x (ISBN 0-405-06946-4). Arno.
Atkinson, Anthony & Stiglitz, Joseph. Lectures on Public Economies. (McGraw-Hill Economics Handbook Ser.). 640p. 1980. text ed. 21.95 (ISBN 0-07-002460-X). McGraw.
Bahl, Roy W. & Burkhead, Jesse, eds. Public Employment & State & Local Government Finance. 264p. 1980. reference 27.50 (ISBN 0-88410-683-7). Ballinger Pub.
Bartlett, Randall. Economic Foundations of Political Power. LC 73-3899. 1973. 12.95 (ISBN 0-02-901870-6). Free Pr.
Beccaria, Cesare B. Discourse on Public Economy & Commerce. LC 73-80244. 1970. Repr. of 1769 ed. lib. bdg. 18.50 (ISBN 0-8337-0211-4). B Franklin.
Bennett, R. J. Geography of Public Finance: Welfare Under Fiscal Federalism & Local Government Finance. 1980. 39.95x (ISBN 0-416-73090-6). Methuen Inc.
Blinder, Alan S., et al. The Economics of Public Finance. (Studies of Government Finance). 14.95 (ISBN 0-8157-0998-6); pap. 6.95 (ISBN 0-8157-0997-8). Brookings.
Boes, D. Economic Theory of Public Enterprise. (Lecture Notes in Economics & Mathematical Systems Ser.: Vol. 188). (Illus.). 142p. 1981. pap. 12.00 (ISBN 0-387-10567-0). Springer-Verlag.
Breton, Albert. The Economic Theory of Representative Government. LC 73-75704. (Treatises in Modern Economics). 232p. 1974. text ed. 12.95x (ISBN 0-202-06064-0). Beresford Bk Serv.
Browning, Edgar K. & Browning, Jacquelene M. Public Finance & the Price System. 1979. text ed. 21.95 (ISBN 0-02-315650-3). Macmillan.
Buchanan, James M. Public Finance in the Democratic Process. 1967. 19.50x (ISBN 0-8078-1014-2). U of NC Pr.
Buchanan, James M. & Flowers, Marilyn R. The Public Finances: An Introductory Textbook. 5th ed. 1980. 19.95x (ISBN 0-256-02333-6). Irwin.
Coe, Charles K. Maximizing Revenue: Minimizing Expenditure. 76p. (Orig.). 1981. pap. 7.50 (ISBN 0-89854-070-4). U of GA Inst Govt.
Crecine, John P., ed. Financing the Metropolis: Public Policy in Urban Economies. LC 72-103479. (Urban Affairs Annual Reviews: Vol. 4). 632p. 1970. 25.00 (ISBN 0-8039-0008-2); pap. 9.95 (ISBN 0-8039-0353-7). Sage.
Dalton, Hugh. Principles of Public Finance. 4th ed. LC 67-27788. 1954. Repr. 12.50x (ISBN 0-678-06512-8). Kelley.
David, Wilfred L., ed. Public Finance, Planning & Economic Development: Essays in Honor of Ursula Hicks. LC 73-77734. (Illus.). 349p. 1973. 28.50x (ISBN 0-8290-0201-4). Irvington.
--Public Finance, Planning & Economic Development: Essays in Honour of Ursula Hicks. 19.95 (ISBN 0-685-58433-X, Pub by St Martins Pr). Cyrco Pr.
Due, John F. Goverment Finance: Economics of the Public Sector. 7th ed. Friedlaender, Ann F., ed. 1981. 20.00 (ISBN 0-256-02492-8). Irwin.
Ecker-Racz, L. L. Politics & Economics of State & Local Finance. (Finance Ser.). 1970. pap. text ed. 9.95 (ISBN 0-13-686048-6). P-H.
Escarraz, Donald R. Price Theory of Value in Public Finance. LC 66-64915. (U of Fla. Social Sciences Monographs: No. 32). 1966. pap. 3.00 (ISBN 0-8130-0075-0). U Presses Fla.
Ferguson, E. James. Power of the Purse: A History of American Public Finance 1776-1790. (Institute of Early American History & Culture Ser.). 1961. Repr. of 1961 ed. 24.50x (ISBN 0-8078-0804-0). U of NC Pr.
Fromm, Gary & Taubman, Paul. Public Economic Theory & Policy. (Illus.). 384p. 1973. text ed. 16.95 (ISBN 0-02-339890-6). Macmillan.
Golembiewski, Robert T. & Rabin, Jack, eds. Public Budgeting & Finance: Readings in Theory & Practice. 2nd ed. LC 73-85768. (Illus.). 515p. 1975. text ed. 17.95 (ISBN 0-87581-162-0). Peacock Pubs.
Gouge, William M. Fiscal History of Texas. LC 68-18226. Repr. of 1852 ed. 17.50x (ISBN 0-678-00364-5). Kelley.
Harberger, Arnold C. Taxation & Welfare. LC 77-99171. (Midway Reprint Ser.). 1978. pap. text ed. 10.00x (ISBN 0-226-31595-9). U of Chicago Pr.
Harris, Seymour E. Economics of Social Security. Repr. of 1941 ed. lib. bdg. 19.50x (ISBN 0-8371-3685-7, HAES). Greenwood.
Haveman, Robert H. The Economics of the Public Sector. 2nd ed. LC 76-186. (Introduction to Economics Ser). 224p. 1976. text ed. 9.95x (ISBN 0-471-36182-8, Pub. by Wiley-Hamilton). Wiley.
Henning, Charles N., et al. Financial Markets & the Economy. 3rd ed. (Illus.). 608p. 1981. text ed. 21.00 (ISBN 0-13-316067-X). P-H.
Herber, Bernard P. Modern Public Finance. 4th ed. 1979. 19.50x (ISBN 0-256-02159-7). Irwin.
Hirsch, Werner Z. Economics of State & Local Governments. 1970. text ed. 17.95 (ISBN 0-07-029042-3, C). McGraw.
Howe, Irving. Beyond the Welfare State. 288p. 1982. 17.95 (ISBN 0-8052-3787-9). Schocken.
Huse, Charles P. Financial History of Boston from May 1, 1822 to January 31, 1909. LC 66-27106. 1967. Repr. of 1916 ed. 10.00 (ISBN 0-8462-0940-3). Russell.
Hyman, D. Economics of Governmental Activity. LC 72-80260. 1973. text ed. 13.95 (ISBN 0-03-085617-5, HoltC). HR&W.
International Monetary Fund. Government Finance Statistics Yearbook, 3 vols. Vol. I, 1977. pap. 10.00 (ISBN 0-686-23213-5); Vol. II, 1978. pap. 10.00 (ISBN 0-686-28636-7); Vol. III, 1979. pap. 10.00 (ISBN 0-686-28637-5). Intl Monetary.
Kearny, John W. Sketch of American Finances: 1789-1835. LC 68-28636. 1968. Repr. of 1887 ed. lib. bdg. 15.00x (ISBN 0-8371-0125-5, KESA). Greenwood.
Leaper, R. A., ed. Health, Wealth & Housing. (Aspects of Social Policy Ser.). 224p. 1980. 28.50x (ISBN 0-631-10391-0, Pub. by Basil Blackwell England); pap. 10.95x (ISBN 0-631-12241-9, Pub. by Basil Blackwell England). Biblio Dist.
Levine, Charles H., et al. The Politics of Betrenchment: How Localities Manage Fiscal Stress. (Sage Library of Social Research: Vol. 130). 250p. 1981. 20.00 (ISBN 0-8039-1688-4); pap. 9.95 (ISBN 0-8039-1689-2). Sage.
Lewis, Wilfred, Jr. Federal Fiscal Policy in the Postwar Recessions. (Studies of Government Finance). 311p. 1962. 9.95 (ISBN 0-8157-5242-3). Brookings.
Lyden, Fremont J. & Miller, Ernest G. Public Budgeting: Program Planning & Implementation. 4th ed. (Illus.). 384p. 1982. 13.95 (ISBN 0-13-737403-8). P-H.
Mandelker, Daniel R., et al. Reviving Cities with Tax Abatement. LC 79-92785. 160p. (Orig.). 1980. pap. text ed. 12.95 (ISBN 0-88285-065-2). Ctr Urban Pol Res.
Meyer, John R. & Quigley, John M., eds. Local Public Finance & the Fiscal Squeeze: A Case Study. LC 76-15619. 1977. 19.50 (ISBN 0-88410-287-4). Ballinger Pub.
Misra, B. Economics of Public Finance. 2nd ed. 1981. 9.00x (ISBN 0-8364-0718-0, Pub. by Macmillan India). South Asia Bks.
--Economics of Public Finance. 1978. 8.50x (ISBN 0-8364-0310-X). South Asia Bks.
Musgrave, Richard & Musgrave, Peggy. Public Finance in Theory & Practice. 3rd ed. (Illus.). 1980. text ed. 22.50 (ISBN 0-07-044122-7). McGraw.
Musgrave, Richard A. The Theory of Public Finance: A Study in Public Economy. 646p. 1981. Repr. of 1959 ed. lib. bdg. 32.50 (ISBN 0-89874-110-6). Krieger.
Musgrave, Richard A. & Musgrave, Peggy B. Public Finance in Theory & Practice. 2nd ed. (Illus.). 832p. 1975. text ed. 19.95 (ISBN 0-07-044121-9, C). McGraw.
Nanjundappa, D. M. Studies in Public Finance. 320p. 1976. pap. 10.75x (ISBN 0-210-22265-4). Asia.
Newcomb, Simon. Critical Examination of Our Financial Policy During the Southern Rebellion. Repr. of 1865 ed. lib. bdg. 15.00 (ISBN 0-8371-0589-7, NEFP). Greenwood.
Pandey, I. M. & Lele, R. K. Financial Management. (Illus.). 1979. text ed. 20.00 (ISBN 0-7069-0703-5, Pub. by Vikas India). Advent NY.
Petersen, John E. & Spain, Catherine L., eds. Essays in Public Finance & Financial Management: State & Local Perspectives. LC 79-24847. 1980. pap. text ed. 9.95x (ISBN 0-934540-03-9). Chatham Hse Pubs.
Pigou, Arthur C. Study in Public Finance. 3rd rev. ed. Repr. of 1947 ed. lib. bdg. 15.00x (ISBN 0-678-07009-1). Kelley.
Pogue, Thomas F. & Sgontz, Larry G. Government & Economic Choice: An Introduction to Public Finance. LC 77-75157. (Illus.). 1978. text ed. 18.95 (ISBN 0-395-25112-5). HM.
Prest, A. R. & Barr, N. A. Public Finance: In Theory & Practice. (Illus.). 568p. 1979. 37.50x (ISBN 0-297-77648-7, Pub. by Weidenfeld & Nicolson England). Biblio Dist.
Ravenstone, Piercy. Thoughts on the Funding System & Its Effects. LC 66-28961. Repr. of 1824 ed. 9.50x (ISBN 0-678-00192-8). Kelley.
Reid, Charles, 3rd. Guide to Residential Financing. Mascari, Claude J., et al, eds. LC 79-92645. 225p. 1979. pap. text ed. cancelled (ISBN 0-9603790-1-0). Rouse & Co.
Rolph, Earl R. The Theory of Fiscal Economics. (California Library Reprint Series: No. 21). 1971. 24.00x (ISBN 0-520-01926-1). U of Cal Pr.
--Theory of Fiscal Economics. LC 76-156206. (Illus.). 1971. Repr. of 1954 ed. lib. bdg. 17.00x (ISBN 0-8371-6156-8, ROFE). Greenwood.
Sandmo, Agnar, ed. Essays in Public Economics. LC 77-7. 1978. 31.95 (ISBN 0-669-01424-9). Lexington Bks.
Seligman, Edwin R. Studies in Public Finance. LC 68-58013. Repr. of 1925 ed. 17.50x (ISBN 0-678-00490-0). Kelley.
Sharp, Ansel M. & Olson, Kent W. Public Finance: The Economics of Government Revenues & Expenditures. (Illus.). 1978. text ed. 17.50 (ISBN 0-8299-0172-8). West Pub.
Shoup, Carl S. Public Finance. LC 69-11227. 652p. 1981. text ed. 39.50x (ISBN 0-932400-02-7). Intervale Pub Co.
Siddiqui, S. A. Public Finance in Islam. 3.95 (ISBN 0-686-18375-4). Kazi Pubns.
Smith, W. L. & Culbertson, J. M., eds. Public Finance & Stabilization Policy. 1974. 53.75 (ISBN 0-444-10682-0, North-Holland). Elsevier.
Tresch, Richard W. Public Finance: A Normative Theory. 1981. text ed. 23.95x (ISBN 0-256-02391-3). Business Pubns.
Turnbull, A. B. Government Budgeting & PPBS: A Programmed Introduction. 1970. pap. 12.95 (ISBN 0-201-07615-2). A-W.
Wheaton, William C., ed. Interregional Movements & Regional Growth. (Papers on Public Economics Ser.: Vol. 2). 253p. (Orig.). 1980. pap. 10.00 (ISBN 0-87766-257-6, 26600). Urban Inst.
Wippern, Ronald F. Cases in Modern Financial Management: Public & Private Sector Perspectives. 1980. 18.95x (ISBN 0-256-02363-8). Irwin.

FINANCE, PUBLIC–ACCOUNTING
see also Tax Accounting
Abraham, Stanley C. The Public Accounting Profession. LC 77-7804. (Illus.). 1978. 19.95 (ISBN 0-669-01606-3). Lexington Bks.
Causey, Denzil Y. Duties & Liabilities of Public Accountants. LC 78-74884. (Illus.). 1979. 19.95 (ISBN 0-87094-185-2). Dow Jones-Irwin.
Crane, Edgar G., Jr. Legislative Review of Government Programs: Tools for Accountability. LC 76-12846. (Special Studies). 1977. text ed. 29.95 (ISBN 0-275-23720-6). Praeger.
Dittenhofer, Mortimer A., ed. Concepts of Government Auditing: A Book of Readings from the Internal Auditor. 1977. pap. text ed. 8.00 (ISBN 0-89413-059-5). Inst Inter Aud.
Funke, Gail S., et al. Assets & Liabilities of Correctional Industries. LC 81-47029. 1981. price not set (ISBN 0-669-04542-X). Lexington Bks.
Geist, Benjamin, ed. State Audit. LC 80-21772. 482p. 1981. 60.00x (ISBN 0-8419-0674-2). Holmes & Meier.
Hay & Engstrom. Plaid for Accounting for Governmental & Nonprofit Entities. 1981. 8.95 (ISBN 0-256-02567-3, 01-1454-01). Learning Syst.
Hay, Leon E. Accounting for Government & Nonprofit Entities. 6th ed. 1980. 23.95x (ISBN 0-256-02329-8). Irwin.
Kerrigan, H. D. Fund Accounting. LC 68-30975. (Accounting Ser.). (Illus.). 1968. text ed. 18.95 (ISBN 0-07-034214-8, C); instructor's manual 10.95 (ISBN 0-07-034212-1); assignment manual 6.95 (ISBN 0-07-034213-X). McGraw.
Lynn, Edward S. & Freeman, Robert J. Fund Accounting: Theory & Practice. 1974. ref. ed. 22.95 (ISBN 0-13-332379-X). P-H.
Michigan Governmental Accounting & Audit Guide. rev. ed. 1978. 5.00 (ISBN 0-686-16236-6). MSU-Inst Comm Devel.
Pomeranz, Felix, et al. Auditing in the Public Sector. 1976. 47.50 (ISBN 0-88262-123-8, 75-22798). Warren.

FINANCE, PUBLIC–BIBLIOGRAPHY
Bogart, Ernest L. & Rawles, William A. Trial Bibliography & Outline of Lectures on the Financial History of the United States. LC 71-75563. Repr. of 1901 ed. lib. bdg. 15.00x (ISBN 0-8371-2157-4, BOTB). Greenwood.
Dewey, Davis R. Financial History of the United States. 12th ed. LC 67-30857. Repr. of 1934 ed. 25.00x (ISBN 0-678-00463-3). Kelley.
Knox, Vera H., ed. Public Finance Information Sources. LC 64-16503. (Management Information Guide Ser.: No. 3). 1964. 36.00 (ISBN 0-8103-0803-7). Gale.
Novotny, Jan M. Library of Public Finance & Economics. 1971. Repr. of 1953 ed. lib. bdg. 23.50 (ISBN 0-8337-2592-0). B Franklin.

FINANCE, PUBLIC–DATA PROCESSING
Konstans, Constantine. Effects of Data Processing Service Bureaus on the Practice of Public Accounting. LC 68-65564. 1968. 7.00 (ISBN 0-87744-023-9). Mich St U Busn.

FINANCE, PUBLIC–LAW
Dunbar, Charles F., ed. Laws of the United States Relating to Currency, Finance & Banking from 1789 to 1891. LC 68-28627. Repr. of 1893 ed. lib. bdg. 20.25x (ISBN 0-8371-4585-6, DULU). Greenwood.
Niskanen, William A., et al. Tax & Expenditure Limitation by Constitutional Amendment: Four Perspectives on the California Initiative. LC 73-9974. 69p. 1973. pap. 2.50x (ISBN 0-87772-170-X). Inst Gov Stud Berk.

FINANCE, PUBLIC–AUSTRALIA
Maxwell, James A. Commonwealth-State Financial Relations in Australia. LC 67-30708. 1967. 12.50x (ISBN 0-522-83829-4, Pub. by Melbourne U Pr). Intl Schol Bk Serv.

FINANCE, PUBLIC–CANADA
Canada-Public Archives. Documents Relating to Canadian Currency, Exchange & Finance During the French Period, 2 Vols. Shortt, Adam, ed. (Fr. & Eng.). 1925. Set. 63.00 (ISBN 0-8337-3256-0). B Franklin.
Strick, John C. Canadian Public Finance. 2nd ed. 1978. pap. text ed. 8.95 (ISBN 0-03-928154-X, Pub. by HR&W Canada). HR&W.

FINANCE, PUBLIC–CHINA
Huang, R. Taxation & Governmental Finance in 16th Century Ming China. LC 73-79311. (Studies in Chinese History, Literature & Institutions). (Illus.). 420p. 1975. 55.00 (ISBN 0-521-20283-3). Cambridge U Pr.
Li Chuan-Shih. Central & Local Finance in China. LC 68-57573. (Columbia University. Studies in the Social Sciences: No. 226). Repr. of 1922 ed. 17.50 (ISBN 0-404-51226-7). AMS Pr.
Young, Arthur N. China's Nation-Building Effort, 1927-1937: The Financial & Economic Record. LC 70-123350. (Publications Ser.: No. 104). (Illus.). 553p. 1971. 22.50 (ISBN 0-8179-6041-4). Hoover Inst Pr.

FINANCE, PUBLIC–CHINA–1949-
Ecklund, George N. Financing the Chinese Government Budget: Mainland China, 1950-1959. (Committee on the Economy of China Monographs). 1966. 5.95x (ISBN 0-202-31001-9). Beresford Bk Serv.

FINANCE, PUBLIC–CONGO, BELGIAN
Stengers, J. Combien le Congo a-t-il Coute a la Belgique. (Fr). Repr. of 1957 ed. 27.00 (ISBN 0-384-57880-2). Johnson Repr.

FINANCE, PUBLIC–EUROPE
Lyon, Bryce & Verhulst, A. E. Medieval Finance: A Comparison of Financial Institutions in Northwestern Europe. LC 67-19657. 100p. 1968. Repr. of 1967 ed. text ed. 8.00x (ISBN 0-87057-102-8, Pub. by Brown U Pr). U Pr of New Eng.
Molho, Anthony. Florentine Public Finances in the Early Renaissance, 1400-1433. LC 70-168431. (Historical Monographs Ser: No. 65). 1972. 12.00x (ISBN 0-674-30665-1). Harvard U Pr.

FINANCE, PUBLIC–FRANCE
see also Intendants
Dakin, Douglas. Turgot & the Ancien Regime in France. 1965. lib. bdg. 20.00x (ISBN 0-374-92033-8). Octagon.
Dent, Julian. Crisis in Finance: Crown, Financiers & Society in Seventeenth-Century France. LC 73-80084. 288p. 1973. 22.50 (ISBN 0-312-17360-1). St Martin.
Henneman, John B. Royal Taxation in Fourteenth-Century France: The Development of War Financing. LC 78-147945. 1971. 26.00x (ISBN 0-691-05188-7). Princeton U Pr.

Lodge, Eleanor. Sully, Colbert & Turgot: A Chapter in French Economic History. LC 71-178939. (Selected Essays in History, Economics & Social Science Ser.). 279p. 1972. Repr. of 1931 ed. lib. bdg. 14.00 (ISBN 0-8337-4237-X). B Franklin.

Lodge, Eleanor C. Sully, Colbert & Turgot. LC 70-110911. 1970. Repr. of 1931 ed. 12.50 (ISBN 0-8046-0893-8). Kennikat.

Susane, G. La Tactique Financiere De Calonne. LC 72-8395. 292p. (Fr.). 1973. Repr. of 1901 ed. 24.00 (ISBN 0-8337-3461-X). B Franklin.

Turgot, Anne R. Life & Writings of Turgot. Stephens, W. Walker, ed. LC 74-161008. (Research & Source Works Ser.: No. 760). 1971. Repr. of 1895 ed. lib. bdg. 19.50 (ISBN 0-8337-4451-8). B Franklin.

FINANCE, PUBLIC–GREAT BRITAIN

Aronson, J. Richard & Schwartz, Eli, eds. Management Policies in Local Government Finance. rev. 2nd ed. LC 81-2934. (Municipal Management Ser.). (Illus.). 512p. 1981. text ed. 32.00x (ISBN 0-87326-022-8). Intl City Mgt.

Burgon, John W. Life & Times of Sir Thomas Gresham, 2 Vols. (Illus.). 1965. Repr. of 1839 ed. Set. 53.00 (ISBN 0-8337-0422-2). B Franklin.

Dietz, Frederick C. English Government Finance, Fourteen Eighty-Five to Fifteen Fifty-Eight. Repr. of 1920 ed. 11.50 (ISBN 0-384-11750-3). Johnson Repr.

Dietz, Fredrick C. English Public Finance. Incl. Vol. 1. English Government Finance, 1485-1558. 210p. 1964. Repr. of 1921 ed. 30.00x (ISBN 0-7146-1299-5); Vol. 2. English Government Finance, 1558-1641. 478p. 1964. Repr. of 1932 ed. 35.00x (ISBN 0-7146-1300-2). 1964 (F Cass Co). Biblio Dist.

Grady, Henry F. British War Finance, 1914-1919. LC 73-76688. (Columbia University. Studies in the Social Sciences: No. 279). Repr. of 1926 ed. 24.50 (ISBN 0-404-51279-8). AMS Pr.

Grellier, J. J. History of the National Debt from the Revolution in 1688 to 1800. LC 73-121224. (Research & Source Works Ser: No. 764). 1971. Repr. of 1810 ed. lib. bdg. 26.00 (ISBN 0-8337-1452-X). B Franklin.

Harriss, G. L. King, Parliament, & Public Finance in Medieval England to 1369. 576p. 1975. 49.50x (ISBN 0-19-822435-4). Oxford U Pr.

Hockley, Graham C. Monetary Policy & Public Finance. LC 70-99928. 1970. lib. bdg. 15.00x (ISBN 0-678-06527-6). Kelley.

Madox, Thomas. History & Antiquities of the Exchequer of the Kings of England, 2 vols. Repr. of 1769 ed. Set. lib. bdg. 79.50x (ISBN 0-8371-1076-9, MAE). Greenwood.

Prestwich, Michael. War, Politics & Finance Under Edward I. 317p. 1972. 17.50x (ISBN 0-87471-116-9). Rowman.

Sandford, C. T. Economics of Public Finance. 2nd ed. LC 77-6680. 1977. text ed. 27.00 (ISBN 0-08-021843-1); pap. text ed. 14.00 (ISBN 0-08-021842-3). Pergamon.

FINANCE, PUBLIC–GREECE

Meritt, Benjamin D. Athenian Calendar in the 5th Century. facs. ed. LC 74-75510. (Select Bibliogrpahies Reprint Ser). 1928. 28.00 (ISBN 0-8369-5012-7). Arno.

FINANCE, PUBLIC–GUATEMALA

Adler, John H. Public Finance & Economic Development in Guatemala. LC 77-138097. (Illus.). xix, 282p. Repr. of 1952 ed. lib. bdg. 15.00 (ISBN 0-8371-5672-6, ADPF). Greenwood.

FINANCE, PUBLIC–INDIA

Bhatia, H. L. Public Finance in India. LC 78-670054. 464p. 1976. 12.00x (ISBN 0-7069-0453-2). Intl Pubns Serv.

Misra, B. Economics of Public Finance. 2nd ed. 1981. 9.00x (ISBN 0-8364-0718-0, Pub. by Macmillan India). South Asia Bks.

Sharma, B. S. Financial Planning in the Indian Public Sector: A Management. 1974. 10.50x (ISBN 0-686-20229-5). Intl Bk Dist.

FINANCE, PUBLIC–LATIN AMERICA

Descartes, S. L. Credit Institutions for Local Authorities in Latin America. LC 73-75403. 81p. 1973. pap. 1.50 (ISBN 0-913480-16-9). Inter Am U Pr.

FINANCE, PUBLIC–NATAL

Konczacki, Zbigniew A. Public Finance & Economic Development of Natal, 1893-1910. LC 67-23301. 1967. 13.75 (ISBN 0-8223-0101-6). Duke.

FINANCE, PUBLIC–NIGERIA

Adedeji, Adebayo. Nigerian Federal Finance: Its Development, Problems & Prospects. LC 77-80848. (Illus.). 1969. 29.50x (ISBN 0-8419-0010-8, Africana). Holmes & Meier.

FINANCE, PUBLIC–PAKISTAN

Andrus, J. Russell & Mohammed, Azizali F. Trade, Finance, & Development in Pakistan. 1966. 12.50x (ISBN 0-8047-0126-1). Stanford U Pr.

FINANCE, PUBLIC–SALVADOR

Wallich, Henry C. & Adler, John H. Public Finance in a Developing Country: El Salvador, a Case Study. LC 68-8339. (Illus.). 1968. Repr. of 1951 ed. lib. bdg. 15.25x (ISBN 0-8371-0259-6, WAPF). Greenwood.

FINANCE, PUBLIC–SINGAPORE

Asher, Mukul & Osborne, Susna, eds. Issues in Public Finance in Singapore. 1981. 22.95 (ISBN 9971-69-007-1, Pub. by Singapore U Pr); pap. 14.00 (ISBN 9971-69-023-3, Pub. by Singapore U Pr). Ohio U Pr.

FINANCE, PUBLIC–UNITED STATES

see also Taxation, State

Cargil, Thomas & Garcia, Gillian. Financial Deregulation & Monetary Control: Historical Perspective & Impact of the 1980 Act. (Publication Ser.: No. 259). (Illus.). 128p. Date not set. pap. text ed. write for info. (ISBN 0-8179-7592-6). Hoover Inst Pr.

Chase, Stuart. Where's the Money Coming From: Problems of Postwar Finance. LC 68-8059. (Illus.). 1968. Repr. of 1943 ed. lib. bdg. 15.00x (ISBN 0-8371-0044-5, CHWM). Greenwood.

Clark, Harold F. The Cost of Government & the Support of Education: An Intensive Study of New York State with Results Applicable Over the Entire Country. LC 79-17668. (Columbia University. Teachers College. Contributions to Education: No. 145). Repr. of 1924 ed. 17.50 (ISBN 0-404-55145-9). AMS Pr.

Coghland, Richard & Sykes, Carolyn. Managing the Money Supply. 224p. 1980. 21.00x (ISBN 0-85941-164-8, Pub. by Woodhead-Faulkner England). State Mutual Bk.

Copeland, Morris A. Trends in Government Financing. LC 75-19710. (National Bureau of Economic Research Ser.). (Illus.). 1975. Repr. 13.00x (ISBN 0-405-07590-1). Arno.

Curran, Donald J. Metropolitan Financing: The Milwaukee Experience, 1920-1970. LC 72-7984. 182p. 1973. 20.00x (ISBN 0-299-06290-2). U of Wis Pr.

Douglas, Charles H. Financial History of Massachusetts from the Organization of the Massachusetts Bay Colony to the American Revolution. LC 71-82251. (Columbia University, Studies in the Social Sciences Ser.: No. 4). 1968. Repr. of 1892 ed. 10.00 (ISBN 0-404-51004-3). AMS Pr.

Due, John F. & Friedlaender, Ann F. Government Finance: Economics of the Public Sector. 7th ed. 1981. text ed. 20.00x (ISBN 0-256-02492-8). Irwin.

Eckstein, Otto. Public Finance. 4th ed. (Foundations of Modern Economics Ser.). (Illus.). 1979. text ed. 14.95 (ISBN 0-13-737452-6); pap. text ed. 9.95 (ISBN 0-13-737445-3). P-H.

Fisher, Louis. Presidential Spending Power. LC 75-4408. 300p. 1975. 25.00x (ISBN 0-691-07575-1); pap. 6.95 (ISBN 0-691-02173-2). Princeton U Pr.

Gardner, Wyland. Government Finance: National, State & Local. LC 77-3572. 1978. 19.95 (ISBN 0-13-360743-7). P-H.

Hammond, Bray. Sovereignty & an Empty Purse: Banks & Politics in the Civil War. LC 79-113003. 1970. 24.00x (ISBN 0-691-04601-8). Princeton U Pr.

Harris, Spencer P., compiled by. Who Audits America. (Corporations & Accountants Ser.). 1979. 38.50 (ISBN 0-933088-03-5); pap. 33.50 (ISBN 0-685-90844-5). Data Financial.

Hockley, Graham. Public Finance: An Introduction. (Illus.). 1979. 32.00 (ISBN 0-7100-0148-7); pap. 15.00 (ISBN 0-7100-0149-5). Routledge & Kegan.

Jewett, Fred E. Financial History of Maine. LC 68-58595. (Columbia University. Studies in the Social Sciences: No. 432). Repr. of 1937 ed. 20.00 (ISBN 0-404-51432-4). AMS Pr.

Legler, John B. Regional Distribution of Federal Receipts & Expenditures in the 19th Century: A Quantative Study. Bruchey, Stuart, ed. LC 76-39833. (Nineteen Seventy-Seven Dissertations Ser.). (Illus.). 1977. lib. bdg. 15.00x (ISBN 0-405-09913-4). Arno.

Levine, Charles H., ed. Fiscal Stress & Public Policy. LC 80-24515. (Sage Yearbook in Politics & Public Policy). 314p. 1980. 20.00 (ISBN 0-8039-1553-5); pap. 9.95 (ISBN 0-8039-1554-3). Sage.

Lindholm, Richard W. & Wignjowijoto, Hortojo. Financing & Managing State & Local Government. LC 78-19227. (Illus.). 1979. 29.95 (ISBN 0-669-02434-1). Lexington Bks.

Ma Yin-Ch'U. Finances of the City of New York. LC 68-56669. (Columbia University, Studies in the Social Sciences: No. 149). Repr. of 1914 ed. 20.00 (ISBN 0-404-51149-X). AMS Pr.

Mandelker, Daniel R., et al. Reviving Cities with Tax Abatement. LC 79-92785. 160p. (Orig.). 1980. pap. text ed. 12.95 (ISBN 0-88285-065-2). Ctr Urban Pol Res.

Maxwell, James A. & Aronson, J. Richard. Financing State & Local Governments. 3rd ed. LC 76-54871. (Studies of Government Finance). 1977. 14.95 (ISBN 0-8157-5512-0); pap. 5.95 (ISBN 0-8157-5511-2). Brookings.

Meltsner, Arnold J. & Kast, Gregory W. Political Feasibility of Reform in School Financing: The Case of California. LC 72-92461. (Special Studies in U.S. Economic, Social & Political Issues). 1973. 27.50x (ISBN 0-685-70526-9). Irvington.

Myers, Margaret G. A Financial History of the United States. LC 70-104900. 1970. 22.50x (ISBN 0-231-02442-8); pap. 7.50x (ISBN 0-231-08309-2). Columbia U Pr.

Noyes, A. D. The War Period of American Finance, 1908-1925. 1973. Repr. of 1926 ed. 25.50 (ISBN 0-384-42130-X). Johnson Repr.

Noyes, Alexander D. Forty Years of American Finance. Bruchey, Stuart, ed. LC 80-1163. (The Rise of Commercial Banking Ser.). 1981. Repr. of 1909 ed. lib. bdg. 38.00x (ISBN 0-405-13672-2). Arno.

Oberman, Joseph & Bingham, Robert. Planning & Managing the Economy of the City: Policy Guidelines for the Metropolitan Mayor. LC 72-79544. (Special Studies in U.S. Economic, Social & Political Issues Ser.). 1972. 29.50x (ISBN 0-275-06160-4). Irvington.

O'Connor, J. F. The Banking Crisis & Recovery Under the Roosevelt Administration. LC 73-171696. (FDR & the Era of the New Deal Ser.). 168p. 1971. Repr. of 1938 ed. lib. bdg. 20.00 (ISBN 0-306-70366-1). Da Capo.

O'Connor, James. The Fiscal Crisis of the State. 200p. 1973. pap. text ed. 6.95 (ISBN 0-312-29330-5). St Martin.

Ott, David J., et al. State & Local Finances in the Last Half of the Seventies. 1975. pap. 5.25 (ISBN 0-8447-3157-9). Am Enterprise.

Pomernanz, Felix, et al. Auditing in the Public Sector. 1976. 47.50 (ISBN 0-88262-123-8, 75-22798). Warren.

Ratner, Sidney, ed. The New American State Papers: Public Finance Subject Set, 32 vols. LC 72-95580. 1973. Set. lib. bdg. 1525.00 (ISBN 0-8420-1610-4). Scholarly Res Inc.

Ripley, William Z. Financial History of Virginia 1609-1776. LC 78-127449. (Columbia Social Science Studies Ser: No. 10). Repr. of 1893 ed. 10.00 (ISBN 0-404-51010-8). AMS Pr.

Rousmaniere, Peter. The Public Money Managers Handbook. (Illus.). 320p. 1981. write for info. (ISBN 0-87251-064-6). Crain Bks.

Selko, Daniel. The Federal Financial System. LC 75-8891. (FDR & the Era of the New Deal Ser.). xii, 606p. 1975. Repr. of 1940 ed. lib. bdg. 59.50 (ISBN 0-306-70708-X). Da Capo.

Sowers, Don C. Financial History of New York State from 1789 to 1912. LC 75-77995. (Columbia University. Studies in the Social Sciences: No. 140). Repr. of 1914 ed. 19.50 (ISBN 0-404-51140-6). AMS Pr.

Spaulding, Elbridge G. Resource of War: The Credit of the Government Made Immediately Available-History of the Legal Tender Paper Money Issued During the Great Rebellion Being a Loan Without Interest & a National Currency. LC 69-19681. (Money Markets Ser). 1971. Repr. of 1869 ed. lib. bdg. 14.75x (ISBN 0-8371-0662-1, SPRW). Greenwood.

Trotter, Alexander. Observations on the Financial Position & Credit of the States of the North American Union As Have Contracted Public Debts. 1971. Repr. of 1839 ed. lib. bdg. 23.50 (ISBN 0-8337-3566-7). B Franklin.

U. S. House Committee on Banking, Currency & Housing. The New York City Fiscal Crisis. LC 77-74954. (American Federalism-the Urban Dimension). (Illus.). 1978. Repr. of 1975 ed. lib. bdg. 20.00x (ISBN 0-405-10498-7). Arno.

U. S. Treasury Department. The National Loans of the United States, from July 4, 1776 to June 30, 1880. 2nd ed. Bayley, Rafael, ed. LC 74-96856. (Research & Source Works Ser: No. 554). 1970. Repr. of 1882 ed. lib. bdg. 26.50 (ISBN 0-8337-0195-9). B Franklin.

U.S. Senate Committee on Government Operations. The Effect of Inflation & Recession on State & Local Governments. LC 77-74957. 1977. lib. bdg. 10.00x (ISBN 0-405-10500-2). Arno.

Van Winter, Pieter. American Finance & Dutch Investment, 1780-1805. Wilkins, Mira, ed. LC 76-46251. (European Business Ser.). (Illus.). 1977. Repr. of 1977 ed. lib. bdg. 68.00x (ISBN 0-405-09860-X). Arno.

Walzer, Norman & Chicoine, David, eds. State & Local Finance in the Nineteen Eighty's: Issues & Trends. 224p. 1981. text ed. 25.00 (ISBN 0-89946-109-3). Oelgeschlager.

Watters, Elise M., ed. Facts & Figures on Government Finance. 21st ed. 328p. (Orig.). pap. 15.00x (ISBN 0-686-30844-1). Tax Found.

Williamson, Charles C. Finances of Cleveland. LC 68-56698. (Columbia University. Studies in the Social Sciences: No. 67). Repr. of 1907 ed. 20.00 (ISBN 0-404-51067-1). AMS Pr.

Wilmerding, Lucius. Spending Power: A History of the Efforts of Congress to Control Expenditures. 1971. Repr. of 1943 ed. 18.50 (ISBN 0-208-01028-9, Archon). Shoe String.

Wood, Frederick A. Finances of Vermont. LC 70-127452. (Columbia University Social Science Studies Ser.: No. 130). Repr. of 1913 ed. 16.50 (ISBN 0-404-51130-9). AMS Pr.

FINANCE CHARGES

see also Interest and Usury

Financial Publishing Company Staff. The Cost of Personal Borrowing in the United States. 10th ed. Gushee, Charles H., ed. (Illus.). 1981. perfect bound 32.00 (ISBN 0-685-87665-9, 830). Finan Pub.

Mors, W. P. Consumer Credit Finance Charges: Rate Information & Quotation. (Financial Research Program Ser.: Studies in Consumer Instalment Financing, No.12). 1965. 8.00x (ISBN 0-87014-128-7, Dist. by Columbia U Pr). Natl Bur Econ Res.

FINANCE COMPANIES, COMMERCIAL

see Commercial Finance Companies; Instalment Plan

FINANCIAL ACCOUNTING

see Accounting

FINANCIAL INSTITUTIONS

see also Banks and Banking; Building and Loan Associations; Commercial Finance Companies; Insurance Companies; Investment Trusts

Adams, T. F. M. & Hoshii, Iwao. A Financial History of the New Japan. LC 75-185642. (Illus.). 547p. 1972. 22.50x (ISBN 0-87011-157-4). Kodansha.

Altman, Edward I. & Sametz, Arnold W. Financial Crises: Institutions & Markets in a Fragile Environment. LC 77-2308. 336p. 1977. 29.95 (ISBN 0-471-02685-9). Ronald Pr.

Blyn, Martin R. & Krooss, Herman E. History of Financial Intermediaries. 1971. text ed. 7.95x (ISBN 0-685-47982-X). Phila Bk Co.

Cohen, Jon S. Finance & Industrialization in Italy, 1894-1914. Bruchey, Stuart, ed. LC 77-81825. (Dissertations in European Economic History Ser.). (Illus.). 1977. lib. bdg. 18.00x (ISBN 0-405-10777-3). Arno.

Cunningham, Dixon C., et al. Cases on Financial Institutions. LC 77-90644. (Finance Ser.). 1979. text ed. 20.95 (ISBN 0-88244-120-5). Grid Pub.

Edmister, Robert O. Financial Institutions Management. (Financial Ser.). 560p. 1980. text ed. 18.95 (ISBN 0-07-018995-1, C); instr's manual 4.95 (ISBN 0-07-018996-X). McGraw.

Fraser, Donald R. & Rose, Peter S., eds. Financial Institutions & Markets in a Changing World. 1980. pap. 12.95x (ISBN 0-256-02201-1). Business Pubns.

Goldsmith, Raymond W. Financial Intermediaries in the American Economy Since 1900. LC 75-19713. (National Bureau of Economic Research Ser.). (Illus.). 1975. Repr. 25.00x (ISBN 0-405-07593-6). Arno.

Hempel, George & Yawitz, Jess. Financial Management of Financial Institutions. (Illus.). 1977 (ISBN 0-13-315978-7). pap. text ed. 10.95 (ISBN 0-13-315960-4). P-H.

Henning, Charles, et al. Financial Markets & the Economy. 2nd ed. (Illus.). 1978. ref. 19.95 (ISBN 0-13-316083-1). P-H.

Kentucky Financial Institutions & Securities Law Annotated. 1975. 37.50 (ISBN 0-8322-0014-X). Banks-Baldwin.

Knowles, James C. The Rockefeller Financial Group. 1974. pap. text ed. 1.60x (ISBN 0-8422-9343-4). Irvington.

Koehn, Michael F. Bankruptcy Risk in Financial Depository Intermediaries: Assessing Regulatory Effects. LC 79-2411. (Arthur D. Little Bk.). (Illus.). 176p. 1979. 20.95- (ISBN 0-669-03169-0). Lexington Bks.

Lees, Francis A. & Eng, Maximo. International Financial Markets: Development of the Present System & Future Prospects. LC 73-13345. (Special Studies). (Illus.). 576p. 1975. pap. text ed. 12.95 (ISBN 0-275-89180-1). Praeger.

Lindholm, Richard W. Money Management & Institutions. 1978. pap. 7.95 (ISBN 0-8226-0334-9). Littlefield.

Mayer, Martin. The Bankers. 608p. 1980. pap. text ed. 3.50 (ISBN 0-345-29569-2). Ballantine.

Morgan, E. Victor, et al. City Lights: Essays on Financial Institutions & Markets in the City of London, No. 19. (Orig.). 1979. technical 5.95 (ISBN 0-255-36119-X). Transatlantic.

Moulton, Harold G. Financial Organization & the Economic System. facsimile ed. LC 75-2652. (Wall Street & the Security Markets Ser.). 1975. Repr. of 1938 ed. 32.00x (ISBN 0-405-06977-4). Arno.

Neufeld, E. P. The Financial System of Canada. LC 70-178200. 635p. 1972. 27.50 (ISBN 0-312-28980-4). St Martin.

Polakoff, Murray A. & Durkin, Thomas A. Financial Institutions & Markets. 2nd ed. LC 80-82758. (Illus.). 673p. 1981. text ed. 23.50 (ISBN 0-395-29191-7). HM.

Prochnow, Herbert V. American Financial Institutions. facs. ed. LC 76-128290. (Essay Index Reprint Ser). 1951. 39.00 (ISBN 0-8369-2017-1). Arno.
Rose, Peter S. & Fraser, Donald R. Financial Institutions. 1980. 18.95x (ISBN 0-256-02205-4). Business Pubns.
Rubel, Stanley M., ed. & intro. by. Source Guide for Borrowing Capital. LC 76-51893. 1977. 49.50 (ISBN 0-914470-09-4). Capital Pub Corp.
Seitz, Neil & Yeager, Frederick. Financial Institution Management. 450p. 1982. text ed. 18.95 (ISBN 0-8359-2022-4); instr's. manual free (ISBN 0-8359-2023-2). Reston.
Shearer, R. & Bond, D. Economics of the Canadian Financial System. 1972. 22.95 (ISBN 0-13-229781-7). P-H.
Taylor, Bernard & De Moubray, Guy, eds. Strategic Planning for Financial Institutions. 348p. 1975. 24.00x (ISBN 0-370-10457-9). Transatlantic.
Tomkins, Cyril, et al. An Economic Analysis of the Financial Leasing Industry. 1979. text ed. 34.25x (ISBN 0-566-00316-3, Pub. by Gower Pub Co England). Renouf.
Wallace, Don, Jr. International Regulation of Multinational Corporations. LC 75-8411. (Special Studies). (Illus.). 1976. text ed. 24.95 (ISBN 0-275-05880-8). Praeger.
Wilson, J. S., ed. Multinational Enterprises. 1974. 40.00 (ISBN 9-0286-0124-4). Heinman.

FINANCIAL JOURNALISM
see Journalism, Commercial

FINANCIAL NEWS
see Newspapers–Sections, Columns, etc.

FINANCIAL RESEARCH
Buckley, John W. Executives Digest of Financial Research-1975. LC 77-9131. 1977. 7.25 (ISBN 0-910586-18-7). Finan Exec.
Chartered Financial Analysts, ed. C.F.A. Readings in Financial Analysis. 4th rev. ed. 1978. pap. 5.00x (ISBN 0-256-02098-1). Irwin.
Financial Publishing Co. Discount & Equivalent Interest Tables No. 948. 42.50 (ISBN 0-685-02540-3). Finan Pub.
--Expanded Bond Values Tables. No. 63. pocket ed. 27.50 (ISBN 0-685-02541-1). Finan Pub.
Hawkins, Robert G., ed. Research in International Business & Finance, Vol. 1. 330p. 1979. 37.50 (ISBN 0-89232-031-1). Jai Pr.
--Research in International Business & Finance, Vol. 2. 350p. 1981. 37.50 (ISBN 0-89232-140-7). Jai Pr.
--Research in International Business & Finance, Vol. 3. 300p. 1981. 37.50 (ISBN 0-89232-245-4). Jai Pr.
Helfert, Erich A. Techniques of Financial Analysis. 5th ed. 285p. 1981. 13.50 (ISBN 0-87094-274-3). Dow Jones-Irwin.
Levich, Richard M. The International Money Market. Altman, Edward I. & Walter, Ingo, eds. LC 78-13841. (Contemporary Studies in Economic & Financial Analysis: Vol. 22). 178p. 1979. 28.50 (ISBN 0-89232-109-1). Jai Pr.
Levy, Haim, ed. Research in Finance, Vol. 1. 1979. lib. bdg. 34.50 (ISBN 0-89232-043-5). Jai Pr.
--Research in Finance, Vol. 3. 225p. 1981. 34.50 (ISBN 0-89232-218-7). Jai Pr.
Marer, Paul. U. S. Financing of East-West Trade: Studies in East European & Soviet Planning, Development, & Trade. (No. 22). 1975. pap. text ed. 8.00 (ISBN 0-89249-030-6). Intl Development.

FINANCIAL STATEMENTS
see also subdivision Accounting under special subjects, e.g. Agriculture–Accounting
American Institute of Certified Public Accountants. Illustrations of Departures from the Auditor's Standard Report. (Financial Report Survey: No. 7). 1975. pap. 8.50 (ISBN 0-685-65410-9). Am Inst CPA.
--Illustrations of the Disclosure of Related Party Transactions. (Financial Report Survey: No. 8). 1975. pap. 8.00 (ISBN 0-685-65409-5). Am Inst CPA.
--Illustrations of the Summary of Operations & Related Management Discussion & Analysis. (Financial Report Survey: No. 6). 1975. pap. 10.00 (ISBN 0-685-65411-7). Am Inst CPA.
Analyzing Financial Statements. 5th ed. 1978. 12.00 (ISBN 0-89982-140-5, 050401); wkbk. 3.00 (ISBN 0-89982-141-3, 050402). Am Bankers.
Backer, Morton. Financial Reporting for Security Investment & Credit Decisions. 9.95 (ISBN 0-686-09779-3, 7049). Natl Assn Accts.
Backer, Morton & McFarland, Walter B. External Reporting for Segments of a Business. 5.95 (ISBN 0-686-09784-X, 6844). Natl Assn Accts.
Ballon, R. J., et al. Financial Reporting in Japan. LC 75-30179. (Illus.). 305p. 1976. 15.00x (ISBN 0-87011-269-4). Kodansha.
Benston, George J. Corporate Financial Disclosure in the UK & the USA. 1976. 21.95 (ISBN 0-347-01133-0, 00409-X, Pub. by Saxon Hse.). Lexington Bks.
Bernstein, Leopold A. The Analysis of Financial Statements. LC 78-55533. 1978. 13.95 (ISBN 0-87094-164-X). Dow Jones-Irwin.
--Financial Statement Analysis: Theory, Application & Interpretation. rev. ed. 1978. 21.95x (ISBN 0-256-02004-3). Irwin.
Briloff, Abraham J. More Debits Than Credits: The Burnt Investor's Guide to Financial Statements. LC 74-15812. (Illus.). 448p. 1976. 15.95 (ISBN 0-06-010476-7, HarpT). Har-Row.
Brown, Clifford D. Emergence of Income Reporting: An Historical Study. LC 71-634897. 1971. pap. 4.25 (ISBN 0-87744-106-5). Mich St U Busn.
Clemens, J. H. Balance Sheets & the Lending Banker. 5th ed. LC 78-670081. 1977. 17.50x (ISBN 0-905118-15-4). Intl Pubns Serv.
Compilation & Review of Financial Statements. (Statements on Standards for Accounting & Review Services Ser.: No. 1). 1978. pap. 1.50 (ISBN 0-686-70226-3). Am Inst CPA.
Daniels, Mortimer B. Corporation Financial Statements. Brief, Richard P., ed. LC 80-1484. (Dimensions of Accounting Theory & Practice Ser.). 1981. Repr. of 1934 ed. lib. bdg. 14.00x (ISBN 0-405-13514-9). Arno.
De Motte Green, Catherine. The Dynamic Balance Sheet: A German Theory of Accounting. Brief, Richard P., ed. LC 80-1497. (Dimensions of Accounting Theory & Practice Ser.). 1981. lib. bdg. 34.00x (ISBN 0-405-13491-6). Arno.
Development & Reporting of Variances. (Accounting Practice Report: No. 15). 2.50 (ISBN 0-686-09796-3, 6232). Natl Assn Accts.
Dicksee, Lawrence R. Business Methods & the War: The Fundamentals of Manufacturing Costs: & Published Balance Sheets & Window Dressing, 3 vols. in 1. Brief, Richard P., ed. LC 80-1487. (Dimensions of Accounting Theory & Practice Ser.). 1981. Repr. of 1927 ed. lib. bdg. 18.00x (ISBN 0-686-73167-0). Arno.
Edwards, James W., et al. Interim Financial Reporting. 9.95 (ISBN 0-686-09775-0, 7253). Natl Assn Accts.
Financial Reporting & Evaluation of Solvency. (Accounting Research Monograph: No. 3). 1978. pap. 8.00 (ISBN 0-685-92045-3). Am Inst CPA.
Flumiani, C. M. How to Read Financial Statements: For Better Stock Market Performance. LC 73-90531. (Illus.). 1975. 42.80 (ISBN 0-913314-33-1). Am Classical Coll Pr.
Foster, George. Financial Statement Analysis. (Illus.). 1978. 22.00 (ISBN 0-13-316273-7). P-H.
Foulke, R. A. Practical Financial Statement Analysis. 6th ed. (Accounting Ser.). 1968. text ed. 18.95 (ISBN 0-07-021655-X, C); solutions to Theory & Problems 4.95 (ISBN 0-07-021652-5). McGraw.
Gibson, Charles H. Cases in Financial Reporting. (Business Ser.). 339p. 1981. pap. text ed. 13.95x (ISBN 0-534-00972-7). Kent Pub Co.
Graham, Benjamin & McGolrick, Charles. The Interpretation of Financial Statements. 3rd rev. ed. LC 74-15829. 128p. 1975. 11.95 (ISBN 0-06-011566-1, HarpT). Har-Row.
Gross, Malvern J. & Jablonsky, Stephen F. Principles of Accounting & Financial Reporting for Nonprofit Organizations. LC 79-4559. 1979. 24.50x (ISBN 0-471-05719-3, Pub. by Wiley-Interscience); instr's manual avail. Wiley.
Hawkins, David F. Corporate Financial Reporting: Text & Cases. rev ed. 1977. 20.95x (ISBN 0-256-01643-7). Irwin.
Helfert, Erich A. Techniques of Financial Analysis. rev. ed. LC 76-49313. (Illus.). 1977. 12.95 (ISBN 0-87094-136-4). Dow Jones-Irwin.
Hoffmaster, Henry R. Financial Statements: How to Read & Interpret Them for Success in the Stock Market. (Illus.). 1980. deluxe ed. 49.45 (ISBN 0-918968-62-3). Inst Econ Finan.
Houston, Lloyd. The New Approach for the Understanding & Interpretation of Financial Statements. (Illus.). 1978. 51.85 (ISBN 0-918968-05-4). Inst Econ Finan.
How to Read a Balance Sheet. (An ILO Programmed Book). 124p. (Thirteenth impression). 1978. 4.55 (ISBN 92-2-100000-1). Intl Labour Office.
How to Read a Financial Statement for Better Stock Market Performance. 1976. 49.75 (ISBN 0-913314-33-1). Inst Econ Finan.
Illustrations of Accounting Policy Disclosure. (Financial Report Survey: No. 1). 1972. pap. 8.00 (ISBN 0-685-36122-5). Am Inst CPA.
Illustrations of Auditors' Reports on Comparitve Financial Statements. (Financial Report Survey Ser.: No. 18). 1979. pap. 9.50 (ISBN 0-686-70236-0). Am Inst CPA.
Illustrations of Disclosure of "Pro Form Calculations". (Financial Report Survey: No. 11). 1976. pap. 8.00 (ISBN 0-685-92031-3). Am Inst CPA.
Illustrations of Disclosure of Subsequent Events. (Financial Report Survey: No. 9). 1976. pap. 8.00 (ISBN 0-685-92029-1). Am Inst CPA.
Illustrations of Disclosure of Unaudited Financial Information in Audited Financial Statements. (Financial Report Survey: No. 13). 1977. pap. 8.00 (ISBN 0-685-92033-X). Am Inst CPA.
Illustrations of Updated Accounting Policy Disclosure. (Financial Report Survey: No. 15). 1978. pap. 8.50 (ISBN 0-685-92035-6). Am Inst CPA.
Keller, T. F. & Zeff, S. A. Financial Accounting Theory Two: Issues & Controversies. 1969. pap. text ed. 10.95 (ISBN 0-07-033496-X, C). McGraw.
Kollaritsch, Felix P. Analysis & Terminology of Financial Statement Items for Highway-Heavy Contractors. 1970. 7.00x (ISBN 0-87776-305-4, AA5). Ohio St U Admin Sci.
Langer, Steven, ed. The Accounting-Financial Report: Industry-Government-Education-Non-Profit, Pt. II. 2nd ed. 1981. pap. 75.00 (ISBN 0-916506-61-4). Abbott Langer Assocs.
--The Accounting-Financial Report: Public Accounting Firms, Pt. I. 2nd ed. 1981. pap. 75.00 (ISBN 0-916506-60-6). Abbott Langer Assocs.
--Available Pay Survey Reports: An Annotated Bibliography, Pts. 2 & 3. 2nd ed. 1980. Pt. 1. pap. 39.50 (ISBN 0-916506-45-2); Pt. 2. pap. 19.50 (ISBN 0-916506-46-0). Abbott Langer Assocs.
Lev, Baruch. Financial Statement Analysis: A New Approach. (Contemporary Topics in Accounting Ser: Foundations of Finance). (Illus.). 288p. 1974. pap. text ed. 8.95 (ISBN 0-13-316364-4). P-H.
McGrath, Phyllis & Walsh, Francis, Jr. Disclosure of Financial Forecasts to Security Analysts & the Public. (Report Ser: No. 602). 23p. (Orig.). 1973. pap. 5.00 (ISBN 0-8237-0016-X). Conference Bd.
--Disclosure of Financial Forecasts to Security Analysts & the Public. (Report Ser: No. 602). 23p. (Orig.). 1973. pap. 5.00 (ISBN 0-8237-0016-X). Conference Bd.
McMullen, Stewart Y. Financial Statements. 7th ed. 1979. 21.95x (ISBN 0-256-02165-1). Irwin.
Management Reports on Financial Statements. (Financial Report Survey Ser.: No. 19). 1980. pap. 9.00 (ISBN 0-686-70242-5). Am Inst CPA.
Mascotte, John P. Finding Commission Dollars in Your Client's Financial Statements. LC 79-88709. (Illus.). 1979. 12.75 (ISBN 0-87218-007-7). Natl Underwriter.
Mautz, R. K. & May, William G. Financial Disclosure in a Competitive Economy. LC 77-95349. 1978. 7.25 (ISBN 0-910586-22-5). Finan Exec.
Metcalf, Richard W. & Titard, Pierre L. Principles of Accounting. LC 75-40638. (Illus.). 1025p. 1976. text ed. 16.95 (ISBN 0-7216-6313-3). HR&W.
Miller, Donald E. Meaningful Interpretation of Financial Statements. rev. ed. LC 72-78301. 1972. 12.50 (ISBN 0-8144-5303-1). Am Mgmt.
--The Meaningful Interpretation of Financial Statements. rev. ed. (Illus.). 1979. pap. 5.95 (ISBN 0-8144-7513-2). Am Mgmt.
Moonitz, Maurice. The Entity Theory of Consolidated Statements. Brief, Richard P., ed. LC 77-87282. (Development of Contemporary Accounting Thought Ser). 1978. Repr. of 1951 ed. lib. bdg. 12.00x (ISBN 0-405-10910-5). Arno.
Myer, John N. Understanding Financial Statements: What the Executive Should Know About the Accountant's Statements. 1968. pap. 1.95 (ISBN 0-451-61676-6, MJ1676, Ment). NAL.
NACM, ed. Credit Clues in Financial Statements. 1975. pap. 3.95 (ISBN 0-934914-20-6). NACM.
Objectives of Financial Statements - Report. 1973. pap. 5.00 (ISBN 0-685-39833-1). Am Inst CPA.
Pattillo, James W. Concept of Materiality in Financial Reporting. LC 75-46325. 1976. 9.00 (ISBN 0-910586-16-0). Finan Exec.
Personal Financial Statements. (Industry Audit Guides). 1968. pap. 4.00 (ISBN 0-685-58484-4). Am Inst CPA.
Rappaport, Alfred & Lerner, Eugene M. Framework for Financial Reporting by Diversified Companies. 3.95 (ISBN 0-686-09780-7, 6948). Natl Assn Accts.
--Segment Reporting for Managers & Investors. 7.95 (ISBN 0-686-09776-9, 7252). Natl Assn Accts.
Rappaport, Louis H. SEC Accounting Practice & Procedure. 3rd ed. 1260p. 1972. 46.95 (ISBN 0-471-06550-1, 77831). Ronald Pr.
Reading & Evaluating Financial Reports. 1977. 24.95 (ISBN 0-935268-00-6). Xerox Learning.
Regulation of Accounting & Financial Reporting: A Growth Industry & a Growing Problem for Industry. 1975. members 5.00 (ISBN 0-686-16534-9); nonmembers 7.00 (ISBN 0-686-16535-7). M & A Products.
Reporting on Comparative Financial Statements. (Statements on Standards for Accounting & Review Services Ser.: No. 2). 1979. pap. 1.50 (ISBN 0-686-70247-6). Am Inst CPA.
Ronen, Joshua & Sorter, George H. Relevant Financial Statements: Original Anthology. new ed. Brief, Richard P., ed. LC 77-87318. (Development of Contemporary Accounting Thought Ser). 1978. lib. bdg. 20.00x (ISBN 0-405-10930-X). Arno.
Senne, Stephen M. Your Financial Report Card. (Illus.). 102p. 1981. pap. 9.95 (ISBN 0-89260-203-1). Hwong Pub.
Sprouse, Robert T. & Swieringa, Robert J. The Essentials of Financial Statement Analysis. (Economics Ser). 480p. (Prog. Bk.). 1972. 12.95 (ISBN 0-201-07170-3). A-W.
Staples, Frederick. The Monthly Financial Statements. LC 72-75990. 139p. 1972. pap. 6.95 (ISBN 0-915026-14-7). Counting Hse.
Stockwell, Herbert G. How to Read a Financial Statement: Adapted Especially to Needs of Credit Men, Bankers & Investors. 443p. 1980. Repr. of 1925 ed. lib. bdg. 30.00 (ISBN 0-8495-5049-1). Arden Lib.
Tracy, John A. How to Read a Financial Report: Wringing Cash Flow & Other Vital Signs Out of the Numbers. LC 79-18853. 1980. 16.50 (ISBN 0-471-05712-6, Pub. by Wiley-Interscience). Wiley.
Unterman, Dr. Israel. Understanding the Balance Sheet & Profit & Loss Statement. rev. ed. LC 73-77431. 1976. 7.95 (ISBN 0-910580-14-6). Farnswth Pub.
Urban Land Institute Real Estate Financial Reporting & Steering Committees & Touche Ross & Company. Real Estate Financial Reporting. LC 72-90085. (Special Report Ser.). 40p. 1972. pap. 4.75 (ISBN 0-87420-555-7). Urban Land.
Vatter, William J. Fund Theory of Accounting & Its Implications for Financial Reports. LC 48-8794. (Midway Reprint Ser). 1975. pap. 6.00x (ISBN 0-226-85151-6). U of Chicago Pr.
--The Fund Theory of Accounting & Its Implications for Financial Reports. Brief, Richard P., ed. LC 77-87291. (Development of Contemporary Accountint Thought Ser). 1978. Repr. of 1947 ed. lib. bdg. 12.00x (ISBN 0-405-10918-0). Arno.
Walker, R. G. Consolidated Statements: History & Analysis. new ed. Brief, Richard P., ed. LC 77-87307. (Development of Contemporary Accounting Thought Ser.). 1978. lib. bdg. 26.00x (ISBN 0-405-10946-6). Arno.
Weaver, David H. & Hanna, J. Marshall. Accounting Ten-Twelve, Part 1: Elements of Financial Records. 3rd ed. (Illus.). (gr. 10-12). 1976. pap. text ed. 4.56 (ISBN 0-07-068901-6, G); indiv. lrng. guides 4.84 (ISBN 0-07-068904-0); working papers & chapter problems 3.12 (ISBN 0-07-068907-5). McGraw.
Wilson, David A., et al. Contemporary Financial Reporting: A Casebook. (Illus.). 1979. pap. 13.95 ref. ed. (ISBN 0-13-170332-3). P-H.

FINANCIAL STATEMENTS–PROGRAMMED INSTRUCTION
Flumiani, C. M. How to Read Financial Statements: For Better Stock Market Performance. LC 73-90531. (Illus.). 1975. 42.80 (ISBN 0-913314-33-1). Am Classical Coll Pr.

FINANCIAL STATEMENTS–GREAT BRITAIN
Benston, George J. Corporate Financial Disclosure in the UK & the USA. 1976. 21.95 (ISBN 0-347-01133-0, 00409-X, Pub. by Saxon Hse.). Lexington Bks.
Edwards, J. R. British Company Legislation & Company Accounts, 1844-1976, 2 vols. original anthology ed. Brief, Richard P., ed. LC 80-1456. (Dimensions of Accounting Theory & Practice Ser.). 1981. lib. bdg. 60.00x (ISBN 0-405-13478-9). Arno.

FINANCIERS
see Capitalists and Financiers

FINCASTLE, VIRGINIA
Worrell, Anne L. A Brief of Wills & Marriages in Montgomery & Fincastle Counties, Virginia, 1733-1831. LC 75-34994. 1979. Repr. of 1932 ed. wrappers 5.00 (ISBN 0-8063-0707-2). Genealog Pub.

FINCH, DANIEL, 1647-1730
Aiken, Wm. A. Conduct of the Earl of Nottingham: 1689-1694. (Yale Historical Pubs., Manuscripts & Edited Texts: No. XVII). 1941. 47.50x (ISBN 0-685-69786-X). Elliots Bks.

FINCH, PETER
Dundy, Elaine. Finch, Bloody Finch: The Life of Peter Finch. (Illus.). 384p. 1980. 14.95 (ISBN 0-03-041796-1). HR&W.

FINCH, ROBERT, 1783-1830
Nitchie, Elizabeth. Reverend Colonel Finch. LC 40-33650. Repr. of 1940 ed. 12.50 (ISBN 0-404-04777-7). AMS Pr.
FINCHES
Bent, Arthur C. Life Histories of North American Cardinals, Grosbeaks, Buntings, Towhees, Finches, Sparrows, & Their Allies, 3 Vols. (Illus.). 1968. pap. 7.95 ea.; Vol. 1. pap. (ISBN 0-486-21977-1); Vol. 2. pap. (ISBN 0-486-21978-X); Vol. 3. pap. (ISBN 0-486-21979-8). Dover.
Enehjelm, Curt A. Australian Finches. Friese, U. Erich, tr. from Ger. Orig. Title: Australische Prachtfinken. (Illus.). 1979. 2.95 (ISBN 0-87666-987-9, KW-O27). TFH Pubns.
Harman, Ian & Vriends, Matthew M. All About Finches. (Illus.). 1978. 9.95 (ISBN 0-87666-965-8, PS-765). TFH Pubns.
Morris, Frank T. Finches of Australia: A Folio. (Illus.). 124p. 65.00 (ISBN 0-7018-1000-9). Eastview.
Roberts, Mervin F. Breeding Zebra Finches. (Illus.). 96p. 1980. 2.95 (ISBN 0-87666-883-X, KW-056). TFH Pubns.
--Society Finches. (Illus.). 1979. 2.95 (ISBN 0-87666-990-9, KW-029). TFH Pubns.
--Society Finches, Breeding. (Illus.). 1979. 2.95 (ISBN 0-87666-991-7, KW-030). TFH Pubns.
--Zebra Finches. (Illus.). 1981. 2.95 (ISBN 0-87666-882-1, KW-055). TFH Pubns.
FINDING LISTS
see Library Catalogs
FINE ARTS
see Art; Arts, the
FINGER ALPHABET
see Deaf–Means of Communication
FINGER GAMES
see Finger Play
FINGER PAINTING
Scott, Guy. Introducing Finger Painting. 1973. 17.95 (ISBN 0-7134-2432-X, Pub. by Batsford England). David & Charles.
FINGER PLAY
Bennett, A. Y. Picture Dictionary, ABCs, Telling Time, Counting Rhymes, Riddles & Finger Plays. (Illus.). (gr. k-3). 1970. 5.95 (ISBN 0-448-02813-1). G&D.
Brown, Marc. Finger Rhymes. LC 80-10173. (Illus.). 32p. (ps-2). 1980. 8.95 (ISBN 0-525-29732-4, Unicorn Bks). Dutton.
Cromwell, Liz & Hibner, Dixie. Finger Frolics: Fingerplays for Young Children. 2nd ed. 1976. pap. 7.95 (ISBN 0-933212-09-7, Dist. by Gryphon House). Partner Pr.
Grayson, Marion. Let's Do Fingerplays. LC 62-10217. (Illus.). (ps-3). 1962. 8.95 (ISBN 0-88331-003-1). Luce.
Poulsson, Emilie. Finger Plays for Nursery & Kindergarten. LC 74-165397. (Illus.). 1971. lib. bdg. 9.50x (ISBN 0-88307-601-2). Gannon.
Self, Margaret, compiled by. Creative Finger Fun. LC 73-88992. 112p. (gr. 1-6). 1974. pap. 1.65 (ISBN 0-8307-0268-7, 50-111-08). Regal.
Self, Margaret, ed. Two Hundred Two Things to Do. LC 68-16267. (Illus., Orig.). (gr. k-2). 1968. pap. 2.95 (ISBN 0-8307-0026-9, 5001102). Regal.
Shely, Patricia, compiled by. All Occasion Finger Plays for Young Children. (Standard Ideas Ser.). (Illus.). 1978. pap. 1.75 (ISBN 0-87239-211-2, 2812). Standard Pub.
--Bible Finger Plays for Young Children. (Standard Ideas Ser.). (Illus.). 1978. pap. 1.75 (ISBN 0-87239-212-0, 2813). Standard Pub.
FINGER-PRESSURE THERAPY
see Shiatsu
FINGER RINGS
see Rings
FINGERPRINTS
Astroms, P. & Eriksson, A. Fingerprints & Archaeology. (Studies in Mediterranean Archaeology Ser.: Vol. XXVIII). 88p. 1981. pap. text ed. 42.00x (ISBN 0-686-72632-4, Pub. by Paul Astroms Sweden). Humanities.
Battley, Harry. Single Finger Prints: A New & Practical Method of Classifying & Filing Single Finger Prints & Fragmentary Impressions. (Illus.). 1931. 42.50x (ISBN 0-686-51311-8). Elliots Bks.
Boy Scouts Of America. Fingerprinting. LC 19-600. (Illus.). 36p. (gr. 6-12). 1964. pap. 0,70x (ISBN 0-8395-3287-3, 3287). BSA.
Field, Annita T. Fingerprint Handbook. (Police Science Ser). (Illus.). 196p. 1976. 14.75 (ISBN 0-398-00562-1). C C Thomas.
Galton, Francis. Finger Prints. 2nd ed. LC 63-23401. 1966. Repr. of 1892 ed. lib. bdg. 12.50 (ISBN 0-306-70910-4). Da Capo.
Herschel, William J. The Origin of Fingerprinting. LC 78-156019. (Illus.). 178p. 1974. Repr. of 1916 ed. 18.00 (ISBN 0-404-09119-9). AMS Pr.
Katz, Marjorie P. Fingerprint Owls & Other Fantasies. LC 72-85648. (Illus.). 64p. 1972. 4.95 (ISBN 0-87131-052-X). M Evans.
Kolb, Patricia A. H.I.T. A Manual for the Classification, Filing, & Retrieval of Palmprints. (Illus.). 112p. 1979. text ed. 16.50 spiral bdg. (ISBN 0-398-03855-4). C C Thomas.
Migne, J. P., ed. Dictionnaire de Paleographie, de Cryptographie, de Dactylologie. (Nouvelle Encyclopedie Theologique Ser.: Vol. 47). 668p. (Fr.). Date not set. Repr. of 1854 ed. lib. bdg. 85.00x (ISBN 0-89241-285-2). Caratzas Bros.
Millimaki, Robert H. Fingerprint Detective. (gr. 4-7). 1973. 10.95 (ISBN 0-397-31484-1, JBL-J). Har-Row.
Olsen, Robert D., Sr. Scott's Fingerprint Mechanics. (Illus.). 480p. 1978. 32.75 (ISBN 0-398-03730-2). C C Thomas.
Rudman, Jack. Fingerprint Technician. (Career Examination Ser.: C-255). (Cloth bdg. avail. on request). pap. 8.00 (ISBN 0-8373-0255-2). Natl Learning.
--Fingerprint Technician Trainee. (Career Examination Ser.: C-286). (Cloth bdg. avail. on request). pap. 8.00 (ISBN 0-8373-0286-2). Natl Learning.
--Senior Fingerprint Technician. (Career Examination Ser.: C-2073). (Cloth bdg. avail. on request). 1977. pap. 10.00 (ISBN 0-8373-2073-9). Natl Learning.
U. S. Government. The Science of Fingerprints. (Illus.). 205p. 1980. pap. 10.00 (ISBN 0-87364-190-6). Paladin Ent.
Wertelecki, Wladimir & Plato, Chris C., eds. Dermatoglyphics Fifty Years Later. LC 79-2595. (Alan R. Liss Ser.: Vol. 15, No. 6). 1979. 76.00 (ISBN 0-8451-1031-4). March of Dimes.
--Dermatoglyphics-Fifty Years Later. LC 79-2595. (Birth Defects: Original Articles Ser.: Vol. XV, No. 6). 826p. 1979. 76.00 (ISBN 0-8451-1031-4). A R Liss.
Wilton, George W. Fingerprints: History, Law & Romance. LC 70-164057. 1971. Repr. of 1938 ed. 24.00 (ISBN 0-8103-3755-X). Gale.
FINGERS
see also Hand; Nails (Anatomy)
FINGERS–ABNORMITIES AND DEFORMITIES
see also Dupuytren's Contracture
FINISHES AND FINISHING
see also Lacquer and Lacquering; Metals–Finishing; Paint; Painting, Industrial; Stains and Staining; Textile Finishing; Varnish and Varnishing; Wood Finishing
Clauser, H. R. Encyclopedia Handbook of Materials, Parts & Finishes. new rev. ed. LC 75-43010. 1976. 35.00 (ISBN 0-87762-189-6). Technomic.
Gillies, M. T., ed. Solventless & High Solids Industrial Finishes: Recent Developments. LC 80-21553. (Chemical Technology Review: No. 179). (Illus.). 342p. 1981. 48.00 (ISBN 0-8155-0828-X). Noyes.
Innes, Jocasta. Paint Magic: The Complete Guide to Decorative Finishes. 240p. 1981. 24.95 (ISBN 0-442-24216-6). Van Nos Reinhold.
O'Neil, Isabel. The Art of the Painted Finish for Furniture & Decoration. LC 70-151928. (Illus.). 1980. pap. 10.95 (ISBN 0-688-06070-6, Quill). Morrow.
Rhoades, Lawrence, ed. Cost Guide for Atomatic Finishing Processes. LC 80-52614. (Illus.). 209p. (Orig.). 1981. pap. 15.50 (ISBN 0-87263-056-0). SME.
Santholzer, R. W. Five Language Dictionary of Surface Coatings, Platings, Product Finishing, Plastics & Rubber. 1969. 60.00 (ISBN 0-08-012336-8). Pergamon.
Soderberg, George A. Finishing Technology. rev. ed. (gr. 10-12). 1969. text ed. 15.96 (ISBN 0-87345-016-7). McKnight.
FINISHING, FURNITURE
see Furniture Finishing
FINITE
see Infinite
FINITE ARITHMETIC
see Modular Arithmetic
FINITE AUTOMATA
see Sequential Machine Theory
FINITE DIFFERENCES
see Difference Equations
FINITE ELEMENT METHOD
Ashwell, D. G. & Gallagher, R. H., eds. Finite Elements for Thin Shells & Curved Members. LC 75-37654. (Studies in Social & Cognitive Development). 268p. 1976. 48.95 (ISBN 0-471-01648-9, Pub. by Wiley-Interscience). Wiley.
Aziz, A. K., ed. The Mathematical Foundations of the Finite Element Method with Applications to Partial Differentail Equations. 1972. 61.00 (ISBN 0-12-068650-3). Acad Pr.
Bathe, K. J., ed. Nonlinear Finite Element Analysis & Adina: Proceedings of the 3rd Adina Conference, Massachussetts, USA, 10-12 June 1981. 206p. 1981. 50.00 (ISBN 0-08-027594-X). Pergamon.
Bathe, Klaus, et al, eds. Formulations & Computational Algorithms in Finite-Element Analysis: U. S. German Symposium. 1977. 52.50x (ISBN 0-262-02127-7). MIT Pr.
Bathe, Klaus-Jurgen. Finite Element Procedures Enengineering Analysis. (Illus.). 736p. 1982. 38.00 (ISBN 0-13-317305-4). P-H.
Bathe, Klaus-Jurgen & Wilson, Edward L. Numerical Methods in Finite Element Analysis. (Illus.). 544p. 1976. 34.95 (ISBN 0-13-627190-1). P-H.
Becker, Eric B., et al. Finite Elements: An Introduction, Vol. I. (Illus.). 256p. 1981. 24.95 (ISBN 0-13-317057-8). P-H.
Belytschko, Ted & Marcal, P. V., eds. Finite Element Analysis of Transient Nonlinear Structural Behavior: AMD, Vol. 14. 200p. 1975. pap. text ed. 20.00 (ISBN 0-685-62566-4, I00094). ASME.
Cheung, Y. K. & Yeo, M. F. A Practical Introduction to Finite Element Analysis. (Civil Engineering Ser.). 1980p. 1979. text ed. 24.95 (ISBN 0-273-01083-2). Pitman Pub MA.
Cook, Robert D. Concepts & Applications of Finite Element Analysis: A Textbook for Beginning Courses in the Finite Method As Used for the Analysis of Displacement, Strain & Stress. LC 74-7053. 402p. 1974. text ed. 30.95 (ISBN 0-471-16915-3). Wiley.
Desai, C. S. Elementary Finite Element Method. (Civil Engineering & Engineering Mechanics Ser.). (Illus.). 1979. ref. ed. 26.95 (ISBN 0-13-256636-2). P-H.
Fairweather, Graeme. Finite Element Galerkin Methods for Differential Equations. (Lecture Notes in Pure & Applied Mathematics Ser.: Vol. 34). 1978. 24.75 (ISBN 0-8247-6673-3). Dekker.
Fenner, Roger T. Finite Element Methods for Engineers. (Illus.). 1976. pap. text ed. 17.50x (ISBN 0-333-18656-7). Scholium Intl.
Gallagher, Richard H. Finite Element Analysis: Fundamentals. (Civil Engr. & Engr. Mechanics Ser.). (Illus.). 416p. 1975. 26.95 (ISBN 0-13-317248-1). P-H.
Galligani, I. & Magenes, E., eds. Mathematical Aspects of Finite Element Methods: Proceedings of the Conference Held in Rome, Dec.10-22, 1975. (Lecture Notes in Mathematics: Vol. 606). 1977. pap. text ed. 24.10 (ISBN 0-387-08342-1). Springer-Verlag.
Girault, V. & Raviart, P. A. Finite Element Approximation of the Navier-Stokes Equations. rev. ed. (Lecture Notes in Mathematics Ser.: Vol. 749). 202p. 1981. pap. 14.00 (ISBN 0-387-09557-8). Springer-Verlag.
Glowinski, R., et al. Energy Methods in Finite Element Analysis. LC 78-13642. (Numerical Methods in Engineering Ser.). 361p. 1979. 61.25x (ISBN 0-471-99723-4, Pub. by Wiley-Interscience). Wiley.
Gudehus, G. Finite Elements in Geomechanics. LC 77-792. (Wiley Series in Numerical Methods of Engineering). 464p. 1977. 78.75x (ISBN 0-471-99446-4, Pub. by Wiley-Interscience). Wiley.
Hinton, E. & Owen, D. R. Finite Element Programming. LC 77-77366. (Computational Mathematics & Application Ser.). 1980. pap. 20.00 (ISBN 0-12-349352-8). Acad Pr.
--Finite Element Programming. (Computational Mathematics & Application Ser.). 1977. 48.50 (ISBN 0-12-349350-1). Acad Pr.
Huebner, Kenneth H. Finite Element Method for Engineers. LC 74-17452. 448p. 1975. 36.50 (ISBN 0-471-41950-8, Pub. by Wiley-Interscience). Wiley.
Irons, Bruce. Techniques of Finite Elements. (Engineering Science Ser.). 529p. 1981. 30.95 (ISBN 0-470-27166-3). Halsted Pr.
Irons, Bruce & Ahmad, Sohrab. Techniques of Finite Elements. LC 79-40994. (Engineering Science Ser.: Civil Engineering). 529p. 1979. 96.95x (ISBN 0-470-26855-7). Halsted Pr.
Martin, Harold C. & Carey, G. F. Introduction to Finite Element Analysis. text ed. 25.50 (ISBN 0-07-040641-3, C); solutions to problems 6.95 (ISBN 0-07-009830-1). McGraw.
Mercier, B. Lectures on Topics in Finite Element Solution of Elliptic Problems. (Tata Institute Lectures on Mathematics). (Illus.). 191p. 1980. pap. 8.00 (ISBN 0-387-09543-8). Springer-Verlag.
Nath, B. Fundamentals of Finite Elements for Engineers. (Illus.). 256p. 1974. text ed. 25.00x (ISBN 0-485-11148-9, Athlone Pr). Humanities.
Norrie, D. H. & De Vries, G. An Introduction to Finite Element Analysis. 1978. 27.50 (ISBN 0-12-521660-2). Acad Pr.
Oden, J. T. & Reddy, J. N. An Introduction to the Mathematical Theory of Finite Elements. LC 76-6953. (Pure & Applied Mathematics Ser.). 429p. 1976. 39.95 (ISBN 0-471-65261-X, Pub. by Wiley-Interscience). Wiley.
Pinder, G. F. & Gray, W. G. Finite Element Simulation in Surface & Subsurface Hydrology. 1977. 43.00 (ISBN 0-12-556950-5). Acad Pr.
Richards, T. H. Energy Methods in Stress Analysis: With an Introduction to Finite Element Techniques. (Ellis Horwood Series in Engineering Science). 1977. 58.95 (ISBN 0-470-98960-2). Halsted Pr.
Robinson, J. Integrated Theory of Finite Element Methods. LC 73-2792. 428p. 1973. 61.50 (ISBN 0-471-72807-1, Pub. by Wiley-Interscience). Wiley.
Rockey, K. C., et al. The Finite Element Method: A Basic Introduction. 239p. 1980. pap. text ed. 21.95x (ISBN 0-470-26979-0). Halsted Pr.
Segerlind, Larry J. Applied Finite Element Analysis. LC 76-6958. 1976. text ed. 28.95 (ISBN 0-471-77440-5). Wiley.
Smith, I. M. Programming the Finite Elements Method with Application to Geomechanics. 300p. 1981. 26.25 (ISBN 0-471-28003-8, Pub. by Wiley-Interscience). Wiley.
Strang, G. & Fix, George J. An Analysis of the Finite Element Method. LC 72-12642. (Illus.). 320p. 1973. ref. ed. 27.00 (ISBN 0-13-032946-0). P-H.
Tong, Pin & Rossettos, John N. Finite Element Method: Basic Technique & Implementation. LC 76-7453. 1976. text ed. 19.95x (ISBN 0-262-20032-5). MIT Pr.
Wachspress, Eugene L. A Rational Finite Element Basis. (Mathematics in Science & Engineering Ser.). 1975. 31.00 (ISBN 0-12-728950-X). Acad Pr.
Whiteman, J. R., ed. The Mathematics of Finite Elements & Applications II: Mafelap 1977. 84.00 (ISBN 0-12-747252-5). Acad Pr.
Zienkiewicz, O. C. Introductory Lectures on the Finite Element Method. (CISM International Centre for Mechanical Sciences Courses & Lectures: Vol. 130). (Illus.). 1978. pap. 13.50 (ISBN 0-387-81202-4). Springer-Verlag.
FINITE FIELDS (ALGEBRA)
see Modular Fields
FINITE GROUPS
see also Modules (Algebra)
Chestnut, D. B. Finite Groups & Quantum Theory. LC 74-9840. 270p. 1974. 25.00 (ISBN 0-471-15445-8). Krieger.
Collins, Michael J., ed. Finite Simple Groups, II. LC 77-149703. 1981. 60.00 (ISBN 0-12-181480-7). Acad Pr.
Conference on Finite Groups, Gainesville, March 1972. Finite Groups: Proceedings. Gagen, T., et al, eds. LC 72-97697. (Mathematical Studies: Vol. 7). 96p. 1973. pap. 22.00 (ISBN 0-444-10451-8, North-Holland). Elsevier.
Conner, P. E. Differentiable Periodic Maps. 2nd ed. (Lecture Notes in Mathematics: Vol. 738). 1979. pap. 10.30 (ISBN 0-387-09535-7). Springer-Verlag.
Conner, Pierre E. Lectures on the Action of a Finite Group. LC 68-57940. (Lecture Notes in Mathematics: Vol. 73). 1968. pap. 10.70 (ISBN 0-387-04243-1). Springer-Verlag.
Curtis, Charles W. & Reiner, Irving. Methods of Representation Theory: With Applications to Finite Groups & Orders, Vol. 1. (Pure & Applied Mathematics Ser.: a Wiley Series of Texts Monographs & Tracts). 912p. 1981. 55.00 (ISBN 0-471-18994-4, Pub. by Wiley-Interscience). Wiley.
--Representation Theory of Finite Groups & Associative Algebras. LC 62-16994. (Pure & Applied Mathematics Ser.). 1962. 53.00 (ISBN 0-470-18975-4, Pub. by Wiley-Interscience). Wiley.
--Representation Theory of Finite Groups & Orders. (Pure & Applied Mathematics: Texts, Monographs & Tracts). 900p. 1981. 55.00 (ISBN 0-471-18994-4, Pub. by Wiley-Interscience). Wiley.
Curzio, M. Institutiones Mathematicae: Some Problems of Sylow Type in Locally Finite Groups. 1981. 17.00 (ISBN 0-12-363605-1). Acad Pr.
Dorn, William S. & McCracken, Daniel D. Introductory Finite Mathematics with Computing. LC 75-30647. 449p. 1976. text ed. 21.95 (ISBN 0-471-21917-7); instructor's manual (ISBN 0-471-01539-3). Wiley.
Feit, Walter. Characters of Finite Groups. 1967. 17.50 (ISBN 0-8053-2434-8, Adv Bk Prog); pap. text ed. 8.50 (ISBN 0-8053-2435-6). Benjamin-Cummings.
Gagen, T. M. Topic in Finite Groups. LC 75-17116. (London Mathematical Society Lecture Note Ser.: No. 16). 80p. 1976. 11.95 (ISBN 0-521-21002-X). Cambridge U Pr.
Gashutz, W. Lectures on Subgroups of Sylow Type in Finite Soluble Groups. Kuhn, U., tr. (Notes on Pure Mathematics Ser.: No. 11). 100p. (Orig.). 1980. pap. text ed. 7.95 (ISBN 0-908160-22-4, 0571). Bks Australia.
Glauberman, G. Factorization in Local Subgroups of Finite Groups. LC 77-13373. (Conference Board of the Mathematical Sciences Ser.: No. 33). 1977. 10.60 (ISBN 0-8218-1683-7, CBMS33). Am Math.
Gorenstein, Daniel. Finite Groups. 2nd ed. xvii, 517p. 1980. 22.50 (ISBN 0-8284-0301-5). Chelsea Pub.
--Finite Simple Groups: An Introduction to Their Classification. (The University Series in Mathematics). 290p. 1981. text ed. price not set (ISBN 0-306-40779-5, Plenum Pr). Plenum Pub.

Gorenstein, Daniel & Harada, Kaichiro. Finite Groups Whose 2-Subgroups Are Generated by at Most 4 Elements. LC 74-11282. (Memoirs: No. 147). 464p. 1974. pap. 13.20 (ISBN 0-8218-1847-3, MEMO-147). Am Math.
Gorenstein, Daniel, ed. Reviews on Finite Groups. LC 74-711. 736p. 1974. 72.00 (ISBN 0-8218-0201-1, REVFINITE). Am Math.
Gruenberg, Karl W. Relation Models of Finite Groups. LC 76-3645. (CBMS Regional Conference Ser. in Mathematics: Vol. 25). 1976. 13.20 (ISBN 0-8218-1675-6, CBMS-25). Am Math.
Jones, Vaughan. Actions of Finite Groups on the Hyperfinite Type II (to the First Power) Factor. LC 80-22560. (Memoirs Ser.: No. 237). 5.20 (ISBN 0-8218-2237-3, MEMO-237). Am Math.
Kegel, O. H. & Wehrfritz, B. A. Locally Finite Groups. (Mathematics Library Ser.). 1973. 27.00 (ISBN 0-444-10406-2, North-Holland). Elsevier.
Keown, R. An Introduction to Group Representation Theory. (Mathematics in Science & Engineering Ser.). 1975. 42.00 (ISBN 0-12-404250-3). Acad Pr.
Lomont, John S. Applications of Finite Groups. 1959. 38.50 (ISBN 0-12-455550-0). Acad Pr.
London Mathematical Society Instructional Conference. Finite Simple Groups: Proceedings. Powell, M. B. & Higman, G., eds. 1971. 50.50 (ISBN 0-12-563850-7). Acad Pr.
Lutzig, George. Representations of Finite Chevally Groups. LC 78-24068. (CBMS Regional Conference Ser. in Mathematics: No. 39). 1978. 10.40 (ISBN 0-8218-1689-6). Am Math.
Norrie, Douglas H. & DeVries, Gerard, eds. The Finite Element Method: Fundamentals & Applications. 1973. 50.00 (ISBN 0-12-521650-5). Acad Pr.
Rector, Robert E. & Zwick, Earl J. Finite Mathematics & Its Applications. LC 78-69547. (Illus.). 1979. text ed. 17.50 (ISBN 0-395-27206-8); inst. manual 0.75 (ISBN 0-395-27207-6). HM.
Scott, William R. & Gross, Fletcher, eds. Proceedings of the Conference on Finite Groups. 1976. 51.00 (ISBN 0-12-633650-4). Acad Pr.
Seminar on Finite Element Analysis, Tokyo, 1973. Theory & Practice in Finite Element Structural Analysis: Proceedings. Yamada, Yoshiaki & Gallagher, Richard H., eds. 754p. 1974. 29.00x (ISBN 0-86008-097-8, Pub. by U of Tokyo Pr). Intl Schol Bk Serv.
Serre, J. P. Linear Representations of Finite Groups. Scott, L., tr. from Fr. LC 76-12585. (Graduate Texts in Mathematics: Vol. 42). 1977. 19.60 (ISBN 0-387-90190-6). Springer-Verlag.
Shatz, Stephen S. Profinite Groups, Arithmetic, & Geometry. LC 77-126832. (Annals of Mathematics Studies: No. 67). 1971. 16.50x (ISBN 0-691-08017-8). Princeton U Pr.
Speiser, A. Die Theorie der Gruppen Von Endlicher Ordnung. (MA Ser.: No. 22). 272p. (Ger.). 1980. 33.00 (ISBN 3-7643-1151-7). Birkhauser.
Srinivasan, B. Representations of Finite Chevalley Groups. (Lecture Notes in Mathematics: Vol. 764). 177p. 1980. pap. text ed. 12.40 (ISBN 0-387-09716-3). Springer-Verlag.
Swan, R. G. & Evans, E. G. K-Theory of Finite Groups & Orders. LC 75-133576. (Lecture Notes in Mathematics: Vol. 149). 1970. pap. 11.20 (ISBN 0-387-04938-X). Springer-Verlag.
Symposia in Pure Mathematics-Madison, Wis.-1970. Representation Theory of Finite Groups & Related Topics: Proceedings, Vol. 21. Reiner, I., ed. LC 79-165201. 1971. 24.80 (ISBN 0-8218-1421-4, PSPUM-21). Am Math.
--Representation Theory of Finite Groups & Related Topics: Proceedings, Vol. 21. Reiner, I., ed. LC 79-165201. 1971. 24.80 (ISBN 0-8218-1421-4, PSPUM-21). Am Math.
Symposia in Pure Mathematics-Pasadena-1960. Institute on Finite Groups, 1960: Proceedings, Vol. 6. LC 50-1183. 1979. Repr. of 1961 ed. 18.40 (ISBN 0-8218-1406-0, PSPUM-6). Am Math.
Symposium on Finite Groups, Urbana, Illinois, Nov. 24, 1967. Proceedings. Repr. of 1969 ed. 8.40 (ISBN 0-8218-0045-0, FIN). Am Math.
Tits, J. Buildings of Spherical Type & Finite BN-Pairs. LC 74-5714. (Lecture Notes in Mathematics: Vol. 386). 229p. 1974. pap. 13.10 (ISBN 0-387-06757-4). Springer-Verlag.
Tsuzuku, T. Finite Groups & Finite Geometrics. (Cambridge Tracts in Mathematics Ser.: No. 78). (Illus.). 250p. Date not set. price not set (ISBN 0-521-22242-7). Cambridge U Pr.
Whiteman, J. R., ed. The Mathematics of Finite Elements & Applications. 1973. 82.50 (ISBN 0-12-747250-9). Acad Pr.

FINITE NUMBER SYSTEMS
see Modules (Algebra)

FINK, MIKE, 1770-1823
Blair, Walter. Mike Fink, King of Mississippi Keelboatmen. LC 74-138143. (Illus.). 1971. Repr. of 1933 ed. lib. bdg. 15.25x (ISBN 0-8371-5600-9, BLMF). Greenwood.
Blair, Walter & Meine, Franklin J. Half Horse Half Alligator: The Growth of the Mike Fink Legend. LC 81-3358. (Illus.). x, 289p. 1981. pap. 5.95x (ISBN 0-8032-6060-1, BB 772, Bison). U of Nebr Pr.
Blair, Walter & Franklin, Meine J., eds. Half Horse Half Alligator: The Growth of the Mike Fink Legend. LC 77-70578. (Intenational Folklore Ser.). Repr. of 1956 ed. lib. bdg. 18.00x (ISBN 0-405-10079-5). Arno.
Blair, Walter & Meine, Franklin J., eds. Half Horse Half Alligator: The Growth of the Mike Fink Legend. LC 81-3358. (Illus.). x, 289p. 1981. Repr. of 1956 ed. price not set (ISBN 0-8032-6060-1, BB 772). U of Nebr Pr.

FINLAND
Benz, A. Finland: Facts About. 1976. pap. 4.50x (ISBN 9-5110-4105-3, F525). Vanous.
Brotherus, V. F. Die Laubmoose Fennoskandias. (Flora Fennica Ser.: Vol. 1). (Illus.). 635p. (Ger.). 1974. Repr. of 1923 ed. lib. bdg. 102.95x (ISBN 3-87429-078-6). Lubrecht & Cramer.
Central Statistical Office of Finland. Statistical Yearbook of Finland, 1979. 75th ed. Laakso, Elia, ed. LC 59-42150. (Illus.). 577p. (Eng, Finnish, Swed.). 1980. vinyl bnd. 38.00x (ISBN 0-8002-2731-X). Intl Pubns Serv.
Finland. (Panorama Bks.). (Illus., Fr.). 3.95 (ISBN 0-685-11188-1). French & Eur.
Lander, Patricia S. In the Shadow of the Factory: Social Change in a Finnish Community. LC 75-37634. 198p. 1976. pap. text ed. 5.95 (ISBN 0-470-01380-X). Halsted Pr.
Nordberg, B. Sociolinguistic Research in Sweden & Finland. 1977. 17.25x (ISBN 90-279-7504-3). Mouton.
Shirer, William L. The Challenge of Scandinavia: Norway, Sweden, Denmark, & Finland in Our Time. LC 76-49145. 1977. Repr. of 1955 ed. lib. bdg. 24.00x (ISBN 0-8371-9345-1, SHCS). Greenwood.

FINLAND-COMMERCE
Finland's Two Thousand Largest Companies. 5th ed. 1976. 42.00x (ISBN 0-8002-1420-X). Intl Pubns Serv.
Sudmen. Fifteen Hundred Largest Companies in Finland. (Illus.). 1975. 19.95x (ISBN 0-8464-1141-5). Beekman Pubs.
Thilman, Borje, ed. The Two Thousand Largest Companies in Finland 1977. 6th rev. ed. 1977. 45.00x (ISBN 951-9102-11-6). Intl Pubns Serv.

FINLAND-DESCRIPTION AND TRAVEL
Finland: The Country, Its People, & Institutions, 6 vols. in 1. LC 77-87706. 1977. Repr. of 1926 ed. 38.50 (ISBN 0-404-16503-6). AMS Pr.
Jones, Michael. Finland, Daughter of the Sea. (Studies in Historical Geography). (Illus.). 1977. 19.50 (ISBN 0-208-01623-6, Archon). Shoe String.
Murray's Hand-Book for Northern Europe: Finland & Russia. LC 70-115567. (Russia Observed, Series I). 1970. Repr. of 1849 ed. 14.00 (ISBN 0-405-03052-5). Arno.
The Nagel Travel Guide to Finland. (Nagel Travel Guide Ser). 1977. 30.00 (ISBN 2-8263-0528-X). Hippocrene Bks.
Nagel's Encyclopedia Guide: Finland. (Illus.). 368p. 1980. 30.00 (ISBN 0-686-74056-4). Masson Pub.
Nickels, Sylvia. The Travellers' Guide to Finland. LC 78-321452. (Travellers' Guide Ser.). (Illus.). 240p. 1979. 10.95 (ISBN 0-224-01281-9, Pub. by Chatto Bodley Jonathan). Merrimack Bk Serv.
Nicol, Gladys. Finland. (Batsford Countries Ser.). Date not set. 12.95 (ISBN 0-8038-2311-8). Hastings.
Sansom, William. The Icicle & the Sun. LC 75-31691. (Illus.). 159p. 1976. Repr. of 1959 ed. lib. bdg. 15.00x (ISBN 0-8371-8442-8, SAICS). Greenwood.
Young, Ernest. Finland: The Land of a Thousand Lakes. LC 77-87707. (Illus.). Repr. of 1912 ed. 35.00 (ISBN 0-404-16502-8). AMS Pr.

FINLAND-ECONOMIC CONDITIONS
Lander, Patricia. In the Shadow of the Factory: Socioeconomic Change in a Finnish Community. 202p. 1976. pap. 8.95x (ISBN 0-87073-020-7). Schenkman.

FINLAND-FOREIGN RELATIONS
Maude, George. The Finnish Dilemma: Neutrality in the Shadow of Power. 1976. 17.50x (ISBN 0-19-218319-2). Oxford U Pr.
Paasivirta, Juhani. Finland & Europe: The Period of Autonomy & the International Crises, 1808-1914. Kirby, D. G., ed. Upton, Anthony F. & Upton, Sirka B., trs. from Finnish. (The Nordic Ser.: Vol. 7). 300p. Date not set. 29.50x (ISBN 0-8166-1046-0). U of Minn Pr.
Schwartz, Andrew J. America & the Russo-Finnish War. LC 74-74344. 103p. 1975. Repr. of 1960 ed. lib. bdg. 15.00 (ISBN 0-8371-7964-5, SCAM). Greenwood.
Vloyantes, John P. Silk Glove Hegemony - Finnish Soviet Relations, 1944-1974. LC 74-27387. 200p. 1975. 12.00x (ISBN 0-87338-174-2). Kent St U Pr.

FINLAND-HISTORY
see also Russo-Finnish War, 1939-1940
De Ullmann, Stephan. Epic of the Finnish Nation. 1977. lib. bdg. 59.95 (ISBN 0-8490-1780-7). Gordon Pr.
Erfurth, Waldemar. Last Finnish War. 1979. 22.00 (ISBN 0-89093-205-0). U Pubns Amer.
Hamalainen, P. K. In Time of Storm: Revolution, Civil War & the Ethnolinguistic Issue in Finland. LC 78-6301. 1979. 40.00 (ISBN 0-87395-375-4). State U NY Pr.
Mazour, Anatole G. Finland Between East & West. LC 75-31771. (Illus.). 298p. 1976. Repr. of 1956 ed. lib. bdg. 19.25x (ISBN 0-8371-8495-9, MAFEW). Greenwood.
Puntila, L. A. The Political History of Finland: 1809-1966. 248p. 1976. 22.50x (ISBN 0-8448-0913-6). Crane-Russak Co.
Soderhjelm, H. The Red Insurrection in Finland in 1918: A Study Based on Documentary Evidence. Fausboll, Anne I., tr. LC 75-39063. (Russian Studies: Perspectives on the Revolution Ser.). 159p. 1976. Repr. of 1919 ed. 16.00 (ISBN 0-88355-443-7). Hyperion Conn.
Thaden, E. C., ed. Russification in the Baltic Provinces & Finland, 1855-1914. LC 80-7557. 1980. 40.00 (ISBN 0-691-05314-6); pap. 17.50 (ISBN 0-691-10103-5). Princeton U Pr.
Tokoi, Oskari. Sisu: Even Through a Stone Wall. 6.00 (ISBN 0-8315-0008-5). Speller.
Upton, Anthony F. The Finnish Revolution. (Nordic Ser.: Vol. 3). 600p. 1981. 39.50x (ISBN 0-8166-0905-5). U of Minn Pr.

FINLAND-JUVENILE LITERATURE
Berry, Erick. The Land & People of Finland. rev. ed. LC 78-37246. (Portraits of the Nations Ser.). (Illus.). (gr. 6 up). 1972. 8.95 (ISBN 0-397-31255-5, JBL-J). Har-Row.

FINLAND-POLITICS AND GOVERNMENT
Cultural Policy in Finland. LC 72-82781. (Studies & Documents on Cultural Policies). (Illus.). 73p. (Orig.). 1972. pap. 5.00 (ISBN 92-3-100965-6, U118, UNESCO). Unipub.
Kirby, D. G. Finland in the Twentieth Century: A History & an Interpretation. LC 79-11651. 1980. 19.75x (ISBN 0-8166-0895-4). U of Minn Pr.
Nousiainen, Jaakko. Finnish Political System. Hodgson, John H., tr. from Fin. LC 76-120320. (Illus.). 1971. 22.50x (ISBN 0-674-30211-7). Harvard U Pr.
Paasivirta, Juhani. Finland & Europe: The Period of Autonomy & the International Crises, 1808-1914. Kirby, D. G., ed. Upton, Anthony F. & Upton, Sirka B., trs. from Finnish. (The Nordic Ser.: Vol. 7). 300p. Date not set. 29.50x (ISBN 0-8166-1046-0). U of Minn Pr.

FINLAND-SOCIAL LIFE AND CUSTOMS
Irwin, John L. The Finns & the Lapps: How They Live & Work. 171p. 1973. text ed. 8.95 (ISBN 0-03-030206-4, HoltC). HR&W.
Lindroos, Maria. Me & My Life. 1980. 7.50 (ISBN 0-682-49558-1). Exposition.
Rajanen, Aini. Of Finnish Ways. LC 80-28932. (Heritage Books). (Illus.). 232p. 1981. 8.95 (ISBN 0-87518-214-3). Dillon.
Ways of Life in Finland: A Preliminary Discussion. 35p. 1980. pap. 5.00 (ISBN 92-808-0142-2, TUNU 070, UNU). Unipub.

FINLEY, ROBERT, 1772-1817
Brown, Isaac V. Biography of the Reverend Robert Finley. LC 73-82178. (Anti-Slavery Crusade in America Ser). 1969. Repr. of 1857 ed. 16.00 (ISBN 0-405-00617-9). Arno.

FINN MAC CUMAILL
Campbell, John G. Fians. LC 79-144457. (Waifs & Strays of Celtic Tradition: Argyllshire Ser.: No. 4). Repr. of 1891 ed. 18.00 (ISBN 0-404-53534-8). AMS Pr.

FINNESBURH-BIBLIOGRAPHY
Fry, Donald K. Beowulf & the Fight at Finnsburh: A Bibliography. LC 70-94760. 160p. 1969. 12.50x (ISBN 0-8139-0268-1, Bibliographical Society, University of Virginia). U Pr of Va.

FINNEY, CHARLES GRANDISON, 1792-1875
Edman, V. Raymond. Finney Lives On. 1970. pap. 3.95 (ISBN 0-87123-150-6, 210150). Bethany Hse.
Finney, Charles G. The Autobiography of Charles G. Finney. Wessel, Helen S., ed. LC 77-2813. 1977. pap. 4.95 (ISBN 0-87123-010-0). Bethany Hse.
Miller, Basil. Charles G. Finney. 1969. pap. 2.95 (ISBN 0-87123-061-5, 200061). Bethany Hse.

FINNISH ARCHITECTURE
see Architecture-Finland

FINNISH FOLK-LORE
see Folk-Lore, Finnish

FINNISH LANGUAGE
Aaltio, M. Finnish for Foreigners, 3 vols. Set. pap. 35.00 (ISBN 0-686-66991-6). Vol. 1 (ISBN 9-5110-0397-6). Vol. 2 (ISBN 9-5110-1483-8). Vol. 3 (ISBN 9-5110-1919-8). Heinman.
Aaltio, M-H. Finnish for Foreigners: Pt 2, Lessons 27 to 40. 8th rev. ed. (Illus.). 192p. 1976. pap. text ed. 18.50x (ISBN 951-1-01483-8, F 562). Vanous.
Aaltio, M. J. Finnish for Foreigners, Pt. 1: Lessons 1-25. 10th ed. (Illus.). 254p. 1976. pap. text ed. 18.50x (ISBN 951-1-00397-6, F561); cassette a, 45.00x cassettes b-e, 100.00x 4 open reels,100.00x 40.00x (ISBN 0-686-66923-1). Vanous.
Atkinson, John A. Finnish Grammar. 132p. 1980. pap. 5.75 (ISBN 0-906191-44-0, Pub. by Findhorn-Thule Scotland). Hydra Bk.
Bell, Aili R. & Koski, Augustus A. FSI Finnish Graded Reader. 1968. pap. text ed. 8.75x (ISBN 0-686-10710-1); 14 cassettes 84.00x (ISBN 0-686-10711-X). Intl Learn Syst.
Berlitz Editors. Finnish for Travellers. rev. ed. LC 75-111363. (Travellers Ser. for English Speakers). (Orig.). 1977. pap. 2.95 (ISBN 0-02-963910-7, Berlitz); cassettepak, 1973 10.95 (ISBN 0-02-962010-4). Macmillan.
Harms, Robert T. Finnish Structural Sketch. LC 64-64593. (Uralic & Altaic Ser: Vol. 42). (Orig.). 1964. pap. text ed. 3.00x (ISBN 0-87750-011-8). Res Ctr Lang Semiotic.
Kallioinen, V. Finnish Conversational Exercises: Elementary Level. pap. 10.00 (ISBN 9-5171-7028-9). Heinman.
Kallioinen, Vilho. Finnish Conversational Exercises. 164p. 1980. pap. 6.50 (ISBN 9-5171-7028-9, Pub. by Findhorn-Thule Scotland). Hydra Bk.
Keresztes, Kalman. Morphemic & Semantic Analysis of the Word Families: Finnish ETE- & Hungarian EL- 'fore' LC 64-64194. (Uralic & Altaic Ser: Vol. 41). (Orig.). 1964. pap. text ed. 4.00x (ISBN 0-87750-010-X). Res Ctr Lang Semiotic.
Learn Finnish for English Speakers. pap. 9.50 (ISBN 0-87557-020-8, 020-8). Saphrograph.
Luthy, Melvin J. Phonological & Lexical Aspects of Coloquial Finnish. (Uralic & Altaic Ser.). x, 94p. 1973. pap. text ed. 9.50x (ISBN 0-87750-173-4). Res Ctr Lang Semiotic.
Nuutinen, Olli. Finnish in Finnish, 4 vols. 365p. 1980. pap. 15.50 (ISBN 9-5171-7150-1, Pub. by Findhorn-Thule Scotland). Hydra Bk.
Paitio, M. H. Finnish for Foreigners, Pt. 3. 1975. 18.50x (ISBN 9-5110-1919-8, F-566). Vanous.
Stoebke, Renate. Verhaltniswo rter in Den Ostseefinnischen Sprachen. LC 67-66160. (Uralic & Altaic Ser: Vol. 93). (Orig.). 1968. pap. text ed. 11.00x (ISBN 0-87750-038-X). Res Ctr Lang Semiotic.
Thomsen, Vilhelm. On the Influence of Germanic Languages on Finnish & Lapp. LC 67-63427. (Uralic & Altaic Ser: Vol. 87). (Ger.). 1967. pap. text ed. 7.00x (ISBN 0-87750-035-5). Res Ctr Lang Semiotic.
Whitney, A. H. Teach Yourself Finnish. (Teach Yourself Ser.). pap. 4.95 (ISBN 0-679-10170-5). McKay.

FINNISH LANGUAGE-DICTIONARIES
Aaltio, Maija H. Finnish Language Book for English Speaking People. 18.50 (ISBN 0-87559-107-8). Shalom.
Alanne, V. S. Finnish Dictionary: Suomalais-Englantilainen, Vol. 1. 3rd ed. 1979. 75.00x (ISBN 9-5100-1069-3, F563). Vanous.
Diccionario Lexicon Finlandes-Espanol, Espanol-Finlandes. 400p. (Finl. -Espn.). leatherette 4.95 (ISBN 84-303-0150-X, S-50405). French & Eur.
Diccionario Lexicon Finlandes-Espanol, Espanol-Finlandes. 400p. (Finl. -Espn.). pap. 4.50 (ISBN 84-303-0149-6, S-50404). French & Eur.
Finnish Pocket Dictionary. 12.50 (ISBN 9-5100-7468-3). Heinman.
Finnish Pocket Dictionary, Finnish-English - English-Finnish. new ed. 465p. (Engl. & Finnish.). 1980. pap. text ed. 13.00x (ISBN 9-5100-7468-3, F559). Vanous.
Hurme, R. & Pesonen, M. Finnish Deluxe Dictionary: English-Finnish. 2nd ed. 1978. 85.00x (ISBN 9-5100-5699-5, F-565). Vanous.
Riikon, E. & Tuomikowski, A. Finnish Dictionary. 10th ed. 1979. text ed. 55.00x (ISBN 9-5110-0343-7, F560). Vanous.
Wuole, A. Finnish-English, English-Finnish Dictionary. 22.50 (ISBN 0-87559-010-1); thumb indexed 26.00 (ISBN 0-87559-011-X). Shalom.
Wuolle, A. Finnish-English, English-Finnish Dictionary, 2 Vols. 11th ed. Set. 35.00 (ISBN 951-0-09469-2). Finnish-Eng (ISBN 9-5100-8500-6). Eng.-Finnish (ISBN 951-0-08500-6). Heinman.
Wuolle, Aino. Finnish Small Dictionary: English-Finnish, Vol. 1. 13th ed. 1980. text ed. 20.00x (ISBN 9-5100-0870-2, F557). Vanous.
--Finnish Small Dictionary: Finnish-English, Vol. 2. 11th ed. 1979. text ed. 20.00x (ISBN 9-5100-0074-4, F558). Vanous.

FINNISH LANGUAGES
see also Estonian Language; Finnish Language; Finno-Ugrian Languages; Votish Language

Luthy, Melvin J. Phonological & Lexical Aspects of Colloquial Finnish. (Uralic & Altaic Ser.: No. 119). 93p. 1973. pap. text ed. 21.25x (ISBN 0-686-27754-6). Mouton.

Raun, Alo. Essays in Finno-Ugric & Finnic Linguistics. (Uralic & Atlaic Ser.: No. 107). 1971. pap. text ed. 8.00x (ISBN 0-87750-152-1). Res Ctr Lang Semiotic.

FINNISH LITERATURE (SELECTIONS EXTRACTS, ETC.)

Dauenhauer, Richard & Binham, Philip, eds. Snow in May: An Anthology of Modern Finnish Writing 1945-1972. LC 74-4967. (Illus.). 389p. 1978. 25.00 (ISBN 0-8386-1583-X). Fairleigh Dickinson.

Ravila, Paavo. Finnish Literary Reader. LC 65-63019. (Uralic & Altaic Ser: Vol. 44). (Orig.). 1965. pap. text ed. 3.50x (ISBN 0-87750-012-6). Res Ctr Lang Semiotic.

FINNISH LITERATURE–HISTORY AND CRITICISM

Ahokas, Jaakko. A History of Finnish Literature. (Uralic & Altaic Ser.: No. 72). 568p. 1973. pap. text ed. 47.00x (ISBN 0-686-27749-X). Mouton.

Harvard University Library. Finnish & Baltic History & Literatures: Classification Schedule, Author & Title Listing, Chronological Listing. LC 72-75829. (Widener Library Shelflist, No. 40). 260p. 1972. 30.00x (ISBN 0-674-30205-2). Harvard U Pr.

FINNISH MYTHOLOGY

see Mythology, Finno-Ugrian

FINNISH POETRY–HISTORY AND CRITICISM

Billson, Charles J. Popular Poetry of the Finns. (Popular Studies in Mythology, Romance & Folklore: No. 5). Repr. of 1900 ed. 5.50 (ISBN 0-404-53505-4). AMS Pr.

Kuusi, Matti, et al. Finnish Folk Poetry: Epic. (Illus.). 1977. lib. bdg. 32.50x (ISBN 0-7735-0289-0). McGill-Queens U Pr.

FINNISH POETRY–TRANSLATIONS INTO ENGLISH

Billson, Charles J. Popular Poetry of the Finns. (Popular Studies in Mythology, Romance & Folklore: No. 5). Repr. of 1900 ed. 5.50 (ISBN 0-404-53505-4). AMS Pr.

Kuusi, Matti, et al. Finnish Folk Poetry: Epic. (Illus.). 1977. lib. bdg. 32.50x (ISBN 0-7735-0289-0). McGill-Queens U Pr.

FINNO-HUNGARIAN LANGUAGES

see Finno-Ugrian Languages

FINNO-RUSSIAN WAR, 1939-1940

see Russo-Finnish War, 1939-1940

FINNO-UGRIAN LANGUAGES

see also Cheremissian Language; Estonian Language; Hungarian Language; Lappish Language; Ural-Altaic Languages; Vogul Language; Votiak Language; Votish Language

Beothy, Erzebet. Bezeichnungen Fur Himmelsrichtungen in Den Finnisch Ugrischen Sprachen. LC 67-63037. (Uralic & Altaic Ser: Vol. 84). 1967. pap. text ed. 9.00x (ISBN 0-87750-033-9). Res Ctr Lang Semiotic.

Budenz, Jozsef. Comparative Dictionary of the Finno-Ugric Elements in the Hungarian Vocabulary. LC 66-64927. (Uralic & Altaic Ser: Vol. 78). (Repr. of 1881 ed). 1966. pap. text ed. 22.00x (ISBN 0-87750-029-0). Res Ctr Lang Semiotic.

Collinder, Bjorn. An Introduction to the Uralic Languages. LC 65-21136. 1965. 24.50x (ISBN 0-520-00256-3). U of Cal Pr.

Gyarmathi, Samuel. Affinitas Linguae Hungaricae Cum Linguis Fennicae Originis, Grammatice Demonstrata, 1799. (Uralic & Altaic Ser: Vol. 95). (Lat). 1968. pap. text ed. 11.00x (ISBN 0-87750-040-1). Res Ctr Lang Semiotic.

Raun, Alo. Essays in Finno-Ugric & Finnic Linguistics. (Uralic & Altaic Ser.: No. 107). 1971. pap. text ed. 8.00x (ISBN 0-87750-152-1). Res Ctr Lang Semiotic.

Sajnovics, Joannis. Demonstratio Idioma Ungarorum & Lapponum Idem Esse. (Uralic & Altaic Ser: Vol. 91). 1967. pap. text ed. 8.00x (ISBN 0-87750-037-1). Res Ctr Lang Semiotic.

Sinor, Denis, ed. Studies in Finno-Ugric Linguistics: In Honor of Alo Raun. (Indiana University Uralic & Altaic Ser.: Vol. 131). 440p. 1977. 70.00 (ISBN 0-933070-00-4). Ind U Res Inst.

FINNO-UGRIAN MYTHOLOGY

see Mythology, Finno-Ugrian

FINNO-UGRIANS

see also Lapps; Ostiaks

Abercromby, John. The Pre- & Proto- Historic Finns, Both Eastern & Western, with the Magic Songs of the West Finns, 2 Vols. LC 70-144523. (Grimm Library: Nos. 9-10). Repr. of 1898 ed. Set. 40.00 (ISBN 0-404-53590-9). AMS Pr.

Vuorela, Toivo. Finno-Ugric Peoples. Atkinson, John, tr. LC 62-63349. (Uralic & Altaic Ser: Vol. 39). (Orig.). 1964. pap. text ed. 13.50x (ISBN 0-87750-008-8). Res Ctr Lang Semiotic.

FINNS IN CANADA

Jalkanen, Ralph J., ed. Finns in North America: A Social Symposium. 230p. 1969. 10.00 (ISBN 0-87013-137-0). Mich St U Pr.

FINNS IN THE UNITED STATES

Engle, Eloise. The Finns in America. LC 77-73740. (In America Bks). (Illus.). (gr. 5 up). 1977. PLB 6.95g (ISBN 0-8225-0229-1). Lerner Pubns.

Hannula, Reino N. Blueberry God: The Education of a Finnish-American. LC 80-54183. 1981. 12.00 (ISBN 0-9605044-0-0). Quality Hill.

Hoglund, Arthur W. Finnish Immigrants in America: Eighteen Eighty to Nineteen Twenty. Scott, Franklyn D., ed. LC 78-15182. (Scandinavians in America Ser.). (Illus.). 1979. Repr. of 1960 ed. lib. bdg. 18.00x (ISBN 0-405-11639-X). Arno.

Hummasti, Paul G. Finnish Radicals in Astoria, Oregon: Nineteen Hundred & Four to Nineteen Forty. Scott, Franklyn D., ed. LC 78-15188. (Scandinavians in America Ser.). 1979. lib. bdg. 22.00x (ISBN 0-405-11641-1). Arno.

Jalkanen, Ralph J., ed. The Faith of the Finns: Historical Perspectives of the Finnish-Lutheran Church in America. xvi, 360p. 1972. 12.50 (ISBN 0-87013-174-5). Mich St U Pr.

--Finns in North America: A Social Symposium. 230p. 1969. 10.00 (ISBN 0-87013-137-0). Mich St U Pr.

Knipping, Mark. Finns in Wisconsin. (Illus.). 1977. pap. 1.25 (ISBN 0-87020-172-7). State Hist Soc Wis.

Kolehmainen, John I. Finns in America. LC 68-19626. (YA) 1968. pap. 2.95 (ISBN 0-8077-1644-8). Tchrs Coll.

Puotinen, Arthur E. Finnish Radicals & Religion in Midwestern Mining Towns: 1865-1914. new ed. Scott, Franklyn D., ed. LC 78-15851. (Scandinavians in America Ser.). (Illus.). 1979. lib. bdg. 24.00x (ISBN 0-405-11657-8). Arno.

Schofer, Jerry P. Urban & Rural Finnish Communities in California, 1860-1960. LC 75-18130. 1975. soft bdg. 8.00 (ISBN 0-88247-366-2). R & E Res Assoc.

Tokoi, Oskari. Sisu: Even Through a Stone Wall. 6.00 (ISBN 0-8315-0008-5). Speller.

Turner, H. Haines. Case Studies of Consumers' Cooperatives. LC 68-58631. (Columbia University. Studies in the Social Sciences: No. 481). Repr. of 1941 ed. 24.50 (ISBN 0-404-51481-2). AMS Pr.

Wuorinen, John H. Finns on the Delaware 1638-1655. LC 38-14748. Repr. of 1938 ed. 17.50 (ISBN 0-404-07057-4). AMS Pr.

FINSEN THERAPY

see Phototherapy

FINSLER SPACE

see Spaces, Generalized

FIORDLAND, NEW ZEALAND

Houghton, Philip. Hidden Water. LC 75-307570. (Illus.). 1974. 9.25x (ISBN 0-340-17739-X). Intl Pubns Serv.

FIORDS

see Fjords

FIOTI LANGUAGE

see Congo Language

FIPA (AFRICAN PEOPLE)

Willis, R. G. Fipa & Related Peoples of South-West Tanzania & North-East Zambia. 1966. 7.50x (ISBN 0-85302-037-X). Intl Pubns Serv.

Willis, Roy G., ed. There Was a Certain Man: Spoken Art of the Fipa. (Library of African Literature). 1979. 24.00x (ISBN 0-19-815146-2). Oxford U Pr.

FIR

see also Balsam Fir; Douglas Fir

FIRBANK, ARTHUR ANNESLEY RONALD, 1886-1926

Brooke, Jocelyn. Ronald Firbank. Incl. John Betjeman. Brook, Jocelyn. pap. 2.95 (ISBN 0-8277-6153-8). British Bk Ctr.

Muir, P. H. A Bibliography of the First Editions of Books by Arthur Annesley Ronald Firbank. LC 73-14822. 1927. Repr. lib. bdg. 10.00 (ISBN 0-8414-5983-5). Folcroft.

Muir, Percival H. A Bibliography of the First Editions of Books by Arthur Annesley Ronald Firbank. 1978. Repr. of 1927 ed. lib. bdg. 12.50 (ISBN 0-8492-6724-2). R West.

Potoker, Edward M. Ronald Firbank. LC 76-92032. (Columbia Essays on Modern Writers Ser.: No. 43). 48p. 1970. pap. 2.00 (ISBN 0-231-03168-8). Columbia U Pr.

FIRE

see also Combustion; Fires; Flame; Fuel; Heat; Heating; Smoke

Adler, Irving. Fire in Your Life. LC 55-9930. (Illus.). (YA) (gr. 5-9). 1955. PLB 8.79 (ISBN 0-381-99991-2, A27060, JD-J). Har-Row.

Bachelard, Gaston. Psychoanalysis of Fire. Ross, A. C., tr. 1964. pap. 3.95x (ISBN 0-8070-6461-0, BP277). Beacon Pr.

Fire Stream Fundamentals. 32p. 1966. pap. 1.00 (ISBN 0-685-58181-0, FSD-4). Natl Fire Prot.

Kozlowski, T. T. & Ahlgren, C. E., eds. Fire & Ecosystems. 1974. 54.50 (ISBN 0-12-424255-3). Acad Pr.

Marat, J. P. Decouvertes Sur le Feau, L'electricite et la Lumiere Constatees Par une Suite D'experiences Nouvelles Qui Viennent D'etre Verifiees Par Mm. les Commissaires De L'academie Des Sciences. Repr. of 1779 ed. 20.00 (ISBN 0-8287-0568-2). Clearwater Pub.

O'Donnell, James J. Fire: Its Many Faces & Moods. LC 80-10123. 192p. (gr. 7 up). 1980. PLB 7.79 (ISBN 0-671-33021-7). Messner.

Sigaut, Francois. L'agriculture et le Feu: Role et Place Du Feu Dans les Techniques De Preparation Du Champ De L'ancienne Agriculture Europeenne. (Cahiers Des Etudes Rurales: No. 1). (Illus.). 320p. (Fr.). 1975. pap. text ed. 23.50x (ISBN 90-2797-982-0). Mouton.

Techniques of Fire Photography. (Illus.). 1978. 16.50 (ISBN 0-685-54503-2, SPP-39SP). Natl Fire Prot.

Turner & McCreery. Chemistry of Fire & Hazardous Materials. 1980. text ed. 18.95 (ISBN 0-205-06912-6, 826912-2). Allyn.

Tuve, Richard L. Principles of Fire Protection Chemistry. Tower, Keith, ed. LC 76-26781. 1976. pap. text ed. 14.95 (ISBN 0-87765-080-2). Natl Fire Prot.

FIRE–JUVENILE LITERATURE

Annenberg, Nathan. Fires! How to Prevent Them; How to Survive Them. rev., 2nd ed. (Illus.). 80p. (gr. 5 up). 1981. pap. 3.95 (ISBN 0-9605888-1-7). Ursa Major.

Bester, Roger. Fireman Jim. (Illus.). 48p. 1981. 9.95 (ISBN 0-517-54290-0). Crown.

Care, R. A. Fire & Fuels. (Illus.). 176p. (gr. 5-8). 1975. 12.50 (ISBN 0-263-05593-0). Transatlantic.

Daub, Edward E. Fire. LC 77-26664. (Read About Ser.). (Illus.). (gr. k-3). 1978. PLB 11.15 (ISBN 0-8393-0080-8). Raintree Child.

Fichter, George S. Disastrous Fires. (First Bks.). (Illus.). 72p. (gr. 4 up). 1981. lib. bdg. 7.40 (ISBN 0-531-04325-8). Watts.

Haines, Gail K. Fire. LC 74-13396. (Illus.). 32p. (gr. 1-5). 1975. PLB 6.48 (ISBN 0-688-32009-0). Morrow.

Pringle, Laurence. Natural Fire, Its Ecology in Forests. LC 79-13606. (Illus.). 64p. (gr. 4-6). 1979. 5.95 (ISBN 0-688-22210-2); PLB 5.71 (ISBN 0-688-32210-7). Morrow.

FIRE (IN RELIGION, FOLK-LORE, ETC.)

Frazer, James G. Myths of the Origin of Fire. LC 76-143348. 1975. Repr. of 1930 ed. 20.00 (ISBN 0-87817-068-5). Hacker.

Furley, William D. Studies in the Use of Fire in the Ancient Greek Religion. rev. ed. Connor, W. R., ed. LC 80-2650. (Monographs in Clasical Studies). (Illus.). 1981. lib. bdg. 29.00 (ISBN 0-405-14037-1). Arno.

Heil, Bob. El En Fuego De las Pruebas. (Span.). 1981. 1.75 (ISBN 0-686-76365-3). Life Pubs Intl.

FIRE, GREEK

see Greek Fire

FIRE BALLS

see Meteors

FIRE COMPANIES

see Fire Departments

FIRE-DAMP

see also Mine Ventilation

FIRE-DEPARTMENT PUMPERS

see Fire-Engines

FIRE DEPARTMENTS

Basic Library of Standards Fire Department Administration, 21 bks. 1974. pap. 40.00 (ISBN 0-685-58188-8, BL-FDA). Natl Fire Prot.

Berenbaum, Esai. Municipal Public Safety: A Guide for the Implementation of Consolidated Police-Fire Services. (Illus.). 104p. 1977. 15.75 (ISBN 0-398-03612-8). C C Thomas.

Bryan, John L. & Picard, Raymond C., eds. Managing Fire Services. LC 79-10067. (Municipal Management Ser.). (Illus.). 1979. text ed. 36.00 (ISBN 0-87326-018-X). Intl City Mgt.

Faria, L. E. Protective Breathing Apparatus. (Illus.). 1975. pap. 5.95 (ISBN 0-87618-132-9). R J Brady.

Fire Service Directory, United States & Canada: 1970-1971. 3rd ed. 118p. 1970. 6.00 (ISBN 0-685-46058-4). Natl Fire Prot.

Getz, Malcolm. Economics of the Urban Fire Department. LC 78-14759. 1979. text ed. 16.50x (ISBN 0-8018-2173-8). Johns Hopkins.

Granito, Anthony R. Fire Officer's Guide to Company Leadership and Operations. LC 75-13631. (Fire Officer's Guide Ser). (Illus.). 282p. 1975. 10.50 (ISBN 0-87765-036-5, F*S*P-43). Natl Fire Prot.

--Fire Service Instructor's Guidebook. Neale, Robert A., ed. LC 76-22898. 1976. pap. 6.50 (ISBN 0-87765-079-9, FSP-49). Natl Fire Prot.

Gratz, David B. Fire Department Management: Scope & Method. (Fire Science Ser). 1972. text ed. 17.95 (ISBN 0-02-474620-7, 47462). Macmillan.

How to Judge Your Fire Department. 132p. 1972. 4.95 (ISBN 0-685-46042-8, FSP-34). Natl Fire Prot.

IFSTA Committee. The Fire Department Company Officer. Carlson, Gene & Orton, Charles, eds. LC 80-85349. (Orig.). 1981. pap. text ed. 8.50 (ISBN 0-87939-043-3). Intl Fire Serv.

--Fire Service Orientation & Indoctrination. Thomas, Charles, et al, eds. (Illus.). 1976. pap. text ed. 7.00 (ISBN 0-87939-012-3). Intl Fire Serv.

--Fire Service Practices for Volunteer Fire Departments. Hudiburg, Everett, ed. (Illus.). 1971. pap. text ed. 7.00 (ISBN 0-87939-011-5). Intl Fire Serv.

--Firefighters Occupational Safety. 1st ed. Laughlin, Jerry & Osterhout, Connie, eds. LC 79-83647. 1979. pap. text ed. 8.50 (ISBN 0-87939-028-X). Intl Fire Serv.

Jacobs, Donald T. Physical Fitness & the Fire Service. LC 76-6714. (Illus.). 1976. spiral bdg. 6.00 (ISBN 0-685-70942-6, FSP-47). Natl Fire Prot.

Jennings, Carrie B. Fire Service of Grand Rapids. (Illus.). 80p. 1971. pap. 4.50 (ISBN 0-912382-08-2). Black Letter.

Johnson, Gus. F.D.N.Y. The Fire Buff's Handbook of the New York Fire Department. (Illus.). 1977. 9.95 (ISBN 0-88279-233-4). Western Islands.

Laughlin, Jerry & Osterhout, Connie, eds. Salvage & Overhaul Practices. 6th ed. LC 79-84252. 1979. pap. text ed. 8.50 (ISBN 0-87939-030-1). Intl Fire Serv.

Lyons, Paul R. Fire Officer's Guide to Elevating Platforms & Aerial Towers. (Get Ahead Ser). (Illus.). 209p. 1974. 8.50 (ISBN 0-87765-022-5, FSP-39). Natl Fire Prot.

--Operating Aerial Ladders. rev ed. (Get Ahead Ser). (Illus.). 253p. 1974. 8.50 (ISBN 0-87765-019-5, FSP-7A). Natl Fire Prot.

--Operating Fire Department Pumpers. (Get Ahead Ser). (Illus.). 282p. 1974. 8.50 (ISBN 0-87765-050-0, FSP-6A). Natl Fire Prot.

McRae. Fire Department Operations with Modern Elevators. 1977. pap. 8.95 (ISBN 0-87618-713-0). R J Brady.

National Fire Protection Association. Successful Public Relations - the What, Why, Who, How, Where & When. LC 74-14277. (Illus.). 116p. 1974. 7.00 (ISBN 0-685-51417-X, FSD-8). Natl Fire Prot.

NFPA Technical Reference Library. Bibliography of Voluntary Standardization. Dean, Amy E., ed. 1978. pap. 3.00 (ISBN 0-87765-112-4, SPP-48). Natl Fire Prot.

Operation of Small Community Fire Departments. 48p. 1968. pap. 2.00 (ISBN 0-685-58187-X, FSD-5). Natl Fire Prot.

Organization for Fire Services. (Zero Ser.). 20p. 1971. pap. 2.75 (ISBN 0-685-46066-5, 4). Natl Fire Prot.

Organization of a Fire Department. (Zero Ser). 1969. pap. 2.00 (ISBN 0-685-58139-X, 4A). Natl Fire Prot.

Page. Effective Company Command for Company Officers in the Professional Fire Service. 6.75 (ISBN 0-685-36849-1). Borden.

Page, James O. Effective Company Command. (Illus.). 160p. 1974. text ed. 6.75 (ISBN 0-685-41127-3, FSP-37). Natl Fire Prot.

--Emergency Medical Services for Fire Departments. Lyons, Paul R., ed. LC 75-15024. (Illus.). 300p. 1975. 7.00 (ISBN 0-87765-038-1). Natl Fire Prot.

Richman, Hal. Truck Company Fire Ground Operations. LC 76-57667. 1977. pap. 11.95 (ISBN 0-87618-796-3). R J Brady.

Rudman, Jack. Deputy Chief Fire Marshall (Uniformed) (Career Examination Ser.: C-2169). (Cloth bdg. avail. on request). 1976. pap. 10.00 (ISBN 0-8373-2169-7). Natl Learning.

--Fire Officer. (Career Examination Ser.: C-1578). (Cloth bdg. avail. on request). pap. 8.00 (ISBN 0-8373-1578-6). Natl Learning.

--Lieutenant, Fire Department. (Career Examination Ser.: C-441). (Cloth bdg. avail. on request). pap. 10.00 (ISBN 0-8373-0441-5). Natl Learning.

Sectional Committee on Protective Equipment. Fire Officer's Guide, Breathing Apparatus for the Fire Service. (Gett Ahead Ser). 120p. 1975. 8.50 (ISBN 0-685-52869-3). Natl Fire Prot.

Walker, W. E., et al. Fire Department Deployment Analysis. LC 79-19522. 704p. 1979. 34.50 (ISBN 0-444-00335-5, Noth Holland). Elsevier.

Walsh, Charles V. & Marks, Leonard. Firefighting Strategy & Leadership. 2nd ed. (Illus.). 1976. text ed. 15.95 (ISBN 0-07-068026-4, G); instructor's manual 3.50 (ISBN 0-07-068027-2). McGraw.

FIRE-DEPARTMENTS–JUVENILE LITERATURE

Beame, Rona. Ladder Company 108. LC 73-7173. (Illus.). 64p. (gr. 3-6). 1973. PLB 6.64 (ISBN 0-671-32642-2). Messner.

Bundt, Nancy. The Fire Station Book. LC 80-16617. (Illus.). 32p. (ps-3). 1981. PLB 6.95 (ISBN 0-87614-126-2). Carolrhoda Bks.

Colby, C. B. Space Age Fire Fighters: New Weapons in the Fireman's Arsenal. LC 73-82034. (Illus.). 48p. (gr. 4-7). 1974. PLB 5.29 (ISBN 0-698-30531-0). Coward.
Loeper, John. By Hook & Ladder. LC 80-36738. (Illus.). 96p. (gr. 4-6). 1981. PLB 7.95 (ISBN 0-689-30816-7). Atheneum.
Petersen, Johanna. Careers with a Fire Department. LC 74-11904. (Early Career Books Ser.). (Illus.). 36p. (gr. 2-5). 1975. PLB 4.95 (ISBN 0-8225-0309-3). Lerner Pubns.

FIRE DEPARTMENTS-LAWS AND LEGISLATION

Bahme, Charles W. Fireman's Law Book. 4th ed. 256p. 1967. 5.50 (ISBN 0-685-46051-7, FSP-3). Natl Fire Prot.
National Fire Codes, 16 vols. LC 38-27236. (Illus.). 1979. Set. pap. 95.00 (ISBN 0-87765-140-X, FC-SET). Natl Fire Prot.
Wallace, Roderick M. & Wallace, Deborah N. Studies on the Collapse of Fire Service in New York City. 1977. pap. text ed. 7.50 (ISBN 0-8191-0358-6). U Pr of Amer.

FIRE DOGS

see Dogs-Breeds-Dalmatians

FIRE-ENGINES

Automotive Fire Apparatus. (Ten Ser). 104p. 1973. pap. 2.00 (ISBN 0-685-44164-4, 19). Natl Fire Prot.
Barr, Jene. Fire Snorkel Number 7. LC 65-15101. (Career Awareness-Community Helpers Ser.). (Illus.). (gr. k-2). 1965. 5.25g (ISBN 0-8075-2442-5). A Whitman.
Bracken, Carolyn, illus. Here Come the Fire Engines! (Golden Sturdy Shape Bks.). 14p. (ps-1). 1981. 2.95 (ISBN 0-686-74868-9, Golden Pr). Western Pub.
Bushey, Jerry. Building a Fire Truck. LC 81-6182. (Illus.). 32p. (gr. k-4). 1981. PLB 6.95 (ISBN 0-87614-170-X, AACR2). Carolrhoda Bks.
Fire Engines. (Puppet Board Books Ser.). bds. 2.50 (ISBN 0-448-02683-X). G&D.
Fulton, Janet. Golden Fire Engine Book. (Golden Play & Learn Bks). (Illus.). (ps). 1969. 2.95 (ISBN 0-307-10739-6, Golden Pr). Western Pub.
Gergely, Tibor, illus. Great Big Fire Engine Book. (Illus.). (gr. k-2). 1950. 1.95 (ISBN 0-307-10470-2, Golden Pr); PLB 7.62 (ISBN 0-307-60470-5). Western Pub.
Hatmon, Paul W. Yesterday's Fire Engines. LC 80-11158. (Superwheels & Thrill Sports Bks.). (Illus.). (YA) (gr. 4 up). 1980. PLB 6.95g (ISBN 0-8225-0430-8). Lerner Pubns.
How to Train Fire Department Drivers. 16p. 1965. 1.00 (ISBN 0-685-46055-X). Natl Fire Prot.
Ingram, Arthur & Bishop, Denis. Fire Engines in Color. (Illus.). 235p. 1980. 9.95 (ISBN 0-7137-0627-9, Pub. by Blandford Fr England). Sterling.
Lichty, Robert. Collecting & Restoring Antique Fire Engines. (Illus.). 224p. 1981. 14.95 (ISBN 0-8306-9700-4, 2099); pap. 9.95 (ISBN 0-8306-2099-0). TAB Bks.
McCall, Walter P., ed. American Fire Engines Since Nineteen Hundred. LC 75-31498. (Automotive Ser.). (Illus.). 1976. 24.95 (ISBN 0-912612-08-8). Crestline.
National Fire Protection Assn. Features of Fire Department Pumpers. Lyons, Paul R., ed. LC 75-37324. (Slide Script Ser). (Illus.). 75p. 1976. 35.00 (ISBN 0-87765-067-5, SL-17). Natl Fire Prot.
Vanderveen, Bart H. Fire & Crash Vehicles from Nineteen Fifty. (Olyslager Auto Library). (Illus.). 72p. 1976. 10.95 (ISBN 0-686-76459-5, Pub. by Warne Pubs England). Motorbooks Intl.
--Fire-Fighting Vechicles, Eighteen Forty to Nineteen Fifty. (Olyslager Auto Library). (Illus.). 80p. 1972. 10.95 (ISBN 0-686-76460-9, Pub. by Warne Pubs England). Motorbooks Intl.

FIRE EXTINCTION

see also Fire Fighters; Fire-Engines; Forest Fires

Air Operations for Forest, Brush & Grass Fires. 2nd ed. LC 75-12409. 68p. 1975. pap. 4.25 (ISBN 0-87765-035-7, FSP-9A). Natl Fire Prot.
Aircraft Hand Fire Extinguishers. (Four Hundred Ser). 1973. pap. 2.00 (ISBN 0-685-58062-8, 408). Natl Fire Prot.
Aircraft Rescue & Fire Fighting Techniques for Fire Departments Using Conventional Fire Apparatus. (Four Hundred Ser). 1968. pap. 2.00 (ISBN 0-685-58060-1, 406M). Natl Fire Prot.
Arco Editorial Board, ed. Fire Administration & Technology. 2nd ed. LC 59-9022. (Orig.). 1976. lib. bdg. 12.00 (ISBN 0-668-01807-0); pap. 10.00 (ISBN 0-668-00604-8). Arco.
Attacking & Extinguishing Interior Fires. 134p. 1960. 5.50 (ISBN 0-685-46059-2, FSP-12). Natl Fire Prot.
Averill, C. F. Sprinkler Systems Design: Past, Present & Future. 1979. 2.50 (ISBN 0-686-25736-7, TR 79-3). Society Fire Protect.
Backes, Nancy. Great Fires of America. Country Beautiful Editors, ed. LC 73-80505. (Illus.). 208p. 1973. 15.95 (ISBN 0-87294-048-9). Country Beautiful.
Bahme, Charles W. Fire Officer's Guide to Extinguishing Systems. (Get Ahead Ser.). 104p. 1970. 5.00 (ISBN 0-685-46047-9, FSP-30). Natl Fire Prot.
--Fire Officer's Guide to Extinguishing Systems. Lyons, Paul R., ed. LC 76-53155. (Fire Officer's Guide Ser.). 1977. text ed. 7.50 (ISBN 0-87765-091-8, FSP-30A). Natl Fire Prot.
Beame, Rona. Ladder Company 108. LC 73-7173. (Illus.). 64p. (gr. 3-6). 1973. PLB 6.64 (ISBN 0-671-32642-2). Messner.
Beatteay, Robert E. Fire Officer's Guide to Waterfront Fires. LC 75-18738. (Fire Officer's Guide Ser). (Illus.). 150p. 1975. 8.50 (ISBN 0-87765-046-2, F*S*P-42). Natl Fire Prot.
Bonadio, Gustave E. Firefighting Hydraulics. 3rd ed. LC 72-88049. 1979. pap. text ed. 8.00 (ISBN 0-668-00572-6). Arco.
Bush, Loren S. & McLaughlin, James. Introduction to Fire Science. Gruber, Harvey, ed. (Fire Science Ser.). 1970. text ed. 13.95x (ISBN 0-02-473900-6). Macmillan.
Carbon Dioxide Extinguishing System. (Ten Ser). 100p. 1973. pap. 2.25 (ISBN 0-685-44156-3, 12). Natl Fire Prot.
Care & Maintenance of Sprinkler Systems. (Ten Ser). 1971. pap. 2.00 (ISBN 0-685-58130-6, 13A). Natl Fire Prot.
Care of Fire Hose. (Ten Ser.). 52p. 1972. pap. 2.00 (ISBN 0-685-46062-2, 198). Natl Fire Prot.
Carlson, Gene & Orton, Charles, eds. Ground Cover Fire Fighting Practices. 2nd ed. (Illus.). 1982. pap. text ed. price not set (ISBN 0-87939-038-7, IFSTA 207). Intl Fire Serv.
Casey, James F. Fire Service Hydraulics. 2nd ed. (Illus.). 1970. 11.00 (ISBN 0-686-12258-5). Fire Eng.
Casey, James F., ed. The Fire Chief's Handbook. 4th ed. (Illus.). 1978. 19.95 (ISBN 0-686-12257-7). Fire Eng.
Clark, William E. Fire Fighting Principles & Practices. (Illus.). 1974. 15.00 (ISBN 0-686-12259-3). Fire Eng.
Colburn, Robert E. Fire Protection & Suppression. Williams, Carlton, ed. (Illus.). 352p. 1975. text ed. 15.95 (ISBN 0-07-011680-6, 11680-6, G); instructor's manual 3.50 (ISBN 0-07-011681-4). McGraw.
Coleman. Management of Fire Service Operations. LC 77-20151. 1978. 13.95 (ISBN 0-87872-129-0). Duxbury Pr.
Committee on Fire Research & Committee on Toxicology. An Appraisal of Halogenated Fire Extinguishing Agents. (Illus.). 360p. 1972. pap. 7.75 (ISBN 0-309-02111-1). Natl Acad Pr.
Committee on Fire Research, National Research Council. Directory of Fire Research. 8th ed. 1978. pap. text ed. 9.50x (ISBN 0-309-02799-3). Natl Acad Pr.
Cozad, Dale. Water Supply for Fire Protection. (Illus.). 304p. 1981. text ed. 18.95 (ISBN 0-13-945964-2). P-H.
Dean, Anabel. Fire! How Do They Fight It? LC 77-17635. (Illus.). 1978. text ed. 8.95 (ISBN 0-664-32626-9). Westminster.
Detecting Fires. (Illus.). 116p. 1975. pap. 5.50 (ISBN 0-87765-033-0, S*P*P-28). Natl Fire Prot.
Didactic Systems, Inc. Management in the Fire Service. Tower, K. & Dean, A. E., eds. LC 7-76527. 1977. text ed. 16.50 (ISBN 0-87765-097-7, TXT-3). Natl Fire Prot.
Dry Chemical Extinguishing Systems. (Ten Ser). 1973. pap. 2.00 (ISBN 0-685-58126-8, 17). Natl Fire Prot.
Erven, Lawrence. Techniques of Fire Hydraulics. (Fire Science Ser). 1972. text ed. 17.95 (ISBN 0-02-473000-9, 47300). Macmillan.
Erven, Lawrence W. Fire Company Apparatus & Procedure. 2nd ed. (Fire Science Ser). (Illus.). 360p. 1974. text ed. 14.95x (ISBN 0-02-474150-7, 47415). Macmillan.
Evaluating Foam Fire Fighting Equipment on Aircraft Rescue & Fire Fighting Vehicles. (Four Hundred Ser). 1974. pap. 2.50 (ISBN 0-685-58233-7, 412). Natl Fire Prot.
Favreau, Donald F. Fire Service Management. (Illus.). 1969. 8.00 (ISBN 0-686-12260-7). Fire Eng.
Fighting Tank Fires with Water. LC 75-37306. (Slide Script Ser.). (Illus.). 60p. 1975. 25.00 (ISBN 0-87765-061-6, SL-2). Natl Fire Prot.
Fire Attack One. (Illus.). 280p. 1966. 7.00 (ISBN 0-685-46043-6, FSP-1). Natl Fire Prot.
Fire Attack Two. (Illus.). 234p. 1968. 7.50 (ISBN 0-685-46045-2, FSP-2). Natl Fire Prot.
Fire Department Ladders, Ground & Aerial. (Ten Ser). 1972. pap. 2.00 (ISBN 0-685-58122-5, 193). Natl Fire Prot.
Fire Department Operations in Protected Properties. (Ten Ser). 1973. pap. 2.00 (ISBN 0-685-58129-2, 13E). Natl Fire Prot.
Fire Fighting Tactics. 112p. 1953. 5.50 (ISBN 0-685-46060-6, FSP-13). Natl Fire Prot.
Fire Hose. (Ten Ser). 1974. pap. 2.00 (ISBN 0-685-58120-9, 196). Natl Fire Prot.
Fire Terminology. 4th ed. 67p. 1970. 4.00 (ISBN 0-685-46056-8, FSD-3A). Natl Fire Prot.
Foam Extinguishing Systems. (Ten Ser). 116p. 1974. pap. 3.75 (ISBN 0-685-44155-5, 11). Natl Fire Prot.
Foam Water Sprinkler & Spray Systems. (Ten Ser). 1974. pap. 2.50 (ISBN 0-685-58127-6, 16). Natl Fire Prot.
Gaines, Glen A. Fire Fighting Operations in Garden Apartments & Townhouses. (Illus.). 144p. 1978. pap. text ed. 10.95 (ISBN 0-87618-885-4). R J Brady.
Gann, Richard G., ed. Halogenated Fire Suppressants. LC 75-25638. (ACS Symposium Ser.: No. 16). 1975. 27.75 (ISBN 0-8412-0297-4). Am Chemical.
Granito, Anthony R. Fire Instructor's Training Guide. (Illus.). 1972. 8.00 (ISBN 0-686-12261-5). Fire Eng.
Guides for Fighting Fires in & Around Petroleum Tanks. 30p. 1975. pap. 2.50 (ISBN 0-87765-049-7). Natl Fire Prot.
Haessler, Walter M. The Extinguishment of Fire. rev. ed. 1974. pap. text ed. 3.75 (ISBN 0-87765-024-1, FSP-40). Natl Fire Prot.
Halogenated Extinguishing Agent Systems: Halcon 1301. (Ten Ser). 84p. 1973. pap. 2.00 (ISBN 0-685-44157-1, 12A). Natl Fire Prot.
Halogenated Fire Extinguishing Agent Systems: Halon 1211. (Ten Ser). 84p. 1973. pap. 2.00 (ISBN 0-685-44161-X, 12B). Natl Fire Prot.
Handling Hose & Ladders. (Illus.). 144p. 5.00 (ISBN 0-685-44147-4, FSP-5). Natl Fire Prot.
Hansen, Jeff. Being a Fire Fighter Isn't Just Squirtin' Water. 1978. 5.95 (ISBN 0-533-03498-1). Vantage.
Hazards of Vaporizing Liquid Extinguishing Agents. (Ten Ser). 1965. pap. 2.00 (ISBN 0-685-58124-1, 182M). Natl Fire Prot.
Hickey, Harry E. Hydraulics for Fire Protection. Hickey, Harry E., ed. LC 79-91611. (Illus.). 340p. 1980. text ed. 16.50 (ISBN 0-87765-170-1, TXT-6). Natl Fire Prot.
High Expansion Foam Systems. (Ten Ser). 1970. pap. 2.00 (ISBN 0-685-58133-0, 11A). Natl Fire Prot.
IFSTA Committee. Essentials of Fire Fighting. Peige, John D., et al, eds. LC 77-75408. (Illus.). 1977. pap. text ed. 18.00 (ISBN 0-87939-000-X). Intl Fire Serv.
--Fire Apparatus Practices. 6th ed. Carlson, Gene & Orton, Charles, eds. LC 80-82822. 1980. pap. text ed. 8.50 (ISBN 0-87939-040-9). Intl Fire Serv.
--Fire Service Ground Ladder Practices. Hudiburg, Everett, ed. (Illus.). 1973. pap. text ed. 7.00 (ISBN 0-87939-002-6). Intl Fire Serv.
--Fire Service Rescue Practices. 5th ed. Carlson, Gene, ed. LC 81-82148. (Illus.). 1981. pap. 8.50 (ISBN 0-87939-044-1). Intl Fire Serv.
--Fire Stream Practices. 6th ed. Carlson, Gene & Orton, Charles, eds. LC 80-80447. (Illus.). 206p. 1980. pap. text ed. 8.50 (ISBN 0-87939-041-7). Intl Fire Serv.
--Fire Ventilation Practices. 6th ed. Carlson, Gene & Orton, Charles, eds. LC 80-84149. 1981. pap. text ed. 7.00 (ISBN 0-87939-039-5). Intl Fire Serv.
--Ground Cover Fire Fighting Practices: 207. Hudiburg, Everett & Thomas, Charles, eds. (Illus.). 1973. pap. text ed. 7.00 (ISBN 0-87939-016-6). Intl Fire Serv.
--Water Supplies for Fire Protection. Laughlin, Jerry & Williams, Connie E., eds. LC 78-58881. (Illus.). 1978. pap. text ed. 8.50 (ISBN 0-87939-029-8). Intl Fire Serv.
IFSTA Committee & Walker, Lorrin. Self-Instruction for IFSTA 200: Essentials of Fire Fighting, SI-200. 1st ed. Carlson, Gene & Orton, Charles, eds. LC 77-75408. (Illus.). 204p. (Orig.). 1980. pap. text ed. 8.00 (ISBN 0-87939-042-5). Intl Fire Serv.
IFSTA Committee Members. Fire Hose Practices. Hudiburg, Everett & Thomas, Charles E., eds. (Illus.). 1974. pap. text ed. 7.00 (ISBN 0-87939-003-4). Intl Fire Serv.
International Symposium on Flammability & Fire Retardants. Fire Retardants: Proceedings. Bhatnagar, Vijay M., ed. LC 74-33842. (Illus.). 350p. 1975. pap. 25.00x (ISBN 0-87762-166-7). Technomic.
Kimball, Warren Y. Effective Streams for Fighting Fires. 88p. 1961. 2.00 (ISBN 0-685-46054-1, FSD-1). Natl Fire Prot.
Kravontka, Stanley J. Communications for Fire Fighting & Evaluation. 1976. 3.25 (ISBN 0-686-17607-3). Society Fire Protect.
Kuvshinoff, B. W., et al, eds. Fire Sciences Dictionary. LC 77-3489. 439p. 1977. 22.00 (ISBN 0-471-51113-7, Pub. by Wiley-Interscience). Wiley.
Lyons, Paul R. Testing Fire Apparatus: Acceptance & Service Tests for Aerial Ladders, Pt. II. LC 78-59790. (Illus.). 50p. (Orig.). 1979. pap. text ed. 65.00 (ISBN 0-87765-136-1, SL-31). Natl Fire Prot.
--Testing Fire Apparatus: Acceptance & Service Tests for Elevating Platforms, Pt. III. LC 78-59790. (Illus.). 54p. (Orig.). 1979. pap. text ed. 65.00 (ISBN 0-87765-137-X). Natl Fire Prot.
Lyons, Paul R., ed. Fire Attack! Horizontal Tanks & Loading Racks. LC 75-15296. (Slide Set Ser.). (Illus.). 65p. 1975. soft cover 35.00 (ISBN 0-87765-044-6); 40 slides incl. (ISBN 0-685-62582-6). Natl Fire Prot.
--Fire Attack Truck Terminals. LC 75-10887. (Slide Set Ser.). (Illus.). 58p. 1975. 35.00 (ISBN 0-87765-034-9); 41 slides incl. (ISBN 0-685-62583-4). Natl Fire Prot.
McGrath, Robert. Emergency Removal of Patients & First Aid Fire Fighting in Hospitals. 3rd ed. (Illus.). 1974. pap. 4.15 (ISBN 0-87912-101-7, 12959). Natl Safety Coun.
Mann, Philip. Incendios De Bomba. Kreps, Georgian, tr. from Eng. (Shape Board Play Book). Orig. Title: Fire Engines. (Illus., Span.). (ps-3). 1981. bds. 3.50 plastic comb bdg (ISBN 0-89828-202-0, 5006SP). Tuffy Bks.
Manning for Fire Attack. 72p. 1969. pap. 2.50 (ISBN 0-685-46044-4, FSD-6). Natl Fire Prot.
Meidl, James. Hazardous Materials Handbook. (Fire Science Ser). 1972. pap. text ed. 12.95x (ISBN 0-02-476370-5, 47637). Macmillan.
Meldrum, D. H. Fighting Fire with Foam: Basics of Effective Systems. 1979. 3.50 (ISBN 0-686-25956-4, TR 79-2). Society Fire Protect.
Mendes, Robert F. Fighting High-Rise Building Fires: Tactics & Logistics. Lyons, Paul R., ed. LC 75-13715. (Illus.). 160p. 1975. 12.50 (ISBN 0-87765-037-3). Natl Fire Prot.
Model Enabling Act for Portable Fire Extinguishers. (Ten Ser). 1969. pap. 2.00 (ISBN 0-685-58134-9, 10L). Natl Fire Prot.
National Fire Protection Association. Hydraulics for the Fire Service: Hydraulic Field Equations, Vol. VI. Lyons, Paul R., ed. LC 78-50007. (Illus.). 72p. (Orig.). 1980. pap. text ed. 42.50 (ISBN 0-87765-171-X, SL-60). Natl Fire Prot.
--Hydraulics for the Fire Sevice: Operating the Pumper, Vol. V. Lyons, Paul R., ed. LC 78-50007. (Illus.). 88p. 1979. text ed. 42.50 (ISBN 0-87765-157-4, SL-51). Natl Fire Prot.
NFPA. The Fire Fighter & Plastics in a Changing Environment. 1977. 35.00 (ISBN 0-87765-093-4, SL-25). Natl Fire Prot.
--Instructor's Manual to Accompany Management in the Fire Service. Tower, K. & Dean, A. E., eds. LC 77-76533. 1977. pap. text ed. 3.50 (ISBN 0-87765-098-5). Natl Fire Prot.
--Thak Vehicle Fire Fighting. Lyons, Paul R., ed. LC 75-24677. (Slide Script Ser: No. SL-1). 52p. 1975. pap. text ed. 25.00 (ISBN 0-87765-048-9); 34 slides incl. (ISBN 0-685-62584-2). Natl Fire Prot.
NFPA Committee on Fire Department Equipment. Fire Apparatus Maintenance. 136p. 1966. 5.00 (ISBN 0-685-46057-6). Natl Fire Prot.
NFPA Forest Committee. Chemicals for Forest Fire Fighting. 2nd ed. 112p. 1967. 3.00 (ISBN 0-685-46049-5). Natl Fire Prot.
--Chemicals for Forest Fire Fighting. 3rd ed. Lyons, Paul, ed. LC 77-814121. 1977. pap. text ed. 6.50 (ISBN 0-87765-104-3, FSP-19A). Natl Fire Prot.
O'Hagan, John T. High Rise Fire & Life Safety. (Illus.). 1977. 16.00 (ISBN 0-686-12263-1). Fire Eng.
Plastics & Plastic Products. LC 75-39854. (Illus.). 126p. 1975. pap. 5.50 (ISBN 0-87765-064-0, SPP-35). Natl Fire Prot.
Proprietary Protective Signaling Systems. (Seventy Ser). 56p. 1974. pap. 3.00 (ISBN 0-685-44175-X, 72D). Natl Fire Prot.
Protection from Exposure Fires. (Eighty-Ninety Ser). 1970. pap. 2.00 (ISBN 0-685-58146-2, 80A). Natl Fire Prot.
Pryor, Andrew J. Browns Ferry Nuclear Plant Fire. 1977. 4.25 (ISBN 0-686-22684-4). Society Fire Protection.
Public Fire Service Communications. (Seventy Ser). 68p. 1973. pap. 2.00 (ISBN 0-685-44176-8, 73). Natl Fire Prot.
Purington, Robert G. Hydraulics for the Fire Service: Pumps & Pumpers, Unit 4. Lyons, Paul R., ed. LC 78-50007. (Illus.). 1979. pap. text ed. 42.50 (ISBN 0-87765-148-5). Natl Fire Prot.
Pyle, Ernest W. New Techniques for Welding & Extending Sprinkler Pipes. 1976. 2.50 (ISBN 0-686-17608-1). Society Fire Protect.
Respiratory Protective Equipment for Fire Fighters. (Ten Ser). 1971. pap. 2.00 (ISBN 0-685-58123-3, 19B). Natl Fire Prot.
Reuter, Margaret. Careers in a Fire Department. LC 77-8151. (Whole Works Ser.). (Illus.). (gr. 3-7). 1977. PLB 10.65 (ISBN 0-8172-0954-9). Raintree Pubs.
Richman, Harold. Engine Company Fireground Operations. LC 74-3389. (Illus.). 1975. pap. 10.95 (ISBN 0-87618-230-9). R J Brady.

Screw Threads & Gaskets for Fire Hose Connections. (Ten Ser). 1974. pap. 2.00 (ISBN 0-685-58131-4, 194). Natl Fire Prot.
Sherad, Shirley E., ed. Fire-Fighting Foams & Foam Systems. LC 77-74657. (Illus.). 1977. pap. 6.00 (ISBN 0-87765-094-2, SPP-44). Natl Fire Prot.
Standard Operating Procedures, Aircraft Rescue & Fire Fighting. (Four Hundred Ser). 140p. 1973. pap. 2.00 (ISBN 0-685-44137-7, 402). Natl Fire Prot.
Standpipes & Hose Systems. (Ten Ser). 1974. pap. 2.00 (ISBN 0-685-58128-4, 14). Natl Fire Prot.
Stephens, Peter J. The Story of Fire Fighting. LC 66-14175. (Story of Science Ser.). (Illus.). (gr. 5-10). 1966. PLB 7.29 (ISBN 0-8178-3722-1). Harvey.
Sylvia, Richard P. Questions & Answers: A Study Guide to Fire Service Hydraulics. 1971. pap. 8.00 (ISBN 0-686-12264-X). Fire Eng.
--Suburban Fire Fighting. (Illus.). 1969. pap. 6.00 (ISBN 0-686-12265-8). Fire Eng.
Synthetic Foam & Combined Agent Systems. (Ten Ser). 1974. pap. 2.00 (ISBN 0-685-58132-2, 11B). Natl Fire Prot.
Tamarin, Alfred. Fire Fighting in America. LC 71-123136. (Illus.). (gr. 4-6). 1971. 8.95 (ISBN 0-02-788820-7). Macmillan.
Torbert, Floyd J. Firefighters the World Over. (Illus.). (gr. 4-6). 1967. reinforced bdg. 5.95 (ISBN 0-8038-2238-3); PLB 3.96 (ISBN 0-8038-2239-1). Hastings.
Training Standard on Initial Fire Attack. (Ten Ser). 1966. pap. 2.00 (ISBN 0-685-58119-5, 197). Natl Fire Prot.
Tuve, Richard L. Principles of Fire Protection Chemistry. Tower, Keith, ed. LC 76-26781. 1976. pap. text ed. 14.95 (ISBN 0-87765-080-2). Natl Fire Prot.
University of Missouri, Division of Fire Training. Combatting Vehicle Fires. Instructional Media Associates, Inc. & National Fire Protection Association, eds. LC 79-720176. (Illus.). 1979. pap. text ed. 49.50 (ISBN 0-87765-145-0). Natl Fire Prot.
Walsh, Charles V. & Marks, Leonard. Firefighting Strategy & Leadership. 2nd ed. (Illus.). 1976. text ed. 15.95 (ISBN 0-07-068026-4, G); instructor's manual 3.50 (ISBN 0-07-068027-2). McGraw.
Whitman, Lawrence E. Fire Safety in the Atomic Age. 1980. 21.95x (ISBN 0-88229-529-2); pap. 11.95x (ISBN 0-88229-732-5). Nelson-Hall.

FIRE EXTINCTION–EXAMINATIONS, QUESTIONS, ETC.

Arco Editorial Board. Battalion & Deputy Chief, F. D. 4th ed. (Orig.). 1969. lib. bdg. 8.50 (ISBN 0-668-02064-4); pap. 6.00 (ISBN 0-668-00515-7). Arco.
--Lieutenant, F. D. 6th ed. LC 73-83373. 1978. pap. 10.00 (ISBN 0-668-00123-2). Arco.
Graham, Frank & Schank, Kenneth. Questions & Answers for Engineers & Firemen's Examinations. 3rd ed. 1979. 10.95 (ISBN 0-672-23327-4). Audel.
McGannon, Robert E. One Thousand Three Hundred Forty Questions & Answers for Firefighters. 3rd ed. LC 79-171440. pap. 4.00 (ISBN 0-668-00857-1). Arco.
Rudman, Jack. Assistant Fire Marshall. (Career Examination Ser.: C-1105). (Cloth bdg. avail on request). pap. 8.00 (ISBN 0-8373-1105-5). Natl Learning.
--Battalion Chief - Fire Department. (Career Examination Ser.: C-81). (Cloth bdg. avail. on request). pap. 10.00 (ISBN 0-8373-0081-9). Natl Learning.
--Captain, Fire Department. (Career Examination Ser.: C-120). (Cloth bdg. avail. on request). pap. 12.00 (ISBN 0-8373-0120-3). Natl Learning.
--Deputy Chief, Fire Department. (Career Examination Ser.: C-195). (Cloth bdg. avail. on request). pap. 10.00 (ISBN 0-8373-0195-5). Natl Learning.
--Fire Administration & Supervision. (Career Examination Ser.: CS-38). (Cloth bdg. avail. on request). pap. 10.00- (ISBN 0-8373-0038-X). Natl Learning.
--Fire Alarm Dispatcher. (Career Examination Ser.: C-256). (Cloth bdg. avail. on request). pap. 8.00 (ISBN 0-8373-0256-0). Natl Learning.
--Fire Control Mechanic. (Career Examination Ser.: C-257). (Cloth bdg. avail. on request). pap. 8.00 (ISBN 0-8373-0257-9). Natl Learning.
--Fire Fighter. (Career Examination Ser.: C-1287). (Cloth bdg. avail. on request). pap. 8.00 (ISBN 0-8373-1287-6). Natl Learning.
--Fire Marshal. (Career Examination Ser.: C-2401). (Cloth bdg. avail. on request). pap. 10.00 (ISBN 0-8373-2401-7). Natl Learning.
--Fireman Examinations - All States. (Career Examination Ser.: C-258). (Cloth bdg. avail. on request). pap. 8.00 (ISBN 0-8373-0258-7). Natl Learning.
--Fireman, Fire Department. (Career Examination Ser.: C-259). (Cloth bdg. avail. on request). pap. 8.00 (ISBN 0-8373-0259-5). Natl Learning.
--Fireman-Laborer. (Career Examination Ser.: C-1289). (Cloth bdg. avail. on request). pap. 8.00 (ISBN 0-8373-1289-2). Natl Learning.
--Housing Fireman. (Career Examination Ser.: C-336). (Cloth bdg. avail. on request). pap. 8.00 (ISBN 0-8373-0336-2). Natl Learning.

FIRE EXTINCTION–HISTORY

Cannon, Donald J., ed. Heritage of Flames. LC 77-43. (The Illustrated History of American Firefighting). (Illus.). 1977. 35.00 (ISBN 0-89528-001-9). Artisan Bks.
Green-Hughes, Evan. A History of Firefighting. 158p. 1980. 37.50x (ISBN 0-903485-61-3, Pub. by Mooreland England). State Mutual Bk.
Lyons, Paul R. Fire in America. LC 75-29598. (Illus.). 1976. 19.95 (ISBN 0-685-68872-0, SPP-33). Natl Fire Prot.

FIRE FIGHTERS

Blumberg, Rhoda. Fire Fighters. rev. ed. (First Bks. Ser). (Illus.). 72p. (gr. 4). 1976. PLB 6.90 (ISBN 0-531-00850-9). Watts.
Broekel, Ray. Fire Fighters. (The New True Books). (Illus.). (gr. k-4). 1981. PLB 9.25 (ISBN 0-516-01620-2). Childrens.
Bugbee, Percy. Men Against Fire. 200p. 1971. 8.00 (ISBN 0-685-46053-3). Natl Fire Prot.
Davis, Robert A. Engineers, Pump Operators, Drivers Handbook, Vol. 1. 1968. pap. 6.50 (ISBN 0-89368-308-6). Davis Pub Co.
--Engineers, Pump Operators, Drivers Handbook, Vol. 2. 1972. pap. 6.50 (ISBN 0-89368-309-4). Davis Pub Co.
--Fire Lieutenant's-Captain's Handbook, Vol. 1. 1966. pap. 7.75 (ISBN 0-89368-305-1). Davis Pub Co.
--Fire Lieutenant's-Captain's Handbook, Vol. 2. 1972. pap. 6.50 (ISBN 0-89368-306-X). Davis Pub Co.
Earnest, Ernest. The Volunteer Fire Company. LC 78-8785. (Illus.). 224p. 1980. pap. 6.95 (ISBN 0-8128-6094-2). Stein & Day.
--The Volunteer Fire Company Book. LC 78-8785. 1979. 10.00 (ISBN 0-8128-2532-2). Stein & Day.
Educational Research Council of America. Firefighters. rev. ed. Muesegaes, Mary & Marchak, John P., eds. (Real People at Work Ser: A). (Illus.). 1976. pap. text ed. 2.25 (ISBN 0-89247-008-9). Changing Times.
Fire Fighter Professional Qualifications. (One Thousand Ser). 1974. pap. 3.50 (ISBN 0-685-58199-3, 1001). Natl Fire Prot.
Firefighter Study Guide. 1st ed. Laughlin, Jerry, et al, eds. LC 79-84380. 1979. pap. 5.00 (ISBN 0-87939-033-6). Intl Fire Serv.
Ford, Robert E. Engineers, Pump Operators, Drivers Handbook, Vol. 3. 1977. pap. 6.00 (ISBN 0-89368-310-8). Davis Pub Co.
--Fire Command Officer's Handbook, Vol. 1. 1978. pap. 6.50 (ISBN 0-89368-311-6). Davis Pub Co.
--Fire Lieutenant's-Captain's Handbook, Vol. 3. 1977. pap. 7.50 (ISBN 0-89368-307-8). Davis Pub Co.
--Firefighter's Entrance Handbook. 1977. pap. 7.00 (ISBN 0-89368-312-4). Davis Pub Co.
Hamilton, Richard & Barnard, Charles N. Twenty Thousand Alarms. LC 74-33553. 256p. 1981. pap. 2.50 (ISBN 0-87216-810-7). Playboy Pbks.
Hardy, Martha. Tatoosh. LC 80-81574. (Illus.). 252p. 1980. pap. 6.95 (ISBN 0-89886-005-9). Mountaineers.
IFSTA Committee. The Fire Service Instructor. 4th ed. Carlson, Gene, ed. LC 81-80268. (Illus.). 1981. pap. text ed. 8.50 (ISBN 0-87939-045-X). Intl Fire Serv.
--Firefighters Occupational Safety. 1st ed. Laughlin, Jerry & Osterhout, Connie, eds. LC 79-83647. 1979. pap. text ed. 8.50 (ISBN 0-87939-028-X). Intl Fire Serv.
Koch, Harry W. Firefighter Entrance Examinations. 1977. 5.00 (ISBN 0-913164-72-0). Ken-Bks.
McGannon, Robert E. Firefighter, F. D. 7th ed. LC 80-25047. 256p. (Orig.). 1981. pap. 8.00 (ISBN 0-668-05170-1, 5170). Arco.
Petersen, Johanna. Careers with a Fire Department. LC 74-11904. (Early Career Books Ser.). (Illus.). 36p. (gr. 2-5). 1975. PLB 4.95 (ISBN 0-8225-0309-3). Lerner Pubns.
Pompilio, Raymond. Volunteers, a Portrait of Small-Town Firefighters. LC 79-11059. (Illus.). 1979. 12.95 (ISBN 0-89594-021-3); pap. 7.95 (ISBN 0-89594-018-3). Crossing Pr.
Public Employee Safety Guide: Fire Department. 20p. 1974. pap. 3.35 (ISBN 0-87912-109-2, 195.93). Natl Safety Coun.
Robinson, Nancy. Firefighters. 64p. (Orig.). (gr. k-3). 1980. pap. 1.50 (ISBN 0-590-05736-7, Schol Pap). Schol Bk Serv.
Scott, Jack D. & Sweet, Ozzie. City of Birds & Beasts: Behind the Scenes at the Bronx Zoo. LC 77-13888. (Illus.). (gr. 6 up). 1978. 8.95 (ISBN 0-399-20633-7). Putnam.
Smith, Betsy. A Day in the Life of a Firefighter. LC 80-54099. (Illus.). 32p. (gr. 4 up). 1981. PLB 6.89 (ISBN 0-89375-444-7); pap. 2.50 (ISBN 0-89375-445-5). Troll Assocs.
Steele, Charles. Guide to Fire Fighter Qualifications Training Programs. Teague, Paul E., ed. LC 77-92424. 1978. pap. text ed. 5.75 (ISBN 0-87765-111-6, FSP-50). Natl Fire Prot.
Tall Bull, Henry & Weist, Tom. Cheyenne Fire Fighters: Modern Indians Fighting Forest Fires. (gr. 4 up). 1973. pap. 1.95 (ISBN 0-89992-016-0). MT Coun Indian.
Tentative Standard for Proctective Clothing for Fire Fighters. 1973. pap. 2.00 (ISBN 0-685-58201-9, 19A-T). Natl Fire Prot.
Tielsch, George & Whisenand, Paul M. Fire Assessment Centers: The New Concept in Promotional Examinations. LC 78-73578. 1978. pap. text ed. 9.50 (ISBN 0-89368-304-3). Davis Pub Co.
Training Reports & Records. (Zero Ser). 1970. pap. 2.00 (ISBN 0-685-58135-7, 9). Natl Fire Prot.
Tuck, Charles A., Jr., ed. Industrial Fire Brigades Training Manual. 5th ed. LC 77-95083. 1978. pap. text ed. 8.50 (ISBN 0-87765-116-7, SPP-13A). Natl Fire Prot.
An Unlikely Firemaster. 170p. 1968. pap. 5.25 (ISBN 0-685-46046-0, FSP-31). Natl Fire Prot.
Wallington, Neil. Fireman: A Personal Account. LC 78-65762. 1979. 17.95 (ISBN 0-7153-7723-X). David & Charles.
--Firemen at War: The Work of London's Firefighters in the Second World War. LC 80-68692. (Illus.). 160p. 1981. 19.95 (ISBN 0-7153-7964-X). David & Charles.

FIRE FIGHTERS–LEGAL STATUS, LAWS, ETC.

Bahme, Charles W. Fireman's Law Book. 4th ed. 256p. 1967. 5.50 (ISBN 0-685-46051-7, FSP-3). Natl Fire Prot.
Morse, H. Newcomb. Legal Insite. 2nd ed. Lyons, Paul R., ed. LC 75-29522. 165p. 1975. pap. 5.50 (ISBN 0-87765-057-8, SPP-20A). Natl Fire Prot.

FIRE FIGHTING

see Fire Extinction

FIRE INSURANCE

see Insurance, Fire

FIRE INVESTIGATION

Aircraft Fire Investigators Manual. (Four Hundred Ser). 1972. pap. 2.00 (ISBN 0-685-58220-5, 422M). Natl Fire Prot.
Bates, Edward B. Elements of Fire & Arson Investigation. 1975. 7.25 (ISBN 0-89368-313-2). Davis Pub Co.
Berrin, Elliott R. Investigative Photography. Date not set. 3.25 (ISBN 0-686-22738-7). Society Fire Protect.
Carroll, John R. Physical & Technical Aspects of Fire & Arson Investigation. (Illus.). 470p. 1979. 32.50 (ISBN 0-398-03785-X). C C Thomas.
Cole, Lee S. The Investigation of Motor Vehicle Fires. 65p. 1980. pap. 5.00 (ISBN 0-939818-04-3). Lee Bks.
Dennett, M. F. Fire Investigation: A Practical Guide for Fire Students & Officers, Insurance Investigators, Loss Adjustors, & Police Officers. (Illus.). 80p. 1980. 17.25 (ISBN 0-08-024741-5); pap. 9.75 (ISBN 0-08-024742-3). Pergamon.
Fire Reporting Field Incident Manual. (Eight Hundred&Nine Hundred Ser). 1973. pap. 2.00 (ISBN 0-685-58216-7, 901AM). Natl Fire Prot.
Fitch, Richard D. & Porter, Edward A. Accidental or Incendiary. 224p. 1975. 14.75 (ISBN 0-398-00582-6). C C Thomas.
Kirk, P. L. Fire Investigation: Including Fire-Related Phenomena: Arson, Explosion, Asphyxiation. LC 69-19240. 255p. 1969. 19.95 (ISBN 0-471-48860-7). Wiley.
Roblee, C. & McKechnie, A. Investigation of Fires. 1981. 14.95 (ISBN 0-13-503169-9). P-H.
Tuck, Charles A., Jr. Analyses of Three Multiple Fatality Penal Institution Fires. 32p. 1978. pap. text ed. 35.00 (ISBN 0-87765-135-3, SL-35). Natl Fire Prot.
Tuck, Charles A., Jr., ed. Fire Incident Data Coding Guide. 1977. pap. 3.50 (ISBN 0-87765-088-8, SPP-42). Natl Fire Prot.

FIRE LOSSES

see Fires; Insurance, Fire

FIRE PREVENTION

see also Fire Extinction; Fire Fighters; Fireproofing; Forest Fires; Lightning Arresters also subdivision Fires and Fire Prevention under various classes of institutions and buildings, e.g. Schools–Fires and Fire Prevention

Aircraft Electrical Systems Maintenance Operations. (Four Hundred Ser). 1968. pap. 2.00 (ISBN 0-685-58061-X, 410A). Natl Fire Prot.
Automatic Fire Detectors. (Seventy Ser.). 1974. pap. 3.00 (ISBN 0-685-58150-0, 72E). Natl Fire Prot.
Auxiliary Protective Signaling Systems. (Seventy Ser). 1974. pap. 3.00 (ISBN 0-685-58063-6, 72B). Natl Fire Prot.
Babcock, Denise L. NFPA Fire Protection Reference Directory, 1979. 4th ed. 1980. pap. 8.00 (ISBN 0-87765-137-X). Natl Fire Prot.
Bahme, Charles W. Fire Officer's Guide to Dangerous Chemicals. Lyons, Paul R., ed. LC 77-76481. (Illus.). 1978. 10.50 (ISBN 0-87765-101-9, FSP-36A). Natl Fire Prot.
--Fire Officer's Guide to Emergency Action. 3rd ed. LC 73-89341. (Get Ahead Ser.). (Illus.). 1976. pap. 7.50 (ISBN 0-685-75458-8, FSP-38). Natl Fire Prot.
--Fire Service & the Law. McKinnon, Gordon P., ed. LC 76-26786. 1976. 8.50 (ISBN 0-87765-081-0, FSP-3A). Natl Fire Prot.
The Baptist Towers Housing for the Elderly Fire. 64p. 1972. pap. 2.50 (ISBN 0-685-46041-X, LS-1). Natl Fire Prot.
Bare, William K. Fundamentals of Fire Prevention. LC 76-23221. (Wiley Ser. in Fire Science). 213p. 1977. text ed. 17.95 (ISBN 0-471-04835-6). Wiley.
--Introduction to Fire Science & Fire Prevention. LC 77-14002. (Wiley Ser. in Fire Science). 290p. 1978. text ed. 17.95 (ISBN 0-471-01708-6); tchrs. manual (ISBN 0-471-03779-6). Wiley.
Barracato, John & Michelmore, Peter. Arson! 1976. 8.95 (ISBN 0-393-08744-1). Norton.
Bhatnagar, Vijay M., ed. Advances in Fire Retardants, Part Two. LC 72-91704. (Progress in Fire Retardancy Ser.: Vol. 3). 200p. 1974. pap. 25.00 (ISBN 0-87762-111-X). Technomic.
--Fire Retardants: Proceeding of the First European Conference on Flammability & Fire Retardants. LC 78-66105. 1979. pap. 35.00 (ISBN 0-87762-264-7). Technomic.
Blanc, Linda-Gay. Fire in Your Home. LC 78-60515. (Illus.). 1978. pap. 1.75 (ISBN 0-87765-131-0, SPP-52). Natl Fire Prot.
Brannigan, Francis, Jr. Fire Hazards in the Construction of Garden Apartments & Town Houses. Tuck, Charles A., ed. LC 76-16714. (Illus.). 1976. incl. tapes & slides 65.00 (ISBN 0-685-73836-1). Natl Fire Prot.
Bugbee, Percy. Principles of Fire Protection. Tower, Keith & Dean, Amy, eds. LC 76-50848. 1978. text ed. 16.50 (ISBN 0-87765-084-5, TXT-4); instructor's manual 3.50 (ISBN 0-87765-122-1, TXT-4A). Natl Fire Prot.
Bush, Loren S. & McLaughlin, James. Introduction to Fire Science. Gruber, Harvey, ed. (Fire Science Ser.). 1970. text ed. 13.95x (ISBN 0-02-473900-6). Macmillan.
Butcher, D. G. & Parnell, A. C. Smoke Control in Fire Safety Design. 1979. 25.00x (ISBN 0-419-11190-5, Pub. by E & FN Spon). Methuen Inc.
Carpets, Clothing, & Furniture. LC 75-29838. (Illus.). 64p. 1975. pap. 4.50 (ISBN 0-87765-060-8, SPP-34). Natl Fire Prot.
Central Station Signaling Systems. (Seventy Ser). 1974. pap. 3.00 (ISBN 0-685-58066-0, 71). Natl Fire Prot.
Clet, Vince. Fire Related Codes, Laws & Ordinances. 1978. text ed. 12.95x (ISBN 0-02-471760-6). Macmillan.
Colburn, Robert E. Fire Protection & Suppression. Williams, Carlton, ed. (Illus.). 352p. 1975. text ed. 15.95 (ISBN 0-07-011680-6, 11680-6, G); instructor's manual 3.50 (ISBN 0-07-011681-4). McGraw.
Commerce & Community Affairs Dept. Fire Protection Administration for Small Communities & Fire Protection Districts. LC 79-93086. (Illus.). 1980. pap. text ed. 15.00 (ISBN 0-87939-037-9). Intl Fire Serv.
Committee on Fire Research, National Research Council. Fire Detection for Life Safety. LC 76-53105. 1977. pap. 7.75 (ISBN 0-309-02600-8). Natl Acad Pr.
Connor, Joseph. Marine Fire Prevention, Fire Fighting & Fire Safety. (Illus.). 404p. 1979. pap. text ed. 9.95 (ISBN 0-87618-994-X). R J Brady.
Construction Library, 23 bks. 964p. includes protective case 45.90 (ISBN 0-685-58053-9, CL-A). Natl Fire Prot.
Critser, James R., Jr. Flame Retardants for Plastics, Rubber & Textiles: Including Indexes & Abstracts 1967 to 1971. Incl. 285.00 (ISBN 0-914428-03-9). (Ser. 2-6771b). 1971. Lexington Data.
Dean, Amy E. & Tower, Keith. Fire Protection Guide on Hazardous Materials. 7th ed. LC 78-59832. 1978. pap. 12.50 (ISBN 0-87765-130-2, SPP-1D). Natl Fire Prot.
Dean, Amy E., ed. Flash Point Index of Trade Liquids. 9th ed. LC 78-54003. 1978. pap. text ed. 5.50 (ISBN 0-87765-127-2, SPP-51). Natl Fire Prot.
--State Fire Marshals Conference Report. LC 77-87129. 1977. pap. text ed. 7.50 (ISBN 0-87765-110-8). Natl Fire Prot.

Design of Buildings for Fire Safety. (Special Technical Publications Ser.). 290p. 1979. 28.00x (ISBN 0-686-76044-1, 685, 04-685000-31). ASTM.
Dixon, Robert G., Jr. Standards Development in the Private Sector: Thoughts on Interest Representation & Procedural Fairness. Dean, Amy E., ed. LC 78-50058. 1978. pap. text ed. 3.00 (ISBN 0-87765-118-3, STD-CSS). Natl Fire Prot.
Earnest, Ernest. The Volunteer Fire Company. LC 78-8785. (Illus.). 224p. 1980. pap. 6.95 (ISBN 0-8128-6094-2). Stein & Day.
Ely, Robert. Fire Officer's Guide: Fire Apparatus Maintenance. Lyons, Paul R., ed. LC 75-15054. (Fire Officer's Guide Ser.). (Illus.). 392p. 1975. 10.50 (ISBN 0-87765-039-X). Natl Fire Prot.
Explosion Prevention Systems. (Sixty Ser). 60p. 1973. pap. 2.00 (ISBN 0-685-44174-1, 69). Natl Fire Prot.
Explosives Motor Vehicle Terminals. (Forty Ser). 1970. pap. 2.00 (ISBN 0-685-58095-4, 498). Natl Fire Prot.
Favreau, Donald F. Guidelines for Fire Service Education Programs in Community & Junior Colleges. 1969. pap. 2.50 (ISBN 0-87117-023-X). Am Assn Comm Jr Coll.
Fire Doors & Windows. (Eighty-Ninety Ser). 108p. 1974. pap. 3.75 (ISBN 0-685-44148-2, 80). Natl Fire Prot.
Fire Hazards in Oxygen Enriched Atmospheres. (Fifty Ser.). 80p. 1974. pap. 4.00 (ISBN 0-685-46068-1, 53M). Natl Fire Prot.
Fire Protection Directory 1979. (Benn Directories Ser.). 1979. 52.50 (ISBN 0-686-52399-7, Pub by Benn Pubns). Nichols Pub.
Fire Protection Guide on Hazardous Materials. 5th ed. 1973. 7.75 (ISBN 0-685-40708-X, SPP-1B). Natl Fire Prot.
Fire Protection Handbook. 13th ed. (Illus.). 2128p. 1969. 29.50 (ISBN 0-685-58184-5, FPH1369). Natl Fire Prot.
Fire Protection Library, 24 bks. 1147p. includes protective case 53.30 (ISBN 0-685-58054-7, FLP-A). Natl Fire Prot.
Fire Protection Standard for Motor Craft. (Three Hundred Ser.). 62p. 1972. pap. 2.00 (ISBN 0-685-46036-3, 302). Natl Fire Prot.
Fire Standards & Safety. 1977. 27.75 (ISBN 0-686-52032-7, 04-614000-31). ASTM.
Ford, Robert, et al. Fire Protection Handbook Study Guide. 1976. pap. 15.00 (ISBN 0-89368-300-0). Davis Pub Co.
Francis, R. L. A Simple Graphical Procedure to Estimate the Minimum Time to Evacuate a Building. 1979. 3.50 (ISBN 0-686-25955-6, TR 79-5). Society Fire Protect.
Gaylor, Harry P. Wildfires: Prevention & Control. LC 74-14269. (Illus.). 1974. pap. 15.95 (ISBN 0-87618-131-0). R J Brady.
Guard Operations in Fire Loss Prevention. (Six Hundred Ser). 1968. pap. 2.00 (ISBN 0-685-58227-2, 601A). Natl Fire Prot.
Guard Service in Fire Loss Prevention. (Six Hundred Ser). 1968. pap. 2.00 (ISBN 0-685-58226-4, 601). Natl Fire Prot.
Gupta, R. S. A Handbook of Fire Technology. 292p. 1981. 15.00x (ISBN 0-86125-113-X, Pub. by Orient Longman India); cloth with jacket 30.00x (ISBN 0-86125-088-5). State Mutual Bk.
Hazardous Locations. (Illus.). 160p. 1974. pap. 4.00 (ISBN 0-685-58192-6, 70C). Natl Fire Prot.
Hickey, Harry E. Hydraulics for Fire Protection. Hickey, Harry E., ed. LC 79-91611. (Illus.). 340p. 1980. text ed. 16.50 (ISBN 0-87765-170-1, TXT-6). Natl Fire Prot.
--Public Fire Safety Organization: A Systems Approach. LC 73-90984. 224p. 1973. 12.50 (ISBN 0-685-40229-0, SPP-21). Natl Fire Prot.
High-Rise Building Fires & Fire Safety. (Illus.). 164p. 1973. pap. 3.50 (ISBN 0-685-44146-6, SPP-18). Natl Fire Prot.
Hilado, Carlos J., ed. Fire Prevention & Suppression, Vol. 10. LC 73-82115. (Fire & Flammability Ser.). 159p. 1974. pap. 20.00 (ISBN 0-87762-134-9). Technomic.
Household Fire Warning Equipment. (Seventy Ser). 1974. pap. 2.00 (ISBN 0-685-58149-7, 74). Natl Fire Prot.
IFSTA Committee. Fire Prevention & Inspection. Hudiburg, Everett & Thomas, Charles, eds. (Illus.). 1974. pap. text ed. 7.00 (ISBN 0-87939-010-7). Intl Fire Serv.
--Forcible Entry, Rope & Portable Extinguisher Practices. Peige, John, et al, eds. LC 77-94425. (Illus.). 1978. pap. text ed. 8.50 (ISBN 0-87939-032-8). Intl Fire Serv.
--Private Fire Protection & Detection Systems. Carlson, Gene P., ed. LC 79-55670. (Illus., Orig.). 1979. pap. 8.00 (ISBN 0-87939-036-0). Intl Fire Serv.
--Public Fire Education. Osterhout, Connie, et al, eds. LC 79-89165. (Illus., Orig.). 1979. pap. 8.50 (ISBN 0-87939-034-4). Intl Fire Serv.
--Water Supplies for Fire Protection. Laughlin, Jerry & Williams, Connie E., eds. LC 78-58881. (Illus.). 1978. pap. text ed. 8.50 (ISBN 0-87939-029-8). Intl Fire Serv.
IFSTA Committee Members. Fire Problems in High Rise Buildings. Peige, John & Williams, Connie, eds. (Illus.). 1976. pap. text ed. 7.00 (ISBN 0-87939-021-2). Intl Fire Serv.
Indoor General Storage. (Two Hundred Ser). 1974. pap. 2.00 (ISBN 0-685-58169-1, 231). Natl Fire Prot.
Industrial Fire Brigades Training Manual. (Illus.). 1968. 5.00 (ISBN 0-685-46050-9, SSP-13). Natl Fire Prot.
Installation, Maintenance & Use of Portable Fire Extinguishers. (Ten Ser). Orig. Title: Installation of Portable Fire Extinguishers. 40p. 1974. pap. 3.00 (ISBN 0-685-44154-7, 10). Natl Fire Prot.
Installation of Sprinkler Systems. (Ten Ser). 180p. 1974. pap. 4.00 (ISBN 0-685-44162-8, 13). Natl Fire Prot.
Institute for Power System. Handbook of Industrial Fire Protection & Security. 600p. 1979. 99.00x (ISBN 0-686-65619-9). State Mutual Bks.
Jensen, Rolf, ed. Fire Protection for the Design Professional. LC 75-9508. 198p. 1975. 29.95 (ISBN 0-8436-0152-3). CBI Pub.
Juillerat, Ernest. Campus Firesafety. new ed. Lyons, Paul R., ed. LC 77-82037. (Illus.). 1977. pap. 8.50 (ISBN 0-87765-106-X, SPP-46). Natl Fire Prot.
Kimball, Warren Y. Fire Service Communications for Fire Attack. LC 78-18839. 1972. 8.50 (ISBN 0-685-40709-8, FSP-35). Natl Fire Prot.
Kuvshinoff, B. W., et al, eds. Fire Sciences Dictionary. LC 77-3489. 439p. 1977. 22.00 (ISBN 0-471-51113-7, Pub. by Wiley-Interscience). Wiley.
Laboratories in Health-Related Institutions. (Fifty Ser). 1973. pap. 2.00 (ISBN 0-685-58087-3, 56C). Natl Fire Prot.
Legal Insight. 112p. 1973. pap. 3.25 (ISBN 0-685-44145-8, SPP-20). Natl Fire Prot.
Life & Property Protection: Proceedings of FRCA Meeting. 1978. pap. 25.00x (ISBN 0-87762-251-5). Technomic.
Life Safety Code. rev. ed. (One Hundred Ser). 250p. 1973. 3.00 (ISBN 0-685-44159-8, 101). Natl Fire Prot.
Local Protective Signaling Systems. (Seventy Ser). 1974. pap. 3.00 (ISBN 0-685-58064-4, 72A). Natl Fire Prot.
Lucht, David A. Fire Prevention Planning & Leadership for Small Communities. Harmon, Ruth L., ed. LC 80-80229. (Illus.). 80p. (Orig.). 1980. pap. text ed. 4.95 (ISBN 0-87765-177-9, FSP-54). Natl Fire Prot.
Lyons, Paul R. Fire Officer's Guide to Operating Aerial Ladders. 4th ed. LC 77-78034. (Fire Officer's Guide Ser.). 1977. text ed. 9.25 (ISBN 0-87765-102-7, FSP-7B). Natl Fire Prot.
--NFPA Fire Protection Reference Directory 1978. LC 77-81422. 1978. pap. 5.00 (ISBN 0-87765-105-1, FSPD-3). Natl Fire Prot.
--Testing Fire Apparatus - One: Acceptance & Service Tests for Pumpers. LC 78-59790. 1979. pap. text ed. 65.00 (ISBN 0-87765-129-9). Natl Fire Prot.
--Testing Fire Apparatus: Acceptance & Service Tests for Aerial Ladders, Pt. II. LC 78-59790. (Illus.). 50p. (Orig.). 1979. pap. text ed. 65.00 (ISBN 0-87765-136-1, SL-31). Natl Fire Prot.
--Testing Fire Apparatus: Acceptance & Service Tests for Elevating Platforms, Pt. III. LC 78-59790. (Illus.). 54p. (Orig.). 1979. pap. text ed. 65.00 (ISBN 0-87765-137-X). Natl Fire Prot.
Lyons, Paul R., ed. Annual Fire Protection Reference Directory. LC 75-24677. 160p. 1975. pap. text ed. 10.00 (ISBN 0-87765-040-3). Natl Fire Prot.
MacGillivray, Lois. Decision-Related Research on the Organization of Service Delivery Systems in Metropolitan Areas: Fire Protection. LC 79-83819. 1979. codebook 34.00 (ISBN 0-89138-985-7). ICPSR.
McKinnon, Gordon P., ed. Instructor's Manual for Principles of Fire Protection. LC 76-27198. 1976. pap. 3.50 (ISBN 0-685-73837-X, IM-FPM). Natl Fire Prot.
McKinnon, Gordon P. & Tower, Keith, eds. Fire Protection Handbook. 14th ed. LC 75-34683. (Illus.). 1300p. 1976. 43.50 (ISBN 0-685-64005-1). Natl Fire Prot.
Management Responsibility for Effects of Fire on Operations. (Zero Ser). 1974. pap. 2.00 (ISBN 0-685-58137-3). Natl Fire Prot.
Manufacture, Transportation, Storage of Fireworks. (Fourty Ser). 52p. 1974. pap. 3.00 (ISBN 0-685-44169-5, 44A). Natl Fire Prot.
Marchant. Design for Fire Safety. 1981. text ed. price not set (ISBN 0-408-00487-8). Butterworth.
Marine Publications Intl. Ltd., ed. Ships Firefighting Manual. 1981. 50.00x (ISBN 0-906314-03-8, Pub. by Marine Pubns Intl England). State Mutual Bk.
Meldrum, D. H. Fighting Fire with Foam: Basics of Effective Systems. 1979. 3.50 (ISBN 0-686-25956-4, TR 79-2). Society Fire Protect.
Melott, Ronald K. Is Energy Conservation Firesafe? 2.50 (ISBN 0-686-12081-7, TR 78-8). Society Fire Protect.
Miller, Curt. Successful Total Home Protection. LC 75-38407. 1976. 12.00 (ISBN 0-912336-22-6); pap. 4.95 (ISBN 0-912336-23-4). Structures Pub.
Model Drafts for Enabling Legislation. (Zero Ser). 1967. pap. 2.00 (ISBN 0-685-58079-2, 2M). Natl Fire Prot.
Morris, John. Managing the Library Fire Risk. 2nd ed. LC 78-22603. (Illus.). 1979. 14.00 (ISBN 0-9602278-1-4). U Cal Risk Management.
National Bureau of Standards. Detector Sensitivity & Siting Requirements for Dwellings: Phase 2. McKinnon, G. P. & Dean, A. E., eds. 1977. pap. 10.00 (ISBN 0-87765-096-9, SPP-43A). Natl Fire Prot.
National Fire Code Supplement, 2 vols. 1978. Set. pap. text ed. 30.00 (ISBN 0-685-66909-2, NFC-S78). Natl Fire Prot.
National Fire Codes, 16 vols. 1976. 90.00 set (ISBN 0-685-68873-9). Natl Fire Prot.
National Fire Codes, Vol.1. 720p. 7.50 (ISBN 0-685-58185-3, FC-1). Natl Fire Prot.
National Fire Codes, Vol.2. 640p. 7.50 (ISBN 0-685-58038-5, FC-2). Natl Fire Prot.
National Fire Codes, Vol.3. 720p. 7.50 (ISBN 0-685-58039-3, FC-3). Natl Fire Prot.
National Fire Codes, Vol.4. 736p. 7.50 (ISBN 0-685-58040-7, FC-4). Natl Fire Prot.
National Fire Codes, Vol.5. 720p. 7.50 (ISBN 0-685-58041-5, FC-5). Natl Fire Prot.
National Fire Codes, Vol.6. 656p. 7.50 (ISBN 0-685-58042-3, FC-6). Natl Fire Prot.
National Fire Codes, Vol.7. 624p. 7.50 (ISBN 0-685-58043-1, FC-7). Natl Fire Prot.
National Fire Codes, Vol.8. 720p. 7.50 (ISBN 0-685-58044-X, FC-8). Natl Fire Prot.
National Fire Codes, Vol.9. 592p. 7.50 (ISBN 0-685-58046-6, FC-9). Natl Fire Prot.
National Fire Codes, Vol.10. 624p. 7.50 (ISBN 0-685-58047-4, FC-10). Natl Fire Prot.
National Fire Codes, 1978, 18 vols. rev. ed. 1978. Set. pap. 90.00 (ISBN 0-685-66908-4, NFC). Natl Fire Prot.
National Fire Protection Association. Danger! Fire Fighters at Work Safety One. LC 79-720640. (Illus.). 1979. pap. text ed. 60.00 (ISBN 0-87765-163-9, SL-53). Natl Fire Prot.
National Fire Protection Association & Urban Institute. Fire Code Inspections & Fire Prevention: What Methods Lead to Success? Tower, Keith & Harmon, Ruth, eds. 1979. pap. 5.00 (ISBN 0-87765-151-5). Natl Fire Prot.
National Fire Protection Association. The Fire Department Safety Program: Safety Two. LC 79-720641. (Illus.). 1979. pap. text ed. 60.00 (ISBN 0-87765-164-7, SL-54). Natl Fire Prot.
--Handling Pipeline Transportation Emergencies. Harmon, Ruth & Tower, Keith, eds. LC 79-720296. 1979. pap. text ed. 115.00 (ISBN 0-87765-149-3). Natl Fire Prot.
--Hydraulics for the Fire Service: Hydraulic Field Equations, Vol. VI. Lyons, Paul R., ed. LC 78-50007. (Illus.). 72p. (Orig.). 1980. pap. text ed. 42.50 (ISBN 0-87765-171-X, SL-60). Natl Fire Prot.
--Hydraulics for the Fire Sevice: Operating the Pumper, Vol. V. Lyons, Paul R., ed. LC 78-50007. (Illus.). 88p. 1979. text ed. 42.50 (ISBN 0-87765-157-4, SL-51). Natl Fire Prot.
National Fire Protection Association's Comm. on Life Safety, et al. NFPA Life Safety Code Handbook. Tasner, Paul & Hill, Mary, eds. LC 77-94009. (Illus.). 1978. 14.50 (ISBN 0-87765-114-0, 101-HBK). Natl Fire Prot.
NFPA & U.S. Department of Transportation. Handling Hazardous Materials Transportation Emergencies. Dean, Amy E., ed. LC 78-54010. 1978. pap. text ed. 350.00 (ISBN 0-87765-126-4, SL-29); wkbk. 10.00 (ISBN 0-87765-125-6, SL-29WB). Natl Fire Prot.
NFPA Guide to OSHA Fire Protection Regulations, 5 vols. rev. 2nd ed. Incl. Vol. 1. NFPA Annotated OSHA Regulations. rev. ed. 15.00 (ISBN 0-685-44151-2); Vol. 2. OSHA-NFPA Standards No. 10-22; Vol. 3. OSHA-NFPA Standards Nos. 24-28; Vol. 4. OSHA-NFPA Standard Nos. 59-80; Vol. 5. OSHA-NFPA Standard Nos. 86a-664. 55.00 set (ISBN 0-685-44150-4). Natl Fire Prot.
NFPA Inspection Manual. 3rd ed. 1970. 6.75 (ISBN 0-685-40707-1, SPP-11A). Natl Fire Prot.
NFPA OSHA Three, 3 vols. rev. ed. Vols. 1, 3, & 4. 35.00 set (ISBN 0-685-44153-9). Natl Fire Prot.
Operation Skyline. 1975. pap. 3.25 (ISBN 0-685-61258-9, S*P*P-27). Natl Fire Prot.
Outdoor General Storage. (Two Hundred Ser). 1970. pap. 2.00 (ISBN 0-685-58170-5, 231A). Natl Fire Prot.
Outside Protection. (Twenty Ser). 56p. 1973. pap. 2.00 (ISBN 0-685-44158-X, 24). Natl Fire Prot.
Powers, W. Robert. Sprinkler Experience in High-Rise Buildings. 1979. 3.25 (ISBN 0-686-26148-8, TR 79-1). Society Fire Protect.
Prevention of Fire & Dust Explosions in Grain Elevators & Bulk Grain Handling Facilities. (Sixty Ser). 1973. pap. 2.00 (ISBN 0-685-58080-6, 61B). Natl Fire Prot.
Prevention of Furnace Explosions in Fuel-Oil & Natural Gas-Fired Watertube Boiler Furnaces with One Burner. (Eighty-Ninety Ser). 68p. 1973. pap. 2.00 (ISBN 0-685-44149-0, 85). Natl Fire Prot.
Prevention of Furnace Explosions in Fuel Oil-Fired Multiple Burner Boiler-Furnace. (Eighty-Ninety Ser.). 84p. 1974. pap. 3.50 (ISBN 0-685-44131-8, 85D). Natl Fire Prot.
Prevention of Furnace Explosions in Natural Gas-Fired Multiple Burner Boiler-Furnaces. (Eighty-Ninety Ser). 68p. 1973. pap. 3.50 (ISBN 0-685-44130-X, 85B). Natl Fire Prot.
Prevention of Furnace Explosions in Pulverized Coal-Fired Multiple Burner Boiler-Furnaces. (Eighty-Ninety Ser). 68p. 1974. pap. 3.50 (ISBN 0-685-44132-6, 85E). Natl Fire Prot.
Private Fire Brigades. (Tenty Ser). 1967. pap. 2.00 (ISBN 0-685-58115-2, 27). Natl Fire Prot.
Protection of Records. (Two Hundred Ser.). 93p. 1970. pap. 2.00 (ISBN 0-685-46035-5, 232). Natl Fire Prot.
Public Employee Safety Guide: Fire Department. 20p. 1974. pap. 3.35 (ISBN 0-87912-109-2, 195.93). Natl Safety Coun.
Public Fire Safety Inspections. 32p. 1967. pap. 2.50 (ISBN 0-685-58183-7, FSP-28). Natl Fire Prot.
Purington, Robert G. Hydraulics for the Fire Service: Unit I- Characteristics of Water. Lyons, Paul R., ed. LC 78-50007. (Illus.). 1978. pap. text ed. 42.50 (ISBN 0-87765-117-5, SL-27). Natl Fire Prot.
--Hydraulics for the Fire Service: Unit II - Water Flow, Friction Loss, Engine Pressure. Lyons, Paul R., ed. LC 78-50007. (Illus.). 1978. pap. text ed. 42.50 (ISBN 0-685-63021-8, SL-28). Natl Fire Prot.
Recommended System for the Indentification of the Fire Hazards of Materials. (Seven Hundred Ser). 1969. pap. 2.00 (ISBN 0-685-58213-2, 704M). Natl Fire Prot.
Remote Station Protective Signaling Systems. (Seventy Ser). 1974. pap. 3.00 (ISBN 0-685-58065-2, 72C). Natl Fire Prot.
Reuter, Margaret. Careers in a Fire Department. LC 77-8151. (Whole Works Ser.). (Illus.). (gr. 3-7). 1977. PLB 10.65 (ISBN 0-8172-0954-9). Raintree Pubs.
Robertson, James C. Introduction to Fire Prevention. (Fire Science Ser.). 1975. text ed. 14.95x (ISBN 0-02-477080-9). Macmillan.
Rosenbauer, Donna. Introduction to Fire Protection Law. Tower, Keith, et al, eds. LC 78-50849. 1978. text ed. 14.95 (ISBN 0-87765-121-3, TXT5); tchrs. manual 3.50 (ISBN 0-87765-123-X, TXT5A). Natl Fire Prot.
Rudman, Jack. Director of Fire Safety. (Career Examination Ser.: C-2396). (Cloth bdg. avail. on request). pap. 10.00 (ISBN 0-8373-2396-7). Natl Learning.
--Fire Inspector. (Career Examination Ser.: C-1288). (Cloth bdg. avail. on request). pap. 8.00 (ISBN 0-8373-1288-4). Natl Learning.
--Fire Prevention Inspector. (Career Examination Ser.: C-287). (Cloth bdg. avail. on request). pap. 8.00 (ISBN 0-8373-0287-0). Natl Learning.
--Fire Safety Officer. (Career Examination Ser.: C-2230). (Cloth bdg. avail. on request). pap. 8.00 (ISBN 0-8373-2230-8). Natl Learning.
--Senior Fire Prevention Inspector. (Career Examination Ser.: C-1765). (Cloth bdg. avail. on request). 1977. pap. 10.00 (ISBN 0-8373-1765-7). Natl Learning.
--Supervising Fire Marshal (Uniformed) (Career Examination Ser.: C-1817). (Cloth bdg. avail. on request). pap. 10.00 (ISBN 0-8373-1817-3). Natl Learning.
Rule, Leonard. Fire. LC 73-161698. (New Citizen Books). (Illus.). 80p. 1973. 10.50x (ISBN 0-85340-229-9). Intl Pubns Serv.
Schaenman, Philip S. & Swartz, Joe. Measuring Fire Protection Productivity in Local Government. LC 73-94246. (Illus.). 108p. 1974. pap. 7.00 (ISBN 0-87765-053-5). Natl Fire Prot.
Scher, Steven. Fire. LC 77-27270. (Illus.). 1978. pap. 7.95 (ISBN 0-8109-2151-0). Abrams.
Seward, Samuel M., et al. Municipal Resource Allocation: Minimizing the Cost of Fire Protection. 1976. 2.50 (ISBN 0-686-64193-0). U CO Busn Res Div.
Sherad, Shirley E., ed. Hazardous Materials Transportation Accidents. LC 78-54633. 1978. pap. text ed. 5.00 (ISBN 0-87765-128-0, SPP-49). Natl Fire Prot.

--Interior Finish & Fire Spread. LC 77-85254. 1977. pap. 7.25 (ISBN 0-87765-108-6, SPP-47). Natl Fire Prot.
Soros, Charles C. & Lyons, Paul R. Safety in the Fire Service. LC 79-84757. (Illus.). 1979. pap. 16.00 (ISBN 0-87765-147-7). Natl Fire Prot.
Standard Methods of Fire Tests for Flame Resistant Textiles & Films. (Seven Hundred Ser). 1969. pap. 2.00 (ISBN 0-685-58210-8, 701). Natl Fire Prot.
Summers, Wilford. NFPA Handbook of the National Electrical Code. Tasner, Paul & Hill, Mary, eds. LC 77-93950. (Illus.). 1978. 15.50 (ISBN 0-87765-115-9, SPP-6B). Natl Fire Prot.
Swartz, Joseph A. Importance of Role Assumption in Behavior of People in Fires. 1979. 3.50 (ISBN 0-686-25735-9, TR 79-4). Society Fire Protect.
Tamarin, Alfred. Fire Fighting in America. LC 71-123136. (Illus.). (gr. 4-6). 1971. 8.95 (ISBN 0-02-788820-7). Macmillan.
Tasner, Paul, et al, eds. Industrial Fire Hazards. LC 79-66427. (Illus.). 1979. 30.00 (ISBN 0-87765-155-8, SPP-57). Natl Fire Prot.
Teague, Paul E. Fire Hazard Properties of Flammable & Combustible Liquids. LC 78-61215. (Illus.). 46p. 1978. pap. text ed. 40.00 (ISBN 0-87765-133-7, SL-34). Natl Fire Prot.
--Firesafety in Hospitals. LC 77-72080. (Illus.). 1977. pap. text ed. 58.50 (ISBN 0-87765-092-6, SL-24). Natl Fire Prot.
Telecommunications Systems. (Illus.). 1975. pap. 3.50 (ISBN 0-685-54122-3). Natl Fire Prot.
Tentative Standard for Evaluating Fire Protection at a New Facility. 1970. pap. 2.00 (ISBN 0-685-58200-0, 5A-T). Natl Fire Prot.
Tentative Standard on Fire Protection for Limited Access Highways, Tunnels, Bridges & Elevated Structures. 1972. pap. 2.00 (ISBN 0-685-58191-8, 502-T). Natl Fire Prot.
Thompson, Norman J. Fire Behavior & Sprinklers. 3rd ed. (Illus.). 167p. 1964. pap. text ed. 3.95 (ISBN 0-87765-052-7, SPP-2). Natl Fire Prot.
Tielsch, George & Whisenand, Paul M. Fire Assessment Centers: The New Concept in Promotional Examinations. LC 78-73578. 1978. pap. text ed. 9.50 (ISBN 0-89368-304-3). Davis Pub Co.
Tower, Keith, ed. Instructor's Manual to Accompany Principles of Fire Protection Chemistry. LC 76-41622. 1976. pap. text ed. 3.50 (ISBN 0-87765-083-7). Natl Fire Prot.
Trade & Technical Press Editors. Handbook of Industrial Fire Protection & Security. 600p. 1976. 83.00x (ISBN 0-85461-059-6, Pub by Trade & Tech England). Renouf.
Trade & Technical Press Ltd, ed. Handbook of Industrial Fire Protection & Security. 105.00x (ISBN 0-85461-059-6). Intl Ideas.
Traister, John E. Design & Application of Security-Fire-Alarm Systems. (Illus.). 176p. 1981. 15.00 (ISBN 0-07-065114-0). McGraw.
Tryon, George H. & McKinnon, Gordon P., eds. NFPA Fire Protection Handbook. 13th ed. LC 62-12655. (Illus.). 2128p. 1969. 29.50 (ISBN 0-87765-021-7, FPH1369). Natl Fire Prot.
Tuck, Charles A., Jr., ed. Fire Incident Data Coding Guide. 1977. pap. 3.50 (ISBN 0-87765-088-8, SPP-42). Natl Fire Prot.
--NFPA Inspection Manual. 4th ed. LC 76-5194. (Illus.). 1976. 12.50 (ISBN 0-685-70941-8, SPP-11B). Natl Fire Prot.
Underdown, G. W. Practical Fire Precautions. 1973. 20.00x (ISBN 0-8464-0742-6). Beekman Pubs.
Underwood, George W. Practical Fire Precautions. 1979. text ed. 50.50x (ISBN 0-566-02124-2, Pub. by Gower Pub Co England). Renouf.
Uniform Coding for Fire Protection. (Eight Hundred & Nine Hundred Ser.). 170p. 1973. pap. 3.50 (ISBN 0-685-44144-X, 901). Natl Fire Prot.
Uniform Marking of Fire Hydrants. (Twenty Ser). 1974. pap. 2.00 (ISBN 0-685-58114-4, 291). Natl Fire Prot.
Urban Institute, NFPA. Procedures for Improving the Measurement of Local Fire Protection Effectiveness. Dean, A. E., ed. LC 77-82347. 1977. pap. text ed. 3.75 (ISBN 0-87765-107-8). Natl Fire Prot.
Vervalin, Charles H., ed. Fire Protection Manual for Hydrocarbon Processing Plants, Vol. 1. 2nd ed. (Illus.). 498p. 1973. 45.50x (ISBN 0-87201-286-7). Gulf Pub.
--Fire Protection Manual for Hydrocarbon Processing Plants, Vol. 2. (Illus.). 300p. 1981. 59.95 (ISBN 0-87201-288-3). Gulf Pub.
Walker, Hubert. Preventive Maintenance Apparatus. (Illus.). 1968. pap. 4.00 (ISBN 0-686-12266-6). Fire Eng.
Wallace, Roderick M. & Wallace, Deborah N. Studies on the Collapse of Fire Service in New York City. 1977. pap. text ed. 7.50 (ISBN 0-8191-0358-6). U Pr of Amer.
Water Charges for Private Fire Protection. (Twenty Ser). 1974. pap. 2.00 (ISBN 0-685-58113-6, 292M). Natl Fire Prot.
Water Spray Fixed Systems. (Ten Ser). 68p. 1973. pap. 2.00 (ISBN 0-685-44163-6, 15). Natl Fire Prot.
Water Tanks for Private Fire Protection. (Twenty Ser.). 137p. 1974. pap. 4.00 (ISBN 0-685-46065-7, 22). Natl Fire Prot.
Wels, Byron. Fire & Theft Security Systems. 2nd ed. (Illus.). 1976. pap. 5.95 (ISBN 0-8306-5956-0). TAB Bks.
Werner, Jane. Smokey the Bear. (Illus.). (ps-3). 1955. PLB 5.00 (ISBN 0-307-60481-0, Golden Pr). Western Pub.
Whitman, Lawrence. Fire Prevention. LC 78-26894. (Illus.). 1979. 21.95x (ISBN 0-88229-359-1). Nelson-Hall.
Whitman, Lawrence E. Fire Safety in the Atomic Age. 1980. 21.95x (ISBN 0-88229-529-2); pap. 11.95x (ISBN 0-88229-732-5). Nelson-Hall.

FIRE PREVENTION–RESEARCH

Bhatnagar, Vijay M. Flammability of Apparel. LC 72-91704. (Progress in Fire Retardancy Ser.: Vol. 7). (Illus.). 230p. 1975. pap. 20.00 (ISBN 0-87762-165-9). Technomic.
Bryan, John L. Fire Suppression & Detection Systems. LC 73-7367. (Fire Science Ser). (Illus.). 320p. 1974. text ed. 18.95 (ISBN 0-02-473920-0, 47392). Macmillan.
Committee on Fire Research. Directory of Fire Research in the United States, 1967-1969. 5th ed. LC 68-60084. 1970. pap. text ed. 14.25 (ISBN 0-309-01763-7). Natl Acad Pr.
--Directory of Fire Research in the U. S. 1969-1971. 6th ed. LC 68-60084. 800p. 1972. pap. 16.00 (ISBN 0-309-02033-6). Natl Acad Pr.
Committee on Fire Research, National Research Council. Directory of Fire Research. 8th ed. 1978. pap. text ed. 9.50x (ISBN 0-309-02799-3). Natl Acad Pr.
Directory of Fire Research in the United States: 1971-1973. 7th ed. LC 74-32544. 1975. pap. 12.75 (ISBN 0-309-02327-0). Natl Acad Pr.
Dixon, Robert G., Jr. Standards Development in the Private Sector: Thoughts on Interest Representation & Procedural Fairness. Dean, Amy E., ed. LC 78-50058. 1978. pap. text ed. 3.00 (ISBN 0-87765-118-3, STD-CSS). Natl Fire Prot.
Erven, Lawrence W. Fire Company Apparatus & Procedure. 2nd ed. (Fire Science Ser). (Illus.). 360p. 1974. text ed. 14.95x (ISBN 0-02-474150-7, 47415). Macmillan.
International Symposium on Flammability & Fire Retardants, 1974. Fire Retardants: Proceedings. Bhatnagar, Vijay M., ed. LC 72-33842. 200p. (Orig.). 1974. pap. 25.00x (ISBN 0-87762-196-9). Technomic.
Plane, Donald R., et al. Simulation of the Denver Fire Department for Development Policy Analysis. 1975. 2.50 (ISBN 0-686-64196-5). U CO Busn Res Div.

FIRE PROOFING

see Fireproofing

FIRE PUMPS

see Fire-Engines

FIRE RESEARCH

see Fire Prevention–Research

FIRE RESISTANT POLYMERS

Bhatnager, Vijay M., ed. Proceedings: 1976 International Symposium on Flammability & Fire Retardants. LC 75-25478. (Illus.). 1977. pap. 25.00x (ISBN 0-87762-215-9). Technomic.
Critser, James R., Jr. Flame, Retardants for Plastics, Rubber, Textiles & Paper. (Ser. 2-7879). 1979. 110.00 (ISBN 0-914428-61-6). Lexington Data.
--Flame Retardants for Plastics, Rubber, Textiles & Paper (July 1975-June 1976) (Ser. 2 - 7576). 1976. 110.00 (ISBN 0-914428-37-3). Lexington Data.
--Flame Retardants for Plastics, Rubber, Textiles & Paper: Series No. 2-7980, July 1979 - June 1980. 136p. 1980. refer. 110.00 (ISBN 0-914428-73-X). Lexington Data.
Hilado, Carlos J., ed. Flammability of Cellulosic Materials, Part 2, Vol. 11. LC 73-82115. (Fire & Flammability Ser.). (Illus.). 1976. pap. 20.00x (ISBN 0-87762-171-3). Technomic.
International Symposium on Flammability & Fire Retardants, 1977. Fire Retardants: Proceedings. Bhatnagar, Vijay M., ed. LC 77-90574. (Illus.). 1977. pap. 35.00x (ISBN 0-87762-246-9). Technomic.
Kuryla, W. C. & Pappa, A. J. Flame Retardency of Polymeric Materials, Vol. 5. 1979. 35.75 (ISBN 0-8247-6778-0). Dekker.
Kuryla, William C. & Papa, Anthony J., eds. Flame Retardancy of Polymeric Materials, Vol. 1. 334p. 1973. 49.75 (ISBN 0-8247-6012-3). Dekker.
--Flame Retardancy of Polymeric Materials, Vol. 2. 256p. 1973. 47.25 (ISBN 0-8247-6013-1). Dekker.
--Flame Retardancy of Polymeric Materials, Vol. 3. 376p. 1975. 47.25 (ISBN 0-8247-6235-5). Dekker.
Lewin, Menachem, et al, eds. Flame-Retardant Polymeric Materials, Vol. 1. 457p. 1975. 49.50 (ISBN 0-306-30840-1, Plenum Pr). Plenum Pub.
National Academy of Sciences. Aircraft: Civil & Military, Vol. 6. LC 77-79218. (Fire Safety Aspects of Polymeric Materials Ser.). 1977. 20.00x (ISBN 0-87762-227-2). Technomic.
--Materials: State of the Art, Vol. 1. LC 77-79218. (Fire Safety Aspects of Polymeric Materials Ser.). 1977. text ed. 15.00x (ISBN 0-87762-222-1). Technomic.
NFPA. The Fire Fighter & Plastics in a Changing Environment. 1977. 35.00 (ISBN 0-87765-093-4, SL-25). Natl Fire Prot.
Yehaskel, A. Fire & Flame Retardant Polymers: Recent Developments. LC 78-70742. (Chemical Technology Review Ser: No. 122). (Illus.). 1979. 45.00 (ISBN 0-8155-0733-X). Noyes.

FIRE-TESTING

Fire Tests of Concrete Joist Floors & Roofs. 25p. 1971. pap. 1.90 (ISBN 0-89312-069-3, RD006B). Portland Cement.
Fire Tests of Concrete Members: An Improved Method for Estimating Thermal Restraint Forces. 33p. 1970. pap. 0.30 (ISBN 0-89312-070-7, RP190B). Portland Cement.
Hilado, Carlos J., ed. Flammability of Fabrics, Vol. 9. LC 73-82115. (Fire & Flammability Ser.). 310p. 1974. pap. 20.00 (ISBN 0-87762-133-0). Technomic.
--Flammability of Solid Plastics, Vol. 7. LC 73-82115. (Fire & Flammability Ser.). 300p. 1974. pap. 20.00 (ISBN 0-87762-131-4). Technomic.
Ignition, Heat Release, & Noncombustibility of Material. 165p. 1972. 10.00 (ISBN 0-8031-0111-2, STP502). ASTM.
Mazzoni, Steve. Safety Considerations of Energy Saving Materials & Devices. 3.25 (ISBN 0-686-12080-9, TR 78-6). Society Fire Protect.
Melott, Ronald K. Is Energy Conservation Firesafe? 2.50 (ISBN 0-686-12081-7, TR 78-8). Society Fire Protect.
Methods of Fire Tests of Roof Coverings. (Two Hundred Ser). 1970. pap. 2.00 (ISBN 0-685-58239-6, 256). Natl Fire Prot.
Prusaczyk, J. E. & Bell, R. H. Fire Performance Characteristics in Rooms As the Result of Increased Insulation. 1978. 4.00 (ISBN 0-686-12079-5, TR 78-2). Society Fire Protect.
Stahl, Joel S. An Analysis of Fire Test Methods for Foam Plastic Insulation Materials. 1978. 4.00 (ISBN 0-686-12078-7, TR 78-4). Society Fire Protect.
Standard Methods of Fire Tests of Building Construction & Materials. (Two Hundred Ser). 1972. pap. 2.00 (ISBN 0-685-58174-8, 251). Natl Fire Prot.
Standard Methods of Fire Tests of Door Assemblies. (Two Hundred Ser). 1972. pap. 2.00 (ISBN 0-685-58175-6, 252). Natl Fire Prot.
Standards for Fire Tests of Window Assemblies. (Two Hundred Ser). 1970. pap. 2.00 (ISBN 0-685-58055-5, 257). Natl Fire Prot.
Zicherman, Joseph B. & Fisher, Fred L. Fire Protection Problems Associates with Cellulose Based Insulation Products. 1978. 3.25 (ISBN 0-686-12077-9, TR 78-7). Society Fire Protect.

FIRE-WORSHIPPERS

see also Fire (In Religion, Folk-Lore, etc.); Zoroastrianism

FIREARMS

see also Air Guns; Gunpowder; Ordnance; Pistols; Revolvers; Rifles; Shooting; Shot-Guns
also names of specific kinds of firearms, e.g. Colt Revolver; Machine Guns; Mauser Rifle; Winchester Rifle

Ackley, P. O. Home Gun Care & Repair. LC 69-16147. 192p. 1974. pap. 6.95 (ISBN 0-8117-2028-4). Stackpole.
Amber, John T., ed. Gun Digest Treasury. 5th ed. (Illus.). 288p. 1977. pap. 7.95 (ISBN 0-695-80841-9). DBI.
Askins, Charles. Askins on Pistols & Revolvers. Bryant, Ted & Askins, Bill, eds. 144p. 1980. text ed. 25.00 (ISBN 0-935998-22-5); pap. 8.95 (ISBN 0-935998-21-7). Natl Rifle Assn.
Automatic & Concealable Firearms: Design Book, Vol. II. (Illus.). 64p. 1979. pap. 12.00 (ISBN 0-87364-177-9). Paladin Ent.
Barker, A. J. Principles of Small Arms. (Illus.). 82p. 1977. pap. 4.00 (ISBN 0-87364-094-2). Paladin Ent.
Barnes, Leslie W. Canada's Guns: An Illustrated History of Artillery. (Illus.). 1979. pap. 9.95 (ISBN 0-660-00137-3, 56297-2, Pub. by Natl Mus Canada). U of Chicago Pr.
Barwick, Humphrey. Concerning the Force & Effect of Manual Weapons of Fire. LC 74-80163. (English Experience Ser.: No. 643). 86p. 1974. Repr. of 1594 ed. 8.00 (ISBN 90-221-0643-8). Walter J Johnson.
Bearse, Ray. Sporting Arms of the World. LC 75-31062. (Outdoor Life Bk.). (Illus.). 1977. 15.95 (ISBN 0-06-010291-8, HarpT). Har-Row.
Bird, Nicholas D. Observer's Book of Firearms. (Observer Bks.). (Illus.). 1978. 3.95 (ISBN 0-684-15199-5, ScribT). Scribner.
Bristow, Allen P. The Search for an Effective Police Handgun. (Illus.). 256p. 1973. 20.00 (ISBN 0-398-02554-1). C C Thomas.
Browne, Bellmore H. Guns & Gunning. (Illus.). Repr. of 1908 ed. pap. 9.95 (ISBN 0-8466-6014-8, SJU14). Shorey.
Burch, Monte. Gun Care & Repair. 1978. 12.95 (ISBN 0-87691-256-0). Winchester Pr.
Cadiou, Yves & Richard, Alphonse. Modern Firearms. (Illus.). 1977. 19.95 (ISBN 0-688-03073-4). Morrow.
Chant, Chris. Armed Forces of the United Kingdom. LC 80-66428. (Illus.). 80p. 1980. 14.95 (ISBN 0-7153-8024-9). David & Charles.
Chapel, Charles E. Complete Guide to Gunsmithing: Gun Care & Repair. rev. ed. (Illus.). 1962. 9.95 (ISBN 0-498-09846-X). A S Barnes.
Corbin, David R. Discover Swaging. LC 78-22085. (Illus.). 288p. 1979. 16.95 (ISBN 0-8117-0497-1). Stackpole.
Courtney, Andrew. Muzzle Loading Today. (Illus.). 96p. (Orig.). 1981. pap. 8.50x (ISBN 0-85242-731-X). Intl Pubns Serv.
Cromwell, Giles. The Virginia Manufactory of Arms. LC 74-8802. 1975. 20.00 (ISBN 0-8139-0573-7). U Pr of Va.
Cullin, William H. How to Conduct Foreign Military Sales: The Eighty-One United States Guide with Fy '81 Update. 1980. loose-leaf 95.00 (ISBN 0-87179-315-6). BNA.
Daehnhardt, Rainer, ed. Espingarda Perfeyta; or the Perfect Gun: Rules for Its Use Together with Necessary Instructions for Its Construction & Precepts for Good Aiming. Neal, W. Keith, tr. from Port. (Illus.). 480p. 1975. 46.00x (ISBN 0-85667-014-6, Pub by Sotheby Parke Bernet England). Biblio Dist.
Davis, John E. An Introduction to Tool Marks, Firearms & the Striagraph. 302p. 1958. pap. 24.50 photocopy ed. spiral (ISBN 0-398-00402-1). C C Thomas.
Dewar, Michael. Internal Security Weapons & Equipment of the World. (Illus.). 1979. (ScribT); encore ed. 4.95 (ISBN 0-684-17258-5). Scribner.
Dunlap, Roy. The Gunowner's Book of Care, Repair & Maintenance. LC 73-92404. (Outdoor Life). (Illus.). 320p. 1974. 12.95 (ISBN 0-06-011137-2, HarpT). Har-Row.
Durham, Douglass. Taking Aim. 1977. 7.95 (ISBN 0-89245-011-8). Seventy Six.
Edsall, James. The Story of Firearm Ignition. 3.50 (ISBN 0-913150-27-4). Pioneer Pr.
--Volcanic Firearms & Their Successors. 2.50 (ISBN 0-913150-28-2). Pioneer Pr.
Educational Research Council of America. Firearms Examiner. Ferris, Theodore N. & Marchak, John P., eds. (Real People at Work Ser.: R). (Illus.). 36p. 1977. 2.25 (ISBN 0-89247-137-9). Changing Times.
Ezell, Edward C. Handguns of the World. (Illus.). 768p. 1981. 24.95 (ISBN 0-8117-0816-0). Stackpole.
Ezelle, Edward C. & Smith, W. H. Small Arms of the World. 11th ed. (Illus.). 672p. 1979. Repr. of 1943 ed. 25.00 (ISBN 0-8117-1558-2). Stackpole.
Fairbairn, W. E. & Sykes, E. A. Shooting to Live. 105p. 1974. Repr. of 1942 ed. 5.95 (ISBN 0-87364-027-6). Paladin Ent.
Foss, Christopher. Infantry Weapons of the World. rev. ed. LC 76-42911. (Illus.). 1979. 12.50 (ISBN 0-684-16246-6, ScribT); encore ed. 4.95 (ISBN 0-684-17183-X). Scribner.
George, John N. English Pistols & Revolvers. 15.00x (ISBN 0-87556-153-5). Saifer.
Grennell, Dean A. ABC's of Reloading. 2nd ed. (Illus.). 288p. 1980. pap. 8.95 (ISBN 0-695-81415-X). DBI.
Guns & Ammo Editors. Guns & Ammo Annual 1982. (Illus.). 288p. (Orig.). 1981. pap. 6.95 (ISBN 0-8227-3019-7). Petersen Pub.
Hacker, Rick. The Muzzleloading Hunter. 224p. 1981. 14.95 (ISBN 0-87691-354-0). Winchester Pr.
Hamilton, T. M. Early Indian Trade Guns: 1625-1775. LC 68-58290. (Contributions of the Museum of the Great Plains Ser.: No. 3). (Illus.). 1968. pap. 2.50 (ISBN 0-685-91360-0). Mus Great Plains.
Hatcher. The Book of the Garand. 15.00 (ISBN 0-88227-014-1). Gun Room.
Hatcher, et al. Firearms Investigation, Identification & Evidence. (Illus.). 548p. 1977. Repr. 24.50 (ISBN 0-8117-0612-5). Stackpole.
Hatcher, Julian S. Hatcher's Notebook. rev. ed. LC 62-12654. (Illus.). 1962. 19.95 (ISBN 0-8117-0795-4). Stackpole.
Hoff, Arne. Dutch Firearms. Stryker, Walter A., ed. (Illus.). 304p. 1978. 105.00x (ISBN 0-85667-041-3, Pub. by Sotheby Parke Bernet England). Biblio Dist.
Hoffschmidt, Edward J. Know Your Gun Set. Incl. Know Your .45 Auto Pistols; Know Your Walther P. 38 Pistols; Know Your Walther P. P. & P. P. K. Pistols; Know Your MI Garand Rifles; Know Your Mauser Broomhandle Pistol; Know Your Anti Tank Rifle. 1976. pap. 4.50 ea. Borden.

Hogg, Brig., frwd. by. The Compleat Gunner. (Illus.). 1976. Repr. 10.50x (ISBN 0-85409-677-9). Charles River Bks.

Hogg, Ian V. The Complete Illustrated Encyclopedia of the World's Firearms. LC 78-56305. (Illus.). 1978. 24.95 (ISBN 0-89479-031-5). A & W Pubs.

Hogg, Ivan V. Guns & How They Work. LC 78-53013. (Illus.). 1979. 16.95 (ISBN 0-89696-023-4). Everest Hse.

Home Workshop Silencers I. (Illus.). 72p. 1980. pap. 12.00 (ISBN 0-87364-193-0). Paladin Ent.

Howe, Walter J. Professional Gunsmithing. (Illus.). 518p. 1946. 24.95 (ISBN 0-8117-1375-X). Stackpole.

Huebner, Siegfried. Silencers for Hand Firearms. Schreier, Konrad & Lund, Peder C., eds. LC 76-13260. (Illus.). 1976. pap. 9.95 (ISBN 0-87364-055-1). Paladin Ent.

Huntington, R. T. Hall's Breechloaders: John H. Hall's Invention & Development of a Breechloading Rifle with Precision-Made Interchangeable Parts, & Its Introduction into the United States Service. LC 71-91843. (Illus.). 369p. 1972. pap. 20.00 softbound (ISBN 0-87387-049-2). Shumway.

Jackson & Whitelaw. European Hand Firearms. 1978. 22.50 (ISBN 0-87556-154-3). Saifer.

James, Garry, ed. Guns for Home Defense. LC 74-25603. (Petersen Books Sports & Hobbies Ser.). (Illus.). 1975. pap. 3.95 (ISBN 0-8227-0088-3). Petersen Pub.

Kennedy, Monty. Checkering & Carving of Gunstocks. rev. ed. (Illus.). 352p. 1952. 21.95 (ISBN 0-8117-0630-3). Stackpole.

Larson, E. Dixon. Remington Tips. 4.95 (ISBN 0-913150-34-7). Pioneer Pr.

Lauber, Georg. How to Build Your Own Flintlock Rifle or Pistol. Seaton, Lionel, tr. from Ger. LC 75-11043. (Sports Library). (Illus.). 1976. pap. text ed. 6.95 (ISBN 0-89149-003-5). Jolex.

--How to Build Your Own Wheellock Rifle or Pistol. Seaton, Lionel, tr. from Ger. LC 75-11042. (Sports Library). (Illus.). 1976. pap. 6.95 (ISBN 0-89149-002-7). Jolex.

Lauber, George. How to Build Your Own Percussion Rifle or Pistol. Seaton, Lionel, tr. from Ger. LC 75-11045. (Sports Library). (Illus.). 1976. pap. 6.95 (ISBN 0-89149-004-3). Jolex.

Lenk, Torsten. Flintlock: Its Origin & Development. 45.00 (ISBN 0-87556-149-7). Saifer.

Lewis, Jack. Law Enforcement Handgun Digest. 3rd ed. (Illus.). 288p. 1980. pap. 8.95 (ISBN 0-695-81413-3). DBI.

Lewis, Jack, ed. Black Powder Gun Digest. 2nd ed. (Illus.). 288p. 1977. pap. 7.95 (ISBN 0-695-80714-5). DBI.

Lindsay, Merrill. Twenty Great American Guns. (Illus.). 34p. 1976. Repr. pap. 1.75 (ISBN 0-686-15689-7). Arma Pr.

Miller, Martin. Collector's Illustrated Guide to Firearms. (Illus.). 1978. 24.95 (ISBN 0-8317-0013-0, Mayflower Bks). Smith Pubs.

Muller, Heinrich. Guns, Pistols, & Revolvers. LC 80-52998. (Illus.). 240p. 1981. 29.95 (ISBN 0-312-35392-8). St Martin.

Murtz, Harold A., ed. Exploded Firearms Drawings. 2nd ed. (Illus.). 288p. 1977. pap. 8.95 (ISBN 0-695-80842-7). DBI.

Myatt, F. An Illustrated Guide to Rifles & Automatic Weapons. LC 80-70977. (Illustrated Military Guides Ser.). (Illus.). 160p. 1981. 8.95 (ISBN 0-668-05229-5, 5229). Arco.

Nation Muzzle Loading Rifle Association. Muzzle Blasts: Early Years Plus Vol. I & II 1939-41. LC 74-11637. 352p. 1974. pap. 18.00 softbound (ISBN 0-87387-069-7). Shumway.

Nonte, George. Black Powder Guide. 2nd ed. (Illus.). 256p. 1976. pap. 6.95 (ISBN 0-695-80659-9). Follett.

Nonte, George C. Handgun Competition. (Illus.). 1978. 14.95 (ISBN 0-87691-253-6). Winchester Pr.

Nonte, George C., Jr. Combat Handguns. Jurras, Lee F., ed. (Illus.). 352p. 1980. 19.95 (ISBN 0-8117-0409-2). Stackpole.

Norton(R.W.) Art Gallery. E. C. Prudhomme: Master Gun Engraver. LC 73-78704. (Illus.). 32p. 1973. pap. 3.00x (ISBN 0-913060-01-1). Norton Art.

Peterson & Elman. The Great Guns. 1977. 10.95 (ISBN 0-448-02069-6, MSP). G&D.

Pollard, Hugh B. The History of Firearms. LC 72-82385. 1974. lib. bdg. 29.50 (ISBN 0-686-57680-2, Artemis); pap. 8.95 (ISBN 0-89102-091-8). B Franklin.

Price, Robert M. Firearms Self-Defense: An Introductory Guide. (Illus.). 200p. 1981. 19.95 (ISBN 0-87364-218-X). Paladin Ent.

Rees, Clair F. Beginner's Guide to Guns & Shooting. (Illus.). 224p. 1978. pap. 7.95 (ISBN 0-695-80945-8). DBI.

Reese, Michael, II. Nineteen Hundred Luger-U.S. Test Trials. 2nd rev. ed. Pioneer Press, ed. LC 71-117532. (Illus.). pap. 4.95 (ISBN 0-913150-35-5). Pioneer Pr.

Richardson, H. L. & Wood, Wallis W. Firearms & Freedom. Date not set. pap. cancelled (ISBN 0-89245-010-X). Seventy Six.

Riling, Ray. Guns & Shooting: A Bibliography. (Illus.). 1981. 75.00 (ISBN 0-686-73396-7). Ray Riling.

Riviere, Bill. The Gunner's Bible. rev ed. LC 73-77415. 192p. 1973. pap. 3.50 (ISBN 0-385-02423-1). Doubleday.

Roberts, Willis J. & Bristow, Allen P. Introduction to Modern Police Firearms. Gourley, Douglas, ed. (Criminal Justice Ser). (Illus.). 1969. text ed. 15.95x (ISBN 0-02-477000-0, 47700). Macmillan.

Rosa, Joseph G. Gunfighter: Man or Myth? (Illus.). 229p. 1980. pap. 5.95 (ISBN 0-8061-1561-0). U of Okla Pr.

Ryan, J. W. Guns, Mortars & Rockets. (Brassey's Battlefield Weapons Systems & Technology: Vol. 2). 160p. 1982. 40.00 (ISBN 0-08-028324-1); pap. 16.00 (ISBN 0-08-028325-X). Pergamon.

Schroeder, Joseph, ed. Gun Digest Book of Gun Accessories. LC 79-54269. (Illus.). 288p. 1979. pap. 8.95 (ISBN 0-695-81313-7). DBI.

Scott, Robert F., ed. Shooter's Bible 1982, No. 73. 576p. 1981. pap. 10.95 (ISBN 0-88317-105-8). Stoeger Pub Co.

Sell. Handguns Americana. 1973. 8.50 (ISBN 0-685-03331-7). Borden.

Smythe, John & Barwick, Humphrey. Bow Vs. Gun. 1976. Repr. 15.00x (ISBN 0-85409-881-X). Charles River Bks.

Stanford, J. K. Complex Gun. 15.00x (ISBN 0-392-00519-0, SpS). Sportshelf.

Stiendler, R. A. Firearms Dictionary. (Illus.). 288p. 1975. pap. 6.95 (ISBN 0-87364-050-0). Paladin Ent.

Stockbridge, V. D. Digest of U. S. Patents Relating to Breech-Loading & Magazine Small Arms, 1836-1873. (Illus.). 1963. 12.50 (ISBN 0-910598-02-9). Flayderman.

Sybertz, Gustav. Technical Dictionary for Weaponry. (Ger. -Eng.). 1969. pap. 120.00 (ISBN 3-7888-0081-X, M-7642, Pub. by Neumann-Neudamm). French & Eur.

Tappan, Mel. Survival Guns. LC 75-17327. 1977. pap. 9.95 (ISBN 0-916172-00-7). Janus Pr.

Thielen, Thomas W. The Complete Guide to Gun Shows. 1980. pap. 6.95 (ISBN 0-686-30707-0). Loompanics.

Thomas, Donald G. Silencer Patents, Vol. III: European Patents 1901-1978. (Illus.). 253p. 1978. pap. 15.00 (ISBN 0-87364-102-7). Paladin Ent.

Truby, J. David, et al. Improvised Modified Firearms, 2 vols. LC 75-26828. 280p. 1975. 19.95 set (ISBN 0-87364-031-4). Paladin Ent.

U. S. Army. Grenade Launcher: M79. (Illus.). pap. 4.00 (ISBN 0-87364-062-4). Paladin Ent.

U.S. Cartridge Company. U. S. Cartridge Company's Collection of Firearms. (Illus.). 6.00 (ISBN 0-911964-22-3). Sycamore Island.

Van Rensselaer, S. American Firearms. (Illus.). 1948. 16.00 (ISBN 0-87282-093-9). Century Hse.

Virgines, George E. Famous Guns & Gunners. LC 77-92857. (Illus.). 1980. 12.95 (ISBN 0-89769-035-4); pap. 6.95 (ISBN 0-89769-010-9). Pine Mntn.

Walker, Ralph T. Black Powder Gunsmithing. (Illus.). 288p. 1978. pap. 8.95 (ISBN 0-695-80943-1). DBI.

Warner, Ken. The Practical Book of Guns. (Illus.). 1978. 14.95 (ISBN 0-87691-274-9). Winchester Pr.

Warner, Ken, ed. Handloader's Digest. 8th ed. (Illus.). 320p. 1981. pap. 9.95 (ISBN 0-910676-33-X). DBI.

--Handloader's Digest Bullet & Powder Update. (Illus.). 128p. 1980. pap. 4.95 (ISBN 0-910676-17-8). DBI.

West, Bill. Know Your Winchesters: General Use, All Models & Types, 1849-1969. (Winchester for Over a Century Ser). (Illus.). 12.00x (ISBN 0-911614-01-X). B West.

--Winchester Encyclopedia. (Winchester for Over a Century Ser). (Illus.). 15.00x (ISBN 0-911614-02-8). B West.

--Winchester Lever-Action Handbook. (Winchester for Over a Century Set). (Illus.). 25.00x (ISBN 0-911614-06-0). B West.

--The Winchester Single Shot. (Winchester for Over a Century Ser). (Illus.). 15.00x (ISBN 0-911614-03-6). B West.

--Winchesters, Cartridges, & History. (Winchester for Over a Century Set). (Illus.). 29.00x (ISBN 0-911614-04-4). B West.

Weston, Paul B. The New Handbook of Handgunning. (Illus.). 112p. 1980. 12.95 (ISBN 0-398-04092-3). C C Thomas.

Willett, Roderick. Gun Safety. LC 78-412108. (Illus.). 1967. 5.25x (ISBN 0-85140-185-6). Intl Pubns Serv.

Williams, John J. Survival Guns & Ammo: Raw Meat. (Illus.). 1979. pap. 19.00 (ISBN 0-686-24791-4). Consumertronics.

Williams, Mason. The Law Enforcement Book of Weapons, Ammunition & Training Procedures: Handguns, Rifles & Shotguns. (Illus.). 544p. 1977. 35.75 (ISBN 0-398-03576-8). C C Thomas.

Wirnsberger, Gerhard. Standard Directory of Proof Marks. Steindler, R. A., tr. from Ger. LC 75-11048. (Illus.). 1976. pap. 5.95 (ISBN 0-89149-006-X). Jolex.

The Women's Gun Pamphlet. 3.00 (ISBN 0-686-74704-6). Crossing Pr.

Wood, J. B. Gun Digest Book of Firearm Assembly - Disassembly: Law Enforcement Weapons, Part VI. (Illus.). 288p. 1981. pap. 9.95 (ISBN 0-910676-31-3). DBI.

Wootters, John. The Complete Book of Practical Handloading. (Illus.). 1976. 13.95 (ISBN 0-87691-215-3). Winchester Pr.

FIREARMS–CATALOGS

Byron, D. The Firearms Price Guide. (Illus.). 1977. pap. 9.95 (ISBN 0-517-53113-5). Crown.

Byron, David. The Firearms Price Guide. rev. ed. (Illus.). 416p. 1980. pap. 9.95 (ISBN 0-517-54065-7, Michelman Books). Crown.

Eighteen-Sixty Two Ordrance Manual. 1.50 (ISBN 0-913150-31-2). Pioneer Pr.

Hawkins, Peter. Guide to Antique Guns & Pistols. (Illus.). 32.50 (ISBN 0-912729-09-0). Newbury Bks Inc.

House of Collectibles, Inc. Official Price Guide to Antique & Modern Firearms. (Collector Ser.). (Illus.). 400p. 1980. pap. 9.95 (ISBN 0-87637-155-1, 155-01). Hse of Collectibles.

Hoxie Bullet Catalog. 0.75 (ISBN 0-913150-32-0). Pioneer Pr.

Quertermouse, Russel C. & Quertermouse, Stephen C. Modern Guns: Identifications & Values. 1979. 11.95 (ISBN 0-517-53800-8). Crown.

Remington Gun Catalog 1877. 1.50 (ISBN 0-913150-17-7). Pioneer Pr.

Sears & Roebuck Ammunition Catalog. (Illus.). soft bdg 1.50 (ISBN 0-686-20760-2). Sand Pond.

Smith Brothers-Boston Mass. 3.00 (ISBN 0-686-20764-5). Sand Pond.

Tarassuk, L. Antique European & American Firearms at the Hermitage Museum. 1973. 15.00 (ISBN 0-685-86582-7, 569080981). State Mutual Bk.

Tarrasuk, Leonid, ed. Antique European & American Firearms at the Hermitage Museum. (Illus., Eng-Rus.). 1976. ltd. ed 40.00 (ISBN 0-686-15685-4). Arma Pr.

Tinkham, Sandra S., ed. Catalog of Tools, Hardware, Firearms, & Vehicles. (Index of American Design Ser.: Pt. 4). (Orig.). 1979. pap. 30.00x (ISBN 0-914146-69-6); incl. color microfiche 260.00x (ISBN 0-914146-68-8). Somerset Hse.

United States Cartridge Co.-Lowell, Mass. 2.50 (ISBN 0-686-20762-9). Sand Pond.

U. S. Cartridge Company's Collection of Firearms. (Illus.). 142p. 1971. 6.00 (ISBN 0-87364-230-9, Sycamore Island). Paladin Ent.

Warner, Ken, ed. Gun Digest Review of Custom Guns. 256p. 1980. pap. 8.95 (ISBN 0-910676-10-0). DBI.

West, Bill. Remington Arms Catalogues, 1877-1899. 1st ed. (Americana Arms Library). (Illus.). 1971. 8.00x (ISBN 0-911614-09-5). B West.

--Stevens Arms Catalogues, 1877-1899. 1st ed. LC 76-143774. (Americana Arms Library). (Illus.). 1971. 8.00x (ISBN 0-911614-11-7). B West.

Winchester Shotshell Catalog 1897. (Illus.). soft bdg 1.25 (ISBN 0-686-20761-0). Sand Pond.

FIREARMS–COLLECTORS AND COLLECTING

Bowman, Hank W. Antique Guns from the Stagecoach Collection. LC 78-75361. (Illus.). 1964. lib. bdg. 3.50 (ISBN 0-668-01917-4). Arco.

Chapel, Charles E. Gun Collector's Handbook of Values: Nineteen Eighty to Eighty-One. 13th rev. ed. (Illus.). 1979. 16.95 (ISBN 0-698-11011-0); pap. 8.95 (ISBN 0-698-11010-2). Coward.

Di Carpegna, N. Firearms in the Princes Odescalchi Collection in Rome. (Illus.). 201p. (Eng.). 1976. Repr. of 1969 ed. 20.00 (ISBN 0-686-14971-8). Arma Pr.

Dixie Gun Works Antique Arms Catalog. 1.50 (ISBN 0-913150-40-1). Pioneer Pr.

Early Firearms of Great Britain & Ireland from the Collection of Clay P. Bedford. LC 77-178856. (Illus.). 1971. 17.50 (ISBN 0-87099-112-4); pap. 4.95 (ISBN 0-87099-113-2). Metro Mus Art.

Flayderman, Norm. Flayderman's Guide to Antique American Firearms. 2nd ed. (Illus.). 576p. 1980. pap. 15.95 (ISBN 0-910676-07-0). DBI.

Gun Digest 1982. 36th ed. LC 44-3588. (Illus.). 448p. (Orig.). 1981. pap. 11.95 (ISBN 0-910676-26-7, 1026). DBI.

Gusler, Wallace B & Lavin, James D. Decorated Firearms, 1540-1870, from the Collection of Clay P. Bedford. LC 76-53750. 1977. 25.00 (ISBN 0-87935-041-5, Colonial Williamsburg Foundation). U Pr of Va.

Hawkins, Peter. Guide to Antique Guns & Pistols. (Illus.). 32.50 (ISBN 0-912729-09-0). Newbury Bks Inc.

Hogg, Ian & Weeks, John. Military Small Arms of the 20th Century. 4th ed. LC 73-83466. (Illus.). 288p. (Orig.). 1981. 10.95 (ISBN 0-910676-28-3, 9146). DBI.

Kennard, A. M. French Pistols & Sporting Guns. (Country Life Collector's Guides Ser). 1972. 4.95 (ISBN 0-600-43594-6). Transatlantic.

Madaus, H. Michael. The Warner Collector's Guide to American Long Arms. (Orig.). 1981. pap. 9.95 (ISBN 0-446-97628-8). Warner Bks.

Murtz, Harold A. Guns Illustrated 1982. 14th ed. LC 69-11342. (Illus.). 288p. (Orig.). 1981. pap. 9.95 (ISBN 0-910676-27-5, 8026). DBI.

Pocket Guide to Guns. (Illus.). 1980. pap. 2.50 (ISBN 0-89145-154-4). Collector Bks.

Quertermous, Russell & Quertermous, Steve. Modern Guns, Identification & Values. 3rd ed. 1980. pap. 11.95 (ISBN 0-89145-146-3). Collector Bks.

Schroeder, Joseph J., ed. Gun Collector's Digest, Vol. III. LC 73-83406. (Illus.). 256p. 1981. pap. 9.95 (ISBN 0-910676-30-5, 5536). DBI.

Serven, Jamese. Rare & Valuable Antique Arms. 1976. 4.95 (ISBN 0-913150-37-1). Pioneer Pr.

Shumaker, P. L. Colt's Variations of the Old Model Pocket Pistol. 1957. 8.95 (ISBN 0-685-07223-1). Borden.

Steinwedel, Louis W. Gun Collector's Fact Book. LC 74-77434. (Illus.). 256p. 1975. pap. 5.95 (ISBN 0-668-03782-2). Arco.

U. S. Cartridge Company's Collection of Firearms. (Illus.). 142p. 1971. 6.00 (ISBN 0-87364-230-9, Sycamore Island). Paladin Ent.

Wilkinson, Frederick. Antique Firearms. (Illus.). 276p. 1980. 17.95 (ISBN 0-8069-9222-0, Pub by Guinness Superlatives England). Sterling.

Wilkinson-Latham, Robert. Antique Guns in Color: Twelve Fifty to Eighteen Sixty-Five. LC 77-26334. (Arco Color Ser.). (Illus.). 1978. 8.95 (ISBN 0-668-04467-5); pap. 6.95 (ISBN 0-668-04478-0). Arco.

FIREARMS–HISTORY

Ayalon, David. Gunpowder & Firearms in the Mamluk Kingdom: A Challenge to Mediaeval Society. 2nd ed. 154p. 1978. 22.50x (ISBN 0-7146-3090-X, F Cass Co). Biblio Dist.

Berger, Michael. Firearms in American History. LC 78-11652. (First Bks.). (Illus.). (gr. 5 up). 1979. PLB 7.40 (ISBN 0-531-02255-2). Watts.

Bianchi, John. Blue Steel & Gunleather. Mason, James D., ed. (Illus.). 213p. 1978. 9.95 (ISBN 0-917714-15-6). Beinfeld Pub.

Blanch, H. J. A Century of Guns: A Sketch of the Leading Types of Sporting & Military Small Arms. (Illus.). 1977. Repr. of 1909 ed. 25.00x (ISBN 0-7158-1156-8). Charles River Bks.

Bowman, Hank W. & Cary, Lucian. Antique Guns. LC 53-13537. (Illus.). 1953. lib. bdg. 4.95 o. s. i. (ISBN 0-668-00328-6); pap. 2.50 (ISBN 0-668-04102-1). Arco.

Brown, M. L. Firearms in Colonial America: The Impact on History & Technology 1492-1792. LC 80-27221. (Illus.). 448p. 1980. 45.00 (ISBN 0-87474-290-0). Smithsonian.

Buchele, William & Shumway, George. Recreating the American Longrifle. 3rd ed. LC 70-105321. (Illus.). 110p. pap. 10.00 (ISBN 0-87387-062-X). Shumway.

Burrell, Brian. Combat Weapons: Handguns & Shoulder Arms of World War 2. (Illus.). 112p. 1974. 9.50 (ISBN 0-902875-35-3). Transatlantic.

Cooper, Jeff. Fireworks: A Gunsite Anthology. LC 80-83992. 1981. 19.95 (ISBN 0-916172-07-4). Janus Pr.

Fuller, Claud E. Breech-Loader in the Service 1816-1917. LC 65-27415. (Illus.). 1965. 14.50 (ISBN 0-910598-03-7). Flayderman.

Fuller, Claude E. & Stewart, Richard D. Firearms of the Confederacy. LC 76-53698. 1977. Repr. of 1944 ed. 25.00x (ISBN 0-88000-103-8). Quarterman.

Gaier, Claude. Four Centuries of Liege Gunmaking. (Illus.). 1977. 80.00 (ISBN 0-686-20478-6). Arma Pr.

Grancsay, Stephen V. & Lindsay, Merrill. Master French Gunsmith's Designs from the XVII to the XIX Centuries. LC 74-99752. (Illus.). 1976. ltd. ed. (1000 copies) 89.00 (ISBN 0-686-15686-2). Arma Pr.

Gusler, Wallace B & Lavin, James D. Decorated Firearms, 1540-1870, from the Collection of Clay P. Bedford. LC 76-53750. 1977. 25.00 (ISBN 0-87935-041-5, Colonial Williamsburg Foundation). U Pr of Va.

Hackley, F. W., et al. History of Modern U.S. Military Small Arms Ammunition: Vol. 2, 1940-1945. 25.00 (ISBN 0-88227-007-9). Gun Room.

Hamilton, T. M., ed. Indian Trade Guns. 10.95 (ISBN 0-913150-43-6). Pioneer Pr.

Helmer, William J. The Gun That Made the Twenties Roar. 16.95 (ISBN 0-88227-012-5). Gun Room.

Hogg, Ian & Batchelor, John. Naval Gun. (Illus.). 1979. 24.95 (ISBN 0-7137-0905-7, Pub. by Blandford Pr England). Sterling.

Holme, N. & Kirby, E. L. Medal Rolls: Twenty-Third Foot Royal Welch Fusiliers, Napoleonic Period. 1979. 39.00 (ISBN 0-686-51595-1, Pub. by Spink & Son England). S J Durst.

Hutslar, Donald A. Gunsmiths of Ohio: 18th & 19th Centuries, Vol. I. LC 72-87114. (Illus.). 448p. casebound 35.00 (ISBN 0-87387-026-3). Shumway.

Jackson, Melvin & De Beer, Charles. Eighteenth Century Gunfounding. LC 73-5882. (Illus.). 200p. 1974. 19.95x (ISBN 0-87474-535-7). Smithsonian.

Kennett, Lee & Anderson, James L. The Gun in America: The Origins of a National Dilemma. LC 74-5990. (Contributions in American History: No. 37). (Illus., Orig.). 1975. lib. bdg. 17.50 (ISBN 0-8371-7530-5, ARF/); pap. text ed. 3.95 (ISBN 0-8371-8715-X, ARF). Greenwood.

Lindsay, Merrill. The New England Gun: The First 200 Years. (Illus.). 208p. 1975. 20.00 (ISBN 0-679-50586-5); pap. 12.50 (ISBN 0-686-14978-5). Arma Pr.

Neal, W. Keith & Back, D. H. L. Great British Gunmakers 1740-1790: The History of John Twigg & the Packington Guns. (Illus.). 424p. 1975. 80.00x (ISBN 0-85667-015-4, Pub. by Sotheby Park Bernet England). Biblio Dist.

North & North. Simeon North: First Official Pistol Maker of the United States. Repr. 9.95 (ISBN 0-88227-001-X). Gun Room.

Oakeshott, Ewart. European Weapons & Armour. (Illus.). 277p. 1980. 29.95 (ISBN 0-686-68855-4). Beinfeld Pub.

Peterson, Harold. Historical Treasury of American Guns: A Remington Sportsmen's Library Bk. pap. 2.95 (ISBN 0-87502-010-0). Benjamin Co.

Pollard, Hugh B. The History of Firearms. LC 72-82385. 1974. lib. bdg. 29.50 (ISBN 0-686-57680-2, Artemis); pap. 8.95 (ISBN 0-89102-091-8). B Franklin.

Reese, Michael, II. Nineteen Hundred Luger-U.S. Test Trials. 2nd rev. ed. Pioneer Press, ed. LC 71-117532. (Illus.). pap. 4.95 (ISBN 0-913150-35-5). Pioneer Pr.

Rosebush, Waldo E. American Firearms & the Changing Frontier. 1962. pap. 3.00 (ISBN 0-910524-01-7). Eastern Wash.

Rywell, Martin. American Antique Pistols. 2.00 (ISBN 0-913150-03-7). Pioneer Pr.

--Confederate Guns. 2.00 (ISBN 0-913150-06-1). Pioneer Pr.

Schreier, Konrad F., Jr. Remington Rolling Block Firearms. Pioneer Press, ed. (Illus.). pap. 3.95 (ISBN 0-913150-39-8). Pioneer Pr.

Serven, James E. Conquering the Frontiers. LC 74-75583. 1974. 19.95 (ISBN 0-910618-39-9). Foun Pubns.

Shelton, Lawrence P. California Gunsmiths. (Illus.). 302p. 1977. casebound 29.65 (ISBN 0-87387-081-6). Shumway.

SIPRI. Anti-Personnel Weapons. LC 77-25754. 1979. 29.95x (ISBN 0-8448-1311-7). Crane-Russak Co.

West, Bill. Marlin & Ballard, Arms & History, 1861-1978. LC 77-77900. (West Arms Library). (Illus.). 1978. 29.00x (ISBN 0-911614-07-9). B West.

--Savage & Stevens, Arms & History, 1849-Date. LC 72-143773. (West Arms Library). (Illus.). 1971. 29.00x (ISBN 0-911614-10-9). B West.

Wilkinson-Latham, Robert. Antique Guns in Color: Twelve Fifty to Eighteen Sixty-Five. LC 77-26334. (Arco Color Ser.). (Illus.). 1978. 8.95 (ISBN 0-668-04467-5); pap. 6.95 (ISBN 0-668-04478-0). Arco.

FIREARMS–IDENTIFICATION

Byron, David. Gunmarks. (Illus.). 1979. 10.00 (ISBN 0-517-53848-2). Crown.

Hill, Richard T. & Anthony, William E. Confederate Longarms & Pistols: A Pictorial Study. Hill, Olivia R., ed. (Illus.). 304p. 1978. 29.95 (ISBN 0-87833-309-6); lib. bdg. 26.95 (ISBN 0-686-28758-4). Confed Arms.

Madaus, H. Michael. The Warner Collector's Guide to American Long Arms. (Orig.). 1981. pap. 9.95 (ISBN 0-446-97628-8). Warner Bks.

Mathews, J. Howard. Firearms Identification: Original Photographs & Other Illustrations of Hand Guns, Vol. 2. (Illus.). 500p. 1973. Repr. of 1962 ed. 56.75 (ISBN 0-398-02356-5). C C Thomas.

--Firearms Identification: Original Photographs & Other Illustrations of Hand Guns, Data on Rifling Characteristics of Hand Guns & Rifles, Vol. 3. Wilimovsky, Allan E., ed. (Illus.). 744p. 1973. 88.00 (ISBN 0-398-02357-3). C C Thomas.

--Firearms Identification: The Laboratory Examination of Small Arms, Rifling Characteristics in Hand Guns, & Notes on Automatic Pistols, Vol. 1. (Illus.). 416p. 1973. Repr. of 1962 ed. 56.75 (ISBN 0-398-02355-7). C C Thomas.

Quertermous, Russell & Quertermous, Steven. Modern Guns. 2nd ed. (Illus.). 416p. 1980. pap. 11.95 (ISBN 0-517-54066-5). Crown.

Quertermouse, Russel C. & Quertermouse, Stephen C. Modern Guns: Identifications & Values. 1979. 11.95 (ISBN 0-517-53800-8). Crown.

Suydam, Charles R. U. S. Cartridges & Their Handguns. (Illus.). 333p. 1976. 15.95 (ISBN 0-917714-04-0); pap. 9.95 (ISBN 0-917714-07-5). Beinfeld Pub.

Wilber, Charles G. Ballistic Science for the Law Enforcement Officer. (Illus.). 324p. 1977. 30.75 (ISBN 0-398-03579-2). C C Thomas.

The World's Submachine Guns: Developments from 1915 to 1963, Vol. I. rev. ed. 1980. 29.95 (ISBN 0-686-15931-4). TBN Ent.

FIREARMS–JUVENILE LITERATURE

Berger, Michael. Firearms in American History. LC 78-11652. (First Bks.). (Illus.). (gr. 5 up). 1979. PLB 7.40 (ISBN 0-531-02255-2). Watts.

Colby, C. B. Civil War Weapons: Small Arms, & Artillery of the Blue & Gray. (Illus.). (gr. 4-7). 1962. PLB 5.29 (ISBN 0-698-30046-7). Coward.

--Firearms by Winchester: A Part of U.S. History. (Illus.). (gr. 4-7). 1957. PLB 5.29 (ISBN 0-698-30079-3). Coward.

--Musket to M-14: Pistols, Rifles & Machine Guns Through the Years. (Illus.). (gr. 4-7). 1960. PLB 5.29 (ISBN 0-698-30246-X). Coward.

--Two Centuries of Weapons: 1776-1976. LC 75-10459. (Illus.). 48p. (gr. 4-7). 1976. PLB 5.29 (ISBN 0-698-30596-5). Coward.

Dolan, Edward F., Jr. Gun Control: A Decision for Americans. LC 78-5576. (Impact Bks). (Illus.). (gr. 7 up). 1978. PLB 7.45 s&l (ISBN 0-531-02202-1). Watts.

Guns. (How & Why Wonder Books Ser.). (gr. 4-6). pap. 1.00 (ISBN 0-448-05047-1). Wonder.

Long, Philip S. Ranch Boy Hunter. Hofmeister, Jane, ed. (Illus.). (gr. 5 up). 1977. pap. 5.00 (ISBN 0-918292-03-4). Griggs Print.

FIREARMS–LAWS AND REGULATIONS

Cook, Philip J. & Lambert, Richard D., eds. Gun Control. (The Annals of the American Academy of Political & Social Science Ser.: No. 455). 250p. 1981. 7.50x (ISBN 0-87761-262-5); pap. 6.00x (ISBN 0-87761-263-3). Am Acad Pol Soc Sci.

Davidson, Bill R. To Keep & Bear Arms. 2nd ed. LC 75-93455. 1979. 12.95 (ISBN 0-87364-145-0, Sycamore Island). Paladin Ent.

Dolan, Edward F., Jr. Gun Control: A Decision for Americans. LC 78-5576. (Impact Bks). (Illus.). (gr. 7 up). 1978. PLB 7.45 s&l (ISBN 0-531-02202-1). Watts.

Gottlieb, Alan. The Rights of Gun Owners. 216p. (Orig.). 1981. pap. 5.95 (ISBN 0-89803-036-6). Green Hill.

Gottlieb, Alan B. The Gun Owner's Political Action Manual. LC 76-48809. 144p. 1976. pap. 1.95 (ISBN 0-916054-09-8). Green Hill.

Gun Control. (Legislative Analyses Ser). 1976. pap. 3.75 (ISBN 0-8447-0175-0). Am Enterprise.

Gun Control Means People Control. LC 74-18763. 1974. 1.75 (ISBN 0-686-15282-4). Ind American.

Kates, Dan B. Restricting Handguns: The Liberal Sceptics Speak Out. 9.95 (ISBN 0-88427-033-5). Green Hill.

Kates, Don B., Jr. Restricting Handguns: The Liberal Skeptics Speak Out. LC 79-12043. 1979. 9.95 (ISBN 0-88427-033-5, Dist. by Caroline Hse); (Dist. by Caroline Hse). North River.

Kennett, Lee & Anderson, James L. The Gun in America: The Origins of a National Dilemma. LC 74-5990. (Contributions in American History: No. 37). (Illus., Orig.). 1975. lib. bdg. 17.50 (ISBN 0-8371-7530-5, ARF/); pap. text ed. 3.95 (ISBN 0-8371-8715-X, ARF). Greenwood.

Krcma, Vaclav. Identification & Registration of Firearms. (Illus.). 200p. 1971. 19.75 (ISBN 0-398-02336-0). C C Thomas.

Kukla, Robert J. Gun Control: A Written Record of Efforts to Eliminate the Private Possession of Firearms in America. LC 73-9505. 448p. 1973. pap. 4.95 (ISBN 0-8117-2057-8). Stackpole.

Shields, Pete. Guns Don't Die -- People Do: The Pros, the Cons, the Facts -- & What Can Be Done to Stop America's Handgun War, by the Foremost Spokesman on the Issue. 1981. 12.95 (ISBN 0-87795-361-9); pap. 5.95 (ISBN 0-87795-347-3). Arbor Hse.

Whisker, James B. The Citizen Soldier & U. S. Military Policy. LC 78-27029. 1979. 7.50 (ISBN 0-88427-035-1, Dist. by Caroline Hse); pap. 4.50 (ISBN 0-88427-036-X, Dist.B by Caroline Hse). North River.

FIREARMS CONTROL

see Firearms–Laws and Regulations

FIREARMS INDUSTRY AND TRADE

see also Gunsmithing; Ordnance

Bleile, C. Roger. American Engravers. (Illus.). 191p. 1980. 29.95 (ISBN 0-917714-29-6). Beinfeld Pub.

Farley, Philip J., et al. Arms Across the Sea. LC 77-91804. 1978. 9.95 (ISBN 0-8157-2746-1); pap. 3.95 (ISBN 0-8157-2745-3). Brookings.

Grancsay, Stephen V. & Lindsay, Merrill. Illustrated British Firearms Patents 1718-1853. limited ed. LC 77-99750. (Illus.). 450p. 1969. 75.00 (ISBN 0-87691-008-8). Arma Pr.

Hanifhen, Frank C. & Engelbrecht, Helmuth C. Merchants of Death: A Study of the International Armaments Industry. LC 79-147546. (Library of War & Peace; Control & Limitation of Arms). lib. bdg. 38.00 (ISBN 0-8240-0327-6). Garland Pub.

Hartzler, Daniel D. Arms Makers of Maryland. LC 74-24434. (Longrifle Ser.). (Illus.). 312p. 1977. 35.00 (ISBN 0-87387-054-9). Shumway.

Kirkland, Turner. Southern Derringers of the Mississippi Valley. 2.00 (ISBN 0-913150-00-2). Pioneer Pr.

Noel-Baker, Philip. The Private Manufacture of Armaments. LC 78-145399. 1971. pap. 6.00 (ISBN 0-486-22736-7). Dover.

Russell, Carl P. Guns on the Early Frontiers: A History of Firearms from Colonial Times Through the Years of the Western Fur Trade. LC 80-12570. xvi, 395p. 1980. 19.50x (ISBN 0-8032-3857-6); pap. 6.95 (ISBN 0-8032-8903-0, BB 747, Bison). U of Nebr Pr.

Smith, Merritt R. Harpers Ferry Armory & the New Technology: The Challenge of Change. LC 76-28022. (Illus.). 1977. 24.50x (ISBN 0-8014-0984-5); pap. 8.95 (ISBN 0-8014-9181-9). Cornell U Pr.

Stockholm International Peace Research Institute (SIPRI) The Arms Trade Registers. LC 75-868. 186p. 1975. text ed. 18.00x (ISBN 0-262-19138-5). MIT Pr.

Stockholm International Peace Research Institute. Arms Trade with the 3rd World. rev. ed. LC 75-15746. 362p. 1975. 29.50x (ISBN 0-8419-0213-5). Holmes & Meier.

West, Bill. Browning Arms & History, 1842-Date. LC 72-81300. (West Arms Library). (Illus.). 380p. 1972. 29.00x (ISBN 0-911614-12-5). B West.

FIREBOARDS

see Dummy Board Figures

FIREFIGHTERS

see Fire Fighters

FIREFLIES–JUVENILE LITERATURE

Hawes, Judy. Fireflies in the Night. LC 63-15088. (A Let's-Read-&-Find-Out Science Bk). (Illus.). (gr. k-3). 1963. (TYC-J); filmstrip with record 11.95 (ISBN 0-690-30067-0); filmstrip with cassette 14.95 (ISBN 0-690-30069-7). Har-Row.

--Fireflies in the Night. LC 63-15088. (Crocodile Paperbacks Ser.). (Illus.). (gr. k-3). 1975. pap. 1.45 (ISBN 0-690-01259-4, TYC-J). Har-Row.

Ryder, Joanne. Fireflies. LC 76-58695. (A Science I Can Read Bk). (Illus.). (gr. k-3). 1977. 6.95 (ISBN 0-06-025153-0, HarpJ); PLB 7.89 (ISBN 0-06-025154-9). Har-Row.

FIREMEN

see Fire Fighters

FIREPLACES

Bortz, Paul. Getting More Heat from Your Fireplace. (Illus.). 144p. 1981. pap. 6.95 (ISBN 0-88266-254-6). Garden Way Pub.

Brann, Donald R. How to Install a Fireplace, Bk. 674. LC 67-15264. (Illus.). 1978. pap. 5.95 (ISBN 0-87733-674-1). Easi-Bild.

Daniels, M. E. Fireplaces & Wood Stoves. LC 76-26948. (Illus.). 1977. 13.95 (ISBN 0-672-52175-X). Bobbs.

--Fireplaces & Wood Stoves. LC 76-26948. (Illus.). 1978. pap. 7.95 (ISBN 0-672-52402-3). Bobbs.

Danz, Ernst & Manges, Axel. Modern Fireplaces. 1979. 29.95 (ISBN 0-8038-0165-3). Hastings.

Danz, Ernst & Menges, Axel. Modern Fireplaces. (Illus.). 1979. 29.95 (ISBN 0-8038-0165-3). Architectural.

Debaigts, Jacques. The Modern Fireplace. 1975. 35.00 (ISBN 0-442-22068-5). Van Nos Reinhold.

Eastman, Wilbur F. & Eastman, Margaret. Planning & Building Your Fireplace. (Illus.). 144p. 1976. o. p. 11.95 (ISBN 0-88266-084-5); pap. 5.95 (ISBN 0-88266-083-7). Garden Way Pub.

Gould, Zack. The Owner-Built Fireplace. 1978. pap. 6.95 (ISBN 0-442-22794-9). Van Nos Reinhold.

Harrington, Geri. Fireplace Stoves, Hearths, & Inserts. LC 80-7587. (Illus.). 192p. 1980. 20.00 (ISBN 0-06-011821-0, HarpT). Har-Row.

--Fireplace Stoves, Hearths, & Inserts: A Guide & Catalog. LC 80-7587. (Illus.). 192p. 1980. pap. 8.95 (ISBN 0-06-090804-1, CN 804, CN). Har-Row.

Jones, Robert E. & Burch, Monte. Fireplaces. Horowitz, Shirley M. & Auer, Marilyn M., eds. LC 80-67153. (Illus.). 128p. (Orig.). 1980. pap. 5.95 (ISBN 0-932944-26-4). Creative Homeowner.

Kern & Magers. Fireplaces. 200p. 7.95 (ISBN 0-686-31218-X). Owner-Builder.

Kern, Ken & Magers, Steve. Fireplaces: The Owner-Builder's Guide. 1978. pap. 7.95 (ISBN 0-684-15885-X, ScribT). Scribner.

Kipp, Jerry. Firefacts: The Consumer's Guide to Wood Heat. 256p. 1980. 14.95 (ISBN 0-914378-61-9); pap. 9.95 (ISBN 0-914378-58-9). Countryman.

Ladd, Paul R. Early American Fireplaces. (Illus.). 1977. 16.95 (ISBN 0-8038-1930-7). Hastings.

Lytle, R. J. & Lytle, Marie-Jeanne. Book of Successful Fireplaces: How to Build, Decorate, & Use Them. 20th ed. LC 77-9166. (A Successful Book). (Illus.). 1977. 13.95 (ISBN 0-912336-52-8); pap. 6.95 (ISBN 0-912336-53-6). Structures Pub.

Morris, David J., Jr. The Wizard's Building, Cleaning & Repairing Fireplace Guide. (Illus.). Date not set. pap. 5.95 (ISBN 0-686-24590-3). ANKH.

Orton, Vrest. The Forgotten Art of Building a Good Fireplace. (Forgotten Arts Ser.). (Illus.). 64p. (Orig.). 1969. pap. 3.95 (ISBN 0-911658-53-X). Yankee Bks.

Presper, Mary. The Joys of Fireplaces & Woodstoves. Reice, Sylvie, ed. LC 78-73323. (Illus.). 1979. pap. 7.95 (ISBN 0-448-14847-1). G&D.

Schuler, Stanley. How to Design & Build a Fireplace. LC 77-3331. (Illus.). 1977. 14.95 (ISBN 0-02-607360-9). Macmillan.

Self, Charles R. Wood Heating Handbook. LC 77-1816. (Illus.). 1977. 8.95 (ISBN 0-8306-7872-7); pap. 5.95 (ISBN 0-8306-6872-1, 872). TAB Bks.

Stedman, Myrtle. Adobe Fireplaces. rev. ed. Smith, James C., Jr., ed. LC 77-78520. (Illus., Orig.). 1977. pap. 2.50 (ISBN 0-913270-32-6). Sunstone Pr.

Sunset, ed. Fireplaces: How to Plan & Build. 4th ed. LC 79-90337. 96p. 1980. pap. 4.95 (ISBN 0-376-01156-4). Sunset-Lane.

Sunset Editors. Building Barbecues. 2nd ed. LC 76-140161. (Illus.). 80p. 1971. pap. 3.95 (ISBN 0-376-01034-7, Sunset Bks). Sunset-Lane.

Taylor, A. D. Campstoves, Fireplaces & Chimneys. (Illus.). 112p. pap. 10.95 (ISBN 0-8466-6055-5, JJU-55). Shorey.

Wright, Lawrence. Home Fires Burning: The History of Domestic Heating & Cooking. 1964. 15.00 (ISBN 0-7100-2332-4). Routledge & Kegan.

FIREPROOF BUILDING

see Building, Fireproof

FIREPROOFING

see also Fire Resistant Polymers; Fire-Testing

Bhatnagar, Vijay M., ed. Advances in Fire Retardant Textiles. LC 72-91704. (Progress in Fire Retardancy Ser.: Vol. 5). 500p. 1974. pap. 45.00 (ISBN 0-87762-143-8). Technomic.

--Advances in Fire Retardants, Part One. LC 72-80324. (Progress in Fire Retardancy Ser: Vol. 2). (Illus.). 250p. 1972. pap. 25.00 (ISBN 0-87762-090-3). Technomic.

--Fire Retardant Polyurethanes: Formulations Handbook, Vol. 8. LC 72-91704. (Progress in Fire Retardancy Ser.). (Illus.). 1977. pap. 19.95x (ISBN 0-87762-217-5). Technomic.

--Fire Retardants: Proceeding of the First European Conference on Flammability & Fire Retardants. LC 78-66105. 1979. pap. 35.00 (ISBN 0-87762-264-7). Technomic.

Bhatnager, Vijay M., ed. Proceedings: 1976 International Symposium on Flammability & Fire Retardants. LC 75-25478. (Illus.). 1977. pap. 25.00x (ISBN 0-87762-215-9). Technomic.

Building Services Library, 15 bks. 1300p. includes protective case 38.70 (ISBN 0-685-58049-0, BSL-A). Natl Fire Prot.

Critser, James R., Jr. Flame, Retardants for Plastics, Rubber, Textiles & Paper. (Ser. 2-7879). 1979. 110.00 (ISBN 0-914428-61-6). Lexington Data.

--Flame Retardants for Plastics, Rubber, Textiles & Paper (July 1974-June 1975) (Ser. 2-7475). 1975. 110.00 (ISBN 0-914428-30-6). Lexington Data.

--Flame Retardants for Plastics, Rubber, Textiles & Paper (July 1976-June 1977) July 1976 - June 1977. (Ser. 2-7677). 1977. 110.00 (ISBN 0-914428-49-7). Lexington Data.

--Flame Retardants for Plastics, Rubber, Textiles & Paper (July 1977-June 1978) (Ser. 2-7778). 1978. 110.00 (ISBN 0-914428-55-1). Lexington Data.

Dean, Amy E., ed. Flash Point Index of Trade Liquids. 9th ed. LC 78-54003. 1978. pap. text ed. 5.50 (ISBN 0-87765-127-2, SPP-51). Natl Fire Prot.

Fire & Smoke Retardant Chemicals Outlook C-004R. 1980. 825.00 (ISBN 0-89336-205-0). BCC.

Fire Protection by Sprinklers. LC 75-21643. (Illus.). 100p. 1975. pap. 4.75 (ISBN 0-87765-047-0, SPP-30). Natl Fire Prot.

Hilado, Carlos J., ed. Flame Retardants, Part 2, Vol. 16. LC 73-82115. (Fire & Flammability Ser.). (Illus.). 1976. pap. 20.00x (ISBN 0-87762-176-4). Technomic.

--Flammability of Fabrics, Vol. 9. LC 73-82115. (Fire & Flammability Ser.). 310p. 1974. pap. 20.00 (ISBN 0-87762-133-0). Technomic.

--Flooring & Floor Covering Materials, Vol. 12. LC 73-82115. (Fire & Flammability Ser.). (Illus.). 1976. pap. 20.00x (ISBN 0-87762-172-1). Technomic.

Lyons, John W. Chemistry & Uses of Fire Retardants. LC 71-112595. 1970. 53.50 (ISBN 0-471-55740-4, Pub. by Wiley-Interscience). Wiley.

Marchant. Design for Fire Safety. 1981. text ed. price not set (ISBN 0-408-00487-8). Butterworth.

Reeves, Wilson A., et al. Fire Resistant Textiles Handbook. LC 73-82116. 250p. 1974. pap. 35.00 (ISBN 0-87762-088-1). Technomic.

Thiery, P. & Goundry, J. H. Fireproofing: Chemistry, Technology, & Applications. (Illus.). 1970. 22.30x (ISBN 0-444-20062-2, Pub. by Applied Science). Burgess-Intl Ideas.

Trade & Technical Press Editors. Handbook of Industrial Fire Protection & Security. 600p. 1976. 83.00x (ISBN 0-85461-059-6, Pub by Trade & Tech England). Renouf.

United Nations Economic Commission for Europe, Timber Committee. Behaviour of Wood Products in Fire: Proceedings, Oxford, 1977. 1977. pap. text ed. 30.00 (ISBN 0-08-021990-X). Pergamon.

FIRES

see also Fire Departments; Fire Extinction; Fire Investigation; Fire Prevention; Forest Fires; also subdivision Fires and Fire Prevention under various classes of institutions and buildings, e.g. Schools–Fires and Fire Prevention; Particular conflagrations are entered under names of place, e.g. London–Fire, 1666

Backes, Nancy. Great Fires of America. Country Beautiful Editors, ed. LC 73-80505. (Illus.). 208p. 1973. 15.95 (ISBN 0-87294-048-9). Country Beautiful.

Best, Richard L. Reconstruction of a Tragedy: The Beverly Hills Supper Club Fire. Dean, Amy E., ed. LC 77-93009. 1978. pap. 5.75 (ISBN 0-87765-113-2, LS-2). Natl Fire Prot.

Bond, Horatio, ed. Fire & the Air War. 1946. pap. text ed. 14.00x (ISBN 0-89126-004-8). MA-AH Pub.

Boy Scouts Of America. Firemanship. LC 19-600. (Illus.). 64p. (gr. 6-12). 1968. pap. 0.70x (ISBN 0-8395-3317-9, 3317). BSA.

Brown, Irving H. Gypsy Fires in America. LC 74-1035. Repr. of 1924 ed. 22.00 (ISBN 0-8103-3942-0). Gale.

Brown, Walter R. & Anderson, Norman D. Historical Catastrophes: Fires. LC 75-5592. (Historical Catastrophes Ser.). (Illus.). 192p. (gr. 5 up). 1976. PLB 7.95 (ISBN 0-201-00826-2, A-W Childrens). A-W.

Bryan, John L. Fire Suppression & Detection Systems. LC 73-7367. (Fire Science Ser). (Illus.). 320p. 1974. text ed. 18.95 (ISBN 0-02-473920-0, 47392). Macmillan.

Cannon, Donald J., ed. Heritage of Flames. LC 77-43. (The Illustrated History of American Firefighting). (Illus.). 1977. 35.00 (ISBN 0-89528-001-9). Artisan Bks.

Canter, David. Fires & Human Behaviour. LC 79-41489. 338p. 1980. 30.00 (ISBN 0-471-27709-6, Pub. by Wiley-Interscience). Wiley.

A Hazard Study: Natural Gas Fires & Explosions. (Illus.). 1974. pap. 2.00 (ISBN 0-685-58193-4, HS-9). Natl Fire Prot.

Kravontka, Stanley J. Elevator Use During Fires in Megastructures. Date not set. 2.50 (ISBN 0-686-22737-9). Society Fire Protect.

LP-Gas Fires & Explosions. 52p. 1961. pap. 1.50 (ISBN 0-685-44152-0, Q55-5). Natl Fire Prot.

Luke, R. H. & McArthur, A. G. Bushfires in Australia. 359p. 1981. 30.00x (ISBN 0-642-02341-7, Pub. by CSIRO Australia). State Mutual Bk.

Palmer, K. N. Dust Explosions & Fires. LC 73-7341. (Powder Technology Ser.). 396p. 1973. text ed. 37.95x (ISBN 0-412-09430-4, Pub. by Chapman & Hall England). Methuen Inc.

Planer, R. Fire Loss Control. (Occupational Safety Ser.: Vol. 3). 1979. 27.50 (ISBN 0-8247-6890-6). Dekker.

Powers, W. Robert. Electrical Fires in New York City - 1976. Date not set. 2.50 (ISBN 0-686-22739-5). Society Fire Protect.

Scher, Steven. Fire. LC 77-27270. (Illus.). 1978. pap. 7.95 (ISBN 0-8109-2151-0). Abrams.

Smallman, Robert E. Firebuilding: With Leader's Guide. (Campcraft Skills Ser.). (Illus.). (gr. 5-12). 1976. pap. text ed. 0.95 (ISBN 0-88441-422-1, 26-212). GS.

Tuck, Charles A., Jr. Analyses of Three Multiple Fatality Penal Institution Fires. 32p. 1978. pap. text ed. 35.00 (ISBN 0-87765-135-3, SL-35). Natl Fire Prot.

FIRES IN SHIPS

see Ships–Fires and Fire Prevention

FIREWOOD

see Wood As Fuel

FIREWORKS

see also Military Fireworks

Barbour, Richard T. Pyrotechnics in Industry. LC 80-11152. (Illus.). 190p. 1981. 19.95 (ISBN 0-07-003653-5). McGraw.

Brauer, Karl O. Handbook of Pyrotechnics. (Illus.). 1974. 37.00 (ISBN 0-8206-0220-5). Chem Pub.

Ellern, Herbert. Military & Civilian Pyrotechnics. 1968. 31.00 (ISBN 0-8206-0085-7). Chem Pub.

Lancaster, Ronald, et al. Fireworks Principles & Practice. (Illus.). 1972. 22.50 (ISBN 0-8206-0216-7). Chem Pub.

McLain, Joseph H. Pyrotechnics. (Illus.). 225p. 1980. 24.50 (ISBN 0-89168-032-2). Franklin Inst.

Manufacture, Transportation, Storage of Fireworks. (Fourty Ser). 52p. 1974. pap. 3.00 (ISBN 0-685-44169-5, 44A). Natl Fire Prot.

Model State Fireworks Law. (Forty Ser). 1974. pap. 2.00 (ISBN 0-685-58097-0, 494L). Natl Fire Prot.

Norton, Robert. The Gunner, Shewing the Whole Practise of Artillerie. LC 73-6155. (No. 617). 1973. Repr. of 1628 ed. 40.00 (ISBN 90-221-0617-9). Walter J Johnson.

Watkins, T. F., et al. Chemical Warfare, Pyrotechnics & the Fireworks Industry. 1968. 16.50 (ISBN 0-08-012811-4); pap. 7.75 (ISBN 0-08-012810-6). Pergamon.

Weingart, George W. Pyrotechnics. (Illus.). 1968. Repr. of 1947 ed. 18.50 (ISBN 0-8206-0112-8). Chem Pub.

FIRMS

see Business Enterprises

FIRST AID FOR ANIMALS

Walker, Ernest P. & Animal Welfare Institute, eds. First Aid & Care of Small Animals. rev. ed. (Illus.). 54p. 1980. pap. text ed. 2.00 (ISBN 0-938414-04-6). Animal Welfare.

FIRST AID IN ILLNESS AND INJURY

see also Accidents; Ambulances; Artificial Respiration; Asphyxia; Bandages and Bandaging; Burns and Scalds; Emergency Medical Services; Medical Emergencies; Resuscitation; Transport of Sick and Wounded

Aaron, James E., et al. First Aid Emergency Care: Prevention & Protection of Injuries. 2nd ed. 1979. pap. text ed. 10.95 (ISBN 0-02-300060-0). Macmillan.

Advice About First Aid, High Blood Pressure, Heart Attack. (Home Adviser Ser.). 80p. (Orig.). 1981. pap. 1.95 (ISBN 0-8326-2404-7, 7054). Delair.

American Medical Association. The AMA Handbook of First Aid & Emergency Care. (Illus.). 256p. 1980. 5.95 (ISBN 0-394-73668-0). Random.

The American Medical Association's Handbook of First Aid & Emergency Care. (Illus.). 1980. pap. 5.95 (ISBN 0-394-73668-0). Random.

American National Red Cross. Advanced First Aid & Emergency Care. 2nd ed. LC 79-53479. (American Red Cross Bks.). (Illus.). 1980. pap. 3.00 (ISBN 0-385-15737-1). Doubleday.

--Advanced First Aid & Emergency Care. LC 73-76727. 320p. 1973. 3.95 (ISBN 0-385-05841-1). Doubleday.

--Basic First Aid, 4 vols. (Illus.). Set. pap. 5.25 slipcased (ISBN 0-385-17211-7). Doubleday.

--Standard First Aid & Personal Safety. 2nd ed. LC 79-53478. (American Red Cross Bks.). 1979. pap. 2.50 (ISBN 0-385-15736-3). Doubleday.

Annarino, Anthony A. & Kahms, Frederick W. First Aid, Safety, & Family Health Emergencies: Study Guide. 2nd ed. 1979. pap. text ed. 6.95x (ISBN 0-8087-0063-4). Burgess.

Arnheim, Daniel D. Dance Injuries: Their Prevention & Care. 2nd ed. LC 79-24524. (Illus.). 1980. pap. text ed. 12.00 (ISBN 0-8016-0311-0). Mosby.

Arnold, Peter. Emergency Handbook: A First Aid Manual for Home & Travel. LC 79-52489. (Illus.). 256p. 1980. 11.95 (ISBN 0-385-15566-2). Doubleday.

Arnold, Peter & Pendagast, Edward L. Emergency Handbook: A First Aid Manual for Home & Travel. 1981. pap. 5.95 (ISBN 0-452-25288-1, Z5288, Plume). NAL.

Arnold, Robert E. What to Do About Bites & Stings of Venomous Animals. LC 72-77647. (Illus.). 125p. 1973. pap. 1.95 (ISBN 0-02-058250-1, Collier). Macmillan.

--What to Do About Bites & Stings of Venomous Animals. 128p. 1973. 9.95 (ISBN 0-02-503250-X). Macmillan.

Baldwin, Shirley. First Aid for the Office & Workplace. (Illus.). 192p. 1982. 15.75 (ISBN 0-87527-258-4). Green.

Barber, Janet & Dillman, Peter. Emergency Patient Care for the EMT: A Guide for the EMT. 1981. 19.95 (ISBN 0-8359-1671-5). Reston.

Bergeron, Dave. First Responders. 450p. 1981. pap. text ed. 12.95 (ISBN 0-87619-998-8). R J Brady.

Boswell, John & Fitzgerald, James, eds. The U. S. Armed Forces First Aid Manual. 1982. 15.95 (ISBN 0-89256-192-0); pap. 8.95 (ISBN 0-89256-201-3). Rawson Wade.

Boy Scouts of America. Emergency Preparedness. LC 19-600. (Illus.). 64p. (gr. 6-12). 1974. pap. 0.70x (ISBN 0-8395-3366-7, 3366). BSA.

--Exploring Emergency Service. (Illus.). 64p. 1971. pap. 3.00x (ISBN 0-8395-6609-3, 6609). BSA.

--First Aid. (Illus.). 56p. (gr. 6-12). 1981. pap. 0.70x (ISBN 0-8395-3276-8). BSA.

--First Aid Skill Book. (Illus.). 32p. (gr. 3-4). 1974. pap. 0.50x (ISBN 0-8395-6588-7, 6588). BSA.

Brennan, William T. & Crowe, James W. Guide to Problems & Practices in First Aid & Emergency Care. 4th ed. 192p. 1981. wire coil (ISBN 0-697-07390-4). Wm C Brown.

Brown, Terry & Hunter, Rob. The Concise Book of Outdoor First Aid. (Illus.). 1978. pap. 2.95 (ISBN 0-7715-9433-X, Pub. by Gage). Vanguard.

--The Concise Book of Survival & Rescue. (Concise Ser.). 1978. pap. 2.95 (ISBN 0-7715-9439-9). Vanguard.

Came-Ross, Luna. Emergency First Aid. (Illus.). 24p. 1981. spiral bound, vinyl slipcase 3.95 (ISBN 0-8256-3241-2, Quick Fox). Music Sales.

Canario, Jack & Mathias, Marilynne. Help! First Steps to First Aid. Katz, Elaine, ed. (Survival Guides Ser.). (Illus.). 64p. (gr. 7 up). 1980. pap. text ed. 2.85 (ISBN 0-915510-46-4). Janus Bks.

Consumer Guide Editors & Mosher, Charles. Emergency First Aid. 96p. 1980. pap. 2.50 (ISBN 0-449-90023-1, Columbine). Fawcett.

Do Carmo, Pamela B. & Patterson, Angelo T. First Aid Principles & Procedures. (Illus.). 256p. 1976. pap. text ed. 9.95 (ISBN 0-13-317933-8). P-H.

Dolan, Joseph P. & Holladay, Lloyd J. First-Aid Management: Athletics, Physical Education, Recreation. LC 73-85694. 1974. 8.95x (ISBN 0-8134-1604-3, 1604). Interstate.

Eastman, Peter F. Advanced First Aid Afloat. 2nd ed. LC 72-78241. (Illus.). 1974. pap. 6.00 (ISBN 0-87033-169-8). Cornell Maritime.

--Advanced First Aid for All Outdoors. LC 76-44658. (Illus.). 1976. pap. 6.00 (ISBN 0-87033-223-6). Cornell Maritime.

Emergency Family First Aid Guide. 1.95 (ISBN 0-671-21427-6, Fireside). S&S.

Erven, Lawrence. First Aid & Emergency Rescue. Gruber, Harvey, ed. LC 71-110984. (Fire Science Ser). (Illus.). 215p. 1970. pap. text ed. 9.95x (ISBN 0-02-474370-4, 47437). Macmillan.

Evans. Emergency Medicine. 1981. text ed. price not set (ISBN 0-407-00172-7). Butterworth.

Family First Aid Guide. (Ideals Guidelines Ser.). 96p. (Orig.). 1981. pap. 2.95 (ISBN 0-8249-4011-3). Ideals.

Feller, Irving & Jones, Claudella A. Teaching Basic Burn Care. LC 75-15373. (Illus.). 1975. plastic 3-ring binder 120.00 (ISBN 0-917478-27-4). Natl Inst Burn.

Folson, Farnham. Extrication & Casualty Handling Techniques. LC 75-19298. (Illus.). 160p. 1975. pap. text ed. 13.50 (ISBN 0-397-59059-8, JBL-Med-Nursing). Har-Row.

Forgey, William W. Wilderness Medicine. LC 79-89027. (Illus.). 1979. cancelled (ISBN 0-934802-03-3); pap. 5.95 (ISBN 0-934802-02-5). ICS Bks.

Frey, R. & Safer, P., eds. Resuscitation & Life Support in Disasters: Relief of Pain & Suffering in Disaster Situations. (Disaster Medicine Ser.: Vol. 2). (Illus.). 320p. 1980. pap. 49.60 (ISBN 0-387-09044-4). Springer-Verlag.

Gibson, D. M. First Aid Homoeopathy in Accidents & Ailments. 1975. pap. 3.95 (ISBN 0-685-76564-4, Pub. by British Homoeopathy Assoc.). Formur Intl.

Grant. First Aid: Boaters & Divers. pap. 4.95 (ISBN 0-686-31265-1). New Century.

Grant, Harvey & Murray, Robert. Course Planning Guide for Emergency Care. 2nd ed. (Illus.). 336p. 1978. pap. text ed. 12.95 (ISBN 0-87618-961-3). R J Brady.

Grant, Sea. First Aid for Boaters & Divers. 128p. 1980. pap. 4.95 (ISBN 0-695-81425-7). New Century.

Green, Martin I. A Sigh of Relief: The First-Aid Handbook for Childhood Emergencies. (Illus.). 1977. pap. 8.95 (ISBN 0-553-01270-3, 01155-3). Bantam.

Hafen, Brent & Karren, Keith. First Aid & Emergency Care Workbook. 2nd new ed. (Illus.). 1980. 10.00x (ISBN 0-89582-024-2). Morton Pub.

Hafen, Brent Q. First Aid for Health Emergencies. 2nd ed. Harrison, Brete C., ed. 587p. 1980. pap. text ed. 12.95 (ISBN 0-8299-0302-X). West Pub.

Hafen, Brent Q. & Peterson, Brenda. First Aid for Health Emergencies. (Illus.). 1977. pap. text ed. 9.95 (ISBN 0-8299-0093-4). West Pub.

Hartunian, Paul. Lifesavers: The Best Free & Almost Free First Aid, Health & Safety Things You Can Get by Mail. LC 81-51355. 50p. (Orig.). 1981. pap. 3.95 (ISBN 0-939038-00-5). Tri-Med.

Haworth, Robert. First Aid for Yachtsmen. (Illus.). 125p. 1975. 11.95x (ISBN 0-8464-1095-8). Beekman Pubs.

Heimlich & Galton. Dr. Heimlich's Home Guide to Emergency Medical Situations. 1980. 10.95 (ISBN 0-671-24947-9, 24947). S&S.

Henderson, John. Emergency Medical Guide. 4th ed. (McGraw Hill Paperbacks). 1978. 15.95 (ISBN 0-07-028168-8, SP); pap. 4.95 (ISBN 0-07-028169-6). McGraw.

Irwin, Vincent & Spira, Michael. Basic Health Education. (Illus.). 1978. pap. text ed. 10.95x (ISBN 0-582-48829-X). Longman.

Johnson, Susan. First Aid for Kids. (Illus.). 128p. 1981. spiral bound 7.95 (ISBN 0-8256-3227-7, Quick Fox). Music Sales.

Jones, William E., ed. Basic First Aid for Horses. (Horse Health & Care Ser.). (Illus.). 1973. pap. 2.95 (ISBN 0-912830-04-2). Printed Horse.

Kalstone, Shirlee & McNamara, Walter. First Aid for Dogs. LC 80-111390. (Illus.). 416p. 1980. 11.95 (ISBN 0-668-04863-8). Arco.

Kean, B. H. & Tucker, Harold A. The Traveler's Health Guide. (Illus.). 236p. 1965. photocopy ed. spiral 19.75 (ISBN 0-398-00989-9). C C Thomas.

--The Traveler's Medical Guide for Physicians. (Illus.). 444p. 1966. photocopy ed. spiral 38.75 (ISBN 0-398-00988-0). C C Thomas.

Kirk, Robert H. & Ellison, Jack S. First Aid & Emergency Care: Guide to Understanding & Action. 2nd ed. 240p. 1980. pap. text ed. 7.95 (ISBN 0-8403-2189-9). Kendall-Hunt.

Kodet, E. Russel & Angier, Bradford. Being Your Own Wilderness Doctor. LC 68-15440. (Illus.). 132p. 1975. pap. 6.95 (ISBN 0-8117-2044-6). Stackpole.

Kornbluth, Alfred. First Aid for Boaters. 1979. 10.00 (ISBN 0-517-53720-6); pap. 5.95 (ISBN 0-517-53721-4). Crown.

Leone, Nicholas C. Cruising Sailors Medical Guide. 1978. 12.50 (ISBN 0-679-50954-2). McKay.

Lobb, Nancy. Everyday First Aid Skills. 1979. pap. 2.50x (ISBN 0-88323-148-4, 235). Richards Pub.

McCarthy, T. First Aid Step by Step. (Illus.). 1977. pap. 11.95x (ISBN 0-433-20451-6). Intl Ideas.

McGrath, Robert. Emergency Removal of Patients & First Aid Fire Fighting in Hospitals. 3rd ed. (Illus.). 1974. pap. 4.15 (ISBN 0-87912-101-7, 12959). Natl Safety Coun.

Madda, Frank C., ed. Outdoor Emergency Medicine. (Illus.). 277p. (Orig.). 1981. pap. 3.95 (ISBN 0-938278-00-2). BioServ Corp.

Marsden, Neville. Diagnosis Before First Aid: A Manual for Emergency Care Workers. (Illus.). 1978. pap. text ed. 6.50 (ISBN 0-443-01639-9). Churchill.

Medical First Aid Guide for Use in Accidents Involving Dangerous Goods. (Illus.). 147p. 1973. 16.50 (ISBN 0-686-70787-7, IMCO). Unipub.

Mitchell Beazly Pub. Ltd. The Pocket Medical Encyclopedia & First Aid Guide. 1979. pap. 3.95 (ISBN 0-671-24671-2). S&S.

Mitchell, Dick. Mountaineering First Aid: A Guide to Accident Response & First Aid Care. 2nd ed. LC 75-25341. (Illus.). 104p. 1975. pap. 3.95 (ISBN 0-916890-33-3). Mountaineers.

Nelson, Louise E. Project-Readiness: A Guide to Family Emergency Preparedness. LC 75-307239. (Illus.). 1975. 10.95 (ISBN 0-88290-036-6). Horizon Utah.

Nisbet, Margaret. How to Book of First Aid & Safety. (How to Bks). (Illus.). 96p. (Orig.). 1981. pap. 3.95 (ISBN 0-686-75064-0, Pub. by Blandford Pr England). Sterling.

--How to Book of First Aid & Safety. (How to Books from Blandford). (Illus.). 96p. (Orig.). 1981. pap. 3.95 (ISBN 0-7137-1054-3, Pub. by Blandford Pr England). Sterling.

Nourse, Alan E. The Outdoorsman's Medical Guide: Common Sense Advice & Essential Health Care for Campers, Hikers, & Backpackers. LC 73-18658. (Illus.). 128p. (YA) 1974. pap. 4.50 (ISBN 0-06-013226-4, TD-194, HarpT). Har-Row.

Oppenheim, Mary L. Aquatic Aid: A Guidebook for Water Satety Instruction. (Illus.). 1981. 7.50 (ISBN 0-682-49764-9). Exposition.

Pappa, John, et al. Foundations of Emergency First Aid Services: Skill Class Workbook. 2nd ed. 96p. 1980. pap. text ed. 5.95 shrink wrap (ISBN 0-8403-2205-4). Kendall-Hunt.

Parcel, Guy S. Basic Emergency Care of the Sick & Injured. 2nd ed. (Illus.). 352p. 1982. pap. text ed. 11.95 (ISBN 0-8016-3754-6). Mosby.

--First Aid in Emergency Care. LC 77-322. (Illus.). 1977. 14.95 (ISBN 0-8016-3400-8); pap. 11.95 (ISBN 0-8016-3757-0). Mosby.

Peige, John, et al, eds. Fire Service First Aid Practices, IFSTA Committee. LC 77-75409. 1977. pap. text ed. 8.50 (ISBN 0-87939-009-3). Intl Fire Serv.
Renouf, Jane & Hulse, Stewart. First Aid for Hill Walkers & Climbers. (Illus.). 169p. 1978. pap. 5.95 (ISBN 0-14-046293-7). Bradt Ent.
Rogers, James H., et al. First Aid & Emergency Medical Care. 128p. 1980. pap. text ed. 6.95 (ISBN 0-8403-2242-9). Kendall-Hunt.
Rubell, Earl B. Yachtsman's Guide to First Aid Afloat. 1980. 8.95 (ISBN 0-686-74212-5). Ziff-Davis Pub.
Rubin, Clifford L. Baby First Aid. 1980. pap. 1.95 (ISBN 0-425-04618-4). Berkley Pub.
Scott, R. W. Handy Medical Guide for Seafarers: Fishermen, Trawlermen & Yachtsmen. (Illus.). 96p. 11.25 (ISBN 0-85238-007-0, FN 52, FNB). Unipub.
--Handy Medical Guide for Seafarers, Fisherman, Trawlermen & Yachtsmen. 1978. 10.00 (ISBN 0-685-63426-4). State Mutual Bk.
Seager, Stephen. Breathe, Little Boy, Breathe: An Emergency Room Doctor's Story. 216p. 1981. 10.95 (ISBN 0-13-081729-5). P-H.
Smith, Ed & Bowser, Milton. Highway Save-Your-Life Kit. pap. 10.00 (ISBN 0-940178-07-9). Sitare Inc.
Survival First Aid: Practical Guide to Life's Preservation in Wars & Cataclysms for Self & Others. Skills &Preparedness. LC 80-84992. (Illus.). 1981. 10.00 (ISBN 0-916508-14-5); pap. 8.00 (ISBN 0-686-69456-2). Happiness Pr.
Thomas, Lowell J. & Sanderson, Joy L. First Aid for Backpackers & Campers. LC 77-212197. (Illus.). 1979. 7.95 (ISBN 0-03-021106-9); pap. 3.95 (ISBN 0-03-021111-5). HR&W.
Thygerson, Alton L. The First Aid Book. (Illus.). 288p. 1982. 10.95 (ISBN 0-13-318006-9). P-H.
--First Aid Practices: Study Guide. (Illus.). 1978. 7.95 (ISBN 0-13-317958-3). P-H.
Vandenburg, Mary Lou. Help! Emergencies That Could Happen to You, & How to Handle Them. LC 75-7007. (Medical Bks for Children). (Illus.). 72p. (gr. 4-7). 1975. PLB 3.95 (ISBN 0-8225-0020-5). Lerner Pubns.
Wachtel, Thomas. Medical Exploring. (Illus.). 256p. (gr. 6-12). 1973. pap. 3.50x (ISBN 0-8395-6618-2, 6618). BSA.
Waisbren, Burton. The Family First Aid Handbook. (Good Health Ser.). (Illus.). 1978. pap. 2.95 (ISBN 0-448-14645-2, Good Health Books). G&D.
Wells, Larry & Giles, Robert. You Can Stay Alive. LC 81-80952. 100p. (Orig.). 1981. pap. 4.95 (ISBN 0-88290-181-8, 4028). Horizon Utah.
Wilson, Judy. Mother Nature's Homestead First Aid. LC 75-7448. (Mother Nature Ser.: No. 4). (Illus.). 192p. (Orig.). pap. 3.95 (ISBN 0-914400-09-6). Oliver Pr.
Young, Carl B., Jr. First Aid for Emergency Crews: A Manual on Emergency First Aid Procedures for Ambulance Crews, Law Enforcement Officers, Fire Service Personnel, Wrecker Drivers, Hospital Staffs, Industry, Nurses. (Illus.). 192p. 1970. 10.75 (ISBN 0-398-02134-1). C C Thomas.

FIRST-BORN CHILDREN
see Children, First-Born

FIRST CHURCH OF CHRIST, SCIENTIST
see Boston–First Church of Christ, Scientist

FIRST COMMUNION
Heeg, Aloysius J. Jesus & I. (gr. 1-2). pap. text ed. 0.80 (ISBN 0-8294-0214-4). Loyola.
McGhee, James. On the Way to Their First Communion: A Handbook for Parents. LC 76-24435. 1976. pap. 6.95 (ISBN 0-8091-1981-1). Paulist Pr.
McIntyre, Marie. Eucharist: Our Communal Celebration. (Illus., Orig.). 1978. pap. 1.95 (ISBN 0-89622-077-X). Twenty-Third.
Montgomery, Mary & Montgomery, Herb. Come to Communion: A Program for First Communion Preparation. 1972. 2.75 (ISBN 0-03-012206-6, 119); parent bklt. 1.65 (ISBN 0-03-012211-2, 120); tchr's. guide 4.35 (ISBN 0-03-012216-3, 121). Winston Pr.
The New Saint Joseph First Communion Cathechism. rev. ed. (Official Baltimore Catechism Ser.). (Illus.). 1.20 (ISBN 0-686-14295-0, 240/05). Catholic Bk Pub.
Thiry, Joan & Burbach, Marilyn. Eucharist Is for Sharing. (gr. 2-5). 1977. duplicating masterbook 12.95 (ISBN 0-686-13699-3). Pflaum Pr.

FIRST EDITIONS
see Bibliography–First Editions

FIRST STREET SCHOOL
Dennison, George. Lives of Children. LC 74-85566. 1970. pap. 2.95 (ISBN 0-394-70863-6, V638, Vin). Random.

FIRTH, SIR CHARLES
Firth, Charles H. Bibliography of the Writings of Sir Charles Firth. LC 74-13083. 1928. lib. bdg. 15.00 (ISBN 0-8414-4244-4). Folcroft.

FIRTH, JOHN RUPERT, 1890-1960
Christie, William M., Jr. Preface to a Neo-Firthian Linguistics. LC 80-21016. (Edward Sapir Monograph Series in Language, Culture, & Cognition: No. 7). viii, 70p. (Orig.). 1980. pap. 6.00x (ISBN 0-933104-11-1). Jupiter Pr.
Mitchell, T. F. Principles of Firthian Linguistics. (Illus.). 232p. 1975. text ed. 19.50x (ISBN 0-582-52455-5). Longman.

FIRUZ SHAH 3RD TAGHLAK, SULTAN OF DELHI, d. 1288
Banerjee, Jamini M. History of Firuz Shah Tughlug: Medieval India. 1967. 6.50x (ISBN 0-8426-1138-X). Verry.

FISCAL EVASION
see Tax Evasion

FISCAL POLICY
see also Monetary Policy
Arrow, Kenneth J. & Kurz, Mordecai. Public Investment, the Rate of Return, & Optimal Fiscal Policy. LC 73-108380. (Resources for the Future Ser). 236p. 1970. 16.50x (ISBN 0-8018-1124-4). Johns Hopkins.
Bangs, Robert B. Financing Economic Development: Fiscal Policy for Emerging Countries. LC 68-27292. 1968. 11.00x (ISBN 0-226-03684-7). U of Chicago Pr.
Buchanan, James M. Fiscal Theory & Political Economy: Selected Essays. 1960. 13.00x (ISBN 0-8078-0795-8). U of NC Pr.
--Public Finance in the Democratic Process. 1967. 19.50x (ISBN 0-8078-1014-2). U of NC Pr.
Burns, Arthur F. Reflections of an Economic Policy Maker: Speeches & Congressional Statements, 1969-1978. 1978. 17.25 (ISBN 0-8447-3319-9); pap. 9.25 (ISBN 0-8447-3333-4). Am Enterprise.
Cargill, Jennifer S. & Alley, Brian. Keeping Track of What You Spend: The Librarian's Guide to Simple Bookkeeping. 1981. write for info. (ISBN 0-912700-79-3). Oryx Pr.
Cook, S. T. & Jackson, P. M., eds. Current Issues in Fiscal Policy. 238p. 1981. pap. 13.50x (ISBN 0-85520-352-8, Pub. by Martin Robertson England). Biblio Dist.
Dauphine Conference on Money & International Money Problems, 3rd, Paris. Stabilization Policies in Interdependent Economies: Proceedings. Salin & Claassen, eds. 1972. 39.00 (ISBN 0-444-10368-6, North-Holland). Elsevier.
Fiscal Measures for Employment Promotion in Developing Countries. 3rd ed. 1974. 14.25 (ISBN 92-2-100160-1). Intl Labour Office.
Friedman, Milton & Heller, Walter H. Monetary Versus Fiscal Policy. 1969. 3.95x (ISBN 0-393-05372-5); pap. 2.95x (ISBN 0-393-09847-8). Norton.
Hansen, Bent. Fiscal Policy in Seven Countries, 1955-1965: Belgium, France, Germany, Italy, Sweden, United Kingdom, United States. 552p. 1969. 11.00x (ISBN 0-686-14783-9). OECD.
Heilbroner, Robert L. & Bernstein, Peter L. Primer on Government Spending. 2nd ed. (Primer Economics Ser). 1970. pap. text ed. 3.95x (ISBN 0-394-30750-X, RanC). Random.
Heller, Walter. New Dimensions of Political Economy. 1967. pap. 3.95x (ISBN 0-393-09755-2). Norton.
Heller, Walter W. New Dimensions of Political Economy. LC 66-23467. (Godkin Lectures Ser.: 1966). 1966. 10.00x (ISBN 0-674-61100-4). Harvard U Pr.
Hicks, Ursula K. Development Finance: Planning & Control. 1965. 8.50x (ISBN 0-19-828151-X). Oxford U Pr.
Kann, Edward. The Currencies of China. (Illus.). 1978. Repr. of 1926 ed. lib. bdg. 39.50 (ISBN 0-915262-22-3). S J Durst.
Kleinsorge, Paul L., ed. Public Finance & Welfare: Essays in Honor of C. Ward Macy. LC 66-4750. 1966. 7.50 (ISBN 0-87114-013-6). U of Oreg Bks.
Krauss, Mel. Fiscal Harmonization in the Benelux Union. 1969. 11.50x (ISBN 0-8002-0815-3). Intl Pubns Serv.
LeLoup, Lance T. The Fiscal Congress: Legislative Control of the Budget. LC 79-6823. (Contributions in Political Science: No. 47). (Illus.). xii, 227p. 1980. lib. bdg. 25.00 (ISBN 0-313-22009-3, LFC/). Greenwood.
Levine, Charles H., ed. Fiscal Stress & Public Policy. LC 80-24515. (Sage Yearbook in Politics & Public Policy). 314p. 1980. 20.00 (ISBN 0-8039-1553-5); pap. 9.95 (ISBN 0-8039-1554-3). Sage.
--Managing Fiscal Stress: The Crisis in the Public Sector. LC 79-27266. (Chatham House Series on Change in American Politics). 1980. pap. text ed. 12.95x (ISBN 0-934540-02-0). Chatham Hse Pubs.
McCracken, Paul W., et al. Fiscal Policy & Business Capital Formation. 1967. pap. 7.25 (ISBN 0-8447-2006-2). Am Enterprise.
Maxwell, James A. Fiscal Policy, Its Techniques & Institutional Setting. LC 68-9710. (Illus.). 1968. Repr. of 1955 ed. lib. bdg. 15.00 (ISBN 0-8371-0165-4, MAFP). Greenwood.
Ott, David J. & Ott, Attiat F. Federal Budget Policy. 3rd ed. (Studies of Government Finance). 1977. 12.95 (ISBN 0-8157-6710-2); pap. 4.95 (ISBN 0-8157-6709-9). Brookings.
Pechman, Joseph A. Federal Tax Policy. 3rd ed. LC 76-54901. (Studies of Government Finance). 1977. 14.95 (ISBN 0-8157-6978-4); pap. 6.95 (ISBN 0-8157-6977-6). Brookings.
--Federal Tax Policy. rev. ed. (Brookings Institute Studies of Government Finance). 1971. pap. text ed. 5.95x (ISBN 0-393-09987-3). Norton.
Peppard, Donald M., Jr. & Roberts, Douglas B. Net Fiscal Incidence in Michigan: Who Pays & Who Benefits? LC 76-620088. 1977. pap. 6.00 (ISBN 0-87744-143-X). Mich St U Busn.
Phelps, Edmund S., ed. Private Wants & Public Needs. rev. ed. (Problems of Modern Economy Ser.). (Orig.). 1965. pap. 4.95x (ISBN 0-393-09496-0, NortonC). Norton.
Reese, Thomas J. The Politics of Taxation. LC 79-8413. (Illus.). xxv, 237p. 1980. lib. bdg. 25.00 (ISBN 0-89930-003-0, RPT/, Quorum Bks). Greenwood.
Snyder, James C. Fiscal Management & Planning in Local Government. LC 76-43218. 1977. 18.95 (ISBN 0-669-01055-3). Lexington Bks.
Stein, Herbert. Fiscal Revolution in America. LC 69-14828. (Studies in Business & Society Ser). 1969. pap. 7.95 (ISBN 0-226-77170-9). U of Chicago Pr.
Swanson, Donald F. Origins of Hamilton's Fiscal Policies. LC 63-63264. (U of Fla. Social Sciences Monographs Ser.: No. 17). 1963. pap. 3.00 (ISBN 0-8130-0222-2). U Presses Fla.
Wagner, Richard E. & Tollison, Robert D. Balanced Budgets, Fiscal Responsibility, & the Constitution. (Cato Public Policy Research Monograph Ser.: No. 1). 64p. (Orig.). 1980. pap. 4.00x (ISBN 0-932790-12-7). Cato Inst.
Wilford, D. Sykes. Monetary Policy & the Open Economy: Mexico's Experience. LC 77-14386. (Praeger Special Studies). 1977. 22.95 (ISBN 0-03-028156-3). Praeger.

FISCAL POLICY–EUROPEAN ECONOMIC COMMUNITY
European Tax Consultants Congress, Strasbourg, October 1978. Fiscalite En Europe: Proceedings. Confederation Fiscale Europeenne, ed. 242p. 1980. pap. 29.00 (ISBN 9-0200-0578-2, Pub. by Kluwer Law Netherlands). Kluwer Boston.

FISCAL POLICY–MATHEMATICAL MODELS
Peacock, Alan & Shaw, G. K. The Economic Theory of Fiscal Policy. 2nd ed. LC 76-15870. 200p. 1976. text ed. 18.95x (ISBN 0-312-23660-3). St Martin.

FISCAL POLICY–GERMANY
Reuss, Frederick G. Fiscal Policy for Growth Without Inflation: The German Experiment. (Goucher College Ser). 335p. 1963. 22.00x (ISBN 0-8018-0553-8). Johns Hopkins.
Roskamp, Karl W. Capital Formation in West Germany. LC 64-22331. (Center for Economic Studies Monographs: No. 3). 1965. 13.95x (ISBN 0-8143-1247-0). Wayne St U Pr.

FISCAL POLICY–GREAT BRITAIN
Sandford, C. T. Economics of Public Finance. 2nd ed. LC 77-6680. 1977. text ed. 27.00 (ISBN 0-08-021843-1); pap. text ed. 14.00 (ISBN 0-08-021842-3). Pergamon.

FISCAL POLICY–LATIN AMERICA
Behrman, J. R. Macroeconomic Policy in a Developing Country: Chilean Experience. (Contributions to Economic Analysis: Vol. 109). 1977. 36.75 (ISBN 0-7204-0548-3, North-Holland). Elsevier.

FISCAL RELATIONS, INTERGOVERNMENTAL
see Intergovernmental Fiscal Relations

FISCHER, BOBBY, 1943-
Darrach, Brad. Bobby Fischer Vs. the Rest of the World. LC 73-81322. 304p. 1974. 25.00x (ISBN 0-8128-1618-8). Stein & Day.
--Bobby Fischer Vs. the Rest of the World. LC 73-81322. 1975. pap. 2.95 (ISBN 0-8128-1850-4). Stein & Day.
Euwe, Max. Bobby Fischer - the Greatest? LC 78-66270. (Illus.). 1979. 9.95 (ISBN 0-8069-4950-3); lib. bdg. 9.29 (ISBN 0-8069-4951-1). Sterling.
How Fischer Plays Chess. LC 75-8435. pap. 4.95 (ISBN 0-89058-011-1). R H M Pr.
Mednis, Edmar. How to Beat Bobby Fischer. Byrne, Robert, ed. LC 74-77932. (Illus.). 256p. 1974. 10.00 (ISBN 0-8129-0469-9). Times Bks.
Reshevsky, Samuel. Samuel Reshevsky's in-Depth Analysis of the Fischer-Spassky Chess Match. LC 72-93887. 1975. 10.00 (ISBN 0-8129-0343-9). Times Bks.
Roberts, Richard, et al, eds. Fischer-Spassky: The New York Times Report on the Chess Match of the Century. LC 72-90465. (Illus.). 281p. 1973. 7.95 (ISBN 0-8129-0302-1). Times Bks.

FISCHER, FRITZ, 1908-
Moses, John A. The Politics of Illusion: The Fischer Controversy in German Historiography. LC 75-9066. 148p. 1975. text ed. 17.50x (ISBN 0-06-495000-X). B&N.

FISCHER, JOHANN CONRAD, 1773-1854
Henderson, William O. J. C. Fischer & His Diary of Industrial England, 1815-1841. LC 66-55759. (Illus.). 1966. 19.50x (ISBN 0-678-05059-7). Kelley.

FISCHER VON ERLACH, J. B., 1656-1723
Aurenhammer, Hans. J. B. Fischer von Erlach. LC 73-83421. 188p. 1974. 15.95x (ISBN 0-674-46988-7). Harvard U Pr.

FISH, HAMILTON, 1808-1893
Davis, J. Bancroft. Mister Fish & the Alabama Claims: A Chapter in Diplomatic History. facsimile ed. (Select Bibliographies Reprint Ser). 1893. 17.00 (ISBN 0-8369-5067-4). Arno.
Nevins, Allan. Hamilton Fish: The Inner History of the Grant Administration, 2 Vols. LC 57-9967. (American Classics Ser.). (Illus.). 1957. 45.00 (ISBN 0-8044-1676-1). Ungar.

FISH
see Fishes

FISH (IN RELIGION, FOLK-LORE, ETC.)
see also Dolphin (In Religion, Folk-Lore, etc.)
Lee, Jenny. A Fish Tale. LC 79-25751. 1980. 9.95 (ISBN 0-915828-17-0). Sufism Reoriented.
Titcomb, Margaret. Native Use of Fish in Hawaii. 2nd ed. 1972. pap. 3.95 (ISBN 0-8248-0592-5). U Pr of Hawaii.
Trevelyan, Marie. Folk-Lore & Folk-Stories of Wales. (Folklore Ser). 20.00 (ISBN 0-685-36521-2). Norwood Edns.

FISH, CANNED
Recommended International Code of Practice for Canned Fish. 1979. pap. 4.50 (ISBN 92-5-100278-9, F1582, FAO). Unipub.
Water Supplies for Fish Processing Plants. (FAO Fisheries Technical Papers Ser.: No. 174). 1979. pap. 7.50 (ISBN 92-5-100685-7, F1595, FAO). Unipub.

FISH AS FOOD
see also Cookery (Sea Food); Sea Food
Billmeyer, Patricia. The Encyclopedia of Wild Game & Fish Cleaning & Cooking. LC 79-54388. 128p. pap. 3.95 (ISBN 0-9606262-0-4). Yesnaby Pubs.
Borgstrom, G., ed. Fish As Food, 4 vols. Incl. Vol. 1. Production, Biochemistry & Microbiology. 1961. 76.50 (ISBN 0-12-118501-X); Vol. 2. Nutrition, Sanitation & Utilization. 1962. 64.00 (ISBN 0-12-118502-8); Vol. 3. Processing, Part 1. 1965. 57.00 (ISBN 0-12-118503-6); Vol. 4. Processing, Part 2. 1965. 57.00 (ISBN 0-12-118504-4). Acad Pr.
Draft Code of Practice for Frozen Fish. 1969. pap. 2.75 (ISBN 0-685-99137-7, IIR7, IIR). Unipub.
FAO. The Fish Resources of the Ocean. Gulland, John, ed. 1978. 37.00x (ISBN 0-685-63412-4). State Mutual Bk.
Gould, Edith & Peters, John A. Testing the Friskness of Frozen Fish. 1978. 16.00x (ISBN 0-685-63459-0). State Mutual Bk.
Kreuzer, Rudolf, ed. Freezing & Irradiation of Fish. (Illus.). 548p. 56.25 (ISBN 0-85238-008-9, FN 50, FNB). Unipub.
Mutkoski, Stephen A. & Schurer, Marcia L. Meat & Fish Management. 1981. text ed. 19.95x (ISBN 0-534-00907-7, Breton Pubs). Wadsworth Pub.
Nakamura, Hiroshi. Tuna: Distribution & Migration. 1978. 12.00x (ISBN 0-685-63462-0). State Mutual Bk.
O'Farrell, R. C. Seafood Fishing for Amateur & Professional. (Illus.). 196p. 15.00 (ISBN 0-85238-097-6, FN 70, FNB). Unipub.
Orr, A. P. & Marshall, S. M. The Fertile Sea. 1978. 20.00 (ISBN 0-685-63407-8). State Mutual Bk.
Papers Presented at the FAO-SIDA Workshop on the Use of Organic Materials As Fertilizers in Africa: Organic Recycling in Africa. 308p. 1981. pap. 20.00 (ISBN 92-5-100945-7, F2096, FAO). Unipub.
Pariser, E. R., et al. Fish Protein Concentrate: Panacea for Protein Malnutrition? LC 77-28112. (International Nutrition Policy Ser.: NO. 3). 1978. text ed. 20.00x (ISBN 0-262-16069-2). MIT Pr.
Recommended International Code of Practice for Frozen Fish. 58p. 1981. pap. 7.50 (ISBN 92-5-100985-6, F2124, FAO). Unipub.
Recommended International Standard for Quick Frozen Fillets of Cod & Haddock. 1972. pap. 4.50 (ISBN 0-685-36317-1, F591, FAO). Unipub.
Recommended International Standard for Quick Frozen Fillets of Ocean Perch. 1972. pap. 4.50 (ISBN 0-685-36318-X, F592, FAO). Unipub.
Recommended International Standard for Quick Frozen Gutted Pacific Salmon. 1970. pap. 4.50 (ISBN 0-685-36320-1, F641, FAO). Unipub.

Report of the EIFAC, IUNS & ICES Working Group on the Standardization of Methodology in Fish Nutrition Research. (EIFAC Technical Paper Ser.: No. 36). 24p. 1980. pap. 8.25 (ISBN 92-5-100918-X, F2048, FAO). Unipub.
Suzuki, T. Fish & Krill Protein: Processing Technology. (Illus.). xiv, 262p. 1981. 46.50x (ISBN 0-85334-954-1). Intl Ideas.
WHO Expert Committee. Fish & Shellfish Hygiene. 62p. 1975. pap. 6.00 (ISBN 0-685-54032-4, F170, FAO). Unipub.

FISH AS LABORATORY ANIMALS

Lewis, William M. Maintaining Fishes for Experimental & Instructional Purposes. LC 62-15001. (Arcturus Books Paperbacks Ser.). 109p. 1963. pap. 3.95 (ISBN 0-8093-0078-8). S Ill U Pr.
Neuhaus, O. W. & Halver, J. E., eds. Fish in Research. LC 74-107020. 1969. 37.50 (ISBN 0-12-515850-5). Acad Pr.

FISH BY-PRODUCTS

see Fishery Products

FISH-CULTURE

see also Animal Introduction; Aquariums; Fish Ponds; Tropical Fish Breeding

Axelrod, Herbert R. Beginning with Mbunas. (Illus., Orig.). 1978. pap. 2.00 (ISBN 0-87666-474-5, PS-762). TFH Pubns.
--Breeding Aquarium Fishes, Bk. 4. (Illus.). 320p. 1976. 12.95 (ISBN 0-87666-451-6, H-963). TFH Pubns.
--Breeding Aquarium Fishes, Bk. 5. (Illus.). 1978. 12.95 (ISBN 0-87666-469-9, H-986). TFH Pubns.
--Breeding Aquarium Fishes, Bk.6. (Illus.). 288p. 1980. 12.95 (ISBN 0-87666-536-9, H-995). TFH Pubns.
Brown, E. Evan & Gratzek, J. B. Fish Farming Handbook. (Illus.). 1980. 24.50 (ISBN 0-87055-341-0). AVI.
Control of Fish Quality. 222p. 1980. 32.00 (ISBN 0-85238-105-0, FN 83, FNB). Unipub.
Davis, H. S. Culture & Diseases of Game Fishes. (Illus.). 1953. 18.50x (ISBN 0-520-00293-8). U of Cal Pr.
Dow, Steven. Breeding Angelfish. (Illus.). 1977. pap. 4.95 (ISBN 0-668-04055-6). Arco.
Educational Research Council of America. Fish Biologist. Kunze, Linda J. & Marchak, John P., eds. (Real People at Work Ser: G). (Illus.). 1974. pap. text ed. 2.25 (ISBN 0-89247-056-9). Changing Times.
Elementary Guide to Fish Culture in Nepal. (Illus.). 131p. 1976. pap. 8.50 (ISBN 0-685-62391-2, F772, FAO). Unipub.
Gerking, Shelby D., ed. Ecology of Freshwater Fish Production. LC 77-92407. 1978. 68.95 (ISBN 0-470-99362-6). Halsted Pr.
Hepher, Dalfour & Pruginin, Yoel. Commercial Fish Farming: With Special Reference to Fish Culture in Israel. LC 80-28593. 250p. 1981. 32.50 (ISBN 0-471-06264-2, Pub. by Wiley-Interscience). Wiley.
Hjul, P., ed. Fish Farming International, No. 2. 1978. 15.00 (ISBN 0-685-63410-8). State Mutual Bk.
Huet, Marcel. Textbook of Fish Culture: Breeding & Cultivation of Fish. (Illus.). 454p. 60.00 (ISBN 0-85238-020-8, FN 16, FNB). Unipub.
Inersen, Edwin S. Farming the Edge of the Sea. 1978. 35.00 (ISBN 0-685-63406-X). State Mutual Bk.
International Directory of Fish Technology Institutes. (Fisheries Technical Paper: No. 152). 1976. pap. 7.50 (ISBN 9-2510-0007-7, F885, FAO). Unipub.
Korringa, P. Farming Marine Fishes & Shrimps: A Multidisciplinary Treatise. (Developments in Aquaculture & Fisheries Science: Vol. 4). 1976. 39.00 (ISBN 0-444-41335-9). Elsevier.
Lewis, William M. Maintaining Fishes for Experimental & Instructional Purposes. LC 62-15001. 109p. 1963. 5.95x (ISBN 0-8093-0077-X). S Ill U Pr.
McNeil, William J. & Himsworth, Daniel C., eds. Salmonid Ecosystems of the North Pacific. LC 80-17800. (Illus.). 348p. pap. 15.00 (ISBN 0-87071-335-3); pap. text ed. 15.00 (ISBN 0-686-68208-4). Oreg St U Pr.
Milne, P. H. Fish & Shellfish Farming in Coastal Waters. 1978. 29.00 (ISBN 0-685-63408-6). State Mutual Bk.
Ostermoeller, Wolfgang. Fish Breeding Recipes. (Illus.). 1973. pap. 5.95 (ISBN 0-87666-071-5, PS-693). TFH Pubns.
Report of the EIFAC Workshop on Mass Rearing of Fry & Fingerlings of Freshwater Fishes. (EIFAC Technical Paper: No. 35). 23p. 1980. pap. 7.50 (ISBN 92-5-100829-9, F 1874, FAO). Unipub.
Report on the Fourth Session of the Cooperative Programme of Research on Aquaculture of the General Fisheries Council for the Mediterranean. (FAO Fisheries Report: No. 232). 32p. 1981. pap. 7.50 (ISBN 92-5-100927-9, F2068, FAO). Unipub.
Standard Techniques for Pelagic Fish Egg & Larva Surveys. (FAO Fisheries Technical Paper Ser.: No. 175). 1978. pap. 8.00 (ISBN 92-5-100515-X, F1439, FAO). Unipub.
Success with Killifish. (Mini Pet Reference Ser.: No.1). (Illus.). 1977. pap. 2.95 (ISBN 0-915096-02-1). Palmetto Pub.
Taverner, John. Certaine Experiments Concerning the Fish & the Fruite. LC 76-6030. (English Experience Ser.: No. 75). 38p. 1968. Repr. of 1600 ed. 7.00 (ISBN 90-221-0075-8). Walter J Johnson.
Terceira, Anthony. Killiefish: Their Care & Breeding. new ed. LC 74-80735. (Illus.). 1974. 9.98 (ISBN 0-914858-00-9). Pisces Pub.
Textbook of Fish Culture: Breeding & Cultivation of Fish. 1978. 40.00x (ISBN 0-685-63460-4). State Mutual Bk.
Thorpe, John, ed. Salmon Ranching. 1981. 78.00 (ISBN 0-12-690660-2). Acad Pr.
Trout Farming Manual. 186p. 1980. 36.75 (ISBN 0-85238-102-6, FN84, FNB). Unipub.
Waters, John F. Sea Farmers. LC 71-98059. (Illus.). 128p. (gr. 6-9). 1970. PLB 7.95 (ISBN 0-8038-6690-9). Hastings.
Workshop on Controlled Reproduction of Cultivated Fishes: Report & Relevant Papers. (EIFAC Technical Paper: No. 25). (Illus.). 180p. 1976. pap. 9.75 (ISBN 0-685-66314-0, FAO). Unipub.

FISH FARMING

see Fish-Culture

FISH HATCHERIES

see Fish-Culture

FISH-HAWKS

see Ospreys

FISH LAW

see Fishery Law and Legislation

FISH MOVEMENT (CHRISTIANITY)

Howell, Robert L. Fish for My People. (Orig.). 1968. pap. 2.50 (ISBN 0-8192-1097-8). Morehouse.

FISH PONDS

Balon, Eugene K. African Fishes of Lake Kariba. (Illus.). 144p. 1974. 4.95 (ISBN 0-87666-073-1, PS-706). TFH Pubns.
Betts, Leonard C. Garden Pools. (Illus.). 1952. pap. 2.50 (ISBN 0-87666-077-4, M513). TFH Pubns.

FISH POPULATIONS

Cushing, D. H. Marine Ecology & Fisheries. LC 74-82218. (Illus.). 228p. 1975. 52.50 (ISBN 0-521-20501-8); pap. 17.50x (ISBN 0-521-09911-0). Cambridge U Pr.
Gulland, J. A. Manual of Methods for Fish Stock Assessment, Pt. 1: Fish Population Analysis. (FAO Manuals in Fisheries Science Ser.: No. 4). (Illus., Orig.). 1969. pap. 12.25 (ISBN 92-5-100204-5, F262, FAO). Unipub.
Gulland, John A., ed. Fish Population Dynamics. LC 75-45094. 1977. 55.95x (ISBN 0-471-01575-X, Pub by Wiley-Interscience). Wiley.
Indo-Pacific Fisheries Council, Special Committee on Management of Indo-Pacific Tuna, Third Session & Indian Ocean Fishery Commission, Committee on Management of Indian Ocean Tuna, Fourth Session, July 18-19, 1975, Mombasa, Kenya. Report: Third Joint Meeting. (No. 174). (Illus.). 47p. 1976. pap. 7.50 (ISBN 0-685-68361-3, F824, FAO). Unipub.
A Review of the World Resources of Mesopelagic Fish. (FAO Fish Tech Paper: No. 193). 151p. 1981. pap. 10.25 (ISBN 92-5-100924-4, F2074, FAO). Unipub.
Stokes, F. Joseph. Handguide to the Coral Reef Fishes of the Caribbean. LC 79-27224. (Illus.). 160p. 1980. 9.95 (ISBN 0-690-01919-X). Har-Row.

FISH TRADE

see also Fishery Products

Ben-Yami, M. Fishing with Light. 1978. 16.00 (ISBN 0-685-63423-X). State Mutual Bk.
Connell, J. J. Control of Fish Quality. 1978. 20.00 (ISBN 0-685-63397-7). State Mutual Bk.
Economics Division FAO. Fishing Ports & Markets. 1978. 38.00 (ISBN 0-685-63421-3). State Mutual Bk.
Firth, Raymond. Malay Fishermen: Their Peasant Economy. (Illus.). 448p. 1975. pap. 4.95x (ISBN 0-393-00775-8, Norton Lib). Norton.
Fishing in Troubled Waters: Research on the Chinese Fishing Industry in West Malaysia. (Asian Folklore & Social Life Monographs: Vol. 100). 1977. 9.00 (ISBN 0-89986-319-1). E Langstaff.
Forrest, David M. Eel Capture, Culture, Processing & Marketing. 1978. 20.00 (ISBN 0-685-63399-3). State Mutual Bk.
Gersuny, Carl, et al. Some Effects of Technological Change on New England Fishermen. (Marine Technical Report Ser.: No. 42). 1975. pap. 1.00 (ISBN 0-938412-14-0). URI MAS.
Hicks, John & Hicks, Regina. Cannery Row: A Pictorial History. LC 72-82748. (A Pictorial History Ser.: Vol. 1). (Illus.). 48p. 1979. pap. 2.95 (ISBN 0-914606-01-8). Creative Bks.
Inersen, Edwin S. Farming the Edge of the Sea. 1978. 35.00 (ISBN 0-685-63406-X). State Mutual Bk.
Jones, Rodney. The Use of Marking Data in Fish Population Analysis. (FAO Fisheries Technical Paper: No. 153). (Illus.). 42p. 1976. pap. 7.50 (ISBN 92-5-100051-4, F886, FAO). Unipub.
Kreuzer, Rudolf, ed. Fish Inspection & Quality Control. 1978. 40.00 (ISBN 0-685-63411-6). State Mutual Bk.
--Freezing & Irradiation of Fish. 1978. 49.00 (ISBN 0-685-63424-8). State Mutual Bk.
MacKnight, C. C. The Voyage to Marege' Macassan Trepangers in Northern Australia. (Illus.). 1976. 27.50x (ISBN 0-522-84088-4, Pub. by Melbourne U Pr). Intl Schol Bk Serv.
The Marketing of Fish & Fishery Products in Europe: No. 4. France. (F. E. R. U. Occasional Paper Ser.: No. 2). 30p. 1981. pap. 8.50 (ISBN 0-686-72374-0, WFA 44, WFA). Unipub.
Mead, John T. Marine Refrigeration & Fish Preservation. rev. ed. LC 80-25359. (Illus.). 1980. 25.00 (ISBN 0-912524-19-7). Busn News.
Motte, G. A. & Iitaka, Y. Evaluation of Trawl Performance by Statistical Inference of the Catch. (Marine Technical Report Ser.: No. 36). 1975. pap. 2.00 (ISBN 0-938412-08-6). URI MAS.
Nowak, W. S. The Marketing of Shellfish. (Illus.). 280p. 22.50 (ISBN 0-85238-010-0, FN 59, FNB). Unipub.
OECD. Financial Support to the Fishing Industry. (Illus.). 161p. (Orig.). 1980. pap. 6.50x (ISBN 92-64-12087-4, 53-80-01-1). OECD.
Sainsbury, John C. Commercial Fishing Methods. 1978. 20.00 (ISBN 0-685-63396-9). State Mutual Bk.
Sullivan, Jeremiah J. & Heggelund, Per O. Foreign Investment in the U. S. Fishing Industry. LC 79-2074. (Pacific Rim Research Ser.: No. 3). 208p. 1979. 21.95 (ISBN 0-669-03066-X). Lexington Bks.
Usui, Atsushi. Eel Culture. 1978. 20.00 (ISBN 0-685-63400-0). State Mutual Bk.
Vibert, R., ed. Fishing with Electricity. 1978. 20.00 (ISBN 0-685-63422-1). State Mutual Bk.
Wolff, Thomas. In Pursuit of Tuna: The Expansion of a Fishing Industry & Its International Ramifications, the End of an Era. (Special Studies: 19). 1980. pap. text ed. 14.95 (ISBN 0-87918-047-1). ASU Lat Am St.

FISH WASTE

see Fishery Products

FISHER, DOROTHEA FRANCES (CANFIELD), 1879-1958

Yates, Elizabeth. Lady from Vermont: Dorothy Canfield Fisher's Life & World. rev. ed. LC 74-148629. Orig. Title: Pebble in a Pool. (Illus.). 1971. pap. 3.95 (ISBN 0-8289-0127-9). Greene.

FISHER, IRVING, 1867-1947

Gayer, A. D., ed. Lessons of Monetary Experience: Essays in Honor of Irving Fisher. LC 70-86089. Repr. of 1937 ed. 19.50x (ISBN 0-678-00643-1). Kelley.

FISHER, VARDIS, 1895-

Chatterton, Wayne. Vardis Fisher: The Frontier & Regional Works. LC 72-619585. (Western Writers Ser: No. 1). (Illus.). 51p. (Orig.). 1972. pap. 2.00 (ISBN 0-88430-000-5). Boise St Univ.
Day, George F. The Uses of History in the Novels of Vardis Fisher. (Vardis Fisher Ser). 1974. lib. bdg. 69.95 (ISBN 0-87700-225-8). Revisionist Pr.
Flora, Joseph M. Vardis Fisher. (Twayne's United States Authors Ser). 1965. pap. 3.45 (ISBN 0-8084-0311-7, T76, Twayne). Coll & U Pr.
--Vardis Fisher. (U. S. Authors Ser.: No. 76). 1965. lib. bdg. 12.50 (ISBN 0-8057-0252-0). Twayne.
Grover, Dorys C. A Solitary Voice: A Collection of Essays on Vardis Fisher. 1973. 69.95 (ISBN 0-87700-198-7). Revisionist Pr.
--Vardis Fisher: The Novelist As Poet. (Vardis Fisher Ser.). 1973. 69.95 (ISBN 0-87700-197-9). Revisionist Pr.
Strong, Lester. The Past in the Present: Essays on Vardis Fisher's Testament of Man. 1979. lib. bdg. 69.95 (ISBN 0-87700-266-5). Revisionist Pr.

FISHER FAMILY

Fisher, Sidney G. Philadelphia Perspective: The Diary of Sidney George Fisher. Wainwright, Nicholas B., ed. 1967. 12.50 (ISBN 0-910732-06-X). Pa Hist Soc.

FISHERIES

see also Cod-Fisheries; Fish Trade; Fishes; Electric Fishing; Fishing Boats; Lobster Fisheries; Trawls and Trawling

Across Beach Operations in the Small-Scale Fishery. (Fisheries Technical Paper: No. 157). 1977. pap. 8.00 (ISBN 92-5-100188-X, F889, FAO). Unipub.
Advisory Committee on Marine Resources Research, First Session, Rome, December 1974. Report. (FAO Fisheries Reports: No. 160). 18p. 1976. pap. 6.00 (ISBN 0-685-67377-4, FAO). Unipub.
Advisory Committee on Marine Resources Research, 8th Session, Sesimbra, Portugal, 1975. Report, Supplement One. (FAO Fisheries Reports: No. 171, Suppl. 1). 136p. 1976. pap. 9.50 (ISBN 0-685-67379-0, F821, FAO). Unipub.
Anderson, Lee G. The Economics of Fisheries Management. LC 76-47384. 1977. text ed. 16.50x (ISBN 0-8018-1913-X). Johns Hopkins.
Anderson, Lee G., ed. Economic Impacts of Extended Fisheries Jurisdiction. LC 76-46025. 1977. 36.00 (ISBN 0-250-40146-0). Ann Arbor Science.
The Artificial Propagation of Warm-Water Finfishes--a Manual for Extension. (FAO Fisheries Technical Paper: No. 201). 183p. 1981. pap. 12.50 (ISBN 92-5-100999-6, F2125, FAO). Unipub.
Aspects of Management of Inland Waters for Fisheries. (Fisheries Technical Paper: No. 161). (Illus.). 43p. 1977. pap. 7.50 (ISBN 92-5-100119-7, F893, FAO). Unipub.
An Assessment of the Fish Stocks & Fisheries of the Campeche Bank. (Western Central Atlantic Fishery Commission Studies: No. 5). 1976. pap. 7.50 (ISBN 92-5-100043-3, F 1213, FAO). Unipub.
Behrendt, Alex. The Management of Angling Waters. (Illus.). 1978. 15.00 (ISBN 0-233-96857-1). Transatlantic.
Biological Monitoring of Inland Fisheries. (Illus., Applied science pub). 1978. pap. 35.70 (ISBN 0-85334-719-0, AS 2, FAO). Unipub.
Blackford, Mansel G. Pioneering a Modern Small Business: Wakefield Seafoods & the Alaskan Frontier. Porter, Glenn, ed. LC 77-7794. (Industrial Development & the Social Fabric Ser.: Vol. 6). 222p. 1979. 29.50 (ISBN 0-686-74079-3). Jai Pr.
Bogdanov, A. S. Soviet-Cuban Fishery Research. 356p. 1973. 27.50x (ISBN 0-7065-1198-0, Pub. by IPST). Intl Schol Bk Serv.
Browning, Robert J. Fisheries of the North Pacific: History, Species, Gear & Processes. rev. ed. (Illus.). 432p. 1980. pap. 24.95 (ISBN 0-88240-128-9). Alaska Northwest.
Carlton, Frank E. Marine Recreational Fisheries, Vol. 3. Clepper, Henry, ed. LC 76-22389. 1978. 15.00 (ISBN 0-686-65030-1). Sport Fishing.
--Marine Recreational Fisheries, Vol. 4. Clepper, Henry, ed. LC 76-22389. 1979. 15.00 (ISBN 0-686-65031-X). Sport Fishing.
--Marine Recreational Fisheries, Vol. 5. Clepper, Henry, ed. LC 76-22389. 1980. 15.00 (ISBN 0-686-70340-5). Sport Fishing.
Childerhose, R. J. & Trim, Marj. Pacific Salmon & Steelhead Trout. LC 78-65830. (Illus.). 166p. 1979. pap. 14.95 (ISBN 0-295-95866-9). U of Wash Pr.
Committee on Fisheries, Ninth Session, Rome, October 15-22, 1974. Report. (FAO Fisheries Reports: No. 154). 39p. 1976. pap. 7.50 (ISBN 0-685-68359-1, F795, FAO). Unipub.
Comparative Studies on Fresh-Water Fisheries. (FAO Fisheries Technical Paper: No. 198). 54p. 1981. pap. 7.50 (ISBN 92-5-100952-X, F2085, FAO). Unipub.
Connell, J. J., ed. Advances in Fish Science & Technology. 528p. 1980. cloth 118.50x (ISBN 0-85238-108-5, Pub. by Fishing News England). State Mutual Bk.
Coordinating Working Party on Atlantic Fishery Statistics, 8th Session. Report. (FAO Fisheries Reports: No. 156). (Illus.). 39p. 1976. pap. 7.50 (ISBN 0-685-74969-X, F797, FAO). Unipub.
Crutchfield, James A. & Pontecorvo, Giulio. The Pacific Salmon Fisheries: A Study of Irrational Conservation. LC 72-75180. (Resources for the Future Ser). (Illus.). 220p. 1969. 14.00x (ISBN 0-8018-1025-6). Johns Hopkins.
Cushing. Science & the Fisheries. (Studies in Biology: No. 85). 1978. 5.95 (ISBN 0-7131-2674-4). Univ Park.
Cushing, D. H. Fisheries Biology: A Study in Population Dynamics. 2nd ed. LC 79-5405. (Illus.). 320p. 1981. 17.50 (ISBN 0-299-08110-9). U of Wis Pr.
--Marine Ecology & Fisheries. LC 74-82218. (Illus.). 228p. 1975. 52.50 (ISBN 0-521-20501-8); pap. 17.50x (ISBN 0-521-09911-0). Cambridge U Pr.
Cushing, David H. Fisheries Resources of the Sea & Their Management. (Science & Engineering Policy Ser). (Illus.). 100p. 1975. 12.95x (ISBN 0-19-858320-6). Oxford U Pr.
--Recruitment & Parent Stock in Fishes. (Washington Sea Grant). 197p. 1973. pap. 10.50 (ISBN 0-295-95311-X). U of Wash Pr.
Dipl-Ling, V. & Bensch, Erhard. Dictionary of Shipbuilding, Shipping & Fisheries. 784p. 1980. vinyl 150.00x (ISBN 0-686-30016-5, Pub. by Collet's). State Mutual Bk.
Directory of Fishing Institutions & Services. (FAO Fisheries Technical Paper Ser.: No. 205). 99p. 1980. pap. 7.50 (ISBN 92-5-001018-4, F2163, FAO). Unipub.

Economic Aspects of the Effects of Pollution on the Marine & Anadromous Fisheries of the Western United States of America. (FAO Fisheries Technical Paper: No. 162). (Illus.). 41p. 1977. pap. 7.50 (ISBN 92-5-100116-2, F894, FAO). Unipub.

Economic Evaluation of Sport & Commercial Fisheries. (EIFAC Technical Paper: No. 26). (Illus.). 1977. pap. 12.75 (ISBN 92-5-000256-4, F767, FAO). Unipub.

Environmental Analysis in Marine Fisheries Research. 1978. pap. 9.75 (ISBN 92-5-100494-3, F1341, FAO). Unipub.

Evaluation of the Fishery Resources of the Eastern Central Atlantic. (FAO Fisheries Reports: No. 183). 1977. pap. 9.00 (ISBN 92-5-100085-9, FAO). Unipub.

Evaluation of the Present State of World Trade in Ornamental Fish. (Fisheries Technical Paper: No. 146). 128p. 1976. pap. 9.00 (ISBN 0-685-68952-2, FAO). Unipub.

Everhart, W. Harry & Youngs, William D. Principles of Fishery Science. 2nd ed. (Illus.). 343p. 1981. 16.50 (ISBN 0-8014-1334-6). Cornell U Pr.

Expanding the Utilization of Marine Fishery Resources for Human Consumption. (Fisheries Reports: No. 175). (Illus.). 47p. 1976. pap. 7.50 (ISBN 0-685-67376-6, F825, FAO). Unipub.

Expert Consultation on Quantitative Analysis in Fishery Industries Development, 6vols. (Fisheries Report: No. 167). 1976. pap. 36.00 (ISBN 0-685-68953-0, FAO). Unipub.

FAO Species Catalogue, Vol. 1: Shrimps & Prawns of the World; an Annotated Catalogue of Species of Interest to Fisheries. (FAO Fisheries Synopsis Ser.: No. 125, Vol. 1). 287p. 1980. pap. 15.50 (ISBN 92-5-100896-5, F1939, FAO). Unipub.

Firth, Frank E. Encyclopedia of Marine Resources. (Illus.). 1969. 29.50 (ISBN 0-442-15610-3); pap. 15.95 (ISBN 0-442-22399-4). Van Nos Reinhold.

Fisheries & Aquatic Sciences in Canada: An Overview. (Fisheries Research Board of Canada Reports Ser.). 53p. 1979. pap. 4.75 (ISBN 0-660-01195-6, SSC 134, SSC). Unipub.

Fisheries in the Food Economy. (FFHC Basic Studies Ser.: No. 19). (Orig.). 1968. pap. 4.25 (ISBN 0-685-09380-8, F177, FAO). Unipub.

Fishery Committee for the Eastern Central Atlantic (CECAF) Working Party on Resources Evaluation, Rome, 1973. Report. (Illus.). 92p. 1976. pap. 7.50 (ISBN 0-685-66351-5, F800, FAO). Unipub.

Fishery Management in Large Rivers. (Fisheries Technical Paper: No. 194). 1979. pap. 7.50 (ISBN 92-5-100764-0, F1637, FAO). Unipub.

Freezing in Fisheries. (FAO Fisheries Technical Paper: No. 167). (Illus.). 1978. pap. 7.50 (ISBN 92-5-100327-0, F899, FAO). Unipub.

General Fisheries Council for the Mediterranean. Proceedings & Technical Papers, Vol. 10. (Orig.). 1970. pap. 6.00 (ISBN 0-685-04910-8, FAO). Unipub.

--Proceedings & Technical Papers, Vol. 11. 71p. (Orig.). 1973. pap. 6.00 (ISBN 0-685-32470-2, FAO). Unipub.

--Report of the First Session of the Working Party on Acoustic Methods for Fish Detection & Abundance Estimation of the General Fisheries Council for the Mediterranean. (FAO Fisheries Report: No. 231). 27p. 1980. pap. 7.50 (ISBN 92-5-100928-7, F2039, FAO). Unipub.

Glossary of Inland Fishery Terms. (EIFAC Occasional Papers: No. 12). 129p. 1979. pap. 8.50 (ISBN 92-5-000724-8, F1558, FAO). Unipub.

Goals & Objectives of Fishery Management. (FAO Fisheries Technical Paper: No. 166). 14p. 1977. pap. 7.50 (ISBN 92-5-100281-9, F898, FAO). Unipub.

Government Consultation on Codes of Practice for Fish & Fishery Products, Rome, October, 1975. Report. (FAO Fisheries Reports: No. 173). 6p. 1976. pap. 7.50 (ISBN 0-685-68360-5, F823, FAO). Unipub.

Government Consultation on Codes of Practice for Fish & Fishery Products. Report. (FAO Fisheries Report: No. 155). 5p. 1976. pap. 7.50 (ISBN 0-685-68965-4, F796, FAO). Unipub.

Gray, Malcom. The Fishing Industries of Scotland 1790-1914: A Study in Regional Adaptation. LC 78-40244. 1978. 26.00x (ISBN 0-19-714105-6). Oxford U Pr.

Gregory, Homer E. & Barnes, Kathleen. North Pacific Fisheries, with Special Reference to Alaska Salmon. 1976. Repr. of 1939 ed. 19.00 (ISBN 0-527-35850-9). Kraus Repr.

Gulland, J. A. Manual of Methods for Fish Stock Assessment, Pt. 1: Fish Population Analysis. (FAO Manuals in Fisheries Science Ser.: No. 4). (Illus., Orig.). 1969. pap. 12.25 (ISBN 92-5-100204-5, F262, FAO). Unipub.

Haley, K. Brian, ed. Applied Operations Research in Fishing. (NATO Conference Series II-Systems Science: Vol. 10). 490p. 1981. 59.50 (ISBN 0-306-40634-9, Plenum Pr). Plenum Pub.

Hannesson, Rognvaldur. Fisheries Economics. 1979. pap. 23.00x (ISBN 82-00-05217-6, Dist. by Columbia U Pr.). Universitet.

Hart, Paul & Pitcher, Tony. Fisheries Ecology. 224p. 1980. 35.00x (ISBN 0-85664-894-9, Pub. by Croom Helm England). State Mutual Bk.

Hazleton, J. E. & Bell, F. W. Recent Developments & Research in Fisheries Economics. LC 66-27364. 288p. 1967. 15.00 (ISBN 0-379-00317-1). Oceana.

Hela, Ilmo & Laevastu, Taivo. Fisheries Oceanography. 1978. 26.00 (ISBN 0-685-63413-2). State Mutual Bk.

Hjul, P., ed. Fish Farming International, No. 2. 1978. 15.00 (ISBN 0-685-63410-8). State Mutual Bk.

Ice in Fisheries. (FAO Fisheries Reports: No. 59, Revision 1). (Illus.). 57p. 1975. pap. 7.50 (ISBN 0-685-55203-9, F779, FAO). Unipub.

Implementation of the International Indian Ocean Fishery Survey & Development Programme. (FAO Fisheries Reports: No. 180). 21p. 1977. pap. 7.50 (ISBN 0-686-67661-0, F828, FAO). Unipub.

Indian Ocean Fishery Comminssion, Fourth Session, Mombasa, Kenya, July 21-25, 1975. Report. (FAO Fisheries Report Ser.: No.166). 27p. 1976. pap. 7.50 (ISBN 0-685-66330-2, F808, FAO). Unipub.

Indian Ocean Fishery Commission. Report: Fourth Session, July 21-25, 1975, Mombasa, Kenya. (FAO Fisheries Reports: No. 166). 27p. 1976. pap. 7.50 (ISBN 0-685-65011-1, F808, FAO). Unipub.

International Cooperation in Fishery Development in Developing Countries. (FAO Fisheries Report Ser: No. 201). 47p. 1978. pap. 7.50 (ISBN 92-5-100482-X, F1414, FAO). Unipub.

International Directory of Fish Technology Institutes. rev. ed. (Fisheries Technical Papers: No. 152, Rev. 1). 114p. 1980. pap. 7.50 (ISBN 92-5-101002-1, F 2031, FAO). Unipub.

Johnson, Ralph W. & Van Cleve, Richard. Management of the High Seas Fisheries of the Northeastern Pacific. (University of Washington Publications in Fisheries Ser.: No. 2). 186p. 1963. pap. 5.00 (ISBN 0-295-95220-2). U of Wash Pr.

Johnstone, Kenneth. The Aquatic Explorers: A History of the Fisheries Research Board of Canada. 1977. 25.00x (ISBN 0-8020-2270-7). U of Toronto Pr.

Kasahara, Hiroshi & Burke, William. North Pacific Fisheries Management. LC 77-86401. (Program of International Studies of Fishery Arrangements. Papers: No. 2). Repr. of 1973 ed. 14.00 (ISBN 0-404-60337-8). AMS Pr.

Konovalov, S. M. Differentiation of Local Populations of Sockeye Salmon Oncorhynchus Nerka. Sagen, Leda V., tr. from Rus. LC 75-14733. (Publications in Fisheries, Ser.: No. 6). (Illus.). 256p. (Orig.). 1975. pap. text ed. 12.50 (ISBN 0-295-95406-X). U of Wash Pr.

Korringa, P. Farming Cupped Oysters of the Genus Crassostrea. (Developments in Aquaculture & Fisheries Science Ser.: Vol. 2). 1976. 39.00 (ISBN 0-444-41333-2). Elsevier.

--Farming Marine Organisms Low in the Food Chain. (Developments in Aquaculture & Fisheries Science: Vol. 1). 1976. 39.00 (ISBN 0-444-41332-4). Elsevier.

--Farming the Flat Oyster of the Genus Ostrea. (Developments in Aquaculture & Fisheries Science Ser.: Vol. 3). 1976. 39.00 (ISBN 0-444-41334-0). Elsevier.

Lackey, Robert T. Fisheries Management. LC 80-20028. 422p. 1980. 34.95 (ISBN 0-470-27056-X). Halsted Pr.

Laevastu, Taivo & Hayes, Murray L. Fisheries Oceanography & Ecology. 1981. 75.00x (ISBN 0-686-75649-5, Pub. by Fishing News England). State Mutual Bk.

Laevastu, Taivo & Larkins, Herbert A. Marine Fisheries Ecosystem: Its Quantitative Evaluation & Management. 1981. 65.00x (ISBN 0-85238-116-6, Pub. by Fishing News England). State Mutual Bk.

Lang, Varley. Follow the Water. LC 61-16637. (Illus.). 1961. 6.95 (ISBN 0-910244-24-3). Blair.

Larssen, A. K. & Jaeger, Sig. The ABC's of Fo'c'sle Living. LC 76-17265. (Illus.). 1976. pap. 4.95 (ISBN 0-914842-11-0). Madrona Pubs.

Lewis, Tracy R. Stochastic Modeling of Ocean Fisheries Resource Management. LC 81-51282. (Illus.). 160p. 1981. 25.00 (ISBN 0-295-95838-3). U of Wash Pr.

Mack, Jerry. Catfish Farming Handbook. LC 76-174495. 1971. 12.95 (ISBN 0-912092-39-4). Educator Bks.

Manual of Fisheries Science, Pt. 2: Methods of Resource Investigation & Their Application. (FAO Fisheries Technical Paper Ser.: No. 115, Rev. 1). 224p. Date not set. pap. 17.50 (ISBN 92-5-100842-6, F854, FAO). Unipub.

Manual of Methods for Fish Stock Assessment, Pt. II: Tables of Yield Functions. rev. ed. (FAO Fisheries Technical Paper Ser.: No. 38, Rev. 1). 1980. pap. 7.50 (ISBN 92-5-000840-6, F848, FAO). Unipub.

Manual of Methods for Fisheries Resource Survey & Appraisal, Pt. 2: The Use of Acoustic Instruments for Fish Detection & Abundance estimation. (FAO Manuals in Fisheries Science Ser.: No. 5). (Illus.). 138p. (Orig.). 1973. pap. 10.00 (ISBN 0-685-32313-7, F263, FAO). Unipub.

Manual of Methods for Fisheries Resource Survey & Appraisal, Part Five: Objectives & Basic Methods. (FAO Fisheries Technical Papers: No.145). (Illus.). 29p. 1976. pap. 7.50 (ISBN 0-685-66356-6, F876, FAO). Unipub.

Manual on Fishermen's Cooperatives. 124p. (Orig.). 1971. pap. 9.25 (ISBN 0-685-30137-0, F264, FAO). Unipub.

Manual on the Identification & Preparation of Fishery Investment Projects. (Fisheries Technical Paper: No. 149). 1976. pap. 7.50 (ISBN 0-685-71575-2, F882, FAO). Unipub.

Marr, John C. Fishery & Resource Management in Southeast Asia. LC 75-36946. (Resources for the Future Ser). 76p. 1976. pap. 5.00x (ISBN 0-8018-1826-5). Johns Hopkins.

Mechanics of Tuna Research & Management. (FAO Fisheries Reports: No. 184). 8p. 1976. pap. 7.50 (ISBN 92-5-100045-X, F832, FAO). Unipub.

Meltzer, Michael. The World of the Small Commercial Fishermen: Their Lives & Their Boats. (Illus.). 1980. pap. 4.95 (ISBN 0-486-23945-4). Dover.

Methods of Measuring Stock Abundance Other Than by the Use of Commercial Catch & Effort Data. 30p. 1978. pap. 7.50 (ISBN 92-5-100397-1, F1323, FAO). Unipub.

Miles, Edward. Organizational Arrangements to Facilitate Global Management of Fisheries. LC 73-20844. (Rff Program of International Studies of Fisheries Arrangements: No. 4). 36p. 1974. pap. 3.00x (ISBN 0-8018-1612-2). Johns Hopkins.

Milne, P. H. Fish & Shellfish Farming in Coastal Waters. 1978. 29.00 (ISBN 0-685-63408-6). State Mutual Bk.

Monitoring of Fish Stock Abundance: The Use of Catch & Effort Data. (FAO Fisheries Technical Paper: No. 155). (Illus.). 1976. pap. 7.50 (ISBN 92-5-100050-6, F888, FAO). Unipub.

Mundt, J. Carl, ed. Limited Entry into the Commercial Fisheries. Institute for Marine Studies. 154p. 1976. pap. 5.50 (ISBN 0-295-95496-5). U of Wash Pr.

OECD. Financial Support to the Fishing Industry. (Illus.). 161p. (Orig.). 1980. pap. 6.50x (ISBN 92-64-12087-4, 53-80-01-1). OECD.

--Review of Fisheries in OECD Member Countries Nineteen Seventy-Nine. (Illus.). 253p. (Orig.). 1980. pap. 12.00x (ISBN 92-64-12103-X). OECD.

O'Farrell, R. C. Seafood Fishing for Amateur & Professional. 1978. 15.00 (ISBN 0-685-63452-3). State Mutual Bk.

Porpoise, Dolphin & Small Whale Fisheries of the World: Status & Problems. (Illus.). 1975. pap. 10.50x (ISBN 2-88032-027-5, IUCN6, IUCN). Unipub.

Report of the ACMRR Working Party on the Scientific Basis of Determining Management Measures. (FAO Fisheries Report Ser.: No. 236). 149p. 1980. pap. 11.75 (ISBN 92-5-100938-4, F2051, FAO). Unipub.

Report of the Eleventh Session of the Committee on Fisheries. (FAO Fisheries Reports Ser: No. 196). 1978. pap. 7.50 (ISBN 92-5-100336-X, F1178, FAO). Unipub.

Report of the Eleventh Session of the European Inland Fisheries Advisory Commission. (FAO Fisheries Report Ser.: No. 248). 56p. 1981. pap. 7.50 (ISBN 92-5-101062-5, F2181, FAO). Unipub.

Report of the FAO-ADAA Workshop on the Management of Small Scale Fishery Enterprises. (Australian Funds Funds-in-Trust Ser). 24p. 1977. pap. 7.50 (ISBN 92-5-100290-8, F1262, FAO). Unipub.

Report of the Fifteenth FAO Regional Conference for Asia & the Pacific. 97p. 1981. pap. 7.50 (ISBN 92-5-100963-5, F2084, FAO). Unipub.

Report of the Fifteenth Session of the General Fisheries Council for the Mediterranean 15. 91p. 1980. pap. 11.25 (ISBN 92-5-101026-9, F2126, FAO). Unipub.

Report of the Fifth Session of the Fishing Committee for the Eastern Central Atlantic (CECAF) (Fisheries Reports: No. 195). 1978. pap. 7.50 (ISBN 92-5-100308-4, FAO). Unipub.

Report of the Fourth Joint Meeting of the Indo-Pacific Fisheries Council & the Indian Ocean Fishery Commission. (Fisheries Report: No. 190). 12p. 1977. pap. 7.50 (ISBN 92-5-100251-7, F838, FAO). Unipub.

Report of the Fourth Session of the Working Party on Resource Evaluation of the CECAF Evaluation of the Fishery Resources of the Eastern Central Atlantic. (FAO Fisheries Reports: No. 220). 203p. pap. 13.25 (ISBN 92-5-100800-0, F1873, FAO). Unipub.

Report of the Joint Meeting of the Western Central Atlantic Fishery Commission Working Party on Assessment of Fishery Resources & Working Party on Stock Assessment of Shrimp & Lobster Resources. (FAO Fisheries Reports Ser.: No. 211). 1979. pap. 7.50 (ISBN 92-5-100675-X, F1543, FAO). Unipub.

Report of the Second Session of the Indian Ocean Fishery Commission Committee for the Development & Management of Fishery Resources of the Gulfs. (FAO Fisheries Report Ser.: No. 223). 19p. 1980. pap. 7.50 (ISBN 92-5-100841-8, F 1895, FAO). Unipub.

Report of the Second Session of the Western Central Atlantic Fishery Commission. (FAO Fishery Reports Ser.: No. 209). 48p. 1979. pap. 7.50 (ISBN 92-5-100665-2, F1537, FAO). Unipub.

Report of the Sixth Session of the Fishery Committee for the Eastern Central Atlantic (CECAF) (FAO Fisheries Report: No. 229). 70p. 1980. pap. 7.50 (ISBN 92-5-100900-7, F1952, FAO). Unipub.

Report of the Sixth Session of the Indian Ocean Fishery Commission. (FAO Fisheries Report: No. 234). 35p. 1981. pap. 7.50 (ISBN 92-5-100930-9, F2088, FAO). Unipub.

Report of the Sixth Session of the Indian Ocean Fishery Commission Executive Committee for the Implementation of the International Indian Ocean Fishery Survey & Development Program. (FAO Fisheries Reports Ser.: No. 198). 17p. 1978. pap. 7.50 (ISBN 92-5-100506-0, F1339, FAO). Unipub.

Report of the Symposium on Finfish Nutrition & Feed Technology. (EIFAC Technical Paper Ser.: No. 31). 1979. pap. 7.50 (ISBN 92-5-100642-3, F1514, FAO). Unipub.

Report of the Technical Consultation of Stock Assessment in the Adriatic. (FAO Fisheries Report Ser.: No. 239). 68p. 1980. pap. 7.50 (ISBN 92-5-100970-8, F2144, FAO). Unipub.

Report of the Tenth Session Coordinating Working Party on Atlantic Fishery Statistics. (FAO Fisheries Report Ser.: No. 242). 65p. pap. 7.50 (ISBN 92-5-101010-2, F2164, FAO). Unipub.

Report of the Tenth Session of the European Inland Fisheries Advisory Commission. (Fisheries Reports Ser.: No. 219). 1979. pap. 7.50 (ISBN 92-5-100771-3, F1638, FAO). Unipub.

Report of the Third Session of the Committee on Resource Management of the General Fisheries Council for the Mediterranean. (FAO Fisheries Report: No. 240). 20p. 1981. pap. 7.50 (ISBN 92-5-100966-X, F2087, FAO). Unipub.

Report of the Third Session of the Western Central Atlantic Fishery Commission. (FAO Fisheries Report Ser.: No. 246). 44p. 1981. pap. 7.50 (ISBN 92-5-101044-7, F2182, FAO). Unipub.

Report of the Thirteenth Session of the Committee on Fisheries. (FAO Fisheries Reports Ser.: No. 228). 51p. 1980. pap. 9.00 (ISBN 92-5-100877-9, F 1896, FAO). Unipub.

Report on the Training Course on Quality Aspects in the Handling & Storage of Fish. (Danish Funds-in-Trust Ser.: No. 143). 26p. 1975. pap. 7.50 (ISBN 0-685-55200-4, F1094, FAO). Unipub.

Report on the Twelfth Session of the Committee on Fisheries. (FAO Fisheries Report Ser.: No. 208). 1979. pap. 7.50 (ISBN 92-5-100656-3, F1518, FAO). Unipub.

Rettig, R. Bruce & Ginter, Jay J., eds. Limited Entry as a Fishery Management Tool. (Washington Sea Grant Ser.). 584p. 1980. pap. 15.00 (ISBN 0-295-95741-7). U of Wash Pr.

Review of Fisheries in OECD Member Countries, 1978. 259p. 1979. 11.00x (ISBN 92-64-11978-7). OECD.

A Review of the Fishery Resources in the Western Central Atlantic. (WECAF Studies Ser: No. 3). (Illus.). 1976. pap. 7.50 (ISBN 92-5-100015-8, F1212, FAO). Unipub.

Ricker, William E. Methods of Estimating Vital Statistics of Fish Populations. LC 48-45487. 1948. pap. 5.00 (ISBN 0-527-75280-0). Kraus Repr.

Royce, William F. Introduction to Fishery Sciences. 351p. 1972. text ed. 22.50 (ISBN 0-12-600950-3). Acad Pr.

Russell-Hunter, W. D. Aquatic Productivity: An Introduction to Some Basic Aspects of Biological Oceanography & Limnology. (Illus.). 1970. text ed. 9.95x (ISBN 0-685-04258-8); pap. 8.95 (ISBN 0-02-404920-4). Macmillan.

Saila, Saul B. & Norton, Virgil J. Tuna: Status, Trends, & Alternative Management Arrangements. LC 73-20846. (Rff Program of International Studies of Fisheries Arrangements: No. 6). 70p. 1974. pap. 3.00x (ISBN 0-8018-1614-9). Johns Hopkins.

Saila, Saul B., ed. Fisheries & Energy Production. LC 74-32513. 1975. 18.95 (ISBN 0-669-98467-1). Lexington Bks.

Smith, M. Estellie. Those Who Live from the Sea: A Study in Maritime Anthropology. (AES Ser.). (Illus.). 1977. text ed. 20.95 (ISBN 0-8299-0139-6). West Pub.

Some Problems of the Management of Shared Stocks. (FAO Fisheries Technical Paper Ser.: No.206). 22p. 1980. pap. 7.50 (ISBN 92-5-101022-6, F2149, FAO). Unipub.

Some Scientific Problems of Multispecies Fisheries: Report of the Expert Consultation on Management of Multispecies Fisheries. (FAO Fisheries Technical Paper Ser: No. 181). 1978. pap. 7.50 (ISBN 92-5-100573-7, F1419, FAO). Unipub.

Stansby, Maurice E. Industrial Fishery Technology. LC 76-3655. 428p. 1976. Repr. of 1963 ed. 22.50 (ISBN 0-88275-305-3). Krieger.

Stroud, Richard H. Marine Recreational Fisheries. Clepper, Henry, ed. 1976. 15.00 (ISBN 0-686-21852-3); pap. 12.00 (ISBN 0-686-21853-1). Sport Fishing.

Stroud, Richard H. & Clepper, Henry, eds. Marine Recreational Fisheries: A Symposium, Vol. 2. LC 76-22389. 1977. 15.00 (ISBN 0-686-22998-3). Sport Fishing.

Sullivan, Jeremiah J. & Heggelund, Per O. Foreign Investment in the U. S. Fishing Industry. LC 79-2074. (Pacific Rim Research Ser.: No. 3). 208p. 1979. 21.95 (ISBN 0-669-03066-X). Lexington Bks.

Symposium on the Oceanography & Fisheries Resources of the Tropical Atlantic, Abidjan, 1966. Proceedings. LC 55-4606. (Illus.). 1969. 18.75 (ISBN 92-3-000749-8, U490, UNESCO). Unipub.

Thomas, Gordon W. Fast & Able, Life Stories of Great Gloucester Fishing Schooners. new ed. Kenyon, Paul B., ed. LC 72-97362. (Illus.). 1973. 4.95 (ISBN 0-930352-01-7). Nelson B Robinson.

Toward a Relevant Science: Fisheries & Aquatic Scientific Resource Needs in Canada. (Fisheries Research Board of Canada Reports Ser: No. 14). 29p. 1978. pap. 5.50 (ISBN 0-685-60676-7, SSC 103, SSC). Unipub.

Trilingual Dictionary of Fisheries Technological Terms-Curing. (FAO Fisheries Ser.: No. 12). 91p. 1980. pap. 11.50 (ISBN 0-686-68188-6, F483, FAO). Unipub.

Types of Parastatal Bodies Concerned with Fisheries Development & Their Financial Responsibilities. (FAO Fisheries Technical Paper Ser: No. 179). 39p. pap. 7.50 (ISBN 92-5-100560-5, F1433, FAO). Unipub.

Welcomme, Robin L. Fisheries Ecology of Floodplain Rivers. (Illus.). 1979. text ed. 50.00x (ISBN 0-582-46310-6). Longman.

Wharton, James. Bounty of the Chesapeake: Fishing in Colonial Virginia. (Illus., Orig.). 1957. pap. 1.95x (ISBN 0-8139-0137-5). U Pr of Va.

White, Donald J. New England Fishing Industry: A Study in Price & Wage Setting. LC 54-7065. (Wertheim Publications in Industrial Relations Ser). (Illus.). 1954. 10.00x (ISBN 0-674-61200-0). Harvard U Pr.

Workshop on the Management of Small-Scale Fishery Enterprises. 28p. 1977. pap. 7.50 (ISBN 92-5-100290-8, F1262, FAO). Unipub.

World List of Aquatic Sciences & Fisheries Serial Titles. (FAO Fisheries Technical Paper Ser.: No. 147, Suppl. 3). 1979. pap. 10.50 (ISBN 92-5-100617-2, F 1490, FAO). Unipub.

Yearbook of Fishery Statistics: Catches & Landings, Vol. 48. 384p. 1980. 43.25 (ISBN 0-686-74541-8, F2147, FAO). Unipub.

Yearbook of Fishery Statistics 1973: Catches & Landings, Vol. 36. 590p. 1975. pap. 34.25 (ISBN 0-685-55205-5, FAO). Unipub.

Yearbook of Fishery Statistics 1973: Fishery Commodities, Vol. 37. 326p. 1975. pap. 19.25 (ISBN 0-685-55204-7, FAO). Unipub.

Yearbook of Fishery Statistics, 1977. (Fishery Commodities Ser.: Vol. 45). 1979. 28.00 (ISBN 92-0-000610-8, F1560, FAO). Unipub.

FISHERIES–BIBLIOGRAPHY

Bibliography of Living Marine Resources. (Regional Fishery Survey & Development Project Ser). 47p. 1977. pap. 7.50 (ISBN 92-5-100200-2, F727, FAO). Unipub.

Douglas, Kimberly & Cowger, Joel D. Maine Department of Marine Resources Index to Publications 1946-1978. (Fisheries Information Ser.: No. 3). (Illus.). 1979. pap. write for info. (ISBN 0-89737-002-3). Maine Dept Marine.

World List of Aquatic Sciences & Fisheries Serial Titles. (FAO Fisheries Technical Paper: No. 147). 128p. 1980. pap. 8.50 (ISBN 92-5-100904-X, F1946, FAO). Unipub.

World List of Aquatic Sciences & Fisheries Serial Titles. (FAO Fisheries Technical Paper: No. 148). 128p. 1980. pap. 7.50 (ISBN 92-5-000882-1, F1947, FAO). Unipub.

World List of Aquatic Sciences & Fisheries Serial Titles. (FAO Fisheries Technical Papers: No.147). 243p. 1976. pap. 16.25 (ISBN 0-685-66345-0, F878, FAO). Unipub.

World List of Aquatic Sciences & Fisheries Serial Titles. (Fisheries Technical Paper Ser.: No. 147, Suppl. 1). 1977. pap. 11.50 (ISBN 92-5-100124-3, F879, FAO). Unipub.

World List of Aquatic Sciences & Fisheries Serial Titles, Suppl. 2. (FAO Fisheries Technical Paper: No. 147). (Illus.). 1978. pap. 10.50 (ISBN 92-5-100341-6, F880, FAO). Unipub.

FISHERIES–EQUIPMENT AND SUPPLIES

see also Fishing–Implements and Appliances

IPFC-IOFC Joint Working Party of Experts on Indian Ocean & Western Pacific Fishery Statistics, 3rd Session. Report. (FAO Fisheries Reports: No. 157). (Illus.). 1976. pap. 7.50 (ISBN 0-685-74970-3, F798, FAO). Unipub.

Tucker, D. G. Sonar in Fisheries: A Forward Look. 1978. 19.50 (ISBN 0-685-63455-8). State Mutual Bk.

FISHERIES–JUVENILE LITERATURE

Brooks, Anita. Picture Book of Fisheries. (Picture Aids to World Geography Ser). (Illus.). (gr. 4-7). 1961. 6.89 (ISBN 0-381-99935-1, A61210, JD-J). Har-Row.

Floethe, Louise L. Fishing Around the World. LC 72-498. (Illus.). 40p. (gr. 1-3). 1972. write for info. (ISBN 0-684-12948-5, ScribJ). Scribner.

Ross, Frank, Jr. Jobs in Marine Science. LC 73-17719. (Exploring Careers Ser.). (Illus.). 96p. (gr. 5 up). 1974. 7.25 (ISBN 0-688-75013-3). Lothrop.

Zim, Herbert S. & Krantz, Lucretia. Commercial Fishing. LC 73-4931. (Illus.). 64p. (gr. 3-7). 1973. 6.75 (ISBN 0-688-20091-5); PLB 6.48 (ISBN 0-688-30091-X); pap. 1.25 (ISBN 0-688-05267-3). Morrow.

FISHERIES–LAW

see Fishery Law and Legislation

FISHERIES–STATISTICS

The Fish Resources of the Eastern Central Atlantic: Part 1, The Resources of the Gulf of Guinea from Angola to Mauritania. (Fisheries Technical Paper: No. 186). 171p. 1981. pap. 11.00 (ISBN 92-5-100851-5, F2028, FAO). Unipub.

Indo-Pacific Fishery Commission Working Party of Experts on Central & Western Pacific Skipjack. (FAO Fisheries Report Ser.: No. 224). 12p. 1980. pap. 7.50 (ISBN 92-5-100843-4, F1892, FAO). Unipub.

Mathematics for Fishery Statisticians. (FAO Fisheries Technical Paper: No. 169). 1978. pap. 12.25 (ISBN 92-5-100314-9, F1241, FAO). Unipub.

Nineteen Seventy-Six Yearbook of Fishery Statistics. (Fisheries Ser. No. 7, Fishery Commodities Vol. 43). 1978. pap. 26.50 (ISBN 92-5-000414-1, F1363, FAO). Unipub.

Nominal Catches, 1964-1974. (CECAF Statistical Bulletin: No. 1). 1977. pap. 12.75 (ISBN 92-5-000095-2, FAO). Unipub.

Report of the Eleventh Session of the Committee on Fisheries. (FAO Fisheries Reports Ser: No. 196). 1978. pap. 7.50 (ISBN 92-5-100336-X, F1178, FAO). Unipub.

Report of the First Session of the Working Party on Fishery Statistics: Fishery Committee for the Eastern Central Atlantic (CECAF) (FAO Fisheries Report Ser.: No. 245). 141p. 1981. pap. 9.50 (ISBN 92-5-101056-0, F2135, FAO). Unipub.

Report of the First Session of the Working Party on Fishery Statistics. (FAO Fishery Reports: No. 212). 1979. pap. 6.00 (ISBN 92-5-100698-9, F1575, FAO). Unipub.

Report of the Second Joint Meeting of the Working Party on Assessment of Fish Resources & the Working Party on Stock Assessment of Shrimp & Lobster Resources (WECAF) (FAO Fisheries Report Ser.: No. 235). 41p. 1981. pap. 7.50 (ISBN 92-5-101049-8, F2143, FAO). Unipub.

Report of the Technical Consultation on the Assessment & Management of the Black Sea Turbot (GFCM) Working Party on Resource Evaluation & Fishery Statistics. 23p. 1980. pap. 9.00 (ISBN 92-5-100879-5, F1964, FAO). Unipub.

Report on the Ninth Session - Coordinating Working Party on Atlantic Fishery Statistics. (Fisheries Report: No. 197). (Illus.). 44p. 1978. pap. 7.50 (ISBN 92-5-100421-8, F1306, FAO). Unipub.

Working Party on Resources Appraisal & Fishery Statistics of the General Fisheries Council for the Mediterranean, 6th Session. Report. (FAO Fisheries Report: No. 182). (Illus.). 1976. pap. 9.25 (ISBN 92-5-100027-1, F203, FAO). Unipub.

Yearbook of Fishery Statistics. annual Incl. Vol. 4, Pt. 1. Production & Craft, 1952-53. 1955; Vol. 5. Production & Fishing Craft, 1954-55. 1956; Vol. 6. Production & Fishing Craft, 1955-56. 1957; Vol. 8. International Trade, 1957. 1959; Vol. 22. Catches & Landings, 1966. 1967. pap. 16.25 (ISBN 0-685-48272-3); Vol. 23. Fishery Commodities, 1966. 1967. pap. 24.00 (ISBN 0-685-48273-1); Vol. 24. Catches & Landings, 1967. 1968. pap. 15.00 (ISBN 0-685-48274-X); Vol. 25. Fishery Commodities, 1967. 1968. pap. 20.00 (ISBN 0-685-48275-8); Vol. 26. Catches & Landings, 1968. 1969. pap. 10.25 (ISBN 0-685-48276-6); Vol. 27. Fishery Commodities, 1968. 1969. pap. 16.25 (ISBN 0-685-48277-4); Vol. 28. Catches & Landings, 1969. 1970. pap. 14.25 (ISBN 0-685-48278-2); Vol. 31. Fishery Commodities, 1970. 1971. pap. 22.25 (ISBN 0-685-48279-0); Vol. 32. Catches & Landings, 1971. 1972. pap. 21.00 (ISBN 0-685-48280-4); Vol. 33. Fishery Commodities, 1971. 1972. pap. 12.00 (ISBN 0-685-48281-2); Vol. 34. Catches & Landings, 1972. 1973. pap. 24.00 (ISBN 0-685-48282-0); Vol. 35. Fishery Commodities, 1972. 1973. pap. 14.50 (ISBN 0-685-48283-9). (Orig., FAO). Unipub.

Yearbook of Fishery Statistics: Catches & Landings, Vol. 42. (Illus.). 1978. 26.50 (ISBN 92-5-000413-3, F1331, FAO). Unipub.

Yearbook of Fishery Statistics: Catches & Landings, 1975, Vol. 40. (FAO Fisheries Ser). (Illus.). 1977. pap. 28.00 (ISBN 0-685-80151-9, F553, FAO). Unipub.

Yearbook of Fishery Statistics: Fishery & Commodities, Vol. 41. (FAO Fisheries Ser). (Illus.). 1977. pap. 20.50 (ISBN 0-685-80152-7, FAO). Unipub.

Yearbook of Fishery Statistics, 1970-1978: Vol. 47, Fishery Commodities. 277p. 1980. 28.25 (ISBN 92-5-000834-1, F 1903, FAO). Unipub.

Yearbook of Fishery Statistics 1974: Catches and Landings, Vol. 38. 1976. pap. 36.00 (ISBN 0-685-68362-1, FAO). Unipub.

Yearbook of Fishery Statistics 1974: Fishery Commodities, Vol. 39. 330p. 1976. 24.00 (ISBN 0-685-68363-X, FAO). Unipub.

Yearbook of Fishery Statistics 1977: Catches & Landings. (Fisheries Ser.: No. 44). 1979. 28.00 (ISBN 92-5-000609-8, F1552, FAO). Unipub.

FISHERIES–AFRICA

Crutchfield, James A. & Lawson, Rowena. West African Marine Fisheries: Alternatives for Management. LC 73-20843. (Rresources for the Future Program of International Studies of Fisheries Arrangements: No. 3). 78p. 1974. pap. 3.00x (ISBN 0-8018-1611-4). Johns Hopkins.

Papers Presented at the FAO-SIDA Workshop on the Use of Organic Materials As Fertilizers in Africa: Organic Recycling in Africa. 308p. 1981. pap. 20.00 (ISBN 92-5-100945-7, F2096, FAO). Unipub.

Report of the Third Session of the Committee for Inland Fisheries of Africa. (Fisheries Reports Ser.: No. 210). 28p. 1979. pap. 7.50 (ISBN 0-685-95366-1, F1548, FAO). Unipub.

Report on the CIDA - FAO - CEDAF Seminar on the Cnanging Law of the Sea & the Fisheries of West Africa. 1979. pap. 10.75 (ISBN 92-5-100634-2, F 1500, FAO). Unipub.

Role of Fishery Technology in the Management & Development of Freshwater Fisheries in Africa. (CIFA Technical Paper Ser.: No. 6). 71p. 1980. pap. 9.00 (ISBN 92-5-100831-0, F 1888, FAO). Unipub.

Symposium on River & Floodplain Fisheries in Africa. (CIFA Technical Papers: No. 5). 1979. pap. 23.75 (ISBN 92-5-000674-8, F1561, FAO). Unipub.

FISHERIES–ASIA

Aquaculture Development in China: Report on an FAO-UNEP Aquaculture Study Tour to the People's Republic of China. 73p. 1980. pap. 7.50 (ISBN 92-5-100811-6, F1861, FAO). Unipub.

Chen, T. P. Aquaculture Practices in Taiwan. 1978. 16.00x (ISBN 0-685-63392-6). State Mutual Bk.

Fisheries & Aquaculture in the People's Republic of China. 32p. 1980. pap. 5.00 (ISBN 0-88936-189-4, IDRC 115, IDRC). Unipub.

Management of Asian Reservoir Fisheries. (FAO Fisheries Technical Paper Ser.: No. 207). 69p. 1980. pap. 7.50 (ISBN 92-5-101023-4, F2156, FAO). Unipub.

FISHERIES–AUSTRALIA

MacKnight, C. C. The Voyage to Marege' Macassan Trepangers in Northern Australia. (Illus.). 1976. 27.50x (ISBN 0-522-84088-4, Pub. by Melbourne U Pr). Intl Schol Bk Serv.

Pownall, Peter. Fisheries of Australia. (Illus.). 160p. 1979. 27.25 (ISBN 0-85238-101-8, FN 79, FNB). Unipub.

--Fisheries of Australia. 1978. 40.00x (ISBN 0-685-63414-0). State Mutual Bk.

FISHERIES–EUROPE

Coull, James R. The Fisheries of Europe. (Advanced Economic Geography Ser.). 1972. lib. bdg. 23.25x (ISBN 0-7135-1612-7). Westview.

Report of the Ninth Session of European Inland Fisheries Commission. (Fisheries Report Ser: No. 178). 1977. pap. 7.50 (ISBN 92-5-000120-7, F826, FAO). Unipub.

FISHERIES–GREAT BRITAIN

Assoc. of Scottish District Salmon Fishery Board. Salmon Fisheries of Scotland. 1978. 11.00 (ISBN 0-685-63451-5). State Mutual Bk.

Edible Crab & Its Fishery in British Waters. 1979. pap. 18.25 (ISBN 0-85238-100-X, FN78, Pub. by FNB). Unipub.

Gray, Malcom. The Fishing Industries of Scotland 1790-1914: A Study in Regional Adaptation. LC 78-40244. 1978. 26.00x (ISBN 0-19-714105-6). Oxford U Pr.

O'Conner, R., et al. Development of the Irish Sea Fishing Industry & Its Regional Implications. 1981. 50.00x (ISBN 0-686-75526-X, Pub. by ESRI Ireland). State Mutual Bk.

The Potential of West Africa & Egypt As Direct Markets for U. K. Produced Fish & Fish Products. (F. E. R. U. Occasional Paper: No. 3). 63p. 1980. pap. 16.00 (ISBN 0-686-75159-0, WFA46, WFA). Unipub.

S. E. Britaines Busse: Or Herring-Fishing Ship, with the States Proclamation Annexed Unto the Same, As Concerning Herring-Fishing. LC 74-80211. (English Experience Ser.: No. 690). 1974. Repr. of 1615 ed. 5.00 (ISBN 90-221-0690-X). Walter J Johnson.

FISHERIES–INDIA

Indian Ocean Fishery Commission. Report of the Sixth Joint Meeting of the Indian Ocean Fishery Commission, Committee on Management of Indian Ocean Tuna. 18p. 1980. pap. 7.50 (ISBN 92-5-100939-2, F2045, FAO). Unipub.

Papers Presented at the Indo-Pacific Fisheries Commission Workshop on Fish Silage Production & Its Use. (FAO Fisheries Report: No. 230). 1980. pap. 7.50 (ISBN 92-5-100921-X, F1940, FAO). Unipub.

FISHERIES–ISLANDS OF THE PACIFIC

Johannes, R. E. Words of the Lagoon: Fishing & Marine Lore in the Palau District of Micronesia. (Illus.). 320p. 1981. 24.95x (ISBN 0-520-03929-7). U of Cal Pr.

Kent, George. The Politics of Pacific Islands Fisheries. (Westview Replica Edition Ser.). 1980. lib. bdg. 23.25x (ISBN 0-89158-683-0). Westview.

Report of the First Session of the Working Party of Experts on Inland Fisheries. (FAO Fisheries Reports Ser.: No. 214). 1979. pap. 7.50 (ISBN 92-5-100747-0, F1621, FAO). Unipub.

FISHERIES–MEDITERRANEAN AREA

Controlled Breeding & Larval Rearing of Selected Mediterranean Marine Species. (General Fisheries Council for the Mediterranean: Studies & Reviews, No. 55). (Illus., Bilingual.). 1977. pap. 11.75 (ISBN 92-5-000059-6, F923, FAO). Unipub.

Data on Fishing Vessels & Gear in the Mediterranean. (GFCM Studies & Reviews Ser.: No. 56). (Illus., Bilingual.). 1978. pap. 12.00 (ISBN 92-5-000350-1, F1257, FAO). Unipub.

General Fisheries Council for the Mediterranean. (Statistical Bulletin: No. 2). 116p. 1980. pap. 7.50 (ISBN 0-686-72310-4, F2065, FAO). Unipub.

General Fisheries Council for the Mediterranean. Proceedings & Technical Papers, Vol. 7. 1964. pap. 30.00 (ISBN 0-685-36297-3, FAO). Unipub.

--Proceedings & Technical Papers, Vol. 8. 1967. pap. 45.00 (ISBN 0-685-36298-1, FAO). Unipub.

General Fisheries Council for the Mediterranean, 13th Session, Rome 1976. Report of the General Fisheries Council for the Mediterranean: Report. 1977. pap. 9.50 (ISBN 92-5-100099-9, F209, FAO). Unipub.

GFCM Statistical Bulletin: Nominal Catches, 1964 - 1974. (General Fisheries Council for the Mediterranean: No. 1). 1976. pap. 6.50 (ISBN 92-5-000026-X, FAO). Unipub.

Report of the Technical Consultation on Stock Assessment in the Balearic & Gulf of Lions Statistical Divisions. (FAO Fisheries Report Ser.: No. 227). 151p. 1980. pap. 10.00 (ISBN 92-5-100894-9, F2145, FAO). Unipub.

FISHERIES–NEWFOUNDLAND

Lounsbury, Ralph G. British Fishery at Newfoundland, 1634-1763. LC 69-19217. 1969. Repr. of 1934 ed. 25.00 (ISBN 0-208-00795-4, Archon). Shoe String.

Reeves, John. History of the Government of the Island of Newfoundland. 1793. 14.00 (ISBN 0-384-50131-1). Johnson Repr.

FISHERIES–NORWAY

Edwards, David J. Salmon & Trout Farming in Norway. 1978. 30.00x (ISBN 0-685-63450-7). State Mutual Bk.

Kobayashi, Teruo. Anglo-Norwegian Fisheries Case of 1951 & the Changing Law of the Territorial Sea. LC 65-64000. (Social Sciences Monographs: No. 26). 1965. pap. 3.00 (ISBN 0-8130-0133-1). U Presses Fla.
S. E. Haugan Consulting. Fish Versus Oil. 1980. 50.00x (ISBN 0-686-69878-9, Pub. by Norwegian Info Norway). State Mutual Bk.
Salmon & Trout Farming in Norway. 1978. 33.75 (ISBN 0-85238-093-3, FN 75, FNB). Unipub.
Underal, Arild. The Politics of International Fisheries Management. 234p. 1981. pap. 20.00x (ISBN 0-686-69763-4). Universitet.
Water Quality Criteria for European Freshwater Fish: Report on the Effect of Zinc & Copper Pollution on the Salmon Fisheries in a River & Lake System in Central Norway. (EIFAC Technical Paper: No. 29). 40p. 1978. pap. 7.50 (ISBN 92-5-100296-7, F770, FAO). Unipub.

FISHERIES–NOVA SCOTIA

Denys, Nicolas. Description - Natural History of the Coasts of North America. Ganong, William F., ed. LC 68-28597. 1968. Repr. of 1908 ed. lib. bdg. 42.25x (ISBN 0-8371-3873-6, DEDH). Greenwood.

FISHERIES–RUSSIA

Bogdanov, A. S. Soviet Fisheries Investigations in the Indian Ocean. Golek, B., ed. Kaner, N., tr. from Rus. (Israel Program for Scientific Translations Ser). (Illus.). iv, 152p. 1972. lib. bdg. 15.00x (ISBN 0-7065-1246-4, Pub. by IPST). Intl Schol Bk Serv.

FISHERIES–TROPICS

Tussing, Arlon & Hiebert, Robin Ann. Fisheries of the Indian Ocean: Issues of International Management & Law of the Sea. LC 73-20845. (Rff Program of International Studies of Fisheries Arrangements: No. 5). 70p. 1974. pap. 3.00x (ISBN 0-8018-1613-0). Johns Hopkins.
Western Central Atlantic Fishery Commission, First Session, Port of Spain, Trinidad & Topago, 1975. Report. (FAO Fisheries Report Ser.: No.172). 31p. 1976. pap. 7.50 (ISBN 0-685-66354-X, F822, FAO). Unipub.

FISHERMEN

Bartlett, Kim. The Finest Kind: The Fisherman of Gloucester. (Illus.). 1977. 8.95 (ISBN 0-393-08797-2). Norton.
--The Finest Kind: The Fishermen of Gloucester. 1979. pap. 2.95 (ISBN 0-380-44339-2, 44339). Avon.
Bauer, Erwin A., ed. Fishermen's Digest. 10th ed. (Illus.). 288p. 1977. pap. 7.95 (ISBN 0-695-80717-X). DBI.
Bibliography for Fishermen's Training. (Fisheries Technical Paper Ser.: No. 184). 1979. pap. 12.00 (ISBN 92-5-100663-6, F1539, FAO). Unipub.
Caldwell, Francis E. Pacific Troller: Life on the Northwest Fishing Grounds. LC 77-10324. (Illus.). 1978. pap. 4.95 (ISBN 0-88240-099-1). Alaska Northwest.
Carey, George. A Faraway Time & Place: Lore of the Eastern Shore. Dorson, Richard M., ed. LC 77-70586. (International Folklore Ser.). (Illus.). 1977. Repr. of 1971 ed. lib. bdg. 16.00x (ISBN 0-405-10086-8). Arno.
Clifford, Harold B. Charlie York: Maine Coast Fisherman. LC 74-81712. (Illus.). 160p. 1974. 10.95 (ISBN 0-87742-043-2). Intl Marine.
Critchfield, Richard. The Golden Bowl Be Broken: Peasant Life in Four Cultures. LC 73-77855. (Illus.). 320p. 1974. 12.50x (ISBN 0-253-13260-6). Ind U Pr.
Curtis, Elwood A. A Wet Butt & a Hungry Gut. LC 74-84152. 1974. 6.95 (ISBN 0-910244-81-2). Blair.
Danowski, Fran. Fishermen's Wives: Coping with an Extraordinary Occupation. LC 80-53352. (Marine Bulletin: No. 37). 1980. 2.00 (ISBN 0-938412-18-3). URI MAS.
Digges, Jeremiah. In Great Waters: The Story of Portugese Fishermen. 1977. lib. bdg. 59.95 (ISBN 0-8490-2043-3). Gordon Pr.
Educational Research Council of America. Fisher. rev. ed. Braverman, Jack R. & Marchak, John P., eds. (Real People at Work Ser: A). (Illus.). 1977. pap. text ed. 2.25 (ISBN 0-89247-006-2). Changing Times.
FAO Manual on Training Fishermen. 1978. 40.00x (ISBN 0-685-63405-1). State Mutual Bk.
Festing, Sally. Fishermen. 1977. 11.95 (ISBN 0-7153-7448-6). David & Charles.
Firth, Raymond. Malay Fishermen: Their Peasant Economy. (Illus.). 448p. 1975. pap. 4.95x (ISBN 0-393-00775-8, Norton Lib). Norton.
Fraser, Raymond. The Fighting Fisherman: The Life of Yvon Durelle. LC 80-703. (Illus.). 1981. 11.95 (ISBN 0-385-15863-7). Doubleday.
Grossinger, Richard. Book of the Cranberry Islands. 320p. (Orig.). 1974. 10.00 (ISBN 0-87685-211-8). Black Sparrow.
Hohmann, Elmo P. The American Whaleman. 1977. lib. bdg. 59.95 (ISBN 0-8490-1418-2). Gordon Pr.
Landale, Zoe. Harvest of Salmon: Adventures in Fishing the B.C. Coast. LC 77-2367. (Illus.). 1977. 12.95 (ISBN 0-919654-75-4, Pub. by Hancock Hse). Universe.
Lang, Varley. Follow the Water. LC 61-16637. (Illus.). 1961. 6.95 (ISBN 0-910244-24-3). Blair.
Meltzer, Michael. The World of the Small Commercial Fisherman: Their Lives & Their Boats. (Illus.). 10.00 (ISBN 0-8446-5792-1). Peter Smith.
Moorhouse, Geoffrey. The Boat & the Town. LC 79-13898. 1979. 10.95 (ISBN 0-316-58060-0). Little.
Orbach, Michael K. Hunters, Seamen & Entrepreneurs: The Tuna Seinermen of San Diego. LC 76-48361. (Illus.). 1978. 18.50x (ISBN 0-520-03348-5). U of Cal Pr.
Peffer, Randall S. The Watermen. LC 79-9896. 1979. 12.95 (ISBN 0-8018-2177-0). Johns Hopkins.
Schwind, Phil. Cape Cod Fisherman. LC 74-19999. (Illus.). 1974. 12.50 (ISBN 0-87742-045-9). Intl Marine.
Scott, R. W. Handy Medical Guide for Seafarers, Fisherman, Trawlermen & Yachtsmen. 1978. 10.00 (ISBN 0-685-63426-4). State Mutual Bk.
Seufert, Francis A. Wheels of Fortune. Vaughan, Thomas, ed. LC 80-81719. (Illus.). 284p. 1981. 19.95 (ISBN 0-87595-083-3); pap. 12.95 (ISBN 0-87595-069-8). Oreg Hist Soc.
Spoehr, Alexander, ed. Maritime Adaptations: Essays on Contemporary Fishing Communities. LC 79-22486. 1980. 12.95x (ISBN 0-8229-1139-6). U of Pittsburgh Pr.
Taylor, Fred J. My Fishing Years. LC 80-85512. (Illus.). 192p. 1981. 22.50 (ISBN 0-7153-8105-9). David & Charles.
Thompson, Ellery. Draggerman's Haul: The Personal History of a Connecticut Fishing Captain. 2nd ed. 1981. pap. 10.00 (ISBN 0-910258-14-7). Book & Tackle.
Van Winkle, Ted. Fred Boynton: Lobsterman, New Harbor Maine. LC 74-29368. (Illus.). 80p. 1975. 10.95 (ISBN 0-87742-050-5). Intl Marine.
Weiner, Sandra. I Want to Be a Fisherman. LC 76-48088. (Illus.). (gr. 3-6). 1977. 8.95 (ISBN 0-02-792520-X, 79252). Macmillan.
Zulaika, Joseba. Terranova: The Ethos & Luck of Deep-Sea Fishermen. LC 80-20931. (Illus.). 160p. 1981. text ed. 14.50x (ISBN 0-89727-016-9). Inst Study Human.

FISHERY LAW AND LEGISLATION

see also Sealing

The Effect of Two-Hundred Mile Limits on Fisheries Management in the Northeast Atlantic. (FAO Fisheries Technical Paper Ser.: No. 183). 19p. 1978. pap. 7.50 (ISBN 92-5-100592-3, F1470, FAO). Unipub.
Fenn, P. T., Jr. The Origin of the Right of Fishery in Territorial Waters. 15.00 (ISBN 0-89020-009-2). Brown Bk.
Hart, Jeffrey A. The Anglo-Icelandic Cod War of 1972-1973: A Case Study of a Fishery Dispute. LC 76-620082. (Research Ser.: No. 29). (Illus.). 1976. pap. 2.00x (ISBN 0-87725-129-0). U of Cal Intl St.
Huntoon, Emery. Intercept & Board. LC 75-20724. (Illus.). 1975. 6.95 (ISBN 0-8323-0251-1); pap. 4.95 (ISBN 0-8323-0252-X). Binford.
Joseph, James & Greenough, Joseph W. International Management of Tuna, Porpoise, & Billfish: Biological, Legal, & Economic Aspects. LC 77-15192. (Illus.). 270p. 1979. 22.50 (ISBN 0-295-95591-0). U of Wash Pr.
Knight, H. Gary. Managing the Sea's Living Resources. LC 76-20042. (Lexington Books Studies in Marine Affairs). 1977. 17.95 (ISBN 0-669-00874-5). Lexington Bks.
Kobayashi, Teruo. Anglo-Norwegian Fisheries Case of 1951 & the Changing Law of the Territorial Sea. LC 65-64000. (Social Sciences Monographs: No. 26). 1965. pap. 3.00 (ISBN 0-8130-0133-1). U Presses Fla.
Koers, Albert W. International Regulation of Marine Fisheries. 1978. 30.00 (ISBN 0-685-63429-9). State Mutual Bk.
Legislation on Coastal State Requirements for Foreign Fishing. (Legislative Study Ser.: No. 21). 411p. 1981. pap. text ed. 27.00 (ISBN 92-5-101038-2, F2035, FAO). Unipub.
Leonard, Leonard L. International Regulation of Fisheries. (Illus.). ix, 201p. Repr. of 1944 ed. 19.50 (ISBN 0-384-32295-6). Johnson Repr.
Lounsbury, Ralph G. British Fishery at Newfoundland, 1634-1763. LC 69-19217. 1969. Repr. of 1934 ed. 25.00 (ISBN 0-208-00795-4, Archon). Shoe String.
McLeod, G. C. Georges Bank: Past, Present, & Future. (Special Studies on Natural Resources & Energy Management). 225p. 1981. lib. bdg. 23.25x (ISBN 0-86531-199-4). Westview.
Recommended International Standard for Canned Crab Meat. 8p. 1978. pap. 4.50 (ISBN 92-5-100358-0, F1362, FAO). Unipub.
Recommended International Standard for Quick Frozen Fillets of Flat Fish. (Joint FAO-WHO Food Standards Programme Codex Alimentarius Commission). 10p. 1978. pap. 4.50 (ISBN 92-5-100359-9, F1397, FAO). Unipub.
Recommended International Standard for Quick Frozen Shrimps or Prawns. 16p. 1978. pap. 4.50 (ISBN 92-5-100360-2, F1370, FAO). Unipub.
Report of the Seventh Session of the Working Party on Resource Appraisal & Fishery Statistics. (FAO Fisheries Reports Ser.: No. 204). 1978. pap. 9.75 (ISBN 92-5-100588-5, F1486, FAO). Unipub.
Report on the CIDA - FAO - CEDAF Seminar on the Cnanging Law of the Sea & the Fisheries of West Africa. 1979. pap. 10.75 (ISBN 92-5-100634-2, F 1500, FAO). Unipub.
Riesenfeld, Stefan A. Protection of Coastal Fisheries Under International Law. (Carnegie Endowment for International Peace Monograph). xii, 296p. Repr. of 1942 ed. 31.00 (ISBN 0-384-50838-3). Johnson Repr.
A Study of Freshwater Fishery Regulation Based on North American Experience. (FAO Fisheries Technical Paper Ser.: No. 180). 46p. 1978. pap. 7.50 (ISBN 92-5-100579-6, F1464, FAO). Unipub.
Tussing, Arlon R., et al, eds. Alaska Fisheries Policy: Economics, Resources, & Management. LC 72-619593. (Illus.). 470p. 1972. pap. 5.00 (ISBN 0-88353-007-4). U Alaska Inst Res.

FISHERY METHODS

see Fisheries

FISHERY PRODUCTS

see also Canning and Preserving; Cold Storage

Brown, E. Evan. World Fish Farming Cultivation & Economics. (Illus.). 1977. lib. bdg. 21.50 (ISBN 0-87055-234-1). AVI.
Chichester, C. O. & Graham, H. D., eds. Microbial Aspects of Fishery Products. 1973. 36.50 (ISBN 0-12-172740-8). Acad Pr.
FAO. The Fish Resources of the Ocean. Gulland, John, ed. 1978. 37.00x (ISBN 0-685-63412-4). State Mutual Bk.
Fish Protein Conference. Economics, Marketing, & Technology of Fish Protein Concentrate: Proceedings. Tannenbaum, Steven & Stillings, Bruce, eds. 1974. 28.00x (ISBN 0-262-20029-5). MIT Pr.
Fishing News Bks. Ltd. Staff, ed. Introduction to Fishery by-Products. 208p. 1981. 40.00x (ISBN 0-85238-115-8, Pub. by Fishing News England). State Mutual Bk.
IPFC-IOFC Ad Hoc Working Party of Scientists, 2nd Session. Stock Assessments of Tuna. (Fisheries Reports: No. 152). (Illus.). 19p. 1975. pap. 7.50 (ISBN 0-685-57608-6, F793, FAO). Unipub.
Kreuzer, Rudolf, ed. Fishery Products. (Illus.). 462p. 1975. 55.00 (ISBN 0-85238-065-8, FN 45, FAO). Unipub.
--Fishery Products. 1978. 59.00 (ISBN 0-685-63415-9). State Mutual Bk.
The Marketing of Fish & Fishery Products in Europe: No. 2, Spain. (Fisheries Economics Research Unit Occasional Paper Ser.: No. 3). 56p. 1980. pap. 6.00 (ISBN 0-686-60080-0, WFA 041, WFA). Unipub.
The Marketing of Fish & Fishery Products in Europe: No. 4. France. (F. E. R. U. Occasional Paper Ser.: No. 2). 30p. 1981. pap. 8.50 (ISBN 0-686-72374-0, WFA 44, WFA). Unipub.
Multilingual Dictionary of Fish & Fish Products. 1978. 60.00 (ISBN 0-85238-086-0, FN 64, FNB). Unipub.
OECD. Multilingual Dictionary of Fish & Fish Products. 1978. 59.00 (ISBN 0-685-63442-6). State Mutual Bk.
OECD, ed. Multilingual Dictionary of Fish & Fish Products. 2nd ed. 446p. 1978. 42.50x (ISBN 0-85238-086-0). Intl Pubns Serv.
Orr, A. P. & Marshall, S. M. The Fertile Sea. 1978. 20.00 (ISBN 0-685-63407-8). State Mutual Bk.
Papers Presented at the Indo-Pacific Fisheries Commission Workshop on Fish Silage Production & Its Use. (FAO Fisheries Report: No. 230). 1980. pap. 7.50 (ISBN 92-5-100921-X, F1940, FAO). Unipub.
The Potential of West Africa & Egypt As Direct Markets for U. K. Produced Fish & Fish Products. (F. E. R. U. Occasional Paper: No. 3). 63p. 1980. pap. 16.00 (ISBN 0-686-75159-0, WFA46, WFA). Unipub.
The Production of Fish Meal & Oil. (FAO Fisheries Technical Paper: No. 142). (Illus.). 54p. 1976. pap. 7.50 (ISBN 92-5-100068-9, F872, FAO). Unipub.
Recommended International Standard for Canned Sardines & Sardine - Type Products. 1979. pap. 4.50 (ISBN 92-5-100673-3, F1573, FAO). Unipub.
Recommended International Standard for Quick Frozen Filets of Hake. 1979. pap. 4.50 (ISBN 92-5-100647-4, F1569, FAO). Unipub.
Report on the CIDA - FAO - CECAF Regional Seminar of Senior Fish Processing Technologists. (FAO Fisheries Report Ser: No. 202). 1978. pap. 7.50 (ISBN 92-5-100561-3, F1417, FAO). Unipub.
Scheuer, Paul J., ed. Marine Natural Products: Chemical & Biological Perspectives, Vol. 4. 1981. 32.00 (ISBN 0-12-624004-3). Acad Pr.
Waterman, J. J. The Production of Dried Fish. (FAO Fisheries Technical Paper: No. 160). 1976. pap. 7.50 (ISBN 0-685-76671-3, F892, FAO). Unipub.
Yearbook of Fishery Statistics 1974: Fishery Commodities, Vol. 39. 330p. 1976. 24.00 (ISBN 0-685-68363-X, FAO). Unipub.

FISHERY PRODUCTS–PRESERVATION

Burgess, G. H., et al. Fish Handling & Processing. (Illus.). 1967. 25.00 (ISBN 0-8206-0045-8). Chem Pub.
Recommended International Standard for Canned Crab Meat. 8p. 1978. pap. 4.50 (ISBN 92-5-100358-0, F1362, FAO). Unipub.
Recommended International Standard for Quick Frozen Fillets of Flat Fish. (Joint FAO-WHO Food Standards Programme Codex Alimentarius Commission). 10p. 1978. pap. 4.50 (ISBN 92-5-100359-9, F1397, FAO). Unipub.
Recommended International Standard for Quick Frozen Shrimps or Prawns. 16p. 1978. pap. 4.50 (ISBN 92-5-100360-2, F1370, FAO). Unipub.

FISHES

see also Aquariums; Fish As Food; Fish-Culture; Fisheries; Fishing; Tropical Fish;
also names of classes, orders, etc. of fishes, e.g. Bass, salmon

Advances in Fish Science & Technology. 512p. 1980. pap. 150.00 (ISBN 0-85238-108-5, FN 87, FNB). Unipub.
Ali, M. A. & Anctil, M. Retinas of Fishes: An Atlas. LC 76-22204. (Illus.). 1976. 65.40 (ISBN 0-387-07840-1). Springer-Verlag.
Allen, Gerald. Anemone Fishes. new ed. 20.00 (ISBN 0-87666-001-4, H-942). TFH Pubns.
Allen, Gerald R. Butterfly & Angelfishes of the World: Atlantic Ocean, Caribbean Sea, Red Sea, Indo-Pacific, Vol. 2. LC 78-17351. 352p. 1980. 35.00 (ISBN 0-471-05618-9, Pub. by Wiley-Interscience). Wiley.
--Butterfly & Angelfishes of the World: Atlantic Ocean, Caribbean Sea, Red Sea, Indo-Pacific, Vol. 2. LC 78-17351. 352p. 1980. 35.00 (ISBN 0-471-05618-9, Pub. by Wiley-Interscience). Wiley.
--Damselfishes. (Illus.). 240p. 1975. 9.95 (ISBN 0-87666-034-0, H-950). TFH Pubns.
Allyn, Rube. Dictionary of Fishes. LC 52-334. (Orig.). pap. 3.95 (ISBN 0-8200-0101-5). Great Outdoors.
Ames, Felicia. Fish You Care For. (Orig.). (RL 5). 1971. pap. 1.25 (ISBN 0-451-04771-0, Y4771, Sig). NAL.
Anderson, Lee. Economic Analysis for Fisheries Management Plans. 300p. 1981. text ed. 49.95 (ISBN 0-250-40389-7). Ann Arbor Science.
Artedi, P. Genera Piscium: Emendata & Aucta. 1967. Repr. of 1792 ed. 60.00 (ISBN 3-7682-0190-2). Lubrecht & Cramer.
--Ichthyolgia. Linnaeus, C., ed. 1961. Repr. of 1738 ed. 50.00 (ISBN 3-7682-0082-5). Lubrecht & Cramer.
Axelrod, Herbert R. Freshwater Fishes, Bk. 1. (Illus.). 320p. 1974. 20.00 (ISBN 0-87666-076-6, PS-713). TFH Pubns.
Axelrod, Herbert R. & Burgess, Dr. Warren. Marine Fishes. (Illus.). 1979. 2.95 (ISBN 0-87666-513-X, KW-031). TFH Pubns.
Axelrod, Herbert R. & Burgess, Warren E. Angelfish. (Illus.). 1979. 2.95 (ISBN 0-87666-516-4, KW-048). TFH Pubns.
Bagenal, T. B. The Observer's Book of Sea Fishes. (The Observer Bks). (Illus.). 1979. 3.95 (ISBN 0-684-16032-3, ScribT). Scribner.
Balon, Eugene, ed. Charrs: Salmonid Fishes of the Genus Salvelinus. (Perspectives in Vertebrate Science: No. 1). (Illus.). 919p. 1980. lib. bdg. 210.50 (ISBN 90-6193-701-9, Pub. by Junk Pubs Netherlands). Kluwer Boston.
Benirschke, K. & Hsu, T. C., eds. Chromosome Atlas: Fish, Amphibians, Reptiles & Birds, Vol. 1. LC 73-166079. (Illus.). 225p. 1972. loose leaf 16.30 (ISBN 0-387-05507-X). Springer-Verlag.
The Biology & Status of Stocks of Small Tunas. (Fisheries Technical Paper: No. 154). 1976. pap. 7.50 (ISBN 92-5-100020-4, F887, FAO). Unipub.
Bloch, E. M. Systema Ichthyologiae: Post Obitum Auctoris Opus Inchoatum Absolvit, J. G. Schneider, 2 vols. in 1. (Illus.). 1967. Repr. of 1801 ed. 100.00 (ISBN 3-7682-7191-9). Lubrecht & Cramer.
Bodie, Scott & Browne, Corinne. Confessions of a Fish Doctor. LC 76-25474. (Illus.). 1977. 7.95 (ISBN 0-911104-83-6). Workman Pub.
Bullen, Frank T. Creatures of the Sea: Sea Birds, Beasts, & Fishes. 1977. lib. bdg. 69.95 (ISBN 0-8490-1682-7). Gordon Pr.

Burgess, Warren E. Butterflyfishes of the World. (Illus.). 1979. 20.00 (ISBN 0-87666-470-2, H-988). TFH Pubns.
Burton, Maurice. The Life of Fishes. LC 77-88434. (Easy Reading Edition of Introduction to Nature Ser.). (Illus.). 1978. lib. bdg. 7.95 (ISBN 0-686-51140-9). Silver.
Cannon, Raymond. How to Fish the Pacific Coast. 3rd ed. LC 67-15740. (Illus.). 160p. 1967. pap. 5.95 (ISBN 0-376-06362-9, Sunset Bks.). Sunset-Lane.
Casier, Edgar. Faune Ichthyologique Du London Clay: Text & Atlas. (Illus.). xiv, 496p. 1966. 87.50x (ISBN 0-565-00654-1, Pub. by British Mus Nat Hist England). Sabbot-Natural Hist Bks.
Casteel, R. W., ed. Fish Remains in Archaeology. 1977. 29.00 (ISBN 0-12-163850-2). Acad Pr.
Cook, Joseph J. The Incredible Atlantic Herring. LC 78-24540. (Illus.). (gr. 4 up). 1979. 5.95 (ISBN 0-396-07647-5). Dodd.
Cook, Joseph J. & Wisner, William L. Coastal Fishing for Beginners. LC 77-6488. (Illus.). (gr. 5 up). 1977. PLB 5.95 (ISBN 0-396-07487-1). Dodd.
Curtis, Brian. Life of the Fish: His Manners & Morals. (Illus.). 6.75 (ISBN 0-8446-1933-7). Peter Smith.
--Life Story of the Fish. 2nd ed. 1949. pap. 4.00 (ISBN 0-486-20929-6). Dover.
Dalrymple, Byron. Complete Guide to Game Fish: A Field Book of Fresh & Saltwater Species. 480p. 1981. 14.95 (ISBN 0-442-21978-4). Van Nos Reinhold.
De Carli, Franco. The World of Fish. Richardson, Jean, tr. LC 79-1436. (Abbeville Press Encyclopedia of Natural Science). (Illus.). 1979. 13.95 (ISBN 0-89659-035-6); pap. 7.95 (ISBN 0-89659-029-1). Abbeville Pr.
Eastman, David. What Is a Fish. LC 81-11373. (Now I Know Ser.). (Illus.). 32p. (gr. k-2). 1982. PLB 7.95 (ISBN 0-89375-660-1); pap. 1.25 (ISBN 0-89375-661-X). Troll Assocs.
Eddy, Samuel & Underhill, James C. Northern Fishes. rev. 3rd ed. LC 73-83729. (Illus.). xx, 414p. 1974. 13.95 (ISBN 0-8166-0674-9). U of Minn Pr.
Encyclopedie Illustree Des Poissons. 600p. (Fr.). 14.95 (ISBN 0-686-57157-6, M-6216). French & Eur.
Fish, Marie Poland & Mowbray, William H. Sounds of Western North Atlantic Fishes: A Reference File of Biological Underwater Sounds. LC 77-106135. (Illus.). 227p. 1970. 20.00x (ISBN 0-8018-1130-9). Johns Hopkins.
Gammon, Clive. A Tide of Fish. 12.50x (ISBN 0-392-06417-0, SpS). Sportshelf.
Goode, G. Brown. Game Fishes of the United States. (Illus.). 1972. Repr. of 1879 ed. 75.00x (ISBN 0-87691-085-1). Winchester Pr.
Gordon, Bernard L. Secret Lives of Fishes. rev. ed. (Illus.). 306p. 1980. pap. text ed. 7.95 (ISBN 0-910258-12-0). Book & Tackle.
Gosline, William A. Functional Morphology & Classification of Teleostean Fishes. LC 77-151454. (Illus.). 1971. pap. text ed. 7.00x (ISBN 0-87022-300-3). U Pr of Hawaii.
Greenberg, Idaz. Guide to Corals & Fishes. (Illus.). 1977. saddlestitched 4.95 (ISBN 0-913008-08-7). Seahawk Pr.
--Waterproof Guide to Corals & Fishes. (Illus.). 1977. soft plastic pages, rust-proof bdg. 8.95 (ISBN 0-913008-07-9). Seahawk Pr.
Greenfield, David, ed. Systemic Ichthyology: A Collection of Readings. 1972. 38.50x (ISBN 0-8422-5024-7); pap. text ed. 12.50x (ISBN 0-8290-0674-5). Irvington.
Greenwood, P. H. & Norman, J. R. A History of Fishes. 3rd ed. 1976. pap. 20.95 (ISBN 0-470-99012-0). Halsted Pr.
Gulland, J. A. The Fish Resources of the Ocean. (Illus.). 255p. 1972. 35.00 (ISBN 0-85238-055-0, FAO). Unipub.
Hempel, Gotthilf. Early Life History of Marine Fish: The Egg Stage. LC 79-14549. (Washington Sea Grant). 86p. 1980. pap. 7.50 (ISBN 0-295-95672-0). U of Wash Pr.
Hocutt, Charles H. & Stauffer, Jay R., Jr., eds. Biological Monitoring of Fish. LC 79-3049. 432p. 1980. 31.95x (ISBN 0-669-03309-X). Lexington Bks.
Hocutt, Charles H., et al. Power Plants: Effects on Fish & Shellfish Behavior. 1980. 25.00 (ISBN 0-12-350950-5). Acad Pr.
Innes, William T. Exotic Aquarium Fishes. 19th ed. (Illus.). 1966. 10.95 (ISBN 0-525-10118-7). Dutton.
International Association of Fish & Wildlife Agencies. Proceedings of the Sixty-Ninth Convention. Blouch, Ralph I., ed. (Orig.). 1980. 11.00 (ISBN 0-932108-04-0). IAFWA.
Jacobs, Kurt. Livebearing Fishes. (Illus.). 495p. (Orig.). 1974. pap. 12.95 (ISBN 0-87666-095-2, PS-705). TFH Pubns.
Jhaveri, S., et al. Abstracts of Methods Used to Assess Fish Quality. (Marine Technical Report Ser.: No. 69). 3.00 (ISBN 0-938412-00-0). URI MAS.
Jocher, Willy. Spawning Problem Fishes. Incl. Book 1 (ISBN 0-87666-146-0, PS-302); Book 2 (ISBN 0-87666-147-9, PS-303). (Illus.). 1972. pap. 2.95 ea. (ISBN 0-685-32894-5). TFH Pubns.
Jordan, David S. Genera of Fishes & a Classification of Fishes. 1963. 35.00x (ISBN 0-8047-0201-2). Stanford U Pr.
Klausewitz, W. Die Erforshung der Ichthyofauna Des Roten Meeres. pap. 6.25 (ISBN 3-7682-7115-3). Lubrecht & Cramer.
Klunzinger, C. B. Synopsis der Fische Des Rothen Meeres, 2 parts in 1 vol. (Illus.). 1964. Repr. of 1871 ed. 50.00 (ISBN 3-7682-7115-3). Lubrecht & Cramer.
Kondo, Riki H. Fishes. (Instant Nature Guides). (Illus.). 1979. pap. 2.95 (ISBN 0-448-12677-X). G&D.
Lagler, Karl F., et al. Ichthyology. 2nd ed. LC 76-50114. 506p. 1977. text ed. 27.95x (ISBN 0-471-51166-8). Wiley.
Lampman, Ben H. Coming of the Pond Fishes. 9.95 (ISBN 0-8323-0341-0). Binford.
Langlois, T. H. A Study of the Small-Mouth Bass, Micropterus dolomieu (Lacepede) in Rearing Ponds in Ohio. 1936. 2.00 (ISBN 0-686-30306-7). Ohio Bio Survey.
Lanham, Url N. The Fishes. LC 62-9366. (Illus.). 116p. 1967. pap. 5.00 (ISBN 0-231-08581-8). Columbia U Pr.
Love, Milton & Cailliet, Gregor M., eds. Readings in Ichthyology. LC 78-16654. (Illus.). 1979. pap. 16.95 (ISBN 0-87620-762-X). Goodyear.
Love, R. M. The Chemical Biology of Fishes: Vol. 2, Advances 1968-1977. 1980. 120.00 (ISBN 0-12-455852-6). Acad Pr.
McNeil, William J. & Himsworth, Daniel C., eds. Salmonid Ecosystems of the North Pacific. LC 80-17800. (Illus.). 348p. pap. 15.00 (ISBN 0-87071-335-3); pap. text ed. 15.00 (ISBN 0-686-68208-4). Oreg St U Pr.
Marshall, N. B. Explorations in the Life of Fishes. LC 75-129122. (Books in Biology Ser: No. 7). 1971. 10.00x (ISBN 0-674-27951-4). Harvard U Pr.
--Life of Fishes. LC 66-11276. (Natural History Ser.). 1966. 15.00x (ISBN 0-87663-121-9). Universe.
Miller, P. J., ed. Fish Phenology: Anabolic Adaptiveness in Teleosts, No. 44. LC 79-40966. (Symposia of the Zoological Society of London). 1980. 60.00 (ISBN 0-12-613344-1). Acad Pr.
Moyle, Peter B. & Cech, Joseph J. Fishes: An Introduction to Ichthyology. (Illus.). 720p. 1982. 27.95 (ISBN 0-13-319723-9). P-H.
Multilingual Dictionary of Fish & Fish Products. 1978. 60.00 (ISBN 0-85238-086-0, FN 64, FNB). Unipub.
Neill, Ian. Trout from the Hills. 12.50x (ISBN 0-392-06403-0, SpS). Sportshelf.
Nelson, J. S. Fishes of the World. LC 76-14959. 1976. 37.00 (ISBN 0-471-01497-4, Pub. by Wiley-Interscience). Wiley.
The New Alchemy Backyard Fish Farm Book. 100p. Date not set. pap. 4.95 (ISBN 0-931790-21-2). Brick Hse Pub.
Nikolsky, G. V. The Ecology of Fishes. rev ed. Orig. Title: The Biology of Fishes. (Illus.). 1978. pap. 4.95 (ISBN 0-87666-505-9, H-999). TFH Pubns.
OECD. Multilingual Dictionary of Fish & Fish Products. 1978. 59.00 (ISBN 0-685-63442-6). State Mutual Bk.
Oren, O. H., ed. Aquaculture of Grey Mullets. LC 79-53405. (International Biological Programme: No. 26). (Illus.). 450p. Date not set. price not set (ISBN 0-521-22926-X). Cambridge U Pr.
Orme, Frank W. Coldwater Fish Cyclopaedia. 1981. 40.00x (ISBN 0-904558-84-3, Pub. by Saiga Pub). State Mutual Bk.
Perlmutter, Alfred. Guide to Marine Fishes. LC 60-14491. (Illus.). 431p. 1961. 25.00x (ISBN 0-8147-0336-4); pap. 12.95x (ISBN 0-8147-6561-0). NYU Pr.
Perymyak, Y. The First Fish. 1977. pap. 0.75 (ISBN 0-8285-1139-X, Pub. by Progress Pubs Russia). Imported Pubns.
Ray, John. Synopsis Methodica Avium & Piscium. Derham, William & Sterling, Keir B., eds. LC 77-81111. (Biologists & Their World Ser.). (Illus., Latin.). 1978. Repr. of 1713 ed. lib. bdg. 26.00x (ISBN 0-405-10695-5). Arno.
Relyea, Kenneth. Inshore Fishes of the Arabian Gulf. (Natural History of the Arabian Gulf Ser.). (Illus.). 96p. 1981. text ed. 19.50x (ISBN 0-04-597003-3). Allen Unwin.
Rice, Don, ed. Fishes, Reptiles & Amphibians: A Picture Sourcebook. 154p. 1981. pap. 9.95 (ISBN 0-442-21196-1). Van Nos Reinhold.
Sato, Torao. A Synopsis of the Sparoid Fish Genus Lethrinus, with the Description of a New Species. 1978. 17.00x (ISBN 0-86008-207-5, Pub. by U of Tokyo Pr). Intl Schol Bk Serv.
Scallops & the Diver-Fisherman. (Illus.). 144p. 1981. pap. 32.00 (ISBN 0-85238-114-X, FN90, FNB). Unipub.
Symposium on Icthygenetics, 1st. Genetics & Mutagenesis of Fish: Proceedings. Schroeder, J. H., ed. LC 73-11601. 330p. 1973. 38.00 (ISBN 0-387-06419-2). Springer-Verlag.
Synopsis of Biological Data on the Walleye: Stizostedion Vitreum. (Fisheries Synopsis Ser.: No. 119). 1979. pap. 11.75 (ISBN 92-5-100757-8, F1622, FAO). Unipub.
Terofol, Fritz. Fishes. (Nature Guide Ser.). (Illus.). 144p. 1979. pap. 5.95 (ISBN 0-7011-2460-1, Pub. by Chatto Bodley Jonathan). Merrimack Bk Serv.
The Theory & Practice of Induced Breeding in Fish. 48p. 1980. pap. 5.00 (ISBN 0-88936-236-X, IDRCTS21, IDRC). Unipub.
Time-Life Television Editors. Fishes of Lakes, Rivers & Oceans. new ed. (Wild, Wild World of Animals Ser). (Illus.). 1978. 10.95 (ISBN 0-913948-20-9). Time-Life.
Walker, Braz. Angelfish. (Illus.). 1974. 5.95 (ISBN 0-87666-755-8, PS-711). TFH Pubns.
WHO Expert Committee. Geneva, 1973. Fish & Shellfish Hygiene: Report. (Technical Report Ser.: No. 550). (Also avail. in French & Spanish). 1974. pap. 2.40 (ISBN 92-4-120550-4). World Health.
Willughby, Francis. De Historia Piscium & Icthyographia ad Amplisimum Virum Dnum: Samuelem Pepys, Presidem Soc. Reg, 2 vols in one. Sterling, Keir B., ed. LC 77-81089. (Biologists & Their World Ser.). (Illus.). 1978. Repr. of 1685 ed. lib. bdg. 44.00x (ISBN 0-405-10667-X). Arno.
Wootton. The Biology of the Sticklebacks. 1977. 47.00 (ISBN 0-12-763650-1). Acad Pr.
Wourms, John P., et al. Genetic Studies of Fish, Vol. 2. LC 74-516. 179p. 1974. text ed. 22.50x (ISBN 0-8422-7207-0). Irvington.
Yearbook of Fishery Statistics 1977: Catches & Landings. (Fisheries Ser.: No. 44). 1979. 28.00 (ISBN 92-5-000609-8, F1552, FAO). Unipub.

FISHES–ANATOMY

see also Electric Organs in Fishes

Gans, Carl & Parsons, Thomas S. A Photographic Atlas of Shark Anatomy: The Gross Morphology of Squalas Acanthias. LC 80-24528. (Illus.). 106p. 1981. spiral bound 8.00 (ISBN 0-226-28120-5). U of Chicago Pr.
Gilbert, Stephen G. Pictorial Anatomy of the Dogfish. LC 74-152331. (Illus.). 66p. (Orig.). 1973. pap. text ed. 6.95 (ISBN 0-295-95148-6). U of Wash Pr.
Harder, Wilhelm. Anatomy of Fishes, 2 pts. Sokoloff, S., tr. from Ger. LC 76-377362. (Illus.). 1975. 180.00x (ISBN 3-510-65067-0). Intl Pubns Serv.
--Anatomy of Fishes, 2 vols. 2nd rev. ed. (Illus.). 1976. Set. text ed. 140.00 (ISBN 3-510-65067-0). Lubrecht & Cramer.
Kindred, James E. Skull of Amiurus. (Illus.). 1919. 9.50 (ISBN 0-384-29415-4). Johnson Repr.
Kusaka, Takaya. The Urohyal of Fishes. (Illus.). 330p. 1974. 65.00x (ISBN 0-86008-102-8, Pub. by U of Tokyo Pr). Intl Schol Bk Serv.
Nybelin, Orvar. On the So Called Postspiracular Bones in Crossopterygians, Brachiopterygians & Actinopterygians. (Acta Regiae Societatis Scientiarum et Litterarum Gothoburgensis Zoologica Ser.: No. 10). 31p. 1976. pap. text ed. 4.00x (ISBN 91-85252-05-0). Humanities.
Tchernavin, V. V. The Feeding Mechanism of a Deep Sea Fish, Chauliodus Sloani Schneider. (Illus.). 1953. pap. 11.50x (ISBN 0-565-00111-6, Pub. by Brit Mus Nat Hist). Sabbot-Natural Hist Bks.

FISHES–BEHAVIOR

Adler, Helmut E. Fish Behavior: Why Fish Do What They Do. (Illus.). 271p. 1975. 20.00 (ISBN 0-87666-162-2, PS-734). TFH Pubns.
Ingle, David, ed. Central Nervous System & Fish Behavior. LC 68-24558. 1968. 15.00x (ISBN 0-226-38054-8). U of Chicago Pr.
Kennleyside, M. H. Diversity & Adaptation in Fish Behaviour. (Zoophysiology Ser.: Vol. 11). (Illus.). 1979. 39.80 (ISBN 0-387-09587-X). Springer-Verlag.
Lateral Line Sense Organs & Their Importance in Fish Behavior. 332p. 1971. 25.00x (ISBN 0-7065-1047-X, Pub. by IPST). Intl Schol Bk Serv.
May, Julian. Fishes We Know. LC 73-4537. (Illus.). (gr. 2-4). 1973. PLB 5.95 (ISBN 0-87191-243-0). Creative Ed.
Reese, Ernst S. & Lighter, Frederick J. Contrasts in Behavior: Adaptations in the Aquatic & Terrestrial Environments. LC 78-8284. 1978. 37.00 (ISBN 0-471-71390-2, Pub. by Wiley-Interscience). Wiley.
Simon, Hilda. Strange Breeding Habits of Aquarium Fish. LC 74-11798. (Illus.). 160p. 1974. 5.95 (ISBN 0-396-07025-6). Dodd.
Sosin, Mark & Clark, John. Through the Fish's Eye. LC 72-97172. (An Outdoor Life Bk.). (Illus.). 256p. 1973. 12.95 (ISBN 0-06-013971-4, HarpT). Har-Row.
Tavolga, W. N., ed. Sound Reception in Fishes. LC 76-13525. (Benchmark Papers in Animal Behavior: Vol. 7). 1976. 48.50 (ISBN 0-12-787516-6); 38.00 set (ISBN 0-685-69401-1). Acad Pr.
Tavolga, William N., ed. Sound Production in Fishes. LC 76-28352. (Benchmark Papers in Animal Behavior: Vol. 9). 1977. 48.50, by subscription 38.00 (ISBN 0-12-787515-8). Acad Pr.
Thresher, Ronald E. Reef Fish: Behaviors & Ecology on the Reef & in the Aquarium. LC 79-28234. (Major Ser.). 17.95 (ISBN 0-915096-09-9). Palmetto Pub.
Wickler, Wolfgang. Breeding Behavior of Aquarium Fishes. (Illus.). 1973. pap. 7.95 (ISBN 0-87666-029-4, PS-306). TFH Pubns.

FISHES–BIBLIOGRAPHY

Check-List of the Fishes of the North-Eastern Atlantic & the Mediterranean: With Supplement. (CLOFAM I & II Ser.). 1077p. 1980. pap. 89.25 (ISBN 92-3-001100-2, U 980, UNESCO). Unipub.
Dean, Bashford. A Bibliography of Fishes, 3 vols. 1973. 160.00 (ISBN 3-87429-036-0). Lubrecht & Cramer.
Huver, Charles W., compiled by. A Bibliography of the Genus Fundulus. (Ser. Seventy). 1973. lib. bdg. 18.00 (ISBN 0-8161-0976-1). G K Hall.
Matthes, H., compiled by. A Bibliography of African Freshwater Fish. 299p. (Orig.). 1974. pap. 24.00 (ISBN 0-685-40090-5, F 89, FAO). Unipub.

FISHES–COLLECTION AND PRESERVATION

Fisher, Jeffrey. The Fish Book: How to Buy, Clean, Catch, Cook & Preserve Them. (Illus.). 128p. 1981. 8.95 (ISBN 0-87523-196-9). Emerson.
Gulland, J. A. Manual of Methods for Fish Stock Assessment, Pt. 1: Fish Population Analysis. (FAO Manuals in Fisheries Science Ser.: No. 4). (Illus., Orig.). 1969. pap. 12.25 (ISBN 92-5-100204-5, F262, FAO). Unipub.
Midgalski, Edward C. How to Make Fish Mounts & Other Fish Trophies: Complete Book of Taxidermy. 2nd ed. LC 80-27829. 212p. 1981. 15.95 (ISBN 0-471-07990-1, Pub. by Wiley-Interscience). Wiley.
Migdalski, Edward C. Fish Mounts & Other Fish Trophies: The Complete Book of Taxidermy. 2nd ed. LC 80-27829. 212p. 1981. 15.95 (ISBN 0-471-07990-1). Wiley.
Phillips, Archie & Phillips, Bubba. How to Mount Fish for Profit or Fun. (Illus.). 144p. 1981. 19.95 (ISBN 0-8117-0787-3). Stackpole.
Preservation of Fish by Irradiation. (Illus., Orig.). 1970. pap. 13.00 (ISBN 92-0-111070-7, ISP196, IAEA). Unipub.
Vierke, Jorg. Dwarf Cichlids. Ahrens, Christa, tr. from Ger. (Illus.). 1979. 2.95 (ISBN 0-87666-509-1, KW-005). TFH Pubns.

FISHES–DISEASES

see also Parasites–Fishes

Anderson, Douglas P. Diseases of Fishes, Book 4: Fish Immunology. Snieszko, S. F. & Axelrod, Herbert R., eds. (Illus.). 240p. 1974. pap. text ed. 12.95 (ISBN 0-87666-036-7, PS-209). Tfh Pubns.
Bodie, Scott & Browne, Corinne. Confessions of a Fish Doctor. LC 76-25474. (Illus.). 1977. 7.95 (ISBN 0-911104-83-6). Workman Pub.
Control of the Spread of Major Communicable Fish Diseases. (Fisheries Reports: No. 192). 44p. 1977. pap. 7.50 (ISBN 92-5-100275-4, F839, FAO). Unipub.
Davis, H. S. Culture & Diseases of Game Fishes. (Illus.). 1953. 18.50x (ISBN 0-520-00293-8). U of Cal Pr.
Doudoroff, Peter. A Critical Review of Recent Literature on Toxicity of Cyanides to Fish. LC 80-68588. 71p. (Orig.). 1980. pap. 3.60 (ISBN 0-89364-039-5, API 847-87000). Am Petroleum.
Dulin, Mark P. Diseases of Marine Aquarium Fishes. (Illus.). 1976. pap. 4.95 (ISBN 0-87666-099-5, PS731). TFH Pubns.
Elkan, E. & Reichenbach-Klinke, H. Color Atlas of the Diseases of Fishes, Amphibians, & Reptiles. (Illus.). 256p. 1974. 20.00 (ISBN 0-87666-028-6, H-948). TFH Pubns.
Geisler, Rolf. Aquarium Fish Diseases. (Illus., Orig.). 1963. pap. 2.00 (ISBN 0-87666-008-1, M516). TFH Pubns.
Goldstein, R. J. Diseases of Aquarium Fishes. (Illus.). pap. 4.95 (ISBN 0-87666-041-3, PS201). TFH Pubns.
Herwig, Nelson. Handbook of Drugs & Chemicals Used in the Treatment of Fish Diseases: A Manual of Fish Pharmacology & Materia Medica. (Illus.). 288p. 1979. text ed. 19.25 (ISBN 0-398-03852-X). C C Thomas.
Kabata, Z. Diseases of Fishes: Crustaceans. pap. 12.95 (ISBN 0-87666-039-1, PS200). TFH Pubns.
Kingsford, Edward. Treatment of Exotic Marine Fish Diseases. 1977. 7.95 (ISBN 0-668-04054-8); pap. 4.95 (ISBN 0-668-04052-1). Arco.

Mawdesley-Thomas, Lionel E., et al. Diseases of Fish. 277p. 1974. text ed. 22.50x (ISBN 0-8422-7178-3). Irvington.
Neish, Gordon A. & Hughes, Gilbert C. Fungal Diseases of Fishes. Axelrod, Herbert R. & Snieszko, Stanislas F., eds. (Diseases of Fishes Ser.). (Illus.). 160p. 12.95 (ISBN 0-87666-504-0, PS-213). TFH Pubns.
Reichenbach-Klinke, H. H. Fish Pathology. (Illus.). 512p. (Orig.). 1973. pap. text ed. 20.00 (ISBN 0-87666-074-X, PS-204). TFH Pubns.
Reichenbach-Klinke, Heinz-Hermann. All About Marine Aquarium Fish Diseases. (Illus.). 1977. pap. 2.95 (ISBN 0-87666-467-2, PS-747). TFH Pubns.
Ribelin, William E. & Migaki, George, eds. Pathology of Fishes. LC 73-15261. 1016p. 1975. pap. 75.00 (ISBN 0-299-06520-0, 652). U of Wis Pr.
Roberts, Ronald J. & Shepherd, C. Jonathan. Handbook of Trout & Salmon Diseases. (Illus.). 172p. 32.00 (ISBN 0-85238-066-6, FN 51, FNB). Unipub.
--Handbook of Trout & Salmon Diseases. 1978. 20.00 (ISBN 0-685-63425-6). State Mutual Bk.
Sarig. Diseases of Fishes: Fish Farming. 12.95 (ISBN 0-87666-040-5, P5203). TFH Pubns.
Schubert, Gottfried. Cure & Recognize Aquarium Fish Diseases. (Illus.). 128p. 1974. pap. 4.95 (ISBN 0-87666-033-2, PS-210). TFH Pubns.
Sinderman, C. J. Principal Diseases of Marine Fish & Shellfish. 1970. 55.50 (ISBN 0-12-645850-2). Acad Pr.
Sindermann, C. J. Diseases of Marine Fishes. (Illus.). pap. 3.95 (ISBN 0-87666-046-4, PS670). TFH Pubns.
Sindermann, Carl J., ed. Disease Diagnosis & Control in North American Marine Aquaculture. (Developments in Aquaculture & Fisheries Science Ser.). 1977. 47.75 (ISBN 0-444-00237-5). Elsevier.
Sniezko, S., et al. Diseases of Fishes: Bacteria. (Illus.). 12.95 (ISBN 0-87666-038-3, PS202). TFH Pubns.
Textbook of Fish Diseases. (Illus.). 12.95 (ISBN 0-87666-037-5, PS667, ED). TFH Pubns.

FISHES–DISTRIBUTION
see Fishes–Geographical Distribution

FISHES–EMBRYOLOGY
see Embryology–Fishes

FISHES–FOOD
Control of Fish Quality. 222p. 1980. 32.00 (ISBN 0-85238-105-0, FN 83, FNB). Unipub.
Fish Feed Technology: Lectures Presented at the FAO - UNDP Training Course in Fish Feed Technology. (Agriculture Development Coordination Programme Ser.). 400p. 1980. pap. 28.00 (ISBN 92-5-100901-5, F1944, FAO). Unipub.
Ivlev, V. S. Experimental Ecology & the Feeding of Fishes. 1961. 32.50x (ISBN 0-685-89751-6). Elliots Bks.
Price, John W. Food Habits of Some Lake Erie Fishes. 1963. 3.00 (ISBN 0-686-30320-2). Ohio Bio Survey.
Sturges, Lena. Fish & Shellfish Cookbook. LC 74-79231. (Family Guide Book Ser). (Illus.). 1974. pap. 1.95 (ISBN 0-8487-0359-6). Oxmoor Hse.

FISHES–GEOGRAPHICAL DISTRIBUTION
see also Fish Populations
Nakamura, Hiroshi. Tuna: Distribution & Migration. 1978. 12.00x (ISBN 0-685-63462-0). State Mutual Bk.

FISHES–JUVENILE LITERATURE
Aliki. The Long Lost Coelacanth & Other Living Fossils. LC 72-83773. (A Let's-Read-&-Find-Out Science Bk.). (Illus.). 40p. (gr. k-3). 1973. 7.95 (ISBN 0-690-50478-0, TYC-J). Har-Row.
Arnold, Caroline. Electric Fish. LC 80-12479. (Illus.). 64p. (gr. 4-6). 1980. 6.95 (ISBN 0-688-22237-4); PLB 6.67 (ISBN 0-688-32237-9). Morrow.
Banister, Keith. A Closer Look at Fish. (gr. 5 up). 1980. PLB 7.45 (ISBN 0-531-03413-5). Watts.
Burger, Carl. All About Fish. (Allabout Ser.: No. 34). (Illus.). (gr. 5-9). 1960. PLB 5.39 (ISBN 0-394-90234-3, BYR). Random.
Cook, Joseph J. & Wisner, William L. Coastal Fishing for Beginners. LC 77-6488. (Illus.). (gr. 5 up). 1977. PLB 5.95 (ISBN 0-396-07487-1). Dodd.
Fishes of Lakes, Rivers, & Oceans. LC 78-51971. (Wild, Wild World of Animals Ser.). (Illus.). 1978. lib. bdg. 11.97 (ISBN 0-686-51169-7). Silver.
Fletcher, Alan M. Fishes & Their Young. LC 73-15119. (Illus.). 48p. (gr. 3-6). 1974. PLB 5.95 (ISBN 0-201-02053-X, A-W Childrens). A-W.
--Fishes Dangerous to Man. LC 71-80502. (Illus.). (gr. 4-7). 1969. PLB 5.95 (ISBN 0-201-02056-4, A-W Childrens). A-W.
--Fishes That Hide. LC 72-467. (Illus.). 48p. (gr. 3-6). 1973. PLB 5.95 (ISBN 0-201-02030-0, A-W Childrens). A-W.
Friedman, Judi. The Eels Strange Journey. LC 75-20136. (A Let's Read & Find Out Science Bk). (Illus.). 40p. (gr. k-3). 1976. PLB 8.79 (ISBN 0-690-01007-9, TYC-J). Har-Row.
Gilbert, Miriam. Science-Hobby Book of Aquariums. rev. ed. LC 67-17406. (Science Hobby Bks). (Illus.). (gr. 5-10). 1968. PLB 4.95 (ISBN 0-8225-0551-7). Lerner Pubns.
Hornblow, Leonora & Hornblow, Arthur. Fish Do the Strangest Things. (Step-up Bks). (Illus.). 1966. 3.95 (ISBN 0-394-80062-1, BYR); PLB 4.99 (ISBN 0-394-90062-6). Random.
Janvier, Jeannine. Fantastic Fish You Can Make. LC 76-19819. (Illus.). (gr. 4 up). 1976. 5.95 (ISBN 0-8069-5406-X); PLB 5.89 (ISBN 0-8069-5407-8). Sterling.
Martin, Dick. The Fish Book. (Illus.). 24p. (gr. k-1). 1976. PLB 5.38 (ISBN 0-307-68982-4, Golden Pr). Western Pub.
May, Julian. Fishes We Know. LC 73-4537. (Illus.). (gr. 2-4). 1973. PLB 5.95 (ISBN 0-87191-243-0). Creative Ed.
Noel, Spike. Fish & the Sea. (Junior Reference Ser.). (Illus.). 64p. (gr. 7 up). 1972. 7.95 (ISBN 0-7136-1239-8). Dufour.
Ommanney, F. The Fishes. (Young Readers Library). (Illus.). 1977. lib. bdg. 7.95 (ISBN 0-686-51090-9). Silver.
Overbeck, Cynthia. The Fish Book. LC 78-7205. (Early Nature Picture Bks). (Illus.). (gr. k-3). 1978. PLB 4.95 (ISBN 0-8225-1110-X). Lerner Pubns.
Pringle, Laurence. The Minnow Family. LC 75-28335. (Illus.). 64p. (gr. 3-7). 1976. 6.25 (ISBN 0-688-22060-6); PLB 6.00 (ISBN 0-688-32060-0). Morrow.
Selsam & Hunt. A First Look at Fish. (gr. k-3). 1976. pap. 1.50 (ISBN 0-590-10288-5). Schol Bk Serv.
Shaw, Evelyn. Fish Out of School. LC 77-105477. (Science I Can Read Books). (Illus.). (ps-3). 1970. 6.95 (ISBN 0-06-025563-3, HarpJ); PLB 7.89 (ISBN 0-06-025564-1). Har-Row.
Shepherd, Elizabeth. Minnows. (Illus.). 64p. (gr. 2-6). 1974. 6.50 (ISBN 0-688-40055-8); PLB 6.24 (ISBN 0-688-50055-2). Lothrop.
Spizzirri Publishing Co. Staff. Fish: An Educational Coloring Book. Spizzirri, Linda, ed. (Illus.). 32p. (gr. 1-8). 1981. pap. 1.25 (ISBN 0-86545-028-5). Spizzirri.
Steinberg, Phil. You & Your Pet: Aquarium Pets. LC 78-54359. (You & Your Pet Bks). (Illus.). (gr. 4 up). 1978. PLB 5.95 (ISBN 0-8225-1255-6). Lerner Pubns.
The Stickleback. (Animal Environment Ser.). (Illus.). (gr. 3-6). 1979. 4.95 (ISBN 0-8120-5363-X). Barron.
Sutton, Felix. Fish. (How & Why Wonder Books Ser.). (Illus.). (gr. 4-6). pap. 1.00 (ISBN 0-448-05066-8). Wonder.
Vevers, Gwynne. Fishes. LC 75-26667. (Illus.). 48p. (gr. 4-9). 1976. PLB 6.95 (ISBN 0-07-067420-5, GB). McGraw.
Waters, John F. Marine Animal Collectors: How Creatures of the Sea Contribute to Science & Our Knowledge of Man. LC 69-15053. (Illus.). (gr. 6-9). 1969. PLB 6.95 (ISBN 0-8038-4648-7). Hastings.
What Is a Fish? (Learning Shelf Kits Ser.). (gr. 2-4). 1978. incl. cassette & tchrs. guide 14.95 (ISBN 0-686-74388-1, 04987). Natl Geog.
White, William, Jr. The Angelfish: Its Life Cycle. LC 75-14511. (Colorful Nature Ser.). (Illus.). 64p. (gr. 5 up). 1975. 9.95 (ISBN 0-8069-3482-4); PLB 9.29 (ISBN 0-8069-3483-2). Sterling.

FISHES–LEGENDS AND STORIES
see also Fishing Stories

FISHES–MIGRATION
Hay, John. The Run. (Illus.). 1979. 9.95 (ISBN 0-393-01269-7); pap. 3.95 (ISBN 0-393-00946-7). Norton.
Joseph, James, et al. Tuna & Billfish: Fish Without a Country. 2nd ed. LC 80-81889. (Illus.). 53p. (Orig.). (gr. 7-12). 1980. pap. 7.95 (ISBN 0-9603078-1-8). Inter-Am Tropical.
Nakamura, Hiroshi. Tuna: Distribution & Migration. 1978. 12.00x (ISBN 0-685-63462-0). State Mutual Bk.

FISHES–NOMENCLATURE
OECD, ed. Multilingual Dictionary of Fish & Fish Products. 2nd ed. 446p. 1978. 42.50x (ISBN 0-85238-086-0). Intl Pubns Serv.

FISHES–PARASITES
see Parasites–Fishes

FISHES–PHYSIOLOGY
The Aging of Fish. (Illus.). 234p. 1975. pap. 30.50 (ISBN 0-9502121-1-3, FAO). Unipub.
Alexander, R. McNeill. Functional Design in Fishes. 3rd ed. (Illus.). 1974. pap. text ed. 7.00 (ISBN 0-09-104751-X, Hutchinson U Lib). Humanities.
Ali, M. A. Vision in Fishes - New Approaches in Research. LC 75-8570. (Nato Advanced Study Institute Ser.: Series A, Life Sciences, Vol. 1). 836p. 1975. 67.50 (ISBN 0-306-35601-5, Plenum Pr). Plenum Pub.
Ali, M. A., ed. Environmental Physiology of Fishes. (NATO Advanced Study Institutes Ser, A-Life Sciences: Vol. 35). 685p. 1981. 69.50 (ISBN 0-306-40574-1, Plenum Pr). Plenum Pub.
Chavin, Walter. Responses of Fish to Environmental Changes. (Illus.). 472p. 1973. text ed. 36.75 (ISBN 0-398-02743-9). C C Thomas.
Hoar, W. S. & Randall, D. J., eds. Fish Physiology. 1969-71. Vol. 1. 63.00, by subscription 54.50 (ISBN 0-12-350401-5); Vol. 2. 63.00, by subscription 54.50 (ISBN 0-12-350402-3); Vol. 3. 63.00, by subscription 54.50 (ISBN 0-12-350403-1); Vol. 4. 63.00, by subscription 54.50 (ISBN 0-12-350404-X); Vol. 5. 70.00, by subscription 60.50 (ISBN 0-12-350405-8); Vol. 6. 70.00, by subscription 60.50 (ISBN 0-12-350406-6); Vol. 7, 1979. 58.00, by subscription 49.50 (ISBN 0-12-350407-4). Acad Pr.
--Fish Physiology Vol. 8: Bioenergetics & Growth. LC 76-84233. 1979. 78.00 (ISBN 0-12-350408-2); subscription 66.50 (ISBN 0-685-86991-1). Acad Pr.
Love, R. The Chemical Biology of Fishes: With a Key to Literature. 1970. 87.00 (ISBN 0-12-455850-X). Acad Pr.
Neuhaus, O. W. & Halver, J. E., eds. Fish in Research. LC 74-107020. 1969. 37.50 (ISBN 0-12-515850-5). Acad Pr.
Reutter, K. Taste Organ in the Bullhead (Teleostei) (Advances in Anatomy, Embryology & Cell Biology: Vol. 55, Pt. 1). (Illus.). 1978. pap. 27.70 (ISBN 0-387-08880-6). Springer-Verlag.
Schuijf, A. & Hawkins, A. D., eds. Sound Reception in Fish. LC 76-54648. (Developments in Aquaculture & Fisheries Science: Vol. 5). 1977. 40.00 (ISBN 0-444-41540-8). Elsevier.
Sharp, Gary D. & Dizon, Andrew E., eds. Physiological Ecology of the Tunas. LC 78-26514. 1979. 42.50 (ISBN 0-12-639180-7). Acad Pr.
Silva, Tony & Kotlar, Barbara. Discus. (Illus.). 98p. 1980. 2.95 (ISBN 0-87666-535-0, KW-097). TFH Pubns.

FISHES–PICTORIAL WORKS
Axelrod, Herbert R., et al. Exotic Marine Fishes. (Illus.). 608p. 1973. 15.00 (ISBN 0-87666-102-9, H938); looseleaf bdg. 20.00 (ISBN 0-87666-103-7, H-938L). Tfh Pubns.
Cohen, Shlomo. The Red Sea Diver's Fish Guide. (Waterproof Fish Guides Ser.). (Illus., Orig., Hebrew.). 1978. 9.95 (ISBN 0-932200-07-9). Seapen Bks.
--The Red Sea Diver's Fish Guide. (Waterproof Fish Guides Ser.). (Illus., Orig., Eng.). 1978. 9.95 (ISBN 0-932200-05-2). Seapen Bks.
Goode, G. Brown. Game Fishes of the United States. (Illus.). 1972. Repr. of 1879 ed. 75.00x (ISBN 0-87691-085-1). Winchester Pr.
Whitehead, P. J. Forty Drawings of Fishes Made by the Artists Who Accompanied Captain James Cook. (Illus.). 1968. text ed. 150.00x (ISBN 0-565-00670-3, Pub. by Brit Mus Nat Hist). Sabbot-Natural Hist Bks.
--The Reeves Collection of Chinese Fish Drawings. (Bulletin of the British Museum Natural History, Historical Ser.: Vol. 3, No. 7). (Illus.). 1969. pap. text ed. 22.00x (ISBN 0-8277-4366-1, Pub. by Brit Mus Nat Hist). Sabbot-Natural Hist Bks.

FISHES–AFRICA
Boulenger, G. A. Fishes of the Nile. 1964. Repr. of 1907 ed. 185.00 (ISBN 3-7682-0241-0). Lubrecht & Cramer.
Brichard, Pierre. Fishes of Lake Tanganyika. (Illus.). 1978. 20.00 (ISBN 0-87666-464-8, H-972). TFH Pubns.
Fryer, G. & Iles, T. D. The Cichlid Fishes of the Great Lakes of Africa, Their Biology & Evolution. (Illus.). 641p. 1981. Repr. of 1972 ed. lib. bdg. 104.50x (ISBN 3-87429-169-3). Lubrecht & Cramer.
Fryer, Geoffrey & Iles, T. D. Cichlids of the Great Lakes of Africa. (Illus.). 1972. 20.00 (ISBN 0-87666-030-8, PS-680). TFH Pubns.
Greenwood, P. H. The Cichlid Fishes of Lake Victoria, East Africa: Biology & Evolution of a Species Flock. (Bulletin of the British Museum Natural History Ser: No. 6). (Illus.). 1974. text ed. 21.50x (ISBN 0-565-00761-0, Pub. by Brit Mus Nat Hist); pap. text ed. 15.00x (ISBN 0-8277-4357-2). Sabbot-Natural Hist Bks.
--The Haplochromine Fishes of the East African Lakes. (Illus.). 1981. 65.00x (ISBN 0-8014-1346-X). Cornell U Pr.
Holden, Michael & Reed, William. West African Freshwater Fish. LC 74-170516. (West African Nature Handbooks). (Illus.). 68p. (Orig.). 1972. pap. 5.00x (ISBN 0-582-60426-5). Intl Pubns Serv.
Jackson, P. B. & Ribbinck, Tony. Mbunas, Malawi Cichlids. (Illus.). 128p. (Orig.). 1975. pap. 5.95 (ISBN 0-87666-454-0, PS-740). TFH Pubns.
Playfair, R. Lambert & Guenther, Albert C. The Fishes of Zanzibar. (Hand Colored Reprint Ser). (Illus.). xiv, 154p. 1971. Repr. of 1866 ed. 125.00 (ISBN 0-912318-00-7). N K Gregg.
Voss, J. Color Patterns of African Cichlids. Orig. Title: Les Livrees Ou Patrons De Coloration Chezles Poissons Chichlides Africains. (Illus.). 128p. 1980. 7.95 (ISBN 0-87666-503-2, PS-755). TFH Pubns.

FISHES–ATLANTIC COAST
Breder, Charles M., Jr. Field Book of Marine Fishes of the Atlantic Coast. (Putnam Nature Field Bks.). (Illus.). 1948. 7.95 (ISBN 0-399-10524-7). Putnam.
Fishes of the Atlantic Coast. pap. 2.95 (ISBN 0-671-79028-5, Wallaby). PB.
Goodson, Gar. The Many Splendored Fishes of Hawaii. Kennedy, Robert D., ed. LC 73-87889. 1977. pap. 4.25 (ISBN 0-916240-00-2). Marquest Colorguide.
--Many Splendored Fishes of the Atlantic Coast. LC 76-3231. 1976. pap. 4.95 (ISBN 0-916240-01-0). Marquest Colorguide.
Hildebrand, Samuel F. & Schroeder, William C. The Fishes of the Chesapeake Bay. LC 72-5565. (Illus.). 388p. 1972. Repr. of 1928 ed. 8.00x (ISBN 0-87474-173-4). Smithsonian.
Perlmutter, Alfred. Guide to Marine Fishes. LC 60-14491. (Illus.). 431p. 1961. 25.00x (ISBN 0-8147-0336-4); pap. 12.95x (ISBN 0-8147-6561-0). NYU Pr.

FISHES–AUSTRALIA
Coleman, Neville. Australian Fisherman's Fish Guide: Angler's Aid to Identification, Location, Habits & Eating Qualities of Australian Sea Fishes. (Illus.). 1978. 10.00x (ISBN 0-85835-231-1). Intl Pubns Serv.
Deas, Walter. Australian Fishes in Color. (Illus.). 1973. 6.00 (ISBN 0-912728-47-7). Newbury Bks.
--Australian Fishes in Colour. LC 70-160558. (Colourful Australia Ser). (Illus.). 32p. 1973. 6.50x (ISBN 0-85179-285-5). Intl Pubns Serv.
Thomson, J. M. A Field Guide to the Common Sea & Estuary Fishes of Ono-Tropical Australia. 144p. 1980. 17.95x (ISBN 0-00-219271-3, Pub. by W Collins Ausftralia). Intl Schol Bk Serv.

FISHES–CANADA
McAllister, D. E. List of Marine Fishes of Canada. 76p. 1960. pap. text ed. 2.00 (ISBN 0-660-02103-X, 56419-3, Pub. by Natl Mus Canada). U of Chicago Pr.
McAllister, D. E. & Coad, Brian W. Fishes of Canada's National Capital Region. (Illus.). 1974. pap. text ed. 5.00x (ISBN 0-660-02014-9, 56345-6, Pub. by Natl Gallery Canada). U of Chicago Pr.
McAllister, D. E. & Crossman, E. J. A Guide to the Freshwater Sport Fishes of Canada. (Illus.). 1973. pap. 4.95 (ISBN 0-660-00048-2, 56365-0, Pub. by Natl Mus Canada). U of Chicago Pr.
Shrimps of the Pacific Coast of Canada. 280p. 1981. 32.50 (ISBN 0-660-10177-7, SSC 148, SSC). Unipub.

FISHES–EUROPE
Blanc, M., et al, eds. European Inland Water Fish: A Multilingual Catalogue. (Illus.). 1972. 29.00 (ISBN 0-85238-056-9, FAO). Unipub.
FAO. European Inland Water Fish. 1978. 35.00 (ISBN 0-685-63401-9). State Mutual Bk.
The Marketing of Fish & Fishery Products in Europe: No. 2, Spain. (Fisheries Economics Research Unit Occasional Paper Ser.: No. 3). 56p. 1980. pap. 6.00 (ISBN 0-686-60080-0, WFA 041, WFA). Unipub.
Water Quality Criteria for European Freshwater Fish: Report on the Effect of Zinc & Copper Pollution on the Salmon Fisheries in a River & Lake System in Central Norway. (EIFAC Technical Paper: No. 29). 40p. 1978. pap. 7.50 (ISBN 92-5-100296-7, F770, FAO). Unipub.
Wheeler, Alwyne. Fishes of the British Isles & North-West Europe. LC 69-19148. 672p. 1969. text ed. 25.00x (ISBN 0-87013-134-6). Mich St U Pr.

FISHES–GREAT BRITAIN
Cacutt, Len. British Freshwater Fishes: The Story of Their Evolution. (Illus.). 202p. 1979. 25.00x (ISBN 0-85664-320-3, Pub. by Croom Helm Ltd England). Biblio Dist.
Cope, Ken. Fishing Canals. LC 79-55994. (Illus.). 1980. 17.95 (ISBN 0-7153-7887-2). David & Charles.
Donovan, Edward. The Natural History of British Fishes: Scientific & General Descriptions of the Most Interesting Species, 2 vols. Sterling, Keir B., ed. LC 77-81091. (Biologists & Their World Ser.). (Illus.). 1978. Repr. of 1808 ed. Set. lib. bdg. 47.00x (ISBN 0-405-10668-8); lib. bdg. 23.50x ea. Vol. 1 (ISBN 0-405-10669-6). Vol. 2 (ISBN 0-405-10670-X). Arno.
Kabata, Z. Parasitic Copepoda of British Fishes. (Illus.). 670p. 1979. 75.00x (ISBN 0-903874-05-9, Pub. by Brit Mus Nat Hist England). Sabbot-Natural Hist Bks.
McDonald, Dan. The Clyde Puffer. LC 77-76092. 1977. 10.50 (ISBN 0-7153-7443-5). David & Charles.
Varley, Margaret. British Freshwater Fishes. 1978. 9.00x (ISBN 0-685-63394-2). State Mutual Bk.

--British Freshwater Fishes: Factors Affecting Their Distribution. (Illus.). 148p. 15.00 (ISBN 0-85238-107-7, FN 4, FNB). Unipub.

Wheeler, Alwyne. Fishes of the British Isles & North-West Europe. LC 69-19148. 672p. 1969. text ed. 25.00x (ISBN 0-87013-134-6). Mich St U Pr.

Woodward, A. Smith. The Fishes of the English Chalk, Part 1-7, Vols. 56-56, 61-65, Nos. 263, 266, 291, 300, 308, 313, 320. Repr. of 1912 ed. Set. pap. 44.50 (ISBN 0-384-69212-5). Johnson Repr.

FISHES-JAPAN

Marr, John, ed. Kuroshio: A Symposium on the Japan Current. 1970. 25.00x (ISBN 0-8248-0090-7, Eastwest Ctr). U Pr of Hawaii.

Masuda, H. & Araga, C. Coastal Fishes of Southern Japan. (Illus.). 379p. (Eng., Jap.). 1976. slipcased 85.00 (ISBN 0-685-76674-8, Tokai). Unipub.

FISHES-LATIN AMERICA

Chirichigno, F. Norma. Clave Para Identificar los Peces Del Peru. (Institut del Mar del Peru Ser.: Informe 44). (Illus.). 388p. (Span.). 1978. pap. text ed. 70.00x (ISBN 3-87429-131-6). Lubrecht & Cramer.

Smith, Nigel J. Man, Fishes, & the Amazon. 176p. 1981. 22.50x (ISBN 0-231-05156-5). Columbia U Pr.

Technical Consultation on the Latin American Hake Industry, Suppl. 1. 1979. pap. 14.75 (ISBN 92-5-100643-1, F1525, FAO). Unipub.

FISHES-NEW ZEALAND

McDowall, R. M. Freshwater Fish in New Zealand. (Mobil New Zealand Nature Ser.). (Illus.). 80p. (Orig.). 1980. pap. 6.95 (ISBN 0-589-01327-0, Pub. by Reed Bks Australia). C E Tuttle.

FISHES-NORTH AMERICA

Carlander, Kenneth D. Handbook of Freshwater Fishery Biology, Vol. 2. 1977. text ed. 19.50x (ISBN 0-8138-0670-4). Iowa St U Pr.

Herbert, Henry W. Frank Forester's Fish & Fishing in the United States & British Provinces of North America. LC 73-125747. (American Environmental Studies). (Illus.). 1970. Repr. of 1850 ed. 22.00 (ISBN 0-405-02672-2). Arno.

Hubbs, Carl L., et al. Memoir VIII: Hydrographic History & Relict Fishes of the North-Central Great Basin. Kessel, Edward L., ed. (Memoirs of the California Academy of Sciences Ser.). (Illus.). 259p. (Orig.). 1974. pap. 15.00 (ISBN 0-940228-11-4). Calif Acad Sci.

McClane, A. J. McClane's Field Guide to Saltwater Fishes to North America. LC 77-14417. pap. 7.95 (ISBN 0-03-021121-2). HR&W.

Mitchell, Robert W., et al. Mexican Eyeless Characin Fishes, Genus Astyanax: Environment, Distribution, & Evolution. (Special Publications: No. 12). (Illus., Orig.). 1977. pap. 5.00 (ISBN 0-89672-038-1). Tex Tech Pr.

Richardson, John. Fauna Boreali-Americana: Zoology of the Northern Parts of British America, the Fish, Pt. 3. Sterling, Keir B., ed. LC 77-81088. (Biologists & Their World Ser.). (Illus.). 1978. Repr. of 1836 ed. lib. bdg. 23.00x (ISBN 0-405-10664-5). Arno.

Walls, Jerry G. Fishes of the Northern Gulf of Mexico. (Illus.). 432p. 1975. 9.95 (ISBN 0-87666-445-1, H960). TFH Pubns.

Whyte, Mal. North American Sealife Coloring Album. (Wildlife Ser.). (Illus.). 1973. pap. 3.50 (ISBN 0-912300-27-2, 27-2). Troubador Pr.

Zim, Herbert S. & Shoemaker, Hurst H. Fishes. (Golden Guide Ser). PLB 10.38 (ISBN 0-307-63508-2, Golden Pr); pap. 1.95 (ISBN 0-307-24498-9). Western Pub.

FISHES-PACIFIC OCEAN

Axelrod, Herbert R. & Burgess, Warren. Pacific Marine Fishes, Bk. 6. (Illus.). 1976. text ed. 20.00 (ISBN 0-87666-128-2, PS-722). TFH Pubns.

--Pacific Marine Fishes, Bk. 7. (Illus.). 1976. text ed. 20.00 (ISBN 0-87666-129-0, PS723). TFH Pubns.

Burgess, Warren E. & Axelrod, Herbert R. Pacific Marine Fishes, Bk. 5. (Illus.). 271p. 1975. 20.00 (ISBN 0-87666-127-4, PS-721). TFH Pubns.

Fowler, H. R. The Fishes of Oceania: With Supplements 1-3. 1967. Repr. of 1881 ed. 150.00 (ISBN 3-7682-0444-8). Lubrecht & Cramer.

Fowler, H. W. Fishes of Guam, Hawaii, Samoa, & Tahiti. Repr. of 1925 ed. pap. 5.00 (ISBN 0-527-02125-3). Kraus Repr.

--The Fishes of Oceania, 1927. (Orig.). Repr. of 1949 ed. pap. 67.00 (ISBN 0-527-01664-0). Kraus Repr.

--Fishes of the Tropical Central Pacific. Repr. of 1927 ed. pap. 5.00 (ISBN 0-527-02141-5). Kraus Repr.

Fowler, H. W. & Ball, S. C. Fishes of Hawaii, Johnston Island, & Wake Island. Repr. of 1925 ed. pap. 5.00 (ISBN 0-527-02129-6). Kraus Repr.

Fowler, Henry W. The Fishes of Oceania, 4 Vols. in 1. (Illus.). Repr. of 1949 ed. 115.50 (ISBN 0-384-16535-4). Johnson Repr.

Gosline, William A. & Brock, Vernon E. Handbook of Hawaiian Fishes. LC 58-11692. (Illus., Orig.). 1960. pap. 7.50 (ISBN 0-87022-302-X). U Pr of Hawaii.

Gotshall, Daniel W. Pacific Coast Inshore Fishes. rev. ed. LC 80-53027. (Illus.). 96p. 1981. 22.95 (ISBN 0-930118-07-3); pap. 11.50 (ISBN 0-930118-06-5). Sea Chall.

--Pacific Coast Inshore Fishes. LC 80-53027. (Illus.). 96p. 1981. pap. 11.50 (ISBN 0-930118-06-5). Western Marine Ent.

--Pacific Coast Inshore Fishes. LC 80-53027. (Illus.). 112p. 1981. pap. 11.50 (ISBN 0-930118-05-7). Western Marine Ent.

Gotshall, Daniel W. & Zimbleman. Fishes of the Pacific Coast: An Underwater Guide, Alaske to the Baja. (Durabooks). (Illus.). 96p. 1974. text ed. 8.95 (ISBN 0-87098-060-2). Livingston.

Guenther, A. Andrew Garrett's Fische der Suedsee, 3 vols. in 1. (Illus.). 1966. 180.00 (ISBN 3-7682-0351-4). Lubrecht & Cramer.

Hobson, Edmund & Chave, Edith H. Hawaiian Reef Animals. LC 72-84060. (Illus.). 1979. pap. 12.95 (ISBN 0-8248-0653-0). U Pr of Hawaii.

Howard, John K. & Ueyanagi, Shoji. Distribution & Relative Abundance of Billfishes (Istiophoridae) of the Pacific Ocean. (Studies in Tropical Oceanography Ser.: No. 2). 1965. 5.50x (ISBN 0-87024-083-8). U Miami Marine.

Indo-Pacific Fisheries Council, Special Committee on Management of Indo-Pacific Tuna, Third Session & Indian Ocean Fishery Commission, Committee on Management of Indian Ocean Tuna, Fourth Session, July 18-19, 1975, Mombasa, Kenya. Report: Third Joint Meeting. (No. 174). (Illus.). 47p. 1976. pap. 7.50 (ISBN 0-685-68361-3, F824, FAO). Unipub.

Johannes, R. E. Words of the Lagoon: Fishing & Marine Lore in the Palau District of Micronesia. (Illus.). 320p. 1981. 24.95x (ISBN 0-520-03929-7). U of Cal Pr.

Jordan, David S. & Evermann, Barton W. The Shore Fishes of Hawaii. LC 73-77578. (Illus.). 1973. pap. 8.50 (ISBN 0-8048-1106-7). C E Tuttle.

Kizevetter, I. V. Chemistry & Technology of Pacific Fish. IPST Staff, tr. from Rus. (Israel Program for Scientific Translations Ser). (Illus.). viii, 304p. 1972. 27.50x (ISBN 0-7065-1271-5, Pub. by IPST). Intl Schol Bk Serv.

Pietschmann, V. Remarks on Pacific Fishes. Repr. of 1930 ed. pap. 5.00 (ISBN 0-527-02179-2). Kraus Repr.

Randall, John E. The Underwater Guide to Hawaiian Reef Fishes. (Illus.). 1980. plastic bdg. 8.95 (ISBN 0-915180-02-2). Harrowood Bks.

Schindler, O. Sexually Mature Larval Hemiramphidae from the Hawaiian Islands. Repr. of 1932 ed. pap. 5.00 (ISBN 0-527-02203-9). Kraus Repr.

Somerton, David & Murray, Craig. Field Guide to the Fish of Puget Sound & the Northwest Coast. LC 75-40884. (Washington Sea Grant Ser.). (Illus.). 80p. 1976. pap. 7.95 (ISBN 0-295-95497-3). U of Wash Pr.

Studies on Skipjack in the Pacific. (FAO Fisheries Technical Papers: No.144). (Illus.). 69p. 1976. pap. 7.50 (ISBN 0-685-66332-9, F874, FAO). Unipub.

Tinker, Spencer W. Fishes of Hawaii. LC 77-93337. (Illus.). 1978. 25.00 (ISBN 0-930492-02-1); soft bdg. 14.95 (ISBN 0-930492-14-5). Hawaiian Serv.

Velasquez, Carmen C. Digenetic Trematodes of Philippine Fishes. 1975. 6.65x (ISBN 0-8248-0444-9). U Pr of Hawaii.

Walford, Lionel A. Marine Game Fishes of the Pacific Coast from Alaska to the Equator. LC 74-80976. 205p. 1975. Repr. of 1937 ed. 15.00x (ISBN 0-87474-153-X). Smithsonian.

FISHES-RED SEA

Cohen, Shlomo. The Red Sea Diver's Fish Guide. (Waterproof Fish Guides Ser.). (Illus., Orig., Hebrew.). 1978. 9.95 (ISBN 0-932200-07-9). Seapen Bks.

--The Red Sea Diver's Fish Guide. (Waterproof Fish Guides Ser.). (Illus., Orig., Eng.). 1978. 9.95 (ISBN 0-932200-05-2). Seapen Bks.

FISHES-TROPICS

see also Tropical Fish

Brittan, Martin. Rasbora. (Illus.). 1972. 9.95 (ISBN 0-87666-136-3, PS-681). TFH Pubns.

Howard, John K. & Starck, Walter A., 2nd. Distribution & Relative Abundance of Billfishes (Istiophoridae) of the Indian Ocean. LC 75-4747. (Studies in Tropical Oceanography Ser: No. 13). (Illus.). 1975. 10.00x (ISBN 0-87024-276-8). U Miami Marine.

Myers, George. Piranhas. 5.95 (ISBN 0-87666-771-X, M539). TFH Pubns.

FISHES-UNITED STATES

Allyn, Rube. Florida Fishes. Allyn, Charles, ed. LC 74-14516. (Illus., Orig.). 1969. pap. 1.95 (ISBN 0-8200-0108-2). Great Outdoors.

Burgess, Warren E. & Axelrod, Herbert R. Pacific Marine Fishes, Bk. 4. (Illus.). 272p. 1974. 20.00 (ISBN 0-87666-126-6, PS-720). TFH Pubns.

Carpenter, Russell & Carpenter, Blyth. Fish Watching in Hawaii. (Illus.). 120p. (Orig.). 1981. 14.95 (ISBN 0-939560-01-1); pap. 9.95 (ISBN 0-939560-00-3). Natural World.

Cross, Frank B. & Collins, Joseph T. Illustrated Guide to Fishes in Kansas. (Public Education Ser.: No. 4). (Illus.). (gr. 4-6). 1976. pap. 1.00 (ISBN 0-89338-000-8). U of KS Mus Nat Hist.

Dahlberg, Michael. Guide to Coastal Fishes of Georgia & Nearby States. LC 73-81624. (Illus.). 200p. 1974. pap. 7.50x (ISBN 0-8203-0333-X). U of Ga Pr.

Economic Impact of the Effects of Pollution on the Coastal Fisheries of the Atlantic & Gulf of Mexico Regions of the United States of America. (FAO Fisheries Technical Paper Ser.: No. 172). (Illus.). 1978. pap. 7.50 (ISBN 92-5-100380-7, F1238, FAO). Unipub.

Fitch, John E. & Lavenberg, Robert J. Marine Food & Game Fishes of California. (California Natural History Guides: No. 28). (Illus.). 1971. pap. 5.95 (ISBN 0-520-01831-1). U of Cal Pr.

--Tidepool & Nearshore Fishes of California. (Illus.). 1976. 14.95x (ISBN 0-520-02844-9); pap. 3.95 (ISBN 0-520-02845-7). U of Cal Pr.

Gordon, Bernard L. The Marine Fishes of Rhode Island. (Illus.). 148p. 1974. 5.00 (ISBN 0-910258-00-7). Book & Tackle.

Hoese, H. Dickson, et al. Fishes of the Gulf of Mexico: Texas, Louisiana & Adjacent Waters. LC 76-51654. (Natural History Ser.: No.1). (Illus.). 346p. 1977. 14.95 (ISBN 0-89096-027-5); pap. 7.95 (ISBN 0-89096-028-3). Tex A&M Univ Pr.

Hubbs, Carl L. & Lagler, Karl F. Fishes of the Great Lakes Region. LC 58-7693. (Illus.). (YA) (gr. 9 up). 1964. 14.00x (ISBN 0-472-08465-8). U of Mich Pr.

Jordan, D. S. & Evermann, B. W. American Food & Game Fishes. (Illus.). 12.50 (ISBN 0-8446-0728-2). Peter Smith.

Jordan, David S. & Evermann, Barton W. The Shore Fishes of Hawaii. LC 73-77578. (Illus.). 1973. pap. 8.50 (ISBN 0-8048-1106-7). C E Tuttle.

Koster, William J. Guide to the Fishes of New Mexico. LC 57-12457. (Illus.). 116p. (Orig.). 1957. pap. 3.00 (ISBN 0-8263-0060-X). U of NM Pr.

McGinnis, S. California Freshwater Fishes. (Illus., Orig.). 1977. pap. cancelled (ISBN 0-685-76991-7). Mad River.

Miller, Daniel J. & Lea, Robert N. Guide to the Coastal Marine Fishes of California. 1976. pap. 2.00x (ISBN 0-931876-13-3, 4065). Ag Sci Pubns.

Moyle, Peter B. Inland Fishes of California. 1976. 20.00 (ISBN 0-520-02975-5). U of Cal Pr.

Naiman, Robert J. & Solt, David L. Fishes in North American Deserts. 360p. 1981. 42.00 (ISBN 0-471-08523-5, Pub. by Wiley-Interscience). Wiley.

Petit, Gedeon D. Effects of Dissolved Oxygen on Survival & Behavior of Selected Fishes of Western Lake Erie. 1973. 3.00 (ISBN 0-686-30329-6). Ohio Bio Survey.

Price, John W. Food Habits of Some Lake Erie Fishes. 1963. 3.00 (ISBN 0-686-30320-2). Ohio Bio Survey.

Rafinesque, Constantine. Ichthyologia Ohiensis, or, Natural History of the Fishes Inhabiting the River Ohio & Its Tributary Streams. LC 72-125760. (American Environmental Studies). 1970. Repr. of 1820 ed. 13.00 (ISBN 0-405-02686-2). Arno.

Shurrager, P. Sheridan. An Ecological Study of the Fishes of the Hocking River. 1932. 1.00 (ISBN 0-686-30301-6). Ohio Bio Survey.

Simpson, James C. & Wallace, Richard L. Fishes of Idaho. LC 78-65345. 1978. 6.50 (ISBN 0-89301-058-8). U Pr of Idaho.

Sisley, Nick. Panfish, U.S.A. 144p. 1981. 12.95 (ISBN 0-87691-333-8). Winchester Pr.

Smith, Jerome V. C. Natural History of the Fishes of Massachusetts. (Illus.). 400p. 1970. boxed 10.75 (ISBN 0-88395-002-2). Freshet Pr.

Smith, Philip W. The Fishes of Illinois. LC 78-12741. 1979. 25.00 (ISBN 0-252-00682-8). U of Ill Pr.

Thompson. Gamefishes of New England. (Illus.). 226p. 1980. 14.95 (ISBN 0-89272-063-8). Down East.

Thomson, Donald A., et al. Reef Fishes of the Sea of Cortez: The Rocky Shore Fishes of the Gulf of California. LC 78-18835. 302p. 1979. 43.50 (ISBN 0-471-86162-6, Pub. by Wiley-Interscience). Wiley.

Titcomb, Margaret. Native Use of Fish in Hawaii. 2nd ed. 1972. pap. 3.95 (ISBN 0-8248-0592-5). U Pr of Hawaii.

Trautman, Milton B. The Fishes of Ohio. rev. 2nd ed. LC 80-29521. (Illus.). 800p. 1981. price not set (ISBN 0-8142-0319-1). Ohio St U Pr.

Werner, Robert G. Freshwater Fishes of New York State: A Field Guide. LC 80-17942. (York State Bks.). (Illus.). 270p. 1980. 20.00s (ISBN 0-8156-2233-3); pap. 11.95 (ISBN 0-8156-2222-8). Syracuse U Pr.

Wydoski, Richard S. & Whitney, Richard R. Inland Fishes of Washington. LC 78-21759. (Illus.). 284p. 1979. 17.50 (ISBN 0-295-95643-7); pap. 8.95 (ISBN 0-295-95644-5). U of Wash Pr.

FISHES, ELECTRIC

see Electric Organs in Fishes

FISHES, FOSSIL

Herre, Albert. Notes on Fishes in the Zoological Museum of Stanford University. 102p. 1974. 6.95 (ISBN 0-912318-02-3). N K Gregg.

Stensio, Erik A. The Downtonian & Devonian Vertebrates of Spitsbergen: Pt. 1, Family Cephalaspidea, Det Norske Videnskaps-Akademii Oslo, Skrifter M Svalbard G Nordishav et, Nr. 12, 2 vols. Gould, Stephen J., ed. LC 79-8553. (History of Paleontology Ser.). (Illus.). 1980. Repr. of 1927 ed. lib. bdg. 70.00x (ISBN 0-405-12746-4); lib. bdg. 35.00x ea. Vol. 1 (ISBN 0-405-12747-2). Vol. 2 (ISBN 0-405-12748-0). Arno.

Traquair, R. H. The Fishes of the Old Red Sandstone, Pt. 2, Nos. 2-4. Repr. of 1914 ed. Set. pap. 16.00 (ISBN 0-384-61370-5). Johnson Repr.

--Ganoid Fishes of British Carboniferous Formations, Pt. 1., Nos. 2-7. Repr. of 1914 ed. Set. pap. 34.50 (ISBN 0-384-61380-2). Johnson Repr.

Woodward, A. Smith. Wealden & Purbeck Fishes, Pts. 1-3. Set. pap. 38.50 (ISBN 0-384-69219-2). Johnson Repr.

FISHES, FRESH-WATER

see also names of classes, orders, etc. of fresh water fishes

Bagenal, T. B. The Observer's Book of Freshwater Fishes. (The Observer Bks). (Illus.). 1979. 3.95 (ISBN 0-684-16025-0, ScribT). Scribner.

Berra, Tim M. An Atlas of Distribution of the Freshwater Fish Families of the World. LC 80-24666. (Illus.). xxviii, 198p. 1981. 26.50x (ISBN 0-8032-1411-1); pap. 12.50x (ISBN 0-8032-6059-8, BB 768, Bison). U of Nebr Pr.

A Bibliography of African Freshwater Fish: Supplement One, 1968-1975. (CIFA Occasional Paper: No. 5). 1977. pap. 7.50 (ISBN 92-5-000092-8, F 737, FAO). Unipub.

Branson, Branley A. & Batch, Donald L. Fishes of the Red River Drainage, Eastern Kentucky. LC 73-80459. (Illus.). 76p. 1974. pap. 5.00x (ISBN 0-8131-1295-8). U Pr of Ky.

Carlander, Kenneth D. Handbook of Freshwater Fishery Biology, Vol. 1. fasc.,3rd ed. (Illus.). 1969. pap. 20.75x (ISBN 0-8138-2335-8). Iowa St U Pr.

Dalrymple, Byron. Complete Guide to Game Fish: A Field Book of Fresh & Saltwater Species. 480p. 1981. 14.95 (ISBN 0-442-21978-4). Van Nos Reinhold.

Eddy, Samuel & Underhill, James C. How to Know the Freshwater Fishes. 3rd ed. (Pictured Key Nature Ser.). 360p. 1978. text ed. write for info. (ISBN 0-697-04751-2); wire coil avail. (ISBN 0-697-04750-4). Wm C Brown.

Everett, Charles. Fresh Water Fishes. (Illus.). 45p. pap. 1.00 (ISBN 0-8323-0126-4). Binford.

Fegely, Thomas D. The World of Freshwater Fish. LC 77-16879. (Illus.). (gr. 5 up). 1978. 6.95 (ISBN 0-396-07562-2). Dodd.

Guidelines for Sampling Fish in Inland Waters. (EIFAC Technical Papers: No. 33). 184p. 1980. pap. 12.00 (ISBN 92-5-100973-2, F 2037, FAO). Unipub.

Lagler, Karl F. Freshwater Fishery Biology. 434p. 1956. text ed. write for info. (ISBN 0-697-04675-3). Wm C Brown.

Lee, D. S., et al. Atlas of North American Freshwater Fishes. LC 80-620039. (Illus.). 854p. 1980. 25.00 (ISBN 0-917134-03-6). NC Natl Hist.

Lloyd, Richard & Alabaster, J. S., eds. Water Quality Criteria for Fresh Water Fish. LC 79-41350. 1980. text ed. 52.50 (ISBN 0-408-10673-5). Butterworth.

McClane, A. J. McClane's Field Guide to Freshwater Fishes of North America. LC 77-11967. (Illus.). 1978. pap. 6.95 (ISBN 0-03-021116-6). HR&W.

McGinnis, S. California Freshwater Fishes. (Illus., Orig.). 1977. pap. cancelled (ISBN 0-685-76991-7). Mad River.

Maitland, Peter S. A Key to British Freshwater Fishes. 1972. 11.00x (ISBN 0-900386-18-5, Pub. by Freshwater Bio). State Mutual Bk.

Morrow, James E. The Freshwater Fishes of Alaska. LC 80-1116. (Illus.). 272p. (Orig.). 1980. pap. 24.95 (ISBN 0-88240-134-3). Alaska Northwest.

Moyle, Peter B. Inland Fishes of California. 1976. 20.00 (ISBN 0-520-02975-5). U of Cal Pr.

Scott, W. B. Freshwater Fishes of Eastern Canada. 2nd ed. LC 67-101255. (Illus.). 1967. pap. 7.50 (ISBN 0-8020-6074-9). U of Toronto Pr.
Sisley, Nick. Panfish, U.S.A. 144p. 1981. 12.95 (ISBN 0-87691-333-8). Winchester Pr.
Walker, Braz. Sharks & Loaches. (Illus.). 160p. 1974. pap. 6.95 (ISBN 0-87666-161-4, PS-718). TFH Pubns.
Water Quality Criteria for European Freshwater Fish. (EIFAC Technical Papers: No. 37). 57p. 1980. pap. 7.50 (ISBN 0-686-74016-5, F 2029, FAO). Unipub.
Water Quality Criteria for European Freshwater Fish: Report on the Effect of Zinc & Copper Pollution on the Salmon Fisheries in a River & Lake System in Central Norway. (EIFAC Technical Paper: No. 29). 40p. 1978. pap. 7.50 (ISBN 92-5-100296-7, F770, FAO). Unipub.

FISHES, TROPICAL
see Tropical Fish

FISHING
see also Bait; Bass Fishing; Electric Fishing; Fishery Law and Legislation; Flies, Artificial; Fly-Casting; Fly Fishing; Ice Fishing; Muskellunge Fishing; River Life; Salmon Fishing; Salt-Water Fishing; Shark Fishing; Spear Fishing; Spin Fishing; Trout Fishing

All-Union Conference, Murmansk, Feb.-Mar., 1968. Fish Behavior & Fishing Techniques: Proceedings. 198p. 1971. 17.50x (ISBN 0-7065-1181-6, Pub. by IPST). Intl Schol Bk Serv.
Allyn, Rube. Fishermen's Handbook. (Orig.). pap. 1.95 (ISBN 0-8200-0103-1). Great Outdoors.
Arnold, Richard. Come Sea Fishing with Me. 9.95x (ISBN 0-392-06448-0, SpS). Sportshelf.
Balfour, Harold. Folk, Fish & Fun. (Illus.). 1979. 14.00x (ISBN 0-900963-85-9, Pub. by Terence Dalton England). State Mutual Bk.
Bashline, L. James, ed. The Eastern Trail. (Illus.). 320p. 1972. 8.95 (ISBN 0-88395-014-6). Freshet Pr.
Bates, Joseph D., Jr. Fishing: An Encyclopedic Guide to Tackle & Tactics for Fresh & Salt Water. 1974. 16.95 (ISBN 0-87690-110-0). Dutton.
--How to Find Fish & Make Them Strike. LC 73-93268. (An Outdoor Life Bk). (Illus.). 224p. 1975. 9.95 (ISBN 0-06-010241-1, HarpT). Har-Row.
Becker, A. C., Jr. The Complete Book of Fishing. LC 76-18477. (Illus.). 217p. 1981. Repr. of 1977 ed. 20.00 (ISBN 0-498-01973-X). A S Barnes.
--The Complete Book of Fishing. LC 76-18477. (Illus.). 1977. 17.50 (ISBN 0-498-01973-X). A S Barnes.
Benedict, J. Nelson, et al. Successful Ocean Game Fishing. Moss, Frank T., ed. LC 72-132081. (Illus.). 20.00 (ISBN 0-87742-013-0). Intl Marine.
Ben-Yami, M. Fishing with Light. (FAO Fishing Manuals). (Illus., Orig.). 1976. pap. 10.50 (ISBN 0-85238-078-X, FAO). Unipub.
Berlin, Sven. Jonah's Dream: A Meditation on Fishing. LC 74-14908. (Illus.). 140p. 1975. 7.95 (ISBN 0-913232-14-9); pap. 2.95 (ISBN 0-913232-78-5). W Kaufmann.
Berners, Juliana. A Treatise on Fishing with a Hook. 9.95 (ISBN 0-88427-038-6). Green Hill.
--A Treatise on Fishing with a Hook. LC 79-20603. (Angling Classics Ser.). 1979. Repr. 9.95 (ISBN 0-88427-038-6, Dist. by Caroline Hse). North River.
Blaisdell, Harold F. The Art of Fishing with Worms & Other Live Bait. 1978. 10.00 (ISBN 0-394-40039-9). Knopf.
Bowring, Dave. How to Fish Streams. (Illus.). 1977. 10.00 (ISBN 0-87691-197-1). Winchester Pr.
Boyd, Lester C. Atlantic Surf Fishing: Maine to Maryland. LC 75-43277. (Illus.). 160p. (Orig.). 1976. pap. 4.95 (ISBN 0-913276-18-9). Stone Wall Pr.
Bradford, Charles. The Brook Trout & the Determined Angler. (Illus.). 72p. 1970. boxed 6.75 (ISBN 0-88395-003-0). Freshet Pr.
Bradner, Enos. Fish-on! LC 76-182889. 3.95 (ISBN 0-87564-610-7). Superior Pub.
Brooks, Joe. Complete Book of Fly Fishing. rev. ed. LC 68-30939. 1968. 9.95 (ISBN 0-498-06963-X). A S Barnes.
Bucknell, Geoffrey. Fishing Days. 9.50x (ISBN 0-392-06580-0, SpS). Sportshelf.
Casson, Paul. Decoys Simplified. (Illus.). 132p. 1973. 14.95 (ISBN 0-88395-016-2). Freshet Pr.
Code of Safety for Fisherman & Fishing Vessels, 2 pts. Incl. Pt. A. Safety & Health Practice for Skippers & Crews. 108p. pap. 13.75 (ISBN 0-686-64932-X, IMCO 42); Pt. B. Safety & Health Requirements for the Construction & Equipment of Fishing Vessels. 158p. pap. 16.50 (ISBN 0-686-64933-8, IMCO 43). 1975 (IMCO). Unipub.
Collins, Peter & Graham, Colin. Coarse Fishing. (Know the Game Ser.). (Illus.). 1975. pap. 2.50 (ISBN 0-7158-0209-7). Charles River Bks.
Cone, Arthur L., Jr. Fishing Made Easy. rev. ed. (Illus.). 336p. 1976. pap. 4.95 (ISBN 0-02-028190-0, Collier). Macmillan.
Congress on Fishing Gear, 3rd, Reykjavik, 1970. Modern Fishing Gear of the World, Three: Fish Finding, Purse Seining, & Aimed Trawling. Kristjonsson, H., ed. (Illus.). 537p. 1972. 46.25 (ISBN 0-85238-054-2, FAO). Unipub.
Consumer Guide Editors. Whole Fishing Catalog. (Illus.). 1978. pap. 7.95 (ISBN 0-671-23023-9, Fireside). S&S.
Cowger, Joel D. Sources of Financial Assistance Available to the Maine Fishing Industry. (Fisheries Information Ser.: No. 2). 1979. pap. write for info (ISBN 0-89737-001-5). Maine Dept Marine.
Crahall, Joseph. The Completest Angling Booke That Ever Was Writ. (Illus.). 256p. 1970. boxed 27.50 (ISBN 0-88395-007-3). Freshet Pr.
Culley, M. B. The Pilchard. 1972. 55.000 (ISBN 0-08-016523-0). Pergamon.
Cushing, D. H. Detection of Fish. 220p. 1973. text ed. 42.00 (ISBN 0-08-017123-0). Pergamon.
Dahlem, Ted. How to Make & Mend Cast Nets. pap. 1.95 (ISBN 0-8200-0608-4). Great Outdoors.
Dalrymple, Byron W. How to Rig & Fish Natural Baits. (Funk & W Bk.). (Illus.). 1977. 7.95 (ISBN 0-308-10289-4); pap. 4.50 (ISBN 0-308-10291-6, TYC-T). T Y Crowell.
Data on Fishing Vessels & Gear in the Mediterranean. (GFCM Studies & Reviews Ser.: No. 56). (Illus., Bilingual.). 1978. pap. 12.00 (ISBN 92-5-000350-1, F1257, FAO). Unipub.
Davies, W. E. Footloose with a Fishing Rod. 7.50x (ISBN 0-392-06479-0, LTB). Sportshelf.
Deindorfer, Robert G. Positive Fishing: The Art of Angling Your Outer Limit. LC 79-67600. 171p. 1981. 10.95 (ISBN 0-87223-660-9). Seaview Bks.
Denny, George. The Dread Fishwish. (Illus.). 1974. 8.95 (ISBN 0-88395-024-3). Freshet Pr.
Doogue, Raymond. Seafishing for Beginners. 1974. 5.95 (ISBN 0-589-00808-0, Pub. by Reed Books Australia). C E Tuttle.
Downey, Earl. How to Fish for Snook. (Orig.). pap. 1.95 (ISBN 0-8200-0104-X). Great Outdoors.
Dunaway, Vic. Modern Saltwater Fishing. 288p. 1975. 11.95 (ISBN 0-87691-168-8). Winchester Pr.
Earp, Samuel A. & Wildeman, William J. The Blue Water Bait Book: Secrets of Successful Big Game Fishing. LC 74-5273. (A Sports Illustrated Bk). (Illus.). 160p. 1974. 8.95 (ISBN 0-316-20330-0). Little.
Eggert, Richard. Fish & Hunt the Backcountry. LC 78-17135. (Illus.). 224p. 1978. 9.95 (ISBN 0-8117-0191-3). Stackpole.
Eisenberg, Lee & Taylor, Decourcy. The Ultimate Fishing Book. (Illus.). 256p. 1981. 40.00 (ISBN 0-395-31767-3). HM.
Elman, Robert. The Fisherman's Field Guide to the Freshwater & Saltwater Gamefish of North America. 1977. 14.95 (ISBN 0-394-41399-7). Knopf.
Evanoff, Vlad. Another Thousand & One Fishing Tips & Tricks. LC 77-123928. (Illus.). 1970. 9.95 (ISBN 0-06-011187-9, HarpT). Har-Row.
--Complete Guide to Fishing. pap. 2.00 (ISBN 0-87980-250-2). Wilshire.
--How to Fish in Salt Water. LC 62-10180. (Large Type Editions Ser.). (Illus.). 210p. 1975. 9.95 (ISBN 0-498-01598-X). A S Barnes.
--One Thousand & One Fishing Tips & Tricks. (Illus.). 1966. 10.95 (ISBN 0-06-070738-0, HarpT). Har-Row.
--One Thousand & One Fishing Tips & Tricks. 1978. pap. 3.95 (ISBN 0-346-12336-4). Cornerstone.
Expert Consultation on Fishing for Squid & Other Cephalopods, Tokyo & Hakodata, Japan, 1975. Report. 11p. 1976. pap. 7.50 (ISBN 0-685-66350-7, F817, FAO). Unipub.
Expert Consultation on Fishing for Squid & Other Cephalopods. Report: Supplement One. (FAO Fisheries Reports: No. 170, Suppl. 1). (Illus.). 1976. pap. 17.00 (ISBN 92-5-100034-4, F818, FAO). Unipub.
Fabian, John. Fishing for Beginners. 1980. pap. 2.95 (ISBN 0-689-70468-2, Aladdin). Atheneum.
Fabian, Leonard. Fishing. (Monarch Illustrated Guide Ser.). (Illus.). 1977. pap. 2.95 (ISBN 0-671-18761-9). Monarch Pr.
Fagerstrom, Stan. Catch More Crappie. (Illus.). 1977. pap. 5.95 (ISBN 0-916682-06-4). Outdoor Empire.
Fichter, George S. & Frances, Phil. Fishing: Guide to Fresh & Saltwater. Zim, Herbert S., ed. (A Golden Guide Ser). 1965. 1.95 (ISBN 0-307-24008-8, Golden Pr). Western Pub.
Field & Stream. Field & Stream Reader. facs. ed. LC 77-128242. (Essay Index Reprint Ser). 1946. 19.50 (ISBN 0-8369-1875-4). Arno.
Fisher, Jeffrey. The Fish Book: How to Buy, Clean, Catch, Cook & Preserve Them. (Illus.). 128p. 1981. 8.95 (ISBN 0-87523-196-9). Emerson.
Fishing Boats & Their Equipment. 182p. 1980. pap. 23.50 (ISBN 0-85238-090-9, FN 81, FNB). Unipub.
Fishing News Bks. Ltd. Staff, ed. Seine Fishing: Bottom Fishing Wih Rope Warps & Wing Trawls. 224p. 1981. 40.00x (ISBN 0-85238-113-1, Pub. by Fishing News England). State Mutual Bk.
Fishing Ports & Markets. (Illus.). 1971. 37.50 (ISBN 0-85238-012-7, FAO). Unipub.
Flick, Art. Art Flicks New Streamside Guide to Naturals & Their Imitations. (Illus.). 176p. 1970. 7.50 (ISBN 0-517-50783-8). Crown.
Forbes, David C. Big-Game Fishing in British Waters. (Illus.). 160p. 1973. 4.95 (ISBN 0-7153-5696-8). David & Charles.
--Successful Roach Fishing. (Illus.). 150p. 1973. 4.50 (ISBN 0-7153-6086-8). David & Charles.
--Successful Sea Angling. (Illus.). 156p. 1971. 3.50 (ISBN 0-7153-5116-8). David & Charles.
Forsberg, Foy. Beginner's Guide to Shorecasting. (Illus.). 183p. 1975. 10.95 (ISBN 0-7207-0753-6). Transatlantic.
Foster, Muriel. Muriel Foster's Fishing Diary. LC 79-21156. (Illus.). 1980. 16.95 (ISBN 0-670-49557-3, Studio). Viking Pr.
Fox, Charles K. The Book of Lures. (Illus.). 256p. 1975. 14.95 (ISBN 0-88395-019-7). Freshet Pr.
Freeman, Jim. California Steelhead Fishing. (Illus.). 96p. 1971. pap. 1.95 (ISBN 0-87701-032-3). Chronicle Bks.
--Shasta Lake Fishing. (Illus.). 80p. 1971. pap. 1.95 (ISBN 0-87701-033-1). Chronicle Bks.
--Trinity River Fishing. (Illus.). 80p. 1971. pap. 1.95 (ISBN 0-87701-030-7). Chronicle Bks.
Fridman, A. L. Theory & Design of Commercial Fishing Gear. Kondor, R., tr. from Rus. (Israel Program for Scientific Translations Ser). (Illus.). x, 490p. 1972. 42.50x (ISBN 0-7065-1249-9, Pub. by IPST). Intl Schol Bk Serv.
Garrison, Chuck. Offshore Fishing: In Southern California & Baja. LC 80-27579. (Illus., Orig.). 1980. pap. 4.95 (ISBN 0-87701-166-4). Chronicle Bks.
Gerlach, Rex. Creative Fly Tying & Fishing. 1974. 13.95 (ISBN 0-87691-122-X). Winchester Pr.
Giles, Ken & Smith, Clive. Match Fishing Our Way. 1978. 13.50 (ISBN 0-7153-7692-6). David & Charles.
Gordon, Sid. How to Fish from Top to Bottom. (Illus.). 384p. 1978. 21.95 (ISBN 0-8117-0837-3); deluxed slipcased ed. 30.00 (ISBN 0-8117-0931-0). Stackpole.
Grey, Zane. Fresh Water Fishing. 298p. Repr. lib. bdg. 15.95x (ISBN 0-89190-762-9). Am Repr-Rivercity Pr.
--Seafishing Yarns. 276p. Repr. lib. bdg. 15.15x (ISBN 0-89190-766-1). Am Repr-Rivercity Pr.
Gryndall, William. Hawking, Hunting, Fouling & Fishing; Newly Corrected by W. Gryndall Faulkener. LC 70-38194. (English Experience Ser.: No. 463). 88p. 1972. Repr. of 1596 ed. 13.00 (ISBN 90-221-0463-X). Walter J Johnson.
Hadson, Alfred. The Fishing Cadet's Handbook. 1978. 10.00 (ISBN 0-685-63420-5). State Mutual Bk.
Haig-Brown, Roderick. Bright Waters, Bright Fish. (Illus.). 160p. 1980. 19.95 (ISBN 0-917304-59-4, Timber Pr). Intl Schol Bk.
--Bright Waters, Bright Fish. 1980. ltd. ed. 75.00 (ISBN 0-918400-05-8, Champoeg Pr). Intl Schol Bk.
--River Never Sleeps. (Sportsmen's Classics Ser.). 352p. 1974. 7.50 (ISBN 0-517-51601-2). Crown.
Haley, K. Brian, ed. Applied Operations Research in Fishing. (NATO Conference Series II-Systems Science: Vol. 10). 490p. 1981. 59.50 (ISBN 0-306-40634-9, Plenum Pr). Plenum Pub.
Hall, Henry M. Idylls of Fishermen: A History of the Literary Species. LC 12-11121. Repr. of 1912 ed. 17.50 (ISBN 0-404-03046-7). AMS Pr.
Hammond, Samuel H. Wild Northern Scene or Sporting Adventures with Rifle & the Rod. (Illus.). 1979. Repr. of 1857 ed. 12.50 (ISBN 0-916346-33-1). Harbor Hill Bks.
Hancock, C. V. Rod in Hand. 9.95x (ISBN 0-392-06434-0, SpS). Sportshelf.
Hardy, Arthur E. Beginner's Guide to Coarse (Bait) Fishing. (Illus.). 128p. 1973. 10.00 (ISBN 0-7207-0585-1). Transatlantic.
--The Sea Angler's First Handbook. 128p. 1975. 8.50 (ISBN 0-7207-0532-0, Pub. by Michael Joseph). Merrimack Bk Serv.
Hayden, Mike. Pier Fishing on San Francisco Bay. LC 81-3799. (Illus.). 116p. (Orig.). 1981. pap. 5.95 (ISBN 0-87701-138-9). Chronicle Bks.
Hill, W. M. Coarse Fishing for New Anglers. LC 74-33154. (Illus.). 112p. 1975. 5.95 (ISBN 0-7153-6443-X). David & Charles.
Hilton, Jack. Quest for Carp. (Illus.). 188p. 1972. 14.00 (ISBN 0-7207-0582-7). Transatlantic.
Hodson, Alfred. The Fishing Cadet's Handbook. (Illus.). 108p. 11.25 (ISBN 0-85238-011-9, FN 44, FNB). Unipub.
Holden, John. Shorefishing. 128p. 1979. 8.50 (ISBN 0-571-11321-4, Pub. by Faber & Faber); pap. 4.50 (ISBN 0-571-11389-3). Merrimack Bk Serv.
Homemade Fishing. 2.95 (ISBN 0-686-31392-5). Outdoor Pubns.
Housby, Trevor. Fishing for Food. pap. 2.95 (ISBN 0-7153-7546-6, Pub. by Batsford England). David & Charles.
Humphrey, William. The Spawning Run. (Illus.). 1979. 7.50 (ISBN 0-440-08204-8, Sey Lawr); pap. 4.95 (ISBN 0-440-08206-4). Delacorte.
International Conference on Safety of Life at Sea, 1960. Incl. Supplement One. 185p. 1976. Repr. of 1970 ed. pap. 12.50 (ISBN 0-686-64930-3, IMCO 02); Supplement Two. 85p. 1978. Repr. of 1974 ed. pap. 11.00 (ISBN 0-686-64931-1, IMCO 03). 512p. 1976. pap. 22.00 (ISBN 0-686-64929-X, IMCO 01, IMCO). Unipub.
Iversen, Edwin S. Farming the Edge of the Sea. 2nd ed. (Illus.). 440p. 50.75 (ISBN 0-85238-079-8, FN 30, FNB). Unipub.
Jenkins, Frances C. Hey Girls, Let's Go Fishing. 1978. 5.00 (ISBN 0-682-49045-8). Exposition.
Jenkins, J. Geraint. Nets & Coracles. LC 74-81005. (Illus.). 352p. 1974. 8.95 (ISBN 0-7153-6546-0). David & Charles.
Johnson, et al. Outdoor Tips: A Remington Sportsmen's Library Bk. pap. 2.95 (ISBN 0-87502-905-1). Benjamin Co.
Judd, Stan. Inshore Fishing: Its Skills, Risks, Rewards. (Illus.). 144p. 15.00 (ISBN 0-85238-096-8, FN 55, FNB). Unipub.
--Inshore Fishing: Its Skills, Risks, Rewards. 1978. 15.00 (ISBN 0-685-63428-0). State Mutual Bk.
Junghanns, George. The Complete Land Angler. (Treasure Hunting Ser.). (Illus.). 1977. pap. write for info. (ISBN 0-686-21782-9). Gauntlet Bks.
Keane, Martin J. Classic Rods & Rodmakers. 1976. 17.95 (ISBN 0-87691-178-5). Winchester Pr.
Kelly, Florence F. Flowing Stream. 59.95 (ISBN 0-8490-0176-5). Gordon Pr.
Ketting, Kees & Peeters, Henk. Two Hundred Fishing Tips: Zander. (Illus.). 88p. (Orig.). 1980. pap. 5.00 (ISBN 0-85242-615-1). Intl Pubns Serv.
Klust, Gerhard. Netting Materials for Fishing Gear. (Illus.). 173p. (Orig.). 1974. pap. 9.00 (ISBN 0-686-77007-2, FAO). Unipub.
Knap, Jerome. Fishing Secrets: One Hundred & One Ways to Improve Your Fishing. (Illus.). 1978. 8.95 (ISBN 0-517-53320-0). Crown.
Kostyunin, Yu N. & Nokonorou, I. V. Trawling & New Methods of Continuous Fishing. (Illus.). 267p. 1971. 20.00x (ISBN 0-7065-1093-3, Pub. by IPST). Intl Schol Bk Serv.
Ku Lien-Chen. Notes on Chinese Fishing. (National Peking University & Chinese Assn. for Folklore, Folklore & Folkliterature Ser.: No. 110). (Chinese.). 6.00 (ISBN 0-89986-188-1). E Langstaff.
Lambuth, Letcher. The Angler's Workshop. 212p. 1979. 49.50x (ISBN 0-918400-01-5, Pub. by Champoeg Pr). Intl Schol Bk Serv.
Lampman, Ben H. A Leaf from French Eddy: On Fish, Anglers & Fisherman. LC 78-15836. (Illus.). 1979. 7.95 (ISBN 0-06-250500-9, HarpR). Har-Row.
Lane, Billy & Graham, Colin. Billy Lanes Encyclopaedia of Float Fishing. (Illus.). 1971. 9.50 (ISBN 0-7207-0514-2). Transatlantic.
Langhenkel, de Boer. Two Hundred Carp Tips. (Illus.). 96p. (Orig.). 1979. pap. 5.00x (ISBN 0-85242-614-3). Intl Pubns Serv.
Larssen, A. K. & Jaeger, Sig. The ABC's of Fo'c'sle Living. LC 76-17265. (Illus.). 1976. pap. 4.95 (ISBN 0-914842-11-0). Madrona Pubs.
Lee, Jasper S. Commercial Catfish Farming. 2nd ed. (Illus.). 1981. 12.50 (ISBN 0-8134-2156-X, 2156). Interstate.
Lyman, Henry. Successful Bluefishing. LC 73-93528. (Illus.). 120p. 1974. 15.00 (ISBN 0-87742-041-6). Intl Marine.
McCafferty, W. Patrick. Aquatic Entomology: The Fisherman's & Ecologists Illustrated Guide to Insects & Their Relatives. 496p. 1981. 50.00 (ISBN 0-686-31440-9). Sci Bks Intl.
McClane, A. J. McClane's Secrets of Successful Fishing. LC 78-24367. (Illus.). 288p. 1980. 12.95 (ISBN 0-03-053271-X); pap. 6.95 (ISBN 0-03-021126-3). HR&W.
Mansfield, Kenneth. Coarse Fishing As a Pastime. 12.50x (ISBN 0-392-06496-0, SpS). Sportshelf.
Marshall, Mel. How to Fish: A Commonsense Approach. (Illus.). 1978. 11.95 (ISBN 0-87691-273-0). Winchester Pr.
--Steelhead. (Illus.). 186p. 1980. 10.95 (ISBN 0-87691-093-2). Winchester Pr.

Martin, A. The Ring-Net Fishermen. 263p. 1981. pap. text ed. 31.25x (ISBN 0-85976-064-2, Pub. by Donald England). Humanities.
Mascall, Leonard. A Booke of Fishing with Hooke & Line (Taken from the Treatise of Fishing with an Angle) LC 72-6017. (English Experience Ser.: No. 542). 92p. 1973. Repr. of 1590 ed. 9.50 (ISBN 90-221-0542-3). Walter J Johnson.
Meyers, Chet & Lindner, Al. Catching Fish. LC 78-6532. (Illus.). 1978. 8.95 (ISBN 0-87518-165-1). Dillon.
Michaelson, John. Tackle Angling. rev. ed. Harris, Brian, ed. (Tackle Ser). (Illus.). 128p. (gr. 9 up). 1975. pap. text ed. 6.95x (ISBN 0-09-120451-8, SpS). Sportshelf.
Millus, Donald. A Contemplative Fishing Guide to the Grand Strand. 1977. pap. 3.95 (ISBN 0-87844-040-2). Sandlapper Store.
Milne, P. H. Fish & Shellfish Farming in Coastal Waters. (Illus.). 208p. 39.50 (ISBN 0-85238-022-4, FN 32, FNB). Unipub.
Mitchell, John. Better Fishing, Freshwater. rev. ed. LC 72-185859. (Better Sports Ser). 1978. 8.50x (ISBN 0-7182-1455-2). Intl Pubns Serv.
--On the Line. 9.50x (ISBN 0-392-06594-0, SpS). Sportshelf.
Moe, Martin. Florida Fishing Grounds. Orig. Title: Off Shore & Coastal Fishing: Florida. (Orig.). pap. 2.95 (ISBN 0-8200-0111-2). Great Outdoors.
Moorhouse, Geoffrey. The Boat & the Town. LC 79-13898. 1979. 10.95 (ISBN 0-316-58060-0). Little.
Moraski, Art. Complete Guide to Walleye Fishing. 1980. pap. 9.95 (ISBN 0-932558-12-7). Willow Creek.
Moss, Frank, ed. The Lore of Sportfishing. 1976. 29.95 (ISBN 0-517-52109-1). Crown.
Moss, Frank T. Successful Striped Bass Fishing. LC 73-93527. (Illus.). 192p. 1974. 15.00 (ISBN 0-87742-040-8). Intl Marine.
Murphy, Brian. The Anglers Companion. LC 78-18808. (Illus.). 1978. 10.00 (ISBN 0-448-22682-0). Paddington.
Norton, Mortimer, ed. Angling Success, by Leading Outdoor Writers. facs. ed. LC 67-30224. (Essay Index Reprint Ser). 1935. 18.00 (ISBN 0-8369-0747-7). Arno.
Oberrecht, Kenn. The Practical Angler's Guide to Successful Fishing. (Illus.). 1978. 12.95 (ISBN 0-87691-250-1). Winchester Pr.
Oberrecht, Kenn & Oberrecht, Pat. Keeping the Catch. 240p. 1981. 14.95 (ISBN 0-87691-339-7). Winchester Pr.
O'Farrell, R. C. Seafood Fishing for Amateur & Professional. (Illus.). 196p. 15.00 (ISBN 0-85238-097-6, FN 70, FNB). Unipub.
Olson, Fred. Exciter Fishing. (Illus.). 1978. 12.50 (ISBN 0-87691-233-1). Winchester Pr.
--Successful Downrigger Fishing. 224p. 1981. 13.95 (ISBN 0-87691-340-0). Winchester Pr.
Ormond, Clyde. Outdoorsman's Handbook. 1975. pap. 1.95 (ISBN 0-425-02893-3, Windhover). Berkley Pub.
Otter Board Design & Performance. (Illus.). 79p. (Orig.). 1975. pap. 4.75 (ISBN 0-685-52330-6, F307, FAO). Unipub.
Ovington, Ray. Freshwater Fishing. 1977. pap. 3.95 (ISBN 0-8015-2837-2, Hawthorn). Dutton.
Parsons, P. Allen. Complete Book of Fresh Water Fishing. LC 63-8071. (Outdoor Life Ser.). (Illus.). 1963. 12.95 (ISBN 0-06-071500-6, HarpT). Har-Row.
Pearsall, R. Is That My Hook in Your Ear. 9.95x (ISBN 0-392-06563-0, SpS). Sportshelf.
Perry, W. H. Fishermen's Handbook. 1980. 60.00x (ISBN 0-686-64736-X, Pub. by Fishing News England). State Mutual Bk.
Perry, W. H., ed. Fishermen's Handbook. 344p. 1980. cloth 29.95x (ISBN 0-85238-106-9, Pub. by Fishing News England). State Mutual Bk.
Piper, John. All About Angling. 1971. 7.50 (ISBN 0-7207-0429-4). Transatlantic.
Pobst, Richard. Fish the Impossible Places. (Illus.). 1974. 9.95 (ISBN 0-88395-025-1). Freshet Pr.
Pratt, Mary M. Better Angling with Simple Science. (Illus.). 144p. 14.25 (ISBN 0-85238-069-0, FN 3, FNB). Unipub.
--Better Angling with Simple Science. 1978. 12.00x (ISBN 0-685-63393-4). State Mutual Bk.
Puddepha, D. N. Coarse Fishing Is Easy. (Illus.). 160p. 1970. 2.50 (ISBN 0-7153-4750-0). David & Charles.
Punola, John A. Fishing & Canoeing the Upper Delaware River. rev. for 1982 ed. (Illus.). 112p. (Orig.). 1981. pap. 4.50 (ISBN 0-939888-02-5). Path Pubns NJ.
Radcliffe, W. Fishing from the Earliest Times. 496p. 1974. 15.00 (ISBN 0-89005-008-2). Ares.
Radcliffe, William. Fishing from the Earliest Times. LC 70-80238. 1969. Repr. of 1921 ed. lib. bdg. 20.95 (ISBN 0-8337-2881-4). B Franklin.
The Rapala Fishing Guide: Secrets from Pros. LC 76-15852. (Illus.). 1976. pap. 2.95 (ISBN 0-686-17472-0). Normark Corp.
Rees, Clair & Wixom, Hartt. The Penny-Pinching Guide to Bigger Fish & Better Hunting. (Illus.). 160p. 1980. 9.95 (ISBN 0-87691-319-2). Winchester Pr.
Regulation of Fishing Effort. (FAO Fisheries Technical Paper: No. 197). 82p. 1981. pap. 7.50 (ISBN 92-5-100947-3, F2067, FAO). Unipub.
Rhead, Louis. Bait Angling for Common Fishes. LC 75-28715. 1976. pap. 3.95 (ISBN 0-8048-1168-7). C E Tuttle.
Richey, David. Complete Guide to Lake Fishing. (Crown - Outdoor Life Bks.). 336p. 1981. 15.95 (ISBN 0-517-54513-6). Crown.
--Dardevle's Guide to Fishing. (Illus.). 1978. 7.95 (ISBN 0-8059-2561-9). Dorrance.
--How to Catch Trophy Freshwater Game Fish. (Illus.). 1979. 11.95 (ISBN 0-517-53836-9). Crown.
Rizzo, Tony. Secrets of a Muskie Guide. 1977. pap. 6.00 (ISBN 0-932558-07-0). Willow Creek.
Romashko, Sandra D. The Sportsfisherman's Handbook: Where, When & How to Catch & Identify All the Recognized Gamefish of the World. LC 76-379974. (Illus.). 64p. (Orig.). 1975. pap. 2.75 (ISBN 0-89317-003-8). Windward Pub.
Rosko, Milt. Salt Water Fishing from Boats. 288p. 1972. pap. 2.45 (ISBN 0-02-029830-7, Collier). Macmillan.
Sainsbury, John C. Commercial Fishing Methods: An Introduction to Vessels & Gear. (Illus.). 120p. 20.75 (ISBN 0-85238-076-3, FN 5, FNB). Unipub.
Sawyer, Frank. Nymphs & the Trout. (Sportsman's Classics Ser.). 272p. 1973. 5.95 (ISBN 0-517-50336-0). Crown.
Scallops & the Diver-Fisherman. (Illus.). 144p. 1981. pap. 32.00 (ISBN 0-85238-114-X, FN90, FNB). Unipub.
Schaldach, William J. Coverts & Casts & Currents & Eddies, 2 vols. (Illus.). 280p. Set. boxed 25.00 (ISBN 0-88395-006-5). Freshet Pr.
Scharp, Hal. Freshwater Angler's Clinic. 1979. 9.95 (ISBN 0-671-24631-3). S&S.
Scott, Jack. Greased Line Fishing. (Illus.). 222p. 1970. boxed 10.75 (ISBN 0-88395-005-7). Freshet Pr.
Seaman, Kenneth. The Complete Chub Angler. LC 76-48822. (Illus.). 1977. 4.95 (ISBN 0-7153-7310-2). David & Charles.
Sehlinger, Bob & Underwood, Wes. A Guide to the Float Fishing Streams of Kentucky. (Illus., Orig.). 1980. pap. 9.95 (ISBN 0-89732-006-9). Thomas Pr.
Seine Fishing. 224p. 1981. pap. 54.50 (ISBN 0-85238-113-1, FN89, FNB). Unipub.
Sharp, Hal. Sportsman's Digest of Fishing. 1953. pap. 3.95 (ISBN 0-06-463247-4, EH 247, EH). Har-Row.
Shepherd. Instructions to Young Anglers. (Illus.). 12.50x (ISBN 0-392-06451-0, SpS). Sportshelf.
Smith, A. Paul. How to Fish for Bass. (Illus.). pap. 1.95 (ISBN 0-8200-0105-8, 114). Great Outdoors.
Sosin, Mark. Practical Light Tackle Fishing. LC 79-7661. (Nick Lyons Bk.). (Illus.). 224p. 1979. 14.95 (ISBN 0-385-15656-1). Doubleday.
Sosin, Mark & Clark, John. Through the Fish's Eye. LC 72-97172. (An Outdoor Life Bk.). (Illus.). 256p. 1973. 12.95 (ISBN 0-06-013971-4, HarpT). Har-Row.
Stewart, Douglas. Fishing Around the Monaro. new ed. 1978. pap. 3.00 (ISBN 0-7081-1811-9, Pub. by ANUP Australia). Bks Australia.
Stewart, R. N. Boys' Book of Angling. 1981. 10.00x (ISBN 0-904558-92-4, Pub. by Saiga Pub). State Mutual Bk.
Stoker, Hugh, et al. Fishing with the Experts. LC 77-91754. 1978. 13.50 (ISBN 0-7153-7543-1). David & Charles.
Stokes, Bill. You Can Catch Fish. LC 76-12478. (Games & Activities Ser.). 48p. (gr. k-3). 1976. 10.65 (ISBN 0-8172-0627-2). Raintree Pubs.
Stone, Peter. Gravel Pit Angling. LC 77-91759. (Illus.). 1978. 17.95 (ISBN 0-7153-7580-6). David & Charles.
Swainbank, Todd, ed. Taking Gamefish: From Dry Flies to Downrigger Freshwater Fishing. LC 79-20982. (Illus.). 1979. 15.95 (ISBN 0-89594-026-4); pap. 8.95 (ISBN 0-89594-025-6). Crossing Pr.
Taylor, Buck. The Complete Guide to Using Depthfinders. (Illus.). 272p. (Orig.). 1981. pap. 9.95 (ISBN 0-940022-00-1). Outdoor Skills.
Tedone, David. Complete Shellfisherman's Guide. (Illus.). 200p. 1981. pap. 7.95 (ISBN 0-933614-09-8). Peregrine Pr.
Three Books on Fishing: Associated with the Complete Angler by Izaac Walton. LC 62-7054. 1962. Repr. of 1659 ed. 22.00x (ISBN 0-8201-1017-5). Schol Facsimiles.
Torbett, Harvey. Coarse Fishing. 12.50x (ISBN 0-392-06501-0, SpS). Sportshelf.
--Sea Fishing. 12.50x (ISBN 0-392-06546-0, SpS). Sportshelf.
Tuna Fishing with Pole & Line. 150p. 1981. pap. 24.50 (ISBN 0-85238-111-5, FN 88, FNB). Unipub.
Underwood, Bob A. Lunker! LC 75-11780. (Illus.). 312p. 1975. 12.95 (ISBN 0-07-065758-0, GB). McGraw.
Vanderweide, Harry. The Book of Maine Fishing Maps. (Illus.). 96p. (Orig.). 1980. pap. 7.95 (ISBN 0-89933-007-X). DeLorme Pub.
Van De Water, Frederick F. In Defense of Worms. 182p. 1970. boxed 5.75 (ISBN 0-88395-000-6). Freshet Pr.
Von Brandt, A. Fish Catching Methods of the World. rev. & enlarged edition ed. (Illus.). 1972. 35.00 (ISBN 0-685-12016-3). Heinman.
Von Brandt, Andres. Fish Catching Methods of the World. 1978. 25.00 (ISBN 0-685-63409-4). State Mutual Bk.
Wade, Charles, ed. Fishing with the Experts. 1977. 9.95 (ISBN 0-285-62189-0, Pub. by Souvenir Pr). Intl Schol Bk Serv.
Walker, Richard. Catching Fish: Knowing Their Feeding Habits. LC 81-65961. (Illus.). 160p. 1981. 19.95 (ISBN 0-686-73221-9). David & Charles.
--The Shell Book of Angling. LC 79-53735. (Illus.). 1979. 22.50 (ISBN 0-7153-7780-9). David & Charles.
--Still Water Angling. new ed. (Illus.). 256p. 1975. 19.95 (ISBN 0-7153-7074-X). David & Charles.
Walton, Izaak. Compleat Angler. 1953. 7.95x (ISBN 0-460-00070-5, Evman); pap. 2.95x (ISBN 0-460-01070-0, Evman). Biblio Dist.
Warner, Dick, et al. Fishing in Ireland: The Complete Guide. 210p. 1981. 20.00x (ISBN 0-904651-32-0, Pub. by Appletree Ireland). State Mutual Bk.
Waterman, Charles F. The Fisherman's World. 1972. 19.95 (ISBN 0-394-41099-8, Co-Pub by Ridge Pr). Random.
--History of Angling. 320p. 1981. 15.95 (ISBN 0-87691-343-5). Winchester Pr.
--Modern Fresh & Salt Water Fly Fishing. LC 70-188598. (Illus.). 1975. 384p. 1974. pap. 3.95 (ISBN 0-02-029910-9, 02991, Collier). Macmillan.
Weeks, Edward. Fresh Waters. LC 67-23839. (Illus.). 1968. 8.95 (ISBN 0-316-92788-0, Pub. by Atlantic Monthly Pr). Little.
Welle-Strand, E. Angling in Norway. (Illus.). 1972. pap. 5.00x (ISBN 0-89918-510-X, N-510). Vanous.
Whitaker, Ralph R. Song of the Outriggers. LC 68-20946. 311p. 1968. 8.95 (ISBN 0-87527-087-5). Fireside Bks.
Willis, Richard, ed. World of Angling. (Illus.). 1977. 4.95 (ISBN 0-285-50291-3, Pub. by Souvenir Pr). Intl Schol Bk Serv.
Willock, Colin. The Angler's Encyclopaedia. 248p. 1975. 14.95 (ISBN 0-7207-0639-4, Pub. by Michael Joseph). Merrimack Bk Serv.
Willock, Colin, ed. ABC of Fishing. (Illus.). 1971. deluxe ed. 15.00 (ISBN 0-233-95921-1). Transatlantic.
Wilson, Loring D. The Handy Sportsman. 1976. 12.95 (ISBN 0-87691-213-7). Winchester Pr.
Wood, E. J. Inshore Dinghy Fishing. (Leisure Plan Bks). pap. 2.95 (ISBN 0-600-40083-2). Transatlantic.
Wrangles, Alan. Sea Fishing for Fun. 1977. 7.50 (ISBN 0-7153-7362-5). David & Charles.
Wrangles, Alan, ed. The Complete Guide to Coarse Fishing. (Illus.). 1973. 15.95 (ISBN 0-7153-5887-1). David & Charles.
--The Complete Guide to Sea Angling. (Illus.). 16.95 (ISBN 0-7153-5886-3). David & Charles.
Wright, D. Macer. A Fish Will Rise. (Illus.). 128p. 1972. 3.50 (ISBN 0-7153-5519-8). David & Charles.
Wright, Leonard M. Where the Fish Are: The New York Times Fish Finding Book. LC 77-79048. (Illus.). 1977. 8.95 (ISBN 0-8129-0717-5). Times Bks.
Yearbook of Fishery Statistics: Catches & Landings, Vol. 48. 384p. 1980. 43.25 (ISBN 0-686-74541-8, F2147, FAO). Unipub.

FISHING–ANECDOTES, FACETIAE, ETC.
see Fishing Stories

FISHING–BIBLIOGRAPHY
Bibliography for Fishermen's Training. (Fisheries Technical Paper Ser.: No. 184). 1979. pap. 12.00 (ISBN 92-5-100663-6, F1539, FAO). Unipub.
Glogan, Joseph. Sportsmans Book of U.S. Records. (Illus.). 96p. (Orig.). 1980. pap. text ed. 2.50 (ISBN 0-937328-00-6). NY Hunting.
Hampton, John F. Modern Angling Bibliography: Books Published on Angling, Fisheries & Fish Culture. 1980. lib. bdg. 49.95 (ISBN 0-8490-3127-3). Gordon Pr.

FISHING–DICTIONARIES
Fisherman's Handbook. (Illus.). 319p. 1980. 37.00 (ISBN 0-85238-106-9, FN85, FNB). Unipub.
Glossary of UK Fishing Gear Terms. 1980. 39.50x (ISBN 0-686-64737-8, Pub. by Fishing News England). State Mutual Bk.
Greenberg, Idaz. Fishwatcher's Field Guide. (Illus.). 1979. plastic card 3.95 (ISBN 0-913008-10-9). Seahawk Pr.
McClane, Albert J. McClane's New Standard Fishing Encyclopedia & International Angling Guide. rev. ed. LC 74-6108. (Illus.). 1176p. 1974. 50.00 (ISBN 0-03-060325-0). HR&W.
Marston, A. N. Encyclopedia of Angling. 2nd ed. 1963. 15.00 (ISBN 0-600-40092-1). Transatlantic.
Schreiner, Jean, et al. Le Nouveau Dictionnaire De la Peche. 384p. (Fr.). 1975. 35.95 (ISBN 0-686-57331-5). French & Eur.

FISHING–FLIES
see Flies, Artificial

FISHING–IMPLEMENTS AND APPLIANCES
see also Fishing Tackle
Clemens, Dale P. Fiberglass Rod Making. 1974. 14.95 (ISBN 0-87691-136-X). Winchester Pr.
Consumer Guide Magazine Editors, ed. Consumer Guide---Complete Guide to Fishing Equipment. (Orig.). 1975. pap. 1.95 (ISBN 0-451-06667-7, J6667, Sig). NAL.
EIFAC Fishing Gear Intercalibration Experiments. 92p. 1980. pap. 9.00 (ISBN 92-5-100864-7, F1954, FAO). Unipub.
Emery, John. How to Build Custom-Made Handcrafted Fishing Rods. LC 77-81170. (Illus.). 1977. pap. 3.95 (ISBN 0-89317-024-0). Windward Pub.
Evanoff, Vlad. Modern Fishing Tackle. (Illus.). 1961. 7.95 (ISBN 0-498-08814-6). A S Barnes.
FAO Catalogue of Fishing Gear Designs. (Illus.). 155p. 1973. 20.00 (ISBN 0-85238-019-4, FN 28, FAO). Unipub.
Fisheries Technology Service. Echo Sounding & Sonar for Fishing. 1980. pap. 20.40x (ISBN 0-85238-110-7, Pub. by Fishing News England). State Mutual Bk.
Garner, John. Modern Inshore Fishing Gear. 1978. 20.00 (ISBN 0-685-63440-X). State Mutual Bk.
Graumont, Raoul & Wenstrom, Elmer. Fisherman's Knots & Nets. LC 48-423. (Illus.). 1948. pap. 6.50 (ISBN 0-87033-024-1). Cornell Maritime.
Hind, J. Anthony, ed. Ships Gear Sixty-Six. 1978. 29.00 (ISBN 0-685-63454-X). State Mutual Bk.
Kristjonsson, Hilmar, ed. Modern Fishing Gear of the World One. 1978. 40.00 (ISBN 0-685-63437-X). State Mutual Bk.
--Modern Fishing Gear of the World Three. 1978. 40.00 (ISBN 0-685-63439-6). State Mutual Bk.
--Modern Fishing Gear of the World Two. 1978. 40.00 (ISBN 0-685-63438-8). State Mutual Bk.
Lewers, Dick. Fishing Knots & Rigs: For Salt & Freshwater. (Illus.). 1976. pap. 3.95 (ISBN 0-589-07127-0, Pub. by Reed Books Australia). C E Tuttle.
--How to Build a Fishing Rod. (Illus.). 80p. (Orig.). 1980. pap. 11.95 (ISBN 0-589-50242-5, Pub. by Reed Books Australia). C E Tuttle.
McNair, Paul C. The Sportsman's Crafts Book. 1978. 12.95 (ISBN 0-87691-263-3). Winchester Pr.
McNally, Tom. Complete Book of Fisherman's Knots. (Illus.). 1975. 7.95 (ISBN 0-686-75268-6); pap. 4.95 (ISBN 0-89149-020-5). Jolex.
Manual of Methods for Fish Stock Assessment, Part III: Selectivity of Fishing Gear. (FAO Fisheries Technical Papers: No.41, Revision 1). (Illus.). 65p. 1976. pap. 7.50 (ISBN 92-5-100409-9, F849, FAO). Unipub.
Modern Fishing Gear of the World, One. 1959. 46.25 (ISBN 0-85238-016-X, FAO). Unipub.
Modern Fishing Gear of the World, Two. 1964. 46.25 (ISBN 0-85238-017-8, FAO). Unipub.
Nedelec, C., ed. FAO Catalogue of Small Scale Fishing Gear. (Illus.). 192p. 33.00 (ISBN 0-85238-077-1, FN 29, FNB). Unipub.
--FAO Catalogue of Small Scale Fishing Gear. 1978. 25.00 (ISBN 0-685-63403-5). State Mutual Bk.
Rizzo, Tony. Secrets of a Muskie Guide. 1977. pap. 6.00 (ISBN 0-932558-07-0). Willow Creek.
Sainsbury, John C. Commercial Fishing Methods: An Introduction to Vessels & Gear. (Illus.). 120p. 20.75 (ISBN 0-85238-076-3, FN 5, FNB). Unipub.
Scharfe, Joachim, ed. FAO Catalogue of Fishing Gear Designs. 1978. 25.00 (ISBN 0-685-63402-7). State Mutual Bk.
Sosin, Mark & Kreh, Lefty. Practical Fishing Knots. LC 72-84294. (Illus.). 176p. 1972. 5.95 (ISBN 0-517-50041-8); pap. 4.95 (ISBN 0-517-52134-2). Crown.
Von Brandt, A. Fish Catching Methods of the World. rev. & enlarged edition ed. (Illus.). 1972. 35.00 (ISBN 0-685-12016-3). Heinman.
Walker, Richard. Dick Walker's Angling: Theory & Practice, Past, Present & to Come. LC 79-51097. (Illus.). 1979. 19.95 (ISBN 0-7153-7814-7). David & Charles.

Wilson, Gloria. More Scottish Fishing Craft & Their Work: Their Work in Great Lining, Small Lining, Seining, Pair Trawling, Drifting, Potting & Trawling. (Illus.). 170p. 13.25 (ISBN 0-85238-048-8, FN 69, FNB). Unipub.

FISHING–JUVENILE LITERATURE

Bartram, Robert. Fishing for Sunfish. LC 76-41251. (Illus.). (gr. 1-4). 1978. 6.95 (ISBN 0-397-31735-2, JBL-J). Har-Row.

Boy Scouts Of America. Fishing. LC 19-600. (Illus.). 64p. (gr. 6-12). 1974. pap. 0.70x (ISBN 0-8395-3295-4, 3295). BSA.

Hofsinde, Robert. Indian Fishing & Camping. (Illus.). (gr. 4-7). 1963. PLB 6.48 (ISBN 0-688-31797-9). Morrow.

Liss, Howard. Fishing Talk for Beginners. LC 77-25258. (Illus.). 96p. (gr. 3 up). 1978. PLB 8.79 (ISBN 0-671-32882-4). Messner.

Matteson, George. Draggermen: Fishing on Georges Bank. LC 78-21767. (Illus.). 144p. (gr. 5 up). 1979. 8.95 (ISBN 0-590-07534-9, Four Winds). Schol Bk Serv.

Mitchell, John. Better Fishing: Freshwater. (Better Ser.). (Illus.). (gr. 7 up). 1979. 15.95x (ISBN 0-7182-1455-2, SpS). Sportshelf.

Neimark, Paul. Fishing. LC 80-27508. (Wilderness World Ser.). (Illus.). 64p. (gr. 3 up). 1981. PLB 9.25 (ISBN 0-516-02452-3). Childrens.

Nentl, Jerolyn & Schroeder, Howard. Fishing. LC 80-10490. (Back to Nature Ser.). (Illus.). (gr. 3-5). 1980. lib. bdg. 6.95 (ISBN 0-89686-070-1). Crestwood Hse.

Shoemaker, Hurst H. Science-Hobby Book of Fishing. rev. ed. LC 68-28033. (Science-Hobby Books). (Illus.). (gr. 5-9). 1968. PLB 4.95 (ISBN 0-8225-0555-X). Lerner Pubns.

Thomas, Art. Fishing Is for Me. LC 80-13442. (Sports for Me Books Ser.). (Illus.). 48p. (gr. 2-5). 1980. PLB 5.95g (ISBN 0-8225-1096-0). Lerner Pubns.

Waters, John F. Fishing. (First Bks.). (Illus.). (gr. 4-6). 1978. PLB 6.90 s&l (ISBN 0-531-01407-X). Watts.

FISHING–ATLANTIC OCEAN

Coordinating Working Party on Atlantic Fishery Statistics, 8th Session. Report. (FAO Fisheries Reports: No. 156). (Illus.). 39p. 1976. pap. 7.50 (ISBN 0-685-74969-X, F797, FAO). Unipub.

Whitaker, Ralph R. Song of the Outriggers: Big Game Fishing on the Ocean Surface. LC 68-20946. (Illus.). 305p. 1968. 8.95 (ISBN 0-87527-087-5). Green.

FISHING–AUSTRALIA

Stewart, Douglas. Fishing Around the Monaro. new ed. 1978. pap. 3.00 (ISBN 0-7081-1811-9, Pub. by ANUP Australia). Bks Australia.

FISHING–BRITISH COLUMBIA

Haig-Brown, Roderick. River Never Sleeps. (Sportsmen's Classics Ser.). 352p. 1974. 7.50 (ISBN 0-517-51601-2). Crown.

Richardson, Lee. Richardson's B.C. Tales of Fly Fishing in British Columbia. (Fly Fishermen Ser.). 1978. 39.50x (ISBN 0-918400-00-7, Pub. by Champoeg Pr). Intl Schol Bk Serv.

Wilson, Doug & Vander Werff, Fred. New Techniques for Catching Bottom Fish. LC 77-17923. (Illus.). 160p. 1977. pap. 4.95 (ISBN 0-916076-16-4). Writing.

FISHING–GREAT BRITAIN

Angling. 1976. pap. 2.50 (ISBN 0-8277-4860-4). British Bk Ctr.

Baverstock, Leslie. The Angling Times Book of the Wye. LC 81-68500. (Illus.). 192p. 1982. 21.95 (ISBN 0-7153-8254-3). David & Charles.

Cope, Ken. Angling Times Book of the Severn. LC 79-51088. (Illus.). 1979. 19.95 (ISBN 0-7153-7791-4). David & Charles.

Edible Crab & Its Fishery in British Waters. 1979. pap. 18.25 (ISBN 0-85238-100-X, FN78, Pub. by FNB). Unipub.

Foster, Muriel. Days on Sea, Loch & River. (Illus.). 124p. 1981. 4.95 (ISBN 0-7181-1788-3, Pub. by Michael Joseph). Merrimack Bk Serv.

Marston, A. N. Encyclopedia of Angling. 2nd ed. 1963. 15.00 (ISBN 0-600-40092-1). Transatlantic.

Smith, Peter. Sea Angling in Southern England. LC 80-85504. (Illus.). 192p. 1981. 22.50 (ISBN 0-7153-8172-5). David & Charles.

Willock, Colin, ed. ABC of Fishing. (Illus.). 1971. deluxe ed. 15.00 (ISBN 0-233-95921-1). Transatlantic.

Wilson, Gloria. More Scottish Fishing Craft & Their Work. 1978. 20.00 (ISBN 0-685-63441-8). State Mutual Bk.

--More Scottish Fishing Craft & Their Work: Their Work in Great Lining, Small Lining, Seining, Pair Trawling, Drifting, Potting & Trawling. (Illus.). 170p. 13.25 (ISBN 0-85238-048-8, FN 69, FNB). Unipub.

FISHING–HAWAII

Carpenter, Russell & Carpenter, Blyth. Fish Watching in Hawaii. (Illus.). 120p. (Orig.). 1981. 14.95 (ISBN 0-939560-01-1); pap. 9.95 (ISBN 0-939560-00-3). Natural World.

Hosaka, Edward. Shore Fishing in Hawaii. pap. 6.95 (ISBN 0-912180-20-X). Petroglyph.

Rizzuto, Jim. Modern Hawaiian Gamefishing. LC 76-58414. (Orig.). 1977. pap. 6.95 (ISBN 0-8248-0481-3). U Pr of Hawaii.

FISHING–INDIA

IPFC-IOFC Joint Working Party of Experts on Indian Ocean & Western Pacific Fishery Statistics, 3rd Session. Report. (FAO Fisheries Reports: No. 157). (Illus.). 1976. pap. 7.50 (ISBN 0-685-74970-3, F798, FAO). Unipub.

FISHING–JAPAN

Kalland, Arne. Shingu: A Japanese Fishing Community. (Scandanavian Institute of Asian Studies Monograph: No. 44). (Orig.). 1980. pap. text ed. 12.50x (ISBN 0-7007-0136-2). Humanities.

FISHING–NEW ZEALAND

Best, Elsdon. Fishing Methods & Devices of the Maori. LC 75-35228. Repr. of 1929 ed. 27.50 (ISBN 0-404-14406-3). AMS Pr.

Ferris, George. Fly Fishing in New Zealand. 116p. 1972. 8.50x (ISBN 0-8002-0076-4). Intl Pubns Serv.

FISHING–NORTH AMERICA

Alaska Magazine Editors, ed. Selected Alaska Hunting & Fishing Tales, Vol. 4. LC 72-92077. 1976. pap. 4.95 (ISBN 0-88240-068-1). Alaska Northwest.

Bradner, Enos. Northwest Angling. 2nd ed. LC 70-81629. (Illus.). 1969. 8.95 (ISBN 0-8323-0125-6). Binford.

Fichter, George S. Fishing the Four Seasons. LC 77-91154. 1978. pap. 7.95 o. p. (ISBN 0-8092-7595-3). Contemp Bks.

Grilli, Sam. Sam Grilli's Complete Guide to Lake Erie Walleye. (Illus.). 160p. (gr. 4-12). 1980. 5.95 (ISBN 0-9604304-0-7); pap. 5.95 (ISBN 0-686-64677-0). Sport Fishing.

Herbert, Henry W. Frank Forester's Fish & Fishing in the United States & British Provinces of North America. LC 73-125747. (American Environmental Studies). (Illus.). 1970. Repr. of 1850 ed. 22.00 (ISBN 0-405-02672-2). Arno.

Knap, Jerome. Where to Fish & Hunt in North America: A Complete Sportsman's Guide. (Illus.). 192p. 8.95 (ISBN 0-919364-78-0, ADON 3513). Pagurian.

Rostlund, Erhard. Freshwater Fish & Fishing in Native North America. Repr. of 1952 ed. pap. 23.00 (ISBN 0-384-52110-X). Johnson Repr.

Sparano, Vin T., ed. The American Fisherman's Fresh & Salt Water Guide. 1976. 12.95 (ISBN 0-87691-214-5). Winchester Pr.

Stearns, Mary Lee. Haida Culture in Custody: The Masset Band. LC 80-50862. (Illus.). 315p. 1980. 24.50 (ISBN 0-295-95763-8). U of Wash Pr.

FISHING–PACIFIC OCEAN

Caldwell, Francis E. The Ebb & the Flood: A History of the Halibut Producers Cooperative. Matsen, Bradford, ed. LC 80-51978. (Illus.). 144p. (Orig.). 1980. pap. 7.95 (ISBN 0-937288-00-4). Waterfront Pr.

--Pacific Troller: Life on the Northwest Fishing Grounds. LC 77-10324. (Illus.). 1978. pap. 4.95 (ISBN 0-88240-099-1). Alaska Northwest.

Cannon, Raymond. How to Fish the Pacific Coast. 3rd ed. LC 67-15740. (Illus.). 160p. 1967. pap. 5.95 (ISBN 0-376-06362-9, Sunset Bks.). Sunset-Lane.

Fisheries & Aquaculture in the People's Republic of China. 32p. 1980. pap. 5.00 (ISBN 0-88936-189-4, IDRC 115, IDRC). Unipub.

Miller, Tom. Angler's Guide to Baja California. Miller, Shirley, ed. (Illus.). 1979. pap. 5.95x (ISBN 0-914622-04-8). Baja Trail.

Squire, James L., Jr. & Smith, Susan E. Sport Fishing in Hawaii, Guam & American Samoa. LC 78-68587. (Illus.). 1979. pap. 7.50 (ISBN 0-8048-1308-6). C E Tuttle.

FISHING–UNITED STATES

Abbott, Henry. Birch Bark Books of Henry Abbott: Sporting Adventures & Nature Observations in the Adirondacks in the Early 1900s. LC 80-11071. (Illus., Repr. of 1914 & 1932 eds.). 1980. 19.95 (ISBN 0-916346-40-4). Harbor Hill Bks.

Apte, Stuart C. Stu Apte's Fishing in the Florida Keys & Flamingo. 2nd ed. LC 76-360969. (Illus.). 80p. 1979. pap. 3.95 (ISBN 0-89317-006-2). Windward Pub.

Bartlett, Kim. The Finest Kind: The Fishermen of Gloucester. 1979. pap. 2.95 (ISBN 0-380-44339-2, 44339). Avon.

Chatham, Russell. Striped Bass on the Fly: A Guide to California Waters. LC 77-71001. (A California Living Book). (Illus.). 1977. pap. 4.50 (ISBN 0-89395-000-9). Cal Living Bks.

Donaldson, Ivan & Cramer, Frederick. Fishwheels of the Columbia. LC 76-173928. (Illus.). 1971. 12.50 (ISBN 0-8323-0007-1). Binford.

Engels, Vincent. Adirondack Fishing in the Nineteen Thirties: A Lost Paradise. (Illus.). 1978. 8.95 (ISBN 0-8156-0144-1). Syracuse U Pr.

Evanoff, Vlad. A Complete Guide to Fishing. rev. ed. LC 80-2251. (Illus.). 1981. 9.95 (ISBN 0-690-04090-3, TYC-J); PLB 9.89 (ISBN 0-690-04091-1). Har-Row.

Farmer, Charles J. Backpack Fishing. LC 73-20839. (Illus.). 224p. 1976. 10.95 (ISBN 0-685-69915-3); pap. 6.95 (ISBN 0-89149-018-3). Jolex.

Fellegy, Joe, Jr. Walleyes & Walleye Fishing. LC 72-89440. (Illus.). 210p. 1973. 8.95 (ISBN 0-87518-054-X). Dillon.

Gilbert, De Witt, ed. The Future of the Fishing Industry of the United States. (University of Washington Publications in Fisheries Ser.: No. 4). (Illus.). 346p. 1968. pap. 15.00 (ISBN 0-295-95204-0). U of Wash Pr.

Goldstein, Robert J. Pier Fishing in North Carolina. LC 78-6506. 1978. pap. 6.95 (ISBN 0-89587-003-7). Blair.

Gresham, Grits. Fishes & Fishing in Louisiana. 1965. 5.00 (ISBN 0-685-08167-2); pap. 4.00 (ISBN 0-685-08168-0). Claitors.

--Fishes & Fishing in Louisiana. 1965. 5.00 (ISBN 0-685-08167-2); pap. 4.00 (ISBN 0-685-08168-0). Claitors.

--Fishing & Boating in Louisiana. 1965. 4.00 (ISBN 0-685-08169-9). Claitors.

--Fishing & Boating in Louisiana. pap. 2.00 (ISBN 0-685-42682-3). Claitors.

Holm, Donald R. One-Hundred One Best Fishing Spots in Oregon. LC 79-109542. (Illus., Orig.). 1970. pap. 5.95 (ISBN 0-87004-204-1). Caxton.

Konizeski, Dick. The Montanans' Fishing Guide: Waters West of the Continental Divide, Vol. 1. LC 75-131414. (Illus.). 310p. 1975. pap. 6.95 (ISBN 0-87842-053-3). Mountain Pr.

--The Montanans' Fishing Guide: West of the Continental Divide, Vol. I. rev. ed. Burk, Dale A., ed. (Illus.). 325p. 1981. pap. 8.95 (ISBN 0-87842-139-4). Mountain Pr.

Lewis, Gordon. Florida Fishing: Fresh & Salt Water. LC 56-11379. (Illus., Orig.). 1957. pap. 2.95 (ISBN 0-8200-0102-3). Great Outdoors.

McTeer, Ed. Adventures in the Woods & Waters of the Low Country. LC 72-91815. 5.95 (ISBN 0-685-30849-9). Beaufort.

Michigan United Conservation Clubs. Trout Streams. 1978. pap. 2.95 (ISBN 0-685-51936-8). Mich United Conserv.

Miller, Tom. Angler's Guide to Baja California. Miller, Shirley, ed. (Illus.). 1979. pap. 5.95x (ISBN 0-914622-04-8). Baja Trail.

Murray, William H. Adventures in the Wilderness. Verner, William K., ed. (Illus.). 1970. Repr. 10.50 (ISBN 0-8156-0071-2, Co-Pub. by Adirondack Museum). Syracuse U Pr.

Neasham, V. Aubrey. Wild Legacy: California Hunting & Fishing Tales. LC 73-78176. (Illus.). 178p. 1973. 6.50 (ISBN 0-8310-7098-6). Howell-North.

Ovington, Ray. America's Best Fresh Water Fishing. LC 77-24740. (Illus.). 1979. 12.50 (ISBN 0-8246-0219-6). Jonathan David.

Reid, Sean, ed. Eastern Washington Freshwater Fishing & Facilities Maps, Vol. 1, No. 2. (Illus.). 1977. pap. 5.95 (ISBN 0-916682-12-9). Outdoor Empire.

--Oregon Freshwater Fishing & Facilities Maps, Vol. 2, No. 1. (Illus.). 1977. pap. 5.95 (ISBN 0-916682-15-3). Outdoor Empire.

--Western Washington Freshwater Fishing & Facilities Maps, Vol. 1, No. 1. (Illus.). 1977. pap. 5.95 (ISBN 0-916682-11-0). Outdoor Empire.

Roush, John H., Jr. Successfully Fishing Lake Tahoe. LC 76-12122. 233p. 1976. 10.00 (ISBN 0-685-77221-7). J H Roush.

Schmidt, Bob. Great Fishing Close to Chicago. LC 77-91188. 1978. pap. 7.95 (ISBN 0-8092-7676-3). Contemp Bks.

Sisley, Nick. Panfish, U.S.A. 144p. 1981. 12.95 (ISBN 0-87691-333-8). Winchester Pr.

Snook, Patricia K. Fishing the Great Lakes. 1979. pap. 6.95 o. p. (ISBN 0-8092-7319-5). Contemp Bks.

Sports Afloat. (Library of Boating Ser.). (Illus.). 1976. 16.95 (ISBN 0-8094-2128-3). Time-Life.

Strung, Norman. Fishing the Headwaters of the Missouri. LC 80-12127. (Illus.). 174p. 1980. pap. 6.95 (ISBN 0-87842-123-8). Mountain Pr.

Wharton, James. Bounty of the Chesapeake: Fishing in Colonial Virginia. (Illus., Orig.). 1957. pap. 1.95x (ISBN 0-8139-0137-5). U Pr of Va.

White, Donald J. New England Fishing Industry: A Study in Price & Wage Setting. LC 54-7065. (Wertheim Publications in Industrial Relations Ser). (Illus.). 1954. 10.00x (ISBN 0-674-61200-0). Harvard U Pr.

Wilcoxson, Kent H. Angler's Guide to Freshwater Fishing in New England. LC 73-76482. (Angler's Guide Ser.). (Illus.). 1974. pap. 5.95 (ISBN 0-89046-065-5). Herman Pub.

--Angler's Guide to Freshwater Fishing in New York State. 2nd ed. LC 76-42142. (Angler's Guide Ser.). (Illus.). 160p. 1977. pap. 4.50 (ISBN 0-89046-064-7). Herman Pub.

Wilson, Doug & Vander Werff, Fred. New Techniques for Catching Bottom Fish. LC 77-17923. (Illus.). 160p. 1977. pap. 4.95 (ISBN 0-916076-16-4). Writing.

Wisconsin Fishing Encyclopedia. 1974. softcover 2.50 (ISBN 0-932558-01-1). Wisconsin Sptm.

FISHING, ELECTRIC

see Electric Fishing

FISHING, PRIMITIVE

see also Harpoons; Indians of North America–Hunting and Fishing

Titcomb, Margaret. Native Use of Fish in Hawaii. 2nd ed. 1972. pap. 3.95 (ISBN 0-8248-0592-5). U Pr of Hawaii.

FISHING BOATS

Blair, Carvel H. & Ansel, Willits D. A Guide to Fishing Boats & Their Gear. LC 68-19048. (Illus.). 1968. 6.00 (ISBN 0-87033-002-0). Cornell Maritime.

Datz, I. Mortimer. Power Transmission & Automation for Ships & Submersibles. 1978. 39.00 (ISBN 0-685-63448-5). State Mutual Bk.

Fishing Boat Designs, Number Two: V-Bottom Boats. (FAO Fisheries Technical Papers: No.134). (Illus.). 22p. 1976. pap. 7.50 (ISBN 0-685-66311-6, F864, FAO). Unipub.

Fishing Boat Designs,Number One: Flat Bottom Boats. rev. ed. (FAO Fisheries Technical Papers: No.117). (Illus.). 15p. 1976. pap. 7.50 (ISBN 0-685-66310-8, F855, FAO). Unipub.

Fishing Boats & Their Equipment. 182p. 1980. pap. 23.50 (ISBN 0-85238-090-9, FN 81, FNB). Unipub.

Fishing Boats of the World-1. (Illus.). 1955. 44.00 (ISBN 0-85238-073-9, FAO). Unipub.

Fishing Boats of the World-2. (Illus.). 1960. 46.25 (ISBN 0-85238-075-5, FAO). Unipub.

Fishing Boats of the World-3. (Illus.). 1967. 46.25 (ISBN 0-85238-043-7, FAO). Unipub.

Fyson, John. FAO Investigates Ferro-Cement Fishing Craft. 1978. 40.00 (ISBN 0-685-63404-3). State Mutual Bk.

Hind, J. Anthony. Stability & Trim of Fishing Vessels. 1978. 19.00 (ISBN 0-685-63456-6). State Mutual Bk.

Hind, J. Anthony, ed. Ships Gear Sixty-Six. 1978. 29.00 (ISBN 0-685-63454-X). State Mutual Bk.

Lowell, Royal. Boatbuilding Down East: How to Build the Maine Lobsterboat. LC 76-52309. (Illus.). 1977. 20.00 (ISBN 0-87742-088-2). Intl Marine.

Merritt, John H. Refrigeration on Fishing Vessels. 1978. 15.00 (ISBN 0-685-63449-3). State Mutual Bk.

Moss, Frank T. Modern Sportfishing Boats. LC 80-84744. (Illus.). 360p. 1981. 30.00 (ISBN 0-87742-122-6). Intl Marine.

Pair Trawling with Small Boats. (FAO Training Ser.: No. 1). 77p. 1981. pap. 8.25 (ISBN 92-5-100627-X, F2095, FAO). Unipub.

Pike, Dag. Fishing Boats & Their Equipment. 1978. 40.00x (ISBN 0-685-63416-7). State Mutual Bk.

Refrigeration on Fishing Vessels. 1979. pap. 26.25 (ISBN 0-85238-095-X, FN24, Pub. by FNB). Unipub.

Thomas, Gordon W. Fast & Able, Life Stories of Great Gloucester Fishing Schooners. new ed. Kenyon, Paul B., ed. LC 72-97362. (Illus.). 1973. 4.95 (ISBN 0-930352-01-7). Nelson B Robinson.

Traung, Jan-Obog, ed. Fishing Boats of the World One. 1978. 38.00 (ISBN 0-685-63417-5). State Mutual Bk.

Traung, Jan-Olof, ed. Mechanization of Small Fishing Craft. 1978. 10.00 (ISBN 0-685-63434-5). State Mutual Bk.

Traung, Jan-Olog, ed. Fishing Boats of the World Three. 1978. 38.00 (ISBN 0-685-63419-1). State Mutual Bk.

--Fishing Boats of the World Two. 1978. 40.00 (ISBN 0-685-63418-3). State Mutual Bk.

FISHING LURES

Almy, Gerald. Tying & Fishing Terrestrials. LC 78-17309. (Illus.). 256p. 1978. 14.95 (ISBN 0-8117-1746-1). Stackpole.

Becker, A. C., Jr. Lure Fishing. LC 73-88250. (Illus.). 1970. 8.50 (ISBN 0-498-07429-3). A S Barnes.

Evanoff, Vlad. Make Your Own Fishing Lures. LC 74-14259. (Illus.). 160p. 1975. 9.95 (ISBN 0-498-01617-X); pap. 6.95 (ISBN 0-498-01981-0). A S Barnes.

Grant, George. The Master Fly Weaver (the Art of Weaving Hair Hackles) 150p. 1980. 50.00x (ISBN 0-918400-03-1, Pub. by Champoeg Pr). Intl Schol Bk Serv.

--Montana Trout Flies. 150p. 1981. 50.00x (ISBN 0-918400-04-X, Pub. by Champoeg Pr). Intl Schol Bk Serv.

Hungerford, Rodger. How to Fish with Lures. (Illus.). 96p. 1978. pap. 5.95 (ISBN 0-589-50080-5, Pub. by Reed Books Australia). C E Tuttle.

Lively, Chauncy K. Chauncy Lively's Flybox: A Portfolio of Modern Trout Flies. (Illus.). 96p. 1980. pap. 9.95 (ISBN 0-8117-2078-0). Stackpole.

Marshall, Mel. How to Make Your Own Lures & Flies. (Funk & W Bk.). (Illus.). 1977. pap. 4.50 (ISBN 0-308-10292-4). T y Crowell.
Picano, Felice. The Lure. 1980. pap. 2.75 (ISBN 0-440-15081-7). Dell.
The Rapala Fishing Guide: Secrets from Pros. LC 76-15852. (Illus.). 1976. pap. 2.95 (ISBN 0-686-17472-0). Normark Corp.
Veniard, John. Fly Dressing Materials. 1978. 13.95 (ISBN 0-87691-267-6). Winchester Pr.
Wilson, Loring D. Encyclopedia of Fishing Lures. LC 78-67468. (Illus.). 1980. 19.95 (ISBN 0-498-02337-0). A S Barnes.

FISHING REGULATIONS
see Fishery Law and Legislation

FISHING STORIES
see also American Wit and Humor-Sports and Games
Ku Wan-Chuan. The Fisherman's Love. Lin Lan, ed. (Tales from the Orient Ser.: No. 17). 5.00 (ISBN 0-89986-241-1). E Langstaff.
Linkert, Lo. Hunter's Fisherman & Other Liars. 2nd ed. (Illus.). 1980. 5.95 (ISBN 0-686-75269-4). Jolex.
McManus, Patrick. They Shoot Canoes, Don't They? 228p. 1981. 10.95 (ISBN 0-03-058646-1). HR&W.
Traver, Robert. Trout Magic. (Sportsmen's Classics Ser.). (Illus.). 220p. 1974. 7.50 (ISBN 0-517-51604-7). Crown.
Woolner, Frank. My New England. LC 72-87870. (Illus.). 176p. 1972. 10.00 (ISBN 0-913276-01-4). Stone Wall Pr.

FISHING TACKLE
Adams, Herbert B. Methods of Historical Study. Repr. of 1884 ed. pap. 11.50 (ISBN 0-384-00336-2). Johnson Repr.
Barnard, Philip. The Tackle Box Fishing Guide. LC 78-69685. (Illus.). 128p. 1981. pap. 7.95 (ISBN 0-498-02254-4). A S Barnes.
Burrell, Leonard F. Beginner's Guide to Home Coarse Tacklemaking. (Illus.). 134p. 1973. 12.95 (ISBN 0-7207-0548-7). Transatlantic.
--Make Your Own Sea-Angling Tackle. (Illus.). 108p. 1976. 12.00 (ISBN 0-7207-0894-X). Transatlantic.
Clemens, Dale P. Advanced Custom Rod Building. (Illus.). 1978. 16.95 (ISBN 0-87691-258-7). Winchester Pr.
FAO Catalog of Fishing Gear Designs. 1978. 30.00 (ISBN 0-85238-098-4, FN28, FNB). Unipub.
Henkin, Harmon. Complete Fisherman's Catalog: A Source Book of Information About Tackle & Accessories. LC 76-56200. 1977. pap. 8.95 (ISBN 0-397-01205-5). Har-Row.
Kimball, Art & Kimball, Scott. Collecting Old Fishing Tackle. LC 80-122941. (Illus.). 1980. 30.00 (ISBN 0-9604906-0-4); pap. 19.00 (ISBN 0-9604906-1-2). Aardvark Pubs.
Marshall, Mel. The Care & Repair of Fishing Tackle. 1976. 12.95 (ISBN 0-87691-183-1). Winchester Pr.
Moss, Frank T. Modern Saltwater Fishing Tackle. LC 76-8780. (Illus.). 1977. 22.50 (ISBN 0-87742-068-8). Intl Marine.
Netherton, Cliff. Angling & Casting: A Manual for Self & Class Instruction. LC 76-10881. (Illus.). 1977. 9.95 (ISBN 0-498-01877-6). A S Barnes.
Pfeiffer, C. Boyd. Tackle Craft. LC 73-82959. (Sportsmen's Classics Ser.). (Illus.). 288p. 1974. 15.00 (ISBN 0-517-50615-7); pap. 7.95 (ISBN 0-517-52136-9). Crown.
Pursell, Thomas. Making Fishing Tackle. LC 76-13065. (Early Craft Books). (Illus.). (gr. k-3). 1976. PLB 3.95 (ISBN 0-8225-0881-8). Lerner Pubns.

FISHPONDS
see Fish Ponds

FISK, CLINTON BOWEN, 1828-1890
Hopkins, Alphonso A. Life of Clinton Bowen Fisk, with a Brief Sketch of John A. Brooks. LC 75-78582. (Illus.). Repr. of 1888 ed. 14.50x (ISBN 0-8371-1419-5, Pub. by Negro U Pr). Greenwood.

FISK, JAMES, 1834-1872
McAlpine, R. W. The Life & Times of Col. James Fisk, Jr. Bruchey, Stuart, ed. LC 80-1329. (Railroads Ser.). (Illus.). 1981. Repr. of 1872 ed. lib. bdg. 45.00x (ISBN 0-405-13803-2). Arno.
Stafford, Marshall P. The Life of James Fisk Jr. Bruchey, Stuart, ed. LC 80-1345. (Railroads Ser.). (Illus.). 1981. Repr. of 1871 ed. lib. bdg. 30.00x (ISBN 0-405-13816-4). Arno.

FISK UNIVERSITY, NASHVILLE
Caliver, Ambrose. Personnel Study of Negro College Students: A Study of the Relations Between Certain Background Factors of Negro College Studens & Their Subsequent Careers in College. LC 73-107470. Repr. of 1931 ed. 10.75x (ISBN 0-8371-3749-7). Greenwood.
Fisk University Library (Nashville) Dictionary Catalog of the Negro Collection of the Fisk University Library, 6 vols. (Library Catalogs Ser.). 1974. Set. lib. bdg. 490.00 (ISBN 0-8161-1055-7). G K Hall.
Richardson, Joe M. History of Fisk University, Eighteen-Sixty Five to Nineteen Forty-Six. LC 79-9736. 1980. 19.50x (ISBN 0-8173-0015-5). U of Ala Pr.

FISKE, JOHN, 1842-1901
Berman, Milton. John Fiske: The Evolution of a Popularizer. LC 62-7334. (Historical Monographs Ser: No. 48). (Illus.). 1961. 15.00x (ISBN 0-674-47551-8). Harvard U Pr.
Fiske, John. Historical Writings of John Fiske, 12 vols. 1902. Repr. Set. 250.00 (ISBN 0-685-43072-3). Norwood Edns.
--The Miscellaneous Writings of John Fiske, 12 vols. 1902. Repr. Set. 150.00 (ISBN 0-685-43086-3). Norwood Edns.
Winston, George P. John Fiske. (U. S. Authors Ser.: No. 197). lib. bdg. 10.95 (ISBN 0-8057-0256-3). Twayne.

FISSION, NUCLEAR
see Nuclear Fission

FISSION DATING METHOD
see Radioactive Dating

FISSION PRODUCTS
see also Radioactive Fallout; Reactor Fuel Reprocessing
Mann, Martin. Peacetime Uses of Atomic Energy. rev. ed. LC 75-5621. (Illus.). 192p. 1975. 8.95 (ISBN 0-690-00118-5). T Y Crowell.
Zysin, Yu. A., et al. Fission Product Yields & Their Mass Distribution. LC 64-10525. 121p. 1964. 35.00 (ISBN 0-306-10691-4, Consultants). Plenum Pub.

FISSIONABLE MATERIALS
see Radioactive Substances

FISTULA, ARTERIOVENOUS
Hamby, Wallace B. Carotid-Cavernous Fistula. (Illus.). 152p. 1966. photocopy ed. spiral 15.75 (ISBN 0-398-00765-9). C C Thomas.

FISTULA, VESICO-VAGINAL
Moir, J. Chassar. The Vesico-Vaginal Fistula. 2nd ed. (Illus.). 1967. text ed. 14.95 (ISBN 0-02-858620-4). Macmillan.

FITCH, JOHN, 1743-1798
Boyd, Thomas. Poor John Fitch: Inventor of the Steamboat. facsimile ed. LC 75-150171. (Select Bibliographies Reprint Ser). 1972. Repr. of 1935 ed. 18.00 (ISBN 0-8369-5684-2). Arno.
Prager, Frank D., ed. The Autobiography of John Fitch. LC 76-8596. (Memoirs Ser.: Vol. 113). (Illus.). 1976. pap. 7.00 (ISBN 0-87169-113-2). Am Philos.
Stevenson, Augusta. John Fitch: Steamboat Boy. LC 66-18417. (Childhood of Famous Americans Ser.). (Illus.). (gr. 3-7). 1966. 3.95 (ISBN 0-672-50101-5). Bobbs.

FITS (ENGINEERING)
see Tolerance (Engineering)

FITTING (ENGINEERING)
see Machine-Shop Practice

FITZGERALD, CHARLES PATRICK, 1902-
Leslie, Donald D., et al, eds. Essays on the Sources for Chinese History. LC 74-10508. xii, 380p. 1975. 19.50x (ISBN 0-87249-329-6). U of SC Pr.

FITZGERALD, EDWARD, 1809-1883
Adams, Morley. Omar's Interpreter. 1978. Repr. of 1911 ed. lib. bdg. 25.00 (ISBN 0-8495-0023-0). Arden Lib.
--Omar's Interpreter: A New Life of Edward Fitzgerald. Repr. of 1911 ed. lib. bdg. 25.00 (ISBN 0-8414-2899-9). Folcroft.
Benson, Arthur C. Edward Fitzgerald. LC 71-131625. 1970. Repr. of 1905 ed. 11.00 (ISBN 0-403-00512-4). Scholarly.
--Edward Fitzgerald. LC 69-13821. Repr. of 1905 ed. lib. bdg. 15.00 (ISBN 0-8371-1069-6, BEEF). Greenwood.
--Edward Fitzgerald. 1973. Repr. of 1905 ed. 9.45 (ISBN 0-8274-1383-1). R West.
--Edward Fitzgerald & "Posh," "Herring Merchants". 1908. 30.00 (ISBN 0-8274-2228-8). R West.
Bentham, George. Edward Fitzgerald, 7 vols. 250.00 (ISBN 0-403-04038-8). Somerset Pub.
Clodd, Edward. Concerning a Pilgrimage to the Grave of Edward Fitzgerald. 1902. 10.00 (ISBN 0-8274-2088-9). R West.
Edward Fitzgerald, 1809-1909: Centenary Celebrations Souvenir. 30.00 (ISBN 0-8274-2225-3). R West.
Fitzgerald, Edward. Fitzgerald to His Friends: Selected Letters of Edward Fitzgerald. Hayter, Alethea, ed. (Illus.). 252p. 1979. 21.95 (ISBN 0-85967-400-2, Pub. by Scolar Pr England); pap. 9.95 (ISBN 0-85967-499-1, Pub. by Scolar Pr England). Biblio Dist.
--The Letters of Edward Fitzgerald, 4 vols. Terhune, Alfred M. & Terhune, Annabelle B., eds. Incl. Vol. 1. 1830-1850. 40.00 (ISBN 0-691-06383-4); Vol. 2. 1851-1866. 40.00 (ISBN 0-691-06386-9); Vol. 3. 1867-1876. 40.00 (ISBN 0-691-06387-7); Vol. 4. 1877-1883. 40.00 (ISBN 0-691-06388-5). LC 78-23221. (Illus.). 1980. Vols 1 & 2. 75.00 set (ISBN 0-686-60726-0); Vols. 3 & 4. 75.00 set (ISBN 0-686-60727-9). Princeton U Pr.
--More Letters of Edward Fitzgerald. 1977. Repr. of 1901 ed. lib. bdg. 22.50 (ISBN 0-8495-1608-0). Arden Lib.
Ganz, Charles. A Fitzgerald Medley. 1973. Repr. of 1933 ed. 30.00 (ISBN 0-8274-0403-4). R West.
Glyde, John. Life of Edward Fitz-Gerald. LC 70-148790. Repr. of 1900 ed. 15.00 (ISBN 0-404-08823-6). AMS Pr.
--Life of Edward Fitz-Gerald. 1973. Repr. of 1900 ed. 25.00 (ISBN 0-8274-1382-3). R West.
Groome, Francis H. Edward Fitzgerald: an Aftermath: With Miscellanies in Verse & Prose. LC 72-5596. (Select Bibliographies Reprint Ser.). 1972. Repr. of 1902 ed. 19.00 (ISBN 0-8369-6911-1). Arno.
Ince, Richard B. Calverley & Some Cambridge Wits of the Nineteenth Century. LC 74-28333. 1929. lib. bdg. 17.50 (ISBN 0-8414-0887-4). Folcroft.
Jackson, Holbrook. Edward Fitzgerald & Omar Kayyam: An Essay & a Bibliography. LC 74-30069. 1972. Repr. of 1899 ed. lib. bdg. 8.50 (ISBN 0-8414-5339-X). Folcroft.
--Edward Fitzgerald & Omar Khayyam. 1980. Repr. lib. bdg. 8.50 (ISBN 0-8492-1274-X). R West.
Jewett, Iran B. Edward Fitzgerald. (English Authors Ser.: No. 205). 1977. lib. bdg. 9.95 (ISBN 0-8057-6675-8). Twayne.
Prideaux, William F. Notes for a Bibliography of Edward FitzGerald. 1901. lib. bdg. 18.50 (ISBN 0-8337-2833-4). B Franklin.
Terhune, Alfred McKinley. The Life of Edward FitzGerald: Translator of the Rubaiyat of Omar Khayyam. LC 79-18964. (Illus.). 1980. Repr. of 1947 ed. lib. bdg. 31.00x (ISBN 0-313-22108-1, TEEF). Greenwood.
Wright, Thomas. Life of Edward Fitzgerald, 2 Vols. LC 70-108556. (Illus.). 1971. Repr. of 1904 ed. 45.00 (ISBN 0-403-00254-0). Scholarly.
Wright, William A., ed. Letters of Edward Fitzgerald, 2 vols. 1977. Repr. of 1894 ed. Set. lib. bdg. 65.00 (ISBN 0-8495-1607-2). Arden Lib.

FITZGERALD, FRANCIS SCOTT KEY, 1896-1940
Allen, Joan M. Candles & Carnival Lights: The Catholic Sensibility of F. Scott Fitzgerald. LC 77-82752. 1978. 20.00x (ISBN 0-8147-0563-4); pap. 8.00x (ISBN 0-8147-0564-2). NYU Pr.
Bessiere, J. Fitzgerald: La Vocation de l'echec. (Collection themes et textes). 256p. (Orig., Fr.). 1972. pap. 6.75 (ISBN 2-03-035002-8, 2682). Larousse.
Bruccoli, Mathew J. & Layman, Richard, eds. Fitzgerald-Hemingway Annual, 1978. 44.00 (ISBN 0-686-63977-4). Bruccoli.
--Fitzgerald-Hemingway Annual, 1979. 44.00 (ISBN 0-686-63978-2). Bruccoli.
Bruccoli, Matthew. Scott & Ernest: The Authority of Failure & the Authority of Success. LC 79-26848. 186p. 1980. pap. 7.95 (ISBN 0-8093-0977-7). S Ill U Pr.
--Some Sort of Epic Grandeur: The Life of F. Scott Fitzgerald. Date not set. 17.95 (ISBN 0-15-183242-0). HarBraceJ.
Bruccoli, Matthew J. Apparatus for F. Scott Fitzgerald's The Great Gatsby: Under the Red, White & Blue. LC 74-4142. (S. C. Apparatus of Definitive Editions: No. 1). 1974. 14.95x (ISBN 0-87249-313-X); deluxe ed. 95.00x (ISBN 0-87249-323-7). U of SC Pr.
--The Last of the Novelists: F. Scott Fitzgerald & "The Last Tycoon". LC 77-4381. (Illus.). 173p. 1977. 9.95 (ISBN 0-8093-0820-7). S Ill U Pr.
--Profile of F. Scott Fitzgerald. LC 75-139588. 1971. pap. text ed. 2.50x (ISBN 0-675-09263-9). Merrill.
--Some Kind of Epic Grandeur: The Life of F. Scott Fitzgerald. LC 80-8740. (Illus.). 384p. 1981. 17.50 (ISBN 0-15-183242-0). HarBraceJ.
--Supplement to F. Scott Fitzgerald: A Descriptive Bibliography. LC 79-21728. (Pittsburgh Ser. in Bibliography). (Illus.). 235p. 1980. 19.95x (ISBN 0-8229-3409-4). U of Pittsburgh Pr.
Bruccoli, Matthew J., ed. The Correspondence of F. Scott Fitzgerald. LC 79-4765. 1980. 25.00 (ISBN 0-394-41773-9). Random.
Bruccoli, Matthew J., intro. by. F. Scott Fitzgerald's Ledger. ltd. ed. LC 72-87563. 1972. 48.00 (ISBN 0-910972-29-X). IHS-PDS.
Bruccoli, Matthew J., ed. Fitzgerald-Hemingway Annual 1969. 18.00 (ISBN 0-685-77405-8). Bruccoli.
--Fitzgerald-Hemingway Annual 1976. 24.00 (ISBN 0-685-84829-9). Bruccoli.
--Fitzgerald Newsletter. rev. ed. LC 79-83380. 1969. 17.00 (ISBN 0-910972-28-1). IHS-PDS.
Bruccoli, Matthew J. & Clark, C. E., eds. Fitzgerald-Hemingway Annual 1970. 18.00 (ISBN 0-685-77406-6). Bruccoli.
Bruccoli, Matthew J. & Clark, C. E. Frazer, Jr., eds. Fitzgerald-Hemingway Annual 1974. 23.00 (ISBN 0-685-84827-2). Bruccoli.
--Fitzgerald-Hemingway Annual 1975. 23.00 (ISBN 0-685-84828-0). Bruccoli.
Bruccoli, Matthew J. & Clark, C. E., Jr., eds. Fitzgerald-Hemingway Annual 1971. 22.00 (ISBN 0-685-77407-4). Bruccoli.
--Fitzgerald-Hemingway Annual 1972. 22.00 (ISBN 0-685-77408-2). Bruccoli.
--Fitzgerald-Hemingway Annual 1973. 20.00 (ISBN 0-685-77409-0). Bruccoli.
Bruccoli, Matthew J. & Layman, Richard, eds. Fitzgerald-Hemingway Annual, 3 vols. Incl. 1977 Annual. 1978 (ISBN 0-8103-0909-2); 1978 Annual. 1979 (ISBN 0-8103-0910-6); 1979 Annual. 1980 (ISBN 0-8103-0911-4). LC 75-83781. (Illus.). 44.00 ea. (Bruccoli Clark). Gale.
Brucoli, F. Scott. The Notebooks of F. Scott Fitzgerald. Bruccoli, Matthew J., ed. LC 78-7094. 1978. 14.95 (ISBN 0-15-167260-1). HarBraceJ.
Bryer, Jackson. Critical Reputation of F. Scott Fitzgerald: A Bibliographical Study. 1967. 18.00 (ISBN 0-208-00412-2, Archon). Shoe String.
Bryer, Jackson, ed. F. Scott Fitzgerald: The Critical Reception. (American Critical Tradition Ser). (Illus.). 1978. lib. bdg. 22.50 (ISBN 0-89102-111-6). B Franklin.
Callaghan, Morley. That Summer in Paris: Memories of Tangled Friendships with Hemingway, Fitzgerald & Some Others. (Illus.). 1979. pap. 3.95 (ISBN 0-14-005074-4). Penguin.
Callahan, John F. The Illusions of a Nation: Myth & History in the Novels of F. Scott Fitzgerald. LC 77-174778. 224p. 1972. 12.50 (ISBN 0-252-00232-6). U of Ill Pr.
Crosland, Andrew. A Concordance to F. Scott Fitzgerald's The Great Gatsby. 52.00 (ISBN 0-685-77426-0). Bruccoli.
Duggan, Margaret M. & Layman, Richard, eds. Fitzgerald-Hemingway Annual 1977. 44.00 (ISBN 0-685-84830-2). Bruccoli.
Eble, Kenneth. F. Scott Fitzgerald. LC 77-429. (Twayne's U. S. Authors Ser.). 187p. 1977. pap. text ed. 4.95 (ISBN 0-672-61503-7). Bobbs.
--F. Scott Fitzgerald. rev ed. (U.S. Authors Ser.: No. 36). 1977. lib. bdg. 9.95 (ISBN 0-8057-7183-2). Twayne.
Eble, Kenneth E. F. Scott Fitzgerald. (Twayne's United States Authors Ser). 1963. pap. 3.45 (ISBN 0-8084-0128-9, T36, Twayne). Coll & U Pr.
Eble, Kenneth E., ed. F. Scott Fitzgerald. 160p. (Orig.). 1973. pap. 1.95 (ISBN 0-07-018857-2, SP). McGraw.
--F. Scott Fitzgerald. 160p. (Orig.). 1973. pap. 1.95 (ISBN 0-07-018857-2, SP). McGraw.
F. Scott Fitzgerald & Ernest Hemingway in Paris. 5.00 (ISBN 0-89723-009-4). Bruccoli.
F. Scott Fitzgerald's Ledger. deluxe ed. 45.00 boxed (ISBN 0-685-77401-5). Bruccoli.
Fahey, William A. F. Scott Fitzgerald & the American Dream. LC 73-4523. (Twentieth-Century American Writers Ser). (gr. 6 up). 1973. 8.95 (ISBN 0-690-00078-2, TYC-J). Har-Row.
Fitzgerald, F. Scott. Afternoon of an Author. (Hudson River Edition Ser.). 1981. 17.50 (ISBN 0-684-16469-8, ScribT). Scribner.
--The Letters of F. Scott Fitzgerald. (Hudson River Edition Ser.). 1981. 30.00 (ISBN 0-684-16476-0, ScribT). Scribner.
--The Notebooks of F. Scott Fitzgerald. Bruccoli, Matthew J., ed. LC 79-18490. 1980. pap. 5.95 (ISBN 0-15-667362-2, Harv). HarBraceJ.
Fitzgerald, Zelda. Save Me the Waltz. 208p. 1974. pap. 1.25 (ISBN 0-451-05603-5, Y5603, Sig). NAL.
Gallo, Rose A. F. Scott Fitzgerald. LC 76-15650. (Modern Literature Ser.). 1978. 10.95 (ISBN 0-8044-2225-7). Ungar.
Kazin, Alfred, ed. F. Scott Fitzgerald: Man & Works. 1962. pap. 1.25 (ISBN 0-02-004100-4, Collier). Macmillan.
Koblas, John J. F. Scott Fitzgerald in Minnesota: His Homes & Haunts. LC 78-21979. 50p. 1978. pap. 3.75 (ISBN 0-87351-134-4). Minn Hist.
Kuehl, John. The Apprentice Fiction of F. Scott Fitzgerald, 1909-1917. (Orig.). 1974. pap. 3.50 (ISBN 0-8135-0790-1). Rutgers U Pr.
LaHood, Marvin J., ed. Tender Is the Night: Essays in Criticism. LC 77-85091. 224p. 1969. 9.50x (ISBN 0-253-35846-9). Ind U Pr.
Lehan, Richard D. F. Scott Fitzgerald & the Craft of Fiction. LC 66-5059. (Crosscurrents-Modern Critiques Ser.). 221p. 1966. 13.95 (ISBN 0-8093-0216-0). S Ill U Pr.
Lockridge, Ernest, ed. Twentieth Century Interpretations of The Great Gatsby. (Orig.). (YA) (gr. 9-12). 1968. 8.95 (ISBN 0-13-363820-0, Spec); pap. 2.95 (ISBN 0-13-363812-X, Spec). P-H.
Long, Robert C. The Achieving of the Great Gatsby: F. Scott Fitzgerald, 1920-1925. LC 77-92572. 224p. 1981. pap. 7.95 (ISBN 0-8387-5026-5). Bucknell U Pr.

Long, Robert E. The Achieving of the Great Gatsby: F. Scott Fitzgerald, 1920-1925. LC 77-92572. 226p. 1979. 16.50 (ISBN 0-8387-2192-3). Bucknell U Pr.
Miller, James E. Fictional Technique of Scott Fitzgerald. LC 76-46979. 1957. lib. bdg. 25.00 (ISBN 0-8414-6189-9). Folcroft.
Miller, James E., Jr. F. Scott Fitzgerald: His Art & His Technique. LC 64-16900. (Gotham Library). 1964. pap. 6.50 (ISBN 0-8147-0309-7). NYU Pr.
Mizener, Arthur. Far Side of Paradise: A Biography of F. Scott Fitzgerald. rev. & enl. ed. (Illus.). pap. 4.95 (ISBN 0-395-08395-8, 46, SenEd). HM.
Mizener, Arthur, ed. F. Scott Fitzgerald: A Collection of Critical Essays. (Orig.). 1963. 10.95 (ISBN 0-13-320853-2, Spec); pap. 2.95 (ISBN 0-13-320846-X, Spec). P-H.
Monarch Notes on Fitzgerald's Great Gatsby. (Orig.). pap. 1.50 (ISBN 0-671-00667-3). Monarch Pr.
Northman, Philip. Great Gatsby Notes. (Orig.). (YA) pap. 1.95 (ISBN 0-8220-0560-3). Cliffs.
Perosa, Sergio. Art of F. Scott Fitzgerald. Matz, Charles, tr. 1968. pap. 2.25 (ISBN 0-472-06142-9, 142, AA). U of Mich Pr.
Piper, Henry D., ed. Fitzgerald's the Great Gatsby: The Novel, the Critics, the Background. (Research Anthologies Ser). (Illus., Orig.). 1970. pap. text ed. 7.95x (ISBN 0-684-41402-3, ScribC). Scribner.
Rao, B. Ramachandra. The American Fictional Hero: An Analysis of the Works of Fitzgerald, Wolfe, Farrell, Dos Passos & Steinbeck. (English Language & Literature Ser.: No. 4). 1979. text ed. 8.95x (ISBN 0-210-40620-8, Pub. by Bahri India). Asia.
Stanley, Linda C. The Foreign Critical Reputation of F. Scott Fitzgerald: An Analysis & Annotated Bibliography. LC 79-7474. 1980. lib. bdg. 25.00 (ISBN 0-313-21444-1, STF/). Greenwood.
Way, Brian. F. Scott Fitzgerald & the Art of Social Fiction. 1980. 25.00 (ISBN 0-312-27950-7). St Martin.
White, Sidney H. Barron's Simplified Approach to Fitzgerald's Great Gatsby. LC 68-8681. 1968. pap. text ed. 1.50 (ISBN 0-8120-0287-3). Barron.

FITZGERALD, FRANCIS SCOTT KEY, 1896-1940–BIBLIOGRAPHY
Bruccoli, Matthew J. F. Scott Fitzgerald: A Descriptive Bibliography. LC 77-181395. (Pittsburgh Ser. in Bibliography). (Illus.). 1972. 25.00x (ISBN 0-8229-3239-3). U of Pittsburgh Pr.
Fitzgerald, F. Scott. Great Gatsby. (Hudson River Edition Ser.). 1981. 15.00 (ISBN 0-684-16498-1, ScribT). Scribner.
Harmon, Robert B., ed. The First Editions of F. Scott Fitzgerald. LC 77-26503. (First Edition Pocket Guides Ser.). 1978. pap. 3.95 (ISBN 0-910720-14-2). Hermes.

FITZGERALD, LORD EDWARD, 1763-1798
Molony, John C. Ireland's Tragic Comedians. LC 73-134117. (Essay Index Reprint Ser). 1934. 17.00 (ISBN 0-8369-1933-5). Arno.

FITZGERALD, ROBERT DAVID, 1902-
Day, A. Grove. Robert D. FitzGerald. (World Authors Ser.: Australia: No. 286). 1974. lib. bdg. 10.95 (ISBN 0-8057-2311-0). Twayne.
FitzGerald, Robert D. Of Places & Poetry. (Illus.). 1976. 14.95x (ISBN 0-7022-1003-X). U of Queensland Pr.

FITZGERALD, ZELDA (SAYRE)
Fitzgerald, F. Scott. The Romantic Egoists: A Pictorial Autobiography from the Albums of Scott & Zelda Fitzgerald. Smith, Scottie F., et al, eds. (Illus.). 1977. Encore Edition. 14.95 (ISBN 0-684-14973-7, ScribT). Scribner.
Fitzgerald, Zelda. Save Me the Waltz. LC 32-30021. (Arcturus Books Paperbacks). 224p. 1967. pap. 6.95 (ISBN 0-8093-0255-1). S Ill U Pr.
Milford, Nancy. Zelda. 1971. pap. 2.50 (ISBN 0-380-00784-3, 40014). Avon.

FITZHERBERT, MARIA ANNE (SMYTHE), 1756-1837
Leslie, Shane, 3rd. Salutation to Five: Mrs. Fitzherbert, Edmund Warre, Sir William Butler, Leo Tolstoy, Sir Mark Sykes. facs. ed. LC 75-126231. (Biography Index Reprint Ser.). 1951. 15.00 (ISBN 0-8369-8027-1). Arno.

FITZHUGH, GEORGE, 1806-1881
Wish, Harvey. George Fitzhugh: Propagandist of the Old South. (Illus.). 1962. 7.50 (ISBN 0-8446-1481-5). Peter Smith.

FITZMAURICE, GEORGE
Fitzmaurice, George. Plays of George Fitzmaurice: Realistic Plays, Vol. 3. Slaughter, Howard K., ed. 1970. 7.50 (ISBN 0-85105-174-X). Dufour.
Gelderman, Carol W. George Fitzmaurice. (English Authors Ser.: No. 252). 1979. lib. bdg. 11.95 (ISBN 0-8057-6741-X). Twayne.
--George Fitzmaurice. (Twayne English Authors Ser.). 1979. lib. bdg. 10.50 (ISBN 0-8057-6741-X). G K Hall.
McGuinness, Arthur E. George Fitzmaurice. (Irish Writers Ser.). 96p. 1975. 4.50 (ISBN 0-8387-7870-4); pap. 1.95 (ISBN 0-8387-7980-8). Bucknell U Pr.
Slaughter, Howard K. George Fitzmaurice & His Enchanted Land. (Irish Theatre Ser.: No. 2). (Illus., Orig.). 1972. pap. text ed. 3.25x (ISBN 0-85105-188-X, Dolmen Pr). Humanities.

FITZPATRICK, THOMAS, 1799?-1854
Hafen, Leroy R. Broken Hand: The Life of Thomas Fitzpatrick, Mountain Man, Guide & Indian Agent. LC 80-23451. (Illus.). xiv, 359p. 1981. pap. 6.50 (ISBN 0-8032-7208-1, BB 753, Bison). U of Nebr Pr.
--Broken Hand: The Life of Thomas Fitzpatrick, Mountain Man, Guide & Indian Agent. rev. ed. 1973. 20.00 (ISBN 0-912094-17-6). Old West.

FITZWILLIAM VIRGINAL BOOK
Naylor, E. W. An Elizabethan Virginal Book. LC 70-87638. (Music Ser). 1970. Repr. of 1905 ed. lib. bdg. 25.00 (ISBN 0-306-71792-1). Da Capo.

FIVE CIVILIZED TRIBES
The Act of Union Between the Eastern & Western Cherokees, the Constitution & Amendments, & the Laws of the Cherokee Nation: Passed During the Session of 1868 & Subsequent Sessions. LC 75-3669. (Constitutions & Laws of the American Indian Tribes Ser. 2: Vol. 3). 1975. Repr. of 1870 ed. 12.00 (ISBN 0-8420-1836-0). Scholarly Res Inc.
Bailey, M. Thomas. Reconstruction in Indian Territory. LC 77-189551. 1972. 13.50 (ISBN 0-8046-9022-7). Kennikat.
The Constitution & Laws of the Cherokee Nation: Passed at Tah-le-Quah, Cherokee Nation, 1839. LC 75-3667. (Constitutions & Laws of the American Indian Tribes Ser. 2: Vol. 1). 1975. Repr. of 1840 ed. 14.00 (ISBN 0-8420-1834-4). Scholarly Res Inc.
Cotterill, R. S. The Southern Indians: The Story of the Civilized Tribes Before Removal. LC 54-5931. (Civilization of the American Indian Ser.: Vol. 38). 259p. 1954. 12.50 (ISBN 0-8061-0286-1); pap. 6.95 (ISBN 0-8061-1171-2). U of Okla Pr.
Debo, Angie. And Still the Waters Run. LC 66-20712. (Illus.). 1966. Repr. of 1940 ed. 9.50 (ISBN 0-87752-026-7). Gordian.
--And Still the Waters Run: The Betrayal of the Five Civilized Tribes. 444p. 1972. 22.00 (ISBN 0-691-04615-8); pap. 4.95 (ISBN 0-691-00578-8). Princeton U Pr.
Gibson, Arrell M. The Chickasaws. (Civilization of the American Indian Ser.: Vol. 109). (Illus.). 320p. 1971. pap. 8.95 (ISBN 0-8061-1042-2). U of Okla Pr.
Jones, Charles C., Jr. Antiquities of the Southern Indians Particularly of the Georgia Tribes. LC 72-5001. (Harvard University. Peabody Museum of Archaeology & Ethnology, Antiquities of the New World: No. 6). (Illus.). Repr. of 1873 ed. 43.50 (ISBN 0-404-57306-1). AMS Pr.
Laws & Joint Resolutions of the Cherokee Nation: Enacted by the National Council During the Regular & Extra Sessions of 1884-5-6. LC 75-3674. (Constitution & Laws of the American Indian Tribes Ser. 2: Vol. 7). 1975. Repr. of 1887 ed. 17.00 (ISBN 0-8420-1840-9). Scholarly Res Inc.
Laws & Joint Resolutions of the Cherokee Nation: Enacted During the Regular & Special Sessions of the Years 1881-2-3. LC 75-3673. (Constitutions & Laws of the American Indian Tribes Ser. 2: Vol. 6). 1975. Repr. of 1884 ed. 22.00 (ISBN 0-8420-1839-5). Scholarly Res Inc.
Laws of the Cherokee Nation: Passed at the Annual Session of the National Council, 1845. LC 75-3668. (Constitutions & Laws of the American Indian Tribes Ser. 2: Vol. 2). 1975. Repr. of 1845 ed. 12.00 (ISBN 0-8420-1835-2). Scholarly Res Inc.
Milligan, Dorothy. The How Book of Being Indian. (Illus.). 142p. 1980. 7.95 (ISBN 0-89015-247-0). Eakin Pubns.
Perdue, Theda. Nations Remembered: An Oral History of the Five Civilized Tribes, 1865-1907. LC 79-6828. (Contributions in Ethnic Studies: No. 1). xxiv, 221p. 1980. lib. bdg. 23.95 (ISBN 0-313-22097-2, PFN/). Greenwood.
Simmons, William H. Notices of East Florida, with an Account of the Seminole Nation of Indians. LC 73-2820. (Bicentennial Floridiana Facsimile & Reprint Ser.). 1973. Repr. of 1822 ed. 6.00 (ISBN 0-8130-0400-4). U Presses Fla.

FIVE YEAR PLAN (RUSSIA)
see Russia–Economic Policy

FIXED COSTS
see Overhead Costs

FIXED IDEAS
see Eccentrics and Eccentricities; Hysteria; Obsessive-Compulsive Neuroses

FIXED WING AIRCRAFT
see Airplanes

FIXTURES (LAW)
see also Personal Property; Real Property

FIXTURES (MECHANICAL DEVICES)
see Jigs and Fixtures

FJORDS
Freeland, Howard J., et al, eds. Fjord Oceanography. (NATO Conference Ser., Ser. IV: Marine Science: Vol. 4). 713p. 1980. 69.50 (ISBN 0-306-40439-7, Plenum Pr). Plenum Pub.

FJORT (AFRICAN TRIBE)
see Bakongo (African Tribe)

FLAGELLA (MICROBIOLOGY)
Ettl, H. Die Gattung Chlamydomonas Ehrenberg (Chlamydomonas und Die Nachstverwandten Gattungen II) (Beihefte Zur Nova Hedwigia: Vol. 49). (Illus.). 1976. pap. 120.00x (ISBN 3-7682-5449-6, Pub. by J. Cramer). Intl Schol Bk Serv.
Sleigh, M. A., ed. Cilia & Flagella. 1974. 79.50 (ISBN 0-12-648150-4). Acad Pr.

FLAGELLANTS AND FLAGELLATION
Gibson, Ian. The English Vice: Beating, Sex & Shame in Victorian England & After. (Illus.). 364p. 1978. 27.50 (ISBN 0-686-26719-2, Pub. by Duckworth England). Biblio Dist.
Henderson, A. Corbin. Brothers of Light: The Penitentes of the Southwest. LC 77-88835. 1977. Repr. of 1937 ed. lib. bdg. 13.50x (ISBN 0-88307-534-2). Gannon.
Rael, Juan B. & Hague, Eleanor. New Mexican Alabado: With Transcription of Music. LC 51-10328. (Stanford University. Stanford Studies in Language & Literature: Vol. 9 Pt. 3). Repr. of 1951 ed. 17.00 (ISBN 0-404-51819-2). AMS Pr.
Weigle, Marta. A Penitente Bibliography. LC 75-40839. 176p. 1976. pap. 8.50x (ISBN 0-8263-0401-X). U of NM Pr.

FLAGELLATA
see also Dinoflagellata; Ebriida

FLAGELLATION
see Corporal Punishment; Flagellants and Flagellation

FLAGEOLET
see also Recorder (Musical Instrument)

FLAGET, BENEDICT JOSEPH, BP., 1763-1850
Spalding, Martin J. Sketches of the Life, Times, Character of Right Reverend Benedict Joseph Flaget, First Bishop of Louisville. LC 71-83441. (Religion in America, Ser. 1). 1969. Repr. of 1852 ed. 17.00 (ISBN 0-405-00266-1). Arno.

FLAGG FAMILY
Flagg, Ernest. Genealogical Notes on the Founding of New England. LC 72-10465. (Illus.). 1973. Repr. of 1926 ed. 17.50 (ISBN 0-8063-0533-9). Genealog Pub.

FLAGLER, HENRY MORRISON, 1830-1913
Martin, Sidney W. Florida's Flagler. LC 49-8401. 280p. 1949. 12.50 (ISBN 0-8203-0064-0). U of Ga Pr.

FLAGS
see also Emblems; Signals and Signaling
Barraclough, E. M. Flags of the World. rev. ed. LC 68-22445. (Illus.). 1979. 30.00 (ISBN 0-7232-2015-8). Warne.
Blair, Margot C. & Ryan, Cathleen. Banners & Flags: How to Sew a Celebration. LC 77-2246. (Illus.). 1977. 16.95 (ISBN 0-15-110560-X); pap. 7.95 (ISBN 0-15-610678-7, Harv). HarBraceJ.
Boros, Ladislav J. Flagorama: Exploring Our World with Flags. LC 73-84143. (gr. 3-10). 1973. pap. 4.50 (ISBN 0-915236-02-8). Focus Quality.
Davis, Brian L. Flags & Standards of the Third Reich: Army, Navy, & Air Force. LC 74-14053. (Illus.). 1975. 15.00 (ISBN 0-668-03620-6). Arco.
Evans, I. O. The Observer's Book of Flags. (Illus.). 1977. 4.95 (ISBN 0-684-14941-9, ScribT). Scribner.
Hope, A. Guy. Symbols of the Nations. 1973. 10.00 (ISBN 0-685-57348-6). Pub Aff Pr.
Hulme, F. Edward. Flags of the World, Their History, Blazonry, & Associations. 1977. lib. bdg. 75.00 (ISBN 0-8490-1843-9). Gordon Pr.
Inglefield, Eric. Flags. LC 79-12912. (Arco Fact Guides in Color). (Illus.). 1979. 6.95 (ISBN 0-668-04804-2). Arco.
Lauckner, Edie. Signs of Celebration. 1978. 2.25 (ISBN 0-570-03770-0, 12-2706). Concordia.
Marxhausen, Joanne. Banners. (A Nice Place to Live Ser.). 1978. pap. 2.25 (ISBN 0-570-07750-8, 12-2709). Concordia.
--See His Banners Go. (Illus.). 32p. 1975. pap. 2.75 (ISBN 0-570-03702-6, 12-2604). Concordia.
Matheson, John R. Canada's Flag: A Search for a Country. (Scholarly Reference Publications). 1980. lib. bdg. 18.50 (ISBN 0-8161-8426-7). G K Hall.
Smith. Flags Through the Ages & Across the World. Date not set. 17.95 (ISBN 0-517-29244-0). Bonanza.
Smith, Whitney. Flags & Arms Across the World. LC 79-13271. (Illus.). 1979. 9.95 (ISBN 0-07-059094-X). McGraw.
Swan, Conrad. Canada: Symbols of Sovereignty. LC 76-20511. 1977. 35.00x (ISBN 0-8020-5346-7). U of Toronto Pr.
Thompson, Brenda & Giesen, Rosemary. Flags. LC 76-22431. (First Fact Books Ser). (Illus.). (gr. k-3). 1977. PLB 4.95 (ISBN 0-8225-1355-2). Lerner Pubns.
Weiskopf, Tom. Go for the Flag. 1969. pap. 3.50 (ISBN 0-8015-3018-0, Hawthorn). Dutton.
Wise, Terence. Military Flags of the World: 1618-1900. LC 77-26286. (Arco Color Ser.). (Illus.). 1978. 8.95 (ISBN 0-668-04472-1); pap. 5.95 (ISBN 0-668-04483-7). Arco.
Wolfe, Betty. The Banner Book. LC 74-80378. (Illus.). 96p. 1974. 6.95 (ISBN 0-8192-1173-7). Morehouse.

FLAGS–UNITED STATES
Blotnick, Elihu & Robinson, Barbara. Free-for-All: The Reds, the Whites & the Blues. (Illus.). 64p. (Orig.). 1981. pap. 6.95 (ISBN 0-915090-02-3). Calif Street.
D'Alessandro, Robert. Glory. pap. 7.95 (ISBN 0-914654-00-4, 8400). Morgan.
Eggenberger, David. Flags of the U.S.A. enl. ed. 1964. 9.95 (ISBN 0-690-30491-9). T Y Crowell.
Furlong, William R. & McCandless, Bryon. So Proudly We Hail: The History of the United States Flag. Langley, Harold D., ed. (Illus.). 256p. (Orig.). 1981. 22.50 (ISBN 0-87474-448-2); pap. 9.95 (ISBN 0-87474-449-0). Smithsonian.
Gibbons, Cromwell. Republic, U.S.A. 1965. 7.50 (ISBN 0-8159-6709-8). Devin.
Livermore, Mary A. My Story of the War: A Woman's Narrative of Four Year's Personal Experience As Nurse in the Union Army. LC 72-2612. (American Women Ser: Images & Realities). (Illus.). 704p. 1972. Repr. of 1889 ed. 30.00 (ISBN 0-405-04466-6). Arno.
Ludlow, Norman H., Jr. U.S. Historic Flag Project Book, 2 vols. (Illus.). 1974. pap. 4.85x (ISBN 0-916706-07-9); Vol. 1. narration (ISBN 0-916706-20-6); Vol. 2. workbook (ISBN 0-916706-21-4). N H Ludlow.
Manwaring, David R. Render Unto Caesar: The Flag-Salute Controversy. LC 62-13563. 1962. 12.50x (ISBN 0-226-50413-1). U of Chicago Pr.
Mastai, Boleslaw & D'Otrange, Marie-Louise. Stars & the Stripes. (Illus.). 1973. 25.00 (ISBN 0-394-47217-9). Knopf.
Mastai, Boleslaw & Mastai, Marie-Louise D. The Stripes & Stars: The Evolution of the American Flag. LC 73-87164. (Illus.). 72p. 1973. pap. 6.95 (ISBN 0-88360-001-3). Amon Carter.
Morris, Robert. The Truth About the American Flag. LC 76-12730. (Illus.). 1976. 10.80 (ISBN 0-9601476-1-6); pap. 7.65 (ISBN 0-9601476-2-4). Wynnehaven.
Quaife, Milo M., et al. History of the United States Flag. LC 64-2613. (Illus.). 1961. 14.95 (ISBN 0-06-013455-0, HarpT). Har-Row.
Shankle, George E. State Names, Flags, Seals, Songs, Birds, Flowers, & Other Symbols. rev. ed. LC 73-109842. (Illus.). 522p. Repr. of 1938 ed. lib. bdg. 23.50x (ISBN 0-8371-4333-0, SHSN). Greenwood.
Six Flags of Texas. (Illus.). 1968. 15.95 (ISBN 0-87244-005-2). Texian.
Smith, Whitney. American Flags from Washington to Lincoln. (Illus.). (gr. 7). pap. 1.00 (ISBN 0-88388-048-2). Bellerophon Bks.
--The Flag Book of the United States. rev. ed. LC 75-18701. (Illus.). 320p. 1975. 12.95 (ISBN 0-688-02977-9). Morrow.
Weaver, Robert B. Our Flag & Other Symbols of Americanism. 76p. (gr. 7-8). 1972. pap. 0.50 (ISBN 0-912530-09-X); test 0.10 (ISBN 0-686-77026-9). Patriotic Educ.

FLAGS–UNITED STATES–JUVENILE LITERATURE
Blassingame, Wyatt. Story of the United States Flag. LC 68-10030. (American Democracy Ser). (Illus.). (gr. 3-6). 1969. PLB 6.48 (ISBN 0-8116-6502-X). Garrard.
Crouthers, David D. Flags of American History. LC 73-8607. (Profile Ser). (gr. 6 up). 1973. 6.95 (ISBN 0-8437-3080-3); PLB 4.39 (ISBN 0-8437-3965-7). Hammond Inc.
Freeman, Mae B. Stars & Stripes: The Story of the American Flag. (Gateway Ser.: No. 34). (Illus.). (gr. 3-7). 1964. PLB 5.99 (ISBN 0-394-90134-7, BYR). Random.
Mayer, Albert I. Story of Old Glory. LC 79-110036. (Cornerstones of Freedom Bks). (Illus.). (gr. 4-8). 1970. PLB 9.25 (ISBN 0-516-04629-2); pap. 2.50 (ISBN 0-516-44629-0). Childrens.
Parrish, Thomas. The American Flag. LC 72-92156. (Illus.). (gr. 5 up). 1973. 7.95 (ISBN 0-671-65204-4, Juveniles). S&S.

FLAGSTAD, KIRSTEN MARIE, 1895-1962
Biancolli, Louis & Farkas, Andrew. The Flagstad Manuscript. LC 76-29935. (Opera Biographies). (Illus.). 1977. Repr. of 1952 ed. lib. bdg. 20.00x (ISBN 0-405-09677-1). Arno.

McArthur, Edwin. Flagstad: A Personal Memoir. (Music Reprint Ser.: 1980). (Illus.). 1980. Repr. of 1965 ed. lib. bdg. 25.00 (ISBN 0-306-76028-2). Da Capo.

FLAGSTAFF, ARIZONA

Roat, Evelyn C. The Museum of Northern Arizona. (MNA Special Publication Ser.: No. 8). 1968. 4.00 (ISBN 0-89734-016-7); pap. 0.60 (ISBN 0-89734-015-9). Mus Northern Ariz.

FLAHERTY, ROBERT JOSEPH, 1884-1951

Flaherty, Frances H. Odyssey of a Film-Maker: Robert Flaherty's Story. LC 77-169343. (Arno Press Cinema Program). (Illus.). 66p. 1972. Repr. of 1960 ed. 8.00 (ISBN 0-405-03918-2). Arno.

Griffith, Richard. World of Robert Flaherty. Repr. of 1953 ed. lib. bdg. 16.25x (ISBN 0-8371-3400-5, GRRF). Greenwood.

--The World of Robert Flaherty. LC 72-166104. 1972. Repr. of 1953 ed. lib. bdg. 25.00 (ISBN 0-306-70296-7). Da Capo.

Weinberg, Herman G. Robert Flaherty & Hans Richter. (Film Ser.). 1979. lib. bdg. 59.95 (ISBN 0-8490-3001-3). Gordon Pr.

FLAKE BOARD

see Particle Board

FLAME

Alkemade, Cornelis T. & Herrmann, Roland. Fundamentals of Analytical Flame Spectroscopy. LC 79-4376. 442p. 1979. 82.95 (ISBN 0-470-26710-0). Halsted Pr.

Gaydon, A. G. The Spectroscopy of Flames. 2nd ed. LC 74-4119. 413p. 1974. text ed. 32.00x (ISBN 0-412-12870-5, Pub. by Chapman & Hall England). Methuen Inc.

Gaydon, A. G. & Wolfhard, H. G. Flames: Their Structure, Radiation & Temperature. 4th ed. LC 78-16087. 449p. 1979. text ed. 49.95x (ISBN 0-412-15390-4, Pub. by Chapman & Hall England). Methuen Inc.

Gray, W. A., et al. Heat Transfer from Flames. (Topics in Fuel Science Ser.). 1977. pap. 9.95 (ISBN 0-236-40044-4, Pub. by Paul Elek). Merrimack Bk Serv.

Lewis, Bernard & Von Elbe, Guenther. Combustion, Flames, & Explosions of Gases. 2nd ed. 1961. 62.00 (ISBN 0-12-446750-4). Acad Pr.

Parsons, M. L., et al. Handbook of Flame Spectroscopy. LC 75-17865. 476p. 1975. 42.50 (ISBN 0-306-30856-8, Plenum Pr). Plenum Pub.

FLAME PHOTOMETRY

Cresser, Malcolm S. Solvent Extraction in Flame Spectroscopic Analysis. 1978. 52.95 (ISBN 0-408-71307-0). Butterworth.

Poluektov, N. S. Techniques in Flame Photometric Analysis. LC 60-16418. (Illus.). 219p. 1961. 35.00 (ISBN 0-306-10645-0, Consultants). Plenum Pub.

Pungor, E. Flame Photometry Theory. (Illus.). 1967. 12.50x (ISBN 0-442-06647-3). Van Nos Reinhold.

FLAME RETARDANT POLYMERS

see Fire Resistant Polymers

FLAMENCO

Berger, Charles. Flamenco Gitano. Carnes, Chris, tr. (Illus.). 108p. 1974. 85.00 (ISBN 0-686-10155-3). Artisan Pr.

The Flamenco Guitar. (Illus.). 200p. 15.00 (ISBN 0-686-09074-8); companion instruction lp 6.98 (ISBN 0-686-09075-6). Peer-Southern.

La Guitarra Flamenco: Spanish Text Edition of 'the Flamenco Guitar' 15.00 (ISBN 0-686-09076-4). Peer-Southern.

FLAMING GORGE RESERVOIR (PROPOSED)

Day, Kent C. & Dibble, David S. Archeological Survey of the Flaming Gorge Reservoir Area, Wyoming-Utah. (Upper Colorado Ser: No. 9). Repr. of 1963 ed. 22.50 (ISBN 0-404-60665-2). AMS Pr.

Flowers, Seville, et al. Ecological Studies of the Flora & Fauna of Flaming Gorge Reservoir Basin, Utah & Wyoming. (Upper Colorado Ser: No. 3). 42.00 (ISBN 0-404-60648-2). AMS Pr.

Purdy, William M. An Outline of the History of the Flaming Gorge Area. (University of Utah Anthropological Papers: No. 37). 1959. pap. 5.00x (ISBN 0-87480-172-9). U of Utah Pr.

--An Outline of the History of the Flaming Gorge Area. (Upper Colorado Ser.: No. 1). Repr. of 1959 ed. 20.00 (ISBN 0-404-60637-7). AMS Pr.

FLAMINGOS

Bent, Arthur C. Life Histories of North American Marsh Birds. (Illus.). 10.50 (ISBN 0-8446-1639-7). Peter Smith.

--Life Histories of North American Marsh Birds. (Illus.). 1927. pap. 6.50 (ISBN 0-486-21082-0). Dover.

Kear, Janet & Duplaix-Hall, Nicole, eds. Flamingos. (Illus.). 1975. 26.00 (ISBN 0-85661-007-0, Pub by T & A D Poyser). Buteo.

FLAMMABILITY TESTING

see Fire-Testing

FLAMMABLE MATERIALS

see Inflammable Materials

FLANAGAN, EDWARD JOSEPH, 1886-1948

Jackson, Sharon. Michael, the Gentle Padre. 1981. 7.95 (ISBN 0-533-04938-5). Vantage.

FLANDERS

Flanders. (Panorama Bks.). (Illus., Fr.). 3.95 (ISBN 0-685-11189-X). French & Eur.

FLANDERS–DESCRIPTION AND TRAVEL

Edwards, G. W. Some Old Flemish Towns. 59.95 (ISBN 0-8490-1078-0). Gordon Pr.

Flandre et Artois touristiques. (Illus.). 1978. text ed. 14.25x (ISBN 2-03-013927-0, 3158). Larousse.

FLANDERS–HISTORY

Froissart, Jean. Chronicle of Froissart, 6 Vols. Bourchier, John, tr. LC 70-168064. (Tudor Translations. First Ser.: Nos. 27-32). Repr. of 1903 ed. Set. 147.00 (ISBN 0-404-51930-X); 24.50 ea. Vol. 1 (ISBN 0-404-51931-8). Vol. 2 (ISBN 0-404-51932-6). Vol. 3 (ISBN 0-404-51933-4). Vol. 4 (ISBN 0-404-51934-2). Vol. 5 (ISBN 0-404-51935-0). Vol. 6 (ISBN 0-404-51936-9). AMS Pr.

--Here Begynneth the First Volum of Sir J. Froyssart. Bourchier, J., tr. LC 72-26004. (English Experience Ser.: No. 257). 644p. 1970. Repr. of 1523 ed. 104.00 (ISBN 90-221-0257-2). Walter J Johnson.

Howaert, J. B. Letters of Ogier Chislain De Busbecq to the Holy Roman Emperor Maximillian Ii. 9.95 (ISBN 0-685-60135-8, Pub by Twayne). Cyrco Pr.

Mendels, Franklin F. Industrialization & Population Pressure in Eighteenth-Century Flanders. Bruchey, Stuart, ed. LC 80-2817. (Dissertations in European Economic History II). (Illus.). 1981. lib. bdg. 29.00x (ISBN 0-405-14001-0). Arno.

FLANDERS FAMILY

Ridlon, G. T. Flanders Family. LC 70-94956. (Saco Valley Settlements Ser). 1970. pap. 1.50 (ISBN 0-8048-0766-3). C E Tuttle.

FLANNAGAN, JOHN BERNARD, 1895?-1942

Baro, Gene. John Flannagan: Sculpture & Works on Paper. LC 74-29627. (Illus.). 1974. soft bdg. 1.50 (ISBN 0-88397-055-4). Intl Exhibit Foun.

FLANNIGAN, KATHERINE MARY (O'FALLON)–FICTION

Freedman, Benedict & Freedman, Nancy. Mrs. Mike. (gr. 7 up). 1968. pap. 1.95 (ISBN 0-425-03643-X, Medallion). Berkley Pub.

--Mrs. Mike. (Illus.). 1947. 8.95 (ISBN 0-698-10260-6). Coward.

FLARES, SOLAR

see Solar Flares

FLASH-LIGHT PHOTOGRAPHY

see Photography, Flash-Light

FLASKS

see Bottles

FLAT RACING

see Horse-Racing

FLATFISHES

Norman, J. R. Systematic Monograph of the Flatfishes, Heterosomata, Vol. 1 Psettodidae, Bothidae, Pleuronectidae. (Illus.). Repr. of 1934 ed. 31.00 (ISBN 0-384-41950-X). Johnson Repr.

Rae, B. Bennet. The Lemon Sole. (Illus.). 108p. 7.00 (ISBN 0-85238-013-5, FNB). Unipub.

--The Lemon Sole. 1978. 12.50 (ISBN 0-685-63430-2). State Mutual Bk.

FLATWARE, SILVER

see Silverware

FLATWORMS

see Platyhelminthes

FLAUBERT, GUSTAVE, 1821-1880

Barnes, Hazel E. Sartre & Flaubert. LC 80-26872. 416p. 25.00 (ISBN 0-226-03720-7). U of Chicago Pr.

Bart, B. F. & Cook, R. F. The Legendary Sources of Flaubert's Saint Julian. LC 77-7892. 1977. 20.00x (ISBN 0-8020-5373-4). U of Toronto Pr.

Bart, B. F., ed. Madame Bovary & the Critics: A Collection of Essays. LC 66-12596. (Gotham Library). 197p. 1966. pap. 4.95x (ISBN 0-8147-0030-6). NYU Pr.

Bart, Benjamin F. Flaubert. LC 67-27410. (Illus.). 1967. pap. 9.95 (ISBN 0-8156-0087-9). Syracuse U Pr.

Blossom, F. A. La Composition De Salammbo, D'apres la Correspondance De Flaubert, 1857-62. (Elliott Monographs: Vol. 3.). 1914. pap. 7.00 (ISBN 0-527-02607-7). Kraus Repr.

Brombert, Victor. Novels of Flaubert, a Study of Themes & Techniques. 1967. 21.50 (ISBN 0-691-06085-1); pap. 6.95 (ISBN 0-691-01290-3). Princeton U Pr.

Buck, Stratton. Gustave Flaubert. (World Authors Ser.: France: No. 3). 1966. pap. 10.95 (ISBN 0-8057-2312-9). Twayne.

Carlut, Charles. Correspondance de Flaubert: Etude et Repertoire Critique. (Fr). 1969. 10.00 (ISBN 0-8142-0010-9). Ohio St U Pr.

Carlut, Charles, et al. A Concordance to Flaubert's L'education Sentimentale, 2 vols. LC 78-68262. (Reference Library of the Humanities: Vol. 125). 1979. Set. lib. bdg. 115.00 (ISBN 0-8240-9795-5). Garland Pub.

--A Concordance to Flaubert's La Tentation de Saint Antoine. LC 79-7914. (Garland Reference Library of the Humanities: No. 180). 1980. lib. bdg. 60.00 (ISBN 0-8240-9547-2). Garland Pub.

--A Concordance to Flaubert's Salammbo, 2 vols. LC 78-68268. (Garland Reference Library of the Humanities: No. 148). 1979. Set. lib. bdg. 100.00 (ISBN 0-8240-9794-7). Garland Pub.

--A Concordance to Flaubert's Trois Contes. LC 79-17347. (Garland Reference Library of the Humaities: No. 178). 1980. lib. bdg. 60.00 (ISBN 0-8240-9548-0). Garland Pub.

Cliff's Notes Editors. Madame Bovary Notes. (Orig.). pap. 2.25 (ISBN 0-8220-0780-0). Cliffs.

Cogny, Pierre. L' Education sentimentale de Flaubert: Le Monde en creux. new ed. (Collection themes et textes). 270p. (Orig., Fr.). 1975. pap. 6.75 (ISBN 2-03-035030-3, 2685). Larousse.

Coleman, A. Flaubert's Literary Development in the Light of His Memories D'un Fou Novembre, & Education Sentimentale. (Elliott Monographs: Vol. 1). 1914. pap. 9.00 (ISBN 0-527-02605-0). Kraus Repr.

Cortland, Peter. Reader's Guide to Flaubert. LC 67-19267. 1968. 4.95 (ISBN 0-87037-027-8). Helios.

Cross, Richard K. Flaubert & Joyce: The Rite of Fiction. LC 73-136197. (Princeton Essays Literature Ser.). 1971. 14.00 (ISBN 0-691-06199-8). Princeton U Pr.

Culler, Jonathan. Flaubert: The Uses of Uncertainty. LC 73-16679. (Novelists & Their World Ser.). 256p. 1974. 19.50x (ISBN 0-8014-0818-0). Cornell U Pr.

Diamond, Marie J. Flaubert: The Problem of Aesthetic Discontinuity. 1975. 12.50 (ISBN 0-8046-9075-8, Natl U). Kennikat.

Dube, Pierre H., et al. A Concordance to Flaubert's Madame Bovary, 2 vols. LC 77-83409. (Library of Humanities Reference Bks.: No. 109). lib. bdg. 100.00 (ISBN 0-8240-9832-3). Garland Pub.

Dumesnil. Gustave Flaubert, l'Homme et l'Oeuvre. 23.50 (ISBN 0-685-34907-1). French & Eur.

Faquet, E. Flaubert. lib. bdg. 59.95 (ISBN 0-8490-0174-9). Gordon Pr.

Fay, P. B. & Coleman, A. Sources & Structure of Flaubert's Salammbo. 1914. pap. 5.00 (ISBN 0-527-02606-9). Kraus Repr.

Ferguson, Walter D. Influence of Flaubert on George Moore. LC 74-10999. 1934. lib. bdg. 10.00 (ISBN 0-8414-4220-7). Folcroft.

Flaubert, G. Letters: Gustave Flaubert. 248p. 1980. Repr. lib. bdg. 40.00 (ISBN 0-8495-1705-2). Arden Lib.

Flaubert, Gustave. Correspondance, 2 vols. 1220p. Vol. 1, 1830-1851. 37.50 (ISBN 0-686-56511-8); Vol. 2, 1851-1858. write for info. French & Eur.

--The Letters of Gustave Flaubert, Eighteen Thirty to Eighteen Fifty-Seven. Steegmuller, Francis, ed. LC 79-13503. (Harvard Paperbacks Ser.). 272p. 1981. pap. 5.95 (ISBN 0-674-52637-6). Harvard U Pr.

--The Letters of Gustave Flaubert: Eighteen Thirty to Eighteen Fifty Seven. Steegmuller, Francis, ed. (Illus.). 267p. 1980. 15.00 (ISBN 0-674-52636-8, Belknap Pr). Harvard U Pr.

Freienmuth Von Helms, E. German Criticism of Gustave Flaubert. LC 70-168138. (Columbia University. Germanic Studies, New Ser.: No. 7). Repr. of 1939 ed. 15.00 (ISBN 0-404-50457-4). AMS Pr.

Gervais, David. Flaubert & Henry James: A Study in Contrasts. 1978. text ed. 23.50x (ISBN 0-06-492375-4). B&N.

Giraud, Raymond. Unheroic Hero in the Novels of Stendahl, Balzac & Flaubert. 1969. lib. bdg. 14.50x (ISBN 0-374-93154-2). Octagon.

Hamilton, A. Sources of the Religious Element in Flaubert's Salammbo. (Elliott Monographs: Vol. 4). 1917. pap. 7.00 (ISBN 0-527-02608-5). Kraus Repr.

Jackson, Joseph F. Louise Colet et Ses Amis Litteraires. LC 72-1613. (Yale Romanic Studies: No. 15). (Fr). Repr. of 1937 ed. 18.00 (ISBN 0-404-53215-2). AMS Pr.

Nadeau, Maurice. The Greatness of Flaubert. Bray, Barbara, tr. 307p. 1972. pap. 6.95 (ISBN 0-87548-325-9, Library Pr). Open Court.

Oliver, Hermia. Flaubert & an English Governess: The Quest for Juliet Herbert. (Illus.). 202p. 1980. 33.50x (ISBN 0-19-815764-9). Oxford U Pr.

Rozen, Arthur. Monarch Notes on Flaubert's Madame Bovary & Three Tales. (Orig.). pap. 1.75 (ISBN 0-671-00560-X). Monarch Pr.

Sarte, Jean-Paul. The Family Idiot: Gustave Flaubert, 1821-1857, Vol. I. Cosman, Carol, tr. LC 81-1694. 1981. 25.00 (ISBN 0-226-73509-5). U of Chicago Pr.

Sartre, Jean-Paul. L' Idiot de la Famille, Gustave Flaubert (1821-1857, 3 tomes. (Bibliotheque de philosophie). Set. 107.20 (ISBN 0-685-36561-1). French & Eur.

Sherman, Stuart, tr. from Fr. The Letters of George Sand & Gustave Flaubert. 1979. 5.95 (ISBN 0-915864-64-9); lib. bdg. 14.95 (ISBN 0-915864-52-5). Academy Chi Ltd.

Sherrington, R. J. Three Novels by Flaubert: A Study of Techniques. 1970. 37.50x (ISBN 0-19-815398-8). Oxford U Pr.

Smalley, Barbara. George Eliot & Flaubert: Pioneers of the Modern Novel. LC 73-85446. ix, 240p. 1974. 13.50x (ISBN 0-8214-0136-X). Ohio U Pr.

Steegmuller, Francis. Flaubert & Madame Bovary: A Double Portrait. 1977. pap. 5.95 (ISBN 0-226-77137-7, P709, Phoen). U of Chicago Pr.

Steegmuller, Francis, ed. & tr. from Fr. Flaubert in Egypt. (Illus.). 1979. lib. bdg. 10.95 (ISBN 0-89733-019-6); pap. 5.95 (ISBN 0-89733-018-8). Academy Chi Ltd.

Tarver, John C. Gustave Flaubert. LC 71-113324. 1970. Repr. of 1895 ed. 14.50 (ISBN 0-8046-1001-0). Kennikat.

Willebrink, George A. The Dossier of Flaubert's un Coeur Simple. 1976. pap. text ed. 37.25x (ISBN 90-6203-409-8). Humanities.

FLAVINS

De Spain, June. The Little Cyanide Cookbook: Delicious Recipes Rich in Vitamin B17. 192p. 1976. pap. text ed. 4.95 (ISBN 0-912986-00-X). Am Media.

Harborne, J. & Mabry, Helga, eds. The Flavonoids. 1975. 88.00 set (ISBN 0-685-72438-7); Pt. 1. 54.50 (ISBN 0-12-324601-6); Pt. 2. 54.50 (ISBN 0-12-324602-4). Acad Pr.

Reichenbach, H., ed. The Flavobacterium-Cytophaga Group. Weeks, O. B. (Illus.). 230p. Date not set. pap. text ed. 55.00 (ISBN 3-527-25919-8). Verlag Chemie.

Yagi, K., ed. Flavins & Flavoproteins: Second International Conference. (Illus.). 1969. 35.00 (ISBN 0-8391-0008-6). Univ Park.

--Reactivity of Flavins. (Illus.). 220p. 1975. 19.50 (ISBN 0-8391-0831-1). Univ Park.

FLAVONES

Farkas, L. & Gabor, M., eds. Flavonoids & Bioflavonoids: Proceedings of the Fifth Hungarian Flavonoid Symposium, Matrafured, Hungary, 1977. 1978. 81.50 (ISBN 0-444-99802-0). Elsevier.

Geissman, Theodore A. Chemistry of Flavonoid Compounds. 1962. 29.95 (ISBN 0-02-341430-8, 34143). Macmillan.

Harborne, Jeffrey B., ed. Comparative Biochemistry of Flavonoids. 1967. 58.50 (ISBN 0-12-324650-4). Acad Pr.

Hungarian Bioflavonoid Symposium, 4th, Hungary, 1973. Topics in Flavonoid Chemistry & Biochemistry: Proceedings. Farkus, L., et al, eds. 1976. 53.75 (ISBN 0-444-99861-6). Elsevier.

Mabry, T. J., et al. Systematic Identification of Flavonoids. LC 72-95565. 1970. 32.70 (ISBN 0-387-04964-9). Springer-Verlag.

FLAVOR

Apt, Charles. Flavor: It's Chemical, Behavioral & Commercial Aspects. LC 77-13274. 1978. lib. bdg. 37.75x (ISBN 0-89158-233-9). Westview.

Bullard, Roger W., ed. Flavor Chemistry of Animal Foods. LC 77-27295. (ACS Symposium Ser.: No. 67). 1978. 19.00 (ISBN 0-8412-0404-7). Am Chemical.

Charalambous, George & Inglett, George E., eds. Flavor of Foods & Beverages: Chemistry & Technology. 1978. 38.00 (ISBN 0-12-169060-1). Acad Pr.

Charalambous, George & Inglett, George, eds. The Quality of Foods & Beverages: Chemistry & Technology, 2 vols, Vols. 1 & 2. 1981. Vol. 1. 29.50 (ISBN 0-12-169101-2); Vol. 2. write for info. (ISBN 0-12-169102-0). Acad Pr.

Hornstein, Irwin, ed. Flavor Chemistry. LC 66-27216. (Advances in Chemistry Ser: No. 56). 1966. 24.00 (ISBN 0-8412-0057-2). Am Chemical.

Jennings, Walter & Shibamoto, Takayuki. Qualitative Analysis of Flavor & Fragrance Volatiles by Glass Capillary Gas Chromtography. LC 79-26034. 1980. 39.00 (ISBN 0-12-384250-6). Acad Pr.

Land, D. G. & Nursten, H. E., eds. Progress in Flavour Research. (Illus.). 1979. 49.60x (ISBN 0-85334-818-9). Intl Ideas.

Margalith, Pinhas. Flavor Microbiology. (Illus.). 336p. 1981. 31.50 (ISBN 0-398-04083-4). C C Thomas.

Scanlan, Richard A., ed. Flavor Quality: Objective Measurement. LC 77-8286. (ACS Symposium Ser: No. 51). 1977. 16.00 (ISBN 0-8412-0378-4). Am Chemical.

FLAVORING ESSENCES

see also Essences and Essential Oils

Dorland, Wayne E. & Rogers, James A. The Fragrance & Flavor Industry. (Illus.). 1977. 30.00 (ISBN 0-9603250-1-8). Dorland Pub Co.

Furia, Thomas E., ed. & tr. Fenaroli's Handbook of Flavor Ingredients, 2 vols. 2nd ed. LC 72-152143. (Handbk. Ser). 1975. Vol. 1, 560p. 59.95 (ISBN 0-87819-534-3); Vol. 2, 944p. 69.95 (ISBN 0-87819-532-7). CRC Pr.

Heath, Henry. Flavor Technology: Profiles, Products, Applications. (Illus.). 1978. lib. bdg. 45.00 (ISBN 0-87055-258-9). AVI.

Heath, Henry B. Source Book of Flavors. (Illus.). 1981. lib. bdg. 79.50 (ISBN 0-87055-370-4). AVI.

Pintauro, N. D. Sweeteners & Enhancers. LC 77-71661. (Food Technology Review Ser.: No. 40). (Illus.). 1977. 39.00 (ISBN 0-8155-0652-X). Noyes.

Supran, Michael K., ed. Lipids As a Source of Flavor. LC 78-9739. (ACS Symposium Ser.: No. 75). 1978. 17.50 (ISBN 0-8412-0418-7). Am Chemical.

Torrey, S., ed. Fragrances & Flavors: Recent Developments. LC 80-12954. (Chemical Technology Review Ser.: No. 156). 335p. 1980. 45.00 (ISBN 0-8155-0798-4). Noyes.

FLAX INDUSTRY

Hoppe, Elisabeth & Edberg, Ragnar. Carding, Spinning, Dyeing: An Introduction to the Traditional Wool & Flax Crafts. (Illus.). 1975. pap. 4.95 (ISBN 0-442-30073-5). Van Nos Reinhold.

FLAXMAN, JOHN, 1755-1826

Bentley, Gerald E., Jr. Early Engravings of Flaxman's Classical Designs. LC 64-25357. (Illus., Orig.). 1964. pap. 5.00 (ISBN 0-87104-066-2). NY Pub Lib.

Bindman, David, ed. John Flaxman. (Illus.). 1980. 24.95 (ISBN 0-500-09139-0). Thames Hudson.

Irwin, David. John Flaxman R.A. LC 79-89678. (Illus.). 280p. 1980. 55.00 (ISBN 0-8478-0263-9). Rizzoli Intl.

FLEAS

Cole, Johanna. Fleas. (Illus.). 64p. (gr. 3-7). 1973. PLB 6.48 (ISBN 0-688-31844-4). Morrow.

Fox, I. Fleas of Eastern United States. 1968. Repr. of 1940 ed. 16.25 (ISBN 0-02-844840-5). Hafner.

Hopkins, G. H. & Rothschild, Miriam. Illustrated Catalogue of the Rothschild Collection of Fleas (Siphonaptera) in the British Museum (Natural History) Incl. Vol. 1. Tungidae & Pulicidae. 362p. 1953. 36.50x (ISBN 0-565-00160-4); Vol. 2. Coptopsyllidae, Vermipsyllidae, Slephanocircidae, Ischnopsyllidae, Hypsophthalmidae & Xiphiopsyllidae. 446p. 1956. 40.00x (ISBN 0-565-00071-3); Vol.3. Hystrichopsyllidae, Acedestiinae, Anomiopsyllinae, Histrichopsyllinae, Neopsyllinae, Rhadinopsyllinae & Stenoponinae. 560p. 1962. 52.50x (ISBN 0-8277-4248-7); Vol. 4. Hystrichopsyllinae, Ctenophthalminae, Dinopsyllinae, Doratopsyllinae, & Listropsyllinae. 550p. 1966. 75.00x (ISBN 0-565-00652-5); Vol. 5. Leptopsyllidae & Ancistropsyllidae. 530p. 1971. 90.00x (ISBN 0-565-00706-8). (Illus., Pub. by Brit Mus Nat Hist). Sabbot-Natural Hist Bks.

Hubbard, Clarence A. Fleas of Western North America, Their Relation to the Public Health. 1968. 23.50 (ISBN 0-02-846120-7). Hafner.

Mardon, D. K. An Illustrated History of the Rothschild Collection of Fleas (siphonaptera) in the British Museum (Natural History) Vol. 6 Pygiopsyllidae. (Illus.). 296p. 1981. 100.00x (ISBN 0-565-00820-X, Pub. by Brit Mus Nat Hist England). Sabbot-Natural Hist Bks.

FLEECE

see Wool

FLEET BALLISTIC MISSILE WEAPONS SYSTEMS

see also Atomic Submarines; Polaris (Missile)

Kuenne, Robert E. Polaris Missile Strike: A General Economic Systems Analysis. LC 66-10715. (Illus.). 1967. 8.00 (ISBN 0-8142-0077-X). Ohio St U Pr.

FLEET PRISON, LONDON

Ashton, John. Fleet: Its River, Prison, & Marriages. LC 68-21753. 1969. Repr. of 1888 ed. 24.00 (ISBN 0-8103-3414-3). Gale.

Harris, Alexander. The Oeconomy of the Fleete. Jessopp, A., ed. 1879. 22.50 (ISBN 0-384-21450-9). Johnson Repr.

FLEET RIVER, LONDON

Ashton, John. Fleet: Its River, Prison, & Marriages. LC 68-21753. 1969. Repr. of 1888 ed. 24.00 (ISBN 0-8103-3414-3). Gale.

FLEMING, ALEXANDER, SIR, 1881-1955

Hughes, W. Howard. Alexander Fleming & Penicillin. 1977. 9.95x (ISBN 0-8448-1089-4). Crane-Russak Co.

Ludovici, L. J. Fleming: Discoverer of Penicillin. 1979. Repr. of 1952 ed. lib. bdg. 25.00 (ISBN 0-8482-1632-6). Norwood Edns.

FLEMING, IAN, 1908-1964

Boyd, Ann. The Devil with James Bond. LC 73-15312. 123p. 1975. Repr. of 1967 ed. lib. bdg. 15.00x (ISBN 0-8371-7182-2, BOJB). Greenwood.

Holbrook, David. The Masks of Hate: The Problem of False Solutions in the Culture of an Acquisitive Society. 276p. 1976. Repr. of 1972 ed. 26.00 (ISBN 0-08-015799-8). Pergamon.

FLEMING, PAUL, 1609-1640

Pyritz, Hans W. Paul Flemings Deutsche Liebeslyrik. Repr. of 1932 ed. 21.50 (ISBN 0-384-48450-6); pap. 18.50 (ISBN 0-685-13548-9). Johnson Repr.

FLEMISH ART

see Art, Flemish

FLEMISH LANGUAGE

see Dutch Language

FLEMISH LITERATURE

Delepiere, Octave. A Sketch of the History of Flemish Literature from the Twelfth Century Down to the Present Time. LC 72-3215. (Studies in European Literature, No. 56). 1972. Repr. of 1860 ed. lib. bdg. 49.95 (ISBN 0-8383-1521-6). Haskell.

De Wit, Joost & Barkan, Stanley H., eds. Fifty Dutch & Flemish Novelists. LC 79-87646. (Illus., Orig.). 1979. 25.00x (ISBN 0-89304-031-2, CCC118); pap. 15.00x (ISBN 0-89304-032-0). Cross Cult.

Meijer, Reinder P. Literature of the Low Countries: A Short History of Dutch Literature in the Netherlands & Belgium. 1971. text ed. 34.50x (ISBN 0-8057-3431-7); pap. text ed. 18.50x (ISBN 0-89197-825-9). Irvington.

Van De Waarsenburg, Hans & Barkan, Stanley H., eds. Five Contemporary Flemish Poets. Holmes, James S., et al, trs. LC 79-87650. (Cross Cultural Review Ser.: No. 3). (Illus., Orig., Dutch-Eng.). 1979. 10.00x (ISBN 0-89304-604-3, CCC120); pap. 4.00x (ISBN 0-89304-605-1). Cross Cult.

FLEMISH MOVEMENT

Clough, Shepard B. History of the Flemish Movement in Belgium. 1967. lib. bdg. 16.00x (ISBN 0-374-91767-1). Octagon.

FLEMISH PAINTING

see Painting, Flemish

FLEMISH PAINTINGS

see Paintings, Flemish

FLEMISH WOOD-ENGRAVINGS

see Wood-Engravings, Flemish

FLESH FOODS

see Animal Food

FLETCHER, JOHN, 1579-1625

Appleton, William W. Beaumont & Fletcher: A Critical Study. LC 74-22014. 1974. Repr. of 1956 ed. lib. bdg. 15.00 (ISBN 0-8414-2982-0). Folcroft.

Bald, Robert C. Bibliographical Studies in the Beaumont & Fletcher Folio of Sixteen Forty-Seven. 1938. lib. bdg. 15.00 (ISBN 0-8414-1790-3). Folcroft.

Beaumont, Francis. The Works of Beaumont & Fletcher. Notes & a Biographical Memoir by Rev. Alexander Dyce. 1976. Repr. of 1843 ed. 72.00 (ISBN 0-403-06489-9, Regency). Scholarly.

Bertram, Paul D. Shakespeare & the "Two Noble Kinsmen". 1965. 21.00 (ISBN 0-8135-0499-6). Rutgers U Pr.

Cone, Mary. Fletcher Without Beaumont: A Study of the Independent Plays of John Fletcher. (Salzburg Studies in English Literature, Jacobean Drama Studies: No. 60). 1976. pap. 25.00x (ISBN 0-391-01348-3). Humanities.

Hatcher, Orie L. John Fletcher: A Study in Dramatic Method. LC 72-8945. (Studies in Drama, No. 39). 1973. Repr. of 1905 ed. lib. bdg. 49.95 (ISBN 0-8383-1682-4). Haskell.

--John Fletcher: A Study of Dramatic Method. 1905. lib. bdg. 7.75 (ISBN 0-8414-5020-X). Folcroft.

Hensman, Bertha. The Shares of Fletcher, Field & Massinger in Twelve Plays of the Beaumont & Fletcher Canon, 2 vols. (Salzburg Studies in English Literature, Jacobean Drama Studies: No.6). 1974. Set. pap. text ed. 50.25x (ISBN 0-391-01406-4). Humanities.

Leech, Clifford. The John Fletcher Plays. 1979. Repr. of 1962 ed. lib. bdg. 5.00 (ISBN 0-89760-502-0, Telegraph). Dynamic Learn Corp.

McKeithan, Daniel M. Debt to Shakespeare in Beaumont & Fletcher Plays. LC 73-128189. 1970. Repr. of 1938 ed. text ed. 8.50 (ISBN 0-87752-070-4). Gordian.

--Debt to Shakespeare in the Beaumont & Fletcher Plays. LC 70-126691. Repr. of 1938 ed. 9.50 (ISBN 0-404-04134-5). AMS Pr.

Makkink, Henri J. Philip Massinger & John Fletcher: A Comparison. LC 68-1145. (Studies in Drama, No. 39). 1969. Repr. of 1927 ed. lib. bdg. 32.95 (ISBN 0-8383-0669-1). Haskell.

Maxwell, Baldwin. Studies in Beaumont, Fletcher & Massinger. 1966. lib. bdg. 16.00x (ISBN 0-374-95396-1). Octagon.

Oliphant, Ernest H. Plays of Beaumont & Fletcher. LC 73-126657. Repr. of 1927 ed. 12.50 (ISBN 0-404-04814-5). AMS Pr.

--Plays of Beaumont & Fletcher. LC 70-93250. 1970. Repr. of 1927 ed. 12.00 (ISBN 0-87753-030-0). Phaeton.

Pearse, Nancy C. John Fletcher's Chastity Plays: Mirrors of Modesty. LC 72-3258. 255p. 1973. 14.50 (ISBN 0-8387-1151-0). Bucknell U Pr.

Sprague, Arthur C. Beaumont & Fletcher on the Restoration Stage. LC 64-14716. (Illus.). 1926. 18.00 (ISBN 0-405-08991-0, Pub. by Blom). Arno.

Thorndike, Ashley H. Influence of Beaumont & Fletcher on Shakespeare. LC 77-182727. Repr. of 1901 ed. 12.50 (ISBN 0-404-06428-0). AMS Pr.

Waith, Eugene M. Pattern of Tragicomedy in Beaumont & Fletcher. LC 69-15694. (Yale Studies in English Ser.: No. 120). 1969. Repr. of 1952 ed. 19.50 (ISBN 0-208-00777-6, Archon). Shoe String.

Wallis, Lawrence B. Fletcher, Beaumont & Company. LC 68-22292. 1968. Repr. of 1947 ed. lib. bdg. 17.50x (ISBN 0-374-98208-2). Octagon.

Wilson, John H. Influence of Beaumont & Fletcher on Restoration Drama. LC 68-57458. (Studies in Drama, No. 39). 1969. Repr. of 1928 ed. lib. bdg. 46.95 (ISBN 0-8383-0645-4). Haskell.

--Influence of Beaumont & Fletcher on the Restoration Stage. LC 67-28847. 1967. Repr. of 1928 ed. 12.00 (ISBN 0-405-09083-8). Arno.

FLETCHER, JOHN GOULD, 1886-1950

De Chasca, Edmund S. John Gould Fletcher & Imagism. LC 77-10795. 1978. 15.50x (ISBN 0-8262-0229-2). U of Mo Pr.

Fletcher, John G. Life Is My Song: The Autobiography of John Gould Fletcher. LC 78-64024. (Des Imagistes: Literature of the Imagist Movement). 416p. Repr. of 1937 ed. 38.50 (ISBN 0-404-17098-6). AMS Pr.

Morton, Bruce. John Gould Fletcher: A Bibliography. LC 79-10897. (The Serif Series of Bibliographies & Checklists: No. 37). 1979. 14.00x (ISBN 0-87338-229-3). Kent St U Pr.

Stephens, Edna B. John Gould Fletcher. (Twayne's United States Authors Ser.). 1967. pap. 3.45 (ISBN 0-8084-0182-3, T118, Twayne). Coll & U Pr.

FLETCHER, JOSEPH FRANCIS, 1905-

Cox, Harvey & Fletcher, Joseph, eds. Situation Ethics Debate. 1968. pap. 2.65 (ISBN 0-664-24814-4). Westminster.

FLETCHER, PHINEAS, 1582-1650

Kastor, Frank S. Giles & Phineas Fletcher. (English Authors Ser.: No. 225). 1978. lib. bdg. 12.50 (ISBN 0-8057-6696-0). Twayne.

Langdale, Abram. Phineas Fletcher: Man of Letters, Science & Divinity. 1968. lib. bdg. 15.00x (ISBN 0-374-94750-3). Octagon.

FLEURE, HERBERT JOHN, b. 1877

Peate, I. C., ed. Studies in Regional Consciousness & Environment: Essays Presented to H. J. Fleure. facs. ed. LC 68-26478. (Essay Index Reprint Ser). (Illus.). 1968. Repr. of 1930 ed. 18.00 (ISBN 0-8369-0917-8). Arno.

FLEURY, ANDRE HERCULE DE, CARDINAL, 1653-1743

Abrege de l'Histoire Ecclesiastique de Fleury. (Holbach & His Friends Ser). 521p. (Fr.). 1974. Repr. of 1767 ed. lib. bdg. 129.00 (ISBN 0-8287-1325-1, 1558). Clearwater Pub.

Wilson, Arthur M. French Foreign Policy During the Administration of Cardinal Fleury: 1726-1743; a Study in Diplomacy & Commercial Development. LC 70-138193. 433p. 1972. Repr. of 1936 ed. lib. bdg. 18.25x (ISBN 0-8371-5333-6, WIFP). Greenwood.

FLEX, WALTER, 1887-1917

Klein, J. Walter Flex, ein Deuter Des Weltkrieges. 1929. pap. 7.00 (ISBN 0-384-29750-1). Johnson Repr.

FLEXURE

see also Elasticity; Girders; Strains and Stresses; Strength of Materials

Plantema, Frederick J. Sandwich Construction: The Bending & Buckling of Sandwich Beams, Plates & Shells. LC 66-17621. 246p. 1966. 19.50 (ISBN 0-471-69106-2, Pub. by Wiley). Krieger.

Rozvany, G. I. Optimal Design of Flexural Systems. 200p. 1976. text ed. 34.00 (ISBN 0-08-020517-8); pap. text ed. 22.00 (ISBN 0-08-020516-X). Pergamon.

FLIES

see also Fruit-Flies; Stone-Flies; Tsetse-Flies

Austen, Ernest E. Illustrations of African Blood-Sucking Flies Other Than Mosquitoes & Tsetse-Flies. 23.00 (ISBN 0-384-02590-0). Johnson Repr.

Bohart, G. E. & Gressitt, J. L. Filth-Inhabiting Flies of Guam. 1951. pap. 15.00 (ISBN 0-527-02312-4). Kraus Repr.

Conklin, Gladys. I Watch Flies. LC 76-26532. (Illus.). (gr. 1-4). 1977. reinforced bdg 6.95 (ISBN 0-8234-0290-8). Holiday.

Dethier, Vincent G. To Know a Fly. LC 62-21838. (Illus.). 1962. pap. 4.50x (ISBN 0-8162-2240-1). Holden-Day.

Freeman, Paul & De Meillon, Botha. Simuliide of the Ethiopian Region. (Illus.). vii, 224p. 1953. Repr. of 1968 ed. 20.00x (ISBN 0-565-00194-9, Pub. by Brit Mus Nat Hist). Sabbot-Natural Hist Bks.

Hall, Jack C. & Evenhuis, Neal L. Flies of the Nearctic Region: Volume V, Part 13: Bombyliidae, No. 1. Griffiths, Graham C., ed. (Illus.). 96p. 1980. pap. text ed. 44.40x (ISBN 3-510-70002-3, Schweizerbart). Lubrecht & Cramer.

Hull, Frank M. Bee Flies of the World: The Genera of the Family Bombyliidae. 1973 ed. LC 73-1581. (Illus.). 687p. 60.00x (ISBN 0-87474-131-9). Smithsonian.

Johnson, Ned K. Character Variation & Evolution of Sibling Species in the Empidonax Difficilis-Flavescens Complex (Aves: Tyrannidae) (University of California Publications in Zoology: Vol. 112). 1980. monograph 12.00x (ISBN 0-520-09599-5). U of Cal Pr.

Laird, Marshall, ed. Blackflies: The Future for Biological Methods in Integrated Control. LC 81-66373. 1981. price not set (ISBN 0-12-434060-1). Acad Pr.

Loosjes, M. Ecology & Genetic Control of the Onion Fly. (Ag. Research Reports: No. 857). 1976. pap. 20.00 (ISBN 90-220-0611-5, Pub. by PUDOC). Unipub.

Pal, R. & Wharton, R. H., eds. Control of Arthropods: Medical & Veterinary Importance. LC 74-4172. 138p. 1974. 32.50 (ISBN 0-306-30790-1, Plenum Pr). Plenum Pub.

Shorrocks, B. Drosophila. (Illus.). 144p. 1980. 12.00 (ISBN 0-08-025941-3). Pergamon.

Stone, Alan. Flies of the Nearctic Region: Volume 1, Handbook, Part 1: History of Nearctic Dipterology. Griffiths, Graham C., ed. (Illus.). 76p. 1981. pap. text ed. 38.80x (ISBN 3-510-7000-15, Schweizerbart). Lubrecht & Cramer.

Strausfeld, N. J. Atlas of an Insect Brain. LC 75-19499. (Illus.). 250p. 1976. 130.20 (ISBN 0-387-07343-4). Springer-Verlag.

Theodor, Oskar. Diptera: Asilidae Insecta II. (Fauna Palaestina Ser.: No. 2). (Illus.). 448p. 1981. text ed. 30.00x (ISBN 0-87474-910-7, Pub. by the Israel Academy of Sciences & Humanities). Smithsonian.

Townes, Henry & Townes, Marjorie. Ichneumon-Flies of America North of Mexico: Seven Subfamily Banchinae, Tribes Lissonotini & Banchini. (Memoir Ser: No. 26). (Illus.). 614p. 1978. 34.00 (ISBN 0-686-30712-7). Am Entom Inst.

West, Luther S. The Housefly: Its Natural History, Medical Importance & Control. (Illus.). 595p. 1951. 32.50x (ISBN 0-8014-0447-9). Comstock.

Zumpt, F. The Stomoxyine Biting Flies of the World (Diptera, Muscidae) Taxonomy, Biology, Economic Importance & Control Measures. (Illus.). 183p. 1973. 65.00x (ISBN 3-437-30146-2). Intl Pubns Serv.

FLIES, ARTIFICIAL

see also Fishing Lures; Fly-Casting

Bates, Joseph D., Jr. Streamers & Bucktails: The Big Fish Flies. LC 79-2163. (Illus.). 1979. 16.95 (ISBN 0-394-41588-4). Knopf.

Blades, William F. Fishing Flies & Flytying. (Illus.). 320p. 1980. 24.95 (ISBN 0-8117-0613-3). Stackpole.

Collyer, David. Fly Dressing Two. LC 81-50000. (Illus.). 224p. 1981. 38.00 (ISBN 0-7153-8145-8). David & Charles.

Collyer, David J. Fly-Dressing. LC 74-20454. (Illus.). 240p. 1975. 25.00 (ISBN 0-7153-6719-6). David & Charles.

Flick, Art, et al, eds. Art Flick's Master Fly-Tying Guide. (Illus.). 220p. 1972. 10.95 (ISBN 0-517-50023-X); pap. 8.95 (ISBN 0-517-52135-0). Crown.

Fling, Paul N. & Puterbaugh, Donald L. The Basic Manual of Fly Tying. LC 77-80194. (Illus.). 1979. pap. 7.95 (ISBN 0-8069-8146-6). Sterling.

Fulsher, Keith. Fishing the Thunder Creek Series. (Illus.). 100p. 1973. 7.95 (ISBN 0-88395-018-9). Freshet Pr.

Gerlach, Rex. Creative Fly Tying & Fishing. 1974. 13.95 (ISBN 0-87691-122-X). Winchester Pr.

Grant, George. The Master Fly Weaver (the Art of Weaving Hair Hackles) 150p. 1980. 50.00x (ISBN 0-918400-03-1, Pub. by Champoeg Pr). Intl Schol Bk Serv.

--Montana Trout Flies. 150p. 1981. 50.00x (ISBN 0-918400-04-X, Pub. by Champoeg Pr). Intl Schol Bk Serv.

Jennings, Preston. Book of Trout Flies. Lyons, Nick, ed. (Illus.). 1970. 7.50 (ISBN 0-517-50204-6). Crown.

Jorgensen, Poul. Dressing Flies for Fresh & Salt Water. (Illus.). 1973. 12.95 (ISBN 0-88395-022-7). Freshet Pr.

--Poul Jorgensen's Modern Trout Flies: --and How to Tie Them. LC 78-3897. (Illus.). 1979. 12.95 (ISBN 0-385-15346-5); pap. 7.95 (ISBN 0-385-15347-3). Doubleday.

--Salmon Flies: Their Character, Style, & Dressing. LC 78-17941. (Illus.). 192p. 1978. 19.95 (ISBN 0-8117-1426-8); deluxe ed. 125.00 (ISBN 0-8117-1694-5). Stackpole.

Laurie, W. H. Scottish Trout Flies. 17.50x (ISBN 0-392-06577-0, SpS). Sportshelf.

Leiser, Eric. The Complete Book of Fly Tying. LC 77-74975. 1977. 13.95 (ISBN 0-394-40047-X). Knopf.
--Fly-Tying Materials. 224p. 1973. 10.00 (ISBN 0-517-50350-6). Crown.
Leonard, J. Edson. The Essential Fly Tier. LC 76-9043. (Illus.). 1976. 12.95 (ISBN 0-13-286120-8). P-H.
--Flies. (Illus.). 1950. 12.00 (ISBN 0-498-08107-9). A S Barnes.
Lively, Chauncy K. Chauncy Lively's Flybox: A Portfolio of Modern Trout Flies. (Illus.). 96p. 1980. pap. 9.95 (ISBN 0-8117-2078-0). Stackpole.
Marshall, Mel. How to Make Your Own Lures & Flies. (Funk & W Bk.). (Illus.). 1977. pap. 4.50 (ISBN 0-308-10292-4). T y Crowell.
Nemes, Sylvester. The Soft-Hackled Fly: A Trout Fishermans' Guide. LC 75-25235. 128p. 1975. 7.95 (ISBN 0-85699-124-4); pap. 4.95 (ISBN 0-85699-125-2). Chatham Pr.
Rice, Freddie & Rice, Freddie. Fly Tying Illustrated: For Nymphs & Lures. LC 76-2150. (Illus.). 112p. 1976. 11.95 (ISBN 0-7153-6952-0). David & Charles.
Robinson, Gilmer G. & Robinson, David L. The Basic Guide to Fly Fishing. LC 78-69639. (Illus.). 1979. 9.95 (ISBN 0-498-02215-3). A S Barnes.
Rosborough, E. H. Tying & Fishing the Fuzzy Nymphs. LC 78-13949. (Illus.). 192p. 1979. 14.95 (ISBN 0-8117-1811-5). Stackpole.
Surette, Dick. Trout & Salmon Fly Index. LC 78-24196. (Illus.). 128p. 1979. pap. 11.95 (ISBN 0-8117-2093-4). Stackpole.
Swisher, Doug & Richards, Carl. Selective Trout. (Illus.). 1971. 10.00 (ISBN 0-517-50304-2); pap. 5.95 (ISBN 0-517-52133-4). Crown.
--Tying the Swisher-Richards Flies. (Illus.). 48p. 1980. pap. 7.95 (ISBN 0-8117-2099-3). Stackpole.
Talleur, Richard. Mastering the Art of Fly-Tying. LC 78-32041. (Illus.). 224p. 1979. 21.95 (ISBN 0-8117-0907-8). Stackpole.
Veniard, John & Downs, Donald. Fly-Tying Problems & Their Answers. (Illus.). 124p. 1972. 5.95 (ISBN 0-517-50787-0). Crown.
Wetzel, Charles M. Trout Flies: Naturals & Imitations. (Illus.). 154p. 1979. 20.00 (ISBN 0-8117-1739-9). Stackpole.
Wulff, Lee. Lee Wulff on Flies. LC 79-5028. (Illus.). 160p. 1980. 14.95 (ISBN 0-8117-0953-1). Stackpole.

FLIES AS CARRIERS OF DISEASE

Greenberg, Bernard. Flies & Disease, 2 vols. Incl. Vol. 1. Ecology Classification & Biotic Associations. LC 68-56210. 1970. 55.00 (ISBN 0-691-08071-2); Vol. 2. Biology & Disease Transmission. LC 68-56310. 1973. 35.00 (ISBN 0-691-08093-3). Set. 70.00 (ISBN 0-685-53050-7). Princeton U Pr.
West, Luther S. The Housefly: Its Natural History, Medical Importance & Control. (Illus.). 595p. 1951. 32.50x (ISBN 0-8014-0447-9). Comstock.

FLIGHT

see also Aeronautics; Flying-Machines; Stability of Airplanes; Wings

Anderson, Eric. Lightplane Vacationing. 1975. pap. 3.95 (ISBN 0-8306-2221-7, 2221). TAB Bks.
Bauer, Harry. The Flying Mystique. (Illus.). 1980. 9.95 (ISBN 0-440-02722-5, E Friede). Delacorte.
Booth, Eugene. In the Air. LC 77-7984. (A Raintree Spotlight Book). (Illus.). (gr. k-3). 1977. PLB 9.30 (ISBN 0-8393-0105-7). Raintree Child.
Buck, Robert N. Weather Flying. rev. ed. (Illus.). 1978. 12.95 (ISBN 0-02-518020-7). Macmillan.
Delmege, J. W. Club Flying. 1966. pap. 3.95 (ISBN 0-8306-2207-1, 2207). TAB Bks.
Dole, Charles E. Flight Theory & Aerodynamcs: A Practical Guide for Operational Safety. LC 81-3009. 336p. 1981. 30.00 (ISBN 0-471-09152-9, Pub. by Wiley-Interscience). Wiley.
Dwiggins, Don. Man-Powered Aircraft. (Illus.). 1979. 9.95 (ISBN 0-8306-9851-5); pap. 5.95 (ISBN 0-8306-2254-3, 2254). TAB Bks.
Dwyer, James. The Private Pilot's Blue Book. LC 76-41837. 9.95 (ISBN 0-8128-2146-7). Stein & Day.
--Private Pilot's Blue Book. LC 76-41837. 1977. 9.95 (ISBN 0-685-81548-X). Macmillan.
Editors of Flying Magazine, ed. I Learned About Flying from That! 1976. 10.95 (ISBN 0-440-04041-8, E Friede). Delacorte.
Etkin, Bernard. Dynamics of Atmospheric Flight. LC 73-165946. (Illus.). 1972. text ed. 38.95 (ISBN 0-471-24620-4). Wiley.
Fillingham, Paul. Basic Guide to Flying. 1977. pap. 5.95 (ISBN 0-8015-0526-7, Hawthorn). Dutton.
Flying Magazine Editors. Back to Basics: Aircraft Construction, Cockpit Mechanics, & Flight Procedures. 1977. 11.95 (ISBN 0-442-22450-8). Van Nos Reinhold.
Garrison, Paul. Cross-Country Flying. (Illus.). 192p. 1980. 9.95 (ISBN 0-8306-9966-X); pap. 5.95 (ISBN 0-8306-2284-5, 2284). TAB Bks.
Garrison, Peter. Long Distance Flying. LC 80-2049. (Illus.). 1981. 13.95 (ISBN 0-385-14595-0). Doubleday.
Gilbert, James, ed. Skywriting. LC 77-99126. 1978. 10.00 (ISBN 0-312-72787-9). St Martin.
Griffin, Jeff W. Cold Weather Flying. (Modern Aviation Ser.). 1980. 9.95 (ISBN 0-8306-9711-X); pap. 5.95 (ISBN 0-8306-2273-X, 2273). TAB Bks.
Grindle, Link. Flying off the Pavement. LC 77-76156. (Illus.). 1977. 12.95 (ISBN 0-918916-02-X); pap. 9.95 (ISBN 0-918916-01-1). Lasenda.
Haldon Books. Flight Maneuver Manual. (Illus.). 1977. spiral bdg. 9.95 (ISBN 0-911720-15-4, Pub. by Haldon Bks). Aviation.
Hartill, William R., ed. World Free Flight Review. (Illus.). 1978. 30.00 (ISBN 0-933066-01-5). World Free Flight.
Lane, Peter. Flight. (Past into Present Ser.). (Illus.). 96p. 1974. 8.50x (ISBN 0-7134-2807-4). Intl Pubns Serv.
Langewiesche, Wolfgang. Stick & Rudder. (Illus.). 1944. 12.95 (ISBN 0-07-036240-8, GB). McGraw.
Learning to Fly. 1976. pap. 2.50 (ISBN 0-8277-4885-X). British Bk Ctr.
Nicklin, Kenneth. Beating the Air. 1978. 6.95 (ISBN 0-533-03716-6). Vantage.
Reay, David A. History of Man-Powered Flight. 1977. text ed. 23.00 (ISBN 0-08-021738-9). Pergamon.
Serjeant. Private Flying for Leisure & Business. 14.95x (ISBN 0-392-06630-0, LTB). Sportshelf.
Sherwin, Kieth. Man-Powered Flight. 1971. 10.75x (ISBN 0-85242-436-1). Intl Pubns Serv.
Smith, Robert T. Advanced Flight Manuevers & Aerobatics. (Illus.). 128p. 1980. 9.95 (ISBN 0-8306-9967-8); pap. 4.95 (ISBN 0-8306-2279-9, 2279). TAB Bks.
Taylor, John W., et al. Air Facts & Feats. LC 77-93306. (Guinness Family of Bks). (Illus.). 1978. 17.95 (ISBN 0-8069-0126-8); lib. bdg. 15.99 (ISBN 0-8069-0127-6). Sterling.
Taylor, Richard L. Fair-Weather Flying. LC 73-20989. (Illus.). 224p. 1974. 12.95 (ISBN 0-02-616700-X). Macmillan.
--Instrument Flying. 1978. 12.95 (ISBN 0-02-616670-4). Macmillan.
Time-Life. The Pathfinders: The Epic of Flight. 1980. 10.95 (ISBN 0-316-20032-8). Little.
Urry, David & Urry, Katie. Flying Birds. LC 74-110974. 1969. 7.95 (ISBN 0-910294-20-8). Brown Bk.
Von Mises, Richard. Theory of Flight. 12.50 (ISBN 0-8446-2599-X). Peter Smith.
Wakeford, Jacqueline. Flytying Techniques. LC 80-1274. (Illus.). 176p. 1981. 29.95 (ISBN 0-385-17306-7, NLB). Doubleday.

FLIGHT–JUVENILE LITERATURE

Engel, Lyle K. The Complete Book of Flying. LC 76-17865. (Illus.). 304p. 1976. 9.95 (ISBN 0-590-17377-4, Four Winds). Schol Bk Serv.
Freedman, Russell. How Birds Fly. LC 77-555. (Illus.). (gr. 4-6). 1977. 8.95 (ISBN 0-8234-0301-7). Holiday.
Gelman, Rita. Why Can't I Fly? (gr. k-3). 1977. pap. 1.50 (ISBN 0-590-10331-8, Schol Pap). Schol Bk Serv.
Gilleo, Alma. Air Travel from the Beginning. LC 77-24134. (From the Beginning Ser.). (Illus.). (gr. 1-4). 1977. PLB 5.95 (ISBN 0-89565-002-9); pap. 2.75 (ISBN 0-686-77017-X). Childs World.
Grey, Jerry. The Facts of Flight. (Franklin Institute Bk). (Illus.). (gr. 7 up). 1973. 4.95 (ISBN 0-664-32526-2); pap. 2.95 (ISBN 0-664-34004-0). Westminster.
Schiff, Barry. Flying. (Golden Guide Ser.). (Illus.). (gr. 7 up). 1971. PLB 10.38 (ISBN 0-307-64345-X, Golden Pr). Western Pub.

FLIGHT–MEDICAL ASPECTS

see Aviation Medicine

FLIGHT–PSYCHOLOGICAL ASPECTS

see Aeronautics–Psychology

FLIGHT, UNPOWERED

see Gliding and Soaring

FLIGHT ATTENDANTS

see Air Lines–Flight Attendants

FLIGHT CREWS

see also Air Lines–Flight Attendants; Air Pilots; Aviation Medicine

FLIGHT ENGINEERING

Aircraft Fueling Ramp Drainage. (Four Hundred Ser). 1973. pap. 2.00 (ISBN 0-685-58234-5, 415). Natl Fire Prot.
Aviation Maintenance Publishers. Airframe Logbook. 77p. 1975. pap. 4.95 (ISBN 0-89100-190-5, EA-AFL-1). Aviation Maintenance.
Aviation Supplies & Academics. Flight Engineer Test. 1979. pap. text ed. 11.95 (ISBN 0-686-73501-3, Pub. by ASA). Aviation.
--Flight Engineer Test Prep Program. 1978. 3-ring binder 36.95 (ISBN 0-686-73502-1, Pub. by ASA). Aviation.
Federal Aviation Administration. Airframe & Powerplant Mechanics Written Exam Airfram (AC-65-22) 1978. pap. text ed. 3.75 (ISBN 0-939158-21-3, Pub. by Natl Flightshops). Aviation.
--Airframe & Powerplant Mechanics Written Exam (AC-65-21) 1978. pap. text ed. 3.75 (ISBN 0-939158-20-5, Pub. by Natl Flightshops). Aviation.
--Airframe & Powerplant Mechanics Written Exam General (AC-65-20) 1978. pap. text ed. 3.75 (ISBN 0-939158-19-1, Pub. by Natl Flightshops). Aviation.
--Flight Engineer, Turbojet-Basic, Written Test Guide (AC 63-3) 1977. pap. text ed. 3.25 (ISBN 0-939158-18-3, Pub. by Natl Flightshops). Aviation.
Flight Engineers Manual. 10th rev. ed. LC 67-30737. 1979. pap. 17.95 (ISBN 0-87219-005-6). Pan Am Nav.
Mises, Richard Von. Theory of Flight. pap. 7.50 (ISBN 0-486-60541-8). Dover.
Vinh, Nguyen X., et al. Hypersonic & Planetary Entry Flight Mechanics. 376p. 1980. 29.95x (ISBN 0-472-10004-1). U of Mich Pr.

FLIGHT RECORDERS

see also Aeronautical Instruments

FLIGHT TESTING OF AIRPLANES

see Airplanes–Flight Testing

FLIGHT TO MARS

see Space Flight to Mars

FLIGHT TO THE MOON

see Space Flight to the Moon

FLIGHT TRACKING

see Artificial Satellites–Tracking

FLIGHT TRAINING

see also Airplanes–Piloting

Advanced Pilot Manual. 1st ed. (Pilot Training Ser.). (Illus.). 480p. 1981. text ed. 18.25 (ISBN 0-88487-068-5, JS314298). Jeppesen Sanderson.
Aviation Supplies & Academics. Airline Transport Pilot, Airplane, Test. 1980. pap. text ed. 9.95 (ISBN 0-686-73498-X, Pub. by ASA). Aviation.
--Answer & Explanation Book for Commercial Pilot, Airplane, Written Test Guide. 1980. pap. text ed. 3.50 (ISBN 0-686-73499-8, Pub. by ASA). Aviation.
--Commercial Pilot Airplane Test. 1980. pap. text ed. 8.95 (ISBN 0-686-73500-5, Pub. by ASA). Aviation.
--Flight Instructor Airplane Test. 1980. pap. text ed. 8.95 (ISBN 0-686-73503-X, Pub. by ASA). Aviation.
--Private Pilots Test. 1980. pap. text ed. 7.95 (ISBN 0-686-73505-6, Pub. by ASA). Aviation.
Colby, C. B. Astronauts in Training: How Our Astronauts Prepare for Space Exploration. (Illus.). (gr. 4-7). 1969. PLB 5.29 (ISBN 0-698-30018-1). Coward.
Commercial Pilot Flight Test Guide (AC 61-55A) 1975. pap. text ed. 1.75 (ISBN 0-939158-10-8, Pub. by Natl Flightshops). Aviation.
Crane, Dale. So You Think You Know...? Quiz Book. (Aviation Training Ser.). (Illus.). 297p. 1980. pap. 6.95 (ISBN 0-89100-071-2, E*A-Q*B). Aviation Maintenance.
Dept. of Aviation Education. Flight Maneuvers: Complete Programmed Course. 2nd ed. LC 67-8780. (Illus.). 332p. 1969. pap. 14.95 (ISBN 0-685-62816-7). Aero Products.
--Manual of Flight: Private & Commercial Pilot. 332p. 1973. pap. 14.95 (ISBN 0-685-62814-0). Aero Products.
Federal Aviation Administration. Advanced Ground Instructor Written Test Guide (AC-143-4) 1980. pap. text ed. 4.00 (ISBN 0-939158-23-X, Pub. by Natl Flightshops). Aviation.
--Aviation Instructor's Handbook (AC-60-14) 1977. pap. text ed. 3.00 (ISBN 0-939158-03-5, Pub. by Natl Flightshops). Aviation.
--Basic Ground Instructor Written Test Guide (AC 143-3) 1980. pap. text ed. 4.25 (ISBN 0-939158-23-X, Pub. by Natl Flightshops). Aviation.
--Flight Instructor, Instrument, Airplane Written Test Guide (AC-61-70A) 1980. pap. text ed. 3.50 (ISBN 0-686-73507-2, Pub. by Natl Flightshops). Aviation.
--Flight Instructor Practical Test Guide (AC 61-58A) 1978. pap. text ed. 1.50 (ISBN 0-939158-12-4, Pub. by Natl Flightshops). Aviation.
--Flight Test Guide, Instrument, Airplane AC 61-56A) 1976. pap. text ed. 0.55 (ISBN 0-686-73508-0, Pub. by Natl Flightshops). Aviation.
--Flight Training Handbook. LC 80-70552. (Illus.). 352p. 1981. 12.95 (ISBN 0-385-17599-X). Doubleday.
--Flight Training Handbook. 2nd ed. (Pilot Training Ser.). (Illus.). 325p. 1980. pap. 7.40 (ISBN 0-89100-165-4, EA-AC61-21A). Aviation Maintenance.
--Fundamentals of Instructing Written Test Guide (AC-61-90) 1979. pap. text ed. 2.25 (ISBN 0-939158-17-5, Pub. by Natl Flightshops). Aviation.
--Student Pilot Guide (AC 61-12J) 1979. pap. text ed. 2.25 (ISBN 0-939158-05-1, Pub. by Natl Flightshops). Aviation.
--Type Rating (Airplane) Flight Test Guide (AC 61-57A) 1975. pap. text ed. 0.70 (ISBN 0-86677-010-0, Pub. by Cooper Aviation). Aviation.
Federal Aviation Administration & Aviation Book Company Editors. IFR Pilot Exam-O-Grams. (Illus.). 96p. 1980. pap. 2.95 (ISBN 0-911721-79-7). Aviation.
Federal Aviation Agency. Pilot Instruction Manual. 7.95 (ISBN 0-385-01046-X). Doubleday.
Flight Instructor Manual. 1st ed. (Pilot Training Ser.). (Illus.). 240p. 1981. pap. text ed. 11.95 (ISBN 0-88487-066-9, JS314126). Jeppesen Sanderson.
Garrison, Peter. Flying Airplanes: The First Hundred Hours. Parke, Robert B., ed. LC 80-7476. (Illus.). 240p. 1980. 11.95 (ISBN 0-385-14594-2). Doubleday.
Goldstein, Avram. VFR Flight Review: A Guide to Better Flying. LC 79-89071. (Illus.). 172p. 1979. pap. 6.50 (ISBN 0-911721-67-3). Pegasus Pr CA.
Haldon Books. Omni in-Flight Interception Excercises. 1976. 12.95 (ISBN 0-686-76783-7, Pub. by Haldon). Aviation.
--Omni in-Flight Orientation Excercises. 1976. pap. 12.95 (ISBN 0-686-74082-3, Pub. by Haldon). Aviation.
--Visualized Flight Maneuvers Check Ride Check List. Orig. Title: Flight Instructor's Check Ride Check List. (Illus.). 60p. 1971. spiral bdg. 5.95 (ISBN 0-911720-43-X, Pub. by Haldon Bks). Aviation.
--Visualized Flight Maneuvers Handbook. (Illus.). 172p. 1980. ringbound softcover 12.95 (ISBN 0-686-71879-8, Pub. by Haldon). Aviation.
Instrument Rating Manual. 1st ed. (Pilot Training Ser.). (Illus.). 344p. 1981. pap. text ed. 17.95 (ISBN 0-88487-069-3, JS314299). Jeppesen Sanderson.
Kershner, William K. Flight Instructor's Manual. 2nd ed. (Illus.). 380p. 1981. pap. 19.95 (ISBN 0-8138-0635-6). Iowa St U Pr.
--Flight Instructor's Manual. (Illus.). 300p. 1974. pap. 14.95 (ISBN 0-8138-0635-6). Iowa St U Pr.
Knauth, Percy. Wind on My Wings. (Illus.). 240p. 1980. 9.95 (ISBN 0-8306-9968-6); pap. 5.95 (ISBN 0-8306-2278-0, 2278). TAB Bks.
Larson, George C. Fly on Instruments. LC 79-7602. (Illus.). 240p. 1980. 12.95 (ISBN 0-385-14619-1). Doubleday.
Macdonald, Sandy. From the Ground up: Training Manual for Pilots. 22nd ed. (Illus.). 1978. pap. 9.95x (ISBN 0-9690054-4-X, Pub. by AvPubns). Aviation.
Maher, Gay D. The Joy of Learning to Fly. 1977. 9.95 (ISBN 0-440-04312-3, E Friede). Delacorte.
Melton, James E. Your Right to Fly. LC 80-82961. (Illus.). 217p. pap. 6.95 (ISBN 0-9604752-0-6). Global Pubns WI.
Multi-Engine Pilot Manual. 1st ed. (Pilot Training Ser.). (Illus.). 128p. 1981. pap. text ed. 13.50 (ISBN 0-88487-070-7, JS314127). Jeppesen Sanderson.
Pilot Manuever's Manual. 1st ed. (Pilot Training Ser.). (Illus.). 210p. 1980. pap. text ed. 7.50 (ISBN 0-88487-065-0, JS314302). Jeppesen Sanderson.
Private Pilot Manual. 1st ed. (Pilot Training Ser.). (Illus.). 400p. 1981. text ed. 14.75 (ISBN 0-88487-067-7, JS314301). Jeppesen Sanderson.
Ramsey, Dan. Budget Flying. (McGraw-Hill Series in Aviation). (Illus.). 176p. 1980. 16.95 (ISBN 0-07-051202-7). McGraw.
Smith, Robert T. Your FAA Flight Exam: Private & Commercial. (Modern Aircraft Ser). (Illus.). 1978. 7.95 (ISBN 0-8306-9893-0); pap. 4.95 (ISBN 0-8306-2248-9, 2248). TAB Bks.
Stoffel, Robert & LaValle, Patrick. Survival Sense for Pilots. LC 80-70906. (Illus.). 160p. 1980. pap. 5.95 (ISBN 0-913724-24-6, Pub. by Emergency Response). Aviation.
Taylor, Richard L. & Guinther, William M. Positive Flying. 1977. 10.00 (ISBN 0-440-07111-9, E Friede). Delacorte.
Taylor, S. E. & Parmar, H. A. Ground Studies for Pilots. Incl. Vol. I. Radio Aids. 3rd ed. 200p. 1979. text ed. 26.50x (ISBN 0-246-11169-0); Vol. II. Plotting & Flight Planning. 130p. 1976. text ed. 19.95x (ISBN 0-246-11176-3); Vol. III. Navigation General. 232p. 1979. text ed. 26.50x (ISBN 0-246-11177-1). Pub. by Granada England). Renouf.
Vasko, Donna M. I'd Rather Be Flying. 100p. (Orig.). 1980. pap. 5.95 (ISBN 0-9604308-0-6). Calligraphy Donna.

FLINDERS RANGE

Flix, Fred. Flinders Ranges Landscapes. LC 76-118391. 1970. 6.50x (ISBN 0-85179-051-8). Intl Pubns Serv.

FLINT, JAMES, 1779-1855
Flint, Timothy. Recollections of the Last Ten Years in the Valley of the Mississippi. 2nd ed. LC 68-24891. (American Scene Ser). 1968. Repr. of 1826 ed. lib. bdg. 39.50 (ISBN 0-306-71136-2). Da Capo.
--Recollections of the Last Ten Years: Passed in Occasional Residences & Journeyings in the Valley of the Mississippi. (American Studies). 1968. Repr. of 1826 ed. 19.50 (ISBN 0-384-16030-1). Johnson Repr.
FLINT, TIMOTHY, 1780-1840
Folsom, James K. Timothy Flint. (Twayne's United States Authors Ser). 1965. pap. 3.45 (ISBN 0-8084-0301-X, T83, Twayne). Coll & U Pr.
Kirkpatrick, John E. Timothy Flint: Pioneer, Missionary, Author, Editor, 1780-1840. LC 68-56780. (Research & Source Works Ser: No. 267). 1968. Repr. of 1911 ed. 21.50 (ISBN 0-8337-1930-0). B Franklin.
FLINT
Shepherd, Walter. Flint: Its Origin, Properties & Uses. (Illus.). 1972. 18.50x (ISBN 0-571-09926-2). Transatlantic.
FLINT IMPLEMENTS
see Stone Implements
FLOATING BODIES
Branley, Franklyn M. Floating and Sinking. LC 67-15396. (A Let's-Read-&-Find-Out Science Bk). (Illus.). (gr. k-3). 1967. (TYC-J); PLB 8.79 (ISBN 0-690-30918-X). Har-Row.
FLOCCULATION
Ives, K. J., ed. The Scientific Basis of Flocculation. 375p. 1978. 36.00x (ISBN 90-286-0758-7). Sijthoff & Noordhoff.
Sonntag, H. & Strenge, K. Coagulation & Stability of Disperse Systems. 139p. 1972. 30.95 (ISBN 0-470-81350-4). Halsted Pr.
FLOGGING
see Corporal Punishment; Flagellants and Flagellation
FLOOD, HENRY, 1732-1791
Lecky, Wm. Edward. Leaders of Public Opinion in Ireland, 2 vols. LC 76-159800. (Europe 1815-1945 Ser.). 720p. 1973. Repr. of 1903 ed. Set. lib. bdg. 59.50 (ISBN 0-306-70574-5). Da Capo.
FLOOD, BIBLICAL
see Deluge
FLOOD CONTROL
see also Flood Dams and Reservoirs
Bosch, Vanden, et al. Urban Watershed Management: Flooding & Water Quality. Bedient, Philip B. & Rowe, Peter G., eds. (Rice University Studies: Vol. 65, No. 1). 205p. 1979. pap. 5.50x (ISBN 0-89263-240-2). Rice Univ.
De Vore, R. William & Haan, Charles T., eds. International Symposium on Urban Storm Water Management: Proceedings. 1978. pap. text ed. 33.50 (ISBN 0-89779-002-2); microfiche 4.50 (ISBN 0-89779-003-0). OES Pubns.
Dougal, Merwin D., ed. Flood Plain Management: Iowa's Experience. LC 75-83320. (Illus.). 1969. 7.95x (ISBN 0-8138-0595-3). Iowa St U Pr.
Frank, Arthur D. Development of the Federal Program of Flood Control on the Mississippi River. LC 68-58572. (Columbia University. Studies in the Social Sciences: No. 323). Repr. of 1930 ed. 21.00 (ISBN 0-404-51323-9). AMS Pr.
Institute of Civil Engineers, UK. Reservoir Flood Standards. 1980. pap. 20.00x (ISBN 0-7277-0023-5, Pub. by Telford England). State Mutual Bk.
Kemper, J. P. Rebellious River. LC 72-2848. (Use & Abuse of America's Natural Resources Ser). 284p. 1972. Repr. of 1949 ed. 15.00 (ISBN 0-405-04514-X). Arno.
Leuchtenburg, William E. Flood Control Politics: The Connecticut River Valley Problem, 1927-1950. LC 73-38834. (FDR & the Era of the New Deal Ser.). (Illus.). 1972. Repr. of 1953 ed. lib. bdg. 32.50 (ISBN 0-306-70446-3). Da Capo.
Mahmood, K., et al, eds. Unsteady Flow in Open Channels, 3 vols. LC 75-9251. 1975. Set. 42.00 (ISBN 0-686-67936-9); Vol. 1. (ISBN 0-918334-09-8); Vol. 2. (ISBN 0-918334-10-1); Vol. 3. (ISBN 0-918334-11-X). WRP.
Penning-Rowsell, E. & Chatterton, J. The Benefits of Flood Alleviation: A Manual of Assessment Techniques. (Illus.). 1978. 80.00 (ISBN 0-566-00190-X, 01796-5, Pub. by Saxon Hse England). Lexington Bks.
Peterson, Elmer. Big Dam Foolishness. 1954. 7.50 (ISBN 0-8159-5107-8). Devin.
World Meteorological Organization. Estimation of Maximum Floods. (Technical Note Ser.). 1969. pap. 45.00 (ISBN 0-685-22303-5, WMO 233, WMO). Unipub.
FLOOD DAMS AND RESERVOIRS
see also Sea-Walls
Chi Ch'ao-Ting. Key Economic Areas in Chinese History. LC 70-104612. (Illus.). Repr. of 1936 ed. 12.50x (ISBN 0-678-00594-X). Kelley.
Institute of Civil Engineers, UK. Reservoir Flood Standards. 1980. pap. 20.00x (ISBN 0-7277-0023-5, Pub. by Telford England). State Mutual Bk.
Peterson, Elmer. Big Dam Foolishness. 1954. 7.50 (ISBN 0-8159-5107-8). Devin.
FLOOD PROTECTION
see Flood Control
FLOODS
see also Flood Control; Reclamation of Land; Rivers;
also subdivision floods under names of rivers, cities, etc.
Baker, Victor R. Paleohydrology & Sedimentology of Lake Missoula Flooding in Eastern Washington. LC 72-89463. (Special Paper: No. 144). (Illus.). 80p. (Orig.). 1973. pap. 7.00x (ISBN 0-8137-2144-X). Geol Soc.
Bartlett, Mable M. The Flood of Thirty-Seven. 1979. 4.50 (ISBN 0-682-49317-1). Exposition.
Berger, Melvin. Disastrous Floods & Tidal Waves. (First Bks.). (Illus.). 72p. (gr. 4 up). 1981. lib. bdg. 7.40 (ISBN 0-531-04326-6). Watts.
Brown, J. P. The Economic Effects of Floods. LC 72-86100. (Lecture Notes in Economics & Mathematical Systems: Vol. 70). v, 87p. 1972. pap. 6.30 (ISBN 0-387-05925-3). Springer-Verlag.
Brown, Walter R. & Brown, Billye. Historical Catastrophes: Floods. LC 74-23684. (Historical Catastrophes Ser.). (Illus.). 192p. (gr. 5 up). 1975. PLB 7.95 (ISBN 0-201-00762-2, 0762, A-W Childrens). A-W.
Burton, Ian, et al. The Human Ecology of Coastal Flood Hazards in Megalopolis. LC 68-57967. (Research Papers Ser.: No. 115). 196p. 1968. pap. 8.00 (ISBN 0-89065-023-3). U Chicago Dept Geog.
Flakkeberg, Ardo. Sea Broke Through. (Illus.). (gr. 5-7). 1960. PLB 5.69 (ISBN 0-394-91591-7). Knopf.
Floods & Their Computation, 2 Vols. (Studies & Reports in Hydrology Ser). (Illus.). 1969. Set. 54.00 (ISBN 92-3-000771-4, UNESCO). Unipub.
Fodor, R. V. Angry Waters: Floods & Their Control. LC 79-24729. (Skylight Ser.). (Illus.). (gr. 2-5). 1980. 4.95 (ISBN 0-396-07799-4). Dodd.
Institute of Civil Engineers, UK. Flood Studies Conference. 106p. 1980. 75.00x (ISBN 0-7277-0014-6, Pub. by Telford England). State Mutual Bk.
--Floods & Reservoir Safety: An Engineering Guide. 1980. pap. 25.00x (ISBN 0-7277-0033-2, By Telford England). State Mutual Bk.
Martin, John H., ed. The Corning Flood: Museum Under Water. LC 77-73627. (Illus.). 1977. pap. 6.00 (ISBN 0-87290-063-0). Corning.
Norel, K. Stand by, Boys! Schoolland, Marian, tr. from Dutch. (Children's Summit Ser.). (Orig.). 1980. pap. 1.65 (ISBN 0-8010-6734-0). Baker Bk.
Schultz, E. F., et al, eds. Floods & Droughts: Proceedings. LC 73-80676. 1973. 21.00 (ISBN 0-918334-03-9). WRP.
Smith, K. & Tobin, G. A. Human Adjustment to Flood Hazard. (Topics in Applied Geography). (Illus.). 1979. pap. text ed. 11.50x (ISBN 0-582-48693-9). Longman.
Stern, Gerald M. The Buffalo Creek Disaster. 1977. pap. 2.95 (ISBN 0-394-72343-0, Vin). Random.
Summers, Dorothy. East Coast Floods. LC 78-62498. (Illus.). 1978. 16.95 (ISBN 0-7153-7456-7). David & Charles.
Tufty, Barbara. One Thousand & One Questions Answered About Earthquakes, Avalanches, Floods, & Other Natural Disasters. LC 78-51736. 1978. lib. bdg. 11.50 (ISBN 0-88307-612-8). Gannon.
--One Thousand and One Questions Answered About Earthquakes, Avalanches, Floods & Other Natural Disasters. Date not set. 8.75 (ISBN 0-8446-5826-X). Peter Smith.
Ward, Roy C. Floods: A Geographical Perspective Paper. (Focal Problems in Geography Ser.). 244p. 1980. pap. text ed. 14.95x (ISBN 0-470-26965-0). Halsted Pr.
World Catalogue of Very Large Floods. (Studies and Reports in Hydrology). (Illus.). 1977. pap. 37.25 (ISBN 92-3-001310-2, UNESCO). Unipub.
FLOOR COVERINGS
see also Carpets; Rugs
Crawshaw, G. H. & Ince, J. Textile Floorcoverings. 84p. 1977. 70.00x (ISBN 0-686-63800-X). State Mutual Bk.
Ellis, Robert. Scribner Book of Floor Coverings: How to Buy Wisely & Install Properly. (Illus.). 1980. 13.95 (ISBN 0-684-16382-9, ScribT). Scribner.
Fairchild Market Research Division. Floor Coverings. (Fact File Ser). 1978. pap. 10.00 (ISBN 0-87005-255-1). Fairchild.
Floor Coverings. (Home & Office Furnishings). 1980. 335.00 (ISBN 0-686-31554-5). Busn Trend.
Hilado, Carlos J., ed. Flooring & Floor Covering Materials, Vol. 12. LC 73-82115. (Fire & Flammability Ser.). (Illus.). 1976. pap. 20.00x (ISBN 0-87762-172-1). Technomic.
Lecher, Helmuth R. How to Install Your Own Floor & Wall Coverings. 1979. 5.95 (ISBN 0-533-03749-2). Vantage.
Nunn, Richard V. Floors & Floorcoverings. LC 74-40861. (Family Guidebooks). (Illus.). 1977. pap. 2.95 (ISBN 0-8487-0451-7). Oxmoor Hse.
Wade, Carlson. Floor Decorating. LC 76-10883. (Illus.). 1979. 15.00 (ISBN 0-498-01810-5). A S Barnes.
FLOOR MATERIALS
see Flooring
FLOORING
see also Floor Coverings
Berkeley, Bernard. Floors: Selection & Maintenance. LC 68-23014. (LTP Publication: No. 13). (Illus.). 1968. 15.00 (ISBN 0-8389-3031-X). ALA.
Hilado, Carlos J., ed. Flooring & Floor Covering Materials, Vol. 12. LC 73-82115. (Fire & Flammability Ser.). (Illus.). 1976. pap. 20.00x (ISBN 0-87762-172-1). Technomic.
Tattersall, Bob. Flooring. (Tricks of the Trade Ser.). (Illus.). 1978. 10.95 (ISBN 0-7207-1045-6). Transatlantic.
FLOORS
see also Flooring
Greener. The Everything Book of Floors, Walls, & Ceilings. (Illus.). 250p. 1980. 14.95 (ISBN 0-8359-1803-3); pap. 7.95 (ISBN 0-8359-1802-5). Reston.
Nunn, Richard V. Floors & Floorcoverings. LC 74-40861. (Family Guidebooks). (Illus.). 1977. pap. 2.95 (ISBN 0-8487-0451-7). Oxmoor Hse.
Schuler, Stanley. The Floor & Ceiling Book. LC 75-37966. (Illus.). 180p. 1976. 8.95 (ISBN 0-87131-201-8). M Evans.
Time Life Books Editors. Floors & Stairways. (Home Repair Ser.). (Illus.). 1978. 10.95 (ISBN 0-8094-2394-4). Time-Life.
FLOORS, CONCRETE
Fire Resistance of Reinforced Concrete Floors. 32p. 1963. pap. 2.00 (ISBN 0-89312-068-5, EB065B). Portland Cement.
Floor Systems Supported by Central Core & Exterior Columns. 30p. 1968. pap. 2.50 (ISBN 0-89312-071-5, EB012D). Portland Cement.
Slab Thickness Design for Industrial Floors on Grade. 1976. pap. 0.75 (ISBN 0-89312-158-4, IS195P). Portland Cement.
FLOORS AND FLOORING
Fairchild Market Research Div. Soft Surface Floor Coverings. (Fact Files Ser.). (Illus.). 75p. 1980. pap. 10.00 (ISBN 0-87005-354-X). Fairchild.
Geary, Don. The How-to Book of Floors & Ceilings. (Illus.). 1978. 8.95 (ISBN 0-8306-8998-2); pap. 5.95 (ISBN 0-8306-7998-7, 998). TAB Bks.
FLORA
see Botany; Plants
FLORA, ANTARCTIC
see Botany-Antarctic Regions
FLORA, ARCTIC
see Botany-Arctic Regions
FLORAL DECORATION
see Flower Arrangement
FLORAL DESIGN
see Design, Decorative-Plant Forms
FLORAL GAMES
Dawson, John C. Toulouse in the Renaissance: The Floral Games, University & Student Life: Etienne Dolet. (Columbia University. Studies in Romance Philology & Literature: No. 33). Repr. of 1923 ed. 18.50 (ISBN 0-404-50633-X). AMS Pr.
FLORENCE
Finn, David, photos by. The Florence Baptistery Doors. LC 80-5365. 328p. 1980. 50.00 (ISBN 0-670-31997-X, Studio). Viking Pr.
Florence. (Panorama Bks.). (Illus., Fr.). 4.50 (ISBN 0-685-11191-1). French & Eur.
Pucci, Eugenio. Dante's Florence Seen Today. 1965. 7.50x (ISBN 0-8002-0738-6). Intl Pubns Serv.
Staley, Edgcumbe. Guilds of Florence. LC 67-12458. (Illus.). 1906. 30.00 (ISBN 0-405-08992-9, Pub. by Blom). Arno.
Stendhal. Rome, Naples et Florence, 3 vols. facsimile ed. Set. 100.00 (ISBN 0-686-55081-1). French & Eur.
Weinstein, Donald. Savonarola & Florence: Prophecy & Patriotism in the Renaissance. LC 76-113013. 1971. 21.00x (ISBN 0-691-05184-4). Princeton U Pr.
FLORENCE-CHURCHES
Luchs, Allison. Cestello: A Cistercian Church of the Florentine Renaissance. LC 76-23642. (Outstanding Dissertations in the Fine Arts - 2nd Series - 15th Century). (Illus.). 1977. Repr. lib. bdg. 63.00 (ISBN 0-8240-2706-X). Garland Pub.
Saalman, Howard. The Bigallo: The Oratory & Residence of the Compagnia Del Bigallo Della Misericordia in Florence. LC 69-18285. (College Art Association Monographs: Vol. 19). (Illus.). 1969. 18.50x (ISBN 0-8147-0370-4). NYU Pr.
Trachtenberg, Marvin. The Campanile of Florence Cathedral: Giotto's Tower. LC 70-124532. (Illus.). 458p. 1971. 45.00x (ISBN 0-8147-8151-9). NYU Pr.
FLORENCE-DESCRIPTION
Bonechi, Edoardo. Florence: A Complete Guide for Visiting the City. 6th ed. (Bonechi Guides-Mercurio Ser.). (Illus.). 208p. 1972. 7.50x (ISBN 0-8002-1424-2). Intl Pubns Serv.
Chiarelli, Renzo. San Lorenzo & the Medici Chapels. (Illus.). 72p. 1971. 5.00x (ISBN 0-8002-1949-X). Intl Pubns Serv.
Cole, Toby, ed. Florence: A Traveler's Anthology. 288p. 1981. 12.95 (ISBN 0-88208-126-8). Lawrence Hill.
Grierson, E. Things Seen in Florence. 1924. 10.00 (ISBN 0-89984-016-7). Century Bookbindery.
Hyman, Isabelle. Fifteenth Century Florentine Studies: The Palazzo Medici & a Ledger for the Church of San Lorenzo. LC 76-23631. (Outstanding Dissertations in the Fine Arts - Fifteenth Century). (Illus.). 1977. Repr. of 1968 ed. lib. bdg. 70.00 (ISBN 0-8240-2700-0). Garland Pub.
McCarthy, Mary. Stones of Florence. LC 59-10257. 130p. 1976. 25.00 (ISBN 0-15-185079-8). HarBraceJ.
Roberts, William. Account of the First Discovery & Natural History of Florida. LC 76-1971. (Bicentennial Floridiana Facsimile & Reprint Ser.). 1976. Repr. of 1763 ed. 8.50 (ISBN 0-8130-0373-3). U Presses Fla.
Whelpton, Barbara. Painters' Florence. (Illus.). 1971. 7.50x (ISBN 0-85307-095-4). Intl Pubns Serv.
Zocchi, Giusseppe. Views of Florence & Tuscany 11. rev. ed. LC 68-59110. (Illus.). 1971. pap. 4.00 (ISBN 0-88397-070-8). Intl Exhibit Foun.
FLORENCE-DESCRIPTION-GUIDEBOOKS
Alter, Richard C. The Tired Tourists Concise Guide to Florence. (Illus.). 68p. pap. 3.00 (ISBN 0-89726-000-7). Foldabook Pub.
Barret, Andre. Florence Observed. 168p. 1974. 24.95 (ISBN 0-19-519750-X). Oxford U Pr.
Florence. LC 73-176706. (Italio Artistica Ser.: No. 9). (Illus.). 128p. 1974. pap. 12.50x (ISBN 0-8002-1423-4). Intl Pubns Serv.
Florence, Pisa, & Siena. LC 73-177329. (Illus.). 80p. 1972. pap. 7.50x (ISBN 0-8002-1425-0). Intl Pubns Serv.
Florence: The Whole City in Color. (Illus.). 64p. 1972. pap. 7.50x (ISBN 0-8002-1426-9). Intl Pubns Serv.
Fusi, Rolando. Looking at Florence. (Illus.). 128p. 1973. pap. 15.00x (ISBN 0-8002-1682-2). Intl Pubns Serv.
Fusi, Rolando & Fusi, Piero. Florence. (Italia Artistica Ser.: No. 26). (Illus.). 158p. (Orig.). 1977. pap. 15.00x (ISBN 0-8002-0011-X). Intl Pubns Serv.
Higson, John W., Jr. A Historical Guide to Florence. LC 72-91632. (Illus.). 1977. pap. 7.95 (ISBN 0-87663-951-1). Universe.
Pucci, Eugenio. All Florence. (Illus.). 1972. 9.95 (ISBN 0-684-12882-9, ScribT). Scribner.
FLORENCE-ECONOMIC CONDITIONS
Brucker, Gene, ed. Society of Renaissance Florence. 1972. pap. 4.95x (ISBN 0-06-131607-5, TB1607, Torch). Har-Row.
Goldthwaite, Richard A. The Building of Renaissance Florence: A Social & Economic History. LC 80-7995. (Illus.). 448p. 1981. text ed. 27.50x (ISBN 0-8018-2342-0). Johns Hopkins.
FLORENCE-FLOOD
Machiavelli, Niccolo. History of Florence & of the Affairs of Italy. 9.00 (ISBN 0-8446-2503-5). Peter Smith.
FLORENCE-GALLERIES AND MUSEUMS
Art in Florence: Masterpieces of Art in Galleries & Museums. (Illus.). 127p. 1973. pap. 12.50x (ISBN 0-8002-1214-2). Intl Pubns Serv.
Berti, Luciano. The Uffizi. (Illus.). 1978. pap. 9.95 (ISBN 0-8467-0453-6, Pub. by Two Continents). Hippocrene Bks.
--Uffizi-All Paintings in 657 Illustrations. 1971. 7.50x (ISBN 0-8002-2117-6). Intl Pubns Serv.
Chiarini, Marco. Pitti Palace: Art & History. (Illus.). 96p. (Orig.). 1973. pap. 15.00x (ISBN 0-8002-2778-6). Intl Pubns Serv.
Lenzini, Margherita. Masterpieces of the Uffizi. (Illus.). 64p. 1974. pap. 7.50x (ISBN 0-8002-1710-1). Intl Pubns Serv.
Orcutt, William D. In Quest of the Perfect Book. LC 79-86577. (Essay & General Literature Index Reprint Ser). (Illus.). 1969. Repr. of 1926 ed. 18.50 (ISBN 0-8046-0582-3). Kennikat.
Pescio, Claudio. Complete Guide for Visiting the Uffizi. Zatta, Merry O., tr. from Italian. (Illus.). 159p. (Orig.). 1979. pap. 10.00x (ISBN 0-8002-2774-3). Intl Pubns Serv.

Ragghianti, Carlo L. UFFIZI: Florence. LC 69-18514. (Great Museums of the World Ser.). (Illus.). 1968. 16.95 (ISBN 0-88225-238-0). Newsweek.

FLORENCE-HISTORY

Becker, Marvin B. Florence in Transition, 2 vols. Incl. Vol. 1. The Decline of the Commune. 263p. 1967 (ISBN 0-8018-0062-5); Vol. 2. Studies in the Rise of the Territorial State. 275p. 1968 (ISBN 0-8018-0063-3). LC 66-28027. 17.50x ea. Johns Hopkins.

British Broadcasting Corporation. City of Florence. (Illus.). 1967. 5.00x (ISBN 0-563-07136-2). Intl Pubns Serv.

Brown, Alison. Bartolomeo Scala, Fourteen Thirty to Fourteen Ninety-Seven, Chancellor of Florence: The Humanist As Bureaucrat. LC 78-70280. 1979. 27.50 (ISBN 0-691-05270-0). Princeton U Pr.

Brucker, Gene. The Civic World of Early Renaissance Florence. LC 76-45891. 1977. text ed. 35.00x (ISBN 0-691-05244-1). Princeton U Pr.

Brucker, Gene, ed. Society of Renaissance Florence. 1972. pap. 4.95x (ISBN 0-06-131607-5, TB1607, Torch). Har-Row.

Brucker, Gene A. Renaissance Florence. (New Dimensions in History-Historical Cities Ser.). 306p. 1969. pap. text ed. 11.50 (ISBN 0-471-11371-9). Wiley.

--Renaissance Florence. LC 74-10921. 320p. 1975. Repr. of 1969 ed. lib. bdg. 15.00 (ISBN 0-88275-184-0). Krieger.

Cochrane, Eric. Florence in the Forgotten Centuries 1527-1800: A History of Florence & the Florentines in the Age of the Grand Dukes. 608p. 1973. 16.00x (ISBN 0-226-11150-4). U of Chicago Pr.

--Florence in the Forgotten Centuries 1527-1800: A History of Florence & the Florentines in the Age of the Grand Dukes. LC 72-90628. xiv, 594p. 1976. pap. 7.95 (ISBN 0-226-11151-2, P663, Phoen). U of Chicago Pr.

Cohn, Samuel K., Jr. The Laboring Classes in Renaissance Florence. (Studies in Social Discontinuity). 1980. 29.50 (ISBN 0-12-179180-7). Acad Pr.

Gardner, E. The Story of Florence. 1976. lib. bdg. 59.95 (ISBN 0-8490-2679-2). Gordon Pr.

Gilbert, Felix. Machiavelli & Guicciardini: Politics & History in Sixteenth Century Florence. LC 63-23405. 1965. 22.50x (ISBN 0-691-05133-X); pap. 8.95 (ISBN 0-691-00771-3). Princeton U Pr.

Goldthwaite, Richard A. The Building of Renaissance Florence: A Social & Economic History. LC 80-7995. (Illus.). 448p. 1981. text ed. 27.50x (ISBN 0-8018-2342-0). Johns Hopkins.

Green, Louis. Chronicle into History: An Essay on the Interpretation of History in Florentine Fourteenth Century Cronicles. LC 71-186249. (Cambridge Studies in Early Modern History). 180p. 1972. 26.95 (ISBN 0-521-08517-9). Cambridge U Pr.

Holmes, Timothy. Vile Florentines. 196p. 1981. 10.95 (ISBN 0-312-84677-0). St Martin.

Kent, Dale. The Rise of the Medici: Faction in Florence 1420-1434. 1978. 59.00x (ISBN 0-19-822520-2). Oxford U Pr.

Landucci, Luca. Florentine Diary from Fourteen Fifteen to Fifteen Forty-Two. LC 76-88827. (Art Histories Collection Ser). (Illus.). Repr. of 1927 ed. 16.00 (ISBN 0-405-02225-5). Arno.

Machiavelli, Niccolo. Florentine History. Bedingfeld, T., tr. LC 73-172705. (Tudor Translations, First Ser.: No. 40). Repr. of 1905 ed. 35.00 (ISBN 0-404-51952-0). AMS Pr.

--Florentine History. 1977. 9.95x (ISBN 0-460-00376-3, Evman). Biblio Dist.

--The History of Florence. 1977. Repr. of 1891 ed. lib. bdg. 30.00 (ISBN 0-8414-6212-7). Folcroft.

Minor, Andrew C. & Mitchell, M. Bonner, eds. Renaissance Entertainment: Festivities for the Marriage of Cosimo I, Duke of Florence, in 1539. LC 68-11348. (Illus.). 1968. 15.00x (ISBN 0-8262-8522-8). U of Mo Pr.

Oliphant, Margaret. The Makers of Florence. 1885. Repr. lib. bdg. 30.00 (ISBN 0-8414-6666-1). Folcroft.

Pazderski, Roman. Alessandro, Duke of Florence. 3.50 (ISBN 0-533-01979-6). Vantage.

Pitti, Buonaccorso & Dati, Gregorio. Two Memoirs of Renaissance Florence: The Diaries of Buonaccorso Pitti & Gregorio Dati. pap. 2.95x (ISBN 0-06-131333-5, TB1333, Torch). Har-Row.

Porter, Bernard H. I Ricordi Di Firenze. 60p. 1981. lib. bdg. 28.50 (ISBN 0-686-68872-4). Porter.

Pottinger, George. The Court of the Medici. 141p. 1978. 13.50x (ISBN 0-8476-6024-9). Rowman.

Rawson, Judith A., ed. & intro. by. Machiavelli: The History of Florence & Other Selections. 1970. text ed. 22.50x (ISBN 0-671-48364-1). Irvington.

Rawson, Judith A., ed. Machiavelli: The History of Florence & Other Selections. (Great History Ser). 1978. 10.95 (ISBN 0-685-60155-2, Pub by Twayne). Cyrco Pr.

Roth, Cecil. Last Florentine Republic, 1527-1530. LC 68-25048. 1968. Repr. of 1925 ed. 13.50 (ISBN 0-8462-1175-0). Russell.

Scaife, Walter B. Florentine Life During the Renaissance. LC 78-64259. (Johns Hopkins University. Studies in the Social Sciences. Extra Volumes: 14). Repr. of 1893 ed. 23.00 (ISBN 0-404-61362-4). AMS Pr.

--Florentine Life During the Renaissance. 1977. lib. bdg. 59.95 (ISBN 0-8490-1844-7). Gordon Pr.

Schevill, Ferdinand. History of Florence: From the Founding of the City Through the Renaissance. rev. ed. LC 60-8571. (Illus.). 1961. 25.00 (ISBN 0-8044-1832-2). Ungar.

Trexler, Richard C. Public Life in Renaissance Florence. LC 80-979. (Studies in Discontinuity). 1980. 45.00 (ISBN 0-12-699550-8). Acad Pr.

Villari, Pasquale. The Two First Centuries of Florentine History. LC 77-153609. Repr. of 1908 ed. 37.50 (ISBN 0-404-09294-2). AMS Pr.

Weinstein, Donald. Savonarola & Florence: Prophecy & Patriotism in the Renaissance. LC 76-113013. 1971. 21.00x (ISBN 0-691-05184-4). Princeton U Pr.

FLORENCE-HISTORY-FICTION

Eliot, George. Romola. (World's Classics Ser: No. 178). 13.95 (ISBN 0-19-250178-X). Oxford U Pr.

FLORENCE-HISTORY-HISTORIOGRAPHY

Gilbert, Felix. Machiavelli & Guicciardini: Politics & History in Sixteenth Century Florence. LC 63-23405. 1965. 22.50x (ISBN 0-691-05133-X); pap. 8.95 (ISBN 0-691-00771-3). Princeton U Pr.

Vile Florentines: The Florence of Dante, Giotto, & Boccaccio. 193p. 1981. 10.95 (ISBN 0-312-84677-0). St Martin.

FLORENCE-SOCIAL LIFE AND CUSTOMS

Brucker, Gene, ed. Society of Renaissance Florence. 1972. pap. 4.95x (ISBN 0-06-131607-5, TB1607, Torch). Har-Row.

Kent, Francis W. Household Lineage in Renaissance Florence: The Family Life of the Capponi, Ginori, & Rucellai. LC 76-3260. 1977. text ed. 23.50 (ISBN 0-691-05237-9). Princeton U Pr.

FLORENCE, COUNCIL OF, 1438-1439

see Ferrara-Florence, Council Of, 1438-1439

FLORICULTURE

see also Annuals (Plants); Bulbs; Florists; Flower Gardening; Flowers; Gardening; Greenhouses; House Plants; Orchid Culture; Perennials; Plant-Breeding; Plant Propagation; Plants, Ornamental; Wild Flower Gardening; Window-Gardening; also particular varieties of plants and flowers, e.g. Aquatic Plants, Chrysanthemums, Climbing Plants, Dahlias, Roses

Brickell, C., et al. Petaloid Monocotyledons: Horticultural & Botanical Research. (Linnean Society Symposium Ser.: No.8). 1980. 71.50 (ISBN 0-12-133950-5). Acad Pr.

Carter, Jack, ed. Sunflower Science & Technology. 1978. write for info. Am Soc Agron.

Janick, Jules. Horticultural Reviews, Vol. 2. (Illus.). 1980. lib. bdg. 33.00 (ISBN 0-87055-352-6). AVI.

Larson, Roy A. Introduction to Floriculture. 1980. text ed. 29.50 (ISBN 0-12-437650-9). Acad Pr.

Laurie, Alex, et al. Commercial Flower Forcing. 7th ed. 1968. text ed. 19.00 (ISBN 0-07-036632-2, C). McGraw.

--Commercial Flower Forcing. 8th ed. (Illus.). 1979. text ed. 20.00 (ISBN 0-07-036633-0, C). McGraw.

Mastalerz, John W. The Greenhouse Environment: The Effect of Environmental Factors on Flower Crops. LC 77-6793. 1977. 28.95 (ISBN 0-471-57606-9). Wiley.

Nehrling, Arno & Nehrling, Irene. Flower Gardening for Flower Arrangement. LC 75-20966. 256p. 1976. pap. 4.00 (ISBN 0-486-23263-8). Dover.

Nelson, Kennard S. Flower & Plant Production in the Greenhouse. 3rd ed. LC 77-79741. (Illus.). (gr. 9-12). 1978. 15.35 (ISBN 0-8134-1965-4). Interstate.

New Cut Flower Crops. 1981. 15.00x (ISBN 0-686-75419-0, Pub. by Grower Bks). State Mutual Bk.

Roest, S. Flowering & Vegetative Propagation of Pyrethrum (Chrysanthemum Cinerariaefolium Vis.) in Vivo & in Vitro. (Agricultural Research Reports Ser.: No. 860). (Illus.). 1976. pap. 14.00 (ISBN 90-220-0622-0, Pub. by PUDOC). Unipub.

FLORICULTURE-EXHIBITIONS

see Flower Shows

FLORIDA

see also names of cities, towns, and geographic areas in Florida, e.g. Miami; Everglades

Barbour, George M. Florida for Tourists, Invalids & Settlers. Peter, Emmett B., Jr., ed. LC 64-19152. (Floridiana Facsimile & Reprint Ser). (Illus.). 1964. Repr. of 1882 ed. 10.75 (ISBN 0-8130-0012-2). U Presses Fla.

Brinton, Daniel G. Notes on the Floridian Penninsula. LC 69-19548. Repr. of 1859 ed. 15.00 (ISBN 0-404-01084-9). AMS Pr.

Carter, Luther J. The Florida Experience: Land & Water Policy in a Growth State. LC 74-6816. (Resources for the Future Ser). 376p. 1976. 22.50x (ISBN 0-8018-1646-7); pap. 5.95 (ISBN 0-8018-1896-6). Johns Hopkins.

Clark, John. The Sanibel Report: Formulation of a Comprehensive Plan Based on Natural Systems. LC 76-56987. (Illus.). 1976. pap. 10.00 (ISBN 0-89164-040-1). Conservation Foun.

Deland, Margaret. Floriday Day. (Illus.). 1978. Repr. of 1889 ed. lib. bdg. 35.00 (ISBN 0-8492-0690-1). R West.

Florida. 28.00 (ISBN 0-89770-085-6). Curriculum Info Ctr.

Florida: A Guide to the Southernmost State. LC 72-84466. 1939. 54.00 (ISBN 0-403-02161-8). Somerset Pub.

Florida Trend Magazine, ed. Florida Facts & Figures Everyone Uses. 17th rev ed. LC 66-13567. (Illus.). 1981. pap. 1.00 (ISBN 0-88251-079-7). Trend House.

Forbes, James G. Sketches, Historical & Topographical, of the Floridas. Covington, James W., ed. LC 64-19158. (Floridiana Facsimile & Reprint Ser). 1964. Repr. of 1821 ed. 9.50 (ISBN 0-8130-0078-5). U Presses Fla.

Frisbie, Louise K. Yesterday's Polk County. LC 75-44454. (Illus.). 1976. 7.95 (ISBN 0-912458-64-X, Pub-by E A Seemann). Imperial Pub Co.

Gaines, George, Jr. & Coleman, David S. Broker Review Outline: Florida. 1981. pap. text ed. 12.50 (ISBN 0-9602004-5-2). G&C Learn.

--Florida Real Estate Principles, Practices, & Law. 5th. ed. 1981. pap. text ed. 10.95 (ISBN 0-9602004-3-6). G&C Learn.

--Salesman Review Outline: Florida. 3rd. ed. 1981. pap. text ed. 5.50 (ISBN 0-9602004-4-4). G&C Learn.

Gifford, John C. On Preserving Tropical Florida. LC 78-126196. (Illus.). 1972. 9.95 (ISBN 0-916224-21-X). Banyan Bks.

Heilprin, Angelo. Explorations on the West Coast of Florida & in the Okeechobee Wilderness. (Illus.). Repr. 8.00 (ISBN 0-87710-364-X). Paleo Res.

Jones, Elise C., ed. Florida Statistical Abstract: 1968. 2nd ed. (LC A67-7393). 1968. pap. 5.50x (ISBN 0-8130-0342-3). U Presses Fla.

--Florida Statistical Abstract: 1969. 3rd ed. (LC A67-7393). 1969. pap. 6.50x (ISBN 0-8130-0343-1). U Presses Fla.

--Florida Statistical Abstract: 1970. 4th ed. (LC A67-7393). 1970. pap. 6.50x (ISBN 0-8130-0344-X). U Presses Fla.

--Florida Statistical Abstract, 1972. annual 6th ed. (Illus., LC A67-7393). 1972. 11.00x (ISBN 0-8130-0404-7). U Presses Fla.

Lanier, Sidney. Florida: Its Scenery, Climate, & History. LC 72-14330. (Bicentennial Floridiana Facsimile & Reprint Ser.). (Illus.). 266p. 1973. Repr. of 1875 ed. 8.50 (ISBN 0-8130-0369-5). U Presses Fla.

Long, Marshall & Wilkinson, Robert, eds. It Was a Beautiful Country: A Southwest Florida Anthology. new ed. LC 73-87597. (Illus.). 64p. 1974. pap. 1.95 (ISBN 0-87208-023-4). Island Pr.

Long, Robert W. & Lakela, Olga. A Flora of Tropical Florida: A Manual of the Seed Plants & Ferns of Southern Peninsular Florida. LC 76-4025. (Illus.). 1976. 45.00x (ISBN 0-916224-06-6). Banyan Bks.

Maloy, Richard H. Your Questions Answered About Florida Divorce Law. LC 77-81168. (Your Questions Answered on Florida Law Ser.). 1977. pap. 1.95 (ISBN 0-89317-023-2). Windward Pub.

--Your Questions Answered About Florida Law & Family Relationships in Life & Death. LC 77-93147. (Your Questions Answered on Florida Law Ser.). 1978. pap. 1.95 (ISBN 0-89317-026-7). Windward Pub.

--Your Questions Answered About Florida Law & Your Continuing Obligations After Divorce. LC 77-93148. (Your Questions Answered on Florida Law Ser.). 1978. pap. 1.95 (ISBN 0-89317-025-9). Windward Pub.

Mullen, Harris H. Florida Close-up: Some Intimate Views of a Very Misunderstood State. LC 72-88084. (Illus.). 104p. (Orig.). 1973. 4.95 (ISBN 0-88251-033-9); pap. 1.50 (ISBN 0-88251-023-1). Trend House.

Pollack, Martin. Welcome to Florida: The Sunshine State. LC 79-63345. 175p. 1979. pap. 11.95 (ISBN 0-936830-00-8). Alliance Pubs.

Read, W. A. Florida Place Names of Indian Origin & Seminole Personal Names. 1977. lib. bdg. 59.95 (ISBN 0-8490-1845-5). Gordon Pr.

Scott, Carroll L. Successful Retirement in Florida. LC 74-31644. (Illus.). 64p. 1974. pap. 2.95 (ISBN 0-915764-00-8). SunRise Hse.

State Industrial Directories Corp. Florida State Industrial Directory 1980. 1980. pap. 65.00 (ISBN 0-89910-039-2). State Indus Dir.

Thompson, Harwood & Ellis. Florida Real Estate Resource Book. 1978. pap. 7.95 ref. ed. (ISBN 0-87909-739-6). Reston.

Thompson, Ralph B., ed. Florida Statistical Abstract, Nineteen Seventy Four. 8th ed. (LC A67-7393). 1974. 12.50x (ISBN 0-8130-0489-6); pap. 8.50 (ISBN 0-8130-0510-8). U Presses Fla.

--Florida Statistical Abstract: Nineteen Seventy-Three. 7th ed. 631p. (LC A67-7393). 1973. 12.50x (ISBN 0-8130-0394-6); pap. 8.50 (ISBN 0-8130-0511-6). U Presses Fla.

--Florida Statistical Abstract 1976. 10th annual ed. (Florida Statistical Abstract). (Illus., LC A67-7393). 15.00x (ISBN 0-8130-0574-4); pap. 9.75 (ISBN 0-8130-0575-2). U Presses Fla.

Tolf, Robert W. How to Survive Your First Six Months in Florida; & Love Every Minute of It. rev. ed. LC 73-84441. (Illus.). 52p. (Orig.). 1979. pap. 1.95 (ISBN 0-88251-074-6). Trend House.

FLORIDA-ANTIQUITIES

Bullen, Ripley P. The Terra Ceia Site, Manatee County, Florida. pap. 5.50 (ISBN 0-384-06299-7). Johnson Repr.

Cushing, Frank H. Explorations of Key Dwellers' Remains on the Gulf Coast of Florida. LC 72-5007. (Antiquities of the New World Ser.: Vol. 13). (Illus.). Repr. of 1896 ed. 16.00 (ISBN 0-404-57313-4). AMS Pr.

Fairbanks, Charles H. Florida Anthropology. Repr. of 1958 ed. pap. 5.50 (ISBN 0-685-02245-5). Johnson Repr.

Fairbanks, George R. History & Antiquities of the City of St. Augustine, Florida. LC 75-15750. (Bicentennial Floridiana Facsimile & Reprint Ser.). 1975. Repr. of 1858 ed. 8.50 (ISBN 0-8130-0403-9). U Presses Fla.

Florida Anthropological Society. Florida Anthropological Society Publications, Nos. 1-5. Set. pap. 27.00 (ISBN 0-384-16110-3). Johnson Repr.

Marx, Robert F. Spanish Treasure in Florida Waters: A Billion Dollar Graveyard. (Illus.). 1979. 12.50case (ISBN 0-913352-06-3). Mariners Boston.

Purdy, Barbara A. Florida's Prehistoric Stone Technology. LC 80-24726. (Illus.). xvi, 165p. 1981. 25.00 (ISBN 0-8130-0697-X). U Presses Fla.

Rouse, Irving. A Survey of Indian River Archeology, Florida. LC 76-43813. (Yale Univ. Publications in Anthropology: No. 45). 376p. Repr. of 1951 ed. 32.50 (ISBN 0-404-15668-1). AMS Pr.

Willey, Gordon R. Archeology of the Florida Gulf Coast. LC 72-5013. (Harvard University. Peabody Museum of Archaeology & Ethnology. Antiquities of the New World: No. 18). (Illus.). Repr. of 1949 ed. 57.50 (ISBN 0-404-57318-5). AMS Pr.

Williams, John L. A View of West Florida, Embracings Its Geography, Topography, & C., with an Appendix Treating of Its Antiquities, Land Titles, & Canals, & Containing a Map Exhibiting a Chart of the Coast, a Plan of Pensacola, & the Entrance of the Harbour. LC 75-45282. (Bicentennial Floridiana Facsimile Ser.). (Illus.). 1976. Repr. of 1827 ed. 8.50 (ISBN 0-8130-0375-X). U Presses Fla.

FLORIDA-DESCRIPTION AND TRAVEL

Baxter, Robert. Baxter's Florida. 1981. 9.95 (ISBN 0-913384-34-8). Rail-Europe-Baxter.

Bowe, Richard J. Pictorial History of Florida. 3rd ed. 1970. 10.00 (ISBN 0-913122-14-9). Mickler Hse.

Burt, Alvin. Florida a Place in the Sun. (Illus.). 244p. 1974. 14.95 (ISBN 0-685-50329-1). Burda Pubns.

Carter, W. Horace. Creatures & Chronicles from Cross Creek. (Illus.). 286p. (Orig.). 1981. pap. text ed. 5.95 (ISBN 0-937866-02-4). Atlantic Pub Co.

Dimock, Anthony Weston & Dimock, Julian A. Florida Enchantments. LC 74-13789. (Illus.). 318p. 1975. Repr. of 1908 ed. 24.00 (ISBN 0-8103-4061-5). Gale.

Federal Writer's Project, Florida. Seeing St. Augustine. LC 73-3605. (American Guide Ser.). Repr. of 1937 ed. 12.50 (ISBN 0-404-57909-4). AMS Pr.

Fletcher, Leslie. Florida's Fantastic Fauna & Flora. LC 77-78032. 1977. pap. 2.50 (ISBN 0-911980-09-1). Beau Lac.

Frisbie, Louise K. Florida's Fabled Inns. LC 78-56754. (Illus.). 1980. 12.95 (ISBN 0-9602960-0-X). Imperial Pub Co.

Gantz, Charlotte O. A Naturalist in Southern Florida. LC 74-126195. (Illus.). 1971. 9.95 (ISBN 0-87024-172-9). U of Miami Pr.

Gilliland, Marion S. The Material Culture of Key Marco, Florida. LC 75-15798. 1976. 15.00 (ISBN 0-8130-0362-8). U Presses Fla.

Grimm, Tom & Grimm, Michele. Florida. LC 77-75963. (This Beautiful World Ser.: Vol. 59). (Illus.). 1977. pap. 4.95 (ISBN 0-87011-315-1). Kodansha.
Guia De la Florida. LC 76-6812. 1976. pap. text ed. 3.50 (ISBN 0-916264-03-3). P de Vosjoli.
Hannau, Hans W. Florida. (Panorama Bks.). (Illus., Fr.). 1964. 3.95 (ISBN 0-685-11192-X). French & Eur.
Harvey, Karen G. St. Augustine & St. Johns County: A Pictoral History. LC 79-19039. (Illus.). 1980. ltd. ed. 24.95 (ISBN 0-89865-025-9); pap. 12.95 (ISBN 0-89865-011-9). Donning Co.
Hill, Jim & Hill, Miriam. Fabulous Florida. 2nd ed. (Illus.). 360p. 1976. pap. 3.95 (ISBN 0-686-11186-9). Ambassador Pubns.
Holland, Claude V. Tortugas Run. 1973. 4.95 (ISBN 0-932092-03-9); pap. 2.98 (ISBN 0-932092-02-0). Hol-Land Bks.
How to Live in Florida on Ten Thousand Dollars a Year, 1981-82. 224p. Date not set. pap. 8.95 (ISBN 0-671-41397-X). Frommer-Pasmantier.
Hudson, L. Frank & Prescott, Gordon R. Lost Treasures of Florida's Gulf Coast. LC 73-9494. (Illus.). 64p. 1973. pap. 2.95 (ISBN 0-8200-1026-X). Great Outdoors.
Lewis, Gordon. Florida Fishing: Fresh & Salt Water. LC 56-11379. (Illus., Orig.). 1957. pap. 2.95 (ISBN 0-8200-0102-3). Great Outdoors.
Lewis, Paul M. Beautiful Florida. Shangle, Robert D., ed. LC 79-1428. (Illus.). 72p. 1979. 14.95 (ISBN 0-915796-71-6); pap. 7.95 (ISBN 0-915796-70-8). Beautiful Am.
McMullen, Edwin W., Jr. English Topographic Terms in Florida, 1563-1874. LC 52-12531. 1953. pap. 5.50 (ISBN 0-8130-0160-9). U Presses Fla.
Marks, H. S. & Riggs, Gene B. Rivers of Florida. 4.95 (ISBN 0-915536-00-5). H S Marks.
Marks, Henry & Riggs, Gene B. Rivers of Florida. (Illus.). 1974. pap. 4.95x (ISBN 0-915536-00-5). Southern Pr.
Marston, Red. Cruising Florida. (Illus.). 1981. 15.00 (ISBN 0-07-120156-4). Ziff-Davis Pub.
Marth, Del. Yesterday's Sarasota. LC 73-80594. (Illus.). 1977. pap. 5.95 (ISBN 0-912458-77-1). E A Seemann.
Marth, Del & Marth, Martha. Florida Almanac 1982. rev. ed. LC 71-618243. 1981. pap. 12.95 (ISBN 0-498-02550-0). A S Barnes.
Matschat, Cecile H. Suwannee River: Strange Green Land. LC 79-5190. (Brown Thrasher Bks.). (Illus.). 295p. 1980. 17.50x (ISBN 0-8203-0508-1); pap. 5.95x (ISBN 0-8203-0496-4). U of Ga Pr.
O'Reilly, John. Boater's Guide to the Upper Florida Keys: Jewfish Creek to Long Key. LC 70-125659. (Illus.). 1970. pap. 3.95 spiral bdg. (ISBN 0-87024-175-3). U of Miami Pr.
Pollack, Martin. Eating-Out Guide to Restaurants in Dade, Broward & Palm Beach Counties. 256p. pap. cancelled. Alliance Pubs.
Robin, C. C. Voyage to Louisiana: 1803-1805. 1966. Repr. of 1807 ed. 20.00 (ISBN 0-911116-20-6). Pelican.
Rolle, Denys. The Humble Petition of Denys Rolle, Esq., Setting Forth the Hardships, Inconveniences, & Grievances Which Have Attended Him in His Attempts to Make a Settlement in East Florida, Humbly Praying Such. LC 77-5133. (Bicentennial Floridiana Facsimile Ser.). 1977. Repr. of 1765 ed. 6.50 (ISBN 0-8130-0417-9). U Presses Fla.
Russell, Franklin. The Okefenokee Swamp. (The American Wilderness Ser.). (Illus.). 1973. 12.95 (ISBN 0-8094-1201-2). Time-Life.
Simmons, William H. Notices of East Florida, with an Account of the Seminole Nation of Indians. LC 73-2820. (Bicentennial Floridiana Facsimile & Reprint Ser.). 1973. Repr. of 1822 ed. 6.00 (ISBN 0-8130-0400-4). U Presses Fla.
Simpson, Charles T. Out of Doors in Florida. 1928. 20.00 (ISBN 0-685-72780-7). Norwood Edns.
--Out of Doors in Florida: The Adventures of a Naturalist. Repr. of 1923 ed. lib. bdg. 35.00 (ISBN 0-8495-5001-7). Arden Lib.
Smiley, Nixon. Florida: Land of Images. LC 72-82931. (Illus.). 1977. pap. 3.95 (ISBN 0-912458-81-X). E A Seemann.
--Yesterday's Florida. LC 74-75296. (Historic States Ser.: No. 1). (Illus.). 256p. 1974. 12.95 (ISBN 0-912458-39-9). E A Seemann.
Stachowicz, Jim. Guide to Florida Campgrounds. Romashko, Sandra, ed. LC 78-157231. (Illus.). 1981. pap. 3.95 (ISBN 0-89317-019-4). Windward Pub.
Steinmetz, Bob. In the Land of Funshine. Smollon, Jim, ed. Orig. Title: Jayhawking Florida Traveler. (Illus.). 72p. 1972. pap. 1.00 (ISBN 0-686-11502-3). Star Pub Fla.
Tolf, Robert W. How to Survive Your First Six Months in Florida; & Love Every Minute of It. rev. ed. LC 73-84441. (Illus.). 52p. (Orig.). 1979. pap. 1.95 (ISBN 0-88251-074-6). Trend House.
Williams, John L. A View of West Florida, Embracings Its Geography, Topography, & C., with an Appendix Treating of Its Antiquities, Land Titles, & Canals, & Containing a Map Exhibiting a Chart of the Coast, a Plan of Pensacola, & the Entrance of the Harbour. LC 75-45282. (Bicentennial Floridiana Facsimile Ser.). (Illus.). 1976. Repr. of 1827 ed. 8.50 (ISBN 0-8130-0375-X). U Presses Fla.

FLORIDA–DESCRIPTION AND TRAVEL–GUIDEBOOKS

Airguide. Airguide Traveler: Bahamas, Florida, Florida Keys, & Sea Islands. (Illus.). 1980. pap. 11.00 (ISBN 0-911721-89-4). Aviation.
Disney's Adventure Guide to Florida. (Fodor's Modern Travel Guides Ser.). 1981. 3.95 (ISBN 0-679-00575-7). McKay.
Firestone, Linda & Morse, Whit. Florida's Enchanting Islands: Sanibel & Captiva. 3rd ed. LC 80-67778. (Illus., Orig.). 1980. pap. 4.95 (ISBN 0-917374-08-8). Good Life VA.
Five Hundred Things to Do in Florida for Free. 140p. Date not set. pap. 3.95 (ISBN 0-695-81564-4). New Century.
Florida: A Guide to the Southernmost State. LC 72-84466. 1939. 54.00 (ISBN 0-403-02161-8). Somerset Pub.
Fodor's Disney's Adventure Guide to Florida. (Fodor Travel Guides Ser.). 64p. (gr. 1-6). 1980. pap. 3.95 (ISBN 0-679-00575-7). McKay.
Fodor's Florida, 1981. 1980. pap. 6.95 (ISBN 0-679-00606-0). McKay.
Ford, Norman D. Florida. 1979. pap. 4.95 (ISBN 0-685-59789-X). Harian.
Grove, Judi. A Vacationer's Guide to Orlando & Central Florida. LC 80-39608. (Illus.). 150p. (Orig.). 1981. pap. 4.95 (ISBN 0-914788-39-6). East Woods.
Grow, Gerald. Florida Parks: A Guide to Camping in Nature. (Illus., Orig.). 1981. pap. 9.95 (ISBN 0-939638-50-9). Longleaf Pubns.
Guide to Florida. (U. S. & Canada Guides). 1981. pap. 6.95 (ISBN 0-528-84470-9). Rand.
Hall, Clarence H. How We Vacationed in Florida on Sixty Four Dollars a Week. 50p. 1979. pap. 2.95 (ISBN 0-9604084-0-1). C H Hall.
Hayes, Edward. The Florida One-Day Trip Book: Fifty-Two off-Beat Excursions in & Around Orlando. (Illus.). 160p. 1981. pap. 4.95 (ISBN 0-914440-50-0). EPM Pubns.
Hill, Jim. Beyond the Beaten Path: A See More Spend Less Guide to Orlando, Walt Disney World & 50 Mile Vicinity. (Illus.). 1978. 1.00 (ISBN 0-686-24070-7). Ambassador Pubns.
A Kosoy Travel Guide to Florida & the South. 3rd ed. (Illus.). 1981. pap. 5.95 (ISBN 0-531-03974-9). Watts.
Marth, Del & Marth, Martha. Florida Almanac. LC 71-618243. (Illus.). 440p. 1980. 4.95 (ISBN 0-498-02454-7). A S Barnes.
Osler, Jack & Griffin, George. Fifty Great Mini-Trips in Florida. rev ed. (Jack Osler's Mini Trips Ser.). (Illus.). Date not set. pap. cancelled (ISBN 0-89645-012-0). Media Ventures.
Perrero, Laurie & Perrero, Louis. Disney World & the Sun & Fun Belt. Romashko, Sandra D., ed. LC 76-46896. (Windward Full Color Travel Guide Ser.). (Illus.). pap. 2.95 (ISBN 0-89317-014-3). Windward Pub.
Rabkin, Richard & Rabkin, Jacob. Nature Guide to Florida. (Illus.). 1978. pap. 7.95 (ISBN 0-916224-44-9). Banyan Bks.
Rambler. Guide to Florida. Patrick, R. W., ed. LC 64-66300. (Floridiana Facsimile & Reprint Ser). (Illus.). 1964. Repr. of 1875 ed. 9.50 (ISBN 0-8130-0193-5). U Presses Fla.
Rand McNally. Guide to Florida. 5th ed. LC 79-656302. (Illus.). 1979. pap. 4.95 (ISBN 0-528-84109-2). Rand.
Rhodes, William W. Rhodes Travel Guide--Florida. Lualdi, Anthony, ed. LC 79-63598. (Illus.). 1979. 9.95 (ISBN 0-933768-00-1); pap. 6.95 (ISBN 0-933768-01-X). Rhodes Geo Lib.
Rowan, Tom. Newcomers Guide to Florida. (Illus.). 1979. pap. 2.95 (ISBN 0-8200-9907-4). Great Outdoors.
Tolf, Robert W. Best Restaurants Florida's Gold Coast. LC 79-3723. (Best Restaurant Ser.). (Illus.). 222p. (Orig.). 1979. pap. 3.95 (ISBN 0-89286-161-4). One Hund One Prods.
Toner, Mike & Toner, Pat. Florida by Paddle & Pack: Forty-Five Wilderness Trails in Central & South Florida. LC 78-25571. (Illus.). 1979. pap. 6.95 (ISBN 0-916224-37-6). Banyan Bks.
Triplett, Kenneth E. & Triplett, Mary R. Free Camping in Florida. 1973. pap. 3.20 (ISBN 0-686-09887-0). Triplett Ents.
Writers Program, Florida. Planning Your Vacation in Florida: Miami & Dade County, Including Miami Beach & Coral Gables. LC 73-3603. Repr. of 1941 ed. 13.50 (ISBN 0-404-57907-8). AMS Pr.

FLORIDA–ECONOMIC CONDITIONS

Bice, David A., et al. A Panorama of Florida. Armstrong, Alfredlene, ed. (Illus.). 320p. 1981. 15.95 (ISBN 0-934750-13-0); text ed. 14.99 (ISBN 0-934750-21-1); pap. 13.95 (ISBN 0-934750-14-9); tchrs. ed. 14.99 (ISBN 0-934750-27-0); wkbk. 3.99 (ISBN 0-934750-22-X); tchrs. wkbk. 4.25 (ISBN 0-934750-23-8). Jalamap.
Blakey, Fred. The Florida Phosphate Industry: A History of the Development & Use of a Vital Mineral. LC 73-82345. (Wertheim Publications in Industrial Relations Ser.). 1973. text ed. 14.00x (ISBN 0-674-30670-8). Harvard U Pr.
Commerce Clearing House. Guidebook to Florida Taxes: 1982. 1982. 10.00 (ISBN 0-686-76125-1). Commerce.
Graham, Bob. Workdays: Finding Florida on the Job. Mahoney, Lawrence, ed. LC 78-4177. (Illus.). 1978. pap. 5.95 (ISBN 0-916224-34-1). Banyan Bks.
Greenhut, M. L. & Colberg, Marshall R. Factors in the Location of Florida Industry. LC 62-63440. (FSU Studies: No. 36). (Illus.). 108p. 1962. 5.25 (ISBN 0-8130-0649-X). U Presses Fla.
Hall, Frances W. Be Careful in Florida. (Illus.). 1979. pap. 1.95 (ISBN 0-8200-9906-6). Great Outdoors.
Kilpatrick, Wylie, ed. Florida's Economy: Past Trends & Prospects for 1970. LC 56-11879. (Illus.). 1956. pap. 2.50 (ISBN 0-8130-0129-3). U Presses Fla.
Smith, Charles A. Some Relationships Existing in School Expenditure Among Florida Counties. LC 72-177776. (Columbia University. Teachers College. Contributions to Education: No. 352). Repr. of 1929 ed. 17.50 (ISBN 0-404-55352-4). AMS Pr.
Thompson, Ralph B., ed. Florida Statistical Abstract, Nineteen Eighty. LC 67-7393. 1980. 20.00x (ISBN 0-8130-0677-5); pap. 11.50 (ISBN 0-8130-0678-3). U Presses Fla.
--Florida Statistical Abstract, 1977. 11th annual ed. (LC A67-7393). 1977. 15.00x (ISBN 0-8130-0597-3). U Presses Fla.
--Florida Statistical Abstract, 1981. (Bureau of Economic & Business Research Ser.). 1981. write for info. (ISBN 0-8130-0715-1); pap. price not set (ISBN 0-8130-0716-X). U Presses Fla.

FLORIDA–HISTORY

Adicks, Richard & Neely, Donna M. Oviedo: Biography of a Town. LC 79-88759. (Illus.). 1979. 15.00x (ISBN 0-9603034-1-3). Oviedo Pub Co.
Adicks, Richard, ed. LeConte's Report on East Florida. LC 77-9286. 1978. 5.00 (ISBN 0-8130-0588-4). U Presses Fla.
Anderson, Edward C. Florida Territory in 1844: The Diary of Master Edward Clifford Anderson USN. Hoole, W. Stanley, ed. LC 76-16071. 1977. 8.50x (ISBN 0-8173-5111-6). U of Ala Pr.
Avant, D. A. Like a Straight Pine Tree: Stories of Reconstruction Days in Alabama & Florida 1855-1971. (Illus.). 124p. 1971. 7.95x (ISBN 0-914570-03-X). L'Avant Studios.
Bacon, Eve. Oakland, the Early Years. LC 74-81080. Orig. Title: History of Oakland, Florida. (Illus.). 1974. 11.75 (ISBN 0-913122-04-1). Mickler Hse.
--Orlando, a Centennial History. Incl. Vol. 1. (Illus.). 1975. 17.76 (ISBN 0-913122-08-4); Vol. 2. (Illus.). 1977. 19.95 (ISBN 0-913122-10-6). LC 75-21374. 2 vol. set 35.00 (ISBN 0-913122-13-0). Mickler Hse.
Bennett, Charles E. Florida's French Revolution. write for info. (ISBN 0-8130-0641-4). U Presses Fla.
Bice, David A., et al. A Panorama of Florida. Armstrong, Alfredlene, ed. (Illus.). 320p. 1981. 15.95 (ISBN 0-934750-13-0); text ed. 14.99 (ISBN 0-934750-21-1); pap. 13.95 (ISBN 0-934750-14-9); tchrs. ed. 14.99 (ISBN 0-934750-27-0); wkbk. 3.99 (ISBN 0-934750-22-X); tchrs. wkbk. 4.25 (ISBN 0-934750-23-8). Jalamap.
Biographical Souvenir of the States of Georgia & Florida, Containing Biographical Sketches of the Representative Public & Many Early Settled Families in These States. LC 75-44662. (Illus.). 1976. Repr. of 1889 ed. 40.00 (ISBN 0-89308-040-3). Southern Hist Pr.
Blackman, E. V. Miami & Dade County, Florida: Its Settlement, Progress & Achievement. LC 77-88898. (Florida County History Ser.). (Illus.). 1977. Repr. of 1921 ed. 22.50 (ISBN 0-913122-12-2). Mickler Hse.
Blackman, William F. History of Orange County, Florida. LC 73-75939. (Florida County History Ser.). (Illus.). 460p. 1973. Repr. of 1927 ed. 22.50 (ISBN 0-913122-03-3). Mickler Hse.
Bowe, Richard J. Pictorial History of Florida. 3rd ed. 1970. 10.00 (ISBN 0-913122-14-9). Mickler Hse.
Brooks, Abbie M. & Sunshine, Silvia. Petals Plucked from Sunny Climes. LC 76-10700. (Bicentennial Floridiana Facsimile & Reprint Ser.). 1976. Repr. of 1880 ed. 13.50 (ISBN 0-8130-0414-4). U Presses Fla.
Brown, Warren J. Florida's Aviation History. 1980. pap. 6.95 (ISBN 0-912522-70-4). Aero-Medical.
Catesby, Mark. Natural History of Carolina, Florida & the Bahama Islands. (Illus.). Repr. 575.00 (ISBN 0-685-88561-5). Johnson Repr.
Chambers, H. E. West Florida & Its Relations to the Historical Cartography of the United States. 1973. Repr. of 1898 ed. pap. 7.00 (ISBN 0-384-08451-6). Johnson Repr.
Chambers, Henry E. West Florida & Its Relations to the Historical Cartography of the United States. LC 78-63863. (Johns Hopkins University. Studies in the Social Sciences. Sixteenth Ser. 1898: 5). Repr. of 1898 ed. 11.50 (ISBN 0-404-61119-2). AMS Pr.
Cox, Merlin & Dovell, J. E. Florida - from Secession to Space Age. Pope, Patricia, ed. LC 74-553. 256p. 1974. 9.95 (ISBN 0-8200-1027-8). Great Outdoors.
Damkohler, E. E. Estero, Florida 1882. LC 67-19575. 1974. pap. 1.00 (ISBN 0-87208-014-5). Island Pr.
Dau, Frederick W. Florida Old & New. LC 74-13957. 1975. Repr. of 1934 ed. 26.00 (ISBN 0-8103-4060-7). Gale.
De Brahm, William G. The Atlantic Pilot. LC 73-18036. (Bicentennial Floridiana Facsimile Ser). (Illus.). 112p. 1974. Repr. of 1772 ed. 6.50 (ISBN 0-8130-0366-0). U Presses Fla.
Dinkins, Lester. Dunellon, Boom Town of the 1890's. (Illus.). 1978. Repr. 4.95 (ISBN 0-8200-1016-2). Great Outdoors.
Doherty, Herbert J., Jr. The Whigs of Florida, Eighteen Forty Five-Eighteen Fifty Four. LC 59-62570. (U of Fla. Social Sciences Monographs: No. 1). 1959. 2.95 (ISBN 0-8130-0064-5). U Presses Fla.
Dunn, Hampton. Yesterday's Tampa. LC 72-82937. (Illus.). 1977. pap. 5.95 (ISBN 0-912458-92-5). E A Seemann.
Eberson, Frederick. Early Medical History of Pinellas Peninsula. LC 78-50560. (Illus.). 1978. 10.00 (ISBN 0-912760-67-2). Valkyrie Pr.
Fradin, Dennis. Florida: In Words & Pictures. LC 80-16681. (Young People's Stories of Our States Ser.). (Illus.). 48p. (gr. 2-5). 1980. PLB 9.25 (ISBN 0-516-03909-1). Childrens.
French, Benjamin F. Historical Collections of Louisiana, Embracing Rare & Valuable Documents Relating to the Natural, Civil, & Political History of That State, 5 vols. LC 72-14380. Repr. of 1853 ed. Set. 150.00 (ISBN 0-404-11050-9); 30.00 ea. Vol. 1 (ISBN 0-404-11051-7). Vol. 2 (ISBN 0-404-11052-5). Vol. 3 (ISBN 0-404-11053-3). Vol. 4 (ISBN 0-404-11054-1). Vol. 5 (ISBN 0-404-11055-X). AMS Pr.
French, Benjamin F., ed. Historical Collections of Louisiana & Florida, 2 vols. LC 72-14374. Repr. of 1875 ed. Set. 55.00 (ISBN 0-404-11096-7); 27.50 ea. Vol. 1 (ISBN 0-404-11097-5). Vol. 2 (ISBN 0-404-11098-3). AMS Pr.
Frisbie, Louise K. Peace River Pioneers. LC 74-81530. (Illus.). 1974. 7.95 (ISBN 0-912458-47-X, Pub. by E A Seemann). Imperial Pub Co.
Fritz, Florence. The Unknown Story of Sanibel & Captiva. 1974. 10.00 (ISBN 0-87012-165-0). McClain.
Gilliland, Marion S. The Material Culture of Key Marco, Florida. LC 75-15798. 1976. 15.00 (ISBN 0-8130-0362-8). U Presses Fla.
Godown, Marian & Rawchuck, Alberta. Yesterday's Ft Myers. LC 75-559. (Historic Cities Ser.: No. 15). (Illus.). 1975. 7.95 (ISBN 0-912458-49-6). E a Seemann.
Griffin, John, intro. by. Narrative of a Voyage to the Spanish Main, in the Ship "Two Friends". The Occupation of Amelia Island, by McGregor. & C.-Sketches of the Province of East Fla; & Anecdotes Illustrative of the Habits & Manners of the Seminole Indians (London 1819) LC 78-9785. (Bicentennial Floridana Facsimile Ser.). 1978. 12.00 (ISBN 0-8130-0416-0). U Presses Fla.
Hahoda, Gloria L. Florida. (States & the Nation Ser.). (Illus.). 1976. 12.95 (ISBN 0-393-05585-X, Co-Pub by AASLH). Norton.
Hamilton, Peter J. Colonial Mobile. Summersell, Charles G., ed. LC 75-19291. (Southern Historical Series: No. 20). 896p. 1976. Repr. of 1910 ed. 25.00 (ISBN 0-8173-5228-7). U of Ala Pr.
Hrdlicka, Ales. The Anthropology of Florida. LC 76-43750. (Pubns. of the Florida State Historical Society: No. 1). Repr. of 1922 ed. 23.50 (ISBN 0-404-15590-1). AMS Pr.
Irving, Theodore. Conquest of Florida Under Hernando De Soto, 2 vols. LC 73-78181. 1974. Repr. 10.00 ea.; Vol. 1. (ISBN 0-87208-017-X); Vol. 2. (ISBN 0-87208-018-8); Set. 17.50 (ISBN 0-87208-036-6). Island Pr.

Jackson, Ronald V. & Teeples, Gary R. Florida Census Index 1830. LC 77-85905. (Illus.). lib. bdg. 14.00 (ISBN 0-89593-025-0). Accelerated Index.
--Florida Census Index 1840. LC 77-85911. (Illus.). lib. bdg. 15.00 (ISBN 0-89593-026-9). Accelerated Index.
--Florida Census Index 1850. LC 77-85910. (Illus.). lib. bdg. 18.00 (ISBN 0-89593-027-7). Accelerated Index.
Johnson, Cecil. British West Florida, 1763-1783. LC 73-131375. (Illus.). 1971. Repr. of 1943 ed. 18.50 (ISBN 0-208-01032-7, Archon). Shoe String.
Kenny, Michael. Romance of the Floridas: The Finding & the Founding. (Illus.). 1971. Repr. of 1934 ed. 13.00 (ISBN 0-403-00767-4). Scholarly.
King & Treat. Florida One Hundred Years Ago. (Sun Historical Ser.). (Illus.). pap. 3.50 (ISBN 0-89540-055-3). Sun Pub.
Lyon, Eugene. The Enterprise of Florida: Pedro Menendez de Aviles & the Spanish Conquest of 1565-1568. LC 76-29612. (Illus.). 1976. 10.00 (ISBN 0-8130-0533-7). U Presses Fla.
McCall, George A. Letters from the Frontiers Written During a Period of Thirty Years Service in the Army of the United States. LC 74-22038. (Bicentennial Floridiana Facsimile & Reprint Ser.). 1974. Repr. of 1868 ed. 13.50 (ISBN 0-8130-0374-1). U Presses Fla.
Marban, Jorge A. La Florida: Cinco Siglos De Historia Hispanica. LC 78-70500. (Hispanic Sudies Collection--Coleccion De Estudios Hispanicos). (Illus.). 1979. pap. 5.95 (ISBN 0-89729-214-6). Ediciones.
Marks, Henry S. Who Was Who in Florida. LC 73-83503. 1973. 14.95 (ISBN 0-87397-039-X). Strode.
Martin, Sidney W. Florida During the Territorial Days. LC 73-19815. (Perspectives in American History Ser.: No. 15). (Illus.). 308p. Repr. of 1944 ed. lib. bdg. 17.50x (ISBN 0-87991-344-4). Porcupine Pr.
Miller, Janice B. Juan Nepomuceno De Quesada: Governor of Spanish East Florida, 1790-1795. LC 81-40589. (Illus.). 196p. (Orig.). 1981. lib. bdg. 19.50 (ISBN 0-8191-1833-8); pap. text ed. 9.50 (ISBN 0-8191-1834-6). U Pr of Amer.
Morris, Allen. Florida Place Names. LC 74-13949. 160p. 1974. 7.95 (ISBN 0-87024-256-3). U of Miami Pr.
Nichols & Woolson. Old Florida. (Sun Historical Ser.). (Illus.). pap. 3.50 (ISBN 0-89540-054-5). Sun Pub.
Parks, Arva M. Florida - the Forgotten Frontier: Florida Through the Lens of Ralph Middleton Munroe. LC 77-11205. (Illus.). 1977. 29.95 (ISBN 0-916224-14-7). Banyan Bks.
Peters, Virginia B. The Florida Wars. (Illus.). 1979. 22.50 (ISBN 0-208-01719-4, Archon). Shoe String.
Phillips, Ulrich B. & Glunt, James D., eds. Florida Plantation Records from Papers of George Noble Jones. LC 74-165409. (American Classics in History & Social Science Ser: No. 197). 1971. Repr. of 1927 ed. lib. bdg. 32.00 (ISBN 0-8337-4674-X). B Franklin.
Powell, Richard R. Compromises of Conflicting Claims: A History of California Law in the Period 1760-1860. LC 77-54938. (Orig.). 1977. lib. bdg. 22.50 (ISBN 0-379-00655-3). Oceana.
Pratt, Theodore. Story of Boca Raton. (Illus.). pap. 1.95 (ISBN 0-8200-1007-3). Great Outdoors.
Proctor, Samuel, ed. Eighteenth-Century Florida & the Caribbean. LC 76-2673. (Papers of the Annual Bicentennial Symposia: No. 2). 1976. 7.00 (ISBN 0-8130-0522-1). U Presses Fla.
--Eighteenth-Century Florida: Life on the Frontier. LC 76-5852. (Papers on the Annual Bicentennial Symposia: No. 3). 1976. 7.00 (ISBN 0-8130-0523-X). U Presses Fla.
--Eighteenth-Century Florida: The Impact of the American Revolution. LC 78-1870. (Papers of the Annual Bicentennail Symposia: No. 5). 1978. 9.00 (ISBN 0-8130-0589-2). U Presses Fla.
Rawlings, Marjorie K. Cross Creek. 279p. 1980. pap. 2.25 (ISBN 0-89176-031-8, 6031). Mockingbird Bks.
Schell, Rolfe F. DeSoto Didn't Land at Tampa. LC 66-17798. (Illus.). 1974. 4.95 (ISBN 0-87208-011-0); pap. 2.95 (ISBN 0-87208-048-X). Island Pr.
--History of Fort Myers Beach, Fla. LC 73-87599. (Illus.). 96p. 1980. 6.95 (ISBN 0-87208-021-8); pap. 3.95 (ISBN 0-87208-022-6). Island Pr.
Shofner, Jerrell H. Daniel Ladd: Merchant Prince of Frontier Florida. LC 77-21789. 1978. 8.50 (ISBN 0-8130-0546-9). U Presses Fla.
--Nor Is It Over Yet: Florida in the Era of Reconstruction, 1863-1877. LC 70-186325. 1974. 12.50 (ISBN 0-8130-0353-9). U Presses Fla.
Siebert, Wilbur H. Loyalists in East Florida, 1774-1785: The Most Important Documents Pertaining Thereto.., 2 vols. LC 72-8750. (American Revolutionary Ser.). Repr. of 1929 ed. Set. lib. bdg. 54.00x (ISBN 0-8398-1881-5). Irvington.
Skinner, W. B., et al. Peoples & Cultures of Early Florida. (Florida Social Studies Ser.). (Illus.). 90p. (gr. 4-9). 1971. pap. text ed. 1.50 (ISBN 0-913122-01-7); teacher's guide avail. (ISBN 0-913122-02-5); package of 25 texts & 1 tchrs' guide 24.70 (ISBN 0-913122-15-7). Mickler Hse.
Smeal, Lee. Florida Historical & Biographical Index. LC 78-53691. (Illus.). Date not set. lib. bdg. price not set (ISBN 0-89593-176-1). Accelerated Index.
Smiley, Nixon. Yesterday's Florida. LC 74-75296. (Historic States Ser.: No. 1). (Illus.). 256p. 1974. 12.95 (ISBN 0-912458-39-9). E A Seemann.
Starr, J. Barton. Tories, Dons, & Rebels: The American Revolution in British West Florida. LC 76-28953. 1976. 8.50 (ISBN 0-8130-0543-4). U Presses Fla.
Swindler, William F. & Frech, Mary, eds. Chronology & Documentary Handbook of the State of Florida. LC 73-567. (gr. 9-12). 1973. PLB 8.50 (ISBN 0-379-16134-6). Oceana.
Tebeau, Charlton W. A History of Florida. LC 80-53678. (Illus.). 1981. 25.00 (ISBN 0-686-76986-4); pap. 16.95 (ISBN 0-87024-073-0). U of Miami Pr.
Tenney, Frank F., Jr. The Enchanting Experience: Naples - Marco Island. Woolfolk, Doug, ed. (Illus.). 112p. 1981. 10.00 (ISBN 0-86518-016-4). Moran Pub Corp.
The Territory of Florida, 1821-1825. (The Territorial Papers of the United States: Vol. 22). Repr. of 1956 ed. 69.50 (ISBN 0-404-01472-0). AMS Pr.
The Territory of Florida, 1824-1828. (The Territorial Papers of the United States: Vol. 23). Repr. of 1958 ed. 69.50 (ISBN 0-404-01473-9). AMS Pr.
The Territory of Florida, 1828-1834. (The Territorial Papers of the United States: Vol. 24). Repr. of 1959 ed. 69.50 (ISBN 0-404-01474-7). AMS Pr.
The Territory of Florida, 1834-1839. (The Territorial Papers of the United States: Vol. 25). Repr. of 1960 ed. 69.50 (ISBN 0-404-01475-5). AMS Pr.
The Territory of Florida, 1839-1845. (The Territorial Papers of the United States: Vol. 26). Repr. of 1962 ed. 69.50 (ISBN 0-404-01476-3). AMS Pr.
Trottman, Rosemary W. The History of Zephyrhills, 1821-1921. 1978. 8.50 (ISBN 0-533-02882-5). Vantage.
Walker, Jonathan. The Trial & Imprisonment of Jonathan Walker at Pensacola, Florida, for Aiding Slaves to Escape from Bondage, with an Appendix Containing a Sketch of His Life. LC 74-19173. (Bicentennial Floridiana Facsimile & Reprint Ser.). 1974. Repr. of 1845 ed. 8.50 (ISBN 0-8130-0371-7). U Presses Fla.
Will, Lawrence E. A Cracker History of Okeechobee. 1978. Repr. 5.00 (ISBN 0-8200-1004-9). Great Outdoors.
--Okeechobee Boats & Skippers. 1978. Repr. 5.00 (ISBN 0-8200-1003-0). Great Outdoors.
--Okeechobee Hurricane. (Illus.). 1978. pap. 4.00 (ISBN 0-8200-1001-4). Great Outdoors.

FLORIDA–HISTORY–BIBLIOGRAPHY

Arthur, Stanley C. Index to the Archives of Spanish West-Florida, 1782-1810. 1975. 17.50 (ISBN 0-686-20873-0). Polyanthos.
Dictionary Catalog of the P. K. Yonge Library of Florida History, the University of Florida, Gainesville. 1977. lib. bdg. 350.00 (ISBN 0-8161-0019-5). G K Hall.

FLORIDA–HISTORY–COLONIAL PERIOD

Barcia Carballido Y Zuniga, Andres Gonzalez de. Barcia's Chronological History of the Continent of Florida: From the Year 1512, in Which Juan Ponce de Leon Discovered Florida, Until the Year 1722. Kerrigan, Anthony, tr. LC 77-106667. 426p. Repr. of 1951 ed. lib. bdg. 39.50x (ISBN 0-8371-3419-6, BAHF). Greenwood.
Campbell, Richard L. Historical Sketches of Colonial Florida. LC 75-14032. (Bicentennial Floridiana Facsimile & Reprint Ser.). 1975. Repr. of 1892 ed. 11.00 (ISBN 0-8130-0370-9). U Presses Fla.
Connor, Jeannette M., ed. Colonial Records of Spanish Florida: Letters & Reports of Governors & Secular Persons, 2 vols. LC 74-19720. Repr. of 1930 ed. Set. 55.00 (ISBN 0-404-12475-5). AMS Pr.
Coxe, Daniel. A Description of the English Province of Carolana, by the Spaniards Call'd Florida, & by the French la Louisiane. LC 76-18184. (Bicentennial Floridiana Facsimile Ser.). (Illus.). 122p. 1976. Repr. of 1722 ed. 8.50 (ISBN 0-8130-0402-0). U Presses Fla.
Curley, Michael J. Church & State in the Spanish Floridas (1783-1822) LC 73-3584. (Catholic University of America. Studies in American Church History: No. 30). Repr. of 1940 ed. 27.50 (ISBN 0-404-57780-6). AMS Pr.
Griffin, John, intro. by. Narrative of a Voyage to the Spanish Main, in the Ship "Two Friends". The Occupation of Amelia Island, by McGregor. & C.-Sketches of the Province of East Fla; & Anecdotes Illustrative of the Habits & Manners of the Seminole Indians (London 1819) LC 78-9785. (Bicentennial Floridana Facsimile Ser.). 1978. 12.00 (ISBN 0-8130-0416-0). U Presses Fla.
Hodge, Frederick W. & Lewis, Theodore H., eds. Spanish Explorers in the Southern United States, 1528-1543. (Original Narratives). (Illus.). 1977. Repr. of 1907 ed. 18.50x (ISBN 0-06-480372-4). B&N.
Howard, Milo B., Jr. & Rea, Robert R., eds. Memoire Justificatif of the Chevalier Montault De Monberaut: Indian Diplomacy in British West Florida, 1763-1765. LC 64-24955. (Southern Historical Ser: Vol. 3). 1965. 12.95x (ISBN 0-8173-5208-2). U of Ala Pr.
Irving, T. Conquest of Florida, by Hernando De Soto. LC 18-4171. Repr. of 1869 ed. 19.00 (ISBN 0-527-44620-3). Kraus Repr.
Kenny, Michael. Romance of the Floridas. LC 70-120573. (Illus.). Repr. of 1934 ed. 15.00 (ISBN 0-404-03656-2). AMS Pr.
Lescarbot, Marc. History of New France, Vol. 1. LC 68-28596. 1968. Repr. of 1907 ed. Vol. 1. lib. bdg. 27.50x (ISBN 0-8371-5039-6, LHFA); Vol. 2. 37.75x (ISBN 0-8371-5040-X, LHFB); Vol. 3. 35.25x (ISBN 0-8371-5041-8, LHFC). Greenwood.
Mowat, Charles L. East Florida As a British Province, 1763-1784. LC 64-66326. (Floridia Facsimile & Reprint Ser.). 1964. Repr. of 1943 ed. 9.50 (ISBN 0-8130-0167-6). U Presses Fla.
Proctor, Samuel, ed. Eighteenth Century Florida & Its Borderlands. LC 74-31385. (Papers of the Annual Bicentennial Symposia: No. 1). (Illus.). xiii, 157p. 1975. 7.75 (ISBN 0-8130-0408-X). U Presses Fla.
--Eighteenth Century Florida & the Revolutionary South. LC 77-23576. (Papers of the Annual Bicentennial Symposia: No. 4). 1978. 7.00 (ISBN 0-8130-0584-1). U Presses Fla.
Rea, Robert R. & Howard, Milo B., eds. The Minutes, Journals, & Acts of the General Assembly of British West Florida. LC 77-13273. 416p. 1979. 45.00x (ISBN 0-8173-5234-1). U of Ala Pr.
Rolle, Denys. The Humble Petition of Denys Rolle, Esq., Setting Forth the Hardships, Inconveniences, & Grievances Which Have Attended Him in His Attempts to Make a Settlement in East Florida, Humbly Praying Such. LC 77-5133. (Bicentennial Floridiana Facsimile Ser.). 1977. Repr. of 1765 ed. 6.50 (ISBN 0-8130-0417-9). U Presses Fla.
Solis De Meras, Gonzalo. Pedro Menendez de Aviles. McAlister, Lyle N., ed. Connor, Jeannette T., tr. LC 64-19155. (Floridiana Facsimile & Reprint Ser). 1964. Repr. of 1567 ed. 16.00 (ISBN 0-8130-0214-1). U Presses Fla.
Vignoles, Charles B. Observations Upon the Floridas. LC 76-39956. (Bicentennial Floridiana Facsimile & Reprint Ser.). 1977. Repr. of 1823 ed. 8.50 (ISBN 0-8130-0421-7). U Presses Fla.
White, David H. Vicente Folch, Governor in Spanish Florida, Seventeen Eighty-Seven to Eighteen Eleven. LC 80-5792. 120p. (Orig.). 1981. text ed. 17.25 (ISBN 0-8191-1598-3); pap. text ed. 7.50 (ISBN 0-8191-1599-1). U Pr of Amer.
Wright, J. Leitch. Florida in the American Revolution. LC 75-15923. (Illus.). 1975. 7.50 (ISBN 0-8130-0524-8). U Presses Fla.

FLORIDA–HISTORY–FICTION

Simms, W. Gilmore. Vasconselos: A Romance of the New World. LC 70-116016. Repr. of 1885 ed. 10.00 (ISBN 0-404-06037-4). AMS Pr.

FLORIDA–JUVENILE LITERATURE

Bailey, Bernadine. Picture Book of Florida. rev. ed. LC 68-4252. (Illus.). (gr. 3-5). 1980. 5.50g (ISBN 0-8075-9510-1). A Whitman.
Carpenter, Allan. Florida. LC 78-8108. (New Enchantment of America State Bks). (Illus.). (gr. 4 up). 1979. PLB 10.60 (ISBN 0-516-04109-6). Childrens.
Fichter, George S. Florida-in Pictures. LC 78-66310. (Visual Geography Ser.). (Illus.). (gr. 5 up). 1979. PLB 4.99 (ISBN 0-8069-1221-9); pap. 2.95 (ISBN 0-8069-1220-0). Sterling.
Fodor's Disney's Adventure Guide to Florida. (Fodor Travel Guides Ser.). 64p. (gr. 1-6). 1980. pap. 3.95 (ISBN 0-679-00575-7). McKay.

FLORIDA–POLITICS AND GOVERNMENT

Colburn, David R. & Sher, Richard K. Florida's Gubernatorial Politics in the Twentieth Century. LC 80-10277. (Illus.). viii, 342p. 1981. 19.95 (ISBN 0-8130-0644-9). U Presses Fla.
Dauer, Manning J., ed. Florida's Politics & Government. LC 80-20723. (Orig.). 1980. pap. 10.00x (ISBN 0-8130-0671-6). U Presses Fla.
Doherty, Herbert J., Jr. The Whigs of Florida, Eighteen Forty Five-Eighteen Fifty Four. LC 59-62570. (U of Fla. Social Sciences Monographs: No. 1). 1959. 2.95 (ISBN 0-8130-0064-5). U Presses Fla.
Flynt, Wayne. Cracker Messiah: Governer Sidney J. Catts of Florida. LC 76-57664. (Southern Biography Ser). (Illus.). 1977. 25.00x (ISBN 0-8071-0263-6). La State U Pr.
Gould Editorial Staff. Criminal Laws of Florida. (Annual). 1979. text ed. 8.50x (ISBN 0-87526-188-4). Gould.
Kelly, Anne E. Modern Florida Government. 395p. 1980. 24.95 (ISBN 0-686-29717-2); pap. 19.95 (ISBN 0-686-29718-0). MDA Pubns FL.
Klingman, Peter D. Josiah Walls: Florida's Black Congressman of Reconstruction. LC 75-45206. 1976. 7.50 (ISBN 0-8130-0399-7). U Presses Fla.
McBrayer, J. T. Examination of Florida Titles. 1958. with 1971 suppl 35.00 (ISBN 0-87215-100-X); 1971 supplement 7.50 (ISBN 0-87215-288-X). Michie-Bobbs.
Marando, Vincent L. & Thomas, Robert D. The Forgotten Governments: County Commissioners As Policy Makers. LC 77-839. (Illus.). 1977. 8.50 (ISBN 0-8130-0569-8). U Presses Fla.
Pelham, Thomas G. State Land-Use Planning & Regulation: Florida, the Model Code, & Beyond. LC 79-2390. (Lincoln Institute of Land Policy Books). 224p. 1979. 23.95 (ISBN 0-669-03062-7). Lexington Bks.
Pittman, Philip. The Present State of the European Settlements on the Mississippi: With a Geographical Description of That River. LC 73-2821. (Bicentennial Floridiana Facsimile & Reprint Ser.). (Illus.). 105p. 1973. Repr. of 1770 ed. 10.00 (ISBN 0-8130-0368-7). U Presses Fla.
TePaske, John J. Governorship of Spanish Florida, 1700-1763. LC 64-18659. 1964. 14.75 (ISBN 0-8223-0173-3). Duke.
Thompson, Arthur W. Jacksonian Democracy on the Florida Frontier. LC 61-63107. (U of Fla. Social Sciences Monographs Ser.: No. 9). 1961. pap. 3.50 (ISBN 0-8130-0225-7). U Presses Fla.
Tschirgi, Harvey D. Investigation of Performance Evaluation in Agencies of the Florida Merit System. LC 66-64091. (Florida State U. Studies: No. 47). 1966. 6.95 (ISBN 0-8130-0484-5). U Presses Fla.
Williamson, Edward C. Florida Politics in the Gilded Age, 1877-1893. LC 75-30634. 1976. 8.00 (ISBN 0-8130-0365-2). U Presses Fla.

FLORIDA–SOCIAL CONDITIONS

Bice, David A., et al. A Panorama of Florida. Armstrong, Alfredlene, ed. (Illus.). 320p. 1981. 15.95 (ISBN 0-934750-13-0); text ed. 14.99 (ISBN 0-934750-21-1); pap. 13.95 (ISBN 0-934750-14-9); tchrs. ed. 14.99 (ISBN 0-934750-27-0); wkbk. 3.99 (ISBN 0-934750-22-X); tchrs. wkbk. 4.25 (ISBN 0-934750-23-8). Jalamap.
Buxbaum, Edwin C. The Greek American Group of Tarpon Springs, Florida: A Study of Ethnic Identification & Acculturation. Cordasco, Francesco, ed. LC 80-843. (American Ethnic Groups Ser.). 1981. lib. bdg. 45.00x (ISBN 0-405-13407-X). Arno.
Dougherty, Molly C. Becoming a Woman in Rural Black Culture: Case Studies in Cultural Anthropology. LC 77-24218. 1978. pap. text ed. 4.95 (ISBN 0-03-014921-5, HoltC). HR&W.
Newton, V. M., Jr. Crusade for Democracy. 1961. 3.50 (ISBN 0-8138-0380-2). Iowa St U Pr.
Osterbind, Carter C. & O'Rand, Angela, eds. Older People in Florida: A Statistical Abstract for the Elderly. 265p. 1979. pap. 10.00 (ISBN 0-8130-0652-X). U Presses Fla.
Scott, Carroll L. Successful Retirement in Florida. rev. ed. (Illus.). Date not set. price not set (ISBN 0-915764-02-4); pap. price not set (ISBN 0-915764-01-6). SunRise Hse.

FLORIDA–SOCIAL LIFE AND CUSTOMS

Fradin, Dennis. Florida: In Words & Pictures. LC 80-16681. (Young People's Stories of Our States Ser.). (Illus.). 48p. (gr. 2-5). 1980. PLB 9.25 (ISBN 0-516-03909-1). Childrens.
Graham, Bob. Workdays: Finding Florida on the Job. Mahoney, Lawrence, ed. LC 78-4177. (Illus.). 1978. pap. 5.95 (ISBN 0-916224-34-1). Banyan Bks.
Miles, Guy, ed. Voices from the Countryside. LC 77-4404. (Illus.). 1977. 6.95 (ISBN 0-916224-13-9). Banyan Bks.
Proctor, Samuel, ed. Eighteenth-Century Florida: Life on the Frontier. LC 76-5852. (Papers on the Annual Bicentennial Symposia: No. 3). 1976. 7.00 (ISBN 0-8130-0523-X). U Presses Fla.

--Eighteenth-Century Florida: The Impact of the American Revolution. LC 78-1870. (Papers of the Annual Bicentennail Symposia: No. 5). 1978. 9.00 (ISBN 0-8130-0589-2). U Presses Fla.

FLORIDA KEYS

Airguide. Airguide Traveler: Bahamas, Florida, Florida Keys, & Sea Islands. (Illus.). 1980. pap. 11.00 (ISBN 0-911721-89-4). Aviation.

Stevenson, George B. Keyguide. (Illus.). 1970. pap. 3.50 (ISBN 0-916224-39-2). Banyan Bks.

Windhorn, Stan & Langley, Wright. Yesterday's Florida Keys. LC 74-7669. (Illus.). pap. 5.95 (ISBN 0-912458-93-3). E A Seemann.

FLORIDA STATE UNIVERSITY, TALLAHASSEE

Campbell, Doak S. University in Transition. LC 64-64161. (Florida State U. Studies: No. 40). 1964. 5.50 (ISBN 0-8130-0478-0). U Presses Fla.

Spielberger, Charles D., ed. Anxiety: Current Trends in Theory & Research, 2 vols. 1972. 30.50 ea. Vol. 1 (ISBN 0-12-657401-4). Vol. 2 (ISBN 0-12-657402-2). Acad Pr.

FLORIDA WAR, 1835-1842

see Indians of North America–Wars–1815-1895

FLORIO, JOHN, 1553-1625

Yates, Frances A. John Florio: The Life of an Italian in Shakespeare's England. 1967. lib. bdg. 18.00x (ISBN 0-374-98835-8). Octagon.

FLORISTS

Cavin, Bram. How to Run a Successful Florist & Plant Store. LC 77-627. (Small Business Ser.). 1977. pap. text ed. 5.95 (ISBN 0-471-04023-1). Wiley.

Educational Research Council of America. Florist. rev. ed. Ferris, Theodore N. & Marchak, John P., eds. (Real People at Work Ser: A). 1976. pap. text ed. 2.25 (ISBN 0-89247-004-6). Changing Times.

Mitchell, H. Retail Floral Shop Management. 1982. text ed. 16.95 (ISBN 0-8359-6676-3); instr's. manual free (ISBN 0-8359-6677-1). Reston.

Pfahl, Peter B. Retail Florist Business. 3rd ed. LC 76-50302. (Illus.). 1977. 16.65 (ISBN 0-8134-1898-4). Interstate.

Rudman, Jack. Florist. (Career Examination Ser.: C-1410). (Cloth bdg. avail. on request). pap. 6.00 (ISBN 0-8373-1410-0). Natl Learning.

Sullivan, Glenn H., et al. Management for Retail Florists: With Applications to Nurseries & Garden Centers. LC 80-15002. (Illus.). 1980. text ed. 22.95x (ISBN 0-7167-1196-6). W H Freeman.

FLORIT, EUGENIO, 1903

Pollin, Alice M., ed. Concordancias de la obra poetica de Eugenio Florit. LC 67-11072. (Spanish). 1967. 22.00x (ISBN 0-8147-0345-3). NYU Pr.

Servodidio, Mirella D. The Quest for Harmony: The Dialectics of Communication in the Poetry of Eugenio Florit. LC 78-66111. 1979. pap. 12.00 (ISBN 0-89295-008-0). Society Sp & Sp-Am.

FLOTATION

Flotation (A.M. Gaudin Memorial Volume) LC 76-19745. 1976. 35.00x (ISBN 0-89520-032-5). Soc Mining Eng.

Froth Flotation. 1962. 16.50x (ISBN 0-89520-029-5). Soc Mining Eng.

Glembotsky, V. A., et al. Flotation. LC 63-21692. (Illus.). 1963. 37.00x (ISBN 0-685-19584-8). Primary.

Leja, Jan. Surface Chemistry of Froth Flotation. 765p. 1981. text ed. 69.50 (ISBN 0-306-40588-1, Plenum Pr). Plenum Pub.

Plaksin, I. N., ed. Flotation Properties of Rare Metal Minerals. LC 67-16333. (Illus.). 1967. 8.75x (ISBN 0-685-19585-6). Primary.

Ranney, M. W., ed. Flotation Agents & Processes: Technology & Applications. LC 80-19191. (Chemical Tech. Rev. 172). (Illus.). 372p. 1981. 48.00 (ISBN 0-8155-0821-2). Noyes.

FLOUNDERS

see Flatfishes

FLOUR

see also Corn; Grain; Oats; Wheat

Shuey, W. C. The Farinograph Handbook. 80p. 1972. saddle stitched 15.00 (ISBN 0-913250-01-5). Am Assn Cereal Chem.

FLOUR AND FEED TRADE

American Feed Manufacturers Association. Feed Manufacturing Technology. Pfost, Harry, ed. 1976. 50.00 (ISBN 0-686-00374-8). AG Pr.

Fance, Wilfred J. The Student's Technology of Breadmaking & Flour Confectionery. (Illus.). 1969. Repr. of 1960 ed. 22.50 (ISBN 0-7100-1363-9). Routledge & Kegan.

Steen, Herman. Flour Milling in America. LC 73-9339. 455p. 1973. Repr. of 1963 ed. lib. bdg. 19.25x (ISBN 0-8371-7008-7, STFM). Greenwood.

FLOUR MILLS

Bennett, Richard & Elton, John. History of Corn Milling, 4 Vols. (Illus.). 1964. Repr. of 1904 ed. Set. 91.00 (ISBN 0-8337-0230-0). B Franklin.

Edgar, William C. The Story of a Grain of Wheat. 1979. Repr. of 1904 ed. lib. bdg. 20.00 (ISBN 0-8495-1332-4). Arden Lib.

Elmen, Paul. Wheat Flour Messiah: Eric Jansson of Bishop Hill. LC 76-28380. (Illus.). 239p. 1976. 7.95x (ISBN 0-8093-0787-1). S Ill U Pr.

An End to Pounding: A New Mechanical Flour Milling System in Use in Africa. 63p. 1980. pap. 5.00 (ISBN 0-88936-246-7, IDRC 152, IDRC). Unipub.

Evans, Oliver. The Young Mill-Wright & Miller's Guide. LC 72-5047. (Technology & Society Ser.). (Illus.). 438p. 1972. Repr. of 1850 ed. 24.00 (ISBN 0-405-04699-5). Arno.

Grist Mills. 1978. 1.50 (ISBN 0-911410-45-7). Applied Arts.

Kuhlman, Charles B. Development of the Flour Milling Industry in the United States. LC 68-56240. Repr. of 1929 ed. 17.50x (ISBN 0-678-00932-5). Kelley.

McGrain, John W. Grist Mills in Baltimore County, Maryland. (Baltimore County Heritage Publication). (Illus.). 40p. 1980. pap. 4.95 (ISBN 0-937076-00-7). Baltimore Co Pub Lib.

Magee, Henry. Miller in Eighteenth Century Virginia. (Williamsburg Craft Ser). (Illus., Orig.). 1958. pap. 1.25 (ISBN 0-910412-19-7). Williamsburg.

Moritz, L. A. Grain-Mills & Flour in Classical Antiquity. Finley, Moses, ed. LC 79-4994. (Ancient Economic History Ser.). (Illus.). 1980. Repr. of 1958 ed. lib. bdg. 21.00x (ISBN 0-405-12381-7). Arno.

Sherfey, Florence. Eastern Washington's Vanished Gristmills & the Men Who Ran Them. (Illus.). 1978. 14.95 (ISBN 0-87770-208-X). Ye Galleon.

Steen, Herman. Flour Milling in America. LC 73-9339. 455p. 1973. Repr. of 1963 ed. lib. bdg. 19.25x (ISBN 0-8371-7008-7, STFM). Greenwood.

FLOW, MULTIPHASE

see Multiphase Flow

FLOW, TWO-PHASE

see Two-Phase Flow

FLOW CHARTS

Arjani, K. A. Structured Programming Flowcharts. 1978. pap. text ed. 6.95 (ISBN 0-89669-000-8). Collegium Bk Pubs.

Bohl, Marilyn. Flowcharting Techniques. 208p. 1971. pap. text ed. 8.95 (ISBN 0-574-16096-5, 13-1440). SRA.

Boillot, Michel H., et al. Essentials of Flowcharting. 2nd ed. 125p. 1979. pap. text ed. write for info. (ISBN 0-697-08129-X). Wm C Brown.

Chapin, Ned. Flowcharts. LC 73-147199. (Auerbach Computer Science Ser.). 1971. pap. 8.00 (ISBN 0-442-80192-0). Van Nos Reinhold.

Edwards, Perry. Flowcharting & Fortran IV. (Illus.). 132p. 1973. pap. text ed. 7.95 (ISBN 0-07-019042-9, G). McGraw.

Edwards, Perry & Broadwell, Bruce. Flowcharting & BASIC. 140p. (Orig.). 1974. pap. text ed. 10.95 (ISBN 0-15-527661-1, HC). HarBraceJ.

Farina, Mario V. Flowcharting. 1970. pap. 10.95 ref. ed. (ISBN 0-13-322750-2). P-H.

Hecht, Matthew S. Flow Analysis of Computer Programs. (Programming Languages Ser.). 1977. 19.95 (ISBN 0-444-00210-3, North Holland). Elsevier.

McQuigg, James D. & Harness, Alta M. Flowcharting. (Modern Mathematics Ser). (Illus.). (gr. 7-12). 1970. pap. 3.21 (ISBN 0-395-03244-X, 2-37422). HM.

Merzkirch, W. Flow Visualization. 1974. 48.50 (ISBN 0-12-491350-4). Acad Pr.

Passen, Barry J. Programming Flowcharting for the Business Data Processing. LC 77-25509. 1978. pap. text ed. 17.95 (ISBN 0-471-01410-9). Wiley.

Schriber, Thomas J. Fundamentals of Flowcharting. LC 79-21692. 1980. Repr. of 1969 ed. lib. bdg. 12.00 (ISBN 0-89874-023-1). Krieger.

Silver, Gerald A. & Silver, J. Introduction to Programming: Programming Logic & Flowcharting. 1975. text ed. 9.60 (ISBN 0-07-057445-6, G); instructor's manual 3.25 (ISBN 0-07-057446-4). McGraw.

Stern, Nancy. Flowcharting: A Tool for Understanding Computer Logic. LC 75-11600. (Self Teaching Guides). 341p. 1975. text ed. 8.95 (ISBN 0-471-82331-7). Wiley.

Structured Analysis & System Specification. 1979. 26.95 (ISBN 0-13-854380-1). P-H.

Westerberg, A. W., et al. Process Flowsheeting. LC 78-51682. (Illus.). 1979. 29.50 (ISBN 0-521-22043-2). Cambridge U Pr.

FLOW DIAGRAMS

see Flow Charts

FLOW GRAPHS

see Flowgraphs

FLOW METERS

American Water Works Association. Water Meters: Selection, Installation, Testing, & Maintenance - M6. 2nd ed. (AWWA Manuals). (Illus.). 112p. 1973. pap. text ed. 8.00 (ISBN 0-89867-064-0). Am Water Wks Assn.

Dowden, R. Rosemary, ed. Fluid Flow Measurement Bibliography. 1972. microfiche 25.00 (ISBN 0-900983-21-3, Dist. by Air Science Co.). BHRA Fluid.

Hayward, Alan T. Flowmeters: A Basic Guide & Source-Book for Users. LC 79-15530. 197p. 1979. 27.95x (ISBN 0-470-26732-1). Halsted Pr.

Instrument Society of America Symposium, 1st, Pittsburgh. Flow - Its Measurement & Control in Science & Industry: Proceedings, 2 pts, Vol. 1, 3 Pts. new ed. Incl. Pt. 1. Flow Characteristics, Joint ASME Fluids Engineering Conference (ISBN 0-87664-228-8); Pt. 2. Flow Measuring Devices (ISBN 0-87664-229-6); Pt. 3. Flow Measurements & Control, Biological Fluid Flows (ISBN 0-87664-230-X). LC 74-77995. 1974. 40.00 ea.. Instru Soc.

PTC 19,5-1972 Application, Part Two of Fluid Meters: Interim Supplement on Instruments & Apparatus. 1972. pap. text ed. 14.00 (ISBN 0-685-30666-6, G00018). ASME.

FLOW OF GAS

see Gas Flow

FLOW OF WATER

see Hydraulics

FLOW PROCESS CHARTS

see Flow Charts

FLOWCHARTS

see Flow Charts

FLOWER, WILLIAM HENRY, SIR, 1831-1899

Lydekker, R. Sir William Flower. Repr. of 1906 ed. 12.00 (ISBN 0-527-58860-1). Kraus Repr.

FLOWER ARRANGEMENT

see also Driftwood Arrangement; Pressed Flower Pictures

Aaronson, Marian. The Art of Flower Arranging. LC 77-579465. (Illus.). 1979. 12.50 (ISBN 0-89955-217-X, Pub. by Grower Books England). Intl Schol Bk Serv.

--Design with Plant Material. (Illus.). 1979. 12.50 (ISBN 0-89955-216-1, Pub. by Grower Books England). Intl Schol Bk Serv.

Adams, Mary. Natural Flower Arranging. (Illus.). 120p. 1981. 22.50 (ISBN 0-7134-2677-2, Pub. by Batsford England). David & Charles.

Ascher, Amalie A. The Complete Flower Arranger. (Illus.). 1974. 15.95 (ISBN 0-671-21666-X); pap. 7.95 (ISBN 0-671-22774-2). S&S.

--The Complete Flower Arranger. 1977. pap. 6.95 (ISBN 0-671-22774-2, Fireside). S&S.

Benz, M. Flowers: Abstract Form II. LC 78-65678. (Illus.). 1979. 47.50 (ISBN 0-911982-11-6). San Jacinto.

Bode, Frances. New Structures in Flower Arrangement. (Illus.). 1968. 5.95 (ISBN 0-8208-0050-3). Hearthside.

Brandenburger, Nelda H. Interpretive Flower Arrangements: How to Express Yourself with Plant Materials, Including Designs to Fit Holiday Occasions, Themes, Moods & Seasons. (Illus.). 1969. 6.95 (ISBN 0-8208-0059-7). Hearthside.

Byrne, Betty. Fell's Beginner's Guide to Flower Arrangement. LC 75-583. 641p. 1976. pap. 4.95 (ISBN 0-8119-0363-X). Fell.

Clark, Virginia. Wedding Flowers, Decorations, & Etiquette. 1970. 8.95 (ISBN 0-8208-0054-6). Hearthside.

Clements, Julia. ABC of Flower Arranging. LC 76-4132. (Illus.). 1976. 6.95 (ISBN 0-8129-0635-7). Times Bks.

--Julia Clement's Flower Arrangements. 1976. pap. 4.50 (ISBN 0-7134-3246-2, Pub. by Batsford England). David & Charles.

--Treasury of Rose Arrangements & Recipes. LC 59-7987. 1959. 3.50 (ISBN 0-8208-0012-0). Hearthside.

Cox, Helen. The Floral Art Book of Reference. LC 70-91462. 1970. text ed. 16.50 (ISBN 0-08-007100-7). Pergamon.

Cutler, Katherine. Flower Arranging for All Occasions. rev. ed. LC 80-2850. (Illus.). 224p. 1981. 12.95 (ISBN 0-385-18508-1). Doubleday.

Cyphers, Emma. New Book of Foliage Arrangements. rev. ed. LC 64-21085. (Illus.). 1965. 4.95 (ISBN 0-8208-0018-X). Hearthside.

Decorations from Dried Flowers & Grasses. 1976. pap. 1.50 (ISBN 0-8277-5705-0). British Bk Ctr.

Designing with Flowers. 1.95 (ISBN 0-686-21172-3). Bklyn Botanic.

Dobson, Eileen. New Zealand Ways with Flowers. 84p. 1980. pap. 4.50 (ISBN 0-85467-012-2, Pub. by Viking Sevenseas New Zealand). Intl Schol Bk Serv.

Dried Flower Designs. 1.95 (ISBN 0-686-21168-5). Bklyn Botanic.

Faurot, Albert. Arranging Tropical Flowers. (Illus.). 1979. pap. 10.75x (ISBN 0-686-25215-2, Pub. by New Day Pub). Cellar.

Feasey, Peggy G. Rubies & Roses: Gems Portrayed in Flowers. LC 72-83077. (Illus.). 1972. Repr. 13.75 (ISBN 0-8048-0507-5). C E Tuttle.

Firth, C. H. An American Garland. 59.95 (ISBN 0-87968-601-4). Gordon Pr.

Flower Arrangement. (Illus.). 60p. 1980. pap. 4.50 (ISBN 0-89955-103-3, Pub. by Shufunotomo Japan). Intl Schol Bk Serv.

Flowers of Dalarna, Swedish Floral Art. (Illus.). 1975. spiral bdg. 4.95 (ISBN 0-9603700-1-3). H E Blanck.

Franklin, Howard. A Flowers Arrangers Guide to Showing. 1979. 14.95 (ISBN 0-7134-3321-3). David & Charles.

Goldson, Rae L. New Trends in Flower Arrangement. (Illus.). 1966. 4.95 (ISBN 0-8208-0052-X). Hearthside.

Groome, Sarah C. Today's Flower Arranging Without Tears. LC 78-67256. (Illus.). 88p. 1978. 8.95 (ISBN 0-8059-2594-5). Dorrance.

Guertner, Beryl. Australian Book of Flower Arrangements. (Illus.). 12.50x (ISBN 0-392-06790-0, ABC). Sportshelf.

Haraszty, Eszter. Living with Flowers. (Illus.). 1980. 16.95 (ISBN 0-87140-641-1). Liveright.

Herrigel, Gustie L. Zen in the Art of Flower Arrangement: An Introduction to the Spirit of the Japanese Art of Flower Arrangement. 1974. 10.00 (ISBN 0-7100-7941-9); pap. 6.00 (ISBN 0-7100-7942-7). Routledge & Kegan.

Hillier, Florence B. Basic Guide to Flower Arranging. (Illus.). 296p. 1974. 16.95 (ISBN 0-07-028907-7, P&RB). McGraw.

Hirsch, Sylvia. Art of Table Setting & Flower Arrangement. rev. ed. (Illus.). 1967. 9.95 (ISBN 0-690-10325-5). T Y Crowell.

Inman, Nancy A. Tropical Flower Arranging: A Practical Guide. LC 72-88931. 1972. 8.25 (ISBN 0-8048-1093-1). C E Tuttle.

Ishimoto, Tatsuo. The Art of Driftwood & Dried Arrangements. (Illus.). 144p. 1951. 4.50 (ISBN 0-517-02565-5). Crown.

Kohler, Julilly H. Plants & Flowers to Decorate Your Home. (Illus.). 1977. 12.95 (ISBN 0-307-49335-0, Golden Pr); pap. 5.95 (ISBN 0-307-49254-0). Western Pub.

Larmie, W. Flower Arranging: Basics to Advanced Design. 1980. 15.95 (ISBN 0-13-322438-4). P-H.

Lewis, Frank. Flower Arrangements. 16.00 (ISBN 0-87245-181-X). Textile Bk.

Love, Diane. Flowers Are Fabulous. 112p. 1975. pap. 7.50 (ISBN 0-02-011770-1, Collier). Macmillan.

--Flowers Are Fabulous: For Decorating. (Illus.). 144p. 1975. 19.95 (ISBN 0-02-575560-9). Macmillan.

McDaniel, G. Floral Design & Arrangement. 250p. 1981. text ed. 16.95 (ISBN 0-8359-2072-0); instr's. manual free (ISBN 0-8359-2073-9). Reston.

McQueen, Sheila. Complete Flower Arranging. 248p. 1980. 15.95 (ISBN 0-8129-0866-X). Times Bks.

--Flower Arranging from Your Garden. LC 77-2468. (Illus.). 1977. 10.95 (ISBN 0-8019-6628-0); pap. 6.95 (ISBN 0-8019-6629-9). Chilton.

MacQueen, Sheila. Your Book of Flower Arranging. 1972. 5.95 (ISBN 0-571-09625-5, Pub. by Faber & Faber). Merrimack Bk Serv.

Moir, May. Flower Sculpture: A Handbook. 1977. pap. 2.95 (ISBN 0-914916-25-4). Topgallant.

Morin, Madeleine. L' Art floral dans votre maison. new ed. (Collection "Flore"). (Illus.). 139p. (Fr.). 1974. 11.50x (ISBN 2-03-074703-3). Larousse.

Otis, Denise & Maia, Ronaldo. Decorating with Flowers. (Illus.). 1978. 45.00 (ISBN 0-8109-0808-5). Abrams.

Page, Phyllis. The Handbook for Flower Arrangers. (Color Ser.). (Illus.). 1965. 9.95 (ISBN 0-7137-0765-8, Pub by Blandford Pr England). Sterling.

Pautz, Phyllis. Decorating with Plant Crafts & Natural Material. LC 70-150912. 1971. 9.95 (ISBN 0-385-08327-0). Doubleday.

Pfahl, Peter & Kalin, Elwood. American Style Flower Arranging. (Illus.). 256p. 1982. 22.95 (ISBN 0-13-029538-8). P-H.

Rosen, Pauline. Bottle Beauty, Guide to Arranging with Bottles. (Illus.). 1968. pap. 3.25 (ISBN 0-9600214-0-X). P Rosen.

Seguy, E. A. Exotic Floral Patterns in Color. (Illus.). 8.75 (ISBN 0-8446-5082-X). Peter Smith.

Shinno, Tat. Flower Arranging by Tat. 1961. 14.50 (ISBN 0-911478-01-9). Tats.

Smith, George. Flower Arranging in House & Garden. 96p. 15.95 (ISBN 0-7207-0958-X, Pub. by Michael Joseph). Merrimack Bk Serv.

Smith, James E. Flower Arranging: A Manual. 1972. 5.50 (ISBN 0-87543-106-2). Lucas.

Smith, Mina. Arranging Flowers. 12.50x (ISBN 0-392-07373-0, LTB). Sportshelf.

Svinicki, Eunice. Flowercraft. (Step-by-Step Crafts Ser.). (Illus.). 1977. (Golden Pr); pap. 1.95 (ISBN 0-307-42020-5). Western Pub.
Taylor, Jean. The Craft of Flower Arrangement. 1976. 9.95 (ISBN 0-09-126770-6, Pub. by Hutchinson); pap. 5.95 (ISBN 0-09-126771-4). Merrimack Bk Serv.
--Creative Flower Arrangement. 1973. 9.95 (ISBN 0-09-113630-X, Pub. by Hutchinson); pap. 5.95 (ISBN 0-09-113631-8). Merrimack Bk Serv.
Thompson, Dorothea. Creative Decorations with Dried Flowers. rev. ed. (Illus.). 160p. 1972. 7.95 (ISBN 0-8208-0033-3). Hearthside.
Tozer, Zibby. The Art of Flower Arranging. (Orig.). 1981. pap. 7.95 (ISBN 0-446-97760-8). Warner Bks.
Webb, Iris, ed. The Complete Guide to Flower & Foliage Arrangement. (Illus.). 256p. 1979. 19.95 (ISBN 0-385-15119-5). Doubleday.
Wheeler, Esther & Lasker, Anabel C. Flowers & Plants for Interior Decoration. 1969. 10.00 (ISBN 0-8208-0065-1). Hearthside.

FLOWER ARRANGEMENT, JAPANESE

Allen, Ellen G. Japanese Flower Arrangement: A Complete Primer. rev. ed. LC 62-21731. (Illus.). 1963. Repr. 8.25 (ISBN 0-8048-0293-9). C E Tuttle.
--Japanese Flower Arrangement in a Nutshell. (Illus., Orig.). pap. 4.50 (ISBN 0-8048-0295-5). C E Tuttle.
Bunnett, Kay. Ikebana Collection: Studies in Sogetsu Ikebana. 67p. 1979. 12.95 (ISBN 0-442-25021-5). Van Nos Reinhold.
Chandler, Billie T. Crafts & Trades of Japan, with Doll & Flower Arrangements. LC 64-24952. (Illus.). 1964. brocade bdg. 5.00 (ISBN 0-8048-0128-2). C E Tuttle.
Creating Japanese Floral Art. Date not set. price not set. Rio Grande.
Davidson, Georgie. Ikebana Simplified. LC 69-12144. (Illus.). 1969. 3.95 (ISBN 0-498-07363-7). A S Barnes.
Flowers & Otherwise. 1979. 2.00 (ISBN 0-932632-02-5). MJG Co.
Fujiwara, Yuchiku. Rikka: The Soul of Japanese Flower Arrangement. Sparnon, Norman, tr. from Japanese. (Illus.). 1976. 22.50 (ISBN 0-8048-1329-9, Pub. by Shufunotomo Co Ltd Japan). C E Tuttle.
Hihara, Koho, et al. Ikebana in Quick & Easy Series. (Illus., Orig.). 1978. pap. 3.95 (ISBN 0-8048-1335-3, Pub. by Shufunotomo Co Ltd Japan). C E Tuttle.
Komoda, Shusul & Pointer, Horst. Ikebana: Spirit & Technique. (Illus.). 224p. 1980. 16.95 (ISBN 0-7137-1040-3, Pub. by Blandford Pr England). Sterling.
Kong, Im W. Oriental Flower Arrangement. (Illus., Eng. & Japanese.). 1979. 9.95 (ISBN 0-8048-1330-2, Pub. by Shufunotomo Co Ltd Japan). C E Tuttle.
Massy, Patricia, ed. & pref. by. The Essentials of Ikebana. (Illus.). 1978. 9.95 (ISBN 0-8048-1326-4, Pub. by Shufunotomo Co Ltd Japan). C E Tuttle.
Mittwer, Henry. Art of Chabana: Flowers for the Tea Ceremony. LC 73-93226. (Illus.). 1973. 12.00 (ISBN 0-8048-1111-3). C E Tuttle.
Neese, Martha & Neese, Marvin. Fun with Flowers. LC 68-27867. (Illus.). 72p. 1980. pap. 8.95 (ISBN 0-8348-0152-3). Weatherhill.
Ohi, Minobu, et al. Flower Arrangement: The Ikebana Way. Steere, William C., ed. & pref. by. (Illus.). 1962. 19.50 (ISBN 0-8048-1325-6, Pub. by Shufunotomo Co Ltd Japan). C E Tuttle.
Reeves, Gearldine. Creating Japanese Floral Art. 96p. Date not set. 8.95 (ISBN 0-89496-033-4); pap. 5.95 (ISBN 0-89496-032-6). Ross Bks.
Sparnon, Norman. A Guide to Japanese Flower Arrangement. (Illus.). 80p. 1969. 8.95 (ISBN 0-8048-1327-2, Pub. by Shufunmoto Co Ltd Japan). C E Tuttle.
Swerda, Patricia. Creating Japanese Shoka. (Illus.). 140p. 1980. pap. 9.50 (ISBN 0-89955-120-3, Pub. by Shufunotomo Japan). Intl Schol Bk Serv.
Teshigahara, Kasumi. Kasumi's Ikebana for All Seasons. (Illus.). 1975. 12.50 (ISBN 0-8048-1328-0, Pub. by Shufunotomo Co Ltd Japan). C E Tuttle.
Teshigahara, Wafu. Ikebana: A New Illustrated Guide to Mastery. LC 80-82782. (Illus.). 159p. 1981. 12.95 (ISBN 0-87011-438-7). Kodansha.
Thomas, Diane. Elegant Silk Ikebana. LC 79-89181. (Illus., Orig.). 1979. pap. 5.95 (ISBN 0-918126-08-8). Hunter Ariz.
--More Silk Ikebana: Fashionable Japanese Silk Flowers Requiring No Sizing. LC 77-77602. 1977. pap. 1.50 (ISBN 0-918126-05-3). Hunter Ariz.
--Silk Ikebana: The Making & Arranging of Japanese Silk Flowers. LC 76-49368. 24p. 1976. pap. 1.50 (ISBN 0-918126-04-5). Hunter Ariz.
Trivedi, Devika. Ikebana. (Illus.). 1976. text ed. 15.00 (ISBN 0-7069-0375-7, Pub. by Vikas India). Advent NY.
Whitaker, Caroline B. The Bride's Book of Flower Arrangement. LC 74-83392. (Illus.). 1974. 15.00 (ISBN 0-8048-1143-1). C E Tuttle.

FLOWER ARRANGEMENT IN CHURCHES

Clements, Julia. Flowers in Praise: Church Flower Arrangements & Festivals. LC 79-57312. (Illus.). 96p. 1980. 24.00 (ISBN 0-7134-3328-0, Pub. by Batsford England). David & Charles.
Moffitt, Oleta S. Arranging Flowers for the Church. rev. ed. 1977. pap. 1.25 (ISBN 0-8006-1837-8, 1-1837). Fortress.
Tolle, Leon J., Jr. Floral Arts for Religious Events. LC 68-20196. (Illus.). 1969. 8.95 (ISBN 0-8208-0062-7). Hearthside.

FLOWER DRAWING

see Flower Painting and Illustration

FLOWER GARDENING

see also Floriculture; Wild Flower Gardening

Adams, William D. Southern Flower Gardening. LC 79-29715. (Illus.). 96p. 1980. pap. 3.95 (ISBN 0-88415-291-X). Pacesetter Pr.
Askwith, Herbert. The Complete Guide to Garden Flowers. (Illus.). 15.00 (ISBN 0-498-09591-6, Encore). A S Barnes.
The Complete Family Flower & Garden Book. (Illus.). 520p. 1981. 8.95 (ISBN 0-686-31186-8, 2541). Playmore & Prestige.
Cooper, W. E. ABC of Flower Growing. (Illus.). 7.50 (ISBN 0-392-06742-0, LTB). Sportshelf.
Crockett, James U. Annuals. (Encyclopedia of Gardening Ser). (Illus.). 1971. 11.95 (ISBN 0-8094-1081-8). Time-Life.
--Crockett's Flower Garden. 1981. 24.95 (ISBN 0-316-16132-2); pap. 14.95 (ISBN 0-316-16133-0). Little.
Crook, H. Clifford. Campanulas. LC 76-46559. (Illus.). 1977. Repr. of 1951 ed. 12.50 (ISBN 0-913728-18-7). Theophrastus.
Crooks, Michael. Growing Flowers. (Practical Gardening Ser.). (Illus.). 112p. (Orig.). 1979. pap. 10.50 (ISBN 0-589-01241-X, Pub. by Reed Bks Australia). C E Tuttle.
Darnell, A. W. Unfamiliar Flowers for Your Garden. LC 75-13001. (Illus.). 1975. pap. 2.75 (ISBN 0-486-23213-1). Dover.
Dawson, Oliver. Herbaceous Border. (Illus.). 144p. 1973. 4.95 (ISBN 0-7153-6211-9). David & Charles.
Genders, Roy. Growing Old-Fashioned Flowers. LC 75-24649. (Illus.). 244p. 1976. 8.95 (ISBN 0-498-01843-1). A S Barnes.
Haraszty, Eszter. Living with Flowers. (Illus.). 1980. 16.95 (ISBN 0-87140-641-1). Liveright.
Hathaway, Polly. Backyard Flowers. (Illus.). (gr. 3 up). 1965. 4.95g (ISBN 0-02-708960-6). Macmillan.
Kramer, Jack. The Old-Fashioned Cutting Garden: Growing Flowers for Pleasure & Profit. (Illus.). 1979. 8.95 (ISBN 0-02-566620-7). Macmillan.
McDonald, Elvin. How to Grow Flowers from Seeds. 1979. pap. 5.95 (ISBN 0-442-80594-2). Van Nos Reinhold.
Pettingill, Amos. The White-Flower-Farm Garden Book. 1977. pap. 6.95 (ISBN 0-316-70400-8). Little.
Shewell-Cooper, W. E. The Compost Flower Grower. 200p. 1975. 12.95 (ISBN 0-7207-0797-8, Pub. by Michael Joseph). Merrimack Bk Serv.
Smith, Bridget A. & Harris, Betty. Color in Rain Country: Growing Flowers in Southeastern Alaska. Ross, John, ed. (Illus.). 64p. 1981. pap. text ed. 11.95 (ISBN 0-939620-00-6). Firsthand.
Thompson, H. C. & Bonnie, Fred. Growing Flowers. LC 74-18642. (Family Guidebooks Ser.). (Illus.). 1975. pap. 1.95 (ISBN 0-8487-0371-5). Oxmoor Hse.
Watts, Leslie. Flower & Vegetable Plant Breeding. (Orig.). 1980. pap. 22.50 (ISBN 0-901361-35-6, Pub. by Grower Bks England). Intl Schol Bk Serv.
Wright, Richardson. The Gardener's Bed Book. Repr. of 1929 ed. 20.00 (ISBN 0-686-20654-1). Lib Serv Inc.

FLOWER LANGUAGE

see also Symbolism of Flowers

Roberts, Victoria S. A Pleasure of Flowers. LC 76-47181. (Illus., Orig.). 1977. pap. 5.95 (ISBN 0-89407-001-0). Strawberry Hill.

FLOWER PAINTING AND ILLUSTRATION

see also Flowers in Art

Anderson, Dennis R. American Flower Painting. (Illus.). 84p. 1980. text ed. 25.00 (ISBN 0-8230-0211-X). Watson-Guptill.
Asker, Randi. Rose Painting in Norway. 2 nd, rev ed. (Illus.). 1971. pap. 14.00x (ISBN 82-09-00382-8, N390). Vanous.
Battershill, Norman. Painting Flowers in Oils. (The Leisure Arts Painting Ser.). 1981. pap. 2.50 (ISBN 0-8008-6196-5, Pentalic). Taplinger.
Blamey, Marjorie & Blamey, Philip. Marjorie Blamey's Flowers of the Countryside. LC 80-81982. (Illus.). 224p. 1980. 25.00 (ISBN 0-688-03685-6). Morrow.
Bohlin, William H. Modern Approach: Flower Painting. 4.47 (ISBN 0-685-57668-X); pap. 1.00 (ISBN 0-685-57669-8). Borden.
Bohlin, William L. Flower Painting. 1967. treasure trove bdg. 4.97 (ISBN 0-685-07318-1); pap. 1.00 (ISBN 0-685-07319-X). Borden.
Campana, D. M. Teacher of Flower & Fruit Painting. (Illus.). 5.95 (ISBN 0-939608-03-0). Campana Art.
Coleridge, Sarah. Painting Flowers in Watercolour. (The Leisure Arts Painting Ser.). 1981. pap. 2.50 (ISBN 0-8008-6197-3, Pentalic). Taplinger.
Dorf, Barbara. Introduction to Still Life & Flower Painting. (Illus.). 184p. 1976. 15.95 (ISBN 0-7207-0885-0). Transatlantic.
Duffield, William. The Art of Flower Painting. (The Library of the Arts). (Illus.). 1977. 37.50 (ISBN 0-89266-070-8). Am Classical Coll Pr.
Goulden, Dorothy. The Illustrated Book of Flowers: A Collection of the Greatest Paintings of Flowers by the Greatest Artists. (Illus.). 1980. deluxe ed. 195.00 (ISBN 0-930582-54-3). Gloucester Art.
Jameson, Kenneth. Flower Painting for Beginners. LC 79-84663. (Start to Paint Ser.). (Illus.). 1979. pap. 3.95 (ISBN 0-8008-2808-9, Pentalic). Taplinger.
Perard, Victor. Drawing Flowers. (Grosset Art Instruction Ser.: Vol. 12). pap. 2.95 (ISBN 0-448-00521-2). G&D.
Reid, Charles. Flower Painting in Oil. (Illus.). 168p. 1976. 19.50 (ISBN 0-8230-1848-2). Watson-Guptill.
--Flower Painting in Watercolor. (Illus.). 1979. 19.50 (ISBN 0-8230-1849-0). Watson-Guptill.
Ryskamp, Charles, pref. by. Flowers in Books & Drawings, Nine Forty to Eighteen Forty. LC 80-83208. (Illus.). 84p. 1980. pap. 6.95 (ISBN 0-87598-072-4). Pierpont Morgan.
Schofield, Heather. Flower Painting Techniques. LC 78-70709. (Art Craft Ser.). (Illus.). 1979. 12.95 (ISBN 0-88332-106-8, 8148). Larousse.
Sibbett, Ed, Jr. Floral Cut & Use Stencils: 54 Full-Size Stencils Printed on Durable Stencil Paper. LC 78-67294. (Cut & Use Stencil Ser.). (Illus.). 1979. pap. 3.00 (ISBN 0-486-23742-7). Dover.
Sweerts, Emmanuel. Early Floral Engravings. Bleiler, E. F., ed. LC 73-76963. (Illus.). 256p. 1976. pap. 6.95 (ISBN 0-486-23038-4). Dover.

FLOWER PRINTS

see Flowers in Art

FLOWER SHOWS

Franklin, Howard. A Flowers Arrangers Guide to Showing. 1979. 14.95 (ISBN 0-7134-3321-3). David & Charles.

FLOWERING OF PLANTS

see Plants, Flowering Of

FLOWERING PLANTS

see Angiosperms

FLOWERING TREES

Donkin, R. A. Manna: An Historical Geography. (Biogeographica Ser.: No. 17). (Illus.). vii, 160p. 1980. lib. bdg. 47.50 (ISBN 90-6193-218-1, Pub. by Junk Pubs Netherlands). Kluwer Boston.
Flowering Trees. 1.95 (ISBN 0-686-21136-7). Bklyn Botanic.
Lancaster, Roy. Arbres, ornements de nos jardins. (Collection "Flore"). (Illus.). 145p. (Fr.). 1974. 11.50x (ISBN 2-03-074704-1). Larousse.
Menninger, Edwin A. Color in the Sky: Flowering Trees in Our Landscape. 260p. 1975. 14.95 (ISBN 0-9600046-3-7). Horticultural.
--Flowering Trees of the World: From Tropics & Warm Climates. 18.95 (ISBN 0-8208-0039-2). Hearthside.
Randhawa, M. S. Flowering Trees. (India - Land & People Ser). (Illus.). 1965. 4.50x (ISBN 0-8426-1483-4). Verry.
Whitehead, Stanley B. The Observer's Book of Flowering Trees & Shrubs for Your Garden. (The Observer Bks). (Illus.). 1979. 3.95 (ISBN 0-684-16029-3, ScribT). Scribner.

FLOWERS

see also Annuals (Plants); Botany; Cookery (Flowers); Everlasting Flowers; Fertilization of Plants; Floriculture; Flower Arrangement; Flower Gardening; Plants; Plants, Flowering of; State Flowers; Wild Flowers; Window-Gardening; also names of flowers, e.g. Carnations, Roses, Violets

Anderson, E. B., et al. The Oxford Book of Garden Flowers. (Illus.). 1963. 29.95 (ISBN 0-19-910002-0). Oxford U Pr.
Anderson, Frank J. Cultivated Flowers. LC 79-64989. (Abbeville Library of Art Ser.). (Illus.). 112p. (Orig.). 1981. pap. 4.95 (ISBN 0-89659-182-4). Abbeville Pr.
Arnberger, Leslie P. Flowers of the Southwest Mountains. 5th ed. Jackson, Earl, ed. LC 74-84444. (Popular Ser.: No. 7). 1974. pap. 2.50 (ISBN 0-911408-00-2). SW Pks Mnmts.
Askwith, Herbert. The Complete Guide to Garden Flowers. (Illus.). 15.00 (ISBN 0-498-09591-6, Encore). A S Barnes.
Baker, K. Wild Flowers of Western Australia. (Illus.). 1973. 6.00 (ISBN 0-912728-45-0). Newbury Bks.
Beek, M. & Foster, D. Wild Flowers of South Australia. (Illus.). 1973. 6.00 (ISBN 0-912728-46-9). Newbury Bks.
Budden, Henry. Bulbous Flowers. (Illus.). 104p. 1980. 15.95x (ISBN 0-19-558055-9). Oxford U Pr.
Burda, ed. Flower of the Month. (Burda Bks.). Date not set. 5.95 (ISBN 0-686-64663-0, B804). Toggitt.
--Sampler of the Month. (Burda Bks.). Date not set. 5.95x (ISBN 0-686-64664-9, B805). Toggitt.
Carr, Samuel, ed. Poetry of Flowers. LC 77-26728. 1977. 7.50 (ISBN 0-8008-6393-3). Taplinger.
Chickering, Carol R. Flowers of Guatemala. LC 72-9278. (Illus.). 180p. 1973. 16.50 (ISBN 0-8061-1081-3); pap. 8.95 (ISBN 0-8061-1368-5). U of Okla Pr.
Clark, Phil. A Flower Lover's Guide to Mexico. 128p. 1978. pap. 4.00 (ISBN 0-912434-06-6). Ocelot Pr.
Clements, E. S. Flowers of Coast & Sierra. 1959. 13.75 (ISBN 0-02-842940-0). Hafner.
Coats, Alice M. Flowers & Their Histories. 1971. 12.50 (ISBN 0-07-011476-5, GB). McGraw.
Compton, Joan. Enjoy Your Flowers. 9.75 (ISBN 0-392-02805-0, LTB). Sportshelf.
Darnell, A. W. Unfamiliar Flowers for Your Garden. (Illus.). 5.50 (ISBN 0-8446-5176-1). Peter Smith.
Davis, P. H. & Cullen, J. The Identification of Flowering Plant Families. LC 78-8125. (Illus.). 1979. 21.50 (ISBN 0-521-22111-0); pap. 5.95x (ISBN 0-521-29359-6). Cambridge U Pr.
Dean, Blanche, et al. Wildflowers of Alabama & Adjoining States. LC 73-10585. (Illus.). 224p. 1973. 12.95 (ISBN 0-8173-1200-5). U of Ala Pr.
Dutton, Joan P. The Flower World of Williamsburg. rev. ed. LC 62-18751. (Illus.). 131p. (Orig.). 1973. pap. 4.00 (ISBN 0-87935-007-5). Williamsburg.
Eichler, A. W. Bluethendiagramme, 2 vols. (Illus.). 1954. 82.50 (ISBN 3-87429-003-4). Lubrecht & Cramer.
Erdtman, G. World Pollen Flora, 4 vols. Incl. Vol. 1. Coriariaceae. 1970. pap.; Vol. 2. Gyrostemonaceae. Prijanto, B. 1970. pap.; Vol. 3. Batidacene. Prijanto, B. 1970. pap.; Vol. 4. Globularioceae. Praglowski, J. & Gyllander, K. 1971. pap.. (Illus.). Set. pap. 39.95 (ISBN 0-02-844210-5). Hafner.
Erickson, Rica, et al. Flowers & Plants of Western Australia. rev. ed. 232p. 1979. 39.95 (ISBN 0-589-50116-X, Pub. by Reed Books Australia). C E Tuttle.
Father. The Language of Flowers. 1976. 5.00 (ISBN 0-517-52555-0, Harmony). Crown.
Faust, Joan L. The New York Times Book of Annuals & Perennials. (Illus.). 1980. 12.50 (ISBN 0-8129-0857-0). Times Bks.
Fish, Margery. Cottage Garden Flowers. 208p. 1980. pap. 7.95 (ISBN 0-571-11463-6, Pub. by Faber& Faber). Merrimack Bk Serv.
Flexner, James T. First Flowers of Our Wilderness. LC 68-8811. 1969. lib. bdg. 13.50 (ISBN 0-88307-094-4). Gannon.
Flora: Enciclopedia Salvat De la Jardineria, 12 vols. 3600p. (Espn.). 1977. Set. 336.00 (ISBN 84-345-3786-9, S-50537). French & Eur.
Fogg, H. G. History of Popular Garden Plants from A to Z. LC 76-44555. (Illus.). 1977. 8.95 (ISBN 0-498-02044-4). A S Barnes.
Friend, Hilderic. The Flowers & Their Story. LC 78-175751. (Illus.). 300p. 1972. Repr. of 1907 ed. 22.00 (ISBN 0-8103-3868-8). Gale.
Hargreaves, Dorothy & Hargreaves, Bob. Hawaii Blossoms. LC 58-46974. (Illus.). 1958. pap. 3.00 (ISBN 0-910690-01-4). Hargreaves.
--Tropical Blossoms of the Caribbean. LC 60-15513. (Illus.). 1960. pap. 3.00 (ISBN 0-910690-03-0). Hargreaves.
Hay, Roy & Synge, Patrick M. The Color Dictionary of Flowers & Plants for Home & Garden. (Illus.). 373p. 1969. 15.00 (ISBN 0-517-50670-X); compact ed. 14.95 (ISBN 0-517-52458-9); pap. 6.95 (ISBN 0-517-52456-2). Crown.
Heiser, Charles B. The Sunflower. LC 74-15906. 1976. 10.95 (ISBN 0-8061-1229-8). U of Okla Pr.
Hultman, G. Eric. Trees, Shrubs & Flowers of the Midwest. LC 77-91186. 1978. o. p. 9.95 (ISBN 0-8092-7693-3); pap. 5.95 (ISBN 0-8092-7692-5). Contemp Bks.
Hutcheson, Gladys. The Flower Book. 96p. 1980. 19.75x (ISBN 0-7050-0071-0, Pub. by Skilton & Shaw England). State Mutual Bk.
Huxley, Anthony & Taylor, William. Flowers of Greece & the Aegean. (Illus.). 1977. 24.00 (ISBN 0-7011-2190-4). Transatlantic.
Kelland, Rufus A. The Illustrated Book in Full Colors of Pansies, Violas & Violets. (Illus.). 117p. 1981. 195.00 (ISBN 0-86650-013-8). Gloucester Art.
McMillan, Mary L. & Jones, Ruth D. Beautiful North Carolina & the World of Flowers. LC 79-91037. (Illus.). 1979. 9.95 (ISBN 0-87716-110-0, Pub. by Moore Pub Co). F Apple.

Mohlenbrock, Robert H. Flowering Plants: Flowering Rush to Rushes. LC 69-16117. (Illustrated Flora of Illinois Ser.). (Illus.). 286p. 1970. 22.95x (ISBN 0-8093-0407-4). S Ill U Pr.
Percival, M. Floral Biology. 1965. 10.50 (ISBN 0-08-010610-2); pap. 7.00 (ISBN 0-08-010609-9). Pergamon.
Perrero, Laurie. World of Tropical Flowers. LC 76-12926. (Illus.). 64p. (Orig.). 1976. pap. 2.75 (ISBN 0-89317-008-9). Windward Pub.
Perry, Frances, ed. Simon & Schuster's Complete Guide to Plants & Flowers. (Illus.). 1976. 17.95 (ISBN 0-671-22246-5); pap. 9.95 (ISBN 0-671-22247-3). S&S.
Pizetti, I. & Cocker, H. Flowers: A Guide for Your Garden, 2 vols. (Illus.). 24.95 set (ISBN 0-517-22044-X). Bonanza.
Polunin, Oleg. The Concise Flowers of Europe. (Illus.). 1972. pap. 8.95x (ISBN 0-19-217630-7). Oxford U Pr.
--Flowers of Greece & the Balkans: A Field Guide. 474p. 1980. 125.00x (ISBN 0-19-217626-9). Oxford U Pr.
Polunin, Oleg & Huxley, Anthony. Flowers of the Mediterranean. LC 79-670242. (Illus.). 260p. 1979. 15.95 (ISBN 0-7011-1029-5, Pub. by Chatto Bodley Jonathan); pap. 9.95 (ISBN 0-7011-2284-6). Merrimack Bk Serv.
Proudley, Brian & Proudley, Valerie. Garden Flowers in Color. (Illus.). 1979. 12.95 (ISBN 0-7137-0911-1, Pub. by Blandford Pr England). Sterling.
Pycraft, David. Observer's Book of Garden Flowers. (Observer Bks.). (Illus.). 1977. 2.95 (ISBN 0-684-15219-3, ScribT). Scribner.
Quality in Cut Flowers. 1981. 12.00x (ISBN 0-686-75424-7, Pub. by Grower Bks). State Mutual Bk.
Reader's Digest Association, London. Encyclopaedia of Garden Plants & Flowers. (Illus.). 1977. 22.50 (ISBN 0-393-08780-8). Norton.
Sattler, Rolf. Organogenesis of Flowers: Photographic Text-Atlas. LC 73-185736. (Illus.). 1973. 37.50x (ISBN 0-8020-1864-5). U of Toronto Pr.
Shinners, Lloyd H. Shinners' Spring Flora of the Dallas-Ft. Worth Area. 2nd rev. ed. Mahler, William F., ed. Orig. Title: Spring Flora of the Dallas-Ft. Worth Area. (Illus.). 1972. pap. 8.50x (ISBN 0-934786-01-1). G Davis.
Smith, L. D. Flowers from Foreign Fields. PLB 59.95 (ISBN 0-8490-0175-7). Gordon Pr.
Sprengel, Christian K. Das Entdectke Geheimnis der Natur Im Bau & der Befruchtung der Blumen. 1973. Repr. of 1793 ed. 50.00 (ISBN 3-7682-0828-1). Lubrecht & Cramer.
Stocken, C. M. Andalusian Flowers & Countryside. pap. 6.95 (ISBN 0-8283-1326-1). Branden.
Summer Flowers for Continuing Bloom. 1.95 (ISBN 0-686-21150-2). Bklyn Botanic.
Taylor, J. Lee. Growing Plants Indoors. LC 76-56951. 1977. pap. 9.95x (ISBN 0-8087-2057-0). Burgess.
Thomas, Barry. Evolution of Plants & Flowers. (Illus.). 120p. 1981. 13.95 (ISBN 0-312-27271-5). St Martin.
Vanishing Flowers Map. pap. 2.50 (ISBN 0-8277-4942-2). British Bk Ctr.
Vilmorin, Roger de. L' Encyclopedie Des Fleurs et Des Jardins, 3 vols. 2000p. (Fr.). 1975. Set. 95.00 (ISBN 0-686-57140-1, M-6197). French & Eur.
Walker, Mary Lu. Mary Lu Walker's Dandelions. 1975. pap. 5.95 (ISBN 0-8091-1882-3); record 6.98 (ISBN 0-8091-7585-1). Paulist Pr.
Watts, Phoebe. Redwood Region Flower Finder. (Illus.). 1979. pap. 1.50 (ISBN 0-912550-08-2). Nature Study.
White, Helen A. & Williams, Maxcine, eds. The Alaska-Yukon Wild Flowers Guide. LC 74-79085. (Illus.). 218p. 1974. pap. 10.95 (ISBN 0-88240-032-0). Alaska Northwest.
Whitlock, Sarah & Rankin, Martha. Dried Flowers: How to Prepare Them. LC 75-17126. 1975. lib. bdg. 8.50x (ISBN 0-88307-598-9). Gannon.
Wilder, Louise B. The Fragrant Garden: A Book About Sweet Scented Flowers & Leaves. 6.00 (ISBN 0-8446-5099-4). Peter Smith.
Wills, Mary M. & Irwin, Howard S. Roadside Flowers of Texas. (Spencer Foundation Ser.: No. 1). 309p. 1961. pap. 5.95 (ISBN 0-292-77009-X). U of Tex Pr.
Withering, William. An Account of the Foxglove & Some of Its Uses. LC 77-6995. 1977. Repr. of 1785 ed. lib. bdg. 30.00 (ISBN 0-89341-146-9). Longwood Pr.

FLOWERS (IN RELIGION, FOLK-LORE, ETC.)

Brush, Bill. Flowers & Plants. LC 12-2710. (A Nice Place to Live Ser.). 1978. pap. 1.95 (ISBN 0-570-07751-6, 12-2710). Concordia.
Flower Lore: The Teachings of Flowers Historical, Legendary, Poetical & Symbolic. LC 79-179690. 1972. Repr. of 1879 ed. 29.00 (ISBN 0-8103-3865-3). Gale.
Friend, Hilderic. Flower Lore. (Illus.). 704p. 1981. pap. 10.95 (ISBN 0-914918-32-X). Para Res.
Heline, Corinne. Magic Gardens. 5th ed. 122p. 1980. pap. 5.95 (ISBN 0-87516-433-1). De Vorss.
Nash, Elizabeth T. One Hundred & One Legends of Flowers. 1977. lib. bdg. 59.95 (ISBN 0-8490-2375-0). Gordon Pr.
Stephenson, Fairfax. Out of the Mouths of Flowers: A Garden Talks with God. LC 78-62585. (Illus.). 1978. 5.00 (ISBN 0-931490-03-0). Gotuit Ent.

FLOWERS-ARRANGEMENT

see Flower Arrangement

FLOWERS-COLLECTION AND PRESERVATION

Cramblit, Joella & Loebel, JoAnn. Flowers Are for Keeping: How to Dry Flowers & Make Gifts & Decorations. LC 79-12892. (Illus.). 128p. (gr. 5 up). 1979. PLB 8.29 (ISBN 0-671-33007-1). Messner.
Crater, Don R. The Dried Guide. LC 81-52464. (Illus.). 64p. (Orig.). 1981. pap. 7.95 (ISBN 0-940654-01-6). Tribune Pub.
Eaton, Marge. Flower Pressing. LC 72-13340. (Early Craft Bks). (Illus.). 36p. (gr. 1-4). 1973. PLB 3.95 (ISBN 0-8225-0855-9). Lerner Pubns.
Flesher, Irene. The Pressed Flower Picture Book. Speiser, W., ed. LC 77-92605. (Illus.). 1978. pap. 7.95 (ISBN 0-8329-0206-3). New Century.
Foster, Laura L. Keeping the Plants You Pick. LC 74-101926. (Illus.). (gr. 4-8). 1970. 8.50 (ISBN 0-690-47140-8, TYC-J). Har-Row.
Foster, Maureen. Preserved Flowers: Practical Methods & Creative Uses. (Illus.). 199p. 1974. 9.75 (ISBN 0-7207-0536-3). Transatlantic.
Karel, Leonard. Dried Flowers from Antiquity to the Present: A History & Practical Guide to Flower Drying. LC 72-10909. 1973. 10.00 (ISBN 0-8108-0512-X). Scarecrow.
Lutz, Earnest L., Sr. How to Embed Flowers in Plastic. (Illus.). (gr. 4 up). 1971. 6.95 (ISBN 0-87961-001-8); pap. 2.95 (ISBN 0-87961-000-X). Naturegraph.
McNamara, Carol. Bloom Succession Calendar. 3.50 (ISBN 0-686-08735-6). HHH Horticult.
Mierhof, Annette. The Dried Flower Book: Growing, Picking, Drying Arranging. (Illus.). 96p. 1981. 26.00 (ISBN 0-525-09573-X); pap. 13.50 (ISBN 0-525-47700-4). Dutton.
Morrison, Winifrede. Drying & Preserving Flowers. 1973. 17.95 (ISBN 0-7134-2324-2, Pub. by Batsford England). David & Charles.
Svinicki, Eunice. Flowercraft. (Step-by-Step Crafts Ser.). (Illus.). 1977. (Golden Pr); pap. 1.95 (ISBN 0-307-42020-5). Western Pub.
Terry, Henry. A Victorian Flower Album. 1981. 35.00 (ISBN 0-7139-1145-X). State Mutual Bk.
Whitlock, Sarah & Rankin, Martha. Dried Flowers: How to Prepare Them. LC 75-17126. 32p. 1975. pap. 1.00 (ISBN 0-486-21802-3). Dover.

FLOWERS-DRYING

see Flowers-Collection and Preservation

FLOWERS-JUVENILE LITERATURE

Billington, Elizabeth T. Adventure with Flowers. LC 66-15814. (Illus.). (gr. 5 up). 1966. 6.95 (ISBN 0-7232-6021-4). Warne.
Daly, Kathleen N. A Child's Book of Flowers. LC 74-16146. 48p. (gr. k-4). 1976. 6.95a (ISBN 0-385-09748-4); PLB (ISBN 0-385-09750-6). Doubleday.
Dowden, Ann O. Look at a Flower. LC 63-12650. (Illus.). (gr. 5 up). 1963. 10.95 (ISBN 0-690-50656-2, TYC-J). Har-Row.
Dowden, Anne O. State Flowers. LC 78-51927. (Illus.). (gr. 5 up). 1978. 8.95 (ISBN 0-690-01339-6, TYC-J); PLB 9.89 (ISBN 0-690-03884-4). Har-Row.
Greenaway, Kate. The Language of Flowers. LC 77-74518. (Illus.). (gr. 1 up). 1977. 5.95 (ISBN 0-7232-2006-9). Warne.
Hutchins, Ross E. This Is a Flower. LC 63-9539. (Illus.). (gr. 5 up). 1963. 5.95 (ISBN 0-396-07181-3). Dodd.
Kirkpatrick, Rena K. Look at Flowers. LC 77-27433. (Look at Science Ser.). (Illus.). (gr. k-3). 1978. PLB 11.15 (ISBN 0-8393-0061-1). Raintree Child.
Lerner, Sharon. I Picked a Flower. LC 67-15699. (Nature Bks for Young Readers). (Illus.). (gr. k-5). 1967. PLB 4.95 (ISBN 0-8225-0261-5). Lerner Pubns.
Little, Brown Editors, ed. Flowers: East Coast Edition. (Explorer's Notebooks). (Illus.). 32p. (Orig.). (gr. 5 up). 1981. pap. 1.95 (ISBN 0-316-52773-4). Little.
--Flowers: West Coast Edition. (Explorer's Notebooks). (Illus.). 32p. (Orig.). (gr. 5 up). 1981. pap. 1.95 (ISBN 0-316-52774-2). Little.
Munari, Bruno. A Flower with Love. LC 74-2095. (Illus.). (gr. 2-6). 1974. PLB 7.89 (ISBN 0-690-00571-7, TYC-J). Har-Row.
Overbeck, Cynthia. Sunflowers. LC 80-27797. (Lerner Natural Science Bks.). (Illus.). (gr. 4-10). 1981. PLB 7.95 (ISBN 0-8225-1457-5). Lerner Pubns.
Rendell, Joan. Your Book of Pressed & Dried Flowers. 64p. (gr. 4 up). 1979. 6.95 (ISBN 0-571-11249-8, Pub. by Faber Faber). Merrimack Bk Serv.
Selsam, Millicent E. & Hunt, Joyce. A First Look at Flowers. LC 76-57063. (First Look at Ser.). (Illus.). (gr. k-3). 1977. PLB 6.85 (ISBN 0-8027-6282-4). Walker & Co.
Tsuchida, Yoshiharu. The Flowers in My Garden. (Fun Time Ser.). (Illus.). 22p. (ps-1). 1981. 2.95 (ISBN 0-89346-195-4). Heian Intl.
Welch, Martha M. Sunflower! LC 80-1008. (Illus.). 64p. (gr. 2-5). 1980. PLB 6.95 (ISBN 0-396-07885-0). Dodd.

FLOWERS-MARKETING

see also Florists

Goodrich, Dana C., Jr. Floral Marketing. LC 80-26287. 1980. 19.95 (ISBN 0-912016-77-9). Lebhar Friedman.
Mitchell, H. Retail Floral Shop Management. 1982. text ed. 16.95 (ISBN 0-8359-6676-3); instr's. manual free (ISBN 0-8359-6677-1). Reston.

FLOWERS-PICTORIAL WORKS

Anderson, Frank J. Abbeville Library of Art Floral Collection: 4 Gatefolds per Volume; Complete Horticultural Instructions. Benjamin, Phyllis, ed. (Illus.). 112p. 1981. pap. 14.85 set (ISBN 0-89659-187-5); pap. 4.95 ea. Abbeville Pr.
Blamey, Marjorie & Blamey, Philip. Marjorie Blamey's Flowers of the Countryside. LC 80-81982. (Illus.). 224p. 1980. 25.00 (ISBN 0-688-03685-6). Morrow.
Della Valle, George. The New, Fully Illustrated Book in Vibrant Colors of the Most Dramatic Flowers in the Universe. (Illus.). 107p. 1982. 49.75 (ISBN 0-89266-322-7). Am Classical Coll Pr.
DeWolf, Gordon. Flora Exotica. LC 72-190443. (Illus.). 1978. pap. 5.95 (ISBN 0-87923-257-9). Godine.
Flesher, Irene. The Pressed Flower Picture Book. Speiser, W., ed. LC 77-92605. (Illus.). 1978. pap. 7.95 (ISBN 0-8329-0206-3). New Century.
Greenaway, Kate, illus. The Illuminated Language of Flowers. LC 78-4697. (Illus.). 1978. 8.95 (ISBN 0-03-044196-X). HR&W.
Hargreaves, Dorothy & Hargreaves, Bob. African Blossoms. LC 72-85425. (Illus.). 64p. 1972. pap. 3.00 (ISBN 0-910690-06-5). Hargreaves.
--Tropical Blossoms of the Pacific. LC 72-113701. (Illus.). 1970. pap. 3.00 (ISBN 0-910690-08-1). Hargreaves.
Penn, Irving. Flowers. (Illus.). 96p. 1980. 35.00 (ISBN 0-517-54074-6, Harmony). Crown.
Rogers, Walter E. Tree Flowers of Forest, Park & Street. (Illus.). 8.00 (ISBN 0-8446-2824-7). Peter Smith.
Sanders, Rosanne. The Remembering Garden. (Clarkson N. Potter Bks.). (Illus.). 1980. 17.95 (ISBN 0-517-54169-6). Potter.

FLOWERS, ARTIFICIAL

see Artificial Flowers

FLOWERS, EVERLASTING

see Everlasting Flowers

FLOWERS, FORCING OF

see Forcing (Plants)

FLOWERS, PAINTING OF

see Flower Painting and Illustration

FLOWERS, PROTECTION OF

see Plants, Protection Of

FLOWERS, STATE

see State Flowers

FLOWERS, SYMBOLISM OF

see Symbolism of Flowers

FLOWERS, WILD

see Wild Flowers

FLOWERS IN ART

see also Design, Decorative-Plant Forms; Flower Painting and Illustration;
also names of specific flowers in art, e.g. Roses in Art

Benz, Morris. Flowers: Geometric Form. rev., 5th ed. LC 80-50568. (Illus.). 336p. 1980. 42.50 (ISBN 0-911982-12-4). San Jacinto.
Chwast, Seymour & Chewning, Emily. The Illustrated Flower. (Illus.). 1977. (Harmony); pap. 6.95 (ISBN 0-517-52913-0). Crown.
Gos, Francois & Baldausky, Karen. Alpine Flower Designs for Artists & Craftsmen. (Illus.). 64p. (Orig.). 1980. pap. 4.00 (ISBN 0-486-23982-9). Dover.
Grace, Princess & Robyns, Gwen. My Book of Flowers. LC 78-68361. (Illus.). 224p. 1980. 24.95 (ISBN 0-385-14076-2). Doubleday.
Greenaway, Kate. Language of Flowers, with Value Guide. LC 66-29515. 1966. 3.50 (ISBN 0-87282-072-6). Century Hse.
Ryskamp, Charles, pref. by. Flowers in Books & Drawings, Nine Forty to Eighteen Forty. LC 80-83208. (Illus.). 84p. 1980. pap. 6.95 (ISBN 0-87598-072-4). Pierpont Morgan.

FLOWERS IN LITERATURE

see also Plant Lore; Roses in Literature

Beisly, Sidney. Shakspere's Garden. LC 79-113551. Repr. of 1864 ed. 17.00 (ISBN 0-404-00727-9). AMS Pr.
Campbell, F. Flowers of Literature: Lord Byron, Coleridge, Burns, Shelley. 1826. Repr. 40.00 (ISBN 0-8274-2351-9). R West.
Colony, Horatio, ed. Flower Myth. 3.75 (ISBN 0-8283-1278-8). Branden.
Crane, Walter. Flowers from Shakespeare's Garden: A Posy from the Plays. (Illus.). 48p. 1980. 9.95 (ISBN 0-02-528650-1). Macmillan.
Koran, Dennis, ed. Panjandrum V: An Anthology of Poetry. (Panjandrum Poetry Journal: No. 5). (Illus.). 1977. pap. 4.00 (ISBN 0-915572-15-X). Panjandrum.
Singleton, Esther. Shakespeare Garden. LC 75-176028. (Illus.). Repr. of 1933 ed. 15.00 (ISBN 0-404-06096-X). AMS Pr.

FLOWERS IN POETRY

see Flowers in Literature

FLOWGRAPHS

Ackers, P., et al. Weirs & Fumes for Flow Measurement. 327p. 1978. 68.25 (ISBN 0-471-99637-8, Pub. by Wiley-Interscience). Wiley.
Busacker, Robert G. & Saaty, T. Finite Graphs & Networks: An Introduction with Applications. (International Pure & Applied Mathematics Ser). 1965. text ed. 18.95 (ISBN 0-07-009305-9, C). McGraw.
Furman, William B. Continuous Flow Analysis: Theory & Practice. (Clinical & Biochemical Analysis Ser.: Vol. 3). 1976. 34.75 (ISBN 0-8247-6320-3). Dekker.
Hecht, Matthew S. Flow Analysis of Computer Programs. (Programming Languages Ser.). 1977. 19.95 (ISBN 0-444-00210-3, North Holland). Elsevier.

FLOWMETERS

see Flow Meters

FLOWOFF

see Runoff

FLOYD COUNTY, GEORGIA

Battey, George M., Jr. History of Rome & Floyd County, Georgia. LC 74-76719. 1969. Repr. of 1922 ed. cloth over bds 25.00 (ISBN 0-87797-003-3); buckram over bds 25.00 (ISBN 0-87797-004-1). Cherokee.

FLU

see Influenza

FLUDD, ROBERT, 1574-1637

Yates, Frances A. Theatre of the World. LC 70-76533. 1969. 11.50x (ISBN 0-226-95004-2). U of Chicago Pr.

FLUID AMPLIFIERS

Brock, T. E., ed. Fluidics Applications Bibliography. 1968. text ed. 24.00 (ISBN 0-900983-00-0, Dist. by Air Science Co.). BHRA Fluid.
Fluidics Quarterly, Vol. 1. (Illus.). 1968-69. 85.00 (ISBN 0-88232-001-7). Delbridge Pub Co.
Fluidics Quarterly, Vol. 2. (Illus.). 1970. 125.00 (ISBN 0-88232-006-8). Delbridge Pub Co.
Fluidics Quarterly, Vol. 3. (Illus.). 1971. 100.00 (ISBN 0-88232-012-2). Delbridge Pub Co.
Fluidics Quarterly, Vol. 9. (Illus.). 1977. 115.00 (ISBN 0-88232-042-4). Delbridge Pub Co.
Humphrey, E. F. & Tarumoto, D. H., eds. Fluidics: A Comprehensive Examination. rev ed. 1968. 28.00 (ISBN 0-88232-000-9). Delbridge Pub Co.
Kirshner, Joseph M. Fluid Amplifiers. 1966. 31.50 (ISBN 0-07-034861-8, P&RB). McGraw.

FLUID AMPLIFIERS-DIRECTORIES

Dummer, Geoffrey W. & Robertson, J. M., eds. Fluidic Components & Equipment, 1968-69. 1969. 105.00 (ISBN 0-08-013446-7). Pergamon.

FLUID BED PROCESSES

see Fluidization

FLUID DYNAMICS

see also Aerodynamics; Boundary Layer; Fluid Amplifiers; Fluid Film Bearings; Fluidization; Gas Dynamics; Hydrodynamics; Ion Flow Dynamics; Laminar Flow; Magnetohydrodynamics; Mass Transfer; Mixing; Molecular Acoustics; Multiphase Flow; Relativistic Fluid Dynamics; Shock Waves; Wakes (Fluid Dynamics); Viscous Flow

AGARD-NATO. Fluid Dynamic Aspects of Space Flight, 2 vols. (Agardographs Ser.: No. 87). 1966. Vol. 1. 93.00x (ISBN 0-677-11560-1); Vol. 2. 74.25x (ISBN 0-677-11570-9); Set. 167.25x (ISBN 0-677-11440-0). Gordon.
American Mathematical Society. Space Mathematics, 3 vols. Rosser, J. B., ed. Incl. Pt.1. (Vol. 5). 1979. 35.20 (ISBN 0-8218-1105-3, LAM-5); Pt. 2. (Vol. 6). 1974. Repr. of 1966 ed. 28.00 (ISBN 0-8218-1106-1, LAM-6); Pt. 3. (Vol. 7). 1966. 29.60 (ISBN 0-8218-1107-X, LAM-7). LC 66-20435. (Lectures in Applied Mathematics Ser). Am Math.
Bain, D. Heavy Current Fluidics. (CISM, International Centre for Mechanical Sciences: Vol. 45). (Illus.). 82p. 1975. pap. 10.00 (ISBN 0-387-81148-6). Springer-Verlag.
Batchelor, George K. Introduction to Fluid Dynamics. (Illus.). 634p. 1967. 71.50 (ISBN 0-521-04118-X); pap. 19.95x (ISBN 0-521-09817-3). Cambridge U Pr.

Beam, R. M., et al. Computational Fluid Dynamics. Keller, Herbert B., ed. LC 78-9700. 1978. 23.60 (ISBN 0-8218-1331-5, SIAM-11). Am Math.
Beck, A., et al. Continuous Flows in the Plane. LC 73-11952. (Grundlehren der Mathematischen Wissenschaften Ser.: Vol. 201). (Illus.). 480p. 1974. 59.40 (ISBN 0-387-06157-6). Springer-Verlag.
Belsterling, Charles A. Fluidic Systems Design. LC 80-12189. 248p. 1981. Repr. of 1971 ed. lib. bdg. write for info. (ISBN 0-89874-169-6). Krieger.
Benedict, Robert P. Fundamentals of Temperature, Pressure, & Flow Measurements. 2nd ed. LC 76-54341. 517p. 1977. 41.00 (ISBN 0-471-06561-7, Pub. by Wiley-Interscience). Wiley.
Bird, R. Byron, et al. Transport Phenomena. LC 60-11717. 780p. 1960. 33.95 (ISBN 0-471-07392-X). Wiley.
Birkhoff, Garrett. Hydrodynamics: A Study in Logic, Fact, & Similitude. LC 77-18143. (Illus.). 1978. Repr. of 1960 ed. lib. bdg. 19.75x (ISBN 0-313-20118-8, BIHY). Greenwood.
Blevins, Robert D. Flow-Induced Vibration. LC 76-56249. 1977. text ed. 19.95x (ISBN 0-442-20828-6). Van Nos Reinhold.
Bock, D. L., ed. Finite-Difference Techniques for Vectorized Fluid Dynamics Calculations. (Springer Ser. Computational Physics). (Illus.). 240p. 1981. 32.00 (ISBN 0-387-10482-8). Springer-Verlag.
Brebbia, C. A. & Connor, J. J. Numerical Methods in Fluid Dynamics. LC 74-83628. 1974. 42.50x (ISBN 0-8448-0524-6). Crane-Russak Co.
Cabannes, H., et al, eds. Sixth International Conference on Numerical Methods in Fluid Dynamics: Proceedings of the Conference, Held in Tbilisi (USSR) June 21-24, 1978. (Lecture Notes in Physics: Vol. 90). 1979. pap. 28.40 (ISBN 0-387-09115-7). Springer-Verlag.
Chao, K. C. & Greenkorn, R. A. Thermodynamics of Fluids: An Introduction to Equilibrium Theory. (Chemical Processing & Engineering Ser.: Vol. 4). 1975. 37.50 (ISBN 0-8247-6258-4). Dekker.
Cheremisinoff, Nicholas. Applied Fluid Flow Measurement. (Engineering Measurement & Instumentation: Vol. 1). 1979. 26.75 (ISBN 0-8247-6871-X). Dekker.
Chung, T. J. Finite Element Analysis in Fluid Dynamics. 1978. text ed. 38.00 (ISBN 0-07-010830-7, C). McGraw.
Collier, J. G. Convective Boiling & Condensation. 2nd ed. (Illus.). 460p. 1981. text ed. 59.50 (ISBN 0-07-011798-5). McGraw.
Corcoran, William H., et al. Momentum Transfer in Fluids. 1956. 47.00 (ISBN 0-12-188050-8). Acad Pr.
Cramer, Kenneth R. & Pai, Shi I. Magnetofluid Dynamics for Engineer & Applied Physicists. (Illus.). 360p. 1973. text ed. 21.00 (ISBN 0-07-013425-1, C). McGraw.
Cranfield Fluidics Conference, 1st. Proceedings. 1965. 24.00 (ISBN 0-686-71058-4). BHRA Fluid.
Cranfield Fluidics Conference, 6th. Proceedings. 1974. 45.00 (ISBN 0-686-71057-6). BHRA Fluid.
Cranfield Fluidics Conference, 7th. Proceedings. 1977. 58.00 (ISBN 0-900983-50-7). BHRA Fluid.
Daily, J. W. & Harleman, D. R. Fluid Dynamics. 1966. 18.95 (ISBN 0-201-01421-1). A-W.
Darby, Ronald. Viscoelastic Fluids: An Introduction to Properties & Behavior. (Chemical Processing & Engineering Ser.: Vol. 9). 1976. 65.00 (ISBN 0-8247-6412-9). Dekker.
Davies, J. T. Turbulence Phenomena: An Introduction to the Eddy Transfer of Momentum, Mass & Heat, Particularly at Interfaces. 1972. 58.50 (ISBN 0-12-206070-9). Acad Pr.
Dragos, L. Magneto-Fluid Dynamics. Hammel, John, ed. Zoita, Vasile, tr. (Illus.). 478p. 1976. 47.00x (ISBN 0-85626-016-9, Pub. by Abacus Pr). Intl Schol Bk Serv.
Drzewiecki, T. M. & Franke, M. E., eds. Twentieth Anniversary of Fluidics Symposium. 225p. 1980. 30.00 (ISBN 0-686-69863-0, G00177). ASME.
Emrich, Raymond J., ed. Fluid Dynamics: Part A. (Methods of Experimental Physics Ser.). 448p. 1981. 50.00 (ISBN 0-12-475960-2). Acad Pr.
Fein, Jay S. Boundary Layers in Homogeneous & Stratified-Rotating Fluids: Notes on Lectures by Allan R. Robinson & Victor Barcilon. LC 78-400. (Florida State University Book Ser.). (Illus.). 1978. 15.25 (ISBN 0-8130-0601-5, 1S-00044, Pub. by U Presses Fla.). Univ Microfilms.
Fifth Intl. Conference on Numerical Methods in Fluid Dynamics. Proceedings. Van De Vooren, A. I. & Zandbergen, P. J., eds. (Lecture Notes in Physics Ser.: Vol. 59). 1976. soft cover 19.40 (ISBN 0-387-08004-X). Springer-Verlag.
Fluidics Quarterly, Vol. 4. (Illus.). 1972. 100.00 (ISBN 0-88232-017-3). Delbridge Pub Co.
Fluidics Quarterly, Vol. 8. (Illus.). 1976. 100.00 (ISBN 0-88232-037-8). Delbridge Pub Co.
Fluidics Quarterly, Vol. 11. (Illus.). 1979. 115.00 (ISBN 0-88232-052-1). Delbridge Pub Co.
Fluidics Quarterly: The Journal of Fluid Control, Vol. 12. (Illus.). 1980. 122.00 (ISBN 0-88232-057-2). Delbridge Pub.
Friedrichs, K. O. Special Topics in Fluid Dynamics. (Notes on Mathematics & Its Applications Ser.). 1966. pap. 19.75x (ISBN 0-677-01005-2). Gordon.
Goldstein, Sydney, ed. Modern Developments in Fluid Dynamics, 2 Vols. (Illus.). 1938. pap. text ed. 5.50 ea.; Vol. 1. pap. text ed. (ISBN 0-486-61357-7); Vol. 2. pap. text ed. (ISBN 0-486-61358-5). Dover.
Greenspan, H. P. The Theory of Rotating Fluids. (Cambridge Monographs on Mechanics & Applied Mathematics). (Illus.). 328p. 1980. pap. 17.95 (ISBN 0-521-29956-X). Cambridge U Pr.
Haugen, Edward B. Probabilistic Mechanical Design. LC 80-13428. 626p. 1980. 42.50 (ISBN 0-471-05847-5, Pub. by Wiley Interscience). Wiley.
Hewitt, B. L., et al, eds. Computational Methods & Problems in Aeronautical Fluid Dynamics. 1976. 105.00 (ISBN 0-12-346350-5). Acad Pr.
Holt, M. Numerical Methods in Fluid Dynamics. LC 76-43304. (Series in Computational Physics). (Illus.). 1977. 40.30 (ISBN 0-387-07907-6). Springer-Verlag.
Holt, Maurice, ed. Basic Developments in Fluid Dynamics, 2 Vols. Vol. 1. 1965. 63.00 (ISBN 0-12-354001-1); Vol. 2, 1968. 42.00 (ISBN 0-12-354002-X). Acad Pr.
Horlock, J. H. Actuator Disk Theory: Discontinuities in Thermo-Fluid Dynamics. (Illus.). 1979. 34.50 (ISBN 0-07-030360-6). McGraw.
Hughes, W. F. & Brighton, J. A. Fluid Dynamics. (Schaum's Outline Ser). (Orig.). 1967. pap. 6.95 (ISBN 0-07-031110-2, SP). McGraw.
Hunt, B., ed. Numerical Methods in Applied Fluid Dynamics. (Inst. of Mathematics & Its Applications Ser.). 1981. 64.00 (ISBN 0-686-72575-1). Acad Pr.
International Conference on Numerical Methods in Fluid Dynamics, 4th, University of Colorado, June 24-28, 1974. Meningiomas Diagnostic & Therapeutic Problems: Proceeding. Richtmyer, R. D., ed. (Lecture Notes in Physics Ser.: Vol. 35). (Illus.). vi, 457p. 1975. pap. 20.30 (ISBN 0-387-07139-3). Springer-Verlag.
International Symposium on Modern Developments in Fluid Dynamics. Proceedings. Rom, J., ed. LC 77-73178. (Illus.). 1977. text ed. 37.50 (ISBN 0-686-24255-6). Soc Indus-Appl Math.
Joseph, D. D. Global Stability of Fluid Motions II. (Tracts in Natural Philosophy: Vol. 28). 1976. 52.90 (ISBN 0-387-07516-X). Springer-Verlag.
--Stability of Fluid Motions 1. (Springer Tracts in Natural Philosophy: Vol. 27). 1976. 52.90 (ISBN 0-387-07514-3). Springer-Verlag.
Karamcheti, Krishnamurty. Principles of Ideal-Fluid Aerodynamics. LC 79-26876. 654p. 1980. Repr. of 1966 ed. lib. bdg. 32.50 (ISBN 0-89874-113-0). Krieger.
Knudsen, James G. & Katz, Donald L. Fluid Dynamics & Heat Transfer. LC 79-9748. 586p. 1979. Repr. lib. bdg. 29.50 (ISBN 0-88275-917-5). Krieger.
Kollmann, W., ed. Computational Fluid Dynamics, Vol. 1. LC 79-17485. 624p. 1980. text ed. 55.00 (ISBN 0-89116-171-6, Co-Pub. with McGraw Intl). Hemisphere Pub.
Kollmann, Wolfgang, ed. Computational Fluid Dynamics, Vol. 2. LC 79-17485. (Illus.). 265p. 1980. text ed. 40.00 (ISBN 0-89116-192-9). Hemisphere Pub.
Leyton, Leonard. Fluid Behaviour in Biological Sciences. (Illus.). 250p. 1975. 79.00x (ISBN 0-19-854126-0). Oxford U Pr.
Lighthill, J. Waves in Fluids. LC 77-8174. (Illus.). 1978. 56.50 (ISBN 0-521-21689-3); pap. 22.95x (ISBN 0-521-29233-6). Cambridge U Pr.
Lydersen, Aksel L. Fluid Flow & Heat Transfer. LC 78-18467. 1979. 59.25 (ISBN 0-471-99697-1); pap. 24.75 (ISBN 0-471-99696-3, Pub. by Wiley-Interscience). Wiley.
McCormack, P. D. & Crane, Lawrence. Physical Fluid Dynamics. 1973. 38.00 (ISBN 0-12-482250-9). Acad Pr.
Marle, Charles. Multiphase Flow in Porous Media. (Illus.). 304p. 1981. pap. 24.95x (ISBN 0-87201-569-6). Gulf Pub.
Marston, C. H., ed. Fluids Engineering in Advanced Energy Systems. 252p. 1978. 30.00 (ISBN 0-685-66800-2, H00122). ASME.
Merzkirch, Wolfgang, ed. Flow Visualization II. LC 81-6406. (Thermal & Fluids Engineering Ser.). (Illus.). 816p. 1981. 90.00 (ISBN 0-89116-232-1). Hemisphere Pub.
Norris, Hosmer, et al. Heat Transfer & Fluid Flow Data Books, 2 vols. (Illus.). 921p. 1981. 350.00 (ISBN 0-931690-02-1). GE Tech Marketing.
Nunge, Richard J. Flow Through Porous Media. LC 78-146798. 248p. 1970. 15.75 (ISBN 0-8412-0111-0). Am Chemical.
Oden, J. T., et al, eds. Finite Element Methods in Flow Problems. (Illus.). 1974. 20.00 (ISBN 0-933958-01-3). UAH Pr.
Research Conference of the National Science Foundation, Troy, New York, July 16-20, 1973 & Lighthill, James. Mathematical Brofluid Dynamics: Proceedings. (CBMS Regional Conference Ser.). (Illus.). 1975. text ed. 24.75 (ISBN 0-686-24247-5). Soc Indus-Appl Math.
Reynolds, W. C. & MacCormack, R. W., eds. Seventh International Conference on Numerical Methods in Fluid Dynamics. Proceedings. (Lecture Notes in Physics Ser.: Vol. 141). 485p. 1981. pap. 28.00 (ISBN 0-387-10694-4). Springer-Verlag.
Rhodes, E. & Scott, D. E., eds. Cocurrent Gas-Liquid Flow. LC 76-80084. 698p. 1969. 57.50 (ISBN 0-306-30404-X, Plenum Pr). Plenum Pub.
Richards, B., ed. Measurement of Unsteady Fluid Dynamic Phenomena. LC 76-11843. (Thermal & Fluids Engineering Series). (Illus.). 450p. 1977. text ed. 44.50 (ISBN 0-89116-012-4, Co-Pub. by McGraw Intl). Hemisphere Pub.
Roache, Patrick J. Computational Fluid Dynamics. rev. ed. 1976. 18.00 (ISBN 0-913478-05-9). Hermosa.
Robinson, Peter G. Marine Engineer's Guide to Fluid Flow. LC 75-25933. (Illus.). 1975. 5.00x (ISBN 0-87033-215-5). Cornell Maritime.
Roedder, Edwin, ed. Fluid Inclusion Research: Proceedings of COFFI, 1973, Vol. 6. 216p. 1973. pap. text ed. 10.00x (ISBN 0-472-02006-4). U of Mich Pr.
--Fluid Inclusion Research: Proceedings of COFFI, 1974, Vol. 7. 300p. 1976. pap. text ed. 10.00x (ISBN 0-472-02007-2). U of Mich Pr.
--Fluid Inclusion Research: Proceedings of COFFI, 1975, Vol. 8. 240p. 1978. pap. text ed. 10.00x (ISBN 0-472-02008-0). U of Mich Pr.
--Fluid Inclusion Research: Proceedings of COFFI, 1975, Vol. 9. 280p. 1978. pap. text ed. 10.00x (ISBN 0-472-02009-9). U of Mich Pr.
Rohsenow, Warren M. & Choi, H. Heat, Mass & Momentum Transfer. (Illus.). 1961. text ed. 27.95 (ISBN 0-13-385187-7). P-H.
Rothfus, Robert R. Working Concepts of Fluid Flow. (Illus.). 96p. (Orig.). pap. 3.75x (ISBN 0-685-23655-2). Bek Tech.
Sabersky, Rolf H., et al. Fluid Flow: First Course in Fluid Mechanics. 2nd ed. 1971. text ed. 25.95 (ISBN 0-02-404970-0). Macmillan.
Second IFAC Symposium on Fluidics. Fluidics Quarterly: Selected Papers, Vol. 3, Issue 4, Pt. 1. 1971. 26.00 (ISBN 0-88232-016-5). Delbridge Pub Co.
Second International Conference on Drag Reduction. Proceedings. pap. 60.00 (ISBN 0-900983-71-X, Dist. by Air Science Co.). BHRA Fluid.
Short Course Held at the Von Karman Institute for Fluid Dynamics, Rhode-St.-Genese, Belgium, Feb. 11-15, 1974. Progress in Numerical Fluid Dynamics. Wirz, H. J., ed. (Lecture Notes in Physics: Vol. 41). 480p. 1975. pap. 21.80 (ISBN 0-387-07408-2). Springer-Verlag.
Sorensen, T. Smith, ed. Dynamics & Instability of Fluid Interfaces. (Lecture Notes in Physics: Vol. 105). 1979. pap. 16.80 (ISBN 0-387-09524-1). Springer-Verlag.
Specialist Symposium on Geophysical Fluid Dynamics, European Geophysical Society, Fourth Meeting, Munich September, 1977. Proceedings. Davies, P. A. & Roberts, P. H., eds. 156p. 1978. 23.25 (ISBN 0-677-40115-9). Gordon.
Stewart, Harry L. & Storer, John M. Fluid Power. 3rd ed. LC 79-9123. 1980. 19.95 (ISBN 0-672-97224-7); instructor's manual 3.33 (ISBN 0-672-97226-3); student manual 8.95 (ISBN 0-672-97225-5); transparency masters 34.95 (ISBN 0-672-97228-X). Bobbs.
Storvick, Truman S. & Sandler, Stanley I., eds. Phase Equilibria & Fluid Properties in the Chemical Industry: Estimation & Correlation. LC 77-13804. (ACS Symposium Ser.: No. 60). 1977. 37.00 (ISBN 0-8412-0393-8). Am Chemical.
Streeter, Victor L. Fluid Dynamics. (Aeronautical Science Ser.). 1948. text ed. 19.95 (ISBN 0-07-062179-9, C). McGraw.
Symposia in Applied Mathematics - College Park Md - 1951. Fluid Dynamics: Proceedings, Vol. 4. Martin, M. H., ed. LC 50-1183. 1953. 20.80 (ISBN 0-8218-1304-8, PSAPM-4). Am Math.
Symposia in Applied Mathematics-New York-1960, et al. Hydrodynamic Instability: Proceedings, Vol. 13. Bellman, R., ed. LC 50-1183. 1962. 22.00 (ISBN 0-8218-1313-7, PSAPM-13). Am Math.
Symposium at Pittsburgh, Penn., June, 1974. Turbulence in Mixing Operations: Theory & Application to Mixing & Reaction. Brodkey, Robert S., ed. 1975. 42.00 (ISBN 0-12-134450-9). Acad Pr.
Symposium, Michigan, 1965. Fluid Mechanics of Internal Flow: Proceedings. Sovran, Gino, ed. 1967. 58.75 (ISBN 0-444-40553-4). Elsevier.
Symposium On The Dynamics Of Fluids And Plasmas. Dynamics of Fluids & Plasmas: Proceedings. Pai, S. I., ed. 1967. 65.00 (ISBN 0-12-544250-5). Acad Pr.
Szekely, Julian. Fluid Flow Phenomena in Metals Processing. 1979. 58.00 (ISBN 0-12-680840-6). Acad Pr.
Tipei, Nicolae. Theory of Lubrication: With Applications to Liquid & Gas-Film Lubrication. Gross, William A., ed. 1962. 22.00x (ISBN 0-8047-0028-1). Stanford U Pr.
Tritton, D. J. Physical Fluid Dynamics. 1977. pap. 13.20x (ISBN 0-442-30132-4). Van Nos Reinhold.
Truesdell, C., ed. Continuum Mechanics, 4 vols. Incl. Vol. 1. Mechanical Foundations of Elasticity. 1966. 35.75x (ISBN 0-677-00820-1); Vol. 2. Rational Mechanics of Materials. 1965. 43.00x (ISBN 0-677-00830-9); Vol. 3. Foundations of Elasticity Theory. 1965. 39.00x (ISBN 0-677-00840-6); Vol. 4. Problems of Nonlinear Elasticity. 1965. 35.75x (ISBN 0-677-00850-3). (International Science Review Ser.). (Illus.). 1965. Gordon.
Turner, J. S. Buoyancy Effects in Fluids. LC 79-7656. (Monographs on Mechanics & Applied Mathematics). (Illus.). 1980. pap. 19.95x (ISBN 0-521-29726-5). Cambridge U Pr.
Von Mises, Richard & Friederichs, K. O. Fluid Dynamics. LC 73-175242. (Applied Mathematical Sciences Ser.: Vol. 5). 360p. 1971. pap. 15.20 (ISBN 0-387-90028-4). Springer-Verlag.
--Fluid Dynamics. LC 73-175242. (Applied Mathematical Sciences Ser.: Vol. 5). 360p. 1971. pap. 15.20 (ISBN 0-387-90028-4). Springer-Verlag.
Von Schwind, J. Geophysical Fluid Dynamics for Oceanographers. 1980. 29.95 (ISBN 0-13-352591-0). P-H.
Ward-Smith, A. J. Internal Fluid Flow: The Fluid Dynamics of Flow in Pipes & Ducts. (Illus.). 618p. 1980. 98.00x (ISBN 0-19-856325-6). Oxford U Pr.
Wasp, Edward J., et al. Solid-Liquid Flow Slurry Pipeline Transportation. (Illus.). 240p. 1979. 39.95x (ISBN 0-87201-809-1). Gulf Pub.
Weigel, F. W. Fluid Flow Through Macromolecular Systems. (Lecture Notes in Physics: Vol. 121). 102p. 1980. pap. 9.80 (ISBN 0-387-09973-5). Springer-Verlag.
Wirz, H. J. & Smolderen, J. J. Numerical Methods in Fluid Dynamics. (McGraw-Hill - Hemisphere Series in Thermal & Fluids Engineering). (Illus.). 1978. text ed. 37.50 (ISBN 0-07-071120-8, C). McGraw.
Woods, L. C. The Thermodynamics of Fluid Systems. (Oxford Engineering Science Ser). (Illus.). 350p. 1975. 74.00x (ISBN 0-19-856125-3). Oxford U Pr.
Yuan, Shao. Foundations of Fluid Mechanics. 1967. text ed. 26.95x (ISBN 0-13-329813-2). P-H.
Zakin, J. L. & Patterson, C. K., eds. Turbulence in Liquids: Proceedings of the Fourth Biennial Symposium on Turbulence in Liquids. LC 76-52537. 1977. lib. bdg. 35.00 (ISBN 0-89500-000-8). Sci Pr.

FLUID FILM BEARINGS

see also Gas-Lubricated Bearings

Gross, William & Matsch, Lee A. Fluid Film Lubrication. Vohr, John H. & Wildman, Manfred, eds. LC 80-36889. 773p. 1980. 38.50 (ISBN 0-471-08357-7, Pub. by Wiley-Interscience). Wiley.
Rohde, S. M., et al, eds. Fundamentals of the Design of Fluid Film Bearings: Bk. No. H00145. 1979. 24.00 (ISBN 0-685-95760-8). ASME.
Trumpler, Paul R. Design of Film Bearings. 1966. 17.95 (ISBN 0-02-421520-1). Macmillan.

FLUID MECHANICS

see also Diaphragms (Mechanical Devices); Fluid Dynamics; Fluids; Hydraulic Engineering; Hydraulics; Hydrodynamics; Hydrometer; Hydrostatics

Albertson, Maurice L., et al. Fluid Mechanics for Engineers. 1960. text ed. 25.95 (ISBN 0-13-322578-X). P-H.
Astarita, G. & Marrucci, G. Principles of Non-Newtonian Fluid Mechanics. 1974. 22.95 (ISBN 0-07-084022-9, C). McGraw.
Au-Yang, M. K. & Brown, S. J., Jr., eds. Fluid-Structure Interaction Phenomena in Pressure Vessel & Piping Systems, Series PVP-PB-026. pap. text ed. 16.00 (ISBN 0-685-86866-4, G00130). ASME.
Au-Yang, M. K., et al, eds. Dynamics of Fluid-Structure Systems in the Energy Industry. (PVP-39). (Orig.). 1979. 30.00 (ISBN 0-685-96305-5, H00153). ASME.

Belsterling, Charles A. Fluidic Systems Design. LC 80-12189. 248p. 1981. Repr. of 1971 ed. lib. bdg. write for info. (ISBN 0-89874-169-6). Krieger.
Binder, Raymond C. Fluid Mechanics. 5th ed. (Illus.). 448p. 1973. ref. ed. 25.95x (ISBN 0-13-322594-1). P-H.
Bober, William & Kenyon, Richard A. Fluid Mechanics. LC 79-12977. 1980. 28.95 (ISBN 0-471-04886-0); solutions manual avail. (ISBN 0-471-04999-9). Wiley.
Brenkert, K. Elementary Theoretical Fluid Mechanics. 348p. 1960. 14.25 (ISBN 0-471-10197-4, Pub by Wiley). Krieger.
Cabannes, H., ed. Pade Approximants Methods & Its Applications to Mechanics. (Lecture Notes in Physics: Vol. 47). 285p. 1976. pap. 15.30 (ISBN 0-387-07614-X). Springer-Verlag.
Chang, Paul K. Control of Flow Separation: Energy Conservation, Operational Efficiency & Safety. new ed. (McGraw-Hill Series in Thermal & Fluids Engineering). (Illus.). 1976. text ed. 47.50x (ISBN 0-07-010513-8, C). McGraw.
Chemical Engineering Magazine. Fluid Movers: Pumps, Compressors, Fans & Blowers. (Chemical Engineering Bks.). (Illus.). 384p. 1980. 24.95 (ISBN 0-07-010769-6, P&RB). McGraw.
Childress, Stephen. Mechanics of Swimming & Flying. LC 80-23364. (Cambridge Studies in Mathematical Biology: No. 2). (Illus.). 170p. Date not set. 37.50 (ISBN 0-521-23613-4); pap. 14.50 (ISBN 0-521-28071-0). Cambridge U Pr.
Chorin, A. J. & Marsden, J. E. A Mathematical Introduction to Fluid Mechanics. (Universitexts Ser.). (Illus.). 1979. pap. 15.20 (ISBN 0-387-90406-9). Springer-Verlag.
Chow, Chuen-Yen. An Introduction to Computational Fluid Mechanics. LC 78-27555. 1979. text ed. 28.95 (ISBN 0-471-15608-6). Wiley.
CISM (International Center for Mechanical Sciences) Fluidic Applications. Belforte, G., ed. (CISM Intl. Centre for Mechanical Sciences, Courses & Lectures Ser.: No. 60). (Illus.). 156p. 1974. pap. 16.90 (ISBN 0-387-81220-2). Springer-Verlag.
--Physiological Fluid Mechanics. Lighthill, J., ed. (CISM Pubns. Ser: No. 111). 59p. 1972. pap. 9.80 (ISBN 0-387-81133-8). Springer Verlag.
Corey, Arthur T. Mechanics of Heterogeneous Fluids in Porous Media. LC 77-71937. 1977. 25.00 (ISBN 0-918334-17-9). WRP.
Croxton, Clive A. Statistical Mechanics of the Liquid Surface. LC 79-40819. 287p. 1980. 75.00 (ISBN 0-471-27663-4, Pub. by Wiley-Interscience). Wiley.
Currie, I. G., ed. Fundamental Mechanics of Fluids. 480p. 1974. text ed. 23.50 (ISBN 0-07-014950-X, C). McGraw.
DeNevers, Noel. Fluid Mechanics. LC 78-91144. (Engineering Ser). 1970. text ed. 24.95 (ISBN 0-201-01497-1). A-W.
Denn, M. Process Fluid Mechanics. 1980. 24.95 (ISBN 0-13-723163-6). P-H.
Douglas, J. F., et al. Fluid Mechanics. (Civil Engineering Ser.). 721p. 1979. text ed. 28.95 (ISBN 0-686-31209-0). Pitman Pub MA.
Duckworth, R. A. Mechanics of Fluids. LC 76-10368. (Introductory Engineering Ser.). (Illus.). 1977. pap. text ed. 13.95x (ISBN 0-582-44138-2). Longman.
Eighth International Conference on Fluid Sealing. Proceedings, 2 vols. Stephens, H. S. & Guy, N. G., eds. (Illus.). 1979. pap. text ed. 71.00 (ISBN 0-900983-93-0, Dist. by Air Science Co.). BHRA Fluid.
Eskinazi, S. Fluid Mechanics & Thermodynamics of Our Environment. 1975. 48.50 (ISBN 0-12-242540-5); lib ed 54.00 (ISBN 0-12-242541-3); microfiche 40.50 (ISBN 0-12-242542-1). Acad Pr.
Eskinazi, Salamon, ed. Vector Mechanics of Fluids & Magneto-Fluids. 1967. 55.00 (ISBN 0-12-242558-8). Acad Pr.
Fitch, E. C. & Surjaatmadja, J. B. Introduction to Fluid Logic. (McGraw-Hill-Hemisphere in Fluids & Thermal Engineering Ser.). (Illus.). 1978. text ed. 26.50 (ISBN 0-07-021126-4, C). McGraw.
Fluidics Quarterly, Vol. 4. (Illus.). 1972. 100.00 (ISBN 0-88232-017-3). Delbridge Pub Co.
Fluidics Quarterly, Vol. 6. (Illus.). 1974. 100.00 (ISBN 0-88232-027-0). Delbridge Pub Co.
Forster. Notes on Numerical Fluid Mechanics, Vol. 2. 1980. 25.00 (ISBN 0-9940012-8-2, Pub. by Vieweg & Sohn Germany). Heyden.
Forster, K., ed. Notes on Numerical Fluid Mechanics: Boundary Algorithms for Multi-Dimensional Inviscid Hyperbolic Flow, No. 1. 1978. casebound 22.00 (ISBN 0-9940011-9-3, Pub. by Vieweg & Sohn Germany). Heyden.
Fourth International Conference on Jet Cutting Technology. Proceedings, 2 vols. Stephens, H. S., ed. (Illus.). 1979. Set. pap. text ed. 68.00 (ISBN 0-900983-79-5, Dist. by Air Science Co.). BHRA Fluid.
Fox, J. A. Introduction to Engineering Fluid Mechanics. 1975. 16.50 (ISBN 0-07-021750-5, C). McGraw.
Fox, Robert W. & McDonald, Alan T. Introduction to Fluid Mechanics. 2nd ed. LC 77-20839. 1978. text ed. 28.95 (ISBN 0-471-01909-7). Wiley.
Francis, J. R. Fluid Mechanics for Engineering Students. 4th ed. 1975. text ed. 25.00x (ISBN 0-7131-3331-7); pap. text ed. 14.95x (ISBN 0-7131-3332-5). Intl Ideas.
Giles, Ronald V. Fluid Mechanics & Hydraulics. (Schaum's Outline Ser). (Orig.). 1962. pap. 6.95 (ISBN 0-07-023234-2, SP). McGraw.
Goldstein, Sidney. Lectures on Fluid Mechanics. LC 60-12712. (Lectures in Applied Mathematics Ser.: Vol. 2A). xvi, 309p. 1976. 36.00 (ISBN 0-8218-0048-5, LAM-2-1). Am Math.
Govinda Rao, N. S. Mechanics of Fluids. 490p. 1981. 20.00x (ISBN 0-86125-671-9, Pub. by Orient Longman India). State Mutual Bk.
Granet, I. Fluid Mechanics for Engineering Technology. 1971. 19.95 (ISBN 0-13-322651-4). P-H.
Granet, Irving. Fluid Mechanics for Engineering Technology. 2nd ed. (Illus.). 416p. 1981. text ed. 19.95 (ISBN 0-13-322610-7). P-H.
Hardison, Thomas B. Fluid Mechanics for Technicians. (Illus.). 272p. 1977. ref. ed. 18.95 (ISBN 0-87909-297-1); students manual avail. Reston.
Heat Transfer & Fluid Mechanics Institute. Proceedings. Incl. 1958 Sessions. viii, 264p. pap. 12.50x (ISBN 0-8047-0422-8); 1959 Sessions. x, 242p. pap. 12.50x (ISBN 0-8047-0423-6); 1960 Sessions. Mason, David M, et al, eds. x, 260p. 12.50x (ISBN 0-8047-0424-4); 1961 Sessions. Binder, Raymond C., et al, eds. xi, 236p. 12.50x (ISBN 0-8047-0425-2); 1962 Sessions. Ehlers, F. Edward, et al, eds. x, 294p. 12.50x (ISBN 0-8047-0426-0); 1963 Sessions. Roshko, Anatol, et al, eds. xii, 280p. 12.50x (ISBN 0-8047-0427-9); 1964 Sessions. Giedt, Warren H. & Levy, Salomon, eds. x, 275p. 12.50x (ISBN 0-8047-0428-7); 1965 Sessions. Charwat, Andrew F., et al, eds. xii, 372p. 16.50x (ISBN 0-8047-0429-5); 1966 Sessions. Saad, Michel A. & Miller, James A., eds. xii, 444p. 17.50x (ISBN 0-8047-0430-9); 1967 Sessions. Libby, Paul A., et al, eds. x, 468p. 17.50x (ISBN 0-8047-0431-7); 1968 Sessions. Emery, Ashley F. & Depew, Creighton A., eds. ix, 272p. 12.50x (ISBN 0-8047-0438-4); 1970 Sessions. Sarpkaya, Turgut, ed. xii, 370p. 15.00x (ISBN 0-8047-0744-8); 1974 Sessions. Davis, Lorin R. & Wilson, Robert E., eds. 17.50x (ISBN 0-8047-0865-7); 1976 Sessions. McKillop, Allan A., et al, eds. 29.50x (ISBN 0-8047-0917-3); 1978 Sessions. Crowe, Clayton T. & Grosshandler, William L., eds. 344p. text ed. 28.50x (ISBN 0-8047-1002-3); 1980 Sessions. Gerstein, Melvin & Choudhury, P. Roy, eds. text ed. 22.50x (ISBN 0-8047-1087-2). (Illus.). Stanford U Pr.
Hirschel. Third Gamm Conference on Numerical Methods in Fluid Mechanics. 1980. 58.00 (ISBN 0-9940013-1-2, Pub. by Vieweg & Sohn Germany). Heyden.
Holland, F. A. Fluid Flow for Chemical Engineers. 1973. 28.50 (ISBN 0-8206-0217-5). Chem Pub.
Horlock, J. H. Fluid Mechanics & Thermodynamics. LC 73-75588. 222p. 1973. Repr. of 1958 ed. 12.50 (ISBN 0-88275-096-8). Krieger.
Hughes, Thomas J. & Marsden, Jerrold E. A Short Course in Fluid Mechanics. LC 76-6802. (Mathematics Lecture Ser.: No. 6). 1976. pap. 7.50x (ISBN 0-914098-15-2). Publish or Perish.
Interflow Eighty: Proceedings, No. 60. 1981. 80.00x (ISBN 0-85295-122-1, Pub. by Inst Chem Eng England). State Mutual Bk.
International Conference on Hydraulics, Pneumatics & Fluidics in Control & Automation. Proceedings. 1977. text ed. 65.00 (ISBN 0-900983-53-1, Dist. by Air Science Co.). BHRA Fluid.
International Symposium on Unsteady Flow in Open Channels. Proceedings. 1977. text ed. 68.00 (ISBN 0-900983-54-X, Dist. by Air Science Co.). BHRA Fluid.
International Symposium, 3rd, December 5-9, 1977. Computing Methods in Applied Sciences & Engineering, 1977, II: Proceedings. Glowinski, R. & Lions, J. L., eds. (Lecture Notes in Physics: Vol. 91). 1979. pap. 18.70 (ISBN 0-387-09119-X). Springer-Verlag.
John, J. & Haberman, W. Introduction to Fluid Mechanics. 2nd ed. 1980. 25.95 (ISBN 0-13-483941-2). P-H.
--Introduction to Fluid Mechanics. 1971. ref. ed. 20.95x (ISBN 0-13-483925-0). P-H.
Kay, J. M. & Nedderman, R. M. An Introduction to Fluid Mechanics & Heat Transfer. 3rd. rev. ed. LC 74-77383. 300p. 1975. 44.50 (ISBN 0-521-20533-6); pap. 17.50x (ISBN 0-521-09880-7). Cambridge U Pr.
Kirschner, Joseph M. & Katz, Silas. Design Theory of Fluidic Components. 1975. 71.50 (ISBN 0-12-410250-6). Acad Pr.
Li, Wen-Hsiung & Lam, Sau-Hai. Principles of Fluid Mechanics. 1964. 20.95 (ISBN 0-201-04240-1). A-W.
Loh, W. H. Modern Developments in Gas Dynamics. LC 69-14561. 386p. 1969. 42.50 (ISBN 0-306-30377-9, Plenum Pr). Plenum Pub.
Lu, P. Introduction to the Mechanics of Viscous Fluids. LC 77-3428. (Thermal & Fluids Engineering Ser.). (Illus.). 1977. Repr. of 1973 ed. text ed. 20.95 (ISBN 0-07-038907-1, C). McGraw.
Lu, Pau-Chang. Fluid Mechanics: An Introductory Course. (Illus.). 1978. text ed. 22.95x (ISBN 0-8138-0685-2). Iowa St U Pr.
Manohar, M. & Krishnamachar, P. Fluid Mechanics. 500p. 1981. text ed. 25.00x (ISBN 0-7069-1188-1, Pub. by Vikas India). Advent NY.
Manwell, A. R. The Generalized Tricomi Equation: With Applications to the Theory of Plane Transonic Flow. (Research Notes in Mathematics Ser.). (Illus.). 1979. pap. cancelled (ISBN 0-8224-8428-5). Pitman Learning.
Mataix, Claudio. Mecanica De Fluidos y Maquinas Hidraulicas. (Span). 1970. pap. text ed. 13.80 (ISBN 0-06-315590-7, IntlDept). Har-Row.
Mathur, K. B. & Epstein, N. Spouted Beds. 1974. 29.50 (ISBN 0-12-480050-5). Acad Pr.
Michell, S. J. Introduction to Fluid & Particle Mechanics. 1970. 41.00 (ISBN 0-08-013313-4); pap. 14.00 (ISBN 0-08-013312-6). Pergamon.
Miller, D. S. Internal Flow Systems. (BHRA Fluid Engineering Ser., Vol. 4). 1978. text ed. 78.00 (ISBN 0-900983-78-7, Dist. by Air Science Co.). BHRA Fluid.
Mironer, Alan. Engineering Fluid Mechanics. (Illus.). 1979. text ed. 19.95 (ISBN 0-07-042417-9, C); 9.50 (ISBN 0-07-042418-7). McGraw.
Monin, A. S. & Yaglom, A. M. Statistical Fluid Mechanics: Mechanics of Turbulence, 2 vols. Lumley, John L., ed. 90.00x set (ISBN 0-262-13158-7); Vol. 1 1971. 50.00x (ISBN 0-262-13062-9, VOL. 1 1971); Vol. 2 1975. 50.00x (ISBN 0-262-13098-X). MIT Pr.
Mott, Robert L. Applied Fluid Mechanics. 2nd ed. (Mechanical Technology Ser.). 1979. text ed. 20.95 (ISBN 0-675-08305-2); instructor's manual 3.95 (ISBN 0-686-67359-X). Merrill.
Mueller, U., et al, eds. Recent Developments in Theoretical & Experimental Fluid Mechanics: Compressible & Incompressible Flows. (Illus.). 1979. 47.30 (ISBN 0-387-09228-5). Springer-Verlag.
Murdock, James. Fluid Mechanics & Its Applications. LC 75-31024. (Illus.). 384p. 1976. text ed. 23.95 (ISBN 0-395-20626-X); solutions manual 2.50 (ISBN 0-395-24216-9). HM.
Narasimhan, S. Engineering Fluid Mechanics, 2 vols. 528p. 1981. 25.00x set (ISBN 0-86125-054-0, Pub. by Orient Longman India). State Mutual Bk.
National Committee for Fluid Mechanics Films. Illustrated Experiments in Fluid Mechanics: The NCFMF Book of Film Notes. 1972. pap. 10.95x (ISBN 0-262-64012-0). MIT Pr.
Olson, Reuben M. Essentials of Engineering Fluid Mechanics. 4th ed. (Illus.). 583p. 1980. text ed. 26.50 scp (ISBN 0-7002-2532-3, HarpC); solutions manual avail. Har-Row.
Parker, J. D., et al. Introduction to Fluid Mechanics & Heat Transfer. (Engineering Ser). 1969. text ed. 25.95 (ISBN 0-201-05710-7). A-W.
Pease, Dudley A. Basic Fluid Power. 1967. ref. ed. 17.95 (ISBN 0-13-061432-7). P-H.
Pennsylvania University Bicentennial Conference. Fluid Mechanics & Statistical Methods in Engineering. Dryden, Hugh & Von Karman, Theodore, eds. LC 68-26203. Repr. of 1941 ed. 11.50 (ISBN 0-8046-0359-6). Kennikat.
Plint, M. A. & Boswirth, L. Fluid Mechanics: A Laboratory Course. 186p. 1978. 30.00x (ISBN 0-85264-245-8, Pub. by Griffin England). State Mutual Bk.
Potter, M. C. & Foss, J. F. Fluid Mechanics. 1975. 29.95 (ISBN 0-8260-7207-0). Wiley.
Prandtl, Ludwig & Tietjens, O. G. Applied Hydro & Aeromechanics. Den Hartog, Jacob P., ed. (Illus.). 1934. pap. text ed. 5.00 (ISBN 0-486-60375-X). Dover.
--Fundamentals of Hydro & Aeromechanics. Rosenhead, L., tr. (Illus.). pap. text ed. 4.00 (ISBN 0-486-60374-1). Dover.
Prasuhn, Alan L. Fundamentals of Fluid Mechanics. (Illus.). 1980. text ed. 24.95 (ISBN 0-13-339507-3). P-H.
Roberson, John A. & Crowe, Clayton T. Engineering Fluid Mechanics. 2nd ed. LC 79-87855. (Illus.). 1980. text ed. 24.50 (ISBN 0-395-28357-4); solutions manual 2.50 (ISBN 0-395-28358-2). HM.
Rogers, Ruth H. Fluid Mechanics. 1978. 28.00 (ISBN 0-7100-8681-4). Routledge & Kegan.
Rouse, Hunter. Elementary Mechanics of Fluids. LC 78-57159. (Illus.). 1978. pap. 5.00 (ISBN 0-486-63699-2). Dover.
Ruzicka, Jaromir & Hansen, Elo H. Flow Injection Analysis. (Analytical Chemistry & Its Applications Monographs). 207p. 1981. 32.50 (ISBN 0-471-08192-2, Pub. by Wiley-Interscience). Wiley.
Schreier, Stefan. Compressible Flow. LC 80-20607. 768p. 1981. 40.00 (ISBN 0-471-05691-X, Pub. by Wiley-Interscience). Wiley.
Second European Conference on Mixing. Proceedings. Stephens, H. S. & Clarke, J. A., eds. 1978. pap. 68.00 (ISBN 0-900983-69-8, Dist. by Air Science Co.). BHRA Fluid.
Second International Conference on Pressure Surges. Proceedings. 1977. text ed. 65.00 (ISBN 0-900983-65-5, Dist. by Air Science Co.). BHRA Fluid.
Shames, Irving H. Mechanics of Fluids. 1962. text ed. 24.50 (ISBN 0-07-056390-X, C); solutions manual 4.95 (ISBN 0-07-056391-8). McGraw.
Shapiro, Ascher H. The Dynamics & Thermodynamics of Compressible Fluid Flow, 2 Vols. (Illus.). 1953-54. Vol. 1. 28.95 (ISBN 0-471-06845-4); Vol. 2. 27.95 (ISBN 0-8260-8075-8). Wiley.
Shinbrot, M. Lectures on Fluid Mechanics. (Notes on Mathematics & Its Applications Ser.). 236p. 1973. 34.25x (ISBN 0-677-01710-3). Gordon.
Stephens, H. S., ed. Papers Presented at the Ninth International Conference on Fluid Sealing. Stapleton, C. A. (Illus.). 500p. 1981. pap. 78.00 (ISBN 0-906085-51-9). BHRA Fluid.
Streeter, Victor L. & Wylie, E. Benjamin. Fluid Mechanics. 7th ed. (Illus.). 1979. text ed. 22.50 (ISBN 0-07-062232-9, C); solutions manual 5.95 (ISBN 0-07-062233-7). McGraw.
Sullivan, James A. Fundamentals of Fluid Mechanics. (Illus.). 1978. ref. ed. 17.95 (ISBN 0-8359-2999-X); students manual avail. Reston.
Sweeney, Eugene T. An Introduction & Literature Guide to Mixing. (BHRA Fluid Engineering Ser., Vol. 5). 1978. pap. 21.00 (ISBN 0-900983-77-9, Dist. by Air Science Co.). BHRA Fluid.
Symposia in Applied Mathematics-Providence, R. I.-1947. Nonlinear Problems in Mechanics of Continua: Proceedings, Vol. 1. Reissner, E., ed. LC 50-1183. 1949. 18.40 (ISBN 0-8218-1301-3, PSAPM-1). Am Math.
Szilard, Rudolph, ed. Hydromechanically Loaded Shells: Proceedings of the 1971 Symposium of the International Association for Shell Structures. LC 72-93559. (Illus.). 900p. 1973. text ed. 55.00x (ISBN 0-8248-0264-0). U Pr of Hawaii.
Turner, J. S. Bouyancy Effects in Fluids. LC 72-76085. (Cambridge Monographs on Mechanics & Applied Mathematics). (Illus.). 350p. 1973. 47.95 (ISBN 0-521-08623-X). Cambridge U Pr.
Van Dyke, M. & Vincenti, W. G., eds. Annual Review of Fluid Mechanics, Vol. 5. LC 74-80866. (Illus.). 1973. text ed. 17.00 (ISBN 0-8243-0705-4). Annual Reviews.
--Annual Review of Fluid Mechanics, Vol. 6. LC 74-80866. (Illus.). 1974. text ed. 17.00 (ISBN 0-8243-0706-2). Annual Reviews.
--Annual Review of Fluid Mechanics, Vol. 7. LC 74-80866. (Illus.). 1975. text ed. 17.00 (ISBN 0-8243-0707-0). Annual Reviews.
--Annual Review of Fluid Mechanics, Vol. 8. LC 74-80866. (Illus.). 1976. text ed. 17.00 (ISBN 0-8243-0708-9). Annual Reviews.
Van Dyke, M. & Wehausen, J. V., eds. Annual Review of Fluid Mechanics, Vol. 9. LC 74-80866. (Illus.). 1977. text ed. 17.00 (ISBN 0-8243-0709-7). Annual Reviews.
--Annual Review of Fluid Mechanics, Vol. 10. LC 74-80866. (Illus.). 1978. text ed. 17.00 (ISBN 0-8243-0710-0). Annual Reviews.
--Annual Review of Fluid Mechanics, Vol. 11. LC 74-80866. (Illus.). 1979. text ed. 17.00 (ISBN 0-8243-0711-9). Annual Reviews.
--Annual Review of Fluid Mechanics, Vol. 12. LC 74-80866. (Illus.). 1980. text ed. 17.00 (ISBN 0-8243-0712-7). Annual Reviews.
Van Dyke, M., et al, eds. Annual Review of Fluid Mechanics, Vol. 13. LC 74-80866. (Illus.). 1981. text ed. 20.00 (ISBN 0-8243-0713-5). Annual Reviews.
--Annual Review of Fluid Mechanics, Vol. 14. LC 74-80866. (Illus.). 469p. 1982. text ed. 20.00 (ISBN 0-8243-0714-3). Annual Reviews.
Van Dyke, Milton. An Album of Fluid Motion. (Illus.). 160p. 1981. text ed. 20.00x (ISBN 0-915760-03-7); pap. text ed. 10.00x (ISBN 0-915760-02-9). Parabolic Pr.
--Perturbation Methods in Fluid Mechanics. LC 75-15072. 1975. 10.00x (ISBN 0-915760-01-0). Parabolic Pr.
Vennard, John K. & Street, Robert L. Elementary Fluid Mechanics. 6th ed. 704p. 1982. text ed. 24.95 (ISBN 0-471-04427-X). Wiley.

--Elementary Fluid Mechanics. 5th ed. LC 74-31232. 740p. 1975. text ed. 28.95 (ISBN 0-471-90587-9). Wiley.
--Elementary Fluid Mechanics: SI Edition. 5th ed. LC 76-4885. 1976. 28.95 (ISBN 0-471-90589-5) (ISBN 0-685-68753-8). Wiley.
Verhulst, F., ed. Asymptotic Analysis: From Theory to Application. (Lecture Notes in Mathematics Ser.: Vol. 711). 1979. pap. 13.10 (ISBN 0-387-09245-5). Springer-Verlag.
Warring, R. H. Fluids for Power Sysytems. (Illus.). 1970. 39.95x (ISBN 0-85461-040-5). Intl Ideas.
Wells, C. Sinclair, ed. Viscous Drag Reduction. LC 77-76496. 500p. 1969. 45.00 (ISBN 0-306-30398-1, Plenum Pr). Plenum Pub.
Welty, James R., et al. Fundamentals of Momentum, Heat & Mass Transfer. 2nd ed. LC 76-16813. 897p. 1976. text ed. 36.95 (ISBN 0-471-93354-6). Wiley.
Whitaker, Stephen. Introduction to Fluid Mechanics. LC 81-1620. 476p. 1981. Repr. of 1968 ed. write for info (ISBN 0-89874-337-0). Krieger.
White, Frank M. Elementary Fluid Mechanics. (Illus.). 1979. text ed. 21.95 (ISBN 0-07-069667-5, C); write for info solution manual (ISBN 0-07-069668-3). McGraw.
Wighton, John L. An Experimentation Approach to the Fluids Laboratory: A Lab Manual. LC 78-23968. (Illus.). 224p. 1979. pap. 6.95 (ISBN 0-910554-26-9). Eng Pr.
Williams, J. Fluid Mechanics. (Problem Solvers). (Illus.). 1974. text ed. 13.50x (ISBN 0-04-519014-3); pap. text ed. 7.50x (ISBN 0-04-519015-1). Allen Unwin.
Wylie, E. Benjamin & Streeter, Victor L. Fluid Transients. (Illus.). 1978. text ed. 34.50x (ISBN 0-07-072187-4, C). McGraw.
Yih, Chia-Shun. Fluid Mechanics. 1979. text ed. 19.80 (ISBN 0-9602190-0-5). West River.

FLUID METERS
see Flow Meters

FLUID POWER TECHNOLOGY
see also Hydraulic Machinery; Pneumatic Control; Pneumatic Machinery
Chemical Engineering Magazine. Fluid Movers: Pumps, Compressors, Fans & Blowers. (Chemical Engineering Bks.). (Illus.). 384p. 1980. 24.95 (ISBN 0-07-010769-6, P&RB). McGraw.
Conference on Fluid Machinery, Fifth. Proceedings, 2 vols. Kisbocskoi, L. & Szabo, A., eds. 1977. 75.00x (ISBN 963-05-0725-0). Intl Pubns Serv.
Design News, ed. Design News Fluid Power Directory. (Design News Directories Ser.). 198p. 1981. pap. 12.00x (ISBN 0-686-73567-6, DNL). Herman Pub.
Esposito, Anthony. Fluid Power with Applications. (Illus.). 1980. text ed. 18.95 (ISBN 0-13-322701-4). P-H.
Fifth Fluid Power Symposium. Proceedings, 2 vols. Stephens, H. S. & Stapleton, C. A., eds. (Illus.). 1979. Set. lib. bdg. 78.00 (ISBN 0-900983-96-5, Dist by Air Science Co.). BHRA Fluid.
Hedges, Charles S. & Womack, R. C. Fluid Power in Plant & Field. (Illus.). 176p. pap. 6.85 (ISBN 0-686-31590-1). Womack Educ Pubns.
Henke, R. W. Introduction to Fluid Mechanics. 1966. 15.95 (ISBN 0-201-02809-3). A-W.
Johnson, Olaf A. Fluid Power for Industrial Use: Vol. 2, Hydraulics, Vol. 2. 224p. 1981. lib. bdg. 12.50 (ISBN 0-89874-048-7). Krieger.
McCloy, D. Control of Fluid Power: Analysis & Design. 2nd rev. ed. LC 80-40027. (Ser. in Engineering Science: Civil Engineering). 505p. 1980. 93.95 (ISBN 0-470-27012-8). Halsted Pr.
McCloy, D. & Martin, H. R. The Control of Fluid Power. LC 72-5349. 1973. 37.95 (ISBN 0-470-58195-6). Halsted Pr.
Merrill, Samuel W. Fluid Power for Aircraft: Modern Hydraulic Technology. 3rd ed. 1974. pap. 10.00 (ISBN 0-914680-01-3). Intermtn Air.
Morgan-Grampian Books, ed. Fluid Power Equipment Locator, 1979-80. 210p. 40.00x (ISBN 0-686-75513-8, Pub. by Morgan-Grampian Bk). State Mutual Bk.
Newton, Donald G. Fluid Power for Technicians. 1971. ref. ed. 14.95 (ISBN 0-13-322685-9). P-H.
Pippenger, John & Hicks, Tyler. Industrial Hydraulics. 3rd ed. (Illus.). 1979. text ed. 19.95 (ISBN 0-07-050140-8, G). McGraw.
Proceedings of the Symposium on Degassing. 1978. pap. 52.00 (ISBN 0-900983-89-2, Dist. by Air Science Co.). BHRA Fluid.
Rohner, Peter. Fluid Power Logic Circuit Design: Analysis, Design Methods & Worked Examples. LC 79-14178. 226p. 1979. 36.95x (ISBN 0-470-26779-8). Halsted Pr.
Stephens, H. S. & Radband, D. Papers Presented at the Sixth Fluid Power Symposium. (Orig.). 1981. pap. 78.00 library ed. (ISBN 0-906085-53-5). BHRA Fluid.
Stephens, H. S. & Jarvis, B., eds. Papers Presented at the Fifth International Symposium on Jet Cutting. (Illus.). 438p. (Orig.). 1980. pap. 99.00x (ISBN 0-906085-41-1). BHRA Fluid.
Stewart, Harry L. Hydraulic & Pneumatic Power for Production. 4th ed. LC 76-28238. (Illus.). 435p. 1977. 20.00 (ISBN 0-8311-1114-3). Indus Pr.
Sullivan, James. Fluid Power: Theory & Applications. (Illus.). 480p. 1975. 18.95 (ISBN 0-87909-272-6); instrs'. manual avail. Reston.
Turnbull, D. E. Fluid Power Engineering. 1975. pap. 19.95 (ISBN 0-408-00199-2). Butterworth.
Wolansky, William D., et al. Fundamentals of Fluid Power. LC 76-13963. (Illus.). 1976. text ed. 21.50 (ISBN 0-395-18956-X); inst. manual 2.25 (ISBN 0-395-18955-1). HM.

FLUID THERAPY
Brooks, Stewart M. Basic Facts of Body Water & Ions. 3rd ed. LC 72-97198. (Illus.). 1973. pap. text ed. 4.95 (ISBN 0-8261-0403-7). Springer Pub.
Ellerbe, Suellyn. Fluid & Blood Component Therapy in the Critically Ill. (Contemporary Issues in Critical Care Nursing). (Illus.). 224p. 1981. lib. bdg. write for info. (ISBN 0-443-08129-8). Churchill.
Shoemaker, William C. & Walker, William F. Fluid-Electrolyte Therapy in Acute Illness. (Illus.). 1970. 25.00 (ISBN 0-8151-7640-6). Year Bk Med.
Taylor, W. H. Fluid Therapy & Disorders of Electrolyte Balance. 2nd ed. (Illus.). 200p. 1970. 9.50 (ISBN 0-632-07430-2, Blackwell). Mosby.

FLUIDIZATION
Blevins, Robert D. Formulas for Natural Frequency & Mode Shape. 1979. text ed. 32.50 (ISBN 0-442-20710-7). Van Nos Reinhold.
Botterill, J. S. Fluid-Bed Heat Transfer: Gas-Fluidized Bed Behavior & Its Influence on Bed Thermal Properties. 1975. 47.50 (ISBN 0-12-118750-0). Acad Pr.
Davidson, J. F., ed. Fluidization. Keairns, D. L. LC 77-82495. (Illus.). 1978. 52.50 (ISBN 0-521-21943-4). Cambridge U Pr.
Davidson, J. F. & Harrison, D., eds. Fluidization. 1972. 110.00 (ISBN 0-12-205550-0). Acad Pr.
Fluidized Bed Combustion. Orig. Title: Wirbelschich Tfeuerung. 145p. 1978. pap. 46.00x (ISBN 3-18-090322-8, Pub. by VDI Verlag Germany). Renouf.
Grace, John R. & Matsen, John M., eds. Fluidization. 597p. 1980. 69.50 (ISBN 0-306-40458-3, Plenum Pr). Plenum Pub.
International Fluidization Conference, 1975. Fluidization Technology: Proceedings, 2 vols. Keairns, Dale L., ed. LC 75-40106. (Thermal & Fluids Engineering Ser.). (Illus.). 1000p. 1976. Set. 119.50 (ISBN 0-89116-162-7, Co-Pub. by McGraw Intl). Hemisphere Pub.
Kunii, Daizo & Levenspiel, Octave. Fluidization Engineering. LC 77-2885. (Illus.). 556p. 1977. Repr. of 1969 ed. lib. bdg. 29.50 (ISBN 0-88275-542-0). Krieger.
Patterson, G. A. Basic Fluid System Analysis: With HP-25 & SR-56 Pocket Calculator Programs. LC 76-21585. 1977. 12.95 (ISBN 0-917410-00-9). Basic Sci Pr.
Roedder, Edwin & Kozlowski, Andrezj, eds. Fluid Inclusion Research: Proceedings of COFFI, Vol. 10, 1977. 270p. 1980. pap. 10.00x (ISBN 0-472-02010-2). U of Mich Pr.
Zabrodsky, S. S. Hydrodynamics & Heat Transfer in Fluidized Beds. 1966. 31.50x (ISBN 0-262-24007-6). MIT Pr.

FLUIDIZED SYSTEMS
see Fluidization

FLUIDS
see also Drops; Fluid Dynamics; Fluid Mechanics; Gases; Hydraulic Engineering; Hydraulic Fluids; Hydrostatics; Liquids; Osmosis; Permeability; Rotating Masses of Fluid; Solvents
Bain, D. C. & Baker, P. J. A Technical & Market Survey of Fluidic Applications. 1969. text ed. 30.00 (ISBN 0-900983-02-7, Dist. by Air Science Co.). BHRA Fluid.
Cole, G. H. An Introduction to the Statistical Theory of Classical Simple Dense Fluids. 1967. 45.00 (ISBN 0-08-010397-9). Pergamon.
Collins, R. Douglas. Illustrated Manual of Fluid & Electrolyte Disorders. LC 76-6131. (Illus.). 190p. 1976. 35.00 (ISBN 0-397-50361-X, JBL-Med-Nursing). Har-Row.
European Federation of Chemical Engineering, 2nd Intl. Conference on Phase Equilibria & Fluid Properties in the Chemical Industry, Berlin, 1980. Phase Equilibria & Fluid Properties in the Chemical Industry: Proceedings, Pts. 1 & 2. (EFCE Publication Ser.: No. 11). 1012p. 1980. text ed. 82.50x (ISBN 3-921567-35-1, Pub. by Dechema Germany). Scholium Intl.
Fifth Cranfield Fluidics Conference. Proceedings. 1972. text ed. 60.00 (ISBN 0-900983-24-8, Dist. by Air Science Co.). BHRA Fluid.
Fifth International Conference on Fluid Sealing. Proceedings. 1971. text ed. 50.00 (ISBN 0-900983-12-4, Dist. by Air Science Co.). BHRA Fluid.
First Fluid Power Symposium. Proceedings. 1969. text ed. 29.00 (ISBN 0-900983-03-5, Dist. by Air Science Co.). BHRA Fluid.
Fisher, I. Z. Statistical Theory of Liquids. Switz, Theodore, tr. LC 64-22249. 1964. pap. 17.50x (ISBN 0-226-25184-5). U of Chicago Pr.
Fluid Mixing: Proceedings, No. 64. 200p. 1981. 70.00x (ISBN 0-85295-135-3, Pub. by Inst Chem Eng England). State Mutual Bk.
Fluidics Quarterly, Vol. 5. (Illus.). 1973. 100.00 (ISBN 0-88232-022-X). Delbridge Pub Co.
Fluidics Quarterly, Vol. 7. (Illus.). 1975. 100.00 (ISBN 0-88232-032-7). Delbridge Pub Co.
Fluidics Quarterly, Vol. 10. (Illus.). 1978. 115.00 (ISBN 0-88232-047-5). Delbridge Pub Co.
Fluidics Quarterly: The Journal of Fluid Control, Vol. 13. (Illus.). 1981. 124.00 (ISBN 0-88232-062-9). Delbridge Pub Co.
Fourth Cranfield Fluidics Conference. Proceedings. 1970. text ed. 60.00 (ISBN 0-900983-08-6, Dist. by Air Science Co.). BHRA Fluid.
Fourth Fluid Power Symposium. Proceedings. 1975. text ed. 56.00 (ISBN 0-900983-45-0, Dist. by Air Science Co.). BHRA Fluid.
Gallagher, R. H., et al, eds. Finite Elements in Fluids, 3 vols. Incl. Vol. 1. Viscous Flow & Hydrodynamics. 290p. 1975. 61.50z (ISBN 0-471-29045-9); Vol. 2. Mathematical Foundations, Aerodynamics, & Lubrication. 287p. 1975. 61.50x (ISBN 0-471-29046-7); Vol. 3. 1978. 61.50x (ISBN 0-471-99630-0). LC 74-13573 (Pub. by Wiley-Interscience). Wiley.
Geiringer, Paul L. Handbook of Heat Transfer Media. LC 76-57170. (Illus.). 272p. 1977. Repr. of 1962 ed. lib. bdg. 18.50 (ISBN 0-88275-498-X). Krieger.
Genet, Edmond C. Memorial on the Upward Motion of Fluids. (Illus.). 7.50 (ISBN 0-8363-0069-6). Jenkins.
Green, Herbert S. The Molecular Theory of Fluids. 8.75 (ISBN 0-8446-0658-8). Peter Smith.
International Conference on Fluid Sealing, 6th. Proceedings. 1973. text ed. 52.00 (ISBN 0-900983-27-2, Dist. by Air Science Co.). BHRA Fluid.
International Symposium on Flow Visualization, Tokyo, Oct. 12-14, 1977. Flow Visualization: Proceedings. new ed. Asanuma, Tsuyoshi, ed. LC 79-12407. (Thermal & Fluids Engineering Ser.). (Illus.). 413p. 1979. text ed. 89.50 (ISBN 0-89116-155-4, Co-Pub. with McGraw Intl). Hemisphere Pub.
Johnson, Julian & Porter, Roger, eds. Liquid Crystals & Ordered Fluids. Incl. Vol. 1. LC 76-110760. 494p. 1970. 42.50 (ISBN 0-306-30466-X); Vol. 2. LC 74-1269. 783p. 1974. 49.50 (ISBN 0-306-35182-X); Vol. 3. 559p. 1978. 45.00 (ISBN 0-306-35183-8). Plenum Pr). Plenum Pub.
Nicksic, Esther. The Plus & Minus of Fluids & Electrolytes. 1981. text ed. 14.95 (ISBN 0-8359-5561-3); pap. text ed. 12.95 (ISBN 0-8359-5560-5). Reston.
Ranney, M. William, ed. Functional Fluids for Industry, Transportation & Aerospace. LC 80-10550. (Chemical Technology Review Ser.: No. 155). (Illus.). 364p. 1980. 45.00 (ISBN 0-8155-0789-5). Noyes.
Reed, T. M. & Gubbins, K. E. Applied Statistical Mechanics. (Chemical Engineering Ser.). (Illus.). 496p. 1973. text ed. 25.95 (ISBN 0-07-051495-X, C); solutions manual o.p. 4.00 (ISBN 0-07-051496-8). McGraw.
Review & Bibliography on Aspects of Fluid Sealing. 1972. text ed. 34.00 (ISBN 0-900983-16-7, Dist. by Air Science Co.). BHRA Fluid.
Riste, T., ed. Ordering in Strongly Fluctuating Condensed Matter Systems. (NATO Advanced Study Institute Ser.: Series B: Physics, Volume 50). 490p. 1980. 55.00 (ISBN 0-306-40341-2, Plenum Pr). Plenum Pub.
Rogers, G. F. & Mahew, Y. R. Thermodynamic & Transport Properties of Fluids SI Units. 3rd. ed. 24p. (Orig.). 1980. pap. 2.50x (ISBN 0-631-12891-3, Pub. by Basil Blackwell England). Biblio Dist.
Seals in Fluid Power Symposium. Proceedings. 1973. pap. 29.00 (ISBN 0-900983-31-0, Dist. by Air Science Co.). BHRA Fluid.
Second Cranfield Fluidics Conference. Proceedings. 1967. text ed. 39.00 (ISBN 0-685-85166-4, Dist. by Air Science Co.). BHRA Fluid.
Second Fluid Power Symposium. Proceedings. 1971. text ed. 47.00 (ISBN 0-900983-11-6, Dist. by Air Science Co.). BHRA Fluid.
Second IFAC Symposium on Fluidics. Fluidics Quarterly: Selected Papers, Vol. 4, Issue 1, Pt. 2. 1971. 26.00 (ISBN 0-88232-018-1). Delbridge Pub Co.
Second Review & Bibliography on Aspects of Fluid Sealing. 1975. text ed. 47.00 (ISBN 0-900983-49-3, Dist. by Air Science Co.). BHRA Fluid.
Seventh International Conference on Fluid Sealing. Proceedings. 1976. text ed. 63.00 (ISBN 0-900983-48-5, Dist. by Air Science Co.). BHRA Fluid.
Tenth Anniversary Fluidics Symposium. Fluidics Quarterly: Special Issue, Vol. 2, Pts. 4 & 5. 1970. Set. 52.00 (ISBN 0-88232-067-X). Pt. 4 (ISBN 0-88232-010-6). Pt. 5 (ISBN 0-88232-011-4). Delbridge Pub Co.
Third Cranfield Fluidics Conference. Proceedings. 1968. text ed. 52.00 (ISBN 0-900983-01-9, Dist. by Air Science Co.). BHRA Fluid.
Third Fluid Power Symposium. Proceedings. 1973. text ed. 52.00 (ISBN 0-900983-30-2, Dist. by Air Science Co.). BHRA Fluid.
Tourret. Performance & Testing of Gear Oils & Transmission Fluids. 1981. 90.00 (ISBN 0-85501-326-5). Heyden.
Trefil, James S. Introduction to the Physics of Fluids & Solids. 320p. 1976. text ed. 28.00 (ISBN 0-08-018104-X). Pergamon.
Turner, J. S. Bouyancy Effects in Fluids. LC 72-76085. (Cambridge Monographs on Mechanics & Applied Mathematics). (Illus.). 350p. 1973. 47.95 (ISBN 0-521-08623-X). Cambridge U Pr.
Vogel, Stephen. Life in Moving Fluids. 368p. 1981. text ed. write for info. (ISBN 0-87150-749-8, 40N 4351). Grant Pr.
Watts, R. O. & McGee, I. J. Liquid State Chemical Physics. LC 76-21793. 350p. 1976. 35.50 (ISBN 0-471-91240-9). Krieger.

FLUIDS-THERAPEUTIC USE
see Fluid Therapy

FLUIDS, DRILLING
see Drilling Muds

FLUORESCENCE
see also Fluorescent Lighting; Fluorimetry; Immunofluorescence; Moessbauer Effect
Chen, R. F. & Edelhoch, H., eds. Biochemical Fluorescence: Concepts, Vol. 1. 424p. 1975. 43.50 (ISBN 0-8247-6222-3). Dekker.
--Biochemical Fluorescence: Concepts, Vol. 2. 336p. 1976. 49.50 (ISBN 0-8247-6223-1). Dekker.
Conference on Particle Induced X-Ray Emissions & Its Applications, Lund, August 23-26, 1976 & Johansson, S. E. Particle Induced X-Ray Emission & Its Analytical Applications: Proceedings. (Nuclear Instruments & Methods: Vol. 142 Pts. 1-2). Date not set. price not set (ISBN 0-7204-0715-X, North-Holland). Elsevier.
Guilbault, G. G. Practical Fluorescence: Theory, Methods, & Techniques. 680p. 1973. 46.75 (ISBN 0-8247-1263-3). Dekker.
Guilbault, G. G., ed. Fluorescence: Theory, Instrumentation, & Practice. 1967. 44.50 (ISBN 0-8247-1260-9). Dekker.
International Symposium on Fluorescin Angiography, Miami, 1970. Photography in Ophthalmology: Proceedings. Ferrer, O., ed. (Modern Problems in Ophthalmology: Vol. 9). 1971. 41.24 (ISBN 3-8055-1165-5). S Karger.
Kottow, Michael H. Anterior Segment Fluorescein Angiography. LC 77-16572. 268p. 1978. 25.00 (ISBN 0-683-04757-4). Krieger.
Passwater, R. A. Guide to Fluorescence Literature. Incl. Vol. 1. LC 67-18073. 367p. 1967. 45.00 (ISBN 0-306-68261-3); Vol. 2. 369p. 1970. 45.00 (ISBN 0-306-68262-1); Vol. 3. LC 67-18075. 358p. 1974. 55.00 (ISBN 0-306-68263-X). IFI Plenum.
Schulman, Stephen G. Fluorescence & Phosphorescence Spectroscopy: Physicochemical Principles & Practice. 1977. text ed. 45.00 (ISBN 0-08-020499-6). Pergamon.
Udenfriend, Sidney. Fluorescence Assay in Biology & Medicine, 2 Vols. (Molecular Biology: Vol. 3). (Illus.). Vol. 1, 1962. 52.50 (ISBN 0-12-705850-8); Vol. 2. 54.50 (ISBN 0-12-705802-8). Acad Pr.
Wehry, E. L. Modern Fluorescence Spectroscopy, Vol. 1. LC 75-43827. (Modern Analytical Chemistry Ser.). (Illus.). 238p. 1976. 29.50 (ISBN 0-306-33903-X, Plenum Pr). Plenum Pub.
Wehry, E. L., ed. Modern Fluorescence Spectroscopy. (Modern Analytical Chemistry Ser.: Vol. 4). 270p. 1981. text ed. 35.00 (ISBN 0-306-40691-8, Plenum Pr). Plenum Pub.
--Modern Fluorescence Spectroscopy, Vol. 2. LC 75-43827. (Modern Analytical Chemistry Ser.). (Illus.). 459p. 1976. 32.50 (ISBN 0-306-33904-8, Plenum Pr). Plenum Pub.

FLUORESCENCE ANALYSIS
see Fluorimetry

FLUORESCENCE MICROSCOPY
see also Fluorescent Antibody Technique

Conference on Quantitative Flourescence Techniques As Applied to Cell Biology, Seattle, Wash. Fluorescence Techniques in Cell Biology: Proceedings. Thaer, A. & Sernetz, M., eds. LC 73-11950. (Illus.). 450p. 1973. 29.00 (ISBN 0-387-06421-4). Springer-Verlag.

FLUORESCENT ANTIBODY TECHNIQUE

Goldman, Morris. Fluorescent Antibody Methods. LC 68-14660. 1968. 44.50 (ISBN 0-12-289050-7). Acad Pr.

Kawamura, A., Jr., ed. Fluorescent Antibody Techniques. 2nd ed. (Illus.). 1977. 29.50 (ISBN 0-8391-0855-9). Univ Park.

Sarker, A. K. Fluorescent Whitening Agents. 1970. 15.00 (ISBN 0-87245-411-8). Textile Bk.

FLUORESCENT LIGHTING

Butler, Keith H. Fluorescent Lamp Phosphors. LC 79-11829. (Illus.). 1980. lib. bdg. 39.50x (ISBN 0-271-00219-0). Pa St U Pr.

Miller, Samuel C. Neon Techniques & Handling: Handbook of Neon Sign & Cold Cathode Lighting. 1977. 21.00 (ISBN 0-911380-41-8). Signs of Times.

FLUORIDATION OF WATER

see Water-Fluoridation

FLUORIDES

see also Water-Fluoridation

Adler, P., et al. Fluorides & Human Health. (Monograph Ser: No. 59). 364p. 1970. 13.60 (ISBN 92-4-140059-5, 423). World Health.

Berndt, Alan F. & Stearns, Robert I. Dental Fluoride Chemistry. (Illus.). 144p. 1978. 14.75 (ISBN 0-398-03753-1). C C Thomas.

Bibliographical Abstracts on Evaluation of Fluorescent Whitening Agents. 1972. 3.25 (ISBN 0-8031-0075-2, STP507). ASTM.

Chambers, Richard D. Fluorine in Organic Chemistry. 410p. 1981. Repr. of 1973 ed. lib. bdg. 35.50 (ISBN 0-89874-345-1). Krieger.

Committee on Animal Nutrition. Effects of Fluorides in Animals. LC 74-4061. (Illus.). 76p. 1974. pap. 4.25 (ISBN 0-309-02219-3). Natl Acad Pr.

Committee On Biological Effects Of Atmospheric Pollutants. Fluorides. LC 70-169178. (Biological Effects of Atmospheric Pollutants Ser). 1971. pap. text ed. 7.75 (ISBN 0-309-01922-2). Natl Acad Pr.

Davies, G. N. Cost & Benefit of Fluoride in the Prevention of Dental Caries. (Offset Pub.: No. 9). (Also avail. in French). 1974. pap. 8.00 (ISBN 92-4-170009-2). World Health.

Gedalia, I., et al. The Role of Fluoride in Bone Structure. LC 72-87824. 1973. 5.00 (ISBN 0-87527-103-0). Green.

Gotzsche, Anne-Lise. The Flouride Question: Panacea or Poison. LC 74-30117. 1975. 25.00 (ISBN 0-8128-1794-X). Stein & Day.

Hawkins, Donald T., et al, eds. Binary Flourides: Free Molecular Structures & Force Fields. a Bibliography, 1957-1975. 238p. 1976. 45.00 (ISBN 0-306-66011-3). IFI Plenum.

Johansen, Erling & Taves, Donald R., eds. Continuing Evaluation of the Use of Fluorides. (AAAS Selected Symposium Ser.: No. 11). (Illus.). 1979. lib. bdg. 28.75x (ISBN 0-89158-439-0). Westview.

Myers, H. M. Fluorides & Dental Fluorosis. (Monographs in Oral Science: Vol. 7). (Illus.). 1978. 23.50 (ISBN 3-8055-1412-3). S Karger.

Newbrun, Ernest, ed. Fluorides & Dental Caries. 2nd ed. (Illus.). 208p. 1978. 15.75 (ISBN 0-398-03448-6). C C Thomas.

Production of Yellow Cake & Uranium Fluorides. 355p. 1981. pap. 45.50 (ISBN 92-0-041080-4, ISP 553, IAEA). Unipub.

Smith, F. A., ed. Pharmacology of Fluorides. (Handbook of Experimental Pharmacology: Vol. 20). (Illus.). 1966-70. Pt. 1. 103.30 (ISBN 0-387-03537-0); Pt. 2. 97.40 (ISBN 0-387-04846-4). Springer-Verlag.

Workshop on Cariostatic Mechanism of Fluorides, Naples, Florida, April 1976. Proceedings. Koenig, K. G., ed. (Caries Research: Vol. 11, Suppl. 1). 1976. 46.25 (ISBN 3-8055-2430-7). S Karger.

FLUORIMETRY

International Commission on Radiation Units & Measurements. Cameras for Image Intensifier Fluorography. LC 73-97641. 7.00 (ISBN 0-913394-08-4). Intl Comm Rad Meas.

Kaufman, Leon. Medical Applications of Fluorescent Excitation Analysis. 176p. 1979. 49.95 (ISBN 0-8493-5507-9). CRC Pr.

Pesez, M. & Bartos, J. Colorimetric & Fluorimetric Analysis of Organic Compounds & Drugs. (Clinical & Biochemical Analysis Ser.: Vol. 1). 688p. 1974. 66.50 (ISBN 0-8247-6105-7). Dekker.

Snell, Forster D. Photometric & Fluorometric Methods of Analysis: Metals, 2 pts. LC 77-25039. 1978. Set. 227.00 (ISBN 0-471-81014-2, Pub. by Wiley-Interscience). Wiley.

Wehry, E. L., ed. Modern Fluorescence Spectroscopy. (Modern Analytical Chemistry Ser.: Vol. 3). 346p. 1981. text ed. 39.50 (ISBN 0-306-40690-X, Plenum Pr). Plenum Pub.

--Modern Fluorescence Spectroscopy. (Modern Analytical Chemistry Ser.: Vol. 4). 270p. 1981. text ed. 35.00 (ISBN 0-306-40691-8, Plenum Pr). Plenum Pub.

White, Charles E. & Argauer, R. J. Fluorescence Analysis: A Practical Approach. 1970. 44.50 (ISBN 0-8247-1781-3). Dekker.

FLUORINE

see also Organofluorine Compounds

Chambers, Richard D. Fluorine in Organic Chemistry. 410p. 1981. Repr. of 1973 ed. lib. bdg. 35.50 (ISBN 0-89874-345-1). Krieger.

Ciba Foundation. Carbon-Fluorine Compounds. (Ciba Foundation Symposium: No. 2). 1972. 30.50 (ISBN 0-444-10373-2, Excerpta Medica). Elsevier.

Committee on Animal Nutrition. Effects of Fluorides in Animals. LC 74-4061. (Illus.). 76p. 1974. pap. 4.25 (ISBN 0-309-02219-3). Natl Acad Pr.

Eagers, R. Y. Toxic Properties of Inorganic Flourine Compounds. 1969. 26.00x (ISBN 0-444-20044-4, Pub. by Applied Science). Burgess-Intl Ideas.

Emeleus, H. J. Chemistry of Fluorine & Its Compounds. (Current Chemical Concepts Monograph Ser). 1969. 27.50 (ISBN 0-12-238150-5). Acad Pr.

Largent, Edward J. Fluorosis: The Health Aspects of Fluorine Compounds. LC 60-16601. 1961. 3.50 (ISBN 0-8142-0079-6). Ohio St U Pr.

Nikolaev, N. S., et al. Analytical Chemistry of Fluorine. LC 72-4101. (Analytical Chemistry of the Elements Ser.). 222p. 1973. 42.95 (ISBN 0-470-63860-5). Halsted Pr.

Simons, J. H., ed. Fluorine Chemistry, 5 vols. 1950-64. Vol. 1. 67.50 (ISBN 0-12-643901-X); Vol. 2. 67.50 (ISBN 0-12-643902-8); Vol. 3. 51.00 (ISBN 0-12-643903-6); Vol. 4. 78.00 (ISBN 0-12-643904-4); Vol. 5. 58.50 (ISBN 0-12-643905-2). Acad Pr.

Tarrant, Paul, ed. Fluorine Chemistry Reviews, Vol. 1. 1967. 49.00 (ISBN 0-8247-1645-0). Dekker.

--Fluorine Chemistry Reviews, Vol. 2. 1968. 36.00 (ISBN 0-8247-1646-9). Dekker.

--Fluorine Chemistry Reviews, Vol. 3. LC 67-30920. 1969. 34.00 (ISBN 0-8247-1647-7). Dekker.

--Fluorine Chemistry Reviews, Vol. 4. 1969. 42.00 (ISBN 0-8247-1648-5). Dekker.

--Fluorine Chemistry Reviews, Vol. 7. 256p. 1974. 47.00 (ISBN 0-8247-6091-3). Dekker.

--Fluorine Chemistry Reviews, Vol. 8. 1977. 43.00 (ISBN 0-8247-6578-8). Dekker.

FLUORINE-PHYSIOLOGICAL EFFECT

see also Water-Fluoridation

Muhler, Joseph C. & Hine, Maynard K., eds. Fluorine & Dental Health: The Pharmacology & Toxicology of Fluorine. LC 72-85274. 216p. 1973. Repr. of 1959 ed. 12.50 (ISBN 0-8046-1703-1). Kennikat.

--Flourine & Dental Health: The Pharmacology & Toxicology of Fluorine. LC 72-85274. 216p. 1973. Repr. of 1959 ed. 12.50 (ISBN 0-8046-1703-1). Kennikat.

Tarrant, Paul, ed. Fluorine Chemistry Reviews, Vol. 5. 1971. 47.00 (ISBN 0-8247-1649-3). Dekker.

FLUOROCARBONS

Aviado, Domingo M. Fluorocarbons. Goldberg, Leon, ed. (Uniscience Ser.). 1976. cancelled (ISBN 0-87819-128-3). CRC Pr.

Banks, R. E., ed. Fluorocarbon & Related Chemistry, Vols. 1-3. Barlow, M. G. Incl. Vol. 1. 1969-70 Literature. 1971. 41.25 (ISBN 0-85186-504-6); Vol. 2. 1971-72 Literature. 1974. 52.25 (ISBN 0-85186-514-3); Vol. 3. 1973-74 Literature. 1976. 96.25 (ISBN 0-85186-524-0). LC 72-78530. Am Chemical.

Markets for Alternatives to Chlorofluocarbons: C-006r. 1979. 700.00 (ISBN 0-89336-206-9). BCC.

Stoel, Thomas B., Jr. & Miller, Alan S. Fluorocarbon Regulation: An International Comparison. LC 79-3178. (Illus.). 320p. 1980. 26.95x (ISBN 0-669-03393-6). Lexington Bks.

Sugden, T. M. & West, T. F., eds. Chlorofluorocarbons in the Environment: The Aerosol Controversy. 183p. 1980. 59.95x (ISBN 0-470-26937-5). Halsted Pr.

FLUOROMETRY

see Fluorimetry

FLUOROSCOPIC DIAGNOSIS

see Diagnosis, Fluoroscopic

FLUTE

see also Recorder (Musical Instrument)

Badger, Alfred G. An Illustrated History of the Flute, & Sketch of the Successive Improvements Made in the Flute. 1976. Repr. 25.00 (ISBN 0-403-06150-4, Regency). Scholarly.

Bate, Philip. The Flute. rev. ed. (Instruments of the Orchestra Ser.). 1980. 17.95 (ISBN 0-393-01292-1). Norton.

--Flute. (Illus.). 1969. 10.00x (ISBN 0-393-02071-1). Norton.

Boehm, Theobald. An Essay on the Construction of Flutes Giving a History & Description of the Most Recent Improvements, with an Explanation of the Principles of Acoustics Applicable to the Manufacture of Wind Instruments. Broadwood, W. S., ed. 1976. Repr. of 1882 ed. 25.00 (ISBN 0-403-06722-7, Regency). Scholarly.

--Flute & Flute-Playing: In Acoustal, Technical & Artistic Aspects. (Illus.). 6.75 (ISBN 0-8446-1697-4). Peter Smith.

--Uber den Flotenbau. (The Flute Library: Vol. 16). (Ger. & Eng.). 1981. 35.00 (ISBN 90-6027-169-6, Pub. by Frits Knuf Netherlands). Pendragon NY.

Boehm, Theobold. Flute & Flute-Playing in Acoustical, Technical & Artistic Aspects. Miller, Dayton C., tr. (Illus.). 1964. pap. 3.00 (ISBN 0-486-21259-9). Dover.

Chapman, F. B. Flute Technique. 4th ed. 1973. pap. 7.75 (ISBN 0-19-318609-8). Oxford U Pr.

Delusse, Charles. L' Art de la Flute Traversiere. (The Flute Library: Vol. 10). 1980. Repr. of 1760 ed. wrappers 35.00 (ISBN 90-6027-207-2, Pub. by Frits Knuf Netherlands). Pendragon NY.

De Vaucanson, J. Le Mecanisme du Fluteur Automate: An Account of the Automation or Image Playing the German Flute. (The Flute Library: Vol. 5). 1979. Repr. of 1742 ed. 37.50 (ISBN 90-6027-211-0, Pub. by Frits Knuf Netherlands); wrappers 25.00 (ISBN 90-6027-210-2, Pub. by Frits Knuf Netherlands). Pendragon NY.

Devienne, F. Nouvelle Methode de Flute. new ed. (The Flute Library: Vol. 7). x, 76p. Repr. of 1800 ed. wrappers 32.50 (ISBN 90-6027-208-0, Pub. by Frits Knuf Netherlands). Pendragon NY.

Dick, Robert. The Other Flute: A Performance Manual of Contemporary Techniques with 33.3 RPM Mono Record. (Illus.). 1975. text ed. 22.50 (ISBN 0-19-322125-X). Oxford U Pr.

Drouet, L. Method of Flute Playing. (The Flute Library: Vol. 17). 1981. Repr. of 1830 ed. write for info. (ISBN 90-6027-390-7, Pub. by Frits Knuf Netherlands); wrappers write for info. (ISBN 90-6027-213-7, Pub. by Frits Knuf Netherlands). Pendragon NY.

Duetti Facili per Flauti in Do: Twenty Nine Easy Duets for Recorder & Flute. pap. 1.95 (ISBN 0-916786-45-5). St George Bk Serv.

Granom, Lewis. Plain & Easy Instructions for Playing the German-Flute. (The Flute Library: Vol. 11). 1981. Repr. of 1770 ed. write for info. (ISBN 90-6027-230-7, Pub. by Frits Knuf Netherlands). Pendragon NY.

Heyde, Herbert. Floteninstrumente Karl-Marx-Universitat zu Leipzig: Musik-instrumenten-Museum, Gesamtkatalog, Band I. (The Flute Library: Vol. 20). 1979. 32.50 (ISBN 90-6027-261-7, Pub. by Frits Knuf Netherlands). Pendragon NY.

Howell, Thomas. Avant-Garde Flute: A Handbook for Composers & Flutists. (New Instrumentation, Vol. 2). (Illus.). 1974. spiral bdg. 14.95x (ISBN 0-520-02305-6). U of Cal Pr.

Hugot, A. & Wunderlich, J. G. Methode de Flute. (The Flute Library: Vol. 3). 1975. Repr. of 1804 ed. 62.50 (ISBN 90-6027-265-X, Pub. by Frits Knuf Netherlands); wrappers 45.00 (ISBN 90-6027-264-1). Pendragon NY.

Mahaut, A. Nieuwe Manier Om Binnen Korte Tijd Op De Dwarsfluit Te Leeren Speelen: Nouvelle Methode Pour Apprendre En Peu De Temps a Jouer De la Flute Traversiere. (The Flute Library: Vol. 4). 36p. 1981. 25.00 (ISBN 90-6027-292-7, Pub. by Frits Knuf Netherlands). Pendragon NY.

Mather, Roger. The Art of Playing the Flute: Breath Control. LC 80-52140. (A Series of Workbooks: Vol. 1). (Illus.). 88p. (Orig.). 1980. pap. 6.95 (ISBN 0-9604640-0-X). Romney Pr.

--The Art of Playing the Flute: Embouchure, Vol. 2. LC 80-52140. (Illus.). 102p. (Orig.). 1981. pap. 8.95 (ISBN 0-9604640-1-8). Romney Pr.

Pellerite, James J. A Notebook of Techniques for a Flute Recital. 1967. pap. text ed. 3.25 (ISBN 0-931200-50-4). Zalo.

--Performance Methods for Flutists. 1968. pap. text ed. 4.75 (ISBN 0-931200-51-2). Zalo.

Putnik, Edwin. Art of Flute Playing. LC 75-146521. (Illus.). 1970. pap. 10.20 (ISBN 0-87487-077-1). Summy.

Quantz, Johann J. On Playing the Flute. Reilly, Edward R., tr. LC 75-10986. (Illus.). 1975. 19.95 (ISBN 0-02-871940-9); pap. 8.95 (ISBN 0-02-871930-1). Schirmer Bks.

Reede, Rien D. Die Flote in der Allgemeine Musikelische Zeitung' (1798-1848) (The Flute Library: Vol. 18). 350p. 1981. write for info. (ISBN 90-6027-324-9, Pub by Frits Knuf Netherlands). Pendragon NY.

Rockstro, Richard S. A Treatise on the Flute. LC 76-22348. (Illus.). 1976. Repr. of 1928 ed. lib. bdg. 50.00 (ISBN 0-89341-007-1). Longwood Pr.

Shepard, Mark. How to Love Your Flute: A Guide to Flutes & Flute-Playing. (Illus.). 1979. pap. 6.95 (ISBN 0-915572-36-2). Panjandrum.

Soussmann, H. Complete Method for the Flute. Popp, W., ed. 144p. (Orig., Eng. & Ger.). (gr. 6-12). 1911. pap. 8.00 (ISBN 0-686-64088-8, 0506). Fischer Inc NY.

Takahashi Flute School, Vol. 1. (The Suzuki Method). 1971. 4.20 (ISBN 0-685-91447-X). Summy.

Thoinan, E. Les Hotteterre et les Chedeville Eighteen & Ninety Four. (The Flute Library: Vol. 19). 37.50 (ISBN 90-6027-355-9, Pub. by Frits Knuf Netherlands). Pendragon NY.

Toff, Nancy. Development of the Modern Flute. LC 78-57562. 1979. 19.95 (ISBN 0-8008-2185-8, Crescendo); pap. 9.95 (ISBN 0-8008-2186-6, Crescendo). Taplinger.

Tromlitz, J. G. Ausfuhrlicher und Grundlicher Unterricht Die Flote Zu Spielen. (The Flute Library: Vol. 1). 60.00 (ISBN 90-6027-358-3, Pub. by Frits Knuf Netherlands); wrappers 45.00 (ISBN 90-6027-357-5). Pendragon NY.

Voorhees, Jerry L. Classifying Flute Fingering Systems of the Nineteenth & Twentieth Centuries. (The Flute Library: Vol. 15). (Illus.). 100p. 1980. 32.50 (ISBN 90-6027-366-4, Pub. by Frits Knuf Netherlands); 22.50 (ISBN 90-6027-365-6). Pendragon NY.

Wagner, Ernst F. Foundation to Flute Playing: An Elementary Method. rev. ed. 120p. (Orig.). (gr. 4-12). 1918. pap. 6.00 (ISBN 0-686-64101-9, 0223). Fischer Inc NY.

Welch, Christopher. History of the Boehm Flute. LC 77-75195. 1977. Repr. of 1886 ed. lib. bdg. 15.00 (ISBN 0-89341-098-5). Longwood Pr.

FLUTE MUSIC

see also Recorder Music

Corrette, M. Methode pour apprende aisement a jouir de la Flute Traversiere. (The Flute Library: Vol. 6). 1978. Repr. of 1740 ed. wrappers 22.50 (ISBN 90-6027-195-5, Pub. by Frits Knuf Netherlands). Pendragon NY.

McGowan, Richard A. Italian Baroque Solo Sonatas for the Recorder & the Flute. LC 77-92345. (Detroit Studies in Music Bibliography Ser.: No. 37). 1978. 7.50 (ISBN 0-911772-90-1). Info Coord.

Quantz, Johann J. On Playing the Flute. Reilly, Edward R., tr. LC 75-10986. (Illus.). 1975. 19.95 (ISBN 0-02-871940-9); pap. 8.95 (ISBN 0-02-871930-1). Schirmer Bks.

Riley, Edward. Riley's Flute Melodies, 2vols. in 1. Hitchcock, H. Wiley, ed. & intro. by. LC 72-14213. (Earlier American Music Ser.: Vol. 18). 200p. 1973. Repr. of 1816 ed. lib. bdg. 17.50 (ISBN 0-306-70565-6). Da Capo.

FLUX (METALLURGY)

see also Slag

FLUXIONS

see Calculus

FLY

see Flies

FLY-CASTING

see also Flies, Artificial

Ball, John W. Casting & Fishing the Artificial Fly. LC 79-140119. (Illus.). 1972. pap. 3.95 (ISBN 0-87004-217-3). Caxton.

Blades, William F. Fishing Flies & Flytying. (Illus.). 320p. 1980. 24.95 (ISBN 0-8117-0613-3). Stackpole.

Hidy, Vernon S. & Sports Illustrated Editors. Sports Illustrated Fly Fishing. rev. ed. LC 74-38908. (Illus.). (YA) 1972. 5.95 (ISBN 0-397-00859-7); pap. 2.95 (ISBN 0-397-00858-9, LP-63). Har-Row.

McKim, John. Fly Tying: Adventures in Fur, Feathers, & Fun. (Illus.). 208p. (Orig.). 1981. pap. 9.95 (ISBN 0-87842-140-8). Mountain Pr.

Netherton, Cliff. Angling & Casting: A Manual for Self & Class Instruction. LC 76-10881. (Illus.). 1977. 9.95 (ISBN 0-498-01877-6). A S Barnes.

--History of the Sport of Casting: People, Events, Records, Tackle & Literature - Early Times. LC 81-65632. (Illus.). 404p. 1981. lib. bdg. 24.95 (ISBN 0-9605960-0-3); pap. 14.95 (ISBN 0-9605960-1-1). Am Casting.

Rice, Freddie. Fly-Tying Illustrated: Wet & Dry Patterns. (Illus.). 168p. 1981. 28.50 (ISBN 0-7134-2363-3, Pub. by Batsford England). David & Charles.

FLY DISEASE

see Trypanosomiasis

FLY FISHING

see also Fly-Casting

Arbona, Fred L., Jr. Mayflies, the Angler, & the Trout. (Illus.). 224p. 1980. 19.95 (ISBN 0-87691-299-4). Winchester Pr.

Atherton, John. The Fly & the Fish. (Illus.). 256p. 1971. boxed 12.95 (ISBN 0-88395-009-X). Freshet Pr.

Barder, Richard. Dry Fly Trouting for Beginners. 1976. 5.95 (ISBN 0-7153-7055-3). David & Charles.

Barnes, George W. How to Make Bamboo Fly Rods. 1977. 11.95 (ISBN 0-87691-237-4). Winchester Pr.

Bay, Kenneth E., ed. The American Fly Tyer's Handbook. (Illus.). 1979. 14.95 (ISBN 0-87691-287-0). Winchester Pr.
Blades, William F. Fishing Flies & Flytying. (Illus.). 320p. 1980. 24.95 (ISBN 0-8117-0613-3). Stackpole.
Burns, Eugene. Advanced Fly Fishing. (Illus.). 288p. 1979. 18.00 (ISBN 0-8117-0040-2). Stackpole.
Cross, Reuben. The Completest Fly Tier. (Illus.). 224p. 1971. 7.95 (ISBN 0-88395-008-1). Freshet Pr.
Dick, Lenox. The Art & Science of Fly Fishing. 1977. pap. 3.95 (ISBN 0-8065-0587-7). Citadel Pr.
Downs, Donald, et al. The Essence of Fly Fishing. (Illus.). 1977. pap. 3.95 (ISBN 0-903330-25-3). Transatlantic.
Esquire, D. J. Secrets of Angling. 62p. 1970. boxed 6.75 (ISBN 0-88395-001-4). Freshet Pr.
Fly Fisherman Magazine, ed. Fly Fisherman's Complete Guide to Fishing with the Fly Rod. (Illus.). 1978. 16.95 (ISBN 0-87165-013-4); pap. 9.95 (ISBN 0-87165-094-0). Ziff-Davis Pub.
Garrison, Everett & Carmichael, Hoagy B. A Master's Guide to Building a Bamboo Fly Rod. LC 77-2831. (Illus.). 384p. 1977. 20.00 (ISBN 0-8117-0352-5). Stackpole.
Haas, Evelyn & Cooper, Gwen. Wade a Little Deeper, Dear. Steinfeld, Naomi, ed. LC 78-75159. (Illus.). 1979. pap. 4.50 (ISBN 0-89395-013-0). Cal Living Bks.
Haig-Brown, Roderick & Haig-Brown, Valerie. The Master & His Fish: From the World of Roderick Haig-Brown. 202p. 1981. 15.00 (ISBN 0-295-95847-2); pap. 7.95 (ISBN 0-295-95875-8). U of Wash Pr.
Hellekson, Terry. Popular Fly Patterns. LC 76-49452. (Illus.). 1975. pap. 11.95 (ISBN 0-87905-065-9). Peregrine Smith.
Hills, John W. History of Fly Fishing for Trout. 256p. 1971. boxed 8.95 (ISBN 0-88395-011-1). Freshet Pr.
Humphreys, Joe. Joe Humphreys's Trout Tactics. (Illus.). 192p. (Orig.). 1981. pap. 12.95 (ISBN 0-8117-2079-9). Stackpole.
Ivens, T. C. Still Water Fly Fishing: A Modern Guide to Angling in Reservoirs & Lakes. 3rd ed. (Illus.). 1971. 12.50 (ISBN 0-233-96128-3). Transatlantic.
Jorgensen, Poul. Modern Fly Dressings for the Practical Angler. 1976. 15.00 (ISBN 0-87691-224-2). Winchester Pr.
--Poul Jorgensen's Modern Trout Flies: --and How to Tie Them. LC 78-3897. (Illus.). 1979. 12.95 (ISBN 0-385-15346-5); pap. 7.95 (ISBN 0-385-15347-3). Doubleday.
Koch, Ed. Fishing the Midge. (Illus.). 164p. 1973. 7.95 (ISBN 0-88395-017-0). Freshet Pr.
LaFontaine, Gary J. Challenge of the Trout. LC 76-8608. (Illus.). 243p. 1976. 12.95 (ISBN 0-87842-058-4). Mountain Pr.
Lee, Art. Fly Fishing: Dry Flies for Trout on Rivers & Streams. LC 81-66449. 1981. 14.95 (ISBN 0-689-10959-8). Atheneum.
--Fly Fishing: Dry Flies for Trout on Rivers & Streams. LC 81-66449. 1981. 10.95 (ISBN 0-689-11221-1). Atheneum.
Leisenring, James & Hidy, Vernon S. Art of Tying the Wet Fly & Fishing the Flymph. (Illus.). 1971. 6.95 (ISBN 0-517-50337-9). Crown.
Leiser, Eric & Boyle, Robert H. Stoneflies for the Angler. LC 81-47478. (Illus.). 192p. 1982. 15.95 (ISBN 0-394-50822-X). Knopf.
Leiser, Eric & Solomon, Larry. The Caddis & the Angler. LC 76-58533. (Illus.). 224p. 1977. 14.95 (ISBN 0-8117-0312-6). Stackpole.
Leonard, Edson. Feather in the Breeze. (Illus.). 1974. 7.95 (ISBN 0-88395-026-X). Freshet Pr.
Leonard, J. Edson. The Essential Fly Tier. LC 76-9043. (Illus.). 1976. 12.95 (ISBN 0-13-286120-8). P-H.
McNally, Tom. Fly Fishing. LC 77-12448. (Outdoor Life Bk.). (Illus.). 1979. 14.95 (ISBN 0-06-012868-2, HarpT). Har-Row.
Malo, John. Fly Fishing for Panfish. LC 80-26788. (Illus.). 150p. 1981. 8.95 (ISBN 0-87518-208-9). Dillon.
Marinaro, Vincent C. In the Ring of the Rise. 1976. limited ed. 12.95 (ISBN 0-517-52550-X). Crown.
--Modern Dry-Fly Code. (Illus.). 1970. 10.00 (ISBN 0-517-50442-1). Crown.
Massy, Carl. Fly Flishing for Trout. (Illus.). 1976. 14.95 (ISBN 0-589-07183-1, Pub. by Reed Books Australia). C E Tuttle.
Mendoza, George. Fishing the Morning Lonely. (Illus.). 1974. 7.95 (ISBN 0-88395-029-4). Freshet Pr.
Michalak, David. Fly-Fishing. LC 75-38445. 1977. 12.00 (ISBN 0-498-01868-7). A S Barnes.
Nixon, Tom. Fly Tying & Fly Fishing for Bass & Panfish. 2nd rev. ed. LC 75-20613. 14.50 (ISBN 0-498-01826-1). A S Barnes.
Quick, James. Fishing the Nymph. (Illus.). 1960. 13.95 (ISBN 0-471-07162-5). Ronald Pr.
Raychard, Al. Al Raychard's Fly Fishing in Maine. LC 80-12126. (Illus.). 176p. (Orig.). 1980. pap. 6.95 (ISBN 0-89621-055-3). Thorndike Pr.
Rice, Freddie. Fly-Tying Illustrated: Wet & Dry Patterns. (Illus.). 168p. 1981. 28.50 (ISBN 0-7134-2363-3, Pub. by Batsford England). David & Charles.
Richards, Carl, et al. Stoneflies. (Illus.). 192p. 1980. 19.95 (ISBN 0-87691-327-3). Winchester Pr.
Robinson, Gilmer G. & Robinson, David L. The Basic Guide to Fly Fishing. LC 78-69639. (Illus.). 1979. 9.95 (ISBN 0-498-02215-3). A S Barnes.
Schuyler, Keith C. Getting Your Start in Flyrod Fishing. 1979. 9.95 (ISBN 0-679-51050-8). McKay.
Schwiebert, Ernest. Nymphs. LC 73-188596. (Illus.). 339p. 1973. 17.95 (ISBN 0-87691-074-6). Winchester Pr.
Shaw, H. Fly-Tying: Materials-Tools-Techniques. 2nd ed. LC 79-18416. 1979. 16.50 (ISBN 0-471-05516-6, Pub. by Wiley-Interscience). Wiley.
Slaymaker, S. R., 2nd. Tie a Fly, Catch a Trout. LC 76-9201. (Illus.). 1976. 9.95 (ISBN 0-06-013983-8, HarpT). Har-Row.
Solomon, Larry, ed. Complete Book of Modern Fly Fishing. (Illus.). 288p. 1979. pap. 7.95 (ISBN 0-695-81312-9). DBI.
Swisher, Doug & Richards, Carl. Fly Fishing Strategy. (Sportsmen's Classics Ser.). (Illus.). 220p. (YA) 1975. 12.95 (ISBN 0-517-52371-X). Crown.
Traver, Robert. Anatomy of a Fisherman. LC 78-13265. (Illus.). 1978. 16.95 (ISBN 0-87905-038-1); pap. 12.95 (ISBN 0-87905-037-3). Peregrine Smith.
Walker, Alf. The Art & Craftsmanship of Fly Fishing. 272p. 1981. 19.95 (ISBN 0-920510-52-3, Pub. by Personal Lib). Everest Hse.
--Fly Fishing Techniques: Basic Fundamentals & Championship Form. (Illus.). 1975. 8.95 (ISBN 0-88932-002-0, ADON 3546). Pagurian.
Wheat, Peter. The Observer's Book of Fly Fishing. (The Observer Bks). (Illus.). 1979. 3.95 (ISBN 0-684-16036-6). Scribner.
Whitlock, Dave & Boyle, Robert, eds. Fly-Tyer's Almanac. (Sportsmen's Classics Ser.). 220p. (YA) 1975. 12.95 (ISBN 0-517-52372-8). Crown.
Wiggin, Maurice. Fly Fishing. (Teach Yourself Ser.). 1974. pap. 4.95 (ISBN 0-679-10430-5). McKay.
Wilson, Loring D. The Fly-Fisherman's Workshop. LC 77-84594. (Illus.). 1979. 9.95 (ISBN 0-498-02182-3). A S Barnes.
--Tying & Fishing the Terrestrials. LC 77-74113. (Illus.). 1978. 12.50 (ISBN 0-498-02069-X). A S Barnes.
Woods, Craig. The Fly Fisherman's Streamside Handbook. 1981. 14.95 (ISBN 0-87165-108-4); pap. 8.95 (ISBN 0-87165-096-7). Ziff-Davis Pub.

FLYING
see Flight

FLYING, FEAR OF
see Fear of Flying

FLYING BOATS
see Seaplanes

FLYING BOMBS
see V-One Bomb; V-Two Rocket

FLYING CLASSES
see Flight Training

FLYING FORTRESS (BOMBERS)
see B-Seventeen Bomber

FLYING-MACHINES
see also Aeronautics; Airplanes; Gliders (Aeronautics); Helicopters; Propellers, Aerial; Rockets (Aeronautics)

Chanute, Octave. Progress in Flying Machines. 1976. Repr. 12.50 (ISBN 0-916494-00-4). Lorenz & Herweg.

FLYING SAUCERS

Barker, Gray. Gray Barker at Giant Rock. (Illus.). 100p. (Orig.). 1975. pap. 6.95 (ISBN 0-685-50455-7). Saucerian.
--Men in Black. (Illus., Orig.). 1979. pap. 7.95 (ISBN 0-685-26705-9). Saucerian.
Barker, Gray, ed. The Strange Case of Dr. M. K. Jessup. 4th ed. (Illus.). 82p. 1975. pap. 7.95 (ISBN 0-685-51759-4). Saucerian.
Bearden, Thomas E. The Excalibur Briefing: Understanding Paranormal Phenomena. LC 78-12936. (A Walnut Hill Bk.). (Illus., Orig.). 1980. pap. 8.95 (ISBN 0-89407-015-0). Strawberry Hill.
Beckley, Timothy G. Book of Space Contacts. 72p. 1981. pap. 7.95 (ISBN 0-938294-05-9). Global Comm.
--Psychic & UFO Revelations in Last Days. 2nd ed. (Illus.). 72p. 1981. pap. 7.95 (ISBN 0-938294-01-6). Global Comm.
Benitez, Juan J. UFOs: Official Documents of the Spanish Government. Creighton, Gordon, tr. 256p. 25.00x (ISBN 0-85978-043-0, Pub. by Spearman England). State Mutual Bk.
Berlitz, Charles & Moore, William L. The Roswell Incident. 1980. 10.00 (ISBN 0-448-21199-8). G&D.
Bernard, Raymond. Hollow Earth. (Illus.). 1969. pap. 6.95 (ISBN 0-685-20197-X). Saucerian.
--Hollow Earth. (Illus.). 1969. 6.95 (ISBN 0-8216-0090-7). Univ Bks.
Billig, Otto. Flying Saucers: Magic in the Skies. 256p. 1981. 16.95x (ISBN 0-87073-833-X). Schenkman.
Binder, Otto O. Flying Saucers Are Watching Us. 1978. pap. 1.50 (ISBN 0-505-51304-8). Tower Bks.
Blum, Ralph & Blum, Judy. Beyond Earth: Man's Contact with Ufo's. 1974. 6.95 (ISBN 0-686-10525-7). Phillips Pub Co.
Blumberg, Rhoda. UFO. (First Books). (Illus.). (gr. 4-6). 1977. PLB 6.90 (ISBN 0-531-00397-3). Watts.
Brandon, Jim. Weird America: A Guide to Places of Mystery in the United States. 1978. pap. 4.95 (ISBN 0-525-47491-9). Dutton.
Branley, Franklyn M. A Book of Flying Saucers for You. LC 72-78278. (Illus.). (gr. 3-6). 1973. PLB 9.89 (ISBN 0-690-15189-6, TYC-J). Har-Row.
Briazack, Norman J. & Mennick, Simon. The UFO Guidebook. 1978. 10.00 (ISBN 0-8065-0636-9). Citadel Pr.
Brom, Elgar. Sagasha: Mysterious Dust from Space. (Illus.). 72p. 1981. pap. 7.95 (ISBN 0-938294-00-8). Global Comm.
Carman, Oneal. God Is Alive & Well. 2nd rev. ed. 1976. 4.75 (ISBN 0-682-48521-7). Exposition.
Cathie, Bruce. Harmonic Thirty-Three. (Illus.). 1968. pap. 6.75 (ISBN 0-589-01055-7, Pub. by Reed Books Australia). C E Tuttle.
Cathie, Bruce L. & Temm, Peter N. UFO & Anti-Gravity. LC 77-8718. (A Walnut Hill Book). (Illus.). 1971. pap. 6.95 (ISBN 0-89407-011-8). Strawberry Hill.
Catoe, Lynn E., ed. UFOs & Related Subjects: An Annotated Bibliography. LC 78-26124. 1979. Repr. of 1969 ed. 44.00 (ISBN 0-8103-2021-5). Gale.
Cazeau, C. J. & Scott, S. D. Exploring the Unknown: Great Mysteries Re-Examined. LC 78-27413. (Illus.). 295p. 1979. 15.95 (ISBN 0-306-40210-6, Plenum Pr). Plenum Pub.
Cohen, Daniel. The Ancient Visitors. LC 75-21220. 224p. (gr. 4-7). 1976. 7.95 (ISBN 0-385-09786-7). Doubleday.
--Creatures from the UFO's. LC 78-7730. (High Interest-Low Vocabulary Book). (Illus.). (gr. 4-9). 1978. 5.95 (ISBN 0-396-07582-7). Dodd.
--Creatures from UFO's. (gr. 4 up). 1979. pap. 1.50 (ISBN 0-671-29951-4). Archway.
--The Great Airship Mystery: A UFO of the 1890's. (Illus.). 256p. 1981. 9.95 (ISBN 0-396-07990-3). Dodd.
Collins, Jim. Unidentified Flying Objects. LC 77-13040. (Great Unsolved Mysteries Ser.). (Illus.). (gr. 4-5). 1977. PLB 10.65 (ISBN 0-8172-1065-2). Raintree Pubs.
Constable, Trevor J. The Cosmic Pulse of Life: The Revolutionary Biological Power Behind UFO's. 432p. 25.00x (ISBN 0-85435-194-9, Pub. by Spearman England). State Mutual Bk.
--The Cosmic Pulse of Life: The Revolutionary Biological Power Behind UFO's. LC 77-72046. (Illus.). 446p. 1977. pap. 9.95 (ISBN 0-8334-1777-0). Steinerbks.
Coundakis, Anthony L. Mannerism on Space Communication. 256p. 1981. 12.50 (ISBN 0-682-49734-7). Exposition.
Drake, Raymond W. Gods or Spacemen? 1976. pap. 1.50 (ISBN 0-451-07192-1, W7192, Sig). NAL.
Druffel, Ann & Rogo, D. Scott. The Tujunga Canyon Contacts: A Continuing "Chain Reaction" of UFO Encounters & Abductions. (Illus.). 264p. 1980. 10.95 (ISBN 0-13-932541-7). P-H.
Dutta, Rex. Flying Saucer Viewpoint. 1972. 8.95 (ISBN 0-7207-0316-6). Transatlantic.
Eden, Jerome. Planet in Trouble: The UFO Assault on Earth. 1973. 8.50 (ISBN 0-682-47822-9). Exposition.
Emenegger, Robert. UFO's Past, Present & Future. Date not set. pap. cancelled (ISBN 0-345-29047-X). Ballantine.
Fitzgerald, Randall. Complete Book of Extraterrestrial Encounters. 1979. pap. 5.95 (ISBN 0-02-095500-6, Collier). Macmillan.
Fort, Charles. New Lands. Del Rey, Lester, ed. LC 75-409. (Library of Science Fiction). 1975. lib. bdg. 17.50 (ISBN 0-8240-1413-8). Garland Pub.
Fowler, R. UFOs: Interplanetary Visitors. 1979. pap. 4.95 (ISBN 0-13-935569-3, Reward). P-H.
Fowler, Raymond E. The Andreasson Affair. LC 78-11659. 1979. 9.95 (ISBN 0-13-036608-0). P-H.
--Casebook of a UFO Investigator. 1981. 10.95 (ISBN 0-13-117432-0). P-H.
Fuller, John G. Incident at Exeter. 272p. Date not set. pap. 1.95 (ISBN 0-425-03929-3). Berkley Pub.
--The Interrupted Journey. 1980. pap. 2.50 (ISBN 0-425-04388-6). Berkley Pub.
--The Interrupted Journey. 1974. pap. 2.50 (ISBN 0-425-03002-4, Medallion). Berkley Pub.
Gansberg, Judith & Gansberg, Alan. Direct Encounters: Personal Histories of UFO Abductees. (Illus.). 1980. 11.95 (ISBN 0-8027-0639-8). Walker & Co.
Gelman, Rita & Seligson, Marcia. UFO Encounters. (gr. 4-6). 1978. pap. 1.25 (ISBN 0-590-05403-1, Schol Pap). Schol Bk Serv.
Goran, Morris. The Modern Myth: Ancient Astronauts & UFOs. LC 76-50190. (Illus.). 1978. 8.95 (ISBN 0-498-02008-8). A S Barnes.
Gurney, Clare & Gurney, Gene. Unidentified Flying Objects. LC 75-105262. (Illus.). (gr. 5-10). 1970. 8.95 (ISBN 0-200-71677-8, B86600, AbS-J). Har-Row.
Haines, Richard F. Observing UFO's: An Investigative Handbook. LC 79-13418. 1980. 21.95x (ISBN 0-88229-540-3); pap. 10.95 (ISBN 0-88229-725-2). Nelson-Hall.
Haines, Richard F., ed. UFO Phenomena & the Behavioral Scientist. LC 79-14878. 464p. 1979. 20.00 (ISBN 0-8108-1228-2). Scarecrow.
Harrison, Sam. The Krone Chronicles: A True Story. LC 80-23505. (Orig.). 1981. pap. 5.95 (ISBN 0-89865-030-5). Donning Co.
Hendry, Allan A. The UFO Handbook-A Guide to Investigating, Evaluating & Reporting UFO Sightings. (Illus.). 1979. pap. 8.95 (ISBN 0-385-14348-6, Dolp). Doubleday.
Hopkins, Budd. Missing Time: A Documented Study of UFO Abductions. 256p. 1981. 12.95 (ISBN 0-399-90102-7). Marek.
Hymers, R. L. Encounters of the Fourth Kind. Orig. Title: UFO's & Bible Prophecy. pap. 1.95 (ISBN 0-89728-028-8, 698609). Omega Pubns OR.
--UFO's & Bible Prophecy. pap. 1.95 (ISBN 0-89728-061-X, 665117). Omega Pubns OR.
Hynek, Allen. The Hynek UFO Report. pap. 1.95 (ISBN 0-440-19201-3). Dell.
Hynek, J. Allen. The UFO Experience: A Scientific Inquiry. LC 76-183827. (Illus.). 256p. 1972. 8.95 (ISBN 0-8092-9130-4). Contemp Bks.
Jacobs, David M. The Ufo Controversy in America. LC 74-11886. (Illus.). 384p. 1975. 15.95x (ISBN 0-253-19006-1). Ind U Pr.
Jessup, M. K. The Case for the UFO. 1973. pap. 32.50 (ISBN 0-685-37599-4). Saucerian.
Keel, John A. Why UFOs. 1978. pap. 1.95 (ISBN 0-532-19183-8). Woodhill.
Kettelkamp, Larry. Investigating UFO's. LC 77-155993. (Illus.). (gr. 5-9). 1971. PLB 6.96 (ISBN 0-688-31768-5). Morrow.
Klass, Philip. UFO's Explained. LC 76-8285. 1976. pap. 2.95 (ISBN 0-394-72106-3, Vin). Random.
Knight, David C. Those Mysteriuos UFO's: The Story of Unidentitied Flying Objects. LC 74-31465. (Finding-Out Book). (Illus.). 64p. (gr. 2-4). 1979. Repr. of 1975 ed. PLB 7.95 (ISBN 0-89490-032-3). Enslow Pubs.
--UFO's: A Pictorial History from Antiquity to the Present. LC 78-23653. (Illus.). 1979. 12.95 (ISBN 0-07-035103-1). McGraw.
Kraspedon, Dino. My Contact with Flying Saucers. 208p. 15.00x (ISBN 0-85435-223-6, Pub. by Spearman England). State Mutual Bk.
Larsen, Sherman J. Close Encounters: A Factual Report on UFOs. LC 78-2322. (Illus.). (gr. 4-12). 1978. PLB 18.25 (ISBN 0-8172-1200-0). Raintree Pubs.
Lindsay, Gordon. Flying Saucers. pap. 0.95 (ISBN 0-89985-199-1). Christ Nations.
Looking at UFOs. (gr. 2-4). 1980. PLB 6.90 (ISBN 0-531-04098-4). Watts.
Looseley, William R. An Account of a Meeting with Denizens of Another World. 1980. 7.95 (ISBN 0-312-00233-5). St Martin.
McCampbell, James M. UFOlogy. new ed. LC 73-93488. (Illus.). 176p. 1976. pap. 4.95 (ISBN 0-89087-144-2). Celestial Arts.
Machlin, Milt. The Total UFO Story. 1979. pap. text ed. 1.95 (ISBN 0-89559-150-2). Dale Books Inc.
Machlin, Milt & Beckley, Tim. UFO. (Illus.). 192p. 1981. pap. 8.95 (ISBN 0-8256-3182-3, Quick Fox). Music Sales.
Mayer, Ann M. & Mayer, Harry F. Who's Out There? UFO Encounters. LC 79-14802. (Illus.). 96p. (gr. 4-6). 1979. PLB 7.29 (ISBN 0-671-32986-3). Messner.
Menzel, Donald H. & Taves, Ernest H. UFO Enigma-the Definitive Explanation of the UFO Phenomenon. LC 76-16255. 1977. 9.95 (ISBN 0-385-03596-9). Doubleday.
Messier, Charles. The Messier Catalogue. Niles, P. H., ed. LC 80-70586. 52p. (Orig.). 1981. pap. 1.50 (ISBN 0-9602738-2-4). Auriga.
Michael X. Venusian Health Magic. 1972. pap. 12.95 (ISBN 0-685-37600-1). Saucerian.
Michel, Aime. Flying Saucers & the Straight-Line Mystery. LC 58-8787. (Illus.). 1958. 12.95 (ISBN 0-87599-077-0). S G Phillips.

Moore, Alvin E. The Mystery of the Skymen. 1979. pap. 15.00 (ISBN 0-685-67589-0). Saucerian.
Ortzen, Len. Strange Stories of UFOs. LC 77-76726. 1977. 7.95 (ISBN 0-8008-7468-4). Taplinger.
Pawlicki, T. How to Build a Flying Saucer: And Other Proposals in Specultive Engineering. 1980. pap. 6.95 (ISBN 0-13-402461-3). P-H.
Peters, Ted. UFOs-God's Chariots? Flying Saucers in Politics, Science & Religion. LC 76-44978. 1977. 7.95 (ISBN 0-8042-2233-9). John Knox.
Pugh, Randall J. & Holiday, F. W. The Dyfed Enigma. 192p. 1979. 16.95 (ISBN 0-571-11412-1, Pub. by Faber & Faber). Merrimack Bk Serv.
Ross, Dave. Making UFOs. (gr. 1-3). 1980. PLB 8.60 (ISBN 0-531-04144-1). Watts.
Rutland, Jonathan. Exploring UFOs. (gr. 3-5). 1980. 6.90 (ISBN 0-531-09176-7); PLB 6.45 (ISBN 0-531-09166-X). Watts.
Rutledge, Harley D. Project Identification: The First Scientific Field Study of UFO Phenomena. (Illus.). 1981. 10.95 (ISBN 0-13-730713-6); pap. 6.95 (ISBN 0-13-730705-5). P-H.
Sachs. The U F O Encyclopedia. 1980. 14.95 (ISBN 0-399-12365-2). Putnam.
Sagan, Carl & Page, Thornton, eds. UFO's: A Scientific Debate. LC 72-4572. (Illus.). 368p. 1973. 16.95 (ISBN 0-8014-0740-0). Cornell U Pr.
--UFO's: A Scientific Debate. (Illus.). 344p. 1974. pap. 3.95 (ISBN 0-393-00739-1, Norton Lib). Norton.
Seagraves, Kelly L. Everything You Always Wanted to Know About Dinosaurs, Flying Saucers, the Beginning & the End. 1980. pap. 3.95 (ISBN 0-89293-003-9). Beta Bk.
Segraves, Kelly L. Great Flying Saucer Myth. 1977. pap. 1.25 (ISBN 0-89293-045-4). Beta Bk.
Sheaffer, Robert. The UFO Verdict: Examining the Evidence. LC 80-84406. (Critiques of the Paranormal Ser.). 275p. 1981. 15.95 (ISBN 0-87975-146-0). Prometheus Bks.
Short, Robert. UFOs: Atlantis to Armeggedon. (Illus.). 72p. 1981. pap. 7.95 (ISBN 0-938294-08-3). Global Comm.
Shuttlewood, Arthur. UFO Prophecy. 2nd ed. (Illus.). 72p. 1981. pap. 8.95 (ISBN 0-938294-03-2). Global Comm.
--UFO Prophecy. 266p. (Orig.). 1978. pap. 7.95 (ISBN 0-910122-42-3, Pub. by Global Commun). Amherst Pr.
--UFO Prophecy. (Orig.). 1978. pap. 7.95 (ISBN 0-910122-42-3). Amherst Pr.
--UFOs: Visions of a New Age. (Illus.). 72p. 1981. pap. 8.95 (ISBN 0-938294-04-0). Global Comm.
Snyder, Gerald S. Are There Alien Beings? The Story of UFOs. LC 80-10453. (Illus.). 160p. (gr. 7 up). 1980. PLB 8.79 (ISBN 0-671-33077-2). Messner.
Somerville, Robert S. UFO Terms. LC 79-63109. (Illus.). 1980. pap. 7.00 (ISBN 0-933938-00-4). UFO Schools.
Soule, Gardner. UFO & IFO: A Factual Report on Flying Saucers. (Illus.). (gr. 5-9). 1967. PLB 5.49 (ISBN 0-399-60647-5). Putnam.
Spencer, John W. No Earthly Explanation. 1974. 6.95 (ISBN 0-686-10168-5). Phillips Pub Co.
Spencer, John Wallace. The UFO Yearbook. 1977. 8.95 (ISBN 0-686-18652-4); pap. 2.25 (ISBN 0-686-18653-2). Phillips Pub Co.
Steiger, Brad. Gods of Aquarius: UFO's & the Transformation of Man. LC 76-20616. (Illus.). 1976. 8.95 (ISBN 0-15-136415-X). HarBraceJ.
Story, Ronald D. UFO's & the Limits of Science. LC 80-25543. (Illus.). 224p. 1981. 12.95 (ISBN 0-688-00144-0). Morrow.
Story, Ronald D., ed. The Encyclopedia of UFOs. LC 77-15174. (Illus.). 1980. 24.95 (ISBN 0-385-13677-3). Doubleday.
--The Encyclopedia of UFOs. LC 77-15174. (Illus.). 1980. pap. 12.95 (ISBN 0-385-11681-0, Dolp). Doubleday.
Stranges, Frank E. My Friend from Beyond Earth. 3rd, rev. ed. (Illus.). 64p. 1981. pap. 4.50x (ISBN 0-686-30008-4). Intl Evang.
Stuart, John. UFO Warning. 1976. pap. 7.95 (ISBN 0-685-81681-8). Saucerian.
Stubbs, U. F. O. Unidentified Flying Object. 1980. 8.95 (ISBN 0-233-97197-1). Andre Deutsch.
Thorne, Ian. UFOs. Schroeder, Howard, ed. LC 78-6529. (Search for the Unknown Ser.). (Illus.). (gr. 4). 1978. PLB 6.95 (ISBN 0-913940-84-4); pap. 2.95 (ISBN 0-89686-005-1). Crestwood Hse.
Trench, Brinsley L. Mysterious Visitors: The UFO Story. LC 72-96748. (Illus.). 192p. 1973. pap. 1.95 (ISBN 0-8128-7001-8). Stein & Day.
UFO Abductions: True Cases of Alien Kidnappings. (Orig.). 1980. pap. 2.25 (ISBN 0-451-09472-7, E9472, Sig). NAL.
Unger, G. Flying Saucers. 1973. lib. bdg. 59.95 (ISBN 0-87968-355-4). Krishna Pr.
Vallee, Jacques. Messengers of Deception. 288p. 1980. pap. 2.95 (ISBN 0-553-13906-1). Bantam.
--The Messengers of Deception. LC 78-73378. 1979. 11.95 (ISBN 0-915904-44-6); pap. 6.95 (ISBN 0-915904-38-1). And-or Pr.
Vance, Adrian. UFO's, the Eye & the Camera. LC 76-48205. (Illus.). 1977. 8.95 (ISBN 0-87929-046-3). Barlenmir.
Vesco, Renato. Intercept but Don't Shoot. 336p. 1981. pap. cancelled (ISBN 0-553-13205-9). Bantam.
White, Dale. Is Something up There: The Story of Flying Saucers. LC 68-17801. (gr. 3-7). 1968. PLB 6.95 (ISBN 0-385-02314-6). Doubleday.
--Is Something Up There? The Story of Flying Saucers. (gr. 7-12). 1970. pap. 1.25 (ISBN 0-590-08740-1, Schol Pap). Schol Bk Serv.
Wilding-White, Ted. All About UFO's. LC 77-17599. (World of the Unknown Ser). (Illus.). (gr. 4-5). 1978. PLB 6.95 (ISBN 0-88436-468-2). EMC.
Willcox, P. J. The UFO Question: Not Yet Answered. LC 75-393401. 1976. 7.95 (ISBN 0-87212-054-6). Libra.
Wilson, Clifford & Weldon, John. Close Encounters: A Better Explanation. LC 77-93674. 1978. pap. 3.95 (ISBN 0-89051-041-5, Pub. by Master Bks). CLP Pubs.

FLYING SAUCERS (GAME)
see Frisbee (Game)

FLYING TIGERS
Toland, John. Flying Tigers. (Landmark Ser: No. 105). (Illus.). (gr. 7-8). 1963. PLB 8.95 (ISBN 0-394-90405-2). Random.

FLYNN, ELIZABETH GURLEY
Flynn, Elizabeth G. The Rebel Girl: An Autobiography. new ed. LC 72-94154. 352p. 1973. pap. 4.50 (ISBN 0-7178-0368-6). Intl Pub Co.
Lamont, Corliss, ed. Trial of Elizabeth Gurley Flynn by the American Civil Liberties Union. (Documents of Civil Liberties, Vol. 1). 1969. 5.95 (ISBN 0-8180-0804-0). Horizon.

FLYNN, ERROL
Casella, Frank A. The Girls Errol Flynn & Me. LC 81-68789. (Illus.). 200p. 1981. text ed. 9.95 (ISBN 0-9606850-0-6). Anthony Pr CA.
Conrad, Earl. Errol Flynn: A Memoir. (Illus.). 1978. 8.95 (ISBN 0-396-07502-9). Dodd.
Flynn, Errol. From a Life of Adventure: The Writings of Errol Flynn. Thomas, Tony, ed. (Illus.). 1980. 12.95 (ISBN 0-8065-0690-3). Citadel Pr.
--My Wicked, Wicked Ways. 1981. pap. 2.75 (ISBN 0-425-04686-9). Berkley Pub.
--My Wicked, Wicked Ways. 1979. pap. 2.75 (ISBN 0-425-04686-9). Berkley Pub.
Freedland, Michael. The Two Lives of Errol Flynn. 1980. pap. 2.95 (ISBN 0-553-14862-1). Bantam.
--The Two Lives of Errol Flynn. LC 79-63012. (Illus.). 1979. 9.95 (ISBN 0-688-03465-9). Morrow.
Godfrey, Lionel. The Life & Crimes of Errol Flynn. LC 77-72302. (Illus.). 1977. 7.95 (ISBN 0-312-48385-6). St Martin.
Higham, Charles. Errol Flynn: The Untold Story. 1981. pap. 3.50 (ISBN 0-440-12307-0). Dell.
--Errol Flynn: The Untold Story. LC 78-22633. (Illus.). 1980. 12.95 (ISBN 0-385-13495-9). Doubleday.
McCarty, Clifford, et al. Films of Errol Flynn. 1971. 12.00 (ISBN 0-685-03372-4); pap. 6.95 (ISBN 0-8065-0237-1). Citadel Pr.

FLYSCH
Enos, Paul. Cloridorme Formation, Middle Ordovician Flysch, Northern Gaspe Peninsula, Quebec. LC 76-81692. (Special Paper: No. 117). (Illus., Orig.). 1969. pap. 3.25x (ISBN 0-8137-2117-2). Geol Soc.
Wallace, David R. Idle Weeds: The Life of a Sandstone Ridge. LC 79-21447. (Illus.). 192p. 1980. 12.95 (ISBN 0-87156-271-5). Sierra.

FM BROADCASTING
Elving, Bruce F. FM Atlas & Station Directory. 7th ed. (Illus.). 1981. write for info. F M Atlas.
--FM Atlas & Station Directory. 6th ed. (Illus.). 1980. pap. 4.50 (ISBN 0-686-65380-7). F M Atlas.

FM RADIO
see Radio Frequency Modulation

FOAM RUBBER
Storage of Cellular Rubber & Plastics. (Two Hundred Ser). 1974. pap. 2.00 (ISBN 0-685-58171-3, 231B). Natl Fire Prot.

FOAMED MATERIALS
see also Foam Rubber; Plastic Foams; Urethane Foam
Akers, R. J., ed. Foams. 1977. 48.00 (ISBN 0-12-047350-X). Acad Pr.
Bakker, Marilyn. Structural Foams, P-006r. 1979. 750.00 (ISBN 0-89336-196-8). BCC.
Bikerman, J. J. Foams. LC 72-94700. (Applied Physics & Engineering: Vol. 10). (Illus.). 320p. 1973. 39.70 (ISBN 0-387-06108-8). Springer-Verlag.
S.P.I. Fifth Structural Foam Conference. Structural Foam '77 - Versatile & Innovative Products: Proceedings. LC 75-25477. (Illus.). 1977. pap. 25.00x (ISBN 0-87762-241-8). Technomic.
U.S. Foamed Plastics Markets & Directory. LC 63-59134. 100p. 1979. pap. 25.00 (ISBN 0-87762-277-9). Technomic.

FOCH, FERDINAND, 1851-1929
King, Jere C. Foch Versus Clemenceau: France & German Dismemberment, 1918-1919. LC 60-11557. (Historical Monographs Ser: No. 44). 1960. 9.00x (ISBN 0-674-30700-3). Harvard U Pr.
Liddell Hart, Basil H. Foch, the Man of Orleans. LC 79-22870. (Illus.). 1980. Repr. of 1932 ed. lib. bdg. 35.00x (ISBN 0-313-22171-5, LHFO). Greenwood.

FOCILLON, HENRI, d. 1943
Grodecki, Louis. Bibliographie Henri Focillon. 1963. 15.00x (ISBN 0-300-00520-2). Yale U Pr.

FOCK, KURT WALDEMAR, 1898-
Feist, Uwe & Weber, Eberhard. Focke Wulf FW 190 A. LC 67-27869. (Aero Ser.: Vol. 18). (Illus.). 1968. pap. 3.00 (ISBN 0-8168-0568-7). Aero.
Nowarra, Heinz J. Focke Wulf 190, a Famous German Fighter. LC 65-15546. (Harleyford Ser). (Illus.). 1965. 18.95 (ISBN 0-8168-6365-2). Aero.

FOCKE-WULF ONE NINETY (FIGHTER PLANES)
Feist, Uwe & Weber, Eberhard. Focke Wulf FW 190 A. LC 67-27869. (Aero Ser.: Vol. 18). (Illus.). 1968. pap. 3.00 (ISBN 0-8168-0568-7). Aero.
Green, William & Swanborough, Gordon. The Focke Wulf: FW 190. LC 76-3455. (Illus.). 1976. 11.95 (ISBN 0-668-04001-7). Arco.
Grinsell, Robert. Focke-Wulf FW 190, Bk. 1. (Crown's World War II Fighter Planes Ser.). 1981. 15.95 (ISBN 0-517-54255-2). Crown.
Nowarra, Heinz J. Focke Wulf 190, a Famous German Fighter. LC 65-15546. (Harleyford Ser). (Illus.). 1965. 18.95 (ISBN 0-8168-6365-2). Aero.
Price, Alfred. Focke Wulf One-Ninety at War. LC 77-8704. (Illus.). 1977. 17.50x (ISBN 0-7110-0768-3). Intl Pubns Serv.
Smith, J. Richard. Focke-Wulf. LC 73-81386. (Aircraft Album Ser., No. 7). (Illus.). 128p. 1974. pap. 4.95 (ISBN 0-668-03349-5). Arco.
--Focke-Wulf. LC 73-81386. (Aircraft Album Ser., No. 7). (Illus.). 128p. 1974. pap. 4.95 (ISBN 0-668-03349-5). Arco.

FOCOLARE MOVEMENT
Lorit, Sergius C. & Grimaldi, Nuzzo. Focolare: After Thirty Years: Insights into the Life of the Focolare Movement. LC 76-18456. (Illus.). 1976. pap. 4.50 (ISBN 0-911782-27-3). New City.
Lubich, Chiara. That All Men Be One: Origins & Life of the Focolare Movement. 1977. pap. 1.95 (ISBN 0-911782-28-1). New City.

FODDER
see Feeds

FOETUS
see Fetus

FOG
see also Smog

FOGAZZARO, ANTONIO
Gallarati-Scotti, Tommaso. Life of Antonio Fogazzaro. LC 73-113311. 1970. Repr. of 1922 ed. 13.50 (ISBN 0-8046-0994-2). Kennikat.

FOGGARA
see Falashas

FOGLIO, FRANK
Foglio, Frank. Hey God! A Large Italian Family's Amazing Experience with God. LC 72-87328. 1972. pap. 3.95 (ISBN 0-88270-007-3). Logos.

FOILS, METAL
see Metal Foils

FOKKER, ANTHONY HERMAN GERARD, 1890-1939
Hegener, Henri. Fokker, the Man & the Aircraft. Robertson, B., ed. LC 61-10595. (Harleyford Ser). (Illus.). 1961. 18.95 (ISBN 0-8168-6370-9). Aero.

FOLDS (GEOLOGY)
Hansen, E. Strain Facies. LC 72-89551. (Minerals, Rocks & Inorganic Materials Ser.: Vol. 2). (Illus.). 1970. 30.80 (ISBN 0-387-05204-6). Springer-Verlag.
Johnson, A. M. Styles of Folding: Mechanics & Mechanisms of Folding of Natural Elastic Materials. (Developments in Geotectonics). 1977. 66.00 (ISBN 0-444-41496-7). Elsevier.
Ramsay, John G. Folding & Fracturing of Rocks. (International Ser. in Earth & Planetary Sciences). (Illus.). 1967. text ed. 28.00 (ISBN 0-07-051170-5, C). McGraw.

FOLEY, HELEN, 1896-1937
Eustace, Cecil J. Infinity of Questions. facs. ed. LC 70-84356. (Essay Index Reprint Ser). 1946. 14.50 (ISBN 0-8369-1080-X). Arno.

FOLIAGE
see Leaves

FOLIC ACID
Adams, Ruth & Murray, Frank. Vitamin B-Twelve & Folic Acid. 176p. (Orig.). 1981. pap. 1.95 (ISBN 0-915962-31-4). Larchmont Bks.
Blakley, R. L. The Biochemistry of Folic Acid & Related Pteridines. (Frontiers of Biology Ser.: Vol. 13). 1969. 53.75 (ISBN 0-444-10146-2, North-Holland). Elsevier.
Botez, M. I. & Reynolds, E. H., eds. Folic Acid in Neurology, Psychiatry, & Internal Medicine. LC 78-57243. 550p. 1979. text ed. 49.50 (ISBN 0-89004-338-8). Raven.
Food & Nutrition Board. Folic Acid: Biochemistry & Physiology in Relation to the Human Nutrition Requirement. LC 77-8182. 1977. pap. text ed. 13.50 (ISBN 0-309-02605-9). Natl Acad Pr.

FOLIOT, GILBERT, d. 1187
Morey, Adrian & Brooke, C. N. Gilbert Foliot & His Letters. (Cambridge Studies in Medieval Life & Thought). 1966. 44.95 (ISBN 0-521-05764-7). Cambridge U Pr.

FOLK ART
see also Art, Primitive; Art Industries and Trade; Arts and Crafts Movement; Children As Artists
American Primitive Art. (Illus.). 1977. 3.00 (ISBN 0-910810-19-2). Johannes.
Ames, Kenneth L. Beyond Necessity: Art in the Folk Tradition. (Illus.). 1978. 14.95x (ISBN 0-393-04499-8). Norton.
Andrews, Ruth, ed. How to Know American Folk Art: Eleven Experts Discuss Many Aspects of the Field. 1977. pap. 6.95 (ISBN 0-525-47460-9). Dutton.
Bartlett, Florence D. The Idea of Folk Art. (Illus.). 1963. pap. 0.95 (ISBN 0-89013-004-3). Museum NM Pr.
Bishop, Robert. Folk Painters of America. 1979. 35.00 (ISBN 0-525-10755-X). Dutton.
--Treasures of American Folk Art. 12.50 (ISBN 0-8109-2218-5). Abrams.
Cahill, Holger. American Folk Art: The Art of the Common Man in America 1750-1900. LC 71-86427. (Museum of Modern Art Publications in Reprint Ser). (Illus.). 1970. Repr. of 1932 ed. 18.00 (ISBN 0-405-01530-5). Arno.
Cannon, Hal, ed. Utah Folk Art: A Catalog of Material Culture. LC 80-13920. (Illus.). 168p. 1980. pap. 10.95 (ISBN 0-8425-1813-4). Brigham.
Celebrate! The Story of the Museum of International Folk Art. (Illus.). 1979. pap. 3.95 (ISBN 0-89013-119-8). Museum NM Pr.
Creekmore, Betsey B. Traditional American Crafts: A Practical Guide to 300 Years of Methods & Materials. LC 68-8517. (Illus.). 1968. 10.00 (ISBN 0-8208-0327-8). Hearthside.
Daniele, Joseph W. Building Colonial Furnishings, Miniatures, & Folk Art. LC 76-17006. (Illus.). 256p. 1976. 17.95 (ISBN 0-8117-0451-3). Stackpole.
Dewhurst, C. Kurt, et al. Artists in Aprons: Folk Art by American Women. (Illus.). 1979. 16.95 (ISBN 0-525-05857-5); pap. 9.95 (ISBN 0-525-47503-6). Dutton.
Dickey, Roland. New Mexico Village Arts. LC 71-107101. (Illus.). 264p. 1970. pap. 5.95 (ISBN 0-8263-0168-1). U of NM Pr.
Doty, Robert M. American Folk Art in Ohio Collections. (Illus.). 1977. 10.00 (ISBN 0-396-07360-3). Dodd.
Ericson, Jack T., ed. Folk Art in America. (Illus.). 1979. pap. 7.95 (ISBN 0-8317-3412-4, Mayflower Bks). Smith Pubs.
Fabian, Monroe. The Pennsylvania-German Decorated Chest. LC 77-91892. (Illus.). 1978. 25.00x (ISBN 0-87663-310-6, Main St). Universe.
Fife, Austin, et al, eds. Forms Upon the Frontier: Folklife & Folk Arts in the United States. (Illus.). 189p. (Orig.). 1969. pap. 5.00 (ISBN 0-87421-036-4). Utah St U Pr.
Folk Arts of the Americas. (Eng.). 1973. pap. 1.00 (ISBN 0-8270-4230-2). OAS.
Fowler, Virginie. Folk Arts Around the World: And How to Make Them. (YA) (gr. 5 up). 1981. 7.95 (ISBN 0-13-323014-7). P-H.
Fried, Frederick & Fried, Mary. America's Forgotten Folk Arts. LC 78-51790. (Illus.). 1978. write for info. (ISBN 0-394-40714-8). Pantheon.
Glubok, Shirley. The Art of the Spanish in the United States & Puerto Rico. LC 75-185218. (Illus.). (gr. 4up). 1972. 9.95 (ISBN 0-02-736130-6). Macmillan.
Groft, Tammis K. The Folk Spirit of Albany. (Illus.). 1978. pap. 6.00 (ISBN 0-939072-00-9). Albany Hist & Art.
Horwitz, Elinor L. The Bird, the Banner, & Uncle Sam: Images of America in Folk & Popular Art. LC 76-16492. (gr. 6 up). 1976. 9.95 (ISBN 0-397-31690-9, JBL-J). Har-Row.
--Contemporary American Folk Artists. LC 75-14353. (Illus.). (gr. 6 up). 1975. 8.50 (ISBN 0-397-31626-7, JBL-J); pap. 3.95 (ISBN 0-397-31627-5). Har-Row.

Howard, Joyce. New Tole & Folk Art Designs: Painting Techniques & Patterns. LC 78-22113. (Creative Crafts Ser.). (Illus.). 1979. 13.95 (ISBN 0-8019-6821-6); pap. 7.95 (ISBN 0-8019-6822-4, 6822). Chilton.
Kauffman, Henry J. Pennsylvania Dutch American Folk Art. rev. & enl. ed. (Illus.). 10.00 (ISBN 0-8446-2354-7). Peter Smith.
--Pennsylvania Dutch American Folk Art. rev. & enl. ed. (Illus.). pap. 5.00 (ISBN 0-486-21205-X). Dover.
Kinney, Jean & Kinney, Cle. Twenty-Three Varieties of Ethnic Art & How You Can Make Each One. LC 76-5409. (Illus.). (gr. 4-7). 1976. 8.95 (ISBN 0-689-30541-9). Atheneum.
LeBlanc, Dotsie L. & Planel, Jacqueline. Le Petit Cajun: Conversations with Andre Rodrigue. (Illus.). 1978. 9.95 (ISBN 0-918784-21-2). Legacy Pub Co.
Lichten, Frances. Folk Art Motifs of Pennsylvania. (Illus.). 6.00 (ISBN 0-8446-5466-3). Peter Smith.
--Folk Art Motifs of Pennsylvania. LC 75-28849. (Pictorial Archive Ser.). (Illus.). 96p. 1976. pap. 3.95 (ISBN 0-486-23303-0). Dover.
Lipman, Jean. American Folk Art in Wood, Metal, & Stone. (Illus.). 8.50 (ISBN 0-8446-4572-9). Peter Smith.
Lipman, Jean & Mevlendyke, Eve. American Folk Decoration. (Illus.). xii, 163p. 1972. pap. 5.00 (ISBN 0-486-22217-9). Dover.
Lipman, Jean, ed. American Folk Painters of Three Centuries. Armstrong, Tom. LC 79-21212. (Illus.). 1980. 35.00 (ISBN 0-933920-05-9); pap. 15.00 museum distribution only (ISBN 0-933920-06-7). Hudson Hills.
Martinez, Eluid L. & Smith, James C., Jr. What Is a New Mexico Santo? LC 77-78519. (Illus.). 1978. pap. 2.95 (ISBN 0-913270-76-8). Sunstone Pr.
Mather, Christine. Baroque to Folk. LC 79-91289. (Illus.). 1980. pap. 4.95 (ISBN 0-89013-129-5). Museum NM Pr.
Morton, Robert. Southern Antiques & Folk Art. Smith, C. Carter, Jr. & Alston, Edith, eds. LC 76-14114. (Illus.). 1976. 34.95 (ISBN 0-8487-0420-7). Oxmoor Hse.
Panyella, August, ed. Folk Art of the Americas. (Illus.). 328p. 1981. 45.00 (ISBN 0-8109-0912-X). Abrams.
Quimby, Ian M. & Swank, Scott T., eds. Perspectives on American Folk Art. (A Winterthur Bk.). (Illus.). 1980. 21.95 (ISBN 0-393-01273-5); pap. 9.95x (ISBN 0-393-95088-3). Norton.
Raycraft, Donald R. Early American Folk & Country Antiques. LC 70-142778. (Illus.). 1971. 11.50 (ISBN 0-8048-0961-5). C E Tuttle.
Rhodes, Lynette I. American Folk Art: From the Traditional to the Naive. LC 77-9240. (Themes in Art Ser.). (Illus.). 120p. 1978. pap. 7.95x (ISBN 0-910386-42-0, Pub. by Cleveland Mus Art). Ind U Pr.
Rogowski, Gini & De Weese, Gene. Making American Folk Art Dolls. (Creative Crafts Ser.). (Illus.). 160p. 1975. pap. 6.95 (ISBN 0-8019-6123-8). Chilton.
Schorsch, Anita. Images of Childhood: An Illustrated Social History. (Illus.). 1979. 14.95 (ISBN 0-8317-4875-3, Mayflower Bks). Smith Pubs.
Slivka, Rose, ed. Crafts of the Modern World. LC 68-8853. (Illus.). 1968. 17.50 (ISBN 0-8180-0102-X). Horizon.
Steinfeldt, Cecilia. Texas Folk Art. 1981. 60.00 (ISBN 0-932012-18-3); ltd. ed. 150.00 (ISBN 0-932012-22-1). Texas Month Pr.
Sun Fu-Hsi. Folk Art: A Special Issue of the "I-Feng". (National Peking University & Chinese Assn. for Folklore, Folklore & Folkliterature Ser.: No. 108). (Chinese.). 6.00 (ISBN 0-89986-186-5). E Langstaff.
Thuro, Catherine. Primitives & Folk Art. (Illus.). 1979. 17.95 (ISBN 0-89145-112-9). Collector Bks.
University of Connecticut at Storrs, William Benton Museum. Nineteenth-Century Folk Painting: Our Spirited National Heritage - Mr. & Mrs. Peter Tillou Collection. (Illus.). 212p. 1974. 14.95 (ISBN 0-517-51766-3). Barre.
Using Folk Entertainments to Promote National Development. 45p. 1981. pap. 4.75 (ISBN 92-3-101773-X, U1064, UNESCO). Unipub.
Vaughan, Betty A. Folk Art Painting: A Bit of the Past & Present. (Illus.). 52p. (Orig.). 1981. pap. 7.95 (ISBN 0-9605172-0-0). BETOM Pubns.
Vidal, Teodoro. Los Milagros en Metal y en Cera De Puerto Rico. 1974. 20.00 (ISBN 0-9600714-1-5). Edns Alba.
Wilder, Michell A. & Breitenbach, E. Santos: The Religious Folk Art of New Mexico. LC 75-11066. 1976. Repr. of 1943 ed. lib. bdg. 30.00 (ISBN 0-87817-169-X). Hacker.
Woodward, Richard B. American Folk Painting: Selections from the Collection of Mr. & Mrs. William E Wiltshire III. LC 77-24971. (Illus.). 110p. 1977. 22.50x (ISBN 0-917046-03-X); pap. 6.95x (ISBN 0-917046-02-1). Va Mus Fine Arts.
Wust, Klaus. Virginia Fraktur: Penmanship As Folk Art. LC 79-189313. (Illus.). 1972. pap. 4.75 (ISBN 0-917968-03-4). Shenandoah Hist.

FOLK ART-AFRICA

Brossert, Helmut T. Folk Art of Asia, Africa & the Americas. (Illus.). 103p. 1975. 52.95 (ISBN 0-8038-2306-1). Hastings.
Finnegan, Ruth H. Limba Stories & Story-Telling. LC 80-25904. (Oxford Library of African Literature). xii, 352p. 1981. Repr. of 1967 ed. lib. bdg. 28.75x (ISBN 0-313-22723-3, FILS). Greenwood.

FOLK ART-ASIA

Baker, Muriel & Lunt, Margaret. Blue & White: Embroideries of Rural China. LC 76-57933. (Illus.). 1977. encore ed 5.95 (ISBN 0-684-16344-6, ScribT). Scribner.
Bossert, Helmuth T. Peasant Art of Europe & Asia. (Illus.). 1977. 35.05 (ISBN 0-8038-5818-3). Hastings.
Brossert, Helmut T. Folk Art of Asia, Africa & the Americas. (Illus.). 103p. 1975. 52.95 (ISBN 0-8038-2306-1). Hastings.
Ecke, Tseng Yu-Ho. Chinese Folk Art. (Illus.). 1977. pap. text ed. 14.00x (ISBN 0-8248-0572-0). U Pr of Hawaii.

FOLK ART-CANADA

Klymasz, Robert B. Continuity & Change: The Ukranian Folk Heritage in Canada. (Illus.). 56p. 1972. pap. 2.95 (ISBN 0-660-00037-7, 563065, Pub. by Natl Mus Canada). U of Chicago Pr.

FOLK ART-EUROPE

Bossert, Helmuth T. Peasant Art of Europe & Asia. (Illus.). 1977. 35.05 (ISBN 0-8038-5818-3). Hastings.
Bossert, Hulmuth T. Folk Art of Europe. (Illus.). 103p. 1976. 52.95 (ISBN 0-8038-2315-0). Hastings.
Brothers Grimm. The Seven Ravens. LC 77-14252. (Illus.). (gr. k-3). 1979. 6.95 (ISBN 0-670-63557-X). Viking Pr.
Sibbett, Ed., Jr. Peasant Designs for Artists & Craftsmen. LC 76-58079. (Dover Needlepoint Ser.). (Illus.). 1977. pap. 3.75 (ISBN 0-486-23478-9). Dover.
Vaughan, Betty A. Folk Art Painting: A Bit of the Past & Present. (Illus.). 52p. (Orig.). 1981. pap. 7.95 (ISBN 0-9605172-0-0). BETOM Pubns.

FOLK ART-GERMANY

Schlee, Ernst. German Folk Art. LC 79-92578. (Illus.). 320p. 1980. 75.00 (ISBN 0-87011-356-9). Kodansha.

FOLK ART-GREAT BRITAIN

Ayres, James. British Folk Art. LC 76-57876. (Illus.). 144p. 1977. 35.00 (ISBN 0-87951-060-9). Overlook Pr.
Lea, Raymond. Country Curiosities: The Rare, the Odd & the Unusual in the English Countryside. LC 73-175029. (Curiosities Ser.). (Illus.). 151p. 1973. 10.00x (ISBN 0-902875-20-5). Intl Pubns Serv.
Pittaway, Andy & Scofield, Bernard. Traditional English Country Crafts & How to Enjoy Them Today. LC 73-18719. 1975. pap. 5.95 (ISBN 0-394-70643-9). Pantheon.
Wymer, Norman. English Town Crafts. (Illus.). 1976. Repr. 20.00x (ISBN 0-7158-1130-4). Charles River Bks.

FOLK ART-GREECE

Vakirtzis, George, et al. Greek Shop Signs. (Illus.). 1979. text ed. 55.00 (ISBN 0-89241-093-0). Caratzas Bros.

FOLK ART-HUNGARY

Fel, Edit. Hungarian Peasant Art. 2nd ed. LC 72-12741. (Illus.). 312p. 1969. 13.50x (ISBN 0-8002-1520-6). Intl Pubns Serv.
Hajdu, Victor. Sungates: A Testimony Carved in Wood. Stein, Rose, tr. (Illus., Hungarian.). 1980. 15.00 (ISBN 0-933652-16-X). Domjan Studio.
Hofer, T & Fel, E. Hungarian Folk Art. (Illus.). 1979. 35.00 (ISBN 0-19-211448-4). Oxford U Pr.
Kolar, Walter W., ed. The Folk Arts of Hungary. LC 80-54019. (Illus.). 190p. (Orig.). 1980. pap. 10.00 (ISBN 0-936922-01-X). Tamburitza.
Kresz, Maria. The Art of the Hungarian Furriers. (Hungarian Folk Art: 9). Orig. Title: Nepi Szucsmunka. (Illus.). 104p. 1979. 8.50x (ISBN 963-13-0417-5). Intl Pubns Serv.
Szalavary, Anne. Hungarian Folk Designs for Embroiderers & Craftsmen. 10.00 (ISBN 0-8446-5824-3). Peter Smith.
--Hungarian Folk Designs for Embroiderers & Craftsmen. (Illus.). 160p. (Orig.). 1980. pap. 4.00 (ISBN 0-486-23969-1). Dover.

FOLK ART-INDIA

Bhavnani, Enakshi. Folk & Tribal Designs of India. (Illus.). 150p. 1974. 20.00x (ISBN 0-8002-0630-4). Intl Pubns Serv.
Bussabarger, Robert F. & Robins, Betty D. Everyday Art of India. LC 68-20951. (Illus., Orig.). 1968. pap. 6.00 (ISBN 0-486-21988-7). Dover.

FOLK ART-ITALY

D'Amato, Alex & D'Amato, Janet. Italian Crafts: Inspirations from Folk Art. LC 76-30523. (Illus.). 160p. 1977. 7.95 (ISBN 0-87131-227-1). M Evans.

FOLK ART-JAPAN

Munsterberg, Hugo. Folk Arts of Japan. LC 58-7496. (Illus.). 1958. 25.00 (ISBN 0-8048-0190-8). C E Tuttle.
Muraoka, Kageo & Okamura, Kichiemon. Folk Arts & Crafts of Japan. Stegmaier, Daphne, tr. from Japanese. LC 72-78600. (Heibonsha Survey of Japanese Art Ser). Orig. Title: Mingei. (Illus.). 176p. 1973. 17.50 (ISBN 0-8348-1009-3). Weatherhill.

FOLK ART-LATIN AMERICA

Folk Arts of the Americas. (Eng.). 1973. pap. 1.00 (ISBN 0-8270-4230-2). OAS.
Parker, Ann & Neal, Avon. Molas: Folk Art of the Cuna Indians. (Illus.). 1977. 29.95 (ISBN 0-517-52911-4). Barre.

FOLK ART-MEXICO

Toor, Frances. Mexican Popular Arts: A Fond Glance at the Craftsmen & Their Handiwork in Ceramics, Textiles, Metals, Glass, Paint, Fibres, & Other Materials. LC 73-78363. (Illus.). 144p. 1973. Repr. of 1939 ed. 12.00x (ISBN 0-87917-034-4). Blaine Ethridge.
Winn, Robert K. V. J. M. y. J. Viva Jesus, Maria y Jose; Mexican Folk Art & Toys from the Collection of Robert K. Winn. (Illus.). 1977. 10.00 (ISBN 0-911536-68-X). Trinity U Pr.

FOLK ART-NORWAY

Stewart, Janice. Folk Arts of Norway. (Illus.). 246p. 1972. pap. 6.95 (ISBN 0-486-22811-8). Dover.
Stewart, Janice S. The Folk Arts of Norway. 2nd enl. ed. (Illus.). 12.50 (ISBN 0-8446-4610-5). Peter Smith.

FOLK ART-OCEANICA

Belen, Hermogenes F. Philippine Creative Handicrafts. (Illus.). (gr. k-4). 1977. 5.75 (ISBN 0-686-09536-7). Cellar.
Handy, Willowdean C. String Figures from the Marquesas & Society Islands. Repr. of 1925 ed. pap. 8.00 (ISBN 0-527-02121-0). Kraus Repr.

FOLK ART-POLAND

Pokropek, Marian. Guide to Folk Art & Folklore in Poland. Paszkiewicz, Magdalena M., tr. from Polish. (Illus.). 307p. 1980. 20.00x (ISBN 83-213-3014-2). Intl Pubns Serv.

FOLK ART-RUSSIA

Halpern, Frieda. Full-Color Russian Folk Needlepoint Designs Charted for Easy Use. (Needlework Ser). (Illus.). 1976. pap. 2.95 (ISBN 0-486-23451-7). Dover.
Klimova, Nina T. Folk Embroidery of the U. S. S. R. LC 80-15453. (Illus.). 128p. 1981. 19.95 (ISBN 0-442-24464-9). Van Nos Reinhold.

FOLK COSTUME

see Costume

FOLK CUSTOMS

see Manners and Customs

FOLK DANCE MUSIC

Chochem, Corinne & Roth, Muriel. Palestine Dances: Folk Dances of Palestine. LC 77-26081. (Illus.). 1978. Repr. of 1941 ed. lib. bdg. 15.00x (ISBN 0-313-20176-5, CHPD). Greenwood.
Rearick, Elizabeth C. Dances of the Hungarians. LC 72-177181. (Columbia University. Teachers College. Contributions to Education: No. 770). Repr. of 1939 ed. 17.50 (ISBN 0-404-55770-8). AMS Pr.
Richardson, J. R. A Selection of Folk Dances, Vol. 1-5. Repr. Vol. 1. 1965. pap. 3.00 (ISBN 0-685-77384-1); Vol. 2. 1966. pap. 3.80 (ISBN 0-08-010842-3); Vol. 3. 1966. pap. 3.80 (ISBN 0-08-011926-3); Vol. 4. 1971. pap. 3.80 (ISBN 0-08-016190-1); Vol. 5. 1978. pap. 3.80 (ISBN 0-08-021589-0). Pergamon.
Tolman, Newton F. & Gilbert, Kay. Nelson Music Collection. pap. 5.95x (ISBN 0-89190-952-4). Am Repr-Rivercity Pr.

FOLK DANCING

see also Folk Music; Play-Party; Square Dancing

Duggan, Ann S., et al. The Folk Dance Library, 5 vols. LC 79-7758. (Dance Ser.). (Illus.). 1980. Repr. of 1948 ed. Set. lib. bdg. 90.00x (ISBN 0-8369-9305-5). Arno.
Dunin, Elsie I. South Slavic Dances in California: A Compendium for the Years 1924-1977. LC 79-63063. 1979. 10.00 (ISBN 0-918660-11-4). Ragusan Pr.
Ellfeldt, Lois E. Folk Dance. (Physical Education Activities Ser.). 72p. 1969. pap. text ed. write for info. (ISBN 0-697-07012-3); tchrs.' manual avail. (ISBN 0-686-66580-5). Wm C Brown.
Gilbert, Cecile. International Folk Dance at a Glance. 2nd ed. LC 73-90229. 1974. spiral bdg. 7.95x (ISBN 0-8087-0727-2). Burgess.
Hall, J. T. Dance! a Complete Guide to Social, Folk, & Square Dancing. LC 79-7766. (Dance Ser.). (Illus.). 1980. Repr. of 1963 ed. lib. bdg. 35.00x (ISBN 0-8369-9294-6). Arno.
Harris, Jane A. & Pittman, Anne M. Dance a While: Handbook of Folk, Square & Social Dance. 5th ed. LC 77-93823. 1978. spiral bdg. 12.95x (ISBN 0-8087-0878-3). Burgess.
Jensen, Mary B. & Jensen, Clayne R. Folk Dancing. LC 73-4771. (Illus.). 148p. 1973. pap. 4.95 (ISBN 0-8425-0458-3). Brigham.
Joukowsky, Anatol M. The Teaching of Ethnic Dance. LC 79-7768. (Dance Ser.). (Illus.). 1980. Repr. of 1965 ed. lib. bdg. 19.00x (ISBN 0-8369-9296-2). Arno.
Kraus, Richard G. Folk Dancing: A Guide for Schools, Colleges, & Recreation Groups. (Illus.). 1962. text ed. 13.95x (ISBN 0-02-366300-6). Macmillan.
La Meri. Total Education in Ethnic Dance. 1977. 16.75 (ISBN 0-8247-6519-2). Dekker.
Lidster, Miriam D. & Tamburini, Dorothy H. Folk Dance Progressions. LC 78-60141, 1978. Repr. of 1965 ed. lib. bdg. 33.75x (ISBN 0-313-20583-3, LIFD). Greenwood.
Mynatt, Constance V. & Kaiman, Bernard D. Folk Dancing for Students & Teachers. 2nd ed. 144p. 1975. write for info. plastic comb (ISBN 0-697-07429-3). Wm C Brown.
Pholeric, Janet J. Folk Dances Around the World, Vol. 1. LC 79-63544. 188p. 1980. 12.00 (ISBN 0-498-02259-5). A S Barnes.
Price, Christine. Dance on the Dusty Earth. LC 78-25714. (Illus.). (gr. 4 up). 1979. 8.95 (ISBN 0-684-16088-9). Scribner.
Richardson, J. R. A Selection of Folk Dances, Vol. 1-5. Repr. Vol. 1. 1965. pap. 3.00 (ISBN 0-685-77384-1); Vol. 2. 1966. pap. 3.80 (ISBN 0-08-010842-3); Vol. 3. 1966. pap. 3.80 (ISBN 0-08-011926-3); Vol. 4. 1971. pap. 3.80 (ISBN 0-08-016190-1); Vol. 5. 1978. pap. 3.80 (ISBN 0-08-021589-0). Pergamon.
Rothgarber, Herbert. Let's Folk Dance. 1980. pap. 3.00 (ISBN 0-918812-10-0). Magnamusic.
Snider, Marcia E. Folk Dance Handbook. (Physical Education Ser.). (Illus., Orig.). 1980. pap. 6.95 (ISBN 0-87663-617-2, Pub. by Hancock Hse). Universe.
Tracey, Hugh. Chopi Musicians. (Illus.). 1970. Repr. of 1948 ed. 36.00x (ISBN 0-19-724182-4). Oxford U Pr.
Using Folk Entertainments to Promote National Development. 45p. 1981. pap. 4.75 (ISBN 92-3-101773-X, U1064, UNESCO). Unipub.

FOLK-DANCING, AMERICAN

Lucero-White, et al. Hispano Culture of New Mexico: An Original Anthology. Cortes, Carlos E., ed. & intro. by. LC 76-5929. (Chicano Heritage Ser.). (Illus.). 1976. 15.00x (ISBN 0-405-09537-6). Arno.
Morrison, James E. Twenty Four Early American Country Dances Cotillions & Reels for the Year, 1976. LC 76-3969. (Illus.). 1976. spiral bdg. 4.50 (ISBN 0-917024-04-4). Country Dance & Song.
National Square Dancing Convention, Tennessee. Recipe Promenade. 1978. 5.00 (ISBN 0-918544-21-1). Wimmer Bks.
Shaw, Lloyd. Cowboy Dances. LC 39-18793. 1952. 5.00 (ISBN 0-87004-153-3). Caxton.

FOLK-DANCING, ASIAN

Vatsyayan, Kapila. Traditions of Indian Folk Dance. (Illus.). 1977. text ed. 18.00x (ISBN 0-8426-1058-8). Verry.

FOLK-DANCING, BRITISH

Breathnach, Breandan. Folk Music & Dances of Ireland. rev. ed. (Illus.). 152p. 1977. pap. 5.95 (ISBN 0-85342-509-4). Irish Bk Ctr.
Hamilton, Jack. English Folk Dancing. (Know the Game Ser.). (Illus.). 1974. pap. 2.50 (ISBN 0-7158-0516-9). Charles River Bks.
Kidson, Frank & Neal, Mary. English Folk-Song & Dance. (Illus.). 178p. 1972. Repr. of 1915 ed. 10.00x (ISBN 0-87471-104-5). Rowman.
--English Folk-Song & Dance. (Illus.). 178p. 1972. Repr. of 1915 ed. 10.00x (ISBN 0-87471-104-5). Rowman.
Smedley, Ronald & Tether, John. Let's Dance-Country Style. 1975. 6.95 (ISBN 0-236-31061-5, Pub. by Paul Elek). Merrimack Bk Serv.
Williams, Iolo. English Folk-Song & Dance. LC 73-7745. 1973. lib. bdg. 20.00 (ISBN 0-8414-9362-6). Folcroft.

FOLK-DANCING, EUROPEAN

Benet, Sula. Song, Dance, & Customs of Peasant Poland. LC 76-44690. Repr. of 1951 ed. 21.50 (ISBN 0-404-15906-0). AMS Pr.
Czompo, Andor. Hungarian Dances. 2nd rev. ed. LC 74-11041. (Illus.). 1980. pap. text ed. 5.95 (ISBN 0-935496-01-7). AC Pubns.
Guilcher, Jean-Michel. La Contredanse et les Renouvellements De la Danse Francaise. (Etudes Europeennes: No. 6). 1969. pap. 25.50x (ISBN 90-2796-263-4). Mouton.
--La Tradition Populaire De Danse En Basse-Bretagne. (Etudes Europeennes: No. 1). 1976. pap. 61.25x (ISBN 90-2797-572-8). Mouton.
Hungarian State Folk Ensemble. LC 75-329067. (Illus.). 100p. 1975. 12.50x (ISBN 0-8002-1523-0). Intl Pubns Serv.
Katzarova-Kukudova, Raina & Djenev, Kiril. Bulgarian Folk Dances. (Illus.). 1976. soft cover 6.95 (ISBN 0-89357-029-X). Slavica.

Lawson, Joan. European Folk Dance. LC 79-7773. (Dance Ser.). 1980. Repr. of 1953 ed. lib. bdg. 34.00x (ISBN 0-8369-9300-4). Arno.
Martin, Gyorgy. Hungarian Folk Dances. LC 74-188808. (Hungarian Folk Art Ser). (Illus.). 83p. 1974. 7.50x (ISBN 0-8002-1518-4). Intl Pubns Serv.
Rearick, Elizabeth C. Dances of the Hungarians. LC 72-177181. (Columbia University. Teachers College. Contributions to Education: No. 770). Repr. of 1939 ed. 17.50 (ISBN 0-404-55770-8). AMS Pr.

FOLK-DANCING, ISRAELI

Chochem, Corinne & Roth, Muriel. Palestine Dances: Folk Dances of Palestine. LC 77-26081. (Illus.). 1978. Repr. of 1941 ed. lib. bdg. 15.00x (ISBN 0-313-20176-5, CHPD). Greenwood.

FOLK-DANCING, LATIN AMERICAN

Folk Songs & Dances of the Americas, 2 Bks. 1969. Bk. 1. pap. 1.00 (ISBN 0-8270-4450-X); Bk. 2. pap. 1.00 (ISBN 0-8270-4455-0). OAS.
Pescador de Umpierre, Paquita. Manual De Bailes Folkloricos. pap. 3.75 (ISBN 0-8477-2501-4). U of PR Pr.

FOLK-DANCING, PHILIPPINE

Friese, Jovita. Philippine Folk Dances from Pangsinan. 1979. 7.95 (ISBN 0-533-03856-1). Vantage.

FOLK-DRAMA

see also Puppets and Puppet-Plays

Brody, Alan. English Mummers & Their Plays: Traces of Ancient Mystery. LC 77-92855. (Folklore & Folklife Ser). (Illus.). 1971. 14.00x (ISBN 0-8122-7611-6). U of Pa Pr.
Collins, Freda. Eight Folk-Tale Plays. 1940. 10.00 (ISBN 0-685-84540-0). Norwood Edns.
Kamerman, Sylvia E., ed. Folk Tale Plays from Round the World. 1982. 12.95 (ISBN 0-8238-0253-1). Plays.
Li Ching-Han. Folk Plays from Ting Hsien. (National Peking University & Chinese Assn. for Folklore, Folklore & Folkliterature Ser.: No. 37-40). (Chinese.). 28.00 (ISBN 0-89986-132-6). E Langstaff.
Stark, Richard B. Music of the Spanish Folk Plays in New Mexico. (Illus.). 1969. 20.00 (ISBN 0-89013-036-1). Museum NM Pr.
Tiddy, Reginald J. Mummers' Play. LC 72-8091. 1923. lib. bdg. 30.00 (ISBN 0-88305-652-6). Norwood Edns.
T'ung Ching-Hsing. Studies on Modern & Ancient Folkplays. (National Peking University & Chinese Assn. for Folklore, Folklore & Folkliterature Ser.: No. 65 & 66). (Chinese.). 12.00 (ISBN 0-89986-155-5). E Langstaff.
Warner, E. The Russian Folk Theatre. (Slavistic Printings & Reprintings: No. 104). 1977. 41.75x (ISBN 90-279-3325-1). Mouton.
Wu Shou-Li. Studies in a Folk-Play-Li-Ching-Chi, No. 7. (Asian Folklore & Social Life Monograph). (Chinese.). 1970. 6.00 (ISBN 0-89986-010-9). E Langstaff.
--Studies on Two Chao-Chow Folk-Plays. (National Peking University & Chinese Assn. for Folklore, Folklore & Folkliterature Ser.: No. 79 & 80). (Chinese.). 16.00 (ISBN 0-89986-164-4). E Langstaff.
Yamamoto, Yoshiko. The Namahage: A Festival in the Northeast of Japan. LC 78-1500. (Illus.). 1978. text ed. 16.00x (ISBN 0-915980-66-5). Inst Study Human.
Yin K'ai. Songs of Folk-Plays from Peiping. (National Peking University & Chinese Assn. for Folklore, Folklore & Folkliterature Ser.: No. 70 & 71). (Chinese.). 14.00 (ISBN 0-89986-158-X). E Langstaff.

FOLK DRAMA–HISTORY AND CRITICISM

Glassie, Henry. All Silver & No Brass: An Irish Christmas Mumming. LC 75-9132. (Illus.). 224p. 1976. 12.50x (ISBN 0-253-30470-9). Ind U Pr.
Miller, George M. The Dramatic Element in the Popular Ballad. LC 76-24125. 1976. Repr. of 1905 ed. lib. bdg. 8.50 (ISBN 0-8414-6131-7). Folcroft.
Sper, Felix. From Native Roots. (Illus.). 6.00 (ISBN 0-910294-03-8). Brown Bk.
Yamamoto, Yoshiko. The Namahage: A Festival in the Northeast of Japan. LC 78-1500. (Illus.). 1978. text ed. 16.00x (ISBN 0-915980-66-5). Inst Study Human.

FOLK LITERATURE

see also Chap-Books; Fairy Tales; Folk-Drama; Folk-Songs; Legends; Nursery Rhymes; Proverbs; Riddles; Tales

Ainsworth, Catherine H. Folktales of America, Vol 1. LC 80-66300. (Folktales & Legends Ser.). 206p. 1980. pap. 10.00 (ISBN 0-933190-08-5). Clyde Pr.
American Proverbs, Maxims & Folk Sayings. (Americana Books Ser.). (Illus.). 1968. 1.50 (ISBN 0-911410-19-8). Applied Arts.
Armistead, Samuel G. & Silverman, Joseph H. Folk-Literature of the Sephardic Jews, Vol. 1. The Judeo-Spanish Ballad Chapbooks of Yacob Abraham Yona. LC 71-78565. 1971. 45.00x (ISBN 0-520-01648-3). U of Cal Pr.
Bain, Robert N., ed. & tr. Cossack Fairy Tales & Folk-Tales. LC 11-132. Repr. of 1894 ed. 14.00 (ISBN 0-527-04404-0). Kraus Repr.
Binner, Vinal O. International Folktales One: A Structured Reader. LC 67-11673. (Contemporary English Ser). (Orig.). 1967. pap. text ed. 6.95 scp (ISBN 0-690-44336-6, HarpC). Har-Row.
Bluestein, Gene. The Voice of the Folk: Folklore & American Literary Theory. LC 70-164443. 192p. 1972. pap. 5.95x (ISBN 0-87023-098-0). U of Mass Pr.
Boas, Franz. Primitive Art. (Illus.). 1962. 8.75 (ISBN 0-8446-1695-8). Peter Smith.
--Primitive Art. (Illus.). 1927. pap. 5.00 (ISBN 0-486-20025-6). Dover.
Christiansen, Reidar T. The Migratory Legends: List of Types with a Systematic Catalogue of the Norwegian Variants. Dorsen, Richard M., ed. LC 77-70585. (International Folklore Ser.). 1977. Repr. of 1958 ed. lib. bdg. 16.00x (ISBN 0-405-10087-6). Arno.
Clarke, Kenneth & Clarke, Mary. The Harvest & the Reapers: Oral Traditions of Kentucky. LC 74-7872. (Kentucky Bicentennial Bookshelf Ser.). 112p. 1974. 6.95 (ISBN 0-8131-0201-4). U Pr of Ky.
Clouston, William A. Flowers from a Persian Garden & Other Papers. Dorsen, Richard M., ed. LC 77-70584. (International Ser.). Repr. of 1890 ed. lib. bdg. 21.00x (ISBN 0-405-10088-4). Arno.
Cohen, Anne B. Poor Pearl, Poor Girl! The Murdered Girl Stereotype in Ballad & Newspaper. LC 73-7919. (American Folklore Society Memoir Ser.: No. 58). (Illus.). 147p. 1973. 7.95 (ISBN 0-292-76409-X); pap. 5.95x (ISBN 0-292-76468-5). U of Tex Pr.
Cullup, Michael, ed. The Stomach & His Friends & Other Stories. (Heinemann Secondary Readers Ser.). 1973. pap. text ed. 3.00x (ISBN 0-435-92510-5). Heinemann Ed.
Falnes, Oscar J. National Romanticism in Norway. LC 68-54263. (Columbia University. Studies in the Social Sciences: No. 386). Repr. of 1933 ed. 21.50 (ISBN 0-404-51386-7). AMS Pr.
Graham, Dougal. Collected Writings of Dougal Graham, Skellat Bellman of Glasgow, 2 Vols. LC 69-16478. 1968. Repr. of 1883 ed. Set. 22.00 (ISBN 0-8103-3535-2). Gale.
Kelly, Eamon. Bless Me Father. 1977. pap. 3.95 (ISBN 0-85342-489-6). Irish Bk Ctr.
Kennedy, Patrick. The Bardic Stories of Ireland. LC 76-53557. 1976. Repr. of 1871 ed. lib. bdg. 30.00 (ISBN 0-8414-5535-X). Folcroft.
Kirtley, Bacil. Motif-Index of Traditional Polynesian Narratives. (Orig.). 1971. pap. text ed. 10.00x (ISBN 0-87022-416-6). U Pr of Hawaii.
Norton, Eloise S. Folk Literature of the British Isles: Readings for Librarians, Teachers, & Those Who Work with Children & Young Adults. LC 78-10324. 1978. lib. bdg. 14.00 (ISBN 0-8108-1177-4). Scarecrow.
Oinas, Felix J., ed. Heroic Epic & Saga: An Introduction to the World's Great Folk Epics. LC 77-9637. (Midland Bks.: No. 211). 448p. 1978. 29.95x (ISBN 0-253-32738-5); pap. 10.95x (ISBN 0-253-20211-6). Ind U Pr.
Parry, Adam & Dorson, Richard M., eds. The Making of Homeric Verse: The Collected Papers of Milman Parry. LC 80-747. (Folklore of the World Ser.). (Illus.). 1980. Repr. of 1971 ed. lib. bdg. 50.00x (ISBN 0-405-13321-9). Arno.
Rothenberg, Jerome, ed. Technicians of the Sacred: A Range of Poetries from Africa, America, Asia & Oceania. LC 67-15391. 1969. pap. 4.95 (ISBN 0-385-07597-9, A06, Anch). Doubleday.
Thompson, Stith. The Folktale. 1977. 24.50x (ISBN 0-520-03359-0); pap. 8.95 (ISBN 0-520-03537-2). U of Cal Pr.
West Lake: A Collection of Folk Tales. 1980. 10.95 (ISBN 0-8351-0726-4). China Bks.
Whedbee, Charles H. Flaming Ship of Ocracoke & Other Tales of the Outer Banks. LC 76-156458. (Illus.). (YA) 1981. 7.95 (ISBN 0-910244-61-8). Blair.

FOLK LITERATURE–THEMES, MOTIVES

see also Literature, Comparative–Themes, Motives

Baughman, Ernest W. Type & Motif-Index of the Folktales of England & North America. 1966. pap. text ed. 65.90x (ISBN 90-2790-046-9). Mouton.
Cook, Arthur B. Zeus: A Study of Ancient Religion, 2 vols. Incl. Vol. 1. Zeus, God of the Bright Sky. LC 64-25839. (Illus.). 885p. Repr. of 1914 ed. 45.00x (ISBN 0-8196-0148-9); Vol. 2. Zeus, God of the Dark Sky: Thunder & Lightning, 2 pts. LC 64-25839. Repr. of 1925 ed. 90.00x set (ISBN 0-8196-0156-X); Vol. 2, Pt. 1. Text & Notes. xliii, 858p; Vol. 2, Pt. 2. Appendixes & Index. (Illus.). 539p. Biblo.
Cross, T. P. Motif-Index of Early Irish Literature. 1952. 30.00 (ISBN 0-527-20700-4). Kraus Repr.
Fouquet, K. Jakob Ayrers Sidea, Shakespeares Tempest und das Maerchen. pap. 7.00 (ISBN 0-384-16500-1). Johnson Repr.
Jones, W. P. The Pastourelle. LC 73-3478. 244p. 1973. Repr. of 1931 ed. lib. bdg. 14.50x (ISBN 0-374-94333-8). Octagon.
Muench, I. Von. Voelkerrecht in programmierter Form mit Vertiefungshinweisen. (Illus.). 445p. 1971. 22.50x (ISBN 3-11-002162-5). De Gruyter.
Newall, Venetia J., ed. Folklore Studies in the Twentieth Century: Proceedings of the Centenary Conference of the Folklore Society. (Illus.). 1980. 85.00x (ISBN 0-8476-3638-0). Rowman.
Peabody, Josephine P. Old Greek Folk Stories. 25.00 (ISBN 0-8274-3973-3). R West.
Potter, Murray A. Sohrab & Rustem, the Epic Theme of a Combat Between Father & Son: A Study of Its Genesis & Use in Literature & Popular Tradition. LC 75-144527. (Grimm Library: No. 14). Repr. of 1902 ed. 11.50 (ISBN 0-404-53557-7). AMS Pr.
Schlauch, Margaret. Chaucer's Constance & Accused Queens. LC 71-93253. 1970. Repr. of 1927 ed. 6.50 (ISBN 0-87752-097-6). Gordian.
Toelken, Barre. The Dynamics of Folklore. LC 78-69536. (Illus.). 1978. text ed. 14.50 (ISBN 0-395-27068-5); inst. manual 0.40 (ISBN 0-395-27069-3). HM.
Williams, Paul V., ed. The Fool & the Trickster: Studies in Honour of Enid Wolsford. (Illus.). 142p. 1979. 21.00x (ISBN 0-8476-6183-0). Rowman.
Wilson, Anne. Traditional Romance & Tale: How Stories Mean. 116p. 1976. 12.50x (ISBN 0-87471-905-4). Rowman.

FOLK-LORE

see also Amulets; Animal Lore; Animals, Legends and Stories Of; Animism; Chap-Books; Charms; Counting-Out Rhymes; Devil; Divining-Rod; Dragons; Dwarfs; Evil Eye; Fables; Fairies; Fairy Tales; Folk Music; Folk-Songs; Ghosts; Grail; Halloween; Incantations; Legends; Leopard Men; Marriage Customs and Rites; Myth; Mythology; Nursery Rhymes; Oral Tradition; Plant Lore; Proverbs; Riddles; Sagas; Story-Telling; Superstition; Tales; Valentines; Vampires; Weather Lore; Werewolves; Witchcraft

Abernethy, Francis, ed. Paisanos: A Folklore Miscellany. 1978. 10.50 (ISBN 0-88426-054-2). Encino Pr.
Adams, Robert J., et al. Introduction to Folklore. rev ed. LC 73-78365. (Illus.). 200p. 1974. pap. text ed. 6.96 (ISBN 0-88429-002-6). Collegiate Pub.
Almqvist, Bo & Dorson, Richard M., eds. Hereditas: Essays & Studies Presented to Professor Seamus O Duilearga. LC 80-737. (Folklore of the World Ser.). (Illus.). 1980. Repr. of 1975 ed. lib. bdg. 39.00x (ISBN 0-405-13301-4). Arno.
Bang, Molly, ed. & illus. The Buried Moon & Other Stories. LC 76-58328. (gr. 4-7). 1977. reinforced bdg. 5.95 (ISBN 0-684-14666-5, ScribJ). Scribner.
Banier, Antoine. The Mythology & Fables of the Ancients, Explain'd from History, 4 vols. LC 75-27885. (Renaissance & the Gods Ser.: Vol. 40). (Illus.). 1976. Repr. of 1740 ed. Set. lib. bdg. 292.00 (ISBN 0-8240-2089-8); lib. bdg. 73.00 ea. Garland Pub.
Baring-Gould, S. Curious Myths of the Middle Ages. 69.95 (ISBN 0-87968-261-2). Gordon Pr.
Baring-Gould, Sabine. Book of Folklore. LC 69-16807. Repr. of 1913 ed. 22.00 (ISBN 0-8103-3603-0). Gale.
Bassett, F. S. The Folk-Lorist. 1978. Repr. of 1973 ed. lib. bdg. 15.00 (ISBN 0-8414-0506-9). Folcroft.
Bassett, Fletcher. Study of Folklore. 1978. 14.50 (ISBN 0-685-86828-1). Porter.
Bassett, Helen W. & Starr, Frederick, eds. International Folk-Lore Congress of the World's Columbian Exposition, July, 1893. LC 80-788. (Folklore of the World Ser.). (Illus.). 1980. Repr. of 1898 ed. lib. bdg. 42.00x (ISBN 0-405-13327-8). Arno.
Beck, Horace P., ed. Folklore in Action: Essays for Discussion in Honor of MacEdward Leach. LC 62-12687. (American Folklore Society Memoirs Ser). Repr. of 1962 ed. 14.00 (ISBN 0-527-01130-4). Kraus Repr.
Ben-Amos, D. & Goldstein, K., eds. Folklore: Performance & Communication. LC 74-80122. (Approaches to Semiotics Ser.: No. 40). (Illus.). 308p. 1975. pap. text ed. 70.50x (ISBN 90-2793-143-7). Mouton.
Bett, Henry. Nursery Rhymes & Tales: Their Origin & History. LC 73-14839. 1924. lib. bdg. 6.50 (ISBN 0-8414-3274-0). Folcroft.
--Nursery Rhymes & Tales, Their Origin & History. LC 68-21756. 1968. Repr. of 1924 ed. 22.00 (ISBN 0-8103-3474-7). Gale.
Bettelheim, Bruno. The Uses of Enchantment: The Meaning & Importance of Fairy Tales. 1977. pap. 3.95 (ISBN 0-394-72265-5, Vin). Random.
Binner, Vinal O. International Folktales Two: A Structured Reader. (Crowell Contemporary English Ser). 1970. pap. text ed. 6.95 scp (ISBN 0-690-44338-2, HarpC). Har-Row.
Blinkenberg, C. The Thunderweapon in Religion & Folklore. 1977. lib. bdg. 59.95 (ISBN 0-8490-2749-7). Gordon Pr.
Boatright, Mody C. Folklore of the Oil Industry. LC 63-21186. 228p. 1980. Repr. of 1963 ed. 6.95 (ISBN 0-87074-007-5). SMU Press.
Boggs, Ralph S. Folklore. 1977. Repr. of 1919 ed. lib. bdg. 10.00 (ISBN 0-8495-0328-0). Arden Lib.
Brett, Bill. There Ain't No Such Animal & Other East Texas Tales. LC 78-21777. (Illus.). 128p. 1979. 8.50 (ISBN 0-89096-068-2). Tex A&M Univ Pr.
Briggs, Katharine M. The Vanishing People: Fairy Lore & Legends. 1979. pap. 3.95 (ISBN 0-394-73740-7). Pantheon.
Brunvand, Jan H. Folklore: A Handbook for Study & Research. LC 75-38016. 178p. 1976. text ed. 12.95 (ISBN 0-312-29715-7); pap. text ed. 4.95 (ISBN 0-312-29750-5). St Martin.
Bulfinch, Thomas. Bulfinch's Mythology. 2nd rev. ed. LC 69-11314. (Illus.). 1970. 11.95 (ISBN 0-690-57260-3). T Y Crowell.
Byer, Carol, illus. Henny Penny. (Illus.). 32p. (gr. k-2). 1981. PLB 5.79 (ISBN 0-89375-490-0); pap. text ed. 1.50 (ISBN 0-89375-491-9). Troll Assocs.
Campbell, Alexander. Albyn's Anthology, 2 vols. (Folklore Ser). 35.00 (ISBN 0-88305-109-5). Norwood Edns.
Cashen, William. Man Folk-Lore. (Folklore Ser.). Repr. 15.00 (ISBN 0-685-43677-2). Norwood Edns.
Chaplin, Dorothea. Mythological Bonds Between East & West. 1976. lib. bdg. 59.95 (ISBN 0-8490-2325-4). Gordon Pr.
Cheney, Thomas, et al, eds. Lore of Faith & Folly. LC 78-161486. 1971. 20.00 (ISBN 0-87480-067-6). U of Utah Pr.
Cheney, Thomas E. The Golden Legacy: A Folk History of J. Golden Kimball. LC 73-89750. 1973. pap. 4.95 (ISBN 0-87905-018-7). Peregrine Smith.
Chodzko, A. B. Fairy Tales of the Slav Peasants & Herdsmen. Repr. of 1896 ed. 20.00 (ISBN 0-527-16900-5). Kraus Repr.
Clark, Mollie. International Folktales Series. Incl. The Bird Catcher & the Crow-Peri: Turkey. LC 73-84508. (RL 3.7) (ISBN 0-8224-9300-4); The Buffalo Stone: North America. LC 73-84505. (RL 3.4) (ISBN 0-8224-9302-0); The Clever Jackal: India. LC 73-84503. (RL 3.3) (ISBN 0-8224-9304-7); Mac-the-Rascal from Mull: Scotland. LC 73-84504. (RL 3.3) (ISBN 0-8224-9306-3); Mink & the Fire: North America. LC 73-84501. (RL 3.2) (ISBN 0-8224-9308-X); The Monkey & the Roaring Rakhas: India. LC 73-84506. (RL 3.6) (ISBN 0-8224-9310-1); Rabbit & Fox: Canada. LC 73-84500. (RL 2.9) (ISBN 0-8224-9312-8); The Remarkable Rat: India. LC 73-84502. (RL 3.2) (ISBN 0-8224-9314-4); Three Marvelous Things: Italy. LC 73-84509. (RL 3.7) (ISBN 0-8224-9316-0); Wu & the Yellow Dragon: China. LC 73-84510. (RL 3.7) (ISBN 0-8224-9318-7). 1973. pap. 3.00 ea. Pitman Learning.
Clarkson, Atelia & Cross, G. B., eds. World Folktales: A Scribner Resource Collection. 1980. 20.00 (ISBN 0-684-16290-3, ScribT). Scribner.
Clodd, Edward. Magic in Names, & in Other Things. LC 67-23906. 1968. Repr. of 1920 ed. 19.00 (ISBN 0-8103-3024-5). Gale.
--Tom Tit Tot. LC 67-23907. 1968. Repr. of 1898 ed. 19.00 (ISBN 0-8103-3459-3). Gale.
Clouston, William A. Popular Tales & Fictions, Their Migrations & Transformations, 2 Vols. LC 67-23920. 1968. Repr. of 1887 ed. Set. 63.00 (ISBN 0-8103-3460-7). Gale.
Coffin, Tristram P. A Proper Book of Sexual Folklore. LC 77-28379. 1978. 8.95 (ISBN 0-8164-9337-5). Continuum.
Cox, G. W. An Introduction to the Science of Comparative Mythology & Folklore. 69.95 (ISBN 0-8490-0420-9). Gordon Pr.
Cox, George W. Introduction to the Science of Comparative Mythology & Folklore. LC 68-20124. 1968. Repr. of 1883 ed. 22.00 (ISBN 0-8103-3425-9). Gale.
--An Introduction to the Science of Comparative Mythology & Folklore. 1976. lib. bdg. 59.95 (ISBN 0-8490-2071-9). Gordon Pr.
Crossley-Holland, Kevin, ed. The Faber Book of Northern Folk-Tales. (Illus.). 157p. (gr. 3-12). 1981. 11.95 (ISBN 0-571-11519-5, Pub. by Faber & Faber). Merrimack Bk Serv.
Daniels, Cora L. & Stevans, C. M., eds. Encyclopedia of Superstitions, Folklore & the Occult Sciences of the World, 3 Vols. LC 70-141151. 1971. Repr. of 1903 ed. 80.00 (ISBN 0-8103-3286-8). Gale.
Davidson, Hilda E. Patterns of Folklore. 133p. 1978. 11.50x (ISBN 0-8476-6092-3). Rowman.

Dorson, Richard, ed. Folklore in the Modern World. (World Anthropology Ser.). 1978. 55.70 (ISBN 0-202-90060-6). Beresford Bk Serv.

Dorson, Richard M. Folklore & Fakelore: Essays Toward a Discipline of Folk Studies. 368p. 1976. 18.50x (ISBN 0-674-30715-1). Harvard U Pr.

--Folktales Told Around the World. (Illus.). xxvi, 622p. 1978. pap. 9.95 (ISBN 0-226-15874-8, P781, Phoen). U of Chicago Pr.

Dorson, Richard M., ed. Folklore & Folklife: An Introduction. LC 77-189038. 512p. 1972. 16.50x (ISBN 0-226-15870-5). U of Chicago Pr.

--Folklore of the World Series, 38 bks. 1980. Set. lib. bdg. 1330.00x (ISBN 0-405-13300-6). Arno.

--International Folklore Ser, 48 bks. (Illus.). 1977. Repr. 1081.00 (ISBN 0-405-10077-9). Arno.

--Studies in Folk Life: Essays in Honor of Iorwerth C. Peate, John G. Jenkins. LC 77-70603. (International Folklore Ser.). 1977. lib. bdg. 22.00x (ISBN 0-405-10102-3). Arno.

Dundes, Alan. The Evil Eye: A Folklore Casebook. 1981. lib. bdg. 30.00 (ISBN 0-8240-9471-9). Garland Pub.

--Folklore Theses & Dissertations in the United States. LC 75-29244. (American Folklore Society Bibliographical & Special Ser: No. 27). 628p. 1976. 22.50x (ISBN 0-292-72413-6). U of Tex Pr.

--Interpreting Folklore. LC 79-2969. (Midland Bks.: No. 240). 320p. 1980. 25.00x (ISBN 0-253-14307-1); pap. 9.95x (ISBN 0-253-20240-X). Ind U Pr.

--Study of Folklore. (Illus.). 1965. text ed. 14.95 (ISBN 0-13-858944-5). P-H.

Dundes, Alen, ed. Varia Folklorica. (World Anthropology Ser.). 1978. 34.75 (ISBN 0-202-90066-5). Beresford Bk Serv.

Durham, Mary E. High Albania. LC 70-135803. (Eastern Europe Collection Ser). 1970. Repr. of 1909 ed. 17.00 (ISBN 0-405-02745-1). Arno.

Eckenstein, Lina. Spell of Words: Studies in Language Bearing on Custom. LC 68-23153. 1969. Repr. of 1932 ed. 19.00 (ISBN 0-8103-3892-0). Gale.

Farrer, Claire R., ed. Women & Folklore. (American Folklore Society Bibliographical & Special Ser: No. 28). 118p. 1976. pap. 3.45x (ISBN 0-292-79006-6). U of Tex Pr.

Favat, F. Andre. Child & Tale: The Origins of Interest. LC 77-6698. (Orig.). 1977. pap. 7.00 (ISBN 0-8141-0595-5). NCTE.

Festing, Gabrielle. From the Land of Princes. (Folklore Ser.). 1904. 30.00 (ISBN 0-685-43836-8). Norwood Edns.

Fife, Austin, et al, eds. Forms Upon the Frontier: Folklife & Folk Arts in the United States. (Illus.). 189p. (Orig.). 1969. pap. 5.00 (ISBN 0-87421-036-4). Utah St U Pr.

Frazer, James G. Garnered Sheaves: Essays, Addresses, Reviews. facs. ed. LC 67-30212. (Essay Index Reprint Ser). 1931. 19.50 (ISBN 0-8369-0457-5). Arno.

Freud, Sigmund & Oppenheim, D. E. Dreams in Folklore. LC 57-14990. 1958. text ed. 12.00 (ISBN 0-8236-1440-9). Intl Univs Pr.

Gaster, Moses. Studies & Texts in Folklore, Magic, Medieval Romance, Hebrew Apocrypha & Samaritan Archaeology, 3 Vols. rev. ed. 1970. Set. 45.00x (ISBN 0-87068-056-0). Ktav.

Gill, Manohar S. Folk Tales of Lahaul. 1977. 9.00x (ISBN 0-7069-0522-9). Intl Bk Dist.

Gollancz, Israel, ed. & tr. Ambales Saga: Hamlet in Iceland. LC 70-178569. Repr. of 1898 ed. 27.50 (ISBN 0-404-56502-6). AMS Pr.

Golther, Wolfgang. Parzival und der Gral in der Dichtung des Mittelalters und der Neuzeit. LC 74-178535. Repr. of 1925 ed. 27.50 (ISBN 0-404-56611-1). AMS Pr.

Gomme, G. L. Folklore As Historical Science. 59.95 (ISBN 0-8490-0177-3). Gordon Pr.

Gomme, George L. Ethnology in Folklore. LC 79-75802. 1969. Repr. of 1892 ed. 19.00 (ISBN 0-8103-3832-7). Gale.

--Folklore As an Historical Science. LC 67-23898. (Illus.). 1968. Repr. of 1908 ed. 24.00 (ISBN 0-8103-3432-1). Gale.

Gorham, Melvin. Curse of the Ring. 1975. pap. 1.50 (ISBN 0-914752-06-5). Sovereign Pr.

Gruffydd, W. J. Folklore & Myth in the Mabinogion. LC 75-34083. 1958. lib. bdg. 6.50 (ISBN 0-8414-4522-2). Folcroft.

Gubernatis, Angelo De. Zoological Mythology, 2 Vols. LC 68-58904. 1968. Repr. of 1872 ed. Set. 39.00 (ISBN 0-8103-3527-1). Gale.

Halliday, W. R. Folklore Studies, Ancient & Modern. LC 76-78175. 1971. Repr. of 1924 ed. 19.00 (ISBN 0-8103-3676-6). Gale.

Hartland, Edwin S. Folklore: What Is It & What Is the Good of It. LC 77-139165. (Popular Studies in Mythology, Romance & Folklore: No. 2). Repr. of 1904 ed. 5.50 (ISBN 0-404-53502-X). AMS Pr.

--Mythology & Folktales: Their Relation & Interpretation. LC 75-144519. (Popular Studies in Mythology, Romance & Folklore: No. 7). Repr. of 1900 ed. 5.50 (ISBN 0-404-53507-0). AMS Pr.

--Science of Fairy Tales: An Inquiry into Fairy Mythology. LC 68-31149. 1968. Repr. of 1891 ed. 26.00 (ISBN 0-8103-3464-X). Gale.

Holy, Ladislav & Stuchlik, M., eds. The Structure of Folk Models. LC 80-41359. (ASA Monographs: No. 20). 1981. 30.00 (ISBN 0-12-353750-9). Acad Pr.

Hopkins, Edward W. Origin & Evolution of Religion. LC 76-79199. 370p. 1969. Repr. of 1923 ed. 15.00x (ISBN 0-8154-0294-5). Cooper Sq.

Hudson, Wilson M., ed. & intro. by. Diamond Bessie & the Shepherds. (Annual Pubns. Ser., No. 36). (Illus.). 170p. 1972. 7.95 (ISBN 0-88426-011-9). Encino Pr.

Jackson, Bruce, ed. Folklore & Society. LC 78-15248. 1978. Repr. lib. bdg. 20.00 (ISBN 0-8414-5402-7). Folcroft.

Judge, Roy. The Jack-in-the-Green: A May Day Custom. (Folklore Society Mistletoe Ser.). (Illus.). 145p. 1978. 18.00x (ISBN 0-8476-6091-5). Rowman.

Jung, Carl G. & Kerenyi, Carl. Essays on a Science of Mythology: The Myths of the Divine Child & the Mysteries of Eleusis. rev. ed. (Bollingen Ser.: Vol. 22). 1969. 12.50 (ISBN 0-691-09851-4); pap. 3.95 (ISBN 0-691-01756-5). Princeton U Pr.

Katz, Elaine S. Folklore for the Time of Your Life. LC 78-55773. (Illus.). 1979. 9.95 (ISBN 0-8487-0488-6). Oxmoor Hse.

Keightley, T. Fairy Mythology. LC 68-26357. (Studies in Shakespeare, No. 24). 1969. Repr. of 1850 ed. lib. bdg. 39.95 (ISBN 0-8383-0281-5). Haskell.

Keightley, Thomas. Fairy Mythology. LC 68-55794. (Bohn's Antiquarian Library Ser). Repr. of 1850 ed. 17.50 (ISBN 0-404-50019-6). AMS Pr.

--Fairy Mythology. rev. ed. (Folklore & Society Ser). 1969. Repr. of 1860 ed. 23.00 (ISBN 0-384-29010-8). Johnson Repr.

Kelchner, Georgia D. Dreams in Old Norse Literature & Their Affinities in Folklore. LC 77-2928. 1977. Repr. of 1935 ed. lib. bdg. 27.50 (ISBN 0-8414-5538-4). Folcroft.

Kellett, Ernst E. Story of Myths. (Folklore & Society Ser). 1969. Repr. of 1927 ed. 15.50 (ISBN 0-384-29025-6). Johnson Repr.

Kelly, Walter K. Curiosities of Indo-European Tradition & Folk-Lore. LC 68-22032. 1969. Repr. of 1863 ed. 22.00 (ISBN 0-8103-3837-8). Gale.

King, E. F. Ten Thousand Wonderful Things. 59.95 (ISBN 0-8490-1184-1). Gordon Pr.

Krappe, Alexander H. Science of Folklore. 1964. pap. 4.25x (ISBN 0-393-00282-9, Norton Lib). Norton.

Laboulaye, Edouard. Last Fairy Tales. Booth, Mary L, tr. LC 76-9900. (Children's Literature Reprint Ser). (Illus.). (gr. 4-6). 1976. Repr. of 1866 ed. 19.50x (ISBN 0-8486-0208-0). Core Collection.

Laing, Jeanie M. Notes on Superstition & Folk Lore. LC 77-19156. 1885. 7.50 (ISBN 0-8414-2260-5). Folcroft.

Lang, Andrew. Custom & Myth. 2nd rev. ed. LC 68-59267. Repr. of 1885 ed. 11.00 (ISBN 0-404-03817-4). AMS Pr.

Laubach, David C. Introduction to Folklore. 192p. (gr. 10-12). 1980. pap. 6.95 (ISBN 0-8104-6039-4). Hayden.

Lawrence, Robert M. Magic of the Horseshoe. LC 68-22034. 1968. Repr. of 1898 ed. 22.00 (ISBN 0-8103-3452-6). Gale.

--The Magic of the Horseshoe & Other Folk-Lore Notes. 1976. lib. bdg. 59.95 (ISBN 0-8490-2195-2). Gordon Pr.

Leichty, E. V. The Series Summa Izbu. LC 66-25697. 24.00 (ISBN 0-685-71732-1). J J Augustin.

Lessa, William A. More Tales from Ulithi Atoll. (U. C. Publications in Folklore & Mythology Studies: Vol. 32). 1980. pap. 16.50x (ISBN 0-520-09615-0). U of Cal Pr.

Long, George. The Folklore Calendar. (Illus.). 240p. 1977. Repr. of 1930 ed. 17.50x (ISBN 0-8476-6062-1). Rowman.

Loomis, C. Grant. White Magic: An Introduction to the Folklore of Christian Legend. 1967. Repr. of 1948 ed. 8.00 (ISBN 0-910956-26-X). Medieval Acad.

Loranth, Alice N., ed. Catalog of Folklore, Folklife & Folk Songs, 3 vols. 2nd ed. 1978. Set. lib. bdg. 245.00 (ISBN 0-8161-0249-X). G K Hall.

Mac Culloch, Edgar. Guernsey: Folklore. 1978. Repr. of 1903 ed. lib. bdg. 40.00 (ISBN 0-8492-1735-0). R West.

McDonald, Susan & Gerrick, David J. Folklore of Kissing Games. 84p. (Orig.). 1981. pap. 3.00 (ISBN 0-916750-77-9). Dayton Labs.

Merin, Jennifer, et al. International Directory of Theatre, Dance, & Folklore Festivals. LC 79-9908. 1979. lib. bdg. 19.95 (ISBN 0-313-20993-6, MTF/). Greenwood.

Metzger, Deena. Skin-Shadows-Silence. 112p. 1975. pap. text ed. 5.00 (ISBN 0-915596-09-1). West Coast.

Morrison, Lillian, ed. Touch Blue. LC 57-10284. (Illus.). (gr. 4 up). 1958. 8.95 (ISBN 0-690-83316-4, TYC-J). Har-Row.

Murray-Aynsley, Harriet G. Symbolism of the East & West. LC 77-141748. (Illus.). 1971. Repr. of 1900 ed. 24.00 (ISBN 0-8103-3395-3). Gale.

Napier, James. Folk-Lore. LC 77-17294. 1977. Repr. of 1879 ed. lib. bdg. 20.00 (ISBN 0-8414-6303-4). Folcroft.

--Folklore: Or, Superstitious Beliefs West of Scotland Within This Country. 190p. 1980. Repr. of 1879 ed. lib. bdg. 22.50 (ISBN 0-8495-4102-6). Arden Lib.

Niemi, Adrian A. The Quest of the Sampo. 1978. 6.95 (ISBN 0-533-03577-5). Vantage.

Oinas, Felix J., ed. Folklore Nationalism & Politics. 1977. pap. 9.95 (ISBN 0-89357-043-5). Slavica.

Owen, Mary A. Voodoo Tales As Told Among the Negroes of the Southwest. facs. ed. LC 70-149874. (Black Heritage Library Collection Ser). 1893. 15.00 (ISBN 0-8369-8754-3). Arno.

Paredes, Americo & Bauman, Richard, eds. Toward New Perspectives in Folklore. LC 74-165922. (American Folklore Society Bibliographical & Special Ser.: No. 23). 197p. 1971. 13.50x (ISBN 0-292-70142-X). U of Tex Pr.

Parry, Adam & Dorson, Richard M., eds. The Making of Homeric Verse: The Collected Papers of Milman Parry. LC 80-747. (Folklore of the World Ser.). (Illus.). 1980. Repr. of 1971 ed. lib. bdg. 50.00x (ISBN 0-405-13321-9). Arno.

Phelps, Ethel J. The Maid of the North & Other Folk Tales Heroines. LC 80-21500. (Illus.). 192p. (gr. 2-6). 1981. 10.95 (ISBN 0-03-056893-5). HR&W.

Popular Studies in Mythology, Romance & Folklore, 15 vols. Repr. of 1908 ed. Set. 88.00 (ISBN 0-404-53500-3). AMS Pr.

Porteous, A. Forest Folklore, Mythology & Romance. 1977. lib. bdg. 59.95 (ISBN 0-8490-1858-7). Gordon Pr.

Purslow, Frank. The Constant Lovers. (Folklore Ser.). 1972. 7.50 (ISBN 0-88305-512-0). Norwood Edns.

--Marrow Bones. (Folklore Ser.). 1965. 7.00 (ISBN 0-88305-508-2). Norwood Edns.

--The Wanton Seed. LC 77-5521. (Folklore Ser.). 1968. 10.00 (ISBN 0-88305-510-4). Norwood Edns.

Raglan, FitzRoy. The Hero: A Study in Tradition, Myth, & Drama. LC 75-23424. 296p. 1975. Repr. of 1956 ed. lib. bdg. 19.25x (ISBN 0-8371-8138-0, RATH). Greenwood.

Ramsey, Eloise. Folklore for Children & Young People. LC 52-10251. Repr. of 1952 ed. 10.00 (ISBN 0-527-01127-4). Kraus Repr.

Richmond, Winthrop E., ed. Studies in Folklore: In Honor of Distinguished Service Professor Stith Thompson. LC 72-163547. (Illus.). 270p. 1972. Repr. of 1957 ed. lib. bdg. 15.00x (ISBN 0-8371-6208-4, RISF). Greenwood.

Robinson, H. S. & Wilson, K. The Encyclopedia of Myths & Legends of All Nations. rev. ed. Picard, Barbara L., ed. 1978. Repr. of 1974 ed. text ed. 19.50x (ISBN 0-7182-0561-8, LTB). Sportshelf.

Rodway, Avril. Fairies. (The Leprechaun Library). (Illus.). 64p. 1981. 3.95 (ISBN 0-399-12610-4). Putnam.

Rosenberg, Bruce A. & Mandel, Jerome, eds. Medieval Literature & Folklore Studies. LC 70-127053. 1971. 27.50 (ISBN 0-8135-0676-X). Rutgers U Pr.

Schneiderman, Leo. The Psychology of Myth, Folklore & Religion. LC 81-9471. 232p. 1981. text ed. 18.95x (ISBN 0-88229-659-0); pap. text ed. 8.95x (ISBN 0-88229-783-X). Nelson-Hall.

Schwab, Gustav. Gods & Heroes. LC 47-873. 1977. pap. 6.95 (ISBN 0-394-73402-5). Pantheon.

Schwarzbaum, Haim. Studies in Jewish & World Folklore. (Fabula Supplement Ser., No. B 3). 1968. 92.00x (ISBN 3-11-000393-7). De Gruyter.

Shah, Idries. World Tales. LC 79-1734. (Illus.). 1979. 19.95 (ISBN 0-15-199434-X). HarBraceJ.

Skeat, Walter. Fables & Folk-Tales from an Eastern Forest. (Folklore Ser). 7.50 (ISBN 0-88305-635-6). Norwood Edns.

Skinner, Charles M. Myths & Legends of Our Own Land, 2 Vols. LC 79-76999. 1969. Repr. of 1896 ed. Set. 26.00 (ISBN 0-8103-3851-3). Gale.

Slator, Lana. Giants & Gnomes Coloring Album. (Illus.). 32p. 1978. pap. 3.50 (ISBN 0-912300-94-9, 94-9). Troubador Pr.

Solomon, Jack & Solomon, Olivia, eds. Zickary Zan: Childhood Folklore. LC 79-1117. (Illus.). 208p. 1980. 14.95 (ISBN 0-8173-0012-0). U of Ala Pr.

Sonntag, Linda. Frogs. (The Leprechaun Library). (Illus.). 64p. 1981. 3.95 (ISBN 0-399-12611-2). Putnam.

Sullivan, J. Cumberland & Westmoreland, Ancient & Modern. (Folklore Ser). 17.50 (ISBN 0-685-36520-4). Norwood Edns.

Sumner, Heywood. The Besom Maker & Other Country Folk Songs. LC 72-6978. 1972. lib. bdg. 5.00 (ISBN 0-88305-602-X). Norwood Edns.

Sutton-Smith, Brian. Folkstories of Children. LC 80-5010. (American Folklore Society Ser.). 1980. 19.95x (ISBN 0-686-61087-3); pap. 12.95x (ISBN 0-8122-1108-1). U of Pa Pr.

Sylva, Carmen & Stretteell, Alma. Legends from River & Mountain. 1977. lib. bdg. 59.95 (ISBN 0-8490-2145-6). Gordon Pr.

Taylor, Archer. The Black Ox: A Study in the History of a Folk-Tale. Dorson, Richard M., ed. LC 80-798. (Folklore of the World Ser.). 1980. Repr. of 1927 ed. lib. bdg. 12.00x (ISBN 0-405-13339-1). Arno.

--Comparative Studies in Folklore: Asia, Europe, America, No. 41. (Asian Folklore & Social Life Monograph). 454p. 1972. 9.20 (ISBN 0-89986-040-0). E Langstaff.

Taylor, Benjamin. Storyology: Essays in Folk-Lore, Sea-Lore, & Plant-Lore. 1979. Repr. of 1900 ed. lib. bdg. 25.00 (ISBN 0-8414-8416-3). Folcroft.

--Storyology: Essays in Folklore, Sea-Lore, & Plant-Lore. 1976. lib. bdg. 59.95 (ISBN 0-8490-2693-8). Gordon Pr.

Thompson, C. J. Hand of Destiny: The Folk-Lore & Superstition of Everyday Life. LC 70-125600. 1970. Repr. of 1932 ed. 26.00 (ISBN 0-8103-3419-4). Gale.

Thompson, Campbell. Semitic Magic: Its Origin & Development. 19.95x (ISBN 0-87068-172-9). Ktav.

Thompson, Stith. Motif-Index of Folk-Literature, 6 Vols. rev. ed. Incl. Vol. 1. 560p. 32.50x (ISBN 0-253-33881-6); Vol. 2. 520p. 32.50x (ISBN 0-253-33882-4); Vol. 3. 520p. 32.50x (ISBN 0-253-33883-2); Vol. 4. 500p. 32.50x (ISBN 0-253-33884-0); Vol. 5. 568p. 32.50x (ISBN 0-253-33885-9); Vol. 6. 896p. 45.00x (ISBN 0-253-33886-7). LC 55-8055. 1955-58. Set. 160.00x (ISBN 0-253-33887-5). Ind U Pr.

Thompson, Stith, ed. Four Symposia on Folklore. LC 76-138. (Indiana University Publications - Folklore Series: No. 8). 340p. 1976. Repr. of 1953 ed. lib. bdg. 21.75x (ISBN 0-8371-8740-0, THFS). Greenwood.

Thorpe, Benjamin, ed. Yule-Tide Stories. LC 68-55557. (Bohn's Antiquarian Library Ser). Repr. of 1853 ed. 24.50 (ISBN 0-404-50024-2). AMS Pr.

Von Sydow, Carl W. Selected Papers on Folklore. Dorson, Richard, ed. LC 77-70623. (International Folklore Ser.). 1977. lib. bdg. 17.00x (ISBN 0-405-10125-2). Arno.

Wilgus, D. K. & Sommer, Carol, eds. Folklore International: Essays in Traditional Literature, Belief, & Custom in Honor of Wayland Debs Hand. LC 67-16249. (Illus.). xiv, 259p. Repr. of 1967 ed. 24.00 (ISBN 0-8103-5023-8). Gale.

Yardley, Edward. Supernatural in Romantic Fiction. LC 76-40241. 1880. lib. bdg. 15.00 (ISBN 0-8414-9761-3). Folcroft.

Yearsley, Macleod. Folklore of Fairy-Tale. LC 68-31517. 1968. Repr. of 1924 ed. 22.00 (ISBN 0-8103-3457-7). Gale.

Zipes, Jack. Breaking the Magic Spell: Radical Theories of Folk & Fairy Tales. LC 79-87883. 1979. text ed. 13.95 (ISBN 0-292-70725-8). U of Tex Pr.

FOLK-LORE–BIBLIOGRAPHY

Danandjaja, James. An Annotated Bibliography of Javanese Folklore. (Occasional Papers Ser.: No. 9). 1972. 10.00 (ISBN 0-686-23624-6, Ctr South & Southeast Asia Studies). Cellar.

Flanagan, Cathleen C. & Flanagan, John T. American Folklore: A Bibliography, 1950-1974. LC 77-23381. 1977. 19.50 (ISBN 0-8108-1073-5). Scarecrow.

Georges, Robert A. & Stern, Stephen. American Immigrant & Ethnic Folklore: An Annotated Bibliography. 1981. lib. bdg. 35.00 (ISBN 0-8240-9307-0). Garland Pub.

International Folklore & Folklife Bibliography, Internationale Volkskundliche Bibliographie, Bibliographie Internationale des Arts et Traditions Populaires, 5 vols. pap. 75.00x 1967-68 (ISBN 3-7749-1118-5); pap. 115.00x 1969-70, 1972 (ISBN 3-7749-1248-3); 1971-72, 1974 130.00x (ISBN 3-7749-1298-X); 1973-74, 1977 130.00x (ISBN 3-7749-1380-3); 1975-76, 1979 130.00x (ISBN 3-7749-1498-2). Intl Pubns Serv.

Ireland, Norma O. Index to Fairy Tales, 1949-1972, Including Folklore, Legends & Myths in Collections. LC 26-11491. (The Useful Reference Ser. of Library Bks: Vol. 101). 1973. lib. bdg. 18.00x (ISBN 0-87305-101-7). Faxon.

McDonald, Margaret R. The Storyteller's Sourcebook: An Index to Folklore Collections for Children. 500p. 1981. 49.95x (ISBN 0-918212-40-5). Neal-Schuman.

Nah-Trang Cong-Huyen-Ton-Nu. Vietnamese Folklore: An Introductory & Annotated Bibliography. (Occasional Papers Ser.: No. 7). 1970. 8.75 (ISBN 0-686-23626-2, Ctr South & Southeast Asia Studies). Cellar.

Perdue, Charles L., Jr., et al. An Annotated Listings of Folklore. 1979. lib. bdg. 30.00 (ISBN 0-8482-5550-X). Norwood Edns.

Pitre, Giuseppe. Bibliografia delle Tradizioni Popolari D'italia, Contre Indici Speciali. LC 72-82380. xx, 603p. 1972. Repr. of 1894 ed. lib. bdg. 43.50 (ISBN 0-8337-2775-3). B Franklin.

Simmons, Merle. Folklore Bibliography for 1973. (Folklore Institute Monograph Ser.: No. 28). 1975. pap. text ed. 12.00x (ISBN 0-87750-189-0). Res Ctr Lang Semiotic.

Simmons, Merle E. Folklore Bibliography for 1974. LC 77-7893. (Folklore Institute Monographs: No. 29). 1977. pap. text ed. 12.00x (ISBN 0-87750-211-0). Res Ctr Lang Semiotic.

--Folklore Bibliography for 1975. LC 79-20051. (Indiana University Folklore Institute Monograph: Vol. 31). 1979. text ed. 17.50x (ISBN 0-89727-000-2). Inst Study Human.

Simmons, Merle E., ed. Folklore Bibliography for Nineteen Seventy-Six. (Indiana University Folklore Institute Monograph Ser. Vol. 33). 240p. 1981. text ed. 17.50x (ISBN 0-89727-023-1). Inst Study Hum.

Ziegler, Elsie B. Folklore: An Annotated Bibliography & Index to Single Editions. LC 73-77289. (The Useful Reference Ser of Library Bks: Vol. 100). 1973. lib. bdg. 12.00x (ISBN 0-87305-100-9). Faxon.

FOLK-LORE–CLASSIFICATION

see also Folk Literature–Themes, Motives

Bassett, Fletcher S. The Folk-Lore Manual. LC 76-49139. 1976. Repr. of 1892 ed. lib. bdg. 15.00 (ISBN 0-8414-1755-5). Folcroft.

Baughman, Ernest W. Type & Motif-Index of the Folktales of England & North America. 1966. pap. text ed. 65.90x (ISBN 90-2790-046-9). Mouton.

Cross, T. P. Motif-Index of Early Irish Literature. 1952. 30.00 (ISBN 0-527-20700-4). Kraus Repr.

Hartland, Edwin S. Legend of Perseus: A Study of Tradition in Story, Custom & Belief, 3 Vols. LC 77-139165. (Grimm Library: Nos. 2, 3, & 5). Repr. of 1896 ed. 35.00 (ISBN 0-404-53570-4). AMS Pr.

FOLK-LORE–DICTIONARIES

Bonnerjea, Biren. Dictionary of Superstitions & Mythology. LC 69-17755. 1969. Repr. of 1927 ed. 24.00 (ISBN 0-8103-3572-7). Gale.

Daniels, Cora L. Encyclopedia of Superstitions, Folklore & the Occult Sciences, 3 vols. 300.00 (ISBN 0-8490-0106-4). Gordon Pr.

Jobes, Gertrude. Dictionary of Mythology, Folklore & Symbols, 2 Vols. LC 61-860. 1961. Set. 50.00 (ISBN 0-8108-0034-9). Scarecrow.

Leach, ed. Funk & Wagnalls Standard Dictionary of Folklore, Mythology & Legend. LC 72-78268. (Funk & W Bk.). 22.95 (ISBN 0-308-40090-9). T Y Crowell.

Radford, Edwin & Radford, Mona A. Encyclopedia of Superstitions. Repr. of 1949 ed. lib. bdg. 19.00x (ISBN 0-8371-2115-9, RASU). Greenwood.

FOLK-LORE–JEWS

see also Folk-Lore, Jewish

Alon, Gedaliah. The Jews in Their Land in the Talmudic Age, Vol. 1. Gershon, Levi, tr. from Hebrew. 324p. 1980. text ed. 23.00x (ISBN 965-223-352-8, Pub. by Magnes Israel). Humanities.

Gaster, Theodore H. Myth, Legend & Custom in the Old Testament: A Comparative Study with Chapters from Sir James G. Frazer's Folklore in the Old Testament, 2 vols. Set. 25.00 (ISBN 0-8446-5189-3). Peter Smith.

FOLK-LORE–JUVENILE LITERATURE

Ainsworth, Catherine H. American Calendar Customs, Vol. I. LC 79-52827. (Calendar Customs & Holidays Ser.). 104p. (Orig.). (gr. 5-12). 1979. pap. 5.00 (ISBN 0-933190-06-9). Clyde Pr.

Anderson, Robin. Sinabouda Lily. (Illus.). (ps-2). 1979. 7.95x (ISBN 0-19-554201-0). Oxford U Pr.

Appiah, Peggy. The Pineapple Child & Other Tales from Ashanti. (Illus.). 176p. (gr. 2-7). 1981. 7.95 (ISBN 0-233-95875-4). Andre Deutsch.

Baker, Betty. No Help at All. LC 76-13223. (Greenwillow Read-Alone Bks.). (Illus.). (gr. 1-4). 1978. 5.95 (ISBN 0-688-80056-4); PLB 5.71 (ISBN 0-688-84056-6). Greenwillow.

Bang, Betsy. The Demons of Rajpur. LC 80-10467. (Illus.). 96p. (gr. 3-6). 1980. 7.95 (ISBN 0-688-80263-X); PLB 7.63 (ISBN 0-688-84263-1). Greenwillow.

Berson, Harold. Joseph & the Snake. LC 78-12317. (Illus.). 32p. (gr. k-3). 1979. 6.95 (ISBN 0-02-709200-3). Macmillan.

Bowden, Joan C. The Bean Boy. LC 78-12150. (Ready-to-Read Ser.). (Illus.). (gr. 1-4). 1979. 6.95 (ISBN 0-02-711800-2). Macmillan.

Carlson, Bernice W. Picture That! LC 76-25813. (Illus.). (gr. k-3). 1977. 7.95 (ISBN 0-687-31419-4). Abingdon.

Carpenter, Francis. Tales of a Chinese Grandmother. 293p. Repr. of 1937 ed. lib. bdg. 15.70x (ISBN 0-89190-481-6). Am Repr-Rivercity Pr.

Carrick, Malcolm. Happy Jack. LC 78-19476. (I Can Read Book). (Illus.). (gr. k-3). 1979. 6.95 (ISBN 0-06-021121-0, HarpJ); PLB 7.89 (ISBN 0-06-021122-9). Har-Row.

Chambless-Rigie, Jane, illus. My First Mother Goose Book. (Golden Storytime Bk. of Learning). 24p. (ps). 1980. 1.50 (ISBN 0-307-11981-5); PLB 6.08 (ISBN 0-307-61981-8). Western Pub.

Chang, Kathleen. The Iron Moonhunter: Bilingual in Chinese & English. LC 77-73783. (Fifth World Tales Ser.). (Illus.). (gr. k-6). pap. 3.95 (ISBN 0-89239-011-5, Imprenta de Libros Infantiles). Childrens Book Pr.

Clark, Mollie. International Folktales Series. Incl. The Bird Catcher & the Crow-Peri: Turkey. LC 73-84508. (RL 3.7) (ISBN 0-8224-9300-4); The Buffalo Stone: North America. LC 73-84505. (RL 3.4) (ISBN 0-8224-9302-0); The Clever Jackal: India. LC 73-84503. (RL 3.3) (ISBN 0-8224-9304-7); Mac-the-Rascal from Mull: Scotland. LC 73-84504. (RL 3.3) (ISBN 0-8224-9306-3); Mink & the Fire: North America. LC 73-84501. (RL 3.2) (ISBN 0-8224-9308-X); The Monkey & the Roaring Rakhas: India. LC 73-84506. (RL 3.6) (ISBN 0-8224-9310-1); Rabbit & Fox: Canada. LC 73-84500. (RL 2.9) (ISBN 0-8224-9312-8); The Remarkable Rat: India. LC 73-84502. (RL 3.2) (ISBN 0-8224-9314-4); Three Marvelous Things: Italy. LC 73-84509. (RL 3.7) (ISBN 0-8224-9316-0); Wu & the Yellow Dragon: China. LC 73-84510. (RL 3.7) (ISBN 0-8224-9318-7). 1973. pap. 3.00 ea. Pitman Learning.

De Blumenthal, Vera. Folk Tales from the Russian. LC 78-74512. (Children's Literature Reprint Ser.). (Illus.). (gr. 4-5). 1979. Repr. of 1903 ed. 16.75x (ISBN 0-8486-0216-1). Core Collection.

De Paola, Tomie. Helga's Dowry. LC 76-54953. (Illus.). 32p. (ps-3). 1977. 8.95 (ISBN 0-15-233701-6, HJ). HarBraceJ.

Domanska, Janina. The Best of the Bargain. LC 76-13010. (Illus.). (gr. k-3). 1977. 8.95 (ISBN 0-688-80062-9); PLB 8.59 (ISBN 0-688-84062-0). Greenwillow.

--A Scythe, A Rooster, & A Cat. LC 80-17445. (Illus.). 32p. (gr. k-3). 1981. 8.95 (ISBN 0-688-80308-3); PLB 8.59 (ISBN 0-688-84308-5). Greenwillow.

Foley, Tom, illus. Sakshi Gopal: A Witness for the Wedding. (Illus.). 16p. (gr. 1-4). 1981. pap. 1.50 (ISBN 0-89647-010-5). Bala Bks.

Ginsburg, Mirra. Little Rystu. LC 76-30485. (Illus.). (gr. k-3). 1978. 7.95 (ISBN 0-688-80097-1); PLB 7.63 (ISBN 0-688-84097-3). Greenwillow.

--Striding Slippers: Adapted from an Udmurt Tale. LC 77-12035. (Illus.). (gr. k-3). 1978. 8.95 (ISBN 0-02-736370-8, 73637). Macmillan.

Grimm Brothers. Mother Holly. LC 77-185753. (Illus.). (gr. k-3). 1972. 7.95 (ISBN 0-690-56363-9, TYC-J). Har-Row.

Gupta, Rupa. Tales from Indian Classics. (Illus.). 136p. (gr. 1-9). 1981. 6.25 (ISBN 0-89744-233-4, Pub. by Hemkunt India). Auromere.

Hearn, Lafcadio, et al. Japanese Fairy Tales. LC 78-74515. (Children's Literature Reprint Ser). (gr. 4-6). 1979. Repr. of 1918 ed. 16.75x (ISBN 0-8486-0218-8). Core Collection.

Hillert, Margaret. Little Red Riding Hood. (Just Beginning-to-Read Ser.). (Illus.). 32p. (gr. 1-6). 1981. PLB 4.39 (ISBN 0-695-41543-3); pap. 1.50 (ISBN 0-695-31543-9). Follett.

--Tom Thumb. (Just Beginning-to-Read Ser.). (Illus.). 32p. (gr. 1-6). 1981. PLB 4.39 (ISBN 0-695-41542-5); pap. 1.50 (ISBN 0-695-31542-0). Follett.

Irving, Washington. Spanish Papers. Irving, Pierre, ed. LC 78-74516. (Children's Literature Reprint Ser.). (gr. 7 up). 1979. Repr. of 1868 ed. 42.50x (ISBN 0-8486-0219-6). Core Collection.

Izawa, T. & Hijkata, S., illus. Jack & the Beanstalk. (Puppet Storybooks). (Illus.). 18p. (gr. k-2). 1981. 3.50 (ISBN 0-448-09758-3). G&D.

Jack & the Beanstalk. Bd. with Treasure Island; Bremen Town Musicians; The Ugly Duckling; Pussin Boots; Thumbelina. (Pocket Pop-Ups Ser.). (Illus.). (ps-5). 1980. Set. 15.00 (ISBN 0-89346-165-2). Heian Intl.

Jameson, Cynthia. Winter Hut. (A Break of Day Bk.). (Illus.). 48p. (gr. 1-3). 1973. PLB 6.59 (ISBN 0-698-30500-0). Coward.

Jones, Gwyn. Scandinavian Legends & Folk-Tales. (Oxford Myths & Legends Ser.). (Illus.). (gr. 4 up). 1979. 10.95 (ISBN 0-19-274124-1). Oxford U Pr.

Knapp, Mary & Knapp, Herbert. One Potato, Two Potato: The Folklore of American Children. 1978. pap. text ed. 4.95x (ISBN 0-393-09039-6). Norton.

Laboulaye, Edouard. Fairy Book: Fairy Tales of All Nations. Booth, Mary L., tr. LC 76-9899. (Children's Literature Reprint Ser). (Illus.). (gr. 4-6). 1976. Repr. of 1870 ed. 19.00x (ISBN 0-8486-0207-2). Core Collection.

Lipson, Greta. Fact, Fantasy, Folklore. (gr. 3-12). 1977. 9.95 (ISBN 0-916456-11-0, GA71). Good Apple.

Lofgren, Ulf. The Boy Who Ate More Than the Giant, & Other Swedish Folktales. LC 78-8653. (Unicef Storycraft Bks.). (Illus.). (ps-3). 1978. 5.95 (ISBN 0-529-05450-7); PLB 5.99 (ISBN 0-529-05451-5). Philomel.

McDowell, John H. Children's Riddling. LC 78-19551. 320p. 1979. 17.50x (ISBN 0-253-15020-5). Ind U Pr.

Mace, Jean. Home Fairy Tales. Booth, Mary L., tr. from Fr. LC 78-74517. (Children's Literature Reprint Ser.). (Illus.). (gr. 4-5). 1979. Repr. of 1867 ed. 24.75x (ISBN 0-8486-0220-X). Core Collection.

McGowen, Tom. Encyclopedia of Legendary Creatures. (Illus.). 72p. (gr. 5 up). 1981. 8.95 (ISBN 0-528-82402-3); PLB 8.97 (ISBN 0-528-80074-4). Rand.

McLenighan, Valjean. Three Strikes & You're Out. (Beginning-to-Read Ser.). 32p. 1980. PLB 4.39 (ISBN 0-695-41462-3); pap. 1.95 (ISBN 0-695-31462-9). Follett.

Mirkovic, Irene. The Greedy Shopkeeper. LC 80-13034. (Illus.). 32p. (gr. k-3). 1980. pap. 2.95 (ISBN 0-15-232552-2, VoyB). HarBraceJ.

--The Greedy Shopkeeper. LC 80-13034. (Illus.). 32p. (gr. k-3). 1980. 7.95 (ISBN 0-15-232551-4, HJ). HarBraceJ.

Moncure, Jane B. The Lad Who Made the Princess Laugh. LC 79-25835. (Illus.). (gr. k-4). 1980. PLB 5.50 (ISBN 0-89565-109-2). Childs World.

--The Shoemaker & the Christmas Elves. (Folk Tales Ser.). (Illus.). 1980. 7.95g (ISBN 0-516-06482-7). Childrens.

Newfeld, Frank. Simon & the Golden Sword. (Illus.). (ps-3). 1979. 5.95 (ISBN 0-19-540270-7). Oxford U Pr.

Obligado, Lilian, illus. Goldilocks & the Three Bears. (Golden Storytime Bk. for Learning). 24p. (gr. 3-6). 1980. 1.50 (ISBN 0-307-11980-7); PLB 6.08 s&l (ISBN 0-307-61980-X). Western Pub.

Obrist, Jurg. They Do Things Right in Albern. LC 78-6598. (Illus.). (ps-3). 1978. 6.95 (ISBN 0-689-30671-7). Atheneum.

Prather, Ray. The Ostrich Girl. LC 78-9710. (Illus.). (gr. 1-3). 1978. reinforced bdg 8.95 (ISBN 0-684-15889-2, ScribJ). Scribner.

Rohermer, Harriet. The Mighty God Viracocha: El Dios Poderoso Viracocha. LC 76-17492. (Illus.). (gr. k-6). pap. 3.95 spanish bilingual ed. (ISBN 0-89239-005-0, Imprenta de Libros Infantiles). Childrens Book Pr.

Rohmer, Harriet. Land of the Icy Death: Tierra De la Muerte Glacial. LC 76-29211. (Fifth World Tales Ser.). (Illus.). (gr. k-6). pap. 3.95 spanish bilingual ed. (ISBN 0-89239-009-3, Imprenta de Libros Infantiles). Childrens Book Pr.

--The Little Horse of Seven Colors: El Caballito De Siete Colores. LC 76-17494. (Fifth World Tales Ser.). (Illus.). (gr. k-6). pap. 3.95 spanish bilingual ed. (ISBN 0-89239-006-9, Imprenta de Libros Infantiles). Childrens Book Pr.

--The Magic Boys: Los Ninos Magicos. LC 75-34916. (Illus.). (gr. k-6). pap. 3.95 spanish bilingual ed. (ISBN 0-89239-001-8, Imprenta de Libros Infantiles). Childrens Book Pr.

--Skyworld Woman: La Mujer del Mundo-Cielo. LC 75-34917. (Fifth World Tales Ser.). (Illus.). (gr. k-6). pap. 3.95 spanish bilingual ed. (ISBN 0-89239-002-6, Imprents de Libros Infantiles). Childrens Book Pr.

--The Treasure of Guatavita: El Tesoro De Guatavita. LC 76-29081. (Fifth World Tales Ser.). (Illus.). (gr. k-6). pap. 3.95 spanish bilingual ed. (ISBN 0-89239-010-7, Imprenta de Libros Infantiles). Childrens Book Pr.

Sandoval, Ruben & Strick, David. Games, Games, Games, Juegos, Juegos, Juegos: Chicano Children at Play--Games & Rhymes. (gr. 1 up). 1977. PLB 6.95 (ISBN 0-385-05438-6). Doubleday.

Schwartz, Alvin. Cross Your Fingers, Spit in Your Hat. LC 73-21912. (Illus.). 160p. (gr. 4 up). 1974. 8.95 (ISBN 0-397-31530-9, JBL-J); pap. 2.95 (ISBN 0-397-31531-7). Har-Row.

--Flapdoodle: Pure Nonsense from American Folklore. LC 79-9618. (Illus.). 128p. (gr. 5up). 1980. 7.95 (ISBN 0-397-31919-3, JBL-J); PLB 7.89 (ISBN 0-397-31920-7); pap. 3.95 (ISBN 0-397-31921-5, JBL-J). Har-Row.

Segovia, Gertrudis. The Spanish Fairy Book. Quinn, Elizabeth V., tr. LC 78-74519. (Children's Literature Reprint Ser.). (gr. 5-7). 1979. Repr. of 1918 ed. 22.50x (ISBN 0-8486-0222-6). Core Collection.

Sheppard-Jones, Elisabeth. Stories of Wales: Told for Children. (Illus.). (gr. 3-6). 1978. pap. 5.00 (ISBN 0-902375-41-5). Academy Chi Ltd.

Smith, Bob. Old African Tales Told Again. (Illus.). (gr. 2-5). 1977. 5.95 (ISBN 0-915864-99-1). Academy Chi Ltd.

Stallman, Birdie. Learning About Dragons. LC 81-4746. (The Learning About Ser.). (Illus.). 48p. (gr. 2-6). Date not set. PLB price not set (ISBN 0-516-06531-9). Childrens.

--Learning About Witches. (The Learning About Ser.). (Illus.). 48p. (gr. 2-6). Date not set. PLB price not set (ISBN 0-516-06536-X). Childrens.

Tester, Sylvia R. Learning About Ghosts. (The Learning About Ser.). (Illus.). 48p. (gr. 2-6). Date not set. PLB price not set (ISBN 0-516-06533-5). Childrens.

Thorne, Ian. Monster Tales of Native Americans. Schroeder, Howard, ed. LC 78-5234. (Search for the Unknown Ser.). (Illus.). (gr. 4). 1978. PLB 6.95 (ISBN 0-913940-85-2); pap. 2.95 (ISBN 0-89686-006-X). Crestwood Hse.

Toye, William, retold by. Mountain Goats of Temlaham. (Illus.). 32p. (ps-3). 1979. pap. 3.95 (ISBN 0-19-540320-7). Oxford U Pr.

Wade, Mary H. Indian Fairy Tales As Told to the Little Children of the Wigwam. LC 78-74523. (Children's Literature Reprint Ser.). (Illus.). (gr. 4-8). 1979. Repr. of 1906 ed. 21.75x (ISBN 0-8486-0225-0). Core Collection.

Watson, Jane W., ed. Rama of the Golden Age. LC 70-126415. (Illus.). (gr. 4-7). 1971. PLB 3.58 (ISBN 0-8116-4206-2). Garrard.

Young, Ed. The Terrible Nung Gwama: A Chinese Folktale. LC 78-18766. (Unicef Storycraft Bks.). (Illus.). (ps-3). 1978. 5.95 (ISBN 0-529-05444-2); PLB 5.99 (ISBN 0-529-05445-0). Philomel.

FOLK-LORE–THEMES, MOTIVES

see also Folk-Lore–Classification

Baev, Gevhard V., et al. World Cultures Arts, & Crafts: Kulturen, Handwerk, Kunst. 388p. (Eng., Fr., Ger.). 1979. 45.00 (ISBN 3-7643-0996-2). Birkhauser.

Baker, Ronald L. Folklore in the Writings of Rowland E. Robinson. 1973. 12.95 (ISBN 0-87972-038-7). Bowling Green Univ.

Baring-Gould, Sabine. Curious Myths of the Middle Ages. Hardy, Edward, ed. (Illus.). 1978. 8.95 (ISBN 0-19-520078-0). Oxford U Pr.

Davidson, H. R., ed. The Journey to the Other World. (Folklore Society Mistletoe Ser.). 149p. 1975. 13.50x (ISBN 0-87471-613-6). Rowman.

Gomme, George L. Folklore Relics of Early Village Life. Dorson, Richard, ed. (International Folklore Ser.). 1977. Repr. of 1883 ed. lib. bdg. 15.00x (ISBN 0-405-10096-5). Arno.

Granger, Byrd H. Motif Index for lost mines & treasures, applied to redaction of Arizona Legends, & to lost mines & treasure legends exterior to Arizona. LC 77-27331. 1978. text ed. 14.50x (ISBN 0-8165-0646-9). U of Ariz Pr.

Laing, Jeanie M. Notes on Superstition & Folk Lore. 106p. 1980. Repr. of 1885 ed. lib. bdg. 15.00 (ISBN 0-8492-1623-0). R West.

FOLK-LORE–THEORY, METHODS, ETC.

Bassett, Fletcher S. The Folk-Lore Manual. LC 76-49139. 1976. Repr. of 1892 ed. lib. bdg. 15.00 (ISBN 0-8414-1755-5). Folcroft.

Ben-Amos, Dan, ed. Folklore Genres. (American Folklore Society Bibliographical & Special Ser.: No. 26). (Illus.). 360p. 1981. pap. 9.95 (ISBN 0-292-72437-3). U of Tex Pr.

Brunvand, Jan H. Guide for Collectors of Folklore in Utah. LC 73-168609. (University of Utah Publications in the American West: Vol. 7). 1971. pap. 10.00 (ISBN 0-87480-084-6). U of Utah Pr.

Dorson, Richard M. American Folklore & the Historian. LC 75-14909. 1971. 8.50x (ISBN 0-226-15868-3). U of Chicago Pr.

Dundes, Alan. Analytic Essays in Folklore. (Studies in Folklore Ser.: No. 2). 1975. pap. text ed. 28.25x (ISBN 90-279-3231-X). Mouton.

--Interpreting Folklore. LC 79-2969. (Midland Bks.: No. 240). 320p. 1980. 25.00x (ISBN 0-253-14307-1); pap. 9.95x (ISBN 0-253-20240-X). Ind U Pr.

Goldstein, Kenneth S. A Guide for Field Workers in Folklore. LC 64-24801. xx, 199p. Repr. of 1964 ed. 15.00 (ISBN 0-8103-5000-9); pap. 9.00 (ISBN 0-8103-5041-6). Gale.

Hughes, Helen M. News & the Human Interest Story. LC 80-19176. (Social Science Classics Ser.). 313p. 1981. text ed. 19.95 (ISBN 0-87855-326-6); pap. text ed. 6.95 (ISBN 0-87855-729-6). Transaction Bks.

Kongas-Maranda, E. & Kongas-Maranda, P. Structural Models in Folklore & Transformational Essays. (Approaches to Semiotics Ser). (Illus.). 145p. 1971. text ed. 28.75x (ISBN 90-2791-705-1). Mouton.

Krohn, Kaarle & Krohn, Julius. Folklore Methodology. Welsch, Roger L., tr. from Ger. (American Folklore Society Bibliographical & Special Ser.: No. 21). Orig. Title: Die Folkloristische Arbeitsmethode. 210p. 1971. pap. text ed. 8.95x (ISBN 0-292-72432-2). U of Tex Pr.

Leach, MacEdward & Glassie, Henry. A Guide for Collectors of Oral Traditions & Folk Cultural Material in Pennsylvania. (Illus., Orig.). 1973. pap. 2.00 (ISBN 0-911124-60-8). Pa Hist & Mus.

Maranda, Pierre & Maranda, Elli K., eds. Structural Analysis of Oral Tradition. LC 71-122380. (Folklore & Folklife Ser). (Illus.). 1971. 20.00x (ISBN 0-8122-7615-9). U of Pa Pr.

FOLK-LORE, AFRICAN

Aardema, Verna. Half-a-Ball-of-Kenki. LC 78-16136. (Illus.). (ps-3). 1979. PLB 8.95 (ISBN 0-7232-6158-X). Warne.

Aardema, Verna, retold by. Who's in Rabbit's House? A Masai Tale. LC 77-71514. (Illus.). 32p. (ps-3). 1979. pap. 2.50 (ISBN 0-8037-9549-1, Pied Piper Book). Dial.

Anozie, S. O., ed. Structuralism & African Folklore. (Studies in African Semiotics Ser.). 1970. pap. 7.00 (ISBN 0-914970-05-4). Conch Mag.

Appel, Joseph H. Africa's White Magic. 1978. Repr. of 1928 ed. lib. bdg. 25.00 (ISBN 0-8492-0089-X). R West.

Arewa, Erastus O. A Classification of the Folktales of the Northern East African Cattle Area by Types. Dorson, Richard M., ed. LC 80-7234. (Folklore of the World Ser.). 1980. lib. bdg. 25.00x (ISBN 0-405-13302-2). Arno.

Awoonor, Kofi. Fire in the Valley: Ewe Folktales. LC 79-88805. 1979. 12.50x (ISBN 0-686-52495-0); pap. text ed. 4.50x (ISBN 0-686-52496-9). NOK Pubs.

Bascom, William, ed. African Dilemma Tales. (World Anthropology Ser.: Vol. 1). 172p. 1975. 12.50x (ISBN 0-202-90001-0). Beresford Bk Serv.

Baskerville, Rosetta G. The King of the Snakes & Other Folk-Lore Stories from Uganda. LC 78-67685. (The Folktale). Repr. of 1922 ed. 14.50 (ISBN 0-404-16054-9). AMS Pr.

Bassey, Linus A., ed. African Wise Sayings. 1980. pap. write for info. African Policy.

Beech, Mervyn W. Suk: Their Language & Folklore. LC 76-75540. (Illus.). Repr. of 1925 ed. 15.75x (ISBN 0-8371-0349-5, Pub. by Negro U Pr). Greenwood.

Bleek, Whilhelm H. & Lloyd, Lucy C. Specimens of Bushman Folklore. LC 78-67687. (The Folktale). (Illus.). Repr. of 1911 ed. 37.00 (ISBN 0-404-16056-5). AMS Pr.

Chatelain, Heli, ed. Folk Tales of Angola: Fifty Tales. LC 69-19354. (Illus., Ki-Mbundu & Eng). Repr. of 1894 ed. 17.50x (ISBN 0-8371-0895-0, Pub. by Negro U Pr). Greenwood.

Christensen, Abigail M. Afro-American Folk Lore. facs. ed. LC 71-157364. (Black Heritage Library Collection Ser). 1892. 8.25 (ISBN 0-8369-8802-7). Arno.

Courlander, Harold. Treasury of African Folklore. 640p. 1975. 14.95 (ISBN 0-517-51670-5). Crown.

Cronise, Florence M. & Ward, Henry W. Cunnie Rabbit, Mr. Spider & Other Beef: West African Folk Tales. LC 72-99363. 1969. Repr. of 1903 ed. lib. bdg. 13.75 (ISBN 0-8411-0034-9). Metro Bks.

Davis, Arthur & Parker, Ben. Brutes & Savages. LC 78-55557. (Illus.). 1978. pap. 1.00 (ISBN 0-912760-73-7). Valkyrie Pr.

Dayrell, Elphinstone. Folk Stories from Southern Nigeria, West Africa. LC 77-76488. Repr. of 1910 ed. 10.50x (ISBN 0-8371-1125-0, Pub. by Negro U Pr). Greenwood.

Doke, Clement M. Lamba Folklore. LC 28-18358. (American Folklore Society Memoirs). Repr. of 1927 ed. 40.00 (ISBN 0-527-01072-3). Kraus Repr.

Dorson, Richard M., ed. African Folklore. LC 77-186052. (Midland Bks: No. 220). 598p. 1979. 18.50x (ISBN 0-253-30250-1); pap. 9.95x (ISBN 0-253-20220-5). Ind U Pr.

Egejuru, Phanuel. Origin & Survival of African Folktales in the New World. 1981. 8.95 (ISBN 0-933184-23-9); pap. 4.95 (ISBN 0-933184-24-7). Flame Intl.

Elliot, Geraldine. The Singing Chameleon: A Book of African Stories Based on Local Custom, Proverbs & Folk-Lore. (Illus.). 1971. Repr. of 1957 ed. 11.95 (ISBN 0-7100-1326-4). Routledge & Kegan.

Ellis, Alfred B. Ewe-Speaking Peoples of the Slave Coast of West Africa. 1964. 16.50 (ISBN 0-910216-01-0). Benin.

--Yoruba-Speaking Peoples of the Slave Coast of West Africa. 1964. 16.50 (ISBN 0-910216-03-7). Benin.

Farrow, Stephen S. Faith, Fancies & Fetish or Yoruba Paganism. LC 76-98718. (Illus.). Repr. of 1926 ed. 12.25x (ISBN 0-8371-2759-9, Pub. by Negro U Pr). Greenwood.

Garcia-Cortez, Julio. Pataki: Leyendas Y Misterios De los Orishas Africanos. LC 79-54684. (Coleccion Ebano Y Canela Ser.). (Illus.). 250p. (Span.). 1980. pap. 14.95 (ISBN 0-89729-236-7). Ediciones.

Gbadamosi, Bakare & Beier, Ulli. Not Even God Is Ripe Enough. (African Writers Ser.). 1968. pap. text ed. 2.50x (ISBN 0-435-90048-X). Heinemann Ed.

Green, Lila. Tales from Africa. LC 78-54623. (The World Folktale Library). (Illus.). 1979. lib. bdg. 7.65 (ISBN 0-686-51162-X). Silver.

Helser, Albert D. Education of Primitive People. LC 75-97403. Repr. of 1934 ed. 14.50x (ISBN 0-8371-2651-7, Pub. by Negro U Pr). Greenwood.

Honeij, James A. South-African Folk Tales. LC 76-78577. Repr. of 1910 ed. 10.25x (ISBN 0-8371-1415-2). Greenwood.

Hurreiz, Sayyid H. Ja'Aliyyin Folktales: An in Interplay of African Arabian & Islamic Elements. LC 76-24190. (Africa Ser.: No. 8). 1977. pap. text ed. 20.00x (ISBN 0-87750-185-8). Res Ctr Lang Semiotic.

Jablow, Alta. Yes & No: The Intimate Folklore of Africa. LC 72-13867. 223p. 1973. Repr. of 1961 ed. lib. bdg. 16.00x (ISBN 0-8371-6757-4, JAYN). Greenwood.

Jacottet, E. The Treasury of Ba-Suto Lore, 2 vols. in 1. LC 78-67723. (The Folktale). Repr. of 1908 ed. 27.50 (ISBN 0-404-16098-0). AMS Pr.

Katongole, G. R. Folklore from the Nile. 1979. 5.95 (ISBN 0-533-03683-6). Vantage.

Keidel, Eudene. African Fables, Bk. 2. (Illus.). 112p. 1981. pap. 3.25 (ISBN 0-8361-1945-2). Herald Pr.

Kell, Gulla & Moody, Ronald, trs. Amadu's Bundle. (African Writers Ser.). 1972. pap. text ed. 3.00 (ISBN 0-435-90118-4). Heinemann Ed.

Lester, Julius. Black Folktales. LC 72-139259. (Illus.). (gr. 3-8). 1970. pap. 2.95 (ISBN 0-394-17178-0, B262, BC). Grove.

Lindfors, Bernth. Folklore in Nigerian Literature. LC 72-91804. 200p. 1974. text ed. 19.75x (ISBN 0-8419-0134-1, Africana). Holmes & Meier.

McNair, John F. & Barlow, Thomas L. Oral Tradition from the Indus. rev. ed. Dorson, Richard M., ed. LC 77-70609. (International Folklore Ser.). (Illus.). 1977. Repr. of 1908 ed. lib. bdg. 10.00x (ISBN 0-405-10108-2). Arno.

Menkin, Larry & Menkin, Chris. Grandpa & the Red Haired Black Giants & Other Far Out Folk Tales from Far Out Africa. (Illus.). 1975. 7.95 (ISBN 0-89002-051-5); pap. 2.95 (ISBN 0-89002-050-7). Northwoods Pr.

Morgan, Fred. Uwharrie Magic. LC 73-86779. 1974. 8.95 (ISBN 0-87716-050-3, Pub. by Moore Pub Co). F Apple.

Mutwa, Vusamazulu C. Indaba My Children. 1971. pap. text ed. 18.25x (ISBN 0-900707-07-0). Humanities.

Mvungi, Martha. Three Solid Stones. (African Writers Ser.). 1975. pap. 2.50x (ISBN 0-435-90159-1). Heinemann Ed.

Obiechina, E. N. Onitsha Market Literature. (African Writers Ser.). 1972. pap. text ed. 4.00x (ISBN 0-435-90109-5). Heinemann Ed.

Parsons, E. W. Folk-Lore from the Cape Verde Islands. LC 24-4017. (American Folklore Society Memoirs). Repr. of 1923 ed. 35.00 (ISBN 0-527-01067-7). Kraus Repr.

Paulitschke, Philipp V. Ethnographie Nordost-Afrikas, 2 Vols. Repr. of 1893 ed. Set. 46.00 (ISBN 0-384-45233-7). Johnson Repr.

Pitcher, Diana. Tokoloshi. (Illus.). (gr. 3 up). 1981. 9.95 (ISBN 0-89742-049-7). Celestial Arts.

--Tokoloshi: African Folk Tales Retold. LC 80-69843. (Illus.). 64p. (gr. 3 up). 1981. 9.95 (ISBN 0-89742-049-7, Dawne-Leigh). Celestial Arts.

Prather, Ray. The Ostrich Girl. LC 78-9710. (Illus.). (gr. 1-3). 1978. reinforced bdg 8.95 (ISBN 0-684-15889-2, ScribJ). Scribner.

Rattray, Robert S. Akan-Ashanti Folk-Tales. LC 78-63214. (The Folktale). (Illus.). Repr. of 1930 ed. 28.00 (ISBN 0-404-16155-3). AMS Pr.

Ross, Mabel & Walker, Barbara K. On Another Day... Tales Told Among the Nkundo of Zaire. (Illus.). 1978. 35.00 (ISBN 0-208-01699-6, Archon). Shoe String.

Scheub, Harold, ed. African Oral Narratives, Proverbs, Riddles, Poetry & Song: An Annotated Bibliography. (Reference Publications Ser.). 1977. lib. bdg. 40.00 (ISBN 0-8161-8034-2). G K Hall.

Smith, Bob. Old African Tales Told Again. (Illus.). (gr. 2-5). 1977. 5.95 (ISBN 0-915864-99-1). Academy Chi Ltd.

Theal, George M. Kaffir Folk-Lore. LC 70-107488. Repr. of 1886 ed. 12.75x (ISBN 0-8371-3790-X, Pub. by Negro U Pr). Greenwood.

--Yellow & Dark-Skinned People of Africa, South of the Zambesi. LC 77-82081. (Illus.). Repr. of 1910 ed. 21.25x (ISBN 0-8371-1557-4). Greenwood.

Todd, Loreto. Some Day Been Dey: West African Pidgin Folktale. (Orig.). 1979. pap. 18.50 (ISBN 0-7100-0024-3). Routledge & Kegan.

Torrend, J. Specimens of Bantu Folk-Lore from Northern Rhodesia. LC 72-78777. (Illus.). Repr. of 1921 ed. 10.75x (ISBN 0-8371-1398-9, Pub. by Negro U Pr). Greenwood.

--Specimens of Bantu Folk-Lore from Northern Rhodesia. LC 72-88947. 192p. 1973. Repr. of 1921 ed. 11.50 (ISBN 0-8046-1768-6). Kennikat.

--Specimens of Bantu Folklore from Northern Rhodesia. 1976. lib. bdg. 69.95 (ISBN 0-8490-2655-5). Gordon Pr.

Weeks, John H. Among the Primitive Bakongo. LC 76-79278. (Illus.). Repr. of 1914 ed. 18.75x (ISBN 0-8371-1453-5, Pub. by Negro U Pr). Greenwood.

Winther, Barbara. Plays from Folktales of Africa & Asia. 1976. 9.95 (ISBN 0-8238-0189-6). Plays.

FOLK-LORE, AFRO-AMERICAN

see Afro-American Folk-Lore

FOLK-LORE, ALGERIAN

Riviere, J. Recueil de contes populaires de la Kabylie du Djurdjura. LC 78-20113. (Collection de contes et de chansons populaires: Vol. 4). Repr. of 1882 ed. 21.50 (ISBN 0-404-60354-8). AMS Pr.

FOLK-LORE, AMERICAN

Abernethy, Francis E. Observations & Reflections on Texas Folklore. (Illus.). 151p. 1972. 7.95 (ISBN 0-88426-010-0). Encino Pr.

Abernethy, Francis E., ed. What's Going on? (Texas Folklore Society Publications: Vol. 40). (Illus.). 1976. 12.50 (ISBN 0-88426-049-6). Encino Pr.

Ainsworth, Catherine H. Folktales of America, Vol. II. LC 80-66300. viii, 209p. (Orig.). 1981. pap. 10.00 (ISBN 0-933190-09-3). Clyde Pr.

--Polish-American Folktales. LC 77-80771. (Folklore Bks.). x, 102p. 1980. 5.00 (ISBN 0-933190-04-2). Clyde Pr.

Anderson, Jean. The Haunting of America: Ghost Stories from Our Past. LC 73-5864. (Illus.). 176p. (gr. 5 up). 1973. 6.95 (ISBN 0-395-17518-6). HM.

Anderson, LaVere. Story of Johnny Appleseed. LC 73-17255. (American Folktales Ser.). (Illus.). (gr. 2-5). 1974. PLB 6.09 (ISBN 0-8116-4040-X). Garrard.

Bauman, Richard & Abrahams, Roger D., eds. And Other Neighborly Names: Social Process & Cultural Image in Texas Folklore. (Illus.). 332p. 1981. text ed. 25.00x (ISBN 0-292-70352-X). U of Tex Pr.

Beck, E. C. They Knew Paul Bunyan. Dorson, Richard M., ed. LC 80-789. (Folklore of the World Ser.). 1980. Repr. of 1956 ed. lib. bdg. 23.00x (ISBN 0-405-13328-6). Arno.

Ben-Amos, Dan, ed. Folklore Genres. (American Folklore Society Bibliographical & Special Ser.: No. 26). (Illus.). 360p. 1975. 14.95x (ISBN 0-292-72415-2). U of Tex Pr.

Bennett, John. The Doctor to the Dead. LC 70-135593. 260p. 1973. Repr. of 1946 ed. 14.75x (ISBN 0-8371-5184-8, Pub. by Negro U Pr). Greenwood.

Bluestein, Gene. The Voice of the Folk: Folklore & American Literary Theory. LC 70-164443. 192p. 1972. pap. 5.95x (ISBN 0-87023-098-0). U of Mass Pr.

Boatright, Mody. Mody Boatright, Folklorist: A Collection of Essays. Speck, Ernest B., ed. LC 73-6908. 2244p. 1973. 9.95x (ISBN 0-292-75007-2). U of Tex Pr.

Boatright, Mody C. Gib Morgan: Minstrel of the Oil Fields. LC 46-815. (Texas Folklore Society Publications: No. 20). (Illus.). 1965. Repr. of 1945 ed. 5.00 (ISBN 0-87074-008-3). SMU Press.

Boatright, Mody C. & Day, Donald, eds. Backwoods to Border. LC 48-18054. (Texas Folklore Society Publications: No. 18). (Illus.). 1967. Repr. of 1943 ed. 6.95 (ISBN 0-87074-011-3). SMU Press.

--From Hell to Breakfast. LC 45-1540. (Texas Folklore Society Publications: No. 19). (Illus.). 1967. Repr. of 1944 ed. 6.95 (ISBN 0-87074-012-1). SMU Press.

Boatright, Mody C., et al, eds. And Horns on the Toads. LC 59-15694. (Texas Folklore Society Publications: No. 29). 1959. 6.95 (ISBN 0-87074-013-X). SMU Press.

--Folk Travelers: Ballads, Tales, & Talk. LC 53-12578. (Texas Folklore Society Publications: No. 25). 1953. 7.95 (ISBN 0-87074-014-8). SMU Press.

--Golden Log. LC 61-17184. (Texas Folklore Society Publications: No. 31). 1962. 5.95 (ISBN 0-87074-015-6). SMU Press.

--Good Tale & a Bonnie Tune. LC 63-10979. (Texas Folklore Society Publications: No. 32). 1964. 6.95 (ISBN 0-87074-016-4). SMU Press.

--Mesquite & Willow. LC 56-12566. (Texas Folklore Society Publications: No. 27). 1957. 5.95 (ISBN 0-87074-018-0). SMU Press.

--Singers & Storytellers. LC 60-15894. (Texas Folklore Society Publications: No. 30). 1961. 7.95 (ISBN 0-87074-019-9). SMU Press.

--Texas Folk & Folklore. LC 54-11299. (Texas Folklore Society Publications: No. 26). (Illus.). 1954. 10.00 (ISBN 0-87074-020-2). SMU Press.

Boatwright, Mody C., et al, eds. Madstones & Twisters. LC 58-9269. (Texas Folklore Society Publication Ser.: No. 28). 180p. 1980. Repr. of 1958 ed. 5.95 (ISBN 0-87074-017-2). SMU Press.

Botkin, B. A. A Treasury of American Folklore. 640p. 1981. pap. 3.95 (ISBN 0-553-14149-X). Bantam.

--A Treasury of New England Folklore. 1947. 7.50 (ISBN 0-517-10918-2). Crown.

Botkin, B. A., ed. Treasury of Western Folklore. rev. ed. 640p. 1975. 9.95 (ISBN 0-517-51684-5). Crown.

Botkin, Benjamin A. Sidewalks of America: Folklore, Legends, Sagas, Traditions, Customs, Songs, Stories, & Sayings of City Folk. LC 76-44361. (Illus.). 1976. Repr. of 1954 ed. lib. bdg. 34.75x (ISBN 0-8371-9312-5, BOSA). Greenwood.

Botkin, Benjamin A., ed. Treasury of American Folklore. (Illus.). (YA) (gr. 10 up). 1944. 9.95 (ISBN 0-517-50766-8). Crown.

--Treasury of Southern Folklore. 1949. 10.00 (ISBN 0-517-50767-6). Crown.

Brandes, Stanley. Metaphors of Masculinity: Sex & Status in Andalusian Folklore. LC 79-5258. (American Folklore Society Ser.). 224p. 1980. 19.95x (ISBN 0-8122-7776-7); pap. 9.95 (ISBN 0-8122-1105-7). U of Pa Pr.

Bratcher, James T. Analytical Index to Publications of the Texas Folklore Society, Vols. 1-36. LC 72-97597. 344p. 1973. 12.50 (ISBN 0-87074-135-7). SMU Press.

Brett, Bill. The Stolen Steers: A Tale of the Big Thicket. LC 76-51651. (Illus.). 116p. 1977. 7.95 (ISBN 0-89096-026-7). Tex A&M Univ Pr.

Brewster, Paul G., ed. Children's Games & Rhymes. LC 75-35063. (Studies in Play & Games: Vol. 1). 1976. Repr. 12.00x (ISBN 0-405-07914-1). Arno.

Brown, Frank C. The Frank C. Brown Collection of North Carolina Folklore, 7 vols. Incl. Vol. 1. Games & Rhymes, Beliefs & Customs, Riddles, Proverbs, Speech, Tales & Legends (ISBN 0-8223-0027-3); Vol. 2. Folk Ballads from North Carolina (ISBN 0-8223-0254-3); Vol. 3. Folk Songs from North Carolina; Vol. 4. The Music of the Ballads; Vol. 5. The/Music of the Folk Songs; Vol. 6. Popular Beliefs & Superstitions from North Carolina, Pt. 1 (ISBN 0-8223-0283-7); Vol. 7. Popular Beliefs & Superstitions from North Carolina, Pt. 2 (ISBN 0-8223-0284-5). LC 58-10967. (Illus.). 1952-64. 19.75 ea.; 125.00 set (ISBN 0-685-22682-4, 58-10967). Duke.

Brown, Virginia P. & Owens, Laurella. Toting the Lead Row: Ruby Pickens Tartt, Alamaba Folklorist. 208p. 1981. 19.95 (ISBN 0-8173-0074-0). U of Ala Pr.

Browne, Ray, ed. A Night with the Hants & Other Alabama Experiences. LC 76-43449. 1976. 12.95 (ISBN 0-87972-075-1); pap. 6.95 (ISBN 0-87972-167-7). Bowling Green Univ.

Brunvand, Jan H. Guide for Collectors of Folklore in Utah. LC 73-168609. (University of Utah Publications in the American West: Vol. 7). 1971. pap. 10.00 (ISBN 0-87480-084-6). U of Utah Pr.

--Study of American Folklore: An Introduction. 2nd ed. 1978. 13.95x (ISBN 0-393-09048-5, NortonC). Norton.

--The Vanishing Hitchhiker: American Urban Legends & Their Meanings. 1981. 14.95 (ISBN 0-393-01473-8). Norton.

Byrne, Donald E. No Foot of Land: Folklore of American Methodist Itinerants. LC 75-1097. (ATLA Monograph: No. 6). (Illus.). 370p. 1975. 15.00 (ISBN 0-8108-0798-X). Scarecrow.

Campa, Arthur. Hispanic Folklore Studies of Arthur Campa: An Original Anthology. Cortes, Carlos E., ed. & intro. by. LC 76-1475. (Chicano Heritage Ser.). (Illus.). 1976. 35.00x (ISBN 0-405-09536-8). Arno.

Carey, George. A Faraway Time & Place: Lore of the Eastern Shore. Dorson, Richard M., ed. LC 77-70586. (International Folklore Ser.). (Illus.). 1977. Repr. of 1971 ed. lib. bdg. 16.00x (ISBN 0-405-10086-8). Arno.

Carey, George C. Maryland Folk Legends & Folk Songs. LC 75-180857. 1971. pap. 4.00 (ISBN 0-87033-158-2, Pub. by Tidewater). Cornell Maritime.

Carey, George G. Maryland Folklore & Folklife. LC 71-142189. (Illus.). 1971. pap. 5.00 (ISBN 0-87033-154-X, Pub. by Tidewater). Cornell Maritime.
Carpenter, Inta G. & Dorson, Richard M., eds. Folklore in the Calumet Region: Special Issue, Indiana Folklore, Vol. 10, No. 2. LC 80-7779. (Folklore of the World Ser.). (Illus.). 1980. Repr. of 1977 ed. lib. bdg. 14.00x (ISBN 0-405-13341-3). Arno.
Center for Southern Folklore. American Folklore Films & Videotapes: an Index. Ferris, Bill & Peiser, Judy, eds. LC 76-6247. (Illus.). 1976. pap. 15.00 (ISBN 0-89267-000-2). Ctr South Folklore.
Chase, Richard. American Folk Tales & Songs. 1971. pap. 3.50 (ISBN 0-486-22692-1). Dover.
--American Folk Tales & Songs. (Illus.). 6.75 (ISBN 0-8446-0057-1). Peter Smith.
--Jack Tales. (Illus.). (gr. 4-6). 1943. 8.95 (ISBN 0-395-06694-8). HM.
Christensen, Mrs. A. M. Afro-American Folklore: Told Round Cabin Fires on the Sea Islands of South Carolina. LC 73-78761. (Illus.). 1892. 10.00x (ISBN 0-8371-1387-3, Pub. by Negro U Pr). Greenwood.
Clarke, Kenneth & Clarke, Mary. The Harvest & the Reapers: Oral Traditions of Kentucky. LC 74-7872. (Kentucky Bicentennial Bookshelf Ser.). 112p. 1974. 6.95 (ISBN 0-8131-0201-4). U Pr of Ky.
Claudel, Calvin A. Fools & Rascals: Louisiana Folktales. 1978. pap. 2.00 (ISBN 0-918784-18-2). Legacy Pub Co.
Clyne, Patricia E. Ghostly Animals of America. LC 77-6487. (Illus.). (gr. 5 up). 1977. 5.95 (ISBN 0-396-07465-0). Dodd.
Cocke, Sarah J. Bypaths in Dixie: Folktales of the South. 1976. lib. bdg. 59.95 (ISBN 0-8490-1562-6). Gordon Pr.
Coffin, Tristram P. Uncertain Glory: Folklore & the American Revolution. LC 77-147812. 1971. 24.00 (ISBN 0-8103-5040-8). Gale.
Coffin, Tristram P. & Cohen, Hennig, eds. Folklore in America. LC 79-97699. 1970. pap. 2.50 (ISBN 0-385-05071-2, A15, Anch). Doubleday.
--The Parade of Heroes-Legendary Figures in American Lore. LC 77-80881. 1978. 12.50 (ISBN 0-385-09711-5, Anchor Pr). Doubleday.
Coffin, Tristram P. & Cohen, Henning, eds. Folklore: From the Working Folk of America. LC 79-97699. (Illus.). 504p. 1973. pap. 3.50 (ISBN 0-385-03881-X, Anch). Doubleday.
Crompton, Anne E. The Lifting Stone. LC 77-10607. (Illus.). (ps-3). 1978. PLB 7.95 (ISBN 0-8234-0325-4). Holiday.
Davidson, Levette J. Guide to American Folklore. LC 74-97313. Repr. of 1951 ed. lib. bdg. 15.00x (ISBN 0-8371-2552-9, DAAF). Greenwood.
Davis, Hubert J. Pon My Honor Hit's the Truth: Tales from the South Western Virginia Mountains. (Illus.). 1973. 4.95 (ISBN 0-930230-19-1). Johnson NC.
--The Silver Bullet & Other American Witch Stories. LC 75-11953. 240p. 1975. 9.95 (ISBN 0-8246-0199-8). Jonathan David.
Davis, Louise. Nashville Tales. (Frontier Tales of Tennessee Ser.: No. 3). 190p. 1981. 12.95 (ISBN 0-88289-303-3). Pelican.
Degh, Linda, ed. Indiana Folklore: A Reader. LC 79-2970. (Midland Bks.: No. 239). (Illus.). 320p. 1980. 20.00x (ISBN 0-253-10986-8); pap. 7.95x (ISBN 0-253-20239-6). Ind U Pr.
Dobie, J. Frank. Coronado's Children: Tales of Lost Mines & Buried Treasures of the Southwest. (Barker Texas History Center Ser.: No. 3). (Illus.). 351p. 1978. 11.95 (ISBN 0-292-71050-X). pap. 5.95 (ISBN 0-292-71052-6). U of Tex Pr.
--Tales of Old-Time Texas. 1955. 10.95 (ISBN 0-316-18801-8); pap. 4.95 (ISBN 0-316-18802-6). Little.
Dobie, J. Frank & Mead, Ben C. I'll Tell You a Tale. (Illus.). 378p. 1981. pap. 8.95 (ISBN 0-292-73821-8). U of Tex Pr.
Dobie, J. Frank, ed. Coffee in the Gourd. (Texas Folklore Society Publications: No. 2). 1969. Repr. of 1923 ed. 5.95 (ISBN 0-87074-039-3). SMU Press.
--Follow De Drinkin' Gou'd. LC 33-1132. (Texas Folklore Society Publications: No. 7). 1965. Repr. of 1928 ed. 5.95 (ISBN 0-87074-040-7). SMU Press.
--Happy Hunting Ground. (Texas Folklore Society Publications: No. 4). (Illus.). 1964. Repr. of 1925 ed. 5.95 (ISBN 0-87074-149-7). SMU Press.
--Man, Bird, & Beast. LC 33-1132. (Texas Folklore Society Publications: No. 8). (Illus.). 1965. Repr. of 1930 ed. 5.95 (ISBN 0-87074-131-4). SMU Press.
--Rainbow in the Morning. LC 74-32243. (Texas Folklore Society Publications: No. 5). 1975. Repr. of 1926 ed. 6.95 (ISBN 0-87074-150-0). SMU Press.
--Texas & Southwestern Lore. LC 33-1131. (Texas Folklore Society Publications: No. 6). 1967. Repr. of 1927 ed. 6.95 (ISBN 0-87074-044-X). SMU Press.
Dobie, J. Frank, et al, eds. Coyote Wisdom. LC 40-499. (Texas Folklore Society Publications: No. 14). (Illus.). 1965. Repr. of 1938 ed. 7.95 (ISBN 0-87074-046-6). SMU Press.
--Mustangs & Cow Horses. 2nd ed. LC 65-3030. (Texas Folklore Society Publications: No. 16). (Illus.). 1965. Repr. of 1940 ed. 10.00 (ISBN 0-87074-047-4). SMU Press.
--Texian Stomping Grounds. LC 41-4871. (Texas Folklore Society Publications: No. 17). 1967. Repr. of 1941 ed. 5.95 (ISBN 0-87074-048-2). SMU Press.
--In the Shadow of History. (Texas Folklore Society Publication Ser.: No. 25). 192p. 1980. Repr. of 1939 ed. 6.95 (ISBN 0-87074-173-X). SMU Press.
Dorson, Richard, ed. America Begins: Early American Writings. LC 72-5802. (Folklore of the World Ser.). (Illus.). 1980. Repr. of 1950 ed. lib. bdg. 39.00x (ISBN 0-8369-2986-1). Arno.
Dorson, Richard M. America in Legend: Folklore from the Colonial Period to the Present. LC 73-7018. (Illus.). 1973. 17.95 (ISBN 0-394-46140-1); pap. 9.95 (ISBN 0-394-70926-8). Pantheon.
--American Folklore. LC 59-12283. (Chicago History of American Civilization Ser.). 4.50 (ISBN 0-226-15859-4, CHAC 4). U of Chicago Pr.
--American Folklore & the Historian. pap. write for info. (ISBN 0-226-15869-1). U of Chicago Pr.
--American Folklore & the Historian. LC 75-14909. 1971. 8.50x (ISBN 0-226-15868-3). U of Chicago Pr.
--Buying the Wind: Regional Folklore in the United States. LC 63-13010. 1964. 15.00x (ISBN 0-226-15861-6). U of Chicago Pr.
--Buying the Wind: Regional Folklore in the United States. LC 63-13010. 573p. 1972. pap. 6.95 (ISBN 0-226-15862-4, P471, Phoen). U of Chicago Pr.
--Land of the Millrats. LC 81-2944. (Illus.). 336p. 1981. text ed. 22.50 (ISBN 0-674-50855-6). Harvard U Pr.
Dorson, Richard M., ed. Davy Crockett: American Comic Legend. LC 77-70590. (International Folklore Ser.). (Illus.). 1977. Repr. of 1939 ed. lib. bdg. 12.00x (ISBN 0-405-10091-4). Arno.
Drake, Samuel A. Book of New England Legends & Folk Lore. LC 69-19881. 1969. Repr. of 1901 ed. 24.00 (ISBN 0-8103-3829-7). Gale.
Dundes, Alan. Analytic Essays in Folklore. (Studies in Folklore Ser.: No. 2). 1975. pap. text ed. 28.25x (ISBN 90-279-3231-X). Mouton.
--Interpreting Folklore. LC 79-2969. (Midland Bks.: No. 240). 320p. 1980. 25.00x (ISBN 0-253-14307-1); pap. 9.95x (ISBN 0-253-20240-X). Ind U Pr.
Dundes, Alan & Pagter, Carl R. Work Hard & You Shall Be Rewarded: Urban Folklore from the Paperwork Empire. LC 77-74429. (Midland Bks: No. 207). (Illus.). 248p. 1978. pap. 3.95 (ISBN 0-253-20207-8). Ind U Pr.
Emrich, Duncan. Folklore on the American Land. LC 72-161865. (Illus.). 1972. 17.50 (ISBN 0-316-23720-5). Little.
Evans, David. Gravel Springs Fife & Drum: An Essay. 1981. cancelled (ISBN 0-89267-006-1). Ctr South Folklore.
Fannin, Angela F. Johnnies, Biffies, Outhouses, Etc. (Illus.). 104p. 1980. write for info. (ISBN 0-89015-259-4). Eakin Pubns.
Ferris, William R., Jr. Mississippi Black Folklore: A Research Bibliography & Discography. LC 70-158331. 61p. 1971. pap. 2.50x (ISBN 0-87805-001-9). U Pr of Miss.
Flanagan, Cathleen C. & Flanagan, John T. American Folklore: A Bibliography, 1950-1974. LC 77-23381. 1977. 19.50 (ISBN 0-8108-1073-5). Scarecrow.
Flanagan, John T., ed. Folklore in American Literature. LC 74-138230. (Illus.). 511p. 1972. Repr. of 1958 ed. lib. bdg. 33.00x (ISBN 0-8371-5587-8, FLFH). Greenwood.
Fleischman, Sid. Jim Bridger's Alarm Clock & Other Tall Tales. (Illus.). (gr. 2-6). 1978. 8.50 (ISBN 0-525-32795-9). Dutton.
Gainer, Patrick W. Witches, Ghosts & Signs, Folklore of the Southern Appalachians. LC 75-29893. 192p. 1975. 7.95 (ISBN 0-89092-006-0). Seneca Bks.
Galdone, Joanna. The Tailypo. LC 77-23289. (ps-4). 1977. 8.95 (ISBN 0-395-28809-6, Clarion). HM.
Gard, Robert E. & Sorden, L. G. Wisconsin Lore. LC 62-12168. 1971. 8.95 (ISBN 0-88361-088-4). Stanton & Lee.
Gardner, E. E. Folklore from the Schoharie Hills, New York. Dorson, Richard M., ed. LC 77-70592. (International Folklore Ser.). 1977. Repr. of 1937 ed. lib. bdg. 21.00x (ISBN 0-405-10094-9). Arno.
Georges, Robert A. Greek-American Folk Beliefs & Narratives: Survivals & Living Tradition. Dorson, Richard M., ed. LC 80-727. (Folklore of the World Ser.). 1980. lib. bdg. 19.00x (ISBN 0-405-13314-6). Arno.
Gilard, Hazel. A Giant Walked Among Them. LC 77-81432. (Half Tall Tales of Paul Bunyan). (Illus.). 1977. 8.00 (ISBN 0-685-89213-1). M Jones.
Gizelis, Gregory. Narrative Rhetorical Devices of Persuasion in the Greek Community of Philadelphia. Dorson, Richard M., ed. LC 80-728. (Folklore of the World Ser.). 1980. lib. bdg. 25.00x (ISBN 0-405-13315-4). Arno.
Glassie, Henry. Pattern in the Material Folk Culture of the Eastern United States. rev. ed. LC 75-160630. (Folklore & Folklife Ser). (Illus.). 1971. 12.50x (ISBN 0-8122-7569-1); pap. 5.95x (ISBN 0-8122-1013-1, Pa Paperbks). U of Pa Pr.
Gravel Springs Fife & Drum: Film Transcript. (Illus.). 1981. cancelled (ISBN 0-89267-007-X). Ctr South Folklore.
Greenway, John. Tales from the United States. LC 78-54626. (The World Folktale Library). (Illus.). 1979. lib. bdg. 7.65 (ISBN 0-686-51166-2). Silver.
Hall, Joseph S. Smoky Mountain Folks & Their Lore. (Illus.). 1964. pap. 1.75 (ISBN 0-9600168-0-5). Hollywood.
Hand, Wayland D., ed. American Folk Legend: A Symposium. (Library Reprint Ser.: No. 98). 1979. Repr. of 1971 ed. 21.50x (ISBN 0-520-03836-3). U of Cal Pr.
Hendricks, George D. Roosters, Rhymes, & Railroad Tracks. LC 80-26473. 200p. 1980. pap. 6.95 (ISBN 0-87074-177-2). SMU Press.
Hines, Donald M. Frontier Folksay. LC 77-16486. 1977. Repr. of 1976 ed. lib. bdg. 25.00 (ISBN 0-8414-4958-9). Folcroft.
Hudson, Wilson M. Hunters & Healers: Folklore Types & Topics. (Texas Folklore Society Ser, Vol. 35). 1971. 7.95 (ISBN 0-88426-021-6). Encino Pr.
Hudson, Wilson M., ed. & intro. by. Diamond Bessie & the Shepherds. (Annual Pubns. Ser., No. 36). (Illus.). 170p. 1972. 7.95 (ISBN 0-88426-011-9). Encino Pr.
Hudson, Wilson M. & Maxwell, Allen, eds. The Sunny Slopes of Long Ago. LC 65-24930. (Texas Folklore Society Publications: No. 33). (Illus.). 1966. 6.95 (ISBN 0-87074-082-2). SMU Press.
Jackson, Bruce. Get Your Ass in the Water & Swim Like Me: Narrative Poetry from Black Oral Tradition. LC 74-81626. 1974. 13.50x (ISBN 0-674-35420-6); pap. 6.95x (ISBN 0-674-35421-4). Harvard U Pr.
Johnson, F. Roy. Legends & Myths of North Carolina's Roanoke Chowan. (Illus.). 1966. 4.95 (ISBN 0-930230-13-2). Johnson NC.
--Supernaturals Among Carolina Folk & Their Neighbors. (Illus.). 256p. (gr. 8-12). 1974. 8.50 (ISBN 0-930230-25-6). Johnson NC.
--Tales from Old Carolina. LC 65-8878. (Illus.). 1980. Repr. of 1965 ed. 7.50 (ISBN 0-930230-38-8). Johnson NC.
Johnson, Jerry M. Country Scrapbook. 1978. 16.95 (ISBN 0-671-22848-X); pap. 5.95 (ISBN 0-671-22895-1). S&S.
Kalin, Berkeley & Robinson, Clayton, eds. Myths & Realities: Conflicting Values in America. (Mississippi Valley Collection Bulletin, No. 5). 78p. 1972. pap. 5.95x (ISBN 0-87870-081-1). Memphis St Univ.
Killion, Ronald G. & Waller, Charles T. A Treasury of Georgia Folklore. LC 72-88901. 267p. 1972. bds. 12.00 (ISBN 0-87797-022-X). Cherokee.
Klein, Barbro S. Legends & Folk Beliefs in a Swedish American Community: A Study in Folklore & Acculturation, 2 vols. Dorson, Richard M., ed. LC 80-730. (Folklore of the World Ser.). 1980. lib. bdg. 68.00x (ISBN 0-405-13343-X). Arno.
Knapp, Mary & Knapp, Herbert. One Potato, Two Potato: The Folklore of American Children. 1978. pap. text ed. 4.95x (ISBN 0-393-09039-6). Norton.
Koch, William E. Folklore from Kansas: Customs, Beliefs, & Superstitions. LC 79-20197. (Illus.). 1980. 20.00 (ISBN 0-7006-0192-9). Regents Pr KS.
Kongas-Maranda, Elli Kaija. Finnish-American Folklore: Quantitative & Qualitative Analysis. Dorson, Richard M., ed. LC 80-732. (Folklore of the World Ser.). 1980. lib. bdg. 45.00x (ISBN 0-405-13319-7). Arno.
Leach, MacEdward & Glassie, Henry. A Guide for Collectors of Oral Traditions & Folk Cultural Material in Pennsylvania. (Illus., Orig.). 1973. pap. 2.00 (ISBN 0-911124-60-8). Pa Hist & Mus.
Lee, H. B. Lost Tales of Appalachia. 1977. 8.00 (ISBN 0-87012-193-6). McClain.
Lisker, Tom. Tall Tales: American Myths. LC 77-11104. (Myth, Magic & Superstition Ser.). (Illus.). (gr. 4-5). 1977. PLB 10.65 (ISBN 0-8172-1039-3). Raintree Pubs.
Lomax, Alan & Crowell, Sidney R. American Folksong & Folklore: A Regional Bibliography. LC 70-181204. 59p. 1942. Repr. 19.00 (ISBN 0-403-03504-X). Scholarly.
Lucero-White, et al. Hispano Culture of New Mexico: An Original Anthology. Cortes, Carlos E., ed. & intro. by. LC 76-5929. (Chicano Heritage Ser.). (Illus.). 1976. 15.00x (ISBN 0-405-09537-6). Arno.
Maclean, Angus. Cuentos: Based on the Folk Tales of the Spanish Californians. (Illus.). 1979. 9.95 (ISBN 0-914330-27-6); pap. 5.95 (ISBN 0-914330-26-8). Pioneer Pub Co.
Massey, Ellen Gray, ed. Bittersweet Country. LC 77-12869. 1978. 12.95 (ISBN 0-385-12960-2, Anchor Pr); pap. 6.95 (ISBN 0-385-12961-0). Doubleday.
Menez, Herminia Q. Folklore Communication Among Filipinos in California. Dorson, Richard M., ed. LC 80-733. (Folklore of the World Ser.). 1980. lib. bdg. 21.00x (ISBN 0-405-13320-0). Arno.
Montell, William L. Ghosts Along the Cumberland: Deathlore in the Kentucky Foothills. LC 74-32241. (Illus.). 283p. 1975. 13.50x (ISBN 0-87049-165-2). U of Tenn Pr.
Mullen, Patrick B. I Heard the Old Fishermen Say: Folklore of the Texas Gulf Coast. LC 78-33. (Illus.). 213p. 1978. 15.00x (ISBN 0-292-73813-7). U of Tex Pr.
Neely, Charles. Tales & Songs of Southern Illinois. 1978. Repr. of 1938 ed. 30.00 (ISBN 0-8492-1946-9). R West.
Parsons, Elsie W., ed. Folk-Lore of the Sea Islands, South Carolina. LC 23-12312. Repr. of 1923 ed. 14.00 (ISBN 0-527-01068-5). Kraus Repr.
Pennsylvania Dutch Folklore. (Pennsylvania Dutch Books Ser.). (Illus.). 1960. 1.50 (ISBN 0-911410-02-3). Applied Arts.
Perdue, Charles L., Jr., et al. An Annotated Listings of Folklore. 1979. lib. bdg. 30.00 (ISBN 0-8482-5550-X). Norwood Edns.
Poulakis, Peter, ed. American Folklore. (American Character Ser). (Also for slow HS students). (gr. 9-12). 1969. pap. text ed. 5.50 (ISBN 0-684-51545-8, SSP16, ScribC). Scribner.
Pound, Louise. Nebraska Folklore. LC 75-36101. 243p. 1976. Repr. of 1960 ed. lib. bdg. 16.00x (ISBN 0-8371-8616-1, PONF). Greenwood.
Preble, Jack. Land of Canaan. 1965. 8.00 (ISBN 0-87012-012-3). McClain.
Puckett, Newbell N. & Hand, Wayland, eds. Popular Beliefs & Superstitions: Urban & Tehnic Folklore from Ohio. (Scholarly Reference Publications Ser.). 1981. lib. bdg. price not set (ISBN 0-8161-8585-9). G K Hall.
Randolph, Vance. Ozark Magic & Folklore. Orig. Title: Ozark Superstition. 1947. pap. 4.50 (ISBN 0-486-21181-9). Dover.
--Ozark Magic & Folklore. Orig. Title: Ozark Superstitions. 7.50 (ISBN 0-8446-0866-1). Peter Smith.
Roberts, Leonard. I Bought Me a Dog. (Illus.). 1976. pap. 1.25 (ISBN 0-686-70692-7). Pikeville Coll.
Sauvageau, Juan. Stories That Must Not Die, Vol. 2. (Illus., Eng. & Span.). 1976. pap. 3.00 (ISBN 0-916378-01-2). PSI Res.
--Stories That Must Not Die, Vol. 3. (Illus.). 1976. pap. 3.00 (ISBN 0-916378-02-0). PSI Res.
--Stories That Must Not Die, Vol. 4. (Illus.). (gr. k-12). 1978. pap. text ed. 3.00 (ISBN 0-916378-11-X). PSI Res.
Schwartz, Henry. Kit Carson's Long Walk & Other True Tales of Old San Diego. LC 80-68570. 112p. (Orig.). 1980. pap. 3.95 (ISBN 0-933362-03-X). Assoc Creative Writers.
Scott, Beth & Norman, Michael. Haunted Wisconsin. LC 80-22151. (Illus.). 256p. (Orig.). 1980. pap. 9.95 (ISBN 0-88361-082-5). Stanton & Lee.
Skinner, Charles M. American Myths & Legends, 2 vols. LC 78-175743. (Illus.). 697p. 1975. Repr. of 1903 ed. Set. 47.00 (ISBN 0-8103-4036-4). Gale.
Stern, Stephen. The Sephardic Jewish Community of los Angeles: A Study in Folklore & Ethnic Identity. Dorson, Richard M., ed. LC 80-734. (Folklore of the World Ser.). 1980. lib. bdg. 35.00x (ISBN 0-405-13324-3). Arno.
Stout, Earl J., ed. Folklore from Iowa. LC 37-19297. (American Folklore Society Memoirs). Repr. of 1936 ed. 23.00 (ISBN 0-527-01081-2). Kraus Repr.
Thigpen, Kenneth A. Folklore & the Ethnicity Factor in the Lives of Romanian-Americans, 2 vols. in one. Dorson, Richard M., ed. (Folklore of the World Ser.). 1980. lib. bdg. 50.00x (ISBN 0-405-13326-X). Arno.
Thompson, H. W. New York State Folktales, Legends & Ballads. Orig. Title: Body,Boots &Britches. (Illus.). 7.00 (ISBN 0-8446-3066-7). Peter Smith.
Thompson, Harold. Body, Boots, & Britches. 2nd ed. 1979. 18.00x (ISBN 0-8156-2218-X); pap. 9.95 (ISBN 0-8156-0160-3). Syracuse U Pr.

Thompson, Stith, ed. Round the Levee. (Texas Folklore Society Publications: No. 1). 1975. Repr. of 1916 ed. 4.95 (ISBN 0-87074-115-2). SMU Press.
Thorne, Ian. Monster Tales of Native Americans. Schroeder, Howard, ed. LC 78-5234. (Search for the Unknown Ser.). (Illus.). (gr. 4). 1978. PLB 6.95 (ISBN 0-913940-85-2); pap. 2.95 (ISBN 0-89686-006-X). Crestwood Hse.
Tully, Marjorie F. & Rael, Juan B. An Annotated Bibliography of Spanish Folklore in New Mexico & Southern Colorado. Dorson, Richard M., ed. LC 77-70628. (International Folkore Ser.). 1977. Repr. of 1950 ed. lib. bdg. 12.00x (ISBN 0-405-10132-5). Arno.
Van Wagenen, Jared, Jr. Golden Age of Homespun. (Illus.). 7.50 (ISBN 0-8446-3107-8). Peter Smith.
Welsch, Roger. Shingling the Fog & Other Plains Lies. LC 79-18730. viii, 160p. 1980. 12.50x (ISBN 0-8032-4709-5); pap. 3.95 (ISBN 0-8032-9700-9, BB 726, Bison). U of Nebr Pr.
Welsch, Roger L., compiled by. Treasury of Nebraska Pioneer Folklore. LC 66-10876. (Illus.). 1966. 19.50 (ISBN 0-8032-0192-3). U of Nebr Pr.
West, John F. Time Was. 1977. Repr. of 1965 ed. writefor info (ISBN 0-686-11108-7). Folkways Pr.
West, Victor R. Folklore in the Works of Mark Twain. LC 74-31097. 1930. lib. bdg. 12.50 (ISBN 0-685-10017-0). Folcroft.
Whedbee, Charles H. Legends of the Outer Banks & Tar Heel Tidewater. LC 66-23049. (Illus.). (gr. 5 up). 1979. 7.95 (ISBN 0-910244-41-3). Blair.
--Outer Banks Mysteries & Seaside Stories. LC 78-58535. 1980. 7.95 (ISBN 0-89587-006-1). Blair.
Whitney, Annie W. & Bullock, Caroline C., eds. Folk-Lore from Maryland. LC 28-9912. Repr. of 1925 ed. 14.00 (ISBN 0-527-01070-7). Kraus Repr.
Wofford, Vera D. Hale County, Facts & Folklore. 18.00 (ISBN 0-686-68989-5). Pioneer Bk Tx.
Writer's Program. South Carolina Folk Tales. LC 76-28225. 1976. Repr. of 1941 ed. lib. bdg. 15.00 (ISBN 0-8414-7821-X). Folcroft.
Wyman, Walker B. Wisconsin Folklore. 96p. Date not set. pap. 4.95 (ISBN 0-686-27304-4). U Pr Wisc River Falls.
Yoder, Don, ed. American Folklife. (Illus.). 312p. 1976. 20.00x (ISBN 0-292-70308-2). U of Tex Pr.

FOLK-LORE, ANDAMAN ISLANDS

Radcliffe-Brown, Alfred R. Andaman Islanders. 1964. pap. text ed. 5.95 (ISBN 0-02-925580-5). Free Pr.

FOLK-LORE, ANTILLES

Parsons, Elsie W., ed. Folk-Lore of the Antilles, French & English, 3 Vols. LC 34-20249. (Fr. & Eng.). Repr. of 1943 ed. Set. 86.00 (ISBN 0-527-01078-2). Kraus Repr.

FOLK-LORE, ARYAN

Halliday, William. Indo-European Folk-Tales & Greek Legend. LC 74-8748. 1933. 17.50 (ISBN 0-8414-4821-3). Folcroft.

FOLK-LORE, ASIAN

Anderson, Walter. Kleinere Arbeiten zur Volkskunde, No. 52. (Asian Folklore & Social Life Monograph). 170p. (Eng. & Ger.). 1973. 4.60 (ISBN 0-89986-049-4). E Langstaff.
Asian Cultural Center. Folktales from Asia for Children Everywhere, Bk. 1. LC 74-82605. (Illus.). 56p. (gr. 1-4). 1975. 6.50 (ISBN 0-8348-1032-8). Weatherhill.
Asian Cultural Center for UNESCO. Folk Tales from Asia for Children Everywhere, Bk. 6. LC 74-82605. (Illus.). 1978. 6.50 (ISBN 0-8348-1037-9). Weatherhill.
Asian Cultural Center for UNESCO, ed. Folk Tales from Asia for Children Everywhere, Bk. 4. LC 74-82605. (gr. 2-5). 1976. 6.50 (ISBN 0-8348-1035-2). Weatherhill.
Birnbaum, Phyllis. Eastern Tradition. LC 79-3783. 320p. 1980. 10.95 (ISBN 0-87223-605-6, Dist. by Har-Row). Seaview Bks.
Bodding, Paul O. Santal Folk Tales, 3 vols. LC 78-67688. (The Folktale). Repr. of 1923 ed. Set. 95.00 (ISBN 0-404-16060-3). AMS Pr.
Busk, Rachel H. Sagas from the Far East. LC 78-67693. (The Folktale). Repr. of 1873 ed. 33.00 (ISBN 0-404-16064-6). AMS Pr.
Coburn, Jewell R. Encircled Kingdom: Legends & Folktales of Laos. LC 79-53838. (Illus.). 100p. 1979. 8.95 (ISBN 0-918060-03-6). Burn-Hart.
Danandjaja, James. An Annotated Bibliography of Javanese Folklore. (Occasional Papers Ser.: No. 9). 1972. 10.00 (ISBN 0-686-23624-6, Ctr South & Southeast Asia Studies). Cellar.
Evans, Ivor H. Studies in Religion, Folklore & Custom in British North Borneo & the Malay Peninsula. (Illus.). 299p. 1970. Repr. of 1923 ed. 35.00x (ISBN 0-7146-2007-6, F Cass Co). Biblio Dist.
Kirtley, Bacil F. A Motif-Index of Polynesian, Melanesian & Micronesian Narratives. Dorson, Richard M., ed. LC 80-729. (Folklore of World Ser.). 1980. lib. bdg. 56.00x (ISBN 0-405-13316-2). Arno.
Lindell, Kristina, et al. Folktales from Kammu Two: A Story-Teller's Tales. (Scandanavian Institute of Asian Studies Monograph: No. 40). (Orig.). 1980. pap. text ed. 10.50x (ISBN 0-7007-0131-1). Humanities.
Nah-Trang Cong-Huyen-Ton-Nu. Vietnamese Folklore: An Introductory & Annotated Bibliography. (Occasional Papers Ser.: No. 7). 1970. 8.75 (ISBN 0-686-23626-2, Ctr South & Southeast Asia Studies). Cellar.
Polevol, S. A. Mongolian Folktales. (National Peking University & Chinese Assn. for Folklore, Folklore & Folkliterature Ser.: No. 97). (Chinese.). 7.00 (ISBN 0-89986-177-6). E Langstaff.
Rafy, K. U. Folk-Tales of the Khasis. LC 77-87050. Repr. of 1920 ed. 16.50 (ISBN 0-404-16851-5). AMS Pr.
Treudley, Mary B. This Stinging Exultation, No. 42. (Asian Folklore & Social Life Monograph). 310p. 1972. 5.90 (ISBN 0-89986-041-9). E Langstaff.
Van Duong, Quyen & Coburn, Jewell R. Beyond the EAST Wind: Legends & Folktales of Vietnam. LC 76-50345. (Illus.). 100p. 1976. 8.95 (ISBN 0-918060-01-X). Burn-Hart.
Wang Chuan. Folktales of Southeastern Asia. (National Peking University & Chinese Assn. for Folklore, Folklore & Folkliterature Ser.: No. 10). (Chinese.). 6.00 (ISBN 0-89986-110-5). E Langstaff.
Winther, Barbara. Plays from Folktales of Africa & Asia. 1976. 9.95 (ISBN 0-8238-0189-6). Plays.
Yung, Lin. A Survey in Zeelandia of Formosa. (Asian Folklore & Social Life Monographs: Vol. 96). 1977. 6.00 (ISBN 0-89986-328-0). E Langstaff.

FOLK-LORE, AUSTRALIAN

Dean, Beth. Folkloric in Australia. (Illus.). 90p. 1981. text ed. 9.95 (ISBN 0-85807-017-0, 3010, Pub. by Pacific Pubns Australia). Bks Australia.
Gordon, Tulo. Milbi: Aboriginal Tales from Queensland's Endeavor River. LC 79-53376. (Illus.). 59p. (Orig.). (gr. 1-4). 1980. text ed. 8.95 (ISBN 0-7081-1299-4, 0548). Bks Australia.
Harney, William E. & Thompson, Patricia. Yarns from an Aussie Bushcook. LC 79-55363. (Illus.). 112p. (Orig.). 1980. pap. 5.00 (ISBN 0-934680-00-0). Cobbers.
Heath, Jeffrey. Nunggubuyu Myths & Ethnographic Texts. (AIAS New Ser.: No. 23). 556p. 1981. pap. text ed. 18.25x (ISBN 0-391-02219-9, Pub. by Australian Inst Australia). Humanities.
Howitt, Alfred W. The Native Tribes of South-East Australia. LC 78-67718. (The Folktale). Repr. of 1904 ed. 65.00 (ISBN 0-404-16095-6). AMS Pr.
Parker, K. Langloh. Australian Legendary Tales. (Illus.). 192p. (gr. 4-7). 1980. 14.95 (ISBN 0-370-10841-8, Pub. by Chatto Bodley Jonathan). Merrimack Bk Serv.
Reed, A. W. Aboriginal Fables. (Illus.). 144p. 1979. pap. 5.95 (ISBN 0-589-07000-2, Pub. by Reed Books Australia). C E Tuttle.
Smith, Patsy A., ed. Folklore of the Australian Railwaymen. 1969. 10.00x (ISBN 0-8426-1546-6). Verry.

FOLK-LORE, BAHAMAS

Curry, Robert. Bahamian Lore. 1976. lib. bdg. 69.95 (ISBN 0-8490-1378-X). Gordon Pr.
Edwards, Charles L. Bahama Songs & Stories. 1976. lib. bdg. 59.95 (ISBN 0-8490-1471-9). Gordon Pr.
--Bahama Songs & Stories: A Contribution to Folklore. LC 9-46. (American Folkore Society Memoirs). Repr. of 1895 ed. 18.00 (ISBN 0-527-01055-3). Kraus Repr.
Parsons, Elsie W. Folk Tales of Andros Island, Bahamas. LC 19-4413. (American Folklore Society Memoirs). Repr. of 1918 ed. 23.00 (ISBN 0-527-01065-0). Kraus Repr.

FOLK-LORE, BASQUE

Monteiro, Mariana. Legends & Popular Tales of the Basque People. 1976. lib. bdg. 59.95 (ISBN 0-8490-2143-X). Gordon Pr.

FOLK-LORE, BENGALI

Bang, Betsy. The Old Woman & the Rice Thief. LC 76-30671. (Illus.). (gr. k-3). 1978. 7.95 (ISBN 0-688-80098-X); PLB 7.63 (ISBN 0-688-84098-1). Greenwillow.
Bhattacharyya, Asutosh. The Sun & the Serpent: Lore of Bengal. 1977. 11.50x (ISBN 0-8364-0087-9). South Asia Bks.
Bodding, Paul O. Santal Folk Tales, 3 vols. LC 78-67688. (The Folktale). Repr. of 1923 ed. Set. 95.00 (ISBN 0-404-16060-3). AMS Pr.
Campbell, A. Santal Folk Tales. LC 78-67700. (The Folktale). Repr. of 1891 ed. 17.00 (ISBN 0-404-16066-2). AMS Pr.
McCulloch, W. Bengali Household Tales. LC 78-63211. (The Folktale). Repr. of 1912 ed. 28.00 (ISBN 0-404-16146-4). AMS Pr.

FOLK-LORE, BRAZILIAN

Cole, Fay C. Traditions of the Tinguian. LC 78-67698. (The Folktale). Repr. of 1915 ed. 22.50 (ISBN 0-404-16069-7). AMS Pr.

FOLK-LORE, BRITISH

Allies, Jabez. On the Ancient British, Roman & Saxon Antiquities & Folk-Lore of Worcestershire. 2nd ed. Dorson, Richard M., ed. LC 77-70577. (International Folklore Ser.). (Illus.). 1977. Repr. of 1852 ed. lib. bdg. 29.00x (ISBN 0-405-10078-7). Arno.
Briggs, Katharine M. Personnel of Fairyland: A Short Account of the Fairy People of Great Britain for Those Who Tell Stories to Children. LC 70-147084. (Illus.). 1971. Repr. of 1953 ed. 19.00 (ISBN 0-8103-3372-4). Gale.
Briggs, Katherine M. The Anatomy of Puck: An Examination of Fairy Beliefs Among Shakespeare's Contemporaries & Successors. Dorson, Richard M., ed. LC 77-70581. (International Folklore Ser.). 1977. Repr. of 1959 ed. lib. bdg. 18.00x (ISBN 0-405-10082-5). Arno.
--British Folktales. (Fairy Tale & Folklore Library). 1980. pap. 5.95 (ISBN 0-394-73993-0). Pantheon.
--The Folklore of the Cotswolds. 1974. 19.95 (ISBN 0-7134-2831-7, Pub. by Batsford England). David & Charles.
Cannan, May W. Grey Ghosts & Voices. 1980. 12.00x (ISBN 0-900093-50-1, Pub. by Roundwood). State Mutual Bk.
Cooper, Derek. Skye. (Illus.). 1970. 22.50 (ISBN 0-7100-6820-4). Routledge & Kegan.
Courtney, Margaret A. Cornish Feasts & Folk-Lore. LC 77-8082. 1977. lib. bdg. 25.00 (ISBN 0-8414-1829-2). Folcroft.
--Cornish Feasts & Folklore. 208p. 1973. Repr. of 1890 ed. 11.50x (ISBN 0-87471-020-0). Rowman.
De Charmoy, Cozette. The True Life of Sweeney Todd. 96p. 1973. 20.00x (ISBN 0-85247-105-X, Pub. by Baberbocchus). State Mutual Bk.
Dickins, Bruce & Ross, Alan S., eds. The Dream of the Rood. (Old English Ser.). 1966. pap. text ed. 1.95x (ISBN 0-89197-567-5). Irvington.
Folklore, Myths & Legends of Britain. (Automobile Association of England Ser.). 1979. 22.95 (ISBN 0-393-01231-X). Norton.
Gordon, I. L., ed. The Seafarer. (Old English Ser.). 1966. pap. text ed. 2.95x (ISBN 0-89197-570-5). Irvington.
Gosset, Adelaide L. Shepherds of Britain: Scenes from Shepherd Life Past & Present. LC 78-174415. (Illus.). Repr. of 1911 ed. 18.00 (ISBN 0-405-08565-6, Pub. by Blom). Arno.
Grattan, J. H. & Singer, Charles. Anglo-Saxon Magic & Medicine. LC 72-190385. 1952. lib. bdg. 35.00 (ISBN 0-8414-1075-5). Folcroft.
Grinsell, Leslie V. Folklore of Prehistoric Sites in Britain. LC 76-8624. (Illus.). 304p. 1976. 12.00 (ISBN 0-7153-7241-6). David & Charles.
Halliwell, James O. The Yorkshire Anthology. LC 72-7051. 1972. lib. bdg. 30.00 (ISBN 0-88305-250-4). Norwood Edns.
Hardwick, Charles. Traditions, Superstitions, & Folk-Lore: Chiefly Lancashire & the North of England: Their Affinity to Others in Widely-Distributed Localities: Their Eastern Origin & Mythical Significance. Dorson, Richard M., ed. LC 80-794. (Forklore of the World Ser.). 1980. Repr. of 1973 ed. lib. bdg. 25.00x (ISBN 0-405-13333-2). Arno.
--Traditions, Superstitions, & Folk-Lore: Chiefly Lancashire & the North of England: Their Affinity to Others in Widely-Distributed Localities: Their Eastern Origin & Mythical Significance. Dorson, Richard M., ed. LC 80-794. (Forklore of the World Ser.). 1980. Repr. of 1973 ed. lib. bdg. 25.00x (ISBN 0-405-13333-2). Arno.
Hartland, Sidney. Welsh Folklore: Its Collection & Study. (Folklore Ser). 10.00 (ISBN 0-685-36463-1). Norwood Edns.
Howells, William. Cambrian Superstitions, Comprising Ghosts, Omens, Witchcraft, & Traditions. LC 77-26988. 1831. 12.50 (ISBN 0-8414-4898-1). Folcroft.
Hull, Eleanor. Folklore of the British Isles. LC 74-12137. 1974. Repr. of 1928 ed. lib. bdg. 25.00 (ISBN 0-8414-4846-9). Folcroft.
Killip, Margaret. The Folklore of the Isle of Man. (Folklore of the British Isles Ser.). (Illus.). 207p. 1976. 16.50x (ISBN 0-87471-771-X). Rowman.
Lanciano, Claude O., Jr. Legends of Lands End. LC 72-18023. (Illus.). 1971. 4.30 (ISBN 0-9603558-1-2). Lands End Bks.
Leather, Ella M. Folk-Lore of Herefordshire. 286p. 1980. lib. bdg. 30.00 (ISBN 0-8414-5758-1). Folcroft.
Macritchie, David. Fians, Fairies & Picts. LC 75-44195. 1976. Repr. of 1893 ed. lib. bdg. 12.50 (ISBN 0-8414-6147-3). Folcroft.
Manley, V. S. Folklore of Warminster: Strange Tales & Belief. (Folklore Ser.). Repr. 7.50 (ISBN 0-685-43672-1). Norwood Edns.
Moore, A. W. The Folk-Lore of the Isle of Man. 192p. 1980. Repr. of 1891 ed. lib. bdg. 10.00 (ISBN 0-8414-6425-1). Folcroft.
Northall, G. English Folk Rhymes. 59.95 (ISBN 0-8490-0110-2). Gordon Pr.
Palmer, Kingsley. The Folklore of Somerset. (Folklore of the British Isles Ser.). 186p. 1976. 15.75x (ISBN 0-87471-807-4). Rowman.
Rinder, E. W. The Shadow of Aryor: Legendary Romances & Folktales of Brittany. LC 78-63219. (The Folktale). 1977. Repr. of 1896 ed. 26.50 (ISBN 0-404-16156-1). AMS Pr.
Rowling, Marjorie. The Folklore of the Lake District. (Folklore of the British Isles Ser.). (Illus.). 184p. 1976. 11.00x (ISBN 0-87471-839-2). Rowman.
Smith, A. H., ed. The Parker Chronicle. (Old English Ser.). 1966. pap. text ed. 8.95x (ISBN 0-89197-569-1). Irvington.
Sternberg, Thomas. The Dialect & Folklore of Northhamptonshire. 200p. 1980. Repr. of 1851 ed. lib. bdg. 20.00 (ISBN 0-8414-7906-2). Folcroft.
Timmer, B. J., ed. Judith. (Old English Ser.). 1966. pap. text ed. 8.95x (ISBN 0-89197-568-3). Irvington.
Tregarthen, Enys. The Doll Who Came Alive. rev. ed. Yates, Elizabeth, ed. LC 70-179780. (Illus.). 80p. (gr. 1-4). 1972. Repr. of 1942 ed. 6.95 (ISBN 0-381-99683-2, A19760, JD-J). Har-Row.
Whitlock, Ralph. The Folklore of Wiltshire. (Folklore of the British Isles Ser.). (Illus.). 205p. 1976. 14.50x (ISBN 0-87471-772-8). Rowman.
Wiltshire Folklore. 8.95 (ISBN 0-8277-7263-7). British Bk Ctr.

FOLK-LORE, BURMESE

Htin Aung. Burmese Folk-Tales. LC 77-87016. Repr. of 1948 ed. 22.00 (ISBN 0-404-16828-0). AMS Pr.
Spiro, Melford E. Burmese Supernaturalism. expanded ed. LC 77-17280. 1978. text ed. 14.95x (ISBN 0-915980-78-9). Inst Study Human.

FOLK-LORE, CANADIAN

Caplan, Ronald. Down North: The Book of Cape Breton's Magazine. LC 78-68351. 1980. 19.95 (ISBN 0-385-14475-X); pap. 12.95 (ISBN 0-385-14476-8). Doubleday.
Fowke, Edith. Folklore of Canada. 1977. 10.95 (ISBN 0-7710-3202-1). McClelland.
Fowke, Edith & Carpenter, Carole H. A Bibliography of Canadian Folklore in English. 232p. 1981. 15.00x (ISBN 0-8020-2394-0). U of Toronto Pr.
Klymasz, Robert B. Ukrainian Folklore in Canada: An Immigrant Complex in Transition. Dorson, Richard M., ed. LC 80-731. (Folklore of the World Ser.). 1980. lib. bdg. 28.00x (ISBN 0-405-13318-9). Arno.
MacMillan, Cycrus, intro. by. Canadian Wonder Tales. 276p. (gr. 4-7). 1980. 9.95 (ISBN 0-370-01279-8, Pub. by Chatto Bodley Jonathan). Merrimack Bk Serv.
Wintemberg, W. J. Folk-Lore of Waterloo County, Ontario. 1979. Repr. of 1950 ed. lib. bdg. 20.00 (ISBN 0-8495-5729-1). Arden Lib.

FOLK-LORE, CELTIC

Henderson, George. Survival in Beliefs Among the Celts. LC 77-3190. (Folklore Ser). 25.00 (ISBN 0-88305-266-0). Norwood Edns.
Jacobs, J. More Celtic Fairy Tales. (Illus.). 6.50 (ISBN 0-8446-2304-0). Peter Smith.
Jacobs, Joseph. Celtic Fairy Tales. LC 67-24223. (Illus.). (ps-6). 1968. pap. 3.50 (ISBN 0-486-21826-0). Dover.
--Celtic Fairy Tales. 59.95 (ISBN 0-87968-823-8). Gordon Pr.
--More Celtic Fairy Tales. LC 67-24224. (ps-6). 1968. pap. 3.00 (ISBN 0-486-21827-9). Dover.
--More Celtic Fairy Tales. 59.95 (ISBN 0-8490-0670-8). Gordon Pr.
Rhys, John. Celtic Folklore, 2 vols. Set. lib. bdg. 250.00 (ISBN 0-87968-099-7). Gordon Pr.
--Celtic Folklore: Welsh & Manx, 2 vols. in 1. LC 72-80504. Repr. of 1901 ed. 44.00 (ISBN 0-405-08885-X, Blom Pubns). Arno.
Rhys, Sir John. Celtic Folklore, Welsh & Manx, 2 vols. xlvi, 718p. Repr. of 1901 ed. 54.00 (ISBN 0-384-50610-0). Johnson Repr.
Rolleston, Thomas W. Myths & Legends of the Celtic Race. (Illus.). 456p. 1973. Repr. of 1934 ed. 22.50 (ISBN 0-685-26066-6). Lemma.
Sjoestedt, Marie-Louise. Gods & Heroes of the Celts. 1976. 69.95 (ISBN 0-8490-1894-3). Gordon Pr.
Soupault, Re, tr. Breton Folktales. 215p. 1974. 12.95 (ISBN 0-7135-1890-1). Transatlantic.
Squire, Charles. Celtic Myth & Legend. new ed. LC 74-26575. (Newcastle Mythology Library: Vol. 1). 450p. 1975. pap. 5.95 (ISBN 0-87877-030-5). Newcastle Pub.
--Celtic Myth & Legend, Poetry & Romance. LC 80-53343. (Newcastle Mythology Library: Vol. 1). 450p. 1980. Repr. of 1975 ed. lib. bdg. 12.95x (ISBN 0-89370-630-2). Borgo Pr.

FOLK-LORE, CHEREMISSIAN

Sebeok, Thomas A. & Ingemann, Frances J. Studies in Cheremis: The Supernatural. (Illus.). Repr. of 1956 ed. pap. 15.50 (ISBN 0-384-54635-8). Johnson Repr.

FOLK-LORE, CHILE

Laval, Ramon A. Cuentos de Pedro Urdemales. LC 78-63205. (The Folktale). Repr. of 1925 ed. 14.50 (ISBN 0-404-16143-X). AMS Pr.

--Cuentos populares en Chile. LC 78-63206. (The Folktale). Repr. of 1923 ed. 25.50 (ISBN 0-404-16144-8). AMS Pr.

FOLK-LORE, CHINESE

Anderson, Eugene & Anderson, Marja L. Mountain & Water: Essays on the Cultural Ecology of South Coastal China, No. 54. (Asian Folklore & Social Life Monograph). 194p. (Chinese.). 1973. 5.50 (ISBN 0-89986-051-6). E Langstaff.

Chang, Kathleen. The Iron Moonhunter: Bilingual in Chinese & English. LC 77-73783. (Fifth World Tales Ser.). (Illus.). (gr. k-6). pap. 3.95 (ISBN 0-89239-011-5, Imprenta de Libros Infantiles). Childrens Book Pr.

Chang Hsiao-Ch'ao. Four Jest Books. (National Peking University & Chinese Assn. for Folklore, Folklore & Folkliterature Ser.: No. 113 &114). (Chinese.). 12.00 (ISBN 0-89986-191-1). E Langstaff.

Chang Nan-Chuang. Ho Tien, Folkliterature with Proverbs. (National Peking University & Chinese Assn. for Folklore, Folklore & Folkliterature Ser.: No. 8). (Chinese.). 6.00 (ISBN 0-89986-108-3). E Langstaff.

Chao Ching-Sheng. Essays on Folk Tales. (Folklore Series of National Sun Yat-Sen University: No. 12). (Chinese.). 5.50 (ISBN 0-89986-082-6). E Langstaff.

Chao Nan-Sing. Jest Books, Thirteen Sixty-Eight to Nineteen Eleven A. D. (National Peking University & Chinese Assn. for Folklore, Folklore & Folkliterature Ser.: No. 7). (Chinese.). 6.00 (ISBN 0-89986-107-5). E Langstaff.

Ch'en Hai-Hung. Cartoons About the Tales of the Snake Bridegroom. (National Peking University & Chinese Assn. for Folklore, Folklore & Folkliterature Ser.: No. 117). (Chinese.). 6.00 (ISBN 0-89986-194-6). E Langstaff.

Ch'en Han-Chang. Essays on Ancient Chinese Folklore. (National Peking University & Chinese Assn. for Folklore, Folklore & Folkliterature Ser.: No. 50). (Chinese.). 6.00 (ISBN 0-89986-141-5). E Langstaff.

Chen Ting-Kuo. Cartoons About the Tales of Filial Piety. (National Peking University & Chinese Assn. for Folklore, Folklore & Folkliterature Ser.: No. 136). (Chinese.). 6.00 (ISBN 0-89986-210-1). E Langstaff.

Chiang Shao-Yuan. The Folklore of Hair, Beard & Nail. (National Peking University & Chinese Assn. for Folklore, Folklore & Folkliterature Ser.: No. 26). (Chinese.). 7.00 (ISBN 0-89986-122-9). E Langstaff.

Chinese Academy of Social Sciences, Institute of Literature, ed. Stories About Not Being Afraid of Ghosts. 2nd ed. Yang, Gladys & Hsien-Yi, Yang, trs. from Chinese. 1979. pap. 2.95 (ISBN 0-8351-0608-X). China Bks.

Ching Wen. More Tales About Other Wise Men. Lin Lan, ed. (Tales from the Orient Ser.: No. 29). (Chinese.). 15.00 (ISBN 0-89986-253-5). E Langstaff.

Ch'iu Chun. Alternate Love Songs. (Folklore Series of National Sun Yat-Sen University: No. 31). (Chinese.). 5.50 (ISBN 0-89986-099-0). E Langstaff.

Chou Ch'i-Ming. Essays on Folklore & Folkliterature. (National Peking University & Chinese Assn. for Folklore, Folklore & Folkliterature Ser.: No. 63). (Chinese.). 6.00 (ISBN 0-89986-153-9). E Langstaff.

Chou Ch'ing-Hwa. Folktales of the Hakka, Taiwan. (National Peking University & Chinese Assn. for Folklore, Folklore & Folkliterature Ser.: No. 55). (Chinese.). 6.00 (ISBN 0-89986-146-6). E Langstaff.

Chu Feng. Folklore of Southern Taiwan. (National Peking University & Chinese Assn. for Folklore, Folklore & Folkliterature Ser.: No. 33). (Chinese.). 6.00 (ISBN 0-89986-128-8). E Langstaff.

Chung Ching-Wen. Essays on Folk-Literature. (Folklore Series of National Sun Yat-Sen University: No. 3). (Chinese.). 5.50 (ISBN 0-89986-073-7). E Langstaff.

--Essays on Folkliterature. (National Peking University & Chinese Assn. for Folklore, Folklore & Folkliterature Ser.: No. 16). (Chinese.). 7.00 (ISBN 0-89986-116-4). E Langstaff.

--Folklore Monthly, 4 vols. (National Peking University & Chinese Assn. for Folklore, Folklore & Folkliterature Ser.: Nos. 18-22). (Chinese.). 26.40 (ISBN 0-89986-118-0). E Langstaff.

--The Golden Frog. Lin Lan, ed. (Tales from the Orient Ser.: No. 6). (Chinese.). 5.00 (ISBN 0-89986-230-6). E Langstaff.

Davis, Mary H. Chinese Fables & Folk Stories. LC 76-48746. 1977. lib. bdg. 20.00 (ISBN 0-8414-3813-7). Folcroft.

Dennys, N. B. The Folk-Lore of China: And Its Affinities with That of the Aryan & Semitic Races. LC 72-84000. Repr. of 1876 ed. 14.00 (ISBN 0-405-08443-9, Blom Pubns). Arno.

Dennys, Nicholas B. The Folk-Lore of China, & Its Affinities with That of the Aryan & Semitic Races. LC 79-89262. (Illus.). iv, 163p. 1972. Repr. of 1876 ed. 24.00 (ISBN 0-8103-3932-3). Gale.

Eberhard, Wolfram. Chinese Fables & Parables, No. 15. (Asian Folklore & Social Life Monograph). 1972. 4.60 (ISBN 0-89986-018-4). E Langstaff.

--Chinese Fairy Tales & Folk Tales. LC 74-9676. 1937. lib. bdg. 25.00 (ISBN 0-8414-3940-0). Folcroft.

--Studies in Chinese Folklore & Related Essays. (Folklore Monographs Ser: Vol. 23). 1970. pap. text ed. 12.00x (ISBN 0-87750-147-5). Res Ctr Lang Semiotic.

--Studies in Hakka Folktales, No. 61. (Asian Folklore & Social Life Monograph). 290p. 1974. 7.00 (ISBN 0-89986-056-7). E Langstaff.

--Studies in Taiwanese Folktales, No. 1. Lou Tsu-K'uang, ed. (Asian Folklore & Social Life Monograph). 1970. 4.60 (ISBN 0-89986-004-4). E Langstaff.

Essays on Folklore, 2 vols. (Chin.). 13.20 (ISBN 0-89986-285-3). E Langstaff.

Fang Ch'eng. Humorous Tales from Ancient China. (National Peking University & Chinese Assn. for Folklore, Folklore & Folkliterature Ser.: No. 95). (Chinese.). 7.00 (ISBN 0-89986-175-X). E Langstaff.

Fisher, W. A String of Chinese Pearls: Ten Tales of Chinese Girls Ancient & Modern. lib. bdg. 59.95 (ISBN 0-87968-518-2). Krishna Pr.

Folk Literature Weekly of Sun Yet-Sen University. (Chin.). 7.70 (ISBN 0-89986-282-9). E Langstaff.

The Folklore Monthly: Szechuan, 2 vols. (Chin.). 15.40 (ISBN 0-89986-286-1). E Langstaff.

Folklore Studies of the Catholic University of Peking: 1942-1947. (English, German, Chinese, & Japanese text). 12.10 ea.; 72.60 set (ISBN 0-89986-289-6). E Langstaff.

Folklore Weekly of National Sun Yet-Sen University, 20 vols. (Chin.). 132.00 (ISBN 0-89986-287-X). E Langstaff.

Frog Rider: Folk Tales from China. 1980. pap. 1.95 (ISBN 0-8351-0777-9). China Bks.

Han, Li & Tzu-Kuang, Hsu. Meng Ch'iu: Famous Episodes from Chinese History & Legend. Watson, Burton, tr. from Chinese. LC 79-89264. 184p. 1980. 15.00 (ISBN 0-87011-278-3). Kodansha.

Hentze, Carl. Chinese Tomb Figures: A Study in the Beliefs & Folklore of Ancient China. LC 70-38072. Repr. of 1928 ed. 94.50 (ISBN 0-404-56934-X). AMS Pr.

Hirasawa, Teito. Taiwanese Folkliterature, 2 vols. (Asian Folklore & Social Life Monographs: Vols. 78-79). (Jap.). 1917. 10.00 (ISBN 0-89986-290-X). E Langstaff.

Hitz, Demi. Under the Shade of the Mulberry Tree. (Illus.). (ps-2). 1979. 8.95 (ISBN 0-13-936476-5). P-H.

Ho Kung-Ch'ao. The Grey King. Lin Lan, ed. (Tales from the Orient Ser.: No. 10). (Chinese.). 5.00 (ISBN 0-89986-234-9). E Langstaff.

Ho Ting-Jui. A Comparative Study of Myths & Legends of Farmosan Aborigines, No. 18. (Asian Folklore & Social Life Monograph). 1972. 5.30 (ISBN 0-89986-020-6). E Langstaff.

Hsuan-Chu. The Melon-King. Lin Lan, ed. (Tales from the Orient Ser.: No. 7). (Chinese.). 5.00 (ISBN 0-89986-231-4). E Langstaff.

Hsu Ju-Chung. Folklore of Kimmen, Fu-Chien. (National Peking University & Chinese Assn. for Folklore, Folklore & Folkliterature Ser.: No 29). (Chinese.). 6.00 (ISBN 0-89986-124-5). E Langstaff.

Jagendorf, M. A. & Weng, Virginia. The Magic Boat & Other Chinese Folk Stories. LC 79-67814. (Illus.). (gr. 4-9). 1980. 9.95 (ISBN 0-8149-0823-3). Vanguard.

Jameson, R. Three Lectures on Chinese Folklore. lib. bdg. 59.95 (ISBN 0-87968-527-1). Krishna Pr.

Jest Books, Nine Sixty to Twelve Seventy-Six A. D. (National Peking University & Chinese Assn. for Folklore, Folklore & Folkliterature Ser.: No. 6). (Chinese.). 6.00 (ISBN 0-89986-106-7). E Langstaff.

Journal of Folklore of Sun Yet-Sen University, 4 vols. (Chin.). Set. 33.00 (ISBN 0-89986-283-7). E Langstaff.

Ku Chieh-Kang. Essays on Ancient Chinese Folkliterature. (National Peking University & Chinese Assn. for Folklore, Folklore & Folkliterature Ser.: No. 51). (Chinese.). 6.00 (ISBN 0-89986-142-3). E Langstaff.

--Essays on Folklore. (National Peking University &Chinese Assn. for Folklore, Folklore & Folkliterature Ser.: No. 17). (Chinese.). 7.00 (ISBN 0-89986-117-2). E Langstaff.

Ku Wan-Chuan. The Fisherman's Love. Lin Lan, ed. (Tales from the Orient Ser.: No. 17). 5.00 (ISBN 0-89986-241-1). E Langstaff.

Ku Wan-Ch'uan. The Red-Flower-Widow. Lin Lan, ed. (Tales from the Orient Ser.: No. 9). (Chinese.). 5.00 (ISBN 0-89986-233-0). E Langstaff.

Levy, Howard S., tr. from Chinese. China's Dirtiest Trickster: Folklore About Hsu Wen-ch'ang (1521-1593) (Sino-Japanese Folklore Translations Ser.: No. 1). (Illus.). 68p. 1974. 8.00 (ISBN 0-686-05428-8). Langstaff-Levy Ent.

Levy, Howard S., tr. Two Chinese Sex Classics. (Asian Folklore & Social Life Nonographs: Vol. 75). 1975. Repr. 6.00 (ISBN 0-686-16298-6). Langstaff-Levy Ent.

Li Su. Folklore Fortnightly. (Chin.). 8.00 (ISBN 0-89986-284-5). E Langstaff.

Li Lin-Tsan. Studies in Mo-So Tribal Stories, No. 3. (Asian Folklore & Social Life Monograph). (Chinese.). 1970. 6.60 (ISBN 0-89986-006-0). E Langstaff.

Lin Heng-Tao. Folklore of Northern Taiwan. (National Peking University & Chinese Assn. for Folklore, Folklore & Folkliterature Ser.: No. 31). (Chinese.). 6.00 (ISBN 0-89986-126-1). E Langstaff.

Liu Fu. Essays on Folkliterature. (National Peking University & Chinese Assn. for Folklore, Folklore & Folkliterature Ser.: No. 61). (Chinese.). 6.00 (ISBN 0-89986-151-2). E Langstaff.

Liu Wan-Chang. Folktales from Canton. (Folklore Series of National Sun Yat-Sen University: No. 6). (Chinese.). 5.50 (ISBN 0-89986-076-1). E Langstaff.

Lou Tsu-K'uang. Essays on Taiwanese Folkliterature. (National Peking University & Chinese Assn. for Folklore, Folklore & Folkliterature Ser.: No. 52). (Chinese.). 6.00 (ISBN 0-89986-143-1). E Langstaff.

Lou Tsu-K-uang. Folktales from Formosa. (National Peking University & Chinese Assn. for Folklore, Folklore & Folkliterature Ser.: No. 11). (Chinese.). 6.00 (ISBN 0-89986-111-3). E Langstaff.

Lou Tsu-K'uang. Legends of Formosa, No. 10. (Asian Folklore & Social Life Monograph). (Chinese.). 1970. 5.90 (ISBN 0-89986-013-3). E Langstaff.

--Sources of Taiwanese Folklore. (National Peking University & Chinese Assn. for Folklore, Folklore & Folkliterature Ser.: No. 64). (Chinese.). 6.00 (ISBN 0-89986-154-7). E Langstaff.

MacGowan, John. Chinese Folklore Tales. LC 74-9650. 1974. Repr. of 1910 ed. lib. bdg. 20.00 (ISBN 0-8414-6146-5). Folcroft.

Mackenzie, Donald A. The Myths of China & Japan. LC 77-6878. 1977. Repr. of 1923 ed. lib. bdg. 45.00 (ISBN 0-89341-149-3). Longwood Pr.

Mi Hsing-Ju. The Fairy Crab. (National Peking University & Chinese Assn. for Folklore, Folklore & Folkliterature Ser.: No. 57). (Chinese.). 6.00 (ISBN 0-89986-148-2). E Langstaff.

Norbeck, Edward. Folklore of the Atayal of Formosa & the Mountain Tribes of Luzon. (Anthropological Papers Ser.: No. 5). (Illus.). 1950. pap. 0.50x (ISBN 0-932206-18-2). U Mich Mus Anthro.

Nott, Stanley C. Chinese Jade Throughout the Ages: A Review of Its Characteristics, Decoration, Folklore & Symbolism. LC 62-8839. (Illus.). 1962. 47.50 (ISBN 0-8048-0100-2). C E Tuttle.

Nowak, Margaret & Durrant, Stephen. The Tale of the Nisan Shamaness: A Manchu Folk Epic. LC 76-49171. (Publications on Asia of the School of International Studies: No. 31). 192p. 1977. 9.95 (ISBN 0-295-95548-1). U of Wash Pr.

Plopper, Clifford H. Chinese Religion Seen Through the Proverbs. LC 79-77385. (Eng. & Chinese.). 1969. 16.50 (ISBN 0-8188-0072-0). Paragon.

Radin, Paul. The Golden Mountain, No. 13. (Asian Folklore & Social Life Monograph). 1971. 4.60 (ISBN 0-89986-016-8). E Langstaff.

Roberts, Moss, ed. Chinese Fairy Tales & Fantasies. (Pantheon Fairy Tale & Folklore Library). (Illus.). 1980. pap. 4.95 (ISBN 0-394-73994-9). Pantheon.

Ryuzo, Nagao. Chinese Folklore: Belief & Marriage, No. 35. (Asian Folklore & Social Life Monograph). (Jap.). 1938. 6.60 (ISBN 0-89986-035-4). E Langstaff.

--Folklore of Manchuria: The Chinese Folkways, No. 36. (Asian Folklore & Social Life Monograph). (Jap.). 1938. 6.60 (ISBN 0-89986-036-2). E Langstaff.

Shanghai Trust Co. A Survey of the Folklore from Shanghai, 1930. (National Peking University & Chinese Assn. for Folklore, Folklore & Folkliterature Ser.: No. 47). (Chinese.). 6.00 (ISBN 0-89986-139-3). E Langstaff.

Shou Shih. The Gluttonous Woman. Lin Lan, ed. (Tales from the Orient Ser.: No. 23). (Chinese.). 5.00 (ISBN 0-89986-247-0). E Langstaff.

Sia Hoon-Seng. Folktales of Fu-Chien. (National Peking University & Chinese Assn. for Folklore, Folklore & Folkliterature Ser.: No.98-100). (Chinese.). 21.00 (ISBN 0-89986-178-4). E Langstaff.

Sun Chia-Hsin. The Elder Brother Ghost. Lin Lan, ed. (Tales from the Orient Ser.: No. 19). (Chinese.). 5.00 (ISBN 0-89986-243-8). E Langstaff.

--Mother Beyond the Clouds. Lin Lan, ed. (Tales from the Orient Ser.: No. 24). 5.00 (ISBN 0-89986-248-9). E Langstaff.

Van Over, Raymond. Taoist Tales. 1973. pap. 2.25 (ISBN 0-451-61650-2, ME1650, Ment). NAL.

Wang Shu-Tan. Folklore of Hsin-Ch'iang. (National Peking University & Chinese Assn. for Folklore, Folklore & Folkliterature Ser.: No. 74). (Chinese.). 6.50 (ISBN 0-89986-160-1). E Langstaff.

Wang T'ung-Chao. Folktales from Shantung. (National Peking University & Chinese Assn. for Folklore, Folklore & Folkliterature Ser.: No. 77). (Chinese.). 6.00 (ISBN 0-89986-162-8). E Langstaff.

Wilhelm, Richard, tr. Chinese Folktales. 215p. 1974. 8.50 (ISBN 0-7135-1813-8). Transatlantic.

Williams, C. A. Outlines of Chinese Symbolism & Art Motives. LC 76-40397. 472p. 1976. pap. 6.00 (ISBN 0-486-23372-3). Dover.

Wu Chia-Ch'ing. Folklore & Folk Literature of Wu-Chin, Chiang-Su, No. 6. (Asian Folklore & Social Life Monograph). (Chinese.). 1970. 6.60 (ISBN 0-89986-009-5). E Langstaff.

Wu Shou-Li. Studies in a Folk-Play-Li-Ching-Chi, No. 7. (Asian Folklore & Social Life Monograph). (Chinese.). 1970. 6.00 (ISBN 0-89986-010-9). E Langstaff.

Wyndham, Robert. Tales the People Tell in China. LC 74-154971. (Illus.). 96p. (gr. 3 up). 1971. PLB 7.29 (ISBN 0-671-32428-4). Messner.

Yang Ch'eng-Chih. Questionary of Folklore. (Folklore Series of National Sun Yat-Sen University: No. 15). (Chinese.). 5.50 (ISBN 0-89986-084-2). E Langstaff.

Yang Hsi-Yao. A Survey of Folklore in Ch'ing Hai. (National Peking University & Chinese Assn. for Folklore, Folklore & Folkliterature Ser.: No. 43). (Chinese.). 6.00 (ISBN 0-89986-135-0). E Langstaff.

Yeh Teh-Chun. Folksongs & Folktales from Huai An. (Folklore Series of National Sun Yat-Sen University: No. 32). (Chinese.). 5.50 (ISBN 0-89986-100-8). E Langstaff.

Young, Ed. The Terrible Nung Gwama: A Chinese Folktale. LC 78-18766. (Unicef Storycraft Bks.). (Illus.). (ps-3). 1978. 5.95 (ISBN 0-529-05444-2); PLB 5.99 (ISBN 0-529-05445-0). Philomel.

Yuan Hsi Kuo & Louise Hsi Kuo. Chinese Folk Tales. LC 75-9082. 1976. pap. 5.95 (ISBN 0-89087-074-8). Celestial Arts.

FOLK-LORE, CZECH

Baudis, J. Czech Folk Tales. Repr. of 1917 ed. 14.00 (ISBN 0-527-05600-6). Kraus Repr.

FOLK-LORE, DANISH

Grundtvig, Svendt. Danish Fairy Tales. Cramer, J. Grant, tr. 5.00 (ISBN 0-8446-4626-1). Peter Smith.

FOLK-LORE, DOMINICAN REPUBLIC

Andrade, M. J., ed. Folk-Lore from the Dominican Republic. LC 33-10559. Repr. of 1930 ed. 25.00 (ISBN 0-527-01075-8). Kraus Repr.

Andrade, Manuel J. Folklore De la Republica Dominicana, 2 vols. 1976. Set. lib. bdg. 250.00 (ISBN 0-8490-1850-1). Gordon Pr.

FOLK-LORE, DUTCH GUIANA

Herskovits, Melville J. & Herskovits, Frances S. Suriname Folk-Lore. LC 71-82365. (Columbia Univ. Contributions to Anthropology Ser.: No. 27). (Illus.). Repr. of 1936 ed. 47.50 (ISBN 0-404-50577-5). AMS Pr.

FOLK-LORE, ENGLISH

Addy, Sidney O. Folk Tales & Superstitions. 163p. 1973. Repr. of 1895 ed. 11.00x (ISBN 0-87471-142-8). Rowman.

Alford, Violet. Introduction to English Folklore. 1978. Repr. of 1952 ed. lib. bdg. 22.50 (ISBN 0-8495-0105-9). Arden Lib.

--Introduction to English Folklore. LC 75-33843. 1975. Repr. of 1952 ed. lib. bdg. 20.00 (ISBN 0-8414-2893-X). Folcroft.

Barrett, W. H. & Garrod, R. P. East Anglian Folklore & Other Tales. (Illus.). 1976. 13.50 (ISBN 0-7100-8300-9). Routledge & Kegan.

Baughman, Ernest W. Type & Motif-Index of the Folktales of England & North America. 1966. pap. text ed. 65.90x (ISBN 90-2790-046-9). Mouton.

Blakeborough, Richard. Legends of Highwaymen & Others. LC 75-154493. (Illus.). 1971. Repr. of 1924 ed. 22.00 (ISBN 0-8103-3373-2). Gale.

--Yorkshire Wit, Character, Folklore & Customs. (Folklore Ser). 20.00 (ISBN 0-685-36428-3). Norwood Edns.

Bloom, J. Harvey. Folk Lore, Old Customs & Superstitions in Shakespeare Land. LC 73-2830. viii, 167p. 1973. Repr. of 1930 ed. 20.00 (ISBN 0-8103-3269-8). Gale.

--Folklore, Old Customs & Superstitions in Shakespeare Land. (Folklore Ser). 10.00 (ISBN 0-88305-055-2). Norwood Edns.

Bloom, James H. Folk Lore, Old Customs & Superstitions in Shakespeare Land. LC 76-29050. 1976. Repr. of 1929 ed. lib. bdg. 20.00 (ISBN 0-8414-1791-1). Folcroft.

Boase, Wendy. The Folklore of Hampshire & the Isle of Wight. (Folklore of British Isles Ser.). (Illus.). 192p. 1976. 17.50x (ISBN 0-87471-784-1). Rowman.

Bord, Janet & Bord, Colin. The Secret Country. 1977. 9.95 (ISBN 0-8027-0559-6). Walker & Co.

Brand, John. Observations on the Popular Antiquities of Great Britain: Chiefly Illustrating the Origin of Our Vulgar & Provincial Customs, Ceremonies & Superstitions. LC 67-23896. 1969. Repr. of 1849 ed. 49.00 (ISBN 0-8103-3256-6). Gale.

Briggs, Katharine M. The Folklore of the Cotswolds. (Folklore of the British Isles Ser.). (Illus.). 208p. 1974. 13.50x (ISBN 0-87471-538-5). Rowman.

Briggs, Katherine M. Pale Hecates Team: Examination of the Beliefs on Witchcraft and Magic Among Shakespeare's Contemporaries & His Immediate Succesors. Dorson, Richard M., ed. LC 77-70582. (International Folklore Ser.). (Illus.). 1977. lib. bdg. 18.00x (ISBN 0-405-10083-3). Arno.

Briscoe, J. P. Nottinghamshire Folk-Lore. (Folklore Ser). 12.50 (ISBN 0-685-36432-1). Norwood Edns.

Brockie, William. Legends & Superstitions of the County of Durham. LC 76-49066. 1976. Repr. of 1886 ed. lib. bdg. 20.00 (ISBN 0-8414-1761-X). Folcroft.

Burland, C. A. Echoes of Magic: A Study of Seasonal Festivals Through the Ages. (Illus.). 234p. 1972. 13.50x (ISBN 0-87471-087-1). Rowman.

Calhoun, Mary. Jack the Wise & the Cornish Cuckoos. LC 77-22714. (Illus.). (gr. k-3). 1978. 7.95 (ISBN 0-688-22132-7); PLB 7.63 (ISBN 0-688-32132-1). Morrow.

Deane, Tony & Shaw, Tony. The Folklore of Cornwall. (Folklore of the British Isles Ser.). 217p. 1975. 16.50x (ISBN 0-87471-695-0). Rowman.

Dorson, Richard M., ed. Peasant Customs & Savage Myths Selections from the British Folklorists, 2 Vols. LC 68-16690. 1969. Set. 25.00x (ISBN 0-226-15867-5); Vol. 1. 13.50x (ISBN 0-226-15865-9); Vol. 2. 12.50x (ISBN 0-226-15866-7). U of Chicago Pr.

EP Books, ed. Folk Lore & Legends of England. 1972. Repr. of 1890 ed. 14.95x (ISBN 0-8464-0418-4). Beekman Pubs.

Firor, Ruth A. Folkways in Thomas Hardy. pap. 2.45 (ISBN 0-498-04069-0, Prpta). A S Barnes.

--Folkways in Thomas Hardy. LC 68-25031. 1968. Repr. of 1931 ed. 11.00 (ISBN 0-8462-1143-2). Russell.

Fish, Lydia M. The Folklore of the Coal Miners of the Northeast of England. LC 76-25433. 1976. Set. lib. bdg. 25.00 (ISBN 0-8414-4209-6). Folcroft.

Gomme, George L. Folklore Relics of Early Village Life. Dorson, Richard, ed. (International Folklore Ser.). 1977. Repr. of 1883 ed. lib. bdg. 15.00x (ISBN 0-405-10096-5). Arno.

Harland, John & Wilkinson, T. T. Lancashire Folk-Lore. (Folklore Ser). 15.00 (ISBN 0-685-36461-5). Norwood Edns.

--Lancashire Legends. LC 73-13529. (Folklore Ser). 15.00 (ISBN 0-88305-262-8). Norwood Edns.

Hartland, Edwin S., ed. English Fairy & Other Folktales. LC 68-21772. 1968. Repr. of 1890 ed. 22.00 (ISBN 0-8103-3465-8). Gale.

Hazlitt, William C. Faiths & Folklore of the British Isles, 2 Vols. LC 64-18758. 1905. Set. 40.00 (ISBN 0-405-08604-0, Blom Pubns); 20.00 ea. Vol. 1 (ISBN 0-405-08605-9). Vol. 2 (ISBN 0-405-08606-7). Arno.

Henderson, William. Folk Lore of the Northern Counties of England & the Borders. 344p. 1973. Repr. of 1866 ed. 15.00x (ISBN 0-87471-141-X). Rowman.

Hewett, Sarah. Nummits & Crummits. (Norwood Folklore Ser.). 12.50 (ISBN 0-88305-256-3). Norwood Edns.

--Nummits & Crummits: Devonshire Customs, Characteristics, & Folklore. 1977. Repr. of 1900 ed. 17.50x (ISBN 0-7158-1170-3). Charles River Bks.

Hole, Christina. British Folk Customs. (Illus.). 1977. 14.95x (ISBN 0-09-127340-4, Pub. by Hutchinson Pub. Group Ltd). Standing Orders.

--Traditions & Customs of Cheshire. LC 73-12972. (Folklore Ser). 10.00 (ISBN 0-88305-260-1). Norwood Edns.

Hunt, Robert, ed. Popular Romances of the West of England. LC 68-56495. 1968. Repr. of 1916 ed. 20.00 (ISBN 0-405-08643-1, Blom Pubns). Arno.

Jacobs, Joseph. English Fairy Tales. (Illus.). (gr. 3-6). 1898. pap. 3.00 (ISBN 0-486-21818-X). Dover.

--The Story of the Three Little Pigs. (Illus.). 32p. (Orig.). (ps-3). 1980. 8.95 (ISBN 0-399-20733-3); pap. 3.95 (ISBN 0-399-20732-5). Putnam.

Jones-Baker, Doris. The Folklore of Hertfordshire. (Folklore of the British Isles Ser.). (Illus.). 240p. 1977. 10.00x (ISBN 0-87471-925-9). Rowman.

Leather, Ella M. The Folk-Lore of Herefordshive. (Folklore Ser). 15.00 (ISBN 0-685-36479-8). Norwood Edns.

Long, George. Folklore Calendar. LC 76-78191. 1970. Repr. of 1930 ed. 21.00 (ISBN 0-8103-3367-8). Gale.

MacCulloch, Edgar. Guernsey Folk Lore. LC 72-7265. (YA) 1972. lib. bdg. 45.00 (ISBN 0-88305-400-0). Norwood Edns.

MacDougall, James, ed. Folk & Hero Tales. LC 75-144456. (Waifs & Strays of Celtic Tradition: Argyllshire Ser.: No. 3). Repr. of 1891 ed. 18.00 (ISBN 0-404-53533-X). AMS Pr.

Marshall, Sybil. Everyman's Book of English Folktales. (Everyman's Library). (Illus.). 260p. 1981. 17.50x (ISBN 0-460-04472-9, Pub. by J. M. Dent England). Biblio Dist.

Meller, Walter C. Old Times. LC 68-26592. (Illus.). 1968. Repr. of 1925 ed. 19.00 (ISBN 0-8103-3453-4). Gale.

Molnar, Agnes, illus. Jack & the Beanstalk. LC 78-12524. (A Goodnight Bk.). (Illus.). (ps-1). 1979. 1.75 (ISBN 0-394-84101-8). Knopf.

Nicholson, Edward W. Folk-Lore in East Yorkshire. LC 72-13994. (Folklore Ser.). 10.00 (ISBN 0-88305-450-7). Norwood Edns.

Nicholson, John. Folk-Lore of East Yorkshire. 168p. 1980. Repr. of 1972 ed. lib. bdg. 20.00 (ISBN 0-8492-1984-1). R West.

Northall, G. F. English Folk-Rhymes: A Collection of Traditional Verses Relating to Places & Persons, Customs, Superstitions, Etc. LC 67-23918. 1967. Repr. of 1892 ed. 26.00 (ISBN 0-8103-3455-0). Gale.

Norton, Eloise S. Folk Literature of the British Isles: Readings for Librarians, Teachers, & Those Who Work with Children & Young Adults. LC 78-10324. 1978. lib. bdg. 14.00 (ISBN 0-8108-1177-4). Scarecrow.

Palmer, Kingsley. Oral Folk Tales of Wessex. 200p. 1973. 6.50 (ISBN 0-7153-5905-3). David & Charles.

Palmer, Roy. The Folklore of Warwickshire. (Folklore of the British Isles Ser.). (Illus.). 208p. 1976. 15.00x (ISBN 0-87471-838-4). Rowman.

Palmer, William T. Odd Yarns of English Lakeland. 1977. Repr. of 1914 ed. lib. bdg. 20.00 (ISBN 0-8414-6844-3). Folcroft.

Parkinson, Thomas. Yorkshire Legends & Traditions. Dorson, Richard M., ed. LC 77-70615. (International Folklore Ser.). 1977. Repr. of 1888 ed. lib. bdg. 14.00x (ISBN 0-405-10117-1). Arno.

Potts, William. Banbury Cross & the Rhyme. LC 76-25535. 1976. Repr. of 1930 ed. lib. bdg. 10.00 (ISBN 0-8414-6737-4). Folcroft.

Raven, Jon. The Folklore of Staffordshire. (Folklore of the British Isles Ser). (Illus.). 223p. 1978. 13.50x (ISBN 0-8476-6021-4). Rowman.

Rosenberg, Bruce A. & Mandel, Jerome, eds. Medieval Literature & Folklore Studies. LC 70-127053. 1971. 27.50 (ISBN 0-8135-0676-X). Rutgers U Pr.

Saxby, Jessie M. Shetland Traditional Lore. (Folklore Ser). 12.50 (ISBN 0-685-36514-X). Norwood Edns.

Simpson, Jacqueline. The Folklore of Sussex. (Folklore of the British Isles Ser.). (Illus.). 187p. 1973. 15.00x (ISBN 0-87471-375-7). Rowman.

Spence, Lewis. The Minor Traditions of British Mythology. LC 72-84001. Repr. of 1948 ed. 24.00 (ISBN 0-405-08989-9). Arno.

Sternberg, Thomas. The Dialect & Folk-Lore of Northamptonshire. LC 73-12997. (Folklore Ser). 12.50 (ISBN 0-88305-625-9). Norwood Edns.

Thiselton-Dyer, Thomas F. British Popular Customs, Present & Past. LC 79-136378. (Bohn's Antiquarian Lib). Repr. of 1875 ed. 12.50 (ISBN 0-404-50006-4). AMS Pr.

--British Popular Customs, Present & Past. LC 67-23908. (Social History Reference Ser.). (Illus.). 1968. Repr. of 1876 ed. 22.00 (ISBN 0-8103-3261-2). Gale.

--English Folk-Lore. LC 75-150242. Repr. of 1878 ed. 24.00 (ISBN 0-8103-3680-4). Gale.

Thoms, William J., ed. Anecdotes & Traditions, Illustrative of Early English History & Literature, Derived from Manuscript Sources. (Camden Society, London. Publications, First Ser.: No. 5). Repr. of 1839 ed. 14.00 (ISBN 0-404-50105-2). AMS Pr.

--Anecdotes & Traditions, Illustrative of Early English History & Literature. Repr. of 1848 ed. 15.50 (ISBN 0-384-60310-6). Johnson Repr.

Tongue, Ruth L. Forgotten Folk-Tales of the English Counties. 1970. 17.50 (ISBN 0-7100-6833-6). Routledge & Kegan.

Whitlock, Ralph. The Folklore of Devon. (Folklore of the British Isles Ser.). (Illus.). 224p. 1977. 13.50x (ISBN 0-87471-954-2). Rowman.

Wimberly, Lowry C. Folklore in the English & Scottish Ballads. 6.00 (ISBN 0-8446-3191-4). Peter Smith.

--Folklore in the English & Scottish Ballads. 1965. pap. 4.00 (ISBN 0-486-21388-9). Dover.

The Witch's Pig: A Cornish Folktale. (gr. k-3). 1977. PLB 7.92 (ISBN 0-688-32092-9). Morrow.

Wright, A. R. English Folklore. LC 73-20004. (Folklore Ser). 7.50 (ISBN 0-88305-771-9). Norwood Edns.

Wright, Elizabeth M. Rustic Speech & Folklore. LC 68-18011. 1968. Repr. of 1913 ed. 22.00 (ISBN 0-8103-3294-9). Gale.

Wright, Thomas. Essays on Subjects Connected with the Literature, Popular Superstitions, & History of England in the Middle Ages, 2 vols. LC 70-80262. (Research & Source Works Ser.: No. 404). 1970. Repr. of 1846 ed. lib. bdg. 36.00 (ISBN 0-8337-3889-5). B Franklin.

FOLK-LORE, EGYPTIAN

Dorson, Richard M., ed. Egyptian Tales & Romances: Pagan, Christian & Muslim. Budge, Ernest A., tr. from Egyptian. LC 80-739. (Folklore of the World Ser.). (Illus.). 1980. Repr. of 1931 ed. lib. bdg. 39.00x (ISBN 0-405-13304-9). Arno.

El-Shamy, Hasan M., ed. Folktales of Egypt. LC 79-9316. (Folktales of the World Ser.). 1980. lib. bdg. 25.00x (ISBN 0-226-20624-6). U of Chicago Pr.

Green, Roger L. Tales of Ancient Egypt. (gr. k-3). 1972. pap. 2.25 (ISBN 0-14-030438-X, Puffin). Penguin.

FOLK-LORE, ESKIMO

Garber, Clark M. Stories & Legends of the Bering Strait Eskimos. LC 74-5835. 260p. 1975. Repr. of 1940 ed. 24.50 (ISBN 0-404-11640-X). AMS Pr.

Hall, Edwin S., Jr. The Eskimo Storyteller: Folktales from Noatak, Alaska. LC 74-17304. (Illus.). 510p. 1975. 21.50x (ISBN 0-87049-160-1). U of Tenn Pr.

Rasmussen, Knud J. Intellectual Culture of the Copper Eskimos. LC 76-21675. (Thule Expedition, 5th, 1921-1924: No. 9). (Illus.). Repr. of 1932 ed. 74.50 (ISBN 0-404-58324-5). AMS Pr.

--Knud Rasmussen's Posthumous Notes on East Greenland Legends & Myths. Osterman, H., ed. LC 74-19913. Repr. of 1939 ed. 27.00 (ISBN 0-404-12296-5). AMS Pr.

--The Netsilik Eskimos. LC 76-21685. (Thule Expedition, 5th, 1921-1924: No. 8, Pts. 1-2). Repr. of 1931 ed. 105.00 (ISBN 0-404-58323-7). AMS Pr.

--Observations on the Intellectual Culture of the Caribou Eskimos. Bd. with Iglulik & Caribou Eskimo Texts. LC 76-22536. (The Fifth Thule Expedition: Vol. 7, No. 2 & No. 3). Repr. of 1930 ed. price not set (ISBN 0-404-58322-9). AMS Pr.

Thalbitzer, W. Legendes & Chants Esquimaux Du Groenland. LC 78-20152. (Collection de contes et de chansons populaires: Vol. 45). Repr. of 1929 ed. 21.50 (ISBN 0-404-60395-5). AMS Pr.

FOLK-LORE, EUROPEAN

Arrowsmith, Nancy & Moorse, George. A Field Guide to the Little People. 1978. pap. 3.95 (ISBN 0-671-79036-6, Wallaby). PB.

Bernheimer, Richard. Wild Men in the Middle Ages. LC 70-120229. 1970. Repr. lib. bdg. 15.50x (ISBN 0-374-90616-5). Octagon.

Bulfinch, Thomas. Bulfinch's Mythology: The Greek & Roman Fables Illustrated. Holme, Bryan, ed. (Illus.). 1979. 15.95 (ISBN 0-670-19464-6, Studio). Viking Pr.

Childers, J. Wesley. Motif-Index of the Cuentos of Juan Timoneda. Dorson, Richard M., ed. LC 80-791. (Folklore of the World Ser.). 1980. Repr. of 1948 ed. lib. bdg. 12.00x (ISBN 0-405-13330-8). Arno.

Cocchiara, Giuseppe. The History of Folklore in Europe. McDaniel, John N., tr. from Ital. LC 80-17823. (Translations in Folklore Studies Ser.). 1981. text ed. 24.00x (ISBN 0-915980-99-1). Inst Study Human.

Kelly, W. K. Curiosities of Indo-European Tradition & Folklore. 59.95 (ISBN 0-87968-977-3). Gordon Pr.

Kryptadia: Recueil de documents pour servir a l'etude des traditions populaires, Vols. 1-12. LC 70-547319. 1970. Repr. of 1883 ed. 375.00 set (ISBN 3-87561-063-6). Maledicta.

Learned, Marion D., ed. Saga of Walther of Aquitaine. Repr. of 1892 ed. lib. bdg. 15.00x (ISBN 0-8371-3903-1, LEWA). Greenwood.

Lockwood, Yvonne R. Yugoslav Folklore: An Annotated Bibliography of Contributions in English. LC 75-38305. 1976. softbound 8.00 (ISBN 0-88247-401-4). R & E Res Assoc.

Luthi, Max. The European Folktale: Form & Nature. Niles, John D., tr. from Ger. (Translations in Folklore Studies). 224p. 1981. text ed. 15.00x (ISBN 0-89727-024-X). Inst Study Human.

Rooth, Anna Birgitta. The Cinderella Cycle. Dorson, Richard M., ed. LC 80-748. (Folklore of the World Ser.). 1980. Repr. of 1951 ed. lib. bdg. 23.00x (ISBN 0-405-13322-7). Arno.

Seidler, Barbara. King Popiel & the Mice. (Young Peoples Ser.). 1976. pap. text ed. 1.00x (ISBN 0-917004-07-8). Kosciuszko.

FOLK-LORE, FILIPINO

Cole, F. C. Traditions of the Tinguian, a Study in Philippine Folk-Lore: The Tinguian Social Religious & Economic Life of a Philippine Tribe. (Chicago Field Museum of Natural History Fieldiana Anthropology Ser). Repr. of 1922 ed. pap. 35.00 (ISBN 0-527-01874-0). Kraus Repr.

Folktales from the Philippines. (Asian Folklore & Social Life Monographs: Vol. 97). 5.50 (ISBN 0-89986-320-5). E Langstaff.

Fuentes, Vilma M. & Edito T. De La Cruz, trs. A Treasury of Mandaya & Mansaka Folk Literature. (Illus.). 130p. (Mandaya, Mansaka.). 1980. 8.50 (ISBN 0-686-28808-4). Cellar.

Menez, Herminia Q. Folklore Communication Among Filipinos in California. Dorson, Richard M., ed. LC 80-733. (Folklore of the World Ser.). 1980. lib. bdg. 21.00x (ISBN 0-405-13320-0). Arno.

Norbeck, Edward. Folklore of the Atayal of Formosa & the Mountain Tribes of Luzon. (Anthropological Papers Ser.: No. 5). (Illus.). 1950. pap. 0.50x (ISBN 0-932206-18-2). U Mich Mus Anthro.

Pil, Teresita V. Philippine Folk Fiction & Tales. 1977. wrps. 5.75x (ISBN 0-686-09443-3). Cellar.

Rohmer, Harriet. Skyworld Woman: La Mujer del Mundo-Ciclo. LC 75-34917. (Fifth World Tales Ser.). (Illus.). (gr. k-6). pap. 3.95 spanish bilingual ed. (ISBN 0-89239-002-6, Imprents de Libros Infantiles). Childrens Book Pr.

FOLK-LORE, FINNISH

Kongas-Maranda, Elli Kaija. Finnish-American Folklore: Quantitative & Qualitative Analysis. Dorson, Richard M., ed. LC 80-732. (Folklore of the World Ser.). 1980. lib. bdg. 45.00x (ISBN 0-405-13319-7). Arno.

Moyne, Ernest J. Raising the Wind: The Legend of Lapland & Finland Wizards in Literature. Kime, Wayne R., ed. (Illus.). 224p. 1981. 18.50 (ISBN 0-87413-146-4). U Delaware Pr.

Synge, Ursula, ed. Land of Heroes: Re-Telling of the Kalevala. LC 77-14489. 224p. (gr. 5 up). 1978. 6.95 (ISBN 0-689-50094-7, McElderry Bk). Atheneum.

Taylor, Archer. The Black Ox: A Study in the History of a Folk-Tale. Dorson, Richard M., ed. LC 80-798. (Folklore of the World Ser.). 1980. Repr. of 1927 ed. lib. bdg. 12.00x (ISBN 0-405-13339-1). Arno.

Vuorela, T. An Atlas of Finnish Folk Culture. 162p. 1981. 55.00 (ISBN 951-717-099-8, Pub. by Findhorn-Thule Scotland). Hydra Bk.

Wilson, William A. Folklore & Nationalism in Modern Finland. LC 75-23895. (Illus.). 288p. 1976. 10.00x (ISBN 0-253-32327-4). Ind U Pr.

FOLK-LORE, FRENCH

Beauquier, C. Faune et flore populaires de Franche-Comte, 2 vols. in 1. LC 78-20142. (Collection de contes et de chansons populaires: Vols. 32-33). Repr. of 1910 ed. 43.00 (ISBN 0-404-60382-3). AMS Pr.

Carriere, Joseph M. Tales from the French Folk-Lore of Missouri. LC 79-128989. (Northwestern University. Humanities Ser.: No. 1). Repr. of 1937 ed. 19.00 (ISBN 0-404-50701-8). AMS Pr.

Delarue, Paul. The Borzoi Book of French Folk Tales. Dorson, Richard M., ed. LC 80-743. (Folklore of the World Ser.). (Illus.). 1980. Repr. of 1956 ed. lib. bdg. 39.00x (ISBN 0-405-13309-X). Arno.

Hassell, James W., Jr. Amorous Games: A Critical Edition of "les Adevineaux Amoureux". LC 73-21840. (American Folklore Society, Bibliographical & Special Ser.: Vol. 25). 312p. 1974. 15.00x (ISBN 0-292-70303-1). U of Tex Pr.

Henri, Gaidoz & Sebillot, Paul. Blason Populaire De la France: Blason Populaire from France. Dorson, Richard M., ed. LC 77-70595. (International Folklore Ser.). (Illus.). 1977. Repr. of 1884 ed. lib. bdg. 22.00x (ISBN 0-405-10093-0). Arno.

Johnson, W. Branch. Folktales of Normandy. (Folklore Ser.). 1929. 20.00 (ISBN 0-685-43831-7). Norwood Edns.
Johnson, William B. Folktales of Provence. LC 74-12479. 1974. Repr. of 1927 ed. lib. bdg. 22.50 (ISBN 0-8414-5304-7). Folcroft.
La Follette, James E. Etude Linguistique De Quatre Contes Folkloriques Du Canada Francais. (Folkloriques Du Canada Francais). 9.50x (ISBN 2-7637-6092-9, Pub. by Laval). Intl Schol Bk Serv.
Lang, Andrew. The Twelve Dancing Princesses. LC 66-10104. (Illus.). 48p. (gr. 1-3). 1980. pap. 2.95 (ISBN 0-03-057493-5). HR&W.
Le Braz, Anatole. Dealings with the Dead: Narratives from "La Legende de la mort en Basse Bretagne". Whitehead, E. A., tr. from Fr. LC 77-87695. Repr. of 1898 ed. 18.50 (ISBN 0-404-16491-9). AMS Pr.
Lubin, Leonard. The White Cat. (Illus.). (gr. 1-3). 1978. 7.95 (ISBN 0-316-53490-0). Little.
Marie-Ursule, Sr. Civilisation Traditionnelle des Lavalois. (Archives De Folklore Ser.: No. 5-6). (Fr). 1951. 10.00x (ISBN 2-7637-0020-9, Pub. by Laval). Intl Schol Bk Serv.
Massignon, Genevieve. Folktales of France. LC 68-14008. (Folktales of the World Ser). 1968. 12.00x (ISBN 0-226-50965-6). U of Chicago Pr.
Paterson, Diane, illus. Stone Soup. (Illus.). 32p. (gr. k-2). 1981. PLB 5.79 (ISBN 0-89375-478-1); pap. text ed. 1.50 (ISBN 0-89375-479-X). Troll Assocs.
Perot, F. Folk-Lore bourbonnais. LC 78-20141. (Collection de contes et de chansons populaires: Vol. 31). Repr. of 1908 ed. 21.50 (ISBN 0-404-60381-5). AMS Pr.
Perrault, Charles. Cinderella. LC 72-93811. (Illus.). 32p. (gr. k-3). 1973. 6.95 (ISBN 0-87888-056-9). Bradbury Pr.
--The Sleeping Beauty. Walker, David, tr. & illus. LC 76-22697. (Illus.). (gr. k-5). 1977. PLB 8.79 (ISBN 0-690-01279-9, TYC-J). Har-Row.
Pineau, L. Le Folk-Lore du Poitou. LC 78-20126. (Collection de contes et de chansons populaires: Vol. 18). Repr. of 1892 ed. 21.50 (ISBN 0-404-60368-8). AMS Pr.
Rolland. Faune Populaire de la France: Noms Vulgaires, Dictons, Proverbes, Legendes, Etc, 7 tomes. Set. 195.00 (ISBN 0-685-36689-8). French & Eur.
Sebillot. Le Folklore de la France, 4 tomes. Set. 148.75 (ISBN 0-685-34001-5). French & Eur.
Sebillot, Paul. Legendes et Curiosites des Metiers. Dorson, Richard M., ed. LC 80-749. (Folklore of the World Ser.). (Illus., Fr.). 1980. Repr. of 1895 ed. lib. bdg. 50.00x (ISBN 0-405-13323-5). Arno.
Thomas, Rosemary H. It's Good to Tell You: French Folk Tales from Missouri. LC 81-50530. 256p. 1981. text ed. 24.00 (ISBN 0-8262-0327-2). U of Mo Pr.

FOLK-LORE, GAELIC

Deeney, Daniel. Peasant Lore from Gaelic Ireland. 1978. 14.50 (ISBN 0-685-86826-5). Porter.
--Peasant Lore from Gaelic Ireland. LC 77-26163. 1978. Repr. of 1900 ed. lib. bdg. 10.00 (ISBN 0-8414-1866-7). Folcroft.
Dunn, Charles W. Highland Settler: A Portrait of the Scottish Gael in Nova Scotia. LC 53-7025. 1953. pap. 5.95 (ISBN 0-8020-6094-3). U of Toronto Pr.
Hyde, Douglas. Beside the Fire: A Collection of Irish Gaelic Folk Stories. LC 78-67719. (Folktale Ser.). Repr. of 1890 ed. 25.00 (ISBN 0-404-16096-4). AMS Pr.
Macnab, Iain. Nicht at Eeine. LC 73-22432. (Folklore Ser.). 1932. 6.50 (ISBN 0-685-43815-5). Norwood Edns.
O Crohan, Tomas. The Islandman. Flower, Robin, tr. (Illus.). 1951. pap. 4.50x (ISBN 0-19-281233-5). Oxford U Pr.

FOLK-LORE, GERMAN

Anglund, Joan W. Nibble Nibble Mousekin: A Tale of Hansel & Gretel. LC 62-14422. (Illus.). (gr. k-3). 1977. pap. 1.95 (ISBN 0-15-257404-2, VoyB). HarBraceJ.
Baumann, Kurt. The Pied Piper of Hamelin. LC 78-62168. (Illus.). (gr. k-4). 1979. 7.95 (ISBN 0-416-30521-0). Methuen Inc.
Borghart, Kees H. Das Nibelungenlied: Die Spuren Mundlichen Ursprungs in Schriftlicher Uberlieferung. (Amsterdamer Publikationen Zur Psrache und Literature Ser.: No. 31). (Orig., Ger.). 1979. pap. text ed. 25.75x (ISBN 90-6203-050-5). Humanities.
Brothers Grimm. The Fisherman & His Wife. Shub, Elizabeth, tr. from Ger. LC 78-8133. (Illus.). (gr. k-3). 1979. 9.50 (ISBN 0-688-86003-6). Greenwillow.
Carpenter, Inta G. A Latvian Storyteller: The Repertoire of Janis Plavnieks. Dorson, Richard M., ed. LC 80-725. (Folklore of the World Ser.). 1980. lib. bdg. 22.00x (ISBN 0-405-13306-5). Arno.
De Regniers, Beatrice S. Red Riding Hood. LC 79-175561. (Illus.). (ps-3). 1972. 5.95 (ISBN 0-689-30036-0). Atheneum.
Gauch, Patricia L. Once Upon a Dinkelsbuhl. LC 76-29356. (Illus.). (gr. k-4). 1977. 6.95 (ISBN 0-399-20560-8). Putnam.
Grimm Brothers. Hansel & Gretel. Crawford, Elizabeth D., tr. from Ger. LC 79-989. (Illus.). 25p. (gr. k-3). 1980. 7.95 (ISBN 0-688-22198-X); PLB 7.63 (ISBN 0-688-32198-4). Morrow.
--Twelve Dancing Princesses. LC 78-8578. (Illus.). (gr. k-3). 1978. 8.95 (ISBN 0-670-73358-X). Viking Pr.
Grimm, Jacob & Grimm, Wilhelm. The Brothers Grimm: Popular Folk Tales. LC 77-17748. (gr. 3-8). 1978. 9.95 (ISBN 0-385-14356-7). Doubleday.
--Deutsche Sagen: German Legends, 2 vols. in 1. Dorson, Richard M., ed. LC 77-70597. (Inter National Folklore Ser.). (Illus.). Repr. of 1891 ed. lib. bdg. 28.00x (ISBN 0-405-10097-3). Arno.
Hobzek, Mildred. We Came a-Marching... One, Two, Three. LC 78-7793. (Illus.). 40p. (ps-3). 1978. PLB 5.95 (ISBN 0-590-07720-1, Four Winds). Schol Bk Serv.
Manheim, Ralph, tr. Grimm's Tales for Young & Old: The Complete Stories. LC 76-56318. 1977. 14.95 (ISBN 0-385-11005-7). Doubleday.
Oppenheimer, Paul, tr. from Ger. A Pleasant Vintage of Till Eulenspiegel. LC 73-184361. (Illus.). 336p. 1972. 20.00x (ISBN 0-8195-4043-9, Pub. by Wesleyan U Pr). Columbia U Pr.
Otto, Svend S., illus. Tom Thumb. (Grimm's Fairy Tales). (Illus.). (gr. 2). 1976. PLB 4.95 (ISBN 0-88332-043-6, 8077). Larousse.
Sandbach, Francis E. Heroic Saga-Cycle of Dietrich of Bern. LC 71-139177. (Popular Studies in Mythology, Romance & Folklore: No. 15). Repr. of 1906 ed. 5.50 (ISBN 0-404-53515-1). AMS Pr.
Schorbach, Karl, ed. Parzifal von Claus Wisse und Philipp Colin (1331 bis 1336) Eine Ergaenzung der Dichtung Wolframs von Eschenbach. (Elsaessische Litteraturdenkmaeler aus dem 14. bis 17. Jahrhundert, Vol. 5). 441p. 1974. Repr. of 1888 ed. 79.50x (ISBN 3-11-002365-2). De Gruyter.
Schwebell, Gertrude C., ed. The Man Who Lost His Shadow, & Nine Other German Fairy Tales. (Illus.). 5.25 (ISBN 0-8446-5243-1). Peter Smith.
Van Woerkom, Dorothy. The Queen Who Couldn't Bake Gingerbread. LC 74-15302. (Illus.). 32p. (gr. k-3). 1975. PLB 5.99 (ISBN 0-394-93033-9). Knopf.
Wakeman, Alan. Hamun & Giben. 1978. 9.50 (ISBN 0-7045-0334-4). State Mutual Bk.

FOLK-LORE, GREEK

Halliday, William. Indo-European Folk-Tales & Greek Legend. LC 74-8748. 1933. 17.50 (ISBN 0-8414-4821-3). Folcroft.
Halliday, William R. Greek & Roman Folklore. LC 63-10289. (Our Debt to Greece & Rome Ser). Repr. of 1930 ed. 7.50x (ISBN 0-8154-0109-4). Cooper Sq.
Hyde, Walter W. Greek Religion & Its Survivals. LC 63-10268. (Our Debt to Greece & Rome Ser). 1963. Repr. of 1930 ed. 7.50x (ISBN 0-8154-0117-5). Cooper Sq.
Imam, Syed M. Folklore of Ancient Greece. 1976. pap. 2.00 (ISBN 0-89684-204-5). Orient Bk Dist.
Moffitt, Frederick J. Tales from Ancient Greece. LC 78-56059. (The World Folktale Library). (Illus.). 1979. lib. bdg. 7.65 (ISBN 0-686-50008-3). Silver.

FOLK-LORE, GREEK (MODERN)

Abbott, George F. Macedonian Folklore. LC 76-51722. 1977. Repr. of 1903 ed. lib. bdg. 40.00 (ISBN 0-8414-2957-X). Folcroft.
Geldart, Edmund M., ed. Folklore of Modern Greece. 1976. lib. bdg. 59.95 (ISBN 0-8490-1851-X). Gordon Pr.
Georges, Robert A. Greek-American Folk Beliefs & Narratives: Survivals & Living Tradition. Dorson, Richard M., ed. LC 80-727. (Folklore of the World Ser.). 1980. lib. bdg. 19.00x (ISBN 0-405-13314-6). Arno.
Gizelis, Gregory. Narrative Rhetorical Devices of Persuasion in the Greek Community of Philadelphia. Dorson, Richard M., ed. LC 80-728. (Folklore of the World Ser.). 1980. lib. bdg. 25.00x (ISBN 0-405-13315-4). Arno.
Legrand, E., tr. Recueil de contes populaires grecs. LC 78-20108. (Collection de contes et de chansons populaires: Vol. 1). Repr. of 1881 ed. 21.50 (ISBN 0-404-60351-3). AMS Pr.

FOLK-LORE, HAITIAN

Barton, Paule. The Woe Shirt. Norman, Howard, tr. from Creole. LC 80-81728. (Illus.). 64p. 1980. 12.50 (ISBN 0-915778-37-8); deluxe ed. 40.00x (ISBN 0-915778-36-X). Penmaen Pr.
Metraux, Alfred. Voodoo in Haiti. LC 77-185327. (Illus.). 1972. pap. 6.95 (ISBN 0-8052-0341-9). Schocken.
Wolkstein, Diane, ed. The Magic Orange Tree: And Other Haitian Folktales. LC 79-22787. (Illus.). 1980. pap. 5.95 (ISBN 0-8052-0650-7). Schocken.

FOLK-LORE, HAUSA

Besmer, Fremont E. Horses, Musicians & Gods: The Bori Cult. 256p. 1981. 35.00x (ISBN 0-89789-020-5). J F Bergin.
Rattray, Robert S., ed. Hausa Folk-Lore, Customs, Proverbs, Etc, 2 Vols. LC 71-79274. (Illus.). 1913. 26.00x (ISBN 0-8371-1464-0, Pub. by Negro U Pr). Greenwood.

FOLK-LORE, HAWAIIAN

Elbert, Samuel H., ed. Selections from Fornander's Hawaiian Antiquities & Folk-Lore. (Illus.). 297p. 1959. pap. 9.50x (ISBN 0-87022-213-9). U Pr of Hawaii.
Emerson, Nathaniel B. Unwritten Literature of Hawaii: The Sacred Songs of the Hula. LC 65-12971. (Illus.). 1965. Repr. pap. 4.95 (ISBN 0-8048-1067-2). C E Tuttle.
Green, Laura. Folktales from Hawaii. lib. bdg. 69.95 (ISBN 0-87968-521-2). Krishna Pr.
Judd, H. P. Hawaiian Proverbs & Riddles. Repr. of 1930 ed. 8.00 (ISBN 0-527-02183-0). Kraus Repr.
Thrum, Thomas G. Hawaiian Folk Tales: A Collection of Native Legends. LC 75-35211. (Illus.). Repr. of 1907 ed. 20.00 (ISBN 0-404-14234-6). AMS Pr.
--More Hawaiian Folk Tales: A Collection of Native Legends & Traditions. LC 75-35212. Repr. of 1923 ed. 28.50 (ISBN 0-404-14235-4). AMS Pr.
Westervelt, William D., ed. Hawaiian Legends of Ghosts & Ghost-Gods. LC 63-22543. (Illus.). 1963. 7.25 (ISBN 0-8048-0238-6). C E Tuttle.

FOLK-LORE, HUNGARIAN

Degh, Linda. People in the Tobacco Belt: Four Lives. Dorson, Richard M., ed. LC 80-792. (Folklore of the World Ser.). (Illus.). 1980. Repr. of 1975 ed. lib. bdg. 25.00x (ISBN 0-405-13331-6). Arno.
Domotor, Tekla. Hungarian Folk Customs. rev. 2nd ed. Elliot, Judith, tr. from Hungarian. LC 75-303594. (Illus.). 103p. (YA) 1977. 7.50x (ISBN 963-13-0164-8). Intl Pubns Serv.
Ortutay. Hungarian Folklore Essays. 1972. 30.00 (ISBN 0-9960005-3-4, Pub. by Kaido Hungary). Heyden.
Redei, K. Zyrian Folklore Texts. 1978. 66.00 (ISBN 0-9960010-2-6, Pub. by Kaido Hungary). Heyden.

FOLK-LORE, INDIAN

Here are entered works on the folk-lore of the American Indians; Collections of Indan tales, legends, or myths are entered under Indians of North America–Legends; Indians of South America–Legends; etc.
see also Totems

Adamson, T., ed. Folk-Tales of the Coast Salish. LC 36-2204. (American Folklore Society Memoirs Ser). Repr. of 1934 ed. 25.00 (ISBN 0-527-01079-0). Kraus Repr.
Applegate, Frank G. Indian Stories from the Pueblos. LC 78-150965. (Beautiful Rio Grande Classics Ser). (Illus.). 1977. 10.00 (ISBN 0-87380-076-1). Rio Grande.
Beauchamp, William M. Iroquois Folk Lore Gathered from the Six Nations of New York. LC 64-8788. (Empire State Historical Publications: No. 31). 1975. Repr. of 1922 ed. 10.00 (ISBN 0-8046-8031-0). Kennikat.
Benedict, Ruth. Tales of the Cochiti Indians. Repr. of 1931 ed. 25.00 (ISBN 0-403-03705-0). Scholarly.
Bierhorst, John, ed. The Girl Who Married a Ghost & Other Tales from the North American Indian. LC 77-21515. (Illus.). (gr. 5 up). 1978. 10.95 (ISBN 0-590-07505-5, Four Winds). Schol Bk Serv.
Boas, Franz. Bella Bella Texts. (Columbia Univ. Contributions to Anthropology Ser.: No. 5). Repr. of 1928 ed. 24.00 (ISBN 0-404-50555-4). AMS Pr.
Boatright, Mody C., ed. The Sky Is My Tipi. LC 49-1690. (Texas Folklore Society Publications: No. 22). (Illus.). 1966. Repr. of 1949 ed. 6.95 (ISBN 0-87074-010-5). SMU Press.
Boy Scouts Of America. Indian Lore. LC 19-600. (Illus.). 96p. (gr. 6-12). 1959. pap. 0.70x (ISBN 0-8395-3358-6, 3358). BSA.
Brinton, D. G. Myths of the New World: A Treatise on the Symbolism & Mythology of the Red Race of America. LC 68-24972. (American History & Americana Ser., No. 47). 1969. Repr. of 1876 ed. lib. bdg. 49.95 (ISBN 0-8383-0918-6). Haskell.
Brinton, Daniel G. The Myths of the New World. LC 71-144901. 331p. 1972. Repr. of 1876 ed. 10.00 (ISBN 0-403-00839-5). Scholarly.
--Myths of the New World: A Treatise on the Symbolism & Mythology of the Red Race of America. 2nd ed. LC 69-13839. 1969. Repr. of 1876 ed. lib. bdg. 15.00x (ISBN 0-8371-2040-3, BRMN). Greenwood.
--Myths of the New World: The Symbolism & Mythology of the Indians of the Americas. LC 72-81594. (Illus.). 348p. 1976. 7.50 (ISBN 0-8334-1742-8, Steinerbooks). Multimedia.
Bruchac, Joseph. Stone Giants & Flying Heads, Adventure Stories from the Iroquois. LC 78-15556. (Children's Stories Ser.). (Illus.). (gr. 5-12). 1979. 6.95 (ISBN 0-89594-006-X); pap. 3.95 (ISBN 0-89594-007-8). Crossing Pr.
Callaway, S. M., et al. Grandfather Stories of the Navajos. LC 68-57898. 77p. pap. 4.50 (ISBN 0-89019-006-2). Navajo Curr.
Carroll, Raymonde. Nukuoro Stories. (Nukuoro Texts Ser.: Vol. 1). 1980. pap. 22.00 (ISBN 0-8357-0551-X, IS-00118, Pub. by U of Mich Pr). Univ Microfilms.
Choate, F. The Indian Fairy Book: From the Original Legends. 1977. lib. bdg. 59.95 (ISBN 0-8490-2053-0). Gordon Pr.
Clark, La Verne H. They Sang for Horses: The Impact of the Horse on Navajo & Apache Folklore. LC 66-18527. (Illus.). 1966. pap. 9.95 (ISBN 0-8165-0091-6). U of Ariz Pr.
Coffer, William E. Where Is the Eagle? 288p. 1981. 16.95 (ISBN 0-442-26163-2). Van Nos Reinhold.
Coffin, Tristram P., ed. Indian Tales of North America: An Anthology for the Adult Reader. LC 61-11866. (American Folklore Soc. Bibliographical & Special Ser.: No. 13). 175p. 1961. pap. 5.95x (ISBN 0-292-73506-5). U of Tex Pr.
Curtis, Natalie. Indians' Book. rev. ed. (Illus.). 1968. pap. 10.00 (ISBN 0-486-21939-9). Dover.
Cushing, Frank H. Zuni Folk Tales. 1977. lib. bdg. 59.95 (ISBN 0-8490-2858-2). Gordon Pr.
De Angulo, Jaime. Indian Tales. (Illus.). 245p. 1962. pap. 3.45 (ISBN 0-8090-0049-0, AmCen). Hill & Wang.
Eastman, Mary. Dahcotah: Or, Life & Legends of the Sioux Around Fort Snelling. facsimile ed. LC 75-95. (Mid-American Frontier Ser.). (Illus.). 1975. Repr. of 1849 ed. 18.00x (ISBN 0-405-06861-1). Arno.
Fletcher, Alice C. Indian Story & Song from North America. LC 76-136396. Repr. of 1900 ed. 9.50 (ISBN 0-404-07880-X). AMS Pr.
Frachtenberg, Leo J. Lower Umpqua Texts & Notes on the Kusan Dialects. LC 72-82341. (Columbia Univ. Contributions to Anthropology Ser.: Vol. 4). 1969. Repr. of 1914 ed. 16.50 (ISBN 0-404-50554-6). AMS Pr.
Gringhuis, Dirk. Lore of the Great Turtle: Indian Legends of Mackinac Retold. LC 73-636148. (Illus.). 96p. (Orig.). 1970. pap. 2.50 (ISBN 0-911872-11-6). Mackinac Island.
Grinnell, George B. Blackfoot Lodge Tales: The Story of a Prairie People. LC 62-4146. 1962. pap. 5.95 (ISBN 0-8032-5079-7, BB 129, Bison). U of Nebr Pr.
--Pawnee Hero Stories & Folktales with Notes on the Origin, Customs & Character of the Pawnee People. LC 61-10153. (Illus.). xiv, 417p. 1961. 21.50x (ISBN 0-8032-0896-0); pap. 7.50 (ISBN 0-8032-5080-0, BB 116, Bison). U of Nebr Pr.
How the Horses Came to Ha'a'ninin: The Boy. 1980. 5.45 (ISBN 0-89992-081-0); pap. 1.95 (ISBN 0-89992-082-9). MT Coun Indian.
Hunt, Ben. Indian Crafts & Lore. 1976. PLB 10.69 (ISBN 0-307-60581-7, Golden Pr); pap. 2.95 (ISBN 0-307-15989-2). Western Pub.
Jacobs, Joseph. Indian Fairy Tales. (Illus.). (ps-4). 1969. pap. 3.50 (ISBN 0-486-21828-7). Dover.
--Indian Fairy Tales. (Illus.). 7.50 (ISBN 0-8446-0723-1). Peter Smith.
Jacobs, Melville. Content & Style of an Oral Literature: Clackamas Chinook Myths & Tales. LC 58-5617. 1959. 12.00x (ISBN 0-226-38973-1). U of Chicago Pr.
--Northwest Sahaptin Texts, 2 Pts. LC 70-82338. (Columbia Univ. Contributions to Anthropology Ser.: Vol. 19). Repr. of 1937 ed. Set. 36.00 (ISBN 0-404-50569-4); 18.00 ea. Vol. 1 (ISBN 0-404-50590-2). Vol. 2 (ISBN 0-404-50591-0). AMS Pr.
Jagendorf, Moritz A. Tales from the First Americans. LC 78-56057. (The World Folktale Library). (Illus.). 1979. lib. bdg. 7.65 (ISBN 0-686-51164-6). Silver.
Leland, Charles G. Algonquin Legends of New England. LC 68-31217. 1968. Repr. of 1884 ed. 26.00 (ISBN 0-8103-3468-2). Gale.
Levi-Strauss, Claude. From Honey to Ashes. (Science of Mythology Ser.). 1980. Repr. of 1973 ed. lib. bdg. 25.00x (ISBN 0-374-94952-2). Octagon.
McDermott, Gerald. Arrow to the Sun: A Pueblo Indian Tale. (Picture Puffin Ser.). (Illus.). (gr. 1 up). 1977. pap. 2.50 (ISBN 0-14-050211-4, Puffin). Penguin.
McElwain, Thomas. Mythological Tales & the Allegany Seneca: A Study of the Socio-Religious Context of Traditional Oral Phenomena in an Iroquois Community. (Stockholm Studies in Comparative Religion Ser.: No. 17). 1978. pap. text ed. 17.75x (ISBN 91-22-00181-6). Humanities.

Menendez, Enrique C. Only the Wind. Armas, Jose, ed. Hernandez, Frances, tr. from Span. (Illus.). 182p. 1980. 9.00 (ISBN 0-918358-05-1); pap. 7.00 (ISBN 0-686-64685-1). Pajarito Pubns.
Mooney, James. Myths of the Cherokee. LC 70-108513. (American Indian History Sers). 1970. Repr. of 1900 ed. 59.00 (ISBN 0-403-00221-4). Scholarly.
Myles, Colette G., ed. The Butterflies Carried Him Home & Other Indian Tales. (Illus.). 65p. 1981. 5.00 (ISBN 0-9605468-1-2). Artmans Pr.
Norman, Howard, tr. Where the Chill Came from: Cree Windigo Tales & Journeys. LC 81-81506. (Illus.). 176p. 1982. 15.00 (ISBN 0-86547-047-2); pap. 7.50 (ISBN 0-86547-048-0). N Point Pr.
Paul, Paula. Geronimo Chino. 1980. 7.95 (ISBN 0-89992-079-9); pap. 4.45 (ISBN 0-89992-080-2). MT Coun Indian.
Piper. Stories from Ugidali: Cherokee Story Teller. 1981. pap. 1.95 (ISBN 0-89992-078-0). MT Coun Indian.
Radin, Paul. Literary Aspects of North American Mythology. 51p. 1980. Repr. of 1915 ed. lib. bdg. 10.00 (ISBN 0-8495-4642-7). Arden Lib.
Rice, Stanley. Ancient Indian Fables & Stories. 1978. Repr. of 1924 ed. lib. bdg. 20.00 (ISBN 0-8492-2395-4). R West.
Roth, Walter E. An Inquiry into the Animism & Folklore of the Guiana Indians. LC 16-9897. (Landmarks in Anthropology Ser). Repr. of 1915 ed. 19.50 (ISBN 0-384-52130-4). Johnson Repr.
Salomon, J. H. The Book of Indian Crafts & Indian Lore. 1977. lib. bdg. 69.95 (ISBN 0-8490-1531-6). Gordon Pr.
Savitri. Tales from Indian Classics: Book I. (Illus.). (gr. 3-9). 1979. 3.00 (ISBN 0-89744-167-2). Auromere.
--Tales from Indian Classics: Book II. (Illus.). (gr. 3-9). 1979. 3.00 (ISBN 0-89744-168-0). Auromere.
--Tales from Indian Classics: Part III. (Illus.). (gr. 3-9). 1979. 3.00 (ISBN 0-89744-169-9). Auromere.
Shankar. Treasury of Indian Tales: Book I. 1979. 3.50 (ISBN 0-89744-170-2). Auromere.
--Treasury of Indian Tales: Book II. 1979. 3.50 (ISBN 0-89744-171-0). Auromere.
Skinner, Alanson B. & Satterlee, John V. Folklore of the Menomini Indians. LC 76-43832. (AMNH. Anthropological Papers: Vol. 13, Pt. 3). Repr. of 1915 ed. 22.00 (ISBN 0-404-15684-3). AMS Pr.
Spencer, Katherine. Reflections of Social Life in the Navaho Origin Myth. LC 76-43850. (Univ. of New Mexico. Publications in Anthropology: No. 3). Repr. of 1947 ed. 13.00 (ISBN 0-404-15705-X). AMS Pr.
Swanton, John R. Haida Texts & Myths: Skidegate Dialect. LC 5-41613. (Landmarks in Anthropology Ser). Repr. of 1905 ed. pap. 28.00 (ISBN 0-384-59020-9). Johnson Repr.
Thompson, Stith, ed. Tales of the North American Indians. LC 66-22898. (Midland Bks.: No. 91). (Illus.). 416p. 1966. pap. 3.95x (ISBN 0-253-20091-1). Ind U Pr.
Trowbridge, C. C. Meearmeear Traditions. Kinietz, Vernon, ed. (Occasional Contributions Ser.: No. 7). (Illus.). 1938. pap. 1.00x (ISBN 0-932206-02-6). U Mich Mus Anthro.
Wade, Mary H. Indian Fairy Tales As Told to the Little Children of the Wigwam. LC 78-74523. (Children's Literature Reprint Ser.). (Illus.). (gr. 4-8). 1979. Repr. of 1906 ed. 21.75x (ISBN 0-8486-0225-0). Core Collection.
White, Elizabeth, pseud. The Sun Girl. LC 78-67324. (Special Publications Ser.). (Illus.). 1978. Repr. of 1941 ed. 4.75 (ISBN 0-89734-046-9). Mus Northern Ariz.
Wilbert, Johannes, ed. Folk Literature of the Selknam Indians: Martin Gusinde's Collection of Selknam Narratives. LC 75-620083. (Latin American Studies: Vol. 32). (Illus.). 266p. 1975. pap. text ed. 9.95 (ISBN 0-87903-032-1). UCLA Lat Am Ctr.

FOLK-LORE, INDIC

Abbott, John. The Keys of Power: A Study of Indian Ritual & Belief. 1974. 10.00 (ISBN 0-8216-0219-5). Univ Bks.
Bahadur, K. P., tr. The Parrot & the Starling. (UNESCO Collection of Representative Works: Indian Ser). 1977. text ed. 21.00x (ISBN 0-8426-1034-0). Verry.
Chaudhury, Bani R. Folk Tales of Rajasthan. LC 72-906833. (Folk Tales of India Ser.: No. 9). 120p. 1972. 3.75x (ISBN 0-8002-0634-7). Intl Pubns Serv.
Chaudhury, P. Roy. Folk Tales of India, 21 vols. (Illus.). 1975. Set. 73.50 (ISBN 0-86578-007-2). Ind-US Inc.
Cowell, E. B. The Jataka; or Stories of the Buddha's Former Births, 3 vols. Repr. of 1895 ed. 21.00x ea. Vol. 1, 1973 (ISBN 0-8002-1612-1). Vol. 2, 1973 (ISBN 0-8002-1613-X). Vol. 3, 1979, Repr. Of 1901 Ed (ISBN 0-8002-1614-8). Intl Pubns Serv.
Crooke, William. Religion & Folklore of Northern India. LC 72-900287. (Illus.). 471p. 1972. Repr. of 1926 ed. 21.50x (ISBN 0-8002-1915-5). Intl Pubns Serv.
Crouch, Marcus. The Ivory City: And Other Stories from India & Pakistan. (Illus.). 192p. (gr. 3-7). 1981. 11.95 (ISBN 0-7207-1188-6, Pub. by Michael Joseph). Merrimack Bk Serv.
Dorson, Richard M., ed. Tales of the Sun: Folklore of Southern India. LC 77-70604. (International Folklore Ser.). 1977. Repr. of 1890 ed. lib. bdg. 18.00x (ISBN 0-405-10103-1). Arno.
Duff, Maggie. Rum Pum Pum. LC 77-12389. (ps-3). 1978. 8.95 (ISBN 0-02-732950-X, 73295). Macmillan.
Elwin, Verrier. Folk-Tales of Mahakoshal. Dorson, Richard M., ed. LC 80-745. (Folklore of the World Ser.). 1980. Repr. of 1944 ed. lib. bdg. 50.00x (ISBN 0-405-13311-1). Arno.
--Tribal Myths of Orissa. Dorson, Richard M., ed. LC 80-746. (Folklore of the World Ser.). 1980. Repr. of 1954 ed. lib. bdg. 65.00x (ISBN 0-405-13312-X). Arno.
Emeneau, Murray B. Kota Texts, 2 vols. in 1. LC 78-67707. (The Folktale). 31.50 (ISBN 0-404-16084-0). AMS Pr.
Frere, Mary E. Old Deccan Days. LC 78-67710. (The Folktale). Repr. of 1868 ed. 28.00 (ISBN 0-404-16087-5). AMS Pr.
Gray, J. E. Indian Tales & Legends. (Myths & Legends Ser.). (gr. 6-12). 1979. Repr. 10.95 (ISBN 0-19-274113-6). Oxford U Pr.
Jacob, K. Folk Tales of Kerala. 275p. 1972. 3.75x (ISBN 0-8002-0632-0). Intl Pubns Serv.
Jacobs, Joseph. Indian Fairy Tales. 59.95 (ISBN 0-8490-0396-2). Gordon Pr.
Kelly, W. K. Curiosities of Indo-European Tradition & Folklore. 59.95 (ISBN 0-87968-977-3). Gordon Pr.
Narayan, R. K. The Ramayana of R. K. Narayan: A Shortened Modern Prose Version of the Indian Epic, Suggested by the Tamil Version of Kamban. LC 79-189514. (Illus.). 192p. 1972. 7.95 (ISBN 0-670-58950-0). Viking Pr.
Natesa Sastri, Sangendi M. Folklore in Southern India, 3 vols. in 1. LC 78-63212. (The Folktale). Repr. of 1888 ed. 26.50 (ISBN 0-404-16148-0). AMS Pr.
Nilakantha. The Elephant-Lore of the Hindus: The Elephant-Sport (Matanga-Lila) of Nilakantha. Edgerton, Franklin, ed. 1931. 32.50x (ISBN 0-686-50042-3). Elliots Bks.
Pakrasi, M. Folk Tales of Assam, Vol. 3. Chaudhury, P. C., ed. (Folk Tales of India Ser.). (Illus.). 1970. 3.50x (ISBN 0-8426-0109-0). Verry.
Penzer, Norman M. Poisen-Damsels & Other Essays in Folklore & Anthropology. Dorson, Richard M., ed. LC 80-669. (Folklore of the World Ser.). 1980. Repr. of 1952 ed. lib. bdg. 27.00x (ISBN 0-405-13336-7). Arno.
Ratnatunga, Manel. Folk Tales of Sri Lanka. (Folk Tales of the World). (Illus.). 119p. 1979. 6.50x (ISBN 0-8002-1007-7). Intl Pubns Serv.
Rice, Stanley P. Ancient Indian Fables & Stories. LC 74-12477. 1974. Repr. of 1924 ed. lib. bdg. 17.50 (ISBN 0-8414-7329-3). Folcroft.
Seethalakshami, K. A. Folk Tales of Himachal Pradesh. (Folk Tales of India Ser.: No. 8). 120p. 1972. 3.75x (ISBN 0-8002-0633-9). Intl Pubns Serv.
Shanta. Nala Damayanti. (Illus.). (gr. 1-9). 1979. pap. 2.00 (ISBN 0-89744-158-3). Auromere.
Stamler, Suzanne. Three Wise Birds. (Jataka Tales for Children Ser.). (Illus.). (gr. 1-6). 1976. pap. write for info. (ISBN 0-913546-68-2). Dharma Pub.
Stutley, Margaret. Ancient Indian Magic & Folklore: An Introduction. LC 79-13211. (Illus.). 1980. 18.50 (ISBN 0-87773-712-6). Great Eastern.
Thomas, Vernon, ed. Folk Tales from India. (Illus.). (gr. 3-10). 1979. 6.25 (ISBN 0-89744-141-9). Auromere.
Vatuk, Ved Prakash. Studies in Indian Folk Traditions. 1979. 13.00x (ISBN 0-8364-0370-3). South Asia Bks.

FOLK-LORE, INDIC-INDEXES

Thompson, Stith & Balys, Jonas. The Oral Tales of India. LC 76-134. (Indiana University Publications - Folklore Series: No. 10). 448p. 1976. Repr. of 1958 ed. lib. bdg. 34.25x (ISBN 0-8371-8739-7, THOT). Greenwood.

FOLK-LORE, IRISH

Andrews, Elizabeth. Ulster Folklore. LC 74-13592. 1974. Repr. of 1913 ed. lib. bdg. 8.50 (ISBN 0-88305-006-4). Norwood Edns.
--Ulster Folklore. 1978. Repr. of 1913 ed. lib. bdg. 20.00 (ISBN 0-8495-0113-X). Arden Lib.
Bourne, Eleanor. The Heritage of Flowers. (The Leprechaun Library). (Illus.). 64p. 1980. 3.95 (ISBN 0-399-12544-2). Putnam.
Brown, Arthur C. Origin of the Grail Legend. LC 65-17878. 1966. Repr. of 1943 ed. 14.00 (ISBN 0-8462-0655-2). Russell.
Christiansen, Reider T. Studies in Irish & Scandinavian Folktales. Dorson, Richard M., ed. LC 80-741. (Folklore of the World Ser.). 1980. Repr. of 1959 ed. lib. bdg. 23.00x (ISBN 0-405-13307-3). Arno.
Colum, Padraic, ed. Treasury of Irish Folklore. rev. ed. (YA) (gr. 9 up). 1969. 9.95 (ISBN 0-517-50294-1). Crown.
Conglinne, Aislinge M. The Vision of McConglinne: A Middle-Irish Wonder Tale. Meyer, Kuno, ed. 212p. 1973. Repr. of 1892 ed. 15.00 (ISBN 0-685-26067-4). Lemma.
Croker, Thomas C. Fairy Legends & Traditions of the South of Ireland, 1825-1828. 1971. text ed. 27.50x (ISBN 0-87696-012-3). Humanities.
Curtin, Jeremiah. Myths & Folk-Lore of Ireland. 1976. Repr. 18.00x (ISBN 0-7158-1090-1). Charles River Bks.
--Myths & Folk Tales of Ireland. LC 69-18206. 256p. 1975. pap. 3.00 (ISBN 0-486-22430-9). Dover.
--Tales of the Fairies & the Ghost-World. LC 75-152760. Repr. of 1895 ed. 14.00 (ISBN 0-405-08416-1, Blom Pubns). Arno.
Danachair, Caoimhin O. A Bibliography of Irish Ethnology & Folk Tradition. 2nd ed. 1978. 32.00 (ISBN 0-85342-490-X). Irish Bk Ctr.
Danaher, Kevin. Folktales of the Irish Countryside. (Illus.). (gr. 5-9). 1970. 4.95 (ISBN 0-87250-242-2); PLB 4.76 (ISBN 0-87250-440-9). D White.
--The Year in Ireland: A Calendar. (Illus.). 1977. pap. 8.95 (ISBN 0-85342-280-X). Irish Bk Ctr.
Deeney, Daniel. Peasant Lore from Gaelic Ireland. 1978. 14.50 (ISBN 0-685-86826-5). Porter.
Fox, Charlotte M. Annals of the Irish Harpers. (Illus.). 320p. 1973. Repr. of 1911 ed. 17.50 (ISBN 0-87696-044-1). Lemma.
Gmelch, George & Kroup, Ben. To Shorten the Road: Traveller Folktales from Ireland. (Illus.). 1978. text ed. 12.50x (ISBN 0-7705-1499-5). Humanities.
Gregory, Isabella A. Irish Folk History Plays, 2 Vols. LC 70-145063. 1971. Repr. of 1912 ed. 39.50 (ISBN 0-403-01006-3). Scholarly.
Gregory, Lady. Cuchulain of Muirthemhe: The Story of the Men of the Red Branch of Ulster. 5th ed. (Coole Edition of the Collected Works of Lady Gregory Ser.). 1970. 17.95x (ISBN 0-19-519477-2). Oxford U Pr.
--Cuchulain of Muirthemne: The Story of the Men of the Red Branch of Ulster Arranged & Put into English. (Coole Edition of the Collected Works of Lady Gregory Ser.: Vol. 2). 272p. 1970. pap. 6.95x (ISBN 0-19-519739-9). Oxford U Pr.
--Kiltartan Books. (Coole Edition of the Collected Works of Lady Gregory Ser.). (Illus.). 1971. 12.00x (ISBN 0-19-519684-8). Oxford U Pr.
--Visions & Beliefs in the West of Ireland. (Coole Edition of the Collected Works of Lady Gregory Ser.: Vol. 1). (Illus.). 1970. 11.25x (ISBN 0-19-519479-9). Oxford U Pr.
Hyde, Douglas. Beside the Fire: A Collection of Irish Gaelic Folk Stories. LC 78-67719. (Folktale Ser.). Repr. of 1890 ed. 25.00 (ISBN 0-404-16096-4). AMS Pr.
Hyde, Douglas, ed. & tr. The Stone of Truth & Other Irish Folk Tales. 126p. 1979. 10.00x (ISBN 0-8476-6232-2). Rowman.
Kelly, Eamon. Bless Me Father. 1977. pap. 3.95 (ISBN 0-85342-489-6). Irish Bk Ctr.
Kennedy, Patrick. Legendary Fictions of the Irish Celts. LC 68-25518. 1968. Repr. of 1866 ed. 22.00 (ISBN 0-8103-3467-4). Gale.
Kiberd, Declan. Synge & the Irish Language. 294p. 1979. 25.00x (ISBN 0-8476-6159-8). Rowman.
Larminie, William, compiled by. West Irish Folk-Tales & Romances. LC 72-4191. (Select Bibliographies Reprint Ser.). 1972. Repr. of 1893 ed. 17.00 (ISBN 0-8369-6888-3). Arno.
MacCumaill, Finn. Fianaigecht. LC 78-72614. (Royal Irish Academy. Todd Lecture Ser.: Vol. 16). Repr. of 1910 ed. 17.00 (ISBN 0-404-60576-1). AMS Pr.
MacDougall, James. Highland Fairy Legends. Calder, George, ed. (Illus.). 117p. 1978. Repr. of 1910 ed. 11.50x (ISBN 0-8476-6041-9). Rowman.
MacManus, D. A. The Middle Kingdom: The Faerie World of Ireland. 1973. pap. text ed. 6.75x (ISBN 0-900675-82-9). Humanities.
MacManus, Diarmuid. Irish Earth Folk. (Illus.). 1959. 6.95 (ISBN 0-8159-5814-5). Devin.
MacManus, Seumas. Donegal Fairy Stories. (Illus.). 6.00 (ISBN 0-8446-2507-8). Peter Smith.
Messenger, Betty. Picking Up the Linen Threads: A Study in Industrial Folklore. LC 77-17978. (Illus.). 287p. 1978. 15.95x (ISBN 0-292-76446-4); pap. 9.95x (ISBN 0-292-76462-6). U of Tex Pr.
Meyer, Kuno, ed. The Death Tales of the Ulster Heroes. LC 78-72612. (Royal Irish Academy. Todd Lecture Ser.: Vol. 14). Repr. 14.50 (ISBN 0-404-60574-5). AMS Pr.
O'Hanlon, John. Irish Folk Lore. LC 76-24888. 1976. Repr. of 1870 ed. lib. bdg. 30.00 (ISBN 0-8414-6536-3). Folcroft.
O'Rahilly, Thomas F. A Miscellany of Irish Proverbs. LC 77-5333. 1977. lib. bdg. 25.00 (ISBN 0-8414-6541-X). Folcroft.
O'Suilleabhain, Sean. Handbook of Irish Folklore. LC 73-129100. 1970. Repr. of 1942 ed. 30.00 (ISBN 0-8103-3561-1). Gale.
O'Suilleabhean, Sean. Irish Folk Custom & Belief. 2nd ed. (Irish Life & Culture Ser.). (Illus.). 1977. pap. 3.50 (ISBN 0-85342-146-3). Irish Bk Ctr.
O'Sullivan, Jean. The Folklore of Ireland. (Illus.). 1975. 8.95 (ISBN 0-8038-2304-5). Hastings.
O'Sullivan, Sean. The Folklore of Ireland. 1974. 19.95 (ISBN 0-7134-2803-1, Pub. by Batsford England). David & Charles.
Rodway, Avril. A Literary Herbal. (The Leprechaun Library). (Illus.). 64p. 1980. 3.95 (ISBN 0-399-12545-0). Putnam.
Ryan, Meda. Biddy Early-the Wise Woman of Clare. 1978. pap. 3.95 (ISBN 0-85342-551-5). Irish Bk Ctr.
Sonntag, Linda. Eggs. (The Leprechaun Library). 64p. 1980. 3.95 (ISBN 0-399-12543-4). Putnam.
Spalding, Henry D. The Lilt of the Irish--an Encyclopedia of Irish Humor & Lore. LC 77-24307. 1978. 12.95 (ISBN 0-8246-0218-8). Jonathan David.
Tymoczko, Maria, tr. Two Death Tales: from the Ulster Cycle: The Death of Cu Roi & the Death of Cu Chulainn. (Dolmen Texts: No. 2). 1980. text ed. 21.25x (ISBN 0-85105-342-4, Dolmen Pr). Humanities.
Wilde, William. Irish Popular Superstitions. 140p. 1973. Repr. of 1852 ed. 10.00x (ISBN 0-87471-154-1). Rowman.
Wood-Martin, W. G. Traces of the Elder Faiths of Ireland, 2 Vols. LC 70-102631. (Irish Culture & History Ser). 1970. Repr. of 1902 ed. Set. 40.00x (ISBN 0-8046-0807-5). Kennikat.
Yeats, W. B., ed. Fairy & Folk Tales of Ireland. 1980. text ed. 11.50x (ISBN 0-900675-59-4). Humanities.
--Representative Irish Tales. 1979. text ed. 23.50x (ISBN 0-391-00987-7); pap. text ed. 8.25x (ISBN 0-391-00988-5). Humanities.
Yeats, William B. Irish Fairy & Folk Tales. LC 76-42706. Repr. of 1918 ed. 26.50 (ISBN 0-404-15376-3). AMS Pr.
Yeats, William B., ed. Fairy & Folk Tales of the Irish Peasantry. 416p. 1973. 12.95 (ISBN 0-02-632640-X). Macmillan.

FOLK-LORE, ITALIAN

Basile, Giovanni B. The Pentamerone of Giambattista Basile, 2 vols. Penzer, N. M., ed. Croce, Benedetto, tr. from It. LC 75-136519. (Illus.). Repr. of 1932 ed. lib. bdg. 55.00x (ISBN 0-8371-5438-3, BAPE). Greenwood.
Calvino, Italo. Italian Folktales. 1981. pap. 9.95 (ISBN 0-394-74909-X). Pantheon.
Clerk, E. M. Fable & Song in Italy. LC 74-9812. 1899. 25.00 (ISBN 0-8414-3509-X). Folcroft.
De Paola, Tomie. The Legend of Old Befana. LC 80-12293. (Illus.). 32p. (gr. k-3). 1980. pap. 3.95 (ISBN 0-15-243817-3, VoyB). HarBraceJ.
--The Legend of Old Befana. LC 80-12293. (Illus.). 32p. (gr. k-3). 1980. 8.95 (ISBN 0-15-243816-5, HJ). HarBraceJ.
Falassi, Alessandro. Folklore by the Fireside: Text & Context of the Tuscan "Vegelia". LC 79-11903. (Illus.). 399p. 1980. 15.00x (ISBN 0-292-72430-6). U of Tex Pr.
Leland, Charles G. Legends of Florence, 2 Vols. LC 68-27173. 1969. Repr. of 1895 ed. 19.00 ea. Vol. 1, First Ser (ISBN 0-8103-3843-2). Vol. 2, Second Ser. (ISBN 0-8103-3844-0); Set. write for info. (ISBN 0-8103-3899-8). Gale.
--Legends of Florence. 1976. lib. bdg. 59.95 (ISBN 0-8490-2146-4). Gordon Pr.
Pitre, Giuseppe. Bibliografia delle Tradizioni Popolari D'italia, Contre Indici Speciali. LC 72-82380. xx, 603p. 1972. Repr. of 1894 ed. lib. bdg. 43.50 (ISBN 0-8337-2775-3). B Franklin.
Salomone-Marino, Salvatore. Customs & Habits of the Sicilian Peasants. Norris, Rosalie N., ed. & tr. from It. LC 80-65583. (Illus.). 256p. 1981. 19.50 (ISBN 0-8386-3010-3). Fairleigh Dickinson.
Spalding, Henry, ed. Joys of Italian Humor & Folklore. LC 80-13750. 360p. 1980. 16.95 (ISBN 0-8246-0255-2). Jonathan David.

FOLK-LORE, JAMAICAN

Beckwith, Martha W. Black Roadways: A Study of Jamaican Folk Life. LC 69-16597. (Illus.). Repr. of 1929 ed. 17.75x (ISBN 0-8371-1144-7, Pub. by Negro U Pr). Greenwood.
--Jamaica Folk-Lore. LC 30-18643. Repr. of 1928 ed. 20.00 (ISBN 0-527-01073-1). Kraus Repr.
Smith, Pamela C. Annancy Stories. LC 78-63221. (The Folktale). Repr. of 1899 ed. 14.50 (ISBN 0-404-16158-8). AMS Pr.

FOLK-LORE, JAPANESE

Ballard, Susan. Fairy Tales from Far Japan. lib. bdg. 59.95 (ISBN 0-87968-477-1). Krishna Pr.
Brenner, Barbara. Little One Inch. (Illus.). 32p. (ps-3). 1977. 6.95 (ISBN 0-698-20408-5). Coward.
Chiba, Reiko. Seven Lucky Gods of Japan. LC 65-25467. (Illus.). 1966. 7.95 (ISBN 0-8048-0521-0). C E Tuttle.
Davis, F. Hadland. Myths & Legends of Japan. 1976. lib. bdg. 59.95 (ISBN 0-8490-2328-9). Gordon Pr.
Dorson, Richard M., ed. Studies in Japanese Folklore. LC 80-744. (Folklore of the World Ser.). (Illus.). 1980. Repr. of 1963 ed. lib. bdg. 30.00x (ISBN 0-405-13310-3). Arno.
Fischer, Sally. The Tale of the Shining Princess. Keene, Donald, tr. LC 80-1943. (Illus.). 72p. 1981. 10.95 (ISBN 0-670-63971-0, Studio). Viking Pr.
Griffis, William E. Japanese Fairy World. LC 78-67714. (The Folktale). (Illus.). Repr. of 1887 ed. 28.00 (ISBN 0-404-16091-3). AMS Pr.
Hauge, Victor & Hauge, Takako. Folk Traditions in Japanese Art. LC 78-66394. (Illus.). 1978. 25.00 (ISBN 0-87011-360-7). Kodansha.
Hearn, Lafcadio. In Ghostly Japan. LC 79-138068. (Illus.). (gr. 9 up). 1971. pap. 3.50 (ISBN 0-8048-0965-8). C E Tuttle.
--Japanese Miscellany. 1954. pap. 5.25 (ISBN 0-8048-0307-2). C E Tuttle.
--Kokoro: Hints & Echoes of Japanese Inner Life. Repr. of 1896 ed. lib. bdg. 17.00x (ISBN 0-8371-1633-3, HEKO). Greenwood.
--Kokoro: Hints & Echoes of Japanese Inner Life. LC 79-184814. 1972. pap. 5.25 (ISBN 0-8048-1035-4). C E Tuttle.
Hearn, Lafcadio, et al. Japanese Fairy Tales. LC 78-74515. (Children's Literature Reprint Ser). (gr. 4-6). 1979. Repr. of 1918 ed. 16.75x (ISBN 0-8486-0218-8). Core Collection.
Lou Tsu-K'uang. Survey of Turkish & Japanese Folklore, No. 53. (Asian Folklore & Social Life Monograph). 162p. (Chinese.). 1973. 4.60 (ISBN 0-89986-050-8). E Langstaff.
Mackenzie, Donald A. The Myths of China & Japan. LC 77-6878. 1977. Repr. of 1923 ed. lib. bdg. 45.00 (ISBN 0-89341-149-3). Longwood Pr.
Mayer, Fanny H. Introducing the Japanese Folk Tales, No. 50. (Asian Folklore & Social Life Monograph). 208p. 1973. 5.30 (ISBN 0-89986-047-8). E Langstaff.
Ozaki, Y. T., ed. Japanese Fairy Tales. 1977. lib. bdg. 59.95 (ISBN 0-8490-2091-3). Gordon Pr.
Varley, H. Paul, tr. from Japanese. A Chronicle of Gods & Sovereigns: Jinno Shotoki of Kitabatake Chikafusa. (Translations from Oriental Classics Ser.). 1980. 22.50x (ISBN 0-231-04940-4). Columbia U Pr.
Wheeler, Post. Tales from the Japanese Storytellers As Collected in the Ho-Dan Zo. Henderson, Harold G., ed. LC 73-90236. 1974. pap. 3.00 (ISBN 0-8048-1132-6). C E Tuttle.
Willig, Rosette F., tr. The Changelings: A Classical Japanese Court Tale. Date not set. price not set. Stanford U Pr.
Yagawa, Sumiko. The Crane Wife. Paterson, Katherine, tr. from Japanese. LC 80-29278. (Junior Bks.). Orig. Title: Tsuru-Nyobo. (Illus.). 32p. (gr. k-3). 1981. 8.95 (ISBN 0-688-00496-2). Morrow.
Yanagita, Kunio. Japanese Folk Tales, No. 37. Mayer, Fanny H., tr. (Asian Folklore & Social Life Monograph). 1938. 5.90 (ISBN 0-89986-037-0). E Langstaff.

FOLK-LORE, JEWISH

Ausubel, Nathan, ed. A Treasury of Jewish Folklore. 544p. 1980. pap. 3.95 (ISBN 0-553-13807-3). Bantam.
--Treasury of Jewish Folklore. 1948. 9.95 (ISBN 0-517-50293-3). Crown.
Bin Gorion, Micha J. & Bin Gorion, Emanuel, eds. Mimekor Yisrael: Classical Jewish Folktales, 3 vols. Lask, I. M., tr. from Heb. LC 74-15713. 1666p. 1976. 50.00x (ISBN 0-253-15330-1). Ind U Pr.
Bousset, Wilhelm. Antichrist Legend: A Chapter in Christian & Jewish Folklore. Keane, A. H., tr. 1976. Repr. of 1896 ed. 33.00 (ISBN 0-685-70615-X, Regency). Scholarly.
Braude, William G. & Kapstein, Israel J., trs. from Heb. Tanna Debe Eliyyahu. 660p. 1980. 27.50 (ISBN 0-8276-0174-3). Jewish Pubn.
Cahan, Judah L. Shtudies Vegn Yidisher Folksshafung. Weinreich, ed. 1952. 5.00 (ISBN 0-914512-05-6). Yivo Inst.
Cohen, A. Ancient Jewish Proverbs. Cranmer-Byng, L. & Kapadia, S. A., eds. 127p. 1980. Repr. of 1911 ed. lib. bdg. 12.50 (ISBN 0-8414-9991-8). Folcroft.
Eichhorn, David M., ed. Joys of Jewish Folklore. LC 80-13936. 534p. 1981. 16.95 (ISBN 0-8246-0254-4). Jonathan David.
Friedlander, Gerald. Jewish Fairy Tales & Stories. LC 78-67711. (The Folktale). (Illus.). Repr. of 1919 ed. 14.50 (ISBN 0-404-16088-3). AMS Pr.
Gaster, Theodor H. The Holy & the Profane: "Evolution of Jewish Folkways". rev ed. LC 80-80325. 1980. pap. 4.95 (ISBN 0-688-06795-6, Quill). Morrow.
Haggart, James A. Israel in Folklore. LC 80-65735. 144p. 1981. pap. 5.00 (ISBN 0-934666-07-5). Artisan Sales.
Hausdorff, David M. A Book of Jewish Curiosities. LC 55-11366. 1979. pap. 5.95 (ISBN 0-8197-0466-0). Bloch.
Higgens, Elford. Hebrew Idolatry & Superstition. 1971. Repr. of 1893 ed. 10.00 (ISBN 0-8046-1150-5). Kennikat.
Jung, Leo. Love & Life. LC 79-87873. 1979. 7.50 (ISBN 0-8022-2355-9). Philos Lib.
Levin, Meyer. Classic Hassidic Tales. (Illus.). 6.50 (ISBN 0-8446-5216-4). Peter Smith.
Noy, Dov. Studies in Jewish Folklore. Date not set. 25.00x (ISBN 0-915938-02-2). Ktav.
Patai, Raphael, et al. Studies in Biblical & Jewish Folklore. LC 72-6871. (Studies in Comparitive Literature, No. 35). 1972. Repr. of 1960 ed. lib. bdg. 42.95 (ISBN 0-8383-1665-4). Haskell.
Rappoport, Angelo S. Folklore of the Jews. LC 71-167125. Repr. of 1937 ed. 22.00 (ISBN 0-8103-3864-5). Gale.
Reinfeld, Fred & Fine, Reuben, eds. A. Alekhine Vs E. D. Bogolijubow: World's Chess Championship, 1934. pap. 2.25 (ISBN 0-486-21813-9). Dover.
Schwarzbaum, Haim. Studies in Jewish & World Folklore. (Fabula Supplement Ser., No. B 3). 1968. 92.00x (ISBN 3-11-000393-7). De Gruyter.
Simon, Solomon. Wandering Beggar. (gr. 3-7). 1942. 4.95 (ISBN 0-87441-127-0). Behrman.
Stern, Stephen. The Sephardic Jewish Community of los Angeles: A Study in Folklore & Ethnic Identity. Dorson, Richard M., ed. LC 80-734. (Folklore of the World Ser.). 1980. lib. bdg. 35.00x (ISBN 0-405-13324-3). Arno.
Thompson, Reginald C. Semitic Magic: Its Origins & Development. LC 73-18858. Repr. of 1908 ed. 24.50 (ISBN 0-404-11361-3). AMS Pr.
Weinreich, Uriel, ed. The Field of Yiddish: Studies in Yiddish Language, Folklore, & Literature. LC 54-12380. 317p. 1954. Repr. 12.50 (ISBN 0-936368-02-0). Lexik Hse.
Winkler, Gershon. The Golem of Prague. (Illus.). 1980. 12.95 (ISBN 0-910818-24-X); pap. 9.95 (ISBN 0-910818-25-8). Judaica Pr.

FOLK-LORE, KOREAN

Bang, Im & Ryuk, Yi. Korean Folk Tales: Imps, Ghosts & Fairies. Gale, James S., tr. LC 62-21538. 1962. pap. 3.25 (ISBN 0-8048-0935-6). C E Tuttle.
In-Sob, Zong, ed. & tr. Folk Tales from Korea. LC 53-12953. 1979. 6.95 (ISBN 0-394-17096-2, E738, Ever). Grove.
Zong, In Sob, compiled by. & tr. Folk Tales from Korea. 176p. 1979. 14.30 (ISBN 0-930878-15-9). Hollym Intl.

FOLK-LORE, LAPPISH

Moyne, Ernest J. Raising the Wind: The Legend of Lapland & Finland Wizards in Literature. Kime, Wayne R., ed. (Illus.). 224p. 1981. 18.50 (ISBN 0-87413-146-4). U Delaware Pr.
Turi, Johan O. Turi's Book of Lappland. (Illus.). 1966. pap. text ed. 8.75x (ISBN 0-391-02064-1). Humanities.

FOLK-LORE, LATIN AMERICAN

Canino, Marcelino J. El Cantar Folklorico De Puerto Rico: Estudio y Florilegio. pap. 5.00 (ISBN 0-8477-0501-3). U of PR Pr.
Canino Salgado, Marcelino. Gozos Devocionales En la Tradicion De Puerto Rico. (UPREX, Folklore: No. 32). pap. 1.85 (ISBN 0-8477-0032-1). U of PR Pr.
De Carvalho-Neto, Paulo. History of Iberoamerican Folklore: Mestizo Cultures. Neutzer, Pollack, tr. 1969. text ed. 10.00x (ISBN 90-62340-03-2). Humanities.
Fernandez-Valledor, Roberto. El Mito De Cofresi En la Narrativa Antillana. LC 77-16653. (Coleccion Mente y Palabra). (Illus.). 1978. 6.25 (ISBN 0-8477-0556-0); pap. 5.00 (ISBN 0-8477-0557-9). U of PR Pr.
Green, Lila. Tales from Hispanic Lands. LC 78-54624. (The World Folktale Library). (Illus.). 1979. lib. bdg. 7.65 (ISBN 0-686-50009-1). Silver.
Rosa-Nieves. Voz Folklorica De Puerto Rico. 1967. 16.95 (ISBN 0-87751-009-1, Pub by Troutman Press). E Torres & Sons.
Roth, Walter E. An Inquiry into the Animism & Folklore of the Guiana Indians. LC 16-9897. (Landmarks in Anthropology Ser). Repr. of 1915 ed. 19.50 (ISBN 0-384-52130-4). Johnson Repr.
Stoddard, Florence J. As Old As the Moon: Cuban Legends & Folklore of the Antillas. 1976. lib. bdg. 59.95 (ISBN 0-8490-1457-3). Gordon Pr.
Wilbert, Johannes, ed. Folk Literature of the Ge Indians. LC 78-620047. (Latin American Studies: Vol. 44). 1979. text ed. 27.50 (ISBN 0-87903-044-5). UCLA Lat Am Ctr.

FOLK-LORE, MALAYAN

Evans, Ivor H. Studies in Religion, Folklore & Custom in British North Borneo & the Malay Peninsula. (Illus.). 299p. 1970. Repr. of 1923 ed. 35.00x (ISBN 0-7146-2007-6, F Cass Co). Biblio Dist.
Knappert, Jan. Malay Myths, & Legends. (Writing in Asia Ser.). (Orig.). 1981. pap. text ed. 7.95 (ISBN 0-686-72738-X, 00255). Heinemann Ed.
McHugh, James N. Hantu Hantu: An Account of Ghost Belief in Modern Malaya. 2nd ed. LC 77-87031. (Illus.). Repr. of 1959 ed. 14.50 (ISBN 0-404-16839-6). AMS Pr.
Skeat, Walter W. Malay Magic: Being an Introduction to the Folklore & Popular Religion of the Malay Peninsula. LC 70-174437. (Illus.). 1973. Repr. of 1900 ed. lib. bdg. 28.00 (ISBN 0-405-08980-5). Arno.

FOLK-LORE, MANX

Cashen, William. William Cashen's Manx Folk-Lore. LC 77-22640. 1977. Repr. of 1912 ed. lib. bdg. 20.00 (ISBN 0-8414-1835-7). Folcroft.
Curghey, M. & Wilkes, J., eds. Bible Chaserick Yn Lught-Thie, the Manx Family Bible. 1979. text ed. 32.00x (ISBN 0-904980-34-0). Humanities.
Gill, Deemster, et al. The Manx National Songbook, Vol. 1. 1979. text ed. 14.50x (ISBN 0-904980-30-8). Humanities.
Moore, A. W. The Folk-Lore of the Isle of Man. LC 73-13528. (Folklore Ser). 10.00 (ISBN 0-685-36492-5). Norwood Edns.
Morrison, Sophia. Manx Fairy Tales. 6.95 (ISBN 0-686-10853-1). British Am Bks.
Rhys, John. Celtic Folklore, 2 vols. Set. lib. bdg. 250.00 (ISBN 0-87968-099-7). Gordon Pr.
Rhys, Sir John. Celtic Folklore, Welsh & Manx, 2 vols. xlvi, 718p. Repr. of 1901 ed. 54.00 (ISBN 0-384-50610-0). Johnson Repr.
Stories in Manx with English Translations. (Manx & Eng.). pap. 2.95 (ISBN 0-686-10859-0). British Am Bks.

FOLK-LORE, MAORI

Best, Elsdon. Forest Lore of the Maori. LC 75-35229. Repr. of 1942 ed. 42.50 (ISBN 0-404-14407-1). AMS Pr.
Clark, Kate M. Maori Tales & Legends. LC 78-67696. (The Folktale). Repr. of 1896 ed. 14.00 (ISBN 0-404-16067-0). AMS Pr.
Cowan, James. Fairy Folk Tales of the Maori. 2nd ed. LC 75-35246. Repr. of 1930 ed. 18.00 (ISBN 0-404-14420-9). AMS Pr.
--Tales of the Maori Bush. LC 75-35248. Repr. of 1934 ed. 24.50 (ISBN 0-404-14422-5). AMS Pr.
Pomare, Maui, et al. Legends of the Maori, 2 vols. LC 75-35265. (Illus.). 1976. Repr. of 1934 ed. Set. 62.50 (ISBN 0-404-14350-4). AMS Pr.
Smith, Stephenson P., ed. The Lore of the Whare-wananga, 2 vols. LC 75-35272. Repr. of 1913 ed. Set. 41.50 (ISBN 0-404-14370-9). AMS Pr.

FOLK-LORE, MEDICAL

see Folk Medicine

FOLK-LORE, MELANESIAN

Hambruch, Paul. Faraulip: Liebesegenden Aus der Sudsee: Love Legends from the South Seas. Dorson, Richard M., ed. LC 77-70600. (International Folklore Ser.). (Illus.). 1977. Repr. of 1924 ed. lib. bdg. 10.00x (ISBN 0-405-10099-X). Arno.
Jensen, Adolf E. Hainuwele: Volkserzahlungen Von der Molukken Insel Ceram. Bolle, Kees W., ed. LC 77-79133. (Mythology Ser.). (Ger.). 1978. Repr. of 1939 ed. lib. bdg. 28.00x (ISBN 0-405-10543-6). Arno.
Johannes, R. E. Words of the Lagoon: Fishing & Marine Lore in the Palau District of Micronesia. (Illus.). 320p. 1981. 24.95x (ISBN 0-520-03929-7). U of Cal Pr.

FOLK-LORE, MEXICAN

Aiken, Riley. Mexican Folktales from the Borderland. (Illus.). 1980. 10.00 (ISBN 0-87074-175-6). SMU Press.
Alexander, Frances, et al, eds. Mother Goose on the Rio Grande: Mexican Folklore. LC 79-50839. (Granger Poetry Library). (Illus.). (gr. k-5). 1979. Repr. of 1944 ed. 14.50x (ISBN 0-89609-151-1). Granger Bk.
Boatright, Mody C., ed. Mexican Border Ballads & Other Lore. LC 48-7407. (Texas Folklore Society Publications: No. 21). (Illus.). 1967. Repr. of 1946 ed. 4.95 (ISBN 0-87074-009-1). SMU Press.
Boudreau, Eugene H. Move Over, Don Porfiro: Tales from the Sierra Madre. LC 75-35308. (Illus.). 96p. 1975. pap. 3.00 (ISBN 0-686-10963-5). Pleasant Hill.
Bullock, J. Benbow. Vaya Con Dios. (Illus.). 150p. 1981. pap. 6.95 (ISBN 0-937024-02-3). Gourmet Guides.
Cornyn, J. H. Mexican Fairy Tales. 59.95 (ISBN 0-8490-0614-7). Gordon Pr.
Diehl, Richard, et al, eds. Tzeltal Tales of Demons & Monsters. Stross, Brian, tr. LC 78-622530. (Museum Briefs Ser.: No. 24). 1978. pap. 2.00 (ISBN 0-913134-24-4). Mus Anthro Mo.
Dobie, J. Frank, ed. Puro Mexicano. LC 35-1517. (Texas Folklore Society Publication Ser.: No. 12). 272p. 1980. Repr. of 1935 ed. 7.95 (ISBN 0-87074-041-5). SMU Press.
--Southwestern Lore. LC 33-1134. (Texas Folklore Society Publications: No. 9). 1965. Repr. of 1931 ed. 6.95 (ISBN 0-87074-042-3). SMU Press.
Feldman, Lawrence H., ed. Love in the Armpit: Tzeltal Tales of Love, Murder & Cannibalism. Stross, Brian, tr. LC 77-151846. (Museum Briefs: No. 23). (Illus.). 1977. pap. text ed. 1.40x (ISBN 0-913134-23-6). Mus Anthro Mo.
Giffords, Gloria. Mexican Folk Retablos: Masterpieces on Tin. LC 72-92107. (Illus.). 1974. 35.00 (ISBN 0-8165-0322-2). U of Ariz Pr.
Hudson, Wilson M., ed. The Healer of Los Olmos & Other Mexican Lore. LC 52-9219. (Texas Folklore Society Publications: No. 24). (Illus.). 1966. Repr. of 1951 ed. 5.95 (ISBN 0-87074-081-4). SMU Press.
Ibarra, Alfredo. Cuentos y leyendas de Mexico. LC 78-67722. (The Folktale). Repr. of 1941 ed. 28.00 (ISBN 0-404-16097-2). AMS Pr.
Radin, Paul & Espinoza, A. M. Folklore de Oaxaca. LC 78-63215. (The Folktale). Repr. of 1917 ed. 28.00 (ISBN 0-404-16299-1). AMS Pr.
Robe, Stanley L., compiled by. Antologia Del Saber Popular. (Monograph Ser.: No.2). 1979. pap. 2.95x (ISBN 0-89551-001-4). UCLA Chicano Stud.
Rohmer, Harriet. The Magic Boys: Los Ninos Magicos. LC 75-34916. (Illus.). (gr. k-6). pap. 3.95 spanish bilingual ed. (ISBN 0-89239-001-8, Imprenta de Libros Infantiles). Childrens Book Pr.
Toor, F. Mexican Folkways. 1976. lib. bdg. 59.95 (ISBN 0-8490-2235-5). Gordon Pr.
Toor, Frances. Treasury of Mexican Folkways. (Illus.). 14.95 (ISBN 0-517-50292-5). Crown.
Tully, Marjorie F. & Rael, Juan B. An Annotated Bibliography of Spanish Folklore in New Mexico & Southern Colorado. Dorson, Richard M., ed. LC 77-70628. (International Folkore Ser.). 1977. Repr. of 1950 ed. lib. bdg. 12.00x (ISBN 0-405-10132-5). Arno.

FOLK-LORE, MOROCCAN

Legey, Francoise. The Folklore of Morocco. Hotz, Lucy, tr. from Fr. LC 77-87639. Repr. of 1935 ed. 23.50 (ISBN 0-404-16428-5). AMS Pr.

FOLK-LORE, NEAR EASTERN

Campbell, Charles G. Tales from the Arab Tribes. Dorson, Richard M., ed. LC 80-790. (Folklore of the World Ser.). (Illus.). 1980. Repr. of 1950 ed. lib. bdg. 20.00x (ISBN 0-405-13329-4). Arno.
Dawkins, Richard M. Forty-Five Stories from the Dodekanese. Dorson, Richard M., ed. LC 80-742. (Folklore of the World Ser.). 1980. Repr. of 1950 ed. lib. bdg. 79.00x (ISBN 0-405-13308-1). Arno.
Drower, Ethel S. Folk-Tales of Iraq. LC 78-63226. (Illus.). 30.50 (ISBN 0-404-16165-0). AMS Pr.
Lorimer, D. L & Lorimer, E. D. Persian Tales. LC 78-63210. (The Folktale). (Illus.). Repr. of 1919 ed. 30.00 (ISBN 0-404-16146-4). AMS Pr.
Travers, P. L. Two Pairs of Shoes. LC 78-3386. (Illus.). (gr. k-3). 1980. 10.95 (ISBN 0-670-73677-5). Viking Pr.

FOLK-LORE, NEGRO

This heading discontinued January 1976. See Afro-American Folk-Lore for later materials.

Abrahams, Roger. Positively Black. LC 69-11358. 1970. pap. text ed. 8.95x (ISBN 0-89197-352-4). Irvington.
Abrahams, Roger D. Deep Down in the Jungle: Negro Narrative Folklore from the Streets of Philadelphia. LC 78-124404. 1970. 24.95x (ISBN 0-202-00109-1); pap. 8.95x (ISBN 0-686-66359-4). Aldine Pub.
--Talking Black. LC 76-77. (Sociolinguistics Ser.). 1976. pap. text ed. 8.95 (ISBN 0-88377-039-3). Newbury Hse.
Adams, E. C. Congaree Sketches. LC 27-13763. Repr. of 1927 ed. 12.00 (ISBN 0-527-00400-6). Kraus Repr.
Brewer, J. Mason, ed. American Negro Folklore. LC 68-10833. 404p. 1974. pap. 4.95 (ISBN 0-8129-6235-4). Times Bks.
Connelly, Marc. Green Pastures, a Play. LC 30-16400. 1959. pap. 4.95 (ISBN 0-03-028805-3). HR&W.
Corrothers, James D. Black Cat Club: Negro Humor & Folk-Lore. LC 72-1047. (Illus.). Repr. of 1902 ed. 18.00 (ISBN 0-404-00023-1). AMS Pr.
Dobie, J. Frank, ed. Follow De Drinkin' Gou'd. LC 33-1132. (Texas Folklore Society Publications: No. 7). 1965. Repr. of 1928 ed. 5.95 (ISBN 0-87074-040-7). SMU Press.
--Tone the Bell Easy. LC 33-1135. (Texas Folklore Society Publications: No. 10). (Illus.). 1965. Repr. of 1932 ed. 5.95 (ISBN 0-87074-045-8). SMU Press.

Dobie, J. Frank, et al, eds. Texian Stomping Grounds. LC 41-4871. (Texas Folklore Society Publications: No. 17). 1967. Repr. of 1941 ed. 5.95 (ISBN 0-87074-048-2). SMU Press.
Fry, Gladys-Marie. Night Riders in Black Folk History. LC 74-34268. (Illus.). 264p. 1975. pap. 7.95x (ISBN 0-87049-238-1). U of Tenn Pr.
Georgia Writers' Program. Drums & Shadows: Survival Studies Among the Georgia Coastal Negroes. LC 73-3018. (Illus.). 274p. 1973. Repr. of 1940 ed. lib. bdg. 16.75x (ISBN 0-8371-6832-5, WRDS). Greenwood.
Gonzales, Ambrose E. With Aesop Along the Black Border. LC 73-97424. Repr. of 1924 ed. 13.75x (ISBN 0-8371-2732-7). Greenwood.
Jackson, Bruce, ed. The Negro & His Folklore in Nineteenth-Century Periodicals. LC 67-21894. (American Folklore Society Bibliographic & Special Ser.: No. 18). 398p. 1967. pap. text ed. 14.50x (ISBN 0-292-75510-4). U of Tex Pr.
Jones, Charles C., Jr. Negro Myths from the Georgia Coast. LC 68-21779. 1969. Repr. of 1888 ed. 22.00 (ISBN 0-8103-3836-X). Gale.
Lester, Julius. Black Folktales. LC 72-139259. (Illus.). (gr. 3-8). 1970. pap. 2.95 (ISBN 0-394-17178-0, B262, BC). Grove.
Owen, Mary A. Voodoo Tales, As Told Among the Negroes of the Southwest. LC 78-78773. (Illus.). Repr. of 1893 ed. 13.00x (ISBN 0-8371-1395-4). Greenwood.
Parsons, Elsie W. Folk Lore of the Sea Islands, South Carolina. LC 79-99401. 1969. Repr. of 1923 ed. lib. bdg. 10.00 (ISBN 0-8411-0071-3). Metro Bks.
Parsons, Elsie W., ed. Folk-Lore of the Sea Islands, South Carolina. LC 23-12312. Repr. of 1923 ed. 14.00 (ISBN 0-527-01068-5). Kraus Repr.
Puckett, N. Niles. Folk Beliefs of the Southern Negro. LC 68-55912. 1968. Repr. of 1926 ed. lib. bdg. 22.50x (ISBN 0-8371-0626-5, PUB&). Greenwood.
Puckett, Newbell N. Folk Beliefs of the Southern Negro. LC 68-55780. (Criminology, Law Enforcement, & Social Problems Ser.: No. 22). (Illus.). 1968. Repr. of 1926 ed. 18.00 (ISBN 0-87585-022-7). Patterson Smith.

FOLK-LORE, NIGERIAN

Arnott, Kathleen. Spiders, Crabs, & Creepy Crawlers: Two African Folktales. LC 78-1057. (Imagination Ser.). (Illus) (gr. k-6). 1978. PLB 6.18 (ISBN 0-8116-4412-X). Garrard.
Simmons, Donald C. Extralinguistic Usages of Tonality in Efik Folklore. LC 79-746. 160p. 1980. 15.00x (ISBN 0-8173-0007-4). U of Ala Pr.
Walker, B. & Walker, W., eds. Nigerian Folk Tales. 9.00 (ISBN 0-8135-0379-5). Brown Bk.
Walker, Barbara K. & Walker, Warren S. Nigerian Folk Tales. 2nd, rev. ed. (Illus.). 1980. 15.00 (ISBN 0-208-01839-5, Archon). Shoe String.

FOLK-LORE, NORWEGIAN

Bringsvaard, T. Phantoms & Fairies. (Tanum of Norway Tokens Ser). (Illus.). 1979. pap. 13.50x (ISBN 82-518-0853-7, N498). Vanous.
Dasent, George W. East O' the Sun & West O' the Moon. (Norwegian Folk Tales). (Illus.). 6.75 (ISBN 0-8446-0573-5). Peter Smith.
Hopp, Zinken. Norwegian Folklore Simplified. (Illus.). (gr. 4-8). 1964. pap. 3.50 (ISBN 0-685-09187-2). Dufour.
Hveberg, H. Of Gods & Giants. (Tanum of Norway Tokens Ser). pap. 9.50x (ISBN 8-2518-0083-8, N430). Vanous.
Schach, Paul & Schach, Paul, trs. from Old Norse. The Saga of Tristram & Isond. LC 73-76351. (Illus.). xxiv, 148p. 1973. 9.50x (ISBN 0-8032-0832-4); pap. 2.25x (ISBN 0-8032-5847-X, BB 608, Bison). U of Nebr Pr.
Volstad, Edith. Folkstories & Fairytales from Norway. (Illus.). 1980. pap. 4.95 (ISBN 0-9603906-1-8). Voldstad Ent.

FOLK-LORE, NOVA-SCOTIAN

Fauset, A. H. Folklore from Nova Scotia. LC 32-8895. (American Folklore Society Memoirs). Repr. of 1931 ed. 14.00 (ISBN 0-527-01076-6). Kraus Repr.

FOLK-LORE, PALESTINE

Hanauer, James E. Folk-Lore of the Holy Land: Moslem, Christian & Jewish. LC 77-22030. 1977. Repr. of 1935 ed. lib. bdg. 25.00 (ISBN 0-8414-4955-4). Folcroft.
--Folklore of the Holy Land. 280p. 1980. Repr. of 1935 ed. lib. bdg. 30.00 (ISBN 0-8492-5272-5). R West.
Vilnay, Zev. Legends of Judaea & Samaria. new ed. LC 74-22895. (The Sacred Land Ser.: Vol. 2). (Illus.). 328p. 1976. 7.50 (ISBN 0-8276-0064-X, 371). Jewish Pubn.

FOLK-LORE, POLISH

Ainsworth, Catherine H. Polish-American Folktales. LC 77-80771. (Folklore Bks.). x, 102p. 1980. 5.00 (ISBN 0-933190-04-2). Clyde Pr.
Benecke, Else C. & Busch, Marie, trs. from Polish. Selected Polish Tales. 1978. Repr. of 1921 ed. lib. bdg. 12.50 (ISBN 0-8495-0417-1). Arden Lib.
Briggs, Maude A. Polish Fairy Tales. 96p. 1979. Repr. of 1920 ed. lib. bdg. 10.00 (ISBN 0-8414-9827-X). Folcroft.
Domanska, Janina. King Krakus & the Dragon. LC 78-12934. (Illus.). (gr. k-3). 1979. 8.95 (ISBN 0-688-80189-7); PLB 8.59 (ISBN 0-688-84189-9). Greenwillow.
Pokropek, Marian. Guide to Folk Art & Folklore in Poland. Paszkiewicz, Magdalena M., tr. from Polish. (Illus.). 307p. 1980. 20.00x (ISBN 83-213-3014-2). Intl Pubns Serv.
Tetmajer, Kazimierz P. Tales of the Tatras. Kennedy, H. E. & Uminska, Zofia, trs. from Pol. LC 79-11094. (Illus.). 1979. Repr. of 1943 ed. lib. bdg. 19.75x (ISBN 0-313-21462-X, TETT). Greenwood.

FOLK-LORE, PUERTO RICAN

Deliz, Monserrate. Songs & Folklore of Puerto Rico. (Puerto Rico Ser.). 1979. lib. bdg. 59.95 (ISBN 0-8490-3007-2). Gordon Pr.
Garcia, David. Fairy Tales of Puerto Rico. (Children's Bks: No. 166). (Illus.). 50p. (gr. 1-5). 1981. 8.95 (ISBN 0-934642-02-8). Puerto Rico Almanacs.
Gordon, Raoul, ed. The Folklore of Puerto Rico. 1976. lib. bdg. 59.95 (ISBN 0-8490-0179-X). Gordon Pr.
Mason, J. Alden. Puerto Rican Folklore. Espinosa, Aurelio M., ed. (Puerto Rico Ser.). 1979. lib. bdg. 59.95 (ISBN 0-8490-2989-9). Gordon Pr.
Ramirez De Arellano, Rafael. Folklore portoriqueno. LC 78-63213. (The Folktale). Repr. of 1926 ed. 25.50 (ISBN 0-404-16154-5). AMS Pr.

FOLK-LORE, ROMAN

Halliday, William R. Greek & Roman Folklore. LC 63-10289. (Our Debt to Greece & Rome Ser). Repr. of 1930 ed. 7.50x (ISBN 0-8154-0109-4). Cooper Sq.

FOLK-LORE, ROMANIAN

Beza, Marcu. Paganism in Roumanian Folklore. LC 74-173102. (Illus.). 1972. Repr. of 1928 ed. lib. bdg. 14.00 (ISBN 0-405-08267-3, Blom Pubns). Arno.
--Paganism in Roumanian Folklore. 1976. lib. bdg. 59.95 (ISBN 0-8490-2397-1). Gordon Pr.
Gaster, Moses. Romanian Bird & Beast Stories. LC 78-67713. (The Folktale). Repr. of 1915 ed. 30.75 (ISBN 0-404-16089-1). AMS Pr.
Nandris, Mabel. Folktales from Roumania. 1976. lib. bdg. 59.95 (ISBN 0-8490-1853-6). Gordon Pr.
Segall, Jacob, ed. Roumanian Folktales Retold from the Original. 1977. lib. bdg. 59.95 (ISBN 0-8490-2544-3). Gordon Pr.
Thigpen, Kenneth A. Folklore & the Ethnicity Factor in the Lives of Romanian-Americans, 2 vols. in one. Dorson, Richard M., ed. (Folklore of the World Ser.). 1980. lib. bdg. 50.00x (ISBN 0-405-13326-X). Arno.
Van Woerkom, Dorothy. Alexandra the Rock-Eater. LC 77-13778. (gr. k-3). 1978. 7.99 (ISBN 0-394-83536-0); 6.99g (ISBN 0-394-93536-5). Knopf.

FOLK-LORE, RUSSIAN

Afanasev, Aleksandr N. Erotic Tales of Old Russia. Perkov, Yury, tr. (Orig., Eng. & Rus.). 1980. pap. 6.95 (ISBN 0-933884-07-9). Berkeley Slavic.
Afanasyev, Alexander, compiled By. Russian Folk Tales: Illustrated by Ivan Bilibin. Chandler, Robert, tr. from Russian. LC 80-50746. (Illus.). 80p. 1980. 14.95 (ISBN 0-394-51353-3). Shambhala Pubns.
Alexander, Alex E. Russian Folklore: An Anthology in English Translation. 1974. 25.00 (ISBN 0-685-47347-3); pap. 12.00 (ISBN 0-686-66993-2). Nordland Pub.
Carey, Claude. Les Proverbes Erotiques Russe: Etudes De Proverbes Recueillis et Non-Publies Par Dal et Simoni. LC 74-159462. (Slavistic Printings & Reprintings Ser.: No. 88). 144p. 1973. text ed. 36.25x (ISBN 90-2792-331-0). Mouton.
Chestnut-Grey: A Russian Folk Tale. 20p. 1977. pap. 0.75 (ISBN 0-8285-1121-7, Pub. by Progress Pubs Russia). Imported Pubns.
Curtin, Jeremiah. Myths & Folktales of the Russians, Western Slavs, & Magyars. 1977. lib. bdg. 59.95 (ISBN 0-8490-2326-2). Gordon Pr.
De Blumenthal, Vera. Folk Tales from the Russian. LC 78-74512. (Children's Literature Reprint Ser.). (Illus.). (gr. 4-5). 1979. Repr. of 1903 ed. 16.75x (ISBN 0-8486-0216-1). Core Collection.
Dietrich, Anton, intro. by. Russian Popular Tales. (Folklore Ser.). 1857. 15.00 (ISBN 0-685-43820-1). Norwood Edns.
Elstob & Barber, trs. Russian Folktales. 213p. 1974. 12.95 (ISBN 0-7135-1653-4). Transatlantic.
Gerber, Adolph. Great Russian Animal Tales. LC 73-140975. (Research & Source Works Ser.: No. 630). 1971. Repr. 19.50 (ISBN 0-8337-1325-6). B Franklin.
Ginsburg, Mirra. Striding Slippers: Adapted from an Udmurt Tale. LC 77-12035. (Illus.). (gr. k-3). 1978. 8.95 (ISBN 0-02-736370-8, 73637). Macmillan.
Jones, Roy G. Language & Prosody of the Russian Folk Epic. (Slavistic Printings & Reprintings Ser: No. 275). (Illus.). 105p. 1972. text ed. 26.25x (ISBN 90-2792-330-2). Mouton.
Klymasz, Robert B. Ukrainian Folklore in Canada: An Immigrant Complex in Transition. Dorson, Richard M., ed. LC 80-731. (Folklore of the World Ser.). 1980. lib. bdg. 28.00x (ISBN 0-405-13318-9). Arno.
Krylov, Ivan A. Krylov's Fables. Pares, Bernard, tr. from Rus. LC 76-23880. (Classics of Russian Literature). 1977. 11.95 (ISBN 0-88355-489-5); pap. 3.95 (ISBN 0-88355-490-9). Hyperion Conn.
Magnus, Leonard A. Russian Folk-Tales with Introduction & Notes. LC 74-6486. 1974. Repr. of 1916 ed. 24.00 (ISBN 0-8103-3654-5). Gale.
Magnus, Leonard A., ed. The Tale of the Armament of Igor, A.D. 1185, a Russian Historical Epic. 1977. lib. bdg. 59.95 (ISBN 0-8490-2727-6). Gordon Pr.
Nagishkin, Dmitri. Folktales of the Amur: Stories from the Russian Far East. Lehrman, Emily, tr. (Illus.). 266p. 1980. 25.00 (ISBN 0-686-62701-6, 0913-8). Abrams.
Oinas, Felix J. & Soudakoff, Stephen. The Study of Russian Folklore. (Indian Univ. Folklore Ser.: No. 25). 341p. 1975. text ed. 60.00x (ISBN 90-2793-147-X). Mouton.
Redei, Karoly. Zyrian Folk Texts. (Illus.). 652p. 1978. 60.00x (ISBN 963-05-1506-7). Intl Pubns Serv.
Reeder, Roberta, ed. Down Along the Mother Volga. LC 74-84293. (Folklore & Folklife Ser). 266p. 1975. 12.50x (ISBN 0-8122-7668-X). U of Pa Pr.
Riordan, James. Tales from Tartary: Russian Tales, Vol. 2. LC 77-27871. (Illus.). (gr. 7 up). 1979. 12.50 (ISBN 0-670-69156-9, Co-Pub. by Kestrel Bks.). Viking Pr.
Ross, Blanche, tr. A Strange Servant: A Russian Folktale. LC 77-4563. (Illus.). (ps-2). 1977. 6.95 (ISBN 0-394-83453-4); PLB 6.99 (ISBN 0-394-93453-9). Knopf.
Sokolov, Yury M. Russian Folklore. Smith, Catherine R., tr. LC 79-134444. (Illus.). 1971. Repr. of 1966 ed. 34.00 (ISBN 0-8103-5020-3). Gale.
Winner, Thomas G. The Oral Art & Literature of Kazakhs of Russian Central Asia. Dorson, Richard M., ed. LC 80-799. (Folklore of the World Ser.). 1980. Repr. of 1958 ed. lib. bdg. 25.00x (ISBN 0-405-13339-1). Arno.
Zeitlin, Ida. Skazki: Tales & Legends of Old Russia. 1979. Repr. of 1926 ed. lib. bdg. 45.00 (ISBN 0-8492-3155-8). R West.
Zenkovsky, Serge. Medieval Russia's Epics, Chronicles, & Tales. rev. ed. 1974. pap. 7.50 (ISBN 0-525-47363-7). Dutton.
Zheleznova, Irina. Folk Tales from Russian Lands. (Illus.). 7.50 (ISBN 0-8446-0974-9). Peter Smith.

FOLK-LORE, SCANDINAVIAN

Annie & Elizakeany. Heroes of Asgard. (Facsimile Classics Ser.). (Illus.). 1979. 6.95 (ISBN 0-8317-4475-8, Mayflower Bks). Smith Pubs.
Arent, A. M., tr. Laxdoela Saga. LC 63-20538. 1964. 8.95x (ISBN 0-89067-039-0). Am Scandinavian.
Austin, P. B. Life & Songs of Carl Michael Bellman. 1967. 12.95x (ISBN 0-89067-048-X). Am Scandinavian.
Bayerschmidt, Carl F. & Hollander, Lee M., eds. Njal's Saga. LC 79-10657. (Illus.). 1979. Repr. of 1956 ed. lib. bdg. 29.25x (ISBN 0-313-20814-X, NJSA). Greenwood.
Christiansen, Reider T. Studies in Irish & Scandinavian Folktales. Dorson, Richard M., ed. LC 80-741. (Folklore of the World Ser.). 1980. Repr. of 1959 ed. lib. bdg. 23.00x (ISBN 0-405-13307-3). Arno.
Craigie, W. A. Scandinavian Folklore. 59.95 (ISBN 0-8490-0996-0). Gordon Pr.
Craigie, William A. Scandinavian Folk-Lore. LC 74-78129. 1970. Repr. of 1896 ed. 30.00 (ISBN 0-8103-3587-5). Gale.
Hague, Kathleen & Hague, Michael. East of the Sun & West of the Moon. LC 80-13499. (Illus.). 48p. (gr. k-3). 1980. pap. 3.95 (ISBN 0-15-224703-3, VoyB). HarBraceJ.
--East of the Sun & West of the Moon. LC 80-13499. (Illus.). 48p. 1980. 9.95 (ISBN 0-15-224702-5, HJ). HarBraceJ.
Hollander, L. M., tr. Viga-Glum's Saga. LC 77-186718. (Library of Scandinavian Literature Ser.: Vol. 14). 1972. 7.50x (ISBN 0-89067-021-8). Am Scandinavian.
Johnston, Alfred W. & Johnston, Amy, eds. Caithness & Sutherland Records. (Viking Society for Northern Research: Old Lore Ser.). Repr. of 1928 ed. 27.50 (ISBN 0-404-60238-X). AMS Pr.
--Old-Lore Miscellany, 10 vols. (Viking Society for Northern Research: Old-Lore Ser.). Repr. of 1946 ed. Set. 275.00 (ISBN 0-404-60220-7). AMS Pr.
Jonsen, George. Favorite Tales of Monsters & Trolls. LC 76-24182. (Pictureback Library Editions). (ps-2). 1978. PLB 4.99 (ISBN 0-394-93477-6, BYR). Random.
Klein, Barbro S. Legends & Folk Beliefs in a Swedish American Community: A Study in Folklore & Acculturation, 2 vols. Dorson, Richard M., ed. LC 80-730. (Folklore of the World Ser.). 1980. lib. bdg. 68.00x (ISBN 0-405-13343-X). Arno.
Laing, Frederick. Tales from Scandinavia. LC 78-56060. (The World Folktale Library). (Illus.). 1979. lib. bdg. 7.65 (ISBN 0-686-51165-4). Silver.
Lindow, John. Swedish Legends & Folktales. LC 77-7830. 1978. 10.95 (ISBN 0-520-03520-8). U of Cal Pr.
Lofgren, Ulf. The Boy Who Ate More Than the Giant, & Other Swedish Folktales. LC 78-8653. (Unicef Storycraft Bks.). (Illus.). (ps-3). 1978. 5.95 (ISBN 0-529-05450-7); PLB 5.99 (ISBN 0-529-05451-5). Philomel.
McGovern, Ann. Half a Kingdom. LC 76-45305. (Illus.). (ps-3). 1977. 6.95 (ISBN 0-7232-6137-7). Warne.
Magnusson, Eirikr & Morris, William, trs. from Icelandic. The Story of Grettir the Strong. 1980. Repr. of 1869 ed. 17.50x (ISBN 0-8154-0517-0). Cooper Sq.
--The Story of the Volsungs & Niblungs: With Certain Songs from the Elder Edda. 275p. 1980. Repr. of 1870 ed. 17.50x (ISBN 0-8154-0518-9). Cooper Sq.
Runeberg, J. L. Tales of Ensign Stal. Stork, C. W., tr. 1938. 4.95x (ISBN 0-89067-007-2). Am Scandinavian.
Schach, Paul & Hollander, Lee M., trs. Eyrbyggja Saga. LC 59-11221. (Landmark Edition). (Illus.). 1959. 11.50x (ISBN 0-8032-0164-8). U of Nebr Pr.
Three Icelandic Sagas. 1950. Repr. 11.50 (ISBN 0-8274-3623-8). R West.

FOLK-LORE, SCOTTISH

Bassin, Ethel. The Old Songs of Skye: Frances Tolmie & Her Circle. Bowman, Derek, ed. 1977. 14.95 (ISBN 0-7100-8546-X). Routledge & Kegan.
Boucher, R. The Kingdom of Fife, Its Ballads & Legends. (Folklore Ser). 15.00 (ISBN 0-8482-7391-5). Norwood Edns.
Campbell, J. L., ed. A Collection of Highland Rites & Customes. (Folklore Society Mistletoe Ser.). 117p. 1975. 11.50x (ISBN 0-87471-676-4). Rowman.
Campbell, John G. Clan Traditions & Popular Tales of the Western Highlands & Islands. Wallace, Jessie & MacIsaac, Duncan, eds. LC 72-144458. (Waifs & Strays of Celtic Tradition: Argyllshire Ser.: No. 5). Repr. of 1895 ed. 14.50 (ISBN 0-404-53535-6). AMS Pr.
--Superstitions of the Highlands & Islands of Scotland. LC 71-173104. (Illus.). Repr. of 1900 ed. 21.00 (ISBN 0-407-80337-8, Blom Pubns). Arno.
--Superstitions of the Highlands & Islands of Scotland. 1970. 24.00 (ISBN 0-8103-3589-1). Gale.
Dalyell, John G. The Darker Superstitions of Scotland. LC 77-26734. 45.00 (ISBN 0-8414-1863-2). Folcroft.
Douglas, George B. & Dorson, Richard M., eds. Scottish Fairy & Folk Tales. LC 77-70591. (International Folklore Ser.). (Illus.). 1977. Repr. of 1901 ed. lib. bdg. 19.00x (ISBN 0-405-10092-2). Arno.
Grant, Anne M. Essays on the Superstitions of the Highlanders of Scotland. LC 76-25997. 1976. Repr. of 1811 ed. Set. lib. bdg. 75.00 (ISBN 0-8414-4530-3). Folcroft.
Henderson, G. The Popular Rhymes, Sayings, & Proverbs of the County of Berwick. LC 77-1079. 1977. Repr. of 1856 ed. lib. bdg. 25.00 (ISBN 0-8414-4946-5). Folcroft.
MacDonald, Alex. Story & Song from Loch Ness-Side. (Folklore Ser). 12.50 (ISBN 0-685-36484-4). Norwood Edns.
McPherson, Joseph M. Primitive Beliefs in the North-East of Scotland. Dorson, Richard M., ed. LC 77-70605. (International Folklore Ser.). 1977. Repr. of 1929 ed. lib. bdg. 18.00x (ISBN 0-405-10109-0). Arno.
Marwick, Ernest W. The Folklore of Orkney & Shetland: Legends, Folk-Tales & Customs. (Folklore of the British Isles Ser.). (Illus.). 215p. 1975. 17.50x (ISBN 0-87471-681-0). Rowman.
Napier, James. Folk Lore: Or Superstitious Beliefs in the West of Scotland. (Folklore Ser). 10.00 (ISBN 0-685-36493-3). Norwood Edns.
--Folklore. 1978. Repr. of 1879 ed. lib. bdg. 22.50 (ISBN 0-8492-1963-9). R West.
--Folklore: Or, Superstitious Beliefs in the West of Scotland. 1977. lib. bdg. 59.95 (ISBN 0-8490-1852-8). Gordon Pr.
Nicholson, Edward W. Golspie. LC 77-12083. 1977. Repr. lib. bdg. 35.00 (ISBN 0-8414-6300-X). Folcroft.

--Golspie: Contributions to Its Folklore. 1978. Repr. of 1897 ed. lib. bdg. 35.00 (ISBN 0-8492-1952-3). R West.

Nicolson, John. Some Folk Tales & Legends of Shetland. LC 76-40418. 1976. Repr. of 1920 ed. lib. bdg. 10.00 (ISBN 0-8414-6295-X). Folcroft.

Quillen, D. G. Homotopical Algebra. (Lecture Notes in Mathematics: Vol. 43). (Orig.). 1967. pap. 10.70 (ISBN 0-387-03914-7). Springer-Verlag.

Ratcliff, Ruth. Scottish Folk Tales. (Illus.). 1977. 12.50 (ISBN 0-584-62393-3). Transatlantic.

--Scottish Folk Tales. 1977. 12.00 (ISBN 0-685-87557-1). State Mutual Bk.

Robertson, R. Macdonald. Selected Highland Folktales. 1977. 11.95 (ISBN 0-7153-7436-2). David & Charles.

Ross, Anne. The Folklore of the Scottish Highlands. (Folklore of the British Isles Ser.). (Illus.). 174p. 1976. 11.50x (ISBN 0-87471-836-8). Rowman.

Shaw, Margaret F. Folksongs & Folklore of South Uist. (Illus.). 1977. text ed. 33.00x (ISBN 0-19-920085-8). Oxford U Pr.

Simpson, Evelyn B. Folk Lore in Lowland Scotland. LC 76-17550. 1976. Repr. of 1908 ed. lib. bdg. 20.00 (ISBN 0-8414-7714-0). Folcroft.

Spence, John. Shetland Folk-Lore. LC 73-8955. 1899. ltd. ed. 12.50 (ISBN 0-88305-622-4). Norwood Edns.

Wilkie, James. Bygone Fife. (Folklore Ser). 20.00 (ISBN 0-685-36528-X). Norwood Edns.

Wimberly, Lowry C. Folklore in the English & Scottish Ballads. 6.00 (ISBN 0-8446-3191-4). Peter Smith.

--Folklore in the English & Scottish Ballads. 1965. pap. 4.00 (ISBN 0-486-21388-9). Dover.

Wood, John M. Witchcraft & Superstitious Record in the Southwestern District of Scotland. LC 76-25108. 1976. 40.00 (ISBN 0-8414-9530-0). Folcroft.

FOLK-LORE, SERBIAN

Mijatovic, Elodie. Serbian Folk Lore. Denton, W., ed. LC 68-56477. 1968. Repr. of 1874 ed. 15.00 (ISBN 0-405-08788-8, Pub. by Blom). Arno.

FOLK-LORE, SIBERIAN

Coxwell, Charles F. Siberian & Other Folk-Tales. LC 78-67702. (The Folktale). Repr. of 1925 ed. 64.50 (ISBN 0-404-16076-X). AMS Pr.

Dioszegi, V., ed. Popular Beliefs & Folklore Tradition in Siberia. (Uralic & Altaic Ser.: No. 57). 1968. text ed. 64.00x (ISBN 0-686-22621-6). Mouton.

FOLK-LORE, SLAVIC

Curtin, Jeremiah. Myths & Folktales of the Russians, Western Slavs, & Magyars. 1977. lib. bdg. 59.95 (ISBN 0-8490-2326-2). Gordon Pr.

Galdone, Joanna. The Little Girl & the Big Bear. (Illus.). 40p. (ps-3). 1980. 8.95 (ISBN 0-395-29029-5, Clarion). HM.

How Quest Sought the Truth. 1974. 10.00 (ISBN 0-686-23320-4). Rochester Folk Art.

Leger, L. Recueil de contes populaires slaves. LC 78-20114. (Collection de contes et de chansons populaires: Vol. 5). Repr. of 1882 ed. 21.50 (ISBN 0-404-60355-6). AMS Pr.

Lockwood, Yvonne R. Yugoslav Folklore: An Annotated Bibliography of Contributions in English. LC 75-38305. 1976. softcover perfect bound 8.00 (ISBN 0-88247-401-4). Ragusan Pr.

Perkowski, Jan L., ed. Vampires of the Slavs. 1976. soft cover 9.95 (ISBN 0-89357-026-5). Slavica.

Strickland, Walter W. Panslavonic Folklore. LC 78-63227. (The Folktale). 1980. 25.00 (ISBN 0-404-16166-9). AMS Pr.

FOLK-LORE, SOUTH AFRICAN

Bleek, Wilhelm H. Reynard the Fox in South Africa. LC 78-67686. (The Folktale). Repr. of 1864 ed. 17.50 (ISBN 0-404-16055-7). AMS Pr.

Honeij, James A. South-African Folk-Tales. LC 78-67717. (The Folktale). Repr. of 1910 ed. 19.00 (ISBN 0-404-16094-8). AMS Pr.

FOLK-LORE, SOUTH AMERICAN

Brett, William H. Legends & Myths of the Aboriginal Indians of British Guiana. LC 78-67691. (The Folktale). Repr. of 1880 ed. 22.00 (ISBN 0-404-16059-X). AMS Pr.

Davis, Arthur & Parker, Ben. Brutes & Savages. LC 78-55557. (Illus.). 1978. pap. 1.00 (ISBN 0-912760-73-7). Valkyrie Pr.

Hartt, Charles F. Amazonian Tortoise Myths. LC 78-67716. (The Folktale). Repr. of 1875 ed. 11.00 (ISBN 0-404-16093-X). AMS Pr.

Niles, Susan A. Theoretical & Analytical Approaches to South American Indian Narrative: An Annotated Bibliography. 1981. lib. bdg. 25.00 (ISBN 0-8240-9308-9). Garland Pub.

Rohermer, Harriet. The Mighty God Viracocha: El Dios Poderoso Viracocha. LC 76-17492. (Illus.). (gr. k-6). pap. 3.95 spanish bilingual ed. (ISBN 0-89239-005-0, Imprenta de Libros Infantiles). Childrens Book Pr.

Rohmer, Harriet. Land of the Icy Death: Tierra De la Muerte Glacial. LC 76-29211. (Fifth World Tales Ser.). (Illus.). (gr. k-6). pap. 3.95 spanish bilingual ed. (ISBN 0-89239-009-3, Imprenta de Libros Infantiles). Childrens Book Pr.

--The Treasure of Guatavita: El Tesoro De Guatavita. LC 76-29081. (Fifth World Tales Ser.). (Illus.). (gr. k-6). pap. 3.95 spanish bilingual ed. (ISBN 0-89239-010-7, Imprenta de Libros Infantiles). Childrens Book Pr.

Thiesen, Eva. Textos Folkloricos De los Bora. (Comunidades y Culturas Peruanas: No. 2). 1975. 2.65x (ISBN 0-88312-648-6). Summer Inst Ling.

Wilbert, Johannes. Yupa Folktales. LC 73-620200. (Latin American Studies Ser. Vol. 24). (Illus.). 1974. 7.95 (ISBN 0-87903-024-0). UCLA Lat Am Ctr.

Wilkins, Harold T. Mysteries of Ancient South America. 1977. lib. bdg. 59.95 (ISBN 0-8490-2312-2). Gordon Pr.

FOLK-LORE, SPANISH

Aragon, Ray J. De. The Legend of La Llorona. LC 79-52953. (Illus.). 1980. 8.95 (ISBN 0-932906-03-6); pap. 5.95 (ISBN 0-932906-02-8). Pan-Am Publishing Co.

Childers, J. Wesley. Motif-Index of the Cuentos of Juan Timoneda. Dorson, Richard M., ed. LC 80-791. (Folklore of the World Ser.). 1980. Repr. of 1948 ed. lib. bdg. 12.00x (ISBN 0-405-13330-8). Arno.

Green, Lila. Tales from Hispanic Lands. LC 78-54624. (The World Folktale Library). (Illus.). 1979. lib. bdg. 7.65 (ISBN 0-686-50009-1). Silver.

Irving, Washington. Spanish Papers. Irving, Pierre, ed. LC 78-74516. (Children's Literature Reprint Ser.). (gr. 7 up). 1979. Repr. of 1868 ed. 42.50x (ISBN 0-8486-0219-6). Core Collection.

Rael, Juan B. Cuentos Espanoles De Colorado y Nuevo Mexico: Spanish Tales from Colorado & New Mexico, Vols. I & II. rev., 2nd ed. LC 77-74170. 1977. Set. lib. bdg. 39.95 (ISBN 0-89013-093-0); Set. pap. text ed. 28.95 slipcase (ISBN 0-89013-095-7); Vol. I. lib. bdg. (ISBN 0-89013-096-5); Vol. I. pap. text ed. (ISBN 0-89013-097-3); Vol. II. lib. bdg. 0 (ISBN 0-89013-098-1); Vol. II. pap. text ed. (ISBN 0-89013-099-X). Museum NM Pr.

--Cuentos Espanoles De Colorado y Nuevo Mejico: Spanish Tales from Colorado & New Mexico, 2 vols. Dorson, Richard M., ed. LC 77-70617. (International Folklore Ser.). 1977. Set. lib. bdg. 80.00x (ISBN 0-405-10119-8); lib. bdg. 40.00x ea. Vol. 1 (ISBN 0-405-10120-1). Vol. 2 (ISBN 0-405-10121-X). Arno.

Segovia, Gertrudis. The Spanish Fairy Book. Quinn, Elizabeth V., tr. LC 78-74519. (Children's Literature Reprint Ser.). (gr. 5-7). 1979. Repr. of 1918 ed. 22.50x (ISBN 0-8486-0222-6). Core Collection.

FOLK-LORE, SUDANESE

Ahmed Al Shahi & Moore, F. C., eds. Wisdom from the Nile: A Collection of Folk-Stories from Northern & Central Sudan. (Illus.). 270p. 1978. text ed. 37.50x (ISBN 0-19-815147-0). Oxford U Pr.

Nalder, Leonard F., ed. Tribal Survey of Mongalla Province. (Illus.). Repr. 12.75 (ISBN 0-8371-2862-5). Greenwood.

FOLK-LORE, SWISS

Obrist, Jurg. They Do Things Right in Albern. LC 78-6598. (Illus.). (ps-3). 1978. 6.95 (ISBN 0-689-30671-7). Atheneum.

FOLK-LORE, TIBETAN

Bischoff, F. A. Kanjur und Seine Kolophone, Pts. 1 & 2. LC 68-19043. 1968. Set. pap. 25.00x (ISBN 0-911706-03-8). Selbstverlag.

Hyde-Chambers, Fredrick & Hyde-Chambers, Audrey. Tibetan Folk Tales. LC 81-50970. (Illus.). 156p. (Orig.). 1981. pap. 6.95 (ISBN 0-394-74886-7). Shambhala Pubns.

O'Connor, W. F. Folk Tales from Tibet. (Folklore Ser). 12.50 (ISBN 0-88305-485-X). Norwood Edns.

--Folk Tales of Tibet. (Folk Tales of the World). (Illus.). 112p. 1979. 6.50x (ISBN 0-8002-1006-9). Intl Pubns Serv.

FOLK-LORE, TURKISH

Basgoz, Ihlan & Tietze, Andreas. Bilmece: A Corpus of Turkish Riddles. (Publications in Folklore Studies Vol. 22). 1974. pap. 38.50x (ISBN 0-520-09145-0). U of Cal Pr.

Basgoz, Ilhan. Turkish Folklore Reader. (Uralic & Altaic Ser: Vol. 120). 1971. pap. text ed. 8.00x (ISBN 0-87750-164-5). Res Ctr Lang Semiotic.

Boratav, Pertev N. & Eberhard, Wolfram. Turkische Volkserzahlung und Die Erzahlerkunst, 2 vols. (Asian Folklore & Social Life Monograph: No. 73). (Ger.). 1975. Set. 9.00 (ISBN 0-89986-069-9). E Langstaff.

Eberhard, Wolfram. Minstrel Tales from Southeastern Turkey. Dorson, Richard M., ed. LC 80-793. (Folklore of the World Ser.). 1980. Repr. of 1955 ed. lib. bdg. 12.00x (ISBN 0-405-13332-4). Arno.

Garnett, Lucy M. The Women of Turkey & Their Folk-Lore, 2 vols. LC 77-87539. Repr. of 1891 ed. 73.50 set (ISBN 0-404-16590-7). AMS Pr.

Lou Tsu-K'uang. Survey of Turkish & Japanese Folklore, No. 53. (Asian Folklore & Social Life Monograph). 162p. (Chinese.). 1973. 4.60 (ISBN 0-89986-050-8). E Langstaff.

Nasr Al-Din. Tales of Nasr-ed-Din Khoja. Barnham, Henry D., tr. from Turkish. LC 77-87632. 1977. Repr. of 1923 ed. 23.00 (ISBN 0-404-16457-9). AMS Pr.

FOLK-LORE, VEI

Ellis, George W. Negro Culture in West Africa: A Social Study of the Negro Group of Vai-Speaking People, with Its Own Invented Alphabet & Written Language. LC 15-1680. 1971. Repr. of 1914 ed. 22.50 (ISBN 0-384-14190-0). Johnson Repr.

FOLK-LORE, WELSH

Bett, Henry. English Myths & Traditions. (Illus.). 144p. 1980. Repr. of 1952 ed. lib. bdg. 17.50 (ISBN 0-8414-2921-9). Folcroft.

Brown, Arthur C. Origin of the Grail Legend. LC 65-17878. 1966. Repr. of 1943 ed. 14.00 (ISBN 0-8462-0655-2). Russell.

Davies, Jonathan C. Folk-Lore of West & Mid-Wales. LC 74-3208. (Folklore Ser). 22.50 (ISBN 0-88305-160-5). Norwood Edns.

--Folklore of West & Mid Wales. 348p. 1980. Repr. of 1911 ed. lib. bdg. 25.00 (ISBN 0-8414-1874-8). Folcroft.

Hess, Gary R. Sam Higginbottom of Allahabad. LC 67-17631. 1967. 7.95x (ISBN 0-8139-0118-9). U Pr of Va.

Jones, Edmund. A Relation of Apparitions of Spirits: Into the Principality of Wales. 2nd ed. LC 77-87687. Repr. of 1780 ed. 18.50 (ISBN 0-404-16485-4). AMS Pr.

Jones, T. Gwynn. Welsh Folklore & Folk-Custom. rev. ed. 1979. Repr. of 1930 ed. 17.50x (ISBN 0-8476-6185-7). Rowman.

Jones, Thomas G. Welsh Folklore & Folk-Custom. 255p. 1980. Repr. of 1930 ed. lib. bdg. 30.00 (ISBN 0-8492-1366-5). R West.

--Welsh Folklore & Folk Custom. LC 77-3195. 1977. lib. bdg. 25.00 (ISBN 0-8414-5319-5). Folcroft.

Lanier, Sidney, ed. Knightly Legends of Wales: Or, the Boy's Mabinogion. LC 76-10202. (Children's Literature Reprint Ser). (Illus.). (gr. 4-6). 1976. Repr. of 1884 ed. 18.75x (ISBN 0-8486-0209-9). Core Collection.

Owen, Elias. Welsh Folk Lore. xii, 359p. 1980. Repr. of 1896 ed. lib. bdg. 30.00 (ISBN 0-8414-6548-7). Folcroft.

--Welsh Folk-Lore. (Folklore Ser). 15.00 (ISBN 0-685-36503-4). Norwood Edns.

--Welsh Folk-Lore: A Collection of Folk-Tales & Legends of North Wales. 1977. Repr. of 1896 ed. 29.00x (ISBN 0-7158-1179-7). Charles River Bks.

Parry-Jones, D. Welsh Legends & Folklore. 59.95 (ISBN 0-8490-1282-1). Gordon Pr.

Parry-Jones, Daniel. Welsh Legends & Fairy Lore. LC 76-10823. 1976. Repr. of 1963 ed. lib. bdg. 17.50 (ISBN 0-8414-6724-2). Folcroft.

Rhys, John. Celtic Folklore, 2 vols. Set. lib. bdg. 250.00 (ISBN 0-87968-099-7). Gordon Pr.

Rhys, Sir John. Celtic Folklore, Welsh & Manx, 2 vols. xlvi, 718p. Repr. of 1901 ed. 54.00 (ISBN 0-384-50610-0). Johnson Repr.

Sheppard-Jones, Elisabeth. Stories of Wales: Told for Children. (Illus.). (gr. 3-6). 1978. pap. 5.00 (ISBN 0-902375-41-5). Academy Chi Ltd.

Simpson, Jacqueline. The Folklore of the Welsh Border. (Folklore of the British Isles Ser.). (Illus.). 210p. 1976. 15.00x (ISBN 0-87471-837-6). Rowman.

FOLK-LORE, WEST INDIAN

Bryan, Ashley. The Dancing Granny. LC 76-25847. (Illus.). (gr. k-3). 1977. 6.95 (ISBN 0-689-30548-6). Atheneum.

Escabi, Pedro, ed. Morovis: Vista Parcial Del Folklore De Puerto Rico. pap. 6.25, incl. record (ISBN 0-8477-2500-6). U of PR Pr.

Flowers, Helen L. A Classification of the Folktales of the West Indies by Types & Motifs. Dorson, Richard M., ed. LC 80-726. (Folklores of the World Ser.). 1980. lib. bdg. 55.00x (ISBN 0-405-13313-8). Arno.

Rohmer, Harriet. The Little Horse of Seven Colors: El Caballito De Siete Colores. LC 76-17494. (Fifth World Tales Ser.). (Illus.). (gr. k-6). pap. 3.95 spanish bilingual ed. (ISBN 0-89239-006-9, Imprenta de Libros Infantiles). Childrens Book Pr.

FOLK-LORE OF AGRICULTURE

Petersen, Eugene T. France at Mackinac. LC 71-435. (Illus.). 44p. (Orig.). 1968. pap. 2.00 (ISBN 0-911872-33-7). Mackinac Island.

FOLK-LORE OF ANIMALS

see Animal Lore

FOLK-LORE OF APES

see Apes (In Religion, Folk-Lore, etc.)

FOLK-LORE OF BEADS

see Beads (In Religion, Folk-Lore, etc.)

FOLK-LORE OF BIRDS

see also Birds in Literature; also names of birds followed by the specification (In Religion, Folk-Lore, etc.)

Ingersoll, Ernest. Birds in Legend, Fable & Folklore. LC 68-26576. 1968. Repr. of 1923 ed. 22.00 (ISBN 0-8103-3548-4). Gale.

Pollard, John. Birds in Greek Life & Myth. (Aspects of Greek & Roman Life Ser.). (Illus.). 1977. 19.95 (ISBN 0-500-40032-6). Thames Hudson.

Rowland, Beryl. Birds with Human Souls: A Guide to Bird Symbolism. LC 77-4230. (Illus.). 1978. 15.00 (ISBN 0-87049-215-2). U of Tenn Pr.

Saxby, Jessie M. Birds of Omen in Shetland, with Notes on the Folklore of the Raven & Owl. (Folklore Ser.). Repr. 6.50 (ISBN 0-685-43668-3). Norwood Edns.

Tyler, Hamilton A. Pueblo Birds & Myths. LC 78-58069. (Civilization of the American Indian Ser: No. 147). (Illus.). 1979. 13.95 (ISBN 0-8061-1483-5). U of Okla Pr.

FOLK-LORE OF BIRTH

see Birth (In Religion, Folk-Lore, etc.)

FOLK-LORE OF BLOOD

see Blood (In Religion, Folk-Lore, etc.)

FOLK-LORE OF CATS

see Cats (In Religion, Folk-Lore, etc.)

FOLK-LORE OF CHILDREN

Brewster, Paul G., ed. Children's Games & Rhymes. LC 75-35063. (Studies in Play & Games: Vol. 1). 1976. Repr. 12.00x (ISBN 0-405-07914-1). Arno.

Brown, Marice C. Amen, Brother Ben: A Mississippi Collection of Children's Rhymes. LC 78-32017. 1979. pap. text ed. 5.00 (ISBN 0-87805-094-9). U Pr of Miss.

Herbert, S. Child-Lore: A Study in Folklore & Psychology. 1976. lib. bdg. 59.95 (ISBN 0-8490-1599-5). Gordon Pr.

Kidd, Dudley. Savage Childhood: A Study of Kafir Children. LC 75-76482. Repr. of 1906 ed. 19.25x (ISBN 0-8371-1135-8). Greenwood.

Opie, Iona & Opie, Peter. Lore & Language of School Children. (Illus.). (gr. 9 up). 1959. 22.00x (ISBN 0-19-827206-5, OPB). Oxford U Pr.

Sandoval, Ruben & Strick, David. Games, Games, Games, Juegos, Juegos, Juegos: Chicano Children at Play--Games & Rhymes. (gr. 1 up). 1977. PLB 6.95 (ISBN 0-385-05438-6). Doubleday.

FOLK-LORE OF COUNTRIES

see Geographical Myths

FOLK-LORE OF DANCING

see Dancing (In Religion, Folk-Lore, etc.)

FOLK-LORE OF DAYS

see Days

FOLK-LORE OF DOGS

see Dogs (In Religion, Folk-Lore, etc.)

FOLK-LORE OF DOLPHINS

see Dolphin (In Religion, Folk-Lore, etc.)

FOLK-LORE OF FELT

see Felt (In Religion, Folk-Lore, etc.)

FOLK-LORE OF FIRE

see Fire (In Religion, Folk-Lore, etc.)

FOLK-LORE OF FISHES

see Fish (In Religion, Folk-Lore, etc.)

FOLK-LORE OF FLOWERS

see Flowers (In Religion, Folk-Lore, etc.)

FOLK-LORE OF GEMS

see Gems (In Religion, Folk-Lore, etc.)

FOLK-LORE OF HARVESTING

see Folk-Lore of Agriculture

FOLK-LORE OF HORNS

see Horns (In Religion, Folk-Lore, etc.)

FOLK-LORE OF HORSES

see Horses (In Religion, Folk-Lore, etc.)

FOLK-LORE OF INITIATIONS

see Initiations (In Religion, Folk-Lore, etc.)

FOLK-LORE OF INSECTS

see also names of insects followed by the specification (In Religion, Folklore, etc.), e.g. Dragonflies (in Religion, Folklore, etc.)

FOLK-LORE OF KINGS AND RULERS

see Kings and Rulers (In Religion, Folk-Lore, etc.)

FOLK-LORE OF MINES

Fish, Lydia M. The Folklore of the Coal Miners of the Northeast of England. LC 76-25433. 1976. Set. lib. bdg. 25.00 (ISBN 0-8414-4209-6). Folcroft.

Gillespie, Angus K. Folklorist of the Coal Fields: George Korson's Life & Work. LC 79-25839. (Illus.). 1980. 16.95 (ISBN 0-271-00255-7). Pa St U Pr.

Granger, Byrd H. Motif Index for lost mines & treasures, applied to redaction of Arizona Legends, & to lost mines & treasure legends exterior to Arizona. LC 77-27331. 1978. text ed. 14.50x (ISBN 0-8165-0646-9). U of Ariz Pr.

Probert, Thomas. Lost Mines & Buried Treasures of the West. LC 76-24596. (Illus.). 1977. 38.50 (ISBN 0-520-03327-2). U of Cal Pr.

Robinson, Richard A. Why Me? Conquest of the Lost Dutchman Mine. 1977. pap. 2.95 (ISBN 0-89412-020-4). Aegean Park Pr.

FOLK LORE OF NUMBERS

see Counting-Out Rhymes

FOLK-LORE OF PLANTS
see Folk-Lore of Trees; Plant Lore
FOLK-LORE OF POLARITY
see Polarity (In Religion, Folk-Lore, etc.)
FOLK-LORE OF RAILROADS
see also John Henry
FOLK-LORE OF SERPENTS
see Serpents (In Religion, Folk-Lore, Etc.)
FOLK-LORE OF STARS
see Stars (In Religion, Folk-Lore, etc.)
FOLK-LORE OF THE BODY
see Body, Human (In Religion, Folk-Lore, etc.)
FOLK-LORE OF THE DEAD
see Dead (In Religion, Folk-Lore, etc.)
FOLK-LORE OF THE MOON
see Moon (In Religion, Folk-Lore, etc.)
FOLK-LORE OF THE SEA

Anderson, Eugene & Anderson, Marja L. Mountain & Water: Essays on the Cultural Ecology of South Coastal China, No. 54. (Asian Folklore & Social Life Monograph). 194p. (Chinese.). 1973. 5.50 (ISBN 0-89986-051-6). E Langstaff.

Baker, Margret. Folklore of the Sea. (Illus.). 1979. 16.95 (ISBN 0-7153-7568-7). David & Charles.

Bassett, Fletcher S. Legends & Superstitions of the Sea & of Sailors, in All Lands & at All Times. LC 70-119444. (Illus.). 1974. Repr. of 1885 ed. 32.00 (ISBN 0-8103-3375-9). Gale.

Beck, Horace. Folklore & the Sea. LC 73-6011. (The American Maritime Library: Vol. 6). (Illus.). 480p. 1973. ltd. ed. 40.00 (ISBN 0-8195-4063-3). Mystic Seaport.

Buss, Reinhard J. The Klabautermann of the Northern Seas: An Analysis of the Protective Spirit of Ships & Sailors in the Context of Popular Belief, Christian Legend & Indo-European Mythology. (U. C. Publ. in Folklore Studies: Vol. 25). pap. 10.00x (ISBN 0-520-09399-2). U of Cal Pr.

Horace. Folklore & the Sea. (Illus.). 463p. 1981. pap. 12.95 (ISBN 0-8195-6052-9, Pub. by Wesleyan U Pr). Columbia U Pr.

Parsons, Kitty. Gloucester Sea Ballads. 2nd, rev. ed. (Illus.). 64p. 1981. pap. 4.95 (ISBN 0-939792-00-1). Fermata.

Smith, Laura A. Music of the Waters. LC 69-16479. 1969. Repr. of 1888 ed. 24.00 (ISBN 0-8103-3552-2). Gale.

Wisner, Bill. Strange Sea Stories & Legends. (Orig.). 1981. pap. 2.95 (ISBN 0-451-11127-3, AE1127, Sig). NAL.

Zeusler, F. A. Sea Drift. 1980. 6.95 (ISBN 0-533-03681-X). Vantage.

FOLK-LORE OF THE SKY
see also Stars (In Religion, Folk-Lore, etc.); Sun (In Religion, Folk-Lore, etc.)

Wainwright, Gerald A. Sky-Religion in Egypt: Its Antiquity & Effects. LC 71-136088. 1971. Repr. of 1938 ed. lib. bdg. 15.00 (ISBN 0-8371-5238-0, WASR). Greenwood.

FOLK-LORE OF THE SUN
see Sun (In Religion, Folk-Lore, etc.)
FOLK-LORE OF TREES
see also Christmas Trees

Helfman, Elizabeth S. Maypoles & Wood Demons: The Meaning of Trees. LC 72-75706. (Illus.). 128p. (gr. 3-7). 1972. 7.95 (ISBN 0-8164-3085-3, Clarion). HM.

Mills, Charles De B. The Tree of Mythology, Its Growth & Fruitage. 1976. lib. bdg. 59.95 (ISBN 0-8490-2765-9). Gordon Pr.

Philpot, J. H. The Sacred Tree: The Tree in Religion & Myth. 1977. lib. bdg. 69.95 (ISBN 0-8490-2553-2). Gordon Pr.

Porteous, Alexander. Forest Folklore, Mythology & Romance. LC 68-26597. 1968. Repr. of 1928 ed. 22.00 (ISBN 0-8103-3456-9). Gale.

FOLK-LORE OF TWINS
see Twins (In Religion, Folk-Lore, etc.)
FOLK-LORE OF VAMPIRES
see Vampires
FOLK-LORE OF WOMEN
see Women (In Religion, Folklore, etc.)
FOLK MEDICINE

Abd Al-Rahman Isma'Il. Folk Medicine in Modern Egypt. LC 77-87651. Repr. of 1934 ed. 19.00 (ISBN 0-404-16407-2). AMS Pr.

--Folk Medicine in Modern Egypt: Being the Relevant Parts of the Tibb al-Rukka, or Old Wives' Medicine, of 'Abd al-Rahman Isma'il. LC 77-87651. (Anthropolgy Ser.). (Illus.). Repr. of 1934 ed. 19.00 (ISBN 0-404-16407-2). AMS Pr.

Aikman, Lonnelle. Nature's Healing Arts: From Folk Medicine to Modern Drugs. LC 76-56997. (Special Publications Ser.: No. 12). (Illus.). 1977. avail. only from natl. geog. 6.95 (ISBN 0-87044-232-5). Natl Geog.

Anderson, John Q., ed. Texas Folk Medicine, Vol. 5. (Texas Folklore Society Paisano Books Ser.). 1970. 9.95 (ISBN 0-88426-013-5). Encino Pr.

Atkinson, Donald T. Magic, Myth & Medicine. LC 72-8510. (Essay Index Reprint Ser.). 1972. Repr. of 1956 ed. 19.00 (ISBN 0-8369-7316-X). Arno.

Black, William G. Folk-Medicine: A Chapter in the History of Culture. LC 74-124308. (Research & Source Ser.: No. 486). 1970. Repr. of 1883 ed. 15.00 (ISBN 0-8337-0298-X). B Franklin.

Bolyard, Judith L. Medicinal Plants & Home Remedies of Appalachia. (Illus.). 160p. 1981. 18.50 (ISBN 0-398-04180-6). C C Thomas.

Brendle, T. R. Folk Medicine of the Pennsylvania Germans: The Non-Occult Cures. LC 71-15633. Repr. of 1935 ed. 15.00x (ISBN 0-678-03753-1). Kelley.

Bridwell, Tom. Anacoluthon. (Orig.). 1980. limited signed ed. 22.50x (ISBN 0-915316-79-X); pap. 4.00x (ISBN 0-915316-78-1). Pentagram.

Camp, John. Magic, Myth & Medicine. LC 73-18793. 200p. 1974. 8.50 (ISBN 0-8008-5046-7). Taplinger.

Cerney, J. Handbook of Unusual & Unorthodox Healing Methods. 1977. pap. 3.45 (ISBN 0-685-80409-7, Reward). P-H.

Early American Home Remedies. (Americana Books Ser.). (Illus.). 1968. 1.50 (ISBN 0-911410-20-1). Applied Arts.

Fabrega, Horacio, Jr. & Silver, Daniel B. Illness & Shamanistic Curing in Zinacantan: An Ethnomedical Analysis. LC 73-80621. 304p. 1973. 15.00x (ISBN 0-8047-0844-4). Stanford U Pr.

Fielder, Mildred. Plant Medicine & Folklore. 1977. pap. 4.95 (ISBN 0-87691-228-5). Winchester Pr.

Frankel, Barbara. Childbirth in the Ghetto: Folk Beliefs of Negro Women in a North Philadelphia Hospital Ward. LC 76-27000. 1977. soft bdg. 10.00 (ISBN 0-88247-418-9). R & E Res Assoc.

Gerrick, David J. & Dietsche, Doreen. Old Time Cures - Farmers Folklore. 104p. (Orig.). 1980. pap. 3.95 (ISBN 0-916750-41-8). Dayton Labs.

Grollig, Francis X., et al, eds. Medical Anthropology. (World Anthropology Ser). (Illus.). 1976. 38.00x (ISBN 0-202-90031-2). Beresford Bk Serv.

Hand, Wayland D. Magical Medicine: The Folkloric Component of Folk Medicine in the Folk Belief, Custom, & Ritual of Non-Primitive Peoples. LC 80-51238. 296p. 1981. 22.50x (ISBN 0-520-04129-1). U of Cal Pr.

Hand, Wayland D., ed. American Folk Medicine: A Symposium. LC 74-30522. 1976. 14.95 (ISBN 0-520-02941-0); pap. 5.95 (ISBN 0-520-04093-7). U of Cal Pr.

Harrison, Ira E. & Cosminsky, Sheila. Traditional Medicine: Implications of Mental Health, Public Health, Maternal & Child Health & Family Planning. LC 75-24105. (Reference Library of Social Science: Vol. 19). 150p. 1975. lib. bdg. 22.00 (ISBN 0-8240-9970-2). Garland Pub.

Hirschhorn, Howard H. Miracle Health Secrets from the Old Country. LC 81-1011. 208p. 1981. 12.95 (ISBN 0-13-585000-2). P-H.

Imperato, Pascal J. African Folk Medicine: Practices & Beliefs of the Bambara & Other Peoples. LC 77-5465. (Illus.). 1977. 16.00x (ISBN 0-912752-08-4). York Pr.

Jarvis, D. C. Arthritis & Folk Medicine. 1978. pap. 2.25 (ISBN 0-449-24160-2, Crest). Fawcett.

--Folk Medicine. 1.95 (ISBN 0-686-29756-3). Cancer Bk Hse.

--Folk Medicine. 1978. pap. 2.50 (ISBN 0-449-24161-0, Crest). Fawcett.

--Folk Medicine: A Vermont Doctor's Guide to Good Health. LC 58-6454. 1958. 5.95 (ISBN 0-03-027410-9). HR&W.

Kemp, Phyllis. Healing Ritual: Studies in the Technique & Tradition of the Southern Slavs. LC 75-23731. Repr. of 1935 ed. 29.00 (ISBN 0-404-13289-8). AMS Pr.

Kiev, Ari. Curanderismo: Mexican-American Folk Psychiatry. LC 67-25331. 1972. pap. 3.95 (ISBN 0-02-917260-8). Free Pr.

Long, Joseph. Psyche Versus Soma: Traditional Healing Choices in Jamaica. (Traditional Healing Ser.). 1981. 17.50 (ISBN 0-932426-20-4). Trado-Medic.

McBride, L. R. Practical Folk Medicine of Hawaii. (Illus.). 1975. pap. 5.50 (ISBN 0-912180-27-7). Petroglyph.

Mackenzie, Dan. The Infancy of Medicine: An Enquiry into the Influence of Folk-Lore Upon the Evolution of Scientific Medicine. (Historia Medicinae Ser.). xiii, 427p. 1981. Repr. of 1927 ed. lib. bdg. 25.00x (ISBN 0-87991-708-3). Porcupine Pr.

McKenzie, Dan. The Infancy of Medicine: Influence of Folklore Upon Scientific Medicine. 1977. lib. bdg. 50.00 (ISBN 0-8490-2057-3). Gordon Pr.

Meyer, Clarence. American Folk Medicine. 1975. pap. 3.95 (ISBN 0-452-25097-8, Z5097, Plume). NAL.

--American Folk Medicine. LC 73-4300. 1973. 3.95 (ISBN 0-685-72759-9, Pub. by NAL). Formur Intl.

Mitchell, Faith. Hoodoo Medicine. 1978. pap. 4.95 (ISBN 0-918408-06-7). Reed & Cannon.

Monahan, Evelyn. Miracle of Metaphysical Healing. 1977. 8.95 (ISBN 0-13-585752-X, Reward); pap. 3.95 (ISBN 0-13-585778-3). P-H.

Page, Robin. Cures & Remedies the Country Way. LC 78-31747. (Country Way Bks.). 1979. 4.95 (ISBN 0-671-40092-4). Summit Bks.

Pitre, Giuseppe. Sicilian Folk Medicine. (Illus.). 320p. 1971. 48.50x (ISBN 0-87291-013-X). Coronado Pr.

Read, Bernard E. Chinese Medicinal Plants from the Pen T'sao Kang Mu. 1977. 7.50 (ISBN 0-89986-317-5). E Langstaff.

--Insect Drugs, Dragon & Snake Drugs, Fish Drugs. 1977. 7.50 (ISBN 0-89986-321-3). E Langstaff.

--Turtle & Shellfish Drugs, Avian Drugs, Minerals & Stones. 1977. 7.50 (ISBN 0-89986-330-2). E Langstaff.

Rinzler, Carol A. The Dictionary of Medical Folklore. LC 78-69518. 1979. 10.00 (ISBN 0-690-01704-9). T Y Crowell.

Solomon, Jack & Solomon, Olivia. Cracklin Bread & Asfidity: Folk Recipes & Remedies. LC 77-13065. (Illus.). 225p. 1979. 14.95 (ISBN 0-8173-8650-5). U of Ala Pr.

Spicer, Edward H., ed. Ethnic Medicine in the Southwest. LC 76-62553. 1977. pap. 6.95x (ISBN 0-8165-0490-3). U of Ariz Pr.

Svenson, Jon-Erik. Compendium of Early American Folk Remedies, Recipes & Advice. 1977. 4.95 (ISBN 0-425-03367-8, Windhover). Berkley Pub.

Thesen, Karen. Country Remedies. LC 78-24701. (Illus.). 1979. pap. 4.95 (ISBN 0-06-090687-1, CN687, CN). Har-Row.

Thomas, Mai, ed. Grannies' Remedies. (Illus.). 1967. 4.95 (ISBN 0-685-11958-0). Heineman.

Trotter, Robert T., 2nd & Chaviro, Juan A. Curanderismo: Mexican American Folk Healing. LC 81-602. (Illus.). 216p. 1981. 16.00 (ISBN 0-8203-0556-1); pap. 8.00 (ISBN 0-8203-0570-7). U of Ga Pr.

Williams, Paul V. Primitive Religion & Healing: A Study of Folk Medicine in North East Brazil. (Folklore Society Mistletoe Ser.). (Illus.). 212p. 1979. 32.50x (ISBN 0-8476-6222-5). Rowman.

FOLK MUSIC
see also Country Music; Folk Dance Music; Folk Dancing; Folk-Songs

Artis, Bob. Bluegrass. 1977. pap. 1.75 (ISBN 0-8439-0452-6, Leisure Bks). Nordon Pubns.

Bartok, Bela. Hungarian Folk Music. Calvocoressi, M. D., tr. LC 78-62328. (Encore Music Editions). (Illus.). 1979. Repr. of 1931 ed. 27.50 (ISBN 0-88355-722-3). Hyperion Conn.

--Hungarian Folk Music. Calvocoressi, M. D., tr. LC 77-87537. Repr. of 1931 ed. 37.00 (ISBN 0-404-16600-8). AMS Pr.

--Rumanian Folk Music, 5 vols. Suchoff, Benjamin, ed. Incl. Vol. 1. Instrumental Melodies. 750p; Vol. 2. Vocal Melodies. 787p; Vol. 3. Texts. 770p. 1967. 385.00x (ISBN 90-247-0622-X). Intl Pubns Serv.

--Turkish Folk Music from Asia Minor. Suchoff, Benjamin, ed. LC 75-23186. (Studies in Musicology). 1976. 21.00 (ISBN 0-691-09120-X). Princeton U Pr.

Bayard, Samuel P., ed. Hill Country Tunes. LC 45-7228. Repr. of 1944 ed. 10.00 (ISBN 0-527-01091-X). Kraus Repr.

Berger, Melvin. The Story of Folk Music. LC 76-18159. (Illus.). (gr. 6 up). 1976. PLB 9.95 (ISBN 0-87599-215-3). S G Phillips.

Blocher, Arlo. Folk. new ed. LC 75-39815. (Illus.). 32p. (gr. 5-10). 1976. PLB 6.89 (ISBN 0-89375-013-1); pap. 2.50 (ISBN 0-89375-029-8). Troll Assocs.

Bobri, V. & Miller, Carl. Two Guitars. 1972. pap. 3.95 (ISBN 0-02-060140-9, Collier). Macmillan.

Breathnach, Breandan. Folk Music & Dances of Ireland. rev. ed. (Illus.). 152p. 1977. pap. 5.95 (ISBN 0-85342-509-4). Irish Bk Ctr.

Chandola, Anoop. Folk Drumming in the Himalayas. LC 76-23549. (Illus.). 1977. 12.50 (ISBN 0-404-15403-4). AMS Pr.

Claire, Vivian. Judy Collins. LC 77-78538. (Illus.). 1977. pap. 3.95 (ISBN 0-8256-3914-X, Quick Fox). Music Sales.

Coleridge-Taylor, S. Twenty-Four Negro Melodies. (Music Reprint Ser.: 1980). 1980. Repr. of 1905 ed. lib. bdg. 22.50 (ISBN 0-306-76023-1). Da Capo.

Cook, Harold E. Shaker Music: A Manifestation of American Folk Culture. LC 71-161507. 312p. 1973. 18.00 (ISBN 0-8387-7953-0). Bucknell U Pr.

Flatt & Scruggs. Folk Music with an Overdrive. pap. 2.50 (ISBN 0-686-09066-7). Peer-Southern.

Gillington, Alice E. Songs of the Open Road. (Folklore Ser). 5.00 (ISBN 0-685-36453-4). Norwood Edns.

Haslund-Christensen, Henning & Cmshevner, Ernst. Music of the Mongols: Eastern Mongolia. LC 79-125045. (Music Ser). 1971. Repr. of 1943 ed. lib. bdg. 25.00 (ISBN 0-306-70009-3). Da Capo.

Hunter, Ilene & Judson, Marilyn. Simple Folk Instruments to Make & to Play. 1980. 4.95 (ISBN 0-671-25432-4). S&S.

Indiana University, Folklore Institute, Archives of Traditional Music. Catalog of the Archives of Traditional Music. 400p. 1976. lib. bdg. 21.00 (ISBN 0-8161-1120-0). G K Hall.

Leach, R. & Palmer, R., eds. Folk Music in School. LC 77-71416. (Resources of Music Ser.). 1978. 17.50 (ISBN 0-521-21595-1); pap. 6.95 (ISBN 0-521-29206-9). Cambridge U Pr.

Mattfield, Julius. The Folk Music of the Western Hemisphere: A List of References in the New York Public Library. Dorson, Richard M., ed. LC 80-796. (Folklore of the World Ser.). 1980. Repr. of 1925 ed. lib. bdg. 12.00x (ISBN 0-405-13335-9). Arno.

Nettl, Bruno. Folk & Traditional Music of the Western Continents. 2nd ed. (Illus.). 272p. 1973. pap. 10.95 (ISBN 0-13-322933-5). P-H.

Nettl, Bruno & Myers, Helen. Folk Music in the United States: An Introduction. 3rd, rev. & exp. ed. LC 76-84. 1976. 8.95 (ISBN 0-8143-1556-9); pap. 4.95 (ISBN 0-685-63511-2). Wayne St U Pr.

Robb, John D. Hispanic Folk Music of New Mexico & the Southwest: A Self-Portrait of the People. LC 78-21392. (Illus.). 1980. 35.00 (ISBN 0-8061-1492-4). U of Okla Pr.

Sandberg, Larry & Weissman, Dick. The Folk Music Sourcebook. (Illus.). 1976. pap. 7.95 (ISBN 0-394-73098-4). Knopf.

Schonzeler, Hans-Hubert. Dvorak: 192p. Date not set. price not set (ISBN 0-7145-2575-8, Pub. by M. Boyars). Merrimack Bk Serv.

Seeger, Pete. The Incompleat Folksinger. 1972. pap. 5.95 (ISBN 0-686-66836-7). S&S.

Silber, Fred & Silber, Irwin, eds. Folksinger's Wordbook. 432p. spiral bdg. 14.95 (ISBN 0-8256-0140-1). Music Sales.

Thede, Marion. The Fiddle Book. LC 66-19062. (Illus., Orig.). 1967. pap. 7.95 (ISBN 0-8256-0145-2, Oak). Music Sales.

Using Folk Entertainments to Promote National Development. 45p. 1981. pap. 4.75 (ISBN 92-3-101773-X, U1064, UNESCO). Unipub.

FOLK-PLAYS
see Folk-Drama
FOLK-PSYCHOLOGY
see Ethnopsychology
FOLK-SONGS
see also Ballads; Carols; Folk-Lore; Lays; National Songs

Alburo, Erlinda K., ed. Cebuano Folksongs One. (Illus.). 1978. pap. 2.00x (ISBN 0-686-24098-7, Pub. by San Carlos). Cellar.

Art Songs & Ballads. pap. 2.00 (ISBN 0-685-22653-0). Polanie.

Asher, Gloria J. Izmirli Proverbs & Songs from the Bronx. 10p. 1976. softcover 1.25 (ISBN 0-686-74365-2). ADELANTRE.

Boni, Margaret & Lloyd, Norman. Fireside Book of Folk Songs. (Illus., New edition with guitar chords). (gr. 5 up). 1966. 17.50 (ISBN 0-671-25836-2). S&S.

Boughton, Rutland. The Reality of Music. LC 72-80495. Repr. of 1934 ed. 14.00 (ISBN 0-405-08294-0, Blom Pubns). Arno.

Chambers, G. B. Folksong-Plainsong: A Study in Origins & Musical Relationships. 2nd ed. 1972. Repr. of 1956 ed. text ed. 9.50x (ISBN 0-85036-178-8). Humanities.

Collection de contes et de chansons populaires, 46 vols. (The Folktale Ser.). Repr. of 1930 ed. Set. 989.00 (ISBN 0-404-60350-5). AMS Pr.

Folk Music Accompaniment for Guitar. pap. 2.95 (ISBN 0-686-09070-5). Peer-Southern.

Garden of Songs: Gwerta de Kantigas. 4p. 1977. softcover 1.00 (ISBN 0-686-74368-7). ADELANTRE.

Glassie, Henry, et al. Folksongs & Their Makers. 179p. 1971. pap. 5.00 (ISBN 0-87972-006-9). Bowling Green Univ.

John, Robert W. & Douglas, Charles N. Playing Social & Recreational Instruments. (Illus.). 144p. 1972. pap. text ed. 10.95 (ISBN 0-13-683680-1). P-H.

Keith, Alexander. Burns & Folk-Song. (Folklore Ser). 5.00 (ISBN 0-685-36473-9). Norwood Edns.

Langstaff, Nancy & Langstaff, John, eds. Jim Along, Josie: A Collection of Folk Songs & Singing Games for Young Children. LC 79-118757. (Illus.). (gr. k up). 1970. 10.50 (ISBN 0-15-240250-0, HJ). HarBraceJ.

Lara, Jesus. Quechua Peoples Poetry. Proser, Maria & Scully, James, eds. LC 76-26704. Orig. Title: Poesia Popular Quechua. 1977. pap. 6.00 (ISBN 0-915306-09-3). Curbstone.

Le Coq, Albert V. Sprichworter und Lieder Aus der Gegend Von Turfan. Repr. of 1911 ed. 13.00 (ISBN 0-384-32000-7). Johnson Repr.

Leisy, James. Good Times Songbook. LC 73-11248. (Illus.). 432p. 1974. 14.95 (ISBN 0-687-15573-8). Abingdon.

Lightfoot, Gordon. The Pony Man. LC 71-184374. (Illus.). 32p. (YA) 1972. lib. bdg. 7.89 (ISBN 0-06-126326-5). Har-Row.

Lomax, Alan. The Folk Songs of North America. (Illus.). 656p. 1975. pap. 8.95 (ISBN 0-385-03772-4, Dolp). Doubleday.

Loranth, Alice N., ed. Catalog of Folklore, Folklife & Folk Songs, 3 vols. 2nd ed. 1978. Set. lib. bdg. 245.00 (ISBN 0-8161-0249-X). G K Hall.

Mahapatra, Sitakant. The Empty Distance Carries... Munda & Oraon Folk - Songs. 1976. lib. bdg. 14.00 (ISBN 0-89253-096-0); flexible bdg. 4.80 (ISBN 0-89253-146-0). Ind-US Inc.

New Troubadours. The New Troubadours Songbook. Crabtree, Philip, et al, eds. (Illus.). 92p. (Orig.). 1981. pap. 10.00 (ISBN 0-936878-02-9). Lorian Pr.

Palmer, R., ed. Room for Company: Folk Songs & Ballads. 1971. piano ed 6.95 (ISBN 0-521-08173-4); pap. 2.95 melody ed (ISBN 0-521-08174-2). Cambridge U Pr.

Randolph, Vance. Ozark Folksongs, 4 vols. Incl. Vol. I. British Ballads & Songs. 464p (ISBN 0-8262-0302-7); Vol. II. Songs of the South & West. 448p (ISBN 0-8262-0303-5); Vol. III. Humorous & Play-Party Songs. 416p (ISBN 0-8262-0304-3); Vol. IV. Religious Songs & Other Items. 464p (ISBN 0-8262-0305-1). LC 79-3611. 1744p. 1980. Set. pap. 49.95 (ISBN 0-8262-0306-X); pap. 12.95 ea. U of Mo Pr.

Sakanishi, Hachiro. Die Volksliedschwebestrophe und Deren Freie Stelle. 146p. 1972. 16.00x (ISBN 0-86008-058-7, Pub by U of Tokyo Pr). Intl Schol Bk Serv.

Seeger, Pete. The Incompleat Folksinger. 1972. pap. 5.95 (ISBN 0-686-66836-7). S&S.

Silverman, Jerry. Liberated Woman's Songbook. Markel, Robert, ed. (Illus.). 1971. pap. 3.95 (ISBN 0-02-082040-2, Collier). Macmillan.

Stedman, Ray C. Folk Psalms of Faith. LC 72-90405. 1973. pap. 2.95 (ISBN 0-8307-0450-7, S264-1-29). Regal.

Von Schmidt, Eric & Rooney, Jim. Baby, Let Me Follow You Down. LC 78-8222. 1979. 8.95 (ISBN 0-385-14456-3, Anch). Doubleday.

Winn, Marie & Miller, Allan. The Fireside Book of Children's Songs. LC 65-17108. (Illus.). (gr. 3 up). 1966. 12.95 (ISBN 0-671-25820-6, Juveniles). S&S.

FOLK-SONGS–BIBLIOGRAPHY

Brunnings, Florence E. Folk Song Index. LC 80-8522. 700p. 1981. lib. bdg. 75.00 (ISBN 0-8240-9462-X). Garland Pub.

Engel, Carl. The Literature of National Music. LC 77-75201. 1977. Repr. of 1879 ed. lib. bdg. 12.50 (ISBN 0-89341-103-5). Longwood Pr.

Stainer, John, ed. Catalogue of English Song Books. LC 77-75178. 1977. Repr. of 1891 ed. lib. bdg. 12.50 (ISBN 0-89341-066-7). Longwood Pr.

FOLK-SONGS–DISCOGRAPHY

Greenway, John. American Folksongs of Protest. LC 75-111635. 1970. Repr. of 1953 ed. lib. bdg. 18.50x (ISBN 0-374-93254-9). Octagon.

Nettel, Reginald. Social History of Traditional Song. LC 70-93274. (Illus.). Repr. of 1954 ed. 15.00x (ISBN 0-678-07506-9). Kelley.

FOLK-SONGS–HISTORY AND CRITICISM

Lomax, Alan, ed. Folk Song Style & Culture. LC 68-21545. 384p. 1978. pap. 6.95 (ISBN 0-87855-640-0). Transaction Bks.

Martinengo-Cesaresco, Evelyn. Essays in the Study of Folksongs. 1976. lib. bdg. 59.95 (ISBN 0-8490-1785-8). Gordon Pr.

Palmer, R. Poverty Knock. LC 73-93391. (Resources of Music Ser.: No. 9). (Illus.). 64p. (gr. 9-11). 1974. pap. text ed. 4.95 (ISBN 0-521-20443-7). Cambridge U Pr.

Seeger, Pete. The Incomplete Folksinger. 1976. pap. 5.95 (ISBN 0-671-22304-6, Fireside). S&S.

FOLK-SONGS–JUVENILE LITERATURE

Bookbinder, David. What Folk Music Is All About. LC 79-229. (Illus.). 320p. (gr. 7 up). 1979. PLB 9.29 (ISBN 0-671-32893-X). Messner.

Kellogg, Steven. There Was an Old Woman. LC 80-15293. (Illus.). 48p. (ps-3). 1980. Repr. of 1974 ed. 8.95 (ISBN 0-590-07779-1, Four Winds). Schol Bk Serv.

Rohmer, Harriet & Perez, Irene. Cuna Song: Cancion De los Cunas. LC 76-29122. (Fifth World Tales Ser.). (Illus.). (gr. k-6). pap. 3.95 spanish bilingual ed. (ISBN 0-89239-008-5, Imprenta de Libros Infantiles). Childrens Book Pr.

Swan, Susan E., illus. The Twelve Days of Christmas. (Illus.). 32p. (gr. k-2). 1981. PLB 5.79 (ISBN 0-89375-474-9); pap. text ed. 1.50 (ISBN 0-89375-475-7). Troll Assocs.

FOLK-SONGS, AFRO-AMERICAN

see Afro-American Songs

FOLK-SONGS, ALBANIAN

Dozon, A. Contes albanais. LC 78-20111. (Collection de contes et de chansons populaires: Vol. 3). Repr. of 1881 ed. 21.50 (ISBN 0-404-60353-X). AMS Pr.

FOLK-SONGS, AMERICAN

see also Ballads, American; Play-Party

The American Songster: As Sung in the Iron Days of 76. (Folklore Ser). 15.00 (ISBN 0-8482-7260-9). Norwood Edns.

Anderson, Sherwood. Mid-American Chants. LC 78-14240. 1978. Repr. of 1918 ed. lib. bdg. 15.00 (ISBN 0-8414-3007-1). Folcroft.

Anonymous. The American Songster: A Collection of Songs. 1978. Repr. of 1840 ed. lib. bdg. 15.00 (ISBN 0-8414-2926-X). Folcroft.

Belden, Henry M., ed. Ballads & Songs Collected by the Missouri Folk-Lore Society. 2nd ed. LC 55-7519. 1955. 15.00x (ISBN 0-8262-0142-3). U of Mo Pr.

Bley, Edgar S. Best Singing Games for Children of All Ages. rev. ed. LC 57-1014. (Illus.). (gr. k-6). 1959. 8.95 (ISBN 0-8069-4450-1); PLB 8.29 (ISBN 0-8069-4451-X). Sterling.

Boatright, Mody C. & Day, Donald, eds. Backwoods to Border. LC 48-18054. (Texas Folklore Society Publications: No. 18). (Illus.). 1967. Repr. of 1943 ed. 6.95 (ISBN 0-87074-011-3). SMU Press.

Boni, Margaret & Lloyd, Norman. Fireside Book of Favorite American Songs. (Illus.). (gr. 3 up). 1963. 15.95 (ISBN 0-671-24771-9). S&S.

Brown, Frank C. The Frank C. Brown Collection of North Carolina Folklore, 7 vols. Incl. Vol. 1. Games & Rhymes, Beliefs & Customs, Riddles, Proverbs, Speech, Tales & Legends (ISBN 0-8223-0027-3); Vol. 2. Folk Ballads from North Carolina (ISBN 0-8223-0254-3); Vol. 3. Folk Songs from North Carolina; Vol. 4. The Music of the Ballads; Vol. 5. The/Music of the Folk Songs; Vol. 6. Popular Beliefs & Superstitions from North Carolina, Pt. 1 (ISBN 0-8223-0283-7); Vol. 7. Popular Beliefs & Superstitions from North Carolina, Pt. 2 (ISBN 0-8223-0284-5). LC 58-10967. (Illus.). 1952-64. 19.75 ea.; 125.00 set (ISBN 0-685-22682-4, 58-10967). Duke.

Browne, Ray B., ed. The Alabama Folk Lyric: A Study in Origins & Media of Dissemination. LC 78-61076. 1979. 25.00 (ISBN 0-87972-129-4). Bowling Green Univ.

Burton, Thomas G., ed. Tom Ashley, Sam McGee, Bukka White: Tennessee Traditional Singers. LC 79-19655. 1981. 14.50 (ISBN 0-87049-260-8). U of Tenn Pr.

Carley, Isabel M. Simple Settings of American Folk Songs: For Orff Ensemble Book 1. 1972. pap. 1.75 (ISBN 0-918812-06-2). Magnamusic.

--Simple Settings of American Folk Songs: For Orff Ensemble Book 2. 1974. pap. 1.75 (ISBN 0-918812-07-0). Magnamusic.

Chase, Richard. American Folk Tales & Songs. 1971. pap. 3.50 (ISBN 0-486-22692-1). Dover.

--American Folk Tales & Songs. (Illus.). 6.75 (ISBN 0-8446-0057-1). Peter Smith.

Cohen, Norm. Long Steel Rail: The Railroad in American Folksong. LC 80-14874. (Music in American Life Ser.). (Illus.). 738p. 1981. 49.95 (ISBN 0-252-00343-8). U of Ill Pr.

Coleman, Satis N. & Bregman, Adolph, eds. Songs of American Folks. facsimile ed. LC 68-57060. (Granger Index Reprint Ser). 1942. 13.00 (ISBN 0-8369-6011-4). Arno.

Cox, John Harrington. Folk-Songs Mainly from West Virginia. Herzog, George & Halpert, Herbert, eds. LC 76-58548. (Music Reprint Series). 1977. Repr. of 1939 ed. lib. bdg. 22.50 (ISBN 0-306-70786-1). Da Capo.

Davis, Arthur K. Folk-Songs of Virginia. LC 79-163676. Repr. of 1949 ed. 26.50 (ISBN 0-404-01987-0). AMS Pr.

Davis, Arthur K., Jr. Traditional Ballads of Virginia. LC 78-79458. (Illus.). 634p. 1969. Repr. of 1929 ed. 10.00 (ISBN 0-8139-0269-X). U Pr of Va.

Dobie, J. Frank, ed. Man, Bird, & Beast. LC 33-1132. (Texas Folklore Society Publications: No. 8). (Illus.). 1965. Repr. of 1930 ed. 5.95 (ISBN 0-87074-131-4). SMU Press.

--Texas & Southwestern Lore. LC 33-1131. (Texas Folklore Society Publications: No. 6). 1967. Repr. of 1927 ed. 6.95 (ISBN 0-87074-044-X). SMU Press.

--Tone the Bell Easy. LC 33-1135. (Texas Folklore Society Publications: No. 10). (Illus.). 1965. Repr. of 1932 ed. 5.95 (ISBN 0-87074-045-8). SMU Press.

Emrich, Duncan. American Folk Poetry: An Anthology. LC 74-3499. (Illus.). 864p. 1974. 24.95 (ISBN 0-316-23722-1). Little.

Flanders, Helen H. & Brown, George. Vermont Folk-Songs & Ballads. LC 68-20768. iv, 256p. 1968. Repr. of 1931 ed. 22.00 (ISBN 0-8103-5010-6). Gale.

Flanders, Helen H. & Olney, Marguerite, eds. Ballads Migrant in New England. facs. ed. LC 68-58825. (Granger Index Reprint Ser). 1953. 15.00 (ISBN 0-8369-6015-7). Arno.

Flanders, Helen H., compiled by. Vermont Chapbook. facs. ed. LC 70-76935. (Granger Index Reprint Ser). 1941. 11.00 (ISBN 0-8369-6016-5). Arno.

Folk-Song Society Of The Northeast. Bulletin of the Folk-Song Society of the Northeast, Nos. 1-12. (American Folklore Society Bibliographical & Special Ser.). Repr. of 1960 ed. 16.00 (ISBN 0-527-01129-0). Kraus Repr.

Folk Songs Out of Wisconsin: An Illustrated Compendium of Words & Music. LC 77-1793. 1977. pap. 6.95 (ISBN 0-87020-165-4). State Hist Soc Wis.

Fowke, Edith & Glazer, Joe. Songs of Work & Protest. Orig. Title: Songs of Work & Freedom. 290p. 1973. Repr. of 1960 ed. 5.00 (ISBN 0-486-22899-1). Dover.

Gainer, Patrick W. Folk Songs from the West Virginia Hills. LC 75-38967. 1975. 15.00 (ISBN 0-89092-001-X). Seneca Bks.

Gillington, Alice E. Song of the Open Road. LC 77-18515. 1978. Repr. of 1911 ed. lib. bdg. 10.00 (ISBN 0-8414-2019-X). Folcroft.

Gray, Roland P., ed. Songs & Ballads of the Maine Lumberjacks. LC 73-75944. 1969. Repr. of 1924 ed. 19.00 (ISBN 0-8103-3835-1). Gale.

Haufrecht, Herbert. Folk Songs in Settings by Master Composers. LC 76-51387. (Paperback Ser.). 1977. pap. 8.95 (ISBN 0-306-80055-1). Da Capo.

Henry, Mellinger E. Folksongs from the Southern Highlands. 6.00 (ISBN 0-685-71711-9). J J Augustin.

Hubbard, Lester A. & Whitelock, Kenly W., eds. Ballads & Songs from Utah. 1961. pap. 25.00 (ISBN 0-87480-134-6). U of Utah Pr.

Hudson, A. P. Folk Tunes from Mississippi. Herzog, George & Halpert, Herbert, eds. LC 76-58548. (Music Reprint Ser.). 1977. Repr. of 1937 ed. lib. bdg. 19.50 (ISBN 0-306-70787-X). Da Capo.

Jackson, George P., ed. Spiritual Folk-Songs of Early America. 8.50 (ISBN 0-8446-2297-4). Peter Smith.

Joyner, Charles W. Folk Song in South Carolina. LC 70-164707. (Tricentennial Booklet: No. 9). (Orig.). 1971. pap. 2.25 (ISBN 0-87249-227-3). U of SC Pr.

Komlos, Katalin, et al. One Hundred & Fifty American Folk Songs to Sing, Read & Play. LC 74-76415. 117p. (gr. k-6). 1974. pap. text ed. 7.50 (ISBN 0-913932-04-3). Boosey & Hawkes.

Langstaff, John, ed. Hi Ho the Rattlin' Bog: And Other Folk Songs for Group Singing. LC 75-76616. (Illus.). (gr. 6 up). 1969. 5.50 (ISBN 0-15-234400-4, HJ). HarBraceJ.

Lingenfelter, Richard E. & Dwyer, Richard A., eds. Songs of the American West. (Illus.). 1968. 30.00 (ISBN 0-520-00753-0). U of Cal Pr.

Linscott, Eloise H., ed. Folk Songs of Old New England. 2nd ed. xxiii, 344p. 1974. Repr. of 1962 ed. 17.50 (ISBN 0-208-01454-3, Archon). Shoe String.

Lomax, John & Lomax, Alan. Folk Song U. S. A. (RL 6). 1975. pap. write for info. (ISBN 0-452-25223-7, Z5223, Plume). NAL.

McIntosh, David S. Folk Songs & Singing Games of the Illinois Ozarks. Whiteside, Dale R., ed. LC 72-75329. 131p. 1974. 8.95x (ISBN 0-8093-0585-2). S Ill U Pr.

McLean, Don, ed. Songs & Sketches of the First Clearwater Crew. (Illus.). 96p. 1970. 7.00 (ISBN 0-88427-000-9). North River.

McRae, Shirley W. Angel at the Door: Traditional Folksongs from the South. (Voice & Orff Instruments). 1981. pap. 6.00 (ISBN 0-918812-16-X). Magnamusic.

Malone, Bill C. Country Music, U.S.A. A Fifty-Year History. LC 68-66367. (American Folklore Society Memoir Ser.: No. 54). (Illus.). 438p. 1969. 15.95 (ISBN 0-292-78377-9); pap. 4.95 (ISBN 0-292-71029-1). U of Tex Pr.

Neely, Charles. Tales & Songs of Southern Illinois. 1978. Repr. of 1938 ed. 30.00 (ISBN 0-8492-1946-9). R West.

Nettl, Bruno & Myers, Helen. Folk Music in the United States: An Introduction. 3rd, rev. & exp. ed. LC 76-84. 1976. 8.95 (ISBN 0-8143-1556-9); pap. 4.95 (ISBN 0-685-63511-2). Wayne St U Pr.

Osman, Alice H. & McConochie, Jean. If You Feel Like Singing: American Folksongs & Activities for Students of English. (English As a Second Language Bk.). (Illus.). 1979. pap. text ed. 3.95x (ISBN 0-582-79724-1); cassettes 11.50x (ISBN 0-582-79725-X); cassette & book 13.50x (ISBN 0-582-78310-0). Longman.

Owens, William A. Texas Folk Songs. rev. ed. LC 51-9126. (Texas Folklore Society Publications: No. 23). (Illus.). 250p. 1976. 15.00 (ISBN 0-87074-157-8). SMU Press.

Paredes, Americo. A Texas-Mexican Cancionero: Folksongs of the Lower Border. LC 75-16393. (Music in American Life Ser.). (Illus.). 240p. 1975. 12.95 (ISBN 0-252-00522-8); pap. 7.95 (ISBN 0-252-00894-4). U of Ill Pr.

Quackenbush, Robert. Skip to My Lou. LC 74-14585. (gr. 3-6). 1975. 8.95 (ISBN 0-397-31613-5, JBL-J). Har-Row.

Robb, John D. Hispanic Folk Music of New Mexico & the Southwest: A Self-Portrait of the People. LC 78-21392. (Illus.). 1980. 35.00 (ISBN 0-8061-1492-4). U of Okla Pr.

Roberts, Leonard W. & Agey, C. Buell. In the Pine: Selected Kentucky Folksongs. 2nd ed. LC 78-56599. 1979. 12.50x (ISBN 0-933302-00-2); pap. 7.95 (ISBN 0-933302-01-0). Pikeville Coll.

Sandburg, Carl. American Songbag. LC 28-681. 1970. pap. 6.95 (ISBN 0-15-605650-X, HB193, Harv). HarBraceJ.

Scarborough, Dorothy. Song Catcher in Southern Mountains. LC 37-4992. Repr. of 1937 ed. 18.50 (ISBN 0-404-05569-9). AMS Pr.

Seeger, Ruth C. American Folk Songs for Children. (Illus.). 192p. 1980. pap. 4.95 (ISBN 0-385-15788-6, Zephyr). Doubleday.

Seeger, Ruth Crawford. American Folk Songs for Children. (gr. 1 up). 12.95a (ISBN 0-385-07210-4); PLB (ISBN 0-385-07316-X). Doubleday.

--American Folk Songs for Christmas. (gr. 1 up). 1953. PLB 7.95 (ISBN 0-385-08299-1). Doubleday.

Sheppard, Muriel E. Cabins in the Laurel. 1935. 12.95 (ISBN 0-8078-0184-4). U of NC Pr.

Siler, Fred & Silber, Irwin, eds. Folksinger's Wordbook: Words to Over 1,000 Songs. 432p. pap. 14.95 (ISBN 0-8256-0146-0, Oak). Music Sales.

Thomas, Will H. Some Current Folksongs of the Negro. 1912. pap. 1.00 (ISBN 0-87074-114-4). SMU Press.

Tolman, Newton F. Quick Tunes & Good Times. (YA) 1972. 5.50 (ISBN 0-87233-018-4). Bauhan.

Wolford, Leah J. The Play-Party in Indiana: Edited & Revised by W. Edson Richmond & William Tillson. Richmond, W. Edson, ed. LC 75-35086. (Studies in Play & Games). (Illus.). 1976. Repr. 14.00x (ISBN 0-405-07933-8). Arno.

FOLK-SONGS, AMERICAN–BIBLIOGRAPHY

Check-List of Recorded Songs in the English Language in the Archive of American Folk Song to July, 1940, 3 Vols in One. LC 78-151055. (Library of Congress Publications in Reprint Ser). 1971. Repr. of 1942 ed. 24.00 (ISBN 0-405-03420-2). Arno.

Lomax, Alan & Crowell, Sidney R. American Folksong & Folklore: A Regional Bibliography. LC 70-181204. 59p. 1942. Repr. 19.00 (ISBN 0-403-03504-X). Scholarly.

Rosenberg, Bruce A. Folksongs of Virginia: A Checklist of the WPA Holdings at Alderman Library, University of Virginia. LC 75-88185. 145p. 1969. 5.95 (ISBN 0-8139-0279-7). U Pr of Va.

Shearin, Hubert G. A Syllabus of Kentucky Folk-Songs. LC 76-25859. 1976. Repr. of 1911 ed. lib. bdg. 10.00 (ISBN 0-8414-3395-X). Folcroft.

U. S. Library of Congress. Division of Music. Archive of American Folk Song. Check-List of Recorded Songs in the English Language in the Archive of American Folk Song to July, 1940, 315 vols. LC 74-26091. Repr. of 1942 ed. Set. 72.50 (ISBN 0-404-13121-2). AMS Pr.

FOLK-SONGS, AMERICAN–HISTORY AND CRITICISM

Boatright, Mody C., et al, eds. Good Tale & a Bonnie Tune. LC 63-10979. (Texas Folklore Society Publications: No. 32). 1964. 6.95 (ISBN 0-87074-016-4). SMU Press.

Brand, Oscar. The Ballad Mongers: Rise of the Modern Folk Song. LC 78-60137. 1979. Repr. of 1962 ed. lib. bdg. 19.25x (ISBN 0-313-20555-8, BRBM). Greenwood.

Bronson, Bertrand H. The Ballad as Song. LC 74-84045. (Illus.). 1969. 25.00x (ISBN 0-520-01399-9). U of Cal Pr.

Combs, Josiah H. Folk-Songs of the Southern United States. Wilgus, D. K., ed. (AFS Bibliographic & Special Ser.: No. 19). 282p. 1967. 9.95x (ISBN 0-292-73692-4). U of Tex Pr.

Cooper, Horton. North Carolina Folklore & Miscellany. (Illus.). 168p. 1972. 7.50 (ISBN 0-930230-18-3). Johnson NC.

Green, Archie. Only a Miner: Studies in Recorded Coal-Mining Songs. LC 78-155499. (Music in American Life Ser). (Illus.). 520p. 1972. 20.00 (ISBN 0-252-00181-8); text ed. 8.95 (ISBN 0-252-00835-9). U of Ill Pr.

Greenway, John. American Folksongs of Protest. LC 75-111635. 1970. Repr. of 1953 ed. lib. bdg. 18.50x (ISBN 0-374-93254-9). Octagon.

Horn, Dorothy D. Sing to Me of Heaven: A Study of Folk & Early American Materials in Three Old Harp Books. LC 74-99212. (Illus.). 1970. 10.00 (ISBN 0-8130-0293-1). U Presses Fla.

Hudson, Arthur P. Folklore Keeps the Past Alive. LC 62-14241. (Mercer University Lamar Lecture Ser: No. 5). 63p. 1962. 5.00x (ISBN 0-8203-0066-7). U of Ga Pr.

Jackson, George P. White & Negro Spirituals, Their Life Span & Kinship. (Music Reprint Ser). (Illus.). xii, 349p. 1975. Repr. of 1944 ed. lib. bdg. 32.50 (ISBN 0-306-70667-9). Da Capo.

FOLK-SONGS, ASIAN

Lefevre-Pontalis, P. Chansons et fetes du Laos. LC 78-20131. (Collection de contes et de chansons populaires: Vol. 22). Repr. of 1896 ed. 21.50 (ISBN 0-404-60372-6). AMS Pr.

Zainnuddin. Songs of Indonesia. 1970. pap. text ed. 3.50x (ISBN 0-686-65419-6, 00508). Heinemann Ed.

FOLK-SONGS, AUSTRALIAN

see also Ballads, Australian

Edwards, Ronald G. Australian Folk Songs. 1980. Repr. of 1972 ed. lib. bdg. 20.00 (ISBN 0-8492-4407-2). R West.

FOLK-SONGS, BRITISH

see also Folk-Songs, English; Folk-Songs, Scottish

Greenway, John. Tales from the British Isles. LC 78-56058. (The World Folktale Library). (Illus.). 1979. lib. bdg. 7.65 (ISBN 0-686-51163-8). Silver.

Haufrecht, Herbert. Folk Songs in Settings by Master Composers. LC 76-51387. (Paperback Ser.). 1977. pap. 8.95 (ISBN 0-306-80055-1). Da Capo.

Kennedy, Peter, ed. Folksongs of Britain & Ireland. LC 75-7571. 1975. 35.00 (ISBN 0-02-870960-8). Schirmer Bks.

Taylor, Tom. Ballads & Songs of Brittany. LC 74-9603. 1865. lib. bdg. 40.00 (ISBN 0-8414-8579-8). Folcroft.

FOLK-SONGS, BULGARIAN

Bernard, Henry. The Shade of the Balkans. 1978. Repr. of 1904 ed. lib. bdg. 40.00 (ISBN 0-8495-0425-2). Arden Lib.

Vikar, L. & Bereczki, G. Chuvash Folksongs. 1978. 60.50 (ISBN 0-9960011-6-6, Pub. by Kaido Hungary). Heyden.

FOLK-SONGS, BURMESE

Maung Myint Thein. Burmese Folk-Songs. (Illus., Orig.). 1970. pap. text ed. 4.50x (ISBN 0-685-69447-X). Paragon.

FOLK-SONGS, CANADIAN

see also Ballads, Canadian

Cass-Beggs, Barbara. Canadian Folk Songs for the Young. 8.50 (ISBN 0-88894-065-3, Pub. by Douglas & McIntyre). Intl Schol Bk Serv.

Creighton, Helen & MacLeod, Calum. Gaelic Songs in Nova Scotia. (Illus.). 1979. pap. 9.50 (ISBN 0-660-00080-6, 56362-6, Pub. by Natl Mus Canada). U of Chicago Pr.

Creighton, Helen & Peacock, Kenneth. Folksongs from Southern New Brunswick. (Illus.). 1971. pap. 7.95 (ISBN 0-660-00045-8, 56348-0, Pub. by Natl Mus Canada). U of Chicago Pr.

Fowke, Edith. Lumbering Songs from the Northern Woods. (American Folklore Society Memoir Ser.: No. 55). 246p. 1970. 9.95x (ISBN 0-292-70018-0). U of Tex Pr.

Gauthier, Dominique, ed. Chansons de Shippagan. (Archives de Folklore Collection Ser). 200p. (Fr.). 1975. pap. 15.00x (ISBN 2-7637-6730-3, Pub. by Laval). Intl Schol Bk Serv.

Gibbon, John M. Canadian Folk Songs (Old & New) LC 74-26593. 1927. lib. bdg. 12.50 (ISBN 0-8414-4579-6). Folcroft.

Macedward, Leach. Folk Ballads & Songs of the Lower Labrador Coast. (Illus.). 1965. pap. 9.00 (ISBN 0-660-00099-7, 56347-2, Pub. by Natl Mus Canada). U of Chicago Pr.

Marius, Barbeau, et al. Come 'a Singing! Canadian Folk-Songs. (Illus.). 1973. pap. 1.95 (ISBN 0-660-00096-2, 56302-2, Pub. by Natl Mus Canada). U of Chicago Pr.

Peacock, Kenneth. Songs of the Newfoundland Outports, 3 vols. (Illus.). 1965. Set. lib. bdg. 35.00x (ISBN 0-660-00150-0, 56507-6, Pub. by Natl Mus Canada); Set. pap. 30.00 (ISBN 0-660-00097-0, 56508-4). U of Chicago Pr.

--Twenty Ethnic Songs from Western Canada. (Illus.). 1966. pap. 5.00 (ISBN 0-660-02053-X, 56524-6, Pub. by Natl Mus Canada). U of Chicago Pr.

Thomas, Phil. Songs of the Pacific Northwest. (Illus.). 176p. 1980. pap. 14.95 (ISBN 0-87663-551-6, Pub. by Hancock Hse). Universe.

FOLK-SONGS, CHINESE

Chang Ch'ien-Ch'ang. Children's Songs from the Hakka of Mei Hsien. (Folklore Series of National Sun Yat-Sen University: No. 26). (Chinese.). 5.50 (ISBN 0-89986-094-X). E Langstaff.

Chang Ch'Ing-Chiu. A Collection of Folksongs of the Po Tribe in Yun-Nan. (National Peking University & Chinese Assn. for Folklore, Folklore & Folkliterature Ser.: No. 44). (Chinese.). 7.00 (ISBN 0-89986-136-9). E Langstaff.

Chou Hui-Ying. Folksongs from the Northwest. (National Peking University & Chinese Assn. for Folklore, Folklore & Folkliterature Ser.: No. 112). (Chinese.). 6.00 (ISBN 0-89986-190-3). E Langstaff.

Chung Ching-Wen. Folksongs of the Tanka of Canton. (National Peking University & Chinese Assn. for Folklore, Folklore & Folkliterature Ser.: No. 3). (Chinese.). 6.00 (ISBN 0-89986-103-2). E Langstaff.

Chu T'ien-Min. Children's Songs from Sixteen Provinces. (National Peking University & Chinese Assn. for Folklore, Folklore & Folkliterature Ser.: No. 134). (Chinese.). 6.00 (ISBN 0-89986-208-X). E Langstaff.

Collection of Myths About the Snake & Pagoda. (National Peking University & Chinese Assn. for Folklore, Folklore & Folkliterature Ser.: No. 135). (Chinese.). 6.00 (ISBN 0-89986-209-8). E Langstaff.

Cumoutier, G. Les Chants et les traditions populaires des Annamites. LC 78-20123. (Collection de contes et de chansons populaires: Vol. 15). Repr. of 1890 ed. 21.50 (ISBN 0-404-60365-3). AMS Pr.

Folksongs Weekly of Peking University, 3 vols. (Chin.). 26.40 (ISBN 0-89986-281-0). E Langstaff.

Fu-Chinese Folk Songs. (Folklore Series of National Sun Yat-Sen University: No. 13). (Chinese.). 5.50 (ISBN 0-89986-083-4). E Langstaff.

Hsueh-Ju. Folksongs from Peking. (National Peking University & Chinese Assn. for Folklore, Folklore & Folkliterature Ser.: No.36). (Chinese.). 6.00 (ISBN 0-89986-131-8). E Langstaff.

Hwa Kwan-Seng. Pai-Hsueh I-Yin Hsuan: Folksongs Collected in 1820. (National Peking University & Chinese Assn. for Folklore, Folklore & Folkliterature Ser.: No. 69). (Chinese.). 6.50 (ISBN 0-89986-157-1). E Langstaff.

Johnson, Kinchen. Folksongs & Children: Songs from Peiping, Nos. 16-17. (Asian Folklore & Social Life Monograph). (Chinese & Eng.). 1971. 9.20 (ISBN 0-89986-019-2). E Langstaff.

Ku Chieh-Kang. Folksongs from Su-Chow. (National Peking University & Chinese Assn. for Folklore, Folklore & Folkliterature Ser.: No. 1). (Chinese.). 8.00 (ISBN 0-89986-101-6). E Langstaff.

Liang Ch'i-Ch'ao. Types of Modern & Ancient Chinese Love-Songs, No. 8. (Asian Folklore & Social Life Monograph). (Chinese.). 1970. 5.90 (ISBN 0-89986-011-7). E Langstaff.

Li Chin-Hui. Children's Songs from Twenty Provinces. (National Peking University & Chinese Assn. for Folklore, Folklore & Folkliterature Ser.: Nos. 59 & 60). (Chinese.). 12.00 (ISBN 0-89986-150-4). E Langstaff.

Liu Ch'ao-Chi. A Survey of Folksongs in Southwestern China. (National Peking University & Chinese Assn. for Folklore, Folklore & Folkliterature Ser.: No. 42). (Chinese.). 6.50 (ISBN 0-89986-134-2). E Langstaff.

Liu Ching-An. Women in Folksongs. (National Peking University &Chinese Assn. for Folklore, Folklore & Folklore Ser.: No. 34). (Chinese.). 6.00 (ISBN 0-89986-129-6). E Langstaff.

Liu Wan-Chang. Children Songs from Southern Canton. (Folklore Series of National Sun Yat-Sen University: No. 23). (Chinese.). 5.50 (ISBN 0-89986-091-5). E Langstaff.

Lo Hsiang-Lin. Folksongs of the Hakka of Kuang-Tung. (National Peking University & Chinese Assn. for Folklore, Folklore & Folkliterature Ser.: No. 111). (Chinese.). 10.00 (ISBN 0-89986-189-X). E Langstaff.

Lou Tsu-K'uang. Folksongs of Shaohsing. (National Peking University & Chinese Assn. for Folklore, Folklore & Folkliterature Ser.: No. 5). (Chinese.). 6.00 (ISBN 0-89986-105-9). E Langstaff.

Pai Shou-Yi. Folksongs from Honan. (Folklore Series of National Sun Yat-Sen University: No. 24). (Chinese.). 5.50 (ISBN 0-89986-092-3). E Langstaff.

Tai Ching-Nung. Folksongs from Huai-Nan. (National Peking University & Chinese Assn. for Folklore, Folklore & Folkliterature Ser.: No. 24). (Chinese.). 6.50 (ISBN 0-89986-120-2). E Langstaff.

Tung Tso-Pin. Studies on the Folksongs with the Theme "He Saw Her". (National Peking University & Chinese Assn. for Folklore, Folklore & Folkliterature Ser.: No. 23). (Chinese.). 6.50 (ISBN 0-89986-119-9). E Langstaff.

Wang I-Chih. Folksongs from Southern Chiang-Su. (Folklore Series of National Sun Yat-Sen University: No. 17). (Chinese.). 5.50 (ISBN 0-89986-086-9). E Langstaff.

Wei Ying-Ch'i. Folksongs of Eastern Fu-Chien. (Folklore Series of National Sun Yat-Sen University: No. 8). (Chinese.). 5.50 (ISBN 0-89986-078-8). E Langstaff.

Yeh Teh-Chun. Folksongs & Folktales from Huai An. (Folklore Series of National Sun Yat-Sen University: No. 32). (Chinese.). 5.50 (ISBN 0-89986-100-8). E Langstaff.

FOLK-SONGS, ENGLISH

see also Ballads, English

Axon, William E. Folk Song & Folk-Speech of Lancashire. (Folklore Ser). 6.00 (ISBN 0-8482-7270-6). Norwood Edns.

Baring-Gould, S. A Garland of Country Song: English Folk Songs with Their Traditional Melodies. 59.95 (ISBN 0-8490-0211-7). Gordon Pr.

Baring-Gould, Sabine & Hitchcock, Gordon, eds. Folk Songs of the West Country. 1974. 5.50 (ISBN 0-7153-6419-7). David & Charles.

Barrett, William A. English Folk Songs Collected, Arranged & Provided with Symphonies & Accompaniments for the Pianoforte. 95p. 1980. Repr. of 1891 ed. lib. bdg. 15.00 (ISBN 0-8492-3758-0). R West.

--English Folk-Songs: Collected, Arranged, & Provided with Symphonies & Accompaniments for the Pianoforte. 1978. Repr. of 1891 ed. lib. bdg. 10.00 (ISBN 0-8414-1720-2). Folcroft.

Chappell, William. Popular Music of the Olden Time, 2 Vols. (Illus.). Set. 11.00 (ISBN 0-8446-1839-X). Peter Smith.

Dean-Smith, Margaret. A Guide to English Folksong Collections. LC 70-181136. 120p. 1954. Repr. 21.00 (ISBN 0-403-01537-5). Scholarly.

DiGeorge, illus. Twelve Days of Christmas. (Illus.). 1967. pap. 1.00 (ISBN 0-685-11987-4). Heineman.

Hill, Geoffry. Wiltshire Folk Songs & Carols. LC 77-26755. 5.00 (ISBN 0-8414-4859-0). Folcroft.

Karasz, Ilonka. Twelve Days of Christmas. LC 49-11875. (Illus.). (gr. 3-6). 1949. 8.95 (ISBN 0-06-023090-8, HarpJ); PLB 9.89 (ISBN 0-06-023091-6). Har-Row.

Karpeles, Maud, ed. Folk Songs from Newfoundland. 1970. 27.50 (ISBN 0-208-01142-0, Archon). Shoe String.

Kidson, Frank & Neal, Mary. English Folk-Song & Dance. (Illus.). 178p. 1972. Repr. of 1915 ed. 10.00x (ISBN 0-87471-104-5). Rowman.

Lloyd, A. L. Folk Song in England. 434p. 1975. 14.95x (ISBN 0-8464-0419-2). Beekman Pubs.

Palmer, R. & Raven, J. The Rigs of the Fair. (Resources of Music Ser.: No. 12). (Illus.). 64p. 1976. 4.95 (ISBN 0-521-20908-0). Cambridge U Pr.

Palmer, Roy. The Painful Plough. LC 76-187081. (Resources of Music Ser.: No. 5). 80p. 1973. 4.95 (ISBN 0-521-08512-8). Cambridge U Pr.

Palmer, Roy, ed. Everyman's Book of English Country Songs. (Illus.). 256p. 1979. 16.95x (ISBN 0-460-12048-4, Pub. by J. M. Dent England). Biblio Dist.

Porter, Enid. The Folklore of East Anglia. (Folklore of the British Isles Ser.). (Illus.). 192p. 1974. 12.50x (ISBN 0-87471-520-2). Rowman.

Purslow, Frank. The Foggy Dew. LC 74-17104. 1975. Repr. of 1974 ed. lib. bdg. 7.00 (ISBN 0-88305-518-X). Norwood Edns.

Sharp, Cecil & Karpeles, Maud, eds. Cecil Sharp's Collection of English Folk Songs, 2 vols. 1500p. 1974. Set. 92.00x (ISBN 0-19-313125-0). Oxford U Pr.

Stubbs, Ken. The Life of a Man: English Folk Songs from the Home Counties. (Folklore Ser.). 1970. 8.00 (ISBN 0-88305-639-9). Norwood Edns.

The Vaughan Williams Memorial Library Catalogue, of the English Folk Song & Dance Society. 783p. 1974. 60.00x (ISBN 0-7201-0368-1, Pub. by Mansell England). Merrimack Bk Serv.

Williams, Alfred. Folksongs of the Upper Thames. LC 68-31150. 1968. Repr. of 1923 ed. 22.00 (ISBN 0-8103-3421-6). Gale.

Williams, Iolo. English Folk-Song & Dance. LC 73-7745. 1973. lib. bdg. 20.00 (ISBN 0-8414-9362-6). Folcroft.

FOLK-SONGS, ENGLISH–HISTORY AND CRITICISM

Bratton, J. S. The Victorian Popular Ballad. 275p. 1975. 19.50x (ISBN 0-87471-760-4). Rowman.

Duncan, Edmondstoune. Story of Minstrelsy. LC 69-16802. (Music Story Ser). 1968. Repr. of 1907 ed. 22.00 (ISBN 0-8103-4240-5). Gale.

Karples, Maud. An Introduction to English Folk Song. 1973. pap. 8.95x (ISBN 0-19-313126-9). Oxford U Pr.

Nettel, Reginald. Social History of Traditional Song. LC 70-93274. (Illus.). Repr. of 1954 ed. 15.00x (ISBN 0-678-07506-9). Kelley.

Sharp, Cecil J. English Folk Song: Some Conclusions. 4th ed. Karpeles, Maud, ed. 1977. Repr. of 1965 ed. 7.95x (ISBN 0-85409-929-8). Charles River Bks.

Stewart, Bob. Where Is St. George: Pagan Imagery in English Folksong. 1977. text ed. 10.50x (ISBN 0-391-00765-3). Humanities.

FOLK-SONGS, EUROPEAN

Bartok, Bela. The Hungarian Folk Song. Suchoff, Benjamin, ed. Calvocoressi, M. D., tr. (Bartok Studies in Musicology). 1980. lib. bdg. 34.00x (ISBN 0-87395-410-6). State U NY Pr.

Bartok, Bela & Suchoff, Benjamin. Rumanian Folk Music, 5 vols. 1967-1975 ed. Teodorescu, E. C., et al, trs. from Rumanian. Incl. Vol. 1. Instrumental Melodies. 75.00 (ISBN 0-685-85187-7); Vol. 2. Vocal Melodies. 75.00 (ISBN 0-685-85188-5); Vol. 3. Texts. 75.00 (ISBN 0-685-85189-3); Vol. 4. Carols & Christmas Songs (Colinde) 150.00 (ISBN 0-685-85190-7); Vol. 5. Maramures County. 85.00 (ISBN 0-685-85191-5). (Bartok Archives Studies in Musicology.). (Illus.). 1978. 460.00 set (ISBN 0-685-85186-9). Heinman.

Busk, Rachel H. The Folk-Songs of Italy: Specimens with Translations & Notes from Each Province & Prefatory Treatise. Dorsen, Richard M., ed. LC 77-70588. (International Folklore Ser.). 1977. Repr. of 1887 ed. lib. bdg. 17.00x (ISBN 0-405-10085-X). Arno.

Vacaresco, Helene. The Bard of the Dimbovitza: Roumanian Folk Songs. Sylva, Carmen & Strettell, Alma, trs. (Folklore Ser.). 1911. 22.50 (ISBN 0-685-43827-9). Norwood Edns.

Vacaresco, Helene, ed. The Bard of the Dimbovitza: Roumanian Folk-Songs. Sylva, Carmen & Strettell, Alma, trs. 1978. Repr. of 1892 ed. lib. bdg. 35.00 (ISBN 0-8495-5508-6). Arden Lib.

FOLK-SONGS, FRENCH

Laforte, Conrad. Poetiques De la Chanson Traditionnelle Francaise. (Archives De Folklore: No. 17). (Illus., Fr.). 1976. pap. 11.50x (ISBN 2-7637-6661-7, Pub. by Laval). Intl Schol Bk Serv.

Ortolo, F. Les Voceri de l'ile de Corse. LC 78-20119. (Collection de contes et de chansons populaires: Vol. 10). 1980. Repr. of 1887 ed. 21.50 (ISBN 0-404-60360-2). AMS Pr.

Poston, Elizabeth & Arma, Paul. Gambit Book of French Folk Songs. LC 79-160414. (Illus.). 150p. (Eng. & Fr.). 1972. 9.95 (ISBN 0-87645-061-3). Gambit.

Young, Russell S. Vieilles Chansons De Nouvelle-France. (Archieves De Folklore). pap. 5.00x (ISBN 2-7637-0021-7, Pub. by Laval). Intl Schol Bk Serv.

FOLK-SONGS, FRENCH-CANADIAN

see Folk-Songs, Canadian

FOLK-SONGS, GERMAN

Eitner, Robert. Das Deutsche Lied Des XV und XVI Jahrhunderts, 2 vols. in 1. LC 71-178529. Repr. of 1876 ed. 37.50 (ISBN 0-404-56542-5). AMS Pr.

Lohre, Heinrich. Von Percy Zum Wunderhorn: Beitraege Zur Geschichte der Wolksliedforschung in Deutschland. (Ger). 14.00 (ISBN 0-384-33415-6); pap. 11.00 (ISBN 0-685-02192-0). Johnson Repr.

FOLK-SONGS, GHEG

see Folk-Songs, Albanian

FOLK-SONGS, GREEK (MODERN)

Beaton, Roderick. Folk Poetry of Modern Greece. LC 79-7644. (Illus.). 272p. 1980. 29.50 (ISBN 0-521-22853-0). Cambridge U Pr.

Frye, Ellen. The Marble Threshing Floor: A Collection of Greek Folksongs. (American Folklore Society Memoir Ser.: No. 57). (Illus.). 343p. 1973. 15.00x (ISBN 0-292-75005-6). U of Tex Pr.

FOLK-SONGS, HAITIAN

Courlander, Harold. Haiti Singing. LC 72-95270. (Illus.). 274p. 1973. Repr. of 1939 ed. lib. bdg. 15.00x (ISBN 0-8154-0461-1). Cooper Sq.

FOLK-SONGS, HAWAIIAN

Roes, Carol. Keiki Songs of Hawaii. (Illus.). 26p. 1966. pap. 1.95 (ISBN 0-930932-16-1). M Loke.

--Song Stories of Hawaii. (Illus.). 24p. 1959. pap. 1.95 (ISBN 0-930932-17-X). M Loke.

Stall, Edna W. The Story of Lauhala. (Illus.). 1974. pap. 3.50 (ISBN 0-912180-24-2). Petroglyph.

FOLK-SONGS, IRISH

see also Ballads, Irish

Boyle, Cathal O., ed. Songs of County Down. 64p. (Orig.). 1979. pap. 2.95 (ISBN 0-686-31625-8, Pub. by Dalton Pubs Ireland). Irish Bk Ctr.

Colum, Padraic, ed. Treasury of Irish Folklore. rev. ed. (YA) (gr. 9 up). 1969. 9.95 (ISBN 0-517-50294-1). Crown.

Gallagher, Elizabeth. Irish Songs & Airs. 5.00 (ISBN 0-8159-5817-X). Devin.

Gregory. Visions & Beliefs in the West of Ireland Collected & Arranged by Lady Gregory: With Two Essays & Notes by W.!. Yeats. 2nd ed. 1976. pap. text ed. 6.95x (ISBN 0-7705-1412-X). Humanities.

Haufrecht, Herbert. Folk Songs in Settings by Master Composers. LC 76-51387. (Paperback Ser.). 1977. pap. 8.95 (ISBN 0-306-80055-1). Da Capo.

Kennedy, Peter, ed. Folksongs of Britain & Ireland. LC 75-7571. 1975. 35.00 (ISBN 0-02-870960-8). Schirmer Bks.

O'Neill, Francis. Irish Folk Music: A Fascinating Hobby with Some Account of Allied Subjects Including O'Farrells Treatise on the Irish or Union Pipes & Touhey's Hints to Amateur Pipers. (Illus.). 359p. 1977. Repr. of 1910 ed. 19.50x (ISBN 0-8476-6063-X). Rowman.

Ranson, Joseph. Songs of the Wexford Coast. LC 73-22152. (Folklore Ser.). 1948. 8.50 (ISBN 0-88305-558-9). Norwood Edns.

FOLK-SONGS, IRISH-HISTORY AND CRITICISM

O'Boyle, Sean. Irish Song Tradition. 1979. text ed. 9.95x (ISBN 0-7705-1507-X). Humanities.

O'Neill, Francis. Irish Folk Music. LC 75-40334. 1975. Repr. of 1910 ed. lib. bdg. 25.00 (ISBN 0-8414-6531-2). Folcroft.

FOLK-SONGS, JAMAICAN

Jekyll, Walter. Jamaican Song & Story. 342p. 1966. pap. 4.00 (ISBN 0-486-21590-3). Dover.

FOLK-SONGS, JAPANESE

Embree, John F., compiled by. Japanese Peasant Songs. LC 44-2122. Repr. of 1943 ed. 10.00 (ISBN 0-527-01090-1). Kraus Repr.

Isaku, Patia R. Mountain Storm, Pine Breeze: Folk Song in Japan. 1981. text ed. 12.95x (ISBN 0-8165-0564-0); pap. 6.50 (ISBN 0-8165-0722-8). U of Ariz Pr.

FOLK-SONGS, JEWISH

Coopersmith, Harry. Companion Volume to the Songs We Sing. 1950. 3.50x (ISBN 0-8381-0210-7). United Syn Bk.

--Songs We Sing. (Illus.). 1950. 22.50x (ISBN 0-8381-0723-0). United Syn Bk.

Rubin, Ruth. Voices of a People: The Story of Yiddish Folksong. 2nd rev. ed. LC 73-6983. (Illus.). 558p. 1973. Repr. of 1963 ed. 9.95 (ISBN 0-07-054194-9, P&RB). McGraw.

Rubin, Ruth, ed. A Treasury of Jewish Folksong. LC 50-14685. (Illus.). 224p. 1976. 12.50 (ISBN 0-8052-3264-8); pap. 6.95 (ISBN 0-8052-0528-4). Schocken.

Slobin, Mark. Tenement Songs: The Popular Music of the Jewish Immigrants. (Music in American Life Ser). (Illus.). 184p. 1982. price not set (ISBN 0-252-00893-6). U of Ill Pr.

Smoira-Roll, Michal. Folk Song in Israel. LC 64-278. 60p. 1963. pap. 8.50 (ISBN 0-913932-32-9). Boosey & Hawkes.

FOLK-SONGS, JEWISH-HISTORY AND CRITICISM

Rubin, Ruth. Voices of a People: The Story of Yiddish Folksong. LC 79-84679. 1979. pap. 6.95 (ISBN 0-8276-0121-2, 445). Jewish Pubn.

FOLK-SONGS, LATIN-AMERICAN

see also Folk-Songs, Haitian, Folk-Songs, Mexican and similar headings

Folk Songs & Dances of the Americas, 2 Bks. 1969. Bk. 1. pap. 1.00 (ISBN 0-8270-4450-X); Bk. 2. pap. 1.00 (ISBN 0-8270-4455-0). OAS.

Hague, Eleanor, ed. Spanish-American Folk-Songs. LC 18-7996. Repr. 10.00 (ISBN 0-527-01062-6). Kraus Repr.

Robb, John D. Hispanic Folk Songs of New Mexico. LC 54-2171. 1979. pap. 6.95 (ISBN 0-8263-0087-1). U of NM Pr.

Rohmer, Harriet & Perez, Irene. Cuna Song: Cancion De los Cunas. LC 76-29122. (Fifth World Tales Ser.). (Illus.). (gr. k-6). pap. 3.95 spanish bilingual ed. (ISBN 0-89239-008-5, Imprenta de Libros Infantiles). Childrens Book Pr.

U. S. Library of Congress Music Division. Bibliography of Latin American Folk Music. LC 72-1794. Repr. of 1942 ed. 16.00 (ISBN 0-404-08305-6). AMS Pr.

FOLK-SONGS, LETTISH

Berzing, Bud. Sex Songs of the Ancient Letts. LC 69-10779. 320p. 1969. 5.95 (ISBN 0-8216-0151-2). Univ Bks.

FOLK-SONGS, MEXICAN

Brinton, D. Rig Veda Americanus: Sacred Songs of the Ancient Mexicans. 1976. lib. bdg. 59.95 (ISBN 0-8490-2524-9). Gordon Pr.

Paredes, Americo. A Texas-Mexican Cancionero: Folksongs of the Lower Border. LC 75-16393. (Music in American Life Ser.). (Illus.). 240p. 1975. 12.95 (ISBN 0-252-00522-8); pap. 7.95 (ISBN 0-252-00894-4). U of Ill Pr.

Robb, John D. Hispanic Folk Music of New Mexico & the Southwest: A Self-Portrait of the People. LC 78-21392. (Illus.). 1980. 35.00 (ISBN 0-8061-1492-4). U of Okla Pr.

Sobek, Maria H. The Bracero Experience: Elitelore Versus Folklore. LC 78-620046. (Latin American Studies: Vol. 43). 1979. text ed. 12.95 (ISBN 0-87903-043-7). UCLA Lat Am Ctr.

FOLK-SONGS, NORWEGIAN

Blom, Jan B. & Nyhus, Sven, eds. Norwegian Folk Music: Vol. VII, Harding Fiddle Music. 320p. 1981. 65.00x (ISBN 82-00-05508-6). Universitet.

FOLK-SONGS, PHILIPPINE

Poethig, Eunice B., ed. Everybody, I Love You: A Philippine Folk Song Book. 1971. wrps. 3.00x (ISBN 0-686-09444-1). Cellar.

FOLK-SONGS, POLISH

Benet, Sula. Song, Dance, & Customs of Peasant Poland. LC 76-44690. Repr. of 1951 ed. 21.50 (ISBN 0-404-15906-0). AMS Pr.

Treasured Polish Folk Rhythms, Songs & Games. 1976. 5.95 (ISBN 0-685-84287-8). Polanie.

FOLK-SONGS, RUSSIAN

see also Byliny

FOLK-SONGS, SCANDINAVIAN

see also Folk-Songs, Norwegian

Jonsson, Bengt R. & Danielson, Eva. The Types of the Scandinavian Medieval Ballad. 1978. 22.00x (ISBN 82-00-01654-4, Dist. by Columbia U Pr). Universitet.

FOLK-SONGS, SCOTTISH

see also Ballads, Scottish

Anonymous. Miscellanea of the Rymour Club Edinburgh. 1978. Repr. of 1973 ed. lib. bdg. 65.00 (ISBN 0-8414-1712-1). Folcroft.

Barbour, John G. Unique Traditions Chiefly of the West & South of Scotland. (Folklore Ser). 12.50 (ISBN 0-685-36424-0). Norwood Edns.

Campbell, J. L. Hebridean Folksongs II. 1977. 39.50x (ISBN 0-19-815214-0). Oxford U Pr.

Chambers, Robert. Popular Rhymes of Scotland. LC 68-58902. 1969. Repr. of 1870 ed. 22.00 (ISBN 0-8103-3828-9). Gale.

Dauney, William. Ancient Scotish Melodies. LC 73-4533. (Maitland Club, Glasgow. Publications: No. 43). Repr. of 1838 ed. 22.00 (ISBN 0-404-53099-0). AMS Pr.

Davie, Cedric T. & McVicar, George, eds. Oxford Scottish Song Book. 1969. 6.20x (ISBN 0-19-330270-5); pap. 4.60 (ISBN 0-19-330271-3); pap. 2.10x melody ed. (ISBN 0-19-330272-1). Oxford U Pr.

Ford, Robert. Vagabond Songs & Ballads in Scotland, 2 vols. LC 74-13895. 1975. Repr. of 1901 ed. Set. lib. bdg. 50.00 (ISBN 0-88305-206-7). Norwood Edns.

McDonald, Patrick. A Collection of Highland Vocal Airs. (Folklore Ser.). Repr. of 1784 ed. 10.00 (ISBN 0-88305-410-8). Norwood Edns.

Shaw, Margaret F. Folksongs & Folklore of South Uist. (Illus.). 1977. text ed. 33.00x (ISBN 0-19-920085-8). Oxford U Pr.

FOLK-SONGS, SCOTTISH-HISTORY AND CRITICISM

Bassin, Ethel. The Old Songs of Skye: Frances Tolmie & Her Circle. Bowman, Derek, ed. 1977. 14.95 (ISBN 0-7100-8546-X). Routledge & Kegan.

Blackie, John S. Scottish Song. LC 70-144563. Repr. of 1889 ed. 24.00 (ISBN 0-404-08579-2). AMS Pr.

Keith, Alexander. Burns & Folk-Song. 1979. Repr. of 1922 ed. lib. bdg. 15.00 (ISBN 0-8495-3028-8). Arden Lib.

--Burns & Folk-Song. LC 76-53558. 1976. Repr. of 1922 ed. lib. bdg. 12.50 (ISBN 0-8414-5536-8). Folcroft.

FOLK-SONGS, SLAVIC

see Folk-Songs, Bulgarian; Folk-Songs, Polish; Folk-Songs, Yugoslav

FOLK-SONGS, SPANISH

see also Alabados

Lummis, Charles F. Land of Poco Tiempo. LC 66-22698. (Illus.). 1981. pap. 5.95 (ISBN 0-8263-0071-5). U of NM Pr.

Rockwell, Anne. Toro Pinto & Other Songs in Spanish. LC 70-146623. (Illus.). (gr. 4-6). 1971. 7.95 (ISBN 0-02-777490-2). Macmillan.

Stark, Richard B. Music of the Spanish Folk Plays in New Mexico. (Illus.). 1969. 20.00 (ISBN 0-89013-036-1). Museum NM Pr.

Writers Program. New Mexico. The Spanish-American Song & Game Book. LC 73-3642. Repr. of 1942 ed. 18.50 (ISBN 0-404-57941-8). AMS Pr.

FOLK-SONGS, TRINIDAD

Connor, Edric, ed. Songs from Trinidad. (YA) (gr. 9 up). 1958. 2.75x (ISBN 0-19-330235-7). Oxford U Pr.

Elder, J. D. Song Games from Trinidad & Tobago. LC 64-25264. (American Folklore Society Bibliographical & Special Ser.: No. 16). 119p. 1965. pap. 3.95x (ISBN 0-292-73508-1). U of Tex Pr.

Warner, Keith Q. Kaiso: The Story of Trinidad Calyso. LC 81-51659. (Illus.). 135p. (Orig.). 1981. 17.00x (ISBN 0-89410-025-4); pap. 8.00x (ISBN 0-89410-026-2). Three Continents.

FOLK-SONGS, TURKISH

Bartok, Bela. Turkish Folk Music from Asia Minor. Suchoff, Benjamin, ed. LC 75-23186. (Studies in Musicology). 1976. 21.00 (ISBN 0-691-09120-X). Princeton U Pr.

Chadwick, Nora K. & Zhirmunsky, Victor. Oral Epics of Central Asia. LC 68-21189. 1969. 78.00 (ISBN 0-521-07053-8). Cambridge U Pr.

FOLK-SONGS, YORUBAN

Ismaili, Rashidah, et al. Womanrise (Anthology) Rivera, Louis R., ed. (Illus.). 128p. (Orig.). 1978. pap. 4.25 (ISBN 0-917886-05-4). Shamal Bks.

FOLK-SONGS, YUGOSLAV

Bartok, Bela. Yugoslav Folk Music, 4 vols. Suchoff, Benjamin, ed. LC 78-8188. 1979. Set. 300.00 (ISBN 0-87395-383-5). State U NY Pr.

Rootham, Helen, ed. Kossovo, Heroic Songs of the Serbs. LC 78-74518. (Children's Literature Reprint Ser.). 1979. Repr. of 1920 ed. 14.50x (ISBN 0-8486-0221-8). Core Collection.

FOLK-TALES

see Folk Literature; Folk-Lore; Legends; Tales

FOLKLORISTS

Dorson, Richard M. British Folklorists: A History. LC 68-16689. (Folktales of the World Ser). 1969. 15.00x (ISBN 0-226-15863-2). U of Chicago Pr.

FOLKWAYS

see Manners and Customs

FOLLIES (ARCHITECTURE)

Goldman, James & Sondheim, Stephen. Follies. 1971. 7.95 (ISBN 0-394-47362-0). Random.

FOLLY

Epstein, Daniel M. The Follies. LC 76-8059. 60p. 1977. 10.00 (ISBN 0-87951-048-X). Overlook Pr.

Erasmus. Praise of Folly. Radice, Betty, tr. (Classics Ser.). 252p. 1971. pap. 2.95 (ISBN 0-14-044240-5). Penguin.

--The Praise of Folly. Dean, Leonard F., ed. 268p. 1969 (ISBN 0-87532-104-6). pap. 2.95 (ISBN 0-87532-105-4). Hendricks House.

Erasmus, Desiderius. The Praise of Folly. Gross, Harvey, ed. Wilson, John, tr. LC 79-65739. (The Mind of Man Ser.). (Illus.). 160p. 1979. hardcover limited ed. 25.00x (ISBN 0-934710-01-5). J Simon.

--Praise of Folly. Hudson, Hoyt H., tr. 1970. 14.00 (ISBN 0-691-07167-5); pap. 4.95 (ISBN 0-691-01969-X). Princeton U Pr.

--Praise of Folly. 1958. pap. 3.95 (ISBN 0-472-06023-6, 23, AA). U of Mich Pr.

--The Praise of Folly. Miller, Clarence H., intro. by. LC 78-13575. 1979. text ed. 17.50 (ISBN 0-300-02279-4); pap. 3.95x (ISBN 0-300-02373-1). Yale U Pr.

FOLZ, HANS

Murdoch, Brian G. Hans Folz & the Adam-Legends. (Amsterdamer Publikationen Zur Sprache und Literatur: No. 28). 1977. pap. text ed. 23.00x (ISBN 90-6203-479-9). Humanities.

FONDUE

see also Cookery, Chafing Dish; Cookery (Dairy Products)

Culinary Arts Institute Staff. Wok, Fondue, & Chafing Dish. LC 78-54625. (Adventures in Cooking Ser.). (Illus.). 1980. pap. 3.95 (ISBN 0-8326-0605-7, 2518). Delair.

Exner. Fondues. Date not set. 8.95 (ISBN 0-8120-5404-0). Barron.

Fabulous Fondues. 1970. 2.95 (ISBN 0-442-82208-1). Peter Pauper.

Hamm, Marie R. Gold Medal Fondue Cookbook. 1979. pap. 1.95 (ISBN 0-449-14238-8, GM). Fawcett.

Kees, Beverly & Flora, Donnie, eds. Fondue on the Menu. 1971. 5.95 (ISBN 0-307-49257-5, Golden Pr). Western Pub.

Moore, Louise. Mastering the Art of Fondue Cooking: Over 100 Original Recipes & Menus. 160p. 6.95 (ISBN 0-919364-71-3, ADON 3519); pap. 2.95 (ISBN 0-919364-70-5, ADON 3521). Pagurian.

FONDA, HENRY

Teichmann, Howard. Fonda: My Life As Told to Howard Teichmann. 1981. 15.95 (ISBN 0-686-73583-8). NAL.

FONDA, JANE

Dowing, David & Herman, Gary. Jane Fonda. (Illus.). 1980. pap. 5.95 (ISBN 0-8256-3944-1, Quick Fox). Music Sales.

Erlanger, Ellen. Jane Fonda. (The Achievers Ser.). (Illus.). (gr. 4-9). 1981. PLB 5.95 (ISBN 0-8225-0485-5). Lerner Pubns.

Fox, Mary V. Jane Fonda: Something to Fight for. LC 79-22102. (Taking Part Ser.). (Illus.). (gr. 3 up). 1980. PLB 6.95 (ISBN 0-87518-189-9). Dillon.

Lavelle, Mike, ed. The Many Faces of Jane Fonda: An A-Z Miscellany. (Illus.). 260p. (Orig.). 1980. pap. 7.95 (ISBN 0-89803-037-4). Caroline Hse.

FONDA FAMILY

Springer, John. Fondas: Films & Careers of Henry, Jane & Peter Fonda. 1970. 10.00 (ISBN 0-8065-0014-X); pap. 6.95 (ISBN 0-8065-0383-1). Citadel Pr.

FONESCA, MANOEL DEODORO DA, 1827-1892

Simmons, Charles W. Marshal Deodoro & the Fall of Dom Pedro Second. LC 66-28493. 1967. 11.50 (ISBN 0-8223-0157-1). Duke.

FONTAINE, CHARLES, 16TH CENTURY

Collins, W. Lucas. La Fontaine & Other French Fabulists. 1973. Repr. of 1882 ed. 25.00 (ISBN 0-8274-1792-6). R West.

Guiton, M. La Fontaine: Poet & Counterpoet. 1970. 5.00 (ISBN 0-8135-0360-4). Brown Bk.

Hawkins, Richmond L. Maistre Charles Fontaine, Parisien. 1916. pap. 16.00 (ISBN 0-527-01100-2). Kraus Repr.

FONTANA, LUCIO

Billeter, Erika. Lucio Fontana, 1899-1968: A Retrospective. LC 77-88448. (Illus.). 1977. softbound 6.98 (ISBN 0-89207-010-2). S R Guggenheim.

FONTANE, THEODOR, 1819-1898

Behrend, E. Theodor Fontanes Roman "Der Stechlin". Repr. of 1929 ed. pap. 7.00 (ISBN 0-384-03770-4). Johnson Repr.

Garland, Henry. The Berlin Novels of Theodor Fontane. 296p. 1980. 42.00x (ISBN 0-19-815765-7). Oxford U Pr.

Gilbert, Mary. Das Gesprach in Fontanes Gesellschaftsromanen. (Ger). Repr. of 1930 ed. 14.00 (ISBN 0-384-18483-9); pap. 11.00 (ISBN 0-685-02255-2). Johnson Repr.

Remak, Joachim. Gentle Critic: Theodor Fontane & German Politics, 1848-1898. LC 64-16920. 1964. 10.95x (ISBN 0-8156-2064-0). Syracuse U Pr.

Robinson, A. R. Theodor Fontane: An Introduction to the Man & His Work. 1976. text ed. 20.00x (ISBN 0-7083-0617-9). Verry.

Shears, Lambert A. Influence of Walter Scott on the Novels of Theodor Fontane. LC 22-10118. (Columbia University. Germanic Studies, Old Ser.: No. 25). Repr. of 1922 ed. 11.50 (ISBN 0-404-50425-6). AMS Pr.

Trebein, Bertha E. Theodor Fontane As a Critic of the Drama. LC 16-14031. (Columbia University. Germanic Studies, Old Ser.: No. 21). Repr. of 1916 ed. 21.50 (ISBN 0-404-50421-3). AMS Pr.

Wegner, Hans G. Theodor Fontane und der Roman Vom Markischen Junker. (Ger). Repr. of 1938 ed. 14.00 (ISBN 0-384-66447-4); pap. 11.00 (ISBN 0-685-02147-5). Johnson Repr.

Wiskott, Ursula. Franzosische Wesenszuge in Theodor Fontanes Personlichkeit & Werk. 200p. Repr. of 1938 ed. 21.50 (ISBN 0-384-68740-7); pap. 18.50 (ISBN 0-685-27497-7). Johnson Repr.

FONTANEL

see Skull

FONTANNE, LYNN

Runkel, Phillip M. Alfred Lunt & Lynn Fontanne: A Bibliography. (Illus.). 1978. pap. 4.50 (ISBN 0-916120-03-1). Carroll Coll.

FONTENELLE, BERNARD LE BOVIER DE, 1657-1757

Le Bovier De Fontenelle, Bernard. Achievement of Bernard le Bovier De Fontenelle. Glanvill, John, et al, trs. LC 74-118361. 1970. Repr. of 1790 ed. 23.00 (ISBN 0-384-16370-X). Johnson Repr.

FONTEYN, MARGOT

Fonteyn, Margot. Margot Fonteyn: Autobiography. 1976. 12.50 (ISBN 0-394-48570-X). Knopf.

FOOD

see also Animal Food; Animals, Food Habits of; Beverages; Cereals As Food; Cookery; Diet; Dietaries; Farm Produce; Fish as Food; Flavoring Essences; Food, Natural; Fruit; Gastronomy; Grain; Markets; Meat; Nutrition; Nuts; Sea Food; Vegetables; Vegetarianism

also headings beginning with the word Food; also particular foods and beverages, e.g. Bread, Milk; also subdivision Food under subjects, e.g. Fishes-Food; Indians of North America-Food

Abelson, Philip H., ed. Food: Politics, Economics, Nutrition & Research. 1976. 22.50 (ISBN 0-12-041652-2); pap. 9.50 (ISBN 0-12-041653-0). Acad Pr.

Ackart, Robert. Souffles, Mousses, Jellies, & Creams. LC 79-55606. 1980. 11.95 (ISBN 0-689-11028-6). Atheneum.

Action Center. Food on Campus. LC 78-947. 1978. pap. 3.95 (ISBN 0-87857-213-9). Rodale Pr Inc.

Adams, Rex. Miracle Medical Foods. 304p. (Orig.). 1981. pap. 2.50 (ISBN 0-446-91940-3). Warner Bks.

--Miracle Medicine Foods. LC 77-6245. 1977. pap. 3.95 (ISBN 0-13-585463-6, Reward). P-H.

Advice About Drugs, Food, Fitness. (Home Adviser Ser.). 80p. (Orig.). 1981. pap. 1.95 (ISBN 0-8326-2408-X, 7050). Delair.

Altobello, Pat & Pierce, Deirdre. The Food Lover's Book of Lists; or the Book Lover's List of Food. (Illus., Orig.). 1979. pap. 4.95 (ISBN 0-452-25201-6, Z5201, Plume). NAL.

Altschul, Aaron A., ed. New Protein Foods Vol. 4. (Food Science & Technology Ser.). 1981. price not set (ISBN 0-12-054804-6). Acad Pr.

Axler, Bruce H. Buying & Using Convenience Foods. 1974. pap. 3.95 (ISBN 0-672-96122-9). Bobbs.

Basic Texts, Vols. 1 & 2. 1978. Set. pap. 27.00 (ISBN 92-5-100568-0, F1556, FAO). Unipub.

Bauer, Cathy & Andersen, Juel. The Tofu Cookbook. 1979. 9.95 (ISBN 0-87857-246-5). Rodale Pr Inc.

BCC Staff. Healthy Foods: Markets, Trends. 1981. 800.00 (ISBN 0-89336-245-X, GA-047). BCC.

Beinhorn, George, ed. Food for Fitness. LC 74-16792. (Illus.). 144p. 1975. pap. 3.95 (ISBN 0-89037-084-2). Anderson World.

Bender, Arnold F. The Facts of Food. (Illus.). 1975. 9.95x (ISBN 0-19-217632-3). Oxford U Pr.

Bennion, Marion. Introductory Foods. 7th ed. (Illus.). 1980. text ed. 18.95 (ISBN 0-02-308170-8). Macmillan.

--The Science of Food. 1980. text ed. 20.95 scp (ISBN 0-06-453532-0, HarpC). Har-Row.

Birch, G. G., et al, eds. Food from Waste. (Illus.). 1976. 67.20x (ISBN 0-85334-659-3, Pub. by Applied Science). Burgess-Intl Ideas.
--Sensory Properties of Food. (Illus.). 1977. 49.70x (ISBN 0-85334-744-1). Burgess-Intl Ideas.
Black, Helen, ed. The Berkeley Co-Op Food Book. (Orig.). 1980. pap. 7.95 (ISBN 0-915950-43-X). Bull Pub.
Border, Barbara. Food Safety & Sanitation. (Careers in Home Economics Ser.). (Illus.). 1979. pap. text ed. 7.44 (ISBN 0-07-006511-X, G); tchr's manual & key 3.00 (ISBN 0-07-006516-0); wkbk 3.00 (ISBN 0-07-006512-8). McGraw.
Boy Scouts of America. Food Systems. LC 19-600. (Merit Badge Ser.). (Illus.). 48p. (gr. 6-12). 1978. pap. 0.70x (ISBN 0-8395-3399-3, 3399). BSA.
Brillat-Savarin, Jean. The Philosopher in the Kitchen. (Handbook Ser.). 384p. 1981. pap. 5.95 (ISBN 0-14-046157-4). Penguin.
Briscoe, Alan. Your Guide to Home Storage. 1974. pap. 1.95 (ISBN 0-88290-041-2). Horizon Utah.
Brown, Jo G. The Good Food Compendium. LC 78-22306. (Illus.). 416p. 1981. pap. 12.95 (ISBN 0-385-13523-8, Dolp). Doubleday.
Cameron, Allan. The Science of Food & Cooking. 3rd ed. (Illus.). 1973. pap. 13.95x (ISBN 0-7131-1791-5). Intl Ideas.
Cameron, Allan G. Food Facts & Fallacies. (Illus.). 168p. (Orig.). 1973. pap. 4.95 (ISBN 0-571-10290-5, Pub. by Faber & Faber). Merrimack Bk Serv.
Carr, Donald E. Deadly Feast of Life. LC 75-135712. 1971. 7.95 (ISBN 0-385-01406-6). Doubleday.
Carson, Byrta, et al. How You Plan & Prepare Meals. 3rd ed. (Illus.). 1979. text ed. 14.24 (ISBN 0-07-010162-0); tchr's ed. 3.64 (ISBN 0-07-060992-6). McGraw.
Carson, Byrta R. & Ramee, Marue C. How You Plan & Prepare Meals. 2nd ed. (gr. 7-12). 1968. text ed. 14.24 (ISBN 0-07-010161-2, W). McGraw.
Chang, K. C, ed. Food in Chinese Culture: Anthropological & Historical Perspectives. LC 75-43312. 1977. 35.00x (ISBN 0-300-01938-6). Yale U Pr.
Charley, Helen. Food Science. 2nd ed. 525p. 1982. text ed. 20.95 (ISBN 0-471-06206-5). Wiley.
--Food Science. LC 80-17047. 530p. 1970. 21.95 (ISBN 0-8260-1925-0). Wiley.
--Food Study Manual. 2nd ed. LC 79-75636. (Illus.). 275p. (Orig.). 1971. 14.95 (ISBN 0-8260-1940-4, 14195). Wiley.
Chichester, C. O., ed. Advances in Food Research, Vol. 27. (Serial Publication). 1981. price not set (ISBN 0-12-016427-2); price not set lib. ed. (ISBN 0-12-016496-5); price not set microfiche (ISBN 0-12-016497-3). Acad Pr.
Chichester, C. O., et al, eds. Advances in Food Research, Vol. 26. LC 48-7808. 1980. 31.00 (ISBN 0-12-016426-4); lib. ed. 40.50 (ISBN 0-12-016494-9); microfiche 21.50 (ISBN 0-12-016495-7). Acad Pr.
--Advances in Food Research, Vol. 25. 1979. 35.50 (ISBN 0-12-016425-6); lib ed. 45.50 (ISBN 0-12-016492-2); microfiche 26.00 (ISBN 0-12-016493-0). Acad Pr.
Cinnamon, Pamela A. & Swanson, Marilyn A. Everything You Always Wanted to Know About Exchange Values for Foods. 1976. 2.75 (ISBN 0-89301-034-0). U Pr of Idaho.
Clydesdale, Fergus M. & Francis, Frederick J. Human Ecological Issues: A Reader. 320p. (Orig.). 1980. pap. text ed. 8.95 (ISBN 0-8403-2197-X). Kendall-Hunt.
Clydesdale, Fergus S. & Francis, F. J. Food, Nutrition & You. (Illus.). 1977. lib. bdg. 13.95 (ISBN 0-13-323048-1); pap. text ed. 9.95 (ISBN 0-13-323030-9). P-H.
Clymer, R. Swinburne. Diet: A Key to Health. 1966. 4.95 (ISBN 0-686-05800-3). Philos Pub.
Commission on International Relations, National Research Council. World Food & Nutrition Study: Interim Report. LC 75-37120. xix, 82p. 1975. pap. 5.50 (ISBN 0-309-02436-6). Natl Acad Pr.
Connolly, Pat. Guide to Living Foods. rev. ed. LC 78-70856. (Illus.). 10.00 (ISBN 0-916764-05-2). Price-Pottenger.
Convience & Take-Away Foods. 120p. 1981. 150.00x (ISBN 0-686-71863-1, Pub. by Euromonitor). State Mutual Bk.
Cooper, Derek. The Bad Food Guide. (Illus.). 1967. 13.95 (ISBN 0-7100-1229-2). Routledge & Kegan.
Crabbe, David & Lawson, Simon, eds. World Food Book. 260p. 1981. 35.00x (ISBN 0-89397-032-8). Nichols Pub.
Cronan, Marion & Atwood, June. First Foods. rev. ed. (gr. 7-9). 1976. text ed. 13.28 (ISBN 0-87002-168-0); tchr's guide free. Bennett IL.
Cronan, Marion L. & Atwood, June. Foods in Homemaking. rev. ed. (Illus.). (gr. 9-12). 1972. text ed. 18.00 (ISBN 0-87002-121-4); tchr's guide free. Bennett IL.
Dasheff, Bill & Dearborn, L. Good Garb. (Orig.). 1980. pap. 9.95 (ISBN 0-440-52588-8, Delta). Dell.
Deatherage, F. E. Food for Life. LC 75-15502. (Illus.). 422p. 1975. 19.50 (ISBN 0-306-30816-9, Plenum Pr). Plenum Pub.
De Kruif, Paul. Hunger Fighters. LC 67-32084. (YA) (gr. 7-12). 1967. pap. 0.95 (ISBN 0-15-642430-4, HPL20, HPL). HarBraceJ.
Dennis, P. O., et al, eds. Food Control in Action. (Illus.). xii, 280p. 1980. 45.00x (ISBN 0-85334-894-4). Burgess-Intl Ideas.
Devine, Marjorie M. & Pimentel, Marcia H. Dimensions of Food: An Introductory Laboratory Manual. 184p. 1975. pap. text ed. 9.50 scp (ISBN 0-06-041656-4, HarpC). Har-Row.
De Voe, Thomas F. The Market Assistant. LC 72-174033. (Illus.). 455p. 1975. Repr. of 1867 ed. 39.00 (ISBN 0-8103-4117-4). Gale.
Doyle, Rodger P. & Redding, James L. The Complete Food Handbook. LC 79-52123. (Illus.). 320p. (Revised & Updated ed.). 1980. pap. 3.50 (ISBN 0-394-17398-8, B431, BC). Grove.
Duckworth, R. B., ed. Water Relations of Foods. (Food Science & Technology Ser.). 1975. 111.00 (ISBN 0-12-223150-3). Acad Pr.
Edwards, D. J. Growing Food. LC 69-18748. (Finding Out About Science Ser). (Illus.). (gr. 3-6). 1969. PLB 8.79 (ISBN 0-381-99835-5, A31710, JD-J). Har-Row.
Eskin, N. A., et al. Biochemistry of Food. 1971. 35.00 (ISBN 0-12-242350-X). Acad Pr.
FAO Commodity Review, 6 vols. (Orig.). pap. 6.00 1962 (ISBN 0-685-36352-X, FAO). pap. 9.00 1964 (ISBN 0-685-36354-6); pap. 6.00 1965 (ISBN 0-685-36355-4); pap. 10.75 1966 (ISBN 0-685-36356-2, F142); pap. 7.25 1967 (ISBN 0-685-36357-0, F143); pap. 14.25 1968 (ISBN 0-685-36358-9). Unipub.
Fennema, Owen. Principles of Food Science, Pt. 1. (Food Sci. Ser.: Vol. 4). 1976. 67.50 (ISBN 0-8247-6350-5). Dekker.
Fetterman, Elsie. Buying Food. (Consumer Casebook Ser.). (Illus.). 80p. (gr. 10-12). 1981. pap. text ed. 5.00 (ISBN 0-87005-268-3). Fairchild.
Fleming, June. The Well-Fed Backpacker. rev. ed. LC 76-12289. (Illus.). 1979. pap. 4.95 (ISBN 0-918480-10-8). Victoria Hse.
Food & Nutrition Board, Natl Research Council. Technology of Fortification of Foods. 114p. 1976. pap. 7.25 (ISBN 0-309-02415-3). Natl Acad Pr.
Food & Nutrition Planning. (Nutrition Consultants Reports Ser: No. 35). 1977. pap. 11.75 (ISBN 92-5-100263-0, F906, FAO). Unipub.
Food for Thought. 1980. 5.95 (ISBN 0-89486-090-9). Hazelden.
Food Legumes: Distribution, Adaptability & Biology of Yield. (FAO Plant Production & Protection Paper: No. 3). 1977. pap. 8.50 (ISBN 92-5-100186-3, F1067, FAO). Unipub.
Francis, F. G. & Clydesdale, F. M. Food Colorimetry: Theory & Applications. (Illus.). 1975. text ed. 45.00 (ISBN 0-87055-183-3). AVI.
Furlong, Marjorie & Pill, Virginia. Edible? Incredible! Pondlife. (Illus.). 1980. lib. bdg. 8.95 (ISBN 0-87961-084-0); pap. 4.95 (ISBN 0-87961-083-2). Naturegraph.
Galvani, Maureen, illus. Where Does Food Come from? (Illus.). 32p. 1980. pap. 1.60 ea. (Pub. by Dinosaur Pubns); pap. in 5 pk. avail. (ISBN 0-85122-197-1). Merrimack Bk Serv.
Gaman, P. M. & Sherrington, K. B. The Science of Food: An Introduction to Food Science, Nutrition & Microbiology. 2nd ed. (Illus.). 224p. 1981. 30.00 (ISBN 0-08-025896-4); pap. 12.50 (ISBN 0-08-025895-6). Pergamon.
Garard, Ira. The Story of Food. LC 73-94093. (Illus., Orig.). 1974. pap. 11.00 (ISBN 0-87055-155-8). AVI.
George, Susan. Feeding the Few: Corporate Control of Food. 79p. 1979. pap. 3.95 (ISBN 0-89758-010-9). Inst Policy Stud.
Golden Chia: Ancient Indian Energy Food. 4.75 (ISBN 0-685-78288-3). Hillside.
Goodwin, Mary T. & Pollen, Gerry. Creative Food Experiences for Children. rev. ed. (Illus.). 256p. 1980. text ed. 12.95 (ISBN 0-89329-028-9). Ctr Sci Public.
--Creative Food Experiences for Children. 2nd rev. ed. (Illus.). 256p. (gr. k-6). 1980. pap. 5.95 (ISBN 0-89329-027-0). Ctr Sci Public.
Grant, Doris. Recipe for Survival: Your Daily Food. LC 73-93654. 224p. 1974. 6.95 (ISBN 0-87983-069-7); pap. 3.95 (ISBN 0-87983-078-6). Keats.
Grigson, Jane. Food with the Famous. LC 79-55605. 1980. 15.95 (ISBN 0-689-11040-5). Atheneum.
Gullett, Walter & Gullett, Jane Fellows. Everyone's Guide to Food Self-Sufficiency. 1981. 10.95 (ISBN 0-87961-096-4); pap. 6.95 (ISBN 0-87961-095-6). Naturegraph.
Hall, Eugene J., ed. The Food We Eat. rev. ed. (Adult ESL Skillbuilders). 64p. 1981. Repr. of 1969 ed. pap. text ed. price not set (ISBN 0-88499-812-6). Inst Mod Lang.
Happel, Margaret. Healthy Eating. Machtiger, B., ed. (The Savers Ser.). (Illus.). 128p. 1981. pap. cancelled (ISBN 0-8329-0228-4). New Century.
Harper, John C. Elements of Food Engineering. (Illus.). 1976. lib. bdg. 17.00 (ISBN 0-87055-218-X). AVI.
Hawthorne, J. & Rolfe, E. J., eds. Low Temperature Biology of Foodstuffs. 1969. 55.00 (ISBN 0-08-013294-4). Pergamon.
Heiser, Charles B., Jr. Seed to Civilization: The Story of Man's Food. LC 73-2949. (Biology Ser.). (Illus.). 1973. pap. text ed. 9.95x (ISBN 0-7167-0594-X). W H Freeman.
Hoff, Johan E. & Janick, Julesintro. by. Food: Readings from Scientific American. LC 73-3138. (Illus.). 1973. text ed. 17.95x (ISBN 0-7167-0876-0); pap. text ed. 9.95x (ISBN 0-7167-0875-2). W H Freeman.
Hooker, Richard J. Food & Drink in America. 1981. 14.95 (ISBN 0-672-52681-6). Bobbs.
International Congress of Food & Science Technology-1st-London, 1962. Food & Science Technology, 5 vols. Leitch, J. M., ed. Incl. Vol. 1. Chemical & Physical Aspects of Foods. 1969; Vol. 2. Biological & Microbiological Aspects of Foods. 1969; Vol. 3. Quality Analysis & Composition of Foods. 1969; Vol. 4. Manufacture & Distribution of Foods. 1969; Vol. 5. Proceedings. 1969. (Illus.). Set. 608.00x (ISBN 0-677-10290-9). Gordon.
Kaplan, Jane R. A Woman's Conflict: The Special Relationship Between Women & Food. 1979. 10.95 (ISBN 0-13-961946-1, Spec); pap. 5.95 (ISBN 0-13-961938-0). P-H.
Katz, Deborah & Goodwin, Mary T. Food: Where Nutrition, Politics & Culture Meet. 1976. pap. 4.50 (ISBN 0-89329-006-8). Ctr Sci Public.
Kaysing, Bill. Eat Well on a Dollar a Day. LC 75-10820. (Illus.). 200p. 1975. pap. 4.95 (ISBN 0-87701-066-8). Chronicle Bks.
Kinder, Faye & Green, Nancy R. Meal Management. 5th ed. (Illus.). 576p. 1978. text ed. 18.95 (ISBN 0-02-364080-4, 36408). Macmillan.
Kinley, David H., et al. Aid As Obstacle: Twenty Questions About Our Foreign Aid & the Hungry. (Illus., Orig.). 1980. pap. 4.95 (ISBN 0-935028-07-2). Inst Food & Develop.
Klinger, Judith L. The Food Inflation Fighters Handbook. (Illus.). 1980. pap. 5.95 (ISBN 0-449-90030-4, Columbine). Fawcett.
Kotschevar, L. H. & McWilliams, Margaret. Understanding Food. LC 69-19238. 684p. 1969. pap. 29.95 (ISBN 0-471-50530-7). Wiley.
Kowtaluk, Helen. Discovering Food. (gr. 9-12). 1978. 7.00 (ISBN 0-87002-270-9); pap. 5.96 (ISBN 0-87002-272-5); student guide 3.96 (ISBN 0-87002-278-4); tchrs. guide 9.04 (ISBN 0-87002-280-6). Bennett IL.
Kowtaluk, Helen & Kopan, Alice. Food for Today. 1977. 15.96 (ISBN 0-87002-181-8); pap. 16.80 tchr. resource guide (ISBN 0-87002-187-7); student activity guide 3.20 (ISBN 0-87002-197-4). Bennett IL.
Kramer, Mary. Illustrated Guide to Foreign & Fancy Foods. LC 75-20972. (Illus.). 1975. pap. 11.95x spiral bdg. (ISBN 0-916434-14-1). Plycon Pr.
Labuza, T. P. & Sloan, A. Elizabeth. Food for Thought. 2nd ed. (Illus.). 1977. pap. text ed. 9.50 (ISBN 0-87055-244-9). AVI.
Lang, George. Lang's Compendium of Culinary Nonsense & Trivia. (Illus.). 1980. 10.00 (ISBN 0-517-54148-3). Potter.
Largen, Velda L. Guide to Good Food. (Illus.). 640p. 1981. 15.96 (ISBN 0-87006-272-7); activity guide 3.20 (ISBN 0-87006-272-7). Goodheart.
Larsen, Egon. Food: Past, Present & Future. 1978. 9.95x (ISBN 0-8448-1304-4). Crane-Russak Co.
Levine, Beverly. Picked This Morning: The California Guide to Fresh Foods. LC 79-23153. (Illus., Orig.). 1980. pap. 6.95 (ISBN 0-87701-173-7). Chronicle Bks.
Lowenberg, Miriam E., et al. Food & People. 3rd ed. LC 78-19172. 1979. text ed. 20.95x (ISBN 0-471-02690-5). Wiley.
McDevitt, Mary Ann K. Fascinating Foods. 1979. pap. 5.00x (ISBN 0-8134-2060-1, 2060); tchr's manual 7.50x (ISBN 0-8134-2059-8, 2059); objective tests 3.50x (ISBN 0-8134-2061-X, 2061). Interstate.
McNutt, Kristen W. & McNutt, David R. Nutrition & Food Choices. LC 77-13636. 1978. text ed. 17.95 (ISBN 0-574-20500-4, 13-3500). SRA.
McWilliams, Margaret. Food Fundamentals. 3rd ed. LC 78-65888. 1979. 22.95x (ISBN 0-471-02691-3). Wiley.
--Fundamentals of Meal Management. LC 78-54660. (The Plycon Home Economics Ser.). 596p. 1978. text ed. 16.95 (ISBN 0-686-75959-1). Burgess.
--Fundamentals of Meal Management. LC 78-54660. (Illus.). 1978. text ed. 16.95 (ISBN 0-8087-3429-6). Plycon Pr.
Magida, Phylis. Eating, Drinking, & Thinking: A Gourmet Perspective. LC 73-86024. 184p. 1973. 16.95 (ISBN 0-911012-91-5). Nelson-Hall.
Marr, John S. The Food You Eat. LC 72-85647. (Illus.). 48p. (gr. 3up). 1973. 4.95 (ISBN 0-87131-053-8). M Evans.
Martin, Margo. The International Gourmet. 1976. 2.95 (ISBN 0-914558-04-8). Georgetown Pr.
Meredith Corp. Editors & Deutsch, Ron. The Family Guide to Better Food & Better Health. 512p. 1973. pap. 2.50 (ISBN 0-553-13259-8, 13259-8). Bantam.
Mohsenin, N. N. Physical Properties of Plant & Animal Materials. 1970. 101.25x (ISBN 0-677-02300-6). Gordon.
Mohsenin, Nuri N. Thermal Properties of Food & Agriculture Materials. 420p. 1980. 53.00 (ISBN 0-677-05450-5). Gordon.
Morr, Mary L. & Irmiter, Theodore F. Introductory Foods. 2nd ed. (Illus.). 368p. 1974. pap. text ed. 8.95 (ISBN 0-02-384100-1). Macmillan.
Moyer, Anne. Better Food for Public Places. LC 76-54336. 1978. pap. 4.95 (ISBN 0-87857-207-4). Rodale Pr Inc.
Mulhauser, Roland. More Vitamins & Minerals with Fewer Calories. LC 77-91210. 1978. pap. 3.95 (ISBN 0-8048-1265-9). C E Tuttle.
Newberry, Lynn & Fisher, M. Frances. The Food Book. LC 80-19009. (Illus.). 368p. 1981. text ed. 14.64 (ISBN 0-87006-299-9). Goodheart.
Newmark, Norma, et al. Food Preparation Principles & Procedures. 6th ed. 334p. 1973. write for info. wire coil (ISBN 0-697-08311-X). Wm C Brown.
Nicholson, Heather J. & Nicholson, Ralph L. Distant Hunger: Agriculture, Food & Human Values. LC 78-60761. (Science & Society: a Purdue University Series in Science Technology, & Human Values: Vol. 3.). (Illus.). 240p. 1979. pap. 3.95 (ISBN 0-931682-00-2). Purdue Univ Bks.
Nuclear Techniques for Increased Food Production. (Freedom from Hunger Campaign Ser.: No. 22). (Orig.). 1969. pap. 4.75 (ISBN 0-685-04919-1, F300, FAO). Unipub.
Nutrition Almanac. LC 75-4193. 1975. pap. 6.95 (ISBN 0-685-72753-X, Pub. by McGraw). Formur Intl.
Ockerman, Herbert W. Source Book for Food Scientists. (Illus.). 1978. lib. bdg. 79.50 (ISBN 0-87055-228-7). AVI.
Olsen, Alfa-Betty & Efron, Marshall. Omnivores: They Said They Would Eat Anything--& They Did. (Affidavit by Mel Brooks). 1979. 8.95 (ISBN 0-670-46570-4). Viking Pr.
Parcells, Hazel. Electro-Magnetic Energy in Foods. 1974. pap. 10.00 (ISBN 0-87516-299-1). De Vorss.
Patti, Charles. Food Book: What You Eat from A-Z. LC 76-179014. 1973. 9.95 (ISBN 0-8303-0118-6). Fleet.
Paul, Pauline C., et al, eds. Food Theory & Applications. LC 79-172953. 1972. text ed. 27.95 (ISBN 0-471-67250-5). Wiley.
Pellegrini, Angelo M. Food-Lover's Garden. LC 76-106621. (Illus.). 1970. pap. 4.95 (ISBN 0-914842-06-4). Madrona Pubs.
Pennington, Jean & Church, Helen N. Food Values of Portions Commonly Used. 13th ed. LC 80-7594. 200p. 1980. 12.95 (ISBN 0-06-010767-7, Harpt); pap. 5.95 (ISBN 0-686-77497-3, CN 819). Har-Row.
Pesticide Residues in Food: 1980 Report. (FAO Plant Production & Protection Paper Ser.: No. 26). 79p. 1981. pap. 7.50 (ISBN 92-5-101058-7, F2180, FAO). Unipub.
Plummer, Mary A. Foods & Nutrition: Syllabus. 1976. pap. text ed. 5.25 (ISBN 0-89420-001-1, 167070); cassette recordings 58.10 (ISBN 0-89420-147-6, 167040). Natl Book.
Priestly, R. J., ed. Effects of Heating on Foodstuffs. (Illus.). 1979. 62.10x (ISBN 0-85334-797-2, Pub. by Applied Science). Burgess-Intl Ideas.
Raw, I., et al. What People Eat. (Illus.). 347p. 1975. pap. 12.95 (ISBN 0-913232-15-7). W Kaufmann.
Rechcigl, Miloslav, Jr., ed. Man, Food & Nutrition. LC 73-81478. (Uniscience Ser). 344p. 1973. 44.95 (ISBN 0-87819-040-6). CRC Pr.
Report of the Fourteenth FAO Regional Conference for the Near East. 1979. pap. 7.50 (ISBN 92-5-100688-1, F1555, FAO). Unipub.
Richards, Aubrey I. Hunger & Work in a Savage Tribe: A Functional Study of Nutrition Among the Southern Bantu. 6.50 (ISBN 0-8446-2801-8). Peter Smith.

Rodale, Robert. Our Next Frontier: A Personal Guide for Tomorrow's Lifestyle. Stoner, Carol, ed. (Illus.). 224p. 1981. 14.95 (ISBN 0-87857-365-8). Rodale Pr Inc.

Rorty, James & Norman, Philip. Tomorrow's Food. 4.95 (ISBN 0-8159-6906-6). Devin.

Roth, June. The Food-Depression Connection. 1979. pap. 4.95 (ISBN 0-8092-7220-2). Contemp Bks.

Sanjur, Diva. Social & Cultural Perspectives in Nutrition. (Illus.). 352p. 1982. text ed. 18.95 (ISBN 0-13-815647-6). P-H.

Scrimshaw, Nevin S. & Altschul, Aaron M., eds. Amino Acid Fortification of Protein Foods. 1971. 30.00x (ISBN 0-262-19091-5). MIT Pr.

Smith, Nathan J. Food for Sport. LC 76-4092. (Berkeley Series in Nutrition). (Illus.). 1976. pap. 5.95 (ISBN 0-915950-03-0). Bull Pub.

Sokolov, Raymond. Fading Feast: A Compendium of Disappearing American Regional Foods. (Illus.). 1981. 17.95 (ISBN 0-374-15213-6). FS&G.

Soup, Stone. The Kitchen Almanac. 1977. pap. 8.95 (ISBN 0-425-03562-X, Windhover). Berkley Pub.

The State of Food & Agriculture, Nineteen Seventy-Eight. (Agricultural Ser.: No. 9). 262p. 1980. pap. 17.00 (ISBN 92-5-100737-3, F1850, FAO). Unipub.

The State of Food & Agriculture 1976. (FAO Agriculture Ser: No. 4). (Illus.). 1978. pap. 17.00 (ISBN 92-5-100181-2, F1224, FAO). Unipub.

Still, Jean. Food Selection & Preparation. 1981. text ed. 16.95x (ISBN 0-02-417510-2). Macmillan.

Thorner, Marvin E. Convenience & Fast Food Handbook. (Illus.). 1973. text ed. 25.50 (ISBN 0-87055-134-5). AVI.

Thypin, Marilyn & Glasner, Lynne. More Food for Our Money: Food Planning, Buying, Nutrition. LC 78-13591. (Consumer Education Ser.). 1979. pap. text ed. 3.50 (ISBN 0-88436-502-6). EMC.

Tilden, J. H. Food: Its Influence As a Factor in Disease & Health. LC 76-2984. 1976. pap. 3.50 (ISBN 0-87983-125-1). Keats.

Time-Life Editors. Foods of the World. 1980. 14.95 (ISBN 0-686-68054-5). Time-Life.

Trillin, Calvin. Alice, Let's Eat. 1978. 7.95 (ISBN 0-394-42500-6). Random.

--Alice, Let's Eat: Further Adventures of a Happy Eater. LC 79-11070. 1979. pap. 1.95 (ISBN 0-394-74171-4, Vin). Random.

--American Fried: Adventures of a Happy Eater. LC 79-11065. 1979. pap. 1.95 (ISBN 0-394-74172-2, Vin). Random.

United States Department of Agriculture. The World Food Situation: Problems & Prospects to 1985, Vol. 2. 1976. 37.50 (ISBN 0-379-00573-5). Oceana.

U.S. Department of Agriculture. Yearbook of Agriculture, 1939: Food & Life; Part 1: Human Nutrition. LC 75-26321. (World Food Supply Ser). (Illus.). 1976. Repr. of 1939 ed. 24.00x (ISBN 0-405-07797-1). Arno.

Vail, Gladys E., et al. Foods. 7th ed. LC 77-74376. (Illus.). 1978. text ed. 18.50 (ISBN 0-395-25521-X); inst. guide 0.90 (ISBN 0-395-25522-8); lab. manual 8.25 (ISBN 0-395-25523-6). HM.

Walcher, D. N., et al, eds. Food, Man, & Society. LC 76-28698. 288p. 1976. 27.50 (ISBN 0-306-30974-2, Plenum Pr). Plenum Pub.

Warfel, M. C. & Waskey, Frank H. The Professional Food Buyer. LC 75-46108. 1979. 26.00 (ISBN 0-8211-2254-1); ten or more copies 22.00 ea. McCutchan.

Wilson, Jose & Leaman, Arthur. The Complete Food Catalogue. (Illus.). 10.95 (ISBN 0-685-85047-1); pap. 6.95 (ISBN 0-03-017701-4). HR&W.

Wolf, Ray. Managing Your Personal Food Supply. LC 76-50569. 1977. 11.95 (ISBN 0-87857-121-3). Rodale Pr Inc.

Woodside, Dave. What Makes Popcorn Pop? LC 80-12712. (Illus.). 160p. (gr. 4-6). 1980. 9.95 (ISBN 0-689-30794-2). Atheneum.

Woodward, Nancy H. The Food Catalog. LC 77-73279. (Illus.). 1977. 19.95 (ISBN 0-88373-065-0). Stonehill Pub Co.

World Food - Hunger Studies. 229p. 1977. 5.00 (ISBN 0-686-63875-1). Inst World Order.

World Food Conference, Ames, Iowa June, 1976. Proceedings. Schaller, Frank, ed. 1977. text ed. 8.50x (ISBN 0-8138-1825-7). Iowa St U Pr.

World Food Congress, 1st, Washington, D. C., 1963. Report, Vol. 1. (Orig.). 1963. pap. 4.00 (ISBN 0-685-02465-2, FAO). Unipub.

World Food Programme: Report of the Eighth Session of the UN - FAO Committee on Food Aid Policies & Programmes. 55p. 1980. pap. 9.00 (ISBN 92-5-100895-7, F1967, FAO). Unipub.

World Meteorological Organization. Weather & Food. 1962. pap. 2.00 (ISBN 0-685-22347-7, WMO). Unipub.

Wrench, G. T. The Wheel of Health: The Sources of Long Life & Health Among the Hunza. LC 72-80274. 147p. 1972. pap. 1.75 (ISBN 0-8052-0355-9). Schocken.

Wright, Carol. The Holiday Cook: Recipes & Shopping Away from Home. LC 80-68682. (Illus.). 160p. 1981. 14.95 (ISBN 0-7153-8017-6). David & Charles.

Wright, Gertrude. Simply Delicious. Kuse, James A., ed. 64p. 1976. pap. 2.95 (ISBN 0-89542-636-6). Ideals.

Yudkin, John. This Nutrition Business. LC 77-10150. 1978. 10.00 (ISBN 0-312-80055-X). St Martin.

Zweifel, Frances W. Pickle in the Middle & Other Easy Snacks. LC 78-19478. (I Can Read Bks.). (Illus.). 64p. (gr. k-3). 1979. 6.95 (ISBN 0-06-027072-1, HarpJ); PLB 7.89 (ISBN 0-06-027073-X). Har-Row.

FOOD-ANALYSIS

see also Flavor; Food-Composition; Food Additives

ACS Committee on Chemistry & Public Affairs. Chemistry & the Food System. LC 80-11194. 1980. 15.00 (ISBN 0-8412-0557-4); pap. 9.00 (ISBN 0-8412-0563-9). Am Chemical.

Amerine, Maynard A., et al. Principles of Sensory Evaluation of Food. (Food and Science Technology Monographs). 1965. 50.00 (ISBN 0-12-056150-6). Acad Pr.

Arsenic & Tin in Foods: Reviews of Commonly Used Methods of Analysis. (FAO Food & Nutrition Paper Ser.: No. 9). 114p. 1980. pap. 10.25 (ISBN 92-5-100727-6, F1898, FAO). Unipub.

Birch, Gordon G., et al. Food Science. 2nd ed. 1977. text ed. 21.00 (ISBN 0-08-021347-2); pap. text ed. 11.25 (ISBN 0-08-021346-4). Pergamon.

Boudreau, James C., ed. Food Taste Chemistry. LC 79-26461. (ACS Symposium Ser.: No. 115). 1979. 25.75 (ISBN 0-8412-0526-4). Am Chemical.

Campbell, Ada M. & Penfield, Marjorie. Experimental Study of Food. 2nd ed. LC 78-69535. (Illus.). 1979. text ed. 19.95 (ISBN 0-395-26666-1). HM.

Charalambous, George, ed. Analysis & Control of Less-Desirable Flavors in Foods & Beverages. 1980. 24.50 (ISBN 0-12-169065-2). Acad Pr.

--Liquid Chromatographic Analysis of Food & Beverages, 2 vols. LC 78-27595. 1979. Vol. 1. 20.00 (ISBN 0-12-169001-6); Vol. 2. 29.00 (ISBN 0-12-169002-4). Acad Pr.

Charalambous, George & Inglett, George, eds. The Quality of Foods & Beverages: Chemistry & Technology, 2 vols, Vols. 1 & 2. 1981. Vol. 1. 29.50 (ISBN 0-12-169101-2); Vol. 2. write for info. (ISBN 0-12-169102-0). Acad Pr.

Charalambous, George & Katz, Ira, eds. Phenolic, Sulfur, & Nitrogen Compounds in Food Flavors. LC 76-16544. (ACS Symposium Ser: No. 26). 1976. 20.50 (ISBN 0-8412-0330-X). Am Chemical.

Committee on Food Stability, National Research Council. Objective Methods for Food Evaluation. LC 76-26723. 1976. pap. 8.75 (ISBN 0-309-02520-6). Natl Acad Pr.

Crook, William G. Tracking Down Hidden Food Allergy. 2nd ed. (Illus.). 104p. (Orig.). 1980. pap. 5.95 (ISBN 0-933478-05-4). Prof Bks.

Dickes, G. J. & Nicholas, P. V. Gas Chromatrography in Food Analysis. 1976. 54.95 (ISBN 0-408-70781-X). Butterworth.

Downey, W. K., ed. Food Quality & Nutrition: Research Priorities for Thermal Processing. (Illus.). 1978. text ed. 71.30x (ISBN 0-85334-803-0, Pub. by Applied Science). Burgess-Intl Ideas.

Earl, Gladys, et al. Make It Metric: Food Principles Laboratory Manual. 1979. text ed. 10.95x spiral bdg. (ISBN 0-8087-0526-1). Burgess.

Educational Research Council of America. FDA Investigator. rev. ed. Kunze, Linda J. & Marchak, John P., eds. (Real People at Work Ser: E). (Illus.). 1976. pap. text ed. 2.25 (ISBN 0-89247-038-0). Changing Times.

Ericksson, C. Maillard Reactions in Food: Proceedings of the International Symposium, Uddevalla, Sweden, September 1979. (Progress in Food & Nutrition Science Ser.: Vol. 5). (Illus.). 500p. 1981. 156.00 (ISBN 0-08-025496-9). Pergamon.

FAO Evaluation of Malthion Residues in Food. 28p. 1980. pap. 7.50 (ISBN 0-686-70033-3, F1977, FAO). Unipub.

FAO-WHO Codex Alimentarius Methods of Analysis for Processed Fruits & Vegetables: Third Series. 14p. 1980. pap. 3.00 (ISBN 92-5-100813-2, F 1886, FAO). Unipub.

FAO-WHO Codex Alimentarius Methods of Analysis for Processed Fruits & Vegetables, Second Series. 12p. (Orig.). 1975. pap. 2.00 (ISBN 0-685-53182-1, FAO). Unipub.

FAO-WHO Evaluation of Chlordane Residues in Food. 68p. 1973. pap. 6.00 (ISBN 0-686-70614-5, F1974, FAO). Unipub.

FAO-WHO Evaluation of Diazinon Residues in Food. 61p. 1973. pap. 6.00 (ISBN 0-686-70615-3, F1975, FAO). Unipub.

FAO-WHO Evaluation of Dichlorvos Residues in Food. 82p. 1973. pap. 6.00 (ISBN 0-686-70616-1, F1979, FAO). Unipub.

FAO-WHO Evaluation of Dieldrin Residues in Food. 99p. 1973. pap. 6.00 (ISBN 0-686-70617-X, F1978, FAO). Unipub.

FAO-WHO Evaluation of Endosulfan Residues in Food. 33p. 1973. pap. 6.00 (ISBN 0-686-70299-9, F1982, FAO). Unipub.

FAO-WHO Evaluation of Ethion Residues in Food. 42p. 1973. pap. 6.00 (ISBN 0-686-70618-8, F1973, FAO). Unipub.

FAO-WHO Evaluation of Parathion Residues in Food. 20p. 1973. pap. 6.00 (ISBN 0-686-70619-6, F1976, FAO). Unipub.

FAO-WHO Evaluation of Phosphamidon Residues in Food. 25p. 1973. pap. 6.00 (ISBN 0-686-70620-X, F1981, FAO). Unipub.

FAO-WHO Evaluation of Residues of Fentin Compounds in Food. 51p. 1973. pap. 6.00 (ISBN 0-686-70621-8, F1980, FAO). Unipub.

FAO-WHO Expert Committee on Food Additives. Rome, 1973, 17th. Toxicological Evaluation of Certain Food Additives with a Review of General Principles & of Specifications: Report. (Technical Report Ser.: No. 539). (Also avail. in French & Spanish). 1974. pap. 2.00 (ISBN 92-4-120539-3). World Health.

Fennema, Owen. Principles of Food Science: Physical Methods of Food Preservation, Pt. 2. (Food Science Ser: Vol. 4). 1975. 56.50 (ISBN 0-8247-6322-X). Dekker.

Filby, Frederick A. A History of Food Adulteration & Analysis. LC 75-23707. 1976. Repr. of 1934 ed. 21.00 (ISBN 0-404-13259-6). AMS Pr.

Fisher, Patty & Bender, A. E. The Value of Food. 3rd ed. (Illus.). 1979. pap. 5.95x (ISBN 0-19-859465-8). Oxford U Pr.

Ford, Robert S. Stale Food vs. Fresh Food: Cause & Cure of Choked Arteries. 6th ed. 48p. 1977. pap. 4.40 (ISBN 0-686-09051-9). Magnolia Lab.

Friberg, Stig, ed. Food Emulsions. (Food Science Ser.: Vol. 5). 1976. 65.00 (ISBN 0-8247-6337-8). Dekker.

Garard, Ira D. Introductory Food Chemistry. (Illus.). 1976. lib. bdg. 27.00 (ISBN 0-87055-206-6); pap. text ed. 17.00 (ISBN 0-87055-288-0). AVI.

Gibson, G. G. & Ioannides, C., eds. Safety Evaluation of Nitrosatable Drugs & Chemicals. (Illus.). 275p. 1981. text ed. 39.50 (ISBN 0-85066-212-5, Pub. by Taylor & Francis England). J K Burgess.

Gould, Wilbur A. Food Quality Assurance. (Illus.). 1977. text ed. 29.50 (ISBN 0-87055-219-8); pap. text ed. 18.50 (ISBN 0-87055-294-5). AVI.

Graham, H. D. Food Colloids. (Illus.). 1977. lib. bdg. 45.00 (ISBN 0-87055-201-5). AVI.

Harris, Robert S. & Karmas, Endel. Nutritional Evaluation of Food Processing. 2nd ed. (Illus.). 1975. text ed. 39.50 (ISBN 0-87055-189-2); pap. 25.00 (ISBN 0-87055-312-7). AVI.

Hart, F. L. & Fisher, H. J. Modern Food Analysis. LC 72-83661. (Illus.). 1971. 70.60 (ISBN 0-387-05126-0). Springer-Verlag.

Horsley, Gaye. Commercial Foods Exposed! 1975. 9.95 (ISBN 0-89036-043-X); pap. 6.95 (ISBN 0-89036-131-2). Hawkes Pub Inc.

Hoyem, T. & Kvale, O., eds. Physical, Chemical & Biological Changes in Food Caused by Thermal Processing. (Illus.). 1977. 87.00x (ISBN 0-85334-729-8). Intl Ideas.

International Commission on Microbiological Specifications for Foods. Microorganisms in Foods: Their Significance & Methods of Enumeration, Vol. 1. 2nd ed. LC 77-17842. 1978. 30.00x (ISBN 0-8020-2293-6). U of Toronto Pr.

International Congress of Food & Science Technology-1st-London, 1962. Food & Science Technology, 5 vols. Leitch, J. M., ed. Incl. Vol. 1. Chemical & Physical Aspects of Foods. 1969; Vol. 2. Biological & Microbiological Aspects of Foods. 1969; Vol. 3. Quality Analysis & Composition of Foods. 1969; Vol. 4. Manufacture & Distribution of Foods. 1969; Vol. 5. Proceedings. 1969. (Illus.). Set. 608.00x (ISBN 0-677-10290-9). Gordon.

Isotope Tracer Studies of Chemical Residues in Food & the Agricultural Environment. (Illus.). 156p. (Orig.). 1974. pap. 13.00 (ISBN 92-0-111274-2, ISP363, IAEA). Unipub.

Jacobs, Morris B. Chemical Analysis of Foods & Food Products. 3rd ed. LC 73-87979. 992p. 1973. Repr. of 1958 ed. 34.50 (ISBN 0-88275-131-X). Krieger.

King, R. D., ed. Developments in Food Analysis Techniques-2. (Illus.). ix, 268p. 1981. 46.00x (ISBN 0-85334-921-5). Burgess-Intl Ideas.

--Developments in Food Analysis Techniques, Vol. 1. (Illus.). 1978. text ed. 71.00x (ISBN 0-85334-755-7, Pub. by Applied Science). Burgess-Intl Ideas.

Kraus, Barbara. Barbara Kraus Guide to Fibers in Foods. 1980. 7.95 (ISBN 0-453-00368-0, H368). NAL.

Larson, Gena. Fundamentals in Foods. 1.50 (ISBN 0-686-29781-4). Cancer Bk Hse.

Lee, Frank A. Basic Food Chemistry. (Illus.). 1975. pap. text ed. 22.00 (ISBN 0-87055-289-9). AVI.

MacLeod, A. J. Instrumental Methods of Food Analysis. LC-72-7618. (Illus.). 802p. 1973. 60.95 (ISBN 0-470-56308-7). Halsted Pr.

McWilliams, Margaret. Experimental Foods Laboratory Manual. 2nd ed. (Illus.). 1977. spiral bdg. 14.95x (ISBN 0-8087-3416-4). Plycon Pr.

Manuals of Food Quality Control: Microbiological Analysis. (FAO Food & Nutrition Paper: No. 14-4). 119p. 1981. pap. 9.50 (ISBN 92-5-100849-3, F2070, FAO). Unipub.

Meloan, Clifton & Pomeranz, Y. Food Analysis Laboratory Experiments. 2nd ed. (Illus.). 1980. pap. 11.50 (ISBN 0-87055-351-8). AVI.

Mondy, Nell I. Experimental Food Chemistry. (Illus.). 1980. pap. text ed. 16.50 (ISBN 0-87055-343-7). AVI.

Nickerson, John T. & Ronsivall, Louis J. Elementary Food Science. 2nd ed. 1980. pap. text ed. 19.00 (ISBN 0-87055-318-6). AVI.

Nineteen Seventy Five Evaluation of Some Pesticide Residues in Food. (Illus.). 1978. pap. 13.75 (ISBN 92-5-100239-8, F 1237, FAO). Unipub.

Nineteen Seventy-Six Evaluation of Some Pesticide Residues in Food. 1978. pap. 17.75 (ISBN 92-5-100442-0, F1345, FAO). Unipub.

OECD Staff. Food Margins Analysis: Aims Methods & Uses. 90p. (Orig.). 1981. pap. 8.00x (ISBN 92-64-12166-8). OECD.

Osborne, D. R. & Voogt, P. The Analysis of Nutrients in Foods. (Food Science & Technology Ser.). 1978. 32.00 (ISBN 0-12-529150-7). Acad Pr.

Pearson, D. Chemical Analysis of Foods. 1977. text ed. 41.00 (ISBN 0-8206-0207-8). Chem Pub.

Pearson, David. Chemical Analysis of Food. 7th ed. (Illus.). 592p. 1976. 49.75 (ISBN 0-443-01411-6). Churchill.

Pomeranz, Y. & Meloan, Clifton E. Food Analysis: Theory & Practice. rev. ed. 1978. 25.00 (ISBN 0-87055-238-4). AVI.

Recommended International Standard for Canned Asparagus. (Codex Alimentarius Commission Reports Ser.). 18p. (Orig.). 1975. pap. 4.50 (ISBN 0-685-53176-7, F597, FAO). Unipub.

Recommended International Standard for Cocoa Butters. (Codex Alimentarius Commission). 12p. 1978. pap. 4.50 (ISBN 0-685-87283-1, F574, FAO). Unipub.

Recommended International Standard for Canned Fruit Cocktail. (Codex Alimentarius Commission). 15p. 1978. pap. 4.50 (ISBN 0-685-87280-7, F573, FAO). Unipub.

Recommended International Standard for Canned Mushrooms. (Codex Alimentarius Commission Reports Ser.). 16p. (Orig.). 1975. pap. 4.50 (ISBN 0-685-53177-5, F596, FAO). Unipub.

Recommended International Standard for Canned Mature Processed Peas. (Codex Alimentarius Commission). 10p. 1978. pap. 4.50 (ISBN 0-685-87281-5, F580, FAO). Unipub.

Recommended International Standard for Canned Pears. (Codex Alimentarius Commission Reports Ser.). 20p. (Orig.). 1975. pap. 4.50 (ISBN 0-685-53181-3, F602, FAO). Unipub.

Recommended International Standard for Canned Strawberries. (Codex Alimentarius Commission Reports Ser.). 18p. (Orig.). 1975. pap. 4.50 (ISBN 0-685-53179-1, F603, FAO). Unipub.

Recommended International Standard for Chocolate. (Codex Alimentarius Commission). 14p. 1978. pap. 4.50 (ISBN 0-685-87282-3, F572, FAO). Unipub.

Recommended International Standard for Pineapple Juice Preserved Exclusively by Physical Means. (Codex Alimentarius Commission). 7p. 1978. pap. 4.50 (ISBN 0-685-87284-X, F575, FAO). Unipub.

Recommended International Standard for Quick Frozen Bilberries. 8p. 1978. pap. 4.50 (ISBN 0-685-87285-8, F577, FAO). Unipub.

Recommended International Standard for Quick Frozen Peaches. (Codex Alimentarius Commission). 11p. 1978. pap. 4.50 (ISBN 0-685-87286-6, F578, FAO). Unipub.

Recommended International Standard for Quick Frozen Spinach. (Codex Alimentarius Commission). 8p. 1978. pap. 4.50 (ISBN 0-685-87287-4, F576, FAO). Unipub.

Recommended International Standards for Concentrated Apple Juice & Concentrated Orange Juice Preserved Exclusively by Physical Means. (Codex Alimentarius Commisssion Reports). 15p. (Orig.). 1974. pap. 4.50 (ISBN 0-685-49915-4, F604, FAO). Unipub.

Report of the Thirteenth Session Codex Alimentarius Commission. 103p. 1981. pap. 7.50 (ISBN 92-5-100912-0, F2071, FAO). Unipub.

Santos, W. J., et al, eds. Nutrition & Food Science: Present Knowledge & Utilization, 3 vols. 1980. 195.00 set (ISBN 0-686-77478-7, Plenum Pr); Vol. 1, 850p. 75.00 (ISBN 0-306-40342-0); Vol. 2, 900p. 79.50 (ISBN 0-306-40343-9); Vol. 3, 760p. 69.50 (ISBN 0-306-40344-7). Plenum Pub.
Sapeika, N. Food Pharmacology. (American Lecture Living Chemistry). (Illus.). 200p. 1969. photocopy ed. spiral 19.50 (ISBN 0-398-01648-8). C C Thomas.
Sharpe, A. N. Food Microbiology. (Illus.). 238p. 1980. 24.75 (ISBN 0-398-04017-6). C C Thomas.
Standardization of Analytical Methodology for Feeds. 128p. 1980. pap. 10.00 (ISBN 0-88936-217-3, IDRC 134, IDRC). Unipub.
Teranishi, Roy. Agricultural & Food Chemistry: Past, Present, Future. (Illus.). 1978. lib. bdg. 45.00 (ISBN 0-87055-231-7). AVI.
Toxicological Evaluation of Some Food Additives Including Anticaking Agents, Antimicrobials, Antioxidants, Emulsifiers & Thickening Agents. (Food Additive Ser.: No. 5). (Also avail. in French). 1974. pap. 9.20 (ISBN 92-4-166005-8). World Health.
Toxicological Evaluation of Some Food Colours, Enzymes, Flavour Enhancers, Thickening Agents & Certain Other Food Additives. (Food Additive Ser.: No. 6). (Also avail. in French). 1975. pap. 5.20 (ISBN 92-4-166006-6). World Health.
Toxicological Evaluation of Some Food Colours, Thickening Agents & Certain Other Substances. (Food Additive Ser.: No. 8). (Also avail. in French). 1975. pap. 4.80 (ISBN 92-4-166008-2). World Health.
Tressler, Donald K. & Sultan, William J. Food Products Formulary, Vol. 2: Cereals, Baked Goods, Dairy & Egg Products. (Illus.). 1975. lib. bdg. 49.50 (ISBN 0-87055-170-1). AVI.
Woods, A. E. & Aurand, L. W. Laboratory Manual in Food Chemistry. (Illus.). 1977. pap. text ed. 11.00 (ISBN 0-87055-220-1). AVI.
Working Conference.Deutsches Krebsforschungszentrum, Heidelberg, Germany.Oct. 13-15, 1971. N-Nitroso Compounds-Analysis & Formation: Proceedings. Bogovski, P., et al, eds. (IARC Scientific Pub.: No. 3). 1972. 10.00 (ISBN 0-686-16787-2). World Health.

FOOD–BACTERIOLOGY
see also Food Poisoning
Ayres, J. C., et al, eds. Chemical & Biological Hazards in Food. (Illus.). 1969. Repr. of 1962 ed. 15.75 (ISBN 0-02-840650-8). Hafner.
Pederson, Carl S. Microbiology of Food Fermentations. 2nd ed. (Illus.). 1979. text ed. 32.00 (ISBN 0-87055-277-5). AVI.
Stumbo, C. R. Thermobacteriology in Food Processing. 2nd ed. (Food, Science & Technology Ser.). 1973. 39.50 (ISBN 0-12-675352-0). Acad Pr.

FOOD–BIBLIOGRAPHY
Commission of European Communities, Directorate-Center for Research-Science & Education, ed. Food: Multilingual Thesaurus. 1979. 4 vols. & index 240.00 (ISBN 0-89664-036-1, Pub. by K G Saur). Gale.
FAO Library Select Catalogue of Books, 1951-58. 1961. 22.50 (ISBN 0-685-09379-4, F 155, FAO). Unipub.
Food & Nutrition: Annotated Bibliography, Author & Subject Index (1945-1972) (Special Index: No. 26). (Orig.). 1974. pap. 8.00 (ISBN 0-685-41433-7, FAO). Unipub.
Food & Nutrition: Annotated Bibliography, Author & Subject Index (1945-1972) (Special Index: No. 26). (Orig.). 1974. pap. 8.00 (ISBN 0-685-41433-7, FAO). Unipub.
Food & Nutrition Bibliography. 11th ed. 1982. pap. 18.00 (ISBN 0-89774-009-2). Oryx Pr.
Food & Nutrition Bibliography. 9th ed. 1980. pap. text ed. 18.00x (ISBN 0-912700-77-7). Oryx Pr.
Food & Nutrition Bibliography. 10th ed. 1981. pap. text ed. 18.00x (ISBN 0-912700-78-5). Oryx Pr.
Freedman, Robert L., compiled by. Human Food Uses: A Cross-Cultural, Comprehensive Annotated Bibliography. LC 81-469. xxxvii, 552p. 1981. lib. bdg. 65.00 (ISBN 0-313-22901-5, FHU/). Greenwood.

FOOD–COMPOSITION
see also Food–Analysis
ACS Committee on Chemistry & Public Affairs. Chemistry & the Food System. LC 80-11194. 1980. 15.00 (ISBN 0-8412-0557-4); pap. 9.00 (ISBN 0-8412-0563-9). Am Chemical.
Adams, Rex. Miracle Medical Foods. 304p. (Orig.). 1981. pap. 2.50 (ISBN 0-446-91940-3). Warner Bks.
Antonetti, Vincent. The Computer Diet. LC 73-80174. (Illus.). 284p. 1973. 6.95 (ISBN 0-87131-122-4). M Evans.
Bender, Arnold & Nash, Tony. Pocket Encyclopedia of Calories & Nutrition. 1979. pap. 3.95 (ISBN 0-671-24839-1). S&S.
Berk, Z. Braverman's Introduction to the Biochemistry of Foods. 2nd ed. 1976. 31.75 (ISBN 0-444-41450-9, North Holland). Elsevier.
Block, Richard J. & Bolling, Diana. The Amino Acid Composition of Proteins & Foods: Analytical Methods & Results. 2nd ed. (Illus.). 584p. 1951. ed. spiral bdg. 48.50photocopy (ISBN 0-398-04210-1). C C Thomas.
Charalambous, George, ed. Analysis & Control of Less-Desirable Flavors in Foods & Beverages. 1980. 24.50 (ISBN 0-12-169065-2). Acad Pr.
Curriculum Planning & Some Current Health Problems. (Educational Studies & Documents, No. 13). 10p. (Orig.). 1974. pap. 2.50 (ISBN 92-3-101129-4, U753, UNESCO). Unipub.
DeMan, J. M. Principles of Food Chemistry. rev. ed. (Illus.). 1980. pap. 21.00 (ISBN 0-87055-287-2). AVI.
Ericksson, C. Maillard Reactions in Food: Proceedings of the International Symposium, Uddevalla, Sweden, September 1979. (Progress in Food & Nutrition Science Ser.: Vol. 5). (Illus.). 500p. 1981. 156.00 (ISBN 0-08-025496-9). Pergamon.
Fisher, Patty & Bender, A. E. The Value of Food. 3rd ed. (Illus.). 1979. pap. 5.95x (ISBN 0-19-859465-8). Oxford U Pr.
Food Composition Table for Use in East Asia. 1979. pap. 25.00 (ISBN 0-685-95365-3, F1546, FAO). Unipub.
Garard, Ira D. Introductory Food Chemistry. (Illus.). 1976. lib. bdg. 27.00 (ISBN 0-87055-206-6); pap. text ed. 17.00 (ISBN 0-87055-288-0). AVI.
Goldbeck, Nikki & Goldbeck, David. The Dieter's Companion: A Guide to Nutritional Self-Sufficiency. LC 75-11585. 384p. 1976. 8.95 (ISBN 0-07-023654-2, GB). McGraw.
Hawthorn, John. Foundations of Food Science. (Illus.). 1981. text ed. 22.95x (ISBN 0-7167-1295-4); pap. text ed. 10.95x (ISBN 0-7167-1296-2). W H Freeman.
Heimann, Werner. Fundamentals of Food Chemistry. (american) ed. (Illus.). 1980. pap. text ed. 30.00 (ISBN 0-87055-356-9). AVI.
Howard, Rosanne B. & Herbold, Nancie. Nutrition in Clinical Care. (Illus.). 1977. text ed. 15.95 (ISBN 0-07-030545-5, HP). McGraw.
Improvement of Food Quality by Irradiation. (Illus.). 188p. (Orig.). 1974. pap. 14.75 (ISBN 92-0-011174-2, ISP370, IAEA). Unipub.
Inglett, G. E. & Charalambous, George, eds. Tropical Foods: Chemistry & Nutrition, Vol. 1. 1979. 29.50 (ISBN 0-12-370901-6). Acad Pr.
Kraus, Barbara. Barbara Kraus Guide to Fiber in Food. (Orig.). 1975. pap. 1.75 (ISBN 0-451-07857-8, E7857, Sig). NAL.
--Barbara Kraus 1980 Calorie Guide to Brand Names & Basic Foods. (Orig.). 1980. pap. 1.50 (ISBN 0-451-09032-2, W9032, Sig). NAL.
--Barbara Kraus 1980 Carbohydrate Guide to Brand Names & Basic Foods. (Orig.). 1980. pap. 1.50 (ISBN 0-451-09033-0, W9033, Sig). NAL.
Liener, I. Toxic Constituents in Plant Foodstuffs. (Food Science & Technology Ser). 1969. 58.50 (ISBN 0-12-449950-3). Acad Pr.
Liener, Irvin E. Toxic Constitutuents of Plant Foodstuffs. 2nd ed. LC 79-51681. (Food Science & Technology Ser.). 1980. 39.50 (ISBN 0-12-449960-0). Acad Pr.
Long, Lucy, et al. Food Products Formulary, Vol. 1: Meats, Poultry, Fish & Shellfish. 2nd ed. (Illus.). 1981. lib. bdg. 49.50 (ISBN 0-87055-392-5). AVI.
McWilliams, Margaret. Experimental Foods Laboratory Manual. (The Plycon Home Economics Ser.). 342p. 1977. spiral 11.95x (ISBN 0-686-75957-5). Burgess.
Manuals of Food Quality Control, 3 vols. Incl. Vol. 1. Food Control Laboratory. 75p. pap. 9.00 (ISBN 92-5-100839-6, F1960); Vol. 2. Additives, Contaminants, Techniques. 317p. pap. 22.00 (ISBN 92-5-100867-1, F1961); Vol. 3. Commodities. 420p. pap. 29.50 (ISBN 92-5-100844-2, F1962). (FAO Food & Nutrition Papers: No. 14). 1980 (FAO). Unipub.
Manuals of Food Quality Control: Microbiological Analysis. (FAO Food & Nutrition Paper: No. 14-4). 119p. 1981. pap. 9.50 (ISBN 92-5-100849-3, F2070, FAO). Unipub.
Medved, Eva. Food in Theory & Practice. LC 77-76340. (The Plycon Home Economics Ser.). 596p. 1978. text ed. 16.95x (ISBN 0-686-75958-3). Burgess.
Meyer, Lillian Hoagland. Food Chemistry. 3rd, rev. ed. (Illus.). 1978. Repr. soft cover 15.00 (ISBN 0-87055-171-X). AVI.
Mondy, Nell I. Experimental Food Chemistry. (Illus.). 1980. pap. text ed. 16.50 (ISBN 0-87055-343-7). AVI.
Morgan-Grampian Books, ed. Food Ingredient & Machinery Survey, 1981. 142p. 1981. 50.00x (ISBN 0-686-75514-6, Pub. by Morgan-Grampian Bk). State Mutual Bk.
Morr, Mary L. & Irmiter, Theodore F. Introductory Foods: A Laboratory Manual of Food Preparation & Evaluation. 3rd ed. (Illus.). 1980. pap. text ed. 9.95 (ISBN 0-02-384120-6). Macmillan.
Nickerson, John T. & Ronsivall, Louis J. Elementary Food Science. 2nd ed. 1980. pap. text ed. 19.00 (ISBN 0-87055-318-6). AVI.
Paul, A. A. & Southgate, D. A. McCance & Widdowson's The Composition of Foods. 4th rev, extended ed. (MRC Special Report: No. 297). 1978. 66.50 (ISBN 0-444-80027-1, North-Holland). Elsevier.
Pellet, P. L. & Shadarevian, Sossy. Food Composition: Tables for Use in the Middle East. 1970. pap. 11.95x (ISBN 0-8156-6032-4, Am U Beirut). Syracuse U Pr.
Robinson, Corinne H. & Lawler, Marilyn R. Normal & Therapeutic Nutrition. 15th ed. (Illus.). 832p. 1977. text ed. 20.95 (ISBN 0-02-402300-0). Macmillan.
Rockland, Louis B. & Stewart, George F., eds. Water Activity: Influences on Food Quality: Proceedings of Second International Symposium on Properties of Water Affecting Food Quality. LC 79-26632. 1980. 60.00 (ISBN 0-12-591350-8). Acad Pr.
Safety Evaluation of Chemicals in Food: Toxicological Data Profiles for Pesticides, Pt. 1: Carbamate & Organophosphorus Insecticides Used in Agriculture & Public Health. (Progress in Standardization: No. 3). (WHO bulletin vol. 52, supp. no. 2). 1975. pap. 4.00 (ISBN 92-4-068522-7). World Health.
Sapeika, N. Food Pharmacology. (American Lecture Living Chemistry). (Illus.). 200p. 1969. photocopy ed. spiral 19.50 (ISBN 0-398-01648-8). C C Thomas.
Schwimmer, Sigmund. Source Book of Food Enzymology. (Illus.). 1981. lib. bdg. 79.50 (ISBN 0-87055-369-0). AVI.
Sharpe, A. N. Food Microbiology. (Illus.). 238p. 1980. 24.75 (ISBN 0-398-04017-6). C C Thomas.
Southgate, D. A., ed. Guidelines for the Preparation of Tables of Food Composition. 80p. 1974. pap. 11.50 (ISBN 3-8055-1780-7). S Karger.
Wade, Carlson. Brand-Name Handbook of Protein, Calories & Carbohydrates. 1977. 8.95 (ISBN 0-13-081307-9, Parker). P-H.
Whitaker, John R. & Tannenbaum, Steven R., eds. Food Proteins. (Illus.). 1977. lib. bdg. 45.00 (ISBN 0-87055-230-9). AVI.
Winter, Ruth. Beware of the Food You Eat. rev. ed. Orig. Title: Poisons in Your Food. 247p. (YA) 1971. 6.95 (ISBN 0-517-50011-6). Crown.

FOOD–CONTAMINATION
see Food Contamination

FOOD–DICTIONARIES
Ashley, Richard & Duggal, Heidi. Dictionary of Nutrition. 1976. pap. 2.50 (ISBN 0-671-83406-1). PB.
Bailey, Adrian. Cooks' Ingredients. Ortiz, Elisabeth L., ed. LC 80-81457. (Illus.). 256p. 1980. 19.95 (ISBN 0-688-03681-3). Morrow.
Bender, A. E. Dictionary of Nutrition & Food Technology. 1977. 28.50 (ISBN 0-8206-0214-0). Chem Pub.
Bender, Arnold E. Dictionary of Nutrition & Food Technology. 4th ed. 1975. text ed. 19.95 (ISBN 0-408-00143-7). Butterworth.
Dahl, C. Food & Menu Dictionary. LC 77-123002. 1972. 12.50 (ISBN 0-8436-0556-1). CBI Pub.
Diccionario de los Alimentos: Vitaminas, Calories, Coccion, Conservacion, Etc. 2nd ed. 758p. (Espn.). 1979. pap. 41.95 (ISBN 84-352-0338-7, S-13671). French & Eur.
Esser, William L. Dictionary of Man's Foods. (Illus.). 1972. pap. 2.95 (ISBN 0-914532-06-5). Natural Hygiene.
FitzGibbon, Theodora. The Food of the Western World. LC 74-24279. (Illus.). 1976. 25.00 (ISBN 0-8129-0427-3). Times Bks.
Gelb, Barbara L. The Dictionary of Food & What's in It for You. 1979. pap. 3.50 (ISBN 0-345-29479-3). Ballantine.
--A Dictionary of Food & What's in It for You. LC 77-20973. (Illus.). 1978. 9.95 (ISBN 0-448-22365-1). Paddington.
Hauser, Gaylord & Berg, Ragnar. Dictionary of Foods. 156p. 1971. pap. 2.25 (ISBN 0-87904-008-4). Lust.
Lapidus, Dorothy F. The Scrutable Feast: A Guide to Eating Authentically in Chinese Restaurants. 1977. pap. 6.95 (ISBN 0-396-07448-0). Dodd.
Lederer, Jean. Encyclopedie Modern De L'hygiene Alimentaire, 4 Vols, 4 vols. (Fr.). 95.00 (ISBN 0-686-57003-0, M-6344). French & Eur.
--Encyclopedie Moderne de l'Hygiene Alimentaire. 750p. (Fr.). 1971. 65.00 (ISBN 0-686-57002-2, M-6343). French & Eur.
--Encyclopedie Moderne De L'hygiene Alimentaire, 1: Exigences Alimentaires De L'homme Normal. Jean Lederer. (Fr.). 1977. 29.95 (M-6345). French & Eur. 198p. (Fr.). 1977. 29.95 (ISBN 0-686-57004-9, M-6345). French & Eur.
--Encyclopedie Moderne de l'Hygiene Alimentaire, 2: Hygiene des Aliments. 282p. (Fr.). 1977. 39.95 (ISBN 0-686-57005-7, M-6346). French & Eur.
--Encyclopedie Moderne De L'hygiene Alimentaire, 3: Technologie et Hygiene Alimentaire. 138p. (Fr.). 1977. 27.50 (ISBN 0-686-57006-5, M-6347). French & Eur.
--Encyclopedie Moderne De L'hygiene Alimentaire, 4: Les Intoxications Alimentaire. 164p. (Fr.). 1977. 27.50 (ISBN 0-686-57007-3, M-6348). French & Eur.
McGraw-Hill Editors. McGraw-Hill Encyclopedia of Food, Agriculture, & Nutrition. (Illus.). 1977. 24.50 (ISBN 0-07-045263-6, P&RB). McGraw.
Montagne, Prosper. Larousse Gastronomique: The Encyclopedia of Food, Wine, & Cooking. Turgeon, Charlotte & Froud, Nina, eds. 1961. 25.00 (ISBN 0-517-50333-6). Crown.
--The New Larousse Gastronomique: The Encyclopedia of Food, Wine, & Cooking. Turgeon, Charlotte, ed. (Illus.). 1977. 25.00 (ISBN 0-517-53137-2). Crown.
Peterson, Martin S. & Johnson, Arnold H. Encyclopedia of Food Science. (Illus.). 1978. lib. bdg. 79.50 (ISBN 0-87055-227-9). AVI.
Root, Waverley. Food: An Informal Dictionary. (Illus.). 1980. 24.95 (ISBN 0-671-22589-8). S&S.
Ward, Artemus. Encyclopedia of Food, Vol. 1. 17.50 (ISBN 0-8446-1464-5). Peter Smith.
Wasserman, Pauline & Wasserman, Sheldon. Don't Ask Your Waiter. LC 77-23434. 1978. 25.00x (ISBN 0-8128-2243-9); pap. 2.95 (ISBN 0-8128-2244-7). Stein & Day.

FOOD–DRYING
Beyer, Bee. Food Drying at Home...the Natural Way. LC 75-38009. (Illus.). 160p. 1976. pap. text ed. 4.95 (ISBN 0-87477-049-1). J P Tarcher.
Bills, Jay & Bills, Shirley. Home Food Dehydrating: Economical "Do-It Yourself" Methods for Preserving, Storing, & Cooking. 1974. pap. 5.95 (ISBN 0-88290-035-8). Horizon Utah.
Borella, Anne. How to Book: Canning, Freezing, Drying. 1977. 1.95 (ISBN 0-87502-051-8). Benjamin Co.
Densley, Barbara. The ABC's of Home Food Dehydration. LC 75-23565. 112p. (Orig.). 1975. pap. 5.50 (ISBN 0-88290-051-X). Horizon Utah.
Hobson, Phyllis. Garden Way's Guide to Food Drying. (Illus.). 224p. (Orig.). 1980. pap. 5.95 (ISBN 0-88266-155-8). Garden Way Pub.
Nichols, Naomi M. Food Drying at Home. 1978. 9.95 (ISBN 0-442-26028-8); pap. 5.95 (ISBN 0-442-26029-6). Van Nos Reinhold.
Spicer, Arnold, ed. Advances in Preconcentration & Dehydration of Foods. LC 74-9512. 526p. 1974. 76.95 (ISBN 0-470-81591-4). Halsted Pr.
Van Arsdel, Wallace B., et al. Food Dehydration, 2 vols. 2nd ed. Incl. Vol. 1. Drying Methods & Phenomena. 34.50 (ISBN 0-87055-137-X); Vol. 2. Practices & Applications. 42.50 (ISBN 0-87055-138-8). (Illus.). 1973. AVI.
Wubben, Pamela G. Drying Foods Naturally: A Handbook for Preserving Foods & Using Them Later. 80p. 1980. pap. 4.50 (ISBN 0-935442-01-4). One Percent.
--The Food Dryer Handbook. 55p. 1980. pap. 3.50 (ISBN 0-935442-02-2). One Percent.

FOOD–FREEZING
see Food, Frozen

FOOD–HISTORY
Burnett, John. Plenty & Want: A Social History of Diet in England from 1815 to the Present Day. 387p. 1979. Repr. of 1966 ed. 15.95 (ISBN 0-85967-461-4, Pub. by Scolar Pr England); pap. 7.95 (ISBN 0-85967-462-2). Biblio Dist.
Fenton, Alexander & Owen, Trefor. Food in Perspective: Third International Conference of Ethnological Food Research. (Illus.). 425p. 1981. text ed. 50.00x (ISBN 0-85976-044-8). Humanities.
Harter, Jim. Food & Drink: A Pictorial Archive from Nineteenth-Century Sources. 10.00 (ISBN 0-8446-5768-9). Peter Smith.
Heiser, Charles B., Jr. Seed to Civilization: The Story of Food. 2nd ed. LC 80-18208. (Illus.). 1981. text ed. 19.95x (ISBN 0-7167-1264-4); pap. text ed. 9.95x (ISBN 0-7167-1265-2). W H Freeman.
Henisch, Bridget Ann. Fast and Feast: Food in Medieval Society. LC 76-15677. (Illus.). 1977. 15.95 (ISBN 0-271-01230-7). Pa St U Pr.
Johnston, James P. A Hundred Years Eating: Food, Drink, & the Daily Diet in Britain Since the Late Nineteenth Century. (Illus.). 1977. 9.95 (ISBN 0-7735-0306-4). McGill-Queens U Pr.

Jones, Evan, ed. A Food Lover's Companion. LC 79-1668. 1979. 13.95 (ISBN 0-06-012288-9, HarpT). Har-Row.

Kinard, Malvina & Crisler, Janet. Loaves & Fishes: Foods from Bible Times. LC 75-19544. (Illus.). 224p. 1975. 8.95 (ISBN 0-87983-110-3); pap. 4.95 (ISBN 0-87983-173-1). Keats.

McLeish, Kenneth. Food & Drink. (Greek & Roman Topics Ser.). (Illus.). 1978. pap. text ed. 3.95x (ISBN 0-04-930007-5). Allen Unwin.

Noel Hume, Audrey. Food. LC 78-4683. (Archaeological Ser.: No. 9). (Illus.). 1978. pap. 2.25 (ISBN 0-87935-045-8). Williamsburg.

Ritchie, Carson I. Food in Civilization: How History Has Been Affected by Human Tastes. LC 81-4288. 192p. 1981. 10.95 (ISBN 0-8253-0037-1). Beaufort Bks NY.

Tannahill, Reay. Food in History. LC 75-160342. (Illus.). 448p. 1974. pap. 8.95 (ISBN 0-8128-1752-4). Stein & Day.

Vickery, Kenton F. Food in Early Greece. 97p. 1980. 12.50 (ISBN 0-89005-339-1). Ares.

Wing, Elizabeth S. & Brown, Antoinette B. Paleonutrition: Prehistoric Foodways. LC 79-21034. (Studies in Archeology). 1979. 19.50 (ISBN 0-12-759350-0). Acad Pr.

FOOD–INSPECTION

see Food Adulteration and Inspection

FOOD–JUVENILE LITERATURE

Abels, Harriette S. Future Food. Schroeder, Howard, ed. LC 80-14823. (Our Future World Ser.). (Illus.). 48p. (Orig.). (gr. 6-9). 1980. PLB 6.95 (ISBN 0-89686-083-3); pap. text ed. 3.25 (ISBN 0-89686-092-2). Crestwood Hse.

Adler, Irving. Food. LC 76-54783. (The Reason Why Ser.). (Illus.). (gr. 2-5). 1977. PLB 8.79 (ISBN 0-381-90051-7, JD-J). Har-Row.

At the Table. (Children's Board Bks.). (Illus.). 1980. 1.50 (ISBN 0-8431-0157-1). Price Stern.

Berger, Melvin & Berger, Gilda. The New Food Book: Nutrition, Diet, Consumer Tips & Foods of the Future. LC 77-7976. (gr. 4-6). 1978. 7.95 (ISBN 0-690-01295-0, TYC-J); PLB 8.79 (ISBN 0-690-03841-0). Har-Row.

Burns, Marilyn. Good for Me! All About Food in 32 Bites. LC 78-6727. (Brown Paper School Book Ser.). (Illus.). (gr. 5 up). 1978. 8.95 (ISBN 0-316-11749-8); pap. 5.95 (ISBN 0-316-11747-1). Little.

Cavanagh, Mary. Favorite Menus. (Illus.). 13p. (gr. 3-5). 1980. pap. 4.95 (ISBN 0-933358-70-9). Enrich.

Daly, Kathleen. My Lunch Box Book. (Carry-Me Books). (Illus.). (ps-3). 1977. PLB 5.38 (ISBN 0-307-68855-0, Golden Pr). Western Pub.

De Paola, Tomie. The Popcorn Book. (gr. k-3). 1979. pap. 1.50 (ISBN 0-590-03142-2, Schol Pap). Schol Bk Serv.

Espeland, Pamela. Why Do We Eat? (Creative's Questions & Answers Library). (Illus.). 32p. (gr. 3-4). Date not set. PLB 5.75 (ISBN 0-87191-747-5); pap. 2.75 (ISBN 0-89812-216-3). Creative Ed.

Gilbert, Sara. You Are What You Eat: A Common-Sense Guide to the Modern American Diet. LC 76-39806. (gr. 5 up). 1977. 8.95 (ISBN 0-02-736020-2, 73602). Macmillan.

Gokay, Nancy H. Sugarbush: Making Maple Syrup. LC 80-17582. (Illus.). 32p. (Orig.). (gr. 3-4). 1980. pap. 3.95 (ISBN 0-910726-95-7). Hillsdale Educ.

Lewis, Alfred. New World of Food. LC 68-14244. (New World Ser.). (Illus.). (gr. 3-9). 1968. PLB 5.95 (ISBN 0-396-06593-7). Dodd.

Peck, Leilani B., et al. Focus on Food. (Illus.). 432p. (gr. 7-9). 1974. text ed. 12.40 (ISBN 0-07-049145-3, W). McGraw.

Perl, Lila. Junk Food, Fast Food, Health Food What America Eats & Why. 192p. (gr. 5 up). 1980. 9.95 (ISBN 0-395-29108-9, Clarion); pap. 4.95 (ISBN 0-395-30060-6). HM.

Riedman, Sarah R. Food for People. rev. ed. LC 75-33193. 1976. 9.95 (ISBN 0-200-00161-2, AbS-J). Har-Row.

Showers, Paul. What Happens to a Hamburger? LC 70-106578. (Crocodile Paperbacks Ser.). (Illus.). (gr. k-3). 1976. pap. 1.45 (ISBN 0-690-01264-0, TYC-J). Har-Row.

Simon, Seymour. About the Food You Eat. LC 79-14395. (Let's-Try-It-Out Ser.). (Illus.). (gr. 1-3). 1979. 6.95 (ISBN 0-07-057457-X). McGraw.

--About the Food You Eat. Date not set. price not set. McGraw.

Weiner, Michael. Bugs in the Peanut Butter: Dangers in Everyday Food. (gr. 7 up). 1976. 6.95 (ISBN 0-316-92860-7). Little.

Wise, William. Fresh, Canned, & Frozen: Food from Past to Future. LC 74-145599. (Finding-Out Book). (Illus.). (gr. 2-4). 1971. PLB 7.95 (ISBN 0-8193-0482-4, Pub. by Parents). Enslow Pubs.

Zim, Herbert S. Your Food & You. (Illus.). (gr. 4-8). 1957. PLB 6.48 (ISBN 0-688-31568-2). Morrow.

FOOD–LAW AND LEGISLATION

see Food Law and Legislation

FOOD–MICROBIOLOGY

see also Food–Bacteriology; Food Poisoning

Ayres, John C., et al. Microbiology of Foods. LC 79-16335. (Food & Nutrition Ser.). (Illus.). 1980. text ed. 22.95x (ISBN 0-7167-1049-8). W H Freeman.

Banwart, George J. Basic Food Microbiology. abr. ed. (Illus.). 1981. pap. text ed. write for info. (ISBN 0-87055-384-4). AVI.

Committee On Food Protection. Evaluation of Public Health Hazards from Microbiological Contamination of Foods. 1964. pap. 3.75 (ISBN 0-309-01195-7). Natl Acad Pr.

De Figueiredo, M. P. & Splittstoesser, D. F. Food Microbiology: Public Health & Spoilage Aspects. (Illus.). 1976. lib. bdg. 39.50 (ISBN 0-87055-209-0). AVI.

Fields, Marion. Fundamentals of Food Microbiology. (Illus.). 1979. text ed. 21.00 (ISBN 0-87055-250-3). AVI.

Frazier, William C. Food Microbiology. 2nd ed. 1967. text ed. 18.00 (ISBN 0-07-021916-8, C). McGraw.

Harrigan, W. F. & McCance, M. E., eds. Laboratory Methods in Food & Dairy Microbiology. 1977. 59.50 (ISBN 0-12-326040-X). Acad Pr.

International Commission on Microbial Specifications for Foods, ed. Microbial Ecology of Foods: The Food Commodities, Vol. II. 1980. 60.00 (ISBN 0-12-363502-0); Set. 51.00 (ISBN 0-686-65843-4). Acad Pr.

International Commission on Microbial Specifications for Foods. Microbial Ecology of Foods: Vol. 1 Factors Affecting Life & Death of Microorganisms. 1980. 29.50 (ISBN 0-12-363501-2); Set. 26.00 (ISBN 0-686-66013-7). Acad Pr.

International Congress of Food & Science Technology-1st-London, 1962. Food & Science Technology, 5 vols. Leitch, J. M., ed. Incl. Vol. 1. Chemical & Physical Aspects of Foods. 1969; Vol. 2. Biological & Microbiological Aspects of Foods. 1969; Vol. 3. Quality Analysis & Composition of Foods. 1969; Vol. 4. Manufacture & Distribution of Foods. 1969; Vol. 5. Proceedings. 1969. (Illus.). Set. 608.00x (ISBN 0-677-10290-9). Gordon.

Mateles, Richard I. & Wogan, Gerald N., eds. Biochemistry of Some Foodborne Microbial Toxins. 1967. 18.00x (ISBN 0-262-13034-3). MIT Pr.

Microbiological Specifications for Foods: Report of the 2nd Joint FAO-WHO Consultation. 1977. pap. 7.50 (ISBN 92-5-100307-6, F1225, FAO). Unipub.

Minor, T. & Marth, E. H. Staphylococci & Their Significance in Foods. 1976. 42.50 (ISBN 0-444-41339-1). Elsevier.

Nickerson, J. & Sinskay, A. Microbiology of Food & Food Processing. 1972. 18.50 (ISBN 0-444-00124-7, North Holland). Elsevier.

Rodricks, Joseph V., ed. Mycotoxins & Other Fungal Related Food Problems. LC 76-4547. (Advances in Chemistry Ser.: No. 149). 1976. 39.00 (ISBN 0-8412-0222-2). Am Chemical.

Speck, Marvin L., ed. Compendium of Methods for the Microbiological Examination of Foods. 1976. 40.00x (ISBN 0-87553-081-8, 020). Am Pub Health.

FOOD–PACKAGING

BCC Staff. Perishable Food Packaging: Markets, Development. (Illus.). 1976. 450.00 (ISBN 0-89336-048-1). BCC.

Crosby, N. T. Food Packaging Materials: Aspects of Analysis & Migration of Contaminants. (Illus.). 190p. 1981. text ed. 28.00 (ISBN 0-85334-926-6, Pub. by Applied Sci England). J K Burgess.

FAO-WHO Codex Alimentarius Sampling Plans for Prepackaged Foods (1969) (Illus.). 15p. (Orig.). 1974. pap. 3.00 (ISBN 0-685-41475-2, FAO). Unipub.

Hersom, A. C. & Hulland, E. D. Canned Foods. 1981. text ed. 40.00 (ISBN 0-8206-0288-4). Chem Pub.

Palling, S. J., ed. Developments in Food Packaging - One. (Illus.). xv, 192p. 1980. 45.00x (ISBN 0-85334-917-7). Burgess-Intl Ideas.

Pintauro, N. D. Food Packaging. LC 78-56010. (Food Technology Review Ser.: No. 47). (Illus.). 1978. 39.00 (ISBN 0-8155-0710-0). Noyes.

Recommended International Code of Practice for the Processing & Handling of Quick-Frozen Foods. 6p. 1978. pap. 4.00 (ISBN 0-685-60671-6, F1426, FAO). Unipub.

Sacharow, Stanley & Griffin, Roger C. Principles of Food Packaging. 2nd ed. (Illus.). 1980. lib. bdg. 35.00 (ISBN 0-87055-347-X). AVI.

Swalm, Charles M., ed. Chemistry of Food Packaging. LC 74-17150. (Advances in Chemistry Ser.: No. 135). 1974. 13.25 (ISBN 0-8412-0205-2). Am Chemical.

U. S. Federal Trade Commission. Chain Stores: Letters from the Chairman of the Federal Trade Commission Transmitting in Response to Senate Resolution No. 224, 3 pts. in 1. LC 75-39243. (Getting & Spending: the Consumer's Dilemma). (Illus.). 1976. Repr. of 1933 ed. 15.00x (ISBN 0-405-08051-4). Arno.

FOOD–PRESERVATION

see also Canning and Preserving; Cold Storage; Fishery Products; Food–Drying; Food, Canned; Food, Frozen; Food Additives; Radiation Sterilization; Vegetables–Preservation

Aston, Graham & Tiffney, John. Guide to Improving Food Hygiene. (Illus.). 1977. pap. 11.95x (ISBN 0-7198-2644-6). Intl Ideas.

Batchelor, Walter D. Gateway to Survival Is Storage. 128p. 1974. pap. 3.95 (ISBN 0-89036-127-4). Hawkes Pub Inc.

Ciobanu, A., et al. Cooling Technology in the Food Industry. Hammel, John, tr. from Romanian. (Illus.). 1976. 44.00x (ISBN 0-85626-018-5, Pub. by Abacus Pr). Intl Schol Bk Serv.

Consumer Guide Editors. Food Preserver. 1979. 12.95 (ISBN 0-671-24591-0, 22227-9); pap. 6.95 (ISBN 0-671-24592-9). S&S.

Copson, David A. Microwave Heating. 2nd ed. (Illus.). 1975. lib. bdg. 49.00 (ISBN 0-87055-182-5). AVI.

Current Trends in the Refrigerated Storage & Transport of Perishable Foodstuffs. 1973. pap. 24.75 (ISBN 0-685-99136-9, IIR31, IIR). Unipub.

Desrosier, Norman W. & Desrosier, John N. Technology of Food Preservation. 4th ed. (Illus.). 1977. pap. 19.00 (ISBN 0-87055-286-4). AVI.

Dotter, Pamela. Preserving Foods. (Guidelines Ser.). (Illus.). 96p. 1980. pap. 2.95 (ISBN 0-89542-905-5). Ideals.

Fields, Marion L. Laboratory Manual in Food Preservation. 1977. 9.50 (ISBN 0-87055-241-4). AVI.

Firth, Grace. A Natural Year. 1973. 6.95 (ISBN 0-671-21205-2). S&S.

Food Preservation by Irradiation, Vol. I. (Illus.). 1978. pap. 61.75 (ISBN 92-0-010278-6, ISP 470-1, IAEA). Unipub.

Food Preservation, Vol. 1: Rural Home Techniques Ser. (Vol. 1). (Illus.). 1976. pap. 9.50 (ISBN 0-685-74256-3, F227, FAO). Unipub.

Ford, Robert S. Stale Food vs. Fresh Food: Cause & Cure of Choked Arteries. 6th ed. 48p. 1977. pap. 4.40 (ISBN 0-686-09051-9). Magnolia Lab.

Frazier, William C. Food Microbiology. 2nd ed. 1967. text ed. 18.00 (ISBN 0-07-021916-8, C). McGraw.

Freezing & Storage of Fish, Poultry, & Meat. 1972. pap. 35.25 (ISBN 0-685-99140-7, IIR26, IIR). Unipub.

Gillies, M. T. Compressed Food Bars. LC 74-82949. (Food Technology Review Ser: No. 18). 116p. 1975. 12.00 (ISBN 0-8155-0547-7). Noyes.

Glanfield, P., compiled by. Applied Cook-Freezing. (Illus.). xii, 203p. 1980. 35.00x (ISBN 0-85334-888-X). Burgess-Intl Ideas.

Guide to Vegetable Gardening & Food Preserving. (Home Improvement Ser.). (Illus.). 112p. 1980. pap. 3.95 (ISBN 0-07-045969-X, GB). McGraw.

Gunther, F. A., ed. Residue Reviews, Vols. 1-11. Incl. Vol. 1. (Illus.). iv, 162p. 1962. 27.20 (ISBN 0-387-02899-4); Vol. 2. (Illus.). iv, 156p. 1963. 27.20 (ISBN 0-387-03047-6); Vol. 3. (Illus.). iv, 170p. 1963. 27.20 (ISBN 0-387-03048-4); Vol. 4. (Illus.). iv, 175p. 1963. 27.20 (ISBN 0-387-03049-2); Vol. 5. Instrumentation for the Detection & Determination of Pesticides & Their Residues in Foods. (Illus.). viii, 176p. 1964. 27.20 (ISBN 0-387-03201-0); Vol. 6. (Illus.). iv, 165p. 1964. 27.20 (ISBN 0-387-03202-9); Vol. 7. vi, 161p. 1964. 19.90 (ISBN 0-387-03203-7); Vol. 8. (Illus.). viii, 183p. 1965. 20.90 (ISBN 0-387-03390-4); Vol. 9. (Illus.). viii, 175p. 1965. 19.90 (ISBN 0-387-03391-2); Vol. 10. With Comprehensive Cumulative Contents, Subjectmatter, & Author Indexes of Volume 1-10. (Illus.). viii, 159p. 1965. 19.90 (ISBN 0-387-03392-0); Vol. 11. (Illus.). viii, 164p. 1965. 20.90 (ISBN 0-387-03393-9). LC 62-18595. (Eng, Fr, Ger.). Springer-Verlag.

--Residue Reviews, Vols. 13-24. Incl. Vol. 13. (Illus.). viii, 136p. 1966. 27.20 (ISBN 0-387-03648-2); Vol. 14. (Illus.). viii, 131p. 1966. 20.90 (ISBN 0-387-03649-0); Vol. 15. (Illus.). vi, 121p. 1966. 19.90 (ISBN 0-387-03650-4); Vol. 16. (Illus.). viii, 158p. 1966. 24.10 (ISBN 0-387-03651-2); Vol. 17. (Illus.). viii, 184p. 1967. 24.10 (ISBN 0-387-03963-5); Vol. 18. (Illus.). viii, 227p. 1967. 37.80 (ISBN 0-387-03964-3); Vol. 19. (Illus.). viii, 155p. 1967. 37.80 (ISBN 0-387-03965-1); Vol. 20. With Cumulative Table of Subjects Covered, Detailed Subject-Matter Index, & Author Index of Volumes 11-20. x, 214p. 1968. 29.00 (ISBN 0-387-04310-1); Vol. 21. (Illus.). viii, 128p. 1968. 29.00 (ISBN 0-387-04311-X); Vol. 22. (Illus.). viii, 120p. 1968. 29.00 (ISBN 0-387-04312-8); Vol. 23. (Illus.). viii, 152p. 1968. 31.20 (ISBN 0-387-04313-6); Vol. 24. vii, 173p. 1968. 31.20 (ISBN 0-387-04314-4). LC 62-18595. (Eng, Fr, Ger.). Springer-Verlag.

--Residue Reviews, Vols. 25-35. Incl. Vol. 25. Special Volume: Seminar on Experimental Approaches to Pesticide Metabolism, Degradation & Mode of Action. United States-Japan Seminar, August 16-19, 1967, Nikko, Japan. (Illus.). x, 364p. 1969. 44.70 (ISBN 0-387-04687-9); Vol. 26. (Illus.). vii, 142p. 1969. 29.00 (ISBN 0-387-04688-7); Vol. 27. (Illus.). vii, 143p. 1969. 29.00 (ISBN 0-387-04689-5); Vol. 28. Insecticide Residues in California Citrus Fruits & Products. (Illus.). vii, 127p. 1969. 29.00 (ISBN 0-387-04690-9); Vol. 29. Special Volume: Symposium on Decontamination of Pesticide Residues in the Environment. Atlantic City Meetings of the ACS, Sept. 1968. (Illus.). viii, 213p. 1969. 35.70 (ISBN 0-387-04691-7); Vol. 30. With Cumulative Table of Subjects Covered, Detailed Subject-Matter Index & Author Index of Vols. 21-30. (Illus.). ix, 169p. 1969. 35.70 (ISBN 0-387-04692-5); Vol. 31. Leaf Structure As Related to Absorption of Pesticides & Other Compounds. Hull, H. M. vii, 155p. 1970. 31.20 (ISBN 0-387-05000-0); Vol. 32. Single-Pesticide Volume: Trianzine Herbicides. (Illus.). 420p. 1970. 35.70 (ISBN 0-387-05235-6); Vol. 33. (Illus.). 160p. 1970. 35.70 (ISBN 0-387-05236-4); Vol. 34. 160p. 1971. 35.70 (ISBN 0-387-05237-2); Vol. 35. (Illus.). viii, 156p. 1971. 35.70 (ISBN 0-387-05238-0). LC 62-18595. (Eng, Fr, Ger.). Springer-Verlag.

--Residue Reviews, Vols. 36-45. Incl. Vol. 36. Chemistry of Pesticides. Melnikov, N. N. (Illus.). xii, 492p. 1971. 40.20 (ISBN 0-387-05373-5); Vol. 37. (Illus.). 144p. 1971. 35.70 (ISBN 0-387-05374-3); Vol. 38. (Illus.). 144p. 1971. 35.70 (ISBN 0-387-05375-1); Vol. 39. The Carbinole Acaricides, Chlorobenzilate & Chloropropylate. 1971. 35.70 (ISBN 0-387-05409-X); Vol. 40. With Cumulative Table of Subjects, Vols. 31-40. (Illus.). 144p. 1971. 35.70 (ISBN 0-387-05410-3); Vol. 41. Rueckstandsberichte. (Illus.). 1972. 17.40 (ISBN 0-387-05568-1); Vol. 42. (Illus.). 1972. 17.40 (ISBN 0-387-05627-0); Vol. 43. (Illus.). 1972. 15.70 (ISBN 0-387-05779-X); Vol. 44. (Illus.). 1973. 31.50 (ISBN 0-387-90058-6); Vol. 45. 1973. 31.50 (ISBN 0-387-90059-4). LC 62-18595. (Eng, Fr, Ger,.). Springer-Verlag.

--Residue Reviews, Vol. 50. x, 192p. 1974. 31.50 (ISBN 0-387-90082-9). Springer-Verlag.

--Residue Reviews, Vol. 51. viii, 203p. 1974. 31.50 (ISBN 0-387-90079-9). Springer-Verlag.

Hertzberg, Ruth, et al. Putting Food By. 2nd ed. LC 74-27454. (Illus.). 448p. 1975. 12.95 (ISBN 0-8289-0252-6); pap. 8.95 (ISBN 0-8289-0251-8). Greene.

--Putting Food by. 2nd ed. 544p. 1976. pap. 3.50 (ISBN 0-553-14564-9). Bantam.

Holm, Don & Holm, Myrtle. Don Holm's Book of Food Drying, Pickling & Smoke Curing. LC 75-28570. 1978. pap. 5.95 (ISBN 0-87004-250-5). Caxton.

Hoyem, T. & Kvale, O., eds. Physical, Chemical & Biological Changes in Food Caused by Thermal Processing. (Illus.). 1977. 87.00x (ISBN 0-85334-729-8). Intl Ideas.

Kerr, Don & Kerr, Vivian. Kerr's Country Kitchen. (Illus.). 164p. 1981. pap. 6.95 (ISBN 0-933614-08-X). Peregrine Pr.

Labuza, Theodore P. Food & Your Well-Being. (Illus.). 1977. pap. text ed. 12.95 (ISBN 0-8299-0129-9); instrs.' manual & study guide 5.95 (ISBN 0-8299-0162-0). West Pub.

McWilliams, Margaret & Paine, Harriet. Modern Food Preservation. LC 77-76339. (The Plycon Home Economics Ser.). 198p. 1977. spiral 11.95x (ISBN 0-686-75962-1). Burgess.

McWilliams, Margaret & Paine, Harriett. Modern Food Preservation. LC 77-76339. (Illus.). 1977. text ed. 11.95x (ISBN 0-916434-25-7). Plycon Pr.

Magallona, E. D., et al. Residue Reviews. (Residue Reviews Ser.: Vol. 56). (Illus.). 160p. 1975. 16.30 (ISBN 0-387-90115-9). Springer-Verlag.

Microbiological Problems in Food Preservation by Irradiation. 1967. pap. 6.50 (ISBN 92-0-111067-7, IAEA). Unipub.
Muller, H. G. & Tobin, G. Nutrition & Food Processing. (american) ed. 1980. pap. 30.00 (ISBN 0-87055-363-1). AVI.
Nichols, Naomi M. Food Drying at Home. 1978. 9.95 (ISBN 0-442-26028-8); pap. 5.95 (ISBN 0-442-26029-6). Van Nos Reinhold.
Nickerson, J. & Sinskay, A. Microbiology of Food & Food Processing. 1972. 18.50 (ISBN 0-444-00124-7, North Holland). Elsevier.
Packard, Vernal S., Jr. Processed Foods & the Consumer: Additives, Labeling, Standards & Nutrition. LC 75-32670. 312p. 1975. 17.50x (ISBN 0-8166-0778-8); pap. text ed. 7.95x (ISBN 0-8166-0784-2). U of Minn Pr.
Peakall, D. B. Residue Reviews, Vol. 54. LC 62-18595. (Illus.). x, 190p. 1975. 29.00 (ISBN 0-387-90099-3). Springer-Verlag.
Pointers on Perishables. (Illus.). 1973. looseleaf bdg 9.95 (ISBN 0-911790-68-3). Prog Grocer.
Prepacked Meat-Eggs-Poultry. 1965. pap. 12.50 (ISBN 0-685-99161-X, IIR29, IIR). Unipub.
Processed Fruit & Vegetables: Trends in World Production & Trade of Citrus Products, Canned Peaches & Apricots, & Tomato Products. (Commodity Bulletin Ser.: No. 47). (Orig.). 1971. pap. 7.25 (ISBN 0-685-02928-X, F334, FAO). Unipub.
Radiation Preservation of Food. 774p. (Orig.). 1972. pap. 61.75 (ISBN 92-0-010373-1, ISP317, IAEA). Unipub.
Reed, Gerald. Enzymes in Food Processing. 2nd ed. 1975. 60.50 (ISBN 0-12-584852-8). Acad Pr.
Refrigeration Applications to Fish, Fruit, & Vegetables in South East Asia. 1974. pap. 17.75 (ISBN 0-685-99171-7, IIR13, IIR). Unipub.
Robinson, James. The Art of Curing, Pickling & Smoking Meat & Fish. 1973. 69.95 (ISBN 0-87968-053-9). Gordon Pr.
Singleton, W. Ralph. Nuclear Radiation in Food & Agriculture. 1958. 12.95x (ISBN 0-442-07608-8). Van Nos Reinhold.
Sonnenschmidt, Fredric H. & Nicolas, Jean F. The Professional Chef's Art of Garde Manger. 2nd ed. LC 72-92377. 1976. 23.95 (ISBN 0-8436-2067-6). CBI Pub.
Stoner, Carol H. Stocking up. rev. ed. LC 77-3942. 1977. 13.95 (ISBN 0-87857-167-1); deluxe ed. 19.95 (ISBN 0-87857-221-X). Rodale Pr Inc.
Tilbury, R. H., ed. Developments in Food Preservatives, No. 1. x, 168p. 1981. 34.00x (ISBN 0-85334-918-5). Intl Ideas.
Time-Life Books Editors. Preserving. (The Good Cook Ser.). (Illus.). 176p. 1981. 12.95 (ISBN 0-8094-2904-7). Time-Life.
Towards an Ideal Refrigerated Food Chain. 1976. pap. 35.25 (ISBN 0-685-99179-2, IIR60, IIR). Unipub.
Turgeon, Charlotte. The Saturday Evening Post Small-Batch Canning & Freezing Cookbook. LC 78-53040. (Illus.). 1978. 8.95 (ISBN 0-89387-020-X); pap. 4.95 (ISBN 0-89387-020-X). Sat Eve Post.
Weight Losses in Foodstuffs. 1970. pap. 24.75 (ISBN 0-685-99182-2, IIR27, IIR). Unipub.
Yepsen, Roger B., Jr., ed. Home Food Systems: Rodale's Catalog of Methods & Tools for Producing, Processing & Preserving Naturally Good Foods. (Illus.). 512p. 1981. 16.95 (ISBN 0-87857-325-9); pap. 13.95 (ISBN 0-87857-320-8). Rodale Pr Inc.

FOOD-PRICES
see Food Prices

FOOD-RADIATION EFFECTS
see Food, Effect of Radiation on

FOOD-TABLES, CALCULATIONS, ETC.
Kraus, Barbara. Barbara Kraus Guide to Calories: 1981 Edition. (Orig.). 1981. pap. 1.75 (ISBN 0-451-09580-4, E9580, Sig). NAL.
Lasota, Marcia. The Fast Food Calorie Guide. (Illus., Orig.). 1980. pap. 3.95 (ISBN 0-933474-09-1, Gabriel Bks). Minn Scholarly.
Pennington, Jean & Church, Helen N. Food Values of Portions Commonly Used. 13th ed. LC 80-7594. 200p. 1980. pap. 5.95 (ISBN 0-06-090819-X, CN819, CN). Har-Row.
Wagner, L. J. Profiles of Foods. (Illus.). 156p. 1973. pap. 5.00 (ISBN 0-9606316-0-7). Profiles Pub.

FOOD-TRANSPORTATION
Kochersperger, Richard H. Food Warehousing & Transportation. LC 78-65886. 1978. 20.00 (ISBN 0-912016-74-4). Lebhar Friedman.
Recommended Conditions for Land Transport of Perishable Foods. 3rd ed. 1974. pap. 4.50 (ISBN 0-685-99166-0, IIR10, IIR). Unipub.
Towards an Ideal Refrigerated Food Chain. 1976. pap. 35.25 (ISBN 0-685-99179-2, IIR60, IIR). Unipub.
Transport of Perishable Produce in Refrigerated Vehicles & Containers. 1974. pap. 23.25 (ISBN 0-685-99180-6, IIR34, IIR). Unipub.

FOOD, ARTIFICIAL
see also Food Substitutes

FOOD, CANNED
Convience & Take-Away Foods. 120p. 1981. 150.00x (ISBN 0-686-71863-1, Pub. by Euromonitor). State Mutual Bk.
Food Processors Institute. Canned Foods: Principles of Thermal Process Control, Acidification & Container Closure Evaluation. rev. 3rd ed. 224p. 1979. pap. 35.00 (ISBN 0-937774-02-2). Food Processors.
International Symposium, Karlsruhe, August 23-24, 1977. How Ready Are Ready-to-Serve Foods? Proceedings. Paulus, K., ed. (Illus.). 1978. pap. 88.75 (ISBN 3-8055-2884-1). S Karger.
Recommended International Standard for Canned Applesauce. (Codex Alimentarius Commission Ser: No. 17). (Orig.). 1970. pap. 4.50 (ISBN 0-685-36281-7, F617, FAO). Unipub.
Recommended International Standard for Canned Fruit Cocktail. (Codex Alimentarius Commission). 15p. 1978. pap. 4.50 (ISBN 0-685-87280-7, F573, FAO). Unipub.
Recommended International Standard for Canned Grapefruit. (Codex Alimentarius Commission Ser: No. 15). (Orig.). 1970. pap. 4.50 (ISBN 0-685-36283-3, F615, FAO). Unipub.
Recommended International Standard for Canned Green Beans & Canned Wax Beans. (Codex Alimentarius Commission Ser: No. 16). (Orig.). 1970. pap. 4.50 (ISBN 0-685-36284-1, F599, FAO). Unipub.
Recommended International Standard for Canned Mature Processed Peas. (Codex Alimentarius Commission). 10p. 1978. pap. 4.50 (ISBN 0-685-87281-5, F580, FAO). Unipub.
Recommended International Standard for Canned Peaches. (Codex Alimentarius Commission Ser: No. 14). (Orig.). 1970. pap. 4.50 (ISBN 0-685-36285-X, F614, FAO). Unipub.
Recommended International Standard for Canned Pineapple. (Codex Alimentarius Commission Ser: No. 42). (Orig.). 1970. pap. 4.50 (ISBN 0-685-36286-8, F583, FAO). Unipub.
Recommended International Standard for Canned Sweet Corn. (Codex Alimentarius Commission Ser: No. 18). (Orig.). 1970. pap. 4.50 (ISBN 0-685-36287-6, F618, FAO). Unipub.
Recommended International Standard for Canned Tomatoes. (Codex Alimentarius Commission Ser: No. 13). (Orig.). 1970. pap. 4.50 (ISBN 0-685-36288-4, F679, FAO). Unipub.
Recommended International Standard for Canned Tropical Fruit Salad. 14p. 1980. pap. 4.50 (ISBN 92-5-100809-4, F 1883, FAO). Unipub.
Recommended International Standard for Fruit & Vegetable Products. (Codex Alimentarius Commission Ser: No. 2). (Orig.). 1969. pap. 3.00 (ISBN 0-685-36282-5, FAO). Unipub.

FOOD, CHEMISTRY OF
see Food-Analysis; Food-Composition

FOOD, COST OF
see Cost and Standard of Living

FOOD, DIETETIC
Bourne, G. H., ed. World Review of Nutrition & Dietetics, Vol. 15. (Illus.). 300p. 1972. 68.50 (ISBN 3-8055-1397-6). S Karger.
Dwivedi, Basant K., ed. Low Calorie & Special Dietary Foods. (Uniscience Ser.). 1978. 46.95 (ISBN 0-8493-5249-5). CRC Pr.
Goldberg, Larry. Goldberg's Diet Catalog. (Illus.). 1977. 17.50 (ISBN 0-02-544480-8). Macmillan.
--Goldberg's Diet Catalog. (Illus.). 1977. pap. 7.95 (ISBN 0-02-059000-8, Collier). Macmillan.
Gormican, Annette. Controlling Diabetes with Diet. (Illus.). 232p. 1976. pap. 10.75 spiral (ISBN 0-398-00705-5). C C Thomas.
Jussawalla, J. M. Natural Dietetics: A Handbook on Food, Nutrition & Health. 1979. text ed. 10.50 (ISBN 0-7069-0806-6, Pub. by Vikas India). Advent NY.
Kronschnabel, Darlene. Low Calorie Cookbook. (Illus.). 64p. (Orig.). 1981. pap. 2.95 (ISBN 0-8249-3003-7). Ideals.

FOOD, DRIED
see also Food-Drying; Food-Preservation
Recommended International Standard for Dessicated Coconut & Dehydrated Fruits & Vegetables Including Edible Fungi. 1972. pap. 3.00 (ISBN 0-685-36290-6, FAO). Unipub.
Recommended International Standard for Dried Edible Fungi. 1970. pap. 4.50 (ISBN 0-685-36293-0, F645, FAO). Unipub.
Recommended International Standard for Dried Fruits. 1969. pap. 3.00 (ISBN 0-685-36294-9, FAO). Unipub.
Recommended International Standard for Dried Glucose Syrup. 1970. pap. 4.50 (ISBN 0-685-36339-2, F674, FAO). Unipub.

FOOD, EFFECT OF RADIATION ON
Application of Food Irradiation in Developing Countries. (Technical Reports Ser.: No. 54). (Orig.). 1966. pap. 11.75 (ISBN 92-0-115066-0, IDC54, IAEA). Unipub.
Aspects of the Introduction of Food Irradiation in Developing Countries. (Illus.). 113p. (Orig.). 1974. pap. 9.75 (ISBN 92-0-111673-X, ISP362, IAEA). Unipub.
Enzymological Aspects of Food Irradiation. (Illus., Orig.). 1969. pap. 8.25 (ISBN 92-0-111169-X, IAEA). Unipub.
Factors Influencing the Economical Application of Food Irradiation. (Illus.). 137p. (Orig.). 1973. pap. 11.50 (ISBN 92-0-111373-0, ISP331, IAEA). Unipub.
Food Irradiation. (Illus., Orig., Eng. , Fr. , Rus. & Span.). 1966. pap. 53.75 (ISBN 92-0-010166-6, ISP127, IAEA). Unipub.
International Acceptance of Irradiated Food: Legal Aspects. (Legal Ser.: No. 11). 1979. pap. 9.75 (ISBN 92-0-176079-5, ISP530, IAEA). Unipub.
Manual of Food Irradiation Dosimetry. (Illus.). 1978. pap. 19.50 (ISBN 92-0-115277-9, IDC 178, IAEA). Unipub.
Microbiological Specifications & Testing Methods for Irradiated Food. (Technical Reports Ser.: No. 104). (Illus., Orig.). 1970. pap. 8.25 (ISBN 92-0-115170-5, ISP168, IAEA). Unipub.
Recommended International General Standard for Irradiated Foods & Recommended International Code of Practice for the Operation of Radiation Facilities for the Treatment of Foods. 19p. 1980. pap. 7.50 (ISBN 0-686-75281-3, F2157, FAO). Unipub.
Training Manual on Food Irradiation Technology & Techniques. (Technical Reports: No. 114). (Illus., Orig.). 1970. pap. 11.75 (ISBN 92-0-115570-0, IDC114, IAEA). Unipub.
Wholesomeness of Irradiated Food. (Food & Nutrition Ser: No. 6). 44p. 1978. pap. 6.25 (ISBN 92-5-100282-7, F495, FAO). Unipub.

FOOD, FRIED
Roth, June. Mac Meals in Minutes. LC 76-53111. (Illus.). 1977. 8.95 (ISBN 0-916752-09-7). Dorison Hse.

FOOD, FROZEN
see also Cookery (Frozen Foods); Home Freezers
Borella, Anne. How to Book: Canning, Freezing, Drying. 1977. 1.95 (ISBN 0-87502-051-8). Benjamin Co.
Burros, Marian & Levine, Lois. Freeze with Ease. LC 65-21466. 1968. pap. 2.95 (ISBN 0-02-009280-6, Collier). Macmillan.
Ciobanu, A., et al. Cooling Technology in the Food Industry. Hammel, John, tr. from Romanian. (Illus.). 1976. 44.00x (ISBN 0-85626-018-5, Pub. by Abacus Pr). Intl Schol Bk Serv.
Controlled Atmosphere Cold Rooms: Storage of Quick Frozen Products. 1968. pap. 9.00 (ISBN 0-685-99131-8, IIR32, IIR). Unipub.
Convience & Take-Away Foods. 120p. 1981. 150.00x (ISBN 0-686-71863-1, Pub. by Euromonitor). State Mutual Bk.
Cox, Pat M. The Home Book of Food Freezing. rev. ed. 352p. 1977. 6.95 (ISBN 0-571-11104-1, Pub. by Faber & Faber). Merrimack Bk Serv.
Current Studies on the Thermophysical Properties of Foodstuffs. 1974. pap. 33.75 (ISBN 0-685-99135-0, IIR24, IIR). Unipub.
Desrosier, Norman W. & Tressler, Donald K. Fundamentals of Food Freezing. (Illus.). 1977. pap. text ed. 18.00 (ISBN 0-87055-290-2). AVI.
Draft Code of Practice for Frozen Fish. 1969. pap. 2.75 (ISBN 0-685-99137-7, IIR7, IIR). Unipub.
Ellis, Audrey. Complete Book of Home Freezing. 9.95 (ISBN 0-600-30148-6). Transatlantic.
--Home Guide to Food Freezing. 1974. 7.50 (ISBN 0-600-34469-X). Transatlantic.
Farm Journal, Editors Of, et al. Farm Journal's Freezing & Canning Cookbook. rev. ed. LC 77-81787. 1978. 10.95 (ISBN 0-385-13444-4). Doubleday.
Fennema, O., et al, eds. Low Temperature Preservation of Foods & Living Matter. (Food Science Ser: Vol. 3). 592p. 1973. 53.50 (ISBN 0-8247-1185-8). Dekker.
Freezing & Storage of Fish, Poultry, & Meat. 1972. pap. 35.25 (ISBN 0-685-99140-7, IIR26, IIR). Unipub.
Frozen Foods. 1969. pap. 21.50 (ISBN 0-685-99141-5, IIR28, IIR). Unipub.
Gould, Edith & Peters, John A. Testing the Friskness of Frozen Fish. 1978. 16.00x (ISBN 0-685-63459-0). State Mutual Bk.
Growing for Freezing. (Illus.). 1977. 8.95 (ISBN 0-02-578230-4). Macmillan.
Harder, Eulalia L. Blast Freezing Quantity Recipes, Vol. II. LC 79-16832. 1979. 18.95 (ISBN 0-8436-2178-8). CBI Pub.
--Blast Freezing System for Quantity Foods, Vol. 1. LC 79-46832. 1979. 24.95 (ISBN 0-8436-2157-5). CBI Pub.
International Symposium, Karlsruhe, August 23-24, 1977. How Ready Are Ready-to-Serve Foods? Proceedings. Paulus, K., ed. (Illus.). 1978. pap. 88.75 (ISBN 3-8055-2884-1). S Karger.
Macmillan. Growing for Freezing. (Illus.). 1977. pap. 5.95 (ISBN 0-02-063380-7, 06338, Collier). Macmillan.
McWilliam, J. Book of Freezing. 1977. Repr. 7.00 (ISBN 0-85941-010-2). State Mutual Bk.
Methods of Analysis for Quick-Frozen Fruits & Vegetables. (Codex Alimentarius Commission: 1st Ser). 6p. 1977. pap. 1.50 (ISBN 0-685-86025-6, FAO). Unipub.
Norwak, Mary. Beginner's Guide to Home Freezing. (Beginners Guide Ser.). 148p. 1973. 12.95 (ISBN 0-7207-0660-2, Pub. by Michael Joseph). Merrimack Bk Serv.
Recommendations for the Processing & Handling of Frozen Foods. 1972. pap. 12.25 (ISBN 0-685-99164-4, IIR8, IIR). Unipub.
Recommended International Code of Practice for Frozen Fish. 58p. 1981. pap. 7.50 (ISBN 92-5-100985-6, F2124, FAO). Unipub.
Recommended International Code of Practice for the Processing & Handling of Quick Frozen Foods: Appendix One Method for Checking Product Temperature. 8p. 1980. pap. 4.50 (ISBN 92-5-100697-0, F2036, FAO). Unipub.
Recommended International Code of Practice for the Processing & Handling of Quick-Frozen Foods. 6p. 1978. pap. 4.00 (ISBN 0-685-60671-6, F1426, FAO). Unipub.
Recommended International Standard for Quick Frozen Blueberries. 11p. 1980. pap. 4.50 (ISBN 92-5-100803-5, F1916, FAO). Unipub.
Recommended International Standard for Quick Frozen Bilberries. 8p. 1978. pap. 4.50 (ISBN 0-685-87285-8, F577, FAO). Unipub.
Recommended International Standard for Quick Frozen Fillets of Cod & Haddock. 1972. pap. 4.50 (ISBN 0-685-36317-1, F591, FAO). Unipub.
Recommended International Standard for Quick Frozen Fillets of Ocean Perch. 1972. pap. 4.50 (ISBN 0-685-36318-X, F592, FAO). Unipub.
Recommended International Standard for Quick Frozen Gutted Pacific Salmon. 1970. pap. 4.50 (ISBN 0-685-36320-1, F641, FAO). Unipub.
Recommended International Standard for Quick Frozen Leek. 12p. 1980. pap. 4.50 (ISBN 92-5-100808-6, F 1885, FAO). Unipub.
Recommended International Standard for Quick Frozen Peas. 1970. pap. 4.50 (ISBN 0-685-36319-8, F647, FAO). Unipub.
Recommended International Standard for Quick Frozen Peaches. (Codex Alimentarius Commission). 11p. 1978. pap. 4.50 (ISBN 0-685-87286-6, F578, FAO). Unipub.
Recommended International Standard for Quick Frozen Strawberries. 1972. pap. 4.50 (ISBN 0-685-36324-4, F593, FAO). Unipub.
Recommended International Standard for Quick Frozen Spinach. (Codex Alimentarius Commission). 8p. 1978. pap. 4.50 (ISBN 0-685-87287-4, F576, FAO). Unipub.
Recommended International Standard Procedures for Thawing of Quick Frozen Fruits & Vegetables & Cooking of Quick-Frozen Vegetables for Examination Purposes. 1972. pap. 4.50 (ISBN 0-685-36322-8, F634, FAO). Unipub.
Recommended International Standards for Quick Frozen Raspberries. (Codex Alimentarius Commission). 8p. 1977. pap. 4.50 (ISBN 0-685-86029-9, F609, FAO). Unipub.
Tressler, Donald K., et al. Freezing Preservation of Foods, 4 vols. 4th ed. Incl. Vol. 1. Principles of Refrigeration; Equipment for Freezing & Transporting Food. 32.00 (ISBN 0-87055-044-6); Vol. 2. Factors Affecting Quality in Frozen Foods. 35.00 (ISBN 0-87055-045-4); Vol. 3. Commercial Freezing Operations; Fresh Foods. 39.00 (ISBN 0-87055-046-2); Vol. 4. Freezing of Precooked & Prepared Foods. 39.00 (ISBN 0-87055-047-0). (Illus.). 1968. AVI.
United Nations Economic Commission for Europe & United Nations, Food & Agricultural Organization. Frozen & Quick-Frozen Food: New Agricultural Production & Marketing Aspects, Proceedings of a Joint Symposium, Budapest, 1977. LC 77-30194. 1977. pap. 35.00 (ISBN 0-08-022031-2). Pergamon.
U. S. Department of Agriculture. Complete Guide to Home Canning, Preserving & Freezing. LC 72-92754. (Illus.). 215p. 1973. pap. 3.50 (ISBN 0-486-22911-4). Dover.
U. S. Dept. of Agriculture. Home Freezing of Fruits & Vegetables. (Illus.). 48p. pap. 5.50 (ISBN 0-8466-6056-3). Shorey.

FOOD, FROZEN-BIBLIOGRAPHY
Consumer Guide: Canning, Preserving & Freezing. rev. ed. 1979. pap. 2.50 (ISBN 0-451-08766-6, E8766, Sig). NAL.

FOOD, HEALTH
see Food, Natural

FOOD, NATURAL
see also Cookery (Natural Foods)
Adams, Ruth. Eating in Eden. 196p. (Orig.). 1976. pap. 1.75 (ISBN 0-915962-16-0). Larchmont Bks.
Adams, Ruth & Murray, Frank. All You Should Know About Health Foods. 352p. pap. 2.50 (ISBN 0-915962-01-2). Larchmont Bks.
--The Good Seeds, the Rich Grains, the Hardy Nuts for a Healthier, Happier Life. rev. ed. 303p. 1973. pap. 1.75 (ISBN 0-915962-07-1). Larchmont Bks.

Bethel, May. Healing Power of Natural Foods. 1978. pap. 3.00 (ISBN 0-87980-363-0). Wilshire.

Blauer, Stephen. Rejuvenation: Dr. Ann Wigmore's Complete Diet & Health Program. 197p. pap. 4.95 (ISBN 0-686-29390-8). Hippocrates.

Bull, Charlotte. Wild Foods: Treats for Your Table. (Illus.). Date not set. 9.95 (ISBN 0-689-11031-6). Atheneum.

Campbell, Diane. Step-by-Step to Natural Food. 6.95 (ISBN 0-686-29883-7). Cancer Bk Hse.

DeKorne, James B. The Survival Greenhouse. 2nd ed. LC 75-39144. (Illus.). 165p. 1978. pap. 7.95 (ISBN 0-915238-20-9). Peace Pr.

Dunlap, James. The Health Food Store Can Save Your Life. 1977. 7.95 (ISBN 0-686-17625-1). World Intl.

Durkin, Mary. The Natural Foods Diet Book. (Good Health Books Ser.). (Illus.). 1978. pap. 2.95 (ISBN 0-448-14822-6). G&D.

Gerras, Charles, ed. Rodale's Naturally Great Food Cookbook. LC 77-10415. 1977. 15.95 (ISBN 0-87857-163-9). Rodale Pr Inc.

Goldbeck, Nikki & Goldbeck, David. The Supermarket Handbook: Access to Whole Foods. 1974. pap. 4.95 (ISBN 0-452-25151-6, Z5151, Plume). NAL.

Goodwin, Stanley J. Can Ice Cream & Oranges Prevent the Common Cold & Influenza? (Illus.). 1979. pap. 2.40 (ISBN 0-686-24961-5). Northland Pubns WA.

Harrison, John B. Good Food Naturally: How to Grow It, Cook It, Keep It. LC 73-77116. 1973. 4.95 (ISBN 0-87983-050-6); pap. 3.95 (ISBN 0-87983-060-3). Keats.

Health Foods. (Food & Beverage Studies). 1980. 450.00 (ISBN 0-686-31518-9). Busn Trend.

Health Quarterly(Plus Two) Editors, ed. What's in It for You? Natural Foods & Your Health Food Store. rev. ed. LC 74-14314. (Pivot Original Health Books). 176p. (Orig.). 1980. pap. 2.95 (ISBN 0-87983-064-6). Keats.

Herbert, Victor & Barrett, Stephen. Vitamins & "Health" Foods: The Great American Hustle. 200p. 1981. 10.95 (ISBN 0-89313-054-0). G F Stickley.

Herz, W., et al, eds. Progress in the Chemistry of Organic Natural Products, Vol. 36. (Illus.). 1979. 115.70 (ISBN 0-387-81472-8). Springer-Verlag.

Hunter, Beatrice T. Beatrice Trum Hunter's Favorite Natural Foods. 1974. 7.95 (ISBN 0-671-21820-4). S&S.

--Fact-Book on Fermented Foods & Beverages. LC 73-76229. (Pivot Original Health Book). 128p. 1973. pap. 1.25 (ISBN 0-87983-055-7). Keats.

Hunter, Kathleen. Health Foods & Herbs. LC 63-15194. (Orig.). 1968. pap. 1.50 (ISBN 0-668-01083-5). Arco.

Kilham, Christopher. The Complete Shopper's Guide to Natural Foods, Vitamins, Supplements, Cosmetics, Kitchenware & Bodycare Tools. LC 80-66696. (Illus.). 172p. 1980. pap. 2.95 (ISBN 0-914398-39-3). Autumn Pr.

Kirban, Salem. The Getting Back to Nature Diet. (Illus.). 1978. pap. 3.95 (ISBN 0-912582-28-6). Kirban.

Kordel, Lelord. You're Younger Than You Think. 1979. pap. 2.50 (ISBN 0-445-04507-8). Popular Lib.

Laughlin, Ruth. Natural Sweets & Treats. new ed. LC 75-17275. (Illus.). 176p. (Orig.). 1975. pap. 5.95 (ISBN 0-912800-17-8). Woodbridge Pr.

Levitt, Eleanor. Wonderful World of Natural Foods. LC 77-151462. (Illus.). 1971. 7.95 (ISBN 0-8208-0227-1). Hearthside.

Matsumoto, Kosai. The Mysterious Japanese Plum: Its Uses for Health, Vigor & Long Life. LC 78-71029. (Lifeline Bks.). (Illus.). 1978. pap. 2.95 (ISBN 0-912800-51-8). Woodbridge Pr.

Natural & Health Food Market, GA-037. 1978. 675.00 (ISBN 0-89336-096-1). BCC.

Norris, P. About Honey: Nature's Elixir for Health. 1980. pap. 1.95 (ISBN 0-87904-043-2). Lust.

Oliver, Martha H. Add a Few Sprouts. LC 75-10539. (Pivot Original Health Bk). 128p. (Orig.). 1975. pap. 1.95 (ISBN 0-87983-104-9). Keats.

Organic Gardening & Farming Staff & Editors. Organically Grown Foods: What They Are & Why You Need Them. LC 72-93099. 1973. pap. 2.95 (ISBN 0-87857-057-8). Rodale Pr Inc.

Peterson, Vicki. The Natural Food Catalog. LC 77-25231. 1978. 10.95 (ISBN 0-668-04538-8); pap. 5.95 (ISBN 0-668-04543-4). Arco.

Phillips, David A. From Soil to Psyche: Total Health for the New Age. LC 77-79907. (Orig.). 1977. pap. 4.95 (ISBN 0-912800-43-7). Woodbridge Pr.

Polunin, Miriam. The Right Way to Eat: To Feel Good-or Even Better. 166p. 1978. 9.50x (ISBN 0-460-04319-6, J M Dent England). Biblio Dist.

Pritzker, Wendy. Natural Foods & Vitamins Handbook. LC 72-88599. 192p. 1974. pap. 1.45 (ISBN 0-668-02740-1). Arco.

Riker, Tom & Roberts, Richard. The First Directory of Natural & Health Foods. LC 79-13757. 1979. 17.95 (ISBN 0-399-12419-5, Perigee); pap. 8.95 (ISBN 0-399-50399-4). Putnam.

Smith, Anne. Eat Your Way to Health. 1.50 (ISBN 0-9601262-1-X). FairMail Serv.

Thompson, Ann. The Organic Baby Food Book. 1973. 6.95 (ISBN 0-671-27107-5). Trident.

Time-Life Books Editors. Wholesome Diet. (Library of Health). (Illus.). 1981. 12.95 (ISBN 0-8094-3766-X). Time-Life.

Weaver, Diana & Weaver, Purcell. Natural Foods Encyclopedia: A Complete Guide to the Preparation & Use of Natural Foods. 1974. 69.95 (ISBN 0-685-51354-8). Revisionist Pr.

Whelan, Elizabeth & Stare, Fredrick J. Panic in the Pantry. LC 75-7952. 1975. pap. 3.95 (ISBN 0-689-70553-0, 236). Atheneum.

Whole Foods Magazine Staff, ed. Whole Foods, Natural Foods Guide. LC 79-19013. (Illus.). 301p. 1979. pap. 8.95 (ISBN 0-915904-46-2). And-Or Pr.

Wigmore, Ann. Be Your Own Doctor: Let Living Food Be Your Medicine. 176p. pap. text ed. 5.95 (ISBN 0-686-29391-6). Hippocrates.

--Recipes for Longer Life. Kimball, Betsy, ed. (Illus.). 181p. pap. text ed. 8.95 (ISBN 0-686-29397-5). Hippocrates.

--Spiritual Diet. (Health Digest Ser.: No. 152). 64p. pap. 1.50 (ISBN 0-686-29396-7). Hippocrates.

--Spiritual-Physical Survival Through Sprouting. (Health Digest Ser.: No. 153). 63p. pap. 1.50 (ISBN 0-686-29395-9). Hippocrates.

Wilson, Frank A. Food Fit for Humans. 1980. 15.00x (ISBN 0-85207-132-9, Pub. by Daniel Co England). State Mutual Bk.

Yntema, Sharon K. Vegetarian Baby: A Sensible Guide for Parents. LC 79-24623. (Illus.). 224p. 1980. 10.95 (ISBN 0-935526-01-3); pap. 5.95 (ISBN 0-935526-02-1). McBooks Pr.

FOOD, ORGANICALLY GROWN

see Food, Natural

FOOD, PURE

see Food Adulteration and Inspection; Food Law and Legislation

FOOD, RAW

see also Vegetarianism

Baker, Elizabeth & Baker, Elton. The Uncook Book: Raw Food Adventures to a New Health High. (Illus.). 198p. 1981. pap. 5.95 (ISBN 0-937766-05-4). Drelwood Pubns.

Buckley, Peter. Eat It Raw. (Illus.). 1978. 5.95 (ISBN 0-396-07479-0). Dodd.

Charmine, Susan E. The Complete Raw Juice Therapy. 1977. pap. 2.95 (ISBN 0-89437-018-9). Baronet.

Gerras, Charles, ed. Feasting on Raw Foods. (Illus.). 336p. (Orig.). 1981. pap. 11.95 (ISBN 0-87857-272-4). Rodale Pr Inc.

--Feasting on Raw Foods. (Illus.). 1980. 14.95 (ISBN 0-87857-271-6); pap. 11.95 (ISBN 0-87857-272-4). Rodale Pr Inc.

Gregory, Dick. Dick Gregory's Natural Diet for Folks Who Eat: Cookin' with Mother Nature. McGraw, James R., ed. LC 72-9096. 185p. 1973. 9.95 (ISBN 0-06-011604-8, HarpT). Har-Row.

--Dick Gregory's Natural Diet for Folks Who Eat: Cookin' with Mother Nature. McGraw, James R. & Fulton, Alvenia M., eds. 192p. 1974. pap. 1.95 (ISBN 0-06-080315-0, P315, PL). Har-Row.

Hunt, Janet. Raw Food Way to Health. 1977. pap. 1.50 (ISBN 0-89437-027-8). Baronet.

Karas, Jim & Griesse, Carolyn. The Raw Foods Diet. 320p. 1981. pap. 8.95 (ISBN 0-8329-0107-5). New Century.

Munroe, Esther. Sprouts to Grow & Eat. LC 74-23609. (Illus.). 128p. 1974. pap. 5.95 (ISBN 0-8289-0226-7). Greene.

Whyte, Karen C. The Original Diet, Raw Vegetarian Guide & Recipe Book: Raw Vegetarian Guide & Recipe Book. LC 77-4415. (Illus.). 1977. pap. 3.95 (ISBN 0-912300-76-0, 76-0). Troubador Pr.

FOOD, SMOKED

see Cookery (Smoked Foods)

FOOD, WILD

see also Cookery (Wild Foods); Game and Game-Birds

Benoliel, Doug. Northwest Foraging: Wild Edibles of the Pacific Northwest. (Illus., With recipes). 1974. pap. 5.95 (ISBN 0-913140-13-9). Signpost Bk Pubns.

Furlong, Marjorie & Pill, Virginia. Wild Edible Fruits & Berries. LC 74-32015. (Illus.). 64p. 1974. 8.95 (ISBN 0-87961-033-6); pap. 4.95 (ISBN 0-87961-032-8). Naturegraph.

Gibbons, Euell & Tucker, Gordon. Euell Gibbons' Handbook of Edible Wild Plants. LC 79-14420. (Illus.). 1979. 9.95 (ISBN 0-915442-82-5, Unilaw); pap. 4.95 (ISBN 0-915442-78-7). Donning Co.

Hall, Alan. The Wild Foods Trailguide. 1976. 8.95 (ISBN 0-03-016741-8); pap. 4.95 (ISBN 0-03-016746-9). HR&W.

Stewart, Hilary. Wild Teas, Coffees, & Cordials. (Illus.). 128p. 1981. pap. 7.95 (ISBN 0-295-95804-9). U of Wash Pr.

Tomikel, John. Edible Wild Plants of Pennsylvania & New York. LC 72-89403. 1973. 5.00 (ISBN 0-910042-14-4); pap. 2.50 (ISBN 0-910042-13-6). Allegheny.

Underhill, J. E. Wild Berries of the Pacific Northwest. (Illus.). 128p. 5.95 (ISBN 0-919654-06-1). Superior Pub.

Urquhart, Judy. Food from the Wild. LC 77-85026. (Penny Pinchers Ser.). 1978. 2.95 (ISBN 0-7153-7545-8). David & Charles.

Van Etta, Marian. Free Food from Twenty-Seven Wild Plants. 1981. pap. 2.95 (ISBN 0-8200-0808-7). Great Outdoors.

FOOD ADDITIVES

Austin, James E., ed. Global Malnutrition & Cereal Grain Fortification. LC 78-21224. 1979. reference 27.50 (ISBN 0-88410-366-8). Ballinger Pub.

BCC Staff. Nutritional Food Additives, GA-040. 1979. 675.00 (ISBN 0-89336-119-4). BCC.

Bicknell, Franklin. Chemicals in Your Food. LC 61-11031. 1970. 8.95 (ISBN 0-87523-130-6). Emerson.

Bigwood, E. J., et al, eds. Food Additives Tables, Parts 1, 2, 3 & 4. 1977. Set. 352.25 (ISBN 0-444-41181-X). Elsevier.

Birch, G. G., ed. Sweetness & Sweeteners. (Illus.). 1971. 26.00x (ISBN 0-85334-503-1, Pub. by Applied Science). Burgess-Intl Ideas.

Block, Zenas. It's All on the Label: Understanding Food, Additives & Nutrition. 1981. pap. 7.95 (ISBN 0-316-09971-6). Little.

Caulfield, Lori. Stop Killing Yourself & Our Children with Additives. 1978. 5.95 (ISBN 0-89200-025-2). Atlantis-by-the-Sea.

Codex Alimentarius Commission. First Supplement to the List of Additives Evaluated for Their Safety-in-Use in Food. 27p. 1975. pap. 3.00 (ISBN 0-685-62844-2, FAO). Unipub.

Committee on Food Protection, NRC. The Use of Chemicals in Food Production, Processing, Storage & Distribution. 40p. 1973. pap. 2.25 (ISBN 0-309-02136-7). Natl Acad Pr.

Connors, C. Keith. Food Additives for Hyperactive Children. 180p. 1980. 18.50 (ISBN 0-306-40400-1, Plenum Pr). Plenum Pub.

Coulston, Frederick, ed. Regulatory Aspects of Carcinogenesis & Food Additives: The Delaney Clause. (Ecotoxicology & Environmental Quality Ser.). 1979. 31.00 (ISBN 0-12-192750-4). Acad Pr.

Counsell, J. N., ed. Xylitol. (Illus.). 1978. text ed. 33.00x (ISBN 0-85334-786-7). Intl Ideas.

Evaluation of Certain Food Additives, 16th Report. 53p. (Orig.). 1973. pap. 4.50 (ISBN 0-685-32312-9, F127, FAO). Unipub.

Evaluation of Certain Food Additives: 20th Report. (Food & Nutrition Ser: No. 1). 32p. 1977. pap. 6.25 (ISBN 92-5-100109-X, F 130, FAO). Unipub.

Evaluation of Food Additives, 14th Report: Specifications for the Identity & Purity of Food Additives & Their Toxicological Evaluation. (FAO Nutrition Meetings Report Ser: No. 48). (Orig.). 1971. pap. 4.50 (ISBN 0-685-02923-9, F 131, FAO). Unipub.

FAO Nutrition Meetings. Specifications for Identity & Purity of Some Food Additives: Including Food Colors, Flavour Enhancers, Thickening Agents, & Others. (FAO Nutrition Meetings Report Ser.: No. 54b). 216p. 1976. pap. 22.00 (ISBN 0-685-66331-0, F1181, FAO). Unipub.

FAO-WHO Expert Committee on Food Additives. Rome, 1974, 18th. Evaluation of Certain Food Additives: Report. (Technical Report Ser.: No. 557). (Also avail. in French & Spanish). 1974. pap. 2.00 (ISBN 92-4-120557-1). World Health.

FAO-WHO Expert Committee on Food Additives. Geneva, 1972, 16th. Evaluation of Certain Food Additives & the Contaminants Mercury, Lead, & Cadmium: Report. (Technical Report Ser.: No. 505). (Also avail. in French & Spanish). 1972. pap. 1.60 (ISBN 92-4-120505-9). World Health.

FAO-WHO Expert Committee on Food Additives. Geneva, 1975, 19th. Evaluation of Certain Food Additives; Some Food Colours, Thickening Agents, Smoke Condensates & Certain Other Substances: Report. (Technical Report Ser.: No. 576). (Also avail. in French & Spanish). 1975. pap. 2.00 (ISBN 92-4-120576-8). World Health.

FAO-WHO Expert Committee on Food Additives. Rome, 1971, 15th. Evaluation of Food Additives. Some Enzymes, Modified Starches & Certain Other Substances; Toxicological Evaluations & Specifications & a Review of the Technological Efficacy of Some Antioxidants: Report. (Technical Report Ser.: No. 488). (Also avail. in French, Russian & Spanish). 1972. pap. 1.60 (ISBN 92-4-120488-5). World Health.

FAO-WHO Expert Committee on Food Additives. Geneva, 1970, 14th. Evaluation of Food Additives: Specifications for the Identity & Purity of Food Additives & Their Toxocological Evaluation: Some Extraction Solvents & Certain Other Substances & a Review of the Technological Efficacy of Some Antimicrobial Agent: Report. (Technical Report Ser.: No. 462). (Also avail. in French, Russian & Spanish). 1971. pap. 2.00 (ISBN 92-4-120462-1). World Health.

FAO - WHO Joint Expert Committee on Food Additives. Evaluation of Mercury, Lead, Cadmium & Food Additives Amaranth, Diethylpyrocarbonate, & Octyl Gallate. (WHO Food Additives Ser: No. 4). 84p. 1972. pap. 2.40 (ISBN 92-4-166004-X). World Health.

--Review of the Technological Efficiency of Some Antioxidants & Synergists. (WHO Food Additives Ser: No. 3). 144p. 1972. pap. 3.20 (ISBN 92-4-166003-1). World Health.

--Specifications for the Identity & Purity of Some Enzymes & Certain Other Substances. (WHO Food Additives Ser: Vol. 2). 174p. 1972. pap. 3.60 (ISBN 92-4-166002-3). World Health.

--Toxicological Evaluation of Some Enzymes, Modified Starches & Certain Other Substances. (WHO Food Additives Ser: Vol. 1). 109p. 1972. pap. 2.40 (ISBN 92-4-166001-5). World Health.

Feingold, Ben F. Why Your Child Is Hyperactive. LC 74-9078. 1974. 9.95 (ISBN 0-394-49343-5, Co-Pub by Bookworks). Random.

Food & Nutrition Board. Food Chemicals Codex. 3rd ed. (Illus.). 768p. 1981. 45.00 (ISBN 0-309-03090-0). Natl Acad Pr.

Food Protection Committee. Use of Human Subjects in Safety Evaluation of Food Chemicals. 1967. pap. 6.25 (ISBN 0-309-01491-3). Natl Acad Pr.

Froehlich, Ronald B. Food Additives, Student Syllabus. pap. text ed. 4.85 (ISBN 0-89420-076-3, 168008); cassette recordings 39.00 (ISBN 0-89420-205-7, 16800O). Natl Book.

Furia, Thomas E., ed. Handbook of Food Additives, CRC. 2nd ed. LC 68-21741. (Handbook Ser.). 432p. 1979. Vol. 1. 64.95 (ISBN 0-8493-0542-X). CRC Pr.

Gray, William D. The Use of Fungi As Food & in Food Processing, Pt. 2. LC 76-141883. (Monotopic Reprint Ser.). 1973. 19.95 (ISBN 0-8493-0118-1). CRC Pr.

Guide to Specifications for General Notices, General Methods, Identification Tests, Test Solutions & Other Reference Materials. (Food & Nutrition Paper Ser: No. 5). 1978. pap. 7.50 (ISBN 92-5-100443-9, F1431, FAO). Unipub.

Houben, Milton & Kropf, William. Dr. Harmful Food Additives: The Eat-Safe Guide. 10.95 (ISBN 0-87949-161-2). Ashley Bks.

How Safe Is Safe? The Design of Policy on Drugs & Food Additives. LC 74-5981. (Academy Forum Ser). 250p. 1974. pap. 8.75 (ISBN 0-309-02222-3). Natl Acad Pr.

Hunter, Beatrice T. Additives Book. rev. ed. LC 79-93436. 144p. 1980. pap. 2.25 (ISBN 0-87983-223-1). Keats.

--Whole-Grain Baking Sampler. LC 74-190457. 320p. 1972. 6.95 (ISBN 0-87983-013-1). Keats.

Inglett, George E., ed. Symposium: Sweeteners: Proceedings. (Illus.). 1974. 24.50 (ISBN 0-87055-153-1). AVI.

Jacobson, Michael F. Eater's Digest: The Consumer's Factbook of Food Additives. LC 75-186030. pap. 3.50 (ISBN 0-385-05341-X). Doubleday.

--How Sodium Nitrite Can Affect Your Health. rev. ed. 1979. pap. 2.00 (ISBN 0-89329-002-5). Ctr Sci Public.

Karki, N., ed. Mechanisms of Toxity & Metabolism: Proceedings of the 6th International Congress of Pharmacology, Helsinki, 1975, Vol. 6. 240p. 1976. text ed. 94.00 (ISBN 0-08-020544-5). Pergamon.

Labuza, Theodore P. Food & Your Well-Being. (Illus.). 1977. pap. text ed. 12.95 (ISBN 0-8299-0129-9); instrs.' manual & study guide 5.95 (ISBN 0-8299-0162-0). West Pub.

Leonard, B. J., ed. Toxicological Aspects of Food Safety: Proceedings of the European Society of Toxicology. (Archives of Toxicol, Suppl: Vol. 1). (Illus.). 1978. pap. 45.10 (ISBN 0-387-08646-3). Springer-Verlag.

List of Additives Evaluated for Their Safety-in-Use in Food. (Codex Alimentarius Commission Reports). 88p. (Orig.). 1974. pap. 4.50 (ISBN 0-685-41476-0, F648, FAO). Unipub.

Lueck, E. Antimicrobial Food Additives: Characteristics, Uses, Effects. (Illus.). 280p. 1980. 39.80 (ISBN 0-387-10056-3). Springer-Verlag.
The Mirage of Safety (Additives) 9.95 (ISBN 0-686-29752-0). Cancer Bk Hse.
Null, Gary & Null, Steven. How to Get Rid of the Poisons in Your Body. LC 76-28699. 192p. 1977. pap. 2.50 (ISBN 0-668-04114-5). Arco.
Packard, Vernal S., Jr. Processed Foods & the Consumer: Additives, Labeling, Standards & Nutrition. LC 75-32670. 312p. 1975. 17.50x (ISBN 0-8166-0778-8); pap. text ed. 7.95x (ISBN 0-8166-0784-2). U of Minn Pr.
Pintauro, N. D. Food Processing Enzymes-Recent Developments. LC 79-84426. (Food Technology Review Ser.: No. 52). (Illus.). 1979. 42.00 (ISBN 0-8155-0748-8). Noyes.
Pintauro, Nicholas D. Nutrition Technology of Processed Foods. LC 75-14912. (Food Technology Review: No. 25). 332p. 1976. 36.00 (ISBN 0-8155-0586-8). Noyes.
Polyphenols in Cereals & Legumes. 72p. 1980. pap. 5.00 (ISBN 0-88936-234-3, IDRC 145, IDRC). Unipub.
Roe, Francis J., ed. Metabolic Aspects of Food Safety. LC 72-142181. 1971. 55.50 (ISBN 0-12-592550-6). Acad Pr.
Specifications for Identity & Purity: Foods Colours-Enzyme Preparation & Other Food Additives. (Food & Nutrition Paper Ser.: No. 7). 1979. pap. 7.50 (ISBN 92-5-100651-2, F1536, FAO). Unipub.
Specifications for Identity & Purity of Food Additives & Their Toxicological Evaluation: Antimicrobial Preservatives & Antioxidants, Vol. 1. 1962. 8.00 (ISBN 0-685-36337-6, FAO). Unipub.
Specifications for Identity & Purity of Food Colours Flavouring Agents & Other Food Additives. 155p. 1980. pap. 12.75 (ISBN 92-5-100812-4, F 1878, FAO). Unipub.
Specifications for Identity & Purity of Some Food Additives. (Food & Nutrition Ser.: No. 1B). 1978. pap. 7.50 (ISBN 92-5-100411-0, F1347, FAO). Unipub.
Specifications for Identity & Purity of Some Food Additives, Including Acids, Bases, Buffers, Flour & Dough Conditioning Agents. (Nutrition Meeting Report Ser: No. 55 B). 1977. pap. 6.00 (ISBN 92-5-100218-5, F1192, FAO). Unipub.
Specifications for Identity & Purity of Thickening Agents, Anticaking Agents, Antimicrobials, Antioxidants & Emulsifiers. (FAO Food & Nutrution Paper Ser.: No. 4). 1978. pap. 21.75 (ISBN 92-5-100503-6, F1425, FAO). Unipub.
Specifications for Identity & Purity Sweeting Agents, Emulsifying Agents, Flavoring Agents & Other Food Additives. (FAO Food & Nutrition Paper Ser.: No. 17). 167p. 1980. pap. 11.75 (ISBN 92-5-100984-8, F2150, FAO). Unipub.
Specifications for the Identity & Purity of Food Additives & Their Toxicological Evaluation: Emulsifiers, Stabilizers, Bleaching & Maturing Agents. (FAO Nutrition Meetings Report Ser: No. 35). 189p. (Orig.). 1974. pap. 8.75 (ISBN 0-685-48300-2, F428, FAO). Unipub.
Specifications for the Identity & Purity of Food Additives & Their Toxicological Evaluation: Food Colours & Some Antimicrobials & Antioxidants. (FAO Nutrition Meetings Report Ser.: No. 38). 25p. (Orig.). 1974. Repr. of 1965 ed. pap. 10.00 (ISBN 0-685-48301-0, F430, FAO). Unipub.
Specifications for the Identity & Purity of Food Additives & Their Toxicological Evaluation: Some Antimicrobials, Antioxidants, Emulsifiers, Stabilizers, Flour-Treatment Agents, Acids, & Bases. (FAO Nutrition Meetings Report Ser.: No. 40). 24p. (Orig.). 1974. Repr. of 1966 ed. pap. 4.50 (ISBN 0-685-48302-9, F431, FAO). Unipub.
Specifications for the Identity & Purity of Food Additives & Their Toxicological Evaluation: Some Emulsifiers & Stabilizers & Certain Other Substances. (FAO Nutrition Meetings Report Ser.: No. 43). 49p. (Orig.). 1974. pap. 4.75 (ISBN 0-685-48303-7, FAO). Unipub.
Specifications for the Identity & Purity of Food Additives & Their Toxicological Evaluation: Some Antibiotics. (FAO Nutrition Meetings Report Ser.: No. 45). 49p. (Orig.). 1969. pap. 4.50 (ISBN 0-685-48304-5, F210, FAO). Unipub.
Specifications for the Identity & Purity of Food Additives & Their Toxicological Evaluation: Some Flavouring Substances & Non-Nutritive Sweetening Agents. (FAO Nutrition Meetings Report Ser.: No. 44). 18p. (Orig.). 1970. Repr. of 1968 ed. pap. 4.50 (ISBN 0-685-48305-3, F433, FAO). Unipub.
Specifications for the Identity & Purity of Some Food Colours, Flavour Enhancers, Thickening Agents & Certain Other Food Additives. (Food Additive Ser.: No. 7). (Also avail. in French). 1976. pap. 8.80 (ISBN 92-4-166007-4). World Health.
Stenberg, A. J., et al. Food Additive Control in the U. S. S. R. (FAO Food Additive Control Ser.: No. 8). (Orig.). 1969. pap. 4.50 (ISBN 0-685-09381-6, F183, FAO). Unipub.
Sullivan, George. Additives in Your Food. 1976. 1.95 (ISBN 0-346-12225-2). Cornerstone.
Taylor, R. J. Food Additives. LC 79-42729. (The Institution of Environmental Sciences Ser.). 126p. 1980. 30.00 (ISBN 0-471-27684-7, Pub. by Wiley Interscience); pap. 13.75 (ISBN 0-471-27683-9). Wiley.
Toxicological Evaluation of Certain Food Additives with a Review of General Principles & of Specifications. (FAO Nutrition Meetings Report Ser.: No. 53). 40p. (Orig.). 1974. pap. 4.50 (ISBN 0-685-50558-8, F466, Fao). Unipub.
Toxicological Evaluation of Some Food Additives; Including Food Colors, Thickening Agents & Others. (FAO Nutrition Meetings Report Ser: No. 55a). (Illus.). 89p. 1977. pap. 9.75 (ISBN 92-5-100060-3, F1217, FAO). Unipub.
Toxocological Evaluation of Some Food Additives, Including Food Colors, Enzymes, Flavour Enhancers, Thickening Agents & Others. (FAO Nutrition Meetings Report Ser: No. 54a). (Illus.). 204p. 1976. pap. 13.25 (ISBN 92-4-166006-6, F1243, FAO). Unipub.
Verrett, Jacqueline & Carper, Jean. Eating May Be Hazardous to Your Health. 240p. 1975. pap. 2.95 (ISBN 0-385-11193-2, Anchor Pr). Doubleday.
Walford, J., ed. Developments in Food Colour - One. (Illus.). ix, 259p. 1980. 45.00x (ISBN 0-85334-881-2, Pub. by Applied Science). Burgess-Intl Ideas.
Whelan, Elizabeth & Stare, Fredrick J. Panic in the Pantry. LC 75-7952. 1975. pap. 3.95 (ISBN 0-689-70553-0, 236). Atheneum.
Wilson, David A. What You Should Know About Sugar & Food Additives. (Orig.). 1975. pap. 2.00 (ISBN 0-934852-14-6, LH-14). Lorien Hse.
Winter, Ruth. A Consumer's Dictionary of Food Additives. 1978. 8.95 (ISBN 0-517-53160-7); pap. 4.95 (ISBN 0-517-53161-5). Crown.
Zweig, Gunter, ed. Analytical Methods for Pesticides, Plant Growth Regulators & Food Additives, 10 vols. Incl. Vol. 1. Principles, Methods & General Applications. 1963. 72.00 (ISBN 0-12-784301-9); Vol. 2. Insecticides. 1964. 72.00 (ISBN 0-12-784302-7); Vol. 3. Fungicides, Nematocides & Soil Fumigants, Rodenticides, & Food & Feed Additives. 1964. 42.00 (ISBN 0-12-784303-5); Vol. 4. Herbicides (Plant Growth Regulators) 1964. 42.00 (ISBN 0-12-784304-3); Vol. 5. 1967. 68.50 (ISBN 0-12-784305-1); Vol. 6. 78.50 (ISBN 0-12-784306-X); Vol. 7. Thin-Layer & Liquid Chromatography & Analysis of Pesticides of International Importance. 1974. 78.50 (ISBN 0-12-784307-8); Vol. 8. Government Regulations, Pheromone Analyses, Additional Pesticides. Zweig, Gunter & Sharma, Joseph, eds. 1976. 72.00 (ISBN 0-12-784308-6); Vol. 10. Newer & Updated Methods. Zweig, Gunter & Sharma, Joseph, eds. 1978. 55.00 (ISBN 0-12-784310-8); Vol. 11. 1980. 46.00 (ISBN 0-12-784311-6). Set. 581.00 (ISBN 0-686-76922-8). Acad Pr.

FOOD ADULTERATION AND INSPECTION
see also Food Contamination; Meat Inspection
Aston, Graham & Tiffney, John. Guide to Improving Food Hygiene. (Illus.). 1977. pap. 11.95x (ISBN 0-7198-2644-6). Intl Ideas.
Filby, Frederick A. A History of Food Adulteration & Analysis. LC 75-23707. 1976. Repr. of 1934 ed. 21.00 (ISBN 0-404-13259-6). AMS Pr.
Food Safety Council, Columbia, U. S. A., ed. Proposed System for Food Safety Assessment: A Comprehensive Report on the Issues of Food Ingredient Testing. new ed. LC 78-40901. (Illus.). 1978. pap. text ed. 23.00 (ISBN 0-08-023752-5). Pergamon.
Giant Food Product Safety & Evaluation Policy. 1976. 1-5 copies 6.50 ea. (ISBN 0-914176-06-4); 6-15 copies 6.25 ea.; 16-25 copies 6.00 ea.; 26 or more copies 5.75 ea. Wash Busn Info.
Goodman, Robert L. A Quick Guide to Food Additives. (Orig.). 1981. pap. price not set (ISBN 0-940988-00-3). Gnosis Pubns.
Graham, Horace D. The Safety of Foods. 2nd ed. (Illus.). 1980. lib. bdg. 54.00 (ISBN 0-87055-337-2). AVI.
Jones, Claire, et al. Pollution: The Food We Eat. LC 74-178673. (Real World of Pollution Ser). (Illus.). (gr. 5-11). 1972. PLB 4.95 (ISBN 0-8225-0634-3). Lerner Pubns.
Kallet, Arthur & Schlink, F. J. One Hundred Million Guinea Pigs: Dangers in Everyday Foods, Drugs, & Cosmetics. LC 75-39252. (Getting & Spending: the Consumer's Dilemma). 1976. Repr. of 1933 ed. 18.00x (ISBN 0-405-08025-5). Arno.
Kreuzer, R., ed. Fish Inspection & Quality Control. (Illus.). 290p. 1972. 39.00 (ISBN 0-85238-051-8, FAO). Unipub.
Lamb, Ruth D. American Chamber of Horrors: The Truth About Food & Drugs. LC 75-39255. (Getting & Spending: the Consumer's Dilemma). (Illus.). 1976. Repr. of 1936 ed. 24.00x (ISBN 0-405-08028-X). Arno.
Manual of Food Quality Control Six: Food for Export. (FAO Food & Nutrition Paper: No. 14-6). 50p. 1980. pap. 9.00 (ISBN 92-5-100836-1, F 1893, FAO). Unipub.
Ninemeier, Jack. Food Service Security Manual: Control of Cash, Food & Beverage. 250p. 1981. 3-ring binder 49.95 (ISBN 0-8436-2250-4). CBI Pub.
Nutrition & Food Preparation & Preventive Care & Maintenance. (Lifeworks Ser.). 1981. 4.96 (ISBN 0-07-037094-X). McGraw.
Puri, Subhash C., et al. Statistical Quality Control for Food & Agricultural Scientists. (Medical Bks.). 1979. lib. bdg. 22.50 (ISBN 0-8161-2177-X, Hall Medical). G K Hall.
Recommended International Code of Hygienic Practice for Food for Infants & Children. 13p. 1980. pap. 7.50 (ISBN 92-5-101014-5, F2158, FAO). Unipub.
Recommended International Standard for Cooked, Cured & Chopped Meat. 1979. pap. 4.50 (ISBN 92-5-100644-X, F1572, FAO). Unipub.
Recommended International Standard for Cocoa Powder (Cocoas) & Dry Sugar Mixtures. 8p. 1980. pap. 4.50 (ISBN 92-5-100852-3, F1915, FAO). Unipub.
Recommended International Standard for Canned Sardines & Sardine - Type Products. 1979. pap. 4.50 (ISBN 92-5-100673-3, F1573, FAO). Unipub.
Recommended International Standard for Food Hygiene. 1969. pap. 3.00 (ISBN 0-685-36299-X, FAO). Unipub.
Recommended International Standard for Quick Frozen Filets of Hake. 1979. pap. 4.50 (ISBN 92-5-100647-4, F1569, FAO). Unipub.
Recommended International Standard for Quick Frozen Lobsters. 1979. pap. 4.50 (ISBN 92-5-100648-2, F1568, FAO). Unipub.
Rha, Chokyun, ed. Theory, Determination & Control of Physical Properties of Food Materials. LC 74-76481. (Food Material Science Ser: No. 1). xi, 315p. 1975. lib. bdg. 68.50 (ISBN 90-277-0468-6, Pub. by Reidel Holland). Kluwer Boston.
Roberts, Howard R. Food Safety. LC 80-25335. 339p. 1981. 39.50 (ISBN 0-471-06458-0, Pub. by Wiley-Interscience). Wiley.
Roe, Francis J., ed. Metabolic Aspects of Food Safety. LC 72-142181. 1971. 55.50 (ISBN 0-12-592550-6). Acad Pr.
Rudman, Jack. Senior Food Inspector. (Career Examination Ser.: C-2051). (Cloth bdg. avail. on request). pap. 10.00 (ISBN 0-8373-2051-8). Natl Learning.
--Supervising Food Inspector. (Career Examination Ser.: C-2055). (Cloth bdg. avail. on request). pap. 10.00 (ISBN 0-8373-2055-0). Natl Learning.
Schlink, F. J. Eat, Drink & Be Wary. LC 75-39273. (Getting & Spending: a Consumer's Dilemma). Repr. of 1935 ed. 18.00x (ISBN 0-405-08045-X). Arno.
Ser-Vol-Tel Institute. Foodservice Safety. (Foodservice Career Education Ser.). 1974. pap. 4.95 (ISBN 0-8436-2008-0). CBI Pub.
Turner, James S. Chemical Feast: Report on the Food & Drug Administration. LC 73-112515. (Ralph Nader Study Group Reports). 1970. 6.95 (ISBN 0-670-21428-0, N2, Grossman). Viking Pr.
Wolfe, Margaret R. Lucius Polk Brown & Progressive Food & Drug Control: Tennessee & New York City,1908-1920. LC 77-6637. 1978. 12.50x (ISBN 0-7006-0163-5). Regents Pr KS.

FOOD AID PROGRAMS
see Food Relief

FOOD ALLERGY
see Allergy

FOOD AND AGRICULTURE ORGANIZATION OF THE UNITED NATIONS
Abbreviations. rev. ed. (Terminology Bulletin Ser: No. 27). 60p. 1976. pap. 9.75 (ISBN 0-685-62390-4, F1196, FAO). Unipub.
Codex Alimentarius Commission. Report of the Twelfth Session. 1979. pap. 7.50 (ISBN 92-5-100628-8, F1511, FAO). Unipub.
Council of the Food & Agriculture Organization, 69th Session. Report. 1976. pap. 7.50 (ISBN 92-5-100090-5, F1133, FAO). Unipub.
FAO Commodity Review & Outlook: 1970-1971. 227p. (Orig.). 1972. pap. 11.25 (ISBN 0-685-24965-4, FAO). Unipub.
FAO Commodity Review & Outlook 1971-1972. (Illus.). 225p. 1973. pap. 18.00 (ISBN 0-685-30142-7, FAO). Unipub.
FAO Conference, 10th Session, Rome, 1959. Report. 1960. pap. 5.50 (ISBN 0-685-36330-9, F360, FAO). Unipub.
FAO Conference, 11th Session, Rome, 1961. Report. 1962. pap. 4.50 (ISBN 0-685-36331-7, F358, FAO). Unipub.
FAO Conference, 12th Session, Rome, 1963. Report. 1964. pap. 4.50 (ISBN 0-685-36332-5, F366, FAO). Unipub.
FAO Conference, 13th Session, Rome, 1965. Report. 1966. pap. 10.00 (ISBN 0-685-36333-3, F365, FAO). Unipub.
FAO Conference, 14th Session, Rome, 1967. Report. 1968. pap. 10.00 (ISBN 0-685-36334-1, F364, FAO). Unipub.
FAO Conference, 15th Session, Rome, 1969. Report. 1969. pap. 8.00 (ISBN 0-685-36335-X, F363, FAO). Unipub.
FAO Conference, 18th Session, Rome, Nov. 8-27,1975. Report. 1976. pap. 17.00 (ISBN 0-685-66336-1, F367, FAO). Unipub.
FAO Photo Library. (Orig.). 1972. pap. 22.50 (ISBN 0-685-36266-3, F156, FAO). Unipub.
Food & Nutrition: Annotated Bibliography, Author & Subject Index (1945-1972) (Special Index: No. 26). (Orig.). 1974. pap. 8.00 (ISBN 0-685-41433-7, FAO). Unipub.
Joint FAO-WHO Expert Committee on Milk Hygiene: Third Report. (FAO Agricultural Studies: No. 83). (Illus., Orig.). 1971. pap. 4.25 (ISBN 0-685-00275-6, FAO). Unipub.
The Propogation of Tropical Fruit Trees. (Horticultural Review Ser.: No. 4). 1978. pap. 24.00 (ISBN 0-85198-351-0, CAB 4, FAO). Unipub.
Report of the Council of FAO: 70th Session. 1977. pap. 12.00 (ISBN 92-5-100216-9, F1131, FAO). Unipub.
Report of the First Session of the United Nations - FAO Committee on Food Aid Policies & Programmes, Rome, 26 April-6 May 1976. 71p. 1976. pap. 5.25 (ISBN 92-5-100065-4, FAO). Unipub.
World Food Congress, 2nd, The Hague, 1970. Report, Vol. 2. (Illus.). 141p. (Orig.). 1971. pap. 14.25 (ISBN 0-685-02921-2, F379, FAO). Unipub.
World Food Programme: Report of the Fifth Session. 1978. pap. 7.50 (ISBN 92-5-100596-6, F1475, FAO). Unipub.

FOOD ANIMALS
see Animal Food

FOOD CHAINS (ECOLOGY)
Blaxter, Kenneth. Food Chains & Human Nutrition. (Illus.). x, 459p. 1980. 65.00x (ISBN 0-85334-863-4, Pub. by Applied Science). Burgess-Intl Ideas.
Krutch, Joseph W. The Great Chain of Life. 1978. pap. 3.95 (ISBN 0-395-25943-6). HM.
Pimm, S. L. Food Web. (Population & Community Biology Ser.). 1981. 29.00x (ISBN 0-412-23100-X, Pub. by Chapman & Hall); pap. 16.00x (ISBN 0-412-23110-7). Methuen Inc.

FOOD CHEMISTRY
see Food-Analysis; Food-Composition

FOOD CONSERVATION
see also Canning and Preserving; Food Contamination
Peel, Dorothy. The Eat-Less-Meat Book. 220p. 1973. 69.95 (ISBN 0-87968-071-7). Gordon Pr.

FOOD CONSUMPTION
Alexis, Marcus, et al. Black Consumer Profiles: Food Purchasing in the Inner City. (Illus.). 106p. 1980. pap. 4.00 (ISBN 0-87712-195-8). U Mich Busn Div Res.
Analysis of Food Consumption Survey Data for Developing Countries. (FAO Food & Nutrition Paper: No. 16). 139p. 1981. pap. 9.50 (ISBN 92-5-100968-6, F2118, FAO). Unipub.
Baxter, M. W. Food in Fiji: The Produce & Processed Foods Distribution Systems. (Development Studies Centre-Monographs: No. 22). 282p. 1980. pap. text ed. 13.95 (ISBN 0-909150-03-6, 0064, Pub. by ANUP Australia). Bks Australia.
Bower, Fay L. Nutrition in Nursing. LC 79-10562. (Nursing Concept Modules Ser.). 1979. pap. 12.50 (ISBN 0-471-04124-6, Pub. by Wiley Med). Wiley.
Changes in Food Habits in Relation to Increase of Productivity. 370p. 1973. 13.75 (ISBN 0-686-70974-8, APO14, APO). Unipub.
Christensen, Raymond P. Efficient Use of Food Resources in the United States. LC 75-26300. (World Food Supply Ser). (Illus.). 1976. Repr. of 1948 ed. 8.00x (ISBN 0-405-07772-6). Arno.
Dressa, Connie M., et al. Food Consumption Profiles of White & Black Persons Aged 1-74 Years: United States, 1971-4. (Series II: No. 210). (Illus.). 1978. pap. text ed. 1.95 (ISBN 0-8406-0143-3). Natl Ctr Health Stats.
Duckham, A. N., et al. Food Production & Consumption. 1977. 58.75 (ISBN 0-7204-0396-0, North-Holland). Elsevier.
McGee, T. G., et al. Food Distribution in the New Herbrides. (Development Studies Centre-Monographs: No. 25). 268p. 1981. pap. text ed. 13.95 (ISBN 0-909150-19-2, 0068, Pub. by ANUP Australia). Bks Australia.
Rao, K. K., ed. Food Consumption & Planning. 1976. 94.00 (ISBN 0-08-016459-5). Pergamon.

Reh, E. Manual on Household Food Consumption Surveys. 1972. pap. 7.25 (ISBN 92-5-100080-8, F266, FAO). Unipub.

Review of Food Consumption Surveys 1977: Europe, North America, Oceania Household Food Consumption by Economic Groups, Vol. 1. (FAO Food & Nutrition Paper: No. 1-1). 1978. pap. 10.50 (ISBN 92-5-100349-1, F1304, FAO). Unipub.

Scheltema, Anne M. & August, Peter. The Food Consumption of the Native Inhabitants of Java & Madura. Hamilton, A. H., tr. LC 75-30080. (Institute of Pacific Relations). 1976. Repr. of 1936 ed. 11.50 (ISBN 0-404-59557-X). AMS Pr.

Talbot, Ross B., ed. World Food Problem & U. S. Food Politics & Policies: Nineteen Seventy-Eight. 1979. pap. text ed. 8.75 (ISBN 0-8138-1155-4). Iowa St U Pr.

Wortman, Sterling & Cummings, Ralph W., Jr. To Feed the World: The Challenge & the Strategy. LC 78-8478. 464p. 1978. pap. text ed. 7.95x (ISBN 0-8018-2137-1). Johns Hopkins.

FOOD CONTAMINATION

see also Radioactive Contamination of Food

Alpert, M. E., et al. Chemical & Radionuclide Food Contamination. (Illus.). 220p. 1973. text ed. 28.50x (ISBN 0-8422-7091-4). Irvington.

Ayres, J. C., et al, eds. Chemical & Biological Hazards in Food. (Illus.). 1969. Repr. of 1962 ed. 15.75 (ISBN 0-02-840650-8). Hafner.

Chen, Edwin. PBB: An American Tragedy. LC 79-15982. 1979. 10.95 (ISBN 0-13-654608-0). P-H.

Christie, A. B. & Christie, Mary C. Food Hygiene & Food Hazards. 2nd ed. (Illus.). 232p. 1977. pap. 5.95 (ISBN 0-571-10902-0, Pub. by Faber & Faber). Merrimack Bk Serv.

Committee On Food Protection. Evaluation of Public Health Hazards from Microbiological Contamination of Foods. 1964. pap. 3.75 (ISBN 0-309-01195-7). Natl Acad Pr.

Crompton, T. R. Additive Migration from Plastics into Food. 1979. 54.00 (ISBN 0-08-022465-2). Pergamon.

FAO-WHO Experts on Pesticide Residues. Geneva, 1968. Pesticide Residues in Food: Report. (Technical Report Ser.: No. 417). (Also avail. in French & Spanish). 1969. pap. 2.00 (ISBN 92-4-120417-6). World Health.

FAO-WHO Experts on Pesticide Residues. Rome, 1970. Pesticide Residues in Food: Report. (Technical Report Ser.: No. 474). (Also avail. in French & Spanish). 1971. pap. 2.00 (ISBN 92-4-120474-5). World Health.

FAO-WHO Experts on Pesticide Residues. Geneva, 1971. Pesticide Residues in Food: Report. (Technical Report Ser.: No. 502). (Also avail. in French, Russian & Spanish). 1972. pap. 1.60 (ISBN 92-4-120502-4). World Health.

FAO-WHO Experts on Pesticide Residues. Rome, 1972. Pesticide Residues in Food: Report. (Technical Report Ser.: No. 525). (Also avail. in french & spanish). 1973. pap. 1.60 (ISBN 92-4-120525-3). World Health.

FAO-WHO Experts on Pesticide Residues. Geneva, 1973. Pesticide Residues in Food: Report. (Technical Report Ser.: No. 545). (Also avail. in French, Russian & Spanish). 1974. pap. 2.40 (ISBN 92-4-120545-8). World Health.

FAO-WHO Experts on Pesticide Residues. Rome, 1975. Pesticide Residues in Food: Report. (Technical Report Ser.: No. 574). (Also avail. in French & Spanish). 1975. pap. 2.40 (ISBN 92-4-120574-1). World Health.

Food & Agriculture Organization. Pesticide Residues in Food: Report of the Joint FAO-Who Meeting, Rome, 1970. (FAO Agricultural Studies: No. 87). (Orig.). 1971. pap. 4.50 (ISBN 0-685-09397-2, F310, FAO). Unipub.

Food & Nutrition Board. Toxicants Occurring Naturally in Foods. rev. 2nd ed. (Illus.). 704p. 1973. 17.25 (ISBN 0-309-02117-0). Natl Acad Pr.

Food & Nutrition Board, National Research Council. Prevention of Microbial & Parasitic Hazard Associated with Processed Foods: A Guide for the Food Processor. 1975. pap. 5.75 (ISBN 0-309-02345-9). Natl Acad Pr.

Gunther, F. A., ed. Residue Reviews, Vols. 1-11. Incl. Vol. 1. (Illus.). iv, 162p. 1962. 27.20 (ISBN 0-387-02899-4); Vol. 2. (Illus.). iv, 156p. 1963. 27.20 (ISBN 0-387-03047-6); Vol. 3. (Illus.). iv, 170p. 1963. 27.20 (ISBN 0-387-03048-4); Vol. 4. (Illus.). iv, 175p. 1963. 27.20 (ISBN 0-387-03049-2); Vol. 5. Instrumentation for the Detection & Determination of Pesticides & Their Residues in Foods. (Illus.). viii, 176p. 1964. 27.20 (ISBN 0-387-03201-0); Vol. 6. (Illus.). iv, 165p. 1964. 27.20 (ISBN 0-387-03202-9); Vol. 7. vi, 161p. 1964. 19.90 (ISBN 0-387-03203-7); Vol. 8. (Illus.). viii, 183p. 1965. 20.90 (ISBN 0-387-03390-4); Vol. 9. (Illus.). viii, 175p. 1965. 19.90 (ISBN 0-387-03391-2); Vol. 10. With Comprehensive Cumulative Contents, Subjectmatter, & Author Indexes of Volume 1-10. (Illus.). viii, 159p. 1965. 19.90 (ISBN 0-387-03392-0); Vol. 11. (Illus.). viii, 164p. 1965. 20.90 (ISBN 0-387-03393-9). LC 62-18595. (Eng, Fr, Ger.). Springer-Verlag.

--Residue Reviews, Vols. 13-24. Incl. Vol. 13. (Illus.). viii, 136p. 1966. 27.20 (ISBN 0-387-03648-2); Vol. 14. (Illus.). viii, 131p. 1966. 20.90 (ISBN 0-387-03649-0); Vol. 15. (Illus.). vi, 121p. 1966. 19.90 (ISBN 0-387-03650-4); Vol. 16. (Illus.). viii, 158p. 1966. 24.10 (ISBN 0-387-03651-2); Vol. 17. (Illus.). viii, 184p. 1967. 24.10 (ISBN 0-387-03963-5); Vol. 18. (Illus.). viii, 227p. 1967. 37.80 (ISBN 0-387-03964-3); Vol. 19. (Illus.). viii, 155p. 1967. 37.80 (ISBN 0-387-03965-1); Vol. 20. With Cumulative Table of Subjects Covered, Detailed Subject-Matter Index, & Author Index of Volumes 11-20. x, 214p. 1968. 29.00 (ISBN 0-387-04310-1); Vol. 21. (Illus.). viii, 128p. 1968. 29.00 (ISBN 0-387-04311-X); Vol. 22. (Illus.). viii, 120p. 1968. 29.00 (ISBN 0-387-04312-8); Vol. 23. (Illus.). viii, 152p. 1968. 31.20 (ISBN 0-387-04313-6); Vol. 24. vii, 173p. 1968. 31.20 (ISBN 0-387-04314-4). LC 62-18595. (Eng, Fr, Ger.). Springer-Verlag.

--Residue Reviews, Vols. 25-35. Incl. Vol. 25. Special Volume: Seminar on Experimental Approaches to Pesticide Metabolism, Degradation & Mode of Action. United States-Japan Seminar, August 16-19, 1967, Nikko, Japan. (Illus.). x, 364p. 1969. 44.70 (ISBN 0-387-04687-9); Vol. 26. (Illus.). vii, 142p. 1969. 29.00 (ISBN 0-387-04688-7); Vol. 27. (Illus.). vii, 143p. 1969. 29.00 (ISBN 0-387-04689-5); Vol. 28. Insecticide Residues in California Citrus Fruits & Products. (Illus.). vii, 127p. 1969. 29.00 (ISBN 0-387-04690-9); Vol. 29. Special Volume: Symposium on Decontamination of Pesticide Residues in the Environment. Atlantic City Meetings of the ACS, Sept. 1968. (Illus.). viii, 213p. 1969. 35.70 (ISBN 0-387-04691-7); Vol. 30. With Cumulative Table of Subjects Covered, Detailed Subject-Matter Index & Author Index of Vols. 21-30. (Illus.). ix, 169p. 1969. 35.70 (ISBN 0-387-04692-5); Vol. 31. Leaf Structure As Related to Absorption of Pesticides & Other Compounds. Hull, H. M. vii, 155p. 1970. 31.20 (ISBN 0-387-05000-0); Vol. 32. Single-Pesticide Volume: Trianzine Herbicides. (Illus.). 420p. 1970. 35.70 (ISBN 0-387-05235-6); Vol. 33. (Illus.). 160p. 1970. 35.70 (ISBN 0-387-05236-4); Vol. 34. 160p. 1971. 35.70 (ISBN 0-387-05237-2); Vol. 35. (Illus.). viii, 156p. 1971. 35.70 (ISBN 0-387-05238-0). LC 62-18595. (Eng, Fr, Ger.). Springer-Verlag.

--Residue Reviews, Vols. 36-45. Incl. Vol. 36. Chemistry of Pesticides. Melnikov, N. N. (Illus.). xii, 492p. 1971. 40.20 (ISBN 0-387-05373-5); Vol. 37. (Illus.). 144p. 1971. 35.70 (ISBN 0-387-05374-3); Vol. 38. (Illus.). 144p. 1971. 35.70 (ISBN 0-387-05375-1); Vol. 39. The Carbinole Acaricides, Chlorobenzilate & Chloropropylate. 1971. 35.70 (ISBN 0-387-05409-X); Vol. 40. With Cumulative Table of Subjects, Vols. 31-40. (Illus.). 144p. 1971. 35.70 (ISBN 0-387-05410-3); Vol. 41. Rueckstandsberichte. (Illus.). 1972. 17.40 (ISBN 0-387-05568-1); Vol. 42. (Illus.). 1972. 17.40 (ISBN 0-387-05627-0); Vol. 43. (Illus.). 1972. 15.70 (ISBN 0-387-05779-X); Vol. 44. (Illus.). 1973. 31.50 (ISBN 0-387-90058-6); Vol. 45. 1973. 31.50 (ISBN 0-387-90059-4). LC 62-18595. (Eng, Fr, Ger,). Springer-Verlag.

--Residue Reviews, Vol. 50. x, 192p. 1974. 31.50 (ISBN 0-387-90082-9). Springer-Verlag.

--Residue Reviews, Vol. 51. viii, 203p. 1974. 31.50 (ISBN 0-387-90079-9). Springer-Verlag.

Hagstad, Harry V. & Hubbert, William T. Food Quality Control: A Syllabus for Veterinary Students. (Illus.). 152p. 1981. pap. text ed. 10.25 (ISBN 0-8138-0701-8). Iowa St U Pr.

Hunter, Beatrice T. How Safe Is Food in Your Kitchen. 96p. 1981. 7.95 (ISBN 0-684-16752-2, ScribT). Scribner.

Institut National De Recherche Chimique Appliguee. Pollution by the Food Processing Industries in the EEC. 193p. 1977. 33.00x (ISBN 0-86010-074-X, Pub. by Graham & Trotman England). State Mutual Bk.

Jones, Claire, et al. Pollution: The Food We Eat. LC 74-178673. (Real World of Pollution Ser). (Illus.). (gr. 5-11). 1972. PLB 4.95 (ISBN 0-8225-0634-3). Lerner Pubns.

Leonard, B. J., ed. Toxicological Aspects of Food Safety: Proceedings of the European Society of Toxicology. (Archives of Toxicol, Suppl: Vol. 1). (Illus.). 1978. pap. 45.10 (ISBN 0-387-08646-3). Springer-Verlag.

Liener, I. Toxic Constituents in Plant Foodstuffs. (Food Science & Technology Ser). 1969. 58.50 (ISBN 0-12-449950-3). Acad Pr.

Liener, Irvin E. Toxic Constitutuents of Plant Foodstuffs. 2nd ed. LC 79-51681. (Food Science & Technology Ser.). 1980. 39.50 (ISBN 0-12-449960-0). Acad Pr.

List of Maximum Levels Recommended for Contaminants by the Joint FAO-WHO Codex Alimentarius Commission. 1979. pap. 4.50 (ISBN 92-5-100693-8, F1603, FAO). Unipub.

List of Maximum Levels Recommended for Contaminants by the Joint FAO-WHO Codes Alimentarius Commission: Second Series. 8p. 1977. pap. 4.50 (ISBN 0-685-81407-6, F664, FAO). Unipub.

List of Maximum Levels Recommended for Contaminants by the Joint FAO-WHO Codex Alimentarius Commission, Ser. 1. 14p. (Orig.). 1975. pap. 4.50 (ISBN 0-685-53180-5, F659, FAO). Unipub.

Lucas, Jack. Our Polluted Food: A Survey of the Risks. LC 75-8700. 237p. 1975. 21.95 (ISBN 0-470-55285-9). Halsted Pr.

Magallona, E. D., et al. Residue Reviews. (Residue Reviews Ser.: Vol. 56). (Illus.). 160p. 1975. 16.30 (ISBN 0-387-90115-9). Springer-Verlag.

Methods of Sampling & Analysis of Contaminants in Food: Report of a Joint FAO-WHO Expert Consultation. 19p. 1978. pap. 7.50 (ISBN 92-5-100572-9, F1472, FAO). Unipub.

Mycotoxin Surveillance: A Guideline. (FAO Food Control Ser: No. 4). 1978. pap. 7.50 (ISBN 92-5-100315-7, F1229, FAO). Unipub.

Natural Resources & the Human Enviroment for Food & Agriculture. (FAO Environment Paper Ser.: No. 1). 62p. 1980. pap. 7.50 (ISBN 92-5-100967-8, F2132, FAO). Unipub.

Peakall, D. B. Residue Reviews, Vol. 54. LC 62-18595. (Illus.). x, 190p. 1975. 29.00 (ISBN 0-387-90099-3). Springer-Verlag.

Pesticide Residues in Food: Evaluations 1977. (Plant Production & Protection Paper Ser.: 10th Supplement). 1979. pap. 28.00 (ISBN 92-5-100666-0, F1534, FAO). Unipub.

Pesticide Residues in Food: FAO Plant Production & Protection. 1978. pap. 7.50 (ISBN 92-5-100578-8, F1510, FAO). Unipub.

Pesticide Residues in Food: Index & Summary, 1965-1978. (Plant Production & Protection Paper Ser.: No. 11). 41p. 1979. pap. 7.50 (ISBN 92-5-100652-0, F1551, FAO). Unipub.

Pesticide Residues in Food: Report of the 1975 Joint Fao-Who Meeting, Geneva, 1975. (FAO Plant Production & Protection Ser: No. 1). 45p. 1976. pap. 6.25 (ISBN 92-5-100040-9, F315, FAO). Unipub.

Pesticide Residues in Food, 1978. (FAO Plant Production & Protection Paper Ser.: No. 15). 1979. pap. 7.50 (ISBN 92-5-100751-9, F1627, FAO). Unipub.

Pesticide Residues in Food 1979. (FAO Plant Production & Protection Paper Ser.: No. 20). 97p. 1980. pap. 7.50 (ISBN 92-5-100922-8, F1936, FAO). Unipub.

Pim, Linda. The Invisible Additives: Environmental Contamination of Food. 288p. 1981. 17.95 (ISBN 0-385-17001-7); pap. 9.95 (ISBN 0-385-17002-5). Doubleday.

Reilly, Conor. Metal Contamination of Food. xvi, 231p. 1980. 42.50x (ISBN 0-85334-905-3). Burgess-Intl Ideas.

Riemann, Hans & Bryan, Frank L., eds. Food-Borne Infections & Intoxication. 2nd ed. LC 79-14935. (Food Science & Technology Ser.). 1979. 66.50 (ISBN 0-12-588360-9). Acad Pr.

Roberts, Howard R. Food Safety. LC 80-25335. 339p. 1981. 39.50 (ISBN 0-471-06458-0, Pub. by Wiley-Interscience). Wiley.

Roe, Francis J., ed. Metabolic Aspects of Food Safety. LC 72-142181. 1971. 55.50 (ISBN 0-12-592550-6). Acad Pr.

Tallian, Laura. Pesticide Jungle. 1.50 (ISBN 0-686-29972-8). Cancer Bk Hse.

Trace Contaminants of Agriculture, Fisheries & Food in Developing Countries. LC 76-8895. (Illus.). 1977. pap. 10.25 (ISBN 92-0-111576-8, ISP454, IAEA). Unipub.

WHO Study Group. Geneva, 1973. Food-Borne Disease; Methods of Sampling & Examination in Surveillance Programmes: Report. (Technical Report Ser.: No. 543). (Also avail. in French & Spanish). 1974. pap. 2.00 (ISBN 92-4-120543-1). World Health.

FOOD CONTROL

see Food Supply

FOOD CUSTOMS

see Food Habits

FOOD DECORATION

see Cookery (Garnishes)

FOOD FOR INVALIDS

see Cookery for the Sick

FOOD FOR SCHOOL CHILDREN

see School Children–Food

FOOD HABITS

see also Diet; Nutrition

Abraham, Sidney, et al. Preliminary Findings of the First Health & Nutrition Examination Survey, U.S., Nineteen Seventy-One to Nineteen Seventy-Two, Dietary Intake & Biochemical Findings. 70p. 1974. pap. 1.25 (ISBN 0-8406-0028-3). Natl Ctr Health Stats.

Arnott, Margaret L., ed. Gastronomy: The Anthropology of Food & Food Habits. (World Anthropology Ser). (Illus.). 1976. 27.00x (ISBN 0-202-90025-8). Beresford Bk Serv.

Brewster, Letitia & Jacobson, Michael. The Changing American Diet. (Illus.). 1978. pap. 2.50 (ISBN 0-89329-007-6). Ctr Sci Public.

Cameron, Allan G. Food-Facts & Fallacies. (Illus.). 168p. 1971. 6.50x (ISBN 0-571-10290-5). Intl Pubns Serv.

Chang, K. C, ed. Food in Chinese Culture: Anthropological & Historical Perspectives. LC 75-43312. 1977. 35.00x (ISBN 0-300-01938-6). Yale U Pr.

Cummings, Richard O. American & His Food: A History of Food Habits in the United States. LC 74-112536. (Rise of Urban America). (Illus.). 1970. Repr. of 1940 ed. 16.00 (ISBN 0-405-02445-2). Arno.

Darby, W. J., ed. Food: the Gift of Osiris. 1977. Vol. 1. 53.00 (ISBN 0-12-203401-5); Vol.2. 53.00 (ISBN 0-12-203402-3); boxed set 83.00 (ISBN 0-12-203450-3). Acad Pr.

Deutsch, Ronald M. The New Nuts Among the Berries. LC 77-70401. 1977. pap. 5.95 (ISBN 0-915950-09-X). Bull Pub.

Dumas, Alexandre. Histoire de la Cuisine. (Illus.). 176p. 1967. 5.95 (ISBN 0-686-55819-7). French & Eur.

Etra, Jonathan, et al. Junk Food: America's Fast Food Miracle. 1980. 17.95 (ISBN 0-8037-4952-X). Dial.

Gifft, Helen, et al. Nutrition, Behavior & Change. LC 79-170033. 1972. ref. ed. 18.95 (ISBN 0-13-627836-1). P-H.

Henisch, Bridget Ann. Fast and Feast: Food in Medieval Society. LC 76-15677. (Illus.). 1977. 15.95 (ISBN 0-271-01230-7). Pa St U Pr.

Kasper, Rick. How to Be Fit & Free. 1978. pap. 3.25 (ISBN 0-8307-0580-5, 54-073-03). Regal.

Khare, Ravindra S. Hindu Hearth & Home. 300p. 1976. 16.00x (ISBN 0-8002-1493-5). Intl Pubns Serv.

Lee, Kay & Lee, Marshall. America's Favorites. (Illus.). 160p. 1980. 17.95 (ISBN 0-399-12514-0). Putnam.

McLaughlin, Terence. If You Like It Don't Eat It: Dietary Fads and Fancies. LC 78-61206. 1979. 10.00x (ISBN 0-87663-332-7). Universe.

Mahoney, Michael J. & Mahoney, Kathryn. Permanent Weight Control: A Total Solution to the Dieter's Dilemma. 192p. 1976. 13.95 (ISBN 0-393-08736-0). Norton.

Manning. Society & Food: The Third World. (Sicon Bks Ser). 1977. 3.95 (ISBN 0-408-71304-6). Butterworth.

Milgram, N. W., et al. Food Aversion Learning. (Illus.). 280p. 1977. 22.50 (ISBN 0-306-31040-6, Plenum Pr). Plenum Pub.

Robson, J. K. R., ed. Food, Ecology and Culture: Readings in the Anthropology of Dietary Habits. 1980. 30.25 (ISBN 0-677-16090-9). Gordon.

Robson, John R., et al. Malnutrition, Its Causation & Control. Set. 63.75x (ISBN 0-677-03140-8). Gordon.

Schwartz, George. Food Power. 1979. 10.95 (ISBN 0-07-055673-3, GB). McGraw.

Schwarzrock, Shirley & Wrenn, C. Gilbert. Food As a Crutch. (Coping with Ser.). (Illus.). (gr. 7-12). 1971. pap. text ed. 1.30 (ISBN 0-913476-18-8). Am Guidance.

Simoons, Frederick J. Eat Not This Flesh: Food Avoidances in the Old World. LC 80-22232. (Illus.). xiii, 241p. 1981. Repr. of 1967 ed. lib. bdg. 29.75x (ISBN 0-313-22772-1, SIEN). Greenwood.

Vasey, George. Illustrations of Eating: Displaying the Omnivorous Character of Man & Exhibiting the Natives of Various Countries at Feeding Time, by a Beef-Eater. 1971. Repr. of 1847 ed. 10.00 (ISBN 0-910330-19-0). Grant Dahlstrom.

Waltz, Julie. Food Habit Management. 1978. pap. text ed. 12.95 (ISBN 0-931836-00-X). Northwest Learn.

Wurtman, Richard J. & Wurtman, Judith J., eds. Determinants of the Availability of Nutrients to the Brain. LC 75-14593. (Nutrition & the Brain Ser: Vol. 1). 336p. 1977. 31.50 (ISBN 0-89004-045-1). Raven.

Wyrwickg,. The Development of Food Preferences. 1981. 12.75 (ISBN 0-398-04483-X). C C Thomas.

Young, P. T. & Chaplin, J. P. Studies of Food Preference, Appetite & Dietary Habit. Incl. Pt. III. Palatability & Appetite in Relation to Bodily Need. pap. 5.00 (ISBN 0-685-23300-6); Pt. V. Techniques for Testing Food Preference, & the Significance of Results Obtained with Different Methods. pap. 5.00 (ISBN 0-685-23301-4); Pt. IX. Palatability Versus Appetite As Determinants of the Critical Concentrations of Sucrose & Sodium Chloride. pap. 5.00 (ISBN 0-527-24933-5); Pt. X. Preferences Adrenalectomized Rats for Salt Solutions of Different Concentrations. pap. 5.00 (ISBN 0-685-23303-0). 1945. Kraus Repr.

FOOD HABITS OF ANIMALS

see Animals, Food Habits of

FOOD HANDLING

Christie, A. B. & Christie, Mary C. Food Hygiene & Food Hazards. 2nd ed. (Illus.). 232p. 1977. pap. 5.95 (ISBN 0-571-10902-0, Pub. by Faber & Faber). Merrimack Bk Serv.

Guthrie, Rufus K. Food Sanitation. 2nd ed. (Illus.). 1980. lib. bdg. 22.50 (ISBN 0-87055-361-5). AVI.

Hess, John L. & Hess, Karen. The Taste of America. 1977. pap. 2.95 (ISBN 0-14-004535-X). Penguin.

Jernigan, Anna K. Food Sanitation: Study Course. LC 73-146936. (Illus.). 67p. 1971. pap. text ed. 6.95x (ISBN 0-8138-0815-4). Iowa St U Pr.

Longree, Karla. Quantity Food Sanitation. 3rd ed. LC 80-11551. 1980. 31.50 (ISBN 0-471-06424-6, Pub. by Wiley Interscience). Wiley.

--Sanitary Techniques in Food Service. LC 81-3047. 235p. 1982. text ed. 13.50 (ISBN 0-471-08820-X). Wiley.

Nickerson, J. & Sinskay, A. Microbiology of Food & Food Processing. 1972. 18.50 (ISBN 0-444-00124-7, North Holland). Elsevier.

Rajagopalan, S. Guide to Simple Sanitary Measures for the Control of Enteric Diseases. (Also avail. in French, supl. with a chapter on food sanitation). 1974. 12.80 (ISBN 92-4-154047-8). World Health.

Rimmer, Peter J. & Drakakis-Smith, David W., eds. Food Shelter & Transport. (Department of Human Geography Publications Ser.). 1978. pap. 8.75 (ISBN 0-7081-0670-6). Bks Australia.

Rudman, Jack. Food Service Worker. (Career Examination Ser.: C-260). (Cloth bdg. avail. on request). pap. 8.00 (ISBN 0-8373-0260-9). Natl Learning.

--Institution Food Administrator. (Career Examination Ser.: C-2121). (Cloth bdg. avail. on request). 1977. pap. 10.00 (ISBN 0-8373-2121-2). Natl Learning.

Scriven, Carl & Stevens, James. Food Equipment Facts. new ed. LC 80-67617. (First Ser.). 429p. (Orig.). 1980. pap. 10.50 (ISBN 0-9604902-0-5); pap. 13.50 ring binder (ISBN 0-686-77532-5). Concept Design.

FOOD INDUSTRY AND TRADE

see also Farm Produce; Food Additives; Food Prices; Food Supply; Produce Trade; Snack Foods;
also individual processed food and processing industries, e.g. Cheese and Dairying; Meat Industry and Trade

Altschul, Aaron A., ed. New Protein Foods. (Food Science & Technology Ser.). 1974. Vol. 1A, 1974. 56.00, by subscription 48.00 (ISBN 0-12-054801-1); Vol. 2B 1976. 48.00, by subscription 42.00 (ISBN 0-12-054802-X). Acad Pr.

Asian Food Processing Industries. 1979. pap. 16.50 (ISBN 92-833-1409-3, APO74, APO). Unipub.

Ayres, John C. & Kirschman, John C., eds. Impact of Toxiology on Food Processing. (Institute of Food Technologists Basic Symposia Ser.). (Illus.). 1981. lib. bdg. 45.00 (ISBN 0-87055-388-7). AVI.

BCC Staff. Plastics in Food Packaging P-034. 1980. 975.00 (ISBN 0-89336-163-1). BCC.

--Specialty Foods Ga-042: New Developments. 1979. text ed. 675.00 (ISBN 0-89336-138-0). BCC.

Bender, A. E. Dictionary of Nutrition & Food Technology. 1977. 28.50 (ISBN 0-8206-0214-0). Chem Pub.

Bender, Arnold. Food Processing & Nutrition. (Food Science & Technology Ser.). 1978. 33.00 (ISBN 0-12-086450-9). Acad Pr.

Bender, Filmore, et al. Systems Analysis for the Food Industry. (Illus.). 1976. pap. text ed. 27.50 (ISBN 0-87055-306-2). AVI.

Bibliography of Food & Agricultural Marketing. (Second Ser: No. 3). 1978. pap. 8.25 (ISBN 92-5-100248-7, F726, FAO). Unipub.

Birch & Blakebrough. Enzymes & Food Processing: An/Industry-University Co-Operation Symposium. Reading, England, April 1980. (Illus.). 295p. text ed. 44.00 (ISBN 0-85334-935-5, Pub. by Applied Sci England). J K Burgess.

Birch, G. G., et al, eds. Enzymes & Food Processing. (Illus.). xii, 295p. 1981. 44.00x (ISBN 0-85334-935-5). Intl Ideas.

Bloom, Gordon F. Productivity in the Food Industry: Problems & Potential. 240p. 1972. 18.50x (ISBN 0-262-02088-2). MIT Pr.

Braton, Norman R. Cryogenic Recycling & Processing. 256p. 1980. 67.95 (ISBN 0-8493-5779-9). CRC Pr.

Breimyer, Harold. Preparing for the Contingency of Intense Pressure on Food - Producing Resources. (Agriculture Committee Ser.). 1981. pap. write for info. (ISBN 0-89068-060-4). Natl Planning.

Brennan, J. G., et al. Food Engineering Operations. 2nd ed. (Illus.). 1976. 61.20x (ISBN 0-85334-694-1, Pub. by Applied Science). Burgess-Intl Ideas.

Bryan, John R. Managing Restaurant Personnel: A Handbook for Food Service Operators. LC 73-94217. (Illus.). 192p. 1974. 12.95 (ISBN 0-912016-33-7). Lebhar Friedman.

Business Communications Co. Convenience Foods & Microwave, GA-044: Directions. 1980. 725.00 (ISBN 0-89336-227-1). BCC.

Business Communications Co., ed. Foods Under Glass, GA-046. 1980. 675.00 (ISBN 0-89336-229-8). BCC.

--Home Do-It Yourself Market. 1980. 675.00 (ISBN 0-89336-232-8, GB-054). BCC.

--New Trends in Food Retailing, GA-045. 1980. 825.00 (ISBN 0-89336-228-X). BCC.

--Retail Fast Foods, GA-038: Business Opportunities. 1980. 675.00 (ISBN 0-89336-236-0). BCC.

Cantor, Sidney M., ed. Use of Sugars & Other Carbohydrates in the Food Industry. LC 55-4135. (Advances in Chemistry Ser: No. 12). 1955. pap. 10.00 (ISBN 0-8412-0013-0). Am Chemical.

Casper, M. E. Energy-Saving Techniques for the Food Industry. LC 77-71931. (Energy Technology Rev. 13; Food Technology Rev. 42). (Illus.). 1977. 39.00 (ISBN 0-8155-0663-5). Noyes.

Cassava Harvesting & Processing. 1979. pap. 5.00 (ISBN 0-88936-188-6, IDRC114, IDRC). Unipub.

Charalambous, George, ed. Analysis of Foods & Beverages: Headspace Techniques. 1978. 34.00 (ISBN 0-12-169050-4). Acad Pr.

Charalambous, George & Inglett, George, eds. The Quality of Foods & Beverages: Chemistry & Technology, 2 vols, Vols. 1 & 2. 1981. Vol. 1. 29.50 (ISBN 0-12-169101-2); Vol. 2. write for info. (ISBN 0-12-169102-0). Acad Pr.

Charm, Stanley E. Fundamentals of Food Engineering. 3rd ed. 1978. pap. text ed. 27.00 (ISBN 0-87055-313-5). AVI.

Chiba, H., et al, eds. Food Science & Technology: Proceedings of the 5th Int'l C. LC 79-20898. (Dev. in Food Science Ser.: Vol. 2). 448p. 1980. 90.25 (ISBN 0-444-99770-9). Elsevier.

Chou, Marylin & Harmon, David P., Jr. Critical Food Issues of the Nineteen Eighties. LC 79-14718. (Pergamon Policy Studies). (Illus.). 1979. 44.00 (ISBN 0-08-024611-7); pap. 9.95 (ISBN 0-08-024639-7). Pergamon.

Christian, Portia, ed. Agricultural Enterprises Management in an Urban-Industrial Society: A Guide to Information Sources. LC 76-27856. (Management Information Guide: No. 34). 1978. 30.00 (ISBN 0-8103-0834-7). Gale.

Clement, Jean-Michel. Dictionnaire des Industries Alimentaires. 361p. (Fr.). 1978. 32.50 (ISBN 0-686-56949-0, M-6071). French & Eur.

Clydesdale, Fergus M. & Francis, Frederick J. Human Ecological Issues: A Reader. 320p. (Orig.). 1980. pap. text ed. 8.95 (ISBN 0-8403-2197-X). Kendall-Hunt.

Code of Ethics for International Trade in Food. 5p. 1979. pap. 7.50 (ISBN 92-5-101004-8, F2159, FAO). Unipub.

Cooperative Processing of Agricultural Products. 52p. 1975. pap. 7.50 (ISBN 0-685-54186-X, 744, FAO). Unipub.

Corley, T. A. Quaker Enterprises in Biscuits: Huntley & Palmers of Reading, 1822-1972. 1972. text ed. 10.50x (ISBN 0-09-111320-2). Humanities.

CRC Handbook of Agricultural Productivity, Vol. II: Animal Productivity. 400p. 1981. 64.95 (ISBN 0-8493-3963-4). CRC Pr.

Crochetti, Gino & Stella, Frank. What's for Dinner Tomorrow? Corporate Views of New Food Products. LC 79-93419. 1979. pap. 5.00 (ISBN 0-918780-15-2). Inform.

Crosby, N. T. Food Packaging Materials: Aspects of Analysis & Migration of Contaminants. (Illus.). 188p. 1981. 28.00x (ISBN 0-85334-926-6). Intl Ideas.

Cross, Jennifer. Supermarket Trap: The Consumer & the Food Industry. rev. ed. LC 75-10806. (Midland Bks.: No. 199). (Illus.). 320p. 1976. 12.50x (ISBN 0-253-35582-6); pap. 3.50x (ISBN 0-253-20199-3). Ind U Pr.

Cushman, Ronald A. & Daggett, Willard. Supermarket Merchandising. (Co-Operative Education Wkbk. Ser). (gr. 7-12). 1976. text ed. 4.50 (ISBN 0-87005-155-5); tchrs' manual 2.50 (ISBN 0-87005-158-X). Fairchild.

Darrah, L. B. Food Marketing. rev. ed. 1971. 27.95 (ISBN 0-8260-2345-2). Wiley.

Davies, R., et al. Intermediate Moisture Foods. (Illus.). 1976. 40.00x (ISBN 0-85334-702-6). Intl Ideas.

Desrosier, Norman W. Rietz Master Food Guide. (Illus.). 1978. pap. text ed. 23.00 (ISBN 0-87055-246-5). AVI.

Desrosier, Norman W. & Desrosier, John N. Economics of New Food Product Development. (Illus.). 1971. 28.50 (ISBN 0-87055-102-7). AVI.

Desrosier, Norman W., ed. Elements of Food Technology. (Illus.). 1977. pap. 19.50 (ISBN 0-87055-284-8). AVI.

Development of Food Marketing Systems for Large Urban Areas, Part Two: Asia and Far East. (Illus.). 79p. 1976. pap. 7.50 (ISBN 0-685-65004-9, F748, FAO). Unipub.

Downey, W. K., ed. Food Quality & Nutrition: Research Priorities for Thermal Processing. (Illus.). 1978. text ed. 71.30x (ISBN 0-85334-803-0, Pub. by Applied Science). Burgess-Intl Ideas.

Doyle, Edwin S. & Mittler, Abe, eds. Control of Critical Points in Food Processing: A Systems Approach. (Illus.). 270p. 1977. text ed. 25.00 (ISBN 0-937774-04-9). Food Processors.

Droms, W. G. Food Store Financial Analysis for Store Operations People. 1981. 14.00 (ISBN 0-201-03159-0). A-W.

Educational Research Council of America. Food Technologist. Ferris, Theodore N. & Marchak, John P., eds. (Real People at Work: Series M). (Illus., Orig.). (gr. 5). 1976. pap. text ed. 2.25 (ISBN 0-89247-102-6). Changing Times.

Energetics of Agriculture & Food Production with Special Emphasis on the Australian Situation. (Bulletin Ser.: No. 288). 20p. 1975. pap. 6.00 (ISBN 0-686-71831-3, CO 42, CSIRO). Unipub.

FAO Production Yearbook, Vol. 33. 309p. 1980. pap. 28.00 (ISBN 92-5-000936-4, F2050, FAO). Unipub.

Farrall, A. W. Food Engineering Systems: Operations, Vol. No. 1. (Illus.). 1976. lib. bdg. 37.50 (ISBN 0-87055-190-6); pap. text ed. 25.00 (ISBN 0-87055-297-X). AVI.

Farrall, Arthur W. Engineering for Dairy & Food Products. 2nd ed. LC 79-1171. (Illus.). 1980. lib. bdg. 28.50 (ISBN 0-88275-859-4). Krieger.

--Food Engineering System, Vol. 2: Utilities. (Illus.). 1979. pap. text ed. 23.50 (ISBN 0-87055-283-X). AVI.

Financial Analysis Group Ltd. Major Food Manufacturing Companies of Europe. 1974. 135.00x (ISBN 0-86010-006-5). Intl Pubns Serv.

Food Machinery. (Machinery Studies). 1979. 295.00 (ISBN 0-686-31535-9). Busn Trend.

Food Processing, GA-041: Developments. 1978. 525.00 (ISBN 0-89336-137-2). BCC.

Food Processors Institute. A Guide for Waste Management in the Food Processing Industry, Vol. II. Warrick, Louis F., ed. 555p. 1979. pap. text ed. 15.00 (ISBN 0-937774-01-4). Food Processors.

--A Guide for Waste Management in the Food Processing Industry, Vol. 1. Katsuyama, Allen M., ed. LC 79-115086. 276p. 1979. pap. text ed. 50.00 (ISBN 0-937774-00-6). Food Processors.

--Principles of Food Processing Sanitation. Katsuyama, Allen, ed. LC 79-57624. 303p. (Orig.). 1980. pap. 40.00 (ISBN 0-937774-03-0). Food Processors.

--Shelf Life - A Key to Sharpening Your Competitive Edge: Proceedings. 64p. (Orig.). 1981. pap. 7.50 (ISBN 0-937774-05-7). Food Processors.

Food Production in the Canadian Environment. (Perspections No. 3). 1978. pap. 4.25 (ISBN 0-660-00515-8, SSC90, SSC). Unipub.

Food Trades Directory & Food Buyer's Yearbook 1981-82. 17th ed. 1981. 125.00x (ISBN 0-686-73787-3). Intl Pubns Serv.

Food Trades Directory & Food Buyers Yearbook, 1979-80. 16th ed. LC 66-83910. 1979. 82.50x (ISBN 0-7079-6912-3). Intl Pubns Serv.

Fox, Brian A. & Cameron, Allan G. Food Science: A Chemical Approach. 3rd ed. 1977. 10.50x (ISBN 0-8448-0938-1). Crane-Russak Co.

Friedland, William H., et al. Manufacturing Green Gold: Capital, Labor, & Technology in the Lettuce Industry. (American Sociological Association on Rose Monograph). (Illus.). Date not set. price not set (ISBN 0-521-24284-3); pap. price not set (ISBN 0-521-28584-4). Cambridge U Pr.

Furia, Thomas E., ed. Handbook of Food Additives, Vol. 2. 2nd ed. (Handbook Ser.). 432p. 1980. 59.95 (ISBN 0-8493-0543-8). CRC Pr.

Garvey, Olive W. Produce or Starve: Bringing up America. LC 76-21117. 240p. 1976. 8.95 (ISBN 0-916054-33-0, Caroline Hse Inc); pap. 4.95 (ISBN 0-916054-34-9). Green Hill.

Giant Food Product Safety & Evaluation Policy. 1976. 1-5 copies 6.50 ea. (ISBN 0-914176-06-4); 6-15 copies 6.25 ea.; 16-25 copies 6.00 ea.; 26 or more copies 5.75 ea. Wash Busn Info.

Glicksman, M. Gum Technology in the Food Industry. (Food Science & Technology Ser). 1969. 68.00 (ISBN 0-12-286350-X). Acad Pr.

Goldblith, S. A., et al, eds. Freeze Drying & Advanced Food Technology. 1975. 113.00 (ISBN 0-12-288450-7). Acad Pr.

Gottlieb, Richard, ed. The American Food Directory, 2 vols. 1600p. 1982. 135.00x (ISBN 0-686-30357-1); pap. 110.00x (ISBN 0-686-30358-X). Grey Hse Pub.

Green, Eric F., et al. Profitable Food & Beverage Management: Planning. 1978. text ed. 19.75x (ISBN 0-8104-9480-9). Hayden.

Green, John H. & Kramer, Amihud. Food Processing Waste Management. (Illus.). 1979. text ed. 46.00 (ISBN 0-87055-331-3). AVI.

Guither, Harold D. The Food Lobbyists: Behind the Scenes of Food & Agri-Politics. LC 79-6734. 352p. 1980. 27.95 (ISBN 0-669-03539-4). Lexington Bks.

Hall, Carl W., et al. Encyclopedia of Food Engineering. (Illus.). 1971. lib. bdg. 79.00 (ISBN 0-87055-086-1). AVI.

Harper, Judson M. Extrusion of Foods. 1981. vol. 1, 224 pgs. 64.95 (ISBN 0-8493-5203-7); vol. 2, 176 pgs. 49.95 (ISBN 0-8493-5204-5). CRC Pr.

Hayward, George S. & York, Glen. Food Store Distributor: A Retail Sales Guide. LC 76-29113. 1977. 14.75 (ISBN 0-912016-57-4). Lebhar Friedman.

Heid, John L. & Joslyn, Maynard A. Fundamentals of Food Processing Operations: Ingredients, Methods & Packaging. (Illus.). 1967. 35.00 (ISBN 0-87055-014-4). AVI.

Heldman, D. R. & Singh, R. P. Food Process Engineering. 2nd ed. (Illus.). 1981. pap. text ed. 26.50 (ISBN 0-87055-380-1). AVI.

Henrickson, Robert L. Meat, Poultry & Seafood Technology. LC 77-25350. (Illus.). 1978. ref. ed. 18.95 (ISBN 0-13-568600-8). P-H.

Herschdoerfer, S. M. Quality Control in the Food Industry. Vol.1. 1967. 61.00 (ISBN 0-12-342901-3); Vol. 2. 1968. 70.50 (ISBN 0-12-342902-1); Vol. 3. 1972. 77.50 (ISBN 0-12-342903-X). Acad Pr.

Hightower, Jim. Eat Your Heart Out: How Food Profiteers Victimize the Consumer. 1976. pap. 1.95 (ISBN 0-394-72094-6, Vin). Random.

Hinich, Melvin J. & Staelin, Richard. Consumer Protection Legislation & the Food Industry. (Policy Studies). 1980. text ed. 16.25 (ISBN 0-08-025093-9). Pergamon.

Horst, Thomas. At Home Abroad: Domestic & Foreign Operations of the American Food-Processing Industry. LC 73-18204. 120p. 1974. text ed. 17.50 (ISBN 0-88410-259-9). Ballinger Pub.

Horwitz, Maxine. Inside the Food Processor. rev. & updated ed. 1981. 8.95 (ISBN 0-686-75132-9). Good Food Bks.

Huddleston, Barbara & McLin, Jon, eds. Political Investments in Food Production: National & International Case Studies. LC 79-5025. 256p. 1979. 19.95x (ISBN 0-253-16219-X); pap. 10.95x (ISBN 0-253-28197-0). Ind U Pr.

Hungate, Lois A. & Sherman, Ralph W. Food & Economics. (Illus.). 1979. pap. text ed. 14.50 (ISBN 0-87055-229-5). AVI.

Inglett, George E. Symposium: Processing Agricultural & Municipal Wastes. (Illus.). 1973. text ed. 23.50 (ISBN 0-87055-139-6). AVI.

Inglett, George E., ed. Fabricated Foods. (Illus.). 395p. 1975. lib. bdg. 25.00 (ISBN 0-87055-179-5). AVI.

Instrumentation in the Food Industry: Including Papers from the Water & Wastewater Industries Division, Minneapolis, Minnesota, 1980, Vol. 3. 60p. pap. text ed. 12.00x (ISBN 0-87664-472-8). Instru Soc.

International Congress of Food & Science Technology-1st-London, 1962. Food & Science Technology, 5 vols. Leitch, J. M., ed. Incl. Vol. 1. Chemical & Physical Aspects of Foods. 1969; Vol. 2. Biological & Microbiological Aspects of Foods. 1969; Vol. 3. Quality Analysis & Composition of Foods. 1969; Vol. 4. Manufacture & Distribution of Foods. 1969; Vol. 5. Proceedings. 1969. (Illus.). Set. 608.00x (ISBN 0-677-10290-9). Gordon.

Johnson, Arnold & Peterson, Martin, eds. Encyclopedia of Food Technology. (Technologic Food Encyclopedia). (Illus.). 1974. 79.50 (ISBN 0-87055-157-4). AVI.

Jowitt, R., ed. Hygenic Design & Operation of Food Plant. (Illus., American edition). 1980. pap. text ed. 27.50 (ISBN 0-87055-345-3). AVI.

Kahrl, W. Introduction to Modern Food & Beverage Service. ref. ed. (Illus.). 240p. 1976. 17.95 (ISBN 0-13-488270-9). P-H.

Kallet, Arthur & Schlink, F. J. One Hundred Million Guinea Pigs: Dangers in Everyday Foods, Drugs, & Cosmetics. LC 75-39252. (Getting & Spending: the Consumer's Dilemma). 1976. Repr. of 1933 ed. 18.00x (ISBN 0-405-08025-5). Arno.

Kelly, Hugh J. Food Service Purchasing: Principles & Practice. new ed. LC 76-49750. 176p. 1976. 18.95 (ISBN 0-912016-55-8). Lebhar Friedman.
Kleeman, Elayne J. & Voltz, Jeanne. How to Turn a Passion for Food into Profit. LC 78-64800. 1979. 9.95 (ISBN 0-89256-086-X). Rawson Wade.
Knight, John & Kotschevar, Lendal H. Quantity Food Production, Planning, & Management. (Illus.). 1979. text ed. 18.95 (ISBN 0-8436-2129-X). CBI Pub.
Komarik, Stephan, et al. Food Products Formulary: Meats, Poultry, Fish & Shellfish. (Illus.). 1974. text ed. 49.50 (ISBN 0-87055-152-3). AVI.
Kotschevar, Lendal H. Quantity Food Production. 3rd ed. (Illus.). 1975. 29.20x (ISBN 0-85334-632-1). Intl Ideas.
--Standards Principles & Techniques in Quantity Food Production. rev. 3rd ed. LC 73-84173. (Illus.). 672p. 1974. 17.95 (ISBN 0-8436-0583-9). CBI Pub.
Kramer, Amihud & Twigg, Bernard. Quality Control for the Food Industry: Vol. 2, Applications. 3rd ed. (Illus.). 1973. text ed. 31.50 (ISBN 0-87055-127-2). AVI.
Kramer, Amihud & Twigg, Bernard A. Quality Control for the Food Industry Vol. 1: Fundamentals. 3rd ed. (Illus.). 1970. text ed. 31.50 (ISBN 0-87055-072-1). AVI.
Kramlich, W. E., et al. Processed Meats. (Illus.). 1973. 32.00 (ISBN 0-87055-141-8). AVI.
Lamb, Ruth D. American Chamber of Horrors: The Truth About Food & Drugs. LC 75-39255. (Getting & Spending: the Consumer's Dilemma). (Illus.). 1976. Repr. of 1936 ed. 24.00x (ISBN 0-405-08028-X). Arno.
Lee, Kay & Lee, Marshall. America's Favorites. (Illus.). 160p. 1980. 17.95 (ISBN 0-399-12514-0). Putnam.
Leed, Theodore W. & German, Gene A. Food Merchandising: Principles & Practices. rev. ed. LC 73-88739. (Illus.). 1979. 18.95 (ISBN 0-912016-77-9). Lebhar Friedman.
Leniger, H. A. & Beverloo, W. A. Food Process Engineering. LC 75-14021. 550p. 1975. lib. bdg. 63.00 (ISBN 90-277-0605-0); pap. 26.35 (ISBN 90-277-0659-X). Kluwer Boston.
Lilley. Information Sources in Agriculture & Food Science. (Butterworths Guides to Information Sources Ser.). 1981. text ed. write for info. (ISBN 0-408-10612-3). Butterworth.
Lillicrap, D. H. Food & Beverage Service. (Illus.). 218p. 1971. pap. 13.95x (ISBN 0-7131-1664-1). Intl Ideas.
Linko, P., et al, eds. Food Process Engineering: Vol. 1 Food Processing Systems. (Illus.). xii, 981p. 1980. 210.00x (ISBN 0-85334-896-0). Burgess-Intl Ideas.
--Food Process Engineering: Volume 2--Enzyme Engineering in Food Processing. (Illus.). vii, 328p. 1980. 75.00x (ISBN 0-85334-897-9). Burgess-Intl Ideas.
Loncin, Marcel & Merson, Richard L. Food Engineering: Principles & Selected Applications. LC 78-31231. (Food Science & Technology Ser.). 1979. 54.00 (ISBN 0-12-454550-5). Acad Pr.
Lynch, R. L. & Lunch, Richard L., eds. Food Marketing. (Career Competencies in Marketing Ser.). (Illus.). 1979. pap. text ed. 5.36 (ISBN 0-07-051483-6, G); teacher's manual & key 3.00 (ISBN 0-07-051484-4). McGraw.
Mallowe, Charles A., Jr. & McLaughlin, Daniel J. Food Marketing & Distribution: Selected Readings. LC 70-134466. 400p. 1971. pap. 12.95 (ISBN 0-912016-08-6). Lebhar Friedman.
Marion, Bruce W., et al. The Food Retailing Industry: Market Structure, Profits, & Prices. LC 78-19751. 1979. 22.95 (ISBN 0-03-046106-5). Praeger.
Matz, Samuel A. Snack Food Technology. (Illus.). 1976. text ed. 39.00 (ISBN 0-87055-193-0). AVI.
Miller, Richard K., et al. Noise Control Soultions for the Food Products Industry. 45.00 (ISBN 0-89671-003-3). Fairmont Pr.
Morgan-Grampian Books, ed. Food Ingredient & Machinery Survey, 1981. 142p. 1981. 50.00x (ISBN 0-686-75514-6, Pub. by Morgan-Grampian Bk). State Mutual Bk.
Muller, H. G. & Tobin, G. Nutrition & Food Processing. 240p. 1980. 35.00x (ISBN 0-85664-540-0, Pub. by Croom Helm England). State Mutual Bk.
Natural & Health Food Market, GA-037. 1978. 675.00 (ISBN 0-89336-096-1). BCC.
Neigoff, Anne. Dinner's Ready. LC 76-150805. (Career Awareness-Community Helpers Ser.). (Illus.). (gr. k-2). 1971. 5.25g (ISBN 0-8075-1594-9). A Whitman.
Non-Profit Food Stores. 1977. pap. 3.00 (ISBN 0-9601626-0-7). Strongforce.
Organization for Economic Cooperation & Development. The Formation of Food Prices & Their Behaviour in Times of Inflation. (Agricultural Products & Markets Ser.). 124p. 1973. 2.50x (ISBN 92-64-11105-0). OECD.
The Organization of Trade in Food Products: An Original Anthology. LC 75-27638. (World Food Supply Ser). (Illus.). 1976. 12.00x (ISBN 0-405-07799-8). Arno.
Ory, Robert L. & St. Angelo, Allen J., eds. Enzymes in Food & Beverage Processing. LC 77-6645. (ACS Symposium Ser: No. 47). 1977. 23.00 (ISBN 0-8412-0375-X). Am Chemical.
Panel, Vienna, March 18-22, 1974. Requirements for the Irradiaton of Food on a Commercial Scale: Proceedings. (Illus.). 216p. 1975. pap. 20.50 (ISBN 92-0-111275-0, ISP394, IAEA). Unipub.
Paul, Pauline C., et al, eds. Food Theory & Applications. LC 79-172953. 1972. text ed. 27.95 (ISBN 0-471-67250-5). Wiley.
Pintauro, N. D. Food Flavoring Processes. LC 76-5100. (Food Technology Review Ser.: No. 32). (Illus.). 1976. 39.00 (ISBN 0-8155-0618-X). Noyes.
--Food Processing Enzymes-Recent Developments. LC 79-84426. (Food Technology Review Ser.: No. 52). (Illus.). 1979. 42.00 (ISBN 0-8155-0748-8). Noyes.
Pitcher, Wayne H., Jr. Immobilized Enzymes for Food Processing. 232p. 1980. 63.95 (ISBN 0-8493-5345-9). CRC Pr.
Potter, Norman N. Food Science. 3rd ed. 1978. text ed. 22.00 (ISBN 0-87055-275-9). AVI.
Powers, Jo Marie. Basics of Quantity Food Production. LC 78-23194. (Service Management Ser.). 1979. text ed. 22.50 (ISBN 0-471-03421-5). Wiley.
Rechcigl, M., ed. Handbook of Nutritive Value of Processed Food: Animal Foodstuffs, Vol. II. 512p. 1981. 68.95 (ISBN 0-686-75117-5). CRC Pr.
--Handbook of Nutritive Value of Processed Food: Food for Human Use, Vol. I. 608p. 1981. 79.95 (ISBN 0-8493-3951-0). CRC Pr.
Rechcigl, Miloslav, Jr. CRC Handbook of Agricultural Productivity, Vol. I: Plant Productivity. 464p. 1981. 72.95 (ISBN 0-8493-3961-8). CRC Pr.
Recommended International Standards for Foods for Infants & Children. (Codex Alimentarius Commission). 33p. 1977. pap. 4.50 (ISBN 0-685-86028-0, F612, FAO). Unipub.
Recommended International Standards for Quick Frozen Raspberries. (Codex Alimentarius Commission). 8p. 1977. pap. 4.50 (ISBN 0-685-86029-9, F609, FAO). Unipub.
Reid, Margaret G. Food for People. LC 75-26312. (World Food Supply Ser). (Illus.). 1976. Repr. of 1943 ed. 38.00x (ISBN 0-405-07790-4). Arno.
Report of the Joint FAO-WHO Food Standards Regional Conference for Asia, Bangkok, 8-15 Dec., 1975. (Codes Alimentarius Commission). (Illus.). 1977. pap. 12.00 (ISBN 0-685-85732-8, FAO). Unipub.
Robbins, P. M. Convenience Foods-Recent Technology. LC 76-24147. (Food Technology Review: No. 37). (Illus.). 1977. 39.00 (ISBN 0-8155-0641-4). Noyes.
Robbins, William. The American Food Scandal. LC 73-19841. 280p. 1974. pap. 3.50 (ISBN 0-688-05299-1). Morrow.
Ronco, William. Food Co-Ops: An Alternative to Shopping in Supermarkets. LC 74-211. 224p. 1974. pap. 3.95 (ISBN 0-8070-0881-8, BP498). Beacon Pr.
Ross, Lynne & McHenry, Roberta. Food Purchasing: Study Course. LC 70-146935. 97p. 1971. pap. text ed. 6.95x (ISBN 0-8138-0810-3). Iowa St U Pr.
Ross, Lynne N. Metric Measurement in Food Preparation & Service. (Illus.). 1978. pap. 4.50 (ISBN 0-8138-0985-1). Iowa St U Pr.
Roth, June. The Food-Depression Connection. 1979. pap. 4.95 (ISBN 0-8092-7220-2). Contemp Bks.
Rutkowski, ed. Advances in Smoking of Foods. 1977. text ed. 27.00 (ISBN 0-08-022002-9). Pergamon.
Schlink, F. J. Eat, Drink & Be Wary. LC 75-39273. (Getting & Spending: a Consumer's Dilemma). Repr. of 1935 ed. 18.00x (ISBN 0-405-08045-X). Arno.
Scriven, Carl & Stevens, James. Food Equipment Facts. new ed. LC 80-67617. (First Ser.). 429p. (Orig.). 1980. pap. 10.50 (ISBN 0-9604902-0-5); pap. 13.50 ring binder (ISBN 0-686-77532-5). Concept Design.
Ser-Vol-Tel Institute. Food Care & Food Storage. (Foodservice Career Education Ser.). 1974. pap. 4.95 (ISBN 0-8436-2014-5). CBI Pub.
Smith, Laura L. & Minor, Lewis J. Food Service Science. (Illus.). 1974. pap. text ed. 21.50 (ISBN 0-87055-382-8). AVI.
The State of Food & Agriculture, 1975. (FAO Agriculture Ser: No. 1). (Illus.). 150p. 1976. pap. 29.00 (ISBN 0-685-76006-5, FAO). Unipub.
Stewart, George & Amerine, Maynard. Introduction to Food Science. (Food Science & Technology Ser). 1973. text ed. 18.95 (ISBN 0-12-670250-0). Acad Pr.
Strang, William A. Restaurant & Food Store Surveys, 1979: Evaluating the Potential for a Small Business Information System in Wisconsin. (Wisconsin Economy Studies: No. 18). (Orig.). 1979. pap. 5.00 (ISBN 0-86603-007-7). Bureau Busn Res U Wis.
Talbot, Ross, ed. The World Food Problem & U.S. Food Politics & Policies 1972-1976. 350p. 1977. pap. text ed. 8.95x (ISBN 0-8138-0040-4). Iowa St U Pr.
Tannenbaum. Nutritional & Safety Aspects of Food Processing. 1979. 45.00 (ISBN 0-8247-6723-3). Dekker.
Tannenbaum, Steven R. & Wang, Daniel I., eds. Single-Cell Protein II. 1974. text ed. 28.00x (ISBN 0-262-20030-9). MIT Pr.
Tilson, Ann & Weiss, Carol H. The Mail Order Food Guide. 1977. 10.95 (ISBN 0-671-22810-2); pap. 4.95 (ISBN 0-671-23077-8). S&S.
Toledo, Romeo T. Fundamentals of Food Process Engineering. (Illus.). 1980. pap. text ed. 25.50 (ISBN 0-87055-338-0). AVI.
Tressler, Donald K. & Woodroof, Jasper G. Food Products Formulary, Vol. 3: Fruit, Vegetable & Nut Products. (Illus.). 1976. lib. bdg. 49.50 (ISBN 0-87055-202-3). AVI.
Tudge, Colin. The Famine Business. LC 76-28063. 1977. 8.95 (ISBN 0-312-28148-X). St Martin.
U. S. Federal Trade Commission. Chain Stores: Letters from the Chairman of the Federal Trade Commission Transmitting in Response to Senate Resolution No. 224, 3 pts. in 1. LC 75-39243. (Getting & Spending: the Consumer's Dilemma). (Illus.). 1976. Repr. of 1933 ed. 15.00x (ISBN 0-405-08051-4). Arno.
U. S. National Commission on Food Marketing. Food from Farmer to Consumer. LC 75-39286. (Getting & Spending: the Consumer's Dilemma). (Illus.). 1976. Repr. of 1966 ed. 15.00x (ISBN 0-405-08052-2). Arno.
Vara, Albert C. Food & Beverage Industries: A Bibliography & Guidebook. LC 70-102058. (Management Information Guide Ser.: No. 16). 1970. 36.00 (ISBN 0-8103-0816-9). Gale.
Woodroof, J. G. & Luh, B. S. Commercial Fruit Processing. (Illus.). 710p. 1975. lib. bdg. 27.00 (ISBN 0-87055-178-7). AVI.
Workshop on the Interfaces Between Agriculture, Nutrition, & Food Science, 1977. Proceedings. 143p. 1979. pap. 7.25 (ISBN 0-686-70590-4, R087, IRRI). Unipub.
World Food Conference, Ames, Iowa June, 1976. Proceedings. Schaller, Frank, ed. 1977. text ed. 8.50x (ISBN 0-8138-1825-7). Iowa St U Pr.

FOOD INDUSTRY AND TRADE–LAW AND LEGISLATION
see Food Law and Legislation

FOOD INDUSTRY AND TRADE–VOCATIONAL GUIDANCE

Ammerman, Gale. Your Future in Food Technology. rev. ed. (Careers in Depth Ser.). 1980. lib. bdg. 5.97 (ISBN 0-8239-0314-1). Rosen Pr.
Cornelius. Food Service Careers. 1979. text ed. 15.60 (ISBN 0-87002-206-7); tchr's guide free; student's guide 2.96 (ISBN 0-87002-165-6). Bennett IL.
Creasy, Donna N. Food Careers. (Home Economics Careers Ser.). (gr. 10-12). 1977. 6.36 (ISBN 0-13-392712-1); pap. 5.12 (ISBN 0-13-392704-0). P-H.
Endres, Joseph G. Opportunities in Food Science & Technology. (gr. 8 up). 1969. pap. 1.25 (ISBN 0-8442-6480-6). Natl Textbk.

FOOD INSPECTION
see Food Adulteration and Inspection

FOOD LAW AND LEGISLATION
see also subdivision Law and legislation under individual foods

Bigwood, E. J. & Gerard, A. Fundamental Principles & Objectives of a Comparative Food Law, 4 vols. Incl. Vol. 1. General Introduction & Field of Application. 1969 (ISBN 3-8055-0669-4); Vol. 2. Elements of Motivation & Elements of Qualification. 1968. pap. text ed. 35.50 (ISBN 3-8055-0670-8); Vol. 3. Elements of Structure & Institutional Elements. 1970. pap. text ed. 36.00 (ISBN 3-8055-0671-6); Vol. 4. Elements of Control & Sanction; Conclusion; Suggested Outline of a. Modern Food Law. 1971. pap. text ed. 52.25 (ISBN 3-8055-1305-4). (Illus.). Set. pap. text ed. 96.00 (ISBN 3-8055-1332-1). S Karger.
Codex Alimentarius Commission. Report of the Twelfth Session. 1979. pap. 7.50 (ISBN 92-5-100628-8, F1511, FAO). Unipub.
Cummings, Richard O. American & His Food: A History of Food Habits in the United States. LC 74-112536. (Rise of Urban America). (Illus.). 1970. Repr. of 1940 ed. 16.00 (ISBN 0-405-02445-2). Arno.
Economics & Sociology Department, Iowa State College. Wartime Farm & Food Policy. LC 75-26304. (World Food Supply Ser). (Illus.). 1976. Repr. of 1943 ed. 31.00x (ISBN 0-405-07783-1). Arno.
Fisher, Patty & Bender, A. E. The Value of Food. 3rd ed. (Illus.). 1979. pap. 5.95x (ISBN 0-19-859465-8). Oxford U Pr.
Food Trades Directory & Food Buyers Yearbook, 1979-80. 16th ed. LC 66-83910. 1979. 82.50x (ISBN 0-7079-6912-3). Intl Pubns Serv.
Hui, Y. H. United States Food Laws, Regulations & Standards. LC 78-26668. 1979. 46.00 (ISBN 0-471-03182-8, Pub by Wiley-Interscience). Wiley.
International Food Standards & National Laws. 1978. pap. 22.00 (ISBN 92-5-000313-7, F1406, FAO). Unipub.
Jackson, Charles O. Food & Drug Legislation in the New Deal. 1970. 14.50x (ISBN 0-691-04598-4). Princeton U Pr.
Joint FAO-IAEA-WHO Expert Committee, Rome, 1964. Technical Basis for Legislation on Irradiated Food: A Report. (Technical Report Ser: No. 316). 56p. (Eng, Fr, Rus, & Span.). 1966. pap. 2.00 (ISBN 92-4-120316-1). World Health.
Manuals of Food Quality Control, 3 vols. Incl. Vol. 1. Food Control Laboratory. 75p. pap. 9.00 (ISBN 92-5-100839-6, F1960); Vol. 2. Additives, Contaminants, Techniques. 317p. pap. 22.00 (ISBN 92-5-100867-1, F1961); Vol. 3. Commodities. 420p. pap. 29.50 (ISBN 92-5-100844-2, F1962). (FAO Food & Nutrition Papers: No. 14). 1980 (FAO). Unipub.
Merrill, Richard A. & Hutt, Peter B. Food & Drug Law, Cases & Materials. LC 80-23167. (University Casebook Ser.). 1028p. 1980. text ed. write for info. (ISBN 0-88277-016-0). Foundation Pr.
North, Hallie B. Commercial Food Patents, U. S. Nineteen Seventy-Nine. (Illus.). 1980. lib. bdg. 30.00 (ISBN 0-87055-358-5). AVI.
An Outline of Food Law (Structure, Principles, Main Provisions) (FAO Legislative Studies: No. 7). 105p. 1975. pap. 13.00 (ISBN 0-685-54196-7, F1020, FAO). Unipub.
Paarlberg, Don. Food & Agricultural Policy. 1978. 15.25 (ISBN 0-8447-2109-3); pap. 7.25 (ISBN 0-8447-2108-5). Am Enterprise.
Recommended International Code of Hygenic Practice for Egg Products. 1979. pap. 4.50 (ISBN 92-5-100544-3, F1517, FAO). Unipub.
Recommended International Code of Practice for the Processing & Handling of Quick-Frozen Foods. 6p. 1978. pap. 4.00 (ISBN 0-685-60671-6, F1426, FAO). Unipub.
Recommended International Standard for Canned Green Peas. (Codex Alimentarius Commission). 16p. 1975. pap. 4.50 (ISBN 0-685-54191-6, F599, FAO). Unipub.
Recommended International Standard for Canned Plums. (Codex Alimentarius Commission). 18p. 1975. pap. 4.50 (ISBN 0-685-54190-8, F600, FAO). Unipub.
Recommended International Standard for Canned Raspberries. (Codex Alimentarius Commission Ser). 16p. 1975. pap. 4.50 (ISBN 0-685-54189-4, F601, FAO). Unipub.
Recommended International Standard for Canned Sardines & Sardine - Type Products. 1979. pap. 4.50 (ISBN 92-5-100673-3, F1573, FAO). Unipub.
Recommended International Standard for Quick Frozen Filets of Hake. 1979. pap. 4.50 (ISBN 92-5-100647-4, F1569, FAO). Unipub.
Recommended International Standard for Quick Frozen Lobsters. 1979. pap. 4.50 (ISBN 92-5-100648-2, F1568, FAO). Unipub.
Recommended International Standards for Cooked Ham & for Cooked Cured Pork Shoulder. 1979. pap. 4.50 (ISBN 92-5-100637-7, F1570, FAO). Unipub.
Report of the Joint FAO-WHO Food Standards Regional Conference for Asia, Bangkok, 8-15 Dec., 1975. (Codes Alimentarius Commission). (Illus.). 1977. pap. 12.00 (ISBN 0-685-85732-8, FAO). Unipub.
Schultz, Harold W. Food Law Handbook. (Illus.). 1981. lib. bdg. 79.50 (ISBN 0-87055-372-0). AVI.
Turner, James S. Chemical Feast: Report on the Food & Drug Administration. LC 73-112515. (Ralph Nader Study Group Reports). 1970. 6.95 (ISBN 0-670-21428-0, N2, Grossman). Viking Pr.
Wiley, Harvey W. The History of a Crime Against the Food Law. LC 75-39281. (Getting & Spending: the Consumer's Dilemma). (Illus.). 1976. Repr. of 1929 ed. 24.00x (ISBN 0-405-08056-5). Arno.
World Food Problems & U. S. Politics & Policies: 1979-1980. 172p. 12.50 (ISBN 0-8138-1926-1). Iowa St U Pr.

FOOD OF ANIMALS
see Animals, Food Habits of

FOOD PLANTS
see Plants, Edible

FOOD POISONING

Boyd, Eldon M. Toxicity of Pure Foods. LC 73-83414. (Uniscience Ser). 260p. 1973. 49.95 (ISBN 0-8493-5026-3). CRC Pr.

Chen, Edwin. PBB: An American Tragedy. LC 79-15982. 1979. 10.95 (ISBN 0-13-654608-0). P-H.

Dack, Gail M. Food Poisoning. rev. ed. LC 55-12510. 1956. 16.00x (ISBN 0-226-13379-6). U of Chicago Pr.

Food & Nutrition Board. Toxicants Occurring Naturally in Foods. rev. 2nd ed. (Illus.). 704p. 1973. 17.25 (ISBN 0-309-02117-0). Natl Acad Pr.

Jemmali, M., ed. Mycotoxins in Foodstuffs-3. 1978. text ed. 26.00 (ISBN 0-08-021194-1). Pergamon.

Jensen, Lloyd B. Poisoning Misadventures: Narrative Excerpts on Food-Borne Diseases & Poisoning for the Physician, Microbiologist, Attorney & Nutritionist. 212p. 1970. 15.75 (ISBN 0-398-00927-9). C C Thomas.

Leonard, B. J., ed. Toxicological Aspects of Food Safety: Proceedings of the European Society of Toxicology. (Archives of Toxicol, Suppl: Vol. 1). (Illus.). 1978. pap. 45.10 (ISBN 0-387-08646-3). Springer-Verlag.

Liener, I. Toxic Constituents in Plant Foodstuffs. (Food Science & Technology Ser). 1969. 58.50 (ISBN 0-12-449950-3). Acad Pr.

Liener, Irvin E. Toxic Constitutuents of Plant Foodstuffs. 2nd ed. LC 79-51681. (Food Science & Technology Ser.). 1980. 39.50 (ISBN 0-12-449960-0). Acad Pr.

Liener, Irvin E., ed. Toxic Constituents of Animal Foodstuffs. (Food Science & Technology Ser.). 1974. 32.50 (ISBN 0-12-449940-6). Acad Pr.

Mackarness, Richard. Living Safely in a Polluted World: How to Protect Yourself & Your Children from Chemicals in Your Food & Environment. LC 80-51062. 256p. 1980. 11.95 (ISBN 0-8128-2741-4). Stein & Day.

Moreau, Claude. Moulds, Toxins & Food. LC 78-8715. 1979. 73.50 (ISBN 0-471-99681-5, Pub. by Wiley-Interscience). Wiley.

Stumbo, C. R., et al. CRC Handbook of Tables of Commercial Thermal Processes for Low-Acid Canned Foods, 2 vols. Date not set. Vol. 1, 560 Pgs. 69.95 (ISBN 0-8493-2961-2); Vol. 2, 544 Pgs. 69.95 (ISBN 0-8493-2963-9). CRC Pr.

Trickett, Jill. The Prevention of Food Poisoning. 1980. 11.85x (ISBN 0-85950-084-5, Pub. by Thornes England). State Mutual Bk.

FOOD PRESERVATION

see Food–Preservation

FOOD PRICES

Artman, Charles E. Food Costs & City Consumers. LC 70-76687. (Columbia University Studies in the Social Sciences: No. 280). Repr. of 1926 ed. 16.50 (ISBN 0-404-51280-1). AMS Pr.

Beard, James. How to Eat Better for Less Money. rev. ed. 1974. pap. 1.95 (ISBN 0-671-81810-4). PB.

Brown, F. E. & Oxenfeldt, A. R. Misperceptions of Economic Phenomena. LC 72-79606. 1972. 16.95x (ISBN 0-89197-851-8); pap. text ed. 7.95x (ISBN 0-89197-852-6). Irvington.

Cinnamon, Pamela A. & Swanson, Marilyn A. Everything You Always Wanted to Know About Exchange Values for Foods. 1976. 2.75 (ISBN 0-89301-034-0). U Pr of Idaho.

Folsom, LeRoi A. Professional Chef & the Recipe Cards. 1974. 44.95 (ISBN 0-8436-0586-3). CBI Pub.

Food Price Policies & Nutrition in Latin America. (Food & Nutrition Bulletin Ser.: Suppl. 3). 170p. 1980. pap. 15.00 (ISBN 92-808-0128-7, TUNU087, UNU). Unipub.

Gupta, Satish C. Food Prices in India. LC 77-917209. (Illus.). 1970. 8.00x (ISBN 0-8002-0631-2). Intl Pubns Serv.

Johnson, D. Gale. Forward Prices for Agriculture. LC 75-26305. (World Food Supply Ser). 1976. Repr. of 1947 ed. 16.00x (ISBN 0-405-07784-X). Arno.

Miller, Jack E. Menu Pricing & Strategy. LC 79-25932. (Illus.). 1980. pap. 14.95 (ISBN 0-8436-2144-3). CBI Pub.

Organization for Economic Cooperation & Development. The Formation of Food Prices & Their Behaviour in Times of Inflation. (Agricultural Products & Markets Ser.). 124p. 1973. 2.50x (ISBN 92-64-11105-0). OECD.

Robbins, William. The American Food Scandal. LC 73-19841. 280p. 1974. pap. 3.50 (ISBN 0-688-05299-1). Morrow.

Samtur, Susan J. & Tuleja, Tad. Cashing in at the Checkout. 1980. pap. 1.95 (ISBN 0-446-90585-2). Warner Bks.

Sherwin, Sally. Seven Steps to Rock-Bottom Food Costs: A Guide to Kitchen Economy. LC 76-12637. (Illus.). 192p. 1976. 6.95 (ISBN 0-688-03069-6); pap. 3.95 (ISBN 0-688-08069-3). Morrow.

Stern, Gloria. How to Start Your Own Food Co-Op: A Guide to Wholesale Buying. pap. 4.95 (ISBN 0-8027-7094-0). Walker & Co.

U. S. Department of Agriculture. How to Buy Food for Economy & Quality. LC 74-26000. (Illus.). 160p. (Orig.). 1975. pap. 1.50 (ISBN 0-486-21913-5). Dover.

Warfel, M. C. & Waskey, Frank H. The Professional Food Buyer. LC 75-46108. 1979. 26.00 (ISBN 0-8211-2254-1); ten or more copies 22.00 ea. McCutchan.

FOOD PROCESSING

see Food Industry and Trade

FOOD PROCESSOR COOKERY

Anderson, Jean. Jean Anderson's Processor Cooking. LC 78-27880. (Illus.). 1979. 14.95 (ISBN 0-688-03389-X). Morrow.

Beard, James & Jerome, Carl. New Recipes for the Cuisinart Food Processor. 4th ed. 96p. 1978. pap. 5.00 (ISBN 0-936662-00-X, FP-250). Cuisinart Cooking.

Better Homes & Gardens Books Editors, ed. Better Homes & Gardens Food Processor Cook Book. (Illus.). 1979. 4.95 (ISBN 0-696-00355-4). Meredith Corp.

Blanchard, Marjorie P. The Woman's Day Food Processor Cookbook. 160p. 1981. 6.95 (ISBN 0-449-90062-2). Fawcett.

Carter, Linda & Culinary Arts Institute Staff. The Food Processor Cookbook. Finnegan, Edward G., ed. LC 78-54620. (Adventures in Cooking Ser). (Illus.). 1980. pap. cancelled (ISBN 0-8326-0607-3, 2517). Delair.

Consumer Guide. The Ultimate Food Processor Cookbook. 1979. 12.95 (ISBN 0-671-24591-0); pap. 6.95 (ISBN 0-671-24592-9). S&S.

Consumer Guide Editors. Food Processor Cookbook. 1977. 13.95 (ISBN 0-671-22675-4); pap. 6.95 (ISBN 0-671-22676-2). S&S.

De Groot, Roy A. Cooking with the Cuisinart Food Processor. LC 76-46586. 1977. 12.95 (ISBN 0-07-016273-5, GB). McGraw.

Dlugosch, Sharon & Battcher, Joyce. Food Processor Recipes for Conventional & Microwave Cooking. LC 78-74899. 1979. pap. 3.95 (ISBN 0-918420-03-2); pap. 12.00 tchrs' manual (ISBN 0-918420-04-0). Brighton Pubns.

The Food Processor Cookbook: Sunbeam. LC 79-65556. (Illus.). 1979. 8.95 (ISBN 0-916752-35-6). Dorison Hse.

Food Processor International Cookbook. 1979. 12.95 (ISBN 0-671-24591-0, Fireside); pap. 6.95 (ISBN 0-671-24592-9). S&S.

Freiman, Jane S. The Art of Food Processor Cooking. 1980. 14.95 (ISBN 0-8092-7005-6); pap. 6.95 (ISBN 0-8092-7004-8). Contemp Bks.

General Electric Co. Cooking with a Food Processor. (Illus.). 1979. 10.95 (ISBN 0-394-50482-8). Random.

Gethers, Judith. The Fabulous Gourmet Food Processor Cookbook. 384p. (Orig.). 1981. pap. 7.95 (ISBN 0-345-29586-2). Ballantine.

Greer, Anne L. The Culinary Renaissance: Creative Food Processor Recipes. 5th rev. ed. 400p. 1979. pap. 9.00 (ISBN 0-936662-01-8, FP-782). Cuisinart Cooking.

Grunes, Barbara. Oriental Express: Chinese Menus for the Food Processor. Horowitz, Maxine, ed. Orig. Title: Cuisine Die Chine. 1979. pap. 5.00 (ISBN 0-932398-01-4). Good Food Bks.

Hemingway, Mary M. & De Lima, Suzanne. Food Processor Magic: Six Hundred Recipes, Basic Techniques, Twists & Turns. 1976. 12.95 (ISBN 0-8038-2321-5). Hastings.

Higson, James D. Building & Remodeling for Energy Savings. LC 77-15079. 1977. pap. 15.00 (ISBN 0-910460-56-6). Craftsman.

Horowitz, Maxine. Inside the Food Processor. Orig. Title: Cuisine by Maxine. (Illus.). pap. 5.95 (ISBN 0-932398-00-6). Good Food Bks.

Jean Anderson's Processor Cooking. 1980. pap. 2.95 (ISBN 0-425-04520-X). Berkley Pub.

Jones, Suzanne S. The Low-Cholesterol Food Processor Cookbook. LC 78-22329. (Illus.). 1980. 9.95 (ISBN 0-385-14745-7). Doubleday.

Mandel, Abby. Abby Mandel's Cuisinart Classroom. McElheny, Ruth, ed. 288p. (Orig.). 1980. pap. 15.00 (ISBN 0-936662-03-4). Cuisinart Cooking.

--Abby Mandel's Cuisinart Classroom. (Illus.). 15.00 (ISBN 0-686-74729-1). Cuisinart Cooking.

--Cuisinart Food Processor Cookbook Hints, Techniques, Menus, Recipes. 5th ed. 112p. pap. 7.00 (ISBN 0-936662-02-6, FP-783). Cuisinart Cooking.

Murphy, Margaret D. Food Processor Cookery. (Illus.). 1979. pap. 4.95 (ISBN 0-89437-078-2). Baronet.

--Food Processor Cookery: Step-by-Step Guide to Success. LC 78-72950. 1978. 8.95 (ISBN 0-916752-30-5). Dorison Hse.

Reingold, Carmel B. Cuisinart: Food Processing Cooking. 1976. pap. 5.95 (ISBN 0-440-51604-8, Delta). Dell.

--Cuisinart Food Processor Cookbook. rev. ed. 1981. pap. 8.95 (ISBN 0-440-51585-8, Delta). Dell.

Rossand, Colette & Herman, Jill H. A Mostly French Food Processor Cookbook. rev. ed. 1980. pap. 2.50 (ISBN 0-451-09537-5, E9537, Sig). NAL.

Rossant, Colette & Herman, Jill. A Mostly French Food Processor Cookbook. (Illus., Orig.). 1977. pap. 4.95 (ISBN 0-452-25158-3, Z5158, Plume). NAL.

Sims, Dorothy. Book of Recipes for the Food Processor. 188p. 1981. 3-ring binder 12.95 (ISBN 0-8256-3190-4, Quick Fox). Music Sales.

Sims, Dorothy & Malone, Barbara. The Food Processor-Microwave Oven Cookbook. (Illus.). 1980. 12.95 (ISBN 0-8256-3189-0, Quick Fox). Music Sales.

Sims, Dorothy & Sims, Dori. The Low Calorie Food Processor Cookbook. (Illus.). 192p. 1980. 14.95 (ISBN 0-8256-3185-8, Quick Fox). Music Sales.

Sims, Dorothy D. The Food Processor Cookbook. 1978. 4.95 (ISBN 0-8256-3142-4, Quick Fox). Music Sales.

Stand-up & Cook Books: Food Processor. (Illus.). 1979. pap. 2.95 (ISBN 0-517-53575-0). Crown.

Stumbo, C. R., et al. CRC Handbook of Tables of Commercial Thermal Processes for Low-Acid Canned Foods, 2 vols. Date not set. Vol. 1, 560 Pgs. 69.95 (ISBN 0-8493-2961-2); Vol. 2, 544 Pgs. 69.95 (ISBN 0-8493-2963-9). CRC Pr.

Sunset Editors. Food Processor Cook Book. LC 77-90721. (Illus.). 80p. 1978. pap. 3.95 (ISBN 0-376-02402-X, Sunset Bks.). Sunset-Lane.

Szilard, Paula & Woo, Juliana J. The Electric Vegetarian: Natural Cooking the Food Processor Way. 1981. 12.95 (ISBN 0-686-77733-6). Johnson VA.

--Electric Vegetarian: Natural Cooking the Food Processor Way. LC 80-83141. 1980. pap. 10.95 (ISBN 0-933472-50-1). Johnson Bks.

Tarr, Yvonne Y. The Great Food Processor Cookbook. 1976. 12.95 (ISBN 0-394-40523-4); pap. 6.95 (ISBN 0-394-73284-7). Random.

Walter, Susan & Biele, Pam. The Food Processor Book. LC 78-53320. (Illus.). 1978. pap. 2.50 (ISBN 0-915942-10-0). Owlswood Prods.

Wicks, Janis. The Food Processor Cookbook. Walsh, Jackie, ed. LC 77-152498. (Illus.). 1977. pap. 3.95 (ISBN 0-911954-41-4). Nitty Gritty.

FOOD RELIEF

Aiken, William & LaFollette, Hugh. World Hunger & Moral Obligation. 224p. 1977. text ed. 12.95 (ISBN 0-13-967968-5); pap. text ed. 9.50 (ISBN 0-13-967950-2). P-H.

Cadet, Melissa L. Food Aid & Policy for Economic Development: An Annotated Bibliography & Directory. LC 80-53500. 178p. (Orig.). 1981. 29.95 (ISBN 0-938398-00-8); pap. 19.95 (ISBN 0-938398-01-6). Trans Tech Mgmt.

Clarkson, Kenneth W. Food Stamps & Nutrition. LC 75-4377. 1975. pap. 4.25 (ISBN 0-8447-3155-2). Am Enterprise.

Cohn, Theodore H. Canadian Food Aid: Domestic & Foreign Policy Implications. (Monograph Ser. in World Affairs). (Illus.). 1979. pap. 4.00x (ISBN 0-87940-061-7). U of Denver Intl.

Dandekar, V. M. The Demand for Food & Conditions Governing Food Aid During Development. (World Food Programme Studies: No. 1). (Orig.). 1965. pap. 4.50 (ISBN 0-685-09376-X, F112, FAO). Unipub.

Dessau, J. Role of Multilateral Food Aid Programs. (World Food Programme Studies: No. 5). (Orig.). 1965. pap. 4.50 (ISBN 0-685-09405-7, F415, FAO). Unipub.

Food Aid & Education. (World Food Programme Studies: No. 6). (Orig.). 1965. pap. 4.50 (ISBN 0-685-09382-4, F185, FAO). Unipub.

Food Aid & Other Forms of Utilization of Agricultural Surpluses: A Review of Programs, Principles & Consultations. (FAO Commodity Policy Studies: No. 15). (Orig.). 1964. pap. 4.50 (ISBN 0-685-09383-2, F186, FAO). Unipub.

Food Stamp Reform. (Legislative Analysis Ser.). 1977. 3.75 (ISBN 0-8447-0186-6). Am Enterprise.

Group Feeding Programs for Southeast Asia. 1977. pap. 7.50 (ISBN 92-5-100255-X, F929, FAO). Unipub.

Lucas, George R., Jr. & Ogletree, Thomas W., eds. Lifeboat Ethics: The Moral Dilemma of World Hunger. LC 76-10002. 192p. 1976. 8.95 (ISBN 0-06-065308-6, HarpR); pap. 4.95x (ISBN 0-06-065309-4, RD170, HarpR). Har-Row.

MacDonald, Maurice. Food Stamps, & Income Maintenance. (Poverty Policy Analysis Ser.). 1977. 16.50 (ISBN 0-12-464050-8); pap. 8.00 (ISBN 0-12-464052-4). Acad Pr.

Manual on Management of Group Feeding Programmes. (FAO Food & Nutrition Paper Ser.). 124p. 1980. pap. 8.50 (ISBN 92-5-100931-7, F2041, FAO). Unipub.

Minear, Larry. New Hope for the Hungry? The Challenge of the World Food Crisis. (Orig.). 1975. pap. 1.95 (ISBN 0-377-00043-4). Friend Pr.

Partnership in Development. (Background Study Ser.: No. 45). 145p. pap. 11.25 (ISBN 0-660-10668-X, SSC159, SSC). Unipub.

Report of the Tenth Session of the United Nations-FAO Committee of Food Aid Policies & Programmes: World Food Programme. 52p. 1980. pap. 7.50 (ISBN 92-5-101034-X, F2151, FAO). Unipub.

Segal, Judith A. Food for the Hungry: The Reluctant Society. LC 79-133455. (Policy Studies in Employment & Welfare: No. 4). (Illus.). 83p. 1970. 7.50x (ISBN 0-8018-1227-5); pap. 2.95x (ISBN 0-8018-1226-7). Johns Hopkins.

Simon, Arthur. Bread for the World. 179p. 1975. pap. 2.95 (ISBN 0-8028-1602-9). Eerdmans.

Sprinkle, Patricia H. Hunger: Understanding the Crisis Through Games, Dramas, & Songs. LC 78-52451. 112p. (Orig.). 1980. pap. 5.95 (ISBN 0-8042-1312-7). John Knox.

Srivastava, Uma K., et al. Food Aid: International Economic Growth. (Illus.). 1975. text ed. 8.25x (ISBN 0-8138-0640-2). Iowa St U Pr.

Stanley, Robert G. Food for Peace. 1973. 29.25 (ISBN 0-677-03650-7). Gordon.

Stevens, Christopher. Food Aid in the Developing World. 1979. 22.50 (ISBN 0-312-29763-7). St Martin.

Toma, Peter A. The Politics of Food for Peace. LC 67-20091. (Institute of Government Research Ser). 1967. 3.95x (ISBN 0-8165-0160-2). U of Ariz Pr.

United States Department of Agriculture. The World Food Situation: Problems & Prospects to 1985, Vol. 2. 1976. 37.50 (ISBN 0-379-00573-5). Oceana.

Venkataramani, M. S. Bengal Famine of Nineteen Forty-Three: The American Response. 1973. 7.00x (ISBN 0-7069-0239-4). Intl Bk Dist.

Wallerstein, Mitchel B. Food for War - Food for Peace: U. S. Food Aid in a Global Context. 320p. 1980. text ed. 30.00x (ISBN 0-262-23106-9). MIT Pr.

World Food Program: Report of the Fourth Session of the U.N.-FAO Committee on Food Aid Policies & Programmes. 48p. 1978. pap. 7.50 (ISBN 92-5-100541-9, F1367, FAO). Unipub.

World Food Program: Report of the Sixth Session of the UN-FAO Committee on Food Aid Policies & Programs. 1979. pap. 7.50 (ISBN 92-5-100692-X, F1557, FAO). Unipub.

FOOD SANITATION

see Food Handling

FOOD SERVICE

Here are entered works on quantity preparation and service of food for outside the home. Works dealing solely with quantity food preparation are entered under Quantity Cookery.

see also Caterers and Catering; Quantity Cookery; Restaurants, Lunchrooms, Etc.; School Lunchrooms, Cafeterias, Etc.

American Society for Hospital Food Service Administrators. Hospital Food Service Management Review. LC 80-11834. 80p. (Orig.). 1980. 10.00 (ISBN 0-87258-323-6, 1410). Am Hospital.

Applied Foodservice Sanitation. 257p. 1981. text ed. write for info. (ISBN 0-669-00792-7); pap. certification course book avail. (ISBN 0-669-02106-7); instr.' guide avail. (ISBN 0-669-02730-8). Wm C Brown.

Avery, Arthur C. A Modern Guide to Foodservice Equipment. LC 79-20831. (Illus.). 1980. text ed. 27.50 (ISBN 0-8436-2179-6). CBI Pub.

Barker, Lewis M., et al, eds. Learning Mechanisms in Food Selection. 632p. 1977. 40.00 (ISBN 0-918954-19-3). Baylor Univ Pr.

BCC Staff. Institutional & Restaurant Foods: Ga-039. 1977. 525.00 (ISBN 0-89336-110-0). BCC.

Birchfield, John C. Foodservice Operations Manual. LC 79-15622. 1979. spiral bd. 49.95 (ISBN 0-8436-2145-1). CBI Pub.

Blair, Eulalia. Breakfast & Brunch Dishes for Food Service Menu Planning. LC 74-34100. (Foodservice Menu Planning Ser.). 256p. 1975. 17.95 (ISBN 0-8436-2057-9). CBI Pub.

Blair, Eulalia C. Mini Meals for Food Service Menu Planning. LC 76-7073. (Foodservice Menu Planning Ser.). 1976. 17.95 (ISBN 0-8436-2102-8). CBI Pub.

Border, Barbara. Food Safety & Sanitation. (Careers in Home Economics Ser.). (Illus.). 1979. pap. text ed. 7.44 (ISBN 0-07-006511-X, G); tchr's manual & key 3.00 (ISBN 0-07-006516-0); wkbk 3.00 (ISBN 0-07-006512-8). McGraw.

Coltman, M. Food & Beverage Cost Control. 1977. 16.95 (ISBN 0-13-323006-6). P-H.

Crawford, H. W. & McDowell, Milton C. Math Workbook for Foodservice-Lodging. 1980. pap. 12.95 (ISBN 0-8436-2197-4); o. p. 11.95 (ISBN 0-8436-0534-0); answer bk. o. p. 1.95 (ISBN 0-8436-0538-3). CBI Pub.

Crawford, Hollie & McDowell, Milton C. Metric Workbook for Food Service & Lodging. LC 76-22181. 224p. 1976. pap. 12.95 (ISBN 0-8436-2103-6); answer book 1.95 (ISBN 0-8436-2168-0). CBI Pub.

Curtis, Bob. Food Service Security: Internal Control. LC 75-33513. 256p. 1975. 18.95 (ISBN 0-912016-50-7). Lebhar Friedman.

Deuel, William K. Kitchen Management for Institutions: Economies in Purchasing, Portioning & Preparation. 1975. 12.95 (ISBN 0-8104-9462-0). Hayden.

Dittmer, Paul R. & Griffin, Gerald C. Principles of Food, Beverage & Labor Cost Control for Hotels & Restaurants. 2nd ed. LC 79-20301. 1979. text ed. 17.95 (ISBN 0-8436-2177-X). CBI Pub.

Dukas, Peter. Planning Profits in the Food and Lodging Industry. 180p. 1976. 14.95 (ISBN 0-8436-2080-3). CBI Pub.

Educational Research Council of America. Chef. rev. ed. Ferris, Theodore N. & Marchak, John P., eds. (Real People at Work Ser: B). (Illus.). 1976. pap. text ed. 2.25 (ISBN 0-89247-015-1). Changing Times.

Eison, Irving L. Strategic Marketing in Food Service: Planning for Change. LC 80-16264. 1980. 18.95 (ISBN 0-912016-89-2). Lebhar Friedman.

Eshbach, Charles E. Food Service Management. 3rd ed. LC 79-20378. 1979. pap. text ed. 12.95 (ISBN 0-8436-2176-1). CBI Pub.

Eshbach, Charles E., ed. Food Service Trends. LC 74-220. 330p. 1974. 16.95 (ISBN 0-8436-0581-2). CBI Pub.

Folsom, LeRoi A. Professional Chef & the Recipe Cards. 1974. 44.95 (ISBN 0-8436-0586-3). CBI Pub.

Goodwin, Mary T. & Pollen, Gerry. Creative Food Experiences for Children. 2nd rev. ed. (Illus.). 256p. (gr. k-6). 1980. pap. 5.95 (ISBN 0-89329-027-0). Ctr Sci Public.

Gottlieb, Leon. The Best of Gottlieb's Bottom Line: A Practical Profit Guide for Today's Food Service Operator. LC 80-16535. 1980. 18.95 (ISBN 0-912016-39-6). Lebhar Friedman.

Griffin, W. R. Food Service: Health, Sanitation & Safety. (Illus.). lab. manual 18.00 (ISBN 0-9601054-4-1). Cleaning Consultant.

Haines, Robert G. Math Principles for Food Service Occupations. LC 77-88118. 1979. pap. text ed. 7.00 (ISBN 0-8273-1680-1); instructor's guide 1.60 (ISBN 0-685-91755-X). Delmar.

Harder, Eulalia L. Blast Freezing System for Quantity Foods, Vol. 1. LC 79-46832. 1979. 24.95 (ISBN 0-8436-2157-5). CBI Pub.

Hardwick, Geraline B. & Kennedy, Robert L. Fundamentals of Quantity Food Preparation: Desserts & Beverages. LC 74-20917. (Illus.). 364p. 1975. 24.95 (ISBN 0-8436-2051-X). CBI Pub.

Hitchcock, Mary J. Foodservice Systems Administration. (Illus.). 1980. text ed. 18.95 (ISBN 0-02-354650-6). Macmillan.

Jernigan, Anna K. & Ross, Lynne N. Food Service Equipment. 2nd ed. (Illus.). 122p. 1980. pap. text ed. 6.75 (ISBN 0-8138-0550-3). Iowa St U Pr.

Jernigan, Anna K., et al. Food Service Management: Study Course. 1977. pap. text ed. 7.50 (ISBN 0-8138-0790-5). Iowa St U Pr.

Kahrl, William L. Advanced Modern Food & Beverage Service. (Illus.). 1977. 16.95x (ISBN 0-13-011353-0). P-H.

--Food Preparation. LC 78-57194. 1978. 5.95 (ISBN 0-912016-72-8). Lebhar Friedman.

--Food Service Cost Control. LC 78-57196. 1978. 5.95 (ISBN 0-912016-69-8). Lebhar Friedman.

--Food Service Equipment. LC 77-95260. 1977. 5.95 (ISBN 0-912016-67-1). Lebhar Friedman.

--The Food Service Productivity & Profit Ideabook. LC 75-8918. (Illus.). 192p. 1975. 16.95 (ISBN 0-8436-0594-4). CBI Pub.

--Food Service Sanitation-Safety. LC 78-57192. 1978. 5.95 (ISBN 0-912016-73-6). Lebhar Friedman.

--Food Service Warehandling. LC 78-50680. 1978. 5.95 (ISBN 0-912016-68-X). Lebhar Friedman.

--Foodservice on a Budget. LC 74-221. 224p. 1974. 18.95 (ISBN 0-8436-0587-1). CBI Pub.

--Improving Food Service. LC 78-57193. 1978. 5.95 (ISBN 0-912016-70-1). Lebhar Friedman.

--Meeting Challenges in Food Service. LC 74-15996. 224p. 1974. 17.95 (ISBN 0-912016-37-X). Lebhar Friedman.

--Menu Planning Merchandising. LC 78-57195. 1978. 5.95 (ISBN 0-912016-71-X). Lebhar Friedman.

--Modern Food Service Planning. LC 75-15518. (The Managing for Profit Ser.). 1975. pap. 5.95 (ISBN 0-912016-51-5). Lebhar Friedman.

--Planning & Operating a Successful Food Service Operation. LC 72-92136. (Chain Store Age Bks.). (Illus.). 1973. 15.95 (ISBN 0-912016-16-7). Lebhar Friedman.

Kazarian, E. A. Food Service Facilities Planning. (Illus.). 1975. text ed. 25.50 (ISBN 0-87055-168-X). AVI.

Kazarian, Edward A. Work Analysis & Design for Hotels, Restaurants & Institutions. 2nd ed. (Illus.). 1979. text ed. 21.50 (ISBN 0-87055-317-8). AVI.

Keiser, Ralph J. & Kallio, Elmer. Controlling & Analyzing Costs in Food Service Operations. LC 73-20156. 291p. 1974. text ed. 21.95 (ISBN 0-471-46710-3). Wiley.

Keister, D. C. Food & Beverage Control. 1977. 18.95 (ISBN 0-13-323022-8). P-H.

Klain, Peter. Food Service Lodging English. (Illus., Prog. Bk.). 1971. pap. 9.95 (ISBN 0-8436-0531-6). CBI Pub.

Knoll, Anne P. Food Service Management: A Human Relations Approach. 1975. 8.95 (ISBN 0-07-035183-X, G); instructor's manual & key 3.50 (ISBN 0-07-035184-8). McGraw.

Kotschevar, Lendal H. Foodservice for the Extended Care Facility. LC 72-75295. 1973. text ed. 22.95 (ISBN 0-8436-0548-0). CBI Pub.

--Quantity Food Purchasing. 2nd ed. LC 74-17407. 684p. 1975. text ed. 29.95 (ISBN 0-471-50524-2). Wiley.

Kotschevar, Lendal H. & Terrell, Margaret E. Food Service Planning: Layout & Equipment. 2nd ed. LC 76-28763. 601p. 1977. 29.95 (ISBN 0-471-50491-2). Wiley.

Kreck, Lothar A. Menus: Analysis & Planning. LC 74-28068. (Illus.). 200p. 1975. 17.95 (ISBN 0-8436-2050-1). CBI Pub.

Lawson, Fred. Designing Commercial Food Service Facilities. (Illus.). 148p. 1974. 24.95 (ISBN 0-8230-7146-4, Whitney Lib). Watson-Guptill.

Le Sueur, Meridel. Women on the Breadlines. LC 78-108080. (Worker Writer Ser.). 1978. pap. text ed. 1.00 (ISBN 0-931122-09-0). West End.

Levinson, Charles. Food & Beverage Operation: Cost Controls & Systems Management. (Illus.). 320p. 1976. 16.95 (ISBN 0-13-322958-0). P-H.

Livingston, G. E. & Chang, Charlotte M., eds. Food Service Systems: Analysis, Design & Implementation. 1980. 35.00 (ISBN 0-12-453150-4). Acad Pr.

Longree, Karla. Sanitary Techniques in Food Service. LC 81-3047. 235p. 1982. text ed. 13.50 (ISBN 0-471-08820-X). Wiley.

Longree, Karla & Blaker, Gertrude G. Sanitary Techniques in Food Service. LC 70-132852. (Illus.). 225p. 1971. pap. text ed. 14.50x (ISBN 0-471-54461-2). Wiley.

--Sanitary Techniques in Food Service. LC 75-42257. 240p. 1976. Repr. of 1971 ed. 12.00 (ISBN 0-88275-372-X). Krieger.

Medved, Eva. Food in Theory & Practice. LC 77-76340. (Illus.). 1978. text ed. 16.95x (ISBN 0-8087-3424-5). Plycon Pr.

Miller, Jack E. Cooperative Education Workbook for Foodservice Hospitality. LC 78-23193. (Illus.). (gr. 11-12). 1978. 11.95 (ISBN 0-8436-2117-6). CBI Pub.

Morgan, William J., Jr. Supervision & Management of Quantity Food Preparation: Principles & Procedures. LC 73-7239. 1974. 24.00x (ISBN 0-8211-1225-2); text ed. 19.50x (ISBN 0-685-72314-3). McCutchan.

--Supervision & Management of Quantity Preparation: Principles & Procedures. 2nd, rev ed. LC 80-83876. (Illus.). 1981. 24.00 (ISBN 0-8211-1254-6); text ed. 19.50 (ISBN 0-686-77732-8). McCutchan.

Morton, I. & Morton, C. Elsevier's Dictionary of Food Science & Technology. 1977. 35.75 (ISBN 0-444-41559-9). Elsevier.

Moyer, Anne. Better Food for Public Places. LC 76-54336. 1977. 8.95 (ISBN 0-87857-155-8). Rodale Pr Inc.

Mutkoski, Stephen A. & Schurer, Marcia L. Meat & Fish Management. 1981. text ed. 19.95x (ISBN 0-534-00907-7, Breton Pubs). Wadsworth Pub.

National Institute for Food Service Industry, et al. Financial Ingredient in Foodservice Management. 211p. 1981. text ed. write for info. (ISBN 0-669-00009-4); instrs.' manual avail. (ISBN 0-915452-29-4); student manual avail. Wm C Brown.

National Institute for Food Service Industry & Axler, Bruce H. Foodservice: A Managerial Approach. 498p. 1981. text ed. avail for info. (ISBN 0-669-00079-5); instrs.' manual avail. (ISBN 0-669-02723-5); student guide avail. (ISBN 0-669-02722-7). Wm C Brown.

Ninemeier, Jack. Food Service Security Manual: Control of Cash, Food & Beverage. 250p. 1981. 3-ring binder 49.95 (ISBN 0-8436-2250-4). CBI Pub.

North, Hallie B. Commercial Food Patents, U.S. Nineteen-Eighty. (Illus.). 1981. lib. bdg. 30.00 (ISBN 0-87055-371-2). AVI.

Peddersen, Ray. Specs: The Comprehensive Foodservice Purchasing and Specification Manual. LC 76-56460. 1977. 99.00 (ISBN 0-8436-2084-6). CBI Pub.

Peddersen, Raymond B. Foodservice & Hotel Purchasing. 460p. 1981. text ed. 21.50 (ISBN 0-8436-2192-3). CBI Pub.

Pedderson, Raymond B., et al, eds. Increasing Productivity in Foodservice. LC 73-84798. 1973. 15.95 (ISBN 0-8436-0560-X). CBI Pub.

Polak, Jeanne E. Food Service for Fitness. 96p. (Orig.). 1981. spiral 7.95 (ISBN 0-8087-3418-0, Feffer & Simons). Burgess.

Poledor, Andrew P. Determining the Feasibility of a Total Convenience Food System. LC 77-14149. 1977. pap. 15.95 (ISBN 0-8436-2160-5). CBI Pub.

Posner, Barbara M. Nutrition & the Elderly. LC 77-17683. 1979. 19.95 (ISBN 0-669-02085-0). Lexington Bks.

Ross, Lynne. Work Simplification in Food Service: Individualized Instruction. LC 73-171164. (Orig., Prog. Bk.). 1972. text ed. 6.95x (ISBN 0-8138-0785-9). Iowa St U Pr.

Rudman, Jack. Assistant Cook. (Career Examination Ser.: C-1101). (Cloth bdg. avail. on request). pap. 8.00 (ISBN 0-8373-1101-2). Natl Learning.

--Food Service Supervisor. (Career Examination Ser.: C-1411). (Cloth bdg. avail. on request). pap. 8.00 (ISBN 0-8373-1411-9). Natl Learning.

Seltz, David. Food Service Marketing & Promotion. LC 76-566430. (Illus.). 1977. 16.95 (ISBN 0-912016-59-0). Lebhar Friedman.

Ser-Vol-Tel Institute. Breakfast Preparation. (Foodservice Career Education Ser.). 1974. pap. 4.95 (ISBN 0-8436-2030-7). CBI Pub.

--Foodservice Safety. (Foodservice Career Education Ser.). 1974. pap. 4.95 (ISBN 0-8436-2008-0). CBI Pub.

--Foodservice Vocabulary. (Foodservice Career Education Ser.). 1975. pap. 4.95 (ISBN 0-8436-2007-2). CBI Pub.

Smith, William O. Food Services. Lynch, Richard, ed. (Career Competencies in Marketing Ser.). (Illus.). (gr. 11-12). 1979. pap. text ed. 5.36 (ISBN 0-07-058541-5); tchr's. manual & key 3.00 (ISBN 0-07-058542-3). McGraw.

Spangler, Alice A. & Mook, Marilyn. Food Consumerism: A Laboratory Manual for Meal Management. (Illus.). 1978. pap. 8.95 (ISBN 0-02-414200-X). Macmillan.

Stokes, John W. How to Manage a Restaurant or Institutional Food Service. 3rd ed. 420p. 1978. text ed. write for info. (ISBN 0-697-08314-4). Wm C Brown.

Stokes, Judy F. Cost-Effective Quality Food Service: An Institutional Guide. LC 78-25871. (Illus.). 336p. 1979. text ed. 29.75 (ISBN 0-89443-083-1). Aspen Systems.

Sweeney, Neil R. Managing People: Techniques for Food Service Operators. new ed. LC 76-7286. 128p. 1976. pap. 13.95 (ISBN 0-912016-54-X). Lebhar Friedman.

Terrell, M. E. Professional Ffod Preparation. 2nd ed. 741p. 1979. 27.50 (ISBN 0-471-85202-3). Wiley.

Thorner, Marvin E. & Manning, Peter B. Quality Control in Food Service. (Illus.). 1976. pap. text ed. 17.50 (ISBN 0-87055-309-7). AVI.

Van Egmond-Pannell, Dorothy. School Foodservice. (Illus.). 1981. pap. text ed. 19.00 (ISBN 0-87055-378-X). AVI.

Villano, Caesar. Food Service Management & Control: The Profitable Approach. (Orig.). 1977. 18.95 (ISBN 0-912016-60-4). Lebhar Friedman.

Villella, Joseph A. The Hospitality Industry-the World of Food Service. (Illus.). 352p. 1975. text ed. 14.50 (ISBN 0-07-067450-7, G); instructor's manual & key 3.50 (ISBN 0-07-067451-5). McGraw.

West, B. B., et al. Food Service in Institutions. 5th ed. 1977. 30.50 (ISBN 0-471-93393-7). Wiley.

Wilkinson, Jule. Complete Book of Cooking Equipment. 2nd ed. LC 80-16554. 336p. 1981. 21.50 (ISBN 0-8436-2186-9). CBI Pub.

Wilkinson, Jule, ed. The Anatomy of Food Service Design 1. LC 75-5730. (Illus.). 224p. 1975. 23.50 (ISBN 0-8436-0569-3). CBI Pub.

--Anatomy of Food Service Design 2. LC 75-5730. (Illus.). 1978. 23.50 (ISBN 0-8436-2105-2). CBI Pub.

--Special Atmosphere Themes for Foodservice. LC 78-184740. 1972. 12.95 (ISBN 0-8436-0536-7). CBI Pub.

FOOD SERVICE–VOCATIONAL GUIDANCE

Anderson, Henry W. The Modern Food Service Industry: An Introductory Guide. 1977. text ed. write for info. (ISBN 0-697-08407-8). Wm C Brown.

Bernbach, Linda. Food Service Supervisor - School Lunch Manager. LC 79-15860. 1980. pap. 8.00 (ISBN 0-668-04819-0, 4819-0). Arco.

Brady, R. J. On the Job Training: A Practical Guide for Food Service Supervisors. (Illus.). 1975. pap. 8.95 (ISBN 0-87618-655-X). R J Brady.

Breithaupt, Herman A. How We Started Students on Successful Foodservice Careers. LC 72-75296. 256p. 1972. 12.95 (ISBN 0-8436-0544-8). CBI Pub.

Cavallaro, Ann. Careers in Food Services. 160p. (YA) 1981. 10.25 (ISBN 0-525-66698-2). Elsevier-Nelson.

Coffman, James P. Introduction to Professional Food Service. rev. ed. 310p. 1974. pap. 16.95 (ISBN 0-8436-2056-0). CBI Pub.

Creasy, Donna N. Food Careers. (Home Economics Careers Ser.). (gr. 10-12). 1977. 6.36 (ISBN 0-13-392712-1); pap. 5.12 (ISBN 0-13-392704-0). P-H.

Fairbrook, Paul. College & University Food Sevice Manual. LC 79-50956. (Illus.). 1979. pap. 17.50 (ISBN 0-9602456-0-X). Colman Pubs.

Freeman, Dorothy R., et al. Very Important People in Food Services. LC 75-28503. (Very Important People Ser). (Illus.). 64p. (gr. 4-12). 1976. PLB 8.65 (ISBN 0-516-07462-8, Elk Grove Bks). Childrens.

Gilbert, Edith. Tabletop the Right Way: An Information & Training Guide for the Professional in the Hospitality Industry. rev ed. LC 80-81206. (Illus.). 54p. 1980. 15.00x (ISBN 0-9600786-4-9). Jet'iquette.

Koch, Harry W. & Currier, Howard E. Food Service & Food Handling Examinations. 1975. 5.00 (ISBN 0-913164-53-4). Ken-Bks.

McKnight Staff. Exploring Careers in Hospitality & Food Service. LC 75-18678. (gr. 8-12). 1975. text ed. 16.64 (ISBN 0-87345-605-X); teacher's guide 30.00 (ISBN 0-87345-606-8). McKnight.

Pelta, Kathy. There's a Job for You in Food Service: A Career Guide. LC 79-52042. (Illus.). 1979. 7.95 (ISBN 0-396-07709-9). Dodd.

Ser-Vo-Tel Institute. Waiter-Waitress. (Foodservice Career Education Ser.). 1974. pap. text ed. 4.95 (ISBN 0-8436-2022-6). CBI Pub.

Ser-Vol-Tel Institute. Busing Attendant. (Foodservice Career Education Ser.). 1974. pap. 4.95 (ISBN 0-8436-2018-8). CBI Pub.

--Counter Service. (Food Service Career Education Ser.). 1974. pap. 4.95 (ISBN 0-8436-2020-X). CBI Pub.

Training Programs for Health Care Workers: Food Service Workers. Incl. Being a Food Service Worker. 276p. student manual 9.95 (ISBN 0-87914-007-0, 9775, 9655); Training the Food Service Worker. 155p. instructor's guide 9.95 (ISBN 0-87914-008-9). 1967. Hosp Res & Educ.

Westbrook, James. Aim for a Job in Restaurants & Food Service. LC 68-26145. (Aim High Vocational Guidance Ser.). (Illus.). (gr. 7 up). 1978. PLB 5.97 (ISBN 0-8239-0099-1). Rosen Pr.

Westbrook, James H. Aim for a Job in Restaurants & Food Service. LC 70-114136. (Career Guidance Ser). 1971. pap. 3.95 (ISBN 0-668-02229-9). Arco.

Winn, Charles S. & Baker, M. C. Exploring Occupations in Food Service & Home Economics. (Careers in Focus Ser.). 1975. text ed. 5.32 (ISBN 0-07-071041-4, G); tchr's manual & key 3.30 (ISBN 0-07-071042-2); wksheet bklet 6.08 (ISBN 0-07-071063-5). McGraw.

FOOD STAMP PLAN

see Food Relief

FOOD SUBSTITUTES

Saltonstall, Maxine. In Lieu of. LC 78-184811. (Illus.). 1972. pap. 1.50 (ISBN 0-8048-1020-6). C E Tuttle.

Specifications for Identity & Purity Sweeting Agents, Emulsifying Agents, Flavoring Agents & Other Food Additives. (FAO Food & Nutrition Paper Ser.: No. 17). 167p. 1980. pap. 11.75 (ISBN 92-5-100984-8, F2150, FAO). Unipub.

FOOD SUPPLY

see also Agriculture–Statistics; Famines; Food–Preservation; Food Consumption; Food Industry and Trade; Meat Industry and Trade; World War, 1939-1945–Food Question

Agricultural Production Team. Report on India's Food Crisis & Steps to Meet It. LC 75-26294. (World Food Supply Ser). 1976. Repr. of 1959 ed. 16.00x (ISBN 0-405-07767-X). Arno.

Aiken, William & LaFollette, Hugh. World Hunger & Moral Obligation. 224p. 1977. text ed. 12.95 (ISBN 0-13-967968-5); pap. text ed. 9.50 (ISBN 0-13-967950-2). P-H.

Allaby, M. World Food Resources: Actual & Potential. (Illus.). 1977. 52.90x (ISBN 0-85334-731-X, Pub. by Applied Science). Burgess-Intl Ideas.

Amin, Galal A. Food Supply & Economic Development with Special Reference to Egypt. LC 67-1159. (Illus.). 1966. 22.50x (ISBN 0-678-05022-8). Kelley.

An Approach to Food-Population Planning. 1978. pap. 7.50 (ISBN 92-5-100563-X, F1471, FAO). Unipub.

Aziz, Sartaj, ed. Hunger, Politics & Markets: The Real Issues in the Food Crisis. LC 75-34674. 130p. 1975. 13.50x (ISBN 0-8147-0559-6); pap. 7.50x (ISBN 0-8147-0560-X). NYU Pr.

Balaam, David N. & Carey, Michael, eds. Food Politics: The Regional Conflict. LC 79-48097. 280p. 1981. write for info. (ISBN 0-916672-52-2). Allanheld.

Baldwin, R. L., ed. Animals, Feed, Food & People: An Analysis of the Role of Animals in Food Production. (AAAS Selected Symposium: No. 42). 150p. 1980. lib. bdg. 16.00x (ISBN 0-89158-779-9). Westview.

Barbour, Ian G., et al, eds. Finite Resources & the Human Future: Population-Food-Energy. LC 76-3864. 144p. 1976. pap. 4.75 (ISBN 0-8066-1526-5, 10-2325). Augsburg.

Barnett, A. Doak. China & the World Food System. LC 79-87912. (Monographs: No. 12). 128p. 1979. 5.00 (ISBN 0-686-28683-9). Overseas Dev Council.

Barrass, Robert. Biology: Food & People. LC 74-21791. 224p. 1975. 18.95 (ISBN 0-312-08050-6). St Martin.

Barrons, Keith C. The Food in Your Future. 1975. 8.95 (ISBN 0-442-20587-2). Van Nos Reinhold.

Beau, Francis N. Quantity Food Purchasing Guide. rev. ed. 1974. pap. 10.95 spiral bdg. (ISBN 0-8436-2046-3). CBI Pub.

Benham, Harvey. Man's Struggle for Food. LC 80-67188. (Illus.). 506p. 1981. lib. bdg. 26.50 (ISBN 0-8191-1518-5); pap. text ed. 16.50 (ISBN 0-8191-1519-3). U Pr of Amer.

Bennett, M. K. The World's Food: A Study of the Interrelations of World Populations, National Diets & Food Potentials. LC 75-26295. (World Food Supply Ser). (Illus.). 1976. Repr. of 1954 ed. 17.00x (ISBN 0-405-07768-8). Arno.

Beresford-Peirse, H. Forests, Food & People. (Freedom from Hunger Campaign Basic Studies: No. 20). (Orig.). 1968. pap. 4.50 (ISBN 0-685-09384-0, F199, FAO). Unipub.

Billions More to Feed. 1978. pap. 6.00 (ISBN 92-5-100229-0, F90, FAO). Unipub.

Biswas, Margaret R. & Biswas, Asit K., eds. Food, Climate & Man. LC 78-15154. (Environmental Science & Technology Ser.: Texts & Monographs). 285p. 1979. 28.00 (ISBN 0-471-03240-9, Pub. by Wiley-Interscience). Wiley.

Black, Herbert. People & Plows Against Hunger: Self-Help Experiment in a Rural Community. LC 75-3825. (Illus.). 160p. (Orig.). 1975. pap. 2.95 (ISBN 0-89046-057-4). Herman Pub.

Blakeslee, LeRoy L., et al. World Food Production, Demand, & Trade. facsimile ed. 428p. 1973. 17.20x (ISBN 0-8138-2435-4). Iowa St U Pr.

Blumberg, Rhoda. Famine. LC 78-6837. (Impact Bks.). (Illus.). (gr. 9 up). 1978. PLB 7.45 s&l (ISBN 0-531-02201-3). Watts.

Board on Agriculture & Renewable Resources, National Research Council. Enhancement of Food Production for the United States: World Food & Nutrition Study. LC 75-37121. xiii, 174p. 1975. pap. 6.00 (ISBN 0-309-02435-8). Natl Acad Pr.

Bobo, Kimberley A., ed. World Food-Hunger Studies. 1977. pap. write for info. Inst World Order.

Bonner, James. The World's People and the World's Food Supply. Head, J. J., ed. (Oxford-Carolina Biology Readers). 16p. (gr. 11-12). pap. 1.50 (ISBN 0-89278-322-2). Carolina Biological.

Borgstrom, Georg. Hungry Planet: The Modern World at the Edge of Famine. 2nd, rev. ed. (Illus.). 576p. 1972. pap. 3.95 (ISBN 0-02-072360-1, Collier). Macmillan.

--Too Many: The Biological Limitations of Our Earth. 1971. pap. 2.95 (ISBN 0-02-072380-6, Collier). Macmillan.

Bradford, Derek. Chemistry & the World Food Problem. (Foreground Chemistry Ser.). 1971. pap. text ed. 5.00x (ISBN 0-435-64298-7). Heinemann Ed.

Brady, N. C., et al, eds. Food for Peace. (Illus.). 1963. 1.00 (ISBN 0-89118-019-2). Am Soc Agron.

Briscoe, Alan K. Timely Tips on Quantity Food Buying. 1974. pap. 1.95 (ISBN 0-88290-044-7). Horizon Utah.

Brown, Lester R. Food or Fuel: New Competition for the World's Cropland. LC 80-50216. (Worldwatch Papers). 1980. pap. 2.00 (ISBN 0-916468-34-8). Worldwatch Inst.

--Increasing World Food Output. LC 75-26298. (World Food Supply Ser). (Illus.). 1976. Repr. of 1965 ed. 10.00x (ISBN 0-405-07770-X). Arno.

--Man, Land & Food. LC 75-26299. (World Food Supply Ser). (Illus.). 1976. Repr. of 1963 ed. 10.00x (ISBN 0-405-07771-8). Arno.

--Our Daily Bread. LC 75-851. (Headline Ser.: No. 225). (Illus.). 1975. pap. 2.00 (ISBN 0-87124-030-0). Foreign Policy.

--The Politics & Responsibility of the North American Breadbasket. (Worldwatch Papers Ser.). 1975. pap. 2.00 (ISBN 0-916468-01-1). Worldwatch Inst.

--The Worldwide Loss of Cropland. LC 78-64454. (Worldwatch Papers). 1978. pap. 2.00 (ISBN 0-916468-23-2). Worldwatch Inst.

Brown, Peter G. & Shue, Henry, eds. Food Policy: The Responsibility of the United States in the Life & Death Choices. LC 76-57803. (Illus.). 1979. pap. text ed. 8.95 (ISBN 0-02-905170-3). Free Pr.

--Food Policy: The Responsibility of the United States in the Life & Death Choices. LC 76-57803. 1977. 14.95 (ISBN 0-02-904980-6). Free Pr.

Caird, James. Landed Interest & the Supply of Food. 4th ed. LC 67-16346. Repr. of 1880 ed. 15.00x (ISBN 0-678-05034-1). Kelley.

--Landed Interests & the Supply of Food. 5th rev ed. 184p. 1967. 24.00x (ISBN 0-7146-1042-9, F Cass Co). Biblio Dist.

Caldwell, Malcolm. Wealth of Some Nations. 192p. 1977. 10.00 (ISBN 0-905762-01-0); pap. 6.00 (ISBN 0-686-71044-4). Lawrence Hill.

Carpenter, Frank G. How the World Is Fed. 1977. lib. bdg. 59.95 (ISBN 0-8490-2021-2). Gordon Pr.

Chopra, R. N. Evolution of Food Policy in India. 1981. 30.00x (ISBN 0-8364-0724-5, Pub. by Macmillan India). South Asia Bks.

Chou, Marilyn, et al. World Food Prospects & Agriculture Potential. LC 76-24346. 1977. text ed. 28.95 (ISBN 0-275-23770-2). Praeger.

Chou, Marylin & Harmon, David P., Jr. Critical Food Issues of the Nineteen Eighties. LC 79-14718. (Pergamon Policy Studies). (Illus.). 1979. 44.00 (ISBN 0-08-024611-7); pap. 9.95 (ISBN 0-08-024639-7). Pergamon.

Chrispeels, Maarten J. & Sadava, David. Plants, Food, & People. LC 76-46498. (Illus.). 1977. text ed. 19.95x (ISBN 0-7167-0378-5); pap. text ed. 9.95x (ISBN 0-7167-0377-7). W H Freeman.

Christensen, Raymond P. Efficient Use of Food Resources in the United States. LC 75-26300. (World Food Supply Ser). (Illus.). 1976. Repr. of 1948 ed. 8.00x (ISBN 0-405-07772-6). Arno.

Clark, Colin. Starvation or Plenty? LC 70-99309. (World Realities Ser). 1970. 4.95 (ISBN 0-8008-7371-8). Taplinger.

Clark, Frederick L. & Pirie, Norman W., eds. Four Thousand Million Mouths. facs. ed. LC 71-117768. (Essay Index Reprint Ser). 1951. 17.00 (ISBN 0-8369-1746-4). Arno.

Clydesdale, Fergus S. & Francis, F. J. Food, Nutrition & You. (Illus.). 1977. lib. bdg. 13.95 (ISBN 0-13-323048-1); pap. text ed. 9.95 (ISBN 0-13-323030-9). P-H.

Cohen, Joel E. Food Webs & Niche Space. (Monographs in Population Biology: No. 11). 1978. text ed. 16.50 (ISBN 0-691-08201-4); pap. text ed. 8.50 (ISBN 0-691-08202-2). Princeton U Pr.

Commission on International Relations. World Food & Nutrition Study: Supporting Papers, 5 vols. 1977. Vol. I. pap. 6.75 (ISBN 0-309-02647-4); Vol. II. pap. 6.75 (ISBN 0-309-02726-8); Vol. III. pap. 7.00 (ISBN 0-309-02730-6); Vol. IV. pap. 6.00 (ISBN 0-309-02727-6); Vol. V. pap. 6.00 (ISBN 0-309-02646-6). Natl Acad Pr.

Committtee on Animal Production. Plant & Animal Products in the U. S. Food System. 1978. pap. 10.75 (ISBN 0-309-02769-1). Natl Acad Pr.

Crookes, William. The Wheat Problem. LC 75-27633. (World Food Supply Ser). (Illus.). 1976. Repr. of 1900 ed. 17.00x (ISBN 0-405-07775-0). Arno.

Dahlberg, Kenneth A., ed. Beyond the Green Revolution: The Ecology & Politics of Global Agricultural Development. LC 78-11271. (Illus.). 270p. 1979. 17.95 (ISBN 0-306-40120-7, Plenum Pr). Plenum Pub.

Dams, T., et al, eds. Food & Population: Priorities in Decision Making. 208p. 1979. text ed. 26.00x (ISBN 0-566-00250-7, Pub. by Gower Pub Co England). Renouf.

Darby, W. J., ed. Food: the Gift of Osiris. 1977. Vol. 1. 53.00 (ISBN 0-12-203401-5); Vol.2. 53.00 (ISBN 0-12-203402-3); boxed set 83.00 (ISBN 0-12-203450-3). Acad Pr.

Deatherage, F. E. Food for Life. LC 75-15502. (Illus.). 422p. 1975. 19.50 (ISBN 0-306-30816-9, Plenum Pr). Plenum Pub.

De Kruif, Paul. Hunger Fighters. LC 67-32084. (YA) (gr. 7-12). 1967. pap. 0.95 (ISBN 0-15-642430-4, HPL20, HPL). HarBraceJ.

Dodd, George. The Food of London. LC 75-27635. (World Food Supply Ser). 1976. Repr. of 1856 ed. 31.00x (ISBN 0-405-07777-7). Arno.

Doubleday, Thomas. True Law of Population: Shewn to Be Connected with the Food of the People. 2nd ed. LC 67-17492. Repr. of 1847 ed. 17.50x (ISBN 0-678-00244-4). Kelley.

Duckham, A. N., et al. Food Production & Consumption. 1977. 58.75 (ISBN 0-7204-0396-0, North-Holland). Elsevier.

Duncan, Elwin R., ed. Dimensions of World Food Problems. (Illus.). 1977. pap. text ed. 9.95x (ISBN 0-8138-1870-2). Iowa St U Pr.

Dunn, James E., et al. Endangered Species. LC 76-27481. (Illus.). 1977. pap. 2.95 (ISBN 0-8054-6117-5). Broadman.

East, Edward M. Mankind at the Crossroads. LC 76-46074. (Anti-Movements in America). 1977. Repr. of 1926 ed. lib. bdg. 21.00x (ISBN 0-405-09947-9). Arno.

Eckholm, Erik P. Losing Ground: Environmental Stress & World Food Prospects. 223p. 1976. 7.95 (ISBN 0-393-06410-7); pap. text ed. 5.95x (ISBN 0-393-09167-8). Norton.

Economics & Sociology Department, Iowa State College. Wartime Farm & Food Policy. LC 75-26304. (World Food Supply Ser). (Illus.). 1976. Repr. of 1943 ed. 31.00x (ISBN 0-405-07783-1). Arno.

Ehrlich, Paul R. & Ehrlich, Anne H. The End of Affluence: A Blueprint for Your Future. 320p. 1974. pap. 2.50 (ISBN 0-345-29049-6). Ballantine.

El-Sherbini, A A. Food Security Issues in the Arab Near East: A Report of the United Nations Economic Commission for Western Asia. LC 79-40254. (Illus.). 1979. 39.50 (ISBN 0-08-023447-X). Pergamon.

Ethyl Corporation. Food for America's Future. LC 72-14156. (Essay Index Reprint Ser.). Repr. of 1960 ed. 15.25 (ISBN 0-518-10009-X). Arno.

FAO Executive Director. Report on the World Food Program. 1965. pap. 4.50 (ISBN 0-685-36329-5, F397, FAO). Unipub.

FAO Studies in Food & Population. (Illus.). 1978. pap. 10.25 (ISBN 92-5-100166-9, FAO). Unipub.

Feeding of Workers in Developing Countries. 1977. pap. 9.50 (ISBN 92-5-100209-6, F905, FAO). Unipub.

Fenton, Alexander & Owen, Trefor. Food in Perspective: Third International Conference of Ethnological Food Research. (Illus.). 425p. 1981. text ed. 50.00x (ISBN 0-85976-044-8). Humanities.

Food & Nutrition Strategies in National Development: Ninth Report of the Joint FAO-WHV Expert Committee on Nutrition, Rome, 1974. (FAO Nutrition Meetings Report Ser: No.56). 64p. (FAO Food & Nutrition Ser., No. 5). 1976. pap. 7.25 (ISBN 92-5-100262-2, P80, FAO). Unipub.

Food Balance Sheets Nineteen Seventy-Five to Seventy-Seven Average & per Caput Food Supplies Nineteen Sixty-One to Sixty-Five Average Nineteen Sixty-Seven to Nineteen Seventy-Seven. 1012p. 1980. pap. 64.00 (ISBN 92-5-101029-3, F2139, FAO). Unipub.

Food Supply Time Series. 1960. pap. 4.75 (ISBN 0-685-36295-7, F192, FAO). Unipub.

Ford, Barbara. Future Food: Alternate Protein for the Year 2000. LC 77-18808. (Illus.). 1978. pap. 4.50 (ISBN 0-688-08299-8). Morrow.

The Fourth World Food Survey. (Statistical Ser. No 11, Food & Nutrition Ser. No. 10). 1978. pap. 7.25 (ISBN 92-5-100429-3, F1359, FAO). Unipub.

Fowler, Kathryn M. Hunger: The World Food Crisis, An NSTA Environmental Materials Guide. 1977. pap. 2.50 (ISBN 0-87355-005-6). Natl Sci Tchrs.

Freudenberger, C. Dean & Minus, Paul M., Jr. A Christian Responsibility in a Hungry World. LC 75-43764. 1976. pap. 2.50 (ISBN 0-687-07567-X). Abingdon.

Gabel, Medard. Ho-Ping Food for Everyone. LC 77-92214. 1979. pap. 9.95 (ISBN 0-385-14082-7, Anch). Doubleday.

George, Henry. Progress & Poverty. LC 79-12191. 1979. 10.00 (ISBN 0-914016-60-1). Phoenix Pub.

George, Susan. How the Other Half Dies: The Real Reasons for World Hunger. LC 76-52614. 328p. 1977. text ed. 12.50 (ISBN 0-916672-07-7); pap. text ed. 6.45 (ISBN 0-916672-08-5). Allanheld.

Gibson, James R. Feeding the Russian Fur Trade: Provisionment of the Okhotsk Seaboard & the Kamchatka Peninsula, 1639-1856. LC 79-81319. (Illus.). 358p. 1969. 27.50x (ISBN 0-299-05230-3). U of Wis Pr.

Githens, Thomas S. & Wood, Carroll E. Food Resources of Africa. (African Handbooks Ser.: Vol. 3). (Illus.). 1943. 3.00 (ISBN 0-686-24087-1). Univ Mus of U PA.

Glassheim, Eliot & Cargille, Charles, eds. Key Issues in Population & Food Policy: Capon Springs Public Policy Conference No. 2. LC 78-63063. (Illus.). 1978. pap. text ed. 14.00 (ISBN 0-8191-0613-5). U Pr of Amer.

Gremillion, Joseph, ed. Food-Energy & the Major Faiths. LC 77-17975. 1978. pap. 9.95 (ISBN 0-88344-138-1). Orbis Bks.

Guidelines for Developing an Effective National Food Control System. (FAO Food Control Ser.: No. 1). 1976. pap. 19.25 (ISBN 0-685-74255-5, F930, FAO). Unipub.

Halacy, D. S. Feast & Famine. (Nature of Man Ser). (Illus.). (gr. 7up). 1971. 6.25 (ISBN 0-8255-4031-3). Macrae.

Halcrow, Harold G. Food Policy for America. (TBD Ser.). (Illus.). 1977. text ed. 19.95 (ISBN 0-07-025550-4, C). McGraw.

Hallock, Richard T. Persepolis Fortification Tablets. (Oriental Institute Pubns. Ser: No. 92). 1969. 50.00x (ISBN 0-226-62195-2, OIP92). U of Chicago Pr.

Harle, Vilho, ed. Political Economy of Food. 346p. 1978. text ed. 30.00x (ISBN 0-566-00206-X, Pub. by Gower Pub Co England). Renouf.

Hartmann, Betsy & Boyce, James. Needless Hunger: Voices from a Bangladesh Village. (Orig.). 1979. pap. 3.00 (ISBN 0-935028-03-X). Inst Food & Develop.

Hedden, W. P. How Great Cities Are Fed. 1977. lib. bdg. 59.95 (ISBN 0-8490-2019-0). Gordon Pr.

Hilliard, Sam B. Hog Meat & Hoecake: Food Supply in the Old South, 1840-1860. LC 75-156778. 309p. 1972. 17.95x (ISBN 0-8093-0512-7). S Ill U Pr.

Hills, Christopher & Nakamura, Hiroshi. Food from Sunlight. new ed. LC 78-9582. (Illus., Orig.). 1978. pap. 14.95 (ISBN 0-916438-13-9). Univ of Trees.

Hollingsworth, Dorothy & Morse, Elisabeth, eds. People & Food Tomorrow: The Scientific, Economic, Political, & Social Factors Affecting Food Supplies in the Last Quarter of the 20th Century. 1976. 29.00x (ISBN 0-85334-701-8). Intl Ideas.

Hopkins, Raymond F. & Puchala, Donald J. Global Food Interdependence: Challenge to Americn Foreign Policy. 1980. 20.00x (ISBN 0-231-04858-0); pap. 7.50x (ISBN 0-231-04859-9). Columbia U Pr.

Hopkins, Raymond F. & Puchala, Donald J., eds. The Global Political Economy of Food. 1979. 17.50 (ISBN 0-299-07750-0); pap. 6.95 (ISBN 0-299-07754-3). U of Wis Pr.

The Hunger Problematique & a Critique of Research. 72p. 1981. pap. 5.00 (ISBN 92-808-0163-5, TUNU 131, UNU). Unipub.

Institute for Food & Development Policy. Food First Resource Guide. (Orig.). 1979. pap. 3.00 (ISBN 0-935028-01-3). Inst Food & Develop.

International Congress of Pesticides Chemistry, 4th, Zurich, July 1978. World Food Production--Environment--Pesticides: Plenary Lectures. Geissbuehler, H., et al, eds. (IUPAC Symposia). 1978. text ed. 30.00 (ISBN 0-08-022374-5). Pergamon.

Iowa State University - Center For Agricultural And Economic Development. Alternatives for Balancing World Food Production & Needs. 1967. 6.95x (ISBN 0-8138-1797-8). Iowa St U Pr.

An Issues Paper: Contributed by the Food Study Group of the GPID Project. 24p. 1980. pap. 5.00 (ISBN 92-808-0054-X, TUNU 020, UNU). Unipub.

Johnson, D. Gale. World Food Problems. 1975. pap. 4.25 (ISBN 0-8447-3165-X). Am Enterprise.

Johnson, D. Gale, ed. World Food Supply, 33 vols. 1976. 635.00x (ISBN 0-405-07766-1). Arno.

Johnston, Bruce F. The Staple Food Economies of Western Tropical Africa. 1958. 15.00x (ISBN 0-8047-0537-2). Stanford U Pr.

King, Clyde L., ed. The World's Food. LC 75-26307. (World Food Supply Ser). (Illus.). 1976. Repr. of 1917 ed. 18.00x (ISBN 0-405-07786-6). Arno.

Knibbs, George H. The Shadow of the World's Future: Or, the Earth's Population Possibilities & the Consequences of the Present Rate of Increase of the Earth's Inhabitants. LC 75-38133. (Demography Ser.). 1976. Repr. of 1928 ed. 10.00x (ISBN 0-405-07986-9). Arno.

Knight, C. Gregory & Wilcox, R. Paul. Triumph or Triage? The World Food Problem in Geographical Persective. Natoli, Salvatore J., ed. LC 76-29265. (Resource Papers for College Geography Ser.). 1977. pap. text ed. 4.00 (ISBN 0-89291-115-8). Assn Am Geographers.

Knight, Henry. Food Administration in India, 1939-47. (Illus.). 1954. 15.00x (ISBN 0-8047-0447-3). Stanford U Pr.

Koerselman, Gary H., ed. Food & Social Policy, I. Dull, Kay E. (Illus.). 1978. text ed. 8.95 (ISBN 0-8138-1090-6). Iowa St U Pr.

Lappe, Frances M. & Collins, Joseph. Food First. 1979. pap. 2.95 (ISBN 0-345-29045-3). Ballantine.

--World Hunger: Ten Myths. rev. ed. 1979. pap. 2.25 (ISBN 0-935028-00-5). Inst Food & Develop.

Lappe, Francis M. & Collins, Joseph. Food First: Beyond the Myth of Scarcity. 1977. 11.95 (ISBN 0-395-25347-0). HM.

Lewicki, T. West African Food in the Middle Ages. LC 72-88615. 288p. 1974. 33.00 (ISBN 0-521-08673-6). Cambridge U Pr.
Linowitz, Sol M. World Hunger: A Challenge to American Policy. LC 80-85486. (Headline Ser.: No. 252). (Illus.). 64p. 1980. pap. 2.00 (ISBN 0-87124-065-3). Foreign Policy.
Lonn, Ella. Salt As a Factor in the Confederacy. LC 65-19663. 324p. 1965. 15.00x (ISBN 0-8173-5209-0). U of Ala Pr.
Lowry, J. H. World Population & Food Supply. 122p. 1970. pap. 8.50x (ISBN 0-8448-0099-6). Crane-Russak Co.
Lucas, George R., Jr. & Ogletree, Thomas W., eds. Lifeboat Ethics: The Moral Dilemma of World Hunger. LC 76-10002. 192p. 1976. 8.95 (ISBN 0-06-065308-6, HarpR); pap. 4.95x (ISBN 0-06-065309-4, RD170, HarpR). Har-Row.
McClintock, David W. U.S. Food: Making the Most of a Global Resource. 1979. lib. bdg. 20.00x (ISBN 0-89158-183-9). Westview.
McGee, Charles T. How to Survive Modern Technology. LC 80-82327. 256p. (Orig.). 1981. pap. 2.95 (ISBN 0-87983-230-4). Keats.
McMillen, Wheeler. Feeding Multitudes. 1981. text ed. write for info. (ISBN 0-8134-2192-6). Interstate.
Manning. Society & Food: The Third World. (Sicon Bks Ser). 1977. 3.95 (ISBN 0-408-71304-6). Butterworth.
Manocha, S. L. Nutrition & Our Overpopulated Planet. (Illus.). 488p. 1975. 31.75 (ISBN 0-398-03180-0); pap. 22.50 (ISBN 0-398-03181-9). C C Thomas.
Marei, Sayed A. The World Food Crisis. 2nd ed. LC 76-4538. 1978. text ed. 10.95x (ISBN 0-582-78077-2). Longman.
Marston, Robert B. War, Famine & Our Food Supply. LC 75-26308. (World Food Supply Ser). (Illus.). 1976. Repr. of 1897 ed. 16.00x (ISBN 0-405-07787-4). Arno.
Marx, Herbert L., Jr., ed. The World Food Crisis. (Reference Shelf Ser: Vol. 47, No. 6). 1975. 6.25 (ISBN 0-8242-0574-X). Wilson.
Mathur, S. C. Agricultural Policy & Food Self-Sufficiency. 1970. 10.50 (ISBN 0-686-20190-6). Intl Bk Dist.
May, Jacques M. & McLellan, Donna L., eds. Studies in Medical Geography, 14 vols. Incl. Vol. 2. Studies in Disease Ecology. (Illus.). 1961. 24.25 (ISBN 0-02-848980-2); Vol. 3. The Ecology of Malnutrition in the Far & Near East. (Illus.). 1961. 21.75 (ISBN 0-02-849010-X); Vol. 4. The Ecology of Malnutrition in Five Countries of Eastern & Central Europe: East Germany,Poland, Yugoslavia, Albania, Greece. (Illus.). 1964. 16.25 (ISBN 0-02-848970-5); Vol. 5. The Ecology of Malnutrition in Middle Africa: Ghana, Nigeria, Republic of the Congo, Rwanda & Burundi & the Former French Equatorial Africa. (Illus.). 1965. 14.25 (ISBN 0-02-848990-X); Vol. 6. The Ecology of Malnutrition in Central & Southern Europe: Austria, Hungary, Romania, Bulgaria & Czechoslovakia. (Illus.). 1966. 16.25 (ISBN 0-02-849000-2); Vol. 7. The Ecology of Malnutrition in Northern Africa: Libya, Tunisia, Algeria, Morocco, Spanish Sahara & Ifni, Mauretania. (Illus.). 1967. 16.25 (ISBN 0-02-848950-0); Vol. 8. The Ecology of Malnutrition in the French-Speaking Countries of West Africa & Madagascar: Senegal, Guinea, Ivory Coast, Togo, Dahomey, Cameroon, Niger, Mali, Upper Volta, & Madagascar. (Illus.). 1968. 18.50 (ISBN 0-02-848960-8); Vol. 9. The Ecology of Malnutrition in Eastern Africa: Equatorial Guinea, the Gambia, Liberia, Sierra Leone, Malawi, Rhodesia, Zambia, Kenya, Tanzania, Uganda, Ethiopia, the French Territory of the Atars & Issas, the Somali Republic & Sudan. 1970. 28.50 (ISBN 0-02-849020-7); Vol. 10. The Ecology of Malnutrition in Seven Countries of Southern Africa and in Portuguese Guinea: The/Republic of South Africa, South West Africa (Namibia), Botswana, Lesotho, Swaziland, Mozambique, Angola, Portuguese Guinea. 1971. 24.00 (ISBN 0-02-848940-3); Vol. 11. The Ecology of Malnutrition in Mexico & Central America. 1972. 21.75 (ISBN 0-02-848930-6); Vol. 12. The Ecology of Malnutrition in the Caribbean. 1973. 26.25 (ISBN 0-02-848920-9); Vol. 13. The Ecology of Malnutrition in Eastern South America. 1975. 36.25 (ISBN 0-02-849060-6); Vol. 14. The Ecology of Malnutrition in Western South America. 1975. 28.50 (ISBN 0-02-849070-3). Hafner.
Mayer, Jean & Dwyer, Johanna, eds. Food & Nutrition Policy in a Changing World. (Illus.). 1978. text ed. 18.95x (ISBN 0-19-502363-3); pap. text ed. 11.95x (ISBN 0-19-502364-1). Oxford U Pr.
Mezerik, Avrahm G., ed. Food & Population. 1963. pap. 15.00 (ISBN 0-685-13198-X, 76). Intl Review.
Miljan, Toivo, et al. Food & Agriculture in Global Perspective: Discussions in the Committee of the Whole of the United States. (Illus.). 260p. 1980. 28.00 (ISBN 0-08-025550-7). Pergamon.
Minear, Larry. New Hope for the Hungry? The Challenge of the World Food Crisis. (Orig.). 1975. pap. 1.95 (ISBN 0-377-00043-4). Friend Pr.
Nair, Kusum. Three Bowls of Rice, India & Japan: A Century of Effort. 1973. 8.50 (ISBN 0-87013-178-8). Mich St U Pr.
National Academy Of Sciences. Prospects of the World Food Supply. 1966. pap. 1.50 (ISBN 0-309-00070-X). Natl Acad Pr.
National Research Council. World Food & Nutrition Study: Potential Contributions of Research, Commission on International Relations. 1977. pap. 10.50 (ISBN 0-309-02628-8). Natl Acad Pr.
Olson, Mancur L., Jr. Economics of Wartime Shortages: A History of British Food Supplies in the Napoleonic War & in World War 1 & World War 2. LC 63-17328. 1963. 12.75 (ISBN 0-8223-0126-1). Duke.
Osborn, Fairfield. Limits of the Earth. LC 76-148640. 1971. Repr. of 1953 ed. lib. bdg. 15.00 (ISBN 0-8371-6005-7, OSLE). Greenwood.
Owens, Owen D. Stones into Bread? LC 77-3890. 1977. pap. 3.95 (ISBN 0-8170-0745-8). Judson.
Pearcy, G. Etzel. World Food Scene. LC 80-80423. (Illus.). 220p. (Orig.). 1980. pap. 13.95 (ISBN 0-686-62774-1). Plycon Pr.
Pearson, Frank A. & Harper, Floyd A. World's Hunger. LC 71-153235. 1971. Repr. of 1945 ed. 12.00 (ISBN 0-8046-1545-4). Kennikat.
Pimentel, David & Pimentel, Marcia. Food, Energy & Society. LC 79-9484. 1979. pap. 16.95x (ISBN 0-470-26840-9). Halsted Pr.
Pimentel, David, ed. World Food, Pest Losses & the Environment. LC 77-90418. (AAAS Selected Symposium Ser.: No. 13). (Illus.). 1978. lib. bdg. 23.25 (ISBN 0-89158-441-2). Westview.
Pontecorvo, Giulio, ed. The Management of Food Policy. LC 75-33468. (Indivual Publications Ser.). (Illus.). 1975. lib. bdg. 12.00x (ISBN 0-405-06680-5). Arno.
Post, John D. The Last Great Subsistence Crisis in the Western World. LC 76-41239. (Illus.). 256p. 1977. 17.00x (ISBN 0-8018-1850-8). Johns Hopkins.
Power, Jonathan & Holenstein, Anne-Marie. World of Hunger: A Strategy for Survival. 1977. 18.75 (ISBN 0-85117-097-8). Transatlantic.
Provisional Food Balance Sheets Seventy-Two to Seventy Four. 1978. pap. 38.25 (ISBN 0-685-60670-8, F1385, FAO). Unipub.
Rajki, Sandor, ed. Proceedings of a Workshop on Agricultural Potentiality Directed by Nutritional Needs. (Illus.). 238p. 1979. 25.00x (ISBN 963-05-1991-7). Intl Pubns Serv.
Raphael, Dana. Breast Feeding & Food Policy in a Hungry World. LC 78-27683. 1979. 23.00 (ISBN 0-12-580950-6). Acad Pr.
Reid, Margaret G. Food for People. LC 75-26312. (World Food Supply Ser). (Illus.). 1976. Repr. of 1943 ed. 38.00x (ISBN 0-405-07790-4). Arno.
Reid, Sue T. & Lyon, David L. Population Crisis: An Interdisciplinary Perspective. 220p. 1972. pap. 4.95x (ISBN 0-673-07629-6). Scott F.
Report of the Council of FAO, 71st Session. 1978. pap. 8.00 (ISBN 92-5-100348-3, F1227, FAO). Unipub.
Report of the Council of Fao, 74th Session. 38p. 1979. pap. 7.50 (ISBN 92-5-100723-3, F1545, FAO). Unipub.
Report of the Eleventh FAO Regional Conference for Europe. 1979. pap. 7.50 (ISBN 92-5-100726-8, F1580, FAO). Unipub.
Report of the Fifteenth FAO Regional Conference for Asia & the Pacific. 97p. 1981. pap. 7.50 (ISBN 92-5-100963-5, F2084, FAO). Unipub.
Report of the First Session of the United Nations - FAO Committee on Food Aid Policies & Programmes, Rome, 26 April-6 May 1976. 71p. 1976. pap. 5.25 (ISBN 92-5-100065-4, FAO). Unipub.
Report on the Second FAO-UNFPA Expert Consultation on Land Resources for Populations of the Future. 369p. 1981. pap. 24.50 (ISBN 92-5-100925-2, F2073, FAO). Unipub.
Root, Waverley. Food of France. (Illus.). 1958. 16.95 (ISBN 0-394-40132-8). Knopf.
Ross, Douglas N., ed. The Challenge of Overpopulation & Food Shortages. LC 76-6742. (Report Ser: No. 684). 61p. (Orig.). 1976. pap. 15.00 (ISBN 0-8237-0118-2). Conference Bd.
Rountree, Estelle & Halverstadt, Hugh, eds. Sometimes They Cry. rev. ed. LC 72-129096. (Illus., Orig.). 1974. pap. 3.50 (ISBN 0-377-00091-4). Friend Pr.
Russell, Edward J. World Population & World Food Supplies. LC 76-23307. (Illus.). 513p. 1976. Repr. of 1954 ed. lib. bdg. 34.50x (ISBN 0-8371-8997-7, RUWP). Greenwood.
Sanderson, Fred. Japan's Food Prospects & Policies. 1978. pap. 3.95 (ISBN 0-8157-7701-9). Brookings.
Schneider, Hartmut. Food Aid for Development. 1979. 6.75x (ISBN 92-64-11862-4). OECD.
Schultz, Theodore W., ed. Food for the World. LC 75-26313. (World Food Supply Ser). (Illus.). 1976. Repr. of 1945 ed. 22.00x (ISBN 0-405-07791-2). Arno.
Scientific American Editors. Food & Agriculture: A Scientific American Book. (Illus.). 1976. text ed. 16.95x (ISBN 0-7167-0382-3); pap. 8.95x (ISBN 0-7167-0381-5). W H Freeman.
Segal, Judith A. Food for the Hungry: The Reluctant Society. LC 79-133455. (Policy Studies in Employment & Welfare: No. 4). (Illus.). 83p. 1970. 7.50x (ISBN 0-8018-1227-5); pap. 2.95x (ISBN 0-8018-1226-7). Johns Hopkins.
Sider, Ronald J. Rich Christians in an Age of Hunger: A Biblical Study. LC 76-45106. 1977. pap. 4.95 (ISBN 0-87784-793-2). Inter-Varsity.
Simon, Arthur. Bread for the World. 179p. 1975. pap. 2.95 (ISBN 0-8028-1602-9). Eerdmans.
Sinha, Radha. Food & Poverty: The Political Ecomomy of Confrontation. LC 76-3727. 220p. 1976. text ed. 21.50x (ISBN 0-8419-0262-3). Holmes & Meier.
Sinha, Radha & Drabek, Gordon, eds. The World Food Problem: Consensus & Conflict. 1978. pap. text ed. 22.00 (ISBN 0-08-024318-5). Pergamon.
Slater, Charles C., et al. Easing Transition in Southern Africa: New Techniques for Policy Planning. LC 79-5018. (A Westview Replica Edition Ser.). (Illus.). 1979. lib. bdg. 20.00x (ISBN 0-89158-481-1). Westview.
Slater, William. Man Must Eat. LC 64-13951. 1964. 5.50x (ISBN 0-226-76185-1). U of Chicago Pr.
Smith, T. Lynn. The Race Between Population & Food Supply in Latin America. LC 75-17375. 194p. 1976. 12.50x (ISBN 0-8263-0366-8). U of NM Pr.
Spitzer, Robert R. No Need for Hunger. 1981. text ed. write for info. (ISBN 0-8134-2193-4). Interstate.
Srivastava, Uma K., et al. Food Aid: International Economic Growth. (Illus.). 1975. text ed. 8.25x (ISBN 0-8138-0640-2). Iowa St U Pr.
Stanley, Robert G. Food for Peace. 1973. 29.25 (ISBN 0-677-03650-7). Gordon.
The State of Food & Agriculture. annual Incl. 1957. pap. 4.25 (ISBN 0-685-48263-4); 1963. pap. 12.00 (ISBN 0-685-48264-2); 1969. pap. 18.00 (ISBN 0-685-48265-0); 1970. pap. 22.25 (ISBN 0-685-48266-9); 1971. pap. 22.25 (ISBN 0-685-48267-7). (Illus., Orig., F1479, FAO). Unipub.
State of Food & Agriculture Nineteen Seventy-Seven. (Agriculture Ser.: No. 8). 1979. pap. 17.00 (ISBN 92-5-100607-5, F1528, FAO). Unipub.
The State of Food & Agriculture 1979. 153p. 1981. pap. 21.75 (ISBN 92-5-100897-3, F2113, FAO). Unipub.
Stouff, Louis. Ravitaillement et Alimentation En Provence Aux XIVe & XVe Siecles. (Civilisations et Societes: No. 20). (Illus.). 1971. pap. 50.00x (ISBN 90-2796-886-1). Mouton.
Strategy for Plenty: The Indicative World Plan for Agricultural Development. (World Food Problems Ser: No. 11). (Orig.). 1970. pap. 4.75 (ISBN 0-685-04925-6, F451, FAO). Unipub.
Talbot, Ross, ed. The World Food Problem & U.S. Food Politics & Policies 1972-1976. 350p. 1977. pap. text ed. 8.95x (ISBN 0-8138-0040-4). Iowa St U Pr.
Talbot, Ross B., ed. World Food Problem & U. S. Food Politics & Policies: 1977. 1978. pap. text ed. 7.50 (ISBN 0-8138-0970-3). Iowa St U Pr.
--World Food Problem & U. S. Food Politics & Policies: Nineteen Seventy-Eight. 1979. pap. text ed. 8.75 (ISBN 0-8138-1155-4). Iowa St U Pr.
Tarrant, John R. Food Policies. LC 79-40740. (Wiley Series on Studies in Environmental Management & Resources Development). 338p. 1980. 48.95 (ISBN 0-471-27656-1, Pub. by Wiley-Interscience). Wiley.
Task Force on World Hunger. And He Had Compassion on Them: The Christian & World Hunger. (Illus.). 1979. pap. text ed. 2.15 (ISBN 0-933140-00-2). Bd of Pubns CRC.
--For My Neighbor's Good: World Hunger & Structural Change. (Illus.). 1980. pap. text ed. 1.65 (ISBN 0-933140-11-8). Bd of Pubns CRC.
The New York Times. Give Us This Day... A Report on the World Food Crisis. LC 75-1038. 1975. 10.00 (ISBN 0-405-06644-9). Arno.
Thomas, Gerald W., et al. Food & Fiber for a Changing World: Third-Century Challenge to American Agriculture. xiv, 225p. 1976. 7.95 (ISBN 0-8134-1817-8). Interstate.
Thomas, W. J., ed. & intro. by. The Demand for Food: An Exercise in Household Budget Analysis. (Illus.). 136p. 1972. text ed. 11.50x (ISBN 0-7190-0512-4). Humanities.
Trzyna, Thaddeus C. & Smith, Joan D. World Food Crisis: An International Directory of Organizations & Information Resources. LC 76-4270. (Who's Doing What Ser.: No. 2). 1977. pap. 20.00x (ISBN 0-912102-21-7). Cal Inst Public.
Tudge, Colin. The Famine Business. LC 76-28063. 1977. 8.95 (ISBN 0-312-28148-X). St Martin.
Tuve, George L. Energy, Environment, Population & Food: Our Four Interdependent Crises. LC 76-40351. 1976. 29.95 (ISBN 0-471-02091-5, Pub. by Wiley-Interscience). Wiley.
--Energy, Environment, Populations & Food: Our Four Interdependant Crises. LC 76-40351. 278p. 1976. 13.50 (ISBN 0-471-02090-7). Krieger.
United Nations-FAO Intergovernmental Committee,Twenty-Eighth Session,Rome,1975. World Food Programme: Report. 48p. 1976. pap. 7.50 (ISBN 0-685-66320-5, F1185, FAO). Unipub.
United States Institute of Inter-American Affairs. Paraguayan Rural Life, Survey of Food Problems, 1943-1945. Reh, Emma, et al, eds. LC 75-90733. (Illus.). 130p. 1975. Repr. of 1946 ed. lib. bdg. 15.50x (ISBN 0-8371-4047-1, PARL). Greenwood.
Valdes, Alberto, ed. Food Security for Developing Countries. 350p. 1981. lib. bdg. 26.25x (ISBN 0-86531-071-8). Westview.
Valentine, William. What Can We Do? A Food, Land, Hunger Action Guide. (Illus., Orig.). 1980. pap. 2.45 (ISBN 0-935028-06-4). Inst Food & Develp.
Values of Growth. LC 75-44724. (Critical Choices for Americans Ser.: Vol. VI). 1976. 13.95 (ISBN 0-669-00418-9). Lexington Bks.
Waldmeir, Joseph, ed. Essays in Honor of Russel B. Nye. 1978. 10.00x (ISBN 0-87013-209-1). Mich St U Pr.
Weston, Burns H., frwd. By. Food-Hunger Macro-Analysis Seminar. (Illus.). 92p. 1977. 2.50 (ISBN 0-686-62578-1). Inst World Order.
Willett, Joseph W. The World Food Situation: Problems & Prospects to 1985, 2 vols, Vols.1 & 2. LC 75-37594. 1976. 55.00 (ISBN 0-685-66659-X). Vol. 1 (ISBN 0-379-00572-7). Vol. 2 (ISBN 0-379-00573-5). Oceana.
Wilson, Harold. War on World Poverty: An Appeal to the Conscience of Mankind. LC 54-19767. 1969. Repr. of 1953 ed. 12.00 (ISBN 0-527-97100-6). Kraus Repr.
Wolf, Ray. Eating Better for Less. LC 77-26011. 1978. pap. 8.95 (ISBN 0-87857-206-6). Rodale Pr Inc.
Woods, Richard G., ed. Future Dimensions of World Food & Populations. (Winrock Ser.). 425p. 1981. lib. bdg. 23.75x (ISBN 0-86531-160-9). Westview.
World Food - Hunger Studies. 229p. 1977. 5.00 (ISBN 0-686-63875-1). Inst World Order.
World Food Conference, Ames, Iowa June, 1976. Proceedings. Schaller, Frank, ed. 1977. text ed. 8.50x (ISBN 0-8138-1825-7). Iowa St U Pr.
World Food Programme: Report of the Eighth Session of the UN - FAO Committee on Food Aid Policies & Programmes. 55p. 1980. pap. 9.00 (ISBN 92-5-100895-7, F1967, FAO). Unipub.
World Food Programme: Report of the Ninth Session. 53p. 1981. pap. 7.50 (ISBN 92-5-100953-8, F2092, FAO). Unipub.
World Food Programs: Report of the 3rd Session of UN-FAO Committee on Food Aid Policy & Programs. (Illus.). 1978. pap. 6.50 (ISBN 92-5-100352-1, F1242, FAO). Unipub.
Wortman, Sterling & Cummings, Ralph W., Jr. To Feed the World: The Challenge & the Strategy. LC 78-8478. 464p. 1978. pap. text ed. 7.95x (ISBN 0-8018-2137-1). Johns Hopkins.
Wynne-Tyson, Jon. Food for a Future: The Complete Case for Vegetarianism. LC 78-65622. 1979. 8.50x (ISBN 0-87663-334-3); pap. 4.95 (ISBN 0-87663-991-0). Universe.

FOOD SUPPLY–JUVENILE LITERATURE

Berger, Melvin & Berger, Gilda. The New Food Book: Nutrition, Diet, Consumer Tips & Foods of the Future. LC 77-7976. (gr. 4-6). 1978. 7.95 (ISBN 0-690-01295-0, TYC-J); PLB 8.79 (ISBN 0-690-03841-0). Har-Row.
Jones, Claire, et al. Pollution: The Population Explosion. LC 71-178675. (Real World of Pollution Ser). (Illus.). (gr. 5-11). 1972. PLB 4.95 (ISBN 0-8225-0633-5). Lerner Pubns.
Perl, Lila. The Global Food Shortage. LC 75-35860. 128p. (gr. 5-9). 1976. PLB 6.96 (ISBN 0-688-32068-6). Morrow.
--Hunter's Stew & Hangtown Fry. LC 77-5366. 176p. (gr. 6 up). 1977. 8.95 (ISBN 0-395-28922-X, Clarion). HM.

Pringle, Laurence. Our Hungry Earth: The World Food Crisis. LC 76-10828. (Science for Survival Ser.). 128p. (gr. 7 up). 1976. 7.95 (ISBN 0-02-775290-9, 77529). Macmillan.

FOOD SUPPLY-STATISTICS

FAO Production Yearbook: 1976, Vol. 30. (FAO Statistics Ser: No. 7). 1978. 18.00 (ISBN 0-686-67966-0, F346, FAO). Unipub.

Food Balance Sheets, 1964-1966. 766p. (Orig.). 1972. pap. 18.00 (ISBN 0-685-25257-4, F191, FAO). Unipub.

FOOD TEXTURE

DeMan, J. M., et al, eds. Rheology & Texture in Food Quality. (Illus.). 1976. lib. bdg. 49.50 (ISBN 0-87055-197-3); pap. text ed. 26.00 (ISBN 0-87055-295-3). AVI.

Kramer, A., et al, eds. Texture Measurement of Foods: Psychophysical Fundamentals-Sensory, Mechanical & Chemical Procedures & Their Interrelationships. LC 72-93271. 175p. 1973. lib. bdg. 34.00 (ISBN 90-277-0307-8, Pub. by Reidel Holland). Kluwer Boston.

Sone, T. Consistency of Foodstuffs. Matsumoto, S., tr. from Japanese. LC 78-183368. Orig. Title: Shokuhin No Nenchosei. (Illus.). 188p. 1972. lib. bdg. 34.00 (ISBN 90-277-0219-5, Pub. by Reidel Holland). Kluwer Boston.

FOOD TRADE

see Farm Produce-Marketing; Food Industry and Trade; Produce Trade

FOODS, CONTAMINATED

see Food Contamination

FOOLS AND JESTERS

see also Clowns

Busby, Olive M. Studies in the Development of the Fool in the Elizabethan Drama. LC 72-39567. Repr. of 1923 ed. 5.00 (ISBN 0-404-07849-4). AMS Pr.

--Studies in the Development of the Fool in the Elizabethan Drama. LC 75-17871. 1923. lib. bdg. 12.50 (ISBN 0-8414-3223-6). Folcroft.

Clouston, William A. Book of Noodles: Stories of Simpletons. LC 67-24351. 1969. Repr. of 1888 ed. 19.00 (ISBN 0-8103-3519-0). Gale.

Doran, John. History of Court Fools. LC 68-3844. (Studies in Comparative Literature, No. 35). 1969. Repr. of 1858 ed. lib. bdg. 49.95 (ISBN 0-8383-0656-X). Haskell.

Lippincott, H. F., ed. A Shakespeare Jestbook: Robert Armin's Foole Upon Foole, a Critical Old-Spelling Edition. (Studies in English Literature, Salzburg Elizabethan & Renaissance Studies: No. 20). (Illus.). 165p. 1973. pap. text ed. 22.75x (ISBN 0-391-01462-5). Humanities.

Welsford, Enid. The Fool, His Social & Literary History. 8.50 (ISBN 0-8446-5832-4). Peter Smith.

FOOT

see also Clubfoot; Podiatry

Arnot, Michelle. Foot Notes: The Complete Guide for Everyone Who Runs, Dances, Walks or Stands on Their Own Two Feet. LC 79-7857. (Illus.). 192p. 1980. pap. 5.95 (ISBN 0-385-14944-1, Dolp). Doubleday.

Bateman & Trott. The Foot & Ankle. 1980. 32.00 (ISBN 0-686-29378-9). Thieme Stratton.

Bateman, James E., ed. Foot Science: A Selection of Papers from the Proceedings of the American Orthopaedic Foot Society, Inc., 1974 & 1975. LC 75-14780. (Illus.). 290p. 1976. text ed. 31.75 (ISBN 0-7216-1580-5). Saunders.

Berkman, Sue, et al. A Doctor Discusses Care of the Feet. (Illus.). 110p. 1979. pap. 2.50 (ISBN 0-685-46330-3). Budlong.

Berkson, Devaki. The Foot Book: Healing with the Integrated Treatment of Foot Reflexology. LC 76-56733. (Funk & W Bk.). (Illus.). 1977. 9.95 (ISBN 0-308-10295-9). T Y Crowell.

Bragg, Paul C. & Bragg, Patricia. Building Strong Feet. 10th ed. pap. 1.75 (ISBN 0-87790-013-2). Health Sci.

Cailliet, Rene. Foot & Ankle Pain. (Illus.). 1968. pap. 7.95 (ISBN 0-8036-1600-7). Davis Co.

Costello, Maurice J. & Gibbs, Richard C. Palms & Soles in Medicine. (American Lecture Dermatology Ser.). (Illus.). 720p. 1967. pap. 60.25 photocopy ed. spiral (ISBN 0-398-00351-3). C C Thomas.

Gerrick, David J. Flatfeet: Man Adapting. (Illus.). 1978. 15.00 (ISBN 0-916750-20-5). Dayton Labs.

Giannestras, Nicholas J., ed. Foot Disorders: Medical & Surgical Management. 2nd ed. LC 72-13759. (Illus.). 699p. 1973. text ed. 37.50 (ISBN 0-8121-0407-2). Lea & Febiger.

Griffin, James M. & Buttell, Louis G., eds. Conservative vs. Surgical Management of Foot Disorders. (Illus.). 1972. 25.75 (ISBN 0-8151-4002-9, Pub. by Symposia Special). Year Bk Med.

Helfet, Arthur J., et al. Disorders of the Foot. 1980. text ed. 31.00 (ISBN 0-397-50430-6, JBL-Med-Nursing). Har-Row.

Hlavac, Harry. The Foot Book: Advice for Athletes. rev. ed. LC 77-78337. (Illus.). 400p. 1977. 14.95 (ISBN 0-89037-119-9). Anderson World.

Hoerr, Normand L., et al. Radiographic Atlas of Skeletal Development of the Foot & Ankle: A Standard of Reference. (Illus.). 176p. 1962. photocopy ed. spiral 22.75 (ISBN 0-398-00850-7). C C Thomas.

Holzenthaler, Jean. My Feet Do. LC 78-13143. (Illus.). (ps-1). 1979. 7.95 (ISBN 0-525-35485-9, Smart Cat). Dutton.

Humphry, George M. The Human Foot & the Human Hand. LC 78-72803. Repr. of 1861 ed. 21.50 (ISBN 0-404-60866-3). AMS Pr.

Krishef, Robert K. Our Remarkable Feet. LC 67-30693. (Medical Bks for Children). (Illus.). (gr. 3-9). 1968. PLB 3.95 (ISBN 0-8225-0018-3). Lerner Pubns.

Kunz, Kevin & Kunz, Barbara. The Complete Guide to Foot Reflexology. (Illus.). 149p. (Orig.). 1980. pap. text ed. 12.95 (ISBN 0-9606070-0-5). RRP.

Levin, Marvin E. & O'Neal, Lawrence W. The Diabetic Foot. 2nd ed. LC 77-7909. (Illus.). 1977. text ed. 37.50 (ISBN 0-8016-2984-5). Mosby.

Mennell, John M. Foot Pain: Diagnosis & Treatment Using Manipulative Techniques. 251p. 1969. 14.95 (ISBN 0-316-56669-1). Little.

Montagne. Atlas of Foot Radiology. 1981. price not set (ISBN 0-89352-097-7). Masson Pub.

Neale, Donald. Common Foot Disorders. (Illus.). 224p. 1981. lib. bdg. 24.00 (ISBN 0-443-01938-X). Churchill.

Roven, Milton D. Non-Disabling Surgical Rehabilitation of the Forefoot. LC 76-176177. (Illus.). 416p. 1976. 32.50 (ISBN 0-87527-123-5). Green.

Rutt. Surgery of the Leg & Foot. (Hackenbroch Ser.). 1980. text ed. write for info. (ISBN 0-7216-4446-5). Saunders.

Schneider, Myles J. & Sussman, Mark D. How to Doctor Your Feet Without the Doctor. 1981. pap. 9.95 (ISBN 0-684-16841-3, ScribT). Scribner.

Shaw, Alan H., ed. The Evaluation & Treatment of Basic Foot Deformities. (Illus.). 1974. 26.00 (ISBN 0-8151-7641-4, Pub. by Symposia Special). Year Bk Med.

Smith, Stephen D. & Di Giovanni, James D., eds. Decision Making in Foot Surgery. LC 76-1049. (Illus.). 1976. text ed. 26.95 (ISBN 0-8151-7832-8, Pub. by Symposia Special). Year Bk Med.

Subotnick, Steven. The Running Foot Doctor. LC 77-73653. (Illus.). 144p. 1977. pap. 4.95 (ISBN 0-89037-117-2); handbk. 6.95 (ISBN 0-89037-116-4). Anderson World.

Tachdjian, Mihran O. The Child's Foot. Date not set. text ed. write for info. (ISBN 0-7216-8734-2). Saunders.

Tillman, K. The Rheumatoid Foot: Diagnosis, Pathomechanics, & Treatment. Goldie, Ian F., tr. from Ger. (Illus.). 116p. 1979. text ed. 29.00 (ISBN 0-88416-304-0). Wright-PSG.

Watson, Elizabeth E. Busy Feet. LC 81-50674. (A Happy Day Bk.). (Illus.). 24p. (Orig.). (ps-1). 1981. pap. 0.98 (ISBN 0-87239-461-1, 3594). Standard Pub.

Weisenfeld, Murry F. & Burr, Barbara. The Foot Book. 1980. 10.00 (ISBN 0-312-29780-7). St Martin.

FOOT-AND-MOUTH DISEASE

European Commission for Control of Foot & Mouth Disease. Report: Twenty-First Session, Rome, April 8-11, 1975. 120p. 1976. pap. 7.50 (ISBN 0-685-65010-3, F1130, FAO). Unipub.

European Commission for the Control of Foot & Mouth Disease, Twenty First Session, Rome, Italy, April 8-11, 1975. Report. 120p. 1976. pap. 7.50 (ISBN 0-685-66329-9, F1130, FAO). Unipub.

Machado, Manuel A., Jr. Aftosa: A Historical Survey of Foot & Mouth Disease & Inter-American Relations. LC 69-11317. 1969. 16.00 (ISBN 0-87395-040-2); microfiche 16.00 (ISBN 0-87395-140-9). State U NY Pr.

Mackowiak, C. & Regamey, R. H., eds. International Symposium on Foot-&-Mouth Disease (II) (Developments in Biological Standardization: Vol. 35). (Illus.). 1977. 57.50 (ISBN 3-8055-2778-0). S Karger.

Report of the Session of the Research Group of the Standing Technical Committee of the European Commission for the Control of Foot & Mouth Disease Held in Brescia, Italy, 6-7 June 1977. 16p. 1978. pap. 7.50 (ISBN 92-5-100343-2, F1236, FAO). Unipub.

Report of the Twenty Second Session of the European Commission for the Control of Foot-&-Mouth Disease. (Illus.). 1978. pap. 8.50 (ISBN 92-5-100319-X, F1245, FAO). Unipub.

FOOT RACING

see Running

FOOT TRAILS

see Trails

FOOTBALL

see also Football Coaching; Passing (Football); Rugby Football; Soccer; Touch Football

Aaseng, Nathan. Football's Cunning Coaches. LC 80-29252. (The Sports Heroes Library). (Illus.). (gr. 4 up). 1981. PLB 6.95g (ISBN 0-8225-1065-0). Lerner Pubns.

--Football's Steadiest Kickers. LC 80-28863. (Sports Heroes Library). (Illus.). (gr. 4 up). 1981. PLB 6.95g (ISBN 0-8225-1069-3). Lerner Pubns.

--Football's Toughest Tight Ends. LC 80-27803. (Sports Heroes Ser.). (Illus.). (gr. 4 up). 1981. PLB 6.95g (ISBN 0-8225-1070-7). Lerner Pubns.

ABC Monday Night Football Book. 1980. pap. cancelled (ISBN 0-201-00058-X). A-W.

Agajanian, Ben & Owens, Paul. The Kicking Game. LC 80-66071. (Illus.). 96p. (Orig.). 1980. pap. 4.95 (ISBN 0-89087-267-8). Celestial Arts.

Allen, George & Weiskopf, Don. Handbook of Winning Football. 1976. text ed. 17.95 (ISBN 0-205-04880-3). Allyn.

American Alliance for Health, Physical Education & Recreation. Flag Football-Speedball Guide 1978-80. (Illus.). 1978. pap. 2.50 (ISBN 0-685-29039-5, 243-26190). AAHPERD.

Attner, Paul. The Terrapins: Maryland Football. LC 75-12204. (College Sports Ser.). 1975. 9.95 (ISBN 0-87397-066-7). Strode.

Barone, Steve. Aztec Uprising. (Illus.). 1975. 7.95 (ISBN 0-89325-000-7). Joyce Pr.

Barrett, Frank & Barrett, Lynn. How to Watch a Football Game. LC 79-3448. (Illus.). 256p. (Orig.). 1980. pap. 7.95 (ISBN 0-03-056958-3). HR&W.

Bebb, Russ. The Big Orange: A Story of Tennessee Football. LC 73-86998. (College Sports Ser.). 1974. 9.95 (ISBN 0-87397-032-2). Strode.

Behee, John & Saylor, Tom. Wave the Flag for Hudson High. LC 77-89960. (Illus.). 1977. pap. 9.95x (ISBN 0-914464-02-7). J & J Bks.

Blanton, J. Neal. Game of the Century. (Illus.). 1970. 12.50 (ISBN 0-8363-0034-3). Jenkins.

Bold, Alan. Scots Football: A Celebration in Verse & Pictures. (Illus.). 1978. text ed. 10.95x (ISBN 0-8464-0824-4); pap. 5.95x (ISBN 0-686-77126-5). Beekman Pubs.

Bolton, Clyde. Alabama Football. (College Sports Ser.: Football). 1981. 10.95 (ISBN 0-87397-020-9). Strode.

--The Crimson Tide: A Story of Alabama Football. LC 72-91388. (College Sports Ser.). 1975. 9.95 (ISBN 0-87397-020-9). Strode.

--War Eagle: A Story of Auburn Football. LC 73-83502. (College Sports Ser.). 1973. 9.95 (ISBN 0-87397-023-3). Strode.

Bouma, Jim & Calpin, John C. The Delaware-Style Wing-T for High School Football. 1975. 10.95 (ISBN 0-13-197822-5, Parker). P-H.

Brock, Ted & Campbell, Jim. First Official NFL Trivia Book. 1980. pap. 1.95 (ISBN 0-451-09541-3, J9541, Sig). NAL.

Broeg, Bob. Ol' Mizzou: A Story of Missouri Football. LC 74-82943. (College Sports Ser.). Orig. Title: Missouri Football. 1974. 9.95 (ISBN 0-87397-051-9). Strode.

Camp, Walter. American Football. LC 74-15732. (Popular Culture in America Ser.). 248p. 1975. Repr. of 1891 ed. 17.00x (ISBN 0-405-06367-9). Arno.

Carlson, Kenneth N. College Football Scorebook. (Illus.). 972p. (Orig.). 1981. pap. 12.95 (ISBN 0-938428-01-2). Res Pubns WA.

Casotti, Fred. Colorado Football: The Golden Buffaloes. (College Sports Ser.). (Illus.). 225p. 1980. 9.95 (ISBN 0-87397-173-6). Strode.

Cebulash, Mel. Football Players Do Amazing Things. LC 73-3686. (Step-up Bk: No. 22). (Illus.). 72p. (gr. 2-5). 1975. 3.95 (ISBN 0-394-82677-9, BYR); PLB 4.99 (ISBN 0-394-92677-3). Random.

Conklin, Mike. Inside Football. 1978. pap. 5.95 (ISBN 0-8092-7585-6). Contemp Bks.

Cook, Ben. Year of the Tide (Alabama Football) LC 80-51066. (College Sports Ser.). (Illus.). 112p. (Orig.). 1980. pap. 5.95 (ISBN 0-87397-171-X). Strode.

Cromartie, Bill. Georgia-Georgia Tech Football. (College Sports Ser.: Football). 1981. 10.95 (ISBN 0-87397-124-8). Strode.

Dawson, P. Defeating Triple Option Offenses with the Backbone Defense. 1974. 10.95 (ISBN 0-13-197277-4). P-H.

DeLuca, Sam. The Football Handbook. LC 78-2876. 1978. 12.50 (ISBN 0-8246-0231-5). Jonathan David.

Devine, Dan & Onofrio, Al. Missouri Power Football. 2nd ed. 1967. text ed. 6.95x (ISBN 0-87543-006-6). Lucas.

Diles, David L. Twelfth Man in the Huddle. LC 76-19529. 1976. 2.95 (ISBN 0-8499-4112-1, 4112-1). Word Bks.

Dolan, Edward F., Jr. Basic Football Strategy. 1978. pap. 2.95 (ISBN 0-346-12344-5). Cornerstone.

Dolson, Frank. The Philadelphia Story: A City of Winners. (Illus.). 310p. 1981. 12.95 (ISBN 0-89651-600-8). Icarus.

Dunn, Jay. The Tigers of Princeton, Old Nassau Football. LC 76-24240. (College Sports Ser.). (Illus.). 1977. 9.95 (ISBN 0-87397-107-8). Strode.

Dyer, Pete. Coaching Football's Split Four-Four Multiple Defense. (Illus.). 1980. 11.95 (ISBN 0-13-139014-7, Parker). P-H.

Ecker, Tom & Calloway, Bill. Athletic Journal's Encylopedia of Football. (Illus.). 1978. 12.95 (ISBN 0-13-050047-X, Parker). P-H.

Etheredge, Randall & Etheridge, Warren. The Football Quiz Book. 124p. 1980. pap. 3.50 (ISBN 0-8015-2720-1, Hawthorn). Dutton.

Eubanks, Lon. University of Illinois Football. LC 76-7853. (College Sports Ser.). 1976. 9.95 (ISBN 0-87397-065-9). Strode.

Evans, Wilbur & McElroy, H. B. The Twelfth Man: A Story of Texas A & M Football. LC 74-81347. (College Sports Ser.). Orig. Title: Texas A & M Football. 1974. 9.95 (ISBN 0-87397-034-9). Strode.

Flynn, George L., ed. Vince Lombardi on Football. 352p. 1981. price not set (ISBN 0-442-22540-7). Van Nos Reinhold.

Football Register 1980. 9.00 (ISBN 0-89204-060-2). Sporting News.

Football Schedules Book. 4.00 (ISBN 0-686-22332-2). NAIA Pubns.

Football Trivia, No. 2. (Orig.). 1982. pap. 1.95 (ISBN 0-440-02684-9). Dell.

Football Trivia Puzzler No. One. (Orig.). 1980. pap. 1.95 (ISBN 0-440-02565-6). Dell.

Ford, Doug. The Wedge. 160p. 1965. pap. 2.95 (ISBN 0-346-12357-7). Cornerstone.

Fox, L. ABC Monday Night Football Book. 1981. pap. 5.95 (ISBN 0-201-10121-1). A-W.

Freeman, Denne. That Good Old Baylor Line. LC 75-260701. (College Sports Ser.). 1975. 9.95 (ISBN 0-87397-063-2). Strode.

Freeman, Denne H. Hook'em Horns: A Story of Texas Football. LC 74-84329. (College Sports Ser.). Orig. Title: Texas Football. 1980. 9.95 (ISBN 0-87397-054-3). Strode.

Frost, David, intro. by. The Bluffer's Guides: Second Series, 5 bks. Incl. Bluff Your Way in Antiques (ISBN 0-517-50027-2); Bluff Your Way in Football (ISBN 0-517-50028-0); Bluff Your Way in Gourmet Food (ISBN 0-517-50029-9); Bluff Your Way in the Theatre (ISBN 0-517-50031-0); Bluff Your Way in Travel (ISBN 0-517-50032-9). 64p. 1972. pap. 1.00 ea. Crown.

Gifford, Thomas. Benchwarmer Bob. new ed. LC 74-13550. (Illus.). 128p. (Orig.). 1974. pap. 3.95 (ISBN 0-685-50666-5). Piper.

Gogolak, Peter & Carter, Joseph. Nothing to Kick About: The Autobiography of a Modern Immigrant. LC 73-3904. (Illus.). 256p. 1973. 6.95 (ISBN 0-396-06820-0). Dodd.

Grambeau, Rodney J., ed. Official National Touch & Flag Football Rules for Men & Women. rev. ed. 1977. soft bdg. 2.00 (ISBN 0-87670-033-4). Athletic Inst.

Grobani, Anton, ed. Guide to Football Literature. LC 75-1478. xvi, 319p. 1975. 26.00 (ISBN 0-8103-0964-5). Gale.

Hardesty, Dan. The Louisiana Tigers: LSU Football. LC 75-12205. (College Sports Ser.). 1975. 9.95 (ISBN 0-87397-064-0). Strode.

Harlow, H. Winning Football with the Strategic Slot. 1969. 10.95 (ISBN 0-13-960831-1, Parker). P-H.

Heard, Robert. Oklahoma Vs. Texas: When Football Becomes War. LC 80-82909. (Illus.). 544p. 1980. 25.00 (ISBN 0-937642-00-2). Honey Hill.

Henry, Orville & Bailey, Jim. The Razorbacks: A Story of Arkansas Football. LC 73-87000. (College Sports Ser.). 1980. 9.95 (ISBN 0-87397-024-1). Strode.

Hodge, Ben, Sr. Good Times with Football. LC 77-81703. (Illus.). 20p. (Span. & Eng.). (gr. 3-4). 4.50 (ISBN 0-912122-11-0); pap. 1.89 (ISBN 0-912122-12-9); Eng. flash cards 3.50 (ISBN 0-912122-25-0); Span. flash cards 3.50 (ISBN 0-912122-26-9). Football Hobbies.

--Skram Runs Kicks & Throws. LC 77-81699. (Illus.). 18p. (gr. 1-2). 1976. 4.50 (ISBN 0-912122-03-X); pap. 1.89 (ISBN 0-912122-04-8). Football Hobbies.

Hollander, Zander. The Complete Handbook of Pro Football, 1981 Edition. (Orig.). 1981. pap. 3.50 (ISBN 0-451-09986-9, E9986, Sig). NAL.

Hollander, Zander, ed. The Complete Handbook of Pro Football: 1980. (Illus.). 275p. (Orig.). (YA) (RL 7). 1980. pap. 2.75 (ISBN 0-451-09359-3, E9359, Sig). NAL.

Holst, Art. Sunday Zebras. 1980. 10.00 (ISBN 0-9605118-0-6). Forest Pub.

Holtz, Lou & Hall, Wally. Lou Holtz in Hog Heaven (Arkansas Football) (College Sports Ser.). 250p. (Orig.). pap. 7.95 (ISBN 0-87397-174-4). Strode.

Hunter, Jim. Clemson Football. (College Sports Ser.: Football). 1981. 10.95 (ISBN 0-87397-194-9). Strode.

--The Gamecocks: South Carolina Football. LC 75-26073. (College Sport Ser.). 1975. 7.95 (ISBN 0-87397-069-1). Strode.

Jannsen, Al. One Way to Play Football: Pro-Athletes. (Illus.). 1979. pap. 3.95 (ISBN 0-89293-081-0). Beta Bk.
Jesse, John. Explosive Muscular Power for Championship Football. LC 68-58253. pap. 4.95 (ISBN 0-87095-032-0). Athletic.
--Explosive Muscular Power for Championship Football. pap. 1.95 (ISBN 0-685-07313-0). Borden.
Joyner, Glenn P. Parents Guide to Football Safety. 1978. pap. text ed. 4.00 (ISBN 0-932800-01-7). Ginseng Pr.
Klein, Dave. The Pro Football Mystique. (Orig.). 1978. pap. 1.95 (ISBN 0-451-08353-9, J8353, Sig). NAL.
Klobuchar, Jim. Will America Accept Love at Halftime? or How to Survive Pro-Football Sunday. pap. 2.95 (ISBN 0-87018-066-5). Ross.
Lentvorsky, Marie G. Read Before Kickoff: Building the High School Football Player. 1978. 6.50 (ISBN 0-533-03630-5). Vantage.
Libby, Bill. O. J. The Story of Football's Fabulous O. J. Simpson. new ed. LC 73-88519. (Putnam Sports Shelf). 160p. (gr. 5 up). 1974. PLB 6.29 (ISBN 0-399-60874-5). Putnam.
Liss, Howard. Football Talk. 1981. pap. write for info. (ISBN 0-671-43472-1). Archway.
--Front Four: Let's Meet at the Quarterback. LC 75-127396. (Illus.). (gr. 7 up). 1970. 5.95 (ISBN 0-87460-238-6). Lion Bks.
Little, Mildred J., et al. Recreational Football: Flag, Touch, & Flicker. (Physical Education Activities Ser.). 112p. 1980. pap. text ed. write for info. (ISBN 0-697-07092-1). Wm C Brown.
Lott, Johnny & Brainard, Kathy. The Complete Book of Fossball. (Illus.). 1980. 9.95 (ISBN 0-8092-5999-0); pap. 5.95 (ISBN 0-8092-5998-2). Contemp Bks.
McCallum, John D. Ivy League Football Since 1872. LC 77-5450. (Illus.). 1977. 17.95 (ISBN 0-8128-2258-7). Stein & Day.
McDonough, John & Owens, Paul T. Don't Hit Him, He's Dead. Celestial Arts, ed. LC 78-54478. (Illus.). 1978. pap. 4.95 (ISBN 0-89087-219-8). Celestial Arts.
McEwen, Tom. The Gators: A Story of Florida Football. LC 74-82944. (College Sports Ser.). Orig. Title: Florida Football. 1974. 9.95 (ISBN 0-87397-025-X). Strode.
Marciani, Louis M. Touch & Flag Football. LC 74-9290. (Illus.). 160p. 1976. 9.95 (ISBN 0-498-01513-0). A S Barnes.
Marcin, Joe, ed. Sporting News National Football Guide. new ed. (Illus., Orig.). 1979. pap. 5.50 (ISBN 0-89204-048-3). Sporting News.
Martz, Jim. Miami(Florida) Football. (College Sports Ser.: Football). 1981. 10.95 (ISBN 0-87397-193-0). Strode.
Mazer, Bill & Fischler, Stan. The Amazin' Bill Mazer's Football Trivia Book. 160p. (Orig.). 1981. pap. 2.59 (ISBN 0-686-73173-5). Warner Bks.
Merrick, Fred. Down on the Farm: A Story of Stanford Football. LC 75-12202. (College Sports Ser.). 1975. 9.95 (ISBN 0-87397-070-5). Strode.
Mills, W. Down the Grid. (Illus.). 9.50 (ISBN 0-392-02710-0, SpS). Sportshelf.
Moore, Jim & Micoleau, T. Football Techniques Illustrated. rev. ed. (Illus.). 1962. 11.50 (ISBN 0-471-07152-8). Ronald Pr.
Mumau, Thad. Go Wolfpack: North Carolina State Football. (College Sports Ser.). (Illus.). 250p. 1980. 9.95 (ISBN 0-87397-179-5). Strode.
Namath, Joe & Oates, Bob, Jr. A Matter of Style. (Illus.). 1973. 12.50 (ISBN 0-316-59690-6). Little.
National Football Guide 1980. 7.50 (ISBN 0-89204-059-9). Sporting News.
National Football League, compiled by. National Football League Nineteen Eighty Media Information Book. (Illus.). 180p. pap. 8.95 (ISBN 0-89480-093-0). Workman Pub.
Neft, D. S., et al. The Complete All-Time Pro Football Register. abr. ed. 192p. 1975. pap. 1.95 (ISBN 0-448-16241-5, Tempo). Ace Bks.
NFL Report, 1981. (Orig.). 1981. pap. 2.95 (ISBN 0-440-06381-7). Dell.
Norinsky, Marvin & Gudmundsson, Margaret. The I Don't Understand Football Book or How to Tackle the Game Painlessly. LC 81-2744. 192p. 1981. pap. 7.95 (ISBN 0-8253-0069-X). Beaufort Bks NY.
Official Nineteen Eighty-One NFL Record Manual. (Orig.). 1981. pap. 3.50 (ISBN 0-440-06577-1). Dell.
Olcott, Jack. Complete Book of Triple Option Football. 1975. 9.95 (ISBN 0-13-158089-2, Parker). P-H.
--Football's Fabulous Forty Defense. 1974. 10.95 (ISBN 0-13-324095-9). P-H.
Olson, O. Charles. Prevention of Football Injuries: Protecting the Health of the Student Athlete. LC 70-157472. 118p. 1971. pap. 5.00 (ISBN 0-8121-0346-7). Lea & Febiger.
Outlar, Jesse. Between the Hedges: A Story of Georgia Football. LC 73-87002. (College Sports Ser.). 1974. 7.95 (ISBN 0-87397-027-6). Strode.
Perry, Will. The Wolverines: A Story of Michigan Football. LC 74-84331. (College Sports Ser.). Orig. Title: Michigan Football. 1974. 9.95 (ISBN 0-87397-055-1). Strode.
Plimpton, George. One More July. 1978. pap. 1.95 (ISBN 0-425-03992-7, Medallion). Berkley Pub.
--Paper Lion. (RL 7). 1974. pap. 1.95 (ISBN 0-451-07668-0, J7668, Sig). NAL.
Pouncey, Temple. Southern Methodist Football: Mustang Mania. (College Sports Ser.). (Illus.). 1980. 9.95 (ISBN 0-87397-176-0). Strode.
Pyke, Frank & Smith, Ross. Football: The Scientific Way. (Illus.). xii, 84p. (Orig.). 1976. pap. 5.00x (ISBN 0-85564-108-8, Pub. by U of W Austral Pr). Intl Schol Bk Serv.
Rappoport, Ken. Great College Football Rivalries. 1978. pap. 1.95 (ISBN 0-448-14624-X, Tempo). Ace Bks.
--The Nittany Lions: A Story of Penn State Football. LC 73-86999. (College Sports Ser.). 1980. 9.95 (ISBN 0-87397-044-6). Strode.
--Notre Dame Football. (College Sports Ser.: Football). 1981. 11.95 (ISBN 0-87397-053-5). Strode.
--Southern Cal Football. (College Sports Ser.: Football). 1981. 11.95 (ISBN 0-87397-033-0). Strode.
--The Syracuse Football Story. LC 75-6096. (College Sports Ser.). 1975. 9.95 (ISBN 0-87397-061-6). Strode.
--The Trojans: A Story of Southern California Football. LC 74-81346. (College Sports Ser.). Orig. Title: Southern Cal Football. 1981. 11.95 (ISBN 0-87397-033-0). Strode.
--Wake Up the Echoes: Notre Dame Football. LC 75-26072. (College Sports Ser.). 1981. 11.95 (ISBN 0-87397-053-5). Strode.
Ray. Football Facts & Fun. pap. 0.50 (ISBN 0-685-07320-3). Borden.
Rice, Homer. Homer Rice on Triple Option Football. 1973. 10.95 (ISBN 0-13-394593-6, Parker). P-H.
Rice, Russ. The Wildcats: Kentucky Football. LC 75-26071. (College Sports Ser.). 1980. 9.95 (ISBN 0-87397-075-6). Strode.
Rippon, Anton. The Story of Aston Villa Football Club. 96p. 1981. 15.00x (ISBN 0-903485-99-0, Pub. by Moorland). State Mutual Bk.
--The Story of the Liverpool Football Club. 96p. 1981. 15.00x (ISBN 0-903485-98-2, Pub. by Moorland). State Mutual Bk.
Rockne, Dick. Bow Down to Washington: A Story of Husky Football. LC 75-12203. (College Sports Ser.). 1975. 9.95 (ISBN 0-87397-073-X). Strode.
Rockne, Knute K. Coaching. LC 70-124591. Repr. of 1925 ed. 15.00 (ISBN 0-404-05377-7). AMS Pr.
Rollow, Copper. Copper Rollow's Bears Nineteen Seventy-Eight Football Book. 224p. (YA) 1978. pap. 1.95 (ISBN 0-916054-71-3). Green Hill.
Rosenthal, Harold. The Fifty Faces of Football. LC 81-66009. 1981. 12.95 (ISBN 0-689-11218-1). Atheneum.
--Five Hundred Five Football Questions Your Friends Can't Answer. 192p. 9.95 (ISBN 0-8027-0661-4); pap. 5.95 (ISBN 0-8027-7163-7). Walker & Co.
Sahadi, Lou. The Raiders: Cinderella Champions of Pro Football. 1981. pap. 12.50 (ISBN 0-385-27192-1, Dist. by Doubleday). Dial.
Schachter, Norm. Close Calls: The Confessions of a NFL Referee. 288p. 1981. 12.95 (ISBN 0-688-00794-5). Morrow.
Schneider, Richard C. Head & Neck Injuries in Football: Mechanisms, Treatment & Prevention. LC 73-4197. 272p. 1973. 22.50 (ISBN 0-683-07573-X). Krieger.
Shapiro, David. One-Hundred Thirty-Five Greatest Pro Running Backs: How They Stack Up Against Each Other. (Illus.). 1978. pap. 7.95 (ISBN 0-9601912-1-6). Sportsminded Pubns.
Sloan, Steve. A Whole New Ball Game. LC 75-24737. (Illus.). 168p. 1975. 5.95 (ISBN 0-8054-5559-0). Broadman.
Snypp, Wilbur. The Buckeyes: A Story of Ohio State Football. LC 74-77737. (College Sports Ser.). Orig. Title: Ohio State Football. 1974. 9.95 (ISBN 0-87397-031-4). Strode.
Sorrels, Bill & Holmes, Charles. Memphis State Football: The Fighting Tigers. (College Sports Ser.). (Illus.). 1981. 10.95 (ISBN 0-87397-175-2). Strode.
Sorrels, William W. The Maroon Bulldogs: Mississippi State Football. LC 75-30454. (College Sports Ser.). 1975. 9.95 (ISBN 0-87397-076-4). Strode.
Stabler, Ken & LaMarre, Tom. Winning Offensive Football. LC 76-11227. (Winning Ser.). (Illus.). 1976. 8.95 (ISBN 0-8092-7991-6); pap. 5.95 (ISBN 0-8092-7990-8). Contemp Bks.
Stabley, Fred. W. The Spartans: A Story of Michigan State Football. LC 75-12206. (College Sports Ser.). 1975. 9.95 (ISBN 0-87397-067-5). Strode.
Staley, C. W. Unfair at Any Gridiron. LC 80-66404. 250p. 1981. 14.95 (ISBN 0-9604324-0-X, 8012 800326). CWS Group Pr.
Sullivan, George. Football Rules Illustrated. (Illus.). 96p. (Orig.). 1981. pap. 4.95 (ISBN 0-346-12526-X). Cornerstone.
Sweeney, George. Tulane: The Green Wave Football. (College Sports Ser.). (Illus.). 250p. 1980. 9.95 (ISBN 0-87397-172-8). Strode.
Tallman, Drew. How to Coach Football's Attacking Defenses. 1973. 10.95 (ISBN 0-13-403774-X, Parker). P-H.
--Winning Play Sequences in Modern Football. LC 73-134519. 1971. 10.95 (ISBN 0-13-961045-6, Parker). P-H.
Tatum, Jack & Kushner, Bill. They Call Me Assassin. LC 79-51202. (Illus.). 1980. 9.95 (ISBN 0-89696-060-9). Everest Hse.
Thomy, Al. The Ramblin' Wreck: A Story of Georgia Tech Football. LC 73-87003. (College Sports Ser.). 1974. 7.95 (ISBN 0-87397-028-4). Strode.
Toomay, Pat. The Crunch. (Illus.). 203p. 1975. 7.95 (ISBN 0-393-08726-3). Norton.
Treat, Roger. Encyclopedia of Football. 16th rev. ed. LC 79-63272. 1979. 17.95 (ISBN 0-498-02421-0). A S Barnes.
Troppmann, Bob. Winning Football Drills for Offensive & Defensive Linemen. 1973. 12.95 (ISBN 0-13-960872-9). P-H.
Trumpy, Bob & Mefford, Bill. Trump! LC 79-20367. (Illus.). 1979. pap. 5.95 (ISBN 0-89865-019-4). Donning Co.
Underwood, John. The Death of an American Game: The Crisis in Football. LC 79-19354. 1979. 10.95 (ISBN 0-316-88735-8). Little.
Unitas, John & Rosenthal, Harold. Playing Pro-Football to Win. (RL 7). 1974. pap. 1.50 (ISBN 0-451-07209-X, W7209, Sig). NAL.
Walker, D. Melvin. Football Forecasting: A System or Two. 1978. 5.95 (ISBN 0-533-03267-9). Vantage.
Weeks, Jim. The Sooners: A Story of Oklahoma Football. LC 74-84330. (College Sports Ser.). Orig. Title: Oklahoma Football. 1974. 9.95 (ISBN 0-87397-030-6). Strode.
Wilkinson, Bud. Sports Illustrated Football Quarterback. LC 75-17678. (Sports Illustrated Ser). (Illus.). 1976. 5.95 (ISBN 0-397-01097-4); pap. 2.95 (ISBN 0-397-01105-9). Lippincott.
Wright, Steve, et al. I'd Rather Be Wright. 192p. 1975. pap. 1.50 (ISBN 0-448-12097-6, Tempo). Ace Bks.
Zalonis, John J. Multiple Belly-Power System for High School Football. 1976. 10.95 (ISBN 0-13-604843-9). P-H.
Zban, Bill. The Five Fundamentals of Ballhandling in Football. new ed. LC 75-38455. (Illus.). 1977. 7.95 (ISBN 0-498-01888-1). A S Barnes.

FOOTBALL–BIOGRAPHY

see also names of individual players, e.g. Bellino, Joseph Michael

Aaseng, Nathan. Football's Crushing Blockers. (Sports Heroes Library). (Illus.). 80p. (gr. 6 up). 1981. PLB 6.95 (ISBN 0-8225-1074-X). Lerner Pubns.
Barnidge, Thomas & Grow, Douglas. The Jim Hart Story. (Illus.). 1977. 6.95 (ISBN 0-8272-1705-6); pap. 4.95 (ISBN 0-8272-1704-8). Bethany Pr.
Biddle, Marcia. Tony Dorsett. LC 80-18302. (Illus.). 192p. (gr. 7 up). 1980. PLB 8.79 (ISBN 0-671-34040-9). Messner.
Blair, Sam. Earl Campbell: The Driving Force. 1980. 8.95 (ISBN 0-8499-0259-2). Word Bks.
Bleier, Rocky & O'Neil, Terry. Fighting Back. rev. ed. LC 75-12865. (Illus.). 240p. 1980. 12.95 (ISBN 0-8128-2767-8). Stein & Day.
--Fighting Back. LC 75-12865. (Illus.). 224p. 1975. 8.95 (ISBN 0-8128-1845-8). Stein & Day.
--Fighting Back. (Illus.). 288p. 1976. pap. 2.75 (ISBN 0-446-95704-6). Warner Bks.
Blount, Roy, Jr. About Three Bricks Shy of a Load. 1981. pap. 2.75 (ISBN 0-345-29110-7). Ballantine.
Bradshaw, Terry & Diles, David. Man of Steel. 1980. pap. 4.95 (ISBN 0-310-39461-9). Zondervan.
Braun, Thomas. Football's Greatest Passer: Fran Tarkenton. (Allstars Ser.). (Illus.). (gr. 2-6). 1977. PLB 5.95 (ISBN 0-87191-583-9). Creative Ed.
Broeg, R. & Ewbank, Weeb. Football Greats. (Illus.). 1977. pap. 4.95 (ISBN 0-8272-1007-8). Bethany Pr.
Broyles, Frank & Bailey, James. Hog Wild: The Autobiography of Frank Broyles. (Illus.). 1979. 13.95 (ISBN 0-87870-065-X). Memphis St Univ.
Burchard, Marshall. Sports Hero: Fran Tarkenton. LC 77-7393. (Sports Hero Ser.). (Illus.). (gr. 3-5). 1977. PLB 6.29 (ISBN 0-399-61096-0). Putnam.
Burchard, S. H. Sports Star: Tony Dorsett. LC 78-52808. (Illus.). (gr. k-3). 1978. 5.25 (ISBN 0-15-278015-7, HJ). HarBraceJ.
Conrad, Dick. Tony Dorsett: From Heisman to Super Bowl in One Year. LC 78-11378. (Sports Stars Ser.). (Illus.). (gr. 2-6). 1979. PLB 7.95 (ISBN 0-516-04305-6); pap. 2.50 (ISBN 0-516-44305-4). Childrens.
Davies, Gerald. Gerald Davies: An Autobiography. (Illus.). 1979. 12.50 (ISBN 0-04-796052-3). Allen Unwin.
De Rosier, John. Chuck Foreman. (Sports Superstars Ser.). (Illus.). (gr. 3-9). 1976. o. p. 5.95 (ISBN 0-87191-543-X); pap. 2.95 (ISBN 0-89812-168-X). Creative Ed.
Devaney, John. The Picture Story of Terry Bradshaw. LC 77-22841. (Illus.). 64p. (gr. 3-6). 1977. PLB 6.97 (ISBN 0-671-32867-0). Messner.
Diles, Dave L. & Bradshaw, Terry. Terry Bradshaw: Man of Steel. 224p. 1980. pap. 4.95 (ISBN 0-310-39461-9, 12025P). Zondervan.
Dolan, Edward F., Jr. & Lyttle, Richard B. Archie Griffin. (gr. 4 up). 1978. pap. 1.25 (ISBN 0-671-29904-2). Archway.
Dressman, Denny. Gerry Faust: From Moeller High to Notre Dame. (Illus.). 224p. 1981. 12.95 (ISBN 0-498-02573-X). A S Barnes.
Feinberg, William H. Ken Stabler. (Sports Superstars Ser). (Illus.). (gr. 3-9). 1978. PLB 5.95 (ISBN 0-87191-670-3); pap. 2.95 (ISBN 0-89812-170-1). Creative Ed.
Gage, Gloria. Fully Alive. LC 80-68884. 160p. (Orig.). 1981. pap. 3.95 (ISBN 0-89636-064-4). Accent Bks.
Glashagel, Jerry, ed. Young Winners Flag Football. (Illus.). 65p. 1980. spiral bdg. 29.95 (ISBN 0-936446-04-8). Youth Sports.
Gutman, Bill. Football Superstars of the '70s. LC 75-12751. (Messner Sports Bks). (Illus.). 192p. (gr. 7 up). 1975. PLB 7.29 (ISBN 0-671-32751-8). Messner.
--Great Linebackers No. 1. 192p. (gr. 5 up). 1974. pap. 0.95 (ISBN 0-448-05712-3, Tempo). Ace Bks.
--Payton, Jones, Haden, Dorsett. pap. 1.50 (ISBN 0-448-14955-9, Tempo). Ace Bks.
Haden, Pat & Kaiser, Robert B. Pat Haden: My Rookie Season with Los Angeles Rams. LC 77-9411. (Illus.). 1977. 8.95 (ISBN 0-688-03224-9). Morrow.
Hahn, James & Hahn, Lynn. Franco Harris: The Quiet Ironman. LC 78-12841. (Champions & Challengers II). (gr. 3-5). 1979. text ed. 5.95 (ISBN 0-88436-447-X); pap. text ed. 3.50 (ISBN 0-88436-448-8). EMC.
--Sayers! The Sports Career of Gale Sayers. Schroeder, Howard, ed. (Sports Legends Ser.). (Illus.). 48p. (gr. 3 up). 1981. PLB 6.95 (ISBN 0-89686-133-3); pap. text ed. 3.25 (ISBN 0-89686-148-1). Crestwood Hse.
Hasegawa, Sam. Coaches. LC 74-23422. (Stars of the NFL Ser.). (gr. 4-12). 1975. PLB 7.95 (ISBN 0-87191-421-2). Creative Ed.
--Terry Bradshaw. (Sports Superstars Ser.). (Illus.). (gr. 3-9). 1977. PLB 5.95 (ISBN 0-87191-542-1); pap. 2.95 (ISBN 0-89812-212-0). Creative Ed.
Hodge, Ben, Sr. Football for Fun: Football in Three Easy Steps. LC 77-81704. (Illus.). 22p. (gr. 5 up). 1976. 4.50 (ISBN 0-912122-07-2); pap. 1.89 (ISBN 0-912122-08-0). Football Hobbies.
--Football for Fun: Football in Three Easy Steps. LC 77-81697. (Illus.). 22p. (Span. & Eng.). (gr. 5 up). 1976. 4.50 (ISBN 0-912122-13-7); pap. 1.89 (ISBN 0-912122-14-5). Football Hobbies.
Kaplan, Richard. Great Linebackers of the NFL. (NFL Punt, Pass & Kick Library: No. 12). (Illus.). (gr. 5-9). 1970. (BYR); PLB 3.69 (ISBN 0-394-90152-5). Random.
Karras, Alex. Alex Karras: My Life in Football, Television, & Movies. LC 78-18138. 1979. 5.95 (ISBN 0-385-12529-1); PLB (ISBN 0-385-12530-5). Doubleday.
Kopay, David & Young, Perry D. David Kopay Story. LC 76-29229. 1977. 8.95 (ISBN 0-87795-145-4). Arbor Hse.
Libby, Bill. Life in the Pit: The Deacon Jones Story. LC 70-129891. 1970. 5.95 (ISBN 0-385-00375-7). Doubleday.
--Star Quarterbacks of the NFL. LC 70-117548. (NFL Punt, Pass & Kick Library: No. 13). (Illus.). (gr. 5-9). 1970. PLB 3.69 (ISBN 0-394-90155-X, BYR). Random.
Lipman, David & Wilks, Ed. The Speed King: Bob Hayes of the Dallas Cowboys. (Putnam Sports Shelf). (gr. 5 up). 1971. PLB 6.29 (ISBN 0-399-60597-5). Putnam.
Lynch, Etta. Tender Tyrant: The Legend of Pete Cawthon. (Illus.). 1976. 12.50 (ISBN 0-685-74784-0). Staked Plains.
McIntyre, Bill. Grambling: Cradle of the Pros. Woolfolk, Doug, ed. (Illus.). 110p. 1980. 12.50 (ISBN 0-86518-015-6). Moran Pub Corp.
Masegawa, Sam. Linebackers. LC 74-23365. (Stars of the NFL Ser.). (gr. 4-12). 1975. PLB 7.95 (ISBN 0-87191-419-0). Creative Ed.

--Quarterbacks. LC 74-23143. (Stars of the NFL Ser.). (gr. 4-12). 1975. PLB 7.95 (ISBN 0-87191-417-4). Creative Ed.
Mendell, Ronald L. & Phares, Timothy B. Who's Who in Football. 1974. 11.95 (ISBN 0-87000-237-6). Arlington Hse.
Miller, David. Father of Football. 1970. 4.95 (ISBN 0-09-104650-5, Pub. by Hutchinson). Merrimack Bk Serv.
Morris, Jeannie. Brian Piccolo: A Short Season. 1972. pap. 2.25 (ISBN 0-440-10889-6). Dell.
Morse, C. A. Running Backs. LC 74-23176. (Stars of the NFL Ser.). (gr. 4-12). 1975. PLB 7.95 (ISBN 0-87191-416-6). Creative Ed.
Musick, Phil. The Tony Dorsett Story. LC 77-17558. (Illus.). 1977. lib. bdg. 7.95 (ISBN 0-89490-011-0); pap. 3.95 (ISBN 0-89490-010-2). Enslow Pubs.
New York Times. The Complete Book of Football: A New York Times Scrapbook History. LC 79-92321. (Sports Ser.). (Illus.). 224p. 1980. 14.95 (ISBN 0-672-52637-9). Bobbs.
Pagna, Tom & Best, Bob. Notre Dame's Era of Ara. LC 76-24238. (Illus.). 1976. 9.95 (ISBN 0-87397-104-3). Strode.
Phillips, Betty Lou. Earl Campbell, Houston Oiler Superstar. 1979. 7.95 (ISBN 0-679-20603-5). McKay.
Plunkett, Jim & Newhouse, Dave. The Jim Plunkett Story: The Saga of a Man Who Came Back. 1981. 12.95 (ISBN 0-87795-326-0). Arbor Hse.
Renick, Marion. The Famous Forward Pass Pair. LC 77-2943. (gr. 3-6). 1977. reinforced bdg. 6.95 (ISBN 0-684-15037-9, ScribJ). Scribner.
Rippon, Anton. The Tottenham Hotspur Story. 96p. 1981. 15.00x (ISBN 0-903485-97-4, Pub. by Moorland). State Mutual Bk.
Sayers, Gale & Silverman, Al. I Am Third. LC 70-119775. (Illus.). 1970. 6.95 (ISBN 0-670-38977-3). Viking Pr.
--I Am Third. (gr. 7 up). pap. 1.95 (ISBN 0-553-12865-5). Bantam.
Shadi, Lou. Ken Stabler & the Oakland Raiders. (gr. 7 up). 1977. pap. 1.25 (ISBN 0-590-11866-8, Schol Pap). Schol Bk Serv.
Slatter, Dave. The Washington Redskins: A Pictorial History. LC 77-15328. (Illus.). 1977. 14.95 (ISBN 0-918908-03-5). JCP Corp VA.
Smith, Jay H. Defensive Linemen. LC 74-23193. (Stars of the NFL Ser.). (gr. 4-12). 1975. PLB 7.95 (ISBN 0-87191-420-4). Creative Ed.
--Receivers. LC 74-23400. (Stars of the NFL Ser.). (gr. 4-12). 1975. PLB 7.95 (ISBN 0-87191-418-2). Creative Ed.
--Roger Staubach. LC 74-13134. (Sports Superstars Ser.). (Illus.). 32p. (gr. 3-6). 1974. PLB 5.95 (ISBN 0-87191-378-X). Creative Ed.
Staubach, Roger, et al. Staubach: First Down, Lifetime to Go. LC 74-81607. 1976. pap. 1.75 (ISBN 0-87680-833-X, 91016, Key-Word Bks). Word Bks.
Stein, Joe & Clark, Diane. Don Coryell Win with Honor. LC 76-28011. (Illus.). 1976. 8.95 (ISBN 0-89325-003-1). Joyce Pr.
Sullivan, George. Roger Staubach: A Special Kind of Quarterback. new ed. (Putnam Sports Shelf Biography Ser.). 160p. (gr. 5 up). 1974. PLB 6.29 (ISBN 0-399-60910-5). Putnam.
Tatum, Jack & Kushner, Bill. They Call Me Assassin. 1980. pap. 2.50 (ISBN 0-380-52480-5, 52480). Avon.
Zeoli, Billy & Hartley, Alan. Tom Landry & the Dallas Cowboys. (Spire Comics Ser.). (Illus.). 32p. (gr. 1 up). 1973. 0.69 (ISBN 0-8007-8504-5). Revell.

FOOTBALL–DEFENSE

Allen. Pass Defense Drills. 1968. 11.50 (ISBN 0-201-00168-3). A-W.
Armey, Charley. Winning Football with the Forty-Three Defense. 1973. 10.95 (ISBN 0-13-961326-9, Parker). P-H.
Buoniconti, Nick & Anderson, Dick. Defensive Football. Bondurant, Bill, ed. LC 73-80752. (Illus.). 1973. 7.95 (ISBN 0-689-10573-8). Atheneum.
Helgeson, Lloyd H. Total Pass Defense. (Illus.). 1977. 10.95 (ISBN 0-13-925628-8, Parker). P-H.
Olcott, Jack. Complete Guide to the Fifty Defenses in Football. 1976. 10.95 (ISBN 0-13-160390-6). P-H.
Pasquini, Duke. Power Six Invert Defense for Winning Football. (Illus.). 1978. 10.95 (ISBN 0-13-686980-7, Parker). P-H.
Porter, Archie. Complete Book of the Man for Man Defense. 1976. 10.95 (ISBN 0-13-157560-0, Parker). P-H.
Reaves, Rhod. Football's "Combo" Defensive System. (Illus.). 1977. 10.95 (ISBN 0-13-324152-1, Parker). P-H.
Sullins, S. E. Complete Book of Multiple Defenses in Football. (Illus.). 1978. 10.95 (ISBN 0-13-158196-1, Parker). P-H.
Sullivan, George. Linebacker! LC 74-2597. (Illus.). 128p. (gr. 5 up). 1974. 5.95 (ISBN 0-396-06958-4). Dodd.
Troppmann, R. Football's Master Defense Guide. 1969. 10.95 (ISBN 0-13-324103-3, Parker). P-H.
Wilkinson, Bud. Sports Illustrated Football Defense. 1973. 5.95 (ISBN 0-397-00833-3); pap. 2.95 (ISBN 0-397-00993-3). Lippincott.

FOOTBALL–DICTIONARIES

Liss, Howard. Football Talk for Beginners. LC 76-102184. (Illus.). 96p. (gr. 4 up). 1970. PLB 7.29 (ISBN 0-671-32241-9). Messner.
Lorimer, Lawrence T. & Devaney, John. The Football Book. LC 77-74461. (Illus.). (gr. 5 up). 1977. PLB 7.99 (ISBN 0-394-93574-8, BYR); pap. 3.95 (ISBN 0-394-83574-3). Random.
Olgin, Joseph. Illustrated Football Dictionary for Young People. (Treehouse Illustrated Sports Dictionaries Ser.). (Illus.). 1978. pap. 2.50 (ISBN 0-13-450874-2). P-H.
Paige, David. Pro Football: An Almanac of Facts & Records. LC 77-857. (Sports Records Ser.). (Illus.). (gr. 3-12). 1977. PLB 6.75 (ISBN 0-87191-604-5). Creative Ed.
Shefski, Bill. Football Language: A Running Press Glossary. LC 77-12492. 1978. lib. bdg. 12.90 (ISBN 0-89471-021-4); pap. 2.95 (ISBN 0-89471-020-6). Running Pr.
Treat, Roger. The Encyclopedia of Football. 16th rev. ed. Palmer, Pete, ed. (Illus.). 1979. pap. 7.95 (ISBN 0-385-15091-1, Dolp). Doubleday.

FOOTBALL–HISTORY

Batty, Eric G., et al, eds. International Football Book, No. 22. (Soccer Ser). (Illus.). 142p. (YA) 1980. text ed. 17.50x (ISBN 0-285-62445-8, SpS). Sportshelf.
Benagh, Jim. Making It to Number One. LC 75-42497. 1976. 10.00 (ISBN 0-396-07210-0). Dodd.
Bonifer & Weaver. Out of Bounds: An Anecdotal History of Notre Dame Football. LC 78-60060. (Illus.). 1978. 15.00 (ISBN 0-87832-043-1). Piper.
Burnes, Robert L. Big Red: The Story of the Football Cardinals. new ed. LC 75-11160. (Illus.). 256p. 1975. lib. bdg. 4.95 (ISBN 0-913656-05-4, Piraeus). Forum Pr MO.
Cohen, Richard M., et al. The Scrapbook History of Pro Football. expanded & updated ed. LC 79-7463. (Illus.). 1979. pap. 10.00 (ISBN 0-672-52614-X). Bobbs.
Cromartie, Bill. Clean Old-Fashioned Hate. LC 77-75764. (College Sports Ser.). 1981. 10.95 (ISBN 0-87397-139-6). Strode.
Cross, George L. Presidents Can't Punt: The OU Football Tradition. (Illus.). 1977. 11.95 (ISBN 0-8061-1419-3). U of Okla Pr.
Durant, John & Etter, Les. Highlights of College Football. (gr. 7 up). 1970. 9.95 (ISBN 0-8038-3013-0). Hastings.
Florence, Mal. Trojan Heritage: A Pictorial History of USC Football. LC 80-84556. (Illus.). 184p. 1980. 16.95 (ISBN 0-938694-01-4). JCP Corp VA.
Forsyth, John D. The Aggies & the 'Horns. Okrent, Daniel, ed. (Illus.). 160p. 1981. 15.95 (ISBN 0-932012-14-0). Texas Month Pr.
Keith, Harold. Oklahoma Kickoff: An Informal History of the First Twenty-Five Years at the University of Oklahoma, & of the Amusing Hardships That Attended Its Pioneering. LC 78-58114. (Illus.). 1978. pap. 9.95 (ISBN 0-8061-1485-1). U of Okla Pr.
Klein, Dave. The Game of Their Lives. (Illus.). (RL 7). 1977. pap. 1.95 (ISBN 0-451-07532-3, J7532, Sig). NAL.
McCallum, John. Big Eight Football: The Story, the Stars, the Stats of America's Toughest Conference. (Encore Edition). (Illus.). 1979. 5.95 (ISBN 0-684-16750-6). Scribner.
Magoun, Francis P., Jr. History of Football from the Beginnings to 1871. pap. 13.50 (ISBN 0-384-35060-7). Johnson Repr.
Michelson, Herb & Newhouse, Dave. Rose Bowl Football: Since 1902. LC 77-8454. (Illus.). 1977. 12.95 (ISBN 0-8128-2168-8). Stein & Day.
Miller, David. Father of Football: The Story of Matt Busby. new ed. (Illus.). 190p. 1971. 12.50x (ISBN 0-392-01167-0, SpS). Sportshelf.
National Football League. Official Encyclopedic History of Professional Football. Bennett, Tom, ed. (Illus.). 384p. 1973. 14.95 (ISBN 0-02-588910-9). Macmillan.
Pagna, Tom & Best, Bob. Notre Dame's Era of Ara. LC 76-24238. (Illus.). 1976. 9.95 (ISBN 0-87397-104-3). Strode.
Rappoport, Ken. Tar Heel, North Carolina Football. LC 76-19968. (College Sports Ser.). (Illus.). 1980. 9.95 (ISBN 0-87397-029-2). Strode.
Rathet, Mike. The Rutledge Book of Football. 128p. 1981. 10.95 (ISBN 0-8317-7597-1, Rutledge Pr). Smith Pubs.
Sellmeyer, Ralph & Davidson, James. The Red Raiders. LC 77-79554. (College Sports Ser.). 1978. 9.95 (ISBN 0-87397-123-X). Strode.
Sorrels, William W. & Cavagnaro, Charles. Ole Miss Rebels, Mississippi Football. LC 76-24239. (Illus.). 1976. 9.95 (ISBN 0-87397-105-1). Strode.
Swinburne, Laurence & Swinburne, Irene. America's First Football Game. LC 78-14865. (Famous Firsts Ser.). (Illus.). 1978. lib. bdg. 7.35 (ISBN 0-686-51096-8). Silver.
Underwood, C. H. Texas Six Man Football. (Illus.). 107p. 1974. pap. 6.95 (ISBN 0-89015-078-8). Eakin Pubns.
Whittingham, Richard. The Chicago Bears: An Illustrated History. rev. ed. LC 79-8734. (Illus.). 1980. 14.95 (ISBN 0-528-81825-2). Rand.
Wizig, Jerry. Eat 'Em up, Cougars, Houston Football. LC 77-79555. (College Sports Ser.). 1981. 9.95 (ISBN 0-87397-122-1). Strode.

FOOTBALL–JUVENILE LITERATURE

Aaseng, Nathan. Football's Breakaway Backs. LC 80-16691. (Sports Heroes Library). (Illus.). 72p. (gr. 4 up). 1980. PLB 6.95g (ISBN 0-8225-1063-4). Lerner Pubns.
--Football's Crushing Blockers. (Sports Heroes Library). (Illus.). 80p. (gr. 6 up). 1981. PLB 6.95 (ISBN 0-8225-1074-X). Lerner Pubns.
--Football's Fierce Defenses. LC 79-16315. (The Sports Heroes Library). (Illus.). (YA) (gr. 4 up). 1980. PLB 6.95g (ISBN 0-8225-1057-X). Lerner Pubns.
--Football's Sure-Handed Receivers. LC 80-17762. (Sports Heroes Library). (Illus.). 72p. (gr. 4 up). 1980. PLB 6.95g (ISBN 0-8225-1064-2). Lerner Pubns.
--Football's Winning Quarterbacks. LC 80-12074. (Sports Heroes Library). (Illus.). (gr. 4 up). 1980. PLB 6.95g (ISBN 0-8225-1062-6). Lerner Pubns.
Antonacci, Robert J. & Barr, Jene. Football for Young Champions. 2nd ed. LC 75-10825. (Illus.). 160p. (gr. 4-6). 1976. PLB 7.95 (ISBN 0-07-002154-6, GB). McGraw.
Baker, Eugene. I Want to Be a Football Player. (I Want to Be Books). (Illus.). 32p. (gr. 1-4). 1972. PLB 7.95 (ISBN 0-516-01796-9). Childrens.
Batson, Larry. Alan Page. LC 74-18256. (Sports Superstars Ser). (Illus.). 32p. (gr. 3-9). 1974. PLB 5.95 (ISBN 0-87191-381-X). Creative Ed.
--An Interview with Alan Page. (Interviews Ser.). (Illus.). (gr. 3-8). 1977. PLB 6.75 (ISBN 0-87191-569-3). Creative Ed.
--An Interview with Jim Plunkett. (Interviews Ser.). (Illus.). (gr. 3-8). 1977. PLB 6.75 (ISBN 0-87191-570-7). Creative Ed.
Beckett, James & Eckes, Dennis. Sport American Football & Basketball Card Price Guide. (Illus.). 160p. (Orig.). (gr. 4 up). 1979. pap. 6.95 (ISBN 0-529-05732-8). Collins Pubs.
Betts, Jerry W. Football Fundamentals for Kids & Parents. LC 77-84561. (Illus.). 1979. 6.95 (ISBN 0-498-02067-3); pap. 4.95 (ISBN 0-498-02304-4). A S Barnes.
Biddle, Marcia. Tony Dorsett. LC 80-18302. (Illus.). 192p. (gr. 7 up). 1980. PLB 8.79 (ISBN 0-671-34040-9). Messner.
Braun, Thomas. Football's Greatest Passer: Fran Tarkenton. (Allstars Ser.). (Illus.). (gr. 2-6). 1977. PLB 5.95 (ISBN 0-87191-583-9). Creative Ed.
--Franco Harris. (Creative Superstars Ser.). (Illus.). (gr. 3-9). 1975. PLB 5.95 (ISBN 0-87191-473-5); pap. 2.75 o. p. (ISBN 0-89812-169-8). Creative Ed.
Brondfield, Jerry. All-Pro Football Stars 1980. 108p. (Orig.). (gr. 7 up). 1980. pap. 1.25 (ISBN 0-590-31623-0, Schol Pap). Schol Bk Serv.
--Kareem Abdul-Jabbar, Magic Johnson & the Los Angeles Lakers. (Illus.). 96p. (Orig.). 1981. pap. 1.25 (ISBN 0-590-31965-5, Schol Pap). Schol Bk Serv.
Burchard, Marshall. Sports Hero: Fran Tarkenton. LC 77-7393. (Sports Hero Ser.). (Illus.). (gr. 3-5). 1977. PLB 6.29 (ISBN 0-399-61096-0). Putnam.
Burchard, S. H. Sports Star: Franco Harris. LC 75-35527. (Sports Star Ser.). (Illus.). 64p. (gr. 1-3). 1976. 6.95 (ISBN 0-15-278000-9, HJ). HarBraceJ.
--Sports Star: "Mean" Joe Greene. LC 76-18130. (Sports Star Ser.). (Illus.). (gr. 1-5). 1976. 5.95 (ISBN 0-15-278009-2, HJ). HarBraceJ.
--Sports Star: "Mean" Joe Greene. LC 76-18130. (Sports Star Ser). (Illus.). (gr. 1-5). 1976. pap. 3.95 (ISBN 0-15-278031-9, VoyB). HarBraceJ.
Cassady, Steve. Super Bowl: Pro Football's Greatest Games. (Illus.). 128p. (Orig.). (gr. 3-7). 1981. pap. 1.50 (ISBN 0-590-31784-9, Schol Pap). Schol Bk Serv.
Christopher, Matt. Catch That Pass! (gr. 3-5). 1974. pap. 0.75 (ISBN 0-671-29612-4). Archway.
Collins, David R. Football Running Backs: Three Ground Gainers. LC 75-23346. (Sports Library). (Illus.). 96p. (gr. 3-6). 1976. PLB 6.48 (ISBN 0-8116-6677-8). Garrard.
Coombs, Charles. Be a Winner in Football. LC 74-5932. 128p. (gr. 5-9). 1974. 7.44 (ISBN 0-688-30119-3); pap. 2.45 (ISBN 0-688-25119-6). Morrow.
Deegan, Paul J. Catching the Football. LC 74-34572. (Creative Education Sports Instructional Bk.). (Illus.). 32p. (gr. 3-9). 1975. PLB 5.95 (ISBN 0-87191-426-3); pap. 2.95 (ISBN 0-89812-133-7). Creative Ed.
--Passing the Football. LC 75-1479. (Creative Education Sports Instructional Bk.). (Illus.). 32p. (gr. 3-6). 1975. PLB 5.95 (ISBN 0-87191-428-X); pap. 2.95 (ISBN 0-89812-132-9). Creative Ed.
--Placekicking & Punting. LC 75-2026. (Creative Education Sports Instructional Bks.). (Illus.). 32p. (gr. 3-6). 1975. PLB 5.95 (ISBN 0-87191-427-1); pap. 2.95 (ISBN 0-89812-134-5). Creative Ed.
De Luca, Sam. Junior Football Playbook. LC 73-80413. (Illus.). 128p. (gr. 4-8). 1973. 5.95 (ISBN 0-8246-0150-5). Jonathan David.
Dickmeyer, Lowell A. Football Is for Me. LC 79-15445. (Sports for Me Bks.). (Illus.). (gr. 2-5). 1979. PLB 5.95g (ISBN 0-8225-1087-1). Lerner Pubns.
Dolan, Edward F., Jr. Basic Football Strategy: An Introduction for Young Players. LC 76-3438. 144p. (gr. 5-9). 1976. 7.95a (ISBN 0-385-03998-0); PLB (ISBN 0-385-04184-5). Doubleday.
Dolan, Edward F., Jr. & Lyttle, Richard B. Archie Griffin. (gr. 4 up). 1978. pap. 1.25 (ISBN 0-671-29904-2). Archway.
--Archie Griffin. LC 76-56279. (gr. 4-7). 1977. 5.95 (ISBN 0-385-12524-0). Doubleday.
Feinberg, William H. Ken Stabler. (Sports Superstars Ser). (Illus.). (gr. 3-9). 1978. PLB 5.95 (ISBN 0-87191-670-3); pap. 2.95 (ISBN 0-89812-170-1). Creative Ed.
Gault, Clare & Gault, Frank. How to Be a Good Football Player. (gr. 4-6). 1974. pap. 0.95 (ISBN 0-590-04841-4, Schol Pap). Schol Bk Serv.
--A Super Fullback for the Super Bowl. (gr. k-3). 1978. pap. 1.25 (ISBN 0-590-11904-4, Schol Pap); pap. 2.95 bk. & record (ISBN 0-590-20608-7). Schol Bk Serv.
Gelman. Great Quarterbacks of Pro Football. (gr. 4-6). 1977. pap. 1.25 (ISBN 0-590-30391-0). Schol Bk Serv.
The Great NFL Fun Book. (gr. 7-12). 1979. pap. 1.95 (ISBN 0-590-12088-3, Schol Pap). Schol Bk Serv.
Gutman, Bill. Football Superstars of the '70s. LC 75-12751. (Messner Sports Bks). (Illus.). 192p. (gr. 7 up). 1975. PLB 7.29 (ISBN 0-671-32751-8). Messner.
--Modern Football Superstars. LC 74-6799. (High Interest-Low Vocabulary Ser.). (Illus.). 128p. (gr. 3-9). 1974. 5.95 (ISBN 0-396-06990-8). Dodd.
Harris, Richard. I Can Read About Football. new ed. LC 76-54398. (Illus.). (gr. 2-5). 1977. pap. 1.25 (ISBN 0-89375-033-6). Troll Assocs.
Heuman, William. Famous Pro Football Stars. LC 67-10443. (Illus.). (gr. 7-9). 1967. 5.95 (ISBN 0-396-05490-0). Dodd.
Hodge, Ben, Sr. Skram Runs, Kicks, & Throws. LC 77-81698. (Illus.). 18p. (Span. & Eng.). (gr. 1-2). 1975. 4.50 (ISBN 0-912122-09-9); pap. 1.89 (ISBN 0-912122-10-2). Football Hobbies.
Hollander, Zander. More Strange but True Football Stories. (NFL Punt, Pass & Kick Library: No. 19). (Illus.). (gr. 5 up). 1973. PLB 4.39 (ISBN 0-394-92607-2, BYR). Random.
Jackson, C. Paul. How to Play Better Football. LC 72-158707. (Illus.). (gr. 3-5). 1972. 8.79 (ISBN 0-690-41567-2, TYC-J). Har-Row.
Libby, Bill. Star Running Backs of the NFL. (NFL Punt, Pass & Kick Library: No. 15). (Illus.). (gr. 5-9). 1971. (BYR); PLB 3.69 (ISBN 0-394-92285-9). Random.
Liss, Howard. Football Talk. (gr. 3-6). 1980. pap. 1.50 (ISBN 0-671-56037-9). Archway.
--Football Talk. (gr. 4-6). 1980. pap. 1.75 (ISBN 0-671-41020-2). PB.
--Football Talk for Beginners. LC 76-102184. (Illus.). 96p. (gr. 4 up). 1970. PLB 7.29 (ISBN 0-671-32241-9). Messner.
--Making of a Rookie. (NFL Punt, Pass & Kick Library: No. 9). (Illus.). (gr. 5-9). 1968. PLB 3.69 (ISBN 0-394-90199-1, BYR). Random.
--They Changed the Game: Football's Great Coaches, Players & Games. LC 75-11512. (Illus.). 160p. (gr. 6up). 1975. 7.95 (ISBN 0-397-31628-3, JBL-J). Har-Row.
Lorimer, Lawrence T. & Devaney, John. The Football Book. LC 77-74461. (Illus.). (gr. 5 up). 1977. PLB 7.99 (ISBN 0-394-93574-8, BYR); pap. 3.95 (ISBN 0-394-83574-3). Random.
Lundgren, Hal. Earl Campbell: The Texas Tornado, Sports Stars. (Illus.). (gr. 2-8). 1981. PLB 7.95 (ISBN 0-516-04316-1); pap. 2.50 (ISBN 0-516-04316-1). Childrens.
McCallum, John D. Getting into Pro Football. (Getting into the Pros Ser.). (Illus.). (gr. 6 up). 1979. PLB 6.90 s&l (ISBN 0-531-02279-X). Watts.
Masegawa, Sam. Linebackers. LC 74-23365. (Stars of the NFL Ser.). (gr. 4-12). 1975. PLB 7.95 (ISBN 0-87191-419-0). Creative Ed.

--Quarterbacks. LC 74-23143. (Stars of the NFL Ser.). (gr. 4-12). 1975. PLB 7.95 (ISBN 0-87191-417-4). Creative Ed.

May, Julian. Dallas Cowboys. LC 74-3241. (Superbowl Champions Ser). 48p. 1974. PLB 6.45 (ISBN 0-87191-327-5); pap. 2.95 (ISBN 0-89812-085-3). Creative Ed.

--The NBA Playoffs. LC 75-17755. (Sports Classics Ser.). (Illus.). 48p. (gr. 4-6). 1975. PLB 8.95 (ISBN 0-87191-448-4). Creative Ed.

--The Oakland Raiders Super Bowl Champions. (Super Bowl Champions Ser.). (Illus.). (gr. 3-9). 1978. PLB 6.45 (ISBN 0-87191-614-2); pap. 2.95 (ISBN 0-89812-091-8). Creative Ed.

--Pittsburgh Steelers. (Super Bowl Champions Ser.). (Illus.). (gr. 3-8). 1977. PLB 6.45 (ISBN 0-87191-454-9); pap. 2.95 (ISBN 0-89812-090-X). Creative Ed.

Morse, A. R. Football's Great Running Back: O. J. Simpson. (Allstars Ser.). (Illus.). (gr. 2-6). 1976. PLB 5.95 (ISBN 0-87191-477-8); pap. 2.95 (ISBN 0-89812-200-7). Creative Ed.

Morse, C. A. Running Backs. LC 74-23176. (Stars of the NFL Ser.). (gr. 4-12). 1975. PLB 7.95 (ISBN 0-87191-416-6). Creative Ed.

Newcombe, Jack. Game of Football. LC 67-10101. (Sports Library Ser). (Illus.). (gr. 3-6). 1967. PLB 6.48 (ISBN 0-8116-6655-7). Garrard.

Olgin, Joseph. Illustrated Football Dictionary for Young People. LC 74-82014. (Illustrated Dictionary Ser.). (Illus.). 128p. (gr. 5 up). 1974. PLB 7.29 (ISBN 0-8178-5182-8). Harvey.

--Illustrated Football Dictionary for Young People. (Treehouse Illustrated Sports Dictionaries Ser.). (Illus.). 1978. pap. 2.50 (ISBN 0-13-450874-2). P-H.

Paulsen, Gary. Tackling, Running, & Kicking--Now & Again. LC 77-7786. (Sports on the Light Side Ser.). (Illus.). (gr. 3-6). 1977. PLB 10.65 (ISBN 0-8172-0966-2). Raintree Pubs.

Phillips, Louis & Markoe, Arnie. Football: Records, Stars, Feats, & Facts. LC 79-87526. (Illus.). (gr. 4-7). 1979. 2.95 (ISBN 0-15-228947-X, HJ). HarBraceJ.

Rainbolt, Richard. Football's Clever Quarterbacks. LC 74-27467. (The Sports Heroes Library). (Illus.). 72p. (gr. 5-11). 1975. PLB 6.95g (ISBN 0-8225-1051-0). Lerner Pubns.

--Football's Rugged Running Backs. LC 74-27469. (The Sports Heroes Library). (Illus.). 72p. (gr. 5-11). 1975. PLB 6.95g (ISBN 0-8225-1052-9). Lerner Pubns.

Ray, Jo A. Careers in Football. LC 72-7649. (Early Career Bks). (Illus.). 36p. (gr. 2-5). 1973. PLB 4.95 (ISBN 0-8225-0314-X). Lerner Pubns.

Roberts, Eric B. From Football to Finance: The Story of Brady Keys Jr. LC 70-151026. (Illus.). 112p. (gr. 7 up). 1971. 4.75 (ISBN 0-15-230265-4, HJ). HarBraceJ.

Roberts, Jim. Football Take Along Game. (gr. 3 up). 1980. pap. 3.95 (ISBN 0-671-41009-1). Wanderer Bks.

Rubin, Bob. Little Men of the NFL. LC 74-5145. (Punt,Pass & Kick Library). (Illus.). 160p. (gr. 5 up). 1974. 3.69 (ISBN 0-394-92807-5, BYR). Random.

Sahadi. Great Pro Running Backs. (gr. 7 up). 1977. pap. 1.25 (ISBN 0-590-00164-7). Schol Bk Serv.

Sayers, Gayle & Griese, Bob. Offensive Football. Bondurant, Bill, ed. (Illus.). 1972. pap. 1.25 (ISBN 0-689-70407-0, Aladdin). Atheneum.

Schoor, Gene. Bart Starr: A Biography. LC 76-56332. (gr. 4-7). 1977. PLB 7.95 (ISBN 0-385-11695-0). Doubleday.

Shadi, Lou. Ken Stabler & the Oakland Raiders. (gr. 7 up). 1977. pap. 1.25 (ISBN 0-590-11866-8, Schol Pap). Schol Bk Serv.

Smith, Jay H. Defensive Linemen. LC 74-23193. (Stars of the NFL Ser.). (gr. 4-12). 1975. PLB 7.95 (ISBN 0-87191-420-4). Creative Ed.

--Receivers. LC 74-23400. (Stars of the NFL Ser.). (gr. 4-12). 1975. PLB 7.95 (ISBN 0-87191-418-2). Creative Ed.

Stainback, Berry. Pro Football Heroes of Today. (Landmark Giant Ser: No. 23). (Illus.). (gr. 5 up). 1973. (BYR); PLB 5.99 (ISBN 0-394-92629-3). Random.

Sullivan, George. Better Football for Boys. new ed. LC 80-12597. (Better Sports Ser.). (Illus.). 64p. (gr. 5 up). 1980. 5.95 (ISBN 0-396-07843-5). Dodd.

--On the Run: Franco Harris. LC 76-10357. (Sports Profiles Ser.). (Illus.). 48p. (gr. 4-11). 1976. PLB 9.30 (ISBN 0-8172-0138-6). Raintree Pubs.

--Pro Football & the Running Back. LC 76-12548. (Illus.). (gr. 5 up). 1976. 5.95 (ISBN 0-396-07335-2). Dodd.

--Pro Football's Greatest Upsets. LC 74-163175. (Sports Library Ser.). (Illus.). 96p. (gr. 3-6). 1972. PLB 6.48 (ISBN 0-8116-6662-X). Garrard.

--This Is Pro Football. rev. ed. LC 75-121980. (Illus.). 96p. (gr. 5 up). 1975. PLB 5.95 (ISBN 0-396-07196-1). Dodd.

--Winning Plays in Pro Football. LC 75-6821. (Illus.). 128p. (gr. 5 up). 1975. PLB 5.95 (ISBN 0-396-07148-1). Dodd.

Swenson, John. The Eagles. (Headliners Ser.). 192p. (Orig.). (gr. 4 up). 1981. pap. 2.25 (ISBN 0-448-17174-0, Tempo). Ace Bks.

Thorne, Ian. Meet the Coaches. (Meet the Players: Football). (Illus.). (gr. 2-4). 1975. PLB 5.95 (ISBN 0-87191-472-7). Creative Ed.

Weber. Pro Football Quiz Book. (gr. 7-12). 1976. pap. 1.25 (ISBN 0-590-00175-2). Schol Bk Serv.

FOOTBALL–OFFENSE

Axman, Steve. Attacking Modern Defenses with Multiple-Formation Veer Offense. (Illus.). 1978. 10.95 (ISBN 0-13-050286-3, Parker). P-H.

Cosner, Ron. Football's Multiple Pro-I Offense. (Illus.). 1979. 10.95 (ISBN 0-13-324137-8, Parker). P-H.

Dyer, Pete. Flip Flop Offense in High School Football. 1967. 10.95 (ISBN 0-13-322446-5, Parker). P-H.

Evans, Bruce. The Swingback-Motion Offense for Winning Football. (Illus.). 1978. 10.95 (ISBN 0-13-879825-7, Parker). P-H.

McClain, Jim R. Football's Multiple Slot-T Attack. 1974. 10.95 (ISBN 0-13-324129-7). P-H.

Metrokotsas, Nick. The Complete Book of Offensive Line Play. 1977. 10.95 (ISBN 0-13-157545-7, Parker). P-H.

Olcott, Jack. Football's Seven Best Offenses. (Illus.). 1978. 10.95 (ISBN 0-13-324699-X, Parker). P-H.

Poff, Mike. Coaches' Guide to Offensive Line Fundamentals & Techniques. LC 80-83977. (Illus.). 160p. (Orig.). 1981. pap. text ed. 5.95 (ISBN 0-918438-62-4). Leisure Pr.

Ray, Gary. Coach's Guide to the Slot One Offense. 1974. 10.95 (ISBN 0-13-139410-X, Parker). P-H.

Rodgers, Pepper & Smith, Homer. Installing Football's Wishbone T Attack. 1974. 10.95 (ISBN 0-13-467712-9, Parker). P-H.

Sayers, Gayle & Griese, Bob. Offensive Football. Bondurant, Bill, ed. LC 72-78293. (Illus.). 1972. 6.95 (ISBN 0-689-10529-0). Atheneum.

Simontonm, Tom. How to Get Top Offensive Power from Available Football Talent. 1975. 10.95 (ISBN 0-13-409748-3). P-H.

Stabler, Ken & LaMarre, Tom. Winning Offensive Football. LC 76-11227. (Winning Ser.). (Illus.). 1976. 8.95 (ISBN 0-8092-7991-6); pap. 5.95 (ISBN 0-8092-7990-8). Contemp Bks.

Tallman. Complete Guide to Football's Option Attacks. 1977. 10.95 (ISBN 0-13-160010-9, Parker). P-H.

Wilkinson, Bud & Sports Illustrated Editors. Sports Illustrated Football Offense. LC 72-2924. (Illus.). 1972. 5.95 (ISBN 0-397-00834-1); pap. 2.95 (ISBN 0-397-00910-0, LP-69). Lippincott.

FOOTBALL–PICTORIAL WORKS

Condon, Dave, et al. Notre Dame Football: The Golden Tradition. (Illus.). 208p. 1981. 21.95 (ISBN 0-89651-510-9). Icarus.

Cromartie, Bill. Clean Old-Fashioned Hate. LC 77-75764. (College Sports Ser.). 1981. 10.95 (ISBN 0-87397-139-6). Strode.

Didinger, Ray. The Professionals: Portraits of NFL Stars by America's Most Prominent Illustrators. 1980. 16.95 (ISBN 0-453-00391-5, H-391). NAL.

Jeffers, Jeff. Rally: The Twelve Greatest Notre Dame Football Comebacks. (Illus.). 250p. 1981. 12.95 (ISBN 0-89651-651-2). Icarus.

Kapral, Frank. Illustrated Guide to Championship Football. 1967. 10.95 (ISBN 0-13-451070-4, Parker). P-H.

Kingsley, D. & Taylor, F. Albion in China: The First British Football Tour to China in Pictures. (Illus.). 1979. pap. 9.00 (ISBN 0-08-024496-3). Pergamon.

Schiffer, Don & Duroska, Lud. Football Rules in Pictures. rev. ed. LC 72-86663. (Sports Handbooks Ser.). (Illus., Orig.). (gr. 7 up). 1969. pap. 3.95 (ISBN 0-448-01785-7). G&D.

Sellmeyer, Ralph & Davidson, James. The Red Raiders. LC 77-79554. (College Sports Ser.). 1978. 9.95 (ISBN 0-87397-123-X). Strode.

Wizig, Jerry. Eat 'Em up, Cougars, Houston Football. LC 77-79555. (College Sports Ser.). 1981. 9.95 (ISBN 0-87397-122-1). Strode.

FOOTBALL–PROGRAMMED INSTRUCTION

Capozzoli, Tom. The Complete Book of Football Instruction. (Illus.). 192p. 1981. 14.95 (ISBN 0-8092-5836-6); pap. 9.95 (ISBN 0-8092-5874-9). Contemp Bks.

Harper, Bill. Pop's Conscience. 1977. pap. 2.95 (ISBN 0-913182-95-8). Grossmont Pr.

FOOTBALL–TRAINING

Allen, George. George Allen's New Handbook of Football Drills. 1974. 10.95 (ISBN 0-13-352716-6). P-H.

Broccoletti, Peter P. & Scanlon, Pat. The Notre Dame Weight Training Program for Football. LC 78-20947. (Illus.). 1979. 12.95 (ISBN 0-89651-502-8); pap. 9.95 (ISBN 0-89651-503-6). Icarus.

Darden, Ellington. Conditioning for Football. LC 77-76074. (Physical Fitness & Sports Medicine Ser). (Illus.). 1978. pap. 4.95 (ISBN 0-89305-011-3). Anna Pub.

Jacobson, Bert. Conditioning for Football the Oklahoma State Way. LC 80-84216. (Fitness America Ser.). (Illus.). 136p. (Orig.). 1981. pap. 4.95 (ISBN 0-918438-71-3). Leisure Pr.

Jesse, John. Explosive Muscular Power for Championship Football. LC 68-58253. pap. 4.95 (ISBN 0-87095-032-0). Athletic.

Kearin, Timothy. Year Around Conditioning for Army Football. LC 80-82965. (Illus.). 128p. (Orig.). 1980. pap. text ed. 4.95 (ISBN 0-918438-60-8). Leisure Pr.

Leighty, James C. How to Develop a Strong High School Kicking Game. 1967. 10.95 (ISBN 0-13-405290-0, Parker). P-H.

O'Connor, Hyla, ed. The Complete NFL Cookbook. 1981. pap. 5.95 (ISBN 0-452-25298-9, Z5298, Plume). NAL.

Riley, Daniel P. Strength Training for Football: The Penn State Way. (Illus.). 1978. pap. text ed. 4.95 (ISBN 0-918438-42-X). Leisure Pr.

Spackman, Robert R., Jr. Conditioning for Football: Pre-Season, Regular Season & Off-Season. (Illus.). 112p. 1968. 11.50 (ISBN 0-398-01819-7). C C Thomas.

Stark, Paul, et al. Total Conditioning for Football-the Pitt Panther Way. (Fitness America - Sports Conditioning Books). (Illus., Orig.). 1979. pap. 4.95 (ISBN 0-918438-51-9). Leisure Pr.

Watson, Bill. Football Fitness. 1973. 6.95 (ISBN 0-09-115780-3, Pub. by Hutchinson); pap. 3.95 (ISBN 0-09-115781-1). Merrimack Bk Serv.

FOOTBALL COACHING

American Alliance for Health, Physical Education & Recreation. What Research Tells the Coach About Football. 1973. 2.50x (ISBN 0-685-41999-1, 241-25476). AAHPERD.

American Football Coaches Assoc., compiled by. Football Coaching. 224p. 1981. 17.95 (ISBN 0-684-17149-X, ScribT). Scribner.

Baran, Dick. Coaching Football's Polypotent Offense. 1974. 10.95 (ISBN 0-13-139055-4). P-H.

Bonham, Aubrey R. Coaching the Flexible Man-to-Man Defense. 1978. 10.95 (ISBN 0-13-139170-4, Parker). P-H.

Capozzoli, Tom. Coaching Football for Young Athletes. (Coaching Ser.). (Illus.). 1980. 14.95 (ISBN 0-8092-7010-2); pap. 7.95 (ISBN 0-8092-7009-9). Contemp Bks.

Coaching Clinic Editors. Illustrated Football Drills from the Coaching Clinic. 1975. 10.95 (ISBN 0-13-451021-6, Parker). P-H.

Davey, Don & Parker, Gary. Hey Dad, We Need a Coach. 1979. pap. 3.95 (ISBN 0-89185-200-X). Anthelion Pr.

Dressman, Denny. Gerry Faust: From Moeller High to Notre Dame. (Illus.). 224p. 1981. 12.95 (ISBN 0-498-02573-X). A S Barnes.

Football. (Coaching Ser.). 1974. 4.50 (ISBN 0-87670-006-7, CFB-SC); pap. 2.50 (ISBN 0-87670-081-4). Athletic Inst.

Friend, John. Coaching Youth League Football. (Coaching Youth League Sports Ser.). 1974. pap. 2.50 (ISBN 0-87670-081-4, CFB-SC). Athletic Inst.

--Youth League Football. LC 79-109498. (Sports Technique Ser.). 1975. pap. 1.95 (ISBN 0-87670-076-8, YFB-SC). Athletic Inst.

Fuoss, Donald E. & Smith, Rowland. Effective Football Coaching. 264p. 1980. text ed. 16.95 (ISBN 0-205-07125-2, 6271251). Allyn.

Hyman, Mervin D. & White, Gordon S., Jr. Joe Paterno: "Football My Way". 1978. pap. 3.95 (ISBN 0-02-029000-4). Macmillan.

Kaplan, David & Griffin, Daniel. The Best of Bum. (Illus.). 64p. 1980. 4.95 (ISBN 0-932012-13-2). Texas Month Pr.

McIntyre, Bill. Grambling: Cradle of the Pros. Woolfolk, Doug, ed. (Illus.). 110p. 1980. 12.50 (ISBN 0-86518-015-6). Moran Pub Corp.

McKay, John H. Football Coaching. (Illus.). 1966. 16.95 (ISBN 0-8260-5885-X). Wiley.

Ray, Gary. Coach's Guide to the Slot One Offense. 1974. 10.95 (ISBN 0-13-139410-X, Parker). P-H.

Reaves, Rhod. Football's "Combo" Defensive System. (Illus.). 1977. 10.95 (ISBN 0-13-324152-1, Parker). P-H.

Rockne, Knute K. Coaching. LC 70-124591. Repr. of 1925 ed. 15.00 (ISBN 0-404-05377-7). AMS Pr.

Rowen. The Coaching of Football Line Play. 1968. pap. text ed. 3.95 (ISBN 0-675-09595-6). Merrill.

Sandusky, Jerry. Developing Linebackers the Penn State Way. LC 80-84214. (Fitness America Ser.). (Illus.). 160p. (Orig.). 1981. pap. text ed. 5.95 (ISBN 0-918438-64-0). Leisure Pr.

Sloan, Steve. A Whole New Ball Game. LC 75-24737. (Illus.). 168p. 1975. 5.95 (ISBN 0-8054-5559-0). Broadman.

Stein, Joe & Clark, Diane. Don Coryell Win with Honor. LC 76-28011. (Illus.). 1976. 8.95 (ISBN 0-89325-003-1). Joyce Pr.

Storey, Edward J. How to Kick a Football. LC 80-83977. (Illus.). 160p. (Orig.). 1981. pap. text ed. 5.95 (ISBN 0-918438-61-6). Leisure Pr.

Strauch, Larry. Coaching Football's Double Slot Attack. (Illus.). 1978. 10.95 (ISBN 0-13-139337-5, Parker). P-H.

Tallman, Drew. Winning Play Sequences in Modern Football. LC 73-134519. 1971. 10.95 (ISBN 0-13-961045-6, Parker). P-H.

Thorne, Ian. Meet the Coaches. (Meet the Players: Football). (Illus.). (gr. 2-4). 1975. PLB 5.95 (ISBN 0-87191-472-7). Creative Ed.

FOOTBALL SCOUTING

Dienhart, Allan. Football Scouting Workbook. pap. 8.95 (ISBN 0-392-07843-0, SpS). Sportshelf.

FOOTBALL STORIES

see also American Wit and Humor–Sports and Games

Bisheff, Steve & National Football League. Los Angeles Rams. LC 73-2759. (Great Teams' Great Years Ser.). (Illus.). 192p. 1973. 8.95 (ISBN 0-02-588940-0). Macmillan.

Good Times with Football. (Illus.). 24p. (gr. 3-4). 1976. 4.50 (ISBN 0-912122-05-6); pap. 1.89 (ISBN 0-912122-06-4). Football Hobbies.

Hollander, Zander, ed. Strange But True Football Stories. (NFL Punt, Pass & Kick Library: No. 8). (Illus.). (gr. 5-9). 1967. 2.95 (ISBN 0-394-80198-9, BYR). Random.

FOOTE, SAMUEL, 1720-1777

Belden, Mary M. Dramatic Work of Samuel Foote. LC 69-15678. (Yale Studies in English Ser.: No. 80). 1969. Repr. of 1929 ed. 13.50 (ISBN 0-208-00768-7, Archon). Shoe String.

Chatten, Elizabeth N. Samuel Foote. (English Authors Ser.: No.284). 1980. lib. bdg. 9.95 (ISBN 0-8057-6779-7). Twayne.

Cooke, William, ed. The Table-Talk & Bon-Mots of Samuel Foote. Repr. of 1902 ed. 20.00 (ISBN 0-8274-4153-3). R West.

Fitzgerald, Percy. Samuel Foote: A Biography. LC 72-84512. 1910. 18.00 (ISBN 0-405-08519-2, Blom Pubns). Arno.

Murray, Grace A. Personalities of the Eighteenth Century: (Samuel Foote, Christopher Smart, William Hazlitt) 230p. 1980. Repr. of 1927 ed. lib. bdg. 25.00 (ISBN 0-8495-3772-X). Arden Lib.

Trefman, Simon. Sam Foote, Comedian, 1720-1777. LC 70-171348. 1971. 12.00x (ISBN 0-8147-8153-5). NYU Pr.

FOOTPATHS

see Trails

FOOTWEAR

see Boots and Shoes

FORAGE PLANTS

see also Cactus; Corn; Grasses; Heather; Legumes; Millet; Pastures; Sorghum; Stock-Ranges

Butler, G. W. & Bailey, R. W., eds. Chemistry & Biochemistry of Herbage, 3 vols. Incl. Vol. 1. 1973. 97.50 (ISBN 0-12-148101-8); Vol. 2. 1974. 68.00 (ISBN 0-12-148102-6); Vol. 3. 1974. 47.00 (ISBN 0-12-148103-4). Acad Pr.

Effect of Selective Consumption on Voluntary Intake & Digestibility of Tropical Forages. 100p. 1980. pap. 48.75 (ISBN 90-220-0729-4, PDC 206, Pudoc). Unipub.

Gibbons, Euell & Tucker, Gordon. Euell Gibbons' Handbook of Edible Wild Plants. LC 79-14420. (Illus.). 1979. 9.95 (ISBN 0-915442-82-5, Unilaw); pap. 4.95 (ISBN 0-915442-78-7). Donning Co.

Heath, Maurice E., et al. Forages: The Science of Grassland Agriculture. 3rd ed. 755p. 1973. 21.95x (ISBN 0-8138-0680-1). Iowa St U Pr.

Humphreys, Ross. Tropical Pastures & Fodder Crops. (Intermediate Tropical Agriculture Ser.). (Illus.). 1978. pap. text ed. 5.50x (ISBN 0-582-60303-X). Longman.

Matches, A. G., ed. Anti-Quality Components of Forages. (Illus.). 1973. pap. 5.00 (ISBN 0-89118-506-2). Crop Sci Soc Am.

Ross, Opal. Fields & Pine Trees. 1977. 8.00 (ISBN 0-87770-184-9); pap. 5.95 (ISBN 0-87770-177-6). Ye Galleon.

Van Keuren, R. W., ed. Systems Analysis in Forage Crops Production & Utilization. (Illus.). 1975. pap. 4.00 (ISBN 0-89118-508-9). Crop Sci Soc Am.

Wheeler, J. L. & Mochrie, R. D. Forage Evaluation Concepts & Techniques. 582p. 1981. 50.00x (ISBN 0-643-02586-3, Pub. by CSIRO Australia). State Mutual Bk.

FORAMINIFERA

Boltovskoy, E., et al, eds. Atlas of Benthic Shelf Foraminfera of the Southwest Atlantic. (Illus.). v, 153p. 1980. lib. bdg. 58.00 (ISBN 90-6193-604-7, Pub. by Junk Pubs Netherlands). Kluwer Boston.

Carpenter, W. B., et al. Introduction to the Study of the Foraminifera. 1965. Repr. of 1862 ed. 37.50 (ISBN 0-934454-52-3). Lubrecht & Cramer.

Cushman, J. A. The Foraminifera of the Mint Spring Calcareous Marl Member of the Marianna Limestone. Repr. of 1922 ed. 4.30 (ISBN 0-934454-37-X). Lubrecht & Cramer.

--A Lower Miocene Foraminifera of Florida. Repr. of 1924 ed. 5.85 (ISBN 0-934454-58-2). Lubrecht & Cramer.

--Upper Cretaceous Foraminifera of the Gulf Coastal Region. Repr. of 1946 ed. 21.80 (ISBN 0-934454-79-5). Lubrecht & Cramer.

--Upper Eocene Foraminifera of the Southeastern U.S. Repr. of 1935 ed. 15.20 (ISBN 0-934454-80-9). Lubrecht & Cramer.

Cushman, J. A. & Cahill, E. D. Miocene Foraminifera of the Coastal Plain of the Eastern U.S. Repr. of 1935 ed. 14.80 (ISBN 0-934454-64-7). Lubrecht & Cramer.

Cushman, J. A. & Cooke, C. W. The Foraminifera of the Bryam Calcareous Marl at Byram, Mississippi & the Byram Calcareous Marl at Mississippi. 1971. 8.30 (ISBN 0-934454-36-1). Lubrecht & Cramer.

--The Foraminifera of the Vicksburg Group. Repr. of 1925 ed. 12.35 (ISBN 0-934454-38-8). Lubrecht & Cramer.

Cushman, Joseph A. Foraminifera: Their Classification & Economic Use. 4th rev. ed. LC 48-9473. (Illus.). 1948. 30.00x (ISBN 0-674-30801-8). Harvard U Pr.

Galloway, J. J. A Manual of Foraminifera. 1961. Repr. of 1933 ed. 25.00 (ISBN 0-934454-60-4). Lubrecht & Cramer.

Hedley, R. H. & Adams, C. G., eds. Foraminifera, Vol. 1. 1974. 45.50 (ISBN 0-12-336401-9). Acad Pr.

--Foraminifera, Vol. 2. 1977. 42.00 (ISBN 0-12-336402-7). Acad Pr.

--Foraminifera, Vol. 3. 1979. 51.50 (ISBN 0-12-336403-5). Acad Pr.

Kleinpell, R. M. Neogene Smaller Foraminifera from Lau, Fiji. Repr. of 1954 ed. pap. 9.00 (ISBN 0-527-02319-1). Kraus Repr.

Loeblich, A. B., et al. Studies in Foraminifera. 1970. 42.00 (ISBN 0-934454-75-2). Lubrecht & Cramer.

Murray, John. British Nearshore Foraminiferids: Keys & Notes for the Identification of the Species. (Synopses of the British Fauna Ser.). 1979. 9.00 (ISBN 0-12-511850-3). Acad Pr.

Murray, John W. An Atlas of British Recent Foraminiferids. 1971. text ed. 65.00x (ISBN 0-435-62430-X). Heinemann Ed.

Orbigny, A. D' Foraminiferes Fossiles Du Bassin Tertiaire De Vienne. 1963. Repr. of 1846 ed. 25.00 (ISBN 0-934454-39-6). Lubrecht & Cramer.

--Memoire Sur les Foraminiferes De la Craie Blanche Du Bassin De Paris. 1964. pap. 4.55 (ISBN 0-934454-63-9). Lubrecht & Cramer.

Williamson, W. C. Recent Foraminifera of Great Britain. 15.50 (ISBN 0-384-68590-0). Johnson Repr.

FORAMINIFERA, FOSSIL

Cushman, J. A. The Foraminifera of the Mint Spring Calcareous Marl Member of the Marianna Limestone. Repr. of 1922 ed. 4.30 (ISBN 0-934454-37-X). Lubrecht & Cramer.

--A Lower Miocene Foraminifera of Florida. Repr. of 1924 ed. 5.85 (ISBN 0-934454-58-2). Lubrecht & Cramer.

--Upper Cretaceous Foraminifera of the Gulf Coastal Region. Repr. of 1946 ed. 21.80 (ISBN 0-934454-79-5). Lubrecht & Cramer.

--Upper Eocene Foraminifera of the Southeastern U.S. Repr. of 1935 ed. 15.20 (ISBN 0-934454-80-9). Lubrecht & Cramer.

Cushman, J. A. & Cahill, E. D. Miocene Foraminifera of the Coastal Plain of the Eastern U.S. Repr. of 1935 ed. 14.80 (ISBN 0-934454-64-7). Lubrecht & Cramer.

Cushman, J. A. & Cooke, C. W. The Foraminifera of the Bryam Calcareous Marl at Byram, Mississippi & the Byram Calcareous Marl at Mississippi. 1971. 8.30 (ISBN 0-934454-36-1). Lubrecht & Cramer.

Cushman, Joseph A. Foraminifera: Their Classification & Economic Use. 4th rev. ed. LC 48-9473. (Illus.). 1948. 30.00x (ISBN 0-674-30801-8). Harvard U Pr.

Galloway, J. J. A Manual of Foraminifera. 1961. Repr. of 1933 ed. 25.00 (ISBN 0-934454-60-4). Lubrecht & Cramer.

Hanna, G. Dallas & Hanna, Marcus A. Foraminifera from the Eocene of Cowlitz River, Lewis County, Washington. (Publications in Geology: 1-4). (Illus.). 7p. 1924. pap. 5.00 (ISBN 0-295-73789-1, UWPG 1-4). U of Wash Pr.

Orbigny, A. D' Foraminiferes Fossiles Du Bassin Tertiaire De Vienne. 1963. Repr. of 1846 ed. 25.00 (ISBN 0-934454-39-6). Lubrecht & Cramer.

Postuma, J. A. Manual of Planktonic Foraminifera. 1971. 83.00 (ISBN 0-444-40909-2). Elsevier.

FORBES, PATRICK, BP. OF ABERDEEN, 1564-1635

Snow, William G. Times, Life & Thought of Patrick Forbes. (Church Historical Society Ser.: No. 54). 1952. 12.50x (ISBN 0-8401-5054-7). Allenson-Breckinridge.

FORBES, WILLIAMINA (STUART), LADY, d. 1810

Scott, Adam. Sir Walter Scott's First Love. LC 72-2013. (English Literature Ser., No. 33). 1972. Repr. of 1896 ed. lib. bdg. 32.95 (ISBN 0-8383-1450-3). Haskell.

FORBIDDEN-COMBINATION CHECK

see Error-Correcting Codes (Information Theory)

FORCE AND ENERGY

see also Dynamics; Energy Transfer; High Pressure Research; Mass (Physics); Mechanics; Motion; Pressure; Quantum Theory

Aho, Arnold J. Materials, Energies & Environmental Design. 1981. lib. bdg. 28.50 (ISBN 0-8240-7178-6). Garland Pub.

Allen, Rodney F. Energy Education: Goals & Practices. LC 79-93115. (Fastback Ser.: No. 139). (Orig.). 1980. pap. 0.75 (ISBN 0-87367-139-2). Phi Delta Kappa.

Andresen, A. F. & Maeland, A., eds. Hydrides for Energy Storage: Proceedings of an International Symposium Held in Norway, Aug. 1977. 1978. text ed. 90.00 (ISBN 0-08-022715-5). Pergamon.

Asher, Maxine K. Ancient Energy: Key to the Universe. LC 78-19497. (Illus.). 1979. 8.95 (ISBN 0-06-060308-9, HarpR). Har-Row.

Balachandran, Sarojini, ed. Energy Statistics: A Guide to Information Sources. LC 80-13338. (Natural World Information Guide Ser.: Vol. 1). 272p. 1980. 36.00 (ISBN 0-8103-1419-3). Gale.

Boustead, I. & Hancock, G. F. Handbook of Industrial Energy Analysis. LC 78-40636. 1979. 76.95 (ISBN 0-470-26492-6). Halsted Pr.

Burk, Creighton A. & Drake, Charles, eds. Impact of the Geosciences on Critical Energy Resources. 1978. lib. bdg. 17.00x (ISBN 0-89158-293-2). Westview.

Campbell, L. J. & Carlton, R. J. Force & Energy: Physics, Bk. 1. (Secondary Science Ser). (Illus., Orig.). (gr. 8-11). 1974. pap. text ed. 6.95 (ISBN 0-7100-7739-4). Routledge & Kegan.

Carey, Helen, ed. Playing with Energy. 106p. (Orig.). 1981. pap. 3.00 (ISBN 0-87355-020-X, 471-14778). Natl Sci Tchrs.

Chigier, N. A., ed. Progress in Energy & Combustion Science, Vol. 6 Complete. (Illus.). 377p. 1981. cancelled (ISBN 0-08-027153-7). Pergamon.

--Progress in Energy & Combustion Science, Vol. 6. (Illus.). 388p. 1981. 119.00 (ISBN 0-08-027153-7). Pergamon.

Chigier, Norman A., ed. Progress in Energy & Combustion Science, Vols. 1-3. Incl. Vol. 1, Pt. 1. pap. 15.50 (ISBN 0-08-019931-3); Vol. 1, Pts. 2-3. pap. 25.00 (ISBN 0-08-021023-6); Vol. 1, Pt. 4. pap. 22.00 (ISBN 0-08-021041-4); Vol. 1, Complete. Pollution Formation & Destruction in Flames. 97.50 (ISBN 0-08-020307-8); Vol. 2, Pt. 1. pap. 14.00 (ISBN 0-08-021211-5); Vol. 2, Pt. 2. pap. 14.00 (ISBN 0-08-021213-1); Vol. 2, Pt. 3. pap. 12.50 (ISBN 0-08-021215-8); Vol. 2, Pt. 4. 97.50 (ISBN 0-08-021217-4); Vol. 2 Complete, 1978. 50.00 (ISBN 0-08-021219-0). LC 75-24822. 1976-78. Pergamon.

Commission of the European Communities, ed. Energy Research & Development Programme, Status Report 1977. 1977. pap. 24.00 (ISBN 90-247-2059-1, Pub. by Martinus Nijhoff Netherlands). Kluwer Boston.

Corey, D. Q. & Maas, J. P. The Energy Couple. (Illus.). 160p. 1980. 9.95 (ISBN 0-398-03964-X). C C Thomas.

Counihan, Martin. A Dictionary of Energy. (Illus.). 200p. 1981. 14.95 (ISBN 0-7100-0847-3). Routledge & Kegan.

Davis, John. Energy-to Use-Abuse. 192p. 1980. softcover 10.00x (ISBN 0-905381-00-9, Pub. by Gresham England). State Mutual Bk.

Eden, Jerome. Orgone Energy: The Answer to Atomic Suicide. LC 72-75477. 1972. 7.50 (ISBN 0-682-47477-0). Exposition.

Emmerich, Werner, et al. Energy Does Matter. (Illus.). 1963. 7.95 (ISBN 0-8027-0096-9). Walker & Co.

Energy. LC 77-19263. (How It Works Ser.). 1978. 9.95 (ISBN 0-668-04555-8, 4555). Arco.

Fowler, John M. Energy-Environment Source Book: Energy, Society, & the Environment; Energy, Its Extraction, Conversion, & Use, 2 vols. rev. ed. (Illus.). 1980. Set. pap. 6.50 (ISBN 0-87355-022-6, 471-14692). Natl Sci Tchrs.

Gattegno, Caleb. Forms of Energy. (The Study of Energy. Vol. 1). 1963. 3.85 (ISBN 0-85225-682-5). Ed Solutions.

Goodman, G. T. & Rowe, W. D., eds. Energy Risk Management. LC 79-42931. 1980. 39.50 (ISBN 0-12-289680-7). Acad Pr.

Hayes, Denis. Energy for Development: Third World Options. LC 77-91821. (Worldwatch Papers). 1977. pap. 2.00 (ISBN 0-916468-14-3). Worldwatch Inst.

Hesse, Mary B. Forces & Fields. LC 74-106693. (Illus.). 318p. Repr. of 1962 ed. lib. bdg. 19.00x (ISBN 0-8371-3366-1, HEFF). Greenwood.

Hoffman, E. J. The Concept of Energy: An Inquiry into Origins & Applications. LC 76-50987. 1977. 60.00 (ISBN 0-250-40153-3). Ann Arbor Science.

Hollander, Jack M., et al, eds. Annual Review of Energy, Vol. 1. (Illus.). 1976. text ed. 17.00 (ISBN 0-8243-2301-7). Annual Reviews.

Hottel, H. C. & Howard, J. B. New Energy Technology - Some Facts & Assessments. 384p. 1972. pap. 4.95 (ISBN 0-262-58019-5). MIT Pr.

International Conference on Energy, 2nd, Washington, D. C., October 1978. Proceedings. Energy Magazine Staff & Business Communications Co., Inc. Staff, eds. 1979. 75.00 (ISBN 0-89336-186-0). BCC.

James, Glenn D. Energy Potpourri-Appendix. (Illus.). 1977. pap. 7.00 (ISBN 0-916898-01-6). Sono Pubs.

Jardine, Jim. Energy. (Science & Technical Readers Ser.). (Orig.). 1980. pap. text ed. 2.95x (ISBN 0-435-29002-9). Heinemann Ed.

Larsen, Egon. New Sources of Energy & Power. 1977. 9.95x (ISBN 0-8448-1043-6). Crane-Russak Co.

Lax, Peter D., ed. Mathematical Aspects of Production & Distribution of Energy. LC 77-7174. (Proceedings of Symposia in Applied Mathematics: No. 21). 1979. Repr. of 1977 ed. with corrections 15.20 (ISBN 0-8218-0121-X, PSAPM-21). Am Math.

Learning Achievement Corporation. Multiplication & Energy & Construction: Division & Medicine. Zak, Therese A., ed. (MATCH Ser.). (Illus.). 144p. 1981. text ed. 5.28 (ISBN 0-07-037112-1, G). McGraw.

Lee, Kaiman & Masloff, Jacqueline. Kaiman's Encyclopedia of Energy Topics, 2 vols. LC 79-104541. (Illus.). 1979. Set. 150.00 (ISBN 0-915250-31-4). Environ Design.

Libowitz, G. G. & Whittingham, M. S., eds. Materials Science in Energy Technology. LC 78-51235. (Materials Science & Technology Ser.). 1979. 58.00 (ISBN 0-12-447550-7). Acad Pr.

Lindsay, B. R., ed. Applications of Energy: Nineteenth Century. (Benchmark Papers in Energy Ser.: Vol. 2). 1976. 54.00 (ISBN 0-12-786961-1). Acad Pr.

Lindsay, R. Bruce, ed. Energy: Historical Development of the Concept. LC 75-30719. (Benchmark Papers on Energy Ser.: Vol 1). 369p. 1975. 48.50 (ISBN 0-12-786963-8). Acad Pr.

Lodge, Oliver. Energy. 1978. Repr. of 1929 ed. lib. bdg. 15.00 (ISBN 0-8414-5751-4). Folcroft.

Measurement of Force & Mass. 181p. 1978. pap. 57.00x (ISBN 0-686-71870-4, Pub. by VDI Verlag Germany). Renouf.

Merklein, Helmut A. & Hardy, W. Carey. Energy Economics. 280p. 1977. 14.95 (ISBN 0-87201-222-0). Gulf Pub.

Miller, David H. Energy at the Surface of the Earth. 1981. 49.50 (ISBN 0-12-497150-4). Acad Pr.

--Energy at the Surface of the Earth: An Introduction to the Energetics of Ecosystems. (International Geophysics Ser.). 1981. 49.50 (ISBN 0-12-497150-4); stud. ed. 25.00 (ISBN 0-12-497152-0). Acad Pr.

Miller, Raymond C. The Force of Energy: A Business History of the Detroit Edison Company. (Illus.). 350p. 1971. 12.50 (ISBN 0-87013-164-8). Mich St U Pr.

Moray, John E. The Sea of Energy. 5th ed. (Illus.). 275p. 1978. Repr. of 1930 ed. 18.50 (ISBN 0-686-30121-8, 264-334); pap. 7.35 (ISBN 0-686-30122-6). Cosray Res.

Morrison, Denton E. Energy: A Bibliography of Social Science & Related Literature. LC 74-4800. (Reference Library of Social Science: No. 9). 185p. 1975. lib. bdg. 23.00 (ISBN 0-8240-1096-5). Garland Pub.

Mott-Smith, Morton. The Concept of Energy Simply Explained. LC 63-19496. 1964. lib. bdg. 9.50 (ISBN 0-88307-626-8). Gannon.

--Concept of Energy Simply Explained. Orig. Title: Story of Energy, Il. 1934. pap. 3.00 (ISBN 0-486-21071-5). Dover.

Nelson, Robert V. Understanding Basic Energy Terms. Ide, Arthur F., ed. LC 79-9940. (E Equals MC Squared Ser.). (Illus.). 67p. 1980. 9.00 (ISBN 0-86663-806-7); pap. 6.25 (ISBN 0-86663-807-5). Ide Hse.

Odum, Howard T. & Odum, Elizabeth C. Energy Basis for Man & Nature. 1976. 18.50 (ISBN 0-07-047531-8, C); pap. 11.95 (ISBN 0-07-047527-X); instructor's manual 2.50 (ISBN 0-07-047534-2). McGraw.

Overman, Michael. Understanding Energy. LC 75-318434. (Understanding Science Ser.). (Illus.). 150p. 1975. 9.00x (ISBN 0-7188-2082-7). Intl Pubns Serv.

Perlmutter, A., et al. Fundamental Interactions at High Energy, Vol. 2. 380p. 1970. 66.00 (ISBN 0-677-14380-X). Gordon.

Pronin, Monica, ed. Energy Index 1979. LC 73-89098. 1980. 125.00 (ISBN 0-89947-006-8). Environ Info.

Reich, Wilhelm. The Murder of Christ: The Emotional Plague of Mankind. 228p. 1953. 5.95 (ISBN 0-374-21625-8); pap. 3.95 (ISBN 0-374-50476-8, N290). FS&G.

Rice-Husk Conversion to Energy. (FAO Agricultural Services Bulletin Ser.: No. 31). (Illus.). 1979. pap. 12.00 (ISBN 92-5-100340-8, F1526, FAO). Unipub.

Rider, Don K. Energy: Hydrocarbon Fuels & Chemical Resources. LC 81-196. 493p. 1981. 34.95 (ISBN 0-471-05915-3, Pub. by Wiley-Interscience). Wiley.

Romer, Robert H. Energy: An Introduction to Physics. LC 75-35591. (Illus.). 1976. 21.95x (ISBN 0-7167-0357-2); tchr's guide avail. W H Freeman.

San Pietro, Anthony G., ed. Biochemical & Photosynthetic Aspects of Energy Production. 1980. 24.50 (ISBN 0-12-618980-3). Acad Pr.

Saperstein, Alvin M. Physics: Energy in the Environment. 384p. 1975. pap. text ed. 14.95 (ISBN 0-316-77070-1); solutions manual free (ISBN 0-316-77072-8). Little.

Savage, N. E. & Wood, R. S. Matter & Energy: General Science, Bk. 1. (Secondary Science Ser). (gr. 8-11). 1972. pap. text ed. 5.75 (ISBN 0-7100-7076-4). Routledge & Kegan.

Scientific American Editors. Energy & Power: A Scientific American Book. LC 75-180254. (Illus.). 1971. pap. text ed. 7.95x (ISBN 0-7167-0938-4). W H Freeman.

Silverman, Sanford L. & Silverman, Martin G. Theory of Relationships. LC 63-13349. 1964. 6.00 (ISBN 0-8022-1571-8). Philos Lib.

Simpson, Jan. Citizens' Energy Directory. 2nd, rev. ed. (Illus.). 185p. 1980. pap. 9.00 (ISBN 0-89988-055-X). Citizens Energy.

Slattery, John C. Momentum, Energy, & Mass Transfer in Continua. 2nd ed. LC 80-22746. 700p. 1981. text ed. 32.50 (ISBN 0-89874-212-9). Krieger.

Smith, Bruce A., ed. A Perspective on Energy Modeling. 1976. pap. text ed. 22.00 (ISBN 0-08-019985-2). Pergamon.

Stoker, H. Stephen, et al. Energy: From Source to Use. 337p. 1975. pap. 7.95x (ISBN 0-673-07947-3). Scott F.

Striedieck, Werner F. Energie: Von der Tretmuhle zum Kernreaktor. LC 65-12034. (Orig., Ger.). 1965. pap. text ed. 4.95x (ISBN 0-89197-141-6). Irvington.

Studies in Atmospheric Energetics Based on Aerospace Probings. Incl. Annual Report-1966. 1967. pap. 5.00 (ISBN 0-299-97024-8); Annual Report-1967. 1968. pap. 7.50 (ISBN 0-299-97025-6); Annual Report-1968. 1969. pap. 5.00 (ISBN 0-299-97026-4). U of Wis Pr.

Swartz, Clifford & Goldfarb, Theodore. A Search for Order in the Physical Universe. LC 73-19743. (Illus.). 1974. text ed. 22.95x (ISBN 0-7167-0345-9). W H Freeman.

Szolsanyi. Energetics in Unit Operations. LC 74-21502. 384p. 1977. 27.50 (ISBN 0-306-30828-2, Plenum Pr). Plenum Pub.

Tarver, Stephen. A Simple Solution to the Energy Problem. 2nd ed. 1976. 3.95 (ISBN 0-686-16522-5). Wyoming Specialties.

Terry, Mark & Witt, Paul. Energy & Order. LC 76-19208. 41p. 1976. pap. text ed. 3.00 (ISBN 0-913890-14-6). Friends Earth.

Veziroglu, Nejat, ed. Hydrogen Energy, Pts. A & B. LC 74-34483. 1369p. 1975. Set. 95.00 (ISBN 0-306-34301-0, Plenum Pr). Plenum Pub.

Warren, Betty. The Energy & Environment Checklist. rev. ed. LC 79-56912. Orig. Title: The Energy & Environment Bibliography. 228p. 1980. pap. 5.95 (ISBN 0-913890-37-5). Friends Earth.

White, Carol. Energy Potential: Toward a New Electromagnetic Field Theory. Cleary, James, tr. 305p. 1978. pap. 7.95 (ISBN 0-918388-04-X, QC665.E4W45, Univ Edns). New Benjamin.

Yergin, Daniel & Hillenbrand, Martin, eds. World Energy: The Crisis & What We Can Do About It. 1982. 13.95 (ISBN 0-395-30517-9). HM.

Youmans, Edward L. The Correlation & Conservation of Forces. Cohen, I. Bernard, ed. LC 80-2152. (Development of Science Ser.). (Illus.). 1981. lib. bdg. 40.00 (ISBN 0-405-13961-6). Arno.

FORCE AND ENERGY–JUVENILE LITERATURE

Adler, Irving. Energy. LC 71-10143. (Reason Why Ser). (Illus.). (gr. 3-6). 1970. PLB 8.79 (ISBN 0-381-99609-3, A23400, JD-J). Har-Row.

Barker, Eric J. & Millard, W. F. Machines & Energy. LC 66-22904. (Science Projects & Experiments for the Junior Scientist). (Illus.). 80p. (gr. 7 up). 1972. PLB 4.50 (ISBN 0-668-01499-7). Arco.

--Nature & Energy. (Science Projects & Experiments). (Illus.). 95p. (gr. 7 up). 1972. PLB 4.50 (ISBN 0-668-01500-4). Arco.
Benczer-Koller, Noemie & Koller, Earl L. Power & Energy. LC 59-13619. (Illus.). (gr. 4-6). 1960. PLB 6.95 (ISBN 0-87396-009-2). Stravon.
Boyd, Waldo T. The World of Energy Storage. LC 76-39936. (Illus.). (gr. 6-8). 1977. PLB 5.29 (ISBN 0-399-61058-8). Putnam.
Breiter, Herta S. Fuel & Energy. LC 77-18560. (Read About Sciences Ser.). (Illus.). (gr. k-3). 1978. PLB 11.15 (ISBN 0-8393-0083-2). Raintree Child.
Energy from the Earth. (Wonders of Learning Kits Ser.). (gr. 3-5). 1980. incl. cassette & tchrs. guide 23.50 (ISBN 0-686-74408-X, 04972). Natl Geog.
Energy from the Sun. (Wonders of Learning Kits Ser.). (gr. 3-5). 1980. incl. cassette & tchrs guide 23.50 (ISBN 0-686-74409-8, 04973). Natl Geog.
Epstein, Sam & Epstein, Beryl. All About Engines & Power. (Allabout Ser.: No. 46). (Illus.). (gr. 5-9). 1962. PLB 5.39 (ISBN 0-394-90245-9). Random.
Freeman, S. David. Energy: The New Era. LC 74-9174. 1974. pap. 2.45 (ISBN 0-394-71316-8, V-316, Vin). Random.
Hellman, Hal. Energy & Inertia. LC 70-106594. (Illus.). 48p. (gr. 2-5). 1970. 3.95 (ISBN 0-87131-046-5). M Evans.
Jugendhandbuch Naturwissen: Energie, Vol. 5. 128p. (Ger.). 1976. pap. 5.95 (ISBN 3-499-16207-5, M-7490, Pub. by Rowohlt). French & Eur.
Legunn, Joel. Motion. Liberty, Gene, ed. LC 73-128852. (Understanding Bks.). Orig. Title: Investigating Motion. (gr. 6-9). 1971. PLB 7.95 (ISBN 0-87191-041-1). Creative Ed.
Mother Earth News Staff. Handbook of Homemade Power. (Illus.). 1974. pap. 3.50 (ISBN 0-553-20077-1). Bantam.
Ruchlis, Hyman. Orbit: Picture Story of Force & Motion. LC 58-5290. (Illus.). (gr. 5 up). 1958. PLB 8.79 (ISBN 0-06-025111-5, HarpJ). Har-Row.
Satchwell, John. Energy at Work. LC 80-85101. (Illus.). (gr. 3-6). 1981. PLB 11.47 (ISBN 0-688-00167-X); pap. 7.95 (ISBN 0-688-00251-X). Lothrop.
Schurr, Sandra. The Power Plug. (Choose-a-Card Ser.). (Illus.). 32p. (gr. 4-6). 1980. pap. text ed. 5.95 (ISBN 0-913916-70-6, IP 70-6). Incentive Pubns.
Wade, Harlan. La Force. Potvin, Claude & Potvin, Rose-Ella, trs. from Eng. (A Book About Ser.). Orig. Title: Strength. (Illus., Fr.). (gr. k-3). 1979. PLB 7.95 (ISBN 0-8172-1453-4). Raintree Pubs.
--La Fuerza. Contreras, Mamie M., tr. from Eng. LC 78-26850. (A Book About Ser.). Orig. Title: Strength. (Illus., Sp.). (gr. k-3). 1979. PLB 7.95 (ISBN 0-8172-1478-X). Raintree Pubs.
Wohlrabe, Raymond A. Fundamental Physical Forces. LC 78-82400. (Introducing Modern Science Ser). (Illus.). (gr. 7 up). 1969. 5.95 (ISBN 0-397-31074-9). Lippincott.

FORCE PUMPS
see Pumping Machinery

FORCED LABOR
see also Contract Labor; Convict Labor; Service, Compulsory Non-Military; Serfdom; Slave Labor
Ferencz, Benjamin B. Less Than Slaves: Jewish Forced Labor & the Quest for Compensation. LC 79-10690. 1979. 15.00x (ISBN 0-674-52525-6). Harvard U Pr.
Klein, Gerda W. All But My Life. 247p. 1971. pap. 4.95 (ISBN 0-8090-1360-6). Hill & Wang.
Kloosterboer, Willemina. Involuntary Labour Since the Abolition of Slavery. LC 76-9771. 1976. Repr. of 1960 ed. lib. bdg. 16.25x (ISBN 0-8371-8887-3, KLIL). Greenwood.
Lasker, Bruno. Human Bondage in Southeast Asia. LC 79-138155. 406p. 1972. Repr. of 1950 ed. lib. bdg. 26.00x (ISBN 0-8371-5612-2, LAHU). Greenwood.
Novak, Daniel A. The Wheel of Servitude: Black Forced Labor After Slavery. LC 77-76334. 144p. 1978. 10.50x (ISBN 0-8131-1371-7). U Pr of Ky.
Ruo-Wang, Bao & Chelminski, Rudolph. Prisoner of Mao. 1976. pap. 2.50 (ISBN 0-14-004112-5). Penguin.
Sherman, William L. Forced Native Labor in Sixteenth-Century Central America. LC 78-13521. (Illus.). 1979. 18.50x (ISBN 0-8032-4100-3). U of Nebr Pr.
Wilson, Walter. Forced Labor in the United States. LC 76-144704. Repr. of 1933 ed. 18.00 (ISBN 0-404-00239-0). AMS Pr.

FORCEPS, OBSTETRIC
Aveling, James H. The Chamberlens & the Midwifery Forceps. LC 75-23677. Repr. of 1882 ed. 19.00 (ISBN 0-404-13230-8). AMS Pr.

FORCING (PLANTS)
see also Greenhouses
Laurie, Alex, et al. Commercial Flower Forcing. 7th ed. 1968. text ed. 19.00 (ISBN 0-07-036632-2, C). McGraw.
--Commercial Flower Forcing. 8th ed. (Illus.). 1979. text ed. 20.00 (ISBN 0-07-036633-0, C). McGraw.

FORD, ARTHUR A.
Montgomery, Ruth. A World Beyond: A Startling Message from the Eminent Psychic Arthur Ford from Beyond the Grave. 1971. 6.95 (ISBN 0-698-10404-8). Coward.
Spraggett, Allen. Arthur Ford: The Man Who Talked with the Dead. 1974. pap. 1.50 (ISBN 0-451-05804-6, W5804, Sig). NAL.
Sullivan, Eileen. Arthur Ford Speaks from Beyond. LC 74-25395. 192p. 1975. 6.95 (ISBN 0-87955-317-0). O'Hara.

FORD, BARNEY
Talmadge, Marian & Gilmore, Iris. Barney Ford, Black Baron. LC 72-12020. (Illus.). 228p. (gr. 7 up). 1973. 5.95 (ISBN 0-396-06751-4). Dodd.

FORD, EDSEL
Greenleaf, William. From These Beginnings: The Early Philanthrophies of Henry & Edsel Ford, 1911-1936. LC 64-1969. 1964. 9.95x (ISBN 0-8143-1233-0). Wayne St U Pr.
Killian, James R., Jr., ed. Proceedings of the Atoms for Peace Awards, 1957-1969: A Memorial to Henry Ford & Edsel Ford. 1978. text ed. 15.00x (ISBN 0-262-11068-7). MIT Pr.

FORD, FORD MADOX, 1873-1939
Andreach, Robert J. The Slain & Resurrected God: Conrad, Ford & the Christian Myth. LC 70-111517. (Gotham Library). 1970. 10.95x (ISBN 0-8147-0456-5); pap. 3.95x (ISBN 0-8147-0494-8). NYU Pr.
Cassell, Richard A. Ford Madox Ford: A Study of His Novels. LC 76-57731. 1977. Repr. of 1962 ed. lib. bdg. 18.00x (ISBN 0-8371-9465-2, CAFF). Greenwood.
Goldring, Douglas. South Lodge. LC 77-18261. 1977. lib. bdg. 25.00 (ISBN 0-8414-4600-8). Folcroft.
Green, R. Ford Madox Ford: Prose & Politics. LC 80-41566. 200p. Date not set. 39.95 (ISBN 0-521-23610-X). Cambridge U Pr.
Harvey, David D. Ford Madox Ford, 1873-1939. LC 76-150411. 1972. Repr. of 1962 ed. text ed. 20.00 (ISBN 0-87752-142-5). Gordian.
Hoffmann, Charles G. Ford Madox Ford. (English Authors Ser.: No. 55). lib. bdg. 10.95 (ISBN 0-8057-1200-3). Twayne.
Huntley, H. Robert. Alien Protagonist of Ford Madox Ford. 1970. 14.00x (ISBN 0-8078-1152-1). U of NC Pr.
Leer, Norman. Limited Hero in the Novels of Ford Madox Ford. vii, 267p. 1966. 6.00 (ISBN 0-87013-104-4). Mich St U Pr.
Lid, R. W. Ford Madox Ford: The Essence of His Art. 1964. 17.50x (ISBN 0-520-00748-4). U of Cal Pr.
MacShane, Frank, ed. Ford Madox Ford: The Critical Heritage. (The Critical Heritage Ser.). 1972. 22.95x (ISBN 0-7100-6957-X). Routledge & Kegan.
Moser, Thomas C. The Life in the Fiction of Ford Madox Ford. LC 80-7548. 360p. 1981. 22.50 (ISBN 0-691-06445-8); pap. 8.95 (ISBN 0-691-10102-7). Princeton U Pr.
Poli, Bernard J. Ford Madox Ford & the Transatlantic Review. LC 67-15880. 1967. 12.00x (ISBN 0-8156-2105-1). Syracuse U Pr.
Sabol, C. Ruth & Bender, Todd K. A Concordance to Ford Madox Ford's The Good Soldier. 1981. lib. bdg. 35.00 (ISBN 0-8240-9371-2). Garland Pub.
Stang, Sondra, ed. The Presence of Ford Madox Ford. (Illus.). 1981. 20.00 (ISBN 0-8122-7794-5). U of Pa Pr.
Stang, Sondra J. Ford Madox Ford. LC 77-41. (Modern Literature Ser.). 1977. 10.95 (ISBN 0-8044-2832-8). Ungar.

FORD, GERALD, PRES. U. S., 1913-
Aaron, Jan. Gerald R. Ford: President of Destiny. LC 74-21356. (Illus.). 140p. 1975. 6.95 (ISBN 0-8303-0147-X). Fleet.
Casserly, John J. The Ford Whitehouse: The Diary of a Speechwriter. LC 77-82185. (Illus.). 1977. 12.50 (ISBN 0-87081-106-1). Colo Assoc.
Claussen, Martin P. Gerald R. Ford of Omaha, Grand Rapids & Alexandria: A Bicentennial Salute, 1637-1974. (Illus.). 40p. 1977. pap. 3.00 (ISBN 0-912680-01-6). Piedmont.
Congressional Quarterly Staff. Presidency, Nineteen Seventy-Five. new ed. LC 74-2658. (Presidency Ser.). 1976. pap. 6.95 (ISBN 0-87187-087-8). Congr Quarterly.
--Presidency, Nineteen Seventy-Four. (Presidency Ser.). 1975. pap. 6.95 (ISBN 0-87187-073-8). Congr Quarterly.
The Cumulated Indexes to the Public Papers of the Presidents of the United States: Gerald R. Ford, 1974-1977. 1980. lib. bdg. 30.00 (ISBN 0-527-20756-X). Kraus Intl.
A Discussion with Gerald R. Ford: The American Presidency. LC 77-80274. 1977. pap. 1.25 (ISBN 0-8447-3257-5). Am Enterprise.
Ford, Gerald R. A Time to Heal: The Autobiography of Gerald R. Ford. LC 78-20162. (Illus.). 1979. 12.95 (ISBN 0-06-011297-2, HarpT). Har-Row.
Hartmann, Jerry. Palace Politics: An Inside Account of the Ford Years. 320p. 1980. 14.95 (ISBN 0-07-026951-3). McGraw.
Lankevich, George. Gerald R. Ford, 1913-... Chronology, Documents, Bibliographical Aids. (Presidential Chronology Ser.). 1977. 15.00 (ISBN 0-379-12084-4). Oceana.
LeRoy, L. David. Biography of Gerald R. Ford. 1974. 2.75 (ISBN 0-87948-036-X). Beatty.
Mercer, Charles. Gerald Ford. LC 74-24332. (Beginning Biographies Ser.). (Illus.). 64p. (gr. k-4). 1975. PLB 5.99 (ISBN 0-399-60944-X). Putnam.
The Nixon-Ford Years. (Political Profile Ser.). 1980. lib. bdg. 55.00 (ISBN 0-87196-454-6). Facts on File.
Reeves, Richard. A Ford, Not a Lincoln. LC 75-22195. 224p. 1975. 8.95 (ISBN 0-15-132302-X). HarBraceJ.
Rothschild, Eric, ed. Gerald Ford & Watergate's Aftermath: 1975-1976. (New York Times School Microfilm Collection Ser.: Guide No. 14). 133p. (gr. 7-12). 1978. pap. 5.50 wkbk (ISBN 0-667-00563-3). Microfilming Corp.
Ter Horst, J. F. Gerald Ford: Past... Present... Future. LC 74-82727. 1974. 11.95 (ISBN 0-89388-191-0). Okpaku Communications.
TerHorst, Jerald F. Gerald Ford & the Future of the Presidency. LC 74-82727. 1974. 11.95 (ISBN 0-89388-191-0). Okpaku Communications.
Weidenfeld, Sheila R. First Lady's Lady: With the Fords at the White House. LC 78-10662. (Illus.). 1979. 11.95 (ISBN 0-399-12292-3). Putnam.
Winter-Berger, Robert N. The Gerald Ford Letters. 235p. 1974. 7.95 (ISBN 0-8184-0204-0). Lyle Stuart.

FORD, GUY STANTON, 1873-1962
Minnesota University - Graduate School. Social Sciences at Mid-Century. facs. ed. LC 68-55852. (Essay Index Reprint Ser). 1952. 12.25 (ISBN 0-8369-0710-8). Arno.

FORD, HENRY, 1863-1947
Burlingame, Roger. Henry Ford. 202p. 1972. pap. 3.95 (ISBN 0-8129-6123-4, QP76). Times Bks.
Dahlinger, John D. & Leighton, Frances S. The Secret Life of Henry Ford. LC 77-15422. (Illus.). 1978. 10.95 (ISBN 0-672-52377-9). Bobbs.
Ervin, Spencer. Henry Ford Vs. Truman H. Newberry: The Famous Senate Election Contest. LC 73-19143. (Politics & People Ser.). 634p. 1974. Repr. 32.00x (ISBN 0-405-05867-5). Arno.
Ford, Henry & Crowther, Samuel. My Life & Work. LC 73-2507. (Big Business; Economic Power in a Free Society Ser.). Repr. of 1922 ed. 17.00 (ISBN 0-405-05088-7). Arno.
Gelderman, Carol. Henry Ford: The Wayward Capitalist. (Illus.). 416p. 1981. 14.95 (ISBN 0-8037-3436-0). Dial.
Greenleaf, William. From These Beginnings: The Early Philanthrophies of Henry & Edsel Ford, 1911-1936. LC 64-1969. 1964. 9.95x (ISBN 0-8143-1233-0). Wayne St U Pr.
Jardim, Anne. First Henry Ford: A Study in Personality & Business Leadership. 1970. 15.00x (ISBN 0-262-10008-8); pap. 4.95 (ISBN 0-262-60005-6). MIT Pr.
Killian, James R., Jr., ed. Proceedings of the Atoms for Peace Awards, 1957-1969: A Memorial to Henry Ford & Edsel Ford. 1978. text ed. 15.00x (ISBN 0-262-11068-7). MIT Pr.
Kimes, Beverly R. The Cars That Henry Ford Built. (Illus.). 1978. 19.95 (ISBN 0-525-07660-3). Dutton.
Lasky, Victor. Never Complain, Never Explain: The Story of Henry Ford. 420p. 1981. 15.00 (ISBN 0-399-90104-3). Marek.
Lewis, David L. The Public Image of Henry Ford: An American Folk Hero & His Company. LC 76-807. (Illus.). 600p. 1976. 25.00 (ISBN 0-8143-1553-4). Wayne St U Pr.
Montgomery, Elizabeth R. Henry Ford: Automotive Pioneer. LC 72-83487. (Americans All Ser). (Illus.). (gr. 3-6). 1969. PLB 6.48 (ISBN 0-8116-4556-8). Garrard.
Nevins, Allan & Hill, Frank E. Ford, 3 vols. Incl. Vol. 1. The Times, the Man, the Company; Vol. 2. Expansion & Challenge, 1915-1933; Vol. 3. Decline & Rebirth: 1933-1962. LC 75-41775. (Companies & Men: Business Enterprise in America Ser.). (Illus.). 1976. Repr. 115.00x (ISBN 0-405-08089-1). Arno.
Nye, David E. Henry Ford: Ignorant Idealist. (National University Publications, American Studies). 1979. 12.50 (ISBN 0-8046-9242-4). Kennikat.
Quackenbush, Robert. Along Came the Model T! How Henry Ford Put the World on Wheels. LC 77-10057. (Illus.). 40p. (gr. k-5). 1978. 6.50 (ISBN 0-590-07714-7, Four Winds). Schol Bk Serv.
Sward, Keith. Legend of Henry Ford. LC 68-16412. 1968. pap. text ed. 5.95x (ISBN 0-689-70191-8, 129). Atheneum.
--Legend of Henry Ford. LC 68-10947. 1968. Repr. of 1948 ed. 10.00 (ISBN 0-8462-1084-3). Russell.
Vidal, Gore, et al. Great American Families. (Illus.). 1977. 15.95 (ISBN 0-393-08752-2). Norton.
Wik, Reynold M. Henry Ford & Grass-Roots America. LC 76-163627. (Illus.). 1972. 10.00 (ISBN 0-472-97200-6). U of Mich Pr.
--Henry Ford & Grass-Roots America. (Illus.). 298p. 1973. pap. 3.95 (ISBN 0-472-06193-3, AA). U of Mich Pr.

FORD, HENRY, 1917-
Burlingame, Roger. Henry Ford. 202p. 1972. pap. 3.95 (ISBN 0-8129-6123-4, QP76). Times Bks.
Kurland, Gerald. Henry Ford: Pioneer in the Automotive Industry. Rahmas, D. Steve, ed. LC 72-81900. (Outstanding Personalities Ser.: No. 42). 32p. (Orig.). (gr. 7-12). 1972. lib. bdg. 2.95 incl. catalog cards (ISBN 0-87157-551-5); pap. 1.50 vinyl laminated covers (ISBN 0-87157-051-3). SamHar Pr.
Post, Dan R., ed. Ford, Closing the Years of Tradition. 1975. 12.00 (ISBN 0-911160-35-3). Post-Era.

FORD, JAMES, d. 1833
Snively, W. D., Jr. & Furbee, Louanna. Satan's Ferryman: A True Tale of the Old Frontier. LC 68-20522. (Illus.). 250p. (gr. 11-12). 1968. text ed. 14.95 (ISBN 0-8044-1875-6). Ungar.

FORD, JOHN, 1586-1640
Ali, Florence. Opposing Absolutes: Conviction & Convention in John Ford's Plays. (Salzburg Studies in English Literature, Jacobean Drama Studies: No.44). 1974. pap. text ed. 25.00x (ISBN 0-391-01295-9). Humanities.
Anderson, Donald K., Jr. John Ford. (English Authors Ser.: No. 129). lib. bdg. 10.95 (ISBN 0-8057-1204-6). Twayne.
Davril, Robert. Le Drame De John Ford. 550p. 1979. Repr. of 1954 ed. lib. bdg. 100.00 (ISBN 0-8495-1051-1). Arden Lib.
Ewing, S. B. Burtonian Melancholy in the Plays of John Ford. LC 77-96156. 1969. Repr. of 1940 ed. lib. bdg. 11.00x (ISBN 0-374-92660-3). Octagon.
Farr, Dorothy M. John Ford & the Caroline Theatre. 1979. text ed. 24.50x (ISBN 0-06-492065-8). B&N.
Huebert, Ronald. John Ford: Baroque English Dramatist. (Illus.). 1978. lib. bdg. 21.95x (ISBN 0-7735-0286-6). McGill-Queens U Pr.
Orbison, Tucker. The Tragic Vision of John Ford. (Salzburg Studies in English Literature, Jacobean Drama Studies: No. 21). 1974. pap. text ed. 25.00x (ISBN 0-391-01492-7). Humanities.
Sargeaunt, Margaret J. John Ford. LC 66-13174. 1966. Repr. of 1935 ed. 7.50 (ISBN 0-8462-0721-4). Russell.
Sensabaugh, George F. Tragic Muse of John Ford. LC 64-14714. Repr. of 1944 ed. 12.00 (ISBN 0-405-08949-X, Blom Pubns). Arno.
Stavig, Mark. John Ford & the Traditional Moral Order. 246p. 1968. 25.00x (ISBN 0-299-04680-X). U of Wis Pr.

FORD, JOHN, 1586-1640–BIBLIOGRAPHY
Tucker, Kenneth. A Bibliography of Writings by & About John Ford & Cyril Tourneur. (Reference Publications Ser.). 1977. lib. bdg. 15.00 (ISBN 0-8161-7834-8). G K Hall.

FORD, JOHN, 1895-1973
Baxter, John. The Cinema of John Ford. LC 79-175640. (International Film Guide Ser.). (Illus.). 208p. 1973. pap. 4.95 (ISBN 0-498-01068-6). A S Barnes.
Bogdanovich, Peter. John Ford. expanded rev. ed. (Cal Ser.: No. 369). 1978. pap. 4.95 (ISBN 0-520-03498-8). U of Cal Pr.
Ford, Dan. Pappy: The Life of John Ford. LC 79-14988. 1979. 12.95 (ISBN 0-13-648493-X). P-H.
McBride, Joseph & Wilmington, Michael. John Ford. LC 75-19281. (Theatre, Film & the Performing Arts Ser.). (Illus.). 234p. 1975. lib. bdg. 18.50 (ISBN 0-306-70750-0); pap. 6.95 (ISBN 0-306-80016-0). Da Capo.
Place, J. A. The Non-Western Films of John Ford. (Illus.). 288p. 1981. pap. 9.95 (ISBN 0-8065-0779-9). Citadel Pr.
--The Non-Western Films of John Ford. (Illus.). 1979. 17.95 (ISBN 0-8065-0643-1). Citadel Pr.
--The Western Films of John Ford. (Illus.). 226p. 1974. text ed. 12.00 (ISBN 0-8065-0445-5). Citadel Pr.
Sarris, Andrew. The John Ford Movie Mystery. LC 75-37286. (Cinema One Ser.: No. 27). (Illus.). 192p. 1976. 8.95x (ISBN 0-253-33167-6). Ind U Pr.
Wootten, A. John Ford Index. (Film Ser.). 1979. lib. bdg. 59.95 (ISBN 0-8490-2952-X). Gordon Pr.

FORD AUTOMOBILE
see Automobiles–Types–Ford

Miller, Ray & Embree, Glenn. Henry's Lady: An Illustrated History of the Model A Ford. LC 72-77244. (The Ford Road Ser: Vol. 2). (Illus.). 300p. 1972. 29.95 (ISBN 0-913056-03-0). Evergreen Pr.
--The V-Eight Affair: An Illustrated History of the Pre-War Ford V-8. LC 70-174898. (The Ford Road Ser: Vol. 3). (Illus.). 303p. 1972. 29.95 (ISBN 0-913056-02-2). Evergreen Pr.
Seidler, Edouard. Let's Call It Fiesta: An Auto-Biography of Ford's Project Bobcat. (Illus.). 1977. pap. 4.95 (ISBN 0-87799-015-8). Aztex.
Sorensen, Lorin. The Ford Road. (Illus.). 191p. 1978. 16.95 (ISBN 0-87938-078-0). Silverado.

FORD FOUNDATION

Magat, Richard. The Ford Foundation at Work: Philanthropic Choices, Methods & Styles. LC 78-24048. (Illus.). 208p. 1979. 14.95 (ISBN 0-306-40129-0, Plenum Pr). Plenum Pub.

FORD MOTOR COMPANY

Arnold, Horace L. & Faurote, Fay L. Ford Methods & the Ford Shops. LC 72-5029. (Technology & Society Ser.). (Illus.). 450p. 1972. Repr. of 1915 ed. 29.00 (ISBN 0-405-04682-0). Arno.
Dominguez, Henry. The Ford Agency: A Pictorial History. 1981. pap. 12.95 (ISBN 0-87938-095-0). Motorbooks Intl.
Ingells, Douglas J. Tin Goose. LC 68-31759. (Illus.). 1968. pap. 4.95 (ISBN 0-8168-8975-9). Aero.
Kimes, Beverly R. The Cars That Henry Ford Built. (Illus.). 1978. 19.95 (ISBN 0-525-07660-3). Dutton.
Meyer, Stephen, III. The Five Dollar Day: Labor Management & Social Control in the Ford Motor Company, 1908-1921. LC 80-22795. (American Social History Ser.). 230p. 1981. text ed. 34.00x (ISBN 0-87395-508-0, MELM); pap. text ed. 9.95x (ISBN 0-87395-509-9, MELM-P). State U NY Pr.
Nevins, Allan & Hill, Frank E. Ford, 3 vols. Incl. Vol. 1. The Times, the Man, the Company; Vol. 2. Expansion & Challenge, 1915-1933; Vol. 3. Decline & Rebirth: 1933-1962. LC 75-41775. (Companies & Men: Business Enterprise in America Ser.). (Illus.). 1976. Repr. 115.00x (ISBN 0-405-08089-1). Arno.
Post, Dan R., ed. Ford, Closing the Years of Tradition. 1975. 12.00 (ISBN 0-911160-35-3). Post-Era.
Seltzer, Lawrence H. Financial History of the American Automobile Industry. LC 77-128076. Repr. of 1928 ed. lib. bdg. 17.50x (ISBN 0-678-03554-7). Kelley.
Sorensen, Lorin. The American Ford. (Fordiana Ser.). (Illus.). 263p. 1975. 49.50 (ISBN 0-87938-079-9). Silverado.
Warnock, C. Gayle. The Edsel Affair. LC 80-81129. (Illus.). 278p. 1980. 16.95 (ISBN 0-9606746-0-8). Pro West.
Wilkins, Mira & Hill, Frank E. American Business Abroad: Ford on Six Continents. LC 64-12747. (Illus.). 1964. 14.95x (ISBN 0-8143-1227-6). Wayne St U Pr.

FORDHAM UNIVERSITY, NEW YORK

Anastasi, Anne, et al. Validation of a Biographical Inventory As a Predictor of College Success. (Research Monograph: No. 1). 1960. pap. 2.50 (ISBN 0-87447-099-4, 200080). College Bd.

FORECASTING

Angoff, Charles, ed. Biology & the Future of Man: Papers by Nathan Hershey & Merril Eisenbud. LC 77-92564. (The Leverton Lecture Ser: No. 6). 52p. 1978. 6.50 (ISBN 0-8386-2222-4). Fairleigh Dickinson.
Ascher, William. Forecasting: An Appraisal for Policy-Makers & Planners. LC 77-21423. (Illus.). 1978. pap. 5.95x (ISBN 0-8018-2273-4). Johns Hopkins.
Baxter, R. & Williams, I. Population Forecasting & Uncertainty at the National & Local Scale. 1978. pap. 11.00 (ISBN 0-08-023112-8). Pergamon.
Bell, Daniel. Coming of Post-Industrial Society: A Venture in Social Forecasting. LC 72-89178. 1973. 18.95x (ISBN 0-465-01281-7); pap. 5.95x (ISBN 0-465-09713-8, CN-5013). Basic.
Bezold, Clement, ed. Anticipatory Democracy: People in the Politics of the Future. LC 77-317. (Illus.). 1978. 12.95 (ISBN 0-394-41236-2). Random.
Bronowski, Jacob. A Sense of the Future: Essays on Natural Philosophy. Ariotti, Piero & Bronowski, Rita, eds. LC 77-9292. 1977. 16.50x (ISBN 0-262-02128-5); pap. 6.95 (ISBN 0-262-52050-8). MIT Pr.
Clarke, I. F., ed. Tale of the Future: From the Beginning to the Present Day. 3rd ed. 1979. pap. 14.00 (ISBN 0-8389-3225-8). ALA.
Darwin, Charles G. The Next Million Years. LC 73-5264. 210p. 1973. Repr. of 1953 ed. lib. bdg. 15.00x (ISBN 0-8371-6876-7, DANM). Greenwood.
Davis, W. Jackson. The Seventh Year: Industrial Civilization in Transition. (Illus.). 1979. 19.95 (ISBN 0-393-05693-7). Norton.
De A'Morelli, Richard. How to Survive the Future. LC 75-5400. 192p. (Orig.). 1975. pap. 1.25 (ISBN 0-89041-037-2, 3037). Major Bks.
Dickson, Paul. The Future File. 1978. pap. 1.95 (ISBN 0-380-42242-5, 42242). Avon.
Dunckel, E. B., et al. Business Environment of the Seventies: A Trend Analysis for Business Planning. 1970. 19.50 (ISBN 0-07-018207-8, P&RB). McGraw.
Encel, Solomon, et al, eds. The Art of Anticipation: Values & Methods in Forecasting. LC 75-34506. 1976. 10.00x (ISBN 0-87663-719-5, Pica). Universe.
Esfandiary, F. M. Up-Wingers. 1977. pap. 1.95 (ISBN 0-445-04094-7). Popular Lib.
Ferkiss, Victor C. Futurology: Promise, Performance, Prospects. LC 77-88625. (Policy Papers Ser.: The Washington Papers, No. 50). 66p. 1977. 4.00 (ISBN 0-8039-0977-2). Sage.
Flumiani, C. M. The Compelling Process of the Historical Inevitabilities at the Close of the 20th Century. (The Institute for Economic & Political World Strategic Studies). (Illus.). 1978. 42.25 (ISBN 0-89266-092-9). Am Classical Coll Pr.
Fowles, Jib, ed. Handbook of Futures Research. LC 77-84767. (Illus.). 1978. lib. bdg. 45.00x (ISBN 0-8371-9885-2, FHF/). Greenwood.
Gilland, B. The Next Seventy Years: Population, Food & Resources. (Illus.). 1979. 19.95x (ISBN 0-85626-176-9, Pub. by Abacus Pr). Intl Schol Bk Serv.
Godet, Michel. The Crisis in Forecasting & the Emergence of the "Prospective" Approach: With Case Studies in Energy & Air Transport. LC 78-10548. (Pergamon Policy Studies). 1979. 16.50 (ISBN 0-08-022487-3). Pergamon.
Goodman, Nelson. Fact, Fiction, & Forecast. 3rd ed. LC 73-11273. 1977. 17.50 (ISBN 0-672-51889-9); pap. text ed. 6.95x (ISBN 0-672-61347-6). Hackett Pub.
Gordon, K. & Hahn, Walter A., eds. Assessing the Future & Policy Planning. LC 72-78920. 350p. 1973. 44.00x (ISBN 0-677-12650-6). Gordon.
Harman, Willis W. An Incomplete Guide to the Future. LC 76-26076. (The Portable Stanford Ser.). (Illus.). 1976. 8.95 (ISBN 0-913374-46-6); pap. 4.95 (ISBN 0-913374-47-4). SF Bk Co.
Harvey, Bill. Our Future: While We Still Have a Choice. Bertisch, Jan & Bragg, Yana, eds. (Illus.). 1979. pap. 6.95 (ISBN 0-918538-07-6). New Age Pr NM.
Hoyle, Geoffrey. Two Thousand & Ten: Living in the Future. LC 73-12832. (Finding-Out Book). (Illus.). 64p. (gr. 2-4). 1974. PLB 7.95 (ISBN 0-8193-0708-4, Pub. by Parents). Enslow Pubs.
Krewer, John. Future Think. (gr. k-3). 1979. 5.95 (ISBN 0-916456-56-0, GA108). Good Apple.
Lasker, Emanuel. The Community of the Future. 1976. lib. bdg. 59.95 (ISBN 0-8490-1650-9). Gordon Pr.
Levenbach, Hans & Cleary, James P. The Forecaster: The Forecasting Process Through Data Analysis. (Illus.). 350p. 1981. text ed. 29.95 (ISBN 0-534-97975-0). Lifetime Learn.
Lindsey, Hal. The Nineteen Eighties Countdown to Armageddon. LC 80-70283. 192p. 1981. pap. 6.95 (ISBN 0-553-01303-3). Bantam.
Linstone, Harold A. & Simmonds, W. H., eds. Futures Research: New Directions. 1977. text ed. 25.50 (ISBN 0-201-04096-4, Adv Bk Prog). A-W.
Mabert, Vincent A. An Introduction to Short Term Forecasting Using the Box-Jenkins Methodology. 1975. pap. text ed. 12.00 (ISBN 0-89806-023-0, 53). Am Inst Indus Eng.
Marien, Michael, et al, eds. Future Survey Annual 2 (1980-81) A Guide to the Recent Literature of Trends, Forecasts, & Policy Proposals. 280p. (Orig.). 1981. pap. 25.00 (ISBN 0-930242-13-0). World Future.
Maude, Barbara. The Turning Tide. 184p. 1975. 9.95 (ISBN 0-571-10766-4, Pub. by Faber & Faber). Merrimack Bk Serv.
Maziarz, E. Value & Values in Evolution: A Symposium. (Current Topics of Contemporary Thought Ser). 1979. 21.50 (ISBN 0-677-15240-X). Gordon.
Merrill, Michael P. Futurology: The Art & Science of Predicting Scientifically the Future. (Illus.). 1979. 47.50 (ISBN 0-89266-205-0). Am Classical Coll Pr.
Montgomery, Douglas C. & Johnson, Lynwood A. Forecasting & Time Series Analysis. 1976. 19.50 (ISBN 0-07-042857-3, P&RB). McGraw.
Morgan, Chris. Future Man. 1981. pap. 6.95 (ISBN 0-86616-005-1). Greene.
--Future Man. (Future Studies Series). (Illus.). 208p. 1979. 16.00 (ISBN 0-8290-0144-1). Irvington.
--Future Man: An Optimistic Look at What the Future Holds for Mankind. 208p. 1981. pap. 6.95 (ISBN 0-86616-005-1). Lewis Pub Co.
Newby, James R. The Creation of a Future. 176p. (Orig.). 1981. pap. 5.95 (ISBN 0-86608-005-8). Zondervan.
O'Neil, Gerard K. Two Thousand Eighty-One: A Hopeful View of the Human Future. 1981. 13.95 (ISBN 0-671-24257-1). S&S.
Parham, William. A Habitation of Devils. LC 81-51729. 280p. 1981. 13.95 (ISBN 0-938264-02-8); pap. 6.95 (ISBN 0-938264-03-6). Veritas Pubns.
Predictions to the Year 2000. LC 79-52912. softcover 1.95 (ISBN 0-912216-16-6). Angel Pr.
Prehoda, Robert W. Your Next Fifty Years. 1980. pap. 5.95 (ISBN 0-441-95220-8). Ace Bks.
Shull, Russell. Wonderfully Made for This Life & the Next. 1980. pap. 0.50 (ISBN 0-910924-70-8). Macalester.
Sullivan, William F. & Claycombe, W. Wayne. Fundamentals of Forecasting. (Illus.). 1977. ref. ed. 18.95 (ISBN 0-87909-300-5). Reston.
Theobald, Robert. Beyond Despair: A Policy Guide to the Communications Era. rev. ed. LC 81-5348. 208p. 1981. 11.95 (ISBN 0-932020-04-6); pap. 7.95 (ISBN 0-932020-05-4). Seven Locks Pr.
Theobald, Robert, et al. Future Quest. (Decisionmakers Bookshelf: Vol. 3). (Illus.). 1977. pap. 1.95 (ISBN 0-931032-03-2). Edison Elec.
Thompson, Alan E. Understanding Futurology: An Introduction to Futures Study. 1979. 14.95 (ISBN 0-7153-7761-2). David & Charles.
Tripp, Maggie, ed. Woman in the Year Two Thousand. 352p. 1976. pap. 2.25 (ISBN 0-440-39709-X, LE). Dell.
Waddington, C. H. The Man-Made Future. LC 77-29043. 1978. 19.95x (ISBN 0-312-51045-4). St Martin.
Wilson, Clifford & Weldon, John. Approaching the Decade of Shock. LC 78-52320. 1978. 6.95 (ISBN 0-89051-044-X, Master Bks). CLP Pubs.
Wollaston, Thomas A. The Incredible Conditions of the World in the Year 2000: An Astonishing Forecast. (Illus.). 131p. 1981. 67.85 (ISBN 0-930008-74-X). Inst Econ Pol.

FORECASTING, BUSINESS

see Business Forecasting

FORECASTING, ECONOMIC

see Economic Forecasting

FORECASTING, SALES

see Sales Forecasting

FORECASTING, TECHNOLOGICAL

see Technological Forecasting

FORECASTING, WEATHER

see Weather Forecasting

FORECASTING THEORY

see Prediction Theory

FORECLOSURE

see also Executions (Law); Mechanics' Liens

Mortgages & Mortgage Foreclosure in New York. rev. ed. 1975. 35.00 (ISBN 0-685-58291-4). Acme Law.

FOREIGN ACCENT

see English Language–Pronunciation by Foreigners

FOREIGN AFFAIRS

see International Relations;
see subdivisions Foreign Relations under names of countries

FOREIGN AID PROGRAM

see Economic Assistance; Technical Assistance

FOREIGN AID TO EDUCATION

see Educational Assistance

FOREIGN AREA STUDIES

see Area Studies

FOREIGN ASSISTANCE

see Economic Assistance

FOREIGN AUTOMOBILES

see Automobiles, Foreign

FOREIGN COMMERCE

see Commerce

FOREIGN CORPORATIONS

see Corporations, Foreign

FOREIGN CORRESPONDENTS

see also Journalists

Fidler, Isaac. Observations on Professions: Literature, Manners, & Emigration in the United States & Canada 1832. LC 73-13129. (Foreign Travelers in America, 1810-1935 Ser.). 446p. 1974. Repr. 23.00x (ISBN 0-405-05452-1). Arno.
Kruglak, Theodore E. Foreign Correspondents. LC 73-20905. 163p. 1974. Repr. of 1955 ed. lib. bdg. 15.00x (ISBN 0-8371-5870-2, KRFC). Greenwood.
Middleton, Drew. Where Has Last July Gone? LC 73-79922. 284p. 1973. 7.95 (ISBN 0-8129-0392-7). Times Bks.

FOREIGN ECONOMIC RELATIONS

see International Economic Relations

FOREIGN EDUCATIONAL ASSISTANCE

see Educational Assistance

FOREIGN ENLISTMENT

see also Mercenary Troops

FOREIGN EXCHANGE

see also Balance of Payments; Foreign Exchange Problem; Sterling Area

Angell, James W. Theory of International Prices. LC 65-19644. Repr. of 1926 ed. 22.50x (ISBN 0-678-00094-8). Kelley.
Beenstock, Michael. The Foreign Exchanges: Theory, Modelling & Policy. LC 78-1372. 1979. 23.50x (ISBN 0-312-29862-5). St Martin.
Bhagwati, Jagdish. Foreign Trade Regimes & Economic Development: Anatomy & Consequences of Exchange Control Regimes, Vol. II. LC 78-18799. (Foreign Trade Regimes & Economic Development Ser.: Vol. XI). 1978. 22.50 (ISBN 0-88410-487-7). Ballinger Pub.
Black, Stanley W. Floating Exchange Rates & National Economic Policy. LC 77-76296. 1977. 17.50x (ISBN 0-300-02124-0). Yale U Pr.
Blake, William. Observations on the Principles Which Regulate the Course of Exchange & on the Present Depreciated State of the Currency, 2 vols. in 1. Bd. with Observations on the Effects Produced by the Expenditure of Government During the Restriction of Cash Payments. 1969. Repr. of 1823 ed. 26.50 (ISBN 0-8337-0304-8). B Franklin.
Blin, Jean, et al. The Impact of Flexible Exchange Rates on International Business. 1981. write for info. (ISBN 0-89068-058-2). Natl Planning.
Brunner, K. & Metlyer, A. H., eds. Policies for Employment, Prices, & Exchange Rates. (Carnegie-Rochester Conference Ser. on Public Policy: Vol. 11). 252p. 1979. 24.50 (ISBN 0-444-85392-8). Elsevier.
Cassel, Gustav. Money & Foreign Exchange After 1914. LC 72-4266. (World Affairs Ser.: National & International Viewpoints). 294p. 1972. Repr. of 1922 ed. 14.00 (ISBN 0-405-04563-8). Arno.
Clare, George. ABC of the Foreign Exchanges. Wilkins, Mira ed. LC 78-3905. (International Finance Ser.). (Illus.). 1978. Repr. of 1895 ed. lib. bdg. 12.00x (ISBN 0-405-11210-6). Arno.
Coninx, Raymond G. Foreign Exchange Dealer's Manual. 168p. 1980. 30.00x (ISBN 0-85941-152-4, Pub. by Woodhead-Faulkner England). State Mutual Bk.
--Foreign Exchange Today. rev. ed. 171p. 1980. 19.95 (ISBN 0-470-27025-X). Halsted Pr.
--Foreign Exchange Today. LC 77-11932. 1978. 19.95 (ISBN 0-470-99315-4). Halsted Pr.
Drummond, Ian. The Floating Pound & the Sterling Area, 1931-1939. LC 80-14539. 352p. 1981. 37.50 (ISBN 0-521-23165-5). Cambridge U Pr.
Eckes, Alfred E., Jr. A Search for Solvency: Bretton Woods & the International Monetary System, 1941-1971. LC 75-14433. 369p. 1975. 17.50x (ISBN 0-292-70712-6). U of Tex Pr.
Einzig, Paul. Dynamic Theory of Forward Exchange. 2nd ed. 1969. 22.50 (ISBN 0-312-22365-X). St Martin.
--Euro-Bond Market. 1969. 18.95 (ISBN 0-312-26705-3). St Martin.
--Exchange Control. LC 75-41085. Repr. of 1934 ed. 18.00 (ISBN 0-404-14733-X). AMS Pr.
--Foreign Exchange Crises. 2nd ed. LC 68-10638. 1970. text ed. 18.95 (ISBN 0-312-29855-2). St Martin.
--History of Foreign Exchange. 2nd ed. LC 74-124951. 1970. 22.50 (ISBN 0-312-37835-1). St Martin.
--Leads & Lags. 1968. 17.95 (ISBN 0-312-47670-1). St Martin.
--Textbook of Foreign Exchange. 1966. 17.95 (ISBN 0-312-79380-4). St Martin.
Ellis, Howard S. Exchange Control in Central Europe. LC 69-13892. Repr. of 1941 ed. lib. bdg. 16.00x (ISBN 0-8371-4462-0, ELEX). Greenwood.
George, Abraham M. Foreign Exchange Management & the Multinational Corporation: A Manager's Guide. LC 78-19738. 1978. 28.95 (ISBN 0-03-046641-5). Praeger.
Goschen, George J. The Theory of the Foreign Exchanges. Wilkins, Mira, ed. LC 78-3918. (International Finance Ser.). 1978. Repr. of 1892 ed. lib. bdg. 12.00x (ISBN 0-405-11221-1). Arno.
Graham, Frank D. Exchange, Prices & Production in Hyper-Inflation: Germany, 1920-1923. LC 66-27086. 1967. Repr. of 1930 ed. 11.00 (ISBN 0-8462-1020-7). Russell.
Grubel, Herbert G. Forward Exchange, Speculation, & the International Flow of Capital. LC 65-21490. 1966. 15.00x (ISBN 0-8047-0269-1). Stanford U Pr.
Grubel, Herbert G., ed. World Monetary Reform: Plans & Issues. 1963. 17.50x (ISBN 0-8047-0169-5). Stanford U Pr.
Haberler, Gottfried. Theory of International Trade. LC 68-4893. (Illus.). Repr. of 1936 ed. 19.50x (ISBN 0-678-08031-3). Kelley.
Harris, Joseph. Essay Upon Money & Coins, Pt. 1. (History of English Economic Thought Ser). 1970. Repr. of 1757 ed. 23.00 (ISBN 0-384-21480-0). Johnson Repr.
Hepworth, Samuel R. Reporting Foreign Operations. Brief, Richard P., ed. LC 80-1494. (Dimensions of Accounting Theory & Practice Ser.). 1981. Repr. of 1956 ed. lib. bdg. 20.00x (ISBN 0-405-13524-6). Arno.
Heywood, John. Foreign Exchange & the Corporate Treasurer. LC 79-50620. 1979. 16.95 (ISBN 0-8144-5556-5). Am Mgmt.

Jacque, Laurent L. Management of Foreign Exchange Risk. LC 77-12281. (Illus.). 1978. 24.95 (ISBN 0-669-01954-2). Lexington Bks.
Kindleberger, Charles P. International Short-Term Capital Movements. LC 65-20927. Repr. of 1937 ed. 15.00x (ISBN 0-678-00116-2). Kelley.
Loosigian, Allan M. Foreign Exchange Futures: A/Guide to International Currency Trading. 350p. 1981. 24.95 (ISBN 0-87094-271-9). Dow Jones-Irwin.
Machlup, Fritz. International Payments, Debts & Gold: Collected Essays. 2nd ed. LC 76-20371. 1976. pap. 12.50x (ISBN 0-8147-5412-0). NYU Pr.
McRae, R. & Walker, D. Foreign Exchange Management. 1981. 24.95 (ISBN 0-13-325357-0). P-H.
Mandich, Donald R., et al, eds. Foreign Exchange Trading Techniques & Controls. LC 76-21912. 1976. 15.00 (ISBN 0-89982-000-X, 230600). Am Bankers.
Miskimin, Harry A. Money, Prices, & Foreign Exchange in Fourteenth Century France. LC 63-7942. 1970. Repr. of 1963 ed. 15.00 (ISBN 0-08-022307-9). Pergamon.
Ohlin, Bertil. Interregional & International Trade. rev. ed. LC 67-17317. (Economic Studies: No. 39). (Illus.). 1967. 16.50x (ISBN 0-674-46000-6). Harvard U Pr.
Perkins, James O. Sterling & Regional Payments System. 1956. 7.50x (ISBN 0-522-83702-6, Pub. by Melbourne U Pr). Intl Schol Bk Serv.
Pither, Raymond F. Manual of Foreign Exchange. 7th ed. 1971. 15.00x (ISBN 0-273-31459-9). Intl Pubns Serv.
Prindl, Andreas R. Foreign Exchange Risk. LC 75-37684. 168p. 1976. 26.25 (ISBN 0-471-01653-5, Pub. by Wiley-Interscience). Wiley.
Riehl, Heinz & Rodriquez, Rita M. Foreign Exchange Markets. (Illus.). 1977. 24.50 (ISBN 0-07-052670-2, P&RB). McGraw.
Robinson, Leland R. Foreign Credit Facilities in the United Kingdom. LC 68-57579. (Columbia University Studies in the Social Sciences: No. 244). Repr. of 1923 ed. 18.50 (ISBN 0-404-51244-5). AMS Pr.
Salera, Virgil. Exchange Control & the Argentine Market. LC 70-76636. (Columbia University. Studies in the Social Sciences: No. 485). Repr. of 1941 ed. 22.50 (ISBN 0-404-51485-5). AMS Pr.
Seyd, Ernest. Bullion & Foreign Exchanges Theoretically & Practically Considered: A Defence of the Double Evaluation with Special Reference to the Proposed System of Universal Coinage. LC 74-36. (Gold Ser.: Vol. 9). 716p. 1974. Repr. of 1868 ed. 37.00x (ISBN 0-405-05921-3). Arno.
Shapiro, Alan C. Foreign Exchange Risk Management. LC 78-10628. 1978. pap. 7.50 (ISBN 0-8144-2229-2). Am Mgmt.
Specific Duties, Inflation & Floating Currencies. (GATT Studies in International Trade: No. 4). 24p. 1978. pap. 6.00 (ISBN 0-685-25469-0, G103, GATT). Unipub.
Stern, Robert M. The Balance of Payments: Theory & Economic Policy. LC 72-78222. 488p. 1973. 29.95x (ISBN 0-202-06059-4). Aldine Pub.
Stern, Siegfried. The United States in International Banking. Bruchey, Stuart & Bruchey, Eleanor, eds. LC 76-5036. (American Business Abroad Ser.). 1976. Repr. of 1952 ed. 28.00x (ISBN 0-405-09302-0). Arno.
Taussig, Frank W. International Trade. LC 66-19696. Repr. of 1927 ed. 19.50x (ISBN 0-678-00157-X). Kelley.
Underwood, Trevor, ed. Foreign Exchange Yearbook, 1979: A Listing of Daily Foreign Exchange & Euro-Currency Deposit Rates for Leading World Currencies. 1979. 35.95 (ISBN 0-470-26694-5). Halsted Pr.
--Foreign Exchange Yearbook 1980. 264p. 1980. 60.95x (ISBN 0-470-26982-0). Halsted Pr.
--Foreign Exchange Yearbook 1981. 264p. 1980. 60.00x (ISBN 0-686-69893-2, Pub. by Woodhead-Faulkner England). State Mutual Bk.
Verbit, Gilbert P. International Monetary Reform & the Developing Countries: The Rule of Law Problem. LC 74-22362. (International Legal Research Program Ser). 336p. 1975. 22.50x (ISBN 0-231-03832-1). Columbia U Pr.
Walker, T. A Guide for Using the Foreign Exchange & Market. LC 80-21975. 372p. 1981. 23.95 (ISBN 0-471-06254-5, Ronald Pr). Wiley.
Walras, Leon. Principe D'une Theorie Mathematique De l'Echange. 20.00 (ISBN 0-8337-3677-9). B Franklin.
Weisweiller, Rudi. Foreign Exchange. 1972. text ed. 10.95x (ISBN 0-04-332045-7). Allen Unwin.
Willey, Russell W. Foreign Exchange: The Accounting, Economics, & Control. LC 77-16521. (Illus.). 1977. text ed. 22.75 (ISBN 0-930950-00-3). Nopoly Pr.
Williamson, John. Exchange Rate Rules. 400p. 1981. 37.50 (ISBN 0-312-27396-7). St Martin.

FOREIGN EXCHANGE–LAW

Miller, Robert & Wood, John B. Exchange Control Forever? (Research Monographs: No. 33). (Orig.). 1979. 5.95 (ISBN 0-255-36117-3). Transatlantic.
Ravenscroft, Donald R. Taxation & Foreign Currency: The Income Tax Consequences of Foreign Exchange Transactions & Exchange Rate Fluctuations. LC 72-81277. (Illus.). 888p. 1973. 50.00x (ISBN 0-915506-15-7). Harvard Law Intl Tax.
Soenen, L. U. Foreign Exchange Exposure Management: A Portfolio Approach. 152p. 1979. 20.00x (ISBN 90-286-0309-3). Sijthoff & Noordhoff.

FOREIGN EXCHANGE–TABLES, ETC.

see Money–Tables, etc.

FOREIGN EXCHANGE PROBLEM

see also Sterling Area

Aliber, Robert Z. Exchange Risk & Corporate International Finance. LC 78-4645. 1978. 24.95 (ISBN 0-470-26307-5). Halsted Pr.
Committee for Economic Development. Strengthening the World Monetary System. LC 73-84800. 87p. 1973. pap. 1.50 (ISBN 0-87186-051-1). Comm Econ Dev.
Dreyer, Jacob S., et al, eds. Exchange Rate Flexibility. 1978. 15.25 (ISBN 0-8447-2124-7); pap. 7.25 (ISBN 0-8447-2123-9). Am Enterprise.
Einzig, Paul. Foreign Exchange Crises. 2nd ed. LC 68-10638. 1970. text ed. 18.95 (ISBN 0-312-29855-2). St Martin.
--Leads & Lags. 1968. 17.95 (ISBN 0-312-47670-1). St Martin.
Fatemi, Nasrollah S., et al. The Dollar Crisis: The United States Balance of Payments & Dollar Stability. LC 63-23017. (Orig.). 1963. 15.00x (ISBN 0-8147-0144-2); pap. 5.95x (ISBN 0-8147-0145-0). NYU Pr.
Flumiani, C. M. The Gyrations of the Dollar & the Deceit of Gold. (Illus.). 1978. deluxe ed. 47.75 (ISBN 0-930008-16-2). Inst Econ Pol.
Haberler, Gottfried, et al. International Payments Problems. 1966. 15.25 (ISBN 0-8447-2001-1); pap. 7.25 (ISBN 0-8447-2000-3). Am Enterprise.
Hinshaw, Randall, ed. The Economics of International Adjustment. LC 78-127351. 208p. 1971. 13.50x (ISBN 0-8018-1204-6). Johns Hopkins.
Johnson, Harry G. & Swoboda, Alexander K. The Economics of Common Currencies. LC 73-76382. 302p. 1973. text ed. 16.50x (ISBN 0-674-23226-7). Harvard U Pr.
Machlup, Fritz. The Alignment of Foreign Exchange Rates. LC 72-169260. (Special Studies in International Economics & Development). 1972. 9.50x (ISBN 0-8290-0384-3); pap. text ed. 4.95x (ISBN 0-89197-655-8). Irvington.
--The Alignment of Foreign Exchange Rates. LC 72-169260. 94p. 1972. 10.00x (ISBN 0-275-28279-1). NYU Pr.
McKinnon, Ronald I. Money in International Exchange: The Convertible Currency System. 1979. text ed. 13.95x (ISBN 0-19-502408-7); pap. text ed. 9.95x (ISBN 0-19-502409-5). Oxford U Pr.
Miles, Marc C. Devaluation, the Trade Balance & the Balance of Payments. (Business Economics & Finance Ser.: Vol. 11). 1978. 24.75 (ISBN 0-8247-6666-0). Dekker.
Minford, P. Substitution Effects, Speculation & Exchange Rate Stability. (Studies in International Economics: Vol. 3). 1978. 36.75 (ISBN 0-444-85055-4, North-Holland). Elsevier.
Murphy, J. Carter, ed. Money in the International Order. LC 64-25692. 1964. 4.00 (ISBN 0-87074-097-0). SMU Press.
Riechel, Klaus-Walter. Economic Effects of Exchange-Rate Changes. new ed. LC 78-58926. 1978. 17.95 (ISBN 0-669-02376-0). Lexington Bks.
Rundell, Walter, Jr. Black-Market Money: The Collapse of U. S. Military Currency Control in World War 2. LC 64-15879. 1964. 10.00 (ISBN 0-8071-0725-5). La State U Pr.
Sohmen, Egon. Flexible Exchange Rates: Theory & Controversy. rev. ed. LC 69-18375. 1969. 9.50x (ISBN 0-226-76781-7). U of Chicago Pr.
Third Paris-Dauphine Conference on Money & International Monetary Problems, March 28-30, 1974. Recent Issues in International Monetary Economics: Proceedings. Claasen, E. M. & Salin, P., eds. LC 75-44183. 1976. 85.50 (ISBN 0-444-11023-2, North-Holland). Elsevier.
Wells, Donald A. Saudi Arabian Revenues & Expenditures: The Potential for Foreign Exchange Savings. LC 74-19945. (Resources for the Future Research Report Ser). 44p. 1974. pap. 4.00x (ISBN 0-8018-1689-0). Johns Hopkins.
Willett, Thomas D. Floating Exchange Rates & International Monetary Reform. LC 77-13327. 1977. pap. 5.25 (ISBN 0-8447-3271-0). Am Enterprise.

FOREIGN EXCHANGE PROBLEM–EUROPE

Krause, Lawrence B. & Salant, Walter S., eds. European Monetary Unification & Its Meaning for the United States. LC 73-1084. 1973. 12.95 (ISBN 0-8157-5032-3). Brookings.

FOREIGN EXCHANGE PROBLEM–GREAT BRITAIN

Carse, Stephen, et al. The Financing Procedures of British Foreign Trade. LC 79-18146. 160p. 1980. 24.95 (ISBN 0-521-22534-5). Cambridge U Pr.
Chalmers, George. Considerations on Commerce, Bullion, & Coin, Circulation & Exchanges. LC 68-55502. Repr. of 1811 ed. 15.00x (ISBN 0-678-00431-5). Kelley.
Minford, P. Substitution Effects, Speculation & Exchange Rate Stability. (Studies in International Economics: Vol. 3). 1978. 36.75 (ISBN 0-444-85055-4, North-Holland). Elsevier.

FOREIGN EXCHANGE PROBLEM–LATIN AMERICA

Coes, Donald V. The Impact of Price Uncertainty: A Study of Brazilian Exchange Rate Policy. LC 78-75067. (Outstanding Dissertations in Economics Ser.). 1979. lib. bdg. 30.00 (ISBN 0-8240-4143-7). Garland Pub.

FOREIGN INCOME, TAXATION OF

see Income Tax–Foreign Income

FOREIGN INVESTMENTS

see Investments, Foreign

FOREIGN LABOR

see Alien Labor

FOREIGN LANGUAGE LABORATORIES

see Language Laboratories

FOREIGN LEGION

see France–Army–Foreign Legion

FOREIGN LICENSING AGREEMENTS

Contractor, Farok J. International Technology Licensing: Compensation, Costs, & Negotiation. LC 80-8768. 208p. 1981. 23.95x (ISBN 0-669-04359-1). Lexington Bks.
Doi, Teruo & Shattuck, Warren L., eds. Patent & Know-How Licensing in Japan & the United States. LC 76-7785. (Asian Law Ser.: No.5). 444p. 1977. 30.00 (ISBN 0-295-95513-9). U of Wash Pr.
Eckstrom, Lawrence J. Licensing in Foreign & Domestic Operations, 3 vols. rev. ed. 1980. looseleaf in post binders pages 187.50 (ISBN 0-87632-075-2). Boardman.
Feinschreiber, Robert, ed. Subpart F: Foreign Subsidiaries & Their Tax Consequences. LC 79-88374. 260p. 1979. 35.00 (ISBN 0-916592-28-6). Panel Pubs.
Hochberg, Irving. Interpretation of Audiometric Results. LC 72-85146. (Studies in Communicative Disorders Ser). 45p. 1973. pap. text ed. 2.50 (ISBN 0-672-61285-2). Bobbs.
Taubman, Joseph. The Joint Venture & Tax Classification. 493p. 1957. 25.00 (ISBN 0-87945-013-4). Fed Legal Pubn.
Telesio, Piero. Foreign Licensing Policy in Multinational Enterprises. (Praeger Special Studies). 21.95 (ISBN 0-03-047476-0). Praeger.
Young, G. Richard & Bradford, Standish, Jr. Joint Ventures: Planning & Action. LC 77-91274. 1977. 3.45 (ISBN 0-910586-20-9). Finan Exec.

FOREIGN LOANS

see Loans, Foreign

FOREIGN MISSIONS

see Missions, Foreign

FOREIGN NEWS

Boyd-Barrett, Oliver. The International News Agencies. LC 80-51779. (Constable Communication & Society Ser.: Vol. 13). (Illus.). 284p. 1980. 25.00 (ISBN 0-8039-1511-X); pap. 12.50 (ISBN 0-8039-1512-8). Sage.
Culbert, David H. News for Everyman: Radio & Foreign Affairs in Thirties America. LC 75-23862. 238p. 1976. lib. bdg. 14.50 (ISBN 0-8371-8260-3, CRC/). Greenwood.
Desmond, Robert W. The Information Process: World News Reporting to the Twentieth Century. LC 77-9491. 1978. text ed. 22.50x (ISBN 0-87745-070-6). U of Iowa Pr.
--The Press & World Affairs. LC 72-4665. (International Propaganda & Communications Ser.). (Illus.). 449p. 1972. Repr. of 1937 ed. 25.00 (ISBN 0-405-04746-0). Arno.
Ghareeb, Edmund, ed. Split Vision: Arab Portrayal in the American Media. LC 77-90775. 171p. 1977. pap. 7.50 (ISBN 0-934484-11-2). Inst Mid East & North Africa.
Hohenberg, John. Foreign Correspondence: The Great Reporters & Their Times. LC 64-22762. 1967. 20.00x (ISBN 0-231-02600-5); pap. 6.50x (ISBN 0-231-08579-6). Columbia U Pr.
Host, David, ed. Citizen & the News. 1962. 4.95 (ISBN 0-87462-406-1). Marquette.
International Press Institute. The Flow of the News. LC 72-4691. (International Propaganda & Communications Ser.). 266p. 1972. Repr. of 1953 ed. 19.00 (ISBN 0-405-04751-7). Arno.
International Press Institute Surveys, Nos. 1-6. Incl. No. 1. Improvement of Information; No. 2. The News from Russia; No. 3. The News from the Middle East; No. 4. Government Pressures on the Press; No. 5. The Press in Authoritarian Countries; No. 6. Professional Secrecy & the Journalist. LC 72-4803. (International Propaganda & Communications Ser.). 657p. 1972. Repr. of 1952 ed. 35.00 (ISBN 0-405-04750-9). Arno.
Le Monde, 2 vols. (Fr.). 1978. Set. lib. bdg. 270.00x (ISBN 0-8287-1389-8). Clearwater Pub.
Richstad, Jim & Anderson, Michael H., eds. Crisis in International News: Policies & Prospects. LC 81-677. 480p. 1981. 28.50x (ISBN 0-231-05254-5); pap. 12.50 (ISBN 0-231-05255-3). Columbia U Pr.
Righter, Rosemary. Whose News? Politics, the Press & the Third World. LC 78-14433. 1978. 12.50 (ISBN 0-8129-0797-3). Times Bks.
Rosenblum, Mort. Coups & Earthquakes: Reporting the World for America. LC 79-1680. 1979. 10.95 (ISBN 0-06-013654-5, HarpT). Har-Row.
Rubin, Barry. International News & the American Media. LC 77-88624. (Washington Papers: No. 49). 71p. 1977. 4.00 (ISBN 0-8039-0976-4). Sage.
Woodward, Julian L. Foreign News in American Morning Newspapers. LC 68-58647. (Columbia University. Studies in the Social Sciences: No. 332). Repr. of 1930 ed. 14.50 (ISBN 0-404-51332-8). AMS Pr.

FOREIGN OFFICES

see also names of individual foreign offices, e.g. United States–Department of State

Buck, Philip W. & Travis, Martin B., Jr., eds. Control of Foreign Relations in Modern Nations. 1957. 13.95x (ISBN 0-393-09528-2, NortonC). Norton.
Moorhouse, Geoffrey. The Diplomats: The Foreign Office Today. 1977. text ed. 18.75x (ISBN 0-224-01323-8). Humanities.

FOREIGN OPINION OF RUSSIA

see Russia–Foreign Opinion

FOREIGN OPINION OF THE UNITED STATES

see United States–Foreign Opinion

FOREIGN POLICY

see International Relations

FOREIGN POPULATION

see Emigration and Immigration

FOREIGN PROPERTY

see Alien Property

FOREIGN RELATIONS

see International Relations

FOREIGN STUDENTS

see Students, Foreign

FOREIGN STUDY

see also Students, Foreign

American Association of School Administrators. American Elementary & Secondary Schools Abroad. rev. ed. 1976. pap. 2.50 (ISBN 0-686-16896-8, 021-00618). Am Assn Sch Admin.
Carter, William D. Study Abroad & Educational Development. (Fundamentals of Education Planning). 49p. (Orig.). 1974. pap. 3.25 (ISBN 92-803-1059-3, UNESCO). Unipub.
Cohen, Gail A., ed. The Learning Traveler Vol. 1: U. S. College-Sponsored Programs Abroad: Academic Year. rev. ed. 186p. 1981. pap. text ed. 8.00 (ISBN 0-87206-108-6). Inst Intl Educ.
Garraty, John A. & Von Klemperer, Lily. The New Guide to Study Abroad: 1981 to 1982. LC 77-11533. 464p. 1980. 16.95 (ISBN 0-06-011423-1, CN849, HarpT); pap. 7.95 (ISBN 0-06-090849-1). Har-Row.
Golay, Frank H. & Lush, Peggy, eds. Directory of the Cornell Southeast Asia Program: 1951-1976. 1976. 3.00 (ISBN 0-87727-103-8, DP 103). Cornell SE Asia.
Hiatt, Thomas A. & Gerzon, Mark F., eds. The Young Internationalists. LC 70-188981. 224p. 1973. 12.00x (ISBN 0-8248-0218-7, Eastwest Ctr). U Pr of Hawaii.
Klineberg, Otto & Hull, W. Frank, IV. At a Foreign University: An International Study of Adaptation & Coping. 22.95 (ISBN 0-03-052486-5). Praeger.
The Learning Traveler Vacation Study Abroad. 182p. 1981. pap. 8.00 (ISBN 0-87206-107-8, IIE28, IIE). Unipub.
McKenzie, James S. A Broad Education Abroad. 1978. 7.95 (ISBN 0-533-03384-5). Vantage.
Overseas Summer Study Programs. 1975. 1.00 (ISBN 0-685-82237-0). Natl Assn Principals.
Rao, G. Lakshmana. Brain Drain & Foreign Students. LC 78-10903. (Illus.). 1979. 25.00x (ISBN 0-312-09437-X). St Martin.
Statistics of Students Abroad; 1962-1968. LC 77-187557. (Statistical Reports & Studies, No. 18). 416p. (Orig.). 1972. pap. 10.00 (ISBN 92-3-000941-5, U633, UNESCO). Unipub.
Sutton, Francis, et al. Internationalizing Higher Education: A United States Approach. (No. 13). 48p. 1974. pap. 1.00 (ISBN 0-89192-151-6). Interbk Inc.
Thomas, W. American Education Abroad. 1973. 11.95 (ISBN 0-02-469910-1). Macmillan Info.

Tomlinson, James C. & Knight, Jenny, eds. Guide to Graduate Studies in Great Britain. LC 74-7351. 1250p. 1974. 60.00x (ISBN 0-87988-007-4). Agathon.

FOREIGN TRADE
see Commerce

FOREIGN TRADE POLICY
see Commercial Policy

FOREIGN TRADE PROMOTION
see also Export Credit; Fairs; Foreign Exchange; Foreign Trade Regulation; Subsidies

Combs, Paul H. Handbook of International Purchasing. 2nd ed. LC 75-31560. 224p. 1976. 17.95 (ISBN 0-8436-1309-2). CBI Pub.

Dyer, John M. & Dyer, Frederick C. Export Financing: Modern U. S. Methods. LC 63-21527. (Business & Economic Ser: No. 6). (Illus.). 1963. 7.95x (ISBN 0-87024-022-6). U of Miami Pr.

Fayerweather, John. International Marketing. 2nd ed. (Foundations of Marketing Ser). 1970. pap. 7.95 ref. ed. (ISBN 0-13-473124-7). P-H.

Kaufman, Burton. Efficiency & Expansion: Foreign Trade Organization in the Wilson Administration, 1913-1921. LC 73-20971. (Contributions in American History: No. 34). 1974. lib. bdg. 16.00 (ISBN 0-8371-7338-8, KEX/). Greenwood.

Siposs, Allan J. Importing: Practical Tips & Ideas. (Illus.). 1979. 25.00x (ISBN 0-686-59709-5). Intl Comm Serv.

FOREIGN TRADE PROMOTION–INDIA

Kacker, Madhav. Marketing Adaptation of U. S. Business Firms in India. 160p. 1974. text ed. 9.00x (ISBN 0-8426-0723-4). Verry.

FOREIGN TRADE REGULATION
see also Commercial Treaties; Customs Administration; Foreign Exchange–Law; Foreign Trade Promotion; Import Quotas; Tariff; Tariff–Law

Agreement on Import Licensing Procedures. 12p. 1980. pap. 2.00 (ISBN 0-686-63029-7, G139, GATT). Unipub.

Agreement on Technical Barriers to Trade. 31p. 1980. pap. 2.75 (ISBN 0-686-63031-9, G136, GATT). Unipub.

Brewster, Kingman, Jr. Antitrust & American Business Abroad. Bruchey, Stuart & Bruchey, Eleanor, eds. LC 76-4768. (American Business Abroad Ser.). 1976. Repr. of 1958 ed. 32.00x (ISBN 0-405-09266-0). Arno.

Bryan, Greyson. Taxing Unfair International Trade Practices: A Study of the U. S. Antidumping & Countervailing Duty Law. LC 80-7571. 1980. 34.95x (ISBN 0-669-03752-4). Lexington Bks.

Export Inspection: Systems in Asia. 1977. pap. 4.50 (ISBN 92-833-2002-6, APO20, APO). Unipub.

Export: Processing Zones in Asia; Some Dimensions. (Illus.). 1977. 10.00 (ISBN 92-833-1039-X, APO21, APO); pap. 10.00 (ISBN 92-833-1040-3). Unipub.

Feinschreiber, Robert, ed. Subpart F: Foreign Subsidiaries & Their Tax Consequences. LC 79-88374. 260p. 1979. 35.00 (ISBN 0-916592-28-6). Panel Pubs.

Franko, Lawrence G. A Survey of the Impact of Manufactured Exports from Industrializing Countries in Asia & Latin America: Must Export-Oriented Growth Be Disruptive? LC 79-91759. 56p. 1979. 4.50 (ISBN 0-89068-051-5). Natl Planning.

A Handbook on Financing U.S. Exports. 3rd ed. 1979. 12.00 (ISBN 0-686-27826-7). M & A Products.

How to Prepare & Process Export-Import Documents. 1978. 25.00 (ISBN 0-685-83441-7). Intl Wealth.

Hutton, J. Bernard. Traitor Trade. (Illus.). 1963. 7.95 (ISBN 0-8392-1120-1). Astor-Honor.

The Impact of the Tokyo Round Agreements on U. S. Export Competitiveness. (Significant Issues Ser.: Vol. II, No. 10). 66p. 1981. pap. 7.50 (ISBN 0-89206-024-7, CSIS 020, CSIS). Unipub.

International Institute for the Unification of Private Law (UNIDROIT) New Directions in International Trade Law: Acts & Proceedings of the Second International Congress on Private Law, Vol. I & II. LC 77-10129. 1977. 75.00 set (ISBN 0-379-00670-7). Oceana.

LaFave, Wayne R. & Hay, Peter, eds. International Trade, Investment, & Organization. LC 66-25556. 1967. 25.00 (ISBN 0-252-74504-3). U of Ill Pr.

Lortie, Pierre. Economic Integration & the Law of Gatt. LC 75-3626. (Special Studies). (Illus.). 202p. 1975. text ed. 25.95 (ISBN 0-275-05230-3). Praeger.

Murr, Alfred. Export-Import Traffic Management & Forwarding. 6th ed. LC 79-18987. 1979. 22.50x (ISBN 0-87033-261-9). Cornell Maritime.

OAS General Secretariat. The United States Generalized System of Preferences: Coverage & Administrative Procedures in Force in 1981. (International Trade & Export Development Program). 59p. 1981. pap. 5.00 (ISBN 0-8270-1324-8). OAS.

Olnek, Jay I. The Invisible Hand: How Free Trade Is Choking the Life Out of America. 1981. 15.00 (ISBN 0-938538-00-4). N Stonington.

Removing Taxes on Knowledge. 1969. pap. 2.50 (ISBN 92-3-100746-7, U545, UNESCO). Unipub.

Schneider, G. W. Export-Import Financing: A Practical Guide. 1974. 34.95 (ISBN 0-471-06578-1). Ronald Pr.

Shaw, Crawford, ed. Legal Problems in International Trade & Investment. LC 62-3307. 1962. 17.50 (ISBN 0-379-12851-9). Oceana.

Simmons, Andre. Sherman Antitrust Act & Foreign Trade. LC 63-63263. (U of Fla. Social Sciences Monographs Ser.: No. 16). 1962. pap. 3.00 (ISBN 0-8130-0204-4). U Presses Fla.

Siposs, Allan J. How to Win the Import Game: Practical Tips & Ideas on Importing. (Illus.). 101p. 1980. pap. 19.95x (ISBN 0-935402-00-4). Intl Comm Serv.

--Importing: Practical Tips & Ideas. (Illus.). 1979. 25.00x (ISBN 0-686-59709-5). Intl Comm Serv.

Stabilization of International Trade in Grains. (FAO Commodity Policy Studies: No. 20). (Orig.). 1971. pap. 10.00 (ISBN 0-685-02918-2, F438, FAO). Unipub.

Stern, Paula. Water's Edge: Domestic Politics & the Making of American Foreign Policy. LC 78-55331. (Contributions in Political Science: No. 15). 1979. lib. bdg. 19.95 (ISBN 0-313-20520-5, SWE/). Greenwood.

UNESCO. Trade Barriers to Knowledge: A Manual of Regulations Affecting Educational, Scientific & Cultural Materials. rev. ed. Repr. of 1955 ed. lib. bdg. 20.50x (ISBN 0-8371-3154-5, UNTB). Greenwood.

U.S. Technology & Export Controls. 1978. 10.00 (ISBN 0-686-27829-1). M & A Products.

Yeats, Alexander J. Trade Barriers Facing Developing Countries. LC 78-10537. 1979. 32.50x (ISBN 0-312-81207-8). St Martin.

Zelko, L. International Value-International Prices. LC 80-50648. 153p. 1980. 17.50 (ISBN 90-286-0040-X). Sijthoff & Noordhoff.

FOREIGN TRADE ZONES
see Free Ports and Zones

FOREIGN VISITORS
see Visitors, Foreign

FOREIGN WORKERS
see Alien Labor

FOREIGNERS
see Aliens; Naturalization; Visitors, Foreign

FOREMAN, BLONNYE

Fletcher, Jesse C. Search for Blonnye Foreman. LC 69-17895. 1969. 3.25 (ISBN 0-8054-7209-6). Broadman.

FOREMEN
see Supervisors, Industrial

FORENAMES
see Names, Personal

FORENSIC CHEMISTRY
see Chemistry, Forensic

FORENSIC DENTISTRY
see Dental Jurisprudence

FORENSIC HEMATOLOGY

Sussman, Leon N. Paternity Testing by Blood Grouping. 2nd ed. (Illus.). 208p. 1976. 22.50 (ISBN 0-398-03523-7). C C Thomas.

FORENSIC MEDICINE
see Medical Jurisprudence

FORENSIC ORATIONS
see also Orations

Blom-Cooper, Louis. Language of the Law, 2 vols. Incl. Literature of the Law. 1967. Set. 29.95 (ISBN 0-02-489130-4). Macmillan.

Dahl, Richard C. & Davis, Robert. Effective Speaking for Lawyers. LC 75-93751. 1969. lib. bdg. 20.00 (ISBN 0-930342-11-9). W S Hein.

Hastings, Arthur & Windes, Russel R. Argumentation & Advocacy. 1965. pap. text ed. 3.75x (ISBN 0-394-30601-5). Random.

Re, Edward D. Brief Writing & Oral Argument. 4th rev. ed. LC 73-11059. 1977. 15.00 (ISBN 0-913338-22-2). Trans-Media Pub.

FORENSIC PHOTOGRAPHY
see Photography, Legal

FORENSIC PSYCHIATRY
Here are entered works on psychiatry as applied in courts of law. Works on the legal status of persons of unsound mind are entered under the heading Insanity–Jurisprudence.
see also Insane, Criminal and Dangerous

Allen, Richard C., et al, eds. Readings in Law and Psychiatry. rev. ed. LC 74-24384. (Illus.). 848p. 1975. 30.00x (ISBN 0-8018-1692-0). Johns Hopkins.

Arens, Richard. Insanity Defense. LC 72-96108. 354p. 1973. 12.50 (ISBN 0-8022-2106-8). Philos Lib.

Asinof, Eliot. The Fox Is Crazy Too. LC 75-17937. 1976. 8.95 (ISBN 0-688-02964-7). Morrow.

Beran, Nancy J. & Toomey, Beverly G., eds. Mentally Ill Offenders & the Criminal Justice System: Issues in Forensic Services. LC 78-19782. 1979. 24.95 (ISBN 0-03-046426-9). Praeger.

Bjerre, Andreas. The Psychology of Murder: A Study in Criminal Psychology. Classen, E., tr. from Swedish. (Historical Foundations of Forensic Psychiatry & Psychology Ser.). 164p. 1980. Repr. lib. bdg. 19.50 (ISBN 0-306-76067-3). Da Capo.

Blinder, Martin. Psychiatry in the Everyday Practice of Law. LC 72-95085. 305p. 1973. 40.00 (ISBN 0-686-05454-7). Lawyers Co-Op.

Bose, Prabodh C. Introduction to Juristic Psychology. (Historical Foundations of Forensic Psychiatry & Psychology Ser.). 426p. 1980. Repr. of 1917 ed. lib. bdg. 39.50 (ISBN 0-686-68561-X). Da Capo.

Bromberg, Walter. The Uses of Psychiatry in the Law: A Clinical View of Forensic Psychiatry. LC 78-22724. (Illus.). 1979. lib. bdg. 25.00 (ISBN 0-89930-000-6, BRP/, Quorum Bks). Greenwood.

Brown, M. Ralph. Legal Psychology. (Historical Foundations of Forensic Psychiatry & Psychology Ser.). (Illus.). 346p. 1980. Repr. of 1926 ed. lib. bdg. 35.00 (ISBN 0-306-76065-7). Da Capo.

Bucknill, John C. & Hammond, William. Insanity & the Law: Two Nineteenth Century Classics. (The Historical Foundations of Forensic Psychiatry & Psychology Ser.). 145p. 1981. Repr. of 1856 ed. lib. bdg. 27.50 (ISBN 0-306-76066-5). Da Capo.

Curran, William J., et al. Modern Legal Medicine, Psychiatry & Forensic Science. LC 79-19477. (Illus.). 1310p. 1980. text ed. 89.50 (ISBN 0-8036-2292-9). Davis Co.

Davey, Herbert. The Law Relating to the Mentally Defective. (Historical Foundations of Forensic Psychiatry & Psychology Ser.). 568p. 1980. Repr. of 1914 ed. lib. bdg. 49.50 (ISBN 0-306-76070-3). Da Capo.

Glueck, Bernard. Studies in Forensic Psychiatry. LC 16-20410. (Criminal Science Monograph: No. 2). 1968. Repr. of 1915 ed. 13.00 (ISBN 0-527-34112-6). Kraus Repr.

Goodwin, John C. Insanity & the Criminal. (Historical Foundations of Forensic Psychiatry & Psychology Ser.). 308p. 1980. Repr. of 1924 ed. lib. bdg. 29.50 (ISBN 0-306-76061-4). Da Capo.

Hoag, Ernest B. & Williams, Edward H. Crime, Abnormal Minds & the Law. (Historical Foundations of Forensic Psychiatry & Psychology Ser.). 405p. 1980. Repr. of 1923 ed. lib. bdg. 35.00 (ISBN 0-306-76060-6). Da Capo.

Hollander, Bernard. The Psychology of Misconduct, Vice, & Crime. (Historical Foundations of Forensic Psychiatry & Psychology Ser.). 220p. 1980. Repr. lib. bdg. 25.00 (ISBN 0-306-76063-0). Da Capo.

Irvine, Lynn M., Jr. & Brelje, Terry B., eds. Law, Psychiatry & the Mentally Disordered Offender, Vol. 1. 164p. 1972. 13.75 (ISBN 0-398-02530-4). C C Thomas.

--Law, Psychiatry & the Mentally Disordered Offender, Vol. 2. 148p. 1973. 13.75 (ISBN 0-398-02645-9). C C Thomas.

Katz, Jay, et al. Psychoanalysis, Psychiatry & Law. LC 65-27757. 1967. text ed. 35.00 (ISBN 0-02-917200-4). Free Pr.

Levitt, Morton & Rubenstein, Ben, eds. Orthopsychiatry & the Law. LC 68-16014. 1968. 9.95x (ISBN 0-8143-1349-3); pap. 4.95x (ISBN 0-8143-1350-7). Wayne St U Pr.

Lubin, Martin. Good Guys, Bad Guys. 312p. Date not set. 12.95 (ISBN 0-07-038913-6). McGraw.

McCarty, Dwight G. Psychology for the Lawyer. (Historical Foundations of Forensic Psychiatry & Psychology Ser.). Date not set. lib. bdg. 49.50 (ISBN 0-306-76068-1). Da Capo.

Macdonald, John M. Psychiatry & the Criminal: A Guide to Psychiatric Examinations for the Criminal Courts. 3rd ed. 524p. 1976. 37.75 (ISBN 0-398-03480-X). C C Thomas.

Mercier, Charles. Criminal Responsibility. (Historical Foundations of Forensic Psychiatry & Psychology Ser.). 256p. 1980. Repr. of 1931 ed. lib. bdg. 25.00 (ISBN 0-306-76064-9). Da Capo.

Polier, Justine Wise. The Rule of Law & the Role of Psychiatry (Isaac Ray Lectures) LC 68-12900. 176p. 1968. 12.00x (ISBN 0-8018-0535-X). Johns Hopkins.

Rieber, R. W., ed. Milestones in the History of Forensic Psychology & Psychiatry: A Book of Readings. Green, Maurice. (The Historical Foundations of Forensic Psychiatry & Psychology Ser.). 250p. 1981. Repr. lib. bdg. 27.50 (ISBN 0-306-76072-X). Da Capo.

Rieber, Robert W. & Vetter, Harold J., eds. The Psychological Foundations of Criminal Justice: Historical Perspectives on Forensic Psychology, Vol. 1. LC 78-18781. (Illus.). 1978. 15.00x (ISBN 0-89444-009-8). John Jay Pr.

Rubin, Sol. Psychiatry & Criminal Law. LC 64-19354. 1965. 12.50 (ISBN 0-379-00225-6). Oceana.

Sadoff, Robert L. Forensic Psychiatry: A Practical Guide for Lawyers & Psychiatrists. (American Lectures in Behavioral Science & Law Ser.). 272p. 1975. 19.75 (ISBN 0-398-03412-5). C C Thomas.

Smith, Selwyn M. & Koranyi, Erwin K. Self-Assessment of Current Knowledge in Forensic & Organic Psychiatry. 1978. spiral bdg. 15.00 (ISBN 0-87488-235-4). Med Exam.

Szasz, Thomas S. Psychiatric Justice. LC 77-18804. 1978. Repr. of 1965 ed. lib. bdg. 25.75x (ISBN 0-313-20196-X, SZPJ). Greenwood.

Weihofen, Henry. Legal Services & Community Mental Health Centers. 74p. 1969. pap. 3.00 (ISBN 0-685-24859-3, P229-0). Am Psychiatric.

Weisstub, David N., ed. Law & Psychiatry in the Canadian Context. 1981. 60.00 (ISBN 0-08-023134-9). Pergamon.

White, W. A. Insanity & the Criminal Law. (Historical Foundations of Forensic Psychiatry & Psychology Ser.). 281p. 1980. Repr. of 1923 ed. lib. bdg. 25.00 (ISBN 0-306-76069-X). Da Capo.

Wright, Fred, et al, eds. Forensic Psychology & Psychiatry. LC 80-17982. (Annals of the New York Academy of Sciences: Vol. 347). 364p. 1980. 58.00x (ISBN 0-89766-084-6); pap. 58.00x (ISBN 0-89766-085-4). NY Acad Sci.

FORENSIC PSYCHOLOGY
see Psychology, Forensic

FOREORDINATION
see Predestination

FOREST CONSERVATION
see also Forest Products; Forest Reserves

Cleveland, Harlan, ed. The Management of Sustainable Growth. LC 80-24162. (Pergamon Policy Studies on International Development). 386p. 1981. 40.00 (ISBN 0-08-027171-5). Pergamon.

Conservation in Arid & Semi-Arid Zones. (Conservation Guide Ser: No. 3). (Illus.). 1977. pap. 9.00 (ISBN 92-5-100130-8, F743, FAO). Unipub.

Eckholm, Erik P. The Other Energy Crisis: Firewood. (Worldwatch Papers). 1975. pap. 2.00 (ISBN 0-916468-00-3). Worldwatch Inst.

Lillard, Richard G. The Great Forest. LC 72-8129. (Illus.). 452p. 1973. Repr. of 1947 ed. lib. bdg. 39.50 (ISBN 0-306-70534-6). Da Capo.

Olson, Sherry H. Depletion Myth: A History of Railroad Use of Timber. LC 70-148940. 1971. 12.50x (ISBN 0-674-19820-4). Harvard U Pr.

Pinkett, Harold T. Gifford Pinchot: Private & Public Forester. LC 74-76830. (Illus.). 1970. 12.50 (ISBN 0-252-00080-3). U of Ill Pr.

Rakestraw, Lawrence. A History of Forest Conservation in the Pacific Northwest, 1891-1913. Bruchey, Stuart, ed. LC 78-56660. (Management in Public Lands in the U. S. Ser.). 1979. lib. bdg. 25.00x (ISBN 0-405-11351-X). Arno.

Roache, Catharine S. What Are Forests for? 44p. 1971. 1.00 (ISBN 0-913478-01-6). Hermosa.

Shands, William E. & Healy, Robert G. The Lands Nobody Wanted: Policy for National Forests in the Eastern United States. LC 77-72771. (Illus.). 1977. 14.50 (ISBN 0-89164-042-8); pap. 10.50 (ISBN 0-89164-043-6). Conservation Foun.

Stephens, Rockwell. One Man's Forest: Managing Your Woodlot for Pleasure & Profit. LC 74-23687. (Illus.). 128p. 1974. pap. 6.95 (ISBN 0-8289-0225-9). Greene.

FOREST ECOLOGY
see also Rain Forests; Woody Plants

Batten, Mary. The Tropical Forest: Ants, Ants, Animals & Plants. LC 73-4196. (Illus.). (gr. 5-9). 1973. 9.95 (ISBN 0-690-00138-X, TYC-J). Har-Row.

Birdseye, Clarence & Birdseye, Eleanor. Growing Woodland Plants. (Illus.). 1972. pap. 3.00 (ISBN 0-486-20661-0). Dover.

Bormann, F. H. & Likens, G. E. Pattern & Process in a Forested Ecosystem: Disturbance, Development & the Steady State Based on the Hubbard Brook Ecosystem Study. LC 78-6015. (Illus.). 1979. 20.80 (ISBN 0-387-90321-6). Springer-Verlag.

Brown, Vinson. Reading the Woods: Seeing More in Nature's Familiar Faces. LC 70-85652. (Illus.). 160p. 1973. pap. 5.95 (ISBN 0-02-062270-8, Collier). Macmillan.

Caras, Roger. The Forest. LC 78-14179. (Illus.). 1979. 8.95 (ISBN 0-03-014436-1). HR&W.

Cousens, John. An Introduction to Woodland Ecology. (Ecology Ser). (Illus.). 155p. (gr. 1-6). 1974. pap. text ed. 6.00x (ISBN 0-05-002775-1). Longman.

Czarnowski, M. S. Productive Capacity of Locality As a Function of Soil & Climate with Particular Reference to Forest Land. LC 64-16087. (University Studies, Biological Science Ser: Vol. 5). (Illus.). 1964. 17.50x (ISBN 0-8071-0422-1). La State U Pr.

Dickson, James G., et al, eds. The Role of Insectivorous Birds in Forest Ecosystems. LC 79-12111. 1979. 31.00 (ISBN 0-12-215350-2). Acad Pr.
Edlin, Herbert L. Trees & Man. LC 76-15972. 269p. 1976. 27.50x (ISBN 0-231-04158-6). Columbia U Pr.
Gehu, J. M., ed. La Vegetation des Forets Caducifoliees Acidiphiles. (Colloques Phytosociologiques Ser.: Vol. 3). (Illus.). 396p. (Fr.). 1975. 48.00x (ISBN 3-7682-0965-2, Pub. by J. Cramer). Intl Schol Bk Serv.
Golley, Frank B., et al. Mineral Cycling in a Tropical Moist Forest Ecosystem. LC 73-89717. 272p. 1975. 20.00x (ISBN 0-8203-0344-5). U of Ga Pr.
Halle, F., et al. Tropical Trees & Forests: An Architectural Analysis. 1978. 72.20 (ISBN 0-387-08494-0). Springer-Verlag.
Holdridge, L. R., et al. Forest Environments in Tropical Life Zones: A Pilot Study. LC 75-129847. 1971. 165.00 (ISBN 0-08-016340-8). Pergamon.
Jackson, James P. The Biography of a Tree. LC 77-2818. (Illus.). 1979. 12.50 (ISBN 0-8246-0216-1). Jonathan David.
Kitazawa, Y., ed. Ecosystem Analysis of the Subalpine Coniferous Forest of the Shigayama IBP Area, Central Japan. (Japan International Biological Program Synthetics Ser.: Vol. 15). 1977. pap. 23.00x (ISBN 0-86008-225-3, Pub. by U of Tokyo Pr). Intl Schol Bk Serv.
Knauth, Percy. The North Woods. (The American Wilderness Ser.). (Illus.). 1972. 12.95 (ISBN 0-8094-1164-4). Time-Life.
Kozlowski, Theodore T. Tree Growth & Environmental Stresses. LC 78-10815. (Geo. S. Long Publication Ser.). (Illus.). 184p. 1979. 10.00 (ISBN 0-295-95636-4). U of Wash Pr.
Lamb, Robert. World Without Trees. LC 78-21868. (Illus.). 1979. 9.95 (ISBN 0-448-22619-7). Paddington.
Lee, Richard. Forest Hydrology. LC 79-19542. 1980. 25.00x (ISBN 0-231-04718-5). Columbia U Pr.
--Forest Microclimatology. LC 77-21961. (Illus.). 276p. 1978. 20.00x (ISBN 0-231-04156-X). Columbia U Pr.
Likens, G. E., et al. Biogeochemistry of a Forested Ecosystem. LC 76-50113. 1977. pap. 11.30 (ISBN 0-387-90225-2). Springer-Verlag.
McCormick, J. Life of the Forest. (Our Living World of Nature Ser.). 1966. 9.95 (ISBN 0-07-044875-2, P&RB); by subscription 3.95 (ISBN 0-07-046001-9). McGraw.
Mattson, W. J., ed. The Role of Arthropods in Forest Ecosystems: Proceedings in Life Sciences. (Illus.). 1977. 20.10 (ISBN 0-387-08296-4). Springer-Verlag.
Meggers, Betty J., et al. Tropical Forest Ecosystems in Africa & South America: A Comparative Review. LC 72-8342. (Illus.). 350p. 1973. pap. 12.50x (ISBN 0-87474-125-4). Smithsonian.
Neal, Ernest G. Woodland Ecology. 2nd ed. LC 54-28260. (Illus.). 1958. 7.95x (ISBN 0-674-95550-1). Harvard U Pr.
Owen, D. F. Animal Ecology in Tropical Africa. 2nd ed. LC 75-46586. (Tropical Ecology Ser). (Illus.). 1976. text ed. 18.95x (ISBN 0-582-44363-6). Longman.
Quinn, John R. The Summer Woodlands. (Illus.). 1980. 9.95 (ISBN 0-85699-140-6). Chatham Pr.
--The Winter Woods. LC 76-18486. (Illus.). 1976. 8.95 (ISBN 0-85699-138-4). Chatham Pr.
Reichle, D. E., ed. Dynamic Properties of Forest Ecosystems. LC 78-72093. (International Biological Programme Ser.: No. 23). (Illus.). 850p. 1981. 110.00 (ISBN 0-521-22508-6). Cambridge U Pr.
A Review-Tropical Woodlands & Forest Ecosystems, Nineteen Eighty. (UNEP Report Ser.: No. 4). 84p. 1980. pap. 9.00 (ISBN 0-686-70046-5, UNEP 030, UNEP). Unipub.
Richards, Paul W. Tropical Rain Forest. LC 79-50507. (Illus.). 1952. 65.50 (ISBN 0-521-06079-6); pap. 22.50 (ISBN 0-521-29658-7). Cambridge U Pr.
Scott, Geoffrey A. Grassland Development in the Gran Pajonal of Eastern Peru: A Study of Soil-Vegetation Nutrient Systems. LC 78-31729. (Hawaii Monographs in Geography: No. 1). 1979. pap. 14.75 (ISBN 0-8357-0369-X, IS-00070, University of Hawaii at Manoa, Department of Geography, Honolulu). Univ Microfilms.
Spurr, Stephen H. & Barnes, Burton V. Forest Ecology. 3rd ed. LC 79-10007. 1980. text ed. 27.95 (ISBN 0-471-04732-5). Wiley.
Stern, K. & Roche, L. Genetics of Forest Ecosystems. (Ecological Studies: Vol. 6). (Illus.). 540p. 1974. 41.80 (ISBN 0-387-06095-2). Springer-Verlag.
Sutton, Ann & Sutton, Myron. Wildlife of the Forests. (Wildlife Habitat Ser.). (Illus.). 1979. 18.95 (ISBN 0-8109-1759-9). Abrams.
Tomlinson, P. B. & Zimmermann, M. H., eds. Tropical Trees As Living Systems. LC 77-8579. (Illus.). 1978. 75.00 (ISBN 0-521-21686-9). Cambridge U Pr.
Troll, Carl. Die Tropischen Gebirge, Ihre Dreidimensionale Klimatische und Pflanzengeographische Zonierung. Repr. of 1959 ed. pap. 15.50 (ISBN 0-384-61680-1). Johnson Repr.
Walker, Laurence C. Ecology & Our Forests. LC 73-39350. (Illus.). 224p. 1973. 9.95 (ISBN 0-498-01159-3). A S Barnes.
Weese, Asa O. Animal Ecology of an Illinois Elm-Maple Forest. pap. 6.00 (ISBN 0-384-66400-8). Johnson Repr.

FOREST ECOLOGY–JUVENILE LITERATURE

Collins, Stephen. Forest & Woodland. LC 60-6114. (Community of Living Things Ser). (Illus.). (gr. 4-8). 1967. PLB 7.45 (ISBN 0-87191-015-2). Creative Ed.
Fegely, Thomas D. The World of the Woodlot. LC 74-25510. (Illus.). (gr. 5 up). 1975. PLB 5.95 (ISBN 0-396-07064-7). Dodd.
Heady, Eleanor B. Trees Are Forever: How They Grow from Seeds to Forests. LC 76-46541. (Finding-Out Book). (Illus.). (gr. 2-4). 1978. PLB 7.95 (ISBN 0-8193-0897-8, Pub. by Parents). Enslow Pubs.
List, Albert, Jr. & List, Ilka. A Walk in the Forest: The Woodlands of North America. LC 76-40171. (Illus.). (gr. 5 up). 1977. 12.95 (ISBN 0-690-00990-9, TYC-J). Har-Row.
Pringle, Laurence. Into the Woods: Exploring the Forest Ecosystem. LC 72-92448. (Illus.). 64p. (gr. 3-6). 1973. 7.95 (ISBN 0-02-775320-4). Macmillan.

FOREST ECONOMICS

see Forests and Forestry–Economic Aspects

FOREST ENTOMOLOGY

see Entomology

FOREST FAUNA

see also Jungle Fauna

Becker, Julie. Animals of the Woods & Forests. LC 77-8253. (Animals Around Us Ser.). (Illus.). (gr. 2-6). 1977. PLB 6.95 (ISBN 0-88436-396-1). EMC.
Friedman, Judi. Noises in the Woods. LC 78-12924. (Illus.). (gr. 1-4). 1979. 7.95 (ISBN 0-525-36023-9, Smart Cat). Dutton.
Johnson, Sylvia A. Animals of the Temperate Forests. LC 75-27757. (Lerner Wildlife Library). (Illus.). 28p. (gr. 4 up). 1976. PLB 5.95 (ISBN 0-8225-1276-9). Lerner Pubns.
--Animals of the Tropical Forests. LC 75-27758. (Lerner Wildlife Library). (Illus.). 28p. (gr. 4 up). 1976. PLB 5.95 (ISBN 0-8225-1278-5). Lerner Pubns.
Kendeigh, S. Charles. Invertebrate Populations of the Deciduous Forest: Fluctuations & Relations to Weather. LC 79-927. (Illinois Biological Monographs: No. 50). (Illus.). 1979. pap. 12.50 (ISBN 0-252-00737-9). U of Ill Pr.
Paulsen, Gary. The Small Ones. LC 76-12635. (Real Animals Ser.). (Illus.). 64p. (gr. 4 up). 1976. PLB 9.85 (ISBN 0-8172-0600-0). Raintree Pubs.
Perry, Richard. Life in Forest & Jungle. LC 74-21573. (The Many Worlds of Wildlife Ser). (Illus.). 256p. 1975. 9.95 (ISBN 0-8008-4799-7). Taplinger.
Quinn, John R. The Summer Woodlands. (Illus.). 1980. 9.95 (ISBN 0-85699-140-6). Chatham Pr.

FOREST FIRES

Air Operations for Forest, Brush & Grass Fires. 2nd ed. LC 75-12409. 68p. 1975. pap. 4.25 (ISBN 0-87765-035-7, FSP-9A). Natl Fire Prot.
Brown, A. A. & Davis, Kenneth P. Forest Fire: Control & Use. 2nd ed. (Forest Resources Ser). (Illus.). 544p. 1973. text ed. 21.00 (ISBN 0-07-008205-7, C). McGraw.
Cohen, Stan B. & Miller, Donald C. Big Burn: Big Burn: the Northwest's Forest Fire of Nineteen Ten. LC 78-51507. (Illus.). 96p. 1978. pap. 4.95 (ISBN 0-933126-04-2). Pictorial Hist.
Forest Fire Control. (FAO Forestry Ser: No. 6). 1953. pap. 7.25 (ISBN 92-5-100488-9, F 1443, FAO). Unipub.
Kurbatskii, N. P., ed. Soviet Progress in Forest Fire Control. LC 64-24390. 38p. 1964. 20.00 (ISBN 0-306-10676-0, Consultants). Plenum Pub.
NFPA Forest Committee. Chemicals for Forest Fire Fighting. 3rd ed. Lyons, Paul, ed. LC 77-814121. 1977. pap. text ed. 6.50 (ISBN 0-87765-104-3, FSP-19A). Natl Fire Prot.
Pringle, Laurence. Natural Fire, Its Ecology in Forests. LC 79-13606. (Illus.). 64p. (gr. 4-6). 1979. 5.95 (ISBN 0-688-22210-2); PLB 5.71 (ISBN 0-688-32210-7). Morrow.
Scott, Jack D. & Sweet, Ozzie. City of Birds & Beasts: Behind the Scenes at the Bronx Zoo. LC 77-13888. (Illus.). (gr. 6 up). 1978. 8.95 (ISBN 0-399-20633-7). Putnam.
Spring, Ira & Fish, Byron. Lookouts: Firewatchers of the Casades & Olympics. (Illus.). 224p. (Orig.). 1981. pap. 8.95 (ISBN 0-89886-014-8). Mountaineers.
Systems for Evaluating & Predicting the Effects of Weather & Climate on Wildland Fires. (Special Environmental Report Ser: No. 11). 40p. 1978. pap. 10.00 (ISBN 92-63-10496-4, W389, WMO). Unipub.

FOREST FLORA

see Forest Ecology; Forests and Forestry

FOREST GENETICS

see also Tree Breeding

Cannell, M. G. & Last, F. T., eds. Tree Physiology & Yield Improvement. 1977. 80.50 (ISBN 0-12-158750-9). Acad Pr.
Forest Genetic Resources: Information, No. 6. (Forestry Occasional Paper: 1977, No. 1). (Illus.). 1977. pap. 8.00 (ISBN 0-685-80147-0, F 917, FAO). Unipub.
The Methodology of Conservation of Forest Genetic Resources: Report on a Pilot Study. (Illus.). 127p. 1976. pap. 11.50 (ISBN 0-685-62394-7, F1136, FAO). Unipub.
Miksche, J. P., ed. Modern Methods in Forest Genetics. LC 76-8828. (Illus.). 1976. 31.60 (ISBN 0-387-07708-1). Springer-Verlag.
Wright, Jonathan W. Introduction to Forest Geneties. 1976. 29.50 (ISBN 0-12-765250-7). Acad Pr.

FOREST INDUSTRIES

see Wood-Using Industries

FOREST INFLUENCES

see also Forests and Forestry; Vegetation and Climate

Beresford-Peirse, H. Forests, Food & People. (Freedom from Hunger Campaign Basic Studies: No. 20). (Orig.). 1968. pap. 4.50 (ISBN 0-685-09384-0, F199, FAO). Unipub.
Kittredge, Joseph. Forest Influences. (Illus.). 6.50 (ISBN 0-8446-4764-0). Peter Smith.

FOREST LAW

see Forestry Law and Legislation

FOREST MACHINERY–DIRECTORIES

Chain Saws in Tropical Forests. (FAO Training Ser.: No. 2). 96p. 1981. pap. 9.25 (ISBN 92-5-100932-5, F2116, FAO). Unipub.

FOREST MANAGEMENT

see Forest Policy; Forests and Forestry

FOREST MENSURATION

see Forests and Forestry–Mensuration

FOREST PLANTING

see Forests and Forestry

FOREST POLICY

see also Forestry Law and Legislation; Forests and Forestry

Bethel, James S. & Massengale, Martin A., eds. Renewable Resource Management for Forestry & Agriculture. LC 78-25994. (Geo. S. Long Publication Ser.). 136p. 1979. 10.00 (ISBN 0-295-95624-0). U of Wash Pr.
Cameron, Jenks. Development of Governmental Forest Control in the United States. (Brookings Institution Reprint Ser). Repr. of 1928 ed. lib. bdg. 21.50x (ISBN 0-697-00153-9). Irvington.
Clawson, Marion. Forests for Whom & for What? LC 74-24399. (Resources for the Future Ser). (Illus.). 192p. 1975. 13.50x (ISBN 0-8018-1698-X); pap. 3.95x (ISBN 0-8018-1751-X). Johns Hopkins.
Clawson, Marion, ed. Forest Policy for the Future: Conflict, Compromise, Consensus. LC 74-13169. (Resources for the Future Working Paper Ser). (Illus.). 366p. 1974. pap. 6.00x (ISBN 0-8018-1674-2). Johns Hopkins.
Cornell University Agricultural Waste Management Conference, 10th, 1978. Best Management Practices for Agriculture & Silviculture: Proceedings. Loehr, Raymond C. & Haith, Douglas A., eds. LC 78-67494. 1979. 35.00 (ISBN 0-250-40271-8). Ann Arbor Science.
Duerr, William A., et al. Forest Resource Management: Decision Making Principles. 1979. text ed. 22.50 (ISBN 0-7216-3223-8). HR&W.
Earl, D. E. Forest Energy & Economic Development. (Illus.). 140p. 1975. 22.50x (ISBN 0-19-854521-5). Oxford U Pr.
Forestry for Local Community Development. (FAO Forestry Paper Ser.: No. 7). 1978. pap. 8.25 (ISBN 92-5-100585-0, F1466, FAO). Unipub.
Mater, Jean. Citizens Involved, Handle with Care! LC 77-12733. (Illus.). 1977. 7.95 (ISBN 0-917304-04-7, Pub. by Timber Pr). Intl Schol Bk Serv.
National Forest Management Proposals. (Legislative Analyses Ser.). 1976. pap. 3.75 (ISBN 0-8447-0178-5). Am Enterprise.
Pinchot, Gifford. Adirondack Spruce, a Study of the Forest in Ne-Ha-Sa-Ne Park. LC 77-125756. (American Environmental Studies). 1971. Repr. of 1907 ed. 10.00 (ISBN 0-405-02682-X). Arno.
--Biltmore Forest. LC 70-125757. (American Environmental Studies). 1970. Repr. of 1893 ed. 9.00 (ISBN 0-405-02683-8). Arno.
Report of the Third Session of the Committee on Forest Development in the Tropics. 183p. 1975. pap. 11.50 (ISBN 0-685-54194-0, F1097, FAO). Unipub.
Spurr, Stephen H. American Forest Policy in Development. LC 76-16648. (Geo. S. Long Pubns. Ser.). 96p. 1976. text ed. 7.95 (ISBN 0-295-95532-5). U of Wash Pr.
The United States Timber Supply Background for Policy: National Policy Conference Proceedings. 1970. write for info. (ISBN 0-686-20724-6). SUNY Environ.
Urban Forestry Conference: Proceedings. 1974. 1.50 (ISBN 0-686-20725-4). SUNY Environ.
Worrell, A. C. Principles of Forest Policy. 1970. text ed. 17.95 (ISBN 0-07-071891-1, C). McGraw.

FOREST PRODUCTS

see also Gums and Resins; Lumber; Lumber Trade; Rubber; Timber; Wood; Wood-Pulp; Wood-Using Industries

Davis, Richard C., compiled by. Inventory of the Records of the National Forest Products Association. (Guides to Forest & Conservation History of North America, No. 3). 1976. pap. 1.25 (ISBN 0-89030-031-3). Forest Hist Soc.
Forest Products Prices Nineteen Sixty-One to Nineteen Eighty. 113p. 1981. pap. 7.50 (ISBN 92-5-001042-7, F2140, FAO). Unipub.
Forest Products Prices Nineteen Sixty to Nineteen Seventy-Seven. (FAO Forestry Papers: No. 13). 84p. 1979. pap. 7.50 (ISBN 92-5-000678-0, F1578, FAO). Unipub.
Gregersen, Hans M. & Contreras, Arnoldo. U. S. Investment in the Forest-Based Sector in Latin America: Problems & Potentials. LC 74-21754. (Resources for the Future). (Illus.). 128p. (Orig.). 1975. pap. 4.50x (ISBN 0-8018-1704-8). Johns Hopkins.
Hillis, W. E. & Brown, A. G. Eucalypts for Wood Production. 434p. 1980. 90.00x (ISBN 0-643-02245-7, Pub. by CSIRO Australia). State Mutual Bk.
Kallio, Edwin & Dickerhoof, Edward. Business Data & Market Information Source Book for the Forest Products Industry. LC 79-63022. 1979. 30.00 (ISBN 0-935018-02-6). Forest Prod.
Panshin, Alex J., et al. Forest Products. 2nd ed. 1962. text ed. 22.00 (ISBN 0-07-048444-9, C). McGraw.
Phillips, F. H. The Pulping & Papermaking Potential of Tropical Hardwoods, Vol. 1. 1980. 10.00x (ISBN 0-643-00339-8, Pub. by CSIRO). State Mutual Bk.
Reese, Richard M. Marketing of a Forest Product: A Chance-Constrained Transportation Model. LC 74-4903. (Studies in Marketing: No. 20). (Illus.). 80p. 1974. pap. 4.00 (ISBN 0-87755-189-8). U of Tex Busn Res.
Sedjo, Roger A. & Radcliffe, Samuel J. Postwar Trends in U.S. Forest Products Trade: A Global, National & Regional View. LC 80-8886. (Resources for the Future Research Paper: R-22). (Illus.). 622p. 1981. pap. text ed. 15.00x (ISBN 0-8018-2635-7). Johns Hopkins.
Sedjo, Roger A., ed. Issues in U.S. International Forest Products Trade: Proceedings of a Workshop. LC 80-8885. (Resources for the Future Research Paper: R-23). (Illus.). 276p. 1981. pap. text ed. 10.50x (ISBN 0-8018-2634-9). Johns Hopkins.
Stewart, G. A. The Potential for Liquid Fuels from Agriculture & Forestry in Australia. 147p. 1980. 35.00x (ISBN 0-643-00353-3, Pub. by CSIRO Australia). State Mutual Bk.
World Forest Products Statistics: A Ten Year Summary, 1954-63. (Orig.). 1965. pap. 10.00 (ISBN 0-685-09416-2, F526, FAO). Unipub.
Yearbook of Forest Products: Nineteen Seventy-Six. (FAO Forestry Ser No. 7, Statistical Ser No. 14). 1978. 29.50 (ISBN 0-685-96153-2, F1400, FAO). Unipub.
Yearbook of Forest Products Nineteen Sixty-Seven to Nineteen Seventy-Eight. (Forestry Ser.: No. 12). 428p. 1980. 40.50 (ISBN 92-5-000888-0, F-1906, FAO). Unipub.
Yearbook of Forest Products Statistics. annual Incl. 1952. pap. 5.25 (ISBN 0-685-48284-7); 1953. pap. 10.25 (ISBN 0-685-48285-5); 1954; 1956; 1957. pap. 10.25 (ISBN 0-685-48288-X); 1961. pap. 10.25 (ISBN 0-685-48289-8); 1964. pap. 15.00 (ISBN 0-685-48290-1); 1965. pap. 15.00 (ISBN 0-685-48291-X); 1966. pap. 8.25 (ISBN 0-685-48292-8). (Orig., FAO). Unipub.
Yearbook of Forest Products, 1966-1977. (Forestry Ser.: No. 8). 1979. 37.00 (ISBN 92-5-000732-9, F1577, FAO). Unipub.
Yearbook of Forest Products 1972: Review 1961-1972. 371p. 1975. 27.00 (ISBN 0-685-55201-2, FAO). Unipub.
Yearbook of Forest Products 1974: 1963-1974. 407p. 1976. 41.00 (ISBN 0-685-68364-8, FAO). Unipub.

FOREST PROTECTION

see also Plants, Protection of; Trees–Diseases and Pests

Smith, W. H. Air Pollution & Forests. (Springer Series on Environmental Management). (Illus.). 379p. 1981. 29.80 (ISBN 0-387-90501-4). Springer-Verlag.

Wilkins, Austin H. Ten Million Acres of Timber: The Remarkable Story of Forest Protection in the Maine Forestry District 1909-1972. (Illus.). xxiv, 312p. 1978. pap. 8.95 (ISBN 0-931474-03-5). TBW Bks.

FOREST RANGERS

see also United States-Forest Service

Colby, C. B. Park Ranger: Equipment, Training & Work of the National Park Rangers. rev. ed. LC 71-150276. (Illus.). (gr. 4-7). 1971. PLB 5.29 (ISBN 0-698-30278-8). Coward.

Crawford, Teri. Protectors of the Wilderness: The First Forest Rangers. LC 78-14492. (Famous Firsts Ser.). (Illus.). 1978. lib. bdg. 7.35 (ISBN 0-686-51114-X). Silver.

Glassman, Henry S. Lead the Way, Rangers - Fifth Ranger Bn. (Illus.). 104p. 1980. pap. 5.95 (ISBN 0-934588-03-1). Ranger Assocs.

Holland, Andy. Switchbacks. Mallory, Cynthia, ed. LC 80-24507. (Illus.). 156p. (Orig.). 1980. pap. 6.95 (ISBN 0-916890-99-6). Mountaineers.

Signy, F. C. History of the Queen's Park Rangers. 12.50x (ISBN 0-392-07910-0, SpS). Sportshelf.

FOREST REPRODUCTION

see Forests and Forestry

FOREST RESERVES

see also Forests and Forestry; National Parks and Reserves; Wilderness Areas

Barnes, William C. Western Grazing Grounds & Forest Ranges. Bruchey, Stuart, ed. LC 78-56685. (Management of Public Lands in the U.S. Ser.). (Illus.). 1979. Repr. of 1913 ed. lib. bdg. 23.00x (ISBN 0-405-11317-X). Arno.

Brockman, C. Frank & Merriam, Lawrence C., Jr. Recreational Use of Wildlands. 2nd ed. (American Forestry Ser.). (Illus.). 336p. 1972. text ed. 17.00 (ISBN 0-07-007981-1, C). McGraw.

Clawson, Marion. The Economics of National Forest Management. LC 76-15939. (Resources for the Future Working Paper Ser: EN-6). (Illus.). 128p. 1976. pap. 4.50x (ISBN 0-8018-1889-3). Johns Hopkins.

--Man, Land & the Forest Environment. LC 76-45999. (Geo. S. Long Publication Ser.). (Illus.). 86p. 1977. 8.95 (ISBN 0-295-95540-6). U of Wash Pr.

Frome, Michael. The National Forests of America. LC 68-22261. (Illus.). 194p. 1968. 15.95 (ISBN 0-87294-024-1). Country Beautiful.

Hilts, Len. National Forest Guide. LC 79-65643. (Illus.). 224p. 1980. pap. 6.95 (ISBN 0-528-84104-1). Rand.

Mid-Atlantic & Southeastern States Public Land Forum: Proceedings. 1969. 5.00 (ISBN 0-686-20719-X). SUNY Environ.

Rakestraw, Lawrence. A History of Forest Conservation in the Pacific Northwest, 1891-1913. Bruchey, Stuart, ed. LC 78-56660. (Management in Public Lands in the U. S. Ser.). 1979. lib. bdg. 25.00x (ISBN 0-405-11351-X). Arno.

Shands, William E. & Healy, Robert G. The Lands Nobody Wanted: Policy for National Forests in the Eastern United States. LC 77-72771. (Illus.). 1977. 14.50 (ISBN 0-89164-042-8); pap. 10.50 (ISBN 0-89164-043-6). Conservation Foun.

Spring, Bob & Spring, Ira. The Redwoods National Park. LC 75-2685. (Illus.). 1975. pap. 2.95 (ISBN 0-87564-618-2). Superior Pub.

Van Name, Willard G. Vanishing Forest Reserves. Bruchey, Stuart, ed. LC 78-56688. (Management of Public Lands in the U. S. Ser.). 1979. Repr. of 1929 ed. lib. bdg. 15.00x (ISBN 0-405-11356-0). Arno.

Van Valkenburgh, Norman J. The Adirondack Forest Preserve. LC 79-12995. 396p. 1979. pap. 30.25 (ISBN 0-8357-0416-5, Pub. by Adirondack Museum, IS-00081). Univ Microfilms.

Wuertz-Schaefer, Karin. Hiking Virginia's National Forests. LC 77-70414. (Illus.). 204p. 1977. pap. 6.95 (ISBN 0-914788-05-1). East Woods.

FOREST SOILS

Bowman, Isaiah. Forest Physiography: Physiography of the United States & Principles of Soils in Relation to Forestry. LC 78-125732. (American Environmental Studies). 1970. Repr. of 1911 ed. 39.00 (ISBN 0-405-02659-5). Arno.

Management Properties of Ferralsols. (Soils Bulletin: No. 23). 120p. 1980. pap. 8.25 (ISBN 0-686-62996-5, F-1165, FAO). Unipub.

Pritchett, William L. Properties & Management of Forest Soils. LC 78-23196. 1979. text ed. 29.95 (ISBN 0-471-03718-4). Wiley.

FOREST SURVEYS

Second FAO - SIDA, Ibadan, Nigeria, 12 August-13 September 1974. Training Course on Forest Inventory: Report. (Illus.). 291p. 1975. pap. 16.25 (ISBN 0-685-62389-0, FAO). Unipub.

Survey of Pine Forests, Honduras: Final Report. 1968. 22.50 (ISBN 0-685-09410-3, F456, FAO). Unipub.

Wilson, A. L. Elementary Forest Surveying & Mapping, Two. 1978. pap. text ed. 7.95 (ISBN 0-88246-136-2). Oreg St U Bkstrs.

Wilson, R. L. Elementary Forest Surveying & Mapping. 1972. pap. text ed. 3.95 (ISBN 0-88246-135-4). Oreg St U Bkstrs.

FOREST VALUATION

see Forests and Forestry-Economic Aspects

FORESTALLING

see Monopolies

FORESTATION

see Forests and Forestry

FORESTERS

see also Forests and Forestry-Vocational Guidance

Baker, Richard & Barbe. Kamiti: A Forester's Dream. (Illus.). 5.50 (ISBN 0-686-05049-5). Wellington.

Eldredge, Inman F. & Demmon, Elwood L. Voices from the South: Recollections of Four Foresters. (Illus.). 1977. pap. 4.95 (ISBN 0-89030-032-1). Forest Hist Soc.

Greeley, William B. Forests & Men. LC 72-2840. (Use & Abuse of America's Natural Resources Ser). 260p. 1972. Repr. of 1951 ed. 15.00 (ISBN 0-405-04508-5). Arno.

Kaufman, Herbert. The Forest Ranger: A Study in Administrative Behavior. LC 60-6650. (Resources for the Future Ser). (Illus.). 259p. 1960. 17.50x (ISBN 0-8018-0327-6); pap. 3.95x (ISBN 0-8018-0328-4). Johns Hopkins.

Kephart, George S. Campfires Rekindled. LC 77-85453. (Illus.). 1977. pap. text ed. 6.95 (ISBN 0-9600496-7-3). Channing Bks.

Rudman, Jack. Forest Ranger. (Career Examination Ser.: C-281). (Cloth bdg. avail. on request). 8.00 (ISBN 0-8373-0281-1). Natl Learning.

FORESTRY AND STATE

see Forest Policy

FORESTRY EDUCATION

see Forestry Schools and Education

FORESTRY ENGINEERING

see also Lumbering

FORESTRY LAW AND LEGISLATION

Cameron, Jenks. The Development of Governmental Forest Control in the United States. LC 79-38096. (Law, Politics, & History Ser). 484p. 1972. Repr. of 1928 ed. lib. bdg. 45.00 (ISBN 0-306-70440-4). Da Capo.

Dana, Samuel T. & Fairfax, Sally K. Forest & Range Policy. 2nd ed. (Illus.). 496p. 1980. text ed. 19.95 (ISBN 0-07-015288-8, P&RB). McGraw.

Forest Industries Committee on Timber Taxation & Valuation, ed. Timber Tax Journal, Vol. 16. 335p. 1980. 25.00x (ISBN 0-914272-19-5, Pub. by Forest Industries). Intl Schol Bk Serv.

Kinney, J. P. The Development of Forest Law in America: A Historical Presentation of the Successive Enactments, by the Legislatures of the Forty-Eight States of the American Union & by the Federal Congress. LC 72-2849. (Use & Abuse of America's Natural Resources Ser). 348p. 1972. Repr. of 1917 ed. 18.00 (ISBN 0-405-04515-8). Arno.

Manwood, John. A Treatise of the Lawes of the Forest. LC 76-57398. (English Experience Ser.: No. 814). 1977. Repr. of 1615 ed. lib. bdg. 51.00 (ISBN 90-221-0814-7). Walter J Johnson.

Merrill, Perry H. Roosevelts Forest Army: A History of the Civilian Conservation Corps, 1933-42. (Illus.). ix, 224p. 1981. 12.95x (ISBN 0-686-29690-7); pap. 8.95x (ISBN 0-686-29691-5). P H Merrill.

Timber Tax Journal, Vol. 15. 418p. 1980. 25.00x (ISBN 0-914272-18-7, Pub. by FICTVT). Intl Schol Bk Serv.

Timber Tax Journal, Volume 13: 1977. 1977. 25.00 (ISBN 0-914272-16-0, Pub. by FICTVT). Intl Schol Bk Serv.

FORESTRY RESEARCH

Hewlett, John D. & Nutter, Wade L. Outline of Forest Hydrology. 1969. pap. 4.95x (ISBN 0-8203-0325-9). U of Ga Pr.

Romberger, J. A. & Mikola, P., eds. International Review of Forestry Research, Vols. 1-3. 1964-70. 47.00 ea. Vol. 1 (ISBN 0-12-365501-3). Vol. 2 (ISBN 0-12-365502-1). Vol. 3 (ISBN 0-12-365503-X). Acad Pr.

FORESTRY SCHOOLS AND EDUCATION

College of Forestry, First 50 Years: 1911-1961. 5.00 (ISBN 0-686-20730-0). SUNY Environ.

Demmon, E. L. Opportunities in Forestry Careers. rev. ed. LC 74-25903. (Illus.). 1975. text ed. 6.60 (ISBN 0-8442-6442-3); pap. text ed. 4.95 (ISBN 0-8442-6441-5). Natl Textbk.

Graves, Henry S. & Guise, C. H. Forest Education. 1932. 37.50x (ISBN 0-686-51388-6). Elliots Bks.

McCulloch, Walter F. Forest Management Education in Oregon. (Studies in Education & Guidance Ser: No. 2). 1949. pap. 3.95 (ISBN 0-87071-042-7). Oreg St U Pr.

Mason, Earl G. Functional Curriculum in Professional Forestry. (Studies in Education & Guidance Ser: No. 1). 1944. pap. 3.95 (ISBN 0-87071-041-9). Oreg St U Pr.

Report of the Eighth Session of FAO Advisory Committee on Forestry Education. 47p. 1980. pap. 9.00 (ISBN 92-5-100480-3, F1968, FAO). Unipub.

World List of Forestry Schools. (FAO Forestry Paper Ser.: No. 3). 1978. pap. 7.50 (ISBN 92-5-000450-8, F1383, FAO). Unipub.

FORESTS, NATIONAL

see Forest Reserves

FORESTS AND FORESTRY

see also Aeronautics in Forestry; Botany-Ecology; Flood Control; Folk-Lore of Trees; Hardwoods; Landscape Gardening; Lumber; Lumber Trade; Lumbering; Natural History-Outdoor Books; Pruning; Rain Forests; Tree Planting; Trees; Wood; Wood-Lots

Agris Forestry. (FAO Forestry Paper: No. 15). 138p. 1980. pap. 8.50 (ISBN 92-5-000810-4, F 1876, FAO). Unipub.

Allison, Philip. The New Forest. 1981. 45.00x (ISBN 0-686-75453-0, Pub. by Cave Pubns England). State Mutual Bk.

American Foresters Society & Wildlife Society. More Than One Way: Choices in Silviculture for American Forests. LC 81-51229. (Illus.). 88p. (Orig.). 1981. pap. 4.00 (ISBN 0-939970-09-0). Soc Am Foresters.

Anderson, David. Forestry Curriculum Guide. LC 75-35415. 1976. pap. 1.95x (ISBN 0-8134-1780-5, 1780). Interstate.

Anderson, David & Smith William, A., eds. Forest & Forestry. 3rd ed. (gr. 10-12). 1981. 15.35 (ISBN 0-8134-2169-1). Interstate.

Armson, K. A. Forest Soils: Properties & Processes. 1977. 25.00x (ISBN 0-8020-2265-0). U of Toronto Pr.

Assmann, E. Principles of Forest Yield Study. 1971. text ed. 79.00 (ISBN 0-08-006658-5). Pergamon.

Baker, Frederick S. Principles of Silviculture. (The American Forestry Ser). 1950. 17.50 (ISBN 0-07-003385-4, C). McGraw.

Baker, Richard S. Dance of the Trees. Rateaver, Bargyla & Rateaver, Gylver, eds. (Conservation Gardening & Farming Ser). pap. write for info. (ISBN 0-685-61012-8). Rateavers.

Bamford, Paul W. Forests & French Sea Power, 1660-1789. LC 57-226. 1956. 17.50x (ISBN 0-8020-7033-7). U of Toronto Pr.

Bernatzky, A. Tree Ecology & Preservation. (Developments in Agricultural & Managed-Forest Ecology Ser.: Vol. 2). 1978. 73.25 (ISBN 0-444-41606-4). Elsevier.

Biology Colloquium, 40th, Oregon State University, 1980. Forests: Fresh Perspectives from Ecosystems Analysis. Proceedings. Waring, Richard H., ed. LC 80-14883. (Illus.). 210p. 1980. pap. 12.00 (ISBN 0-87071-179-2). Oreg St U Pr.

Bowman, Isaiah. Forest Physiography: Physiography of the United States & Principles of Soils in Relation to Forestry. LC 78-125732. (American Environmental Studies). 1970. Repr. of 1911 ed. 39.00 (ISBN 0-405-02659-5). Arno.

Braun, E. L. Deciduous Forests of Eastern North America. 1967. Repr. of 1950 ed. 27.25 (ISBN 0-02-841910-3). Hafner.

Brockman, C. Frank & Merriam, Lawrence C., Jr. Recreational Use of Wild Lands. 3rd ed. (M-H Series in Forest Resources). (Illus.). 1979. text ed. 17.00 (ISBN 0-07-007982-X, C). McGraw.

Cable Logging Systems. (FAO Forestry Paper Ser.: No. 24). 104p. 1981. pap. 7.50x (ISBN 92-5-101046-3, F2178, FAO). Unipub.

Cameron, Jenks. Development of Governmental Forest Control in the United States. (Brookings Institution Reprint Ser). Repr. of 1928 ed. lib. bdg. 21.50x (ISBN 0-697-00153-9). Irvington.

Caras, Roger. The Forest. 1980. pap. 4.95 (ISBN 0-395-29611-0). HM.

Clarkson, Roy B., et al. Forest Plants of the Monangahela National Forest. 1980. pap. 8.95 (ISBN 0-910286-82-5). Boxwood.

Clawson, Marion. The Economics of U. S. Nonindustrial Private Forests. LC 79-2196. 1979. pap. 8.95x (ISBN 0-8018-2282-3). Resources Future.

--Man, Land & the Forest Environment. LC 76-45999. (Geo. S. Long Publication Ser.). (Illus.). 86p. 1977. 8.95 (ISBN 0-295-95540-6). U of Wash Pr.

Clepper, Henry. Professional Forestry in the United States. LC 70-171107. (Resources for the Future Ser). 346p. 1971. 22.50x (ISBN 0-8018-1331-X). Johns Hopkins.

Collins, Bobby & White, Fred. Elementary Forestry. 1981. text ed. 16.95 (ISBN 0-8359-1647-2); instr's. manual free (ISBN 0-8359-1646-4). Reston.

Dana, Samuel T. & Fairfax, Sally K. Forest & Range Policy. 2nd ed. (Illus.). 496p. 1980. text ed. 19.95 (ISBN 0-07-015288-8, P&RB). McGraw.

Danov, Christo. Alttrakien. LC 73-75484. 1976. 104.75x (ISBN 3-11-003434-4). De Gruyter.

Davis, Kenneth P. Forest Management. 2nd ed. 1966. text ed. 20.50 (ISBN 0-07-015531-3, C). McGraw.

Digby, Margaret & Edwardson, T. E. The Organisation of Forestry Co-Operatives. 250p. 1976. 25.00x (ISBN 0-85042-010-5, Pub. by Plunkett Found England). State Mutual Bk.

Dilworth, J. R. Variable Plot Cruising. 1976. pap. text ed. 3.50 (ISBN 0-88246-030-7). Oreg St U Bkstrs.

The Directory of Agricultural & Forestry Equipment Manufacturers in Western Europe. 1981. 150.00x (ISBN 0-686-75441-7, Pub. by European Directories England). State Mutual Bk.

Douglas, David. Douglas of the Forests: The North American Journals of David Douglas. Davies, John, ed. LC 80-12535. (Illus.). 194p. 1980. 14.95 (ISBN 0-295-95707-7). U of Wash Pr.

Douglas, J. Sholto & Hart, Robert A. Forest Farming. LC 78-5774. 1978. 8.95 (ISBN 0-87857-228-7). Rodale Pr Inc.

Duerr, William A., ed. Timber! Problems, Prospects, Policies. LC 72-1160. 252p. 1973. 8.95x (ISBN 0-8138-1700-5). Iowa St U Pr.

Duffey, Eric. The Forest World. LC 79-91274. (Illus.). 224p. 1980. 18.95 (ISBN 0-89479-060-9). A & W Pubs.

Eckholm, Erik. Planting for the Future: Forestry for Human Needs. LC 79-62890. (Worldwatch Papers). 1979. pap. 2.00 (ISBN 0-916468-25-9). Worldwatch Inst.

Economic Analysis of Forestry Projects. (FAO Forestry Paper Ser.: No. 17, Suppl. 1). 243p. 1980. pap. 15.75 (ISBN 92-5-100830-2, F1959, FAO). Unipub.

Economics of U. S. Nonindustrial Private Forests in the United States. (Resources for the Future Ser.). 1979. pap. 8.95x (ISBN 0-8018-2282-3). Johns Hopkins.

Edlin, Herbert L. Trees & Man. LC 76-15972. 269p. 1976. 27.50x (ISBN 0-231-04158-6). Columbia U Pr.

Establishment Techniques for Forest Plantations. (FAO Forestry Paper Ser.: No. 8). 1979. pap. 12.00 (ISBN 92-5-100535-4, F 1491, FAO). Unipub.

Forbes, Reginald D., et al, eds. Forestry Handbook. (Illus.). 1955. 37.50 (ISBN 0-8260-3155-2, Pub. by Wiley-Interscience). Wiley.

Forest Fertilization. LC 72-92357. (Bibliographic Ser.: No. 258, Supplement 1). 1975. pap. 25.00 (ISBN 0-87010-042-4). Inst Paper Chem.

Forest Influences. (FAO-Forestry Ser.: No. 9). 307p. 1980. pap. 18.00 (ISBN 92-5-100722-5, F 1880, FAO). Unipub.

Forest Pest Control: An Assessment of Present & Alternative Technologies, 5 vols, Vol Iv. (Pest Control Ser.). 1976. pap. 7.00 (ISBN 0-309-02413-7). Natl Acad Pr.

Forest Resources in the Asia & Far East Region. (Illus.). 100p. 1976. pap. 12.00 (ISBN 0-685-68954-9, F909, FAO). Unipub.

Forest Tree Seed Directory, 1975. 283p. 1975. pap. 24.00 (ISBN 0-685-61018-7, F197, FAO). Unipub.

Forest Utilization Contracts on Public Land. (Forestry Paper Ser.: No. 1). 1978. pap. 14.00 (ISBN 92-5-100356-4, F1307, FAO). Unipub.

Forest Watershed Management, No. 46. 1963. write for info. (ISBN 0-686-20717-3). SUNY Environ.

Forestry for Rural Communities. 56p. 1981. pap. 7.50 (ISBN 0-686-72309-0, F2024, FAO). Unipub.

Fountain, Paul. The Great Mountains & Forests of South America. 1976. lib. bdg. 59.95 (ISBN 0-8490-1902-8). Gordon Pr.

Ginns, Patsy M. Rough Weather Makes Good Timber: Carolinians Recall. LC 76-20765. 189p. 1977. 11.50 (ISBN 0-8078-1288-9); pap. 6.50 (ISBN 0-8078-4071-8). U of NC Pr.

Grey, Gene W. & Deneke, Frederick J. Urban Forestry. LC 78-5275. 279p. 1978. text ed. 23.50 (ISBN 0-471-01515-6). Wiley.

Guide to Safety & Health in Forestry Work. 3rd ed. (Illus.). 1971. 8.55 (ISBN 92-2-100975-0). Intl Labour Office.

Guise, Cedric H. Management of Farm Woodlands. 2nd ed. (American Forestry Ser.). 1960. text ed. 20.95 (ISBN 0-07-025179-7, C). McGraw.

Guthrie, John A. & Armstrong, George R. Western Forest Industry: An Economic Outlook. (Resources for the Future Ser). 324p. 1961. 22.50x (ISBN 0-8018-0245-8). Johns Hopkins.

Hampton, Charles M. Dry Land Log Handling & Sorting: Planning, Construction, & Operation of Log Yards. LC 80-80437. (A Forest Industries Bk). (Illus.). 216p. 1981. pap. 45.00 (ISBN 0-87930-081-7). Miller Freeman.

Harlow, William M. Ways of the Woods. 1979. 8.50 (ISBN 0-935050-00-0). Am Forestry.

Harvesting Man-Made Forests in Developing Countries: A Manual on Techniques, Roads, Production & Costs. (Illus.). 1977. pap. 21.00 (ISBN 92-5-100128-6, F931, FAO). Unipub.

Hays, Edward. Twelve & One-Half Keys. Turkle, Thomas, ed. (Illus.). 152p. (Orig.). 1981. pap. 4.95 (ISBN 0-939516-00-4). Forest Peace.
Heekin, William D., compiled by. Inventory of the Papers of William R. Schofield. (Guides to Forest & Conservation History of North America: No. 4). 1977. pap. 1.25 (ISBN 0-89030-035-6). Forest Hist Soc.
Hough, Lynn H. Vital Control: Forest Essays, First Series. LC 70-117809. (Essay Index Reprint Ser). 1934. 17.00 (ISBN 0-8369-1756-1). Arno.
Howes, K. M. & Rummery, R. A. Integrating Agriculture & Forestry. 238p. 1981. 30.00x (ISBN 0-643-02431-X, Pub. by CSIRO Australia). State Mutual Bk.
Husch, Bertram, et al. Forest Mensuration. 2nd ed. (Illus.). 1972. 24.50 (ISBN 0-471-06834-9). Wiley.
Ise, John. The United States Forest Policy. LC 72-2845. (Use & Abuse of America's Natural Resources Ser). 400p. 1972. Repr. of 1920 ed. 19.00 (ISBN 0-405-04511-5). Arno.
Jackson, James P. Pulse of the Forest. 1980. 14.00 (ISBN 0-686-72415-1). Am Forestry.
Jacobi, C. Vocabulaire Forestier Francais, Allemand, Danois. 207p. (Fr., Ger. & Dan.). 1907. pap. 12.50 (ISBN 0-686-56985-7, M-6322). French & Eur.
James, N. D. The Forester's Companion. 3rd ed. (Illus.). 400p. 1981. 25.00x (ISBN 0-631-12796-8, Pub by Basil Blackwell England); pap. 9.95x (ISBN 0-631-12797-6). Biblio Dist.
--The Forester's Companion. 2nd ed. 372p. 1979. (Pub. by Basil Blackwell); pap. 8.95x (ISBN 0-631-10811-4). Biblio Dist.
Jepsen, Stanley M. Trees & Forests. LC 69-17393. (Illus.). 1969. 8.95 (ISBN 0-498-06913-3). A S Barnes.
Khatib, Ahmad. Chihabi's Dictionary of Agricultural & Forestry Terms: English-Arabic. 1978. 40.00x (ISBN 0-86685-072-4). Intl Bk Ctr.
Kinch, Michael P., compiled by. Forestry Theses Accepted by Colleges & Universities in the United States July 1973-June 1976. (Bibliographic Ser.: No. 15). 1978. pap. 5.00 (ISBN 0-87071-135-0). Oreg St U Pr.
--Forestry Theses Accepted by Colleges & Universities in the United States July 1966-June 1973. (Bibliographic Ser.: No. 14). 1979. pap. 5.00 (ISBN 0-87071-134-2). Oreg St U Pr.
Laacke, R. J., ed. California Forest Soils: A Guide for Professional Foresters & Resource Managers & Planners. LC 79-62985. (Illus., Orig.). 1979. pap. text ed. 5.00x (ISBN 0-931876-32-X, 4094). Ag Sci Pubns.
Laarman, Jan, et al. Choice of Technology in Forestry: A Philippine Case Study. (Illus.). 1981. pap. 9.00x (ISBN 0-686-30446-2, Pub. by New Day Philippines). Cellar.
Lillard, Richard G. The Great Forest. LC 72-8129. (Illus.). 452p. 1973. Repr. of 1947 ed. lib. bdg. 39.50 (ISBN 0-306-70534-6). Da Capo.
Litschauer, R. Vocabularium Polyglottum Vitae Silvarum. 126p. (Lat., Eng., Ger., Fr., Span. & Rum.). 1955. 21.50 (ISBN 0-686-56473-1, M-7679, Pub. by P. Parey). French & Eur.
McCormick, J. Life of the Forest. (Our Living World of Nature Ser.). 1966. 9.95 (ISBN 0-07-044875-2, P&RB); by subscription 3.95 (ISBN 0-07-046001-9). McGraw.
Metro, Andre. Dictionnaire Forestier Multilingue. 434p. (Fr.). 1976. 79.95 (ISBN 0-686-57047-2, M-6409). French & Eur.
Minckler, Leon S. Woodland Ecology: Environmental Forestry for the Small Owner. 2nd ed. (Illus.). 230p. 1980. pap. 9.95 (ISBN 0-8156-0154-9). Syracuse U Pr.
Mitchell, Alan. The International Book of the Forest. 1981. 35.00 (ISBN 0-671-41004-0). S&S.
Moslemi, A. A. Particleboard, Vol. 1: Materials. LC 74-2071. (Illus.). 256p. 1974. 18.95x (ISBN 0-8093-0655-7). S Ill U Pr.
--Particleboard, Vol. 2: Technology. LC 74-2071. (Illus.). 252p. 1974. 18.95x (ISBN 0-8093-0656-5). S Ill U Pr.
Mountain Forest Roads & Harvesting. (FAO Forestry Papers Ser.: No. 14). 1979. pap. 17.75 (ISBN 92-5-100725-X, F1593, FAO). Unipub.
Muir, John. Steep Trails. Bade, William F., ed. LC 18-18667. (Illus.). 1970. pap. 20.00 (ISBN 0-910220-19-0). Larlin Corp.
Namkoong, Gene. Introduction to Quantitative Genetics in Forestry. 342p. 1981. text ed. 38.00 (ISBN 0-7194-0067-8, Pub. by Castle Hse England); pap. text ed. 21.00 (ISBN 0-7194-0068-6). J K Burgess.
Nash, Andrew J. Statistical Techniques in Forestry. 2nd ed. 6.00x (ISBN 0-685-52947-9). Lucas.
North American Forest Soils Conf., 4th. Forest Soils & Forest Land Management: Proceedings. Bernier, B. & Winget, C. H., eds. (Illus.). 675p. 1975. 27.50x (ISBN 2-7637-6716-8, Pub. by Laval). Intl Schol Bk Serv.
North American Forestry Commission, 8th Session. Report. (Illus., Orig.). 1976. pap. 7.50 (ISBN 92-5-100025-5, F111, FAO). Unipub.
Olson, Sherry H. Depletion Myth: A History of Railroad Use of Timber. LC 70-148940. 1971. 12.50x (ISBN 0-674-19820-4). Harvard U Pr.
Planning a Forest Inventory. (FAO Forest Ser: No. 4). 1978. pap. 7.25 (ISBN 92-5-100486-2, F 1446, FAO). Unipub.
Planning Forest Roads & Harvesting Systems. (FAO Paper Ser.: No. 2). (Illus.). 1978. pap. 10.50 (ISBN 92-5-100407-2, F1343, FAO). Unipub.
Productivity of Forest Ecosystems: Proceedings of the Brussels Symposium, 1969. (Illus.). 707p. 1972. 59.50 (ISBN 92-3-000897-4, U493, UNESCO). Unipub.
Public Forestry Administration in Latin America. (FAO Forestry Paper Ser.: No. 25). 178p. 1981. pap. 12.00 (ISBN 92-5-101051-X, F2179, FAO). Unipub.
Raphael, Ray. Tree Talk: The People & Politics of Timber. (Illus.). 304p. (Orig.). 1981. pap. 12.00 (ISBN 0-933280-10-6). Island Ca.
Reifsnyder, William E. & Lull, Howard W. Radiant Energy in Relation to Forests. LC 77-10239. (U. S. Department of Agriculture. Technical Bulletin: 1344). Repr. of 1965 ed. 15.00 (ISBN 0-404-16217-7). AMS Pr.
Report of the Conference of FAO: 20th Session, 1979. 234p. 1980. pap. 24.00 (ISBN 92-5-100892-2, F-1904, FAO). Unipub.
Report of the Council of FAO: 76th Session. 91p. 1980. pap. 9.00 (ISBN 92-5-100871-X, F-1910, FAO). Unipub.
Report of the Council of FAO: 77th Session. 35p. 1980. pap. 9.00 (ISBN 92-5-100889-2, F1909, FAO). Unipub.
Report of the Fifteenth Session of the Intergovernmental Group on Jute Kenaf & Allied Fibres to the CCP. 18p. 1980. pap. 9.00 (ISBN 92-5-100863-9, F1908, FAO). Unipub.
Report of the Tenth Session of the Asia-Pacific Forestry Commission. 33p. 1978. pap. 7.50 (ISBN 92-5-100370-X, F1349, FAO). Unipub.
Robbie, T. A. Teach Yourself Forestry. Date not set. 7.50x (ISBN 0-392-08216-0, SpS). Sportshelf.
Roth, Filibert. Forest Regulation. 1925. 3.95x (ISBN 0-685-21784-1). Wahr.
Rudman, Jack. Forester. (Career Examination Ser.: C-289). (Cloth bdg. avail. on request). pap. 8.00 (ISBN 0-8373-0289-7). Natl Learning.
--Forestry Technician. (Career Examination Ser.: C-1424). (Cloth bdg. avail. on request). pap. 8.00 (ISBN 0-8373-1424-0). Natl Learning.
--Senior Forestry Technician. (Career Examination Ser.: C-2715). (Cloth bdg. avail. on request). 1980. pap. 12.00 (ISBN 0-8373-2715-6). Natl Learning.
Safety & Health in Forestry Work: ILO Code of Practice. 1969. 5.15 (ISBN 92-2-100017-6). Intl Labour Office.
St. Barbe Baker, Richard. My Life My Trees. 192p. 1981. pap. 5.75 (ISBN 0-905249-40-2, Pub. by Findhorn-Thule Scotland). Hydra Bk.
Saltman, David. Paper Basics: Forestry, Manufacture, Selection, Purchasing, Mathematics & Metrics, Recycling. 1978. text ed. 10.95x (ISBN 0-442-25121-1). Van Nos Reinhold.
Sands, Anne, ed. Riparian Forests in California. LC 80-53162. (Illus.). 121p. pap. 4.00x (ISBN 0-931876-41-9, 4101). Ag Sci Pubns.
Shands, William E., et al. National Forest Policy: From Conflict Toward Consensus. LC 79-89875. 1979. pap. 4.00 (ISBN 0-89164-054-1). Conservation Foun.
Sharpe, Grant W., et al. Introduction to Forestry. 4th ed. (Forest Resources Ser.). 1976. text ed. 18.50 (ISBN 0-07-056480-9, C). McGraw.
Shidei, T. & Kira, T., eds. Primary Productivity of Japanese Forests--Productivity of Terrestrial Communities. (Japan International Biological Program Synthetics Ser.: Vol. 16). 1977. pap. 32.50x (ISBN 0-86008-226-1, Pub. by U of Tokyo Pr). Intl Schol Bk Serv.
Shirley, Hardy L. Forestry & Its Career Opportunities. 3rd ed. (Forest Resources Ser). (Illus.). 544p. 1973. text ed. 17.95 (ISBN 0-07-056978-9, C). McGraw.
Silvicultural Aspects of Woodlands, No. 42. 1958. 0.50 (ISBN 0-686-20715-7). SUNY Environ.
Smith, David M. Practice of Silviculture. 7th ed. LC 62-16244. 1962. 27.95x (ISBN 0-471-80017-1). Wiley.
Society of American Foresters. Forests for People. (SAF Convention Proceedings). (Illus.). 361p. (Orig.). 1977. pap. 12.00 (ISBN 0-939970-04-X). Soc Am Foresters.
--SAF Convention Proceedings Ser. Evans, H. H., ed. (Convention Proceedings Ser.). (Illus.). 320p. (Orig.). 1980. pap. 15.00 (ISBN 0-939970-06-6). Soc Am Foresters.
Sonnenfeld, Jeffrey A. Corporate Views of the Public Interest: The Perceptions of the Forest Products Industry. 200p. 1981. 19.95 (ISBN 0-86569-060-X). Auburn Hse.
Springer, John S. Forest Life & Forest Trees. rev. ed. (Illus.). 292p. 1971. Repr. of 1851 ed. 7.50x (ISBN 0-912274-08-5). O'Brien.
Standiford, Richard B. & Ramcher, Shirley I., eds. Cumulative Effects on Forest Management on California Watersheds: An Assessment of Status & Need for Information. 109p. (Orig.). Date not set. pap. price not set (ISBN 0-931876-48-6). Ag Sci Pubns.
Stoddard, Charles H. Essentials of Forestry Practice. 3rd ed. LC 78-6652. 387p. 1978. text ed. 19.95 (ISBN 0-471-07262-1). Wiley.
--The Small Private Forest in the United States. LC 77-86414. Repr. of 1961 ed. 17.50 (ISBN 0-404-60345-9). AMS Pr.
Sutton, Ann & Sutton, Myron. Wildlife of the Forests. (Wildlife Habitat Ser.). (Illus.). 1979. 18.95 (ISBN 0-8109-1759-9). Abrams.
Symposium on Forest Meteorology. Proceedings. 233p. 1980. pap. text ed. 10.00 (ISBN 92-63-00527-3, W447, WMO). Unipub.
U. S. Dept. of Agriculture-Forest Service. Timber Resources for America's Future: Forest Resource Report No. 14. LC 72-2872. (Use & Abuse of America's Natural Resources Ser). 728p. 1972. Repr. of 1958 ed. 31.00 (ISBN 0-405-04538-7). Arno.
U. S. Senate. A National Plan for American Forestry, 2 vols. Brouchey, Stuart, ed. LC 78-53554. (Development of Public Land Law in the U. S. Ser.). (Illus.). 1979. Repr. of 1933 ed. lib. bdg. 98.00x (ISBN 0-405-11389-7). Arno.
V. Weck, Johannes. Woerterbuch der Forstwirtschaft. (Ger., Eng., Fr., Span. & Rus., Dictionary of Forestry). 1966. 99.50 (ISBN 3-405-10494-7, M-7005). French & Eur.
Weck, J. Dictionary of Forestry. 1966. 85.50 (ISBN 0-444-40626-3). Elsevier.
Wilkins, Austin H. Ten Million Acres of Timber: The Remarkable Story of Forest Protection in the Maine Forestry District 1909-1972. (Illus.). xxiv, 312p. 1978. pap. 8.95 (ISBN 0-931474-03-5). TBW Bks.
Yavchenko, P. Interrelations of Forest & Bog. 1981. 50.00x (ISBN 0-686-76646-6, Pub. by Oxford & IBH India). State Mutual Bk.
Yearbook of Forest Products, 1973: Review 1962-1973. 371p. 1975. 36.00 (ISBN 0-685-57599-3, FAO). Unipub.

FORESTS AND FORESTRY–BIBLIOGRAPHY

Kinch, Michael P., compiled by. Forestry Theses Accepted by Colleges & Universities in the United States 1956-June 1966. (Bibliographic Ser.: No. 13). 1978. pap. 5.00 (ISBN 0-87071-133-4). Oreg St U Pr.
Osborn, Katherine H. Forestry Theses Accepted by Colleges & Universities in the United States, Supplement 1953-55. (Bibliographic Ser: No. 5). 1957. pap. 3.50 (ISBN 0-87071-125-3). Oreg St U Pr.
Yale University - Henry S. Graves Memorial Library. Dictionary Catalogue of the Yale Forestry Library, 12 Vols. 1962. Set. lib. bdg. 1140.00 (ISBN 0-8161-0631-2). G K Hall.

FORESTS AND FORESTRY–ECOLOGY

see Forest Ecology

FORESTS AND FORESTRY–ECONOMIC ASPECTS

see also Forest Policy

Beresford-Peirse, H. Forests, Food & People. (Freedom from Hunger Campaign Basic Studies: No. 20). (Orig.). 1968. pap. 4.50 (ISBN 0-685-09384-0, F199, FAO). Unipub.
Clawson, Marion. The Economics of National Forest Management. LC 76-15939. (Resources for the Future Working Paper Ser: EN-6). (Illus.). 128p. 1976. pap. 4.50x (ISBN 0-8018-1889-3). Johns Hopkins.
Cornell University Agricultural Waste Management Conference, 10th, 1978. Best Management Practices for Agriculture & Silviculture: Proceedings. Loehr, Raymond C. & Haith, Douglas A., eds. LC 78-67494. 1979. 35.00 (ISBN 0-250-40271-8). Ann Arbor Science.
Duerr, William A. Economic Problems of Forestry in the Appalachian Region. LC 49-8873. (Economic Studies: No. 84). (Illus.). 1949. 16.50x (ISBN 0-674-22950-9). Harvard U Pr.
Earl, D. E. Forest Energy & Economic Development. (Illus.). 140p. 1975. 22.50x (ISBN 0-19-854521-5). Oxford U Pr.
Economics of Forestry: A Bibliography for the United States & Canada, 1955-1959, No. 45. 1.50 (ISBN 0-686-20716-5). SUNY Environ.
Fernow, Bernhard E. Economics of Forestry: A Reference Book for Students of Political Economy & Professional & Lay Students of Forestry. LC 72-2836. (Use & Abuse of America's Natural Resources Ser). 536p. 1972. Repr. of 1902 ed. 25.00 (ISBN 0-405-04505-0). Arno.
Financial Maturity of the Eastern White Pine, No. 91. 1.50 (ISBN 0-686-20702-5). SUNY Environ.
Forests & the Economy of Lewis County, New York, No. 33. 1956. 0.75 (ISBN 0-686-20708-4). SUNY Environ.
Gregersen, Hans M. & Contreras, Arnoldo. U. S. Investment in the Forest-Based Sector in Latin America: Problems & Potentials. LC 74-21754. (Resources for the Future). (Illus.). 128p. (Orig.). 1975. pap. 4.50x (ISBN 0-8018-1704-8). Johns Hopkins.
Gregory, G. Robinson. Forest Resource Economics. 548p. 1972. 25.50 (ISBN 0-8260-3605-8, 40503). Wiley.
Heinsdijk, D. Forest Assessment. 359p. 1975. 48.00 (ISBN 90-220-0550-X, Pub. by PUDOC). Unipub.
Madas, Andras. World Consumption of Wood. LC 76-350270. 130p. 1974. 18.00x (ISBN 963-05-0183-X). Intl Pubns Serv.
Massie, Michael & Haring, Robert C. The Forest Economy of Haines, Alaska: A Study of Current Forest Utilization, Forest Management & Utilization Alternatives & Resultant Economic Impact. (Joint Institute of Social & Economic Research Ser.: No. 20). (Illus.). 203p. 1969. pap. 5.00 (ISBN 0-295-95117-6). U of Wash Pr.
Openshaw, K. Cost & Financial Accounting in Forestry. 1977. text ed. 33.00 (ISBN 0-08-021456-8); pap. text ed. 15.00 (ISBN 0-08-021455-X). Pergamon.
Reese, Richard M. Marketing of a Forest Product: A Chance-Constrained Transportation Model. LC 74-4903. (Studies in Marketing: No. 20). (Illus.). 80p. 1974. pap. 4.00 (ISBN 0-87755-189-8). U of Tex Busn Res.
Report of the FAO-Norway Seminar on Storage, Transport & Shipping of Wood. 1978. pap. 15.00 (ISBN 92-5-100351-3, F1249, FAO). Unipub.
Roth, Filibert. Forest Valuation. 1926. 3.95x (ISBN 0-685-21785-X). Wahr.
Rumsey, Fay & Duerr, William A. Social Sciences in Forestry: A Book of Readings. LC 74-24518. (Illus.). 409p. 1975. pap. text ed. 9.95 (ISBN 0-7216-7839-4). HR&W.
State Taxation of Forest & Land Resources: Symposium Proceedings. (Lincoln Institute Monograph: No. 80-6). 149p. 1980. pap. text ed. 12.00 (ISBN 0-686-29507-2). Lincoln Inst Land.
Vardaman, James M. Tree Farm Business Management. 2nd ed. LC 78-1610. 1978. 20.50 (ISBN 0-471-07263-X, Pub. by Wiley-Interscience). Wiley.
Worrell, Albert C. Economics of American Forestry. LC 59-6780. (Illus.). 1959. 20.50 (ISBN 0-471-96096-9). Wiley.

FORESTS AND FORESTRY–JUVENILE LITERATURE

Blatchford, Noel. Your Book of Forestry. (Illus.). 48p. (gr. 4 up). 1980. 8.95 (ISBN 0-571-11456-3, Pub. by Faber & Faber). Merrimack Bk Serv.
Boy Scouts Of America. Forestry. LC 19-600. (Illus.). 64p. (gr. 6-12). 1971. pap. 0.70x (ISBN 0-8395-3302-0, 3302). BSA.
Editions les Belles Images Staff, ed. Hidden in the Woods. (Butterfly Bks). (Illus., Orig.). (gr. 2-6). 1977. pap. 1.50 (ISBN 0-8467-0332-7, Pub. by Two Continents). Hippocrene Bks.
A Forest-Products Community: Crosset, Arkansas. (gr. 2). 1974. pap. text ed. 4.12 (ISBN 0-205-03888-3, 8038880); tchr's. guide 12.00 (ISBN 0-205-03884-0, 8038848). Allyn.
Heady, Eleanor B. Trees Are Forever: How They Grow from Seeds to Forests. LC 76-46541. (Finding-Out Book). (Illus.). (gr. 2-4). 1978. PLB 7.95 (ISBN 0-8193-0897-8, Pub. by Parents). Enslow Pubs.
Life in the Woods. (Wonders of Learning Kits Ser.). (gr. 3-5). 1980. incl. cassette & tchrs. guide 23.50 (ISBN 0-686-74398-9, 04962). Natl Geog.
Paige, David. A Day in the Life of a Forest Ranger. LC 78-68809. (Illus.). 32p. (gr. 4-8). 1980. PLB 6.89 (ISBN 0-89375-227-4); pap. 2.50 (ISBN 0-89375-231-2). Troll Assocs.
Sabin, Francene. Wonders of the Forest. (Illus.). 32p. (gr. 2-4). 1981. PLB 7.29 (ISBN 0-89375-572-9); pap. text ed. 1.95 (ISBN 0-89375-573-7). Troll Assocs.
Selsam, Millicent E. Birth of a Forest. LC 63-17281. (Illus.). (gr. 3-7). 1964. PLB 8.79 (ISBN 0-06-025276-6, HarpJ). Har-Row.
--See Through the Forest. LC 56-5191. 48p. (gr. 3-6). 1956. PLB 8.79 (ISBN 0-06-025351-7, HarpJ). Har-Row.
Simons, Barbara B. A Visit to the Forest. LC 78-5439. (Adventures in Nature Ser). (Illus.). (gr. 2-6). 1978. lib. bdg. 6.95 (ISBN 0-916392-22-8); pap. 3.95 (ISBN 0-916392-21-X). Oak Tree Pubns.

FORESTS AND FORESTRY–LAW

see Forestry Law and Legislation

FORESTS AND FORESTRY–MENSURATION

see also Lumber Trade–Tables and Ready-Reckoners

Chapman, Herman H. & Meyer, Walter H. Forest Mensuration. (The American Forestry Ser). (Illus.). 1949. 19.95 (ISBN 0-07-010647-9, C). McGraw.

Dilworth, J. R. Log Scaling & Timber Cruising. 1981. pap. text ed. 9.00 (ISBN 0-88246-031-5). Oreg St U Bkstrs.

Husch, Bertram, et al. Forest Mensuration. 2nd ed. (Illus.). 1972. 24.50 (ISBN 0-471-06834-9). Wiley.

FORESTS AND FORESTRY-PICTORIAL WORKS

Emsley, Michael. Rain Forests & Cloud Forests. (Illus.). 1979. 45.00 (ISBN 0-8109-1551-0). Abrams.

FORESTS AND FORESTRY-STATISTICS

World Forest Inventory, 1963. (Orig.). 1966. pap. 9.00 (ISBN 0-685-09415-4, F508, FAO). Unipub.

FORESTS AND FORESTRY-STUDY AND TEACHING

see Forestry Schools and Education

FORESTS AND FORESTRY-SURVEYING

see Forest Surveys

FORESTS AND FORESTRY-VOCATIONAL GUIDANCE

Educational Research Council of America. Forester. rev. ed. Ferris, Theodore N. & Marchak, John P., eds. (Real People at Work Ser: C). (Illus.). 1976. pap. text ed. 2.25 (ISBN 0-89247-028-3). Changing Times.

Hanaburgh, David H. Your Future in Forestry. LC 75-114121. (Career Guidance Ser). 1971. pap. 3.95 (ISBN 0-668-02245-0). Arco.

--Your Future in Forestry. LC 77-84173. (Careers in Depth Ser). (Illus.). (gr. 7 up). 1979. PLB 5.97 (ISBN 0-8239-0172-6). Rosen Pr.

McCulloch, W. F. Forester on the Job. 1972. pap. text ed. 7.95 (ISBN 0-88246-081-1). Oreg St U Bkstrs.

Rudman, Jack. Principal Forestry Technician. (Career Examination Ser.: C-2716). (Cloth bdg. avail. on request). 1980. pap. 14.00 (ISBN 0-8373-2716-4). Natl Learning.

Shirley, Hardy L. Forestry & Its Career Opportunities. 3rd ed. (Forest Resources Ser). (Illus.). 544p. 1973. text ed. 17.95 (ISBN 0-07-056978-9, C). McGraw.

FORESTS AND FORESTRY-AFRICA

African Forestry Commission, 4th Session. Report. 34p. 1976. pap. 7.50 (ISBN 92-5-100039-5, F1104, FAO). Unipub.

Forestry Administrative Problems in Selected African Countries. 1978. pap. 7.50 (ISBN 92-5-100331-9, F 1240, FAO). Unipub.

Report on the Information Mission of Forest Operations in Africa. 25p. 1978. pap. 7.50 (ISBN 92-5-100498-6, F1346, FAO). Unipub.

Savanna Afforestation in Africa. (Illus.). 1978. pap. 21.00 (ISBN 92-5-100273-8, F1176, FAO). Unipub.

Shantz, Homer L. & Marbut, Curtis F. Vegetation & Soils of Africa. LC 70-170848. Repr. of 1923 ed. 19.00 (ISBN 0-404-05953-8). AMS Pr.

Tree Planting Practices in African Savannas. (Forestry Development Papers: No. 19). (Illus.). 185p. 1975. pap. 15.75 (ISBN 0-685-57605-1, F479, FAO). Unipub.

FORESTS AND FORESTRY-ASIA

Bamboo Research in Asia. 228p. 1981. pap. 15.00 (ISBN 0-88936-267-X, IDRC 159, IDRC). Unipub.

Development & Forest Resources in Asia & Far East Region: Trends & Perspectives 1961-1991. (Illus.). 1977. pap. 11.50 (ISBN 92-5-100212-6, 747, FAO). Unipub.

Forest Resources in the Asia & Far East Region. (Illus.). 100p. 1976. pap. 12.00 (ISBN 0-685-68954-9, F909, FAO). Unipub.

Report on the FAO-SIDA Workshop on Forestry Development Planning for Countries of the Near East & South Asia. 26p. 1978. pap. 7.50 (ISBN 92-5-100417-X, F 1325, FAO). Unipub.

Report on the FAO-SIDA Workshop on Forestry Development Planning for Countries of Southeast Asia. (Swedish Funds-in-Trust Ser). 33p. 1977. pap. 7.50 (ISBN 92-5-100291-6, F1220, FAO). Unipub.

Richardson, S. D. Forestry in Communist China. (Illus.). 256p. 1966. 17.50x (ISBN 0-8018-0555-4). Johns Hopkins.

Sagreiya, K. P. Forests & Forestry. (India - Land & People Ser). (Illus.). 1967. 4.25x (ISBN 0-8426-1498-2). Verry.

Stainton, J. D. Forests of Nepal. (Illus.). 1972. 21.75 (ISBN 0-02-852700-3). Hafner.

Whitmore, T. C., ed. Tree Flora of Malaya: A Manual for Foresters, Vol. 1. (Illus.). 471p. 1972. text ed. 40.75x (ISBN 0-582-72412-0). Humanities.

FORESTS AND FORESTRY-AUSTRALIA

Lhuede, E. P. & Davern, W. A. Noise Levels in Australian Sawmills. 1980. 10.00x (ISBN 0-643-00348-7, Pub. by CSIRO Australia). State Mutual Bk.

Mack, J. J. Australian Methods for Mechanically Testing Small Clear Specimens of Timber. 1980. 10.00x (ISBN 0-643-00333-9, Pub. by CSIRO Australia). State Mutual Bk.

--The Withdrawal Resistance of Plain Steel Nails & Screws in Australian Timbers. 1980. 10.00x (ISBN 0-643-00329-0, Pub. by CSIRO Australia). State Mutual Bk.

Old, K. M. Phytophthora & Forest Management in Australia. 118p. 1980. 35.00x (ISBN 0-643-02523-5, Pub. by CSIRO Australia). State Mutual Bk.

Phytophthora & Forest Management in Australia. 114p. 1979. pap. 7.25 (ISBN 0-686-71838-0, CO 55, CSIRO). Unipub.

The Potential for Liquid Fuels from Agriculture & Forestry in Australia. 147p. 1979. pap. 9.00 (ISBN 0-686-71840-2, CO 25, CSIRO). Unipub.

Shepherd, K. R. & Richter, H. V., eds. Forestry in National Developments: Production Systems, Conservation, Foreign Trade & Aid. (Development Studies Centre - Monograph: No. 17). (Orig.). 1980. pap. 13.95 (ISBN 0-7081-1822-4, 0414, Pub. by ANUP Australia). Bks Australia.

Stewart, G. A. The Potential for Liquid Fuels from Agriculture & Forestry in Australia. 147p. 1980. 35.00x (ISBN 0-643-00353-3, Pub. by CSIRO Australia). State Mutual Bk.

FORESTS AND FORESTRY-CANADA

Lower, Arthur R. North American Assault on the Canadian Forest: A History of the Lumber Trade Between Canada & the United States. LC 68-57620. (Illus.). 1969. Repr. of 1938 ed. lib. bdg. 18.00x (ISBN 0-8371-0543-9, LOLT). Greenwood.

Mullins, E. J. & McKnight, T. S., eds. Canadian Woods: Their Properties & Uses. 3rd ed. 400p. 1981. 27.50 (ISBN 0-8020-2430-0). U of Toronto Pr.

FORESTS AND FORESTRY-CHINA

China: Forestry Support for Agriculture. (FAO Forestry Papers Ser.: No. 12). 115p. 1979. pap. 8.00 (ISBN 92-5-100695-4, F1554, FAO). Unipub.

FORESTS AND FORESTRY-COMMONWEALTH OF NATIONS

Browne, Frances G. Pests & Diseases of Forest Plantation Trees: An Annotated List of the Principle Species Occurring in the British Commonwealth. 1968. 89.00x (ISBN 0-19-854367-0). Oxford U Pr.

FORESTS AND FORESTRY-EUROPE

Forest Resources in the European Region. (Illus.). 35p. 1977. pap. 7.50 (ISBN 92-5-100038-7, F910, FAO). Unipub.

Fraas, Karl N. Geschichte Der Landbau-Und Forstwissenschaft. Repr. of 1865 ed. 41.50 (ISBN 0-384-16660-1). Johnson Repr.

Heske, Franz. German Forestry. 1938. 47.50x (ISBN 0-686-51394-0). Elliots Bks.

Phillips, Roger. Trees in Britain, Europe, & North America. (Illus.). 224p. 1978. 29.95x (ISBN - 08464-1147-4). Beekman Pubs.

FORESTS AND FORESTRY-GREAT BRITAIN

Cross, Arthur L. Eighteenth Century Documents Relating to the Royal Forests, the Sheriffs & Smuggling. 1973. lib. bdg. 16.50x (ISBN 0-374-91935-6). Octagon.

Leutscher, Alfred. Epping Forest: The Story of an Ancient British Woodland. LC 74-76194. 1975. 4.95 (ISBN 0-7153-6662-9). David & Charles.

Ryle, George. Forest Service: First Forty-Five Years of the Forestry Commission of Great Britain. LC 69-11237. (Illus.). 1969. 14.95x (ISBN 0-678-05675-7). Kelley.

Whitlock, Ralph. Historic Forests of England. LC 79-1924. (Illus.). 188p. 1980. 20.00 (ISBN 0-498-02429-6). A S Barnes.

Woodward, Guy H. & Woodward, Grace S. The Secret of Sherwood Forest: Oil Production in England During World War Two. LC 72-12546. (Illus.). 275p. 1973. 13.95 (ISBN 0-8061-1094-5). U of Okla Pr.

FORESTS AND FORESTRY-HONDURAS

Survey of Pine Forests, Hondouras: Final Report. 1968. 22.50 (ISBN 0-685-09410-3, F456, FAO). Unipub.

FORESTS AND FORESTRY-INDIA

Chowdhury, K. A., et al. Ancient Agriculture & Forestry in North India. (Illus.). 1978. text ed. 15.95x (ISBN 0-210-40604-6). Asia.

FORESTS AND FORESTRY-NEW ZEALAND

Baker, Richard S. & Barbe. Land of Tane: New Zealand Forests. 1956. 5.95 (ISBN 0-686-00581-3). Wellington.

FORESTS AND FORESTRY-NORTH AMERICA

Atlas of Forestry in New York, No. 41. 1958. 2.50 (ISBN 0-686-20714-9). SUNY Environ.

Carroll, Charles F. The Timber Economy of Puritan New England. LC 73-7122. (Illus.). xiv, 221p. 1973. pap. 15.00x (ISBN 0-87057-142-7, Pub. by Brown U Pr). U Pr of New Eng.

Daniel, Glenda & Sullivan, Jerry. A Sierra Club Naturlist's Guide to the North Woods of Michigan, Wisconsin, & Minnesota. (Naturalist's Guide Ser.). (Illus.). 384p. 1981. 24.95 (ISBN 0-87156-248-0); pap. 10.95 (ISBN 0-87156-277-4). Sierra.

Forest Acreage & Timber Volume in Franklin County, New York, No. 38. 1956. 1.50 (ISBN 0-686-20712-2). SUNY Environ.

Forest Acreage & Timber Volume in the Adirondack & Catskill Regions, No. 35. 1956. 0.80 (ISBN 0-686-20709-2). SUNY Environ.

Forest Acreage & Timber Volume of Clinton County, New York, No. 36. 1956. 0.75 (ISBN 0-686-20710-6). SUNY Environ.

Forest Acreage & Timber Volume of Essex County, New York, No. 37. 1956. 1.50 (ISBN 0-686-20711-4). SUNY Environ.

Forest Volume Estimation & Yield Prediction. (FAO Forestry Paper Ser.: Vol. 22, Nos. 1 & 2). 1980. Set. pap. 19.25 (ISBN 92-5-100923-6, F2138, FAO). Vol. 1, Volume Estimation, 98p. Vol. 2, Yield Prediction, 194p. Unipub.

Forests & the Economy of Lewis County, New York, No. 33. 1956. 0.75 (ISBN 0-686-20708-4). SUNY Environ.

Future Technological Needs of the U. S. Pulp & Paper Industries: Proceedings. 1973. 5.00 (ISBN 0-686-20722-X). SUNY Environ.

The Genus Peniophora in New York State & Adjacent Regions. 1960. 1.10 (ISBN 0-686-20695-9). SUNY Environ.

McIntosh, Robert P. The Forests of the Catskill Mountains. 1977. pap. 3.50x (ISBN 0-685-85607-0). Hope Farm.

May, Julian. Forests That Change Color. Publication Associates, ed. LC 77-156059. (Investigating the Earth Ser). (Illus.). (gr. 4-8). 1972. PLB 5.95 (ISBN 0-87191-060-8). Creative Ed.

Pfleger, Robert E. Green Leaves: A History of the Davey Tree Expert Company. LC 76-51129. (Illus.). 1977. casebound 9.95 (ISBN 0-87106-081-7). Globe Pequot.

Smith, David C. A History of Lumbering in Maine, 1861-1960. 1972. 15.00 (ISBN 0-89101-024-6). U Maine Orono.

Society of American Foresters. Forest Cover Types of the United States & Canada. Eyre, F. H., ed. LC 80-54185. Orig. Title: Forest Cover Types of North America (Exclusive of Mexico) 1954. (Illus.). 148p. (Orig.). 1980. pap. 7.50 (ISBN 0-686-30697-X). Soc Am Foresters.

--Forestry for America's Future. LC 77-79252. (SAF Convention Proceedings). (Illus.). 1977. pap. 8.00 (ISBN 0-939970-03-1). Soc Am Foresters.

--Forestry Issues in Urban America. (SAF Convention Proceedings). (Illus.). 287p. (Orig.). 1975. pap. 5.00 (ISBN 0-939970-01-5). Soc Am Foresters.

--Land-Use Allocation: Processes, People, Politics, Professionals. Evans, H. H., ed. (SAF Convention Proceedings Ser.). (Illus.). 298p. (Orig.). 1981. pap. 17.00 (ISBN 0-939970-07-4). Soc Am Foresters.

--North America's Forests: Gateway to Opportunity. Evans, H. H., ed. (SAF Convention Proceedings Ser.). (Illus.). 496p. (Orig.). 1979. pap. 15.00 (ISBN 0-939970-05-8). Soc Am Foresters.

--Sound American Forestry. (SAF Convention Proceedings). (Illus.). 261p. (Orig.). 1972. pap. 3.00 (ISBN 0-939970-00-7). Soc Am Foresters.

Wood, Richard G. A History of Lumbering in Maine, 1820-1861. 1972. 12.50 (ISBN 0-89101-023-8). U Maine Orono.

FORESTS AND FORESTRY-TROPICS

Manual of Forest Inventory with Special Reference to Mixed Tropical Forests. (Illus.). 200p. 1975. pap. 13.00 (ISBN 0-685-54182-7, F1025, FAO). Unipub.

Transportation of Tropical Wood Products: Proceedings. 1971. 10.00 (ISBN 0-686-20721-1). SUNY Environ.

Troll, Carl. Die Tropischen Gebirge, Ihre Dreidimensionale Klimatische und Pflanzengeographische Zonierung. Repr. of 1959 ed. pap. 15.50 (ISBN 0-384-61680-1). Johnson Repr.

Tropical Hardwoods Conference: Proceedings. 1969. 10.00 (ISBN 0-686-20720-3). SUNY Environ.

FORGERY

see also Checks; Counterfeits and Counterfeiting; Literary Forgeries and Mystifications

Ames, Daniel T. Ames on Forgery, Its Detection & Illustration with Numerous Causes Celebres. (Illus.). 293p. 1981. Repr. of 1901 ed. lib. bdg. 27.50x (ISBN 0-8377-0208-9). Rothman.

Baker, J. Newton. Law of Disputed & Forged Documents. (Illus.). 1955. 35.00 (ISBN 0-87215-079-8). Michie-Bobbs.

Baudin, Robert. Confessions of a Promiscuous Counterfeiter. LC 78-22243. 1979. 9.95 (ISBN 0-15-121853-6). HarBraceJ.

Boaden, James. Inquiry into the Authenticity of Various Pictures & Prints. 1824. Repr. 5.00 (ISBN 0-8274-2574-0). R West.

Boyer, Brian. Prince of Thieves: Memoirs of the World's Greatest Forger. 239p. 1975. 8.95 (ISBN 0-8037-5387-X). Dial.

Osborn, Albert S. Problem of Proof: Especially As Exemplified in Disputed Documents Trials. LC 75-20212. 1975. Repr. of 1926 ed. 41.95x (ISBN 0-88229-300-1). Nelson-Hall.

--Questioned Documents. 2nd ed. LC 74-78841. (Illus.). 1072p. 1974. Repr. of 1926 ed. 27.95x (ISBN 0-88229-190-4). Nelson-Hall.

Saudek, Robert. Anonymous Letters. LC 75-38671. (Foundations of Criminal Justice Ser.). (Illus.). Repr. of 1933 ed. 14.00 (ISBN 0-404-09182-2). AMS Pr.

Sternitzky, Julius L. Forgery & Fictitious Checks. (Illus.). 128p. 1955. photocopy ed. spiral 12.75 (ISBN 0-398-04418-X). C C Thomas.

Williamson, Doris M. & Meenach, Antoinette E. Cross-Check System for Forgery & Question Document Examination. LC 81-1974. (Illus.). 136p. 1981. text ed. 21.95 (ISBN 0-88229-430-X). Nelson-Hall.

FORGERY OF ANTIQUITIES

see also Antiquities; Forgery of Works of Art

FORGERY OF WORKS OF ART

see also Literary Forgeries and Mystifications; Precious Stones, Artificial

Cescinsky, Herbert. Gentle Art of Faking Furniture. LC 65-12295. (Illus.). 1967. pap. 7.95 (ISBN 0-486-21862-7). Dover.

Drachsler, Leo M. & Torczyner, Harry, eds. Forgery in Art & the Law. 61p. 1956. pap. 5.00 (ISBN 0-87945-012-6). Fed Legal Pubn.

Fleming, S. J. Authenticity in Art: The Scientific Detection of Forgery. LC 75-27303. (Illus.). 164p. 1976. 16.50x (ISBN 0-8448-0752-4). Crane-Russak Co.

Keating, Tom, et al. The Fake's Progress-Tom Keating's Story. (Illus.). 1978. 11.95 (ISBN 0-09-129420-7, Pub. by Hutchinson). Merrimack Bk Serv.

Kurtz, O. Art Forgeries & How to Examine Paintings Scientifically. (Illus.). 1979. deluxe ed. 57.45 (ISBN 0-930582-32-2). Gloucester Art.

Lee, Ruth W. Antique Fakes & Reproductions. rev. ed. (Illus.). 15.00 (ISBN 0-910872-07-4). Lee Pubns.

Norman, Geraldine, ed. The Tom Keating Catalogue: Illustrations to "the Fake's Progress". (Illus.). 1978. 22.95 (ISBN 0-09-129610-2, Pub. by Hutchinson). Merrimack Bk Serv.

Sachs, Samuel, 2nd & Johnson, Kathryn C. Fakes & Forgeries. (Illus.). 1973. 7.00 (ISBN 0-685-67981-0). Minneapolis Inst Arts.

Voelkle, William. The Spanish Forger. LC 78-60193. (Illus.). 77p. 1978. 35.00 (ISBN 0-87598-065-1); pap. 19.50 (ISBN 0-87598-054-6). Pierpont Morgan.

Waldron, Ann. True or False? Amazing Art Forgeries. (Illus.). 128p. 1981. PLB 8.95 (ISBN 0-8038-7220-8). Hastings.

FORGETFULNESS

see Memory

FORGING

see also Blacksmithing; Dies (Metal-Working); Drawing (Metal Work); High Energy Forming; Rolling (Metal-Work)

Garcia Mercadal, Jose. Diccionario Lengua Espanola Forja. 24th ed. 488p. (Espn.). 1977. 4.50 (ISBN 84-7105-026-9, S-50034). French & Eur.

Mueller, E. Hydraulic Forging Presses. 3rd ed. (Illus.). 1968. 49.80 (ISBN 0-387-04286-5). Springer-Verlag.

Serrano Mesa, Eleesbaan. Diccionario Ingles-Espanol, Espanol-Ingles Forja. 17th ed. 488p. (Eng.-Span.). 1977. 4.50 (ISBN 84-7105-098-6, S-50352). French & Eur.

Smith, Dale. Forage Management in the North. 3rd ed. 272p. 1981. perfect bdg. 10.95 (ISBN 0-8403-2377-8, 40237701). Kendall-Hunt.

Smith, Robert E. Forging & Welding. rev. ed. (Illus.). (gr. 7 up). 1956. text ed. 14.00 (ISBN 0-87345-120-1). McKnight.

FORGIVENESS OF SIN

see also Absolution; Confession; Penance; Repentance

Augsberger. Livre Para Perdoar. (Portuguese Bks.). 1979. 1.30 (ISBN 0-8297-0735-2). Life Pubs Intl.

Augsburger, David. Caring Enough to Forgive. LC 80-50545. 1981. pap. 4.95 (ISBN 0-8307-0749-2). Regal.

--Caring Enough to Forgive-Caring Enough Not to Forgive. 160p. (Orig.). 1981. pap. 4.95 (ISBN 0-8361-1965-7). Herald Pr.

Benko, Stephen. Meaning of Sanctorum Communio. LC 64-55292. (Studies in Historical Theology: No. 3). 1964. pap. 6.95x (ISBN 0-8401-0178-3). Allenson-Breckinridge.

Bright, Bill. How to Experience God's Love & Forgiveness. (Transferable Concepts Ser.). 63p. 1981. pap. 1.25 (ISBN 0-918956-89-7). Campus Crusade.

Cornwall, Judson. Let Us Enjoy Forgiveness. 1978. pap. 3.95 (ISBN 0-8007-0945-4). Revell.

Hall, Howard, et al. Come, Be Reconciled. LC 74-33576. 160p. (gr. k-12). 1975. pap. 5.95 (ISBN 0-8091-1876-9). Paulist Pr.

Hosier, Helen K. It Feels Good to Forgive. ev. ed. 176p. 1980. pap. 3.95 (ISBN 0-89081-251-9). Harvest Hse.

Hunter, Robert G. Shakespeare & the Comedy of Forgiveness. LC 65-15096. 1965. 17.50x (ISBN 0-231-02757-5). Columbia U Pr.

Keysor, Charles W. Forgiveness Is a Two-Way Street. 132p. 1981. pap. 3.95 (ISBN 0-88207-338-9). Victor Bks.

Koplik, William & Brady, Joan. Celebrating Forgiveness. 96p. 1981. pap. 7.95 (ISBN 0-89622-137-7). Twenty-Third.

Murray, Andrew. Confession & Forgiveness. pap. 2.50 (ISBN 0-310-29732-X). Zondervan.

Ogilvie, Lloyd J. Loved & Forgiven. LC 76-29889. 1977. pap. 2.50 (ISBN 0-8307-0442-6, S313-1-03). Regal.

Start Loving: The Miracle of Forgiving. 1977. lib. bdg. 8.95 (ISBN 0-8161-6476-2, Large Print Bks). G K Hall.

Taylor, Michael J., ed. Mystery of Sin & Forgiveness. LC 70-140284. 1971. pap. 3.95 (ISBN 0-8189-0198-5). Alba.

Williams, Ferelith E. My Book About Forgiveness. 1976. 24 copy pre pack 22.80 (ISBN 0-00-599540-X, PK540). Collins Pubs.

FORM (ESTHETICS)

Abell, Walter. Representation & Form. LC 79-138573. (Illus.). 1971. Repr. of 1936 ed. lib. bdg. 16.75x (ISBN 0-8371-5772-2, ABRF). Greenwood.

Anderson, John M. The Realm of Art. LC 67-16195. 1967. 11.95x (ISBN 0-271-73124-9); pap. 6.95x (ISBN 0-271-01180-7). Pa St U Pr.

Burnham, Jack. Structure of Art. rev. ed. LC 75-143195. 1970. 12.50 (ISBN 0-8076-0596-4); pap. 5.95 (ISBN 0-8076-0595-6). Braziller.

Jacobus, L. A. Aesthetics & the Arts. 1968. pap. text ed. 9.95 (ISBN 0-07-032215-5, C). McGraw.

Kahler, Erich. The Disintegration of Form in the Arts. LC 68-12888. 1968. 6.95 (ISBN 0-8076-0441-0); pap. 3.95 (ISBN 0-8076-0442-9). Braziller.

Mugniani, Joseph. Hidden Elements of Drawing. (Illus.). 212p. 1974. pap. text ed. 10.95 (ISBN 0-442-25722-8). Van Nos Reinhold.

Pearce, Peter. Structure in Nature Is a Strategy for Design. LC 77-26866. 1978. 45.00x (ISBN 0-262-16064-1); pap. 12.50 (ISBN 0-262-66045-8). MIT Pr.

Ritterbush, Philip C. Art of Organic Forms. LC 68-33165. (Illus.). 1968. 17.50x (ISBN 0-87474-068-1). Smithsonian.

Slattery, Sr. M. Francis. Hazard, Form, & Value. LC 77-161073. 1971. 8.95x (ISBN 0-8143-1455-4). Wayne St U Pr.

Spencer-Brown, G. Laws of Form. 1979. pap. 4.95 (ISBN 0-525-47544-3). Dutton.

Wasserman, Burton. Exploring the Visual Arts. Horn, George F. & Rainey, Sarita R., eds. LC 76-19938. (Books in Art Education). (Illus.). 1976. 13.95 (ISBN 0-87192-085-9). Davis Mass.

Williams, Christopher. Origins of Form. (Illus.). 160p. (Orig.). 1981. pap. 12.95 (ISBN 0-8038-5394-7). Hastings.

Woelfflin, Heinrich. Sense of Form in Art. LC 57-12877. (Illus., Orig.). pap. 4.95 (ISBN 0-8284-0153-5). Chelsea Pub.

FORM (PHILOSOPHY)

see also Structuralism

Gandillac, Maurice, et al. Entretiens Sur les Notions De Genese et De Structure: Centre Culturel International De Cerisy-la-Salle, Juillet-Aout 1959. (Congres et Colloques: No. 9). 1965. pap. 23.50x (ISBN 90-2796-094-1). Mouton.

Happ, Heinz H. Studien zum aristotelischen Materie-Begriff. 953p. 1971. 134.50x (ISBN 3-11-001796-2). De Gruyter.

Porter, Gene L. Nature of Form in Process. LC 69-14357. 1969. 4.50 (ISBN 0-8022-2004-5). Philos Lib.

Santayana, George. The Realm of Matter: Book Second of "Realms of Being". LC 72-11746. 209p. 1974. Repr. of 1930 ed. lib. bdg. 15.00x (ISBN 0-8371-6701-9, SARF). Greenwood.

Schuman, David. The Ideology of Form. LC 77-15815. 1978. 19.95 (ISBN 0-669-02059-1). Lexington Bks.

Whyte, Lancelot L. Accent on Form: An Anticipation of the Science of Tomorrow. LC 72-10702. 198p. 1973. Repr. of 1954 ed. lib. bdg. 15.00 (ISBN 0-8371-6622-5, WHAF). Greenwood.

FORM, LITERARY

see Literary Form

FORM, MUSICAL

see Musical Form

FORM AND MATTER

see Hylomorphism

FORM CRITICISM (BIBLE)

see Bible–Criticism, Form

FORM IN BIOLOGY

see Morphology

FORM LETTERS

Minnick, Sally. Dear World: A Collection of Form Letters for You to Use & Enjoy. Date not set. cancelled (ISBN 0-686-70423-1). Green Hill.

Vermes, Jean C. Secretary's Book of Instant Letters. LC 72-156169. 1971. 10.95 (ISBN 0-13-797506-6, Parker). P-H.

FORM PERCEPTION

Allington. Beginning to Learn About Shapes & Sizes. Date not set. lib. bdg. 7.99 (ISBN 0-8172-1277-9). Raintree Pubs.

Allington, Richard L. Shapes. LC 79-19852. (Beginning to Learn About Ser.). (Illus.). (gr. k-2). 1979. PLB 10.65 (ISBN 0-8172-1277-9). Raintree Pubs.

Barrett, Peter & Barrett, Susan. The Circle Sarah Drew. Incl. The Line Sophie Drew. LC 76-174716 (ISBN 0-87592-029-2); The Square Ben Drew (ISBN 0-87592-049-7). LC 72-89449. (Illus.). 32p. (ps-2). 1973. 4.75 ea. (ISBN 0-87592-012-8). Scroll Pr.

Cornsweet, Tom N. Visual Perception. 1970. text ed. 22.95 (ISBN 0-12-189750-8). Acad Pr.

Goldmeier, Erich. Similarity in Visually Perceived Forms. LC 72-83230. (Psychological Issues Monograph: No. 29, Vol. 8, No. 1). 1972. text ed. 11.00x (ISBN 0-8236-6077-X). Intl Univs Pr.

Holmes, Kenneth. Basic Shapes...Plus. (Illus.). 24p. (gr. k-3). 1980. pap. 4.25 (ISBN 0-933358-63-6). Enrich.

Magarian, Judith A. Measurement Comparisons. (Illus.). 24p. (gr. k-3). 1980. pap. 4.25 (ISBN 0-933358-64-4). Enrich.

Ranucci, Ernest. Seeing Shapes. 1973. pap. 5.95 wkbk. (ISBN 0-88488-038-9). Creative Pubns.

Rock, Irvin. Orientation & Form. 1974. 22.50 (ISBN 0-12-591250-1). Acad Pr.

Shape & Colors, No. 1. (Shapes & Colors Ser.). 1980. 1.95 (ISBN 0-8431-0165-2). Price Stern.

Shapes & Colors, No. 3. (Shapes & Colors Ser.). 1980. 1.95 (ISBN 0-8431-0167-9). Price Stern.

Shapes & Colors, No. 4. (Shapes & Colors Ser.). 1980. 1.95 (ISBN 0-8431-0168-7). Price Stern.

Shapp, Martha & Shapp, Charles. Let's Find Out About What's Big & What's Small. LC 74-2992. (Let's Find Out Bks). (Illus.). 48p. (gr. k-3). 1975. PLB 6.45 (ISBN 0-531-00106-7). Watts.

--Let's Find Out About What's Light & What's Heavy. LC 74-2991. (Let's Find Out Bks). (Illus.). 48p. (gr. k-3). 1975. PLB 6.45 (ISBN 0-531-00107-5). Watts.

FORM PSYCHOLOGY

see Gestalt Psychology

FORMA PAUPERIS

see In Forma Pauperis

FORMAL GARDENS

see Gardens

FORMAL LANGUAGES

see also L Systems

Aguilar, R. Formal Languages & Programming. 1976. 19.50 (ISBN 0-444-11084-4, North-Holland). Elsevier.

Aho, Alfred V., ed. Currents in the Theory of Computing. (Illus.). 256p. 1973. ref. ed. 17.95 (ISBN 0-13-195651-5). P-H.

Arbib, M. A., et al. A Basis for Theoretical Computer Science. (Computer Science Texts & Monographs). (Illus.). 224p. 1981. 17.50 (ISBN 0-387-90573-1). Springer-Verlag.

Bobrow, Leonard S. & Arbib, Michael A. Discrete Mathematics: Applied Algebra for Computer & Information Science. LC 73-77936. (Illus.). 1974. 24.50 (ISBN 0-7216-1768-9). Hemisphere Pub.

Book, Ronald V., ed. Formal Language Theory: Perspectives & Open Problems. 1980. 25.00 (ISBN 0-12-115350-9). Acad Pr.

Cleaveland, J. Craig & Uzgalis, Robert C. Grammars for Programming Languages. LC 76-25909. (Programming Language Ser.: Vol. 4). (Illus.). 1977. 18.95 (ISBN 0-444-00187-5, North Holland); pap. 10.95 (ISBN 0-444-00199-9). Elsevier.

Colloquium on Automata, Languages & Programming, 2nd, University of Saarbrucken, 1974. Proceedings. Loeckx, J., ed. (Lecture Notes in Computer Science Ser.: Vol. 14). viii, 611p. 1974. pap. 26.20 (ISBN 0-387-06841-4). Springer-Verlag.

Engelfriet, J. Simple Program Schemes & Formal Languages. (Lecture Notes in Computer Science Ser.: Vol. 20). vii, 254p. 1974. pap. 14.90 (ISBN 0-387-06953-4). Springer-Verlag.

Foster, J. M. Automatic Syntactic Analysis. (Computer Monograph Ser). 1970. 17.95 (ISBN 0-444-19725-7). Elsevier.

Gruska, J., ed. Mathematical Foundations of Computer Science 1977: Proceedings, 6th Symposium, Tatranska Lmnica, Sept. 5-9, 1977. LC 77-10135. (Lecture Notes in Computer Science: Vol. 53). 1977. pap. 23.40 (ISBN 0-387-08353-7). Springer-Verlag.

Guessarian, Irene. Algebraic Semantics. (Lecture Notes in Computer Science Ser.: Vol. 99). 158p. 1981. pap. 11.80 (ISBN 0-387-10284-1). Springer-Verlag.

Hartmanis, Juris. Feasible Computations & Provable Complexity Properties. (CBMS-NSF Regional Conference Ser.: Vol. 30). (Orig.). 1978. pap. text ed. 7.75 (ISBN 0-89871-027-8). Soc Indus-Appl Math.

McNaughton, Robert. Elementary Computability, Formal Languages & Automata. (Illus.). 464p. 1982. text ed. 24.95 (ISBN 0-13-253500-9). P-H.

Milner, R. A Calculus of Communicating Systems. (Lecture Notes in Computer Science Ser.: Vol. 92). 260p. 1981. pap. 11.80 (ISBN 0-387-10235-3). Springer-Verlag.

Salomaa, Arto. Formal Languages. (ACM Monograph Ser). 1973. 43.00 (ISBN 0-12-615750-2). Acad Pr.

Second GI Conference, Karlsruhe, May 20-23, 1975. Automata Theory & Formal Languages. Brakhage, H., ed. (Lecture Notes in Computer Science Ser.: Vol. 33). viii, 292p. 1975. pap. 14.70 (ISBN 0-387-07407-4). Springer-Verlag.

Weihrauch, K., ed. Theoretical Computer Science: 4th GI Conference Aachen, March 26 - 28, 1979. (Lecture Notes in Computer Science: Vol. 67). 1979. pap. 16.80 (ISBN 0-387-09118-1). Springer-Verlag.

FORMALDEHYDE

Formaldehyde & Other Aldehydes. 1981. 11.50 (ISBN 0-309-03146-X). Natl Acad Pr.

Meyer, Beat. Urea-Formaldehyde Resins. (Illus.). 1979. text ed. 34.50 (ISBN 0-201-04558-3). A-W.

Walker, J. Frederick. Formaldehyde. 3rd ed. LC 74-14555. 728p. 1975. Repr. of 1964 ed. 36.50 (ISBN 0-88275-218-9). Krieger.

FORMALIN

see Formaldehyde

FORMALISM (RUSSIAN LITERATURE)

Eagle, Herb. Russian Formalist Film Theory. (Michigan Slavic Materials Ser.: No. 19). 1981. pap. 7.00 (ISBN 0-930042-42-5). Mich Slavic Pubns.

Pike, Christopher, ed. The Futurists, the Formalists & the Marxist Critique. Andrew, Joe & Pike, Christopher, trs. from Rus. 265p. 1979. text ed. 20.00x (ISBN 0-906133-14-9). Humanities.

Thompson, Ewa M. Russian Formalism & Anglo-American New Criticism: A Comparative Study. (De Proprietatibus Litterarum, Ser. Major: No. 8). 160p. 1971. text ed. 27.50x (ISBN 90-2791-845-7). Mouton.

FORMAN FAMILY

Liehm, Antonin J. The Milos Forman Stories. LC 73-92806. 191p. 1975. 20.00 (ISBN 0-87332-051-4). M E Sharpe.

FORMAT OF BOOKS

see Books–Format

FORMER JEOPARDY

see Double Jeopardy

FORMICIDAE

see Ants

FORMOSA

see Taiwan

FORMS (BUSINESS)

see Business–Forms, Blanks, etc.

FORMS (LAW)

Here are entered works on and collections of legal forms in general. Forms relating to special topics or branches of law are entered under the specific heading.

see also Contracts–Forms; Conveyancing; Legal Composition

Baldwin's Ohio Legal Forms: An Encyclopedia of Legal & Business Forms, 6 vols. (Baldwin's Ohio Practice Ser.). 1962. Set. 275.00 (ISBN 0-8322-0003-4). Banks-Baldwin.

Bates, James D. Minnesota Legal Forms: Probate. Mason Publishing Staff, ed. 184p. 1981. ring binder 19.95 (ISBN 0-917126-98-X). Mason Pub.

Dacey, Norman F. How to Avoid Probate. (Illus.). 1965. pap. 10.95 (ISBN 0-517-06428-6). Crown.

Dann, D. Forms in Your Life. 1977. pap. 2.50 (ISBN 0-671-18771-6). Monarch Pr.

Dawson, Townes L. Mounce's Legal Forms Workbook. 6th ed. 272p. 1979. pap. text ed. write for info. (ISBN 0-697-08207-5). Wm C Brown.

Gilmer, Wesley, ed. Kentucky Legal Forms, 6 vols. 1975. Set. 260.00 (ISBN 0-8322-0016-6). Banks-Baldwin.

Gore, Thomas P., et al. Gore's Forms for Tennessee Annotated, 4 vols. 3rd ed. 1970. 80.00 (ISBN 0-87215-088-7). Michie-Bobbs.

Gouldman, W. Clyde & Hess, Amy M. Virginia Forms. 1978. 60.00 (ISBN 0-87215-205-7). Michie-Bobbs.

Grimes, John S. Thompson on Real Property, 24 vols. Set. 350.00 (ISBN 0-672-83972-5, Bobbs-Merrill Law); 1981 cum. suppl. 100.00 (ISBN 0-672-84139-8). Michie-Bobbs.

Hyman, Marvin. Basic Legal Forms: With Commentary. LC 80-53751. 1981. 47.50 (ISBN 0-88262-536-5). Warren.

Jones, Leonard A. Jones Legal Forms, 3 Vols. 10th ed. 1962. Set. 75.00 (ISBN 0-672-81252-5, Bobbs-Merrill Law). Michie-Bobbs.

Kass, Louis A. Enforcement of Money Judgments. 1964. pap. 3.50x (ISBN 0-87526-031-4). Gould.

Louisiana Formulary, Annotated, 2 Vols. 3rd ed. 1970. pap. 35.00 (ISBN 0-672-81516-8, Bobbs-Merrill Law). Michie-Bobbs.

McNutt, Robert D. West's Book of Legal Forms. 162p. 1981. pap. text ed. 5.95 (ISBN 0-8299-0516-2). West Pub.

Mattox, Rick E. Minnesota Legal Forms-Criminal Law. 237p. 1981. ring binder 25.00 (ISBN 0-917126-84-X). Mason Pub.

Miller, John M. Minnesota Legal Forms-Commercial Real Estate. Mason Publishing Staff, ed. 268p. 1981. ring binder 19.95 (ISBN 0-917126-89-0). Mason Pub.

Miller, Thomas F. Minnesota Legal Forms-Creditors' Remedies. Mason Editorial Staff, ed. 150p. 1981. 3-ring binder 19.95 (ISBN 0-917126-95-5). Mason Pub.

Minahan, John C. & Wagner, Michael P. Nebraska Legal Forms: Bankruptcy, 1981-82. 175p. 1981. looseleaf bdg. 19.95 (ISBN 0-86678-029-7). Mason Pub.

Montrose, J. L. Precedent in English Law & Other Essays. 374p. 1968. 25.00x (ISBN 0-7165-0503-7, Pub. by Irish Academic Pr Ireland). Biblio Dist.

Nebraska Legal Forms, 1981-82, 10 vols. 175p. 1981. 195.00 (ISBN 0-86678-021-1). Mason Pub.

Newell, Robert L. Minnesota Legal Forms: Law Office Systems. Mason Publishing Staff, ed. 221p. 1981. 24.00 (ISBN 0-917126-99-8). Mason Pub.

Parella, Robert E. & Miller, Joel E. Modern Trust Forms & Checklists with Commentary, 2 vols. LC 79-56181. 1980. Repr. Set. 96.00 (ISBN 0-88262-275-7). Vol. 1: Modern Trust Forms(1970) Vol. 2: Modern Trust Checklists(1975) Warren.

Phayre, Thomas. A Newe Boke of Presidentes in Maner of a Register. LC 73-6100. (English Experience Ser.: No. 569). 1973. Repr. of 1543 ed. 21.00 (ISBN 90-221-0569-5). Walter J Johnson.

Smith, Robert S. Lawyer's Model Letter Book. 1978. 34.95 (ISBN 0-13-526897-4, Busn). P-H.

Stoneking, Gary E. Minnesota Legal Forms-Personal Injury. Mason Publishing Staff, ed. 148p. 1981. ring binder 19.95 (ISBN 0-917126-93-9). Mason Pub.

Wagner, Michael P. Minnesota Legal Forms: Bankruptcy. Mason Publishing Staff, ed. 353p. 1981. ring binder 25.00 (ISBN 0-917126-92-0). Mason Pub.

FORMS (MATHEMATICS)

see also Automorphic Forms; Partitions (Mathematics)

Clebsch, Rudolph F., tr. Vorlesungen Ueber Geometrie Mit Besonderer Benutzung der Vortrage Von Clebsch, 2 Vols. in 3 Pts. (Bibliotheca Mathematica Teubneriana Ser. 43-44). (Ger). 1969. Repr. Set. 107.00 (ISBN 0-384-09295-0). Johnson Repr.

Dreben, Burton & Goldfarb, Warren D. Decision Problem: Solvable Classes of Quantificational Formulas. LC 79-18456. (Illus.). 1980. text ed. 27.50 (ISBN 0-201-02540-X); pap. text ed. write for info (ISBN 0-201-02539-6). A-W.

Elliott, Edwin B. Algebra of Quantics. 2nd ed. LC 63-11320. 11.95 (ISBN 0-8284-0184-5). Chelsea Pub.

Greenberg, Marvin J. Lectures on Forms in Many Variables. (Math Lecture Notes Ser.: No. 31). 1969. pap. 8.50 (ISBN 0-8053-3553-6, Adv Bk Prog). Benjamin-Cummings.

Gunning, Robert C. Lectures on Modular Forms. (Annals of Mathematics Studies: No. 48). (Orig.). pap. 8.50x (ISBN 0-691-07995-1). Princeton U Pr.

Hellinger, Ernst & Toeplitz, Otto. Integralgleichungen. LC 54-2866. (Ger). 14.95 (ISBN 0-8284-0089-X). Chelsea Pub.

Slebodzinski, Wladyslaw. Exterior Forms & Their Applications. (Eng.). 1971. 15.75 (ISBN 0-02-852380-6). Hafner.

Weil, A. Dirichlet Series & Automorphic Forms. LC 72-151320. (Lecture Notes in Mathematics: Vol. 189). 1971. pap. 11.80 (ISBN 0-387-05382-4). Springer-Verlag.

FORMS, AUTOMORPHIC

see Automorphic Forms

FORMS, BINARY

see also Forms, Quadratic

Linnik, Ju. V. Dispersion Method in Binary Additive Problems. LC 63-15660. (Translations of Mathematical Monographs: Vol. 4). 1979. Repr. of 1963 ed. 34.00 (ISBN 0-8218-1554-7, MMONO-4). Am Math.

Salmon, George. Modern Higher Algebra. 5th ed. LC 64-13786. 9.95 (ISBN 0-8284-0150-0). Chelsea Pub.

FORMS, DIFFERENTIAL

see Differential Forms

FORMS, QUADRATIC

see also Diophantine Analysis

Baeza, R. Quadratic Forms Over Semilocal Rings. (Lecture Notes in Mathematics Ser.: Vol. 655). 1978. pap. 12.80 (ISBN 0-387-08845-8). Springer-Verlag.
Cassels, J. W. Rational Quadratic Forms. (London Mathematical Society Monograph). 1979. 63.50 (ISBN 0-12-163260-1). Acad Pr.
Dickson, Leonard E. Studies in the Theory of Numbers. LC 61-13494. 9.95 (ISBN 0-8284-0151-9). Chelsea Pub.
Jones, Burton W. The Arithmetic Theory of Quadratic Forms. (Carus Monograph: No. 10). 212p. 1950. 12.50 (ISBN 0-88385-010-9). Math Assn.
Lam, T. Y. The Algebraic Theory of Quadratic Forms. LC 72-11103. (Math Lecture Notes Ser.: No. 54). 350p. 1973. text ed. 15.00 (ISBN 0-8053-5664-9, Adv Bk Prog); pap. text ed. 12.50 (ISBN 0-8053-5665-7, Adv Bk Prog). Benjamin-Cummings.
Milnor, J. & Husemoller, D. Symmetric Bilinear Forms. LC 72-90190. (Ergebuisse der Mathematik und Ihrer Greuzgebiete: Vol. 73). (Illus.). 147p. 1973. 25.00 (ISBN 0-387-06009-X). Springer-Verlag.
O'Meara, O. T. Introduction to Quadratic Forms. 3rd ed. LC 73-10503. (Grundlehren der Mathematischen Wissenschaften: Vol. 117). (Illus.). xi, 342p. 1973. 40.20 (ISBN 0-387-02984-2). Springer-Verlag.
Simon, Barry. Quantum Mechanics for Hamiltonians Defined As Quadratic Forms. LC 73-146648. (Princeton Ser. in Physics). 1971. 16.00 (ISBN 0-691-08090-9). Princeton U Pr.

FORMS OF ADDRESS

Dinneen, L. Titles of Addresses in Christian Greek Epistolography. 114p. 1980. 15.00 (ISBN 0-89005-376-6). Ares.
Measures, Howard. Styles of Address: A Manual of Usage in Writing & in Speech. 3rd ed. LC 72-85142. (Griffin Ser). 150p. 1970. pap. 4.95 (ISBN 0-312-77385-4, S70905). St Martin.
Montaigne-Smith, Patrick, ed. Debrett's Peerage & Baronetage. LC 42-17925. 2336p. 1980. 112.50x (ISBN 0-905649-20-6). Intl Pubns Serv.

FORMULA TRANSLATION (COMPUTER PROGRAM LANGUAGE)

see FORTRAN (Computer Program Language)

FORMULARIES

see Medicine-Formulae, Receipts, Prescriptions

FORMULAS (MATHEMATICS)

see Mathematics-Formulae

FORNCETT MANOR, ENGLAND

Davenport, Frances G. Economic Development of a Norfolk Manor, 1085-1585. LC 67-16349. (Illus.). Repr. of 1906 ed. 19.50x (ISBN 0-678-05041-4). Kelley.

FORNER, JUAN PABLO

Laughrin, Sr. M. Fidelia. Juan Pablo Forner As a Critic. LC 79-94173. (Catholic University of America. Studies in Romance Languages & Literatures: No. 26). Repr. of 1943 ed. 19.00 (ISBN 0-404-50326-8). AMS Pr.
Smith, Gilbert. Juan Pablo Forner. LC 75-33832. (World Authors Ser.,: Spain: No. 377). 1976. lib. bdg. 12.50 (ISBN 0-8057-6170-5). Twayne.

FORNOVO, BATTLE OF, 1495

Benedetti, Alessandro. Diary of the Caroline War. Schullian, Dorothy M., tr. LC 66-21028. (Renaissance Text Ser.: Vol. 1). Orig. Title: Diaria De Bello Carolina. 15.00 (ISBN 0-8044-1105-0). Ungar.

FORREST, EDWIN, 1806-1872

Alger, William R. Life of Edwin Forest, 2 vols. LC 76-84505. 1877. Set. 28.50 (ISBN 0-405-08198-7, Pub. by Blom); 14.50 ea. Vol. 1 (ISBN 0-405-08199-5). Vol. 2 (ISBN 0-405-08200-2). Arno.
Barrett, Lawrence. Edwin Forrest. LC 71-91894. 1881. 12.00 (ISBN 0-405-08238-X, Pub. by Blom). Arno.
--Edwin Forrest. 1881. 10.00 (ISBN 0-403-00242-7). Scholarly.
Moses, Montrose J. Fabulous Forrest. LC 72-91909. (Illus.). Repr. of 1929 ed. 16.00 (ISBN 0-405-08801-9, Pub. by Blom). Arno.
Rees, James. The Life of Edwin Forrest. LC 77-92447. 1978. Repr. of 1874 ed. lib. bdg. 40.00 (ISBN 0-89341-376-3). Longwood Pr.

FORREST, JOHN, SIR, 1847-1918

Crowley, F. K. Forrest, Eighteen Forty-Seven to Nineteen Eighteen, Vol. 1: Apprenticeship to Premiership, 1847-1891. (Illus.). 1971. 25.00x (ISBN 0-7022-0698-9). U of Queensland Pr.

FORREST, NATHAN BEDFORD, 1821-1877

Henry, Robert S. First with the Most Forrest. LC 73-10875. (Illus.). 558p. 1974. Repr. of 1944 ed. lib. bdg. 27.50x (ISBN 0-8371-7044-3, HEFM). Greenwood.
Mathes, J. Harvey. General Forrest. (Great Commanders Ser.). (Illus.). 395p. 1976. Repr. of 1902 ed. 22.50 (ISBN 0-937130-05-2). Burke's Bk Store.

FORSTER, EDWARD MORGAN, 1879-1970

Borrello, Alfred. E. M. Forster: An Annotated Bibliography of Secondary Materials. LC 73-7990. (Author Bibliographies Ser.: No. 11). 1973. 10.00 (ISBN 0-8108-0668-1). Scarecrow.
--An E. M. Forster Glossary. LC 74-188548. 1972. 12.00 (ISBN 0-8108-0475-1). Scarecrow.
Brander, Laurence, ed. E. M. Forster: A Critical Study. 1979. 16.95x (ISBN 0-8464-0080-4); pap. 9.95 (ISBN 0-8464-0081-2). Beekman Pubs.
Brown, E. K. Rhythm in the Novel. LC 77-14165. 1978. 9.95x (ISBN 0-8032-1150-3); pap. 3.25x (ISBN 0-8032-6050-4, BB 667, Bison). U of Nebr Pr.
Cavaliero, Glen. A Reading of E. M. Forster. 187p. 1979. 21.50x (ISBN 0-8476-6191-1). Rowman.
Cecil, David. Poets & Story-Tellers. 201p. 1980. Repr. of 1968 ed. lib. bdg. 30.00 (ISBN 0-8495-0852-5). Arden Lib.
Colmer, J. Forster: A Passage to India. (Studies in English Literature Ser.). 1967. pap. text ed. 3.95x (ISBN 0-7131-5111-0). Dynamic Learn Corp.
Colmer, John. E. M. Forster: The Personal Voice. 256p. 1975. 19.50x (ISBN 0-7100-8209-6). Routledge & Kegan.
Das, G. K. E. M. Forster's India. LC 77-2901. 170p. 1978. 16.50x (ISBN 0-87471-977-1). Rowman.
Das, G. K. & Beer, John, eds. E. M. Forster: A Human Exploration; Centenary Essays. LC 79-84339. 1979. 27.50x (ISBN 0-8147-1768-3). NYU Pr.
Devlin, Laura K. Looking Inward: Studies in James Joyce, E.M. Forster, & the Twentieth Century Novel. 1980. lib. bdg. 59.95 (ISBN 0-87700-269-X). Revisionist Pr.
Finkelstein, Bonnie B. Forster's Women: Eternal Differences. LC 74-18418. 183p. 1975. 12.50x (ISBN 0-231-03893-3). Columbia U Pr.
Forster, E. M. Commonplace Book. facsimile, limited ed. (Illus.). 300p. 1979. ltd. ed., slipcase 300.00x (ISBN 0-85967-492-4, Pub. by Scolar Pr England). Biblio Dist.
--E. M. Forster's Letters to Donald Windham. 1975. wrappers, ltd. ed. 35.00x (ISBN 0-917366-04-2). S Campbell.
--Only Connect Letters to Indian Friends. 127p. 1979. text ed. 8.00x (ISBN 0-8426-1695-0). Verry.
Furbank, P. N. E. M. Forster: A Life. LC 78-53882. (Illus.). 1978. 19.95 (ISBN 0-15-128759-7). HarBraceJ.
Gardner, Philip, ed. E. M. Forster: The Critical Heritage. (The Critical Heritage Ser). 518p. 1973. 38.50x (ISBN 0-7100-7641-X). Routledge & Kegan.
Gilbert, Sandra. Monarch Notes on Forster's Passage to India & Howards End. (Orig.). pap. 1.95 (ISBN 0-671-00712-2). Monarch Pr.
Kelvin, Norman. E. M. Forster. LC 67-10282. (Crosscurrents-Modern Critiques Ser.). 208p. 1967. 7.95 (ISBN 0-8093-0265-9). S Ill U Pr.
Levine, June P. Creation & Criticism: A Passage to India. LC 78-134772. 1971. 14.50x (ISBN 0-8032-0758-1). U of Nebr Pr.
Lewis, Robin J. E. M. Forster's Passages to India. LC 79-843. 168p. 1979. 17.50x (ISBN 0-231-04508-5). Columbia U Pr.
Macaulay, Dame Rose. The Writings of E. M. Forster. LC 73-12868. 1974. Repr. of 1938 ed. lib. bdg. 20.00 (ISBN 0-8414-6014-0). Folcroft.
McConkey, James. Novels of E. M. Forster. LC 74-143882. 1971. Repr. of 1957 ed. 15.00 (ISBN 0-208-00464-5, Archon). Shoe String.
McDowell, Frederick P., compiled by. E. M. Forster: An Annotated Bibliography of Writings About Him. LC 73-18797. (Annotated Secondary Bibliography Series on English Literature in Transition 1880-1920). 672p. 1976. 30.00 (ISBN 0-87580-046-7). N Ill U Pr.
The Manuscripts of a Passage to India. LC 78-26698. (The Abinger Edition of E. M. Forster Ser.). 1979. text ed. 97.50x (ISBN 0-8419-0470-7). Holmes & Meier.
Martin, J. S. E. M. Forster, the Endless Journey. LC 76-4755. (British Authors Ser). 1976. 26.50 (ISBN 0-521-21272-3); pap. 7.95x (ISBN 0-521-29082-1). Cambridge U Pr.
Martin, Richard. The Love That Failed: Ideal & Reality in the Writings of E. M. Forster. (Studies in English Literature: No. 84). 1974. text ed. 24.00x (ISBN 90-2792-679-4). Mouton.
Ostrander, Norma. Passage to India Notes. (Orig.). pap. 1.95 (ISBN 0-8220-0985-4). Cliffs.
Pinchin, Jane L. Alexandria Still: Forster, Durrell & Carafy. LC 76-3014. 1976. 18.50 (ISBN 0-691-06283-8). Princeton U Pr.
Rose, Martial. E. M. Forster. (Literary Critiques Ser). (Illus.). 1970. lib. bdg. 4.95 (ISBN 0-668-02356-2). Arco.
Sahni, Chaman L. E. M. Forster: The Religious Dimension. 160p. 1981. text ed. write for info. (ISBN 0-391-02201-6). Humanities.
Shahana, V. A., ed. Focus on Forster's "A Passage to India". Indian Essays in Criticism. 137p. 1975. text ed. 8.50x (ISBN 0-391-01071-9). Humanities.
Shahane, V. A. E. M. Forster: A Study in Double Vision. 130p. (Orig.). 1980. pap. 4.95 (ISBN 0-89684-086-7, Pub. by Arnold Heinemann India). Orient Bk Dist.
Shahane, V. R., ed. Focus on Forster's "A Passage to India". Indian Essays in Criticism. LC 76-900437. 1976. 9.50x (ISBN 0-88386-748-6). South Asia Bks.
Shahane, Vasant A. Approaches to E. M. Forester. 1981. 10.25 (ISBN 0-391-02200-8). Humanities.
Shusterman, David. Quest for Certitude in E. M. Forster's Fiction. LC 72-6784. (Studies in Fiction, No. 34). 1972. Repr. of 1965 ed. lib. bdg. 33.95 (ISBN 0-8383-1662-X). Haskell.
Stone, Wilfred. The Cave & the Mountain: A Study of E. M. Forster. (Illus.). 1966. 18.95x (ISBN 0-8047-0263-2). Stanford U Pr.
Trilling, Lionel. E. M. Forster. LC 79-3367. 160p. 1980. 12.95 (ISBN 0-15-128759-7). HarBraceJ.
--E. M. Forster. rev. ed. LC 64-23845. 1964. pap. 5.95 (ISBN 0-8112-0210-0, NDP189). New Directions.
Widdowson, Peter. E. M. Forster's Howards End: Fiction As History. (Text & Context Ser.). 1977. pap. text ed. 8.75x (ISBN 0-85621-068-4); pap. text ed. 4.50x (ISBN 0-85621-067-6). Humanities.

FORSTER, GEORG, 1754-1794

Saine, Thomas P. Georg Forster. (World Authors Ser.: Germany: No. 215). lib. bdg. 10.95 (ISBN 0-8057-2316-1). Twayne.

FORSTER, MAX, b. 1869

Schoffler, Herbert. Bibliographie der Wissenschaftlichen Veroffentlichungen Max Forsters. Repr. of 1939 ed. pap. 7.00 (ISBN 0-384-54230-1). Johnson Repr.

FORSYTH, PETER TAYLOR, 1848-1921

Hunter, Archibald M. P. T. Forsyth: Per Crucem Ad Lucem. 1974. pap. text ed. 3.95x (ISBN 0-8401-1146-0). Allenson-Breckinridge.
Miller, Donald G., et al. P. T. Forsyth: The Man, the Preachers' Theologian & Prophet for the Twentieth Century. (Pittsburgh Theological Monograph Ser.: No. 36). 1981. pap. write for info. (ISBN 0-915138-48-4). Pickwick.
Rodgers, John H. Theology of P. T. Forsyth. 1965. 12.50x (ISBN 0-8401-2040-0). Allenson-Breckinridge.

FORT APACHE INDIAN RESERVATION

Basso, K. H. The Cibecue Apache. LC 70-100384. (Case Studies in Cultural Anthropology). 1970. pap. text ed. 5.95 (ISBN 0-03-083171-7, HoltC). HR&W.

FORT BENTON, MONTANA

Bell, W. S. Old Fort Benton. facs. ed. 32p. Repr. of 1909 ed. pap. 3.50 (ISBN 0-8466-0084-6, SJS84). Shorey.

FORT BLISS, TEXAS

Metz, Leon C. & McKinney, Millard G. Fort Bliss, An Illustrated History. Mangan, Frank, ed. (Illus.). 1981. 30.00 (ISBN 0-930208-10-2). Mangan Bks.

FORT CASPAR, WYOMING

see Caspar, Fort, Wyoming

FORT COLLINS, COLORADO

Swanson, Evadene B. Fort Collins Yesterdays. LC 74-83114. (Illus.). 254p. 1975. 10.00 (ISBN 0-9600862-1-8); pap. 7.50 (ISBN 0-9600862-2-6). E Swanson.

FORT DALLES

see Dalles, Fort

FORT DUQUESNE, PENNSYLVANIA

Darlington, Mary C., ed. Fort Pitt & Letters from the Frontier. LC 72-106087. (First American Frontier Ser). (Illus.). 1971. Repr. of 1892 ed. 16.00 (ISBN 0-405-02842-3). Arno.

FORT FAMILY

Montgomery, Robert & Barnwell, John. Most Delightful Golden Islands. LC 77-76733. 1969. Repr. of 1717 ed. cloth over bds 5.00 (ISBN 0-87797-007-6). Cherokee.

FORT HARE, SOUTH AFRICA-UNIVERSITY COLLEGE

Kerr, Alexander. Fort Hare Nineteen Fifteen to Nineteen Forty-Eight: The Evolution of an African College. LC 68-22137. (Illus.). 1968. text ed. 8.50x (ISBN 0-903983-04-4). Humanities.

FORT LEAVENWORTH

see Leavenworth, Fort

FORT MCKAVETT, TEXAS

Bierschwale, Margaret. Fort McKavett, Texas. (Illus.). 1966. 15.00 (ISBN 0-685-05001-7). A Jones.

FORT PITT, PENNSYLVANIA

Darlington, Mary C., ed. Fort Pitt & Letters from the Frontier. LC 72-106087. (First American Frontier Ser). (Illus.). 1971. Repr. of 1892 ed. 16.00 (ISBN 0-405-02842-3). Arno.

FORT SILL, OKLAHOMA

Nye, Wilbur S. Carbine & Lance: The Story of Old Fort Sill. rev. centennial ed. 1937. 14.95 (ISBN 0-8061-0856-8). U of Okla Pr.

FORT SMITH, ARKANSAS-HISTORY

Bearss, Edwin C. & Gibson, A. M. Fort Smith: Little Gibralter on the Arkansas. 1979. pap. 8.95 (ISBN 0-8061-1232-8). U of Okla Pr.

FORT SNELLING, MINNESOTA

Ziebarth, Marilyn F. & Ominsky, Alan. Fort Snelling: Anchor Post of the Northwest. LC 70-121443. (Minnesota Historic Sites Pamphlet Ser.: No. 4). (Illus.). 36p. 1979. Repr. of 1970 ed. pap. 2.50 (ISBN 0-87351-061-5). Minn Hist.

FORT SUMTER

see Sumter, Fort

FORT UNION, NEW MEXICO

Harper, Frank B. Fort Union & Its Neighbors on the Upper Missouri. (Illus.). 36p. Repr. pap. 5.00 (ISBN 0-8466-0216-4, SJS216). Shorey.

FORT WARREN

see Warren, Fort

FORT WORTH, TEXAS

Amon Carter Museum. Amon Carter Museum: Nineteen Sixty-One to Nineteen Seventy-Seven. LC 77-81806. (Illus.). 47p. 1977. pap. 3.50 (ISBN 0-88360-028-5). Amon Carter.
Pirtle, Caleb. Fort Worth: The Civilized West. Blakey, Ellen S. & Silvey, Larry P., eds. LC 80-66338. (The American Portrait Ser.). (Illus.). 240p. 1980. 24.95 (ISBN 0-932986-11-0). Continent Herit.
Sanders, Leonard. How Fort Worth Became the Texasmost City. LC 73-87509. (Illus.). 224p. 1973. 17.50 (ISBN 0-88360-002-1). Amon Carter.
Williams, Mack H. In Old Fort Worth. (Illus.). 126p. 1977. 14.95 (ISBN 0-939348-00-4). News-Tribune.

FORT WORTH AND DENVER CITY RAILWAY COMPANY

Overton, Richard C. Gulf to Rockies. LC 76-100234. Repr. of 1953 ed. lib. bdg. 17.75x (ISBN 0-8371-3035-2, OVGR). Greenwood.
--Gulf to Rockies: The Heritage of the Fort Worth & Denver-Colorado & Southern Railways, 1861-1898. LC 53-10833. (Illus.). 424p. 1953. pap. text ed. 14.95x (ISBN 0-292-72712-7). U of Tex Pr.

FORTIFICATION

see also Castles; Earthwork; Intrenchments; Military Architecture; Mounds; also subdivision Defenses under countries, e.g. Great Britain-Defenses; also names of specific forts, e.g. Fort Ticonderoga

Agnew, Brad. Fort Gibson: Terminal on the Trail of Tears. LC 78-21391. (Illus.). 1980. 15.95 (ISBN 0-8061-1521-1). U of Okla Pr.
De La Croix, Horst. Military Considerations in City Planning: Fortifications. LC 72-143398. (Planning & Cities Ser). (Illus.). 1971. 7.95 (ISBN 0-8076-0585-9); pap. 3.95 (ISBN 0-8076-0584-0). Braziller.
Forde-Johnston, J. Hillforts of the Iron Age in England & Wales: A Survey of the Surface Evidence. (Illus.). 331p. 1976. 55.00x (ISBN 0-87471-802-3). Rowman.
Haas, Irvin. Citadels, Ramparts, & Stockades: America's Historic Forts. LC 78-74583. (Illus.). 1979. 11.95 (ISBN 0-89696-038-2). Everest Hse.
Hale, J. R. Renaissance Fortificaton: Art or Engineering? (Illus.). 1978. 9.95 (ISBN 0-500-55009-3). Thames Hudson.
Harding, D., ed. Hillforts: Later Prehistoric Earthworks in Britain & Ireland. 1976. 94.50 (ISBN 0-12-324750-0). Acad Pr.
Harris, W. Stuart. Dead Towns of Alabama. LC 76-29655. (Illus.). 176p. 1977. 9.95 (ISBN 0-8173-5232-5). U of Ala Pr.
Hart, Herbert M. Tour Guide to Old Forts of New Mexico, Arizona, Nevada, Utah, Colorado, Vol. 2. (Illus.). 65p. (Orig.). 1981. pap. 3.95 (ISBN 0-87108-581-X). Pruett.
--Tour Guide to Old Forts of Oregon, Idaho, Washington, California, Vol. 3. (Illus.). 65p. (Orig.). 1981. pap. 3.95 (ISBN 0-87108-582-8). Pruett.
--Tour Guide to Old Forts of Texas, Kansas, Nebraska, Oklahoma, Vol. 4. (Illus.). 65p. (Orig.). 1981. pap. 3.95 (ISBN 0-87108-583-6). Pruett.
--Tourguide to Old Forts of Montana, Wyoming North & South Dakota, Vol. 4. (Illus.). 150p. 1980. pap. 3.95 (ISBN 0-87108-570-4). Pruett.
Ive, Paul. The Practise of Fortification. LC 68-54649. (English Experience Ser.: No. 29). 40p. 1968. Repr. of 1589 ed. 9.50 (ISBN 90-221-0029-4). Walter J Johnson.
Ivers, Larry E. Colonial Forts of South Carolina, 1670-1775. LC 71-113805. (Tricentennial Booklet: No. 3). (Illus., Orig.). 1970. pap. 2.25 (ISBN 0-87249-135-8). U of SC Pr.
Jones, Michael J. Roman Port-Defenses to A.D. One Hundred Seventeen. 1975. 15.00x (ISBN 0-904531-24-4, Pub. by BAR). State Mutual Bk.
Lamb, R. G. Iron Age Promontory Forts in the Northern Isles. 114p. 1980. 24.00x (ISBN 0-86054-087-1, Pub. by BAR). State Mutual Bk.
Lawrence, Arnold W. Greek Aims in Fortification. (Illus.). 552p. 1979. 98.00x (ISBN 0-19-814824-0). Oxford U Pr.
Mahan, Dennis H. Complete Treatise on Field Fortification. Repr. of 1836 ed. lib. bdg. 21.75 (ISBN 0-8371-0557-9, MAFF). Greenwood.

Norwood, Richard. Fortification, or Architecture Military. LC 72-6019. (English Experience Ser.: No. 545). 1973. Repr. of 1628 ed. 15.00 (ISBN 90-221-0545-8). Walter J Johnson.

O'Neil, Bryan H. Castles & Cannon. LC 74-30843. (Illus.). 121p. 1975. Repr. of 1960 ed. lib. bdg. 15.00 (ISBN 0-8371-7933-5, ONCC). Greenwood.

Osborne, Milton E. Strategic Hamlets in South Viet-Nam: A Survey & a Comparison. 1965. pap. 2.50 (ISBN 0-87727-055-4, DP 55). Cornell SE Asia.

Peterson, Harold L. Forts in America. LC 64-17210. (Illus.). (gr. 3-7). 1964. reinforced bdg. 5.95 (ISBN 0-684-12890-X, ScribJ). Scribner.

Scorpan, C. Limes Scythiae: Topographical & Stratigraphical Research on the Late Roman Fortifications on the Lower Danube. 238p. 45.00x (ISBN 0-86054-102-9, Pub. by BAR). State Mutual Bk.

Thrapp, Dan L., ed. Dateline Fort Bowie: Charles Fletcher Lummis Reports on an Apache War. LC 78-58091. (Illus.). 1979. 10.95 (ISBN 0-8061-1494-0). U of Okla Pr.

Venkatarama, Ayyar. Records of Fort St. George. Repr. of 1928 ed. pap. 5.00 (ISBN 0-8466-0137-0, SJS137). Shorey.

FORTRAN (COMPUTER PROGRAM LANGUAGE)

see also GASP (Computer Program Language); SIMSCRIPT (Computer Program Language)

Ageloff, Roy & Mojena, Richard. Applied Fortran Seventy-Seven Featuring Structured Programming. 624p. 1981. pap. text ed. 15.95x (ISBN 0-534-00961-1), Wadsworth Pub.

--Fundamentals of Fortran for Management. 1979. text ed. 16.95x (ISBN 0-534-00710-4). Wadsworth Pub.

Alexander, Daniel E. & Messer, Andrew C. FORTRAN Four Pocket Handbook. 96p. (Orig.). 1972. pap. 3.95 (ISBN 0-07-001015-3, SP). McGraw.

Anderson, Decima M. Computer Programming: Fortran Four. (Illus., Orig.). 1966. pap. 14.50 (ISBN 0-13-164822-5). P-H.

Balfour, A. & Marwick, D. H. Programming in Standard Fortran 77. LC 79-7450. 1979. 16.95 (ISBN 0-444-19465-7, North Holland). Elsevier.

Basso, David T. & Schwartz, Ronald D. Programming in FORTRAN, WATFOR, WATFIV. (Corporate Science Ser.). 352p. 1980. 12.95 (ISBN 0-87626-638-3). Winthrop.

Bauer, C. R. & Peluso, A. P. Basic FORTRAN IV with WATFOR & WATFIV. 1974. 13.95 (ISBN 0-201-00411-9) (ISBN 0-686-67380-8). A-W.

Beech, Graham. Fortran IV in Chemistry: An Introduction to Computer-Assisted Methods. LC 75-2488. 303p. 1975. 54.00 (ISBN 0-471-06165-4, Pub. by Wiley-Interscience). Wiley.

Bent, Robert J. & Sethares, George C. Fortran. LC 80-28581. 448p. (Orig.). 1981. pap. text ed. 16.95 (ISBN 0-8185-0436-6). Brooks-Cole.

Boguslavsky, Boris. Elementary Computer Programming in Fortran IV. 2nd ed. (Illus.). 1980. pap. text ed. 17.95 (ISBN 0-8359-1648-0). Reston.

Boillot, Michael. Understanding Fortran. (Illus.). 1978. pap. text ed. 12.50 (ISBN 0-8299-0205-8). West Pub.

Boillot, Michel. Understanding FORTRAN. 2nd ed. (Illus.). 520p. 1981. pap. text ed. 15.50 (ISBN 0-8299-0355-0). West Pub.

Boyle, Thomas A. Enough Fortran. 2nd ed. 1976. pap. text ed. 3.75 (ISBN 0-918876-01-X). Tech Direct.

Breuer, Hans. Dictionary for Computer Languages. (Automatic Programming Information Centre Studies in Data Processing: Vol. 6). 1966. 62.00 (ISBN 0-12-132950-X). Acad Pr.

Brown, Gary D. Fortran to PL-One Dictionary, PL-One to Fortran Dictionary. LC 74-30147. 288p. 1975. 19.50 (ISBN 0-471-10796-4, Pub. by Wiley-Interscience). Wiley.

Burkhard, R. E. & Derigs, U. Assignment & Matching Problems: Solution Methods with FORTRAN-Programs. (Lecture Notes in Economics & Mathematical Systems Ser.: Vol. 184). 148p. 1981. pap. 15.00 (ISBN 0-387-10267-1). Springer-Verlag.

Calderbank, V. J. Course in Programming in FORTRAN IV. 1969. pap. 6.95x (ISBN 0-412-20640-4, Pub. by Chapman & Hall). Methuen Inc.

Carnahan, Brice & Wilkes, James O. Digital Computing & Numerical Methods with Fortran LV Watfor & Watfiv Programming. LC 72-13010. 496p. 1973. text ed. 29.95x (ISBN 0-471-13500-3). Wiley.

Carver, D. K. Introduction to Business Data Processing: With Basic, Fortran & Cobol Programming. 2nd ed. LC 78-19131. 1979. text ed. 22.50 (ISBN 0-471-03091-0). wkbk. 9.95 (ISBN 0-471-03998-5). Wiley.

Chirlian, Paul M. Introduction to Structured FORTRAN. 1979. pap. 13.95 (ISBN 0-916460-07-X, Pub. by Matrix). Intl Schol Bk Serv.

Chopra, M. G. & Kumar, Ram. Fortran IV Programming. 248p. 1980. text ed. 20.00 (ISBN 0-7069-1040-0, Pub. by Vikas India). Advent NY.

A Clear Introduction to Fortran IV. 2nd ed. LC 77-21300. (Illus.). 1979. pap. text ed. 12.95 (ISBN 0-87872-175-4). Duxbury Pr.

Cohen, Doron J. & Brillinger, Peter C. Introduction to Data Structures & Non-Numeric Computation. (Illus.). 656p. 1972. ref. ed. 22.95 (ISBN 0-13-479899-6). P-H.

Cole, J. W. Perry. ANSI FORTRAN IV: A Structured Programming Approach. 450p. 1978. pap. text ed. write for info. (ISBN 0-697-08125-7); instrs.' manual avail. (ISBN 0-686-52439-X). Wm C Brown.

Computer Usage Company Inc. & Weiss, E. A. Computer Usage - Three Sixty Fortran Programming. 1969. pap. text ed. 15.95 (ISBN 0-07-012381-0, C). McGraw.

Conway & Archer. Programming for Poets: A Gentle Intro Using Fortran (WATF IV) 1979. 12.95 (ISBN 0-87626-728-2). Winthrop.

Cooper, Laura G. & Smith, Marilyn Z. Standard Fortran: A Problem-Solving Approach. LC 72-4395. 288p. (Orig.). 1973. pap. text ed. 13.95 (ISBN 0-395-14028-5). HM.

Couger, Daniel & Shannon, Loren E. Plaid for Fortran: A Beginners Approach. 1977. pap. 5.50 (ISBN 0-256-01986-X, 14-0826-02). Learning Syst.

Cress, P., et al. Fortran IV with Watfor & Watfiv. 1970. ref. ed. 15.95x (ISBN 0-13-329433-1). P-H.

--Strucured FORTRAN with Watfiv-S. 1980. pap. 15.95 (ISBN 0-13-854752-1). P-H.

Davis, Gordon B. & Hoffmann, Thomas R. Fortran: A Structured, Disciplined Approach. (Illus.). 1978. text ed. 12.95 (ISBN 0-07-015901-7, C); instructor's manual 7.95 (ISBN 0-07-015902-5). McGraw.

Davis, W. S. Computers & Business Information Processing & FORTRAN: Getting Started. 1981. 16.95 (ISBN 0-201-13298-2). A-W.

--Information Processing Systems & FORTRAN: Getting Started. 1981. 20.95 (ISBN 0-201-13296-6). A-W.

Davis, William S. Fortran-Getting Started. 1980. pap. text ed. 5.95 (ISBN 0-201-03104-3). A-W.

Dawson, John A. & Unwin, David J. Computing for Geographers. LC 75-37400. 1976. 16.95x (ISBN 0-8448-0871-7). Crane-Russak Co.

Day, A. C. Compatible Fortran. LC 77-95444. (Illus.). 1979. 16.95 (ISBN 0-521-22027-0). Cambridge U Pr.

--Fortran Techniques. LC 72-78891. (Illus.). 104p. 1972. 16.95 (ISBN 0-521-08549-7); pap. 6.95x (ISBN 0-521-09719-3). Cambridge U Pr.

Dickson, T. R. The Computer & Chemistry: An Introduction to Programming & Numerical Methods. LC 68-16758. (Illus.). 1968. text ed. 17.95x (ISBN 0-7167-0141-3). W H Freeman.

Didday, Rich & Page, Rex. Fortran for Humans. 2nd ed. 1977. pap. text ed. 13.95 (ISBN 0-8299-0125-6). West Pub.

Didday, Rich L., et al. Fortran for Business People. (Illus.). 1978. pap. text ed. 14.50 (ISBN 0-8299-0101-9). West Pub.

Didday, Richard & Page, Rex. Fortran for Humans. 3rd ed. (Illus.). 450p. 1981. pap. text ed. 14.95 (ISBN 0-8299-0356-9). West Pub.

Dimitry, D. L. & Mott, T. H., Jr. Introduction to Fortran Four Programming. LC 66-16969. 1966. pap. text ed. 12.95 (ISBN 0-03-059490-1, HoltC). HR&W.

Dock, V. Thomas. Structured FORTRAN IV Programing. (Data Processing & Information System Ser.). (Illus.). 1979. pap. text ed. 14.95 (ISBN 0-8299-0249-X). West Pub.

Dorn, William S. & McCracken, Daniel D., eds. Numerical Methods with Fortran IV Case Studies. LC 77-37365. 477p. 1972. 29.95 (ISBN 0-471-21918-5). Wiley.

Duchane, Emma, ed. User's Manual, Advanced Fortran IV Utilities for Data General Computers. (Illus.). viii, 223p. 1980. pap. 20.00 (ISBN 0-938876-03-1). Entropy Ltd.

Dunn, W. L. Introduction to Digital Computer Problems Using Fortran IV. 1969. text ed. 15.95 (ISBN 0-07-018285-X, C). McGraw.

Edwards, Perry & Broadwell, Bruce. Data Processing: Computers in Action with Fortran. 496p. 1980. text ed. 20.95x (ISBN 0-534-00805-4); wkbk. 7.95x (ISBN 0-534-00879-8). Wadsworth Pub.

Evett, Jack & Pinckney, Richard P. Fortran Programming with Applications to Engineering: An Introductory Fortran Manual. LC 80-22695. 208p. 1981. pap. 5.95 (ISBN 0-910554-32-3). Eng Pr.

Farina, Mario V. Fortran IV Self-Taught. 1966. pap. 14.95 (ISBN 0-13-329722-5). P-H.

Fegan, Richard C. & Brosche, Susan L. Fortran Computer Programming for Statistics: A Manual. 1979. pap. 7.95 (ISBN 0-13-329326-2). P-H.

Fletcher, L. S. & Shoup, T. E. Introduction to Engineering Including Fortran Programming. (Illus.). 1978. pap. 14.95 ref. ed. (ISBN 0-13-501858-7). P-H.

Ford, Donald H. Standard Fortran Programming. 3rd ed. (Irwin-Dorsey Ser. in Information Processing). 1978. pap. 12.50x (ISBN 0-256-01998-3). Irwin.

Forsythe, Alexandra I., et al. Computer Science: Programming in FORTRAN IV with WATFOR-WATFIV. LC 74-96044. 1975. pap. 8.95 (ISBN 0-471-26685-X). Wiley.

FORTRAN for IBM System-360. 1968. pap. text ed. 10.95 (ISBN 0-574-16104-X, 15-0600); guide 2.25 (ISBN 0-574-16105-8, 15-0601). SRA.

Friedman, F. L. & Koffman, E. B. Problem Solving & Structured Programming in FORTRAN. 2nd ed. 1981. pap. 15.95 (ISBN 0-201-02461-6); write for info. wkbk. (ISBN 0-201-02465-9). A-W.

Friedmann, J., et al. Fortran IV. 2nd ed. (Wiley Self Teaching Guide Ser.). 544p. 1980. pap. 10.95 (ISBN 0-471-07771-2). Wiley.

Fuller, W. R. Fortran Programming: A Supplement for Calculus Course (Universitext) LC 77-12129. (Illus.). 1977. pap. text ed. 10.70 (ISBN 0-387-90283-X). Springer-Verlag.

Gleason, G. Essentials of Fortran. LC 72-90224. 1973. pap. text ed. 10.95 (ISBN 0-03-091400-0, HoltC). HR&W.

Gonzalez, Richard F. & McMillan, Claude, Jr. Machine Computation: An Algorithmic Approach. (Irwin-Dorsey Information Processing Ser). 1971. text ed. 17.95x (ISBN 0-256-00234-7). Irwin.

Gottfried, Byron S. Fortran IV Programmer's Reference Guide. (QPI Ser.). 1973. pap. 1.95 (ISBN 0-934644-16-0). Quantum Pubs.

--Programming with Fortran IV. (QPI Ser.). 1972. pap. 6.95 (ISBN 0-934644-01-2). Quantum Pubs.

Green, Leroy. Introduction to BASIC & FORTRAN: A Comparative Analysis. LC 77-18446. 1977. pap. 13.50 (ISBN 0-8357-0289-8, SS-00055). Univ Microfilms.

Guernsey, Elwood W. Workbook in Basic Computer Programming (Fortran 4) (Illus.). 192p. 1973. pap. 17.75 (ISBN 0-398-02592-4). C C Thomas.

Hammond, Robert, et al. Introduction to Fortran IV. 2nd ed. (Illus.). 1978. text ed. 9.95 (ISBN 0-07-025897-X, C); solutions manual 4.95 (ISBN 0-07-025898-8). McGraw.

Hare, Van C., Jr. Introduction to Programming: A BASIC Approach. 1970. text ed. 17.95 (ISBN 0-15-543600-7, HC); instructor's manual avail. (ISBN 0-15-543601-5, HC). HarBraceJ.

Haskell, Richard E. FORTRAN Programming Using Structured Flowcharts. LC 77-23931. 320p. 1978. pap. text ed. 12.95 (ISBN 0-574-21135-7, 13-4135). SRA.

--FORTRAN Programming Using Structured Flowcharts. LC 77-23931. 320p. 1978. pap. text ed. 12.95 (ISBN 0-574-21135-7, 13-4135). SRA.

Healy, J. J. & DeBruzzi, D. J. Basic FORTRAN IV Programming. rev. ed. 1975. pap. 13.95 (ISBN 0-201-02827-1). A-W.

Hill, Louis A., Jr. Structured Programming in FORTRAN. (Illus.). 512p. 1981. text ed. 14.95 (ISBN 0-13-854612-6). P-H.

Hirsch, Seymour C. BASIC Programming: Self-Taught. (Illus.). 1980. pap. text ed. 12.95 (ISBN 0-8359-0432-6). Reston.

Holden, Herbert L. Introduction to Fortran Four. (Illus.). 1970. pap. 8.95 (ISBN 0-02-355990-X). Macmillan.

Holt, R. C. & Hume, J. N. Fundamentals of Structured Programming Using FORTRAN with SF-K & WATFIV-S. (Illus.). 1977. pap. text ed. 12.95 (ISBN 0-87909-302-1); case ed. 14.95 (ISBN 0-8359-7131-7). Reston.

Honess, Brian C. Structured Business Problem Solving with Fortran. 300p. 1981. text ed. 15.95 (ISBN 0-205-07332-8); tchrs' ed. free (ISBN 0-205-07328-X). Allyn.

Hughes, Joan. Programming the IBM 1130. LC 69-16045. 1969. 26.95x (ISBN 0-471-42040-9). Wiley.

Hume, J. N. & Holt, R. C. Programming FORTRAN Seventy-Seven. (Illus.). 1979. pap. text ed. 14.95 (ISBN 0-8359-5671-7). Reston.

Jacobs, Zeney P., et al. Communicating with the Computer: Introductory Experiences, Fortran IV. (gr. 9-12). 1973. text ed. 11.40 (ISBN 0-205-03819-0, 2038196); tchrs'. guide 4.40 (ISBN 0-205-03820-4, 203820X). Allyn.

James, M. L., et al. Applied Numerical Methods for Digital Computation with Fortran & CSMP. 2nd ed. 1977. text ed. 27.50 scp (ISBN 0-7002-2499-8, HarpC); solutions manual free (ISBN 0-06-363255-1). Har-Row.

Jamison, Robert V. Fortran IV Programming: Based on the IBM System 1130. LC 70-96241. (Illus.). 1970. text ed. 17.95 (ISBN 0-07-032270-8, G); instructor's manual 2.95 (ISBN 0-07-032274-0). McGraw.

Katzan, Harry, Jr. Fortran Seventy-Seven. 1978. text ed. 18.50x (ISBN 0-442-24278-6). Van Nos Reinhold.

Kaufman, Roger. FORTRAN Coloring Book. LC 78-998. 1978. pap. 8.95 (ISBN 0-262-61026-4). MIT Pr.

Kazmier, Leonard J. & Philippakis, A. S. Fundamentals of E. D. P. & Fortran. 1970. text ed. 13.50 (ISBN 0-07-033416-1, C); instructor's manual restricted 1.95 (ISBN 0-07-033419-6). McGraw.

Kennedy, Michael & Solomon, Martin B. Ten Statement Fortran Plus Fortran Four. 2nd ed. (Illus.). 400p. 1975. pap. text ed. 15.95 (ISBN 0-13-903385-8). P-H.

Khailany, A. Business Programming in FORTRAN VI & ANSI FORTRAN: A Structured Approach. 1981. pap. 13.95 (ISBN 0-13-107607-8). P-H.

--Business Programming in FORTRAN VI & ANSI FORTRAN: A Structured Approach. 1981. pap. 13.95 (ISBN 0-13-107607-8). P-H.

Kreitzberg, Charles & Shneiderman, Ben. Elements of Fortran Style: Techniques for Effective Programming. (Illus.). 121p. 1972. pap. text ed. 9.95 (ISBN 0-15-522156-6, HC). HarBraceJ.

Kreitzberg, Charles B. & Shneiderman, Ben. FORTRAN Programming: A Spiral Approach. (Illus.). 368p. (Orig.). 1975. pap. text ed. 15.95 (ISBN 0-15-528012-0, HC); instructor's manual avail. (ISBN 0-15-528013-9). HarBraceJ.

Kuo, Shan S. Assembler Language for FORTRAN, COBOL & PL-1 Programmers. new ed. LC 73-2138. 1974. text ed. 20.95 (ISBN 0-201-03954-0). A-W.

--Computer Applications of Numerical Methods. LC 78-164654. 1972. text ed. 18.95 (ISBN 0-201-03956-7). A-W.

Land, A. H. & Powell, S. Fortran Codes for Mathematical Programming: Linear, Quadratic & Discrete. LC 73-2789. 249p. 1973. 36.95 (ISBN 0-471-51270-2, Pub. by Wiley-Interscience). Wiley.

Ledgard, Henry F. Programming Proverbs for FORTRAN Programmers. LC 74-22074. (Computer Programming Ser.). (Illus.). 144p. (Orig.). 1975. pap. text ed. 8.95x (ISBN 0-8104-5820-9). Hayden.

Ledgard, Henry F. & Chmura, Louis J. FORTRAN with Style. (Computer Programming Ser.). (gr. 12 up). 1978. pap. text ed. 8.95x (ISBN 0-8104-5682-6). Hayden.

Lee, John A. Numerical Analysis for Computers. 1966. 14.95x (ISBN 0-442-17003-3). Van Nos Reinhold.

Lee, R. M. A Short Course in Basic Fortran IV Programming: Based on the IBM System,360-370. 2nd, rev. ed. 1972. 13.50 (ISBN 0-07-036998-4, C). McGraw.

Lewis, William E. Problem-Solving Principles for FORTRAN Programmers: Applied Logic, Psychology & Grit. (Problem-Solving Principles Ser.). 177p. pap. 9.95 (ISBN 0-8104-5430-0). Hayden.

Lipschutz, Seymour & Poe, Arthur. Schaum's Outline of Programming with Fortran IV. (Schaum's Outline Ser.). 1978. pap. 5.95 (ISBN 0-07-037984-X, SP). McGraw.

McCalla, Thomas R. Introduction to Numerical Methods & FORTRAN Programming. LC 66-28745. 1967. 26.75 (ISBN 0-471-58125-9, Pub. by Wiley-Interscience). Wiley.

McCameron, Fritz A. Fortran IV. 3rd ed. 1978. pap. 12.95x (ISBN 0-256-02036-1). Irwin.

McCracken, Daniel. A Simplified Guide to Fortran Programming. LC 74-876. 288p. 1974. text ed. 16.95 (ISBN 0-471-58292-1). Wiley.

McCracken, Daniel D. Fortran with Engineering Applications. LC 67-17343. (Illus.). 1967. pap. 19.95 (ISBN 0-471-58236-0, Pub. by Wiley-Interscience). Wiley.

--A Guide to Fortran IV Programming. 2nd ed. LC 72-4745. (Illus.). 256p. 1972. pap. 16.95 (ISBN 0-471-58281-6). Wiley.

--Guide to Fortran Programming. LC 61-16618. 1961. pap. 12.50 (ISBN 0-471-58212-3, Pub. by Wiley-Interscience). Wiley.

McCuen, R. Fortran Programming for Civil Engineers. 1975. pap. 16.95 (ISBN 0-13-329417-X). P-H.

McKinley, Joe W. Beginning Fortran. 250p. 1980. pap. 9.95 (ISBN 0-916460-11-8, Pub. by Matrix). Intl Schol Bk Serv.

Malley, John, Jr. & Stair, Ralph. Essentials of FORTRAN Programming. 1981. pap. 3.95 (ISBN 0-256-02390-5). Irwin.

Mann, Richard A. Fortran Four Primer. LC 77-188187. 1972. pap. text ed. 12.50 scp (ISBN 0-7002-2412-2, HarpC); solutions manual scp 4.50 (ISBN 0-685-23390-1). Har-Row.

--An IBM Eleven Thirty Fortran Primer. 2nd ed. 1974. pap. text ed. 16.50 scp (ISBN 0-7002-2455-6, HarpC); sol. man. scp 3.95 (ISBN 0-686-77049-8). Har-Row.

Manning, W. A. & Garnero, R. S. Fortran IV Problem Solver. 1970. 13.50 (ISBN 0-07-039918-2, C). McGraw.

Marateck, Samuel L. Fortran. 1977. 13.95 (ISBN 0-12-470460-3); instr' manual 1978 3.00 (ISBN 0-12-470462-X). Acad Pr.
Marxer & Hartford. Elements of Computer Programming (Fortran) LC 75-153725. (Illus.). 224p. 1973. 8.00 (ISBN 0-8273-0413-7); tchr's manual 2.00 (ISBN 0-8273-0414-5). Delmar.
May, Phillip T. Programming Business Applications in Fortran IV. LC 72-7634. 1973. pap. text ed. 14.25 (ISBN 0-395-14047-1, 3-34905); solutions man. pap. 1.50 (ISBN 0-395-17159-8, 3-34906). HM.
Meek, B. Fortran, Pl-1 & the Algols. 1979. 19.95 (ISBN 0-444-19464-9, North Holland). Elsevier.
Meissner, Loren P. & Organick, Elliot I. FORTRAN Seventy-Seven: Featuring Structured Programming. 3rd ed. LC 78-74689. 1980. pap. text ed. 13.95 (ISBN 0-201-05499-X). A-W.
Merchant & Sturgul. Applied Fortran Program W Standard Fortan, Watfor, Watfiv & Structured Watfiv. 1977. 16.95x (ISBN 0-534-00497-0). Wadsworth Pub.
Merchant, Michael. Fortran Seventy-Seven: Language & Style. 464p. 1981. pap. text ed. 15.95x (ISBN 0-534-00920-4). Wadsworth Pub.
Merchant, Michael J. ABC's of FORTRAN Programming. 1979. pap. text ed. 15.95x (ISBN 0-534-00634-5). Wadsworth Pub.
Merriam, C. W., 3rd. Fortran Computer Programs. LC 77-14792. 1978. 24.95 (ISBN 0-669-01995-X). Lexington Bks.
Monro, Donald M. Computing with Fortran: A Practical Course. 1978. pap. 16.95 (ISBN 0-7131-2546-2, Pub. by Edward Arnold). Intl Schol Bk Serv.
Moore, J. WATFIV. 1975. pap. 14.95 (ISBN 0-87909-876-7). Reston.
Moore, John B. & Maleka, Leo. Structured FORTRAN. 2nd ed. 567p. 1981. text ed. 19.95 (ISBN 0-8359-7104-X); pap. text ed. 15.95 (ISBN 0-8359-7103-1); soln. manual avail. (ISBN 0-8359-7105-8). Reston.
Mullish, Henry. Introduction to Computer Programming. (Notes on Mathematics & Its Applications Ser.). (Orig.). 1966. 33.50x (ISBN 0-677-01160-1); pap. 27.00x (ISBN 0-677-01165-2). Gordon.
Murrill, Paul W. & Smith, Cecil L. Fortran Four Programming for Engineers & Scientists. 2nd ed. LC 73-1689. (Illus.). 322p. 1973. pap. text ed. 16.50 scp (ISBN 0-7002-2419-X, HarpC); solution manual scp 4.95 (ISBN 0-685-28248-1). Har-Row.
--An Introduction to Fortran Four Programming: A General Approach. 2nd ed. 300p. 1975. pap. text ed. 16.50 scp (ISBN 0-7002-2469-6, HarpC); scp solutions manual 3.95 (ISBN 0-7002-2479-3). Har-Row.
Nanney, T. Ray. Computing: A Problem-Solving Approach Using FORTRAN Seventy-Seven. (Illus.). 432p. 1981. text ed. 17.95 (ISBN 0-13-165209-5). P-H.
National Computing Centre Ltd., ed. APSE User Manual. 130p. 1970. 25.00x (ISBN 0-85012-018-7). Intl Pubns Serv.
Nickerson, Robert C. Fundamentals of Fortran Programming. 2nd ed. (Illus.). 1980. text ed. 13.95 (ISBN 0-87626-301-5). Winthrop.
Organick, Elliot I. & Meissner, Loren P. Fortran Four: Standard Fortran Watfor-Watfiv. 1975. text ed. 13.95 (ISBN 0-201-05503-1). A-W.
Page, Rex & Didday, Richard. FORTRAN Seventy-Seven for Humans. (Illus.). 1980. pap 14.95 (ISBN 0-8299-0271-6); instrs.' manual avail. (ISBN 0-8299-0615-0). West Pub.
Page, Rex L. & Didday, Richard L. WATFIV for Humans. LC 76-3433. (Illus.). 630p. 1976. pap. text ed. 14.95 (ISBN 0-8299-0100-0). West Pub.
Parker, James L. & Bohl, Marilyn. FORTRAN Programming & WATFIV. LC 73-77126. (Illus.). 284p. 1973. pap. text ed. 12.95 (ISBN 0-574-17070-7, 13-0070). SRA.
Pennington, Ralph H. Introductory Computer Methods & Numerical Analysis. 2nd ed. (Illus.). 1970. text ed. 20.95 (ISBN 0-02-393830-7). Macmillan.
Petersen, T. M. Elementary FORTRAN. (Illus.). 176p. 1976. pap. text ed. 10.95x (ISBN 0-7121-0548-4, Pub. by Macdonald & Evans England). Intl Ideas.
Poch, Udo W. & Chattergy, Rahul. Top-Down Modular Programming in Fortran with Watfiv. (Illus.). 1980. text ed. 13.95 (ISBN 0-87626-879-3). Winthrop.
Pollack, Seymour V. Guide to Fortran IV. LC 65-8201. 260p. 1966. 17.50x (ISBN 0-231-02904-7). Columbia U Pr.
Radford, A. S. Computer Programming-Fortran. (Teach Yourself Ser.). 1975. pap. 4.95 (ISBN 0-679-10378-3). McKay.
Ralston, Anthony. Fortran Four Programming: A Concise Exposition. 1971. text ed. 13.50 (ISBN 0-07-051164-0, C). McGraw.
Ramden, H. JCL & Advanced FORTRAN Programming. 1976. 34.25 (ISBN 0-444-41415-0). Elsevier.
Ratzer, Gerald. A FORTRAN Seventy-Seven Course. 144p. 1981. pap. text ed. 7.95 (ISBN 0-8403-2427-8). Kendall-Hunt.
Rice, J. R. Introduction to Computing with FORTRAN. LC 73-2437. 1973. text ed. 16.95 (ISBN 0-03-086217-5, HoltC). HR&W.
Rogowski, Stephen J. Computer Clippings. 1976. 7.95 (ISBN 0-88488-058-3). Creative Pubns.
Rohl, J. S. Programming in Fortran. 128p. 1973. 15.00x (ISBN 0-7190-0555-8, Pub. by Manchester U Pr England). State Mutual Bk.
Rosenblatt, Lisa & Rosenblatt, Judah. Simplified Fortran Programming: With Companion Problems. 1973. pap. text ed. 8.95 (ISBN 0-201-06511-8). A-W.
Rule, Wilfred P. Programacion Fortran IV. (Orig.). 1976. text ed. 9.00x (ISBN 0-06-316996-7, IntlDept). Har-Row.
SAS Institute Inc., ed. SAS Programmer's Guide, 1981 Edition. (SAS Programmer's Guide). 208p. (Orig.). 1980. pap. 9.95 (ISBN 0-917382-17-X). SAS Inst.
Sass, C. Joseph. FORTRAN Four Programming & Applications. LC 72-93537. 328p. 1974. pap. text ed. 12.95x (ISBN 0-8162-7473-8). Holden-Day.
Schallert, William F. & Clark, Carol R. Programming in FORTRAN. LC 78-74039. 1979. pap. text ed. 13.95 (ISBN 0-201-06716-1). A-W.
Schick, William & Merz, Charles. Fortran for Engineering. (Illus.). 384p. 1972. text ed. 14.95 (ISBN 0-07-055276-2, C); solutions manual 2.50 (ISBN 0-07-055277-0). McGraw.
Schmidt, B. GPSS FORTRAN. LC 80-40968. (Computing Ser.). 523p. 1980. 39.00 (ISBN 0-471-27881-5, Pub. by Wiley-Interscience). Wiley.
Schott, Brian. RISKM: A FORTRAN Computer Program. (Research Monograph: No. 66 B). 1975. 50.00 (ISBN 0-88406-100-0). Ga St U Busn Pub.
Sears, Joel L. Optimization Techniques in Fortran. (Illus.). 96p. (Orig.). 1979. pap. text ed. 10.00 (ISBN 0-89433-034-9). Petrocelli.
--Optimization Techniques in Fortran. 1979. 10.00 (ISBN 0-07-091042-1, P&RB). McGraw.
Seeds, H. Fortran IV for Business & General Applications. LC 74-34058. 422p. 1975. 16.95 (ISBN 0-471-77109-0, Pub. by Wiley-Interscience). Wiley.
Seeds, Harice L. Structured Fortran Seventy-Seven for Business & General Applications. LC 81-125. 528p. 1981. text ed. 16.95 (ISBN 0-471-07836-0). Wiley.
Selfridge, Oliver. A Primer for FORTRAN IV: On-Line. 1972. pap. 7.95x (ISBN 0-262-69035-7). MIT Pr.
Silver, Gerald A. & Silver, Joan B. Simplified ANSI FORTRAN IV Programming. 2nd ed. (Illus.). 335p. 1976. pap. text ed. 14.95 (ISBN 0-15-581040-5, HC). HarBraceJ.
Slater, L. J. First Step in Basic FORTRAN. 104p. 1971. pap. 4.95x (ISBN 0-412-10120-3, Pub. by Chapman & Hall England). Methuen Inc.
Slater, Lucy J. More Fortran Programs for Economists. (Department of Applied Economics, Occasional Papers: No. 3). (Illus.). 150p. 1972. 15.95x (ISBN 0-521-09722-3). Cambridge U Pr.
Smith, Robert E. & Johnson, Dora E. Fortran Autotester. (Prog. Bk.). 1962. pap. 13.00 (ISBN 0-471-80337-5, Pub. by Wiley-Interscience). Wiley.
Spencer, Donald D. FORTRAN Programming. 1980. pap. 8.95 (ISBN 0-686-65745-4); tchr's manual 4.95 (ISBN 0-686-65746-2); wkbk 3.95 (ISBN 0-89218-018-8). Camelot Pub.
--Problem Solving with FORTRAN. LC 76-26040. (Illus.). 1977. pap. text ed. 14.95 (ISBN 0-13-720094-3). P-H.
Standard FORTRAN Programming Manual. 150p. 1980. 27.50 (ISBN 0-85012-239-2). Intl Pubns Serv.
Stark, Peter. Computer Programming Handbook. LC 75-24688. 518p. 1975. 12.95 (ISBN 0-8306-5752-5); pap. 11.95 (ISBN 0-8306-4752-X, 752). TAB Bks.
Steingraber, Jack. FORTRAN Fundamentals: A Short Course. (Computer Programming Ser.). (Illus.). 96p. 1975. pap. text ed. 6.50 (ISBN 0-8104-5860-8). Hayden.
Stuart, Frederic. Watfor Watfiv FORTRAN Programming. LC 78-162424. 239p. 1971. pap. 18.95 (ISBN 0-471-83471-8). Wiley.
Stuart, Frederick. Fortran Programming. rev. ed. LC 68-30922. 371p. 1970. 23.95 (ISBN 0-471-83466-1). Wiley.
--Introductory Computer Programming. 155p. 1966. text ed. 8.50 (ISBN 0-471-83475-0, Pub. by Wiley). Krieger.
Sturgul, John R. & Merchant, M. J. Applied Fortran Four Programming. 2nd ed. 1977. pap. text ed. 16.95x (ISBN 0-534-00440-7). Wadsworth Pub.
Taylor, Fred I. & Smith, Steve L. Digital Signal Processing in Fortran. LC 75-28940. 192p. 1976. 27.95 (ISBN 0-669-00330-1). Lexington Bks.
Tremblay, Jean P. & Bunt, Richard B. Structured Fortran WATFIV-S Programming. 1979. pap. text ed. 13.50 (ISBN 0-07-065171-X). McGraw.
Understanding FORTRAN. 1981. 2.50 (ISBN 0-88284-148-3). Alfred Pub.
Vickers, Frank D. FORTRAN IV: A Modern Approach. 2nd ed. 1978. pap. text ed. 7.95 (ISBN 0-8403-1829-4). Kendall-Hunt.
Wagener, Jerrold L. Principles of Fortran Seventy-Seven Programming. LC 79-17421. 1980. pap. text ed. 16.95 (ISBN 0-471-04474-1); tchr's manual (ISBN 0-471-07831-X). Wiley.
Walker, Henry M. Problems for Computer Solutions Using Fortran. (Illus.). 1980. pap. text ed. 12.95 (ISBN 0-87626-654-5). Winthrop.
Watters, John. FORTRAN Programming. (Computer Programming Ser). (Illus.). 354p. 1968. 10.50x (ISBN 0-435-77800-5). Intl Pubns Serv.
Wilf. Programming for a Digital Computer in the Fortran Language. 1969. 6.50 (ISBN 0-201-08639-5). A-W.
Worth, T. Non-Technical Fortran. 1976. pap. 15.95 (ISBN 0-13-623678-2). P-H.
Wu, Nesa L. Business Programming in FORTRAN IV. 2nd ed. 377p. 1977. pap. text ed. write for info. (ISBN 0-697-08123-0); solutions manual avail. (ISBN 0-686-67598-3). Wm C Brown.
Zinsmeister, George E., et al. Fortran on Time-Sharing. LC 78-26269. 103p. 1979. pap. 4.95x (ISBN 0-910554-27-7). Eng Pr.

FORTRAN (COMPUTER PROGRAM LANGUAGE)-PROGRAMMED INSTRUCTION

Brainerd, Walter S., et al. Fortran Seventy-Seven Programming. 1978. pap. text ed. 14.50 scp (ISBN 0-06-042394-3, HarpC). Har-Row.
Couger, J. Daniel & Shannon, Loren E. Fortran IV: A Programmed Instruction Approach. 3rd ed. 1976. pap. 12.50x (ISBN 0-256-01632-1). Irwin.
Dock, V. Thomas. Structured FORTRAN IV Programing. (Data Processing & Information System Ser.). (Illus.). 1979. pap. text ed. 14.95 (ISBN 0-8299-0249-X). West Pub.
Keys, William J. & Cashman, Thomas J. Introduction to Computer Programming - Basic Fortran IV: A Practical Approach. (Illus.). 1972. pap. text ed. 12.95x (ISBN 0-88236-151-1). Anaheim Pub Co.
Lewis, Robert J. & Hart, David G. Business FORTRAN: A Structured Approach. 480p. 1980. pap. text ed. 16.95x (ISBN 0-534-00778-3). Wadsworth Pub.
Rule, Wilfred. FORTRAN: A Practical Approach with Style & Structure. 3rd ed. 1980. write for info. (ISBN 0-87150-290-9, 2292). Prindle.

FORTRESSES (BOMBERS)

see Boeing Bombers

FORTS

see Fortification

FORTUNA, GODDESS

Patch, Howard R. Goddess Fortuna in Medieval Literature. 1968. Repr. lib. bdg. 13.00x (ISBN 0-374-96308-8). Octagon.
--The Tradition of the Goddess Fortuna in Medieval Philosophy & Literature. Repr. of 1922 ed. lib. bdg. 10.00 (ISBN 0-8414-6751-X). Folcroft.
--The Tradition of the Goddess Fortuna in Roman Literature & in the Transitional Period. 1980. Repr. of 1912 ed. lib. bdg. 10.00 (ISBN 0-686-62403-3). Norwood Edns.
--The Tradition of the Goddess Fortuna in Roman Literature & in the Transitional Period. LC 76-41188. 1976. Repr. of 1922 ed. lib. bdg. 10.00 (ISBN 0-8414-6753-6). Folcroft.

FORTUNE, AMOS, 1709 or 1710-1801

Yates, Elizabeth. Amos Fortune, Free Man. (gr. 7 up). 1967. 8.95 (ISBN 0-525-25570-2). Dutton.

FORTUNE

see also Chance; Fate and Fatalism; Probabilities; Success

Gunther, Max. Luck Factor. 1977. 7.95 (ISBN 0-02-546580-5). Macmillan.

FORTUNE-TELLING

see also Astrology; Clairvoyance; Crystal-Gazing; Divination; Dreams; Palmistry

Chinese Fortune Telling. 80p. 1980. pap. 4.95 (ISBN 0-89955-112-2, Pub. by Shufunotomo Japan). Intl Schol Bk Serv.
Cohen, Daniel. The Magic Art of Foreseeing the Future. LC 72-6882. (Illus.). 192p. (gr. 7 up). 1973. 5.95 (ISBN 0-396-06718-2). Dodd.
Foli. Fortune Telling with Cards. pap. 3.00 (ISBN 0-87980-035-6). Wilshire.
Landau, Elaine. Occult Visions: A Mystical Gaze into the Future. LC 79-16873. (Illus.). 160p. (gr. 7 up). 1979. PLB 7.79 (ISBN 0-671-32930-8). Messner.
Leek, Sybil. Sybil Leek Book of Fortune Telling. 1969. pap. 2.95 (ISBN 0-02-029160-4, Collier). Macmillan.
LeNormand. Fortune Telling Cards & Key. 3.95 (ISBN 0-685-21947-X). Wehman.
Long, Max F. Tarot Card Symbology. 2nd ed. Wingo, E. Otha, ed. (Illus.). 1972. pap. 8.50x (ISBN 0-910764-03-4). Huna Res Inc.
Madame Fabia, ed. The Book of Fortune Telling. (Illus.). 512p. 1975. pap. 3.95 (ISBN 0-668-03603-6). Arco.
Martello, Leo L. It's in the Cards. pap. 2.00 (ISBN 0-686-00692-5). Key Bks.
--It's Written in the Cards. pap. 0.75 (ISBN 0-685-06567-7). Assoc Bk.
Scouezec. Diccionario De Atres Adivinatorias. 226p. (Espn.). 1973. pap. 7.95 (ISBN 84-270-0220-3, S-50042). French & Eur.
Sherman, Harold. How to Foresee & Control Your Future. 240p. 1978. pap. 1.75 (ISBN 0-449-13927-1, GM). Fawcett.
Shimano, Jimmei. Oriental Fortune Telling. LC 65-18960. (Illus.). (gr. 9 up). 1965. pap. 5.50 (ISBN 0-8048-0448-6). C E Tuttle.
Showers, Paul. Fortune Telling for Fun. LC 80-2549. 349p. 1980. Repr. of 1971 ed. lib. bdg. 10.95x (ISBN 0-89370-607-8). Borgo Pr.
--Fortune Telling for Fun. 1971. pap. 3.95 (ISBN 0-87877-007-0, T-7). Newcastle Pub.
Vickers, Peggy. The Home Book of Fortune Telling. 1977. pap. 1.75 (ISBN 0-89041-136-0, 3136). Major Bks.
Ward, Margarete. Gong Hee Fot Choy. 80p. 1981. pap. 4.95 (ISBN 0-89087-331-3). Celestial Arts.
Your Complete Guide to Fate & Fortune. (Illus.). 1979. pap. 2.95 (ISBN 0-89437-068-5). Baronet.

FORTUNES

see Income; Wealth

FORUMS (DISCUSSION AND DEBATE)

Bormann, Ernest G. Discussion & Group Methods: Theory & Practice. 2nd ed. (Auer Ser.). 395p. 1975. text ed. 18.95 scp (ISBN 0-06-040863-4, HarpC); instructor's manual free (ISBN 0-06-360845-6). Har-Row.
Dobbins, Gaines S. Learning to Lead. LC 68-12342. (Orig.). 1968. pap. 3.50 (ISBN 0-8054-3208-6). Broadman.
Ford, LeRoy. Using the Panel in Teaching & Training. McCormick, Joe, tr. LC 79-127196. (Multi-Media Teaching & Training Ser.). (Orig.). 1971. pap. 3.95 (ISBN 0-8054-3414-3). Broadman.
Hall, Dale M. Dynamics of Group Action. LC 64-22544. (Illus.). 1964. 10.00 (ISBN 0-8134-0457-6). Interstate.
Johnson, Mary C. Discussion Dynamics: A Classroom Analysis. LC 78-6865. 1979. pap. text ed. 11.95 (ISBN 0-88377-115-2). Newbury Hse.
Leypoldt, Martha M. Forty Ways to Teach in Groups. (Orig.). 1967. pap. text ed. 2.75 (ISBN 0-8170-0376-2). Judson.
Miles, Matthew B. Learning to Work in Groups. 2nd ed. 360p. 1981. pap. text ed. 12.95x (ISBN 0-8077-2586-2). Tchrs Coll.
NASSP. Workshops: Laboratories for Student Leaders. 1974. pap. 3.00 (ISBN 0-88210-057-2). Natl Assn Principals.
Pask, G. Conversation Theory. new ed. 1976. 47.00 (ISBN 0-444-41424-X). Elsevier.
Philadelphia Macro-Analysis Collective of Movement Ofor a New Society. Organizing Macro-Analysis Seminars: Study & Action for a New Society. 76p. (Orig.). 1980. pap. 4.95 (ISBN 0-86571-009-0); reading unit 1.75 (ISBN 0-86571-010-4). New Soc Pubs.
Shenson, Howard L. How to Create & Market Successful Seminars. Date not set. 27.00 (ISBN 0-686-30968-5). Everest Hse.
Simpson, Douglas B. & Podsakoff, Philip M. Workshop Management: A Behavioral & Systems Approach. (Illus.). 152p. 1975. 17.50 (ISBN 0-398-03364-1). C C Thomas.
Stanford, Gene & Stanford, Barbara D. Learning Discussion Skills Through Games. LC 78-105863. (Illus.). 80p. (Orig.). 1969. pap. 1.95 (ISBN 0-590-09016-X, Citation). Schol Bk Serv.

FORWARDERS, FREIGHT

see Freight Forwarders

FORWARDING MERCHANTS

Official Forwarding Agents Directory, 1980. Orig. Title: Offizielles Spediteur-Adressbuch. (Illus.). 1032p. (Orig.). 1979. pap. 62.50x (ISBN 0-8002-2390-X). Intl Pubns Serv.

FOSCOLO, NICCOLO UGO, 1778-1827

Cambon, Glauco. Ugo Foscolo: Poet of Exile. LC 79-3193. 360p. 1980. 21.50x (ISBN 0-691-06424-5). Princeton U Pr.
Umstead, Douglas R. Ugo Foscolo. (World Authors Ser.: No. 115). 10.95 (ISBN 0-8057-2320-X). Twayne.

FOSDICK, HARRY EMERSON, 1878-1964

Fosdick, Harry E. A Pilgrimage to Palestine. Davis, Moshe, ed. LC 77-70688. (America & the Holy Land Ser.). 1977. Repr. of 1927 ed. lib. bdg. 22.00x (ISBN 0-405-10247-X). Arno.

Scruggs, Julius R. Baptist Preachers with Social Consciousness: A Comparative Study of Martin Luther King Jr. & Harry Emerson Fosdick. 72p. 1979. 5.00 (ISBN 0-8059-2501-5). Dorrance.

FOSS FAMILY

Ridlon, G. T. Foss Family. LC 74-94957. (Saco Valley Settlements Ser).*1970. pap. 1.50 (ISBN 0-8048-0767-1). C E Tuttle.

Skalley, Michael. Eighty Years of Towboating: The History of Foss Launch & Tug Company. (Illus.). 224p. 1981. 19.95 (ISBN 0-686-73376-2). Madrona Pubs.

FOSSIL BOTANY

see Paleobotany

FOSSIL MAN

see also Australopithecines

Andrews, Roy C. On the Trail of Ancient Man. 1926. 30.00 (ISBN 0-8495-0227-6). Arden Lib.

Bishop, Walter W. Geological Background to Fossil Man: Recent Research in the Gregory Rift Valley, East Africa. 1978. 75.00x (ISBN 0-8020-2302-9). U of Toronto Pr.

Black, Davidson. On a Lower Molar Hominid Tooth from the Chou Kou Tien Deposit. LC 77-86443. (China. Geological Survey. Palaeontologia Sinica. Ser. D.: Vol. 7, Fasc. 1). 1977. 12.50 (ISBN 0-404-16686-5). AMS Pr.

--On an Adolescent Skull of Sinanthropus Pekinensis: In Comparison with an Adult Skull of the Same Species & with Other Hominid Skulls, Recent & Fossil. LC 77-86442. (China. Geological Survey. Palaeontologia Sinica. Ser. D.: Vol. 7, Fasc. 2). Repr. of 1930 ed. 23.00 (ISBN 0-404-16685-7). AMS Pr.

Black, Davidson, ed. Fossil Man in China. LC 73-38049. Repr. of 1933 ed. 32.00 (ISBN 0-404-56903-X). AMS pr.

Chia Lan-Po. Cave Home of Peking Man. (Illus.). 1975. pap. 1.95 (ISBN 0-8351-0024-3). China Bks.

Clark, W. E. The Fossil Evidence for Human Evolution: An Introduction to the Study of Paleoanthropology. 3rd rev. ed. Campbell, Bernard G., ed. LC 78-529. (Illus.). 1979. 16.00x (ISBN 0-226-10937-2); pap. 4.95 (ISBN 0-226-10938-0, P502, Phoen). U of Chicago Pr.

Day, M. H. The Fossil History of Man. rev. ed. Head, J. J., ed. LC 76-62979. (Carolina Biology Readers Ser.). (Illus.). (gr. 11 up). 1977. pap. 1.65 (ISBN 0-89278-232-3, 45-9632). Carolina Biological.

Greis, Noel P. Early Man. Reed, Suzanne W., ed. LC 74-80541. (Science Ser.). (Illus., Orig.). (gr. 6-9). 1975. pap. text ed. 3.25 (ISBN 0-88301-151-4). Pendulum Pr.

Lugenbeal, Edward. Who Killed Adam? A Look at the Major Types of Fossil Man. LC 78-8513. (Flame Ser.). 1978. pap. 0.95 (ISBN 0-8127-0186-0). Review & Herald.

Martin, Henri. L' Homme fossile de la Quina. LC 78-72703. (Illus.). Repr. of 1923 ed. 41.00 (ISBN 0-404-18272-0). AMS Pr.

Matiegka, Jindrich. Homo Predmostensis, fosilni Clovek z Predmosti na Morave, 2 vols. LC 78-72704. Repr. of 1938 ed. Set. 72.50 (ISBN 0-404-18273-9). Vol. 1 (ISBN 0-404-18274-7). Vol. 3 (ISBN 0-404-18275-5). AMS Pr.

The Stone Age of Mount Carmel, 2 vols. Incl. Vol. 1. Excavations at the Wady el-Mughara. Garrod, D. A. & Bate, D. M. (ISBN 0-404-16651-2); Vol. 2. The Fossil Human Remains from the Levalloiso-Mousterian. McCown, T. D. & Keith, Arthur. (ISBN 0-404-16652-0). LC 77-86432. Repr. of 1839 ed. Set. 125.00 (ISBN 0-404-16650-4). AMS Pr.

Weidenreich, F. The Skull of Sinanthropus Pekinensis. (Paleontologia Sinica). (Illus.). 1943. pap. 15.00 (ISBN 0-934454-88-4). Lubrecht & Cramer.

Weiner, J. S. The Piltdown Forgery. (Illus.). 240p. 1981. pap. 4.00 (ISBN 0-486-24075-4). Dover.

FOSSILS

see Paleontology

FOSSILS, LIVING

see Living Fossils

FOSTER, ABIGAIL KELLEY, 1810-1887–JUVENILE LITERATURE

Bacon, Margaret H. I Speak for My Slave Sister: The Life of Abby Kelley Foster. LC 74-4042. (gr. 5-12). 1974. 8.95 (ISBN 0-690-00515-6, TYC-J). Har-Row.

Bernard, Joel. Authority, Autonomy & Radical Commitment: Stephen & Abby Kelley Foster. 39p. 1981. pap. 6.00 (ISBN 0-912296-50-X, Dist. by U Pr of Va). Am Antiquarian.

FOSTER, STEPHEN COLLINS, 1826-1864

Bernard, Joel. Authority, Autonomy & Radical Commitment: Stephen & Abby Kelley Foster. 39p. 1981. pap. 6.00 (ISBN 0-912296-50-X, Dist. by U Pr of Va). Am Antiquarian.

Foster, Stephen. Stephen Foster Song Book. 224p. (Orig.). 1974. 8.95 (ISBN 0-486-23086-4); pap. 5.00 (ISBN 0-486-23048-1). Dover.

Howard, John T. Stephen Foster: America's Troubadour. 7.50 (ISBN 0-8446-2275-3). Peter Smith.

--Stephen Foster: America's Troubadour. (Apollo Eds.). pap. 2.95 (ISBN 0-8152-0032-3, A32). T Y Crowell.

Milligan, H. V. Stephen Collins Foster. 69.95 (ISBN 0-87968-313-9). Gordon Pr.

Morneweck, Evelyn F. Chronicles of Stephen Foster's Family, 2 vols. LC 72-154716. (Illus.). 1973. Repr. of 1944 ed. Set. 42.50x (ISBN 0-8046-1742-2). Kennikat.

Whittlesey, W. R. & Sonneck, O. G. Catalogue of First Editions of Stephen C. Foster. LC 76-155233. (Music Ser). 1971. Repr. of 1915 ed. lib. bdg. 15.00 (ISBN 0-306-70162-6). Da Capo.

FOSTER, GEORGE MURPHY (POPS), 1892?-1969

Drucker, Malka & Foster, George. The George Foster Story. rev. ed. LC 80-11437. (Illus.). 128p. (gr. 5 up). 1980. 7.95 (ISBN 0-8234-0413-7). Holiday.

FOSTER, GREGORY, 1949-1972

Silverman, Al. Foster & Laurie. 1974. 7.95 (ISBN 0-316-79116-4). Little.

FOSTER CARE, INSTITUTIONAL

see Children–Institutional Care

FOSTER DAY CARE

see Day Care Centers

FOSTER HOME CARE

see also Adoption; Children–Institutional Care

Amstutz, Beverly. Moccasins & Sneakers. (Illus.). 24p. (gr. k-7). 1980. pap. 2.50x (ISBN 0-937836-02-8). Precious Res.

--Sharing Is Fun. (Illus.). 22p. (gr. k-9). 1979. pap. 2.25x (ISBN 0-937836-00-1). Precious Res.

Bryant, Bradford A. Special Foster Care: A History & Rationale. (Orig.). 1980. pap. text ed. 4.50 (ISBN 0-9604068-0-8). People Places.

C W LA Standards for Foster Family Service. rev. ed. LC 73-93884. 1975. pap. text ed. 7.50 (ISBN 0-87868-114-0). Child Welfare.

Carbino, Rosemarie. Foster Parenting: An Updated Review of the Literature. 49p. (Orig.). 1980. pap. text ed. 4.90 (ISBN 0-87868-178-7). Child Welfare.

Cautley, Patricia W. New Foster Parents. 288p. 1980. 19.95 (ISBN 0-87705-495-9). Human Sci Pr.

--New Foster Parents: The First Experience. LC 80-10937. 288p. 1980. 19.95x (ISBN 0-87705-495-9). Human Sci Pr.

Children, Family & Foster Care: New Insights from Research in New York City. 1976. 3.00 (ISBN 0-86671-029-9). Comm Coun Great NY.

Conversations No. 1 - to Foster Parents: from: Mary Reistroffer: What You Always Wanted to Discuss About Foster Care but Didn't Have the Chance or the Time to Bring up. LC 72-166581. 41p. 1971. pap. 2.90 (ISBN 0-87868-087-X, F-41). Child Welfare.

Conversations No. 2 - to Foster Parents: from Mary Reistroffer: What's So Special About Teenagers. LC 75-75120. 42p. 1972. pap. 2.90 (ISBN 0-87868-095-0, F-42). Child Welfare.

Costin, Lela B. & Gruener, Jennette R. The Licensing of Family Homes in Child Welfare: A Guide for Instructors & Trainees. LC 65-12939. 1965. 8.95x (ISBN 0-8143-1266-7). Wayne St U Pr.

Crist, Evamae B. Take This House. (Illus.). 1977. pap. 2.25 (ISBN 0-8361-1817-0). Herald Pr.

CWLA Standards for Homemaker Service for Children. LC 59-12714. 45p. 1959. pap. 7.50 (ISBN 0-87868-067-5, HM-11). Child Welfare.

Dennis, Muriel, ed. Chosen Children. 6.95 (ISBN 0-89107-154-7). Good News.

Dickerson, Martha U. Our Four Boys. pap. 6.95 (ISBN 0-686-31409-3). NACAC.

--Our Four Boys: Foster Parenting Retarded Teenagers. 1978. pap. 7.95 (ISBN 0-8156-0155-7). Syracuse U Pr.

Fanshel, David. Toward More Understanding of Foster Parents. LC 74-28598. 1975. soft bdg. 12.00 (ISBN 0-88247-319-0). R & E Res Assoc.

Fanshel, David & Shinn, Eugene. Children in Foster Care: A Longitudinal Investigation. LC 77-2872. (Social Work & Social Issues Ser.). 520p. 1978. 27.50x (ISBN 0-231-03576-4). Columbia U Pr.

Felker, Evelyn. Raising Other People's Kids: Successful Child-Rearing in the Restructured Family. 160p. (Orig.). 1981. pap. 4.95 (ISBN 0-8028-1868-4). Eerdmans.

Felker, Evelyn H. Foster Parenting Young Children: Guidelines from a Foster Parent. LC 73-93885. 1974. pap. 4.55 (ISBN 0-87868-119-1). Child Welfare.

Foster Family Care for Emotionally Disturbed Children. 72p. 1962. pap. 4.55 (ISBN 0-87868-049-7, F-20). Child Welfare.

Geiser, Robert L. The Illusion of Caring: Children in Foster Care. LC 73-6246. (Illus.). 192p. 1973. 9.95 (ISBN 0-8070-2378-7); pap. 4.95 (ISBN 0-8070-2379-5, BP490). Beacon Pr.

George, V. Foster Care: Theory & Practice. (International Library of Sociology & Social Reconstruction). 1970. text ed. 11.25x (ISBN 0-7100-6800-X). Humanities.

Grossbard, Hyman. Cottage Parents - What They Have to Be, Know, & Do. LC 60-53475. 29p. 1960. pap. 2.25 (ISBN 0-87868-064-0, I-22). Child Welfare.

Group Homes in Perspective. 48p. (Eight papers reprinted from "Child welfare"). 1964. pap. 3.95 (ISBN 0-87868-055-1, GH-12). Child Welfare.

Gruber, Alan R. Children in Foster Care: Destitute, Neglected...Betrayed. LC 77-521. 1977. 22.95 (ISBN 0-87705-265-4). Human Sci Pr.

Hester, Glenn & Nygren, Bruce. Child of Rage. 8.95 (ISBN 0-8407-5245-8). Warner Bks.

--Child of Rage. 192p. 1981. 8.95 (ISBN 0-8407-5245-8). Nelson.

Holman, Robert. Trading in Children: A Study of Private Fostering. (International Library of Social Policy). (Illus.). 374p. 1973. 32.50x (ISBN 0-7100-7538-3). Routledge & Kegan.

Horejsi, Charles R. Foster Family Care: A Handbook for Social Workers, Allied Professionals, & Concerned Citizens. (Illus.). 384p. 1979. text ed. 21.75 (ISBN 0-398-03898-8). C C Thomas.

Hubbell, Ruth. Foster Care & Families: Conflicting Values & Policies. (Family Impact Seminar Ser.). 200p. 1981. 15.00x (ISBN 0-87722-206-1). Temple U Pr.

Hutchinson, Dorothy. Cherish the Child: Dilemmas of Placement. Kemp, Maude V., ed. LC 72-4076. 1972. 10.00 (ISBN 0-8108-0496-4). Scarecrow.

Jenkins, Shirley & Norman, Elaine. Beyond Placement: Mothers View Foster Care. LC 75-15916. (Social Work & Social Issues Ser.). 149p. 1975. 13.50x (ISBN 0-231-03812-7). Columbia U Pr.

--Filial Deprivation & Foster Care. LC 72-3564. 296p. 1972. 16.00x (ISBN 0-231-03575-6). Columbia U Pr.

Kaplan, Bert L. & Seitz, Martin. The Practical Guide to Foster Family Care. 112p. 1980. lexotone 9.75 (ISBN 0-398-04033-8). C C Thomas.

Keith-Lucas, Alan & Sanford, Clifford W. Group Child Care As a Family Service. LC 76-40411. 1977. 17.00x (ISBN 0-8078-1303-6). U of NC Pr.

Kline, Draza & Overstreet, Helen-Mary F. Foster Care of Children: Nurture & Treatment. LC 78-186386. (Studies of the Child Welfare League of America). 316p. 1972. 17.50x (ISBN 0-231-03601-9); pap. 8.00x (ISBN 0-231-08337-8). Columbia U Pr.

Lawder, Elizabeth A., et al. Five Models of Foster Family Group Homes. LC 74-75756. (Orig.). 1974. pap. 6.00 (ISBN 0-87868-122-1). Child Welfare.

Lind, Miriam S. No Crying He Makes. pap. 1.50 (ISBN 0-686-31408-5). NACAC.

McCoin, John. Adult Foster Homes: Their Managers & Residents. 1982. in prep. (ISBN 0-89885-087-8). Human Sci Pr.

McDaniel, Deborah. Foster Care in the 1980s. 174p. 1981. pap. 13.80 (ISBN 0-08-028096-X). Pergamon.

Maluccio, Anthony N. & Sinanoglu, Paula A., eds. The Challenge of Partnership: Working with Parents of Children in Foster Care. (Orig.). 1981. 14.00 (ISBN 0-87868-181-7); pap. 8.95 (ISBN 0-686-77616-X). Child Welfare.

Mandell, Betty R. Where Are the Children? 128p. 1973. 17.95 (ISBN 0-669-88963-6). Lexington Bks.

New Approaches to Homemaker Service. 48p. (Ten papers reprinted from "Child Welfare"). 1968. pap. 2.25 (ISBN 0-87868-069-1, HM-13). Child Welfare.

Parfit, Jessie, ed. Community's Children. 1967. pap. text ed. 2.50x (ISBN 0-582-32417-3). Humanities.

Payne, C. J. & White, K. J., eds. Caring for Deprived Children: International Case Studies of Residential Setting. 1979. 19.95 (ISBN 0-312-12166-0). St Martin.

Pearson, Dawn G., as told to. Foster Mother: The Mary Romano Story. 1979. pap. 4.00 (ISBN 0-89502-034-3). FEB.

Pers, Jessica S. Government As Parent: Administering Foster Care in California. LC 76-25050. 1976. pap. 5.50x (ISBN 0-87772-215-3). Inst Gov Stud Berk.

Prosser, Hilary. Perspectives on Foster Care. (General Ser.). 1978. pap. text ed. 20.75x (ISBN 0-85633-147-3, NFER). Humanities.

Reistroffer, Mary. Conversations No. 3: Foster Parents & Social Workers: on the Job. LC 73-93881. 1974. pap. 2.80 (ISBN 0-87868-111-6). Child Welfare.

Rutter, Barbara A. A Way of Caring: The Parents Guide to Foster Family Care. LC 78-51720. 1978. pap. text ed. 4.50 (ISBN 0-87868-127-2). Child Welfare.

Sarason, Irwin G. A Guide for Foster Parents. LC 75-38739. 40p. 1976. pap. 4.95 (ISBN 0-87705-281-6); five or more 1.95 (ISBN 0-686-57797-3). Human Sci Pr.

Satre, Elizabeth D. The Story of Ellen: How Love Transforms a Troubled Child. LC 78-66952. 1979. pap. 2.95 (ISBN 0-8066-1691-1, 10-6045). Augsburg.

Shapiro, Deborah. Agencies & Children: A Child Welfare Network's Investment in Its Clients. 240p. 1976. text ed. 12.50x (ISBN 0-231-03578-0). Columbia U Pr.

Slingerland, W. H. Child-Placing in Families: Manuel for Students & Social Workers. LC 74-1705. (Children & Youth Ser.: Vol. 22). (Illus.). 267p. 1974. Repr. of 1919 ed. 18.00x (ISBN 0-405-05982-5). Arno.

Stein, Theodore J., et al. Children in Foster Homes: Achieving Continuity of Care. LC 78-16927. 1978. 28.95 (ISBN 0-03-046421-8). Praeger.

Stevenson, Olive. Someone Else's Child: A Book for Foster Parents of Young Children. 2nd ed. 1977. pap. 6.50 (ISBN 0-7100-8706-3). Routledge & Kegan.

Stone, Helen D. & Hunzeker, Jeanne M. Creating a Foster Parent-Agency Handbook. LC 74-81975. 1974. pap. 4.30 (ISBN 0-87868-123-X). Child Welfare.

--Education for Foster Family Care: Models & Methods for Social Workers & Foster Parents. LC 74-25269. 1974. pap. 7.95 (ISBN 0-87868-112-4). Child Welfare.

Taylor, Joseph L., et al. A Group Home for Adolescent Girls: Practice & Research. LC 76-27209. 1976. pap. 6.60 (ISBN 0-87868-164-7). Child Welfare.

Timms, Noel, ed. The Receiving End: Consumer Accounts of Social Help for Children. 102p. 1973. 7.50x (ISBN 0-7100-7549-9). Routledge & Kegan.

Triseliotis, John, ed. New Developments in Foster Care & Adoption. 1980. 27.00x (ISBN 0-7100-0368-4); pap. 13.50 (ISBN 0-7100-0461-3). Routledge & Kegan.

Van Senden Theis, Sophie. How Foster Children Turn Out: A Study & Critical Analysis of 910 Children Placed in Foster Homes, Who Are Now Eighteen Years of Age or Over. LC 74-1708. (Children & Youth Ser.: Vol. 19). 240p. 1974. Repr. of 1924 ed. 15.00x (ISBN 0-405-05985-X). Arno.

Werner, Ruth M. Public Financing of Voluntary Agency Foster Care Programs. LC 76-54383. (Orig.). 1976. pap. 4.50 (ISBN 0-87868-163-9). Child Welfare.

Wolins, Martin. Selecting Foster Parents: The Ideal & the Reality. LC 63-19855. 1964. 17.50x (ISBN 0-231-02514-9). Columbia U Pr.

FOUCAULD, CHARLES EUGENE, VICOMTE DE, 1858-1916

Lorit, Sergius C. Charles De Foucauld: The Silent Witness. 1977. 2.50 (ISBN 0-911782-29-X). New City.

FOUCAULT'S PENDULUM

see also Earth–Rotation

FOUCHE, JOSEPH, DUC D'OTRANTE, 1759-1820

Cubberly, Ray E. The Role of Fouche During the Hundred Days. LC 78-626285. 1969. 3.50 (ISBN 0-87020-136-0, Logmark Eds). State Hist Soc Wis.

Forssell, Nils. Fouche, the Man Napoleon Feared. LC 71-112299. Repr. of 1928 ed. 19.50 (ISBN 0-404-02514-5). AMS Pr.

FOULAHS

see Fulahs

FOULIS PRESS

Duncan, William J., ed. Notices & Documents Illustrative of the Literary History of Glasgow During the Greater Part of Last Century. (Maitland Club. Glasgow. Publications: No. 14). Repr. of 1831 ed. 18.00 (ISBN 0-404-52947-X). AMS Pr.

FOULKE, WILLIAM DUDLEY, 1848-1935

Foulke, William D. Fighting the Spoilsmen: Reminiscenses of the Civil Service Reform Movement. LC 73-19146. (Politics & People Ser.). 356p. 1974. Repr. 18.00x (ISBN 0-405-05870-5). Arno.

FOUND OBJECTS (ART)

see also Assemblage (Art); Collage

Comins, Jeremy. Art from Found Objects. LC 74-8220. (Illus.). 128p. (gr. 5 up). 1974. 7.25 (ISBN 0-688-41646-2); PLB 6.96 (ISBN 0-688-51646-7). Lothrop.

Stribling, Mary L. Art from Found Materials: Discarded & Natural: Techniques, Design Inspiration. (Illus.). 1970. pap. 5.95 (ISBN 0-517-54307-9). Crown.

FOUNDATION GARMENTS

see also Corset

Kunzle, David. Fashion & Fetishism: A Social History of the Corset, Tight-Lacing & Other Forms of Body-Sculpture in the West. (Illus.). 300p. 1981. 27.50x (ISBN 0-8476-6276-4). Rowman.

FOUNDATIONS

see also Basements; Coffer-Dams; Compressed Air; Concrete; Earthwork; Masonry; Piling (Civil Engineering); Soil Mechanics; Walls

American Society of Civil Engineers, compiled by. Research Conference on Shear Strength of Cohesive Soils. 1174p. 1966. pap. text ed. 37.50 (ISBN 0-87262-004-2). Am Soc Civil Eng.
--Shotcrete for Ground Support. 776p. 1977. pap. text ed. 24.00 (ISBN 0-87262-091-3). Am Soc Civil Eng.
--Subsurface Exploration for Underground Excavation & Heavy Construction. 414p. 1974. pap. text ed. 13.50 (ISBN 0-87262-105-7). Am Soc Civil Eng.
--Subsurface Investigation for Design & Construction for Foundations of Buildings. (Manuel & Report on Engineering Practice Ser.: No. 56). 68p. 1976. pap. text ed. 6.00 (ISBN 0-87262-230-4). Am Soc Civil Eng.
Arya, Suresh C., et al. Design of Structures & Foundations for Vibrating Machines. 200p. 1979. 29.95x (ISBN 0-87201-294-8). Gulf Pub.
Atkinson, J. H. Foundations & Slopes. 384p. 1981. 32.50 (ISBN 0-470-27246-5). Halsted Pr.
Barker, John. Dictionary of Soil Mechanics & Foundation Engineering. 1981. pap. text ed. 22.00x tent. (ISBN 0-86095-885-X). Longman.
--Dictionary of Soil Mechanics & Foundation Engineering. 1981. pap. text ed. 30.00x (ISBN 0-86095-885-X). Longman.
Behavior of Deep Foundations. (Special Technical Publications Ser.). 610p. 1979. soft cover 49.50x (ISBN 0-686-76088-3, 670, 04-670000-38). ASTM.
Bell, F. G. Foundation Engineering in Difficult Ground. 1978. 79.95 (ISBN 0-408-00311-1). Butterworth.
Bowles, J. Foundation Analysis & Design. 3rd ed. 1982. price not set (ISBN 0-07-006770-8). McGraw.
Brown, Robert W. Residential Foundations: Design, Behavior & Repair. LC 78-12069. 1979. text ed. 13.95x (ISBN 0-442-20937-1). Van Nos Reinhold.
Carson, Arthur B. Foundation Construction. 1965. 32.50 (ISBN 0-07-010167-1, P&RB). McGraw.
Chellis, Robert D. Pile Foundations. 2nd ed. (Soil Mechanic Foundations Library). (Illus.). 1961. 37.50 (ISBN 0-07-010751-3, P&RB). McGraw.
Chen, F. H. Foundations on Expansive Soils. (Developments in Geotechnical Engineering Ser.: Vol. 12). 1976. 46.50 (ISBN 0-444-41393-6). Elsevier.
Degree Problems in Soil Mechanics & Foundation Engineering. 1977. pap. 5.95 (ISBN 0-408-00296-4). Butterworth.
Foundation Analysis & Design. 2nd ed. (Illus.). 1977. text ed. 26.50 (ISBN 0-07-006750-3, C). McGraw.
Hanna, T. H. Foundation Instrumentation. new ed. LC 72-90015. (Ser. on Rock & Soil Mechanics). (Illus.). 400p. 1973. 35.00 (ISBN 0-87849-006-X). Trans Tech.
Institute of Civil Engineers. Diaphragm Walls & Anchorages. 234p. 1980. 79.00x (ISBN 0-7277-0005-7, Pub. by Telford England). State Mutual Bk.
Johnson, Sidney M. & Kavanagh, Thomas C. Design of Foundations for Buildings. LC 68-18576. (Modern Structure Ser.). 1968. 32.00 (ISBN 0-07-032583-9, P&RB). McGraw.
Kezdi, A. & Lazanyi, I, eds. Proceedings of the Fifth Budapest Conference on Sil Mechanics & Foundation Engineering. 1976. 40.00 (ISBN 0-9960005-0-X, Pub. by Kiado Hungary). Heyden.
Leonards, G. A., ed. Foundation Engineering. (Civil Engineering Ser.). 1962. 48.50 (ISBN 0-07-037198-9, P&RB). McGraw.
McCarthy, David. Essentials of Soil Mechanics & Foundations. 640p. 1982. text ed. 21.95 (ISBN 0-686-76718-7); solutions manual free (ISBN 0-8359-1782-7). Reston.
McCarthy, David F. Essentials of Soil Mechanics & Foundations. (Illus.). 576p. 1977. text ed. 18.95 (ISBN 0-87909-221-1); students manual avail. Reston.
Peck, Ralph B., et al. Foundation Engineering. 2nd ed. LC 73-9877. 544p. 1974. 29.95 (ISBN 0-471-67585-7). Wiley.
Reimbert, M. & Reimbert, A. Study of Passive Resistance in Foundation Structures: Part 2. LC 74-77789. (Rock & Soil Mechanics Ser). (Illus.). 200p. 1976. text ed. 30.00x (ISBN 0-87849-013-2). Trans Tech.
Richart, F. E., Jr., et al. Vibrations of Soils & Foundations. (Civil Engineering Ser) 1970. ref. ed. 25.95 (ISBN 0-13-941716-8). P-H.
Schnabel, Harry, Jr. Tiebacks in Foundation Engineering & Construction. (Illus.). 192p. 1981. price not set (ISBN 0-07-055516-8, P&RB). McGraw.
Scott, C. R. Introduction to Soil Mechanics & Foundations. 3rd ed. (Illus.). xi, 405p. 1980. pap. text ed. 18.00x (ISBN 0-85334-873-1). Intl Ideas.
Scott, Ronald F. Foundation Analysis. (Civil Engineering & Engineering Mechanics Ser.). (Illus.). 496p. 1981. text ed. 29.95 (ISBN 0-13-329169-3). P-H.
Simons & Menzies. Short Course in Foundation Engineering. 1977. 19.95 (ISBN 0-408-00295-6). Butterworth.
Smith, G. N. & Pole, E. L. Elements of Foundation Design. 250p. 1981. lib. bdg. 32.50 (ISBN 0-8240-7274-X). Garland Pub.
Szechy, K. & Varga, L. Foundation Engineering. (Illus.). 1979. 52.00 (ISBN 0-9960010-7-7, Pub. by Kiado Hungary). Heyden.
--Foundation Engineering: Soil Exploration & Spread Foundations. LC 79-318873. (Illus.). 1978. 50.00x (ISBN 963-05-1489-3). Intl Pubns Serv.
Teng, Wayne C. Foundation Design. (Illus.). 1962. ref. ed. 27.95x (ISBN 0-13-329805-1). P-H.
Tomlinson, M. J. Foundation Design & Construction. 4th ed. (Civil Engineering Ser.). 793p. 1980. text ed. 55.00 (ISBN 0-273-08455-0). Pitman Pub MA.
Tschebotarioff, Gregory P. Foundations, Retaining & Earth Structures: The Art of Design Construction & Its Scientific Basis in Soil Mechanics. 2nd ed. (Illus.). 704p. 1973. 34.50 (ISBN 0-07-065377-1, P&RB). McGraw.
Vollmer, Ernst. Encyclopaedia of Hydraulics, Soil & Foundation Engineering. 1967. 73.25 (ISBN 0-444-40615-8). Elsevier.
Winterkorn, Hans F. & Fang, F. Y., eds. Foundation Engineering Handbook. 736p. 1975. text ed. 42.50x (ISBN 0-442-29564-2). Van Nos Reinhold.
Zeevaert, Leonardo. Foundation Engineering for Difficult Subsoil Conditions. LC 79-17288. 670p. 1979. Repr. of 1973 ed. lib. bdg. 27.50 (ISBN 0-89874-010-X). Krieger.

FOUNDATIONS (ENDOWMENTS)
see Charitable Uses, Trusts and Foundations; Endowments
Foundation Center. Foundation Grants to Individuals. 3rd ed. 1981. pap. 15.00 (ISBN 0-87954-048-6). Foundation Ctr.

FOUNDATIONS OF ARITHMETIC
see Arithmetic–Foundations

FOUNDATIONS OF GEOMETRY
see Geometry–Foundations

FOUNDING
see also Brass Founding; Bronze; Die Casting; Metal Castings; Metal-Work; Molding (Founding); Pattern-Making; Precision Casting; Type and Type-Founding
Aspin, B. Terry. The Backyard Foundry. (Illus., Orig.). 1978. pap. 7.50x (ISBN 0-85242-603-8). Intl Pubns Serv.
--Foundrywork for the Amatuer. 94p. 6.50x (ISBN 0-85344-105-7). Intl Pubns Serv.
Beeley, P. R. Foundry Technology. 1972. text ed. 51.95 (ISBN 0-408-70348-2). Butterworth.
Berman, Harold. Encyclopedia of Bronzes, Sculptors & Founders: 1800-1930. LC 74-78612. (Abage Encyclopedia Ser.: Vols. 1-4). 1974-79. Set. lib. bdg. 210.00 (ISBN 0-917350-05-7); Vol. 1. lib. bdg. 45.00 (ISBN 0-917350-01-4); Vol. 2. lib. bdg. 50.00 (ISBN 0-917350-02-2); Vol. 3. lib. bdg. 55.00 (ISBN 0-917350-03-0); Vol. 4. lib. bdg. 60.00 (ISBN 0-917350-04-9). Abage.
Brunhuber, E. Giesserei - Fachwoerterbuch. 802p. (Ger., Eng., Fr. & It., Dictionary of Foundry). 1977. 120.00 (ISBN 3-7949-0283-1, M-7424, Pub. by Fachverlag, Schiele & Schon). French & Eur.
--Giesserei - Lexikon 1978. 960p. (Ger.). 1977. 62.50 (ISBN 3-7949-0282-3, M-7425, Pub. by Fachverlag, Schiele & Schon). French & Eur.
Cannon, Bill. How to Cast Small Metal & Rubber Parts. (Illus.). 1979. 9.95 (ISBN 0-8306-9869-8); pap. 5.95 (ISBN 0-8306-1105-3, 1105). TAB Bks.
Choate, Sharr. Creative Casting. (Arts & Crafts Ser). (Illus.). 1966. 12.95 (ISBN 0-517-02445-4). Crown.
Clarke, Carl D. Molding & Casting: Its Technique & Application. 3rd ed. (Illus.). 380p. 1972. 18.00 (ISBN 0-685-25470-4). Standard Arts.
Foundry Services Ltd. Foundryman's Handbook. 8th ed. 1976. text ed. 13.75 (ISBN 0-08-018020-5). Pergamon.
Foundry Type: Specimen Book. pap. 10.00 (ISBN 0-87100-201-9). Morgan.
Information Sources on the Foundry Industry. rev. ed. (UNIDO Guides to Information Sources Ser.: No.5). 87p. pap. 4.00 (ISBN 0-686-70502-5, UN). Unipub.
Longden, E. Densening & Chilling in Foundary Work. 178p. 1954. 10.95x (ISBN 0-85264-040-4, Pub. by Griffin England). State Mutual Bk.
McCombe, C., ed. Foundry Year Book 1979. (Illus.). 508p. (Orig.). 1979. pap. 30.00x (ISBN 0-86108-043-2). Intl Pubns Serv.
Pearson, H. L. Projects for the School Foundry. (Illus.). 1970. 15.95x (ISBN 0-291-39673-9). Intl Ideas.
Seminar on Engineering Equipment for Foundries & Advanced Methods of Producing Such Equipment, Geneva, 1977. Engineering Equipment for Foundries: Proceedings. United Nations Economic Commission for Europe, Geneva, ed. (Illus.). 1979. text ed. 81.00 (ISBN 0-08-022421-0). Pergamon.
Simons, E. N. Dictionary of Foundry Work. (Illus.). 192p. 1972. text ed. 10.00x (ISBN 0-8464-0333-1). Beekman Pubs.
Smith, Robert E. Patternmaking & Founding. (gr. 9 up). 1959. pap. 5.00 (ISBN 0-87345-020-5). McKnight.
Standke, Wolfgang, compiled by. Foundry Dictionary: German-English & English-German. 1971. 21.50x (ISBN 3-87260-002-8). Intl Pubns Serv.
Strauss, K. Applied Science in the Casting of Metals. 1970. 50.00 (ISBN 0-08-015711-4). Pergamon.
Sylvia, J. Gerin. Cast Metals Technology. LC 74-153067. 1972. text ed. 18.95 (ISBN 0-201-07395-1). A-W.
Taylor, F., et al. Foundry Engineering. LC 59-11811. 407p. 1959. 31.95 (ISBN 0-471-84843-3). Wiley.
Vocabulary de la Fonderie, Francais-Anglais. (Fr.-Eng., French-English Vocabulary of Foundries). pap. 14.95 (ISBN 0-686-56719-6, M-6557). French & Eur.
Vocabulary de la Fonderie, Francais-Anglais. (Fr.-Eng., French-English Vocabulary of Foundries). pap. 12.50 (ISBN 0-686-56720-X, M-6556). French & Eur.

FOUNDLINGS
see also Adoption; Orphans and Orphan-Asylums
Brophy, A. Blake. Foundlings on the Frontier: Racial & Religious Conflict in Arizona Territory, 1904-1905. LC 79-187824. (Southwest Chronicles). 1972. pap. 2.00 (ISBN 0-8165-0319-2). U of Ariz Pr.

FOUNDRY PRACTICE
see Founding

FOUNTAIN, ALBERT JENNINGS, 1838-1896
Gibson, Arrell M. Life & Death of Colonel Albert Jennings Fountain. LC 65-11229. (Illus.). 1975. Repr. of 1965 ed. 15.95 (ISBN 0-8061-0647-6); pap. 6.95 (ISBN 0-8061-1231-X). U of Okla Pr.

FOUNTAINS
MacDougall, Elisabeth B. & Miller, Naomi. Fons Sapientiae: Garden Fountains in Illustrated Books, Sixteen-Eighteenth Centuries. LC 77-76011. (Illus.). 1977. pap. 5.00x (ISBN 0-88402-073-8, Ctr Landscape Arch). Dumbarton Oaks.
Miller, Naomi. French Renaissance Fountains. LC 76-23645. (Outstanding Dissertations in the Fine Arts - 16th Century). (Illus.). 1977. Repr. of 1966 ed. lib. bdg. 63.00 (ISBN 0-8240-2713-2). Garland Pub.
Wiles, Bertha H. Fountains of Florentine Sculptors & Their Followers from Donatello to Bernini. LC 79-143370. (Illus.). 1975. Repr. of 1933 ed. 40.00 (ISBN 0-87817-089-8). Hacker.

FOUQUET, JEAN, 1415-1480
Melet-Sanson, J. Fouquet. (Artists Watercolor Ser.). (Illus.). (gr. 10-12). 1978. 10.95 (ISBN 0-8120-5280-3, Screpel). Barron.

FOUR-COLOR PROBLEM
Saaty, Thomas L. & Kainen, Paul C. The Four-Color Problem: Assaults & Conquest. (Illus.). 1977. text ed. 22.00x (ISBN 0-07-054382-8, C). McGraw.

FOUR INDIAN KINGS
Bond, Richmond P. Queen Anne's American Kings. 1972. lib. bdg. 14.00x (ISBN 0-374-90783-8). Octagon.

FOURIER, FRANCOIS MARIE CHARLES, 1772-1837
Alhaiza, Adolphe. Historique De L'ecole Societaire Fondee Par Charles Fourier Suivi D'un Resume De la Doctrine Fourieriste et Du Sommaire Du Gerantisme Elucide. 152p. 1981. Repr. of 1894 ed. lib. bdg. 70.00 (ISBN 0-8287-1550-5). Clearwater Pub.
Barthes, Roland. Sade, Fourier, Loyola. 1971. 14.95 (ISBN 0-686-53941-9). French & Eur.
Brisbane, Albert. Association: Or, a Concise Exposition of the Practical Part of Fourier's Social Science. LC 72-2947. (Communal Societies in America Ser). Repr. of 1843 ed. 11.50 (ISBN 0-404-10713-3). AMS Pr.
--Social Destiny of Man. LC 68-18217. Repr. of 1840 ed. 14.50x (ISBN 0-678-00471-4). Kelley.
--Social Destiny of Man: Or Association & Reorganization of Industry. LC 68-56752. 1967. Repr. of 1840 ed. 15.00 (ISBN 0-8337-0376-5). B Franklin.
--Theory of the Functions of the Human Passions. LC 75-304. (The Radical Tradition in America Ser). (Illus.). 166p. 1975. Repr. of 1856 ed. 17.00 (ISBN 0-88355-209-4). Hyperion Conn.
Godwin, Parke. A Popular View of the Doctrines of Charles Fourier. Bd. with Democracy, Constructive & Pacific. 55p. LC 77-187451. (The American Utopian Adventure Ser). 120p. Repr. of 1844 ed. lib. bdg. 15.00x (ISBN 0-87991-006-2). Porcupine Pr.
--A Popular View of the Doctrines of Charles Fourier. 2nd ed. LC 72-2951. Repr. of 1844 ed. 10.00 (ISBN 0-404-10716-8). AMS Pr.
Riasanovsky, Nicholas V. The Teaching of Charles Fourier. LC 77-84043. 1969. 24.00x (ISBN 0-520-01405-7). U of Cal Pr.
Silberling, E. Dictionnaire De Sociologie Phalansterienne: Guide Des Oeuvres Completes De Charles Fourier. 1964. Repr. of 1911 ed. 29.50 (ISBN 0-8337-3266-8). B Franklin.
Zeldin, David. Educational Ideas of Charles Fourier. LC 67-31331. 1969. 22.50x (ISBN 0-678-05019-8). Kelley.
--Educational Ideas of Charles Fourier, 1772-1837. 167p. 1969. 24.00x (ISBN 0-7146-1451-3, F Cass Co). Biblio Dist.

FOURIER, JEAN BAPTISTE JOSEPH, BARON, 1768-1830
Herivel, John. Joseph Fourier: The Man & the Physicist. (Illus.). 362p. 1975. 64.00x (ISBN 0-19-858149-1). Oxford U Pr.

FOURIER ANALYSIS
see also Fourier Series; Fourier Transformations; Functions, Orthogonal; Orthogonal Polynomials
Argabright, Loren & De Lamadrid, Jesus G. Fourier Analysis of Unbounded Measures on Locally Compact Abelian Groups. LC 74-6499. (Memoirs: No. 145). 1974. pap. 7.60 (ISBN 0-8218-1845-7, MEMO-145). Am Math.
Fourier Coefficients of Automorphic Forms. (Lecture Notes in Mathematics Ser.: Vol. 865). 201p. 1981. pap. 14.00 (ISBN 0-387-10839-4). Springer-Verlag.
Rees, C., et al, eds. Theory & Applications of Fourier Analysis. (Pure & Applied Mathematics Ser.: Vol. 59). 1980. 37.50 (ISBN 0-8247-6903-1). Dekker.
Stein, Elias M. & Weiss, Guido. Introduction to Fourier Analysis on Euclidean Spaces. LC 73-106394. (Mathematical Ser.: No. 32). 1971. 22.00x (ISBN 0-691-08078-X). Princeton U Pr.
Taibleson, M. H. Fourier Analysis on Local Fields. LC 74-32047. (Mathematical Notes Ser.: No. 15). 308p. 1977. 16.00x (ISBN 0-691-08165-4). Princeton U Pr.
Triebel, Hans. Fourier Analysis. LC 77-555434. 1977. pap. 9.50x (ISBN 0-8002-0808-0). Intl Pubns Serv.

FOURIER INTEGRALS
see Fourier Series

FOURIER SERIES
see also Almost Periodic Functions; Harmonic Analysis; Harmonic Functions
Balabanian, Norman. Fourier Series. 1976. pap. 6.95x (ISBN 0-916460-17-7, Pub. by Matrix). Intl Schol Bk Serv.
Bari, N. K., et al. Series & Approximation. (Translations Ser.: Vol. 3). 1962. 20.80 (ISBN 0-8218-1603-9, TRANS 1-3). Am Math.
Bloomfield, Peter. Fourier Analysis of Time Series: An Introduction. LC 75-34294. (Probability & Mathematical Statistics Ser.). 258p. 1976. 27.50 (ISBN 0-471-08256-2, Pub. by Wiley-Interscience). Wiley.
Boas, R. P., Jr. Integrability Theorems for Trigonometric Transforms. (Ergebnisse der Mathematik und Ihrer Grenzgebiete: Vol. 38). 1967. 13.40 (ISBN 0-387-03780-2). Springer-Verlag.
Bochner, Salomon. Fouriersche Integrale. LC 49-22695. (Ger). 8.95 (ISBN 0-8284-0042-3). Chelsea Pub.
Campbell, G. A. & Foster, R. M. Fourier Integrals for Practical Applications. 1947. 10.95 (ISBN 0-442-01451-1, Pub. by Van Nos Reinhold). Krieger.
Carslaw, Horatio S. Introduction to the Theory of Fourier's Series & Integrals. 3rd ed. (Illus.). 1952. pap. 6.00 (ISBN 0-486-60048-3). Dover.
Challifour, John L. Generalized Functions & Fourier Analysis: An Introduction. (Math Lecture Notes Ser.: No. 49). 188p. 1972. 15.00 (ISBN 0-8053-1876-3, Adv Bk Prog); (Adv Bk Prog). Benjamin-Cummings.
Chazarain, J. Fourier Integral Operators & Partial Differential Equations. (Lecture Notes in Mmathematics: Vol. 459). 372p. 1975. pap. 17.50 (ISBN 0-387-07180-6). Springer-Verlag.
Churchill, Ruel V. & Brown, James W. Fourier Series & Boundary Value Problems. 3rd ed. 1978. text ed. 19.95 (ISBN 0-07-010843-9, C). McGraw.
Coifman, Ronald & Weiss, Guido. Transference Methods in Analysis. LC 77-24098. (Conference Board of the Mathematical Sciences Ser.: No. 31). 1977. 11.20 (ISBN 0-8218-1681-0, CBMS 31). Am Math.
Dym, H. & McKean, H. P. Fourier Series & Integrals. (Probability & Mathematical Statistics Ser). 1972. 44.50 (ISBN 0-12-226450-9). Acad Pr.
Edwards, R. Fourier Series: A Modern Introduction. LC 79-11932. (Graduate Texts in Mathematics: Pt. 1, Vol. 64). 1979. 17.60 (ISBN 0-387-90412-3). Springer-Verlag.
Gelbart, Stephen S. Fourier Analysis on Matrix Space. LC 52-42839. (Memoirs: Vol. 108). 1971. pap. 6.40 (ISBN 0-8218-1808-2, MEMO-108). Am Math.
Gowar, N. W. & Baker, J. Fourier Series. 139p. 1974. 16.50x (ISBN 0-8448-0408-8). Crane-Russak Co.

Hirschman, I. I. Decomposition of Walsh & Fourier Series. LC 52-42839. (Memoirs: No. 15). 1980. pap. 10.80 (ISBN 0-8218-1215-7, MEMO-15). Am Math.
Kawata, Tatsuo. Fourier Analysis in Probability Theory. (Probability & Mathematical Statistics Ser). 1972. 66.50 (ISBN 0-12-403650-3). Acad Pr.
Kufner, A. & Kadlec, J. Fourier Series. 372p. 1971. 15.95 (ISBN 0-592-03944-7). Butterworth.
Levinson, Norman. Gap & Density Theorems. LC 41-6147. (Colloquium, Pbns. Ser.: Vol. 26). 1963. Repr. of 1940 ed. 19.60 (ISBN 0-8218-1026-X, COLL-26). Am Math.
Lighthill, M. J. Introduction to Fourier Analysis & Generalized Functions. (Cambridge Monographs on Mechanics & Applied Mathematics). 18.95 (ISBN 0-521-05556-3); pap. text ed. 7.95 (ISBN 0-521-09128-4). Cambridge U Pr.
Marcus, Michael B. & Pisier, Gilles. Random Fourier Series with Application to Harmonic Analysis. LC 81-47145. (Annals of Mathematical Studies: No.101). 192p. 1981. 17.50x (ISBN 0-691-08289-8); pap. 7.00x (ISBN 0-691-08292-8). Princeton U Pr.
Mozzochi, C. J. On the Pointwise Convergence of Fourier Series. LC 79-162399. (Lecture Notes in Mathematics: Vol. 199). 1971. pap. 8.20 (ISBN 0-387-05475-8). Springer-Verlag.
Oberhettinger, Fritz. Fourier Expansions: A Collection of Formulas. 1973. 25.00 (ISBN 0-12-523640-9). Acad Pr.
Olevsky, A. M. Fourier Series with Respect to General Orthogonal Systems, Vol. 86. LC 74-32297. (Ergebnisse der Mathematik und Ihrer Grenzgebiete). 160p. 1975. 42.60 (ISBN 0-387-07103-2). Springer-Verlag.
Papoulis, Athanasios. Fourier Integral & Its Applications. (Electronic Science Ser.). 1962. text ed. 24.95 (ISBN 0-07-048447-3, C). McGraw.
Rogosinski, Werner. Fourier Series. 2nd ed. LC 50-6214. 6.95 (ISBN 0-8284-0067-9). Chelsea Pub.
Spiegel, Murray R. Fourier Analysis. 1974. pap. text ed. 5.95 (ISBN 0-07-060219-0, SP). McGraw.
Steklov Institute of Mathematics, Academy of Sciences, U S S R, No. 99. Limits of Interdeterminacy in Measure of Trigonometric & Orthogonal Series: Proceedings. 1968. 19.60 (ISBN 0-8218-1899-6, STEKLO-99). Am Math.
Stuart, R. D. Introduction to Fourier Analysis. 128p. 1966. pap. text ed. 7.95x (ISBN 0-412-20200-X, Pub. by Chapman & Hall England). Methuen Inc.
Titchmarsh, Edward C. Introduction to the Theory of Fourier Integrals. 2nd ed. 1948. 59.00x (ISBN 0-19-853320-9). Oxford U Pr.
Tolstov, Georgi P. Fourier Series. Silverman, Richard A., tr. from Russian. LC 75-41883. 352p. 1976. pap. 5.00 (ISBN 0-486-63317-9). Dover.
Wainger, Stephen. Special Trigonometric Series in k-Dimensions. LC 52-42839. (Memoirs: No. 59). 1965. pap. 7.20 (ISBN 0-8218-1259-9, MEMO-59). Am Math.
Walsh, Thomas. On Summability Methods for Conjugate Fourier-Steilties Integrals in Several Variables & Generalizations. LC 73-2729. (Memoirs: No. 131). 1973. pap. 9.60 (ISBN 0-8218-1831-7, MEMO-131). Am Math.
Wiener, Norbert. Fourier Integral & Certain of Its Applications. 1933. pap. text ed. 3.50 (ISBN 0-486-60272-9). Dover.
Wilcox, Howard & Myers, David L. An Introduction to Lebesgue Integration & Fourier Analysis. LC 77-12013. 168p. 1978. 13.50 (ISBN 0-88275-614-1). Krieger.
Young, Robert M. An Introduction to Nonharmonic Fourier Series. LC 79-6807. (Pure & Applied Ser.). 1980. 32.00 (ISBN 0-12-772850-3). Acad Pr.
Zygmund, A. Trigonometric Series. LC 77-82528. 1977. 79.50 (ISBN 0-521-07477-0). Cambridge U Pr.

FOURIER TRANSFORMATIONS
see also Digital Filters (Mathematics)
Amoros, J. L. & Amoros, M. Molecular Crystals: Their Transforms & Diffuse Scattering. 479p. 1968. text ed. 26.00 (ISBN 0-471-02555-0, Pub. by Wiley). Krieger.
Bell, R. J. Introductory Fourier Transform Spectroscopy. 1972. 43.00 (ISBN 0-12-085150-4). Acad Pr.
Berenstein, C. A. & Dostal, M. A. Analytically Uniform Spaces & Their Applications to Convolution Equations. LC 70-189386. (Lecture Notes in Mathematics: Vol. 256). 137p. 1972. pap. 6.20 (ISBN 0-387-05746-3). Springer-Verlag.
Bochner, S. & Chandrasekharan, K. Fourier Transforms. 1949. pap. 10.00 (ISBN 0-527-02735-9). Kraus Repr.
Bracewell, R. The Fourier Transform & Its Applications. 2nd ed. (Electrical Engineering Ser.). (Illus.). 1978. text ed. 24.50 (ISBN 0-07-007013-X, C); solutions manual 10.95 (ISBN 0-07-007014-8). McGraw.
Brigham, E. Oran. Fast Fourier Transform. (Illus.). 304p. 1973. ref. ed. 23.95 (ISBN 0-13-307496-X). P-H.
Challifour, John L. Generalized Functions & Fourier Analysis: An Introduction. (Math Lecture Notes Ser.: No. 49). 188p. 1972. 15.00 (ISBN 0-8053-1876-3, Adv Bk Prog); (Adv Bk Prog). Benjamin-Cummings.
Champeney, D. C. Fourier Transforms & Their Physical Applications. (Techniques of Physics Ser.: No. 1). 1972. 40.50 (ISBN 0-12-167450-9). Acad Pr.
Donoghue, William F. Distributions & Fourier Transforms. (Pure & Applied Mathematics Ser.: Vol. 32). 1969. 50.00 (ISBN 0-12-220650-9). Acad Pr.
Ehrenpreis, Leon. Fourier Analysis in Several Complex Variables. (Pure & Applied Mathematics Ser.). 1970. 49.00 (ISBN 0-471-23400-1, Pub. by Wiley-Interscience). Wiley.
Ferraro, John R., ed. Fourier Transform: Applications to Chemical Systems, Vol. 1. 1978. 39.50 (ISBN 0-12-254101-4). Acad Pr.
Ferraro, John R. & Basile, Louis J., eds. Fourier Transform Infared Spectroscopy, Vol. 3: Techniques Using Fourier Transform Interferometry. 1981. price not set (ISBN 0-12-254103-0). Acad Pr.
--Fourier Transform Infrared Spectroscopy: Applications to Chemical Systems, Vol. 2. LC 78-26956. 1979. 37.50 (ISBN 0-12-254102-2). Acad Pr.
Gaskill, Jack D. Linear Systems, Fourier Transforms & Optics. LC 78-1118. (Pure & Applied Optics Ser.). 1978. 35.00x (ISBN 0-471-29288-5, Pub. by Wiley-Interscience). Wiley.
Griffiths, Peter R. Chemical Infrared Fourier Transform Spectroscopy. LC 75-6505. (Chemical Analysis Ser: Vol. 43). 340p. 1975. 39.50x (ISBN 0-471-32786-7, Pub by Wiley-Interscience). Wiley.
Hermann, Robert. Fourier Analysis on Groups & Partial Wave Analysis. (Math Lecture Notes Ser.: No. 32). 1969. 19.50 (ISBN 0-8053-3940-X, Adv Bk Prog); pap. 9.50 (ISBN 0-8053-3941-8, Adv Bk Prog). Benjamin-Cummings.
Mattson, James S., et al, eds. Infrared Correlation & Fourier Transform Spectroscopy. (Computers in Chemistry & Instrumentation: Vol. 7). 1976. 39.50 (ISBN 0-8247-6369-6). Dekker.
Maurice, D. Convolution & Fourier Transforms for Communications Engineers. LC 75-34082. 189p. 1976. 27.95x (ISBN 0-470-57770-3). Halsted Pr.
Mullen, K. & Pregosin, P. S. Fourier Transform Nuclear Magnetic Resonance Techniques: A Practical Approach. 1977. 28.00 (ISBN 0-686-75175-2). Acad Pr.
Oberhettinger. Fourier Transformations of Distributions & Their Inverses: A Collection of Tables. 1973. 37.50 (ISBN 0-12-523650-6). Acad Pr.
Paley, Raymond E. & Wiener, Norbert. Fourier Transforms in the Complex Domain. LC 35-3273. (Colloquium, Pbns. Ser.: Vol. 19). 1978. Repr. of 1934 ed. 27.60 (ISBN 0-8218-1019-7, COLL-19). Am Math.
Peled, Abraham & Liu, Bede. Digital Signal Processing: Theory, Design & Implemetation. LC 76-17326. 1976. text ed. 26.95 (ISBN 0-471-01941-0). Wiley.
Rabiner, Lawrence R. & Rader, Charles M. Digital Signal Processing. LC 72-90358. (IEEE Press Selected Reprint Ser.). 500p. 1972. pap. text ed. 17.50 (ISBN 0-471-70291-9, Pub by Wiley-Interscience). Wiley.
Rudin, W. Fourier Analysis on Groups. (Pure & Applied Mathematics Ser.). 1962. 57.50 (ISBN 0-470-74481-2). Wiley.
Silberger, A. J. P G L-2, Over the P-Adics: Its Representations, Spherical Functions, & Fourier Analysis. LC 70-139951. (Lecture Notes in Mathematics: Vol. 166). 1970. pap. 11.20 (ISBN 0-387-05193-7). Springer-Verlag.
Szmydt, Zofia. Fourier Transformation & Linear Differential Equations. new ed. PWN, Polish Scientific Pb., ed. (Symposia of the Intl. Astronomical Union: No. 71). 1976. lib. bdg. 47.50 (ISBN 90-277-0622-0, Pub. by Reidel Holland). Kluwer Boston.
Wrinch. Fourier Transforms & Structure Factors. pap. 3.00 (ISBN 0-686-60368-0). Polycrystal Bk Serv.

FOURNIER, ALAIN, 1886-1914
Champigny, Robert R. Portrait of a Symbolist Hero. 1954. 12.00 (ISBN 0-527-16100-4). Kraus Repr.
Loize. Alain Fournier: Sa Vie et le Grand Meaulnes. 26.15 (ISBN 0-685-37148-4). French & Eur.
Peguy, Charles & Alain-Fournier. Correspondance (1910-1914) 160p. 1973. 12.95 (ISBN 0-686-54856-6). French & Eur.

FOURTEENTH CENTURY
Lerner, Robert E. Age of Adversity: The Fourteenth Century. (Development of Western Civilization Ser.). (Illus.). 133p. (Orig.). 1968. pap. text ed. 3.45x (ISBN 0-8014-9846-5). Cornell U Pr.
Snell, F. J. The Fourteenth Century. 1978. Repr. of 1923 ed. lib. bdg. 40.00 (ISBN 0-8414-7924-0). Folcroft.
Tuchman, Barbara. A Distant Mirror. 1980. pap. 8.95 (ISBN 0-345-29542-0). Ballantine.
Utley, Francis L., ed. Forward Movement of the Fourteenth Century. LC 60-14642. (Illus.). 1962. 6.00 (ISBN 0-8142-0124-5). Ohio St U Pr.

FOURTH DIMENSION
Here are entered only philosophical and imaginative works. Mathematical works are entered under the heading Hyperspace.
see also Space and Time
Abbott, Edwin A. Flatland: A Romance of Many Dimensions. 5th rev. ed. 1963. 7.50x (ISBN 0-06-480005-9). B&N.
--Flatland: A Romance of Many Dimensions. 5th rev ed. 1963. pap. 2.95 (ISBN 0-06-463210-5, EH 210, EH). Har-Row.
--Flatland: A Romance of Many Dimensions. 2nd ed. 1884. pap. 2.00 (ISBN 0-486-20001-9). Dover.
Bragdon, Claude. Primer of Higher Space. 180p. 1972. pap. 2.65 (ISBN 0-912358-06-8). Omen Pr.
Hinton, Charles H. The Fourth Dimension. LC 75-36840. (Occult Ser.). 1976. Repr. of 1912 ed. 15.00x (ISBN 0-405-07953-2). Arno.
Hinton, Howard C. Scientific Romances: First & Second Series, 2 vols, in 1. LC 75-36841. (Occult Ser.). 1976. Repr. of 1922 ed. 23.00x (ISBN 0-405-07954-0). Arno.
Manning, Henry. The Fourth Dimension Simply Explained. 8.00 (ISBN 0-8446-2522-1). Peter Smith.
Ouspensky, P. D. New Model of the Universe. 1934. 8.95 (ISBN 0-394-43819-1). Knopf.
--Tertium Organum: A Key to the Enigmas of the World. LC 76-128440. 1970. pap. 3.95 (ISBN 0-394-70864-4, V639, Vin). Random.
Rucker, Rudolf V. Geometry, Relativity & the Fourth Dimension. LC 76-22240. (Illus.). 1977. pap. text ed. 2.75 (ISBN 0-486-23400-2). Dover.

FOURTH DISEASE
see Rubella

FOURTH OF JULY
Boyd, Helen M. The True Horoscope of the U. S. LC 75-7188. 1975. 7.25 (ISBN 0-88231-007-0). Asi Pubs Inc.
Dalgliesh, Alice. The Fourth of July Story. (Illus.). (gr. k-4). 1956. reinforced bdg. 8.95 (ISBN 0-684-13164-1, ScribJ); (ScribJ). Scribner.
Graves, Charles P. Fourth of July. LC 63-13625. (Holiday Books Ser). (Illus.). (gr. 2-5). 1963. PLB 6.87 (ISBN 0-8116-6550-X). Garrard.
Phelan, Mary K. Fourth of July. LC 65-25909. (Holiday Ser.). (Illus.). (gr. k-3). 1966. PLB 7.89 (ISBN 0-690-31415-9, TYC-J). Har-Row.
Schultz, Ellen. I Can Read About July Fourth, Seventeen Seventy Six. new ed. LC 78-68470. (Illus.). (gr. 3-5). 1979. pap. 1.25 (ISBN 0-89375-211-8). Troll Assocs.

FOWL PEST
see Newcastle Disease

FOWLES, JOHN
Olshen, Barry. John Fowles: A Reference Guide. (Reference Bks.). 1980. lib. bdg. 12.00 (ISBN 0-8161-8187-X). G K Hall.
Olshen, Barry N. John Fowles. LC 78-3149. (Modern Literature Ser.). 1978. 10.95 (ISBN 0-8044-2665-1). Ungar.
Wolf, Peter. John Fowles, Magus & Moralist. 2nd ed. LC 79-50516. 208p. 1979. 12.00 (ISBN 0-8387-5001-X). Bucknell U Pr.

FOWLING
see also Decoys (Hunting); Duck Shooting; Falconry; Waterfowl Shooting
Bauer, Erwin A. Duck Hunter's Bible. LC 65-15543. pap. 2.95 (ISBN 0-385-04373-2). Doubleday.
Begbie, Eric. Modern Wildfowling. 1981. 40.00x (ISBN 0-904558-76-2, Pub. by Saiga Pub). State Mutual Bk.
Bell, Bob. Hunting the Long Tailed Bird. (Illus.). 224p. 1975. 14.95 (ISBN 0-88395-027-8). Freshet Pr.
Duffey, David. Bird Hunting Tactics. 1978. pap. 5.95 (ISBN 0-932558-08-9). Willow Creek.
Gryndall, William. Hawking, Hunting, Fouling & Fishing; Newly Corrected by W. Gryndall Faulkener. LC 70-38194. (English Experience Ser.: No. 463). 88p. 1972. Repr. of 1596 ed. 13.00 (ISBN 90-221-0463-X). Walter J Johnson.
Rice, F. Phillip & Dahl, John I. Game Bird Hunting. rev. ed. LC 65-14985. (Funk & W Bk.). (Illus.). 1977. pap. 4.50 (ISBN 0-308-10323-8). T y Crowell.
Williams, Lovett E., Jr. The Book of the Wild Turkey. 204p. 1981. 15.95 (ISBN 0-87691-337-0). Winchester Pr.
Woods, Shirley E., Jr. Gunning for Upland Birds & Wildfowl. (Illus.). 1976. 10.00 (ISBN 0-87691-219-6). Winchester Pr.

FOWLS
see Poultry

FOX, CHARLES JAMES, 1749-1806
Cannon, J. Fox-North Coalition. LC 70-85715. 1970. 35.50 (ISBN 0-521-07606-4). Cambridge U Pr.
Derry, John W. Charles James Fox. 1972. 42.00 (ISBN 0-7134-1118-X, Pub. by Batsford England). David & Charles.
Lascelles, Edward C. Life of Charles James Fox. LC 78-96183. 1970. Repr. of 1936 ed. lib. bdg. 16.00x (ISBN 0-374-94788-0). Octagon.
Oliver, Robert T. Four Who Spoke Out. LC 75-101831. (Biography Index Reprint Ser). 1946. 17.00 (ISBN 0-8369-8005-0). Arno.
Trevelyan, George M. Early History of Charles James Fox. 1973. lib. bdg. 15.00 (ISBN 0-8414-8431-7). Folcroft.
Trevelyan, George O. Early History of Charles James Fox. LC 79-158852. Repr. of 1880 ed. 31.00 (ISBN 0-404-06524-4). AMS Pr.
Walpole, B. C. Charles James Fox. 1978. Repr. lib. bdg. 25.00 (ISBN 0-8492-2953-7). R West.

FOX, GEORGE, 1624-1691
Brinton, Howard H. Religion of George Fox: As Revealed in His Epistles. LC 68-57978. (Orig.). 1968. pap. 0.70x (ISBN 0-87574-161-4). Pendle Hill.
Fogelklou-Norlind, Emilia. Atonement of George Fox. Mather, Eleanore P., ed. LC 75-84675. (Orig.). 1969. pap. 0.70x (ISBN 0-87574-166-5). Pendle Hill.
Fox, George. George Fox's Book of Miracles. Cadbury, Henry J., ed. LC 73-735. 161p. 1973. Repr. of 1948 ed. lib. bdg. 12.50x (ISBN 0-374-92825-8). Octagon.
--The Journal of George Fox, 2 vols. Penney, Norman, ed. LC 73-8978. 1973. Repr. of 1911 ed. Set. lib. bdg. 55.00x (ISBN 0-374-92826-6). Octagon.
Jones, Rufus M. The Journal of George Fox. 576p. 1976. pap. 3.95 (ISBN 0-913408-24-7). Friends United.
Vernon, Louise A. Key to the Prison. LC 86-11054. (Illus.). (gr. 4-9). 1968. 2.95 (ISBN 0-8361-1813-8). Herald Pr.
Yolen, Jane. Friend: The Story of George Fox & the Quakers. LC 74-171865. 192p. (gr. 6 up). 1972. 6.95 (ISBN 0-395-28932-7, Clarion). HM.

FOX, GUSTAVUS VASA, 1821-1883
Loubat, Joseph F. Gustavus Fox's Mission to Russia in 1866. LC 70-115559. (Russia Observed, Series I). 1970. Repr. of 1873 ed. 18.00 (ISBN 0-405-03045-2). Arno.
Thompson, Robert M. & Wainwright, Richard, eds. Confidential Correspondence of Gustavus Vasa Fox, Assistant Secretary of the Navy, 1861-1865: New York Historical Society, Ix, X, 2 vols. LC 20-7659. (Illus.). 1918. Set. 16.00x (ISBN 0-685-73893-0). U Pr of Va.

FOX, JOHN, JR., 1863-1919
Titus, Warren I. John Fox, Jr. (United States Authors Ser.). 1971. lib. bdg. 8.95x (ISBN 0-89197-811-9); pap. text ed. 4.95x (ISBN 0-8290-0014-3). Irvington.

FOX, WILLIAM, 1879-
Sinclair, Upton. Upton Sinclair Presents William Fox. LC 78-124037. (Literature of Cinema, Ser. 1). Repr. of 1933 ed. 12.00 (ISBN 0-405-01637-9). Arno.

FOX
see Foxes

FOX-HUNTING
Bradley, Cuthbert. Fox Hunting from Shire to Shire with Many Noted Packs. (Illus.). 1979. Repr. of 1912 ed. lib. bdg. 75.00 (ISBN 0-8492-3729-7). R West.
British Horse Society & Pony Club. Riding to Hounds. 1976. pap. 1.95 (ISBN 0-8120-0756-5). Barron.
Clayton, Michael. A Hunting We Will Go. 6.00 (ISBN 0-85131-178-4, Dist. by Sporting Book Center). J A Allen.
Cone, Carl B. Hounds in the Morning: Sundry Spots of Merry England: Excerpts from the Sporting Magazine, 1792-1836. LC 81-51017. (Illus.). 1981. 16.00 (ISBN 0-8131-1411-X). U Pr of Ky.
Duke Of Beaufort. Fox Hunting. LC 79-56043. (Illus.). 236p. 1980. 29.95x (ISBN 0-7153-7896-1). David & Charles.
Fox Hunting, Five Minute Lectures. (British Horse Society Ser.). Date not set. pap. 2.25 (ISBN 0-8120-2097-9). Barron.
Goeldner, Christian T. The Thoroughbred Field Hunter. LC 75-20593. (Illus.). 184p. 1976. 9.95 (ISBN 0-498-01767-2). A S Barnes.
Itzkowitz, David C. Peculiar Privilege: A Social History of English Fox-Hunting 1753-1885. 1977. text ed. 22.00x (ISBN 0-391-00689-4). Humanities.
Kidd, Jane. Drag Hunting. 1978. 5.25 (ISBN 0-85131-285-3, Dist. by Sporting Book Center). J A Allen.

Lewis, Collin A. Hunting in Ireland. (Illus.). 26.25 (ISBN 0-85131-213-6, Dist. by Sporting Book Center). J A Allen.

Longrigg, Roger. The History of Fox Hunting. (Illus.). 272p. 1975. 29.95 (ISBN 0-517-52003-6). Potter.

Moore, Daphne. Famous Foxhunters. 1981. 35.00x (ISBN 0-904558-46-0, Pub. by Saiga Pub). State Mutual Bk.

Slater, Kitty. Hunt Country of America. rev. ed. LC 72-92318. (Illus.). 247p. 1974. 15.00 (ISBN 0-668-02788-6). Arco.

Watson, J. N. The Book of Foxhunting. LC 77-8511. (Illus.). 1977. 12.95 (ISBN 0-668-04356-3, 4356). Arco.

Williams, John. An Introduction to Hunting. (Illus.). pap. 5.25 (ISBN 0-85131-200-4, Dist. by Sporting Book Center). J A Allen.

Woolner, Lionel R., ed. The Hunting of the Hare. (Illus.). 6.10 (ISBN 0-85131-122-9, Dist. by Sporting Book Center). J A Allen.

FOX INDIANS

see Indians of North America–Northwest, Old

FOXE, JOHN, 1516-1587

Foxe, John. The English Sermons of John Foxe. LC 77-29100. 1978. Repr. of 1578 ed. 39.00x (ISBN 0-8201-1267-4). Schol Facsimiles.

Mozley, James F. John Foxe & His Book. LC 76-120651. 1970. Repr. of 1940 ed. lib. bdg. 14.50x (ISBN 0-374-95977-3). Octagon.

Olsen, V. Norskov. John Foxe & the Elizabethan Church. 1973. 26.75x (ISBN 0-520-02075-8). U of Cal Pr.

FOXES

see also Red Fox

Burkett, Molly & Burkett, John. Foxes Three. LC 75-15649. (Illus.). 160p. (gr. 3-6). 1975. 7.95 (ISBN 0-397-31630-5, JBL-J). Har-Row.

Caius, John. Of Englishe Dogges, the Diversities & the Properties. Fleming, A., tr. LC 73-26240. (English Experience Ser.: No. 110). 44p. 1969. Repr. of 1576 ed. 8.00 (ISBN 90-221-0110-X). Walter J Johnson.

Committee On Animal Nutrition. Nutrient Requirements of Mink & Foxes. (Nutrient Requirements of Domestic Animals Ser.). 1968. pap. 3.50 (ISBN 0-309-01676-2). Natl Acad Pr.

Edwards, Mary L. In Woods & Meadows. 1978. 7.95 (ISBN 0-533-03698-4). Vantage.

Johnson, Fred. The Foxes. Bourne, Russell & Lawrence, Bonnie S., eds. LC 73-83781. (Ranger Rick's Best Friends Ser.: No. 1). (Illus.). 32p. (gr. 1-6). 1973. 2.00 (ISBN 0-912186-04-6). Natl Wildlife.

Johnston, Johanna. The Fabulous Fox: An Anthology of Fact & Fiction. LC 78-21031. (Illus.). (gr. 5 up). 1979. 5.95 (ISBN 0-396-07652-1). Dodd.

Livermore, Elaine. Follow the Fox. (gr. k-3). 1981. 7.95 (ISBN 0-395-31672-3). HM.

McDearmon, Kay. Foxes. (A Skylight Bk.). (Illus.). (gr. 3-5). 1981. PLB 5.95 (ISBN 0-396-07972-5). Dodd.

May, Julian. Cactus Fox. LC 78-156051. (Illus.). (gr. 3-6). 1972. PLB 7.95 (ISBN 0-87191-078-0). Creative Ed.

Pfloog, Jan. The Fox Book. (Illus.). 24p. (gr. k-1). 1976. PLB 5.38 (ISBN 0-307-68978-6, Golden Pr). Western Pub.

Roach, Marilynne. Dune Fox. (Illus.). (gr. 1-3). 1977. 6.95 (ISBN 0-316-74870-6, Atlantic-Little, Brown). Little.

Taketazu, Minoru. Fox Family. LC 79-9286. (Illus.). 1979. 25.00 (ISBN 0-8348-1039-5). Weatherhill.

FOXES–LEGENDS AND STORIES

Dudley, Ernest. For Love of a Wild Thing. LC 74-80816. 224p. 1974. 10.00 (ISBN 0-8397-2325-3). Eriksson.

Johnston, Tony. Five Little Foxes & the Snow. LC 76-50579. (Illus.). (gr. k-4). 1977. 6.95 (ISBN 0-399-20557-8). Putnam.

Lippincott, Joseph W. Little Red the Fox. rev. ed. (Illus.). (gr. 4-6). 1953. 5.95 (ISBN 0-397-30239-8). Har-Row.

FOXES IN ART

Varty, Kenneth. Reynard the Fox: A Study of the Fox in Medieval Enlish Art. 1967. text ed. 25.00x (ISBN 0-391-01055-7, Leicester). Humanities.

FOXHOLES

see Intrenchments

FOYT, A. J., 1935-

Braun, Thomas. A. J. Foyt: Superstars. LC 76-12627. 1974. PLB 5.95 (ISBN 0-87191-282-1). Creative Ed.

Kupper, Mike. Driven to Win: A. J. Foyt. LC 75-19276. (Sports Profiles Ser.). (Illus.). 48p. (gr. 4-11). 1975. PLB 9.30 (ISBN 0-8172-0120-3). Raintree Pubs.

Libby, Bill. A. J. Foyt: Racing Champion. LC 78-767. (Sports Shelf Ser.). (Illus.). (gr. 6-8). 1978. PLB 6.29 (ISBN 0-399-61123-1). Putnam.

Olney, Ross R. A. J. Foyt: The Only Four Time Winner. LC 77-86364. (Star People Ser.). (Illus.). (gr. 4 up). 1978. PLB 5.99 (ISBN 0-8178-5792-3). Harvey.

FRA ANGELICO (GIOVANNI DA FIESOLE), 1387-1455

Pope-Hennessey, John. Fra Angelico. rev. ed. LC 74-9200. (Illus.). 296p. 1974. 60.00x (ISBN 0-8014-0855-5). Cornell U Pr.

Serti, Luciano, ed. Fra Angelico. (Art Library Ser.: Vol. 22). (Illus., Orig.). 1969. pap. 3.50 (ISBN 0-448-00471-2). G&D.

FRACTIONS

Clark, Clara E. & Lytle, Gretchen B. Beginning Fractions. (The Basic Skills in Math Ser.). (Illus.). 1975. tchr's manual 3.25 (ISBN 0-89170-008-0). Laurel Pub.

Daniel, Charlie & Daniel, Becky. Freaky Fractions. (gr. 1-5). 1978. 4.95 (ISBN 0-916456-19-6, GA77). Good Apple.

Dennis, J. Richard. Fractions Are Parts of Things. LC 73-127603. (Illus.). 40p. (gr. 2-5). 1971. 7.95 (ISBN 0-690-31520-1, TYC-J); PLB 8.79 (ISBN 0-690-31521-X); pap. 1.45 (ISBN 0-690-31522-8, TYC-J). Har-Row.

Driscoll, P., et al. Fractions. West, K. & Johnston, D., eds. (Math Skills for Daily Living Ser.). (Illus.). 40p. (gr. 7-12). 1979. pap. text ed. 3.95x (ISBN 0-87453-092-X, 82092). Denoyer.

Fair, Jan. Electric Drill-Fractions. (Electric Drill Set Ser.). (Illus.). (gr. 5-12). 1975. tchrs. ed. 24.95 (ISBN 0-88488-077-X). Creative Pubns.

Frank, Marge. Fraction Action. (Choose-a-Card Ser.). (Illus.). 32p. (gr. 3-6). 1981. pap. text ed. 5.95 (ISBN 0-86530-015-1, IP 151). Incentive Pubns.

Gatje, Charles T. & Gatje, John F. A Math Activity Packet for Fractions. (Orig.). 1976. pap. text ed. 1.50 (ISBN 0-937534-01-3). G&G Pubs.

Gregorich, Barbara & Odom, Clark. Fractions. LC 79-730045. (Illus.). 1978. 135.00 (ISBN 0-89290-094-6, A510-SATC). Soc for Visual.

Howett, J. Basic Skills with Fractions. 128p. 1980. pap. text ed. 3.00 (ISBN 0-8428-2117-1). Cambridge Bk.

Jenkins, Lee & McLean, Peggy. Fraction Tile Program. (Illus., Orig.). (gr. 2-9). 1972. pap. 2.95 student's bk. (ISBN 0-918932-17-3); tchr's bk. 2.95 (ISBN 0-918932-18-1); manipulative bk. 3.50 (ISBN 0-918932-19-X); acrylic tiles 23.50 (ISBN 0-686-67783-8). Activity Resources.

Learning Achievement Corporation. Fractions & Food: Fractions, Decimals & Electronic Communications. Zak, Therese A., ed. (MATCH Ser.). (Illus.). 144p. 1981. text ed. 5.28 (ISBN 0-07-037113-X, G). McGraw.

Loose, Frances F. Fractions, Book 1: Reusable Edition. (gr. 4). 1973. wkbk. 6.00x (ISBN 0-89039-064-9). Ann Arbor Pubs.

--Fractions, Book 2: Reusable Edition. (gr. 4-6). 1973. wkbk. 6.50x (ISBN 0-89039-066-5). Ann Arbor Pubs.

--Fractions: Teacher's Guide. 1973. 2.00x (ISBN 0-89039-067-3). Ann Arbor Pubs.

Mick, Beverly J. Multiplication Facts & Basic Fractions. (gr. 5-12). 1981. Set. 8.50 (ISBN 0-932786-01-4); Bk. 1. 4.25 (ISBN 0-932786-02-2); Bk. 2. 4.25 (ISBN 0-932786-03-0). Bellefontaine.

Rasmussen, Steven. Key to Fractions Series. Incl. Bk. 1. Fraction Concepts. 40p (ISBN 0-913684-91-0); Bk. 2. Multiplying & Dividing. 40p (ISBN 0-913684-92-9); Bk. 3. Adding & Subtracting. 40p (ISBN 0-913684-93-7). (gr. 4 up). 1980. pap. 0.95 ea. Key Curr Project.

Singer, Bertrand B. Mathematics at Work: Decimals. (gr. 9-12). 1977. pap. text ed. 9.95 (ISBN 0-07-057489-8, G); answer key 1.95 (ISBN 0-07-057490-1). McGraw.

--Mathematics at Work: Fractions. (Illus.). (gr. 9-12). 1977. pap. 6.95 (ISBN 0-07-057487-1, G); answer key 1.95 (ISBN 0-07-057488-X). McGraw.

Smart, Margaret & Tuel, Patricia. Focus on Fractions, 3 vols. (Illus.). (gr. 6-9). 1977. pap. text ed. 4.50 ea.; Set. 12.95 (ISBN 0-918932-69-6). Vol. 1 (ISBN 0-918932-14-9). Vol. 2 (ISBN 0-918932-15-7). Vol. 3 (ISBN 0-918932-16-5). Activity Resources.

Swienciki, Lawrence W. Adventures with Arithmetic, Fractions. (Illus.). 48p. (Orig.). (gr. 7-12). 1974. wkbk. 4.95 (ISBN 0-88488-000-1). Creative Pubns.

FRACTIONS–PROGRAMMED INSTRUCTION

Bezuszka, Stanley, et al. Fraction Action 1. (Motivated Math Project Activity Booklets). 47p. (Orig.). (gr. 5-8). 1976. pap. text ed. 2.00 (ISBN 0-917916-12-3). Boston Coll Math.

--Fraction Action 2. (Motivated Math Project Activity Booklets). 68p. (Orig.). (gr. 7-12). 1976. pap. text ed. 2.00 (ISBN 0-917916-13-1). Boston Coll Math.

Gatje, Charles T. & Gatje, John F. A MAP for Fractions. Marcos, Rafael, tr. (Orig., Span.). (gr. 5 up). 1981. pap. text ed. 1.75 (ISBN 0-937534-07-2). G&G Pubs.

Sorracco, Lionel J., Jr. Math House Proficiency Review Tapes: Operations with Whole Numbers & Fractions, Unit A. (YA) (gr. 7 up). 1980. manual & cassettes 179.50 (ISBN 0-917792-03-3). Math Hse.

FRACTIONS, CONTINUED

see also Processes, Infinite

Jones, William B. & Thron, W. J. Continued Fractions: Analytic Theory & Applications. (Encyclopedia of Mathematics & Applications Ser.: Vol. II). (Illus.). 450p. 1980. cancelled (ISBN 0-201-13510-8). A-W.

Moore, Charles G. An Introduction to Continued Fractions. LC 64-18579. (gr. 9-12). 1964. pap. 2.50 (ISBN 0-87353-064-0). NCTM.

Olds, Carl D. Continued Fractions. LC 61-12185. (New Mathematical Library: No. 9). 1975. pap. 6.50 (ISBN 0-88385-609-3). Math Assn.

Shohat, J. A. & Tamarkin, J. D. Problem of Moments. LC 51-96. (Mathematical Surveys Ser.: No. 1). 1963. Repr. of 1943 ed. 25.60 (ISBN 0-8218-1501-6, SURV-1). Am Math.

Wall, H. S. Analytic Theory of Continued Fractions. LC 66-24296. 14.95 (ISBN 0-8284-0207-8). Chelsea Pub.

FRACTURE MECHANICS

see also Brittleness; Materials–Fatigue; Metals–Fracture; Polymers and Polymerization–Fracture; Yield-Line Analysis

Allgower, M., et al, eds. ASIF - Technique for Internal Fixation of Fractures. 1976. ring binder 269.60 (ISBN 0-387-92105-2). Springer-Verlag.

Bonis, L. J., et al, eds. Fracture of Metals, Polymers & Glasses. (Fundamental Phenomena in the Materials Science Ser.: Vol. 4). 310p. 1967. 32.50 (ISBN 0-306-38604-6, Plenum Pr). Plenum Pub.

Bradt, Richard C., et al, eds. Fracture Mechancis of Ceramics, 4 vols. Incl. Vol. 1. 443p. 1974. 42.50 (ISBN 0-306-37591-5); Vol. 2. 494p. 1974. 42.50 (ISBN 0-306-37592-3); Vol. 3. Flaws & Testing. 528p. 1978. 45.00 (ISBN 0-306-37593-1); Vol. 4. Crack Growth & Microstructure. 504p. 1978. 45.00 (ISBN 0-306-37594-X). LC 73-20399 (Plenum Pr). Plenum Pub.

Broek, D. Elementary Engineering Fracture Mechanics. rev. ed. 450p. 1978. 60.00x (ISBN 90-286-0208-9); pap. 20.00x (ISBN 90-286-0218-6). Sijthoff & Noordhoff.

Burke & Weiss, eds. Application of Fracture Mechanics to Design. (Sagamore Army Materials Research Conference: Vol. 22). 1979. 39.50 (ISBN 0-306-40040-5, Plenum Pr). Plenum Pub.

Burridge, Robert, ed. Fracture Mechanics. LC 78-24473. (SIAM-AMS Proceedings: Vol. 12). 1979. 16.80 (ISBN 0-8218-1332-3). Am Math.

Caddell, Robert M. Deformation & Fracture of Solids. (Illus.). 1980. text ed. 27.95 (ISBN 0-13-198309-1). P-H.

Chell, G. G., ed. Developments in Fracture Mechanics-1. (Illus.). 1979. 57.00x (ISBN 0-85334-858-8, Pub. by Applied Science). Burgess-Intl Ideas.

Cherepanov, C. P. Mechanics of Brittle Fracture. 1979. 110.00 (ISBN 0-07-010739-4). McGraw.

Conway, J. B. Numerical Methods for Creep & Rupture Analysis. 1967. 45.25 (ISBN 0-677-01090-7). Gordon.

Crack Arrest Methodology & Applications. (Special Technical Publications Ser.). 452p. 1980. 44.75x (ISBN 0-686-76045-X, 711, 04-711000-30). ASTM.

Cyclic Stress-Strain Behavior: Analysis, Experimentation & Failure Prediction. 1973. 28.00 (ISBN 0-8031-0078-7, STP519). ASTM.

Developments in Fracture Mechanics Test Methods Standardization. 1977. 24.75 (ISBN 0-686-52035-1, 04-632000-30). ASTM.

Easterling, K., ed. Mechanisms of Deformation & Fracture: Proceedings of the Interdisciplinary Conference, Held at the University of Lulea-Sweden, 20-22, September 1978. (Strength & Fracture of Materials & Structures). 1979. 89.00 (ISBN 0-08-024258-8). Pergamon.

Effects of Environment & Complex Load History on Fatigue Life. 1970. 22.00 (ISBN 0-8031-0032-9, 04-462000-30). ASTM.

Fatigue Crack Growth Under Spectrum Loads. 1976. 34.50 (ISBN 0-686-52028-9, 04-595000-30). ASTM.

Ford, Hugh, et al. Fracture Mechanics in Design & Service. (Phil Trans of the Royal Soc., Series A: Vol. 299). (Illus.). 239p. 1981. lib. bdg. 67.00x (ISBN 0-85403-152-9, Pub. by Royal Soc London). Scholium Intl.

Fracture Analysis. 1974. 22.75 (ISBN 0-686-52044-0, 04-560000-30). ASTM.

Fracture Mechanics. (Special Technical Publications Ser.). 587p. 1980. 53.25x (ISBN 0-686-76046-8, 700, 04-700000-30). ASTM.

Fracture Mechanics. (Special Technical Publications Ser.). 802p. 1979. 60.00x (ISBN 0-686-31513-8, 677, 04-677000-30). ASTtM.

Fracture Mechanics Applied to Brittle Measurements. (Special Technical Publications Ser.). 232p. 1979. 25.00x (ISBN 0-686-76047-6, 678, 04-678000-30). ASTM.

Fracture Toughness. (Special Technical Publications Ser.). 191p. 1972. 18.25x (ISBN 0-686-76049-2, 514, 04-514000-30). ASTM.

Fracture Toughness & Slow-Stable Cracking. 1974. 25.25 (ISBN 0-686-52045-9, 04-559000-30). ASTM.

Fracture Toughness Testing & Its Applications. 1965. 19.50 (ISBN 0-8031-0105-8, STP381). ASTM.

Garrett, G. G. & Marriott, D. L., eds. Engineering Applications of Fracture Analysis: Proceedings of the First National Conference on Fracture Held in Johannesburg, South Africa, 1979. LC 80-41074. (International Ser. on the Strength & Fractures of Materials & Structures). (Illus.). 440p. 1980. 60.00 (ISBN 0-08-025437-3). Pergamon.

Hertzberg, Richard W. Deformation & Fracture Mechanics of Engineering Materials. LC 76-10812. 580p. 1976. 32.95 (ISBN 0-471-37385-0). Wiley.

Jayatilaka, Ayal De S. Fracture of Engineering Brittle Materials. (Illus.). 1979. 64.60x (ISBN 0-85334-825-1, Pub. by Applied Science). Burgess-Intl Ideas.

Kobayashi, Albert S., ed. Experimental Techniques in Fracture Mechanics. LC 72-13967. (Society for Experimental Stress Analysis Ser.: No. 1). (Illus.). 160p. 1973. 7.50x (ISBN 0-8138-0710-7). Iowa St U Pr.

--Experimental Techniques in Fracture Mechanics, No. 2. (Society for Experimental Stress Analysis Ser.: No.2). (Illus.). 216p. 1975. text ed. 8.95x (ISBN 0-8138-0735-2). Iowa St U Pr.

Larsson, L. H., ed. Advances in Elasto-Plastic Fracture Mechanics. (Illus.). xi, 428p. 1980. 45.00x (ISBN 0-85334-889-8, Pub. by Applied Science). Burgess-Intl Ideas.

Latzko, D. G., ed. Post-Yield Fracture Mechanics. (Illus.). 1979. 63.00x (ISBN 0-85334-775-1). Intl Ideas.

Lawn, B. R. & Wilshaw, T. R. Fracture of Brittle Solids. LC 74-12970. (Solid State Science Ser). (Illus.). 160p. 1975. 47.00 (ISBN 0-521-20654-5); pap. 17.50x (ISBN 0-521-09952-8). Cambridge U Pr.

Liebowitz, H., ed. Combined Nonlinear & Linear (Micro & Macro) Fracture Mechanics: Applications to Modern Engineering Structures - Selected Papers, U.S.-Japan Seminar. 1976. pap. text ed. 46.00 (ISBN 0-08-019982-8). Pergamon.

--Progress in Fatigue & Fracture, Vol. 8 No. 1. 1976. text ed. 60.00 (ISBN 0-08-020866-5). Pergamon.

Liebowitz, Harold A. A Treatise on Fracture, 7 vols. Incl. Vol. 1. Microscopic & Macroscopic Fundamentals of Fracture. 1969. 71.50 (ISBN 0-12-449701-2); Vol. 2. Mathematical Fundamentals of Fracture. 1969. 86.50 (ISBN 0-12-449702-0); Vol. 3. Engineering Fundamentals & Environmental Effects. 1971. 86.50 (ISBN 0-12-449703-9); Vol. 4. 1969. 58.50 (ISBN 0-12-449704-7); Vol. 5. 1969. 67.00 (ISBN 0-12-449705-5); Vol. 6. 1969. 67.00 (ISBN 0-12-449706-3); Vol. 7. 1972. 111.50 (ISBN 0-12-449707-1). Set. 355.00 (ISBN 0-685-23225-5). Acad Pr.

Mechanics of Crack Growth. 1976. 45.25 (ISBN 0-686-52042-4, 04-590000-30). ASTM.

Panasyuk, V. V. Limiting Equilibrium of Brittle Solids with Fractures. LC 75-135093. 325p. 1969. 34.50 (ISBN 0-686-01972-5). Mgmt Info Serv.

Parker, A. P. Mechanics of Fracture & Fatigue: An Introduction. 1981. 29.95x (ISBN 0-419-11460-2, Pub. by E & FN Spon); pap. 14.95x (ISBN 0-419-11470-X). Methuen Inc.

Part-Through Crack Fatigue Life Prediction. (Special Technical Publications Ser.). 226p. 1979. 26.25x (ISBN 0-686-76041-7, 687, 04-687000-30). ASTM.

Parton, V. Elastic-Plastic Fracture Mechanics. 233p. 1978. 10.00 (ISBN 0-8285-0678-7, Pub. by Mir Pubs Russia). Imported Pubns.

Perrone, N. & Atluri, S. N., eds. Nonlinear & Dynamic Fracture Mechanics, Bk. No. G00152. LC 79-54425. (Applied Mechanics Division Ser.: Vol. 35). 220p. 1979. 30.00 (ISBN 0-686-62962-0). ASME.

Progress in Flow Growth & Fracture Toughness Testing. 1973. 33.25 (ISBN 0-8031-0084-1, STP536). ASTM.

Radon, J. C. Fracture & Fatigue - Elasto-Plasticity, Thin Sheet & Micro-Mechanisms: Proceedings of the Third European Colloquium on Fracture, London, 8-10 September 1980. LC 80-40915. (Illus.). 450p. 1980. 60.00 (ISBN 0-08-026161-2). Pergamon.

Rolfe, Stan & Barson, John. Fracture & Fatigue Control in Structures: Applications of Fracture Mechanics. (Illus.). 1977. text ed. 34.95 (ISBN 0-13-329953-8). P-H.

Second European Colloquium on Fracture (EFC) (Fracture Mechanisms & Analysis of Failures Ser.). 395p. 1978. pap. 100.00x (ISBN 3-18-140618-X, Pub. by VDI Verlag Germany). Renouf.

Sih, G. C. & Tamus, V. P. Fracture of Composite Materials. 429p. 1979. 35.00x (ISBN 90-286-0289-5). Sijthoff & Noordhoff.

Sih, G. C., ed. Analytical & Experimental Fracture Mechanics. Mirabile, M. 970p. 1981. 87.50x (ISBN 90-286-0890-7). Sijthoff & Noordhoff.
--Fracture Mechanics & Technology, 2 vols. 1636p. 1977. 125.00x (ISBN 90-286-0934-2). Sijthoff & Noordhoff.
Sih, G. C. & Theocaris, P. S., eds. Mixed Mode Crack Propagation. 410p. 1981. 50.00x (ISBN 90-286-2691-3). Sijthoff & Noordhoff.
Smith, R. A., ed. Fracture Mechanics, Current Status, Future Prospects: Proceedings of a Conference Held at Cambridge University, March 16, 1979. (Illus.). 128p. 1979. 55.00 (ISBN 0-08-024766-0). Pergamon.
Stress Analysis & Growth of Cracks. 307p. 1972. 27.50x (ISBN 0-686-76050-6, 513, 04-513000-30). ASTM.
Tetelman, A. S. & McEvily, A. J. Fracture of Structural Materials. LC 67-12573. (Wiley Series on the Science & Technology of Materials). 697p. 1967. 46.50 (ISBN 0-471-85350-X, Pub. by Wiley-Interscience). Wiley.
Yokobori, T. Interdisciplinary Approach to Fractures & Strength of Solids. 1968. 68.75 (ISBN 0-677-61320-2). Gordon.

FRACTURE OF METALS
see Metals–Fracture

FRACTURE OF POLYMERIC MATERIALS
see Polymers and Polymerization–Fracture

FRACTURE OF SOLIDS
see Fracture Mechanics

FRACTURES
see also Bones; Pseudarthrosis; Surgery; X-Rays also subdivision Fracture or Wounds and injuries under particular bones etc, e.g. Skull–Wounds and Injuries

Adams, John C. Outline of Fractures. 7th ed. LC 77-30525. (Illus.). 1978. pap. text ed. 16.25 (ISBN 0-443-01633-X). Churchill.
American College of Surgeons. Early Care of the Injured Patient. 2nd ed. LC 76-8566. (Illus.). 1976. text ed. 17.00 (ISBN 0-7216-1161-3). Saunders.
Apley, A. Graham. System of Orthopedics & Fractures. 5th ed. 1977. 56.95 (ISBN 0-407-40653-0). Butterworth.
Bohler, Lorenz & Bohler, Jorg. The Treatment of Fractures. 1966. with 406pp. suppl. 90.50 (ISBN 0-8089-0063-3). Grune.
Bohler, Lorenz, et al. The Treatment of Fractures. LC 55-5445. (Illus.). 1956-58. Vol. 2, 450pps. 1957. 55.25 (ISBN 0-8089-0065-X); Vol. 3, 816pps, 1958. 68.00 (ISBN 0-8089-0066-8). Grune.
Cameron, Bruce M. Shaft Fractures & Pseudarthroses. (Illus.). 128p. 1966. ed. spiral bdg. 17.50photocopy (ISBN 0-398-00276-2). C C Thomas.
Cave, Edwin F., et al. Trauma Management. (Illus.). 2251p. 1974. 90.00 (ISBN 0-8151-1454-0). Year Bk Med.
Chapchal, G., ed. Fractures in Children. (Reconstruction Surgery & Traumatology Ser.: Vol. 17). (Illus.). 1979. 47.50 (ISBN 3-8055-3013-7). S Karger.
Charnley, John. Closed Treatment of Common Fractures. 3rd ed. 1970. 30.00 (ISBN 0-443-00119-7). Churchill.
Clissold, Grace K. The Body's Response to Trauma: Fractures. LC 72-97905. (Illus.). 1973. pap. text ed. 7.50 (ISBN 0-8261-1350-8). Springer Pub.
Connolly, John F., ed. DePalma's the Management of Fractures & Dislocations: An Atlas, 2 vols. 3rd ed. (Illus.). 2000p. Date not set. Set. text ed. price not set (ISBN 0-7216-2666-1); Vol. 1. price not set (ISBN 0-7216-2702-1); Vol. 2. price not set (ISBN 0-7216-2703-X). Saunders.
DePalma, Anthony F. Management of Fractures & Dislocations: An Atlas, 2 vols. 2nd ed. LC 69-12877. (Illus.). 1970. Set. 75.00 (ISBN 0-686-66532-5); 37.50 ea.; Vol. 1. (ISBN 0-7216-3027-8); Vol. 2. (ISBN 0-7216-3028-6). Saunders.
Devers, Michael. Stress Fractures. (Illus.). 245p. 1975. text ed. 52.65 (ISBN 0-443-01146-X). Churchill.
Francois, D. Advances in Fracture Research: Proceedings of the 5th International Conference on Fracture, 1981, Cannes, France. LC 80-41879. (International Series on the Strength & Fracture of Materials & Structures). 3000p. 1981. 450.00 (ISBN 0-08-025428-4); pap. 375.00 (ISBN 0-08-024776-8). Pergamon.
Gozna, Eric R. & Harrington, Ian J. Biomechanics of Musculoskeletal Injury. 150p. 1981. lib. bdg. 19.95 (ISBN 0-683-03728-5). Williams & Wilkins.
Hartman, J. Ted. Fracture Management: A Practical Approach. LC 77-24292. (Illus.). 338p. 1978. text ed. 21.50 (ISBN 0-8121-0601-6). Lea & Febiger.
Heppenstall, R. Bruce, ed. Fracture Treatment & Healing. LC 77-79395. (Illus.). 1087p. 1980. text ed. 75.00 (ISBN 0-7216-4638-7). Saunders.
Killey, H. C. Fractures of the Mandible. 1976. 9.95 (ISBN 0-8151-5035-0). Year Bk Med.
--Fractures of the Middle Third of the Facial Skeleton. 1977. 10.95 (ISBN 0-8151-5042-3). Year Bk Med.
Koostra, G. Femoral Shaft Fractures in Adults. 1973. 14.25x (ISBN 90-232-1123-5, Pub by Van Gorcum). Intl Schol Bk Serv.
Kuntscher, Gerhard. Practice of Intramedullary Nailing. (Illus.). 388p. 1967. photocopy ed. 35.75 (ISBN 0-398-01067-6). C C Thomas.
Letournel, E. & Judet, R. Fracture to the Acetabulum. (Illus.). 420p. 1981. 151.80 (ISBN 0-387-09875-5). Springer-Verlag.
Matter, Peter & Rittman, Willy-Werner. The Open Fracture. (Illus.). 1978. 47.50 (ISBN 0-8151-5779-7). Year Bk Med.
Morris, James M. & Blickenstaff, Loren D. Fatigue Fractures: A Clinical Study. (Illus.). 232p. 1967. photocopy ed. spiral 22.50 (ISBN 0-398-01351-9). C C Thomas.
Mueller, M. E., et al. Manual of Internal Fixation. 2nd rev. ed. LC 78-20743. (Illus.). 1979. 123.90 (ISBN 0-387-09227-7). Springer-Verlag.
Radin, E. L., et al. Practical Biomechanics for the Orthopedic Surgeon. 168p. 1979. 24.50 (ISBN 0-686-74422-5, Pub. by Wiley Med). Wiley.
Rang, Mercer. Children's Fractures. LC 74-8276. 240p. 1974. text ed. 32.50 (ISBN 0-397-50338-5). Har-Row.
Rockwood, Charles A., Jr. & Green, David P., eds. Fractures, 2 vols. LC 74-32299. 1500p. 75. 120.00 (ISBN 0-397-50339-3). Har-Row.
Sarmiento, A. & Latta, L. Closed Functional Treatment of Fractures. (Illus.). 608p. 1981. 148.00 (ISBN 0-387-10384-8). Springer-Verlag.
Schultz, Robert J. The Language of Fractures. LC 75-43698. 408p. 1976. Repr. of 1972 ed. 29.50 (ISBN 0-88275-369-X). Krieger.
Segmuller, Gottfried. Surgical Stabilization of the Skeleton of the Hand. (Illus.). 170p. 1977. pap. 22.50 (ISBN 0-683-07751-1). Krieger.
Unthoff, H. K., ed. Current Concept of Internal Fixation of Fractures. (Illus.). 460p. 1980. 49.50 (ISBN 0-387-09846-1). Springer-Verlag.
Venable, Charles S. & Stuck, Walter G. The Internal Fixation of Fractures. (Illus.). 252p. 1947. photocopy ed. spiral 25.50 (ISBN 0-398-04450-3). C C Thomas.
Weber, B. G., ed. Treatment of Fractures in Children & Adolescents. LC 79-16985. (Illus.). 1979. 123.90 (ISBN 0-387-09313-3). Springer-Verlag.
Wilson, J. N., ed. Watson-Jones Fractures & Joint Injuries, 2 vols. rev. 5th ed. LC 75-7549. (Illus.). 1976. text ed. 150.00 (ISBN 0-443-01105-2). Churchill.

FRACTURES–JUVENILE LITERATURE

Nourse, Alan E. Fractures, Dislocations & Sprains. LC 78-6855. (First Bks). (Illus.). (gr. 4 up). 1978. PLB 6.90 s&l (ISBN 0-531-01494-0). Watts.
Wolff, Angelika. Mom, I Broke My Arm. LC 69-18646. (Illus.). (gr. k-3). 1969. PLB 6.87 (ISBN 0-87460-121-5). Lion Bks.

FRACTURES, SPONTANEOUS

Clissold, Grace K. The Body's Response to Trauma: Fractures. LC 72-97905. (Illus.). 1973. pap. text ed. 7.50 (ISBN 0-8261-1350-8). Springer Pub.

FRAENKEL, MICHAEL, 1896-1957

Lowenfels, Walter & McCord, Howard. Life of Fraenkel's Death. (Illus., Orig.). 1969. pap. 3.00 (ISBN 0-87422-008-4). Wash St U Pr.

FRAGMENTARY BOOKS
see Unfinished Books

FRAGONARD, JEAN HONORE, 1732-1806

Fragonard. (Artists Ser.). (Illus.). 1977. pap. 5.95 (ISBN 0-8120-0871-5). Barron.
Wakefield, David. Fragonard. 1981. 27.00x (ISBN 0-905368-01-0, Pub. by Jupiter England). State Mutual Bk.
--Fragonard. (Illus.). 1977. 15.95 (ISBN 0-8467-0246-0, Pub. by Two Continents); pap. 9.95 (ISBN 0-8467-0245-2). Hippocrene Bks.

FRAMES (STRUCTURES)
see Structural Frames

FRAMING (BUILDING)
see also Roofs

Elliot, Stewart. Timber Frame Raising. LC 79-84581. 129p. (Orig.). 1979. pap. 9.95 (ISBN 0-932302-01-7). Brick Hse Pub.
Jones, R. Framing, Sheathing & Insulation. LC 73-1847. 235p. 1973. pap. 7.00 (ISBN 0-8273-0096-4); answer book 1.60 (ISBN 0-8273-0097-2). Delmar.
Kani, Gaspar. Analysis of Multistory Frames. Hyman, Charles J., tr. LC 57-6114. 1967. 8.50 (ISBN 0-8044-4486-2). Ungar.
National Building Agency (NBA) & Timber Research & Development Assoc. (T.R.A.D.A.) Manual of Timber Frame Housing: A Simplified Method. (Illus.). 1980. text ed. 32.00x (ISBN 0-86095-815-9). Longman.

FRAMING OF PICTURES
see Picture Frames and Framing

FRANCE, ANATOLE (PSEUD. JACQUES ANATOLE THIBAULT, 1844-1924)

Brousson, Jean J. Anatole France Himself. Pollock, John, tr. 1973. 20.00 (ISBN 0-8274-0075-6). R West.
Dargan, Edwin P. Anatole France, Eighteen Forty-Four to Eighteen Ninety-Six. (Illus.). Repr. of 1937 ed. lib. bdg. 37.50x (ISBN 0-87991-511-0). Porcupine Pr.
George, W. L. Anatole France. 1973. Repr. of 1915 ed. 15.00 (ISBN 0-8274-0399-2). R West.
Gisell, Paul. Anatole France & His Circle. Repr. of 1922 ed. 25.00 (ISBN 0-8274-3786-2). R West.
Lion, Jacques & Martin, Andre. Contributions Bibliographiques sur Anatole France. LC 73-21639. 96p. 1974. Repr. lib. bdg. 17.50 (ISBN 0-8337-4651-0). B Franklin.
May, James L. Anatole France. LC 70-103205. 1970. Repr. of 1924 ed. 13.00 (ISBN 0-8046-0842-3). Kennikat.
Pouquet, Jeanne M. The Last Salon: Anatole France & His Muse. 1973. Repr. of 1927 ed. 20.00 (ISBN 0-8274-0999-0). R West.
Segur, Nicolas. Conversations with Anatole France. 1977. lib. bdg. 59.95 (ISBN 0-8490-1673-8). Gordon Pr.
Shanks, Lewis P. Anatole France. LC 70-103210. 1970. Repr. of 1919 ed. 11.00 (ISBN 0-8046-0847-4). Kennikat.
--Anatole France. 35.00 (ISBN 0-87968-623-5). Gordon Pr.
Smith, Helen B. The Skepticism of Anatole France. 35.00 (ISBN 0-8490-1057-8). Gordon Pr.
--The Skepticism of Anatole France. LC 76-46532. 1973. Repr. of 1927 ed. 20.00 (ISBN 0-8492-2403-9). R West.
Stewart, Herbert L. Anatole France. LC 72-1324. (Select Bibliographies Reprint Ser.). 1972. Repr. of 1927 ed. 21.00 (ISBN 0-8369-6837-9). Arno.
Tylden-Wright, David. Anatole France. LC 67-102216. (Illus.). 1967. 10.50x (ISBN 0-8002-0661-4). Intl Pubns Serv.

FRANCE
see also names of cities, towns and geographic areas in France

Barres, Maurice. The Undying Spirit of France. 1917. 14.50x (ISBN 0-686-51322-3). Elliots Bks.
Beck, Haig, ed. France: Ad Profiles. LC 78-68794. (Illus.). 1979. pap. 9.95 (ISBN 0-8478-0223-X). Rizzoli Intl.
Blond, Georges. Dreams of France. (Illus.). 120p. 1969. 13.50x (ISBN 0-8002-0756-4). Intl Pubns Serv.
Castellio, Sebastian. Advice to a Desolate France: 1562. new ed. Valkhoff, Maurius F., ed. Valkhoff, Wouter, tr. from Fr. LC 75-16650. xiv, 50p. (Eng.). 1975. 12.95 (ISBN 0-915762-00-5). Patmos Pr.
Cobb, Richard. Tour de France. 1978. text ed. 17.50x (ISBN 0-8419-7101-3). Holmes & Meier.
Codevilla, Angelo. Modern France. LC 74-56. 272p. 1974. 12.95 (ISBN 0-87548-150-7). Open Court.
De Martonne, E. Geographical Regions of France. Brentnall, H. C., tr. 1968. text ed. 9.95x (ISBN 0-435-34225-8). Heinemann Ed.
Dollfus, Jean. France: Its Geography & Growth. 128p. 1972. 15.25 (ISBN 0-7195-1898-9). Transatlantic.
Flower, J. E. France Today. 4th ed. 1980. pap. 9.95x (ISBN 0-416-74010-3). Methuen Inc.
Flower, J. E., ed. France Today: Introductory Studies. 3rd ed. LC 76-858560. 200p. 1977. pap. 8.95x (ISBN 0-416-85700-0). Methuen Inc.
Fox, Edward W. History in Geographic Perspective: The Other France. LC 79-140754. (Illus.). 1972. pap. 2.45x (ISBN 0-393-00650-6, Norton Lib). Norton.
France Specialized Catalogue, 1980. (Illus.). 52p. 1980. pap. 12.00x (ISBN 0-936668-00-8). Orzano Pub Co.
Gibbons, H. A. France & Ourselves. 59.95 (ISBN 0-8490-0189-7). Gordon Pr.
Hansen, Niles M. France in the Modern World. (Illus., Orig.). 1969. pap. 3.95x (ISBN 0-442-09742-5, SL42, Srchl). Van Nos Reinhold.
Huddleston, Sisley. A History of France. 1929. Repr. 15.00 (ISBN 0-685-43216-5). Norwood Edns.
Hueffer, Oliver M. French France. 1929. 10.00 (ISBN 0-8495-2360-5). Arden Lib.
Mason, Caroline A. The Spell of France. 1812. Repr. 10.00 (ISBN 0-685-43351-X). Norwood Edns.
Maurois, Andre. France. (Coll. Les Peintres Du Livre). 39.40 (ISBN 0-685-36936-6). French & Eur.
--La France change de visage, les fertus necessaires. (Coll. L'Air du Temps). pap. 6.25 (ISBN 0-685-36937-4). French & Eur.
Palay, Simin. Dictionnaire Du Bearnais et Du Gascon Modernes. 1044p. (Fr.). 1974. 95.00 (ISBN 0-686-56867-2, M-6645). French & Eur.
Peyrefitte, Alain. The Trouble with France. LC 81-47489. 352p. 1981. 17.95 (ISBN 0-394-51750-4). Knopf.
Propositions Pour la Creation du Parc National Ivoirien De Tai. (Illus.). 1973. pap. 7.50x (ISBN 2-88032-041-0, IUCN58, IUCN). Unipub.
Regional Problems & Policies in OECD Countries: Vol. 1, France, Italy, Ireland, Denmark, Sweden, Japan. 1976. 7.00x (ISBN 92-64-11486-6). OECD.
Sedgwick, Henry D. France. 1930. Repr. 25.00 (ISBN 0-685-43462-1). Norwood Edns.
Stein, Henri. Dictionnaire Topographique de la France. Hubert, J., ed. 738p. (Fr.). 1954. pap. 25.00 (ISBN 0-686-57226-2, M-6525). French & Eur.
Tingey, F. The North of France: Picardy & Artois. (History, People & Places Ser.). (Illus.). 160p. 1979. pap. 7.95 (ISBN 0-88254-558-2, Pub by Spurbooks England). Hippocrene Bks.
Trudel, Marcel. Atlas De la Nouvelle-France: Atlas of New France. 2nd ed. 1973. 9.00x (ISBN 2-7637-6402-9, Pub. by Laval). Intl Schol Bk Serv.

FRANCE–AIR FORCE

Farre, Henry. Sky Fighters of France: Aerial Warfare, Nineteen Fourteen to Nineteen Eighteen. Gilbert, James, ed. Rush, Catharine, tr. LC 79-7252. (Flight: Its First Seventy-Five Years Ser.). (Illus.). 1979. Repr. of 1919 ed. lib. bdg. 16.00x (ISBN 0-405-12164-4). Arno.
Hall, James N. High Adventure: A Narrative of Air Fighting in France. Gilbert, James, ed. LC 79-7267. (Flight: Its First Seventy-Five Years Ser.). 1979. Repr. of 1918 ed. lib. bdg. 20.00x (ISBN 0-405-12177-6). Arno.

FRANCE–ANTIQUITIES

Hemingway, M. F. The Initial Magdalenian in France. 502p. 70.00x (ISBN 0-86054-104-5, Pub. by BAR). State Mutual Bk.
Laville, Henri, et al. Rock Shelters of the Perigord: Geological Stratigraphy & Archaeological Succession. LC 80-511. (Studies in Archaeology). 1980. 29.50 (ISBN 0-12-438750-0). Acad Pr.
Movius, Hallam L., Jr. Excavation of Abri Pataud, les Eyzies (Dordogne) Stratigraphy. LC 76-52630. (American School of Prehistoric Bulletins Ser.: No. 31). (Illus.). 1977. pap. 30.00 (ISBN 0-87365-534-6). Peabody Harvard.
Nash, Daphne. Settlement & Coinage in Central Gaul, c. 200-50 B.C. 1978. 40.00x (ISBN 0-86054-006-5, Pub. by BAR). State Mutual Bk.

FRANCE–ARMY
see also France–History, Military

Ambler, John S. French Army in Politics, 1945-1962. LC 65-26274. 1966. 6.50 (ISBN 0-8142-0018-4). Ohio St U Pr.
Aron, Jean P., et al. Anthropologie Du Conscrit Francais D'apres les Comptes Numeriques et Sommaires Du Recrutement De L'armee, 1819-1826: Presentation Cartographique. (Civilisation et Societes: No. 28). 1972. 41.75 (ISBN 90-2797-167-6). Mouton.
Bankwitz, Philip C. Maxime Weygand & Civil-Military Relations in Modern France. LC 67-22860. (Historical Studies: No. 81). 1967. 20.00x (ISBN 0-674-55701-8). Harvard U Pr.
Bukhari, Emil. Napoleon's Guards Cavalry. (Men-at-Arms Ser.). (Illus.). 48p. 1979. pap. 7.95 (ISBN 0-85045-288-0). Hippocrene Bks.
Bukhari, Emir. Napoleon's Line Chasseurs. (Men-at-Arms Ser.). (Illus.). 48p. 1977. pap. 7.95 (ISBN 0-85045-269-4). Hippocrene Bks.
De Ville, Winston. Louisiana Troops, Seventeen Twenty-Seventeen-Seventy. LC 67-10538. (Illus.). 1965. pap. 10.00 (ISBN 0-8063-0463-4). Genealog Pub.
Gohier, Urbain D. Armee Contre la Nation. LC 72-147547. (Library of War & Peace; Control & Limitation of Arms). lib. bdg. 38.00 (ISBN 0-8240-0328-4). Garland Pub.
Hicks, James E. French Military Weapons, 1717-1938. LC 64-16389. (Illus.). 1964. 9.50 (ISBN 0-910598-05-3). Flayderman.
Jaures, Jean L. Democracy & Military Service. LC 70-147769. (Library of War & Peace; Control & Limitation of Arms). lib. bdg. 38.00 (ISBN 0-8240-0467-1). Garland Pub.
Kennett, Lee. French Armies in the Seven Years' War: A Study in Military Organization & Administration. LC 67-18529. 1967. 12.75 (ISBN 0-8223-0096-6). Duke.
Lefferts, Charles. Uniforms of the American, British, French & German Armies in the War of the American Revolution, 1775-1783. rev. ed. LC 70-27396. (Illus.). 304p. 1971. Repr. of 1926 ed. 8.00 (ISBN 0-87364-232-5). Paladin Ent.
Macdonald, Alexander, ed. Papers Relative to the Royal Guard of Scottish Archers in France. LC 79-175588. (Maitland Club, Glasgow. Publications: No. 36). Repr. of 1835 ed. 11.50 (ISBN 0-404-53007-9). AMS Pr.

Moch, Gaston. Armee D'une Democratie. LC 72-147555. (Library of War & Peace; Control & Limitation of Arms). lib. bdg. 38.00 (ISBN 0-8240-0334-9). Garland Pub.
Ralston, David B. Army of the Republic: The Place of the Military in the Political Evolution of France, 1871-1914. 1967. 17.50x (ISBN 0-262-18021-9). MIT Pr.
Scott, Samuel F. The Response of the Royal Army to the French Revolution: The Role & Development of the Line Army, 1793-1878. 1978. 45.00x (ISBN 0-19-822534-2). Oxford U Pr.
Thorburn, W. A. French Army Regiments & Uniforms. LC 76-13825. (Illus.). 1976. pap. 3.95 (ISBN 0-88254-411-X). Hippocrene Bks.

FRANCE–ARMY–FOREIGN LEGION

Chadzynski, Martin & Lakland, Carli. The Runaway! LC 79-14284. (gr. 7 up). 1979. 7.95 (ISBN 0-07-010360-7). McGraw.
Murray, Simon. Legionnaire: My Five Years in the French Foreign Legion. LC 78-14215. 1979. 9.95 (ISBN 0-8129-0798-1). Times Bks.
Szajkowski, Soza. Jews in the French Foreign Legion. 20.00x (ISBN 0-87068-285-7). Ktav.
Thomas, Nigel. The French Foreign Legion. LC 77-283. (History Makers Ser.). (Illus.). (YA) 1977. 6.95 (ISBN 0-312-30465-X). St Martin.
Windrow, Martin. French Foreign Legion. LC 73-833335. (Men-at-Arms Ser). (Illus.). 40p. 1973. pap. 7.95 (ISBN 0-88254-160-9). Hippocrene Bks.

FRANCE–ARMY–LAFAYETTE ESCADRILLE

Genet, E. C. An American for Lafayette: The Diaries of E. C. C. Genet, Lafayette Escadrille. Brown, Walt, Jr., ed. 227p. 1981. price not set (ISBN 0-8139-0893-0). U Pr of Va.
Hall, Bert & Niles, John J. One Man's War: The Story of the Lafayette Escadrille. Gilbert, James, ed. LC 79-7266. (Flight: Its First Seventy-Five Years Ser.). (Illus.). 1979. Repr. of 1929 ed. lib. bdg. 30.00x (ISBN 0-405-12176-8). Arno.
Parsons, Edwin C. I Flew with the Lafayette Escadrille. LC 74-169432. (Literature & History of Aviation Ser). 1971. Repr. of 1963 ed. 21.00 (ISBN 0-405-03775-9). Arno.

FRANCE–ASSEMBLEE NATIONALE, 1871-1942

Gooch, Robert K. French Parliamentary Committee System. LC 69-19226. 1969. Repr. of 1935 ed. 18.50 (ISBN 0-208-00803-9, Archon). Shoe String.
Howard, John E. Parliament & Foreign Policy in France. LC 74-6110. 172p. 1974. Repr. of 1948 ed. lib. bdg. 15.00x (ISBN 0-8371-7503-8, HOPF). Greenwood.
Rothney, John. Bonapartism After Sedan. LC 68-9752. (Illus.). 360p. 1969. 22.50x (ISBN 0-8014-0473-8). Cornell U Pr.
Warwick, Paul. The French Popular Front: A Legislative Analysis. LC 76-22952. (Illus.). 1977. lib. bdg. 16.00x (ISBN 0-226-86914-8). U of Chicago Pr.
Williams, Philip M. The French Parliament: Politics in the Fifth Republic. LC 75-32655. 1977. Repr. of 1968 ed. lib. bdg. 15.00x (ISBN 0-8371-8558-0, WIFPP). Greenwood.

FRANCE–BIBLIOGRAPHY

Chambers, Frances. France. (World Bibliographical Ser.: No. 13). 175p. 1980. 31.50 (ISBN 0-903450-25-9). ABC Clio.
Fondation des Sciences Politiques, Paris, France. Bibliographie Courante D'Articles de Periodiques Posterieurs a 1944 Sur les Problemes Politiques, Economiques et Sociaux: Dixieme Supplement, 2 vols. (Library Catalogs Bib.Guides). Orig. Title: Index to Post-1944 Periodical Articles on Political Economic & Social Problems - Tenth Supplement. 1979. Set. lib. bdg. 275.00 (ISBN 0-8161-0298-8). G K Hall.
Institut National De la Statistique et Des Etudes Economiques. Annuaire Statistique De la France 1979. 84th ed. LC 79-39079. (Illus.). 920p. (Fr.). 1979. 80.00x (ISBN 0-8002-2274-1). Intl Pubns Serv.
Mery, Raymond, ed. Annuaire De la Presse et De la Publicite 1980. 93rd ed. LC 75-648916. Orig. Title: Annuaire De la Presse Francaise et Etrangere. 874p. (Fr.). 1979. 87.50x (ISBN 0-8002-2474-4). Intl Pubns Serv.
Patrick, Alison. The Men of the First French Republic: Political Alignments in the National Convention of 1792. LC 72-4018. (Illus.). 425p. 1972. 27.50x (ISBN 0-8018-1305-0). Johns Hopkins.

FRANCE–BIOGRAPHY

Bernen, Robert. In the Heat of the Sun. 133p. 1981. 17.50 (ISBN 0-241-10521-8, Pub. by Hamish Hamilton England). David & Charles.
Bertocci, Philip A. Jules Simon: Republican Anticlericalism & Cultural Politics in France, 1848-1886. LC 77-14668. 1978. 17.00x (ISBN 0-8262-0239-X). U of Mo Pr.
Bloch, Marc. Memoirs of War, Nineteen Fourteen to Nineteen Fifteen. Fink, Carole, tr. from Fr. LC 79-6849. Orig. Title: Souvenirs De Guerre. (Illus.). 184p. 1980. 15.00 (ISBN 0-8014-1220-X). Cornell U Pr.
Bourneuf, Roland. St. Denys Garneau et Ses Lectures Europeennes. 1969. pap. 8.50 (ISBN 2-7637-6387-1, Pub. by Laval). Intl Schol Bk Serv.
Bradford, Gamaliel. Daughters of Eve. LC 72-85989. (Essay & General Literature Index Reprint Ser). 1969. Repr. of 1930 ed. 13.50 (ISBN 0-8046-0542-4). Kennikat.
Campan, Madame. Memoirs of Marie Antoinette. Waller, A. R., ed. 442p. 1981. Repr. of 1823 ed. lib. bdg. 40.00 (ISBN 0-89987-116-X). Darby Bks.
Chaytor, H. J. Savaric De Mavleon. 1939. 20.00 (ISBN 0-8274-3326-3). R West.
Cox, Trenchard. Jehan Foucquet, Native of Tours. LC 72-7072. (Select Bibliographies Reprint Ser.). 1972. Repr. of 1931 ed. 31.00 (ISBN 0-8369-6926-X). Arno.
Delisle, Leopold V., ed. Rouleaux Des Morts Du IXe Au XVe Siecle. 1866. 35.50 (ISBN 0-384-11361-3); pap. 31.00 (ISBN 0-384-11360-5). Johnson Repr.
De Pougy, Liane. My Blue Notebooks. Athill, Diana, tr. from Fr. LC 79-1659. (Illus.). 1979. 15.00 (ISBN 0-06-011083-X, HarpT). Harper Row.
Dictionnaire des Groupes Industriels et Financiers en France. 360p. (Fr.). 1978. 17.95 (ISBN 0-686-57102-9, M-6127). French & Eur.
Dictionnaire des Personnages de Tous les Temps et de Tous les Pays. 81.50 (ISBN 0-685-36081-4). French & Eur.
Dunoyer, Alphonse. The Public Prosecutor of the Terror: Antoine Quentin Fouquier-Tinville. 1977. lib. bdg. 59.95 (ISBN 0-8490-2489-7). Gordon Pr.
Durel, Lionel C. L' Oeuvre D'Andre Mareschal. 1973. pap. 11.50 (ISBN 0-384-13390-8). Johnson Repr.
Fowler, Carolyn. A Knot in the Thread: The Life & Work of Jacques Roumain. LC 76-53817. 1980. 12.95 (ISBN 0-88258-057-4). Howard U Pr.
Gallaher, John G. The Iron Marshal: A Biography of Louis N. Davout. LC 75-37956. (Illus.). 432p. 1976. 24.95x (ISBN 0-8093-0691-3). S Ill U Pr.
Gold, Arthur & Fizdale, Robert. Misia: The Life of Misia Sert. LC 80-27340. (Illus.). 340p. 1981. Repr. pap. 8.95 (ISBN 0-688-00391-5, Quill). Morrow.
Hamerton, Philip G. Modern Frenchmen: Five Biographies. LC 72-4579. (Essay Index Reprint Ser.). Repr. of 1878 ed. 22.00 (ISBN 0-8369-2947-0). Arno.
Herold, J. Christopher. Mistress to an Age: A Life of Madame De Stael. 1979. pap. 6.95 (ISBN 0-517-53783-4). Crown.
James, George P. Mary of Burgundy; or, the Revolt of Ghent, 3 vols. in 2. LC 79-8141. Repr. of 1833 ed. Set. 84.50 (ISBN 0-404-61940-1). Vol. 1 (ISBN 0-404-61941-X). Vol. 2 (ISBN 0-404-61942-8). AMS Pr.
Lafranche, Gaston M. The Intimate Memoirs of Louise Renee De Kerouaille, Duchess of Portsmouth & Aubigny. (The Great Women of History Library). (Illus.). 94p. 1981. 27.15 (ISBN 0-89266-275-1). Am Classical Coll Pr.
Lee, S. H., ed. The Boke of Duke Huon of Burdeux, Pts. 1-4. Bourchier, John, tr. (EETS, ES Ser.: Nos. 40-41). Repr. of 1887 ed. Pts. 1-2. 33.00 (ISBN 0-527-00249-6); Pts. 3-4. 14.00 (ISBN 0-527-00250-X). Kraus Repr.
Le Maingre, Jean. Le Livre des faicts du bon messire Jean le Maingre. LC 79-8367. Repr. of 1851 ed. 18.50 (ISBN 0-404-18351-4). AMS Pr.
McGowan, Francis X. The Story of Sain Odile, the Pearl of Alsace. 1979. Repr. of 1899 ed. lib. bdg. 12.50 (ISBN 0-8495-3514-X). Arden Lib.
Martin, Benjamin F., Jr. Count Albert De Mun: Paladin of the Third Republic. LC 78-1739. 1978. 24.00x (ISBN 0-8078-1325-7). U of NC Pr.
Masson, Madeleine. I Never Kissed Paris Goodbye. 1979. 19.95 (ISBN 0-241-89872-2, Pub by Hamish Hamilton). David & Charles.
Nowinski, Judith. Baron Dominique Vivant Denon, 1747-1825: Hedonist & Scholar in a Period of Transition. LC 78-86651. (Illus.). 280p. 1970. 18.00 (ISBN 0-8386-7470-4). Fairleigh Dickinson.
Ojala, Jeanne A. Auguste De Colbert: Aristocratic Survival in an Era of Upheaval, 1793-1809. 1979. 20.00x (ISBN 0-87480-129-X). U of Utah Pr.
Pearson, Hesketh. Henry of Navarre: The King Who Dared. LC 76-23244. 1976. Repr. of 1963 ed. lib. bdg. 18.75x (ISBN 0-8371-9015-0, PEHN). Greenwood.
Peguy, Charles. Saints de France. pap. 1.95 (ISBN 0-685-37039-9). French & Eur.
Prevost, M. M. & D'Amat, Roman, eds. Dictionnaire De Biographie Francaise, 13 vols. 1,300.00 (ISBN 0-685-99755-3). Adler.
Raitt, A. W. The Life of Villiers de L'Isle-Adam. (Illus.). 400p. 1981. 72.00 (ISBN 0-19-815771-1). Oxford U Pr.
Sainte-Beuve, C. A. Portraits of the Eighteenth Century: Historic & Literary, 2 Vols. Wormeley, Katherine P., tr. LC 64-15699. (Illus.). 1964. 38.00 (ISBN 0-8044-2759-3). Ungar.
--Portraits of the Seventeeth Century: Historic & Literary, 2 Vols. Wormeley, Katherine P., tr. (Illus.). 1964. 38.00 (ISBN 0-8044-2756-9). Ungar.
Sarolea, Charles. French Renascence. LC 73-110920. 1970. Repr. of 1916 ed. 12.50 (ISBN 0-8046-0902-0). Kennikat.
Schneider, Joyce A. Flora Tristan: Feminist, Socialist & Free Spirit. LC 80-20067. 256p. (gr. 7-9). 1980. 8.95 (ISBN 0-688-22250-1); PLB 8.59 (ISBN 0-688-32250-6). Morrow.
Sichel, Edith. Women & Men of the French Renaissance. LC 74-110923. (Illus.). 1970. Repr. of 1901 ed. 14.50 (ISBN 0-8046-0905-5). Kennikat.
Siegchrist, Mark. Rough in Brutal Print: The Legal Sources of Browning's "Red Cotton Night-Cap Country". 200p. 1981. 15.00 (ISBN 0-8142-0327-2). Ohio St U Pr.
Sleight, W. Charles Lecorgne: The Deaf Mute of Normandy. PLB 59.95 (ISBN 0-87968-842-4). Gordon Pr.
Smith, Albert. The Marchioness of Brinvilliers: The Poisoner of the Seventeenth Century. 1978. Repr. of 1886 ed. lib. bdg. 45.00 (ISBN 0-8495-4839-X). Arden Lib.
Storrs, Richars D. Bernard of Clairvaux. 69.75 (ISBN 0-87968-723-1). Gordon Pr.
Tyler, Sidney F. A Rainbow of Time & of Space: Orphans of the Titanic. 64p. 1981. pap. 5.95 (ISBN 0-89404-062-6). Aztex.
Watson, Paul B. Some Women of France. LC 73-90691. (Essay Index Reprint Ser). 1936. 19.50 (ISBN 0-8369-1433-3). Arno.
Who's Who in France - Dictionnaire Biographique, 1981-82. 15th ed. LC 54-17054. 1621p. (Fr.). 1981. 167.50x (ISBN 2-85784-015-2). Intl Pubns Serv.
Wright, Gordon. Insiders & Outliers: The Individual in History. (Illus.). 152p. 1981. price not set (ISBN 0-7167-1339-X); pap. price not set (ISBN 0-7167-1340-3). W H Freeman.

FRANCE–CHURCH HISTORY

Aulard, Alphonse. Christianity & the French Revolution. 1966. 18.50 (ISBN 0-86527-025-2). Fertig.
Chevalier, Jules. Visite Pastorale Du Diocese De Die Par Charls-Jacques De Leberon...1664. 200p. (Fr.). 1981. Repr. of 1913 ed. lib. bdg. 85.00 (ISBN 0-8287-1503-3). Clearwater Pub.
Delisle, Leopold V., ed. Rouleaux Des Morts Du IXe Au XVe Siecle. 1866. 35.50 (ISBN 0-384-11361-3); pap. 31.00 (ISBN 0-384-11360-5). Johnson Repr.
Galpern, A. N. The Religions of the People in Sixteenth-Century Champagne. (Historical Studies: No. 92). 1976. 19.50x (ISBN 0-674-75836-6). Harvard U Pr.
Gregorius, Saint Histoire Ecclesiastique Des Francs, 4 vols. 1967. 126.00 (ISBN 0-384-19875-9); pap. 108.00 (ISBN 0-384-19874-0). Johnson Repr.
--Zehn Bucher Frankischer Geschichte, 3 vols. 4th ed. Hellmann, S., ed. Von Geisebrecht, Wilhel M, tr. 1911-1913. pap. 28.00 ea. Johnson Repr.
Gregory Bishop Of Tours. History of the Franks. Brehaut, Ernest, ed. 1965. lib. bdg. 20.00x (ISBN 0-374-90950-4). Octagon.
Haag. La France Protestante: Biographies Historiques, 12 tomes. Set. 113.75 (ISBN 0-685-36098-9). French & Eur.
Histoire du Catholicisme en France, 3 tomes. Incl. Tome I. Des origines a la chretiente medievale (du IIe a la fin du XIIe siecle) Palanque & Delaruelle. 7.50 (ISBN 0-685-36063-6); Tome II. Sous les Rois Tres Chretiens (Du XIIIe au XVIIIe Siecle) Delaruelle & Latreilla. 8.50 (ISBN 0-685-36064-4); Tome III. La Periode Contemporaine (du XVIIIe Siecle a nos Jours) Latreille & Remona. 9.50 (ISBN 0-685-36065-2). French & Eur.
La Gorce, Pierre F. Histoire religieuse de la Revolution francaise, 5 Vols. LC 71-88239. (Fr). Repr. of 1923 ed. Set. 142.50 (ISBN 0-404-03810-7); 28.00 ea. Vol. 1 (ISBN 0-404-03811-5). Vol. 2 (ISBN 0-404-03812-3). Vol. 3 (ISBN 0-404-03813-1). Vol. 4 (ISBN 0-404-03814-X). Vol. 5 (ISBN 0-404-03815-8). AMS Pr.
Matthew, Donald. The Norman Monasteries & Their English Possessions. LC 78-26293. (Oxford Historical Ser.). 1979. Repr. of 1962 ed. lib. bdg. 18.75x (ISBN 0-313-20847-6, MANM). Greenwood.
Neale, J. E. The Age of Catherine de Medici. 1978. pap. 6.50 (ISBN 0-224-60566-6, Pub. by Chatto Bodley Jonathan). Merrimack Bk Serv.
Palm, Franklin C. Politics & Religion in Sixteenth-Century France: A Study of the Career of Henry of Montmorency-Damville, Uncrowned King of the South. 8.50 (ISBN 0-8446-0835-1). Peter Smith.
Perrens, Francois T. Libertins en France au Dix-Septieme Siecle. LC 72-168701. 428p. (Fr.). 1973. Repr. of 1896 ed. lib. bdg. 29.00 (ISBN 0-8337-2728-1). B Franklin.
Phillips, Charles S. Church in France, 1789-1848. LC 66-24748. 1966. Repr. of 1929 ed. 9.00 (ISBN 0-8462-0795-8). Russell.
--Church in France, 1848-1907. LC 66-24749. 1967. Repr. of 1936 ed. 10.00 (ISBN 0-8462-0775-3). Russell.
Rebillon, Armand, ed. Departement d'ille-et Vilaine. LC 74-29230. Repr. of 1913 ed. 65.00 (ISBN 0-404-58701-1). AMS Pr.
Robinet, Jean F. Le Mouvement religieux a Paris pendant la Revolution: 1789-1801, 2 vols. LC 70-174331. (Collection de documents relatifs a l'histoire de Paris pendant la Revolution francaise). Repr. of 1898 ed. Set. 106.50 (ISBN 0-404-52567-9); 53.25 ea. Vol. 1 (ISBN 0-404-52568-7). Vol. 2 (ISBN 0-404-52569-5). AMS Pr.
Schwartz, Hillel. The French Prophets: The History of a Millenarian Group in Eighteenth-Century England. LC 78-65459. (Illus.). 1980. 31.50x (ISBN 0-520-03815-0). U of Cal Pr.
Seguy, J. Les Assemblees Anabaptistes-Mennonites De France. 1977. 89.00x (ISBN 90-279-7524-8). Mouton.
Simard, Jean. Une Iconographie Du Clerge Francais Au XVIIe Siecle: Les Devotins De L'ecole Francaise et les Sources De L'imagerie Religience En France. (Illus.). 1977. pap. 15.50x (ISBN 2-7637-6768-0, Pub. by Laval). Intl Schol Bk Serv.
Stoddard, Whitney S. The Facade of Saint-Gilles-du-Gard: Its Influence on French Sculpture. LC 72-3696. (Illus.). 384p. 1973. 40.00x (ISBN 0-8195-4056-0, Pub. by Wesleyan U Pr); pap. 14.95 (ISBN 0-8195-6068-5). Columbia U Pr.
Tackett, T. Priest & Parish in Eighteenth-Century France. 1977. 25.00 (ISBN 0-691-05243-3). Princeton U Pr.
Wakefield, Walter L. Heresy, Crusade, & Inquisition in Southern France, 1100-1250. 1974. 28.50x (ISBN 0-520-02380-3). U of Cal Pr.

FRANCE–CIVILIZATION

Bagley, Charles R. & Diller, George E. France d'autrefois et d'aujourd'hui. 2nd ed. LC 61-13001. (Fr., Fr). 1961. 12.95x (ISBN 0-89197-177-7); pap. text ed. 4.95x (ISBN 0-89197-178-5). Irvington.
Barres, Maurice. Les Traits Eternels De la France. 1918. 14.50x (ISBN 0-685-89791-5). Elliots Bks.
Bernanos, Georges. La France contre les Robots. 3.95 (ISBN 0-685-37218-9). French & Eur.
Boussard, Jacques. Civilization of Charlemagne. (World University Library Ser.). (Illus., Orig.). 1968. pap. 3.95 (ISBN 0-07-006710-4, SP). McGraw.
Carlut, C. & Bree, G. France De Nos Jours. 3rd ed. 1968. text ed. 5.95 (ISBN 0-02-319320-4). Macmillan.
Comeau, Raymond, et al. Ensemble: Culture et Societe. LC 76-49630. 1977. pap. text ed. 10.95 (ISBN 0-03-018271-9, HoltC). HR&W.
Curtius, Ernst Robert. Civilization of France: an Introduction. facsimile ed. Wyon, Olive, tr. LC 70-148877. (Select Bibliographies Reprint Ser). Repr. of 1932 ed. 16.00 (ISBN 0-8369-5648-6). Arno.
Dappagne, A. Trois Aspects du francais contemporain. (Langue vivante). (Fr). pap. 8.25 (ISBN 0-685-14087-3, 3629). Larousse.
Dostert, L. & Lindenfeld, J. Francais, Cours Moyen, Civilisation. 1961. text ed. 6.95 (ISBN 0-02-815500-9). Glencoe.
Durant, Will & Durant, Ariel. Age of Louis Fourteenth. (Story of Civilization: Vol. 8). (Illus.). 1963. 25.95 (ISBN 0-671-01215-0). S&S.
Feuillerat, Albert. French Life & Ideals. 1925. 34.50x (ISBN 0-685-89753-2). Elliots Bks.
Franklin, Afred L. Dictionnaire Historique Des Arts, Metiers Et Professions Exerces Dans Paris Depuis Le Treizieme Siecle. (Biblio. & Ref. Ser.: No. 198). 1968. Repr. of 1906 ed. 49.00 (ISBN 0-8337-1231-4); 40.00 (ISBN 0-685-06747-5). B Franklin.
Gaxotte, Pierre. Age of Louis Fourteenth. Shaw, Michael, tr. 1970. Repr. of 1958 ed. 7.95 (ISBN 0-02-542880-2). Macmillan.
Guerard, Albert. French Civilization. 59.95 (ISBN 0-8490-0197-8). Gordon Pr.
Guerard, Albert L. French Civilization from Its Origins to the Close of the Middle Ages. LC 76-76562. 328p. Repr. of 1921 ed. 13.50x (ISBN 0-8154-0298-8). Cooper Sq.
--French Civilization in the Nineteenth Century. LC 74-132943. (History of French Civilization Ser.: Vol. III). 1971. Repr. of 1918 ed. lib. bdg. 13.50x (ISBN 0-8154-0357-7). Cooper Sq.

Hardre, Jacques. La France et la Civilisation. (Illus., Orig.). 1969. text ed. 19.50 scp (ISBN 0-06-042609-8, HarpC). Har-Row.
Havens, George R. The Age of Ideas: From Reaction to Revolution in Eighteenth Century France. (Illus.). 1955. 34.50x (ISBN 0-89197-651-5). Irvington.
Hess, John L. Vanishing France. LC 74-77944. (Illus.). 176p. 1975. 12.50 (ISBN 0-8129-0483-4). Times Bks.
Kruger, Fritz. Die Hochpyrenaen, 6 vols. LC 77-87689. Repr. of 1939 ed. 235.00 set (ISBN 0-404-16570-2). AMS Pr.
Lee, Vara G. Reign of Women in Eighteenth Century France. (Illus.). 192p. 1975. 11.95x (ISBN 0-87083-990-X); pap. 5.95x (ISBN 0-87073-992-1). Schenkman.
Mandrou, Robert. Introduction to Modern France. 1977. pap. 5.95x (ISBN 0-06-131627-X, TB1627, Torch). Har-Row.
--Introduction to Modern France, 1500-1640: An Essay in Historical Psychology. Hallmark, R. E., tr. LC 75-28239. (Illus.). 285p. 1976. text ed. 23.50x (ISBN 0-8419-0245-3). Holmes & Meier.
Metraux, Rhoda B. & Mead, Margaret. Themes in French Culture: A Preface to a Study of French Community. LC 77-87694. Repr. of 1954 ed. 15.00 (ISBN 0-404-16490-0). AMS Pr.
Mueller, Theodore & Niedzielski, Henri. Basic French. Incl. Premiers Pas. pap. text ed. 4.40x (ISBN 0-89197-670-1); Pratique de la grammaire. pap. text ed. 8.20x (ISBN 0-89197-671-X); Introduction a la culture. pap. text ed. 3.10x (ISBN 0-89197-672-8). (Fr.). 1974. Set. pap. text ed. 15.70x (ISBN 0-89197-673-6); tchr's manual avail. (ISBN 0-685-77774-X); Set. 29 audio tapes 232.00x (ISBN 0-8290-0141-7). Irvington.
Painter, Sidney. French Chivalry: Chivalric Ideas & Practices in Medieval France. (YA) (gr. 9-12). 1957. pap. 4.95 (ISBN 0-8014-9061-8, CP67). Cornell U Pr.
Shenkan, A. & Besnard, M. Au Fil Des Jours: Lectures En Francais. 1971. pap. text ed. 6.95x (ISBN 0-02-409650-4). Macmillan.
Taine, Hippolyte A. The Ancient Regime. 8.00 (ISBN 0-8446-1434-3). Peter Smith.
--The Ancient Regime: Les Oricines De la France Contemporaine. Durand, John, tr. LC 79-38368. (Select Bibliographies Reprint Ser.). Repr. of 1881 ed. 21.00 (ISBN 0-8369-6785-2). Arno.
--The Modern Regime, 2 vols. 8.00 ea. (ISBN 0-8446-1436-X). Peter Smith.
Tilley, Arthur A., ed. Modern France: A Companion to French Studies. LC 66-27168. (Illus.). 1967. Repr. of 1922 ed. 25.00 (ISBN 0-8462-0890-3). Russell.
Wiley, William L. Formal French. LC 67-17322. (Illus.). 1967. 15.00x (ISBN 0-674-30900-6). Harvard U Pr.
Williams, Roger L. Gaslight & Shadow: The World of Napoleon III, 1851-1870. LC 77-11624. 1977. Repr. of 1957 ed. lib. bdg. 20.75x (ISBN 0-8371-9821-6, WIGA). Greenwood.
Wright, Charles H. The Background of Modern French Literature. facsimile ed. LC 79-37360. (Select Bibliographies Reprint Ser). Repr. of 1926 ed. 25.00 (ISBN 0-8369-6707-0). Arno.

FRANCE–CIVILIZATION–HISTORY

Beauroy, Jacques, et al, eds. The Wolf & the Lamb: Popular Culture in France, from the Old Regime to the Twentieth Century. (Stanford French & Italian Studies: No. 3). (Illus.). 1977. pap. 24.50 (ISBN 0-915838-31-1). Anma Libri.
Ford, Ford M. Between Saint Denis & Saint George. LC 73-153640. (English Literature Ser., No. 33). 1971. Repr. lib. bdg. 38.95 (ISBN 0-8383-1244-6). Haskell.
Harding, Frank J. Matthew Arnold, The Critic & France. 1979. Repr. of 1964 ed. lib. bdg. 30.00 (ISBN 0-8495-2349-4). Arden Lib.
--Matthew Arnold, the Critic & France. LC 76-50106. 1977. Repr. of 1964 ed. lib. bdg. 25.00 (ISBN 0-8414-4721-7). Folcroft.
Picavet, Francois J. Les Idealogues: Scientific, Philosophical, & Religious Theories in France Since 1789. LC 74-25774. (European Sociology Ser.). 646p. 1975. Repr. 36.00x (ISBN 0-405-06528-0). Arno.
Stone, Donald. France in the Sixteenth Century. LC 75-46622. 180p. 1976. Repr. of 1969 ed. lib. bdg. 16.25x (ISBN 0-8371-8734-6, STFS). Greenwood.
Tyler, William R. Dijon & the Valois Dukes of Burgundy. LC 70-160507. (Centers of Civilization Ser.: Vol. 29). (Illus.). 1971. 5.95x (ISBN 0-8061-0979-3). U of Okla Pr.

FRANCE–COLONIES

Betts, Raymond F. Assimilation & Association in French Colonial Theory 1890-1914. LC 70-130622. (Columbia University Social Science Studies Ser.: No. 604). Repr. of 1961 ed. 17.50 (ISBN 0-404-51604-1). AMS Pr.
Cohen, William B. Rulers of Empire: The French Colonial Service in Africa. LC 76-137405. (Publications Ser.: No. 95). 1971. 11.95 (ISBN 0-8179-1951-1). Hoover Inst Pr.
Cooke, James J. The New French Imperialism, 1880-1910: The Third Republic & Colonial Expansion. (Library of Politics & Society Ser.). 224p. 1973. 18.50 (ISBN 0-208-01320-2, Archon). Shoe String.
Decalo, Samuel. Historical Dictionary of Niger. LC 79-15704. (African Historical Dictionaries Ser.: No. 20). 376p. 1979. 19.00 (ISBN 0-8108-1229-0). Scarecrow.
De Francis, J. Colonialism & Language Policy in Vietnam. 1977. 25.00x (ISBN 90-279-7643-0). Mouton.
Delavignette, Robert. Freedom & Authority in French West Africa. 152p. 1968. 26.00x (ISBN 0-7146-1652-4, F Cass Co). Biblio Dist.
Delzvignette, Robert. Robert Delzvignette on the French Empire: Selected Writings. Cohen, William B., tr. from Fr. Cohen, William, ed. LC 77-1339. 1977. lib. bdg. 13.00x (ISBN 0-226-14191-8). U of Chicago Pr.
Fanon, Frantz. Wretched of the Earth. Farrington, Constance, tr. 1965. pap. 2.95 (ISBN 0-394-17327-9, B342, BC). Grove.
Garrett, Mitchell B. French Colonial Question, 1789-1791. LC 72-100292. Repr. of 1916 ed. 10.00x (ISBN 0-8371-2925-7, Pub. by Negro U Pr). Greenwood.
Lescarbot, Marc. Nova Francia, or the Description of That Part of New France, Which Is One Continent with Virginia. Erondelle, Pierre E., tr. LC 77-7415. (English Experience Ser.: No. 877). 1977. Repr. of 1609 ed. lib. bdg. 31.00 (ISBN 90-221-0877-5). Walter J Johnson.
Levy, Roger. French Interests & Policies in the Far East. LC 75-30110. (Institute of Pacific Relations). 1976. Repr. of 1941 ed. 21.50 (ISBN 0-404-59540-5). AMS Pr.
Lokke, Carl L. France & the Colonial Question. LC 75-76632. (Columbia University. Studies in the Social Sciences: No. 365). Repr. of 1932 ed. 12.50 (ISBN 0-404-51365-4). AMS Pr.
--France & the Colonial Question: A Study of Contemporary French Opinion, 1763-1801. 1972. lib. bdg. 14.50x (ISBN 0-374-95081-4). Octagon.
Mitchell, Harold P. Europe in the Caribbean. LC 73-75777. (Illus.). xi, 211p. 1973. Repr. of 1963 ed. lib. bdg. 10.00x (ISBN 0-8154-0479-4). Cooper Sq.
Morris-Jones, W. H. & Fischer, Georges, eds. Decolonisation & After: The British & French Experience. (Studies in Commonwealth Politics & History: No. 7). 369p. 1980. 29.50x (ISBN 0-7146-3095-0, F Cass Co). Biblio Dist.
Newton, Arthur P., ed. Sea Commonwealth, & Other Papers. Imperial Studies Ser. facs. ed. LC 68-22114. (Essay Index Reprint Ser). 1919. 11.75 (ISBN 0-8369-0742-6). Arno.
Power, Thomas F., Jr. Jules Ferry & the Renaissance of French Imperialism. 1966. lib. bdg. 15.00x (ISBN 0-374-96555-2). Octagon.
Priestley, Herbert I. France Overseas. 1966. lib. bdg. 24.00x (ISBN 0-374-96593-5). Octagon.
--France Overseas. 1966. lib. bdg. 24.00x (ISBN 0-374-96593-5). Octagon.
Roberts, W. Adolphe. French in the West Indies. LC 70-141373. (Illus.). 1971. Repr. of 1942 ed. 16.00x (ISBN 0-8154-0377-1). Cooper Sq.
Saint-Vallier, Jean B. Estat Present De l'Eglise et De la Colonie Francoise Dans la Nouvelle France. Repr. of 1688 ed. 16.00 (ISBN 0-384-52995-X). Johnson Repr.
Southworth, Constant. The French Colonial Venture. Wilkins, Mira, ed. LC 76-29740. (European Business Ser.). (Illus.). 1977. Repr. of 1931 ed. lib. bdg. 19.00x (ISBN 0-405-09757-3). Arno.
Thompson, Virginia M. French Indo-China. 1967. lib. bdg. 30.00x (ISBN 0-374-97866-2). Octagon.
Thwaites, Reuben G. France in America, 1497-1763. Repr. of 1905 ed. lib. bdg. 15.00x (ISBN 0-8371-4106-0, THFA). Greenwood.
Turmeau De La Morandiere. Appel Des Etrangers Dans Nos Colonies. Repr. of 1763 ed. 16.50 (ISBN 0-8287-0840-1). Clearwater Pub.

FRANCE–COMMERCE

Blanqui, Jerome A. & De Girardin, Emile. De la liberte du Commerce et la protection de l'industrie. LC 76-146244. (Research & Source Works Ser: No. 857). 1971. Repr. of 1847 ed. lib. bdg. 18.50 (ISBN 0-8337-0310-2). B Franklin.
Boiteau, Dieudonne A. Les Traites de commerce. (Research & Source Works Ser., History, Economics & Social Science). 1971. Repr. of 1863 ed. 32.50 (ISBN 0-8337-0332-3). B Franklin.
Bottin Professions 1979, 6 vols. LC 76-647504. 1979. Set. 275.00x (ISBN 0-8002-2365-9). Intl Pubns Serv.
Buyer's Guide to the French Ready-to-Wear Industry (Guide D' Achats Du Pret-a Porter) 1978-79, 2 vols. 1978. Set. 15.00x (ISBN 0-8002-2360-8). Intl Pubns Serv.
Conseil General Du Commerce. Session De 1845-1846. Rapport Presente Par M. Schneider, D'autun, Au Nom De la Commission Chargee D'examiner la Loi Du 22 Mars 1841, Sur le Travail Des Enfants Dans les. (Conditions of the 19th Century French Working Class Ser.). 16p. (Fr.). 1974. Repr. of 1846 ed. 20.00 (ISBN 0-8287-1351-0, 1078). Clearwater Pub.
Des Cilleuls, Alfred. Histoire et Regime De la Grande Industrie En France Au 17e et 18e Siecles. LC 70-126407. (Research & Source Works: No. 5). 1970. Repr. of 1898 ed. lib. bdg. 25.00 (ISBN 0-8337-0575-X). B Franklin.
Dunham, Arthur L. Anglo-French Treaty of Commerce of 1860 & the Progress of the Industrial Revolution in France. LC 75-151546. (Illus.). 1971. Repr. of 1930 ed. 18.00 (ISBN 0-8462-1580-2). Russell.
--Anglo-French Treaty of Commerce of 1860. LC 77-159180. 1971. Repr. of 1930 ed. lib. bdg. 20.00x (ISBN 0-374-92411-2). Octagon.
Dutot, Charles. Political Reflections on the Finances & Commerce of France. LC 76-146461. Repr. of 1739 ed. lib. bdg. 22.50x (ISBN 0-678-00842-6). Kelley.
Franko, Lawrence & Stephenson, Sherry. French Export Behavior in Third World Markets, Vol. II. LC 80-66695. (Significant Issues Ser.: No. 6). 96p. 1980. 4.00 (ISBN 0-686-70747-8). CSI Studies.
Girard, Albert. Commerce Francais a Seville Et Cadiz Au Temps De Habsbourg, 3 pts. in 1. 1967. Repr. of 1932 ed. 36.50 (ISBN 0-8337-1358-2). B Franklin.
John Crerar Library. Catalogue of French Economic Documents from the Sixteenth, Seventeenth & Eighteenth Centuries. (Bibliography & Reference Ser.: No. 222). (Fr). 1969. Repr. of 1918 ed. 18.50 (ISBN 0-8337-0734-5). B Franklin.
Kaeppelin, Paul. Compagnie Des Indes Orientales et Francois Martin: Etude sur l'Histoire du Commerce et Des Establissements Francais dans l'Inde Sous Louis 14th. Repr. of 1664 ed. 40.50 (ISBN 0-8337-1891-6). B Franklin.
Marshall, R. T. The French Building Industry. 1981. 40.00x (ISBN 0-686-75648-7, Pub. by Surveyors Tech Serv). State Mutual Bk.
Masson, Paul. Histoire Du Commerce Francais Dans Le Levant Au Dix-Huitieme Siecle. LC 12-23170. 1967. Repr. of 1911 ed. 62.50 (ISBN 0-8337-2287-5). B Franklin.
Miquelon, Dale. Dugard of Rouen: French Trade to Canada & the West Indies, 1729-1770. 1978. 21.95x (ISBN 0-7735-0299-8). McGill-Queens U Pr.
Nussbaum, Frederick L. Commercial Policy in the French Revolution: A Study of the Career of G. J. A. Ducher. LC 79-111782. Repr. of 1923 ed. 15.00 (ISBN 0-404-04807-2). AMS Pr.
Pigeonneau, Henri. Histoire Du Commerce De la France, 2 Vols. LC 71-121592. (Research & Source Works Ser.: No. 506). (Fr). 1970. Repr. of 1888 ed. Set. lib. bdg. 50.50 (ISBN 0-8337-2769-9). B Franklin.
Puryear, Vernon J. France & the Levant: From the Bourbon Restoration to the Peace of Kutiah. 1968. Repr. of 1941 ed. 18.50 (ISBN 0-208-00721-0, Archon). Shoe String.
Wilson, Arthur M. French Foreign Policy During the Administration of Cardinal Fleury: 1726-1743; a Study in Diplomacy & Commercial Development. LC 70-138193. 433p. 1972. Repr. of 1936 ed. lib. bdg. 18.25x (ISBN 0-8371-5333-6, WIFP). Greenwood.

FRANCE–CONSEIL D'ETAT

Freedeman, Charles E. Conseil d'Etat in Modern France. LC 68-59225. (Columbia University. Studies in the Social Sciences: No. 603). Repr. of 1961 ed. 18.50 (ISBN 0-404-51603-3). AMS Pr.
Hamson, Charles J. Executive Discretion & Judicial Control: An Aspect of the French Conseil D'Etat. LC 79-1606. 1980. Repr. of 1954 ed. 18.50 (ISBN 0-88355-909-9). Hyperion Conn.

FRANCE–CONSTITUTIONAL HISTORY

Brissaud, J. B. History of French Public Law. (Continental Legal History Ser: Vol. 9). lviii, 581p. 1969. Repr. of 1915 ed. 22.50x (ISBN 0-8377-1932-1). Rothman.
Brissaud, Jean B. History of French Public Law. Garner, James W., tr. LC 68-54746. (Continental Legal History Ser., No. 9). Repr. of 1915 ed. 22.50x (ISBN 0-678-04510-0). Kelley.
Church, William F. Constitutional Thought in Sixteenth Century France. LC 77-86273. 1969. Repr. of 1941 ed. lib. bdg. 20.00x (ISBN 0-374-91596-2). Octagon.
Cuny, L. Role De Dupont De Nemours En Matiere Fiscale a l'Assemblee Constituante. LC 74-132533. (Research & Source Works Ser.: No. 823). (Fr). 1971. Repr. of 1909 ed. lib. bdg. 22.50 (ISBN 0-8337-0741-8). B Franklin.
Hotman, Francis. Francogallia by Francis Hotman. Salmon, J. H. & Giesey, R., eds. LC 73-172835. (Studies in the History & Theory of Politics). (Illus.). 608p. 1972. 59.95 (ISBN 0-521-08379-6). Cambridge U Pr.
Hotman, Francois. Franco-Gallia. 1977. lib. bdg. 59.95 (ISBN 0-8490-1863-3). Gordon Pr.
Saint-Just, Antoine L. Esprit De la Revolution et De la Constitution De France. 182p. 1981. Repr. of 1791 ed. lib. bdg. 80.00 (ISBN 0-8287-1569-6). Clearwater Pub.
Weiss, Jean-Jacques. Combat Constitutionnel: 1868-1886. 334p. (Fr.). 1981. Repr. lib. bdg. 135.00 (ISBN 0-8287-1570-X). Clearwater Pub.

FRANCE–CONVENTION NATIONALE, 1792-1795

Nussbaum, Frederick L. Commercial Policy in the French Revolution: A Study of the Career of G. J. A. Ducher. LC 79-111782. Repr. of 1923 ed. 15.00 (ISBN 0-404-04807-2). AMS Pr.
Patrick, Alison. The Men of the First French Republic: Political Alignments in the National Convention of 1792. LC 72-4018. (Illus.). 425p. 1972. 27.50x (ISBN 0-8018-1305-0). Johns Hopkins.
Sydenham, M. J. The Girondins. LC 72-4006. 252p. 1973. Repr. of 1961 ed. lib. bdg. 19.75x (ISBN 0-8371-6433-8, SYGI). Greenwood.

FRANCE–COURT AND COURTIERS

Batiffol, Louis. Marie De Medicis & the French Court in the Seventeenth Century. Davis, H. W., ed. King, Mary, tr. from Fr. LC 72-137368. (Select Bibliographies Reprint Ser.). 1972. Repr. of 1908 ed. 17.00 (ISBN 0-8369-5569-2). Arno.
Bingham, Denis A. Marriages of the Bourbons, Two Vols. LC 70-113557. (Illus.). Repr. of 1890 ed. Set. 45.00 (ISBN 0-404-00890-9); 23.00 ea. Vol. 1 (ISBN 0-404-00891-7). Vol. 2 (ISBN 0-404-00892-5). AMS Pr.
Brooks, Geraldine. Dames & Daughters of the French Court. facs. ed. LC 68-8443. (Essay Index Reprint Ser). 1904. 17.00 (ISBN 0-8369-0256-4). Arno.
Douet-D'Arcq, Louis C. Comptes De l'Hotel Des Rois De France Au Quatorzieme et Quinzieme Siecles. 1865. 35.50 (ISBN 0-384-12421-6); pap. 31.00 (ISBN 0-384-12420-8). Johnson Repr.
Douet-D'Arcq, Louis C., ed. Comptes De L'argenterie Des Rois De France Au Quatorzieme Siecle. 1851. 28.00 (ISBN 0-384-12410-0); pap. 23.00 (ISBN 0-384-12411-9). Johnson Repr.
Elliot, Frances. Old Court Life in France, 2 vols. 1893. 75.00 set (ISBN 0-932062-54-7). Sharon Hill.
Ford, Franklin L. Robe & Sword: The Regrouping of the French Aristocracy After Louis 14. LC 52-12261. (Historical Studies: No. 64). (Illus.). 1953. 14.00x (ISBN 0-674-77415-9). Harvard U Pr.
Hall, Geoffrey F. Moths Round the Flame. LC 72-93343. (Essay Index Reprint Ser). 1935. 29.00 (ISBN 0-8369-1413-9). Arno.
Marguerite De Valois. Memoires et Lettres De Marguerite De Valois. Gessard, M. F., ed. 35.50 (ISBN 0-384-35398-3); pap. 31.00 (ISBN 0-384-35388-6). Johnson Repr.
Petersen-Dyggve, Holgern. Trouveres et Protecteurs De Trouveres Dans les Cours Seigneuriales De France. LC 80-2168. Repr. of 1942 ed. 41.50 (ISBN 0-404-19032-4). AMS Pr.
Scully, Terence. Le Court D'amours De Mahieu le Poirier et la Suite Aonyme De la Court D'amours. 279p. 1976. pap. text ed. 7.00 (ISBN 0-88920-032-7, Pub. by Laurier U Pr). Humanities.
Wiley, William L. Gentleman of Renaissance France. LC 75-152622. (Illus.). 1971. Repr. of 1954 ed. lib. bdg. 16.00x (ISBN 0-8371-6169-X, WIGR). Greenwood.

FRANCE–DEFENSES

Bury, J. P. Gambetta & the National Defense. LC 70-80531. 1970. Repr. of 1936 ed. 23.50 (ISBN 0-86527-077-5). Fertig.
Bury, John P. Gambetta - the National Defence: A Republican Dictatorship in France. LC 77-114490. (Illus.). 1971. Repr. of 1936 ed. lib. bdg. 15.25x (ISBN 0-8371-4818-9, BUGN). Greenwood.
Jaures, Jean L. Democracy & Military Service. LC 70-147769. (Library of War & Peace; Control & Limitation of Arms). lib. bdg. 38.00 (ISBN 0-8240-0467-1). Garland Pub.
Young, Robert J. In Command of France: French Foreign Policy & Military Planning, 1933-1940. LC 78-4875. (Illus.). 1978. 18.50x (ISBN 0-674-44536-8). Harvard U Pr.

FRANCE–DESCRIPTION AND TRAVEL

Allen, Zachariah. The Practical Tourist; or, Sketches of the State of the Useful Arts, & of Society, Scenery in Great Britain, France & Holland, 2 vols. in 1. LC 73-38258. (The Evolution of Capitalism Ser.). 896p. 1972. Repr. of 1832 ed. 39.00 (ISBN 0-405-04111-X). Arno.

Alpes, Savoie, Dauphine. (Michelin Travel Guides). (Fr.). pap. 5.95 (ISBN 0-685-36087-3). French & Eur.
Beaujeu-Garnier, J. France. LC 75-28288. (World's Landscapes). (Illus.). 160p. 1975. pap. text ed. 9.50x (ISBN 0-582-48178-3). Longman.
Belloc, Hillare. The Path to Rome. 1981. pap. text ed. 5.95 (ISBN 0-89526-884-1). Regnery-Gateway.
Bloch, Marc. Ile-De-France: The Country Around Paris. Anderson, J. E., tr. LC 70-148715. (Illus.). 175p. 1971. 15.00x (ISBN 0-8014-0640-4). Cornell U Pr.
Bourgogne. (Michelin Travel Guides). (Fr.). pap. 5.95 (ISBN 0-685-36088-1). French & Eur.
Brunet, Roger, ed. Decouvrir la France, 7 vols. Incl. Vol. 1. Bretagne, Normandie, Poitou, Vendee, Charentes (ISBN 2-03-013351-5, 3578); Vol. 2. Paris, Bassin parisien, Pays de Loire (3579); Vol. 3. Nord, Alsace, Lorraine, Bourgogne (3581); Vol. 4. Franche-Comte, Auvergne, Lyonnais, Alpes (3582); Vol. 5. Languedoc, Provence, Cote d'azur, Corse (3583); Vol. 6. Limousin, Bassin aquitain, Pyrenees, Pays basque et catalan (3584); Vol. 7. La France d'outre-Mer, la France maintenant (3585). (Illus.). 336p. 1972. 78.25 ea. Larousse.
--Decouvrir la France, 18 vols, Vols. 1-5 & 10-22. Incl. Vol. 1. La Bretagne (ISBN 2-03-013801-0); Vol. 2. La Maine et la Normandie; Vol. 3. Poitou, Charentes, Vendee; Vol. 4. Paris (ISBN 2-03-013804-5); Vol. 5. Champagne, Picardie, Ile de France; Vol. 10. Bourgogne et Franche Comte; Vol. 11. L'Auvergne et le Boubonnais; Vol. 12. En Pays lyonnais (ISBN 2-03-013812-6); Vol. 13. Les Alpes (ISBN 2-03-013813-4); Vol. 14. Bas Languedoc, Cevennes, Causses, Languedoc (ISBN 2-03-013814-2); Vol. 15. La Provence; Vol. 16. Cote d'azur, la Corse (ISBN 2-03-013816-9); Vol. 17. Limousin, Perigord, Quercy, Bouergue; Vol. 18. L' Aquitaine (ISBN 2-03-013818-5); Vol. 19. Le Midi toulousain; Vol. 20. Pyrenees du Pays Basque au Pays Catalan; Vol. 21. La France d'outremer; Vol. 22. La France maintenant (ISBN 2-03-013822-3). (Illus.). 1972. 22.50 ea. Larousse.
Buttimer, Anne. Society & Milieu in the French Geographic Tradition. LC 72-158112. (Monograph: No. 6). 4.95 (ISBN 0-89291-085-2). Assn Am Geographers.
Chamberlain, Narcissa & Chamberlain, Narcisse. The Flavor of France. (Illus.). 1978. 14.95 (ISBN 0-8038-2326-6). Hastings.
Cooper, J. F. Gleanings in Europe, 2 Vols. Spiller, Robert E., ed. Repr. of 1928 ed. Set. 34.00 (ISBN 0-527-19400-X). Kraus Repr.
Cooper, James F. Gleanings in Europe: Italy. (The Writings of James Fenimore Cooper Ser.). (Illus.). 377p. 1981. pap. text ed. 8.95x (ISBN 0-87395-460-2, COGI-P). State U NY Pr.
Cooper, James Fenimore. Gleanings in Europe: France. Spiller, Robert E., ed. 1979. Repr. of 1928 ed. lib. bdg. 40.00 (ISBN 0-8492-4022-0). R West.
Cox, Thornton. Thornton Cox Traveller's Guide to France. (Illus.). 1975. pap. 4.95 (ISBN 0-8038-7156-2). Hastings.
Cunff, Madeleine Le. Sur le Vif. (Illus., Fr.). 1977. pap. text ed. 5.75 (ISBN 0-88436-454-2). EMC.
De Loy Jameson, Raymond, pseud. Trails of the Troubadors. LC 78-102837. 1970. Repr. of 1927 ed. 12.50 (ISBN 0-8046-0752-4). Kennikat.
Dibdin, Thomas F. Bibliographical, Antiquarian, & Picturesque Tour in France & Germany, 3 Vols. 2nd ed. LC 76-111768. Repr. of 1829 ed. Set. 80.00 (ISBN 0-404-02130-1). AMS Pr.
Dollfus, Jean. France. (Geography & Growth Ser). (Illus.). 1969. 12.50x (ISBN 0-7195-1898-9). Intl Pubns Serv.
Dordogne: Michelin Travel Guides. (Fr.). pap. 5.95 (ISBN 0-685-36089-X). French & Eur.
Edwards, G. W. Vanished Halls & Cathedrals of France. 69.95 (ISBN 0-8490-1255-4). Gordon Pr.
Eliot, John. The Survey, or Topographical Description of France. with a New Mappe. LC 79-84104. (English Experience Ser.: No. 923). (Illus.). 116p. 1979. Repr. of 1592 ed. lib. bdg. 11.50 (ISBN 90-221-0923-2). Walter J Johnson.
French Farm & Village Holiday Guide 1981. 320p. 1981. pap. 8.95 (ISBN 0-906318-05-X, HM 24, DUO). Unipub.
Garrick, David. Journal of David Garrick Describing His Visit to France & Italy in 1763. Stone, G. W., Jr., ed. 1939. pap. 6.00 (ISBN 0-527-32560-0). Kraus Repr.
Gold, Mary J. Crossroads Marseilles Nineteen Forty. LC 79-8551. (Illus.). 1980. 15.95 (ISBN 0-385-15618-9). Doubleday.
Gougaud, Henri & Gouvion, Colette. France Observed. (Observed Ser.). (Illus.). 1978. 24.95 (ISBN 0-19-519968-5). Oxford U Pr.
Hamilton, Ronald. The Holiday History of France. 1978. 8.95 (ISBN 0-7011-1686-2, Pub. by Chatto Bodley Jonathan). Merrimack Bk Serv.
Harvard Student Agencies. Let's Go, France: The Budget Guide 1981 to 1982 Edition. (Illus.). 352p. 1981. pap. 5.95 (ISBN 0-525-93144-9). Dutton.
House, J. W. France: An Applied Geography. (Illus.). 1978. 35.00x (ISBN 0-416-15080-2). Methuen Inc.
Hugo, Victor. Voyages en France et Belgique, 1834-1837. Gely, Claude, ed. (Illus.). 388p. 1974. 32.50 (ISBN 0-686-54048-4). French & Eur.
Hurlimann, Martin. France. new ed. Valery, Paul, ed. (Illus.). 1968. 12.95 (ISBN 0-670-32645-3, Studio). Viking Pr.
James, Henry. Little Tour in France. LC 78-94312. (Illus.). Repr. of 1900 ed. 12.50 (ISBN 0-404-03546-9). AMS Pr.
--A Little Tour in France. 59.95 (ISBN 0-8490-0546-9). Gordon Pr.
Kelly, Reine C. A Descriptive Analysis of Gascon. (Janua Linguarum Ser. Practica: No. 138). 1973. pap. text ed. 40.00x (ISBN 90-2792-388-4). Mouton.
Kerouac, Jack. Satori in Paris. 1966. pap. 2.25 (ISBN 0-394-17437-2, B135, BC). Grove.
Kleinholz, Frank. The Flowering Rock: Ile De Brehat. LC 74-171455. (Illus.). 1971. 10.00 (ISBN 0-916224-20-1); pap. 7.50 (ISBN 0-916224-55-4). Banyan Bks.
Lanier, Alison R. Update -- France. LC 80-83928. (Country Orientation Ser.). 1980. pap. text ed. 25.00x (ISBN 0-933662-41-6). Intercult Pr.
Lenard, Yvone. Fenetres Sur la France. new ed. (Verbal-Active French Ser.). (Illus.). (gr. 11-12). 1976. text ed. 15.68 (ISBN 0-06-582101-7, SchDept); tchr's ed. 22.36 (ISBN 0-06-582205-6); wkbk. 4.00 (ISBN 0-06-582303-6); tests 3.56 (ISBN 0-06-582603-5); tchrs. test ed. 4.00 (ISBN 0-06-582701-5); tapes 216.04 (ISBN 0-06-582802-X). Har-Row.
Liholiho, Alexander. Journal of Prince Alexander Liholiho: Voyages Made to the United States, England, & France in 1849-50. Adler, Jacob, ed. LC 67-27052. (Personal Diary, Photos, Index, Notes, 188p). 1967. 10.00 (ISBN 0-87022-009-8). U Pr of Hawaii.
Longnon, Auguste H. Les Noms De Lieu De la France: Leur Origine Leur Signification, Leurs Transformation. LC 75-140989. 1973. Repr. of 1920 ed. lib. bdg. 49.00 (ISBN 0-8337-2142-9). B Franklin.
Marty, Fernand. Vivre en France. (Illus.). 1975. text ed. 5.95 (ISBN 0-88332-000-2, 5450). Larousse.
Mauger. Scenes de la Vie Francaise. 6.95 (ISBN 0-685-36697-9). French & Eur.
Michaud, G. Nouveau Guide France: Manuel De Civilization Francaise. 9.90 (ISBN 0-685-20239-9). Schoenhof.
Montgolfier, Bernard de. Dictionnaire des Chateaux de France. 2nd ed. 250p. (Fr.). 1970. pap. 6.95 (ISBN 0-686-56837-0, M-6615). French & Eur.
Moreau, Daniel, ed. La France. new ed. (Collection monde et voyages). (Illus.). 159p. (Fr.). 1973. 21.00x (ISBN 2-03-053107-3, 3896). Larousse.
Newman, William M. Charters of St-Fursy of Peronne. 1977. 16.00 (ISBN 0-910956-59-6). Medieval Acad.
Paris: Michelin Travel Guides. (Fr.). pap. 4.95 (ISBN 0-685-36091-1). French & Eur.
Pillement, Georges. Unknown France, 4 vols. Incl. Vol. 1. From Paris to the Riviera. 236p. 1963; Vol. 2. The French Alps, the Riviera. 176p. 1963; Vol. 3. The Roads to Spain. 256p. 1964; Vol. 4. The Valley of the Loire, Brittany. 250p. 1965. LC 66-41729. (Unknown Guides Ser). (Illus.). 12.50x ea. Intl Pubns Serv.
Pyrenees. (Michelin Travel Guides). (Fr.). pap. 5.95 (ISBN 0-685-36092-X). French & Eur.
Rivages de France. (Illus.). 1978. text ed. 63.75x (ISBN 2-03-013271-3, 3120). Larousse.
Rivages de la Mediterranee. (Illus.). 1978. text ed. 18.95x (ISBN 2-03-013904-1, 3183). Larousse.
Rivages de l'Atlantique. (Beautes de la France). (Illus.). 1978. 24.25x (ISBN 2-03-013909-2, 3188). Larousse.
Senior, Nassau W. Journals Kept in France & Italy from 1848 to 1852. LC 70-126608. (Europe 1815-1945 Ser.). 654p. 1973. Repr. of 1871 ed. lib. bdg. 59.50 (ISBN 0-306-70055-7). Da Capo.
Smollett, Tobias. Tobias Smollett: Travels Through France & Italy. facsimile ed. Felsenstein, Frank, ed. 45.00x (ISBN 0-19-812611-5). Oxford U Pr.
Southey, Robert. Journals of a Residence in Portugal, 1800-1801, & a Visit to France. Cabral, Adolfo, ed. LC 78-16176. (Illus.). 1978. Repr. of 1960 ed. lib. bdg. 31.00 (ISBN 0-313-20590-6, SOJR). Greenwood.
Spender, Stephen. European Witness. LC 74-138186. 246p. 1972. Repr. of 1946 ed. lib. bdg. 15.00 (ISBN 0-8371-5643-2, SPEW). Greenwood.
--European Witness. LC 74-138186. 246p. 1972. Repr. of 1946 ed. lib. bdg. 15.00 (ISBN 0-8371-5643-2, SPEW). Greenwood.
Stendhal. Memoires d'un Touriste, 3 vols. Abravanel, Ernest & Del Litto, Victor, eds. (Illus.). 9.95 ea. French & Eur.
--Memoires d'un Touriste, 3 vols. facsimile ed. 1929. Set. 150.00 (ISBN 0-686-55071-4). French & Eur.
--Memoirs of a Tourist. Seager, Allan, tr. (Illus.). 1962. 14.95x (ISBN 0-8101-0231-5). Northwestern U Pr.
Verne, Jules. Geographie Ilustree de la France et de Ses Colonies: Avec: Lavallee, Theophile. Etude sur la Geographie Generale de la France. facsimile ed. 816p. 1976. 100.00 (ISBN 0-686-55917-7). French & Eur.
Villages pittoresques. (Beautes de la France). (Illus.). 1978. 24.25x (ISBN 2-03-013908-4, 3187). Larousse.
White, Freda. Three Rivers of France. 3rd ed. 236p. 1979. 9.95 (ISBN 0-571-04779-3, Pub. by Faber & Faber); pap. 4.50 (ISBN 0-571-04780-7). Merrimack Bk Serv.
--West of the Rhone. (Illus.). 240p. 1980. 8.95 (ISBN 0-571-05804-3, Pub by Faber & Faber). Merrimack Bk Serv.
Wildman, Frederick S., Jr. A Wine Tour of France: A Convivial Guide to French Vintages & Vineyards. 1976. pap. 3.95 (ISBN 0-394-71755-4, Vin). Random.
Young, Arthur. Travels During the Years 1787, 1788, & 1789, 2 Vols. 2nd ed. LC 79-115008. Repr. of 1794 ed. Set. 145.00 (ISBN 0-404-07068-X). Vol. 1 (ISBN 0-404-07069-8). Vol. 2 (ISBN 0-404-07070-1). AMS Pr.
Young, Elisabeth L. Family Afoot. (Illus.). 1978. 7.95 (ISBN 0-8138-0615-1, 0615-1). Iowa St U Pr.

FRANCE–DESCRIPTION AND TRAVEL–GUIDEBOOKS

Baedecker. The Baedecker Guide to France. (The Baedecker Travel Ser.). 1981. 19.95 (ISBN 0-13-055822-2); pap. 11.95 (ISBN 0-13-055814-1). P-H.
Bristow, Philip. Through the French Canals. 200p. 1980. 18.00 (ISBN 0-245-53403-2, Pub. by Nautical England). State Mutual Bk.
Brown, Karen A. French Country Inns & Chateau Hotels. LC 77-82024. (Illus., Orig.). 1977. pap. 7.95 (ISBN 0-930328-01-9). Travel Pr.
Cox, Thornton. Southern France. (Thornton Cox's Travellers' Guide Ser.). Date not set. pap. 4.95 (ISBN 0-8038-7156-2). Hastings.
Dollarwise Guide to France, 1981-82. 496p. 1981. pap. 6.95 (ISBN 0-671-41425-9). Frommer-Pasmantier.
Evans, Craig. On Foot Through Europe: A Trail Guide to France & the Benelux Nations. Whitney, Stephen, ed. (Illus.). 496p. 1980. lib. bdg. 13.95 (ISBN 0-933710-17-8); pap. 7.95 (ISBN 0-933710-16-X). Foot Trails.
Fodor's Budget France, 1981. 1980. pap. 4.95 (ISBN 0-679-00654-0). McKay.
Fodor's France, 1981. 1980. 13.95 (ISBN 0-679-00685-0); pap. 10.95 (ISBN 0-679-00686-9). McKay.
French Farm & Village Holiday Guide, 1980. 320p. 1980. pap. 4.95 (ISBN 0-686-61372-4, HM 3, DUO). Unipub.
French Farm & Village Holiday Guide 1979. 1979. pap. 4.95 (ISBN 0-906318-01-7, HM 1, DUO). Unipub.
French Pilot, Vol.1. 224p. 1980. 30.00x (ISBN 0-686-69883-5, Pub. by Nautical England). State Mutual Bk.
Guide to France. (Foreign Guides). 1981. pap. 6.95 (ISBN 0-528-84536-5). Rand.
Harvard Student Agencies. Let's Go, France: The Budget Guide 1980 to 1981 Edition. (Illus.). 1980. pap. 4.95 (ISBN 0-525-93088-4). Dutton.
Kay, F. George. France. LC 79-89185. (A Rand McNally Pocket Guide). (Illus., Orig.). 1980. pap. 3.95 (ISBN 0-528-84290-0). Rand.
Lands, Neil. Beyond the Dordogne. (History, People & Places Ser.). (Illus.). 1978. pap. 7.95 (ISBN 0-904978-88-5). Hippocrene Bks.
--Dordogne. (History, People & Places Ser.). (Illus.). 1978. 12.50 (ISBN 0-902875-94-9). Hippocrene Bks.
--Languedoc-Roussillon. (History, People & Places Ser.). (Illus.). 1978. 12.50 (ISBN 0-904978-00-1). Hippocrene Bks.
Liley, John. France, the Quiet Way: A Guide to Its Waterways. (Illus.). 159p. 1975. 17.95x (ISBN 0-8464-0425-7). Beekman Pubs.
Michelin Green Travel Guide: Camping En France. 4.95 (ISBN 0-685-11373-6). French & Eur.
Michelin Green Travel Guide: Cote L'atlantique. (Illus., Fr.). 4.95 (ISBN 0-685-11375-2). French & Eur.
Michelin Guides & Maps. Dictionnaire des Communes de France (Guide to French Townships) 1979. 45.00 (ISBN 2-06-007500-9). Michelin.
--Michelin Green Guide to Bourgogne. 16th ed. (Fr.). 1980. pap. 7.95 (ISBN 2-06-003060-9). Michelin.
--Michelin Green Guide to Cote De L'atlantique. 9th ed. (Green Guide Ser.). (Fr.). 1978. pap. 7.95 (ISBN 2-06-003330-6). Michelin.
--Michelin Green Guide to Nord De la France. 4th ed. (Green Guide Ser.). (Fr.). 1977. pap. 7.95 (ISBN 2-06-003420-5). Michelin.
Michelin Guides & Maps Dept. Michelin Green Guide to French Riviera. 7th ed. (Green Guide Ser.). (Avail. in Fr.). pap. 7.95 (ISBN 2-06-013300-9). Michelin.
--Michelin Green Guide to Normandy. 5th ed. (Green Guide Ser.). (Avail. in Fr.). pap. 7.95 (ISBN 2-06-013480-3). Michelin.
Michelin Guides & Maps Division. Camping Caravanning in France. (Annual Ser.). 1980. pap. 7.95 (ISBN 2-06-006101-6). Michelin.
--Michelin Green Guide to Chateaux Loire. 6th ed. (Green Guide Ser.). (Avail. in Fr., Ger.). pap. 7.95 (ISBN 2-06-013210-X). Michelin.
Michelin Red Guide to France. (Red Guide Ser.). 1981. pap. 14.95 (ISBN 2-06-006401-5). Michelin.
The Nagel Travel Guide to the Chateaux of the Loire. (Nagel Travel Guide Ser.). (Illus.). 192p. 1975. 16.00 (ISBN 2-8263-0104-7). Hippocrene Bks.
Nagel's Encyclopedia Guide: French & Italian Riviera. (Illus.). 640p. 1973. 23.00 (ISBN 2-8263-0045-8). Masson Pub.
Robson, Malcom. French Pilot, Vol. 2. 256p. 1980. 33.00x (ISBN 0-245-53382-6, Pub. by Nautical England). State Mutual Bk.
Root, Waverley. The Food of France. 1977. pap. 5.95 (ISBN 0-394-72428-3, Vin). Random.
Shaw, M. B. Your Guide to South West France. 1968. 5.25x (ISBN 0-8002-0787-4). Intl Pubns Serv.
Verstappen, Peter, ed. Rand McNally Guide to France. LC 78-70557. 1981. pap. 6.95 (ISBN 0-528-84536-5). Rand.
Young, Edward, ed. The Shell Guide to France. (Illus.). 1979. 22.95 (ISBN 0-393-08842-1). Norton.
The Young Traveler's Guide to France. 1979. pap. 4.95 (ISBN 0-906318-02-5, HM2, DUO). Unipub.

FRANCE–ECONOMIC CONDITIONS

Bonvallet, des Brosses. Richesses et Resources De la France... 305p. 1981. Repr. of 1789 ed. lib. bdg. 120.00 (ISBN 0-8287-1575-0). Clearwater Pub.
Bouchard, Leon. Systeme financier de l'ancienne monarchie. 1971. Repr. of 1891 ed. lib. bdg. 29.00 (ISBN 0-8337-0341-2). B Franklin.
Cameron, Rondo. France & the Economic Development of Europe, 1800-1914. 586p. 1975. Repr. of 1961 ed. lib. bdg. 35.00x (ISBN 0-374-91252-1). Octagon.
Caron, Francois. An Economic History of Modern France. Bray, Barbara, tr. from Fr. (Columbia Economic History of the Modern World). 360p. 1979. 18.50x (ISBN 0-231-03860-7). Columbia U Pr.
Caron, Francois & Graeme, Holmes. The Performance of the French Economy: 1870-1939. (Studies in Economic & Social History Ser.). 1975. pap. text ed. 1.75x (ISBN 0-333-15092-9). Humanities.
Carre, Antonio. Necker et la question des grains a la fin du XVIIIe siecle. LC 79-147152. 220p. 1973. Repr. of 1903 ed. 21.00 (ISBN 0-8337-0481-8). B Franklin.
Case, Lynn M., ed. French Opinion on the United States & Mexico: Extracts from the Reports of the Procureurs Generaux. LC 69-19212. 1969. Repr. of 1936 ed. 22.50 (ISBN 0-208-00791-1, Archon). Shoe String.
Chaboseau, Augustin. De Babeuf a la Commune. LC 70-101232. (Research & Source Works: No. 389). (Fr). 1970. Repr. of 1911 ed. text ed. 14.00 (ISBN 0-8337-0508-3). B Franklin.
Clapham, John H. Economic Development of France & Germany 1815-1914. 4th ed. 1935. 50.50 (ISBN 0-521-04664-5); pap. 15.95 (ISBN 0-521-09150-0, 150). Cambridge U Pr.
Clark, John G. La Rochelle & the Atlantic Economy During the Eighteenth Century. LC 80-29275. (Illus.). 304p. 1981. text ed. 24.00x (ISBN 0-8018-2529-6). Johns Hopkins.
Clough, Shepard B. France: A History of National Economics, 1789-1939. LC 65-25882. 1964. Repr. lib. bdg. 25.00x (ISBN 0-374-91748-5). Octagon.
Clout, H. C. Themes in the Historical Geography of France. 1977. 78.50 (ISBN 0-12-175850-8). Acad Pr.
Cole, Arthur H. & Watts, George B. The Handicrafts of France As Recorded in the Description Des Arts et Metiers, 1761-1788. (Kress Library of Business & Economics: No. 8). (Illus.). 1952. pap. 5.00x (ISBN 0-678-09903-0, Baker Lib). Kelley.

D'Avenel, Georges. Fortune Privee a Travers Sept Siecles. LC 68-56732. (Research & Source Works Ser.: No. 212). (Fr). 1968. Repr. of 1895 ed. 26.50 (ISBN 0-8337-4062-8, 60). B Franklin.
Deloche, Maximin. La Crise Economique Au Seizeime Siecle et la Crise Actuelle. LC 71-132525. (Research & Source Works Ser.: No. 623). 1971. Repr. of 1922 ed. lib. bdg. 16.50 (ISBN 0-8337-0831-7). B Franklin.
Demographic, Social, Educational & Economic Data for France, 1833-1925: Historical Population, Economic & Social Data: France,1901-1921. 1979. codebook 20.00 (ISBN 0-89138-978-4). ICPSR.
Desmars, J. Un Precurseur D'Adam Smith en France: J. J. L. Graslin (1727-1790) LC 77-159696. 257p. (Fr.). 1973. Repr. of 1900 ed. 20.50 (ISBN 0-8337-0840-6). B Franklin.
Dictionnaire des Groupes Industriels et Financiers en France. 360p. (Fr.). 1978. 17.95 (ISBN 0-686-57102-9, M-6127). French & Eur.
Du Buisson, Paul U. Lettres Critiques et Politiques Sur les Colonies et le Commerce Des Villes Maritimes De France: Adressees a G. T. Raynal. 281p. 1981. Repr. of 1785 ed. lib. bdg. 110.00 (ISBN 0-8287-1555-6). Clearwater Pub.
Duby, Georges. The Early Growth of the European Economy: Warriors & Peasants from the Seventh to the Twelfth Centuries. Clarke, Howard B., tr. from Fr. LC 73-16955. (World Economic History Ser.). 292p. 1974. 22.50x (ISBN 0-8014-0814-8); pap. 6.95 (ISBN 0-8014-9169-X). Cornell U Pr.
Ducrocq, Theophile G. Etudes D'histoire Financiere et Monetaire. LC 75-132536. (Research & Source Works: No. 559). (Fr). 1970. Repr. of 1887 ed. lib. bdg. 23.50 (ISBN 0-8337-0939-9). B Franklin.
Dulles, Eleanor L. The French Franc: 1914-1928. Wilkins, Mira, ed. LC 78-3910. (International Finance Ser.). (Illus.). 1978. Repr. of 1929 ed. lib. bdg. 36.00x (ISBN 0-405-11214-9). Arno.
Dunham, Arthur L. The Industrial Revolution in France, 1815-1848. 1955. 10.00 (ISBN 0-682-47037-6, University). Exposition.
Dupin, Charles. Des Forces Productives et Commerciales De la France. (Conditions of the 19th Century French Working Class Ser.). (Fr.). 1974. Repr. of 1827 ed. lib. bdg. 180.50x (ISBN 0-8287-0300-0, 1153). Clearwater Pub.
Du Puynode, M. Gustave. Grandes Crises Financieres De La France. LC 70-166961. (History, Economics & Social Science Ser.: No. 287). (Fr). 1971. Repr. of 1876 ed. lib. bdg. 26.50 (ISBN 0-8337-0973-9). B Franklin.
Fairchilds, Cissie C. Poverty & Charity in Aix-en-Provence, 1640-1789. LC 75-36930. (Studies in Historical & Political Science: Ninety-Fourth Series No. 1 (1976)). (Illus.). 226p. 1976. 15.00x (ISBN 0-8018-1677-7). Johns Hopkins.
Fierain, Jacques. Les Raffineries De Sucre Des Ports En France: XIX Debut De XX Siecles. Bruchey, Stuart, ed. LC 77-77169. (Dissertations in European Economic History Ser.). (Fr.). 1977. lib. bdg. 42.00x (ISBN 0-405-10783-8). Arno.
Golob, Eugene O. Meline Tariff: French Agriculture & Nationalist Economic Policy. LC 68-58582. (Columbia University. Studies in the Social Sciences: No. 506). Repr. of 1944 ed. 21.50 (ISBN 0-404-51506-1). AMS Pr.
Hammond, Charles. Factors Affecting Economic Growth in France: 1913-1938. Bruchey, Stuart, ed. LC 80-2807. (Dissertations in European Economic History II). (Illus.). 1981. lib. bdg. 18.00x (ISBN 0-405-13991-8). Arno.
Hatton, Ragnhild, ed. Louis the Fourteenth & Absolutism. LC 75-45158. (Illus.). 1976. 17.50x (ISBN 0-8142-0255-1). Ohio St U Pr.
Kemp, Tom. The French Economy: Nineteen-Thirteen to Nineteen Thirty-Nine. LC 79-189810. 176p. 1972. text ed. 17.95 (ISBN 0-312-30450-1). St Martin.
Le Goff, T. J. Vannes & Its Region: A Study of Town & Country in Eighteenth-Century France. (Illus.). 496p. 1981. 74.00x (ISBN 0-19-822515-6). Oxford U Pr.
Lodge, Eleanor. Sully, Colbert & Turgot: A Chapter in French Economic History. LC 71-178939. (Selected Essays in History, Economics & Social Science Ser.). 279p. 1972. Repr. of 1931 ed. lib. bdg. 14.00 (ISBN 0-8337-4237-X). B Franklin.
Lodge, Eleanor C. Sully, Colbert & Turgot. LC 70-110911. 1970. Repr. of 1931 ed. 12.50 (ISBN 0-8046-0893-8). Kennikat.
Lowe, Joseph. Present State of England in Regard to Agriculture, Trade & Finance. 2nd ed. LC 66-21682. Repr. of 1823 ed. 25.00x (ISBN 0-678-00320-3). Kelley.
Lublinskaya, Alexandra D. French Absolutism: The Crucial Phase, 1620-1629. (Illus.). 1968. 44.50 (ISBN 0-521-07117-8). Cambridge U Pr.
Marczewski, Jan. Inflation & Unemployment in France: A Quantitative Analysis. LC 77-25490. (Praeger Special Studies). 1978. 23.95 (ISBN 0-03-040921-7). Praeger.
Marx, Karl. Class Struggles in France. 2nd ed. 220p. 1967. 3.50 (ISBN 0-935534-07-5); pap. 1.25 (ISBN 0-935534-08-3). NY Labor News.
Merriman, John, ed. French Cities in the Nineteenth Century. LC 81-2520. 256p. 1981. text ed. 28.50x (ISBN 0-8419-0464-2). Holmes & Meier.
Norman, Hilda. Swindlers & Rogues in French Drama. LC 68-26280. 1968. Repr. of 1928 ed. 12.00 (ISBN 0-8046-0337-5). Kennikat.
O'Brien, Patrick & Keyder, Caglar. Economic Growth in Britain & France 1780-1914: Two Paths to the Twentieth Century. 1978. text ed. 27.50x (ISBN 0-04-330288-2). Allen Unwin.
Price, Roger. An Economic History of Modern France Seventeen Thirty to Nineteen Fourteen. 1981. 27.50x (ISBN 0-312-23322-1). St Martin.
--The Economic Modernisation of France Seventeen Thirty to Eighteen Eighty. LC 75-14447. 235p. 1975. 19.50 (ISBN 0-470-69722-9, Pub. by Wiley). Krieger.
--The Economic Modernization of France, 1730-1880. LC 75-14447. 1975. 27.95 (ISBN 0-470-69722-9). Halsted Pr.
Pris, Claude. Une Grande Entreprise Francaise Sous L'ancien-Regime: La Manufacture Royale Des Glaces Des Saint-Gobain, 1665-1830. Bruchey, Stuart, ed. LC 80-2824. (Dissertations in European Economic History II). (Illus.). 1981. lib. bdg. 60.00x (ISBN 0-686-73125-5). Arno.
Roblot, R. French Business Taxation. (European Commercial Law Library: No. 2). 1974. pap. text ed. 14.95x (ISBN 0-8464-0429-X). Beekman Pubs.
Saly, Pierre. La Politique Des Grands Travaux En France: 1929-1939. Bruchey, Stuart, ed. LC 77-77184. (Dissertations in European Economic History Ser.). (Fr.). 1977. lib. bdg. 27.00 (ISBN 0-405-10797-8). Arno.
Schuker, Stephen A. The End of French Predominance in Europe - the Financial Crisis of Nineteen Twenty Four & the Adoption of the Dawes Plan. LC 75-38799. 400p. 1976. 24.50x (ISBN 0-8078-1253-6). U of NC Pr.
See, Henri. Economic & Social Conditions in France During the Eighteenth Century. LC 68-9200. 1968. Repr. of 1927 ed. 11.50x (ISBN 0-8154-0203-1). Cooper Sq.
Smith, Michael S. Tariff Reform in France, Eighteen Sixty to Nineteen Hundred: The Politics of Economic Interest. LC 79-25272. 288p. 1980. 20.00x (ISBN 0-8014-1257-9). Cornell U Pr.
Stearns, Peter N. Paths to Authority: The Middle Class & the Industrial Labor Force in France, 1820-48. LC 78-16223. 1978. 12.95 (ISBN 0-252-00633-X). U of Ill Pr.
Thuillier, Andre. Economie et societe nivernaises: Au debut du XIX siecle. LC 73-79514. (Civilisations et Societes Ser: No. 39). 484p. (Orig., Fr.). 1974. pap. text ed. 50.00x (ISBN 90-2797-317-2). Mouton.
White, Harry D. The French International Accounts: 1880-1913. Wilkins, Mira, ed. LC 78-3956. (International Finance Ser.). (Illus.). 1978. Repr. of 1933 ed. lib. bdg. 23.00x (ISBN 0-405-11257-2). Arno.

FRANCE–ECONOMIC CONDITIONS–BIBLIOGRAPHY

Boissonnade, Prosper. Etudes relatives a l'histoire economique de la Revolution francaise. 1967. Repr. of 1906 ed. 22.50 (ISBN 0-8337-0331-5). B Franklin.
John Crerar Library. Catalogue of French Economic Documents from the Sixteenth, Seventeenth & Eighteenth Centuries. (Bibliography & Reference Ser.: No. 222). (Fr). 1969. Repr. of 1918 ed. 18.50 (ISBN 0-8337-0734-5). B Franklin.

FRANCE–ECONOMIC CONDITIONS–1945-

Carre, J. J., et al. French Economic Growth. Hatfield, John P., tr. from French. LC 74-82775. Orig. Title: Croissance Francaise. 608p. 1975. 22.50x (ISBN 0-8047-0878-9). Stanford U Pr.
Clout, Hugh D. The Geography of Post-War France: A Social & Economic Approach. 180p. 1972. text ed. 18.50 (ISBN 0-08-016765-9); pap. text ed. 7.75 (ISBN 0-08-016766-7). Pergamon.
Coffey, Peter. The Social Economy of France. LC 73-85269. 160p. 1974. 17.95 (ISBN 0-312-73220-1). St Martin.
Luthy, Herbert. France Against Herself. Mosbacher, Eric, tr. LC 74-20277. 476p. 1975. Repr. of 1955 ed. lib. bdg. 25.50x (ISBN 0-8371-7854-1, LUFA). Greenwood.
Marceau, Jane. Class & Status in France: Economic Change & Social Immobility, 1945-1975. 1977. 29.95x (ISBN 0-19-827217-0). Oxford U Pr.
Savage, Dean. Founders, Heirs, & Managers: French Industrial Leadership in Transition. LC 79-13929. (Sage Library of Social Research: Vol. 91). 228p. 1979. 20.00 (ISBN 0-8039-1150-5); pap. 9.95 (ISBN 0-8039-1151-3). Sage.
Stigum, Marcia L. The Impact of the European Economic Community on the French Cotton & Electrical Engineering Industries. Bruchey, Stuart, ed. LC 80-2830. (Dissertations in European Economic History II). (Illus.). 1981. lib. bdg. 24.00x (ISBN 0-405-14012-6). Arno.
White, Andrew D. Fiat Money Inflation in France. LC 80-13239. (Cato Paper Ser.: No. 11). Orig. Title: Paper Money Inflation in France. 96p. 1980. pap. 4.00x (ISBN 0-932790-13-5). Cato Inst.

FRANCE–ECONOMIC POLICY

Beik, Paul H. Judgment of the Old Regime. LC 44-2365. (Columbia University Studies in the Social Sciences: No. 509). Repr. of 1944 ed. 18.50 (ISBN 0-404-51509-6). AMS Pr.
Clough, Shepard B. France: A History of National Economics, 1789-1939. LC 65-25882. 1964. Repr. lib. bdg. 25.00x (ISBN 0-374-91748-5). Octagon.
Cohen, Stephen S. Modern Capitalist Planning: The French Model. new ed. 1977. 28.50x (ISBN 0-520-02793-0); pap. 8.95x (ISBN 0-520-02892-9, CAMPUS 141). U of Cal Pr.
Cole, Charles W. French Mercantilism, 1683-1700. 1965. lib. bdg. 17.00x (ISBN 0-374-91824-4). Octagon.
--French Mercantilist Doctrines Before Colbert. LC 79-96178. 1970. Repr. of 1931 ed. lib. bdg. 14.50x (ISBN 0-374-91805-8). Octagon.
De Graziani, Vincenzo G. The Franco-German Coalition & the Emergence of a New International Superpower: Its Effects Upon the Future Course of History. (Illus.). 1979. deluxe ed. 55.75 (ISBN 0-930008-31-6). Inst Econ Pol.
Dollfus, Jean. France. (Geography & Growth Ser). (Illus.). 1969. 12.50x (ISBN 0-7195-1898-9). Intl Pubns Serv.
French Export Behaviour in Third World Markets. (Significant Issues Ser.: Vol. II, No. 6). 96p. 1980. pap. 10.00 (ISBN 0-89206-021-2, CSIS014, CSIS). Unipub.
Harlow, John S. French Economic Planning. 1966. 4.95x (ISBN 0-87745-010-2); pap. 3.95x (ISBN 0-87745-011-0). U of Iowa Pr.
Joubleau, Felix. Etudes Sur Colbert Ou Exposition, ou Exposition du Systeme D'economique Politique Suivie En France De 1661 a 1683, 2 Vols. LC 74-153032. (Research & Source Works Ser.: No. 674). 1971. Repr. of 1856 ed. lib. bdg. 53.00 (ISBN 0-8337-1879-7). B Franklin.
Landry, Adolphe. Essai Economique Sur les Mutations Des Monnaies Dans L'ancienne France De Philippe le Bel a Charles Sept. LC 79-171948. (Research & Source Work Ser.: No. 826). (Fr). 1971. Repr. of 1910 ed. lib. bdg. 26.50 (ISBN 0-8337-1998-X). B Franklin.
Lord, Guy. The French Budgetary Process. LC 70-186113. 1973. 32.50x (ISBN 0-520-02196-7). U of Cal Pr.
Lutz, Vera. French Planning. 1965. pap. 5.25 (ISBN 0-8447-3049-1). Am Enterprise.
Miskimin, Harry A. Money, Prices, & Foreign Exchange in Fourteenth Century France. LC 63-7942. 1970. Repr. of 1963 ed. 15.00 (ISBN 0-08-022307-9). Pergamon.
Moulton, Harold G. & Lewis, Cleona. The French Debt Problem. LC 25-17675. 1971. Repr. of 1925 ed. 27.00 (ISBN 0-384-40237-2, S885). Johnson Repr.
Palm, Franklin C. The Economic Policies of Richelieu. (Illinois Studies in the Social Sciences: Vol. 9, No. 4). Repr. of 1922 ed. 9.50 (ISBN 0-384-44640-X). Johnson Repr.
Sargent, Arthur J. Economic Policy of Colbert. LC 68-57918. (Research & Source Works Ser.: No. 310). 1968. Repr. of 1899 ed. 20.50 (ISBN 0-8337-3126-2). B Franklin.
Spooner, Frank C. International Economy & Monetary Movements in France, 1493-1725. rev. abr. ed. LC 70-145894. (Economic Studies: No. 138). (Illus.). 1972. 17.50x (ISBN 0-674-45840-0). Harvard U Pr.
Tissier, Pierre. The Government of Vichy. LC 74-65. 347p. 1974. Repr. of 1942 ed. lib. bdg. 16.75x (ISBN 0-8371-7372-8, TIGV). Greenwood.
White, Andrew D. Fiat Money Inflation in France. LC 80-13239. (Cato Paper Ser.: No. 11). Orig. Title: Paper Money Inflation in France. 96p. 1980. pap. 4.00x (ISBN 0-932790-13-5). Cato Inst.
White, Harry D. The French International Accounts: 1880-1913. Wilkins, Mira, ed. LC 78-3956. (International Finance Ser.). (Illus.). 1978. Repr. of 1933 ed. lib. bdg. 23.00x (ISBN 0-405-11257-2). Arno.

FRANCE–ETATS GENERAUX

Hyslop, Beatrice F. French Nationalism in 1789 According to the General Cahiers. 1968. Repr. lib. bdg. 15.50 (ISBN 0-374-94085-1). Octagon.
--Guide to the General Cahiers of 1789, with the Texts of Unedited Cahiers. 1968. lib. bdg. 17.50x (ISBN 0-374-94104-1). Octagon.
Major, J. Russell. The Deputies to the Estates General in Renaissance France. LC 74-8957. (Studies Presented to the International Commission for the History of Representative & Parlimentary Institutions Ser.: No. 21). (Illus.). 201p. 1974. Repr. of 1960 ed. lib. bdg. 15.00 (ISBN 0-8371-7597-6, MAEG). Greenwood.
--Representative Government in Early Modern France. LC 79-14711. 800p. 1980. text ed. 50.00x (ISBN 0-300-02300-6). Yale U Pr.
Major, James R. The Estates General of Fifteen Sixty. (Princeton Studies in History: Vol. 6). Repr. of 1951 ed. 10.00 (ISBN 0-384-35090-9). Johnson Repr.
Picot, Georges M. Histoire Des Etats Generaux, 5 Vols. 2nd ed. (Fr). 1969. Repr. of 1888 ed. 165.00 (ISBN 0-8337-2756-7). B Franklin.

FRANCE–ETATS GENERAUX–TIERS ETAT

Sieyes, Emmanuel & Sainte Beuve, Charles A. Qu'est-Ce Que le Tiers Etat? & Sieyes, 2 vols. in one. Mayer, J. P., ed. LC 78-67389. (European Political Thought Ser.). (Fr.). 1979. Repr. of 1885 ed. lib. bdg. 10.00x (ISBN 0-405-11740-X). Arno.

FRANCE–EXECUTIVE DEPARTMENTS

Fleurian, Dominique de. Dictionnaire National des Communes de France. 20th ed. Simond, Jacques & Frenay, Jacques, eds. 1150p. (Fr.). 1977. 39.95 (ISBN 0-686-57184-3, M-6254). French & Eur.

FRANCE–FOREIGN RELATIONS

Albrecht-Carrie, Rene. France, Europe & the Two World Wars. LC 74-6775. 346p. 1975. Repr. of 1961 ed. lib. bdg. 19.75x (ISBN 0-8371-7568-2, ALFR). Greenwood.
Barker, Nancy N. Distaff Diplomacy: The Empress Eugenie & the Foreign Policy of the Second Empire. 268p. 1967. 12.50x (ISBN 0-292-73694-0). U of Tex Pr.
Barker, Nancy N., ed. French Legation in Texas, 2 vols. (Illus.). 1971-73. 12.00 ea. Vol. 1 (ISBN 0-87611-026-X). Vol. 2 (ISBN 0-87611-030-8). Tex St Hist Assn.
Butterfield, Herbert. The Peace Tactics of Napoleon, 1806-1808. LC 70-159170. viii, 395p. 1972. Repr. of 1929 ed. lib. bdg. 22.50x (ISBN 0-374-91130-4). Octagon.
Cameron, Rondo. France & the Economic Development of Europe, 1800-1914. 586p. 1975. Repr. of 1961 ed. lib. bdg. 35.00x (ISBN 0-374-91252-1). Octagon.
Carroll, E. Malcolm. French Public Opinion & Foreign Affairs, 1870-1914. 1964. Repr. of 1931 ed. 19.50 (ISBN 0-208-00414-9, Archon). Shoe String.
Cowan, Laing G. France & the Saar, 1680-1948. LC 50-3112. (Columbia University Studies in the Social Sciences: No. 561). Repr. of 1950 ed. 20.00 (ISBN 0-404-51561-4). AMS Pr.
Dull, Jonathan R. The French Navy & American Independence: A Study of Arms & Diplomacy, 1774-1787. LC 75-2987. 448p. 1975. 30.00 (ISBN 0-691-06920-4). Princeton U Pr.
Ekberg, Carl J. The Failure of Louis XIV's Dutch War. LC 78-21955. 20.00x (ISBN 0-8078-1347-8). U of NC Pr.
French Export Behaviour in Third World Markets. (Significant Issues Ser.: Vol. II, No. 6). 96p. 1980. pap. 10.00 (ISBN 0-89206-021-2, CSIS014, CSIS). Unipub.
Galarneau, Claude & Lavoie, Elvoie. France et Canada Francais Du 16 Au 20 Siecle. (Cahiers De L'institut D'histoire Ser.: No. 7). (Fr). 1966. pap. 8.50x (ISBN 2-7637-6263-8, Pub. by Laval). Intl Schol Bk Serv.
Gombin, Richard. Les Socialistes et la Guerre: La S.F.I.O. et la Politique Etrangere Francaise Entre les Deux Guerres Mondiales. (Illus.). 1970. pap. 19.50x (ISBN 90-2796-427-0). Mouton.
Hatton, Ragnhild, ed. Louis the Fourteenth & Europe. LC 75-45334. (Illus.). 1976. 17.50x (ISBN 0-8142-0254-3). Ohio St U Pr.
Howard, John E. Parliament & Foreign Policy in France. LC 74-6110. 172p. 1974. Repr. of 1948 ed. lib. bdg. 15.00x (ISBN 0-8371-7503-8, HOPF). Greenwood.
--Parliament & Foreign Policy in France. LC 74-6110. 172p. 1974. Repr. of 1948 ed. lib. bdg. 15.00x (ISBN 0-8371-7503-8, HOPF). Greenwood.
Hughes, Judith M. To the Maginot Line: The Politics of French Military Preparations in the 1920's. LC 70-156139. (Historical Monographs Ser: No. 64). (Illus.). 1971. 15.00x (ISBN 0-674-89310-7). Harvard U Pr.
Hytier, Adrienne D. Two Years of French Foreign Policy: Vichy, 1940-1942. LC 74-7448. (Etudes D'histoire Economique Politique et Sociale: No. 25). 402p. 1974. Repr. of 1958 ed. lib. bdg. 21.00x (ISBN 0-8371-7551-8). Greenwood.
--Two Years of French Foreign Policy: Vichy, 1940-1942. LC 74-7448. (Etudes D'histoire Economique Politique et Sociale: No. 25). 402p. 1974. Repr. of 1958 ed. lib. bdg. 21.00x (ISBN 0-8371-7551-8). Greenwood.

Jusserand, Jean J. What Me Befell. (Select Bibliographies Reprint Ser.). 1972. Repr. of 1933 ed. 22.00 (ISBN 0-8369-6831-X). Arno.
Levy, Roger. French Interests & Policies in the Far East. LC 75-30110. (Institute of Pacific Relations). 1976. Repr. of 1941 ed. 21.50 (ISBN 0-404-59540-5). AMS Pr.
Marshall, D. Bruce. The French Colonial Myth & Constitution: Making in the Fourth Republic. LC 71-99833. (Illus.). 352p. 1973. 27.50x (ISBN 0-300-01212-8). Yale U Pr.
Medzini, Meron. French Policy in Japan During the Closing Years of the Tokugawa Regime. (East Asian Monographs Ser: No. 41). 1971. pap. 9.00x (ISBN 0-674-32230-4). Harvard U Pr.
Nere, J. Foreign Policy of France. (Foreign Policies of the Great Powers). 1975. 26.00x (ISBN 0-7100-7968-0). Routledge & Kegan.
Oncken, Hermann. Napoleon Third & the Rhine: The Origin of the War of 1870-1871. Zeydel, Edwin H., tr. LC 66-24743. 1967. Repr. of 1928 ed. 8.00 (ISBN 0-8462-0966-7). Russell.
Paleologue, Maurice. Three Critical Years, 1904-05-06. 6.00 (ISBN 0-8315-0015-8). Speller.
Pallain, G., ed. Ambassade De Talleyrand: A Londres. LC 72-12238. (Europe 1815-1945 Ser.). 464p. 1973. Repr. of 1891 ed. lib. bdg. 49.50 (ISBN 0-306-70575-3). Da Capo.
Porter, Charles W. The Career of Theophile Delcasse. LC 74-11938. 356p. 1975. Repr. of 1936 ed. lib. bdg. 19.50x (ISBN 0-8371-7720-0, POTD). Greenwood.
Puryear, Vernon J. France & the Levant: From the Bourbon Restoration to the Peace of Kutiah. 1968. Repr. of 1941 ed. 18.50 (ISBN 0-208-00721-0, Archon). Shoe String.
Ragsdale, Hugh. Detente in the Napoleonic Era: Bonaparte & the Russians. LC 79-28494. (Illus.). 196p. 1980. 17.50x (ISBN 0-7006-0201-1). Regents Pr KS.
Roosen, William J. The Age of Louis XIV: The Rise of Modern Diplomacy. LC 76-7842. 250p. 1976. text ed. 15.25x (ISBN 0-87073-580-2); pap. text ed. 8.95x (ISBN 0-87073-581-0). Schenkman.
Schoonmaker, E. D. Our Genial Enemy, France. 69.95 (ISBN 0-8490-0783-6). Gordon Pr.
Schuman, Frederick L. War & Diplomacy in the French Republic: An Inquiry into Political Motivations & the Control of Foreign Policy. LC 68-9635. 1970. Repr. of 1931 ed. 19.50 (ISBN 0-86527-204-2). Fertig.
--War & Diplomacy in the French Republic. LC 71-11468. 1970. Repr. of 1931 ed. 29.50 (ISBN 0-404-05623-7). AMS Pr.
Serfaty, Simon. France, DeGaulle, & Europe: The Policy of the Fourth & Fifth Republics Toward the Continent. LC 68-15453. 176p. 1968. 12.00x (ISBN 0-8018-0584-8). Johns Hopkins.
Serfaty, Simon, ed. The Foreign Policies of the French Left. LC 79-53137. (Westview Special Studies in West European Politics & Society). 1979. lib. bdg. 16.50x (ISBN 0-89158-652-0). Westview.
Singh, R. John. French Diplomacy in the Caribbean & the American Revolution. 1977. 10.00 (ISBN 0-682-48891-7, University). Exposition.
Slawecki, Leon M. French Policy Towards the Chinese in Madagascar. (Foreign Area Studies Ser.: No. 13). (Illus.). 1971. 18.50 (ISBN 0-208-01251-6). Shoe String.
Sullivan, Marianna P. France's Vietnam Policy: A Study in French-American Relations. LC 77-94749. (Contributions in Political Science: No. 12). 1978. lib. bdg. 17.50 (ISBN 0-313-20317-2, SUV/). Greenwood.
Wandycz, Piotr S. France & Her Eastern Allies, 1919-1925. LC 74-10474. (Illus.). 454p. 1974. Repr. of 1962 ed. lib. bdg. 27.75 (ISBN 0-8371-7687-5, WAFH). Greenwood.
Werth, Alexander. France & Munich. LC 68-9632. 1969. Repr. of 1939 ed. 27.50 (ISBN 0-86527-071-6). Fertig.
--The Twilight of France, 1933-1940. 24.00 (ISBN 0-86527-199-2). Fertig.
Wilson, Arthur M. French Foreign Policy During the Administration of Cardinal Fleury: 1726-1743; a Study in Diplomacy & Commercial Development. LC 70-138193. 433p. 1972. Repr. of 1936 ed. lib. bdg. 18.25x (ISBN 0-8371-5333-6, WIFP). Greenwood.
Wolfers, Arnold. Britain & France Between Two Wars: Conflicting Strategies of Peace from Versailles to World War Two. 1966. pap. 5.95 (ISBN 0-393-00343-4, Norton Lib). Norton.
Young, Robert J. French Foreign Policy, Nineteen Eighteen to Nineteen Forty-Five: A Guide to Research & Research Materials. Kimmich, Christoph M., ed. LC 80-53892. 242p. 1981. lib. bdg. 17.50 (ISBN 0-8420-2178-7). Scholarly Res.

FRANCE–FOREIGN RELATIONS–1945-

Cerny, Phillip G. The Politics of Grandeur. LC 79-50232. 1980. 35.50 (ISBN 0-521-22863-8). Cambridge U Pr.
De Carmoy, Guy. Foreign Policies of France, Nineteen Forty-Four to Nineteen Sixty-Eight. Halperin, Elaine P., tr. LC 71-85446. 1970. 16.50x (ISBN 0-226-13991-3). U of Chicago Pr.
DePorte, Anton W. DeGaulle's Foreign Policy: 1944-1946. LC 67-29624. 1968. 16.50x (ISBN 0-674-19550-7). Harvard U Pr.
Deutsch, Karl W. Arms Control & the Atlantic Alliance. 167p. 1967. text ed. 8.50 (ISBN 0-471-21140-0, Pub. by Wiley). Krieger.
Grosser, Alfred. French Foreign Policy Under de Gaulle. LC 77-21747. 1977. Repr. of 1967 ed. lib. bdg. 18.00x (ISBN 0-8371-9795-3, GRFR). Greenwood.
Kohl, Wilfrid L. French Nuclear Diplomacy. LC 71-153846. 1972. 25.00 (ISBN 0-691-07540-9). Princeton U Pr.
Kolodziej, Edward A. French International Policy Under de Gaulle & Pompidou: The Politics of Grandeur. LC 73-20791. 576p. 1974. 38.50x (ISBN 0-8014-0829-6). Cornell U Pr.
Kulski, Wladyslaw W. De Gaulle & the World: The Foreign Policy of the Fifth French Republic. LC 66-28137. 1966. 14.95x (ISBN 0-8156-0052-6). Syracuse U Pr.
Macridis, Roy C., ed. De Gaulle: Implacable Ally. LC 75-41500. 248p. 1976. Repr. of 1966 ed. lib. bdg. 16.75x (ISBN 0-8371-8710-9, DEIA). Greenwood.
Morse, Edward L. Foreign Policy & Interdependence in Gaullist France. LC 72-5391. (Center of International Studies). 388p. 1973. 24.50 (ISBN 0-691-05209-3). Princeton U Pr.
Poincare, Raymond. The Memoirs of Raymond Poincare, 4 vols. Arthur, George, tr. LC 70-160452. Repr. of 1931 ed. Set. 110.00 (ISBN 0-404-09090-7); 27.50 ea. Vol. 1 (ISBN 0-404-09091-5). Vol. 2 (ISBN 0-404-09092-3). Vol. 3 (ISBN 0-404-09093-1). Vol. 4 (ISBN 0-404-09094-X). AMS Pr.
Schoenbrun, David. As France Goes. LC 55-8033. 1968. pap. 3.25 (ISBN 0-689-70174-8, 128). Atheneum.
Tint, Herbert. French Foreign Policy Since the Second World War. LC 72-83418. 1973. 17.95 (ISBN 0-312-30485-4). St Martin.
Young, Robert J. In Command of France: French Foreign Policy & Military Planning, 1933-1940. LC 78-4875. (Illus.). 1978. 18.50x (ISBN 0-674-44536-8). Harvard U Pr.

FRANCE–FOREIGN RELATIONS–AFRICA

Brown, Roger Glenn. Fashoda Reconsidered: The Impact of Domestic Politics on French Policy in Africa, 1893-1898. LC 70-94393. (Studies in Historical & Political Sciences Ser: Eighty-Eight Series No.1 (1970)). 168p. 1970. 12.00x (ISBN 0-8018-1098-1). Johns Hopkins.
Perkins, Kenneth J. Quaids, Captains, Colons: French Military Administration in the Colonial Maghrib 1844-1934. LC 80-13114. 225p. 1981. text ed. 24.50x (ISBN 0-8419-0564-9, Africana). Holmes & Meier.
White, Dorothy S. Black Africa & De Gaulle; from the French Empire to Independence. LC 79-1733. (Illus.). 1979. 16.95x (ISBN 0-271-00214-X). Pa St U Pr.
Williams, A. Britain & France in the Middle East & North Africa. 1969. 6.95 (ISBN 0-312-09765-4). St Martin.

FRANCE–FOREIGN RELATIONS–ALGERIA

Smith, Tony. The French Stake in Algeria, 1945-1962. (Illus.). 1978. 22.50x (ISBN 0-8014-1125-4). Cornell U Pr.

FRANCE–FOREIGN RELATIONS–ARGENTINE REPUBLIC

Cady, John F. Foreign Intervention in the Rio De La Plata 1838-50: A Study of French, British, & American Policy in Relation to the Dictator Juan Manuel Rosas. LC 71-100817. (BCL Ser. II). Repr. of 1929 ed. 24.00 (ISBN 0-404-01360-0). AMS Pr.

FRANCE–FOREIGN RELATIONS–CONFEDERATE STATES OF AMERICA

Case, Lynn M. & Spencer, Warren F. The United States & France: Civil War Diplomacy. LC 75-105108. 680p. 1974. 25.00x (ISBN 0-8122-7604-3). U of Pa Pr.
Willson, Beckles. John Slidell & the Confederates in Paris, 1862-65. LC 77-111089. (Illus.). Repr. of 1932 ed. 23.50 (ISBN 0-404-06992-4). AMS Pr.

FRANCE–FOREIGN RELATIONS–EUROPE

Charlton, Sue E. The French Left & European Integration. (Monograph Ser. in World Affairs, Vol. 9: 1971-72 Ser., Pt. D). 4.00 (ISBN 0-87940-032-3). U of Denver Intl.
Gladwyn, Hubert M. Europe After De Gaulle. Crozier, Brian, ed. LC 70-86972. (World Realities Ser). (Orig.). 1969. 4.95 (ISBN 0-8008-2520-9). Taplinger.

FRANCE–FOREIGN RELATIONS–GERMANY

Gooch, G. P. Germany & the French Revoluton. 543p. 1965. Repr. 35.00x (ISBN 0-7146-1477-7, F Cass Co). Biblio Dist.
Gooch, George P. Franco-German Relations, 1871-1914. LC 66-24694. 1967. Repr. of 1923 ed. 5.00 (ISBN 0-8462-0830-X). Russell.
McDougall, Walter A. France's Rhineland Policy, 1914-1924: The Last Bid for a Balance of Power in Europe. LC 77-85550. 1978. 31.00 (ISBN 0-691-05268-9). Princeton U Pr.
Mitchell, Allan. Bismarck & the French Nation: 1848-1890. LC 72-167692. 1971. 24.50x (ISBN 0-672-53510-6). Irvington.
Pottinger, Evelyn A. Napoleon Third & the German Crisis, 1865-1866. LC 66-18253. (Historical Studies: No. 75). 1966. 12.50x (ISBN 0-674-60050-9). Harvard U Pr.
Pryce-Jones, David. Paris in the Third Reich: A History of the German Occupation, 1940-1944. LC 80-21256. (Illus.). 304p. 1981. 25.00 (ISBN 0-03-045621-5). HR&W.
Reynaud, Louis. Histoire Generale De L'influence Francaise En Allemagne. 3rd ed. LC 77-172643. (Research & Source Works Ser.: No. 852). 576p. (Fr.). 1972. Repr. of 1924 ed. lib. bdg. 34.50 (ISBN 0-8337-4337-6). B Franklin.
Wienefeld, Robert H. Franco-German Relations, 1878-1885. LC 78-64133. (Johns Hopkins University. Studies in the Social Sciences. Forty-Seventh Ser. 1929: 4). Repr. of 1929 ed. 19.50 (ISBN 0-404-61246-6). AMS Pr.

FRANCE–FOREIGN RELATIONS–GREAT BRITAIN

Cartwright, John. Commonwealth in Danger. 1968. Repr. of 1795 ed. 24.50 (ISBN 0-8337-0486-9). B Franklin.
Choiseul, Etienne F., ed. Memoire Historique Sur la Negociation De la France et De l'Angleterre. 1761. 12.50 (ISBN 0-384-08930-5). Johnson Repr.
Cobban, Alfred. Ambassadors & Secret Agents: The Diplomacy of the First Earl of Malmesbury at the Hague. LC 78-59012. (Illus.). 1979. Repr. of 1954 ed. 21.00 (ISBN 0-88355-687-1). Hyperion Conn.
Correspondance Diplomatique De Bertrand De Salignac De la Mothe-Fenelon, 7 vol. set. LC 73-168014. (Bannatyne Club, Edinburgh Publications Ser.: No. 67). 345.00 (ISBN 0-404-52780-9). AMS Pr.
Coville, Alfred, et al, eds. Studies in Anglo-French History During the Eighteenth, Nineteenth & Twentieth Centuries. facs. ed. LC 67-23197. (Essay Index Reprint Ser). 1935. 15.00 (ISBN 0-8369-0343-9). Arno.
De Salignac Fenelon, Bertrand. Correspondance diplomatique, 7 Vols. LC 73-168014. (Bannatyne Club, Edinburgh. Publications: No. 67). Repr. of 1840 ed. Set. 345.00 (ISBN 0-404-52780-9). AMS Pr.
Gates, Eleanor M. End of the Affair: The Collapse of the Anglo-French Alliance. LC 80-23585. 496p. 1981. 28.50x (ISBN 0-520-04292-1). U of Cal Pr.
Harrison, Royden, ed. English Defence of the Commune: 1871. 292p. 1971. text ed. 7.75x (ISBN 0-391-00237-6). Humanities.
Korr, Charles P. Cromwell & the New Model Foreign Policy. 1975. 23.50x (ISBN 0-520-02281-5). U of Cal Pr.
Laprade, William T. England & the French Revolution, 1789-1797. LC 77-109922. Repr. of 1909 ed. 12.50 (ISBN 0-404-03878-6). AMS Pr.
Lee, Maurice, Jr. James First & Henri Fourth: An Essay in English Foreign Policy, 1603-1610. LC 74-100377. (Illus.). 1970. 14.50 (ISBN 0-252-00084-6). U of Ill Pr.
Legg, L. Wickham. Matthew Prior: A Study of His Public Career & Correspondence. LC 72-5135. x, 348p. 1972. Repr. of 1921 ed. lib. bdg. 17.50x (ISBN 0-374-94890-9). Octagon.
Lord, Walter E. England & France in the Mediterranean 1660-1830. LC 73-110902. 1970. Repr. of 1901 ed. 14.00 (ISBN 0-8046-0894-6). Kennikat.
Rolo, P. J. Entente Cordiale: The Origins & Negotiations of the Anglo-French Agreements of April 8, 1904. LC 77-86588. 1970. 18.95 (ISBN 0-312-25690-6). St Martin.
Savelle, Maxwell H. Diplomatic History of the Canadian Boundary, 1749-1763. LC 68-27084. (Relations of Canada & the U. S. Ser). (Illus.). 1968. Repr. of 1940 ed. 8.00 (ISBN 0-8462-1213-7). Russell.
Spears, Edward. Fulfillment of a Mission: Syria & Lebanon, 1941-1944. 1978. 19.00 (ISBN 0-208-01695-3, Archon). Shoe String.
Teulet, Jean B. Papiers D'etat, 3 Vols. LC 70-176146. (Bannatyne Club, Edinburgh. Publications: No. 107). Repr. of 1860 ed. 210.00 (ISBN 0-404-52870-8). AMS Pr.
Thomas, R. T. Britain & Vichy: The Dilemma of Anglo-French Relations, 1940-42. (The Making of the Twentieth Century Ser.). 1979. 19.95 (ISBN 0-312-09822-7). St Martin.

FRANCE–FOREIGN RELATIONS–HOLY ROMAN EMPIRE

Bradford, William, ed. Correspondence of the Emperor Charles Fifth. Repr. of 1850 ed. 27.50 (ISBN 0-404-00926-3). AMS Pr.

FRANCE–FOREIGN RELATIONS–ISRAEL

Crosbie, Sylvia K. A Tacit Alliance: France & Israel from the Suez to the Six Day War. (Studies of the Middle East Institute, Columbia University). 304p. 1974. 21.00 (ISBN 0-691-07557-3). Princeton U Pr.

FRANCE–FOREIGN RELATIONS–ITALY

Case, Lynn M. Franco-Italian Relations, 1860-1865. LC 75-121289. (BCL Ser. I). Repr. of 1932 ed. 24.50 (ISBN 0-404-01405-4). AMS Pr.

FRANCE–FOREIGN RELATIONS–LATIN AMERICA

Robertson, William S. France & Latin-American Independence. 1967. lib. bdg. 30.00x (ISBN 0-374-96878-0). Octagon.

FRANCE–FOREIGN RELATIONS–MEXICO

Barker, Nancy N. French Experience in Mexico, Eighteen Twenty-One to Eighteen Sixty-One: A History of Constant Misunderstanding. LC 78-12935. 1979. 18.00x (ISBN 0-8078-1339-7). U of NC Pr.
Lally, Frank E. French Opposition to the Mexican Policy of the Second Empire. LC 78-64141. (Johns Hopkins University. Studies in the Social Sciences. Forty-Ninth Ser. 1931: 3). Repr. of 1931 ed. 18.00 (ISBN 0-404-61253-9). AMS Pr.
Maissin, Eugene. French in Mexico & Texas, 1838-1839. Sheppherd, J. L., tr. (Illus.). 1961. 35.00 (ISBN 0-685-05002-5). A Jones.

FRANCE–FOREIGN RELATIONS–MOROCCO

Barlow, Ima C. Agadir Crisis. 1971. Repr. of 1940 ed. 25.00 (ISBN 0-208-01023-8, Archon). Shoe String.

FRANCE–FOREIGN RELATIONS–NEAR EAST

Charriere, Ernest, compiled by. Negociations de la France dans le Levant, 4 Vols. 1965. Repr. of 1848 ed. Set. 261.00 (ISBN 0-8337-0544-X). B Franklin.
Cumming, Henry H. Franco-British Rivalry in the Post-War Near East: The Decline of French Influence. LC 79-2854. (Illus.). 229p. 1981. Repr. of 1938 ed. 19.75 (ISBN 0-8305-0029-4). Hyperion Conn.
Shorrock, William I. French Imperialism in the Middle East: The Failure of Policy in Syria & Lebanon, 1900-1914. LC 75-32078. 224p. 1976. 25.00x (ISBN 0-299-07030-1). U of Wis Pr.
Tanenbaum, Jan K. France & the Arab Middle East, 1914-1920. LC 78-68379. (Transactions Ser.: Vol. 68, Pt. 7). 1978. pap. 6.00 (ISBN 0-87169-687-8). Am Philos.
Zeine, Zeine N. The Struggle for Arab Independence. 2nd ed. LC 77-5149. 280p. 1977. lib. bdg. 25.00x (ISBN 0-88206-002-3). Caravan Bks.

FRANCE–FOREIGN RELATIONS–RUSSIA

Niven, Alexander C. Napoleon & Alexander I: A Study in Franco-Russian Relations, 1807-1812. LC 78-60628. 1978. pap. text ed. 6.50 (ISBN 0-8191-0561-9). U Pr of Amer.
Oliva, L. Jay. Misalliance: A Study of French Policy in Russia During the Seven Years' War. LC 64-10779. 218p. 1964. 8.95x (ISBN 0-8147-0328-3). NYU Pr.
Ragsdale, Hugh. Detente in the Napoleonic Era: Bonaparte & the Russians. LC 79-28494. (Illus.). 196p. 1980. 17.50x (ISBN 0-7006-0201-1). Regents Pr KS.

FRANCE–FOREIGN RELATIONS–SCOTLAND

Macdonald, Alexander, ed. Papers Relative to the Royal Guard of Scottish Archers in France. LC 79-175588. (Maitland Club, Glasgow. Publications: No. 36). Repr. of 1835 ed. 11.50 (ISBN 0-404-53007-9). AMS Pr.
Teulet, Jean B., ed. Relations Politiques de la France et de l' Espagne avec l' Ecosse au Seizieme Siecle, 5 vols. Incl. Vol. 1. Correspondences Francaises 1515-1560. 47.50 (ISBN 0-404-52891-0); Vol. 2. Correspondences Francaises 1559-1573. 47.50 (ISBN 0-404-52892-9); Vol. 3. Correspondences Francaises 1575-1585. 47.50 (ISBN 0-404-52893-7); Vol. 4. Correspondences Francaises 1585-1603. 47.50 (ISBN 0-404-52894-5); Vol. 5. Correspondences Espagnoles 1562-1588. 47.50 (ISBN 0-404-52895-3). (Bannatyne Club, Edinburgh. Publications: No. B). (Fr.). Repr. of 1862 ed. 237.50 set (ISBN 0-404-52890-2). AMS Pr.

FRANCE–FOREIGN RELATIONS–SPAIN

Jensen, DeLamar. Diplomacy & Dogmatism: Bernardino De Mendoza & the French Catholic League. LC 63-20769. (Illus.). 1964. 17.50x (ISBN 0-674-20800-5). Harvard U Pr.

FRANCE–FOREIGN RELATIONS–TUNISIA

Mezerik, Avrahm G., ed. Tunisian-French Dispute. 1961. pap. 15.00 (ISBN 0-685-13211-0, 67). Intl Review.

FRANCE–FOREIGN RELATIONS–UNITED STATES

Ames, Herman, et al, eds. X, Y, Z Letters. (BCL History Ser). 1899. 6.00 (ISBN 0-403-00035-1). Scholarly.

Bowman, Albert H. The Struggle for Neutrality: Franco-American Diplomacy During the Federalist Era. LC 73-21917. 1974. 18.50x (ISBN 0-87049-152-0). U of Tenn Pr.

Carroll, Daniel B. Henri Mercier & the American Civil War. LC 77-132235. 1971. 28.00x (ISBN 0-691-04585-2). Princeton U Pr.

Case, Lynn M. & Spencer, Warren F. The United States & France: Civil War Diplomacy. LC 75-105108. 680p. 1974. 25.00x (ISBN 0-8122-7604-3). U of Pa Pr.

Corwin, E. S. French Policy & the American Alliance of 1778. 7.50 (ISBN 0-8446-0559-X). Peter Smith.

Corwin, Edward S. French Policy & the American Alliance of 1778. LC 77-121599. (Research & Source Works Ser: No. 476). 1970. Repr. of 1916 ed. lib. bdg. 21.00 (ISBN 0-8337-0687-X). B Franklin.

Duroselle, Jean B. France & the United States: From the Beginnings to the Present Day. Coltman, Derek, tr. from Fr. LC 78-1467. (United States & the World: Foreign Perspectives Ser.). 1978. lib. bdg. 18.00x (ISBN 0-226-17408-5). U of Chicago Pr.

Eccles, W. J. France in America. LC 72-79657. (New American Nation Ser.). (Illus.). 1972. 16.95x (ISBN 0-06-011152-6, HarpT). Har-Row.

Fish, Hamilton. Lafayette in America During & After the Revolutionary War: And Other Essays on Franco-American Relations. 1977. 6.95 (ISBN 0-533-02314-9). Vantage.

Hill, Peter P. William Vans Murray, Federalist Diplomat: The Shaping of Peace with France, 1797-1801. LC 71-150347. 1971. 12.95x (ISBN 0-8156-0078-X). Syracuse U Pr.

Langer, William R. Our Vichy Gamble. 1965. Repr. of 1947 ed. 25.00 (ISBN 0-208-00409-2, Archon). Shoe String.

Leffler, Melvyn P. The Elusive Quest: America's Pursuit of European Stability & French Security, 1919-1933. LC 78-9782. 1979. 24.50x (ISBN 0-8078-1333-8). U of NC Pr.

Morris, Gouverneur. Diary & Letters of Gouverneur Morris, 2 Vols. Morris, Anne C., ed. LC 70-98691. (American Public Figures Ser). 1969. Repr. of 1888 ed. lib. bdg. 95.00 (ISBN 0-306-71835-9). Da Capo.

--Diary of the French Revolution, 2 vols. Davenport, Beatrix C., ed. LC 70-110859. (Illus.). 1972. Repr. of 1939 ed. lib. bdg. 53.00x (ISBN 0-8371-4528-7, MOFR). Greenwood.

--A Diary of the French Revolution, 2 vols. facsimile ed. Davenport, Beatrix C., ed. LC 71-157348. (Select Bibliographies Reprint Ser). Repr. of 1939 ed. Set. 60.00 (ISBN 0-8369-5809-8). Arno.

Perkins, James B. France in the American Revolution. LC 78-122844. (Research & Source Ser.: No. 504). 1970. Repr. of 1911 ed. 29.00 (ISBN 0-8337-2725-7). B Franklin.

Phillips, Paul C. West in the Diplomacy of the American Revolution. LC 66-24750. 1967. Repr. of 1913 ed. 8.50 (ISBN 0-8462-0947-0). Russell.

Reeves, Jesse S. The Napoleonic Exiles in America: A Study in Diplomatic History, 1815-1819. LC 78-63910. (Johns Hopkins University. Studies in the Social Sciences. Twenty-Third Ser. 1905: 9-10). Repr. of 1905 ed. 16.50 (ISBN 0-404-61162-1). AMS Pr.

Savard, Pierre. Jules-Paul Tardivel, la France et les Etats-Unis, 1851-1905. (Cahiers De L'institut D'histoire: No. 8). (Fr). 1967. pap. 12.50x (ISBN 0-7746-6188-7, Pub. by Laval). Intl Schol Bk Serv.

Shulim, Joseph I. Old Dominion & Napoleon Bonaparte. LC 68-59263. (Columbia University. Studies in the Social Sciences: No. 572). Repr. of 1952 ed. 18.50 (ISBN 0-404-51572-X). AMS Pr.

Stinchcombe, William. The XYZ Affair. LC 80-544. (Contributions in American History: No. 89). (Illus.). 167p. 1980. lib. bdg. 23.95 (ISBN 0-313-22234-7, SXY/). Greenwood.

Stinchcombe, William C. American Revolution & the French Alliance. LC 69-18862. (Illus.). 1969. 14.95x (ISBN 0-8156-2134-5). Syracuse U Pr.

Strauss, David. Menace in the West: The Rise of French Anti-Americanism in Modern Times. LC 77-94748. (Contributions in American Studies: No. 40). 1978. lib. bdg. 22.50x (ISBN 0-313-20316-4, SMW/). Greenwood.

Turner, Frederick J., ed. Correspondence of the French Ministers to the United States, 1791-1797. LC 75-75268. (American History, Politics & Law Ser). 1969. Repr. of 1904 ed. lib. bdg. 95.00 (ISBN 0-306-71315-2). Da Capo.

FRANCE–GENEALOGY

Newman, William M. Les Seigneurs De Nesle En Picardie (12e Siecle a 1286) Leurs Chartes et Leur Histoire. (Memoirs Ser.: Vol. 91). 1971. 32.50 (ISBN 0-87169-091-8). Am Philos.

Potier De Courcy, Pol. Continuation De L'histoire Genealogique et Chronologique De la Maison Royale De France Du Pere Anselme, 3 Vols. (Fr). 1969. Repr. of 1868 ed. Set. 215.50 (ISBN 0-384-47374-1). Johnson Repr.

FRANCE–HISTORICAL GEOGRAPHY

Demangeon, Albert. Sources de la Geographie de la France au Archives Nationales. 1969. Repr. of 1905 ed. 18.50 (ISBN 0-8337-0832-5). B Franklin.

Moreau, Joseph. Dictionnaire De Geographie Historique De la Gaule et De la France. 426p. (Fr.). 1972. pap. 37.50 (ISBN 0-686-56815-X, M-6593). French & Eur.

FRANCE–HISTORIOGRAPHY

Archambault, Paul. Seven French Chroniclers: Witnesses to History. LC 73-16652. 224p. 1974. 12.00x (ISBN 0-8156-0099-2). Syracuse U Pr.

Campbell, Stuart L. The Second Empire Revisited: A Study in French Historiography. LC 77-20247. 1978. 17.00 (ISBN 0-8135-0856-8). Rutgers U Pr.

Church, William F. Louis the Fourteenth in Historical Thought. (Historical Controversies Ser.). 128p. 1976. pap. text ed. 2.95x (ISBN 0-393-09211-9). Norton.

Farmer, Paul. France Reviews Its Revolutionary Origins. 1963. lib. bdg. 13.00x (ISBN 0-374-92698-0). Octagon.

Flint, Robert. The Philosophy of History in France & Germany. 631p. 1971. Repr. of 1874 ed. 57.50x (ISBN 0-8002-1333-5). Intl Pubns Serv.

Fredericq, Paul. The Study of History in Germany & France. LC 78-63795. (Johns Hopkins University. Studies in the Social Sciences. Eighth Ser. 1890: 5-6). Repr. of 1890 ed. 11.50 (ISBN 0-404-61060-9). AMS Pr.

Huppert, George. The Idea of Perfect History: Historical Erudition & Historical Philosophy in Renaissance France. LC 70-94396. 1970. 14.50 (ISBN 0-252-00076-5). U of Ill Pr.

Keylor, William R. Academy & Community: The Foundation of the French Historical Profession. LC 74-81867. 352p. 1975. text ed. 18.50x (ISBN 0-674-00255-5). Harvard U Pr.

Ricoeur, Paul. The Contribution of French Historiography to French History. (Zaharoff Lectures Ser.). 56p. 1980. pap. 8.95x (ISBN 0-19-952249-9). Oxford U Pr.

Stoianovich, Traian. French Historical Method: The "Annales" Paradigm. LC 75-38425. 1976. 22.50x (ISBN 0-8014-0861-X). Cornell U Pr.

FRANCE–HISTORY

Adams, George B. The Growth of the French Nation. 1896. 25.00 (ISBN 0-8482-7274-9). Norwood Edns.

Bachrach, Bernard S., ed. Liber Historae Francorum. 123p. 1973. 5.00x (ISBN 0-87291-058-X). Coronado Pr.

Baughan, Michalina, et al. Social Change in France. 1980. 22.50x (ISBN 0-312-73161-2). St Martin.

Beauregard, J. Histoire de France illustree. 1968. 15.00 (ISBN 0-08-013198-0); pap. 7.00 (ISBN 0-08-013197-2). Pergamon.

Beauroy, Jacques, et al, eds. The Wolf & the Lamb: Popular Culture in France, from the Old Regime to the Twentieth Century. (Stanford French & Italian Studies: No. 3). (Illus.). 1977. pap. 24.50 (ISBN 0-915838-31-1). Anma Libri.

Belaval, Yvon. Histoire de la Philosophie: De la Renaissance a la Revolution, Vol. 2. (Historique Ser.). 1168p. 48.95 (ISBN 0-686-56455-3). French & Eur.

--Histoire de la Philosophie: Du XIX Siecle a nos Jours, Vol. 3. (Historique Ser.). 1408p. 52.50 (ISBN 0-686-56456-1). French & Eur.

Bernier, Olivier. Pleasure & Privilege: Life in France, Naples & America. LC 79-6174. (Illus.). 304p. 1981. 14.95 (ISBN 0-385-15780-0). Doubleday.

Blaze, Francois H. L' Academie Imperiale De Musique: Histoire Litteraire, Musicale, Politique et Galant De Ce Theatre, De 1645 a 1855, 2 vols. LC 80-2258. Repr. of 1855 ed. 95.00 (ISBN 0-404-18804-4). AMS Pr.

Bouvier, Jean & Girault, Rene. L' Imperialisme Francais d'Avant 1914: Recueil De Textes. (Savoir Historique Ser.: No. 10). (Fr.). 1976. pap. text ed. 34.10x (ISBN 90-279-7992-8). Mouton.

Bricaire De La Dixmerie, Nicolas. La Sibyle Gauloise Ou la France Telle Qu'elle Fut, Telle Qu'elle Est, Telle, a Peu Pres, Qu'elle Pourra Etre. 302p. 1981. Repr. of 1775 ed. lib. bdg. 120.00 (ISBN 0-8287-1552-1). Clearwater Pub.

Brichant, Colette. La France Au Cours Des Ages. (Illus.). 480p. 1972. text ed. 22.00 (ISBN 0-07-007712-6, C). McGraw.

Briggs, Robin. Early Modern France, 1560-1715. (Illus.). 1977. 8.95x (ISBN 0-19-215815-5, OPUS 82); pap. 7.50x (ISBN 0-19-289040-9). Oxford U Pr.

Buchon, Jean A., ed. Collection Des Chroniques Nationales Francaises, 47 vols. LC 79-180448. Repr. of 1829 ed. Set. 1034.00 (ISBN 0-404-56550-6); 22.00 ea. AMS Pr.

Butor, Michel. La Banlieue de Paris a l'Aurore, mouvement brownien. (Coll. Huit). 18.50 (ISBN 0-685-37243-X). French & Eur.

Centre de Recherche pour un Tresor de la Langue Francaise. Tresor de la Francaise: Dictionnaire du XIXe et du XXe Siecles (1789-1960, 4 vols. Set. 175.00 (ISBN 0-685-36650-2). French & Eur.

Charlton, D. G., ed. France: Companion to French Studies. (Illus.). 1979. 37.95x (ISBN 0-416-72300-4). Methuen Inc.

Chenon, Emile. Etude Sur L'Histoire Des Alleux En France Avec une Carte Des Pays Allodiaux. LC 80-2036. 1981. Repr. of 1888 ed. 33.00 (ISBN 0-404-18557-6). AMS Pr.

Clark, John G. La Rochelle & the Atlantic Economy During the Eighteenth Century. LC 80-29275. (Illus.). 304p. 1981. text ed. 24.00x (ISBN 0-8018-2529-6). Johns Hopkins.

Clout, H. C. Themes in the Historical Geography of France. 1977. 78.50 (ISBN 0-12-175850-8). Acad Pr.

Cobban, Alfred. History of Modern France: 3 Vols, Vol. 1. 1715-1799. Vol. 2. 1799-1871. Vol. 3. 1871-1962. rev. ed. (Orig.). (YA) (gr. 9 up). 1966. Vol. 1. pap. 3.50 (ISBN 0-14-020403-2, Pelican); Vol. 2. pap. 3.50 (ISBN 0-14-020525-X, Pelican); Vol. 3. pap. 3.50 (ISBN 0-14-020711-2, Pelican). Penguin.

Cohen, William B. The French Encounter with Africans: White Response to Blacks, 1530 to 1880. LC 79-84260. (Illus.). 384p. 1980. 22.50x (ISBN 0-253-34922-2). Ind U Pr.

Cormier, Louis-Phillipe. Lettres a Pierre Margry De 1844-86. (Cahiers De L'institut D'historie: No. 10). (Fr). pap. 7.50x (ISBN 2-7637-6278-6, Pub. by Laval). Intl Schol Bk Serv.

Cuvier, Bon Georges. Recueil Des Eloges Historiques Lus Dans les Seances Publiques De France. 1981. Repr. lib. bdg. 490.00 (ISBN 0-8287-1460-6). Clearwater Pub.

De Castries, Duc. The Lives of the Kings & Queens of France. LC 79-2205. (Illus.). 1979. 20.00 (ISBN 0-394-50734-7). Knopf.

De Fenin, Pierre. Memoires. 1837. 28.00 (ISBN 0-384-15455-7); pap. 23.00 (ISBN 0-384-15460-3). Johnson Repr.

Delzvignette, Robert. Robert Delzvignette on the French Empire: Selected Writings. Cohen, William B., tr. from Fr. Cohen, William, ed. LC 77-1339. 1977. lib. bdg. 13.00x (ISBN 0-226-14191-8). U of Chicago Pr.

Denis, Ernest. Fin De l'Independance Boheme, 2 vols. LC 76-151601. (BCL Ser. I). Repr. of 1890 ed. Set. 57.50 (ISBN 0-404-02087-9). AMS Pr.

Deslandres, Maurice. Histoire Constitutionnelle de la France de 1789 a 1970, 3 vols. Mayer, J. P., ed. LC 78-67346. (European Political Thought Ser.). (Fr.). 1979. Repr. of 1937 ed. Set. lib. bdg. 125.00x (ISBN 0-405-11692-6). Arno.

Duby, G. Histoire de la France. 1978. pap. text ed. 33.95 (ISBN 2-03-079951-3, 3916). Larousse.

Du Cange, Charles D. Les Familles d'Outre-Mer. LC 70-173996. (Research & Source Works Ser.: No. 864). 1006p. (Fr.). 1972. Repr. of 1869 ed. lib. bdg. 47.50 (ISBN 0-8337-0932-1). B Franklin.

Fisher, M. F. A Considerable Town. LC 77-20369. 1978. 8.95 (ISBN 0-394-42711-4). Knopf.

Forster, Robert & Ranum, Orest. Rural Society in France. Forster, Elborg & Ranum, Patricia, trs. from Fr. LC 76-47373. (Selections from the Annales, Economics, Societies, Civilizations Ser: Vol. 3). (Illus.). 1977. text ed. 14.00x (ISBN 0-8018-1916-4); pap. 3.50 (ISBN 0-8018-1917-2). Johns Hopkins.

Funck-Brentano, Frantz, ed. National History of France. 10 Vols. in 11. LC 74-168076. Repr. of 1938 ed. Set. 330.00 (ISBN 0-404-50790-5); 30.00 ea. AMS Pr.

Gasquet, Amedee L. Etudes Byzantines: L'Empire Byzantin et la Monarchie Franque. 484p. 1972. Repr. of 1888 ed. lib. bdg. 30.50 (ISBN 0-8337-1291-8). B Franklin.

Gouraud, Charles. Histoire De la Politique Commerciale De la France et De Son Influence Sur les Progres De la Richesse Publique Depuis le Moyen Age Jusqu'a Nos Jours, 2 vols. LC 79-171408. (Research & Source Works Ser.: No. 851). (Fr.). 1972. Repr. of 1854 ed. lib. bdg. 49.00 (ISBN 0-8337-1400-7). B Franklin.

Guerard, Albert. France: A Modern History. rev. & enl. ed. LC 69-19782. (Illus.). 632p. 1969. 12.50x (ISBN 0-472-08390-2). U of Mich Pr.

Guerard, Albert L. France, a Short History. 1946. 8.50x (ISBN 0-393-05229-X, NortonC). Norton.

Guizot, Francois P. Essais Sur L'histoire de France. x1865 ed. Mayer, J. P., ed. LC 78-67354. (European Political Thought Ser.). (Fr.). 1979. lib. bdg. 26.00x (ISBN 0-405-11700-0). Arno.

Guizot, Francois P., ed. History of France from the Earliest Times to the Year Eighteen Forty-Eight, 8 Vols. Black, Robert, tr. LC 73-91786. (Illus.). Repr. of 1881 ed. Set. 276.00 (ISBN 0-404-03010-6); 34.50 ea. AMS Pr.

Hallie, Philip P. Lest Innocent Blood Be Shed: The Story of the Village of Le Chambon & How Goodness Happened There. LC 77-11825. (Illus.). 1980. pap. 4.95 (ISBN 0-06-090805-X, CN 805, CN). Har-Row.

Hamilton, Ronald. A Holiday History of France. (Illus.). 248p. 1971. 10.00x (ISBN 0-7011-1686-2). Intl Pubns Serv.

Harrigan, Patrick. Lyceens et Collegiens Sous le Second Empire. LC 79-15711. (Illus.). 240p. (Orig., Fr.). 1979. pap. 21.00 (ISBN 2-901725-06-6, IS-00083, Pub. by Maison Science France). Univ Microfilms.

Hassall, Arhur. France: Mediaeval & Modern. 1919. Repr. 20.00 (ISBN 0-685-43042-1). Norwood Edns.

Hayes, Carlton J. France: A Nation of Patriots. 1971. lib. bdg. 25.00x (ISBN 0-374-93753-2). Octagon.

Heggoy, Alf A. & Cooke, James J., eds. Proceedings of the Fourth Meeting of the French Colonial Historical Society. LC 79-63751. 1979. pap. text ed. 9.50 (ISBN 0-8191-0738-7). U Pr of Amer.

Higonnet, Patrice L. Pont-De-Montvert: Social Structure & Politics in a French Village 1700-1914. LC 70-133209. (Historical Studies: No. 85). (Illus.). 1971. 11.50x (ISBN 0-674-68960-7). Harvard U Pr.

Jackson, J. H. A Short History of France from Early Times to 1972. 2nd ed. (Illus.). 260p. 1974. 34.95 (ISBN 0-521-20485-2); pap. 8.95x (ISBN 0-521-09864-5). Cambridge U Pr.

Landry, Adolphe. Essai Economique Sur les Mutations Des Monnaies Dans L'ancienne France De Philippe le Bel a Charles Sept. LC 79-171948. (Research & Source Work Ser.: No. 826). (Fr). 1971. Repr. of 1910 ed. lib. bdg. 26.50 (ISBN 0-8337-1998-X). B Franklin.

Lavisse, Ernest, ed. Histoire De France, Depuis les Origines Jusqu'a la Revolution, 18 pts. in 9 vols. LC 73-89549. (Illus.). Repr. of 1911 ed. Set. 415.00 (ISBN 0-404-03900-6); 47.50 ea. AMS Pr.

Leroy-Ladurie, Emmanuel. The Territory of the Historian. LC 78-31362. 1979. Repr. of 1973 ed. lib. bdg. 21.00 (ISBN 0-226-47327-9). U of Chicago Pr.

Levitine, George. The Dawn of Bohemianism: The Barbu Rebellion & Primitivism in Neoclassical France. LC 77-13892. (Illus.). 1978. 22.50x (ISBN 0-271-00527-0). Pa St U Pr.

Lot, Ferdinand. L' Impot Foncier et la Capitation Personnelle Sous le Bas-Empire et a l'epoque Franque. LC 80-2018. Date not set. Repr. of 1928 ed. 21.50 (ISBN 0-404-18576-2). AMS Pr.

Lucas, Colin R. The Structure of the Terror. (Oxford Historical Monographs). 1973. 42.00x (ISBN 0-19-821843-5). Oxford U Pr.

Luce, Simeon. Histoire De Bertrand Du Gueselin et De Son Epoque. LC 78-63505. Repr. of 1876 ed. 37.50 (ISBN 0-404-17154-0). AMS Pr.

Luchaire, Achille. Social France at the Time of Philip Augustus. 1970. lib. bdg. 13.50x (ISBN 0-88307-190-8). Gannon.

Magoun, F. P., Jr. & Smyser, H. M., trs. Walter of Aquitaine: Materials for the Study of His Legend. (Connecticut College Monograph: No. 4). viii, 62p. 1950. pap. 2.00 (ISBN 0-686-08958-8). Conn Coll Bkshp.

Marx. Civil War in France. 1977. 3.95 (ISBN 0-8351-0562-8); pap. 2.25 (ISBN 0-8351-0044-8). China Bks.

Maurois, Andre. La Conquete de l'Angleterre par les normands. (Coll. Le Memorial des Siecles). 17.50 (ISBN 0-685-34318-9). French & Eur.

--France. (Illus.). 27.50 (ISBN 0-686-55492-2). French & Eur.

--Histoire de la France. 34.90 (ISBN 0-685-36939-0). French & Eur.

Melanges Gustave Glotz, 2 vols. (Illus.). xxvi, 941p. Repr. of 1932 ed. Set. 77.00 (ISBN 0-384-18825-7). Johnson Repr.

Mettam, Roger S. & Johnson, Douglas. French History & Society: The Wars of Religion to the Fifth Republic. LC 75-2861. 168p. 1974. pap. text ed. 3.95x (ISBN 0-416-81620-7). Methuen Inc.

Michel, Francisque X. Histoire Du Commerce et De la Navigation a Bordeaux, Principalement Sous L'administration Anglaise, 2 Vols. LC 79-133550. (Social Science Ser). 1971. Repr. of 1867 ed. Set. 63.00 (ISBN 0-8337-2384-7). B Franklin.

Michelet, Jules. The People. 59.95 (ISBN 0-8490-0810-7). Gordon Pr.

Moreton-Macdonald, John R. History of France, 3 Vols. LC 76-142245. Repr. of 1915 ed. Set. 92.50 (ISBN 0-404-04430-1). Vol. 1 (ISBN 0-404-04431-X). Vol. 2 (ISBN 0-404-04432-8). Vol. 3 (ISBN 0-404-04433-6). AMS Pr.

Mounier, Jean J. On the Influence Attributed to Philosophers, Free-Masons, & to the Illuminati, on the Revolution of France. LC 74-13148. 280p. (Eng.). 1974. Repr. of 1801 ed. 28.00x (ISBN 0-8201-1135-X). Schol Facsimiles.

Mousnier, Roland E. The Institutions of France Under the Absolute Monarchy, Fifteen Ninety-Eight to Seventeen Eighty-Nine: Society & the State. Pearce, Brian, tr. from Fr. LC 78-26857. 1980. Repr. of 1974 ed. lib. bdg. 45.00x (ISBN 0-226-54327-7). U of Chicago Pr.

Munro, William B. Crusaders of New France: A Chronicle of the Fleur-De-Lys in the Wildnerness. Repr. of 1918 ed. 20.00 (ISBN 0-685-43335-8). Norwood Edns.

Newman, William M. Charters of St-Fursy of Peronne. 1977. 16.00 (ISBN 0-910956-59-6). Medieval Acad.

Osburn, Charles B. Guide to French Studies: Supplement, with Cumulative Indexes. LC 68-12638. 1972. 13.50 (ISBN 0-8108-0493-X). Scarecrow.

Parmele, Mary P. A Short History of France. Repr. of 1905 ed. 30.00 (ISBN 0-685-43323-4). Norwood Edns.

Peguy, Charles. La Republique... Notre Royaume de France. pap. 7.95 (ISBN 0-685-37037-2). French & Eur.

Pellissier, Georges. Les Ecrivains Politiques en France Avant le Revolution. Mayer, J. P., ed. LC 78-67374. (European Political Thought Ser.). (Fr.). 1979. Repr. of 1884 ed. lib. bdg. 10.00x (ISBN 0-405-11724-8). Arno.

Perkins, James B. Richelieu & the Growth of French Power. facsimile ed. LC 70-157353. (Select Bibliographies Reprint Ser). Repr. of 1900 ed. 29.00 (ISBN 0-8369-5814-4). Arno.

Perrot, Jean-Claude. Genese D'une Ville Moderne: Caen Au XVIII Siecle. (Civilisations et Societes: No. 44). (Illus.). 548p. (Orig.). 1976. pap. text ed. 100.00x (ISBN 90-2797-995-2). Mouton.

Pickles, Dorothy M. France Between the Republics. LC 79-122000. 1971. Repr. of 1946 ed. 13.00 (ISBN 0-8462-1371-0). Russell.

Sanfacon, Roland. Defrichements, Peuplement et Institutions Seigneuriales En Haut-Poitou Du 10th & 13th Siecle. (Cahiers De L'institut D'histoire Ser.: No. 9). (Fr). 1967. pap. 9.50x (ISBN 2-7637-6170-4, Pub. by Laval). Intl Schol Bk Serv.

Sarolea, Charles. The French Renascence. 1916. Repr. 25.00 (ISBN 0-685-43303-X). Norwood Edns.

Schoenbrun, David. Soldiers of the Night: The Story of the French Resistance. 1981. pap. 7.95 (ISBN 0-452-00565-5, F 565, Mer). NAL.

Seignobos, Charles. The Evolution of the French People. 382p. 1974. Repr. of 1938 ed. lib. bdg. 22.50x (ISBN 0-374-97272-9). Octagon.

Sharatt, P., ed. French Renaissance Studies. 1976. 17.00x (ISBN 0-85224-276-X, Pub. by Edinburgh U Pr Scotland). Columbia U Pr.

Sheridan, George J., Jr. The Social & Economic Foundations of Association Among the Silk Weavers of Lyons, 1852-1870. Bruchey, Stuart, ed. LC 80-2829. (Dissertations in European Economic History Ii). (Illus.). 1981. lib. bdg. 65.00x (ISBN 0-405-14013-4). Arno.

Smith, Bonnie G. Ladies of the Leisure Class: The Bourgeoises of Northern France in the Nineteenth Century. LC 81-47157. (Illus.). 325p. 1981. 25.00x (ISBN 0-691-05330-8); pap. 9.95x (ISBN 0-691-10121-3). Princeton U Pr.

Smith, Michael S. Tariff Reform in France, Eighteen Sixty to Nineteen Hundred: The Politics of Economic Interest. LC 79-25272. 288p. 1980. 20.00x (ISBN 0-8014-1257-9). Cornell U Pr.

Spiers, Victor. History & Literature of France in Synoptic Tables & Essays on the Chief Characters & Epochs. 1978. lib. bdg. 40.00 (ISBN 0-8495-4877-2). Arden Lib.

Studies in French Language, Literature & History. facs. ed. LC 76-80400. (Essay Index Reprint Ser). 1949. 15.00 (ISBN 0-8369-1067-2). Arno.

Swords, Liam, ed. Irish-French Connection Fifteen Seventy-Eight to Nineteen Seventy-Eight. (Orig.). 1979. pap. text ed. 6.25x (ISBN 0-391-01706-3). Humanities.

Taine, Hippolyte A. The Origins of Contemporary France. Gargan, Edward T., ed. LC 73-87311. (Classic European Historians Ser). xlvi, 446p. 1974. 15.00x (ISBN 0-226-78934-9). U of Chicago Pr.

Tilley, Arthur A., ed. Modern France: A Companion to French Studies. LC 66-27168. (Illus.). 1967. Repr. of 1922 ed. 25.00 (ISBN 0-8462-0890-3). Russell.

Timayenis, Telemachus T. The Original Mr. Jacobs: Startling Expose. Grob, Gerald, ed. LC 76-46107. (Anti-Movements in America). 1977. Repr. of 1888 ed. lib. bdg. 18.00x (ISBN 0-405-09978-9). Arno.

Tollemer, Abbe A. Un Sire De Gouberville: Gentilhomme Campagnard Au Cotentin De 1553 a 1562. 2nd ed. (Reeditions: No. 10). 1972. 58.50x (ISBN 0-686-21793-4). Mouton.

Vachon, Andre. Administration De la Nouvelle France: Administration of New France 1627-1760. 1970. pap. 2.00x (ISBN 2-7637-6475-4, Pub. by Laval). Intl Schol Bk Serv.

Vexler, Robert I. France: A Chronology & Fact Book. LC 75-34433. (World Chronology Ser.). 160p. 1977. 8.50x (ISBN 0-685-52544-9). Oceana.

Wright, Gordon. France in Modern Times. 3rd ed. 500p. 1981. pap. text ed. 12.95x (ISBN 0-393-95153-7). Norton.

--Insiders & Outliers: The Individual in History. (Illus.). 152p. 1981. price not set (ISBN 0-7167-1339-X); pap. price not set (ISBN 0-7167-1340-3). W H Freeman.

FRANCE–HISTORY–BIBLIOGRAPHY

Cioranescu, Alexandre. Bibliographie de la litterature francaise du 17e siecle, 3 Vols. 1965-67. Pt. 1. 29.90 (ISBN 0-685-99752-9); Pt. 2. 36.00 (ISBN 0-685-99753-7); Pt. 3. 32.70 (ISBN 0-685-99754-5). Adler.

Heinz, Grete & Peterson, Agnes F. The French Fifth Republic, Continuity & Change, 1966-1970: A Bibliography. LC 73-88379. (Bibliographical Ser.: No. 54). 125p. 1974. 11.95 (ISBN 0-8179-2541-4). Hoover Inst Pr.

Molinier, Auguste E. Les Sources de l'histoire de France: Des Origines aux Guerres d'Italie, 6 vols. Incl. Table General Par Marie Louis Felix Alphonse Polain. vii, 218p. 1964. Repr. of 1901 ed. Set. 185.00 (ISBN 0-8337-2428-2). B Franklin.

Vexler, Robert I. France: A Chronology & Fact Book. LC 75-34433. (World Chronology Ser.). 160p. 1977. 8.50x (ISBN 0-685-52544-9). Oceana.

FRANCE–HISTORY–DICTIONARIES

Lalanne, Ludovic. Dictionnaire Historique De la France, 2 Vols. 2nd ed. 1967. Repr. of 1877 ed. 93.00 (ISBN 0-8337-1985-8). B Franklin.

Marion, Marcel, ed. Dictionnaire Des Institutions De la France Aux Dix-Septieme et Dix-Huitieme Siecles. LC 68-6230. (Bibliography & Reference Ser.: No. 214). 1968. Repr. of 1923 ed. 39.00 (ISBN 0-8337-2216-6). B Franklin.

FRANCE–HISTORY–SOURCES

Basin, Thomas. Histoire Des Regnes De Charles VII et De Louis XI, 4 Vols. Repr. of 1855 ed. Set. 126.50 (ISBN 0-384-03510-8); Set. pap. 108.00 (ISBN 0-685-13455-5). Johnson Repr.

The Boke of Noblesse: Addressed to King Edward the Fourth on His Invasion of France in 1475. LC 73-80201. 95p. 1972. Repr. of 1860 ed. lib. bdg. 25.50 (ISBN 0-8337-2524-6). B Franklin.

Delisle, Leopold V., ed. Rouleaux Des Morts Du IXe Au XVe Siecle. 1866. 35.50 (ISBN 0-384-11361-3); pap. 31.00 (ISBN 0-384-11360-5). Johnson Repr.

De Mornay, Charlotte A. Memoires 2 Vols. 1869. Set. 55.50 (ISBN 0-384-40148-1); Set. pap. 46.00 (ISBN 0-384-40149-X). Johnson Repr.

De Salignac Fenelon, Bertrand. Correspondance diplomatique, 7 Vols. LC 73-168014. (Bannatyne Club, Edinburgh. Publications: No. 67). Repr. of 1840 ed. Set. 345.00 (ISBN 0-404-52780-9). AMS Pr.

Douet-D'Arcq, Louis C. Comptes De l'Hotel Des Rois De France Au Quatorzieme et Quinzieme Siecles. 1865. 35.50 (ISBN 0-384-12421-6); pap. 31.00 (ISBN 0-384-12420-8). Johnson Repr.

Douet-D'Arcq, Louis C., ed. Comptes De L'argenterie Des Rois De France Au Quatorzieme Siecle. 1851. 28.00 (ISBN 0-384-12410-0); pap. 23.00 (ISBN 0-384-12411-9). Johnson Repr.

Guizot, Francois P., ed. Collections Des Memoires Relatifs a L'histoire De France, 31 Vols. LC 75-88788. (Fr). Repr. of 1835 ed. Set. 930.00 (ISBN 0-404-02970-1); 30.00 ea. AMS Pr.

Gutwirth, Madelyn, et al, eds. Sources et Reflets De l'Histoire De France. (Illus., Fr). 1972. pap. text ed. 7.95x (ISBN 0-19-501465-0). Oxford U Pr.

Lesure, Michel. Les Sources De L'histoire De Russie Aux Archives Nationales. (Etudes Sur L'histoire, L'economie et la Sociologie Des Pays Slaves: No. 15). 1970. pap. 39.50 (ISBN 90-2796-295-2). Mouton.

Masson, Gustave. Early Chroniclers of Europe: France. LC 70-156388. (Research & Source Works Ser.: No. 738). 1971. Repr. of 1879 ed. lib. bdg. 21.00 (ISBN 0-8337-2290-5). B Franklin.

Mornet, Daniel. Sentiment De la Nature En France De J. J. Rousseau a Bernardin De Saint-Pierre. LC 70-164483. (Research & Source Works Ser.: No. 59). 31.50 (ISBN 0-8337-2468-1). B Franklin.

Napoleon First. Correspondance De Napoleon Ier, Supplement: Lettres Curieuses Omises Par le Comite De Publication, Rectifications. LC 77-173013. 1975. Repr. of 1887 ed. 20.00 (ISBN 0-404-07148-1). AMS Pr.

Roland de la Platiere, Marie J. An Appeal to Impartial Posterity, 2 vols. LC 74-37718. Repr. of 1798 ed. 40.00 set (ISBN 0-404-56826-2); 20.50 ea. AMS Pr.

Vexler, Robert I. France: A Chronology & Fact Book. LC 75-34433. (World Chronology Ser.). 160p. 1977. 8.50x (ISBN 0-685-52544-9). Oceana.

FRANCE–HISTORY–TO 987

see also Carlovingians; Latin Empire, 1204-1261

Bullough, Donald. The Age of Charlemagne. 1965. 19.95 (ISBN 0-236-17790-7, Pub. by Paul Elek); pap. 7.95 (ISBN 0-236-17696-X). Merrimack Bk Serv.

Cabaniss, Allen, ed. Son of Charlemagne: A Contemporary Life of Louis the Pious. LC 61-1398. 1961. 14.00x (ISBN 0-8156-2031-4). Syracuse U Pr.

Dhondt, Jan. Etudes Sur la Naissance Des Principautes Territoriales En France, IXe-IXe Siecle. LC 80-2033. Repr. of 1948 ed. 38.50 (ISBN 0-404-18560-6). AMS Pr.

Dill, Samuel. Roman Society in Gaul in the Merovingian Age. 566p. 1970. Repr. of 1926 ed. 22.50x (ISBN 0-87471-319-6). Rowman.

Easton, Stewart C. & Wieruszowski, Helene. The Era of Charlemagne: Frankish State & Society. LC 79-4518. (Anvil Ser.). 192p. 1979. pap. 4.95 (ISBN 0-88275-905-1). Krieger.

Funck-Brentano, Frantz. Earliest Times. LC 77-168074. (National History of France: No. 1). Repr. of 1927 ed. 30.00 (ISBN 0-404-50791-3). AMS Pr.

Gregorius, Saint Histoire Ecclesiastique Des Francs, 4 vols. 1967. 126.00 (ISBN 0-384-19875-9); pap. 108.00 (ISBN 0-384-19874-0). Johnson Repr.

--Zehn Bucher Frankischer Geschichte, 3 vols. 4th ed. Hellmann, S., ed. Von Geisebrecht, Wilhel M, tr. 1911-1913. pap. 28.00 ea. Johnson Repr.

Gregory - Bishop Of Tours. History of the Franks. Brehaut, Ernest, tr. (Columbia University Records of Civilization Ser). 1969. pap. 6.95x (ISBN 0-393-09845-1, NortonC). Norton.

Gregory Bishop Of Tours. History of the Franks. Brehaut, Ernest, ed. 1965. lib. bdg. 20.00x (ISBN 0-374-90950-4). Octagon.

Halphen, L. Charlemagne & the Carolingian Empire. (Europe in the Middle Ages; Select Studies: Vol. 3). 1978. 49.00 (ISBN 0-444-11078-X, North-Holland). Elsevier.

Lewis, Archibald R. The Development of Southern French & Catalan Society Seven Eighteen to Ten Fifty. LC 80-2019. 1981. Repr. of 1965 ed. 47.50 (ISBN 0-404-18575-4). AMS Pr.

McKeon, Peter R. Hincmar of Laon: A Study of Carolingian Politics in the Age of Charles the Bald. LC 78-12418. 1978. 17.00 (ISBN 0-252-00536-8). U of Ill Pr.

Richer. Richer: Histoire De Son Temps, 2 Vols. Repr. of 1845 ed. Set. 61.50 (ISBN 0-384-50734-4); Set. pap. 54.00 (ISBN 0-384-50735-2). Johnson Repr.

Rural Settlement in Central Gaul in the Roman Period. 1980. 60.00x (ISBN 0-86054-081-2, Pub. by BAR). State Mutual Bk.

Simonde De Sismondi, Jean C. The French Under the Merovingians. Bellingham, W., tr. Bd. with The French Under the Carlovingians. LC 79-178563. Repr. of 1850 ed. 34.50 (ISBN 0-404-56669-3). AMS Pr.

Wemple, Suzanne F. Women in Frankish Society: Marriage & the Cloister 500 to 900. LC 80-54051. 352p. 1981. 22.50 (ISBN 0-8122-7798-8). U of Pa Pr.

FRANCE–HISTORY–TO 987–SOURCES

Loisel, S. Essai sur la Legislation Economique des Carolingines d'apres les Capitulaires. LC 71-140988. (Social Science Ser). 1971. Repr. of 1904 ed. 23.50 (ISBN 0-8337-2136-4). B Franklin.

FRANCE–HISTORY–CAPETIANS, 987-1328

Here are entered works on the period from The Capetians to 1328 as a whole, as well as those on any part of the period.

Asimov, Isaac. The Shaping of France. LC 72-75604. (Illus.). 288p. (gr. 7 up). 1972. 5.95 (ISBN 0-395-13891-4). HM.

Brumont, Francis. La Burebs L'Epoque De Philippe II. Bruchey, Stuart, ed. LC 77-81824. (Dissertations in European Economic History). (Illus., Fr.). 1977. lib. bdg. 20.00x (ISBN 0-405-10776-5). Arno.

Fawtier, Robert. Capetian Kings of France: Monarchy & Nation, 987-1328. (Illus.). 1960. pap. 7.95 (ISBN 0-312-11900-3). St Martin.

Guillaume De Nangis. Chronique Latine De Guillaume De Nangis 1113 a 1300, 2 Vols. Geraud, H., ed. Set. 71.00 (ISBN 0-384-20360-4); Set. pap. 61.50 (ISBN 0-384-20361-2). Johnson Repr.

Hallam, Elizabeth M. Capetian France, 937-1328. (Illus.). 366p. 1980. text ed. 45.00x cased (ISBN 0-582-48909-1). Longman.

Ilardi, Vincent, ed. Dispatches with Related Documents of Milanese Ambassadors in France (Mar. 11- June 29 1466, Vol. III. Fata, Frank J., tr. LC 68-20933. 445p. 1980. 35.00 (ISBN 0-87580-069-6). N Ill U Pr.

--Dispatches with Related Documents of Milanese Ambassadors in France & Burgundy 1450-1483. Incl. Vol. I 1450-1460. 390p. 1970 (ISBN 0-8214-0067-3); Vol. II 1460-1461. 486p. 1971 (ISBN 0-8214-0082-7). LC 68-20933. 35.00 ea. N Ill U Pr.

Jeanroy, Alfred, et al. Lais et Descorts Francais Du Treizieme Siecle. LC 73-178540. (Fr.). Repr. of 1901 ed. 27.50 (ISBN 0-404-56622-7). AMS Pr.

Mitchell, John H. Court of the Connectable: A Study of a French Administrative Tribunal During the Reign of Henry Iv. 1947. 34.50x (ISBN 0-686-51365-7). Elliots Bks.

Newman, William M. Le Domaine Royal Sous les Premiers Capetiens (987-1180) LC 80-2014. Repr. of 1937 ed. 36.00 (ISBN 0-404-18581-9). AMS Pr.

Painter, Sidney. Scourge of the Clergy: Peter of Dreux, Duke of Brittany. LC 76-96188. 1970. Repr. of 1937 ed. lib. bdg. 13.00x (ISBN 0-374-96175-1, Dist. by NYGS). Octagon.

Richer. Richer: Histoire De Son Temps, 2 Vols. Repr. of 1845 ed. Set. 61.50 (ISBN 0-384-50734-4); Set. pap. 54.00 (ISBN 0-384-50735-2). Johnson Repr.

Von Strassburg, Gottfried. Thirteenth Century, the Story of Tristan & Iseult, 2 Vols. 1971. Repr. of 1899 ed. Set. 29.50 (ISBN 0-403-00996-0). Scholarly.

FRANCE–HISTORY–MEDIEVAL PERIOD, 987-1515

Here are entered works on the medieval period as whole as well as those on any part of this period.

Asimov, Isaac. The Shaping of France. LC 72-75604. (Illus.). 288p. (gr. 7 up). 1972. 5.95 (ISBN 0-395-13891-4). HM.

Basin, Thomas. Histoire Des Regnes De Charles VII et De Louis XI, 4 Vols. Repr. of 1855 ed. Set. 126.50 (ISBN 0-384-03510-8); Set. pap. 108.00 (ISBN 0-685-13455-5). Johnson Repr.

Beech, George T. A Rural Society in Medieval France: The Gatine of Poitou in the Eleventh & Twelfth Centuries. LC 78-64241. (Johns Hopkins University. Studies in the Social Sciences. Eighty-Second Ser. 1964: 1). Repr. of 1964 ed. 17.00 (ISBN 0-404-61346-2). AMS Pr.

Brussel, Nicolas. Nouvel Examen de l'usage General des Fiefs en France Pendant le XI, le XII, le XIII & XIV Siecle, 2 vols. LC 79-8359. Repr. of 1750 ed. Set. 175.00 (ISBN 0-404-18337-9). AMS Pr.

Charles, the Duke of Orleans. England & France in the Fifteenth Century. Pyne, Henry, tr. LC 78-63491. Repr. of 1870 ed. 27.50 (ISBN 0-404-17139-7). AMS Pr.

De Comines, Philippe. History of Comines, 2 Vols. Danett, Thomas, tr. (Tudor Translations, First Ser.: Nos. 17-18). Repr. of 1897 ed. Set. 70.00 (ISBN 0-404-51890-7); 35.00 ea. Vol. 1 (ISBN 0-404-51891-5). Vol. 2 (ISBN 0-404-51892-3). AMS Pr.

De Commynes, Philippe. Memoirs of Philippe De Commynes, Vol. 1, Bks 1-5 & Vol. 2, Bks. 6-8. Kinser, Samuel, ed. Cazeaux, Isabelle, tr. from Fr. LC 68-9363. (Illus.). 1969. Vol. 1. 19.50x (ISBN 0-87249-224-9); Vol. 2. 19.50x (ISBN 0-87249-224-9); Set. 37.50x (ISBN 0-87249-199-4). U of SC Pr.

Delpech, Henri M. La Tactique au XIII siecle, 2 vols. LC 78-63493. Repr. of 1886 ed. Set. 110.00 (ISBN 0-404-17140-0). AMS Pr.

De Monstrelet, Enguerrend. Chronique D'Enguerrand De Monstrelet, 6 Vols. Douet D'Arcq, L., ed. 1857-62. Set. 212.50 (ISBN 0-384-39781-6); Set. pap. 185.00 (ISBN 0-384-39780-8). Johnson Repr.

De Nogent, Guibert. Self & Society in Medieval France. pap. 4.95x (ISBN 0-06-131471-4, TB1471, Torch). Har-Row.

D'Escouchy, Mathieu. Chronique De Mathieu D'Escouchy, 3 Vols. 1863-1864. Set. 106.00 (ISBN 0-384-14650-3); Set. pap. 92.50 (ISBN 0-384-14651-1). Johnson Repr.

Devailly, Guy. Le Berry Du Xe Siecle Au Milieu Du XIIIe: Etude Politique, Religieuses, Sociale & Economique. (Civilisations & Societes: No. 19). (Illus.). 1973. pap. 58.50x (ISBN 90-2797-235-4). Mouton.

Didier, Noel. Le Droit Des Fiefs Dans la Coutume De Hainaut Au Moyen Age. LC 80-2032. Repr. of 1945 ed. 29.50 (ISBN 0-404-18561-4). AMS Pr.

Douet-D'Arcq, Louis C. Comptes De l'Hotel Des Rois De France Au Quatorzieme et Quinzieme Siecles. 1865. 35.50 (ISBN 0-384-12421-6); pap. 31.00 (ISBN 0-384-12420-8). Johnson Repr.

Douet-D'Arcq, Louis C., ed. Choix De Pieces Inedites Relatives Au Regne De Charles Six, 2 Vols. 1863-1864. 63.50 (ISBN 0-384-12400-3); pap. 54.00 (ISBN 0-384-12401-1). Johnson Repr.

--Comptes De L'argenterie Des Rois De France Au Quatorzieme Siecle. 1851. 28.00 (ISBN 0-384-12410-0); pap. 23.00 (ISBN 0-384-12411-9). Johnson Repr.

Duvernoy, Emile & Harmand, Rene. Le Tournoi de Chauvency en 1285: Etude sur la societe et les moeurs chevaleresques au XIII Siecle. LC 79-8361. Repr. of 1905 ed. 13.50 (ISBN 0-404-18343-3). AMS Pr.

Faral, Edmond. Jongleurs En France Au Moyen Age. LC 79-140971. (Reseach & Source Works Ser: No. 606). 1971. Repr. of 1910 ed. 23.50 (ISBN 0-8337-1099-0). B Franklin.

Finn, R. Weldon. The Norman Conquest & Its Effects on the Economy, 1066-1086. (Illus.). 1970. 20.00 (ISBN 0-208-01154-4, Archon). Shoe String.

Froissart, Jean. Chronicle of Froissart, 6 Vols. Bourchier, John, tr. LC 70-168064. (Tudor Translations. First Ser.: Nos. 27-32). Repr. of 1903 ed. Set. 147.00 (ISBN 0-404-51930-X); 24.50 ea. Vol. 1 (ISBN 0-404-51931-8). Vol. 2 (ISBN 0-404-51932-6). Vol. 3 (ISBN 0-404-51933-4). Vol. 4 (ISBN 0-404-51934-2). Vol. 5 (ISBN 0-404-51935-0). Vol. 6 (ISBN 0-404-51936-9). AMS Pr.

--Here Begynneth the First Volum of Sir J. Froyssart. Bourchier, J., tr. LC 72-26004. (English Experience Ser.: No. 257). 644p. 1970. Repr. of 1523 ed. 104.00 (ISBN 90-221-0257-2). Walter J Johnson.

Funck-Brentano, Frantz. Middle Ages. LC 70-168075. (National History of France: No. 2). Repr. of 1930 ed. 30.00 (ISBN 0-404-50792-1). AMS Pr.

Guillaume De Nangis. Chronique Latine De Guillaume De Nangis 1113 a 1300, 2 Vols. Geraud, H., ed. Set. 71.00 (ISBN 0-384-20360-4); Set. pap. 61.50 (ISBN 0-384-20361-2). Johnson Repr.

Henneman, John B., ed. The Medieval French Monarchy. (European Problem Studies). 148p. 1973. pap. 5.50 (ISBN 0-03-086630-8, Pub. by HR&W). Krieger.

Ladurie, Emmanuel L. Montaillou: The Promised Land of Error. Bray, Barbara, tr. from Fr. (Illus.). 1979. pap. 4.95 (ISBN 0-394-72964-1, Vin). Random.

--Montaillou: The Promised Land of Error. LC 77-6124. 1978. 20.00 (ISBN 0-8076-0875-0). Braziller.

Lewis, P. S. Later Medieval France: The Polity. 1968. 17.95 (ISBN 0-312-47250-1). St Martin.

Luce, Simeon, ed. Chronique Des Quatre Premiers Valois, 1327-1393. 1962. 28.00 (ISBN 0-384-08996-8); pap. 23.00 (ISBN 0-384-08995-X). Johnson Repr.

Masson, Gustave. The Story of the Nations: the Story of Mediaeval France: From the Reign of Hughes Capet to the Beginning of the Eighteenth Century. 354p. 1980. Repr. of 1888 ed. lib. bdg. 40.00 (ISBN 0-8495-3793-2). Arden Lib.

Petit-Dutaillis, C., ed. The French Communes in the Middle Ages. (Europe in the Middle Ages Selected Studies: Vol. 6). 1978. 31.75 (ISBN 0-7204-0550-5, North-Holland). Elsevier.

Rogozinski. Power, Caste & Law: Social Conflict in Fourteenth-Century Montpellier. 1980. write for info. (ISBN 0-910956-72-3). Medieval Acad.

Rose, J. H. The Revolutionary & Napoleonic Era. 387p. 1980. Repr. of 1894 ed. lib. bdg. 40.00 (ISBN 0-89760-737-6). Telegraph Bks.

Sarolea, Charles. The French Renascence. 302p. 1980. lib. bdg. 40.00 (ISBN 0-89760-825-9, Telegraph). Dynamic Learn Cor Corp.

Stoddard, E. C. Bertrand Du Guesclin Constable of France: His Life & Times. (Illus.). 301p. 1980. Repr. of 1897 ed. lib. bdg. 35.00 (ISBN 0-89987-761-3). Darby Bks.

Strayer, Joseph R. The Reign of Philip the Fair. LC 79-3232. 1980. 35.00 (ISBN 0-691-05302-2); pap. 13.50 (ISBN 0-691-10089-6). Princeton U Pr.

Tiphaigne De La Roche, Charles-Francois. Historie Des Galligenes, Ou Memoire De Duncan. Repr. of 1765 ed. 55.50 (ISBN 0-8287-0824-X). Clearwater Pub.

Tuchman, Barbara W. A Distant Mirror: The Calamitous Fourteenth Century. LC 78-5988. (Illus.). 1978. 17.95 (ISBN 0-394-40026-7). Knopf.

Werner, Karl F. Untersuchungen zur Fruhzeit des franzosischen Furstentums (9-10 Jahrhundert. LC 79-8375. Repr. of 1960 ed. 18.50 (ISBN 0-404-18357-3). AMS Pr.

FRANCE–HISTORY–MEDIEVAL PERIOD, 987-1515–FICTION

Here are entered historical fiction on the medieval period. For biographical fiction see the names of the kings or other histrocial figues, e.g. Louis 11th King of France–Fiction.

Fagniez, Gustave C. Etudes sur l'Industrie et la Classe Industrielle a Paris aux 13e et au 14e Siecle. LC 73-126393. (Research & Source Works: No. 566). (Fr). 1970. Repr. of 1877 ed. 32.50 (ISBN 0-8337-1096-6). B Franklin.

Lang, Andrew. Monk of Fife. LC 68-59287. Repr. of 1895 ed. 10.00 (ISBN 0-404-03847-6). AMS Pr.

Scott, Walter. Quentin Durward. (Classics Ser). (gr. 9 up). pap. 2.50 (ISBN 0-8049-0132-5, CL-132). Airmont.

FRANCE–HISTORY–16TH CENTURY

Here are entered works on the 16th century as well as those on any part of it except the wars of the huguenots, for which see below.

Baird, Henry M. History of the Rise of the Huguenots of France, 2 Vols. LC 79-130236. Repr. of 1879 ed. Set. 90.00 (ISBN 0-404-00520-9); 45.00 ea. Vol. 1 (ISBN 0-404-00521-7). Vol. 2 (ISBN 0-404-00522-5). AMS Pr.

Brandt de Galametz, Rodolphe. La Taxe des pauvres a Abbeville en 1588, precedee d'une etude sur l'assistance publique avant cette epoque. 1981. Repr. of 1884 ed. lib. bdg. 65.00 (ISBN 0-8287-1578-5). Clearwater Pub.

Compayre, Gabriel, ed. Histoire critique des doctrines de l'education en France depuis le 16e siecle, 2 vols. (Fr.). 1981. Repr. of 1904 ed. Set. lib. bdg. 340.00 (ISBN 0-8287-1535-1). Vol. 1, 457 Pgs (ISBN 0-8287-1536-X). Vol. 2, 437 Pgs. Clearwater Pub.

Davis, Natalie Z. Society & Culture in Early Modern France: Eight Essays by Natalie Zemon Davis. LC 74-82777. (Illus.). 1975. 17.50x (ISBN 0-8047-0868-1); pap. 5.95 (ISBN 0-8047-0972-6, SP-142). Stanford U Pr.

De Gontaut, Armand. The Letters & Documents of Armand De Gontaut, Baron De Biron, Marshal of France: 1524-1592, 2 vols. Ehrman, Sidney H., ed. LC 76-29405. Repr. of 1936 ed. Set. 57.50 (ISBN 0-404-15351-8). AMS Pr.

Deloche, Maximin. La Crise Economique Au Seizeime Siecle et la Crise Actuelle. LC 71-132525. (Research & Source Works Ser.: No. 623). 1971. Repr. of 1922 ed. lib. bdg. 16.50 (ISBN 0-8337-0831-7). B Franklin.

De Valois, Marguerite. The Revealing Intimate Memoirs of Marguerite De Valois. (Illus.). 1978. Repr. of 1831 ed. deluxe ed. 39.75 (ISBN 0-930582-11-X). Gloucester Art.

Febvre, Lucien. Life in Renaissance France. Rothstein, Marian, tr. from Fr. LC 77-7454. 1979. 8.95x (ISBN 0-674-53175-2); pap. 3.95x (ISBN 0-674-53180-9). Harvard U Pr.

Harding, Robert R. Anatomy of a Power Elite: The Provincial Governors of Early Modern France. LC 78-4125. (Historical Publications Ser.: No. 120). 1978. 25.00x (ISBN 0-300-02202-6). Yale U Pr.

Huppert, George. Les Bourgeois Gentilshommes: An Essay on the Definitions of Elites in Renaissance France. LC 76-22954. 1977. lib. bdg. 18.50x (ISBN 0-226-36099-7). U of Chicago Pr.

Marguerite De Valois. Memoires et Lettres De Marguerite De Valois. Gessard, M. F., ed. 35.50 (ISBN 0-384-35398-3); pap. 31.00 (ISBN 0-384-35388-6). Johnson Repr.

Masson, Gustave. The Story of the Nations: the Story of Mediaeval France: From the Reign of Hughes Capet to the Beginning of the Eighteenth Century. 354p. 1980. Repr. of 1888 ed. lib. bdg. 40.00 (ISBN 0-8495-3793-2). Arden Lib.

Pare, Ambroise. Life & Time of Ambroise Pare. Packard, Francis R., ed. LC 79-160607. (Illus.). Repr. of 1921 ed. 18.00 (ISBN 0-405-08834-5, Pub. by Blom). Arno.

Rothrock, George A. The Huguenots: A Biography of a Minority. LC 78-23476. (Illus.). 1979. 18.95x (ISBN 0-88229-277-3). Nelson-Hall.

Salmon, J. H. Society in Crisis: France in the Sixteenth Century. LC 75-5141. (Illus.). 300p. 1975. 25.00 (ISBN 0-312-73815-3). St Martin.

Stone, Donald. France in the Sixteenth Century. LC 75-46622. 180p. 1976. Repr. of 1969 ed. lib. bdg. 16.25x (ISBN 0-8371-8734-6, STFS). Greenwood.

Tilley, Arthur A. Dawn of the French Renaissance. LC 68-10951. (Illus.). 1968. Repr. of 1918 ed. 16.50 (ISBN 0-8462-1069-X). Russell.

Von Ranke, Leopold. Civil Wars & Monarchy in France, in the Sixteenth & Seventeenth Centuries, 2 vols in 1. Garvey, M. A., tr. LC 70-153634. Repr. of 1852 ed. 42.50 (ISBN 0-404-09254-3). AMS Pr.

FRANCE–HISTORY–16TH CENTURY–FICTION

Here is entered historical fiction on the 16th century. For biographical fiction, drama, etc. see names of rulers or other historical figures.

Merimee, Prosper. A Chronicle of the Reign of Charles Nine. Saintsbury, George, tr. from Fr. LC 75-4910. xvi, 309p. 1975. Repr. of 1890 ed. 21.50 (ISBN 0-86527-226-3). Fertig.

FRANCE–HISTORY–WARS OF THE HUGUENOTS, 1562-1598

Adams, John. Discourses on Davila. LC 70-87665. (American Constitutional & Legal History Ser.). 260p. 1973. Repr. of 1805 ed. lib. bdg. 25.00 (ISBN 0-306-71761-1). Da Capo.

Armstrong, Edward. The French Wars of Religion: Their Political Aspects. 2nd ed. LC 70-139896. (Illus.). 1971. Repr. of 1904 ed. 10.00 (ISBN 0-8462-1548-9). Russell.

Baird, Henry M. Huguenots & Henry of Navarre, 2 Vols. LC 76-130987. Repr. of 1903 ed. Set. 57.50 (ISBN 0-404-00540-3). Vol. 1 (ISBN 0-404-00541-1). Vol. 2 (ISBN 0-404-00542-X). AMS Pr.

Benedict, Philip. Rouen During the Wars of Religion. LC 79-50883. (Cambridge Studies in Early Modern History). (Illus.). 324p. 1981. 39.50 (ISBN 0-521-22818-2). Cambridge U Pr.

The King's Edict or Decree Upon the Pacification of the Troubles. LC 72-183. (English Experience Ser.: No. 170). 22p. 1969. Repr. of 1568 ed. 8.00 (ISBN 90-221-0170-3). Walter J Johnson.

Maugis, Edquard. Histoire Du Parlement De Paris De l'Avenememt Des Rois Valois a la Mort D'Henri Quatre, 3 Vols. 1967. Repr. of 1913 ed. 92.50 (ISBN 0-8337-2304-9). B Franklin.

Neale, J. E. The Age of Catherine de Medici. 1978. pap. 6.50 (ISBN 0-224-60566-6, Pub. by Chatto Bodley Jonathan). Merrimack Bk Serv.

Neale, John E. Age of Catherine De Medici. pap. 3.50x (ISBN 0-06-131085-9, TB1085, Torch). Har-Row.

Palm, Franklin C. Calvinisim & the Religious Wars. LC 78-80579. 1971. Repr. 16.50 (ISBN 0-86527-020-1). Fertig.

Ranke, Leopold. Civil Wars & Monarchy in France: In the Sixteenth & Seventeenth Centuries; a History of France Principally During That Period, 2 vols. Garvey, M. A., tr. LC 78-38365. (Select Bibliographies Reprint Ser). Repr. of 1852 ed. 32.00 (ISBN 0-8369-6782-8). Arno.

FRANCE–HISTORY–BOURBONS, 1589-1789

Here are entered works on the history of France from 1589 to 1789 as a whole as well as those on any portion of it. For books about individual kings, etc. see under the names of kings etc. e.g. Louis 12th King of France; Richelieu.

Argenson, Rene L. Journal et Memoires Du Marquis D'Argenson, 9 Vols. Set. 318.50 (ISBN 0-384-01912-9); Set. pap. 277.00 (ISBN 0-384-01914-5). Johnson Repr.

Ashley, Maurice. Louis the Fourteenth & the Greatness of France. 1965. pap. 5.95 (ISBN 0-02-901080-2). Free Pr.

Baird, Henry M. The Huguenots & the Revocation of the Edict of Nantes, 2 vols. LC 76-161752. Repr. of 1895 ed. Set. 74.50 (ISBN 0-404-08003-0). AMS Pr.

Balsama, George D. The Politics of National Despair: French Royalism in the Post-Reformation Era. 1977. pap. text ed. 7.75 (ISBN 0-8191-0142-7). U Pr of Amer.

Bamford, Paul W. Fighting Ships & Prisons: The Mediterranean Galleys of France in the Age of Louis XIV. LC 72-92334. 412p. 1973. 20.00x (ISBN 0-8166-0655-2). U of Minn Pr.

Barbier, Edmond J. Journal Historique et Anecdotique Du Regne De Louis XV, 4 Vols. Set. 141.50 (ISBN 0-384-03391-1); Set. pap. 123.00 (ISBN 0-384-03390-3). Johnson Repr.

Batiffol, Louis. Century of the Renaissance. (National History of France: No. 3). Repr. of 1935 ed. 30.00 (ISBN 0-404-50793-X). AMS Pr.

--Marie De Medicis & the French Court in the Seventeenth Century. Davis, H. W., ed. King, Mary, tr. from Fr. LC 72-137368. (Select Bibliographies Reprint Ser.). 1972. Repr. of 1908 ed. 17.00 (ISBN 0-8369-5569-2). Arno.

Behrens, C. B. The Ancien Regime. (History of European Civilization Library). (Illus.). 215p. 1967. pap. text ed. 8.95 (ISBN 0-15-502750-6, HC). HarBraceJ.

Boulenger, Jacques R. Seventeenth Century. LC 70-181913. (National History of France: No. 4). Repr. of 1933 ed. 30.00 (ISBN 0-404-50794-8). AMS Pr.

Cameron, Iain A. Crime & Represssion in the Auvergne & Guyenne, 1720-1790. LC 80-41953. (Illus.). 256p. Date not set. price not set (ISBN 0-521-23882-X). Cambridge U Pr.

Crouse, Nellis M. French Pioneers in the West Indies, 1624-1664. 1972. lib. bdg. 15.00x (ISBN 0-374-91937-2). Octagon.

De Beauvais-Nangis, Nicolas D. Memoires Du Marquis De Beauvais-Nangis et Journal Du Proces Du Marquis De La Boulaye. 1862. 35.50 (ISBN 0-384-03695-3); pap. 31.00 (ISBN 0-685-13509-8). Johnson Repr.

De Segur, Louis. Memoirs & Recollections of Count Louis Philippe De Segur. LC 73-115584. (Russia Observed, Series I). 1970. Repr. of 1827 ed. 45.00 (ISBN 0-405-03061-4). Arno.

Egret, Jean. The French Pre-Revolution, 1787-1788. Camp, Wesley D., tr. from Fr. LC 77-78776. (Illus.). 1978. Repr. of 1972 ed. lib. bdg. 24.00x (ISBN 0-226-19142-7). U of Chicago Pr.

Fenton, Geoffrey, tr. A Discourse of the Civile Warres in Fraunce, Drawn into Englishe by G. Fenton. LC 76-26510. (English Experience Ser.: No. 248). 1970. Repr. of 1570 ed. 20.00 (ISBN 90-221-0248-3). Walter J Johnson.

Ford, Franklin L. Robe & Sword: The Regrouping of the French Aristocracy After Louis 14. LC 52-12261. (Historical Studies: No. 64). (Illus.). 1953. 14.00x (ISBN 0-674-77415-9). Harvard U Pr.

Fox-Genovese, Elizabeth. The Origins of Physiocracy: Economic Revolution & Social Order in Eighteenth-Century France. LC 75-36999. (Illus.). 312p. 1976. 20.00x (ISBN 0-8014-1006-1). Cornell U Pr.

Golden, Richard M. The Godly Rebellion: Parisian Cures & the Religious Fronde, 1652-1662. LC 80-25282. 264p. 1981. 22.50x (ISBN 0-8078-1466-0). U of NC Pr.

Goubert, Pierre. The Ancien Regime: French Society 1600-1750. Cox, Steve, tr. from Fr. 1974. pap. 4.95x (ISBN 0-06-131822-1, TB1822, Torch). Har-Row.

--Clio Parmi les Hommes: Recueil D'articles. (Civilisations et Societes: No. 52). (Fr.). 1976. pap. text ed. 24.50x (ISBN 90-2797-833-6). Mouton.

--Louis the Fourteenth & the Twenty Million Frenchmen. 352p. 1972. pap. 3.95 (ISBN 0-394-71751-1, V751, Vin). Random.

Grant, Arthur J. The French Monarchy (1483-1789, 2 vols. LC 75-41118. Repr. of 1925 ed. Set. 30.00 (ISBN 0-404-14930-8). AMS Pr.

Grant, Charles. The Battle of Fontenoy. (Illus.). 1976. 10.00 (ISBN 0-86002-056-8). Hippocrene Bks.

Green, Frederick C. Eighteenth-Century France: Six Essays. LC 64-21609. 9.00 (ISBN 0-8044-1315-0); pap. 4.95 (ISBN 0-8044-6221-6). Ungar.

Hall, Geoffrey F. Moths Round the Flame. LC 72-93343. (Essay Index Reprint Ser). 1935. 29.00 (ISBN 0-8369-1413-9). Arno.

Hall, Thadd E. France & the Eighteenth-Century Corsican Question. LC 71-161629. 1971. 12.00x (ISBN 0-8147-3359-X). NYU Pr.

Hilton, Wendy. Dance of Court & Theatre: The French Noble Style 1690-1725. LC 78-70248. (Illus.). 1981. 35.00x (ISBN 0-916622-09-6). Princeton Bk Co.

Hufton, Olwen H. The Poor of Eighteenth-Century France 1750-1789. (Illus.). 1979. pap. 11.00x (ISBN 0-19-822558-X). Oxford U Pr.

Isherwood, Robert M. Music in the Service of the King: France in the Seventeenth Century. LC 72-3842. (Illus.). 422p. 1973. 30.00x (ISBN 0-8014-0734-6). Cornell U Pr.

Jordan, David P. The King's Trial: Louis XVI vs. the French Revolution. LC 78-54797. 1979. 14.95 (ISBN 0-520-03684-0); pap. 5.95 (ISBN 0-520-04399-5, CAL 497). U of Cal Pr.

Kaplan, S. L. Bread, Politics & Political Economy in the Reign of Louis XV. (International Archives of the History of Ideas Ser: No. 86). 1977. lib. bdg. 105.00 (ISBN 90-247-1873-2, Pub. by Martinus Nijhoff Netherlands); Vol. 1 & 2. lib. bdg. 52.50 ea. Kluwer Boston.

Klaits, J. Printed Propaganda Under Louis the Fourteenth: Absolute Monarchy & Public Opinion. 1976. 25.00 (ISBN 0-691-05238-7). Princeton U Pr.

La Fayette, Marie-Madeleine de. Memoires de la Cour de France, Pour les Annees 1688-1689. new ed. 176p. 1962. 12.50 (ISBN 0-686-54265-7). French & Eur.

Lot, Myrrha. La Femme et l'amour au XII Siecle. LC 78-63503. Repr. of 1909 ed. 27.50 (ISBN 0-404-17153-2). AMS Pr.

Lougee, C. C. Le Paradis Des Femmes: Women, Salons, & Social Stratification in Seventeenth-Century France. 1976. 22.50 (ISBN 0-691-05239-5). Princeton U Pr.

Louis Fourteenth. King's Lessons in Statecraft: Louis Fourteenth. Wilson, Herbert, tr. LC 77-110913. 1970. Repr. of 1924 ed. 12.00 (ISBN 0-8046-0895-4). Kennikat.

Lublinskaya, Alexandra D. French Absolutism: The Crucial Phase, 1620-1629. (Illus.). 1968. 44.50 (ISBN 0-521-07117-8). Cambridge U Pr.

McLynn, Francis. France & the Jacobite Rising of Seventeen Forty-Five. 256p. 1981. 26.50x (ISBN 0-85224-404-5, Pub. by Edinburgh U Pr Scotland). Columbia U Pr.

McManners, J. French Ecclesiastical Society Under the Ancient Regime: A Study of Angers in the Eighteenth Century. 428p. 1960. 42.00x (ISBN 0-7190-0340-7, Pub. by Manchester U Pr England). State Mutual Bk.
Maland, David. Culture & Society in Seventeenth Century France. 1970. 40.00 (ISBN 0-7134-1520-7, Pub. by Batsford England). David & Charles.
Masson, Gustave. The Story of the Nations: the Story of Mediaeval France: From the Reign of Hughes Capet to the Beginning of the Eighteenth Century. 354p. 1980. Repr. of 1888 ed. lib. bdg. 40.00 (ISBN 0-8495-3793-2). Arden Lib.
Mazarin, Jules. Lettres Du Cardinal Mazarin a la Reine, a la Princesse Palatine. 35.50 (ISBN 0-384-36195-1); pap. 31.00 (ISBN 0-384-36185-4). Johnson Repr.
Meuvret, Jean. Le Probleme des Subsistances a l'epoque Louis XIV. 1: La Production des Cereales dans la France du XVIIe et du XVIIIe Siecle Texte-Notes, 2 pts. (Civilisations et Societes Ser.: No. 50). 1977. pap. 31.75x set (ISBN 0-686-26041-4). Mouton.
Moheau. Recherches et Considerations Sur la Population De la France, Seventeen Seventy-Eight. Repr. of 1912 ed. lib. bdg. 20.00x (ISBN 0-87991-805-5). Porcupine Pr.
Mole, Mathieu. Memoires: De Mathieu Mole Procureur General, Premier President Au Parlement De Paris et Garde Des Sceaux De France, 4 Vols. 154.00 (ISBN 0-384-39556-2); pap. 135.50 (ISBN 0-384-39557-0). Johnson Repr.
Moreau, Celestin, ed. Choix De Mazarinades, 2 Vols. 1853. Set. 77.00 (ISBN 0-384-40103-1); Set. pap. 67.50 (ISBN 0-685-13377-X). Johnson Repr.
Le Nouvelles Ephemerides Economique, December,1779 to June, 1786, 9 vols. 2100p. (Fr.). 1976. Repr. Set. lib. bdg. 310.00x (ISBN 0-8287-1392-8). Clearwater Pub.
Ranum, Orest. Paris in the Age of Absolutism. LC 79-2603. (Midland Bks.: No. 238). (Illus.). 336p. 1980. 17.50x (ISBN 0-253-19677-9); pap. 6.95x (ISBN 0-253-20238-8). Ind U Pr.
Registres De l'Hotel de Ville de Paris Pendant la Fronde, 3 vols. 1481p. 1846-48. Repr. Set. 106.00 (ISBN 0-384-44800-3); Set. pap. 92.50 (ISBN 0-685-27512-4). Johnson Repr.
Saint Simon, L. Memoires Completes et authentiques, 22 tomes. Chervel, ed. Set. pap. 350.00 (ISBN 0-685-01988-8). French & Eur.
Shepherd, Robert P. Turgot & the Six Edicts. LC 74-147488. (Columbia University Social Science Studies Ser.: No. 47). Repr. of 1903 ed. 18.50 (ISBN 0-404-51047-7). AMS Pr.
Sheppard, Thomas F. Lourmarin in the Eighteenth Century: A Study of a French Village. LC 75-126802. (Studies in Historical & Political Science: Eighty-Eighth Series No. 2 (1970)). (Illus.). 1971. 16.00x (ISBN 0-8018-1132-5). Johns Hopkins.
Les Soupirs De la France Esclave: 1689-1690. 64.50 (ISBN 0-8287-0786-3). Clearwater Pub.
Stryienski, Casimir. Eighteenth Century. LC 16-17721. (National History of France: No. 5). Repr. of 1923 ed. 30.00 (ISBN 0-404-50795-6). AMS Pr.
Van Kley, Dale. The Jansenists & the Expulsion of the Jesuits from France, 1757-1765. LC 74-26390. (Historical Publications, Miscellany Ser.: No. 107). 272p. 1975. 20.00x (ISBN 0-300-01748-0). Yale U Pr.
Voltaire. Le Siecle de Louis XIV, 2 vols. Adam, Antoine, ed. 1966. pap. 4.95 ea. French & Eur.
Voltaire, Francois M. De. Age of Louis Fourteenth. 1958. 8.95x (ISBN 0-460-00780-7, Evman). Biblio Dist.
Wilson, Arthur M. French Foreign Policy During the Administration of Cardinal Fleury: 1726-1743; a Study in Diplomacy & Commercial Development. LC 70-138193. 433p. 1972. Repr. of 1936 ed. lib. bdg. 18.25x (ISBN 0-8371-5333-6, WIFP). Greenwood.
Wood, C. T. Philip the Fair & Boniface VIII: State vs. Papacy. LC 76-23207. (European Problem Ser.). 124p. 1976. pap. 5.50 (ISBN 0-88275-454-8). Krieger.
Young, Arthur. Travels in France During the Years 1787, 1788, 1789. Kaplow, Jeffry, ed. 10.00 (ISBN 0-8446-3223-6). Peter Smith.

FRANCE–HISTORY–BOURBONS–FICTION

Here is entered historical fiction on the period between 1589 and 1789, or any part of it. For Biographical fiction, drama, etc. see names of kings or other historical figures, e.g. Louis 14th King of France–Fiction.

Dumas, Alexandre. Man in the Iron Mask. (Classics Ser). (gr. 9 up). 1967. pap. 1.95 (ISBN 0-8049-0150-3, CL-150). Airmont.
--Three Musketeers. (Classics Ser). (gr. 8 up). pap. 2.50 (ISBN 0-8049-0127-9, CL-127). Airmont.
--Three Musketeers. 1966. 14.95x (ISBN 0-460-00081-0, Evman). Biblio Dist.
--Three Musketeers. (Illus.). (gr. 4-6). 1953-59. il. jr. lib. 5.95 (ISBN 0-448-05824-3); deluxe ed. 8.95 (ISBN 0-448-06024-8). G&D.
Dumas, Alexandre, Sr. Trois Mousquetaires. Samaran, ed. 1961. pap. 9.95 (ISBN 0-685-11605-0). French & Eur.
--Vingt Ans Apres, 2 tomes. (Coll. GF). 1961. Set. pap. 9.00 (ISBN 0-685-11621-2). French & Eur.
Lewis, Janet. Ghost of Monsieur Scarron. LC 65-16520. 378p. 1959. 20.00 (ISBN 0-8040-0076-X); pap. 8.95 (ISBN 0-8040-0133-2). Swallow.

FRANCE–HISTORY–17TH CENTURY

see France–History–Bourbons, 1589-1789

FRANCE–HISTORY–1789-1815

Ballard, Colin R. Napoleon: An Outline. facsimile ed. LC 76-179503. (Select Bibliographies Reprint Ser). Repr. of 1924 ed. 19.00 (ISBN 0-8369-6632-5). Arno.
Barbaroux, Charles O. Memoires De Robert Guillemard, Sergent En Retraite, Suivis De Documents Historiques, 2 Vols. Repr. of 1826 ed. Set. 30.00 (ISBN 0-404-07537-1); 15.00 ea. Vol. 1 (ISBN 0-404-07538-X). Vol. 2 (ISBN 0-404-07539-8). AMS Pr.
Behrens, C. B. The Ancien Regime. (History of European Civilization Library). (Illus.). 215p. 1967. pap. text ed. 8.95 (ISBN 0-15-502750-6, HC). HarBraceJ.
Cameron, Iain A. Crime & Represssion in the Auvergne & Guyenne, 1720-1790. LC 80-41953. (Illus.). 256p. Date not set. price not set (ISBN 0-521-23882-X). Cambridge U Pr.
Cobb, Richard C. Police & the People: French Popular Protest, 1789-1820. 414p. 1970. 34.50x (ISBN 0-19-821479-0); pap. 5.95x (ISBN 0-19-881297-3, OPB). Oxford U Pr.
Duke Des Cars, ed. Memoirs of the Duchess De Tourzel: Governess to the Children of France During the Years 1789, 1790, 1791, 1792, 1793 & 1795, 2 vols. 1977. Repr. of 1886 ed. lib. bdg. 65.00 (ISBN 0-8495-1003-1). Arden Lib.
Dupre, Huntley. Lazare Carnot, Republican Patriot. LC 75-29217. (Perspectives in European Hist. Ser.: No. 5). viii, 343p. Repr. of 1940 ed. lib. bdg. 19.50x (ISBN 0-87991-612-5). Porcupine Pr.
Garmen, Douglas, tr. The Memoirs of Chancellor Pasquier 1767-1815. LC 68-9353. (Illus.). 292p. 1968. 18.00 (ISBN 0-8386-6981-6). Fairleigh Dickinson.
Glover, Michael. The Napoleonic Wars: An Illustrated History 1792-1815. LC 78-74016. (Illus.). 1979. 22.50 (ISBN 0-88254-473-X). Hippocrene Bks.
Godechot, Jacques. The Counter Revolution: Doctrine & Action, 1789-1804. Attanasio, Salvator, tr. from Fr. LC 70-159820. 416p. 1981. pap. 7.95 (ISBN 0-691-00788-8). Princeton U Pr.
--Counter-Revolution, Doctrine & Action, Seventeen Eighty-Nine to Eighteen Four. LC 70-159820. 1971. 25.00 (ISBN 0-86527-035-X). Fertig.
Haythornthwaite, Philip. Weapons & Equipment of the Napoleonic Wars. (Illus.). 1979. 24.95 (ISBN 0-7137-0906-5, Pub by Blandford Pr England). Sterling.
Kerr, Wilfrid B. The Reign of Terror Seventeen Ninety-Three to Seventeen Ninety-Four: The Experiment of the Democratic Republic & the Rise of the Bourgeoisie. (Perspectives in European History: No. 24). (Illus.). Repr. of 1927 ed. lib. bdg. 27.50x (ISBN 0-87991-631-1). Porcupine Pr.
Lewis, Gwynne. The Second Vendee: The Continuity of Counter-Revolution in the Department of the Gard 1789-1815. (Illus.). 1978. 45.00x (ISBN 0-19-822544-X). Oxford U Pr.
Lyons, M. France Under the Directory. (Illus.). 256p. 1975. 35.50 (ISBN 0-521-20785-1); pap. 10.50x (ISBN 0-521-09950-1). Cambridge U Pr.
Mowat, Robert B. Diplomacy of Napoleon. LC 76-139931. 1971. Repr. of 1924 ed. 14.50 (ISBN 0-8462-1539-X). Russell.
Parlange, Michel. Les Signaux De la Defense Des Cotes En Belgique, Aux Pays-Bas et En Allemagne Sous L'occupation Francaise, 1794-1814. 1968. pap. 27.50x (ISBN 0-686-21822-1). Mouton.
Phillips, Roderick. Family Breakdown in Late Eighteenth Century France: Divorces in Rouen 1792-1803. (Illus.). 288p. 1981. 55.00x (ISBN 0-19-822572-5). Oxford U Pr.
Pinkney, David H., ed. Napoleon: Historical Enigma. LC 77-76609. (Problems in Civilization Ser). 1969. pap. text ed. 3.95x (ISBN 0-88273-403-2). Forum Pr MO.
Rude, George. Revolutionary Europe 1783-1815. (History of Europe Ser.). pap. 5.50x (ISBN 0-06-131272-X, TB1272, Torch). Har-Row.
Scott, Samuel F. The Response of the Royal Army to the French Revolution: The Role & Development of the Line Army, 1793-1878. 1978. 45.00x (ISBN 0-19-822534-2). Oxford U Pr.
Shepherd, Robert P. Turgot & the Six Edicts. LC 74-147488. (Columbia University Social Science Studies Ser.: No. 47). Repr. of 1903 ed. 18.50 (ISBN 0-404-51047-7). AMS Pr.

FRANCE–HISTORY–1789-1900

Agulhon, Maurice. Marianne into Battle: Republican Imagery & Symbolism in France, 1789-1880. Lloyd, Janet, tr. (Co-Publication with the Maison Des Sciences De L'homme). (Illus.). 224p. Date not set. 39.50 (ISBN 0-521-23577-4); pap. 14.95 (ISBN 0-521-28224-1). Cambridge U Pr.
Alger, John G. Paris in 1789-1794, Farewell Letters of Victims of the Guillotine. LC 78-113540. Repr. of 1902 ed. 34.50 (ISBN 0-404-00323-0). AMS Pr.
Anderson, Frank M. The Constitution & Other Select Documents. 1978. Repr. of 1904 ed. lib. bdg. 75.00 (ISBN 0-8495-0132-6). Arden Lib.
Barberet, J. Les Greves et la Loi sur les Coalitions. (Conditions of the 19th Century French Working Class Ser.). 189p. (Fr.). 1974. Repr. of 1873 ed. lib. bdg. 55.00x (ISBN 0-8287-0055-9, 1104). Clearwater Pub.
Benoiston De Chateauneuf. Recherches sur les Consommations de Tout Genre de la Ville de Paris-Comparees a Ce Qu'Elles Etaient en 1789. (Conditions of the 19th Century French Working Class Ser.). 157p. (Fr.). 1974. Repr. of 1821 ed. lib. bdg. 48.00x (ISBN 0-8287-0079-6, 1120). Clearwater Pub.
Bernstein, Samuel. Essays in Political & Intellectual History. facs. ed. LC 73-86729. (Essay Index Reprint Ser). 1955. 16.00 (ISBN 0-8369-1171-7). Arno.
Blanqui, Adolphe. Des Classes Ouvrieres En France Pendant L'annee 1848. (Conditions in the 19th Century French Working Class Ser.). 255p. (Fr.). 1974. Repr. of 1849 ed. lib. bdg. 73.75x (ISBN 0-8287-0096-6, 1117). Clearwater Pub.
Bonaparte, Louis-Napoleon. Extinction du Pauperisme. (Conditions of the 19th Century French Working Class Ser.). 31p. (Fr.). 1974. Repr. of 1848 ed. 22.50x (ISBN 0-8287-1375-8, 1116). Clearwater Pub.
Bouquet, Louis. Le Travail des Enfants et des Filles Mineures dans l'Industrie. (Conditions of the 19th Century French Working Class Ser.). 356p. (Fr.). 1974. Repr. of 1885 ed. lib. bdg. 93.50x (ISBN 0-8287-0129-6, 1106). Clearwater Pub.
Bourgeois, E. History of Modern France, 1815-1913, 2 vols. 1972. lib. bdg. 42.50x (ISBN 0-374-90847-8). Octagon.
Boyer, Adolphe. De l'Etat des Ouvriers et de Son Amelioration par l'Organisation du Travail. (Conditions of the 19th Century French Working Class Ser.). 141p. (Fr.). 1974. Repr. of 1841 ed. lib. bdg. 44.50x (ISBN 0-8287-0133-4, 1105). Clearwater Pub.
Bury, J. P. T. France 1814-1940. 1962. pap. 4.95 (ISBN 0-498-04070-4, Prpta). A S Barnes.
Cere, Paul. Les Population Dangereuses et les Miseres Sociales. (Conditions of the 19th Century French Working Class Ser.). 378p. (Fr.). 1974. Repr. of 1872 ed. lib. bdg. 104.75x (ISBN 0-8287-0173-3, 1093). Clearwater Pub.
Cerfbeer, Auguste-Edouard. Des Societes De Bienfaisance Mutuelle. (Conditions of the 19th Century French Working Class Ser.). 113p. (Fr.). 1974. Repr. of 1836 ed. lib. bdg. 38.00x (ISBN 0-8287-0174-1, 1059). Clearwater Pub.
Chamborant, C. G. De. Du Pauperisme, Ce Qu'Il Etait dans L'antiquite et Ce Qu'Il Est de Nos Jours. (Conditions of the 19th Century French Working Class Ser.). 496p. (Fr.). 1974. Repr. of 1842 ed. lib. bdg. 127.00 (ISBN 0-8287-0177-6, 1097). Clearwater Pub.
Cherbuliez, A. E. Etudes sur les Causes de la Misere. (Conditions of the 19th Century French Working Class Ser). 352p. (Fr.). 1974. Repr. of 1853 ed. lib. bdg. 91.00x (ISBN 0-8287-0185-7, 1082). Clearwater Pub.
--Richesse ou Pauvrete. Exposition des Causes et des Effets de la Distribution Actuelle des Richesses Sociales. (Conditions of the 19th Century French Working Class Ser.). 184p. (Fr.). 1974. Repr. of 1841 ed. lib. bdg. 56.00x (ISBN 0-8287-0186-5, 1056). Clearwater Pub.
Chevalier, Michel. Questions des Travailleurs: L'amelioration du Sort des Ouvriers. Les Salaires, l'Organisation du Travail. (Conditions of the 19th Century French Working Class Ser.). 32p. (Fr.). 1974. Repr. of 1848 ed. lib. bdg. 23.00x (ISBN 0-8287-0189-X, 1001). Clearwater Pub.
Chevallier, Emile. Les Salaires au Dix-Neuvieme Siecle. (Conditions of the 19th Century French Working Class Ser.). 299p. (Fr.). 1974. Repr. of 1887 ed. lib. bdg. 79.50x (ISBN 0-8287-0190-3, 1094). Clearwater Pub.
Clement, Ambroise. Recherches sur les Causes de l'Indigence. (Conditions of the 19th Century French Working Class Ser.). 368p. (Fr.). 1974. Repr. of 1846 ed. lib. bdg. 95.00x (ISBN 0-8287-0204-7, 1002). Clearwater Pub.
Cobb, Richard C. Police & the People: French Popular Protest, 1789-1820. 414p. 1970. 34.50x (ISBN 0-19-821479-0); pap. 5.95x (ISBN 0-19-881297-3, OPB). Oxford U Pr.
Cochin, Augustin. La Condition des Ouvriers Francais d'apres les Dernier Travaux. (Conditions of the 19th Century French Working Class Ser.). 48p. (Fr.). 1974. Repr. of 1862 ed. lib. bdg. 24.50x (ISBN 0-8287-0208-X, 1107). Clearwater Pub.
Compagnon, A. Les Classes Laborieuses. Leur Condition Actuelle, Leur Avenir par la Reorginisation du Travail. (Conditions of the 19th Century French Working Class Ser.). 354p. (Fr.). 1974. Repr. of 1858 ed. lib. bdg. 91.50x (ISBN 0-8287-0215-2, 1076). Clearwater Pub.
Cooke, James J. France: 1789-1962. (Modern History Reference Ser.). 287p. 1975. 19.50 (ISBN 0-208-01510-8, Archon). Shoe String.
Corbon, Anthime. De l'Enseignement Professionnel, quatrieme edition. (Conditions of the 19th Century French Working Class Ser.). 192p. (Fr.). 1974. Repr. lib. bdg. 55.50x (ISBN 0-8287-0226-8, 1144). Clearwater Pub.
--Le Secret du Peuple de Paris. (Conditions of the 19th Century French Working Class Ser.). 412p. (Fr.). 1974. Repr. of 1863 ed. lib. bdg. 95.50x (ISBN 0-8287-0227-6, 1084). Clearwater Pub.
Coste, Adolphe. Hygiene Sociale contre le Pauperisme. (Conditions of the 19th Century French Working Class Ser.). 543p. (Fr.). 1974. Repr. of 1882 ed. lib. bdg. 134.00x (ISBN 0-8287-0228-4, 1085). Clearwater Pub.
Daubie, Julie. La Femme Pauvre Au Dix-Neuvieme Siecle. Condition Economique. Condition Professionnelle, 3 vols. (Conditions of the 19th Century French Working Class Ser.). (Fr.). 1974. Repr. of 1869 ed. Set. lib. bdg. 205.00x (ISBN 0-8287-0249-7). Vol. 1 (1139). Vol. 2 (1140). Vol. 3 (1141). Clearwater Pub.
De Cellier, Florent. Histoire des Classes Ouvrieres en France depuis la Conquete de la Gaule jusqu'a Nos Jours. (Conditions of the 19th Century French Working Class Ser.). 486p. (Fr.). 1974. Repr. of 1859 ed. lib. bdg. 121.00 (ISBN 0-8287-0252-7, 1004). Clearwater Pub.
Delesalle, Paul. Les Conditions de Travail Chez les Ouvriers en Instruments de Precision de Paris. (Conditions of the 19th Century French Working Class Ser.). 35p. (Fr.). 1974. Repr. of 1899 ed. lib. bdg. 21.00 (ISBN 0-8287-0255-1, 1122). Clearwater Pub.
De Madre, Ad. Des Ouvriers et Des Moyens D'ameliorer Leur Condition Dans les Villes. (Conditions of the 19th Century French Working Class Ser.). 140p. (Fr.). 1974. Repr. of 1863 ed. lib. bdg. 44.00x (ISBN 0-8287-0257-8, 1087). Clearwater Pub.
Du Cellier, Florent. Les Classes Ouvrieres en France depuis 1789. (Conditions of the 19th Century French Working Class Ser.). 96p. (Fr.). 1974. Repr. of 1857 ed. lib. bdg. 34.50 (ISBN 0-8287-0284-5, 1003). Clearwater Pub.
Duchatel, M. T. La Charite dans ses Rapports avec l'Etat Moral, et le Bien-Etre des Classes Inferieures de la Societe. (Conditions of the 19th Century French Working Class Ser.). 431p. (Fr.). 1974. Repr. of 1829 ed. lib. bdg. 108.50 (ISBN 0-8287-0285-3, 1005). Clearwater Pub.
Ducpetiaux, Edouard. De la Condition Physique et Morale des Jeunes Ouvriers et des Moyens de l'Ameliorer. (Conditions of the 19th Century French Working Class Ser.). 472p. (Fr.). 1974. Repr. of 1843 ed. lib. bdg. 118.00 (ISBN 0-8287-0287-X, 1161). Clearwater Pub.
Du Mesnil. L' Hygenie a Paris. l'Habitation du Pauvre. (Conditions of the 19th Century French Working Class Ser.). 233p. (Fr.). 1974. Repr. of 1890 ed. lib. bdg. 65.00x (ISBN 0-8287-0700-6, 1172). Clearwater Pub.
Du Mesnil & Mangenot. Etude d'Hygiene et d'Economie Sociale. Enquete sur les Logements, Professions, Salaires et Budgets. (Conditions of the 19th Century French Working Class Ser.). 166p. (Fr.). 1974. Repr. of 1899 ed. lib. bdg. 50.00x (ISBN 0-8287-0295-0, 1114). Clearwater Pub.
Dumont, A. A. Les Habitations Ouvrieres dans les Grands Centre Industries et Plus Particulierments dans la Region du Nord. (Conditions of the 19th Century French Working Class Ser.). 268p. (Fr.). 1974. Repr. of 1905 ed. lib. bdg. 72.50x (ISBN 0-8287-0297-7, 1054). Clearwater Pub.
Dunn-Pattison, R. P. Napoleon's Marshals. (Illus.). 373p. 1977. Repr. of 1909 ed. 26.50x (ISBN 0-8476-6060-5). Rowman.
Dupin, Charles. Du Travail des Enfants Qu'Emploient les Ateliers, les Usines, et les Manufactures. (Conditions of the 19th Century French Working Class Ser.). (Fr.). 1974. Repr. of 1847 ed. lib. bdg. 84.00x (ISBN 0-8287-0301-9, 1118). Clearwater Pub.

--Des Forces Productives et Commerciales De la France. (Conditions of the 19th Century French Working Class Ser.). (Fr.). 1974. Repr. of 1827 ed. lib. bdg. 180.50x (ISBN 0-8287-0300-0, 1153). Clearwater Pub.

Dupont. Les Ouvriers. Histoire Populaire Illustree des Travailleurs au Dix-Neuvieme Siecle. (Conditions of the 19th Century French Working Class Ser.). 600p. (Fr.). 1974. Repr. of 1890 ed. lib. bdg. 146.00x (ISBN 0-8287-0302-7, 1151). Clearwater Pub.

Dupont-White, Charles. Essai sur les Relations du Travail avec le Capital. (Conditions of the 19th Century French Working Class Ser.). 444p. (Fr.). 1974. Repr. of 1846 ed. lib. bdg. 111.00 (ISBN 0-8287-0303-5, 1007). Clearwater Pub.

Durand. De la Conditions des Ouvriers de Paris de 1789 jusqu'en 1841. (Conditions of the 19th Century French Working Class Ser.). 287p. (Fr.). 1974. Repr. of 1841 ed. lib. bdg. 77.00x (ISBN 0-8287-0305-1, 1009). Clearwater Pub.

Dutens, J. M. Essai Comparatif sur la Formation et la Distribution du Revenu de la France en 1815 et 1835. (Conditions of the 19th Century French Working Class Ser.). 182p. (Fr.). 1974. Repr. of 1842 ed. lib. bdg. 53.50x (ISBN 0-8287-0307-8, 1010). Clearwater Pub.

Dutouquet, H. E. De la Condition des Classes Pauvres a la Campagne, des Moyens les plus Efficaces de l'Ameliorer. (Conditions of the 19th Century French Working Class Ser.). 112p. (Fr.). 1974. Repr. of 1846 ed. lib. bdg. 38.00x (ISBN 0-8287-0308-6, 1011). Clearwater Pub.

Esterno, F. C. De la Misere, de Ses Causes, de Ses Remedies. (Conditions of the 19th Century French Working Class Ser.). 259p. (Fr.). 1974. Repr. of 1842 ed. lib. bdg. 83.00x (ISBN 0-8287-0319-1, 1012). Clearwater Pub.

Fix, Theodore. Observations sur l'Etat des Classes Ouvrieres. (Conditions of the 19th Century French Working Class Ser.). 416p. (Fr.). 1974. Repr. of 1846 ed. lib. bdg. 105.50 (ISBN 0-8287-0343-4, 1013). Clearwater Pub.

Fodere, F. E. Essai Historique et Moral sur la Pauvrete des Nations, la Population, la Mendicite, les Hopitaux et les Enfants Trouves. (Conditions of the 19th Century French Working Class Ser.). 628p. (Fr.). 1974. Repr. of 1825 ed. lib. bdg. 152.50x (ISBN 0-8287-0347-7, 1014). Clearwater Pub.

Fregier, H. A. Des Classes Dangereuses De la Societe Dans les Grandes Villes et Des Moyens De les Rendre Meilleures, 2 vols. (Conditions of the 19th Century French Working Class Ser.). (Fr.). 1974. Repr. of 1840 ed. Set. lib. bdg. 115.00 (ISBN 0-8287-0354-X, 1015, 1037). Clearwater Pub.

Gatti de Gamond, Zoe. Pauperisme et Association. (Conditions of the 19th Century French Working Class Ser.). 176p. (Fr.). 1974. Repr. of 1847 ed. lib. bdg. 52.00x (ISBN 0-8287-0366-3, 1058). Clearwater Pub.

Gerando, J. M. De la Bienfaisance Publique, 4 vols. (Conditions of the 19th Century French Working Class Ser.). (Fr.). 1974. Repr. of 1839 ed. lib. bdg. 950.00x set (ISBN 0-8287-0372-8). Vol. 1 (1188). Vol. 2 (1189). Vol. 3 (1190). Vol. 4 (1191). Clearwater Pub.

Gerando, J. M. de. Le Visiteur du Pauvre. (Conditions of the 19th Century French Working Class Ser.). 170p. (Fr.). 1974. Repr. of 1820 ed. lib. bdg. 51.00x (ISBN 0-8287-0373-6, 1017). Clearwater Pub.

Gillet. Quelques Reflexions sur l'Emploi des Enfants dans les Fabriques et sur les Moyens d'en Prevenir les Abus. (Conditions of the 19th Century French Working Class Ser.). 84p. (Fr.). 1974. Repr. of 1840 ed. lib. bdg. 31.50x (ISBN 0-8287-0377-9, 1150). Clearwater Pub.

Girardin, Emile de. L' Abolition de la Misere par l'Elevation des Salaires. (Conditions of the 19th Century French Working Class). 160p. (Fr.). 1974. Repr. of 1850 ed. lib. bdg. 48.50 (ISBN 0-8287-0251-9, 1018). Clearwater Pub.

Granier, Camille. Essai de Bibliographie Charitable. (Conditions of the 19th Century French Working Class Ser.). 458p. (Fr.). 1974. Repr. of 1891 ed. lib. bdg. 115.00 (ISBN 0-8287-0392-2, 1090). Clearwater Pub.

Guepin, Ange. Nantes au Dix-Neuvieme Siecle. Statistique Topographique, Industrielle et Morale: Hygenie Physique et Morale. (Conditions of the 19th Century French Working Class Ser.). 203p. (Fr.). 1974. Repr. of 1835 ed. lib. bdg. 58.00x (ISBN 0-8287-0402-3, 1187). Clearwater Pub.

Lehning, James R. Peasants of Marlhes: Economic Development & Family Organization in Nineteenth-Century France. LC 79-18707. xiv, 218p. 1980. 19.50x (ISBN 0-8078-1411-3). U of NC Pr.

Lough, John & Lough, Munel. An Introduction to Nineteenth Century France. (Illus.). 1978. text ed. 14.50x (ISBN 0-582-35118-9); pap. text ed. 7.50x (ISBN 0-582-35119-7). Longman.

Maitron, Jean. Dictionnaire Biographique du Movement Ouvrier Francais: De la Revolution Francaise a la Fondation de la Premiere Internationale (1789-1864, 3 tomes. Incl. Tome I. De A a C. 16.95 (ISBN 0-685-36060-1); Tome II. De D a L. 19.95 (ISBN 0-685-36061-X); Tome III. De M a Z. 19.95 (ISBN 0-685-36062-8). French & Eur.

Meuvret, Jean. Le Probleme des Subsistances a l'epoque Louis XIV. I: La Production des Cereales dans la France du XVIIe et du XVIIIe Siecle Texte-Notes, 2 pts. (Civilisations et Societes Ser.: No. 50). 1977. pap. 31.75x set (ISBN 0-686-26041-4). Mouton.

Nodier, Charles. History of the Secret Societies of the Army, & of the Military Conspiracies Which Had As Their Object the Destruction of the Government of Bonaparte. LC 78-14740. 1978. Repr. of 1815 ed. 26.00x (ISBN 0-8201-1318-2). Schol Facsimiles.

Parker, Harold T. The Bureau of Manufacturers During the French Revolution & Under Napoleon. LC 77-88658. 1979. 14.95 (ISBN 0-89089-076-5). Carolina Acad Pr.

Plamenatz, John P. The Revolutionary Movement in France: Eighteen Fifteen to Eighteen Seventy-One. LC 78-14135. 1980. Repr. of 1952 ed. 17.50 (ISBN 0-88355-809-2). Hyperion Conn.

Stein, Robert. The French Slave Trade in the Eighteenth Century: An Old Regime Business. LC 79-3970. 1979. 20.00 (ISBN 0-299-07910-4). U of Wis Pr.

Stryienski, Casimir. Eighteenth Century. LC 16-17721. (National History of France: No. 5). Repr. of 1923 ed. 30.00 (ISBN 0-404-50795-6). AMS Pr.

Woodward, Ernest L. French Revolutions. LC 78-21044. 1979. Repr. of 1934 ed. lib. bdg. 19.75x (ISBN 0-313-20851-4, WOFR). Greenwood.

FRANCE–HISTORY–REVOLUTION, 1789-1799

see also Girondists; Jacobins; Vendean War, 1793-1800

Acton, John E. Lectures on the French Revolution. Figgis, John N. & Laurence, Reginald V., eds. LC 78-108814. (BCL Ser.: No. II). Repr. of 1910 ed. 24.50 (ISBN 0-404-00284-6). AMS Pr.

Acton, Lord. Lectures on the French Revolution. 59.95 (ISBN 0-8490-0499-3). Gordon Pr.

Alger, John G. Paris in 1789-1794, Farewell Letters of Victims of the Guillotine. LC 78-113540. Repr. of 1902 ed. 34.50 (ISBN 0-404-00323-0). AMS Pr.

Arbois de Joubainville, Paul, ed. Cahiers de doleances des bailliages de Longuyon, Longwy et de Villiers-la-Montagne pour les Etats-generaux de 1789. LC 74-29619. (Collection de la Commission d'histoire economique et sociale de la Revolution francaise). Repr. of 1952 ed. 21.00 (ISBN 0-404-58603-1). AMS Pr.

Aulard, Alphonse. Christianity & the French Revolution. 1966. 18.50 (ISBN 0-86527-025-2). Fertig.

Aulard, Francois V. Paris pendant la reaction thermidorienne et sous le Directoire, 5 vols. LC 70-161713. (Collection de documents relatifs a l'histoire de Paris pendant la Revolution francaise). Repr. of 1902 ed. Set. 266.25 (ISBN 0-404-52570-9); 53.25 ea. AMS Pr.

Balencie, Gaston, ed. Departement des Hautes-Pyrenees: Cahiers de doleances de la senechaussee de Bigorre pour les Etats-generaux de 1789. LC 74-29249. (Collection de la Commission d'histoire economique et sociale de la Revolution francaise). Repr. of 1926 ed. 45.00 (ISBN 0-404-58602-3). AMS Pr.

Barante, Amable G. Histoire de la Convention Nationale, 6 vols. LC 77-161739. Repr. of 1853 ed. 27.50 ea.; 165.00 (ISBN 0-404-07780-3). AMS Pr.

Bax, Ernest B. Last Episodes of the French Revolution. LC 74-159489. (World History Ser., No. 48). 1971. lib. bdg. 51.95 (ISBN 0-8383-1282-9). Haskell.

Bearman, Graham. The French Revolution. (History Broadsheets Ser.). (Illus.). 1977. pap. text ed. 6.95x (ISBN 0-435-31749-0). Heinemann Ed.

Beik, Paul H. The French Revolution Seen from the Right. p ed. LC 70-80523. 1971. Repr. of 1956 ed. 17.50 (ISBN 0-86527-074-0). Fertig.

Belloc, Hilaire. The French Revolution. 1979. Repr. of 1911 ed. lib. bdg. 20.00 (ISBN 0-8495-0515-1). Arden Lib.

Beraud, Henri. Twelve Portraits of the French Revolution. facs. ed. Boyd, M., tr. LC 68-16909. (Essay Index Reprint Ser). 1928. 18.00 (ISBN 0-8369-0197-5). Arno.

Berland, Just. Departement de la Marne: Les dommages de guerre apres Valmy. LC 74-29238. (Collection de la Commission d'histoire economique et sociale de la Revolution francaise). Repr. of 1931 ed. 32.00 (ISBN 0-404-58604-X). AMS Pr.

Bienvenu, Richard, ed. Ninth of Thermidor: The Fall of Robespierre. (Problems in European History Series). (Orig.). 1968. pap. 3.50x (ISBN 0-19-500832-4). Oxford U Pr.

Birch, Una. Secret Societies & the French Revolution. 1976. lib. bdg. 59.95 (ISBN 0-8490-2585-0). Gordon Pr.

Blanc, Louis. Histoire de la Revolution francaise, 12 Vols. LC 79-39452. (Fr). Repr. of 1862 ed. Set. 270.00 (ISBN 0-404-07150-3); 22.50 ea. AMS Pr.

Bloch, Camille, ed. Departement du Loiret: Cahiers de doleances du bailliage d'Orleans pour les Etats-generaux de 1789, 2 vols. LC 74-29232. (Collection de la Commission d'histoire economique et sociale de la Revolution francaise). Repr. of 1907 ed. Set. 98.00 (ISBN 0-404-58605-8). AMS Pr.

Blossier, Albert, ed. Departement du Calvados: Comite du Calvados. Cahiers de doleances du bailliage de Honfleur pour les Etats-generaux de 1789. LC 74-29217. (Collection de la Commission d'histoire economique et sociale de la Revolution francaise). Repr. of 1913 ed. 18.00 (ISBN 0-404-58722-4). AMS Pr.

Boissonnade, Prosper, ed. Departement de la Charente: Cahiers de doleances de la senechaussee d'Angouleme et du siege royal de Cognac pour les Etats-generaux de 1789. LC 74-29218. (Collection de la Commission d'histoire economique et sociale de la Revolution francaise). Repr. of 1907 ed. 38.00 (ISBN 0-404-58608-2). AMS Pr.

--Departement de la Vienne: Cahiers de doleances de la senechaussee de Civray pour les Etats-generaux de 1789. LC 74-29259. (Collection de la Commission d'histoire economique et sociale de la Revolution francaise). Repr. of 1925 ed. 31.00 (ISBN 0-404-58609-0). AMS Pr.

Bondurand, Edouard B., ed. Departement du Gard: Cahiers de doleances de la senechaussee de Nimes pour les Etats-generaux de 1789, 2 vols. LC 74-29222. (Collection de la Commission d'histoire economique et sociale de la Revolution francaise). Repr. of 1909 ed. Set. 92.00 (ISBN 0-404-58610-4). AMS Pr.

Bourgin, Georges, ed. Le Partage des communaux: Documents sur la preparation de la loi du 10 juin 1793. LC 74-29271. (Collection de la Commission d'histoire economique et sociale de la Revolution francaise). Repr. of 1908 ed. 55.00 (ISBN 0-404-58614-7). AMS Pr.

Bourgin, Hubert, ed. L' Industrie siderurgique en France au debut de la Revolution. LC 74-29269. (Collection de la Commission d'histoire economique et sociale de la Revolution francaise). Repr. of 1920 ed. 40.00 (ISBN 0-404-58613-9). AMS Pr.

Brace, Richard M. Bordeaux & the Gironde, 1789-1794. LC 68-10905. 1968. Repr. of 1947 ed. 10.00 (ISBN 0-8462-1072-X). Russell.

Bridrey, Emile, ed. Departement de la Manche: Cahiers de doleances du bailliage de Cotentin (coutances et secondaires) pour les Etats-generaux de 1789, 3 vols. LC 74-29236. (Collection de la Commission d'histoire economique et sociale de la Revolution francaise). Repr. of 1914 ed. Set. 160.00 (ISBN 0-404-58616-3). AMS Pr.

Brinton, Crane. Decade of Revolution, 1789-1799. (Rise of Modern Europe Ser). pap. 6.95x (ISBN 0-06-133018-3, TB3018, Torch). Har-Row.

Brown, Philip A. French Revolution in English History. 234p. 1965. Repr. 25.00x (ISBN 0-7146-1458-0, F Cass Co). Biblio Dist.

Bruchet, Max, ed. Departement de la Haute-Savoie: L'abolition des droits seigneuriaux en Savoie 1761-1793 documents. LC 74-29252. (Collection de la Commission d'histoire economique et sociale de la Revolution francaise). Repr. of 1908 ed. 50.00 (ISBN 0-404-58615-5). AMS Pr.

Bruun, Geoffrey. Saint-Just: Apostle of the Terror. 1966. Repr. of 1932 ed. 16.00 (ISBN 0-208-00531-5, Archon). Shoe String.

Burke, Edmund. Reflections on the Revolution in France. O'Brien, Conor C., ed. (Pelican Classics Ser.). 1976. pap. 2.50 (ISBN 0-14-040003-6, Pelican). Penguin.

Carlyle, Thomas. French Revolution, 2 vols. in 1. Date not set. 15.95x (ISBN 0-460-10031-9, Evman). Biblio Dist.

Carol, Raymond L. Two Rebel Priests of the French Revolution. LC 75-18135. 1975. soft bdg. 9.00 (ISBN 0-685-64835-4). R & E Res Assoc.

Cathelineau, Leonce, ed. Departement des Deux-Sevres: Cahiers de doleances des senechaussees de Niort et de Saint-Maixent, et des communautes et corporations de Niort et Saint-Maixent pour les Etats-generaux de 1789. LC 74-29258. (Collection de la Commission d'histoire economique et sociale de la Revolution francaise). Repr. of 1912 ed. 35.00 (ISBN 0-404-58620-1). AMS Pr.

Censer, Jack Richard. Prelude to Power: The Parisian Radical Press, 1789-1791. LC 76-7968. (Illus.). 208p. 1976. 14.50x (ISBN 0-8018-1816-8). Johns Hopkins.

Chaboseau, Augustin. De Babeuf a la Commune. LC 70-101232. (Research & Source Works: No. 389). (Fr). 1970. Repr. of 1911 ed. text ed. 14.00 (ISBN 0-8337-0508-3). B Franklin.

Challamel, Augustin. Les Clubs contre-revolutionnaires. LC 72-38038. (Collection de documents relatifs a l'histoire de Paris pendant la Revolution francaise). Repr. of 1895 ed. 53.25 (ISBN 0-404-52552-0). AMS Pr.

Chandler, David. Dictionary of the Napoleonic Wars. (Illus.). 1979. 40.00 (ISBN 0-02-523670-9). Macmillan.

Charlety, Sebastien, ed. Departement du Rhone: Documents relatifs a la vente des biens nationaux. LC 74-29250. (Collection de la Commission d'histoire economique et sociale de la Revolution francaise). Repr. of 1906 ed. 50.00 (ISBN 0-404-58621-X). AMS Pr.

Chassin, Charles L. Les Volontaires nationaux pendant la Revolution, 3 vols. LC 70-38040. Repr. of 1906 ed. Set. 159.75 (ISBN 0-404-52600-4); 53.25 ea.; Vol. 1. (ISBN 0-404-52601-2); Vol. 2. (ISBN 0-404-52602-0); Vol. 3. (ISBN 0-404-52603-9). AMS Pr.

Cobb, Richard. Armees Revolutionnaires, 2 Vols. (Societe Mouvements Sociaux et Ideologies Etudes 3: No. 3). 1961. Set. pap. text ed. 70.00x (ISBN 90-2796-235-9). Mouton.

Cobb, Richard C. Reactions to the French Revolution. 1972. 22.00x (ISBN 0-19-212187-1). Oxford U Pr.

Cobban, Alfred. The Myth of the French Revolution. 1978. Repr. of 1955 ed. lib. bdg. 10.00 (ISBN 0-8495-0906-8). Arden Lib.

Cobban, Alfred B. Social Interpretation of the French Revolution. LC 64-21535. 1968. 24.95 (ISBN 0-521-04679-3); pap. 7.50xx (ISBN 0-521-09548-4). Cambridge U Pr.

Connelly, Owen. French Revolution: Napoleonic Era. LC 77-85509. 1979. text ed. 15.95 (ISBN 0-03-091558-9, HoltC). HR&W.

Croker, John W. Essays on the Early Period of the French Revolution. LC 78-114146. Repr. of 1857 ed. 34.50 (ISBN 0-404-01858-0). AMS Pr.

Curtis, Eugene W. Saint-Just, Colleague of Robespierre. LC 73-14540. xi, 402p. 1973. Repr. of 1935 ed. lib. bdg. 25.00x (ISBN 0-374-92010-9). Octagon.

Dawson, Philip. Provinicial Magistrates & Revolutionary Politics in France, 1789-1795. LC 74-182816. (Historical Monographs Ser: No. 66). (Illus.). 416p. 1972. 20.00x (ISBN 0-674-71960-3). Harvard U Pr.

Defresne, A. Departement de Seine-et-Oise: Les subsistances dans le district de Versailles de 1788 a l'an V, 2 vols. LC 74-29254. (Collection de la Commission d'histoire economique et sociale de la Revolution francaise). Repr. of 1922 ed. Set. 72.00 (ISBN 0-404-58622-8). AMS Pr.

Desmoulins, Camille. Oeuvres, 2 Vols in 1. LC 72-164282. Repr. of 1838 ed. 42.50 (ISBN 0-404-07124-4). AMS Pr.

De Tocqueville, Alexis. The European Correspondence with Gobineau. Lukacs, John, ed. & tr. 7.50 (ISBN 0-8446-1152-2). Peter Smith.

Dippel, Horst. Germany & the American Revolution, 1770-1800: A Sociohistorical Investigation of Late Eighteenth-Century Political Thinking. Uhlendorf, Bernhard A., tr. LC 77-367. (Institute of Early American History & Culture Ser.). (Illus.). 1977. 24.50x (ISBN 0-8078-1301-X). U of NC Pr.

Donat, Jean. Une Communaute rurale a la fin de l'ancien regime. LC 74-29621. (Collection de la Commission d'histoire economique et sociale de la Revolution francaise). Repr. of 1926 ed. 21.00 (ISBN 0-404-58625-2). AMS Pr.

Dorvaux, N., ed. Departement de la Moselle: Cahiers de doleances des bailliages des generalites de Metz et Nancy pour les Etats-generaux de 1789. LC 74-29242. (Collection de la Commission de l'histoire economique et sociale de la Revolution francaise). Repr. of 1922 ed. 27.00 (ISBN 0-404-58626-0). AMS Pr.

Douarche, Aristide. Les Tribunaux civils de Paris pendant la Revolution: 1791-1800, 2 vols. LC 71-164777. (Collection de documents relatifs a l'histoire de Paris pendant la Revolution francaise). Repr. of 1907 ed. Set. 106.50 (ISBN 0-404-52553-9); 53.25 ea. Vol. 1 (ISBN 0-404-52554-7). Vol. 2 (ISBN 0-404-52555-5). AMS Pr.

Dowden, Edward. French Revolution & English Literature. LC 67-27592. Repr. of 1901 ed. 12.50 (ISBN 0-8046-0114-3). Kennikat.

Doyle, William. Origins of the French Revolution. 272p. 1981. 37.50 (ISBN 0-19-873020-9); pap. 14.95 (ISBN 0-19-873021-7). Oxford U Pr.

Dubreuil, Leon, ed. Departement des Cotes-du-Nord: Les vicissitudes du domaine congeable en Basse-Bretagne a l'epoque de la Revolution, 2 vols. in 1. LC 74-29220. (Collection de la Commission d'histoire economique et sociale de la Revolution francaise). Repr. of 1915 ed. 39.00 (ISBN 0-404-58627-9). AMS Pr.

Dunoyer, Alphonse. The Public Prosecutor of the Terror: Antoine Quentin Fouquier-Tinville. 1977. lib. bdg. 59.95 (ISBN 0-8490-2489-7). Gordon Pr.

Dupre, Huntley. Lazare Carnot, Republican Patriot. LC 75-29217. (Perspectives in European Hist. Ser.: No. 5). viii, 343p. Repr. of 1940 ed. lib. bdg. 19.50x (ISBN 0-87991-612-5). Porcupine Pr.

Erdant, Alexandre. Les Revolutionnaires De L'A. B. C. 281p. 1981. Repr. of 1854 ed. lib. bdg. 115.00 (ISBN 0-8287-1556-4). Clearwater Pub.

Evrard, Fernand. Versailles, ville du roi 1770-1789: Etude d'economie urbaine, suivie du texte des cahiers des corps et communautes de metiers de Versailles. LC 74-29273. (Collection de la Commission d'histoire economique et sociale de la Revolution francaise). Repr. of 1935 ed. 45.00 (ISBN 0-404-58628-7). AMS Pr.

Farmer, Paul. France Reviews Its Revolutionary Origins. 1963. lib. bdg. 13.00x (ISBN 0-374-92698-0). Octagon.

Fauchet, Joseph. Le Despotisme Decrete Par L'assemblee Nationale. (Rousseauism, 1788-1797). 1978. Repr. lib. bdg. 26.00x (ISBN 0-8287-0332-9). Clearwater Pub.

Forrest, Alan. The French Revolution & the Poor. LC 80-29105. 280p. 1981. 25.00x (ISBN 0-312-30524-9). St Martin.

--Society & Politics in Revolutionary Bordeaux. (Oxford Historical Monographs). 320p. 1975. 42.00x (ISBN 0-19-821859-1). Oxford U Pr.

Fourastie, Victor, ed. Departement du Lot: Cahiers de doleances de la senechaussee de Cahors pour les Etats-generaux de 1789. LC 74-29234. (Collection de la Commission d'histoire economique et sociale de la Revolution francaise). Repr. of 1908 ed. 28.00 (ISBN 0-404-58633-3). AMS Pr.

Fournier, Joseph, ed. Departement des Bouches-du-Rhone: Cahiers de doleances de la senechausse de Marseille pour les Etats-generaux de 1789. LC 74-29215. (Collection de la Commission d'histoire economique et sociale de la Revolution francaise). Repr. of 1908 ed. 44.00 (ISBN 0-404-58634-1). AMS Pr.

France. Assemblee nationale constituante, 1789-1791. Comite des finances. Proces-verbaux, 2 vols. in 1. LC 74-29268. (Collection de la Commission d'histoire economique et sociale de la Revolution francaise). Repr. of 1923 ed. 44.00 (ISBN 0-404-58635-X). AMS Pr.

France. Assemblee nationale constituante, 1789-1791. Comite de mendicite. Proces-verbaux et rapports du Comite de mendicite de la Constituante 1790-1791. LC 74-29270. (Collection de la Commission d'histoire economique et sociale de la Revolution francaise). Repr. of 1911 ed. 62.00 (ISBN 0-404-58638-4). AMS Pr.

France. Commission des subsistances et approvisionnements. La Commission des subsistances de l'an II: Proces-verbaux et actes. LC 74-29272. (Collection de la Commission d'histoire economique et sociale de la Revolution francaise). Repr. of 1925 ed. 60.00 (ISBN 0-404-58644-9). AMS Pr.

France. Commission d'histoire economique de la Revolution francaise. Cahiers de doleances des bailliages de generalites de Metz et de Nancy pour les Etats-generaux de 1789; premier serie: Departement de Meurthe-et-Moselle, 4 vols. LC 74-29241. Repr. of 1934 ed. 165.00 (ISBN 0-404-58600-7). AMS Pr.

France. Ministere de l'interieur. Correspondance du ministre de l'interieur relative au commerce, aux subsistances et a l'administration generale. LC 74-29279. (Collection de la Commission d'histoire economique et sociale de la Revolution francaise). Repr. of 1917 ed. 55.00 (ISBN 0-404-58645-7). AMS Pr.

Frey, Lucius J. Philosophie Sociale Dediee Au Peuple Francais...Par un Citoyen De la Section De la Republique Francaise, Ci-Devant Du Roule. (Rousseauism, 1788-1797). 1978. Repr. lib. bdg. 73.00x (ISBN 0-8287-0357-4). Clearwater Pub.

Gandihon, Alfred A., ed. Departement du Cher: Cahiers de doleances du bailliage de Bourges et des bailliages secondaires de Vierzon et d'Henrichemont pour les Etats-generaux de 1789. LC 74-29219. (Collection de la Commission d'histoire economique et sociale de la Revolution francaise). Repr. of 1910 ed. 60.00 (ISBN 0-404-58646-5). AMS Pr.

Gardiner, Bertha M. The French Revolution. 1883. Repr. 10.00 (ISBN 0-685-43466-4). Norwood Edns.

Garrett, Clarke. Respectable Folly: Millenarians and the French Revolution in France and England. LC 74-24378. 252p. 1975. 16.00x (ISBN 0-8018-1618-1). Johns Hopkins.

Gaxotte, Pierre. The French Revolution. Phillips, Walter A., tr. 1978. Repr. of 1932 ed. lib. bdg. 40.00 (ISBN 0-8492-4911-2). R West.

Gerbaux, Fernand, ed. Proces-verbaux des Comites d'agriculture et de commerce de la Constituante, de la Legislative et de la Convention, 5 vols. in 4. LC 74-29275. (Collection de la Commission d'histoire economique et sociale de la Revolution francaise). Repr. of 1910 ed. Set. 225.00 (ISBN 0-404-58647-3). AMS Pr.

Gershoy, Leo. Era of the French Revolution, Seventeen Eighty-Nine to Seventeen Ninety-Nine. (Orig.). 1957. pap. 5.95x (ISBN 0-442-00022-7, 22, Anv). Van Nos Reinhold.

Godard, M., ed. Departement de la Haute-Saone: Cahiers de doleances du bailliage d'Amont, 2 vols. LC 74-29251. (Collection de la Commission d'histoire economique et sociale de la Revolution francaise). Repr. of 1927 ed. Set. 70.00 (ISBN 0-404-58652-X). AMS Pr.

Gooch, G. P. Germany & the French Revoluton. 543p. 1965. Repr. 35.00x (ISBN 0-7146-1477-7, F Cass Co). Biblio Dist.

Gottschalk, Louis R. Jean Paul Marat: A Study in Radicalism. LC 67-16987. 1967. pap. 12.50x (ISBN 0-226-30532-5). U of Chicago Pr.

Greenlaw, Ralph W. The Social Origins of the French Revolution. pap. 4.95x (ISBN 0-669-91116-X). Heath.

Greer, Donald. The Incidence of the Terror During the French Revolution: A Statistical Interpretation. 1935. 7.00 (ISBN 0-8446-1211-1). Peter Smith.

Guillaume, Paul, ed. Departement des Hautes-Alpes: Recueil des reponses faites par les communautes de l'election de Gap au questionnaire envoye par la commission intermediaire des etats du Dauphine. LC 74-29213. (Collection de la Commission d'histoire economique et sociale de la Revolution francaise). Repr. of 1908 ed. 44.00 (ISBN 0-404-58655-4). AMS Pr.

Guillou, Adolphe, ed. Departement d'Ille-et-Vilaine: Documents relatifs a la vente des biens nationaux. LC 74-29228. (Collection de la Commission d'histoire economique et sociale de la Revolution francaise). Repr. of 1911 ed. 60.00 (ISBN 0-404-58656-2). AMS Pr.

Hampson, Norman. Social History of the French Revolution. LC 64-20652. 1963. pap. 8.50 (ISBN 0-8020-6060-9). U of Toronto Pr.

Harris, Seymour E. Assignats. LC 74-98625. Repr. of 1930 ed. 23.00 (ISBN 0-404-03136-6). AMS Pr.

Hazen, Charles D. The French Revolution & Napoleon. 1979. Repr. of 1917 ed. lib. bdg. 25.00 (ISBN 0-8482-4482-6). Norwood Edns.

Henderson, Ernest F. Symbol & Satire in the French Revolution: With 171 Illustrations. 1977. lib. bdg. 69.95 (ISBN 0-8490-2724-1). Gordon Pr.

Hibbert, Christopher. Days of the French Revolution. LC 81-9666. (Illus.). 384p. 1981. Repr. 10.95 (ISBN 0-688-03704-6); pap. 6.95 (ISBN 0-688-00746-5). Morrow.

Higgins, E. L., ed. The French Revolution As Told by Contemporaries. LC 74-79396. 463p. 1975. Repr. of 1939 ed. lib. bdg. 20.00x (ISBN 0-8154-0492-1). Cooper Sq.

Historical Tales of the Days of the Great Revolution. 1978. Repr. of 1858 ed. lib. bdg. 35.00 (ISBN 0-8492-0069-5). R West.

Holtman, Robert B. The Napoleonic Revolution. LC 67-11308. 1979. pap. 5.95x (ISBN 0-8071-0487-6). La State U Pr.

Hyslop, Beatrice F. French Nationalism in 1789 According to the General Cahiers. 1968. Repr. lib. bdg. 15.50 (ISBN 0-374-94085-1). Octagon.

--Repertoire critique des cahiers de doleances pour les Etats-generaux de 1789, 2 vols. LC 74-29276. (Collection de la Commission d'histoire ecoonomique et sociale de la Revolution francaise). Repr. of 1933 ed. Set. 60.00 (ISBN 0-404-58719-4). AMS Pr.

Jackson, T. A., ed. Essays on the French Revolution. Zak, William, tr. LC 73-103238. 1970. Repr. of 1945 ed. 12.50 (ISBN 0-8046-0874-1). Kennikat.

James, C. L. History of the French Revolution. lib. bdg. 59.95 (ISBN 0-8490-1997-4). Gordon Pr.

Jaures, Jean. Histoire Socialiste De la Revolution Francaise, 8 Vols. LC 71-170843. Repr. of 1927 ed. Set. 220.00 (ISBN 0-404-07320-4); 27.50 ea. AMS Pr.

Johnson, D. French Society & the Revolution. LC 76-1136. (Past and Present Publications Ser.). 300p. 1976. 26.95 (ISBN 0-521-21275-8). Cambridge U Pr.

Johnston, R. M. The French Revolution. 1909. Repr. 15.00 (ISBN 0-685-43052-9). Norwood Edns.

Jouanne, Rene, ed. Departement de l'Orne: Cahiers de doleances des Corps et corporations de la ville d'Alencon pour les Etats-generaux de 1789. LC 74-29247. (Collection de la Commission d'histoire economique et sociale de la Revolution francaise). Repr. of 1929 ed. 18.00 (ISBN 0-404-58658-9). AMS Pr.

Kellett, E. E. The French Revolution. Repr. 10.00 (ISBN 0-685-43228-9). Norwood Edns.

Kim, Kyung-Won. Revolution & International System: A Study in the Breakdown of International Stability. LC 76-92521. 1970. 10.95x (ISBN 0-8147-0233-3). NYU Pr.

Kropotkin, Peter. The Great French Revolution. Dryhurst, N. F., tr. from Fr. LC 75-163336. (Studies in the Libertarian & Utopian Tradition). 1971. 10.00x (ISBN 0-8052-3421-7); pap. 4.50 (ISBN 0-8052-0317-6). Schocken.

La Gorce, Pierre F. Histoire religieuse de la Revolution francaise, 5 Vols. LC 71-88239. (Fr). Repr. of 1923 ed. Set. 142.50 (ISBN 0-404-03810-7); 28.00 ea. Vol. 1 (ISBN 0-404-03811-5). Vol. 2 (ISBN 0-404-03812-3). Vol. 3 (ISBN 0-404-03813-1). Vol. 4 (ISBN 0-404-03814-X). Vol. 5 (ISBN 0-404-03815-8). AMS Pr.

Lanjalley, Paul & Corriez, Paul. Histoire De la Revolution Du 18 Mars. LC 78-171657. Repr. of 1871 ed. 37.00 (ISBN 0-404-07139-2). AMS Pr.

Laprade, William T. England & the French Revolution, 1789-1797. LC 77-109922. Repr. of 1909 ed. 12.50 (ISBN 0-404-03878-6). AMS Pr.

Laurent, Gustave, ed. Departement de la Marne: Cahiers De Doleances Pour les Etats-Generaux De 1789, 5 vols. LC 74-29239. (Collection de la Commission d'histoire economique et sociale de la Revolution francaise). Repr. of 1930 ed. Set. 275.00 (ISBN 0-404-58659-7). AMS Pr.

LeBon, Gustave. The French Revolution & the Psychology of Revolution. LC 78-62691. (Social Science Classics Ser.). 337p. 1980. 19.95 (ISBN 0-87855-310-X); pap. 6.95 (ISBN 0-87855-697-4). Transaction Bks.

Lecky, William H. The French Revolution. 1904. 20.00 (ISBN 0-685-43888-0). Norwood Edns.

Lefebvre, Georges. Coming of the French Revolution. Palmer, Robert R., tr. 1947. 17.50 (ISBN 0-691-05112-7); pap. 5.95 (ISBN 0-691-00751-9). Princeton U Pr.

--The French Revolution, 2 vols. Incl. Vol. 1. From Its Origins to 1793. Evans, Elizabeth M., tr. 20.00x (ISBN 0-231-02342-1); pap. 6.00x (ISBN 0-231-08598-2); Vol. 2. From 1793 to 1799. Stewart, John H. & Friguglietti, James, trs. 20.00x (ISBN 0-231-02519-X); pap. 6.00x (ISBN 0-231-08599-0). LC 64-11939. 1962-64. Columbia U Pr.

--Great Fear of Seventeen Eighty-Nine: Rural Panic in Revolutionary France. White, Joan, tr. 1973. pap. 1.95 (ISBN 0-394-71939-5, Vin). Random.

Lefebvre, Georges, ed. Departement du Nord: Documents ratifs a l'histoire des substances dans le district de Berques pendant la Revolution 1789-an V, 2 vols. LC 74-29244. (Collection de la Commission d'histoire economique et sociale de la Revolution francaise). Repr. of 1921 ed. Set. 105.00 (ISBN 0-404-58665-1). AMS Pr.

--Questions agraires au temps de la terreur. LC 74-29277. (Collection de la Commission d'histoire economique et sociale de la Revolution francaise). Repr. of 1932 ed. 20.00 (ISBN 0-404-58668-6). AMS Pr.

Legg, L. Wickham. Select Documents Illustrative of the History of the French Revolution, 2 vols. 1973. lib. bdg. 45.00x set (ISBN 0-374-94891-7). Octagon.

Leith, James A. Idea of Art as Propaganda in France, 1750-1799: A Study in the History of Ideas. LC 65-1875. (Romance Ser.). 1965. 15.00x (ISBN 0-8020-5151-0). U of Toronto Pr.

Le Moy, A., ed. Departement de Maine-et-Loire: Cahiers de doleances des Corporations de la ville d'Angers et des paroisses de la senechaussee particuliere d'Angers pour les Etats-generaux de 1789. LC 74-29235. (Collection de la Commission d'histoire economique et sociale de la Revolution francaise). Repr. of 1916 ed. 60.00 (ISBN 0-404-58669-4). AMS Pr.

Le Parquier, E., ed. Departement de la Seine-Inferieure: Cahiers de doleances du bailliage d'Arques (secondaires de Caudebec) pour les Etats-generaux de 1789, 2 vols. in 1. LC 74-29255. (Collection de la Commission d'histoire economique et sociale de la Revolution francaise). Repr. of 1922 ed. 50.00 (ISBN 0-404-58670-8). AMS Pr.

--Departement de la Seine-Inferieure: Cahiers de doleances du bailliage du Havre (secondaire de Caudebec) pour les Etats-generaux de 1789. LC 74-29256. (Collection de la Commission d'histoire economique et sociale de la Revolution francaise). Repr. of 1929 ed. 25.00 (ISBN 0-404-58671-6). AMS Pr.

--Departement de la Seine-Inferieure: Cahiers de doleances du bailliage de Neufchatel-en-Bray. LC 74-29257. (Collection de la Commission d'histoire economique et sociale de la Revolution francaise). Repr. of 1908 ed. 22.00 (ISBN 0-404-58672-4). AMS Pr.

Lesprand, P., ed. Departement de la Moselle: Cahiers de doleances des prevotes bailliageres de Sarrebourg et de Phalsbourg, et du bailliage de Lixheim pour les Etats-generaux de 1789. LC 74-29243. (Collection de la Commission d'histoire economique et sociale de la Revolution francaise). Repr. of 1938 ed. 20.00 (ISBN 0-404-58673-2). AMS Pr.

Lesueur, F., ed. Departement de Loir-et-Cher: Cahiers de doleances du bailliage secondaire de Romorantin pour les Etats-generaux de 1789, 2 vols. LC 74-29233. (Collection de la Commission d'histoire economique et sociale de la Revolution francaise). Repr. of 1908 ed. Set. 85.00 (ISBN 0-404-58674-0). AMS Pr.

Lorain, C., ed. Departement de la Haute-Marne: Les subsistances en cereales dans le district de Chaumont de 1788 a l'an V, 2 vols. LC 74-29240. (Collection de la Commission d'histoire economique et sociale de la Revolution francaise). Repr. of 1912 ed. Set. 120.00 (ISBN 0-404-58677-5). AMS Pr.

Lowell, Edward J. Eve of the French Revolution. LC 72-1016. Repr. of 1892 ed. 29.50 (ISBN 0-404-07145-7). AMS Pr.

Madelin, Louis. Figures of the Revolution. facs. ed. Curtis, R., tr. LC 68-22221. (Essay Index Reprint Ser). 1929. 16.50 (ISBN 0-8369-0663-2). Arno.

--Figures of the Revolution. LC 68-16297. 1968. Repr. of 1929 ed. 12.50 (ISBN 0-8046-0290-5). Kennikat.

--French Revolution. LC 73-181954. (National History of France: No. 6). Repr. of 1938 ed. 30.00 (ISBN 0-404-50796-4). AMS Pr.

Mahan, Alfred T. Influence of Sea Power Upon the French Revolution & Empire, 2 Vols. 1898. 34.00 (ISBN 0-403-00193-5). Scholarly.

--Influence of Sea Power Upon the French Revolution & Empire 1793-1812, 2 Vols. 10th ed. LC 69-10127. (Illus.). 1968. Repr. of 1898 ed. Set. lib. bdg. 35.25x (ISBN 0-8371-2666-5, MASP). Greenwood.

Manceron, Claude. The Twilight of the Old Order. Wolf, Patricia, tr. 1977. 15.95 (ISBN 0-394-48902-0). Knopf.

Marion, M., ed. Departement de la Gironde: Documents relatifs a la vente des biens nationaux, 2 vols. LC 74-29227. (Collection de la Commission d'histoire economique et sociale de la Revolution francaise). Repr. of 1912 ed. Set. 100.00 (ISBN 0-404-58680-5). AMS Pr.

Martin, E., ed. Departement des Vosges: Cahier des doleances du bailliage de Mirecourt. LC 74-29260. (Collection de la Commission d'histoire economique et sociale de la Revolution francaise). Repr. of 1928 ed. 23.00 (ISBN 0-404-58683-X). AMS Pr.

Martin, Henri, ed. Departement de la Haute-Garonne: Documents relatifs a la vente des biens nationaux...District de Saint-Gaudens. LC 74-29225. (Collection de la Commission d'histoire economique et sociale de la Revolution francaise). Repr. of 1924 ed. 45.00 (ISBN 0-404-58684-8). AMS Pr.

--Departement de la Haute-Garonne: Documents relatifs a la vente des biens nationaux. LC 74-29226. (Collection de la Commission d'histoire economique et sociale de la Revolution francaise). Repr. of 1916 ed. 50.00 (ISBN 0-404-58685-6). AMS Pr.

Mathiez, Albert. Fall of Robespierre & Other Essays. LC 68-55329. Repr. of 1927 ed. lib. bdg. 15.00x (ISBN 0-678-00428-5). Kelley.

--Proces De Corruption Sous la Terreur: L'affaire De la Compagnie Des Indes. (Illus.). 1971. Repr. of 1920 ed. lib. bdg. 26.50 (ISBN 0-8337-2299-9). B Franklin.

--Proces De Corruption Sous la Terreur: L'affaire De la Compagnie Des Indes. (Illus.). 1971. Repr. of 1920 ed. lib. bdg. 26.50 (ISBN 0-8337-2299-9). B Franklin.

--Requisitions De Grains Sous la Terreur. (Revue D'histoire Economique et Sociale: Vol. 8). (Fr.). 1973. Repr. of 1920 ed. lib. bdg. 15.00 (ISBN 0-8337-2298-0). B Franklin.

Maurel, Blanche, ed. Cahiers de doleances de la colonie de Saint-Dominique pour les Etats-generaux de 1789. LC 74-29267. (Collection de la Commission d'histoire economique et sociale de la Revolution francaise). Repr. of 1933 ed. 28.00 (ISBN 0-404-58686-4). AMS Pr.

Mayer, J. P., ed. Considerations sur les Principaux Evenemens de la Revolution Francoise, Madame la Baronne Stael, 3 vols. in 2. LC 78-67391. (European Political Thought Ser.). (Fr.). 1979. Repr. of 1818 ed. lib. bdg. 74.00x (ISBN 0-405-11742-6); lib. bdg. 37.00 ea. Vol. 1 (ISBN 0-405-11743-4). Vol. 2 (ISBN 0-405-11744-2). Arno.

--The Impact of the Eighteenth Brumaire: An Original Anthology. LC 78-67322. (European Political Thought Ser.). (Ger. & Eng.). 1979. lib. bdg. 32.00x (ISBN 0-405-11672-1). Arno.

Meikle, Henry W. Scotland & the French Revolution. LC 68-56255. Repr. of 1912 ed. 15.00x (ISBN 0-678-00588-5). Kelley.

Michelet. Histoire de la Revolution Francaise: Livres I a VIII, Vol. 1. 1568p. 41.50 (ISBN 0-686-56541-X). French & Eur.

--Histoire de la Revolution Francaise: Livres IX a XXI - Tableau Chronologique, Vol. 2. 1696p. 42.95 (ISBN 0-686-56542-8). French & Eur.

Michelet, Jules. Histoire de la Revolution Francaise, 2 tomes. Walter, ed. (Bibliotheque de la Pleiade). Set. 75.00 (ISBN 0-685-34946-2). French & Eur.

--History of the French Revolution. Wright, Gordon, ed. Cocks, Charles, tr. (Classical European Historians Ser.). 1967. 15.00x (ISBN 0-226-52332-2). U of Chicago Pr.

--History of the French Revolution. Wright, Gordon, ed. Cocks, Charles, tr. LC 67-15315. 1967. pap. 8.50x (ISBN 0-226-52333-0, P257, Phoen). U of Chicago Pr.

Morris, Gouverneur. Diary & Letters of Gouverneur Morris, 2 Vols. Morris, Anne C., ed. LC 70-98691. (American Public Figures Ser). 1969. Repr. of 1888 ed. lib. bdg. 95.00 (ISBN 0-306-71835-9). Da Capo.

--Diary of the French Revolution, 2 vols. Davenport, Beatrix C., ed. LC 70-110859. (Illus.). 1972. Repr. of 1939 ed. lib. bdg. 53.00x (ISBN 0-8371-4528-7, MOFR). Greenwood.

--A Diary of the French Revolution, 2 vols. facsimile ed. Davenport, Beatrix C., ed. LC 71-157348. (Select Bibliographies Reprint Ser). Repr. of 1939 ed. Set. 60.00 (ISBN 0-8369-5809-8). Arno.

Morris, William O. The French Revolution & First Empire. Repr. of 1892 ed. 10.00 (ISBN 0-685-43337-4). Norwood Edns.

Morton, J. B. Brumaire: The Rise of Bonaparte. (Select Bibliographies Reprint Ser.). Repr. of 1948 ed. 20.75 (ISBN 0-518-19075-7). Arno.

Moulin, Paul, ed. Departement des Bouches-du-Rhone: Documents Relatifs a la vente des biens nationaux, 4 vols. LC 74-29216. (Collection de la Commission d'histoire economique et sociale de la Revolution francaise). Repr. of 1911 ed. Set. 180.00 (ISBN 0-404-58687-2). AMS Pr.

Mourlot, Felix, ed. Departement de l'Orne: Recueil des documents d'ordre economique contenus dans les registres de deliberations des municipalites du district d'Alencon, 1788-an IV, 3 vols. LC 74-29248. (Collection de la Commission d'histoire economique et Sociale de la Revolution francaise). Repr. of 1911 ed. 150.00 (ISBN 0-404-58692-9). AMS Pr.

Palmer, R. R. The School of the French Revolution: A Documentary History Ofthe College of Louis-le-Grand & Its Director, Jean-Francois Champagne, 1762-1814. 1975. 21.50 (ISBN 0-691-05229-8). Princeton U Pr.

--World of the French Revolution. 1972. pap. 4.95x (ISBN 0-06-131620-2, TB1620, Torch). Har-Row.

Palmer, Robert R. Twelve Who Ruled: The Year of the Terror in the French Revolution. 1941. 18.50x (ISBN 0-691-05119-4); pap. 5.95 (ISBN 0-691-00761-6). Princeton U Pr.

Patrick, Alison. The Men of the First French Republic: Political Alignments in the National Convention of 1792. LC 72-4018. (Illus.). 425p. 1972. 27.50x (ISBN 0-8018-1305-0). Johns Hopkins.

Pfeiffer, Laura B. Uprising of June Twentieth, 1792. LC 78-115360. Repr. of 1913 ed. 14.50 (ISBN 0-404-05019-0). AMS Pr.

Phillips, W. Alison. The French Revolution. 1929. Repr. 10.00 (ISBN 0-685-43319-6). Norwood Edns.

Plechanoff, George. The Bourgeois Revolution. 3rd ed. Kuhn, Henry, tr. 1968. pap. text ed. 0.50 (ISBN 0-935534-05-9). NY Labor News.

Poree, Charles, ed. Departement de l'Yonne: Cahiers de doleances du bailliage de Sens pour les Etats-generaux du 1789. LC 74-29264. (Collection de la Commission d'histoire economique et sociale de la Revolution francaise). Repr. of 1908 ed. 60.00 (ISBN 0-404-58696-1). AMS Pr.

--Departement de l'Yonne: Cahiers des cures et des communautes ecclesiastiques du bailliage d'Auxerre de 1789. LC 74-29265. (Collection de la Commission d'histoire economique et sociale de la Revolution francaise). Repr. of 1927 ed. 40.00 (ISBN 0-404-58697-X). AMS Pr.

--Departement de l'Yonne: Documents relatifs a la vente des biens nationaux dans le district de Sens, 2 vols. LC 74-29266. (Collection de la Commission d'histoire economique et sociale de la Revolution francaise). Repr. of 1913 ed. Set. 105.00 (ISBN 0-404-58698-8). AMS Pr.

Powers, Elizabeth. The Journal of Madame Royale. LC 75-43990. (Illus.). 192p. (gr. 5 up). 1976. PLB 7.39 (ISBN 0-8027-6252-2). Walker & Co.

Rebillon, Armand, ed. Departement d'ille-et Vilaine. LC 74-29230. Repr. of 1913 ed. 65.00 (ISBN 0-404-58701-1). AMS Pr.

Robison, Georgia. Revelliere-Lepeaux, Citizen Director, 1753-1824. LC 72-8923. 308p. 1971. Repr. of 1938 ed. lib. bdg. 15.00x (ISBN 0-374-96893-4). Octagon.

Roland de la Platiere, Marie. The Private Memoirs of Madame Roland. 2nd ed. LC 78-37719. (Women of Letters Ser). (Illus.). Repr. of 1901 ed. 24.50 (ISBN 0-404-56829-7). AMS Pr.

Ross, Steven T., ed. The French Revolution: Conflict or Continuity? LC 77-21289. (European Problem Studies). 138p. 1978. pap. text ed. 5.50 (ISBN 0-88275-633-8). Krieger.

Rude, George. Crowd in the French Revolution. (Illus.). 1959. pap. text ed. 4.95x (ISBN 0-19-500370-5). Oxford U Pr.

Rutkoff, Peter M. Revanche & Revision: The Ligue des Patriotes & the Origins of the Radical Right in France, 1882-1900. LC 80-39575. x, 182p. 1981. text ed. 16.50x (ISBN 0-8214-0589-6). Ohio U Pr.

Sagnac, Philippe, ed. Les Comites des droits feodaux et de legislation et l'abolition du regime seigneurial 1780-1793. LC 74-29278. (Collection de la Commission d'histoire economique et sociale de la Revolution francaise). Repr. of 1907 ed. 60.00 (ISBN 0-404-58702-X). AMS Pr.

Saint-Just, Antoine L. Esprit De la Revolution et De la Constitution De France. 182p. 1981. Repr. of 1791 ed. lib. bdg. 80.00 (ISBN 0-8287-1569-6). Clearwater Pub.

Salvemini, Gaetano. French Revolution. 1962. pap. 2.25x (ISBN 0-393-00179-2, Norton Lib). Norton.

Savina, Jean, ed. Departement du Finistere: Cahiers de doleances des senechaussees de Quimper et de Concarneau pour les Etats-generaux de 1789, 2 vols. in 1. LC 74-29221. (Collection de la Commission d'histoire economique et sociale de la Revolution francaise). Repr. of 1927 ed. 35.00 (ISBN 0-404-58706-2). AMS Pr.

Scherr, Marie. Charlotte Corday & Certain Men of the Revolutionary Torment. LC 79-100512. Repr. of 1929 ed. 22.50 (ISBN 0-404-05588-5). AMS Pr.

Schwab, Leon, ed. Departement des Vosges: Documents relatifs a la vente des biens nationaux. District de Remiremont. LC 74-29263. (Collection de la Commission d'histoire economique et sociale de la Revolution francaise). Repr. of 1913 ed. 33.00 (ISBN 0-404-58708-9). AMS Pr.

--Departement des Vosges: Documents relatifs a la vente des biens nationaux. District d'Epinal. LC 74-29262. (Collection de la Commission d'histoire economique et sociale de la Revolution francaise). Repr. of 1911 ed. 33.00 (ISBN 0-404-58707-0). AMS Pr.

See, Henri E., ed. Departement d'Ille-et-Vilaine: Cahiers de doleances de la senechaussee de Rennes pour les Etats-generaux de 1789, 4 vols. LC 74-29231. (Collection de la Commission d'histoire economique et sociale de la Revolution francaise). Repr. of 1912 ed. Set. 205.00 (ISBN 0-404-58709-7). AMS Pr.

Sloane, William M. The French War & the Revolution. 1893. Repr. 15.00 (ISBN 0-685-43288-2). Norwood Edns.

Smyth, W. Lectures on the History of the French Revolution, 2 vols. new ed. LC 71-175988. Repr. of 1855 ed. Set. 41.00 (ISBN 0-404-06145-1). Vol. 1 (ISBN 0-404-06146-X). Vol. 2 (ISBN 0-404-06147-8). AMS Pr.

Sobel, Robert. French Revolution: A Concise History & Interpretation. 7.00 (ISBN 0-8446-0922-6). Peter Smith.

Soboul, A. The Sans-Culottes: The Popular Movement & Revolutionary Government, 1793-1794. 1980. 16.00 (ISBN 0-691-05320-0); pap. 4.95 (ISBN 0-691-00782-9). Princeton U Pr.

Soboul, Albert. The French Revolution, 1787-1799: From the Storming of the Bastille to Napoleon. 1975. pap. 5.95 (ISBN 0-394-71220-X, Vin). Random.

--The Parisian Sans-Culottes & the French Revolution, 1793-94. Lewis, Gwynne, tr. from Fr. LC 78-26780. 1979. Repr. of 1964 ed. lib. bdg. 22.50x (ISBN 0-313-20913-8, SOTP). Greenwood.

--A Short History of the French Revolution, 1789-1799. Symcox, Geoffrey, tr. 1977. 22.75x (ISBN 0-520-02855-4); pap. 4.95x (ISBN 0-520-03419-8). U of Cal Pr.

Stephens, Henry M., ed. The Principal Speeches of the Statesmen & Orators of the French Revolution, 1784-1795, 2 vols. 1973. lib. bdg. 75.00x set (ISBN 0-374-97623-6). Octagon.

Sydenham, M. J. The First French Republic, 1792-1804. 1974. 28.50x (ISBN 0-520-02577-6). U of Cal Pr.

--The Girondins. LC 72-4006. 252p. 1973. Repr. of 1961 ed. lib. bdg. 19.75x (ISBN 0-8371-6433-8, SYGI). Greenwood.

Szajkowski, Soza. Jews & the French Revolution of 1789, 1830 & 1848. 1969. 45.00x (ISBN 0-87068-112-5). Ktav.

Taine, Hippolyte A. The French Revolution, 3 vols. 8.00 ea. (ISBN 0-8446-1435-1). Peter Smith.

--The Origins of Contemporary France. Gargan, Edward T., ed. LC 73-87311. (Classic European Historians Ser.). 1978. pap. text ed. 5.00x (ISBN 0-226-78935-7). U of Chicago Pr.

Tames, Richard. The French Revolution. Killingray, Margaret, et al, eds. (Wolrd History Ser.). (Illus.). 32p. (gr. 10). 1980. Repr. lib. bdg. 5.95 (ISBN 0-89908-136-3); pap. text ed. 1.95 (ISBN 0-89908-111-8). Greenhaven.

Their Gracious Pleasure, Vol. 3. LC 80-36724. (The French Revolution Ser.). (Illus.). 480p. 1981. 19.95 (ISBN 0-394-50155-1). Knopf.

Thiers, Louis A. The History of the French Revolution, 5 vols. facs. new ed. Shoberl, Frederick, tr. LC 78-179541. (Select Bibliographies Reprint Ser.). (Illus.). Repr. of 1881 ed. Set. 175.00 (ISBN 0-8369-6670-8). Arno.

Thompson, J. M. The French Revolution. 2nd ed. (Illus.). 544p. 1966. pap. 10.95x (ISBN 0-631-11921-3, Pub. by Basil Blackwell). Biblio Dist.

--Leaders of the French Revolution. (Illus.). 272p. 1968. pap. 9.95x (ISBN 0-631-11931-0, Pub. by Basil Blackwell). Biblio Dist.

Thompson, James M., ed. English Witnesses of the French Revolution. LC 71-110925. 1970. Repr. of 1938 ed. 12.50 (ISBN 0-8046-0907-1). Kennikat.

Tocqueville, Alexis De. The European Revolution & Correspondence with Gobineau. Lukacs, John, ed. & tr. LC 74-9040. 340p. 1975. Repr. of 1959 ed. lib. bdg. 22.75x (ISBN 0-8371-7603-4, TOER). Greenwood.

Toulouse. Comite des subsistances, 1793-1795. Le Comite des subsistances de Toulouse 12 aout 1793-mars 1795: Correspondance et deliberations. LC 74-29223. (Collection de la Commission d'histoire economique et sociale de la Revolution francaise). Repr. of 1912 ed. 32.00 (ISBN 0-404-58714-3). AMS Pr.

Tuckerman, Bayard. Life of General Lafayette, 2 Vols. LC 72-177575. Repr. of 1889 ed. Set. 45.00 (ISBN 0-404-07187-2). Vol. 1 (ISBN 0-404-07188-0). Vol. 2 (ISBN 0-404-07189-9). AMS Pr.

Vernier, Jules J., ed. Departement de l'Aube: Cahiers de doleances du bailliage de Troyes (principal et secondaires) et du bailliage de Bar-sur-Seine pour les Etats-generaux de 1789, 3 vols. LC 74-29214. (Collection de la Commission d'histoire economique et sociale de la Revolution francaise). Repr. of 1911 ed. Set. 160.00 (ISBN 0-404-58715-1). AMS Pr.

Vicomterie De Saint-Sanson. Les Droits Du Peuple Sur L'assemblee Nationale. (Rousseauism, 1788-1797). 1978. Repr. lib. bdg. 62.00x (ISBN 0-8287-0859-2). Clearwater Pub.

Villette, Charles-Michel. Protestation D'un Serf Du Mont-Jura, Contre L'assemblee Des Notables. Repr. of 1789 ed. 5.00 (ISBN 0-8287-0871-1). Clearwater Pub.

Voegelin, Eric. From Enlightenment to Revolution. Hallowell, John H., ed. LC 74-81864. ix, 307p. 1975. 16.75 (ISBN 0-8223-0326-4). Duke.

Voeu Sur la Derniere Classe Du Peuple a L'assemblee Des Notables. Repr. of 1787 ed. 7.00 (ISBN 0-8287-0874-6). Clearwater Pub.

Webster, Nesta. The French Revolution: A Study in Democracy. 75.00 (ISBN 0-8490-0199-4). Gordon Pr.

Webster, Nesta H. French Revolution. 1975. pap. 6.00 (ISBN 0-913022-15-2). Angriff Pr.

Whitham, J. Mills. Biographical History of the French Revolution. facs. ed. LC 68-24860. (Essay Index Reprint Ser). 1968. Repr. of 1931 ed. 20.50 (ISBN 0-8369-0989-5). Arno.

--Men & Women of the French Revolution. facs. ed. LC 68-20346. (Essay Index Reprint Ser). 1933. 18.50 (ISBN 0-8369-0990-9). Arno.

Williams, Gwyn A. Artisans & Sans-Culottes. LC 69-14476. (Foundations of Modern History Ser). 1969. pap. text ed. 3.95x (ISBN 0-393-09832-X, NortonC). Norton.

Williams, Helen M. Letters from France, 8 vols. in 2. LC 75-22224. 2050p. 1975. 150.00x set (ISBN 0-8201-1158-9). Schol Facsimiles.

Wilson, R. McNair. Women of the French Revolution. 75.00 (ISBN 0-8490-1324-0). Gordon Pr.

Woloch, Isser. Jacobin Legacy: The Democratic Movement Under the Directory. LC 76-83689. 1960. 30.00x (ISBN 0-691-06183-1). Princeton U Pr.

Wright, D., ed. The French Revolution: Introductory Documents. 1974. pap. 8.95x (ISBN 0-7022-0923-6). U of Queensland Pr.

Wright, D. G. Revolution & Terror in France 1789-95. (Seminar Studies in History). 146p. 1974. pap. text ed. 5.50x (ISBN 0-582-35209-6). Longman.

FRANCE–HISTORY–REVOLUTION, 1789-1799–BIBLIOGRAPHY

Boissonnade, Prosper. Etudes relatives a l'histoire economique de la Revolution francaise. 1967. Repr. of 1906 ed. 22.50 (ISBN 0-8337-0331-5). B Franklin.

Gliozzo, Charles A. Bibliography of Ecclesiastical History of the French Revolution. LC 73-154506. (Bibliographia Tripotamopolitana: No. 6). 1972. 8.00 (ISBN 0-931222-05-2). C E Barbour.

Horward, Donald D. The French Revolution & Napoleon Collection at Florida State University: A Bibliographical Guide. LC 72-89895. 450p. 1972. 12.50 (ISBN 0-686-02405-2). Friends Fla St.

Paris Commune, 1789-1794. Actes de la Commune de Paris pendant la Revolution, 9 vols. LC 73-15863. (Second Ser.). Repr. of 1955 ed. Set. 479.25 (ISBN 0-404-52630-6); 53.25 ea. AMS Pr.

Posner, Charles. Reflections on the Revolution in France: 1968. 6.75 (ISBN 0-8446-0852-1). Peter Smith.

Thompson, Lawrence S. A Bibliography of French Revolutionary Pamphlets on Microfiche. LC 74-18197. 653p. 1974. 25.00x (ISBN 0-87875-047-9). Whitston Pub.

Weiner, Margery. The French Exiles, 1789-1815. LC 75-15941. (Illus.). 240p. 1975. Repr. of 1961 ed. lib. bdg. 15.00x (ISBN 0-8371-8220-4, WEFE). Greenwood.

FRANCE–HISTORY–REVOLUTION, 1789-1799–CAUSES AND CHARACTER

Alengry, Frank. Condorcet: Guide de la Revolution francaise, theoricien du droit constitutionnel et precurseur de la science sociale. LC 79-159691. xxiii, 891p. (Fr.). 1972. Repr. of 1904 ed. lib. bdg. 43.00 (ISBN 0-8337-3925-5). B Franklin.

Annales De la Confederation Universelle Des Amis De la Verite. (Le Cercle Social). (Fr.). 1978. lib. bdg. 23.75x (ISBN 0-8287-1327-8). Clearwater Pub.

Beik, Paul H. The French Revolution Seen from the Right. p ed. LC 70-80523. 1971. Repr. of 1956 ed. 17.50 (ISBN 0-86527-074-0). Fertig.

Bergeron, Louis. France Under Napoleon. Palmer, R. R., tr. from Fr. LC 81-47115. (Illus.). 240p. 1981. 18.75 (ISBN 0-691-05333-2); pap. 5.95x (ISBN 0-691-00789-6). Princeton U Pr.

Billington, James H. Fire in the Minds of Men. LC 79-2750. 677p. 1980. 25.00 (ISBN 0-465-02405-X). Basic.

Buonarroti, Philippe. History of Babeuf's Conspiracy for Equality. O'Brien, Bronterre, tr. LC 64-7661. Repr. of 1836 ed. 25.00x (ISBN 0-678-00087-5). Kelley.

Burke, Edmond. Reflections on the Revolution in France. Bd. with The Rights of Man. Paine, Thomas (Anchor). Doubleday. pap. 3.95 (ISBN 0-385-08190-1, Anch). Doubleday.

Burke, Edmund. Reflections on the Revolution in France. Mahoney, Thomas H., ed. 1955. pap. 6.95 (ISBN 0-672-60213-X, LLA46). Bobbs.

Cobb, Richard C. Reactions to the French Revolution. 1972. 22.00x (ISBN 0-19-212187-1). Oxford U Pr.

Cobban, Alfred. Myth of the French Revolution. LC 74-7278. 1955. lib. bdg. 10.00 (ISBN 0-8414-3581-2). Folcroft.

Comparative Display of the Different Opinions of the Most Distinguished British Writers on the Subject of the French Revolution, 3 Vols. LC 76-131515. Repr. of 1811 ed. Set. 112.50 (ISBN 0-404-01800-9); 37.50 ea. Vol. 1 (ISBN 0-404-01801-7). Vol. 2 (ISBN 0-404-01802-5). Vol. 3 (ISBN 0-404-01803-3). AMS Pr.

De Tocqueville, Alexis. Old Regime & the French Revolution. Gilbert, Stuart, tr. 8.00 (ISBN 0-8446-1973-6). Peter Smith.

Doyle, William. Origins of the French Revolution. 272p. 1981. 37.50 (ISBN 0-19-873020-9); pap. 14.95 (ISBN 0-19-873021-7). Oxford U Pr.

Elton, Godfrey. The Revolutionary Idea in France, 1789-1871. 1969. 7.00 (ISBN 0-86527-170-4). Fertig.

Elton, Godfrey E. Revolutionary Idea in France, 1789-1871. 2nd ed. LC 74-147116. Repr. of 1931 ed. 17.50 (ISBN 0-404-02325-8). AMS Pr.

Fay, Bernard. Revolutionary Spirit in France and America. Guthrie, Ramon, tr. LC 66-26824. Repr. of 1927 ed. 16.50x (ISBN 0-8154-0067-5). Cooper Sq.

Furet, Francois M. Interpreting the French Revolution. Forster, Elborg, tr. LC 80-42290. 224p. Date not set. price not set (ISBN 0-521-23574-X); pap. price not set (ISBN 0-521-28049-4). Cambridge U Pr.

Gentz, Friedrich Von. The Origin & Principles of the American Revolution, Compared with the Origin & Principles of the French Revolution. Loss, Richard, ed. LC 77-16175. 1977. Repr. of 1800 ed. lib. bdg. 20.00 (ISBN 0-8201-1302-6). Schol Facsimiles.

Gomel, Charles. Causes Financieres De la Revolution Francaise, 2 vols. 1892-93. Set. 55.00 (ISBN 0-8337-1374-4); 30.00 ea. (ISBN 0-8337-1374-4). B Franklin.

Halevy, Elie. The Growth of Philosophic Radicalism, 3 pts. rev. ed. Incl. Pt. 1. The Youth of Bentham; Pt. 2. The Evolution of the Utilitarian Doctrine from 1789 to 1815; Pt. 3. Philosophic Radicalism. LC 72-85214. xix, 554p. Repr. of 1952 ed. 13.50x (ISBN 0-678-08005-4). Kelley.

Johnson, D. French Society & the Revolution. LC 76-1136. (Past and Present Publications Ser.). 300p. 1976. 26.95 (ISBN 0-521-21275-8). Cambridge U Pr.

Kropotkin, Peter. The Great French Revolution. Dryhurst, N. F., tr. from Fr. LC 75-163336. (Studies in the Libertarian & Utopian Tradition). 1971. 10.00x (ISBN 0-8052-3421-7); pap. 4.50 (ISBN 0-8052-0317-6). Schocken.

Lefebvre, Georges. Great Fear of Seventeen Eighty-Nine: Rural Panic in Revolutionary France. White, Joan, tr. 1973. pap. 1.95 (ISBN 0-394-71939-5, Vin). Random.

Lichtenberger, Andre. Socialisme Au Dix-Huitieme Siecle. LC 67-27835. (Fr). Repr. of 1895 ed. 22.50x (ISBN 0-678-00329-7). Kelley.

Mallet Du Pan, Jacques. Considerations on the Nature of the French Revolution & on the Causes Which Prolong Its Duration. LC 74-13491. xxii, 114p. 1975. Repr. of 1793 ed. 17.50 (ISBN 0-86527-032-5). Fertig.

Michelet. Histoire de la Revolution Francaise: Livres I a VIII, Vol. 1. 1568p. 41.50 (ISBN 0-686-56541-X). French & Eur.

--Histoire de la Revolution Francaise: Livres IX a XXI - Tableau Chronologique, Vol. 2. 1696p. 42.95 (ISBN 0-686-56542-8). French & Eur.

Michelet, Jules. History of the French Revolution. Wright, Gordon, ed. Cocks, Charles, tr. (Classical European Historians Ser.). 1967. 15.00x (ISBN 0-226-52332-2). U of Chicago Pr.

--History of the French Revolution. Wright, Gordon, ed. Cocks, Charles, tr. LC 67-15315. 1967. pap. 8.50x (ISBN 0-226-52333-0, P257, Phoen). U of Chicago Pr.

Paine, Thomas. Rights of Man. 1935. 9.95x (ISBN 0-460-00718-1, Evman). Biblio Dist.

--Rights of Man. 1976. pap. 3.95 (ISBN 0-8065-0548-6). Citadel Pr.

Parker, Harold T. Cult of Antiquity & the French Revolutionaries. 1965. lib. bdg. 11.00x (ISBN 0-374-96251-0). Octagon.

Roberts, J. M. The French Revolution. 1979. pap. text ed. 5.95 (ISBN 0-19-289069-7). Oxford U Pr.

Rogers, Cornwell B. Spirit of Revolution in Seventeen Eighty Nine: A Study of Public Opinion As Revealed in the Political Songs & Other Popular Literature. Repr. of 1949 ed. lib. bdg. 15.75x (ISBN 0-8371-1632-5, ROSR). Greenwood.

Roustan, Marius. The Pioneers of the French Revolution. LC 68-9659. 1970. Repr. of 1926 ed. 20.00 (ISBN 0-86527-150-X). Fertig.

Scott, John A., ed. The Defense of Gracchus Babeuf Before the High Court of Vendome: Essay by Herbert Marcuse. Scott, John A., tr. LC 67-11244. (Illus.). 120p. 1967. 10.00x (ISBN 0-87023-024-7). U of Mass Pr.

Slavin, Morris & Smith, Agnes M., eds. Bourgeois, Sans-Culottes, & Other Frenchmen: (Essays on the French Revolution in Honor of John Hall Stewart) 139p. 1981. text ed. 11.00x (ISBN 0-88920-097-1, Pub. by Laurier U Pr). Humanities.

Stourm, Rene. Finances de l'Ancient Regime et de la Revolution, 2 Vols. LC 68-56718. (Research & Source Works Ser.: No. 203). (Fr). 1968. Repr. of 1885 ed. Set. 55.50 (ISBN 0-8337-3429-6). B Franklin.

Tierney, Brian, et al, eds. The Origins of the French Revolution: Popular Misery, Social Ambitions, or Philosophical Ideas? 3rd ed. (Historical Pamphlets). 1977. pap. text ed. 1.95x (ISBN 0-394-32058-1). Random.

Tocqueville, Alexis de. Old Regime & the French Revolution. Mayer, J. P. & Kerr, A. P., eds. LC 55-10160. 1955. pap. 3.50 (ISBN 0-385-09260-1, A60, Anch). Doubleday.

Van Duzer, Charles H. Contributions of the Ideologues to French Revolutionary Thought. LC 78-64160. (Johns Hopkins University. Studies in the Social Sciences. Fifty-Third Ser. 1935: 4). Repr. of 1935 ed. 18.50 (ISBN 0-404-61270-9). AMS Pr.

Wollstonecraft, Mary. An Historical & Moral View of the Origin & Progress of the French Revolution & the Effect It Has Produced in Europe. LC 74-28416. 530p. 1975. Repr. of 1794 ed. lib. bdg. 55.00x (ISBN 0-8201-1149-X). Schol Facsimiles.

FRANCE–HISTORY–REVOLUTION, 1789-1799–FICTION

Dickens, Charles. Tale of Two Cities. Woodcock, George, ed. (English Library Ser). 1970. pap. 1.95 (ISBN 0-14-043054-7). Penguin.

--Tale of Two Cities. (Classics Ser). (gr. 9 up). 1964. pap. 1.95 (ISBN 0-8049-0021-3, CL-21). Airmont.

--Tale of Two Cities. (Literature Ser). (gr. 7-12). 1969. pap. text ed. 4.00 (ISBN 0-87720-716-X). AMSCO Sch.

--Tale of Two Cities. pap. 1.95 (ISBN 0-440-98465-3, LFL). Dell.

--Tale of Two Cities. 1958. 10.95x (ISBN 0-460-00102-7, Evman); pap. 2.50x (ISBN 0-460-01102-2, Evman). Biblio Dist.

--Tale of Two Cities. (Illus.). (gr. 4-6). 1948. il. jr. lib. 5.95 (ISBN 0-448-05823-5); deluxe ed. 8.95 (ISBN 0-448-06023-X). G&D.

--Tale of Two Cities. (Illus.). (gr. 9 up). 1962. 4.95 (ISBN 0-02-730530-9); PLB 4.94 (ISBN 0-02-730540-6). Macmillan.

--Tale of Two Cities. 1962. pap. 1.25 (ISBN 0-02-050400-4, Collier). Macmillan.

--Tale of Two Cities. (RL 7). 1960. pap. 1.95 (ISBN 0-451-51490-4, CJ1490, Sig Classics). NAL.

France, Anatole. The Gods Are Athirst. 349p. 1980. Repr. of 1978 ed. lib. bdg. 22.50 (ISBN 0-8414-1995-7). Folcroft.

Sabatini, Rafael. Scaramouche. 10.95 (ISBN 0-395-08142-4). HM.

Trease, Geoffrey. Victory at Valmy. LC 60-15072. (gr. 7-11). 1960. 7.95 (ISBN 0-8149-0427-0). Vanguard.

FRANCE–HISTORY–REVOLUTION, 1789-1799–FOREIGN PUBLIC OPINION

Godechot, Jacques. Counter-Revolution, Doctrine & Action, Seventeen Eighty-Nine to Eighteen Four. LC 70-159820. 1971. 25.00 (ISBN 0-86527-035-X). Fertig.

Hazen, Charles D. Contemporary American Opinion of the French Revolution. 1964. 7.75 (ISBN 0-8446-1228-6). Peter Smith.

--Contemporary American Opinion of the French Revolution. 59.95 (ISBN 0-87968-936-6). Gordon Pr.

--Contemporary American Opinion of the French Revolution. LC 78-64261. (Johns Hopkins University. Studies in the Social Sciences. Extra Volume: 16). Repr. of 1897 ed. 11.50 (ISBN 0-404-61364-0). AMS Pr.

Sears, Louis M. George Washington & the French Revolution. LC 73-8258. 378p. 1973. Repr. of 1960 ed. lib. bdg. 17.00x (ISBN 0-8371-6975-5, SEGW). Greenwood.

Story, G. D., ed. British Reactions to the French Revolution, 1789-1815. (Themes in Modern History Ser., Documentary Research Folder No. 2). 1972. 6.95 (ISBN 0-7022-0807-8). U of Queensland Pr.

Thompson, James M., ed. English Witnesses of the French Revolution. LC 71-110925. 1970. Repr. of 1938 ed. 12.50 (ISBN 0-8046-0907-1). Kennikat.

FRANCE–HISTORY–REVOLUTION, 1789-1799–INFLUENCE ON LITERATURE

Cestre, Charles. La Revolution Francaise et les Poetes Anglais, 1789-1809. 1972. Repr. of 1906 ed. lib. bdg. 50.00 (ISBN 0-8414-0108-X). Folcroft.

Dowden, Edward. The French Revolution & English Literature. LC 76-22533. Repr. of 1897 ed. lib. bdg. 25.00 (ISBN 0-8414-3714-9). Folcroft.

Hancock, Albert E. French Revolution & the English Poets: Study in Historical Criticism. LC 67-27605. 1967. Repr. of 1899 ed. 12.50 (ISBN 0-8046-0193-3). Kennikat.

FRANCE–HISTORY–REVOLUTION, 1789-1799–PHILOSOPHY

see France–History–Revolution, 1789-1799–Causes and Character

FRANCE–HISTORY–REVOLUTION, 1789-1799–PICTORIAL WORKS

Dowd, David L. Pageant-Master of the Republic. facs. ed. LC 72-75507. (Select Bibliographies Reprint Ser). 1948. 22.00 (ISBN 0-8369-5005-4). Arno.

FRANCE–HISTORY–REVOLUTION, 1789-1799–SOURCES

Annales De la Confederation Universelle Des Amis De la Verite. (Le Cercle Social). (Fr.). 1978. lib. bdg. 23.75x (ISBN 0-8287-1327-8). Clearwater Pub.

La Bien Informe. (Le Cercle Social). (Fr.). 1978. lib. bdg. 1235.00x (ISBN 0-8287-1334-0). Clearwater Pub.

Bonneville, Nicolas De, ed. Le Tribun Du Peuple. (Le Cercle Social). (Fr.). 1978. lib. bdg. 65.00x (ISBN 0-8287-1425-8). Clearwater Pub.

--Le Vieux Tribun Du Peuple. (Le Cercle Social). (Fr.). 1978. lib. bdg. 79.00x (ISBN 0-8287-1431-2). Clearwater Pub.

--Le Vieux Tribun Du Peuple et Sa Bouche De Fer. (Le Cercle Social). (Fr.). 1978. lib. bdg. 145.00x (ISBN 0-8287-1430-4). Clearwater Pub.

Bulletin De la Bouche De Fer. (Le Cercle Social). (Fr.). 1978. lib. bdg. 22.35x (ISBN 0-8287-1338-3). Clearwater Pub.

Cercle Social. (Le Cercle Social). (Fr.). 1978. lib. bdg. 206.00x (ISBN 0-8287-1340-5). Clearwater Pub.

Chassin, Charles L. Les Elections et les cahiers de Paris en 1789, 4 vols. LC 76-38039. Repr. of 1889 ed. Set. 213.00 (ISBN 0-404-52590-3); 53.25 ea.; Vol. 1. (ISBN 0-404-52591-1); Vol. 2. (ISBN 0-404-52592-X); Vol. 3. (ISBN 0-404-52593-8); Vol. 4. (ISBN 0-404-52594-6). AMS Pr.

La Chronique Du Mois Ou les Cahiers Patriotiques. (Le Cercle Social). (Fr.). 1978. lib. bdg. 533.00x (ISBN 0-8287-1345-6). Clearwater Pub.

Ellery, Eloise. Brissot De Warville: A Study in the History of the French Revolution. LC 71-130601. (Research & Source Works: No. 536). 1970. Repr. of 1915 ed. 20.50 (ISBN 0-8337-1032-X). B Franklin.

Fauchet, Claude & Bonneville, Nicolas De, eds. La Bouche De Fer. (Le Cercle Social). (Fr.). 1978. lib. bdg. 615.25x (ISBN 0-8287-1335-9). Clearwater Pub.

France: Commission d'Histoire Economique et Sociale de la Revolution Francaise. Collection de Documents, 99 vols. in 65 sets. 1975. Repr. of 1953 ed. Complete Set. 4250.00 (ISBN 0-404-58600-7). AMS Pr.

Gilchrist, W. & Murray, W. J., eds. Press in the French Revolution. LC 77-150256. 1971. 28.50x (ISBN 0-89197-596-9). Irvington.

Hyslop, Beatrice F. Guide to the General Cahiers of 1789, with the Texts of Unedited Cahiers. 1968. lib. bdg. 17.50x (ISBN 0-374-94104-1). Octagon.

Lorthe, Gabriel A. De. Eloge De J. J. Rousseau Mis Au Concours De 1790. (Rousseauism: 1788-1797). (Fr.). 1978. Repr. of 1790 ed. lib. bdg. 33.50x (ISBN 0-8287-0554-2). Clearwater Pub.

Madame De Stael. Lettres Sur les Ouvrages et la Caractere De J. J. Rousseau. (Rousseauism: 1788-1797). (Fr.). 1978. Repr. of 1788 ed. lib. bdg. 42.00x (ISBN 0-8287-0793-6). Clearwater Pub.

Mathiez, Albert. Requisitions De Grains Sous la Terreur. (Revue D'histoire Economique et Sociale: Vol. 8). (Fr.). 1973. Repr. of 1920 ed. lib. bdg. 15.00 (ISBN 0-8337-2298-0). B Franklin.

Mercier, Louis S. De J. J. Rousseau, Considere Comme L'un Des Premiers Auteurs De la Revolution. (Rousseauism: 1788-1797). (Fr.). 1978. Repr. of 1791 ed. lib. bdg. 170.00x (ISBN 0-8287-0601-8). Clearwater Pub.

Monti, Laura V., compiled by. French Revolutionary Pamphlets at the University of Florida. LC 74-182319. v, 166p. 1971. 8.50 (ISBN 0-8130-0350-4). U Presses Fla.

Morisse, Avocat. Essai Sur la Nature et L'exercice De L'autorite Du Peuple Dans un Etat. (Rousseauism: 1788-1797). (Fr.). 1978. Repr. of 1789 ed. lib. bdg. 39.00x (ISBN 0-8287-0642-5). Clearwater Pub.

Regnault-Warin, Jean-Joseph. Elements De Politique. (Rousseauism: 1788-1797). (Fr.). 1978. Repr. of 1792 ed. lib. bdg. 63.50x (ISBN 0-8287-0711-1). Clearwater Pub.

Robiquet, Paul. Le Personnel municipal de Paris pendant la Revolution. LC 73-174332. (Collection de documents relatifs a l'histoire de Paris pendant la Revolution francaise). Repr. of 1890 ed. 53.25 (ISBN 0-404-52557-1). AMS Pr.

Saige, Joseph. Code National, Ou Manuel Francais a L'usage Des 3 Orders, et Principalement Des Deputes Aux Prochains Etats Generaux. (Rousseauism: 1788-1797). (Fr.). 1978. Repr. of 1789 ed. lib. bdg. 58.00x (ISBN 0-8287-0748-0). Clearwater Pub.

Salaville, Jean-Babtise. De L'organisation D'un Etat Monarchique Ou Considerations Sur les Vices De la Monarchie Francaise et Sur la Necessite De Lui Donner une Constitution. (Rousseauism: 1788-1797). (Fr.). 1978. Repr. of 1789 ed. lib. bdg. 49.00x (ISBN 0-8287-0756-1). Clearwater Pub.

Thiery, Avocat. Eloge De J. J. Rousseau, Qui a Concouru Pour le Prix D'eloquence De L'academie Francaise, En L'annee 1791. (Rousseauism: 1788-1797). (Fr.). 1978. Repr. of 1791 ed. lib. bdg. 30.50x (ISBN 0-8287-0817-7). Clearwater Pub.

Thompson, Lawrence S. A Bibliography of French Revolutionary Pamphlets on Microfiche. LC 74-18197. 653p. 1974. 25.00x (ISBN 0-87875-047-9). Whitston Pub.

Wolfe, Martin, et al, eds. Maclure Collection of French Revolutionary Materials. LC 64-24489. 1966. 50.00x (ISBN 0-8122-7378-8). U of Pa Pr.

FRANCE–HISTORY–CONSULATE AND EMPIRE, 1799-1815

see also Continental System of Napoleon; Trafalgar (Cape), Battle Of, 1805; Waterloo, Battle Of, 1815

Aulard, Francois V. Paris sous le Consulat, 4 vols. LC 74-161714. (Collection de documents relatifs a l'histoire de Paris pendant la Revolution francaise). Repr. of 1909 ed. Set. 213.00 (ISBN 0-404-52580-6); 53.25 ea.; Vol. 1. (ISBN 0-404-52581-4); Vol. 2. (ISBN 0-404-52582-2); Vol. 3. (ISBN 0-404-52583-0); Vol. 4. (ISBN 0-404-52584-9). AMS Pr.

Barante, Amable G. Histoire du directoire de la Republique francaise, 3 vols. LC 71-161740. Repr. of 1855 ed. Set. 110.00 (ISBN 0-404-07770-6); Vol. 1. (ISBN 0-404-07771-4); Vol. 2. (ISBN 0-404-07772-2); Vol. 3. (ISBN 0-404-07773-0). AMS Pr.

Burton, June. Napoleon & Clio: Historical Writing, Teaching, & Thinking During the First Empire. LC 77-88659. 1979. 11.95 (ISBN 0-89089-077-3). Carolina Acad Pr.

Chateaubriand, Rene de. Napoleon. 1969. 7.95 (ISBN 0-686-54372-6). French & Eur.

Connelly, Owen. The Epoch of Napoleon. LC 77-13473. 208p. 1978. pap. text ed. 6.25 (ISBN 0-88275-622-2). Krieger.

--Napoleon's Satellite Kingdoms. LC 66-10336. 1970. pap. 2.95 (ISBN 0-02-906600-X). Free Pr.

Deutsch, Harold C. The Genesis of Napoleonic Imperialism. LC 75-25811. (Perspectives in European Hist. Ser.: No. 4). 460p. Repr. of 1938 ed. lib. bdg. 25.00x (ISBN 0-87991-611-7). Porcupine Pr.

Jaunez-Sponville, Pierre-Ignace & Bugnet, Nicolas. La Philosophie de Ruravebohni, 2 vols. (Utopias in the Enlightenment Ser.). 575p. (Fr.). 1974. Repr. of 1809 ed. Set. lib. bdg. 154.00x (ISBN 0-8287-0462-7). Clearwater Pub.

Johnson, David. Napoleon's Cavalry & Its Leaders. LC 78-5596. (Illus.). 1978. text ed. 24.50x (ISBN 0-8419-0390-5). Holmes & Meier.

Lefebvre, Georges. Napoleon: From Eighteen Brumaire to Tilsit, 1799-1807. Stockhold, Henry F., tr. LC 68-29160. 337p. 1969. 20.00x (ISBN 0-231-02558-0). Columbia U Pr.

--Napoleon: From Tilsit to Waterloo, 1807-1815. Anderson, J. E., tr. LC 74-79193. 414p. 1969. 20.00x (ISBN 0-231-03313-3). Columbia U Pr.

Madelin, Louis. Consulate & Empire, 2 Vols. LC 34-10700. (National History of France: No. 7). Repr. of 1936 ed. Set. 60.00 (ISBN 0-404-50810-3); 30.00 ea. Vol. 1 (ISBN 0-404-50808-1). Vol. 2 (ISBN 0-404-50809-X). AMS Pr.

Mahan, Alfred T. Influence of Sea Power Upon the French Revolution & Empire, 2 Vols. 1898. 34.00 (ISBN 0-403-00193-5). Scholarly.

--Influence of Sea Power Upon the French Revolution & Empire 1793-1812, 2 Vols. 10th ed. LC 69-10127. (Illus.). 1968. Repr. of 1898 ed. Set. lib. bdg. 35.25x (ISBN 0-8371-2666-5, MASP). Greenwood.

Napoleon I. Memoirs of the History of France During the Reign of Napoleon: Dictated by the Emperor at St. Helena to the General Who Shared His Captivities, 4 vols. Date not set. Repr. of 1823 ed. Set. 75.00 (ISBN 0-685-33292-6). Fertig.

Parker, Harold T. The Bureau of Manufacturers During the French Revolution & Empire, & Under Napoleon. LC 77-88658. 1979. 14.95 (ISBN 0-89089-076-5). Carolina Acad Pr.

Petre, F. Loraine. Napoleon's Conquest of Prussia, 1806. LC 77-72679. 1977. 14.95 (ISBN 0-88254-435-7). Hippocrene Bks.

Phipps, Ramsay W. The Armies of the First French Republic & the Rise of the Marshals of Napoleon I, 5 vols. LC 79-23801. (Illus.). 1980. Repr. of 1939 ed. Set. lib. bdg. 200.00x (ISBN 0-313-22208-8, PHAR). Greenwood.

Sloane, William M. Life of Napoleon Bonaparte, 4 Vols. (Illus.). Repr. of 1910 ed. Set. 130.00 (ISBN 0-404-06100-1); 32.50 ea. Vol. 1 (ISBN 0-404-06101-X). Vol. 2 (ISBN 0-404-06102-8). Vol. 3 (ISBN 0-404-06103-6). Vol. 4 (ISBN 0-404-06104-4). AMS Pr.

Stendhal. Napoleon, 2 vols. Abravanel, Ernest & Del Litto, Victor, eds. (Illus.). 1970. 9.95 ea. French & Eur.

--Napoleon, 2 vols. facsimile ed. Set. 100.00 (ISBN 0-686-55074-9). French & Eur.

Sutherland, Christine. Maria Walewska: Napoleon's Great Love. (Illus.). 1979. 9.95 (ISBN 0-670-28473-4, The Vendome Pr). Viking Pr.

Sydenham, M. J. The First French Republic, 1792-1804. 1974. 28.50x (ISBN 0-520-02577-6). U of Cal Pr.

Walsh, Henry H. Concordat of 1801. LC 34-12835. (Columbia University. Studies in the Social Sciences: No. 387). Repr. of 1933 ed. 21.00 (ISBN 0-404-51387-5). AMS Pr.

Warner, Richard. Napoleon's Enemies. (Illus.). 1977. 14.95 (ISBN 0-85045-172-8). Hippocrene Bks.

Young, Arthur. Travels in France & Italy. Date not set. 8.95x (ISBN 0-460-00720-3, Evman). Biblio Dist.

FRANCE–HISTORY–CONSULATE AND EMPIRE, 1799-1815–BIBLIOGRAPHY

Bridge, John S. A History of France from the Death of Louis Sixteenth, 5 vols. 1972. lib. bdg. 97.50x (ISBN 0-374-90984-9). Octagon.

Sloane, William M. Life of Napoleon Bonaparte, 4 Vols. (Illus.). Repr. of 1910 ed. Set. 130.00 (ISBN 0-404-06100-1); 32.50 ea. Vol. 1 (ISBN 0-404-06101-X). Vol. 2 (ISBN 0-404-06102-8). Vol. 3 (ISBN 0-404-06103-6). Vol. 4 (ISBN 0-404-06104-4). AMS Pr.

FRANCE–HISTORY–RESTORATION, 1814-1830

Artz, Frederick B. France Under the Bourbon Restoration, 1814-1830. LC 63-11027. (Illus.). 1963. Repr. of 1931 ed. 22.00 (ISBN 0-8462-0380-4). Russell.

Bezucha, Robert J. The Lyon Uprising of 1834: Social & Political Conflict in the Early July Monarchy. LC 74-75780. (Studies in Urban History). 288p. 1974. text ed. 15.00x (ISBN 0-674-53965-6). Harvard U Pr.

Lucas-Dubreton, Jean. Restoration & the July Monarchy. LC 29-16694. (National History of France: No. 8). Repr. of 1929 ed. 30.00 (ISBN 0-404-50798-0). AMS Pr.

Macaulay, Thomas B. Napoleon & the Restoration of the Bourbons: The Complete Portion of Macaulay's Projected History of France from the Restoration of the Bourbons to the Accession of Louis Phillipe. LC 77-7107. 117p. 1977. 15.00x (ISBN 0-231-04376-7). Columbia U Pr.

Porch, Douglas. Army & Revolution: France 1815-1848. (Illus.). 198p. 1974. 15.00x (ISBN 0-7100-7460-3). Routledge & Kegan.

Resnick, Daniel P. The White Terror & the Political Reaction After Waterloo. LC 66-18254. (Historical Studies: No. 77). 1966. 7.00x (ISBN 0-674-95190-5). Harvard U Pr.

Stearns, Peter N. Paths to Authority: The Middle Class & the Industrial Labor Force in France, 1820-48. LC 78-16223. 1978. 12.95 (ISBN 0-252-00633-X). U of Ill Pr.

Stewart, J. H. The Restoration Era in France 1814-1830. 4.75 (ISBN 0-8446-3013-6). Peter Smith.

FRANCE–HISTORY–RESTORATION, 1814-1830 BIBLIOGRAPHY

Wilson, R. McNair. Women of the French Revolution. LC 72-110928. 1970. Repr. of 1936 ed. 12.50 (ISBN 0-8046-0910-1). Kennikat.

FRANCE–HISTORY–1830-1848

Blanc, Louis. History of Ten Years, 1830-1840, 2 Vols. LC 68-56841. Repr. of 1845 ed. 50.00x (ISBN 0-678-00448-X). Kelley.

Dumas, Alexandre. Les Barricades de Juillet: Avec: 20 Pages du Petit Journal Illustre. 192p. 1975. 7.95 (ISBN 0-686-55837-5). French & Eur.

Pinkney, D. H. The French Revolution of 1830. Halsey, F. D., tr. 1972. 28.00 (ISBN 0-691-05202-6). Princeton U Pr.

Porch, Douglas. Army & Revolution: France 1815-1848. (Illus.). 198p. 1974. 15.00x (ISBN 0-7100-7460-3). Routledge & Kegan.

Stearns, Peter N. Paths to Authority: The Middle Class & the Industrial Labor Force in France, 1820-48. LC 78-16223. 1978. 12.95 (ISBN 0-252-00633-X). U of Ill Pr.

FRANCE–HISTORY–FEBRUARY REVOLUTION, 1848

Amann, Peter H. Revolution & Mass Democracy: The Paris Club Movement of 1848. LC 74-2959. 320p. 1975. 24.00 (ISBN 0-691-05223-9). Princeton U Pr.

De Luna, Frederick A. French Republic Under Cavaignac 1848. 1969. 28.00x (ISBN 0-691-05171-2). Princeton U Pr.

De Tocqueville, Alexis. The Recollections of Alexis De Tocqueville. Mayer, J. P., ed. De Mattos, Alexander, tr. LC 78-13685. 1979. Repr. of 1949 ed. lib. bdg. 20.50x (ISBN 0-313-21052-7, TRRE). Greenwood.

Elton, Godfrey. The Revolutionary Idea in France, 1789-1871. 1969. 7.00 (ISBN 0-86527-170-4). Fertig.

Elton, Godfrey E. Revolutionary Idea in France, 1789-1871. 2nd ed. LC 74-147116. Repr. of 1931 ed. 17.50 (ISBN 0-404-02325-8). AMS Pr.

Lamartine, Alphonse M. History of the French Revolution of 1848, 2 Vols in 1. LC 73-171645. Repr. of 1854 ed. 34.50 (ISBN 0-404-07138-4). AMS Pr.

Marx, Karl. Eighteenth Brumaire of Louis Bonaparte. LC 63-23036. 1963. pap. 1.75 (ISBN 0-7178-0056-3). Intl Pub Co.

Polisensky, Josef. Aristocrats & the Crowd in the Revolutionary Year Eighteen Forty-Eight: A Contribution to the History of Revolution & Counter-Revolution. Snider, Frederick, tr. LC 79-14765. 1980. 34.00 (ISBN 0-87395-398-3); pap. 12.95 (ISBN 0-87395-449-1). State U NY Pr.

Price, Roger, ed. Eighteen Forty Eight in France. LC 74-11607. (Documents of Revolution Ser.). (Illus.). 180p. 1975. 19.50x (ISBN 0-8014-0934-9); pap. 4.95 (ISBN 0-8014-9149-5). Cornell U Pr.

Senior, Nassau W. Journals Kept in France & Italy from 1848 to 1852. LC 70-126608. (Europe 1815-1945 Ser.). 654p. 1973. Repr. of 1871 ed. lib. bdg. 59.50 (ISBN 0-306-70055-7). Da Capo.

Story, D. & Hayes, J. J., eds. The Revolution of 1848 in France. (Themes in Modern History Ser.; Documentary Research Folder: No. 3). 1973. 6.95x (ISBN 0-7022-0837-X). U of Queensland Pr.

Zeldin, Theodore. France, Eighteen Forty-Eight to Nineteen Forty-Five: Anxiety & Hypocrisy. 448p. (Orig.). 1981. pap. 9.95 (ISBN 0-19-285106-3, GB 647). Oxford U Pr.

FRANCE–HISTORY–SECOND REPUBLIC, 1848-1852

Arnaud, Rene. Second Republic & Napoleon Third. LC 70-158271. Repr. of 1930 ed. 30.00 (ISBN 0-404-50799-9). AMS Pr.

Calman, Alvin R. Ledru-Rollin & the Second French Republic. 1980. lib. bdg. 27.00x (ISBN 0-374-91239-4). Octagon.

De Hegermann-Lindencrone, L. In the Courts of Memory: Eighteen Fifty-Eight to Eighteen Seventy-Five. (Music Reprint Ser.). viii, 450p. 1980. Repr. of 1911 ed. lib. bdg. 32.50 (ISBN 0-306-76012-6). Da Capo.

Forstenzer, Thomas R. French Provincial Police & the Fall of the Second Republic: Social Fear & Counterrevolution. LC 80-8549. 384p. 1981. 25.00x (ISBN 0-691-05318-9). Princeton U Pr.

Hemmings, D. W. Culture & Society in France: Eighteen Forty-Eight to Eighteen Ninety-Eight. 1971. 40.00 (ISBN 0-7134-1522-3, Pub. by Batsford England). David & Charles.

La Gorce, Pierre F. Histoire De la Seconde Republique, 2 Vols. LC 76-171635. Repr. of 1914 ed. Set. 67.50 (ISBN 0-404-07135-X). Vol. 1 (ISBN 0-404-07136-8). Vol. 2 (ISBN 0-404-07137-6). AMS Pr.

--Histoire Du Second Empire, 7 Vols. LC 77-90101. (Fr.). Repr. of 1905 ed. Set. 241.50 (ISBN 0-404-01960-9); 34.50 ea. AMS Pr.

Margadant, Ted W. French Peasants in Revolt: The Insurrection of Eighteen Fifty One. LC 79-84001. 1979. 25.00 (ISBN 0-691-05284-0). Princeton U Pr.

Marx, Karl. Class Struggles in France Eighteen Forty-Eight to Eighteen Fifty. 143p. 1972. pap. 0.75 (ISBN 0-8285-0019-3, Pub. by Progress Pubs Russia). Imported Pubns.

--Class Struggles in France, 1848-1850. LC 64-19792. 1964. pap. 2.25 (ISBN 0-7178-0030-X). Intl Pub Co.

--Eighteenth Brumaire of Louis Bonaparte. LC 63-23036. 1963. pap. 1.75 (ISBN 0-7178-0056-3). Intl Pub Co.

--Las Luchas De Clases En Francia De 1848-1850. 166p. (Span.). 1979. pap. 1.50 (ISBN 0-8285-1484-4, Pub. by Progress Pubs Russia). Imported Pubns.

Price, Roger. The French Second Republic: A Social History. 1972. 32.00 (ISBN 0-7134-1117-1, Pub. by Batsford England). David & Charles.

Senior, Nassau W. Journals Kept in France & Italy from 1848 to 1852. LC 70-126608. (Europe 1815-1945 Ser.). 654p. 1973. Repr. of 1871 ed. lib. bdg. 59.50 (ISBN 0-306-70055-7). Da Capo.

Tchernoff, J. Associations et Societes Secretes Sous la Deuxieme Republique, 1848-1851. LC 77-176137. Repr. of 1905 ed. 27.50 (ISBN 0-404-07185-6). AMS Pr.

Zeldin, Theodore. France, Eighteen Forty-Eight to Nineteen Forty-Five: Anxiety & Hypocrisy. 448p. (Orig.). 1981. pap. 9.95 (ISBN 0-19-285106-3, GB 647). Oxford U Pr.

--France, Eighteen Forty-Eight to Nineteen Forty-Five: Ambition & Love. 1979. pap. 8.95 (ISBN 0-19-285090-3, GB 587, GB). Oxford U Pr.

--France, 1848-1945: Intellect, Taste, & Anxiety, Vol. 2. (Oxford History of Modern Europe Ser.). 1977. text ed. 59.00x (ISBN 0-19-822125-8). Oxford U Pr.

FRANCE–HISTORY–SECOND EMPIRE, 1852-1870

Arnaud, Rene. Second Republic & Napoleon Third. LC 70-158271. Repr. of 1930 ed. 30.00 (ISBN 0-404-50799-9). AMS Pr.

Brown, Marvin L., Jr. Louis Veuillot. LC 77-82882. 1977. 15.00 (ISBN 0-87716-070-8, Pub. by Moore Pub Co). F Apple.

Campbell, Stuart L. The Second Empire Revisited: A Study in French Historiography. LC 77-20247. 1978. 17.00 (ISBN 0-8135-0856-8). Rutgers U Pr.

Case, Lynn M., ed. French Opinion on the United States & Mexico: Extracts from the Reports of the Procureurs Generaux. LC 69-19212. 1969. Repr. of 1936 ed. 22.50 (ISBN 0-208-00791-1, Archon). Shoe String.

Gooch, George P. The Second Empire. LC 75-1151. (Illus.). 324p. 1975. Repr. of 1960 ed. lib. bdg. 19.75x (ISBN 0-8371-7985-8, GOSE). Greenwood.

Harrigan, Patrick J. Mobility, Elites, & Education in French Society of the Second Empire. 203p. 1980. text ed. 9.75x (ISBN 0-88920-087-4, Pub. by Laurier U Pr). Humanities.

Hemmings, D. W. Culture & Society in France: Eighteen Forty-Eight to Eighteen Ninety-Eight. 1971. 40.00 (ISBN 0-7134-1522-3, Pub. by Batsford England). David & Charles.

Napoleon, 3rd. The Second Empire & Its Downfall. facsimile ed. Wilson, Herbert, tr. LC 74-126266. (Select Bibliographies Reprint Ser). Repr. of 1925 ed. 16.00 (ISBN 0-8369-5464-5). Arno.

Sencourt, Robert. Napoleon III: The Modern Emperor. LC 71-38366. (Select Bibliographies Reprint Ser.). Repr. of 1933 ed. 22.00 (ISBN 0-8369-6783-6). Arno.

Simpson, Frederick A. Louis Napoleon & the Recovery of France. LC 75-8490. (Illus.). 400p. 1975. Repr. of 1951 ed. lib. bdg. 21.75x (ISBN 0-8371-8153-4, SILN). Greenwood.

Thompson, James M. Louis Napoleon & the Second Empire. (Illus.). 1967. pap. 2.95 (ISBN 0-393-00403-1, Norton Lib). Norton.

Walker, Mack, ed. Plombieres: Secret Diplomacy & the Rebirth of Italy. (Problems in European History Series). (Orig.). 1968. pap. 4.95x (ISBN 0-19-501096-5). Oxford U Pr.

Williams, Roger L. Gaslight & Shadow: The World of Napoleon III, 1851-1870. LC 77-11624. 1977. Repr. of 1957 ed. lib. bdg. 20.75x (ISBN 0-8371-9821-6, WIGA). Greenwood.

Zeldin, Theodore. France, Eighteen Forty-Eight to Nineteen Forty-Five: Anxiety & Hypocrisy. 448p. (Orig.). 1981. pap. 9.95 (ISBN 0-19-285106-3, GB 647). Oxford U Pr.

--France, Eighteen Forty-Eight to Nineteen Forty-Five: Ambition & Love. 1979. pap. 8.95 (ISBN 0-19-285090-3, GB 587, GB). Oxford U Pr.

--France, 1848-1945: Intellect, Taste, & Anxiety, Vol. 2. (Oxford History of Modern Europe Ser.). 1977. text ed. 59.00x (ISBN 0-19-822125-8). Oxford U Pr.

FRANCE–HISTORY–CRIMEAN WAR, 1853-1856

see Crimean War, 1853-1856

FRANCE–HISTORY–FRANCO-GERMAN WAR, 1870-1871

see Franco-German War, 1870-1871

FRANCE–HISTORY–THIRD REPUBLIC, 1870-1940

Barrows, Susanna. Distorting Mirrors: Visions of the Crowd in Late Nineteenth-Century France. LC 81-3014. (Historical Publications, Miscellany Ser.: No. 127). 224p. 1981. text ed. 20.00x (ISBN 0-300-02588-2). Yale U Pr.

Brogan, D. W. Development of Modern France 1870-1939, 2 vols. rev. ed. Set. 20.00 (ISBN 0-8446-0515-8). Peter Smith.

--France Under the Republic. LC 74-11934. 744p. 1974. Repr. of 1940 ed. lib. bdg. 45.50x (ISBN 0-8371-7718-9, BRFU). Greenwood.

Bruun, Geoffrey. Clemenceau. (Illus.). 1968. Repr. of 1943 ed. 17.50 (ISBN 0-208-00152-2, Archon). Shoe String.

Cobban, Alfred. Ambassadors & Secret Agents: The Diplomacy of the First Earl of Malmesbury at the Hague. LC 78-59012. (Illus.). 1979. Repr. of 1954 ed. 21.00 (ISBN 0-88355-687-1). Hyperion Conn.

Earle, Edward M., ed. Modern France: Problems of the Third & Fourth Republics. LC 64-10387. (Illus.). 1964. Repr. of 1951 ed. 17.50 (ISBN 0-8462-0462-2). Russell.

Elwitt, Sanford. The Making of the Third Republic: Class & Politics in France, 1868-1884. LC 73-90866. 330p. 1975. 22.50 (ISBN 0-8071-0077-3). La State U Pr.

Fiaux, Louis. Histoire De la Guerre Civile De 1871. LC 76-168020. Repr. of 1879 ed. 47.50 (ISBN 0-404-07126-0). AMS Pr.

Gimpl, Caroline Ann. The Correspondant & the Founding of the French Third Republic. LC 74-5773. 239p. 1974. Repr. of 1959 ed. lib. bdg. 15.00x (ISBN 0-8371-7517-8, GITR). Greenwood.

--The Correspondant & the Founding of the French Third Republic. LC 74-5773. 239p. 1974. Repr. of 1959 ed. lib. bdg. 15.00x (ISBN 0-8371-7517-8, GITR). Greenwood.

Hanagan, Michael P. The Logic of Solidarity: Artisans & Industrial Workers in Three French Towns, 1871-1914. LC 79-13181. (The Working Class in European History Ser.). (Illus.). 280p. 1980. 15.00 (ISBN 0-252-00758-1). U of Ill Pr.

Hanotaux, Gabriel. Contemporary France, 4 vols. facsimile ed. Tarver, John C. & Sparvel-Bayly, E., trs. LC 77-150185. (Select Bibliographies Reprint Ser). Repr. of 1909 ed. 140.00 (ISBN 0-8369-5698-2). Arno.

Hemmings, D. W. Culture & Society in France: Eighteen Forty-Eight to Eighteen Ninety-Eight. 1971. 40.00 (ISBN 0-7134-1522-3, Pub. by Batsford England). David & Charles.

Martin, Benjamin F., Jr. Count Albert De Mun: Paladin of the Third Republic. LC 78-1739. 1978. 24.00x (ISBN 0-8078-1325-7). U of NC Pr.

Mazgaj, Paul. The Action Francaise & Revolutionary Syndicalism. LC 79-4229. 1979. 19.00x (ISBN 0-8078-1316-8). U of NC Pr.

Osgood, Samuel. French Royalism Under the Third & Fourth Republics. LC 79-2289. 1981. Repr. of 1961 ed. 19.00 (ISBN 0-88355-965-X). Hyperion Conn.

Recouly, Raymond. Third Republic. Buckley, E. F., tr. LC 28-23849. (National History of France: No. 10). Repr. of 1928 ed. 30.00 (ISBN 0-404-50800-6). AMS Pr.

Sedgwick, Alexander. Third French Republic, 1870-1914. LC 68-13384. (AHM Europe Since 1500 Ser. 4). (Orig.). 1969. pap. 5.95x (ISBN 0-88295-763-5). Harlan Davidson.

Weber, Eugen. Peasants into Frenchmen: The Modernization of Rural France, 1870-1914. LC 75-7486. 1976. 25.00x (ISBN 0-8047-0898-3); pap. 8.95x (ISBN 0-8047-1013-9). Stanford U Pr.

Wienefeld, Robert H. Franco-German Relations, 1878-1885. LC 78-64133. (Johns Hopkins University. Studies in the Social Sciences. Forty-Seventh Ser. 1929: 4). Repr. of 1929 ed. 19.50 (ISBN 0-404-61246-6). AMS Pr.

Wright, Charles H. History of the Third French Republic. facsimile ed. LC 71-109638. (Select Bibliographies Reprint Ser). 1916. 17.00 (ISBN 0-8369-5247-2). Arno.

Zeldin, Theodore. France, Eighteen Forty-Eight to Nineteen Forty-Five: Anxiety & Hypocrisy. 448p. (Orig.). 1981. pap. 9.95 (ISBN 0-19-285106-3, GB 647). Oxford U Pr.

--France, Eighteen Forty-Eight to Nineteen Forty-Five: Ambition & Love. 1979. pap. 8.95 (ISBN 0-19-285090-3, GB 587, GB). Oxford U Pr.

--France, 1848-1945: Intellect, Taste, & Anxiety, Vol. 2. (Oxford History of Modern Europe Ser.). 1977. text ed. 59.00x (ISBN 0-19-822125-8). Oxford U Pr.

FRANCE–HISTORY–COMMUNE, 1871

see Paris–History–Commune, 1871

FRANCE–HISTORY–20TH CENTURY

Andrews, William G. & Hoffman, Stanley, eds. The Impact of the Fifth Republic on France. LC 80-14651. 270p. pap. text ed. 7.95x (ISBN 0-87395-440-8). State U NY Pr.

Bury, J. P. T. France 1814-1940. 1962. pap. 4.95 (ISBN 0-498-04070-4, Prpta). A S Barnes.

Cairns, John C. & Davison, Will, eds. Contemporary France: Illusion, Conflict & Regeneration. (Modern Scholarship on European History Ser.). (Illus.). 1978. 12.95 (ISBN 0-531-05398-9); pap. 6.95 (ISBN 0-531-05608-2). Watts.

De Francis, J. Colonialism & Language Policy in Vietnam. 1977. 25.00x (ISBN 90-279-7643-0). Mouton.

De Gaulle, Charles. Discours et Messages, 5 tomes. Incl. Tome I. Pendant la Guerre (Juin 1940-Janv. 1946; Tome II. Dans L'attente (Fev. 46-Avr. 58; Tome III. Vers le Renouveau (Mai 58-Juill. 62; Tome IV. Pour l'Effort (Aout 62-Dec. 65; Tome V. Vers le Terme (Jano. 66-Avril 69. 24.50 ea. French & Eur.

--La France et Son Armee. 14.95 (ISBN 0-685-34131-3). French & Eur.

--Memoires d'Espoir, 2 tomes. Incl. Tome I. Le Renouveau (1958-1962; Tome II. L' Effort (1962. 11.95 ea. French & Eur.

Demographic, Social, Educational & Economic Data for France, 1833-1925: Historical Population, Economic & Social Data: France,1901-1921. 1979. codebook 20.00 (ISBN 0-89138-978-4). ICPSR.

Dreyfus, Alfred. Five Years of My Life. Mortimer, James, tr. (Select Bibliographies Reprint Ser). Repr. of 1901 ed. 22.00 (ISBN 0-8369-5836-5). Arno.

Mandrou, Robert. Introduction to Modern France. 1977. pap. 5.95x (ISBN 0-06-131627-X, TB1627, Torch). Har-Row.

Paul, Harry W. The Second Ralliement, the Rapprochement Between Church & State in France in the Twentieth Century. 1967. 11.95 (ISBN 0-8132-0321-X). Cath U Pr.

Stein, Louis. Beyond Death & Exile: The Spanish Republicans in France, 1939-1955. LC 79-12797. (Illus.). 1979. 20.00x (ISBN 0-674-06888-2). Harvard U Pr.

Tint, Herbert. France Since Nineteen Eighteen. 2nd ed. 1980. 19.95 (ISBN 0-312-30315-7). St Martin.

--France Since Nineteen Eighteen. 1970. 24.00 (ISBN 0-7134-1505-3, Pub. by Batsford England). David & Charles.

Wendell, Barrett. The France of Today. 1908. 15.00 (ISBN 0-686-17713-4). Quality Lib.

Zeldin, Theodore. France 1848-1945: Ambition, Love & Politics, Vol. 1. (Oxford History of Modern Europe Ser). (Illus.). 828p. 1973. 49.00x (ISBN 0-19-822104-5). Oxford U Pr.
--France, 1848-1945: Intellect, Taste, & Anxiety, Vol. 2. (Oxford History of Modern Europe Ser.). 1977. text ed. 59.00x (ISBN 0-19-822125-8). Oxford U Pr.

FRANCE-HISTORY-1914-1940

Adamthwaite, Anthony P. France & the Coming of the Second World War. (Illus.). 456p. 1977. 30.00x (ISBN 0-7146-3035-7, F Cass Co). Biblio Dist.
Andrew, Christopher M. & Kanya-Forstner, A. S. The Climax of French Imperial Expansion, 1914-1924. LC 80-53435. 304p. 1981. 29.50x (ISBN 0-8047-1101-1). Stanford U Pr.
Bloch, Marc. Memoirs of War, Nineteen Fourteen to Nineteen Fifteen. Fink, Carole, tr. from Fr. LC 79-6849. Orig. Title: Souvenirs De Guerre. (Illus.). 184p. 1980. 15.00 (ISBN 0-8014-1220-X). Cornell U Pr.
Bond, Brian. France & Belgium, Nineteen Thirty-Nine to Nineteen Forty. Frankland, Noble & Dowling, Christopher, eds. LC 79-52237. (The Politics & Strategy of the Second World War Ser.). 208p. 1979. 13.50 (ISBN 0-87413-157-X). U Delaware Pr.
Gunsburg, Jeffrey A. Divided & Conquered: The French High Command & the Defeat of the West, Nineteen Forty. LC 78-22725. (Contributions in Military History: No. 18). (Illus.). 1979. lib. bdg. 25.00 (ISBN 0-313-21092-6, GDC/). Greenwood.
Helias, Pierre-Jakez. The Horse of Pride: Life in a Brenton Village. Guicharnaud, June, tr. from Fr. LC 78-6929. (Illus.). 369p. 1980. 22.50x (ISBN 0-300-02036-8); pap. 6.95x (ISBN 0-300-02599-8, Y-374). Yale U Pr.
Irvine, William D. French Conservatism in Crisis: The Republican Federation of France in the 1930s. LC 78-27254. (Illus.). 1979. text ed. 22.50x (ISBN 0-8071-0555-4). La State U Pr.
King, Jere C. Generals & Politicians: Conflict Between France's High Command, Parliament, & Government, 1914-1918. LC 74-112325. 1971. Repr. of 1951 ed. lib. bdg. 18.50x (ISBN 0-8371-4713-1, KIGP). Greenwood.
Remond, Rene & Bourdin, Janine, eds. Edouard Daladier, Chef de Gouvernement avril 1938-septembre 1939. 1977. lib. bdg. 31.25x (ISBN 2-7246-0378-8); pap. text ed. 23.75x (ISBN 2-7246-0377-X). Clearwater Pub.
Roy, Jules. The Trial of Marshal Petain. 278p. 1968. 6.95 (ISBN 0-571-08538-5, Pub. by Faber & Faber). Merrimack Bk Serv.
Schuker, Stephen A. The End of French Predominance in Europe - the Financial Crisis of Nineteen Twenty Four & the Adoption of the Dawes Plan. LC 75-38799. 400p. 1976. 24.50x (ISBN 0-8078-1253-6). U of NC Pr.
Trotsky, Leon. The Crisis of the French Section (1935-1936) Allen, Naomi & Breitman, George, eds. Vogt, Marilyn, et al, trs. from Russ. Fr. 1977. 17.00 (ISBN 0-87348-519-X); pap. 4.95 (ISBN 0-87348-520-3). Path Pr NY.
--Leon Trotsky on France. Salner, David, ed. LC 78-59267. (Illus.). 1979. lib. bdg. 17.00 (ISBN 0-913460-65-6); pap. 4.95 (ISBN 0-913460-66-4). Monad Pr.

FRANCE-HISTORY-GERMAN OCCUPATION, 1940-1945

Bond, Brian. France & Belgium, Nineteen Thirty-Nine to Nineteen Forty. Frankland, Noble & Dowling, Christopher, eds. LC 79-52237. (The Politics & Strategy of the Second World War Ser.). 208p. 1979. 13.50 (ISBN 0-87413-157-X). U Delaware Pr.
Gordon, Bertram. Collaborationism in France During the Second World War. LC 79-25281. (Illus.). 1980. 22.50x (ISBN 0-8014-1263-3). Cornell U Pr.
Halls, W. D. The Youth of Vichy France. 528p. 1981. 63.00x (ISBN 0-19-822577-6). Oxford U Pr.
Huddleston, Sisley. France, the Tragic Years. (Americanist Classics Ser). 1965. pap. 1.00 pocketsize (ISBN 0-88279-016-1). Western Islands.
Karslake, Basil. Nineteen Forty, The Last Act: The Story of the British Forces in France After Dunkirk. (Illus.). 1979. 25.00 (ISBN 0-208-01810-7, Archon). Shoe String.
Kedward, H. R. Resistance in Vichy France. (Illus.). 1978. 37.50x (ISBN 0-19-822529-6). Oxford U Pr.
Marrus, Michael R. & Paxton, Robert O. Vichy France & the Jews. 1981. 20.00 (ISBN 0-686-73004-6). Basic.
Paxton, Robert O. Vichy France: Old Guard & New Order, 1940-1944. 426p. 1975. pap. 5.95 (ISBN 0-393-00794-4, N794, Norton Lib). Norton.
Whitcomb, Philip W., tr. France During the German Occupation, 1940-1944: A Collection of 292 Statements on the Government of Marechal Petain & Pierre Laval, 3 Vols. 1959. 45.00x set (ISBN 0-8047-0507-0). Stanford U Pr.
Wolf, Jacqueline. Take Care of Josette: A Memoir in Defense of Occupied France. 192p. 1981. 9.95 (ISBN 0-531-09861-3). Watts.
Zeldin, Theodore. France, Eighteen Forty-Eight to Nineteen Forty-Five: Ambition & Love. 1979. pap. 8.95 (ISBN 0-19-285090-3, GB 587, GB). Oxford U Pr.

FRANCE-HISTORY-GERMAN OCCUPATION, 1940-1945-SOURCES

De Montherlant, Henry. Textes Sous une Occupation (1940-1944) pap. 6.95 (ISBN 0-685-36989-7). French & Eur.

FRANCE-HISTORY-1945-

Andrews, William G. & Hoffmann, Stanley, eds. The Fifth Republic at Twenty. 500p. 1980. 34.00 (ISBN 0-686-61728-2, ANFR). State U NY Pr.
Bernanos, Georges. Francais, Si Vous Saviez (1945-1948) 4.95 (ISBN 0-685-37217-0). French & Eur.
Huddleston, Sisley. France, the Tragic Years. (Americanist Classics Ser). 1965. pap. 1.00 pocketsize (ISBN 0-88279-016-1). Western Islands.
Isenberg, Irwin, ed. France Under De Gaulle. (Reference Shelf Ser: Vol. 39, No. 1). 1967. 6.25 (ISBN 0-8242-0094-2). Wilson.
Labat, Joseph, et al, eds. La France En Mutation. 1979. pap. text ed. 12.95 (ISBN 0-88377-160-8). Newbury Hse.
Marshall, D. Bruce. The French Colonial Myth & Constitution: Making in the Fourth Republic. LC 71-99833. (Illus.). 352p. 1973. 27.50x (ISBN 0-300-01212-8). Yale U Pr.
Osgood, Samuel. French Royalism Under the Third & Fourth Republics. LC 79-2289. 1981. Repr. of 1961 ed. 19.00 (ISBN 0-88355-965-X). Hyperion Conn.
Sorum, Paul C. Intellectuals & Decolonization in France. LC 76-56186. 1977. 19.50x (ISBN 0-8078-1295-1). U of NC Pr.
Writing on the Wall: France, May 1968. LC 78-25997. 1979. 24.95x (ISBN 0-312-89485-6). St Martin.

FRANCE-HISTORY, MILITARY

Adamthwaite, Anthony P. France & the Coming of the Second World War. (Illus.). 456p. 1977. 30.00x (ISBN 0-7146-3035-7, F Cass Co). Biblio Dist.
Baxter, Douglas C. Servants of the Sword: French Intendants of the Army, 1630-70. LC 75-40115. 288p. 1976. 17.50 (ISBN 0-252-00291-1). U of Ill Pr.
Bukhari, Emir Salah. Napoleon's Cavalry. LC 79-10364. (Illus.). 1979. Repr. 20.00 (ISBN 0-89141-090-2). Presidio Pr.
Challener, Richard D. French Theory of the Nation in Arms, 1866-1939. LC 64-66394. 1965. Repr. of 1952 ed. 8.50 (ISBN 0-8462-0565-3). Russell.
Contamine, Philippe. Guerre, Etat & Societe a la Fin Du Moyen Age: Etudes Sur les Armees Des Rois De France, 1337-1494. (Civilisation & Societes: No. 24). (Illus.). 1972. 58.50x (ISBN 90-2796-991-4). Mouton.
De Gaulle, Charles. The Edge of the Sword. LC 75-26731. 128p. 1975. Repr. of 1960 ed. lib. bdg. 15.00x (ISBN 0-8371-8366-9, GAES). Greenwood.
De Louvois, Marquis Letters of Louvois Selected from the Years 1681-1684. Hardre, Jacques, ed. (Studies in the Romance Languages & Literatures: No. 10). 1949. pap. 21.00x (ISBN 0-8078-9010-3). U of NC Pr.
Dickerman, Edmund H. Bellievre & Villeroy: Obellievre & Villeroy. LC 70-127365. (Illus.). xii, 200p. 1971. 12.00x (ISBN 0-87057-131-1, Pub. by Brown U Pr). U Pr of New Eng.
Furniss, E. S. De Gaulle & the French Army: A Crisis in Civil Military Relations. (Twentieth Century Fund Ser.). Repr. of 1964 ed. 5.00 (ISBN 0-527-02818-5). Kraus Repr.
Haythornthwaite, Philip. Weapons & Equipment of the Napoleonic Wars. (Illus.). 1979. 24.95 (ISBN 0-7137-0906-5, Pub by Blandford Pr England). Sterling.
Hughes, Judith M. To the Maginot Line: The Politics of French Military Preparations in the 1920's. LC 70-156139. (Historical Monographs Ser: No. 64). (Illus.). 1971. 15.00x (ISBN 0-674-89310-7). Harvard U Pr.
Humble, Richard. Napoleon's Peninsular Marshals: A Reassessment. LC 74-3874. (Illus.). 256p. 1974. 10.95 (ISBN 0-8008-5465-9). Taplinger.
Johnson, David. Napoleon's Cavalry & Its Leaders. LC 78-5596. (Illus.). 1978. text ed. 24.50x (ISBN 0-8419-0390-5). Holmes & Meier.
Kelly, George A. Lost Soldiers: The French Army & Empire in Crises, 1947-1962. 1965. 17.50x (ISBN 0-262-11014-8). MIT Pr.
Lefebvre, Georges. Napoleon: From Eighteen Brumaire to Tilsit, 1799-1807. Stockhold, Henry F., tr. LC 68-29160. 337p. 1969. 20.00x (ISBN 0-231-02558-0). Columbia U Pr.
--Napoleon: From Tilsit to Waterloo, 1807-1815. Anderson, J. E., tr. LC 74-79193. 414p. 1969. 20.00x (ISBN 0-231-03313-3). Columbia U Pr.
O'Callaghan, J. C. History of the Irish Brigades in the Service of France. 674p. 1969. Repr. of 1870 ed. 35.00x (ISBN 0-7165-0068-X, Pub. by Irish Academic Pr Ireland). Biblio Dist.
Porch, Douglas. The March to the Marne: The French Army 1871-1914. LC 81-10139. 304p. Date not set. price not set (ISBN 0-521-23883-8). Cambridge U Pr.
Quimby, Robert S. Background of Napoleonic Warfare: The Theory of Military Tactics in Eighteenth-Century France. LC 68-59257. (Columbia University. Studies in the Social Sciences: No. 596). Repr. of 1957 ed. 19.50 (ISBN 0-404-51596-7). AMS Pr.
Riehn, Richard K. French Imperial Army, 1813, 1814 & Waterloo. 1959. pap. 3.50 (ISBN 0-912364-01-7). Imrie-Risley.
--French Infantry & Artillery, 1795-1812. 1963. pap. 1.95 (ISBN 0-912364-02-5). Imrie-Risley.
Sherwig, John M. Guineas & Gunpowder: British Foreign Aid in the Wars with France, 1793-1815. LC 69-12736. (Illus.). 1969. 20.00x (ISBN 0-674-36775-8). Harvard U Pr.

FRANCE-HISTORY, NAVAL

Auphan, Gabriel & Mordal, Jacques. The French Navy in World War Two. Sabalot, Captain, tr. LC 75-38376. (Illus.). 413p. 1976. Repr. of 1959 ed. lib. bdg. 29.50x (ISBN 0-8371-8660-9, AUFN). Greenwood.
Bamford, Paul W. Forests & French Sea Power, 1660-1789. LC 57-226. 1956. 17.50x (ISBN 0-8020-7033-7). U of Toronto Pr.
Mahan, Alfred T. Influence of Sea Power Upon the French Revolution & Empire, 2 Vols. 1898. 34.00 (ISBN 0-403-00193-5). Scholarly.
--Influence of Sea Power Upon the French Revolution & Empire 1793-1812, 2 Vols. 10th ed. LC 69-10127. (Illus.). 1968. Repr. of 1898 ed. Set. lib. bdg. 35.25x (ISBN 0-8371-2666-5, MASP). Greenwood.

FRANCE-IMPRINTS

French Books in Print, 2 vols. 6th ed. (Fr.). 1977. Set. 95.00 (ISBN 0-685-87728-0). Paris Pubns.

FRANCE-INDUSTRIES

Audiganne, Armand. Les Populations ouvrieres et les industries de la France, 2 Vols. 2nd ed. (Research & Source Works Ser., History, Economics & Social Science). 1971. Repr. of 1860 ed. lib. bdg. 48.00 (ISBN 0-8337-0124-X). B Franklin.
Bairoch, Paul. Revolution Industrielle et Sous-Developpement. 4th ed. (Le Savoir Historique: No. 9). 1974. pap. 19.50x (ISBN 90-2797-295-8). Mouton.
Blanqui, Jerome A. & De Girardin, Emile. De la liberte du Commerce et la protection de l'industrie. LC 76-146244. (Research & Source Works Ser: No. 857). 1971. Repr. of 1847 ed. lib. bdg. 18.50 (ISBN 0-8337-0310-2). B Franklin.
Cole, Arthur H. & Watts, George B. The Handicrafts of France As Recorded in the Description Des Arts et Metiers, 1761-1788. (Kress Library of Business & Economics: No. 8). (Illus.). 1952. pap. 5.00x (ISBN 0-678-09903-0, Baker Lib). Kelley.
Des Cilleuls, Alfred. Histoire et Regime De la Grande Industrie En France Au 17e et 18e Siecles. LC 70-126407. (Research & Source Works: No. 5). 1970. Repr. of 1898 ed. lib. bdg. 25.00 (ISBN 0-8337-0575-X). B Franklin.
Dumont, A. A. Les Habitations Ouvrieres dans les Grands Centre Industries et Plus Particulierments dans la Region du Nord. (Conditions of the 19th Century French Working Class Ser.). 268p. (Fr.). 1974. Repr. of 1905 ed. lib. bdg. 72.50x (ISBN 0-8287-0297-7, 1054). Clearwater Pub.
Dunham, Arthur L. Anglo-French Treaty of Commerce of 1860 & the Progress of the Industrial Revolution in France. LC 75-151546. (Illus.). 1971. Repr. of 1930 ed. 18.00 (ISBN 0-8462-1580-2). Russell.
--The Industrial Revolution in France, 1815-1848. 1955. 10.00 (ISBN 0-682-47037-6, University). Exposition.
Ehrmann, Henry W. Organized Business in France. LC 81-4161. (Illus.). xx, 514p. 1981. Repr. of 1957 ed. lib. bdg. 45.00x (ISBN 0-313-23035-8, EHOB). Greenwood.
Geiger, Reed G. Anzin Coal Company, 1800-1833: Big Business in the Early Stages of the French Industrial Revolution. LC 74-77774. 345p. 18.00 (ISBN 0-87413-108-1). U Delaware Pr.
Levasseur, Emile. Histoire Des Classes Ouvrieres et De L'industrie En France De 1789-1870, 2 Vols. 2nd ed. LC 78-92175. (Fr). Repr. of 1904 ed. Set. 105.00 (ISBN 0-404-03977-4). AMS Pr.
Nef, John U. Industry & Government in France & England, 1540-1640. 1957. pap. 3.95 (ISBN 0-8014-9053-7, CP53). Cornell U Pr.
--Industry & Government in France & England, 1540-1640. LC 68-25045. 1968. Repr. of 1940 ed. 8.00 (ISBN 0-8462-1172-6). Russell.
Rose, Michael. French Industrial Studies. 148p. 1977. text ed. 25.50x (ISBN 0-566-00207-8, Pub. by Gower Pub Co England). Renouf.
Sheahan, John. Promotion & Control of Industry in Postwar France. LC 63-7592. 1963. 16.00x (ISBN 0-674-71550-0). Harvard U Pr.
Stearns, Peter N. Revolutionary Syndicalism & French Labor. 1971. 13.00 (ISBN 0-8135-0688-3). Rutgers U Pr.
Tuppen, John N. France. (Studies in Industrial Geography Ser.). 224p. 1980. lib. bdg. 23.75x (ISBN 0-86531-048-3, Pub. by Dawson Pub). Westview.

FRANCE-INTELLECTUAL LIFE

Church, William F., ed. Influence of the Enlightenment on the French Revolution. 2nd ed. (Problems in European Civilization Ser). 1973. pap. text ed. 4.95x (ISBN 0-669-82024-5). Heath.
Darnton, Robert. Mesmerism & the End of the Enlightenment in France. LC 68-25607. (Illus.). 1968. 12.50x (ISBN 0-674-56950-4). Harvard U Pr.
--Mesmerism: The End of the Enlightenment in France. LC 68-25607. (Illus.). 1971. pap. 5.95 (ISBN 0-8052-0269-2). Schocken.
Debray, Regis. Teachers, Writers, Celebrities: The Intellectuals of Modern France. 251p. 1981. text ed. 19.95 (ISBN 0-8052-7086-8, Pub. by NLB England). Schocken.
Demiashkevich, Michael. The National Mind: English, French, German. 1979. Repr. of 1938 ed. lib. bdg. 45.00 (ISBN 0-8495-1104-6). Arden Lib.
Feuillerat, Albert. French Life & Ideals. 1925. 34.50x (ISBN 0-685-89753-2). Elliots Bks.
Furet, Francois, ed. Livre et Societe Dans la Rance Du XVIIIE, Tome 2. (Civilisations et Societes: No. 16). 1970. pap. 19.50x (ISBN 90-2796-285-5). Mouton.
Hillgarth, J. N. Ramon Lull & Lullism in Fourteenth-Century France. (Oxford-Warburg Ser.). 1971. 75.00x (ISBN 0-19-824348-0). Oxford U Pr.
Hirsh, Arthur. The French New Left: An Intellectual History from Sartre to Gorz. 250p. 1981. 17.50 (ISBN 0-89608-087-0); pap. 7.00 (ISBN 0-89608-086-2). South End Pr.
Lehmann, A. G. The Symbolist Aesthetic in France, 1885-1895. 2nd ed. 328p. 1968. 30.25x (ISBN 0-631-10380-5, Pub. by Basil Blackwell). Biblio Dist.
Lovett, Clara M. Giuseppe Ferrari & the Italian Revolution. LC 78-24099. 1979. 19.00x (ISBN 0-8078-1354-0). U of NC Pr.
Martin, Kingsley. The Rise of French Liberal Thought: A Study of Political Ideas from Bayle to Condorcet. 2nd ed. Mayer, J. P., ed. LC 80-11662. xviii, 316p. 1980. Repr. of 1954 ed. lib. bdg. 25.50x (ISBN 0-313-22368-8, MARF). Greenwood.
Morley, Grace L. Le Sentiment De la Nature En France Dans la Premiere Moitie Du Dix-Septieme Siecle. LC 75-168927. (Research & Source Works Ser). 211p. (Fr.). 1972. Repr. of 1926 ed. lib. bdg. 21.00 (ISBN 0-8337-4292-2). B Franklin.
Mornet, Daniel. French Thought in the Eighteenth Century. Levin, Lawrence M., tr. 1969. Repr. of 1929 ed. 19.50 (ISBN 0-208-00750-4, Archon). Shoe String.
--Sciences De la Nature En France Au Dix-Auitieme Siecle. LC 76-172194. (Research and Source Works Ser: No. 854). 1971. Repr. of 1911 ed. lib. bdg. 21.50 (ISBN 0-8337-4295-7). B Franklin.
Park, Julian, ed. Culture of France in Our Time. Repr. of 1954 ed. lib. bdg. 16.75x (ISBN 0-8371-3236-3, PACF). Greenwood.
Picavet, Francois J. Ideologues: Essai Sur L'histoire Des Idees et Des Theories Scientifiques, Philosophiques, Religieuses, Etc. En France Depuis 1789. LC 78-168278. (Philosophy Monographs: No. 70). (Fr). 1971. Repr. of 1891 ed. lib. bdg. 34.00 (ISBN 0-8337-4322-8). B Franklin.
Renan, Ernest. Reforme Intellectuelle et Morale. Charvet, P. E., ed. LC 68-54434. (Illus., Fr.). 1968. Repr. of 1950 ed. lib. bdg. 15.00x (ISBN 0-8371-0635-4, RELR). Greenwood.
Saillant, Las Teyrie Du. Bibliographie Generale des Travaux Historiques et Archeologiques Publies Par les Societes Savantes en France Depuis les Origines, 6 vols. LC 66-20686. 4529p. (Fr.). 1972. Repr. Set. lib. bdg. 30.50 (ISBN 0-8337-2015-5). B Franklin.
Saisselin, Remy G. The Literary Enterprise in Eighteenth Century France. 1979. 14.95x (ISBN 0-8143-1618-2). Wayne St U Pr.
Shattuck, Roger. Banquet Years. (Orig.). 1968. pap. 3.95 (ISBN 0-394-70415-0, Vin). Random.
--Banquet Years: The Origins of the Avant-Garde in France, 1885 to World War One. rev. ed. LC 79-152213. (Essay Index Reprint Ser.). Repr. of 1968 ed. 35.00 (ISBN 0-8369-2826-1). Arno.
Sorum, Paul C. Intellectuals & Decolonization in France. LC 76-56186. 1977. 19.50x (ISBN 0-8078-1295-1). U of NC Pr.

Spender, Stephen. European Witness. LC 74-138186. 246p. 1972. Repr. of 1946 ed. lib. bdg. 15.00 (ISBN 0-8371-5643-2, SPEW). Greenwood.

Von Mohrenschildt, Dimitri S. Russia in the Intellectual Life of Eighteenth-Century France. LC 71-159255. x, 326p. 1971. Repr. of 1936 ed. lib. bdg. 16.00x (ISBN 0-374-98088-8). Octagon.

Wade, Ira C. The Structure & Form of the French Enlightment. Incl. Vol. 1. Esprit Philosophique. text ed. 50.00 (ISBN 0-691-05256-5); Vol. 2. Esprit Revolutionnaire. text ed. 30.00 (ISBN 0-691-05257-3). LC 77-72139. 1977. Set. text ed. 70.00 (ISBN 0-685-80551-4). Princeton U Pr.

Wade, Ira O. Clandestine Organization & Diffusion of Philosophic Ideas in France from 1700 to 1750. 1967. Repr. lib. bdg. 16.50x (ISBN 0-374-98094-2). Octagon.

--Intellectual Origins of the French Enlightenment. LC 70-132244. 1971. 33.00x (ISBN 0-691-06052-5). Princeton U Pr.

Wright, Charles H. The Background of Modern French Literature. facsimile ed. LC 79-37360. (Select Bibliographies Reprint Ser). Repr. of 1926 ed. 25.00 (ISBN 0-8369-6707-0). Arno.

FRANCE–JUVENILE LITERATURE

Bishop, Claire H. Here Is France. LC 69-20376. (Illus.). 240p. (gr. 7 up). 1969. 6.95 (ISBN 0-374-32970-2). FS&G.

Bragdon, Lillian J. The Land & People of France. rev. ed. LC 78-37605. (Portraits of the Nations Ser.). (Illus.). (gr. 6 up). 1972. lib. bdg. 8.95 (ISBN 0-397-31297-0, JBL-Med-Nursing). Har-Row.

Cairns, T. Power for the People. LC 76-30607. (Cambridge Introduction to the History of Mankind Ser.: Bk. 8). (Illus.). 1978. 5.95 (ISBN 0-521-20902-1). Cambridge U Pr.

Creed, Virginia. France. rev. ed. LC 77-83911. (World Culture Ser). (Illus.). 168p. (gr. 6 up). 1978. text ed. 9.95 ea. 1-4 copies (ISBN 0-88296-188-8); text ed. 7.96 ea. 5 or more copies; tchrs'. guide 8.94 (ISBN 0-88296-369-4). Fideler.

Creed, Virginia & Douglas Jackson, W. A. France & Soviet Union. rev. ed. LC 77-83892. (World Cultures Ser.). (Illus.). 298p. (gr. 6 up). 1978. text ed. 12.43 ea. 1-4 copies (ISBN 0-88296-154-3); text ed. 9.94 ea. 5 or more copies; tchrs'. guide 8.94 (ISBN 0-88296-369-4). Fideler.

Goldstein, Frances. Children's Treasure Hunt Travel to Belgium & France. LC 80-85012. (Children's Treasure Hunt Travel Guide Ser.). (Illus.). 230p. (Orig.). (gr. k-12). 1981. pap. 5.95 (ISBN 0-933334-02-8). Paper Tiger Pap.

Holbrook, Sabra. The French Founders of North America & Their Heritage. LC 75-13574. (gr. 6 up). 1976. 7.95 (ISBN 0-689-30490-0). Atheneum.

--Growing up in France. LC 79-22101. (Illus.). (gr. 6-9). 1980. 8.95 (ISBN 0-689-30745-4). Atheneum.

Holland, John. Come to France. (Come to Ser.). (Illus.). (gr. 4-6). 1979. PLB 7.45 s&l (ISBN 0-531-09156-2, Warwick Press). Watts.

Lifschitz, Danielle. France. LC 75-44867. (Macdonald Countries). (Illus.). (gr. 7 up). 1976. PLB 7.95 (ISBN 0-382-06099-7, Pub. by Macdonald Ed). Silver.

Sterling Publishing Company Editors. France in Pictures. LC 65-24384. (Visual Geography Ser). (Illus., Orig.). (gr. 5 up). 1965. PLB 4.99 (ISBN 0-8069-1057-7); pap. 2.95 (ISBN 0-8069-1056-9). Sterling.

Weiss, Hugh. Week in Daniel's World: France. LC 69-18809. (Face to Face Bks.). (Illus.). (gr. k-3). 1969. 4.95g (ISBN 0-685-16355-5, CCPr); (CCPr). Macmillan.

FRANCE–KINGS AND RULERS

Barnett, Correlli. Bonaparte. (Illus.). 224p. 1978. 19.95 (ISBN 0-8090-3049-7). Hill & Wang.

Connelly, Owen. The Epoch of Napoleon. LC 77-13473. 208p. 1978. pap. text ed. 6.25 (ISBN 0-88275-622-2). Krieger.

De Castries, Duc. The Lives of the Kings & Queens of France. LC 79-2205. (Illus.). 1979. 20.00 (ISBN 0-394-50734-7). Knopf.

De Mailles, Jacques. History of Bayard the Good. LC 79-8370. Repr. of 1883 ed. 42.50 (ISBN 0-404-18353-0). AMS Pr.

Grant, Arthur J. The French Monarchy (1483-1789, 2 vols. LC 75-41118. Repr. of 1925 ed. Set. 30.00 (ISBN 0-404-14930-8). AMS Pr.

Mansel, Philip. Louis XVIII. 460p. 70.00x (ISBN 0-85634-093-6, Pub. by Muller Ltd). State Mutual Bk.

Newman, William M. The Kings, the Court & Royal Power in France in the Eleventh Century. LC 80-2030. Repr. of 1929 ed. 24.50 (ISBN 0-404-18582-7). AMS Pr.

Rowen, Herbert H. The King's State: Proprietary Dynasticism in Early Modern France. 256p. 1980. 19.50 (ISBN 0-8135-0893-2). Rutgers U Pr.

Stendhal, pseud. A Life of Napoleon. LC 76-13154. 1977. Repr. of 1956 ed. 18.50 (ISBN 0-86527-272-7). Fertig.

Thornton-Cook, Elsie. Royal Line of France: The Story of the Kings & Queens of France. facs. ed. LC 67-26789. (Essay Index Reprint Ser). 1934. 19.50 (ISBN 0-8369-0939-9). Arno.

Willert, P. F. Henry of Navarre & the Hugenots in France. 1978. Repr. of 1893 ed. lib. bdg. 40.00 (ISBN 0-8495-5634-1). Arden Lib.

FRANCE–LAWS, STATUTES, ETC.

Kroell, Maurice. L Immunite Franque. LC 80-2021. Repr. of 1910 ed. 39.50 (ISBN 0-404-18573-8). AMS Pr.

Michel, Henry. La Loi Falloux: Four Janvier, Eighteen Forty-Nine - Fifteen Mars Eighteen Fifty. ii, 524p. (Fr.). 1981. Repr. of 1906 ed. 200.00 (ISBN 0-8287-1498-3). Clearwater Pub.

FRANCE–MAPS

Eliot, John. The Survey, or Topographical Description of France. with a New Mappe. LC 79-84104. (English Experience Ser.: No. 923). (Illus.). 116p. 1979. Repr. of 1592 ed. lib. bdg. 11.50 (ISBN 90-221-0923-2). Walter J Johnson.

Michelin Guides & Maps Division. France Motorway Atlas. 4th ed. pap. 3.95 (ISBN 0-686-10140-5). Michelin.

FRANCE–MILITARY POLICY

Challener, Richard D. French Theory of the Nation in Arms, 1866-1939. LC 64-66394. 1965. Repr. of 1952 ed. 8.50 (ISBN 0-8462-0565-3). Russell.

France, Ministere de la Guerre. Rules & Regulations for the Field Exercise & Manoeuvres of the French Infantry: Issued August 1, 1791, 2 vols. 2nd ed. MacDonald, John, tr. from Fr. LC 68-54795. (Illus.). Repr. of 1806 ed. cancelled (ISBN 0-8371-2336-4). Greenwood.

Furniss, E. S. De Gaulle & the French Army: A Crisis in Civil Military Relations. (Twentieth Century Fund Ser.). Repr. of 1964 ed. 5.00 (ISBN 0-527-02818-5). Kraus Repr.

Jaures, Jean L. Democracy & Military Service. LC 70-147769. (Library of War & Peace; Control & Limitation of Arms). lib. bdg. 38.00 (ISBN 0-8240-0467-1). Garland Pub.

Joshua, Wynfred & Hahn, Walter F. Nuclear Politics: America, France, & Britain. LC 73-83411. (The Washington Papers: No. 9). 80p. 1973. 4.00 (ISBN 0-8039-0282-4). Sage.

Martin, Michel L. Warriors to Managers: The French Military Establishment Since 1945. LC 79-28114. (Illus.). 424p. 1981. 29.00x (ISBN 0-8078-1421-0). U of NC Pr.

Ruehl, Lothar. La Politique Militaire De la Cinquieme Republique. (Cahiers Ser.: No. 193). (Fr.). 1977. lib. bdg. 27.50x (ISBN 2-7246-0351-6, Pub by Presses de la Fondation Nationale des Sciences Politiques); pap. text ed. 19.00 (ISBN 2-7246-0328-1). Clearwater Pub.

FRANCE–MORAL CONDITIONS

Renan, Ernest. Reforme Intellectuelle et Morale. Charvet, P. E., ed. LC 68-54434. (Illus., Fr.). 1968. Repr. of 1950 ed. lib. bdg. 15.00x (ISBN 0-8371-0635-4, RELR). Greenwood.

FRANCE–NAVY

Cobden, R. Three Panics: An Historical Episode. 3rd. ed. Repr. of 1862 ed. 12.00 (ISBN 0-527-18230-3). Kraus Repr.

Labayle-Couhat, Jean. French Warships of World War One. LC 74-193971. (Illus.). 304p. 1974. 13.00x (ISBN 0-7110-0445-5). Intl Pubns Serv.

McTaggart, David & Hunter, Robert. Greenpeace III: Journey into the Bomb. LC 78-71083. (Illus.). 1979. 10.95 (ISBN 0-688-03385-7). Morrow.

FRANCE–NOBILITY

Balon, Joseph. Etudes Franques, I: Aux Origines De la Noblesse. LC 80-2202. Repr. of 1963 ed. 16.50 (ISBN 0-404-18551-7). AMS Pr.

Bitton, Davis. French Nobility in Crisis, 1560-1640. LC 69-13177. 1969. 10.00x (ISBN 0-8047-0684-0). Stanford U Pr.

De Castries, Duc. The Lives of the Kings & Queens of France. LC 79-2205. (Illus.). 1979. 20.00 (ISBN 0-394-50734-7). Knopf.

Ford, Franklin L. Robe & Sword: The Regrouping of the French Aristocracy After Louis 14. LC 52-12261. (Historical Studies: No. 64). (Illus.). 1953. 14.00x (ISBN 0-674-77415-9). Harvard U Pr.

Forster, Robert. The Nobility of Toulouse. LC 79-159186. 212p. 1971. Repr. of 1960 ed. lib. bdg. 14.00x (ISBN 0-374-92817-7). Octagon.

Lafranche, Gaston M. The Intimate Memoirs of Louise Renee De Kerouale, Duchess of Portsmouth & Aubigny. (The Great Women of History Library). (Illus.). 94p. 1981. 27.15 (ISBN 0-89266-275-1). Am Classical Coll Pr.

Martin, Charlotte B. The World & the Aristocrat. LC 75-138162. 175p. 1972. Repr. of 1954 ed. lib. bdg. 15.00 (ISBN 0-8371-5619-X, MAWO). Greenwood.

Royalty, Peerage & Aristocracy of the World: Annuaire de la Noblesse de France, Vol. 90. LC 6-44325. (Illus.). 730p. 1967. 32.50x (ISBN 0-9503480-1-5). Intl Pubns Serv.

Sereville, Etienne De & Saint-Simon, F. de. Dictionnaire de la Noblesse Francais. 1214p. (Fr.). 1975. 95.00 (ISBN 0-686-56753-6, M-6513). French & Eur.

Sereville, Etienne de & Saint-Simon, Fernand de. Supplement au Dictionnaire de la Noblesse Francaise. 668p. 1977. 65.00 (ISBN 0-686-56752-8, M-6514). French & Eur.

Tuchman, Barbara W. A Distant Mirror: The Calamitous Fourteenth Century. LC 78-5988. (Illus.). 1978. 17.95 (ISBN 0-394-40026-7). Knopf.

FRANCE–PARLEMENT (AIX)

Beik, Paul H. Judgment of the Old Regime. LC 44-2365. (Columbia University Studies in the Social Sciences: No. 509). Repr. of 1944 ed. 18.50 (ISBN 0-404-51509-6). AMS Pr.

Kettering, Sharon. Judicial Politics & Urban Revolt in Seventeenth-Century France: The Parlement of Aix, 1629-1659. LC 77-85543. 1978. 27.00 (ISBN 0-691-05267-0). Princeton U Pr.

FRANCE–PARLEMENT (PARIS)

Ducoudray, Gustave. Les Origines du Parlement de Paris et la Justice aux Treizieme et Quatorzieme Siecles, 2 vols. 1969. 61.50 (ISBN 0-8337-0938-0). B Franklin.

Hardy, James D., Jr. Judicial Politics in the Old Regime: The Parlement of Paris During the Regency. LC 67-21375. 1967. 17.50 (ISBN 0-8071-0521-X). La State U Pr.

Maugis, Edquard. Histoire Du Parlement De Paris De l'Avenement Des Rois Valois a la Mort D'Henri Quatre, 3 Vols. 1967. Repr. of 1913 ed. 92.50 (ISBN 0-8337-2304-9). B Franklin.

Moote, A. Lloyd. Revolt of the Judges: The Parlement of Paris & the Fronde, 1643-1652. LC 78-155003. 1971. 28.00 (ISBN 0-691-05191-7). Princeton U Pr.

Penniman, Howard R., ed. French National Assembly Elections of 1978. 1980. pap. 7.25 (ISBN 0-8447-3372-5). Am Enterprise.

Stone, Bailey S. Parlement of Paris, 1774-1789. LC 79-27732. x, 227p. 1981. 19.00x (ISBN 0-8078-1442-3). U of NC Pr.

FRANCE–POLITICS AND GOVERNMENT

see also Intendants

Anderson, M. Government in France: An Introduction to the Executive Power. 1970. 23.00 (ISBN 0-08-015562-6); pap. 11.25 (ISBN 0-08-015561-8). Pergamon.

Ashford, Douglas E. British Dogmatism & French Pragmatism: Central-Local Policy Making in the Welfare State. (New Local Government Ser.: No. 22). (Illus.). 432p. 1981. text ed. 60.00x (ISBN 0-04-352096-0). Allen Unwin.

Beck, Thomas. French Legislators 1800-1834: A Study in Quantitative History. LC 73-83059. 1975. 26.75x (ISBN 0-520-02535-0). U of Cal Pr.

Becquart-Leclerq, Jeanne, ed. Paradoxes du Pouvoir Local. (Travaux et Recherches Ser: No. 38). 1977. lib. bdg. 28.75x (ISBN 2-7246-0346-X, Pub. by Presses De la Foundation Nationale Sciences Politiques); pap. text ed. 20.00x (ISBN 2-7246-0339-7). Clearwater Pub.

Berger, Suzanne. French Political System. (Patterns of Government Ser.). 1974. pap. text ed. 6.95 (ISBN 0-394-31818-8). Random.

--Peasants Against Politics: Rural Organization in Britanny, 1911-1967. LC 73-174541. (Center for International Affairs Ser). (Illus.). 508p. 1972. 15.00x (ISBN 0-674-65925-2). Harvard U Pr.

Blondel, Jean. Government of France. 4th ed. (Orig.). 1974. pap. text ed. 8.95 scp (ISBN 0-690-00062-6, HarpC). Har-Row.

Bottin Administraitif 1980. LC 66-43255. 1980. 55.00x (ISBN 2-7039-0464-9). Intl Pubns Serv.

Bottin Communes, 1979. 1400p. 1979. 45.00x (ISBN 0-686-59625-0). Intl Pubns Serv.

Buthman, W. C. The Rise of Integral Nationalism in France with Special Reference to the Ideas & Activities of Charles Maurras. LC 78-120239. 1970. Repr. lib. bdg. 20.00x (ISBN 0-374-91128-2). Octagon.

Campagne, Alexandre A. Principes D'un Bon Gouvernement Ou Reflexions Morales et Politiques Tendantes a Procurer le Bonheur De L'homme et Celui Des Societes Politiques. 510p. 1981. Repr. of 1768 ed. lib. bdg. 240.00 (ISBN 0-8287-1553-X). Clearwater Pub.

Cerny, Philip & Schain, Martin, eds. French Politics & Public Policy. 1980. write for info. (ISBN 0-312-30509-5). St Martin.

Chapman, Brian. Introduction to French Local Government. LC 78-59010. (Illus.). 1979. Repr. of 1953 ed. 18.50 (ISBN 0-88355-685-5). Hyperion Conn.

Constant, Alphonse L. Le Testament De la Liberte. 219p. 1981. Repr. of 1848 ed. lib. bdg. 95.00 (ISBN 0-8287-1554-8). Clearwater Pub.

Constant, Benjamin. Ecrits et Discours Politiques, 2 vols. (Illus.). 256p. Set. 29.95 (ISBN 0-686-54610-5). French & Eur.

De Graziani, Vincenzo G. The Franco-German Coalition & the Emergence of a New International Superpower: Its Effects Upon the Future Course of History. (Illus.). 1979. deluxe ed. 55.75 (ISBN 0-930008-31-6). Inst Econ Pol.

De Maistre, Joseph. Considerations on France. Lebrun, Richard A., ed. & tr. from Fr. 216p. 1974. 13.50x (ISBN 0-7735-0182-7). McGill-Queens U Pr.

De Tarr, Francis. The French Radical Party: From Herriot to Mendes-France. LC 80-18231. (Illus.). xx, 264p. 1980. Repr. of 1961 ed. lib. bdg. 25.00x (ISBN 0-313-22608-3, DEFR). Greenwood.

Dioudonnat, Pierre-Marie & Bragadir, Sabine. Dictionnaire des 10,000 Dirigeants Politiques Francais. 756p. (Fr.). 1978. 69.50 (ISBN 0-686-56727-7, M-6164). French & Eur.

Doyle, William. The Parliament of Bordeaux & the End of the Old Regime: 1771-1790. LC 74-77768. 1974. text ed. 27.50 (ISBN 0-312-59675-8). St Martin.

Elbow, Matthew H. French Corporative Theory, 1789-1948. 1966. lib. bdg. 13.00x (ISBN 0-374-92527-5). Octagon.

Fanon, Frantz. Les Damnes de la Terre. (Petite Coll. Maspero). pap. 5.50 (ISBN 0-685-33977-7). French & Eur.

Godechot. Les Institutions De la France Sous la Revolution et l'Empire. 42.95 (ISBN 0-685-36097-0). French & Eur.

Goodnow, Frank J., ed. Comparative Administrative Law: An Analysis of the Administrative Systems of the U. S., England, France & Germany. 1970. Repr. of 1893 ed. Set. text ed. 44.50 (ISBN 0-8337-1384-1). B Franklin.

Grevisse. Code de Dictees Francaises. 11.95 (ISBN 0-685-36703-7). French & Eur.

Guerard, Albert L. Beyond Hatred: The Democratic Ideal in France & America. LC 71-89035. Repr. of 1925 ed. 13.75x (ISBN 0-8371-1918-9, Pub. by Negro U Pr). Greenwood.

Hayward, Jack. The One & Indivisible French Republic. (Comparative Modern Government Ser.). 306p. 1974. 10.95x (ISBN 0-393-05506-X); pap. 5.95x (ISBN 0-393-09325-5). Norton.

Higonnet, Patrice L. Pont-De-Montvert: Social Structure & Politics in a French Village 1700-1914. LC 70-133209. (Historical Studies: No. 85). (Illus.). 1971. 11.50x (ISBN 0-674-68960-7). Harvard U Pr.

Hotman, Francis. Francogallia by Francis Hotman. Salmon, J. H. & Giesey, R., eds. LC 73-172835. (Studies in the History & Theory of Politics). (Illus.). 608p. 1972. 59.95 (ISBN 0-521-08379-6). Cambridge U Pr.

Hotman, Francois. Franco-Gallia. 1977. lib. bdg. 59.95 (ISBN 0-8490-1863-3). Gordon Pr.

Howard, John E. Parliament & Foreign Policy in France. LC 74-6110. 172p. 1974. Repr. of 1948 ed. lib. bdg. 15.00x (ISBN 0-8371-7503-8, HOPF). Greenwood.

Jacobs, Dan N., et al. Comparative Politics: Introduction to the Politics of Britain, the United Kingdom, France, Germany, & the Soviet Union. 320p. 1982. pap. text ed. 9.95x (ISBN 0-934540-05-5). Chatham Hse Pubs.

Jaures, Jean L. Democracy & Military Service. LC 70-147769. (Library of War & Peace; Control & Limitation of Arms). lib. bdg. 38.00 (ISBN 0-8240-0467-1). Garland Pub.

Lalanne, Ludovic. Dictionnaire Historique De la France, 2 Vols. 2nd ed. 1967. Repr. of 1877 ed. 93.00 (ISBN 0-8337-1985-8). B Franklin.

Lean, E. Tangye. Napoleonists: A Study in Political Disaffection, 1760-1960. 1970. 17.00x (ISBN 0-19-215184-3). Oxford U Pr.

Maier, Charles S. & White, Dan S., eds. Thirteenth of May: The Advent of De Gaulle's Republic. (Problems in European History Ser). (Orig.). 1968. pap. 4.95x (ISBN 0-19-500959-2). Oxford U Pr.

Manceron, Claude. The Wind From America, Vol. 2. LC 78-54928. (Illus.). 1978. 17.95 (ISBN 0-394-49883-6). Knopf.

Marinetti, F. T. Mots En Liberte Futuristes. soft 15.00x (ISBN 0-87556-216-7). Saifer.

Mauriac, Francois. Memoires Politiques. 1967. 14.95 (ISBN 0-686-55469-8). French & Eur.

Muret, Charlotte T. French Royalist Doctrines Since the Revolution. LC 72-8904. x, 326p. 1971. Repr. of 1933 ed. lib. bdg. 15.50x (ISBN 0-374-96025-9). Octagon.

Padover, Saul K. French Institutions: Values & Politics. LC 78-5634. (Hoover Studies: No. 2). 1978. Repr. of 1954 ed. lib. bdg. 16.75x (ISBN 0-313-20459-4, PAFI). Greenwood.

Partin, Malcolm O. Waldeck-Rousseau, Combes, & the Church, 1899-1905: The Politics of Anticlericalism. LC 74-76167. (Duke Historical Publication Ser). 1969. 15.75 (ISBN 0-8223-0130-X). Duke.

Peguy, Charles. Notre Patrie. 12p. 1915. 2.95 (ISBN 0-686-54861-2). French & Eur.

Picot, Georges M. Histoire Des Etats Generaux, 5 Vols. 2nd ed. (Fr.). 1969. Repr. of 1888 ed. 165.00 (ISBN 0-8337-2756-7). B Franklin.

Poincare, Raymond. How France Is Governed. Miall, Bernard, tr. LC 79-110909. 1970. Repr. of 1913 ed. 15.00 (ISBN 0-8046-0901-2). Kennikat.

Remond, Rene. Right Wing in France: From 1815 to De Gaulle. rev. ed. Laux, James M., tr. LC 72-87940. 1969. 10.00 (ISBN 0-8122-7490-3). U of Pa Pr.

Renouvin, Pierre. Forms of War Government in France. (Economic & Social History of the World War Ser.). 1927. 47.50x (ISBN 0-685-69856-4). Elliots Bks.

Ridley, F. & Blondel, J. Public Administration in France. new ed. 1969. 25.00x (ISBN 0-7100-2037-6). Routledge & Kegan.

Safran, William. French Polity. LC 76-58487. (Comparative Studies of Political Life Ser.). 1977. pap. text ed. 10.95x (ISBN 0-582-28102-4). Longman.

Schonfeld, William R. Obedience & Revolt: French Behavior Toward Authority. LC 75-23616. (Sage Library of Social Research: Vol. 22). 256p. 1976. 20.00x (ISBN 0-8039-0515-7); pap. 9.95 (ISBN 0-8039-0516-5). Sage.

See, Henri. Idees Politiques en France Au XVIIe. Mayer, J. P., ed. LC 78-67385. (European Political Thought Ser.). (Fr.). 1979. Repr. of 1923 ed. lib. bdg. 22.00x (ISBN 0-405-11737-X). Arno.

--Les Idees politiques en France au XVIIIe siecle. Mayer, J. P., ed. LC 78-11738. (European Political Thought Ser.). (Fr.). 1979. Repr. of 1920 ed. lib. bdg. 18.00x (ISBN 0-405-11738-8). Arno.

Sharp, Walter R. French Civil Service: Bureaucracy in Transition. LC 74-137268. Repr. of 1931 ed. 28.50 (ISBN 0-404-05954-6). AMS Pr.

Shennan, J. H. Government & Society in France, 1461-1661. (Historical Problems: Studies & Documents). 1969. text ed. 21.00x o. p. (ISBN 0-04-901014-X); pap. text ed. 8.95x (ISBN 0-04-901015-8). Allen Unwin.

Siegfried, A. France: A Study in Nationality. 122p. 1980. Repr. of 1930 ed. lib. bdg. 20.00 (ISBN 0-89760-826-7). Telegraph Bks.

Siegfried, Andre. France: A Study in Nationality. 1978. Repr. of 1930 ed. lib. bdg. 27.50 (ISBN 0-8495-4900-0). Arden Lib.

Social & Political France. (YFS Ser.: No. 15). 1955. pap. 6.00 (ISBN 0-527-01723-X). Kraus Repr.

Stone, Bailey S. Parlement of Paris, 1774-1789. LC 79-27732. x, 227p. 1981. 19.00x (ISBN 0-8078-1442-3). U of NC Pr.

Suleiman, E. N. Politics, Power & Bureaucracy in France: The Administrative Elite. LC 72-6524. 1974. 32.00x (ISBN 0-691-07552-2); pap. 12.50x (ISBN 0-691-10022-5). Princeton U Pr.

Suleiman, Ezra N., ed. Politics & Society in Contemporary France. 186p. (Orig.). 1977. pap. text ed. 4.00 (ISBN 0-87855-679-6). Transaction Bks.

Taine, Hippolyte A. The Ancient Regime. 8.00 (ISBN 0-8446-1434-3). Peter Smith.

--The Ancient Regime: Les Oricines De la France Contemporaine. Durand, John, tr. LC 79-38368. (Select Bibliographies Reprint Ser.). Repr. of 1881 ed. 21.00 (ISBN 0-8369-6785-2). Arno.

--The Modern Regime, 2 vols. 8.00 ea. (ISBN 0-8446-1436-X). Peter Smith.

Thomas, Ruth. Broadcasting & Democracy in France. 1976. 19.95x (ISBN 0-8464-0217-3). Beekman Pubs.

Weill, Georges J. Histoire Du Parti Republicain En France De 1814 a 1870. 2nd ed. LC 78-158214. Repr. of 1928 ed. 31.00 (ISBN 0-404-07194-5). AMS Pr.

Westfall, Gloria. French Official Publications. LC 80-40418. (Guides to Official Publications: Vol. 6). (Illus.). 223p. 1980. 35.00 (ISBN 0-08-021838-5). Pergamon.

Zeldin, Theodore. France Eighteen Forty-Eight to Nineteen Forty-Five: Politics & Anger. (Illus.). 1979. pap. 8.95 (ISBN 0-19-285082-2, GB578, GB). Oxford U Pr.

--Political System of Napoleon 3rd. (Illus.). 1971. pap. 4.95x (ISBN 0-393-00580-1, Norton Lib). Norton.

FRANCE–POLITICS AND GOVERNMENT–BIBLIOGRAPHY

Lindsay, Robert O. & Neu, John, eds. French Political Pamphlets, Fifteen Forty-Seven to Sixteen Forty-Eight: A Catalog of Major Collections in American Libraries. LC 78-84953. 522p. 1969. 35.00 (ISBN 0-299-04990-6). U of Wis Pr.

Lipkowitz, Marcel. French Royal & Administrative Acts, Twelve Fifty-Six to Seventeen Ninety-Four: A Subject Guide to the New York Public Library Collection of Sixteen Thousand Pamphlets Now on Microfilm. 1979. 65.00 (ISBN 0-89235-011-3). Res Pubns Conn.

Welsh, Doris V., ed. Checklist of French Political Pamphlets, 1560-1644. 176p. 1950. pap. 1.50 (ISBN 0-685-18883-3). Newberry.

--Second Checklist of French Political Pamphlets, 1560-1653. 1955. pap. 1.50 (ISBN 0-685-18890-6). Newberry.

FRANCE–POLITICS AND GOVERNMENT–TO 1328

Flach, Jacques. Origines De L'ancienne France, 4 Vols. LC 69-18612. (Research & Source Works: No. 391). (Fr). 1970. Repr. of 1917 ed. Set. text ed. 135.00 (ISBN 0-8337-1148-2). B Franklin.

Ganshof, Francois L. Frankish Institutions Under Charlemagne. 1970. pap. 3.95 (ISBN 0-393-00500-3, Norton Lib). Norton.

--Frankish Institutions Under Charlemagne. Lyon, Bryce & Lyon, Mary, trs. LC 68-29166. 107p. 1968. text ed. 12.00x (ISBN 0-87057-108-7, Pub. by Brown U Pr). U Pr of New Eng.

Strayer, J. R. Administration of Normandy Under Saint Louis. 1932. 20.00 (ISBN 0-527-01686-1). Kraus Repr.

Wood, Charles T. French Apanages & the Capetian Monarchy, 1224-1328. LC 66-13186. (Historical Monographs Ser: No. 59). 1966. 8.95x (ISBN 0-674-32001-8). Harvard U Pr.

FRANCE–POLITICS AND GOVERNMENT–1328-1589

Bonney, Richard. Political Change in France Under Richelieu & Mazarin, 1624-1661. (Illus.). 1977. text ed. 64.00x (ISBN 0-19-822537-7). Oxford U Pr.

Kelley, Donald R. Francois Hotman: A Revolutionary's Ordeal. LC 72-735. 358p. 1973. 25.00 (ISBN 0-691-05206-9). Princeton U Pr.

Keohane, Nannerl O. Philosophy & the State in France: The Renaissance to the Enlightenment. LC 79-3219. 1980. 30.00x (ISBN 0-691-07611-1); pap. 12.50 ltd. ed. (ISBN 0-691-10078-0). Princeton U Pr.

Palm, Franklin C. Politics & Religion in Sixteenth-Century France: A Study of the Career of Henry of Montmorency-Damville, Uncrowned King of the South. 8.50 (ISBN 0-8446-0835-1). Peter Smith.

Seyssel, Claude De. The Monarchy of France. Hexter, J. H., tr. from Fr. Kelley, Donald R., ed. Sherman, Michael, tr. from Fr. LC 80-23554. 1981. text ed. 16.95x (ISBN 0-300-02516-5). Yale U Pr.

Stoddard, E. C. Bertrand Du Guesclin Constable of France: His Life & Times. (Illus.). 301p. 1980. Repr. of 1897 ed. lib. bdg. 35.00 (ISBN 0-89987-761-3). Darby Bks.

Sutherland, Nicola M. The French Secretaries of State in the Age of Catherine De Medici. LC 75-40996. (Illus.). 1977. Repr. of 1962 ed. lib. bdg. 21.75x (ISBN 0-8371-8707-9, SUFS). Greenwood.

Weill, George J. Theories Sur Le Pouvoir Royal En France Pendant Les Guerres De Religion. 1966. 20.00 (ISBN 0-8337-3722-8). B Franklin.

FRANCE–POLITICS AND GOVERNMENT–1589-1789

Church, William F. Richelieu & Reason of State. LC 76-181518. 582p. 1972. 36.00 (ISBN 0-691-05199-2). Princeton U Pr.

Coveney, P. J., ed. France in Crisis, 1620-1675. 273p. 1977. 22.50x (ISBN 0-87471-916-X). Rowman.

Dakin, Douglas. Turgot & the Ancien Regime in France. 1965. lib. bdg. 20.00x (ISBN 0-374-92033-8). Octagon.

De Saint-Simon, Louis, pseud. Historical Memoirs of the Duc De Saint-Simon, 3 vols. Norton, Lucie, tr. from Fr. Incl. Vol. 1 1691-1709. 550p. 1967 (ISBN 0-241-89084-5); Vol. 2. 1710-1715. 524p. 1968 (ISBN 0-241-89085-3); Vol. 3. 1715-1723. 576p. 1972 (ISBN 0-241-89086-1). LC 67-95163. (Illus.). 10.00x ea. Intl Pubns Serv.

Gruder, Vivian R. Royal Provincial Intendants: A Governing Elite in Eighteenth Century France. 1968. 22.50x (ISBN 0-8014-0164-X). Cornell U Pr.

Hardy, James D., Jr. Judicial Politics in the Old Regime: The Parlement of Paris During the Regency. LC 67-21375. 1967. 17.50 (ISBN 0-8071-0521-X). La State U Pr.

Hatton, Ragnhild, ed. Louis the Fourteenth & Absolutism. LC 75-45158. (Illus.). 1976. 17.50x (ISBN 0-8142-0255-1). Ohio St U Pr.

--Louis the Fourteenth & Europe. LC 75-45334. (Illus.). 1976. 17.50x (ISBN 0-8142-0254-3). Ohio St U Pr.

Hayden, J. M. France & the Estates General of 1614. LC 73-82456. (Studies in Early Modern History). (Illus.). 320p. 1974. 42.95 (ISBN 0-521-20325-2). Cambridge U Pr.

Hill, Henry B., tr. Political Testament of Cardinal Richelieu: The Significant Chapters & Supporting Selections. (Illus.). 1961. 15.00x (ISBN 0-299-02420-2); pap. 5.95 (ISBN 0-299-02424-5). U of Wis Pr.

Hyslop, Beatrice F. Guide to the General Cahiers of 1789, with the Texts of Unedited Cahiers. 1968. lib. bdg. 17.50x (ISBN 0-374-94104-1). Octagon.

Iiams, Thomas M. Peacemaking from Vergennes to Napoleon. LC 79-14922. 240p. 1979. lib. bdg. 12.50 (ISBN 0-88275-997-3). Krieger.

Kettering, Sharon. Judicial Politics & Urban Revolt in Seventeenth-Century France: The Parlement of Aix, 1629-1659. LC 77-85543. 1978. 27.00 (ISBN 0-691-05267-0). Princeton U Pr.

King, James E. Science & Rationalism in the Government of Louis Fourteenth, 1661-1683. LC 74-159202. 337p. 1971. Repr. of 1950 ed. lib. bdg. 20.00x (ISBN 0-374-94585-3). Octagon.

Levy, Darline G. The Ideas & Careers of Simon-Nicolas-Henri Linguet: A Study in Eighteenth-Century French Politics. LC 79-24109. (Illus.). 360p. 1980. 30.00 (ISBN 0-252-00311-X). U of Ill Pr.

Overbury, Thomas. Sir T. Overbury His Observations in His Travailes. LC 70-26399. (English Experience Ser.: No. 154). 28p. 1969. Repr. of 1626 ed. 7.00 (ISBN 90-221-0154-1). Walter J Johnson.

Rothney, John, ed. Brittany Affair & the Crisis of the Ancien Regime. (Problems in European History Ser). 1969. pap. 5.95x (ISBN 0-19-501040-X). Oxford U Pr.

Rousseau, Jean-Jacques. Du Contrat Social. Bd. with Discours sur les Sciences et les Arts; Discours sur l'Origine de l'Inegalite; Lettre a M. D'Alembert; Considerations sur le Gouvernement de Pologne; Lettre a Mgr. de Beaumont. (Coll. Prestige). 21.95 (ISBN 0-685-34055-4). French & Eur.

Rowen, Herbert H. The King's State: Proprietary Dynasticism in Early Modern France. 256p. 1980. 19.50 (ISBN 0-8135-0893-2). Rutgers U Pr.

Scott, Samuel F. The Response of the Royal Army to the French Revolution: The Role & Development of the Line Army, 1793-1878. 1978. 45.00x (ISBN 0-19-822534-2). Oxford U Pr.

Shennan, J. H. Philippe, Duke of Orleans: Regent of France, 1715-1723. (Illus.). 1979. 16.95 (ISBN 0-500-87009-8). Thames Hudson.

Stankiewicz, W. J. Politics & Religion in Seventeenth-Century France. LC 76-2075. 269p. 1976. Repr. of 1960 ed. lib. bdg. 18.00x (ISBN 0-8371-8770-2, STPR). Greenwood.

Wood, James B. The Nobility of the Election of Bayeux, Fourteen Sixty-Three to Sixteen Sixty-Six: Continuity Through Change. LC 79-3235. (Illus.). 1980. 16.00x (ISBN 0-691-05294-8). Princeton U Pr.

FRANCE–POLITICS AND GOVERNMENT–1789-1870

Bagge, Dominique. Les Idees Politiques En France Sous la Restauration. Mayer, J. P., ed. LC 78-67327. (European Political Thought Ser.). 1979. lib. bdg. 30.00x (ISBN 0-405-11674-8). Arno.

Collins, Irene. Napoleon & His Parliaments, Eighteen Hundred to Eighteen Fifteen. 1979. 22.50x (ISBN 0-312-55892-9). St Martin.

Constant, Benjamin. De l'Esprit de Conquete. 72p. 1947. 4.95 (ISBN 0-686-54609-1). French & Eur.

Gomel, Charles. Histoire Financiere De la Legislative & De la Convention, 2 vols. LC 76-6475. 1902-05. Repr. 55.00 (ISBN 0-8337-1374-4). B Franklin.

Iiams, Thomas M. Peacemaking from Vergennes to Napoleon. LC 79-14922. 240p. 1979. lib. bdg. 12.50 (ISBN 0-88275-997-3). Krieger.

Levy, Darline G. The Ideas & Careers of Simon-Nicolas-Henri Linguet: A Study in Eighteenth-Century French Politics. LC 79-24109. (Illus.). 360p. 1980. 30.00 (ISBN 0-252-00311-X). U of Ill Pr.

Paris Assemblee Electorale. Assemblee Electorale De Paris, 18 Novembre 1790-15, Juin 1791. LC 79-173488. (Collection de documents relatifs a l'histoire de Paris pendant la Revolution francaise). Repr. of 1890 ed. 53.25 (ISBN 0-404-52614-4). AMS Pr.

--Assemblee Electorale De Paris, 2 Septembre 1792. LC 75-38036. Repr. of 1905 ed. 53.25 (ISBN 0-404-52616-0). AMS Pr.

Scott, Samuel F. The Response of the Royal Army to the French Revolution: The Role & Development of the Line Army, 1793-1878. 1978. 45.00x (ISBN 0-19-822534-2). Oxford U Pr.

FRANCE–POLITICS AND GOVERNMENT–1789-1900

Allison, John M. Thiers & the French Monarchy. (Illus.). 1968. Repr. of 1926 ed. 22.50 (ISBN 0-208-00017-8, Archon). Shoe String.

Un Citoyen Aux Etats-Generaux. Repr. of 1788 ed. 9.50 (ISBN 0-8287-1346-4). Clearwater Pub.

Favre, Jules. Government of the National Defence from the Thirtieth of June to the Thirty First of October, 1870. Clark, H., tr. Repr. of 1873 ed. 26.00 (ISBN 0-404-07125-2). AMS Pr.

Gomel, Charles. Histoire Financiere De l'Assemblee Constituante, 2 vols. LC 70-6433. 1896-97. Repr. 55.00 (ISBN 0-8337-1374-4). B Franklin.

Gooch, Robert K. Parliamentary Government in France: Revolutionary Origins, 1789-1791. LC 70-139924. 1971. Repr. of 1960 ed. 13.50 (ISBN 0-8462-1559-4). Russell.

Gruder, Vivian R. Royal Provincial Intendants: A Governing Elite in Eighteenth Century France. 1968. 22.50x (ISBN 0-8014-0164-X). Cornell U Pr.

Guizot, Francois P. Democracy in France. LC 74-19357. v, 82p. 1974. Repr. of 1849 ed. 13.75 (ISBN 0-86527-040-6). Fertig.

Hudson, Nora E. Ultra-Royalism & the French Restoration. LC 73-670. 209p. 1973. Repr. of 1936 ed. lib. bdg. 13.50x (ISBN 0-374-94027-4). Octagon.

Kent, Sherman. The Election of Eighteen Twenty-Seven in France. LC 75-3702. (Historical Studies: No. 91). 224p. 1975. text ed. 12.50x (ISBN 0-674-24321-8). Harvard U Pr.

Resnick, Daniel P. The White Terror & the Political Reaction After Waterloo. LC 66-18254. (Historical Studies: No. 77). 1966. 7.00x (ISBN 0-674-95190-5). Harvard U Pr.

Schapiro, J. Salwyn. Liberalism & the Challenge of Fascism. 1964. lib. bdg. 20.00x (ISBN 0-374-97087-4). Octagon.

Sedgwick, Alexander C. Ralliement in French Politics, 1890-1898. LC 65-12828. (Historical Studies: No. 74). 1965. 8.50x (ISBN 0-674-74751-8). Harvard U Pr.

Soltau, Roger H. French Political Thought in the Nineteenth Century. LC 59-12366. 1959. Repr. of 1931 ed. 20.00 (ISBN 0-8462-0277-8). Russell.

Spitzer, Alan B. Old Hatreds & Young Hopes: The French Carbonari Against the Bourbon Restoration. LC 76-139722. (Historical Monographs Ser: No. 63). 1971. 18.50x (ISBN 0-674-63220-6). Harvard U Pr.

Thiers, Adolphe. Discours parlementaires de M. Thiers, 16 Vols. LC 74-176147. Repr. of 1889 ed. Set. 275.00 (ISBN 0-404-07520-7); 17.50 ea. AMS Pr.

Thiers, Louis A. Memoirs, 1870-1873. LC 79-80598. 834p. 1973. Repr. of 1915 ed. 25.00 (ISBN 0-86527-329-4). Fertig.

Van Deusen, Glyndon G. Sieyes: His Life & His Nationalism. LC 68-58632. (Columbia University. Studies in the Social Sciences: No. 362). Repr. of 1932 ed. 16.50 (ISBN 0-404-51362-X). AMS Pr.

FRANCE–POLITICS AND GOVERNMENT–REVOLUTION, 1789-1799

Cloots, Jean-Baptiste. Republique Universelle, ou Adresse aux Tyrannicides. LC 72-147425. (Library of War & Peace; Proposals for Peace, a History). lib. bdg. 38.00 (ISBN 0-8240-0217-2). Garland Pub.

Gentz, Friedrich Von & Possony, Stefan T. Three Revolutions: The French & American Revolutions Compared, & Reflections on the Russian Revolutions. Adams, John Q., tr. from German. LC 75-3866. 1976. Repr. of 1959 ed. lib. bdg. 15.00x (ISBN 0-8371-8090-2, GETR). Greenwood.

Hunt, Lynn A. Revolution & Urban Politics in Provincial France: Troyes & Reims, 1786-1790. LC 76-48016. 1978. 11.50x (ISBN 0-8047-0940-8). Stanford U Pr.

Hyslop, Beatrice F. French Nationalism in 1789 According to the General Cahiers. 1968. Repr. lib. bdg. 15.50 (ISBN 0-374-94085-1). Octagon.

Marechal, Sylvain. Dame Nature a la Barre De L'assemblee Nationale. Repr. of 1791 ed. 9.50 (ISBN 0-8287-0578-X). Clearwater Pub.

Rose, R. Enrages: Socialists of the French Revolution. 1965. pap. 4.00x (ISBN 0-424-05650-X, Pub. by Sydney U Pr). Intl Schol Bk Serv.

Sagnac, Philippe. La Legislation civile de la Revolution, 1789-1804. LC 75-174800. Repr. of 1898 ed. 29.50 (ISBN 0-404-07168-6). AMS Pr.

FRANCE–POLITICS AND GOVERNMENT–1848-1852

Dommanget, Maurice. Auguste Blanqui & la Revolution De 1848. 1972. pap. 22.25x (ISBN 90-2796-939-6). Mouton.

--Auguste Blanqui, Au Debut De la IIIe Republique (1871-80) Derniere Prison et Ultimes Combats. 1971. pap. 12.75x (ISBN 90-2796-272-3). Mouton.

--Auguste Blanqui, Des Origines a la Revolution De 1848: Premiers Combats et Premieres Prisons. (Societe, Mouvements Sociaux & Ideologies, Documents & Temoignages: No. 5). 1969. pap. 25.50x (ISBN 90-2797-011-4). Mouton.

Marx, Karl. Class Struggles in France, 1848-1850. LC 64-19792. 1964. pap. 2.25 (ISBN 0-7178-0030-X). Intl Pub Co.

Merriman, John M. The Agony of the Republic: Repression of the Left in Revolutionary France, 1848-1851. LC 77-10434. 1978. 25.00x (ISBN 0-300-02151-8). Yale U Pr.

Price, R. D. French Second Republic: A Social History. LC 70-173282. 1972. 22.50x (ISBN 0-8014-0686-2). Cornell U Pr.

Zeldin, Theodore. France Eighteen Forty-Eight to Nineteen Forty-Five: Taste & Corruption. 448p. 1980. pap. 8.95 (ISBN 0-19-285100-4, GB 620). Oxford U Pr.

FRANCE–POLITICS AND GOVERNMENT–1852-1870

Bagehot, Walter. Collected Works of Walter Bagehot, Vols. 3 & 4. St. John Stevas, Norman, ed. LC 66-1165. 1968. Set. 50.00x (ISBN 0-674-14002-8). Harvard U Pr.

Hutton, Patrick H. The Cult of the Revolutionary Tradition: The Blanquists in French Politics, 1864-1893. LC 80-28850. 264p. 1981. 24.50x (ISBN 0-520-04114-3). U of Cal Pr.

Renan, Ernest. Reforme Intellectuelle et Morale. Charvet, P. E., ed. LC 68-54434. (Illus., Fr.). 1968. Repr. of 1950 ed. lib. bdg. 15.00x (ISBN 0-8371-0635-4, RELR). Greenwood.

Simpson, Frederick A. Louis Napoleon & the Recovery of France. LC 75-8490. (Illus.). 400p. 1975. Repr. of 1951 ed. lib. bdg. 21.75x (ISBN 0-8371-8153-4, SILN). Greenwood.

Zeldin, Theodore. France Eighteen Forty-Eight to Nineteen Forty-Five: Taste & Corruption. 448p. 1980. pap. 8.95 (ISBN 0-19-285100-4, GB 620). Oxford U Pr.

FRANCE–POLITICS AND GOVERNMENT–1870-

McMillan, James. Housewife or Harlot: The Woman Question in France Under the Third Republic. 1980. 25.00 (ISBN 0-312-39347-4). St Martin.

Siegfried, Andre. Tableau Politique De la France De L'ouest Sous la Troisieme Republique: The Political Map of Western France Under the Third Republic. LC 74-25784. (European Sociology Ser.). 566p. 1975. Repr. 31.00x (ISBN 0-405-06537-X). Arno.

Singer, Barnett. Modern France: Mind, Politics, Society, 1870-1970. LC 80-24177. 212p. 1981. 16.95 (ISBN 0-295-95791-3). U of Wash Pr.

Zeldin, Theodore. France Eighteen Forty-Eight to Nineteen Forty-Five: Taste & Corruption. 448p. 1980. pap. 8.95 (ISBN 0-19-285100-4, GB 620). Oxford U Pr.

FRANCE–POLITICS AND GOVERNMENT–1870-1940

Acomb, Evelyn M. French Laic Laws: 1879-1889. LC 67-18747. 1968. Repr. lib. bdg. 16.00 (ISBN 0-374-90038-8). Octagon.

Anderson, R. D. France, 1870-1914: Politics & Society. 1977. 22.50x (ISBN 0-7100-8575-3). Routledge & Kegan.

Brogan, D. W. France Under the Republic. LC 74-11934. 744p. 1974. Repr. of 1940 ed. lib. bdg. 45.50x (ISBN 0-8371-7718-9, BRFU). Greenwood.

Bury, J. P. Gambetta & the National Defense. LC 70-80531. 1970. Repr. of 1936 ed. 23.50 (ISBN 0-86527-077-5). Fertig.

Bury, John P. Gambetta - the National Defence: A Republican Dictatorship in France. LC 77-114490. (Illus.). 1971. Repr. of 1936 ed. lib. bdg. 15.25x (ISBN 0-8371-4818-9, BUGN). Greenwood.

Farmer, Paul. France Reviews Its Revolutionary Origins. 1963. lib. bdg. 13.00x (ISBN 0-374-92698-0). Octagon.

Freycinet, Charles L. Souvenirs, Eighteen Seventy-Eight to Eighteen-Ninety-Three. LC 73-258. (Europe 1815-1945 Ser.). 524p. 1973. Repr. of 1913 ed. lib. bdg. 49.50 (ISBN 0-306-70560-5). Da Capo.

Friedman, Lee M. Zola & the Dreyfus Case. (World History Ser., No. 48). (Illus.). 1970. pap. 12.95 (ISBN 0-8383-0092-8). Haskell.

Gohier, Urbain D. Armee Contre la Nation. LC 72-147547. (Library of War & Peace; Control & Limitation of Arms). lib. bdg. 38.00 (ISBN 0-8240-0328-4). Garland Pub.

Hanotaux, Gabriel. Contemporary France, 4 vols. facsimile ed. Tarver, John C. & Sparvel-Bayly, E., trs. LC 77-150185. (Select Bibliographies Reprint Ser). Repr. of 1909 ed. 140.00 (ISBN 0-8369-5698-2). Arno.

Hutton, Patrick H. The Cult of the Revolutionary Tradition: The Blanquists in French Politics, 1864-1893. LC 80-28850. 264p. 1981. 24.50x (ISBN 0-520-04114-3). U of Cal Pr.

Joughin, Jean T. Paris Commune in French Politics, 1871-1880: The History of the Amnesty of 1880, 2 vols. in 1. LC 72-84991. 529p. 1973. Repr. of 1955 ed. 23.00 (ISBN 0-8462-1703-1). Russell.

Judt, T. Socialism in Provence Eighteen Seventy-One to Nineteen Fourteen. LC 78-16419. (Illus.). 1979. 42.50 (ISBN 0-521-22172-2); pap. 14.95x (ISBN 0-521-29598-X). Cambridge U Pr.

Locke, Robert R. French Legitimists & the Politics of Moral Order in the Early Third Republic. 336p. 1974. text ed. 23.00x (ISBN 0-691-05215-8). Princeton U Pr.

Mitchell, Allan. German Influence in France After Eighteen Seventy: The Formation of the French Republic. LC 78-31677. 1979. 19.95x (ISBN 0-8078-1357-5); pap. text ed. 9.95x (ISBN 0-8078-1374-5). U of NC Pr.

Paul-Boncour, Joseph. Recollections of the Third Republic. 6.00 (ISBN 0-8315-0050-6). Speller.

Ralston, David B. Army of the Republic: The Place of the Military in the Political Evolution of France, 1871-1914. 1967. 17.50x (ISBN 0-262-18021-9). MIT Pr.

Rothney, John. Bonapartism After Sedan. LC 68-9752. (Illus.). 360p. 1969. 22.50x (ISBN 0-8014-0473-8). Cornell U Pr.

Schapiro, J. Salwyn. Liberalism & the Challenge of Fascism. 1964. lib. bdg. 20.00x (ISBN 0-374-97087-4). Octagon.

Schechter, Betty. Dreyfus Affair: A National Scandal. (Illus.). (gr. 7 up). 1965. 3.50 (ISBN 0-395-07092-9). HM.

Schuman, Frederick L. War & Diplomacy in the French Republic: An Inquiry into Political Motivations & the Control of Foreign Policy. LC 68-9635. 1970. Repr. of 1931 ed. 19.50 (ISBN 0-86527-204-2). Fertig.

--War & Diplomacy in the French Republic. LC 71-11468. 1970. Repr. of 1931 ed. 29.50 (ISBN 0-404-05623-7). AMS Pr.

Scott, John A. Republican Ideas & the Liberal Tradition in France, 1870-1914. 1966. lib. bdg. 14.00x (ISBN 0-374-97202-8). Octagon.

Sedgwick, Alexander C. Ralliement in French Politics, 1890-1898. LC 65-12828. (Historical Studies: No. 74). 1965. 8.50x (ISBN 0-674-74751-8). Harvard U Pr.

Soltau, Roger H. French Parties & Politics, 1871-1921 with a Supplementary Chapter, 1922-1930. LC 65-18832. 1965. Repr. of 1930 ed. 6.00 (ISBN 0-8462-0571-8). Russell.

Weber, Eugen. Action Francaise: Royalism & Reaction in Twentieth-Century France. LC 62-15267. 1962. 25.00x (ISBN 0-8047-0134-2). Stanford U Pr.

--The Nationalist Revival in France. (California Library Reprint Series: No. 7). 1968. 25.75x (ISBN 0-520-01321-2). U of Cal Pr.

Zola, Emile. La Republique en Marche. 660p. 1956. 8.95 (ISBN 0-686-55799-9). French & Eur.

FRANCE–POLITICS AND GOVERNMENT–20TH CENTURY

Earle, Edward M., ed. Modern France: Problems of the Third & Fourth Republics. LC 64-10387. (Illus.). 1964. Repr. of 1951 ed. 17.50 (ISBN 0-8462-0462-2). Russell.

Ehrman, Henry W. Politics in France. 3rd ed. (Ser. in Comparative Politics). 1976. pap. text ed. 9.95 (ISBN 0-316-22292-5). Little.

Frears, J. R. Political Parties & Elections in the French 5th Republic. LC 77-82043. 1978. 18.95 (ISBN 0-312-62331-3). St Martin.

Gallaher, John G. The Students of Paris & the Revolution of Eighteen Forty-Eight. LC 79-27580. 150p. 1980. 9.95x (ISBN 0-8093-0953-X). S Ill U Pr.

Hanley, D. L., et al. Contemporary France: Politics & Society Since 1945. (Illus.). 1979. 25.00x (ISBN 0-7100-0308-0); pap. 12.50 (ISBN 0-7100-0309-9). Routledge & Kegan.

Hauss, Charles. The New Left in France: The Unified Socialist Party. LC 77-94753. (Contributions in Political Science: No. 9). (Illus.). 1978. lib. bdg. 19.95 (ISBN 0-313-20113-7, HNL/). Greenwood.

Kuisel, Richard F. Capitalism & the State in Modern France: Renovation & Economic Management in the Twentieth Century. 352p. Date not set. price not set (ISBN 0-521-23474-3). Cambridge U Pr.

Leffler, Melvyn P. The Elusive Quest: America's Pursuit of European Stability & French Security, 1919-1933. LC 78-9782. 1979. 24.50x (ISBN 0-8078-1333-8). U of NC Pr.

Liddendale, David W. The Parliament of France. LC 79-1633. 1980. Repr. of 1954 ed. 23.50 (ISBN 0-88355-937-4). Hyperion Conn.

Macridis, Roy C., ed. De Gaulle: Implacable Ally. LC 75-41500. 248p. 1976. Repr. of 1966 ed. lib. bdg. 16.75x (ISBN 0-8371-8710-9, DEIA). Greenwood.

Mendes France, Pierre. A Modern French Republic. Carter, Anne, tr. from Fr. LC 75-2698. 205p. 1975. Repr. of 1963 ed. lib. bdg. 15.00 (ISBN 0-8371-8026-0, MEMF). Greenwood.

Micaud, Charles A. French Right & Nazi Germany, 1933-1939. 1964. lib. bdg. 16.00x (ISBN 0-374-95586-7). Octagon.

Moraze, Charles. French & the Republic. Demorest, Jean-Jacques, tr. LC 75-153260. (French Civilization Ser). 1971. Repr. of 1958 ed. 13.00 (ISBN 0-8046-1578-0). Kennikat.

Pickles, Dorothy M. French Politics: The First Years of the Fourth Republic. LC 72-122001. 1971. Repr. of 1953 ed. 15.00 (ISBN 0-8462-1464-4). Russell.

Schalk, David. The Spectrum of Political Engagement: Mounier, Benda, Nizan, Brasillach, Sartre. LC 78-70318. 1979. 15.00x (ISBN 0-691-05275-1). Princeton U Pr.

Serfaty, Simon, ed. The Foreign Policies of the French Left. LC 79-53137. (Westview Special Studies in West European Politics & Society). 1979. lib. bdg. 16.50x (ISBN 0-89158-652-0). Westview.

Simone, Andre. J'accuse: The Men Who Betrayed France. LC 68-26224. 1969. Repr. of 1940 ed. 12.50 (ISBN 0-8046-0422-3). Kennikat.

Talbott, John. France Since Nineteen Thirty. (New York Times Book Ser.). 1972. 7.95 (ISBN 0-531-06325-9); pap. 2.95 (ISBN 0-531-06425-5). Watts.

Touraine, Alain. May Movement: Revolt & Reform. Mayhew, Leonard F., tr. LC 76-103977. 1979. 28.50x (ISBN 0-394-46256-4); pap. text ed. 9.95x (ISBN 0-89197-626-4). Irvington.

FRANCE–POLITICS AND GOVERNMENT–1914-1940

Daladier, Edouard. In Defense of France. facsimile ed. LC 74-156637. (Essay Index Reprint Ser). Repr. of 1939 ed. 16.00 (ISBN 0-8369-2352-9). Arno.

Greene, Nathanael. From Versailles to Vichy: The Third French Republic 1919-1940. LC 75-101945. (AHM Europe Since 1500 Ser.). 1970. pap. 5.95x (ISBN 0-88295-737-6). Harlan Davidson.

Irvine, William D. French Conservatism in Crisis: The Republican Federation of France in the 1930s. LC 78-27254. (Illus.). 1979. text ed. 22.50x (ISBN 0-8071-0555-4). La State U Pr.

King, Jere C. Generals & Politicians: Conflict Between France's High Command, Parliament, & Government, 1914-1918. LC 74-112325. 1971. Repr. of 1951 ed. lib. bdg. 18.50x (ISBN 0-8371-4713-1, KIGP). Greenwood.

Larmour, Peter J. The French Radical Party in the 1930's. 1964. 15.00x (ISBN 0-8047-0206-3). Stanford U Pr.

McDougall, Walter A. France's Rhineland Policy, 1914-1924: The Last Bid for a Balance of Power in Europe. LC 77-85550. 1978. 31.00 (ISBN 0-691-05268-9). Princeton U Pr.

Marcus, John T. French Socialism in the Crisis Years, 1933-1936. LC 75-28666. 1976. Repr. of 1958 ed. lib. bdg. 15.50x (ISBN 0-8371-8480-0, MAFRS). Greenwood.

Tanenbaum, Jan K. General Maurice Sarrail, 1856-1929. LC 73-17109. (Illus.). 300p. 1974. 20.00x (ISBN 0-8078-1222-6). U of NC Pr.

Trachtenberg, Marc. Reparation in World Politics: France & European Economic Diplomacy, 1916-1923. LC 79-26898. 1980. 25.00x (ISBN 0-231-04786-X). Columbia U Pr.

Trotsky, Leon. The Crisis of the French Section (1935-1936) Allen, Naomi & Breitman, George, eds. Vogt, Marilyn, et al, trs. from Russ. Fr. 1977. 17.00 (ISBN 0-87348-519-X); pap. 4.95 (ISBN 0-87348-520-3). Path Pr NY.

--Leon Trotsky on France. Salner, David, ed. LC 78-59267. (Illus.). 1979. lib. bdg. 17.00 (ISBN 0-913460-65-6); pap. 4.95 (ISBN 0-913460-66-4). Monad Pr.

Warwick, Paul. The French Popular Front: A Legislative Analysis. LC 76-22952. (Illus.). 1977. lib. bdg. 16.00x (ISBN 0-226-86914-8). U of Chicago Pr.

Werth, Alexander. France & Munich. LC 68-9632. 1969. Repr. of 1939 ed. 27.50 (ISBN 0-86527-071-6). Fertig.

--The Twilight of France, 1933-1940. 24.00 (ISBN 0-86527-199-2). Fertig.

Wright, Gordon. Raymond Poincare & the French Presidency. 1967. Repr. lib. bdg. 17.50x (ISBN 0-374-98797-1). Octagon.

Yates, Louis A. U.S. & French Security, 1917-1921: A Study in American Diplomatic History. 10.95 (ISBN 0-685-60150-1, Pub by Twayne). Cyrco Pr.

FRANCE–POLITICS AND GOVERNMENT–1940-1945

Christian, William A. Divided Island: Faction & Unity on Saint Pierre. LC 69-12720. (Illus.). 1969. 12.50x (ISBN 0-674-21285-1). Harvard U Pr.

Farmer, Paul. Vichy: Political Dilemma. 1977. Repr. of 1955 ed. lib. bdg. 22.50x (ISBN 0-374-92700-6). Octagon.

Paxton, Robert O. Vichy France: Old Guard & New Order, 1940-1944. 426p. 1975. pap. 5.95 (ISBN 0-393-00794-4, N794, Norton Lib). Norton.

Tissier, Pierre. The Government of Vichy. LC 74-65. 347p. 1974. Repr. of 1942 ed. lib. bdg. 16.75x (ISBN 0-8371-7372-8, TIGV). Greenwood.

Waterfield, Gordon. What Happened to France. LC 72-1303. (Select Bibliographies Reprint Ser.). 1972. Repr. of 1940 ed. 14.00 (ISBN 0-8369-6839-5). Arno.

FRANCE–POLITICS AND GOVERNMENT–1945-

Ambler, John S. French Army in Politics, 1945-1962. LC 65-26274. 1966. 6.50 (ISBN 0-8142-0018-4). Ohio St U Pr.

Andrews, William G. French Politics & Algeria: The Process of Policy Formation 1954-1962. LC 62-15310. (Orig.). 1962. pap. text ed. 9.95x (ISBN 0-89197-179-3). Irvington.

Flanner, Janet. Paris Journal: Vol. I, 1944-1965. Shawn, William, ed. LC 76-45462. 1977. pap. 8.95 (ISBN 0-15-670950-3, Harv). HarBraceJ.

--Paris Journal: Vol. 2, 1965-1971. Shawn, William, ed. LC 76-45462. 1977. pap. 4.95 (ISBN 0-15-670951-1, Harv). HarBraceJ.

Furniss, Edgar S., Jr. France, Troubled Ally. LC 74-2667. 512p. 1974. Repr. of 1960 ed. lib. bdg. 23.50x (ISBN 0-8371-7421-X, FUFR). Greenwood.

Goguel, Francois. France Under the Fourth Republic. Pierce, Roy, tr. LC 76-139923. (Illus.). 1971. Repr. of 1952 ed. 12.00 (ISBN 0-8462-1558-6). Russell.

Johnson, R. W. The Long March of the French Left. 350p. 1981. 22.50x (ISBN 0-312-49645-1). St Martin.

Luthy, Herbert. France Against Herself. Mosbacher, Eric, tr. LC 74-20277. 476p. 1975. Repr. of 1955 ed. lib. bdg. 25.50x (ISBN 0-8371-7854-1, LUFA). Greenwood.

MacRae, D., Jr. Parliament Parties & Society in France: 1946-1958. 1967. 19.95 (ISBN 0-312-59710-X). St Martin.

Pickles, Dorothy M. Algeria & France. LC 75-35340. 1976. Repr. lib. bdg. 16.25x (ISBN 0-8371-8564-5, PIAF). Greenwood.

--France: The Fourth Republic. LC 75-3870. 1976. Repr. of 1958 ed. lib. bdg. 16.50x (ISBN 0-8371-8089-9, PIFR). Greenwood.

Romains, Jules. Examen de Conscience des Francais. 168p. 1954. 3.95 (ISBN 0-686-55306-3). French & Eur.

Schoenbrun, David. As France Goes. LC 55-8033. 1968. pap. 3.25 (ISBN 0-689-70174-8, 128). Atheneum.

Simmons, Harvey G. French Socialists in Search of a Role, 1956-1967. LC 75-87023. 1970. 22.50x (ISBN 0-8014-0540-8). Cornell U Pr.

Talbott, John. The War Without a Name: France in Algeria, 1954-1962. LC 80-344. 320p. 1980. 12.95 (ISBN 0-394-50909-9). Knopf.

Williams, Philip. Wars, Plots & Scandals in Post-War France. LC 77-96105. 1970. 31.95 (ISBN 0-521-07741-9). Cambridge U Pr.

Williams, Philip M. & Harrison, Martin. De Gaulle's Republic. LC 78-23520. 1979. Repr. of 1960 ed. lib. bdg. 20.50x (ISBN 0-313-21085-3, WIDG). Greenwood.

Wright, Gordon. The Reshaping of French Democracy. LC 68-9654. 1970. Repr. of 1948 ed. 18.50 (ISBN 0-86527-167-4). Fertig.

Wright, Vincent. The Government & Politics of France. LC 78-9274. 1978. text ed. 21.45x (ISBN 0-8419-0409-X); pap. text ed. 9.75x (ISBN 0-8419-0410-3). Holmes & Meier.

FRANCE–POLITICS AND GOVERNMENT–1958-

Andrews, William G. & Hoffman, Stanley, eds. The Impact of the Fifth Republic on France. LC 80-14651. 270p. pap. text ed. 7.95x (ISBN 0-87395-440-8). State U NY Pr.

Blondel, Jean. Contemporary France. 1974. pap. 5.95x (ISBN 0-416-81610-X). Methuen Inc.

--Government of France. 4th ed. (Orig.). 1974. pap. text ed. 8.95 scp (ISBN 0-690-00062-6, HarpC). Har-Row.

Bottin Administratif - 1980. 174th ed. LC 66-43255. 1302p. 1980. 55.00x (ISBN 2-7039-0477-0). Intl Pubns Serv.

Charlot, Jean. The Gaullist Phenomenon: The Gaullist Movement in the Fifth Republic. (Studies in Political Science). 1971. text ed. 32.50x (ISBN 0-04-320069-9). Allen Unwin.

Frears, J. C. & Parodi, Jean-Luc. War Will Not Take Place: The French Parliamentary Elections March 1978. LC 79-527. (Illus.). 1979. text ed. 20.00x (ISBN 0-8419-0478-2). Holmes & Meier.

Frears, J. R. France in the Giscard Presidency. 224p. 1981. text ed. 24.50x (ISBN 0-04-354025-2); pap. text ed. 10.95x (ISBN 0-04-354026-0). Allen Unwin.

--Parties & Elections in the French Fifth Republic. LC 77-82033. (Illus.). 1977. 17.95 (ISBN 0-312-59750-9). St Martin.

Heinz, Grete & Peterson, Agnes F. French Fifth Republic: Establishment & Consolidation, 1958-1965. LC 70-92497. (Bibliographical Ser.: No. 44). 1970. 11.95 (ISBN 0-8179-2441-8). Hoover Inst Pr.

Hermens, Ferdinand A. Fifth Republic. 1960. pap. 1.95x (ISBN 0-268-00098-0). U of Notre Dame Pr.

Johnson, Richard. The French Communist Party Versus the Students: Revolutionary Politics in May-June 1968. LC 72-181533. 288p. 1972. 17.50x (ISBN 0-300-01525-9); pap. 3.95x (ISBN 0-300-01563-1, Y-252). Yale U Pr.

Laponce, J. A. The Government of the Fifth Republic. LC 76-2005. (Illus.). 415p. 1976. Repr. of 1961 ed. lib. bdg. 24.00x (ISBN 0-8371-8763-X, LAGF). Greenwood.

McInnes, Neil. French Politics Today: The Future of the Fifth Republic. LC 77-90942. (The Washington Papers: No. 51). 71p. 1977. 4.00x (ISBN 0-8039-0978-0). Sage.

Macridis, Roy & Brown, Bernard. The De Gaulle Republic: Quest for Unity. LC 76-7417. 1976. Repr. of 1960 ed. lib. bdg. 32.50 (ISBN 0-8371-8848-2, MADG). Greenwood.

Micaud, Charles A. Communism & the French Left. 308p. 1980. Repr. of 1963 ed. lib. bdg. 17.50x (ISBN 0-374-95585-9). Octagon.

Morse, Edward L. Foreign Policy & Interdependence in Gaullist France. LC 72-5391. (Center of International Studies). 388p. 1973. 24.50 (ISBN 0-691-05209-3). Princeton U Pr.

Nana-Sinkam, Samuel. Pays Candidats Au Processus De Developement: Capacite d'Absorption Assistance Exterieure et Modeles de Vroissache Economique. (Illus.). 581p. (Fr.). 1975. text ed. 74.00x (ISBN 90-2797-965-0). Mouton.

Penniman, Howard R., ed. France at the Polls: The Presidential Election of 1974. LC 75-15146. 1975. pap. 8.25 (ISBN 0-8447-3171-4). Am Enterprise.

--French National Assembly Elections of 1978. 1980. pap. 7.25 (ISBN 0-8447-3372-5). Am Enterprise.

Philip, Andre. Counsel from an Ally: Reflections on Changes Within the Atlantic Community. LC 66-14033. 1966. 2.50 (ISBN 0-8262-0045-1). U of Mo Pr.

Pickles, Dorothy. The Government & Politics of France, Vol. 2: Politics. 500p. 1973. 26.00x (ISBN 0-416-75540-2); pap. 12.50x (ISBN 0-416-75550-X). Methuen Inc.

Pickles, Dorothy M. The Fifth French Republic. LC 75-32461. 222p. 1976. Repr. of 1960 ed. lib. bdg. 14.75x (ISBN 0-8371-8544-0, PIFF). Greenwood.

Pierce, Roy. French Politics & Political Institutions. 2nd ed. (Harper's Comparative Government Ser.). (Illus.). 1973. pap. text ed. 9.95 scp (ISBN 0-06-045234-X, HarpC). Harper Row.

Servan-Schreiber, Jean-Jacques. Spirit of May. 1969. 4.95 (ISBN 0-07-056315-2, GB). McGraw.

Soustelle, Jacques. New Road for France. 6.95 (ISBN 0-8315-0047-6). Speller.

Sulzberger, C. L. The Test: De Gaulle & Algeria. LC 74-6097. 228p. 1974. Repr. of 1962 ed. lib. bdg. 15.00x (ISBN 0-8371-7492-9, SUTT). Greenwood.

Thomas, Ruth. Broadcasting & Democracy in France. LC 77-90540. (International & Comparative Broadcasting Ser.). 1978. 15.00x (ISBN 0-87722-110-3). Temple U Pr.

Tilly, Charles. The Vendee: A Sociological Analysis of the Counter-Revolution of 1973. LC 64-21247. (Illus.). 1976. 17.50x (ISBN 0-674-93300-1); pap. 7.95x (ISBN 0-674-93302-8). Harvard U Pr.

Wahl, Nicholas. The Fifth Republic: France's New Political System. LC 78-24135. 1979. Repr. of 1959 ed. lib. bdg. 14.50x (ISBN 0-313-21217-1, WAFI). Greenwood.

Williams, Philip. French Politicians & Elections, 1951-1968. (Illus.). 1970. 41.50 (ISBN 0-521-07709-5); pap. 12.50x (ISBN 0-521-09608-1). Cambridge U Pr.

Williams, Philip M. The French Parliament: Politics in the Fifth Republic. LC 75-32655. 1977. Repr. of 1968 ed. lib. bdg. 15.00x (ISBN 0-8371-8558-0, WIFPP). Greenwood.

--The French Parliament 1958-1967. (Studies in Political Science). 1968. pap. text ed. 7.50x (ISBN 0-04-320045-1). Allen Unwin.

Wilson, Frank L. French Democratic Left, 1963-1969: Toward a Modern Party System. LC 74-143787. 1971. 12.50x (ISBN 0-8047-0765-0). Stanford U Pr.

Wright, Vincent, ed. Conflict & Consensus in France. 1979. 25.00x (ISBN 0-7146-3119-1, F Cass Co). Biblio Dist.

FRANCE–POPULATION

Angeville, A. d' Essai Sur la Statistique De la Population Francaise: Consideree Sous Quelque-Uns De Ses Rapports Physiques et Moraux. (Reeditions: No. 6). 1970. 65.30 (ISBN 0-686-20911-7). Mouton.

Bastide, R., et al. Les Haitiens en France. (Publications de l'Institut d'Etudes et de Recherches Interethniques et Interculturelles Ser.: No. 4). (Illus.). 229p. (Fr.). 1975. pap. text ed. 29.00x (ISBN 90-2797-515-9). Mouton.

Brion De Latour, Louis. Tableau De la Population De la France. Repr. of 1789 ed. 11.50 (ISBN 0-8287-0139-3). Clearwater Pub.

Dyer, Colin. Population & Society in Twentieth Century France. LC 77-2908. (Illus.). 1978. text ed. 31.00x (ISBN 0-8419-0308-5); pap. text ed. 13.50x (ISBN 0-8419-6209-X). Holmes & Meier.

Messance. Recherches Sur la Population Des Generalites D'auvergne, De Lyon, De Rouen... Repr. of 1766 ed. 46.00 (ISBN 0-8287-0607-7). Clearwater Pub.

Newell, William Henry. Population Change & Agricultural Development in 19th Century France. Bruchey, Stuart, ed. LC 77-77783. (Dissertations in European Economic History Ser.). (Illus.). 1977. lib. bdg. 20.00x (ISBN 0-405-10796-X). Arno.

Sauvy, Alfred. Les Principaux Demographes Francais Au XVIII Siecle, 12 vols. (Principal French Demographic Works of the 18th Century Ser.). (Fr.). 1976. Repr. of 1682 ed. lib. bdg. 295.00x set (ISBN 0-8287-1399-5). Clearwater Pub.

Spengler, Joseph. France Faces Depopulation: Postlude Edition, Nineteen Thirty-Six to Nineteen Seventy-Six. 1979. 17.75 (ISBN 0-8223-0422-8). Duke.

Spengler, Joseph J. France Faces Depopulation. LC 69-10158. (Illus.). 1968. Repr. of 1938 ed. lib. bdg. 16.75x (ISBN 0-8371-0235-9, SPFD). Greenwood.

Van De Walle, Etienne. The Female Population of France in the Nineteenth Century: A Reconstruction of 82 Departments. (Office of Population Research, Princeton University). 512p. 1974. text ed. 35.00x (ISBN 0-691-09360-1). Princeton U Pr.

FRANCE–PRESIDENTS

Wright, Gordon. Raymond Poincare & the French Presidency. 1967. Repr. lib. bdg. 17.50x (ISBN 0-374-98797-1). Octagon.

FRANCE–RACE QUESTION

Cohen, William B. The French Encounter with Africans: White Response to Blacks, 1530 to 1880. LC 79-84260. (Illus.). 384p. 1980. 22.50x (ISBN 0-253-34922-2). Ind U Pr.

Freeman, Gary P. Immigrant Labor & Racial Conflict in Industrial Societies: The French & British Experience, 1945-1975. LC 78-70292. 1979. 25.00x (ISBN 0-691-07603-0). Princeton U Pr.

FRANCE–RELATIONS (GENERAL) WITH FOREIGN COUNTRIES

Aron, Raymond & Heckscher, August. Diversity of Worlds. LC 72-12631. 178p. 1973. Repr. of 1957 ed. lib. bdg. 15.00 (ISBN 0-8371-6686-1, ARDW). Greenwood.

Bastide, Charles. Anglo-French Entente in the 17th Century. LC 78-146136. (Research & Source Works Ser.: No. 825). 1971. Repr. of 1914 ed. lib. bdg. 21.00 (ISBN 0-8337-0185-1). B Franklin.

De Graziani, Vincenzo G. The Franco-German Coalition & the Emergence of a New International Superpower: Its Effects Upon the Future Course of History. (Illus.). 1979. deluxe ed. 55.75 (ISBN 0-930008-31-6). Inst Econ Pol.

Dufrenoy, Marie-Louise. L' Orient Romanesque En France, 1704-1789: Tome III, L'idee De Progres L'orient. 509p. (Fr.). 1975. pap. text ed. 40.00x (ISBN 90-6203-108-0). Humanities.

Echeverria, Durand. Mirage in the West: A History of the French Image of American Society to 1815. 1966. lib. bdg. 17.50x (ISBN 0-374-92489-9). Octagon.

--Mirage in the West: A History of the French Image of American Society to 1815. LC 56-8379. 1957. pap. 6.95 (ISBN 0-691-00560-5). Princeton U Pr.

Farguharson, J. B. & Holt, S. C. Europe from Below: An Assessment of Franco-German Popular Contacts. LC 75-591. 224p. 1975. 19.95 (ISBN 0-312-26915-3). St Martin.

Fay, Bernard. Revolutionary Spirit in France and America. Guthrie, Ramon, tr. LC 66-26824. Repr. of 1927 ed. 16.50x (ISBN 0-8154-0067-5). Cooper Sq.

Jarrett, Derek. The Begetters of Revolution. 320p. 1973. 17.50x (ISBN 0-87471-136-3). Rowman.

Jones, Howard M. America & French Culture, 1750-1848. LC 73-3015. (Illus.). 615p. 1973. Repr. of 1927 ed. lib. bdg. 29.50x (ISBN 0-8371-6834-1, JOAF). Greenwood.

Jusserand, Jean A. With Americans of Past & Present Days. facsimile ed. LC 73-156669. (Essay index Reprint Ser). Repr. of 1916 ed. 19.50 (ISBN 0-8369-2555-6). Arno.

Mitchell, Allan. German Influence in France After Eighteen Seventy: The Formation of the French Republic. LC 78-31677. 1979. 19.95x (ISBN 0-8078-1357-5); pap. text ed. 9.95x (ISBN 0-8078-1374-5). U of NC Pr.

Pickles, Dorothy M. Algeria & France. LC 75-35340. 1976. Repr. 186p. lib. bdg. 16.25x (ISBN 0-8371-8564-5, PIAF). Greenwood.

Tout, Thomas F. France & England: Their Relations in the Middle Ages & Now. LC 74-5775. (U of Manchester Historical Ser.). 168p. 1975. Repr. of 1922 ed. lib. bdg. 15.00x (ISBN 0-8371-7514-3, TOFE). Greenwood.

Von Mohrenschildt, Dimitri S. Russia in the Intellectual Life of Eighteenth-Century France. LC 71-159255. x, 326p. 1971. Repr. of 1936 ed. lib. bdg. 16.00x (ISBN 0-374-98088-8). Octagon.

Willis, F. Roy. France, Germany, & the New Europe, 1945-1967. rev. ed. 1968. 25.00x (ISBN 0-8047-0241-1). Stanford U Pr.

FRANCE–RELATIONS (GENERAL) WITH FOREIGN COUNTRIES–BIBLIOGRAPHY

Fay, Bernard. Bibliographie Critique Des Ouvrages Francais Relatifs Aux Etats-Unis 1770-1800. LC 68-56725. 1968. 15.00 (ISBN 0-8337-1102-4). B Franklin.

FRANCE–RELIGION

see France–Church History

FRANCE–SOCIAL CONDITIONS

Babeau, Albert A. Ville sous l'ancien regime, 2 Vols. 2nd ed. Repr. of 1884 ed. Set. 49.50 (ISBN 0-404-07516-9). Vol. 1 (ISBN 0-404-07517-7). Vol. 2 (ISBN 0-404-07518-5). AMS Pr.

Baughan, Michalina, et al. Social Change in France. 1980. 22.50x (ISBN 0-312-73161-2). St Martin.

Beech, George T. A Rural Society in Medieval France: The Gatine of Poitou in the Eleventh & Twelfth Centuries. LC 78-64241. (Johns Hopkins University. Studies in the Social Sciences. Eighty-Second Ser. 1964: 1). Repr. of 1964 ed. 17.00 (ISBN 0-404-61346-2). AMS Pr.

Beer, William R. The Unexpected Rebellion: Ethnic Activism in Contemporary France. LC 79-3515. 1980. 20.00x (ISBN 0-8147-1029-8). NYU Pr.

Bernanos, Georges. Nous Autres Francais: Essai. pap. 4.95 (ISBN 0-685-37223-5). French & Eur.

Blondel, Jean. Contemporary France. 1974. pap. 5.95x (ISBN 0-416-81610-X). Methuen Inc.

Bourdieu, Pierre & Passeron, Jean-Claude. The Inheritors: French Students & Their Relation to Culture with a New Epilogue, Nineteen Seventy-Nine. Nice, Richard, tr. from Fr. LC 78-31532. (Illus.). 1979. lib. bdg. 15.00x (ISBN 0-226-06739-4). U of Chicago Pr.

Buttimer, Anne. Society & Milieu in the French Geographic Tradition. LC 72-158112. (Monograph: No. 6). 4.95 (ISBN 0-89291-085-2). Assn Am Geographers.

Cahm, Eric. Politics & Society in Contemporary France, 1789-1971: A Documentary History. 716p. 1972. 42.50x (ISBN 0-8448-0248-4). Crane-Russak Co.

Cobb, Richard C. Police & the People: French Popular Protest, 1789-1820. 414p. 1970. 34.50x (ISBN 0-19-821479-0); pap. 5.95x (ISBN 0-19-881297-3, OPB). Oxford U Pr.

--Reactions to the French Revolution. 1972. 22.00x (ISBN 0-19-212187-1). Oxford U Pr.

Cobban, Alfred B. Social Interpretation of the French Revolution. LC 64-21535. 1968. 24.95 (ISBN 0-521-04679-3); pap. 7.50xx (ISBN 0-521-09548-4). Cambridge U Pr.

Coffey, Peter. The Social Economy of France. LC 73-85269. 160p. 1974. 17.95 (ISBN 0-312-73220-1). St Martin.

Collins, Irene, ed. Government & Society in France: Eighteen-Fourteen to Eighteen Forty-Eight. LC 78-143997. (Documents of Modern History Ser). 1971. text ed. 17.95 (ISBN 0-312-34160-1). St Martin.

Delisle, Leopold V. Etudes sur la Condition de la Classe Agricole et l'Etat de l'Agriculture en Normandie au Moyen Age. 1965. Repr. of 1906 ed. 45.00 (ISBN 0-8337-0820-1). B Franklin.

Demographic, Social, Educational & Economic Data for France, 1833-1925: Historical Population, Economic & Social Data: France,1901-1921. 1979. codebook 20.00 (ISBN 0-89138-978-4). ICPSR.

Desert, Gabriel. Une Societe Rurale Au XIX Siecle: Les Paysans Du Calvados, 1815-1895. Bruchey, Stuart, ed. LC 77-77166. (Dissertations in European Economic History Ser.). (Illus., Fr.). 1977. lib. bdg. 53.00x (ISBN 0-405-10780-3). Arno.

Duby, Georges. Hommes & Structures Du Moyen Age: Racueil d'articles. (Le Savoir Historique: No. 1). (Illus.). 1973. pap. 19.50x (ISBN 90-2797-191-9). Mouton.

Dyer, Colin. Population & Society in Twentieth Century France. LC 77-2908. (Illus.). 1978. text ed. 31.00x (ISBN 0-8419-0308-5); pap. text ed. 13.50x (ISBN 0-8419-6209-X). Holmes & Meier.

Evans, David O. Social Romanticism in France, 1830-1848. LC 77-96180. 1969. Repr. of 1951 ed. lib. bdg. 11.00x (ISBN 0-374-92641-7, Dist. by NYGS). Octagon.

Fagniez, Gustave C. Etudes sur l'Industrie et la Classe Industrielle a Paris aux 13e et au 14e Siecle. LC 73-126393. (Research & Source Works: No. 566). (Fr). 1970. Repr. of 1877 ed. 32.50 (ISBN 0-8337-1096-6). B Franklin.

Forster, Robert, ed. Deviants & the Abandoned in French Society: Selections from the Annales Economies, Societies, Civilizations, Vol. 14. Ranum, Orest. LC 77-17253. (Illus.). 1978. text ed. 15.00x (ISBN 0-8018-1991-1); pap. 4.95 (ISBN 0-8018-1992-X). Johns Hopkins.

Fregier, H. A. Des Classes Dangereuses De la Societe Dans les Grandes Villes et Des Moyens De les Rendre Meilleures, 2 vols. (Conditions of the 19th Century French Working Class Ser.). (Fr.). 1974. Repr. of 1840 ed. Set. lib. bdg. 115.00 (ISBN 0-8287-0354-X, 1015, 1037). Clearwater Pub.

Funck-Brentano, Frantz. The Old Regime in France. LC 68-9656. 1970. Repr. 22.50 (ISBN 0-86527-141-0). Fertig.

Girardin, Emile de. L' Abolition de la Misere par l'Elevation des Salaires. (Conditions of the 19th Century French Working Class). 160p. (Fr.). 1974. Repr. of 1850 ed. lib. bdg. 48.50 (ISBN 0-8287-0251-9, 1018). Clearwater Pub.

Guizot, Francois P. Democracy in France. LC 74-19357. v, 82p. 1974. Repr. of 1849 ed. 13.75 (ISBN 0-86527-040-6). Fertig.

Le Goff, T. J. Vannes & Its Region: A Study of Town & Country in Eighteenth-Century France. (Illus.). 496p. 1981. 74.00x (ISBN 0-19-822515-6). Oxford U Pr.

Lewis, P. S. Later Medieval France: The Polity. 1968. 17.95 (ISBN 0-312-47250-1). St Martin.

Marceau, Jane. Class & Status in France: Economic Change & Social Immobility, 1945-1975. 1977. 29.95x (ISBN 0-19-827217-0). Oxford U Pr.

Maurice, Marc & Delomenie, Dominique. Mode De Vie et Espaces Sociaux: Processus D'urbanisation et Differenciation Sociale Dans Deux Zones Urbaines De Marseille. (La Recherche Urbaine: No. 11). (Illus., Orig., Fr.). 1976. pap. text ed. 15.50x (ISBN 0-686-22641-0). Mouton.

Mendras, Henri. Vanishing Peasant: Innovation & Change in French Agriculture. Lerner, Jean, tr. from Fr. Orig. Title: Fin Des Paysans. 1971. 20.00x (ISBN 0-262-13065-3). MIT Pr.

Michelet, Jules. The People. McKay, John P., tr. from Fr. & intro. by. LC 72-91078. 245p. 1973. 14.95 (ISBN 0-252-00321-7); pap. 4.95 (ISBN 0-252-00331-4). U of Ill Pr.

Mousnier, Roland E. The Institutions of France Under the Absolute Monarchy, Fifteen Ninety-Eight to Seventeen Eighty-Nine: Society & the State. Pearce, Brian, tr. from Fr. LC 78-26857. 1980. Repr. of 1974 ed. lib. bdg. 45.00x (ISBN 0-226-54327-7). U of Chicago Pr.

Petonnet, Colette. Those People: The Subculture of a Housing Project. Smidt, Rita, tr. from Fr. LC 72-825. (Contributions in Sociology: No. 10). 1973. lib. bdg. 14.95 (ISBN 0-8371-6393-5, PTP/). Greenwood.

Price, R. D. French Second Republic: A Social History. LC 70-173282. 1972. 22.50x (ISBN 0-8014-0686-2). Cornell U Pr.

Roustan, Marius. The Pioneers of the French Revolution. LC 68-9659. 1970. Repr. of 1926 ed. 20.00 (ISBN 0-86527-150-X). Fertig.

Rubin, James H. Realism & Social Vision in Courbet & Proudhon. LC 80-17559. (Essays on the Arts: No. 10). (Illus.). 270p. 1980. 18.50x (ISBN 0-691-03960-7); pap. 8.95x (ISBN 0-691-00327-0). Princeton U Pr.

Say, Jean-Baptiste. Olbie: Ou Essai sur les Moyens de Reformer les Moeurs d'une Nation. (Utopias in the Enlightenment Ser.). 141p. (Fr.). 1974. Repr. of 1800 ed. lib. bdg. 44.00x (ISBN 0-8287-0763-4, 055). Clearwater Pub.

See, Henri. Economic & Social Conditions in France During the Eighteenth Century. LC 68-9200. 1968. Repr. of 1927 ed. 11.50x (ISBN 0-8154-0203-1). Cooper Sq.

Shennan, J. H. Government & Society in France, 1461-1661. (Historical Problems: Studies & Documents). 1969. text ed. 21.00x o. p. (ISBN 0-04-901014-X); pap. text ed. 8.95x (ISBN 0-04-901015-8). Allen Unwin.

Sheridan, George J., Jr. The Social & Economic Foundations of Association Among the Silk Weavers of Lyons, 1852-1870. Bruchey, Stuart, ed. LC 80-2829. (Dissertations in European Economic History Ii). (Illus.). 1981. lib. bdg. 65.00x (ISBN 0-405-14013-4). Arno.

Suleiman, Ezra N., ed. Politics & Society in Contemporary France. 186p. (Orig.). 1977. pap. text ed. 4.00 (ISBN 0-87855-679-6). Transaction Bks.

Weber, Eugen. Peasants into Frenchmen: The Modernization of Rural France, 1870-1914. LC 75-7486. 1976. 25.00x (ISBN 0-8047-0898-3); pap. 8.95x (ISBN 0-8047-1013-9). Stanford U Pr.

Wood, Mary M. Spirit of Protest in Old French Literature. LC 17-30250. (Columbia University. Studies in Romance Philology & Literature: No. 21). Repr. of 1917 ed. 19.00 (ISBN 0-404-50621-6). AMS Pr.

Wright, Gordon. Rural Revolution in France: The Peasantry in the Twentieth Century. (Illus.). 1964. 12.50x (ISBN 0-8047-0190-3). Stanford U Pr.

Zeldin, Theodore. France, Eighteen Forty-Eight to Nineteen Forty-Five: Ambition & Love. 1979. pap. 8.95 (ISBN 0-19-285090-3, GB 587, GB). Oxford U Pr.

FRANCE-SOCIAL LIFE AND CUSTOMS

Argenson, Rene L. Journal et Memoires Du Marquis D'Argenson, 9 Vols. Set. 318.50 (ISBN 0-384-01912-9); Set. pap. 277.00 (ISBN 0-384-01914-5). Johnson Repr.

Barthes, Roland. Mythologies. 1957. 16.95 (ISBN 0-686-53938-9); pap. 5.95 (ISBN 0-686-53939-7). French & Eur.

Borrmans, M. Statut Personnel et Famille Au Maghreb De 1940 a Nos Jours. 77.75x (ISBN 90-279-7713-5). Mouton.

Briere, Eloise, et al. A French Cultural Reader. 1980. pap. 7.95 (ISBN 0-394-32642-3). Random.

Cobb, Richard C. Reactions to the French Revolution. 1972. 22.00x (ISBN 0-19-212187-1). Oxford U Pr.

Cooper, J. F. Gleanings in Europe, 2 Vols. Spiller, Robert E., ed. Repr. of 1928 ed. Set. 34.00 (ISBN 0-527-19400-X). Kraus Repr.

Cooper, James F. Gleanings in Europe: Italy. (The Writings of James Fenimore Cooper Ser.). (Illus.). 377p. 1981. pap. text ed. 8.95x (ISBN 0-87395-460-2, COGI-P). State U NY Pr.

Cooper, James Fenimore. Gleanings in Europe: France. Spiller, Robert E., ed. 1979. Repr. of 1928 ed. lib. bdg. 40.00 (ISBN 0-8492-4022-0). R West.

Deyon, Pierre. Amiens, Capitale Provinciale: Etude Sur la Societe Urbaine Au 17e Siecle. (Civilisations & Societes: No. 2). 1967. pap. 58.50x (ISBN 90-2796-073-9). Mouton.

Douet-D'Arcq, Louis C., ed. Choix De Pieces Inedites Relatives Au Regne De Charles Six, 2 Vols. 1863-1864. 63.50 (ISBN 0-384-12400-3); pap. 54.00 (ISBN 0-384-12401-1). Johnson Repr.

Ducros, Louis. French Society in the Eighteenth Century. De Geijer, W., tr. (Illus.). 1927. 22.50 (ISBN 0-8337-0941-0). B Franklin.

Dupeux, Georges. French Society, 1789-1970. Wait, Peter, tr. LC 75-46320. 294p. 1976. text ed. 25.00x (ISBN 0-416-65250-6). Methuen Inc.

Edeine, Bernard. La Sologne: Contribution Aux Etudes D'ethnologie Metropolitaine, 2 vols. 1974. 107.75x (ISBN 90-2797-253-2). Mouton.

--La Sologne: Documents de Litterature Traditionnelle, Vol. 3. (Illus.). 342p. (Fr.). 1975. text ed. 90.00x (ISBN 90-2797-735-6). Mouton.

Farnsworth, William O. Uncle & Nephew in the Old French Chansons De Geste. LC 70-168008. (Columbia University. Studies in Romance Philology & Literature: No. 14). Repr. of 1913 ed. 22.00 (ISBN 0-404-50614-3). AMS Pr.

Febvre, Lucien. Life in Renaissance France. Rothstein, Marian, tr. from Fr. LC 77-7454. 1979. 8.95x (ISBN 0-674-53175-2); pap. 3.95x (ISBN 0-674-53180-9). Harvard U Pr.

Fedden, Katharine. Manor Life in Old France: From the Journal of the Sire De Gouberville for the Years 1549-1562. LC 70-168013. Repr. of 1933 ed. 21.00 (ISBN 0-404-02374-6). AMS Pr.

Guizot, Francois P., ed. Memoirs to Illustrate the History of My Time, 8 Vols. Cole, John W., tr. LC 72-168212. Repr. of 1867 ed. Set. 260.00 (ISBN 0-404-08040-5); 32.50 ea. AMS Pr.

Holmes, Urban T., Jr. Daily Living in the Twelfth Century: Based on the Observations of Alexander Neckam in London & Paris. (Illus.). 1952. pap. 7.95x (ISBN 0-299-00854-1). U of Wis Pr.

Huizinga, J. Waning of the Middle Ages. LC 54-4529. pap. 3.95 (ISBN 0-385-09288-1, A42, Anch). Doubleday.

Huizinga, Johan. Waning of the Middle Ages: Study of the Forms of Life, Thought & Art in France & the Netherlands in the 14th & 15th Centuries. (Illus.). 1924. 25.00 (ISBN 0-312-85540-0). St Martin.

Keating, Louis C. Studies on the Literary Salon in France, 1550-1615. 1941. pap. 12.00 (ISBN 0-527-01114-2). Kraus Repr.

Lemieux, Vincent. Parente et Politique l'Organisation Sociale Dans l'Ile D'Orleans. 250p. (Fr.). 1971. 12.00 (ISBN 2-7637-6464-9, Pub. by Laval). Intl Schol Bk Serv.

Le Play, Frederick. La Reforme Sociale En France Deduite De L'observation Comparee Des Peuples Europeens: Social Reform in France Deduced from the Comparative Observation of the European Peoples, 2 vols. in one. LC 74-25766. (European Sociology Ser.). 936p. 1975. Repr. 51.00x (ISBN 0-405-06520-5). Arno.

Levitine, George. The Dawn of Bohemianism: The Barbu Rebellion & Primitivism in Neoclassical France. LC 77-13892. (Illus.). 1978. 22.50x (ISBN 0-271-00527-0). Pa St U Pr.

Luchaire, Achille. Social France at the Time of Philip Augustus. 1976. lib. bdg. 59.95 (ISBN 0-8490-2617-2). Gordon Pr.

--Social France at the Time of Phillip Augustus. 1929. 25.00 (ISBN 0-685-43863-5). Norwood Edns.

Mandrou, Robert. Introduction to Modern France, 1500-1640: An Essay in Historical Psychology. Hallmark, R. E., tr. LC 75-28239. (Illus.). 285p. 1976. text ed. 23.50x (ISBN 0-8419-0245-3). Holmes & Meier.

Maranda, Pierre. French Kinship Structure & History. (Janua Linguarum Ser. Practica: No. 169). 1974. pap. text ed. 36.25x (ISBN 0-686-22562-7). Mouton.

Miller, J. Dale & Loiseau, Maurice. USA-France Culture Capsules. 1977. pap. text ed. 5.95 (ISBN 0-88377-151-9). Newbury Hse.

Moore, John C. Love in Twelfth Century France. LC 75-170268. (Orig.). 1972. 12.00x (ISBN 0-8122-7648-5); pap. 5.95x (ISBN 0-8122-1027-1, Pa Paperbks). U of Pa Pr.

Roustan, Marius. The Pioneers of the French Revolution. LC 68-9659. 1970. Repr. of 1926 ed. 20.00 (ISBN 0-86527-150-X). Fertig.

Schneider, Pierre. World of Watteau. (Library of Art). (Illus.). 1967. 15.95 (ISBN 0-8094-0238-6). Time-Life.

Singer, Barnett. Modern France: Mind, Politics, Society, 1870-1970. LC 80-24177. 212p. 1981. 16.95 (ISBN 0-295-95791-3). U of Wash Pr.

Some Aspects of French Cultural Policy. 1970. pap. 3.25 (ISBN 92-3-100801-3, UNESCO). Unipub.

Sterne, Laurence. A Sentimental Journey Through France & Italy by Mr. Yorick. rev. ed. Stout, Gardner D., Jr., ed. (Illus.). 1967. 30.00x (ISBN 0-520-01228-3). U of Cal Pr.

--Sentimental Journey Through France & Italy. Petrie, Graham, ed. (English Library Ser.). 1967. pap. 2.50 (ISBN 0-14-043026-1). Penguin.

Suleiman, Ezra N. Elites in French Society: The Politics of Survival. LC 78-51195. 1978. text ed. 22.00 (ISBN 0-691-07597-2); pap. 9.75 (ISBN 0-691-10071-3). Princeton U Pr.

Taine, Hippolyte A. The Ancient Regime. 8.00 (ISBN 0-8446-1434-3). Peter Smith.

--The Ancient Regime: Les Oricines De la France Contemporaine. Durand, John, tr. LC 79-38368. (Select Bibliographies Reprint Ser.). Repr. of 1881 ed. 21.00 (ISBN 0-8369-6785-2). Arno.

--The Modern Regime, 2 vols. 8.00 ea. (ISBN 0-8446-1436-X). Peter Smith.

Valette, Jean-Paul & Valette, Rebecca. Contacts: Langue et Culture Francaises. LC 75-32873. 1976. text ed. 17.35 (ISBN 0-395-20690-1); tchrs. ed. 18.40 (ISBN 0-395-20689-8); wkbk. cahier d'exercices 5.55 (ISBN 0-395-20692-8). HM.

Wylie, Laurence W. Village in the Vaucluse. 3rd ed. (Illus.). 1974. 18.50x (ISBN 0-674-93937-9); pap. 5.95 (ISBN 0-674-93936-0). Harvard U Pr.

Zeldin, Theodore. France Eighteen Forty-Eight to Nineteen Forty-Five: Intellect & Pride. 368p. 1980. pap. 8.95 (ISBN 0-19-285096-2, GB600, GB). Oxford U Pr.

FRANCE-STATISTICS

Demographic, Social, Educational & Economic Data for France, 1833-1925: Vital Statistics for France, 1836-1925. LC 79-63207. 1979. codebook 20.00 (ISBN 0-89138-979-2). ICPSR.

Lebrun, Francois. Les Hommes et la Mort En Anjou Aux 17e et 18e Siecles: Essai De Demographie et De Psychologie Historiques. (Civilisations et Societes: No. 25). (Illus.). 1971. pap. 56.25x (ISBN 90-2796-904-3). Mouton.

Sandier, S. Comparison of Health Expenditures in France & the United States. Shipp, Audrey, ed. 60p. 1981. pap. text ed. 1.95 (ISBN 0-8406-0224-3). Natl Ctr Health Stats.

Spengler, Joseph J. France Faces Depopulation. LC 69-10158. (Illus.). 1968. Repr. of 1938 ed. lib. bdg. 16.75x (ISBN 0-8371-0235-9, SPFD). Greenwood.

FRANCE COMBATTANTE

Burman, Ben L. Generals Wear Cork Hats: An Amazing Adventure That Made World History. LC 63-18337. (Illus.). 1963. 5.00 (ISBN 0-8008-3150-0). Taplinger.

Spears, Edward. Fulfillment of a Mission: Syria & Lebanon, 1941-1944. 1978. 19.00 (ISBN 0-208-01695-3, Archon). Shoe String.

White, Dorothy S. Seeds of Discord: De Gaulle, Free France, & the Allies. LC 64-16922. (Illus.). 1964. 14.95x (ISBN 0-8156-0038-0). Syracuse U Pr.

FRANCE IN LITERATURE

France & World Literature: YFS, No. 6. 1950. pap. 6.00 (ISBN 0-527-01714-0). Kraus Repr.

Maurice, A. B. The Paris of the Novelists. 59.95 (ISBN 0-8490-0801-8). Gordon Pr.

Maurice, Arthur B. The Paris of the Novelists. LC 74-153276. (Illus.). 299p. 1973. Repr. of 1919 ed. 16.00 (ISBN 0-8046-1736-8). Kennikat.

FRANCESCA, PIERO DELLA

see Franceschi, Pietro Di Benedetto Dei, 1416-1492

FRANCESCHI, PIETRO DI BENEDETTO DEI, 1416-1492

Clark, Kenneth. Piero Della Francesca. 2nd ed. LC 81-66150. (Cornell-Phaidon Bks.). (Illus.). 240p. 1981. 75.00 (ISBN 0-8014-1423-7, Pub. by Phaidon England). Cornell U Pr.

Gilbert, Creighton. Change in Piero Della Francesca. LC 62-19124. (Illus.). 5.00 (ISBN 0-685-71754-2). J J Augustin.

Kenneth, Clark. Piero Della Francesca. (Illus.). 212p. 1981. 75.00 (ISBN 0-8014-1423-7). Cornell U Pr.

Lavin, Marilyn A. Piero della Francesca's Baptism of Christ. LC 81-3371. (Publications in the History of Art Ser.: No. 29). (Illus.). 204p. 1981. 27.50x (ISBN 0-300-02619-6). Yale U Pr.

Stokes, Adrian D. Art & Science: A Study of Alberti, Pierodella Francesca & Giorgione. LC 50-2168. 75p. 1949. Repr. 29.00 (ISBN 0-403-07226-3). Somerset Pub.

FRANCESCO D'ASSISI, SAINT, 1182-1226

Alimenti, Dane. Warriors for Love. Bertagni, Ted & Kocka, David, trs. 1979. cancelled (ISBN 0-8199-0760-X). Franciscan Herald.

Armstrong, Edward A. St. Francis, Nature Mystic: The Derivation & Significance of the Nature Stories in the Franciscan Legend. LC 74-149949. 1973. 24.50x (ISBN 0-520-01966-0); pap. 5.95 (ISBN 0-520-03040-0). U of Cal Pr.

Bach, Lester. Take Time for Sunsets. 1975. 6.95 (ISBN 0-8199-0565-8). Franciscan Herald.

Bishop, Morris. St. Francis of Assisi. (Library of World Biography). 1974. pap. 3.95 (ISBN 0-316-09666-0). Little.

Brown, Raphael. True Joy from Assisi. 1978. 8.95 (ISBN 0-8199-0688-3). Franciscan Herald.

Butler, Salvator, tr. We Were with St. Francis. 164p. 1976. pap. 4.95 (ISBN 0-8199-0603-4). Franciscan Herald.

Celano, Thomas. St. Francis of Assisi. 1963. 11.95 (ISBN 0-8199-0097-4); pap. 4.95 (ISBN 0-8199-0098-2). Franciscan Herald.

Chesterton, G. K. Saint Francis of Assisi. LC 57-1230. 1957. pap. 2.45 (ISBN 0-385-02900-4, D50, Im). Doubleday.

--St. Francis of Assisi. 1979. Repr. lib. bdg. 25.00 (ISBN 0-8495-0933-5). Arden Lib.

Christiani, Leon. St. Francis of Assisi. LC 74-79802. 1975. 4.95 (ISBN 0-8198-0494-0). Dghtrs St Paul.

Clissold, Stephen, compiled by. The Wisdom of St. Francis & His Companions. LC 78-27504. (Wisdom Books). 1979. pap. 3.75 (ISBN 0-8112-0721-8, NDP477). New Directions.

Coulton, G. G. Two Saints: St. Bernard & St. Francis. 1923. lib. bdg. 10.00 (ISBN 0-8414-3513-8). Folcroft.

Cunningham, Lawrence. Saint Francis of Assisi. LC 81-47419. (Illus.). 128p. 1981. 19.95 (ISBN 0-06-061651-2, HarpR); prepub. 14.95 pre-Dec (ISBN 0-686-72764-9). Har-Row.

Cunningham, Lawrence S. Saint Francis of Assisi. LC 76-14219. (World Authors Ser: No. 409). 1976. lib. bdg. 12.50 (ISBN 0-8057-6249-3). Twayne.

De La Bedoyere, Michael. Francis: A Biography of the St. of Assisi. (Fountain Religious Paperbacks Ser.). 1976. pap. 2.50 (ISBN 0-00-624453-X, FA4453). Collins Pubs.

Doyle, Eric. Saint Francis & the Song of Brotherhood. 1981. pap. 5.95 (ISBN 0-8164-2300-8). Seabury.

Egan, Maurice F. The Life of St. Francis & the Soul of Modern Man. (Illus.). 1979. 27.75 (ISBN 0-89266-149-6). Am Classical Coll Pr.

Englebert, Abbe Omer. St. Francis of Assisi. 1965. 8.50 (ISBN 0-8199-0099-0, L38735). Franciscan Herald.

Englebert, Omer. Saint Francis of Assisi: A Biography. abr. ed. 1979. pap. 2.95 (ISBN 0-89283-071-9). Servant.

Erikson, Joan M. Saint Francis & His Four Ladies. LC 71-127178. (Illus.). 1970. 6.95 (ISBN 0-393-05427-6). Norton.

Esser, Cajetan. Rule & Testament of St. Francis. LC 77-5318. 1977. 7.95 (ISBN 0-8199-0674-3). Franciscan Herald.

Flood, David & Matura, Thadee. The Birth of a Movement. LaChance, Paul & Schwartz, Paul, trs. 168p. 1975. 6.95 (ISBN 0-8199-0567-4). Franciscan Herald.

Floristan, Casiano & Duquoc, Christian. Francis of Assisi: An Example, Vol. 149. (Concilium 1981). 128p. (Orig.). 1981. pap. 6.95 (ISBN 0-8164-2349-0). Seabury.

Fortini, Arnaldo. Francis of Assisi. Moak, Helen, tr. 900p. 1980. 29.50 (ISBN 0-8245-0003-2). Crossroad NY.

Franciscan Education. (Franciscan Educational Conferences Ser). 1929. pap. 1.00 (ISBN 0-685-77548-8). Franciscan Herald.

Garner, Robert H. The Way of St. Francis. 1981. 6.95 (ISBN 0-8062-1605-0). Carlton.

Gemelli, Agostino. Message of St. Francis. 1976. 3.95 (ISBN 0-8199-0072-9). Franciscan Herald.

Habig, Marion A., ed. English Omnibus of Sources: St. Francis of Assisi. new ed. 1977. 18.95 (ISBN 0-8199-0658-1). Franciscan Herald.

--St. Francis of Assisi: Omnibus of Sources of the Life of St.Francis. Brown, Raphael & Fahy, B., trs. (Illus.). 1828p. 1975. 25.00 (ISBN 0-8199-0440-6). Franciscan Herald.

Hansen, Warren N. St. Francis of Assisi: Patron of the Environment. LC 72-139973. (Illus.). 1971. 4.95 (ISBN 0-8199-0508-9). Franciscan Herald.

Hegener, Mark. Poverello: St. Francis of Assisi. pap. 0.95 (ISBN 0-8199-0358-2). Franciscan Herald.

Holl, Adolf & Heinegg, Peter. The Last Christian: A Biography of Francis Assisi. LC 79-7868. 288p. 1980. 12.95 (ISBN 0-385-15499-2). Doubleday.

Isabell, Damian, ed. Workbook for Franciscan Studies: Companion Guide to Omnibus of Sources. 1976. pap. text ed. 8.50 (ISBN 0-8199-0574-7). Franciscan Herald.

Jorgensen, Johannes. Saint Francis of Assisi. pap. 3.50 (ISBN 0-385-02875-X, D22, Im). Doubleday.

Kazantzakis, Nikos. Saint Francis. 1963. pap. 5.95 (ISBN 0-671-21247-8, Touchstone Bks). S&S.

Leclerc, Eloi. The Canticle of Creatures: An Interpretive Study. O'Connell, Matthew J. & Motte, Mary M., trs. 280p. 1977. 6.95 (ISBN 0-8199-0441-4). Franciscan Herald.

--Exile & Tenderness. 1965. 3.95 (ISBN 0-8199-0019-2, L38136). Franciscan Herald.

Line, Francis R. & Line, Helen E. Man with a Song. 1978. 8.95 (ISBN 0-8199-0756-1). Franciscan Herald.

Longpre, Ephrem. Poor Man's Peace: St. Francis of Assisi. 1968. 4.95 (ISBN 0-8199-0017-6). Franciscan Herald.

Meyer, James. Social Ideals of St. Francis. 2.75 (ISBN 0-8199-0296-9, L38825). Franciscan Herald.

Nicholson, D. H. The Mysticism of St. Francis of Assissi. 1977. lib. bdg. 59.95 (ISBN 0-8490-2319-X). Gordon Pr.

Nigg, Walter. Francis of Assisi. (Illus.). 240p. 1975. 12.95 (ISBN 0-8199-0586-0). Franciscan Herald.

O'Brien, Isidore. Francis of Assisi: Mirror Christ. 1978. 6.95 (ISBN 0-8199-0691-3). Franciscan Herald.

Petry, Ray C. Francis of Assisi. LC 41-25932. Repr. of 1941 ed. 11.50 (ISBN 0-404-05017-4). AMS Pr.

Raymond, Ernest. In the Steps of St. Francis. 380p. 1975. pap. 4.95 (ISBN 0-8199-0557-7). Franciscan Herald.

Sabatier, Paul. Life of St. Francis of Assisi. 1977. lib. bdg. 59.95 (ISBN 0-8490-2167-7). Gordon Pr.

Sabatini, Rafael. Heroic Lives. facs. ed. LC 70-99648. (Essay Index Reprint Ser). 1934. 17.50 (ISBN 0-8369-2071-6). Arno.

A Short Life of St. Francis. LC 77-6661. 1977. pap. text ed. 3.95 (ISBN 0-8199-0675-1). Franciscan Herald.

Subercaseaux, Pedro E. Life of Saint Francis. 1977. buckram 25.00 (ISBN 0-8199-0615-8). Franciscan Herald.

Telaki, Isabella. St. Francis, the Troubadour of Assisi. 1973. pap. 2.25 (ISBN 0-686-18873-X). Benziger Sis.

Timmermans, Felix. The Perfect Joy of St. Francis. 280p. 1974. pap. 2.95 (ISBN 0-385-02378-2, Im). Doubleday.

Van Corstanje. Francis: Bible of the Poor. 1977. 5.95 (ISBN 0-8199-0661-1). Franciscan Herald.

Van Corstanje, Auspicius. Covenant with God's Poor. 3.95 (ISBN 0-8199-0014-1). Franciscan Herald.

Van Doornik, N. Francis of Assisi: A Prophet for Our Time. 1978. 7.95 (ISBN 0-8199-0695-6). Franciscan Herald.

Van Moorselaar, Corinne. Francis & the Animals. Hegener, Mark, ed. Smith, David, tr. LC 77-7391. (Illus., Dutch.). (gr. 3). 1977. 3.50x (ISBN 0-685-81231-6). Franciscan Herald.

Von Galli, Mario. Living Our Future: St. Francis of Assisi & the Church Tomorrow. new ed. (Illus.). 239p. 1976. pap. 4.95 (ISBN 0-8199-0439-2). Franciscan Herald.

Vorreux, Damien. First Encounter with Francis of Assisi. Schwartz, Paul & Lachance, Paul, trs. from Fr. 1979. pap. 6.95 (ISBN 0-8199-0698-0). Franciscan Herald.

FRANCESCO D'ASSISI, SAINT, 1182-1226-ART

Fortini, Arnaldo. Francis of Assisi. Moak, Helen, tr. 900p. 1980. 29.50 (ISBN 0-8245-0003-2). Crossroad NY.

FRANCESCO D'ASSISI, SAINT, 1182-1226-BIBLIOGRAPHY

Englebert, Abbe Omer. St. Francis of Assisi. 1965. 8.50 (ISBN 0-8199-0099-0, L38735). Franciscan Herald.

FRANCESCO D'ASSISI, SAINT, 1182-1226–FICTION

Brown, Raphael, tr. Little Flowers of St. Francis. 1971. pap. 2.95 (ISBN 0-385-07544-8, Im). Doubleday.

Johnson, Jan. Brother Francis: A Story About Saint Francis of Assisi. (Stories About Christian Heroes Ser). (gr. 1-5). 1977. pap. 1.95 (ISBN 0-03-022131-5). Winston Pr.

FRANCESCO D'ASSISI, SAINT, 1182-1226–JUVENILE LITERATURE

Bulla, Clyde R. Song of Saint Francis. LC 52-6739. (Illus.). (gr. 2-5). 1952. 10.95 (ISBN 0-690-75222-9, TYC-J). Har-Row.

Chavez, Fray A. Song of Francis. LC 73-75205. (Illus.). 64p. 1973. 6.50 (ISBN 0-87358-105-9). Northland.

Darian, Mujana. St. Francis & You. LC 79-88515. (gr. 1-4). 1979. pap. 4.95 (ISBN 0-87973-363-2). Our Sunday Visitor.

De Paola, Tomie. St. Francis of Assisi. (Illus.). 48p. (ps). 1982. PLB 10.95 (ISBN 0-8234-0435-8). Holiday.

FRANCESCO D'ASSISI, SAINT, 1182-1226–POETRY

Hermann, Placid. Seraph of Love. 2.50 (ISBN 0-8199-0128-8, L38775). Franciscan Herald.

Patterson, Elizabeth B., ed. Saint Francis & the Poet. 5.00 (ISBN 0-8159-6802-7). Devin.

Thom, Sr. M. Thaddeus. Two Prayers for Two Stones. 1976. 4.95 (ISBN 0-8199-0616-6). Franciscan Herald.

FRANCHISE

see Elections; Suffrage

FRANCHISES (RETAIL TRADE)

Alexander, Sandy. Franchising & You. (Illus.). 1970. pap. 5.95 (ISBN 0-685-04149-2). Lawrence.

Auslander, M. Arthur. Protecting & Profiting from Your Business Ideas. LC 68-30897. (Orig.). 1969. pap. 2.95 (ISBN 0-87576-021-X). Pilot Bks.

Church, Nancy S. Future Opportunities in Franchising: A Realistic Appraisal. LC 79-18545. 1979. pap. 3.50 (ISBN 0-87576-086-4). Pilot Bks.

DeBanks, M. Henward & Ginalski, William. The Franchise Option: Expanding Your Business Through Franchising. LC 80-65946. (Illus.). 187p. 1980. 34.50 (ISBN 0-936898-00-3). Franchise Group.

Finn, Richard. Your Fortune in Franchises. 1980. pap. 4.95 (ISBN 0-8092-7448-5). Contemp Bks.

Fowler, Robert A. & Hummel, T. W., eds. Buyerism: How to Buy a Franchise or Small Business. new ed. 1979. pap. 5.95 (ISBN 0-685-48362-2). WWWWW Info Serv.

Franchise Annual. 190p. 1980. 16.00 (ISBN 0-686-62457-2). B Klein Pubns.

Franchise Opportunities: A Business of Your Own. 13th rev. ed. LC 77-18404. (Illus.). 352p. 1980. pap. 7.95 (ISBN 0-8069-8886-X). Sterling.

Friedlander, Mark, Jr. & Gurney, Gene. Handbook of Successful Franchising. 1981. 19.95 (ISBN 0-442-22986-0). Van Nos Reinhold.

Glickman, Gladys. Franchising. 100.00 (ISBN 0-685-02522-5). Bender.

Green, Michael L., ed. Franchise Handbook. rev. ed. 1981. 13.20 (ISBN 0-89552-027-3); pap. text ed. 8.95 (ISBN 0-89552-026-5). DMR Pubns.

--Franchise Handbook. 1978. pap. 6.95 (ISBN 0-89552-020-6). DMR Pubns.

Gross, Harry. Franchise Investigation & Contract Negotiation. rev. ed. LC 67-29579. 1979. pap. 2.50 (ISBN 0-87576-001-5). Pilot Bks.

Hackett, Donald W. Franchising: The State of the Art. LC 77-21643. (Monograph Ser.: No. 9). 1977. 10.00 (ISBN 0-87757-101-5). Am Mktg.

Hammond, Alexander. Franchisee Rights: A Self Defense Manual for Dealers, Distributors, Wholesalers, & Other Franchisees. LC 79-90436. 360p. 1979. write for info. (ISBN 0-916592-33-2). Panel Pubs.

Head, Victor. Sponsorship: The Newest Marketing Skill. 160p. 1980. 39.00x (ISBN 0-85941-151-6, Pub. by Woodhead-Faulkner England). State Mutual Bk.

Heard, Niel. How the Value Added Tax Can Boost Our Economy. LC 71-132263. (Orig.). 1970. pap. 2.00 (ISBN 0-87576-031-7). Pilot Bks.

Hicks, Tyler G. Franchise Riches Success Kit. 2nd ed. 876p. 1981. pap. 99.50 (ISBN 0-914306-40-5). Intl Wealth.

Hunter, Richard J., Jr. Franchising: Legal & Financial Aspects. 400p. 1982. write for info. (ISBN 0-89651-215-0). Icarus.

Hutchison, T. W. Markets & the Franchise. (Institute of Economic Affairs, Occasional Papers Ser.: No. 10). pap. 2.50 (ISBN 0-255-69590-X). Transatlantic.

Jones, Thomas B. A Franchising Guide for Blacks. LC 73-12907. 48p. (Orig.). 1973. pap. 2.00 (ISBN 0-87576-004-X). Pilot Bks.

Lewis, Mack O. How to Franchise Your Business. rev. ed. LC 74-8015. 1980. 3.50 (ISBN 0-87576-007-4). Pilot Bks.

Mendelsohn, M. The Guide to Franchising. 2nd ed. LC 78-40961. 1978. 27.50 (ISBN 0-08-022466-0). Pergamon.

Mockler, Robert J. & Easop, Harrison. Guidelines for More Effective Planning & Management of Franchise Systems. LC 68-66049. (Research Monograph: No. 42). 1968. spiral bdg. 7.00 (ISBN 0-88406-056-X). Ga St U Busn Pub.

Modica, Alfred J. Franchising. (Illus.). 192p. 1981. pap. 12.95 (ISBN 0-8256-3203-X, Quick Fox). Music Sales.

Norback, Peter & Norback, Craig. The Dow Jones-Irwin Guide to Franchises. LC 78-55302. 1979. 14.95 (ISBN 0-87094-169-0). Dow Jones-Irwin.

Norback, Peter G. & Norback, Craig T. The Dow Jones-Irwin Guide to Franchises. rev. ed. 271p. 1981. 16.95 (ISBN 0-87094-270-0). Dow Jones-Irwin.

Pilot's Question & Answer Guide to Successful Franchising. rev. ed. LC 79-103723. (Orig.). 1978. pap. 2.00 (ISBN 0-87576-005-8). Pilot Bks.

Representing the Franchiser & Franchisee, 1979. (Commercial Law & Practice Course Handbook Ser. 1978-79: Vol. 205). 20.00 (ISBN 0-685-94315-1, A4-3035). PLI.

Scherer, Daniel J. Financial Security & Independence Through a Small Business Franchise. rev. ed. LC 67-29580. 1977. pap. 2.50 (ISBN 0-87576-002-3). Pilot Bks.

Schwartz, David J. The Franchise System for Establishing Independent Retail Outlets. LC 60-62926. (Research Monograph: No. 14). 1959. spiral bdg. 5.00 (ISBN 0-88406-031-4). Ga St U Busn Pub.

Seltz, D. D. The Complete Handbook of Franchising. 1982. price not set (ISBN 0-201-07136-3). A-W.

Seltz, David, ed. How to Get Started in Your Own Franchise Business. rev. ed. LC 79-27945. 1980. 19.95 (ISBN 0-87863-172-0). Farnswth Pub.

Seltz, David D. Treasury of Business Opportunities...Featuring Over 400 Ways to Make a Fortune Without Leaving Your House. LC 76-47103. 1976. 15.00 (ISBN 0-87863-097-X). Farnswth Pub.

Small, Anne & Levy, Robert S. Woman's Guide to Her Own Franchised Business. rev. ed. LC 67-25561. 1979. pap. 2.50 (ISBN 0-87576-003-1). Pilot Bks.

Small, Samuel & Pilot Books Staff. Directory of Franchising Organizations 1981. LC 62-39831. 1981. pap. 3.50 (ISBN 0-87576-000-7). Pilot Bks.

State Business Franchise Disclosure & Relationship Laws, As of May, 1978. 1978. pap. 8.50 (ISBN 0-685-39490-5). Commerce.

Vaughn, Charles L. Franchising. 2nd & rev. ed. LC 78-24841. (Illus.). 304p. 1979. 22.95 (ISBN 0-669-02852-5). Lexington Bks.

FRANCHISES, MUNICIPAL

see Municipal Franchises

FRANCHISES, TAXATION OF

see Corporations–Taxation

FRANCIA, JOSE GASPAR RODRIGUEZ, DICTATOR OF PARAGUAY, d. 1840

Rengger, Johann R. & Longchamps, M. Reign of Doctor Joseph Gaspard Roderick De Francia, in Paraguay. LC 70-130334. (Latin-American History & Culture Ser). 1971. Repr. of 1827 ed. 12.50 (ISBN 0-8046-1394-X). Kennikat.

Robertson, John P. & Robertson, W. P. Letters on Paraguay Comprising an Account of a Four Years' Residence in That Republic, Under the Government of the Dictator Francia, 3 Vols. 2nd ed. LC 74-128429. Repr. of 1839 ed. Set. 65.00 (ISBN 0-404-05390-4); 22.50 ea. AMS Pr.

White, Richard A. Paraguay's Autonomous Revolution, 1810-1840. LC 78-55707. 1978. 12.95x (ISBN 0-8263-0486-9). U of NM Pr.

FRANCIS OF ASSISI, SAINT

see Francesco D'Assisi, Saint, 1182-1226

FRANCIS OF SALES

see Francois De Sales, Saint, Bishop of Geneva, 1567-1622

FRANCISCAN RECOLLETS

see Recollets (Franciscan)

FRANCISCAN SISTERS

Flood, David. Franciscan Women. 64p. 1976. pap. 0.95 (ISBN 0-8199-0593-3). Franciscan Herald.

Mary in the Franciscan Order: Proceedings Third National Meeting of Franciscan Teaching Sisterhoods, Vol. 3. 1955. 4.00 (ISBN 0-686-11578-3). Franciscan Inst.

FRANCISCANS

see also Recollets (Franciscan)

Bacigalupo, Leonard. The Franciscans & Italian Immigration in America. LC 76-50676. 1977. 4.50 (ISBN 0-682-48741-4, University). Exposition.

Bettoni, Efrem. Nothing for Your Journey. 1959. 2.50 (ISBN 0-8199-0669-7, L38565). Franciscan Herald.

Boehner, Philotheus. Conferences for Franciscan Religious. (Spirit & Life Ser). 1966. 2.00 (ISBN 0-686-11571-6). Franciscan Inst.

Breton, Valentine. Franciscan Spirituality. pap. 1.50 (ISBN 0-8199-0035-4, L38225). Franciscan Herald.

Brooke, Rosalind B., ed. The Coming of the Friars. (Historical Problems: Studies & Documents Ser.: Vol.24). 224p. 1975. text ed. 16.50x (ISBN 0-06-490700-7). B&N.

Ciampi, Luke. Watering the Seed. 1977. 5.95 (ISBN 0-685-71934-0). Franciscan Herald.

Communications & the Franciscan Message. (Franciscan Educational Conferences). 1959. pap. 4.50 (ISBN 0-685-77536-4). Franciscan Herald.

Crosby, J. Bearing Witness. 3.75 (ISBN 0-685-10960-7, L38022). Franciscan Herald.

De Aspurz-Iriarte, Lazaro. The Franciscan Calling. Kelly, Sr. Marie, tr. 300p. 1975. 6.95 (ISBN 0-8199-0538-0). Franciscan Herald.

Douie, Decima L. The Nature & the Effect of the Heresy of the Fraticelli. LC 77-84715. Repr. of 1932 ed. 25.50 (ISBN 0-404-16121-9). AMS Pr.

Esser, Cajetan. Order of St. Francis. 1959. 0.95 (ISBN 0-8199-0081-8, L38595). Franciscan Herald.

--Origins of the Order of Friars Minor. (Orig.). 1970. 12.50 (ISBN 0-8199-0414-7). Franciscan Herald.

Esser, Cajetan & Grau, E. Love's Reply. 1963. 4.95 (ISBN 0-685-10969-0, L38405); pap. 3.95 (ISBN 0-8199-0067-2, L38406). Franciscan Herald.

Fleming, John V. An Introduction to the Franciscan Literature of the Middle Ages. 1977. 10.95 (ISBN 0-8199-0651-4). Franciscan Herald.

Flood, David & Matura, Thadee. The Birth of a Movement. LaChance, Paul & Schwartz, Paul, trs. 168p. 1975. 6.95 (ISBN 0-8199-0567-4). Franciscan Herald.

Franciscan Approach to Theology. (Franciscan Educational Conferences Ser). 1957. pap. write for info. (ISBN 0-685-77538-0). Franciscan Herald.

Franciscan Education. (Franciscan Educational Conferences Ser). 1929. pap. 1.00 (ISBN 0-685-77548-8). Franciscan Herald.

Franciscan Educational Conference - 43rd. Holy Eucharist & Christian Unity. 1962. pap. 4.50 (ISBN 0-8199-0300-0, L38270). Franciscan Herald.

Franciscan Educational Conference - 44th. Elements of Franciscan Formation. 1963. 4.50 (ISBN 0-685-10964-X, L38134). Franciscan Herald.

Franciscan Ideals & Family Problems. (Franciscan Educational Conferences Ser). 1960. pap. 4.50 (ISBN 0-685-77535-6). Franciscan Herald.

Franciscan Life Today. (Franciscan Educational Conferences Ser). 1956. pap. 3.75 (ISBN 0-685-77539-9). Franciscan Herald.

Gasnick, Roy, compiled By. The Francis Book: A Celebration of the Universal Saint. (Illus.). 320p. 1980. 19.95 (ISBN 0-02-542760-1, Collier); pap. 12.95 (ISBN 0-02-003200-5). Macmillan.

Guidance Through Franciscan Spirituality. (Franciscan Educational Conferences Ser). 1948. pap. 3.50 (ISBN 0-685-77545-3). Franciscan Herald.

Habig, Marion A., ed. Vitam Alere, Franciscan Readings. (Tau Ser.). 1979. 5.95 (ISBN 0-8199-0769-3). Franciscan Herald.

Harkins, Conrad L., ed. Franciscan Studies. (Annual review). 12.00 (ISBN 0-686-12038-8). Franciscan Inst.

Jeffrey, David L. The Early English Lyric & Franciscan Spirituality. LC 74-78478. (Illus.). xvi, 306p. 1975. 19.50x (ISBN 0-8032-0845-6). U of Nebr Pr.

Lapsanski, Duane V. The First Franciscans & the Gospel. 1976. 6.95 (ISBN 0-8199-0568-2). Franciscan Herald.

Marquard, Philip. Formation of Lay Franciscans. 1973. pap. 1.50 (ISBN 0-8199-0470-8). Franciscan Herald.

Marshall, John F. Conferences on the Our Father. (Spirit & Life Ser). 1967. 2.00 (ISBN 0-686-11573-2). Franciscan Inst.

Muller, Francis J. De Parolcia Domui Religiosae Commissa. 1956. 3.50 (ISBN 0-686-11580-5). Franciscan Inst.

Musser, Benjamin F. Franciscan Poets. facs. ed. LC 67-26768. (Essay Index Reprint Ser). 1933. 15.25 (ISBN 0-8369-0732-9). Arno.

Muzzey, D. S. The Spiritual Franciscans. 59.95 (ISBN 0-8490-1113-2). Gordon Pr.

Ozanam, Frederick. Franciscan Poets of the Thirteenth Century. LC 68-26288. 1969. Repr. of 1914 ed. 13.75 (ISBN 0-8046-0342-1). Kennikat.

Romb, Anselm. Franciscan Charism. 1976 ed. 3.00 (ISBN 0-685-77515-1); pap. 1.95 (ISBN 0-685-77516-X). Franciscan Herald.

Salimbene Di Adam. From Saint Francis to Dante: Translations from the Chronicle of the Franciscan Salimbene (1221-88) Coulton, G. G., ed. & tr. from It. LC 68-10910. 462p. 1972. pap. 5.95x (ISBN 0-8122-1053-0, Pa Paperbks). U of Pa Pr.

Van Corstanje, Auspicius. Covenant with God's Poor. 3.95 (ISBN 0-8199-0014-1). Franciscan Herald.

Wolter, Allan B. Life in God's Love. 1958. pap. 1.75 (ISBN 0-8199-0059-1, L38375). Franciscan Herald.

FRANCISCANS–BIBLIOGRAPHY

Adams, Eleanor B. Bio-Bibliography of Franciscan Authors in Colonial Central America. (Bibliographical Ser.). 1953. 10.00 (ISBN 0-88382-101-X). AAFH.

FRANCISCANS–MISSIONS

Bacigalupo, Leonard F. The American Franciscan Missions in Central America. LC 80-68205. 480p. 1980. 14.50 (ISBN 0-933402-20-1); pap. 8.95 (ISBN 0-933402-21-X). Charisma Pr.

Dawson, Christopher. Mission to Asia. (Medieval Academy Reprints for Teaching Ser.). 228p. 1981. pap. 6.00x (ISBN 0-8020-6436-1). U of Toronto Pr.

Habig, Marion A. In Journeyings Often: Franciscan Pioneers in the Orient. (Spirit & Life Ser). 1953. 6.50 (ISBN 0-686-11564-3). Franciscan Inst.

O'Rourke, Thomas P. The Franciscan Missions in Texas (1690-1793) LC 73-3559. (Catholic University of America. Studies in American Church History: No. 5). Repr. of 1927 ed. 14.50 (ISBN 0-404-57755-5). AMS Pr.

Willeke, Bernward H. Imperial Government & Catholic Missions in China During the Years 1784-1785. (Missiology Ser). 1948. 3.00 (ISBN 0-686-11584-8). Franciscan Inst.

FRANCISCANS–PRAYER-BOOKS AND DEVOTIONS

Boehner, Philotheus. Walter Burleigh De Puritate Artis Logicae Tractatus Langios. Incl. Tractatus Brevior. (Text Ser). 1955. 6.00 (ISBN 0-686-17965-X). Franciscan Inst.

Francis, Mary. Blessed Are You. (Spirit & Life Ser). 1976. 3.50 (ISBN 0-686-17961-7). Franciscan Inst.

FRANCISCANS–SECOND ORDER

see Poor Clares

FRANCISCANS–THIRD ORDER

Esser, Cajetan. Origins of the Order of Friars Minor. (Orig.). 1970. 12.50 (ISBN 0-8199-0414-7). Franciscan Herald.

Habig, Marion A. & Hegener, Mark. Short History of the Third Order. pap. 1.95 (ISBN 0-8199-0107-5, L38805). Franciscan Herald.

Lummis, Charles F. Land of Poco Tiempo. LC 66-22698. (Illus.). 1981. pap. 5.95 (ISBN 0-8263-0071-5). U of NM Pr.

Rome Hath Spoken: Encyclicals on the Third Order. 1958. pap. 1.50 (ISBN 0-8199-0095-8, L38695). Franciscan Herald.

Van Corstanje, Auspicius. The Third Order for Our Times. 1974. 2.50 (ISBN 0-8199-0487-2). Franciscan Herald.

Wolter, Allan B. The Book of Life: An Explanation of the Rule of the Third Order Regular of Saint Francis. (Spirit & Life Ser). 1954. pap. 2.50 (ISBN 0-686-11566-X). Franciscan Inst.

FRANCISCANS IN AMERICA

Adams, Eleanor B., ed. The Missions of New Mexico, 1776: A Description by Fray Francisco Atanasio Dominguez with Other Contemporary Documents. LC 55-12223. 1975. Repr. of 1956 ed. 35.00 (ISBN 0-8263-0373-0); deluxe ed. 100.00 (ISBN 0-8263-0418-4). U of NM Pr.

Griffen, William B. Indian Assimilation in the Franciscan Area of Nueva Vizcaya. LC 78-14546. (Anthropological Papers: No. 33). 1979. pap. 6.75x (ISBN 0-8165-0584-5). U of Ariz Pr.

Phelan, John L. The Millennial Kingdom of the Franciscans in the New World. 2nd rev ed. 1970. 21.75x (ISBN 0-520-01404-9). U of Cal Pr.

FRANCISCANS IN CHINA

Dawson, Christopher H., ed. The Mongol Mission. LC 78-63334. (The Crusades & Military Orders: Second Ser.). Repr. of 1955 ed. 26.50 (ISBN 0-404-17008-0). AMS Pr.

Pfeilschifter, B. & Schmalz, N. Shen-Fu's Story. 3.50 (ISBN 0-8199-0130-X, L38787). Franciscan Herald.

FRANCISCANS IN FRANCE

Burr, David. Persecution of Peter Olivi. LC 76-24254. (Transactions Ser.: Vol. 66, Pt. 5). 1976. pap. 6.00 (ISBN 0-87169-665-7). Am Philos.

FRANCISCANS IN THE UNITED STATES

Bolton, Herbert E. Fray Juan Crespi, Missionary Explorer on the Pacific Coast, 1769-1774. LC 78-158616. Repr. of 1927 ed. 29.50 (ISBN 0-404-01838-6). AMS Pr.

Morales, Francisco. Ethnic & Social Background of the Franciscan Friars in Seventeenth Century Mexico. (Monograph Ser.). 1973. 20.00 (ISBN 0-88382-060-9). AAFH.

Palou, Francisco. Historical Memoirs of New California, 4 Vols. Bolton, Herbert E., ed. & tr. LC 66-11363. (Illus.). 1966. Repr. of 1926 ed. Set. 65.00 (ISBN 0-8462-0658-7). Russell.

Truman, Stanley R. Missions. LC 80-66674. (Illus.). 96p. 1980. 38.95 (ISBN 0-910312-43-5). Calif Hist.

FRANCISCO XAVIER, SAINT, 1506-1552

Benziger, Marieli. St. Francis Xavier: A Sixteenth-Century Nobleman. pap. 2.25 (ISBN 0-686-18871-3). Benziger Sis.

Daughters of St. Paul. Flame in the Night. 1967. 3.00 (ISBN 0-8198-0234-4). Dghtrs St Paul.

Gowen, Herbert H. Five Foreigners in Japan. facs. ed. LC 67-28735. (Essay Index Reprint Ser). 1936. 18.00 (ISBN 0-8369-0491-5). Arno.

Hammer, Sahue. Indonesia & India, Fifteen Forty-Five to Fifteen Forty-Nine. 726p. (Orig.). 1980. 33.00 (ISBN 0-8294-0356-6). Loyola.

Schurhammer, Georg. Francis Xavier, His Life, His Times. Costelloe, M. Joseph, tr. Incl. Vol. 1. Europe, 1506-1541. 1973. 22.00 (ISBN 0-686-28511-5); Vol. 2. India, 1541-1545. 1977. 28.00 (ISBN 0-686-28512-3). LC 72-88247. (Illus.). Jesuit Hist.

FRANCK, CESAR AUGUSTE, 1822-1890

Davies, Laurence. Cesar Franck & His Circle. LC 77-4231. (Music Reprint Ser.). (Illus.). 1977. Repr. of 1970 ed. lib. bdg. 27.50 (ISBN 0-306-77410-0). Da Capo.

--Franck. (The Master Musicians Ser.). (Illus.). 160p. 1973. 11.00x (ISBN 0-460-03134-1, Pub. by J. M. Dent England). Biblio Dist.

Vallas, Leon. Cesar Franck. LC 73-5210. (Illus.). 283p. 1973. Repr. of 1951 ed. lib. bdg. 16.50x (ISBN 0-8371-6873-2, VACF). Greenwood.

FRANCK, FREDERICH, 1909-

Franck, Frederick. Art As a Way: A Return to the Spiritual Roots. LC 81-7853. (Illus.). 160p. (Orig.). 1981. pap. 9.95 (ISBN 0-8245-0076-8). Crossroad NY.

--Pilgrimage to Now - Here. LC 73-78933. (Illus.). 192p. 1974. pap. 3.95x (ISBN 0-88344-387-2). Orbis Bks.

--Zen of Seeing. 1973. pap. 5.95 (ISBN 0-394-71968-9, V968, Vin). Random.

FRANCO BAHAMONDE, FRANCISCO, 1892-1975

Ellwood, Sheelagh M., ed. Spain in Franco's Shadow: Interviews on Contemporary Politics, Society, Economics, & Culture. 250p. 1981. text ed. 25.95x (ISBN 0-918294-13-4). Karz Pub.

Fox, Hugh. The Guernica Cycle: The Year Franco Died. 64p. 1981. 12.00 (ISBN 0-916156-60-5); pap. 4.00 (ISBN 0-916156-61-3). Cherry Valley.

May, Harry S. Francisco Franco: The Jewish Connection. 1978. pap. text ed. 9.00 (ISBN 0-8191-0363-2). U Pr of Amer.

FRANCO-CHINESE WAR

see Chinese-French War, 1884-1885

FRANCO-ENGLISH WAR, 1755-1763

see United States-History-French and Indian War, 1755-1763

FRANCO-GERMAN WAR, 1870-1871

see also Paris-History

Bury, J. P. Gambetta & the National Defense. LC 70-80531. 1970. Repr. of 1936 ed. 23.50 (ISBN 0-86527-077-5). Fertig.

Bury, John P. Gambetta - the National Defence: A Republican Dictatorship in France. LC 77-114490. (Illus.). 1971. Repr. of 1936 ed. lib. bdg. 15.25x (ISBN 0-8371-4818-9, BUGN). Greenwood.

Calleo, David. The German Problem Reconsidered. LC 78-9683. 208p. 1980. pap. 6.95 (ISBN 0-521-29966-7). Cambridge U Pr.

Decsy, Janos. Prime Minister Gyula Andrassy's Influence on Habsburg Foreign Policy. (East European Monographs: No. 52). 1979. 12.00x (ISBN 0-914710-44-3). East Eur Quarterly.

De Mauni, Roger. Franco-Prussian War. Clarke, David S., ed. (Military Memoirs Ser.). 1970. 14.50 (ISBN 0-208-01081-5, Archon). Shoe String.

Gazley, John G. American Opinion of German Unification, 1848-1871. LC 77-130939. (Columbia University Social Science Studies Ser.: No. 267). 1970. Repr. of 1926 ed. 10.00 (ISBN 0-404-51267-4). AMS Pr.

Halperin, S. William. Diplomat Under Stress. LC 63-13065. 1963. 7.00x (ISBN 0-226-31441-3). U of Chicago Pr.

Hemmings, D. W. Culture & Society in France: Eighteen Forty-Eight to Eighteen Ninety-Eight. 1971. 40.00 (ISBN 0-7134-1522-3, Pub. by Batsford England). David & Charles.

Howard, Michael. The Franco-Prussian War: The German Invasion of France 1870-71. 1979. Repr. of 1961 ed. text ed. 26.00x (ISBN 0-246-63587-8). Humanities.

Lord, Robert H. Origins of the War of 1870: New Documents from the German Archives. LC 65-17907. 1966. Repr. of 1924 ed. 8.50 (ISBN 0-8462-0608-0). Russell.

Mitchell, Allan. German Influence in France After Eighteen Seventy: The Formation of the French Republic. LC 78-31677. 1979. 19.95x (ISBN 0-8078-1357-5); pap. text ed. 9.95x (ISBN 0-8078-1374-5). U of NC Pr.

Ollivier, Emile. The Franco-Prussian War & Its Hidden Causes. facsimile ed. Ives, George B., tr. LC 71-140369. (Select Bibliographies Reprint Ser). Repr. of 1912 ed. 26.00 (ISBN 0-8369-5612-5). Arno.

Oncken, Hermann. Napoleon Third & the Rhine: The Origin of the War of 1870-1871. Zeydel, Edwin H., tr. LC 66-24743. 1967. Repr. of 1928 ed. 8.00 (ISBN 0-8462-0966-7). Russell.

Peel, Peter H. British Public Opinion & the Wars of German Unification: 1864-1871. 537p. 1978. 19.95 (ISBN 0-940990-00-8). Intl Res Inst.

Raymond, Dora N. British Policy & Opinion During the Franco-Prussian War. LC 21-20208. (Columbia University. Studies in the Social Sciences: No. 227). 1921. 27.50 (ISBN 0-404-51227-5). AMS Pr.

Sumner, Charles. Addresses on War. Bd. with Letters to Charles Sumner on His Oration on the True Grandeur of Nations. Ford, Washington C., ed. LC 74-147699. (Library of War & Peace; Proposals for Peace: a History). lib. bdg. 38.00 (ISBN 0-8240-0226-1). Garland Pub.

Von Blumenthal, Leonhard. Journals of Field Marshall Count Von Blumenthal for 1866 & 1870-71. Gillespie-Addison, A. D., tr. LC 71-136412. Repr. of 1903 ed. 15.00 (ISBN 0-404-00914-X). AMS Pr.

Von Verdy Du Vernois, Julius A. With the Royal Headquarters in Eighteen Seventy to Eighteen Seventy-One. LC 68-54812. (Illus.). 1968. Repr. of 1897 ed. lib. bdg. 14.50x (ISBN 0-8371-0392-4, VERH). Greenwood.

--With the Royal Headquarters in Eighteen Seventy to Seventy-One. LC 79-142243. Repr. of 1897 ed. 21.50 (ISBN 0-404-06757-3). AMS Pr.

FRANCO-GERMAN WAR, 1870-1871–FICTION

Howard, Michael. Franco-Prussian War: The German Invasion of France, 1870-1871. 1981. pap. 11.00x (ISBN 0-416-30750-7). Methuen Inc.

Zola, Emile. Debacle. 1968. 9.95 (ISBN 0-236-17783-4, Pub. by Paul Elek). Merrimack Bk Serv.

FRANCO-PROVENCAL DIALECTS

see also Provencal Language

Adams, George C. Words & Descriptive Terms for "Woman" & "Girl" in French & Provencal & Border Dialects. (Studies in the Romance Languages & Literatures: No. 11). 1949. pap. 7.00x (ISBN 0-8078-9011-1). U of NC Pr.

Jochnowitz, George. Dialect Boundaries & the Question of Franco-Provencal. (Janua Linguarum Ser. Practica: No. 147). 1973. pap. text ed. 45.00x (ISBN 90-2792-480-5). Mouton.

Woodard, Clement M. Words for "Horse" in French & Provencal. (Language Dissertation Ser.: No. 29). 1939. pap. 6.00 (ISBN 0-527-00775-7). Kraus Repr.

FRANCO-PRUSSIAN WAR, 1870-1871

see Franco-German War, 1870-1871

FRANCO-RUSSIAN ALLIANCE

Langer, William L. Franco-Russian Alliance, 1890-1894. 1967. Repr. lib. bdg. 25.00x (ISBN 0-374-94769-4). Octagon.

Michon, Georges. The Franco Russian Alliance, 1891-1917. LC 68-9610. 1969. Repr. of 1929 ed. 25.00 (ISBN 0-86527-072-4). Fertig.

FRANCO-TEXAN LAND COMPANY

Taylor, Virginia H. The Franco-Texan Land Company. (M. K. Brown Range Life Ser.: No. 7). (Illus.). 345p. 1969. 15.00 (ISBN 0-292-78417-1). U of Tex Pr.

FRANCOIS 1ST, KING OF FRANCE, 1494-1547

Hackett, Francis. Francis the First. LC 68-8334. (Illus.). 1968. Repr. of 1935 ed. lib. bdg. 18.25x (ISBN 0-8371-0093-3, HAFF). Greenwood.

Wilkinson, Burke. Francis in All His Glory. LC 70-182106. (Illus.). 288p. (gr. 7 up). 1972. 5.95 (ISBN 0-374-32457-3). FS&G.

FRANCOIS DE SALES, SAINT, BISHOP OF GENEVA, 1567-1622

Rivet, Mother Mary M. Influence of the Spanish Mystics on the Works of Saint Francis De Sales. LC 79-115355. (Catholic University of America. Studies in Romance Languages & Literatures: No. 22). Repr. of 1941 ed. 15.00 (ISBN 0-404-50322-5). AMS Pr.

Streebing, Cecilian. Devout Humanism As a Style. LC 70-128930. (Catholic University. Romance Literature: No. 50). Repr. of 1954 ed. 17.50 (ISBN 0-404-50350-0). AMS Pr.

Vincent, Francis. Le Travail du style chez St. Francois de Sales. 115p. (Fr.). 1981. Repr. of 1923 ed. lib. bdg. 55.00 (ISBN 0-8287-1519-X). Clearwater Pub.

FRANCS-TIREURS

see Guerrillas

FRANJU, GEORGES, 1912-

Durgnat, Raymond. Franju. movie ed. LC 68-31139. 1967. 9.95x (ISBN 0-520-00366-7); pap. 1.95 (ISBN 0-520-00367-5, CAL171). U of Cal Pr.

FRANK, ANNE, 1929-1945

Felderer, Ditlieb. Anne Frank's Diary: A Hoax. 1981. lib. bdg. 59.95 (ISBN 0-686-73176-X). Revisionist Pr.

--Anne Frank's Diary: A Hoax. (Illus.). 100p. (Orig.). 1980. pap. 5.00 (ISBN 0-911038-57-4, 335, Dist. by Inst Hist Rev.). Noontide.

Frank, Anne. Anne Frank: The Diary of a Young Girl. pap. 2.50 (ISBN 0-671-80243-7); enriched classic edition 2.25 (ISBN 0-671-82748-0). WSP.

Monarch Notes on Frank's Diary of a Young Girl. (Orig.). pap. 1.95 (ISBN 0-671-00561-8). Monarch Pr.

Schnabel, Ernst. Anne Frank: A Portrait in Courage. LC 53-12702. 1967. pap. 0.65 (ISBN 0-15-607530-X, HPL16, HPL). HarBraceJ.

FRANK, GLENN, 1887-1940

Larsen, Lawrence H. The President Wore Spats: A Biography of Glenn Frank. LC 65-63009. (Illus.). 1965. 4.50 (ISBN 0-87020-056-9). State Hist Soc Wis.

FRANK, JACOB, 1726?-1791

Mandel, Arthur. The Militant Messiah or the Flight from the Ghetto: The Story of Jacob Frank & the Frankist Movement. LC 79-443. 1979. text ed. 10.00x (ISBN 0-391-00973-7). Humanities.

FRANK, JEROME NEW, 1889-1957

Rosenberg, J. Mitchell. Jerome Frank: Jurist & Philosopher. LC 76-100581. 1970. 8.75 (ISBN 0-8022-2328-1). Philos Lib.

Volkomer, Walter E. Passionate Liberal: The Political & Legal Ideas of Jerome Frank. LC 74-580407. 1970. 15.00x (ISBN 90-247-0561-4). Intl Pubns Serv.

FRANK, LEO MAX, 1884-1915

Dinnerstein, L. The Leo Frank Case. LC 68-199750. 248p. 1968. 16.00x (ISBN 0-231-03067-3). Columbia U Pr.

FRANK, WALDO DAVID, 1889-1967

Carter, Paul J. Waldo Frank. (Twayne's United States Authors Ser). 1967. pap. 3.45 (ISBN 0-8084-0313-3, T125, Twayne). Coll & U Pr.

Munson, Gorham B. Waldo Frank: A Study. LC 75-23023. 1975. lib. bdg. 15.00 (ISBN 0-8414-6124-4). Folcroft.

Trachtenberg, Alan, ed. Memoirs of Waldo Frank. LC 73-123541. (Illus.). 304p. 1973. 15.00x (ISBN 0-87023-081-6). U of Mass Pr.

FRANKENHEIMER, JOHN, 1930-

Pratley, Gerald. Cinema of John Frankenheimer. LC 69-14893. (Film Guide Ser.). (Illus.). 1969. pap. 4.95 (ISBN 0-498-07413-7). A S Barnes.

FRANKFURT AM MAIN

Estienne, Henri. Frankfort Book Fair. Thompson, James W., tr. (Bibliography & Reference Ser.: No. 145). (Lat & Eng). 1968. Repr. of 1911 ed. 29.00 (ISBN 0-8337-3519-5). B Franklin.

Heyn, Udo. Private Banking & Industrialization: The Case of Frankfurt Am Main, 1825-1875. Bruchey, Stuart, ed. LC 80-2810. (Dissertations in European Economic History II). (Illus.). 1981. lib. bdg. 38.00x (ISBN 0-405-13994-2). Arno.

Slater, Phil. Origin & Significance of the Frankfurt School, a Marxist Perspective. (International Library of Sociology). 1980. pap. 7.95 (ISBN 0-7100-0490-7). Routledge & Kegan.

Soliday, Gerald L. A Community in Conflict: Frankfurt Society in the Seventeenth & Early Eighteenth Centuries. LC 73-89285. (Illus.). 270p. 1974. text ed. 15.00x (ISBN 0-87451-092-9). U Pr of New Eng.

Whittingham, William. A Brieff Discours off the Troubles Begonne at Franckford. LC 71-38228. (English Experience Ser.: No. 492). 210p. 1972. Repr. of 1574 ed. 13.00 (ISBN 90-221-0492-3). Walter J Johnson.

FRANKFURT BOOK FAIR

Who's Who at the Frankfurt Book Fair Nineteen Seventy-Nine. (An International Publisher's Guide). 425p. 1979. pap. 19.80 (ISBN 0-89664-132-5). K G Saur.

FRANKFURTER, FELIX, 1882-1965

Frankfurter, Felix. Felix Frankfurter Reminisces. LC 78-5896. 1978. Repr. of 1960 ed. lib. bdg. 23.50x (ISBN 0-313-20466-7, FRFF). Greenwood.

Hirsch, H. N. The Enigma of Felix Frankfurter. LC 80-68184. 320p. 1981. 14.95 (ISBN 0-465-01979-X). Basic.

Jacobs, Clyde. Justice Frankfurter & Civil Liberties. LC 74-1331. (Civil Liberties in American History Ser.). 265p. 1974. Repr. of 1961 ed. lib. bdg. 25.00 (ISBN 0-306-70585-0). Da Capo.

Konefsky, Samuel J. The Constitutional World of Mr. Justice Frankfurter: Some Representative Opinions. Konefsky, Samuel J., ed. 1971. Repr. of 1949 ed. 16.25 (ISBN 0-02-847990-4). Hafner.

Kurland, Philip B. Mr. Justice Frankfurter & the Constitution. LC 77-133259. 1971. 15.00x (ISBN 0-226-46405-9). U of Chicago Pr.

Lash, Joseph P., ed. From the Diaries of Felix Frankfurter. 366p. 1975. 12.50 (ISBN 0-393-07488-9). Norton.

Mendelson, Wallace. Justices Black & Frankfurter: Conflict in the Court. 2nd ed. LC 61-5781. 1966. 8.00x (ISBN 0-226-51980-5). U of Chicago Pr.

FRANKL, VIKTOR EMIL

Leslie, Robert C. Jesus & Logotherapy. LC 65-11077. (Series AD). 1968. pap. 2.25 (ISBN 0-687-19927-1, Apex). Abingdon.

FRANKLIN, BENJAMIN, 1706-1790

Aldridge, Alfred O. Benjamin Franklin & Nature's God. LC 67-13409. 1967. 13.75 (ISBN 0-8223-0002-8). Duke.

--Franklin & His French Contemporaries. LC 76-21244. 260p. 1976. Repr. of 1957 ed. lib. bdg. 18.50x (ISBN 0-8371-9007-X, ALFF). Greenwood.

Aldridge, Alfred Owen. Franklin & his French Contemporaries. LC 56-10778. 1957. 11.00x (ISBN 0-8147-0003-9). NYU Pr.

Alico, Stella H. Benjamin Franklin - Martin Luther King Jr. (Pendulum Illustrated Biography Ser.). (Illus.). (gr. 4-12). 1979. text ed. 5.00 (ISBN 0-88301-365-7); pap. text ed. 1.95 (ISBN 0-88301-353-3); wkbk 1.25 (ISBN 0-88301-377-0). Pendulum Pr.

Amacher, Richard E. Benjamin Franklin. (Twayne's United States Authors Ser). 1962. pap. 3.45 (ISBN 0-8084-0059-2, T12, Twayne). Coll & U Pr.

Autobiography of Benjamin Franklin. (Literature Ser.). (gr. 10-12). 1970. pap. text ed. 3.58 (ISBN 0-87720-721-6). AMSCO Sch.

Baker, Jim. Benjamin Franklin: The Uncommon Man. (Illus.). 1976. pap. 1.00 (ISBN 0-914482-13-0). Ohio Hist Soc.

Barbour, Brian M., ed. Benjamin Franklin: A Collection of Critical Essays. (Twentieth Century Views Ser.). 1979. text ed. 10.95 (ISBN 0-13-074856-0, Spec); pap. 3.95 (ISBN 0-13-074849-8). P-H.

Bigelow, ed. Works of Ben Franklin, 12 vols. 275.00 (ISBN 0-403-04349-2). Somerset Pub.

Block, Seymour S. Benjamin Franklin: His Wit, Wisdom & Women. 448p. 1975. 14.50 (ISBN 0-8038-0767-8). Hastings.

Bowen, Catherine D. The Most Dangerous Man in America: Scenes from the Life of Benjamin Franklin. 1974. 10.95 (ISBN 0-316-10396-9, Pub. by Atlantic Monthly Pr). Little.

Buxbaum, Melvin H. Benjamin Franklin & the Zealous Presbyterians. LC 74-14932. 320p. 1974. 17.95x (ISBN 0-271-01176-9). Pa St U Pr.

Clark, William B. Ben Franklin's Privateers: A Naval Epic of the American Revolution. LC 74-90485. Repr. of 1956 ed. lib. bdg. 15.00x (ISBN 0-8371-2262-7, CLFP). Greenwood.

Conner, Paul W. Poor Richard's Politicks: Benjamin Franklin & His New American Order. LC 80-21490. xiv, 285p. 1980. Repr. of 1965 ed. lib. bdg. 27.50x (ISBN 0-313-22695-4, COPRP). Greenwood.

Country Beautiful Editors. The Spirit of Early America: The Life & Words of Benjamin Franklin. (Home Library Ser.). (Illus.). 1976. 9.95 (ISBN 0-87294-093-4). Country Beautiful.

Country Beautiful Editors, ed. The Most Amazing American: Benjamin Franklin. LC 73-75989. (Illus.). 160p. 1973. 15.95 (ISBN 0-87294-035-7). Country Beautiful.

Crane, Verner W. Benjamin Franklin & A Rising People. (Library of American Biography). 219p. 1962. pap. text ed. 4.95 (ISBN 0-316-16012-1). Little.

Crowther, James G. Famous American Men of Science. facs. ed. LC 69-18925. (Essay Index Reprint Ser). 1937. 25.00 (ISBN 0-8369-0040-5). Arno.

Currey, Cecil B. Road to Revolution: Benjamin Franklin in England 1765-1775. (Illus.). 10.00 (ISBN 0-8446-1931-0). Peter Smith.

Day, Kenneth. William Caxton & Charles Knight. (Illus.). 240p. pap. 8.95 (ISBN 0-913720-06-2). Sandstone.

De Meyer, John. Benjamin Franklin Calls on the President. 1939. 10.00 (ISBN 0-8274-1924-4). R West.

Duane, William, ed. Letters to Benjamin Franklin, from His Family & Friends, 1751-1790. facs. ed. (Select Bibliographies Reprint Ser). 1858. 16.00 (ISBN 0-8369-5325-8). Arno.

Eliot, Charles W. Four American Leaders. LC 73-14550. (Franklin, Washington, Channing, Emerson). 1907. lib. bdg. 17.50 (ISBN 0-8414-3916-8). Folcroft.

Fay, Bernard. Franklin: The Apostle of Modern Times. 1929. 30.00 (ISBN 0-8274-2370-5). R West.

--Two Franklins. LC 70-93277. Repr. of 1933 ed. 18.50 (ISBN 0-404-02372-X). AMS Pr.

Ford, Paul L. Franklin Bibliography: A List of Book Written by or Relating to Benjamin Franklin. 1966. Repr. of 1889 ed. 31.50 (ISBN 0-8337-1187-3). B Franklin.

--The Many-Sided Franklin. LC 73-38353. (Select Bibliographies Reprint Ser). Repr. of 1898 ed. 34.00 (ISBN 0-8369-6770-4). Arno.
--The Many Sided Franklin. 1899. 30.00 (ISBN 0-8274-2671-2). R West.
--Who Was the Mother of Franklin's Son? An Historical Conundrum, Hitherto Given up-Now Partly Answered. LC 78-182127. (Historical Printing Club, Publications: No. 26). 16p. 1972. Repr. of 1889 ed. lib. bdg. 10.00 (ISBN 0-8337-1203-9). B Franklin.
Franklin, Benjamin. Autobiography & Other Writings. Nye, Russel B., ed. LC 58-59440. (YA) (gr. 9 up). 1958. pap. 3.95 (ISBN 0-395-05130-4, 3-47666, RivEd, A32). HM.
--Autobiography & Selected Writings. Wecter, Dixon & Ziff, Larzer, eds. LC 59-14521. (Rinehart Editions). 1949. pap. text ed. 5.95 (ISBN 0-03-009890-4, HoltC). HR&W.
--Autobiography & Selected Writings. (YA) 1950. pap. 3.25 (ISBN 0-394-30918-9, T18, Mod LibC). Modern Lib.
--Autobiography of Benjamin Franklin. (Classics Ser.). (gr. 8 up). pap. 1.25 (ISBN 0-8049-0071-X, CL-71). Airmont.
--Autobiography of Benjamin Franklin. 1962. pap. 2.95 (ISBN 0-02-002910-1, Collier). Macmillan.
--Autobiography of Benjamin Franklin. Labaree, Leonard W., et al, eds. (Illus.). 1964. 25.00x (ISBN 0-300-00648-9); pap. 5.45x (ISBN 0-300-00147-9, Y117). Yale U Pr.
--The Autobiography of Benjamin Franklin: A Genetic Text. Lemay, J. A. & Zall, P. M., eds. LC 78-25907. 352p. 1981. 28.00x (ISBN 0-87049-256-X). U of Tenn Pr.
--Benjamin Franklin Autobiography & Selections from his Other Writings. Schneider, Herbert W., ed. LC 52-14644. 1952. pap. 5.50 (ISBN 0-672-60003-X, AHS2). Bobbs.
--The Papers of Benjamin Franklin, 18 vols. Incl. Vol. 1. January 6, 1706 Through December 31, 1734. Labaree, Leonard W., ed. (Illus.). lxxxviii, 400p. 1959 (ISBN 0-300-00650-0); Vol. 2. January 1, 1735 Through December 31, 1744. Labaree, Leonard W., ed. (Illus.). xxv, 471p. 1960 (ISBN 0-300-00651-9); Vol. 3. January 1, 1745 Through June 30, 1750. Labaree, Leonard W., ed. (Illus.). xxv, 513p. 1961 (ISBN 0-300-00652-7); Vol. 4. July 1, 1750 Through June 30, 1753. Labaree, Leonard W., ed. (Illus.). xxviii, 544p. 1961 (ISBN 0-300-00653-5); Vol. 5. July 1, 1753 Through March 31, 1755. Labaree, Leonard W., ed. (Illus.). xxvi, 575p. 1962 (ISBN 0-300-00654-3); Vol. 6. April 1, 1755 Through September 24, 1756. Labaree, Leonard W., ed. (Illus.). xxix, 581p. 1963 (ISBN 0-300-00655-1); Vol. 7. October 1, 1756 Through March 31, 1758. Lambaree, Leonard W., ed. (Illus.). xxvi, 427p. 1963 (ISBN 0-300-00657-8); Vol. 8. April 1, 1758 Through December 31, 1759. Labaree, Leonard W., ed. (Illus.). xxiv, 489p. 1965 (ISBN 0-300-00658-6); Vol. 9. January 1, 1760 Through December 31, 1761. Labaree, Leonard W., ed. (Illus.). xxvi, 429p. 1966 (ISBN 0-300-00659-4); Vol. 10. January 1, 1762 Through December 31, 1763. Labaree, Leonard W., ed. (Illus.). xxix, 459p. 1966 (ISBN 0-300-00660-8); Vol. 11. January 1, 1764 Through December 31, 1764. Labaree, Leonard W., ed. (Illus.). xxviii, 593p. 1967 (ISBN 0-300-00661-6); Vol. 12. January 1, 1765 Through December 31, 1765. Labaree, Leonard W., ed. (Illus.). 1968 (ISBN 0-300-01073-7); Vol. 13. January 1, 1766 Through December 31, 1766. Labaree, Leonard W., ed. (Illus.). 544p. 1969 (ISBN 0-300-01132-6); Vol. 14. January 1, 1767 Through December 31, 1767. Labaree, Leonard W., ed. (Illus.). 600p. 1970 (ISBN 0-300-01317-5); Vol. 15. January 1, 1768 Through December 31, 1768. Willcox, William B., ed. (Illus.). 1972 (ISBN 0-300-01469-4); Vol. 16. Papers of Benjamin Franklin: January 1 1769 Through December 31, 1769. Willcox, William B., ed. LC 59-12697. (Illus.) (ISBN 0-300-01570-4); Vol. 17. January 1, 1770 Through December 31, 1770. (Illus.). 1973 (ISBN 0-300-01596-8); Vol. 18. January 1, 1771 Through December 31, 1771. Willcox, William B., ed. LC 59-12697. 1974 (ISBN 0-300-01685-9); Vol. 19. January 1, 1792 Through December 31, 1772. 1976 (ISBN 0-300-01865-7); Vol. 20. January 1, 1773 Through December 31, 1773. 1976 (ISBN 0-300-01966-1); Vol. 21. January 1, 1774 Through March 22, 1775. 1978 (ISBN 0-300-02224-7). LC 59-12697. 27.50x ea. Yale U Pr.
--The Papers of Benjamin Franklin: March 23, 1775 Through October 27, 1776, Vol. 22. Willcox, William B., ed. 800p. 1981. price not set. Yale U Pr.
--The Sayings of Poor Richard: The Prefaces, Proverbs & Poems of Benjamin Franklin. Leicester, Paul, compiled by. LC 74-23378. 1975. Repr. of 1890 ed. 24.50 (ISBN 0-8337-1198-9). B Franklin.
Franklin's Wit & Wisdom. 2.95 (ISBN 0-442-82228-6). Peter Pauper.
Goodman, Nathan G., ed. The Ingenious Dr. Franklin: Selected Scientific Letters of Benjamin Franklin. LC 74-81751. 256p. 1974. 15.00 (ISBN 0-8122-7680-9); pap. 5.95x (ISBN 0-8122-1067-0). U of Pa Pr.
Granger, Bruce I. Benjamin Franklin: An American Man of Letters. LC 76-8167. 1976. pap. 5.95 (ISBN 0-8061-1336-7). U of Okla Pr.
Graves, Charles P. Benjamin Franklin. (Illus.). (gr. 2-6). pap. 0.95 (ISBN 0-440-40499-1, YB). Dell.
Griggs, Edward H. American Statesmen: An Interpretation of Our History & Heritage. LC 76-121474. (Essay Index Reprint Ser). 1927. 19.50 (ISBN 0-8369-1810-X). Arno.
Hale, Edward E. Franklin in France, 2 Vols. LC 77-108349. (Research & Source Works Ser.: No. 409). 1970. Repr. of 1887 ed. lib. bdg. 53.50 (ISBN 0-8337-1536-4). B Franklin.
Hall, Max. Benjamin Franklin & Polly Baker. (Institute of Early American History & Culture Ser.). 1960. 13.50x (ISBN 0-8078-0783-4). U of NC Pr.
Hanna, William S. Benjamin Franklin & Pennsylvania Politics. 1964. 12.50x (ISBN 0-8047-0209-8). Stanford U Pr.
Jacobs, Wilbur R. Benjamin Franklin: Statesman-Philosopher or Materialist? LC 76-3663. (American Problem Studies). 126p. 1976. pap. text ed. 5.50 (ISBN 0-88275-407-6). Krieger.
Johansen, Bruce E. The Forgotten Founders: Benjamin Franklin, the Iroquois & the Rationale for American Revolution. 200p. 1981. 10.95 (ISBN 0-87645-111-3). Gambit.
Lemay, J. A., ed. The Oldest Revolutionary: Essays on Benjamin Franklin. LC 75-41618. 176p. 1976. 16.00x (ISBN 0-685-63233-4). U of Pa Pr.
Lokken, Roy N., ed. Meet Dr. Franklin. 2nd ed. 295p. 1981. 20.00 (ISBN 0-89168-035-7). Franklin Inst Pr.
Lopez, Claude-Anne. Mon Cher Papa: Franklin & the Ladies of Paris. (Illus.). 1966. 25.00x (ISBN 0-300-00725-6). Yale U Pr.
Lopez, Claude-Anne & Herbert, Eugenia W. The Private Franklin: The Man & His Family. (Illus.). 361p. 1975. 11.95 (ISBN 0-393-07496-X). Norton.
MacLaurin, Lois M. Franklin's Vocabulary. 1928. 35.00 (ISBN 0-8274-2371-3). R West.
McMaster, John B. Benjamin Franklin. LC 80-23681. (American Men & Women of Letters Ser.). 300p. 1980. pap. 4.95 (ISBN 0-87754-161-2). Chelsea Hse.
--Benjamin Franklin As a Man of Letters. LC 70-125706. (American Journalists). 1970. Repr. of 1887 ed. 19.00 (ISBN 0-405-01687-5). Arno.
--Benjamin Franklin As Man of Letters. 59.95 (ISBN 0-87968-722-3). Gordon Pr.
Morse, John T., Jr., ed. Benjamin Franklin. LC 74-128926. (American Statesmen: No. 1). Repr. of 1898 ed. 23.50 (ISBN 0-404-50851-0). AMS Pr.
Newcomb, Benjamin H. Franklin & Galloway: A Political Partnership. LC 72-75205. 360p. 1972. 25.00x (ISBN 0-300-01506-2). Yale U Pr.
Oswald, John C. Benjamin Franklin, Printer. LC 74-3020. 1974. Repr. of 1917 ed. 28.00 (ISBN 0-8103-3642-1). Gale.
Parton, James. Life & Times of Benjamin Franklin, 2 vols. LC 72-126603. (American Scene Ser). (Illus.). 1971. Repr. of 1864 ed. Set. lib. bdg. 95.00 (ISBN 0-306-70048-4). Da Capo.
Pepper, William. The Medical Side of Benjamin Franklin. (Illus.). 137p. 1970. Repr. of 1910 ed. 15.00 (ISBN 0-87266-039-7). Argosy.
Rowe. Biographical Sketch: Writings of Benjamin Franklin. 6.95 (ISBN 0-89315-003-7). Lambert Bk.
Russell, Phillips. Benjamin Franklin-the First Civilized American. 1926. 20.00 (ISBN 0-8274-1925-2). R West.
--Benjamin Franklin: The First Civilized American. 1979. Repr. of 1926 ed. lib. bdg. 30.00 (ISBN 0-8495-4564-1). Arden Lib.
Sappenfield, James A. A Sweet Instruction: Franklin's Journalism As a Literary Apprenticeship. LC 73-7808. (New Horizons in Journalism Ser.). 247p. 1973. 8.95x (ISBN 0-8093-0610-7). S Ill U Pr.
Schiereth, Thomas J. The Cosmopolitan Ideal in Enlightenment Thought. LC 76-22405. 1977. text ed. 13.95x (ISBN 0-268-00720-9). U of Notre Dame Pr.
Scudder, Evarts S. Benjamin Franklin: a Biography. facsimile ed. LC 79-150199. (Select Bibliographies Reprint Ser). Repr. of 1939 ed. 19.00 (ISBN 0-8369-5712-1). Arno.
Seeger, Raymond J. Benjamin Franklin. LC 73-7981. 200p. 1973. 16.50 (ISBN 0-08-017648-8). Pergamon.
Sellers, Charles C. Benjamin Franklin in Portraiture. LC 62-8663. 1962. 35.00x (ISBN 0-300-00893-7). Yale U Pr.
Skaggs, Merrill M. Autobiography of Benjamin Franklin Notes. pap. 1.95 (ISBN 0-8220-0216-7). Cliffs.
Stourzh, Gerald. Benjamin Franklin & American Foreign Policy. 2nd ed. 1954. 12.50x (ISBN 0-226-77634-4); pap. 3.25 (ISBN 0-226-77635-2). U of Chicago Pr.
Van Doren, Carl. Benjamin Franklin & Jonathan Edwards. 1979. Repr. of 1920 ed. lib. bdg. 20.00 (ISBN 0-8495-5525-6). Arden Lib.
--Jane Mecom. LC 78-122067. (Illus.). Repr. of 1950 ed. 15.00x (ISBN 0-678-03174-6). Kelley.
Van Doren, Carl C. Benjamin Franklin. LC 73-8566. (Illus.). 845p. 1973. Repr. of 1938 ed. lib. bdg. 47.25x (ISBN 0-8371-6964-X, VABF). Greenwood.
Weems, Mason L. The Life of Benjamin Franklin. LC 75-31137. Repr. of 1822 ed. 21.00 (ISBN 0-404-13611-7). AMS Pr.
Wendel, Thomas. Benjamin Franklin & the Politics of Liberty. Cadenhead, I. E., ed. LC 73-7133. (Shapers of History Ser.). (gr. 11 up). 1974. pap. text ed. 3.50 (ISBN 0-8120-0459-0). Barron.
Wetzel, W. A. Benjamin Franklin As an Economist. Repr. of 1895 ed. pap. 7.00 (ISBN 0-384-66959-X). Johnson Repr.
Wetzel, William A. Benjamin Franklin As an Economist. LC 78-63842. (Johns Hopkins University. Studies in the Social Sciences. Thirteenth Ser. 1895: 9). Repr. of 1895 ed. 11.50 (ISBN 0-404-61100-1). AMS Pr.
Wright, Esmond. Benjamin Franklin - American Independence. (Men & Their Times Ser). 1967. 4.00x (ISBN 0-8426-1599-7). Verry.
Zall, P. M., ed. Ben Franklin Laughing: Anecdotes from Original Sources by & About Benjamin Franklin. 1980. 12.95 (ISBN 0-520-04026-0). U of Cal Pr.

FRANKLIN, BENJAMIN, 1706-1790-BIBLIOGRAPHY

Ford, Paul L. Franklin Bibliography: A List of Books Written by, or Relating to Benjamin Franklin. LC 77-13526. 1977. Repr. of 1889 ed. lib. bdg. 25.00 (ISBN 0-89341-455-7). Longwood Pr.
Miller, C. William. Benjamin Franklin's Philadelphia Printing: A Descriptive Bibliography. LC 72-83464. (Memoirs Ser.: Vol. 102). 1974. 35.00 (ISBN 0-87169-102-7). Am Philos.

FRANKLIN, BENJAMIN, 1706-1790-FICTION

Zochert, Donald. Murder in the Hellfire Club. LC 78-4702. 1979. 8.95 (ISBN 0-03-022441-1). HR&W.

FRANKLIN, BENJAMIN, 1706-1790-JUVENILE LITERATURE

Aliki. The Many Lives of Benjamin Franklin. (Illus.). (ps-2). 1977. PLB 6.95 (ISBN 0-13-556019-5). P-H.
Asimov, Isaac. Kite That Won the Revolution. (gr. 7 up). 1963. 3.95 (ISBN 0-395-06560-7). HM.
Bourne, Miriam A. What Is Papa up to Now? (Break-of-Day Ser). (Illus.). 64p. (gr. k-3). 1977. PLB 6.59 (ISBN 0-698-30658-9). Coward.
Cousins, Margaret. Ben Franklin of Old Philadelphia. LC 81-806. (Landmark Paperback Ser.: No. 10). 160p. (gr. 5-9). 1981. pap. 2.95 (ISBN 0-394-84928-0). Random.
D'Aulaire, Ingri & D'Aulaire, Edgar Parin. Benjamin Franklin. (gr. 1-4). 1950. 9.95a (ISBN 0-385-07219-8); PLB (ISBN 0-385-07603-7). Doubleday.
Donovan, Frank R. & Bell, Whitfield J. Many Worlds of Benjamin Franklin. LC 63-21834. (American Heritage Junior Library). (Illus.). 153p. (gr. 5 up). 1963. 9.95 (ISBN 0-8281-0390-9, J013-0). Am Heritage.
Franklin, Benjamin. The Autobiography & Selected Writings. Lemisch, Jesse, ed. & intro. by. pap. 2.50 (ISBN 0-451-51463-7, CE1463, Sig Classics). NAL.
Fritz, Jean. What's the Big Idea, Ben Franklin? LC 75-25902. (Illus.). 48p. (gr. 2-6). 1976. 6.95 (ISBN 0-698-20365-8). Coward.
Gross, Ruth. A Book About Benjamin Franklin. (Illus.). (gr. k-3). 1975. pap. 1.25 (ISBN 0-590-10119-6, Schol Pap). Schol Bk Serv.
Johnson, Spencer. The Value of Saving: The Story of Benjamin Franklin. LC 78-8652. (ValueTales Ser). (Illus.). (gr. k-6). 1978. 6.95 (ISBN 0-916392-17-1, Dist. by Oak Tree Pubns). Value Comm.
Kurland, Gerald. Benjamin Franklin: America's Universal Man. Rahmas, D. Steve, ed. LC 72-190250. (Outstanding Personalities Ser: No. 33). 32p. (Orig.). (gr. 7-12). 1972. lib. bdg. 2.95 incl. catalog cards (ISBN 0-87157-533-7); pap. 1.50 vinyl laminated covers (ISBN 0-87157-033-5). SamHar Pr.
Scarf, Maggi. Meet Benjamin Franklin. (Step-up Books). (Illus.). (gr. 2-6). 1968. PLB 4.99 (ISBN 0-394-90070-7, BYR). Random.
Tottle, John. Benjamin Franklin. (gr. 4-6). 1958. 4.36 (ISBN 0-395-01748-3, Piper). HM.
Wayne, Bennett, ed. The Founding Fathers. LC 74-19112. (Target Books Ser). (Illus.). 168p. (gr. 5-12). 1975. PLB 7.29 (ISBN 0-8116-4912-1). Garrard.

FRANKLIN, ISAAC, 1789-1846

Stephenson, Wendell H. Isaac Franklin: Slave Trader & Planter of the Old South. (Illus.). 8.50 (ISBN 0-8446-0929-3). Peter Smith.

FRANKLIN, JOHN, SIR, 1786-1847

Collinson, Richard. Journal of H.M.S. Enterprise on the Expedition in Search of Sir John Franklin's Ships by Behring Strait: 1850-55. LC 74-5830. 1976. Repr. of 1889 ed. 37.50 (ISBN 0-404-11636-1). AMS Pr.
Hooper, William H. Ten Months Among the Tents of the Tuski. LC 74-5847. (Illus.). Repr. of 1853 ed. 31.00 (ISBN 0-404-11652-3). AMS Pr.

FRANKLIN, MILES

Mathew, Ray. Miles Franklin. Date not set. pap. 3.50x (ISBN 0-392-09494-0, SpS). Sportshelf.

FRANKLIN, WILLIAM, 1730-1813

Ford, Paul L. Who Was the Mother of Franklin's Son? An Historical Conundrum, Hitherto Given up-Now Partly Answered. LC 78-182127. (Historical Printing Club, Publications: No. 26). 16p. 1972. Repr. of 1889 ed. lib. bdg. 10.00 (ISBN 0-8337-1203-9). B Franklin.

FRANKLIN (STATE)

Williams, Samuel C. History of the Lost State of Franklin. rev. ed. LC 73-19813. (Perspectives in American History Ser.: No. 23). (Illus.). 378p. Repr. of 1933 ed. lib. bdg. 19.50x (ISBN 0-87991-348-7). Porcupine Pr.

FRANKLIN, TENNESSEE, BATTLE OF, 1864

Field, Henry M. Bright Skies & Dark Shadows. LC 77-114876. (Select Bibliographies Reprint Ser). 1890. 17.00 (ISBN 0-8369-5280-4). Arno.

FRANKLIN AND MARSHALL COLLEGE, LANCASTER, PENNSYLVANIA

Andrews, F. Emerson. Foundation Watcher. LC 73-7398. 1973. 7.50 (ISBN 0 685 40252 5). Franklin & Marsh.
Barron's Profile of Franklin & Marshall College. (College Profiles Ser.). 1978. pap. text ed. 2.50 (ISBN 0-8120-1211-9). Barron.
Douglas, Henry K. The Douglas Diary: Student Days at Franklin & Marshall College 1856-1858. Klein, Frederic S. & Carrill, John H., eds. LC 73-89382. (Illus.). 1973. 7.95 (ISBN 0-910626-00-6). Franklin & Marsh.
Klein, Frederic S. Since Seventeen Eighty-Seven: The Franklin & Marshall College Story. 1968. 2.00 (ISBN 0-685-10974-7): pap. 1.00 (ISBN 0-685-10975-5). Franklin & Marsh.

FRANKLIN COUNTY, NEW YORK

Forest Acreage & Timber Volume in Franklin County, New York. No. 38. 1956. 1.50 (ISBN 0-686-20712-2). SUNY Environ.

FRANKLIN COUNTY, VIRGINIA

Wingfield, Marshall. Franklin County, Virginia: A History. LC 64-7910. 309p. 1964. 12.50 (ISBN 0-685-65091-X). Va Bk.
--Pioneer Families of Franklin County, Virginia. 373p. 1964. 18.50 (ISBN 0-685-65092-8). Va Bk.

FRANKLIN INSTITUTE, PHILADELPHIA

McMahon, A. Michal & Morris, Stephanie A. Technology in Industrial America: The Committee on Science & the Arts of the Franklin Institute. Guide to the Records of the Committee on Science & the Arts of the Franklin Institute, 1824-1900. LC 77-77872. 40.00 (ISBN 0-8420-2123-X). Scholarly Res Inc.
Sinclair, Bruce A. Philadelphia's Philosopher Mechanics: A History of the Franklin Institute, 1824-1865. LC 74-6843. (History of Technology Ser). (Illus.). 352p. 1974. 22.50x (ISBN 0-8018-1636-X). Johns Hopkins.

FRANKLIN PRESS AND THE HIGHLAND MACONIAN

Jones, Weimar. My Affair with a Weekly. LC 60-13610. 1960. 2.75 (ISBN 0-910244-19-7). Blair.

FRANKS

Gregorius, Saint Histoire Ecclesiastique Des Francs, 4 vols. 1967. 126.00 (ISBN 0-384-19875-9); pap. 108.00 (ISBN 0-384-19874-0). Johnson Repr.
Gregory - Bishop Of Tours. History of the Franks. Brehaut, Ernest, tr. (Columbia University Records of Civilization Ser). 1969. pap. 6.95x (ISBN 0-393-09845-1, NortonC). Norton.
The History of the Franks: Gregory of Tours. 1976. pap. 4.95 (ISBN 0-14-044295-2). Penguin.
Lasko, Peter. Kingdom of the Franks. (Illus.). 1972. pap. 3.95 (ISBN 0-07-036499-0, SP). McGraw.
Los, F. J. The Franks. Wardle, John P., tr. from Dutch. 112p. 1940. pap. 3.50x (ISBN 0-911038-79-5, N League). Noontide.

FRANZ JOSEPH 1ST, EMPEROR OF AUSTRIA, 1830-1916

Clark, Chester W. Franz Joseph & Bismarck: The Diplomacy of Austria Before the War of 1866. LC 68-15113. 1968. Repr. of 1934 ed. 16.00 (ISBN 0-8462-1232-3). Russell.

Hallberg, Charles W. Franz Joseph & Napoleon Third, 1852-1864: A Study of Austro-French Relations. 1972. lib. bdg. 22.50x (ISBN 0-374-93380-4). Octagon.
Mahaffy, Robert. Francis Joseph His Life & Times: An Essay in Politics. 59.95 (ISBN 0-8490-0190-0). Gordon Pr.
Murad, Anatol. Franz Joseph I of Austria & His Empire. LC 68-17233. (Illus.). 259p. 1968. text ed. 24.50x (ISBN 0-8290-0172-7). Irvington.
--Franz Joseph I of Austria & His Empire. 9.95 (ISBN 0-685-60126-9, Pub by Twayne). Cyrco Pr.

FRASCONI, ANTONIO
Frasconi, Antonio. Antonio Frasconi's World. 1974. pap. 5.95 (ISBN 0-685-42855-9). Macmillan.
--Frasconi: Against the Grain. (Illus.). 200p. 1975. 14.95 (ISBN 0-02-551100-9); pap. 7.95 (ISBN 0-02-000600-4, 00060). Macmillan.

FRASER, AMY STEWART
Fraser, Amy S. The Hills of Home. (Illus.). 250p. 1973. 15.00 (ISBN 0-7100-7414-X). Routledge & Kegan.

FRASER'S MAGAZINE
Thrall, Miriam M. Rebellious Fraser's: Nol Yorke's Magazine in the Days of Maginn, Thackeray & Carlyle. LC 35-1070. Repr. of 1934 ed. 19.50 (ISBN 0-404-06458-2). AMS Pr.

FRATERNAL BENEFIT SOCIETIES
see Friendly Societies

FRATERNAL ORGANIZATIONS
see Friendly Societies; Greek Letter Societies

FRATERNITIES
see Greek Letter Societies; Secret Societies

FRAUD
see also Checks; Forgery; Impostors and Imposture; Mistake (Law); Swindlers and Swindling; Whiskey Frauds
Anderson, Kent, ed. Television Fraud: The History & Implications of the Quiz Show Scandals. LC 77-94755. (Contributions in American Studies: No. 39). lib. bdg. 22.50x (ISBN 0-313-20321-0, ATF/). Greenwood.
Bane, Charles A. The Electrical Equipment Conspiracies: The Treble Damage Actions. LC 73-75126. (Illus.). 554p. 1973. 17.50 (ISBN 0-87945-023-1). Fed Legal Pubns.
Bigelow, Melville M. The Law of Fraud & the Procedure Pertaining to the Redress Thereof. lix, 696p. 1981. Repr. of 1877 ed. lib. bdg. 45.00x (ISBN 0-8377-0317-4). Rothman.
Blum, Richard H. Deceivers & Deceived: Observations on Confidence Men & Their Victims, Informants & Their Quarry, Political & Industrial Spies & Ordinary Citizens. (Illus.). 340p. 1972. 24.50 (ISBN 0-398-02235-6). C C Thomas.
Bromberg, A. Securities Law: Fraud, SEC 10b-5. 1967. pap. text ed. 160.00 (ISBN 0-07-007998-6, P&RB). McGraw.
Brooks, Collin & Brief, Richard P., eds. The Royal Mail Case: Rex V. Lord Kylsant, & Another. LC 80-1475. (Dimensions of Accounting Theory & Practice Ser.). 1981. Repr. of 1933 ed. lib. bdg. write for info. Arno.
Cohen, Daniel. Frauds & Hoaxes & Swindles. (YA) (gr. 7-12). pap. 1.50 (ISBN 0-440-92699-8, LE). Dell.
Comstock, Anthony. Frauds Exposed; or, How People Are Deceived & Robbed, & Youth Corrupted. LC 69-16234. (Criminology, Law Enforcement, & Social Problems Ser.: No. 79). (Illus.). 1969. Repr. of 1880 ed. 25.00 (ISBN 0-87585-079-0). Patterson Smith.
Curtis, Bob. Security Control: External Theft. LC 76-163714. (Security Control Ser.). 1971. 18.95 (ISBN 0-912016-11-6). Lebhar Friedman.
Elliot, Robert K. & Willingham, John. Management Fraud: Deterents & Detection. (Illus.). 1980. 25.00 (ISBN 0-89433-135-3). Petrocelli.
Elliott, Robert K. & Willingham, John J. Management Fraud: Detection & Deterrence. 300p. 1980. 25.00 (ISBN 0-07-091072-3). McGraw.
Evans, D. Morier. Facts, Failures, & Frauds Revelations, Financial, Mercantile, Criminal. LC 68-24163. Repr. of 1859 ed. 25.00x (ISBN 0-678-00394-7). Kelley.
Feld, Lipman G. Bad Checks & Fraudulent Identity. 1978. pap. 6.50 (ISBN 0-934914-02-8). NACM.
Friedman, Paul. And If Defeated Allege Fraud: Stories. LC 77-141520. 1971. 4.95 (ISBN 0-252-00159-1). U of Ill Pr.
Glick, Rush G. & Newsom, Robert S. Fraud Investigation: Fundamentals for Police. (Illus.). 358p. 1974. text ed. 17.75 (ISBN 0-398-03070-7). C C Thomas.
Harding, T. Swann. The Popular Practice of Fraud. LC 75-39246. (Getting & Spending: the Consumer's Dilemma). 1976. Repr. of 1935 ed. 21.00x (ISBN 0-405-08020-4). Arno.
How to Reduce Business Losses from Employee Theft & Customer Fraud. LC 78-5093. (Almar Report). 1978. 3.00 (ISBN 0-930256-03-4). Almar.
Hull, Burling. The Billion Dollar Bait. (Illus.). 1977. pap. 6.50x varnished (ISBN 0-686-00150-8). Volcanda Educ.
Klein, John F. & Montague, Arthur. Check-Forgers. LC 77-14869. 1978. 16.95 (ISBN 0-669-01993-3). Lexington Bks.
Kwitny, Jonathan. Fountain Pen Conspiracy. 1973. 12.95 (ISBN 0-394-47935-1). Knopf.
Nash, Jay R. Hustlers & Con Men: An Anecdotal History of the Confidence Man & His Games. LC 75-38602. (Illus.). 384p. 1976. 14.95 (ISBN 0-87131-188-7). M Evans.
Oughton, Frederick. Fraud & White Collar Crime. 1971. 8.95 (ISBN 0-236-15409-5, Pub. by Paul Elek). Merrimack Bk Serv.
Roberts, David. Great Exploration Hoaxes. Michaelman, Herbert, ed. 192p. 1981. 10.95 (ISBN 0-517-54075-4, Michaelman Books). Crown.
Russell, Harold. Foozles & Frauds. LC 76-58739. 1977. text ed. 16.00 (ISBN 0-89413-044-7). Inst Inter Aud.
Stamp, Edward, et al. Notable Financial Causes Celebres. original anthology ed. Brief, Richard P., ed. LC 80-1466. (Dimensions of Accounting Theory & Practice Ser.). 1981. lib. bdg. 20.00x (ISBN 0-405-13488-6). Arno.
Suthers, John W. & Shupp, Gary L. Fraud & Deceit: How to Stop Being Ripped off. 192p. 1981. pap. 6.95 (ISBN 0-668-05318-6, 5318). Arco.
Thomas, John L. Law of Lotteries, Frauds & Obscenity in the Mails. xviii, 358p. 1980. Repr. of 1903 ed. lib. bdg. 32.50x (ISBN 0-8377-1202-5). Rothman.
Verplanck, Gulian C. An Essay on the Doctrine of Contracts. LC 77-37992. (American Law Ser.: The Formative Years). 244p. 1972. Repr. of 1825 ed. 10.00 (ISBN 0-405-04039-3). Arno.

FRAUDS, LITERARY
see Literary Forgeries and Mystifications

FRAUDULENT CONVEYANCES
see also Debtor and Creditor

FRAZER, JAMES GEORGE, SIR, 1854-1941
Besterman, Theodore. A Bibliography of Sir James George Frazer. 1977. Repr. of 1934 ed. lib. bdg. 27.50 (ISBN 0-8482-0317-8). Norwood Edns.
Gaster, Theodore H. Myth, Legend & Custom in the Old Testament: A Comparative Study with Chapters from Sir James G. Frazer's Folklore in the Old Testament, 2 vols. Set. 25.00 (ISBN 0-8446-5189-3). Peter Smith.
Malinowski, Bronislaw. Scientific Theory of Culture. 1944. 9.95x (ISBN 0-8078-0433-9). U of NC Pr.
Vickery, John B. The Literary Impact of The Golden Bough. LC 72-4049. 428p. 1973. 31.00x (ISBN 0-691-06243-9); pap. 8.95 (ISBN 0-691-01331-4). Princeton U Pr.

FRAZIER, WALT, 1945-
Batson, Larry. Walt Frazier. LC 74-2013. (Creative Superstars Ser.). 32p. 1974. PLB 5.95 (ISBN 0-87191-348-8); pap. 2.95 (ISBN 0-89812-179-5). Creative Ed.
--Walt Frazier. LC 74-2013. (Creative Superstars Ser.). 32p. 1974. PLB 5.95 (ISBN 0-87191-348-8); pap. 2.95 (ISBN 0-89812-179-5). Creative Ed.
Burchard, S. H. Sports Star: Walt Frazier. LC 75-11781. (Sports Star Ser). (Illus.). 64p. (gr. 1-5). 1975. 4.95 (ISBN 0-15-277999-X, HJ). HarBraceJ.
--Sports Star: Walt Frazier. LC 75-11781. (Sports Star Ser.). (Illus.). (gr. 1-5). 1975. pap. 3.95 (ISBN 0-15-278035-1, VoyB). HarBraceJ.

FREAKS
see Monsters

FREDERIC, HAROLD, 1856-1898
Franchere, Hoyt C. & O'Donnell, Thomas F. Harold Frederic. (Twayne's United States Authors Ser). 1961. pap. 3.45 (ISBN 0-8084-0149-1, T3, Twayne). Coll & U Pr.
Garner, Stanton. Harold Frederic. (Pamphlets on American Writers Ser: No. 83). (Orig.). 1969. pap. 1.25x (ISBN 0-8166-0545-9, MPAW83). U of Minn Pr.
Garner, Stanton, et al, eds. The Correspondence of Harold Frederic, Vol. 1. LC 76-8562. (Harold Frederic Edition Ser.). 1977. text ed. 22.00 (ISBN 0-912646-15-2). Tex Christian.

FREDERICH WILHELM 1ST, KING OF PRUSSIA, 1688-1740
Ergang, Robert R. The Potsdam Fuhrer, Frederick William First, Father of Prussian Militarism. 1973. lib. bdg. 16.00x (ISBN 0-374-92623-9). Octagon.
Johnson, Hubert C. Frederick the Great & His Officials. LC 74-84085. (Illus.). 328p. 1975. 25.00x (ISBN 0-300-01755-3). Yale U Pr.

FREDERICK 1ST, GERMAN EMPEROR
see Friedrich 1st, Barbarossa, Emperor of Germany, 1121-1190

FREDERICK 2ND, GERMAN EMPEROR
see Friedrich 2nd, Emperor of Germany, 1194-1250

FREDERICK 3RD, GERMAN EMPEROR
see Friedrich 3rd, Emperor of Germany, 1831-1888

FREDERICK, THE GREAT, KING OF PRUSSIA
see Friedrich 2nd, Der Grosse, King of Prussia, 1712-1786

FREDERICK COUNTY, MARYLAND
Hitselberger, Mary F. & Dern, John P. Bridge in Time: The Complete 1850 Census of Frederick County, Maryland. LC 78-71854. (Illus.). 1978. 25.00 (ISBN 0-913186-07-4). Monocacy.
Holdcraft, Jacob M. More Names in Stone: Cemetery Inscriptions from the Peripheral Areas of Frederick County, Maryland. (Illus.). 1976. Repr. of 1972 ed. 5.00 (ISBN 0-913186-04-X). Monocacy.
Rice, Millard M. New Facts & Old Families - from the Records of Frederick County, Maryland. LC 75-43342. (Illus.). 1976. 9.00 (ISBN 0-913186-06-6). Monocacy.
Scharf, John T. History of Western Maryland: Including Biographical Sketches of Their Representative Men, 2 Vols. LC 68-26127. (Illus.). 1968. Repr. of 1882 ed. Set. 85.00 (ISBN 0-8063-7965-0). Regional.
Williams, Thomas J. & McKinsey, Folger. History of Frederick County, Maryland, 2 vols. LC 67-28098. (Illus.). 1979. Repr. of 1910 ed. 60.00 (ISBN 0-8063-7973-1). Regional.

FREDERICKSBURG, BATTLE OF, 1862
Army of the Potomac: Part 1. LC 76-41427. (Civil War Monographs). 1977. lib. bdg. 41.00 (ISBN 0-527-17550-1); pap. 35.00 (ISBN 0-527-17548-X). Kraus Repr.
Army of the Potomac: Part 2. LC 76-41428. (Civil War Monographs). 1977. lib. bdg. 34.00 (ISBN 0-527-17551-X); pap. 28.00 (ISBN 0-527-17552-8). Kraus Repr.

FREDHOLM'S EQUATION
see Integral Equations

FREDONIAN INSURRECTION, 1826-1827
Pattie, James O. The Personal Narrative of James O. Pattie of Kentucky. Flint, Timothy, ed. LC 72-9464. (The Far Western Frontier Ser.). (Illus.). 314p. 1973. Repr. of 1831 ed. 15.00 (ISBN 0-405-04992-7). Arno.

FREDYSIS EIRIKSDOTTIR, fl. 1014-POETRY
Scott, Winfield Townley. The Dark Sister. LC 57-11574. 115p. 1958. 5.00x (ISBN 0-8147-0378-X). NYU Pr.

FREE AGENCY
see Free Will and Determinism

FREE BANKING
Duncombe, Charles. Duncombe's Free Banking. LC 68-27852. Repr. of 1841 ed. 17.50x (ISBN 0-678-00530-3). Kelley.
Hildreth, Richard. Banks, Banking, & Paper Currencies. LC 68-28635. 1968. Repr. of 1840 ed. lib. bdg. 15.00 (ISBN 0-8371-0475-0, HIBB). Greenwood.

FREE CHURCHES
see Dissenters, Religious

FREE COINAGE
see Currency Question; Silver Question

FREE DIVING
see Skin Diving

FREE ELECTRON THEORY OF METALS
see also Electric Conductivity; Electrons-Emission; Fermi Surfaces
Barnard, R. D. Thermoelectricity in Metals & Alloys. LC 72-10919. 259p. 1973. 32.95 (ISBN 0-470-05053-5). Halsted Pr.
Brandt, N. B. & Chudinov, S. M. Electronic Structure of Metals. 336p. 1973. 5.75 (ISBN 0-8285-0778-3, Pub. by Mir Pubs Russia). Imported Pubns.
Faber, T. E. Introduction to the Theory of Liquid Metals. LC 76-184903. (Cambridge Monographs in Physics). (Illus.). 600p. 1972. 71.50 (ISBN 0-521-08477-6). Cambridge U Pr.
O'Sullivan, W. J., et al, eds. Low Temperature Physics - LT-13, 4 vols. Incl. Vol. 1. Quantum Fluids. 669p. 47.50 (ISBN 0-306-35121-8); Vol. 2. Quantum Crystals & Magnetism. 668p. 52.50 (ISBN 0-306-35122-6); Vol. 3. Superconductivity. 834p. 52.50 (ISBN 0-686-66919-3); Vol. 4. Electronic Properties, Instrumentation, & Measurement. 684p. 52.50 (ISBN 0-306-35124-2). LC 73-81092. (Illus.). 1974 (Plenum Pr). Plenum Pub.
Platzman, P. M. & Wolff, P. A. Waves & Interactions in Solid State Plasmas. (Solid State Physics: Suppl. 13). 1973. 26.50 (ISBN 0-12-607773-8). Acad Pr.
Raymond, Kenneth N., ed. Bioinorganic Chemistry II. LC 77-22225. (Advances in Chemistry Ser.: No. 162). 1977. 54.50 (ISBN 0-8412-0359-8). Am Chemical.

FREE ENERGY RELATIONSHIP, LINEAR
see Linear Free Energy Relationship

FREE ENTERPRISE
see Laissez-Faire

FREE FALL-PHYSIOLOGICAL EFFECT
see Weightlessness

FREE HARBORS
see Free Ports and Zones

FREE LOVE
see also Unmarried Couples
Andrews, Stephen P., ed. Love, Marriage, & Divorce, & the Sovereignty of the Individual. LC 78-67573. (Free Love in America). Repr. of 1853 ed. 14.50 (ISBN 0-404-60962-7). AMS Pr.
Bird, Joseph W. & Bird, Lois F. Freedom of Sexual Love. LC 67-10377. 1970. pap. 2.75 (ISBN 0-385-04341-4, Im). Doubleday.
Butler, Francelia & Bakker, Jan. Marxism, Feminism & Free Love: The Story of the Ruskin Commonwealth. (Illus.). 140p. 1981. Repr. lib. bdg. 12.95x (ISBN 0-87991-034-8). Porcupine Pr.
Chase, Warren. The Fugitive Wife. LC 78-22162. (Free Love in America). Repr. of 1861 ed. 19.50 (ISBN 0-404-60959-7). AMS Pr.
Clay, James A. A Voice from the Prison. LC 78-67580. (Free Love in America). Repr. of 1856 ed. 28.50 (ISBN 0-404-60957-0). AMS Pr.
Craddock, Ida C. Heavenly Bridegrooms, 3 vols. in 1. Incl. Right Marital Living; Helps to Happy Wedlock, No. 1, for Husbands. LC 78-22600. (Free Love in America). Repr. of 1918 ed. 28.50 (ISBN 0-404-60991-0). AMS Pr.
Croly, David G. The Truth About Love. 2nd ed. LC 78-22167. (Free Love in America). Repr. of 1872 ed. 24.50 (ISBN 0-404-60971-6). AMS Pr.
Davis, Andrew J. The Reformer. LC 78-67577. (Free Love in America). Repr. of 1868 ed. 35.00 (ISBN 0-404-60956-2). AMS Pr.
Dixon, William H. Spiritual Wives, Vol. 1 & 2. LC 72-134428. Repr. of 1868 ed. Set. 49.50 (ISBN 0-404-08471-0). Vol. 1 (ISBN 0-404-08472-9). Vol. 2 (ISBN 0-404-08473-7). AMS Pr.
Ellis, John B. Free Love & Its Votaries. LC 77-134430. Repr. of 1870 ed. 35.00 (ISBN 0-404-08474-5). AMS Pr.
Foote, Edward B. Dr. Foote's Replies to the Alphites. LC 78-22173. (Free Love in America). Repr. of 1882 ed. 19.50 (ISBN 0-404-60988-0). AMS Pr.
Harmon, Moses, et al. The Moses Harman Circle: Selected Pamphlets, 6 vols. in 1. LC 78-22165. (Free Love in America). Repr. of 1905 ed. 33.50 (ISBN 0-404-60970-8). AMS Pr.
Hennequin, Victor A. Love in the Phalanstery. James, Henry, Sr., tr. LC 78-72345. (Free Love in America). Repr. of 1849 ed. 11.50 (ISBN 0-404-60960-0). AMS Pr.
Heywood, Ezra, et al. Heywood Vs. Comstock: Selected Pamphlets, 4 parts in 1 vol. LC 78-22178. (Free Lovee in America). Repr. of 1878 ed. 17.50 (ISBN 0-404-60968-6). AMS Pr.
Kent, Austin. Free Love. LC 78-72347. (Free Love in America). Repr. of 1857 ed. 17.50 (ISBN 0-404-60958-9). AMS Pr.
Lazarus, Max E. Love Vs. Marriage, Pt. 1. LC 78-72349. (Free Love in America). Repr. of 1852 ed. 19.50 (ISBN 0-404-60961-9). AMS Pr.
Lenderman. Lenderman's Adventures Among the Spiritualists & Free Lovers. LC 78-72350. (Free Love in America). Repr. of 1857 ed. 27.50 (ISBN 0-404-60986-4). AMS Pr.
Miller, George N. After the Sex Struck: Or, Zugassent's Discovery. LC 78-72353. (Free Love in America). Repr. of 1895 ed. 18.50 (ISBN 0-404-60992-9). AMS Pr.
Nichols, Mary S. Mary Lyndon: Or, Revelations of a Life. An Autobiography. LC 78-72356. (Free Love in America). Repr. of 1855 ed. 32.50 (ISBN 0-404-60985-6). AMS Pr.
Nichols Monthly: A Magazine of Social Science & Progressive Literature, Vols. 1-3. (Free Love in America). Repr. of 1854 ed. Set. 84.50 (ISBN 0-404-60976-7). AMS Pr.
Proceedings of the Free Convention, Held at Rutland, Vermont, July 25th, 26th, & 27th, 1858. LC 78-22163. (Free Love in America). Repr. of 1858 ed. 19.00 (ISBN 0-404-60963-5). AMS Pr.
Ruedebusch, Emil. The Old & the New Ideal. LC 78-72361. (Free Love in America). Repr. of 1896 ed. 29.50 (ISBN 0-404-60974-0). AMS Pr.
Sears, Hal D. The Sex Radicals: Free Love in High Victorian America. LC 76-49946. (Illus.). 1977. 15.00x (ISBN 0-7006-0148-1). Regents Pr KS.
Severance, Juliet H. A Discussion of the Social Question. LC 78-22169. (Free Love in America). Repr. of 1891 ed. 12.50 (ISBN 0-404-60973-2). AMS Pr.
The Social Revolutionist: Rising Sun Association. Greenville, Ohio, Jan. 1856-Dec. 1857, 23 nos. in 2 vols. (Free Love in America Ser.). Set. 59.50 (ISBN 0-404-60979-1). AMS Pr.
Stoehr, Taylor. Free Love in America: A Documentary History. LC 77-15911. (No. 3). 30.00 (ISBN 0-404-16034-4). AMS Pr.

Vartorella, William F., ed. Berlin Heights: Free Love & the New Faith in Ohio, 1857-1871. LC 78-22170. (Free Love in America). 1979. 27.50 (ISBN 0-404-60978-3). AMS Pr.
Webber, Charles W. Yieger's Cabinet. LC 78-22171. (Free Love in America). Repr. of 1853 ed. 22.50 (ISBN 0-404-60984-8). AMS Pr.

FREE MATERIAL

Aubrey, Ruth H. Selected Free Materials for Classroom Teachers. 6th ed. LC 77-90627. 1978. pap. 5.95 (ISBN 0-8224-6560-4). Pitman Learning.
Diffor, John C., ed. Educators Guide to Free Filmstrips. 32st rev. ed. LC 50-11650. 1980. pap. 13.00 (ISBN 0-87708-102-6). Ed Prog.
Free Stuff Editors, ed. Free Stuff for Home & Garden. (Illus.). 130p. (Orig.). 1981. pap. 2.95 (ISBN 0-915658-27-5). Meadowbrook Pr.
--Free Stuff for Parents. (Illus.). 110p. (Orig.). 1980. pap. 2.95 (ISBN 0-915658-25-9). Meadowbrook Pr.
--Free Stuff for Travelers. 130p. (Orig.). 1981. pap. 2.95 (ISBN 0-915658-29-1). Meadowbrook Pr.
Gale, Barry & Gale, Linda. The National Career Directory: An Occupational Information Handbook. LC 78-5511. 1979. pap. 5.95 (ISBN 0-668-04510-8). Arco.
Horkheimer, Foley A. & Alley, Louis E., eds. Educators Guide to Free Health, Physical Education & Recreation Materials. 13th rev. ed. LC 68-57948. 1980. pap. 16.50 (ISBN 0-87708-109-3). Ed Prog.
Keenan, Linda, ed. Educators Index of Free Materials. 89th rev. ed. LC 44-32700. 1980. 39.50 (ISBN 0-87708-090-9). Ed Prog.
Kenworthy, Leonard S. Free & Inexpensive Materials on World Affairs. LC 68-56447. 1969. pap. text ed. 3.50x (ISBN 0-8077-1608-1). Tchrs Coll.
Nehmer, Kathleen S., ed. Elementary Teachers Guide to Free Curriculum Materials. 37th rev. ed. LC 44-52255. 1980. pap. 15.00 (ISBN 0-87708-104-2). Ed Prog.
Nehmer, Kathleen S., et al, eds. Educators Grade Guide to Free Teaching Aids. 26th rev. ed. LC 56-2444. 1980. looseleaf 33.25 (ISBN 0-87708-105-0). Ed Prog.
Saalheimer, Harriet. Super Treasury of Valuable Things You Can Get Free or for Next to Nothing. 1976. 9.95 (ISBN 0-13-876052-7, Parker). P-H.
Saterstrom, Mary H. & Renner, John W., eds. Educators Guide to Free Science Materials. 21th rev. ed. LC 61-919. 1980. pap. 15.50 (ISBN 0-87708-106-9). Ed Prog.
Suttles, Patricia H., et al, eds. Educators Guide to Free Social Studies Materials. 20th rev. ed. LC 61-65910. 1980. pap. 16.75 (ISBN 0-87708-107-7). Ed Prog.
Trevarrow, W. M. The Book of Free Books. LC 79-54261. (Illus.). 156p. (Orig.). 1979. pap. 4.95 (ISBN 0-89196-042-2, Domus Bks). Quality Bks IL.

FREE METHODIST CHURCH

Bastian, Donald N. Belonging! Adventures in Church Membership. 1978. pap. 4.95 (ISBN 0-89367-044-8). Light & Life.

FREE PORTS AND ZONES

Export: Processing Zones in Asia; Some Dimensions. (Illus.). 1977. 10.00 (ISBN 92-833-1039-X, APO21, APO); pap. 10.00 (ISBN 92-833-1040-3). Unipub.
Waldmann, Raymond J., ed. U S Foreign Trade Zones. (Orig.). 1981. pap. 45.00 (ISBN 0-933678-02-9). Transnatl Invest.

FREE SCHOOLS

see also Open Plan Schools

Carr, John C., et al. Pygmalion or Frankenstein? Alternative Schooling in American Education. LC 76-2929. 1977. pap. text ed. 7.95 (ISBN 0-201-00898-X). A-W.
Deal, Terrence & Nolan, Robert, eds. Alternative Schools: Ideologies, Realities, Guidelines. LC 78-18505. (Illus.). 1978. 20.95x (ISBN 0-88229-383-4); pap. 11.95x (ISBN 0-88229-613-2). Nelson-Hall.
Erikson, Aase & Gantz, Joseph. Partnership in Urban Education: An Alternative School. new ed. LC 73-89103. 100p. 1974. pap. 7.00 (ISBN 0-87812-054-8). Pendell Pub.
Graubard, Allen. Free the Children: Radical Reform & the Free School Movement. LC 72-3401. 1972. 24.00x (ISBN 0-394-47132-6). Irvington.
Love, Robert. How to Start Your Own School. LC 72-90275. 176p. 1975. pap. 1.95 (ISBN 0-916054-01-2). Green Hill.
Ramage, Burr J. Local Government & Free Schools in South Carolina. LC 78-63741. (Johns Hopkins University. Studies in Social Sciences. First Ser. 1882-1883: 12). Repr. of 1883 ed. 11.50 (ISBN 0-404-61011-0). AMS Pr.
Smith, Vernon, et al. Optional Alternative Public Schools. LC 74-83880. (Fastback Ser.: No. 42). (Orig.). 1974. pap. 0.75 (ISBN 0-87367-042-6). Phi Delta Kappa.
Swidler, Ann. Organization Without Authority: Dilemmas of Social Control in Free Schools. LC 79-16575. 1980. text ed. 12.50x (ISBN 0-674-64340-2). Harvard U Pr.

FREE SOIL PARTY

Blue, Frederick J. The Free Soilers: Third Party Politics, 1848-54. LC 72-86408. 384p. 1973. 18.00 (ISBN 0-252-00308-X). U of Ill Pr.
Gardiner, Oliver C. Great Issue: Or the Three Presidential Candidates. LC 71-107475. Repr. of 1848 ed. 10.50x (ISBN 0-8371-3753-5, Pub. by Negro U Pr). Greenwood.
Smith, Theodore C. Liberty & Free Soil Parties in the Northwest. LC 76-28555. (Anti-Slavery Crusade in America Ser). 1969. Repr. of 1897 ed. 15.00 (ISBN 0-405-00661-6). Arno.
--Liberty & Free-Soil Parties in the Northwest. LC 66-24761. (Illus.). 1967. Repr. of 1897 ed. 8.50 (ISBN 0-8462-0968-3). Russell.

FREE SPEECH

see Liberty of Speech

FREE THOUGHT

see also Bible–Evidences, Authority, Etc.; Rationalism; Religious Liberty; Skepticism

Besant, Annie. The Freethinker's Textbook: Christianity, Its Evidences, Its Origin, Its Morality, Its History, Pt. 2. 3rd ed. LC 77-169205. (Atheist Viewpoint Ser). 288p. 1972. Repr. 15.00 (ISBN 0-405-03803-8). Arno.
Blanshard, Paul, ed. Classics of Free Thought. LC 77-73846. (Skeptic's Bookshelf Ser.). 190p. 1977. 12.95 (ISBN 0-87975-071-5); pap. 5.95 (ISBN 0-87975-079-0). Prometheus Bks.
Bury, John B. A History of Freedom of Thought. LC 74-30844. 246p. 1975. Repr. of 1952 ed. lib. bdg. 15.25x (ISBN 0-8371-7935-1, BUHF). Greenwood.
Cohen, Chapman. Essays in Freethinking, Vols. II & III. 1981. pap. 4.00 ea.; pap. 4.00 (ISBN 0-686-73828-4). Am Atheist.
--Essays in Freethinking, Vol. 1. 1980. pap. 4.00 (ISBN 0-686-70309-X). Am Atheist.
Courtney, Janet E. Freethinkers of the Nineteenth Century. facs. ed. LC 67-30182. (Essay Index Reprint Ser). 1920. 18.00 (ISBN 0-8369-0342-0). Arno.
Ingersoll, Robert G. Works of Robert G. Ingersoll, 12 Vols. LC 70-170063. Repr. of 1929 ed. Set. 390.00 (ISBN 0-404-03490-X); 32.50 ea. AMS Pr.
Lewis, Joseph. Atheism & Other Addresses. LC 72-161333. (Atheist Viewpoint Ser). (Illus.). 510p. 1972. Repr. of 1960 ed. 24.00 (ISBN 0-405-03800-3). Arno.
Lieberstein, Stanley H. Who Owns What Is in Your Head? How to Protect Your Ideas. 320p. pap. 6.95 (ISBN 0-8015-8576-7, Hawthorn). Dutton.
Macdonald, George E. Fifty Years of Freethought, Being the Story of the Truth Seeker with the Natural History of Its Third Editor, 2 vols. in 1. LC 76-161334. (Atheist Viewpoint Ser). (Illus.). 1224p. 1972. Repr. of 1931 ed. 55.00 (ISBN 0-405-03793-7). Arno.
The Movement: Anti-Persecution Gazette & Register of Progress. Bd. with The Circular of the Anti-Persecution Union. (No. 1 (May 1, 1845) - no. 4 (August 1, 1845)). LC 79-120546. (No. 1 (1843) - No. 68 (1845)). Repr. 35.00x (ISBN 0-678-00679-2). Kelley.
Powys, Llewelyn. Rats in the Sacristy. facs. ed. LC 67-30226. (Essay Index Reprint Ser). 1937. 15.00 (ISBN 0-8369-0798-1). Arno.
Proceedings & Addresses at the Freethinkers' Convention Held at Watkins, N. Y., 1878. LC 73-119051. (Civil Liberties in American History Ser). 1970. Repr. of 1878 ed. lib. bdg. 39.50 (ISBN 0-306-71937-1). Da Capo.
Robertson, J. M. A Short History of Freethought, Ancient & Modern. LC 74-169215. (Atheist Viewpoint Ser). 464p. 1972. Repr. of 1957 ed. 22.00 (ISBN 0-405-03804-6). Arno.
Russell, Bertrand. Why I Am Not a Christian & Other Essays on Religion & Related Subjects. 1967. pap. 3.95 (ISBN 0-671-20323-1, Touchstone Bks). S&S.
Spink, John S. French Free-Thought from Gassendi to Voltaire. Repr. of 1960 ed. lib. bdg. 15.25x (ISBN 0-8371-0663-X, SPFF). Greenwood.
Stephen, L. Essays on Freethinking & Plainspeaking. LC 75-41262. Repr. of 1905 ed. 25.50 (ISBN 0-404-14789-5). AMS Pr.
Swancara, Frank. Obstruction of Justice by Religion: A Treatise on Religious Barbarities of the Common Law, & a Review of Judicial Oppressions of the Non-Religious in the U.S. LC 70-139581. (Civil Liberties in American History Ser). (Illus.). 1970. Repr. of 1936 ed. lib. bdg. 29.50 (ISBN 0-306-71964-9). Da Capo.
Tribe, David. One Hundred Years of Freethought: A Survey of the Intellectual Climate in the Last Hundred Years. 1967. text ed. 7.25x (ISBN 0-236-30837-8). Humanities.
Warren, Sidney. American Freethought, Eighteen Sixty to Nineteen Fourteen. LC 66-20711. 1966. Repr. of 1943 ed. 10.00 (ISBN 0-87752-116-6). Gordian.

FREE TRADE AND PROTECTION

see also Balance of Trade; Free Ports and Zones; Import Quotas; Laissez-Faire; Mercantile System; Reciprocity; Supply and Demand; Tariff; also subdivisions Commercial Policy and Economic Policy under names of countries

Armitage-Smith, George. Free-Trade Movement & Its Results. LC 77-95061. (Select Bibliographies Reprint Ser). 1903. 24.00 (ISBN 0-8369-5063-1). Arno.
Balassa, Bela, et al. Studies in Trade Liberalization: Problems and Prospects for the Industrial Countries. LC 77-147366. 352p. 1967. 22.50x (ISBN 0-8018-0051-X). Johns Hopkins.
Balassa,Bela & Associates. The Structure of Protection in Developing Countries. LC 77-147366. (World Bank Ser). (Illus.). 384p. 1971. 25.00x (ISBN 0-8018-1257-7). Johns Hopkins.
Bastiat, Frederic. Economic Sophisms. 271p. 1968. pap. 3.00 (ISBN 0-910614-14-8). Foun Econ Ed.
Bober, G. F. Protection & the Law. (Contemporary Consumer Ser.). text ed. 4.24 (ISBN 0-07-006210-2, G); tchr's. manual & key 4.50 (ISBN 0-07-006211-0). McGraw.
Burn, Duncan & Epstein, Barbara. Realities of Free Trade. 1972. text ed. 12.95x (ISBN 0-04-382016-6). Allen Unwin.
Carey, Henry C. Harmony of Interests: Agricultural, Manufacturing & Commercial. LC 68-18572. Repr. of 1851 ed. 15.00x (ISBN 0-678-00246-0). Kelley.
Carey, Matthew. Essays on Political Economy. LC 66-21660. Repr. of 1822 ed. 22.50x (ISBN 0-678-00285-1). Kelley.
Churchill, Winston S. For Free Trade. LC 76-26306. 1977. Repr. of 1906 ed. 16.50 (ISBN 0-917684-06-0); lib. bdg. 15.00 (ISBN 0-685-87406-0). Churchilliana.
Colton, Calvin. Public Economy for the United States. 2nd ed. LC 68-30517. Repr. of 1848 ed. 19.50x (ISBN 0-678-00513-3). Kelley.
Corden, W. M. Theory of Protection. (Illus.). 1971. 17.95x (ISBN 0-19-828171-4). Oxford U Pr.
--Trade Policy & Economic Welfare. (Illus.). 400p. 1974. text ed. 48.00x (ISBN 0-19-828199-4); pap. text ed. 17.95x (ISBN 0-19-828401-2). Oxford U Pr.
Cox, Harold. Economic Liberty. Repr. of 1920 ed. lib. bdg. 15.00 (ISBN 0-8414-2401-2). Folcroft.
Dew, Thomas R. Lectures on the Restrictive System. LC 68-55701. Repr. of 1829 ed. 13.50x (ISBN 0-678-00441-2). Kelley.
Eiselen, Malcolm R. The Rise of Pennsylvania Protectionism. LC 73-18438. (Perspectives in American History Ser.: No. 8). 287p. Repr. of 1932 ed. lib. bdg. 17.50x (ISBN 0-87991-342-8). Porcupine Pr.
English, H. Edward, ed. Regional Adjustment Aspects of Trade Liberalization. LC 73-79292. 1973. 15.00x (ISBN 0-8020-3307-5). U of Toronto Pr.
Franck, Thomas M. & Weisband, Edward, eds. A Free Trade Association. LC 68-29429. (Studies in Peaceful Change: Vol. 2). 1968. 10.00x (ISBN 0-8147-0153-1). NYU Pr.
Greeley, Horace. Essays Designed to Elucidate the Science of Political Economy. LC 73-38258. (The Evolution of Capitalism Ser.). 388p. 1972. Repr. of 1870 ed. 20.00 (ISBN 0-405-04122-5). Arno.
Hirst, Margaret E. Life of Friedrich List & Selections from His Writings. LC 65-16266. Repr. of 1909 ed. 17.50x (ISBN 0-678-00068-9). Kelley.
Hobson, John A. International Trade. LC 66-21676. Repr. of 1904 ed. 12.50x (ISBN 0-678-00179-0). Kelley.
List, Friedrich. National System of Political Economy. LC 65-26368. Repr. of 1885 ed. 19.50x (ISBN 0-678-00154-5). Kelley.
Lloyd, Lewis E. Tariffs: The Case for Protection. 5.00 (ISBN 0-8159-6902-3). Devin.
McCulloch, John R., ed. Select Collection of Scarce & Valuable Tracts on Commerce. LC 65-16985. Repr. of 1859 ed. 32.50x (ISBN 0-678-00146-4). Kelley.
Marx, Karl. Free Trade. 5th ed. 1966. pap. 0.50 (ISBN 0-935534-34-2). NY Labor News.
Misselden, Edward. Free Trade. LC 67-26245. Repr. of 1622 ed. 15.00x (ISBN 0-678-00305-X). Kelley.
--Free Trade, or, the Means to Make Trade Flourish. LC 70-25644. (English Experience Ser.: No. 267). 136p. 1970. Repr. of 1622 ed. 16.00 (ISBN 90-221-0267-X). Walter J Johnson.
North, Dudley. Discourses Upon Trade: Principally Directed to the Cases of the Interest, Coinage, Clipping, Increase of Money. (History of English Economic Thought Ser). 1970. Repr. of 1691 ed. 12.50 (ISBN 0-384-41960-7). Johnson Repr.
Patten, Simon N. The Economic Basis of Protection. LC 73-2528. (Big Business; Economic Power in a Free Society Ser.). Repr. of 1890 ed. 8.00 (ISBN 0-405-05107-7). Arno.
Pejovich, Svetozar, ed. Governmental Controls & the Free Market: The U. S. Economy in the 1970's. LC 76-17976. 240p. 1976. 19.50x (ISBN 0-89096-020-8). Tex A&M Univ Pr.
Permezel, P. Idees des Physiocrates en Matiere de Commerce International. LC 72-12957. 249p. (Fr.). 1973. Repr. of 1907 ed. lib. bdg. 22.50 (ISBN 0-8337-2727-3). B Franklin.
Phillips, Willard. Propositions Concerning Protection & Free Trade. LC 67-29515. Repr. of 1850 ed. 15.00x (ISBN 0-678-00369-6). Kelley.
Protection or Free Trade? Date not set. pap. price not set (ISBN 0-911312-53-6). Schalkenbach.
Rae, John. Statement of Some New Principles on the Subject of Political Economy. LC 65-10366. 19.50x (ISBN 0-678-00065-4). Kelley.
Raguet, Condy. Principles of Free Trade. 2nd ed. LC 68-56569. Repr. of 1840 ed. 19.50x (ISBN 0-678-00529-X). Kelley.
Schmitz, W., ed. Convertibility, Multilateralism & Freedom: World Economic Policy in the Seventies. Essays in Honour of Reinhard Kamitz. LC 76-186940. 400p. 1972. 37.80 (ISBN 0-387-81056-0). Springer-Verlag.
Semmel, Bernard. Rise of Free Trade Imperialism. LC 71-112473. 1970. 41.50 (ISBN 0-521-07725-7). Cambridge U Pr.
Stern, Clarence A. Protectionist Republicanism: Republican Tariff Policy in the McKinley Period. 1971. pap. 1.50 (ISBN 0-9600116-4-1). Stern.
Stewart, Andrew. The American System: Speeches on the Tariff Question, & on Internal Improvements. (The Neglected American Economists Ser.). 1974. lib. bdg. 50.00 (ISBN 0-8240-1019-1). Garland Pub.
Taft, Charles P. Trade Barriers & the National Interest, Together with Relevant Selections from the Writings of Jno. E. Owens. LC 55-14719. 1955. 2.50 (ISBN 0-87074-109-8). SMU Press.
Taussig, Frank W. Some Aspects of the Tariff Question. 3rd ed. LC 68-58025. Repr. of 1931 ed. lib. bdg. 12.50x (ISBN 0-678-00734-9). Kelley.
--Some Aspects of the Tariff Question: An Examination of the Development of American Industries Under Protection. LC 72-137297. Repr. of 1931 ed. 13.00 (ISBN 0-404-06348-9). AMS Pr.
Taussiq, Frank W. Some Aspects of the Tariff Question: An Examination of the Development of American Industries Under Protection. Repr. of 1931 ed. lib. bdg. 20.00x (ISBN 0-8371-1044-0, TATO). Greenwood.
Thomas, Parakunnel J. Mercantilism & the East India Trade. LC 66-5362. Repr. of 1926 ed. 19.50x (ISBN 0-678-05197-6). Kelley.
Travis, William P. Theory of Trade & Protection. LC 64-16070. (Economic Studies: No. 121). (Illus.). 1964. 15.00x (ISBN 0-674-88305-5). Harvard U Pr.
Tucker, Josiah. The Elements of Commerce & the Theory of Taxes. (History of English Economic Thought Ser). 1970. Repr. of 1755 ed. 38.50 (ISBN 0-384-61903-7). Johnson Repr.
Vanderlint, Jacob. Money Answers All Things. (History of English Economic Thought Ser). Repr. of 1734 ed. 38.50 (ISBN 0-384-63883-X). Johnson Repr.
--Money Answers All Things. 1970. Repr. of 1734 ed. 28.00x (ISBN 0-8464-0640-3). Beekman Pubs.
Walker-Smith, Derek. Protectionist Case in the 1840's. LC 72-111294. Repr. of 1933 ed. 11.50x (ISBN 0-678-00614-8). Kelley.
Wonnacott, Ronald J. & Wonnacott, Gordon P. Free Trade Between the United States & Canada: The Potential Economic Effects. LC 67-17323. (Economic Studies: No. 129). 1967. 18.50x (ISBN 0-674-31900-1). Harvard U Pr.

FREE TRADE AREAS

see Customs Unions

FREE VERSE

see also Imagist Poetry

Binyon, Laurence. Tradition & Reaction in Modern Poetry. LC 74-5434. 1926. lib. bdg. 5.00 (ISBN 0-8414-3159-0). Folcroft.
Fraser, G. S. Metre, Rhyme, & Free Verse. (Critical Idiom Ser.). 1970. pap. text ed. 5.50x (ISBN 0-416-17300-4). Methuen Inc.
Nelson, Cary. Our Last First Poets: Vision & History in Contemporary American Poetry. LC 81-5082. 226p. 1981. 15.95 (ISBN 0-252-00885-5). U of Ill Pr.
Riding, Laura & Graves, R. Survey of Modernist Poetry. LC 76-95444. (Studies in Poetry, No. 38). 1969. Repr. of 1927 ed. lib. bdg. 37.95 (ISBN 0-8383-1200-4). Haskell.
Rosenblum, Martin J. Protractive Verse: Movement for Free Verse Prosody. 50p. (Orig.). 1976. pap. text ed. 4.00 (ISBN 0-89018-001-6). Lionhead Pub.

Sutton, Walter. American Free Verse: The Modern Revolution on Poetry. LC 72-93980. 256p. 1973. pap. 3.95 (ISBN 0-8112-0473-1, NDP351). New Directions.
Winters, Yvor. Primitivism & Decadence. LC 70-92994. (Studies in Comparative Literature, No. 35). 1969. Repr. of 1937 ed. lib. bdg. 32.95 (ISBN 0-8383-1213-6). Haskell.

FREE WILL AND DETERMINISM
see also Decision-Making (Ethics); Freedom (Theology); God–Will; Inhibition; Necessity (Philosophy); Pelagianism; Responsibility
Alexander, Patrick P. Mill & Carlyle. 1866. lib. bdg. 10.00 (ISBN 0-8414-2968-5). Folcroft.
Arieti, Silvano. The Will to Be Human. LC 72-78504. 288p. 1972. 8.95 (ISBN 0-8129-0285-8). Times Bks.
Augustine, Saint On Free Choice of the Will. Benjamin, A. S. & Hackstaff, L. H., trs. LC 63-16932. (Orig.). 1964. pap. 4.95 (ISBN 0-672-60368-3, LLAS150). Bobbs.
Bergson, Henri. Time & Free Will. (Muirhead Library of Philosophy). 1971. text ed. 20.00x (ISBN 0-04-194002-4). Humanities.
Berofsky, Bernard. Determinism. LC 70-112994. 1971. 20.00 (ISBN 0-691-07169-1). Princeton U Pr.
Berofsky, Bernard, ed. Free Will & Determinism. (Orig.). 1966. pap. text ed. 14.50 scp (ISBN 0-06-040648-8, HarpC). Har-Row.
Best, W. E. Free Grace vs Free Will. 1977. pap. 2.95 (ISBN 0-8010-0703-8). Baker Bk.
Bledsoe, Albert T. An Examination of President Edwards' Inquiry into the Freedom of the Will. LC 75-3003. Repr. of 1845 ed. 18.00 (ISBN 0-404-59047-0). AMS Pr.
Boyle, Joseph M., Jr., et al. Free Choice: A Self-Referential Argument. LC 76-645. 232p. 1976. text ed. 15.95x (ISBN 0-268-00940-6). U of Notre Dame Pr.
Bramhall, John. Castigations of Mr. Hobbes. Wellek, Rene, ed. LC 75-11199. (British Philosophers & Theologians of the 17th & 18th Centuries: Vol. 6). 1976. Repr. of 1658 ed. lib. bdg. 42.00 (ISBN 0-8240-1755-2). Garland Pub.
--A Defence of True Liberty from Ante-Cedent & Extrinsical Necessity. an Answer to Hobbes' a Treatise of Liberty & Necessity. Wellek, Rene, ed. LC 75-11200. (British Philosophers & Theologians of the 17th & 18th Centuries: Vol. 7). 1976. Repr. of 1655 ed. lib. bdg. 42.00 (ISBN 0-8240-1756-0). Garland Pub.
Campbell, Charles A. In Defense of Free Will. (Muirhead Library of Philosophy). 1967. text ed. 12.00x (ISBN 0-04-170003-1). Humanities.
Clark, Gordon H. Religion, Reason & Revelation. pap. 3.50 (ISBN 0-934532-04-4). Presby & Reformed.
Compton, Arthur H. Freedom of Man. LC 70-95117. Repr. of 1935 ed. lib. bdg. 15.00x (ISBN 0-8371-2543-X, COFM). Greenwood.
D'Angelo, Edward. Problem of Freedom & Determinism. LC 68-63295. 1968. 6.00x (ISBN 0-8262-7713-6). U of Mo Pr.
Davis, Lawrence. Theory of Action. (Foundations of Philosophy Ser.). 1979. ref. 10.95 (ISBN 0-13-913152-3); pap. text ed. 7.95 (ISBN 0-13-913145-0). P-H.
Day, Jeremiah. An Examination of President Edwards' Inquiry on the Freedom of the Will. LC 75-3125. Repr. of 1841 ed. 28.00 (ISBN 0-404-59125-6). AMS Pr.
--An Inquiry Respecting the Self-Determining Power of the Will: Or, Contingent Volition. LC 75-950. Repr. of 1838 ed. 18.00 (ISBN 0-404-59001-2). AMS Pr.
Easterbrook, James. The Determinants of Free Will: A Psychological Analysis of Responsible, Adjustive Behavior. (Personality & Psychopathology Ser.). 1978. 28.00 (ISBN 0-12-227550-0). Acad Pr.
Edwards, Jonathan. A Dissertation Concerning Liberty & Necessity. LC 73-21786. 1974. Repr. of 1797 ed. lib. bdg. 22.50 (ISBN 0-8337-1003-6). B Franklin.
--Freedom of the Will. Ramsey, Paul, ed. (Works of Jonathan Edwards Ser.: Vol. 1). (Illus.). 1957. 37.50x (ISBN 0-300-00848-1). Yale U Pr.
--Freedom of the Will. Kaufman, Arnold S. & Frankena, William K., eds. LC 68-22308. 1969. 24.50x (ISBN 0-672-51063-4); pap. text ed. 12.95x (ISBN 0-672-60360-8). Irvington.
Erasmus, Desiderius & Luther, Martin. Discourse on Free Will. Winter, Ernst F., tr. LC 60-53363. (Milestones of Thought Ser.). 8.00 (ISBN 0-8044-5353-5); pap. 3.95 (ISBN 0-8044-6140-6). Ungar.
Gibbs, Benjamin. Freedom & Liberation. LC 76-12234. 1976. 15.95 (ISBN 0-312-30415-3). St Martin.
Glover, Jonathan. Responsibility. (International Library of Philosophy and Scientific Method). 1970. text ed. 23.25x (ISBN 0-391-00097-7). Humanities.
Haddock, Frank C. Scientific Training of One's Will for the Achievement of Success. (Illus.). 117p. 1981. 32.65 (ISBN 0-89920-018-4). Am Inst Psych.
Hampshire, Stuart. Freedom of Mind & Other Essays. 1971. 17.00x (ISBN 0-691-07176-4). Princeton U Pr.
Hazard, Rowland G. Causation & Freedom in Willing: Together with Man a Creative First Cause, & Kindred Papers. Hazard, Caroline, ed. LC 75-3165. Repr. of 1889 ed. 25.50 (ISBN 0-404-59170-1). AMS Pr.
--Freedom of the Mind in Willing: Or, Every Being That Wills a Creative First Cause. LC 75-3169. 1976. Repr. of 1864 ed. 33.00 (ISBN 0-404-59173-6). AMS Pr.
Heschel, Abraham J. The Insecurity of Freedom: Essays on Human Existence. LC 66-16293. 330p. 1972. pap. 4.50 (ISBN 0-8052-0361-3). Schocken.
Hook, Sidney, ed. Determinism & Freedom. 1969. pap. 2.95 (ISBN 0-02-065590-8, Collier). Macmillan.
Kenny, Anthony. Freewill & Responsibility: Four Lectures. 1978. 12.50x (ISBN 0-7100-8998-8). Routledge & Kegan.
Knox, Malcolm. Action. LC 68-25993. (Muirhead Library of Philosophy). 1968. text ed. 8.25x (ISBN 0-04-170020-1). Humanities.
Laird, John. On Human Freedom. 1947. text ed. 3.50x (ISBN 0-391-02019-6). Humanities.
Lamont, Corliss. Freedom of Choice Affirmed. 214p. 1969. pap. 3.95 (ISBN 0-87975-085-5). Prometheus Bks.
Larkin, Maurice. Man & Society in Nineteenth-Century Realism: Determinism & Literature. 201p. 1977. 22.75x (ISBN 0-87471-956-9). Rowman.
Lucas, John R. Freedom of the Will. 1970. 29.95x (ISBN 0-19-824343-X). Oxford U Pr.
Luther, Martin. Bondage of the Will. Packer, J. I. & Johnston, O. R., trs. 1970. 10.95 (ISBN 0-8007-0028-7). Revell.
--Christian Liberty. Grimm, Harold J., ed. Lambert, W. A., tr. from Ger. 1943. pap. 0.75 (ISBN 0-8006-0182-3, 1-182). Fortress.
McTaggart, John. Some Dogmas of Religion. LC 68-57622. (Illus.). 1969. Repr. of 1906 ed. lib. bdg. 15.50x (ISBN 0-8371-0587-0, MCDR). Greenwood.
--Some Dogmas of Religion. LC 7-7484. 1968. Repr. of 1906 ed. 14.00 (ISBN 0-527-60000-8). Kraus Repr.
Maritain, Jacques. Freedom & the Modern World. O'Sullivan, Richard, tr. LC 77-150414. 1971. Repr. of 1936 ed. text ed. 9.00 (ISBN 0-87752-147-6). Gordian.
Melden, Abraham I. Free Action. (Studies in Philosophical Psychology). 1961. text ed. 10.25x (ISBN 0-7100-3838-0). Humanities.
Miller, David L. Modern Science & Human Freedom. Repr. of 1959 ed. lib. bdg. 14.25x (ISBN 0-8371-2101-9, MIMS). Greenwood.
Morris, Herbert, ed. Freedom & Responsibility: Readings in Philosophy & Law. 1961. 15.00x (ISBN 0-8047-0067-2). Stanford U Pr.
O'Higgins. Determinism & Freewill. (International Archives of the History of the Ideas Ser: No. 18). 1976. pap. 26.00 (ISBN 90-247-1776-0, Pub. by Martinus Nijhoff Netherlands). Kluwer Boston.
O'Sullivan, P. N. Intentions, Motives & Human Action: An Argument for Free Will. 1977. text ed. 18.25x (ISBN 0-7022-1351-9). Humanities.
Planck, Max K. Where Is Science Going? Murphy, James, tr. LC 75-41215. (Prologue by Albert Einstein). Repr. of 1932 ed. 18.50 (ISBN 0-404-14696-1). AMS Pr.
Price, Richard. A Free Discussion of the Doctrine of Materialism and Philosophical Necessity, 1778. Wellek, Rene, ed. LC 75-11247. (British Philosophers & Theologians of the 17th & 18th Centuries Ser.). 1978. lib. bdg. 42.00 (ISBN 0-8240-1798-6). Garland Pub.
Read, Leonard E. Seeds of Progess. 128p. 1980. 3.00 (ISBN 0-910614-65-2); pap. 1.00 (ISBN 0-910614-66-0). Foun Econ Ed.
Reid, Thomas. Essays on the Active Powers of the Human Mind. 1969. pap. 3.95 (ISBN 0-262-68013-0). MIT Pr.
Rickaby, Joseph J. Free Will & Four English Philosophers. facs. ed. LC 74-84333. (Essay Index Reprint Ser). 1906. 15.50 (ISBN 0-8369-1103-2). Arno.
Ricoeur, Paul. Freedom & Nature: The Voluntary & the Involuntary. Kohak, E. V., tr. (Studies in Phenomenology & Existential Philosophy Ser). 1966. 22.95x (ISBN 0-8101-0208-0); pap. 10.95x (ISBN 0-8101-0534-9). Northwestern U Pr.
Rupp, E. Gordon & Watson, Philip S. Luther & Erasmus: Free Will & Salvation. (Library of Christian Classics). 1978. softcover 8.95 (ISBN 0-664-24158-1). Westminster.
Rychlak, Joseph F. Discovering Free Will & Personal Responsibility. LC 78-31709. 1979. 13.95x (ISBN 0-19-502687-X); pap. text ed. 7.95x (ISBN 0-686-66190-7). Oxford U Pr.
Sayre, Kenneth M. Moonflight. LC 76-30422. 1977. 16.25 (ISBN 0-268-01340-3, IS-00025, Pub. by Univ. of Notre Dame Press). Univ Microfilms.
Schmidt, Paul F. Rebelling, Loving & Liberation: A Metaphysics of the Concrete. LC 73-152513. 208p. 1971. 10.00 (ISBN 0-912998-00-8); pap. 4.00 (ISBN 0-912998-01-6). Hummingbird.
Schopenhauer, Arthur. Essay on the Freedom of the Will. Kolenda, Konstantin, tr. LC 59-11675. 1960. pap. 3.95 (ISBN 0-672-60248-2, LLA70). Bobbs.
--World As Will & Representation, 2 vols. Payne, E. F., tr. Set. 22.00 (ISBN 0-8446-2885-9). Peter Smith.
Schuller, Robert H. Discover Freedom. (Orig.). 1978. pap. 1.25 (ISBN 0-89081-155-5). Harvest Hse.
Steiner, Rudolf. Philosophy of Freedom. Wilson, Michael, tr. from Ger. 226p. 1973. pap. 5.50 (ISBN 0-910142-52-1). Anthroposophic.
Venden, Morris L. Salvation by Faith & Your Will. LC 78-7597. (Horizon Ser.). 1978. pap. 4.50 (ISBN 0-8127-0190-9). Review & Herald.
Von Wright, Georg H. Causality & Determinism. 128p. 1974. 15.00x (ISBN 0-231-03758-9). Columbia U Pr.
Weinberg, George. The Pliant Animal. 256p. 1981. 10.95 (ISBN 0-312-61751-8). St Martin.
Westbrook, Perry D. Free Will & Determinism in American Literature. LC 77-89785. 275p. 1979. 18.50 (ISBN 0-8386-2150-3). Fairleigh Dickinson.
Wicklund, Robert A. Freedom & Reactance. LC 74-4004. 1974. 12.95x (ISBN 0-470-94255-X). Halsted Pr.
Williams, Clifford. Free Will & Determinism: A Dialogue. LC 79-24164. 1980. lib. bdg. 12.50 (ISBN 0-915144-78-6); pap. text ed. 2.25 (ISBN 0-915144-77-8). Hackett Pub.
Wolff, Robert. Philosophy: A Modern Encounter. LC 76-25427. 1976. text ed. 15.95 (ISBN 0-13-663385-4); pap. text ed. 14.50 (ISBN 0-13-663377-3). P-H.
Zavalloni, Roberto. Self-Determination: The Psychology of Personal Freedom. 1962. 6.95 (ISBN 0-8199-0127-X, L38765). Franciscan Herald.

FREE ZONES
see Free Ports and Zones

FREEBOOTERS
see Buccaneers; Pirates

FREED SLAVES
see Freedmen

FREEDMAN'S SAVINGS AND TRUST COMPANY, WASHINGTON, D.C.
Fleming, Walter L. Freedman's Savings Bank: A Chapter in the Economic History of the Negro Race. LC 75-109324. Repr. of 1927 ed. 10.75x (ISBN 0-8371-3590-7, Pub. by Negro U Pr). Greenwood.
Osthaus, Carl R. Freedmen, Philanthropy & Fraud: A History of the Freedman's Savings Bank. LC 75-23214. (Blacks in the New World Ser). 270p. 1976. 15.00 (ISBN 0-252-00305-5). U of Ill Pr.

FREEDMEN
see also Slavery
Bentley, George. History of the Freedmen's Bureau. LC 73-120227. 1970. Repr. of 1955 ed. lib. bdg. 17.50x (ISBN 0-374-90584-3). Octagon.
Berlin, Ira. Slaves Without Masters: The Free Negro in the Antebellum South. LC 74-4761. 448p. 1975. 15.00 (ISBN 0-394-49041-X). Pantheon.
Bruce, Philip A. Plantation Negro As a Freeman. 1970. Repr. of 1889 ed. 11.00 (ISBN 0-87928-010-7). Corner Hse.
Child, Lydia M. Freedmen's Book. LC 68-28989. (American Negro: His History & Literature Ser., No. 1). (Illus.). 1968. Repr. of 1865 ed. 13.00 (ISBN 0-405-01809-6). Arno.
Cohen, David W. & Greene, Jack P., eds. Neither Slave nor Free: The Freedman of African Descent in the Slave Societies of the New World. LC 79-184238. (Symposia in Comparative History Ser.). 357p. 1972. 22.50x (ISBN 0-8018-1374-3); pap. 5.45x (ISBN 0-8018-1647-5). Johns Hopkins.
De Forest, John W. Union Officer in the Reconstruction. Potter, David M. & Croushore, James H., eds. LC 68-12523. 1968. Repr. of 1948 ed. 15.00 (ISBN 0-208-00097-6, Archon). Shoe String.
Donald, Henderson H. Negro Freedman: Life Conditions of the American Negro in the Early Years After Emancipation. LC 70-160846. 1971. Repr. of 1952 ed. lib. bdg. 13.50x (ISBN 0-8154-0388-7). Cooper Sq.
Eaton, John. Grant, Lincoln & the Freedman. LC 70-78763. (Illus.). Repr. of 1907 ed. 17.50x (ISBN 0-8371-1388-1, Pub. by Negro U Pr). Greenwood.
Franklin, John H. Free Negro in North Carolina, 1790-1860. LC 70-81492. (Illus.). 1969. Repr. of 1943 ed. 10.00 (ISBN 0-8462-1403-2). Russell.
Free People of Color: On the Condition of the Free People of Color in the United States(Present Condition of the Free Colored People in the United States. LC 75-92232. (American Negro: His History & Literature, Ser. No. 3). 1970. Repr. of 1853 ed. 7.50 (ISBN 0-405-01928-9). Arno.
French, Mrs. A. M. Slavery in South Carolina, & the Ex-Slaves. LC 75-82051. (Illus.). Repr. of 1862 ed. 14.50x (ISBN 0-8371-1472-1). Greenwood.
Handler, Jerome S. The Unappropriated People: Freedmen in the Slave Society of Barbados. LC 73-18489. (Illus.). 238p. 1974. 16.00x (ISBN 0-8018-1565-7). Johns Hopkins.
Haviland, Laura S. Woman's Life-Work: Labors & Experiences of Laura S. Haviland. LC 78-82198. (Anti-Slavery Crusade in America Ser). 1969. Repr. of 1889 ed. 24.00 (ISBN 0-405-00638-1). Arno.
Jones, Jacqueline. Soldiers of Light & Love: Northern Teachers & Georgia Blacks, 1865-1873. LC 79-27129. (Fred W. Morrison Ser. in Southern Studies). xiii, 273p. 1980. 17.50x (ISBN 0-8078-1435-0). U of NC Pr.
Litwack, Leon F. North of Slavery: The Negro in the Free States, 1790-1860. LC 61-10869. 1961. 14.00x (ISBN 0-226-48585-4). U of Chicago Pr.
--North of Slavery: The Negro in the Free States, 1790-1860. LC 61-10869. 1965. pap. 4.95 (ISBN 0-226-48586-2, P179, Phoen). U of Chicago Pr.
McKay, Mrs. C. E. Stories of Hospital & Camp. facsimile ed. LC 70-37312. (Black Heritage Library Collection). Repr. of 1876 ed. 15.50 (ISBN 0-8369-8949-X). Arno.
Magdol, Edward. A Right to the Land: Essays on the Freedmen's Community. LC 76-39707. (Contributions in American History: No. 61). (Illus.). 1977. lib. bdg. 16.95x (ISBN 0-8371-9409-1, MFC/). Greenwood.
Montesano, Phillip. Some Aspects of the Free Negro Question in San Francisco. LC 73-78054. pap. 7.00 (ISBN 0-88247-232-1). R & E Res Assoc.
Morris, Robert C. Reading, 'Writing, & Reconstruction: The Education of Freedmen in the South, 1861-1870. LC 80-25370. (Illus.). 1981. lib. bdg. 25.00x (ISBN 0-226-53928-8). U of Chicago Pr.
Nieman, Donald G. To Set the Law in Motion: The Freedmen's Bureau & the Legal Rights of Blacks, 1865-1868. LC 79-12536. (KTO Studies in American History Ser.). 1979. lib. bdg. 23.00 (ISBN 0-527-67235-1). Kraus Intl.
Oubre, Claude F. Forty Acres & a Mule: The Freedmen's Bureau & Black Land Ownership. LC 78-2687. 1978. 17.50x (ISBN 0-8071-0298-9). La State U Pr.
Schurz, Carl. Report on the Condition of the South. LC 74-92238. (American Negro: His History & Literature, Ser No. 3). 1970. Repr. of 1865 ed. 7.50 (ISBN 0-405-01938-6). Arno.
Slaughter, Linda W. Freedmen of the South. 1869. 12.00 (ISBN 0-527-83500-5). Kraus Repr.
Smith, James L. Autobiography of James L. Smith. LC 72-97456. Repr. of 1881 ed. 10.00x (ISBN 0-8371-2685-1, Pub. by Negro U Pr). Greenwood.
Swint, Henry L. Northern Teacher in the South, 1862-1870. 1967. lib. bdg. 15.00x (ISBN 0-374-97676-7). Octagon.
Towne, Laura M. Letters & Diary of Laura M. Towne: Written from the Sea Islands of South Carolina, 1862-1884. Holland, Rupert S., ed. LC 70-97415. Repr. of 1912 ed. 15.75x (ISBN 0-8371-2654-1, Pub. by Negro U Pr). Greenwood.
Vaughan, Walter R. Vaughan's Freedmen's Pension Bill. facsimile ed. LC 72-173620. (Black Heritage Library Collection). Repr. of 1891 ed. 16.75 (ISBN 0-8369-8913-9). Arno.
Waterbury, M. Seven Years Among the Freedmen. 2nd, rev. & enl ed. LC 79-178484. (Black Heritage Library Collection). Repr. of 1890 ed. 16.50 (ISBN 0-8369-8934-1). Arno.
Webster, Laura J. Operation of the Freedmen's Bureau in South Carolina, 2 pts in 1 vol. LC 72-81490. (Illus.). 1970. Repr. of 1916 ed. 7.75 (ISBN 0-8462-1399-0). Russell.
White, Howard A. Freedmen's Bureau in Louisiana. LC 70-103131. 1970. 17.50x (ISBN 0-8071-0919-3). La State U Pr.
Woolfolk, George R. The Free Negro in Texas, 1800-1860: A Study in Cultural Compromise. LC 76-48791. 1976. 20.00 (ISBN 0-8357-0192-1, SS-00020). Univ Microfilms.

FREEDMEN IN ROME
Weaver, P. R. Familia Caesaris: A Social Study of the Emperor's Freedmen & Slaves. LC 76-171686. (Illus.). 1972. 42.95 (ISBN 0-521-08340-0). Cambridge U Pr.

FREEDMEN IN THE UNITED STATES
see Freedmen

FREEDOM
see Liberty; Slavery

FREEDOM (THEOLOGY)
Brown, Delwin. To Set at Liberty: Christian Faith & Human Freedom. LC 80-21783. 144p. (Orig.). 1981. pap. 6.95 (ISBN 0-88344-501-8). Orbis Bks.
Cone, James H. Black Theology of Liberation. LC 74-120333. 1970. pap. 4.50 (ISBN 0-397-10098-1). Har-Row.
Guardini, Romano. Freedom, Grace, & Destiny. Murray, John, tr. from Ger. LC 75-8786. 384p. 1975. Repr. of 1961 ed. lib. bdg. 14.50x (ISBN 0-8371-8111-9, GUFG). Greenwood.
Hawkinson, James R., ed. Bound to Be Free. 150p. 1975. 6.95 (ISBN 0-910452-40-7); pap. 5.45 (ISBN 0-910452-25-3). Covenant.
Hummel, Charles. Becoming Free. pap. 0.50 (ISBN 0-87784-137-3). Inter-Varsity.
Johann, Robert O., ed. Freedom & Value. LC 76-13969. 1976. 15.00 (ISBN 0-8232-1010-3); pap. 8.00 (ISBN 0-8232-1011-1). Fordham.
Junker, Bill. Freedom Bound. LC 75-2930. 128p. 1976. pap. 1.95 (ISBN 0-8054-5553-1). Broadman.
Kappen, Sebastian. Jesus & Freedom. LC 76-25927. 1977. 8.95x (ISBN 0-88344-232-9); pap. 3.95x (ISBN 0-88344-233-7). Orbis Bks.
Kasemann, Ernst. Jesus Means Freedom. Clarke, Frank, tr. from Ger. LC 75-94357. 168p. (Orig.). 1972. pap. 2.95 (ISBN 0-8006-1235-3, 1-1235). Fortress.
McLean, George F., ed. Freedom. LC 77-153528. (Proceedings of the American Catholic Philosophical Association: Vol. 50). 1976. pap. 8.00 (ISBN 0-918090-10-5). Am Cath Philo.
Martin, Everett D. Liberty. 307p. 1981. Repr. of 1930 ed. lib. bdg. 20.00 (ISBN 0-8495-3828-9). Arden Lib.
Palmer, Otto. Rudolf Steiner on His Book, The Philosophy of Freedom. Spock, Marjorie, tr. from Ger. 1975. 4.50 (ISBN 0-910142-68-8). Anthroposophic.
Paoli, Arturo. Freedom to Be Free. Quinn, Charles U., tr. from It. LC 72-93340. 320p. 1973. pap. 4.95x (ISBN 0-88344-143-8). Orbis Bks.
Perry, Ralph B. The Free Man & the Soldier. facsimile ed. LC 73-24250. (Select Bibliographies Reprint Ser.). Repr. of 1916 ed. 16.00 (ISBN 0-8369-5438-6). Arno.
Robinson, John A. Christian Freedom in a Permissive Society. LC 75-110149. 1970. pap. 2.95 (ISBN 0-664-24887-X). Westminster.
Russell, Letty M. Human Liberation in a Feminist Perspective: A Theology. LC 74-10613. 1974. pap. 5.95 (ISBN 0-664-24991-4). Westminster.
Schaeffer, Francis A. Back to Freedom & Dignity. pap. 2.25 (ISBN 0-87784-439-9). Inter-Varsity.
Schrank, Jeffrey. Freedom Now & When? (Infinity Ser.: No. 11). 1972. text ed. 2.50 (ISBN 0-03-004091-4, 247); tchr's. guide by Kathy Gearin 1.15 (ISBN 0-03-004096-5, 248). Winston Pr.
Smith, Gerard. Freedom in Molina. 1966. 2.25 (ISBN 0-8294-0070-2). Loyola.
Topel, John. The Way to Peace: Liberation Through the Bible. LC 78-9148. 1979. pap. 7.95 (ISBN 0-88344-704-5). Orbis Bks.
Trungpa, Chogyam. The Myth of Freedom & the Way of Meditation. LC 75-40264. (Clear Light Ser.). (Illus., Orig.). 1976. pap. 5.95 (ISBN 0-394-73180-8). Shambhala Pubns.
Wright, Elliott. Go Free. 128p. (Orig.). 1973. pap. 1.75 (ISBN 0-377-03011-2). Friend Pr.

FREEDOM OF ASSEMBLY
see Assembly, Right of

FREEDOM OF ASSOCIATION
see also Assembly, Right Of; Trade-Unions
Freedom of Association: An International Survey. vii, 598p. 1975. 8.55 (ISBN 92-2-101269-7). Intl Labour Office.
Freedom of Association: Digest of Decisions of Freedom of Association Committee of Governing Body. 2nd rev. ed. 1976. 11.40 (ISBN 92-2-101457-6). Intl Labour Office.
Horn, Robert A. Groups & the Constitution. LC 78-156942. (Stanford University. Stanford Studies in History, Economics, & Political Science: No. 12). Repr. of 1956 ed. 18.50 (ISBN 0-404-50975-4). AMS Pr.
Kalven, Harry, Jr. Negro & the First Amendment. LC 66-29115. 1966. pap. 2.45 (ISBN 0-226-42315-8, P240, Phoen). U of Chicago Pr.
Kurland, Philip B. Free Speech & Association: The Supreme Court & the First Amendment. 1976. pap. 6.95 (ISBN 0-226-46403-2). U of Chicago Pr.
Munoz Amato, Pedro. Problemas De Derecho Civil En la Administracion Del Personal Del Estado Libre Asociado. pap. 1.10 (ISBN 0-8477-2211-2). U of PR Pr.

FREEDOM OF CONTRACT
see Liberty of Contract

FREEDOM OF DECISION (ETHICS)
see Decision-Making (Ethics)

FREEDOM OF INFORMATION
see also Government and the Press; Government Information; Liberty of Speech; Liberty of the Press; Moving-Pictures-Censorship; Radio Broadcasting
AECT Intellectual Freedom Commitee. Media, the Learner & Intellectual Freedom: A Handbook. (Orig.). 1979. pap. 7.95 (ISBN 0-89240-034-X). Assn Ed Comm Tech.
Barron, Jerome A. Freedom of the Press for Whom?: The Right of Access to Mass Media. LC 72-75387. (Midland Bks.: No. 178). 384p. 1973. pap. 3.95x (ISBN 0-253-20178-0). Ind U Pr.
Berninghausen, David K. The Flight from Reason: Essays on Intellectual Freedom in the Academy, the Press, & the Library. LC 74-23236. 189p. 1975. pap. text ed. 7.50 (ISBN 0-8389-0192-1). ALA.
Busha, Charles H. Freedom Versus Suppression & Censorship. LC 72-91672. (Research Studies in Library Science: No. 8). 250p. 1972. lib. bdg. 15.00x (ISBN 0-87287-057-X). Libs Unl.
Chadwick, O. Catholicism & History. LC 77-77740. 1978. 18.95 (ISBN 0-521-21708-3). Cambridge U Pr.
Chenery, William L. Freedom of the Press. LC 77-14294. 1978. Repr. of 1955 ed. lib. bdg. 24.50x (ISBN 0-8371-9835-6, CHFP). Greenwood.
Ernst, M. L. The First Freedom. LC 73-166324. (Civil Liberties in American History Ser.). 316p. 1971. Repr. of 1946 ed. lib. bdg. 29.50 (ISBN 0-306-70242-8). Da Capo.
Fascell, Dante B., ed. International News: Freedom Under Attack. LC 78-66210. (Illus.). 320p. 1979. 17.50x (ISBN 0-8039-1229-3). Sage.
Gordon, Andrew C. & Heinz, John P., eds. Public Access to Information. LC 78-63009. 462p. 1979. Repr. text ed. 19.95 (ISBN 0-87855-278-2). Transaction Bks.
Goren, Dina. Secrecy & the Right to Know. LC 79-115395. 1980. 17.50x (ISBN 965-20-0003-5, Pub. by Turtledove Pub Ltd Israel). Intl Schol Bk Serv.
Halperin, Morton H. & Adler, Allan, eds. The Nineteen Eighty-Two Edition of Litigation Under the Federal Freedom of Information Act & Privacy Act. 400p. 1981. pap. 25.00 (ISBN 0-86566-023-9). Ctr Natl Security.
Houdek, Frank G. The Freedom of Information Act: A Comprehensive Bibliography of Law Related Materials. rev. ed. (Tarlton Law Library Legal Bibliography Ser.: No. 22). 61p. 1981. 15.00 (ISBN 0-686-75484-0). U of Tex Tarlton Law Lib.
How to Use the Freedom of Information Act. 1975. pap. 2.75 (ISBN 0-915598-11-6). Church of Scient Info.
Lacy, Dan. Freedom & Communications. 2nd ed. LC 65-19107. (Windsor Ser: No. 7). 1965. pap. 3.95 (ISBN 0-252-72430-5). U of Ill Pr.
Lawrence, John S. & Timberg, Bernard, eds. Fair Use & Free Inquiry: Copyright Law & the New Media. (Communication & Information Science Ser.). 1980. 32.50 (ISBN 0-89391-028-7). Ablex Pub.
Lillico, Joris. Freedom Handbook. 36p. 1978. pap. 2.50 (ISBN 0-931116-03-1). Ralston-Pilot.
Newton, V. M., Jr. Crusade for Democracy. 1961. 3.50 (ISBN 0-8138-0380-2). Iowa St U Pr.
Rourke, Francis E. Secrecy & Publicity: Dilemmas of Democracy. 236p. 1961. pap. 2.95x (ISBN 0-8018-0565-1). Johns Hopkins.
Sherick, L. G. How to Use the Freedom of Information Act: FOIA. LC 78-7353. 1978. lib. bdg. 7.95 (ISBN 0-668-04643-0); pap. 3.50 (ISBN 0-668-04651-1). Arco.
Siebert, Fredrick S. The Rights & Privileges of the Press. LC 70-100243. xvii, 429p. Repr. of 1934 ed. lib. bdg. 17.75x (ISBN 0-8371-4021-8, SIRP). Greenwood.
Using the Freedom of Information Act: A Step by Step Guide. 20p. 1981. pap. 1.50 (ISBN 0-86566-022-0). Ctr Natl Security.
Wrone, David R., ed. The Legal Proceedings of Harold Weisberg v. General Services Administration Civil Action 2052-73 Together with the January 22 & 27 Warren Commission Transcripts. (Freedom of Information Act & Political Assassinations Ser.: Vol. 1). (Illus., Orig.). pap. 8.95 (ISBN 0-932310-00-1, Foundation Pr.). U of Wis-Stevens Point.

FREEDOM OF MOVEMENT
Goodwin-Gill, Guy S. International Law & the Movement of Persons Between States. 1978. 49.50x (ISBN 0-19-825333-8). Oxford U Pr.
Kaufmann, Corinne K. Creative Rhythmic Movement for Children. 1976. 7.95 (ISBN 0-685-74220-2). Plantagenet Pr.

FREEDOM OF RELIGION
see Religious Liberty

FREEDOM OF SPEECH
see Liberty of Speech

FREEDOM OF SPEECH IN THE CHURCH
see Liberty of Speech in the Church

FREEDOM OF TEACHING
see Teaching, Freedom Of

FREEDOM OF THE PRESS
see Liberty of the Press

FREEDOM OF THE SEAS
Crecraft, Earl W. Freedom of the Seas. facsimile ed. LC 70-102232. (Select Bibliographies Reprint Ser). 1935. 24.00 (ISBN 0-8369-5117-4). Arno.
Janis, Mark W. Sea Power & the Law of the Sea. LC 76-11973. (Lexington Books Studies of Marine Affairs). (Illus.). 1976. 15.95 (ISBN 0-669-00717-X). Lexington Bks.

FREEDOM OF THE WILL
see Free Will and Determinism

FREEDOM OF WORSHIP
see Religious Liberty

FREEHOLD
see Land Tenure; Real Property

FREEMAN, DANIEL, 1826-1908-POETRY
Jaffe, Dan. Dan Freeman. LC 67-13150. (Illus.). 1967. pap. 2.95 (ISBN 0-8032-5101-7, BB 371, Bison). U of Nebr Pr.

FREEMAN, ELIZABETH
Felton, Harold W. Mumbet: The Story of Elizabeth Freeman. LC 74-108785. (Illus.). (gr. 3-7). 1970. PLB 6.95 (ISBN 0-396-06558-9). Dodd.

FREEMAN, JOSEPH, 1897-1965
Freeman, Joseph. An American Testament. LC 72-13741. x, 678p. 1972. Repr. lib. bdg. 32.50x (ISBN 0-374-92887-8). Octagon.

FREEMAN, LAWRENCE, 1906-
Freeman, Bud. You Don't Look Like a Musician. LC 73-89352. 135p. 1974. 5.95 (ISBN 0-913642-05-3). Balamp Pub.

FREEMAN, LEGH RICHMOND
Heuterman, Thomas H. Movable Type: Biography of Legh R. Freeman. 1979. text ed. 11.50x (ISBN 0-8138-0890-1). Iowa St U Pr.
Wright, Elizabeth. Independence in All Things, Neutrality in Nothing. LC 73-88669. (Illus.). 1973. 10.00 (ISBN 0-87930-023-X). Miller Freeman.

FREEMAN, MARY ELEANOR (WILKINS) 1852-1930
Foster, Edward. Mary E. Wilkins Freeman. 238p. 1956. 9.00 (ISBN 0-87532-058-9). Hendricks House.
Neilson, Francis. The Story of the Freeman. 59.95 (ISBN 0-87700-011-5). Revisionist Pr.
Westbrook, Perry. Mary Wilkins Freeman. (Twayne's United States Author Ser). 1967. pap. 3.45 (ISBN 0-8084-0217-X, T122, Twayne). Coll & U Pr.
Westbrook, Perry D. Mary Wilkins Freeman. (United States Authors Ser.). 1968. lib. bdg. 7.95x (ISBN 0-89197-838-0); pap. text ed. 2.95x (ISBN 0-8290-0017-8). Irvington.

FREEMAN (MAGAZINE) NEW YORK, 1920-1924
Roberts, Allen E. Key to Freemasonry's Growth. LC 76-107026. 1977. Repr. 7.50 (ISBN 0-685-65770-1). Macoy Pub.

FREEMAN'S FARM, BATTLE OF, 1777
see Saratoga Campaign, 1777

FREEMASONS
Bailey, Foster. The Spirit of Masonry. rev. ed. 143p. 1979. pap. 3.50 (ISBN 0-85330-135-2). Lucis.
Bede, Elbert. Five-Fifteen Minute Talks. LC 72-81262. 1972. text ed. 4.50 (ISBN 0-685-88785-5, M-91). Macoy Pub.
--The Landmarks of Freemasonry. pap. text ed. 3.00 (ISBN 0-685-88795-2, M-69). Macoy Pub.
--Three-Five-Seven Minute Talks on Freemasonry. 1978. pap. text ed. 3.50 (ISBN 0-685-88817-7, M-306). Macoy Pub.
Blackmer, Rollin C. The Lodge & the Craft. 1976. s.p. 7.95 (ISBN 0-685-70959-0). Macoy Pub.
Blakemore, Louis B. Masonic Lodge Methods. 1981. Repr. of 1953 ed. text ed. 11.50 (ISBN 0-685-88798-7, M-76). Macoy Pub.
Blanchard, J. Standard Freemasonry. 3.95 (ISBN 0-685-22116-4). Wehman.
Cahill, E. Freemasonry & the Anti-Christian Movement. 59.95 (ISBN 0-8490-0195-1). Gordon Pr.
Cass. Negro Freemasonry & Segregation. 4.00 (ISBN 0-685-19494-9). Powner.
Cass, D. A. Negro Freemasonry. 4.95 (ISBN 0-685-22057-5). Wehman.
Castells, F. Genuine Secrets of Freemasonry. 7.95 (ISBN 0-685-21955-0). Wehman.
--Origin of Masonic Degrees. 1960. 6.95 (ISBN 0-685-22066-4). Wehman.
Chase, Jackson H. Cryptic Masonry. Repr. of 1981 ed. s.p. soft cover 3.50 (ISBN 0-685-70960-4). Macoy Pub.
Clymer, R. Swinburne. Mysticism of Masonry. 1924. 4.95 (ISBN 0-686-00820-0). Philos Pub.
Coil, Henry W. Coil's Masonic Encyclopedia. LC 60-53289. lib. bdg. 31.50 (ISBN 0-685-88779-0, M-316). Macoy Pub.
--A Comprehensive View of Freemasonry. (Illus.). 1973. Repr. of 1954 ed. text ed. 7.95 (ISBN 0-685-88780-4, M-314). Macoy Pub.
--Conversation on Free Masonry. 1980. Repr. soft cover 12.50 (ISBN 0-686-68272-6). Macoy Pub.
Crawford, George W. Prince Hall & His Followers. LC 74-144591. Repr. of 1914 ed. 11.50 (ISBN 0-404-00145-9). AMS Pr.
Denslow, William R. Ten Thousand Famous Freemasons, 4 vols. 1979. Repr. Set. pap. 29.95 slip cover (ISBN 0-686-68268-8). Macoy Pub.
Diccionario Enciclopedico de la Masoneria. (Span.). 40.95 (ISBN 0-686-56654-8, S-14860). French & Eur.
Edwards, Lewis. Masonic Speechmaking. 1960. 3.95 (ISBN 0-685-22034-6). Wehman.
Freemasons & Freemasonry Extract from National Union Catalog: Pre 1956 Imprints, Vol. 184. 199p. 1973. text ed. 52.50 (ISBN 0-686-30822-0, Pub. by Mansell England). Merrimack Bk Serv.
Garver, William L. Brother of the Third Degree. 12.00 (ISBN 0-685-07211-8). Borden.
Goranson, Dean N. Freemasonry: A Remarkable Technique. 1980. 5.75 (ISBN 0-8062-1531-3). Carlton.
Hall, Manly P. Freemasonry of the Ancient Egyptians. 6.95 (ISBN 0-89314-406-1). Philos Res.
--The Lost Keys of Freemansonry: Or, the Secret of Hiram Abiff. rev. and enl. ed. 1981. Repr. 8.50 (ISBN 0-685-69542-5). Macoy Pub.
--Lost Keys of Freemasonry. 4.75 (ISBN 0-89314-500-9). Philos Res.
--Masonic Orders of Fraternity. 5.75 (ISBN 0-89314-536-X). Philos Res.
--The Secret Teachings of All Ages: An Encyclopedia Guide to Masonic, Hermetic, Quabbalistic & Rosicrucian Symbolic Philosophy. (Illus.). 1978. pap. cancelled (ISBN 0-685-54894-5). Bolder Bks.
Hammond, William E. What Masonry Means. 1978. Repr. of 1939 ed. 4.50 (ISBN 0-685-88820-7, M-311). Macoy Pub.
Haywood, H. L. More About Masonry. rev. ed. 1980. softcover 5.95 (ISBN 0-686-74285-0, M081). Macoy Pub.
Haywood, H. L., ed. The Great Teachings of Masonry. 1971. Repr. of 1921 ed. text ed. 4.50 (ISBN 0-685-88790-1, M-90). Macoy Pub.
--How to Become a Masonic Lodge Officer. 1975. Repr. of 1958 ed. 5.00 (ISBN 0-685-88792-8, M-77). Macoy Pub.
Inman, H. F. Masonic Problems. 4.50 (ISBN 0-685-22031-1). Wehman.
Janes, William H. Masonic Musical Manual. 1969. pap. 3.00 (ISBN 0-685-88799-5, M-44). Macoy Pub.
Jones, Bernard E. Freemason's Guide. 11.95 (ISBN 0-685-21951-8). Wehman.
Ludendorff, Erich. Destruction of Free Masonry Through Revelation of Their Secrets. Koester, J. Elisabeth, tr. from German. LC 77-79972. (Illus.). 1977. pap. 4.95 (ISBN 0-911038-01-9). Noontide.
McCoy, Winston. Fellow-Crafts Ritual. 1981. 4.95 (ISBN 0-8062-1608-5). Carlton.
Mackey, Albert G. Jurisprudence of Freemasonry. 4.00 (ISBN 0-685-19480-9). Powner.
--Masonic Jurisprudence. 1980. Repr. s.p. 12.00 (ISBN 0-685-70957-4). Macoy Pub.
Mackey's Masonic Encyclopedia of Freemasonry, 3 vols. 1976. Repr. 45.00 set (ISBN 0-685-69545-X). Macoy Pub.
Macoy, Robert. Worshipful Master's Assistant. 1980. Repr. s.p. 11.95 (ISBN 0-685-70954-X). Macoy Pub.
Makrakis, Apostolos. Freemasonry Known by the Masonic Diploma. Cummings, Denver, tr. 135p. (Orig.). 1956. pap. 3.00x (ISBN 0-938366-42-4). Orthodox Chr.
Masonic Quiz: Ask Me Another, Brother. 4.00 (ISBN 0-685-19487-6). Powner.
Mellor, Allec. Dictionnaire de la Franc-Maconnerie et des Francs-Macons. 400p. (Fr.). 1971. 27.50 (ISBN 0-686-57043-X, M-6403). French & Eur.
More Light. 3.50 (ISBN 0-685-19492-2). Powner.
Morgan, William. Freemasonry Exposed. 2.50 (ISBN 0-685-19475-2). Powner.
Morris, Robert. Freemasonry in the Holy Land: Handmarks of Hiram's Builders. Davis, Moshe, ed. LC 77-70731. (America & the Holy Land Ser.). (Illus.). 1977. Repr. of 1872 ed. lib. bdg. 35.00x (ISBN 0-405-10270-4). Arno.
Muir, Ada. Book of Nodes & Part of Fortune. 1975. pap. 1.50 (ISBN 0-685-70968-X). Macoy Pub.
Nettl, Paul. Mozart & Masonry. LC 78-114564. (Music Ser). 1957. Repr. of 1957 ed. lib. bdg. 17.50 (ISBN 0-306-71922-3). Da Capo.
Newton, Joseph F. The Men's House: Masonic Papers & Addresses. 1969. text ed. 5.00 (ISBN 0-685-88800-2, M-86). Macoy Pub.
Newton, Joseph F., ed. The Religion of Masonry: An Interpretation. 1969. text ed. 4.25 (ISBN 0-685-88806-1, M-87). Macoy Pub.
Petersen, William. Masonic Quiz. 4.50 (ISBN 0-685-22032-X). Wehman.
Pick, F. Freemason's Pocket Reference. 4.50 (ISBN 0-685-21952-6). Wehman.
Pocket Lexicon of Freemasonry. 1.50 (ISBN 0-685-19495-7). Powner.

Pollard, Stewart M. Tied to Masonic Apron Strings. Cook, Lewis C., ed. pap. 3.50 (ISBN 0-685-88818-5, M-322). Macoy Pub.

Pott, Constance M. Francis Bacon & His Secret Society. LC 71-174282. Repr. of 1891 ed. 32.50 (ISBN 0-404-05096-4). AMS Pr.

Reid, Elmer T. Practical Guide for Royal Arch Chapter Officers & Companions. (Illus.). 1970. pap. text ed. 1.75 (ISBN 0-685-88804-5, M-63). Macoy Pub.

Roberts, Allen E. How to Conduct a Leadership Seminar. 11p. 1970. pap. 1.00 (ISBN 0-685-88793-6, M-57). Macoy Pub.

Robison, John. Proofs of a Conspiracy. 1967. pap. 3.95 (ISBN 0-88279-121-4). Western Islands.

Ronayne. Freemasonry Handbook. 4.95 (ISBN 0-685-21949-6). Wehman.

Ronayne, E. Chapter Masonry. 3.50 (ISBN 0-685-21895-3). Wehman.

Ronayne, Edmond. Blue Lodge & Chapter. 1947. 7.00 (ISBN 0-685-19465-5). Powner.

--Chapter Degrees. 4.00 (ISBN 0-685-19469-8). Powner.

--Mah Hah Bone. 7.00 (ISBN 0-685-19485-X). Powner.

--Master's Carpet. 4.00 (ISBN 0-685-19490-6). Powner.

Shepherd, Silas H., et al. Little Masonic Library, 5 vols. 1977. Repr. text ed. 27.50 (ISBN 0-685-88796-0, M-5). Macoy Pub.

Simons, George E. The Standard Monitor. 1978. Repr. 5.75 (ISBN 0-685-70970-1). Macoy Pub.

Steinmetz, George H. Freemasonry: Its Hidden Meaning. 1976. Repr. s.p. 6.75 (ISBN 0-685-70958-2). Macoy Pub.

Upton, William H. Negro Masonry. LC 70-144696. Repr. of 1902 ed. 16.00 (ISBN 0-404-00218-8). AMS Pr.

Voorhis, H. V., compiled by. Facts for Freemasons. 1978. 9.50 (ISBN 0-685-87982-8, M-65). Macoy Pub.

Ward, J. M. Hiram Abiff. 7.95 (ISBN 0-685-21968-2). Wehman.

Willets, Walter E. Master's Book of Short Speeches. 1980. Repr. s.p. soft cover 2.00 (ISBN 0-685-70961-2). Macoy Pub.

Wilson-Ludlam, Mae. The Power Trio. 1976. soft cover 6.95 (ISBN 0-685-70963-9). Macoy Pub.

Worthy Matron's Year Book. 1981. Repr. s.p. 10.00 (ISBN 0-685-70953-1). Macoy Pub.

Wright, Dudley. Roman Catholicism & Freemasonry. 1977. lib. bdg. 69.95 (ISBN 0-8490-2531-1). Gordon Pr.

FREEMASONS–FICTION

Easter, Robert S. The Sword of Slomon. 1962. text ed. 3.50 (ISBN 0-685-88816-9, M-318). Macoy Pub.

FREEMASONS–HISTORY

Ancient Masonry: Lessons 6-18. 1980. pap. 9.00 (ISBN 0-87887-347-3). Church of Light.

Coil, Henry W. Freemasonry Through Six Centuries, 2 vols. 1976. Repr. of 1966 ed. 20.00 (ISBN 0-685-74612-7, M-83). Macoy Pub.

Darrah, D. D. History & Evolution of Freemasonry. 4.95 (ISBN 0-685-21969-0). Wehman.

Darrah, Delmore D. History & Evolution of Freemasonry. (Illus.). 1951. 4.00 (ISBN 0-685-19479-5). Powner.

Grimshaw, William H. Official History of Free Masonry Among the Colored People in North America. LC 74-91257. (Illus.). Repr. of 1903 ed. 20.50x (ISBN 0-8371-2051-9, Pub. by Negro U Pr). Greenwood.

--Official History of Freemasonry Among the Colored People in North America. facs. ed. LC 74-157370. (Black Heritage Library Collection Ser). 1903. 20.50 (ISBN 0-8369-8808-6). Arno.

Gwynne, H. A., intro. by. The Cause of World Unrest. 1978. pap. 5.00x (ISBN 0-911038-40-X). Noontide.

Haywood, H. L., ed. Famous Masons & Masonic Presidents. 1968. Repr. of 1944 ed. text ed. 4.00 (ISBN 0-685-88783-9, M-79). Macoy Pub.

--The Newly Made Mason: What He & Every Mason Should Know About Masonry. (Illus.). 1978. Repr. of 1973 ed. text ed. 10.00 (ISBN 0-685-88801-0, M-80). Macoy Pub.

Headings, Mildred J. French Freemasonry Under the Third Republic. LC 78-64206. (Johns Hopkins University. Studies in the Social Sciences. Sixty-Sixth Ser. 1948: 1). Repr. of 1949 ed. 26.00 (ISBN 0-404-61311-X). AMS Pr.

Katz, Jacob. Jews & Freemasons in Europe, 1723-1939. Oschry, Leonard, tr. from Heb. LC 71-115475. 1970. 16.00x (ISBN 0-674-47480-5). Harvard U Pr.

Lipson, Dorothy Ann. Freemasonry in Federalist Connecticut, 1789-1835. 1977. text ed. 25.00 (ISBN 0-691-04646-8). Princeton U Pr.

Macbride, A. S. Speculative Masonry Its Mission, Its Evolution & Its Landmarks. 1971. Repr. of 1924 ed. text ed. 4.50 (ISBN 0-685-88814-2, M-89). Macoy Pub.

Newton, Joseph F. The Builders: A Story and Study of Freemasonry. 1979. Repr. 10.00 (ISBN 0-685-69541-7). Macoy Pub.

--Short Talks on Masonry. 1979. Repr. of 1969 ed. text ed. 6.95 (ISBN 0-685-88813-4, M-85). Macoy Pub.

Pick, F. History of Freemasonry. 4.50 (ISBN 0-685-21970-4). Wehman.

Pick, Fred L. & Knight, Norman. Pocket History of Freemasonry. 5th ed. 1969. 13.50x (ISBN 0-584-10256-9). Intl Pubns Serv.

Roberts, Allen E. House Undivided: The Story of Freemasonry & the Civil War. LC 61-14452. 1976. 8.95 (ISBN 0-685-65769-8). Macoy Pub.

Van der Veur, Paul W. Freemasonry in Indonesia from Radermacher to Soekanto, 1762-1961. LC 76-620040. (Papers in International Studies: Southeast Asia: No. 40). (Illus.). 1976. pap. 4.00 (ISBN 0-89680-026-1). Ohio U Ctr Intl.

Walker, Joseph A., Jr. Black Square & Compass: 200 Years of Prince Hall Freemasmry. rev. ed. LC 79-112352. 1981. 12.50 (ISBN 0-686-73815-2). Macoy Pub.

FREEMASONS–KNIGHTS TEMPLARS

see also Templars

Blanchard, J. Knight Templarism. rev. ed. 5.50 (ISBN 0-685-22013-3). Wehman.

Cook, E. H. Knight Templarism. 4.50 (ISBN 0-685-19481-7). Powner.

FREEMASONS–LAWS, DECISIONS, ETC.

Mackey, A. G. Jurisprudence of Freemasonry. 4.95 (ISBN 0-685-22001-X). Wehman.

Masonic Addresses & Writings of Roscoe Pound. (Illus.). 1978. Repr. of 1953 ed. text ed. 13.50 (ISBN 0-685-88797-9, M-68). Macoy Pub.

FREEMASONS–MONITORS

see Freemasons–Rituals

FREEMASONS–NEGRO

Williams, Loretta J. Black Freemasonry & Middle-Class Realities. LC 79-48029. (University of Missouri Studies: Vol. 69). 176p. 1980. 15.00x (ISBN 0-8262-0308-6). U of Mo Pr.

FREEMASONS–POETRY

Brunke, Ottillie S. Chapter Ceremonies & Poems. pap. text ed. 1.50 (ISBN 0-685-88778-2, S-192). Macoy Pub.

FREEMASONS–RITUALS

Blue Lodge Enlightenment. 3.50 (ISBN 0-685-19466-3). Powner.

Brunke, Ottillie S. Chapter Ceremonies & Poems. pap. text ed. 1.50 (ISBN 0-685-88778-2, S-192). Macoy Pub.

Ceremonies, Heroines of Jericho. 1.75 (ISBN 0-685-19468-X). Powner.

Cook, E. A. Scottish Rite Masonry, 2 vols. Set. 14.50 (ISBN 0-685-22097-4). Wehman.

Duncan, M. C. Masonic Ritual. rev. ed. 4.95 (ISBN 0-685-22033-8). Wehman.

Duncan, Malcolm. Masonic Ritual & Monitor, 2 Pts. 1946. 2.50 ea.; 1 vol. ed. 4.00 (ISBN 0-685-19489-2). Powner.

Duncan, Malcolm C. Duncan's Masonic Ritual & Monitor. new ed. 288p. 1976. pap. 3.95 (ISBN 0-679-50626-8). McKay.

Heroines of Jerico Ritual. 1.75 (ISBN 0-685-19478-7). Powner.

King, Ethel L. Amaranth Ceremonies. 1969. Repr. of 1950 ed. 2.00 (ISBN 0-685-88776-6, S-87). Macoy Pub.

Lester. Look to the East. 3.50 (ISBN 0-685-22017-6). Wehman.

Lester, Ralph P. Look to the East. 3.00 (ISBN 0-685-19484-1). Powner.

Lodge of Sorrows. pap. 1.00 (ISBN 0-685-19483-3). Powner.

Macoy Publishing & Masonic Supply Co. Book of the Scarlet Line; Heroines of Jericho Ritual & Ceremonies. 1978. Repr. of 1948 ed. text ed. 4.50 (ISBN 0-685-88777-4, S-77). Macoy Pub.

Macoy, Robert. The Adoptive Rite. 1981. Repr. 5.00 (ISBN 0-685-69540-9). Macoy Pub.

Masonic Burial Service. 1.50 (ISBN 0-685-19486-8). Powner.

Maxwell, Geraldine Boldt. Royal Matron's Treasury of Addresses & Ceremonies, No. 2. 1975. soft cover 3.50 (ISBN 0-685-70962-0). Macoy Pub.

Richardson, J. Masonic Monitor. 4.50 (ISBN 0-685-22030-3). Wehman.

Richardson, Jabez. Monitor of Freemasonry. 3.25 (ISBN 0-685-19491-4). Powner.

Ronayne, E. Ma-Ha-Bone: Ritual. 7.95 (ISBN 0-685-22019-2). Wehman.

Ronayne, Edmond. Handbook of Freemasonry. 4.00 (ISBN 0-685-19476-0); pap. 3.00 (ISBN 0-685-19477-9). Powner.

Scottish Rite Masonry, 2 Vols. Set. 8.50 (ISBN 0-685-19498-1). Powner.

Simons, George E. Standard Monitor. 2.75 (ISBN 0-685-19502-3). Powner.

Standard Freemasonry. (Illus.). 4.00 (ISBN 0-685-19501-5). Powner.

Welcomes & Ceremonies for the Year's Program. 1980. Repr. s.p. soft cover 1.25 (ISBN 0-685-70955-8). Macoy Pub.

What to Say. rev. and enl. ed. 1980. Repr. 5.00 (ISBN 0-685-69544-1). Macoy Pub.

Worshipful Master's Assistant. 3.50 (ISBN 0-685-19506-6). Powner.

FREEMASONS–SYMBOLISM

Buck, Jirah D. Symbolism of Freemasonry. 4.00 (ISBN 0-685-19503-1). Powner.

Claudy, Carl H., ed. Foreign Countries: A Gateway to the Interpretation & Development of Certain Symbols of Freemasonry. 1971. Repr. of 1925 ed. text ed. 4.50 (ISBN 0-685-88786-3, M-88). Macoy Pub.

Hall, Manly P. Occult Anatomy of Man. pap. 1.75 (ISBN 0-89314-338-3). Philos Res.

Horne, Alex. King Solomon's Temple in the Masonic Tradition. 1974. pap. 5.00 (ISBN 0-87980-275-8). Wilshire.

Mackey, A. G. Symbolism of Freemansonry. 4.95 (ISBN 0-685-22122-9). Wehman.

Mackey, Albert G. Symbolism of Freemasonry. 4.00 (ISBN 0-685-19504-X). Powner.

Percival, Harold W. Masonry & Its Symbols, in Light of "Thinking & Destiny". LC 52-2237. 1979. pap. 3.00 (ISBN 0-911650-07-5). Word Foun.

Roberts, Allen E. The Craft & Its Symbols. LC 73-89493. 1981. Repr. 6.00 (ISBN 0-685-65768-X). Macoy Pub.

Steinmetz, George H. The Lost Word: Its Hidden Meaning. 1976. Repr. 6.75 (ISBN 0-685-69543-3). Macoy Pub.

--The Royal Arch: Its Hidden Meaning. 1979. Repr. of 1946 ed. text ed. 6.95 (ISBN 0-685-88808-8, M-302). Macoy Pub.

FREEMASONS–TEMPLARS

see Freemasons–Knights Templars

FREEMASONS–FRANCE

Headings, Mildred J. French Freemasonry Under the Third Republic. LC 78-64206. (Johns Hopkins University. Studies in the Social Sciences. Sixty-Sixth Ser. 1948: 1). Repr. of 1949 ed. 26.00 (ISBN 0-404-61311-X). AMS Pr.

FREEMASONS–GREAT BRITAIN–ROYAL ARCH MASONS

Jones, B. E. Freemason Royal Arch. 10.95 (ISBN 0-685-21950-X). Wehman.

Sheville & Gould. Guide to the Royal Arch Chapter. 1980. Repr. 8.50 (ISBN 0-685-69546-8). Macoy Pub.

FREEMASONS AND CATHOLIC CHURCH

see also Anti-Clericalism

DePoncins, Leon V. Freemasonry & the Vatican. 59.95 (ISBN 0-8490-0196-X). Gordon Pr.

Thornton, Mary C. The Church & Freemasonry in Brazil, 1872-1875. LC 73-2647. 287p. 1973. Repr. of 1948 ed. lib. bdg. 17.50x (ISBN 0-8371-6816-3, THCF). Greenwood.

FREESIAS

Smith, Denis. Freesias. 90p. 1980. pap. 9.95 (ISBN 0-901361-25-9, Pub. by Grower Bks England). Intl Schol Bk Serv.

FREETOWN, SIERRA LEONE

Banton, Michael. West African City: A Study of Tribal Life in Freetown. (International African Institute Ser.). 1957. 24.50x (ISBN 0-19-724102-6). Oxford U Pr.

Harrell-Bond, Barbara, et al. Community Leadership & the Transformation of Freetown, 1801-1976. 1978. 40.00x (ISBN 90-279-7525-6). Mouton.

FREEWAYS

see Express Highways

FREEZE-DRYING

Copson, David A. Microwave Heating. 2nd ed. (Illus.). 1975. lib. bdg. 49.00 (ISBN 0-87055-182-5). AVI.

Freeze-Drying of Biological Materials. 1973. pap. 12.50 (ISBN 0-685-99139-3, IIR40, IIR). Unipub.

Freezing Frozen Storage & Freeze-Drying. 1979. pap. 28.75 (ISBN 0-685-90709-0, IIR 17, IIR). Unipub.

Goldblith, S. A., et al, eds. Freeze Drying & Advanced Food Technology. 1975. 113.00 (ISBN 0-12-288450-7). Acad Pr.

Gutcho, M. H. Freeze Drying Processes for the Food Industry. LC 77-71930. (Food Technology Review Ser.: No. 41). (Illus.). 1977. 39.00 (ISBN 0-8155-0662-7). Noyes.

Hower, Rolland O. Freeze-Drying Biological Specimens: A Laboratory Manual. LC 78-10750. (Illus.). 196p. 1979. 25.00x (ISBN 0-87474-532-2). Smithsonian.

Mellor, J. D. Fundamentals of Freeze Drying. 1979. 60.00 (ISBN 0-12-490050-X). Acad Pr.

Recent Developments in Freeze-Drying, 2 vols. 1969. Vol. 1. pap. 12.50 (ISBN 0-685-99183-0, IIR41, IIR); Vol. 2. pap. 14.50 (ISBN 0-685-99184-9, IIR42). Unipub.

Sunset Editors. Canning, Freezing & Drying. 2nd ed. LC 80-53480. (Illus.). 128p. 1981. pap. 4.95 (ISBN 0-376-02213-2, Sunset Books). Sunset-Lane.

FREEZING

see Cryobiology; Home Freezers; Ice; Refrigeration and Refrigerating Machinery

FREEZING AND OPENING OF RIVERS, LAKES, ETC.

see Ice on Rivers, Lakes, Etc.

FREEZING OF FOOD

see Food, Frozen

FREEZING OF HUMAN BODIES

see Cryonics

FREEZING OF SEMEN

see Semen, Frozen

FREEZING POINTS OF SOLUTIONS

see Molecular Weights

FREGE, GOTTLOB, 1848-1925

Angelelli, I. Studies on Gottlob Frege & Traditional Philosophy. 291p. 1967. lib. bdg. 34.00 (ISBN 90-277-0067-2, Pub. by Reidel Holland). Kluwer Boston.

Anscombe, G. E. & Geach, Peter T. Three Philosophers. 162p. 1961. text ed. 11.50x (ISBN 0-8014-0016-3). Cornell U Pr.

Birjukov, B. V. Two Soviet Studies on Frege. Angelelli, Ignacio, tr. from Rus. (Sovietica Ser.: No. 15). 101p. 1964. lib. bdg. 18.50 (ISBN 90-277-0072-9, Pub by Reidel Holland). Kluwer Boston.

Dummett, Michael. Frege Philosophy of Language. LC 80-29692. 752p. 1981. text ed. 40.00 (ISBN 0-674-31930-3). Harvard U Pr.

--The Interpretation of Frege's Philosophy. LC 77-12777. 1980. text ed. 40.00x (ISBN 0-674-45975-X). Harvard U Pr.

Heintz, John. Subjects & Predicables. LC 73-81805. (Janua Linguarum, Ser. Minor: No. 79). 103p. 1973. pap. text ed. 20.00x (ISBN 90-2792-539-9). Mouton.

Klemke, E. D., ed. Essays on Frege. LC 68-18205. 1968. pap. 8.95 (ISBN 0-252-72435-6). U of Ill Pr.

Resnik, Michael. Frege & the Philosophy of Mathematics. 240p. 1980. 16.50x (ISBN 0-8014-1293-5). Cornell U Pr.

Sluga, Hans. Gottlob Frege. (Arguments of the Philosophers). 224p. 1980. 35.00 (ISBN 0-7100-0474-5). Routledge & Kegan.

Thiel, C. Sense & Reference in Frege's Logic. Blakeley, T. J., tr. from Ger. 172p. 1968. lib. bdg. 26.00 (ISBN 90-277-0088-5, Pub. by Reidel Holland). Kluwer Boston.

FREIDANK

Rapp, Catherine. Burgher & Peasant. LC 75-140039. (Catholic University Studies in German Ser.: No. 7). Repr. of 1936 ed. 17.00 (ISBN 0-404-50227-X). AMS Pr.

FREIGHT AND FREIGHTAGE

see also Bills of Lading; Breakage, Shrinkage, etc. (Commerce); Charter-Parties; Freight Forwarders; Railroads–Freight; Stowage

Boyle, David H. How to Succeed in Big Time Trucking. (Orig.). 1979. pap. 6.95 (ISBN 0-913668-97-4). Ten Speed Pr.

Broehl, Wayne G., Jr. Trucks, Trouble & Triumph: The Norwalk Truck Line Company. LC 75-41749. (Companies & Men: Business Enterprises in America). (Illus.). 1976. Repr. of 1954 ed. 21.00x (ISBN 0-405-08066-2). Arno.

Button, K. J. & Pearman, A. D. The Economics of Urban Freight Transport. 1981. text ed. 40.00x (ISBN 0-8419-5060-1). Holmes & Meier.

Davis, Grant M. & Dillard, John E., Jr. Increasing Motor Carrier Productivity: An Empirical Analysis. LC 77-7821. (Praeger Special Studies). 1977. text ed. 20.95 (ISBN 0-03-022641-4). Praeger.

European Conference of Ministers of Transport, 20th Round Table. Demand for Freight Transport. 86p. 1973. 2.50x (ISBN 92-821-1013-3). OECD.

Felton, John R. The Economics of Freight Car Supply. LC 78-15970. (Illus.). xii, 118p. 1978. 9.50x (ISBN 0-8032-1950-4). U of Nebr Pr.

Friedlaender, Ann F. The Dilemma of Freight Transport Regulation. LC 69-18820. (Studies in the Regulation of Economic Activity). 216p. 1969. 11.95 (ISBN 0-8157-2936-7). Brookings.

Harper, Donald V. Transportation in America: Users, Carriers, Government. (Illus.). 1978. ref. 19.95 (ISBN 0-13-930214-X). P-H.

International Symposium on Transport & Handling in the Pulp & Paper Industry, 2nd, Rotterdam, Netherlands, Oct. 1976. Transport & Handling in the Pulp & Paper Industry, Vol. 2: Proceedings. Kalish, John E. & Haas, Leonard E., eds. LC 74-20162. (A Pulp & Paper Bk.). (Illus.). 309p. 1977. 37.50 (ISBN 0-87930-065-5). Miller Freeman.

Jane's Freight Containers 1977. Date not set. 72.50x (ISBN 0-531-03262-0). Key Bk Serv.

Jane's Freight Containers 1980. Date not set. 125.00x (ISBN 0-531-03934-X). Key Bk Serv.

Keller, J. J., & Assocs., Inc. Freight Claims Manual. Nelson, Harold C., ed. LC 78-71118. 1979. 45.00 (ISBN 0-934674-22-1, 6M). J J Keller.

--Freight Security Manual. McDowell, George B., ed. LC 79-64975. 1979. 45.00 (ISBN 0-934674-23-X, 7M). J J Keller.

Kneafsey, James T. Transportation Economic Analysis. LC 74-2203. (Illus.). 1975. 21.95x (ISBN 0-669-93211-6). Lexington Bks.

Lass, William E. From the Missouri to the Great Salt Lake: An Account of Overland Freighting. LC 75-183071. (Nebraska State Historical Publications Ser.: Vol. 26). (Illus.). 1972. 7.95 (ISBN 0-686-18151-4). Nebraska Hist.

Lowe, David. Costing & Pricing Goods Vehicle Operations. LC 75-307091. (Illus.). 195p. 1975. 19.50x (ISBN 0-85038-120-7). Intl Pubns Serv.

Moore, Thomas G. Freight Transportation Regulation: Surface Freight & the Interstate Commerce Commission. 1972. pap. 3.00 (ISBN 0-8447-3088-2). Am Enterprise.

Motor Carrier Entry Regulation in Texas. (Policy Research Project Report: No. 24). 1978. 3.00 (ISBN 0-89940-617-3). LBJ Sch Public Affairs.

Motor Freight Terminals. (Five Hundred Ser). 1973. pap. 2.00 (ISBN 0-685-58225-6, 513). Natl Fire Prot.

Newborne, M. J. A Guide to Freight Consolidation for Shippers. LC 76-10119. 1977. pap. 5.25 (ISBN 0-87408-004-5). Traffic Serv.

Newbourne, Malcolm J. The Transportation & Distribution Manager's Guide to Time Sharing. new ed. Marshall, Kenneth, ed. LC 79-88410. 1979. 25.00 (ISBN 0-87408-016-9). Traffic Serv.

Pierce, Jack. The Freight Train Book. LC 79-91307. (Illus.). (ps-3). 1980. PLB 6.95g (ISBN 0-87614-123-8). Carolrhoda Bks.

Possinger, Callie, ed. The Official Directory of Industrial & Commercial Traffic Executives-1982 Edition. LC 72-626342. (Illus.). 500p. 1981. 45.00 (ISBN 0-87408-021-5). Traffic Serv.

Reebie Associates, et al. Transguide: A Guide to Sources of Freight Transportation Information. LC 80-53144. 392p. 1980. 40.00 (ISBN 0-9604776-0-8). Reebie Assoc.

Rudman, Jack. Freight Rate Specialist. (Career Examination Ser.: C-973). (Cloth bdg. avail.on request). pap. 6.00 (ISBN 0-8373-0973-5). Natl Learning.

Sullivan, George. How Does It Get There? LC 73-10345. (Illus.). 112p. (gr. 5 up). 1973. 5.95 (ISBN 0-664-32535-1). Westminster.

Transport of Dangerous Goods. rev. ed. 1978. pap. 20.00 (ISBN 0-685-33032-X, 77.VIII.1). UN.

Wilson, George W. Economic Analysis of Intercity Freight Transportation. LC 79-3131. 352p. 1980. 25.00x (ISBN 0-253-36915-0). Ind U Pr.

FREIGHT AND FREIGHTAGE–VOCATIONAL GUIDANCE

Lerner, Mark. Careers in Trucking. LC 79-18675. (Early Career Bks.). (Illus.). (gr. 2-5). 1979. PLB 4.95 (ISBN 0-8225-0341-7). Lerner Pubns.

FREIGHT AND FREIGHTAGE–RUSSIA

Williams, E. W. Freight Transportation in the Soviet Union. (National Bureau of Economic Research, A-76). 1962. 17.50x (ISBN 0-691-04131-8). Princeton U Pr.

Williams, Ernest W., Jr. Freight Transportation in the Soviet Union, Including Comparisons with the United States. (General Ser.: No. 76). 1962. 12.00 (ISBN 0-691-04131-8, Dist. by Princeton U Pr). Natl Bur Econ Res.

FREIGHT FORWARDERS

see also Carriers

Official Freight Forwarders Directory 1981-Offizielles Spediteur Adressbuch 1981: Annuaire Officiel Des Transitaires 1981. 952p. (Ger.). 1980. pap. 67.50x (ISBN 3-87154-156-7). Intl Pubns Serv.

Ullman, Gerald H. Ocean Freight Forwarder, the Exporter & the Law. LC 67-25958. 1967. 6.00x (ISBN 0-87033-072-1). Cornell Maritime.

Wood, Frances & Wood, Dorothy. I Hauled These Mountains in Here. LC 76-187948. (Illus.). 1977. 9.95 (ISBN 0-87004-233-5). Caxton.

FREIGHT HANDLING

see Freight and Freightage; Railroads–Freight

FREIGHT PLANES

see Transport Planes

FREIGHT RATES

see Freight and Freightage

FREIGHT SHIPS

see Cargo Ships

FREIGHT VESSELS

see Cargo Ships

FREIGHTERS

see Cargo Ships

FREIRE, PAULO, 1921-

Collins, Denis E. Paulo Freire: His Life, Works & Thought. LC 77-83567. 104p. 1977. pap. 2.95 (ISBN 0-8091-2056-9). Paulist Pr.

Grabowski, Stanley, ed. Paulo Freire: A Revolutionary Dilemma for the Adult Educator. LC 72-7971. (Occasional Papers Ser., No. 32). 75p. (Orig.). 1972. pap. 6.00 (ISBN 0-87060-054-0). Syracuse U Cont Ed.

Mackie, Robert, ed. Literacy & Revolution: The Pedagogy of Paulo Freire. 172p. 1981. pap. 7.95 (ISBN 0-8264-0055-8). Continuum.

FREMONT, JESSIE (BENTON) 1824-1902–FICTION

Stone, Irving. Immortal Wife. LC 54-6846. 1948. 10.95 (ISBN 0-385-04219-1). Doubleday.

FREMONT, JOHN CHARLES, 1813-1890

Bartlett, Ruhl J. John C. Fremont & the Republican Party. LC 73-87663. (American Scene Ser). 1970. Repr. of 1930 ed. lib. bdg. 19.50 (ISBN 0-306-71763-8). Da Capo.

Brandon, William. The Men & the Mountain: Fremont's Fourth Expedition. LC 73-20901. (Illus.). 337p. 1974. Repr. of 1955 ed. lib. bdg. 16.50x (ISBN 0-8371-5873-7, BRME). Greenwood.

Carvalho, Solomon N. Incidents of Travel & Adventure in the Far West, with Colonel Fremont's Last Expedition Across the Rocky Mountains. LC 72-9434. (The Far Western Frontier Ser.). 384p. 1973. Repr. of 1857 ed. 18.00 (ISBN 0-405-04964-1). Arno.

Montaignes, Francois Des. The Plains. Mower, Nancy & Russell, Don, eds. LC 70-177341. (American Exploration & Travel Ser.: Vol. 60). 200p. 1972. 10.95x (ISBN 0-8061-0998-X). U of Okla Pr.

Nevins, Allan. Fremont: Pathmarker of the West, 2 vols. Incl. Vol. 1. Fremont, the Explorer. xi, 344p; Vol. 2. Fremont in the Civil War. (Illus.). x, 394p. LC 61-7088. (American Classics Ser.). Set. 40.00 (ISBN 0-8044-1671-0). Ungar.

Spence, Mary L. & Jackson, Donald, eds. The Expeditions of John Charles Fremont, Vol. 2: The Bear Flag Revolt & the Court Martial. (Illus.). 501p. 1973. 30.00 (ISBN 0-252-00249-0). U of Ill Pr.

Syme, Ronald. John Fremont: Last American Explorer. LC 74-4198. (Illus.). 192p. (gr. 5-9). 1974. 6.95 (ISBN 0-688-20120-2). Morrow.

Talbot, Theodore. Soldier in the West: Letters of Theodore Talbot During His Services in California, Mexico, & Oregon, 1845-53. Hine, Robert V. & Lottinville, Savoie, eds. LC 74-177337. (The American Exploration & Travel Ser.: Vol. 61). (Illus.). 200p. 1972. 11.95 (ISBN 0-8061-1002-3). U of Okla Pr.

FREMONT RIVER

Morss, Noel. Ancient Culture of the Fremont River in Utah. 1931. pap. 6.00 (ISBN 0-527-01226-2). Kraus Repr.

FRENCH, PETE

French, Giles. Cattle Country of Peter French. 2nd ed. LC 64-23094. (Illus.). 1972. pap. 5.95 (ISBN 0-8323-0280-5). Binford.

THE FRENCH ACADEMY

Vincent, Leon H. The French Academy. 1979. Repr. of 1901 ed. lib. bdg. 20.00 (ISBN 0-8492-2823-9). R West.

FRENCH AND INDIAN WAR, 1755-1763

see United States–History–French and Indian War, 1755-1763

FRENCH ARCHITECTURE

see Architecture–France

FRENCH ART

see Art, French

FRENCH AUTHORS

see Authors, French

FRENCH BALLADS AND SONGS

see also Folk-Songs, French; Songs, French

Picker, Martin. The Chanson Albums of Marguerite of Austria. 1965. 62.50x (ISBN 0-520-01009-4). U of Cal Pr.

Wilkins, Nigel. One Hundred Ballades. LC 69-10342. 1969. 42.00 (ISBN 0-521-07146-1). Cambridge U Pr.

FRENCH BROAD RIVER VALLEY

Dykeman, Wilma. The French Broad. LC 54-9347. (Illus.). 1965. 8.50 (ISBN 0-87049-056-7). U of Tenn Pr.

FRENCH-CANADIAN FOLK-SONGS

see Folk-Songs, Canadian

FRENCH-CANADIAN LITERATURE

Beaulieu, Andre & Hamelin, Jean. La Presse Quebecoise: Des Origines Anos Jours. 1973. pap. 14.50x (ISBN 2-7637-6658-7, Pub. by Laval). Intl Schol Bk Serv.

Bouchard, Rene, ed. Culture Populaire et Litteratures Au Quebec. (Stanford French & Italian Studies: Vol. 19). 308p. (Fr.). 1980. pap. 20.00 (ISBN 0-915838-20-6). Anma Libri.

Fraser, Ian F. Spirit of French Canada: A Study of the Literature. LC 70-168135. Repr. of 1939 ed. 17.50 (ISBN 0-404-02548-X). AMS Pr.

Lamarche, Gustave. Oeuvres Theatrales: Tome Premier, Theatre Varie. (Vie Des Lettres Quebecoises). 572p. (Fr.). 1971. 17.50x (ISBN 2-7637-6620-X, Pub. by Laval); pap. 12.50x (ISBN 0-7746-6620-X). Intl Schol Bk Serv.

Lamontagne, Leopold, ed. Le Canada Francais D'aujourd' Hui. (Illus.). 161p. (Fr.). 1970. 8.50x (ISBN 2-7637-6426-6, Pub. by Laval). Intl Schol Bk Serv.

Lemire, Maurice. Grands Themes Nationalistes Du Roman Historique Canadien-Francais. (Vie Des Lettres Quebecoises Ser.: No. 8). 281p. (Fr.). 1970. 12.50x (ISBN 2-7637-0004-7, Pub. by Laval); pap. 10.00x (ISBN 2-7637-6358-8, Pub. by Laval). Intl Schol Bk Serv.

Tougas, Gerard. History of French-Canadian Literature. 2nd ed. Cook, Alta L., tr. from Fr. LC 76-7977. 1976. Repr. of 1966 ed. lib. bdg. 18.00x (ISBN 0-8371-8858-X, TOHF). Greenwood.

Warwick, Jack. Long Journey: Literary Themes of French Canada. LC 68-117293. (Romance Ser.). 1968. 17.50x (ISBN 0-8020-5198-7). U of Toronto Pr.

FRENCH-CANADIAN LITERATURE–BIBLIOGRAPHY

Hayne, David M. & Tirol, Marcel. Bibliographie Critique Du Roman Canadien-Francais: 1837-1900. 141p. (Fr.). 1969. pap. 3.50x (ISBN 2-7637-6369-3, Pub. by Laval). Intl Schol Bk Serv.

FRENCH-CANADIAN POETRY

Blais, Jacques. De L'Ordre et De L'Aventure: La Poesie au Quebec de 1934 a 1944. (Vie Des Lettres Quebecoises Ser.: No. 14). 420p. (Fr.). 1975. pap. 15.00x (ISBN 2-7637-6722-2, Pub. by Laval). Intl Schol Bk Serv.

La Poesie Nationaliste au Canada Francais (1606-1867) (Vie Des Lettres Quebecoises Ser.: No. 13). 450p. (Fr.). 1975. pap. 15.00x (ISBN 2-7637-6674-9, Pub. by Laval). Intl Schol Bk Serv.

FRENCH-CANADIAN POETRY–TRANSLATIONS INTO ENGLISH

Roy, George R., ed. & tr. Twelve Modern French Canadian Poets. LC 76-26074. 1976. Repr. of 1958 ed. lib. bdg. 15.00x (ISBN 0-8371-9018-5, ROTM). Greenwood.

FRENCH-CANADIAN TALES

see Tales, French-Canadian

FRENCH-CANADIANS

see also Acadians; Canada–English-French Relations

Armstrong, Elizabeth H. Crisis of Quebec, Nineteen Fourteen to Nineteen Eighteen. LC 77-158270. (BCL Ser.: No. 2). Repr. of 1937 ed. 17.50 (ISBN 0-404-00384-2). AMS Pr.

Basham, Richard. Crisis in Blanc & White: Urbanization & Ethnic Identity in French Canada. LC 77-7182. (Illus.). 304p. 1978. pap. 7.95 (ISBN 0-87073-571-3). Schenkman.

Cappon, Paul. Conflit Entre les Neo-Canadiens et les Francophones de Montreal. (Centre International de Recherche sur le Bilinguisme). 288p. (Fr.). 1975. pap. 13.50x (ISBN 2-7637-6721-4, Pub. by Laval). Intl Schol Bk Serv.

Dionne, N. E. Le Parler Populaire des Canadiens Francais. (Langue Francaise au Quebec-Lexicologie et Lexicographie). 696p. (Fr.). 1974. 18.50x (ISBN 2-7637-6724-9, Pub. by Laval). Intl Schol Bk Serv.

Dionne, Narcisse-Eutrope. Canadiens-Francais: Origine Des Familles Emigrees De France D'Espagne, De Suisse Etc. LC 73-76767. 1969. Repr. of 1914 ed. 22.50 (ISBN 0-8063-0095-7). Genealog Pub.

Dumond, Fernand, et al, eds. Ideologies an Canada Francais 1850-1900 (Ideologies of French Canada 1850-1900) (I Histoire et Sociologie De Al Culture Ser). 326p. 1971. 12.50x (ISBN 2-7637-6481-9, Pub. by Laval). Intl. Schol Bk Serv.

Facultede Sciencesdel'universite Laval. Cri D'alarme: La Civilisation Scientifique et les Canadiens Francais. 1963. pap. 2.50x (ISBN 2-7637-6591-2, Pub. by Laval). Intl Schol Bk Serv.

Garigue, Phillip. A Bibliographical Introduction to the Study of French Canada. LC 77-11621. 1977. Repr. of 1956 ed. lib. bdg. 14.50x (ISBN 0-8371-9807-0, GABI). Greenwood.

Holbrook, Sabra. The French Founders of North America & Their Heritage. LC 75-13574. (gr. 6 up). 1976. 7.95 (ISBN 0-689-30490-0). Atheneum.

Hughes, Everett C. French Canada in Transition. 1963. 11.00x (ISBN 0-226-35924-7). U of Chicago Pr.

--French Canada in Transition. 1963. pap. 2.95 (ISBN 0-226-35925-5, P139, Phoen). U of Chicago Pr.

Miner, Horace. St. Denis: A French-Canadian Parish. LC 63-13068. (Illus.). 1963. 11.00x (ISBN 0-226-52992-4). U of Chicago Pr.

--Saint Denis: A French-Canadian Parish. LC 63-13068. 1963. pap. 4.45 (ISBN 0-226-52993-2, P108, Phoen). U of Chicago Pr.

Nute, Grace L. Voyageur. LC 55-12180. (Illus.). 289p. 1955. Repr. of 1931 ed. 7.50 (ISBN 0-87351-012-7). Minn Hist.

Oury, G. M. Madame de la Peltrie et Ses Fondations Canadiennes. (Illus.). 164p. (Fr.). 1974. pap. 6.00 (ISBN 2-7637-6697-8, Pub. by Laval). Intl Schol Bk Serv.

Wessel, Bessie B. Ethnic Survey of Woonsocket, Rhode Island. LC 74-129418. (American Immigration Collection, Ser. 2). (Illus.). 1970. Repr. of 1931 ed. 12.50 (ISBN 0-405-00572-5). Arno.

FRENCH CLOVER

see Alfalfa

FRENCH DRAMA (COLLECTIONS)

Here are entered collections of drama in French. For English translations see subdivision Translations into English.

see also Moralities, French

Bishop, Tom, ed. L' Avant-Garde Theatrale: French Theatre Since 1950. LC 74-29373. 1975. 15.00x (ISBN 0-8147-0985-0); pap. 7.00x (ISBN 0-8147-0986-9). NYU Pr.

Borgerhoff, Joseph L., ed. Nineteenth Century French Plays. (Fr). 1978. Repr. of 1931 ed. 34.50x (ISBN 0-89197-319-2). Irvington.

Bree, G. & Kroff, A. Y. Twentieth Century French Drama. 1969. text ed. 18.95 (ISBN 0-02-313820-3). Macmillan.

Chiari, Joseph. Contemporary French Theatre: The Flight from Naturalism. LC 76-128187. 1970. Repr. of 1958 ed. text ed. 9.50 (ISBN 0-87752-126-3). Gordian.

Dabney, Lancaster E. Claude Billard, Minor French Dramatist of the Early Seventeenth Century. 1973. pap. 11.50 (ISBN 0-384-10641-2). Johnson Repr.

Faguet, Emile. Drame Ancien, Drame Moderne. LC 74-168695. (Research & Source Works Ser: No. 8). 280p. (Theater & Drama; No. 25). 1972. Repr. of 1924 ed. lib. bdg. 20.50 (ISBN 0-8337-4093-8). B Franklin.

Fournier, Edouard, ed. Theatre Francais Avant La Renaissance, 1430-1550. 1965. Repr. of 1872 ed. 32.00 (ISBN 0-8337-1225-X). B Franklin.

Grant, Elliott M., ed. Four French Plays of the Twentieth Century. Repr. of 1949 ed. lib. bdg. 15.00x (ISBN 0-8371-2212-0, GRFF). Greenwood.

Harden, Arthur R., ed. Trois pieces medievales: Le Jeu d'Adam, le Miracle de Theophile, la Farce du Cuvier. LC 67-20813. (Medieval French Literature Ser). (Orig., Fr.). 1967. pap. text ed. 8.95x (ISBN 0-89197-455-5). Irvington.

Paulson, Michael G. The Fallen Crown: Three French Mary Stuart Plays of the Seventeenth Century. LC 79-6812. 207p. 1980. text ed. 17.00 (ISBN 0-8191-0959-2); pap. text ed. 9.25 (ISBN 0-8191-0960-6). U Pr of Amer.

Sartre, John-Paul, et al. Four Contemporary French Plays. 1967. 3.95 (ISBN 0-394-60090-8, M90). Modern Lib.

Stone, Donald, ed. Four Renaissance Tragedies. Incl. Jephte ou le Voeu. Buchanan, George; Abraham Sacrifiant. De Beze, Theodore; Didon: Se Sacrifiant. Jodelle, Etienne; Saul le Furieux. De La Taille, Jean. LC 66-4592. (Texts from the Romance Languages Ser: No. 3). xxx, 224p. 1966. pap. text ed. 2.50x (ISBN 0-674-31550-2). Harvard U Pr.

Theatre comique au moyen age. (Documentation thematique). (Illus., Fr.). pap. 2.95 (ISBN 0-685-14082-2, 322). Larousse.

FRENCH DRAMA–BIBLIOGRAPHY

Brenner, Clarence D. Bibliographical List of Plays in the French Language, Seventeen Hundred to Seventeen Eighty-Nine. LC 76-43909. (Music & Theatre in France in the 17th & 18th Centuries). Repr. of 1947 ed. 27.50 (ISBN 0-404-60152-9). AMS Pr.

Mason, Hamilton. French Theatre in New York: 1899-1939. LC 40-14965. Repr. of 1940 ed. 19.45 (ISBN 0-404-04224-4). AMS Pr.

Thompson, Lawrence S. Bibliography of French Plays on Microcards. 1967. 27.50 (ISBN 0-208-00301-0, Archon). Shoe String.

Wicks, C. Beaumont, ed. Parisian Stage, 5 vols. LC 50-2939. 1950-79. Vol. 1. pap. 5.00x (ISBN 0-8173-9502-4); Vol. 3. pap. 9.20x (ISBN 0-8173-9504-0); Vol. 5. pap. 16.75x (ISBN 0-8173-9506-7). U of Ala Pr.

FRENCH DRAMA–HISTORY AND CRITICISM

Abraham, Claude, et al, eds. Le Theatre Complet De Tristan L'hermite. LC 73-7453. 859p. 1975. 25.00 (ISBN 0-8173-8600-9). U of Ala Pr.

Actors Roles at the Comedie Francaise According to the Reports Des Comedies Francoises Qui Se Peuvent Jouer En Sixteen Eighty-Five: Comedie Francaise, Paris. pap. 10.50 (ISBN 0-384-44826-7). Johnson Repr.

Affron, Charles. Stage for Poets: Studies in the Theatre of Hugo & Musset. LC 75-153847. (Princeton Essays in Literature Ser.). 1972. 18.00 (ISBN 0-691-06201-3). Princeton U Pr.

Alasseur, Claude. La Comedie Francaise Au XVIIIe: Etude Economique. (Civilisation et Societes: No. 3). 1967. pap. 14.70x (ISBN 90-2796-074-7). Mouton.

Allard, Louis. La Comedie De Moeurs En France Au Dixneuvieme Siecle. LC 23-17333. (Harvard Studies in Romance Languages Monographs: Vol. 5). 1923. pap. 28.00 (ISBN 0-527-01103-7). Kraus Repr.

Arden, Heather. Fools' Play. LC 78-73603. 1980. 34.50 (ISBN 0-521-22513-2). Cambridge U Pr.

Arvin, Neil C. Eugene Scribe & the French Theatre, 1815-1860. LC 67-13422. 1924. 18.00 (ISBN 0-405-08216-9, Pub. by Blom). Arno.

Baichelor. Existence et Imagination: Essai sur le Theatre de Montherlant. Laredu, tr. (Fr.). 14.50 (ISBN 0-685-37000-3). French & Eur.

Baudin, Maurice. Les Batards Au Theatre En France De la Renaissance a la Fin Du XVIII Siecle. Repr. of 1932 ed. pap. 11.50 (ISBN 0-384-03555-8). Johnson Repr.

Bennetton, Norman A. Social Significance of the Duel in 17th Century French Drama. 1973. Repr. of 1938 ed. pap. 11.50 (ISBN 0-384-03903-0). Johnson Repr.

Besant, Walter. The French Humorists. 1975. Repr. of 1877 ed. 15.50 (ISBN 0-8274-4068-5). R West.

Branford, Kester A. A Study of Jean-Jacques Bernard's Theatre De L'inexprime. LC 76-58424. (Romance Monographs: No. 24). 1977. 20.00x (ISBN 84-399-6422-6). Romance.

Brereton, Geoffrey. French Comic Drama from the Sixteenth to the Eighteenth Century. 1977. text ed. 22.95x (ISBN 0-416-78220-5); pap. text ed. 15.95x (ISBN 0-416-80710-0). Methuen Inc.

--French Tragic Drama in the Sixteenth & Seventeenth Centuries. (Illus.). 320p. 1973. 18.95x (ISBN 0-416-07630-0); pap. 12.95x (ISBN 0-416-78920-X). Methuen Inc.

Carlson, Marvin. The French Stage in the Nineteenth Century. LC 72-3981. 1972. 11.50 (ISBN 0-8108-0516-2). Scarecrow.

Carnahan, David H. Prologue in the Old French & Provencal Mystery. LC 68-55160. (Studies in French Literature, No. 45). 1969. Repr. of 1905 ed. lib. bdg. 46.95 (ISBN 0-8383-0519-9). Haskell.

Carter, Lawson A. Zola & the Theater. LC 77-6784. (Yale Romantic Studies, English Ser.). 1977. Repr. of 1963 ed. lib. bdg. 20.25x (ISBN 0-8371-9659-0, CAZO). Greenwood.

Chasles, Emile. Comedie en France au seizieme siecle. LC 71-168279. (Theatre & Drama Ser.: No. 21). (Fr). 1971. Repr. of 1862 ed. 19.00 (ISBN 0-8337-0546-6). B Franklin.

Chiari, Joseph. Contemporary French Theatre: The Flight from Naturalism. LC 76-128187. 1970. Repr. of 1958 ed. text ed. 9.50 (ISBN 0-87752-126-3). Gordian.

Cook, Albert. French Tragedy: The Power of Enchantment. LC 80-39611. xiv, 124p. 1981. 12.95x (ISBN 0-8040-0548-6). Swallow.

Daniel, May. French Drama of the Unspoken. LC 72-191858. 1953. lib. bdg. 20.00 (ISBN 0-8414-2435-7). Folcroft.

Daniels, May. The French Drama of the Unspoken. LC 77-2374. (Edinburgh University Pubns. Language & Literature: No. 3). 1977. Repr. of 1953 ed. 19.25x (ISBN 0-8371-9464-4, DAFD). Greenwood.

Diderot, Denis & Green, F. C. Diderot's Writings on the Theatre. LC 76-43916. (Music & Theatre in France in the 17th & 18th Centuries). Repr. of 1936 ed. 22.50 (ISBN 0-404-60157-X). AMS Pr.

Faral, Edmond. Mimes Francais Du Xiiie Siecle: Contribution a L'histoire Du Theatre Comique Au Moyen Age. LC 77-178533. Repr. of 1910 ed. 20.00 (ISBN 0-404-56599-9). AMS Pr.

Fowlie, Wallace. Dionysus in Paris: A Guide to Contemporary French Theatre. (Illus.). 8.50 (ISBN 0-8446-0096-2). Peter Smith.

Frank, Grace. Medieval French Drama. 1954. 29.50x (ISBN 0-19-815317-1). Oxford U Pr.

Gautier, Theophile. Histoire de l'Art Dramatique en France Depuis Vingt-Cing Ans, 6 vols. facsimile ed. 1968. Repr. of 1859 ed. Set. 350.00 (ISBN 0-686-55904-5). French & Eur.

Gochberg. Stage of Dreams: The Dramatic Art of Alfred de Musset (1828-1834) (Hist. des Idees et Crit. Litt.). 26.50 (ISBN 0-685-34954-3). French & Eur.

Gossip, C. J. An Introduction to French Classical Tragedy. 1982. 28.50x (ISBN 0-389-20163-4). B&N.

Grannis, Valleria B. Dramatic Parody in Eighteenth Century France. (Studies in Comparative Literature: No. 5). 428p. Repr. of 1931 ed. lib. bdg. 22.50x (ISBN 0-87991-504-8). Porcupine Pr.

Green, Frederick C. Literary Ideas in Eighteenth Century France & England: A Critical Survey. LC 65-23576. 1965. 18.00 (ISBN 0-8044-2299-0). Ungar.

--Minuet: A Critical Survey of French & English Literary Ideas in the 18th Century. LC 75-158504. 1971. Repr. of 1935 ed. 35.00 (ISBN 0-403-01296-1). Scholarly.

Gretry, Andre E. Reflexions d'un solitaire, 4 vols. Solvay, Lucien & Closson, Ernest, eds. LC 76-43920. (Music & Theatre in France in the 17th & 18th Centuries). Repr. of 1922 ed. Set. 105.00 (ISBN 0-404-60190-1). AMS Pr.

Grossvogel, David I. Twentieth Century French Drama. LC 65-7487. 378p. 1958. pap. 6.00x (ISBN 0-231-08522-2). Columbia U Pr.

--Twentieth Century French Drama. LC 68-16434. 1966. Repr. of 1961 ed. 9.00 (ISBN 0-87752-048-8). Gordian.

Guicharnaud, Jacques & Guicharnaud, June. Modern French Theatre: From Giraudoux to Genet. rev. ed. (Romantic Studies, Second Ser: No. 7). (Illus.). 1975. pap. 5.95x (ISBN 0-300-00106-1). Yale U Pr.

Harvey, H. G. Theatre of the Basoche: The Contribution of the Law Societies to French Mediaeval Comedy. 1941. pap. 16.00 (ISBN 0-527-01115-0). Kraus Repr.

Hawkins, Frederick. Annals of the French Stage from Its Origin to the Death of Racine, 2 Vols. LC 68-24949. (Studies in Drama, No. 39). 1969. Repr. of 1884 ed. lib. bdg. 79.95 (ISBN 0-8383-0161-4). Haskell.

--Annals of the French Stage from Its Origin to the Death of Racine. 1968. Repr. of 1884 ed. 29.00 (ISBN 0-403-08982-4). Scholarly.

--French Stage in the Eighteenth Century, 2 Vols. LC 68-24950. (Studies in Drama, No. 39). 1969. Repr. of 1888 ed. Set. lib. bdg. 79.95 (ISBN 0-8383-0162-2). Haskell.

--French Stage in the Eighteenth Century, 2 Vols. rev. ed. 1968. Repr. of 1888 ed. Set. 32.00 (ISBN 0-403-00085-8). Scholarly.

Hawkins, Frederick W. Annals of the French Stage from Its Origin to the Death of Racine, 2 Vols. LC 68-57607. (Illus.). 1969. Repr. of 1884 ed. lib. bdg. 31.50x (ISBN 0-8371-2172-8, HAFS). Greenwood.

--French Stage in the Eighteenth Century, 2 Vols. LC 68-57608. (Illus.). 1969. Repr. of 1888 ed. lib. bdg. 34.00x (ISBN 0-8371-2746-7, HASE). Greenwood.

Herzel, Roger W. The Original Casting of Moliere's Plays. Beckerman, Bernard, ed. LC 81-7538. (Theater & Dramatic Studies: No. 1). 1981. price not set (ISBN 0-8357-1209-5, Pub. by UMI Res Pr). Univ Microfilms.

Hill, L. A. Tudors in French Drama. 1973. Repr. of 1932 ed. 13.00 (ISBN 0-384-23257-4). Johnson Repr.

Hobson, Harold. French Theatre Since Eighteen Thirty. 1979. 17.95 (ISBN 0-7145-3650-4). Riverrun NY.

--French Theatre Today. LC 65-16240. 1953. 19.00 (ISBN 0-405-08631-8). Arno.

Howarth, W. D., et al, eds. Form & Content in Seventeenth-Century French Drama. 1982. 65.00x (ISBN 0-86127-216-1, Pub. by Avebury Pub England). State Mutual Bk.

Joannides, A. Comedie-Francaise de Seize Cent Quatre Vingt a Dix-neuf Cent: Dictionnaire General des Pieces et des Auteurs. LC 75-171947. (Bibliography & Reference Ser.: No. 440). 462p. (Essays in Literature & Criticism, No. 171). 1972. Repr. of 1901 ed. lib. bdg. 26.50 (ISBN 0-8337-4190-X). B Franklin.

Jourdain, Eleanor F. Dramatic Theory & Practice in France 1690-1808. LC 68-20232. 1968. Repr. of 1921 ed. 15.00 (ISBN 0-405-08675-X). Arno.

Kurz, Harry. European Characters in French Drama of the Eighteenth Century. LC 72-1018. (Columbia University. Studies in Romance Philology & Literature: No. 17). Repr. of 1916 ed. 19.50 (ISBN 0-404-50617-8). AMS Pr.

--European Characters in French Drama of the Eighteenth Century. 1978. Repr. of 1916 ed. 25.00 (ISBN 0-8492-1467-X). R West.

Lancaster, Henry C. French Tragedy in the Time of Louis Fifteenth & Voltaire, 2 vols. 1973. lib. bdg. 42.50x (ISBN 0-374-94720-1). Octagon.

--French Tragi-Comedy. LC 66-29465. 1966. Repr. of 1907 ed. 8.50 (ISBN 0-87752-059-3). Gordian.

--History of French Dramatic Literature in the Seventeenth Century, 9 vols. Incl. Pt. 1, Vol. 1. The Pre-Classical Period. 1610-1634. 15.00 (ISBN 0-685-22670-0); Pt. 1, Vol. 2. The Pre-Classical Period. 1610-1634. 15.00 (ISBN 0-685-22671-9); Pt. 2, Vol. 1. The Period of Corneille. 1635-1651. 15.00 (ISBN 0-685-22672-7); Pt. 2, Vol. 2. The Period of Corneille. 1635-1651. 15.00 (ISBN 0-685-22673-5); Pt. 3, Vol. 1. The Period of Moliere. 1652-1672. 15.00 (ISBN 0-685-22674-3); Pt. 3, Vol. 2. The Period of Moliere. 1652-1672. 15.00 (ISBN 0-685-22675-1); Pt. 4, Vol. 1. The Period of Racine. 1673-1700. 16.00 (ISBN 0-685-22676-X); Pt. 4, Vol. 2. The Period of Racine. 1673-1700. 16.00 (ISBN 0-685-22677-8); Pt. 5. Recapitulation. 1610-1700. 10.00 (ISBN 0-685-22678-6). LC 66-20028. 3698p. 1966. Repr. of 1942 ed. 125.00 (ISBN 0-87752-060-7). Gordian.

--Sunset: A History of Parisian Drama in the Last Years of Louis XIV, 1701-1715. LC 76-29737. 1976. Repr. of 1945 ed. lib. bdg. 24.00x (ISBN 0-8371-9278-1, LASH). Greenwood.

Landois, Paul. First French Tragedie Bourgeoise: Sylvie. 1973. Repr. of 1954 ed. 11.50 (ISBN 0-384-31237-3). Johnson Repr.

Lanson, Gustave. Esquisse D'une Histoire De la Tragedie Francaise. LC 20-11323. (Columbia University. Studies in Romance Philology & Literature: No. 27). Repr. of 1920 ed. 17.00 (ISBN 0-404-50627-5). AMS Pr.

Lawton, Harold W., ed. Handbook of French Renaissance Dramatic Theory. LC 72-6199. 147p. (Lat., Eng. & Fr.). 1973. Repr. of 1949 ed. lib. bdg. 15.00x (ISBN 0-8371-6457-5, LAFR). Greenwood.

Levy, Sydney. The Play of the Text: Max Jacob's le Cornet a Des. LC 80-52298. 169p. 1981. 18.00x (ISBN 0-299-08510-4). U of Wis Pr.

Lockert, Lacy. Studies in French-Classical Tragedy. LC 59-298. 1958. 10.00 (ISBN 0-8265-1049-3). Vanderbilt U Pr.

Lough, John. Seventeenth-Century French Drama: The Background. (Illus.). 1979. 18.95x (ISBN 0-19-815757-6). Oxford U Pr.

McBride, Robert. Aspects of Seventeenth-Century French Drama & Thought. 190p. 1979. 21.50x (ISBN 0-8476-6137-7). Rowman.

McKean, Sr. M. Faith. Interplay of Realistic & Flamboyant Art Elements in the French Mysteres. LC 74-94196. (Catholic University of America Studies in Romance Languages & Literatures Ser: No. 60). Repr. of 1959 ed. 17.50 (ISBN 0-404-50360-8). AMS Pr.

McKee, Kenneth N. Role of the Priest on the Parisian Stage During the French Revolution. pap. 11.50 (ISBN 0-384-34886-6). Johnson Repr.

Magnon, Jean. Tite, Tragi-Comedie: A Critical Edition. 1973. pap. 11.50 (ISBN 0-384-35045-3). Johnson Repr.

Marsan, Jules. Pastorale Dramatique En France a la Fin Du Seizieme & Au Commencement Du Dix-Septieme Siecle. LC 79-159703. (Research & Source Works Ser.: No. 745). (Illus.). 1971. Repr. of 1905 ed. lib. bdg. 32.50 (ISBN 0-8337-4254-X). B Franklin.

Mason, Hamilton. French Theatre in New York. 1940. 20.00 (ISBN 0-685-84576-1). Norwood Edns.

Matthews, Brander. French Dramatists of the Nineteenth Century. LC 68-20240. 1968. Repr. of 1901 ed. 15.00 (ISBN 0-405-08782-9, Pub. by Blom). Arno.

Matthews, J. H. Theatre in Dada & Surrealism. LC 73-16286. 312p. 1974. 14.95x (ISBN 0-8156-0097-6). Syracuse U Pr.

Maxwell, Ian R. French Farce & John Heywood. LC 76-42464. 1976. Repr. of 1946 ed. lib. bdg. 25.00 (ISBN 0-8414-6080-9). Folcroft.

Melcher, Edith. Stage Realism in France Between Diderot & Antoine. LC 73-84757. vi, 189p. 1976. Repr. of 1928 ed. 14.00 (ISBN 0-8462-1738-4). Russell.

Menestrier, Claude-Francois. Traite des tournois, joustes, carrousels et autres spectacles publics. LC 76-43926. (Music & Theatre in France in the 17th & 18th Centuries). Repr. of 1669 ed. 49.50 (ISBN 0-404-60174-X). AMS Pr.

Mongredien, Georges & Robert, Jean. Dictionnaire Biographique des Comediens Francais du 17e Siecle. 2nd ed. 240p. (Fr.). 1972. 19.95 (ISBN 0-686-56808-7, M-6586). French & Eur.

Music & Theatre in France in the 17th & 18th Centuries - le Grand Siecle: Basic Collection for Musical, Theatrical, Literary & Cultural Historians, 37 titles in 48 vols. Repr. 1275.00 (ISBN 0-404-60100-6). AMS Pr.

Norman, Hilda. Swindlers & Rogues in French Drama. LC 68-26280. 1968. Repr. of 1928 ed. 12.00 (ISBN 0-8046-0337-5). Kennikat.

Paulson, Michael G. The Fallen Crown: Three French Mary Stuart Plays of the Seventeenth Century. LC 79-6812. 207p. 1980. text ed. 17.00 (ISBN 0-8191-0959-2); pap. text ed. 9.25 (ISBN 0-8191-0960-6). U Pr of Amer.

Pellet, E. J. A Forgotten French Dramatist, Gabriel Gilbert. 1973. Repr. of 1931 ed. pap. 27.00 (ISBN 0-384-45678-2). Johnson Repr.

Petersen, Christine E. Doctor in French Drama: 1700-1775. LC 39-2239. Repr. of 1938 ed. 17.00 (ISBN 0-404-04996-6). AMS Pr.

Pianfetti, Alice T. The Theatre of Nicolas Drouin. LC 76-16239. 1977. 12.00 (ISBN 0-8022-2184-X). Philos Lib.

Profession of King in 17th Century French Drama. 1973. Repr. of 1941 ed. 11.50 (ISBN 0-384-03556-6). Johnson Repr.

Pronko, Leonard C. Avant Garde: The Experimental Theater in France. LC 77-26017. (Illus.). 1978. Repr. of 1962 ed. lib. bdg. 19.75x (ISBN 0-313-20096-3, PRAV). Greenwood.

Reichenburg, Louisette. Contribution a l'histoire de la "querelle des Bouffons". LC 76-43938. (Music & Theatre in France in the 17th & 18th Centuries). Repr. of 1937 ed. 14.50 (ISBN 0-404-60188-X). AMS Pr.

Reyes, M. Philomene de los. The Biblical Theme in Modern Drama. 1979. text ed. 12.50x (ISBN 0-8248-0633-6, Pub. by U of Philippines Pr); pap. text ed. 8.50x (ISBN 0-8248-0644-1, Pub. by U of Philippines Pr). U Pr of Hawaii.

Riccoboni, Luigi. A General History of the Stage from Its Origin....with Two Essays: On the Art of Speaking in Public, & a Comparison Between the Ancient & Modern Drama. LC 76-43937. (Music & Theatre in France in the 17th & 18th Centuries). Repr. of 1754 ed. 27.50 (ISBN 0-404-60187-1). AMS Pr.

Smith, Hugh A. Main Currents of Modern French Drama. facs. ed. LC 68-22946. (Essay Index Reprint Ser). 1925. 18.00 (ISBN 0-8369-0883-X). Arno.

--Main Currents of Modern French Drama. 1978. Repr. of 1925 ed. lib. bdg. 30.00 (ISBN 0-8414-7897-X). Folcroft.

States, Bert O. The Shape of Paradox: An Essay on Waiting for Godot. (Quantum Bk.). 1978. 14.50x (ISBN 0-520-03549-6); pap. 2.65 (ISBN 0-520-03572-0). U of Cal Pr.

Wade, Ira O. Philosophe in the French Drama of the Eighteenth Century. (Elliott Monographs: Vol. 18). 1926. pap. 9.00 (ISBN 0-527-02621-2). Kraus Repr.

Waxman, Samuel M. Antoine & the Theatre Libre. LC 63-23192. Repr. of 1926 ed. 15.00 (ISBN 0-405-09056-0). Arno.

White, Kenneth S. Man's New Shapes: French Avant-Garde Drama's Metamorphoses. LC 79-62911. 1979. pap. text ed. 6.50 (ISBN 0-8191-0717-4). U Pr of Amer.

Whitehead, F., ed. Le Chanson De Roland. (French Texts Ser.). 175p. 1975. pap. text ed. 9.95x (ISBN 0-631-00390-8, Pub. by Basil Blackwell). Biblio Dist.

Whiting, B. J. Proverbs in the Earlier English Drama. LC 70-86290. 1969. Repr. of 1938 ed. lib. bdg. 25.00x (ISBN 0-374-98513-8). Octagon.

Zamparelli, Thomas L. The Theater of Claude Billard: A Study in Post-Renaissance Dramatic Esthetics, Vol. 9. 188p. 1978. pap. 7.00 (ISBN 0-912788-08-9). Tulane Romance Lang.

FRENCH DRAMA–TRANSLATIONS INTO ENGLISH

Benedikt, Michael & Wellwarth, George E., eds. Modern French Theatre: The Avant-Garde, Dada & Surrealism. Benedikt, Michael & Wellwarth, George E., trs. 1966. pap. 5.95 (ISBN 0-525-47176-6). Dutton.

Bermel, Albert, ed. Three Popular French Comedies. LC 75-1959. x, 187p. 1975. 10.50 (ISBN 0-8044-2041-6); pap. 4.95 (ISBN 0-8044-6044-2). Ungar.

Guicharnaud, J., ed. Seventeenth Century French Drama. Bishop, Morris & Muir, Kenneth, trs. Incl. Tartuffe. Moliere, Jean B; The Would Be Gentleman. Moliere, Jean B; Precious Damsels. Moliere, Jean B; Phaedra. Racine, Jean B; Athaliah. Racine, Jean B; Cid. Corneille, Pierre. (YA) 1976. pap. 3.95 (ISBN 0-394-30977-4, 30977, Mod LibC). Modern Lib.

Lockert, Lacy, tr. Chief Rivals of Corneille & Racine. LC 56-14366. 1956. 10.00 (ISBN 0-8265-1047-7). Vanderbilt U Pr.

Obey, Andre. Andre Obey: Three Plays: One for the Wind, Noah, & The Phoenix. Suther, Judith D. & Clowney, Earle D, trs. LC 79-10498. pap. 8.00 (ISBN 0-912646-21-7); 2 vols. together 14.00 (ISBN 0-912646-23-3). Tex Christian.

The Play of Adam. 1976. 12.00 (ISBN 0-686-23382-4). Classical Folia.

Robles, Emmanuel. Three Plays by Emmanuel Robles: Plaidoyer Pour un Rebelle (Case for a Rebel), L'Horloge (the Clock), & Porfirio. Kilker, James A., tr. from Fr. LC 77-24662. (Illus.). 223p. 1977. 15.00x (ISBN 0-8093-0822-3). S Ill U Pr.

FRENCH DRAWINGS

see Drawings, French

FRENCH EQUATORIAL AFRICA

see Africa, French-Speaking Equatorial

FRENCH ESSAYS

Bossuet. Sermons. new ed. (Documentation thematique). (Illus., Fr.). 1975. pap. 2.50 (ISBN 0-685-65684-5, 41). Larousse.

Bronte, Emily J. Five Essays Written in French. 1978. Repr. of 1948 ed. lib. bdg. 10.00 (ISBN 0-8495-0433-3). Arden Lib.

Dale, John B. & Dale, Magdalene L. Lectures Francaises. 1973. pap. text ed. 8.95x (ISBN 0-669-86454-4). Heath.

De Rougemont, Denis. The Growl of Deeper Waters. Hazo, Samuel & Luey, Beth, trs. LC 75-33422. 1976. 10.95 (ISBN 0-8229-3315-2). U of Pittsburgh Pr.

Sitney, P. Adams, ed. The Gaze of Orpheus: & Other Literary Essays. Davis, Lydia, tr. from Fr. 216p. 1981. 20.00 (ISBN 0-930794-37-0); pap. 8.95 (ISBN 0-930794-38-9). Station Hill Pr.

FRENCH FARCES

Cohen, Gustave, ed. Recueil De Farces Francaises Inedites Du Quinzieme Siecle. 1949. 20.00 (ISBN 0-910956-21-9). Medieval Acad.

Farce de Maistre Pathelin. (Documentation thematique). (Fr). pap. 2.95 (ISBN 0-685-13916-6, 345). Larousse.

Fournier, Edouard, ed. Theatre Francais Avant La Renaissance, 1430-1550. 1965. Repr. of 1872 ed. 32.00 (ISBN 0-8337-1225-X). B Franklin.

Lancaster, H. Carrington, ed. Five French Farces 1655-1694. (Johns Hopkins University Studies in Romance Literatures and Languages: Vol. 19). 1970. Repr. of 1937 ed. 11.50 (ISBN 0-384-31170-9). Johnson Repr.

FRENCH FICTION (COLLECTIONS)

Here are entered collections of fiction in French. For English translations see subdivision Translations into English.

see also Short Stories, French

Federman, Raymond, ed. Cinq Nouvelles Nouvelles. LC 70-115011. (Illus., Orig., Fr.). 1970. pap. text ed. 6.95x (ISBN 0-89197-079-7). Irvington.
LeSage, Laurent. French New Novel: An Introduction & a Sampler. LC 62-20758. 1962. 13.95x (ISBN 0-271-73065-X). Pa St U Pr.

FRENCH FICTION–BIBLIOGRAPHY

Baldner, Ralph W. Bibliography of Seventeenth-Century French Prose Fiction. 197p. 1967. 18.00x (ISBN 0-87352-016-5). Modern Lang.
Williams, Ralph C. Bibliography of the Seventeenth Century Novel in France. xiv, 355p. 1964. Repr. of 1931 ed. 25.00 (ISBN 0-900470-44-5). Oak Knoll.

FRENCH FICTION–HISTORY AND CRITICISM

Atkinson, Geoffrey. Extraordinary Voyage in French Literature, 2 vols. Incl. Vol. 1. Before 1700; Vol. 2. 1700-1720. Repr. of 1920 ed. Set. 33.00 (ISBN 0-8337-0115-0). B Franklin.
Atkinson, Geoffroy. Extraordinary Voyage in French Literature Before 1700. LC 70-161705. (Columbia University. Studies in Romance Philology & Literature: No. 26). Repr. of 1920 ed. 18.00 (ISBN 0-404-50626-7). AMS Pr.
Bowen, Ray. The Novels of Ferdinand Fabre. 1977. lib. bdg. 59.95 (ISBN 0-8490-2362-9). Gordon Pr.
Brombert, Victor. The Intellectual Hero: Studies in the French Novel 1880-1955. LC 61-8673. (Midway Reprint Ser). 256p. 1974. pap. text ed. 12.00x (ISBN 0-226-07545-1). U of Chicago Pr.
Brooks, Peter. Novels of Worldliness, Crebillon, Marivaux, Laclos, Stendhal. LC 68-56303. 1969. 21.50 (ISBN 0-691-06154-8). Princeton U Pr.
Caillet, E. The Themes of Magic in Nineteenth Century French Fiction. 59.95 (ISBN 0-8490-1188-4). Gordon Pr.
Cailliet, Emile. The Themes of Magic in Nineteenth Century French Fiction. LC 80-22976. (Studies in Comparative Literature: No. 2). 228p. Repr. of 1932 ed. lib. bdg. 16.00x (ISBN 0-87991-501-3). Porcupine Pr.
Cook, Mercer. The Haitian Novel. 59.95 (ISBN 0-8490-0275-3). Gordon Pr.
Cruickshank, John, ed. The Novelist As Philosopher: Studies in French Fiction, Nineteen Thirty-Five to Nineteen Sixty. LC 77-28882. 257p. 1978. Repr. of 1962 ed. lib. bdg. 22.00x (ISBN 0-313-20271-0, CRNP). Greenwood.
Frohock, W. M., et al. Image & Theme: Studies in Modern French Fiction - Bernanos, Malraux, Sarraute, Gide, Martin Du Gard. Keane, Susan, ed. LC 79-95931. 1969. pap. 4.50x (ISBN 0-674-44395-0). Harvard U Pr.
Frohock, Wilbur M. Style & Temper: Studies in French Fiction, 1925-1960. LC 67-3155. 1967. 8.95x (ISBN 0-674-85335-0). Harvard U Pr.
Gibson, Robert. The Land Without a Name: Alain-Fournier & His World. LC 75-4392. (Illus.). 320p. 1975. text ed. 27.50 (ISBN 0-312-46515-7). St Martin.
Gleason, Judith I. This Africa: Novels by West Africans in English & French. (Northwestern University African Studies Ser.: No. 14). 1965. 11.95x (ISBN 0-8101-0103-3). Northwestern U Pr.
Green, Frederick C. French Novelists, Manners & Ideas: From the Renaissance to the Revolution. LC 64-21610. 1964. pap. 3.45 (ISBN 0-8044-6222-4). Ungar.
Guedeville, Nicolas. Critique Generale des Aventures de Telemarque. (Utopias in the Enlightenment Ser.). 87p. (Fr.). 1974. Repr. of 1700 ed. 25.00x (ISBN 0-8287-0401-5, 037). Clearwater Pub.
Heath, Stephen. The Nouveau Roman: A Study in the Practice of Writing. LC 72-83512. 312p. 1972. 15.00x (ISBN 0-87722-050-6). Temple U Pr.
Hicks, Benjamin E. Plots & Characters in Classic French Fiction. (Plots & Characters Ser.). 288p. 1981. 27.50 (ISBN 0-208-01703-8, Archon). Shoe String.
Horst, C. H. Van Der. Blandin De Cornouaille: Introduction, Edition, Diplomatique, Glossaire. (Publications de L'institut D'etudes Francaises et Occitanes De L'universite D'utrecht: No. 4). 1974. pap. text ed. 55.00x (ISBN 90-2797-984-7). Mouton.
Hubbard, Louise J. Individual & the Group in French Literature Since 1914. (Catholic University of America Studies in Romance Languages & Literatures Ser: No. 52). Repr. of 1955 ed. 16.00 (ISBN 0-404-50352-7). AMS Pr.
Lemaitre, Jules. Theatrical Impressions. LC 75-102847. 1970. Repr. of 1924 ed. 14.00 (ISBN 0-8046-0757-5). Kennikat.
LeSage, Laurent. French New Novel: An Introduction & a Sampler. LC 62-20758. 1962. 13.95x (ISBN 0-271-73065-X). Pa St U Pr.
Levin, Harry. Gates of Horn: A Study of Five French Realists. 1963. 18.95 (ISBN 0-19-500620-8). Oxford U Pr.
--Gates of Horn: A Study of Five French Realists. 1966. pap. 5.95 (ISBN 0-19-500727-1, GB). Oxford U Pr.
Loutfi, Martine A. Litterature et Colonialisme: L'expansion Coloniale Vue Dans la Litterature Romanesque Francaise, 1871-1914. 1971. pap. 15.75 (ISBN 90-2796-918-3). Mouton.
Mauriac, Francois. Le Roman. LC 75-41191. (Fr.). Repr. of 1928 ed. 12.75 (ISBN 0-404-14766-6). AMS Pr.
Mercier, Vivian. New Novel: From Queneau to Pinget. LC 75-125158. 432p. 1971. 10.00 (ISBN 0-374-22165-0); pap. 2.95 (ISBN 0-374-50983-2). FS&G.
Miller, Nancy K. The Heroine's Text: Readings in the French & English Novel, 1722-1782. 1980. 18.50x (ISBN 0-231-04910-2). Columbia U Pr.
Minogue, Valerie. Nathalie Sarraute: The War of the Words. 156p. 1981. 22.00x (ISBN 0-85224-405-3, Pub. by Edinburgh U Pr Sctland). Columbia U Pr.
Oppenheim, Lois. Intentionality & Intersubjectivity: A Phenomenological Study of Butor's La Modification. LC 79-53399. (French Forum Monographs: No. 16). 189p. 1980. pap. 11.50 (ISBN 0-917058-15-1). French Forum.
Peyre, Henri. French Novelists of Today. rev. & enl. ed. Orig. Title: Contemporary French Novel, Orig. (YA) (gr. 9 up). 1967. pap. 5.50 (ISBN 0-19-500742-5, GB). Oxford U Pr.
Raoul, Valerie. The French Fictional Journal: Fictional Narcissism-Narcissistic Fiction. (Romance Ser.). 176p. 1980. 12.50x (ISBN 0-8020-5497-8). U of Toronto Pr.
Ratner, Moses. Theory & Criticism of the Novel in France from L'Astree to 1750. LC 79-151555. 1971. Repr. of 1938 ed. 9.00 (ISBN 0-8462-1586-1). Russell.
Real, Terry. Monarch Notes on Dumas' the Three Musketeers. (Monarch Notes). (Orig.). 1977. pap. 1.50 (ISBN 0-671-00980-X). Monarch Pr.
Reck, Rima D. Literature & Responsibility: The French Novelist in the Twentieth Century. LC 69-18482. 1969. 22.50x (ISBN 0-8071-0301-2). La State U Pr.
Roudiez, Leon S. French Fiction Today: A New Direction. LC 70-185392. 1972. 28.00 (ISBN 0-8135-0724-3). Rutgers U Pr.
Saintsbury, George E. Essays on French Novelists, 2 vols. LC 73-15913. 1974. Repr. of 1891 ed. lib. bdg. 75.00 (ISBN 0-8414-7677-2). Folcroft.
--History of the French Novel to the Close of the 19th Century, 2 Vols. LC 64-23461. (1964. Repr. of 1917-19 ed). Set. 25.00 (ISBN 0-8462-0519-X). Russell.
Sayre, Robert. Solitude in Society: A Sociological Study in French Literature. LC 77-16265. 1978. 14.00x (ISBN 0-674-81761-3). Harvard U Pr.
Showalter, English, Jr. The Evolution of the French Novel, 1641-1782. LC 78-37577. 1972. 25.00 (ISBN 0-691-06229-3). Princeton U Pr.
Stambolian, George, ed. Twentieth-Century French Fiction: Essays for Germaine Bree. 1975. 20.00 (ISBN 0-8135-0786-3). Rutgers U Pr.
Stephens, Winifred. French Novelists of To-Day, First Ser. facs. ed. LC 68-20338. (Essay Index Reprint Ser). 1914. 16.00 (ISBN 0-8369-0904-6). Arno.
--French Novelists of To-Day, Second Ser. facs. ed. LC 68-20339. (Essay Index Reprint Ser). 1915. 16.00 (ISBN 0-8369-0905-4). Arno.
Turk, Edward B. Baroque Fiction-Making: A Study of Gomberville's Polexandre. (Studies in the Romance Languages & Literatures: No. 196). 1978. pap. text ed. 11.50x (ISBN 0-8078-9196-7). U of NC Pr.
Turnell, Martin. Art of French Fiction. LC 59-9491. 1968. pap. 2.95 (ISBN 0-8112-0211-9, NDP251). New Directions.
--The Rise of the French Novel. LC 77-26792. 1978. pap. 8.95 (ISBN 0-8112-0716-1, NDP474). New Directions.
Ullmann, Stephen. The Image in the Modern French Novel: Gide, Alain-Fournier, Proust, Camus. LC 77-23234. 1977. Repr. of 1963 ed. lib. bdg. 19.25x (ISBN 0-8371-9459-8, ULIM). Greenwood.
Wells, Benjamin W. A Century of French Fiction. 1978. Repr. of 1898 ed. lib. bdg. 40.00 (ISBN 0-89760-907-7, Telegraph). Dynamic Learn Corp.
Zola, Emile. Experimental Novel & Other Essays. Sherman, Belle M., tr. LC 74-890. (Studies in Fiction, No. 34). 1893. lib. bdg. 39.95 (ISBN 0-8383-0697-7). Haskell.
--Le Roman Experimental. Guedj, Aime, ed. 1971. 4.50 (ISBN 0-686-55801-4). French & Eur.

FRENCH FICTION–TRANSLATIONS FROM ENGLISH–HISTORY AND CRITICISM

Smith, Thelma M. & Miner, Ward L. Transatlantic Migration: The Contemporary American Novel in France. LC 68-29749. (Illus.). 1968. Repr. of 1955 ed. lib. bdg. 14.25x (ISBN 0-8371-0232-4, SMCA). Greenwood.
Streeter, Harold W. Eighteenth Century English Novel in French Translation. LC 69-13251. 1969. Repr. of 1936 ed. 15.00 (ISBN 0-405-09011-0, Pub. by Blom). Arno.

FRENCH FICTION–TRANSLATIONS INTO ENGLISH

Macklin, Alys E., ed. Twenty-Nine Tales from the French. facsimile ed. Herrick, Robert, tr. & intro. by. LC 72-157785. (Short Story Index Reprint Ser.). Repr. of 1922 ed. 17.00 (ISBN 0-8369-3897-6). Arno.

FRENCH FOLK-LORE

see Folk-Lore, French

FRENCH FOLK-SONGS

see Folk-Songs, French

FRENCH GUIANA

Allison-Booth, William. Devils Island: Revelations of the French Penal Settlements in Guiana. LC 71-162504. (Illus.). 1971. Repr. of 1931 ed. 22.00 (ISBN 0-8103-3761-4). Gale.

FRENCH HORN

see Horn (Musical Instrument)

FRENCH IN FOREIGN COUNTRIES

Brebion, Antoine. Bibliographie des voyages dans l'Indochine francaise du 9e au 19e siecle. LC 78-132542. (Bibliography & Reference Ser.: No. 395). (Geography & Discovery Ser., No. 8). 1971. Repr. of 1910 ed. lib. bdg. 24.00 (ISBN 0-8337-0359-5). B Franklin.
--Livre d'or du Cambodge de la Cochinchine et de l'Annam, 1625-1910 et bibliographie. LC 72-147145. (Research & Source Works Ser.: No. 665). 1971. Repr. of 1910 ed. lib bdg. 14.00 (ISBN 0-8337-0360-9). B Franklin.
Childs, Frances W. French Refugee Life in the United States, 1790-1800: An American Chapter of the French Revolution. LC 78-15085. (Perspectives in American History Ser.: No. 47). (Illus.). Repr. of 1940 ed. lib. bdg. 15.00x (ISBN 0-87991-371-1). Porcupine Pr.
Dodwell, Henry H. Dupleix & Clive: The Beginning of Empire. 1968. Repr. of 1920 ed. 18.50 (ISBN 0-208-00713-X, Archon). Shoe String.
Dunn, William E. Spanish & French Rivalry in the Gulf Region of the U. S., 1678-1702: The Beginnings of Texas & Pensacola. facsimile ed. (Select Bibliographies Reprint Ser). Repr. of 1917 ed. 18.00 (ISBN 0-8369-5792-X). Arno.
Ennis, Thomas E. French Policy & Developments in Indochina. LC 72-94980. (Illus.). x, 230p. 1973. Repr. of 1936 ed. 16.00 (ISBN 0-8462-1722-8). Russell.
Ewert, Alfred. The French Language. 2nd ed. (Great Language Ser.). 1943. text ed. 11.50x (ISBN 0-571-07019-1). Humanities.
Forbes, Allan. The Boston French. (Illus.). 1976. Repr. 7.50 (ISBN 0-686-20855-2). Polyanthos.
Fosdick, Lucian J. The French Blood in America. LC 73-279. (Illus.). 1973. Repr. of 1906 ed. 17.50 (ISBN 0-8063-0552-5). Genealog Pub.
Harvey, Daniel C. French Regime in Prince Edward Island. LC 72-113193. Repr. of 1926 ed. 21.50 (ISBN 0-404-03153-6). AMS Pr.
Hendrickson, Dyke. Quiet Presence. pap. 6.95 (ISBN 0-930096-06-1). G Gannett.
Kellogg, Louise P. French Regime in Wisconsin & the Northwest. LC 68-31296. 1968. Repr. of 1925 ed. 18.50x (ISBN 0-8154-0127-2). Cooper Sq.
Kloss, Heinz. Les Droits Linguistiques des Franco-Americans aux Etats-Unis. (International Center for Research on Bilingualism Ser.). 81p. (Fr.). 1971. pap. 4.50x (ISBN 2-7637-6610-2, Pub. by Laval). Intl Schol Bk Serv.
Kunz, Virginia B. French in America. LC 66-10146. (In America Bks). (Illus.). (gr. 5-11). 1966. PLB 6.95g (ISBN 0-8225-0204-6). Lerner Pubns.
McAvoy, Thomas T. Catholic Church in Indiana, Seventeen Eighty-Nine to Eighteen Thirty-Four. LC 41-6425. (Columbia University. Studies in the Social Sciences: No. 471). Repr. of 1940 ed. 20.00 (ISBN 0-404-51471-5). AMS Pr.
McCullogh, Flavia M., Sr. The Basques in the Northwest: Thesis. LC 74-76670. 1974. soft bdg. 7.00 (ISBN 0-88247-262-3). R & E Res Assoc.
Mackworth, Cecily. English Interludes: Mallarme, Verlaine, Paul Valery, Valery Larbaud in London 1860-1912. (Illus.). 232p. 1975. 18.50 (ISBN 0-7100-7878-1). Routledge & Kegan.
Maxwell, Thomas R. The Invisible French: The/French in Metropolitan Toronto. 174p. 1977. text ed. 11.00 (ISBN 0-88920-029-7, Pub. by Laurier U Pr Canada); pap. text ed. 7.00 (ISBN 0-88920-028-9). Humanities.
Murat, Ines. Napoleon & the American Dream. Frenaye, Frances, tr. from Fr. 256p. 1981. 17.50x (ISBN 0-8071-0770-0). La State U Pr.
Osborne, Milton E. French Presence in Cochinchina & Cambodia: Rule & Response 1859-1905. LC 78-87021. 1969. 22.50x (ISBN 0-8014-0512-2). Cornell U Pr.
Picot, Emile. Francais Italianisants Au Seizieme Siecle, 2 Vols. LC 68-56740. (Research & Source Works Ser.: No. 221). (Fr). 1968. Repr. of 1907 ed. 42.50 (ISBN 0-8337-2755-9). B Franklin.
Pula, James S. The French in America, 1488-1974: A Chronology & Fact Book. LC 75-14292. (Ethnic Chronology Ser.). 160p. 1975. text ed. 8.50 (ISBN 0-379-00515-8). Oceana.
Rey, Emmanuel. Colonies Franques De Syrie Aux Dix-Septieme & Dix-Huitieme Siecles. LC 75-168087. Repr. of 1883 ed. 32.50 (ISBN 0-404-05285-1). AMS Pr.
Stoddard, Theodore L. French Revolution in San Domingo. LC 74-111588. Repr. of 1914 ed. 21.25x (ISBN 0-8371-4614-3, Pub. by Negro U Pr). Greenwood.
Taylor, Virginia H. The Franco-Texan Land Company. (M. K. Brown Range Life Ser.: No. 7). (Illus.). 345p. 1969. 15.00 (ISBN 0-292-78417-1). U of Tex Pr.
Theriault, George F. Experiment in Survival: A Study of the Franco-Americans in New England. Cordasco, Francesco, ed. LC 80-900. (American Ethnic Groups Ser.). (Illus.). 1981. lib. bdg. 50.00x (ISBN 0-405-13460-6). Arno.
Thompson, Virginia M. French Indo-China. 1967. lib. bdg. 30.00x (ISBN 0-374-97866-2). Octagon.
Thwaites, Reuben G. France in America: Fourteen Ninety-Seven to Seventeen Sixty-Three. LC 68-31299. 1968. Repr. of 1905 ed. 11.50x (ISBN 0-8154-0236-8). Cooper Sq.
--France in America, 1497-1763. Repr. of 1905 ed. lib. bdg. 15.00x (ISBN 0-8371-4106-0, THFA). Greenwood.
Volney, C. F. View of the Soil & Climate of the United States of America. Brown, C. B., tr. (Contributions to the History of Geology). (Illus.). 1968. 29.00 (ISBN 0-02-854250-9). Hafner.
Von Mohrenschildt, Dimitri S. Russia in the Intellectual Life of Eighteenth-Century France. LC 71-159255. x, 326p. 1971. Repr. of 1936 ed. lib. bdg. 16.00x (ISBN 0-374-98088-8). Octagon.
Weiner, Margery. The French Exiles, 1789-1815. LC 75-15941. (Illus.). 240p. 1975. Repr. of 1961 ed. lib. bdg. 15.00x (ISBN 0-8371-8220-4, WEFE). Greenwood.
Wimmer, Geraldine. Social & Economic Aspects of French Activities in Early California: Thesis. LC 74-77168. 1974. Repr. of 1940 ed. soft bdg. 7.00 (ISBN 0-88247-269-0). R & E Res Assoc.
Ziadeh, Nicola. Origins of Nationalism in Tunsia. (Arab Background Ser.). Repr. of 1969 ed. 8.00x (ISBN 0-685-77110-5). Intl Bk Ctr.

FRENCH LANGUAGE

Ashby, William J. Clitic Inflection in French: An Historical Perspective. 1977. pap. text ed. 14.25x (ISBN 90-6203-469-1). Humanities.
Asher, John A. Amis et Amis, an Exploratory Survey. LC 77-21930. Repr. of 1952 ed. lib. bdg. 8.50 (ISBN 0-8414-1704-0). Folcroft.
Assimil Junior. (Fr.). 15.00 (ISBN 0-685-36086-5). French & Eur.
Bagley, Charles R. & Diller, George E. France d'autrefois et d'aujourd'hui. 2nd ed. LC 61-13001. (Fr., Fr). 1961. 12.95x (ISBN 0-89197-177-7); pap. text ed. 4.95x (ISBN 0-89197-178-5). Irvington.
Barnett, F. J., et al, eds. History & Structure of French: Essays in Honour of Professor T. B. W. Reid. 268p. 1972. 17.50x (ISBN 0-87471-125-8). Rowman.
Belle, R. & Haas, A. F. Promenades en France. 3rd ed. LC 56-11937. 1972. pap. text ed. 12.50 (ISBN 0-03-080294-6, HoltC). HR&W.
Benamou, Michael & Ionesco, Eugene. Mise En Train: Premiere Annee De Francais. (gr. 11-12). 1969. text ed. 19.95 (ISBN 0-02-307970-3); wkbk. 5.95 (ISBN 0-02-307980-0). Macmillan.
Benamou, Michel & Carduner, Jean. Le Moulin a paroles. 2nd ed. LC 71-126958. (Illus.). 336p. (Fr.). 1971. pap. text ed. 10.95 (ISBN 0-471-06450-5); tapes avail. (ISBN 0-471-00024-8). Wiley.
Blume, Eli. Review Text in French First Year. 2nd ed. (Illus., Orig.). (gr. 7-12). 1967. pap. text ed. 4.83 (ISBN 0-87720-451-9). AMSCO Sch.
--Review Text in French Three Years. 2nd ed. (Orig.). (gr. 11-12). 1980. pap. text ed. 6.33 (ISBN 0-87720-471-3). AMSCO Sch.
--Review Text in French Two Years. 2nd ed. (Illus., Orig.). (gr. 7-12). 1966. pap. text ed. 5.33 (ISBN 0-87720-454-3). AMSCO Sch.
Bottke, K. Brief Oral French Review. 3rd ed. 1964. pap. 8.95 (ISBN 0-13-082040-7). P-H.
Boudreault, M. Rythme et Melodie De la Phrase Parlee En France et Au Quebec: Language et Literature Francaises Au Canada No. 4. 1968. pap. 8.50x (ISBN 2-7637-6343-X, Pub. by Laval). Intl Schol Bk Serv.

Brookes, H. F. & Fraenkel, C. E. Life in France. 1976. pap. text ed. 6.50x (ISBN 0-435-37102-9). Heinemann Ed.
Brosman, Catharine S., et al. Studies in French in Honor of Andre Bourgeois. (Rice University Studies: Vol. 59, No. 3). 100p. 1973. pap. 3.25x (ISBN 0-89263-217-8). Rice Univ.
Cadoux, R. Vous et Moi: Premier Pas. 1970. 6.84 (ISBN 0-02-268300-3). Macmillan.
Caput, Jean-Pol. La Langue francaise, Vol. 2. (Collection "L"). 287p. (Orig., Fr.). 1975. pap. 13.95 (ISBN 2-03-036009-0). Larousse.
Chatman, Seymour, et al, eds. A Semiotic Landscape - Panorama Semiotique. (Approaches to Semiotics Ser.: No. 29). (Fr.). 1979. text ed. 147.00x (ISBN 90-279-7928-6). Mouton.
Churchman, Phillip H. A First Book in French. (Illus.). 1935. text ed. 3.00x (ISBN 0-911090-05-3). Pacific Bk Supply.
Combe, T. G. & Rickard, P. French Language: History, Practice, & Stylistics. 1970. 14.95x (ISBN 0-245-59995-9). Intl Ideas.
Courtney, G. J. Je Vous Presente. (Illus.). 1970. pap. text ed. 2.50x (ISBN 0-582-36008-0). Longman.
Cox, Richard G. Singer's Manual of German & French Diction. 1970. pap. text ed. 6.95 (ISBN 0-02-870650-1). Schirmer Bks.
Cunff, Madeleine Le. Sur le Vif. (Illus., Fr.). 1977. pap. text ed. 5.75 (ISBN 0-88436-454-2). EMC.
De La Bruyere, Jean. Caracteres, 2 Vols. (Documentation thematique). (Illus., Fr.). pap. 2.95 ea. Larousse.
De Rivarol, Antoine. Discours sur l'universalite de la langue francaise. (Classiques Larousse). (Illus., Fr.). pap. 1.95 (ISBN 0-685-13892-5, 277). Larousse.
Deschamps, Philippe. Analyse Raisonnee De la Langue Francaise. (Fr). 1955. pap. 2.50x (ISBN 2-7637-0093-4, Pub. by Laval). Intl Schol Bk Serv.
Dietiker, Simone R. Franc-Parler. 2nd ed. 1980. text ed. 17.95x (ISBN 0-669-02491-0); instrs.' guide 6.95 (ISBN 0-669-02494-5); wkbk. 6.95 (ISBN 0-669-02492-9); tapes-reels 45.00 (ISBN 0-669-02496-1); cassettes 45.00 (ISBN 0-669-02497-X); demo tape (ISBN 0-669-02498-8); tapescript (ISBN 0-669-02495-3). Heath.
Dubois, Jean & Lagane, Rene, eds. Comment apprendre le francais. new ed. (Orig., Fr.). 1976. pap. 9.25 (ISBN 2-03-041300-3). Larousse.
Dulac, Colette. Shortcut to French. (gr. 9 up). 1977. pap. text ed. 4.75 (ISBN 0-88345-300-2); cassettes 30.00 (ISBN 0-685-79306-0). Regents Pub.
Edwards, S. A. French Structure in Review. 3rd ed. 1979. pap. text ed. 8.95x (ISBN 0-669-02327-2). Heath.
En France comme si Vous y Etiez. (gr. 10-12). text ed. 14.95 (ISBN 0-685-36071-7). French & Eur.
Fanelli, Maresa. Aujourd'hui. 2nd ed. 1980. text ed. 16.95 (ISBN 0-669-02503-8); wkbk. 5.95 (ISBN 0-669-02504-6); tapes-reels 55.00 (ISBN 0-669-02506-2); cassettes cancelled (ISBN 0-669-02507-0); demo tape (ISBN 0-669-02508-9); tapescript (ISBN 0-669-02505-4). Heath.
Favre de Vaugelas, Cl. Nouvelles Remarques sur la Langue Francaise. (Linguistics 13th-18th Centuries Ser.). 651p. (Fr.). 1974. Repr. lib. bdg. 173.00x (ISBN 0-8287-0335-3, 71-5014). Clearwater Pub.
--Remarques sur la Langue Francaise. (Linguistics 13th-18th Centuries Ser.). 664p. (Fr.). 1974. Repr. of 1647 ed. lib. bdg. 160.50x (ISBN 0-8287-0336-1, 71-5013). Clearwater Pub.
Fellows, Otis, et al. A Livre Ouvert: Premieres Lectures En Francais. 1970. text ed. 7.50 (ISBN 0-02-336860-8). Macmillan.
Fenelon, Francois. Lettre a l'Academie. (Classiques Larousse). (Illus., Fr.). pap. 2.95 (ISBN 0-685-13967-0, 97). Larousse.
Finocchiaro, Mary & Cadoux, Remunda. Living French: Advanced Course. 10.95 (ISBN 0-517-00260-4). Crown.
Foreign Service Institute. French Basic Course, Vol. 2, Pts. A & B. 572p. (Fr.). 1980. Pt. A. 170.00x (ISBN 0-88432-023-5, F260); Pt. B. 160.00x (ISBN 0-88432-024-3); 53 audicassettes incl. J Norton Pubs.
--French Phonology. 394p. (Fr.). 1980. 60.00x (ISBN 0-88432-032-4, F250); 8 audiocassettes incl. J Norton Pubs.
Gautier, J. M. L' Exotisme Americain dans l'Oeuvre de Chateaubriand. 66p. 1951. 21.00x (ISBN 0-7190-1208-2, Pub. by Manchester U Pr England). State Mutual Bk.
Greimas, A. J. L' Ancien Francais. 271p. (Orig.). 1974. bds. 27.50 (ISBN 2-03-070335-4, 3609). Larousse.
Guillou, J. & Vitols, M. Le Francais Contemporain. LC 75-140658. 1972. pap. text ed. 15.95 (ISBN 0-03-081347-6, HoltC). HR&W.
Hayes, Walter M. & Killeen, Veronica A. Introductory French Program, 2 Bks. (Prog. Bk.). (gr. 9-12). 1970. Set. pap. 13.00 (ISBN 0-8294-0197-0); 15 tapes s.p. 85.00 (ISBN 0-685-04188-3). Loyola.
Henried, Doris E. Le Francais Intensif. 1976. pap. 8.95x (ISBN 0-442-23260-8); tapes 95.00 (ISBN 0-442-23261-6); cassettes 59.95 (ISBN 0-442-23262-4). D Van Nostrand.
Holt Staff. Voici la Francais. 1968. film tape script 55.00 (ISBN 0-03-072075-3). HR&W.
Jean, B. & Montaigne, F. Mouret. Descartes et Pascal Par la Dissertation. 196p. 1971. 21.00x (ISBN 0-686-63844-1, Pub. by Manchester U Pr England). State Mutual Bk.
Kellenberger, Hunter. Influence of Accentuation on French Word Order. (Elliott Monographs: Vol. 30). 1932. pap. 7.00 (ISBN 0-527-02633-6). Kraus Repr.
L'Universelle Bordas, 10 vols. (Fr.). 1976. 495.00 set (ISBN 0-686-70324-3). Pergamon.
McArthur, D. G. Les Constructions Verbales du Francais Contemporain. 94p. 1971. 24.00x (ISBN 0-7190-1250-3, Pub. by Manchester U Pr England). State Mutual Bk.
MacDonald, Ian. Get to Know France. 1975. pap. text ed. 5.00x (ISBN 0-435-37555-5). Heinemann Ed.
Malecot, A. Contribution a L'etude De la Force D'articulation En Francais. 1977. 11.25x (ISBN 90-279-3176-3). Mouton.
Mauger & Brueziere. Le Francais Accelere. (gr. 10-12). text ed. 6.50 (ISBN 0-685-36068-7). French & Eur.
--Le Francais et la Vie, Vol I. (gr. 10-12). text ed. 8.95 (ISBN 0-685-36069-5); tchrs manual free (ISBN 0-685-36070-9). French & Eur.
Mauger & Gougenheim. Le Francais Elementaire, 2 vols. Incl. Vol. 1. text ed. 5.25 (ISBN 0-685-35622-1); Vol. 2. text ed. 4.95 (ISBN 0-685-35623-X). (gr. 4-6). ea tchr's manuals in Eng. 7.50. French & Eur.
Mayer, Edgar N. Structure of French. 1969. pap. 8.95x (ISBN 0-87081-074-X). Colo Assoc.
Michaud, G. Guide France. 7.95 (ISBN 0-685-36082-2). French & Eur.
Mok, Q. I. Contribution a L'etude Des Categories Morphologiques Du Genre et Du Nombre Dans le Francais Parle Actuel. (Janua Linguarum, Series Practica: No. 100). 1968. pap. 29.00x (ISBN 90-2790-675-0). Mouton.
Moody, Marvin D. A Classification of Noun De Noun Construction in French. 1973. pap. text ed. 55.00x (ISBN 90-2792-434-1). Mouton.
Noblitt, James S. Nouveau Point De Vue. 1978. text ed. 17.95x (ISBN 0-669-96545-6); instr's manual 1.95 (ISBN 0-669-00335-2); wkbk. 6.95 (ISBN 0-669-96552-9); Sets. reels 60.00 (ISBN 0-669-96560-X); cassettes 60.00 (ISBN 0-669-00250-X). Heath.
Palmeri, Joseph & Milligan, E. E. French for Reading Knowledge. 2nd ed. (Fr). 1969. text ed. 12.95x (ISBN 0-442-24121-6). Van Nos Reinhold.
Patterson, W. R. Colloquial French. 16th ed. (Tribner's Colloquial Manuals). 1950. pap. 4.95 (ISBN 0-7100-6384-9). Routledge & Kegan.
Petit Larousse illustre 1980. (Illus.). 1979. 29.95 (ISBN 0-685-94503-0, 2280). Larousse.
Rickard, Peter. Langue Francaise au Seizieme Siecle. (Illus., Fr.). 1968. 74.00 (ISBN 0-521-06921-1). Cambridge U Pr.
Rudman, Jack. French. (Undergraduate Program Field Test Ser.: UPFT-9). (Cloth bdg. avail. on request). pap. 9.95 (ISBN 0-8373-6009-9). Natl Learning.
Rundle, Stanley. Cracking the Language Code: French. 1974. 19.95 (ISBN 0-87243-050-2, Pub. by Octavo Pr). Templegate.
Runte, Hans R. & Valdman, Albert, eds. Identite Culturelle et Francophonie Dans les Ameriques. (Indiana University Publications: Collogue 2). (Fr.). 1976. pap. text ed. 15.00x (ISBN 0-87750-201-3). Res Ctr Lang Semiotic.
Sauvageot, A. Francais ecrit, francais parle. (Langue vivante). (Fr). pap. 8.25 (ISBN 0-685-13928-X, 3623). Larousse.
Schulz, Charles M. Increvable Charlie Brown. (Illus., Fr., For, Language Fr). 1971. pap. 1.50 (ISBN 0-03-086014-8). HR&W.
Secretan, D. E. La Pratique Du Francais Cours Superieur. 208p. 1970. 21.00x (ISBN 0-7190-0424-1, Pub. by Manchester U Pr England). State Mutual Bk.
Secretan, D. E. & Dervaux, J. C. La Pratique Du Francais Cours Superieur. 200p. 1972. 15.00x (ISBN 0-7190-0490-X, Pub. by Manchester U Pr England). State Mutual Bk.
Seibert, Louise C. & Crocker, Lester G., eds. Le Fils Du Fauconnier. (Fr.). 1963. pap. text ed. 7.95x (ISBN 0-684-41431-7, ScribC). Scribner.
Stern, A. Z. & Reif, Joseph A., eds. Useful Expressions in French. (Useful Expressions Ser.). 64p. (Orig.). 1980. pap. 2.00 (ISBN 0-86628-006-5). Ridgefield Pub.
Stowell, William A. Old-French Titles of Respect in Direct Address. LC 79-8373. Repr. of 1908 ed. 26.50 (ISBN 0-404-18355-7). AMS Pr.
Symposium on Cultural Indentity & French Speaking in the Americas, University of Indiana, Bloomington. Identie Culturelle et Francopone Dans les Ameriques: Proceedings. Snyder, Emile & Valdman, Albert, eds. (Fr. & Eng.). 1977. 21.50x (ISBN 2-7637-6794-X, Pub. by Laval). Intl Schol Bk Serv.
Tabouret-Keller, Andree, ed. Regional Language in France. (International Journal of the Sociology of Language: No. 25). 1980. pap. text ed. 21.00x (ISBN 90-279-3068-6). Mouton.
Tucker, G. French Speaker's Skill with Grammatical Gender. 1977. 21.25x (ISBN 90-279-3195-X). Mouton.
Valdman, Albert. Introduction to French Phonology & Morphology. LC 76-1888. 1976. pap. text ed. 10.95 (ISBN 0-88377-054-7). Newbury Hse.
Valette, Jean P. & Valette, Rebecca M. C'est Comme Ca: Manuel De Lecture et De Communication. 1978. pap. text ed. 8.95x (ISBN 0-669-01162-2). Heath.
Valette, Jean-Paul & Valette, Rebecca. Contacts: Langue et Culture Francaises. LC 75-32873. 1976. text ed. 17.35 (ISBN 0-395-20690-1); tchrs. ed. 18.40 (ISBN 0-395-20689-8); wkbk. cahier d'exercices 5.55 (ISBN 0-395-20692-8). HM.
Vaugelas. Remarques sur la langue francaise. new ed. (Nouveaux Classiques Larousse). (Illus., Fr.). 1976. pap. 2.95 (ISBN 0-685-66287-X, 332). Larousse.

FRENCH LANGUAGE–TO 1500

Crabb, Daniel M. Comparative Study of Word Order in Old Spanish & Old French Prose Works. LC 78-94189. (Catholic University of America Studies in Romance Languages & Literatures Ser: No. 51). Repr. of 1955 ed. 14.50 (ISBN 0-404-50351-9). AMS Pr.
De La Halle, Adam. The Chansons of Adam De la Halle. Marshall, L. L., ed. 148p. 1971. 12.00x (ISBN 0-7190-0461-6, Pub. by Manchester U Pr England). State Mutual Bk.
Einhorn, E. C. Old French: A Concise Handbook. 210p. 1975. 29.50 (ISBN 0-521-20343-0); pap. 12.50x (ISBN 0-521-09838-6). Cambridge U Pr.
Fotitch, Tatiana. Narrative Tenses in Chretien De Troyes: A Study in Syntax & Stylistics. LC 75-94180. (Catholic University of America Studies in Romance Languages & Literatures Ser: No. 38). 1969. Repr. of 1950 ed. 14.50 (ISBN 0-404-50338-1). AMS Pr.
Gardner, Rosalyn & Green, Marion. A Brief Description of Middle French Syntax. (Studies in the Romance Languages & Literatures: No. 29). 1958. pap. 9.00x (ISBN 0-8078-9029-4). U of NC Pr.
Garey, H. B. Historical Development of Tenses from Late Latin to Old French. 1955. pap. 6.00 (ISBN 0-527-00797-8). Kraus Repr.
Garvey, Sr. M. Calixta. Syntax of the Declinable Words in the Roman De la Rose. LC 74-94208. (Catholic University in Romance Languages & Literatures Ser: No. 13). Repr. of 1936 ed. 20.00 (ISBN 0-404-50313-6). AMS Pr.
Laubscher, G. G. Syntactical Causes of Case Reduction in Old French. (Elliott Monographs: Vol. 7). 1921. pap. 9.00 (ISBN 0-527-02611-5). Kraus Repr.
Levy, Raphael. Contribution a la Lexicographie Francaise Selon D'anciens Textes D'origies Juive. (Fr.). 1960. 35.00 (ISBN 0-89366-103-1). Ultramarine Pub.
Murray, Joseph P. Selective English Old-French Glossary As a Basis for Studies in Old French Onomatology & Synonymics. LC 77-128932. (Carl Ser.: No. 40). Repr. of 1950 ed. 16.00 (ISBN 0-404-50340-3). AMS Pr.
Rohlfs, Gerhard. From Vulgar Latin to Old French: An Introduction to the Study of Old French. Almazan, Vincent & McCarthy, Lillian, trs. from Ger. LC 71-98131. 1970. text ed. 16.95x (ISBN 0-8143-1409-0). Wayne St U Pr.
Studer, Paul & Waters, E. G. Historical French Reader: Medieval Period. 1924. 22.50x (ISBN 0-19-815327-9). Oxford U Pr.
Yedlicka, Leo C. Expressions of the Linguistic Area of Repentance & Remorse in Old French. LC 76-94175. (Catholic University of America Studies in Romance Languages & Literatures Ser: No. 28). 1969. Repr. of 1945 ed. 28.00 (ISBN 0-404-50328-4). AMS Pr.

FRENCH LANGUAGE–TO 1500–DICTIONARIES

Benoit De Sainte - More. Roman De Troie, 6 Vols. Repr. of 1904 ed. Set. 161.50 (ISBN 0-384-03915-4); Set. pap. 138.50 (ISBN 0-384-03916-2). Johnson Repr.
De Gorog, Ralph. Lexique Francais Moderne - Ancien Francais. LC 72-91996. 487p. 1973. 20.00x (ISBN 0-8203-0312-7). U of Ga Pr.
Godefroy, Frederic. Lexique De L'ancien Francais. 544p. (Fr.). 1976. 39.95 (ISBN 0-686-57305-6, M-6282). French & Eur.

FRENCH LANGUAGE–ABBREVIATIONS

see Abbreviations

FRENCH LANGUAGE–BUSINESS FRENCH

Cummins, Patricia. Commercial French. (Illus.). 320p. 1982. 17.95 (ISBN 0-13-152710-X). P-H.
De Renty, Ivan. Lexique de l'anglais des affaires. new ed. 320p. 1973. pap. 7.95 (ISBN 0-88332-247-1, 4100). Larousse.
Dinsale, W. A. & Pearce, E. A. French for Insurance Officials. 3rd ed. Jory, G. A., ed. 1976. pap. 12.50x (ISBN 0-8002-0804-8). Intl Pubns Serv.
Fontenilles, Alfred & Heimerdinger, Mark C. Le Francais Des Affaires. 1981. pap. text ed. 7.95x (ISBN 0-02-338700-9). Macmillan.
Mauger, G., et al. Le Francais commercial, 3 vols. Vol. 1. pap. text ed. 7.50 (ISBN 2-03-040404-7, 3760); Vol. 2. pap. text ed. 8.50 (ISBN 2-03-040405-5, 3761); Vol. 3. pap. text ed. 7.50 (ISBN 0-685-13927-1, 3762). Larousse.
Paton, Roderick. Business Case Studies (French) (Illus.). 125p. (Fr.). 1980. pap. text ed. 7.95x (ISBN 0-582-35283-5). Longman.

FRENCH LANGUAGE–COMPOSITION AND EXERCISES

Barton, Francis B. & Sirich, Edward H. Simplified French Review: Grammar & Composition. 1941. 10.95x (ISBN 0-89197-409-1); pap. text ed. 4.95x (ISBN 0-89197-410-5). Irvington.
Bauer, Camille. France Actuelle. rev. ed. (Illus.). 1971. text ed. 10.50 (ISBN 0-395-04150-3, 3-03207). HM.
Benamou, Michel & Carduner, Jean. Le Moulin a paroles. 2nd ed. LC 71-126958. (Illus.). 336p. (Fr.). 1971. pap. text ed. 10.95 (ISBN 0-471-06450-5); tapes avail. (ISBN 0-471-00024-8). Wiley.
--Le Moulin a paroles. 2nd ed. LC 71-126958. (Illus.). 336p. (Fr.). 1971. pap. text ed. 10.95 (ISBN 0-471-06450-5); tapes avail. (ISBN 0-471-00024-8). Wiley.
Besnard, M. & Coursodon, J. P. Ecritures: Techniques de Composition. 1972. 10.95 (ISBN 0-02-309150-9). Macmillan.
Blume, Eli. Cours superieur de francais. (Orig.). (gr. 11-12). 1970. pap. text ed. 5.75 (ISBN 0-87720-460-8); wkbk. 6.75 (ISBN 0-87720-462-4). AMSCO Sch.
Breunig, L. C., et al. Forme et Fond. 1964. text ed. 10.95 (ISBN 0-02-314210-3). Macmillan.
Brunetti, Mendor. Read, Write, Speak French. (Orig.). (gr. 9-12). 1963. pap. 2.95 (ISBN 0-553-14168-6). Bantam.
Cadoux, Remunda. Invitation Au Francais: Vous et Moi, Level One. 1970. 8.20 (ISBN 0-02-268500-6). Macmillan.
Clarke, K. & Holt Editorial Staff. A la francaise. (Secondary French Ser: Level 1). (gr. 7-9). text ed. 11.96 (ISBN 0-03-000941-3, HoltC); tchrs' manual. s.p. 4.50 (ISBN 0-685-28997-4); exercise manual, flashcards, projectuals,study packets, testing program avail. (ISBN 0-685-28998-2); 5 films 955.00, avail. sep (ISBN 0-685-28999-0); guides 0.36 ea.; records, tapes, cassetttes avail. (ISBN 0-685-29001-8). HR&W.
Cochrane, Rollin. ETC. - Problemes Du Francais Ecrit. LC 72-9378. (Illus.). 304p. 1973. text ed. 11.95 (ISBN 0-13-289983-3). P-H.
Coveney, J., ed. International Organization Documents for Translation from French. 93p. 1972. 16.00 (ISBN 0-08-016287-8). Pergamon.
D'Alelio, Ellen & Dufau, Micheline. En Avant: A Progressive Review of French. 398p. 1972. pap. text ed. 11.95 (ISBN 0-15-522567-7, HC); instructor's manual avail. (ISBN 0-15-522568-5, HC); tapes, 15 reels 200.00 (ISBN 0-15-522569-3, HC). HarBraceJ.
Darbelnet, John. Pensee & Structure. 2nd ed. LC 68-19906. (Fr). 1977. text ed. 11.95x (ISBN 0-684-14882-X, ScribC); wkbk. 7.95x (ISBN 0-684-15932-5, ScribC); wkbk. 5.95 (ISBN 0-684-15091-3, ScribC). Scribner.
Daudon, Rene. French in Review. 2nd ed. 1962. text ed. 12.95 (ISBN 0-15-528850-4, HC); tapes, 10 reels 125.00 (ISBN 0-15-528851-2, HC). HarBraceJ.
Dostert, L. & Lindenfeld, J. Francais, Cours Moyen, Civilisation. 1961. text ed. 6.95 (ISBN 0-02-815500-9). Glencoe.
Etude de l'expression francaise: Cours elementaire I - le francais. (Illus., Fr.). 1969. 7.25 (ISBN 0-685-13911-5, 4019). Larousse.
Frautschi, Richard L. & Bouygues, Claude. Pour et Contre: Manuel De Conversations Graduees. 2nd ed. LC 78-20794. 1979. pap. text ed. 16.50 scp (ISBN 0-06-042164-9, HarpC). Har-Row.
Joiner, Elizabeth G., et al. First-Year French. LC 76-58859. 1977. text ed. 19.95 (ISBN 0-03-015006-X, HoltC); tchr's manual 5.95 (ISBN 0-03-022751-8); lab manual 7.50 (ISBN 0-03-015111-2); tape program 350.00 (ISBN 0-03-015026-4). HR&W.
Kendris, Christopher. Beginning to Write in French: A Workbook in French Composition. rev. ed. 1982. pap. text ed. 3.50 (ISBN 0-8120-2261-0). Barron.

--Beginning to Write in French: A Workbook in French Composition. LC 65-25685. (gr. 7-12). 1971. pap. text ed. 3.50 (ISBN 0-8120-0234-2). Barron.
Langellier, Alice, et al. Chez Les Francais. (Secondary French Ser: Level 2). (Follows Ecouter et Parler or Deuxieme Etape). (gr. 7-12). 1969. text ed. 13.32 (ISBN 0-03-080350-0, HoltC); tchrs' ed 13.60 (ISBN 0-03-080355-1); wkbk. 2.80 (ISBN 0-685-12191-7); photos 24.00 (ISBN 0-685-12192-5); tests 0.80 (ISBN 0-685-12193-3); records 11.04 (ISBN 0-685-12194-1); tapes 7.5 or 3.75 ips s.p. 110.00 ea. HR&W.
Limouzy, Pierre & Bourgeacq, Jacques A. Manuel De Composition Francaise. (Fr). 1970. text ed. 12.95 (ISBN 0-394-30363-6, RanC); tchr's ed o.p. free (ISBN 0-394-30695-3). Random.
Malecot, Andre. Fundamental French: Language & Culture. LC 63-10567. (Illus.). 1963. 18.50x (ISBN 0-89197-184-X); pap. text ed. 8.95x (ISBN 0-89197-766-X). Irvington.
Max, Stefan. Dialogues et Situations. 2nd ed. 1979. text ed. 15.95 (ISBN 0-669-01788-4); cahier de travaux practiques 5.95 (ISBN 0-669-01789-2); cahier de travaux practiques 4.95 (ISBN 0-669-01907-0); cassettes 35.00 (ISBN 0-669-01908-9); demonstration tape avail.; transcript avail. (ISBN 0-669-01906-2). Heath.
Mondelli, Rudolph J. & Francois, Pierre. French Conversational Review Grammar. 3rd ed. (Fr). 1972. pap. text ed. 15.95x (ISBN 0-442-23762-6); tapes 125.00 (ISBN 0-442-23763-4). Van Nos Reinhold.
O'Hair, L. & Ropert, M. French Exercises for Schools. 3rd ed. 1973. Repr. 7.50x (ISBN 0-522-83893-6, Pub. by Melbourne U Pr). Intl Schol Bk Serv.
Richardson, G. & Lord, M. M. Salut, Les Jeunes. (Illus., Fr. & Eng.). (gr. 7-9). 1966. text ed. 4.95 (ISBN 0-312-69825-9, S01795). St Martin.
Ritchie, Robert L. & Simons, C. J. Essays in Translation from French. text ed. 27.50x (ISBN 0-521-06092-3). Cambridge U Pr.
Wellek, Susanne & Bass, Nelly. Paul et Marie a l'Ecole. (Illus.). (gr. 5 up). 1950. text ed. 8.50 (ISBN 0-8044-0800-9). Ungar.
Whitmarsh, W. F. Examination French. 1978. pap. text ed. 3.25x (ISBN 0-582-33109-9). Longman.

FRENCH LANGUAGE–CONVERSATION AND PHRASE BOOKS

see also French Language–Self Instruction; French Language–Text-Books for Children

Adrienne. Le Gimmick, Francais Parle. 1977. 9.95 (ISBN 0-393-04438-6); pap. 4.95 (ISBN 0-393-04474-2). Norton.
Arnold, Julius. Student's Guide to Basic French. 2nd ed. 184p. (gr. 9-11). 1980. pap. text ed. 5.50 (ISBN 0-88334-021-6). Ind Sch Pr.
Atkinson, David. Menu French. (International Ser. in Hospitality Management). (Illus.). 96p. 1980. 15.00 (ISBN 0-08-024309-6); pap. 6.75 (ISBN 0-08-024308-8). Pergamon.
Benedeit. The Anglo-Norman Voyage of St. Brendan. Short, T. & Merrilees, B., eds. 144p. 1979. 12.00x (ISBN 0-7190-0735-6, Pub. by Manchester U Pr England). State Mutual Bk.
Betourne, Henriette D., et al. Direct French Conversation, 2 Bks. (Orig., Fr.). (YA) (gr. 9 up). 1966. Bk. 1. pap. text ed. 2.75 (ISBN 0-88345-040-2, 17470); Bk. 2. pap. text ed. 2.75 (ISBN 0-88345-041-0, 17471). Regents Pub.
Bonar, Lore S., et al. Say It in Another Language: Phrases in Spanish, French, Japanese, Swahili, & German. (YA) 1976. pap. text ed. 2.50 pkg. of 20 (ISBN 0-88441-414-0, 26-814). GS.
Bonnell, Peter & Sedwick, Frank. Conversation in French: Points of Departure. 3rd ed. (Orig.). 1981. pap. text ed. write for info. (ISBN 0-442-24468-1). D Van Nostrand.
--Conversation in French: Points of Departure. 2nd ed. 1976. pap. text ed. 6.95x (ISBN 0-442-20725-5). Van Nos Reinhold.
Bourdillon, F. W. Aucassin et Nicolete. 128p. 1919. 9.00x (ISBN 0-7190-0387-3, Pub. by Manchester U Pr England). State Mutual Bk.
Bryan, Anne-Marie & Duche, Jean. Pour Parler: Manual De Conversation Francaise. 2nd ed. (Illus.). 1977. text ed. 14.95 (ISBN 0-13-686386-8); exercises de laboratoire 6.95 (ISBN 0-13-686394-9); tapes 100.00 (ISBN 0-13-686378-7). P-H.
Carton, Dana & Caprio, Anthony. En Francais: Practical Conversational French. 2nd ed. 1980. text ed. write for info. (ISBN 0-442-21215-1); write for info. instr's. manual (ISBN 0-442-21218-6); write for info. tape (ISBN 0-442-21219-4); write for info. cassette (ISBN 0-442-21220-8). D Van Nostrand.
--En Francais: Practical Conversational French. 1976. pap. 11.95 (ISBN 0-442-21468-5); tapes 85.00 (ISBN 0-442-21467-7); cassettes 54.95 (ISBN 0-442-21469-3). D Van Nostrand.
Cohen, Leon J. Listen & Learn French. 3.00 (ISBN 0-486-20875-3); with records 12.95 (ISBN 0-486-98875-9). Dover.
--Say It in French. (Orig.). pap. 1.35 (ISBN 0-486-20803-6). Dover.
--Say It in French. LC 55-13819. 1962. lib. bdg. 8.50x (ISBN 0-88307-555-5). Gannon.
Constant, H. B. Adolphe. Rudler, G., ed. 128p. 1941. 9.00x (ISBN 0-7190-0142-0, Pub. by Manchester U Pr England). State Mutual Bk.
Cote, D. G., et al. Deuxieme Etape. (Secondary French Ser: Level 1). (Follows Premiere Etape & leads into either Nous les Jeunes & Ce Monde des Francais, or Chez les Francais & Ce Monde des Francais, or Parler et Lire). (gr. 7). 1970. text ed. 8.64 (ISBN 0-03-084953-5, HoltC); tchrs' ed. 12.00 (ISBN 0-685-03759-2); 5 films 955.00 (ISBN 0-685-03760-6); film guides 0.36 ea.; flash cards 60.00 (ISBN 0-685-03762-2); projectuals 132.00 (ISBN 0-685-03763-0); exercise manual 1.36 (ISBN 0-685-03764-9); testing prog. 1.20 (ISBN 0-685-03765-7); records 4.60 (ISBN 0-685-03766-5). HR&W.
Du Wes, Giles. An Introduction for to Lerne, to Rede, to Pronounce & to Speke French Trewly. 1972. Repr. of 1532 ed. 19.50x (ISBN 0-8002-1281-9). Intl Pubns Serv.
Ellison, Al. Ellison's French Menu Reader. 1977. 2.95 (ISBN 0-930580-00-1). Ellison Ent.
Follett Instant French Conversation Guide. 2.50 (ISBN 0-695-84196-3). New Century.
France--a Hugo Phrase Book. (Hugo's Language Courses Ser.: No. 560). 1970. pap. 1.50 (ISBN 0-8226-0560-0). Littlefield.
Frautschi, Richard L. & Bouygues, Claude. Pour et Contre: Manuel De Conversations Graduees. 2nd ed. LC 78-20794. 1979. pap. text ed. 16.50 scp (ISBN 0-06-042164-9, HarpC). Har-Row.
French in Twenty Lessons. rev. ed. (Cortina Method Language Ser). (Illus.). 6.95 (ISBN 0-385-00070-7). Doubleday.
French Review. pocket ed. 150p. (gr. 7-12). 1982. pap. text ed. 2.50 (ISBN 0-8120-2194-0). Barron.
Gallo & Sedwick. French for Careers: Conversational Perspectives. (Illus., Orig.). 1980. pap. text ed. 8.95 (ISBN 0-442-23883-5). D Van Nostrand.
Gerber & Storzer. French Conversation Through Idioms. 1982. pap. 6.95 (ISBN 0-8120-2107-X). Barron.
Haac, Oscar A. & Bieler, Arthur. Actualite et Avenir: A Guide to France & to French Conversation. LC 74-30489. (Illus.). 256p. 1975. pap. text ed. 9.95 (ISBN 0-13-003855-5). P-H.
Hamlyn French Phrase Book. pap. 2.95 (ISBN 0-600-33608-5, 8143). Larousse.
Harris, J. & Leveque, A. Intermediate Conversational French. 3rd ed. LC 79-172937. 1972. text ed. 19.95 (ISBN 0-03-088063-7, HoltC); tchrs' manual avail.; lab manual 6.50 (ISBN 0-03-088235-4); tapes 200.00 (ISBN 0-03-088603-1). HR&W.
Hoffman, Leon-Francois. La Pratique du Francais Parle. LC 72-7530. 93p. 1973. pap. text ed. 6.50 (ISBN 0-684-13208-7); cassettes 4.95 (ISBN 0-684-13696-1). Scribner.
Holloway Staff. French. (Harper Phrase Books for the Traveler Ser.). (Orig.). 1977. pap. 1.00 (ISBN 0-8467-0309-2, Pub. by Two Continents). Hippocrene Bks.
Hope, Q. M. Spoken French in Review. 3rd ed. 1974. 14.95 (ISBN 0-02-356950-6), wkbk. 1.95 (ISBN 0-02-357090-3). Macmillan.
Hughes, Charles A. Grosset's French Phrase Book & Dictionary for Travelers. (Orig.). 1971. pap. 2.95 (ISBN 0-448-00651-0). G&D.
Humphreys, R. A. Colloquial French. rev. ed. (Trubner's Colloquial Manuals). (Illus.). 192p. 1981. pap. 6.95 (ISBN 0-7100-0450-8). Routledge & Kegan.
Joslin, Sesyle & Haas, Irene. There Is a Dragon in My Bed. LC 61-6118. (Illus.). (gr. k-3). 1966. 4.95 (ISBN 0-15-285146-1, HJ). HarBraceJ.
Langellier, Alice, et al. Ce Monde Des Francais. (Secondary French Ser: Level 2). (Follows Nous les Jeunes or Chez les Francaise, leads into Lire, Parler et Ecrire). (gr. 7-12). 1970. text ed. 13.32 (ISBN 0-03-084234-4, HoltC); tchrs' ed. 8.28 (ISBN 0-03-084235-2); exercise manual 2.46 (ISBN 0-685-03753-3); tests 1.60 (ISBN 0-685-03754-1); prog. practice 14.00 (ISBN 0-685-03755-X); tapes s.p. 90.00 (ISBN 0-685-03756-8). HR&W.
Lenard, Yvone & Hester, Ralph. L' Art De la Conversation. 1967. text ed. 16.50 scp (ISBN 0-06-043966-1, HarpC); scp tapes 175.00 (ISBN 0-06-047460-2); texte de bande sohores o.p. 1.25 (ISBN 0-06-363966-1). Har-Row.
Lentz, M. M., et al. French in the Office. 2nd ed. 1978. pap. text ed. 4.50x (ISBN 0-582-35153-7). Longman.
Listen & Learn French. (Listen & Learn Ser.). 1981. Incl. 3 Cassettes & Manual. 14.95 (ISBN 0-486-99900-9). Dover.
Living French: Cassette Edition. 1969. 14.95, with 2 cassettes plus dictionary & manual (ISBN 0-517-00896-3). Crown.
Logan, Gerald E. & Leroux, Michele. French Conversational Practice. 1975. tchr's bk 5.95 (ISBN 0-88377-046-6); student's bk 4.95 (ISBN 0-88377-045-8). Newbury Hse.
A Lytell Treatise for to Lerne Englisshe & Frensshe. LC 73-6167. (English Experience Ser.: No. 630). 27p. 1973. Repr. of 1497 ed. 6.00 (ISBN 90-221-0630-6). Walter J Johnson.
Mueller, Theodore & Niedzielski, Henri. Basic French. Incl. Premiers Pas. pap. text ed. 4.40x (ISBN 0-89197-670-1); Pratique de la grammaire. pap. text ed. 8.20x (ISBN 0-89197-671-X); Introduction a la culture. pap. text ed. 3.10x (ISBN 0-89197-672-8). (Fr.). 1974. Set. pap. text ed. 15.70x (ISBN 0-89197-673-6); tchr's manual avail. (ISBN 0-685-77774-X); Set. 29 audio tapes 232.00x (ISBN 0-8290-0141-7). Irvington.
Muyskens, Judith. First Year French. 1981. text ed. 17.95x (ISBN 0-394-32638-5); wkbk. 5.95 (ISBN 0-394-32639-3); lab manual 5.95 (ISBN 0-394-32640-7). Random.
Norman, Jill & Orteu, Henri. French Phrase Book. (Orig., Bilingual). 1968. pap. 2.50 (ISBN 0-14-002706-8). Penguin.
Nouveau Larousse des debutants. (Fr.). 16.25 (ISBN 2-03-020146-4, 3750). Larousse.
Okin, Josee & Schmitt, Conrad J. Let's Speak French, Bks. 1-3. 1966. Bks. 1-2. text ed. 5.28x ea. (W). Bk. 1 O. P (ISBN 0-07-047642-X). Bk. 2 (ISBN 0-07-047644-6). Bk. 3. text ed. 11.72x (ISBN 0-07-047638-1); tchrs. guide bks. 1 & 2 8.08x (ISBN 0-07-047645-4). Bk. 3 O. P. tchrs. guide 9.32x (ISBN 0-07-047639-X). McGraw.
--Let's Speak French: Lectures. 1967. text ed. 11.72 (ISBN 0-07-047640-3, W); cassettes 99.00 (ISBN 0-07-097187-0). McGraw.
Parlons Francais. Vols. 1-3. 7.95 (ISBN 0-88499-069-9); tapebks. vols. 1 & 2 5.95 ea.; readers vols. 1 & 2 6.95 ea.; cassette sets vols. 1 & 2 115.00 ea.; tape sets vols. 1 & 2 225.00 ea. Inst Mod Lang.
Pirz, Therese. Speak French to Your Baby. (Illus.). (gr. 5-8). Date not set. spiral bdg. 12.95 (ISBN 0-9606140-0-1). Chou-Chou.
Popper, Evelyn. Les Images et les Mots. rev ed. 1971. 4.80 (ISBN 0-02-826040-6). Glencoe.
R. D. Cortina Company. Conversational French in Twenty Lessons. 382p. 1980. pap. 4.95 (ISBN 0-06-463601-1, EH 601). Har-Row.
Rassias, John A. & De Lachapelle-Skubly, Jacqueline. Le Francais: Depart-Arrivee. 577p. 1980. text ed. 20.95 scp (ISBN 0-06-045316-8, HarpC); instrs'. manual avail. (ISBN 0-06-365328-1); scp student wkbk. 7.50 (ISBN 0-06-045317-6); scp tapes 310.00 (ISBN 0-06-047493-9). Har-Row.
Rosenberg. Topical French. 1977. pap. text ed. 3.50x (ISBN 0-582-35902-3). Longman.
Thomas, Pierre. Conversation et Vocabulaire: Cours Soixante-Quinze. (Fr.). 1948. pap. 3.00x (ISBN 0-910408-06-8). Coll Store.
Uzan, Bernard F. & Kany, Charles E. Spoken French for Students & Travelers. 2nd ed. 1978. pap. text ed. 6.95x (ISBN 0-669-00878-8). Heath.
Vaillancourt, Sarah. Perspectives Francaises One. LC 80-12737. (Illus.). 1980. text ed. 9.56 (ISBN 0-88436-754-1); pap. text ed. 6.50 (ISBN 0-88436-755-X). EMC.
Verga, G. L' Malavoglia. Woolf, M. D., ed. 336p. 1972. 12.00x (ISBN 0-7190-0470-5, Pub. by Manchester U Pr England). State Mutual Bk.
Weiman, Ralph. Living French. (YA) (gr. 6-12). 1955. 14.95, with 4 lp records conversation manual & dictionary (ISBN 0-517-00129-2). Crown.
Wellek, Susanne & Bass, Nelly. Rire et Apprendre. 3rd ed. (Illus.). (gr. 1-4). 8.50 (ISBN 0-8044-0806-8); tchrs. manual 1.95 (ISBN 0-8044-0807-6). Ungar.
Whitehead, F., ed. La Chastelaire De Vergi. 86p. 1951. 9.00x (ISBN 0-7190-0136-6, Pub. by Manchester U Pr England). State Mutual Bk.

FRENCH LANGUAGE–DIALECTS

Bouchard, Rene, ed. Culture Populaire et Litteratures Au Quebec. (Stanford French & Italian Studies: Vol. 19). 308p. (Fr.). 1980. pap. 20.00 (ISBN 0-915838-20-6). Anma Libri.
Conwell, Marilyn & Juilland, Alphonse. Louisiana French Grammar, Vol. 1, Phonology, Morphology, & Syntax. (Janua Linguarum, Ser. Practica: No. 1). 1963. text ed. 45.00x (ISBN 90-2790-621-1). Mouton.
Highfield, Arnold R. The French Dialect of St. Thomas U.S. Virgin Islands: A Descriptive Grammar with Texts & Glossary. 350p. 1979. pap. 10.50 (ISBN 0-89720-026-8). Karoma.
Juneau, Marcel. Problems De Lexicologie Quebecoise: Prolegomenes a un Tresor De la Langue Francaise Au Quebec. (Fr.). 1978. 19.00 (ISBN 2-7637-6819-9, Pub. by Laval). Intl Schol Bk Serv.
Locke, W. N. Pronunciation of the French Spoken at Brunswick, Maine. (Publications of the American Dialect Society: No. 12). 201p. 1949. pap. 7.50x (ISBN 0-8173-0612-9). U of Ala Pr.
Millardet, George. Etude De Dialectologie Landaise et Developpement Des Phenomenes Additionnels. Repr. of 1910 ed. 17.70 (ISBN 0-384-38880-9). Johnson Repr.
--Petit Atlas Linguistique D'une Region Des Landes. Repr. of 1910 ed. 35.50 (ISBN 0-384-38882-5). Johnson Repr.
Morgan, Raleigh, Jr. The Regional French of County Beauce, Quebec. LC 74-78061. (Janua Linguarum, Series Practica: No. 177). 128p. 1975. pap. text ed. 26.25x (ISBN 90-2793-107-0). Mouton.
Rice, James. A Cajun Alphabet. LC 76-28490. (Illus.). 1976. 9.95 (ISBN 0-88289-136-7). Pelican.
Vintila-Radulescu, Ioana. Le Creole Francais. (Janua Linguarum, Series Critica: No. 17). 211p. (Fr.). 1976. pap. text ed. 29.50x (ISBN 90-2793-154-2). Mouton.
Woodard, Clement M. Words for "Horse" in French & Provencal. (Language Dissertation Ser.: No. 29). 1939. pap. 6.00 (ISBN 0-527-00775-7). Kraus Repr.

FRENCH LANGUAGE–DIALECTS–BIBLIOGRAPHY

Dulong, Gaston. Bibliographie Linguistique Du Canada Francais. (Fr). 1966. pap. 5.00x (ISBN 2-7637-6246-8, Pub. by Laval). Intl Schol Bk Serv.

FRENCH LANGUAGE–DICTIONARIES

Albertini, Jean. Dictionnaire Francais-Corse. 349p. (Fr.-Cors.). 1974. pap. 32.50 (ISBN 0-686-56891-5, M-6001). French & Eur.
Alpha Encyclopedie, 17 vols. 6240p. (Fr.). Set. 650.00 (ISBN 0-686-56892-3, M-6002). French & Eur.
Bailleul, Pere C. Petit Dictionnaire Bambara-Francais Francais-Bambara. 1981. 100.00x (ISBN 0-686-75433-6, 0-86127-220-X, Pub. by Avebury Pub England). State Mutual Bk.
Bailly, Anatolc. Dictionnaire Abrege Grec-Francais. 1012p. (Gr.-Fr.). 1969. pap. 22.95 (ISBN 0-686-56906-7, M-6019). French & Eur.
--Dictionnaire Grec-Francais. 2230p. (Gr.-Fr.). 1967. pap. 47.50 (ISBN 0-686-56907-5, M-6020). French & Eur.
Baldinger, Kurt. Dictionnaire Etymologique De L'Ancien Francais. 80p. (Fr.). 1971. 17.50x (ISBN 2-7637-6606-4, Pub by Laval). Intl Schol Bk Serv.
Benac. Dictionnaire des Synonymes. 15.75 (ISBN 0-685-36658-8). French & Eur.
Bonnard, Henry, et al. Dictionnaire Syntagmatique Du Francais. 412p. 1980. 13.50 (ISBN 0-89955-118-1, Pub. by Shufunotomo Japan). Intl Schol Bk Serv.
Bornecque, Henri & Cauet, Fernand. Dictionnaire Latin-Francais. 560p. (Fr.-Lat.). 1953. 25.00 (ISBN 0-686-56926-1, M-6044). French & Eur.
Calfa, Ambroise. Dictionnaire Armenien-Francais, 2 vols. 1038p. (Arm.-Fr.). 1973. Set. pap. 49.95 (ISBN 0-686-56934-2, M-6056). French & Eur.
Cassells. French Concise Dictionary. 1977. 8.95 (ISBN 0-02-052267-3). Macmillan.
Ceccaldi, Mathieu. Dictionnaire Corse-Francais, Pierre d'Evisa. 464p. (Cors.-Fr.). 1974. pap. 29.95 (ISBN 0-686-56944-X, M-6066). French & Eur.
Centre de Recherche Pour un Tresor de la Langue Francaise, ed. Dictionnaire des Frequences, Vocabulaire Litteraire Des 19th et 20th Siecles, 4 vols. 2284p. (Fr.). 1976. pap. 110.00 (ISBN 0-686-56841-9, M-6620). French & Eur.
Centre National De la Recherche Scientifique & Imbs, Paul, eds. Tresor De la Langue Francaise: Dictionnaire De la Langue Du 19th et Du 20th Siecle (1789-1960, 14 vols. 2000p. (Fr.). 1972. 55.00x ea. Intl Pubns Serv.
Clapin, Sylva. Dictionnaire Canadien-Francais. 394p. (Canadien Fr.). 1974. 17.50 (ISBN 0-686-56809-5, M-6587). French & Eur.
D'Alembert, Jean. Discours Preliminaire (Plan of the French Encyclopedia) 59.95 (ISBN 0-8490-0049-1). Gordon Pr.
Dauzat, A., et al. Nouveau Dictionnaire etymologique. (Fr) 27.50 (ISBN 2-03-020210-X, 3612). Larousse.
Davau, Maurice & Lallemand, Maurice. Dictionnaire du Francais Vivant. 1360p. (Fr.). 1972. pap. 26.50 (ISBN 0-686-56975-X, M-6102). French & Eur.
Deak, Etienne & Deak, Simone. Dictionnaire des Americanismes. 6th ed. 928p. (Fr.). 1974. 25.00 (ISBN 0-686-56976-8, M-6103). French & Eur.
Denizeau, Claude. Dictionnaire des Parlers Arabes de Syrie, Liban et Palestine. 581p. (Fr.-Arab.). 1961. pap. 49.95 (ISBN 0-686-57090-1, M-6112). French & Eur.
Dictionanaire Francais-Breton. (Fr. -Bret.). 1979. 15.00 (ISBN 0-686-56718-8, M-6141). French & Eur.
Dictionnaire Breton-Francais, Francais-Breton. (Fr. -Bret.). 1979. 29.95 (ISBN 0-686-56717-X, M-6118). French & Eur.

Dictionnaire des Communes (de France) 20.95 (ISBN 0-685-36659-6). French & Eur.
Dictionnaire des Mots Contemporains. (Fr.). 1979. pns (M-6128). French & Eur.
Dictionnaire du francais contemporain: Manuel et travaux pratique. (Fr.). 18.95 (ISBN 0-685-92177-8, 4078). Larousse.
Dictionnaire Francais-Francais des Mots Rare et Precieux. 8.50 (ISBN 0-685-36677-4). French & Eur.
Dictionnaire Francais-Serbo-Croate. 632p. (Fr.-Serbo-Croatian.). pap. 19.95 (ISBN 0-686-57109-6, M-6142). French & Eur.
Dictionnaire Quillet De la Langue Francais, 4 vols. 2132p. (Fr.). Set. 195.00 (ISBN 0-686-57114-2, M-6153). French & Eur.
Dordillon, Ildefonse. Dictionnaire De la Langue Des Iles Marquises. 598p. (Fr. & Marq.). 1932. 27.50 (ISBN 0-686-56819-2, M-6597). French & Eur.
Dubois, C. Pluri Dictionnaire. new ed. (Illus.). 1974. 31.50x (ISBN 2-03-020124-3, 3677). Larousse.
Dubois, J. & Giacomo, M. Dictionnaire de linguistique. 516p. (Fr.). 1974. 27.50 (ISBN 2-03-020299-1, 1002). Larousse.
Dubois, Jean & Lagane, Rene. Dictionnaire du Francais Classique. 608p. (Fr.). 1971. 22.50 (ISBN 0-686-57298-X, F-133960). French & Eur.
Dubois, Jean, ed. Lexis: Dictionnaire De la Langue Francaise. 2032p. (Fr.). 1975. 47.50 (ISBN 0-686-57019-7, M-6376). French & Eur.
--Lexis-Dictionnaire de la Largue francaise. 1979. 56.25 (ISBN 0-686-60644-2, 2427). Larousse.
Dubois, Jean, et al. Dictionnaire du Francais Contemporain. new ed. 1246p. (Fr.). 1976. 25.00 (ISBN 0-686-57127-4, M-6175). French & Eur.
Dulong, Gaston. Dictionnaire Correctif Du Francais Au Canada. (Fr). 1968. pap. 3.00x (ISBN 2-7637-6363-4, Pub. by Laval). Intl Schol Bk Serv.
Dupre, Paul. Encyclopedie Du Bon Francais Dans L'usage Contemporain, 3 vols. 2900p. (Fr.). 1959. Set. 160.00 (ISBN 0-686-57128-2, M-6179). French & Eur.
Dupuis, Hector & Legare, Romain. Dictonnaire des Synonymes et des Antonymes. 608p. (Fr.). 1975. 22.50 (ISBN 0-686-57129-0, M-6180). French & Eur.
Edon, Georges. Dictionnaire Francais-Latin. (Fr.-Lat.). 37.50 (ISBN 0-686-57201-7, M-6703). French & Eur.
Elihai, Yohanan. Dictionnaire de l'Arabe Parle Palestinien. 418p. (Fr.-Arab.). 1974. pap. 22.50 (ISBN 0-686-57132-0, M-6185). French & Eur.
Encyclopedie Francaise Permanente, 22 vols. (Fr.). Set. 1750.00 (ISBN 0-686-57273-4, F-12790). French & Eur.
Esnault. Dictionnaire des Argots Francais. 16.50 (ISBN 0-685-36663-4). French & Eur.
Faine, Jules. Dictionnaire Francais-Creole. 480p. (Fr.-Creo.). 1975. pap. 39.95 (ISBN 0-686-57291-2, M-4608). French & Eur.
Ferrar, H., et al, eds. The Concise Oxford French Dictionary. 912p. 1980. 22.50 (ISBN 0-19-864126-5). Oxford U Pr.
Franklin, Afred L. Dictionnaire Historique Des Arts, Metiers Et Professions Exerces Dans Paris Depuis Le Treizieme Siecle. (Biblio. & Ref. Ser.: No. 198). 1968. Repr. of 1906 ed. 49.00 (ISBN 0-8337-1231-4); 40.00 (ISBN 0-685-06747-5). B Franklin.
French Dictionary. (Teach Yourself Ser.). 1977. pap. 5.95 (ISBN 0-679-10245-0). McKay.
French Duden, Pictorial Dictionary. (Illus.). 20.50 (ISBN 3-4110-0972-1). Adler.
Gaffiot, Felix. Dictionnaire Abrege Latin-Francais. 1720p. (Lat.-Fr.). 1970. pap. 15.95 (ISBN 0-686-57186-X, M-6258). French & Eur.
--Dictionnaire Latin-Francais. (Lat.-Fr.). 1967. pap. 32.50 (ISBN 0-686-57187-8, M-6259). French & Eur.
Galisson, R. & Coste, D., eds. Dictionnaire De Didactique des Largues. 612p. (Fr.). 1976. 22.50 (ISBN 0-686-56813-3, M-6591). French & Eur.
Gamillscheg, Ernst. Etymologisches Woerterbuch der Franzoesischen Sprache. 2nd ed. (Fr. & Ger.). 1969. 195.00 (ISBN 0-686-56604-1, M-7370, Pub. by Carl Winter). French & Eur.
Genouvrier, Emile, et al. Nouveau Dictionnaire des Synonymes. (Fr.). 1977. 19.95 (ISBN 0-686-57192-4, M-6266). French & Eur.
Georgin, Ch. Dictionnaire Grec-Francais. (Gr.-Fr.). pap. 14.95 (ISBN 0-686-57194-0, M-6268). French & Eur.
Giraudeau, A. & Gore, Francis. Dictionnaire Francais-Tibetain (Tibet Oriental) 310p. (Fr.-Tib.). 1956. 49.95 (ISBN 0-686-57301-3, M-6275). French & Eur.
Guilbert. Le Vocabulaire de L'astronautique: Enquete Linguistique a travers la Presse d'information a L'occasion De Cinq Exploits de Cosmonautes. (Publ. de l'Univ. de Rouen Fac. des Lettres et Sc. Hum.). 15.95 (ISBN 0-685-36683-9). French & Eur.
Hatzfeld, et al. Dictionnaire General de la Langue Francaise: Du commencement du XVIIe sielce a nos jours, 2 tomes. Set. 73.90 (ISBN 0-685-36651-0). French & Eur.
Hatzfeld, Adophe & Darmesteter, Arsene. Dictionnaire General de la Langue Francaise du Commencement du 17e Siecle Jusqu' a Nos Jours, 2 vols. 1468p. (Fr.). 1964. Set. 89.95 (ISBN 0-686-57290-4, F-134240). French & Eur.
Isaacs, Alan, ed. Multilingual Commercial Dictionary. 1980. 22.50 (ISBN 0-87196-425-2). Facts on File.
Juilland, A., et al. Frequency Dictionary of French Words. LC 73-142752. (Romance Languages & Their Structures, First Ser. F-1). 1970. text ed. 101.25x (ISBN 90-2791-553-9). Mouton.
Kendris, Christopher. Dictionary of Five Hundred & One French Verbs: Fully Conjugated in All Tenses. LC 73-90072. 1970. 10.75 (ISBN 0-8120-6077-6); pap. 4.50 (ISBN 0-8120-0395-0). Barron.
L-1 Dictionaire Encyclopedique. (Illus.). 1520p. (Fr.). 1980. 99.95 (ISBN 2-03-020127-8). Larousse.
Larousse. Nouveau Petit Larousse. 29.95 (ISBN 0-685-20242-9). Schoenhof.
Larousse And Co. Dictionnaire du francais contemporain. (Fr). 27.50 (ISBN 0-685-13872-0, 3745). Larousse.
--Dictionnaire du vocabulaire essentiel. (Illus., Fr.). pap. 12.25 (ISBN 0-685-13873-9, 3753). Larousse.
--Larousse classique. (Illus., Fr.). 28.25 (ISBN 0-685-13957-3, 3747). Larousse.
--Larousse de poche. (Fr.). pap. 6.95 (ISBN 2-03-020166-9, 1008). Larousse.
--Larousse des debutants. (Illus., Fr.). 12.25 (ISBN 2-03-020151-0, 3752). Larousse.
--Larousse pour tous. (Fr). 11.50 (ISBN 0-685-13965-4, 3751). Larousse.
--Nouveau Larousse elementaire. (Illus., Fr.). 23.95 (ISBN 0-685-14003-2). Larousse.
--Nouveau Petit Larousse en couleurs. (Illus., Fr.). 1974. 83.00 (ISBN 2-03-020111-1, 3676). Larousse.
--Petit Dictionnaire francais Larousse. (Illus., Fr.). 10.50 (ISBN 0-685-14034-2, 3754). Larousse.
--Plus Petit Larousse. (Fr). plastic bdg. 6.25 (ISBN 0-685-14044-X, 3756). Larousse.
Larousse encyclopedique des debutants. new ed. 144p. (Fr.). 1975. 16.50 (ISBN 2-03-020145-6). Larousse.
Lebaigue, Charles. Dictionnaire Latin-Francais. 1382p. (Fr. & Lat.). 33.50 (ISBN 0-686-56999-7, M-6340). French & Eur.
Le Maistre. Dictionnaire Jersias-Francais, 2 tomes. Set. 86.50 (ISBN 0-685-36662-6). French & Eur.
Lhande, Pierre. Dictionnaire Basque Francais. 1117p. (Basq. Fr.). 1938. 79.95 (ISBN 0-686-57020-0, M-6377). French & Eur.
Littre. Dictionnaire de la Langue Francaise. Beaujean & Geraud-Venzac, eds. 24.95 (ISBN 0-685-36652-9). French & Eur.
Littre, Emile. Dictionnaire De La Langue Francaise, 7 tomes. 21.95 (ISBN 0-685-11141-5); Set. 245.00 (ISBN 0-685-11142-3). French & Eur.
Mai-Aru & Anisson du Perron, J. Dictionnaire Francais-Tahitien et Tahitien-Francais. 380p. (Fr.-Tahi.). 1973. 17.50 (ISBN 0-686-57025-1, M-6383). French & Eur.
Malzac, R. P. Dictionnaire Francais-Malgache. 861p. (Fr.-Mada.). 1953. pap. 32.50 (ISBN 0-686-57030-8, M-6390). French & Eur.
Mirambel, Andre. Petit Dictionnaire Francais-Grec Moderne et Grec Moderne-Francais. 486p. (Fr.-Mod. Gr.). 1969. 29.95 (ISBN 0-686-57051-0, M-6413). French & Eur.
Niobey, G. Dictionnaire analogique. (Fr) 26.50 (ISBN 0-685-13850-X, 3608). Larousse.
Nougayrol, Pierre, et al. Dictionnaire Elementaire Creole Haitien-Francais. Bentolila, Alain, ed. 511p. (Hait.-Fr.). 1976. 29.95 (ISBN 0-686-57060-X, M-6430). French & Eur.
Pessoneaux, Emile. Dictionnaire Grec-Francais. 896p. (Fr.-Gr.). 1953. 35.95 (ISBN 0-686-57071-5, M-6443). French & Eur.
Petit Robert. (Fr.). Vol. 1. 49.95 (ISBN 0-685-26781-4); Vol. 2. 65.00 (ISBN 0-686-66707-7). French & Eur.
Piat. Dictionnaire Francais-Langue d'Oc. 1000p. (Fr.). 75.00 (ISBN 0-686-56730-7, M-6451). French & Eur.
Quicherat, Louis. Dictionnaire Francais-Latin. (Fr.-Lat.). 1967. pap. 35.00 (ISBN 0-686-57202-5, M-6472). French & Eur.
Reinhorn, Marc. Dictionnaire Laotien-Francais, 2 vols. 2000p. (Fr.-Lao.). 1970. Set. 85.00 (ISBN 0-686-57204-1, M-6481). French & Eur.
Robert. Dictionnaire Alphabetique et Analogique De la Langue Francaise, 7 vols. (Illus.). Set. 437.50 (ISBN 0-685-11140-7). French & Eur.
Robert, Paul. Le Micro-Robert: Dictionnaire Du Francais Primordial. 1231p. (Fr.). 1971. 14.95 (ISBN 0-686-57209-2, M-6487). French & Eur.
Robert, Paul, ed. The Robert Dictionaries. Incl. Le Micro Robert en Poche, 2 vols. 1171p; Le Micro Robert, 2 vols. in 1. 1230p; Le Petit Robert. rev. ed. 1972p. 44.50x (ISBN 0-684-15802-7); Le Grand Robert, 7 vols. 6530p. Set. 295.00x (ISBN 0-684-14004-7); o.p. suppl. only (ISBN 0-684-14085-3); Dictionnaire Universel des Noms Propres, 4 vols. (Illus.). 3200p. 1974 (ScribC). Scribner.
Schneider, Lucien. Dictionnaire Esquimau-Francais Du Parler De l'Ungava et Contrees Limitrophes. 437p. 1970. 17.50x (ISBN 2-7637-6315-4, Pub. by Laval). Intl Schol Bk Serv.
Servotte, Jozef V. Commercial & Financial Dictionary in Four Languages: French-Dutch-English-German. rev. 4th ed. Orig. Title: Dictionnaire Commercial et Financier en 4 Langues. 968p. 1972. 52.50x (ISBN 90-02-11109-6). Intl Pubns Serv.
Societe Du Paler Francais Au Canada. Glossaire Du Parler Francais Au Canada. LC 68-143461. 710p. (Fr.). 1968. 25.00 (ISBN 0-686-57223-8, M-6521). French & Eur.
Switzer, Robert, ed. World-Wide French Dictionary. 1978. pap. 2.95 (ISBN 0-449-30849-9, Prem). Fawcett.
Thomas, A. V. Dictionnaire des difficultes de la langue francaise. (Fr) 23.50 (ISBN 0-685-13865-8, 3611). Larousse.
Tisserant, Ch. Dictionnaire Banda-Francais. 611p. (Banda-Fr.). 1931. 32.50 (ISBN 0-686-56789-7, M-6585, Pub. by Institut Ethnologie). French & Eur.
Vest-Pocket French. pap. 2.95 (ISBN 0-8329-1532-7). New Century.
Wartburg, Walter von. Franzoesisch Etymologisches Woerterbuch. 2nd ed. (Fr.). 1984. 38.50 (ISBN 3-16-926772-8, M-7414, Pub. by Francke). French & Eur.
World-Wide French Dictionary. pap. 3.95 (ISBN 0-686-31299-6). New Century.
World-Wide French Dictionary: Indexed. 5.95 (ISBN 0-686-31298-8). New Century.

FRENCH LANGUAGE–DICTIONARIES–ARABIC

Blachere, Regis & Chouemi, Moustafa. Dictionnaire Arabe-Francais-Anglais, 1, Pts. 1-12. (Arab., Fr. & Eng.). 1967. 195.00 (ISBN 0-686-56918-0, M-6034). French & Eur.
--Dictionnaire Arabe-Francais-Anglais, 2, Pts. 13-24. (Arab., Fr. & Eng.). 1970. 210.00 (ISBN 0-686-56919-9, M-6035). French & Eur.
Blachere, Regis, et al. Dictionnaire Arabe-Francais-Anglais - Arabic-French-English Dictionary: Classical & Modern Language, 3 vols. LC 72-203569. 1512p. 1967-72. Vol. 1. 80.00x (ISBN 0-8002-1363-7); Vol. 2. 90.00x (ISBN 0-8002-1364-5); Vol. 3. 95.00x (ISBN 0-8002-1366-1). Intl Pubns Serv.
Cherbonneau. French Arabic Dictionary, 2 vols. Set. 30.00x (ISBN 0-86685-103-8). Intl Bk Ctr.
Dozy. Dictionary Noms de Vetements Chez Arabes. 20.00x (ISBN 0-86685-104-6). Intl Bk Ctr.
Gasselin, E. Dictionnaire Francais-Arabe(Arabe Parle-Arabe Grammatical, 2 vols. 1974. Repr. of 1880 ed. text ed. 60.00x (ISBN 0-8426-0757-9). Verry.
Hakki, Mamdouh. Dictionnaire Des Terms Juridiques et Commerciaux (Francais-Arabe) 1973. 20.00x (ISBN 0-86685-108-9). Intl Bk Ctr.
Henni, Mustapha. Dictionary Des Terms Economiques et Commerciaux (French-English-Arabic) 25.00x (ISBN 0-86685-111-9). Intl Bk Ctr.
Kazirmski. Arabe Francais Dictionnaire, 2 vols. 70.00x (ISBN 0-86685-110-0). Intl Bk Ctr.
Naggary-Bey, M. Dictionnaire Francais-Arabe, 6 vols. in 3. 1974. 75.00x set (ISBN 0-8426-0756-0). Verry.
Sabek, Jerwan. English-French-Arabic Trilingual Dictionary. 35.00 (ISBN 0-86685-116-X). Intl Bk Ctr.
Saisse, Louis. Dictionaire Francais-Arabe. 1980. pap. 8.95x (ISBN 0-86685-112-7). Intl Bk Ctr.
Wahba, Magdi. A Dictionary of Literary Terms (English-French-Arabic) 1974. 30.00x (ISBN 0-86685-117-8). Intl Bk Ctr.

FRENCH LANGUAGE–DICTIONARIES–DUTCH

Grootaers, Ludovic. Dictionnaire Classique: Francais-Neerlandais, Neerlandais-Francais. 22nd ed. 1050p. (Fr.-Dutch.). 1969. 29.95 (ISBN 0-686-57317-X, M-6300). French & Eur.
--Le Nouveau Dictionnaire Francais-Neerlandais, Nederlands-Francais. 18th ed. 826p. (Fr.-Dutch.). 1969. 65.00 (ISBN 0-686-57318-8, M-6301). French & Eur.

FRENCH LANGUAGE–DICTIONARIES–ENGLISH

Atkins, B. T., et al, eds. Colins Robert Dictionary: French-English-English-French. Duval, A. & Milnet, R. C. 16.95 (ISBN 0-686-28358-9, CFD1); thumb index avail. (ISBN 0-00-433479-5). Collins Pubs.
Beaudet, Albert. Dictionnaire Anglais-Francais Des Nouveautes Linguistics. (Eng. & Fr.). 1971. 7.50x (ISBN 0-8002-0199-X). Intl Pubns Serv.
Blachere, Regis & Chouemi, Moustafa. Dictionnaire Arabe-Francais-Anglais, 1, Pts. 1-12. (Arab., Fr. & Eng.). 1967. 195.00 (ISBN 0-686-56918-0, M-6034). French & Eur.
--Dictionnaire Arabe-Francais-Anglais, 2, Pts. 13-24. (Arab., Fr. & Eng.). 1970. 210.00 (ISBN 0-686-56919-9, M-6035). French & Eur.
Blachere, Regis, et al. Dictionnaire Arabe-Francais-Anglais - Arabic-French-English Dictionary: Classical & Modern Language, 3 vols. LC 72-203569. 1512p. 1967-72. Vol. 1. 80.00x (ISBN 0-8002-1363-7); Vol. 2. 90.00x (ISBN 0-8002-1364-5); Vol. 3. 95.00x (ISBN 0-8002-1366-1). Intl Pubns Serv.
Camille, Cl. & Dehaine, M. Dictionnaire de l'Informatique, Francais-Anglais. 248p. (Fr.-Eng.). 1972. 22.50 (ISBN 0-686-56936-9, M-6058). French & Eur.
Cassells. French-English Dictionary. 1977. standard 14.95 (ISBN 0-02-052261-4); index 16.95 (ISBN 0-02-052262-2). Macmillan.
Cassell's Compact French-English, English-French Dictionary. 1981. pap. price not set (ISBN 0-440-31128-4, LE). Dell.
Chaffurin, L. & Mergault, J. Dictionnaire bilingue Larousse, francais-anglais, anglais-francais. (Apollo). (Fr. & Eng.). 10.50 (ISBN 0-685-13856-9, 3767). Larousse.
Chauffurin, L. Petit Dictionnaire bilingue Larousse, francais-anglais et English-French. (Adonis). (Fr. & Eng.). plastic bdg. 6.25 (ISBN 0-685-14032-6, 3768). Larousse.
Colpron, Gilles. Les Anglicismes au Quebec. 247p. (Fr.-Eng.). 1979. 17.50 (ISBN 0-686-56957-1, M-6080). French & Eur.
Cortina. Cortina-Ace Basic French Dictionary. (Foreign Language Dictionary Ser.). 384p. 1981. pap. 2.50 (ISBN 0-441-05001-8). Ace Bks.
Cotgrave, Randle. Dictionarie of the French & English Tongues. LC 51-4027. Repr. 27.50x (ISBN 0-87249-023-8). U of SC Pr.
--A Dictionarie of the French & English Tongues. LC 77-171741. (English Experience Ser.: No. 367). 992p. 1971. Repr. of 1611 ed. 105.00 (ISBN 90-221-0367-6). Walter J Johnson.
--Dictionary of the French & English Tongues. 1971. Repr. of 1611 ed. 128.00 (ISBN 0-685-05204-4). Adler.
Cruikshank, Eleanor P. French-English Instant Vocabulary Francais-Anglais. 88p. 1980. pap. 4.00 (ISBN 0-9605284-0-7). Cruikshank.
Cusset, Francis. English-French & French-English Technical Dictionary. rev. ed. 1967. 28.50 (ISBN 0-8206-0043-1). Chem Pub.
Deak, Etienne & Deak, Simone. Dictionary of Colorful French Slanguage & Colloquialisms. (Illus.). 1961. pap. 4.75 (ISBN 0-525-47087-5). Dutton.
Delamarre. Dictionnaire Francais-Anglais et Anglais-Francais des Termes Techniques De Medecine. 49.95 (ISBN 0-685-36680-4). French & Eur.
Delmas-Harrap. Dictionnaire des affaires francais-anglais, anglais-francais. 65.50 (ISBN 0-685-36681-2). French & Eur.
Dictionary of Idioms French-English: Dictionnaire des locutions. 33.95 (ISBN 2-03-021101-X, 3681). Larousse.
Dictionnaire Des Techniques Aerospatiales. LC 72-315260. 406p. (Eng. & Fr.). 1971. 32.50x (ISBN 0-8002-1216-9). Intl Pubns Serv.
Douglas, J. H., et al, eds. Cassell's Concise French-English, English-French Dictionary. abr. ed. LC 77-7667. 1977. 6.95 (ISBN 0-02-522670-3). Macmillan.
Dubois, M. M. Dictionnaire moderne Larousse francais-anglais et anglais-francais. new rev. ed. 25.00 (ISBN 0-88332-003-7, 3769). Larousse.
Dubois, Marguerite-Marie. Dictionnaire de Locutions, Francais-Anglais. 392p. (Fr.-Eng.). 1973. 22.50 (ISBN 0-686-57125-8, M-6173). French & Eur.
Dubois-Charlier, F., et al. Dictionnaire d'anglais. 868p. (Fr.). 1975. pap. text ed. 11.50 (ISBN 2-03-040531-0). Larousse.
Falconer, William. Universal Dictionary of the Marine. LC 72-87321. (Illus.). Repr. of 1780 ed. lib. bdg. 24.50x (ISBN 0-678-05655-2). Kelley.
Farmer, John S., ed. Vocabula Amatoria: French-English Dictionary of Erotica. 1965. 10.00 (ISBN 0-8216-0160-1). Univ Bks.
French-English Chemical Terminology: An Introduction to Chemistry in French & English. (Illus.). 590p. 1968. 22.50x (ISBN 0-8002-1432-3). Intl Pubns Serv.

Gerber, Barbara & Storzer, Gerald. French Idioms on the Way. (Illus.). 1982. pap. 4.95 (ISBN 0-8120-2108-8). Barron.

Gieber, Robert L. An English-French Glossary of Educational Terminology. LC 80-5652. 212p. 1980. lib. bdg. 18.00 (ISBN 0-8191-1344-1); pap. text ed. 9.25 (ISBN 0-8191-1345-X). U Pr of Amer.

Girard, Denis. Dictionnaire Francais-Anglais et Anglais-Francais. 1464p. (Fr.-Eng.). 1972. 27.50 (ISBN 0-686-57300-5, M-6274). French & Eur.

Girard, Denis, et al, eds. Cassell's French Dictionary. LC 77-7669. 1977. indexed 13.95 (ISBN 0-02-522620-7); plain 12.50 (ISBN 0-02-522610-X). Macmillan.

Gladstone. Vocabulaire De Medecine et Des Sciences Connexes Anglais-Francais-Anglais. 21.95 (ISBN 0-685-36682-0). French & Eur.

Hall, Robert A., Jr. & Langbaum, Francesca V. French Vest Pocket Dictionary. 1954. pap. 2.50 (ISBN 0-394-40054-2). Random.

Hamlyn French-English Dictionary. 1977. pap. 3.95 (ISBN 0-600-36563-8, 8086). Larousse.

Harrap's French-English Dictionary of Slang & Colloquialisms. (Fr.-Eng.). 1975. 14.95 (ISBN 0-686-57323-4, M-6308). French & Eur.

Harrap's New Standard Francais-Anglais, 2: J A07 Z. 1162p. (Fr.-Eng.). 1972. 32.50 (ISBN 0-8442-1898-7, M-6310). French & Eur.

Harrap's Standard Anglais-Francais. 1530p. (Fr.-Eng.). 1970. 49.95 (ISBN 0-686-57324-2, M-6311). French & Eur.

Harrop's New Standard Francais-Anglais, 1: A-I. (Fr.-Eng.). 1972. 32.50 (ISBN 0-8442-1876-6, M-6309). French & Eur.

Hochman, ed. Kettridge's English-French - French-English Dictionary. 1971. pap. 2.95 (ISBN 0-451-11038-2, AE1038, Sig). NAL.

Hughes, Charles A. Ace's French Phrase Book & Dictionary. (Ace's Foreign Phrase Bk). 192p. 1981. pap. 1.95 (ISBN 0-441-25207-9). Ace Bks.

Hugo Pocket Dictionary: French-English, English-French. 1973. 3.50 (ISBN 0-8226-0503-1, 503). Littlefield.

Institute for Language Study. Vest Pocket French. (Illus.). 128p. (Fr.). Date not set. pap. 1.95 (ISBN 0-06-464901-6, BN 4900, BN). Har-Row.

Jeans Pocket Dictionaries: French-English. 224p. (Orig.). 1981. pap. 1.95 (ISBN 0-8437-1725-4). Hammond Inc.

Kelly, L. L. Cle Du Francais. 1970. text ed. 12.95 (ISBN 0-02-362310-1); wkbk. 3.40x (ISBN 0-685-14880-7). Macmillan.

Kettridge. French-English, English-French Dictionary of Commercial & Financial Terms. 21.50 (ISBN 0-685-36684-7). French & Eur.

Kettridge, J. O. French-English & English-French Dictionary of Commercial & Financial Terms, Phrases & Practice. 2nd ed. 1969. Repr. of 1968 ed. 30.00 (ISBN 0-7100-1671-9). Routledge & Kegan.

--French-English & English-French Dictionary of Financial & Mercantile Terms Phrases & Practice. 1971. Repr. of 1934 ed. 20.00 (ISBN 0-7100-1667-0). Routledge & Kegan.

--French-English & English-French Dictionary of Technical Terms & Phrases, 2 vols. Incl. Vol. 1. French-English. 40.00 (ISBN 0-7100-1672-7); Vol. 2. English-French. 40.00 (ISBN 0-7100-1673-5). 1970. Repr. of 1959 ed. Set. 70.00 (ISBN 0-685-25619-7). Routledge & Kegan.

Kettridge, Julius O. Dictionary of Technical Terms, 2 vols. (Fr. -Eng-Eng. -Fr.). Set. 55.50 (ISBN 0-685-11207-1). French & Eur.

--Financial & Mercantile Dictionary. (Fr. & Eng.). 13.95 (ISBN 0-685-11187-3). French & Eur.

Langbaum, Francesca L., ed. The Random House Basic Dictionary French. 1981. pap. 1.50 (ISBN 0-345-29617-6). Ballantine.

Langenscheidt Staff, ed. Langenscheidt's New Pocket French Dictionary: French-English, English-French. (Langenscheidt Pocket Dictionaries Ser.). 640p. 1970. 5.95 (ISBN 0-685-31331-X). Hippocrene Bks.

Langenscheidt's Lilliput French-English Dictionary. 640p. (Eng. & Fr.). 1972. 1.50 (ISBN 0-685-31354-9). Hippocrene Bks.

Larousse And Co. Larousse de poche francais-espagnol, et espanol-frances. (Fr. & Span.). pap. 5.95 (ISBN 0-685-13961-1, 1010). Larousse.

--Mon Premier Larousse francais-anglais, anglais-francais en couleurs. (Fr. & Eng.). (gr. 6-9). 28.95 (ISBN 2-03-051431-4, 3794). Larousse.

Larousse Bi-Lingual French-English, English French Dictionary. (Apollo). 10.50 (ISBN 2-03-020903-1, 3767). Larousse.

Larousse De Poche. pap. 2.95 (ISBN 0-671-48896-1). PB.

Larousse French-English Dictionary. 1981. pap. 2.95 (ISBN 0-686-72054-7). PB.

Larousse Modern French-English, English-French Dictionary. 25.00 (ISBN 2-03-020602-4, 3769). Larousse.

Lipton, Gladys. French Bilingual Dictionary: Compact Ed. LC 78-20788. (Illus.). (gr. 7-12). 1979. pap. 3.25 (ISBN 0-8120-2007-3). Barron.

Mansion, J. E. Harrap's Concise Student French & English Dictionary. new ed. Collin, P. H., et al, eds. (gr. 9-12). 1978. Repr. text ed. 9.95 (ISBN 0-8442-1872-3, 1872-4). Natl Textbk.

--Harrap's New Collegiate French & English Dictionary. rev. ed. Ledesert, D. H., ed. LC 75-182800. (gr. 9-12). 1967. Repr. text ed. 14.95 (ISBN 0-8442-1873-1, 1873-4). Natl Textbk.

--Harrap's New Standard French & English Dictionary, Part One, French-English (A-I) rev. ed. Ledesert, D. H. & Ledesert, R. P., eds. 1972. Repr. text ed. 32.50 (ISBN 0-8442-1876-6, 1874-4). Natl Textbk.

--Harrap's New Standard French & English Dictionary, Part One, French-English (J-Z) rev. ed. Ledesert, D. H. & Ledesert, R. P., eds. 1972. Repr. 32.50 (ISBN 0-8442-1884-7, 1875-4). Natl Textbk.

--Harrap's Standard French & English Dictionary, Part 2, English-French (A-Z) rev. ed. 1962. Repr. text ed. 49.50 (ISBN 0-8442-1898-7, 1876-4). Natl Textbk.

--Harrap's Super-Mini French & English Dictionary. abridged ed. Forbes, Patricia & Ledesert, Margaret, eds. (gr. 7-12). 1977. pap. 2.75 (ISBN 0-8442-1871-5, 1871-4). Natl Textbk.

Mansion, J. E., ed. Harrap's New Standard French & English Dictionary, English-French, Vol. 3, A-K, Vol. 4, L-Z. 1600p. 1981. 80.00 set (ISBN 0-524-11899-X). Bowker.

Marcy, Teresa & Marcy, Michel. Cortina-Grosset Basic French Dictionary. Berberi, Dilaver & Berberi, Edel A., eds. LC 73-18522. 384p. 1975. pap. 3.50 (ISBN 0-448-14031-4). G&D.

Nouveau Larousse francais-anglais, English-French. (Mars). 24.00 (ISBN 2-03-020812-4, 4083). Larousse.

Patterson, A. M. German-English Dictionary for Chemists. 3rd ed. 1950. 23.50 (ISBN 0-471-66990-3, Pub. by Wiley-Interscience). Wiley.

Perreau & Langford. Concise French-American Dictionary of Figurative & Idiomatic Language. 17.95 (ISBN 0-685-36686-3). French & Eur.

Petit, Charles & Savage, William. Dictionnaire Classique Anglais-Francais et Francais-Anglais. 686p. (Eng.-Fr.). 1967. pap. 27.50 (ISBN 0-686-57072-3, M-6444). French & Eur.

Piraux. Dictionaire Francais-Anglais d'electro-technique et d'electronique. 32.50 (ISBN 0-685-36687-1). French & Eur.

Piraux, H. French-Eng., Eng-French Dictionary of Electrotechnic Electronics & Allied Fields, 2 Vols. Set. 90.00 (ISBN 0-685-12017-1). Heinman.

Pocket Bi-Lingual French-English English-French. 6.25 (ISBN 2-03-020410-2, 3768). Larousse.

Putnam's Contemporary French Dictionary. 1977. pap. 2.25 (ISBN 0-425-04361-4, Medallion). Berkley Pub.

Quemner. Dictionaire Juridique Francais-Anglais, Anglais-Francais, 2 vols. in 1. 75.00 (ISBN 0-685-36688-X). French & Eur.

Rudler, G. & Anderson, N. C., eds. French-English, English-French Gem Dictionary. (Gem Foreign Language Ser.). 1952. 2.95 (ISBN 0-00-458617-4, G2). Collins Pubs.

Rudler, Gustave, et al, eds. Putnam's Contemporary French Dictionary. LC 72-88105. (Fr. & Eng.). 1972. 2.95 (ISBN 0-399-11042-9). Putnam.

--Putnam's Contemporary French Dictionary. LC 72-88105. (Fr. & Eng.). 1972. 2.95 (ISBN 0-399-11042-9). Putnam.

Sabek, Jerwan. English-French-Arabic Trilingual Dictionary. 35.00 (ISBN 0-86685-116-X). Intl Bk Ctr.

Steiner, Roger, ed. Bantam New College French & English Dictionary. 736p. (Orig.). 1972. pap. 2.75 (ISBN 0-553-14890-7). Bantam.

Steiner, Roger J. The New College French & English Dictionary. (gr. 7-12). 1972. pap. text ed. 7.17 (ISBN 0-87720-463-2). AMSCO Sch.

Switzer, Richard & Gochberg, Herbert S., eds. Follett Vest-Pocket French Dictionary. rev. ed. (Orig.). 2.50 (ISBN 0-695-89050-6). New Century.

Unwin, Kenneth. Langenscheidt's Standard French Dictionary: French-English, English-French. Orig. Title: Standard French Dictionary. 1216p. 1974. 11.95 (ISBN 0-88254-285-0). Hippocrene Bks.

Vinay, Jean P. Everyman's French-English, English-French Dictionary. 1972. Repr. of 1962 ed. 12.50x (ISBN 0-460-03017-5). Intl Pubns Serv.

Weiman, Ralph. Living French. (YA) (gr. 6-12). 1955. 14.95, with 4 lp records conversation manual & dictionary (ISBN 0-517-00129-2). Crown.

FRENCH LANGUAGE–DICTIONARIES–GERMAN

Bertaux, Pierre. Franzosisch-Deutsches, Deutsch-Franzosisches Woerterbuch, Vol. 1. (Ger. & Fr.). 1966. 52.00 (ISBN 3-87097-000-6, 7411, Pub. by Brandstetter). French & Eur.

--Franzosisch-Deutsches, Deutsch-Franzosisches Woerterbuch, Vol. 2. (Ger. & Fr.). 1966. 52.00 (ISBN 3-87097-001-4, 7412, Pub. by Brandstetter). French & Eur.

Dubois, F. & Werny, P. Dictionnaire Francais-Allemand des Locutions. (Fr.-Ger.). 1976. 23.95 (ISBN 0-686-57124-X, M-6172). French & Eur.

Eckel, Denis & Manfred, Hofer. Dictionnaire Allemand-Francais et Francais-Allemand. 1324p. (Fr.-Ger.). 1970. 25.95 (ISBN 0-686-57131-2, M-6184). French & Eur.

Grappin, P. Dictionnaire moderne Larousse, francais-allemand et allemand-francais. (Fr. & Ger.). 39.95 (ISBN 2-03-020603-2, 3778). Larousse.

Knauer, Karl. Bertelsmann Woerterbuch Duetsch-Franzoesisch, Franzoesisch-Deutsch. 640p. (Ger. -Fr.). 1974. 17.50 (ISBN 3-570-01486-X, M-7307, Pub. by Bertelsmann Lexikon VVA). French & Eur.

Larousse And Co. Interprete Larousse, francais-allemand et allemand-francais. pap. 3.95 (ISBN 0-685-13946-8, 3782). Larousse.

--Larousse de poche, francais-allemand et allemand-francais. pap. 5.95 (ISBN 0-685-13959-X). Larousse.

Pinloche, A. & Jolivet, A. Dictionnaire bilingue Larousse, francais-alemand et allemand-francais. (Apollo). (Fr. & Ger.). 10.50 (ISBN 0-685-13853-4, 3779). Larousse.

Roepke, F. Franzosisch - Deutsches Glossarium. 540p. (Ger. & Fr) 1964. 36.00 (ISBN 3-7819-2007-0, M-7413, Pub. by Fritz Knapp Verlag). French & Eur.

Rotteck, ed. Dictionnaire Allemand-Francais, Francais-Allemand. 980p. (Fr.-Ger.). 1970. pap. 7.50 (ISBN 0-686-57093-6, M-6115). French & Eur.

Weis, E. & Mattutat, H. Woerterbuch der Franzoesischen und Deutschen Sprache, Vol. 1. (Fr. -Ger.). 18.95 (ISBN 3-215-01824-1, M-7004). French & Eur.

--Woerterbuch der Franzoesischen und Deutschen Sprache, Vol. 2. (Ger. -Fr.). 18.95 (ISBN 3-215-01825-X, M-7003). French & Eur.

Weis, Erich & Mattutat, Heinrich. Dictionnaire Allemand-Francais. 570p. (Ger & Fr.). 1977. 29.95 (ISBN 0-686-57259-9, M-6570). French & Eur.

--Dictionnaire Francais-Allemand et Allemand-Francais. 1022p. (Fr & Ger.). 1977. 55.00 (ISBN 0-686-57260-2, M-6571). French & Eur.

FRENCH LANGUAGE–DICTIONARIES–HEBREW

Cohn, M. M. Dictionnaire francais-hebreu. (Fr. & Heb.). 29.00 (ISBN 0-685-13874-7). Larousse.

Cohn, Marc M. Dictionnaire Francais-Hebreu. 760p. (Fr.-Heb.). 1966. 27.50 (ISBN 0-686-56955-5, M-6077). French & Eur.

--Nouveau Dictionnaire Hebreu-Francais. 792p. (Fr.-Heb.). 1974. 32.50 (ISBN 0-686-56956-3, M-6078). French & Eur.

Nouveau Dictionnaire francais-hebreu. 1973. 26.00 (ISBN 0-685-55772-3). Larousse.

Nouveau dictionnaire hebreu-francais. 1973. 39.25 (ISBN 0-685-55771-5). Larousse.

FRENCH LANGUAGE–DICTIONARIES–ITALIAN

Dictionnaire Garzanti Francais-Italien, Italien-Francais. 2046p. (Fr.-It.). 1969. 39.95 (ISBN 0-686-57110-X, M-6143). French & Eur.

Ghiotti, et al. Dictionnaire Italien-Francais, Francais-Italien de la Langue d'Aujourd'hui. (Fr.-It.). 1976. 27.50 (ISBN 0-686-57196-7, M-6270). French & Eur.

Larousse And Co. Interprete Larousse, francais-italien et italien-francais. (Fr. & It.). pap. 3.95 (ISBN 0-685-13947-6, 3787). Larousse.

--Larousse de poche, francais-italien et italien-francais. (Fr. & It.). pap. 5.98 (ISBN 0-685-13960-3, 1012). Larousse.

Padovani, G. & Silvestri, R. Dictionnaire bilingue Larousse, francais-italien et italien-francais. (Apollo). (Fr.). 10.50 (ISBN 0-685-13854-2, 3784). Larousse.

Rouede, Pierre & Rouede, Denise. Dictionnaire Italien-Francais et Francais-Italien. 1256p. (Fr.-It.). 1970. 25.00 (ISBN 0-686-57211-4, M-6493). French & Eur.

FRENCH LANGUAGE–DICTIONARIES–POLYGLOT

Renoux, Y. & Yates, J. Glossary of International Treaties. 1970. 29.50 (ISBN 0-444-40813-4). Elsevier.

Violette, Louis. Dictionnaire Samoa-Francais-Anglais et Francais-Samoa-Anglais. LC 75-35215. Repr. of 1879 ed. 44.50 (ISBN 0-404-14238-9). AMS Pr.

FRENCH LANGUAGE–DICTIONARIES–PORTUGUESE

Da Fonseca, F. Peixoto. Dictionnaire bilingue Larousse, francais-portugais et portugais-francais. (Apollo). (Fr. & Port.). 10.50 (ISBN 2-03-020909-0, 3791). Larousse.

Fournier, J. & Laborde, G. Le Mot et L'idee, Francais-Portugais, Portugais-Francais. 120p. (Fr.-Port.). 6.95 (ISBN 0-686-57185-1, M-6256). French & Eur.

FRENCH LANGUAGE–DICTIONARIES–PROVENCAL

Mistral, Frederic. Le Tresor de Felibridge: Dictionnaire Provencal-Francais, 2 vols. 2375p. (Fr.). Set. 195.00 (ISBN 0-686-56736-6, M-6414). French & Eur.

FRENCH LANGUAGE–DICTIONARIES–RUSSIAN

Dictionnaire bilingue francais-russe et russe-francais. 10.50 (ISBN 2-03-020904-X, 2715, Apollo). Larousse.

FRENCH LANGUAGE–DICTIONARIES–SPANISH

Alcala-Zamora. Alcala-Zamora, Diccionario Frances-Espanol, Espanol-Frances. 960p. (Espn. -Fr.). pap. 9.95 (ISBN 84-303-0094-5, S-50399). French & Eur.

--Alcala-Zamora, Diccionario Frances-Espanol, Espanol-Frances. 960p. (Espn. -Fr.). 12.25 (ISBN 84-303-0093-7, S-50400). French & Eur.

Amador, E. M. Martinez. Diccionario Frances-Espanol, Espanol-Frances. 1568p. (Espn. -Fr.). 1974. 47.95 (ISBN 84-303-0091-0, S-13282). French & Eur.

--Diccionario Manual Amador Frances-Espanol y Espanol-Frances. 944p. (Espn. -Fr.). 1975. 17.95 (ISBN 84-303-0100-3, S-50401). French & Eur.

Arimany Coma, Miguel. Diccionari Practic Catala-Frances. 2nd ed. 256p. (Cata. -Espn.). 1977. pap. 5.25 (ISBN 84-7211-048-6, S-50413). French & Eur.

Azkue, Resurreccion M. Diccionario Vasco-Espanol-Frances, 2 vols. (Espn., Vasco & Fr.). Set. leatherette 68.00 (ISBN 84-248-0015-X, S-12384). French & Eur.

Cuyas Armengol, Arturo. Diccionario De Bolsillo Frances-Espanol, Espagnol-Francais. 670p. (Espn. -Fr.). 1971. pap. 3.50 (ISBN 84-7183-048-5, S-50391). French & Eur.

--Diccionario Manual Frances-Espanol, Espagnol-Francais. 36th ed. 830p. (Espn. -Fr.). 1977. 5.95 (ISBN 84-7183-047-7, S-50390). French & Eur.

Denis, Serge & Maraval, Marcel. Dictionnaire Espagnol-Francais. 1774p. (Fr.-Eng.). 1968. pap. 26.50 (ISBN 0-686-56983-0, M-6110). French & Eur.

Denis, Serge, et al. Le Dictionnaire Espagnol-Francais et Francais-Espagnol. new ed. 904p. (Span.-Fr.). 1976. 36.95 (ISBN 0-686-56984-9, M-6111). French & Eur.

De Toro, M. & Gisbert. Dictionnaire bilingue Larousse, francais-espagnol, espanol-frances. (Apollo). (Fr. & Span.). 10.50 (ISBN 0-685-13857-7, 3774). Larousse.

Diccionario Cuyas: Spanish-French, French-Spanish. 5.50x (ISBN 0-686-00850-2). Colton Bk.

Diccionario Universal Herder Frances-Espanol, Espanol-Frances. 5th ed. 368p. (Fr. -Espn.). 1977. leatherette 4.50 (ISBN 84-254-0780-X, S-12394). French & Eur.

Diez Mateo, Felix & Hochleitner, Frida. Diccionario Manual Frances-Espanol, Espanol-Frances. 992p. (Espn. -Fr.). 1971. 9.95 (ISBN 84-239-4721-1, S-50389). French & Eur.

Garcia-Pelayo, R. & Testas, J. Dictionnaire moderne Larousse, francais-espagnol et espagnol-francais. (Span. & Fr.). 39.95 (ISBN 2-03-020601-6, 3773). Larousse.

Gimenez Sales, Miguel. Diccionario Espanol-Frances, Espagnol-Francais. 736p. (Espn. -Fr.). 1975. pap. 3.95 (ISBN 84-02-04265-1, S-50394). French & Eur.

Gimeno, E. Diccionario Lexicon Frances-Espanol, Espanol-Frances. 384p. (Fr. -Espn.). 1975. leatherette 3.75 (ISBN 84-303-0099-6, S-31393). French & Eur.

Haensch, Gunther. Diccionario Manual Herder Frances-Espanol, Espanol-Frances. 644p. (Espn. -Fr.). 1976. 16.75 (ISBN 84-254-1049-5, S-50392). French & Eur.

Larousse And Co. Interprete Larousse, French-Spanish & Spanish-French. (Fr. & Span.). pap. 3.95 (ISBN 0-685-13948-4, 3777). Larousse.

--Petit Dictionnaire bilingue Larousse, francais-espagnol, espanol-frances. (Adonis). (Fr & Span). plastic bdg. 5.95 (ISBN 0-685-14033-4, 3775). Larousse.

Salva, Vicente & Larrieu, Robert, eds. Dictionnaire Espagnol-Francais et Francais-Espagnol. 1580p. (Fr.-Span.). 1951. 22.50 (ISBN 0-686-57295-5, F-140811). French & Eur.

Seco. Manual de Gramatica Espanola. pap. 7.50 (ISBN 0-686-27679-5). Colton Bk.

Vox--Diccionario Abreviado Frances-Espanol, Espanol-Frances. 8th ed. 672p. (Fr. -Espn.). 1978. leatherette 7.25 (ISBN 84-7153-216-6, S-12414). French & Eur.
Vox--Diccionario Manual Frances-Espanol, Espanol-Frances. 7th ed. 922p. (Fr. -Espn.). 1979. leatherette 14.95 (ISBN 84-7153-186-0, S-12418). French & Eur.
Vox--Diccionario Superior Frances-Espanol, Espanol-Frances. 1224p. (Fr. -Espn.). 1977. leatherette 18.95 (ISBN 84-7153-187-9, S-31577). French & Eur.

FRENCH LANGUAGE–DICTIONARIES, JUVENILE

Didier, Marcel. Mes 10,000 Mots. (Fr.). (gr. 3-6). 1977. text ed. 14.95 (ISBN 0-8120-5207-2). Barron.
Eastman, Philip D. The Cat in the Hat Beginner Book Dictionary in French. (ps-2). 1965. (BYR); PLB 8.99 (ISBN 0-394-91063-X). Random.
Lamblin, Simone. Le Larousse des enfants. (Illus., Fr.). (gr. 3 up). 1979. 33.75 (ISBN 2-03-051421-7). Larousse.
Mon Grand Dictionnaire Francais-Anglais. 13.50 (ISBN 0-685-11402-3). French & Eur.

FRENCH LANGUAGE–ETYMOLOGY

Bloch & Von Wartburg. Dictionnaire Etymologique De la Langue Francaise. 65.00 (ISBN 0-685-36657-X). French & Eur.
Bloch, Oscar & Wartburg, Walther Von. Dictionnaire Etymologique de la Langue Francaise. 6th ed. 684p. (Fr.). 1975. 62.50 (ISBN 0-686-57293-9, C-1016). French & Eur.
Dauzat, A., et al. Nouveau Dictionnaire etymologique. (Fr). 27.50 (ISBN 2-03-020210-X, 3612). Larousse.
Dauzat, Albert. Nouveau Dictionnaire Etymologique. 6th ed. 856p. (Fr.). 1971. 23.50 (ISBN 0-686-57269-6, F-135950). French & Eur.
Dubois, Jean. Vocabulaire politique et social en France de 1869 a 1872. (Fr). pap. 11.95x (ISBN 0-685-14095-4). Larousse.
Fortrin, David. Evolution Du Langage Agricole Franco-Canadien. (Fr). 1968. pap. 7.50x (ISBN 2-7637-6354-5, Pub. by Laval). Intl Schol Bk Serv.
Jenkins, Thomas A. Word-Studies in French & English, 1st Ser. 1933. pap. 6.00 (ISBN 0-527-00818-4). Kraus Repr.
Losique, Serge. Dictionnaire Etymologique des Noms de Pays et de Peuples. 243p. (Fr.). 1971. pap. 22.50 (ISBN 0-686-57294-7, F-35990). French & Eur.

FRENCH LANGUAGE–EXAMINATIONS, QUESTIONS, ETC.

Cabat, Louis, et al. Barron's How to Prepare for the College Board Achievement Tests - French. LC 75-151972. (gr. 11-12). 1971. pap. 3.95 (ISBN 0-8120-0068-4). Barron.
Frizzle, Arnold L. Study of Some of the Influences of Regents Requirements & Examinations in French. LC 70-176789. (Columbia University. Teachers College. Contributions to Education: No. 964). Repr. of 1950 ed. 17.50 (ISBN 0-404-55964-6). AMS Pr.
Kendris, Christopher & Newmark, Maxim, eds. Barron's Regents Exams & Answers French Level 3 (Comprehensive French) rev ed. 250p. (gr. 9-12). 1981. pap. 3.50 (ISBN 0-8120-0198-2). Barron.
Kretschmer, F. A. Graduate School Foreign Language Test: French. 3rd ed. (Orig.). 1971. lib. bdg. 5.50 (ISBN 0-668-01578-0); pap. 4.95 (ISBN 0-668-01461-X). Arco.
Rudman, Jack. French. (National Teachers Examination Ser.: NT-19). (Cloth bdg. avail. on request). pap. 9.95 (ISBN 0-8373-8429-X). Natl Learning.
--French. (Graduate Record Examination Ser.: GRE-6). (Cloth bdg. avail. on request). 9.95 (ISBN 0-8373-5206-1). Natl Learning.
--French. (College Level Examination Ser.: CLEP-44). 1976. 14.95 (ISBN 0-8373-5394-7); pap. 9.95 (ISBN 0-8373-5344-0). Natl Learning.
--French - Jr. H.S. (Teachers License Examination Ser.: T-20). (Cloth bdg. avail. on request). pap. 10.00 (ISBN 0-8373-8020-0). Natl Learning.
--French - Sr. H.S. (Teachers License Examination Ser.: T-21). (Cloth bdg. avail. on request). pap. 10.00 (ISBN 0-8373-8021-9). Natl Learning.
--Graduate School Foreign Language Test (GSFLT) French. (Admission Test Ser.: ATS-28A). (Cloth bdg. avail. on request). pap. 9.95 (ISBN 0-685-60572-8). Natl Learning.
Warner, et al. Barron's How to Prepare for the College Board Achievement Tests - French. 3rd ed. 1981. pap. 7.95 (ISBN 0-8120-0941-X). Barron.
Warner, Pearl. Barron's How to Prepare for the College Board Achievement Tests -- French. rev. ed. LC 75-151972. (gr. 11-12). 1981. pap. text ed. 7.95 (ISBN 0-8120-0941-X). Barron.

FRENCH LANGUAGE–GLOSSARIES, VOCABULARIES, ETC.

Byrne, L. S. & Churchill, E. L. A Comprehensive French Grammar: With Classified Vocabularies. 515p. (Orig.). 1980. pap. 15.95x (ISBN 0-631-12594-9, Pub. by Basil Blackwell England). Biblio Dist.
Dunn, Oscar. Glossaire Franco-Canadian. (Langue Francaise Au Quebec 3e Section: Lexicologie et Lexicographie 4). 1978. Repr. of 1880 ed. 12.00x (ISBN 2-7637-6779-6, Pub. by Laval). Intl Schol Bk Serv.
Holmes, Urban T. & Scholberg, Kenneth R., eds. French & Provencal Lexicography. LC 64-17108. 1964. 7.50 (ISBN 0-8142-0064-8). Ohio St U Pr.
Juilland, Alphonse. Dictionnaire Inverse De la Langue Francaise. (Janua Linguarum, Ser. Practica: No. 7). 1965. text ed. 101.25x (ISBN 90-2790-626-2). Mouton.
Keeler, Sr. Mary J. Etude sur la poesie et sur le vocabulaire de Loys Papon. LC 75-94199. (Catholic University of America. Studies in Romance Languages & Literatures: No. 3). 16.00 (ISBN 0-404-50303-9). AMS Pr.
Roepke, F. Franzosisch - Deutsches Glossarium. 540p. (Ger. & Fr.). 1964. 36.00 (ISBN 3-7819-2007-0, M-7413, Pub. by Fritz Knapp Verlag). French & Eur.

FRENCH LANGUAGE–GRAMMAR

Atkinson, James C. The Two Forms of Subject Inversion in Modern French. (Janua Linguarum Ser. Practica: No. 168). 1973. pap. text ed. 18.25x (ISBN 90-2792-481-3). Mouton.
Balas, Robert S. & Rice, Donald. Qu'est-Ce Qui Se Passe? Conversation--Revision De Grammaire. (Illus.). 1979. pap. text ed. 11.95 (ISBN 0-528-64030-5); instructor's manual free (ISBN 0-528-64031-3); wkbk. 6.50 (ISBN 0-528-64032-1); tape set 150.00x (ISBN 0-528-64033-X); sample tape free (ISBN 0-528-64034-8). Rand.
Barton, Francis B. & Sirich, Edward H. Simplified French Review: Grammar & Composition. 1941. 10.95x (ISBN 0-89197-409-1); pap. text ed. 4.95x (ISBN 0-89197-410-5). Irvington.
Benamou, Michael & Ionesco, Eugene. Mise En Train: Premiere Annee De Francais. (gr. 11-12). 1969. text ed. 19.95 (ISBN 0-02-307970-3); wkbk. 5.95 (ISBN 0-02-307980-0). Macmillan.
Benamou, Michel & Carduner, Jean. Le Moulin a paroles. 2nd ed. LC 71-126958. (Illus.). 336p. (Fr.). 1971. pap. text ed. 10.95 (ISBN 0-471-06450-5); tapes avail. (ISBN 0-471-00024-8). Wiley.
Betourne, Henriette D., et al. Direct French Conversation, 2 Bks. (Orig., Fr.). (YA) (gr. 9 up). 1966. Bk. 1. pap. text ed. 2.75 (ISBN 0-88345-040-2, 17470); Bk. 2. pap. text ed. 2.75 (ISBN 0-88345-041-0, 17471). Regents Pub.
Blume, Eli. Cours superieur de francais. (Orig.). (gr. 11-12). 1970. pap. text ed. 5.75 (ISBN 0-87720-460-8); wkbk. 6.75 (ISBN 0-87720-462-4). AMSCO Sch.
Brichant, Collette. French Grammar: The Key to Reading. (Orig.). 1968. pap. text ed. 9.95 (ISBN 0-13-331264-X). P-H.
Brown, Thomas H. French: Listening, Speaking, Reading, Writing. 3rd ed. (Illus., Fr.). 1977. text ed. 16.95 (ISBN 0-07-008396-7, C); instructor's manual 4.50 (ISBN 0-07-008397-5); cahier d'exercises 5.95 (ISBN 0-07-008398-3); tapes 325.00 (ISBN 0-07-008399-1). McGraw.
--Langue et Litterature: A Second Course in French. 2nd ed. (Illus.). 448p. 1974. text ed. 18.00x (ISBN 0-07-008400-9, C); instructor's manual 3.95 (ISBN 0-07-008401-7); 6.50x (ISBN 0-07-008402-5). McGraw.
Bryan, Anne M. & Hull, Alexander. Situations: Une Grammaire Pour Aujourd'hui. 288p. 1973. pap. text ed. 10.95 (ISBN 0-13-810697-5); tapes 79.00 (ISBN 0-13-810705-X). P-H.
Buffier. Grammaire Francaise sur un Plan Nouveau. (Linguistics 13th-18th Centuries Ser.). 494p. (Fr.). 1974. Repr. of 1709 ed. lib. bdg. 123.50 (ISBN 0-8287-0149-0, 71-5030). Clearwater Pub.
--Suite de la Grammaire Francaise sur un Plan Nouveau. (Linguistics 13th-18th Centuries Ser.). 608p. (Fr.). 1974. Repr. of 1728 ed. lib. bdg. 148.00x (ISBN 0-8287-0150-4, 71-5031). Clearwater Pub.
Bullock, Hazel J. Grammaire Francaise: Methode Orale. 1949. 22.50x (ISBN 0-89197-493-8); pap. text ed. 12.50x (ISBN 0-89197-775-9). Irvington.
Butturff, Diane & Coffman, Mary. French: Language & Life Styles. new ed. (Illus.). 512p. 1975. text ed. 15.95 (ISBN 0-07-009455-1, C); instructor's manual 3.95 (ISBN 0-07-009456-X); cahier d'exercises 5.95 (ISBN 0-07-009457-8). McGraw.
Byrne, L. S. & Churchill, E. L. A Comprehensive French Grammar: With Classified Vocabularies. 515p. (Orig.). 1980. pap. 15.95x (ISBN 0-631-12594-9, Pub. by Basil Blackwell England). Biblio Dist.
Cadoux, Remunda. Invitation Au Francais: Vous et Moi, Level One. 1970. 8.20 (ISBN 0-02-268500-6). Macmillan.
Carlut, Charles & Meiden, Walter. French for Oral & Written Review. 2nd ed. LC 75-20021. 1976. pap. text ed. 14.95 (ISBN 0-03-089726-2, HoltC); practice manual 7.50 (ISBN 0-03-089803-X); tapes 400.00 (ISBN 0-03-017436-8). HR&W.
Coffman, Mary. Schaum's Outline of French Grammar. (Schaum's Outline Ser.). 288p. 1980. pap. 4.95 (ISBN 0-07-011553-2, SP). McGraw.
Coffman, Mary E. French Grammar. (Schaum Outline Ser.). 1973. 3.95 (ISBN 0-07-011552-4, SP). McGraw.
Colbert, Roman. Brief French Reference Grammar. 1972. pap. text ed. 10.95x (ISBN 0-442-21615-7). Van Nos Reinhold.
Comeau, Raymond F., et al. Ensemble: Grammaire. LC 76-49636. 1977. pap. text ed. 12.95 (ISBN 0-03-018256-5, HoltC). HR&W.
Cremona, J. A. Barron's Card Guide to French Grammar. 1963. pap. text ed. 1.75 (ISBN 0-8120-5042-8). Barron.
Darbelnet, John. Pensee & Structure. 2nd ed. LC 68-19906. (Fr). 1977. text ed. 11.95x (ISBN 0-684-14882-X, ScribC); wkbk. 7.95x (ISBN 0-684-15932-5, ScribC); wkbk. 5.95 (ISBN 0-684-15091-3, ScribC). Scribner.
Daudon, Rene. French in Review. 2nd ed. 1962. text ed. 12.95 (ISBN 0-15-528850-4, HC); tapes, 10 reels 125.00 (ISBN 0-15-528851-2, HC). HarBraceJ.
Donahue-Gaudet. Le Vocalisme et le Consonantisme Francais. 14.95 (ISBN 0-685-36654-5). French & Eur.
Donaldson, Weber D. French Reflexive Verbs: A Case Grammar Description. (Janua Linguarum Ser. Practica: No. 194). 1973. pap. text ed. 32.50x (ISBN 90-2792-503-8). Mouton.
Donaldson-Evans, Lancelot K. Love's Fatal Glance: A Study of Eye Imagery in the Poets of the Ecole lyonnaise. LC 80-10415. (Romance Monographs: No. 39). 155p. 1980. 16.00 (ISBN 84-499-3694-2). Romance.
Dubois, Jean. Grammaire de base. new ed. (Orig., Fr.). 1976. pap. 7.25 (ISBN 2-03-040166-8). Larousse.
--Grammaire structurale du francais, 3 vols. Incl. Vol. 1. Nom et pronom. 192p (3630); Vol. 2. Verbe. 192p (3631); Vol. 3. Phrase et transformations. 180p (3632). (Fr.). pap. 14.50 ea. Larousse.
Duff, Charles. The Basis & Essentials of French. (Quality Paperback: No. 247). 122p. (Orig.). 1972. pap. 1.75 (ISBN 0-8226-0247-4). Littlefield.
--French for Beginners. 1955. pap. 3.95 (ISBN 0-06-463252-0, EH 252, EH). Har-Row.
Dumont, Francis M. French Grammar. 2nd ed. 1969. pap. 3.95 (ISBN 0-06-460035-1, CO 35, COS). Har-Row.
Du Terme, Laurence. The Flower De Luce Planted in England, Wherein Is Contained the Pronuntiation & Understanding of the French Tongue. LC 72-5977. (English Experience Ser.: No. 505). 68p. 1973. Repr. of 1619 ed. 6.00 (ISBN 90-221-0505-9). Walter J Johnson.
Etude de l'expression francaise: Cours elementaire I - le francais. (Illus., Fr.). 1969. 7.25 (ISBN 0-685-13911-5, 4019). Larousse.
French in Twenty Lessons. rev. ed. (Cortina Method Language Ser). (Illus.). 6.95 (ISBN 0-385-00070-7). Doubleday.
Gendron, Jean D. Phonetique Orthophonique a l'Usage Des Canadiens Francais. 2nd ed. (Fr). 1968. pap. 7.95x (ISBN 2-7637-6171-2, Pub. by Laval). Intl Schol Bk Serv.
Glossaire Du Parler Francais Au Canada. (Fr). 1968. 22.50x (ISBN 2-7637-6414-2, Pub. by Laval). Intl Schol Bk Serv.
Grevisse. Le Bon Usage: Grammaire Francaise. 29.95 (ISBN 0-685-36692-8). French & Eur.
Grevisse, M. Le Bon Usage. (Fr). 59.95 (ISBN 0-685-20226-7). Schoenhof.
--Nouveaux Exercices Francais. (gr. 10-12). text ed. 11.95 (ISBN 0-685-36072-5); tchrs. manual 13.95 (ISBN 0-685-36073-3). French & Eur.
--Precis de Grammaire Francaise. (gr. 10-12). text ed. 11.25 (ISBN 0-685-36074-1). French & Eur.
Gross, Maurice. Grammaire transformationelle du francais: Syntaxe du nom. 1978. pap. text ed. 20.95 (ISBN 2-03-070343-5, 3633). Larousse.
Harmer, Lewis. Uncertainties in French Grammar. Rickard, P. & Combe, G. S., eds. LC 78-58793. 1980. 80.00 (ISBN 0-521-22233-8). Cambridge U Pr.
Harris, J. & Leveque. Basic Conversational French. 6th ed. LC 77-112964. 1978. text ed. 19.95 (ISBN 0-03-022735-6, HoltC). HR&W.
Heise, Edward T. & Muller, Rene F. Conversational Introduction to French. 2nd ed. 1967. text ed. 17.50 scp (ISBN 0-06-042748-5, HarpC); scp tapes 180.00 (ISBN 0-06-042747-7). Har-Row.
Hoffman, Leon-Francois. La Pratique du Francais Parle. LC 72-7530. 93p. 1973. pap. text ed. 6.50 (ISBN 0-684-13208-7); cassettes 4.95 (ISBN 0-684-13696-1). Scribner.
Hoffmann, Leon-Francois. L' Essential de la Grammaire Francaise. 2nd ed. (Fr). (gr. 11 up). 1973. pap. text ed. 10.95x (ISBN 0-684-13086-6, ScribC). Scribner.
Keating, L. Clark. Carnet de Voyage. LC 59-6575. (Illus., Fr.). 1959. text ed. 12.95x (ISBN 0-89197-691-4); pap. text ed. 6.95x (ISBN 0-89197-692-2). Irvington.
Langellier, Alice, et al. Chez Les Francais. (Secondary French Ser: Level 2). (Follows Ecouter et Parler or Deuxieme Etape). (gr. 7-12). 1969. text ed. 13.32 (ISBN 0-03-080350-0, HoltC); tchrs' ed 13.60 (ISBN 0-03-080355-1); wkbk. 2.80 (ISBN 0-685-12191-7); photos 24.00 (ISBN 0-685-12192-5); tests 0.80 (ISBN 0-685-12193-3); records 11.04 (ISBN 0-685-12194-1); tapes 7.5 or 3.75 ips s.p. 110.00 ea. HR&W.
Larousse & Co. Grammaire Larousse du francais contemporain. (Fr). 18.00 (ISBN 2-03-070031-2, 3746). Larousse.
Lassere. Est Ce "a" ou "de", 2 vols. text ed. 5.50 vol 1 repertoire (ISBN 0-685-36075-X); text ed. 5.50 vol 2 exercices (ISBN 0-685-36076-8). French & Eur.
Lenard, Yvone. Jeunes Voix, Jeunes Visages. (Verbal-Active French Ser.). text ed. 12.76 (ISBN 0-06-582100-9, SchDept); tchr's ed 22.32 (ISBN 0-06-582204-8); wkbk 4.00 (ISBN 0-06-582300-1); tests 3.56 (ISBN 0-06-582602-7); tchrs.' tests 3.56 (ISBN 0-06-582700-7); tapes 252.84 (ISBN 0-06-582801-1); study prints 48.08 (ISBN 0-06-582800-3). Har-Row.
--Tresors Du Temps. (Verbal-Active French Ser.). text ed. 15.68 (ISBN 0-06-582102-5, SchDept); tchr's. ed. 12.36 (ISBN 0-06-582206-4). Har-Row.
Levitt, Jesse. Grammaire Des Grammaires of Girault-Duvivier: A Study of Nineteen Century French. (Janua Linguarum Ser. Major: No. 19). 1968. text ed. 64.00x (ISBN 90-2790-611-4). Mouton.
Linaberry, Paul & Meras, Edmond A. French Reference Grammar & Review Composition. 1963. 8.95x (ISBN 0-913298-28-X). S F Vanni.
Luker, Benjamin F. Use of the Infinitive Instead of a Finite Verb in French. LC 16-16932. (Columbia University. Studies in Romance Philology & Literature: No. 18). Repr. of 1916 ed. 14.50 (ISBN 0-404-50618-6). AMS Pr.
Madrigal, Magarita & Launay, Pierre. Invitation to French. new ed. 1961. pap. 3.95 (ISBN 0-671-21030-0, Fireside). S&S.
Madrigal, Margarita & Dulac, Colette. Madrigal's Magic Key to French. LC 58-11321. 1958. 12.95 (ISBN 0-385-05120-4). Doubleday.
Malecot, Andre. Fundamental French: Language & Culture. LC 63-10567. (Illus.). 1963. 18.50x (ISBN 0-89197-184-X); pap. text ed. 8.95x (ISBN 0-89197-766-X). Irvington.
Mansion, J. E., ed. Harrap's a Grammar of Present Day French. 2nd ed. Date not set. pap. text ed. 3.95 (ISBN 0-684-15539-7, ScribT). Scribner.
Mansion, Jean E. French Reference Grammar for Schools & Colleges. LC 72-98855. 1971. Repr. of 1928 ed. lib. bdg. 15.00 (ISBN 0-8371-3125-1, MAFG). Greenwood.
Mauger. Grammaire Pratique du Francais d Aujourd Hui, Lanque Parlee, Laugue Ecrite. (Coll. F). 12.95 (ISBN 0-685-36653-7). French & Eur.
Metz, Mary. Reflets Du Monde Francais. (Level 3). (gr. 9-12). 1971. text ed. 14.95 (ISBN 0-07-041718-0, C); inst. manual 14.95 (ISBN 0-07-041722-9); wkbk 5.95 (ISBN 0-07-041719-9). McGraw.
Metz, Mary S. Reflets Du Monde Francais. 2nd ed. 1978. text ed. 15.50 (ISBN 0-07-041791-1, C). McGraw.
Micks, Wilson. Review of Basic French. (Orig.). (YA) (gr. 9 up). 1960. pap. 4.95x (ISBN 0-19-500986-X). Oxford U Pr.
Mondelli, Rudolph J. & Francois, Pierre. French Conversational Review Grammar. 3rd ed. (Fr). 1972. pap. text ed. 15.95x (ISBN 0-442-23762-6); tapes 125.00 (ISBN 0-442-23763-4). Van Nos Reinhold.
Moody, Marvin D. The Interior Article in De-Compounds in French: Agent De Police Versus Agent De la Police. LC 79-5432. 1980. pap. text ed. 6.00 (ISBN 0-8191-0881-2). U Pr of Amer.
Mueller, Theodore & Niedzielski, Henri. Basic French. Incl. Premiers Pas. pap. text ed. 4.40x (ISBN 0-89197-670-1); Pratique de la grammaire. pap. text ed. 8.20x (ISBN 0-89197-671-X); Introduction a la culture. pap. text ed. 3.10x (ISBN 0-89197-672-8). (Fr.). 1974. Set. pap. text ed. 15.70x (ISBN 0-89197-673-6); tchr's manual avail. (ISBN 0-685-77774-X); Set. 29 audio tapes 232.00x (ISBN 0-8290-0141-7). Irvington.

Nachtmann, Francis W. French Review for Reading Improvement. (Orig.). 1966. pap. text ed. 9.95 (ISBN 0-02-385940-7). Macmillan.
Nebel, Cecile & Fales, Frederick F. French Grammar. (College Outlines Ser.). pap. 4.95 (ISBN 0-671-08032-6). Monarch Pr.
O'Brien, Katherine L., et al. Advanced French. 365p. 1965. 19.50x (ISBN 0-471-00400-6). Wiley.
Okin, Josee & Schmitt, Conrad J. Francais: Commencons. 1970. text ed. 11.60 (ISBN 0-07-047500-8, W); tchr's. ed. 10.96 (ISBN 0-07-047501-6). tapes 360.00 (ISBN 0-07-047503-2); tests 72.00 (ISBN 0-07-047505-9); Webster master replacements 36.00 (ISBN 0-07-047506-7); filmstrips 80.00 (ISBN 0-07-047504-0). McGraw.
--Francais: Continuons. (gr. 8-10). 1970. text ed. 11.60 (ISBN 0-07-047515-6, W); tchr's. ed. 11.96 (ISBN 0-07-047516-4); wkbk. 4.40 (ISBN 0-07-047517-2); tests 72.00 (ISBN 0-07-047520-2); test replacements 36.00 (ISBN 0-07-047521-0); filmstrips 80.00 (ISBN 0-07-047519-9); tapes 346.64 (ISBN 0-07-047518-0). McGraw.
Ollivier, Jacqueline. Grammaire Francaise. (Fr.). 1978. pap. text ed. 11.95 (ISBN 0-15-529675-2, HC). HarBraceJ.
Ostyn, Paul & Le Texier, Bernard. Fluent Spoken French. 1974. text ed. 20.50 scp (ISBN 0-06-044945-4, HarpC); instructor's manual free (ISBN 0-06-364946-2); scp wkbk. o.p. 7.50 (ISBN 0-06-044946-2); scp tapes 260.00 (ISBN 0-06-047466-1). Har-Row.
Ostyn, Paul & Melka-Teichroew, Francine. La France Vous Parle. 314p. 1981. text ed. 15.50 scp (ISBN 0-06-044947-0, HarpC). Har-Row.
Owens, John H. French for Freshman, 3 Vols. rev. ed. 1960. Vol. 1. pap. 4.75 (ISBN 0-87506-014-5); Vol. 2. pap. 7.00 (ISBN 0-87506-015-3); Vol. 3. pap. 5.75 (ISBN 0-87506-016-1). Campus.
Palmeri, Joseph. Conversational & Cultural French. (Fr.). 1966. text ed. 15.95 (ISBN 0-13-171900-9). P-H.
Patterson, W. R. Colloquial French. 16th ed. (Tribner's Colloquial Manuals). 1950. pap. 4.95 (ISBN 0-7100-6384-9). Routledge & Kegan.
Politzer, Robert, et al. La France: Une Tapisserie. 2nd ed. (Illus.). 496p. 1972. text ed. 16.80 (ISBN 0-07-050384-2, W); instructor's manual 2.20 (ISBN 0-07-050385-0); tapes 348.00 (ISBN 0-07-097890-5); tests 60.00 (ISBN 0-07-050387-7). McGraw.
Politzer, Robert L. & Hagiwara, Michio P. Active Review of French: Selected Patterns, Vocabulary & Pronunciation Problems for Speakers of English. LC 63-155633. 1963. pap. 16.95 (ISBN 0-471-00438-3); tapes avail. (ISBN 0-471-00439-1). Wiley.
Purkis, Helen M. French Course for West Africa, 4 bks. 1962-65. Bk. 1. text ed. 5.95x (ISBN 0-521-06009-5); Bk. 2. text ed. 5.95x (ISBN 0-521-06010-9); Bk. 3. text ed. 5.95x (ISBN 0-521-06011-7); Bk. 4. text ed. 5.95x (ISBN 0-521-06012-5). Cambridge U Pr.
Ranieri, Helene. Let's "Unhook" the French Verbs & Seventy Seven Quick Grammar, Syntax & Pronunciaton "Tips". 1978. 10.50 (ISBN 0-686-24058-8). APSA.
Resnick, Seymore. Essential French Grammar. LC 63-1378. 1965. lib. bdg. 9.50x (ISBN 0-88307-575-X). Gannon.
Resnick, Seymour. Essential French Grammar. (Orig.). 1963. pap. 2.00 (ISBN 0-486-20419-7). Dover.
Richardson, Henry B. Outline of French Grammar with Vocabularies. rev. ed. 1950. text ed. 12.50x (ISBN 0-89197-327-3); pap. text ed. 4.95x (ISBN 0-89197-328-1). Irvington.
Ryding, William W. Petite Revision de Grammaire Francaise. 247p. 1975. text ed. 16.95 scp (ISBN 0-06-045686-8, HarpC). Har-Row.
Salkoff, Morris. Analyse Syntaxique Du Francais-Grammaire En Chaine. 1980. 28.00 (ISBN 90-272-3111-7, LIS 2). Benjamins North Am.
Waldinger, Renee & Corbiere-Gille, Gisele. Promenades. Litteraires & Grammaticales. 1966. text ed. 12.95x (ISBN 0-669-28662-1); tapes. 6 reels o. p. 30.00 (ISBN 0-669-33977-6). Heath.
Waugh, Linda R. A Semantic Analysis of Word Order: Position of the Adjective in French. (Cornell Linguistic Contributions Ser.: No. 1). 1977. text ed. 29.00x (ISBN 90-04-04572-4). Humanities.

FRENCH LANGUAGE-GRAMMAR, COMPARATIVE

Heatwole, O. W. A Comparative Practical Grammar of French, Spanish & Italian. 1977. 8.95x (ISBN 0-913298-39-5); pap. 6.50 (ISBN 0-913298-26-3). S F Vanni.
Notley, Edwin A. A Comparative Grammar of the French, Italian, Spanish & Portuguese Languages. 1977. lib. bdg. 69.95 (ISBN 0-8490-1652-5). Gordon Pr.

FRENCH LANGUAGE-GRAMMAR, GENERATIVE

Gross, M. Grammaire transformationelle du francais: Syntaxe du verbe. (Fr). pap. 14.50 (ISBN 0-685-13931-X). Larousse.

FRENCH LANGUAGE-GRAMMAR, HISTORICAL

Arnauld, Antoine & Lancelot, Claude. General & Rational Grammar: The Port-Royal Grammar. Rieux, Jacques & Rollin, Bernard E., eds. LC 74-84245. (Janua Linguarum, Series Minor: No. 208). 197p. 1975. pap. text ed. 34.10x (ISBN 90-2793-004-X). Mouton.
Price, Glanville. The French Language: Present & Past. 302p. 1971. pap. 17.50x (ISBN 0-8448-0035-X). Crane-Russak Co.

FRENCH LANGUAGE-HISTORY

Bibbesworth, Walter De. Le Traite De Walter De Bibbesworth Sur la Langue Francaise, Quatorzieme Siecle. (Linguistics, 13th-18th Centuries Ser.). 203p. (Fr.). 1974. Repr. of 1929 ed. lib. bdg. 58.00x (ISBN 0-8287-0088-5, 71-5001). Clearwater Pub.
Brunot. Histoire de la Langue Francaise des Origines a nos Jours, 13 tomes. Incl. Tome I. De L'epoque Latine a la Renaissance. 29.95 (ISBN 0-685-36636-7); Tome II. Le XVIe Siecle. 25.50 (ISBN 0-685-36637-5); Tome III. La Formation de la langue classique, 2 pts. Set. 59.95 (ISBN 0-685-36638-3); Tome IV. La Langue Classique (1660-1715, 2 pts. Set. 59.95 (ISBN 0-685-36639-1); Tome V. Le Francais en France et hors De France au XVIIe Siecle. 29.95 (ISBN 0-685-36640-5); Tome VI. Le XVIIIe Siecles, 4 pts. Set. 118.95 (ISBN 0-685-36641-3); Tome VII. La Propagation du Francais en France jusqu'a la Fin de L'ancien Regime. 29.95 (ISBN 0-685-36642-1); Tome VIII. Le Francais hors de France au XVIIIe Siecle, 3 pts. en 2 pts. Set. 59.95 (ISBN 0-685-36643-X); Tome IX. La Revolution et l'Empire, 2 pts. Set. 59.95 (ISBN 0-685-36644-8); Tome X. La Langue Classique dans la Tourmente, 2 pts. Set. 59.95 (ISBN 0-685-36645-6); Tome XI. Le Francais au-dehors sous la Revolution, le Consulat et l'Empire. 29.95 (ISBN 0-685-36646-4); Tome XII. L'Epoque Romantique. Bruneau. 29.95 (ISBN 0-685-36647-2); Tome XIII. L'Epoque Realiste. Bruneau. 59.95 (ISBN 0-685-36648-0). French & Eur.
Brunot, Ferdinand. Histoire de la Langue Francaise des Origines a Nos Jours, 13 vols. in 22 pts. Repr. of 1972 ed. Set. per pt. 26.50 (ISBN 0-686-57670-5). Adler.
Catach. L' Orthographe Francaise a L'epoque de la Renaissance. (Publ. Romanes et Franc.). 72.00 (ISBN 0-685-36649-9). French & Eur.
Combe, T. G. & Rickard, P. French Language: History, Practice, & Stylistics. 1970. 14.95x (ISBN 0-245-59995-9). Intl Ideas.
Du Bellay, Joachim. Defense et illustration de langue francaise. (Documentation thematique). 2.95 (ISBN 0-685-36191-8, 101). Larousse.
Dubois, Jean. Vocabulaire politique et social en France de 1869 a 1872. (Fr). pap. 11.95x (ISBN 0-685-14095-4). Larousse.
Duron, J. Langue francaise, langue humaine. (Langue Vivante Ser). (Fr). pap. 8.25 (ISBN 0-685-13956-5, 3626). Larousse.
Hugo, V. Choix De Poems. Gaudon, J., ed. 214p. 1957. 10.00x (ISBN 0-7190-0146-3, Pub. by Manchester U Pr England). State Mutual Bk.
Lemieux, Germain. Placide-Eustache: Sources et Parallelles Du Conte-Type 938. (Les Archives De Folklore Ser.: No. 10). (Illus.). 214p. 1970. pap. 9.50x (ISBN 2-7637-6383-9, Pub by Laval). Intl Schol Bk Serv.
Mackenzie, Fraser, et al, eds. Studies in French Language Literature & History. 258p. 1980. Repr. of 1949 ed. lib. bdg. 50.00 (ISBN 0-89760-736-8). Telegraph Bks.
Mauger. Cours de Langue et de Civilisation Francaise a L'usage des Etrangers, 4 tomes. Incl. Tome 1. 6.25 (ISBN 0-685-36693-6); Tome II. 6.25 (ISBN 0-685-36694-4); Tome III. 7.50 (ISBN 0-685-36695-2); Tome IV. 8.95 (ISBN 0-685-36696-0). French & Eur.
Les Plus Anciens Monuments de la Langue Francaise. (Societe des Anciens Textes Francais). 67.50 (ISBN 0-685-34016-3). French & Eur.
Pope, M. K. From Latin to Modern French. 600p. 35.00x (ISBN 0-7190-0176-5, Pub. by Manchester U Pr England). State Mutual Bk.
Rickard, P., ed. Chrestomathie de la Langue Francaise au Quinzieme Siecle. LC 74-12976. 464p. 1976. 115.00 (ISBN 0-521-20685-5). Cambridge U Pr.
Rickard, Peter. A History of the French Language. 1978. 13.95x (ISBN 0-09-118740-0, Pub by Hutchinson); pap. 6.95x (ISBN 0-09-118741-9). Merrimack Bk Serv.
--A History of the French Language. (Modern Languages Ser). 174p. 1974. (Hutchinson U Lib); pap. text ed. 9.25x (ISBN 0-09-118741-9). Humanities.
Von Wartburg, Walter. Evolution et Structure De la Langue Francaise. 22.50 (ISBN 3-7720-0013-4). Adler.

FRENCH LANGUAGE-IDIOMS, CORRECTIONS, ERRORS

Denoeu, Francois & Sices, David. Two Thousand & One French & English Idioms: Idiotismes Francais et Anglais 2001. 1982. pap. text ed. 7.50 (ISBN 0-8120-0435-3). Barron.
Gerber, Barbara & Storzer, Gerald. French Idioms on the Way. (Illus.). 1982. pap. 4.95 (ISBN 0-8120-2108-8). Barron.
Gerber, Barbara L. & Storzer, Gerald H. Dictionary of Modern French Idioms, 2 vols. LC 76-24743. (Reference Library of the Humanities Ser.: Vol. 63). 1977. Set. lib. bdg. 110.00 (ISBN 0-8240-9935-4). Garland Pub.
Kelly, Reine C. Expressions Idiomatiques en Francais Vivant. 192p. 1974. pap. text ed. 10.95 (ISBN 0-15-526450-8, HC). HarBraceJ.
Kettridge, J. O. French Idioms & Figurative Phrases. pap. 7.50 (ISBN 0-87557-024-0, 024-0). Saphrograph.
Miller, J. Dale & Essig, Kaylinda B. Seven Hundred French Idioms. LC 75-28039. (Illus.). 266p. 1976. pap. 7.95 (ISBN 0-8425-0085-5). Brigham.
Resnick, Seymour & Kurz, Doriane. Embarrassing Moments in French & How to Avoid Them. LC 53-9731. (gr. 11-12). 1953. text ed. 6.50 (ISBN 0-8044-0469-0); pap. 3.95 (ISBN 0-8044-6706-4). Ungar.
Thomas, A. V. Dictionnaire des difficultes de la langue francaise. (Fr). 23.50 (ISBN 0-685-13865-8, 3611). Larousse.

FRENCH LANGUAGE-LEXICOGRAPHY

Matore, G. Histoire des dictionnaires francais. (Langue Vivante Ser). (Fr). pap. 11.95 (ISBN 0-685-13937-9, 3625). Larousse.
Sauvageot, A. Portrait du vocabulaire francais. (Langue vivante). (Fr). pap. 8.25 (ISBN 0-685-14055-5, 3627). Larousse.
Vincent, Leon H The French Academy. 1974. Repr. of 1901 ed. lib. bdg. 20.00 (ISBN 0-8414-9198-4). Folcroft.
Wooldridge, Terence R. Les Debuts De la Lexicographie Francaise: Estienne, Nicot et 'le Thresor De la Langue Francoyse' (1606) LC 77-3960. (Romance Ser). 1977. 37.50x (ISBN 0-8020-5392-0). U of Toronto Pr.

FRENCH LANGUAGE-MORPHOLOGY

Gertner, Michael H. The Morphology of the Modern French Verb. (Janua Linguarum Ser. Practica: No. 204). 1973. pap. 29.00x (ISBN 90-2792-504-6). Mouton.
Giraud, J. & Pamart, J. Riverain. Les Nouveaux mots dans le vent. 271p. (Fr.). 1974. pap. 11.95 (ISBN 2-03-070334-6, 2717). Larousse.
Tranel, Bernard. Concreteness in Generative Phonology: Evidence from French. LC 80-51243. 400p. 1980. 29.50x (ISBN 0-520-04165-8). U of Cal Pr.

FRENCH LANGUAGE-OLD FRENCH

see French Language-To 1500

FRENCH LANGUAGE-ORTHOGRAPHY AND SPELLING

Beaugrand. Manuel Pratique de Composition Francaise. 6.50 (ISBN 0-685-36705-3). French & Eur.
Catach. L' Orthographe Francaise a L'epoque de la Renaissance. (Publ. Romanes et Franc.). 72.00 (ISBN 0-685-36649-9). French & Eur.
Etiemble. L' Art d'ecrire. 16.50 (ISBN 0-685-36551-4). French & Eur.
Grevisse. Code de L'orthographe. 11.50 (ISBN 0-685-36702-9). French & Eur.

FRENCH LANGUAGE-PHONETICS

Burroughs, Eliane. French Phonetics. (gr. 8-12). 1972. pap. text ed. 10.00 (ISBN 0-8449-1601-3). Learning Line.
Delattre, Pierre. Les Difficultes Phonetiques Du Francais. (Fr.). 1948. pap. 3.00x (ISBN 0-910408-02-5). Coll Store.
--Principes De Phonetique Francaise a l' Usage Des Etudiants Anglo-Americains. (Fr.). 1951. pap. 3.00x (ISBN 0-910408-01-7). Coll Store.
--Studies in French & Comparative Phonetics. (Janua Linguistica, Ser. Major: No. 18). (Fr. & Eng.). 1966. text ed. 55.00x (ISBN 90-2790-610-6). Mouton.
Du Terme, Laurence. The Flower De Luce Planted in England, Wherein Is Contained the Pronuntiation & Understanding of the French Tongue. LC 72-5977. (English Experience Ser.: No. 505). 68p. 1973. Repr. of 1619 ed. 6.00 (ISBN 90-221-0505-9). Walter J Johnson.
FSI Introduction to French Phonology. 1977. pap. text ed. 6.50x (ISBN 0-686-10738-1); cassettes 60.00x (ISBN 0-686-10739-X). Intl Learn Syst.
Gendron, Jean D. Phonetique Pratique. (Fr). 1961. pap. 2.50x (ISBN 2-7637-6001-5, Pub. by Laval). Intl Schol Bk Serv.
Guitard, Lucien & Marandet, Leon. French Pronunciation Illustrated. text ed. 3.25x (ISBN 0-521-05156-8). Cambridge U Pr.
Haden, Ernest F. Physiology of French Consonant Changes. 1938. pap. 8.00 (ISBN 0-527-00772-2). Kraus Repr.
Klausenburger, Juergen. French Prosodics & Phonotactics: An Historical Typology. 102p. 1970. 20.00x (ISBN 3-484-52027-2). Intl Pubns Serv.
Malecot, Andre. Introduction a la Phonetique Francaise. (Janua Linguarum Ser.: No. 15). 1977. pap. 13.50x (ISBN 90-2793-395-2). Mouton.
Martinet, Andre. Phonology As Functional Phonetics. LC 76-41785. 1949. lib. bdg. 12.50 (ISBN 0-8414-6157-0). Folcroft.
Nitze, William A. & Wilkins, Ernest H. A Handbook of French Phonetics. 1945. pap. text ed. 12.95x (ISBN 0-89197-781-3). Irvington.
Peyrollaz, M. & De Tovar, M. Bara. Manuel de phonetique et de diction francaises a l'usage des etrangers. (Fr). pap. 7.25 (ISBN 0-88332-246-3, 3759). Larousse.
Schmidt-Mackery, Llonka. Phonetique Pratique De L'allemand. (Fr). 1965. pap. 3.00x (ISBN 2-7637-6206-9, Pub. by Laval). Intl Schol Bk Serv.
Shipman, G. R. Vowel Phonemes of Meigret. 1953. pap. 6.00 (ISBN 0-527-01450-8). Kraus Repr.
Straka, Georges. Album Phonetique. (Fr). 1965. 6.00x (ISBN 2-7637-6169-0, Pub. by Laval). Intl Schol Bk Serv.
Tranel, Bernard. Concreteness in Generative Phonology: Evidence from French. LC 80-51243. 400p. 1980. 29.50x (ISBN 0-520-04165-8). U of Cal Pr.
Valdman, Albert. Introduction to French Phonology & Morphology. LC 76-1888. 1976. pap. text ed. 10.95 (ISBN 0-88377-054-7). Newbury Hse.
Van Den Berghe, Christian L. La Phonostylistique Du Francais. (De Propietatibus Litterarum, Series Practice: No. 68). 1976. text ed. 101.25x (ISBN 90-2793-303-0). Mouton.

FRENCH LANGUAGE-PROGRAMMED INSTRUCTION

Berlitz, Charles. French Step by Step. LC 78-73614. 1979. 9.95 (ISBN 0-89696-026-9). Everest Hse.
--Passport to French. 1974. pap. 1.95 (ISBN 0-451-11060-9, AJ1060, Sig). NAL.
Burroughs, Eliane. Programmed French Reading & Writing I. 1971. pap. text ed. 7.00 incl. tchrs' manual & test (ISBN 0-8449-1700-1). Learning Line.
--Programmed French Reading & Writing II. 1964. pap. text ed. 7.00 incl. tchrs' manual & test (ISBN 0-8449-1704-4). Learning Line.
--Programmed French Reading & Writing III. 1972. pap. text ed. 7.00 incl. tchrs' manual & test (ISBN 0-8449-1708-7). Learning Line.
Dietiker, Simone R. En Bonne Forme. 2nd ed. 416p. 1978. pap. text ed. 12.95x (ISBN 0-669-00863-X). Heath.
Jassey, William, ed. French: Three Thousand One Hundred Steps to Master Vocabulary. LC 67-188C1. (Prog. Bk.). 1969. pap. 2.95 (ISBN 0-668-01680-9). Arco.
Mayer, Edgar N. Structure of French: A Programmed Course on the Linguistic Structure of French. (Prog. bk). 1969. pap. text ed. 8.95x (ISBN 0-89197-429-6). Irvington.
Simenon, Georges. Meurtre D'un Etudiant. Ernst, F., ed. LC 73-135358. (Fr). (gr. 9-12). 1971. text ed. 10.95 (ISBN 0-03-084993-4, HoltC). HR&W.

FRENCH LANGUAGE-PRONUNCIATION

Arnold, William H. French Diction for Singers & Speakers. LC 74-27328. Repr. of 1912 ed. 14.50 (ISBN 0-404-12854-8). AMS Pr.
Barret. Methode de prononciation de francais. 20.50 (ISBN 0-685-36698-7). French & Eur.
Bras, Monique. Your Guide to French Pronunciation. (Illus.). 231p. 1975. pap. text ed. 14.50 (ISBN 2-03-043101-X, 3819). Larousse.
Delattre, Pierre. Advanced Training in French Pronunciation. 1949. pap. 3.00x (ISBN 0-910408-03-3); record 7.75 (ISBN 0-910408-04-1). Coll Store.
Leon. Exercises Systematiques de Prononciation Francaise. 7.50 (ISBN 0-685-36701-0). French & Eur.
--Prononciation du Francais Standard. (Coll. Linguistique Appliquee). 16.50 (ISBN 0-685-36699-5); 4 magnetic tapes 59.95 (ISBN 0-685-36700-2). French & Eur.
Martinet, Andre & Walter, Henriette. Dictionnaire De la Prononciation Francaise Dans Son Usage Reel. (Fr.). 1977. lib. bdg. 59.00x (ISBN 0-685-74923-1). Clearwater Pub.
--Dictionnaire de la Prononciation Francaise Dans Son Usage Reel. 932p. (Fr.). 1973. 95.00 (ISBN 0-686-56802-8, M-4739). French & Eur.
Thomas, Pierre. Elements of Oral Practice: Cours Soixante-Seize. (Fr.). 1958. pap. 3.00x (ISBN 0-910408-07-6). Coll Store.
Tory, G., ed. Champ Fleury. Ives, George B., tr. 1927. 70.00 (ISBN 0-527-90600-X). Kraus Repr.
Tory, Geofroy. Champ Fleury. Ives, George B., tr. (Illus.). pap. 3.50 (ISBN 0-486-21807-4). Dover.

Valdman, Albert, et al. Drillbook of French Pronunciation. 2nd ed. (Orig.). 1970. text ed. 19.50 scp (ISBN 0-06-046741-X, HarpC); scp tapes 285.00 (ISBN 0-06-047474-2). Har-Row.
Warnant, Leon. Dictionnaire de la Prononciation Francaise, Vol. 1. 3rd ed. (Fr.). 1968. pap. 35.00 (ISBN 0-686-56824-9, M-6602). French & Eur.
Wierenga, Leanne. French Diction for the Singer: A Phonetics Workbook. LC 77-81950. 1977. 4.95 (ISBN 0-934286-07-8). Kenyon.

FRENCH LANGUAGE-PROVINCIALISMS

Adams, George C. Words & Descriptive Terms for "Woman" & "Girl" in French & Provencal & Border Dialects. (Studies in the Romance Languages & Literatures: No. 11). 1949. pap. 7.00x (ISBN 0-8078-9011-1). U of NC Pr.
Juneau, Marcel. Contribution a l'Histoire De la Prononciation Francais Au Quebec: D'Apres Des Graphies Des Documents d'Archives. (Fr.). 1972. 12.50x (ISBN 2-7637-6602-1, Pub by Laval). Intl Schol Bk Serv.
Tory, G., ed. Champ Fleury. Ives, George B., tr. 1927. 70.00 (ISBN 0-527-90600-X). Kraus Repr.
Tory, Geofroy. Champ Fleury. Ives, George B., tr. (Illus.). pap. 3.50 (ISBN 0-486-21807-4). Dover.

FRENCH LANGUAGE-READERS

see also French Language-Text-Books for Children

Aspland, Clifford W., ed. A Medieval French Reader. 436p. 1979. text ed. 39.00x (ISBN 0-19-872035-1); pap. text ed. 19.50x (ISBN 0-19-815761-4). Oxford U Pr.
Barson, J. G. & Chenetier. Textuellement. LC 73-2099. 1974. pap. text ed. 11.95 (ISBN 0-03-007006-6, HoltC). HR&W.
Baudelaire, Charles. Oeuvres critiques: Petits Poemes en prose. (Nouveaux Classiques Larousse). (Fr). pap. 2.95 (ISBN 0-685-14010-5, 20). Larousse.
--Petits poemes en prose: Oeuvres critiques. (Nouveaux Classiques Larousse). (Fr). pap. 2.95 (ISBN 0-685-14037-7, 20). Larousse.
Bauer, Camille. France Actuelle. rev. ed. (Illus.). 1971. text ed. 10.50 (ISBN 0-395-04150-3, 3-03207). HM.
Bauer, Camille & Bond, Otto F. Graded French Reader, Deuxieme Etape. 2nd ed. 240p. 1981. pap. text ed. 7.95 (ISBN 0-686-72926-9). Heath.
Bauer, Camille & Bond, Otto, eds. Graded French Reader: Premiere Etape. 3rd ed. 1978. pap. text ed. 6.95x (ISBN 0-669-00876-1). Heath.
Beaujour, M. & Ehrmann, J. France Contemporaine. 1965. text ed. 10.95 (ISBN 0-02-307770-0). Macmillan.
Benoit. Le Dejeuner De Sousceyrac. (Easy Readers Ser. B). 1978. pap. text ed. 3.75 (ISBN 0-88436-293-0). EMC.
Bieler, Arthur, et al. Perspectives De France. abr. rev. ed. (Illus.). 1972. text ed. 17.95 (ISBN 0-13-660571-0); wkbk. 8.95 (ISBN 0-13-660803-5); tapes 175.00 (ISBN 0-13-660779-9). P-H.
Block, Phyllis R. First-Year French: Debuts Litteraires. LC 76-58856. 1977. pap. text ed. 7.95 (ISBN 0-03-015011-6, HoltC). HR&W.
Boucher, John G. & Paris, Robert L. Contrastes. (Fr.). (gr. 7-12). 1972. text ed. 14.80 (ISBN 0-205-03368-7, 3633683); tchrs'. guide 5.12 (ISBN 0-205-03369-5, 3633691); wkbk. 5.60 (ISBN 0-205-03370-9, 3633705); ans. bk. 2.40 (ISBN 0-205-03371-7, 3633713). Allyn.
Bragger, Jeannette & Shupp, Robert P. First-Year French: Debuts Culturels. LC 77-433. 1977. pap. text ed. 7.50 (ISBN 0-03-015016-7, HoltC). HR&W.
Bree, G. & Markow-Totevy, G. Contes et Nouvelles, 1950-1970. rev. ed. LC 72-106166. (gr. 10-12). 1970. pap. text ed. 11.95 (ISBN 0-03-081344-1, HoltC). HR&W.
Breunig, L. C., et al. Forme et Fond. 1964. text ed. 10.95 (ISBN 0-02-314210-3). Macmillan.
Brichant, Colette D. Premier Guide de France: The First Year Reader. (Illus.). 1978. pap. text ed. 10.95 (ISBN 0-13-695460-X). P-H.
Brichant, Collette, ed. French for the Humanities. 1968. pap. text ed. 9.95 (ISBN 0-13-331199-6). P-H.
Brodin, Pierre & Ernst, F. Gens De France. (Secondary French Ser: Level 4). (gr. 7-12). 1968. text ed. 17.00 (ISBN 0-03-068720-9, HoltC); 3 tapes 7.5 ips double track s.p. o.s.i. 30.00 (ISBN 0-685-12255-7). HR&W.
Brunetti, Mendor. Read, Write, Speak French. (Orig.). (gr. 9-12). 1963. pap. 2.95 (ISBN 0-553-14168-6). Bantam.
Burne, J. R. Caisse De Joseph. 1966. text ed. 2.25x (ISBN 0-521-04388-3). Cambridge U Pr.
Campbell, Hugh D. & Bauer, Camille. Programmed French Readers, 4 bks. Incl. Contes pour Debutants. 1965. pap. text ed. 6.10 (ISBN 0-685-23331-6, 3-08300); Arsene Lupin. 1965. pap. text ed. 6.60 (ISBN 0-685-23332-4, 3-08301); La Robe et le Couteau. 1966. pap. text ed. 6.60 (ISBN 0-395-04264-X, 3-08310); La Dynamite. 1970. pap. text ed. 6.10 (ISBN 0-395-04265-8, 3-08315). HM.
Carlut, Charles & Marks, E., eds. Recits De Nos Jours. 1964. pap. text ed. 2.95x (ISBN 0-685-15834-9). Macmillan.
Cauvin, Jean-Pierre & Baker, Mary J. Panache Litteraire: Textes Du Monde Francophone. 1978. pap. text ed. 10.95 scp (ISBN 0-06-041205-4, HarpC). Har-Row.
Cazziol, Roger J. Gloire D'Afrique. (Illus.). 1971. text ed. 2.25x (ISBN 0-521-08181-5). Cambridge U Pr.
--Kone. (Illus.). 1971. text ed. 2.25x (ISBN 0-521-07955-1). Cambridge U Pr.
--Vacances Au Senegal. (Illus.). 1971. text ed. 2.25x (ISBN 0-521-08180-7). Cambridge U Pr.
Chatagnier, Louis J., et al. Images de la France contemporaine. (Illus.). 211p. 1965. text ed. 5.00x (ISBN 0-8354-2079-5); tchrs' key 1.00 (ISBN 0-8354-2080-9). Intl Film.
Chretien de Troyes. Yvain: Ou le Chevalier au lion. (Documentation thematique). (Fr). pap. 2.95 (ISBN 0-685-14099-7, 48). Larousse.
Cocteau, Jean. Les Enfants Terribles. (Easy Readers, B). (Illus.). 1977. pap. text ed. 3.75 (ISBN 0-88436-286-8). EMC.
Comeau, Raymond F., et al. Ensemble: Litterature. LC 76-48930. 1977. pap. text ed. 10.95 (ISBN 0-03-018266-2, HoltC). HR&W.
Conroy, Joseph F. Le Monstre dans le Metro et d'Autres Merveilles. (gr. 7-12). 1974. wkbk. 4.58 (ISBN 0-87720-469-1). AMSCO Sch.
Corbiere. Amours jaunes. (Documentation thematique). (Fr). pap. 2.95 (ISBN 0-685-13797-X, 61). Larousse.
Daninos, Pierre. Carnets Du Major W. Marmaduke Thompson. (Illus.). 1963. pap. text ed. 5.95x (ISBN 0-521-04767-6). Cambridge U Pr.
DeRocher, Francoise & DeRocher, Gregory. Options: Apercus de la France. LC 79-27245. 1980. pap. text ed. 8.50 (ISBN 0-471-04260-9). Wiley.
Derrida, Jacques. Limited Inc: Supplement to Glyph 2. LC 77-14309. 1977. pap. text ed. 4.00x (ISBN 0-8018-2044-8). Johns Hopkins.
Diderot, Denis. Fils naturel: Les Entretiens. (Documentation thematique). (Fr). pap. 2.95 (ISBN 0-685-13921-2, 84). Larousse.
--Neveu de rameau. (Documentation thematique). (Fr). pap. 2.95 (ISBN 0-685-13999-9, 85). Larousse.
--Poesie dramatique. (Nouveaux Classiques Larousse). (Fr). pap. 2.95 (ISBN 0-685-14048-2, 86). Larousse.
Dostert, L. & Decaux, M. Francais, Cours Avance, Styles Litteraires. 1964. text ed. 7.20 (ISBN 0-02-815560-2). Glencoe.
Dumont, Jean-Louis & Pomerantz, Donald. Paroles Du Terroir. (Illus., Fr.). 1967. pap. text ed. 4.95x (ISBN 0-442-21755-2). Van Nos Reinhold.
Ellis, M. Leroy, ed. Prose Classique. LC 65-14565. 1966. pap. text ed. 11.95 (ISBN 0-471-00151-1). Wiley.
Fanelli, Maresa. Histoires et Idees. 1978. pap. text ed. 8.95x (ISBN 0-669-01532-6). Heath.
Les Farfeluches choisissent un metier: The Farfeluches Choose a Career. (Illus.). (gr. 8). 1978. 8.95 (ISBN 0-88332-101-7, 2906). Larousse.
Forster, Arthur B. & Lenoir, Lucille, eds. French Songs, Poems & Proverbs. 1934. pap. text ed. 1.45x (ISBN 0-89197-502-0). Irvington.
Fotos, John T. & Shaw, Edward P. Dix Contes. (Orig., Fr.). 1961. pap. text ed. 3.25x (ISBN 0-685-15015-1). Macmillan.
France, Anatole. Le Livre De Mon Ami. (Easy Readers, A). 1978. pap. text ed. 2.90 (ISBN 0-88436-289-2). EMC.
French Reader. (Teach Yourself Ser). 1971. 2.95 (ISBN 0-679-10247-7). McKay.
Galland, Joseph S. Ten Favorite French Stories. (Fr.). 1935. 12.50x (ISBN 0-89197-506-3); pap. text ed. 6.95x (ISBN 0-89197-962-X). Irvington.
Galpin, A. M. & Milligan, E. E. French Prose: An Intermediate Reader. 1965. text ed. 8.50 (ISBN 0-02-340250-4). Macmillan.
Gibson, Alexander D., ed. Anthologie. LC 66-28097. (Orig., Fr.). 1967. pap. 5.95 (ISBN 0-672-63008-7). Odyssey Pr.
Gide, Andre. Symphonie Pastorale. O'Brien, Justin & Shackleton, M., eds. 1954. pap. text ed. 5.95x (ISBN 0-669-27383-X). Heath.
Giono, Jean. Regain. 192p. 1958. 3.95 (ISBN 0-686-53986-9). French & Eur.
Gode, Alexander. French at Sight. LC 62-17089. (gr. 9-12). text ed. 7.50 (ISBN 0-8044-0182-9); pap. 3.45 (ISBN 0-8044-6181-3). Ungar.
Gree, Alain & Camps, Luis. Les Farfeluches a la campagne. (Illus.). 1973. 8.95 (ISBN 0-88332-234-X, 2914). Larousse.
--Les Farfeluches a la maison. (Illus.). 1973. 8.95 (ISBN 0-88332-235-8, 2915). Larousse.
--Les Farfeluches a l'ecole. (Illus.). 1973. 8.95 (ISBN 0-88332-236-6, 2907). Larousse.
--Les Farfeluches au bord de la mer. (Illus.). 1973. 8.95 (ISBN 0-88332-237-4, 2913). Larousse.
--Les Farfeluches au cirque. (Illus.). 1973. 8.95 (ISBN 0-88332-238-2, 2916). Larousse.
--Les Farfeluches au marche. (Illus.). 1973. 8.95 (ISBN 0-88332-239-0, 2909). Larousse.
--Les Farfeluches prennent le train. (Illus.). 1973. 8.95 (ISBN 0-88332-242-0, 2918). Larousse.
--Les Farfeluches sur la route. (Illus.). 1973. 8.95 (ISBN 0-88332-243-9, 2917). Larousse.
Guillat, R. Tipiti le rouge-gorge: Cours elementaire. (Lectures Suivies Ser). (Fr). text ed. 5.95 (ISBN 0-686-66472-8, 3990). Larousse.
Guth, Paul. Le Naif Aux Quarante Enfants. (Easy Readers, C). 1979. pap. 3.75 (ISBN 0-88436-294-9). EMC.
Haac, Oscar A. & Bieler, Arthur. Actualite et Avenir: A Guide to France & to French Conversation. LC 74-30489. (Illus.). 256p. 1975. pap. text ed. 9.95 (ISBN 0-13-003855-5). P-H.
Hameau, Marie-Anne. Je Lis Tu Lis, 3 bks. (gr. 4-6). Bk. 1. text ed. 5.95 (ISBN 0-685-35643-4); Bk. 2. text ed. 5.95 (ISBN 0-685-35644-2); text ed. 6.50 (ISBN 0-685-35645-0). Bk. 3. French & Eur.
Harris, J. & Leveque, A. Basic French Reader. 3rd ed. LC 76-106167. 1970. text ed. 10.95 (ISBN 0-03-080025-0, HoltC). HR&W.
Hathorn, R. Le Francais Partout 6. Wright, W., ed. (YA) (gr. 12). 1978. text ed. 8.25 (ISBN 0-03-929287-8, Pub. by HR&W Canada); Tchr's Ed. 7.50 (ISBN 0-03-929290-8); Cahier D'exercices. 4.38 (ISBN 0-03-929288-6). HR&W.
Hester, Claudie F., et al. Initiation a la Culture Francaise. 4th ed. (Illus.). 1977. text ed. 17.50 scp (ISBN 0-06-045011-8, HarpC). Har-Row.
Hope, Quentin M. Reading French for Comprehension. 1965. text ed. 8.95 (ISBN 0-02-357000-8). Macmillan.
Hughes, Dorothy. Madeleine. (Fr.). (YA) (gr. 9-12). 1958. 1.75x (ISBN 0-685-14286-8); pap. 1.40x (ISBN 0-8338-0033-7). M Jones.
Irvin, Leon P. & King, Donald L. Vingt et un Contes. 3rd ed. 1964. pap. text ed. 11.50 scp (ISBN 0-06-043220-9, HarpC). Har-Row.
James, C. D. Twentieth Century French Reader. 1966. 8.00 (ISBN 0-08-011232-3); pap. 6.70 (ISBN 0-08-011231-5). Pergamon.
Jarvis, Gilbert A., et al. Passeport Pour la France: A Beginning Reader for Communication. LC 76-46537. 1977. pap. text ed. 10.50 (ISBN 0-03-015486-3, HoltC). HR&W.
Katz, Eve, ed. La France En Metamorphose. 224p. 1976. pap. text ed. 11.50 scp (ISBN 0-06-043564-X, HarpC). Har-Row.
Keating, L. Clark & Clubb, William G. Journal Parisien. LC 55-6942. 1955. text ed. 12.95x (ISBN 0-89197-512-8); pap. text ed. 6.95x (ISBN 0-89197-815-1). Irvington.
Keating, L. Clark & Moraud, Marcel I. Cultural Graded Readers, Elementary Series, 3 vols. Incl. Lafitte. 1958; Moliere. 1958. pap. text ed. 2.50x (ISBN 0-442-31815-4); Voltaire. 1968. pap. text ed. 2.50x (ISBN 0-442-21816-8). (Fr.). D Van Nostrand.
Kenan, Lucette R. Chez les Francais. (Illus., Orig., Fr.). 1967. pap. text ed. 8.95 (ISBN 0-15-506501-7, HC). HarBraceJ.
Kincaid, Mary. Contes Francais, 3 bks. Incl. Bk. 1. La Parure. 24p (ISBN 0-911168-23-0). tape (ISBN 0-911168-26-5); Bk. 2. Carmen. 32p (ISBN 0-911168-22-2). tape (ISBN 0-911168-25-7); Bk. 3. Episodes des Miserables. 24p (ISBN 0-911168-24-9). tape (ISBN 0-911168-27-3). (Illus., Fr.). 1965. pap. 0.50 ea.; tape recordings 8.95 ea. Prakken.
Kirkland, Catherine J. & Knox, Edward C. A mon avis. (Orig., Fr.). 1977. pap. text ed. 8.95 (ISBN 0-15-500362-3, HC); student manual 4.95 (ISBN 0-15-500363-1). HarBraceJ.
Kopp, Richard D. & Fraser, Theodore P. Readings in French Literature. 1975. pap. text ed. 8.80 (ISBN 0-395-13638-5). HM.
Kretsch, Robert W. Images et Reflets Litteraires. 1967. text ed. 8.95 (ISBN 0-07-035491-X, C). McGraw.
Kuhn, Reinhard, ed. L' Espirit Moderne Dans la Litterature Francaise. (Fr.). 1972. pap. 6.95x (ISBN 0-19-501529-0). Oxford U Pr.
Lafitte, Lucette. Eau Trouble. 1963. text ed. 2.95x (ISBN 0-521-05506-7). Cambridge U Pr.
Langellier, Alice & Langellier, Paul. Billet Circulaire. LC 66-12110. 1966. pap. text ed. 3.95x (ISBN 0-89197-516-0). Irvington.
Lannois, Georges, ed. Pages francaises. 1969. 14.50 (ISBN 0-08-006379-9). Pergamon.
Learn French the BBC Way: Book 1. (gr. 7-12). 1977. pap. text ed. 5.95 (ISBN 0-8120-0723-9); tape 5.20 (ISBN 0-8120-0743-3); tchr's manual 2.00 (ISBN 0-8120-0745-X). Barron.
Learn French the BBC Way: Book 2. (gr. 8-12). 1978. pap. text ed. 5.95 (ISBN 0-8120-0724-7); tape 5.20 (ISBN 0-8120-0744-1); tchr's manual 2.00 (ISBN 0-8120-0746-8). Barron.
Lee, Simon & Ricks, David, eds. Penguin French Reader. (Orig., Bilingual.). (YA) (gr. 9 up). 1967. pap. 1.95 (ISBN 0-14-002656-8). Penguin.
Lenard, Yvone. Parole et Pensee: Introduction au Francais D'aujord'hui. 3rd ed. (Illus.). 1977. text ed. 20.95 scp (ISBN 0-06-043963-7, HarpC); tchrs'. guide free (ISBN 0-06-363965-3); scp lab manual 8.50 (ISBN 0-06-043972-6); scp tapes 310.00 (ISBN 0-06-047486-6). Har-Row.
Madrigal, Margarita & Dulac, Colette. Open Door to French. (gr. 7-10). 1963. pap. text ed. 2.95 (ISBN 0-88345-121-2, 17476). Regents Pub.
Martineau, Richard & Girolami, Anne-Marie. Vient De Paraitre. LC 74-20593. 1975. pap. text ed. 4.25 (ISBN 0-88436-174-8). EMC.
Maurois, Michelle. Contes De Michelle Maurois. Meiden, Walter, ed. (Fr). 1966. pap. text ed. 9.35 (ISBN 0-395-04878-8, 3-37424). HM.
Merimee, Prosper. Carmen: La Venus d'Ille. (Nouveaux Classiques Larousse). (Fr). pap. 2.95 (ISBN 0-685-13817-8, 180). Larousse.
--Venus d'Ille: Carmen. (Documentation thematique). (Fr). pap. 2.95 (ISBN 0-685-14090-3, 180). Larousse.
Miller, Minnie M., ed. First Readings in French Literature. (Fr.). 1940. 18.50x (ISBN 0-89197-597-7). Irvington.
Milligan, Edward E. Beginning Readings in French. (Orig.). 1961. pap. text ed. 7.95x (ISBN 0-685-14720-7). Macmillan.
--Introductory French Reader. 1963. pap. text ed. 8.95 (ISBN 0-02-381470-5). Macmillan.
Moore, Olin H. & Meiden, Walter. Onze Contes. LC 57-674. (Fr). 1957. pap. text ed. 7.70 (ISBN 0-395-04941-5, 3-38350). HM.
Morrison, Veronique, et al, eds. Tout a Fait Francais. (Illus.). 1979. pap. text ed. 4.95x (ISBN 0-393-09005-1). Norton.
Mortimer, Mildred P., ed. Contes Africains. LC 71-168855. (Illus., Orig.). 1972. pap. text ed. 7.20 (ISBN 0-395-12078-0, 3-39210). HM.
Muyskens, Judith. A French Literary Reader. 1981. pap. text ed. 7.95x (ISBN 0-394-32641-5). Random.
Nelson, Roy J., ed. Reading Expository French: From Modern Authors. (Orig., Fr.). 1965. pap. text ed. 11.50 scp (ISBN 0-06-044790-7, HarpC). Har-Row.
Ostyn, Paul & Melka-Teichroew, Francine. La France Vous Parle. 314p. 1981. text ed. 15.50 scp (ISBN 0-06-044947-0, HarpC). Har-Row.
Otten, Anna, ed. Voix et silences: Les Meilleures pieces radiophoniques francaises. Incl. Silences de Paris. Camus, Albert & Vedres, V.; Une L'arme. Forest, Jean & Clair, Rene.; C'est vrai mais il ne faut pas le croire. Aveline, Claude; Frederic General. Constant, Jacques; Interview. Pinget, Robert. LC 68-11212. (Illus., Fr.). 1968. pap. text ed. 5.95x (ISBN 0-89197-466-0). Irvington.
Peyrazat, Jean E. Histoires Droles. (Illus.). (gr. 9-10). 1972. pap. text ed. 2.95 (ISBN 0-88345-063-1, 18069); 2 tapes o.p. 15.00 (ISBN 0-685-59048-8, 58265); 2 cassettes 25.00 (ISBN 0-685-59049-6, 58422). Regents Pub.
Pimsleur, Paul. C'est la Vie. 2nd ed. LC 75-35331. (Illus., Fr.). 1976. pap. text ed. 8.95 (ISBN 0-15-505891-6, HC). HarBraceJ.
Politzer, R., et al. France: Une Tapisserie. 1965. text ed. 12.20 (ISBN 0-07-050382-6, W); teachers' ed. 9.60 (ISBN 0-07-050383-4); tests 56.00 (ISBN 0-07-050391-5). McGraw.
Pryor, E. Voyage en Provence. (Illus.). 1977. pap. text ed. 3.00x (ISBN 0-582-36038-2); cassette 10.50x (ISBN 0-582-37170-8). Longman.
Reed, Muriel. Visites Chez les Francais. Carre, Jeffrey J. & Carre, Marie-Rose, eds. (Illus., Orig., Fr.). 1966. pap. text ed. 8.95 (ISBN 0-13-942250-1). P-H.
Saint-Exupery, Antoine De. Petit Prince. rev. ed. Miller, John R., ed. LC 47-151. (Fr). (gr. 11). 1975. pap. 5.00 (ISBN 0-395-24005-0). HM.
Sareil, J. & Sareil, J. Romanciers Du Vingtieme Siecle. LC 73-106169. 1970. pap. text ed. 9.95 (ISBN 0-03-081481-2, HoltC). HR&W.
Sareil, Jean. Les Cent Femmes. (Illus.). (gr. 11 up). 1972. pap. text ed. 5.95 (ISBN 0-88345-092-5, 18083). Regents Pub.
Sartre, Jean-Paul. Huis Clos. Hardre, Jacques & Daniel, George B., eds. (Orig., Fr.). (gr. 10-12). 1962. pap. text ed. 8.95 (ISBN 0-13-444679-8). P-H.
Sas, Louis F., ed. Grands Savants Francais: Lectures Scientifiques. (Illus., Orig., Fr.,.). 1961. pap. text ed. 3.95x (ISBN 0-89197-189-0). Irvington.
Schwarz, M. Variete Du Conte Francais. (Fr). (gr. 9-12). 1972. pap. text ed. 14.95 (ISBN 0-03-085702-3, HoltC). HR&W.
Seibert, Louise C. & Crocker, Lester G., eds. Histoire D'une Revanche. (Orig., Fr.). 1963. pap. text ed. 7.95x (ISBN 0-684-41430-9, ScribC). Scribner.
Sempe, J. J. & Goscinny, R. Aventures Du Petit Nicholas. Kaplan, C., ed. 1966. 5.96 (ISBN 0-685-14571-9). Macmillan.
Sidwell, Duncan. Expedition Two Thousand Sixty-One. LC 73-145608. (Illus.). 1971. text ed. 2.95x (ISBN 0-521-08087-8). Cambridge U Pr.

Simenon, Georges. Choix De Simenon. Lindsay, Frank W. & Nazzaro, Anthony M., eds. (Illus., Fr.). 1972. pap. 8.95x (ISBN 0-13-133033-0). P-H.
--Maigret et le Fantome. (Easy Readers, B). (Illus.). 1977. pap. text ed. 3.75 (ISBN 0-88436-287-6). EMC.
Smith, Eunice C. & Savacool, John K., eds. Voix Du Siecle. (Fr.). pap. text ed. 8.95 (ISBN 0-15-595006-1, HC). HarBraceJ.
Stack, Edward M. Reading French in the Arts & Sciences. 3rd ed. 265p. 1979. pap. text ed. 8.80 (ISBN 0-395-27505-9). HM.
Steckman & Sklarew. Amusettes. (Illus.). (gr. 7-9). 1973. pap. text ed. 3.75 (ISBN 0-88345-185-9, 18082). Regents Pub.
Therio, Adrien & Burks, James F., eds. Temoins du Monde Francais. LC 68-12127. (Illus., Orig., Fr.). (YA) (gr. 9 up). 1968. pap. text ed. 8.95x (ISBN 0-89197-446-6). Irvington.
Troyat, Henri. La Tete Sur les Epaules. (Easy Readers, C). (Illus.). pap. text ed. 3.75 (ISBN 0-88436-285-X). EMC.
Valette, Rebecca. Nouvelles Lectures Libres. 256p. 1981. pap. text ed. 9.95 (ISBN 0-669-04753-8). Heath.
Voltaire. Candide. rev. ed. Havens, G. R., ed. (Fr). 1969. pap. 9.95 (ISBN 0-03-080120-6, HoltC). HR&W.
Weckselmann, David & Bevan, Elizabeth. Tunde et Ses Amis, 2 bks. 1962-65. text ed. 2.25x ea. Vol. 1 (ISBN 0-521-06757-X). Vol. 2 (ISBN 0-521-06758-8). Cambridge U Pr.
Wellek, Susanne & Bass, Nelly. Paul et Marie a l'Ecole. (Illus.). (gr. 5 up). 1950. text ed. 8.50 (ISBN 0-8044-0800-9). Ungar.
Wiley, W. Leon & Grubbs, Henry A. Minimum French. 1935. text ed. 11.95x (ISBN 0-89197-634-5); pap. text ed. 4.95x (ISBN 0-89197-610-8). Irvington.

FRENCH LANGUAGE–READERS (HISTORY)

Beauregard, J. Histoire de France illustree. 1968. 15.00 (ISBN 0-08-013198-0); pap. 7.00 (ISBN 0-08-013197-2). Pergamon.
Carlut, C. & Bree, G. France De Nos Jours. 3rd ed. 1968. text ed. 5.95 (ISBN 0-02-319320-4). Macmillan.

FRENCH LANGUAGE–READERS (SCIENCE)

Hyland, Jean S. Reading Proficiency in French: Humanities. (Fr). 1970. pap. text ed. 6.95x (ISBN 0-442-22601-2). Van Nos Reinhold.
--Reading Proficiency in French: Physical Sciences. (Illus.). 1969. pap. text ed. 6.95x (ISBN 0-442-22598-9). Van Nos Reinhold.

FRENCH LANGUAGE–RHETORIC

Barrette, Paul & Fol, Monique. Certain Style Ou un Style Certain. 1969. pap. 8.95x (ISBN 0-19-500824-3). Oxford U Pr.
Davidson, Hugh M. Audience, Words, & Art: Studies in Seventeenth-Century French Rhetoric. LC 65-18737. 1965. 5.00 (ISBN 0-8142-0043-5). Ohio St U Pr.
Frohock, Wilbur M. French Literature: An Approach Through Close Reading. 4th ed. 1970. 5.50 (ISBN 0-87774-000-3). Schoenhof.
Houston, John P. The Traditions of French Prose Style: A Rhetorical Study. LC 80-27871. 352p. 1981. 30.00x (ISBN 0-8071-0858-8). La State U Pr.

FRENCH LANGUAGE–RIME–DICTIONARIES

Warnant, Leon. Dictionnaire des rimes orales et ecrites. new ed. 553p. (Fr.). 1972. 23.50 (ISBN 2-03-020271-1, 3546). Larousse.

FRENCH LANGUAGE–SELF INSTRUCTION

see also French Language–Conversation and Phrase Books

Adams, J. & Wilson, N. S. Teach Yourself French. (Teach Yourself Ser.). pap. 3.50 (ISBN 0-679-10172-1). McKay.
Adrienne. French in Thirty-Two Lessons. (Gimmick Ser.). 1979. 10.95 (ISBN 0-393-04520-X); pap. 5.95 (ISBN 0-393-04531-5). Norton.
Berlitz Schools Of Languages. Self-Teacher: French. 1958. 8.95 (ISBN 0-448-01421-1). G&D.
Cherel, Albert O. Frances Sin Esfuerzo. 11.95 (ISBN 0-685-11201-2). French & Eur.
--Francese Senza Sforzo. 9.95 (ISBN 0-685-11202-0). French & Eur.
--Franzosisch Ohne Muhe. 9.95 (ISBN 0-685-11205-5). French & Eur.
--French Without Toil. 11.95 (ISBN 0-685-11209-8); records 75.00 (ISBN 0-686-66422-1); 75.00, 3 sets cassette (ISBN 0-686-66423-X). French & Eur.
Ernst, Frederic. New French Self-Taught. 390p. (Fr.). 1982. pap. text ed. 5.05 (ISBN 0-06-463614-3, EH 614, BN). Har-Row.
French in Twenty Lessons. (Cortina Language Ser.). (Illus.). 1977. pap. 3.95 (ISBN 0-385-13007-4, Dolp). Doubleday.
Jackson, Eugene & Rubio, Antonio. French Made Simple. LC 73-9033. pap. 3.50 (ISBN 0-385-08691-1, Made). Doubleday.
Jenkins, Edward S. Teach Yourself French Grammar. (Teach Yourself Ser.). pap. 3.95 (ISBN 0-679-10173-X). McKay.
Lemaitre, Joseph. French: How to Speak & Write It. (Illus.). 1962. pap. 4.00 (ISBN 0-486-20268-2). Dover.
Madrigal, Margarita & Dulac, Collette. See It & Say It in French. (Orig.). pap. 1.95 (ISBN 0-451-08941-3, E8941, Sig). NAL.
Martin, Genevieve A. Living French for Spanish-Speaking People. 14.95, with 4 lp records conversation manual & dictionary (ISBN 0-517-50821-4). Crown.
Wilson, N. Scarlyn. Teach Yourself Everyday French. (Teach Yourself Ser.). pap. 3.95 (ISBN 0-679-10168-3). McKay.
--Teach Yourself First French. (Teach Yourself Ser.). 1969. pap. 3.95 (ISBN 0-679-10215-9). McKay.

FRENCH LANGUAGE–SLANG

Caradec, Francois. Dictonnaire Du Francais Argotique et Populaire. 255p. (Fr.). 1977. pap. 6.95 (ISBN 0-686-56879-6, M-4968). French & Eur.

FRENCH LANGUAGE–STUDY AND TEACHING

Adler-Golden, Rachel & Gordon, Debbie. Beginning French for Preschoolers: A Montessori Handbook. LC 80-83136. (Illus.). 85p. 1981. pap. text ed. 6.00 (ISBN 0-915676-04-4). Montessori Wkshps.
American Association of Teachers of French. FLES: Foreign Language Teaching Techniques in FLES & Bilingual Settings. Kunkle, John F. & Cipriani, Anita A., eds. (Reports of the FLES Committee). 184p. (Orig.). 1973. pap. 5.00x (ISBN 0-87352-166-8). Modern Lang.
--FLES: Goals & Guides. Lipton, Gladys C. & Spaar-Rauch, Virginia, eds. (Reports of the FLES Committee). ix, 75p. (Orig.). 1971. pap. 5.00x (ISBN 0-87352-164-1). Modern Lang.
--FLES: USA Success Stories. Lipton, Gladys C. & Bourque, Edward H., eds. (Reports of the FLES Committee). 85p. (Orig.). 1972. pap. 5.00x (ISBN 0-87352-165-X). Modern Lang.
Barrette, Paul & Braun, Theodore. First French: Le Francais Non sans Peine. rev. ed. 1970. 12.95x (ISBN 0-673-05113-7). Scott F.
--Second French: Le Francais Non sans Peine. 1968. 12.95x (ISBN 0-673-05110-2). Scott F.
Boucher, John G. & Hurtgen, Andre O. Encore. (Allyn & Bacon French Program Ser.). (gr. 9-12). 1976. text ed. 15.12 (ISBN 0-205-04903-6, 3649032); tchrs'. guide 5.12 (ISBN 0-205-04904-4, 3649040). Allyn.
Burstall, Clare. Primary French in the Balance: Main Report. (Research Reports Ser.). 304p. 1974. pap. text ed. 18.00x (ISBN 0-85633-052-3, NFER). Humanities.
Cadoux, R. L' Envolee, Level 3. 1972. 9.08 (ISBN 0-02-268660-6). Macmillan.
--Notre Monde, Level 2. 1971. 8.56 (ISBN 0-02-268580-4). Macmillan.
--Vous et Moi: En Avant. 1970. 6.84 (ISBN 0-02-268400-X). Macmillan.
Carroll, John B. The Teaching of French As a Foreign Language in Eight Countries. LC 75-17945. (International Studies in Evaluation, Vol. 5). 1975. 19.95 (ISBN 0-470-13602-2). Halsted Pr.
Cazziol, R. J. Paul et Remi. (Illus.). 40p. (Fr.). 1974. pap. text ed. 2.25x (ISBN 0-521-20433-X). Cambridge U Pr.
--Safari En Cote d'Ivoire. (Illus.). 40p. 1974. pap. 2.25x (ISBN 0-521-20434-8). Cambridge U Pr.
Champion, Jacques. Les Langues Africaines et la Francophonie: Essai D'une Pedagogie Du Francais En Afrique Noire Par une Analyse Typologique De Fautes. (Illus.). 1974. pap. 22.25x (ISBN 90-2797-605-8). Mouton.
Charbonneau, Gerard & Seguin, Hubert. Workbook in Everyday French, 2 bks. rev. ed. 213p. (gr. 9-11). 1971. Bk. 1. pap. text ed. 4.75 (ISBN 0-88345-167-0, 17479); Bk. 2. pap. text ed. 4.75 (ISBN 0-88345-168-9, 17480); answer key 2.75 (ISBN 0-685-38985-5). Regents Pub.
Cote, D. G., et al. Ecouter Et Parler. rev. ed. (Secondary French Ser: Level 1). (gr. 7-12). 1968. text ed. 13.28 (ISBN 0-03-069500-7, HoltC); tchrs' ed. 7.60 (ISBN 0-685-12236-0); 5 films s.p. 955.00, avail. sep. (ISBN 0-685-12237-9); film guides 0.36 ea.; flashcards 60.00 (ISBN 0-685-12239-5); projectuals 132.00 (ISBN 0-685-12240-9); exercise manual 2.60 (ISBN 0-685-12241-7); unit quizzes 1.16 (ISBN 0-685-12242-5); records 8.28 (ISBN 0-685-12243-3). HR&W.
Coulon, R., et al. Le Francais a Travers les Sciences Humaines. (Fr., Prog. Bk.). 1972. pap. text ed. 4.95x (ISBN 0-582-35892-2); 5 tapes 45.00x (ISBN 0-582-37840-0). Longman.
Cummins, Patricia. Commercial French. (Illus.). 320p. 1982. 17.95 (ISBN 0-13-152710-X). P-H.
Davis, Margaret B. French. (Blue Book Ser). pap. 1.25 (ISBN 0-671-18121-1). Monarch Pr.
De Harven, Emile. Suivez la Piste. LC 77-10091. 1972. pap. 3.75 (ISBN 0-912022-30-2). EMC.
Dubois, Jean & Lagane, Rene. La Nouvelle Grammaire du francais. 272p. (Orig., Fr.). 1973. pap. 10.95 (ISBN 2-03-040165-X, 3772). Larousse.
Dunkel, Harold B. & Pillet, Roger A. French in the Elementary School. LC 62-12631. 1962. 6.50x (ISBN 0-226-17222-8). U of Chicago Pr.
Etmekjian, James. Pattern Drills in Language Teaching. LC 66-12597. 307p. 1966. 10.95x (ISBN 0-8147-0140-X). NYU Pr.
Foreign Service Institute. Advanced French, 2 pts. 567p. 1980. Pt. A. text & cassettes 170.00x (ISBN 0-88432-067-7, Audio-Forum); Pt. B. text & cassettes 160.00 (ISBN 0-88432-068-5). J Norton Pubs.
Le Francais En Faculte. (Scottish Universities French Language Research Project Ser.). 1981. 15.00x (ISBN 0-340-23890-9, Pub. by Hodder & Stoughton England). State Mutual Bk.
French Made Easy. Date not set. 4.95 (ISBN 0-686-75978-8, 2505). Barron.
French Sixteen to Nineteen: A New Perspective. (Study Group, Hampshire). 1981. 9.00x (ISBN 0-340-25528-5, Pub. by Hodder & Stoughton England). State Mutual Bk.
French Without a Teacher. pap. 0.75 (ISBN 0-685-02611-6, 0054520X). Stein Pub.
Gourevitch, D. & Stadler, E. M. Premiers Textes Litteraires. 2nd ed. LC 74-83346. 242p. 1975. text ed. 9.50 (ISBN 0-471-00811-7). Wiley.
Grew, James H. & Olivier, Daniel D. One Thousand & One Pitfalls in French. LC 73-7323. (gr. 9up). 1974. pap. text ed. 3.95 (ISBN 0-8120-0471-X). Barron.
Hellstrom, Sten-Gunnar, et al. Rendez-Vous en France. 1972. pap. text ed. 4.75 (ISBN 0-912022-28-0); exercise bk 4.25 (ISBN 0-912022-29-9). EMC.
Helstrom, Jo & Metz, Mary. Le Francais a Decouvrir: Learning French the Modern Way, Level 1. 3rd ed. (Illus.). 432p. (gr. 9). 1972. text ed. 12.80 (ISBN 0-07-027960-8); tchr's. ed. 13.32 (ISBN 0-07-027961-6); wkbk. 3.64 (ISBN 0-07-027962-4); filmstrips, tapes, tests & dupl. masters avail. McGraw.
Instant French. pap. 2.50 (ISBN 0-686-31294-5). New Century.
Knight, R. C. & George, F. W. Advice to the Student of French. 3rd ed. 108p. 1977. pap. 7.50x (ISBN 0-686-28464-X, Pub. by Basil Blackwell). Biblio Dist.
Langellier, Alice, et al. Nous les Jeunes. (Secondary French Ser: Level 2). (gr. 7-12). 1974. text ed. 11.96 s.p. (ISBN 0-03-000951-0, HoltC); tchrs' manual. s.p. 6.64 (ISBN 0-03-006151-2); exercise manual 2.80, testing program 1.60 (ISBN 0-685-28992-3); filmstrips with bklet s.p. 73.50 (ISBN 0-685-28993-1); bklet sep. s.p. 4.50 (ISBN 0-685-28994-X); filmstrip tapes s.p. 50.00 (ISBN 0-685-28995-8); tape prog. price not set (ISBN 0-685-28996-6). HR&W.
Lopes, Albert R. & Yarbro, J. D. Bonjour: One Minute Dialogues in French. (Fr.). 1947. pap. text ed. 1.65x (ISBN 0-89197-521-7). Irvington.
Mayer, Edgar N. Structure of French: A Programmed Course on the Linguistic Structure of French. (Prog. bk). 1969. pap. text ed. 8.95x (ISBN 0-89197-429-6). Irvington.
Metz, Mary & Helstrom, Jo. Le Francais a Vivre, Learning French the Modern Way, Level 2. 3rd ed. (Illus.). (gr. 10-12). 1972. text ed. 13.32 (ISBN 0-07-041710-5, W); tchr's. ed. 14.60 (ISBN 0-07-041711-3); wkbk. 3.96 (ISBN 0-07-041712-1). McGraw.
Morton, Jacqueline. English Grammar for Students of French. LC 79-87578. 1979. pap. 4.50 (ISBN 0-934034-00-1). Olivia & Hill.
National Association of Independent Schools. A Teacher's Notebook: French. 1974. pap. 4.75 (ISBN 0-934338-03-5). NAIS.
Okin, Josee P. & Schmitt, Conrad J. Le Francais: Continuons. 2nd ed. (Illus.). 288p. (Fr.). (gr. 8-10). 1975. text ed. 10.60 (ISBN 0-07-047741-8, W); tchr's. ed. 11.92 (ISBN 0-07-047742-6); wkbk. 3.44 (ISBN 0-07-047743-4); cassette tapes 240.00 (ISBN 0-07-097988-X); reel-to-reel tapes 360.00 (ISBN 0-07-097986-3); test pkg. 72.00 (ISBN 0-07-047744-2); test replacements 36.00 (ISBN 0-07-047745-0); filmstrips 80.00 (ISBN 0-07-097987-1). McGraw.
Ortali, R. Entre Nous. 1972. text ed. 10.95 (ISBN 0-02-389510-1). Macmillan.
Politzer, Robert L. Teaching French: An Introduction to Applied Linguistics. 2nd ed. LC 65-14561. 1965. text ed. 16.95 (ISBN 0-471-00430-8). Wiley.
Rey, Jean-Noel & Santoni, Georges. Quand les Francais Parlent. 1975. text ed. 11.95 (ISBN 0-88377-042-3). Newbury Hse.
Rivers, Wilga. A Practical Guide to the Teaching of French. 375p. 1975. pap. text ed. 6.95x (ISBN 0-19-501911-3). Oxford U Pr.
Rolland, Barbara, et al. Le Francais: Langue & Culture. 2nd ed. 1979. text ed. 13.95x (ISBN 0-442-27040-2). D Van Nostrand.
Sandberg, Karl C. & Tatham, Eddison C. French for Reading: A Programmed Approach for Graduate Degree Requirements. 1972. text ed. 14.95 (ISBN 0-13-331603-3). P-H.
Sareil, Jean & Ryding, William. Au Jour le Jour: A French Review. 2nd ed. LC 73-18083. 240p. 1974. text ed. 13.95 (ISBN 0-13-052977-X). P-H.

FRENCH LANGUAGE–SYNONYMS

Bailly, R. Dictionnaire des synonymes. (Fr). 23.50 (ISBN 0-685-13870-4, 3621). Larousse.
Benac, Henri. Dictionnaire Des Synonymes. 1026p. (Fr.). 1975. pap. 18.95 (ISBN 0-686-56880-X, M-4558). French & Eur.
Denis-Papin, Maurice. Dictionnaire Analogique et de Synonymes Pour la Resolution des Problemes des Mots Croises. 6th ed. (Fr.). 1970. pap. 6.95 (ISBN 0-686-56786-2, M-6582, Pub. by Albin Michel). French & Eur.

FRENCH LANGUAGE–SYNTAX

Gardner, Rosalyn & Green, Marion. A Brief Description of Middle French Syntax. (Studies in the Romance Languages & Literatures: No. 29). 1958. pap. 9.00x (ISBN 0-8078-9029-4). U of NC Pr.
Georgin. Comment s'exprimer en Francais. 9.50 (ISBN 0-685-36704-5). French & Eur.
Guillaune, Gustave. Structure Semiologigue et Structure Physique De la Langue Francaise, Vol. 2. 276p. 1974. 11.50x (ISBN 2-7637-6701-X, Pub. by Laval). Intl Schol Bk Serv.
Harris, Martin. The Evolution of French Syntax: A Comparative Approach. (Longman Linguistics Library). (Illus.). 1978. text ed. 22.00x (ISBN 0-582-55047-5); pap. text ed. 13.50x (ISBN 0-582-55048-3). Longman.
Jensen, Frede. The Syntax of the Old French Subjunctive. LC 73-79890. (Janua Linguarum, Ser. Practica: No. 220). 134p. (Orig.). 1974. pap. text ed. 35.00x (ISBN 90-2792-691-3). Mouton.
Kayne, Richard S. French Syntax: The Transformational Cycle. LC 75-4681. (Current Studies in Linguistics Ser.: No. 6). 464p. 1975. text ed. 27.50x (ISBN 0-262-11055-5). MIT Pr.
Le Bidois. Syntaxe du Francais Moderne, 2 tomes. Set. 35.90 (ISBN 0-685-36655-3). French & Eur.
Molho. Semantique et Poetique. (Coll. Ducros, Ser Minor). 5.95 (ISBN 0-685-36656-1). French & Eur.
Ruwet, Nicolas. Problems in French Syntax: Transformational - Generative Studies. Robins, Sheila M., tr. from Fr. (Linguistics Library). 1976. text ed. 22.00x (ISBN 0-582-55058-0). Longman.
Sturges, Hale, et al. Une Fois Pour Toutes: Revision Des Structures Essentielles De la Langue Francais. (Illus.). 1976. pap. text ed. 6.50x (ISBN 0-88334-079-8). Ind Sch Pr.

FRENCH LANGUAGE–TECHNICAL FRENCH

Locke, William N. Scientific French: A Concise Description of the Structural Elements of Scientific & Technical French. LC 78-11669. 124p. 1979. pap. 6.50 (ISBN 0-88275-771-7, Pub. by Wiley). Krieger.

FRENCH LANGUAGE–TERMS AND PHRASES

Bonnard, H., et al. Modern French Usage: A Student Guide. 1971. 7.95 (ISBN 0-02-312100-9). Macmillan.
Dictionaire des Expressions et Locutions Figurees. (Fr.). 1979. pns (M-6126). French & Eur.
Kettridge, J. O. French for English Idioms & Figurative Phrases. 1966. Repr. of 1940 ed. 16.00 (ISBN 0-7100-1669-7). Routledge & Kegan.
--French Idioms & Figurative Phrases: With Many Quotations. 1970. Repr. of 1949 ed. 18.00 (ISBN 0-7100-1668-9). Routledge & Kegan.
Pei, Mario & Fisher, John. Getting Along in French. 1976. pap. 1.50 (ISBN 0-06-080388-6, P388, PL). Har-Row.
Rat, M. Dictionnaire des locutions francaises. (Fr). 23.50 (ISBN 0-685-13866-6, 3613). Larousse.
Swann, Harvey J. French Terminologies in the Making. LC 18-23121. (Columbia University. Studies in Romance Philology & Literature: No. 24). Repr. of 1918 ed. 22.00 (ISBN 0-404-50624-0). AMS Pr.
Tinsley, Sr. Lucy. French Expressions for Spirituality & Devotion: A Semantic Study. LC 73-94185. (Catholic University of America Studies in Romance Languages & Literature Ser: No. 47). Repr. of 1953 ed. 25.00 (ISBN 0-404-50347-0). AMS Pr.
Tyard, Pontus De. Modeles de Phrases suivis d'un recueil de modeles de lettres d'amour. Lapp, John C., ed. (Studies in the Romance Languages & Literatures: No. 70). 1967. pap. 7.00x (ISBN 0-8078-9070-7). U of NC Pr.

FRENCH LANGUAGE–TEXT-BOOKS FOR CHILDREN

see also French Language–Conversation and Phrase Books; French Language–Dictionaries, Juvenile; French Language–Readers

Burroughs, Eliane. Modern French A, 2 bks. (gr. 8-12). 1966. pap. text ed. 7.00 each (ISBN 0-686-57756-6); tchr's manual & test avail. Learning Line.

--Modern French B, 3 bks. (gr. 8-12). 1966. pap. text ed. 7.00 each (ISBN 0-686-57757-4); tchr's manual & test avail. Learning Line.

Conroy, Joseph F. Adventure en Normandie. LC 81-7784. (A L'aventure! Ser). (Illus.). 40p. (Orig., French.). (gr. 7-12). 1981. pap. 1.95 (ISBN 0-88436-855-6, 121052). EMC.

--Danger sur la Cote d'azur. LC 81-7820. (A L'aventure! Ser.). (Illus.). 40p. (Orig., French.). (gr. 7-12). 1981. pap. 1.95 (ISBN 0-88436-857-2, 121054). EMC.

--Destination: France! LC 81-7816. (A L'aventure! Ser.). (Illus.). 40p. (Orig., French.). (gr. 7-12). 1981. pap. 1.95 (ISBN 0-88436-854-8, 121051). EMC.

--Sur la Route de la Contrebande. LC 81-7817. (A L'aventure! Ser.). (Illus.). 40p. (French.). (gr. 7-12). pap. 1.95 (ISBN 0-88436-856-4, 121053). EMC.

Cooper, Eve. Petit Monde, Teacher's Guide. rev ed. Mitchell, William, ed. (Le Francais Partout Ser.). 1978. write for info. (ISBN 0-685-46784-8, HoltC). HR&W.

Cooper, Lee & McIntosh, Clifton. Fun with French. (Illus.). (gr. 3 up). 1963. 8.95 (ISBN 0-316-15607-8). Little.

Cote, D. G., et al. Deuxieme Etape. (Secondary French Ser: Level 1). (Follows Premiere Etape & leads into either Nous les Jeunes & Ce Monde des Francais, or Chez les Francais & Ce Monde des Francais, or Parler et Lire). (gr. 7). 1970. text ed. 8.64 (ISBN 0-03-084953-5, HoltC); tchrs' ed. 12.00 (ISBN 0-685-03759-2); 5 films 955.00 (ISBN 0-685-03760-6); film guides 0.36 ea.; flash cards 60.00 (ISBN 0-685-03762-2); projectuals 132.00 (ISBN 0-685-03763-0); exercise manual 1.36 (ISBN 0-685-03764-9); testing prog. 1.20 (ISBN 0-685-03765-7); records 4.60 (ISBN 0-685-03766-5). HR&W.

--Premiere Etape. (Secondary French Ser: Level 1). (gr. 7). 1970. text ed. 4.68 (ISBN 0-685-03793-2, HoltC); tchrs' ed. 12.00 (ISBN 0-685-03794-0); 5 films s.p. 955.00, avail. sep. (ISBN 0-685-03795-9); film guides 0.36 ea.; flashcards 60.00 (ISBN 0-685-03797-5); projectuals 132.00 (ISBN 0-685-03798-3); exercise manual 1.36 (ISBN 0-685-03799-1); testing prog. 1.00 (ISBN 0-685-03800-9); records 4.60 (ISBN 0-685-03801-7). HR&W.

Les Farfeluches au zoo. (Les Farfeluches Ser.). (Illus.). (gr. 1). 1976. 8.95 (ISBN 0-88332-240-4, 2905). Larousse.

Gree, Alain. Les Farfeluches font des achats. (Illus., Fr.). (gr. k-3). 1979. 8.95 (ISBN 0-88332-114-9). Larousse.

Halioua, et al. Adventures En Ville. LC 79-63579. (gr. 9-12). 1979. pap. text ed. write for info. (ISBN 0-395-27833-3). HM.

Jacob, Suzanne. Children's Living French. (Living Language Courses Ser). (Illus.). (gr. k-5). 1960. lesson manual & bilingual picture dictionary 14.95 (ISBN 0-517-00135-7). Crown.

Kahn, Michele. My Everyday French Word Book. 44p. (gr. 1-6). 1981. 7.95 (ISBN 0-8120-5344-3). Barron.

Langellier, Alice, et al. Ce Monde Des Francais. (Secondary French Ser: Level 2). (Follows Nous les Jeunes or Chez les Francaise, leads into Lire, Parler et Ecrire). (gr. 7-12). 1970. text ed. 13.32 (ISBN 0-03-084234-4, HoltC); tchrs' ed. 8.28 (ISBN 0-03-084235-2); exercise manual 2.46 (ISBN 0-685-03753-3); tests 1.60 (ISBN 0-685-03754-1); prog. practice 14.00 (ISBN 0-685-03755-X); tapes s.p. 90.00 (ISBN 0-685-03756-8). HR&W.

Potter, Beatrix. Famille flopsaut: The Flopsy Bunnies. (Fr.). (gr. 3-7). bds. 4.50 (ISBN 0-7232-0655-4). Warne.

--Jeannot lapin: Benjamin Bunny. (gr. 3-7). bds. 4.50 (ISBN 0-7232-0651-1). Warne.

--Jeremie Peche-a-la-Ligne: Jeremy Fisher. (Fr.). (gr. 3-7). bds. 4.50 (ISBN 0-7232-0656-2). Warne.

--Noisy-Noisette: Squirrel Nutkin. (Fr.). (gr. 3-7). Date not set. bds. 4.50 (ISBN 0-7232-0654-6). Warne.

--Pierre Lapin: Peter Rabbit. (Illus., Fr.). (gr. 3-7). Date not set. bds. 4.50 (ISBN 0-7232-0650-3). Warne.

--Poupette-A-L'Epingle: Mrs. Tiggy-Winkle. (Fr.). (gr. 3-7). Date not set. bds. 4.50 (ISBN 0-7232-0652-X). Warne.

--Sophie Canetang: Jemima Puddle-Duck. (Fr.). (gr. 3-7). Date not set. bds. 4.50 (ISBN 0-7232-0653-8). Warne.

--Toto Le Minet: Tom Kitten. (Fr.). (gr. 3-7). bds. 4.00 (ISBN 0-7232-0657-0). Warne.

Rich, Beatrice. ABCDEFGHIJKLMNOPQRSTUVWXYZ in Eng & French. (Illus.). 64p. (gr. k-2). 1981. PLB 7.95 (ISBN 0-87460-353-6). Lion Bks.

Schneider, Margery J. & Grimbert, Joan T. Two Hundred & Fifty Conjugated French Verbs. 264p. (Orig.). 1981. pap. 2.50 (ISBN 0-8092-5846-3). Contemp Bks.

Slack, Anne, et al. French for Communication, One. LC 77-87429. (Illus., Gr. 9). 1978. text ed. 12.16 (ISBN 0-395-20159-4). HM.

FRENCH LANGUAGE–TEXT-BOOKS FOR FOREIGNERS

see also French Language–Conversation and Phrase Books; French Language–Self Instruction

Assimil. Assimil Language Courses: For Dutch Speaking People Who Want to Learn French - Frans Zondar Moeite. 12.95 (ISBN 0-686-56180-5); accompanying records & tapes 75.00 (ISBN 0-686-56181-3). French & Eur.

--Assimil Language Courses: For English Speaking People Who Want to Learn French - French Without Toil. 11.95 (ISBN 0-686-56150-3); accompanying records & tapes 75.00 (ISBN 0-686-56151-1). French & Eur.

--Assimil Language Courses: For English Speaking People Who Want to Learn French - Let's Learn French. 15.95 (ISBN 0-686-56152-X); accompanying records & tapes 75.00 (ISBN 0-686-56153-8). French & Eur.

--Assimil Language Courses: For French Speaking People Who Want to Learn Corsican - Le Corse Sans Peine. 13.95 (ISBN 0-686-56102-3); accompanying records & tapes 75.00 (ISBN 0-686-56103-1). French & Eur.

--Assimil Language Courses: For German Speaking People Who Want to Learn French - Franzosisch Ohne Muhe. 11.95 (ISBN 0-686-56140-6); accompanying records & tapes 75.00 (ISBN 0-686-56141-4). French & Eur.

--Assimil Language Courses: For Italian Speaking People Who Want to Learn French -Il Francese Senza Sforzo. 11.95 (ISBN 0-686-56162-7); accompanying records & tapes 75.00 (ISBN 0-686-56163-5). French & Eur.

--Assimil Language Courses: For Portuguese Speaking People Who Want to Learn French - O Frances Sem Custo. 11.95 (ISBN 0-686-56128-7); accompanying records & tapes 75.00 (ISBN 0-686-56129-5). French & Eur.

--Assimil Language Courses: For Spanish Speaking People Who Want to Learn French - El Frances Sin Esfuerzo. 11.95 (ISBN 0-686-56120-1); accompanying records & tapes 75.00 (ISBN 0-686-56121-X). French & Eur.

--Assimil Language Courses: For Yugoslav Speaking People Who Want to Learn French - Francuski Bez Muke. 12.95 (ISBN 0-686-56168-6); accompanying records & tapes 75.00 (ISBN 0-686-56169-4). French & Eur.

Assimil, ed. French Without Toil. 1957. 9.50x (ISBN 2-7005-0028-8); 3 cassettes 70.00 (ISBN 0-686-09278-3); 12 records 70.00x (ISBN 0-686-28531-X); bk. & cassettes 79.00x (ISBN 0-686-28532-8). Intl Learn Syst.

Bernstein, Mary. Auditory & Reading Comprehension Exercises in French. (gr. 10-12). 1964. pap. 1.25 (ISBN 0-88345-021-6, 17466); tchrs. ed. 2.50 (ISBN 0-88345-022-4, 17467). Regents Pub.

Biggs, P. & Dalwood, C. Les Orleanais ont la Parole. (Illus.). 1977. pap. text ed. 4.00x (ISBN 0-582-33121-8); tchr's ed. 4.50x (ISBN 0-582-33122-6); tapes 17.50x (ISBN 0-582-37746-3). Longman.

Blume, Eli. French Workbook, Book 1. (gr. 9 up). 1977. wkbk. 6.00 (ISBN 0-87720-993-6). AMSCO Sch.

--French Workbook, Book 2. (gr. 10-11). 1977. wkbk. 6.25 (ISBN 0-87720-994-4). AMSCO Sch.

--Workbook in French First Year. 2nd ed. (Illus., Orig.). (gr. 8-11). 1967. wkbk. 6.00 (ISBN 0-87720-452-7). AMSCO Sch.

--Workbook in French Three Years. 2nd. ed. (Illus., Orig.). (gr. 10-12). 1978. wkbk. 6.75 (ISBN 0-87720-459-4). AMSCO Sch.

--Workbook in French Two Years. 3rd ed. (Orig.). (gr. 10-11). 1979. pap. text ed. 7.92 (ISBN 0-87720-470-5). AMSCO Sch.

Cherel, Albert O. Frances Sem Custo. 9.95 (ISBN 0-685-11200-4). French & Eur.

--Francuski Bez Muke. (Assimil Textbks). 11.95 (ISBN 0-685-11203-9). French & Eur.

--Frans Zonder Moeite. 11.95 (ISBN 0-685-11204-7). French & Eur.

Cherel, Jean L. Let's Learn French, Book 1. (Illus.). 1976. 12.50x (ISBN 2-7005-0066-0); Set. 3 cassettes 70.00x (ISBN 0-686-19968-5); 10 records 70.00x (ISBN 0-686-28608-1); book & cassettes 79.00x (ISBN 0-686-28609-X). Intl Learn Syst.

Conroy, Joseph F. Adventure en Normandie. LC 81-7784. (A L'aventure! Ser). (Illus.). 40p. (Orig., French.). (gr. 7-12). 1981. pap. 1.95 (ISBN 0-88436-855-6, 121052). EMC.

--Danger sur la Cote d'azur. LC 81-7820. (A L'aventure! Ser.). (Illus.). 40p. (Orig., French.). (gr. 7-12). 1981. pap. 1.95 (ISBN 0-88436-857-2, 121054). EMC.

--Destination: France! LC 81-7816. (A L'aventure! Ser.). (Illus.). 40p. (Orig., French.). (gr. 7-12). 1981. pap. 1.95 (ISBN 0-88436-854-8, 121051). EMC.

--Sur la Route de la Contrebande. LC 81-7817. (A L'aventure! Ser.). (Illus.). 40p. (French.). (gr. 7-12). pap. 1.95 (ISBN 0-88436-856-4, 121053). EMC.

Cossard, Monique & Salazar, Robert. FSI French Basic Course, Units 1-12. 1976. pap. text ed. 12.50x (ISBN 0-686-10712-8); Units 1-6. 19 cassettes 114.00x (ISBN 0-686-10713-6); Units 7-12. 29 cassettes 174.00x (ISBN 0-686-10714-4). Intl Learn Syst.

--FSI French Basic Course, Units 13-24. 1976. pap. text ed. 9.75x (ISBN 0-686-10715-2); Units 13-18. 29 cassettes 174.00x (ISBN 0-686-10716-0); Units 19-24. 24 cassettes 144.00x (ISBN 0-686-10717-9). Intl Learn Syst.

Decouvrir la France, 4 vols, Vols. 6-9. Incl. Vol. 6. Pays de Loire; Vol. 7. Le Nord; Vol. 8. L'Alsace; Vol. 9. Les Vosges et la Lorraine. 22.50 ea. Larousse.

DeRocher, Francoise & DeRocher, Gregory. Options: Apercus de la France. LC 79-27245. 1980. pap. text ed. 8.50 (ISBN 0-471-04260-9). Wiley.

Foreign Service Institute. French Basic Course, 2 pts. (Fr.). 1979. Vol. 1, Pt. A, 194p. 11 audio cassettes incl. 115.00x (ISBN 0-88432-021-9, F170); Vol. 1, Pt. B, 290p. 29 audio cassettes incl. 149.00x (ISBN 0-88432-022-7, F181). J Norton Pubs.

Frances En Veinte Lecciones, for Spanish Speaking Readers. rev. ed. (Cortina Method Language Ser). (Illus.). 6.95 (ISBN 0-385-00071-5). Doubleday.

French in Africa: A Guide to the Teaching of French in a Foreign Language. 230p. 1975. pap. 10.50 (ISBN 92-3-101038-7, UNESCO). Unipub.

French in Three Months. (Hugo's Language Courses Ser.: No. 523). 1971. pap. 3.50 (ISBN 0-8226-0523-6). Littlefield.

Gande, Maureen & Gande, Anthony. L' Affaire Du Pneu Degonfle. 1969. pap. 2.50x (ISBN 0-435-37351-X). Heinemann Ed.

--La Clef. 1969. pap. text ed. 2.50x (ISBN 0-435-37352-8). Heinemann Ed.

--Mystere au Bois de Boulogne. 1969. pap. text ed. 2.50x (ISBN 0-435-37350-1). Heinemann Ed.

Grevisse, Maurice. Grevisse's Correct French: A Practical Guide. Kendris, Christopher, tr. from Fr. (gr. 11-12). Date not set. pap. text ed. 8.95 (ISBN 0-8120-2169-X). Barron.

Hargreaves, P. H., et al. French Once a Week Book, 2 bks. 1976. pap. 5.25x ea. (Pub. by Basil Blackwell); Bk. 1, Repr. Of 1961 Ed. pap. (ISBN 0-631-97290-0); Bk. 2, Repr. Of 1962 Ed. pap. (ISBN 0-631-97300-1). Biblio Dist.

Helstrom, Jo & Metz, Mary S. Le Francais a Decouvrir. 4th ed. LC 77-12172. (Illus.). 1978. text ed. 12.80 (ISBN 0-07-027966-7, W); tchr's. ed. 13.32 (ISBN 0-07-027967-5); wkbk. 3.64 (ISBN 0-07-027968-3); tests 74.40 (ISBN 0-07-027969-1); filmstrips 113.36 (ISBN 0-07-097690-2); tapes, cassettes & dupl. masters avail. McGraw.

Hendrix, William. Beginning French. 5th ed. LC 77-93107. (Illus.). 1978. pap. text ed. 15.75 (ISBN 0-395-25739-5); wkbk. 6.60 (ISBN 0-395-25740-9); tapes 207.28 (ISBN 0-395-25741-7). HM.

Hoffmann, Leon-Francois. Travaux Pratiques. 2nd ed. LC 73-8687. 1973. pap. text ed. 8.95x (ISBN 0-684-13577-9, ScribC). Scribner.

Kendris, Christopher & Wald, Heywood. French Now! A Level One Worktext. LC 78-243. 1980. pap. 7.95 (ISBN 0-8120-0473-6). Barron.

Madrigal, Margarita & Dulac, Colette. First Steps in French. (Illus.). (gr. 4-7). 1964. pap. text ed. 2.75 (ISBN 0-88345-176-X, 17473). Regents Pub.

Mauger, Gaston. Cours De Langue et De Civilization Francaises, 4 Vols. (Fr) Vol. 1. 7.00 (ISBN 0-685-20231-3); Vol. 2. 7.00 (ISBN 0-685-20232-1); Vol. 3. 7.50 (ISBN 0-685-20233-X); Vol. 4. 9.90 (ISBN 0-685-20234-8). Schoenhof.

Methode Orange, Bk 1. (Methode Orange Ser.). (Illus.). (gr. 7-12). 1979. text ed. 5.25 (ISBN 0-88345-407-6). Regents Pub.

Metz, Mary S. & Helstrom, Jo. Le Francais a Vivre. 4th ed. Rebisz, Jacqueline, ed. (Illus.). (gr. 9-12). 1978. text ed. 13.32 (ISBN 0-07-041755-5, W); tchr's. ed. 14.60 (ISBN 0-07-041756-3); wkbk. 3.96 (ISBN 0-07-041757-1). McGraw.

Moore, S., et al. Longman Audio-Visual French. (Illus.). write for info. (ISBN 0-686-19163-3). Longman.

Okin, Josee P. & Schmitt, Conrad J. Le Francais: Commencons. 2nd ed. LC 74-18343. (Illus.). 288p. (gr. 7). 1975. text ed. 10.60 (ISBN 0-07-047731-0, W); tchr's. ed. 11.92 (ISBN 0-07-047732-9); wkbk. 3.44 (ISBN 0-07-047733-7); cassette tapes 240.00 (ISBN 0-07-097983-9); exampak 8.00 (ISBN 0-07-047746-9); reel-to-reel tapes 360.00 (ISBN 0-07-097981-2); test pkg. 72.00 (ISBN 0-07-047734-5); test replacements 36.00 (ISBN 0-07-047735-3); filmstrips 80.00 (ISBN 0-07-097982-0). McGraw.

Patterson, W. R. Learn French for English Speakers. 230p. pap. 8.50 (ISBN 0-87557-023-2, 023-2). Saphrograph.

Purkis, Helen M. French Course for West Africa, 4 bks. 1962-65. Bk. 1. text ed. 5.95x (ISBN 0-521-06009-5); Bk. 2. text ed. 5.95x (ISBN 0-521-06010-9); Bk. 3. text ed. 5.95x (ISBN 0-521-06011-7); Bk. 4. text ed. 5.95x (ISBN 0-521-06012-5). Cambridge U Pr.

Reboullet, et al. Methode Orange, Bk 1. (Methode Orange Ser.). (Illus., Fr.). (gr. 7-12). 1979. pap. text ed. 4.25 (ISBN 0-88345-406-8). Regents Pub.

--Methode Orange - Workbook 1. (Methode Orange Ser.). (Illus., Fr.). (gr. 7-12). 1979. pap. text ed. 2.75 (ISBN 0-88345-408-4); tchrs' manual 5.95 (ISBN 0-88345-411-4); cassettes 70.00 (ISBN 0-686-60844-5); slides 120.00 (ISBN 0-686-60845-3). Regents Pub.

--Methode Orange 2. (Methode Orange Ser.). (Illus.). 143p. (gr. 7-12). 1979. pap. text ed. 4.25 (ISBN 0-88345-415-7, 18933). Regents Pub.

Staaks, Walter. French Verb Usage: A Direct Approach for American Students. 1971. pap. 3.95x (ISBN 0-673-07600-8). Scott F.

Three Hundred & One French Verbs. Date not set. 2.50 (ISBN 0-686-75970-2, 2496). Barron.

Two Thousand & One Words You Need to Know to Pass Any Test in French. Date not set. 3.95 (ISBN 0-686-75969-9, 2465). Barron.

Vaillancourt, Sarah. Perspectives Francaises, No. 2. LC 81-3311. (Illus.). 400p. (Fr.). 1981. text ed. 9.50 (ISBN 0-88436-756-8); pap. text ed. 6.50 (ISBN 0-88436-757-6, FRA125021). EMC.

Valette, Jean-Paul & Valette, Rebecca. Contacts: Langue et Culture Francaises. 2nd ed. (Illus.). 528p. 1981. text ed. 18.00 (ISBN 0-395-29328-6); tchrs. ed. 19.00 (ISBN 0-395-29329-4); wkbk 5.55 (ISBN 0-395-29330-8); reel-to-reel 250.00 (ISBN 0-395-29331-6); write for info. sample cassette (ISBN 0-395-29332-4). HM.

FRENCH LANGUAGE–VERB

Bescherelle. Art De Conjuguer: Huit Milles Verses. (Fr). 7.00 (ISBN 0-685-20225-9). Schoenhof.

Bescherelle, Louis. Le Nouveau Bescherelle: L'Art De Conjuguer. 7.50 (ISBN 0-685-11014-1). French & Eur.

Caput, J. P. & Caput, J. Dictionnaire des verbes francais. (Fr). 27.50 (ISBN 0-685-13871-2, 3622). Larousse.

Foley, James. Theoretical Morphology of the French Verb. iv, 292p. 1979. 28.00 (ISBN 90-272-0502-7, LIS 1). Benjamins North Am.

Fourel, M. Exercices de Verbes. Incl. No. 1. 60p. 1969 (ISBN 0-87774-031-3); No. 2. 86p. 1969; No. 3. 102p. 1969 (ISBN 0-87774-033-X); No. 4. 75p. 1967 (ISBN 0-87774-034-8). (Fr.). pap. text ed. 3.50 ea. Schoenhof.

French Verbs Simplified. (Hugo's Language Courses Ser.: No. 550). 1970. pap. 1.50 (ISBN 0-8226-0550-3). Littlefield.

Kendris, Christopher. Diccionario De 201 Verbos Franceses Conjugados En Todos Sus Tiempos y Personas. LC 68-8677. (Orig., Span. & Fr.). 1972. pap. 3.95 (ISBN 0-8120-0393-4). Barron.

--Dictionary of Five Hundred & One French Verbs: Fully Conjugated in All Tenses. LC 73-90072. 1970. 10.75 (ISBN 0-8120-6077-6); pap. 4.50 (ISBN 0-8120-0395-0). Barron.

--Two Hundred & One French Verbs Fully Conjugated in All the Tenses. LC 62-18770. (Orig.). 1963. text ed. 6.50 (ISBN 0-8120-6046-6); pap. text ed. 2.50 (ISBN 0-8120-0209-1). Barron.

Levy & Fleder. How to Use French Verbs. LC 75-22441. (Orig.). (gr. 11 up). 1977. pap. text ed. 4.95 (ISBN 0-8120-0599-6). Barron.

Ranieri, Helene. Let's "Unhook" the French Verbs (and 77 Quick Grammar, Syntax & Pronunciation "Tips") 2nd, rev. ed. LC 77-85156. (Illus.). 1974. 9.50 (ISBN 0-686-24866-X). H Ranieri.

Schogt, Henry C. Le Systeme Verbal Du Francais Contemporain. (Janua Linguarum, Series Practica: No. 79). 1968. pap. 17.50x (ISBN 90-2790-673-4). Mouton.

Strutz. Two Hundred & One Franzoische Verben. Date not set. pap. 3.95 (ISBN 0-8120-0689-5). Barron.

Szymanski, Jeanette R. Ecrivons les Verbes - Let's Write Verbs. LC 78-60629. 1978. pap. text ed. 9.00 (ISBN 0-8191-0560-0). U Pr of Amer.

Tolentino, Jaime M. Le Verbe Francais: Five Tomes in One Volume. LC 78-14928. (Illus.). 1979. text ed. 12.00 (ISBN 0-8477-3322-X). U of PR Pr.

FRENCH LANGUAGE–VERSIFICATION

Kastner, Leon E. A History of French Versification. 312p. 1980. Repr. of 1903 ed. lib. bdg. 40.00 (ISBN 0-8492-1472-6). R West.

Keeler, Sr. Mary J. Etude sur la poesie et sur le vocabulaire de Loys Papon. LC 75-94199. (Catholic University of America. Studies in Romance Languages & Literatures: No. 3). 16.00 (ISBN 0-404-50303-9). AMS Pr.
Klausenburger, Juergen. French Prosodics & Phonotactics: An Historical Typology. 102p. 1970. 20.00x (ISBN 3-484-52027-2). Intl Pubns Serv.
Langlois, Ernest. De Artibus Rhetoricae Rhythmicae, Sive. De Artibus Poeticis in Francia Ante Litterarum Renovationem Editis, Quibus Versificationis Nostrae Leges Explicantur. LC 72-86908. 119p. 1972. Repr. of 1890 ed. lib. bdg. 20.50 (ISBN 0-8337-2005-8). B Franklin.
Legouis, Emile. Short Parallel Between French & English Versification. LC 76-41176. 1925. lib. bdg. 6.00 (ISBN 0-8414-5653-4). Folcroft.
Martinon, Philippe. Strophes; Etudes Historiques et Critiques Sur les Formes De la Poesie Lyrique En France Depuis la Renaissance. 1969. Repr. of 1912 ed. 36.50 (ISBN 0-8337-2271-9). B Franklin.
Patterson, Warner F. Three Centuries of French Poetic Theory: A Critical History of the Chief Arts of Poetry in France, 1328-1630, Pts. 1 & 2 In 3 Vols. LC 65-17917. 1966. Repr. of 1935 ed. Set. 32.50 (ISBN 0-8462-0668-4). Russell.
Scott, Clive. The French Verse-Art. LC 79-50508. 1980. 37.50 (ISBN 0-521-22689-9). Cambridge U Pr.

FRENCH LANGUAGE–VOCABULARY

Gabillon, Aime. All in French - a Picture Book of Words & Phrases: Tout En Francais - un Livre Illustre De Mots et De Phrases. (Illus.). (gr. 1-3). 1976. 5.95 (ISBN 0-601-08508-6). Hamlyn-Amer.
Matore, Georges. Dictionnaire du Vocabulaire Essentiel. 5th ed. 360p. (Fr.). 1970. pap. 10.95 (ISBN 0-686-56874-5, M-6652). French & Eur.
Sauvageot, A. Portrait du vocabulaire francais. (Langue vivante). (Fr). pap. 8.25 (ISBN 0-685-14055-5, 3627). Larousse.
Savard, Jean-Guy & Richards, Jack. Les Indices D'utilite De Vocabulaire Fondamental Francais. 169p. 1970. pap. 5.00x (ISBN 2-7637-6460-6, Pub. by Laval). Intl Schol Bk Serv.

FRENCH LANGUAGE–WORDS–HISTORY

Kirk-Greene, C. W. E. French False Friends. 272p. 1981. 18.95 (ISBN 0-7100-0741-8). Routledge & Kegan.

FRENCH LEGENDS

see Legends, French

FRENCH LETTERS

Aquin De Chateau-Lyon, Pierre-Louis. Siecle litteraire de Louis XV; ou, lettres sur les hommes celebres, 2 vols. in 1. LC 76-43913. (Music & Theatre in France in the 17th & 18th Centuries). Repr. of 1754 ed. 34.00 (ISBN 0-404-60156-1). AMS Pr.
Bowen, Marjorie, ed. Some Famous Love Letters. LC 78-14213. 1978. Repr. of 1937 ed. lib. bdg. 30.00 (ISBN 0-8414-1659-1). Folcroft.
Daudet, Alphonse. Lettres de Mon Moulin. deluxe ed. 428.00 (ISBN 0-685-34889-X). French & Eur.
De Saint-Exupery, Antoine. Lettres a sa Mere. pap. 4.95 (ISBN 0-685-37088-7). French & Eur.
--Lettres de Jeunesse (1923-1931) pap. 4.95 (ISBN 0-685-37089-5). French & Eur.
Grente, George F. Dictionnaire des Lettres Francaises, 19e Siecle: L-Z. 568p. (Fr.). 1973. 79.95 (ISBN 0-686-57315-3, M-6297). French & Eur.
Grente, Georges F. Dictionnaire des Lettres Francaises, le 19e Siecle: A-K. 549p. (Fr.). 1971. 75.00 (ISBN 0-686-57314-5, M-6296). French & Eur.
Grente, Georges Francois. Dictionnaire Des Lettres Francaises (le Moyen Age) 768p. (Fr.). 1972. 79.95 (ISBN 0-686-56780-3, M-6577). French & Eur.
--Dictionnaire Des Lettres Francaises, 18e Siecle (A-K, 2 vols. 672p. (Fr.). 1960. 75.00 (ISBN 0-686-56782-X, M-6578). French & Eur.
--Dictionnaire des Lettres Francaises, 18e siecle (L-Z, 2 vols. 568p. (Fr.). 1973. 75.00 (ISBN 0-686-56784-6, M-6580). French & Eur.
Hastings, W. S. Balzac's Letters to His Family. 59.95 (ISBN 0-87968-700-2). Gordon Pr.
Hawkins, Richmond L., ed. Newly Discovered French Letters of the Seventeenth, Eighteenth & Nineteenth Centuries. 1933. pap. 16.00 (ISBN 0-527-01107-X). Kraus Repr.
Jean-Aubry, Georges. Une Amitie Exemplaire: Villiers De L'isle-Adam et Stephane Mallarme. LC 80-205. (Symbolists Ser.). (Illus., Fr.). Repr. of 1942 ed. 18.50 (ISBN 0-404-16300-9). AMS Pr.
Lentin, A, ed. Voltaire & Catherine the Great: Selected Correspondence. Orig. Title: Fr. (Illus.). 196p. 1974. 12.00 (ISBN 0-89250-099-9). Orient Res Partners.
Leroy, Pierre. Letters from My Friend Teilhard De Chardin. Lucas, Mary, tr. from Fr. LC 80-81883. (Illus.). 224p. 1980. pap. 6.95 (ISBN 0-8091-2292-8). Paulist Pr.
Mallarme, Stephane. Correspondance, 3 tomes. Mondor, ed. Incl. Tome I. 1862-1871. 13.50 (ISBN 0-685-34936-5); Tome II. 1871-1885. 13.95 (ISBN 0-685-34937-3); Tome III. 1886-1889. 17.50 (ISBN 0-685-34938-1). French & Eur.
Prevert, Jacques. Lettres des Iles Baladar. pap. 3.40 (ISBN 0-685-37051-8). French & Eur.
Proust, Marcel. A un Ami, G. de Lauris: Correspondance Inedite, 1903-1922. 5.50 (ISBN 0-685-37055-0). French & Eur.
--Choix de Lettres. 8.50 (ISBN 0-685-37057-7). French & Eur.
--Chroniques. pap. 3.95 (ISBN 0-685-37058-5). French & Eur.
--Correspondance avec sa Mere. pap. 6.95 (ISBN 0-685-37065-8). French & Eur.
--Lettre a la N. R. F. (Cahiers Marcel Proust). pap. 5.95 (ISBN 0-685-37067-4). French & Eur.
--Lettres a Bibesco. 11.95 (ISBN 0-685-37066-6). French & Eur.
--Lettres a Reynaldo Hahn. pap. 6.50 (ISBN 0-685-37068-2). French & Eur.
--Lettres Retrouvees. 6.95 (ISBN 0-685-37069-0). French & Eur.
Rybalka. Boris Vian. (Bibliotheque des Lettres Modernes). 15.50 (ISBN 0-685-36633-2). French & Eur.
Sand, George, pseud. Correspondance Generale, 9 tomes. Lubin, ed. Incl. Tome I. (1812-1831) pap. 24.50 (ISBN 0-685-34977-2); Tome II. (Juin 1832-Juin 1835) pap. 24.50 (ISBN 0-685-34978-0); Tome III. (Juillet 1835-Avril 1837 pap. 24.50 (ISBN 0-685-34979-9); Tome IV. (Mai 1837-Mars 1840) pap. 24.50 (ISBN 0-685-34980-2); Tome V. (Avril 1840-Decembre 1842) pap. 24.50 (ISBN 0-685-34981-0); Tome V I. (1843-Juin 1845) pap. 25.95 (ISBN 0-685-34982-9); Tome VII. (Juillet 1845-Juillet 1847) pap. 22.95 (ISBN 0-685-34983-7); Tome VIII. (Juillet 1847-Decembee 1848) pap. 22.95 (ISBN 0-685-34984-5); Tome IX. (1849-1850) pap. 29.95 (ISBN 0-685-34985-3). (Class. Garnier). French & Eur.
Sand, George. Correspondance Generale, 9 tomes. Lubin, ed. Incl. Tome I. (1812-1831) 30.65 (ISBN 0-685-34986-1); Tome II. (Juin 1832-Juin 1835) 30.65 (ISBN 0-685-34987-X); Tome III. (Juillet 1835-Avril 1837) 30.65 (ISBN 0-685-34988-8); Tome IV. (Mai 1837-Mars 1840) 32.50 (ISBN 0-685-34989-6); Tome V. (Avril 1840-Decembre 1842) 33.25 (ISBN 0-685-34990-X); Tome VI. (1843-Juin 1845) 34.95 (ISBN 0-685-34991-8); Tome VII. (Juillet 1845-Juillet 1847) 34.95 (ISBN 0-685-34992-6); Tome VIII. (Juillet 1847-Decembre 1848) 38.50 (ISBN 0-685-34993-4); Tome IX. (1849-1850) 64.65 (ISBN 0-685-34994-2). (Coll. Prestige). French & Eur.
Sevigne. Letters of Madame De Sevigne to Her Daughter & Her Friends, 2vols. 1974. Repr. of 1927 ed. lib. bdg. 85.00 (ISBN 0-8414-8121-0). Folcroft.
Teilhard De Chardin, Pierre. Accomplir L'homme: Lettres Inedites 1926-1952. 15.95 (ISBN 0-685-36586-7). French & Eur.
--Ecrits du Temps de Guerre (1916-1919) 17.50 (ISBN 0-685-36587-5). French & Eur.
--Genese d'une Pensee: Lettres 1914-1919. 15.90 (ISBN 0-685-36590-5). French & Eur.
--Lettres a Leontine Zanta. pap. 10.50 (ISBN 0-685-36594-8). French & Eur.
--Lettres d'Egypte (1905-1908) pap. 7.95 (ISBN 0-685-36595-6). French & Eur.
--Lettres d'Hastings et de Paris (1908-1914) 15.75 (ISBN 0-685-36596-4). French & Eur.
Teilhard De Chardin, Pierre & De Labac. Lettres Intimes a Auguste Valensin Bruno de Solages et Hanri de Labac. 18.95 (ISBN 0-685-36597-2). French & Eur.
Valery, Paul. Lettres a Quelques-uns. pap. 6.25 (ISBN 0-685-36617-0). French & Eur.
Wormeley, Katharine P., ed. The Correspondence of Madame, Princess Palatine, Mother of the Regent; of Marie - Adelaide De Savoie, Duchesses De Bourgogne; & of Madame De Maintenon, in Relation to Saint-Cyr. 1978. Repr. of 1902 ed. lib. bdg. 40.00 (ISBN 0-8492-2891-3). R West.

FRENCH LETTERS–HISTORY AND CRITICISM

Irvine, Lyn L. Ten Letter-Writers. facs. ed. LC 68-16942. (Essay Index Reprint Ser). 1932. 15.00 (ISBN 0-8369-0560-1). Arno.
Smith, Mabell S. The Spirit of French Letters. 374p. 1980. Repr. of 1912 ed. lib. bdg. 25.00 (ISBN 0-89760-819-4, Telegraph). Dynamic Learn Corp.

FRENCH LITERATURE (COLLECTIONS)

Here are entered collections of French Literature in French. For translations into English see subdivision Translations into English.
see also Encyclopedists; French-Canadian Literature

Adams, A., et al. Litterature francaise, 2 Vols. (Illus., Fr.). 76.50 ea. Larousse.
Artaud, Antonin. Artaud: Four Texts. Eshleman, Clayton, tr. from Fr. (Illus.). 100p. 1981. 12.95 (ISBN 0-915572-57-5); pap. 6.95 (ISBN 0-915572-56-7). Panjandrum.
Bernanos, Georges. Essais et Ecrits de Combat. Bridel & Chabot, eds. Incl. Saint-Dominique; Jeanne, Relapse et Sainte; La Grande Peur Des Bien-Pensants; Les Grands Cimetieres Sous la Lune; Scandale de la Verite; Nous Autres Francais; Les Enfants Humilies; Articles (1909-1939. (Bibliotheque de la Pleiade). 35.50 (ISBN 0-685-37212-X). French & Eur.
Bree, G. Twentieth Century French Literature. 1962. text ed. 8.95x (ISBN 0-685-16158-7). Macmillan.
Calder, John, intro. by. A Nouveau Roman Reader. 1979. 11.95 (ISBN 0-7145-3719-5); pap. 5.95 (ISBN 0-7145-3720-9). Riverrun NY.
Catel, Jean. Rythme et Langage Dans la L'Edition Des "Leaves of Grass". 1979. Repr. of 1930 ed. lib. bdg. 30.00 (ISBN 0-8482-0469-7). Norwood Edns.
Chapman, Frederic, ed. Novels & Short Stories of Anatole France, 19 vols. 1980. Set. lib. bdg. 425.00 (ISBN 0-8495-0790-1). Arden Lib.
Cholakian, Patricia F. & Cholakian, Rouben C., eds. The Early French Novella: An Anthology of Fifteenth & Sixteenth Century Tales. LC 79-171179. 1972. 19.00 (ISBN 0-87395-090-9); pap. 7.95 (ISBN 0-87395-220-0); microfiche 19.00 (ISBN 0-87395-190-5). State U NY Pr.
Clouard, Henri & Leggewie, Robert, eds. Anthologie De la Litterature Francaise, 2 vols. 2nd ed. 860p. 1975. Vol. 1. pap. text ed. 12.95x (ISBN 0-19-501877-X); Vol. 2. pap. text ed. 12.95x (ISBN 0-19-501878-8). Oxford U Pr.
Colette. Looking Backwards. Le Vay, David, tr. from Fr. LC 74-29051. 216p. 1975. 8.95x (ISBN 0-253-14900-2). Ind U Pr.
Delarue & Teneze. Le Conte Populaire Francais: Catalogue Raisonne des Versions de France et des Pays d'Outremer de Langue Francaise. 33.95 (ISBN 0-685-33999-8). French & Eur.
France, Anatole. On Life & Letters, First Series. facsimile ed. Chapman, F., ed. LC 77-156643. (Essay Index Reprint Ser). Repr. of 1910 ed. 19.00 (ISBN 0-8369-2357-X). Arno.
--On Life & Letters, Fourth Series. facsimile ed. Chapman, F., ed. LC 77-156643. (Essay Index Reprint Ser). Repr. of 1924 ed. 20.00 (ISBN 0-8369-2360-X). Arno.
--On Life & Letters, Second Series. facsimile ed. Chapman, F., ed. LC 77-156643. (Essay Index Reprint Ser). Repr. of 1914 ed. 19.50 (ISBN 0-8369-2358-8). Arno.
--On Life & Letters, Third Series. facsimile ed. Chapman, F., ed. LC 77-156643. (Essay Index Reprint Ser). Repr. of 1924 ed. 20.00 (ISBN 0-8369-2359-6). Arno.
Frey, Linda, et al. The Gods Are Athirst: Anatole France. LC 78-31742. 1978. lib. bdg. 22.50 (ISBN 0-8482-0846-3). Norwood Edns.
Gautier, J. M. L' Exotisme Americain dans l'Oeuvre de Chateaubriand. 66p. 1951. 21.00x (ISBN 0-7190-1208-2, Pub. by Manchester U Pr England). State Mutual Bk.
Guerard, A. L. Five Masters of French Romance. 326p. 1980. Repr. lib. bdg. 25.00 (ISBN 0-89760-311-7). Telegraph Bks.
Historiens et memorialistes du seizieme siecle. (Classiques Larousse). (Illus., Fr.). pap. 1.95 (ISBN 0-685-13939-5, 114). Larousse.
James, Henry. Literary Reviews & Essays. LC 58-8375. 1979. pap. 4.95 (ISBN 0-394-17098-9, B428, BC). Grove.
Jean, B. & Montaigne, F. Mouret. Descartes et Pascal Par la Dissertation. 196p. 1971. 21.00x (ISBN 0-686-63844-1, Pub. by Manchester U Pr England). State Mutual Bk.
Jensen, Russell C. Preliminary Survey of the French Collection: Finding Aids to the Microfilmed Manuscript Collection of the Genealogical Society of Utah, No. 5. 433p. 1981. pap. 25.00x (ISBN 0-87480-171-0). U of Utah Pr.
Lagarde, A. & Michard, L. Collection Litteraire, 6 vols. Incl. Vol. 1. Moyen Age. 9.60 (ISBN 0-685-58371-6); Vol. 2. Seizieme Siecle. 9.60 (ISBN 0-685-58372-4); Vol. 3. Dix-Septieme Siecle. 10.90 (ISBN 0-685-58373-2); Vol. 4. Dix-Huitieme Siecle. 12.25 (ISBN 0-685-58374-0); Vol. 5. Dix-Neuvieme Siecle. 13.65 (ISBN 0-685-58375-9); Vol. 6. Vingtieme Siecle. 17.25 (ISBN 0-685-58376-7). (Fr.). Schoenhof.
Moore, Will G., et al, eds. French Mind: Studies in Honour of Gustave Rudler. facsimile ed. LC 75-167386. (Essay Index Reprint Ser). Repr. of 1952 ed. 19.50 (ISBN 0-8369-2464-9). Arno.
Palache, John. Four Novelists of the Old Regime: Crebillon, Laclos, Diderot, Restif De La Bretonne. LC 73-132443. (Studies in French Literature, No. 45). 1970. Repr. of 1926 ed. lib. bdg. 53.95 (ISBN 0-8383-1193-8). Haskell.
Saintsbury, George. Miscellaneous Essays. LC 72-39114. (Essay Index Reprint Ser.). Repr. of 1892 ed. 22.00 (ISBN 0-8369-2718-4). Arno.
Secretan, D. E. La Pratique Du Francais Cours Superieur. 208p. 1970. 21.00x (ISBN 0-7190-0424-1, Pub. by Manchester U Pr England). State Mutual Bk.
Secretan, D. E. & Dervaux, J. C. La Pratique Du Francais Cours Superieur. 200p. 1972. 15.00x (ISBN 0-7190-0490-X, Pub. by Manchester U Pr England). State Mutual Bk.
Sommer, H. Oskar, ed. Aventures Ou la Queste Del Saint Graal: La Mort le Roi Artus. (Vulgate Version of the Arthurian Romances: No. 6). Repr. of 1913 ed. 57.50 (ISBN 0-404-17636-4). AMS Pr.
Wells, Benjamin. Modern French Literature. 1973. lib. bdg. 25.00 (ISBN 0-8414-9665-X). Folcroft.
Weston, Jessie L., tr. Guingamor, Lanval, Tyolet, le Bisclareret. (Fr). Repr. of 1900 ed. 14.00 (ISBN 0-404-00474-1). AMS Pr.
Yale University - French Dept. Contes Modernes. 3rd ed. 1972. pap. text ed. 8.50 scp (ISBN 0-06-047301-0, HarpC). Har-Row.

FRENCH LITERATURE (COLLECTIONS)–TO 1500

Gauthier, J. D., ed. French Twenty Bibliography: Provencal Supplement No. 1, Critical & Biographical References to Provencal Literature Since 1850. (Orig.). 1976. pap. 12.00 (ISBN 0-933444-32-X). French Inst.
Paris, Gaston. Mediaeval French Literature facsmile ed. LC 78-154160. (Select Bibliographies Reprint Ser). Repr. of 1903 ed. 15.00 (ISBN 0-8369-5776-8). Arno.

FRENCH LITERATURE (SELECTIONS: EXTRACTS, ETC.)

Alden, Douglas W., ed. Introduction to French Masterpieces. (Fr.). 1948. 22.95x (ISBN 0-89197-240-4); pap. text ed. 8.95x (ISBN 0-89197-241-2). Irvington.
Alexander, Ian W., et al. Studies in Romance Philology & French Literature Presented to John Orr by Pupils, Colleagues & Friends. 315p. 1980. lib. bdg. 65.00 (ISBN 0-89760-627-2, Telegraph). Dynamic Learn Corp.
Bishop, Morris. A Survey of French Literature, 2 vols. rev. ed. Incl. Vol. 1. The Middle Ages to 1800. 462p (ISBN 0-15-584963-8, HC); Vol. 2. The Nineteenth & Twentieth Centuries. 462p (ISBN 0-15-584964-6, HC). 1965. text ed. 17.95 ea. (HC). HarBraceJ.
Bradley, Robert F. & Michell, R. B. Eight Centuries of French Literature: Chanson de Roland to Sartre. (Fr., Fr) 1951. 34.50x (ISBN 0-89197-134-3); pap. text ed. 18.50x (ISBN 0-8290-0372-X). Irvington.
Clouard, Henri & Leggewie, Robert, eds. French Writers of Today. (Illus.). 336p. (Fr.). 1965. pap. 7.95x (ISBN 0-19-500853-7). Oxford U Pr.
Lemaitre, Jules. Literary Impressions. Evans, A. W., tr. 320p. 1980. Repr. of 1921 ed. lib. bdg. 30.00 (ISBN 0-89987-502-5). Darby Bks.
Maman, Andre, et al. France: Ses Grandes Heures Litteraires. (Level 4 or 5). (gr. 9-12). 1968. text ed. 15.95 (ISBN 0-07-039851-8, C); inst. manual 4.95 (ISBN 0-07-039852-6); exercises 5.95 (ISBN 0-07-039853-4); tapes 150.00 (ISBN 0-07-097885-9). McGraw.
Nelson, Robert J. & Oxenhandler, Neal, eds. Aspects of French Literature. LC 61-5992. (Fr.). 1961. 34.50x (ISBN 0-89197-037-1); pap. text ed. 16.95x (ISBN 0-89197-038-X). Irvington.
Steinhauer, Harry & Walter, Felix, eds. Omnibus of French Literature, 2 Vols. 1941. text ed. 8.95x ea. Vol. 1 (41691). Vol. 2 (41698). Macmillan.

FRENCH LITERATURE–AFRICAN AUTHORS

see African Literature (French)

FRENCH LITERATURE–BIBLIOGRAPHY

Alden, Douglas W., ed. French Twenty Bibliography: Critical & Biographical References for the Study of French Literature Since 1885, Index to Nos. 26-30. LC 77-648803. (Orig.). 1981. pap. 26.00x (ISBN 0-933444-38-9). French Inst.
--French Twenty Bibliography: Critical & Biographical References for the Study of French Literature Since 1885, No. 32. LC 77-648803. (Orig.). 1981. pap. 42.00x (ISBN 0-933444-37-0). French Inst.
Alden, Douglas W. & Brooks, Richard A., eds. A Critical Bibliography of French Literature: Vol. VI, Twentieth Century, 3 pts. 1979. 150.00x (ISBN 0-8156-2204-X). Syracuse U Pr.

Alden, Douglas W., et al, eds. French Twenty Bibliography: Critical & Biographical References for the Study of French Literature Since 1885, Nos. 1-31. Incl. Nos. 1-9. 1949-1957. pap. 4.00x ea.; No. 1. 1949. pap. (ISBN 0-933444-02-8); No. 2, 1950. pap. (ISBN 0-933444-03-6); No. 3. 1951. pap. (ISBN 0-933444-04-4); No. 4. 1952. pap. (ISBN 0-933444-05-2); No. 5. 1953. pap. (ISBN 0-933444-06-0); No. 6. 1954. pap. (ISBN 0-933444-07-9); No. 7. 1955. pap. (ISBN 0-933444-08-7); No. 8. 1956. pap. (ISBN 0-933444-09-5); No. 9. 1957. pap. (ISBN 0-933444-10-9); No. 10. 1958. Incl. Index To Nos. 1-10. pap. 7.00x (ISBN 0-933444-11-7); Nos. 11-16. pap. 6.00x ea.; No. 11. 1959. pap. (ISBN 0-933444-12-5); No. 12. 1960. pap. (ISBN 0-933444-13-3); No. 13. 1961. pap. (ISBN 0-933444-14-1); No. 14. 1962. pap. (ISBN 0-933444-15-X); No. 15. 1963. pap. (ISBN 0-933444-16-8); No. 16. 1964. pap. (ISBN 0-933444-17-6); Nos. 17-20. pap. 12.00x ea.; No. 17. 1965. pap. (ISBN 0-933444-18-4); No. 18. 1966. pap. (ISBN 0-933444-19-2); No. 19. 1967. pap. (ISBN 0-933444-20-6); No. 20. 1968. pap. (ISBN 0-933444-21-4); General Index to Nos. 11-20. Tussing, Ruth-Elaine, et al, eds. 1969. pap. 15.00x (ISBN 0-933444-22-2); No. 21. 1969. pap. 12.00x (ISBN 0-933444-23-0); Nos. 22-24. pap. 18.00x ea.; No. 22. 1970. pap. (ISBN 0-933444-24-9); No. 23. 1971. pap. (ISBN 0-933444-25-7); No. 24. 1972. pap. (ISBN 0-933444-26-5); No. 25. 1973. pap. 24.00x (ISBN 0-933444-27-3); Index to Nos. 21-25. Tussing, Ruth-Elaine, ed. 1974. pap. 26.00x (ISBN 0-933444-28-1); Nos. 26-27. pap. 30.00x ea. (ISBN 0-685-96993-2); No. 26. 1974. pap. (ISBN 0-933444-29-X); No. 27. 1975. pap. (ISBN 0-933444-30-3); Nos. 28-31. Annual Serial: No. 28, 1976. pap. 36.00x (ISBN 0-933444-31-1); Annual Serial: No. 29, 1977. pap. 42.00x (ISBN 0-933444-33-8); No. 30, 1978. pap. 42.00x (ISBN 0-933444-34-6); No. 31, 1979. pap. 42.00 (ISBN 0-933444-36-2). (Orig., Nos. 1-20, LC 49-3084; nos. 21-30, LC 77-648803. Nos. 1-20 originally published as French Seven Bibliography). 1949-79. Set. pap. 360.00x (ISBN 0-933444-01-X). French Inst.

Atkinson, Geoffroy. Litterature geographique francaise de la Renaissance, 2 vols. in 1. LC 68-7028. (Bibliography & Reference Ser.: No. 213). (Illus.). 1968. Repr. of 1927 ed. with supplement 45.50 (ISBN 0-8337-0113-4). B Franklin.

Baker, Robert K. Introduction to Library Research in French Literature. LC 77-18074. (A Westview Special Study Ser.). 1978. lib. bdg. 23.75x (ISBN 0-89158-060-3); pap. text ed. 9.00 (ISBN 0-89158-082-4). Westview.

Bassan, Fernande, et al. An Annotated Bibliography of French Language & Literature. LC 75-24079. (Reference Library of the Humanities: Vol. 26). 300p. 1975. lib. bdg. 33.00 (ISBN 0-8240-9986-9). Garland Pub.

Brooks, Richard A., ed. Critical Bibliography of French Literature, Vol. 4a: The Eighteen Century-Supplement. LC 47-3282. 1968. 34.95x (ISBN 0-8156-2009-8). Syracuse U Pr.

Cabeen, David C. & Brody, Jules, eds. Critical Bibliography of French Literature, Vol. 3: The Seventeenth Century. LC 47-3282. 1961. 34.95x (ISBN 0-8156-2007-1). Syracuse U Pr.

Cabeen, David C. & Havens, George R., eds. Critical Bibliography of French Literature, Vol. 4: The Eighteenth Century. LC 47-3282. 1951. text ed. 34.95x (ISBN 0-8156-2008-X). Syracuse U Pr.

Cabeen, David C. & Holmes, Urban T., eds. Critical Bibliography of French Literature, Vol. 1: The Medieval Period. LC 47-3282. 1952. 34.95x (ISBN 0-8156-2005-5). Syracuse U Pr.

Cabeen, David C. & Schutz, Alexander H., eds. Critical Bibliography of French Literature, Vol. 2: The Sixteenth Century. LC 47-3282. 1956. 34.95x (ISBN 0-8156-2006-3). Syracuse U Pr.

Cioranesco. Bibliographie De la Litterature Francaise Du XVIIe Siecle, 3 Vols. Tome 1, A-C. 49.95 (ISBN 0-685-11047-8); Tome 2, D-M. 59.95 (ISBN 0-685-11048-6); Tome 3, N-Z. Tables. 54.95 (ISBN 0-685-11049-4). French & Eur.

--Bibliographie de la Litterature Francaise du 18eme Siecle, 3 tomes. Tome 1, A-D. 59.95 (ISBN 0-686-52227-3); Tome 2, E-Q. 54.95 (ISBN 0-686-52228-1); Tome 3, R-Z. 54.95 (ISBN 0-686-52229-X). French & Eur.

Cioranescu, A. Bibliographie de la litterature francaise du 18e siecle, 3 vols. 2266p. Pt. 1. 29.90 (ISBN 0-685-99776-6); Pt. 2. 32.70 (ISBN 0-686-66719-0); Pt. 3. 32.70 (ISBN 0-686-66720-4). Adler.

Cioranescu, Alexandre. Bibliographie de la litterature francaise du 17e siecle, 3 Vols. 1965-67. Pt. 1. 29.90 (ISBN 0-685-99752-9); Pt. 2. 36.00 (ISBN 0-685-99753-7); Pt. 3. 32.70 (ISBN 0-685-99754-5). Adler.

De Rothschild, James E. Catalogue Des Livres Composant la Bibliotheque De Feu M. le Baron Rothschild, 5 Vols. Picot, Emile, ed. Repr. of 1884 ed. 215.00 (ISBN 0-8337-3070-3). B Franklin.

Fay, Bernard. Bibliographie Critique Des Ouvrages Francais Relatifs Aux Etats-Unis 1770-1800. LC 68-56725. 1968. 15.00 (ISBN 0-8337-1102-4). B Franklin.

Federn, Robert. Repertoire Bibliographique De la Litterature Francaise Des Origines a 1911, 2 vols. 612p. Repr. of 1913 ed. 46.00 (ISBN 0-384-15401-8). Johnson Repr.

Frere, Edouard B. Manuel Du Bibliographe Normand, ou, Dictionnaire Bibliographique et Historique Contenant, 2 Vols. 1964. Repr. of 1860 ed. 73.00 (ISBN 0-8337-1245-4). B Franklin.

Griffin, Lloyd W., et al. Modern French Literature & Language: A Bibliography of Homage Studies. LC 75-26480. 175p. 1976. 21.50 (ISBN 0-299-06990-7, IS-00003, Pub. by U of Wis. Pr.). Univ Microfilms.

Harvard University Library. French Literature: Classification Schedule, Author & Title Listing, Chronological Listing, 2 vols. LC 72-93949. (Widener Library Shelflist Ser.: No. 47-48). 1973. Set. text ed. 75.00x (ISBN 0-674-32215-0). Harvard U Pr.

Jensen, Russell C. Preliminary Survey of the French Collection: Finding Aids to the Microfilmed Manuscript Collection of the Genealogical Society of Utah, No. 5. 433p. 1981. pap. 25.00x (ISBN 0-87480-171-0). U of Utah Pr.

Kempton, Richard. French Literature: An Annotated Guide to Selected Bibliographies. LC 80-24230. (Selected Bibliographies in Language & Literature Ser.: No. 2). 42p. (Orig.). 1981. pap. 4.50x (ISBN 0-87352-951-0). Modern Lang.

Klapp. Bibliographie d'historie Litteraire Francaise, 9 tomes. 450.00 set (ISBN 0-685-36709-6). French & Eur.

Mahaffey, Denis, ed. Concise Bibliography of French Literature. LC 75-7801. 286p. 1976. 25.00 (ISBN 0-85935-008-8). Bowker.

Miller, Joan M. French Structuralism: An Annotated Bibliography. LC 78-68283. 1981. lib. bdg. 55.00 (ISBN 0-8240-9780-7). Garland Pub.

Peyre, Henri. Bibliographie critique de l'hellenisme en France de 1843 a 1870. LC 72-1698. (Yale Romanic Studies: No. 6). Repr. of 1932 ed. 14.00 (ISBN 0-404-53206-3). AMS Pr.

Scholberg, Henry & Divien, Emmanuel. Bibliographie des Francais dans l'Inde. 216p. 1975. lib. bdg. 12.50 (ISBN 0-88253-738-5). Ind-US Inc.

Stambolian, George, ed. Twentieth-Century French Fiction: Essays for Germaine Bree. 1975. 20.00 (ISBN 0-8135-0786-3). Rutgers U Pr.

Starr, William T. French Six Bibliography: Critical & Biographical References for the Study of Nineteenth Century French Literature, No. 1-7, 1954-1967. (Orig.). 1945-69. Set. pap. 25.00x (ISBN 0-933444-00-1). French Inst.

Tchemerzine, Avenir. Bibliographie D'Edtions Originales & Rares D'Auteurs Francais Des Xve, Xvie, Xviie, Xviiie Siecles Contenant Environ 6,000 Fac-Similes De Titres & Gravures. LC 73-87061. (Illus.). 420p. (Fr., Originally published in 10 vols. & reprinted in reduced format in 1 vol.). 1973. Repr. of 1927 ed. 105.00x (ISBN 0-914146-03-3). Somerset Hse.

Thieme, Hugo P. Bibliographie De la Litterature Francaise De 1800 a 1930, 3 vols. LC 33-11487. 2370p. (Fr.). 1971. Repr. of 1933 ed. Set. 200.00x (ISBN 0-8002-1234-7). Intl Pubns Serv.

Vicaire, Georges. Manuel de L'amateur de Livres du Dix-Neuvieme Siecle, Eighteen-One to Eighteen Ninty-Three, 8 vols. LC 79-144832. (Fr., X1894-1920). 1973. Repr. of 1884 ed. Set. lib. bdg. 297.00 (ISBN 0-8337-3644-2). B Franklin.

--Manuel de L'amateur de Livres du Dix-Neuvieme Siecle, Eighteen-One to Eighteen Ninty-Three, 8 vols. LC 79-144832. (Fr., X1894-1920). 1973. Repr. of 1884 ed. Set. lib. bdg. 297.00 (ISBN 0-8337-3644-2). B Franklin.

--Manuel De L'Amateur De Livres Du XIXe Siecle, 1801-1893. LC 73-87062. 500p. 1973. Repr. lib. bdg. 98.50x (ISBN 0-914146-03-3). Somerset Hse.

Viollet-Le Duc, Emmanuel L. Catalogue Des Livres Composant la Bibliotheque Poetique de M. Vidlet-le Duc Auec Des Notes Bibliographiques, 2 Vols in 1. 1967. Repr. of 1847 ed. 45.50 (ISBN 0-8337-3656-6). B Franklin.

Wade, Ira O. Clandestine Organization & Diffusion of Philosophic Ideas in France from 1700 to 1750. 1967. Repr. lib. bdg. 16.50x (ISBN 0-374-98094-2). Octagon.

FRENCH LITERATURE–DICTIONARIES

Barbier. Dictionnaire Des Ouvrages Anonymes, 4 Vols. Set. 325.00 (ISBN 0-685-11143-1). French & Eur.

Bonnefoy, Claude, et al. Dictionaire De Litterature Contemporaire. 22.50 (ISBN 2-7113-0077-3). Gaylord Prof Pubns.

--Dictionnaire de Litterature Francais Contemporaine. 411p. (Fr.). 1977. 35.00 (ISBN 0-686-56924-5, M-6042). French & Eur.

Bouty, Michel. Dictionnaire des Oeuvres et Des Themes de la Litterature Frncaise. 351p. (Fr.). 1972. pap. 8.95 (ISBN 0-686-56855-9, M-6633). French & Eur.

Braun, Sidney, ed. Dictionary of French Literature. 1958. 10.00 (ISBN 0-8022-0169-5). Philos Lib.

Braun, Sidney D., ed. Dictionary of French Literature. LC 70-138576. (Illus.). 1971. Repr. of 1958 ed. lib. bdg. 21.00x (ISBN 0-8371-5775-7, BRDF). Greenwood.

Dictionnaire des Oeuvres: Index. 5th ed. (Fr.). 1969. 295.00 (ISBN 0-686-56851-6, M-6629). French & Eur.

Engler, Winfried. Lexikon der Franzoesischen Literatur. (Ger.). 1974. 27.50 (ISBN 3-520-38801-4, M-7259). French & Eur.

Grente, S. I. Le Dictionnaire des lettres francaises. Incl. Le Moyen Age. 71.75 (ISBN 0-685-42270-4); pap. 64.75 (ISBN 0-685-42271-2); Le 18e Siecle, 2 pts. 68.25 ea.; pap. 59.25 ea.; Le 19e Siecle, 2 pts. 138.95 set (ISBN 0-686-66957-6); pap. 120.50 set (ISBN 0-686-66958-4). Adler.

Harvey, Paul & Heseltine, Janet E., eds. Oxford Companion to French Literature. (YA) (gr. 9 up). 1959. 49.50 (ISBN 0-19-866104-5). Oxford U Pr.

LeSage, Laurent & Yon, André. Dictionnaire Des Critiques Litteraires: Guide De la Critique De la Vingtieme Siecle. LC 68-8181. (Fr.). 1969. 14.95x (ISBN 0-271-00081-3). Pa St U Pr.

Reid, Joyce M. The Concise Oxford Dictionary of French Literature. rev. abr. ed. Orig. Title: The Oxford Companion to French Literature. 1976. 15.95 (ISBN 0-19-866118-5). Oxford U Pr.

FRENCH LITERATURE–EXPLICATION

Ferguson, Rachel. Celebrated Sequels. 1934. 17.50 (ISBN 0-686-18155-7). Havertown Bks.

FRENCH LITERATURE–HISTORY AND CRITICISM

see also Pleiade

Adam, Jean-Michel. Linguistique et discours litteraire. new ed. (Collection L). (Orig., Fr.). 1976. pap. text ed. 19.95 (ISBN 0-685-66283-7). Larousse.

Alcover, Madeleine, et al. Studies in French. (Rice University Studies: Vol. 63, No. 1). 133p. 1977. pap. 4.25x (ISBN 0-89263-231-3). Rice Univ.

Aldington, Richard. A Book of Characters from Theophrastus Joseph Hall, Sir Thomas Overbury, Nicolas Breton, John Earle, Thomas Fuller, & Other English Authors; Jean De la Bruyere, Vauvenargues, & Other French Authors. 559p. 1980. Repr. of 1924 ed. lib. bdg. 50.00 (ISBN 0-8482-0049-7). Norwood Edns.

--French Studies & Reviews. facs. ed. LC 67-23172. (Essay Index Reprint Ser). 1926. 15.00 (ISBN 0-8369-0142-8). Arno.

--Literary Studies & Reviews. facs. ed. LC 68-16901. (Essay Index Reprint Ser). 1924. 15.00 (ISBN 0-8369-0143-6). Arno.

Anglade, Joseph. Histoire Sommaire De la Litterature Meridionale Au Moyen Age. LC 74-38486. Repr. of 1921 ed. 21.50 (ISBN 0-404-08343-9). AMS Pr.

Baker, Susan R. Collaboration et Originalite chez la Rochefoucauld. LC 79-21085. (U. of Fla. Humanities Monographs: No. 48). 135p. (Orig.). 1980. pap. 9.00 (ISBN 0-8130-0657-0). U Presses Fla.

Barberis, P. Pere Goriot de Balzac: Ecriture, structures, significations. new ed. (Collection themes et textes). 296p. (Orig., Fr.). 1972. pap. 6.75 (ISBN 2-03-035010-9, 2681). Larousse.

Baring, Maurice. Punch & Judy & Other Essays. facs. ed. LC 68-16904. (Essay Index Reprint Ser). 1968. Repr. of 1924 ed. 18.00 (ISBN 0-8369-0172-X). Arno.

Barre, Andre. Symbolisme: essai historique sur le mouvement symboliste en France de 1885 a 1900. 1967. Repr. of 1911 ed. 25.50 (ISBN 0-8337-3970-0). B Franklin.

Beauchemin, Normand. Recherches Sur L'accent D'apres les Poemes D'alain Grandbois, Etude Acoustique et Statistique Langue et Litterature Francaises Au Canada. 1970. pap. 8.50x (ISBN 2-7637-6431-2, Pub. by Laval). Intl Schol Bk Serv.

Bellimin-Noel, J. Le Texte et l'avant-texte: Les Brouillons d'un poeme de Milosz. new ed. (Collection L). 144p. (Orig., Fr.). 1972. pap. 8.95 (ISBN 2-03-036003-1). Larousse.

Bersani, Leo. Balzac to Beckett: Center & Circumference in French Fiction. 1970. 15.95 (ISBN 0-19-501264-X). Oxford U Pr.

Besant, Walter. French Humorists: From the Twelfth to the Nineteenth Century. facsimile ed. LC 74-38774. (Essay Index Reprint Ser). Repr. of 1874 ed. 23.00 (ISBN 0-8369-2635-8). Arno.

Betham Edwards. French Men Women & Books. 1973. Repr. of 1911 ed. 15.00 (ISBN 0-8274-1802-7). R West.

Beys, C. De & Protzman, M. I. Les Illustres Fous of Charles Beys: A Critical Ed. pap. 16.50 (ISBN 0-384-04089-6). Johnson Repr.

Biblio (Catologue-Dictionnaire Des Ouvrages Parus En Francais Dans le Monde) annual Incl. 1934 a 1969. 65.00 (ISBN 0-685-35985-9); 1970. 77.50 (ISBN 0-685-35986-7); Les/Livres de l'Annee Biblio. 1971. 98.75 (ISBN 0-685-35987-5); 1972. 108.00 (ISBN 0-685-35988-3); 1973. 169.00 (ISBN 0-685-35989-1); 1974. 360.00 (ISBN 0-685-35990-5); 1975. 360.00 (ISBN 0-685-35991-3); 1976. 385.00 (ISBN 0-685-35992-1). French & Eur.

Bisson, L. A. Proust & Hardy: Incidence or Coincidence in Studies in French Language Literature & History Presented to R. L. Graeme Ritchie. 1949. Repr. 40.00 (ISBN 0-8274-3920-2). R West.

Blanchard, J. M. & Gavronsky, S. La Litterature Francaise: le Milieu et le Moment, Vol. 1: Le Moyen Age. 1972. pap. 6.95 (ISBN 0-02-310680-8). Macmillan.

Boase, Alan M. Fortunes of Montaigne: A History of the Essays in France, 1580-1669. 1970. Repr. lib. bdg. 25.00 (ISBN 0-374-90725-0). Octagon.

Boissier, Gaston. Great French Writers: Madame De Sevigne. 154p. 1980. Repr. of 1887 ed. lib. bdg. 25.00 (ISBN 0-8495-0476-7). Arden Lib.

Bouche, Claude. Lautreamont: Du lieu commun a la parodie. new ed. (Collection themes et textes). 253p. (Orig.). 1974. pap. 6.75 (ISBN 2-03-035024-9, 2615). Larousse.

Braun, Sidney D. & Lainoff, Seymour, eds. Transatlantic Mirrors: Essays in Franco-American Literary Relations. (United States Authors Ser.). 1978. lib. bdg. 15.00 (ISBN 0-8057-9008-X). Twayne.

Braunrot, Bruno. L' Imagination Poetique Chez du Bartas: Elements de Sensibilite Baroque dans la "Creation du Monde.". (Studies in the Romance Languages & Literatures: No. 135). 1973. pap. 9.00x (ISBN 0-8078-9135-5). U of NC Pr.

Brunet. Supplement aux supercheries litteraires. 43.75 (ISBN 0-685-35982-4). French & Eur.

Brunetiere, F. Manual of French Literature. LC 71-127998. (Studies in French Literature, No. 45). 1970. Repr. of 1898 ed. lib. bdg. 59.95 (ISBN 0-8383-1149-0). Haskell.

Brunetieve, F. Essays in French Literature. 59.95 (ISBN 0-8490-0127-7). Gordon Pr.

Busby, Keith. Gauvain in Old French Literature. (Degre Second Ser.: No. 2). 425p. 1980. pap. text ed. 48.50x (ISBN 90-6203-831-X). Humanities.

Butler, Kathleen T. History of French Literature, 2 Vols. LC 66-24676. (Illus.). 1966. Repr. of 1923 ed. Set. 20.00 (ISBN 0-8462-0785-0). Russell.

Calin, William. Crown, Cross & "Fleur-De-Lis". (Stanford French & Italian Studies: No. 6). 1977. pap. 15.00 (ISBN 0-915838-34-6). Anma Libri.

Carrere, Jean. Degeneration in the Great French Masters. facs. ed. McCabe, J., tr. LC 67-26722. (Essay Index Reprint Ser). 1922. 18.00 (ISBN 0-8369-0277-7). Arno.

Castex, P. & Surer, P. Manuel Des Etudes Litteraires Francaises, 6 tomes. (Illus.). Tome 1, Moyen Age. 5.95 (ISBN 0-685-11344-2); Tome, 2 16e Siecle. 5.95 (ISBN 0-685-11345-0); Tome 3, 17e Siecle. 7.95 (ISBN 0-685-11346-9); Tome 4, 18e Siecle. 7.95 (ISBN 0-685-11347-7); Tome 5, 19e Siecle. 8.95 (ISBN 0-685-11348-5); Tome 6, 20e Siecle. 8.95 (ISBN 0-685-11349-3). French & Eur.

Caxton, William, ed. Quatre fils Aimon, 2 pts. (EETS, ES Ser.: Nos. 44-45). Repr. of 1885 ed. Pt. 1. 17.00 (ISBN 0-527-00253-4); Pt. 2. 20.00 (ISBN 0-527-00254-2). Kraus Repr.

Cazelles, Brigitte. La Faiblesse Chez Gautier De Coinci. (Stanford French & Italian Studies: No. 14). (Fr.). 1978. pap. 20.00 (ISBN 0-915838-27-3). Anma Libri.

Clement, Nemours H. Romanticism in France. 1938. pap. 28.00 (ISBN 0-527-17800-4). Kraus Repr.

Cocteau, Jean. The Grand Ecart. Galantiere, Lewis, tr. from Fr. LC 74-22403. 153p. 1977. Repr. of 1925 ed. 17.50 (ISBN 0-86527-257-3). Fertig.

Cohn, Robert G. Modes of Art: A Critical Work. (Stanford French & Italian Studies: No. 1). 1976. pap. 20.00 (ISBN 0-915838-29-X). Anma Libri.

Conlon, Denis, ed. Richard Sans Peur. (Studies in the Romance Languages & Literatures). (Orig.). 1978. pap. 9.00x (ISBN 0-8078-9192-4). U of NC Pr.

Cormier, Raymond J., ed. Voices of Conscience: Essays on Medieval & Modern French Literature in Memory of James D. Powell & Rosemary Hodgins. LC 76-15343. 1976. 19.50x (ISBN 0-87722-090-5). Temple U Pr.

Costa, John. Le Conflict Moral dans les Oeuvres Romanesques de Jean-Pierre Camus: 1584-1652. LC 74-2068. (Illus.). 70p. (Fr.). 1976. lib. bdg. 18.50 (ISBN 0-89102-031-4). B Franklin.

Crawford, Virginia M. Studies in Foreign Literature: (Daudet, Huysmans, Verhaeren, Maeterlinck, & D'annunzio) 1908. Repr. 20.00 (ISBN 0-8274-3535-5). R West.

Crichfield, Grant. Three Novels of Madame De Duras: Ourika, Edouard, Olivier. (De Proprietatibus Litterarum, Series Practica: No. 114). 67p. (Orig.). 1975. pap. text ed. 15.75x (ISBN 90-2793-316-2). Mouton.

Cruickshank, John, ed. French Literature & Its Background, 6 vols. Incl. Vol. 1. Sixteenth Century. (No. 138). 238p. 1968; Vol. 2. Seventeenth Century. (No. 171). 240p. 1969. 9.95x (ISBN 0-19-285028-8); Vol. 3. Eighteenth Century. (No. 139). 232p. 1968. 9.95x (ISBN 0-19-285021-0); Vol. 4. Early Nineteenth Century. (No. 172). 250p. 1969. 11.95x (ISBN 0-19-285029-6); Vol. 5. Late Nineteenth Century. (No. 173). 238p. 1969. 5.95x (ISBN 0-19-285033-4); Vol. 6. Twentieth Century. (No. 184). 350p. 1970. 11.50x (ISBN 0-19-285043-1). (Oxford Paperbacks Ser). Oxford U Pr.

Daniel, George B., ed. Renaissance & Other Studies in Honor of William Leon Wiley. (Studies in the Romance Languages & Literatures: No. 72). 1968. pap. 13.50x (ISBN 0-8078-9072-3). U of NC Pr.

De Bury, Yetta B. French Literature of To-Day. 1973. Repr. of 1898 ed. 20.00 (ISBN 0-8274-1405-6). R West.

De Grandpre. Histoire de la Litterature Francaise du Quebec, 4 tomes. Set. 144.50 (ISBN 0-685-35932-8). French & Eur.

De Ligne. Oeuvres Choisies du Prince De Ligne: Nouvelle Anthologie Critique. Guy, Basil, ed. (Stanford French & Italian Studies: No. 13). (Fr.). 1978. pap. 20.00 (ISBN 0-915838-28-1). Anma Libri.

Delille, Edward. Some French Writers. facsimile ed. LC 78-37526. (Essay Index Reprint Ser). Repr. of 1893 ed. 16.00 (ISBN 0-8369-2543-2). Arno.

De Man. Allegories of Reading. LC 79-64075. 1979. 19.50x (ISBN 0-300-02322-7). Yale U Pr.

De Musset, Alfred. Chandelier: Un Caprice. (Documentation thematique). 2.95 (ISBN 0-685-36195-0, 260). Larousse.

Derche. Etudes de Textes Francais, 6 tomes. Set. 47.90 (ISBN 0-685-36706-1). French & Eur.

Doody, Terrence. Confession & Community in the Novel. LC 79-26388. 256p. 1980. 14.95x (ISBN 0-8071-0662-3). La State U Pr.

Dowden, Edward. A History of French Literature. (Select Bibliographies Reprint Ser). Repr. of 1897 ed. 22.00 (ISBN 0-8369-6644-9). Arno.

--A History of French Literature. 1973. lib. bdg. 30.00 (ISBN 0-8414-2498-5). Folcroft.

Drevet. Bibliographie de la Litterature Francaise (1940-1948) 85.95 (ISBN 0-685-35967-0). French & Eur.

Du, Gerard & Lecherbonnier, Bernard. Le Surrealisme: Theories, themes, techniques. new ed. (Collection themes et textes). 288p. (Orig., Fr.). 1972. pap. 6.75 (ISBN 2-03-035004-4, 2691). Larousse.

Duchemin. Chateaubriand: Essais de Critique et d'Histoire. 23.75 (ISBN 0-685-34885-7). French & Eur.

Duclaux, Agnes M. Twentieth Century French Writers. facs. ed. LC 67-22089. (Essay Index Reprint Ser). 1920. 22.00 (ISBN 0-8369-1330-2). Arno.

Dufourcq. Le Livre de l'Orgue Francais (1589-1789, 2 tomes. Set. 218.75 (ISBN 0-685-35984-0). French & Eur.

Duhamel, Georges. In Defence of Letters. LC 68-16293. 1968. Repr. of 1939 ed. 12.00 (ISBN 0-8046-0121-6). Kennikat.

Duisit, Lionel. Satire, Parodie, Calembour. (Stanford French & Italian Studies: No. 11). (Fr.). 1978. pap. 20.00 (ISBN 0-915838-26-5). Anma Libri.

Edwards, Matilda B. French Men, Women & Books: A Series of Nineteenth-Century Studies. facs. ed. LC 67-26737. (Essay Index Reprint Ser). 1911. 15.00 (ISBN 0-8369-0407-9). Arno.

Egger, E. L' Hellenisme En France, 2 Vols. 1964. Repr. of 1869 ed. 50.50 (ISBN 0-8337-1022-2). B Franklin.

The Egoist: Special Imagist Number. LC 78-64018. (Des Imagistes: Literature of the Imagist Movement). Repr. of 1915 ed. 11.00 (ISBN 0-404-17093-5). AMS Pr.

Ellis, Havelock. From Rousseau to Proust. facs. ed. LC 68-24851. (Essay Index Reprint Ser). 1968. Repr. of 1935 ed. 18.00 (ISBN 0-8369-0412-5). Arno.

Engel-Janosi, Friedrich. Four Studies in French Romantic Historical Writing. LC 78-64220. (Johns Hopkins University. Studies in the Social Sciences. Seventy-First Ser. 1953: 2). Repr. of 1955 ed. 17.50 (ISBN 0-404-61324-1). AMS Pr.

Faguet, Emile. A Literary History of France. 1907. Repr. 40.00 (ISBN 0-8274-2955-X). R West.

Fairlie, Alison. Imagination & Language. LC 80-40307. (Illus.). 400p. Date not set. 72.00 (ISBN 0-521-23291-0). Cambridge U Pr.

Fisher, Mary. A Group of French Critics. LC 73-37155. (Essay Index Reprint Ser.). Repr. of 1897 ed. 18.00 (ISBN 0-8369-2496-7). Arno.

Foster, Mrs. A. F. French Literature. 1979. Repr. of 1860 ed. lib. bdg. 40.00 (ISBN 0-8482-3958-X). Norwood Edns.

Foster, Mrs. A. French Literature. 1860. Repr. 30.00 (ISBN 0-8274-2372-1). R West.

Foulet, Alfred & Speer, Mary B. On Editing Old French Texts. (Edward C. Armstrong Monographs on Medieval Literature Ser.). 1979. 14.00x (ISBN 0-7006-0182-1). Regents Pr KS.

Fowlie, Wallace. Climate of Violence: The French Literary Tradition from Beaudelaire to the Present. 1967. 6.95 (ISBN 0-02-540410-5). Macmillan.

--Guide to Contemporary French Literature from Valery to Sartre. 8.25 (ISBN 0-8446-2077-7). Peter Smith.

France, Anatole. Latin Genius. facsimile ed. Chapman, F. & May, J. L., eds. LC 78-177957. (Essay Index Reprint Ser). Repr. of 1924 ed. 19.50 (ISBN 0-8369-2497-5). Arno.

--La Vie Litteraire. 5th ed. 336p. 1950. 8.95 (ISBN 0-686-55882-0). French & Eur.

Gallop, Jane. Intersections: A Reading of Sade with Bataille, Blanchot, & Klossowski. LC 80-23117. viii, 135p. 1981. 13.95x (ISBN 0-8032-2110-X). U of Nebr Pr.

Gardiner, L. J. Outlines of French Literature. 1973. Repr. of 1927 ed. 20.00 (ISBN 0-8274-0194-9). R West.

Genest, Emile. Les Belles Citations de la Litterature Francaise. 1923. Repr. 45.00 (ISBN 0-8274-1923-6). R West.

Genette, Gerard. Figures of Discourse. Sheridan, Alan, tr. from French. 320p. 1981. 20.00x (ISBN 0-231-04984-6). Columbia U Pr.

Genouvrier. Linguistique et enseignement du francais. 13.95 (ISBN 2-03-042171-5, 4539). Larousse.

Giraud. Manuel de Bibliographie Litteraire pour les XVIe, XVIIe, XVIIIe Siecles Francais (1921-1935, 2 tomes. 15.50 ea.; Set. 35.75 (ISBN 0-685-35966-2). French & Eur.

--Mots dans le vent. 11.25 (ISBN 0-685-36202-7, 2727). Larousse.

Glidden, Hope H. The Storyteller As Humanist: The Serees of Guillaume Bouchet. LC 80-70809. (French Forum Monographs: No. 25). 200p. (Orig.). 1981. pap. 12.50 (ISBN 0-917058-24-0). French Forum.

Goller, Karl H., ed. The Alliterative Morte Arthure: A Reassessment of the Poem. (Arthurian Studies: II). 186p. 1981. 37.50x (ISBN 0-85991-075-X, Pub. by Boydell & Brewer). Biblio Dist.

Gosse, Edmund W. French Profiles. LC 70-108638. (Essay Index Reprint Ser). 1913. 19.50 (ISBN 0-8369-1574-7). Arno.

--French Profiles. 1973. Repr. of 1913 ed. 19.00 (ISBN 0-8274-1379-3). R West.

Gracq, Julien. Preferences. 256p. 1961. 17.50 (ISBN 0-686-54024-7). French & Eur.

Graham, Victor E. & Johnson, W. McAllister. Estienne Jodelle, Le Recueil de Inscriptions, 1558: A Literary & Iconographical Exegesis. LC 79-163818. (Illus.). 1972. 25.00x (ISBN 0-8020-1752-5). U of Toronto Pr.

Greimas, A. Essais de semiotique poetique: Avec des etudes sur Apollinaire, Bataille, Hugo, Jarry, Mallarme, Michaux, Nerval, Rimbaud, Roubaud. (Collection L). 240p. (Orig., Fr.). 1972. pap. 13.95 (ISBN 2-03-036002-3, 2666). Larousse.

Groueff, S. L' Homme et la mer. (Collection maitrise du monde). 64.50x (ISBN 0-685-36200-0, 2278). Larousse.

Guy, Henry. Essai Sur la Vie & les Oeuvres Litteraires Du Trouvere Adam De la Hale. LC 79-101989. 605p. 1898. Repr. 32.50 (ISBN 0-8337-1498-8). B Franklin.

Guyer, Foster E. The Main Stream of French Literature. 1973. Repr. of 1932 ed. 25.00 (ISBN 0-8274-0185-X). R West.

Harding, James. Lost Illusions: Paul Leautaud & His World. (Illus.). 230p. 12.50 (ISBN 0-8386-1744-1). Fairleigh Dickinson.

Harper, George M. Masters of French Literature. facs. ed. LC 68-22095. (Essay Index Reprint Ser). 1901. 16.00 (ISBN 0-8369-0512-1). Arno.

Hatzfeld, Helmut A. Literature Through Art: A New Approach to French Literature. (Studies in the Romance Languages & Literatures: No. 86). 1969. pap. 13.50x (ISBN 0-8078-9086-3). U of NC Pr.

Histoire des Spectacles. (Encylopedie de la Pleiade). 32.50 (ISBN 0-685-35933-6). French & Eur.

Hocking, Elton. Ferdinand Brunetiere: The Evolution of a Critic. 1979. Repr. of 1936 ed. lib. bdg. 40.00 (ISBN 0-8492-5323-3). R West.

Howarth, W. D., et al. French Literature from Sixteen Hundred to the Present. LC 75-2864. 161p. 1974. pap. text ed. 3.95x (ISBN 0-416-81640-1). Methuen Inc.

Huddleston, Sisley. Bohemian Literary & Social Life in Paris. 1973. Repr. of 1928 ed. 30.00 (ISBN 0-8274-0346-1). R West.

Hudson, William H. Short History of French Literature. LC 72-103227. 1970. Repr. of 1919 ed. 13.75 (ISBN 0-8046-0864-4). Kennikat.

--Short History of French Literature. 1973. lib. bdg. 20.00 (ISBN 0-8414-5199-0). Folcroft.

Hutson, C. W. A History of French Literature. 353p. 1980. Repr. of 1889 ed. lib. bdg. 30.00 (ISBN 0-89760-330-3). Telegraph Bks.

Hytier. Questions de Litterature. Etudes Valeryennes et Autres. 23.50 (ISBN 0-685-36629-4). French & Eur.

Hytier, Jean. Questions De Litterature. LC 68-4151. 1967. 20.00x (ISBN 0-231-03123-8). Columbia U Pr.

James, Henry. French Poets & Novelists. LC 77-13419. 1973. lib. bdg. 30.00 (ISBN 0-8414-5284-9). Folcroft.

--Literary Reviews & Essays on American, English, & French Literature. Mordell, Albert, ed. (Orig.). 1957. pap. 4.95 (ISBN 0-8084-0202-1, L6). Coll & U Pr.

James, Joseph A., ed. Octavien de Saint Gelais, Sejour D'Honneur. (Studies in the Romance Languages & Literatures: No. 181). 1978. pap. 19.50x (ISBN 0-8078-9181-9). U of NC Pr.

Jasinski. L' Engagement de Benjamin Constant. 21.50 (ISBN 0-685-34886-5). French & Eur.

Jones, P. Mansell. French Introspectives. LC 76-103228. 1970. Repr. of 1937 ed. 12.00 (ISBN 0-8046-0865-2). Kennikat.

Jones, Percy M. French Introspectives, from Montaigne to Andre Gide. Repr. of 1937 ed. lib. bdg. 15.00x (ISBN 0-8371-3113-8, JOFI). Greenwood.

Kastner, L. E. & Atkins, Henry G. Short History of French Literature. LC 70-103229. 1970. Repr. of 1925 ed. 15.00 (ISBN 0-8046-0866-0). Kennikat.

--Short History of French Literature. 1973. Repr. of 1925 ed. 20.00 (ISBN 0-8274-1378-5). R West.

--A Short History of French Literature: From the Origins to the Present Day. 1977. Repr. lib. bdg. 25.00 (ISBN 0-8482-1462-5). Norwood Edns.

Keeler, Jerome, Sr. Catholic Literary France: From Verlaine to the Present Time. 1938. Repr. 25.00 (ISBN 0-8274-2011-0). R West.

Keeler, Sr. Mary J. Catholic Literary France from Verlaine to the Present Time. LC 76-90649. (Essay Index Reprint Ser). 1938. 17.00 (ISBN 0-8369-1219-5). Arno.

Kerr, Cynthia B. L' Amour, L'amitie et la Fourberie: Une Etude Des Premieres Comedies De Corneille. (Stanford French & Italian Studies: Vol. 20). 152p. (Fr.). 1980. pap. 20.00 (ISBN 0-915838-19-2). Anma Libri.

King, Preston. Fear of Power: An Analysis of Antistatism in Three French Writers. 139p. 1967. 23.50x (ISBN 0-7146-1559-5, F Cass Co). Biblio Dist.

Konstantinovic. Vercors, Ecrivain et Dessinateur. (Bibliotheque Franc. et Romane. Et. Litter.). 10.95 (ISBN 0-685-36631-6). French & Eur.

Kritzman, Lawrence D. Destruction-Decouverte: Le Fontionnement de la Rhetorique dans les Essais de Montaigne. LC 80-66329. (French Forum Monographs: No. 21). 187p. (Orig.). 1980. pap. 12.50 (ISBN 0-917058-20-8). French Forum.

Lagarde & Michara. Textes et Litterature. Incl. Moyen Age. 7.95 (ISBN 0-685-35942-5); XVIe Siecle. 8.95 (ISBN 0-685-35943-3); XVIIe Siecle. 9.50 (ISBN 0-685-35944-1); XVIIIe Siecle. 9.50 (ISBN 0-685-35945-X); XIXe Siecle. 11.50 (ISBN 0-685-35946-8); XXe Siecle. 15.50 (ISBN 0-685-35947-6). French & Eur.

Lancaster, Henry C. Adventures of a Literary Historian: A Collection of His Writings Presented to H. C. Lancaster by His Former Students & Other Friends in Anticipation of His Sixtieth Birthday November 10, 1942. facs. ed. LC 68-14907. (Essay Index Reprint Ser). 1942. 19.50 (ISBN 0-8369-0605-5). Arno.

Langlois, Walter G., ed. The Persistent Voice: Essays on Hellenism in French Literature Since the 18th Century In Honor of Henri M. Peyre. LC 71-150982. 1971. 12.00x (ISBN 0-8147-4952-6). NYU Pr.

Lanson & Tuffrau. Manuel Illustre D'histoire De La Litterature Francaise. (Illus.). 13.95 (ISBN 0-685-11351-5). French & Eur.

La Queriere, Yves de. Celine et les mots: Etude stylistique des effets de mots dans le Voyage au bout de la nuit. LC 70-160050. (Studies in Romance Languages: No. 7.). 172p. 1973. 10.00x (ISBN 0-8131-1268-0). U Pr of Ky.

Larousse and Co. La Rochefoucauld: Maximes. (Documentation thematique). 2.95 (ISBN 0-685-36192-6, 123). Larousse.

Laufer, R. Introduction a la textologie: Verification...etablissement, edition des textes. (Collection L). 160p. (Orig., Fr.). 1972. pap. 13.95 (ISBN 2-03-036006-6). Larousse.

Law, B. W. & Law, R. G. From Reason to Romanticism. LC 72-4541. (Studies in French Literature, No. 45). 1972. Repr. of 1960 ed. lib. bdg. 31.95 (ISBN 0-8383-1595-X). Haskell.

Lawler, James, ed. Essays in French Literature, Nos. 4-8. Incl. No. 4. 1967; No. 5. 1968; No. 6. 1969; No. 7. 1970; No. 8. 1971. pap. 3.50x ea. (Pub. by U of W Austral Pr). Intl Schol Bk Serv.

Lebel, Maurice. Explications De Textes Francais et Anglais. (Fr). 1953. 3.50x (ISBN 2-7637-0106-X, Pub. by Laval). Intl Schol Bk Serv.

Le Corbusier. Oeuvres Completes, 9 tomes. Incl. Tome I. (1910-1929) 27.50 (ISBN 0-685-35993-X); Tome II. (1929-1934) 27.50 (ISBN 0-685-35994-8); Tome III. (1934-1938) 27.50 (ISBN 0-685-35995-6); Tome IV. (1938-1946) 27.50 (ISBN 0-685-35996-4); Tome V. (1947-1951) 38.50 (ISBN 0-685-35997-2); Tome VI. (1952-1957) 38.50 (ISBN 0-685-35998-0); Tome VII. (1957-1965) 38.50 (ISBN 0-685-35999-9); Tome Recapitulatif (1910-1965) 47.50 (ISBN 0-685-36000-8); Dernieres Oeuvres. 47.50 (ISBN 0-685-36001-6). French & Eur.

Legge, James G. Chanticleer: A Study of the French Muse. 395p. 1980. Repr. of 1935 ed. lib. bdg. 20.00 (ISBN 0-8482-1638-5). Norwood Edns.

Lehrmann, C. The Jewish Element in French Literature. LC 75-120998. 295p. 1971. 15.00 (ISBN 0-8386-7725-8). Fairleigh Dickinson.

Lemaitre, ed. Le Litterature Francaise, 5 tomes. Incl. Tome I. Du Moyen Age a L'age Baroque. 29.95 (ISBN 0-685-36710-X); Tome II. Des Classiques aux Philosophes. 29.95 (ISBN 0-685-36711-8); Tome III. Les Evolutions du XIXe Siecle. 29.95 (ISBN 0-685-36712-6); Tome IV. Les Metamorphoses du XXe Siecle. 29.95 (ISBN 0-685-36713-4); Tome V. La Litterature Aujourd'hui. 17.50 (ISBN 0-685-36714-2). (Bibliotheque des Connaissances Essentielles). French & Eur.

La Librairie Francaise, Tables Decennales, 7 tomes. Incl. 1946-1955, 3 tomes. Set. 175.00 (ISBN 0-685-35973-5); 1956-1965, 4 tomes. Set. 275.00 (ISBN 0-685-35974-3). (Cercle de la librairie). French & Eur.

Lockwood, Helen D. Tools & the Man. LC 21-12534. Repr. of 1927 ed. 14.75 (ISBN 0-404-03999-5). AMS Pr.

Lough, John. Writer & Public in France: From the Middle Ages to the Present Day. 1978. text ed. 49.50x (ISBN 0-19-815749-5). Oxford U Pr.

Lucas, Frank L. Studies French & English. facs. ed. LC 69-17583. (Essay Index Reprint Ser). 1934. 17.00 (ISBN 0-8369-0084-7). Arno.

McArthur, D. G. Les Constructions Verbales du Francais Contemporain. 94p. 1971. 24.00x (ISBN 0-7190-1250-3, Pub. by Manchester U Pr England). State Mutual Bk.

Mackenzie, Fraser, et al, eds. Studies in French Language Literature & History. 258p. 1980. Repr. of 1949 ed. lib. bdg. 50.00 (ISBN 0-89760-736-8). Telegraph Bks.

McQueen, Priscilla L. Around the World in Twenty Legends. (Basic Readers Ser.). 1970. tchrs. wkbk. 2.00 (ISBN 0-685-36208-6); wkbk. 1.50 (ISBN 0-685-36209-4). McQueen.

--Carousel of Stories. (Basic Readers Ser.). 1970. 9.31 (ISBN 0-917186-13-3); stu. wkbk. 6.38 (ISBN 0-917186-14-1). McQueen.

--Imagine That. (Basic Readers Ser.). 1970. tchrs. wkbk. 2.00 (ISBN 0-685-36210-8); wkbk. 1.50 (ISBN 0-685-36211-6). McQueen.

--Our Own Country. (Basic Readers Ser.). 1970. tchrs. wkbk. 2.00 (ISBN 0-685-36212-4); wkbk. 1.50 (ISBN 0-685-36213-2). McQueen.

Malcles. Les Sources du Travail Bibliographique, 3 tomes. Incl. Tome I. Bibliographies Generales. 22.50 (ISBN 0-685-35977-8); Tome II. Bibliographies Specialisees; Sciences Humaines, 2 pts. Set. 46.50 (ISBN 0-685-35978-6); Tome III. Bibliographies Specialisees; Sciences Exactes et Techniques. 22.50 (ISBN 0-685-35979-4). French & Eur.

Malory, Sir Thomas. Morte Darthur. Field, P. J., ed. LC 77-22498. (London Medieval & Renaissance Ser.). 1978. text ed. 29.00x (ISBN 0-8419-0333-6). Holmes & Meier.

Marcus, Millicent. An Allegory of Form: Literary Self-Conciousness in the "Decameron". (Stanford French & Italian Studies: No. 18). 1979. pap. 20.00 (ISBN 0-915838-21-4). Anma Libri.

Martin Du Gard, Roger, pseud. The Postman. Russell, John, tr. from Fr. LC 74-13052. 156p. 1975. Repr. of 1955 ed. 15.50 (ISBN 0-86527-333-2). Fertig.

Mason, Germaine. Concise Survey of French Literature. Repr. of 1959 ed. lib. bdg. 15.00 (ISBN 0-8371-2464-6, MAFL). Greenwood.

--A Concise Survey of French Literature. (Quality Paperback: No. 141). (Orig.). 1966. pap. 3.50 (ISBN 0-8226-0141-9). Littlefield.

Masson, Gustave. French Literature. 1973. Repr. of 1888 ed. 20.00 (ISBN 0-8274-0754-8). R West.

Mauriac, Francois. Men I Hold Great. LC 78-132088. 1971. Repr. of 1951 ed. 12.00 (ISBN 0-8046-1416-4). Kennikat.

Maurois, Andre. De Proust a Camus. 13.50 (ISBN 0-685-36931-5). French & Eur.

--Dialogues sur le Commandement. pap. 8.95 (ISBN 0-685-36932-3). French & Eur.

Micro Robert. 13.50 (ISBN 0-685-36078-4). French & Eur.

Millward. L' Oeuvre de Pierre Loti et l'Esprit Fin de Siecle. 9.50 (ISBN 0-685-34266-2). French & Eur.

Mitchell, Jane T. A Thematic Analysis of Mme. D'Aulnoy's "Contes De Fees". LC 78-6947. (Romance Monographs: No. 30). 1978. 16.00x (ISBN 84-399-8448-0). Romance.

Moliere. Dom Juan Ou le Festin De Pierre. Howarth, W. D., ed. (French Texts Ser.). 100p. 1975. pap. text ed. 9.95x (ISBN 0-631-00580-3, Pub. by Basil Blackwell). Biblio Dist.

Montherlant, Henry de. Port-Royal. Griffiths, Richard, ed. (French Texts Ser.). 97p. 1976. pap. text ed. 11.25x (ISBN 0-631-00730-X, Pub. by Basil Blackwel). Biblio Dist.

Mouillaud, G. Le Rouge et le noir de Stendhal: Le Roman possible. new ed. (Collection themes et textes). 240p. (Orig., Fr.). 1973. pap. 6.75 (ISBN 2-03-035014-1, 2658). Larousse.

Nash, Jerry C. Concordance De la "Delie" De Maurice Sceve, 2 vols. LC 76-14560. (North Carolina Studies in the Romance Languages & Literatures,174). 1976. 58.00 (ISBN 0-8357-0430-0, IS-00011, Pub. by North Carolina Studies in the Romance Languages & Literatures); Vol. 1. (ISBN 0-8078-9174-6); Vol. 2. (ISBN 0-8078-9177-0). Univ Microfilms.

Nesselroth. Lautreamont's Imagery: A Stylistic Approach. 14.95 (ISBN 0-685-34929-2). French & Eur.

Nisard, Charles. Histoire Des Livres Populaires, 2 Vols. 2nd ed. (Illus.). 1964. Repr. of 1864 ed. 55.50 (ISBN 0-8337-2562-9). B Franklin.

Nitze, William A. & Dargan, E. Preston. A History of French Literature. 1922. 85.00 (ISBN 0-8274-1165-0). R West.

O'Connell, David. The Instructions of Saint Louis: A Critical Text. (Studies in the Romance Languages & Literatures). 104p. 1980. pap. 8.00 (ISBN 0-8078-9216-5). U of NC Pr.

Owen, Dorothy L. Piers Plowman: A Comparison with Some Earlier & Contemporary French Allegories. LC 72-194998. 1912. lib. bdg. 20.00 (ISBN 0-8414-9235-2). Folcroft.

Paris, Gaston. Melanges De Litterature Francais Du Moyen Age Publies Par Mario Roques. (Fr). 1910-12. 40.50 (ISBN 0-8337-4311-2). B Franklin.

Paris, Gaston B. La Litterature Francaise Au Moyen Age (Eleventh to Fourteenth Centuries) LC 73-178583. Repr. of 1914 ed. 30.00 (ISBN 0-404-56658-8). AMS Pr.

Partridge, Eric. Critical Medley. facsimile ed. LC 73-148894. (Select Bibliographies Reprint Ser). Repr. of 1926 ed. 17.00 (ISBN 0-8369-5680-X). Arno.

Petit Littre. 32.50 (ISBN 0-685-36077-6). French & Eur.

Peyre, Henri. Historical & Critical Essays. LC 68-12702. 1968. 18.50x (ISBN 0-8032-0145-1). U of Nebr Pr.

Peyre, Henri M., ed. Essays in Honor of Albert Feuillerat. facs. ed. LC 75-99633. (Essay Index Reprint Ser). 1943. 19.50 (ISBN 0-8369-1650-6). Arno.

Pitou, S. La Calprenede's Faramond. 1973. Repr. of 1938 ed. pap. 13.00 (ISBN 0-384-46640-0). Johnson Repr.

Ploetz, Richard A. A Manual of French Literature. 1973. Repr. of 1878 ed. 45.00 (ISBN 0-8274-1133-2). R West.

Ponton, Sr. Jeanne. Religieuse Dans La Litterature Francaise. (Fr). 1969. 9.50x (ISBN 2-7637-6348-0, Pub. by Laval). Intl Schol Bk Serv.

Poulet, Georges. Studies in Human Time. Coleman, Elliot, tr. LC 78-13572. 1979. Repr. of 1956 ed. lib. bdg. 22.50x (ISBN 0-8371-9348-6, POSH). Greenwood.

Premont, Laurent. Le Mythe De Promethee Dans la Litterature Francaise Contemporaire, 1900-1960. (Fr). 1964. pap. 7.50x (ISBN 2-7637-6088-0, Pub. by Laval). Intl Schol Bk Serv.

Priddin, Deirdre. Art of the Dance in French Literature from Theophile Gautier to Paul Valery. 1952. text ed. 4.00x (ISBN 0-391-01947-3). Humanities.

La Princesse de Cleves: Le Roman paradoxal. new ed: (Collection themes et textes). 192p. (Orig., Fr.). 1972. pap. 6.75 (ISBN 2-03-035017-6, 2663). Larousse.

Querard. La France Litteraire ou Dictionanaire Bibliographique des Savants, Historiens et Gens de Lettres de la France, 12 tomes. Set. 350.00 (ISBN 0-685-35981-6). French & Eur.

--La Litterature Francaise Contemporaine, 6 tomes. Set. 262.50 (ISBN 0-685-35980-8). French & Eur.

--Ls Supercheries litteraires devoiles, 3 tomes. Set. 150.00 (ISBN 0-685-35983-2). French & Eur.

Le Quillet Flammarion. 13.95 (ISBN 0-685-36079-2). French & Eur.

Read, Herbert E. Sense of Glory: Essays in Criticism. facs. ed. LC 67-26773. (Essay Index Reprint Ser). 1930. 15.00 (ISBN 0-8369-0814-7). Arno.

Rees, Garnet. Baudelaire, Sartre & Camus: Lectures & Commentaries. 86p. 1976. pap. text ed. 10.00x (ISBN 0-7083-0601-2). Verry.

Renouard. Imprimeurs et Libraires Parisiens Du XVIe Siecle. Incl. Tome I. Abada Avril. 135.00 (ISBN 0-685-35948-4); Tome II. Baaleu Banville. 165.00 (ISBN 0-685-35949-2). French & Eur.

--Repertoire Des Imprimeurs Parisiens, Libraires, Foundeurs De Caracteres et Correcteurs De l'Imprimerie Depius l'Introduction De l'Imprimerie (1470) Jusqu'a la Fin Du Xvie Siecle. 61.95 (ISBN 0-685-35952-2). French & Eur.

Repertoire des Livres de Langue Francaise Disponibles (1972, 2 tomes. Set. 95.00 (ISBN 0-685-35972-7). French & Eur.

Ridge, G. R. The Hero in French Decadent Literature. LC 61-17538. 5.00 (ISBN 0-910294-23-2). Brown Bk.

--The Hero in French Romantic Literature. LC 59-14610. 5.00 (ISBN 0-910294-24-0). Brown Bk.

Robinson, Christopher. French Literature in the 19th Century. LC 79-79571. (Comparative Literature Ser.). 1978. text ed. 17.50x (ISBN 0-06-495943-0). B&N.

Rochester, Myrna B. Rene Crevel: Le Pays des Miroirs Absolus. (Stanford French & Italian Studies: No. 12). 1979. pap. 20.00 (ISBN 0-915838-25-7). Anma Libri.

Romains, Jules. Saints de Notre Calendrier. 256p. 1952. 4.95 (ISBN 0-686-55290-3). French & Eur.

Ronsard. Oeuvres poetiques. (Documentation thematique). 2.95 (ISBN 0-685-36194-2, 202). Larousse.

Rozenberg, Paul. Le Romantisme anglais: Le Defi des vulnerables. new ed. (Collection L). 287p. (Orig., Fr.). 1973. pap. 13.95 (ISBN 2-03-036010-4). Larousse.

St. Pierre. Romantisme europeen, 2 vols. (Documentation thematique). 2.95 ea. Larousse.

Saintsbury, George. Primer of French Literature. 1912. Repr. 15.00 (ISBN 0-8274-3202-X). R West.

--A Short History of French Literature. 1978. Repr. of 1882 ed. lib. bdg. 35.00 (ISBN 0-89760-800-3, Telegraph). Dynamic Learn Corp.

--A Short History of French Literature. 1977. Repr. of 1882 ed. lib. bdg. 30.00 (ISBN 0-8482-2554-6). Norwood Edns.

--Specimens of French Literature from Villon to Hugo. 1892. Repr. 40.00 (ISBN 0-8274-3481-2). R West.

Saintsbury, George E. Collected Essays & Papers 1875-1920, 4 Vols. (English Literary Reference Ser). Repr. of 1924 ed. Set. 65.50 (ISBN 0-384-53070-2). Johnson Repr.

--Essays on French Novelists. 460p. 1980. Repr. of 1891 ed. lib. bdg. 35.00 (ISBN 0-8482-6215-8). Norwood Edns.

--French Literature & Its Masters. Cairns, Huntington, ed. LC 77-163540. (Illus.). 326p. 1946. Repr. lib. bdg. 18.75x (ISBN 0-8371-6202-5, SAFL). Greenwood.

--Prefaces & Essays. LC 72-99722. (Essay Index Reprint Ser). 1933. 25.00 (ISBN 0-8369-1377-9). Arno.

Sarolea, Charles. French Renascence. LC 73-110920. 1970. Repr. of 1916 ed. 12.50 (ISBN 0-8046-0902-0). Kennikat.

Sartre, Jean-Paul. Qu'est-Ce que la litterature? (Coll. Idees). pap. 4.50 (ISBN 0-685-36564-6). French & Eur.

Schofer, Peter, et al, eds. Poemes, Pieces, Prose: Introduction a l'analyse De textes litteraires francais. (Illus.). 768p. (Fr.). 1973. pap. text ed. 12.95x (ISBN 0-19-501643-2). Oxford U Pr.

Sergeant, Elizabeth S. French Perspectives. 1916. Repr. 20.00 (ISBN 0-8274-2373-X). R West.

Sherzer, Dina. Structure De la Trilogie De Beckett: Molloy, Malone Meurt, L'innommable. (Approaches to Semiotics Ser: No. 38). 100p. 1976. text ed. 23.75x (ISBN 0-686-22619-4). Mouton.

Smith, Horatio. Masters of French Literature. 338p. 1981. Repr. of 1937 ed. lib. bdg. 35.00 (ISBN 0-89987-772-9). Darby Bks.

--Masters of French Literature. facs. ed. LC 69-17589. (Essay Index Reprint Ser). 1937. 13.00 (ISBN 0-8369-0092-8). Arno.

Smith, Mabell. The Spirit of French Letters. 1973. Repr. of 1912 ed. 15.00 (ISBN 0-8274-0891-9). R West.

Spiers, Victor. History & Literature in France; in Synoptic Tables & Essays on the Chief Characters & Epochs. 1973. Repr. of 1899 ed. 20.00 (ISBN 0-8274-0879-X). R West.

--History & Literature of France in Synoptic Tables & Essays on the Chief Characters & Epochs. 1978. lib. bdg. 40.00 (ISBN 0-8495-4877-2). Arden Lib.

Stambolian, George & Marks, Elaine, eds. Homosexualities & French Literature: Cultural Contexts, Critical Texts. LC 78-25659. 1979. 24.50x (ISBN 0-8014-1186-6). Cornell U Pr.

Strachey, G. L. Landmarks in French Literature. 1912. Repr. 15.00 (ISBN 0-8274-2795-6). R West.

Styles, meubles et decors, 2 vols. 51.25x ea. Larousse.

Talbot, Lucien. Recueils De Textes Francais a Expliquer. 4th ed. (Fr). 1960. 2.95x (ISBN 2-7637-6115-1, Pub. by Laval). Intl Schol Bk Serv.

Talvart. Bibliographie des Auteurs Modernes de Langue Francaise (1801-1962) Incl. Tome XV. Michaux-Mirbeau; Tome XVI. Index Alphabetique des Titres des Ouvrages Decrits de A a L; Tome XVII. Index des Titres, M-Z. Index des Noms dAuteurs. 65.00 (ISBN 0-685-35962-X); Tome XVIII. Mir-Mon; Tome XIX. Mong-Mont. French & Eur.

Thieme, Hugo P. Essai Sur l'Histoire Du Vers Francais. LC 70-168703. (Essays in Literature & Criticism Ser.: No. 148). (Fr). 1971. Repr. of 1916 ed. lib. bdg. 26.50 (ISBN 0-8337-3506-3). B Franklin.

Thimann, I. C. A Short History of French Literature. 1967. 15.00 (ISBN 0-08-012011-3); pap. 7.00 (ISBN 0-08-012010-5). Pergamon.

Thomas, Patrick A. L' Oeuvre De Jacques De Baisieux: Edition Critique. (Studies in French Literature: No. 3). 1972. pap. 32.50x (ISBN 90-2792-530-5). Mouton.

Tiefenbrun, Susan. A Structural Stylistic Analysis of la Princesse De Cleves. (De Proprietatibus Litterarum Series Practica: No. 25). 185p. (Orig.). 1976. pap. text ed. 35.00x (ISBN 90-2793-263-8). Mouton.

Tilley, Arthur A., ed. Modern France: A Companion to French Studies. LC 66-27168. (Illus.). 1967. Repr. of 1922 ed. 25.00 (ISBN 0-8462-0890-3). Russell.

Turnell, Martin. The Novel in France: Mme. De Lafayette, Laclos, Constant, Stendhal, Balzac, Flaubert, Proust. LC 72-297. (Essay Index Reprint Ser.). Repr. of 1951 ed. 30.00 (ISBN 0-8369-2831-8). Arno.

Turquet-Milnes, G. From Pascal to Proust. LC 76-52955. (Studies in French Literature, No. 45). 1977. lib. bdg. 32.95 (ISBN 0-8383-2131-3). Haskell.

Van Laun, Henri. History of French Literature, 3 vols. 1973. Repr. of 1876 ed. 100.00 set (ISBN 0-8274-0796-3). R West.

--History of French Literature, 3 vols. Repr. of 1876 ed. 75.00 (ISBN 0-686-19850-6). Ridgeway Bks.

Voltaire. Lettres philosophiques. (Documentation thematique). 2.95 (ISBN 0-685-36196-9, 265). Larousse.

Ware, J. N. The Vocabulary of Bernardin De Saint-Pierre & Its Relation to the French Romantic School. Repr. of 1927 ed. 11.50 (ISBN 0-384-65803-2). Johnson Repr.

Wilkinson, William C. Classic French Course in English. 1973. Repr. of 1887 ed. 20.00 (ISBN 0-8274-0680-0). R West.

Wilson, N. Scarlyn. The French Classic Age. 1973. lib. bdg. 20.00 (ISBN 0-8414-9749-4). Folcroft.

Winkelman, J. H. Die Bruckenpachter und Die Turmwachterepisode Im "Trierer Floyris" und in der "Version Rrstperatique" Des Altfranzosischen Florisromans. (Amsterdamer Publikationen Zur Sprache und Literatur: No. 27). (Orig., Ger.). 1977. pap. text ed. 26.00x (ISBN 90-6203-499-3). Humanities.

Woodbridge, B. M. Gatien De Courtilz, Sieur Du Verger: Etude Sur un Precurseur Du Roman Realiste En France. Repr. of 1925 ed. 17.00 (ISBN 0-384-69156-0). Johnson Repr.

Wright, C. H. A History of French Literature, 2 vols. lib. bdg. 50.00 (ISBN 0-8414-9625-0). Folcroft.

Wright, Charles H. History of French Literature. LC 68-24951. (Studies in French Literature, No. 45). 1969. Repr. of 1926 ed. lib. bdg. 72.95 (ISBN 0-8383-0263-7). Haskell.

Yale University French Department. Studies by Members of the French Department of Yale University. LC 72-1658. (Yale Romance Studies: No. 18). Repr. of 1941 ed. 24.00 (ISBN 0-404-53218-7). AMS Pr.

Zell, Hans & Silver, Helene. Reader's Guide to African Literature. LC 76-83165. 1971. text ed. 16.00x (ISBN 0-8419-0018-3, Africana); pap. text ed. 9.50x (ISBN 0-8419-0019-1, Africana). Holmes & Meier.

FRENCH LITERATURE–HISTORY AND CRITICISM–TO 1500

Barrow, Sarah F. The Medieval Society Romances. LC 73-13967. 141p. 1973. Repr. of 1924 ed. lib. bdg. 13.50x (ISBN 0-374-90416-2). Octagon.

Brereton, Georgine E. & Ferrier, Janet M., eds. Le Menagier De Paris: A Critical Edition. 600p. 1981. 99.00x (ISBN 0-19-815748-7). Oxford U Pr.

Brody, Jules, ed. The Eye of the Beholder: Essays in French Literature by Nathan Edelman. LC 74-6813. 222p. 1974. 14.50x (ISBN 0-8018-1621-1). Johns Hopkins.

Bruckner, Matilda T. Narrative Invention in Twelfth-Century French Romance: The Convention of Hospitality (1160-1200) LC 79-53400. (French Forum Monographs: No. 17). 232p. 1980. pap. 11.50 (ISBN 0-917058-16-X). French Forum.

Chatelain, Henri L. Recherches sur le vers francais au quinzieme siecle: rimes, metres et strophes. LC 79-149950. (Research & Source Works Ser.: No. 725). 1971. Repr. of 1908 ed. lib. bdg. 26.50 (ISBN 0-8337-0550-4). B Franklin.

Cook, Robert F. Chanson D'antioche, Chanson de Geste: Le Cycle de la Croisade Est-Ii Epique? vi, 107p. 1979. 14.00 (ISBN 90-272-1712-2, PUMRL 2). Benjamins North Am.

Crosland, Jessie. Old French Epic. LC 73-117589. (Studies in French Literature, No. 45). 1970. Repr. of 1951 ed. lib. bdg. 36.95 (ISBN 0-8383-1022-2). Haskell.

Crosland, Jessie, tr. Medieval French Literature. LC 76-17313. 1976. Repr. of 1956 ed. lib. bdg. 17.50x (ISBN 0-8371-8971-3, CRMF). Greenwood.

Davis, Betty J. The Storytellers in Marguerite de Navarre's Heptameron. LC 77-93406. (Monographs: No. 9). 203p. (Orig.). 1978. pap. 9.50x (ISBN 0-917058-08-9). French Forum.

Faral, Edmond. Jongleurs En France Au Moyen Age. LC 79-140971. (Reseach & Source Works Ser: No. 606). 1971. Repr. of 1910 ed. 23.50 (ISBN 0-8337-1099-0). B Franklin.

Holmes, Urban T., Jr. History of Old French Literature from the Origins to 1300. LC 62-10230. (With rev. bibliographical supplement). 1962. Repr. of 1938 ed. 20.00 (ISBN 0-8462-0201-8). Russell.

Jones, Lowanne. The Cort D'amor: A Thirteenth-Century Allegorical Art of Love. (Studies in the Romance Languages & Literatures: No. 185). (Orig.). 1978. pap. 14.00x (ISBN 0-8078-9185-1). U of NC Pr.

Kilgour, Raymond L. The Decline of Chivalry, As Shown in the French Literature of the Late Middle Ages. 1937. 8.50 (ISBN 0-8446-1262-6). Peter Smith.

Koch, Sr. M. Pierre. Analysis of the Long Prayers in Old French Literature with Special Reference to the Biblical Creed Narrative Prayers. LC 70-94168. (Catholic University of America Studies in Romance Languages & Literatures Ser: No. 19). Repr. of 1940 ed. 18.00 (ISBN 0-404-50319-5). AMS Pr.

Kotin, Armine A. The Narrative Imagination: Comic Tales by Philippe de Vigneulles. LC 77-76329. (Studies in Romance Languages: No. 18). 152p. 1977. 13.50x (ISBN 0-8131-1369-5). U Pr of Ky.

Lancaster, Charles M., ed. & tr. Saints & Sinners in Old Romance: Poems of Feudal France & England. 2nd ed. LC 72-139930. (Illus., With new translations). 1971. Repr. of 1942 ed. 18.50 (ISBN 0-8462-1541-1). Russell.

Leclercq, Jean. Monks & Love in Twelfth-Century France: Psycho-Historical Essays. 156p. 1979. text ed. 28.50x (ISBN 0-19-822546-6). Oxford U Pr.

Maddox, Donald. Structure & Sacring: The Systematic Kingdom in Chretien's Erec. LC 77-93405. (Monographs: No. 8). 221p. (Orig.). 1978. pap. 9.50x (ISBN 0-917058-07-0). French Forum.

Marie De France. French Mediaeval Romances from the Lays of Marie De France. Mason, Eugene, tr. from Fr. LC 75-41188. Repr. of 1924 ed. 17.00 (ISBN 0-404-14571-X). AMS Pr.

Martino, Pierre. Orient Dans la Litterature Francaise Au Dixseptieme et Au Dixhuitieme Siecle. LC 77-170953. (Essays in Literature & Criticism Ser.: No. 154). 1906. 26.50 (ISBN 0-8337-4256-6). B Franklin.

Meiss, Millard & Beatson, Elizabeth H. La Vie de Nostre Benoit Sauveur Ihesuscrist & La Saincte Vie de Nostre Dame: translatee a la requeste de tres hault et puissant prince Iehan, duc de Berry. LC 76-16657. (College Art Association Monographs: Vol. 32). 1977. 22.50x (ISBN 0-8147-5410-4). NYU Pr.

Pei, Mario A. French Precursors of the Chanson De Roland. LC 48-9636. Repr. of 1948 ed. 14.00 (ISBN 0-404-04967-2). AMS Pr.

Rickard, P. Britain in Medieval French Literature, 1100-1500. 1956. 14.00 (ISBN 0-527-75250-9). Kraus Repr.

Rossman, Vladimir. Perspectives of Irony in Medieval French Literature. (De Proprietatibus Litterarum, Ser Maior: No. 35). 198p. (Orig.). 1975. pap. text ed. 32.50x (ISBN 90-2793-291-3). Mouton.

Schobben, J. G. La Part Du Pseudo-Turpin Dans les "Croniques & Conquests De Charlemaine" De David Aubert. (Publications De L'institut D'etudes Francaises & Occitanes De L'universite D'utrecht: No. 2). 1970. pap. 22.50x (ISBN 90-2791-272-6). Mouton.

Scholz, Bernard W. & Rogers, Barbara, trs. from Lat. Carolingian Chronicles: Royal Frankish Annals & Nithard's Histories. 1972. pap. 2.95 (ISBN 0-472-06186-0, 186, AA). U of Mich Pr.

Smith, Nathaniel B. Figures of Repetition in the Old Provencal Lyric: A Study in the Style of the Troubadours. (Studies in the Romance Languages & Literatures Ser: No. 176). 1976. pap. 17.50x (ISBN 0-8078-9176-2). U of NC Pr.

Studies in French Language & Mediaeval Literature. facs. ed. LC 70-84340. (Essay Index Reprint Ser). 1939. 24.25 (ISBN 0-8369-1109-1). Arno.

Vincent, P. R. The Jeu De Saint Nicolas of Jean Bodel of Arras: A Literary Analysis. Repr. of 1954 ed. 11.50 (ISBN 0-384-64610-7). Johnson Repr.

Wood, Mary M. Spirit of Protest in Old French Literature. LC 17-30250. (Columbia University. Studies in Romance Philology & Literature: No. 21). Repr. of 1917 ed. 19.00 (ISBN 0-404-50621-6). AMS Pr.

Yedlicka, Leo C. Expressions of the Linguistic Area of Repentance & Remorse in Old French. LC 76-94175. (Catholic University of America Studies in Romance Languages & Literatures Ser: No. 28). 1969. Repr. of 1945 ed. 28.00 (ISBN 0-404-50328-4). AMS Pr.

FRENCH LITERATURE–HISTORY AND CRITICISM–16TH CENTURY

Benouis, Mustapha K. Le Dialogue Philosophique Dans la Litterature Francaise Du Seizieme Siecle. (De Proprietatibus Litterarum, Ser. Maior: No. 31). 1976. write for info (ISBN 90-279-3201-8). Humanities.

--Le Dialoque Philosophique Dans la Litterature Francaise Du Seizieme Siecle. (De Proprietatibus Litterarum, Series Maior: No. 31). 1976. text ed. 48.25x (ISBN 90-2793-201-8). Mouton.

Cave, Terence. The Cornucopian Text: Problems of Writing in the French Renaissance. 1979. 54.00x (ISBN 0-19-815752-5). Oxford U Pr.

Cottrell, Robert D. Sexuality-Textuality: A Study of the Fabric of Montaigne's "Essais". LC 81-2085. 197p. 1981. 15.00 (ISBN 0-8142-0326-4). Ohio St U Pr.

Davis, Betty J. The Storytellers in Marguerite de Navarre's Heptameron. LC 77-93406. (Monographs: No. 9). 203p. (Orig.). 1978. pap. 9.50x (ISBN 0-917058-08-9). French Forum.

Hanisch, Gertrude S. Love Elegies of the Renaissance: Marot, Louise Labe & Ronsard. (Stanford French & Italian Studies: No. 15). 1979. pap. 20.00 (ISBN 0-915838-24-9). Anma Libri.

Keating, Louis C. Studies on the Literary Salon in France, 1550-1615. 1941. pap. 12.00 (ISBN 0-527-01114-2). Kraus Repr.

Kotin, Armine A. The Narrative Imagination: Comic Tales by Philippe de Vigneulles. LC 77-76329. (Studies in Romance Languages: No. 18). 152p. 1977. 13.50x (ISBN 0-8131-1369-5). U Pr of Ky.

La Charite, Raymond C. Recreation, Reflection, & Re-Creation: Perspectives on Rabelais' Pantagruel. LC 79-53402. (French Forum Monographs: No. 19). 140p. 1980. pap. 11.50 (ISBN 0-917058-18-6). French Forum.

Lapp, John C. The Brazen Tower: Essays on Mythological Imagery in French Renaissance & Baroque, 1550-1670. (Stanford French & Italian Studies: No. 7). 1978. pap. 20.00 (ISBN 0-915838-35-4). Anma Libri.

Lenient, Charles F. Satire En France, Ou la Litterature Militante Au Seizieme Siecle, 2 vols. 3rd rev. ed. 1966. Repr. of 1886 ed. 36.50 (ISBN 0-8337-2067-8). B Franklin.

Richardson, L. McDowell. The Forerunners of Feminism in French Literature of the Renaissance. 1973. Repr. of 1929 ed. 15.50 (ISBN 0-685-30642-9). Johnson Repr.

Rouillard, Clarence D. The Turk in French History, Thought & Literature, 1520-1660. LC 71-180375. (Appendix 1. A Bibliography of Pamphlets Relating to the Turks, 1481 to 1660). Repr. of 1940 ed. 39.00 (ISBN 0-404-56321-X). AMS Pr.

Stone, Donald. France in the Sixteenth Century. LC 75-46622. 180p. 1976. Repr. of 1969 ed. lib. bdg. 16.25x (ISBN 0-8371-8734-6, STFS). Greenwood.

Tilley, Arthur A. Dawn of the French Renaissance. LC 68-10951. (Illus.). 1968. Repr. of 1918 ed. 16.50 (ISBN 0-8462-1069-X). Russell.

The Web of Metaphor: Studies in the Imagery of Montaigne's Essais. LC 77-93404. (Monographs: No. 7). 191p. (Orig.). 1978. pap. 9.50x (ISBN 0-917058-06-2). French Forum.

West, Albert H. Influence Francaise Dans la Poesie Burlesqu En Angleterre Entre 1660 et 1700. LC 76-144834. (Bibliotheque De la Revue De Litterature Comparee: Vol. 74). Repr. of 1937 ed. 22.50 (ISBN 0-8337-3751-1). B Franklin.

FRENCH LITERATURE–HISTORY AND CRITICISM–17TH CENTURY

Abraham, Claude K. Enfin Malherbe: The Influence of Malherbe on French Lyric Prosody, 1605-1674. LC 70-160042. 368p. 1971. 18.00x (ISBN 0-8131-1254-0). U Pr of Ky.

Boas, George. The Happy Beast in French Thought of the Seventeenth Century. 1966. lib. bdg. 14.00x (ISBN 0-374-90722-6). Octagon.

Boileau-Despreaux, Nicolas. Selected Criticism. Dilworth, Ernest, tr. from Fr. LC 65-26530. 1965. pap. text ed. 3.95x (ISBN 0-672-60471-X). Irvington.

Borgerhoff, Elbert B. Freedom of French Classicism. LC 68-27051. (Illus.). 1968. Repr. of 1950 ed. 8.50 (ISBN 0-8462-1193-9). Russell.

Brereton, Geoffrey. French Tragic Drama in the Sixteenth & Seventeenth Centuries. (Illus.). 320p. 1973. 18.95x (ISBN 0-416-07630-0); pap. 12.95x (ISBN 0-416-78920-X). Methuen Inc.

Brody, Jules, ed. The Eye of the Beholder: Essays in French Literature by Nathan Edelman. LC 74-6813. 222p. 1974. 14.50x (ISBN 0-8018-1621-1). Johns Hopkins.

Bunch, William A. Jean Mairet. (World Authors Ser.: France: No. 358). 1975. lib. bdg. 10.95 (ISBN 0-8057-2565-2). Twayne.

Chambers, Frank. Prosateurs Francais XVIE Siecle. 1976. pap. 12.95x (ISBN 0-669-00016-7). Heath.

The Comic Novels of Charles Sorel: A Study of Structure, Characterization & Disguise. (French Forum Monographs: No. 32). 135p. (Orig.). 1981. pap. 10.00 (ISBN 0-917058-31-3). French Forum.

Cruickshank, John, ed. French Literature & Its Background, 6 vols. Incl. Vol. 1. Sixteenth Century. (No. 138). 238p. 1968; Vol. 2. Seventeenth Century. (No. 171). 240p. 1969. 9.95x (ISBN 0-19-285028-8); Vol. 3. Eighteenth Century. (No. 139). 232p. 1968. 9.95x (ISBN 0-19-285021-0); Vol. 4. Early Nineteenth Century. (No. 172). 250p. 1969. 11.95x (ISBN 0-19-285029-6); Vol. 5. Late Nineteenth Century. (No. 173). 238p. 1969. 5.95x (ISBN 0-19-285033-4); Vol. 6. Twentieth Century. (No. 184). 350p. 1970. 11.50x (ISBN 0-19-285043-1). (Oxford Paperbacks Ser). Oxford U Pr.

DeJean, Joan. Libertine Strategies: Freedom & the Novel in Seventeenth Century France. LC 81-38431. 240p. 1981. 17.50x (ISBN 0-8142-0325-6). Ohio St U Pr.

France, Peter. Rhetoric & Truth in France: Descartes to Diderot. 1972. 24.95x (ISBN 0-19-815709-6). Oxford U Pr.

Guizot, Francois P. Corneille & His Times. LC 76-153271. 1971. Repr. of 1852 ed. 17.50 (ISBN 0-8046-1569-1). Kennikat.

Hanisch, Gertrude S. Love Elegies of the Renaissance: Marot, Louise Labe & Ronsard. (Stanford French & Italian Studies: No. 15). 1979. pap. 20.00 (ISBN 0-915838-24-9). Anma Libri.

Horowitz, Louise K. Love & Language: A Study of the Classical French Moralist Writers. LC 76-57232. 1977. 12.50x (ISBN 0-8142-0233-0). Ohio St U Pr.

Ivker, Barry. An Anthology & Analysis of 17th & 18th Century French Libertine Fiction. 1977. pap. 18.50 (ISBN 0-8357-0259-6, SS-00033). Univ Microfilms.

Lancaster, H. Carrington, ed. Five French Farces 1655-1694. (Johns Hopkins University Studies in Romance Literatures and Languages: Vol. 19). 1970. Repr. of 1937 ed. 11.50 (ISBN 0-384-31170-9). Johnson Repr.

Lanson, Gustave. Origenes et Premieres Manifestations de l'Esprit Philosophique dans la Litterature Francaise de 1675 a 1748. 1910. 29.50 (ISBN 0-8337-4215-9). B Franklin.

Lapp, John C. The Brazen Tower: Essays on Mythological Imagery in French Renaissance & Baroque, 1550-1670. (Stanford French & Italian Studies: No. 7). 1978. pap. 20.00 (ISBN 0-915838-35-4). Anma Libri.

MacLean, Ian. Woman Triumphant: Feminism in French Literature 1610-1652. (Illus.). 1977. 54.00x (ISBN 0-19-815741-X). Oxford U Pr.

Moliere. L' Ecole des Femmes & la Critique de L'ecole des Femmes. Howarth, W. D., ed. (Blackwell's French Text Ser.). 142p. 1968. pap. text ed. 9.95x (ISBN 0-631-00630-3, Pub. by Basil Blackwell). Biblio Dist.

Reese, H. Reese. La Mesnardiere's Poetique 1639: Sources & Dramatic Theories. 1973. Repr. of 1937 ed. pap. 18.50 (ISBN 0-384-50113-3). Johnson Repr.

Rosenfield, Leonora. From Beast Machine to Man Machine: Animal Soul in French Letters from Descartes to La Mettrie. 1968. lib. bdg. 25.00x (ISBN 0-374-96955-8). Octagon.

Stegmann, A. Les Caracteres de la Bruyere: Bible de l'honnete homme. new ed. (Collection themes et textes). 224p. (Orig., Fr.). 1972. pap. 5.95 (ISBN 2-03-035008-7, 2667). Larousse.

Voltaire. Le Siecle de Louis XIV, 2 vols. Adam, Antoine, ed. 1966. pap. 4.95 ea. French & Eur.

West, Albert H. Influence Francaise Dans la Poesie Burlesqu En Angleterre Entre 1660 et 1700. LC 76-144834. (Bibliotheque De la Revue De Litterature Comparee: Vol. 74). Repr. of 1937 ed. 22.50 (ISBN 0-8337-3751-1). B Franklin.

Williams, Ralph C. Bibliography of the Seventeenth Century Novel in France. xiv, 355p. 1964. Repr. of 1931 ed. 25.00 (ISBN 0-900470-44-5). Oak Knoll.

FRENCH LITERATURE–HISTORY AND CRITICISM–18TH CENTURY

Atkinson, Geoffroy & Keller, Abraham C. Prelude to the Enlightenment: French Literature, 1690-1740. LC 70-114416. 221p. 1971. 12.95 (ISBN 0-295-95082-X). U of Wash Pr.

Bussy, Carvel De. Conferences De Litterature Francaise: XVIIIe Siecle. LC 78-66098. (Fr.). 1979. pap. text ed. 10.00 (ISBN 0-9602260-0-1). C de Bussy.

Couperus, M. C. Un Periodique Francais En Hollande: Le Glaneur Historique, 1731-33. (Publications De L'institut D'etudes Francaises & Occitanes De L'universite D'utrecht: No. 6). 1971. pap. 59.00x (ISBN 90-2792-221-7). Mouton.

Davidson, Hugh M. Audience, Words, & Art: Studies in Seventeenth-Century French Rhetoric. LC 65-18737. 1965. 5.00 (ISBN 0-8142-0043-5). Ohio St U Pr.

Dufrenoy, Marie-Louise. L' Orient Romanesque en Frances: 1704-1789, Tomes I & II. 1978. pap. text ed. 40.00x (ISBN 9-0620-3108-0). Humanities.

Fellows, Otis E. & Torrey, Norman L. Age of Enlightenment. 2nd ed. LC 73-147121. 1971. text ed. 18.95 (ISBN 0-13-018465-9). P-H.

Fierobe, Claude. Charles Robert Maturin (1780-1824) L'homme et L'oeuvre. 1974. pap. text ed. 24.25x (ISBN 2-85939-022-7). Humanities.

Fox, J. H., et al, eds. Studies in Eighteenth-Century French Literature Presented to Robert Niklaus. 345p. 1975. 50.00x (ISBN 0-85989-050-3, Pub. by Exeter Univ England). State Mutual Bk.

France, Peter. Rhetoric & Truth in France: Descartes to Diderot. 1972. 24.95x (ISBN 0-19-815709-6). Oxford U Pr.

George, Albert J. The Development of French Romanticism: The Impact of the Industrial Revolution on Literature. LC 77-10903. 1977. Repr. of 1955 ed. lib. bdg. 16.25x (ISBN 0-8371-9806-2, GEDF). Greenwood.

Green, Frederick C. Eighteenth-Century France: Six Essays. LC 64-21609. 9.00 (ISBN 0-8044-1315-0); pap. 4.95 (ISBN 0-8044-6221-6). Ungar.

--Minuet: A Critical Survey of French & English Literary Ideas in the 18th Century. LC 75-158504. 1971. Repr. of 1935 ed. 35.00 (ISBN 0-403-01296-1). Scholarly.

Hastings, H. Man & Beast in French Thought of the 18th Century. 1973. Repr. of 1936 ed. 22.50 (ISBN 0-384-21748-6). Johnson Repr.

Ivker, Barry. An Anthology & Analysis of 17th & 18th Century French Libertine Fiction. 1977. pap. 18.50 (ISBN 0-8357-0259-6, SS-00033). Univ Microfilms.

Jacoebee, W. Pierre. La Persuasion De la Charite: Themes, Formes et Structure Dans les Jornaux et Oeuvres Diverses De Marivaux. (Orig., Fr.). 1976. pap. text ed. 20.00x (ISBN 90-6203-239-7). Humanities.

Lanson, Gustave. Origenes et Premieres Manifestations de l'Esprit Philosophique dans la Litterature Francaise de 1675 a 1748. 1910. 29.50 (ISBN 0-8337-4215-9). B Franklin.

LeSage, Laurent & Yon, Andre. Dictionnaire Des Critiques Litteraires: Guide De la Critique De la Vingtieme Siecle. LC 68-8181. (Fr.). 1969. 14.95x (ISBN 0-271-00081-3). Pa St U Pr.

Mornet, Daniel. French Thought in the Eighteenth Century. Levin, Lawrence M., tr. 1969. Repr. of 1929 ed. 19.50 (ISBN 0-208-00750-4, Archon). Shoe String.

--Romantisme En France Au Dix-Huitieme Siecle. LC 76-159705. (Research & Source Works Ser: No. 853). 1971. Repr. of 1912 ed. lib. bdg. 21.50 (ISBN 0-8337-4294-9). B Franklin.

Mylne, Vivienne. The Eighteenth-Century French Novel: Techniques of Illusion. LC 81-3911. 302p. Date not set. price not set (ISBN 0-521-23864-1); pap. price not set (ISBN 0-521-28266-7). Cambridge U Pr.

Peyre, Henri. What Is Romanticism? Roberts, Roda P., tr. from Fr. LC 75-42374. 1977. 15.50x (ISBN 0-8173-7003-X). U of Ala Pr.

Roberts, Warren. Morality & the Social Class in Eighteenth Century French Literature & Painting. LC 79-185732. (Illus.). 1974. 22.50x (ISBN 0-8020-5250-9). U of Toronto Pr.

Rolland, Romain, et al. French Thought in the Eighteenth Century. facsimile ed. LC 70-152172. (Essay Index Reprint Ser). Repr. of 1953 ed. 24.00 (ISBN 0-8369-2316-2). Arno.

Rosbottom, Ronald C. Choderlos de Laclos. (World Authors Ser.: France: No. 502). 1978. 13.95 (ISBN 0-8057-6343-0). Twayne.

Szenczi, Miklos J., ed. Studies in Eighteenth-Century Literature. LC 75-313202. 387p. 1975. 25.00x (ISBN 963-05-0243-7). Intl Pubns Serv.

Tilley, Arthur A. From Montaigne to Moliere; or the Preparation for the Classical Age of French Literature. 2nd ed. LC 78-102549. 1970. Repr. of 1923 ed. 10.00 (ISBN 0-8462-1475-X). Russell.

Van Roosbroeck, G. L. Persian Letters Before Montesquieu. 1932. 19.00 (ISBN 0-8337-4458-5). B Franklin.

Vinet, Alexander. History of French Literature in the Eighteenth Century. LC 70-103237. 1970. Repr. of 1854 ed. 17.50 (ISBN 0-8046-0873-3). Kennikat.

Von Mohrenschildt, Dimitri S. Russia in the Intellectual Life of Eighteenth-Century France. LC 71-159255. x, 326p. 1971. Repr. of 1936 ed. lib. bdg. 16.00x (ISBN 0-374-98088-8). Octagon.

Wright, Charles H. French Classicism. (Harvard Studies in Romance Languages: Vol. 4). 1920. pap. 12.00 (ISBN 0-527-01102-9). Kraus Repr.

FRENCH LITERATURE–HISTORY AND CRITICISM–19TH CENTURY

Atkinson, Geoffroy. The Sentimental Revolution: French Writers of 1690-1740. Keller, Abraham C., ed. LC 64-18424. 200p. 1966. 10.50 (ISBN 0-295-74024-8). U of Wash Pr.

Babbitt, Irving. The Master of Modern French Criticism. LC 76-56408. 1977. Repr. of 1912 ed. lib. bdg. 24.00x (ISBN 0-8371-9415-6, BAMF). Greenwood.

Balakian, Anna. The Symbolist Movement: A Critical Appraisal. LC 77-76044. 320p. 1977. 17.50x (ISBN 0-8147-0993-1); pap. 8.00x (ISBN 0-8147-0994-X). NYU Pr.

Blaze De Bury, Yetta. French Literature of Today. LC 68-8223. 1969. Repr. of 1898 ed. 12.50 (ISBN 0-8046-0103-8). Kennikat.

Bowen, Barbara C., ed. Four Farces: L'obstination Des Femmes; le Cuvier: le Paste et la Tarte; Maistre Pierre Pathelin. (French Texts Ser.). 156p. 1967. pap. 10.00x (ISBN 0-631-00670-2, Pub. by Basil Blackwell). Biblio Dist.

Brandes, Georg M. French Romantics. LC 60-12189. (Main Currents in 19th Century Literature Ser.: Vol. 5). 1966. Repr. of 1905 ed. 10.00 (ISBN 0-8462-0687-0). Russell.

--Revolution & Reaction in Nineteenth Century French Literature. LC 60-12189. (Main Currents in 19th Century Literature Ser.: Vol. 3). 1960. Repr. of 1901 ed. 8.00 (ISBN 0-8462-0133-X). Russell.

Cambiaire, Celestin P. Influence of Edgar Allen Poe in France. 1971. Repr. of 1927 ed. 23.00 (ISBN 0-403-00894-8). Scholarly.

Chartier, Armand B. Barbey D'Aurevilly. (World Authors Ser.: France: No. 468). 1977. lib. bdg. 12.50 (ISBN 0-8057-6305-8). Twayne.

Clark, Sr. M. Ursula. Cult of Enthusiasm in French Romanticism. LC 70-94179. (Catholic University of America. Studies in Romance Languages & Literatures: No. 37). Repr. of 1950 ed. 19.00 (ISBN 0-404-50337-3). AMS Pr.

Dakyns, Jannie R. The Middle Ages in French Literature 1851-1900. new ed. (Oxford Modern Languages & Literature Monographs). 364p. 1973. 29.95x (ISBN 0-19-815522-0). Oxford U Pr.

Daudet, Alphonse. Suffering Eighteen Eighty-Seven to Eighteen Ninety-Five. 1934. 22.50x (ISBN 0-686-51319-3). Elliots Bks.

Debre, Moses. Image of the Jew in French Literature from 1800 to 1908. Hirschler, Gertrude, tr. 1970. 15.00x (ISBN 0-87068-075-7). Ktav.

De Gourmont, Remy. Book of Masks. facs. ed. Lewis, J., tr. LC 67-26745. (Essay Index Reprint Ser). 1921. 15.00 (ISBN 0-8369-0490-7). Arno.
Evans, David O. Social Romanticism in France, 1830-1848. LC 77-96180. 1969. Repr. of 1951 ed. lib. bdg. 11.00x (ISBN 0-374-92641-7, Dist. by NYGS). Octagon.
Freilich, Joan. Paul Claudel's le Soulier De Satin: A Stylistic, Structuralist, & Psychoanalytic Interpretation. LC 72-75739. (Illus.). 300p. 1973. 25.00x (ISBN 0-8020-5279-7). U of Toronto Pr.
Frierson, William C. Influence du naturalism francais sur les romanciers anglais de 1885 a 1900. LC 77-148781. Repr. of 1925 ed. 23.50 (ISBN 0-404-08799-X). AMS Pr.
Furst, Lillian R. Counterparts: The Dynamics of Franco-German Literary Relationships, 1770-1895. LC 77-2407. 1977. text ed. 13.50x (ISBN 0-8143-1582-8). Wayne St U Pr.
Gaboriau, Emile. Monsieur Lecoq. Bleiler, E. F., ed. (Illus.). 5.50 (ISBN 0-8446-5188-5). Peter Smith.
Green, F. C., compiled by. French Short Stories of the Nineteenth & Twentieth Centuries. 1961. 8.95x (ISBN 0-460-00896-X, Evman). Biblio Dist.
Guerard, Albert L. Five Masters of French Romance: Anatole France, Pierre Loti, Paul Bourget, Maurice Barres, & Romain Rolland. 326p. 1981. Repr. of 1916 ed. lib. bdg. 35.00 (ISBN 0-89987-309-X). Darby Bks.
Harding, Frank J. Matthew Arnold, The Critic & France. 1979. Repr. of 1964 ed. lib. bdg. 30.00 (ISBN 0-8495-2349-4). Arden Lib.
--Matthew Arnold, the Critic & France. LC 76-50106. 1977. Repr. of 1964 ed. lib. bdg. 25.00 (ISBN 0-8414-4721-7). Folcroft.
James, Henry. Literary Reviews & Essays, on American, English & French Literature. Mordell, Albert, ed. LC 73-137249. Repr. of 1957 ed. 17.50 (ISBN 0-404-04408-5). AMS Pr.
James, Henry, Jr. French Poets & Novelists. facsimile ed. LC 70-38773. (Essay Index Reprint Ser). Repr. of 1878 ed. 23.00 (ISBN 0-8369-2660-9). Arno.
Lerner, Michael G. Pierre Loti. (World Authors Ser.: France: No. 285). 1974. lib. bdg. 12.50 (ISBN 0-8057-2546-6). Twayne.
Lipschutz, Ilse H. Spanish Painting & the French Romantics. LC 74-172322. (Studies in Romance Languages: No. 32). (Illus.). 1972. 22.50x (ISBN 0-674-83110-1). Harvard U Pr.
Lockwood, Helen D. Tools & the Man. LC 21-12534. Repr. of 1927 ed. 14.75 (ISBN 0-404-03999-5). AMS Pr.
Maurois, Andre. De La Bruyere a Proust: Lecture Mon Doux Plaisir. (Coll. Les Grands Evenements Litteraires). 11.95 (ISBN 0-685-36929-3). French & Eur.
Mickel, Emanuel J., Jr. The Artificial Paradises: The Influence of Opium & Hashish on the Literature of French Romanticism & "les Fleurs du Mal". (Studies in the Romance Languages & Literatures: No. 84). 1969. pap. 10.50x (ISBN 0-8078-9084-7). U of NC Pr.
Minor, Lucian. The Militant Hack Writer: French Popular Literature 1800-1848 - Its Influence, Artistic & Political. 1975. 10.95 (ISBN 0-87972-105-7); pap. 5.95 (ISBN 0-87972-106-5). Bowling Green Univ.
Mitchell, Robert L., ed. Pre-Text, Text, Context: Essays on Nineteenth-Century French Literature. LC 80-11801. 302p. 1980. 20.00x (ISBN 0-8142-0305-1). Ohio St U Pr.
Pellissier, Georges. Literary Movement in France During the Nineteenth Century. facsimile ed. LC 71-150197. (Select Bibliographies Reprint Ser). Repr. of 1897 ed. 26.00 (ISBN 0-8369-5710-5). Arno.
Peyre, Henri. What Is Romanticism? Roberts, Roda P., tr. from Fr. LC 75-42374. 1977. 15.50x (ISBN 0-8173-7003-X). U of Ala Pr.
Porter, Laurence M. The Literary Dream in French Romanticism: A Psychoanalytic Interpretation. LC 79-14035. 1979. 16.95x (ISBN 0-8143-1627-1). Wayne St U Pr.
Sabin, Margery. English Romanticism & the French Tradition. 1976. 15.00x (ISBN 0-674-25686-7, SAER). Harvard U Pr.
Sainte-Beuve, Charles-Augustin. Chateau-Briand et Son Groupe Litteraire Sous L'Empire, 2 vols. Allem, Maurice, ed. 7.95 ea. French & Eur.
Saurat, Denis. Modern French Literature 1870-1940. LC 79-103234. 1971. Repr. of 1946 ed. 11.75 (ISBN 0-8046-1191-2). Kennikat.
St Aubyn, F. C. Charles Peguy. (World Authors Ser.: France: No. 467). 1977. lib. bdg. 12.50 (ISBN 0-8057-6304-X). Twayne.
Symons, Arthur. Studies in Two Literatures. 1978. Repr. of 1924 ed. lib. bdg. 25.00 (ISBN 0-8495-4847-0). Arden Lib.
--Studies in Two Literatures. LC 76-20002. (The Decadent Consciousness Ser.: Vol. 25). 1977. Repr. of 1897 ed. lib. bdg. 38.00 (ISBN 0-8240-2774-4). Garland Pub.
--The Symbolist Movement in Literature. LC 77-11488. (Symbolists Ser). 208p. 1980. Repr. of 1899 ed. 17.50 (ISBN 0-404-16348-3). AMS Pr.
--Symbolist Movement in Literature. LC 79-166209. (Studies in Comparative Literature, No. 35). 1971. lib. bdg. 49.95 (ISBN 0-8383-1316-7). Haskell.
Terdiman, Richard. The Dialectics of Isolation: Self & Society in the French Novel from the Realists to Proust. LC 75-18187. (Romantic Studies, Second Ser.: No. 25). 288p. 1976. 17.50x (ISBN 0-300-01888-6). Yale U Pr.
Thibault, Pierre. Savoir et Pouvoir: Philosophie Thomiste et Politique Clericale au XIXe Siecle. (Fr.). 1972. 12.50x (ISBN 2-7637-6603-X, Pub by Laval). Intl Schol Bk Serv.
Thorold, Algar. Six Masters in Disillusion. LC 75-113325. 1971. Repr. of 1909 ed. 11.00 (ISBN 0-8046-1364-8). Kennikat.
Turquet-Milnes, Gladys R. The Influence of Baudelaire in France & England. LC 77-1298. 1977. Repr. of 1913 ed. lib. bdg. 30.00 (ISBN 0-8414-8627-1). Folcroft.
Vicaire, Georges. Manuel de L'amateur de Livres du Dix-Neuvieme Siecle, Eighteen-One to Eighteen Ninty-Three, 8 vols. LC 79-144832. (Fr., X1894-1920). 1973. Repr. of 1884 ed. Set. lib. bdg. 297.00 (ISBN 0-8337-3644-2). B Franklin.
Weinberg, B. French Realism: The Critical Reaction, 1830-1870. 1937. pap. 14.00 (ISBN 0-527-95200-1). Kraus Repr.
Whitridge, Arnold. Critical Ventures in Modern French Literature. facs. ed. LC 67-22066. (Essay Index Reprint Ser). 1924. 10.25 (ISBN 0-8369-0993-3). Arno.
Wright, Charles H. The Background of Modern French Literature. facsimile ed. LC 79-37360. (Select Bibliographies Reprint Ser). Repr. of 1926 ed. 25.00 (ISBN 0-8369-6707-0). Arno.
Zola, Emile. Experimental Novel & Other Essays. Sherman, Belle M., tr. LC 74-890. (Studies in Fiction, No. 34). 1893. lib. bdg. 39.95 (ISBN 0-8383-0697-7). Haskell.
--Le Roman Experimental. Guedj, Aime, ed. 1971. 4.50 (ISBN 0-686-55801-4). French & Eur.

FRENCH LITERATURE–HISTORY AND CRITICISM–20TH CENTURY

Alden, Douglas W., ed. French Twenty Bibliography: Critical & Biographical References for the Study of French Literature Since 1885, Index to Nos. 26-30. LC 77-648803. (Orig.). 1981. pap. 26.00x (ISBN 0-933444-38-9). French Inst.
Babbitt, Irving. The Masters of Modern French Criticism. 426p. 1981. Repr. of 1912 ed. lib. bdg. 40.00 (ISBN 0-8495-0469-4). Arden Lib.
Cagnon, Maurice, ed. Ethique et Esthetique Dans la Litterature Francaise Du XXe Siecle. (Stanford French & Italian Studies: No. 10). 1978. pap. 20.00 (ISBN 0-915838-38-9). Anma Libri.
Cobb, Richard. Promenades: An Historian's Appreciation of Modern French Literature. 160p. 1980. 16.95x (ISBN 0-19-211758-0). Oxford U Pr.
Davies, Jane D. Le Compagnon Du Petit Prince: Cahier D'Exercises Sur le Texte De Sainte-Exupery. 1975. pap. text ed. 5.95 (ISBN 0-15-550448-7, HC); instructor's man. avail. (ISBN 0-15-550449-5). HarBraceJ.
Doubrovsky, Serge. The New Criticism in France. Coltman, Derek, tr. from Fr. 1973. 15.00x (ISBN 0-226-16040-8). U of Chicago Pr.
Dumas Ribadeau, Francois. These Moderns: Some Parisian Closeups. LC 71-113308. 1971. Repr. of 1932 ed. 12.50 (ISBN 0-8046-1357-5). Kennikat.
Fay, Bernard. Since Victor Hugo: French Literature of Today. LC 66-25911. 1927. 11.50 (ISBN 0-8046-0141-0). Kennikat.
Field, F. Three French Writers & the Great War. LC 35-22982. 1975. 23.50 (ISBN 0-521-20916-1). Cambridge U Pr.
Fiser, Emeric. Le Symbole litteraire: Essai sur la signification du symbole chez Wagner, Baudelaire, Mallarme, Bergson, et Marcel Proust. LC 77-10260. Repr. of 1941 ed. 27.50 (ISBN 0-404-16315-7). AMS Pr.
Flower, J. E., et al. Writers & Politics in Modern Britain, France, & Germany. LC 77-7595. 1977. text ed. 29.50x (ISBN 0-8419-0320-4). Holmes & Meier.
Flower, John E. Literature & the Left in France. LC 76-2895. Date not set. text ed. 28.50x (ISBN 0-06-492135-2). B&N.
Fowlie, Wallace. Clowns & Angels: Studies in Modern French Literature. LC 72-93684. 162p. 1973. Repr. of 1943 ed. lib. bdg. 11.00x (ISBN 0-8154-0467-0). Cooper Sq.
Green, F. C., compiled by. French Short Stories of the Nineteenth & Twentieth Centuries. 1961. 8.95x (ISBN 0-460-00896-X, Evman). Biblio Dist.
Haft, Cynthia. The Theme of the Nazi Concentration Camp in French Literature. (New Babylon Studies in the Social Sciences: No. 12). 1973. 22.50x (ISBN 90-2797-190-0). Mouton.
Keylor, William R. Jacques Bainville & the Renaissance of Royalist History in Twentieth Century France. LC 79-10604. 1979. 24.95x (ISBN 0-8071-0465-5). La State U Pr.
Lemaitre, Georges E. From Cubism to Surrealism in French Literature. LC 77-18121. (Illus.). 1978. Repr. of 1947 ed. lib. bdg. 22.00x (ISBN 0-313-20112-9, LEFC). Greenwood.
Lerner, Michael G. Pierre Loti. (World Authors Ser.: France: No. 285). 1974. lib. bdg. 12.50 (ISBN 0-8057-2546-6). Twayne.
Matthews, J. H. Benjamin Peret. LC 74-30229. (World Authors Ser.: France: No. 359). 1975. lib. bdg. 12.50 (ISBN 0-8057-2691-8). Twayne.
Maurois, Andre. De Gide a Sartre. 8.95 (ISBN 0-685-36928-5). French & Eur.
Mehlman, Jeffrey. A Structural Study of Autobiography: Proust, Leiris, Sartre, Levi-Strauss. LC 74-6648. 264p. 1974. 22.50x (ISBN 0-8014-0886-5). Cornell U Pr.
Michaud, Regis. Modern Thought & Literature in France. facs. ed. LC 67-23248. (Essay Index Reprint Ser). 1934. 15.75 (ISBN 0-8369-0707-8). Arno.
O'Brien, Justin. The French Literary Horizon. 1967. 22.00 (ISBN 0-8135-0562-3). Rutgers U Pr.
O'Flaherty, Kathleen. The Novel in France, 1945-1965: A General Survey. 168p. 1973. text ed. 5.00x (ISBN 0-8426-0501-0). Verry.
O'Rourke, Brian. The Conscience of the Race: Sex & Religion in Irish & French Novels 1941-1973. 72p. 1980. 10.00x (ISBN 0-906127-22-X, Pub. by Irish Academic Pr Ireland). Biblio Dist.
O'Rourke, Maire. Charles Du Bos: "Exaltation" & Creative Criticism with Special Reference to the Period 1919-1927". LC 77-17699. 1977. 20.25 (ISBN 0-8357-0283-9, SS-00047). Univ Microfilms.
Paris. Bibliotheque Nationale. Cinquantenaire du symbolisme: Exposition de manuscrits autographes, estamps, peintures, sculptures, editions rares, portraits, objets d'art. LC 77-11471. (Symbolists Ser.). (Illus., Fr.). Repr. of 1936 ed. 27.50 (ISBN 0-404-16333-5). AMS Pr.
Peyre, Henri. French Literary Imagination & Dostoevsky & Other Essays. LC 74-28294. (Studies in the Humanities: No. 10). 176p. 1975. 12.95x (ISBN 0-8173-7324-1). U of Ala Pr.
Picon, Gaetan. Contemporary French Literature: 1945 & After. Scott, Kelvin & Martin, Graham, trs. from Fr. LC 72-89056. 236p. 1974. 11.50 (ISBN 0-8044-3255-4). Ungar.
Popkin, Debra & Popkin, Michael, eds. Modern French Literature, 2 vols. LC 76-15655. (Library of Literary Criticism Ser.). 1977. Set. 60.00 (ISBN 0-8044-3256-2). Ungar.
Qui-Phiet, Tran. Faulkner & the French New Novelist. LC 80-66067. (Scholarly Monographs). 85p. 1980. pap. 7.50 (ISBN 0-8408-0503-9). Carrollton Pr.
Raynaud, Ernest. La Melee symboliste, 3 vols. in 1. LC 77-11474. Repr. of 1922 ed. 37.50 (ISBN 0-404-16336-X). AMS Pr.
Riordan, Sr. Francis E. Concept of Love in the French Catholic Literary Revival. LC 76-94183. (Catholic University of America Studies in Romance Languages & Literature Ser: No. 42). Repr. of 1952 ed. 19.00 (ISBN 0-404-50342-X). AMS Pr.
Robinson, Christopher. French Literature in the Twentieth Century. (Comparative Literature Ser.). 288p. 1981. 15.00x (ISBN 0-389-20121-9). B&N.
Roudiez, Leon S., ed. Contemporary French Literature: Essays by Justin O'Brien. LC 77-127052. 1971. 21.00 (ISBN 0-8135-0661-1). Rutgers U Pr.
--Contemporary French Literature: Essays by Justin O'Brien. LC 77-127052. 1971. 21.00 (ISBN 0-8135-0661-1). Rutgers U Pr.
Sartre, Jean-Paul. Saint Genet. pap. 4.95 (ISBN 0-452-25153-2, Z5153, Plume). NAL.
St Aubyn, F. C. Charles Peguy. (World Authors Ser.: France: No. 467). 1977. lib. bdg. 12.50 (ISBN 0-8057-6304-X). Twayne.
Tollinchi, Esteban. La Conciencia Proustiana. LC 77-12535. (Coleccion Mente y Palabra). 1978. 6.25 (ISBN 0-8477-0552-8); pap. 5.00 (ISBN 0-8477-0553-6). U of PR Pr.
Turquet-Milnes, Gladys R. Some Modern French Writers: A Study in Bergsonism. facs. ed. LC 68-24858. (Essay Index Reprint Ser). 1968. Repr. of 1921 ed. 16.00 (ISBN 0-8369-0954-2). Arno.
Von Franz, Marie-Louise. Puer Aeternus. 2nd ed. LC 80-28090. (Illus.). 304p. 1981. 15.00 (ISBN 0-938434-03-9); pap. 10.50 (ISBN 0-938434-01-2). Sigo Pr.

FRENCH LITERATURE–LIBRARY RESOURCES

Lake, Carlton. Baudelaire to Beckett: A Century of French Art & Literature. (Illus.). 1976. 20.00 (ISBN 0-87959-019-X); pap. 12.50 (ISBN 0-87959-020-3). U of Tex Hum Res.

FRENCH LITERATURE–STUDY AND TEACHING

Bourgeois, Andre, et al. Studies in French Literature. (Rice University Studies: Vol. 57, No. 2). 127p. 1971. pap. 3.25x (ISBN 0-89263-208-9). Rice Univ.
Fowlie, Wallace. Pantomime, a Journal of Rehearsals. LC 74-29632. 246p. 1975. Repr. of 1951 ed. lib. bdg. 15.25x (ISBN 0-8371-7981-5, FOPA). Greenwood.
Fraser, Theodore P. & Whipple, Alan L. Le Pot au Feu. (Illus.). 218p. (gr. 7-10). 1975. pap. text ed. 4.75x (ISBN 0-88334-068-2). Ind Sch Pr.
Frohock, Wilbur M. French Literature: An Approach Through Close Reading. 4th ed. 1970. 5.50 (ISBN 0-87774-000-3). Schoenhof.
Houston, John P. Fictional Technique in France, 1802-1927: An Introduction. LC 72-181568. 1972. 12.50x (ISBN 0-8071-0041-2). La State U Pr.
Johnson, H. H. A Short Introduction to the Study of French Literature. 1973. lib. bdg. 20.00 (ISBN 0-8414-5385-3). Folcroft.
Jones, Percy M. The Assault on French Literature & Other Essays. LC 75-26214. 197p. 1976. Repr. of 1963 ed. lib. bdg. 15.00x (ISBN 0-8371-8401-0, JOAFL). Greenwood.
Morize, Andre. Problems & Methods of Literary History. LC 66-13475. 1922. 12.00x (ISBN 0-8196-0168-3). Biblo.
Nelson, Robert J. & Oxenhandler, Neal, eds. Aspects of French Literature. LC 61-5992. (Fr.). 1961. 34.50x (ISBN 0-89197-037-1); pap. text ed. 16.95x (ISBN 0-89197-038-X). Irvington.
Osburn, Charles B. Present State of French Studies: A Collection of Research Reviews. LC 78-149990. 1971. 30.00 (ISBN 0-8108-0373-9). Scarecrow.
Peyrazat, Jean E. Classics in French Literature: Simplified & Adapted for Classroom Use. Incl. Bk. 1. Contes Choisis. De Maupassant, Guy. 1967. pap. text ed. 2.75 (ISBN 0-88345-032-1, 17468); Bk. 2. Eugenie Grandet. De Balzac, Honore. 1967. pap. text ed. 2.75 (ISBN 0-88345-050-X, 17472); Bk. 3. Les Miserables. Hugo, Victor. 1967. pap. text ed. 2.75 (ISBN 0-88345-093-3, 17475); Bk. 4. Le Comte De Monte-Cristo. Dumas, Alexandre. 1969. pap. text ed. 2.75 (ISBN 0-88345-118-2, 17474); Bk. 5. Paul et Virginie. De Saint-Pierre, Bernardin. 1970. pap. text ed. 2.75 (ISBN 0-88345-126-3, 17478). (gr. 9-12). Regents Pub.

FRENCH LITERATURE–TRANSLATIONS FROM ENGLISH

Blassneck, Marce. Frankreich Als Vermittler Englisch-Deutscher Einflusse Im Siebzehnten und Achtzehnten Jahrhundert. 1934. pap. 10.00 (ISBN 0-384-04685-1). Johnson Repr.
Catel, Jean. Rhythme et Language Dans la Primiere Edition Des Leaves of Grass. 1930. lib. bdg. 17.50 (ISBN 0-8414-3377-1). Folcroft.

FRENCH LITERATURE–TRANSLATIONS INTO ENGLISH

Benedikt, Michael, ed. The Poetry of Surrealism: An Anthology. LC 74-8014. 1975. pap. 5.95 (ISBN 0-316-08898-6). Little.
Bowe, Forrest & Daniels, Mary F., eds. French Literature in Early American Translation: A Bibliographical Survey of Books & Pamphlets Printed in the United States from 1668 Through 1820. (Reference Library of the Humanities: Vol. 77). (Illus., LC 76-052680). 1977. lib. bdg. 63.00 (ISBN 0-8240-9893-5). Garland Pub.
Chapman, P. A. An Anthology of Seventeenth Century French Literature. 1927. 25.00 (ISBN 0-686-17673-1). Quaker City.
De Maupassant, Guy. Pierre & Jean. LC 76-48441. (Library of World Literature Ser.). 1978. Repr. of 1923 ed. lib. bdg. 19.50 (ISBN 0-88355-578-6). Hyperion Conn.
Grieder, Josephine. Translations of French Sentimental Prose Fiction in Late Eighteenth-Century England: The History of a Literary Vogue. LC 74-81963. ix, 127p. 1975. 8.95 (ISBN 0-8223-0327-2). Duke.
Morris, William. Old French Romances, Done into English. LC 75-113680. (Short Story Index Reprint Ser.). 1896. 15.00 (ISBN 0-8369-3409-1). Arno.
Robertson, D. W., Jr. Literature of Medieval England. LC 75-95827. 1970. text ed. 17.50 (ISBN 0-07-053158-7, C). McGraw.
Shirley, Janet, ed. Garnier's Becket: Translated from the 12th Century Vie Saint Thomas le Martyr de Cantorbire of Gannier of Pont-Sainte Maxence. (Illus.). 191p. 1975. 20.00x (ISBN 0-87471-798-1). Rowman.
Stabler, Arthur, ed. Four French Renaissance Plays. (Illus.). 1978. pap. 10.00 (ISBN 0-87422-014-9). Wash St U Pr.

Voltaire. Voltaire: The Age of Louis XIV & Other Selected Writings. Brumfit, J. H., ed. & intro. by. 1963. text ed. 20.00x (ISBN 0-8290-0219-7). Irvington.

FRENCH LITERATURE-CANADA
see French-Canadian Literature

FRENCH MUSIC
see Music, French

FRENCH NATIONAL CHARACTERISTICS
see National Characteristics, French

FRENCH PAINTING
see Painting, French

FRENCH PAINTINGS
see Paintings, French

FRENCH PHILOLOGY

Die Auseinandersetzungen an der Pariser Universitaet im Xiii Jahrhundert. (Miscellanea Mediaevalia Ser, Vol. 10). 1976. 78.00x (ISBN 3-11-005986-X). De Gruyter.

Studies in French Language & Mediaeval Literature. facs. ed. LC 70-84340. (Essay Index Reprint Ser). 1939. 24.25 (ISBN 0-8369-1109-1). Arno.

Studies in French Language, Literature & History. facs. ed. LC 76-80400. (Essay Index Reprint Ser). 1949. 15.00 (ISBN 0-8369-1067-2). Arno.

FRENCH PHILOLOGY-BIBLIOGRAPHY

Golden, H. H. & Simches, S. O. Modern French Literature & Language. Repr. of 1953 ed. 9.00 (ISBN 0-527-34300-5). Kraus Repr.

FRENCH PHILOSOPHY
see Philosophy, French

FRENCH POETRY (COLLECTIONS)
Here are entered collections of Poetry in French. For translations into English see subdivision Translations into English.
see also Chansons De Geste; French-Canadian Poetry; Lays; Romances; Troubadours

Abbot, Claude C., ed. Early Mediaeval French Lyrics. 1979. Repr. of 1932 ed. lib. bdg. 25.00 (ISBN 0-8495-0218-7). Arden Lib.

Angus, Frances R. French Poetry: An Anthology 1100-1925. 1977. Repr. of 1928 ed. 15.00 (ISBN 0-89984-040-X). Century Bookbindery.

Appelbaum, Stanley, ed. French Poetry: A Selection from Charles D'orleans to Yves Bonnefoy. (Illus., Fr. & Eng.). 4.75 (ISBN 0-8446-0100-4). Peter Smith.

Aspinwall, Dorothy. Modern Verse Translations from French. 220p. 1981. 9.95 (ISBN 0-89962-020-5). Todd & Honeywell.

Baudelaire, Charles, et al. Baudelaire, Rimbaud & Verlaine: Selected Verse & Prose Poems. Bernstein, Joseph M., ed. 1962. pap. 4.95 (ISBN 0-8065-0196-0, 67). Citadel Pr.

Benamou, Michel & Calin, William, eds. Aux Portes Du Poeme: Supervielle, Aragon, Eluard, Reverdy. (Orig.). 1964. pap. text ed. 2.50x (ISBN 0-685-14674-X). Macmillan.

Bennett, Betty T., ed. British War Poetry in the Age of Romanticism: 1793-1815. LC 75-31144. (Romantic Context: Poetry 1789-1830 Ser.: Vol. 1). 1977. lib. bdg. 47.00 (ISBN 0-8240-2100-2). Garland Pub.

Bergens, A. & Noakes, D., eds. Prevert Vous Parle. (Fr.). 1968. pap. 8.95 (ISBN 0-13-699231-5). P-H.

Boase, Alan M., ed. Poetry of France, Vol. 2: 1600-1800. 385p. 1973. 16.95x (ISBN 0-416-17110-9); pap. 8.50x (ISBN 0-416-77630-2). Methuen Inc.

Broome, P. & Chesters, G., eds. An Anthology of Modern French Poetry. LC 75-40769. 224p. 1976. 36.00 (ISBN 0-521-20793-2); pap. 8.95x (ISBN 0-521-20929-3). Cambridge U Pr.

Bullen, Keith & Cromer, John, eds. Salamander. facsimile ed. LC 79-103084. (Granger Index Reprint Ser). 1947. 15.00 (ISBN 0-8369-6099-8). Arno.

Chiari, Joseph, ed. Harrap Anthology of French Poetry. LC 70-131247. 1970. Repr. of 1958 ed. text ed. 12.50 (ISBN 0-87752-017-8). Gordian.

Comfort, W. W. French Romantic Prose. 1977. Repr. of 1928 ed. 20.00 (ISBN 0-89984-167-8). Century Bookbindery.

De Normandie, Guillaume. Le Bestiare. LC 73-180441. Repr. of 1892 ed. 31.50 (ISBN 0-404-56615-4). AMS Pr.

Ferrante, Joan M., tr. from Fr. Guillaume D'Orange: Four Twelfth-Century Epics. LC 74-4421. (Records of Civilization Ser). 311p. 1974. 18.50x (ISBN 0-231-03809-7). Columbia U Pr.

Flint, F. S. Some Modern French Poets. Bd. with The Younger French Poets. LC 78-64029. (Des Imagistes: Literature of the Imagist Movement). Repr. of 1920 ed. 14.00 (ISBN 0-404-17108-7). AMS Pr.

Gavronsky, Serge. Poems & Texts: An Anthology of French Poems. 1969. 7.50 (ISBN 0-8079-0150-4). October.

Giese, Frank S. & Wilder, Warren F. French Lyric Poetry: An Anthology. LC 64-7849. 1965. pap. 5.50 (ISBN 0-672-63038-9). Odyssey Pr.

--French Lyric Poetry: An Anthology. LC 64-7849. 1965. pap. 5.50 (ISBN 0-672-63038-9). Odyssey Pr.

Gray, Floyd, ed. Anthologie de la Poesie Francaise du Seizieme Siecle. LC 67-10343. (Fr.). 1977. 29.50x (ISBN 0-89197-026-6); pap. text ed. 18.95x (ISBN 0-89197-659-0). Irvington.

Grubbs, H. A. & Kneller, J. W. Introduction a la Poesie Francaise. 275p. 1962. 15.95 (ISBN 0-471-00217-8). Wiley.

Hackett, C. A. An Anthology of Modern French Poetry from Baudelaire to the Present. 305p. 1981. Repr. of 1953 ed. lib. bdg. 35.00 (ISBN 0-89984-288-7). Century Bookbindery.

Hackett, C. A., ed. New French Poetry: An Anthology. 219p. 1973. (Pub. by Basil Blackwell); pap. 12.50x (ISBN 0-631-14500-1, Pub. by Basil Blackwell). Biblio Dist.

Hackett, Cecil A. Anthology of Modern French Poetry. rev. ed. 1964. text ed. 8.95x (ISBN 0-685-14635-9). Macmillan.

Henning, George. Representative French Lyrics of the Nineteenth Century. 1977. Repr. of 1935 ed. 15.00 (ISBN 0-89984-199-6). Century Bookbindery.

Horn & Rimenhild. Horn et Rimenhild. LC 72-1055. (Bannatyne Club, Edinburgh. Publications: No. 80). Repr. of 1845 ed. 47.50 (ISBN 0-404-52804-X). AMS Pr.

Houston, John P. & Houston, Mona T., trs. French Symbolist Poetry: An Anthology. LC 79-3381. (Midland Bks.: No. 250). 288p. 1980. 25.00x (ISBN 0-253-16725-6); pap. 10.95x (ISBN 0-253-20250-7). Ind U Pr.

Hurtgen, Andre O., ed. Poemes Pour le Cours Avance Nineteen Eighty-One to Nineteen Eighty-Two. (Illus.). 154p. (Orig.). 1979. pap. text ed. 4.95x (ISBN 0-88334-117-4). Ind Sch Pr.

Jargy, Simon. La Poesie Populaire Traditionnelle Chanteau Proche-Orient Arabe, I: Les Textes. (Le Monde D'outre-Mer Passe et Present, Documents: No. 14). 1970. pap. 35.50x (ISBN 0-686-21239-8). Mouton.

Jeanroy, Alfred, ed. Joies Du Gai Savoir: Recueil De Poesies Couronnees Par Le Consistoire Dela Gaie Science, 1324-1484. Repr. of 1914 ed. 26.00 (ISBN 0-384-27090-5). Johnson Repr.

Kastner, L. E. A History of French Versification. LC 73-14807. 1903. Repr. lib. bdg. 25.00 (ISBN 0-8414-5474-4). Folcroft.

Lawler, James R., ed. Anthology of French Poetry. 3rd ed. 1969. pap. 5.95x (ISBN 0-19-500342-X). Oxford U Pr.

Lawton, Frederick. Anthology of French Poetry. 1977. Repr. of 1906 ed. 7.50 (ISBN 0-89984-211-9). Century Bookbindery.

Legge, J. F. Chanticleer: A Study of the French Muse. LC 68-26298. 1969. Repr. of 1935 ed. 15.00 (ISBN 0-8046-0266-2). Kennikat.

Lucas, St. John & Jones, P. M., eds. Oxford Book of French Verse, Thirteenth Century to Twentieth Century. 2nd ed. (Fr). 1957. 24.95 (ISBN 0-19-812109-1). Oxford U Pr.

Mallarme, Stephane. Mallarme et le symbolisme, auteurs et oeuvres. (Nouveaux Classiques Larousse). (Illus., Fr.). pap. 2.95 (ISBN 0-685-13978-6, 165). Larousse.

Martin, G. D., ed. & tr. Anthology of Contemporary French Poetry. (Edinburgh Bilingual Library: No. 5). 234p. 1971. 10.95x (ISBN 0-292-71006-2); pap. 5.50x (ISBN 0-292-71004-6). U of Tex Pr.

Palfrey, Thomas R. & Will, Samuel F., eds. Petite Anthologie: Poesies Francaises. (Orig., Fr.). 1961. pap. text ed. 3.95x (ISBN 0-89197-337-0). Irvington.

Parmee, Douglas. Fifteen French Poets, 1820-1950. 1974. pap. text ed. 8.95x (ISBN 0-582-35901-5). Longman.

Parton, James. A Book of French Poetry. 1977. Repr. of 1887 ed. 20.00 (ISBN 0-89984-085-X). Century Bookbindery.

--A Book of French Poetry: From A.D. Fifteen Fifty to the Present Time. 1979. Repr. of 1887 ed. lib. bdg. 30.00 (ISBN 0-8492-2183-8). R West.

Pocock, G. Corneille & Racine. LC 72-97886. 352p. 1973. 47.50 (ISBN 0-521-20197-7); pap. 12.50x (ISBN 0-521-09814-9). Cambridge U Pr.

Robertson, William. A Century of French Verse. Repr. of 1895 ed. 20.00 (ISBN 0-686-18760-1). Scholars Ref Lib.

--A Century of French Verse. 1977. Repr. of 1895 ed. 20.00 (ISBN 0-89984-103-1). Century Bookbindery.

Saintsbury, George. French Lyrics. 1977. Repr. of 1890 ed. 25.00 (ISBN 0-89984-106-6). Century Bookbindery.

Still, Gloria, ed. Serving Blood: New Poems by French Women. LC 79-67297. (Wampeter Firsts Ser.: No. 2). (Illus.). 1980. pap. 3.95 (ISBN 0-931694-06-X). Wampeter Pr.

Terry, Patricia & Garronsky, Serge. Modern French Poetry: A Bilingual Anthology. Terry, Patricia & Garronsky, Serge, trs. from Fr. 192p. 1975. 15.00x (ISBN 0-231-03957-3); pap. 7.00x (ISBN 0-231-03958-1). Columbia U Pr.

Thrley, Wilfred, tr. The French Muse: Fifty Examples with Biographical & Critical Notes. 1978. Repr. of 1947 ed. lib. bdg. 20.00 (ISBN 0-8495-5121-8). Arden Lib.

Weinberg, Bernard, ed. French Poetry of the Renaissance. LC 64-19796. (Arcturus Books Paperbacks). 260p. (Fr). 1964. pap. 6.95 (ISBN 0-8093-0135-0). S Ill U Pr.

Woledge, Brian, et al, eds. Penguin Book of French Verse. (Penguin Poets Ser.). 704p. 1975. pap. 5.95 (ISBN 0-14-042182-3). Penguin.

FRENCH POETRY-TO 1500
see also Rondeaus

Anglade, Joseph, ed. Leys D'amors, Manuscrit Inedit De L'academie Des Jeux Floraux, 4 Vols. Repr. of 1919 ed. 67.50 (ISBN 0-384-32499-1). Johnson Repr.

Carman, J. Neale, tr. From Camelot to Joyous Guard: The Old French La Mort le Roi Artu. LC 73-18242. xxii, 172p. 1974. 7.50x (ISBN 0-7006-0121-X). Regents Pr KS.

Chansonnier D'Arras, Reproduction En Phototypie. 1925. 28.00 (ISBN 0-384-08465-6); pap. 23.00 (ISBN 0-384-08475-3). Johnson Repr.

Chatelain, Henri L. Recherches sur le vers francais au quinzieme siecle: rimes, metres et strophes. LC 79-149950. (Research & Source Works Ser.: No. 725). 1971. Repr. of 1908 ed. lib. bdg. 26.50 (ISBN 0-8337-0550-4). B Franklin.

Currey, R. N., tr. Formal Spring. facsimile ed. LC 76-80372. (Granger Index Reprint Ser). 1950. 15.00 (ISBN 0-8369-6054-8). Arno.

Johnson, Phyllis & Cazelles, Brigitte. Le Vain Siecle Guerpir: A Literary Approach to Sainthood Through Old French Hagiography of the Twelfth Century. (Studies in the Romance Languages & Literatures). 1978. 19.50x (ISBN 0-8078-9205-X). U of NC Pr.

Parsons, Rosamond H. Anglo-Norman Books of Courtesy & Nurture. (English Literature Ser., No. 33). 1970. pap. 12.95 (ISBN 0-8383-0059-6). Haskell.

FRENCH POETRY-BIBLIOGRAPHY

Barre, Andre. Le Symbolisme: bibliographie de la poesie symboliste. (Bibliography & Reference Ser: No. 140). 1968. Repr. of 1911 ed. 23.50 (ISBN 0-8337-0169-X). B Franklin.

--Symbolisme: essai historique sur le mouvement symboliste en France de 1885 a 1900. 1967. Repr. of 1911 ed. 25.50 (ISBN 0-8337-3970-0). B Franklin.

Langfors, Arthur I. Incipit Des Poemes Francais Anterieurs Au Seizieme Siecle: Repertoire Bibliographique. LC 77-133547. (Fr). 1970. Repr. of 1917 ed. 32.50 (ISBN 0-8337-2004-X). B Franklin.

Linker, Robert W. A Bibliography of Old French Lyrics. LC 79-11948. (Romance Monographs: No. 31). 1979. 40.00x (ISBN 84-499-2809-5). Romance.

Martinon, Philippe. Strophes; Etudes Historiques et Critiques Sur les Formes De la Poesie Lyrique En France Depuis la Renaissance. 1969. Repr. of 1912 ed. 36.50 (ISBN 0-8337-2271-9). B Franklin.

Mendes, Catulle. Mouvement Poetique Francais De 1867 a 1900. LC 73-156389. (Bibliography & Reference Ser: No. 414). 1971. Repr. of 1903 ed. lib. bdg. 39.00 (ISBN 0-8337-2359-6). B Franklin.

FRENCH POETRY-DICTIONARIES

Peterson-Dyggve, Holger. Onomastique Des Trouveres. LC 72-82372. 255p. (Fr.). 1973. Repr. of 1934 ed. lib. bdg. 23.50 (ISBN 0-8337-4320-1). B Franklin.

FRENCH POETRY-HISTORY AND CRITICISM

Apollinaire, Guillaume. Alcools. Rees, Garnet, ed. (French Poets Ser.). 192p. 1975. text ed. 24.75x (ISBN 0-485-14708-4, Athlone Pr); pap. text ed. 11.75x (ISBN 0-485-12708-3, Athlone Pr). Humanities.

Bailey, John C. Claims of French Poetry: Nine Studies in the Greater French Poets. facs. ed. LC 67-30195. (Essay Index Reprint Ser). 1909. 18.00 (ISBN 0-8369-0168-1). Arno.

Balakian, Anna. Literary Origins of Surrealism: A New Mysticism in French Poetry. 1966. 11.50x (ISBN 0-8147-0024-1); pap. 6.00x (ISBN 0-8147-0025-X). NYU Pr.

Belloc, Hilaire. Avril. facsimile ed. (Essay Index Reprint Ser). 1904. 17.00 (ISBN 0-8369-1339-6). Arno.

Besant, Walter. Studies in Early French Poetry. LC 72-13206. (Essay Index Reprint Ser.). Repr. of 1868 ed. 18.00 (ISBN 0-8369-8147-2). Arno.

Bishop, Michael, ed. The Language of Poetry: Crisis & Solution, Studies in Modern Poetry of French Expression, 1945 to the Present. 268p. 1980. pap. text ed. 34.25x (ISBN 90-6203-681-3). Humanities.

Bithell, Jethro, tr. Contemporary French Poetry. 227p. 1980. Repr. lib. bdg. 20.00 (ISBN 0-89760-041-X). Telegraph Bks.

Brereton, Geoffrey. Introduction to French Poets. 2nd ed. 1979. pap. 11.95x (ISBN 0-416-76630-7). Methuen Inc.

Broome, P. & Chesters, G. The Appreciation of Modern French Poetry: 1850 to 1950. LC 75-40768. 176p. 1976. 29.50 (ISBN 0-521-20792-4); pap. 8.50 (ISBN 0-521-20930-7). Cambridge U Pr.

Cardinal, Roger, ed. Sensibility & Creation: Studies in Twentieth-Century French Poetry. LC 76-40876. 1977. text ed. 20.00x (ISBN 0-06-490957-3). B&N.

Carter, Marion E. Role of the Symbol in French Romantic Poetry. LC 77-94178. (Catholic University of America. Studies in Romance Languages & Literatures: No. 32). Repr. of 1946 ed. 14.50 (ISBN 0-404-50332-2). AMS Pr.

Cary, Henry F. The Early French Poets. LC 72-103219. 1970. Repr. of 1923 ed. 11.50 (ISBN 0-8046-0856-3). Kennikat.

Caws, Mary A., ed. About French Poetry from Dada to "Tel Quel". Text & Theory. LC 74-10962. 298p. 1974. text ed. 14.95x (ISBN 0-8143-1520-8). Wayne St U Pr.

Caws, Mary Ann. The Inner Theatre of Recent French Poetry: Cendrars, Tzara, Peret, Artaud, Bonnefoy. LC 72-166364. (Princeton Essays in Literature). 132p. 1972. 15.50 (ISBN 0-691-06212-9). Princeton U Pr.

Chiari, Joseph. Contemporary French Poetry. facs. ed. LC 68-20289. (Essay Index Reprint Ser). 1952. 15.00 (ISBN 0-8369-0301-3). Arno.

Chisholm, Alan R. Towards Herodiade: A Literary Genealogy. LC 77-10255. Repr. of 1934 ed. 22.50 (ISBN 0-404-16310-6). AMS Pr.

Clark, John E. Elegie: The Fortunes of a Classical Genre in Sixteenth Century France. (Studies in French Literature Ser.: No. 23). 268p. 1975. pap. text ed. 43.25x (ISBN 90-2793-132-1). Mouton.

Clements, Robert J. Critical Theory & Practice of the Pleiade. LC 68-16770. 1969. Repr. lib. bdg. 16.50x (ISBN 0-374-91691-8). Octagon.

Cohen, Helen L. Lyric Forms from France. 1973. Repr. of 1922 ed. lib. bdg. 35.00 (ISBN 0-8414-3045-4). Folcroft.

Cohn, Robert G. Mallarme's Un coup de des: An Exegesis. LC 77-10256. Repr. of 1949 ed. 27.50 (ISBN 0-404-16311-4). AMS Pr.

Coleman. Maurice Sceve: Poet of Love. LC 74-31794. 212p. 1975. 44.50 (ISBN 0-521-20745-2). Cambridge U Pr.

Coleman, Dorothy. The Gallo-Roman Muse. LC 79-71. 1979. 32.50 (ISBN 0-521-22254-0). Cambridge U Pr.

Collie, Michael. Jules Laforgue. (Athlone French Poets Ser). 160p. 1977. text ed. 18.75x (ISBN 0-485-14606-1, Athlone Pr); pap. text ed. 6.25x (ISBN 0-485-12206-5). Humanities.

Cornell, Kenneth. Post-Symbolist Period: French Poetic Currents, 1900-1920. 1970. Repr. of 1958 ed. 15.00 (ISBN 0-208-00822-5, Archon). Shoe String.

Dawson, John C. Toulouse in the Renaissance: The Floral Games, University & Student Life: Etienne Dolet. (Columbia University. Studies in Romance Philology & Literature: No. 33). Repr. of 1923 ed. 18.50 (ISBN 0-404-50633-X). AMS Pr.

De Mourgues, Odette. Metaphysical Baroque & Precieux Poetry. LC 73-1144. 1953. lib. bdg. 20.00 (ISBN 0-8414-1850-0). Folcroft.

Diderot, Denis. De la poesie dramatique. new ed. (Nouveaux Classiques Larousse). (Illus.). 1976. pap. 2.95 (ISBN 0-685-66282-9, 86). Larousse.

Donaldson-Evans, Lancelot K. Love's Fatal Glance: A Study of Eye Imagery in the Poets of the Ecole lyonnaise. LC 80-10415. (Romance Monographs: No. 39). 155p. 1980. 16.00 (ISBN 84-499-3694-2). Romance.

Dubos, Jean B. Critical Reflections on Poetry, Painting & Music, 3 vols. LC 78-3659. (Music & Theatre in France in the 17th & 18th Centuries). Repr. of 1748 ed. Set. 74.50 (ISBN 0-404-60170-7). AMS Pr.

Fowlie, Wallace. Mid-Century French Poets. (International Studies & Translations Ser.). 1980. 7.00 (ISBN 0-8057-5822-4). Twayne.

Freeman, Michelle A. The Poetics of Translatio Studii & Conjointure: Chretien de Troyes's Cliges. LC 78-54262. (Monographs: No. 12). 201p. (Orig.). 1979. pap. 11.50x (ISBN 0-917058-11-9). French Forum.

Frey, John A. Motif Symbolism in the Disciples of Mallarme. LC 73-94193. (Catholic University of America Studies in Romance Languages & Literatures Ser: No. 55). Repr. of 1957 ed. 17.50 (ISBN 0-404-50355-1). AMS Pr.

Gautier, Theophile. Les Grotesques. facsimile ed. 1969. 65.00 (ISBN 0-686-55903-7). French & Eur.

Gibson, R., compiled by. Modern French Poets on Poetry. LC 78-73241. 1979. 32.50 (ISBN 0-521-05078-2). Cambridge U Pr.

Grant, Elliott M. French Poetry & Modern Industry, 1830-1870. 1927. pap. 13.00 (ISBN 0-527-01104-5). Kraus Repr.

Greene, Robert W. Six French Poets of Our Time: A Critical & Historical Study. LC 78-70927. (Princeton Essays in Literature Ser.). 1979. 12.50 (ISBN 0-691-06390-7). Princeton U Pr.

Greimas, A. Essais de semiotique poetique: Avec des etudes sur Apollinaire, Bataille, Hugo, Jarry, Mallarme, Michaux, Nerval, Rimbaud, Roubaud. (Collection L). 240p. (Orig., Fr.). 1972. pap. 13.95 (ISBN 2-03-036002-3, 2666). Larousse.

Grubbs, H. A. & Kneller, J. W. Introduction a la Poesie Francaise. 275p. 1962. 15.95 (ISBN 0-471-00217-8). Wiley.

Hagiwara, M. P. French Epic Poetry in the Sixteenth Century. (De Proprietatibus Litterarum, Ser.Major: No. 20). 1972. text ed. 22.25x (ISBN 0-686-22532-5). Mouton.

Heroet, et al. La Borderie et Autres Divins Poetes Opuscules D'amour (Lyon, 1547) Introduction, Description Du Texte Presente et Bibliographie Par M.A. Screech. (Classiques De la Renaisance En France French Renaissance Classics: No. 9). 1970. 36.25x (ISBN 90-2796-439-4). Mouton.

Hester, Ralph M. A Protestant Baroque Poet: Pierre Poupo. (Studies in French Literature: No. 10). 1970. 36.25x (ISBN 90-2790-537-1). Mouton.

Heylbut, Rose. English Opinions of French Poetry, Sixteen Sixty to Seventeen Fifty. LC 23-11065. (Columbia University. Studies in Romance Philology & Literature: No. 36). Repr. of 1923 ed. 17.50 (ISBN 0-404-50636-4). AMS Pr.

Holyoake, S. J. An Introduction to French Sixteenth Century Poetic Theory. 224p. 1972. 18.00x (ISBN 0-7190-0475-6, Pub. by Manchester U Pr England). State Mutual Bk.

Houston, John P. Demonic Imagination: Style & Theme in French Romantic Poetry. LC 69-15051. 15.00x (ISBN 0-8071-0306-3). La State U Pr.

--French Symbolism & the Modernist Movement. LC 79-23479. 320p. 1980. 20.00x (ISBN 0-8071-0593-7). La State U Pr.

Hunt, Herbert J. The Epic in Nineteenth Century France: A Study in Heroic & Humanitarian Poetry from Les Martyrs to Les Siecles Mort. 1976. lib. bdg. 69.95 (ISBN 0-8490-1779-3). Gordon Pr.

Hyder, Clyde K., ed. Swinburne As Critic. (The Routledge Critics Ser.). 1972. 25.00x (ISBN 0-7100-7343-7). Routledge & Kegan.

Ince, W. N. Heredia. (French Poets Ser.). 1979. text ed. 30.00x (ISBN 0-485-14607-X, Athlone Pr); pap. text ed. 11.25x (ISBN 0-485-12207-3). Humanities.

Jackson, Elizabeth R. Worlds Apart: Structural Parallels in Poetry of Paul Valery, Saint-John Perse, Benjamin Peret & Rene Char. (De Proprietatibus Litterarum Series Practica: No. 106). 256p. 1976. pap. text ed. 46.25x (ISBN 90-2793-394-4). Mouton.

Kahn, Gustave. Symbolistes et decadents. LC 77-10272. Repr. of 1902 ed. 37.50 (ISBN 0-404-16324-6). AMS Pr.

Langfors, Arthur I. Incipit Des Poemes Francais Anterieurs Au Seizieme Siecle: Repertoire Bibliographique. LC 77-133547. (Fr). 1970. Repr. of 1917 ed. 32.50 (ISBN 0-8337-2004-X). B Franklin.

Lawler, J. R. Language of French Symbolism. 1969. 14.50 (ISBN 0-691-06167-X). Princeton U Pr.

Legge, J. E. Chanticleer: A Study of the French Muse. 59.95 (ISBN 0-87968-835-1). Gordon Pr.

Legge, J. F. Chanticleer: A Study of the French Muse. LC 68-26298. 1969. Repr. of 1935 ed. 15.00 (ISBN 0-8046-0266-2). Kennikat.

Legouis, Emile. Defense De la Poesie Francaise a L'usage Des Lecturs Anglais. 1973. Repr. of 1912 ed. 20.00 (ISBN 0-8274-0159-0). R West.

Lenient, Charles F. Poesie Patriotique En France Au Moyen Age. LC 75-168698. (Essays in Literature & Criticism Ser.: No. 151). 1968. Repr. of 1891 ed. 29.00 (ISBN 0-8337-2066-X). B Franklin.

Le Sage, Laurent. Rhumb Line of Symbolism: French Poets from Sainte-Beuve to Valery, Presentation & Selected Texts. LC 77-8020. 1978. text ed. 15.95x (ISBN 0-271-00513-0). Pa St U Pr.

Lewisohn, Ludwig. Poets of Modern France. LC 78-103231. 1970. Repr. of 1918 ed. 12.00 (ISBN 0-8046-0868-7). Kennikat.

Lloyd, Rosemary H. Baudelaire et Hoffmann. LC 78-58796. (Fr.). 1979. 38.00 (ISBN 0-521-22459-4). Cambridge U Pr.

Lowell, Amy. Six French Poets: Studies in Contemporary Literature. facs. ed. LC 67-28737. (Essay Index Reprint Ser). 1915. 19.50 (ISBN 0-8369-0626-8). Arno.

MacCombie, John. The Prince & the Genie: A Study of Rimbaud's Influence on Claudel. LC 70-164440. 1972. 10.00x (ISBN 0-87023-089-1). U of Mass Pr.

Marmontel, Jean F. Poetique Francoise, 2 vols. (Classics in Art & Literary Criticism Ser). Repr. of 1763 ed. 54.00 (ISBN 0-384-35410-6). Johnson Repr.

Marni, Archimede. Allegory in French Heroic Poem of the 17th Century. LC 72-122994. (Studies in French Literature, No. 45). 1970. Repr. of 1936 ed. lib. bdg. 49.95 (ISBN 0-8383-1127-X). Haskell.

Matthews, J. H. Surrealist Poetry in France. LC 71-96815. 1969. 12.95x (ISBN 0-8156-2144-2). Syracuse U Pr.

Mauriac, Francois. La Vie et la Mort d'un Poete. pap. 7.50 (ISBN 0-685-34308-1). French & Eur.

Maynard, Theodore. The Connection Between the Ballade Chaucer's Modification of It, Rime Royal, & the Spenserian Stanza. LC 73-7718. 1934. Repr. lib. bdg. 20.00 (ISBN 0-8414-5943-6). Folcroft.

Minta, Stephen. Love Poetry in 16th Century France: A Study in Themes & Traditions. LC 77-16716. 1977. text ed. 21.25x (ISBN 0-391-00828-5). Humanities.

Montagu, Elizabeth. Essay on the Writings & Genius of Shakespeare Compared with the Greek & French Dramatic Poets: 1785-1839. 292p. 1970. Repr. of 1839 ed. 25.00x (ISBN 0-7146-2515-9, F Cass Co). Biblio Dist.

Mulhauser, Ruth E. Maurice Sceve. LC 76-28722. (World Authors Ser: France: No. 424). 1977. lib. bdg. 12.50 (ISBN 0-8057-6264-7). Twayne.

Nalbantian, Suzanne. The Symbol of the Soul from Holderlin to Yeats: A Study in Metonymy. LC 76-25550. 151p. 1976. 17.50x (ISBN 0-231-04148-9). Columbia U Pr.

Noske, Frits R. French Song from Berlioz to DuParc: The Origins & Development of the Melodie. Benton, Rita, tr. LC 68-11171. (Illus.). 1970. pap. 6.95 (ISBN 0-486-22104-0). Dover.

Patterson, Warner F. Three Centuries of French Poetic Theory: A Critical History of the Chief Arts of Poetry in France, 1328-1630, Pts. 1 & 2 In 3 Vols. LC 65-17917. 1966. Repr. of 1935 ed. Set. 32.50 (ISBN 0-8462-0668-4). Russell.

Petersen-Dyggve, Holger N. Personnages Historiques Figurant Dans la Poesie Lyrique Francaise Des XII et XIIIe Siecles. LC 80-2166. 1981. 67.50 (ISBN 0-404-19031-6). AMS Pr.

Pieri, Marius. Petrarquisme Au Seizieme Siecle: Petrarque et Ronsard, Ou l'Influence De Petrarque Sur la Pleiade Francaise. (Research & Source Works Ser: No. 179). 1967. Repr. of 1896 ed. 22.50 (ISBN 0-8337-2763-X). B Franklin.

Piore, Nancy K. Lightning: The Poetry of Rene Char. LC 80-22001. (Illus.). 150p. 1981. 17.95x (ISBN 0-930350-08-1). NE U Pr.

Ponge, Francis. Le Parti Pris Des Choses. Higgins, Ian, ed. (Athlone French Poets Ser.). 1979. text ed. 27.50x (ISBN 0-485-14714-9, Athlone Pr); pap. text ed. 13.00x (ISBN 0-485-12212-X, Athlone Pr). Humanities.

Porter, Laurence M. The Renaissance of the Lyric in French Romanticism: Elegy, "Poeme," & Ode. LC 78-52832. (Monographs: No. 10). 145p. (Orig.). 1978. pap. 9.50x (ISBN 0-917058-09-7). French Forum.

Quainton, Malcolm. Ronsard's Ordered Chaos: Visions of Flux & Stability in the Poetry of Pierre de Ronsard. 252p. 1980. 25.00x (ISBN 0-389-20023-9). B&N.

Quennell, Peter. Baudelaire & the Symbolists. LC 76-111315. (Essay & General Literature Index Reprint Ser). 1970. Repr. of 1929 ed. 11.50 (ISBN 0-8046-0935-7). Kennikat.

Raymond, Marcel. Influence De Ronsard Sur La Poesie Francaise, 1550-1585, 2 vols. LC 76-168702. (Research & Source Works Ser.: No. 841). 1927. 44.50 (ISBN 0-8337-2907-1). B Franklin.

Rice, Richard A. Rousseau & the Poetry of Nature in Eighteenth Century France. LC 74-9920. 1925. 10.00 (ISBN 0-8414-7313-7). Folcroft.

Robertson, William J. A Century of French Verse: Brief Biographical & Critical Notices of Thirty-Three French Poets of the Nineteenth Century. LC 77-11481. (Symbolists Ser.). 392p. Repr. of 1895 ed. 32.50 (ISBN 0-404-16342-4). AMS Pr.

Roinard, P. M. & Michelet, V. E. La Poesie symboliste. LC 77-11482. Repr. of 1909 ed. 40.00 (ISBN 0-404-16343-2). AMS Pr.

Rubin, David L. The Knot of Artifice: A Poetic of the French Lyric in the Early Seventeenth Century. LC 80-26260. 119p. 1981. 11.00 (ISBN 0-8142-0322-1). Ohio St U Pr.

Rudmose-Brown, T. B. French Literary Studies. LC 68-8218. 1969. Repr. of 1917 ed. 10.00 (ISBN 0-8046-0396-0). Kennikat.

Saltus, Edgar E. Parnassians Personally Encountered. 1st ed. 1923. boxed, limited to 200 copies 17.50x (ISBN 0-686-17411-9). R S Barnes.

Seaman, David W. Concrete Poetry in France. Foster, Stephen, ed. (Studies in Fine Arts: the Avant-Garde: No. 18). 1981. price not set (ISBN 0-8357-1253-2, Pub. by UMI Res Pr). Univ Microfilms.

Shipley, Joseph T., ed. Modern French Poetry: An Anthology. LC 72-8283. (Granger Index Reprint Ser). 1972. Repr. of 1926 ed. 22.00 (ISBN 0-8369-6394-6). Arno.

Stavan, Henry A. La Lyrisme Dana la Poesie Francaise De a 1760 a 1820s: Analyae et Textes De Quelques Auteurs. (De Probristatibus Litterarua Practica Ser.: No. 94). 1976. pap. text ed. 38.75x (ISBN 90-2793-265-4). Mouton.

Stephan, Philip. Paul Verlaine & the Decadence Eighteen Eighty-Two to Ninety. 216p. 1974. 17.50x (ISBN 0-87471-563-6). Rowman.

Thrley, Wilfred, tr. The French Muse: Fifty Examples with Biographical & Critical Notes. 1978. Repr. of 1947 ed. lib. bdg. 20.00 (ISBN 0-8495-5121-8). Arden Lib.

Trout, John M. The Voyage of Prudence: The World View of Alan of Lille. LC 79-66473. 1979. pap. text ed. 9.00 (ISBN 0-8191-0840-5). U Pr of Amer.

Valery, Paul. Charmes ou Poemes. Whiting, Charles G., ed. (French Poets Ser.). 146p. 1973. text ed. 16.25x (ISBN 0-485-14701-7, Athlone Pr); pap. text ed. 8.75x (ISBN 0-485-12701-6, Athlone Pr). Humanities.

Van Der Vat, Daniel G. Fabulous Opera. LC 67-30820. (Studies in Comparative Literature, No. 35). 1969. Repr. of 1936 ed. lib. bdg. 48.95 (ISBN 0-8383-0724-8). Haskell.

Verlaine, Paul. Sagesse. Chadwick, Charles, ed. (Athlone French Poets Ser.). 1973. (Athlone Pr); pap. text ed. 4.50x (ISBN 0-485-12704-0, Athlone Pr). Humanities.

Verlaine, Paul M. Les Poetes maudits. LC 77-11495. (Symbolists Ser.). (Illus., Fr.). Repr. of 1888 ed. 16.50 (ISBN 0-404-16354-8). AMS Pr.

Wilson, D. B., ed. French Renaissance Scientific Poetry. (Renaissance Library). 1974. text ed. 19.50x (ISBN 0-485-13808-5, Athlone Pr). Humanities.

FRENCH POETRY–HISTORY AND CRITICISM–TO 1500

Cooke, Thomas D. The Old French & Chaucerian Fabliaux: A Study of Their Comic Climax. LC 77-77861. 1978. 15.00x (ISBN 0-8262-0225-X). U of Mo Pr.

Cooke, Thomas D. & Honeycutt, Benjamin L., eds. The Humor of the Fabliaux: A Collection of Critical Essays. LC 74-82563. 208p. 1974. 15.00x (ISBN 0-8262-0168-7). U of Mo Pr.

Denomme, Robert T. The French Parnassian Poets. LC 72-185260. (Crosscurrents-Modern Critiques Ser.). 160p. 1972. 6.95 (ISBN 0-8093-0575-5). S Ill U Pr.

Faral, Edmond. Recherches Sur les Sources Latines Des Contes et Romans Courtois Du Moyen Age. LC 72-178580. Repr. of 1913 ed. 27.50 (ISBN 0-404-56600-6). AMS Pr.

Parsons, Rosamond H. Anglo-Norman Books of Courtesy & Nurture. (English Literature Ser., No. 33). 1970. pap. 12.95 (ISBN 0-8383-0059-6). Haskell.

Quennell, Peter. Baudelaire & the Symbolists. facsimile ed. LC 72-142689. (Essay Index Reprint Ser). Repr. of 1954 ed. 16.00 (ISBN 0-8369-2423-1). Arno.

FRENCH POETRY–TRANSLATIONS INTO ENGLISH

Aspinwall, Dorothy B. French Poems in English Verse, Eighteen Fifty to Nineteen Seventy. LC 73-1782. 113p. 1973. lib. bdg. 10.00 (ISBN 0-8108-0599-5). Scarecrow.

Beckett, Samuel. Collected Poems in English & French. LC 77-77855. 1977. 10.00 (ISBN 0-394-42200-7, GP796). Grove.

Betham-Edwards, M. French Fireside Poetry: With Metrical Translations. Miall, Bernard, ed. 1979. Repr. of 1921 ed. lib. bdg. 20.00 (ISBN 0-8492-3741-6). R West.

Brickell, Alfred. Few, but Roses: Poems from the French. 1977. Repr. of 1924 ed. 15.00 (ISBN 0-89984-242-9). Century Bookbindery.

Char, Rene. Leaves of Hypnos. Corman, Cid, tr. 1973. pap. 5.95 (ISBN 0-685-78993-4, Pub. by Mushinsha Bks). SBD.

Chedid, Andree. Contemporary French Women Poets: A Bilingual Critical Anthology. Hermey, Carl W., ed. LC 76-3065. (Perivale Translation Series No. 4). 207p. 1977. pap. 6.95 (ISBN 0-912288-08-6). Perivale Pr.

Currey, R. N., tr. Formal Spring. facsimile ed. LC 76-80372. (Granger Index Reprint Ser). 1950. 15.00 (ISBN 0-8369-6054-8). Arno.

Harrison, Robert. Gallic Salt: Eighteen Fabliaux Translated from the Old French. LC 72-97748. 1974. 27.50x (ISBN 0-520-02418-4). U of Cal Pr.

Hellman, Robert & O'Gorman, Richard, trs. from Fr. Fabliaux: Ribald Tales from the Old French. LC 75-3993. (Illus.). 196p. 1976. Repr. of 1965 ed. lib. bdg. 14.75x (ISBN 0-8371-7414-7, HEFA). Greenwood.

Legge, J. F. Chanticleer: A Study of the French Muse. LC 68-26298. 1969. Repr. of 1935 ed. 15.00 (ISBN 0-8046-0266-2). Kennikat.

Lewisohn, Ludwig. Poets of Modern France. LC 78-103231. 1970. Repr. of 1918 ed. 12.00 (ISBN 0-8046-0868-7). Kennikat.

MacIntyre, C. F., tr. French Symbolist Poetry. bilingual ed. 1958. pap. 2.95 (ISBN 0-520-00784-0, CAL21). U of Cal Pr.

Mackworth, Cecily, ed. Mirror for French Poetry, 1840-1940. facs. ed. LC 71-76946. (Granger Index Reprint Ser). 1947. 15.00 (ISBN 0-8369-6027-0). Arno.

Martin, Dorothy, tr. Sextette: Translations from the French Symbolists. LC 80-10539. (Symbolists Ser.). Repr. of 1928 ed. 18.50 (ISBN 0-404-16331-9). AMS Pr.

Martin, G. D., ed. & tr. Anthology of Contemporary French Poetry. (Edinburgh Bilingual Library: No. 5). 234p. 1971. 10.95x (ISBN 0-292-71006-2); pap. 5.50x (ISBN 0-292-71004-6). U of Tex Pr.

Moro, Cesar. Love till Death. Lefevre, Frances, tr. 140p. 5.00 (ISBN 0-931106-05-2). TVRT.

Mowrer, Paul S. Choice of French Poems. 1969. 4.00 (ISBN 0-8233-0134-6). Golden Quill.

Shapiro, Norman, ed. Negritude: Black Poetry from Africa & the Caribbean. 1970. 7.50 (ISBN 0-8079-0149-0); pap. 4.95 (ISBN 0-8079-0164-4). October.

Shapiro, Norman R., tr. The Comedy of Eros: Medieval French Guides to the Art of Love. LC 78-143327. (Illus.). 1971. 10.00 (ISBN 0-252-00146-X). U of Ill Pr.

Taylor, Simon W. & Lucie-Smith, Edward, eds. French Poetry Today: A Bilingual Anthology. LC 71-163335. 1972. 10.00x (ISBN 0-8052-3426-8). Schocken.

Terry, Patricia & Garronsky, Serge. Modern French Poetry: A Bilingual Anthology. Terry, Patricia & Garronsky, Serge, trs. from Fr. 192p. 1975. 15.00x (ISBN 0-231-03957-3); pap. 7.00x (ISBN 0-231-03958-1). Columbia U Pr.

Theobald, John. The Lost Wine: Seven Centuries of French into English Lyrical Poetry. (Illus.). 600p. 1981. 25.00 (ISBN 0-914676-36-9, Star & Elephants Bks). Star & Elephant.

FRENCH POETRY–TRANSLATIONS INTO SPANISH

Mallarme, Stephane. Igitur. Hirschman, Jack, tr. from Fr. LC 74-22857. 1974. pap. 6.00 (ISBN 0-915148-04-8). Press Pegacycle.

FRENCH PRIMERS

see French Language–Text-Books for Children

FRENCH PROPAGANDA

see Propaganda, French

FRENCH PROSE LITERATURE

Cohen, Helen L. Lyric Forms from France. 1973. Repr. of 1922 ed. lib. bdg. 35.00 (ISBN 0-8414-3045-4). Folcroft.

Galpin, A. M. & Milligan, E. E. French Prose: An Intermediate Reader. 1965. text ed. 8.50 (ISBN 0-02-340250-4). Macmillan.

Houston, John P. The Traditions of French Prose Style: A Rhetorical Study. LC 80-27871. 352p. 1981. 30.00x (ISBN 0-8071-0858-8). La State U Pr.

FRENCH PROTESTANTS

see Huguenots; Protestants in France

FRENCH REVOLUTION

see France–History–Revolution, 1789-1799

FRENCH SALONS

see Salons

FRENCH SATIRE

see Satire, French

FRENCH SCIENCE

see Science, French

FRENCH SCULPTURE

see Sculpture–France

FRENCH SHORTHAND

see Shorthand, French

FRENCH SONGS

see Songs, French

FRENCH SPOLIATION CLAIMS

McLemore, Richard A. Franco-American Diplomatic Relations, 1816-1836. LC 76-159074. 1971. Repr. of 1941 ed. 12.50 (ISBN 0-8046-1669-8). Kennikat.

FRENCH TALES

see Tales, French

FRENCH WIT AND HUMOR

Besant, Walter. The French Humorists: From the Twelfth to the Ninteenth Century. Date not set. Repr. of 1873 ed. lib. bdg. 40.00 (ISBN 0-8495-0378-7). Arden Lib.

--French Humorists: From the Twelfth to the Nineteenth Century. facsimile ed. LC 74-38774. (Essay Index Reprint Ser). Repr. of 1874 ed. 23.00 (ISBN 0-8369-2635-8). Arno.

Flaubert, Gustave. Dictionary of Accepted Ideas. LC 68-15880. 1954. pap. 3.95 (ISBN 0-8112-0054-X, NHDP230). New Directions.

Lee, Elizabeth, ed. The Humour of France. 1978. Repr. of 1893 ed. lib. bdg. 30.00 (ISBN 0-8492-1583-8). R West.

Mankin, Paul & Szogyi, Alex. Anthologie d'humour Francais. 1970. pap. 6.95x (ISBN 0-673-05111-0). Scott F.

FRENCH WIT AND HUMOR, PICTORAL
see also Caricatures and Cartoons–France

Rothe, Hans, ed. Daumier on War. LC 77-9349. (Paperback Ser.). (Illus.). 1977. pap. 6.95 (ISBN 0-306-80079-9). Da Capo.

Sine. French Cat. (Illus.). 1958. 1.50 (ISBN 0-671-27290-X, Fireside). S&S.

FRENEAU, PHILIP MORIN, 1752-1832

Adkins, Nelson F. Philip Freneau & the Cosmic Enigma. LC 75-139892. 1971. Repr. of 1949 ed. 8.00 (ISBN 0-8462-1528-4). Russell.

Austin, Mary S. Philip Freneau, the Poet of the Revolution. Vreeland, Helen K., ed. LC 67-23885. 1968. Repr. of 1901 ed. 19.00 (ISBN 0-8103-3040-7). Gale.

Axelrad, Jacob. Philip Freneau: Champion of Democracy. 492p. 1966. 18.50x (ISBN 0-292-73605-3). U of Tex Pr.

Bowden, Mary W. Philip Freneau. (U. S. Authors Ser.: No. 260). 1976. lib. bdg. 9.95 (ISBN 0-8057-7161-1). Twayne.

Forman, Samuel E. Political Activities of Philip Freneau. LC 77-125693. (American Journalists Ser). 1970. Repr. of 1902 ed. 10.00 (ISBN 0-405-01670-0). Arno.

--The Political Activities of Phillip Freneau. LC 78-63891. (Johns Hopkins University. Studies in the Social Sciences. Twentieth Ser. 1902: 9-10). Repr. of 1902 ed. 11.50 (ISBN 0-404-61145-1). AMS Pr.

Leary, Lewis. That Rascal Freneau. 1964. lib. bdg. 25.00x (ISBN 0-374-94845-3). Octagon.

Marsh, Philip M. Freneau's Published Prose: A Bibliography. (Author Bibliographies Ser.: No. 5). 1970. 10.00 (ISBN 0-8108-0289-9). Scarecrow.

Paltsits, Victor-H. Bibliography of the Separate & Collected Works of Philip Freneau. LC 72-191120. 1903. lib. bdg. 11.45 (ISBN 0-8414-9241-7). Folcroft.

--Bibliography of the Separate & Works of Philip Preneau Seventeen Fifty-Two to Eighteen Thirty-Two. 1967. Repr. of 1903 ed. 19.00 (ISBN 0-8337-2664-1). B Franklin.

Vitzthum, Richard C. Land & Sea: The Lyric Poetry of Philip Freneau. LC 77-93379. 1978. 12.50x (ISBN 0-8166-0860-1). U of Minn Pr.

FREQUENCIES OF OSCILLATING SYSTEMS
see also Doppler Effect; Radio Frequency

Frerking, Marvin E. Crystal Oscillator Design & Temperature Compensation. 1978. text ed. 18.95x (ISBN 0-442-22459-1). Van Nos Reinhold.

Kartaschoff, P. Frequency & Time. (Monographs in Physical Measurement Ser.). 1978. 41.50 (ISBN 0-12-400150-5). Acad Pr.

MacFarlane, A. G., ed. Frequency: Response Methods in Control Systems. LC 79-90572. 1979. 43.95 (ISBN 0-87942-125-8). Inst Electrical.

Ord, J. K. Families of Frequency Distributions. 1972. pap. 16.25 (ISBN 0-02-849910-7). Hafner.

Penfield, Paul, Jr. Frequency-Power Formulas. (Press Research Monographs: No. 8). 1960. 15.00x (ISBN 0-262-16005-6). MIT Pr.

Skudrzyk, Eugen. Simple & Complex Vibratory Systems. LC 66-18222. (Illus.). 1968. 24.50x (ISBN 0-271-73127-3). Pa St U Pr.

FREQUENCY ANALYSIS (DYNAMICS)
see Frequencies of Oscillating Systems

FREQUENCY CHANGERS
see also Frequency Multipliers

Heller, Samuel. Frequency Changers: Rotating Type-Designing, Reconnecting & Testing with Design of Induction Regulators. LC 68-57467. (Illus., Orig.). 1968. 15.00 (ISBN 0-911740-05-8). Datarule.

Manassewitsch, Vadim. Frequency Synthesizers: Theory & Design. 2nd ed. LC 80-13345. 544p. 1980. 38.00 (ISBN 0-471-07917-0, Pub. by Wiley Interscience). Wiley.

FREQUENCY CONVERTERS
see Frequency Changers

FREQUENCY CURVES

Elderton, W. P. & Johnson, N. L. Systems of Frequency Curves. LC 69-10571. Orig. Title: Frequency Curves & Correlation. (Illus.). 1969. 32.95 (ISBN 0-521-07369-3). Cambridge U Pr.

Haberman, Shelby J. The Analysis of Frequency Data. LC 74-7558. (Statistical Research Monographs). (Midway Reprints). 1974. pap. text ed. 15.00x (ISBN 0-226-31185-6). U of Chicago Pr.

FREQUENCY DISTRIBUTION
see Distribution (Probability Theory)

FREQUENCY MODULATION, RADIO
see Radio Frequency Modulation

FREQUENCY MODULATION BROADCASTING
see FM Broadcasting

FREQUENCY MULTIPLIERS

Gyugyi, L. & Pelly, B. R. Static Power Frequency Changers: Theory, Performance & Application. LC 76-6088. 512p. 1976. 45.50x (ISBN 0-471-67800-7, Pub. by Wiley-Interscience). Wiley.

FREQUENCY OF OSCILLATION
see Frequencies of Oscillating Systems

FRERE, JOHN HOOKHAM, 1769-1846

Eichler, Albert. John Hookham Frere, Sein Leben und Sein Werke. 1905. pap. 21.00 (ISBN 0-384-14035-1). Johnson Repr.

FRESCO PAINTING
see Mural Painting and Decoration

FRESH WATER
see Drinking Water; Saline Waters–Demineralization

FRESH-WATER BIOLOGY
see also Aquarium Plants; Aquariums; Aquatic Plants; Fresh-Water Fauna; Fresh-Water Flora; Limnology

Bardach, John E., et al. Aquaculture: The Farming & Husbandry of Freshwater & Marine Organisms. LC 72-2516. 976p. 1972. pap. 26.00 (ISBN 0-471-04826-7, Pub. by Wiley-Interscience). Wiley.

Barica, J. & Mur, L., eds. Hypertrophic Ecosystems. (Developments in Hydrobiology Ser.: No. 2). 330p. 1981. PLB 87.00 (ISBN 90-6193-752-3, Pub. by Junk Pubs. Netherlands). Kluwer Boston.

Benson, Carol E. & Rushforth, Samuel R. The Algal Flora of Huntington Canyon Utah, U. S. A. (Bibliotheca Phycologia: Band 18). (Illus.). 1976. pap. 32.50x (ISBN 3-7682-0954-7, Pub. by J. Cramer). Intl Schol Bk Serv.

Cadbury, B. Bartram. Fresh & Salt Water. LC 60-6114. (Community of Living Things Ser). (Illus.). (gr. 4-8). 1967. PLB 7.45 (ISBN 0-87191-017-9). Creative Ed.

Cairns, John, Jr., ed. The Structure & Function of Fresh-Water Microbial Communities. 1971. 5.00x (ISBN 0-8139-0541-9). U Pr of Va.

Cash, J. & Hopkinson, J. British Freshwater Rhizopoda & Heliozoa, 5 Vols. 1905-21. Set. 77.00 (ISBN 0-384-07835-4). Johnson Repr.

Clegg, John. Your Book of Freshwater Life. (Illus.). (gr. 7 up). 1968. 5.95 (ISBN 0-571-08399-4). Transatlantic.

Division Of Biology And Agriculture. Eutrophication: Causes, Consequences, Correctives. LC 68-62704. 1969. text ed. 14.75 (ISBN 0-309-01700-9). Natl Acad Pr.

Edmondson, W. T., et al. Freshwater Biology. 2nd ed. LC 59-6781. (Illus.). 1959. 78.50 (ISBN 0-471-23298-X). Wiley.

Fassett, Norman C. Manual of Aquatic Plants. rev. ed. 416p. 1957. 15.00x (ISBN 0-299-01450-9). U of Wis Pr.

Freshwater Biological Association, Cumbria England. Catalogue of the Library of the Freshwater Biological Association. 1979. lib. bdg. 630.00 (ISBN 0-8161-0289-9). G K Hall.

Johannsen, Oskar A. Aquatic Diptera. LC 78-7782. (Illus.). 370p. 1969. Repr. of 1937 ed. 17.50 (ISBN 0-911836-01-2). Entomological Repr.

Jones, Gwynfryn. A Guide to Methods for Estimating Microbial Numbers & Biomass in Fresh Water. 1979. 25.00x (ISBN 0-900386-37-1, Pub. by Freshwater Bio). State Mutual Bk.

Knight, Maxwell. British Amphibians, Reptiles & Pond Dwellers. 1978. pap. 9.95 (ISBN 0-86025-820-3). State Mutual Bk.

Kofoid, Charles A. The Plankton of the Illinois River, 1894-1899: Quantitative Investigations & General Results, Pt.1. Egerton, Frank N., 3rd, ed. LC 77-74235. (History of Ecology Ser.). (Illus.). 1978. Repr. of 1903 ed. lib. bdg. 35.00x (ISBN 0-405-10404-9). Arno.

Krogh, August. Osmotic Regulation in Aquatic Animals. 7.50 (ISBN 0-8446-2408-X). Peter Smith.

Macam, T. T. & Worthington, E. B. Life in Lakes & Rivers. 1972. pap. 2.25 (ISBN 0-531-06040-3, Fontana Pap). Watts.

Maitland, Peter S. Biology of Fresh Waters. (Tertiary Level Biology Ser.). 244p. 1980. pap. text ed. 27.95x (ISBN 0-470-26986-3). Halsted Pr.

Mellanby, Helen. Animal Life in Fresh Water. 6th ed. LC 75-17181. 308p. 1963. pap. text ed. 10.95x (ISBN 0-412-21360-5, Pub. by Chapman & Hall England). Methuen Inc.

Morgan, Ann. Field Book of Ponds & Streams. (Putnam's Nature Field Bks.). (Illus.). (gr. 7 up). 1930. 6.95 (ISBN 0-399-10291-4). Putnam.

Muenscher, W. C. Aquatic Plants of the United States. (HANH Ser.). (Illus.). 384p. 1944. 25.00x (ISBN 0-8014-0306-5). Comstock.

Muller, Paul, ed. Verhandlungen der Gesellschaft Fur Okologie, Gottingen 1976. 1977. pap. 60.50 (ISBN 90-6193-568-7, Pub. by Junk Pubs Netherlands). Kluwer Boston.

Needham, James G. & Lloyd, J. T. The Life of Inland Waters: An Elementary Textbook of Fresh-Water Biology for Students. 2nd ed. (Illus.). 438p. 1930. photocopy ed. spiral 19.75 (ISBN 0-398-04378-7). C C Thomas.

Needham, James G. & Needham, Paul R. A Guide to the Study of Fresh-Water Biology: With Special Reference to Aquatic Insects & Other Invertebrate Animals. (Illus.). 88p. 1930. photocopy ed. spiral 19.75 (ISBN 0-398-04377-9). C C Thomas.

--Guide to the Study of Freshwater Biology. 5th ed. LC 62-20742. (Illus.). 1962. pap. 5.95x (ISBN 0-8162-6310-8). Holden-Day.

Prescott, G. W. How to Know the Freshwater Algae. 3rd ed. (Pictured Key Nature Ser.). 300p. 1978. write for info. wire coil (ISBN 0-697-04754-7); text ed. write for info (ISBN 0-697-04755-5). Wm C Brown.

Russian-English Glossary of Hydrobiology. 113p. 1958. 35.00 (ISBN 0-306-10599-3, Consultants). Plenum Pub.

Sculthorpe, C. Duncan. Biology of Aquatic Vascular Plants. (Illus.). 1967. 39.95 (ISBN 0-312-07945-1). St Martin.

Stroud, Richard H. & Clepper, Henry, eds. Black Bass Biology & Management. 1975. 25.00 (ISBN 0-686-21850-7); pap. 20.00 (ISBN 0-686-21851-5). Sport Fishing.

Time Life Books Editors. Beavers & Other Pond Dwellers. (Wild, Wild World of Animals). (Illus.). 1978. 10.95 (ISBN 0-913948-16-0). Time-Life.

Uhlmann, Dietrich. Hydrobiology: A Text for Engineers & Scientists. LC 77-24258. 1979. 57.25 (ISBN 0-471-99557-6, Pub. by Wiley-Interscience). Wiley.

Usinger, Robert L. Life of Rivers & Streams. (Illus.). 1967. 9.95 (ISBN 0-07-066690-3, P&RB); pap. 3.95 (ISBN 0-07-046008-6). McGraw.

Willoughby, L. C. Freshwater Biology. LC 76-20405. (Studies in the Biological Sciences Ser.). (Illus.). 1977. 12.50x (ISBN 0-87663-721-7). Universe.

Winberg, G. G. Methods for the Estimation of Production of Aquatic Animals. 1971. 29.00 (ISBN 0-12-758350-5). Acad Pr.

Wong, Herbert H. & Vessel, Matthew F. Pond Life: Watching Animals Find Food. LC 72-105875. (Illus.). (gr. k-4). 1970. PLB 6.95 (ISBN 0-201-08732-4, A-W Childrens). A-W.

--Pond Life: Watching Animals Grow Up. LC 72-118993. (gr. k-4). 1970. PLB 6.95 (ISBN 0-201-08730-8, A-W Childrens). A-W.

Woods, Cedric S. Freshwater Life in Ireland. 1974. 7.00x (ISBN 0-7165-2280-2, Pub. by Irish Academic Pr Ireland); pap. 2.50x o. p. (ISBN 0-7165-2281-0). Biblio Dist.

FRESH-WATER BIOLOGY–JUVENILE LITERATURE

Bartlett, Margaret F. Clean Brook. LC 60-8257. (A Let's-Read-&-Find-Out Science Bk). (Illus.). (gr. k-3). 1960. PLB 8.79 (ISBN 0-690-19556-7, TYC-J). Har-Row.

Becker, Julie. Animals of the Ponds & Streams. LC 77-8497. (Animals Around Us Ser.). (Illus.). (gr. 2-6). 1977. PLB 6.95 (ISBN 0-88436-398-8). EMC.

Cooper, Elizabeth K. Science on the Shores & Banks. (Illus.). (gr. 5-9). 1960. 4.95 (ISBN 0-15-270843-X, HJ). HarBraceJ.

--Science on the Shores & Banks. LC 60-8411. (Illus.). (gr. 7-9). 1966. pap. 1.50 (ISBN 0-15-679609-0, AVB38, VoyB). HarBraceJ.

Crosby, Alexander L. Pond Life. LC 64-12627. (Junior Science Books Ser). (Illus.). (gr. 2-5). 1964. PLB 6.09 (ISBN 0-8116-6169-5). Garrard.

Klots, Elsie B. The New Field Book of Freshwater Life. LC 66-15583. (Putnam's Nature Field Bks.). (Illus.). 1966. 7.95 (ISBN 0-399-10288-4); pap. 4.50 (ISBN 0-399-12155-2). Putnam.

Life in a Pond. (Wonders of Learning Kits Ser.). (gr. 3-5). 1979. incl. cassette & tchrs guide 23.50 (ISBN 0-686-74404-7, 04968). Natl Geog.

Muirhead-Thompson, R. C. Pesticides & Fresh Water Fauna. 1971. 36.00 (ISBN 0-12-509760-3). Acad Pr.

Paysan, Klaus. Creatures of Pond & Pool. LC 77-102893. (Nature & Man Ser). (Illus.). (gr. 5-12). 1971. PLB 8.95g (ISBN 0-8225-0562-2). Lerner Pubns.

Reid, George K. Pond Life. Zim, Herbert S., ed. (Golden Guide Ser). (Illus.). (gr. 7 up). 1967. PLB 10.38 (ISBN 0-307-63535-X, Golden Pr); pap. 1.95 (ISBN 0-307-24017-7). Western Pub.

Sabin, Francene. Wonders of the Pond. (Illus.). 32p. (gr. 2-4). 1981. PLB 7.29 (ISBN 0-89375-576-1); pap. text ed. 1.95 (ISBN 0-89375-577-X). Troll Assocs.

FRESH-WATER ECOLOGY
see also Marsh Ecology; Pond Ecology; Thermal Pollution of Rivers, Lakes, etc.

Amos, William H. Life of the Pond. (Our Living World of Nature Ser). 1967. 9.95 (ISBN 0-07-001586-4, P&RB); by subscription 3.95 (ISBN 0-07-046009-4). McGraw.

Andrews, W. Guide to the Study of Freshwater Ecology. 1971. 11.36 (ISBN 0-13-370866-7); pap. text ed. 8.16 (ISBN 0-13-370759-8). P-H.

Bick, H. Ciliated Protozoa: An Illustrated Guide to the Species Used As Biological Indicators in Fresh Water Biology. 198p. 1972. pap. 9.60 (ISBN 92-4-154028-1, 1308). World Health.

Biro. Human Impacts on Life in Fresh Waters. 1980. 22.50 (ISBN 0-9960013-5-2, Pub. by Kaido Hungary). Heyden.

Burton, Robert. Ponds: Their Wildlife & Upkeep. LC 77-76100. 1977. 5.95 (ISBN 0-7153-7390-0). David & Charles.

Curds, C. R. & Hawkes, H. A., eds. Ecological Aspects of Used Water Treatment, Vol. 1. 1975. 56.00 (ISBN 0-12-199501-1). Acad Pr.

Good, Ralph E., et al, eds. Freshwater Wetlands: Ecological Processes & Management Potential. 1978. 27.00 (ISBN 0-12-290150-9). Acad Pr.

Hart, C. W. & Fuller, Samuel. Pollution Ecology of Freshwater Invertebrates. 1974. 46.50 (ISBN 0-12-328450-3). Acad Pr.

Hynes, H. B. Ecology of Running Waters. 1970. 30.00x (ISBN 0-8020-1689-8). U of Toronto Pr.

Leadley-Brown, Alison. Ecology of Fresh Water. LC 75-156140. (Illus.). 1971. 7.95x (ISBN 0-674-22447-7). Harvard U Pr.

Le Cren, E. D. & Lowe-McConnell, R. H., eds. The Functioning of Freshwater Ecosystems. LC 79-50504. (International Biological Programme Ser.: No. 22). (Illus.). 1980. 95.00 (ISBN 0-521-22507-8). Cambridge U Pr.

Moss, Brian. The Ecology of Fresh Waters. 360p. 1980. pap. 27.95x (ISBN 0-470-26942-1). Halsted Pr.

Ogden, C. G. An Atlas of Freshwater Testate Amoebae. (Illus.). 228p. 1980. text ed. 49.50x (ISBN 0-19-858502-0). Oxford U Pr.

Reid, Gecrge K. Ecology of Inland Waters & Estuaries. 2nd ed. 1976. 21.95x (ISBN 0-442-17605-8). Van Nos Reinhold.

Ward, James V. & Stanford, Jack A., eds. The Ecology of Regulated Streams. LC 79 21632. 412p. 1979. 35.00 (ISBN 0-306-40317-X, Plenum Pr). Plenum Pub.

Weller, Milton W. Freshwater Marshes: Ecology & Wildlife Management. (Illus.). 160p. 1981. 22.50x (ISBN 0-8166-1061-4); pap. 8.95 (ISBN 0-8166-1062-2). U of Minn Pr.

FRESH-WATER FAUNA
see also Aquariums; Fishes, Fresh-Water; Insects, Aquatic

Baker, F. C. The Fresh Water Mollusca of Wisconsin. 1973. pap. 100.00 (ISBN 3-7682-0764-1). Lubrecht & Cramer.

Boulenger, G. A. Fishes of the Nile. 1964. Repr. of 1907 ed. 185.00 (ISBN 3-7682-0241-0). Lubrecht & Cramer.

Brauer, A. Die Suesswasserfauna Deutchlands. (Illus.). 1961. Repr. of 1909 ed. 175.00 (ISBN 3-7682-0045-0). Lubrecht & Cramer.

Ellis, A. E. British Freshwater Bivalve Mollusca: Keys & Notes for the Identification of the Species. (A Volume in the Synopses of the British Fauna Ser.). 1978. pap. 8.50 (ISBN 0-12-236950-5). Acad Pr.

Evanoff, Vlad. Fresh-Water Fisherman's Bible. rev. ed. LC 79-7684. (Outdoor Bible Ser.). (Illus.). 1980. pap. 3.95 (ISBN 0-385-14405-9). Doubleday.

Forel, Francois A. La Faune Profonde Des Lacs Suisses: The Bottom Fauna of Swiss Lakes. Egerton, Frank N., 3rd, ed. LC 77-74224. (History of Ecology Ser.). 1978. Repr. of 1884 ed. lib. bdg. 14.00x (ISBN 0-405-10394-8). Arno.

McDowall, R. M. New Zealand Freshwater Fishes: A Guide and Natural History. (Illus.). 230p. 1978. text ed. 27.50x (ISBN 0-87474-632-9, Pub. by Heinemann New Zealand). Smithsonian.

Ogden, C. G. An Atlas of Freshwater Testate Amoebae. (Illus.). 228p. 1980. text ed. 49.50x (ISBN 0-19-858502-0). Oxford U Pr.

Pennak, Robert W. Fresh-Water Invertebrates of the United States. 2nd ed. LC 78-8130. 1978. 34.50 (ISBN 0-471-04249-8, Pub. by Wiley-Interscience). Wiley.

Stamm, Douglas R. Under Water: The Northern Lakes. 128p. 1977. pap. 7.95 (ISBN 0-299-07264-9). U of Wis Pr.

Wesenberg-Lund, C. Biologie der Suesswassertiere: Wirbellose Tiere. (Illus.). 1967. 80.00 (ISBN 3-7682-0426-X). Lubrecht & Cramer.

Whitford, L. A. & Schumacher, George. Manual of Freshwater Algae. 15.00 (ISBN 0-916822-01-X). Sparks Pr.

FRESH-WATER FLORA
see also Phytoplankton

Aquatic Plants of Australia. 1973. pap. 36.00x (ISBN 0-522-84044-2, Pub. by Melbourne U Pr). Intl Schol Bk Serv.

Haslam, S. M. River Plants. LC 76-46857. (Illus.). 1978. 90.00 (ISBN 0-521-21493-9); pap. 22.95x (ISBN 0-521-29172-0). Cambridge U Pr.

Hotchkiss, Neil. Common Marsh, Underwater & Floating-Leaved Plants of the United States & Canada. (Illus.). 9.50 (ISBN 0-8446-4558-3). Peter Smith.

Magee, Dennis W. Freshwater Wetlands: A Guide to Common Indicator Plants of the Northeast. LC 80-26876. (Illus.). 240p. 1981. lib. bdg. 20.00x (ISBN 0-87023-316-5); pap. text ed. 8.95x (ISBN 0-87023-317-3). U of Mass Pr.
Wright, D. Macer. The Fly Fishers Plants: Their Value in Trout Waters. (Illus.). 1973. 4.95 (ISBN 0-7153-6116-3). David & Charles.

FREUD, SIGMUND, 1856-1939

Amacher, Peter. Freud's Neurological Education & Its Influence on Psychoanalytic Theory. LC 65-19461. (Psychological Issues Monograph: No. 16, Vol. 4, No. 4). (Orig.). 1966. text ed. 11.00 (ISBN 0-8236-2040-9). Intl Univs Pr.
Anzieu, D. Freud's Self-Analysis & the Discovery of Psychoanalysis, Vols. 1 & 2. 1982. Set. text ed. write for info. (ISBN 0-8236-2044-1). Vol. 1 (ISBN 0-8236-2045-X). Vol. 2 (ISBN 0-8236-2046-8). Intl Univs Pr.
Arlow, Jacob A. Legacy of Sigmund Freud. LC 56-9746. 1956. text ed. 15.00 (ISBN 0-8236-2980-5). Intl Univs Pr.
Axelrod, Charles D. Studies in Intellectual Breakthrough: Freud, Simmel, & Buber. LC 78-53177. 1979. lib. bdg. 10.00x (ISBN 0-87023-256-8). U of Mass Pr.
Bartels, Martin. Selbstbewusstsein und Unbewusstes: Studien Zu Freud und Heidegger. (Quellen und Studien Zur Philosophie Ser.: Vol. 10). 1976. 48.75x (ISBN 3-11-005778-6). De Gruyter.
Bersani, Leo. Baudelaire & Freud. LC 76-55562. (Quantum Ser.). 1978. 12.95x (ISBN 0-520-03402-3); pap. 2.65 (ISBN 0-520-03535-6). U of Cal Pr.
Bocock, Robert. Freud & Modern Society: An Outline & Analysis of Freud's Sociology. LC 77-19118. 1978. text ed. 25.50x (ISBN 0-8419-0364-6); pap. text ed. 14.50x (ISBN 0-8419-0365-4). Holmes & Meier.
Brandell, Gunnar. Freud-A Man of His Century. White, Iain, tr. LC 78-5347. 1979. text ed. 18.25x (ISBN 0-391-00871-4). Humanities.
Brill, A. A. Psychoanalysis, Its Theories & Practical Application. LC 78-180559. (Medicine & Society in America Ser). 346p. 1972. Repr. of 1913 ed. 16.00 (ISBN 0-405-03939-5). Arno.
Brill, Abraham A. Freud's Contribution to Psychiatry. 5.00 (ISBN 0-8446-1738-5). Peter Smith.
Brivic, Sheldon R. Joyce Between Freud & Jung. (National University Publications, Literary Criticism Ser.). 1980. 15.00 (ISBN 0-8046-9249-1). Kennikat.
Clouzet, Maryse. Sigmund Freud: A New Appraisal. LC 72-9606. 141p. 1974. Repr. of 1963 ed. lib. bdg. 15.00x (ISBN 0-8371-6593-8, CLSF). Greenwood.
Dalbiez, Roland. Psychoanalytical Method & the Doctrine of Freud, 2 vols. facsimile ed. Lindsay, T. F., tr. from Fr. (Select Bibliographies Reprint Ser). Repr. of 1941 ed. 43.00 (ISBN 0-8369-6715-1). Arno.
Decker, Hannah. Freud in Germany: Revolution & Reaction in Science, 1893-1907. LC 77-20062. (Psychological Issues Ser.: Mono. 41). 1977. text ed. 19.50 (ISBN 0-8236-2023-9); pap. text ed. 11.00 (ISBN 0-8236-2022-0). Intl Univs Pr.
De Luca, Anthony. Freud & Future Religious Experience. LC 75-3782. 290p. 1976. 12.50 (ISBN 0-8022-2173-4). Philos Lib.
De Luca, Anthony J. Freud & Future Religious Experience. (Quality Paperback Ser: No. 330). 1977. pap. 4.95 (ISBN 0-8226-0330-6). Littlefield.
Doolittle, Hilda. Tribute to Freud. 208p. 1975. pap. 2.95 (ISBN 0-07-027731-1, SP). McGraw.
Dunlap, Knight. Mysticism, Freudianism & Scientific Psychology. facsimile ed. (Select Bibliographies Reprint Ser). Repr. of 1920 ed. 16.00 (ISBN 0-8369-5838-1). Arno.
Eissler, K. R. Talent & Genius: The Fictitious Case of Tausk Contra Freud. LC 70-162813. 388p. 1971. 12.95 (ISBN 0-8129-0222-X). Times Bks.
Eissler, Kurt R. Leonardo Da Vinci: Psychoanalytic Notes on the Enigma. LC 61-11610. (Illus.). 1961. text ed. 25.00 (ISBN 0-8236-3000-5). Intl Univs Pr.
Engelman, Edmund. Berggasse Nineteen: Sigmund Freud's Home & Offices, Vienna, 1938; the Photographs of Edmund Engelman. LC 80-23056. 1981. pap. 15.00 (ISBN 0-226-20847-8). U of Chicago Pr.
Engelman, Edmund, photos by. Berggasse Nineteen: Sigmund Freud's Home & Offices, Vienna 1938. LC 76-7686. 1976. 30.00 (ISBN 0-465-00656-6). Basic.
Eysenck, Hans J. & Wilson, Glenn D. The Experimental Studies of Freudian Theories. 1973. 33.00x (ISBN 0-416-78010-5). Methuen Inc.
Fancher, Raymond E. Psychoanalytic Psychology: The Development of Freud's Thought. LC 73-1273. (Illus.). 1973. pap. 5.95x (ISBN 0-393-09356-5). Norton.
Feffer, Melvin. The Structure of Freudian Thought: The Problem of Immutability & Discontinuity in Developmental Theory. 1981. pap. text ed. 17.50 (ISBN 0-8236-6185-7). Intl Univs Pr.
Ferraro, Armando. A Trilogy of Freud's Major Fallacies. LC 77-94260. 1979. 12.50 (ISBN 0-533-03584-8). Vantage.
Fine, Reuben. Development of Freud's Thought: From the Beginnings (1886-1899) Through Id Psychology (1900-1914) to Ego Psychology (1914-1939) rev ed. LC 73-77279. 320p. 1973. 25.00x (ISBN 0-87668-085-6). Aronson.
Fisher, Seymour & Greenberg, Roger P. The Scientific Credibility of Freud's Theories & Therapy. LC 76-7685. (Illus.). 1977. text ed. 22.50x (ISBN 0-465-07385-9). Basic.
Fisher, Seymour & Greenberg, Roger, eds. The Scientific Evaluation of Freud's Theories & Therapy: A Book of Readings. LC 77-90537. 1978. text ed. 25.00x (ISBN 0-465-07388-3). Basic.
Foster, R. E. The Influence of Freud on the Autobiographical Novel. 59.95 (ISBN 0-8490-0407-1). Gordon Pr.
Fox, Seymour. Freud & Education. (American Lectures in Philosophy Ser.). 272p. 1975. text ed. 16.50 (ISBN 0-398-03009-X). C C Thomas.
Freeman, Lucy. Freud Rediscovered. LC 79-52251. 1980. 11.95 (ISBN 0-87795-227-2). Arbor Hse.
Freeman, Lucy & Strean, Herbert S. Freud & Women. LC 81-40460. 250p. 1981. 10.95 (ISBN 0-8044-5374-8). Ungar.
French Freud, No. 48. 1973. pap. 10.00 (ISBN 0-527-01737-X). Kraus Repr.
Freud, Ernst, et al. Sigmund Freud: His Life in Pictures & Words. Trollope, Christiane, tr. LC 78-53882. (Helen & Kurt Wolff Bks). (Illus.). 1978. 39.95 (ISBN 0-15-182546-7). HarBraceJ.
Freud, Sigmund. The Complete Psychological Works: Standard Edition, 24 vols. Strachey, James, ed. & tr. from Ger. 1976. 495.00 set (ISBN 0-393-01128-3). Norton.
--Freud: Dictionary of Psychoanalysis. Fodor, Nandor & Gaynor, Frank, eds. Repr. of 1950 ed. lib. bdg. 15.00x (ISBN 0-8371-2135-3, FRP/). Greenwood.
Frey-Rohn, Liliane. From Freud to Jung. 368p. 1976. pap. 3.95 (ISBN 0-440-54715-6, Delta). Dell.
--From Freud to Jung. LC 73-77114. 1974. 16.00 (ISBN 0-913430-24-2). C G Jung Foun.
Fromm, Erich. Greatness & Limitations of Freud's Thought. 1981. pap. 2.95 (ISBN 0-451-61995-1, ME1995, Ment). NAL.
--The Greatness & Limitations of Freud's Thought. LC 79-2730. 1980. 9.95 (ISBN 0-06-011389-8, HarpT). Har-Row.
--Sigmund Freud's Mission: An Analysis of His Personality & Influence. 7.00 (ISBN 0-8446-4544-3). Peter Smith.
Gay, Peter. Freud, Jews & Other Germans: Masters & Victims in Modernist Culture. 1978. 15.95x (ISBN 0-19-502258-0). Oxford U Pr.
Gedo, John E. & Pollock, George H., eds. Freud: The Fusion of Science & Humanism: The Intellectual History of Psychoanalysis. LC 75-792. (Psychological Issues Monograph: No. 34-35, Vol. 9, No. 2-3). 400p. 1975. text ed. 22.00x (ISBN 0-8236-2031-X); pap. text ed. 16.50 (ISBN 0-8236-2030-1). Intl Univs Pr.
George, Diana H. Blake & Freud. LC 80-11244. (Illus.). 288p. 1980. 17.50x (ISBN 0-8014-1286-2). Cornell U Pr.
Gorlich, Bernard, ed. Der Stachel Freud: Eine Kontroverse Zwischen Otto Fenichel, Erich Fromm und Herbert Marcuse. (Edition Suhrkamp: 961). 369p. (Orig., Ger.). 1980. pap. text ed. 8.45 (ISBN 3-518-10961-8, Pub. by Suhrkamp Verlag Germany). Suhrkamp.
Grinstein, Alexander. Sigmund Freud's Dreams. LC 79-2485. 475p. 1980. text ed. 22.50 (ISBN 0-8236-6074-5). Intl Univs Pr.
Grinstein, Alexander, ed. Sigmund Freuds Writings: A Comprehensive Bibliography. LC 76-46812. 1977. text ed. 22.50 (ISBN 0-8236-6076-1). Intl Univs Pr.
Grunfeld, Frederic V. Prophets Without Honor: A Background to Freud, Kafka, Einstein & Their World. 1980. pap. 5.95x (ISBN 0-07-025087-1). McGraw.
Guttman, Samuel, et al, eds. The Concordance to the Standard Edition of the Complete Psychological Works of Sigmund Freud. (Scholarly Reference Publications). 1980. lib. bdg. 525.00 (ISBN 0-8161-8383-X). G K Hall.
Hale, Nathan G., Jr. Freud & the Americans: The Origin & Foundation of the Psychoanalytic Movement in America, 1876-1918. 1971. 19.50 (ISBN 0-19-501427-8). Oxford U Pr.
Hall, Calvin S. A Primer of Freudian Psychology. 1978. Repr. of 1954 ed. lib. bdg. 14.50x (ISBN 0-374-93386-3). Octagon.
Hitschmann, Edward. Freud's Theories of the Neuroses. Payne, C. R., tr. (Nervous & Mental Disease Monographs: No. 17). 1913. 15.50 (ISBN 0-384-23480-1). Johnson Repr.
Hoffman, Frederick J. Freudianism & the Literary Mind. 1977. Repr. of 1957 ed. lib. bdg. 26.75 (ISBN 0-8371-9713-9, HOFL). Greenwood.
Holt, Edwin B. The Freudian Wish & Its Place in Ethics. 1915. 11.50 (ISBN 0-384-24060-7). Johnson Repr.
Homans, Peter. Theology After Freud: An Interpretive Inquiry. LC 76-84162. 1970. 18.50x (ISBN 0-672-51245-9); pap. text ed. 6.95x (ISBN 0-672-60802-2). Irvington.
Izenberg, G. N. The Existentialist Critique of Freud: The Crisis of Autonomy. 1976. 25.00 (ISBN 0-691-07214-0). Princeton U Pr.
Jahoda, Marie. Freud & the Dilemmas of Psychology. LC 80-17140. vi, 186p. 1981. pap. 4.50x (ISBN 0-8032-7553-6, BB 759, Bison). U of Nebr Pr.
--Freud & the Dilemmas of Psychology. LC 76-46853. 1977. 12.50x (ISBN 0-465-02561-7). Basic.
Jones, Ernest. Life & Work of Sigmund Freud. abr. ed. Trilling, Lionel L. & Marcus, Steven, eds. LC 61-15950. 1961. 17.95 (ISBN 0-465-04014-4); pap. 5.95 (ISBN 0-465-09700-6, CN50000). Basic.
--The Life & Work of Sigmund Freud, 3 vols. Incl. Vol. 1. The Formative Years & the Great Discoveries, 1856-1900. 428p. 1953 (ISBN 0-465-04016-0); Vol. 2. Years of Maturity, 1901-1919. 512p. 1955 (ISBN 0-465-04017-9); Vol. 3. The Last Phase, 1919-1939. 537p. 1957 (ISBN 0-465-04018-7). LC 53-8700. (Illus.). 45.00x set (ISBN 0-465-04015-2); 16.00x ea. Basic.
Kalin, Martin G. The Utopian Flight from Unhappiness: Freud Against Marx on Social Progress. (Quality Paperback: No. 314). 231p. 1975. pap. 3.50 (ISBN 0-8226-0314-4). Littlefield.
Kanzer, Mark & Glenn, Jules, eds. Freud & His Patients. LC 79-51909. (Downstate Psycholanalytic Institute Twenty Fifth Anniversary Ser.: Vol. II). 1979. 25.00 (ISBN 0-87668-367-7). Aronson.
--Freud & His Patients, Vol. 2 Of 4 Vols. LC 79-51910. 375p. Date not set. 25.00 (ISBN 0-686-72800-9). Aronson.
--Freud & His Self Analysis. LC 79-51908. (Downstate Psychoanalytic Institute Twenty-Fifth Anniversary Ser.: Vol. I). 308p. 1979. 25.00x (ISBN 0-87668-366-9). Aronson.
Kaufmann, Walter. Discovering the Mind: Freud Versus Adler & Jung. LC 80-25767. 1981. 14.95 (ISBN 0-07-033313-0). McGraw.
Kline, Paul. Fact & Fantasy in Freudian Theory. 2nd ed. (Methuen's Manuals of Modern Psychology Ser.). 1981. 42.95x (ISBN 0-416-72640-2). Methuen Inc.
--Fact & Fantasy in Freudian Theory. (Methuen's Manuals of Modern Psychology Ser.). 1979. text ed. 27.50 (ISBN 0-416-15060-8). Methuen Inc.
Kung, Hans. Freud & the Problem of God. Quinn, Edward, tr. LC 78-25581. (Terry Lecture Ser.). 136p. 1980. pap. 3.95 (ISBN 0-300-02597-1, Y-237). Yale U Pr.
--Freud & the Problem of God. Quinn, Edward, tr. (Terr Lecture Ser.). 1979. 14.50 (ISBN 0-300-02350-2). Yale U Pr.
LaPiere, Richard T. The Freudian Ethic. LC 74-6710. 299p. 1974. Repr. of 1959 ed. lib. bdg. 15.75x (ISBN 0-8371-7543-7, LAFE). Greenwood.
Laplanche, Jean. Life & Death in Psychoanalysis. Mehlman, Jeffrey, tr. LC 75-36928. (Illus.). 160p. 1976. 11.50x (ISBN 0-8018-1637-8). Johns Hopkins.
Leavy, Stanley A., tr. Freud Journal of Lou Andreas-Salome. 1973. pap. 5.95x (ISBN 0-465-09506-2, TB5007). Basic.
Levin, Kenneth. Freud's Early Psychology of the Neuroses: A Historical Perspective. LC 77-15734. 1978. 15.95 (ISBN 0-8229-3366-7). U of Pittsburgh Pr.
Levitt, Morton. Freud & Dewey on the Nature of Man. LC 76-138157. 180p. 1972. Repr. of 1960 ed. lib. bdg. 15.00x (ISBN 0-8371-5614-9, LEFD). Greenwood.
Lewin, Bertram D. Dreams & the Uses of Regression. LC 58-9230. (The New York Psychoanalytic Institute Freud Anniversary Lecture Ser.). 1963. text ed. 10.00 (ISBN 0-8236-1460-3). Intl Univs Pr.
Lewis, Helen B. Freud & Modern Psychology: The/Emotional Basis of Mental Illness, Vol. 1. (Emotions Personality & Psychotherapy Ser.). 240p. 1981. 19.50 (ISBN 0-306-40525-3, Plenum Pr). Plenum Pub.
Lichtman, Richard. Production of Desire: The Integration of Psychoanalysis into Marxist Theory. 320p. 1981. text ed. 20.00 (ISBN 0-686-74620-1). Free Pr.
McGuire, William, ed. The Freud-Jung Letters: The Correspondence Between Sigmund Freud & C. G. Jung. Manheim, Ralph & Hull, R. F., trs. LC 76-166373. (Bollingen Ser.: No. 94). 650p. 1974. 30.00 (ISBN 0-691-09890-5); pap. 9.95 (ISBN 0-691-01810-3). Princeton U Pr.
Mahony, Patrick J. Freud As a Writer. 1980. 17.50 (ISBN 0-8236-2018-2). Intl Univs Pr.
Meisel, Perry. Freud: A Collection of Critical Essays. (Twentieth Century Views Ser.). 256p. 1981. 13.95 (ISBN 0-13-331405-7, Spec); pap. 5.95 (ISBN 0-13-331397-2). P-H.
Meynell, Hugo. Freud, Marx & Morals. (New Studies in Practical Philosophy). 222p. 1981. 23.00 (ISBN 0-389-20045-X). B&N.
Monarch Notes on Freud's the Interpretation of Dreams & Other Works. (gr. 7-12). pap. 2.25 (ISBN 0-671-00986-9). Monarch Pr.
Morris, Nat, pseud. A Man Possessed: The Case History of Sigmund Freud. LC 73-92383. 7.95 (ISBN 0-911238-53-0); pap. 2.45 (ISBN 0-911238-57-3). Regent House.
Mujeeb-Ur Rahman, Mohammed, ed. The Freudian Paradigm: Psychoanalysis & Scientific Thought. LC 73-89486. 1977. 25.95x (ISBN 0-911012-89-3); pap. 13.95x (ISBN 0-88229-461-X). Nelson-Hall.
Nelson. The Voice of Sigmund Freud. 1980. 8.95 (ISBN 0-87705-464-9). Human Sci Pr.
Nelson, Benjamin, ed. Freud & the Twentieth Century. 6.75 (ISBN 0-8446-2097-1). Peter Smith.
New York Academy Of Medicine. Freud & Contemporary Culture. facs. ed. Galdston, Iago, ed. LC 77-142674. (Essay Index Reprint Ser). 1957. 11.00 (ISBN 0-8369-2112-7). Arno.
Nye, Robert D. Three Psychologies: Perspectives from Freud, Skinner & Rogers. 2nd ed. LC 80-25716. 170p. (Orig.). 1981. pap. text ed. 7.95 (ISBN 0-8185-0438-2). Brooks-Cole.
--Three Views of Man: Perspectives from Sigmund Freud, B. F. Skinner, & Carl Rogers. LC 74-27872. 1975. pap. text ed. 7.95 (ISBN 0-685-52380-2). Brooks-Cole.
Orlando, Francesco. Toward a Freudian Theory of Literature: With an Analysis of Racine's Phedre. Lee, Charmaine, tr. from Ital. LC 78-7577. 1979. text ed. 16.00x (ISBN 0-8018-2102-9). Johns Hopkins.
Paley, Alan L. Sigmund Freud, Father of Psychoanalysis. new ed. Rahmas, D. Steve, ed. LC 74-14694. (Outstanding Personalities Ser.). 32p. 1974. lib. bdg. 2.95 incl. catalog cards (ISBN 0-686-11500-7); pap. 1.50 vinyl laminated covers (ISBN 0-686-11501-5). SamHar Pr.
Philp, Howard L. Freud & Religious Belief. LC 72-12635. 140p. 1974. Repr. of 1956 ed. lib. bdg. 15.00x (ISBN 0-8371-6682-9, PHFR). Greenwood.
--Freud & Religious Belief. LC 72-12635. 140p. 1974. Repr. of 1956 ed. lib. bdg. 15.00x (ISBN 0-8371-6682-9, PHFR). Greenwood.
Pickering, George. Creative Malady. 1974. 13.95 (ISBN 0-19-519800-X). Oxford U Pr.
Podwal, Mark. Freud's Da Vinci. 1977. 9.95 (ISBN 0-89545-002-X); pap. 4.95 (ISBN 0-89545-003-8). Images Graphiques.
Rainey, Reuben M. Freud As Student of Religion: Perspectives on the Background & Development of His Thought. LC 75-17536. (American Academy of Religion. Dissertation Ser.: No. 7). 1975. pap. 7.50 (ISBN 0-89130-012-0, 010107). Scholars Pr Ca.
Reik, Theodor. From Thirty Years with Freud. Winston, Richard, tr. from Ger. LC 75-8725. (Illus.). 241p. 1975. Repr. of 1940 ed. lib. bdg. 14.50x (ISBN 0-8371-8047-3, REFT). Greenwood.
Ricoeur, Paul. Freud & Philosophy: An Essay on Interpretation. Savage, Denis, tr. LC 70-89907. (Terry Lectures Ser). 1970. 35.00x (ISBN 0-300-01165-2); pap. 9.95 (ISBN 0-300-02189-5). Yale U Pr.
Rieff, Phillip. Freud: The Mind of the Moralist. 3rd ed. LC 78-69967. 1979. 15.00x (ISBN 0-226-71640-6); pap. 6.95 (ISBN 0-226-71639-2, P777, Phoen). U of Chicago Pr.
Roazen, Paul. Freud & His Followers. 656p. 1975. pap. 5.95 (ISBN 0-452-00440-3, F440, Mer). NAL.
--Sigmund Freud. (Makers of Modern Social Science Ser). (Illus.). 1973. 6.95 (ISBN 0-13-332361-7, Spec). P-H.
Rosenfeld, Israel. Freud: Character & Consciousness. 5.95 (ISBN 0-8216-0080-X). Univ Bks.
Rosenzweig, Saul. Freud & the Kingmaker: The Visit to America - The Letters of Sigmund Freud & G. S. Hall, 1908 to 1923 & Freud's Five Lectures at Clark University. LC 78-65156. 1981. 13.50 (ISBN 0-930172-03-5). Rana Hse.
--The Rosenzweig Picture-Frustration (P-F) Study--Basic Manual. LC 77-95428. 1978. 8.00 (ISBN 0-930172-02-7). Rana Hse.
Ruitenbeek, Hendrik, ed. Freud As We Knew Him. LC 72-6471. 550p. 1973. 17.50x (ISBN 0-8143-1488-0). Wayne St U Pr.
Ruitenbeek, Hendrik M. Freud & America. 1966. 4.95 (ISBN 0-02-605920-7). Macmillan.
Rushdoony, Rousas. Freud. (Modern Thinkers Ser.). 1975. pap. 2.00 (ISBN 0-87552-583-0). Presby & Reformed.

Sachs, Hanns. Freud, Master & Friend. facs. ed. LC 78-133531. (Select Bibliographies Reprint Ser). 1944. 15.00 (ISBN 0-8369-5563-3). Arno.
Schellenberg, James A. Masters of Social Psychology: Freud, Mead, Lewin, & Skinner. 1979. pap. 3.95 (ISBN 0-19-502622-5, GB 590, GB). Oxford U Pr.
Schneider, Louis. The Freudian Psychology & Veblen's Social Theory. LC 73-19119. 270p. 1974. Repr. of 1948 ed. lib. bdg. 14.00x (ISBN 0-8371-7308-6, SCFP). Greenwood.
Schur, Max. Freud: Living & Dying. LC 71-143379. 1972. text ed. 30.00 (ISBN 0-8236-2025-5); pap. text ed. 7.95 (ISBN 0-8236-8052-5, 022025). Intl Univs Pr.
Sears, Robert R. Survey of Objective Studies of Psychoanalytic Concepts. LC 79-4476. 1979. Repr. of 1943 ed. lib. bdg. 17.25x (ISBN 0-313-21249-X, SESO). Greenwood.
Shakow, David & Rapaport, David. Influence of Freud on American Psychology. LC 64-21456. (Psychological Issues Monograph: No. 13, Vol. 4, No. 1). (Orig.). 1964. text ed. 13.50 (ISBN 0-8236-2656-3); pap. text ed. 11.00 (ISBN 0-8236-2652-0). Intl Univs Pr.
Smith, Joseph H., ed. The Literary Freud: Mechanisms of Defense & the Poetic Will. LC 79-19104. (Psychiatry & the Humanities Ser.: Vol. 4). 1980. 30.00x (ISBN 0-300-02405-3). Yale U Pr.
Spector, Jack J. The Aesthetics of Freud: A Study in Psychoanalysis & Art. LC 70-168347. (McGraw-Hill Paperbacks). (Illus.). 288p. 1974. pap. 3.95 (ISBN 0-07-060015-5, SP). McGraw.
Stafford-Clark, David. What Freud Really Said. LC 66-24900. (What They Really Said Ser). 1971. 7.50x (ISBN 0-8052-3283-4); pap. 4.95 (ISBN 0-8052-0290-0). Schocken.
Stannard, David E. Shrinking History: On Freud & the Failure of Psychohistory. (Illus.). 1980. 12.95 (ISBN 0-19-502735-3). Oxford U Pr.
Steadman, Ralph. Sigmund Freud. 1980. pap. 6.95 (ISBN 0-671-25431-6, Touchstone). S&S.
--Sigmund Freud. LC 79-10784. (Illus.). 1979. 17.95 (ISBN 0-448-22980-3). Paddington.
Strauss, Allan R., Jr. A Critical Study of Freud's Concept of Unconscious Mental Processes with Special Reference to Gestalt Psychology. (Illus.). 160p. 1980. 12.50 (ISBN 0-682-49602-2, University). Exposition.
Strupp, Hans H. Introduction to Freud & Modern Psychoanalysis. LC 67-18385. (Orig.). (YA) 1967. text ed. 7.95 (ISBN 0-8120-6058-X); pap. text ed. 2.50 (ISBN 0-8120-0276-8). Barron.
Sulloway, Frank J. Freud, Biologist of the Mind: Beyond the Psychoanalytic Legend. 20.00 (ISBN 0-686-68084-7). Basic.
Turkle, Sherry. Psychoanalytic Politics: Freud's French Revolution. LC 78-54494. 1978. 12.50 (ISBN 0-465-06607-0). Basic.
Wallace, Edwin R., IV. Freud & Anthropology. (Psychological Issues Monograph: No. 54). 1981. write for info. (ISBN 0-8236-2010-7). Intl Univs Pr.
Wittels, Fritz. Sigmund Freud: His Personality, His Teaching & His School. facsimile ed. Paul, Eden & Paul, Cedar, trs. from Ger. LC 79-161001. (Select Bibliographies Reprint Ser). Repr. of 1924 ed. 18.00 (ISBN 0-8369-5869-1). Arno.
Wollheim, Richard. Sigmund Freud. 316p. 1981. pap. 7.95 (ISBN 0-521-28385-X). Cambridge U Pr.
Zilboorg, Gregory. Sigmund Freud: His Exploration of the Mind of Man. LC 70-128069. Repr. of 1951 ed. 12.50x (ISBN 0-678-02750-1). Kelley.
Zweig, Stefan. Mental Healers: Franz Anton Mesmer, Mary Baker Eddy, Sigmund Freud. LC 62-19082. 12.50 (ISBN 0-8044-2995-2); pap. 6.95 (ISBN 0-8044-6996-2). Ungar.

FREUD, SIGMUND, 1856-1939-JUVENILE LITERATURE

Hollitscher, Walter. Sigmund Freud: An Introduction. facsimile ed. LC 72-119931. (Select Bibliographies Reprint Ser). Repr. of 1947 ed. 13.00 (ISBN 0-8369-5374-6). Arno.
Neimark, Anne E. Sigmund Freud: The World Within. LC 76-187464. (Illus.). (gr. 7 up). 1976. 6.95 (ISBN 0-15-274164-X, HJ). HarBraceJ.

FREWEN, MORETON

Leslie, Shane. Studies in Sublime Failure. LC 70-117817. (Essay Index Reprint Ser). 1932. 18.00 (ISBN 0-8369-1670-0). Arno.

FREYTAG, GUSTAV, 1816-1895

Mayrhofer, O. Gustav Freytag und das Junge Deutschland. pap. 7.00 (ISBN 0-384-36160-9). Johnson Repr.
Ulrich, P. Gustav Freytags Romantechnik. Repr. of 1907 ed. pap. 7.00 (ISBN 0-384-62640-8). Johnson Repr.

FRIARS

see also Carmelites; Dominicans; Franciscans; Monasticism and Religious Orders

Brusher, Joseph. Consecrated Thunderbolt: A Life of Fr. Peter C. Yorke of San Francisco. pap. 4.95 (ISBN 0-686-31705-X). Alba.
Fish, Simon. A Supplicacyon for the Beggers. LC 72-5989. (English Experience Ser.: No. 515). 16p. 1973. Repr. of 1529 ed. 6.00 (ISBN 90-221-0515-6). Walter J Johnson.
Kennard, Joseph S. Friar in Fiction, Sincerity in Art, & Other Essays. facs. ed. LC 68-20313. (Essay Index Reprint Ser). 1923. 18.00 (ISBN 0-8369-0588-1). Arno.
Leutenegger, Benedict, tr. Life of Fray Antonio Margil De Jesus. (Illus.). 1967. 10.00 (ISBN 0-88382-254-7). AAFH.

FRIARS, BLACK

see Dominicans

FRIARS, GRAY

see Franciscans

FRIARS MINOR

see Franciscans

FRIARS PREACHERS

see Dominicans

FRICTION

see also Aerodynamic Heating; Bearings (Machinery); Internal Friction; Lubrication and Lubricants; Mechanical Wear; Rolling Contact; Surfaces (Technology)

Charnley, J. Low Friction Arthroplasty of the Hip: Theory & Practice. (Illus.). 1979. 52.80 (ISBN 0-387-08893-8). Springer-Verlag.
Kragelsky, I. V. Methods of Calculating Friction & Wear. 100.00 (ISBN 0-08-027320-3). Pergamon.
Kragelsky, I. V., et al. Friction & Wear: Calculation Methods. LC 80-41669. (Illus.). 450p. 1981. 100.00 (ISBN 0-08-025461-6); pap. 60.00 (ISBN 0-08-027320-3). Pergamon.
Newman, L. B. Friction Materials: Recent Advances. LC 77-15219. (Chemical Technology Review Ser.: No. 100). (Illus.). 1978. 36.00 (ISBN 0-8155-0688-0). Noyes.
Postnikov, S. N. Electrophysical & Electrochemical Phenomena in Friction, Cutting, & Lubrication. Teague, Ben, tr. 1978. text ed. 21.50x (ISBN 0-442-26624-3). Van Nos Reinhold.
Pugh, B. Friction & Wear: A Trilogy Text for Students. 19.95 (ISBN 0-408-00097-X); pap. 6.95 (ISBN 0-408-00098-8). Butterworth.
Rabinowicz, Ernest. Friction & Wear of Materials. LC 65-12704. (Ser. on the Science & Technology of Materials). (Illus.). 1965. 33.00 (ISBN 0-471-70340-0). Wiley.
Sarkar, A. D. Friction & Wear. LC 80-40526. 1980. 86.50 (ISBN 0-12-619260-X). Acad Pr.

FRIEDEL-CRAFTS REACTION

Roberts. A Century of Friedel-NCrafts Alkylations & Re-Arrangements. Date not set. price not set (ISBN 0-8247-6433-1). Dekker.

FRIEDMAN, BRUCE JAY, 1930-

Schulz, Max F. Bruce Jay Friedman. (U. S. Authors Ser.: No. 219). 1974. lib. bdg. 10.95 (ISBN 0-8057-0290-3). Twayne.

FRIEDRICH 1ST, BARBAROSSA, EMPEROR OF GERMANY, 1121-1190

Munz, Peter. Frederick Barbarossa: A Study in Medieval Politics. LC 69-20392. (Illus.). 442p. 1969. 27.50x (ISBN 0-8014-0511-4). Cornell U Pr.
Otto of Freising. Deeds of Frederick Barbarossa. Mierow, Christopher, tr. 1966. pap. 7.45x (ISBN 0-393-09697-1, NortonC). Norton.

FRIEDRICH 2ND, EMPEROR OF GERMANY, 1194-1250

Boulle, Pierre. L' Etrange Croisade de Frederic II. 9.95 (ISBN 0-686-54099-9). French & Eur.
Bowen, Marjorie. Sundry Great Gentlemen: Some Essays in Historical Biography. facs. ed. LC 68-29192. (Essay Index Reprint Ser). 1968. Repr. of 1928 ed. 18.00 (ISBN 0-8369-0230-0). Arno.
De Novare, Philip. The Wars of Frederick the Second Against the Ibelins in Syria and Cyprus. La Monte, John L., ed. ix, 230p. 1976. Repr. of 1936 ed. lib. bdg. 18.00x (ISBN 0-374-94663-9). Octagon.
Kantorowicz, Ernst. Frederick the Second, 1194-1250. Lorimer, E. O., tr. LC 57-9408. (Illus.). 1957. 24.50 (ISBN 0-8044-1468-8). Ungar.
Kington-Oliphant, Thomas L. History of Frederick the Second, Emperor of the Romans, 2 vols. LC 76-29844. Repr. of 1862 ed. Set. 86.00 (ISBN 0-404-15430-1). AMS Pr.
Masson, Georgina. Frederick II of Hohenstaufen. 1973. lib. bdg. 18.50x (ISBN 0-374-95297-3). Octagon.
Poschinger, Margarete. Life of the Emperor Frederick. LC 78-145242. Repr. of 1901 ed. 32.00 (ISBN 0-403-01157-4). Scholarly.
Van Cleve, Thomas C. The Emperor Frederick Second of Hohenstaufen, Immutator Mundi. (Illus.). 618p. 1972. 49.00x (ISBN 0-19-822513-X). Oxford U Pr.

FRIEDRICH 3RD, EMPEROR OF GERMANY, 1831-1888

Allinson, A. R., ed. War Diary of the Emperor Frederick the Third, 1870-1871. LC 77-114529. (Illus.). 1971. Repr. of 1926 ed. lib. bdg. 22.75x (ISBN 0-8371-4824-3, FRWD). Greenwood.
Von Poschinger, Margaret E. Life of the Emperor Frederick. LC 72-151599. Repr. of 1901 ed. 31.50 (ISBN 0-404-05089-1). AMS Pr.

FRIEDRICH 2ND, DER GROSSE, KING OF PRUSSIA, 1712-1786

Barker, Thomas, ed. Frederick the Great & the Making of Prussia. LC 76-23215. (European Problem Studies). 116p. 1976. pap. 5.50 (ISBN 0-88275-456-4). Krieger.
Carlyle, Thomas. History of Frederich Second of Prussia Called Frederick the Great. Clive, John, ed. LC 79-82375. (Classic European Historians Ser). 1969. pap. 3.45 (ISBN 0-226-09297-6, P344, Phoen). U of Chicago Pr.
Gaxotte, Pierre. Frederick the Great. Bell, R. A., tr. from Fr. LC 75-16845. (Illus.). 420p. 1975. Repr. of 1942 ed. lib. bdg. 22.75x (ISBN 0-8371-8269-7, GAFG). Greenwood.
Goldsmith, Margaret. Frederick the Great. 218p. 1980. Repr. of 1929 ed. lib. bdg. 20.00 (ISBN 0-89760-314-1). Telegraph Bks.
Henderson, W. O. Studies in Economic Policy of Frederick the Great. 205p. 1963. 25.00x (ISBN 0-7146-1321-5, F Cass Co). Biblio Dist.
Hubatsch, Walther. Frederick the Great: Absolutism & Administration. Hattan, Ragnhild, ed. (Men in Office Ser.). (Illus.). 1977. 16.95 (ISBN 0-500-87002-0). Thames Hudson.
Lavisse, Ernest. Youth of Frederick the Great. LC 71-172308. Repr. of 1892 ed. 24.75 (ISBN 0-404-03891-3). AMS Pr.
Macaulay, Thomas B. Essay on Frederic the Great. LC 73-137257. Repr. of 1893 ed. 8.50 (ISBN 0-404-04100-0). AMS Pr.
Mitford, Nancy. Frederick the Great. LC 73-116435. (Illus.). 1970. 20.00 (ISBN 0-06-012986-7, HarpT). Har-Row.
Reddaway, William. Frederick the Great & the Rise of Prussia. LC 68-25262. (Studies in German Literature, No. 13). 1969. Repr. of 1904 ed. lib. bdg. 37.95 (ISBN 0-8383-0232-7). Haskell.
Reddaway, William F. Frederick the Great & the Rise of Prussia. Repr. of 1904 ed. lib. bdg. 15.75x (ISBN 0-8371-1974-X, REFG). Greenwood.
--Frederick the Great & the Rise of Prussia. 1904. Repr. 75.00 (ISBN 0-403-00037-8). Scholarly.
Reiners, Ludwig. Frederick the Great. 1960. 13.95 (ISBN 0-85496-251-4). Dufour.
Ritter, Gerhard. Frederick the Great: A Historical Profile. Paret, Peter, tr. & intro. by. 1968. 19.50x (ISBN 0-520-01074-4); pap. 5.95x (ISBN 0-520-02775-2). U of Cal Pr.
Simon, Edith. The Making of Frederick the Great. LC 76-51768. (Illus.). 1977. Repr. of 1963 ed. lib. bdg. 20.25x (ISBN 0-8371-9440-7, SIMF). Greenwood.
Temperly, H. W. Frederick the Great & Kaiser Joseph. 2nd ed. (Illus.). 274p. 1968. 24.00x (ISBN 0-7146-1518-8, F Cass Co). Biblio Dist.
Tuttle, Herbert. History of Prussia, 4 Vols. LC 76-140031. Repr. of 1896 ed. 17.50 ea. Vol. 1 (ISBN 0-404-06671-2). Vol. 2 (ISBN 0-404-06672-0). Vol. 3 (ISBN 0-404-06673-9). Vol. 4 (ISBN 0-404-06674-7). Set. 70.00 (ISBN 0-404-06670-4). AMS Pr.

FRIEDRICH 2ND, DER GROSSE, KING OF PRUSSIA, 1712-1786-FICTION

Frank, Bruno. Days of the King. Lowe-Porter, H. T., tr. LC 75-121550. (Short Story Index Reprint Ser). 1927. 12.00 (ISBN 0-8369-3506-3). Arno.

FRIEDRICH WILHELM, ELECTOR OF BRANDENBURG, CALLED THE GREAT ELECTOR, 1620-1688

Maurice, Charles E. Life of Frederick William the Great Elector of Brandenburg. LC 81-2946. (Illus.). 191p. 1981. Repr. of 1926 ed. lib. bdg. 22.50x (ISBN 0-313-23069-2, MAFW). Greenwood.

FRIEL, BRIAN

Maxwell, D. E. S. Brian Friel. LC 76-125299. (Irish Writers Ser.). 110p. 1973. 4.50 (ISBN 0-8387-7753-8); pap. 1.95 (ISBN 0-8387-7666-3). Bucknell U Pr.

FRIEND FAMILY

Olsen, Evelyn G. Indian Blood. (Illus.). 1967. 10.00 (ISBN 0-87012-047-6). McClain.

FRIENDLINESS

see Friendship

FRIENDLY SOCIETIES

Baernreither, Joseph M. English Associations of Working Men. Taylor, A., tr. LC 66-28040. 1966. Repr. of 1889 ed. 26.00 (ISBN 0-8103-3078-4). Gale.
Beveridge, William H. & Wells, Alan F., eds. The Evidence for Voluntary Action, Being Memoranda by Organisations & Individuals & Other Materials Relevant to Voluntary Action. LC 78-5650. (Illus.). 1978. Repr. of 1949 ed. lib. bdg. 24.00x (ISBN 0-313-20485-3, BEEV). Greenwood.
Ferguson, Charles W. Fifty Million Brothers: A Panorama of American Lodges & Clubs. LC 71-125596. 1979. Repr. of 1937 ed. lib. bdg. 23.50x (ISBN 0-8371-5188-0, FMB&). Greenwood.
Friendly Societies: Seventeen Ninety-Eight to Eighteen Thirty-Nine. LC 72-2528. (British Labour Struggles Before 1850 Ser). (7 pamphlets). 1972. 10.00 (ISBN 0-405-04421-6). Arno.
Pratt, John T. The Law Relating to Friendly Societies. Berkowitz, David S. & Thorne, Samuel E., eds. LC 77-86656. (Classics of English Legal History in the Modern Era Ser.: Vol. 40). 160p. 1979. lib. bdg. 40.00 (ISBN 0-8240-3089-3). Garland Pub.
Schmidt, Alvin J. Fraternal Organizations. LC 79-6187. (Greenwood Encyclopedia of American Institutions). xxxiii, 410p. 1980. lib. bdg. 35.00 (ISBN 0-313-21436-0, SFR/). Greenwood.
Silverman, Phyllis R. Mutual Help Groups: Organization & Development. LC 80-22341. (Sage Human Services Guides: Vol. 16). 144p. 1980. pap. 8.00 (ISBN 0-8039-1519-5). Sage.

FRIENDLY VISITING

see also Social Case Work

Cabot, Richard C. Social Work: Essays on the Meeting-Ground of Doctor & Social Worker. LC 76-180561. (Medicine & Society in America Ser). 224p. 1972. Repr. of 1919 ed. 12.00 (ISBN 0-405-03940-9). Arno.
Richmond, Mary E. Friendly Visiting Among the Poor, a Handbook for Charity Workers. LC 69-16244. (Criminology, Law Enforcement, & Social Problems Ser.: No. 92). (With intro. added). 1969. Repr. of 1899 ed. 10.00 (ISBN 0-87585-092-8). Patterson Smith.

FRIENDS, SOCIETY OF

see also Inner Light; Seekers (Sect)

Applegarth, Albert C. Quakers in Pennsylvania. Repr. of 1892 ed. pap. 7.00 (ISBN 0-384-01765-7). Johnson Repr.
--Quakers in Pennsylvania. LC 78-63813. (Johns Hopkins University. Studies in the Social Sciences. Tenth Ser. 1892: 8-9). Repr. of 1892 ed. 11.50 (ISBN 0-404-61076-5). AMS Pr.
Battey, Thomas C. The Life & Adventures of a Quaker Among the Indians. 339p. 1972. Repr. of 1875 ed. 12.50 (ISBN 0-87928-025-5). Corner Hse.
Braithwaite, William C. The Beginnings of Quakerism. (Illus.). 562p. 1981. Repr. of 1923 ed. lib. bdg. 65.00 (ISBN 0-8495-0625-5). Arden Lib.
Brinton, Anna, ed. Then & Now. facs. ed. LC 72-128214. (Essay Index Reprint Ser). 1960. 19.50 (ISBN 0-8369-1905-X). Arno.
Brinton, Howard. Ethical Mysticism in the Society of Friends. LC 67-31429. (Orig.). 1967. pap. 0.70x (ISBN 0-87574-156-8). Pendle Hill.
Brinton, Howard H. Guide to Quaker Practice. LC 43-11899. (Orig.). 1943. pap. 1.75 (ISBN 0-87574-020-0). Pendle Hill.
--How They Became Friends. LC 61-12670. (Orig.). 1961. pap. 0.70x (ISBN 0-87574-114-2). Pendle Hill.
--Meeting House & Farm House. LC 72-80096. (Orig.). 1972. pap. 0.70x (ISBN 0-87574-185-1). Pendle Hill.
--Quaker Doctrine of Inward Peace. LC 64-23230. (Orig.). 1948. pap. 0.95 (ISBN 0-87574-044-8). Pendle Hill.
--Quaker Journals: Varieties of Religious Experience Among Friends. LC 78-188399. (Illus., Orig.). 1972. 4.75 (ISBN 0-87574-952-6). Pendle Hill.
Bronner, Edwin B. Quakerism & Christianity. LC 67-18689. (Orig.). 1967. pap. 0.70x (ISBN 0-87574-152-5). Pendle Hill.
Carroll, Kenneth. Quakerism on the Eastern Shore. LC 70-112986. (Illus.). 1970. 12.50x (ISBN 0-938420-15-1). Md Hist.
Cartland, Fernando G. Southern Heroes, or the Friends in Wartime. Bd. with Conscript Quakers. Foster, Ethan. (Library of War & Peace; Conscrip. & Cons. Object.). lib. bdg. 38.00 (ISBN 0-8240-0424-8). Garland Pub.
Dubois, Rachel D. Deepening Quaker Faith & Practice: Through the Use of Three-Session Quaker Dialogue. (Illus.). 56p. 1976. pap. 1.50 (ISBN 0-913408-22-0). Friends United.
Elliott, Errol T. Life Unfolding. LC 75-9806. 172p. 1975. pap. 4.95 (ISBN 0-913408-17-4). Friends United.
Ferguson, Henry. Essays in American History. LC 68-26266. 1969. Repr. of 1894 ed. 12.00 (ISBN 0-8046-0144-5). Kennikat.
Foulds, Elfrida V. The Story of Quakerism. LC 55-15148. Repr. of 1954 ed. lib. bdg. 17.00x (ISBN 0-8371-9171-8, FOSQ). Greenwood.
Frost, William J. The Quaker Family in Colonial America. (Griffin Paperback Ser). 1973. 17.95 (ISBN 0-312-65765-X); pap. 6.95 (ISBN 0-312-65800-1). St Martin.
Gorman, George. The Society of Friends. 1978. pap. 2.90 (ISBN 0-08-021412-6). Pergamon.
Gummere, Amelia M. Quaker: A Study in Costume. LC 68-56494. (Illus.). 1968. Repr. of 1901 ed. 18.00 (ISBN 0-405-08585-0, Blom Pubns). Arno.
Gurney, Joseph J. A Peculiar People: The Rediscovery of Primitive Christianity. LC 79-50100. 1979. pap. 11.95 (ISBN 0-913408-48-4). Friends United.

Hancock, Thomas. Principles of Peace: Exemplified by the Conduct of the Society of Friends in Ireland, 1798. LC 70-147620. (Library of War & Peace; Non-Resis. & Non-Vio.). lib. bdg. 38.00 (ISBN 0-8240-0377-2). Garland Pub.
Hilty, Hiram H. Friends in Cuba. (Illus.). 1977. pap. 4.95 (ISBN 0-913408-33-6). Friends United.
Hinshaw, William W. Encyclopedia of American Quaker Genealogy, 6 vols. Incl. Vol. 1. North Carolina Yearly Meeting. 1185p. (Includes supplement by Thomas W. Marshall). 1978. Repr. of 1948 ed. 50.00 (ISBN 0-8063-0178-3); Vol. 3. New York Monthly Meetings. 540p. 1969. Repr. of 1940 ed. 30.00 (ISBN 0-8063-0180-5); Vols. 4 & 5. Ohio. Marshall, Thomas W., ed. 1973. Repr. of 1946 ed. Vol. 4. 60.00 (ISBN 0-8063-0548-7); Vol. 5. 50.00 (ISBN 0-8063-0549-5); Vol. 6. Virginia. Marshall, Thomas W., ed. 1973. Repr. of 1950 ed. LC 68-31728. 1969. Genealog Pub.
Hintz, Howard W. Quaker Influence in American Literature. Repr. of 1940 ed. lib. bdg. 15.00 (ISBN 0-8371-3945-7, HIGA). Greenwood.
Hull, William I. William Penn & the Dutch Quaker Migration to Pennsylvania. LC 79-112826. (Swarthmore College Monographs on Quaker History: No. 2). 1970. Repr. of 1935 ed. 18.50 (ISBN 0-8063-0432-4). Genealog Pub.
Hutchinson, Dorothy. Unless One Is Born Anew. LC 65-26994. (Orig.). 1965. pap. 0.70x (ISBN 0-87574-143-6). Pendle Hill.
James, Sydney V. People Among Peoples: Quaker Benevolence in Eighteenth Century America. LC 62-20248. (Center for the Study of the History of Liberty in America Ser). 1963. 20.00x (ISBN 0-674-66050-1). Harvard U Pr.
Jones, Rufus M. The Faith & Practice of the Quakers. 181p. 1980. pap. 3.95 (ISBN 0-913408-57-3). Friends United.
Jones, Thomas E. Light on the Horizon: The Quaker Pilgrimage of Tom Jones. LC 74-14286. 200p. 1973. 3.95 (ISBN 0-913408-13-1). Friends United.
Jorns, Auguste. Quakers As Pioneers in Social Work. LC 68-8232. 1969. Repr. of 1931 ed. 12.50 (ISBN 0-8046-0244-1). Kennikat.
--Quakers As Pioneers in Social Work. Brown, Thomas K., tr. LC 69-14934. (Criminology, Law Enforcement, & Social Problems Ser.: No. 27). 1969. Repr. of 1931 ed. 8.50 (ISBN 0-87585-027-8). Patterson Smith.
Kavanaugh, John, ed. Quaker Approach to Contemporary Problems. Repr. of 1953 ed. lib. bdg. 15.00x (ISBN 0-8371-4432-9, KAGA). Greenwood.
Kenworthy, Leonard S. Quakerism: A Study Guide on the Religious Society of Friends. LC 81-80656. 224p. 1981. pap. 5.00 (ISBN 0-932970-21-4). Prinit Pr.
--Sixteen Quaker Leaders Speak. LC 79-50101. 1979. pap. 2.95 (ISBN 0-913408-49-2). Friends United.
Laughlin, Sceva B., ed. Beyond Dilemmas. LC 79-86035. (Essay & General Literature Index Reprint Ser). 1969. Repr. of 1937 ed. 13.50 (ISBN 0-8046-0567-X). Kennikat.
Loukes, Harold. Quaker Contribution. 1965. 2.95 (ISBN 0-02-575280-4). Macmillan.
Maurer, Herrymon, ed. Pendle Hill Reader. facsimile ed. LC 74-142668. (Essay Index Reprint Ser). Repr. of 1950 ed. 16.00 (ISBN 0-8369-2415-0). Arno.
Mekeel, Arhtur J. The Relation of the Quakers to the American Revolution. LC 79-66173. 1979. pap. text ed. 12.50 (ISBN 0-8191-0792-1). U Pr of Amer.
Nevaskar, Balwant S. Capitalists Without Capitalism: The Jains of India & the Quakers of the West. LC 72-98709. (Contributions in Sociology: No. 6). 1971. lib. bdg. 14.00 (ISBN 0-8371-3297-5, NCA/). Greenwood.
Newby, James R. Reflections from the Light of Christ: 5 Quaker Classics. LC 80-7477. 126p. 1980. 6.95 (ISBN 0-913408-55-7). Friends United.
Peck, George. Simplicity: A Rich Quaker's View. LC 72-97851. (Orig.). 1973. pap. 0.70x (ISBN 0-87574-189-4). Pendle Hill.
Penn, W. Select Works, 3 Vols. 4th ed. Fothergill, J., ed. LC 73-154550. Repr. of 1825 ed. Set. 66.00 (ISBN 0-527-70550-0). Kraus Repr.
Penn, William, et al. Quaker Classics in Brief: Penn, Barclay, & Penington. Brinton, Anna C., et al, eds. LC 78-57741. 153p. 1978. pap. 2.75 (ISBN 0-87574-904-6). Pendle Hill.
Proud, Robert. The History of Pennsylvania, 2 Vols. LC 66-25101. 1967. Repr. of 1797 ed. 20.00 ea. Vol. 1 (ISBN 0-87152-031-1). Vol. 2 (ISBN 0-87152-032-X). Set. 40.00 (ISBN 0-87152-305-1). Reprint.
Steere, Douglas V. Prayer & Worship. LC 78-70480. 1978. pap. 2.50 (ISBN 0-913408-44-1). Friends United.
Sykes, Marjorie. Quakers in India. (Illus.). 176p. 1980. pap. 12.95 (ISBN 0-04-275003-2). Allen Unwin.
Watkins, Owen. The Puritan Experience: Studies in Spiritual Autobiography. LC 70-150987. 1972. 12.00x (ISBN 0-8052-3425-X). Schocken.
Weeks, Stephen B. Southern Quakers & Slavery: A Study in Institutional History. LC 78-64260. (Johns Hopkins University. Studies in the Social Sciences. Extra Volumes: 15). Repr. of 1896 ed. 31.00 (ISBN 0-404-61363-2). AMS Pr.
Woody, Thomas. Quaker Education in the Colony & State of New Jersey. LC 76-89256. (American Education: Its Men, Institutions & Ideas, Ser. 1). 1969. Repr. of 1923 ed. 29.00 (ISBN 0-405-01494-5). Arno.
Woolman, John. The Journal of John Woolman. 256p. 1972. pap. 4.95 (ISBN 0-8065-0294-0). Citadel Pr.
--Journal of John Woolman & a Plea for the Poor. 7.00 (ISBN 0-8446-0297-3). Peter Smith.
Wright, Luella M. Literary Life of the Early Friends, 1650-1725. LC 32-25426. Repr. of 1932 ed. 19.50 (ISBN 0-404-07046-9). AMS Pr.
Yarrow, C. H. Quaker Experiences in International Conciliation. LC 78-7415. 1978. 15.00x (ISBN 0-300-02260-3). Yale U Pr.
Yolen, Jane. Friend: The Story of George Fox & the Quakers. LC 74-171865. 192p. (gr. 6 up). 1972. 6.95 (ISBN 0-395-28932-7, Clarion). HM.
Young, Mildred B. The Candle, the Lantern, the Daylight. LC 61-15103. (Orig.). 1961. pap. 0.70x (ISBN 0-87574-116-9). Pendle Hill.
Yungblut, John. Quakerism of the Future: Mystical, Prophetic & Evangelical. LC 74-81830. (Orig.). 1974. pap. 0.70x (ISBN 0-87574-194-0). Pendle Hill.

FRIENDS, SOCIETY OF-AMERICAN FRIENDS SERVICE COMMITTEE

Jones, Mary H. Swords into Ploughshares. LC 70-109757. (Illus.). 1971. Repr. of 1937 ed. lib. bdg. 16.75x (ISBN 0-8371-4247-4, JOSP). Greenwood.
Wilson, Raymond E. Uphill for Peace. LC 77-29428. 1974. 7.95 (ISBN 0-913408-16-6). Friends United.

FRIENDS, SOCIETY OF-BIBLIOGRAPHY

Smith, J. Bibliotheca Anti-Quakeriana, & Bibliotheca Quakeristica, 2 vols. in 1. 1873-1883. 22.00 (ISBN 0-527-84060-2). Kraus Repr.
--Descriptive Catalogue of Friends' Books, 3 Vols. with Suppl. LC 1-10200. 1867-1893. Set. 102.00 (ISBN 0-527-84100-5). Kraus Repr.
Swathmore College. Catalog of the Friends Historical Library Book & Serial Collection, Swathmore College. 1981. lib. bdg. cancelled (ISBN 0-8161-0376-3). G K Hall.

FRIENDS, SOCIETY OF-BIOGRAPHY

Best, Mary A. Rebel Saints. facs. ed. LC 68-55839. (Essay Index Reprint Ser). 1925. 16.00 (ISBN 0-8369-0205-X). Arno.
Brinton, Anna C. Quaker Profiles: Silhouettes 1750-1850. LC 64-8697. (Illus., Orig.). 1964. pap. 1.50 (ISBN 0-87574-902-X). Pendle Hill.
Chalkley, Thomas. The Journal of Thomas Chalkley. LC 75-31088. (Incl. a collection of author's works). Repr. of 1808 ed. 45.00 (ISBN 0-404-13506-4). AMS Pr.
Dalglish, Doris N. People Called Quakers. facsimile ed. LC 78-90628. (Essay Index Reprint Ser). 1938. 15.00 (ISBN 0-8369-1254-3). Arno.
Deutsch, Alfred D., ed. Journal of William Edmundson. LC 74-6439. 1974. pap. 1.00 (ISBN 0-913408-11-5). Friends United.
Elliot, Errol T. Quaker Profiles from the American West. LC 72-5126. 1972. pap. 2.95 (ISBN 0-913408-05-0). Friends United.
Raistrick, Arthur. Quakers in Science & Industry. LC 68-18641. (Illus.). Repr. of 1950 ed. 17.50x (ISBN 0-678-05622-6). Kelley.
Wahl, Albert J. Jessie Herman Holmes. LC 79-63127. text ed. 10.95 (ISBN 0-913408-50-6). Friends United.

FRIENDS, SOCIETY OF-DOCTRINAL AND CONTROVERSIAL WORKS

Brinton, Howard. Light & Life in the Fourth Gospel. LC 76-128679. (Orig.). 1971. pap. 0.70x (ISBN 0-87574-179-7). Pendle Hill.
Brinton, Howard H. Evolution & the Inward Light. LC 77-137101. (Orig.). 1970. pap. 0.70x (ISBN 0-87574-173-8). Pendle Hill.
Broyn, Severyn. Quaker Testimonies & Economic Alternatives. LC 80-80915. 35p. pap. 1.25 (ISBN 0-87574-231-9). Pendle Hill.
Evans, William & Evans, Thomas, eds. The Friends' Library: Comprising Journals, Doctrinal Treatises & Other Writings of the Members of the Religious Society of Friends, 14 vols. Repr. of 1850 ed. 595.00 set (ISBN 0-404-07100-7); 42.50 ea. AMS Pr.
Fox, George. The Works of George Fox, Vols. 1-8. Incl. Vols. 1 & 2. A Journal or Historical Account of the Life, Travels, Sufferings, Christian Experiences & Labour of Love in the Work of the Ministry, of That Ancient, Eminent, & Faithful Servant of Jesus Christ, George Fox. LC 75-16194. Vol. 1 (ISBN 0-404-09351-5). Vol. 2 (ISBN 0-404-09352-3); Vol. 3. The Great Mystery of the Great Whore Unfolded. LC 75-16195. 616p (ISBN 0-404-09353-1); Vols. 4-6. Gospel Truth Demonstrated, in a Collection of Doctrinal Books, Given Forth by That Faithful Minister of Jesus Christ, George Fox. LC 75-16199. Vol. 4 (ISBN 0-404-09354-X). Vol. 5 (ISBN 0-404-09355-8). Vol. 6 (ISBN 0-404-09356-6); Vols. 7 & 8. A Collection of Many Select & Christian Epistles, Letters & Testimonies. LC 75-16207. Vol. 7 (ISBN 0-404-09357-4). Vol. 8 (ISBN 0-404-09358-2). Repr. of 1831 ed. Set. 260.00 (ISBN 0-404-09350-7); 32.50 ea. AMS Pr.
Frost, William J. The Quaker Origins of Antislavery. LC 79-11744. (Illus.). 303p. 1979. lib. bdg. 25.00 (ISBN 0-8482-3961-X). Norwood Edns.
Hall, Francis B. Quaker Worship in North America. LC 79-53170. 1979. pap. 4.95 (ISBN 0-913408-53-0). Friends United.
Silcock, Thomas H. Words & Testimonies. LC 72-80097. (Orig.). 1972. pap. 0.70x (ISBN 0-87574-186-X). Pendle Hill.
Ullmann, Richard K. Between God & History: The Human Situation Exemplified in Quaker Thought & Practice. 1959. text ed. 5.25x (ISBN 0-391-01957-0). Humanities.
Wilson, Dan. An Opening Way. LC 61-11637. (Orig.). 1961. pap. 0.70x (ISBN 0-87574-113-4). Pendle Hill.

FRIENDS, SOCIETY OF-EDUCATION

Brinton, Howard. The Pendle Hill Idea. LC 50-11234. (Orig.). 1950. pap. 1.25 (ISBN 0-87574-055-3). Pendle Hill.
Brinton, Howard H. Quaker Education in Theory & Practice. rev. ed. LC 58-12843. (Orig.). 1940. pap. 6.75 (ISBN 0-87574-009-X). Pendle Hill.
Castle, David. Toward Caring: People Building in the Family. 1973. pap. 1.00 (ISBN 0-913408-09-3). Friends United.
Heath, Douglas. Why a Friends School. LC 75-81158. (Orig.). 1969. pap. 0.70x (ISBN 0-87574-164-9). Pendle Hill.
Hinshaw, Ed & Adams, Charlie. Toward Caring: Cases & Letters for Dialogue. 1972. pap. 1.00 (ISBN 0-913408-04-2). Friends United.
Hole, Helen. Things Civil & Useful. LC 78-60560. 1978. 7.95 (ISBN 0-913408-40-9). Friends United.
Homan, Walter J. Children & Quakerism. LC 70-169387. (Family in America Ser). 180p. 1972. Repr. of 1939 ed. 12.00 (ISBN 0-405-03864-X). Arno.
Loukes, Harold. Friends & Their Children: A Study in Quaker Education. LC 79-12928. 1979. Repr. of 1958 ed. lib. bdg. 15.00x (ISBN 0-313-21150-7, LOFT). Greenwood.
Stewart, W. A. Quakers & Education. LC 76-115330. 1971. Repr. of 1953 ed. 12.50 (ISBN 0-8046-1121-1). Kennikat.
Wilcox, Wilma M. Quaker Volunteer: An Experience in Palestine. LC 77-80232. (Illus.). 1977. pap. 2.50 (ISBN 0-913408-34-4). Friends United.
Woody, Thomas. Early Quaker Education in Pennsylvania. LC 72-89255. (American Education: Its Men, Institutions & Ideas, Ser. 1). 1969. Repr. of 1920 ed. 15.50 (ISBN 0-405-01493-7). Arno.
--Early Quaker Education in Pennsylvania. LC 77-177623. (Columbia University. Teachers College. Contributions to Education: No. 105). Repr. of 1920 ed. 17.50 (ISBN 0-404-55105-X). AMS Pr.

FRIENDS, SOCIETY OF-FICTION, JUVENILE

Vernon, Louise A. Key to the Prison. LC 86-11054. (Illus.). (gr. 4-9). 1968. 2.95 (ISBN 0-8361-1813-8). Herald Pr.

FRIENDS, SOCIETY OF-HISTORY

Bacon, Margaret H. As the Way Opens: The Story of Quaker Women in America. LC 80-67786. 1980. pap. 8.95 (ISBN 0-913408-58-1). Friends United.
--Quiet Rebels: The Story of the Quakers in America. 1969. 12.50x (ISBN 0-465-06790-5). Basic.
Benjamin, Philip S. The Philadelphia Quakers in the Industrial Age, 1865-1920. LC 75-22967. 309p. 1976. 19.50x (ISBN 0-87722-086-7). Temple U Pr.
Best, Mary A. Rebel Saints. facs. ed. LC 68-55839. (Essay Index Reprint Ser). 1925. 16.00 (ISBN 0-8369-0205-X). Arno.
Bowden, James. The History of the Society of Friends in America, 2 vols. in 1. LC 73-38440. (Religion in America, Ser. 2). 870p. 1972. Repr. of 1854 ed. 44.00 (ISBN 0-405-04061-X). Arno.
--The History of the Society of Friends in America. 1976. Repr. of 1850 ed. 33.00 (ISBN 0-685-70604-4, Regency). Scholarly.
Brinton, Howard H. Friends for Three Hundred Years. LC 52-5424. (Orig.). 1965. pap. 3.00 (ISBN 0-87574-903-8). Pendle Hill.
--The Religious Philosophy of Quakerism. LC 73-80041. 1979. pap. 2.75 (ISBN 0-87574-953-4, 953). Pendle Hill.
Brock, Peter. Pioneers of the Peaceable Kingdom: The Quaker Peace Testimony from the Colonial Era to the First World War. pap. 8.95 (ISBN 0-691-00573-7). Princeton U Pr.
Bronner, Edwin B. English View of American Quakerism. LC 71-107345. (Memoirs Ser., Vol. 79). (Illus.). 1970. pap. 3.50 (ISBN 0-87169-079-9). Am Philos.
Elkinton, Russell J. & Clark, Robert A. The Quaker Heritage in Medicine. (Illus.). 1978. pap. 3.95 (ISBN 0-910286-68-X). Boxwood.
Elliot, Errol T. Quakers on the American Frontier. 1969. 4.95 (ISBN 0-913408-00-X). Friends United.
Endy, Melvin. William Penn & Early Quakerism. LC 72-7798. 420p. 1973. 29.50x (ISBN 0-691-07190-X). Princeton U Pr.
Gorman, George. The Society of Friends. 1978. pap. 2.90 (ISBN 0-08-021412-6). Pergamon.
Gragg, Larry D. Migration in Early America: The Virginia Quaker Experience. (Studies in American History & Culture III: No. 13). 133p. 1980. 24.95 (ISBN 0-8357-1095-5, Pub. by UMI Res Pr). Univ Microfilms.
Hall. Long Road to Freedom. LC 78-60562. 1978. pap. 6.50 (ISBN 0-913408-41-7). Friends United.
Hirst, Margaret E. The Quakers in Peace & War: An Account of Their Peace Principles & Practice. LC 73-137545. (Peace Movement in America Ser). 560p. 1972. Repr. of 1923 ed. lib. bdg. 26.95x (ISBN 0-89198-073-3). Ozer.
Jones, Rufus M. The Later Periods of Quakerism, 2 vols. LC 74-109758. 1921. Repr. Set. lib. bdg. 41.50x (ISBN 0-8371-4248-2, JOQU). Greenwood.
Lloyd, Arnold. Quaker Social History: Sixteen Sixty-Nine to Seventeen Thirty-Eight. LC 79-4398. 1979. Repr. of 1950 ed. lib. bdg. 19.50x (ISBN 0-313-20943-X, LLQU). Greenwood.
Myers, Albert C. Immigration of the Irish Quakers into Pennsylvania, 1682-1750, with Their Early History in Ireland. LC 77-92027. (Illus.). 1969. Repr. of 1902 ed. 17.50 (ISBN 0-8063-0252-6). Genealog Pub.
--Quaker Arrivals at Philadelphia, 1682-1750. LC 70-77321. 1978. Repr. of 1902 ed. 9.50 (ISBN 0-8063-0253-4). Genealog Pub.
Penn, William. The Rise & Progress of the People Called Quakers. 1977. pap. 2.95 (ISBN 0-913408-32-8). Friends United.
Pringle, Cyrus. Civil War Diary of Cyrus Pringle: Record of Quaker Conscience. LC 62-18328. Orig. Title: Record of a Quaker Conscience. (Orig.). 1962. pap. 0.70x (ISBN 0-87574-122-3). Pendle Hill.
Reynolds, Reginald. The Wisdom of John Woolman: With a Selection from His Writings As a Guide to the Seekers of Today. LC 79-8724. xii, 178p. 1981. Repr. of 1948 ed. lib. bdg. 22.50x (ISBN 0-313-22190-1, REJW). Greenwood.
Russell, Elbert. History of Quakerism. LC 79-53169. 612p. 1980. pap. 14.95 (ISBN 0-913408-52-2). Friends United.
Simkin, Robert L. & Simkin, Margaret. Letters from Szechwan. 1978. text ed. 8.95 (ISBN 0-914064-08-8); pap. text ed. 6.95 (ISBN 0-914064-09-6). Celo Pr.
The Story of Quakerism. rev. ed. LC 77-71638. (Illus.). 1977. pap. 5.95 (ISBN 0-913408-31-X). Friends United.
Tolles, Frederick. Quakers & the Atlantic Culture. 1980. Repr. of 1960 ed. lib. bdg. 14.00x (ISBN 0-374-97949-9). Octagon.
Tolles, Frederick B. Meeting House & Counting House. (Illus.). 1963. pap. 4.95 (ISBN 0-393-00211-X, Norton Lib). Norton.
Trueblood, D. Elton. People Called Quakers. LC 66-15046. 1971. pap. 5.95 (ISBN 0-913408-02-6). Friends United.
Weeks, Stephen B. Southern Quakers & Slavery: A Study in Institutional History. 1968. Repr. of 1896 ed. text ed. 22.50x (ISBN 0-87503-004-1). Humanities.
Wilson, Robert H. Philadelphia Quakers, Sixteen Eighty-One to Nineteen Eighty-One. (Illus.). 136p. 1981. 14.95 (ISBN 0-916838-45-5); pap. 6.95 (ISBN 0-916838-46-3). Schiffer.
Worrall, Arthur J. Quakers in the Colonial Northeast. LC 79-63086. 248p. 1980. text ed. 15.00 (ISBN 0-87451-174-7). U Pr of New Eng.

FRIENDS, SOCIETY OF-SERMONS

Jones, Rufus M. Thou Dost Open up My Life. LC 63-11819. (Orig.). 1963. pap. 0.70x (ISBN 0-87574-127-4). Pendle Hill.
Tuke, Samuel, ed. Epistles of George Fox. LC 78-24657. 1979. pap. 2.95 (ISBN 0-913408-46-8). Friends United.

FRIENDS, SOCIETY OF-GREAT BRITAIN
Benezet, Anthony. Observations of the Enslaving, Importing & Purchasing of Negroes: With Some Advice Thereon, Extracted from the Epistle of the Yearly-Meeting of the People Called Quakers Held at London in the Year 1748. 1976. Repr. of 1760 ed. 25.00 (ISBN 0-403-06626-3, Regency). Scholarly.
Crowther-Hunt, Norman. Two Early Political Associations: The Quakers & the Dissenting Deputies in the Age of Sir Robert Walpole. LC 78-23805. 1979. Repr. of 1961 ed. lib. bdg. 18.75x (ISBN 0-313-21036-5, HUTW). Greenwood.
Raistrick, Arthur. Quakers in Science & Industry. LC 68-18641. (Illus.). Repr. of 1950 ed. 17.50x (ISBN 0-678-05622-6). Kelley.
Vann, Richard T. Social Development of English Quakerism 1655-1755. LC 79-78524. 1969. 14.00x (ISBN 0-674-81290-5). Harvard U Pr.
Wright, Luella M. Literary Life of the Early Friends, 1650-1725. LC 32-25426. Repr. of 1932 ed. 19.50 (ISBN 0-404-07046-9). AMS Pr.
FRIENDS FINDERS INSTITUTE, LOS ANGELES, CALIFORNIA
Thornton, Alice B. How Come You're Not Married. 1966. 5.95 (ISBN 0-8158-0200-5). Chris Mass.
FRIENDS OF GOD (GOTTESFREUNDE)
Jones, Rufus M. The Flowering of Mysticism: The Friends of God in the Fourteenth Century. 1971. Repr. of 1940 ed. 15.75 (ISBN 0-02-847290-X). Hafner.
Seesholtz, Anna G. Friends of God: Practical Mystics of the Fourteenth Century. 1970. Repr. of 1934 ed. 14.50 (ISBN 0-404-05697-0). AMS Pr.
FRIENDS OF THE LIBRARY
see also Library Associations
FRIENDSHIP
see also Love; Sympathy
Anderson, Colena M. Friendship's Bright Shinings. (Large Print Ser.). 1976. kivar 4.95 (ISBN 0-310-20037-7). Zondervan.
Bald, R. C. Literary Friendships in the Age of Wordsworth. 1968. lib. bdg. 17.50x (ISBN 0-374-90342-5). Octagon.
Bell, Robert R. Worlds of Friendship. (Sociological Observations Ser.: Vol. 12). 200p. 1981. 20.00 (ISBN 0-8039-1723-6); pap. 9.95 (ISBN 0-686-75129-9). Sage.
Berger, Terry. Special Friends. LC 79-13059. (Illus.). 64p. (gr. 3-5). 1979. PLB 7.97 (ISBN 0-671-33091-8). Messner.
Block, Joel. Friendship. 256p. 1981. 4.95 (ISBN 0-02-075590-2, Collier). Macmillan.
--Friendship: How to Give It, How to Get It. 1980. 10.95 (ISBN 0-02-511760-2). Macmillan.
--The Nature of Friendship. 1981. 10.00 (ISBN 0-02-511760-2). MacMillan.
Bolotin, David. Plato's Dialogue on Friendship: An Interpretation of the "Lysis," with a New Translation. LC 79-4041. 1979. 15.00x (ISBN 0-8014-1227-7). Cornell U Pr.
Bond, John, ed. Friends Search for Wholeness. LC 78-62765. 1978. pap. 8.95 (ISBN 0-913408-42-5). Friends United.
Brady, Mari. Please Remember Me. (gr. 7-9). 1978. pap. 1.50 (ISBN 0-671-56032-8). Archway.
Brenton, Myron. Friendship. LC 74-78533. 1974. 6.95 (ISBN 0-8128-1727-3). Stein & Day.
--Friendship. LC 74-78533. 1975. pap. 2.45 (ISBN 0-8128-1854-7). Stein & Day.
Briscoe, Jill. Thank You for Being a Friend. 192p. (Orig.). 1981. pap. 5.95 (ISBN 0-310-21851-9). Zondervan.
Brownlow, Leroy. Flowers of Friendship. 1974. gift ed. 4.95 (ISBN 0-915720-04-3). Brownlow Pub Co.
Carpenter, Edward. An Anthology of Friendship. 1935. lib. bdg. 40.00 (ISBN 0-8414-1553-6). Folcroft.
Crothers, Samuel M., intro. by. Book of Friendship. facsimile ed. LC 76-98079. (Granger Index Reprint Ser). 1910. 17.00 (ISBN 0-8369-6074-2). Arno.
Cumberland, Gerald. Written in Friendship. 1973. lib. bdg. 15.00 (ISBN 0-8414-2427-6). Folcroft.
Cummins, Robert. Friendship. 1972. pap. 3.25 (ISBN 0-88489-034-1). St Marys.
Dawlwy, Harold H., Jr. Friendship: How to Make & Keep Friends. (Illus.). 176p. 1980. 9.95 (ISBN 0-13-330860-X, Spec); pap. 4.95 (ISBN 0-13-330852-9). P-H.
Dear Friend. 1974. 2.95 (ISBN 0-442-82536-6). Peter Pauper.
Drier, Patricia, compiled by. The Blessings of Friendship. 1979. pap. 4.50 (ISBN 0-8378-5026-6). Gibson.
Drimmer, Frederick, compiled by. A Friend Is Someone Special. LC 75-16038. 44p. 1976. boxed 3.00 (ISBN 0-8378-2101-0). Gibson.
Duck, Steven. The Study of Acquaintance. 1977. 24.95 (ISBN 0-566-00160-8, 01085-5, Pub. by Saxon Hse England). Lexington Bks.
Emerson, Ralph W. On Love & Friendship. 2.95 (ISBN 0-442-82199-9). Peter Pauper.
Feinberg, Paul. Friends. (Illus.). 96p. 1980. pap. 5.95 (ISBN 0-8256-3184-X, Quick Fox). Music Sales.
Foot, Hugh C., et al. Friendship & Social Relations in Children. LC 79-40637. 1980. 56.25 (ISBN 0-471-27628-6, Pub. by Wiley-Interscience). Wiley.
Francis, Mary. But I Have Called You Friends. 1974. 4.95 (ISBN 0-8199-0500-3). Franciscan Herald.
Friendship Is Forever. 1978. 2.95 (ISBN 0-442-82584-6). Peter Pauper.
Gift of Friendship. (Gifts of Gold Ser.). 1970. 3.50 (ISBN 0-442-82483-1). Peter Pauper.
Gould, Shirley. Challenge of Friendship: Helping Your Child Become a Friend. 124p. 1981. 16.95 (ISBN 0-8015-1172-0, Hawthorn). Dutton.
Hall, Manly P. Friendship, Love & Beauty. pap. 2.00 (ISBN 0-89314-301-4). Philos Res.
Hallinan, P. K. That's What a Friend Is. 32p. (gr. k-6). 1981. pap. 2.50 (ISBN 0-8249-8006-9). Ideals.
Hay, Gilbert. Friendship Is... 1970. pap. 1.00 (ISBN 0-671-10458-6, Fireside). S&S.
Hearn, Janice W. Making Friends, Keeping Friends. LC 78-22231. 1979. 7.95 (ISBN 0-385-14900-X, Galilee). Doubleday.
Heart of a Friend. 2.95 (ISBN 0-442-82251-0). Peter Pauper.
Hinnebusch, Paul. Friendship in the Lord. LC 73-90411. 144p. 1974. pap. 2.25 (ISBN 0-87793-065-1). Ave Maria.
Hutter, Horst. Politics As Friendship: The Origins of Classical Notions of Politics in the Theory & Practce of Friendship. 204p. 1978. text ed. 12.75 (ISBN 0-88920-067-X, Pub. by Laurier U Pr Canada). Humanities.
Inrig, Gary. Quality Friendship. 192p. (Orig.). 1981. pap. 2.95 (ISBN 0-8024-2891-6). Moody.
James, Muriel & Savary, Louis. The Heart of Friendship. LC 74-25702. 1978. pap. 4.95 (ISBN 0-06-064113-4, RD 254, HarpR). Har-Row.
Kiesling, Christopher. Celibacy, Prayer & Friendship: A Making-Sense-Out-of-Life Approach. LC 77-25084. 1978. pap. 5.95 (ISBN 0-8189-0365-1). Alba.
Krahn, Fernando. The Great Ape. LC 78-9053. (Illus.). (gr. k-3). 1978. 5.95 (ISBN 0-670-34840-6, Co-Pub by Kestrel Bks). Viking Pr.
Leefeldt, Christine & Callenbach, Ernest. The Art of Friendship. 1980. pap. 2.75 (ISBN 0-425-04674-5). Berkley Pub.
--The Art of Friendship. LC 79-1893. 1979. 8.95 (ISBN 0-394-50460-7). Pantheon.
Lepp, Ignace. Ways of Friendship. 1968. 8.95 (ISBN 0-02-570410-9). Macmillan.
Malone, John. Straight Women-Gay Men: A Special Relationship. 1980. 8.95 (ISBN 0-8037-8174-1). Dial.
Meilaender, Gilbert. Friendship: A Study in Theological Ethics. LC 81-50459. 128p. 1981. text ed. 9.95 (ISBN 0-268-00956-2). U of Notre Dame Pr.
Miller, E. Lorraine. Friendship. LC 77-79105. (Aware Bear Ser.). (Illus.). 1977. 3.50 (ISBN 0-89566-000-8). Miller Ent.
Nash, Bruce. So, You Think You Know Your Best Friend? Schneider, Meg, ed. 32p. (Orig.). (gr. 3-7). 1981. pap. 1.95 (ISBN 0-671-44428-X). Wanderer Bks.
Naylor, Phyllis R. Getting Along with Your Friends. LC 79-22999. (Illus.). (gr. 4-7). 1980. 6.95g (ISBN 0-687-14122-2). Abingdon.
Nekrasov, A. Friends. (Illus.). 55p. 1977. 2.50 (ISBN 0-8285-1146-2, Pub. by Progress Pubs Russia). Imported Pubns.
O'Dell, William F. How to Make Lifetime Friends with Peers & Parents. 1978. 5.50 (ISBN 0-682-49093-8, Banner). Exposition.
Ogilvie, Lloyd J. The Beauty of Friendship. LC 80-80463. 1980. pap. 4.95 (ISBN 0-89081-243-8). Harvest Hse.
On Friendship. 1970. 2.95 (ISBN 0-442-82357-6). Peter Pauper.
Oxenbury, Helen. Friends. (Baby Board Bks.). (Illus.). 14p. (ps). 1981. boards 3.50 (ISBN 0-671-42111-5, Little Simon). S&S.
Ransome, Arthur. The Book of Friendship: Anthology. 40.00 (ISBN 0-686-18754-7). Scholars Ref Lib.
Reader, Dennis J. Coming Back Alive. LC 79-5147. (Illus.). 256p. (gr. 7 up). 1981. 8.95 (ISBN 0-394-84359-2); PLB 8.99 (ISBN 0-394-94359-7). Random.
Reisman, John M. Anatomy of Friendship. 1981. pap. 6.95 (ISBN 0-86616-004-3). Greene.
--Anatomy of Friendship. LC 79-12857. 1979. 14.50 (ISBN 0-89197-646-9). Irvington.
Richards, Arlene K. & Willis, Irene. Boy Friends, Girl Friends, Just Friends. LC 78-14257. (gr. 7 up). 1979. 7.95 (ISBN 0-689-30695-4). Atheneum.
Ripple, Paula. Called to Be Friends. LC 80-67402. 160p. (Orig.). 1980. pap. 3.95 (ISBN 0-87793-212-3). Ave Maria.
Ross, Pat. Meet M & M. LC 79-190. (I Am Reading Bks.). (Illus.). 48p. (gr. 1-4). 1980. 4.95 (ISBN 0-394-84184-0); PLB 5.99 (ISBN 0-394-94184-5). Pantheon.
Rubin, Zick. Children's Friendship. (Developing Child Ser.). 150p. 1980. 8.95x (ISBN 0-674-11618-6); pap. 3.95 (ISBN 0-674-11619-4). Harvard U Pr.
Schutz, Susan P., ed. The Language of Friendship. LC 74-29431. (Illus.). 64p. (Orig.). 1975. pap. 3.95 (ISBN 0-88396-010-9). Blue Mtn Pr CO.
Scoby, Joan & McGrath, Lee P. What Is a Friend. 1971. pap. 1.95 (ISBN 0-671-10539-6, Fireside). S&S.
Smith, Charles G. Spenser's Theory of Friendship. 1939. lib. bdg. 11.00 (ISBN 0-8414-1579-X). Folcroft.
Sparks, James A. Friendship After Forty. LC 80-10629. 144p. 1980. 7.95 (ISBN 0-687-13520-6). Abingdon.
Thomas, Ianthe. Hi, Mrs. Mallory! LC 78-3013. (Illus.). (gr. k-3). 1979. 7.95 (ISBN 0-06-026128-5, HarpJ); PLB 7.89 (ISBN 0-06-026129-3). Har-Row.
Walley, Dean. Friendship Is a Very Special Thing. 1979. pap. 2.50 (ISBN 0-8378-5032-0). Gibson.
Welter, Paul. How to Help a Friend. 1978. pap. 4.95 (ISBN 0-8423-1521-7). Tyndale.
West, Uta. If Love Is the Answer, What Is the Question? 1977. 8.95 (ISBN 0-07-069476-1, GB). McGraw.
What Is a Friend? 1972. 2.95 (ISBN 0-442-82455-6). Peter Pauper.
Woods, Ralph L., compiled by. Friendship. LC 69-16102. (Illus.). 1969. boxed 4.95 (ISBN 0-8378-1715-3). Gibson.
Words of Comfort. 1968. 2.95 (ISBN 0-442-82469-6). Peter Pauper.
Ziegler, Sandra. Friends: A Handbook About Getting Along Together. LC 80-17529. (Living the Good Life Ser.). (Illus.). 112p. (Orig.). (gr. 1-6). 1980. pap. 5.95 (ISBN 0-89565-174-2). Childs World.
FRIES REBELLION, 1789-1799
Davis, William W. Fries Rebellion, 1798-1799. LC 78-90171. (Mass Violence in America). Repr. of 1899 ed. 8.50 (ISBN 0-405-01305-1). Arno.
FRIESE-GREENE, WILLIAM
Allister, Ray. Friese-Greene: Close-Up of an Inventor. LC 71-169339. (Arno Press Cinema Program). (Illus.). 212p. 1972. Repr. of 1948 ed. 14.00 (ISBN 0-405-03908-5). Arno.
Rossi, Alice S., ed. The Feminist Papers: From Adams to De Beauvoir. 600p. 1973. 22.50x (ISBN 0-231-03795-3). Columbia U Pr.
FRIESIAN LANGUAGE
Markey, Thomas L. Frisian. (Contributions to the Sociology of Language Ser.: No. 30). 1979. text ed. 40.00x (ISBN 90-279-3128-3). Mouton.
FRIESIAN PHILOLOGY
Hewett, W. T. The Frisian Language & Literature. 59.95 (ISBN 0-87968-162-4). Gordon Pr.
FRIGATE-BIRDS
see also Steganopodes
FRIGIDITY (PSYCHOLOGY)
Baisden, Major J., Jr. The World of Rosaphrenia: The Sexual Psychology of the Female. LC 72-178852. 224p. 1971. 6.95 (ISBN 0-912984-01-5). Allied Res Soc.
Hirsch, Edwin W. Impotence & Frigidity. pap. 3.00 (ISBN 0-87980-084-4). Wilshire.
MacVaugh, Gilbert S. Frigidity: Its Cure with Hypnosis. LC 78-26958. 1979. 44.00 (ISBN 0-08-021748-6). Pergamon.
Stekel, Wilhelm. Frigidity in Woman in Relation to Her Love Life, 2 Vols. 1943. 14.95x (ISBN 0-87140-843-0). Liveright.
FRINGE BENEFITS
see Non-Wage Payments
FRINGE METHOD, MOIRE
see Moire Method
FRINGILLIDAE
see Finches
FRISBEE (GAME)
Poynter, Dan & Danna, Mark. Frisbee Players' Handbook. 3rd ed. LC 77-79101. (Illus.). 1980. pap. text ed. 6.95 (ISBN 0-915516-20-9); pap. 9.95 with disc (ISBN 0-915516-15-2); pap. 6.95 without disc (ISBN 0-915516-19-5). Para Pub.
Roddick, D. Frisbee Disc Basics. 1980. 8.95 (ISBN 0-13-331322-0). P-H.
Schmitz, Dorothy C. The Fabulous Frisbee. Schroeder, Howard, ed. LC 78-7416. (Funseekers Ser.). (Illus.). (gr. 3-4). 1978. PLB 6.95 (ISBN 0-913940-88-7); pap. 3.25 (ISBN 0-89686-009-4). Crestwood Hse.
Schumacher, Craig. Frisbee Fun. (Creative Games, Projects & Activities Ser.). (Illus.). 40p. (gr. 4-8). 1979. PLB 5.95 (ISBN 0-87191-674-6); pap. 2.95 (ISBN 0-89812-046-2). Creative Ed.
Tips, Charles. Frisbee by the Masters. LC 76-55832. (Illus., Orig.). 1977. pap. 5.95 (ISBN 0-89087-142-6). Celestial Arts.
Tips, Charles & Roddick, Dan. Frisbee Disc Sports & Games. LC 78-67849. (Illus.). 1979. pap. 5.95 (ISBN 0-89087-233-3). Celestial Arts.
FRISBIE (GAME)
see Frisbee (Game)
FRISCH, MAX, 1911-
Butler, Michael. The Novels of Max Frisch. 1976. text ed. 14.50x (ISBN 0-391-00687-8). Humanities.
Dahms, Erna M. Zeit und Zeiterlebnis in den Werken Max Frischs: Bedeutung und Technische Darstellung. (Quellen und Forschungen zur Sprachund und Kulturgeschichte der Germanischen Voelker). 1976. 40.00x (ISBN 3-11-006679-3). De Gruyter.
Frisch, Max. Sketchbook 1966-1971. Skelton, Geoffrey, tr. LC 73-19649. (Helen & Kurt Wolff Bk). 1974. 10.00 (ISBN 0-15-182892-X). HarBraceJ.
Groot, Cegienas De. Zeitgestaltung Im Drama Max Frischs: Die Vergegenwartigungstechnik in "Santa Cruz", "Die Chinesische Mauer" und "Biografie". (Amsterdamer Publikationen Zur Sprache und Literature Ser.: No. 33). (Orig., Ger.). 1979. pap. text ed. 33.00x (ISBN 90-6203-150-1). Humanities.
Kiernan, Doris. Existenziale Themen Bei Max Frisch. (Quellen und Forschungen Zur Sprache und Kulturgeschichte der Germanischen Voelker: No. 73). 1978. 34.50x (ISBN 3-11-007406-0). De Gruyter.
Petersen, Carol. Max Frisch. LaRue, Charlotte, tr. LC 72-153124. (Modern Literature Ser.). 10.95 (ISBN 0-8044-2692-9). Ungar.
Probst, Gerhard F. & Bodine, Jay F., eds. Essays on Max Frisch. LC 80-5181. 1982. price not set (ISBN 0-8131-1438-1). U Pr of Ky.
FRISIAN LANGUAGE
see Friesian Language
FROBISHER, MARTIN, SIR, 1535-1594
Best, George. The Three Voyages of Martin Frobisher: In Search of a Passage to Cathaia & India by the Northwest, A.D. 1576-78. Collinson, Richard, ed. (Hakluyt Society, First Ser.: No. 38). (Illus.). 1964. 32.00 (ISBN 0-8337-0271-8). B Franklin.
Settle, Dionyse. A True Reporte of the Laste Voyage by Capteine Frobisher. LC 79-6343. (English Experience Ser.: No. 88). 48p. 1969. Repr. of 1577 ed. 11.50 (ISBN 90-221-0088-X). Walter J Johnson.
FROEBEL, FRIEDRICH WILHELM AUGUST, 1782-1852
Bowen, H. Courthope. Froebel & Education Through Self-Activity. (Educational Ser.). 1909. Repr. 15.00 (ISBN 0-8482-7377-X). Norwood Edns.
Bulow, B. von Marenholz. Reminiscences of Friedrich Froebel. Mann, Mrs. Horace, tr. 359p. 1980. Repr. of 1877 ed. lib. bdg. 30.00 (ISBN 0-8492-2833-6). R West.
Cole, Percival R. Herbart & Froebel: An Attempt at Synthesis. LC 70-176659. (Columbia University. Teachers College. Contributions to Education: No. 14). Repr. of 1907 ed. 17.50 (ISBN 0-404-55014-2). AMS Pr.
Downs, Robert B. Friedrich Froebel. (World Leaders Ser.: No. 74). 1978. lib. bdg. 10.95 (ISBN 0-8057-7668-0). Twayne.
Froebel, Friedrich. Froebel Letters. Heinemann, Arnold H., ed. (Educational Ser.). 1893. Repr. 15.00 (ISBN 0-685-43015-4). Norwood Edns.
Macvannel, John A. The Educational Theories of Herbart & Froebel. LC 72-177043. (Columbia University. Teachers College. Contributions to Education: No. 4). Repr. of 1905 ed. 17.50 (ISBN 0-404-55004-5). AMS Pr.
FROEBEL SYSTEM OF EDUCATION
see Kindergarten
FROGS
Billings, Charlene W. Spring Peepers Are Calling. LC 78-7735. (Illus.). (gr. 2-5). 1979. 5.95 (ISBN 0-396-07584-3). Dodd.
Cole, Joanna. A Frog's Body. LC 80-10705. (Illus.). 48p. (gr. k-3). 1980. 6.95 (ISBN 0-688-22228-5); PLB 6.67 (ISBN 0-688-32228-X). Morrow.
Cornelius, Carol. Hyla(Peep) Crucifer: The Story of the Spring Peeper Frog. LC 78-640. (Illus.). (ps-4). 1978. PLB 5.95 (ISBN 0-913778-98-2). Childs World.
Dickerson, Mary C. Frog Book. (Illus.). 1969. pap. 6.50 (ISBN 0-486-21973-9). Dover.
--The Frog Book: North American Toads & Frogs, with a Study of the Habits & Life Histories of Those of the Northeastern States. (Illus.). 13.50 (ISBN 0-8446-0582-4). Peter Smith.
Donaldson, Gerald. Frogs. 127p. 1980. 14.95 (ISBN 0-442-22650-0). Van Nos Reinhold.
Ecker. The Anatomy of the Frog. Haslam, G., tr. from Ger. 1971. 57.50 (ISBN 90-6123-240-6). Lubrecht & Cramer.
Gilbert, Stephen G. Pictorial Anatomy of the Frog. LC 65-14843. (Illus.). 71p. 1965. pap. 6.95 (ISBN 0-295-73878-2). U of Wash Pr.

Knobler, Susan. The Tadpole & the Frog. LC 74-83422. (Books Without Words Ser.). (Illus.). 32p. (ps-4). 1974. PLB 4.48 (ISBN 0-8178-5302-2). Harvey.
Llinas, R. & Precht, W., eds. Frog Neurobiology: A Handbook. LC 75-46505. 1976. 245.20 (ISBN 0-387-07606-9). Springer-Verlag.
Lutz, Bertha & Lutz, Guaeter. Brazilian Species of "Hyla". LC 70-39502. (Illus.). 286p. 1973. 25.00x (ISBN 0-292-70704-5). U of Tex Pr.
Minkoff, Eli. C. A Laboratory Guide to Frog Anatomy. LC 74-22206. 176p. 1975. pap. text ed. 7.75 (ISBN 0-08-018315-8). Pergamon.
Parker, H. W. Monograph of the Frogs of the Family Microhylidae. Repr. of 1934 ed. 15.50 (ISBN 0-384-44850-X). Johnson Repr.
Saiga Editors. Lizards & Frogs. 1981. 10.00x (ISBN 0-86230-004-5, Pub. by Saiga Pub). State Mutual Bk.
Sonntag, Linda. Frogs. (The Leprechaun Library). (Illus.). 64p. 1981. 3.95 (ISBN 0-399-12611-2). Putnam.
Tyler, Michael J. Frogs. LC 75-42538. (Australian Naturalist Library Ser.). (Illus.). 1976. 17.50 (ISBN 0-8008-3063-6). Taplinger.
Underhill, Raymond A. Laboratory Anatomy of the Frog. 4th ed. (Laboratory Anatomy Ser.). 75p. 1980. write for info. wire coil (ISBN 0-697-04645-1). Wm C Brown.
Von Filek, Werner. Frogs in the Aquarium. new ed. Orig. Title: Frosche im Aquarium. (Illus.). 96p. (Orig.). 1973. pap. 5.95 (ISBN 0-87666-191-6, PS690). TFH Pubns.
Waldie, Jerome & Frobish, Nestle J. Fair Play for Frogs: The Waldie-Frobish Papers. LC 76-27418. 1977. 7.95 (ISBN 0-15-129961-7). HarBraceJ.
Wells, Thomas A. The Frog: A Dissection Manual. (YA) (gr. 9-12). pap. 2.00 (ISBN 0-486-61717-3). Dover.
Wright, Albert H. & Wright, Anna A. Handbook of Frogs & Toads of the United States & Canada. 3rd ed. (HANH Ser.). (Illus.). 652p. 1949. 34.50x (ISBN 0-8014-0462-2). Comstock.
Zimmerman, Helmut. Tropical Frogs. (Illus.). 1979. 2.95 (ISBN 0-87666-926-7, KW-028). TFH Pubns.

FROGS–JUVENILE LITERATURE

Blassingame, Wyatt. Wonders of Frogs & Toads. LC 74-25523. (Wonders Ser.). (Illus.). (gr. 3-7). 1975. PLB 5.95 (ISBN 0-396-07086-8). Dodd.
Cleveland, David. The Frog on Robert's Head. (Illus.). (gr. 1-4). Date not set. 8.95 (ISBN 0-686-76705-5). Coward.
Dallinger, Jane. Frogs & Toads. LC 80-27667. (Lerner Natural Science Bks.). (Illus.). (gr. 4-10). 1981. PLB 7.95 (ISBN 0-8225-1454-0). Lerner Pubns.
Hogan, Paula Z. The Frog. LC 78-21240. (Life Cycles Ser.). (Illus.). (gr. k-3). 1979. PLB 11.15 (ISBN 0-8172-1253-1). Raintree Pubs.
Hogeweg, M. & Moonen, Ries. The Green Frog. (Animal Environment Ser.). (Illus.). (gr. 3-6). 1979. 4.95 (ISBN 0-8120-5362-1). Barron.
Lane, Margaret. The Frog. LC 81-1228. 32p. (ps-4). 1981. Repr. of 1981 ed. 7.95 (ISBN 0-8037-2711-9). Dial.
McClung, Robert M. Peeper, First Voice of Spring. LC 77-2410. (Illus.). (gr. 1-5). 1977. PLB 6.96 (ISBN 0-688-32116-X). Morrow.
May, Julian. Life Cycle of a Bullfrog. LC 73-1186. (Illus.). (gr. 2-4). 1973. PLB 5.95 (ISBN 0-87191-233-3). Creative Ed.
Morris, Dean. Frogs & Toads. LC 77-8116. (Read About Ser.). (Illus.). (gr. k-3). 1977. PLB 11.15 (ISBN 0-8393-0003-4). Raintree Child.
Ommanney, F. D. Frogs, Toads & Newts. LC 74-9513. (Illus.). 48p. (gr. 2-7). 1974. 6.95 (ISBN 0-07-047705-1, GB). McGraw.
Oxford Scientific Films. Common Frog. new ed. LC 78-24038. (Illus.). (gr. 1 up). 1979. 7.95 (ISBN 0-399-20675-2). Putnam.
Perry, Phyllis J. Let's Look at Frogs. (Nature & Science Bk.). (Illus.). (gr. k-6). PLB 5.95 (ISBN 0-513-00471-8). Denison.
Schultz, Ellen. I Can Read About Frogs & Toads. new ed. LC 78-73714. (Illus.). (gr. 2-5). 1979. pap. 1.25 (ISBN 0-89375-210-X). Troll Assocs.
Simon, Hilda. Frogs & Toads of the World. LC 75-14095. (Illus.). 128p. (gr. 4-6). 1975. 7.95 (ISBN 0-397-31634-8). Lippincott.
Turner, Edward & Turner, Clive. Frogs & Toads. Brenner, Barbara, ed. LC 76-13653. (Young Naturalist Ser.). (Illus.). 80p. (gr. 3-7). 1976. PLB 9.30 (ISBN 0-8172-0331-1). Raintree Pubs.
Zim, Herbert S. Frogs & Toads. (Illus.). (gr. 3-7). 1950. PLB 6.48 (ISBN 0-688-31316-7). Morrow.

FROHLICH, HERBERT

Haken, H. & Wagner, M., eds. Cooperative Phenomena. LC 73-79119. (Illus.). xv, 460p. 1973. 85.90 (ISBN 0-387-06203-3). Springer-Verlag.

FROISSART, JEAN, 1338-1410

McGregor, Rob R. The Lyric Poems of Jehan Froissart: A Critical Edition. (Studies in the Romance Languages & Literatures: No. 143). 1976. pap. 21.00x (ISBN 0-8078-9143-6). U of NC Pr.
Palmer, J. J. Froissart: Historian. (Illus.). 256p. 1981. 47.50x (ISBN 0-8476-7029-5). Rowman.
Shears, F. S. Froissart, Chronicler & Poet. 1930. lib. bdg. 25.00 (ISBN 0-8414-0493-3). Folcroft.

FROMENTIN, EUGENE, 1820-1876

Evans, Arthur R., Jr. The Literary Art of Eugene Fromentin: A Study in Style and Motif. 166p. 1964. 25.00x (ISBN 0-8018-0191-5). Johns Hopkins.
Mickel, Emanuel J., Jr. Eugene Fromentin. (World Authors Ser.: No. 640). 15.95 (ISBN 0-8057-6484-4). Twayne.

FROMM, ERICH, 1900-1980

Funk, Rainer. Erich Fromm: The Courage to Be Human. 320p. 1982. 19.50 (ISBN 0-8264-0061-2). Continuum.
Gotesky, Rubin. Personality: The Need for Liberty & Rights. 1967. 3.50 (ISBN 0-87212-012-0). Libra.
Hammond, Guyton B. Man in Estrangement: Paul Tillich & Erich Fromm Compared. LC 65-18546. 1965. 7.50 (ISBN 0-8265-1075-2). Vanderbilt U Pr.

FRONDE

see also Mazarinades

Knachel, Philip A. England & the Fronde: The Impact of the English Civil War & Revolution on France. (Monographs). 1978. 17.50x (ISBN 0-918016-33-9). Folger Bks.
Moote, A. Lloyd. Revolt of the Judges: The Parlement of Paris & the Fronde, 1643-1652. LC 78-155003. 1971. 28.00 (ISBN 0-691-05191-7). Princeton U Pr.
Westrich, Sal Alexander. The Ormee of Bordeaux: A Revolution during the Fronde. LC 79-166485. (Studies in Historical & Political Science: Eighty-Ninth Series No. 2 (1971)). 192p. 1972. 12.00x (ISBN 0-8018-1306-9). Johns Hopkins.

FRONT POPULAIRE

Warwick, Paul. The French Popular Front: A Legislative Analysis. LC 76-22952. (Illus.). 1977. lib. bdg. 16.00x (ISBN 0-226-86914-8). U of Chicago Pr.

FRONTAL LOBOTOMY

Winter, Arthur, ed. Surgical Control of Behavior: A Symposium. (Illus.). 100p. 1971. 11.25 (ISBN 0-398-02091-4). C C Thomas.

FRONTENAC, LOUIS DE BUADE DE, COMPTE, 1620-1698

Syme, Ronald. Frontenac of New France. (Illus.). (gr. 5-9). 1969. 6.95 (ISBN 0-688-21318-9). Morrow.

FRONTIER AND PIONEER LIFE

see also Cowboys; Indians of North America–Captivities; Overland Journeys to the Pacific; Pioneers; Ranch Life; West

Abernethy, Thomas P. Three Virginia Frontiers. 6.50 (ISBN 0-8446-1001-1). Peter Smith.
Allen, Harry C. Bush & Backwoods. LC 75-9110. 153p. 1975. Repr. of 1959 ed. lib. bdg. 15.00 (ISBN 0-8371-8135-6, ALBB). Greenwood.
American Geographical Society Of New York. Pioneer Settlement. facsimile ed. LC 74-90599. (Essay Index Reprint Ser). 1932. 28.00 (ISBN 0-8369-1241-1). Arno.
Andrews, Matthew P. Social Planning by Frontier Thinkers. 1944. 10.00 (ISBN 0-685-72796-3). Norwood Edns.
Arter, Jared M. Echoes from a Pioneer Life. facsimile ed. LC 72-170688. (Black Heritage Library Collection). Repr. of 1922 ed. 12.50 (ISBN 0-8369-8877-9). Arno.
Atherton, Lewis E. The Pioneer Merchant in Mid-America. LC 75-77700. (American Scene Ser). 1969. Repr. of 1939 ed. 19.50 (ISBN 0-306-71338-1). Da Capo.
Audubon, John J. Delineations of American Scenery & Character. LC 70-125730. (American Environmental Studies). 1970. Repr. of 1926 ed. 18.00 (ISBN 0-405-02655-2). Arno.
Bailey, Hugh C. John Williams Walker: A Study in the Political, Social & Cultural Life of the Old Southwest. LC 64-14073. (Southern Historical Ser: Vol. 2). 1964. 18.95x (ISBN 0-8173-5207-4). U of Ala Pr.
Bartlett, Richard A. Great Surveys of the American West. LC 62-16475. (The American Exploration & Travel Ser.: Vol. 38). (Illus.). 464p. 1980. pap. 9.95 (ISBN 0-8061-1653-6). U of Okla Pr.
--The New Country: A Social History of the American Frontier 1776-1890. LC 74-79619. (Illus.). 495p. 1976. pap. 8.95 (ISBN 0-19-502021-9, 452, GB). Oxford U Pr.
Bell, Horace. On the Old West Coast: Being Further Reminiscences of a Ranger. Bartlett, Lanier, ed. LC 76-1242. (Chicano Heritage Ser.). (Illus.). 1976. Repr. of 1930 ed. lib. bdg. 23.00x (ISBN 0-405-09485-X). Arno.
Billington, Ray A. America's Frontier Culture: Three Essays. LC 77-89510. (Essays on the American West Ser.: No. 3). 100p. 1977. 5.00 (ISBN 0-89096-036-4). Tex A&M Univ Pr.
Blair, Walter & Meine, Franklin J. Half Horse Half Alligator: The Growth of the Mike Fink Legend. LC 81-3358. (Illus.). x, 289p. 1981. pap. 5.95x (ISBN 0-8032-6060-1, BB 772, Bison). U of Nebr Pr.
Blair, Walter & Meine, Franklin J., eds. Half Horse Half Alligator: The Growth of the Mike Fink Legend. LC 81-3358. (Illus.). x, 289p. 1981. Repr. of 1956 ed. price not set (ISBN 0-8032-6060-1, BB 772). U of Nebr Pr.
Bowman, Isaiah. The Pioneer Fringe. facsimile ed. LC 71-160960. (Select Bibliographies Reprint Ser.). Repr. of 1931 ed. 35.00 (ISBN 0-8369-5828-4). Arno.
Boynton, Percy H. Rediscovery of the Frontier. LC 75-118636. 184p. 1970. Repr. of 1931 ed. lib. bdg. 11.50x (ISBN 0-8154-0327-5). Cooper Sq.
--Rediscovery of the Frontier. LC 74-14617. 1931. lib. bdg. 15.00 (ISBN 0-8414-9871-7). Folcroft.
--Rediscovery of the Frontier. LC 31-28011. (Illus.). 1969. Repr. of 1931 ed. lib. bdg. 15.00x (ISBN 0-8371-0480-7, BORE). Greenwood.
Brackenridge, R. Douglas. Beckoning Frontiers: A Biography of James Woodin Laurie. (Illus.). 1976. 10.00 (ISBN 0-911536-61-2). Trinity U Pr.
Branch, Douglas E. Westward: The Romance of the American Frontier. LC 76-92485. 626p. Repr. of 1930 ed. 17.50x (ISBN 0-8154-0311-9). Cooper Sq.
Bridges, Martin F. This Time & Place. 1979. 8.95 (ISBN 0-87881-077-3). Mojave Bks.
Brown, Jesse & Willard, A. M. The Black Hills Trails: A History of the Struggles of the Pioneers... facsimile ed. LC 75-83. (Mid-American Frontier Ser.). (Illus.). 1975. Repr. of 1924 ed. 33.00x (ISBN 0-405-06852-2). Arno.
Burright, Orrin U. The Sun Rides High: Pioneering Days in Oklahoma, Kansas & Missouri. 1974. 8.95 (ISBN 0-89015-022-2). Eakin Pubns.
Byington, Margaret. Homestead, the Households of a Milltown. 1980. pap. 6.95x (ISBN 0-8229-8250-1). U of Pittsburgh Pr.
Carroll, Peter N. Puritanism & the Wilderness: The Intellectual Significance of the New England Frontier, 1629-1700. LC 78-84673. 1969. 17.50x (ISBN 0-231-03253-6). Columbia U Pr.
Chapin, Henry. To the End of West. 1970. pap. 3.95 (ISBN 0-87233-017-6). Bauhan.
Clark, Thomas D. The Rampaging Frontier. LC 75-17477. 350p. 1976. Repr. of 1939 ed. lib. bdg. 15.00x (ISBN 0-8371-8313-8, CLRF). Greenwood.
Clark, Walter V. Ox-Bow Incident. 6.75 (ISBN 0-8446-0060-1). Peter Smith.
Cochran, Alice C. Miners, Merchants & Missionaries: The Roles of Missionaries & Pioneer Churches in the Colorado Gold Rush & Its Aftermath, 1858-1870. LC 80-16895. (ATLA Monographs: No. 15). x, 287p. 1980. 15.00 (ISBN 0-8108-1325-4). Scarecrow.
Cody, W. F. Story of the Wild West & Camp-Fire Chats: A Full & Complete History of the Renowned Pioneer Quartette, Boone, Crocket, Carson, & Buffalo Bill. facsimile ed. LC 75-109620. (Select Bibliographies Reprint Ser). 1888. 42.00 (ISBN 0-8369-5229-4). Arno.
Cook, James H. Fifty Years on the Old Frontier As Cowboy, Hunter, Guide, Scout, & Ranchman. LC 57-5951. (Illus.). 310p. 1981. pap. 8.95 (ISBN 0-8061-0364-7). U of Okla Pr.
Corbusier. Verde to San Carlos. LC 68-24017. (Illus.). 1971. 8.95 (ISBN 0-912762-16-0); deluxe ed. 40.00 (ISBN 0-912762-17-9). King.
Cummins, D. Duane & White, William G. The American Frontier. rev. ed. (Inquiries into American History Ser.). (gr. 11-12). 1972. pap. text ed. 4.28 (ISBN 0-02-641220-9, 64122); tchr's. ed. 5.28 (ISBN 0-02-641250-0, 64125). Glencoe.
Curti, Merle. The Making of an American Community: A Case Study of Democracy in a Frontier County. 1959. 19.50x (ISBN 0-8047-0534-8). Stanford U Pr.
Darlington, William M., ed. Christopher Gist's Journals. LC 65-27166. 296p. Repr. of 1893 ed. 17.50 (ISBN 0-405-03671-X). Arno.
Davis, James E. Frontier America, 1800-1840: A Comparative Demographic Analysis of the Settlement Process. LC 77-77031. (Illus.). 1977. 15.50 (ISBN 0-87062-120-3). A H Clark.
Doetsch, Raymond N. Journey to the Green & Golden Lands: The Epic of Survival on the Wagon Trail. 1976. 11.50 (ISBN 0-8046-9142-8, Natl U). Kennikat.
Dunbar, Seymour. History of Travel in America, 4 Vols. LC 68-23283. (Illus.). 1968. Repr. of 1915 ed. Set. lib. bdg. 81.75x (ISBN 0-8371-0063-1, DUHT). Greenwood.
Durham, Philip & Jones, Everett, eds. Frontier in American Literature. LC 68-31708. 1969. pap. 8.95 (ISBN 0-672-63040-0). Odyssey Pr.
Ebbutt, Percy G. Emigrant Life in Kansas. facsimile ed. LC 75-96. (Mid-American Frontier Ser.). (Illus.). 1975. Repr. of 1886 ed. 15.00x (ISBN 0-405-06862-X). Arno.
The English in the Pacific Northwest: The/English in the Pacific Northwest. LC 81-620029. (Illus.). 1981. pap. 5.00 (ISBN 0-917048-52-0). Wash St Hist Soc.
Faragher, John M. Women & Men on the Overland Trail. LC 78-10290. (Yale Historical Publications, Miscellany Ser.: No. 121). 304p. 1980. 25.00x (ISBN 0-300-02267-0); pap. 6.50x (ISBN 0-300-02605-6). Yale U Pr.
Farrar, Elizabeth R. Recollections of Seventy Years. Baxter, Annette K., ed. LC 79-8791. (Signal Lives Ser.). 1980. Repr. of 1866 ed. lib. bdg. 30.00x (ISBN 0-405-12838-X). Arno.
Farrelly, Alan & Morrison, Ron. New Frontiers: The Newest Survey of Australian Potential, Power, Production & Problems. (Illus.). 1970. 11.50x (ISBN 0-8426-1257-2). Verry.
Favour, Alpheus H. Old Bill Williams, Mountain Man. LC 62-10767. (Illus.). 234p. 1981. pap. 5.95 (ISBN 0-8061-1698-6). U of Okla Pr.
Fisher, Jon. The Last Frontiers on Earth: Strange Places Where You Can Live Free. 1980. pap. 6.95 (ISBN 0-686-30626-0). Loompanics.
--The Last Frontiers on Earth: Strange Places Where You Can Live Free. 1980. pap. 6.95 (ISBN 0-686-30708-9). Loompanics.
Flandrau, Grace. Verendrye Overland Quest of Pacific. Repr. of 1925 ed. pap. 7.25 (ISBN 0-8466-0213-X, SJS213). Shorey.
Fowler, William W. Woman on the American Frontier. LC 73-12867. 1974. Repr. of 1878 ed. 34.00 (ISBN 0-8103-3702-9). Gale.
Giles, Janice H. Janice Holt Giles Frontier Set, 4 bks. Incl. The Believers; Hannah Fowler; Johnny Osage; The Kentuckians. 1980. Set. lib. bdg. 58.00 (ISBN 0-686-62740-7, Large Print Bks). G K Hall.
Gladstone, T. H. Englishman in Kansas; or, Squatter Life & Border Warfare. LC 74-155700. 1971. 21.50x (ISBN 0-8032-0800-6); pap. 3.95 (ISBN 0-8032-5742-2, BB 536, Bison). U of Nebr Pr.
Harris, Gertrude. Foods of the Frontier. LC 72-77565. (Illus.). 192p. 1972. pap. 4.95 (ISBN 0-912238-25-9). One Hund One Prods.
Helms, Mary W. & Loveland, Franklin O., eds. Frontier Adaptations in Lower Central America. LC 76-25073. 192p. 1976. text ed. 16.00x (ISBN 0-915980-55-X). Inst Study Human.
Hochbaum, H. Albert. Canvasback on a Prairie Marsh. LC 80-22699. (Illus.). xvii, 207p. 1981. 15.95x (ISBN 0-8032-2300-5); pap. 5.95 (ISBN 0-8032-7200-6, BB 681, Bison). U of Nebr Pr.
Hofstadter, Richard & Lipset, Seymour M., eds. Turner & Sociology of the Frontier. LC 68-22859. pap. 4.50x (ISBN 0-465-08769-8). Basic.
Hollon, W. Eugene. Frontier Violence: Another Look. LC 73-87617. (Illus.). 288p. 1976. pap. 4.95 (ISBN 0-19-502098-7, 475, GB). Oxford U Pr.
Hoople, Cheryl G. As I Saw It: Women Who Lived the American Adventure. LC 78-51324. (Illus.). 1978. 8.95 (ISBN 0-8037-0339-2). Dial.
Horsman, Reginald. The Frontier in the Formative Years, 1783-1815. LC 76-94404. (Histories of the American Frontier Ser). (Illus.). 253p. 1979. pap. 8.95x (ISBN 0-8263-0313-7). U of NM pr.
Howard, Helen A. American Frontier Tales. 280p. Date not set. 12.95 (ISBN 0-87842-120-3). Mountain Pr.
Hult, Ruby E. Steamboats in the Timber. 2nd enl. ed. LC 68-58896. (Illus.). 1968. 8.95 (ISBN 0-8323-0022-5). Binford.
Humphrey, William. Ah, Wilderness: The Frontier in American Literature. (Literature Ser.: No. 2). 1977. 3.00 (ISBN 0-87404-057-4). Tex Western.
Jacobs-Bond, Carrie. The Roads of Melody. Baxter, Annette K., ed. LC 79-8776. (Signal Lives Ser.). (Illus.). 1980. Repr. of 1927 ed. lib. bdg. 24.00x (ISBN 0-405-12825-8). Arno.
Jeffrey, Julie R. Frontier Women: The Trans-Mississippi West 1840-1880. Foner, Eric, ed. 256p. 1979. 11.95 (ISBN 0-8090-4803-5); pap. 5.95 (ISBN 0-8090-0141-1). Hill & Wang.
Johnston, Charles H. Famous Scouts. facsimile ed. LC 79-38743. (Essay Index Reprints - Famous Leaders Ser.). Repr. of 1910 ed. 23.00 (ISBN 0-8369-2661-7). Arno.
Kalman, Harold. Pioneer Churches. 1976. 27.50 (ISBN 0-393-08754-9). Norton.
Katz, William Loren. The Black West. rev. ed. LC 72-93397. 352p. 1973. 6.95 (ISBN 0-385-00380-3, Anch). Doubleday.

Klose, Nelson. Concise Study Guide to the American Frontier. LC 64-15180. (Illus.). 1964. pap. 4.95x (ISBN 0-8032-5110-6, BB 190, Bison). U of Nebr Pr.
Knox, Daryl K. Pioneers in a Frontier Land: The Strabane Knoxes & Other Families. LC 78-108863. 165p. 1978. 11.00 (ISBN 0-9605790-0-1). D Knox.
Lamar, Howard & Thompson, Leonard, eds. The Frontier in History: North America & Southern Africa Compared. (Illus.). 336p. 1981. text ed. 37.50x (ISBN 0-300-02624-2); pap. 7.95x (ISBN 0-300-02742-7, Y-406). Yale U Pr.
Langford, J. O. & Gipson, Fred. Big Bend: A Homesteader's Story. (Illus.). 191p. 1981. pap. 6.95 (ISBN 0-292-70734-7). U of Tex Pr.
Leckie, William H. The Military Conquest of the Southern Plains. (Illus.). 1963. 14.95 (ISBN 0-8061-0570-4). U of Okla Pr.
Lewis, Faye C. Nothing to Make a Shadow. (Illus.). 1972. pap. 9.45 facsimile ed. (ISBN 0-8138-2445-1). Iowa St U Pr.
Leyburn, James G. Frontier Folkways. LC 79-122402. 1970. Repr. of 1935 ed. 19.50 (ISBN 0-208-00961-2, Archon). Shoe String.
Lockley, Fred. The Lockley Files, Vol. 2: Bullwhackers, Muleskinners, Pioneers, Prospectors, 49ers, Indian Fighters, Trappers, Ex-Barkeepers, Authors, Preachers, Poets & Near-Poets, & All Sorts & Conditions of Men. LC 81-50845. 368p. 1981. pap. 8.95 (ISBN 0-931742-09-9). Rainy Day Oreg.
--The Lockley Files, Vol. 3: Visionaries, Mountain Men, & Empire Builders. LC 81-50845. 1981. pap. price not set (ISBN 0-931742-10-2). Rainy Day Oreg.
Logan, Bob. Denim & Dogwood. (Illus.). 96p. 1981. 5.95 (ISBN 0-89962-049-3). Todd & Honeywell.
Lyon, William H. Pioneer Editor in Missouri, 1808-1860. LC 64-17647. 1965. 10.00x (ISBN 0-8262-0037-0). U of Mo Pr.
McConnel, John L. Western Characters: Or, Types of Border Life in the Western States. facsimile ed. LC 75-110. (Mid-American Frontier Ser.). (Illus.). 1975. Repr. of 1853 ed. 22.00x (ISBN 0-405-06877-8). Arno.
McKnight, Charles. Our Western Border, Its Life, Combats, Adventures, Forays, Massacres, Captivities, Scouts, Red Chiefs, Pioneers, Women, One Hundred Years Ago, Carefully Written & Compiled. (Rediscovering America Ser). (Illus.). Repr. of 1876 ed. 42.50 (ISBN 0-384-34890-4, R174). Johnson Repr.
Martin, John D. Christopher Dock: Pioneer Schoolmaster on Skippack. 1971. pap. 2.45x (ISBN 0-87813-906-0). Christian Light.
Mason, Bernard S. Primitive & Pioneer Sports for Recreation Today: Rope Spinning, Lariat Throwing, Tumblesticks, Whip Cracking, Boomerangs, Log Rolling, Boomabirds, Tomahawks, Darts, Blowguns, & Many Others. LC 76-162516. (Illus.). 342p. 1975. Repr. of 1937 ed. 24.00 (ISBN 0-8103-4029-1). Gale.
Mayer, Frank B. With Pen & Pencil on the Frontier in 1851: The Diary & Sketches of Frank Blackwell Mayer. facsimile ed. LC 75-103. (Mid-American Frontier Ser.). (Illus.). 1975. Repr. of 1932 ed. 13.00x (ISBN 0-405-06871-9). Arno.
Mays, Lois B. Settlers of the Okefenokee. 208p. 1975. 6.95x (ISBN 0-9601606-0-4). Okefenokee Pr.
Metcalf, Samuel L. A Collection of Some of the Most Interesting Narratives of Indian Warfare in the West. LC 75-7060. (Indian Captivities Ser.: Vol. 38). 1977. Repr. of 1821 ed. lib. bdg. 44.00 (ISBN 0-8240-1662-9). Garland Pub.
Miller, David H. & Steffen, Jerome O., eds. The Frontier: Comparative Studies. LC 76-62507. (Illus.). 1977. 15.95x (ISBN 0-8061-1376-6). U of Okla Pr.
Morison, James. By Sea to San Francisco, Eighteen Forty Nine-Eighteen Fifty: The Journal of Dr. James Morison. White, Lonnie J. & Gillaspie, William R., eds. LC 76-40153. (Memphis State University Press Primary Source Ser). (Orig.). 1977. pap. 6.95x (ISBN 0-87870-036-6). Memphis St Univ.
Morning Dove. Cogewea, the Half-Blood. LC 80-29687. xxx, 302p. 1981. 17.95x (ISBN 0-8032-3069-9); pap. 6.25 (ISBN 0-8032-8110-2, BB 754, Bison). U of Nebr Pr.
Olds, Sarah E. Twenty Miles from a Match: Homesteading in Western Nevada. LC 78-13766. (Illus.). xiii, 182p. 1978. 5.50 (ISBN 0-87417-052-4). U of Nev Pr.
O'Neil, Paul. The Frontiersmen. LC 76-47101. (Old West Ser.). (Illus.). (gr. 5 up). 1977. 12.96 (ISBN 0-8094-1547-X, Pub. by Time-Life). Silver.
--The Frontiersmen. (Old West Ser.). 1977. 14.95 (ISBN 0-8094-1545-3). Time-Life.
Parish, Peggy. Let's Be Early Settler's with Daniel Boone. LC 67-14068. (Activities Bk). (Illus.). (gr. 1-5). 1967. PLB 8.79 (ISBN 0-06-024648-0, HarpJ). Har-Row.
Paschal, George W. Ninety-Four Years - Agnes Paschal. LC 74-2356. 366p. 1974. Repr. of 1871 ed. 18.00 (ISBN 0-87152-184-9). Reprint.
Peyton, John L. Adventures of My Grandfather. LC 65-27156. 270p. Repr. of 1867 ed. 12.50 (ISBN 0-405-03680-9). Arno.
Pierce, Charles W. Pioneer Life in Southeast Florida. Curl, Donald W., ed. LC 70-122290. 1981. 10.95 (ISBN 0-87024-304-7). U of Miami Pr.
Porter, Kenneth W. The Negro on the American Frontier. LC 77-135872. Repr. of 1971 ed. 15.00 (ISBN 0-405-01983-1). Arno.
Reid, Agnes J. Letters of Long Ago. (Utah, the Mormons & the West Ser.: No. 2). 93p. 1973. 9.50 (ISBN 0-87480-158-3, Tanner). U of Utah Pr.
Reps, John W. Town Planning in Frontier America. LC 68-20877. 336p. 1981. pap. 9.95 (ISBN 0-8262-0316-7). U of Mo Pr.
Ridlon, G. T. The Gibson Family. LC 71-94959. (Saco Valley Settlements Ser). 1970. pap. 1.50 (ISBN 0-8048-0769-8). C E Tuttle.
--The Goodenow Family. LC 76-94960. (Saco Valley Settlements Ser). 1970. pap. 1.50 (ISBN 0-8048-0770-1). C E Tuttle.
--The Gookin & Googin Family. LC 70-94961. (Saco Valley Settlements Ser). 1970. 1.50 (ISBN 0-8048-0771-X). C E Tuttle.
--The Gordon Family. LC 74-94965. (Saco Valley Settlements Ser). 1970. pap. 2.50 (ISBN 0-8048-0775-2). C E Tuttle.
--The Graffam Family. LC 73-94962. (Saco Valley Settlements Ser). 1970. pap. 1.50 (ISBN 0-8048-0772-8). C E Tuttle.
--The Grant Family. LC 77-94963. (Saco Valley Settlements Ser). 1970. pap. 1.50 (ISBN 0-8048-0773-6). C E Tuttle.
--The Haley Family. LC 73-109424. (Saco Valley Settlements Ser). 1970. pap. 4.00 (ISBN 0-8048-0777-9). C E Tuttle.
--The Hamlin Family. LC 77-10925. (Saco Valle y Settlements Ser.). 1970. pap. 2.00 (ISBN 0-8048-0778-7). C E Tuttle.
--The Hancock Family. LC 73-113906. (Saco Valley Settlements Ser). 1970. pap. 2.00 (ISBN 0-8048-0779-5). C E Tuttle.
--The Hastie & Hasty Family. LC 70-113908. (Saco Valley Settlements Ser). 1970. pap. 2.00 (ISBN 0-8048-0780-9). C E Tuttle.
--The Higgins & Hagen Family. LC 79-113910. (Saco Valley Settlements Ser). 1970. pap. 1.50 (ISBN 0-8048-0781-7). C E Tuttle.
--The Hobson Family. LC 76-113912. (Saco Valley Settlements Ser). 1970. pap. 3.75 (ISBN 0-8048-0782-5). C E Tuttle.
--The Howard Family. LC 70-113913. (Saco Valley Settlements Ser). 1970. pap. 2.00 (ISBN 0-8048-0783-3). C E Tuttle.
--The Hubart-Hubbard Family. LC 73-113914. (Saco Valley Settlements Ser). 1970. pap. 1.50 (ISBN 0-8048-0784-1). C E Tuttle.
--The Huntress Family. LC 77-113915. (Saco Valley Settlements Ser). 1970. pap. 1.50 (ISBN 0-8048-0785-X). C E Tuttle.
--The Hutchinson Family. LC 70-113916. (Saco Valley Settlements Ser). 1970. pap. 1.50 (ISBN 0-8048-0786-8). C E Tuttle.
--The Ingalls Family. LC 74-113917. (Saco Valley Settlements Ser). 1970. pap. 4.50 (ISBN 0-8048-0787-6). C E Tuttle.
--The Jameson Family. LC 78-113918. (Saco Valley Settlements Ser.). 1970. pap. 2.00 (ISBN 0-8048-0788-4). C E Tuttle.
--The Jenkins & Junkins Family. LC 71-113919. (Saco Valley Settlements Ser). 1970. pap. 2.00 (ISBN 0-8048-0789-2). C E Tuttle.
--The Jose Family. LC 76-113920. (Saco Valley Settlements Ser). 1970. pap. 1.50 (ISBN 0-8048-0790-6). C E Tuttle.
--The Killpatrick & Gillpatrick Family. LC 70-113921. (Saco Valley Settlements Ser). 1970. pap. 4.50 (ISBN 0-8048-0791-4). C E Tuttle.
--The Lane Family. LC 76-116484. (Saco Valley Settlements Ser). 1970. pap. 3.00 (ISBN 0-8048-0793-0). C E Tuttle.
--The Larrabee Family. LC 79-116482. (Saco Valley Settlements Ser). 1970. pap. 10.00 (ISBN 0-8048-0792-2). C E Tuttle.
--The Leavitt Family. LC 73-116486. (Saco Valley Settlements Ser). 1970. pap. 2.50 (ISBN 0-8048-0794-9). C E Tuttle.
--The Lewis Family. LC 70-116488. (Saco Valley Settlements Ser). 1970. pap. 2.50 (ISBN 0-8048-0795-7). C E Tuttle.
--The Lord Family. LC 79-116490. (Saco Valley Settlements Ser). 1970. pap. 2.75 (ISBN 0-8048-0796-5). C E Tuttle.
--The Macarthur Family. LC 72-116491. (Saco Valley Settlements Ser). 1970. pap. 2.00 (ISBN 0-8048-0797-3). C E Tuttle.
--The Macdonald Family. LC 77-120390. (Saco Valley Settlements Ser). 1970. pap. 2.00 (ISBN 0-8048-0798-1). C E Tuttle.
--McKenney Family. LC 73-123900. (Saco Valley Settlements Ser.). 1970. pap. 3.50 (ISBN 0-8048-0803-1). C E Tuttle.
--The Mansfield Family. LC 74-120392. (Saco Valley Settlements Ser). 1970. pap. 1.50 (ISBN 0-8048-0799-X). C E Tuttle.
--The Marr Family. LC 71-120394. (Saco Valley Settlements Ser). 1970. pap. 2.75 (ISBN 0-8048-0801-5). C E Tuttle.
--The Martin Family. LC 75-120395. (Saco Valley Settlements Ser). 1970. pap. 2.50 (ISBN 0-8048-0802-3). C E Tuttle.
--The Means Family. LC 77-123901. (Saco Valley Settlements Ser). 1970. pap. 2.00 (ISBN 0-8048-0804-X). C E Tuttle.
--The Meeds & Meads Family. LC 70-123902. (Saco Valley Settlements Ser). 1970. pap. 1.50 (ISBN 0-8048-0805-8). C E Tuttle.
--The Merrifield Family. LC 74-123903. (Saco Valley Settlements Ser). 1970. pap. 4.00 (ISBN 0-8048-0806-6). C E Tuttle.
--The Merrill Family. LC 78-123904. (Saco Valley Settlements Ser). 1970. pap. 3.50 (ISBN 0-8048-0807-4). C E Tuttle.
--The Messervey & Meserve Family. LC 71-123905. (Saco Valley Settlements Ser). 1970. pap. 3.50 (ISBN 0-8048-0808-2). C E Tuttle.
--The Milliken Family. LC 75-123906. (Saco Valley Settlements Ser). 1970. pap. 12.50 (ISBN 0-8048-0809-0). C E Tuttle.
--The Mitchell Family. LC 79-123907. (Saco Valley Settlements Ser). 1970. pap. 1.50 (ISBN 0-8048-0810-4). C E Tuttle.
--The Moses Family. LC 72-123908. (Saco Valley Settlements Ser). 1970. pap. 2.50 (ISBN 0-8048-0811-2). C E Tuttle.
--The Mulvey Family. LC 76-123909. (Saco Valley Settlements Ser). 1970. pap. 1.50 (ISBN 0-8048-0812-0). C E Tuttle.
--The Nason Family. LC 73-123910. (Saco Valley Settlements Ser). 1970. pap. 2.50 (ISBN 0-8048-0813-9). C E Tuttle.
--The Newbegin Family. LC 76-130412. (Saco Valley Settlements Ser). 1970. pap. 2.50 (ISBN 0-8048-0814-7). C E Tuttle.
--The Norton Family. LC 70-130413. (Saco Valley Settlements Ser). 1970. pap. 2.00 (ISBN 0-8048-0815-5). C E Tuttle.
--The O'Brien Family. LC 73-130414. (Saco Valley Settlements Ser). 1970. pap. 1.50 (ISBN 0-8048-0816-3). C E Tuttle.
--The Osgood Family. LC 77-130415. (Saco Valley Settlements Ser). 1970. pap. 2.00 (ISBN 0-8048-0817-1). C E Tuttle.
--The Parker Family. LC 75-133872. (Saco Valley Settlements Ser). 1970. pap. 1.50 (ISBN 0-8048-0818-X). C E Tuttle.
--The Patten Family. LC 79-133873. (Saco Valley Settlements Ser). 1970. pap. 2.00 (ISBN 0-8048-0819-8). C E Tuttle.
--The Patterson Family. LC 72-133874. (Saco Valley Settlements Ser). 1970. pap. 3.50 (ISBN 0-8048-0820-1). C E Tuttle.
--The Pease Family. LC 76-133875. (Saco Valley Settlements Ser). 1970. pap. 1.50 (ISBN 0-8048-0821-X). C E Tuttle.
--The Pennell Family. LC 70-133876. (Saco Valley Settlements Ser). 1970. pap. 2.00 (ISBN 0-8048-0822-8). C E Tuttle.
--The Pike Family. LC 77-133878. (Saco Valley Settlements Ser). 1970. pap. 1.50 (ISBN 0-8048-0824-4). C E Tuttle.
--The Pingree Family. LC 70-133879. (Saco Valley Settlements Ser). 1970. pap. 1.50 (ISBN 0-8048-0825-2). C E Tuttle.
--The Plaisted Family. LC 75-133880. (Saco Valley Settlements Ser). 1970. pap. 2.00 (ISBN 0-8048-0826-0). C E Tuttle.
--The Poingdestre-Pendexter Family. LC 73-133877. (Saco Valley Settlements Ser). 1970. pap. 4.00 (ISBN 0-8048-0823-6). C E Tuttle.
--The Rankin Family. LC 79-133881. (Saco Valley Settlements Ser). 1970. pap. 2.00 (ISBN 0-8048-0827-9). C E Tuttle.
Sanford, Mollie D. Mollie: The Journal of Mollie Dorsey Sanford in Nebraska & Colorado Territories, 1857-1866. LC 75-8764. (Pioneer Heritage Series: Vol. 1). xii, 199p. 1976. pap. 3.95 (ISBN 0-8032-5826-7, BB 607, Bison). U of Nebr Pr.
Seattle Art Museum. Lewis & Clark's America, 2 vols. boxed. LC 76-23167. (Seattle Art Museum). (Illus.). 192p. 1976. pap. 12.50 (ISBN 0-295-95524-4). U of Wash Pr.
Simms, W. Gilmore. Border Beagles: A Tale of Mississippi. rev. ed. LC 71-119151. Repr. of 1855 ed. 24.50 (ISBN 0-404-06007-2). AMS Pr.
--Guy Rivers: A Tale of Georgia. rev. ed. LC 71-116011. Repr. of 1885 ed. 14.50 (ISBN 0-404-06034-X). AMS Pr.
Smith, Coho & Logan, Iva Roe. Cohographs. (Illus.). 1976. 15.00 (ISBN 0-87706-071-1); pap. 12.50 (ISBN 0-87706-072-X). Branch-Smith.
Smith, William R. Observations on the Wisconsin Territory. facsimile ed. LC 75-122. (Mid-American Frontier Ser.). 1975. Repr. of 1838 ed. 11.00x (ISBN 0-405-06887-5). Arno.
Sosin, Jack M. The Revolutionary Frontier, 1763-1783. LC 67-11811. (Histories of the American Frontier Ser.). (Illus.). 241p. 1974. pap. 8.95x (ISBN 0-8263-0331-5). U of NM Pr.
Spence, Vernon G. Judge Legett of Abilene: A Texas Frontier Profile. LC 77-89508. (Centennial Ser. of Association of Former Students: No. 5). 304p. 1977. 12.95 (ISBN 0-89096-041-0). Tex A&M Univ Pr.
Steffa, Don. Tales of Noted Frontier Character "Soapy" Smith. Repr. of 1908 ed. pap. 3.50 (ISBN 0-8466-0193-1, SJS193). Shorey.
Steffen, Jerome O., ed. Mid-American Frontier, 47 vols. (Illus.). 1975. Set. 1335.00x (ISBN 0-405-06845-X). Arno.
Stoll, Elmo & Stoll, Mark. The Pioneer Catalogue of Country Living. (Illus.). 1981. pap. 6.95 (ISBN 0-920510-13-2, Pub. by Personal Lib). Everest Hse.
Streeter, Floyd B. The Kaw: Heart of a Nation. facsimile ed. LC 75-124. (Mid-American Frontier Ser.). (Illus.). 1975. Repr. of 1941 ed. 21.00x (ISBN 0-405-06889-1). Arno.
Swanson, Budington. The Long Land. 1977. 10.00 (ISBN 0-931068-07-X). Purcells.
Sweet, William W. Religion on the American Frontier, 4 vols. Incl. Vol. 1. The Baptists, 1783-1830. 652p. Repr. of 1931 ed. 37.50x (ISBN 0-8154-0222-8); Vol. 2. The Presbyterians, 1783-1840. (Illus.). 939p. 1964. Repr. of 1936 ed. 37.50x (ISBN 0-8154-0223-6); Vol. 3. The Congregationalists, 1783-1850. (Illus.). 435p. 1964. Repr. of 1934 ed. 37.50x (ISBN 0-8154-0224-4); Vol. 4. The Methodists, 1783-1840. (Illus.). 800p. 1964. Repr. of 1946 ed. 37.50x (ISBN 0-8154-0225-2). LC 63-21092. 1964. Repr. of 1946 ed. Cooper Sq.
Tome, Philip. Pioneer Life or Thirty Years a Hunter: Being Scenes & Adventures in the Life of Philip Tome. LC 78-146424. (First American Frontier Ser). (Illus.). 1971. Repr. of 1854 ed. 15.00 (ISBN 0-405-02893-8). Arno.
Tryon, Warren S., ed. My Native Land: Life in America, 1790-1870. 1961. pap. 3.95 (ISBN 0-226-81313-4, P61, Phoen). U of Chicago Pr.
Turner, Frederick J. The Frontier in American History. LC 75-22065. 400p. 1976. Repr. of 1920 ed. 11.50 (ISBN 0-88275-347-9). Krieger.
--Significance of the Frontier in American History. Simonson, Harold P., ed. LC 63-12915. (Milestones of Thought Ser). pap. 2.95 (ISBN 0-8044-6919-9). Ungar.
Utley, Robert M. Frontiersmen in Blue: The United States Army & the Indian, 1848-1865. LC 80-27796. (Illus.). xvi, 416p. 1981. 23.50x (ISBN 0-8032-4550-5); pap. 9.95 (ISBN 0-8032-9550-2, BB 769, Bison). U of Nebr Pr.
Volwiler, Albert T. George Croghan & the Westward Movement, 1741-1782. LC 77-137274. Repr. of 1926 ed. 26.50 (ISBN 0-404-06779-4). AMS Pr.
Walsh, Margaret. The American Frontier Revisited. (Studies in Economic & Social History). (Illus.). 1980. pap. text ed. 5.00x (ISBN 0-391-02098-6). Humanities.
Wayne, Bennett, ed. Men of the Wild Frontier. LC 73-13615. (Target Ser.). (Illus.). 168p. (gr. 5-12). 1974. PLB 7.29 (ISBN 0-8116-4905-9). Garrard.
Weslager, C. A. The Log Cabin in America: From Pioneer Days to the Present. (Illus.). 1969. 23.00 (ISBN 0-8135-0596-8). Rutgers U Pr.
Wesley, Edgar B. Guarding the Frontier: A Study of Frontier Defense from 1815 to 1825. LC 70-110883. (Illus.). xi, 217p. Repr. of 1935 ed. lib. bdg. 15.00 (ISBN 0-8371-4567-8, WEGF). Greenwood.
--Guarding the Frontier, a Study of Frontier Defense from 1815-1825. LC 71-145365. (Illus.). 1971. Repr. of 1935 ed. 14.00 (ISBN 0-403-01270-8). Scholarly.
Wolfskill, George & Palmer, Stanley, eds. Essays on Frontiers in World History. (Walter Prescott Webb Memorial Lectures Ser.: No. 14). 168p. 1981. text ed. 15.00x (ISBN 0-292-72033-5). U of Tex Pr.
Woodmason, Charles. Carolina Backcountry on the Eve of the Revolution: The Journal & Other Writings of Charles Woodmason, Anglican Itinerant. Hooker, Richard J., ed. (Institute of Early American History & Culture Ser.). 1969. 17.95 (ISBN 0-8078-0643-9); pap. 6.00x (ISBN 0-8078-4035-1). U of NC Pr.
Wright, J. E. & Corbett, Doris S. Pioneer Life in Western Pennsylvania. LC 40-10730. (Illus.). 1968. pap. 5.95 (ISBN 0-8229-6044-3). U of Pittsburgh Pr.

FRONTIER AND PIONEER LIFE–BIBLIOGRAPHY

Paul, Rodman W. The Frontier & the American West. Etulain, Richard W., ed. LC 76-11622. (Goldentree Bibliographies in American History). 1977. pap. text ed. 12.95x (ISBN 0-88295-542-X). Harlan Davidson.

Vail, R. W. Voice of the Old Frontier. LC 78-120673. 1970. Repr. lib. bdg. 17.50x (ISBN 0-374-98068-3). Octagon.

FRONTIER AND PIONEER LIFE–JUVENILE LITERATURE

Andrist, Ralph K. & Hanna, Archibald. California Gold Rush. LC 61-10677. (American Heritage Junior Library). (Illus.). 153p. (gr. 5 up). 1961. 9.95 (ISBN 0-8281-0388-7, JOO6-0). Am Heritage.

Heard, J. Norman. Black Frontiersmen: Adventures of Negroes Among American Indians, 1528-1918. LC 79-89317. (Illus.). (gr. 6 up). 1969. 7.95 (ISBN 0-381-99799-5, A09050, JD-J). Har-Row.

Hilton, Suzanne. Getting There: Frontier Travel Without Power. LC 79-23196. 1980. 9.95 (ISBN 0-664-32657-9). Westminster.

Johnston, Charles H. Famous Frontiersmen & Heroes of the Border. facsimile ed. LC 72-152178. (Essay Index Reprints - Famous Leaders Ser.). Repr. of 1913 ed. 23.00 (ISBN 0-8369-2231-X). Arno.

Lathrop, West. Keep the Wagons Moving. (Illus.). (gr. 10-12). 1955. PLB 5.39 (ISBN 0-394-91299-3). Random.

Lyons, Grant. Mustangs, Six-Shooters & Barbed Wire: How the West Was Really Won. LC 80-26715. (Illus.). 96p. (gr. 3-5). 1981. PLB 8.29 (ISBN 0-671-32996-0). Messner.

Meadowcroft, Enid L. By Wagon & Flatboat. LC 38-32408. (Illus.). (gr. 5 up). 1938. 8.95 (ISBN 0-690-16502-1, TYC-J). Har-Row.

Perl, Lila. Hunter's Stew & Hangtown Fry. LC 77-5366. 176p. (gr. 6 up). 1977. 8.95 (ISBN 0-395-28922-X, Clarion). HM.

Seidman, Laurence. The Fools of '49: The California Gold Rush, 1848-1856. LC 74-164. (A Living History Library Bk.). (gr. 6 up). 1976. 7.95 (ISBN 0-394-82685-X). Knopf.

Steele, William O. Westward Adventure: The True Stories of Six Pioneers. LC 62-9479. (Illus.). (gr. 4-6). 1962. 5.95 (ISBN 0-15-294999-2, HJ). HarBraceJ.

Strait, Treva A. The Price of Free Land. LC 78-24287. (Illus.). (gr. 4-6). 1979. 8.95 (ISBN 0-397-31836-7). Lippincott.

Tunis, Edwin. Frontier Living. LC 75-29639. (Illus.). 168p. (gr. 7 up). 1976. 14.95 (ISBN 0-690-01064-8, TYC-J). Har-Row.

FRONTIER AND PIONEER LIFE–AFRICA, SOUTH

Lamar, Howard & Thompson, Leonard, eds. The Frontier in History: North America & Southern Africa Compared. (Illus.). 336p. 1981. text ed. 37.50x (ISBN 0-300-02624-2); pap. 7.95x (ISBN 0-300-02742-7, Y-406). Yale U Pr.

FRONTIER AND PIONEER LIFE–ALASKA

Anderson, Doris. Ways Harsh & Wild. 10.95 (ISBN 0-88894-027-0, Pub. by Douglas & McIntyre); pap. 6.50 (ISBN 0-88894-140-4, Pub. by Douglas & McIntyre). Intl Schol Bk Serv.

Barber, Olive. Meet Me in Juneau. LC 60-53461. (Illus.). 1960. 8.95 (ISBN 0-8323-0079-9). Binford.

Black, Martha L. My Ninety Years. Whyard, Flo, ed. LC 76-3117. (Northern History Library). (Illus.). 1976. pap. 7.95 (ISBN 0-88240-062-2). Alaska Northwest.

Brower, Charles D. Fifty Years Below Zero. LC 42-22432. (Illus.). 1942. 8.95 (ISBN 0-396-02379-7). Dodd.

McKeown, Martha F. Trail Led North. (Illus.). 1960. 8.95 (ISBN 0-8323-0090-X). Binford.

Murie, Margaret E. Two in the Far North. 2nd ed. LC 78-16407. (Illus.). 1978. pap. 6.95 (ISBN 0-88240-111-4). Alaska Northwest.

FRONTIER AND PIONEER LIFE–CANADA

Angier, Bradford & Angier, Vena. At Home in the Woods: Living the Life of Thoreau Today. (Illus.). 9.50 (ISBN 0-911378-02-2). Sheridan.

Burke, Stanley & Peterson, Roy. Blood, Sweat & Bears. 7.50 (ISBN 0-88894-117-X, Pub. by Douglas & McIntyre). Intl Schol Bk Serv.

Cole, Jean M. Exile in the Wilderness: The Life of Chief Factor Archibald McDonald, 1790-1853. LC 79-5361. (Illus.). 288p. 1980. 15.95 (ISBN 0-295-95704-2). U of Wash Pr.

De Goutiere, Justin. The Pathless Way. pap. 6.50 (ISBN 0-88894-006-8, Pub. by Douglas & McIntyre). Intl Schol Bk Serv.

Farrow, Moira. Nobody Here but Us Pioneers of the North. pap. 7.50 (ISBN 0-88894-087-4, Pub. by Douglas & McIntyre). Intl Schol Bk Serv.

Gould, Ed. Ralph Edwards of Lonesome Lake. (Illus.). 1979. 17.00x (ISBN 0-87663-320-3, Pub. by Hancock Hse); pap. 7.95 (ISBN 0-87663-639-3, Pub. by Hancock Hse). Universe.

Guillet, Edwin C. Pioneer Arts & Crafts. 2nd ed. LC 72-415879. (Photos). 1968. pap. 3.50 (ISBN 0-8020-6081-1). U of Toronto Pr.

--Pioneer Days in Upper Canada. LC 66-37656. (Illus.). 1964. pap. 6.50 (ISBN 0-8020-6031-5). U of Toronto Pr.

--Pioneer Farmer & Backwoodsman, 2 Vols. LC 63-24314. (Illus.). 1963. boxed 37.50 (ISBN 0-8020-1753-3). U of Toronto Pr.

--Pioneer Settlements in Upper Canada. (Illus.). 1970. pap. 5.00 (ISBN 0-8020-6110-9). U of Toronto Pr.

--Pioneer Travel. LC 66-4464. (Illus.). 1966. pap. 5.00 (ISBN 0-8020-6052-8). U of Toronto Pr.

Harris, Lorraine. Halfway to the Goldfields. pap. 9.50 (ISBN 0-88894-062-9, Pub. by Douglas & McIntyre). Intl Schol Bk Serv.

McBurney, Margaret & Byers, Mary. Homesteads: Early Buildings & Families from Kingston to Toronto. (Illus.). 1979. 15.00 (ISBN 0-8020-2357-6). U of Toronto Pr.

Moodie, Susanna. Roughing It in the Bush. LC 70-104530. Repr. of 1852 ed. lib. bdg. 16.50x (ISBN 0-8398-1266-3). Irvington.

Patterson, R. M. Far Pastures. (Illus.). 299p. 1963. pap. 1.95 (ISBN 0-686-74144-7). Superior Pub.

Pritchett, John P. Black Robe & Buckskin. 1960. 3.00 (ISBN 0-8084-0063-0). Coll & U Pr.

Roberts, Sarah E. Alberta Homestead: Chronicle of a Pioneer Family. Roberts, Lathrop E., ed. (M. K. Brown Range Life Ser.: No. 10). (Illus.). 282p. 1971. 12.50 (ISBN 0-292-70143-8). U of Tex Pr.

Sharp, Paul F. Whoop-up Country: The Canadian-American West, 1865-1885. LC 73-3166. (Illus.). 368p. 1978. pap. 8.95 (ISBN 0-8061-1484-3). U of Okla Pr.

Stowe, Leland. Crusoe of Lonesome Lake. (YA) 1957. 8.95 (ISBN 0-394-42092-6). Random.

Traill, Catherine P. The Young Emigrants, or Pictures of Canada. (Early Children's Bks). Repr. of 1826 ed. 14.50 (ISBN 0-384-61350-0). Johnson Repr.

Turner, Trudy & McVeigh, Ruth. Fogswamp: Living with Swans in the Wilderness. (Illus.). 1977. 15.00x (ISBN 0-919654-63-0, Pub. by Hancock Hse); pap. 7.95 (ISBN 0-87663-636-9). Universe.

Wicks, Walter. Memories of the Skeena. (Illus.). 1976. 11.00x (ISBN 0-919654-62-2, Pub. by Hancock Hse). Universe.

FRONTIER AND PIONEER LIFE–INDIANA

Cox, Sandford C. Recollections of the Early Settlement of the Wabash Valley. facs. ed. LC 78-117870. (Select Bibliographies Reprint Ser). 1860. 15.00 (ISBN 0-8369-5323-1). Arno.

Hall, Baynard R. The New Purchase: Or, Seven & a Half Years in the Far West. facsimile ed. LC 75-101. (Mid-American Frontier Ser.). 1975. Repr. of 1843 ed. 35.00x (ISBN 0-405-06869-7). Arno.

Johnson, Howard. A Home in the Woods: Pioneer Life in Indiana. LC 77-74426. (Illus.). 104p. 1978. Repr. of 1951 ed. 8.95x (ISBN 0-253-32842-X). Ind U Pr.

FRONTIER AND PIONEER LIFE–KENYA

Huxley, Elspeth. Settlers of Kenya. LC 74-33894. (Illus.). 126p. 1975. Repr. of 1948 ed. lib. bdg. 15.00x (ISBN 0-8371-5457-X, HUSK). Greenwood.

FRONTIER AND PIONEER LIFE–NEW MEXICO

French, William. Further Recollections of a Western Ranchman: New Mexico 1883-1889, Vol. II. (Illus.). 1965. 20.00 (ISBN 0-87266-012-5). Argosy.

Poe, Sophie A. Buckboard Days. Cunningham, Eugene, ed. (Illus.). 304p. 1981. 14.95 (ISBN 0-8263-0572-5); pap. 8.95 (ISBN 0-8263-0573-3). U of NM Pr.

FRONTIER AND PIONEER LIFE–NEW YORK (STATE)

Cooper, William. Guide in the Wilderness. facs. ed. LC 79-140352. (Select Bibliographies Reprint Ser). 1810. 10.00 (ISBN 0-8369-5595-1). Arno.

FRONTIER AND PIONEER LIFE–NEW ZEALAND

Scholefield, Guy H., ed. Richmond-Atkinson Papers, 2 vols. (Illus.). 1960. 16.50x (ISBN 0-8426-1502-4). Verry.

FRONTIER AND PIONEER LIFE–NORTHWEST, OLD

Allman, C. B. Lewis Wetzel, Indian Fighter. (Illus.). 1961. 7.50 (ISBN 0-8159-6107-3). Devin.

Blair, Walter. Mike Fink, King of Mississippi Keelboatmen. LC 74-138143. (Illus.). 1971. Repr. of 1933 ed. lib. bdg. 15.25x (ISBN 0-8371-5600-9, BLMF). Greenwood.

Blegen, Theodore C. Grass Roots History. LC 75-85987. 1969. Repr. of 1947 ed. 13.50 (ISBN 0-8046-0602-1). Kennikat.

Brunson, Alfred. A Western Pioneer: Or, Incidents of the Life & Times of Rev. Alfred Brunson.., 2 vols. in 1. facsimile ed. LC 75-89. (Mid-American Frontier Ser.). 1975. Repr. of 1872 ed. 46.00x (ISBN 0-405-06856-5). Arno.

Doddridge, Joseph. Notes, on the Settlement & Indian Wars, of the Western Parts of Virginia & Pennsylvania, from the Year 1763 Until the Year 1783 Inclusive. LC 75-7062. (Indian Captivities Ser.: Vol. 40). 1977. Repr. of 1824 ed. lib. bdg. 44.00 (ISBN 0-8240-1664-5). Garland Pub.

Drache, Hiram M. The Challenge of the Prairie. LC 70-632775. 1970. 10.95 (ISBN 0-8134-1994-8). Interstate.

Eckert, Allan W. The Frontiersmen. 1967. 17.50 (ISBN 0-316-20856-6). Little.

Flandrau, Grace. Frontier Days Along the Upper Missouri. (Illus.). 40p. Repr. pap. 5.25 (ISBN 0-8466-0209-1, SJS209). Shorey.

Frost, John. Pioneer Mothers of the West; or, Daring & Heroic Deeds of American Women, Comprising Thrilling Examples of Courage, Fortitude, Devotedness & Self-Sacrifice. LC 74-3950. (Women in America Ser). (Illus.). 360p. 1974. Repr. of 1869 ed. 21.00x (ISBN 0-405-06097-1). Arno.

Fuller, Clark. Pioneer Paths. (Illus.). 1974. 10.00 (ISBN 0-931068-03-7). Purcells.

Isackson, Maxine B. The Sandhills Beckon. 1977. 10.00 (ISBN 0-931068-08-8). Purcells.

Morris, Lucy W., ed. Old Rail Fence Corners: Frontier Tales Told by Minnesota Pioneers. 344p. 1976. 8.50 (ISBN 0-87351-108-5); pap. 5.50 (ISBN 0-87351-109-3). Minn Hist.

Olson, David C. Life on the Upper Michigan Frontier. LC 74-76304. 250p. 1974. 8.95 (ISBN 0-8283-1544-2). Branden.

O'Meara, Walter. Guns at the Forks. LC 79-4000. (Illus.). 1979. pap. 5.95 (ISBN 0-8229-5309-9). U of Pittsburgh.

FRONTIER AND PIONEER LIFE–NORTHWESTERN STATES

Blue, John S. History & Tales of a Pioneer. (Illus.). 194p. 1980. 25.00x (ISBN 0-9604474-0-7). Jasper County.

Boller, Henry A. Among the Indians: Four Years on the Upper Missouri, 1858-1862. Quaife, Milo M., ed. LC 76-100810. (Illus.). xvi, 370p. 1972. pap. 4.50 (ISBN 0-8032-5714-7, BB 514, Bison). U of Nebr Pr.

Burt, Struthers M. Powder River: Let'er Buck. LC 73-144923. (Illus.). 1971. Repr. of 1938 ed. 29.00 (ISBN 0-403-00886-7). Scholarly.

Dimsdale, Thomas J. Vigilantes of Montana. (Western Frontier Library: No. 1). 1978. Repr. of 1953 ed. pap. 4.95 (ISBN 0-8061-1379-0). U of Okla Pr.

Donaldson, Thomas C. Idaho of Yesterday. LC 70-104218. Repr. of 1941 ed. lib. bdg. 25.00x (ISBN 0-8371-3335-1, DOID). Greenwood.

McCurdy, James G. Indian Days at Neah Bay. Newell, Gordon, ed. (Northwest Historical Classics Ser.). (Illus.). 123p. 1981. text ed. 10.95 (ISBN 0-939806-03-7); pap. text ed. 7.95 (ISBN 0-939806-04-5). Hist Soc Seattle.

Nesmith, James W. Two Addresses. 1978. 7.95 (ISBN 0-87770-200-4); pap. 4.95 (ISBN 0-87770-202-0). Ye Galleon.

Newell, Gordon. Westward to Alki. LC 76-56785. (Illus.). 1977. 10.95 (ISBN 0-87564-807-X). Superior Pub.

Reinhart, Herman F. The Golden Frontier: The Recollections of Herman Francis Reinhart, 1851-1869. Nunis, Doyce B., Jr., ed. (Personal Narratives of the West Ser.: No. 2). (Illus.). 381p. 1962. 14.95x (ISBN 0-292-73251-1). U of Tex Pr.

Riddle, George W. Early Days in Oregon. facsimile ed. (Illus.). pap. 8.50 (ISBN 0-8466-0188-5, SJS188). Shorey.

Roosevelt, Theodore. Ranch Life in the Far West. 1978. pap. 5.95 (ISBN 0-89646-034-7). Outbooks.

Russell, Osborne. Journal of a Trapper. Haines, Aubrey L., ed. LC 56-52. (Illus.). xxiv, 203p. 1965. 14.50x (ISBN 0-8032-0897-9); pap. 3.50 (ISBN 0-8032-5166-1, BB 316, Bison). U of Nebr Pr.

Sharp, Paul F. Whoop-up Country: The Canadian-American West, 1865-1885. LC 73-3166. (Illus.). 368p. 1978. pap. 8.95 (ISBN 0-8061-1484-3). U of Okla Pr.

Sheller, Roscoe. Ben Snipes: Northwest Cattle King. 4th ed. LC 57-13209. (Illus.). 1966. pap. 5.95 (ISBN 0-8323-0250-3). Binford.

Van Dusen, W. W. Blazing the Way: Pioneer Experiences in Idaho, Washington & Oregon. Repr. of 1905 ed. pap. 14.00 (ISBN 0-8466-0233-4, SJS233). Shorey.

Watt, Roberta F. Four Wagons West. (Illus.). 1966. 8.95 (ISBN 0-8323-0045-4); pap. 5.95 (ISBN 0-8323-0294-5). Binford.

White, Helen M., ed. Ho! for the Gold Fields: Northern Overland Wagon Trains of the 1860s. LC 66-64828. (Illus.). 289p. 1966. 8.50 (ISBN 0-87351-030-5). Minn Hist.

Wicks, Walter. Memories of the Skeena. (Illus.). 1976. 11.00x (ISBN 0-919654-62-2, Pub. by Hancock Hse). Universe.

FRONTIER AND PIONEER LIFE–ROCKY MOUNTAINS

Blair, Edward. Palace of Ice: A History of Leadville's Ice Palace, 1895-1896. 1978. 2.00 (ISBN 0-913488-03-8). Timberline Bks.

Marsh, James B. Four Years in the Rockies: or, the Adventures of Isaac P. Rose. LC 72-9459. (The Far Western Frontier Ser.). 266p. 1973. Repr. of 1884 ed. 15.00 (ISBN 0-405-04987-0). Arno.

Smith, Duane A. Rocky Mountain Mining Camps: The Urban Frontier. LC 67-24522. (Illus.). xii, 304p. 1974. pap. 3.50 (ISBN 0-8032-5792-9, BB 582, Bison). U of Nebr Pr.

Villard, Henry. The Past & the Present of the Pike's Peak Gold Regions. LC 76-87629. (The American Scene Ser). (Illus.). 186p. 1972. Repr. of 1932 ed. lib. bdg. 22.50 (ISBN 0-306-71804-9). Da Capo.

West, Elliott. The Saloon on the Rocky Mountain Mining Frontier. LC 78-24090. (Illus.). 1979. 14.50 (ISBN 0-8032-4704-4). U of Nebr Pr.

FRONTIER AND PIONEER LIFE–SOUTHWEST, NEW

Austin, Mary. Land of Little Rain. (Illus.). 7.00 (ISBN 0-8446-0465-8). Peter Smith.

Bieber, Ralph P. & Hafen, Leroy R., eds. Southwest Historical Series, 12 vols. (Illus.). Repr. lib. bdg. 195.00x (ISBN 0-87991-309-6). Porcupine Pr.

Cleaveland, Agnes M. No Life for a Lady. LC 75-25302. 366p. 1976. Repr. of 1941 ed. 15.00 (ISBN 0-88307-519-9). Gannon.

Gillmor, Frances & Wetherill, Louisa W. Traders to the Navajos: The Story of the Wetherills of Kayenta. LC 52-9210. 1965. pap. 6.95 (ISBN 0-8263-0040-5). U of NM Pr.

Horn, Tom. Life of Tom Horn, Government Scout & Interpreter, Written by Himself, Together with His Letters & Statements by His Friends: A Vindication. (Western Frontier Library: No. 26). 1964. pap. 4.95 (ISBN 0-8061-1044-9). U of Okla Pr.

Laune, Seigniora R. Sand in My Eyes. LC 74-82365. (Illus.). 256p. 1974. Repr. of 1956 ed. 7.50 (ISBN 0-87358-130-X). Northland.

Miller, Joseph, ed. Arizona Cavalcade. (Illus.). 1962. 8.95 (ISBN 0-8038-0320-6). Hastings.

Nunis, Doyce. Josiah Belden, 1841 California Overland Pioneer. LC 62-11494. (Illus.). 1962. 6.95 (ISBN 0-934612-04-8). Talisman.

Perkins, William. Three Years in California: Journal of Life at Sonora, 1849-1852. 1964. 18.95 (ISBN 0-520-01000-0). U of Cal Pr.

Robinson, W. Stitt. The Southern Colonial Frontier: 1607-1763. LC 78-21432. (Histories of the American Frontier Ser). 1979. pap. 8.95x (ISBN 0-8263-0503-2). U of NM Pr.

Sonnichsen, C. L., ed. Billy King's Tombstone: The Private Life of an Arizona Boom Town. LC 42-10170. (Southwest Chronicles). 1972. 7.50 (ISBN 0-8165-0396-6); pap. 6.50 (ISBN 0-8165-0375-3). U of Ariz Pr.

Thorp, N. Howard & Clark, Neil M. Pardner of the Wind. LC 77-7243. (Illus.). 1977. 18.50x (ISBN 0-8032-0938-X); pap. 4.75 (ISBN 0-8032-5875-5, BB 638, Bison). U of Nebr Pr.

Yount, George C. George C. Yount & His Chronicles of the West. Camp, C. L., ed. 280p. 1966. limited ed 35.00 (ISBN 0-912094-08-7). Old West.

FRONTIER AND PIONEER LIFE–SOUTHWEST, OLD

Boatright, Mody C. & Day, Donald, eds. From Hell to Breakfast. LC 45-1540. (Texas Folklore Society Publications: No. 19). (Illus.). 1967. Repr. of 1944 ed. 6.95 (ISBN 0-87074-012-1). SMU Press.

Churchill, E. Richard. The McCartys. 1978. 2.00 (ISBN 0-913488-02-X). Timberline Bks.

Dick, Everett. The Dixie Frontier. LC 73-19957. 374p. 1974. Repr. lib. bdg. 24.00x (ISBN 0-374-92157-1). Octagon.

Dobie, J. Frank, et al, eds. Texian Stomping Grounds. LC 41-4871. (Texas Folklore Society Publications: No. 17). 1967. Repr. of 1941 ed. 5.95 (ISBN 0-87074-048-2). SMU Press.

Ganzhorn, Jack. I've Killed Men: An Epic of Early Arizona. (Illus.). 1959. 6.50 (ISBN 0-8159-5821-8). Devin.

Geiser, Samuel W. Naturalists of the Frontier. rev. ed. LC 48-7357. (Illus.). 1948. 5.95 (ISBN 0-87074-059-8). SMU Press.

Hale, Will. Twenty-Four Years a Cowboy & Ranchman in Southern Texas & Old Mexico. (Western Frontier Library: No. 12). (Illus.). 1976. pap. 4.95 (ISBN 0-8061-1272-7). U of Okla Pr.

McCurdy, Frances L. Stump, Bar & Pulpit: Speechmaking on the Missouri Frontier. LC 74-93050. 1969. 9.00x (ISBN 0-8262-0081-8). U of Mo Pr.

Preece, Harold. Lone Star Man: The Life of Ira Aten. 1960. 7.50 (ISBN 0-8038-4255-4). Hastings.

Robinson, W. Stitt. The Southern Colonial Frontier: 1607-1763. LC 78-21432. (Histories of the American Frontier Ser). 1979. pap. 8.95x (ISBN 0-8263-0503-2). U of NM Pr.

Rohrbough, Malcolm J. The Trans-Appalachian Frontier. (Illus.). 1978. 22.50x (ISBN 0-19-502209-2). Oxford U Pr.

--The Trans-Appalachian Frontier. (Illus.). 1978. 22.50x (ISBN 0-19-502209-2). Oxford U Pr.

Snively, W. D., Jr. & Furbee, Louanna. Satan's Ferryman: A True Tale of the Old Frontier. LC 68-20522. (Illus.). 250p. (gr. 11-12). 1968. text ed. 14.95 (ISBN 0-8044-1875-6). Ungar.

Thorpe, Thomas B. Mysteries of the Backwoods. LC 71-104579. (Illus.). Repr. of 1846 ed. lib. bdg. 15.00x (ISBN 0-8398-1958-7). Irvington.

Webb, Walter P. Texas Rangers: A Century of Frontier Defense. new ed. 606p. 1965. 14.95 (ISBN 0-292-73400-X). U of Tex Pr.

FRONTIER AND PIONEER LIFE-TEXAS

Caffey, David L. The Old Home Place: Farming on the West Texas Frontier. (Illus.). 224p. 1981. 11.95 (ISBN 0-89015-283-7). Eakin Pubns.

Casey, Clifford B. A Bakers Dozen: We Were Thirteen, the Caseys of Tuscola, Taylor County, Texas. (Illus.). 1974. 9.75 (ISBN 0-933512-21-X). Pioneer Bk Tx.

Cook, James H. Fifty Years on the Old Frontier As Cowboy, Hunter, Guide, Scout, & Ranchman. LC 57-5951. 310p. 1957. 14.95 (ISBN 0-8061-0364-7). U of Okla Pr.

Coward, Margaret, ed. The Gaines County Story. (Illus.). 1974. 12.50 (ISBN 0-933512-18-X). Pioneer Bk Tx.

Gillett, James B. Six Years with the Texas Rangers, 1875 to 1881. Quaife, Milo M., ed. LC 76-4495. (Illus.). 1976. 17.50x (ISBN 0-8032-0889-8); pap. 5.95 (ISBN 0-8032-5844-5, BB 624, Bison). U of Nebr Pr.

God, Grass & Grit: History of the Sherman County Trade Area. (Illus.). 1971. Vol. I 1971. 12.50 (ISBN 0-686-77319-5). Vol. II 1975. 12.50 (ISBN 0-933512-23-6). Pioneer Bk Tx.

Holman, David & Persons, Billie. Buckskin & Homespun: Frontier Clothing in Texas, 1820-1870. (Illus.). 130p. 1979. 120.00 (ISBN 0-911796-06-1). Beacham.

Laine, Tanner. Cattle Call. (Illus.). 1975. 12.50 (ISBN 0-933512-22-8). Pioneer Bk Tx.

Ligon, Robert L. Just Dad - a Pioneer History of the Southwest. Ligon, Ernest M., ed. LC 76-45578. (Illus.). 1976. pap. 5.95 (ISBN 0-915744-06-6). Character Res.

Poe, Sophie A. Buckboard Days. Cunningham, Eugene, ed. (Illus.). 304p. 1981. 14.95 (ISBN 0-8263-0572-5); pap. 8.95 (ISBN 0-8263-0573-3). U of NM Pr.

Rathjen, Frederick W. The Texas Panhandle Frontier. LC 73-7602. (M. K. Brown Range Life Ser.: No. 12). (Illus.). 298p. 1973. 14.95 (ISBN 0-292-78007-9). U of Tex Pr.

Reagan County Historical Society & Werst, Mike, eds. The Reagan County Story. (Illus.). 1974. 12.50 (ISBN 0-933512-19-8). Pioneer Bk Tx.

Smith, Erwin E. & Haley, J. Evetts. Life on the Texas Range. LC 52-13181. (M. K. Brown Range Life Ser.: No. 14). (Illus.). 1973. 19.95 (ISBN 0-292-74605-9); pap. 9.95 (ISBN 0-292-74623-7). U of Tex Pr.

Smithers, W. D. Chronicles of the Big Bend: A Photographic Memoir of Life on the Border. LC 75-16939. (Illus.). 250p. 1976. 12.95 (ISBN 0-89052-016-X). Madrona Pr.

Spence, Vernon G. Pioneer Women of Abilene. (Illus.). 128p. 1981. 9.95 (ISBN 0-89015-281-0). Eakin Pubs.

Spiller, Wayne, compiled by. A Handbook of McCulloch County History, Vol. I. (Illus.). 1976. 16.95 (ISBN 0-933512-24-4). Pioneer Bk Tx.

Warwick, Mrs. Clyde W., ed. The Randall County Story: From 1541 to 1910. (Illus.). 1969. 12.50 (ISBN 0-933512-03-1). Pioneer Bk Tx.

White, Owen P. My Texas 'tis of Thee. facsimile ed. LC 76-169568. (Short Story Index Reprint Ser.). Repr. of 1936 ed. 16.00 (ISBN 0-8369-4031-8). Arno.

Wilhelm, Hubert G. Organized German Settlement & Its Effects on the Frontier of South-Central Texas. Cordasco, Francesco, ed. LC 80-905. (American Ethnic Groups Ser.). (Illus.). 1981. lib. bdg. 25.00x (ISBN 0-405-13464-9). Arno.

Wylie, Rosa L. History of Van Horn & Culberson County, Texas. (Illus.). 1973. 8.50 (ISBN 0-933512-31-7). Pioneer Bk Tx.

FRONTIER AND PIONEER LIFE-THE WEST

see also Frontier and Pioneer Life-Northwest, Old; Frontier and Pioneer Life-Northwestern States; Frontier and Pioneer Life-Southwest, New; Frontier and Pioneer Life-Southwest, Old

Adams, Andy. Log of a Cowboy: A Narrative of the Old Trail Days. LC 3-12817. (Illus.). x, 387p. 1964. 21.50x (ISBN 0-8032-1000-0); pap. 3.50 (ISBN 0-8032-5000-2, 192, Bison). U of Nebr Pr.

Albert, Herman W. Odyssey of a Desert Prospector. (Western Frontier Library: No. 35). 1974. pap. 5.95 (ISBN 0-8061-1180-1). U of Okla Pr.

Alter, J. Cecil. Jim Bridger. (Illus.). 1979. Repr. of 1962 ed. 15.95 (ISBN 0-8061-0546-1). U of Okla Pr.

Anderson, Charles G. In Search of the Buffalo: The Story of J. Wright Mooar. (Illus.). 1974. 5.95 (ISBN 0-933512-20-1). Pioneer Bk Tx.

Arnold, Mary E. & Reed, Mabel. In the Land of the Grasshopper Song: Two Women in the Klamath River Indian Country in 1908-09. LC 80-12556. (Illus.). iv, 313p. 1980. 17.95x (ISBN 0-8032-1804-4); pap. 5.95 (ISBN 0-8032-6703-7, BB 740, Bison). U of Nebr Pr.

Beckwourth, James P. & Bonner, Thomas D. The Life & Adventures of James P. Beckwourth. LC 73-88092. (Illus.). xvi, 649p. 1972. pap. 10.95 (ISBN 0-8032-0724-7) (ISBN 0-8032-6061-X, BB 773, Bison). U of Nebr Pr.

Billington, Ray A. Far Western Frontier: Eighteen Thirty to Eighteen Sixty. (New American Nation Ser.). (Illus.). pap. 4.95x (ISBN 0-06-133012-4, TB 3012, Torch). Har-Row.

Blacker, Irwin R., ed. Old West in Fact. 1962. 15.00 (ISBN 0-8392-1081-7). Astor-Honor.

Blair, Edward & Churchill, E. Richard. Everybody Came to Leadville. 1978. 2.00 (ISBN 0-913488-00-3). Timberline Bks.

Blair, Kay R. Ladies of the Lamplight. 1978. 2.00 (ISBN 0-913488-01-1). Timberline Bks.

Blasingame, Ike. Dakota Cowboy: My Life in the Old Days. LC 58-11667. (Illus.). 1964. 18.50x (ISBN 0-8032-0906-1); pap. 3.45 (ISBN 0-8032-5015-0, BB 191, Bison). U of Nebr Pr.

Blegen, Theodore C. & Davidson, Sarah A., eds. Iron Face. 1950. 10.00 (ISBN 0-686-30160-9). Caxton Club.

Boatright, Mody C. & Day, Donald, eds. Backwoods to Border. LC 48-18054. (Texas Folklore Society Publications: No. 18). (Illus.). 1967. Repr. of 1943 ed. 6.95 (ISBN 0-87074-011-3). SMU Press.

Bonner, T. D. Life & Adventures of James P. Beckwourth. 1965. Repr. 12.50 (ISBN 0-87018-003-7). Ross.

Bonner, T. D., ed. Life & Adventures of James P. Beckwourth, Mountaineer, Scout & Pioneer & Chief of the Crow Nation of Indians. LC 69-18563. (American Negro: His History & Literature Ser., No. 2). 1969. Repr. of 1856 ed. 19.00 (ISBN 0-405-01850-9). Arno.

Buffalo Bill, pseud. Buffalo Bill's True Tales. (Illus.). 24p. 1977. Repr. of 1879 ed. pap. 2.50 (ISBN 0-89646-022-3). Outbooks.

Campbell, Walter S. Mountain Men. LC 77-99620. (Essay Index Reprint Ser). 1937. 25.00 (ISBN 0-8369-1397-3). Arno.

Carson, Kit. Kit Carson's Autobiography. Quaife, Milo M., ed. LC 66-4130. (Illus.). 1966. pap. 3.95 (ISBN 0-8032-5031-2, BB 325, Bison). U of Nebr Pr.

Chapman, Arthur. The Reader of Romantic Adventure in Business. LC 70-164522. (Illus.). 320p. 1971. Repr. of 1932 ed. 12.50x (ISBN 0-8154-0391-7). Cooper Sq.

Chisholm, James. South Pass, 1868: James Chisholm's Journal of the Wyoming Gold Rush. Homsher, Lola M., ed. LC 60-12692. (Pioneer Heritage Ser.: Vol. 3). (Illus.). vi, 245p. 1960. pap. 2.95 (ISBN 0-8032-5824-0, BB 606, Bison). U of Nebr Pr.

Chrisman, Harry E. Lost Trails of the Cimarron. LC 61-14370. (Illus.). 313p. 1964. pap. 7.95 (ISBN 0-8040-0615-6, SB). Swallow.

Churchill, E. Richard. Doc Holliday, Bat Masterson, Wyatt Earp: Their Colorado Careers. 1978. 2.00 (ISBN 0-913488-05-4). Timberline Bks.

Clark, Thomas D., ed. Indiana University: Midwestern Pioneer, Historical Documents Since 1816, Vol. 4. LC 74-126207. 1977. 15.00x (ISBN 0-253-37501-0). Ind U Pr.

Clarke, Mary W. The Slaughter Ranches & Their Makers. (Illus.). Date not set. 12.95 (ISBN 0-686-70086-4). Jenkins.

Cody, William F. Life & Adventures of 'Buffalo Bill' facsimile ed. LC 74-169755. (Select Bibliographies Reprint Ser). Repr. of 1917 ed. 26.00 (ISBN 0-8369-5975-2). Arno.

--The Life of Hon. William F. Cody: Known As Buffalo Bill, the Famous Hunter, Scout, & Guide. LC 78-18732. (Illus.). xviii, 365p. 1978. 21.50x (ISBN 0-8032-1406-5); pap. 4.95 (ISBN 0-8032-6303-1, BB 686, Bison). U of Nebr Pr.

Collins, Dennis. Indians Last Fight or the Dull Knife Raid. LC 72-1004. Repr. of 1915 ed. 25.00 (ISBN 0-404-07122-8). AMS Pr.

Connelley, William E. Wild Bill & His Era: The Life & Adventures of James Butler Hickok. LC 76-187842. (Illus.). xii, 244p. 1972. Repr. of 1933 ed. 10.00x (ISBN 0-8154-0413-1). Cooper Sq.

Crawford, Thomas E. West of the Texas Kid, Eighteen Eighty-One to Nineteen Ten: Recollections of Thomas Edgar Crawford, Cowboy, Gun Fighter, Rancher, Hunter, Miner. Dykes, Jeff C., ed. (Western Frontier Library: No. 20). (Illus.). 1962. bds. 6.95 (ISBN 0-8061-0513-5); pap. 3.95 (ISBN 0-8061-1117-8). U of Okla Pr.

Crockett, David. Narrative of the Life of David Crockett of the State of Tennessee. LC 72-177358. (Tennesseana Editions Ser.). 1973. 9.95 (ISBN 0-87049-119-9). U of Tenn Pr.

Dick, Everett. Tales of the Frontier: From Lewis & Clark to the Last Roundup. LC 62-14664. (Illus.). 1963. 20.00x (ISBN 0-8032-0038-2); pap. 5.95 (ISBN 0-8032-5744-9, BB 539, Bison). U of Nebr Pr.

Doddridge, Joseph. Notes on the Settlement & Indian Wars. 1976. Repr. of 1824 ed. 15.00 (ISBN 0-87012-001-8). McClain.

Dykstra, Robert R. Cattle Towns. LC 68-12677. (Illus.). 1970. pap. text ed. 6.95x (ISBN 0-689-70253-1, 166). Atheneum.

Flower, George. The Errors of Emigrants. facsimile ed. LC 75-100. (Mid-American Frontier Ser.). 1975. Repr. of 1841 ed. 9.50x (ISBN 0-405-06868-9). Arno.

Frink, Maurice & Barthelmess, Casey E. Photographer on an Army Mule. (Illus.). 1966. Repr. of 1965 ed. 16.95 (ISBN 0-8061-0669-7). U of Okla Pr.

Gard, Wayne. Frontier Justice. (Illus.). 324p. 1981. 17.50 (ISBN 0-8061-0194-6); pap. 8.95 (ISBN 0-8061-1755-9). U of Okla Pr.

--Great Buffalo Hunt. LC 59-11049. (Illus.). 1968. pap. 5.95 (ISBN 0-8032-5067-3, BB 390, Bison). U of Nebr Pr.

Gillespie, Charles B. A Miner's Sunday, 1849. Jones, William R., ed. (Illus.). 18p. 1976. Repr. of 1891 ed. pap. 2.00 (ISBN 0-89646-005-3). Outbooks.

Goetzmann, William H. The Mountain Man. LC 78-51924. (Illus.). 64p. 1979. pap. 12.95 (ISBN 0-8032-7004-6, Buffalo Bill Hist. Ctr.). U of Nebr Pr.

Grimmett, Robert G. Cabal of Death. LC 77-15675. 1977. 7.50 (ISBN 0-89301-047-2). U Pr of Idaho.

Hafen, LeRoy & Hafen, Ann W. Reports from Colorado, 1859-65. (Illus.). 1961. 15.00 (ISBN 0-87062-040-1). A H Clark.

Hafen, LeRoy R. & Hafen, Ann W. Handcarts to Zion. LC 59-14279. (Illus.). 1969. 10.00 (ISBN 0-87062-027-4). A H Clark.

Hale, Will. Twenty-Four Years a Cowboy & Ranchman in Southern Texas & Old Mexico. (Western Frontier Library: No. 12). (Illus.). 1976. pap. 4.95 (ISBN 0-8061-1272-7). U of Okla Pr.

Hall, James. Letters from the West. LC 67-10123. 1967. Repr. of 1828 ed. 41.00x (ISBN 0-8201-1024-8). Schol Facsimiles.

Hardin, John W. Life of John Wesley Hardin As Written by Himself. (Western Frontier Library: No. 16). (Illus.). 1977. pap. 3.95 (ISBN 0-8061-1051-1). U of Okla Pr.

Hatch, Elvin. Biography of a Small Town. LC 79-313. 1979. 22.50x (ISBN 0-231-04694-4). Columbia U Pr.

Hine, Robert V. Community on the American Frontier: Separate but Not Alone. LC 80-5238. (Illus.). 292p. 1980. 12.50 (ISBN 0-8061-1678-1). U of Okla Pr.

Holm, Lewis N. Stepson of the Forest: An Anniversary Pioneer Story & Autobiography. (Illus.). 1977. 5.50 (ISBN 0-533-02567-2). Vantage.

Horan, James D. The Authentic Wild West: The Lawmen. (The Authentic Wild West Ser.). (Illus.). 352p. 1980. 15.95 (ISBN 0-517-54176-9). Crown.

--The Great American West. rev. ed. (Illus.). 1978. 14.95 (ISBN 0-517-53491-6). Crown.

Horn, Huston. The Pioneers. (The Old West Ser.). (Illus.). 1974. 14.95 (ISBN 0-8094-1475-9). Time-Life.

--The Pioneers. LC 73-94242. (The Old West). (Illus.). (gr. 5 up). 1974. kivar 12.96 (ISBN 0-8094-1477-5, Pub. by Time-Life). Silver.

Hoyt, Edward J. Buckskin Joe: Being the Unique & Vivid Memoirs of Edward Jonathan Hoyt, 1840-1918. Shirley, Glenn, ed. LC 65-24306. (Illus.). 1966. 9.95 (ISBN 0-8032-0081-1). U of Nebr Pr.

Hughes, Alton. Pecos: A History of the Pioneer West. LC 78-61694. (Illus.). 1978. 14.95 (ISBN 0-933512-28-7). Pioneer Bk Tx.

Inman, H. & Cody, W. F. Great Salt Lake Trail. (Illus.). 1897. Repr. 12.50 (ISBN 0-87018-030-4). Ross.

Inman, Henry. Old Santa Fe Trail. 1897. Repr. 12.50 (ISBN 0-87018-031-2). Ross.

Kelly, Luther S. Yellowstone Kelly: The Memoirs of Luther S. Kelly. Quaife, M. M., ed. LC 26-9001. (Illus.). xiv, 300p. 1973. pap. 6.50 (ISBN 0-8032-5784-8, BB 571, Bison). U of Nebr Pr.

Lamar, Howard R. The Trader on the American Frontier: Myth's Victim. LC 76-51650. (Essays on the American West Ser.-Elma Dill Russell Spencer: No.2). (Illus.). 56p. 1977. 5.00 (ISBN 0-89096-033-X). Tex A&M Univ Pr.

Leakey, John & Yost, Nellie S. West That Was: From Texas to Montana. LC 58-14110. (Illus.). 1965. pap. 2.95 (ISBN 0-8032-5117-3, BB 304, Bison). U of Nebr Pr.

Lemay, J. Leo. The Frontiersman from Lout to Hero: Notes on the Significance of the Comparative Method & the Stage Theory in Early American Literature & Culture. 1979. pap. 3.50 (ISBN 0-912296-39-9, Dist. by U Pr of Va). Am Antiquarian.

The Life & Travels of Josiah Mooso: A Life on the Frontier Among Indians & Spaniards, Not Seeing the Face of a White Woman for 15 Years. LC 75-7124. (Indian Captivities Ser.: Vol. 97). 1976. Repr. of 1888 ed. lib. bdg. 44.00 (ISBN 0-8240-1721-8). Garland Pub.

McCarthy, Frank C. Frank C. McCarthy: The Old West. limited ed. LC 81-80256. (Illus.). 168p. 1981. pre pub price - leather-bound, gold-embossed slipcase 850.00 (ISBN 0-86713-001-6). Greenwich CT.

McDermott, John F., ed. The Frontier Re-Examined. LC 67-12990. (Illus.). 1967. 12.00 (ISBN 0-252-72491-7). U of Ill Pr.

Majors, Alexander. Seventy Years on the Frontier. 1893. Repr. 10.00 (ISBN 0-87018-040-1). Ross.

Marshall, Thomas M., ed. The Life & Papers of Frederick Bates, 2 vols. in 1. facsimile ed. LC 75-109. (Mid-American Frontier Ser.). 1975. Repr. of 1926 ed. 39.00x (ISBN 0-405-06876-X). Arno.

Mattes, Merrill J. The Great Platte River Road: The Covered Wagon Mainline Via Fort Kearny to Fort Laramie. 2nd ed. LC 79-627916. (Nebraska State Historical Society Publications Ser.: Vol. 25). (Illus.). 1979. pap. 8.95 (ISBN 0-686-26254-9). Nebraska Hist.

Mattes, Merrill J., ed. Indians, Infants & Infantry. (Illus.). 304p. 1960. 7.50 (ISBN 0-912094-01-X). Old West.

Meriwether, David. My Life in the Mountains & on the Plains: A Newly Discovered Autobiography. Griffen, Robert A., ed. (American Exploration & Travel Ser.: No. 46). 1966. Repr. of 1965 ed. 16.95 (ISBN 0-8061-0668-9). U of Okla Pr.

Merriam, H. G., ed. Way Out West: Recollections & Tales. LC 68-31372. 1970. Repr. of 1969 ed. 15.95 (ISBN 0-8061-0833-9). U of Okla Pr.

Metcalf, P. Richard, ed. The American People on the Western Frontier. new ed. LC 72-95871. (American People Ser.). 175p. (Orig.). (gr. 9-12). 1973. PLB 7.95 (ISBN 0-88301-089-5); pap. 2.50 (ISBN 0-88301-073-9). Pendulum Pr.

Miller, Ronald D. Shady Ladies of the West. 8.50 (ISBN 0-87026-023-5). Westernlore.

Monaghan, James. Overland Trail. facs. ed. LC 73-107726. (Essay Index Reprint Ser). 1947. 25.00 (ISBN 0-8369-1999-8). Arno.

Mondy, Robert W. Pioneers & Preachers: Stories of the Old Frontier. LC 79-16906. (Illus.). 1980. 23.95x (ISBN 0-88229-619-1); pap. 13.95 (ISBN 0-88229-722-8). Nelson-Hall.

Murbarger, Nell. Sovereigns of the Sage: True Stories of People & Places in the Great Sagebrush Kingdom of the Western United States. (Illus.). 1977. pap. 7.95 (ISBN 0-918080-22-3). Treasure Chest.

Nelson, Bruce. Land of the Dacotahs. LC 65-108129. (Illus.). 1964. pap. 3.95 (ISBN 0-8032-5145-9, BB 176, Bison). U of Nebr Pr.

Nelson, John Y. Fifty Years on the Trail, a True Story of Western Life: The Adventures of John Young Nelson, As Described to Harrington O'Reilly. (Western Frontier Library: No. 22). (Illus.). 1969. Repr. of 1963 ed. 7.95 (ISBN 0-8061-0572-0). U of Okla Pr.

New Spain & the Anglo - American West: Historical Contributions Presented to Herbert Eugene Bolton, 2 Vols. in 1. LC 33-3181. 1968. Repr. of 1932 ed. 24.00 (ISBN 0-527-66950-4). Kraus Repr.

Norman, William M. A Portion of My Life. LC 59-13119. (Illus.). 1959. 6.95 (ISBN 0-910244-15-4). Blair.

North, Luther. Man of the Plains: Recollections of Luther North, 1856-1882. Danker, Donald F., ed. LC 61-6409. (Pioneer Heritage Ser.: Vol. 4). (Illus.). 1961. 16.50 (ISBN 0-8032-0131-1). U of Nebr Pr.

Nunis, Doyce. Josiah Belden, 1841 California Overland Pioneer. LC 62-11494. (Illus.). 1962. 6.95 (ISBN 0-934612-04-8). Talisman.

O'Neil, Paul. The End & the Myth. Time-Life Books, ed. LC 78-26389. (The Old West). (Illus.). 1979. 14.95 (ISBN 0-8094-2312-X). Time-Life.

O'Neill, Paul. The End & the Myth. (The Old West Ser.). (Illus.). 1979. lib. bdg. 12.96 (ISBN 0-686-51083-6). Silver.

Pappas, Martha R., ed. Heroes of the American West. (American Character Ser). (Illus.). (gr. 9-12). 1969. pap. text ed. 5.50 (ISBN 0-684-51542-3, SSP21, ScribC). Scribner.

Parkman, Frances. Oregon Trail. Feltskog, E. N., ed. (Illus.). 854p. 1969. 27.50 (ISBN 0-299-05070-X). U of Wis Pr.

Parkman, Francis. Oregon Trail. (Classics Ser). (gr. 6 up). 1964. pap. 1.50 (ISBN 0-8049-0037-X, CL-37). Airmont.

--Oregon Trail. (RL 8). pap. 1.75 (ISBN 0-451-51377-0, CE1377, Sig Classics). NAL.

Paxson, Frederic L. Last American Frontier. LC 75-115693. (Illus.). 402p. 1970. Repr. of 1910 ed. lib. bdg. 13.50x (ISBN 0-8154-0324-0). Cooper Sq.

Peters, DeWitt C. Life & Adventures of Kit Carson, the Nestor of the Rocky Mountains from Facts Narrated by Himself. LC 76-109631. (Select Bibliographies Reprint Ser). 1858. 30.00 (ISBN 0-8369-5240-5). Arno.

Phares, Ross. Bible in Pocket, Gun in Hand: The Story of Frontier Religion. LC 64-11375. 1971. pap. 3.95 (ISBN 0-8032-5725-2, BB 524, Bison). U of Nebr Pr.

--Cavalier in the Wilderness: The Story of the Explorer & Trader Louis Juchereau De St. Denis. 7.75 (ISBN 0-8446-0846-7). Peter Smith.
Pioneer Circuses of the West. 8.50 (ISBN 0-686-74360-1). Westernlore.
Powell, H. M. Santa Fe Trail to California, 1849-1852. Watson, Douglas S., ed. LC 79-174284. (Illus.). Repr. of 1931 ed. lib. bdg. 125.00 (ISBN 0-404-05099-9). AMS Pr.
Powers, Bob. South Fork Country. LC 72-180832. (Illus.). 1972. 18.95 (ISBN 0-87026-020-0). Westernlore.
Reiter, J. The Women. LC 78-1346. (The Old West Ser.). (Illus.). 1978. lib. bdg. 12.96 (ISBN 0-686-51082-8). Silver.
Remington, Frederick. Pony Tracks. (Western Frontier Library: No. 19). (Illus.). 1977. pap. 3.95 (ISBN 0-8061-1248-4). U of Okla Pr.
Richmond, Robert W. & Mardock, Robert W., eds. Nation Moving West: Readings in the History of the American Frontier. LC 66-10446. x, 366p. 1966. 20.00x (ISBN 0-8032-0152-4); pap. 3.50x (ISBN 0-8032-5157-2, BB 336, Bison). U of Nebr Pr.
Rickey, Don, Jr. Forty Miles a Day on Beans & Hay: The Enlisted Soldier Fighting the Indian Wars. (Illus.). 1977. pap. 7.95 (ISBN 0-8061-1113-5). U of Okla Pr.
Ridge, Martin & Billington, Ray A., eds. America's Frontier Story: A Documentary History of Westward Expansion. LC 79-28118. 668p. 1980. pap. text ed. 14.50 (ISBN 0-89874-090-8). Krieger.
Riley, Glenda. Frontierswomen, the Iowa Experience. (Illus.). 1981. 18.95 (ISBN 0-8138-1470-7). Iowa St U Pr.
Robinson, Chandler A. J. Evetts Haley: Passing of the Old West. Date not set. 12.50 (ISBN 0-8363-0160-9). Jenkins.
Rolle, Andrew F. Immigrant Upraised: Italian Adventurers & Colonists in an Expanding America. LC 68-10302. (Illus.). 1968. 17.95x (ISBN 0-8061-0810-X). U of Okla Pr.
Ross, Nancy. Westward the Women. LC 76-117832. (Essay Index Reprint Ser). 1944. 16.00 (ISBN 0-8369-1846-0). Arno.
Rounds, Glen. The Treeless Plains. (Illus.). 96p. (gr. 4-6). 1967. 8.95 (ISBN 0-8234-0122-7). Holiday.
Royce, Sarah. A Frontier Lady: Recollections of the Gold Rush & Early California. Gabriel, Ralph H., ed. LC 76-44263. (Illus.). 1977. 10.95x (ISBN 0-8032-0909-6); pap. 2.45 (ISBN 0-8032-5856-9, BB 634, Bison). U of Nebr Pr.
Ruede, Howard. Sod-House Days. Ise, J., ed. LC 66-17858. 248p. Repr. of 1937 ed. 11.00x (ISBN 0-8154-0200-7). Cooper Sq.
Russell, Carl P. Guns on the Early Frontiers: A History of Firearms from Colonial Times Through the Years of the Western Fur Trade. LC 80-12570. xvi, 395p. 1980. 19.50x (ISBN 0-8032-3857-6); pap. 6.95 (ISBN 0-8032-8903-0, BB 747, Bison). U of Nebr Pr.
Sandoz, Mari. Old Jules. LC 35-27361. 1962. pap. 4.95 (ISBN 0-8032-5173-4, BB 100, Bison). U of Nebr Pr.
Sanford, Mollie D. Mollie: Journal of Mollie Dorsey Sanford in Nebraska & Colorado Territories, 1857-1866. LC 59-13675. (Pioneer Heritage Ser: Vol. 1). 1959. 13.75x (ISBN 0-8032-0162-1). U of Nebr Pr.
Santee, Ross. Men & Horses. LC 76-57158. (Illus.). 1977. 16.50x (ISBN 0-8032-0919-3); pap. 3.50 (ISBN 0-8032-5859-3, BB 639, Bison). U of Nebr Pr.
Saturday Evening Post Editors. The Saturday Evening Post Saga of the American West. LC 80-67057. (Illus.). 144p. 1980. 15.95 (ISBN 0-89387-043-9). Curtis Pub Co.
The Saturday Evening Post Saga of the American West. LC 80-67057. (Illus.). 1980. 13.95 (ISBN 0-89387-043-9). Sat Eve Post.
Savage, William W. & Thompson, Stephen I., eds. The Frontier: Comparative Studies, Vol. II. LC 76-62507. (Illus.). 1979. 14.95 (ISBN 0-8061-1514-9). U of Okla Pr.
Schaefer, Jack. Monte Walsh. LC 80-25036. x, 442p. 1981. 21.50x (ISBN 0-8032-4124-0); pap. 7.50 (ISBN 0-8032-9121-3, BB 755, Bison). U of Nebr Pr.
Shepherd, William. Prairie Experiences in Handling Cattle & Sheep. facsimile ed. LC 70-165807. (Select Bibliographies Reprint Ser.). Repr. of 1885 ed. 16.00 (ISBN 0-8369-5964-7). Arno.
Silliman, Eugene L. We Seized Our Rifles. (Illus.). 200p. 1981. 10.95 (ISBN 0-87842-121-1). Mountain Pr.
Smith, Dwight L., ed. Western Life in the Stirrups. 1965. 10.00 (ISBN 0-686-30161-7). Caxton Club.
Smith, Marguerite E. & Stubblefield, Mildred S. Pioneer Heritage: The Smith Family. (Illus.). 1977. 9.95 (ISBN 0-533-02626-1). Vantage.
Snyder, Joel. American Frontiers: The Photographs of Timothy H. O'Sullivan, 1867-1874. (Illus.). 128p. 1981. 35.00 (ISBN 0-89381-083-5). Aperture.
Sonnichsen, C. L., ed. Billy King's Tombstone: The Private Life of an Arizona Boom Town. LC 42-10170. (Southwest Chronicles). 1972. 7.50 (ISBN 0-8165-0396-6); pap. 6.50 (ISBN 0-8165-0375-3). U of Ariz Pr.
Sprague, William F. Women & the West: A Short Social History. LC 72-2624. (American Women Ser: Images & Realities). (Illus.). 304p. 1972. Repr. of 1940 ed. 15.00 (ISBN 0-405-04480-1). Arno.
Steffen, Jerome O. Comparative Frontiers: A Proposal for Studying the American West. LC 79-20315. 128p. 1980. 10.95 (ISBN 0-8061-1617-X). U of Okla Pr.
Stewart, Elinore P. Letters of a Woman Homesteader. LC 61-16191. 1961. pap. 3.50 (ISBN 0-8032-5193-9, BB 115, Bison). U of Nebr Pr.
Stork, Byron C. Rawhide & Haywire. (Illus.). 1959. 4.25 (ISBN 0-87164-007-4). William-F.
Streeter, Floyd B. Prairie Trails & Cow Towns. (Illus.). 1963. 6.95 (ISBN 0-8159-6510-9). Devin.
Todd, Edgeley W., ed. A Doctor on the California Trail: Diary of Dr. John Hudson Wayman from Indiana to the Gold Fields in 1852. ltd. ed. (Illus.). 132p. 1971. 15.00 (ISBN 0-912094-16-8). Old West.
Toponce, Alexander. Reminiscences of Alexander Toponce. LC 71-145507. (Illus.). 1971. 7.95x (ISBN 0-8061-0954-8). U of Okla Pr.
Vail, R. W. Voice of the Old Frontier. LC 78-120673. 1970. Repr. lib. bdg. 17.50x (ISBN 0-374-98068-3). Octagon.
Van Every, Dale. The Final Challenge: The American Frontier, 1804-1845. LC 76-1431. (Frontier People of America Ser.). 1976. Repr. of 1964 ed. 15.00x (ISBN 0-405-05544-7). Arno.
Van Nuys, Laura B. Family Band: From the Missouri to the Black Hills, 1881-1900. LC 61-17253. (Pioneer Heritage Ser: Vol. 5). (Illus.). 1962. 16.95x (ISBN 0-8032-0186-9). U of Nebr Pr.
Vestal, Stanley. Short Grass Country. Repr. of 1941 ed. lib. bdg. 15.00 (ISBN 0-8371-2978-8, VESG). Greenwood.
Visscher, William L. Pony Express. 2nd ed. 3.00 (ISBN 0-685-19496-5). Powner.
Ward, Don & Dykes, J. C. Cowboys & Cattle Country. LC 61-18251. (American Heritage Junior Library). (Illus.). 153p. (gr. 5 up). 1961. 9.95 (ISBN 0-8281-0389-5, J008-0). Am Heritage.
Ward, Don, ed. Bits of Silver: Western Anthology. 1961. 8.95 (ISBN 0-8038-0687-6). Hastings.
Wheeler, Keith. The Townsmen. (The Old West Ser). (Illus.). 240p. 1975. 14.95 (ISBN 0-8094-1488-0). Time-Life.
Wiltsee, Ernest A. The Pioneer Miner & the Pack Mule Express. LC 76-4134. (Illus.). 160p. 1976. Repr. 35.00x (ISBN 0-88000-084-8). Quarterman.
Wright, Robert M. Dodge City. facsimile ed. LC 75-132. (Mid-American Frontier Ser.). (Illus.). 1975. Repr. of 1913 ed. 22.00x (ISBN 0-405-06897-2). Arno.
Wyman, Walker D. California Emigrant Letters. LC 78-175936. (Illus.). Repr. of 1952 ed. 17.50 (ISBN 0-404-07059-0). AMS Pr.

FRONTIER AND PIONEER LIFE–THE WEST–FICTION

Steele, James W. Frontier Army Sketches. LC 73-99567. 1969 (ISBN 0-8263-0159-2). pap. 7.95 (ISBN 0-8263-0233-5). U of NM Pr.

FRONTIER FORMALITIES

see International Travel Regulations

FRONTIERS

see Boundaries

FROST, JOHN, 1784-1877

Williams, David. John Frost: A Study in Chartism. LC 73-93275. Repr. of 1939 ed. 17.50x (ISBN 0-678-07502-6). Kelley.

FROST, ROBERT, 1874-1963

Barry, Elaine. Robert Frost. LC 72-79942. (Modern Literature Ser.). 1973. 10.95 (ISBN 0-8044-2016-5). Ungar.
--Robert Frost on Writing. 1974. 14.00 (ISBN 0-8135-0692-1); pap. 3.95 (ISBN 0-8135-0789-8). Rutgers U Pr.
Bober, Natalie S. A Restless Spirit: The Story of Robert Frost. LC 80-23930. (Illus.). 224p. (gr. 6 up). 1981. PLB 10.95 (ISBN 0-689-30801-9). Atheneum.
Borroff, Marie. Language & the Poet: Verbal Artistry in Frost, Stevens, & Moore. LC 78-14567. (Illus.). 1979. lib. bdg. 15.00x (ISBN 0-226-06651-7). U of Chicago Pr.
Clemens, Cyril. A Chat with Robert Frost. LC 7-860. 1977. lib. bdg. 6.50 (ISBN 0-8414-3567-7). Folcroft.
Coffin, Robert P. New Poetry of New England: Frost & Robinson. LC 64-12140. 1964. Repr. of 1938 ed. 10.00 (ISBN 0-8462-0414-2). Russell.
Cook, Reginald L. Robert Frost: A Living Voice. LC 74-78982. (New England Writers Ser.). 360p. 1974. 15.00 (ISBN 0-87023-165-0). U of Mass Pr.
Cox, James M., ed. Robert Frost: A Collection of Critical Essays. 1962. 10.95 (ISBN 0-13-331512-6, Spec). P-H.
Cox, Sidney. Swinger of Birches: A Portrait of Robert Frost. 1961. pap. 0.95 (ISBN 0-02-002190-9, Collier). Macmillan.
--A Swinger of Birches: A Portrait of Robert Frost. LC 54-6902. 1957. 14.00x (ISBN 0-8147-0105-1). NYU Pr.
Crane, Joan St. C., compiled by. Robert Frost: A Descriptive Catalogue of Books & Manuscripts in the Clifton Waller Barrett Library, University of Virginia. LC 73-89904. (Illus.). 150p. 1974. 17.50x (ISBN 0-8139-0509-5). U Pr of Va.
Doyle, John R., Jr. Poetry of Robert Frost: An Analysis. 1965. 9.75 (ISBN 0-02-843990-2). Hafner.
Evans, William R. Robert Frost & Sidney Cox: Forty Years of Friendship. LC 80-54464. 310p. 1981. 17.50 (ISBN 0-87451-195-X). U Pr of New Eng.
Ford, Caroline. Less Traveled Road, Study of Robert Frost. LC 74-12496. 1935. lib. bdg. 8.50 (ISBN 0-8414-4238-X). Folcroft.
Francis, Robert. Frost: A Time to Talk, Conversations & Indiscretions Recorded by Robert Francis. LC 72-77570. (New England Writers Ser.). 104p. 1972. 7.50x (ISBN 0-87023-106-5). U of Mass Pr.
Frost, Lesley. New Hampshire's Child: Derry Journals of Lesley Frost. LC 69-12099. (Illus.). 1969. 29.00 (ISBN 0-87395-043-7); microfiche 29.00 (ISBN 0-87395-143-3). State U NY Pr.
Frost, Robert. Robert Frost: Farm-Poultryman--The Story of Robert Frost's Career As a Breeder & Fancier of Hens. Lathem, Edward C. & Thompson, Lawrance, eds. LC 64-638. 116p. 1963. 10.00 (ISBN 0-87451-032-5). U Pr of New Eng.
Gerber, Philip L. Robert Frost. (Twayne's United States Authors Ser). 1966. pap. 3.45 (ISBN 0-8084-0266-8, T107, Twayne). Coll & U Pr.
--Robert Frost. (U. S. Authors Ser.: No. 107). 1966. lib. bdg. 9.95 (ISBN 0-8057-0296-2). Twayne.
Grant, Douglas. Robert Frost & His Reputation. LC 77-7604. 1977. Repr. of 1965 ed. lib. bdg. 8.50 (ISBN 0-8414-4595-8). Folcroft.
Greiner, Donald J. & Sanders, Charles. Robert Frost: The Poet & His Critics. (Poet & His Critics Ser.: No. 1). 1974. 20.00 (ISBN 0-8389-0191-3). ALA.
Harris, Kathryn G. Robert Frost: Studies of the Poetry. 196p. 1979. lib. bdg. 18.95 (ISBN 0-8161-8397-X). G K Hall.
Isaacs, Elizabeth. Introduction to Robert Frost. LC 72-4617. (American Literature Ser., No. 49). 1972. Repr. of 1962 ed. lib. bdg. 49.95 (ISBN 0-8383-1593-3). Haskell.
Jones, Dewitt & Bradley, David. Robert Frost, a Tribute to the Source. LC 78-10444. (Illus.). 176p. 1979. 20.00 (ISBN 0-03-046326-2). HR&W.
Kemp, John C. Robert Frost & New England: The Poet As Regionalist. LC 78-70301. 1979. 15.00 (ISBN 0-691-06393-1). Princeton U Pr.
Lathem, Edward C. & Thompson, Lawrance. Robert Frost & the Lawrence Massachusetts, "High School Bulletin". 1966. 20.00x (ISBN 0-8139-0460-9, Dist. by U Pr of Va). Grolier Club.
--Robert Frost & the Lawrence Massachusetts, "High School Bulletin": The Beginning of a Literary Career. LC 66-29452. (Illus.). 94p. 1966. 20.00x (ISBN 0-8139-0460-9, Grolier Club). U Pr of Va.
Lentricchia, Frank & Lentricchia, Melissa C. Robert Frost: A Bibliography, 1913-1974. LC 75-44093. (Author Bibliographies Ser.: No. 25). 1976. 11.00 (ISBN 0-8108-0896-X). Scarecrow.
Lentriccia, Frank. Robert Frost: Modern Poetics & the Landscapes of Self. LC 74-83787. 1975. 12.50 (ISBN 0-8223-0329-9). Duke.
Longo, Lucas. Robert Frost: Twentieth Century Modern American Poet Laureate. Rahmas, D. Steve, ed. LC 70-190239. (Outstanding Personalities Ser: No. 21). 32p. (Orig.). (gr. 7-9). 1972. lib. bdg. 2.95 incl. catalog cards (ISBN 0-87157-521-3); pap. 1.50 vinyl laminated covers (ISBN 0-87157-021-1). SamHar Pr.
Mertins, Louis. Robert Frost: Life & Talks-Walking. (Illus.). 1966. Repr. of 1965 ed. 22.50x (ISBN 0-8061-0653-0). U of Okla Pr.
Mertins, M. Louis & Mertins, Esther P. The Intervals of Robert Frost: A Critical Bibliography. LC 73-94144. (Illus.). vi, 91p. 1976. Repr. of 1947 ed. 11.00 (ISBN 0-8462-1787-2). Russell.
Munson, Gorham B. Robert Frost: A Study in Sensibility & Good Sense. LC 72-10857. (Studies in Poetry, No. 38). 1969. Repr. of 1927 ed. lib. bdg. 49.95 (ISBN 0-8383-0788-4). Haskell.
Nitchie, George W. Human Values in the Poetry of Robert Frost. LC 60-10813. xi, 242p. 1960. 14.50 (ISBN 0-8223-0123-7); pap. 8.75 (ISBN 0-8223-0358-2). Duke.
--Human Values in the Poetry of Robert Frost: A Study of a Poet's Convictions. LC 78-4612. 242p. 1978. Repr. of 1960 ed. 9.50 (ISBN 0-87752-199-9). Gordian.
Orton, Urest. Vermont Afternoons with Robert Frost. LC 70-134029. 64p. 1981. pap. 4.50 (ISBN 0-686-73717-2). Academy Bks.
Poirier, Richard. Robert Frost. LC 76-57259. (The Work of Knowing). 1977. 14.95 (ISBN 0-19-502216-5). Oxford U Pr.
--Robert Frost: The Work of Knowing. 1979. pap. 5.95 (ISBN 0-19-502615-2, GB 586, GB). Oxford U Pr.
Potter, James L. Robert Frost Handbook. LC 79-9145. 1980. text ed. 15.95x (ISBN 0-271-00230-1). Pa St U Pr.
Sharma, T. R. S. Robert Frost's Poetic Style. 1981. text ed. 15.00x (ISBN 0-391-01794-2). Humanities.
Smyth, Daniel. Robert Frost Speaks. 158p. 18.95x (ISBN 0-8290-0203-0). Irvington.
--Robert Frost Speaks. 9.95 (ISBN 0-685-60140-4, Pub by Twayne). Cyrco Pr.
Sweeney, John D. & Lindroth, James. Monarch Notes on Frost's Poetry. (Orig.). pap. 1.50 (ISBN 0-671-00783-1). Monarch Pr.
Tharpe, Jac, ed. Frost: Centennial Essays. LC 73-93331. 1974. 17.50x (ISBN 0-87805-055-8). U Pr of Miss.
--Frost: Centennial Essays II. LC 76-26665. 1976. 12.00x (ISBN 0-87805-026-4). U Pr of Miss.
--Frost: Centennial Essays III. LC 78-3548. (Illus.). 1978. 15.00x (ISBN 0-87805-047-7). U Pr of Miss.
Thompson, Lawrance. Robert Frost. rev. ed. (Pamphlets on American Writers Ser: No. 2). (Orig.). 1964. pap. 1.25x (ISBN 0-8166-0192-5, MPAW2). U of Minn Pr.
Thompson, Lawrance & Winnick, R. H. Robert Frost: A Biography. Lathem, Edward C., ed. LC 80-28337. (Illus.). 592p. 1981. 25.00 (ISBN 0-03-050921-1). HR&W.
Thompson, Lawrance R. Fire & Ice: The Art & Thought of Robert Frost. LC 61-15326. 1961. Repr. of 1942 ed. 13.00 (ISBN 0-8462-0283-2). Russell.
Thompson, Lawrence. Emerson & Frost, Critics of Their Times. LC 73-182. 1940. lib. bdg. 10.00 (ISBN 0-8414-1381-9). Folcroft.
--Robert Frost: A Chronological Survey. LC 74-9991. 1973. lib. bdg. 10.00 (ISBN 0-8414-8583-6). Folcroft.
Thompson, Lawrence R. Robert Frost: A Chronological Survey. 58p. 1980. Repr. of 1936 ed. lib. bdg. 10.00 (ISBN 0-8495-5815-8). Arden Lib.
Vail, Dennis. Robert Frost's Imagery & the Poetic Consciousness. (Graduate Studies: No. 12). (Orig.). 1976. pap. 4.00 (ISBN 0-89672-022-5). Tex Tech Pr.
Van Egmond, Peter. The Critical Reception of Robert Frost: Reference Bks. 1974. lib. bdg. 20.00 (ISBN 0-8161-1105-7). G K Hall.
Vogel, Nancy. Robert Frost, Teacher. LC 73-89797. vii, 99p. 1974. pap. 3.95 (ISBN 0-87367-759-5). Phi Delta Kappa.
Wagner, Linda, ed. Robert Frost: The Critical Reception. 1977. 21.50 (ISBN 0-89102-096-9); pap. 8.95 (ISBN 0-685-81130-1). B Franklin.

FROST

see also Frost Protection; Frozen Ground; Ice; Refrigeration and Refrigerating Machinery

Killian, H. Cold & Frost Injuries: Rewarming Damages. (Disaster Medicine: Vol. 3). (Illus.). 260p. 1981. pap. 65.70 (ISBN 0-387-08991-8). Springer-Verlag.

FROST PROTECTION

Protection of Plants Against Adverse Weather. (Technical Note Ser.). (Orig.). 1972. pap. 12.00 (ISBN 0-685-02934-4, 281, WMO). Unipub.
Techniques of Frost Prediction & Methods of Frost & Cold Protection. 1978. pap. 37.00 (ISBN 92-63-10487-5, W403, WMO). Unipub.
World Meteorological Organization. Protection Against Frost Damage. (Technical Note Ser.). 1968. pap. 11.00 (ISBN 0-685-22333-7, WMO). Unipub.

FROSTINGS, CAKE

see Icings, Cake

FROTHINGHAM, DAVID, 1765-ca. 1814

Diamond, Beatrice. Episode in American Journalism. LC 64-15546. 1964. 11.50 (ISBN 0-8046-0108-9). Kennikat.

FROTTAGE

see Rubbings

FROUDE, JAMES ANTHONY, 1818-1894

Burrow, John W. A Liberal Descent: Victorian Historians & the English Past. LC 81-3912. 336p. Date not set. price not set (ISBN 0-521-24079-4). Cambridge U Pr.
Dunn, Waldo H. Froude & Carlyle: A Study of the Froude - Carlyle Controversy. LC 68-26221. 1969. Repr. of 1933 ed. 15.00 (ISBN 0-8046-0124-0). Kennikat.

Goetzman, Robert. James Anthony Froude: A Bibliography of Studies. LC 75-24080. (Reference Library of the Humanities: Vol. 27). 1977. lib. bdg. 22.50 (ISBN 0-8240-9985-0). Garland Pub.

Paul, Herbert. The Life of Froude. 1973. Repr. of 1905 ed. 25.00 (ISBN 0-8274-1236-3). R West.

Salmon, Charles S. Caribbean Confederation: A Plan for the Union of the Fifteen British West Indian Colonies. LC 73-89057. Repr. of 1888 ed. 11.00x (ISBN 0-8371-1833-6, Pub. by Negro U Pr). Greenwood.

Wilson, D. Mr. Froude & Mr. Carlyle. LC 75-122460. (English Biography Ser., No. 31). 1970. Repr. of 1898 ed. lib. bdg. 54.95 (ISBN 0-8383-0904-6). Haskell.

FROZEN ASSETS

see Liquidity (Economics)

FROZEN FOOD

see Food, Frozen

FROZEN FOOD COOKERY

see Cookery (Frozen Foods)

FROZEN GROUND

see also Ice-Wedge Polygons; Patterned Ground

Brown, Roger J. Permafrost in Canada: Its Influence on Northern Development. LC 70-464841. (Illus.). 1970. 22.50x (ISBN 0-8020-1602-2). U of Toronto Pr.

Building Research Advisory Board. Permafrost. 2nd ed. (Illus.). 744p. 1973. 44.50 (ISBN 0-309-02115-4). Natl Acad Pr.

--Permafrost: Russian Papers. 1978. pap. 18.00 (ISBN 0-309-02746-2). Natl Acad Pr.

Johnston, G. H. Permafrost: Engineering Design & Construction. 540p. 1981. 37.50 (ISBN 0-471-79918-1, Pub. by Wiley-Interscience). Wiley.

Jumikis, Alfred R. Thermal Geotechnics. 1977. 42.00 (ISBN 0-8135-0824-X). Rutgers U Pr.

Linell, Kenneth A. & Tedrow, C. F. Soil & Permafrost Surveys in the Arctic. (Monographs on Soil Survey). (Illus.). 250p. 1981. 49.50 (ISBN 0-19-857557-2). Oxford U Pr.

Pewe, Troy L. Permafrost & Its Effect on Life in the North. LC 52-19235. (Illus.). 1970. pap. 2.95 (ISBN 0-87071-141-5). Oreg St U Pr.

Tsytovich, N. A. Mechanics of Frozen Ground. 1975. 45.00 (ISBN 0-07-065410-7, P&RB). McGraw.

Vigdorchik, Michael. Submarine Permafrost on the Alaskan Continental Shelf. (Westview Special Studies in Earth Science). 1979. lib. bdg. 25.75 (ISBN 0-89158-659-8). Westview.

FROZEN SEMEN

see Semen, Frozen

FROZEN SPERM

see Semen, Frozen

FROZEN STARS

see Black Holes (Astronomy)

FRUCTOSEDIPHOSPHATASE

McGilvery, R. W. & Pogell, B. M., eds. Fructose -One, Six-Diphosphates & Its Role in Gluconeogenesis. 1964. 5.50 (ISBN 0-934454-40-X). Lubrecht & Cramer.

FRUIT

see also Berries; Citrus Fruits; Cookery (Fruit); Fruit-Culture; Fruit Juices;
also particular fruits, e.g. Apple, Orange

Allen, Betty M. Common Malaysian Fruits. (Malaysian Nature Handbooks). (Illus.). 1975. 7.50x (ISBN 0-582-72409-0). Intl Pubns Serv.

Appel, Louise. Lexique Anglais-Francais Des Fruits et Legumes. rev. ed. 128p. (Eng.-Fr.). 1974. pap. 2.95 (ISBN 0-686-56897-4, M-6007). French & Eur.

Bager, Bertel. Nature As Designer: A Botanical Art Study. (Illus.). 1966. pap. 7.95 (ISBN 0-442-22017-0). Van Nos Reinhold.

Blanchet, Francoise & Doornekamp, Rinke. What to Do with...Fruit. LC 77-89095. (Children's Cookery Ser.). (gr. 3-8). 1979. 2.95 (ISBN 0-8120-5257-9). Barron.

Carcione, Joe & Lucas, Bob. The Greengrocer. LC 72-85171. (Illus.). 1978. pap. 5.95 (ISBN 0-87701-113-3). Chronicle Bks.

Carrol, Frieda. Pick Your Own Fruits & Vegetables & More. LC 80-70861. 1981. 14.95 (ISBN 0-939476-12-6); pap. 9.95 (ISBN 0-939476-11-8). Biblio Pr GA.

Ceres. Herbs & Fruit for Dieting. LC 80-53452. (Everybodys Home Herbal Ser.). 64p. 1981. pap. 1.95 (ISBN 0-394-74837-9). Shambhala Pubns.

Crispo, Dorothy. The Story of Our Fruits & Vegetables. pap. 3.50 (ISBN 0-8159-6826-4). Devin.

Cyphers, Emma H. Fruit & Vegetable Arrangements. rev. ed. 4.50 (ISBN 0-8208-0014-7). Hearthside.

Day, Jenifer W. What Is a Fruit? (Child's Golden Science Bks.). (Illus.). (gr. k-4). 1976. PLB 6.92 (ISBN 0-307-61801-3, Golden Pr). Western Pub.

De Verteuil, Maurice. Maurice's Tropical Fruits Cookbook. pap. 1.95 (ISBN 0-8200-0806-0). Great Outdoors.

Flood, R. B. Home Fruit & Vegetable Production. LC 78-4214. 1978. 10.00 (ISBN 0-8108-1132-4). Scarecrow.

Gide. Fruits of the Earth. 1970. 2.95 (ISBN 0-442-82234-0). Peter Pauper.

Goldman, Ethel. I Like Fruit. LC 68-56699. (Nature Bks for Young Readers). (Illus.). (gr. k-5). 1969. PLB 4.95 (ISBN 0-8225-0270-4). Lerner Pubns.

Goor, Asaph & Nurock, Max. The Fruits of the Holy Land. (Illus.). 1978. 16.95 (ISBN 0-89955-235-8, Pub. by IPST). Intl Schol Bk Serv.

Gunn, Charles R. & Dennis, John V. World Guide to Tropical Drift Seeds & Fruits. LC 75-36255. (Illus.). 256p. 1976. 17.50 (ISBN 0-8129-0616-0, Demeter). Times Bks.

Harrison, S. G., et al. Oxford Book of Food Plants. (Illus.). 1969. 17.95 (ISBN 0-19-910006-3). Oxford U Pr.

Hedrick, U. P. Fruits for the Home Garden. (Illus.). 224p. 1973. pap. 3.50 (ISBN 0-486-22944-0). Dover.

--Fruits for the Home Garden. (Illus.). 5.50 (ISBN 0-8446-4753-5). Peter Smith.

International Standardisation of Fruit & Vegetables: Peaches. rev. ed. 40p. 1979. 9.00x (ISBN 92-64-01994-4). OECD.

Kadans, Joseph N. Encyclopedia of Fruits, Vegetables, Nuts & Seeds for Healthful Living. 1973. 9.95 (ISBN 0-13-275412-6, Reward); pap. 3.95 (ISBN 0-13-275420-7). P-H.

McCoy, Doyle. Roadside Wild Fruits of Oklahoma. LC 79-6705. (Illus.). 96p. (Orig.). 1980. pap. 8.95 (ISBN 0-8061-1626-9). U of Okla Pr.

Martin, Dick. The Apple Book. (Illus.). 24p. (ps-4). 1964. PLB 5.38 (ISBN 0-307-68904-2, Golden Pr). Western Pub.

Martin, Franklin W., et al. Cultivation of Neglected Tropical Fruits with Promise. (Studies in Tropical Agriculture). 1980. lib. bdg. 59.95 (ISBN 0-8490-3074-9). Gordon Pr.

Miller, Erston V. & Munger, James I. Good Fruits & How to Buy Them. (Illus., Orig.). 1967. 4.50 (ISBN 0-910286-22-1); pap. 2.95 (ISBN 0-910286-04-3). Boxwood.

Mitgutsch, Ali. From Seed to Pear. LC 81-83. (Carolrhoda Start to Finish Bks.). Orig. Title: Vom Kern Zur Birne. (Illus.). 24p. (ps-3). 1981. PLB 5.95 (ISBN 0-87614-163-7). Carolrhoda Bks.

Peterson, Maude G. How to Know Wild Fruits. LC 72-95943. (Illus.). 1973. pap. text ed. 4.00 (ISBN 0-486-22943-2). Dover.

Popenoe, Wilson. Manual of Tropical & Subtropical Fruits: Excluding the Banana, Coconut, Pineapple, Citrus Fruits, Olive & Fig. (Illus.). 1974. Repr. 15.95 (ISBN 0-02-850280-9). Hafner.

Processed Fruits & Vegetables. (Food & Beverage Studies). 280p. 1980. 350.00 (ISBN 0-686-31520-0). Busn Trend.

The Propogation of Tropical Fruit Trees. (Horticultural Review Ser.: No. 4). 1978. pap. 24.00 (ISBN 0-85198-351-0, CAB 4, FAO). Unipub.

Salunkhe, D. K. Storage, Processing & Nutritional Quality of Fruits & Vegetables. LC 74-20660. (Monotopic Reprint Ser.). 176p. 1974. Repr. 19.95 (ISBN 0-8493-0123-8). CRC Pr.

Samson, J. A. Tropical Fruits. LC 74-40498. (Tropical Agriculture Ser.). (Illus.). 288p. 1980. text ed. 38.00x (ISBN 0-582-46032-8). Longman.

Selsam, Millicent E. The Apple & Other Fruits. (Illus.). 48p. (gr. k-3). 1973. PLB 7.92 (ISBN 0-688-30089-8). Morrow.

Seymour, John. The Self-Sufficient Gardener: A Complete Guide to Growing & Preserving All Your Own Food. LC 78-19223. 1979. 15.95 (ISBN 0-385-14670-1). Doubleday.

Shewell-Cooper, W. E. Plants, Flowers & Herbs of the Bible. LC 76-58772. (Illus.). 180p. 1977. 7.95 (ISBN 0-87983-166-9); pap. 3.95 (ISBN 0-87983-147-2). Keats.

Simmons, Alan F. Potted Orchards: Growing Fruit in Small Spaces. (Illus.). 192p. 1975. 4.95 (ISBN 0-7153-6666-1). David & Charles.

Singh, Ranjit. Fruits. (India-Land & People Ser). 1969. 4.50x (ISBN 0-8426-1536-9). Verry.

Stefferud, Alfred. Wonders of Seeds. LC 35-27284. (gr. 5-9). 1956. 4.95 (ISBN 0-15-299466-1, HJ). HarBraceJ.

Turner, Nancy J. & Szczawinski, Adam F. Edible Wild Fruits & Nuts of Canada. (Illus.). 1979. pap. 9.95 spiral bdg. (ISBN 0-660-00128-4, 56328-6, Pub. by Natl Mus Canada). U of Chicago Pr.

Vegetables & Fruit, 4 vols. (National Peking University & Chinese Assn. for Folklore, Folklore & Folkliterature Ser.: Suppl. 1, Vols. 9-12). (Chinese.). 1974. Set. 50.00 (ISBN 0-89986-218-7). E Langstaff.

Westwood, Melvin N. Temperate-Zone Pomology. LC 77-26330. (Illus.). 1978. text ed. 29.95x (ISBN 0-7167-0196-0). W H Freeman.

FRUIT-DISEASES AND PESTS

see also Fruit-Flies; Insects, Injurious and Beneficial; Plant Diseases; Scale-Insects;
also subdivision Diseases and Pests under particular fruits, and names of diseases and pests

Bethell, Richard S., ed. Pear Pest Management. LC 78-67293. 1978. 3-ring polymer bndr. 20.00x (ISBN 0-931876-26-5, 4086). Ag Sci Pubns.

Frazier, N. W., ed. Virus Diseases of Small Fruits & Grapevines. 1970. 7.50x (ISBN 0-931876-21-4, 4056). Ag Sci Pubns.

Hall, E. G. & Scott, K. J. Storage & Market Diseases of Fruit. (Illus.). 1978. pap. 3.50x (ISBN 0-643-00217-0, Pub. by CSIRO). Intl Schol Bk Serv.

International Organization of Citrus Virologists, 2nd Conference. Proceedings. Price, W. C., ed. LC 61-64183. 1961. 10.00 (ISBN 0-8130-0189-7). U Presses Fla.

Klotz, Leo J. Color Handbook of Citrus Diseases. LC 73-620140. 1973. pap. 5.00x (ISBN 0-931876-06-0, 4015). Ag Sci Pubns.

Storage & Market Diseases of Fruit: Collected Supplements I-XXIV Reprinted from CSIRO Food Research Quarterly. 52p. 1977. pap. 6.50 (ISBN 0-686-71846-1, CO 39, CSIRO). Unipub.

Toms, A. M. & Dahl, M. H. Pests & Diseases of Fruit & Vegetables in the Garden. (Color Ser.). 1976. 8.95 (ISBN 0-7137-0771-2, Pub by Blandford Pr England). Sterling.

FRUIT-MARKETING

Here are entered works on the marketing of fruit from the point of view of the farmer. Works on the marketing of fruit from the point of view of the commodity dealer are entered under the heading Fruit trade.

Burrows, Fredrika A. Cannonball & Cranberries. LC 76-3143. (Illus.). 1976. 4.95 (ISBN 0-88492-011-9); pap. 2.50 (ISBN 0-88492-012-7). W S Sullwold.

Lloyd, John W. Co-Operative & Other Organized Methods of Marketing California Horticultural Products. (Illinois Studies in the Social Sciences: Vol. 8, No. 1). Repr. of 1919 ed. 9.50 (ISBN 0-384-33185-8). Johnson Repr.

Storage & Market Diseases of Fruit: Collected Supplements I-XXIV Reprinted from CSIRO Food Research Quarterly. 52p. 1977. pap. 6.50 (ISBN 0-686-71846-1, CO 39, CSIRO). Unipub.

Watts, Gilbert S. How to Make a Million Dollars from a Fruit & Vegetables Roadside Market. (Illus.). 1977. Repr. 39.75 (ISBN 0-89266-054-6). Am Classical Coll Pr.

FRUIT-PESTS

see Fruit-Diseases and Pests

FRUIT-PRESERVATION

Fitzley, George, ed. Growing & Preserving Your Own Fruits & Vegetables. LC 75-4569. (Illus.). 240p. 1975. 9.95 (ISBN 0-8246-0198-X). Jonathan David.

Flack, Dora D. Fun with Fruit Preservation: Leather, Drying, & Other Methods. LC 74-78025. (Illus.). 98p. 1973. pap. 5.50 (ISBN 0-88290-023-4). Horizon Utah.

Goodenough, P. W. & Atkin, R. K. Quality of Stored & Processed Vegetables & Fruit. LC 81-66382. 1981. 62.00 (ISBN 0-12-289740-4). Acad Pr.

Hanson, L. P. Commercial Processing of Fruits. LC 75-32117. (Food Technology Review Ser: No. 30). (Illus.). 302p. 1976. 36.00 (ISBN 0-8155-0608-2). Noyes.

Jagtiani, Duru, ed. Fruit Preservation. 128p. 1980. text ed. 10.50 (ISBN 0-7069-1039-7, Pub. by Vikas India). Advent NY.

McBean, D. M. Drying & Processing Tree Fruits. (Illus.). 20p. 1977. pap. 1.50x (ISBN 0-643-00181-6, Pub. by CSIRO). Intl Schol Bk Serv.

Phelan, Chas. Dried Fruit: Its Care, Protection from Worms, Packing, Storing, Etc. facs. ed. Repr. of 1902 ed. pap. 4.95 (ISBN 0-8466-6049-0, SJU49). Shorey.

Preservation of Fruit & Vegetables by Radiation. 1968. pap. 9.75 (ISBN 92-0-111068-5, ISP149, IAEA). Unipub.

Recommended International Standard for Apple Juice Preserved Exclusively by Physical Means. 1972. pap. 4.50 (ISBN 0-685-36321-X, F589, FAO). Unipub.

Recommended International Standard for Canned Pears. (Codex Alimentarius Commission Reports Ser.). 20p. (Orig.). 1975. pap. 4.50 (ISBN 0-685-53181-3, F602, FAO). Unipub.

Recommended International Standard for Canned Strawberries. (Codex Alimentarius Commission Reports Ser.). 18p. (Orig.). 1975. pap. 4.50 (ISBN 0-685-53179-1, F603, FAO). Unipub.

Recommended International Standard for Orange, Grapefruit & Lemon Juices Preserved Exclusively by Physical Means. 1972. pap. 4.50 (ISBN 0-685-36312-0, F588, FAO). Unipub.

Recommended International Standards for Quick Frozen Raspberries. (Codex Alimentarius Commission). 8p. 1977. pap. 4.50 (ISBN 0-685-86029-9, F609, FAO). Unipub.

Rice, Eddy. How to Grow, Preserve & Store All the Food You Need. (Illus.). 1977. 10.95 (ISBN 0-87909-350-1). Reston.

Seymour, John. The Self-Sufficient Gardener: A Complete Guide to Growing & Preserving All Your Own Food. LC 78-19223. 1979. 15.95 (ISBN 0-385-14670-1). Doubleday.

FRUIT-STORAGE

Cooling & Ripening of Fruits in Relation to Quality. 1973. pap. 24.75 (ISBN 0-686-52755-0, IIR25, IIR). Unipub.

Haard, Norman F. & Salunkhe, D. K. Postharvest Biology & Handling of Fruits & Vegetables. (Illus.). 1975. text ed. 27.50 (ISBN 0-87055-187-6). AVI.

Packing Stations for Fruits & Vegetables. 1973. pap. 17.75 (ISBN 0-685-99159-8, IIR6, IIR). Unipub.

Ryall, A. Lloyd & Lipton, Werner J. Handling, Transporation & Storage of Fruits & Vegetables, Vol. 1. 2nd ed. (Illus.). 1979. text ed. 55.00 (ISBN 0-87055-264-3). AVI.

Storage & Market Diseases of Fruit: Collected Supplements I-XXIV Reprinted from CSIRO Food Research Quarterly. 52p. 1977. pap. 6.50 (ISBN 0-686-71846-1, CO 39, CSIRO). Unipub.

FRUIT-VARIETIES

Brooks, Reid M. & Olmo, Harold P. Register of New Fruit & Nut Varieties. 2nd rev. & enl. ed. LC 76-100017. 512p. 1972. 25.75x (ISBN 0-520-01638-6). U of Cal Pr.

Peterson, Mary E. How to Know Wild Fruits. (Illus.). 6.50 (ISBN 0-8446-4791-8). Peter Smith.

FRUIT, FORCING OF

see Forcing (Plants)

FRUIT-CULTURE

see also Berries; Dwarf Fruit Trees; Fungi in Agriculture; Grafting; Horticulturists; Nurseries (Horticulture); Olive Industry and Trade; Plant Propagation; Pruning; Viticulture;
also names of fruits

Abraham, George. Green Thumb Book of Fruit & Vegetable Gardening. LC 78-85000. (Illus.). 1969. 11.95 (ISBN 0-13-365189-4). P-H.

Alexander, D. M. Some Avocado Varieties for Australia, 1980. 10.00x (ISBN 0-643-02276-7, Pub. by CSIRO Australia). State Mutual Bk.

Allen, Betty M. Common Malaysian Fruits. (Malaysian Nature Handbooks). (Illus.). 1975. 7.50x (ISBN 0-582-72409-0). Intl Pubns Serv.

Alth, Max. How to Farm Your Backyard the Mulch Organic Way. (Illus.). 1977. 9.95 (ISBN 0-07-001128-1, P&RB). McGraw.

Bailey, Liberty H. Sketch of the Evolution of Our Native Fruits. LC 72-89072. (Rural America Ser.). 1973. Repr. of 1898 ed. 26.00 (ISBN 0-8420-1473-X). Scholarly Res Inc.

Beatty, Virginia L. & Consumer Guide Editors. Consumer Guide Rating & Raising Vegetables: A Practical Guide for Growing Vegetables, Herbs, Fruits & Sprouts. 8.95 (ISBN 0-671-22361-5); pap. 4.95 (ISBN 0-671-22362-3). S&S.

Clarke, Harold. Growing Berries & Grapes at Home. 384p. 1976. pap. 4.50 (ISBN 0-486-23274-3). Dover.

Control of Bitter Pit & Breakdown by Calcium in the Apples Cox's Orange Pippin & Jonathan. (Agricultural Research Reports Ser.: No. 711). 43p. 1968. pap. 4.00 (ISBN 0-686-71855-0, PDC 173, Pudoc). Unipub.

Crockett, James U. Vegetables & Fruits. (The Encyclopedia of Gardening Ser.). (Illus.). 1972. 12.95 (ISBN 0-8094-1069-9); lib. bdg. avail. (ISBN 0-685-27455-1). Time-Life.

Drying & Processing Tree Fruits. 52p. 1976. pap. 6.00 (ISBN 0-686-71829-1, CO 40, CSIRO). Unipub.

Edwards, Ray. Growing Soft Fruits. 1980. pap. 4.50 (ISBN 0-7153-7903-8). David & Charles.

The Expert Gardener: A Treatise Containing Certaine Necessary, Secret, & Ordinary Knowledges in Grafting. LC 74-80178. (English Experience Ser.: No. 659). (Illus.). 54p. 1974. Repr. of 1640 ed. 6.00 (ISBN 90-221-0659-4). Walter J Johnson.

Fogg, H. G. Soft Fruit Growing. 160p. 1981. pap. 12.00x (ISBN 0-906379-01-6, Pub. by Jupiter England). State Mutual Bk.

Geiser, Samuel W. Horticulture & Horticulturists in Early Texas. LC 46-161. 1945. pap. 1.00 (ISBN 0-87074-058-X). SMU Press.

Genders, Roy. Growing Soft Fruit. (Gardening Farming Ser.). (Illus.). 128p. 1977. 7.95 (ISBN 0-7207-0951-2, Pub. by Michael Joseph). Merrimack Bk Serv.

--Simple Fruit Growing. (Illus.). Date not set. pap. 2.95 (ISBN 0-8120-0908-8). Barron.

Gilbert, Zoe. Fruit Growing in Southern Africa. 1980. 25.00x (ISBN 0-686-69982-3, Pub. by Bailey & Swinton South Africa). State Mutual Bk.

Graham, J. J. Observations on the Alewife, Pomolobus Pseudoharengus (Wilson), in Fresh Water. (Scholarly Reprint Ser.). 1978. Repr. of 1956 ed. 10.00x (ISBN 0-8020-7093-0). U of Toronto Pr.

Griggs, William H. & Iwakiri, Ben T. Asian Pear Varieties in California. 1977. pap. 3.00x (ISBN 0-931876-00-1, 4068). Ag Sci Pubns.

Hill, Lewis. Fruit & Berries for the Home Garden. 1977. 11.95 (ISBN 0-394-40059-3). Knopf.
Janick, Jules & Moore, James N. Advances in Fruit Breeding. LC 73-76916. (Illus.). 640p. 1975. 30.00 (ISBN 0-911198-36-9). Purdue.
Lee, Hollis. Nuts, Berries & Grapes. (Country Home & Small Farm Guides). 96p. 1981. 5.95 (ISBN 0-442-27229-4); pap. 2.95 (ISBN 0-442-27228-6). Van Nos Reinhold.
--Nuts, Berries & Grapes. (Country Home & Small Farm Guides Ser.). (Illus.). 1978. pap. 2.95 (ISBN 0-88453-009-4). Barrington.
--Orchard Handbook. (Country Home & Small Farm Guides). 96p. 1981. 5.95 (ISBN 0-442-27227-8); pap. 2.95 (ISBN 0-442-27225-1). Van Nos Reinhold.
--Orchard Handbook. (Country Home & Small Farm Guides Ser.). 1978. pap. 2.95 (ISBN 0-88453-007-8). Barrington.
Leeg, Elizabeth. Container Farming. LC 75-16641. (Illus.). 160p. (Orig.). 1975. pap. 1.25 (ISBN 0-89041-022-4, 3022). Major Bks.
Logsdon, Gene. Successful Berry Growing. 1977. pap. 3.95 (ISBN 0-87857-182-5). Rodale Pr Inc.
Mascall, Leonard. A Booke of the Arte & Manner How to Plant & Graffe All Sortes of Trees. LC 74-80200. (English Experience Ser.: No. 679). 90p. 1974. Repr. of 1572 ed. 13.00 (ISBN 90-221-0679-9). Walter J Johnson.
Nijjar, G. S. Fruit Breeding in India. 219p. 1981. 15.00x (ISBN 0-686-76637-7, Pub. by Oxford & IBH India). State Mutual Bk.
Ortho Books Editorial Staff, ed. All About Growing Fruits & Berries. LC 76-29250. (Illus.). 1977. pap. 4.95 ea.; pap. midwest-northeast ed. (ISBN 0-917102-29-0); pap. west ed. (ISBN 0-917102-28-2); pap. south ed. (ISBN 0-917102-30-4). Ortho.
Popenoe, Wilson. Manual of Tropical & Subtropical Fruits: Excluding the Banana, Coconut, Pineapple, Citrus Fruits, Olive & Fig. (Illus.). 1974. Repr. 15.95 (ISBN 0-02-850280-9). Hafner.
Ramos, David. Prune Orchard Management. LC 80-71944. (Illus.). 144p. (Orig.). 1981. pap. 10.00x (ISBN 0-931876-45-1). AG Sci Pubns.
Reichenbach, Ethel K. The Life of a Cranberry Grower. (Illus.). 70p. 1981. 6.95 (ISBN 0-533-04719-6). Vantage.
Rice, Eddy. How to Grow, Preserve & Store All the Food You Need. (Illus.). 1977. 10.95 (ISBN 0-87909-350-1). Reston.
Scheer, Arnold H. & Juergenson, E. M. Approved Practices in Fruit & Vine Production. 2nd ed. (Illus.). 550p. 1976. 14.00 (ISBN 0-8134-1704-X, 1704). Interstate.
Schuler, Stanley. Gardens Are for Eating. 1971. 9.95 (ISBN 0-02-607410-9). Macmillan.
Shewell-Cooper, W. E. The Compost Fruit Grower. 200p. 1975. 13.95 (ISBN 0-7207-0757-9, Pub. by Michael Joseph). Merrimack Bk Serv.
Shoemaker, James S. Small Fruit Culture. 5th ed. (Illus.). 1978. lib. bdg. 22.00 (ISBN 0-87055-248-1). AVI.
Simmons, Alan. Simmon's Manual of Fruit. 1979. 19.95 (ISBN 0-7153-7607-1). David & Charles.
Smith, J. Russell. Tree Crops. 1978. pap. 5.95 (ISBN 0-06-090610-3, CN 610, CN). Har-Row.
Steffel, Edwin, ed. Home Growing. LC 77-256. (Illus.). 1977. 19.95 (ISBN 0-312-38836-5). St Martin.
Sturrock, David. Fruits for Southern Florida. 196p. 1980. pap. 7.95 (ISBN 0-9600046-2-9). Horticultural.
Taverner, John. Certaine Experiments Concerning the Fish & the Fruite. LC 76-6030. (English Experience Ser.: No. 75). 38p. 1968. Repr. of 1600 ed. 7.00 (ISBN 90-221-0075-8). Walter J Johnson.
Westwood, Melvin N. Temperate-Zone Pomology. LC 77-26330. (Illus.). 1978. text ed. 29.95x (ISBN 0-7167-0196-0). W H Freeman.

FRUIT-CULTURE–GREAT BRITAIN

Neuteboom, Dan I. Cox Production in England. (Illus.). 1979. pap. 6.95 (ISBN 0-901361-20-8, Pub. by Grower Books England). Intl Schol Bk Serv.

FRUIT-CULTURE–HAWAII

Miller, Carey D., et al. Fruits of Hawaii: Description, Nutritive Value, & Recipes. 4th ed. 1976. pap. 4.95 (ISBN 0-8248-0448-1). U Pr of Hawaii.

FRUIT-FLIES

Ashburner, M. & Novitski, E., eds. The Genetics & Biology of Drosophila. Incl. Vol. 1, 3 pts. 1976. Pt. A. 82.50 (ISBN 0-12-064901-2); Pt. B. 60.50 (ISBN 0-12-064902-0); Pt. C. 82.50 (ISBN 0-12-064903-9); Vol. 2, 5 pts. 1978-79. Pt. A. 107.00 (ISBN 0-12-064940-3); Pt. B. 86.50 (ISBN 0-12-064941-1); Pt. C. 93.00 (ISBN 0-12-064942-X); Pt. D. 124.50 (ISBN 0-12-064943-8); Pt. E. write for info. (ISBN 0-12-064944-6). Acad Pr.
Clark, Arnold M., et al. Aging in Insects. (Aging Ser.). 201p. 1976. text ed. 24.50x (ISBN 0-8422-7269-0). Irvington.
Controlling Fruit Flies by the Sterile-Insect Technique. (Illus.). 175p. 1976. pap. 17.25 (ISBN 92-0-111575-X, ISP392, IAEA). Unipub.
Demerec, M. & Kaufmann, B. P. Drosophila Guide: Introduction to the Genetics & Cytology of Drosophila melanogaster. rev. ed. (Illus.). 47p. 1969. lab manual 2.50 (ISBN 0-87279-950-6). Carnegie Inst.
King, Robert C. Ovarian Development in Drosophila Melanogaster. 1970. 42.00 (ISBN 0-12-408150-9). Acad Pr.
Lindsley, Dan L. & Grell, E. H. Genetic Variations of Drosophila melanogaster. LC 68-15915. (Illus.). 472p. 1968. 16.50 (ISBN 0-87279-638-8, 627). Carnegie Inst.
Lints, F. A., et al. Aging in Drosophila. (Aging Ser.). 179p. 1977. text ed. 24.50x (ISBN 0-8422-7244-5). Irvington.
Siddiqui, O., et al, eds. Development & Neurobiology of Drosophila. (Basic Life Sciences Ser.: Vol. 16). 485p. 1980. 49.50 (ISBN 0-306-40559-8, Plenum Pr). Plenum Pub.
Sterile-Male Technique for Control of Fruit Flies. (Illus., Orig.). 1970. pap. 13.00 (ISBN 92-0-111570-9, ISP276, IAEA). Unipub.
Strickberger, M. W. Experiments in Genetics with Drosophila. LC 62-16158. 144p. 1962. pap. 14.95x (ISBN 0-471-83373-8). Wiley.

FRUIT JARS, GLASS

see Glass Fruit Jars

FRUIT JUICES

Bedford, Stewart. Stress & Tiger Juice: How to Manage Your Stress & Improve Your Life & Health. LC 79-92277. 128p. 1980. 9.95x (ISBN 0-935930-00-0); pap. 5.95x (ISBN 0-935930-01-9). Scott Pubns CA.
Brandt, Johanna. The Grape Cure. 192p. 1971. pap. 2.25 (ISBN 0-87904-002-5). Lust.
Charmine, Susan E. The Complete Raw Juice Therapy. 1977. pap. 2.95 (ISBN 0-89437-018-9). Baronet.
Fruit Juice Processing. (Agricultural Services Bulletin Ser.: No. 13). (Illus.). 1976. pap. 7.50 (ISBN 92-5-100174-X, F708, FAO). Unipub.
Hanssen, Maurice. The Blender & Juicer Book. 1977. pap. 1.50 (ISBN 0-89437-029-4). Baronet.
Kirschner, H. E. Live Food Juices. 3.00 (ISBN 0-686-29769-5). Cancer Bk Hse.
Kramer, Jackie. The Juicer Cookbook. 1978. pap. 5.95 (ISBN 0-346-12366-6). Cornerstone.
Krop, J. J. The Mechanism of Cloud Loss in Orange Juice. (Agricultural Research Reports: No. 830). (Illus.). vi, 107p. 1975. pap. 14.00 (ISBN 90-220-0545-3, Pub. by PUDOC). Unipub.
Lovewisdom, Johnny. Modern Juice Therapy. pap. 2.00 (ISBN 0-933278-08-X). OMango.
Lust, John B. Raw Juice Therapy. 1978. 4.95 (ISBN 0-87904-026-2). Lust.
Nelson, Philip E. & Tressler, Donald K. Fruit & Vegetable Juice Processing Technology. 3rd ed. (Illus.). 1980. text ed. 49.50 (ISBN 0-87055-362-3). AVI.
Newman, Laura. Make Your Juicer Your Drug Store. LC 66-125414. (Illus.). 192p. 1978. pap. 2.50 (ISBN 0-87904-001-7). Lust.
Recommended International Standard for Apple Juice Preserved Exclusively by Physical Means. 1972. pap. 4.50 (ISBN 0-685-36321-X, F589, FAO). Unipub.
Recommended International Standard for Orange, Grapefruit & Lemon Juices Preserved Exclusively by Physical Means. 1972. pap. 4.50 (ISBN 0-685-36312-0, F588, FAO). Unipub.
Recommended International Standards for Concentrated Apple Juice & Concentrated Orange Juice Preserved Exclusively by Physical Means. (Codex Alimentarius Commisssion Reports). 15p. (Orig.). 1974. pap. 4.50 (ISBN 0-685-49915-4, F604, FAO). Unipub.
Recommened International Standards for Apricot, Peach & Pear Nectars Preserved Exclusively by Physical Means. (Codex Alimentarius Commission Ser.: No. 44). (Orig.). 1972. pap. 4.50 (ISBN 0-685-36280-9, F587, FAO). Unipub.
Tressler, Donald K., et al. Freezing Preservation of Foods, 4 vols. 4th ed. Incl. Vol. 1. Principles of Refrigeration; Equipment for Freezing & Transporting Food. 32.00 (ISBN 0-87055-044-6); Vol. 2. Factors Affecting Quality in Frozen Foods. 35.00 (ISBN 0-87055-045-4); Vol. 3. Commercial Freezing Operations; Fresh Foods. 39.00 (ISBN 0-87055-046-2); Vol. 4. Freezing of Precooked & Prepared Foods. 39.00 (ISBN 0-87055-047-0). (Illus.). 1968. AVI.

FRUIT PAINTING AND ILLUSTRATION

Campana, D. M. Teacher of Flower & Fruit Painting. (Illus.). 5.95 (ISBN 0-939608-03-0). Campana Art.

FRUIT PESTS

see Fruit–Diseases and Pests

FRUIT TRADE

see also Citrus Fruit Industry; Fruit–Marketing; Olive Industry and Trade

Adams, Frederick U. Conquest of the Tropics: The Story of the Creative Enterprises Conducted by the United Fruit Company. Bruchey, Stuart & Bruchey, Eleanor, eds. LC 76-4766. (American Business Abroad Ser.). (Illus.). 1976. Repr. of 1914 ed. 27.00x (ISBN 0-405-09263-6). Arno.
Atkinson, D., et al, eds. Mineral Nutrition of Fruit Trees. LC 79-41647. (Studies in the Agricultural & Food Sciences). 1980. text ed. 79.95 (ISBN 0-408-10662-X). Butterworth.
Demand Interrelationship Between Major Fruits. (FAO Commodity Policy Studies, No. 19). (Illus., Orig.). 1969. pap. 4.50 (ISBN 0-685-04906-X, F113, FAO). Unipub.
Deupree, Robert G. The Wholesale Marketing of Fruits & Vegetables in Baltimore. LC 78-64175. (Johns Hopkins University. Studies in the Social Sciences. Fifty-Seventh Ser. 1939: 2). Repr. of 1939 ed. 16.00 (ISBN 0-404-61284-9). AMS Pr.
Freeman, Donald B. Rail Movement of Fruit in Queensland: A Study of Patterns & Trends in the Transport of a Perishable Commodity. (Illus.). 1971. 14.95x (ISBN 0-7022-0616-4). U of Queensland Pr.
Henri. Tropical Fruit Processing Industry: Case Studies of the Industry in Developing Countries. 1976. 12.50x (ISBN 92-64-11489-0). OECD.
Karnes, Thomas. Tropical Enterprise: Standard Fruit & Steamship Company in Latin America. LC 78-9641. 1979. 25.00x (ISBN 0-8071-0395-0). La State U Pr.
Lloyd, John W. Co-Operative & Other Organized Methods of Marketing California Horticultural Products. (Illinois Studies in the Social Sciences: Vol. 8, No. 1). Repr. of 1919 ed. 9.50 (ISBN 0-384-33185-8). Johnson Repr.
Price, David, ed. Kemp's Fruit Trades World Directory 1978-79. LC 75-648560. 1978. pap. text ed. 35.00x (ISBN 0-905255-41-0). Intl Pubns Serv.
Recommended International Standard for Canned Pears. (Codex Alimentarius Commission Reports Ser.). 20p. (Orig.). 1975. pap. 4.50 (ISBN 0-685-53181-3, F602, FAO). Unipub.
Recommended International Standard for Canned Strawberries. (Codex Alimentarius Commission Reports Ser.). 18p. (Orig.). 1975. pap. 4.50 (ISBN 0-685-53179-1, F603, FAO). Unipub.
Recommended International Standard for Jams (Fruit Preserves) & Jellies & Recommended International Standard for Citrus Marmalade. (Illus.). 20p. 1978. pap. 4.50 (ISBN 92-5-100432-3, F1365, FAO). Unipub.
Report of the Seventh Session of the Intergovernmental Group on Bananas. 17p. 1981. pap. 7.50 (ISBN 92-5-100950-3, F2091, FAO). Unipub.
Ryall, A. L. & Pentzer, Wilbur T. Handling, Transportation & Storage of Fruits & Vegetables: Fruits & Tree Nuts, Vol. No. 2. (Illus.). 1974. lib. bdg. 55.00 (ISBN 0-87055-165-5). AVI.

FRUIT TREES

see also Dwarf Fruit Trees

Atkinson, D., et al, eds. Mineral Nutrition of Fruit Trees. LC 79-41647. (Studies in the Agricultural & Food Sciences). 1980. text ed. 79.95 (ISBN 0-408-10662-X). Butterworth.
Drying & Processing Tree Fruits. 52p. 1976. pap. 6.00 (ISBN 0-686-71829-1, CO 40, CSIRO). Unipub.
Fruit Trees & Shrubs. 1.95 (ISBN 0-686-21159-6). Bklyn Botanic.
Logsdon, Gene. Organic Orcharding: A Grove of Trees to Live in. Wallace, Dan, ed. (Illus.). 424p. (Orig.). 1981. 16.95 (ISBN 0-87857-356-9). Rodale Pr Inc.
Mohlenbrock. Growing Tropical Fruit Trees. (Illus.). 1979. pap. 2.95 (ISBN 0-8200-0409-X). Great Outdoors.
The Propogation of Tropical Fruit Trees. (Horticultural Review Ser.: No. 4). 1978. pap. 24.00 (ISBN 0-85198-351-0, CAB 4, FAO). Unipub.
Stefanile, Felix. A Fig Tree in America. 1970. 6.00 (ISBN 0-685-01012-0, Pub. by Elizabeth Pr). SBD.
Teskey, Benjamin J. & Shoemaker, James S. Tree Fruit Production. 3rd ed. (Illus.). 1978. text ed. 23.50 (ISBN 0-87055-265-1). AVI.
Wilson, Edward E. & Ogawa, Joseph M. Fungal, Bacterial, & Certain Nonparasitic Diseases of Fruit & Nut Crops in California. LC 79-63107. 1979. 18.00x (ISBN 0-931876-29-X, 4090). Ag Sci Pubns.

FRUIT TREES, TRAINING OF

see Espaliers

FRUITS

see Fruit

FRUSTRATION

see also Control (Psychology)

Bailes, Frederick. Is There a Cure for Frustration? 1972. pap. 0.75 (ISBN 0-87516-129-4). De Vorss.
Barker, Roger, et al. Frustration & Regression: An Experiment with Young Children. LC 75-34765. (Studies in Play & Games). (Illus.). 1976. Repr. of 1941 ed. 19.00x (ISBN 0-405-07934-6). Arno.
Conaway, Judith. I'll Get Even. LC 77-23455. (Moods & Emotions Ser.). (Illus.). (gr. k-3). 1977. PLB 10.25 (ISBN 0-8172-0964-6). Raintree Pubs.
Dollard, John, et al. Frustration & Aggression. LC 79-26458. 1980. Repr. of 1939 ed. lib. bdg. 19.00x (ISBN 0-313-22201-0, DOFR). Greenwood.
Hauck, Paul A. Overcoming Frustration & Anger. LC 73-20285. 1974. pap. 3.95 (ISBN 0-664-24983-3). Westminster.
Janis, Irving L. Stress & Frustration. 1971. pap. text ed. 9.95 (ISBN 0-15-583942-X, HC). HarBraceJ.
Lembo, John M. How to Cope with Your Fears & Frustrations. LC 76-52139. 1977. 6.95 (ISBN 0-87212-091-0). Libra.
Prater, Arnold. How to Win Over Frustration. 128p. (Orig.). 1980. pap. 2.25 (ISBN 0-89081-252-7). Harvest Hse.
Schuller, Robert H. Discover Your Opportunities. (Orig.). 1978. pap. 1.25 (ISBN 0-89081-142-3). Harvest Hse.
Tester, Sylvia R. Frustrated. (What Does It Mean Ser.). (Illus.). (ps-2). 1980. 7.95g (ISBN 0-516-06444-4). Childrens.
Wilson, Pauline. College Women Who Express Futility. LC 79-177629. (Columbia University. Teachers College. Contributions to Education: No. 956). Repr. of 1950 ed. 17.50 (ISBN 0-404-55956-5). AMS Pr.
Wright, Norman. Answer to Anger & Frustration. LC 76-51531. (Answer Ser.). 1977. pap. 1.25 (ISBN 0-89081-030-3, 0303). Harvest Hse.

FRY, CHRISTOPHER

Fry, Christopher. Can You Find Me? (Illus.). 1978. 13.95 (ISBN 0-19-211751-3). Oxford U Pr.
Roy, Emil. Christopher Fry. LC 68-10119. (Crosscurrents-Modern Critiques Ser.). 189p. 1968. 6.95 (ISBN 0-8093-0315-9). S Ill U Pr.

FRY, ELIZABETH (GURNEY), 1780-1845

Johnson, Jan. The Angel of the Prison: A Story About Elizabeth Fry. (Stories About Christian Heroes Ser). (gr. 1-5). 1977. pap. 1.95 (ISBN 0-03-022121-8). Winston Pr.
Johnson, Spencer. The Value of Kindness: The Story of Elizabeth Fry. 2nd ed. LC 76-55339. (ValueTales). (Illus.). (gr. k-6). 1976. 6.95 (ISBN 0-916392-09-0, Dist. by Oak Tree Pubns.). Value Comm.
Pitman, Emma R. Elizabeth Fry. Repr. of 1884 ed. lib. bdg. 15.00x (ISBN 0-8371-1005-X, PIEF). Greenwood.
--Elizabeth Fry. (Women Ser.). 1889. 20.00 (ISBN 0-685-43714-0). Norwood Edns.
Rose, June. Elizabeth Fry: A Biography. 1980. 22.50 (ISBN 0-312-24248-4). St Martin.
Whitney, Janet. Elizabeth Fry: Quaker Heroine. LC 72-83752. (Illus.). Repr. of 1937 ed. 17.00 (ISBN 0-405-09072-2). Arno.
--Elizabeth Fry: Quaker Heroine. Repr. of 1937 ed. lib. bdg. 20.00 (ISBN 0-8495-5909-X). Arden Lib.
--Elizabeth Fry: Quaker Heroine. 1977. Repr. of 1936 ed. 20.00 (ISBN 0-8274-4290-4). R West.

FRY, WILLIAM HENRY, 1813-1864

Upton, William T. William Henry Fry. LC 73-20224. (Music Ser.). 346p. 1974. Repr. of 1954 ed. lib. bdg. 32.50 (ISBN 0-306-70625-3). Da Capo.

FRYE, NORTHROP

Denham, Robert D. Northrop Frye: An Enumerative Bibliography. LC 73-20345. (Author Bibliographies Ser.: No. 14). 1974. 10.00 (ISBN 0-8108-0693-2). Scarecrow.
--Northrop Frye & Critical Method. 1978. text ed. 14.95x (ISBN 0-271-00546-7). Pa St U Pr.

FRYE, WALTER, 15TH CENTURY

Kenney, Sylvia W. Walter Frye & the Contenance Angloise. (Music Reprint Ser.). 1980. Repr. of 1964 ed. 22.50 (ISBN 0-306-76011-8). Da Capo.

FRYE FAMILY

Ridlon, G. T. Frye Family. LC 78-94958. (Saco Valley Settlements Ser). 1970. pap. 2.00 (ISBN 0-8048-0768-X). C E Tuttle.

FRYER, JOHN, 1839-1928

Bennett, Adrian A. John Fryer: The Introduction of Western Science & Technology into Nineteenth-Century China. LC 68-4092. (East Asian Monograph Ser.: No. 24). 1967. pap. 9.00x (ISBN 0-674-47650-6). Harvard U Pr.

FRYING

Ager, Anne. Tefal Super Fryer Cookbook. (Illus.). 1979. pap. 2.95 (ISBN 0-09-131951-X, Pub. by Hutchinson). Merrimack Bk Serv.
Hoffman, Mable. Mini Deep-Fry Cookery. LC 77-83277. (Illus.). 1977. 5.95 (ISBN 0-912656-81-6). H P Bks.
Methven, Barbara. Mini-Fryer Cookery. (Illus.). 1978. 8.95 (ISBN 0-517-53238-7). Crown.

Roth, June. Mac Meals in Minutes. LC 76-53111. (Illus.). 1977. 8.95 (ISBN 0-916752-09-7). Dorison Hse.
Ser-Vol-Tel Institute. Fry Cooking. (Foodservice Career Education Ser.). 1974. pap. 4.95 (ISBN 0-8436-2028-5). CBI Pub.
Sunbeam Cook & Serve. 1981. cancelled (ISBN 0-916752-43-7). Green Hill.

FUCHS, ERNST, 1903-
Fuchs, Ernst. Ernst Fuchs. (Contemporary Art Ser.). (Illus.). 1979. 65.00 (ISBN 0-8109-0903-0). Abrams.

FUCHSIA
Barnes, Bill, et al. The New A to Z on Fuchsias. (Illus.). 1976. 11.95 (ISBN 0-686-19065-3). Natl Fuchsia.
Jennings, K. & Miller, V. Growing Fuchsias. (Illus.). 170p. 1981. Repr. 17.50x (ISBN 0-85664-890-6, Pub. by Croom Helm LTD England). Biblio Dist.
Munz, Phillip A. Revision of the Genus Fuchsia: Onagraceae. LC 44-30622. 1971. Repr. of 1943 ed. 11.50 (ISBN 0-384-40590-8). Johnson Repr.
Proudley, Brian & Proudley, Valerie. Fuchsias in Color. (Illus.). 206p. 1981. 12.95 (ISBN 0-8069-9736-2, Pub. by Blandford Pr England). Sterling.
Wilson, Stanley. Fuchsias. 290p. 1977. pap. 10.95 (ISBN 0-571-11047-9, Pub. by Faber & Faber). Merrimack Bk Serv.

FUCUS
Esper, E. J. Icones Fucorum Cum Characteribus Systematicis Synonymis Auctorum & Descriptionibus Novarum Specierum. 1966. Repr. of 1797 ed. 120.00 (ISBN 3-7682-0262-3). Lubrecht & Cramer.

FUEL
see also Biomass Energy; Charcoal; Coal; Coke; Heating; Lignite; Liquid Fuels; Motor Fuels; Peat; Petroleum As Fuel; Smoke; Synthetic Fuels; Wood As Fuel
AIP Conference. Physics & the Energy Problem, 1974: Proceedings, No. 19. Fiske, Milan D. & Havens, William W., eds. LC 73-94416. 428p. 1974. text ed. 18.00 (ISBN 0-88318-118-5). Am Inst Physics.
Anderson, Larry L. & Tillman, David A. Synthetic Fuels from Coal: Overview & Assessment. LC 79-17786. 158p. 1979. 23.00 (ISBN 0-471-01784-1, Pub. by Wiley-Interscience). Wiley.
Applied Science Publishers Ltd London, ed. Metabolism of Hydrocarbons, Oils, Fuels & Lubricants. (Illus.). 1976. 50.40x (ISBN 0-85334-703-4). Intl Ideas.
Battelle Columbus Laboratories. Preliminary Environmental Assessment of Biomass Conversion to Synthetic Fuels. 346p. 1980. pap. 34.95 (ISBN 0-89934-049-0, B049-PP). Solar Energy Info.
BCC Staff. Fuel & Lubricant Additives. 1981. 950.00 (ISBN 0-89336-239-5, C-027). BCC.
Breiter, Herta S. Fuel & Energy. LC 77-18560. (Read About Sciences Ser.). (Illus.). (gr. k-3). 1978. PLB 11.15 (ISBN 0-8393-0083-2). Raintree Child.
Brown, Lester R. Food or Fuel: New Competition for the World's Cropland. LC 80-50216. (Worldwatch Papers). 1980. pap. 2.00 (ISBN 0-916468-34-8). Worldwatch Inst.
Campbell, Ian M. Energy & the Atmosphere: A Physical-Chemical Approach. LC 76-57689. 1977. 55.95 (ISBN 0-471-99482-0); pap. 23.00 (ISBN 0-471-99481-2, Pub. by Wiley-Interscience). Wiley.
Clean Fuel Supply. 1978. 6.25x (ISBN 92-64-11827-6). OECD.
Commoner, Barry & Boksenbaum, Howard, eds. Energy & Human Welfare: Alternative Technologies for Power Production, Vol. 2. LC 75-8987. 1975. 14.95 (ISBN 0-02-468430-9). Macmillan Info.
Conference on Non-Fossil Fuel & Non-Nuclear Fuel Energy Strategies, Honolulu, USS, January 1979. Renewable Energy Prospects: Proceedings. Bach, W., et al, eds. 340p. 1980. 57.50 (ISBN 0-08-024252-9). Pergamon.
Cowser, K. E. & Richmond, C. E., eds. Synthetic Fossil Fuel Technologies: Potential Health & Environmental Effects. 288p. 1980. 29.50 (ISBN 0-250-40358-7). Ann Arbor Science.
Cusumano, James A. & Farkas, Adalbert, eds. Catalysis in Coal Conversion. LC 77-25620. 1978. 31.50 (ISBN 0-12-199935-1). Acad Pr.
Equipment & Supplies for Fuel Exploration, E-010. 1979. 675.00 (ISBN 0-89336-166-6). BCC.
Fabrication of Water Reactor Fuel Elements. 1978. pap. 75.75 (ISBN 9-2005-0079-X, ISP499, IAEA). Unipub.
Francis, W. & Peters, M. C. Fuels & Fuel Technology. 2nd ed. (Illus.). 608p. 1980. 105.00 (ISBN 0-08-025249-4); pap. 34.50 (ISBN 0-08-025250-8). Pergamon.
Friedel, R. A. Spectrometry of Fuels. LC 70-112726. 344p. 1970. 37.50 (ISBN 0-306-30442-2, Plenum Pr). Plenum Pub.
Fry, L. John. Practical Building of Methane Power Plants for Rural Energy Independence. Knox, D. Anthony, ed. LC 76-16224. (Illus.). 1974. pap. text ed. 12.00 (ISBN 0-9600984-1-0). L J Fry.
Gilchrist, J. D. Fuel, Furnaces & Refractories. 1977. text ed. 32.00 (ISBN 0-08-020430-9); pap. text ed. 12.75 (ISBN 0-08-020429-5). Pergamon.
Goodger, E. M. Alternative Fuels: Chemical Energy Resources. LC 80-11796. 238p. 1980. 48.95x (ISBN 0-470-26952-9). Halsted Pr.
Gyftopoulos, Elias, et al. Potential Fuel Effectiveness in Industry. LC 74-16497. (Ford Foundation's Energy Policy Project). 112p. 1974. text ed. 16.50 (ISBN 0-88410-309-9); pap. text ed. 7.95 (ISBN 0-88410-311-0). Ballinger Pub.
Harter, Walter. Coal: The Rock That Burns. LC 78-27745. (Illus.). (gr. 6 up). 1979. 7.95 (ISBN 0-525-66609-5). Elsevier-Nelson.
Hollaender, A., et al, eds. Trends in the Biology of Fermentations for Fuels & Chemicals. (Basic Life Sciences Ser.). 580p. 1981. 65.00 (ISBN 0-306-40752-3, Plenum Pr). Plenum Pub.
Kaplan & Lebowitz. The Student Scientist Explores Energy & Fuels. rev. ed. LC 74-34077. (gr. 7-12). 1981. PLB 7.97 (ISBN 0-8239-0338-9). Rosen Pr.
Kasem, A. Three Clean Fuels from Coal. 1979. 375.00 (ISBN 0-8247-6923-6). Dekker.
Klass, Donald L., ed. Biomass As a Nonfossil Fuel Source. LC 80-26044. (ACS Symposium Ser.: No. 144). 1981. 42.00 (ISBN 0-8412-0599-X). Am Chemical.
Klein. Sandstone Depositional Models for Exploration for Fossil Fuels. 2nd ed. 120p. 1981. 24.95 (ISBN 0-686-76188-X); pap. 18.95 (ISBN 0-686-76189-8). Burgess.
Macrae, J. C. An Introduction to the Study of Fuel. 1966. 29.50 (ISBN 0-444-40380-9). Elsevier.
Methane Digesters for Fuel Gas & Fertilizer. (Illus.). 1973. pap. text ed. 4.00 (ISBN 0-9600984-2-9). L J Fry.
Nathan, R. A., ed. Fuels from Sugar Crops. 137p. 1980. pap. 14.95 (ISBN 0-930978-91-9, B.036). Solar Energy Info.
Nathan, Richard A., ed. Fuels from Sugar Crops: Systems Study for Sugarcane, Sweet Sorghum, & Sugar Beets. LC 78-19127. (DOE Critical Review Ser.). 148p. 1978. pap. 4.75 (ISBN 0-686-75556-1); microfiche 3.00 (ISBN 0-686-75557-X). DOE.
National Industrial Fuel Efficiency Service Ltd. Fuel Economy Handbook. 300p. 1979. 27.50x (ISBN 0-86010-130-4, Pub. by Graham & Trotman England). State Mutual Bk.
Nixon, Hershell H. & Lowery, Joan. Oil & Gas: From Fossils to Fuel. LC 77-1671. (Let Me Read Bk.). (Illus.). 64p. (gr. 1-4). 1977. 5.95 (ISBN 0-15-257700-9, HJ). HarBraceJ.
Platt, Hugh. A New, Cheape & Delicate Fire of Cole-Balles. LC 72-7838. (English Experience Ser.: No. 550). 32p. 1972. Repr. of 1603 ed. 7.00 (ISBN 90-221-0550-4). Walter J Johnson.
Pugh, Brinley. Fuel Calorimetry. 196p. 1966. 22.50 (ISBN 0-306-30654-9, Plenum Pr). Plenum Pub.
Ranney, M. W. Fuel Additives for Internal Combustion Engines--Recent Developments. LC 78-57662. (Chemical Technology Review Ser. No. 112, Energy Technology Review Ser. No. 30). 1978. 39.00 (ISBN 0-8155-0709-7). Noyes.
Redmayne, R. Fuel. 1979. Repr. of 1929 ed. lib. bdg. 12.50 (ISBN 0-8495-4623-0). Arden Lib.
--Fuel: Its Origin & Use. 1979. Repr. of 1929 ed. lib. bdg. 12.50 (ISBN 0-8492-2399-7). R West.
Reed, C. B. Fuels, Minerals & Human Survival. LC 74-21575. 1978. softcover 12.50 (ISBN 0-250-40256-4). Ann Arbor Science.
Rice, Dale. Energy from Fossil Fuels. (A Look Inside Ser.). (Illus.). 48p. (gr. 4 up). 1982. PLB 11.55 (ISBN 0-8172-1417-8). Raintree Pubs.
Robinson, Colin. Policy for Fuel. (Institute of Economic Affairs, Occasional Papers Ser.: No. 31). pap. 2.50 (ISBN 0-255-27607-9). Transatlantic.
Rocks, Lawrence. Fuels for Tomorrow. 190p. 1980. 23.50 (ISBN 0-87814-135-9). Pennwell Pub.
Rose, J. W. & Cooper, J., eds. Technical Data on Fuel: S. I. Units. 7th rev. ed. LC 77-24872. 1978. 97.95 (ISBN 0-470-99239-5). Halsted Pr.
Short, W., et al. Questions & Answers on Cutting Fuel Costs. 104p. 1975. 11.00x (ISBN 0-86010-019-7, Pub. by Graham & Trotman England). State Mutual Bk.
Solar Energy Research Institute. Fuel from Farms: A Guide to Small-Scale Ethanol Production. 161p. 1980. 29.95 (ISBN 0-89934-050-4, B947-PP); pap. 17.95 (ISBN 0-89934-051-2, B047-PP). Solar Energy Info.
Storage, Handling & Movement of Fuel & Related Components at Nuclear Power Plants. (Technical Reports Ser.: No. 189). 1979. pap. 10.50 (ISBN 92-0-125279-X, IDC189, IAEA). Unipub.
Weisz, P. B. & Marshall, J. F., eds. Fuels from Biomass. 136p. 1980. 375.00 (ISBN 0-8247-6964-3). Dekker.
Williams, J. R., et al. Ethanol, Methanol, & Gasohol. (Illus.). 200p. 1981. 18.75 (ISBN 0-250-40382-X). Ann Arbor Science.
Wilson, Richard. Health Effects of Fossil Fuel Burning: Assessment & Mitigation. 1980. 35.00 (ISBN 0-88410-714-0). Ballinger Pub.

FUEL–AUSTRALIA
Economics of Sulfur Recovery from Fossil Fuels. 12.50 (ISBN 0-686-05703-1). Environ Sci Serv.

FUEL CELLS
Bagotskii, V. S. & Vasil'ev, Yu B., eds. Fuel Cells: Their Electrochemical Kinetics. LC 64-66348. 121p. 1966. 30.00 (ISBN 0-306-10741-4, Consultants). Plenum Pub.
Baker, Bernard S., ed. Fuel Cell Systems II. LC 76-99924. (Advances in Chemistry Ser: No. 90). 1969. 34.50 (ISBN 0-8412-0091-2). Am Chemical.
--Hydrocarbon Fuel Cell Technology: A Symposium. (Illus.). 1966. 74.50 (ISBN 0-12-074250-0). Acad Pr.
Breiter, M. W. Electrochemical Processes in Fuel Cells. LC 69-17789. (Illus.). 1969. 29.00 (ISBN 0-387-04418-3). Springer-Verlag.
Crouthamel, C. E. & Recht, H. L., eds. Regenerative EMF Cells. LC 67-25567. (Advances in Chemistry Ser: No. 64). 1967. 25.75 (ISBN 0-8412-0065-3). Am Chemical.
Fuel Cells: A Bibliography, Mid-Sixties to Nineteen Seventy-Six. 1977. write for info. DOE.
Fuel Cells: A Bibliography, Nineteen Seventy-Seven to June Nineteen Eighty. 1980. write for info. DOE.
Mitchell, Will, Jr., ed. Fuel Cells. (Chemical Technology, Vol. 1). 1963. 55.00 (ISBN 0-12-500301-3). Acad Pr.
Noyes, R. Fuel Cells for Public Utility & Industrial Power. LC 77-89632. (Energy Technology Review Ser.: No. 18). (Illus.). 1978. 42.00 (ISBN 0-8155-0676-7). Noyes.
Oniciu, L. Fuel Cells. Hammel, John, tr. from Romanian. 1976. 25.00x (ISBN 0-85626-014-2, Pub. by Abacus Pr). Intl Schol Bk Serv.
Sandstede, G., ed. From Electrocatalysis to Fuel Cells. LC 79-38116. (Illus.). 441p. 1972. 20.00 (ISBN 0-295-95178-8). U of Wash Pr.
Snyder, Nathan W., ed. Energy Conversion for Space Power. (Progress in Astronautics & Aeronautics Ser.: Vol. 3). (Illus.). 1961. 24.50 (ISBN 0-12-535103-8). Acad Pr.
Vielstich, W. Fuel Cells. LC 76-114088. 501p. 1970. 63.50 (ISBN 0-471-90695-6, Pub. by Wiley-Interscience). Wiley.
Young, George J. & Linden, Henry R., eds. Fuel Cell Systems. LC 65-16399. (Advances in Chemistry Ser: No. 47). 1965. 28.75 (ISBN 0-8412-0048-3). Am Chemical.

FUEL ELEMENTS
see Nuclear Fuel Elements

FUEL OIL
see Petroleum As Fuel

FUEL OIL BURNERS
see Oil Burners

FUEL PUMPS
see also Automobiles–Fuel Systems
Pulverized Fuel Systems. (Sixty Ser). Orig. Title: Installation & Operation of Pulverized Fuel Systems. 68p. 1973. pap. 2.00 (ISBN 0-685-44173-3, 60). Natl Fire Prot.

FUEL TRADE
see also Coal Trade; Coke; Wood
Bates, R. W. & Fraser, N. M. Investment Decisions in the Nationalized Fuel Industries. LC 74-76575. (Illus.). 208p. 1974. 29.50 (ISBN 0-521-20455-0). Cambridge U Pr.
BCC Staff. Utility Engineering. rev. ed. 1977. 650.00 (ISBN 0-89336-003-1, E-028). BCC.
Johnson, Charles J. Coal Demand in the Electric Utility Industry, Nineteen Forty-Six to Nineteen Ninety. Bruchey, Stuart, ed. LC 78-22689. (Energy in the American Economy Ser.). (Illus.). 1979. lib. bdg. 20.00x (ISBN 0-405-11992-5). Arno.
Posner, Michael V. Fuel Policy: A Study in Applied Economics. 356p. 1973. text ed. 21.00x (ISBN 0-333-05554-3). Verry.
Striner, Herbert E. An Analysis of the Bituminous Coal Industry in Terms of Total Energy Supply & a Synthetic Oil Program. Bruchey, Stuart, ed. LC 78-22752. (Energy in the American Economy Ser.). (Illus.). 1979. lib. bdg. 21.00x (ISBN 0-405-12016-8). Arno.

FUEL TRADE–GREAT BRITAIN
Tugendhat, George. Freedom for Fuel. (Institute of Economic Affairs, Hobart Papers Ser.: No. 21). pap. 2.50 (ISBN 0-685-20586-X). Transatlantic.

FUENTES, CARLOS
Duran, Gloria. The Archetypes of Carlos Fuentes: From Witch to Androgyne. 240p. 1980. 22.50 (ISBN 0-208-01775-5, Archon). Shoe String.
Sanchez Reyes, Carmen. Carlos Fuentes y "La Region Mas Transparente". (UPREX, Estudios Literarios: No. 45). 272p. (Orig.). 1975. pap. 1.85 (ISBN 0-8477-0045-3). U of PR Pr.

FUERTES, LOUIS AGASSIZ, 1874-1927
Marcham, Frederick G., ed. Louis Agassiz Fuertes & the Singular Beauty of Birds. LC 76-156537. (Illus.). 1971. 40.00 (ISBN 0-06-012775-9, HarpT). Har-Row.
Sutton, George M. To a Young Bird Artist: Selected Letters from Louis Agassiz Fuertes to George Miksch Sutton. LC 79-4754. (Illus.). 1979. 9.95 (ISBN 0-8061-1589-0). U of Okla Pr.

FUGGER, JAKOB, 1459-1525
Matthews, George T., ed. & intro. by. The Fugger Newsletter. 7.50 (ISBN 0-8446-0201-9). Peter Smith.

FUGGER FAMILY
Ehrenberg, Richard. Capital & Finance in the Age of the Renaissance. LC 63-22259. Repr. of 1928 ed. 19.50x (ISBN 0-678-00015-8). Kelley.
Von Klarwill, Victor, ed. The Fugger News-Letters. facsimile ed. De Chary, Pauline, tr. LC 79-140360. (Select Bibliographies Ser). Repr. of 1924 ed. 23.00 (ISBN 0-8369-5603-6). Arno.
--The Fugger News-Letters: Second Series; Being a Further Selection from the Fugger Papers. facsimile ed. Byrne, L. S., tr. LC 72-140361. (Select Bibliographies Ser). Repr. of 1926 ed. 26.00 (ISBN 0-8369-5604-4). Arno.

FUGITIVE SLAVE LAW OF 1850
see also Christiana, Pennsylvania–Riot, 1851; Compromise of 1850
Bearse, Austin. Reminiscences of Fugitive Slave Law Days in Boston. LC 74-82170. (Anti-Slavery Crusade in America Ser). 1969. Repr. of 1880 ed. 11.00 (ISBN 0-405-00609-8). Arno.
Campbell, Stanley W. Slave Catchers: Enforcement of the Fugitive Slave Law, 1850-1860. 1972. pap. 1.95x (ISBN 0-393-00626-3, Norton Lib). Norton.
--Slave Catchers: Enforcement of the Fugitive Slave Law, 1850-1860. LC 79-109463. 1970. 16.00x (ISBN 0-8078-1141-6). U of NC Pr.
Elliott, E. N., ed. Cotton Is King, & Pro-Slavery Arguments. (Basic Afro-American Reprint Library). Repr. of 1860 ed. 35.00 (ISBN 0-384-14175-7). Johnson Repr.
--Cotton Is King & Pro-Slavery Arguments. LC 68-55884. Repr. of 1850 ed. 35.00x (ISBN 0-8371-4847-2, Pub. by Negro U Pr). Greenwood.
Hosmer, William. Higher Law, in Its Relations to Civil Government, with Particular Reference to Slavery & the Fugitive Slave Law. LC 69-18993. (Illus.). Repr. of 1852 ed. 11.50x (ISBN 0-8371-0929-9, Pub. by Negro U Pr). Greenwood.
May, Samuel. Fugitive Slave Law & Its Victims. facs. ed. LC 77-133161. (Black Heritage Library Collection Ser). 1861. 10.25 (ISBN 0-8369-8716-0). Arno.
Parker, Theodore. Boston Kidnapping: A Discourse to Commemorate the Rendition of Thomas Simms. LC 70-82208. (Anti-Slavery Crusade in America Ser). 1969. Repr. of 1852 ed. 7.50 (ISBN 0-405-00646-2). Arno.
--Trial of Theodore Parker. LC 70-100297. Repr. of 1855 ed. 13.25x (ISBN 0-8371-2912-5). Greenwood.
--Trial of Theodore Parker: For the Misdemeanor of a Speech in Fanenil Hall Against Kidnapping. facs. ed. LC 70-154087. (Black Heritage Library Collection Ser). 1855. 13.75 (ISBN 0-8369-8798-5). Arno.
Shipherd, Jacob R. History of the Oberlin-Wellington Rescue. LC 71-97437. Repr. of 1859 ed. 14.75x (ISBN 0-8371-2729-7, Pub. by Negro U Pr). Greenwood.
Wisconsin - Supreme Court. Unconstitutionality of the Fugitive Slave Act. LC 74-109991. Repr. of 1855 ed. 12.00x (ISBN 0-8371-4125-7). Greenwood.

FUGITIVE SLAVES IN THE UNITED STATES
see Slavery in the United States–Fugitive Slaves

FUGITIVES
Bradbury, John M. The Fugitives. 1958. pap. 3.95 (ISBN 0-8084-0139-4, L15). Coll & U Pr.

FUGITIVES FROM JUSTICE
see also Escapes
Worker, Dwight & Worker, Barbara. Escape! LC 77-78676. 1977. 8.95 (ISBN 0-913374-76-8). SF Bk Co.

FUGUE
see also Canon (Music)
Gedalge, Andre. Treatise on Fugue. Levin, A., tr. 1964. 18.00 (ISBN 0-910648-02-6). Gamut Music.

Kirkendale, Warren. Fugue & Fugato in Rococo & Classical Chamber Music. rev. ed. Bent, Margaret & Kirkendale, Warren, trs. LC 78-50394. 1979. 23.75 (ISBN 0-8223-0416-3). Duke.
Mann, Alfred. The Story of Fugue. LC 81-4183. (Illus.). x, 341p. 1981. Repr. of 1958 ed. lib. bdg. 29.75x (ISBN 0-313-22623-7, MASF). Greenwood.
--Study of Fugue. (Illus.). 1966. pap. 5.95x (ISBN 0-393-09675-0, NortonC). Norton.
Oldroyd, George. Technique & Spirit of Fugue: An Historical Study. (YA) (gr. 9 up). 1948. pap. 16.75 (ISBN 0-19-317311-5). Oxford U Pr.
Prout, E. Fugue. LC 68-25301. (Studies in Music, No. 42). 1969. Repr. of 1891 ed. lib. bdg. 48.95 (ISBN 0-8383-0313-7). Haskell.
Prout, Ebenezer. Fugue. LC 71-108527. 1970. Repr. of 1891 ed. 12.00 (ISBN 0-403-00328-8). Scholarly.
--Fugue. 4th ed. Repr. of 1891 ed. lib. bdg. 15.00x (ISBN 0-8371-1872-7, PRFU). Greenwood.
Thiman, Eric. Fugue for Beginners. (YA) (gr. 9 up). 1966. 3.90 (ISBN 0-19-321770-8). Oxford U Pr.
Tovey, Donald F. Companion to the Art of Fugue of J. S. Bach. 1931. 6.00 (ISBN 0-19-323151-4). Oxford U Pr.
Verrall, John W. Fugue & Invention in Theory & Practice. LC 66-23124. (Illus.). 1966. text ed. 8.95x (ISBN 0-87015-152-5). Pacific Bks.

FUGUES
see Canons, Fugues, etc.

FUJI, MOUNT
Hokusai, Katsushika & Jones, Easley S. Hokusai's Views of Mt. Fuji. LC 65-12269. (Illus.). 1965. 9.50 (ISBN 0-8048-0253-X). C E Tuttle.

FUKIEN, CHINA (PROVINCE)-HISTORY
Rawski, Evelyn S. Agricultural Change & the Peasant Economy of South China. LC 77-173407. (East Asian Ser: No. 66). (Illus.). 280p. 1972. 15.00x (ISBN 0-674-01210-0). Harvard U Pr.

FUKUZAWA, YUKICHI, 1834-1901
Blacker, Carmen. Japanese Enlightenment. (University of Cambridge Oriental Pubns). 1964. 32.50 (ISBN 0-521-04267-4). Cambridge U Pr.
Fukuzawa, Yukichi. Autobiography. Kiyooka, E., tr. from Jap. LC 66-15468. (Illus.). 407p. 1966. 22.50 (ISBN 0-231-02884-9); pap. 10.00x (ISBN 0-231-08373-4). Columbia U Pr.
Kiyooka, Eiichi, tr. The Autobiography of Yukichi Fukuzawa. 407p. (Japanese.). 1980. pap. text ed. 10.00x (ISBN 0-231-08373-4). Columbia U Pr.
Oxford, Wayne H. Speeches of Fukuzawa. 1973. 24.50 (ISBN 0-89346-094-X, Pub. by Hokuseido Pr). Heian Intl.

FULAH EMPIRE
Adeleye, R. A. Power & Diplomacy in Northern Nigeria, 1804-1906. (Ibadan History Ser). (Illus.). 1971. text ed. 11.50x (ISBN 0-391-00169-8). Humanities.
Hiskett, Mervyn. The Sword of Truth: The Life & Times of the Shehu Usuman Dan Fodlo. (Illus.). 192p. 1973. pap. 3.00x (ISBN 0-19-501647-5). Oxford U Pr.
Last, Murray. Sokoto Caliphate. LC 67-16974. (Ibadan History Ser.). (Illus.). 1967. pap. text ed. 8.00x (ISBN 0-582-64504-2). Humanities.

FULAH LANGUAGE
Swift, Lloyd B., et al. FSI Fula Basic Course. 1975. pap. text ed. 6.95x (ISBN 0-686-10718-7); 29 cassettes 174.00x (ISBN 0-686-10719-5). Intl Learn Syst.

FULAHS
Azarya, Victor. Aristocrats Facing Change: The Fulbe in Guinea, Nigeria, & Cameroon. LC 77-15025. (Illus.). 1978. lib. bdg. 19.00x (ISBN 0-226-03356-2). U of Chicago Pr.
Riesman, Paul. Freedom in Fulani Social Life: An Introspective Ethnography. Fuller, Martha, tr. LC 76-25630. 1977. lib. bdg. 25.00x (ISBN 0-226-71741-0). U of Chicago Pr.
--Societe & Liberte Chez les Peul Djelgobe De Haute-Volta: Essai D'anthropologie Introspective. (Cahiers De L'homme, Nouvelle Serie: No. 14). (Illus.). 1974. pap. 23.50x (ISBN 90-2797-322-9). Mouton.
Whitaker, C. S., Jr. Politics of Tradition: Continuity & Change in Northern Nigeria, 1946-1966. LC 68-56323. (Center of International Studies Ser). 1969. 28.50x (ISBN 0-691-03079-0). Princeton U Pr.

FULBRIGHT, JOHN WILLIAM, 1905-
Lynn, Naomi B. & McClure, Arthur F. The Fulbright Premise: Senator J. William Fulbright's Views on Presidential Power. LC 72-14248. 224p. 1973. 14.50 (ISBN 0-8387-1358-0). Bucknell U Pr.

FULFILLMENT (ETHICS)
see Self-Realization

FULGENTIUS, FABIUS PLANCIADES
Friebel, Otto. Fulgentius, der Mythograph und Bischof. pap. 12.50 (ISBN 0-384-16880-9). Johnson Repr.
Whitbread, Leslie G., tr. Fulgentius the Mythographer. LC 70-165263. 1972. 15.00 (ISBN 0-8142-0161-X). Ohio St U Pr.

FULGENTIUS, SAINT, BP. OF RUSPA, 468-533
Friebel, Otto. Fulgentius, der Mythograph und Bischof. pap. 12.50 (ISBN 0-384-16880-9). Johnson Repr.

FULL EMPLOYMENT POLICIES
see also Deficit Financing; Employment Agencies; Employment Stabilization; Government Spending Policy; Labor Supply; Public Works; Unemployed
Anderson, Howard J., ed. Major Employment-Law Principles Established by the EEOC, the OFCCP, & the Courts. 110p. 1981. pap. text ed. 12.50 (ISBN 0-87179-342-3). BNA.
Brunner, K. & Metlyer, A. H., eds. Policies for Employment, Prices, & Exchange Rates. (Carnegie-Rochester Conference Ser. on Public Policy: Vol. 11). 252p. 1979. 24.50 (ISBN 0-444-85392-8). Elsevier.
Bullock, Paul. CETA's New Thrust: Employment Policy & Politics. (Monograph Ser.: No. 28). 200p. 1981. write for info. (ISBN 0-89215-113-7). U Cal LA Indus Rel.
Bullock, Paul, ed. A Full Employment Policy for America: Papers Presented at a UCLA Symposium. 1974. 3.00 (ISBN 0-89215-044-0). U Cal LA Indus Rel.
Burchardt, F. A., ed. Economics of Full Employment. LC 67-16340. Repr. of 1944 ed. lib. bdg. 11.50x (ISBN 0-678-00212-6). Kelley.
Conference of the Universities. Policies to Combat Depression: Proceedings. LC 75-19701. (National Bureau of Economic Research Ser.). (Illus.). 1975. Repr. 24.00x (ISBN 0-405-07581-2). Arno.
Fechter, Alan. Public Employment Programs. LC 75-10561. 1975. pap. 3.25 (ISBN 0-8447-3160-9). Am Enterprise.
Gartner, Alan, et al, eds. A Full Employment Program for the 1970's. LC 75-36408. (Praeger Special Studies Ser.). 160p. 1976. text ed. 11.95 (ISBN 0-275-22810-X). Praeger.
Goals for Full Employment & How to Achieve Them Under the Full Employment & Balanced Growth Act of 1978. 1978. 2.00 (ISBN 0-685-90104-1). Conf Econ Prog.
Gordon, Robert A. Goal of Full Employment. LC 67-26636. 204p. 1967. 9.50 (ISBN 0-471-31605-9). Krieger.
International Labour Conference, 56th Session. World Employment Programme: Report IV. 2nd ed. (The Employment Prospects for the 1970's Employment Policies in Developing Countries; International Action & the Role of the ILO). 1973. 3.00 (ISBN 92-2-100137-7). Intl Labour Office.
Keyserling, Leon H. & Conference on Economic Progress Staff. Full Employment Without Inflation. (Illus.). 1975. 2.00 (ISBN 0-685-64407-3). Conf Econ Prog.
--Key Policies for Full Employment. (Illus.). 1962. 0.50 (ISBN 0-685-88930-0). Conf Econ Prog.
--Toward Full Employment Within Three Years. (Illus.). 1976. 2.00 (ISBN 0-685-88931-9). Conf Econ Prog.
Lerner, Abba P. Economics of Employment. LC 77-18756. (Economics Handbook Ser.). 1978. Repr. of 1951 ed. lib. bdg. 33.50x (ISBN 0-313-20181-1, LEEE). Greenwood.
Levison, Andrew. The Full Employment Alternative. LC 79-17768. 1980. 10.95 (ISBN 0-698-10814-0). Coward.
Lord Beveridge. Full Employment in a Free Society. 1960. text ed. 55.00x (ISBN 0-04-331004-4). Allen Unwin.
McGaughey, William, Jr. A Shorter Workweek in the 1980's. LC 80-54666. 320p. (Orig.). 1981. pap. 6.95 (ISBN 0-9605630-0-8). Thistlerose.
Manpower Adjustment Programmes, 3 vols. Incl. Vol. 1. France, Federal Republic of Germany, United Kingdom. 1967. 5.70 (ISBN 92-2-100978-5); Vol. 2. Sweden, U. S. S. R., United States. 1967. 5.70 (ISBN 92-2-100979-3); Vol. 3. Canada, Italy, Japan. 1968. 4.55 (ISBN 92-2-100147-4). Intl Labour Office.
Palmer, John L., ed. Creating Jobs: Public Employment Programs & Wage Subsidies. (Studies in Social Economics). 1978. 17.95 (ISBN 0-8157-6892-3); pap. 6.95 (ISBN 0-8157-6891-5). Brookings.
Pierson, Frank C. The Minimum Level of Unemployment & Public Policy. 194p. 1980. text ed. 8.50 (ISBN 0-911558-76-4); pap. text ed. 5.50 (ISBN 0-911558-75-6). Upjohn Inst.
Prager, Audrey & Gettleman, Barry. Job Creation in the Community: An Evaluation of Locally Initiated Employment Projects in Massachusetts. 1977. 17.50 (ISBN 0-89011-506-0, EMT 114). Abt Assoc.
Scott, Maurice & Laslett, Robert A. Can We Get Back to Full Employment? LC 78-10635. 1979. text ed. 24.95x (ISBN 0-8419-0460-X). Holmes & Meier.
Sen, Amartya. Employment, Technology & Development. (Economic Development Ser.). 204p. 1975. text ed. 22.50x (ISBN 0-19-877052-9); pap. text ed. 5.95x (ISBN 0-19-877053-7). Oxford U Pr.
Shapiro, E. & White, W., eds. Capital for Productivity & Jobs. 1977. 11.95 (ISBN 0-13-113498-1, Spec); pap. 5.95 (ISBN 0-13-113480-9, Spec). P-H.
U. S. Congress - Joint Economic Committee. Relationship of Prices to Economic Stability & Growth. 1958-1959. Repr. lib. bdg. 29.50x (ISBN 0-8371-2897-8, REOP). Greenwood.

FULLER, BUCKMINISTER
Snyder, Robert. Buckminster Fuller: An Autobiographical Monologue Scenario. 1980. 15.95 (ISBN 0-312-10678-5). St Martin.

FULLER, HENRY BLAKE, 1857-1929
Bowron, Bernard R., Jr. Henry B. Fuller of Chicago. LC 70-140915. (Contributions in American Studies, No. 11). (Illus.). 1974. lib. bdg. 16.00x (ISBN 0-8371-5820-6, BHF/). Greenwood.
Pilkington, John, Jr. Henry Blake Fuller. LC 69-18504. (United States Authors Ser.). 1970. lib. bdg. 8.95x (ISBN 0-8057-0300-4); pap. text ed. 4.95x (ISBN 0-8290-0005-4). Irvington.
Silet, Loring. Henry Blake Fuller & Hamlin Garland: A Reference Guide. (Reference Publications). 1977. lib. bdg. 14.00 (ISBN 0-8161-7988-3). G K Hall.

FULLER, MARGARET
see Ossoli, Sarah Margaret (Fuller) Marchesa d', 1810-1850

FULLER, MELVILLE WESTON, 1833-1910
King, Willard L. Melville Weston Fuller: Chief Justice of the United States, 1888-1910. LC 67-12152. 1967. pap. 3.95 (ISBN 0-226-43579-2, P258, Phoen). U of Chicago Pr.

FULLER, RICHARD BUCKMINSTER, 1895-
Applewhite, Edgar J. The Cosmic Fishing. 1977. 10.95 (ISBN 0-02-502710-7, 50271). Macmillan.
Hatch, Alden. Buckminster Fuller. 288p. 1976. pap. 3.25 (ISBN 0-440-54408-4, Delta). Dell.
Lord, Athena V. Pilot for Spaceship Earth: R. Buckminster Fuller, Architect, Inventor & Poet. LC 77-12629. (Illus.). (gr. 5 up). 1978. 8.95 (ISBN 0-02-761420-4, 76142). Macmillan.
Robertson, Donald W. Mind's Eye of Richard Buckminster Fuller. 1976. 7.00 (ISBN 0-533-23314-3). Robertson.

FULLER, THOMAS, 1608-1661
Addison, William. Worthy Doctor Fuller. LC 71-106707. Repr. of 1951 ed. lib. bdg. 14.75x (ISBN 0-8371-3437-4, ADDF). Greenwood.
Houghton, Walter E., Jr. Formation of Thomas Fuller's Holy & Profane States. (Harvard Studies in English: Vol. 19). 1969. Repr. of 1938 ed. 19.50 (ISBN 0-384-24390-8). Johnson Repr.
Jessop, Augustus. Wise Words & Quaint Counsels of Thomas Fuller: Selected & Arranged with a Short Sketch of the Author's Life. 1979. Repr. of 1892 ed. lib. bdg. 45.00 (ISBN 0-8492-5602-X). R West.

FULLERS EARTH
see also Filters and Filtration
Hasruddin Siddiqui, M. K. Bleaching Earths. 1968. 19.50 (ISBN 0-08-012738-X). Pergamon.

FULLING (TEXTILES)
see Textile Finishing

FULTON, ROBERT, 1765-1815
Dickinson, Henry W. Robert Fulton, Engineer & Artist. facsimile ed. LC 77-148879. (Select Bibliographies Reprint Ser). Repr. of 1913 ed. 24.00 (ISBN 0-8369-5649-4). Arno.
Henry, Joanne L. Robert Fulton: Steamboat Builder. LC 74-18326. (Discovery Ser). (Illus.). 80p. (gr. 2-5). 1975. PLB 6.09 (ISBN 0-8116-6317-5). Garrard.
Hutcheon, Wallace S., Jr. Robert Fulton: Pioneer of Undersea Warfare. LC 80-81094. 192p. 1981. 17.95 (ISBN 0-87021-547-7). Naval Inst Pr.
LeBoeuff, Randall, Jr. Some Notes on the Life of Robert Fulton. (Illus.). 1971. 0.50 (ISBN 0-913344-11-7). South St Sea Mus.
Parsons, W. Barclay. Robert Fulton & the Submarine. LC 23-5456. Repr. of 1922 ed. 16.00 (ISBN 0-404-04888-9). AMS Pr.

FUMIGATION
see also Disinfection and Disinfectants
Standards on Fumigation. 1973. pap. 2.00 (ISBN 0-685-58082-2, 57). Natl Fire Prot.
User Guide to Dust & Fume Collection. 1981. 30.00x (ISBN 0-85295-125-6, Pub. by Inst Chem Eng England). State Mutual Bk.
A User Guide to Dust & Fume Control. 130p. 1981. 30.00x (ISBN 0-686-75382-8, Pub. by Inst Chem Eng England). State Mutual Bk.

FUNCTION ALGEBRAS
Glicksberg, I. Recent Results on Function Algebras. LC 75-38927. (CBMS Regional Conference Series in Mathematics: No. 11). 38p. 1972. 8.80 (ISBN 0-8218-1660-8, CBMS-11). Am Math.
Rudin, Walter. Function Theory in Polydiscs. (Math Lecture Notes Ser.: No. 41). 1969. 17.50 (ISBN 0-8053-8350-6, Adv Bk Prog); pap. 8.50 (ISBN 0-8053-8351-4, Adv Bk Prog). Benjamin-Cummings.
Simon, Barry. Functional Integration & Quantum Physics. (Pure & Applied Mathematics Ser.). 1979. 37.50 (ISBN 0-12-644250-9). Acad Pr.

FUNCTION SPACES
see also Functional Analysis
Baker, J. & Cleaver, C., eds. Banach Spaces of Analytic Functions, Kent 1976: Proceedings of a Conference Held at Kent State University July 12-16, 1976. LC 77-11202. (Lecture Notes in Mathematics: Vol. 604). 1977. pap. text ed. 10.70 (ISBN 0-387-08356-1). Springer-Verlag.
Bekken, O. B., et al, eds. Spaces of Analytic Functions. (Lecture Notes in Mathematics Ser.: Vol. 512). 1976. pap. 12.70 (ISBN 0-387-07682-4). Springer-Verlag.
Fisher, S. W. & Jerome, J. W. Minimum Norm Extremals in Function Spaces: With Applications to Classical & Modern Analysis. (Lecture Notes in Mathematics: Vol. 479). viii, 209p. (Orig.). 1975. pap. 12.60 (ISBN 0-387-07394-9). Springer-Verlag.
Hamilton, R. S. Harmonic Maps of Manifolds with Boundary. (Lecture Notes in Mathematics Ser.: Vol. 471). 168p. 1975. pap. 10.90 (ISBN 0-387-07185-7). Springer-Verlag.
Katz, M. B. Questions of Uniqueness & Resolution in Reconstruction of 2-D & 3-D Objects from Their Projections. (Lecture Notes in Biomathematics: Vol. 26). 1979. pap. 11.30 (ISBN 0-387-09087-8). Springer-Verlag.
Kluvanek, I. & Knowles, G. Vector Measures & Control Systems. (Mathematics Studies: Vol. 20). 180p. 1976. pap. text ed. 24.50 (ISBN 0-7204-0362-6, North-Holland). Elsevier.
Smart, D. R. Fixed Point Theorems. LC 73-79314. (Tracts in Mathematics Ser.: No. 66). (Illus.). 160p. 1974. 23.95 (ISBN 0-521-20289-2). Cambridge U Pr.

FUNCTION TESTS (MEDICINE)
see also Heart Function Tests; Pulmonary Function Tests
Bach-Y-Rita, Paul, ed. Recovery of Function. 278p. 1980. pap. text ed. 29.95 (ISBN 0-8391-4111-4). Univ Park.
Blatter, Joerg. Grothendieck Spaces in Approximation Theory. LC 52-42839. (Memoirs: No. 120). 1972. pap. 7.20 (ISBN 0-8218-1820-1, MEMO-120). Am Math.
Evans, D. M. Special Tests & Their Meanings. 12th rev. ed. (Illus.). 272p. 1981. pap. 7.95 (ISBN 0-571-18034-5, Pub. by Faber & Faber). Merrimack Bk Serv.
Galen, P. S. & Gambino, S. R. Beyond Normality: The Predictive Value & Efficiency of Medical Diagnosis. LC 75-25915. 1975. 26.00x (ISBN 0-471-29047-5, Pub. by Wiley Medical). Wiley.
Horvath, Milton, ed. Adverse Effects of Environmental Chemicals & Psychotropic Drugs, Vol. 2. 1976. 50.25 (ISBN 0-444-41498-3). Elsevier.
Mellerowicz, Harald. Ergometry: Basics of Medical Exercise Testing. Smodlaka, Vojin N., ed. Rice, Allan L., tr. from Ger. LC 80-11140. (Illus.). 432p. 1981. text ed. 49.00 (ISBN 0-8067-1241-4). Urban & S.

FUNCTION TESTS, PULMONARY
see Pulmonary Function Tests

FUNCTIONAL ANALYSIS
see also Approximation Theory; Digital Filters (Mathematics); Distributions, Theory of (Functional Analysis); Function Spaces; Functor Theory; Hardy Spaces; Hilbert Algebras; Integral Equations; Perturbation (Mathematics); Spectral Theory (Mathematics); Topological Algebras; Vector Spaces
Abrahamson, M. Functionalism. LC 77-6828. 1978. pap. 9.95 ref. (ISBN 0-13-331900-8). P-H.
Abramov, L. M., et al. Ten Papers in Functional Analysis & Measure Theory. LC 51-5559. (Translations Ser.: No. 2, Vol. 49). 1966. 21.20 (ISBN 0-8218-1749-3, TRANS 2-49). Am Math.
Agranovic, Z. S., et al. Thirteen Papers on Functional Analysis. LC 51-5559. (Translations Ser.: No. 2, Vol. 90). 1970. 26.80 (ISBN 0-8218-1790-6, TRANS 2-90). Am Math.
Ahiezer, N. I. & Krein, M. G. Some Questions in the Theory of Moments. LC 63-22077. (Translations of Mathematical Monographs: Vol. 2). 1974. Repr. of 1962 ed. 25.60 (ISBN 0-8218-1552-0, MMONO-2). Am Math.
Aizerman, M. A., et al. Sixteen Papers on Differential & Difference Equations, Functional Analysis, Games & Control. LC 51-5559. (Translations Ser.: No. 2, Vol. 87). 1970. 30.80 (ISBN 0-8218-1787-6, TRANS 2-87). Am Math.

Aleksandrov, A. D., et al. Ten Papers on Differential Equations & Functional Analysis. LC 51-5559. (Translations Ser.: No. 2, Vol. 68). 1968. 29.60 (ISBN 0-8218-1768-X, TRANS 2-68). Am Math.

Altman. Contractors & Contractor Direction Theory & Applications: A New Approach to Solving Equations, Vol. 32. (Lecture Notes in Pure & Applied Math). 1977. 29.75 (ISBN 0-8247-6672-5). Dekker.

Anderson, R. D., ed. Symposium on Infinite Dimensional Topology. LC 69-17445. (Annals of Mathematic Studies, 69). 230p. 1972. text ed. 17.50 (ISBN 0-691-08087-9). Princeton U Pr.

Arnol'd, V. I., et al. Fourteen Papers on Functional Analysis & Differential Equations. LC 51-5559. (Translations Ser.: No. 2, Vol. 61). 1967. 33.20 (ISBN 0-8218-1761-2, TRANS 2-61). Am Math.

--Thirteen Papers on Functional Analysis & Differential Equations. LC 51-5559. (Translations Ser.: No. 2, Vol. 79). 1968. 30.00 (ISBN 0-8218-1779-5, TRANS 2-79). Am Math.

Asimow, L. & Ellis, A. J. Convexity, Theory & Its Application in Functional Analysis. LC 80-40648. (London Mathematical Society Monographs: No. 16). 1981. 56.00 (ISBN 0-12-065340-0). Acad Pr.

Aubin, Jean-Pierre. Applied Functional Analysis. LC 78-20896. (Pure & Applied Mathematics: Texts, Monographs & Tracts). 1979. 30.00 (ISBN 0-471-02149-0, Pub. by Wiley-Interscience). Wiley.

Bachman, George & Narici, Lawrence. Functional Analysis. 1966. text ed. 22.95 (ISBN 0-12-070250-9). Acad Pr.

Bahtin, I. A., et al. Eleven Papers on Differential Equations, Functional Analysis & Measure Theory. LC 51-5559. (Translations, Ser: No. 2, Vol. 51). 1966. 34.00 (ISBN 0-8218-1751-5, TRANS 2-51). Am Math.

Beltrami, E. J. Algorithmic Approach to Nonlinear Analysis & Optimization. (Mathematics in Science & Engineering Ser.: Vol. 63). 1970. 40.50 (ISBN 0-12-085560-7). Acad Pr.

Berberian, S. K. Lectures in Functional Analysis & Operator Theory. (Graduate Texts in Mathematics: Vol. 15). 370p. 1974. 20.50 (ISBN 0-387-90080-2). Springer-Verlag.

Berezanskii, Ju. M. Expansions in Eigenfunctions of Selfadjoint Operators. LC 67-22347. (Translations of Mathematical Monographs: Vol. 17). 1968. 58.40 (ISBN 0-8218-1567-9, MMONO-17). Am Math.

Berezanskii, Ju. M., et al. Nine Papers on Functional Analysis. (Translations Ser.: No. 2, Vol. 93). 1970. 26.80 (ISBN 0-8218-1793-0, TRANS 2-93). Am Math.

Berezin, F. A., et al. Eight Papers on Differential Equations & Functional Analysis. LC 51-5559. (Translations, Ser.: No. 2, Vol. 56). 1966. 32.00 (ISBN 0-8218-1756-6, TRANS 2-56). Am Math.

Besov, O. V., et al. Nine Papers on Functional Analysis & Numerical Analysis. (Translations Ser.: No. 2, Vol. 40). 1964. 22.00 (ISBN 0-8218-1740-X, TRANS 2-40). Am Math.

Besov, Oleg V., et al. Integral Representations of Functions & Imbedding Theorems, 2 vols. (Scripta Ser. in Mathematics). 1979. 19.95 ea. Vol. 1 (ISBN 0-470-26540-X). Vol. 2 (ISBN 0-470-26593-0). Halsted Pr.

Bierstedt, K. & Fuchssteiner, B., eds. Functional Analysis: Surveys & Recent Results: Proceedings of the Conference, Paderborn, Federal Republic of Germany, November, 1976. (North-Holland Mathematics Studies: Vol. 27). 1978. 34.25 (ISBN 0-444-85057-0, North-Holland). Elsevier.

Blackman, P. F. Introduction to State-Variable Analysis. 1978. 26.95 (ISBN 0-333-14680-8, Pub. by Macmillan Pr). Intl Schol Bk Serv.

Blackorby, C. & Primont, D. Duality, Separability & Functional Structure: Theory & Economic Applications. (Dynamic Economic Ser.). 1978. 36.00 (ISBN 0-444-00235-9, North-Holland). Elsevier.

Bonic, Robert A. Linear Functional Analysis. (Notes on Mathematics & Its Applications Ser.). 1969. 34.25x (ISBN 0-677-02050-3). Gordon.

Borok, V. M., et al. Eight Papers on Functional Analysis & Partial Differential Equations. LC 51-5559. (Translations, Ser.: No. 2, Vol. 5). 1957. 24.80 (ISBN 0-8218-1705-1, TRANS 2-5). Am Math.

Brodskii, M. S., et al. Nine Papers on Partial Differential Equations & Functional Analysis. LC 51-5559. (Translations Ser.: No. 2, Vol. 65). 1967. 32.00 (ISBN 0-8218-1765-5, TRANS 2-65). Am Math.

--Thirteen Papers on Functional Analysis & Partial Differential Equations. LC 51-5559. (Translations Ser.: No. 2, Vol. 47). 1965. 22.40 (ISBN 0-8218-1747-7, TRANS 2-47). Am Math.

Brown, A. & Pearcy, C. Introduction to Operator Theory, Vol. 1: Elements of Functional Analysis. LC 77-23438. (Graduate Texts in Mathematics: Vol. 55). (Illus.). 1977. 27.30 (ISBN 0-387-90257-0). Springer-Verlag.

Cekanovskii, E. R., et al. Five Papers on Functional Analysis. LC 51-5559. (Translations Ser.: No. 2, Vol. 62). 1967. 31.20 (ISBN 0-8218-1762-0, TRANS 2-62). Am Math.

Cesari, Lamberto, et al, eds. Nonlinear Functional Analysis & Differential Equations: Proceedings of the Michigan State University Conference. (Lecture Notes in Pure and Applied Math Ser.: Vol. 19). 1976. 38.75 (ISBN 0-8247-6452-8). Dekker.

Chazel, Francois. La Theorie Analytique De le Societe Dans L'oeuvre De Talcott Parsons Societe, Mouvements Sociaux et Ideologies. (Premiere Serie Etudes: No. 16). 1974. pap. 19.50x (ISBN 90-2797-306-7). Mouton.

Clancey, K. Seminormal Operators. (Lecture Notes in Mathematics: Vol. 742). 1979. pap. 9.50 (ISBN 0-387-09547-0). Springer-Verlag.

Collatz, Lothar. Functional Analysis & Numerical Mathematics. Oser, H., tr. 1966. 52.50 (ISBN 0-12-180450-X). Acad Pr.

Conference Held at Manheim, 21-25 July, 1975. Categorical Topology: Proceedings. Binz, E., ed. (Lecture Notes in Mathematics: Vol. 540). 1976. soft cover 28.40 (ISBN 0-387-07859-2). Springer-Verlag.

Conference on Functional Analysis & Related Fields, University of Chicago, 1968. Proceedings. Browder, Felix E., ed. LC 74-79552. (Illus.). 1970. 38.00 (ISBN 0-387-05104-X). Springer-Verlag.

Conference on K-Theory & Operator Algebras, University of Georgia, Athens, Ga., Apr. 21-25, 1975. K-Theory & Operator Algebras: Proceedings. Morrel, B. B. & Singer, I. M., eds. (Lecture Notes in Mathematics: Vol. 575). 1977. soft cover 10.10 (ISBN 0-387-08133-X). Springer-Verlag.

Cooper, J. B. Saks Spaces & Applications to Functional Analysis. (North-Holland Mathematics Studies: Vol. 28). 1978. pap. 34.25 (ISBN 0-444-85100-3, North-Holland). Elsevier.

Curtain, Ruth & Pritchard, A. J., eds. Functional Analysis in Modern Applied Mathematics. 1977. 48.00 (ISBN 0-12-196250-4). Acad Pr.

Davies, E. B., ed. Quantum Theory of Open Systems. 1976. 29.00 (ISBN 0-12-206150-0). Acad Pr.

Davis, Martin. A First Course in Functional Analysis. (Notes on Mathematics & Its Applications Ser). (Orig.). 1966. 20.50x (ISBN 0-677-01155-5). Gordon.

Deimling, K. Ordinary Differential Equations in Banach Spaces. (Lecture Notes in Mathematics: Vol. 596). 1977. 10.10 (ISBN 0-387-08260-3). Springer-Verlag.

DeVito, Carl L. Functional Analysis. (Pure & Applied Mathematics Ser.). 1978. 16.50 (ISBN 0-12-213250-5). Acad Pr.

Djairo Guedes De Figuerido, ed. Functional Analysis-Proceedings of the Sao Paulo Symposium. (Lecture Notes in Pure and Applied Mathematics Ser.: Vol. 18). 1976. 33.75 (ISBN 0-8247-6334-3). Dekker.

Dubinskii, Ju. A., et al. Nine Papers on Functional Analysis & Partial Differential Equations. (Translations Ser.: No. 2, Vol. 67). 1968. 31.20 (ISBN 0-8218-1767-1, TRANS 2-67). Am Math.

Erdelyi, I., ed. Operator Theory & Functional Analysis. (Research Notes in Mathematics Ser.: No. 38). 176p. (Orig.). 1979. pap. text ed. 17.95 (ISBN 0-273-08450-X). Pitman Pub MA.

Fell, J. M, et al. Induced Representations & Banach-Algebraic Bundles. (Lecture Notes in Mathematics: Vol. 582). 1977. soft cover 17.40 (ISBN 0-387-08147-X). Springer-Verlag.

Filippov, N. D., et al. Ten Papers on Algebra & Functional Analysis. LC 51-5559. (Translations Ser.: No. 2, Vol. 96). 1970. 26.80 (ISBN 0-8218-1796-5, TRANS 2-96). Am Math.

Fomenko, V. T., et al. Twelve Papers on Functional Analysis & Geometry. LC 51-5559. (Translations Ser.: No. 2, Vol. 85). 1969. 28.80 (ISBN 0-8218-1785-X, TRANS 2-85). Am Math.

Gabasov, R. & Kirillova, F. M., eds. Optimal Linear Systems: Methods of Functional Analysis. (Mathematical Concepts & Methods in Science & Engineering Ser.: Vol. 15). 300p. 1978. 29.50 (ISBN 0-306-40119-3, Plenum Pr). Plenum Pub.

Garnir, H. G., et al, eds. Functional Analysis & Its Applications. (Lecture Notes in Mathematics: Vol. 399). xvii, 565p. 1974. pap. 24.10 (ISBN 0-387-06869-4). Springer-Verlag.

Germain, P. & Nayroles, B., eds. Applications of Methods of Functional Analysis to Problems in Mechanics. LC 76-5454. (Lecture Notes in Mathematics Ser: Vol. 503). 1976. pap. 23.10 (ISBN 0-387-07629-8). Springer-Verlag.

Girsanov, I. V. Lectures on Mathematical Theory of Extremum Problems. Louvish, D., tr. from Rus. LC 72-80360. (Lecture Notes in Economics & Mathematical Systems: Vol. 67). (Illus.). 139p. 1972. pap. 7.30 (ISBN 0-387-05857-5). Springer-Verlag.

Glimm, J., et al. Lectures in Modern Analysis & Applications - Two. Taam, C. T., ed. LC 76-94096. (Lecture Notes in Mathematics: Vol. 140). 1970. pap. 10.70 (ISBN 0-387-04929-0). Springer-Verlag.

Gohberg, I. & Kal, M., eds. Topics in Functional Analysis: Essays Dedicated to M. G. Krein on the Occasion of His 70th. Birthday. (Adv. in Mathematics Supplementary Studies: Vol. 3). 1978. 58.00 (ISBN 0-12-287150-2). Acad Pr.

Graff, Richard A. Elements of Non-Linear Functional Analysis. LC 78-14727. (Memoirs: No. 206). 1980. Repr. of 1978 ed. 9.60 (ISBN 0-8218-2206-3). Am Math.

Griffel, D. H. Applied Functional Analysis. (Mathematics & Its Applications). 420p. 1981. 89.95 (ISBN 0-470-27196-5). Halsted Pr.

Groetsch, C. W. Elements of Applicable Functional Analysis. (Pure & Applied Mathematics Ser.: Vol. 55). 1980. 24.75 (ISBN 0-686-74341-5). Dekker.

Haug, Edward J. & Arora, Jasbir S. Applied Optimal Design: Mechanical & Structural Systems. LC 79-11437. 1979. 33.50 (ISBN 0-471-04170-X, Pub. by Wiley-Interscience). Wiley.

Hermes, Henry & La Salle, Joseph. Functional Analysis & Time Optimal Control. (Mathematics in Science & Engineering Ser.: Vol. 56). 1969. 25.50 (ISBN 0-12-342650-2). Acad Pr.

Herve, M. Analytic & Plurisubharmonic Functions in Finite & Infinite Dimensional Spaces. (Lecture Notes in Mathematics: Vol. 198). 1971. pap. 8.20 (ISBN 0-387-05472-3). Springer-Verlag.

Heuser, Harro. Functional Analysis. 464p. 1982. 47.50 (ISBN 0-471-28052-6, Pub. by Wiley-Interscience). Wiley.

Hille, Einar. Einar Hille: Classical Analysis & Functional Analysis: Selected Papers. Kallman, Robert R., ed. LC 74-18465. (Mit Press Mathematicians of Our Time Ser.: Vol. 2). 752p. 1975. 40.00x (ISBN 0-262-08080-X). MIT Pr.

Hille, Einar & Phillips, R. S. Functional Analysis & Semigroups. rev. ed. LC 58-102. (Colloquium Pbns. Ser.: Vol. 31). 1974. Repr. of 1957 ed. 30.40 (ISBN 0-8218-1031-6, COLL-31). Am Math.

Hogbe-Nlend, H. Bornologies & Functional Analysis. (North-Holland Mathematical Studies: Vol. 25). 1977. 24.25 (ISBN 0-7204-0712-5, North-Holland). Elsevier.

Holmes, R. B. A Course on Optimization & Best Approximation. (Lecture Notes in Mathematics: Vol. 257). 233p. 1972. pap. 7.50 (ISBN 0-387-05764-1). Springer-Verlag.

Hutson, V. & Pym, J. S. Applications of Functional Analysis & Operator Theory. (Mathematics in Science & Engineering Ser.). 1980. 45.50 (ISBN 0-12-363260-9). Acad Pr.

Il'in, V. P., ed. Boundary Value Problems of Mathematical Physics & Related Aspects of Function Theory, Pt. 1. LC 69-12506. (Seminars in Mathematics Ser.: Vol. 5). 96p. 1969. 29.50 (ISBN 0-306-18805-8, Consultants). Plenum Pub.

International Seminar, Trieste. Control Theory & Topics in Functional Analysis: Proceedings, 2 vols. (Illus.). 1976. Vol. 2. pap. 32.50 (ISBN 92-0-130176-6, ISP415-2, IAEA); Vol. 3. pap. 40.75 (ISBN 9-2013-0276-2, ISP415-3). Unipub.

Kantorovich, L. V. & Akilov, G. P. Functional Analysis. 2nd ed. 800p. 1981. 100.00 (ISBN 0-08-023036-9); pap. 25.00 (ISBN 0-08-026486-7). Pergamon.

Kolmogorov, A. N. & Fomin, S. V. Introductory Real Analysis. Silverman, Richard A., ed. & tr. from Rus. LC 74-18669. 416p. 1975. pap. 5.00 (ISBN 0-486-61226-0). Dover.

Korovkin, P. P. Linear Operators & Approximation Theory. (Russian Monographs & Texts on the Physical Sciences Ser). 1961. 48.50x (ISBN 0-677-20170-2). Gordon.

Krasnosel'Ski, M. A. & Rutickii, Y. B. Convex Functions & Orlicz Spaces. (Russian Monographs & Texts on the Physical Sciences Ser). 1962. 57.25x (ISBN 0-685-88496-1). Gordon.

Krein, M. G., et al. Functional Analysis & Measure Theory. rev. ed. (Translations Ser.: No. 1, Vol. 10). 1980. 41.60 (ISBN 0-8218-1610-1, TRANS 1-10). Am Math.

LaGrange, Joseph-Louis. Lecons Sur le Calcul Des Fonctions. Repr. of 1806 ed. 138.00 (ISBN 0-8287-0485-6). Clearwater Pub.

--Theorie Des Fonctions Analytiques Contenant les Principes Du Calcul Differentiel. 81.00 (ISBN 0-8287-0487-2). Clearwater Pub.

Langenbach, A. Monotone Potentialoperatoren in Theorie & Anwendung. (Ger.). 1977. 37.80 (ISBN 3-540-08071-6). Springer-Verlag.

Larsen, Ronald. Functional Analysis: An Introduction. (Pure & Applied Mathematics Ser: Vol. 15). 520p. 1973. 22.50 (ISBN 0-8247-6042-5). Dekker.

Leigh, J. R. Functional Analysis & Linear Control Theory. (Mathematics in Science & Engineering Ser.). 1981. 29.00 (ISBN 0-686-72571-9). Acad Pr.

Limaye, B. V. Functional Analysis. LC 80-84533. 400p. 1981. 17.95 (ISBN 0-470-26933-2). Halsted Pr.

Lloyd, N. G. Degree Theory. LC 77-3205. (Tracts in Mathematics Ser.: No. 73). (Illus.). 1978. 35.50 (ISBN 0-521-21614-1). Cambridge U Pr.

Lusternik, L. A. & Sobolev, V. J. Elements of Functional Analysis. (Russian Monographs Ser.). (Illus.). 1962. 57.75x (ISBN 0-677-20270-9). Gordon.

Machade, S., ed. Functional Analysis, Holomorphy, & Approximation Theory: Proceedings. (Lecture Notes in Mathematics Ser.: Vol. 843). 636p. 1981. pap. 36.00 (ISBN 0-387-10560-3). Springer-Verlag.

McKennon, Kelly. Multipliers, Positive Functionals, Positive-Definite Functions & Fourier-Stieltjes Transforms. LC 52-42839. (Memoirs: No. 111). 1971. pap. 6.40 (ISBN 0-8218-1811-2, MEMO-111). Am Math.

Maddox, I. J. Elements of Functional Analysis. LC 71-85726. 1970. text ed. 29.95 (ISBN 0-521-07617-X); pap. 12.50x (ISBN 0-521-29266-2). Cambridge U Pr.

Mandrigues, Debra. Introductory Functional Analysis with Applications. LC 77-2560. 1978. text ed. 34.95 (ISBN 0-471-50731-8). Wiley.

Massera, Jose L. & Schaffer, Juan J. Linear Differential Equations & Function Spaces. (Pure & Applied Mathematics Ser.: Vol. 2). 1966. 60.00 (ISBN 0-12-478650-2). Acad Pr.

Mathai, A. M. & Saxena, R. K. The H-Function with Applications in Statistics & Other Disciplines. 192p. 1978. 14.95 (ISBN 0-470-26380-6). Halsted Pr.

Mathesius, Vilem. A Functional Analysis of Present Day English on a General Linguistic Basis. Vachek, Josef, ed. Duskova, Libuse, tr. from Czech. (Janua Linguarum, Series Practica: No. 208). 228p. 1975. pap. text ed. 40.75x (ISBN 90-2793-077-5). Mouton.

MRC Symposium-1971. Contributions to Nonlinear Functional Analysis: Proceedings. Zarantonello, Eduardo H., ed. 1971. 29.50 (ISBN 0-12-775850-X). Acad Pr.

Nachbin. An Introduction to Functional Analysis. (Lecture Notes in Pure & Applied Mathematics Ser.: Vol. 60). 184p. 1981. 19.75 (ISBN 0-8247-6984-8). Dekker.

Nagel, A. & Stein, E. M. Lectures on Pseudo-Differential Operators: Regularity Theorems & Applications to Non-Elliptic Problems. LC 79-19388. (Mathematical Notes Ser.: No. 24). 6.75 (ISBN 0-691-08247-2). Princeton U Pr.

Nashed, M. Z., ed. Functional Analysis Methods in Numerical Analysis: Proceeding, St. Louis, Mo., 1977. (Lecture Notes in Mathematics: Vol. 701). 1979. pap. 16.80 (ISBN 0-387-09110-6). Springer-Verlag.

Nine Papers on Analysis. LC 77-11203. (Translation Ser.: No. 2, Vol. 110). 1977. 40.40 (ISBN 0-8218-3060-0, TRANS2-110). Am Math.

Novozhilov, Y. V. & Tulub, A. V. The Method of Functionals in the Quantum Theory of Fields. (Russian Tracts on the Physical Sciences Ser). 1961. 16.00x (ISBN 0-677-20410-8). Gordon.

Nowinski, J. L. Applications of Functional Analysis in Engineering. (Mathematical Concepts & Methods in Science & Engineering Ser.: Vol.22). 299p. 1981. 37.50 (ISBN 0-306-40693-4, Plenum Pr). Plenum Pub.

Ogden, J. T. Applied Functional Analysis: A First Course for Students of Mechanics & Engineering Science. LC 78-541. (Illus.). 1979. ref. 29.95 (ISBN 0-13-040162-5). P-H.

Packel, Edward W. Functional Analysis: A Short Course. Anderson, Richard D. & Rosenberg, Alex, eds. 192p. 1980. Repr. of 1974 ed. lib. bdg. 12.50 (ISBN 0-89874-019-3). Krieger.

Pelczynski, Aleksander. Banach Spaces of Analytic Functions & Absolutely Summing Operators. LC 77-9884. (Conference Board of the Mathematical Sciences Ser.: No. 30). 1980. Repr. of 1977 ed. 8.20 (ISBN 0-8218-1680-2, CBMS30). Am Math.

Plemelj, J. Problems in the Sense of Riemann & Klein. 175p. 1964. 11.50 (ISBN 0-470-69125-5, Pub. by Wiley). Krieger.

Rall, Louis B., ed. Nonlinear Functional Analysis & Applications: Proceedings. 1971. 27.00 (ISBN 0-12-576350-6). Acad Pr.

Rellich, Franz. Perturbation Theory of Eigenvalue Problems. (Notes on Mathematics & Its Applications Ser). (Orig.). 1969. 29.25x (ISBN 0-677-00680-2). Gordon.

Rudin, Walter. Functional Analysis. LC 71-39686. (McGraw-Hill Series in Higher Mathematics). 1972. text ed. 25.00 (ISBN 0-07-054225-2, C). McGraw.

Sard, Arthur. Linear Approximation. LC 63-11988. (Mathematical Surveys Ser.: No. 9). 1963. 35.60 (ISBN 0-8218-1509-1, SURV-9). Am Math.

Sawyer, W. W. A First Look at Numerical Functional Analysis. (Oxford Applied Mathematics & Computing Science Ser.). (Illus.). 1978. pap. 9.95x (ISBN 0-19-859629-4). Oxford U Pr.

Schwartz, Jacob T. Nonlinear Functional Analysis. (Notes on Mathematics & Its Applications Ser.). 1969. 33.00x (ISBN 0-677-01500-3). Gordon.

Segal, I. E. & Kunze, R. A. Integrals & Operators. 2nd rev ed. LC 77-16682. (Grundlehren der Mathematischen Wissenschaften: Vol. 228). 1978. Repr. 37.80 (ISBN 0-387-08323-5). Springer-Verlag.

Seminar on Functional Operators & Equations, Zurich, 1965-66. Proceedings. Targonski, G. I., ed. (Lecture Notes in Mathematics: Vol. 33). 1967. pap. 10.70 (ISBN 0-387-03904-X). Springer-Verlag.

Simon, Barry. Trace Ideals & Their Applications. LC 78-20867. (London Mathematical Society Lecture Notes Ser.: No. 35). 1979. pap. 16.95x (ISBN 0-521-22286-9). Cambridge U Pr.

Singer, Ivan. The Theory of Best Approximation & Functional Analysis: Proceedings. (CBMS Regional Conference Ser.: Vol. 13). (Orig.). 1974. pap. text ed. 9.00 (ISBN 0-686-24264-5). Soc Indus-Appl Math.

Sobolev, Sergei L., tr. Applications of Functional Analysis in Mathematical Physics. LC 63-15658. (Translations of Mathematical Monographs: Vol. 7). 1969. Repr. of 1963 ed. 22.40 (ISBN 0-8218-1557-1, MMONO-7). Am Math.

Steklov Institute of Mathematics, Academy of Sciences, U S S R, No. 96. Automatic Programming, Numerical Methods & Functional Analysis: Proceedings. Faddeeva, V. N., ed. 1970. 41.20 (ISBN 0-8218-1896-1, STEKLO-96). Am Math.

Steklov Institute of Mathematics, Academy of Sciences, U.S.S.R., No. 114. Some Questions in Constructive Functional Analysis: Proceedings. LC 73-21929. 238p. 1974. 59.20 (ISBN 0-8218-3014-7, STEKLO-114). Am Math.

Steklov Institute of Mathematics, Academy of Sciences, U S S R, No. 77. Theory & Applications of Differentiable Functions of Several Variables: Proceedings. Nikol'skii, S. M., ed. 1967. 40.00 (ISBN 0-8218-1877-5, STEKLO-77). Am Math.

Steklov Institute of Mathematics, Academy of Sciences, U S S R, No. 89. Theory & Applications of Differentiable Functions of Several Variables, 2: Proceedings. Nikol'skii, S. M., ed. 1968. 58.40 (ISBN 0-685-05637-6, STEKLO-89). Am Math.

Swaminathan, S., ed. Fixed Point Theory & Its Applications. 1976. 23.50 (ISBN 0-12-678650-X). Acad Pr.

Tammi, O. Extremum Problems for Bounded Univalent Functions. (Lecture Notes in Mathematics: Vol. 646). 1978. pap. 15.60 (ISBN 0-387-08756-7). Springer-Verlag.

Taylor, A. & Lay, D. Introduction to Functional Analysis. 2nd ed. 467p. 1980. 28.95 (ISBN 0-471-84646-5). Wiley.

Thirty-Five Scientific Communications from the All-Union Conference on Functional Analysis & Its Applications & Five Papers on Analysis. LC 51-5559. (Translations Ser.: No. 2, Vol. 16). 1960. 31.20 (ISBN 0-8218-1716-7, TRANS 2-16). Am Math.

Treves, Francois. Linear Partial Differential Equations with Constant Coefficients. (Mathematics & Its Applications Ser). 1966. 104.00x (ISBN 0-677-01190-3). Gordon.

Van Rooij. Non-Archimedian Functional Analysis. 1978. 29.50 (ISBN 0-8247-6556-7). Dekker.

Varga, Richard S. Functional Analysis & Approximation Theory in Numerical Analysis: Proceedings. (CBMS Regional Conference Ser.: Vol. 3). (Orig.). 1971. pap. text ed. 5.50 (ISBN 0-686-24246-7). Soc Indus-Appl Math.

Von Neumann, J. Functional Operators, Vol. 2, Geometry Of Orthogonal Spaces. (Annals of Mathematics Studies). Repr. of 1950 ed. pap. 7.00 (ISBN 0-527-02738-3). Kraus Repr.

Von Neumann, John. Functional Operators: Measures & Integrals. (Annals of Mathematics Studies: No. 21). (Orig.). 1950. pap. 16.50x (ISBN 0-691-07966-8). Princeton U Pr.

Voronovskaja, E. V. Functional Method & Its Applications. LC 70-138816. (Translations of Mathematical Monographs: Vol. 28). 1970. 34.40 (ISBN 0-8218-1578-4, MMONO-28). Am Math.

Wilansky, A. Topics in Functional Analysis. (Lecture Notes in Mathematics: Vol. 45). 1967. pap. 10.70 (ISBN 0-387-03916-3). Springer-Verlag.

Wilde, Carroll O., ed. Functional Analysis: Proceedings. 1970. 30.00 (ISBN 0-12-751750-2). Acad Pr.

Wong, Y. C. The Topology of Uniform Convergence on Order-Bounded Sets. (Lecture Notes in Mathematics: Vol. 531). 1976. soft cover 9.90 (ISBN 0-387-07800-2). Springer-Verlag.

Zemanian, A. H. Realizability Theory for Continuous Linear Systems. (Mathematics in Science & Engineering Ser.: Vol. 97). 1972. 40.00 (ISBN 0-12-779550-2). Acad Pr.

FUNCTIONAL CALCULUS

see Functional Analysis

FUNCTIONAL EQUATIONS

see also Differential-Difference Equations; Functional Analysis; Functional Equations; Integral Equations; Invariant Imbedding; Programming (Mathematics)

Aczel, J. Lectures on Functional Equations & Their Applications. (Mathematics in Science & Engineering). 1966. 59.50 (ISBN 0-12-043750-3). Acad Pr.

--On Applications & Theory of Functional Equations. 1969. 15.00 (ISBN 0-12-043756-2). Acad Pr.

Beran, M. Statistical Continuum Theory. 424p. 1968. 21.00 (ISBN 0-470-06861-2, Pub. by Wiley). Krieger.

Carico, Charles C. Functions & Relations. 1974. pap. 4.95x (ISBN 0-534-00315-X). Wadsworth Pub.

Hale, Jack & Meyer, K. R. Class of Functional Equations of Neutral Type. LC 52-42839. (Memoirs: No. 76). 1967. 7.20 (ISBN 0-8218-1276-9, MEMO-76). Am Math.

Japan - United States Seminar on Ordinary Differential & Functional Equations, Kyoto, 1971. Proceedings. Urabe, M., ed. (Lecture Notes in Mathematics: Vol. 243). viii, 332p. 1972. pap. 10.20 (ISBN 0-387-05708-0). Springer-Verlag.

Langlands, R. P. On the Functional Equations Satisfied by Eisenstein Series. (Lecture Notes in Mathematics: Vol. 544). 1976. soft cover 17.00 (ISBN 0-387-07872-X). Springer-Verlag.

Prouse, G. & Amerio, L. Almost-Periodic Functions & Functional Equations. LC 72-112713. viii, 183p. 1975. 18.40 (ISBN 0-387-90119-1). Springer-Verlag.

Schmitt, Klaus, ed. Delay & Functional Differential Equations & Their Applications. 1972. 56.50 (ISBN 0-12-627250-6). Acad Pr.

Truesdell, Clifford A. Unified Theory of Special Functions. 1948. pap. 10.00 (ISBN 0-527-02734-0). Kraus Repr.

Warga, J. Optimal Control of Differential & Functional Equations. 1972. 56.00 (ISBN 0-12-735150-7). Acad Pr.

FUNCTIONALS

see Functional Analysis

FUNCTIONS

see also Asymptotic Expansions; Calculus; Convergence; Distributions, Theory of (Functional Analysis); Riemann Surfaces

Abel, Niels H. Oeuvres Completes, 2 vols in 1. Sylow, L. & Lie, S., eds. Set. 54.00 (ISBN 0-384-00103-3). Johnson Repr.

Abramowitz, Milton & Stegun, Irene A., eds. Handbook of Mathematical Functions with Formulas, Graphs & Mathematical Tables. (Illus.). 1964. pap. 14.95 (ISBN 0-486-61272-4). Dover.

Ahiezer, N. I., et al. Fifteen Papers on Real & Complex Functions, Series, Differential & Integral Equations. LC 51-5559. (Translations Ser.: No. 2, Vol. 86). 1970. 29.20 (ISBN 0-8218-1786-8, TRANS 2-86). Am Math.

Aleksandrov, A. D., et al. Eleven Papers on Topology, Function Theory, & Differential Equations. LC 51-5559. (Translations Ser.: No. 2, Vol. 1). 1955. 23.20 (ISBN 0-8218-1701-9, TRANS 2-1). Am Math.

Allendoerfer, Carl B., et al. Elementary Functions. 1976. text ed. 14.95 (ISBN 0-07-001371-3, C); instructor's manual 3.50 (ISBN 0-07-001374-8). McGraw.

Andreev, A. E., et al. Twelve Papers on Function Theory, Probability, & Differential Equations. LC 51-5559. (Translations Ser.: No. 2, Vol. 8). 1957. 36.80 (ISBN 0-8218-1708-6, TRANS 2-8). Am Math.

Arson, I. S., et al. Eighteen Papers on Logic & Theory of Functions. LC 51-5559. (Translations, Ser.: No. 2, Vol. 83). 1969. 28.00 (ISBN 0-8218-1783-3, TRANS 2-83). Am Math.

Bear, H. S. Elementary Functions. 2nd ed. LC 76-184867. 1976. 8.95 (ISBN 0-685-65371-4). Page-Ficklin.

Bieberach, Ludwig, tr. Lehrbuch der Funktionentheorie, 2 Vols. (Bibliotheca Mathematica Teubneriana Ser: Nos. 21, 22). Repr. of 1921 ed. Set. 38.50 (ISBN 0-384-04244-9). Johnson Repr.

Bohr, Harald. Almost Periodic Functions. LC 47-5500. 1980. 8.50 (ISBN 0-8284-0027-X). Chelsea Pub.

Bonar, D. D. On Annular Functions. (Math. Forschungsberichte, No.24). (Illus.). 1971. pap. 15.00 (ISBN 0-685-37412-2). Adler.

Bruckner, A. M. Differentiation of Real Functions. (Lecture Notes in Mathematics: Vol. 659). 1978. pap. 13.90 (ISBN 0-387-08910-1). Springer-Verlag.

Burago, Yu D. & Maz'ya, V. G., eds. Potential Theory & Function Theory for Irregular Regions. LC 69-15004. (Seminars in Mathematics Ser.: Vol. 3). 68p. 1969. 25.00 (ISBN 0-306-18803-1, Consultants). Plenum Pub.

Caratheodory, Constantin. Vorlesungen Ueber Reelle Funktionen. 3rd ed. LC 63-11321. (Ger). 1968. 19.95 (ISBN 0-8284-0038-5). Chelsea Pub.

Carter, David S. & Vogt, Andrew. Two Articles: Collinearity-Preserving Functions Between Affine Desarguesian Planes. LC 80-20427. (Memoirs: No. 235). 1980. 6.40 (ISBN 0-8218-2235-7). Am Math.

Cernikov, S. N., et al. Twelve Papers on Algebra & Real Functions. LC 51-5559. (Translations Ser.: No. 2, Vol. 17). 1961. 26.00 (ISBN 0-8218-1717-5, TRANS 2-17). Am Math.

Chandrasekharan, K. Arithmetical Functions. LC 72-102384. (Die Grundlehren der Mathematischen Wissenschaften: Vol. 167). (Illus.). 1970. 34.40 (ISBN 0-387-05114-7). Springer-Verlag.

Christy, Dennis T. Elementary Functions. (Illus.). 1978. text ed. 18.95 scp (ISBN 0-06-041297-6, HarpC); free answers to even number excercises (ISBN 0-06-361191-0). Har-Row.

Cohn, L. Analytic Theory of the Harishchandra C-Function. LC 74-23331. (Lecture Notes in Mathematics Ser.: Vol. 429). 167p. 1975. pap. 9.50 (ISBN 0-387-07017-6). Springer-Verlag.

Conference on Constructive Theory of Functions, Budapest, 1969. Proceedings: Approximation Theory. Alexits-Steckin, G., ed. 538p. 1971. 48.50 (ISBN 0-685-27554-X). Adler.

Conway, J. B. Functions of One Complex Variable. 2nd ed. (Graduate Texts in Mathematics: Vol. 11). (Illus.). 1979. 24.00 (ISBN 0-387-90328-3). Springer-Verlag.

Eremin, I. I., et al. Twelve Papers on Real & Complex Function Theory. LC 51-5559. (Translations Ser.: No. 2, Vol. 88). 1970. 32.40 (ISBN 0-8218-1788-4, TRANS 2-88). Am Math.

Fichtenholz, G. M. Functional Series. (Pocket Mathematical Library Ser.). 1970. 25.25x (ISBN 0-677-20950-9). Gordon.

Fitts, Gary. Module XI: Graphing Functions. Ablon, Leon J., ed. LC 76-62884. (Ser. in Mathematics Modules). 1977. pap. 4.95 (ISBN 0-8465-0265-8). Benjamin-Cummings.

Fitts, Gary, ed. Module X: Functions & Word Problems. Ablon, Leon J. LC 76-1055. (Mathematics Modules Ser.). 1976. pap. 3.95 (ISBN 0-8465-0264-X). Benjamin-Cummings.

Fobes, Melcher P. Elementary Functions: Backdrop for Calculus. 510p. 1973. text ed. 14.95 (ISBN 0-02-338500-6). Macmillan.

Froman, Robert. A Game of Functions. LC 74-2266. (Young Math Ser). (Illus.). 40p. (gr. k-3). 1974. (TYC-J); PLB 8.79 (ISBN 0-690-00545-8). Har-Row.

Gelfand, I. M., et al. Functions & Graphs. (Pocket Mathematical Library Ser.). 1968. 18.75x (ISBN 0-677-20690-9). Gordon.

Gel'fond, A. O., et al. Twelve Papers on Number Theory & Function Theory. LC 51-5559. (Translations Ser.: No. 2, Vol. 19). 1962. 23.60 (ISBN 0-8218-1719-1, TRANS 2-19). Am Math.

Hardy, F. Lane. Precalculus Mathematics. 2nd ed. LC 75-148246. 1971. text ed. 18.95 (ISBN 0-675-09251-5). Merrill.

Hardy, Godfrey H. Pure Mathematics. 1959. text ed. 59.50 (ISBN 0-521-05203-3); pap. text ed. 17.50 (ISBN 0-521-09227-2, 227). Cambridge U Pr.

Hughes-Hallett, Deborah. The Math Workshop: Elementary Functions. 1980. text ed. 15.95 (ISBN 0-393-09033-7); tchrs'. manual avail. (ISBN 0-393-09028-0). Norton.

Iooss, G. & Joseph, D. Elementary Stability & Bifurcation Theory. (Undergraduate Texts in Mathematics Ser.). (Illus.). 286p. 1981. 22.00 (ISBN 0-387-90526-X). Springer-Verlag.

Jahnke, Eugene & Emde, Fritz. Tables of Functions with Formulae & Curves. 4th ed. (Ger & Eng). 1945. pap. text ed. 5.00 (ISBN 0-486-60133-1). Dover.

Johnson, Richard E., et al. College Algebra. 2nd ed. LC 72-94886. 562p. 1973. pap. text ed. 15.95 (ISBN 0-8465-3396-0); tchr's guide 2.95 (ISBN 0-8465-3397-9, 53397); study guide 3.95 (ISBN 0-8465-0297-6). Benjamin-Cummings.

Jones, D. S. The Theory of Generalised Functions. LC 80-41830. 500p. Date not set. price not set (ISBN 0-521-23723-8). Cambridge U Pr.

Jones, T. A. & Montgomery, R. M. Calculus & Elementary Functions One. LC 74-108107. (School Mathematics Project Ser). (Illus.). 1970. text ed. 11.95x (ISBN 0-521-07712-5). Cambridge U Pr.

Klentos, Gus & Newmyer, Joseph, Jr. Elementary Functions: Algebra & Analytic Geometry. 448p. 1975. pap. text ed. 17.50 (ISBN 0-675-08827-5); media: audiocassettes 160.00, 2-6 sets, 100.00 ea., 7 or more sets, 75.00 ea. (ISBN 0-675-08774-0); instructor's manual 3.95 (ISBN 0-686-67047-7). Merrill.

Knopp, Konrad. Elements of the Theory of Functions. Bagemihl, Frederick, tr. 1952. pap. text ed. 2.75 (ISBN 0-486-60154-4). Dover.

--Problem Book in the Theory of Functions, 2 vols. Incl. Vol. 1. Problems in the Elementary Theory of Functions. Bers, Lipman, tr (ISBN 0-486-60158-7); Vol. 2. Problems in the Advanced Theory of Functions (ISBN 0-486-60159-5). 1968. pap. text ed. 3.00 ea. Dover.

Korn, Henry R. & Liberi, Albert W. An Elementary Approach to Functions. (Illus.). 1977. text ed. 15.95 (ISBN 0-07-035401-4, C); write for info instructor's manual (ISBN 0-07-035402-2); student guide 4.95 (ISBN 0-07-035403-0). McGraw.

--An Elementary Approach to Functions. (Illus.). 1977. text ed. 15.95 (ISBN 0-07-035401-4, C); write for info instructor's manual (ISBN 0-07-035402-2); student guide 4.95 (ISBN 0-07-035403-0). McGraw.

Korovkin, P. P. Limits & Continuity. (Pocket Mathematical Library Ser). 1969. 34.75x (ISBN 0-677-20740-9). Gordon.

Ladyzhenskaya, O. A., ed. Boundary Value Problems of Mathematical Physics & Related Aspects of Function Theory, Part 3. LC 69-12506. (Seminars in Mathematics Ser.: Vol. 11). 79p. 1970. 25.00 (ISBN 0-306-18811-2, Consultants). Plenum Pub.

Lighthill, M. J. Introduction to Fourier Analysis & Generalized Functions. (Cambridge Monographs on Mechanics & Applied Mathematics). 18.95 (ISBN 0-521-05556-3); pap. text ed. 7.95 (ISBN 0-521-09128-4). Cambridge U Pr.

Lukacs, Eugene & Laha, R. G. Applications of Characteristic Functions. (Griffin's Statistical Monographs & Courses Ser: Vol. 14). 1964. pap. 12.95 (ISBN 0-02-848540-8). Hafner.

Natanson, I. P. Constructive Function Theory, 3 vols. Incl. Vol. 1. Uniform Approximation. Obolensky, Alexis N., tr. viii, 232p. 12.50 (ISBN 0-8044-4695-4); Vol. 2. Approximation in Mean. Schulenberger, John R., tr. 176p. 12.00 (ISBN 0-8044-4696-2); Vol. 3. Interpolation & Approximation Quadratures. Schulenberger, John R., tr. 180p. 12.00 (ISBN 0-8044-4697-0). LC 64-15689. Ungar.

--Theory of Functions of a Real Variable, 2 vols. Boron, Leo F. & Hewitt, Edwin, eds. Boron, Leo F. & Hewitt, Edwin, trs. LC 54-7420. 278p. Vol. 2. 13.00 (ISBN 0-8044-4703-9). Ungar.

Nevanlinna, R. Analytic Functions. Emig, P., tr. (Grundlehren der Mathematischen Wissenschaften: Vol. 162). (Illus.). 1970. 41.70 (ISBN 0-387-04834-0). Springer-Verlag.

Nikol'skii, N. K., ed. Investigations in Linear Operators & Function Theory, Pt. 1. LC 74-37620. (Seminars in Mathematics Ser.: Vol. 19). 138p. 1972. 25.00 (ISBN 0-306-18819-8, Consultants). Plenum Pub.

Osgood, William F. Funktionentheorie, 2 Vols. LC 63-11319. (Ger). Vol. 1. 12.50 (ISBN 0-8284-0193-4); Vol. 2. 17.50 (ISBN 0-8284-0182-9). Chelsea Pub.

Paley, Raymond E. & Wiener, Norbert. Fourier Transforms in the Complex Domain. LC 35-3273. (Colloquium, Pbns. Ser.: Vol. 19). 1978. Repr. of 1934 ed. 27.60 (ISBN 0-8218-1019-7, COLL-19). Am Math.

Pontrjagin, L. S., ed. Theory of Functions & Its Applications. LC 77-10017. (Steklov Institute of Mathematics, Proceedings: No. 134). 1977. 72.00 (ISBN 0-8218-3034-1, STEKLO 134). Am Math.

Pringsheim, Alfred. Vorlesungen Uber Zahlen & Funktionenlehre, 2 Vols. (Bibliotheca Mathematica Teubneriana Ser: Nos. 28-29). (Ger). 1969. Repr. of 1916 ed. Set. 100.00 (ISBN 0-384-47885-9). Johnson Repr.

Puri, M. L., ed. Nonparametric Techniques in Statistical Inference. LC 74-116750. (Illus.). 1970. 86.50 (ISBN 0-521-07817-2). Cambridge U Pr.

Rice, John R. The Approximation of Linear Functions, 2 vols, Vols. 1 & 2. 1964-69. Vol. 1: Linear Theory. 14.50 (ISBN 0-201-06430-8, Adv Bk Prog); Vol. 2: Nonlinear & Multivariate Theory. 18.00 (ISBN 0-201-06432-4, Adv Bk Prog). A-W.

Riesz, Frigyes & Sz-Nagy, Bela. Functional Analysis. Boron, Leo. F, tr. LC 55-8437. xii, 468p. 25.00 (ISBN 0-8044-4821-3); appendix 2.50 (ISBN 0-8044-4822-1). Ungar.

Rivlin, Theodore J. An Introduction to the Approximation of Functions. 160p. 1981. pap. 3.50 (ISBN 0-486-64069-8). Dover.

Rodin, R. & Sario, L. Principal Functions. (Illus.). xviii, 347p. 1975. 13.80 (ISBN 0-387-90129-9). Springer-Verlag.

Rose, I. H. Elementary Functions: A Precalculus Primer. 324p. 1973. text ed. 12.95x (ISBN 0-673-07625-3). Scott F.
Schaeffer, A. C. & Spencer, D. C. Coefficient Regions for Schlicht Functions. Bd. with The Region of Values of the Derivative of a Schlicht Function. Grad, Arthur. LC 51-944. (Colloquium Pubns. Ser.: Vol. 35). 1950. 20.00 (ISBN 0-8218-1035-9, COLL-35). Am Math.
Schober, G. Univalent Functions: Selected Topics. (Lecture Notes in Mathematics: Vol. 478). v, 200p. 1975. pap. 12.60 (ISBN 0-387-07391-4). Springer-Verlag.
Siegel, C. L. Topics in Complex Function Theory, 3 vols. Incl. Vol. 1. Elliptical Functions & Uniformization Theory. 1969. 31.00 (ISBN 0-471-79070-2); Vol. 2. Automorphic Functions & Abelian Integrals. 1972. 31.00 (ISBN 0-471-79080-X); Vol. 3. Abelian Functions & Modular Functions of Several Variables. Tretkoff, M. & Gottschling, E., trs. 244p. 1973. 39.95 (ISBN 0-471-79090-7). LC 69-19931. (Pure & Applied Mathematics Ser., Pub. by Wiley-Interscience). Wiley.
Smith, Karl J. Precalculus Mathematics: A Functional Approach. Wisner, Robert J., ed. LC 78-6279. (Contemporary Undergraduate Mathematics Ser.). (Illus.). 1979. text ed. 18.95 (ISBN 0-8185-0269-X). Brooks-Cole.
Sprecher, David A. Precalculus Mathematics: An Elementary Functions Approach. (Illus.). 1974. text ed. 20.95 scp (ISBN 0-06-046394-5, HarpC); ans. to even numbered exercises avail. (ISBN 0-06-366390-2). Har-Row.
Steckin, S. B. Approximation of Functions by Polynomials & Splines. LC 81-2805. (STEKLO Ser.: No. 1981/1/145). Date not set. 80.00 (ISBN 0-8218-3049-X). Am Math.
Steklov Institute of Mathematics, Academy of Sciences, U S S R, No. 88. Approximation of Functions in the Mean: Proceedings. Steckin, S. B., ed. 1969. 25.60 (ISBN 0-8218-1888-0, STEKLO-88). Am Math.
Steklov Institute of Mathematics, Academy of Sciences, U S S R, No. 101 & Babenko, K. I. On the Theory of Extremal Problems for Univalent Functions of Class S: Proceedings. 1974. 78.40 (ISBN 0-8218-3001-5, STEKLO-101). Am Math.
Steklov Institute of Mathematics, Vol. 109. Approximation of Periodic Functions: Proceedings. Steckin, S. B., ed. LC 74-11473. 1974. 35.60 (ISBN 0-8218-3009-0, STEKLO-109). Am Math.
Talman, James D. Special Functions: A Group Theoretical Approach Based on Lectures by Eugene P. Wigner. (Mathematical Physics Monographs: No. 11). 1968. pap. 9.50 (ISBN 0-8053-9261-0, Adv Bk Prog). Benjamin-Cummings.
Titchmarsh, Edward C. Theory of Functions. 2nd ed. 1939. 17.95x (ISBN 0-19-853349-7). Oxford U Pr.
Todd, J. Introduction to the Constructive Theory of Functions. (International Ser. of Numerical Mathematics: No. 1). 127p. 1963. 26.50 (ISBN 3-7643-0186-4). Birkhauser.
Treves, Francois. Linear Partial Differential Equations with Constant Coefficients. (Mathematics & Its Applications Ser.). 1966. 104.00x (ISBN 0-677-01190-3). Gordon.
Voronovskaja, E. V. Functional Method & Its Applications. LC 70-138816. (Translations of Mathematical Monographs: Vol. 28). 1970. 34.40 (ISBN 0-8218-1578-4, MMONO-28). Am Math.
Walsh, J. L. Interpolation & Approximation by Rational Functions in the Complex Domain. rev. ed. LC 60-3978. (Colloquium Pbns. Ser.: Vol. 20). 1966. 39.60 (ISBN 0-8218-1020-0, COLL-20). Am Math.
Walsh, Joseph L. Location of Critical Points of Analytic & Harmonic Functions. LC 50-12177. (Colloquium Pbns. Ser.: Vol. 34). 1950. 20.00 (ISBN 0-8218-1034-0, COLL-34). Am Math.
Whittaker, Edmund T. & Watson, George N. A Course of Modern Analysis. 4th ed. 1927. 74.50 (ISBN 0-521-06794-4); pap. text ed. 19.95x (ISBN 0-521-09189-6). Cambridge U Pr.
Yaqub, Adil. Elementary Functions. 368p. 1975. text ed. 17.50 (ISBN 0-395-17093-1); instructors manual pap. 2.25 (ISBN 0-395-17871-1). HM.

FUNCTIONS (FUNCTIONAL ANALYSIS)
see Distributions, Theory of (Functional Analysis)

FUNCTIONS, ABELIAN
see also Geometry, Algebraic

Hejhal, Dennis A. Theta Functions, Kernel Functions, & Abelian Integrals. LC 72-6824. (Memoirs: No. 129). 116p. 1972. pap. 7.60 (ISBN 0-685-29912-0, MEMO-129). Am Math.
Lang, Serge. Introduction to Algebraic & Abelian Functions. LC 72-1765. 1972. text ed. 16.50 (ISBN 0-201-04163-4, Adv Bk Prog). A-W.

FUNCTIONS, ALGEBRAIC

Appell, Paul, et al. Theorie Des Fonctions Algebriques, Vol. 1. 3rd ed. LC 72-114210. 1977. text ed. 29.50 (ISBN 0-8284-0285-X). Chelsea Pub.
--Theorie Des Fonctions Algebriques et Leurs Integrales: Volume II. LC 72-114210. text ed. 25.00 (ISBN 0-8284-0299-X). Chelsea Pub.
Artin, E. Algebraic Numbers & Algebraic Functions. 1968. pap. 32.50 (ISBN 0-677-00635-7). Gordon.
Bear, H. S. Algebra & Elementary Functions. 2nd ed. LC 76-184869. (Page-Ficklin Math Ser). 1976. pap. text ed. 13.95x (ISBN 0-8087-2855-5). Burgess.
--Algebra & Elementary Functions. 2nd ed. LC 70-184868. 1976. pap. 9.95 (ISBN 0-685-65372-2). Page-Ficklin.
Chernoff, P. R. & Marsden, J. E. Properties of Infinite Dimensional Hamiltonian Systems. LC 74-22373. (Lecture Notes in Mathematics Ser.: Vol. 425). iv, 160p. 1975. pap. 10.50 (ISBN 0-387-07011-7). Springer-Verlag.
Davenport, J. H. On the Integration of Agebraic Function. (Lecture Notes in Computer Science Ser.: Vol. 102). 197p. 1981. pap. 11.80 (ISBN 0-387-10290-6). Springer-Verlag.
Deuring, M. Lectures on the Theory of Algebraic Functions of One Variable. LC 72-97679. (Lecture Notes in Mathematics: Vol. 314). 151p. 1973. pap. 8.80 (ISBN 0-387-06152-5). Springer-Verlag.
Eichler, Martin. Introduction to the Theory of Algebraic Numbers & Functions. (Pure & Applied Mathematics: Vol. 23). 1966. 55.00 (ISBN 0-12-233650-X). Acad Pr.
Hensel, Kurt & Landsberg, G. Algebraische Funktionen. LC 65-11624. (Ger). 1965. 29.50 (ISBN 0-8284-0179-9). Chelsea Pub.
Kaluznin, Lev & Poschel, Reinhard. Funktionen und Relationenalgebren. (Mathematische Reihe: No. 67). (Illus., Ger.). 1979. 42.00 (ISBN 3-7643-1038-3). Birkhauser.
Knopfmacher. Analytic Arithmetic of Algebraic Function Fields. (Lecture Notes Ser.: Vol. 50). 1979. 16.50 (ISBN 0-8247-6907-4). Dekker.
Kutepov, A. Problem Book: Algebra & Elementary Functions. 439p. 1978. 5.30 (ISBN 0-8285-0737-6, Pub. by Mir Pubs Russia). Imported Pubns.
Lang, Serge. Introduction to Algebraic & Abelian Functions. LC 72-1765. 1972. text ed. 16.50 (ISBN 0-201-04163-4, Adv Bk Prog). A-W.
Mergener, Robert J. Functions: An Approach to Algebra & Trigonometry. 2nd ed. 1978. pap. text ed. 18.50 (ISBN 0-8403-2339-5). Kendall-Hunt.
Nash, J. C. Compact Numerical Methods for Computers: Linear Algebra & Functional Minimization. LC 78-10144. 1979. 32.95x (ISBN 0-470-26559-0). Halsted Pr.
Oman, Robert M. Graphing Algebraic Functions. 1979. pap. 2.45 (ISBN 0-931660-02-5). R Oman Pubns.
Peitgen, H. O. & Walther, H. O., eds. Functional Differential Equations & Approximations of Fixed Points. (Lecture Notes in Mathematics: Vol. 730). 1979. pap. 24.20 (ISBN 0-387-09518-7). Springer-Verlag.
Picard, Emile & Simart, G. Theorie Des Fonctions Algebriques De Deux Variables Independantes 2 Vols. in 1. LC 67-31156. (Fr). 1971. 29.00 (ISBN 0-8284-0248-5). Chelsea Pub.
Rickart, C. E. Natural Functions Algebras. (Universitexts). 240p. 1980. pap. 15.50 (ISBN 0-387-90449-2). Springer-Verlag.
Schilling, O. F. Theory of Valuations. 3rd ed. LC 50-12178. (Mathematical Surveys Ser.: No. 4). 1978. Repr. of 1950 ed. 30.40 (ISBN 0-8218-1504-0, SURV-4). Am Math.
Stockton, Doris S. Essential Algebra with Functions. 600p. 1973. pap. 11.95x (ISBN 0-673-07862-0). Scott F.

FUNCTIONS, ALMOST PERIODIC
see Almost Periodic Functions

FUNCTIONS, ANALYTIC
see Analytic Functions

FUNCTIONS, AUTOMORPHIC

Baily, Walter L., Jr. Introductory Lectures on Automorphic Forms. LC 72-4034. (Publications of the Mathematical Society of Japan Series, No. 12). 272p. 1973. lib. bdg. 18.00 (ISBN 0-691-08123-9). Princeton U Pr.
Borel, A., ed. Automorphic Forms, Representations & L-Functions, 2 vols. LC 78-21184. (Proceedings of Symposia in Pure Mathematics: Vol. 33). 1980. 38.00 set (ISBN 0-686-52415-2, PSPUM-33); Pt. 1. 22.40 (ISBN 0-8218-1435-4); Pt. 2. 22.40 (ISBN 0-685-99018-4). Am Math.
Ford, Lester R. Automorphic Functions. LC 52-8647. 14.95 (ISBN 0-8284-0085-7). Chelsea Pub.
Fricke, Robert & Klein, Felix. Vorlesungen Ueber Die Theorie der Automorphen Funktionen, 2 Vols. Repr. of 1912 ed. 61.50 (ISBN 0-384-16870-1). Johnson Repr.
Harvey, W. J., ed. Discrete Groups and Automorphic Functions. 1978. 64.50 (ISBN 0-12-329950-0). Acad Pr.
Jacquet, H. Automorphic Forms on GL 2, Pt. 2. LC 76-108338. (Lecture Notes in Mathematics: Vol. 278). 142p. 1972. pap. 6.30 (ISBN 0-387-05931-8). Springer-Verlag.
Kra, Irwin. Automorphic Forms & Kleinian Groups. LC 72-187423. (Math Lecture Notes Ser.: No. 51). xiv, 464p. 1972. text ed. 23.50 (ISBN 0-8053-2342-2, Adv Bk Prog); pap. text ed. 13.50 (ISBN 0-8053-2343-0, Adv Bk Prog). Benjamin-Cummings.
Lax, Peter D. & Phillips, Ralph S. Scattering Theory for Automorphic Functions. LC 76-3028. (Annals of Mathematics Studies: No. 87). 260p. 1976. 22.00x (ISBN 0-691-08179-4); pap. 10.50x (ISBN 0-691-08184-0). Princeton U Pr.
Lehner, Joseph. Discontinuous Groups & Automorphic Functions. LC 63-110987. (Mathematical Surveys Ser.: Vol. 8). 1974. Repr. of 1964 ed. 30.00 (ISBN 0-8218-1508-3, SURV-8). Am Math.
Pyatekskii-Shapiro, I. I. Automorphic Functions & the Geometry of Classical Domains. (Mathematics & Its Applications Ser.). 1969. 44.00x (ISBN 0-677-20310-1). Gordon.
Raghunathan, M. S. Discrete Subgroups of Lie Groups. LC 71-189389. (Ergebnisse der Mathematik und Ihrer Grenzgebiete: Vol. 68). 240p. 1972. 27.20 (ISBN 0-387-05749-8). Springer-Verlag.
Shimura, G. Automorphic Functions & Number Theory. LC 68-25132. (Lecture Notes in Mathematics: Vol. 54). (Orig.). 1968. pap. 10.70 (ISBN 0-387-04224-5). Springer-Verlag.

FUNCTIONS, BESSELIAN
see Bessel's Functions

FUNCTIONS, BETA

Hamilton-Miller, J. M. T. & Smith, J. T., eds. Beta Lactamases. 1979. 70.50 (ISBN 0-12-321550-1). Acad Pr.
Pearson, K. Tables of the Incomplete Beta-Function. 505p. 1968. 60.00x (ISBN 0-85264-704-2, Pub. by England Griffin). State Mutual Bk.
Pearson, Karl. Tables of the Incomplete Beta Function. 205p. 1968. lib. bdg. 35.95x (ISBN 0-521-05922-4, Pub. by Charles Griffin & Co Ltd England). Lubrecht & Cramer.

FUNCTIONS, CHARACTERISTIC
see also Distribution (Probability Theory)

FUNCTIONS, CHEBYSHEV'S
see Chebyshev Polynomials

FUNCTIONS, CIRCULAR
see Trigonometrical Functions

FUNCTIONS, CONTINUOUS

Burckel, R. B. Characterization of C(X) Among Its Subalgebras. (Lecture Notes in Pure & Applied Mathematics Ser: Vol. 6). 176p. 1972. 19.75 (ISBN 0-8247-6038-7). Dekker.
De Vore, R. A. The Approximation of Continuous Functions by Positive Linear Operators. LC 72-91891. (Lecture Notes in Mathematics: Vol. 293). viii, 289p. 1972. pap. 9.40 (ISBN 0-387-06038-3). Springer-Verlag.
Owen, T. C. Characterization of Organic Compounds by Chemical Methods: An Introductory Laboratory Textbook. 256p. 1969. 9.95 (ISBN 0-8247-1510-1). Dekker.
Semadeni, Zbigniew. Banach Spaces of Continuous Functions, Vol. 1. 1972. 24.75 (ISBN 0-02-855730-1). Hafner.
Zalcman, L. Analytic Capacity & Rational Approximation. LC 68-19414. (Lecture Notes in Mathematics: Vol. 50). (Orig.). 1968. pap. 10.70 (ISBN 0-387-04220-2). Springer-Verlag.

FUNCTIONS, COULOMB
see Coulomb Functions

FUNCTIONS, ELLIPTIC
see also Functions, Modular; Functions of Complex Variables

Apostol, T. M. Modular Functions & Dirichlet Series in Number Theory. Gehring, F. W. & Moore, C. C., eds. LC 76-10236. (Graduate Texts in Mathematics: Vol. 41). 1976. 20.80 (ISBN 0-387-90185-X). Springer-Verlag.
Byrd, P. F. & Friedman, M. D. Handbook of Elliptic Integrals for Engineers & Scientists. 2nd ed. LC 72-146515. (Die Grundlehren der Mathematischen Wissenschaften: Vol. 67). (Illus.). 1971. 39.80 (ISBN 0-387-05318-2). Springer-Verlag.
Ciarlet, P. G. The Finite Element Method for Elliptic Problems. (Studies in Mathematics & Its Applications). 1978. 63.50 (ISBN 0-444-85028-7, North-Holland). Elsevier.
Cross, B. H. Arithmetic on Elliptic Curves with Complex Multiplication. (Lecture Notes in Mathematics Ser.: Vol. 776). 1980. pap. 9.80 (ISBN 0-387-09743-0). Springer-Verlag.
Du Val, P. Elliptic Functions & Elliptic Curves. (Condon Mathematical Society Lecture Notes Ser.: No. 9). (Illus.). 200p. 1972. 26.50 (ISBN 0-521-20036-9). Cambridge U Pr.
Fricke, Robert. Die Elliptischen Funktionen und Ihre Anwendungen, 2 Vols. LC 5-33590. 1971. Repr. of 1922 ed. Set. 69.00 (ISBN 0-384-16860-4). Johnson Repr.
Lang, S. Elliptic Curves: Diophantine Analysis. LC 77-21139. (Grundlehren der Mathematischen Wissenschaften: Vol 231). 1978. 39.30 (ISBN 0-387-08489-4). Springer-Verlag.
Lang, Serge. Elliptic Functions. LC 72-1767. 350p. 1973. text ed. 26.50 (ISBN 0-201-04162-6, Adv Bk Prog). A-W.
Masser, D. W. Elliptic Functions & Transcendence. (Lecture Notes in Mathematics: Vol. 437). xiv, 143p. 1975. pap. 10.00 (ISBN 0-387-07136-9). Springer-Verlag.
Neville, Eric H. Elliptic Functions: A Primer. Langford, W. J., ed. 211p. 1972. text ed. 25.00 (ISBN 0-08-016369-6). Pergamon.
Rauch, H. E. & Lebowitz, A. Elliptic Functions, Theta Functions & Riemann Surfaces. 304p. 1973. 20.50 (ISBN 0-683-07187-4, Pub. by Wiley). Krieger.
Schoeneberg, B. Elliptic Modular Functions: An Introduction. Smart, J. R. & Schwandt, E., trs. from Ger. LC 73-8486. (Grundlehren der Mathematischen Wissenschaften: Vol. 203). (Illus.). 233p. 1974. 37.00 (ISBN 0-387-06382-X). Springer-Verlag.
Selfridge, R. G. & Maxfield, J. E. Table of the Incomplete Elliptic Integral of the Third Kind. 1958. 10.00 (ISBN 0-486-60501-9). Dover.
Tannery, Jules & Molk, Jules. Elements de la Theorie des Fonctions Elliptiques, 4 vols. in 2. 2nd ed. LC 70-113152. 1145p. (Fr.). 1972. Set. text ed. 39.50 (ISBN 0-8284-0257-4). Chelsea Pub.
Weber, Heinrich. Lehrbuch der Algebra, Vols. 1, 2, & 3. 3rd ed. LC 61-6890. 1979. Repr. of 1962 ed. Set. text ed. 85.00 (ISBN 0-8284-0144-6). Chelsea Pub.
Weil, A. Elliptic Functions According to Eisenstein & Kronecker. LC 75-23200. (Ergebnisse der Mathematik und Ihrer Grenzgebiete: Vol. 88). 105p. 1976. 19.70 (ISBN 0-387-07422-8). Springer-Verlag.

FUNCTIONS, ENTIRE
see also Value Distribution Theory

Boas, Ralph P., Jr. Entire Functions. (Pure and Applied Mathematics Ser.: Vol. 5). 1954. 39.50 (ISBN 0-12-108150-8). Acad Pr.
Evgrafov, M. A. Asymptotic Estimates & Entire Functions. (Russian Tracts on the Physical Sciences Ser.). (Illus.). 1962. 39.00x (ISBN 0-677-20070-6). Gordon.
Holland, A. S. Introduction to the Theory of Entire Functions. (Pure & Applied Mathematics Ser.). 1973. 40.50 (ISBN 0-12-352750-3). Acad Pr.
Levin, Boris J. Distribution of Zeros of Entire Functions. rev. ed. LC 80-36891. (Translations of Mathematical Monographs: Vol. 5). 1980. 26.80 (ISBN 0-8218-4505-5, MMONO-5). Am Math.
Ronkin, L. I. Introduction to the Theory of Entire Functions of Several Variables. LC 74-12068. (Translations of Mathematical Monographs: Vol. 44). 1974. 50.80 (ISBN 0-8218-1594-6, MMONO-44). Am Math.
Steklov Institute of Mathematics, Academy of Sciences, USSR, No. 118. On Integral Functionals with Variable Domain of Integration: Proceedings. Daniljuk, I. I., ed. 1976. 33.60 (ISBN 0-8218-3018-X, STEKLO-118). Am Math.
Stoll, Wilhelm. Holomorphic Functions of Finite Order in Several Variables. LC 74-8213. (CBMS Regional Conference Series in Mathematics: No. 21). 1974. 10.00 (ISBN 0-8218-1671-3, CBMS-21). Am Math.
Symposia in Pure Mathematics-San Diego-1966. Entire Functions & Related Parts of Analysis: Proceedings, Vol. 11. Chern, S. S., et al, eds. LC 68-10458. 1968. 33.20 (ISBN 0-8218-1411-7, PSPUM-11). Am Math.
Valiron, Georges. Theory of Integral Functions. LC 51-7375. 9.95 (ISBN 0-8284-0056-3). Chelsea Pub.

FUNCTIONS, EXPONENTIAL

Barndorff-Nielsen, O. Information & Exponential Families in Statistical Theory. LC 77-9943. (Probability & Mathematical Statistics, Tracts). 238p. 1978. 47.25 (ISBN 0-471-99545-2, Pub. by Wiley-Interscience). Wiley.
Levinson, Norman. Gap & Density Theorems. LC 41-6147. (Colloquium, Pbns. Ser.: Vol. 26). 1963. Repr. of 1940 ed. 19.60 (ISBN 0-8218-1026-X, COLL-26). Am Math.
Paley, Raymond E. & Wiener, Norbert. Fourier Transforms in the Complex Domain. LC 35-3273. (Colloquium, Pbns. Ser.: Vol. 19). 1978. Repr. of 1934 ed. 27.60 (ISBN 0-8218-1019-7, COLL-19). Am Math.

FUNCTIONS, GAMMA

Farrell, Orin J. & Ross, Bertram. Solved Problems in Analysis: As Applied to Gamma, Beta, Legendre and Bessel Function. 7.50 (ISBN 0-8446-0091-1). Peter Smith.
Nielsen, Niels. Die Gammafunktion, 2 vols. in 1. Incl. Integrallogarithmus. LC 64-13785. (Ger.). 1965. 16.50 (ISBN 0-8284-0188-8). Chelsea Pub.

Pearson, K. Tables of the Incomplete Gamma-Function. 164p. 1965. 30.00x (ISBN 0-85264-703-4, Pub. by Griffin England). State Mutual Bk.

Pearson, Karl. Tables of the Incomplete Gamma Function. 164p. 1965. lib. bdg. 17.50x (ISBN 0-521-05924-0, Pub. by Charles Griffin & Co Ltd England). Lubrecht & Cramer.

FUNCTIONS, GENERALIZED
see Distributions, Theory of (Functional Analysis)

FUNCTIONS, GREEN'S
see Green's Functions

FUNCTIONS, HARMONIC
see Harmonic Functions

FUNCTIONS, HOLOMORPHIC
see Analytic Functions

FUNCTIONS, HYPERBOLIC
see Functions, Exponential

FUNCTIONS, HYPERGEOMETRIC

Buchholz, H. Confluent Hypergeometric Function with Special Emphasis on Its Applications. Lichtblau, H. & Wetzel, K., trs. LC 69-16291. (Springer Tracts in Natural Philosophy: Vol. 15). 1969. 40.20 (ISBN 0-387-04715-8). Springer-Verlag.

Erdelyi, Arthur & Swanson, Charles A. Asymptotic Forms of Whittaker's Confluent Hypergeometric Functions. LC 52-42839. (Memoirs: No. 25). 1967. pap. 7.20 (ISBN 0-8218-1225-4, MEMO-25). Am Math.

Exton, Harold. Handbook of Hypergeometric Integrals: Theory Applications, Tables, Computer Programs. (Mathematics & Its Applications Ser.). 1978. 59.95 (ISBN 0-470-26342-3). Halsted Pr.

--Multiple Hypergeometric Functions & Applications. LC 76-20720. 1976. 41.95 (ISBN 0-470-15190-0). Halsted Pr.

Lieberman, Gerald J. & Owen, Donald B. Tables of the Hypergeometric Probability Distribution. 1961. 28.50x (ISBN 0-8047-0057-5). Stanford U Pr.

Mathai, A. M. & Saxena, R. K. Generalized Hypergeometric Functions with Applications in Statistics & Physical Sciences. LC 73-13489. (Lecture Notes in Mathematics: Vol. 348). pap. 15.70 (ISBN 0-387-06482-6). Springer-Verlag.

FUNCTIONS, INTEGRAL
see Functions, Entire

FUNCTIONS, INVERSE

Nashed, M. Z., ed. Recent Applications of Generalized Inverses. (Research Notes in Mathematics Ser.: No. 23). (Illus.). 1979. pap. cancelled (ISBN 0-685-96564-3). Pitman Learning.

Sabatier, P. C., ed. Applied Inverse Problems: Lectures Presented at the RCP 264 in Montpellier. (Lecture Notes in Physics: Vol. 85). 1979. pap. 22.60 (ISBN 0-387-09094-0). Springer-Verlag.

FUNCTIONS, LAME'S
see Lame's Functions

FUNCTIONS, LIAPUNOV
see Liapunov Functions

FUNCTIONS, MATHIEU
see Mathieu Functions

FUNCTIONS, MEROMORPHIC
see also Value Distribution Theory

Andreotti, A. & Stoll, W. Analytic & Algebraic Dependence of Meromorphic Functions. (Lecture Notes in Mathematics: Vol. 234). iii, 390p. 1971. pap. 10.20 (ISBN 0-387-05670-X). Springer-Verlag.

McDonald, Alvis E. A Multiplicity-Independent, Global Iteration for Meromorphic Functions. LC 75-130610. 116p. 1969. 19.00 (ISBN 0-686-01953-9). Mgmt Info Serv.

Namba, M. Families of Meromorphic Functions on Compact Riemann Surfaces. (Lecture Notes in Mathematics: Vol. 267). 284p. 1980. pap. 16.30 (ISBN 0-387-09722-8). Springer-Verlag.

Weyl, Hermann. Meromorphic Functions & Analytic Curves. 1943. pap. 13.00 (ISBN 0-527-02728-6). Kraus Repr.

Wu, Hung-Hsi. Equidistribution Theory of Holomorphic Curves. LC 78-100997. (Annals of Mathematics Studies: No. 64). 1970. 15.00 (ISBN 0-691-08073-9). Princeton U Pr.

FUNCTIONS, MODULAR

Apostol, T. M. Modular Functions & Dirichlet Series in Number Theory. Gehring, F. W. & Moore, C. C., eds. LC 76-10236. (Graduate Texts in Mathematics: Vol. 41). 1976. 20.80 (ISBN 0-387-90185-X). Springer-Verlag.

Gunning, Robert C. Lectures on Modular Forms. (Annals of Mathematics Studies: No. 48). (Orig.). pap. 8.50x (ISBN 0-691-07995-1). Princeton U Pr.

International Summer School, Univ. of Antwerp, RUCA, July-Aug., 1972. Modular Functions of One Variable Four: Proceedings. Birch, B. J. & Kuyk, W., eds. (Lecture Notes in Mathematics: Vol. 476). v, 151p. (Orig.). 1975. pap. text ed. 10.90 (ISBN 0-387-07392-2). Springer-Verlag.

International Summer School, University of Antwerp, 1972. Modular Functions of One Variable 3: Proceedings. Kuyk, W. & Serre, J. P., eds. LC 73-13491. (Lecture Notes in Mathematics: Vol. 350). 1973. pap. 15.75 (ISBN 0-387-06483-4). Springer-Verlag.

Klein, Felix & Fricke, Robert. Vorlesungen Ueber Die Theorie der Elliptischen Modulfunktionen, 2 Vols. 1890-1892. 69.00 (ISBN 0-384-29734-X). Johnson Repr.

Rankin, R. A. Modular Forms & Functions. LC 76-11089. (Illus.). 1977. 68.50 (ISBN 0-521-21212-X). Cambridge U Pr.

Serre, J. P. & Zigler, D. B., eds. Modular Functions of One Variable V: Proceedings. LC 77-22148. (Lecture Notes in Mathematics: Vol. 601). 1977. pap. text ed. 14.50 (ISBN 0-387-08348-0). Springer-Verlag.

FUNCTIONS, MONOGENIC
see Analytic Functions

FUNCTIONS, ORTHOGONAL
see also Orthogonal Polynomials; Series, Orthogonal

Ahmed, N. & Rao, K. R. Orthogonal Transforms for Digital Signal Processing. LC 73-18912. (Illus.). 280p. 1975. text ed. 30.70 (ISBN 0-387-06556-3). Springer-Verlag.

Geramita & Seberry. Orthogonal Designs: Quad. Forms & Had. Matrices. (Lecture Notes in Pure & Applied Mathematics Ser.: Vol. 45). 1979. 39.75 (ISBN 0-8247-6774-8). Dekker.

Harmuth, H. F. Transmission of Information by Orthogonal Functions. 2nd ed. LC 73-166296. (Illus.). 400p. 1972. 24.30 (ISBN 0-387-05512-6). Springer-Verlag.

Jackson, Dunham. Fourier Series & Orthogonal Polynomials. (Carus Monograph: No. 6). 234p. 1941. 12.50 (ISBN 0-88385-006-0). Math Assn.

Milin, Isaak M. Univalent Functions & Orthonormal Systems. LC 77-1198. (Translations of Mathematical Monographs: Vol. 49). 1977. 39.60 (ISBN 0-8218-1599-7, MMONO-49). Am Math.

Olevsky, A. M. Fourier Series with Respect to General Orthogonal Systems, Vol. 86. LC 74-32297. (Ergebnisse der Mathematik und Ihrer Grenzgebiete). 160p. 1975. 42.60 (ISBN 0-387-07103-2). Springer-Verlag.

Sansone, G., et al. Orthogonal Functions. rev. ed. LC 75-11888. 424p. 1977. Repr. of 1959 ed. 21.50 (ISBN 0-88275-303-7). Krieger.

FUNCTIONS, POLYHEDRAL
see also Groups, Theory Of

FUNCTIONS, POTENTIAL
see Differential Equations, Partial; Harmonic Analysis; Potential, Theory Of; Spherical Harmonics

FUNCTIONS, RECURSIVE
see Recursive Functions

FUNCTIONS, REGULAR
see Analytic Functions

FUNCTIONS, SPECIAL
see also names of special functions, e.g. Functions, Orthogonal

Advanced Seminar, the University of Wisconsin, Madison, March-April, 1975. Theory & Application of Special Functions: Proceedings. Askey, Richard A., ed. (University of Wisconsin Mathematics Research Center Publications: No. 35). 1975. 22.00 (ISBN 0-12-064850-4). Acad Pr.

Askey, Richard. Orthogonal Polynomials & Special Functions. (CBMS Regional Conference Ser.: Vol. 21). (Orig.). 1975. pap. text ed. 10.65 (ISBN 0-89871-018-9). Soc Indus-Appl Math.

Dieudonne, Jean. Special Functions & Linear Representations of Lie Groups. (CBMS Regional Conference Ser. in Mathematics: No. 42). 1980. 9.40 (ISBN 0-8218-1692-6). Am Math.

Feinsilver, P. J. Special Functions, Probability Semigroups, & Hamiltonian Flows. (Lecture Notes in Mathematics Ser.: Vol. 696). 1979. pap. 10.50 (ISBN 0-387-09100-9). Springer-Verlag.

Geronimus, Ja L. & Szego, Gabor. Two Papers on Special Functions. LC 76-30843. (Translations Ser. 2: Vol. 108). 1977. 28.80 (ISBN 0-8218-3058-9, TRANS2108). Am Math.

Higgins, J. R. Completeness & Basis Properties of Sets of Special Functions. LC 76-19630. (Cambridge Tracts in Mathematics Ser.: No. 72). (Illus.). 1977. 47.50 (ISBN 0-521-21376-2). Cambridge U Pr.

Lebedev, N. N. Special Functions & Their Applications. rev. ed. Silverman, Richard A., tr. from Rus. LC 72-86228. 320p. 1972. pap. 5.00 (ISBN 0-486-60624-4). Dover.

Luke, Yudell L. Special Functions & Their Approximations, 2 Vols. LC 68-23498. (Mathematics in Science & Engineering Ser.,: Vol. 53). 1969. Vol. 1. 55.00 (ISBN 0-12-459901-X); Vol. 2. 63.00 (ISBN 0-12-459902-8). Acad Pr.

McBride, E. B. Obtaining Generating Functions. LC 72-138811. (Springer Tracts in Natural Philosophy: Vol. 21). 1971. 29.00 (ISBN 0-387-05255-0). Springer-Verlag.

Olver, F. W. J. Asymptotics & Special Functions. (Computer Science & Applied Mathematics Ser.). 1974. 60.00 (ISBN 0-12-525850-X). Acad Pr.

Rainville, Earl D. Special Functions. LC 70-172380. (Illus.). xii, 365p. 1972. Repr. of 1960 ed. text ed. 12.95 (ISBN 0-8284-0258-2). Chelsea Pub.

Sneddon, I. N. Special Functions of Mathematical Physics & Chemistry. 3rd ed. (Longman Mathematical Texts Ser.). (Illus.). 176p. 1980. pap. text ed. 14.50x (ISBN 0-582-44396-2). Longman.

Symposia on Special Functions & Wave Propagation, Washington, D.C., 1969. Studies in Applied Mathematics Six: Special Functions & Wave Propagation. Proceedings. Ludwig, Donald & Olver, Frank W., eds. (Illus.). 1970. text ed. 11.75 (ISBN 0-686-24261-0). Soc Indus-Appl Math.

Vilenkin, N. Ja. Special Functions & the Theory of Group Representations. LC 68-19438. (Translations of Mathematical Monographs: Vol. 22). 1978. Repr. of 1968 ed. 34.80 (ISBN 0-8218-1572-5, MMONO-22). Am Math.

FUNCTIONS, SPHEROIDAL
see also Mathieu Functions

Connett, W. C. & Schwartz, Alan Lee. The Theory of Ultraspherical Multipliers. LC 76-58958. (Memoirs: No. 183). 1977. 10.80 (ISBN 0-8218-2183-0). Am Math.

John, F. Plane Waves & Spherical Means Applied to Partial Differential Equations. (Illus.). 172p. 1981. pap. 18.00 (ISBN 0-686-73036-4). Springer-Verlag.

Meixner, J., et al. Mathieu Functions & Spheroidal Functions & Their Mathematical Foundations. (Lecture Notes in Mathematics: Vol. 837). 126p. 1981. pap. 9.80 (ISBN 0-387-10282-5). Springer-Verlag.

FUNCTIONS, SYMMETRIC
see Symmetric Functions

FUNCTIONS, THETA

Accola, R. D. Riemann Surfaces, Theta Functions, & Abelian Automorphisms Groups. LC 75-25928. (Lecture Notes in Mathematics: Vol. 483). iii, 105p. 1975. pap. text ed. 9.50 (ISBN 0-387-07398-1). Springer-Verlag.

Auslander, L. Lecture Notes on Nil-Theta Functions. LC 77-16471. (Conference Board of the Mathematical Sciences Ser.: No. 34). 1977. 8.40 (ISBN 0-8218-1684-5, CBMS34). Am Math.

Baker, Henry F. Abel's Theorem & the Allied Theory, Including the Theory of the Theta Functions. 1976. Repr. of 1897 ed. 89.00 (ISBN 0-403-06225-X, Regency). Scholarly.

Fay, J. D. Theta Functions of Riemann Surfaces. (Lecture Notes in Mathematics: Vol. 352). 137p. 1973. pap. 9.10 (ISBN 0-387-06517-2). Springer-Verlag.

Gunning, R. C. Riemann Surfaces & Generalized Theta Functions. (Illus.). 1976. 26.30 (ISBN 0-387-07744-8). Springer-Verlag.

Hejhal, Dennis A. Theta Functions, Kernel Functions, & Abelian Integrals. LC 72-6824. (Memoirs: No. 129). 116p. 1972. pap. 7.60 (ISBN 0-685-29912-0, MEMO-129). Am Math.

Krazer, Adolph. Lehrbuch der Thetafunktionen. LC 75-113132. (Ger). 1970. Repr. of 1903 ed. 19.50 (ISBN 0-8284-0244-2). Chelsea Pub.

Lion, Gerard & Vergne, Michele, eds. The Weil Representation, Maslov Index & Theta Series. (Progress in Mathematics Ser.: No. 6). 346p. 1980. pap. text ed. 18.00 (ISBN 3-7643-3007-4). Birkhauser.

Rauch, H. E. & Farkas, H. M. Theta Functions with Applications to Riemann Surfaces. 244p. 1974. 15.95 (ISBN 0-683-07196-3, Pub. by W & W). Krieger.

Rauch, H. E. & Lebowitz, A. Elliptic Functions, Theta Functions & Riemann Surfaces. 304p. 1973. 20.50 (ISBN 0-683-07187-4, Pub. by Wiley). Krieger.

FUNCTIONS, TRANSCENDENTAL
see also names of specific transcendental functions, e.g. Bellel Functions; Functions, Gamma

Erdelyi, A. Higher Transcendental Functions, Vol. 2. 1980. Repr. of 1953 ed. lib. bdg. write for info. (ISBN 0-89874-069-X). Krieger.

Erdelyi, Arthur, et al. Higher Transcendental Functions, 3 Vols. text ed. 21.50 ea. (P&RB). Vol. 1 (ISBN 0-07-019545-5). Vol. 2 (ISBN 0-07-019546-3). Vol. 3 O.p (ISBN 0-07-019547-1). McGraw.

--Tables of Integral Transforms, Vol. 1. (Illus.). 1954. text ed. 32.50 (ISBN 0-07-019549-8, P&RB). McGraw.

FUNCTIONS, TRIGONOMETRICAL
see Trigonometrical Functions

FUNCTIONS, ZETA

Edwards, Harold M. Riemann's Zeta Function. (Pure & Applied Mathematics: A Series of Monographs & Textbooks, Vol. 59). 1974. 43.00 (ISBN 0-12-232750-0). Acad Pr.

Godement, R. & Jacquet, H. Zeta Functions of Simple Algebras. LC 72-76391. (Lecture Notes in Mathematics: Vol. 260). 197p. 1972. pap. 7.00 (ISBN 0-387-05797-8). Springer-Verlag.

Hunter, R. J. Zeta Potential in Colloid Science. 1981. price not set (ISBN 0-12-361960-2). Acad Pr.

Koblitz, H. P-Adic Numbers, P-Adic Analysis & Zeta-Functions. LC 77-21869. (Graduate Texts in Mathematics: Vol.58). (Illus.). 1977. 16.30 (ISBN 0-387-90274-0). Springer-Verlag.

FUNCTIONS OF COMPLEX VARIABLES
see also Analytic Functions; Banach Spaces; Boundary Value Problems; Functions, Elliptic; Functions, Entire; Functions of Real Variables; Functions of Several Complex Variables; Global Analysis (Mathematics); Hardy Spaces

Abramov, L. M., et al. Fourteen Papers on Logic, Algebra, Complex Variables & Topology. LC 51-5559. (Translations Ser.: No. 2, Vol. 48). 1965. 26.80 (ISBN 0-8218-1748-5, TRANS 2-48). Am Math.

Adjan, S., et al. Eleven Papers on Number Theory, Algebra & Functions of a Complex Variable. LC 51-5559. (Translations, Ser.: No. 2, Vol. 46). 1965. 22.00 (ISBN 0-8218-1746-9, TRANS 2-46). Am Math.

Ahlfors, Lars. Conformal Invariants. (Higher Mathematics Ser.). (Illus.). 168p. 1973. 22.00 (ISBN 0-07-000659-8, C). McGraw.

Alenicyn, Ju. E., et al. Fifteen Papers on Series & Functions of Complex Variables. LC 51-5559. (Translations Ser.: No. 2, Vol. 43). 1964. 23.60 (ISBN 0-8218-1743-4, TRANS 2-43). Am Math.

Ash, Robert B. Complex Variables. 1971. text ed. 22.95 (ISBN 0-12-065250-1). Acad Pr.

Azarin, V. S., et al. Thirteen Papers on Functions of Real & Complex Variables. LC 51-5559. (Translations Ser.: No. 2, Vol. 80). 1969. 30.80 (ISBN 0-8218-1780-9, TRANS 2-80). Am Math.

Bazilevic, I. E., et al. Thirteen Papers on Algebra, Topology, Complex Variables, & Linear Programming. LC 51-5559. (Translations Ser.: No. 2, Vol. 71). 1968. 26.80 (ISBN 0-8218-1771-X, TRANS 2-71). Am Math.

Beardon, A. F. Complex Analysis: The Argument Principle in Analysis & Topology. LC 78-8540. 239p. 1979. 48.95 (ISBN 0-471-99671-8, Pub. by Wiley-Interscience). Wiley.

Bieberbach, Ludwig. Conformal Mapping. LC 53-7209. 6.95 (ISBN 0-8284-0090-3); pap. 2.95 o. p. (ISBN 0-8284-0176-4). Chelsea Pub.

Brannan, D. A. & Clunie, J. G., eds. Aspects of Contemporary Complex Analysis. LC 80-40887. 1981. 108.00 (ISBN 0-12-125950-1). Acad Pr.

Caratheodory, Constantin. Theory of Functions. 2nd ed. LC 60-16838. Vol. 1. 12.95 (ISBN 0-8284-0097-0); Vol. 2. 12.95 (ISBN 0-8284-0106-3). Chelsea Pub.

Carin, V. S., et al. Nine Papers on Foundations, Algebra, Topology, Functions of a Complex Variable. (Translations Ser.: No. 2, Vol. 15). 1960. 24.80 (ISBN 0-8218-1715-9, TRANS 2-15). Am Math.

Carrier, George F., et al. Functions of a Complex Variable: Theory & Technique. 1966. 22.00 (ISBN 0-07-010089-6, C). McGraw.

Chevalley, Claude C. Introduction to the Theory of Algebraic Functions of One Variable. LC 51-4714. (Mathematical Surveys Ser.: No. 6). 1979. Repr. of 1971 ed. 22.40 (ISBN 0-8218-1506-7, SURV-6). Am Math.

Churchill, Ruel V. & Brown, James W. Complex Variables & Applications. 3rd ed. (Illus.). 352p. 1974. text ed. 21.00 (ISBN 0-07-010855-2, C). McGraw.

Complex Analysis & Its Applications, 3 vols. 1977. Set. pap. 80.25 (ISBN 0-685-79710-4, ISP428-1-2-3, IAEA). Unipub.

Copson, E. T. Introduction to the Theory of Functions of a Complex Variable. (Illus.). 1935. pap. 19.95x (ISBN 0-19-853145-1). Oxford U Pr.

Cunningham, J. Complex Variable Methods in Science & Technology. (Illus.). 1965. 8.95x (ISBN 0-442-31788-3). Van Nos Reinhold.

Dzrbasjan, M. M., et al. Seventeen Papers on Functions of Complex Variables. LC 51-5559. (Translations Ser.: No. 2, Vol. 32). 1963. 26.80 (ISBN 0-8218-1732-9, TRANS 2-32). Am Math.

Funciones De Variable Compleja. rev. ed. (Serie De Matematica: No. 8). (Span.). 1973. pap. 1.25 (ISBN 0-8270-6260-5). OAS.

Gilbert, R. P. Function Theoretic Methods in Partial Differential Equations. (Mathematics in Science & Engineering Ser: Vol. 54). 1969. 52.50 (ISBN 0-12-283050-4). Acad Pr.

Goluzin, G. M. Geometric Theory of Functions of a Complex Variable. LC 70-82894. (Translations of Mathematical Monographs: Vol. 26). 1969. 62.00 (ISBN 0-8218-1576-8, MMONO-26). Am Math.

Greenleaf, Frederick P. Introduction to Complex Variables. LC 70-180179. (Illus.). 1972. 16.95 (ISBN 0-7216-4260-8). HR&W.

Hawkins, F. M. & Hawkins, J. Q. Complex Numbers & Elementary Complex Functions. 1970. 32.50x (ISBN 0-677-61110-2). Gordon.

Heins, Maurice. Complex Function Theory. (Pure & Applied Mathematics Ser.: Vol. 28). 1968. text ed. 24.95 (ISBN 0-12-337950-4). Acad Pr.

Jameson, G. J. First Course on Complex Functions. (Mathematics Ser.). 148p. 1970. text ed. 10.95x (ISBN 0-412-09710-9, Pub. by Chapman & Hall England). Methuen Inc.

Kirwan, W. E. & Zalcman, L., eds. Advances in Complex Function Theory. LC 75-45187. (Lecture Notes in Mathematics Ser: Vol. 505). 1976. pap. 12.70 (ISBN 0-387-07548-8). Springer-Verlag.

Krzyz, J. G. Problems in Complex Variable Theory. (Modern Analytic & Computational Methods in Science & Mathematics: Vol. 36). 1972. 24.95 (ISBN 0-444-00098-4, North Holland). Elsevier.

Kyrala, A. Applied Functions of a Complex Variable. LC 74-176285. 374p. 1972. 36.50 (ISBN 0-471-51129-3, Pub. by Wiley-Interscience). Wiley.

--Applied Functions of Complex Variables. LC 74-176285. 394p. 1972. 35.00 (ISBN 0-686-76784-5). Krieger.

Landkof, N. S. Foundations of Modern Potential Theory. Doohovskoy, A. P., tr. from Rus. LC 77-186131. (Grundlehren der Mathematischen Wissenschaften: Vol. 180). 440p. 1972. 52.20 (ISBN 0-387-05394-8). Springer-Verlag.

Lang, Serge R. Complex Analysis. LC 76-15463. (Illus.). 1977. text ed. 19.95 (ISBN 0-201-04137-5). A-W.

Levinson, Norman. Gap & Density Theorems. LC 41-6147. (Colloquium, Pbns. Ser.: Vol. 26). 1963. Repr. of 1940 ed. 19.60 (ISBN 0-8218-1026-X, COLL-26). Am Math.

Levinson, Norman & Redheffer, Raymond. Complex Variables. LC 76-113833. (Illus.). 1970. text ed. 24.95x (ISBN 0-8162-5104-5); sol. man. 2.95 (ISBN 0-8162-5114-2). Holden-Day.

McCullough, Thomas A. & Phillips, Keith. Foundations of Analysis in the Complex Plane. LC 72-87153. 1973. text ed. 18.50x (ISBN 0-03-009105-5). Irvington.

Marden, Morris. Geometry of Polynomials. rev. ed. LC 49-48816. (Mathematical Surveys Ser.: Vol. 3). 1966. 29.60 (ISBN 0-8218-1503-2, SURV-3). Am Math.

Marsden, Jerrold E. Basic Complex Analysis. LC 72-89894. (Illus.). 1973. text ed. 23.95x (ISBN 0-7167-0451-X). W H Freeman.

Morse, Marston. Topological Methods in the Theory of Functions of a Complex Variable. 1947. pap. 7.00 (ISBN 0-527-02731-6). Kraus Repr.

Neri, U. Singular Integrals. LC 76-166077. (Lecture Notes in Mathematics: Vol. 200). 1971. pap. text ed. 11.20 (ISBN 0-387-05502-9). Springer-Verlag.

Paliouras, John D. Complex Variables for Scientists & Engineers. (Illus.). 416p. 1975. text ed. 24.95 (ISBN 0-02-390550-6). Macmillan.

Polya, George & Latta, Gordon. Complex Variables. LC 73-14882. 352p. 1974. text ed. 27.95 (ISBN 0-471-69330-8). Wiley.

Silverman, Richard A. Complex Analysis with Applications. 304p. 1974. 23.95x (ISBN 0-13-164806-3). P-H.

Smirnov, Vladimir I. & Lebedev, N. A. Functions of a Complex Variable. LC 68-20049. 1968. 19.50x (ISBN 0-262-19046-X). MIT Pr.

Spiegel, Murray R. Complex Variables. (Orig.). 1964. pap. 6.95 (ISBN 0-07-060230-1, SP). McGraw.

Steklov Institute of Mathematics, Academy of Sciences, U S S R, No. 94. External Problems of the Geometric Theory of Functions: Proceedings. Alenicyn, J. E., ed. 1969. 38.40 (ISBN 0-8218-1894-5, STEKLO-94). Am Math.

Stolzenberg, G. Volumes, Limits & Extensions of Analytic Varieties. (Lecture Notes in Mathematics: Vol. 19). (Orig.). 1966. pap. 10.70 (ISBN 0-387-03602-4). Springer-Verlag.

Symposia in Pure Mathematics-San Diego-1966. Entire Functions & Related Parts of Analysis: Proceedings, Vol. 11. Chern, S. S., et al, eds. LC 68-10458. 1968. 33.20 (ISBN 0-8218-1411-7, PSPUM-11). Am Math.

Tall, D. O. Functions of a Complex Variable, 2 vols. (Library of Mathematics). 1970. Vol. 1. pap. 2.95 (ISBN 0-7100-6567-1); Vol. 2. pap. 2.95 (ISBN 0-7100-6785-2); pap. 6.50 set (ISBN 0-685-25621-9). Routledge & Kegan.

Valiron, Georges. Theory of Integral Functions. LC 51-7375. 9.95 (ISBN 0-8284-0056-3). Chelsea Pub.

FUNCTIONS OF REAL VARIABLES

see also Functions of Complex Variables

Alexsandrov, Paul S. Introduction to the Theory of Sets & Functions. write for info. (ISBN 0-685-07980-5). Chelsea Pub.

Artemiadis, Nicolas. Real Analysis. LC 75-29189. 594p. 1976. 15.00x (ISBN 0-8093-0727-8). S Ill U Pr.

Azarin, V. S., et al. Thirteen Papers on Functions of Real & Complex Variables. LC 51-5559. (Translations Ser.: No. 2, Vol. 80). 1969. 30.80 (ISBN 0-8218-1780-9, TRANS 2-80). Am Math.

Bernstein, Serge & Poussin, Charles D. Approximation, 2 Vols. in 1. LC 69-16996. (Fr). 13.95 (ISBN 0-8284-0198-5). Chelsea Pub.

Boas, Ralph P., Jr. A Primer of Real Functions. 2nd ed. LC 60-10307. (Carus Monograph: No. 13). 196p. 1972. 12.50 (ISBN 0-88385-013-3). Math Assn.

Fleming, W. H. Functions of Several Variables. 2nd ed. LC 76-40029. (Undergraduate Texts in Mathematics). (Illus.). 1977. Repr. 20.70 (ISBN 3-540-90206-6). Springer-Verlag.

Goldberg, Richard R. Methods of Real Analysis. 2nd ed. LC 75-30615. 1976. text ed. 25.95 (ISBN 0-471-31065-4). Wiley.

Golovkin, K. K., et al. Four Papers on Functions of Real Variables. LC 51-5559. (Translations Ser.: No. 2, Vol. 81). 1969. 30.80 (ISBN 0-8218-1781-7, TRANS 2-81). Am Math.

Handscomb, D. C., ed. Multivariate Approximation. 1979. 36.50 (ISBN 0-12-323350-X). Acad Pr.

Karlin, Samuel. Total Positivity: Vol. 1. 1968. 25.00x (ISBN 0-8047-0314-0). Stanford U Pr.

Kolmogorov, A. N. & Fomin, S. V. Introductory Real Analysis. Silverman, Richard A., ed. & tr. from Rus. LC 74-18669. 416p. 1975. pap. 5.00 (ISBN 0-486-61226-0). Dover.

Natanson, I. P. Theory of Functions of a Real Variable, 2 vols. Boron, Leo F. & Hewitt, Edwin, eds. LC 61-14620. 278p. Vol. 1. 13.50 (ISBN 0-8044-4702-0). Ungar.

Olmsted, John M. Intermediate Analysis: An Introduction to Theory of Functions of One Real Variable. LC 56-5844. (Illus.). 1956. 34.50x (ISBN 0-89197-796-1); pap. text ed. 18.50x (ISBN 0-8290-0385-1). Irvington.

Shapiro, Victor L. Topics in Fourier & Geometric Analysis. LC 52-42839. (Memoirs: No. 39). 1968. pap. 8.40 (ISBN 0-8218-1239-4, MEMO-39). Am Math.

Spiegel, Murray R. Real Variables. 1969. pap. 6.95 (ISBN 0-07-060221-2, SP). McGraw.

Stein, E. M. Singular Integrals & Differentiability Properties of Functions. (Mathematical Ser.: No. 30). 1971. 20.00 (ISBN 0-691-08079-8). Princeton U Pr.

Steklov Institute of Mathematics, Academy of Sciences, U S S R, No. 77. Theory & Applications of Differentiable Functions of Several Variables: Proceedings. Nikol'skii, S. M., ed. 1967. 40.00 (ISBN 0-8218-1877-5, STEKLO-77). Am Math.

Steklov Institute of Mathematics, Academy of Sciences, U S S R, No. 89. Theory & Applications of Differentiable Functions of Several Variables, 2: Proceedings. Nikol'skii, S. M., ed. 1968. 58.40 (ISBN 0-685-05637-6, STEKLO-89). Am Math.

Vulikh, B. Z. A Brief Course in the Theory of Functions of a Real Variable. 357p. 1976. 5.40 (ISBN 0-8285-0702-3, Pub. by Mir Pubs Russia). Imported Pubns.

Walsh, Thomas. On Summability Methods for Conjugate Fourier-Steilties Integrals in Several Variables & Generalizations. LC 73-2729. (Memoirs: No. 131). 1973. pap. 9.60 (ISBN 0-8218-1831-7, MEMO-131). Am Math.

Williamson, Richard, et al. Calculus of Vector Functions. 3rd ed. LC 75-167788. (Illus.). 576p. 1972. ref. ed. 25.95 (ISBN 0-13-112367-X). P-H.

FUNCTIONS OF SEVERAL COMPLEX VARIABLES

see also Analytic Continuation; Automorphic Forms

Ehrenpreis, Leon. Fourier Analysis in Several Complex Variables. (Pure & Applied Mathematics Ser.). 1970. 49.00 (ISBN 0-471-23400-1, Pub. by Wiley-Interscience). Wiley.

Grauert, H. & Remmert, R. Theory of Stein Spaces. LC 79-1430. (Grundlehren der Mathematischen Wissenschaften: Vol. 236). (Illus.). 1979. 41.80 (ISBN 0-387-90388-7). Springer-Verlag.

Handscomb, D. C., ed. Multivariate Approximation. 1979. 36.50 (ISBN 0-12-323350-X). Acad Pr.

International Mathematical Conference, College Park, 1970. Several Complex Variables 2: Proceedings. Horvath, J., ed. (Lecture Notes in Mathematics: Vol. 185). 1971. pap. 11.20 (ISBN 0-387-05372-7). Springer-Verlag.

Kujala, Robert O. & Vitter, Albert L., III, eds. Value Distribution Theory: Deficit & Bezout Estimates, Pt. B. (Pure & Applied Mathematics Ser: Vol. 25). 288p. 1973. 26.25 (ISBN 0-8247-6125-1). Dekker.

Lelong, P. Fonctions Plurisousharmoniques et Formes Differentielles Positives. (Cours & Documents de Mathematiques & de Physique Ser.). 1968. 18.75x (ISBN 0-677-50220-6). Gordon.

--Plurisubharmonic Functions & Positive Differential Forms. (Notes on Mathematics & Its Applications Ser.). 1969. 18.75 (ISBN 0-677-30220-7). Gordon.

Narasimhan, Raghavan. Several Complex Variables. LC 75-166949. (Chicago Lectures in Mathematics Ser). (Orig.). 1971. text ed. 10.00x (ISBN 0-226-56816-4); pap. text ed. 7.00 (ISBN 0-226-56817-2). U of Chicago Pr.

Ronkin, L. I. Introduction to the Theory of Entire Functions of Several Variables. LC 74-12068. (Translations of Mathematical Monographs: Vol. 44). 1974. 50.80 (ISBN 0-8218-1594-6, MMONO-44). Am Math.

Wells, R. O., ed. Several Complex Variables: Proceedings, 2 pts. LC 77-23168. (Proceedings of Symposia in Pure Mathematics: Vol. 30). 1977. Set. 64.40 (ISBN 0-685-74775-1, PSPUM-30); Pt. 1. 35.60 (ISBN 0-8218-0249-6, PSPUM 30-1); Pt. 2. 35.60 (ISBN 0-8218-0250-X, PSPUM 30-2). Am Math.

Wermer, J. Banach Algebras & Several Complex Variables. (Graduate Texts in Mathematics Ser.: Vol. 35). 185p. 1976. 19.70 (ISBN 0-387-90160-4). Springer-Verlag.

FUNCTOR THEORY

see also Categories (Mathematics)

Arbib, Michael A. & Manes, Ernest G., eds. Arrows, Structures & Functors: The Categorical Imperative. 1975. 22.50 (ISBN 0-12-059060-3). Acad Pr.

Dubuc, E. J. Kan Extensions in Enriched Category Theory. LC 77-131542. (Lecture Notes in Mathematics: Vol. 145). 1970. pap. 8.20 (ISBN 0-387-04934-7). Springer-Verlag.

Lane, S. Mac, ed. Coherence in Categories. LC 72-87920. (Lecture Notes in Mathematics: Vol. 281). vii, 235p. 1972. pap. 7.90 (ISBN 0-387-05963-6). Springer-Verlag.

Lehrberger, John. Functor Analysis of Natural Language. LC 74-82387. (Janua Linguarum, Ser. Minor: No. 197). 155p. 1974. pap. text ed. 27.50x (ISBN 90-2793-342-1). Mouton.

Michor, P. W. Functors & Categories of Banach Spaces: Tensor Products, Operator Ideals & Functors on Categories of Banach Spaces. (Lecture Notes in Mathematics: Vol. 651). 1978. pap. 9.20 (ISBN 0-387-08764-8). Springer-Verlag.

Midwest Category Seminar, 1st. Reports. Benabou, J., et al, eds. (Lecture Notes in Mathematics: Vol. 47). (Orig.). 1967. pap. 10.70 (ISBN 0-387-03918-X). Springer-Verlag.

Moss, R. M. F. & Thomas, C. B. Algebraic K-Theory & Its Geometric Applications. LC 74-97991. (Lecture Notes in Mathematics). 1969. pap. 10.70 (ISBN 0-387-04627-5). Springer-Verlag.

Quine, Willard V. Algebraic Logic & Predicate Functors. LC 71-157092. 1971. pap. text ed. 1.25x (ISBN 0-672-61267-4). Irvington.

Schubert, H. Categories. Gray, J., tr. from Ger. LC 72-83016. 390p. 1972. 45.60 (ISBN 0-387-05783-8). Springer-Verlag.

Sidney Category Theory Seminar, 1972-1973. Category Seminar: Proceedings. Kelly, G. M., ed. (Lecture Notes in Mathematics Ser.: Vol. 420). 650p. 1975. pap. 17.50 (ISBN 0-387-06966-6). Springer-Verlag.

FUNCTORIAL REPRESENTATION

see Functor Theory

FUND RAISING

see also Federations, Financial (Social Service)

The A-V Connection 1981: The Guide to Federal Funds for Audio-Visual Programs. 22.00 (ISBN 0-686-74730-5). ALA.

Ayer Press Staff. Ayer Fund-Raising Dinner Guide: 1974. 1974. 8.90 (ISBN 0-910190-03-8). Ayer Pr.

Blanshard, Paul, Jr. The KRC Fund Raisers Manual. 39.00 (ISBN 0-686-24202-5). Public Serv Materials.

--KRC Fund Raiser's Manual: A Guide to Personalized Fund Raising. (KRC on Fund Raising Ser.). 1974. 38.95 (ISBN 0-917440-02-1). K R C Dev.

Blume, H. Fund-Raising. (Orig.). 1977. pap. 7.95 (ISBN 0-7100-8549-4). Routledge & Kegan.

Brakely, George A., Jr. Tested Ways to Successful Fund Raising. (Illus.). 176p. 1980. 16.95 (ISBN 0-8144-5531-X). Am Mgmt.

Broce, Thomas E. Fund Raising: The Guide to Raising Money from Private Sources. LC 78-21388. (Illus.). 1979. 15.95 (ISBN 0-8061-1531-9). U of Okla Pr.

Bronzan, Robert T. Public Relations, Promotions, & Fund-Raising for Athletic & Physical Education Programs. LC 76-10950. 580p. 1977. text ed. 25.50 (ISBN 0-471-01540-7). Wiley.

Brose, E. F. Twenty New Ways to Get the Minister Out of Moneyraising. 1976. 2.50 (ISBN 0-686-22747-6). Sharing Co.

Brownrigg, W. Grant. Corporate Fund Raising: A Practical Plan of Action. LC 76-58748. (Illus.). 74p. (Orig.). 1978. pap. text ed. 12.50 (ISBN 0-915400-10-3). Am Council Arts.

Carter, Virginia L., ed. Annual Fund Ideas. 48p. 1979. pap. 10.50 (ISBN 0-89964-016-8). CASE.

Compton, Everald. Ten Steps to Successful Fund Raising. 1978. text ed. 9.00x (ISBN 0-7223-1155-9). Verry.

Conrad, Daniel L. How to Solicit Big Gifts. 1978. 3 ring binder with cassette tape program 195.00 (ISBN 0-916664-04-X). Public Management.

--Techniques of Fund-Raising. 1974. 25.00 (ISBN 0-8184-0169-9). Lyle Stuart.

Conrad, Daniel L. & Institute for Fund Raising Research & Development Staff. Successful Fund Raising Techniques. 2nd ed. LC 76-49799. 1976. pap. 35.00 (ISBN 0-916664-03-1). Public Management.

Conrad, Daniel L. & Research & Development Staff of the Institute for Fund Raising. The Grants Planner. LC 76-54604. 1976. 37.50 (ISBN 0-916664-02-3). Public Management.

The Corporate Fund Raising Directory 1980-1981. 1980. 19.75 (ISBN 0-686-27210-2). Public Serv Materials.

Cover, Nelson, compiled by. A Guide to Successful Phonathons. 100p. 1980. pap. 14.50 (ISBN 0-89964-049-4). CASE.

Crohn, Richard J. KRC Portfolio of Fund Raising Letters. (KRC on Fund Raising Ser.). 1973. 39.95 (ISBN 0-917440-01-3). K R C Dev.

Crohn, Richard J. & Keller, Mitchell. KRC Guide to Direct Mail Fund Raising. (KRC on Fund Raising Ser.). 1977. 39.50 (ISBN 0-917440-04-8). K R C Dev.

Cumerford, William R. Fund Raising: A Professional Guide. LC 77-93555. 1978. 29.95 (ISBN 0-918214-02-5). F E Peters.

Cutlip, Scott M. Fund Raising in the United States. LC 64-8261. 1965. 12.50 (ISBN 0-910294-21-6). Brown Bk.

Daniels, Ellen S., ed. How to-Raise Money: Special Events for Arts Organizations. 32p. 1981. pap. 3.00 (ISBN 0-915400-30-8). Am Council Arts.

Darnbrough, Ann & Kinrade, Derek. Fund-Raising & Grant-Aid: A Practical & Legal Guide for Charities & Voluntary Organisations. 160p. 1980. 24.00x (ISBN 0-85941-075-7, Pub. by Woodhead-Faulkner England). State Mutual Bk.

Davis, King E. Fund Raising in the Black Community: History, Feasibility, & Conflict. LC 75-25586. 1975. 10.00 (ISBN 0-8108-0870-6). Scarecrow.

Dermer, Joseph. The New How-to-Raise-Funds-from-Foundations. 9.95 (ISBN 0-686-24206-8). Public Serv Materials.

Dermer, Joseph, ed. America's Most Successful Fund Raising Letters. 14.75 (ISBN 0-686-24210-6). Public Serv Materials.

Dexter, Kerry. Bazaars, Fairs & Festivals: A How-to Book. 1978. pap. 4.50 (ISBN 0-8192-1238-5). Morehouse.

Doyle, Alfreda. Guide for Fundraisers. 52p. 1981. pap. text ed. 5.00 (ISBN 0-939476-30-4). Bibliotheca.

Drotning, Phillip T. Putting the Fun in Fund Raising: Five Hundred Ways to Raise Money for Charity. 1979. o. p. 10.95 (ISBN 0-8092-7627-5). Contemp Bks.

Evanson, Roy. Promoting Fund Raising. (Clipping Art Ser.). 1975. 3.95 (ISBN 0-916068-01-3). Groupwork Today.

Georgi, Charlotte. Foundations, Grants & Fund-Raising: A Selected Bibliography. 1976. pap. 5.00x (ISBN 0-911798-15-3). UCLA Mgmt.

Getting Your Share: An Introduction to Fundraising. 1976. 2.00 (ISBN 0-686-17661-8). Women's Action.

Golden, Hal. The Grant Seekers: The Foundation Fund Raising Manual. LC 76-13235. 224p. 1976. lib. bdg. 17.00 (ISBN 0-379-00685-5). Oceana.

Gurin, Maurice G. What Volunteers Should Know for Successful Fund Raising. LC 80-51637. (Illus.). 144p. 1980. 10.00 (ISBN 0-8128-2739-2). Stein & Day.

Hicks, Tyler G. Raising Money from Grants & Other Sources Success Kit. 2nd ed. 496p. 1981. pap. 99.50 (ISBN 0-914306-45-6). Intl Wealth.

Hopkins, Bruce. Charity Under Siege: Government Regulation of Fund Raising. LC 80-23987. 274p. 1980. 43.50 (ISBN 0-471-08170-1, Pub. by Ronald). Wiley.

Jacob, John J. Mehr Bargeld Im Betrieb - Woher und Wie? 1977. 16.50 (ISBN 0-89532-000-2). United Seabears.

Knowles, Helen. How to Succeed in Fund Raising Today. LC 74-20200. 256p. 1975. 10.95 (ISBN 0-87027-151-2); pap. 6.95 (ISBN 0-87027-150-4). Wheelwright.

The KRC Portfolio of Fund Raising Letters. 39.95 (ISBN 0-686-24203-3). Public Serv Materials.

Lant, Jeffrey L. Development Today: A Guide for Nonprofit Organizations. (Nonprofit Technical Assistance Ser.: No. 1). 200p. (Orig.). 1981. pap. text ed. 24.95 (ISBN 0-940374-01-3). JLA Pubns.

Lawe, Theodore M. How to Secure & Manage Foundation & Federal Funds in the 1980's. LC 80-81753. 185p. (Orig.). 1980. pap. text ed. 12.95 (ISBN 0-9604706-0-3, 92142). MRDC Educ Inst.
Leibert, Edwin R. & Sheldon, Bernice E. Handbook of Special Events for Nonprofit Organizations: Tested Ideas for Fund Raising & Public Relations. (Illus.). 1972. 12.95 (ISBN 0-8096-1809-5, Assn Pr). New Century.
Lesjack, John J. How to Stage a Successful Gold Rush Carnival. (Illus.). 1978. pap. 4.40 (ISBN 0-88409-080-9). Creative Bk Co.
Long, David F. How to Organize & Raise Funds for Small Non-Profit Organizations. 283p. 1979. 19.95 (ISBN 0-916068-09-9); pap. 10.95 (ISBN 0-916068-12-9). Groupwork Today.
Longacre, Paul. Fund-Raising Projects with a World Hunger Emphasis. LC 80-83771. 72p. 1980. pap. 1.95 (ISBN 0-8361-1940-1). Herald Pr.
Lord, James G. Philanthropy & Marketing: New Strategies for Fund Raising. 203p. 1981. lib. bdg. 47.50 (ISBN 0-939120-00-3); 3-ring notebook 47.50 (ISBN 0-939120-01-1). Third Sector.
Marshall, Sol H. Fund-Raising with Your Own Cookbook. 1980. pap. 4.40 (ISBN 0-88409-084-1). Creative Bk Co.
Marshall, Sol H., ed. Money to Run the Show. 1980. pap. 8.80 (ISBN 0-88409-100-7). Creative Bk Co.
Mirkin, Howard R. The Complete Fund Raising Guide. 13.50 (ISBN 0-686-24209-2). Public Serv Materials.
Mitiguy, Nancy. The Rich Get Richer & the Poor Write Proposals. LC 79-624731. (Illus., Orig.). 1978. pap. 6.00x (ISBN 0-934210-02-0). Citizen Involve.
Morgan, James W. Successful Fund Raising: Proven Ways to Raise Money for Your Organization. (Designed to accompany "Proposal Format For Successful Private Sector Investments"). 1976. 19.95 (ISBN 0-686-16388-5); Set. 22.95 (ISBN 0-686-16389-3). Grantsman Ent.
National Catholic Development Conference. Bibliography of Fund Raising & Philanthropy. LC 75-12128. 1975. 22.50, incl. 1976 & 1977 supplements (ISBN 0-9603196-0-3). Natl Cath Dev.
Newman, Edwin S. Law of Philanthropy. LC 55-5958. (Legal Almanac Ser: No. 38). (Orig.). 1955. 5.95 (ISBN 0-379-11038-5). Oceana.
Orlich, Donald C. & Orlich, Patricia R. The Art of Writing Successful R & D Proposals. 1979. pap. 9.40 (ISBN 0-913178-51-9, Pub. by Two Continents). Hippocrene Bks.
Ott, Tony W. Fund Raising & Non-Profit Organization Management Publications: An Annotated Buyer's & Researcher's Bibliography. 125p. 1980. 15.00 (ISBN 0-938606-01-8). Grant Admin.
Pendleton, Niel. Fund Raising: A Guide for Non-Profit Organizations. (Illus.). 192p. 1981. 13.95 (ISBN 0-13-332163-0, Spec); pap. 5.95 (ISBN 0-13-332155-X). P-H.
Perri & Ardman. The Woman's Day Book of Fund Raising. 1980. 11.95 (ISBN 0-312-88646-2). St Martin.
Petersen, Sheila. Successful Community Fundraising: A Complete How-to Guide. LC 79-83688. (Illus.). 1979. pap. 7.95 (ISBN 0-89803-003-X). Caroline Hse.
Porter, Robert, ed. United Arts Fundraising: Nineteen Eighty Campaign Analysis. (Illus.). 80p. (Orig.). 1981. pap. 15.00 (ISBN 0-915400-29-4). Am Council Arts.
Public Management Institute Staff. Direct Mail Fund Raising. LC 80-80195. 400p. 1980. 47.50 (ISBN 0-916664-26-0). Public Management.
--Evaluation Handbook. LC 80-80196. 400p. 1980. 47.50 (ISBN 0-916664-25-2). Public Management.
--How to Build a Big Endowment. LC 80-65011. 400p. 1980. 75.00 (ISBN 0-916664-17-1). Public Management.
--How to Conduct a Needs Assessment. LC 80-80197. 1980. ring binder 47.50 (ISBN 0-916664-24-4). Public Management.
--How to Get Better Results from Groups. Date not set. price not set ring binder. Public Management.
--Improving Results from Direct Mail Appeals. Date not set. price not set ring binder. Public Management.
--Successful Seminars, Conferences & Workshops. LC 80-65013. 400p. 1980. 37.50 (ISBN 0-916664-19-8). Public Management.
Pulling, Lisa. KRC Desk Book for Fund Raisers. (KRC on Fund Raising Ser.). 1980. pap. text ed. 37.95 (ISBN 0-917440-05-6). K R C Dev.
Rowes, Barbara. Earning Money in Ways You Never Thought of. 96p. (Orig.). (gr. 7 up). 1980. pap. 1.25 (ISBN 0-590-31337-1, Schol Pap). Schol Bk Serv.
Russell, John M. Giving & Taking: Across the Foundation Desk. LC 77-4865. 1977. pap. text ed. 4.95 (ISBN 0-8077-2526-9). Tchrs Coll.
Schneiter, Paul H. The Art of Asking: A Handbook for Raising Money Successfully. LC 77-78993. pap. 7.95 (ISBN 0-8027-7153-X). Walker & Co.
Seymour, Harold J. Designs for Fund-Raising: Principles, Patterns, Techniques. 1966. 15.95 (ISBN 0-07-056354-3, P&RB). McGraw.
Sheridan, Philip G. Fund Raising for the Small Organization. LC 68-4053. 240p. 1968. 5.95 (ISBN 0-87131-050-3). M Evans.
Soroker, Gerald S. Fund Raising for Philanthropy. 9.95 (ISBN 0-686-09115-9). Pitt Jewish Foun.
Tatum, Liston. The KRC Computer Book for Fund Raisers. (K R C on Fund Raising Ser.). 368p. 1975. 38.50 (ISBN 0-917440-03-X). K R C Dev.
--The KRC Computer Book for Fund Raisers. 38.50 (ISBN 0-686-24204-1). Public Serv Materials.
Taylor, Bernard P. Guide to Successful Fund Raising: For Authentic Charitable Purposes. rev. 2nd ed. 154p. (Orig.). 1981. pap. 8.95 (ISBN 0-916068-14-5). Groupwork Today.
Vecchitto, Daniel W., et al, eds. A Introduction to Planned Giving: Fund Raising Through Bequests, Charitable Remainder Trusts, Gift Annuities & Life Insurance. (Nonprofit Technical Assistance Ser.: No. 2). 200p. (Orig.). 1981. pap. 24.95 (ISBN 0-940374-02-1). JLA Pubns.
Warner, Irving R. The Art of Fund Raising. LC 74-1869. (Illus.). 188p. 1975. 10.95 (ISBN 0-06-014526-9, HarpT). Har-Row.
Weenink, Allan D. Art of Church Canvass. LC 78-69998. 1978. pap. 4.95 (ISBN 0-87983-172-3). Keats.

FUNDAMENTAL EDUCATION

Bowren, Fay F. & Zintz, Miles V. Teaching Reading in Adult Basic Education. 432p. 1977. pap. text ed. write for info. (ISBN 0-697-06150-7). Wm C Brown.
Joffe, Irwin L. Reading Skills for Successful Living. 1979. pap. text ed. 8.95x (ISBN 0-534-00618-3). Wadsworth Pub.

FUNDAMENTAL THEOLOGY

see Apologetics

FUNDAMENTALISM

see also Evangelicalism; Modernism; Modernist-Fundamentalist Controversy

Barr, James. Fundamentalism. 1978. pap. 9.50 (ISBN 0-664-24191-3). Westminster.
Bridges, Horace J. God of Fundamentalism & Others Studies. facs. ed. LC 79-86733. (Essay Index Reprint Ser). 1925. 17.00 (ISBN 0-8369-1249-7). Arno.
Clabaugh, Gary K. Thunder on the Right: The Protestant Fundamentalists. LC 74-9551. 283p. 1974. 14.95x (ISBN 0-88229-108-4). Nelson-Hall.
Cole, Stewart G. History of Fundamentalism. LC 70-138107. 1971. Repr. of 1931 ed. lib. bdg. 19.50x (ISBN 0-8371-5683-1, COHF). Greenwood.
Cooper, John C. Religious Pied Pipers. 128p. 1981. pap. 5.95 (ISBN 0-8170-0907-8). Judson.
Gasper, Louis. The Fundamentalist Movement. (Twin Brooks Ser.). 181p. (Orig.). 1981. pap. 5.95 (ISBN 0-8010-3769-7). Baker Bk.
Hamann, Henry P. The Bible Between Fundamentalism & Philosophy. LC 80-65558. 80p. 1980. pap. 3.50 (ISBN 0-8066-1803-5, 10-0701). Augsburg.
Malachy, Yona. American Fundamentalism & Israel: The Relation of Fundamentalist Churches to Zionism & the State of Israel. 178p. 1978. pap. text ed. 9.25x (ISBN 0-686-74305-9, Pub. by Magnus Israel). Humanities.
Marsden, George M. Fundamentalism & American Culture: The Shaping of Twentieth Century Evangelicalism, 1870-1925. (Illus.). 320p. 1980. 19.95 (ISBN 0-19-502758-2). Oxford U Pr.
Packer, James I. Fundamentalism & the Word of God. 1958. pap. 2.95 (ISBN 0-8028-1147-7). Eerdmans.
Sandeen, Ernest R. Roots of Fundamentalism: British & American Millenarianism 1800-1930. (Twin Brooks). 1978. pap. 5.95 (ISBN 0-8010-8147-5). Baker Bk.
Torrey, R. A., et al. The Fundamentals, 4 vols. Set. 35.00 (ISBN 0-8010-8809-7). Baker Bk.
Valbracht, Louis H. The Follies of Fundamentalism. 1974. 3.15 (ISBN 0-89536-066-7). CSS Pub.

FUNDS

see Finance

FUNDULUS HETEROCLITUS

Pickford, Grace E., et al. Studies on the Blood Serum of the Euryhaline Cyprinodont Fish, Fundulus Heteroclitus, Adapted to Fresh or to Salt Water. (Transactions of the Connecticut Academy of Arts & Sciences Ser.: Vol. 43). 1969. pap. 9.00 (ISBN 0-208-00907-8). Shoe String.
Shepherd, Elizabeth. Minnows. (Illus.). 64p. (gr. 2-6). 1974. 6.50 (ISBN 0-688-40055-8); PLB 6.24 (ISBN 0-688-50055-2). Lothrop.

FUNDUS OCULI

Albert, Daniel M. Jaeger's Atlas of Diseases of the Ocular Fundus. LC 75-180175. (Illus.). 165p. 1972. 50.00 (ISBN 0-7216-1085-4). Saunders.
Bito, L. & Davson, H., eds. The Ocular & Cerebrospinal Fluids: Experimental Eye Research Supplement. 1978. 66.50 (ISBN 0-12-102550-0). Acad Pr.
Chester, Edward M. The Ocular Fundus in Systemic Disease: A Clinical Pathological Correlation. (Illus.). 245p. 1973. 52.50 (ISBN 0-8151-1657-8). Year Bk Med.
Nover, Arno. The Ocular Fundus: Methods of Examination & Typical Findings. 4th ed. Blodi, Frederick C., tr. (Illus.). 196p. 1981. text ed. 35.00 (ISBN 0-8121-0788-8). Lea & Febiger.
Sorsby, A. Diseases of the Fundus Oculi. 1976. 54.95 (ISBN 0-407-00023-2). Butterworth.

FUNERAL DIRECTORS

see Undertakers and Undertaking

FUNERAL MUSIC

see also Requiems

Girard, Sharon. Funeral Music & Customs in Venezuela. (Special Studies: No. 22). (Illus.). 1981. pap. 8.95 (ISBN 0-87918-050-1). ASU Lat Am St.
Gregory Nazianzen, St. & Ambrose, St. Funeral Orations. (Fathers of the Church Ser: Vol. 22). 18.00 (ISBN 0-8132-0022-9). Cath U Pr.

FUNERAL MUSIC-HISTORY AND CRITICISM

Girard, Sharon. Funeral Music & Customs in Venezuela. (Special Studies: No. 22). 99p. 1980. pap. text ed. 8.95 (ISBN 0-87918-050-1). ASU Lat Am St.

FUNERAL RITES AND CEREMONIES

see also Ancestor Worship; Cremation; Dead; Funeral Service; Mourning Customs

Bendann, E. Death Customs: An Analytical Study of Burial Rites. 59.95 (ISBN 0-8490-0010-6). Gordon Pr.
Bendann, Effie. Death Customs: An Analytical Study of Burial Rites. 1971. 24.00 (ISBN 0-8103-3733-9). Gale.
Bernardin, Joseph B. Burial Services: Revised & Updated. 1980. casebound 12.95 (ISBN 0-8192-1267-9). Morehouse.
Bernstein, Joanne E. & Gullo, Stephen V. When People Die. (gr. k-3). 1977. 9.95 (ISBN 0-525-42545-4). Dutton.
Blackwood, Andrew W. The Funeral. (Source Book for Ministers Ser.). 1972. pap. 4.95 (ISBN 0-8010-0576-0). Baker Bk.
Book of the Dead. The Chapters of Coming Forth by Day, 3 vols. LC 73-18833. Repr. of 1910 ed. 49.50 set (ISBN 0-404-11303-6). AMS Pr.
Bowman, LeRoy E. The American Funeral: A Study in Guilt, Extravagance, & Sublimity. LC 72-14083. 181p. 1973. Repr. of 1959 ed. lib. bdg. 15.00x (ISBN 0-8371-6749-3, BOFU). Greenwood.
Budge, E. A. Mummy. 2nd ed. LC 64-13391. (Illus.). 1894. 15.00x (ISBN 0-8196-0139-X). Biblo.
Budge, E. Wallis. The Liturgy of Funerary Offerings: The Egyptian Texts with English Translations. LC 72-83744. (Illus.). Repr. of 1909 ed. 15.00 (ISBN 0-405-08322-X, Blom Pubns). Arno.
Ch'en Kou-Chun. Studies in Marriage & Funerals of Taiwan Aborigines, No. 4. (Asian Folklore & Social Life Monograph). (Chinese.). 1970. 6.60 (ISBN 0-89986-007-9). E Langstaff.
Consumer Reports, ed. Funerals: Consumers' Last Rights. 1978. 14.95 (ISBN 0-393-08816-2). Norton.
Continental Assocation of Funeral & Memorial Societies, Inc & Memorial Society Association of Canadacompiled by. Handbook for Funeral & Memorial Societies. Fleming, Peggy, ed. LC 72-7963. 1976. pap. 3.50 (ISBN 0-686-18088-7). Continent Assn Funeral.
Cumont, Franz. Recherches sur le Symbolisme Funeraire des Romains. facsimile ed. LC 75-10632. (Ancient Religion & Mythology Ser.). (Illus., Fr.). 1976. Repr. of 1942 ed. 43.00x (ISBN 0-405-07007-1). Arno.
Curl, James S. The Victorian Celebration of Death: The Architecture & Planning of the 19th-Century Necropolis. LC 70-184048. 1972. 17.00 (ISBN 0-8103-2000-2). Gale.
Dickerson, Robert B., Jr. Final Placement: A Guide to the Deaths, Funerals, & Burials of Famous Americans. Irvine, Keith, ed. LC 81-52598. (Illus.). 252p. 1981. 19.95 (ISBN 0-917256-18-2). Ref Pubns.
Ellis, Hilda R. Road to Hel: A Study of the Conception of the Dead in Old Norse Literature. LC 68-23286. (Illus.). 1968. Repr. of 1943 ed. lib. bdg. 15.00 (ISBN 0-8371-0070-4, ELRH). Greenwood.
Girard, Sharon. Funeral Music & Customs in Venezuela. (Special Studies: No. 22). (Illus.). 1981. pap. 8.95 (ISBN 0-87918-050-1). ASU Lat Am St.
Goody, Jack. Death, Property, & the Ancestors: A Study of the Mortuary Customs of the LoDagaa of West Africa. (Illus.). 1962. 25.00x (ISBN 0-8047-0068-0). Stanford U Pr.
Gorer, Geoffrey. Death, Grief, & Mourning. Kastenbaum, Robert, ed. LC 76-19573. (Death & Dying Ser.). (Illus.). 1977. Repr. of 1965 ed. lib. bdg. 18.00x (ISBN 0-405-09571-6). Arno.
Huntington, R. & Metcalf, P. Celebrations of Death. LC 79-478. (Illus.). 1979. 27.50 (ISBN 0-521-22531-0); pap. 7.95x (ISBN 0-521-29540-8). Cambridge U Pr.
International Committee on English in the Liturgy, tr. Rite of Funerals. blue cloth 6.50 (ISBN 0-686-14315-9, 350/22). Catholic Bk Pub.
Irion, Paul E. The Funeral & the Mourners. LC 53-11337. (Abingdon Reprint Library). 1979. pap. 3.25 (ISBN 0-687-13820-5). Abingdon.
Ku Chieh-Kang. Marriage & Funerals of Su-Chow. Bd. with Marriage & Funerals of Canton. Liu Wan-Chang. (Folklore Series of National Sun Yat-Sen University: No. 21). (Chinese.). 5.50 (ISBN 0-89986-065-6). E Langstaff.
Lewis, Oscar. Death in the Sanchez Family. 1969. 7.95 (ISBN 0-394-42160-4). Random.
Long, Charlotte R. The Ayia Triadha Sarcophagus: A Study of Late Minoan & Mycenaean Funerary Practices & Beliefs. (Studies in Mediterranean Archaelogy: No. XLI). (Illus.). 1974. pap. text ed. 29.50x (ISBN 91-85058-59-9). Humanities.
McPherson, Thomas. American Funeral Cars & Ambulances Since 1900. Dammann, George H., ed. LC 73-80009. (Automotive Ser.). (Illus.). 352p. 1973. 19.95 (ISBN 0-912612-05-3). Crestline.
Margolis, Otto S., et al. Grief & the Meaning of the Funeral. 1975. 11.50x (ISBN 0-8422-7267-4). Irvington.
Mitford, Jessica. The American Way of Death. 1978. pap. 4.95 (ISBN 0-671-24415-9, Touchstone Bks). S&S.
--American Way of Death. 1979. pap. 2.95 (ISBN 0-449-23985-3, Crest). Fawcett.
Morley, John. Death, Heaven & the Victorians. LC 78-173852. (Illus.). 1972. 19.95 (ISBN 0-8229-1103-5). U of Pittsburgh Pr.
Nibley, Hugh. The Message of Joseph Smith Papyri: An Egyptian Endowment. LC 75-18734. 305p. 1975. 14.95 (ISBN 0-87747-485-0). Deseret Bk.
Papagno, Noella C. The Hairdresser at the Funeral Home: Desairology Handbook Questions & Answers. LC 80-82330. 30p. (Orig.). 1981. spiral bound 5.95 (ISBN 0-686-73674-5). JJ Pub FL.
Pine, Vanderlyn R., et al, eds. Acute Grief & the Funeral. (Illus.). 328p. 1976. 21.75 (ISBN 0-398-03434-6). C C Thomas.
Poovey, W. A., ed. Planning a Christian Funeral: A Minister's Guide. LC 78-52198. 1978. pap. 3.95 (ISBN 0-8066-1668-7, 10-4990). Augsburg.
Rock, Joseph F. The Zhi Ma Funeral Ceremony of the Na-Khi of South-West China. Repr. of 1955 ed. 23.00 (ISBN 0-384-51600-9). Johnson Repr.
Rosenblatt, Paul C., et al. Grief & Mourning in Cross-Cultural Perspective. LC 76-29270. (Comparative Studies Ser.). 242p. 1976. pap. 7.00x (ISBN 0-87536-334-2). HRAFP.
Rutherford, Richard. The Death of a Christian: The Rite of Funerals. (Studies in the Reformed Rites of the Catholic Church: Vol. 7). 1980. pap. 9.95 (ISBN 0-916134-40-7). Pueblo Pub Co.
Simmons, William S. Cautantowwit's House: An Indian Burial Ground on the Island of Conanicut in Narragansett Bay. LC 77-111456. (Illus.). 198p. 1970. text ed. 12.00x (ISBN 0-87057-122-2, Pub. by Brown U Pr). U Pr of New Eng.
Tashjian, Dickran & Tashjian, Ann. Memorials for Children of Change: The Art of Early New England Stonecarving. LC 73-6006. (Illus.). 336p. 1974. 27.95x (ISBN 0-8195-4061-7, Pub. by Wesleyan U Pr). Columbia U Pr.
Tegg, William. The Last Act: Being the Funeral Rites of Nations & Individuals. LC 72-10592. (Illus.). 404p. 1973. Repr. of 1876 ed. 24.00 (ISBN 0-8103-3172-1). Gale.
Toynbee, J. M. Death & Burial in the Roman World. Scullard, H. H., ed. LC 77-120603. (Aspects of Greek & Roman Life Ser). (Illus.). 336p. 1971. 22.50x (ISBN 0-8014-0593-9). Cornell U Pr.
Wagner, Johannes, ed. Reforming the Rites of Death. LC 68-20845. (Concilium Ser.: Vol. 32). 189p. 6.95 (ISBN 0-8091-0123-8). Paulist Pr.
Weever, John. Ancient Funerall Monuments Within the United Monarchie of Great Britaine, Ireland & the Islands Adjacent. LC 79-84145. (Engilsh Experience Ser.). 910p. 1979. Repr. of 1631 ed. lib. bdg. 125.00 (ISBN 90-221-0961-5). Walter J Johnson.

Zamzow, Dale. Build Your Own Coffin. (Illus.). Date not set. pap. 5.95 (ISBN 0-917982-13-4). Cougar Bks.

FUNERAL SERMONS

Allen, R. Earl. Funeral Source Book. (Preaching Helps Ser.). (Orig.). 1974. pap. 2.50 (ISBN 0-8010-0076-9). Baker Bk.

Bedwell, B. L. Sermons for Funeral Ocassions. 1960. pap. 1.50 (ISBN 0-686-21507-9). Firm Foun Pub.

Best Funeral Sermons. 1972. 3.50 (ISBN 0-89536-016-0). CSS Pub.

Bossuet, Jacques-Benigne. Oraisons funebres et sermons, 2 vols. (Classiques Larousse). (Illus., Fr.). pap. 1.95 ea. Larousse.

Coniaris, Anthony M. Sixty-One Talks for Orthodox Funerals. 1969. pap. 4.95 (ISBN 0-937032-02-6). Light & Life Pub Co MN.

D'Alembert, Jean. Eulogies. 59.95 (ISBN 0-8490-0137-4). Gordon Pr.

Editorial Staff, ed. Through the Valley of the Shadow. 118p. 1976. pap. 5.30 (ISBN 0-89536-232-5). CSS Pub.

Erdman, F. E., et al. Sixty Funeral Messages. (Pocket Pulpit Library). 1979. pap. 2.45 (ISBN 0-8010-3310-1). Baker Bk.

Ford, W. Herschel. Simple Sermons for Funeral Services. pap. 3.95 (ISBN 0-310-24461-7). Zondervan.

Wallis, Charles L., ed. Funeral Encyclopedia. (Source Bks for Ministers Ser.). 1973. pap. 5.95 (ISBN 0-8010-9539-5). Baker Bk.

Wood, Charles R., ed. Sermon Outlines for Funeral Services. (Easy-To-Use Sermon Outline Ser). 1970. pap. 1.95 (ISBN 0-8254-4007-6). Kregel.

FUNERAL SERVICE

see also Funeral Rites and Ceremonies

Biddle, Perry H., Jr. Abingdon Funeral Manual. LC 75-33059. 256p. 1976. 6.95 (ISBN 0-687-00469-1). Abingdon.

Bolding, Amy. A Sourcebook of Comfort. (Pocket Pulpit Library Ser). 1979. pap. 1.95 (ISBN 0-8010-0520-5). Baker Bk.

Champlin, Joseph M. Through Death to Life. LC 78-74436. 88p. 1979. pap. 1.45 (ISBN 0-87793-175-5). Ave Maria.

Christensen, James L. Complete Funeral Manual. 1967. 7.95 (ISBN 0-8007-0049-X). Revell.

--Funeral Services. 1959. 7.95 (ISBN 0-8007-0104-6). Revell.

--Funeral Services for Today. 1977. 7.95 (ISBN 0-8007-0856-3). Revell.

Consumer Reports, ed. Funerals: Consumers' Last Rights. 1978. 14.95 (ISBN 0-393-08816-2). Norton.

Hickman, Hoyt, ed. A Service of Death & Resurrection: The Ministry of the Church at Death. 1979. pap. 3.95 (ISBN 0-687-38075-8). Abingdon.

Hutton, Samuel W. Minister's Funeral Manual. 1968. 4.95 (ISBN 0-8010-4021-3). Baker Bk.

Irion, Paul E. The Funeral: Vestige or Value? Kastenaum, Robert, ed. LC 76-19578. (Death & Dying Ser.). 1977. Repr. lib. bdg. 16.00x (ISBN 0-405-09575-9). Arno.

Lamont, Corliss. Humanist Funeral Service. LC 77-76001. 48p. 1977. 6.95 (ISBN 0-87975-093-6); pap. 2.95 (ISBN 0-87975-090-1). Prometheus Bks.

Margolis, O. S., et al, eds. Thanatology Course Outlines: Funeral Service. 200p. 1976. 12.50x (ISBN 0-685-53681-5). Irvington.

Martin, Edward A. Psychology of Funeral Service. 6th ed. text ed. 12.50 (ISBN 0-686-20530-8). E A Martin.

Wagner, Johannes, ed. Reforming the Rites of Death. LC 68-20845. (Concilium Ser.: Vol. 32). 189p. 6.95 (ISBN 0-8091-0123-8). Paulist Pr.

Wallis, Charles L., ed. Funeral Encyclopedia. (Source Bks for Ministers Ser.). 1973. pap. 5.95 (ISBN 0-8010-9539-5). Baker Bk.

FUNGAL GENETICS

see Fungi–Genetics

FUNGAL TOXINS

see Mycotoxins

FUNGI

see also Ascomycetes; Bacteriology; Basidiomycetes; Discomycetes; Gasteromycetes; Lichens; Molds (Botany); Mushrooms; Myxomycetes; Phycomycetes; Pyrenomycetes; Soil Micro-Organisms; Truffles; Thermophilic Fungi

Ainsworth, G. C. Ainsworth & Bisby's Dictionary of the Fungi, Including the Lichens. 6th ed. LC 74-883641. (Illus.). 673p. 1971. 27.50x (ISBN 0-85198-075-9). Intl Pubns Serv.

Ainsworth, Geoffrey C. & Sussman, A. S., eds. Fungi: An Advanced Treatise, 4 vols. LC 65-15769. Vol. 1. 1965. 72.00 (ISBN 0-12-045601-X); Vol.2. 1966. 72.00 (ISBN 0-12-045602-8); Vol. 3. 1968. 72.00 (ISBN 0-12-045603-6); Vol. 4A. 1973. 72.00 (ISBN 0-12-045604-4); Vol. 4b, 1973. 60.50 (ISBN 0-12-045644-3); Set. 280.00 (ISBN 0-685-05128-5). Acad Pr.

Alexopoulos, Constantine J. & Bold, Harold C. Algae & Fungi. 1967. pap. 9.95 (ISBN 0-02-301700-7, 30170). Macmillan.

Arx, J. A. von. Pilzkunde: Ein Kurzer Abriss der Mykologie Unter Besonderer Beruecksichtigung der Pilze in Reinkultur. 3rd ed. (Illus.). 1976. 14.75 (ISBN 3-7682-1067-7). Lubrecht & Cramer.

Baldwin, Richard S. The Fungus Fighters: Two Women Scientists & Their Discovery. (Illus.). 1981. 14.95 (ISBN 0-8014-1355-9). Cornell U Pr.

Bataille, F. Les Reactions Macrochimiques Chez les Champignons Suives D'Indications Sur la Morphologie Des Spores. 1969. Repr. of 1948 ed. 20.00 (ISBN 3-7682-0654-8). Lubrecht & Cramer.

Batra, Lekh R., ed. Insect-Fungus Symbiosis: Nutrition, Mutualism & Commensalism. LC 78-20640. (Illus.). 276p. 1979. text ed. 29.95 (ISBN 0-470-26671-6). Halsted Pr.

Berlese, A. N. Icones Fungorum Omnium Hucusque Cognitorum: Ad usum sylloges Saccardianae accomodatae, 4 vols. 1968. 180.00 (ISBN 3-7682-0575-4). Lubrecht & Cramer.

Bessey, Ernest A. Morphology & Taxonomy of Fungi. (Illus.). 1973. Repr. of 1950 ed. 18.50 (ISBN 0-02-841320-2). Hafner.

Bigelow, H. E. & Thiers, H. D., eds. Studies on Higher Fungi. (Beihefte Zur Nova Hedwigia Ser.: Vol. 51). (Illus.). 372p. 1975. pap. 100.00x (ISBN 3-7682-5451-8, Pub. by J. Cramer). Intl Schol Bk Serv.

Brandenburger, W. Vademekum Zum Sammeln Parasitischer Pilze. (Ger.). 1963. pap. 12.95 (ISBN 3-8001-3412-8, M-7136). French & Eur.

Brodie, H. J. The Bird's Nest Fungi. LC 75-18476. 1975. 25.00x (ISBN 0-8020-5307-6). U of Toronto Pr.

Brodie, Harold J. Fungi: Delight of Curiosity. 1978. 15.00 (ISBN 0-8020-2289-8). U of Toronto Pr.

Burnett, J. H. & Trinci, A. P., eds. Fungal Walls & Hyphal Growth. LC 78-72082. (Illus.). 1980. 68.50 (ISBN 0-521-22499-3). Cambridge U Pr.

Byrde, R. J. & Willetts, H. J. Brown Rot Fungi of Fruit: Their Biology & Control. 1977. text ed. 19.50 (ISBN 0-08-019740-X). Pergamon.

Christensen, Clyde M. Molds & Man: An Introduction to the Fungi. 3rd ed. (Illus.). 1965. 15.00x (ISBN 0-8166-0348-0). U of Minn Pr.

Clements, Frederic E. & Shear, Cornelius L. Genera of Fungi. (Illus.). 1965. Repr. of 1931 ed. 22.50 (ISBN 0-02-842980-X). Hafner.

The Coelomycetes. 694p. 1981. 115.00 (ISBN 0-85198-446-0, CAB 7, CAB). Unipub.

Coker, William C. The Club & Coral Mushrooms (Clavarious) of the United States & Canada. LC 74-82202. (Illus.). 320p. 1975. pap. 5.95 (ISBN 0-486-23101-1). Dover.

Cole, G. T. & Kendrick, B. Biology of Conidial Fungi, 2 vols. 1981. Vol. 1. 49.00 (ISBN 0-12-179501-2); Vol. 2. 68.50 (ISBN 0-12-179502-0); Set. 100.00 (ISBN 0-686-77698-4). Acad Pr.

Cole, Garry T. & Samson, Robert A. Patterns of Development in Conidial Fungi. 190p. 1979. text ed. 67.95 (ISBN 0-273-08407-0). Pitman Pub MA.

Cooke, Roderic. The Biology of Symbiotic Fungi. LC 76-56175. 1977. 41.50 (ISBN 0-471-99467-7, Pub. by Wiley-Interscience). Wiley.

Cooke, W. Bridge. Ecology of Fungi. 288p. 1979. 74.95 (ISBN 0-8493-5343-2). CRC Pr.

Corda, A. C. Icones Fungorum Hucusque Cognitorum. 1963. 190.00 (ISBN 3-7682-7050-5). Lubrecht & Cramer.

Corner, E. J. Monograph of Clavaria & Allied Genera. (Annals of Botany Ser.: Memoir 1). 1967. Repr. of 1950 ed. lib. bdg. 27.50x (ISBN 0-934454-85-X). Lubrecht & Cramer.

De Schweinitz, L. D. Synopsis Fungorum Carolinae Superioris: Secumdum Observationes. (Bibliotheca Mycologica: Band 49). (Illus.). 1978. pap. 16.00x (ISBN 3-7682-1065-0, Pub. by J Cramer). Intl Schol Bk Serv.

Dube, H. C. An Introduction to Fungi. 400p. 1980. 24.00x (ISBN 0-686-69933-5, Pub. by Croom Helm England). State Mutual Bk.

--A Textbook of Fungi, Bacteria & Viruses. 1978. 12.50 (ISBN 0-7069-0587-3, Pub. by Vikas India). Advent NY.

Duddington, C. L. Beginner's Guide to the Fungi. 176p. 1972. 6.95 (ISBN 0-7207-0448-0, Pub. by Michael Joseph). Merrimack Bk Serv.

Findlay, W. P. Observer's Book of Mushrooms, Toadstools, & Other Common Fungi. (Observer Bks.). (Illus.). 1977. 3.95 (ISBN 0-684-15201-0, ScribT). Scribner.

--Wayside & Woodland Fungi. LC 68-10154. (Illus.). 1967. 20.00 (ISBN 0-7232-0008-4). Warne.

Fries, Elias M. Systema Mycologicum, Sistens Fungorum Ordines, Genera et Species, 6 vols. in 4. 115.50 (ISBN 0-384-16960-0). Johnson Repr.

Funder, Sigurd. Practical Mycology: Manual for Identification of Fungi. 3rd, rev. ed. (Illus.). 1968. 14.75 (ISBN 0-02-844880-4). Hafner.

Griffin, David H. Fungal Physiology. 392p. 1981. 32.50 (ISBN 0-471-05748-7, Pub. by Wiley-Interscience). Wiley.

Grund, D. W. & Harrison, K. A. Nova Scotian Boletes. (Bibliotheca Mycologica Ser.: No. 47). 1976. text ed. 30.00 (ISBN 3-7682-1062-6). Lubrecht & Cramer.

Hawker, Lilian E. Fungi: An Introduction. 1966. pap. text ed. 5.75x (ISBN 0-09-078992-X, Hutchinson U Lib). Humanities.

--Physiology of Fungi. (Illus.). 1968. Repr. of 1950 ed. 40.00 (ISBN 3-7682-0530-4). Lubrecht & Cramer.

--Physiology of Reproduction in Fungi. LC 70-164676. 1972. Repr. of 1957 ed. 12.00 (ISBN 0-02-845820-6). Hafner.

Heath, I. B., ed. Nuclear Division in the Fungi. 1978. 25.00 (ISBN 0-12-335950-3). Acad Pr.

Hoffman, P. Genetische Grundlagen der Artbildung in der Gattung Polyporus. (Bibliotheca Mycologica Ser.: No. 65). (Illus.). 1978. pap. text ed. 15.00x (ISBN 3-7682-1210-6). Lubrecht & Cramer.

Horak, E. Fungi Austroamericani. pap. 6.00 (ISBN 3-7682-0226-7). Lubrecht & Cramer.

Ingold, Cecil T. Biology of Fungi. 3rd rev. ed. (Hutchinson Biology Monographs). (Illus., Orig.). 1973. pap. text ed. 10.50x (ISBN 0-09-105120-7, Hutchinson U Lib). Humanities.

International Congress of Botany, Edinburgh, 1964. Incompatability in Fungi: A Symposium. Raper, J. R. & Esser, K., eds. (Illus.). viii, 124p. 1965. pap. 27.10 (ISBN 0-387-03334-3). Springer Verlag.

Karling, J. S. Chytridiomycetarum Iconographia: Illustrated & Descriptive Guide to the Chytridiomycetous Genera with a Suppl. of the Hyphochytriomycetes. (Illus.). 1978. lib. bdg. 100.00 (ISBN 3-7682-1111-8). Lubrecht & Cramer.

--The Simple Biflagellate Holocarpic Phycomycetes. 2nd ed. (Illus.). 1981. lib. bdg. 60.00x (ISBN 0-686-31663-0). Lubrecht & Cramer.

Karling, John S. Chytridiomycetarum Iconographia. (Illus.). 1978. 100.00 (ISBN 3-7682-1111-8, Pub. by J Cramer). Intl Schol Bk Serv.

Kavaler, Lucy. Mushrooms, Moulds & Miracles: The Strange World of Fungi. 5.95 (ISBN 0-686-05401-6). British Am Bks.

Kohlmeyer, J. Index Alphabecticus Klotzschii & Rabenhorstii Herbarii Mycologici. 1962. pap. 20.00 (ISBN 3-7682-5404-6). Lubrecht & Cramer.

Kohlmeyer, J. E. Icones Fungorum Maris, 7 parts. 1969. 100.00 (ISBN 3-7682-2000-1). Lubrecht & Cramer.

Largent, David L. The Genus Leptonia. (Bibliotheca Mycologica: Band 55). (Illus.). 1978. 32.00x (ISBN 3-7682-1114-2, Pub. by J Cramer). Intl Schol Bk Serv.

Mehrotra, B. S. The Fungi. 1981. 17.00x (ISBN 0-686-76638-5, Pub. by Oxford & IBH India). State Mutual Bk.

Meinhardt, F. Untersuchungen Zur Genetik Des Fortpflanzungsverhaltens und der Fruchtkoerper- und Antibiotikabbildung Des Basidiomyceten Agrocybe Aegerita. (Bibliotheca Mycologica: No. 75). (Illus.). 128p. (Ger.). 1981. pap. text ed. 20.00x (ISBN 3-7682-1275-0). Lubrecht & Cramer.

Metlitsky, L. V. & Ozeretskovskaya, O. L. Plant Immunity. LC 68-25383. 114p. 1968. 29.50 (ISBN 0-306-30344-2, Plenum Pr). Plenum Pub.

Moser, M. Fungorum Rariorum Icones Coloratae, Part 7. (Illus.). 1979. pap. text ed. 17.50x (ISBN 3-7682-0413-8, J. Cramer Verlag). Lubrecht & Cramer.

Nag Raj, T. R. & DiCosmo, F. A Monograph of Herknessia & Mastigosporella with Notes on Associated Teleomorphs, Vol. 80. (Bibliotheca Mycologica). (Illus.). 160p. 1981. text ed. 25.00x (ISBN 3-7682-1300-5, Pub. by Cramer Germany). Lubrecht & Cramer.

Neuner, Andreas. Mushrooms & Fungi. LC 78-316610. (Nature Guides Ser.). (Illus.). 144p. 1979. pap. 5.95 (ISBN 0-7011-2328-1, Pub. by Chatto Bodley Jonathan). Merrimack Bk Serv.

New York Botanical Garden. Mycologia Index: Volumes 1-58, 1909-1966. LC 57-51730. (Mycologia Ser). 1968. 20.00 (ISBN 0-89327-215-9). NY Botanical.

Persoon, Christiaan H. Synopsis Methodica Fungorum, 3 vols. in 1. 1952. Repr. of 1808 ed. incl. index botanicus 38.50 (ISBN 0-384-45820-3). Johnson Repr.

Petersen, R. H. Ramaria, Subgenus Lentoramaria, with Emphasis on North American Taxa. (Bibliotheca Mycologica Ser.: No. 43). 1975. text ed. 25.00 (ISBN 3-7682-0961-X). Lubrecht & Cramer.

Petrak, F. & Sydow, H. Die Gattungen der Pyrenomyceten, Sphaeropsideen und Melanconieen, Pt. 1. (Feddes Repertorium: Beiheft 27). 551p. (Ger.). 1979. Repr. of 1926 ed. lib. bdg. 90.00x (ISBN 3-87429-071-9). Lubrecht & Cramer.

Quintanilha, A. La Probleme De la Sexualite Chez les Champignons: Recherches Sur le Genre Coprinus. (Illus.). 1968. pap. 20.00 (ISBN 3-7682-0556-8). Lubrecht & Cramer.

Ramsbottom, J. Fungi: An Introduction to Mycology. 1979. Repr. of 1929 ed. lib. bdg. 12.50 (ISBN 0-8495-4608-7). Arden Lib.

Rattan, S. S. Resupinate Aphyllophorales of the Northwestern Himalayas. (Bibliotheca Mycologica Ser.: No. 60). (Illus.). 1977. lib. bdg. 60.00x (ISBN 3-7682-1172-X). Lubrecht & Cramer.

Recommended International Standard for Fresh Fungus "Chantarelle". (Codex Alimentarius Commission Ser: No. 40). (Orig.). 1970. pap. 4.50 (ISBN 0-685-36296-5, F646, FAO). Unipub.

Reid, Derek A. A Monograph of the Stipitate Steroid Fungi. (Illus.). 1965. pap. 80.00 (ISBN 3-7682-5418-6). Lubrecht & Cramer.

Remler, P. Ascomyceten auf Ericaceen in den Ostalpen. (Bibliotheca Mycologica: No. 68). (Illus., Ger.). 1980. lib. bdg. 40.00x (ISBN 3-7682-1248-3). Lubrecht & Cramer.

Ricken, H. Vademecum Fuer Pilzfreunde: Taschenbuch Zur Bequemen Bestimmung Aller in Mittel-Europa Vorkommenden Ansehnlichen Pilzkoerper. 1969. Repr. of 1920 ed. pap. 20.00 (ISBN 3-7682-0603-3). Lubrecht & Cramer.

Robinson, Peter M. Practical Fungal Physiology. LC 78-4243. 1978. pap. 13.25 (ISBN 0-471-99656-4, Pub. by Wiley-Interscience). Wiley.

Rolfe, R. T. & Rolfe, F. W. The Romance of the Fungus World. (Illus.). Repr. of 1925 ed. 19.50 (ISBN 0-384-51830-3). Johnson Repr.

--The Romance of the Fungus-World: An Account of Fungus Life in Its Numerous Guises, Both Real & Legendary. LC 74-81401. (Illus.). 352p. 1974. pap. 3.50 (ISBN 0-486-23105-4). Dover.

Romagnesi, H. Petit Atlas Des Champignons, 2 vols. (Illus.). 1964. Vols. 1 & 2. 25.00 (ISBN 0-934454-91-4). Lubrecht & Cramer.

Saccardo, Pier A. Sylloge Fungorum Omnium Hucusque Cognitorum, Vols. 1-25. Repr. of 1931 ed. Set. 1625.00 (ISBN 0-384-52831-7); Set. pap. 1500.00 (ISBN 0-384-52830-9); Vols. 1-4, 6, 7, 10, 11, 18-21. pap. 55.00 ea.; Vols. 5, 8, 9, 12-14, 16, 17, 19, 20, 23, 25. pap. 60.00 ea.; Vol. 15. pap. 35.00 suppl. to vols. 1-4 (ISBN 0-685-13610-8); Vols. 22, 24 In 2 Pts, Ea. pap. 95.00 ea.; Vol. 26. 175.00 (ISBN 0-685-13612-4). Johnson Repr.

Samuels, Gary J. A Revision of the Fungi Formerly Classified As Nectria Subgenus Hyphonectria. LC 66-6394. (Memoirs of the New York Botanical Garden Ser.: Vol. 26, No. 3). 1976. pap. 12.00 (ISBN 0-89327-008-3). NY Botanical.

Schroeter, J. Die Pilze Schlesiens, 2 vols. (Illus.). 1973. Repr. of 1908 ed. Set. 125.00 (ISBN 3-7682-0761-7). Lubrecht & Cramer.

Sivanesan, A. The Genus Venturia. (Illus.). 1979. 20.00x (ISBN 3-7682-1167-3, Pub. by J Cramer). Intl Schol Bk Serv.

Smith, J. E., ed. Fungal Biotechnology, No. 3. (British Mycological Society Symposia Ser.). 1980. 32.50 (ISBN 0-12-652950-7). Acad Pr.

Smith, John E. & Berry, David, eds. Filamentous Fungi. Incl. Vol. 1. Industrial Mycology. LC 75-2101. 340p. 64.00 (ISBN 0-470-80187-5); Vol. 2. Biosynthesis & Metabolism. LC 75-41613. 87.95 (ISBN 0-470-15005-X); Vol. 3. Developmental Mycology. LC 75-2101. 60.95 (ISBN 0-470-99352-9). (Filamentous Fungi Ser.: Vols. 1-3). 1975-78. Halsted Pr.

Soothill, Eric & Fairhurst, Alan. The New Field Guide to Fungi. (Illus.). 1979. 22.00 (ISBN 0-7181-1620-8). Transatlantic.

Stevens, F. L. Hawaiian Fungi. Repr. of 1925 ed. pap. 16.00 (ISBN 0-527-02122-9). Kraus Repr.

Stevens, Frank L. The Genus Meliola in Porto Rico. (University of Illinois Biological Monographs: Vol. 2, No. 4). Repr. of 1916 ed. pap. 6.00 (ISBN 0-384-58110-2). Johnson Repr.

Sydow, Hans & Sydow, Paul. Monographia Uredinearum: Seu Specierum Omnium As Hunc Usque Diem Cognitarum Descripto & Adumbratio Systematica, Vols. 1-4. pap. 400.00 (ISBN 3-7682-0730-7). Lubrecht & Cramer.

Turner, W. B. Fungal Metabolites. 1971. 68.00 (ISBN 0-12-704550-3). Acad Pr.

Von Arx, J. A. A Revision of the Fungi Described As Gloesporium. 1970. 40.00 (ISBN 3-7682-0667-X). Lubrecht & Cramer.

Watling, Roy & Gregory, Norma. Census Catalogue of World Members of the Bolbitiaceae. (Bibliotheca Mycologica). 300p. 1981. lib. bdg. 40.00x (ISBN 3-7682-1279-3). Lubrecht & Cramer.

Weber, Darrell J., ed. The Fungal Spore: Form & Function. LC 75-3889. 912p. 1976. 49.50 (ISBN 0-686-74188-9). Krieger.

Webster, John. Introduction to Fungi. 2nd ed. LC 79-52856. (Illus.). 1980. 79.50 (ISBN 0-521-22888-3); pap. 21.95x (ISBN 0-521-29699-4). Cambridge U Pr.

--Introduction to Fungi. LC 77-93714. (Illus.). 1970. text ed. 29.95x (ISBN 0-521-07640-4); pap. 16.95x (ISBN 0-521-29232-8). Cambridge U Pr.

Weete, John D. Fungal Lipid Biochemistry. LC 94-8457. (Monographs in Lipid Research: Vol. 1). (Illus.). 393p. 1974. 35.00 (ISBN 0-306-35801-8, Plenum Pr). Plenum Pub.

Wicklow & Carroll. The Fungal Community: Its Organization & Role in the Ecosystem. 864p. 1981. 85.00 (ISBN 0-686-72768-1). Dekker.

Wolf, Frederick A. & Wolf, Frederick T. Fungi, 2 Vols. (Illus.). 1969. Repr. of 1948 ed. Set. 45.00 (ISBN 0-02-854910-4). Hafner.

Wylie, Thomas & Morehouse, Lawrence, eds. Mycotoxic Fungi, Mycotoxins, Mycotoxicoses, Vol. 3. 1978. 45.00 (ISBN 0-8247-6552-4). Dekker.

Zainal, A. S. Micro-Morphological Studies of Soft Rot Fungi in Wood. (Bibliotheca Mycologica: No. 70). (Illus.). 1980. lib. bdg. 30.00 (ISBN 3-7682-1252-1). Lubrecht & Cramer.

FUNGI–BIBLIOGRAPHY

Lindau, Gustav. Thesaurus Litteraturae Mycologicae et Lichenologicae, 5 Vols. Repr. of 1917 ed. 231.00 (ISBN 0-384-32706-0); pap. 192.50 (ISBN 0-384-32707-9). Johnson Repr.

Uellner, W. Fungorum Libri Bibliothecae Joachim Schliemann. (Books & Prints of 4 Centuries). 1976. 30.00 (ISBN 3-7682-1075-8). Lubrecht & Cramer.

Watling, Roy, ed. A Literature Guide to the Identification of Mushrooms. 120p. (Orig.). 1980. pap. 6.95 (ISBN 0-916422-18-6). Mad River.

FUNGI–CLASSIFICATION

Kreisel, Hans. Grundzuege Eines Natuerlichen Systems der Pilze. (Illus.). 1969. pap. 20.00 (ISBN 3-7682-0630-0). Lubrecht & Cramer.

Oudemans, C. A. Enumeratio Systematica Fungorum, 5 vols. 250.00 (ISBN 0-934454-30-2). Lubrecht & Cramer.

Peterson, Ronald H., ed. Evolution in the Higher Basidiomycetes: An International Symposium. LC 73-100410. 1971. 26.50x (ISBN 0-87049-109-1). U of Tenn Pr.

FUNGI–ECONOMIC ASPECTS

see also Fungi, Pathogenic; Fungi in Agriculture; Mushrooms; Mushrooms, Edible

FUNGI–GENETICS

Arx, J. A. von. The Genera of Fungi Sporulating in Pure Culture. 3rd rev. ed. (Illus.). 410p. 1981. lib. bdg. 50.00x (ISBN 3-7682-0693-9). Lubrecht & Cramer.

Baroni, T. J. A Revision of the Genus Rhodocybe Maire (Agaricales) rev. ed. (Nova Hedwigia Beiheft). (Illus.). 300p. 1981. text ed. 60.00x (ISBN 3-7682-5467-4). Lubrecht & Cramer.

Burnett, J. H. Mycogenetics: An Introduction to the General Genetics of Fungi. LC 74-13143. 375p. 1975. 57.50 (ISBN 0-471-12445-1, Pub. by Wiley-Interscience); pap. 15.25 (ISBN 0-471-12446-X). Wiley.

Esser, Karl & Kuenen, Rudolf. Genetics of Fungi. Steiner, Erich, tr. 1967. 62.60 (ISBN 0-387-03784-5). Springer-Verlag.

Fincham, J. R. A Study of Genetic Recombination. rev. ed. Head, J. J., ed. LC 77-75593. (Carolina Biology Readers Ser.). (Illus.). (gr. 11 up). 1982. pap. 1.65 (ISBN 0-89278-202-1, 45-9602). Carolina Biological.

Ingold, Cecil T. Fungal Spores: Their Liberation & Dispersal. 310p. 1971. 26.00x (ISBN 0-19-854115-5). Oxford U Pr.

Lakhanpal, T. N. & Mukerji, K. G. Taxonomy of the Indian Myxomycetes. (Bibliotheca Mycologica: No. 78). (Illus.). 532p. 1981. lib. bdg. 60.00x (ISBN 3-7682-1287-4). Lubrecht & Cramer.

Von Arx, J. Genera of Fungi Sporulating in Pure Culture. rev., 2nd ed. (Illus.). 1976. 40.00x (ISBN 3-7682-0693-9, Pub. by J. Cramer). Intl Schol Bk Serv.

Zehr, Douglas R. Assessment of Variation in Scampania Nemorosa & Selected Related Species (Hepatophyta) (Bryophytorum Bibliotheca: No. 15). (Illus.). 140p. 1980. pap. 20.00x (ISBN 3-7682-1282-3). Lubrecht & Cramer.

FUNGI–AUSTRALIA

Cunningham, G. H. The Gasteromycetes of Australia & New Zealand. (Bibliotheca Mycologica 67). 1979. Repr. of 1942 ed. lib. bdg. 40.00 (ISBN 3-7682-1231-9). Lubrecht & Cramer.

FUNGI–EUROPE

Jahn, H. Die resupinaten Phellinus-Arten in Mittel-Europa. Mit Hinweisen Auf Die Resupinaten Incnotus Arten, Vol. 81. (Bibliotheca Mycologica). (Illus., Ger.). 1981. pap. text ed. 19.75x (ISBN 3-7682-1307-2, Pub. by Cramer Germany). Lubrech & Cramer.

--Mitteleuropaeische Porlinge (Poly. S. Lato) & Ihr Vorkommen in Westfalen. (Illus.). 1970. pap. 15.00 (ISBN 3-7682-0698-X). Lubrecht & Cramer.

Kibby, Geoffrey. Mushrooms & Toadstools: A Field Guide. (Illus.). 256p. 1979. text ed. 23.00x (ISBN 0-19-217688-9). Oxford U Pr.

Telleria, M. T. Contribucion Al Estudio De los Aphyllophorales Espanoles: With Key to Species in English. (Bibliotheca Mycologica: No. 74). (Illus.). 474p. (Span.). 1981. lib. bdg. 50.00x (ISBN 3-7682-1274-2). Lubrecht & Cramer.

FUNGI–FINLAND

Karsten, P. A. Mycologia Fennica: 1871-78, 4 parts in 1 vol. 1967. 180.00 (ISBN 3-7682-0353-0). Lubrecht & Cramer.

Karsten, Peter A. Mycologia Fennica, 4 Vols. in 1. 1871-1879. 138.50 (ISBN 0-384-28665-8). Johnson Repr.

--Symbolae Ad Mycologiam Fennicam. 1870-1895. 61.50 (ISBN 0-384-28690-9). Johnson Repr.

FUNGI–GREAT BRITAIN

Berkeley, M. J. & Broome, C. E. Notices of British Fungi: 1841-45, 35 papers bd. in 1 vol. (Bibl. Myco.: Vol. 1). 1967. 70.00 (ISBN 3-7682-0456-1). Lubrecht & Cramer.

Grove, W. B. British Stem-&-Leaf-Fungi: Coelomysycetes, 2 vols. (Illus.). 1967. Set. pap. 50.00 (ISBN 3-7682-0500-2). Lubrecht & Cramer.

Rea, C. British Basidomysetaceae: A Handbook to the Larger British Fungi. 1968. pap. 50.00 (ISBN 3-7682-0561-4). Lubrecht & Cramer.

FUNGI–NEW ZEALAND

Cunningham, G. H. The Gasteromycetes of Australia & New Zealand. (Bibliotheca Mycologica 67). 1979. Repr. of 1942 ed. lib. bdg. 40.00 (ISBN 3-7682-1231-9). Lubrecht & Cramer.

Horak, E. Fungi Agaracini Nova Zelandiae. 1973. 50.00 (ISBN 3-7682-5443-7). Lubrecht & Cramer.

FUNGI–NORTH AMERICA

Burt, E. A. Thelephoraceae of North America. (Illus.). 1966. 35.75 (ISBN 0-02-842320-8). Hafner.

Cibula, William G. An Ecological & Taxonomic Study of Selected Higher Fungi in Northeastern Ohio. 1974. 4.00 (ISBN 0-686-30338-5). Ohio Bio Survey.

Coker, W. C. & Couch, J. N. The Gastromycetes of the Eastern U. S. & Canada. 1969. pap. 32.00 (ISBN 3-7682-0602-5). Lubrecht & Cramer.

Coker, William C. & Couch, John N. The Gasteromycetes of the Eastern United States & Canada. LC 73-91490. (Illus.). 447p. 1974. pap. 6.95 (ISBN 0-486-23033-3). Dover.

Grund, Darryl W. & Harrison, Kenneth A. Nova Scotian Boletes. (Bibliotheca Mycologica: Band 47). (Illus.). 1976. text ed. 25.00x (ISBN 3-7682-1062-6, Pub. by J. Cramer). Intl Schol Bk Serv.

Hesler, L. R. & Smith, Alexander H. North American Species of Hygrophorus. LC 62-20535. (Illus.). 1963. 21.50x (ISBN 0-87049-039-7). U of Tenn Pr.

McIlvaine, Charles & Macadam, Robert K. One Thousand American Fungi. (Illus.). 13.50 (ISBN 0-8446-4781-0). Peter Smith.

Miller, O. K., Jr. & Farr, D. F. An Index of the Common Fungi of North America (Synonymy & Common Names) 1975. pap. 18.75 (ISBN 3-7682-0974-1). Lubrecht & Cramer.

Miller, Orson K., Jr. & Farr, David F. An Index of the Common Fungi of North America (Synonymy & Common Names) (Bibliotheca Mycologica: Vol. 44). 1976. plasticized bds. 15.00x (ISBN 3-7682-0974-1, Pub. by J. Cramer). Intl Schol Bk Serv.

Overholts, Lee O. Polyporaceae of the United States, Alaska, & Canada. Lowe, Josiah L., ed. (Illus.). 1953. 20.00x (ISBN 0-472-08714-2). U of Mich Pr.

Petersen, Ronald H. Ramaria Subgenus Lentoramaria with Special Emphasis on North American Taxa. (Bibliotheca Mycologica Ser.: Vol. 43). (Illus.). 176p. 1975. pap. 20.00x (ISBN 3-7682-0961-X, Pub. by J. Cramer). Intl Schol Bk Serv.

Pomerleau, R. & Jackson, H. A. Champignons de l'Est du Canada et des Etats-Unis. (Illus.). 1951. 10.00 (ISBN 0-934454-21-3). Lubrecht & Cramer.

Schweinitz, L. D. Synopsis Fungorum in America Boreali Media Degentium. 1962. Repr. of 1834 ed. 50.00 (ISBN 3-7682-0117-1). Lubrecht & Cramer.

Seymour, A. B. Host Index of the Fungi of North America. (Bibl. Myco. Ser.: No.2). 1967. pap. 50.00 (ISBN 3-7682-0461-8). Lubrecht & Cramer.

Stevenson, J. An Account of Fungus Exiccati Containing Material from the Americas. 1971. 100.00 (ISBN 3-7682-5436-4). Lubrecht & Cramer.

Tilden, J. The Myxophyceae of North America & Adjacent Regions. (Bibl. Phyco.: Vol. 4). (Illus.). 1968. pap. 40.00 (ISBN 3-7682-0546-0). Lubrecht & Cramer.

Tomentelloid Fungi of North America, No. 93. 1968. 2.00 (ISBN 0-686-20703-3). SUNY Environ.

Von Schweinitz, L. D. Synopsis Fungorum Carolinea Superioris. 1976. Repr. of 1822 ed. 20.00 (ISBN 3-7682-1065-0). Lubrecht & Cramer.

FUNGI–SOUTH AMERICA

Dennis, R. Fungus Flora of Venezuela & Adjacent Countries. 1970. 52.80 (ISBN 3-7682-0692-0). Lubrecht & Cramer.

Moser, Meinhard & Horak, Egon, eds. Cortinarius Fr. und Nahe Verwandte Gattungen in Suedamerica. (Beihefte zur Nova Hedwigiia Ser.: Vol. 52). (Illus.). 714p. (Ger.). 1975. pap. 100.00x (ISBN 0-686-67202-X, Pub. by J. Cramer). Intl Schol Bk Serv.

Singer, R. The Genera Marasmiellus, Crepidotus & Simocybe in the Neotropics. 1973. 100.00 (ISBN 3-7682-5444-5). Lubrecht & Cramer.

Singer, Rolf. Mycoflora Australis. 1969. pap. 80.00 (ISBN 3-7682-5429-1). Lubrecht & Cramer.

FUNGI, EDIBLE

see Mushrooms, Edible; Truffles

FUNGI, MARINE

see Marine Fungi

FUNGI, PATHOGENIC

see also Fungi, Phytopathogenic; Medical Mycology; Mycotoxins; Rusts (Fungi)

Christensen, Clyde M. Molds, Mushrooms, & Mycotoxins. LC 74-21808. (Illus.). 292p. 1975. 15.00x (ISBN 0-8166-0743-5). U of Minn Pr.

Duffy, Thomas J. & Vergeer, Paul P. California Toxic Fungi. LC 77-76180. (Toxicology Monograph: No. 1). (Illus.). 1977. 2.00 (ISBN 0-918942-00-4). Mycological.

Frey, Dorothea, et al. Color Atlas of Pathogenic Fungi. (Illus.). 1979. 42.95 (ISBN 0-8151-3277-8). Year Bk Med.

International Congress on Microbiology, 12th, Munich, 1978. Fungal Viruses: Proceedings. Molitoris, H. P., ed. (Proceddings in Life Sciences Ser.). (Illus.). 1979. 31.90 (ISBN 0-387-09477-6). Springer-Verlag.

Larone, Davise H. Medically Important Fungi: A Guide to Identification. (Illus.). 1976. pap. 13.75x (ISBN 0-06-141513-8, Harper Medical). Har-Row.

Long Ashton Research Station Symposium, University of Bristol, Sept. 1971. Fungal Pathogenicity & the Plant's Response: Proceedings. Byrde, R. J. & Cutting, C. V, eds. 1973. 107.00 (ISBN 0-12-148850-0). Acad Pr.

Moore, W. C. British Parasitic Fungi. 1959. 68.50 (ISBN 0-521-05758-2). Cambridge U Pr.

Prevention of Mycotoxins. (Food & Nutrition Ser.: No. 10). 1979. pap. 7.50 (ISBN 92-5-100703-9, F1628, FAO). Unipub.

Rodricks, Joseph V., ed. Mycotoxins & Other Fungal Related Food Problems. LC 76-4547. (Advances in Chemistry Ser.: No. 149). 1976. 39.00 (ISBN 0-8412-0222-2). Am Chemical.

Stevens, Frank L. Parasitic Fungi from British Guiana & Trinidad. (University of Illinois Biological Monographs: Vol. 8, No. 3). Repr. of 1924 ed. pap. 6.00 (ISBN 0-384-58120-X). Johnson Repr.

FUNGI, PHYTOPATHOGENIC

Boyce, John S. Forest Pathology. 3rd ed. (American Forestry Ser.). (Illus.). 1961. text ed. 22.00 (ISBN 0-07-006898-4, C). McGraw.

Christensen, Clyde M. & Kaufmann, Henry H. Grain Storage: The Role of Fungi in Quality Loss. LC 70-76174. (Illus.). 1969. 10.95x (ISBN 0-8166-0518-1). U of Minn Pr.

Cronartium Ribicola: Its Growth & Reproduction in the Tissues of the Eastern White Pine, No. 86. 1964. 1.50 (ISBN 0-686-20698-3). SUNY Environ.

Cummins, George B. Rust Fungi on Legumes & Composites in North America. LC 78-60541. 1978. pap. 8.95x (ISBN 0-8165-0653-1). U of Ariz Pr.

Garrett, S. D. Pathogenic Root-Infecting Fungi. LC 72-10024. (Illus.). 1970. 42.50 (ISBN 0-521-07786-9). Cambridge U Pr.

Gilbertson, Robert L. Fungi That Decay Ponderosa Pine. LC 74-77206. 1974. pap. 9.50x (ISBN 0-8165-0361-3). U of Ariz Pr.

Holliday, Paul. Fungus Diseases of Tropical Crops. LC 79-41602. (Illus.). 500p. 1980. 125.00 (ISBN 0-521-22529-9). Cambridge U Pr.

Mace, M. E. & Bell, A. A., eds. Fungal Wilt Diseases of Plants. 1981. 58.00 (ISBN 0-12-464450-3). Acad Pr.

Stevens, Frank L. The Fungi Which Cause Plant Disease. (Illus.). Repr. of 1913 ed. 38.50 (ISBN 0-384-58100-5). Johnson Repr.

FUNGI, POISONOUS

see Fungi, Pathogenic

FUNGI IMPERFECTI

Barnett, Horace L. & Hunter, Barry B. Illustrated Genera of Imperfect Fungi. 3rd ed. LC 71-163710. 1972. spiral bdg. 12.95x (ISBN 0-8087-0266-1). Burgess.

FUNGI IN AGRICULTURE

see also Fungi, Phytopathogenic; Fungicides; Plant Diseases

Kampmeijer, P. & Zadoks, J. C. Epimul, a Simulator of Foci & Epidemics in Mixtures of Resistant & Susceptible Plants, Mosaics & Multilines. 1977. pap. 8.00 (ISBN 90-220-0636-0, Pub. by PUDOC). Unipub.

FUNGICIDES

Biolog. Gesellschaft in D. Dt. Demokratischen Republik, Sektion Mikrobiologie. Mechanisms of Action of Fungicides & Antibiotics: Wirkungs Mechanismus Von Fungiziden & Antibiotika. (Illus.). 443p. (Eng. & Ger.). wrappers 30.00 (ISBN 0-685-42268-2). Adler.

Fungi of Pulp & Paper in New York, No. 87. 1.75 (ISBN 0-686-20699-1). SUNY Environ.

Lukens, R. J. Chemistry of Fungicidal Action. LC 70-154308. (Molecular Biology, Biochemistry, & Biophysics Ser.: Vol. 10). (Illus.). 1972. 18.70 (ISBN 0-387-05405-7). Springer-Verlag.

Marsh, R. W., ed. Systemic Fungicides. 2nd ed. LC 76-49542. (Illus.). 1977. text ed. 40.00x (ISBN 0-582-44167-6). Longman.

--Systemic Fungicides. LC 72-4058. 321p. 1972. pap. 24.95 (ISBN 0-470-57250-7). Halsted Pr.

Nene, Y. L. & Thapliyal, P. N. Fungicides in Plant Disease Control. 1981. 25.00 (ISBN 0-686-76639-3, Pub. by Oxford & IBH India). State Mutual Bk.

Page, B. G. & Thomson, W. T. The Nineteen Eighty-One Insecticide, Herbicide, Fungicide Quick Guide. 140p. 1981. pap. 12.00 (ISBN 0-913702-11-0). Thomson Pub Ca.

Ramulu, U. S. Chemistry of Insecticides & Fungicides. 342p. 1981. 25.00x (ISBN 0-686-72944-7, Pub. by Oxford & IBH India); 15.25x (ISBN 0-686-72945-5). State Mutual Bk.

Siegel, Malcolm R. & Sisler, Hugh D., eds. Antifungal Compounds: Discovery & Development, Vol. 1. 1977. 72.50 (ISBN 0-8247-6557-5). Dekker.

--Antifungal Compounds, Vol. 2: Interactions in Biological & Ecological Systems. 1977. 79.50 (ISBN 0-8247-6558-3). Dekker.

Thomson, W. T. Agricultural Chemicals Book IV: Fungicides - 1981. rev. ed. 175p. 1981. pap. 13.50 (ISBN 0-913702-14-5). Thomson Pub Ca.

Torgeson, Dewayne C., ed. Fungicides: An Advanced Treatise, Vols. 1-2. 1967. Vol. 1. 78.50 (ISBN 0-12-695601-4). Vol. 2. 78.50 (ISBN 0-12-695602-2). Acad Pr.

Zehr, Eldon I., ed. Methods for Evaluating Plant Fungicides, Nematicides, & Bactericides. LC 78-63414. 76p. 1978. lib. bdg. 15.00 (ISBN 0-89054-025-X). Am Phytopathol Soc.

FUNGOUS DISEASES

see Medical Mycology

FUNGUS DISEASES OF PLANTS

see Fungi, Phytopathogenic

FUNICULAR RAILROADS

see Railroads, Cable

FUNK, JOHN FRETZ, BP. 1835-1930

Wenger, J. C. Bless the Lord, O My Soul. LC 64-23575. (Illus.). 1964. 6.95 (ISBN 0-8361-1497-3). Herald Pr.

FUNNIES

see Comic Books, Strips, etc.

FUR

see also Fur Garments

Bachrach, Max. Fur - a Practical Treatise: Geography of the Fur World. 1977. lib. bdg. 75.00 (ISBN 0-8490-1873-0). Gordon Pr.

Ewing, Elizabeth. Fur in Dress. (Illus.). 192p. 1981. 42.00 (ISBN 0-7134-1741-2, Pub. by Batsford England). David & Charles.

Kaplan, David G. World of Furs. LC 75-153567. (Illus.). 256p. 1974. 15.00 (ISBN 0-87005-098-2). Fairchild.

Nilsson, Greta, et al. Facts About Furs. rev. ed. Animal Welfare Institute, tr. LC 80-65265. (Illus.). 257p. 1980. pap. text ed. 4.00 (ISBN 0-938414-02-X). Animal Welfare.

Patton, Mary A. Designing with Leather & Fur (Real & Fake) 1972. 8.95 (ISBN 0-8208-0346-4). Hearthside.

FUR-BEARING ANIMALS

see also Fur Farming; Fur Trade; also Names of Fur-Bearing Animals

Coues, Elliott. Fur-Bearing Animals of North America. LC 79-125735. (American Environmental Studies). (Illus.). 1970. Repr. of 1877 ed. 18.00 (ISBN 0-405-02660-9). Arno.

Geary, Steve M. Fur Trapping in North America. LC 81-3592. (Illus.). 160p. 1981. 12.95 (ISBN 0-498-02563-2). A S Barnes.

McCracken, Harold & Van Cleve, Harry. Trapping. (Illus.). 1974. 8.95 (ISBN 0-498-08272-5). A S Barnes.

Rue, Leonard L. Furbearing Animals of North America. (Illus.). 352p. 1981. 19.95 (ISBN 0-517-53942-X, Michelman Books). Crown.

FUR COATS

see Fur Garments

FUR FARMING

see also names of Fur-Bearing Animals

Harding, A. R. Fur Farming. rev ed. (Illus.). 442p. 1979. pap. 5.00 (ISBN 0-936622-08-3). A R Harding Pub.

FUR GARMENTS
Arnim, Faye. Fur Craft: How to Glamorize Your Wardrobe with Fur. pap. 2.00 (ISBN 0-686-00679-8). Key Bks.
Ewing, Elizabeth. Fur in Dress. (Illus.). 192p. 1981. 42.00 (ISBN 0-7134-1741-2, Pub. by Batsford England). David & Charles.
Fur Storage, Fumigation & Cleaning. (Eighty-Ninety Ser). 1969. pap. 2.00 (ISBN 0-685-58145-4, 81). Natl Fire Prot.
Kresz, Maria. The Art of the Hungarian Furriers. (Hungarian Folk Art: 9). Orig. Title: Nepi Szucsmunka. (Illus.). 104p. 1979. 8.50x (ISBN 963-13-0417-5). Intl Pubns Serv.
Schwebke, Phyllis W. & Krohn, Margaret B. How to Sew Leather, Suede & Fur. (Illus.). 160p. 1974. pap. 3.95 (ISBN 0-02-011930-5, Collier). Macmillan.
FUR SEAL
see Sealing
FUR TRADE
see also Fur Garments;
also Names of Fur-Bearing Animals
Berry, Don. A Majority of Scoundrels. new ed. 1977. pap. 2.95 (ISBN 0-89174-028-7). Comstock Edns.
Bryce, George. Remarkable History of the Hudson's Bay Company: Induding That of the French Traders of Northwestern Canada, & of the Astor Fur Companies. (Research & Source Works Ser.: No. 171). (Illus.). 1968. 29.50 (ISBN 0-8337-0407-9). B Franklin.
Campbell, Marjorie W. Fur Trade. (Canadian Jackdaw Ser: No. C5). (Illus.). 1968. 6.95 (ISBN 0-670-33278-X, Grossman). Viking Pr.
Campbell, Walter S. Mountain Men. LC 77-99620. (Essay Index Reprint Ser). 1937. 25.00 (ISBN 0-8369-1397-3). Arno.
Chittenden, Hiram M. American Fur Trade in the Far West, 2 vols. LC 73-21914. (Illus.). Repr. of 1935 ed. Set. lib. bdg. 37.50x (ISBN 0-678-01035-8). Kelley.
Cleland, Robert G. This Reckless Breed of Men: The Trappers & Fur Traders of the Southwest. LC 75-46376. 1976. pap. 7.95 (ISBN 0-8263-0415-X). U of NM Pr.
Coman, Katharine. Economic Beginnings of the Far West: How We Won the Land Beyond the Mississippi, 2 vols. Incl. Vol. 1. Explorers & Colonizers; Vol. 2. American Settlers. LC 67-29510. Repr. of 1912 ed. Set. 37.50x (ISBN 0-678-00422-6). Kelley.
Davidson, Gordon C. North West Company. LC 66-27059. (Illus.). 1967. Repr. of 1918 ed. 30.00 (ISBN 0-8462-0894-6). Russell.
De Voto, Bernard. Across the Wide Missouri. (Illus.). pap. 7.95 (ISBN 0-395-08374-5, 25, SenEd). HM.
Douglas, Walter B. Manuel Lisa. Nasatir, Abraham P., ed. (Illus.). 1964. Repr. of 1911 ed. 12.50 (ISBN 0-87266-006-0). Argosy.
Educational Research Council of America. Furrier. rev. ed. Ferris, Theodore N. & Marchak, John P., eds. (Real People at Work Ser: E). (Illus.). 1976. pap. text ed. 2.25 (ISBN 0-89247-030-5). Changing Times.
Fogdall, Alberta B. Royal Family of the Columbia. (Illus.). 1978. 14.95 (ISBN 0-87770-168-7). Ye Galleon.
Franchere, Gabriel. Adventure at Astoria, Eighteen Ten to Eighteen Fourteen. Franchere, Hoyt C., tr. (American Exploration & Travel Ser.: No. 53). (Illus.). 1967. 9.95 (ISBN 0-8061-0747-2). U of Okla Pr.
Fuchs, Victor R. Economics of the Fur Industry. LC 73-76661. (Columbia University. Studies in the Social Sciences: No. 593). Repr. of 1957 ed. 16.50 (ISBN 0-404-51593-2). AMS Pr.
Gates, Charles M., ed. Five Fur Traders of the Northwest: Narrative of Peter Pond & the Diaries of John Macdonell et Al. LC 65-63528. 296p. 1971. Repr. of 1933 ed. 7.25 (ISBN 0-87351-024-0). Minn Hist.
Geary, Steve M. Fur Trapping in North America. LC 81-3592. (Illus.). 160p. 1981. 12.95 (ISBN 0-498-02563-2). A S Barnes.
Gilma, Rhoda R. The Fur Trade. (Wisconsin Stories Ser.). 16p. pap. 1.25 (ISBN 0-686-76159-6). State Hist Soc Wis.
Gilman, Rhoda R., et al. Red River Trails: Oxcart Routes between St. Paul & the Selkirk Settlement, 1820-1870. LC 78-11045. (Illus.). 104p. 1979. pap. 6.75 (ISBN 0-87351-133-6). Minn Hist.
Gowans, Fred R. Rocky Mountain Rendezvous: A History of the Fur Trade Rendezvous 1825-1840. LC 77-8225. (Illus.). 1977. 8.95 (ISBN 0-8425-0791-4); pap. 6.95 (ISBN 0-8425-0787-6). Brigham.
Harding, A. R. Fur Buyer's Guide. (Illus.). 366p. pap. 4.00 (ISBN 0-936622-07-5). A R Harding Pub.
Henry, Alexander. Travels & Adventures in Canada & the Indian Territories Between the Years 1760 & 1776. LC 75-7053. (Indian Captivities Ser.: Vol. 31). 1976. Repr. of 1809 ed. lib. bdg. 44.00 (ISBN 0-8240-1655-6). Garland Pub.
Howay, Frederic William. A List of Trading Vessels in the Maritime Fur Trade, 1785-1825. (Alaska History Ser.: No. 2). 1973. pap. 8.50x (ISBN 0-919642-51-9). Limestone Pr.
Innis, Harold A. Fur Trade in Canada: An Introduction to Canadian Economic History. rev. ed. LC 57-2937. 1956. pap. 10.00 (ISBN 0-8020-6001-3). U of Toronto Pr.
Irving, Washington. Astoria. LC 67-25439. (Illus.). 1967. 10.00 (ISBN 0-8323-0101-9). Binford.
Johnson, Ida A. The Michigan Fur Trade. LC 74-155928. Repr. of 1919 ed. 12.00 (ISBN 0-912382-07-4). Black Letter.
Krech, Shepard, ed. Indians, Animals, & the Fur Trade: A Critique of Keepers of the Game. LC 81-1351. 176p. 1981. text ed. 12.00x (ISBN 0-8203-0563-4). U of Ga Pr.
Lavender, David. The Trans-Canada Canoe Trail. LC 77-4864. (American Trail Ser.). 1977. 11.50 (ISBN 0-07-036678-0, GB). McGraw.
Long, John. Voyages & Travels of an Indian Interpreter & Trader Describing the Manners & Customs of the North American Indians. (American Studies). 1969. Repr. of 1791 ed. 14.00 (ISBN 0-384-33570-5). Johnson Repr.
Luttig, John C. Journal of a Fur Trading Expedition on the Upper Missouri, 1812-1813. (Illus.). 1964. Repr. of 1920 ed. 12.50 (ISBN 0-87266-019-2). Argosy.
McDonald, Lois H. Fur Trade Letters of Francis Ermatinger. LC 80-65050. (Northwest Historical Ser.: Vol. 15). (Illus.). 317p. 1980. 29.00 (ISBN 0-87062-130-0). A H Clark.
MacKay, Douglas. Honourable Company. facs. ed. LC 73-124242. (Select Bibliographies Reprint Ser). 1936. 23.00 (ISBN 0-8369-5430-0). Arno.
Martin, Calvin. Keepers of the Game: Indian-Animal Relationship & the Fur Trade. LC 77-78381. 1978. 10.95 (ISBN 0-520-03519-4). U of Cal Pr.
Mitchell, Elaine A. Fort Timiskaming & the Fur Trade. LC 76-51782. 1977. 22.50x (ISBN 0-8020-2234-0). U of Toronto Pr.
Morgan, Dale L. Jedediah Smith & the Opening of the West. LC 53-10550. (Illus.). 1964. pap. 5.95 (ISBN 0-8032-5138-6, BB 184, Bison). U of Nebr Pr.
Morse, Eric W. Fur Trade Canoe Routes of Canada: Then & Now. rev ed. (Illus.). 1979. pap. 6.00 (ISBN 0-8020-6384-5). U of Toronto Pr.
Musgrove, Bill & Blair, Gerry. Fur Trapping. (Illus.). 1979. 12.95 (ISBN 0-87691-284-6). Winchester Pr.
Norton, Thomas E. & Frank, Robert. The Fur Trade in Colonial New York, 1686-1776. LC 73-2047. 266p. 1974. 25.00x (ISBN 0-299-06420-4). U of Wis Pr.
Nute, Grace L. Caesars of the Wilderness: Medard Chouart, Sieur des Groseilliers & Pierre Esprit Radisson, 1618-1710. 386p. 1978. 12.50 (ISBN 0-87351-127-1); pap. 6.50 (ISBN 0-87351-128-X). Minn Hist.
--Voyageur. LC 55-12180. (Illus.). 289p. 1955. Repr. of 1931 ed. 7.50 (ISBN 0-87351-012-7). Minn Hist.
Nute, Grace Lee. Caesars of the Wilderness: Medard Chouart, Sieurdes Groseilliers & Pierre Espirt Radisson, 1618-1710. Wilkins, Mira, ed. LC 76-29750. (European Business Ser.). (Illus.). 1977. Repr. of 1943 ed. lib. bdg. 24.00x (ISBN 0-405-09766-2). Arno.
Ogden, Adele. The California Sea Otter Trade: 1784-1848. (California Library Reprint Ser.). 1975. 24.00x (ISBN 0-520-02806-6). U of Cal Pr.
Phillips, Paul C. & Smurr, J. W. The Fur Trade, 2 Vols. (Illus.). 1967. Repr. of 1961 ed. 50.00 (ISBN 0-8061-0497-X). U of Okla Pr.
Ray, Arthur J. Indians in the Fur Trade: Their Role As Trappers, Hunters, & Middle Man in the Lands Southwest of Hudson Bay, 1660-1860. LC 73-89848. (Illus.). 1974. pap. 8.50 (ISBN 0-8020-6226-1). U of Toronto Pr.
Ray, Arthur J. & Judd, Carol, eds. Old Trails & New Directions: Papers of the Third North American Fur Trade Conference. 1979. 30.00x (ISBN 0-8020-5468-4). U of Toronto Pr.
Russell, Carl P. Firearms, Traps & Tools of the Mountain Men. LC 77-81984. (Illus.). 448p. 1977. pap. 8.95 (ISBN 0-8263-0465-6). U of NM Pr.
--Guns on the Early Frontiers: A History of Firearms from Colonial Times Through the Years of the Western Fur Trade. LC 80-12570. xvi, 395p. 1980. 19.50x (ISBN 0-8032-3857-6); pap. 6.95 (ISBN 0-8032-8903-0, BB 747, Bison). U of Nebr Pr.
Russell, Osborne. Journal of a Trapper. Haines, Aubrey L., ed. LC 56-52. (Illus.). xxiv, 203p. 1965. 14.50x (ISBN 0-8032-0897-9); pap. 3.50 (ISBN 0-8032-5166-1, BB 316, Bison). U of Nebr Pr.
Sandoz, Mari. Beaver Men. (American Procession Ser). (Illus.). 1975. Repr. of 1964 ed. 10.95 (ISBN 0-8038-0674-4). Hastings.
Saum, Lewis O. The Fur Trader & the Indian. LC 65-23915. (Illus.). 336p. (gr. 9 up). 1965. 13.95 (ISBN 0-295-73793-X); pap. 3.95 (ISBN 0-295-74031-0). U of Wash Pr.
--The Fur Trader & the Indian. LC 65-23915. (Illus.). 336p. (gr. 9 up). 1965. 13.95 (ISBN 0-295-73793-X); pap. 3.95 (ISBN 0-295-74031-0). U of Wash Pr.
Simpson, George. Fur Trade & Empire: George Simpson's Journal, 1824-1825. rev. ed. Merk, Frederick, ed. LC 68-15646. 1968. 20.00x (ISBN 0-674-33500-7, Belknap Pr). Harvard U Pr.
Tikhmenev, P. A. A History of the Russian American Company. Pierce, Richard A. & Donnelly, Alton S., eds. Donnelly, Alton S., tr. from Russian. LC 77-73318. (Illus.). 576p. 1978. 35.00 (ISBN 0-295-95564-3). U of Wash Pr.
Turner, Frederick J. Character & Influence of the Indian Trade in Wisconsin: A Study of the Trading Post As an Institution. 1891. 16.50 (ISBN 0-8337-3579-9). B Franklin.
--The Character & Influence of the Indian Trade in Wisconsin: A Study of the Trading Post As an Institution. Miller, David & Miller, Harry M., eds. LC 76-47331. 1977. 9.95 (ISBN 0-8061-1335-9). U of Okla Pr.
Vandiveer, Clarence A. Fur-Trade & Early Western Exploration. LC 73-145876. (Illus.). 1971. Repr. of 1929 ed. lib. bdg. 14.50x (ISBN 0-8154-0381-X). Cooper Sq.
Wallace, William S., ed. Documents Relating to the North West Company. LC 68-28610. 1968. Repr. of 1934 ed. lib. bdg. 33.00x (ISBN 0-8371-5060-4, WADR). Greenwood.
Weber, David J. The Taos Trappers: The Fur Trade in the Far Southwest, 1540-1846. 260p. 1980. pap. 6.95 (ISBN 0-8061-1702-8). U of Okla Pr.
White, Bruce M., compiled by. The Fur Trade in Minnesota: An Introductory Guide to Manuscript Sources. 61p. 1977. pap. 4.50 (ISBN 0-87351-121-2). Minn Hist.
Wishart, David J. The Fur Trade of the American West, 1807-1840: A Geographical Synthesis. LC 78-62915. (Illus.). 1979. 15.00 (ISBN 0-8032-4705-2). U of Nebr Pr.
Woodward, Arthur. The Denominators of the Fur Trade. (Illus.). 1979. 12.00 (ISBN 0-87026-041-3). Westernlore.
Yount, George C. George C. Yount & His Chronicles of the West. Camp, C. L., ed. 280p. 1966. limited ed 35.00 (ISBN 0-912094-08-7). Old West.
FUR TRADE–JUVENILE LITERATURE
Jones, Evan & Morgan, Dale L. Trappers & Mountain Men. LC 61-6561. (American Heritage Junior Library). (Illus.). 153p. (gr. 5 up). 1961. PLB 12.89 (ISBN 0-06-023056-8, Dist. by Har-Row). Am Heritage.
FURNACES
see also Electric Furnaces; Kilns; Solar Furnaces
Ben David, Eliezer. Out of the Iron Furnace. Feitman, Yaakov, tr. from Heb. LC 74-84829. 1975. 5.95 (ISBN 0-88400-040-0). Shengold.
Cone, Carroll. Energy Management for Industrial Furnaces. LC 80-10435. 1980. 32.50 (ISBN 0-471-06037-2, Pub. by Wiley-Interscience). Wiley.
Dolezal, R. Large Boiler Furnaces: Theory, Construction & Control. 1967. 58.75 (ISBN 0-444-40176-8). Elsevier.
Fulop, Christina & Harris, Ralph. Marketing for Central Heating. (Institute of Economic Affairs, Research Monographs: No. 4). pap. 2.50 (ISBN 0-255-69588-8). Transatlantic.
Gasoline Blow Torches & Plumber's Furnaces. (Thirty Ser). 1974. pap. 2.00 (ISBN 0-685-58104-7, 393). Natl Fire Prot.
Gilchrist, J. D. Fuel, Furnaces & Refractories. 1977. text ed. 32.00 (ISBN 0-08-020430-9); pap. text ed. 12.75 (ISBN 0-08-020429-5). Pergamon.
Glinkov, M. A. & Glinkov, G. M. A General Theory of Funaces. 1980. 7.20 (ISBN 0-8285-1799-1, Pub. by Mir Pubs Russia). Imported Pubns.
Khalil, ed. Flow, Mixing & Heat Transfer in Furnaces. 1978. 45.00 (ISBN 0-08-022695-7). Pergamon.
Ovens & Furnaces, Design, Location & Equipment. (Eighty-Ninety Ser). 156p. 1973. pap. 2.50 (ISBN 0-685-44133-4, 86A). Natl Fire Prot.
Perniak, Y. Campfire to Furnace. 16p. 1975. pap. 0.75 (ISBN 0-8285-1120-9, Pub. by Progress Pubs Russia). Imported Pubns.
Prevention of Furnace Explosions in Fuel-Oil & Natural Gas-Fired Watertube Boiler Furnaces with One Burner. (Eighty-Ninety Ser). 68p. 1973. pap. 2.00 (ISBN 0-685-44149-0, 85). Natl Fire Prot.
Prevention of Furnace Explosions in Natural Gas-Fired Multiple Burner Boiler-Furnaces. (Eighty-Ninety Ser). 68p. 1973. pap. 3.50 (ISBN 0-685-44130-X, 85B). Natl Fire Prot.
Prevention of Furnace Explosions in Pulverized Coal-Fired Multiple Burner Boiler-Furnaces. (Eighty-Ninety Ser). 68p. 1974. pap. 3.50 (ISBN 0-685-44132-6, 85E). Natl Fire Prot.
Reed, Robert D. Furnace Operations. 3rd ed. 230p. 1981. 19.50 (ISBN 0-87201-301-4). Gulf Pub.
Trinks, W. Industrial Furnaces, 2 vols. Incl. Vol. 1. Principals of Design & Operation. 5th ed. 1961 (ISBN 0-471-89034-0); Vol. 2. Fuels, Furnace Types & Furnace Equipment: Their Selection & Influence Upon Furnace Operation. 4th ed. 1967 (ISBN 0-471-89068-5). LC 61-11493. 46.50 ea. (Pub. by Wiley-Interscience). Wiley.
White, Bill. Build Your Own Woodburning Furnace. LC 78-66818. (Illus.). 1978. pap. 3.50 (ISBN 0-9601794-2-9). FireBuilders.
--Convert Your Oil Furnace to Wood. 2nd ed. LC 76-58642. (Illus.). 1977. 3.50 (ISBN 0-9601794-1-0). FireBuilders.
FURNITURE
see also Built-In Furniture; Chairs; Church Furniture; Garden Ornaments and Furniture; Home Workshops; Hospitals–Furniture, Equipment, etc.; Implements, Utensils, etc.; Interior Decoration; Library Fittings and Supplies; Mirrors; Schools–Furniture, Equipment, etc.; Tables; Upholstery; Veneers and Veneering; Wood-Carving
Alth, Max & Alth, Charlotte. The Furniture Buyer's Handbook: How to Buy, Arrange, Maintain & Repair Furniture. (Illus.). 1980. 14.95 (ISBN 0-8027-0636-3); pap. 9.95 (ISBN 0-8027-7155-6). Walker & Co.
--Making Plastic Pipe Furniture. 224p. 1981. 13.95 (ISBN 0-89696-087-0); pap. 8.95 (ISBN 0-89696-133-8). Everest Hse.
--Rattan Furniture: A Home Craftsman's Guide Including Repair of Wicker. (Illus.). 1979. 12.95 (ISBN 0-8015-4788-1, Hawthorn). Dutton.
Andrews, J. Price Guide to Antique Furniture. (Illus.). 1978. 39.50 (ISBN 0-902028-70-7). Apollo.
Burton, E. Milby. Charleston Furniture, 1700-1825. 2nd ed. LC 73-120917. Orig. Title: Contributions from the Charleston Museum: XII. (Illus.). 1970. lib. bdg. 19.50 (ISBN 0-87249-198-6). U of SC Pr.
Cescinsky, H. Gentle Art of Faking Furniture. (Illus.). 12.50 (ISBN 0-8446-1830-6). Peter Smith.
Constock, Helen. American Furniture: Seventeenth, Eighteenth & Nineteen Century Styles. (Illus.). 336p. 1980. Repr. 29.95 (ISBN 0-916838-28-5). Schiffer.
Corbin, Patricia. All About Wicker. (Illus.). 1978. pap. 8.95 (ISBN 0-525-47495-1). Dutton.
Curtis, Tony, ed. Furniture. (Illus.). 1978. 3.95 (ISBN 0-902921-46-0). Apollo.
Dal Fabbro, Mario. How to Make Children's Furniture & Play Equipment. 2nd ed. (Illus.). 192p. 1974. 12.95 (ISBN 0-07-015186-5, P&RB). McGraw.
Davis, Frank. The Plain Man's Guide to Second Hand Furniture. 104p. 1971. 6.95 (ISBN 0-7181-0936-8, Pub. by Michael Joseph). Merrimack Bk Serv.
--The Plain Man's Guide to Second-Hand Furniture. 1972. 8.95 (ISBN 0-7181-0936-8). Transatlantic.
Fairchild Market Research Division. Household Furniture & Bedding. (Fact File Ser.). (Illus.). 60p. 1980. pap. 10.00 (ISBN 0-87005-346-9). Fairchild.
Garner, Philippe. Twentieth Century Furniture. 224p. 1980. 24.95 (ISBN 0-442-25421-0). Van Nos Reinhold.
Haweis, Mrs. E. The Art of Decoration. LC 76-17761. (Aesthetic Movement Ser.: Vol. 17). 1977. Repr. of 1889 ed. lib. bdg. 44.00x (ISBN 0-8240-2466-4). Garland Pub.
Hennessey, James & Papanek, Victor. Nomadic Furniture Two. LC 73-18725. 1974. pap. 5.95 (ISBN 0-394-70638-2). Pantheon.
Hepplewhite, George. Cabinet-Maker & Upholsterer's Guide. LC 69-19164. 1969. pap. 5.00 (ISBN 0-486-22183-0). Dover.
Hill, Conover. Value Guide to Antique Oak Furniture. (Illus.). 1978. pap. 7.95 (ISBN 0-89145-007-6). Collector Bks.
Himmelheber, Georg. Biedermeier Furniture. 198p. 1974. 48.00 (ISBN 0-571-08719-1, Pub. by Faber & Faber). Merrimack Bk Serv.
Hope, Thomas. Household Furniture & Interior Decoration: Executed from Designs by Thomas Hope. (Illus.). 1970. Repr. of 1807 ed. 16.50 (ISBN 0-685-04855-1). Transatlantic.
Idleman, H. K. Housing, Furniture & Appliances. (Contemporary Consumer Ser.). 1974. text ed. 4.24 (ISBN 0-07-031701-1, G); tchr's manual & key 4.95 (ISBN 0-07-031702-X). McGraw.
Ince & Mayhew. Universal Systems of Household Furniture 1762. 16.50 (ISBN 0-85458-618-0). Transatlantic.
Katz, Laszlo. Art of Woodworking & Furniture Appreciation. 2nd ed. (Illus.). 1980. 39.50 (ISBN 0-686-00808-1). PFC.

Linsley, Leslie. New Ideas for Old Furniture. (Illus.). 176p. 1980. 15.95 (ISBN 0-690-01756-1). T Y Crowell.
Martindale, Wight, Jr. We Do It Every Day: The Story Behind the Success of Levitz Furniture. LC 72-86727. 1972. text ed. 12.00 (ISBN 0-87005-139-3). Fairchild.
Nutting, Wallace. Windsor Handbook. LC 73-77579. (Illus.). 1973. pap. 4.95 (ISBN 0-8048-1105-9). C E Tuttle.
Pain, Howard. The Heritage of Country Furniture. 1978. 49.95 (ISBN 0-442-29828-5). Van Nos Reinhold.
Philip, P. & Atterbury, P. World Furniture. (Illus.). Date not set. 30.00 (ISBN 0-686-68700-0, Mayflower Bks). Smith Pubs.
Pile, John F. Modern Furniture. LC 78-5440. 1979. 28.25 (ISBN 0-471-02667-0, Pub. by Wiley-Interscience). Wiley.
Rubin, Cynthia & Rubin, Jerome. Mission Furniture: Making It, Decorating with It, Its History & Place in the Antique Market. LC 79-24376. (Illus.). 160p. (Orig.). 1980. pap. 8.95 (ISBN 0-87701-169-9). Chronicle Bks.
Salomonsky, Verna C. Masterpieces of Furniture. (Illus.). 11.50 (ISBN 0-8446-2856-5). Peter Smith.
--Masterpieces of Furniture in Photographs & Measured Drawings. rev. ed. (Illus.). 1953. pap. 5.00 (ISBN 0-486-21381-1). Dover.
Selection of Furniture. 1972. pap. 1.25 (ISBN 0-686-14999-8, 261-08412). Home Econ Educ.
Shea, John G. Contemporary Furniture. 208p. 1980. pap. 10.95 (ISBN 0-442-20172-9). Van Nos Reinhold.
Sieber, Roy. African Furniture & Household Objects. LC 79-5340. (Illus.). 280p. 1980. 37.50x (ISBN 0-253-11927-8); pap. 20.00x (ISBN 0-253-28242-X). Ind U Pr.
Singleton, Esther & Sturgis, Russell. Furniture of Our Forefathers. LC 68-56505. (Illus.). 1969. Repr. of 1901 ed. 35.00 (ISBN 0-405-08975-9, Pub. by Blom). Arno.
Smith, Nancy A. Old Furniture: Understanding the Craftsman's Art. (Illus.). 1976. pap. 6.95 (ISBN 0-316-79932-7). Little.
Vedder, Alan C. Furniture of Spanish New Mexico. LC 76-50322. (Illus.). 96p. 1977. 14.95 (ISBN 0-913270-67-9). Sunstone Pr.
Watson, Aldren A. Country Furniture. LC 73-18013. (Illus.). (gr. 7-12). 1974. 13.95 (ISBN 0-690-00190-8, TYC-J). Har-Row.
--Country Furniture. 1976. pap. 4.95 (ISBN 0-452-25130-3, Z5130, Plume). NAL.
Weiss, Jeffrey. Pine. LC 80-7832. (Illus.). 128p. (Orig.). 1980. pap. 8.95 (ISBN 0-06-090814-9, CN 814, CN). Har-Row.
Wilk, Christopher. Marcel Breuer: Furniture & Interior Design. LC 81-81191. (Illus.). 192p. 1981. 22.50 (ISBN 0-87070-264-5); pap. 12.50 (ISBN 0-87070-263-7). Museum Mod Art.
Wise, Herbert H. & Weiss, Jeffrey. Made with Oak. (Illus.). 96p. 1975. pap. 6.95 (ISBN 0-8256-3052-5, Quick Fox). Music Sales.

FURNITURE–BUILDING

see Furniture Making

FURNITURE–CATALOGS

Aaronson, Joseph. The Encyclopedia of Furniture. 1970. 53.00 (ISBN 0-7134-0802-2, Pub. by Batsford England). David & Charles.
Andrews, John. The Price Guide to Antique Furniture. 2nd ed. (Price Guide Ser.). (Illus.). 290p. 1979. Repr. of 1968 ed. 39.50 (ISBN 0-902028-70-7). Antique Collect.
--The Price Guide to Victorian, Edwardian & 1920's Furniture. (Price Guide Ser.). (Illus.). 218p. 1980. 39.50 (ISBN 0-902028-89-8). Antique Collect.
--The Price Guide to Victorian Furniture. (Price Guide Ser.). (Illus.). 346p. 1973. 21.50 (ISBN 0-902028-18-9). Antique Collect.
Conran's Catalog, 1981. (Illus.). 1981. pap. 3.00 (ISBN 0-686-30378-4, Mayflower Bks). Smith Pubs.
Delehanty, Suzanne & Pincus-Witten, Robert. Improbable Furniture. (Illus.). 48p. 1977. pap. 7.00 (ISBN 0-88454-022-7). U of Pa Contemp Art.
Foa, Linda & Brin, Geri. Kids' Stuff: Guide to the Best in Children's Furnishings. LC 78-14343. (Illus.). 1979. 17.95 (ISBN 0-394-41558-2); pap. 8.95 (ISBN 0-394-73658-3). Pantheon.
Gray, Stephen. Limbert Furniture. (Mission Furniture Catalogues Ser.: No. 4). 128p. 1981. pap. 9.95 (ISBN 0-940326-04-3). Turn of Cent.
Gray, Stephen, ed. Lifetime Furniture. (Mission Furniture Catalogues Ser.: No. 2). 112p. 1981. pap. 11.95 (ISBN 0-940326-02-7). Turn of Cent.
--Quaint Furniture. (Mission Furniture Catalogues Ser.: No. 1). 80p. 1981. pap. 8.95 (ISBN 0-940326-01-9). Turn of Cent.
--Roycroft Furniture. (Mission Furniture Catalogues: No. 3). 52p. 1981. pap. 6.50 (ISBN 0-940326-03-5). Turn of Cent.
Grotz, George. The Current Antique Furniture Style & Price Guide. LC 77-27673. 1979. 9.95 (ISBN 0-385-13165-8, Dolp). Doubleday.
Hennessey, James & Papanek, Victor. Nomadic Furniture One. LC 72-342. 1973. pap. 5.95 (ISBN 0-394-70228-X). Pantheon.
Nutting, W. Checklist of E. A. Reproductions. LC 73-96940. 1969. 3.95 (ISBN 0-87282-087-4). Century Hse.
Oehlberg, Barbara E. Buyer's Guide to Home Furnishings: The Market of Obsolescence. 1978. 6.95 (ISBN 0-533-03117-6). Vantage.
Stickley, Gustav. Stickley Craftsman Furniture Catalogs: Unabridged Reprints of Two Mission Furniture Catalogs-"Craftsman Furniture Made by Gustav Stickley" & "the Work of L. & J. G. Stickley". (Illus.). Date not set. 10.00 (ISBN 0-8446-5821-9). Peter Smith.
Stickley, Gustav, et al. Stickley Craftsman Furniture Catalogs. Orig. Title: Craftsman Furniture Made by Gustav Stickley the Work of L. & J.G. Stickley. 192p. 1979. pap. 5.00 (ISBN 0-486-23838-5). Dover.
Thonet. Thonet Bentwood & Other Furniture: The 1904 Illustrated Catalogue. 16.50 (ISBN 0-8446-5825-1). Peter Smith.
Thonet Co. Thonet Bentwood & Other Furniture: The 1904 Illustrated Catalogue & Supplements. (Illus.). 154p. 1980. pap. 8.95 (ISBN 0-486-24024-X). Dover.

FURNITURE–COLLECTORS AND COLLECTING

Andrews, John. The Price Guide to Antique Furniture. 2nd ed. (Price Guide Ser.). (Illus.). 290p. 1979. Repr. of 1968 ed. 39.50 (ISBN 0-902028-70-7). Antique Collect.
--The Price Guide to Victorian Furniture. (Price Guide Ser.). (Illus.). 346p. 1973. 21.50 (ISBN 0-902028-18-9). Antique Collect.
Antique Furniture Handbooks. Incl. Handbook No. 1. 3.95 (ISBN 0-87282-003-3); Handbook No. 2. 3.95 (ISBN 0-87282-004-1); Handbook No. 3. (ISBN 0-87282-005-X); Handbook No. 4. (ISBN 0-87282-006-8); Handbook No. 5. (ISBN 0-87282-007-6); Handbook No. 6. (ISBN 0-87282-008-4); Handbook No. 7. (ISBN 0-87282-009-2). 5.00 ea., nos. 1-4; 3.95 ea., nos. 5-7. Century Hse.
Antiques Magazine & Winchester, Alice, eds. Living with Antiques: A Treasury of Private Homes in America. 1963. 15.00 (ISBN 0-525-14793-4). Dutton.
Bishop, Robert. How to Know American Antique Furniture. 1973. pap. 8.50 (ISBN 0-525-47337-8). Dutton.
Blundell, Peter & Dunning, Phil. Marketplace Guide to Victorian Furniture. (Illus.). 1981. 17.95 (ISBN 0-89145-166-8). Collector Bks.
Blundell, Peter S. Marketplace Guide to Oak Furniture Styles & Values. (Illus.). 1980. 17.95 (ISBN 0-89145-141-2). Collector Bks.
Colonial, Williamsburg. The Williamsburg Collection of Antique Furnishing. LC 73-86811. 1974. 6.95 (ISBN 0-03-089492-1). HR&W.
Colonial Williamsburg Foundation Staff. The Williamsburg Collection of Antique Furnishings. LC 73-86811. (Decorative Art Ser). (Illus.). 128p. (Orig.). 1974. pap. 4.50 (ISBN 0-87935-017-2). Williamsburg.
Dolz, Renate. Furniture. (Collectors Library). 1977. pap. 2.50 (ISBN 0-445-04099-8). Popular Lib.
Farnam, Anne, et al. Furniture Collections of the Essex Institute. (E. I. Museum Booklet Ser.). (Illus.). 64p. (Orig.). 1981. 4.95 (ISBN 0-88389-102-6). Essex Inst.
Grotz, George. New Antiques. rev. ed. LC 73-78710. 1970. 7.95 (ISBN 0-385-01980-7). Doubleday.
Hayden, Arthur. Chats on Old Furniture: A Practical Guide for Collectors. 1979. Repr. of 1905 ed. lib. bdg. 65.00 (ISBN 0-8492-5346-2). R West.
Hyde, Bryden B. Bermuda's Antique Furniture & Silver. LC 76-157116. (Illus.). 1971. 15.00x (ISBN 0-938420-03-8). Md Hist.
Kane, Patricia E. Three Hundred Years of American Seating Furniture. Chairs & Beds from the Mabel Brady Garvan & Other Collections at Yale University. LC 75-9097. 1976. 29.95 (ISBN 0-8212-0678-8, 844225). NYGS.
McNerney, Kathryn. Victorian Furniture, Our American Heritage. (Illus.). 1981. 8.95 (ISBN 0-89145-164-1). Collector Bks.
Marsh, Moreton. Easy Expert in American Antiques: Knowing, Finding, Buying & Restoring Early American Furniture. rev. ed. LC 78-9050. Orig. Title: The Easy Expert in Collecting & Restoring American Antiques. 1978. 12.95 (ISBN 0-397-01287-X); pap. 7.95 (ISBN 0-397-01288-8). Har-Row.
Miller, Edgar G., Jr. American Antique Furniture, 2 vols. (Illus.). Set. 32.50 (ISBN 0-8446-2589-2). Peter Smith.
--American Antique Furniture, 2 Vols. (Illus.). 1966. pap. 8.95 ea.; Vol. 1. pap. (ISBN 0-486-21599-7); Vol. 2. pap. (ISBN 0-486-21600-4). Dover.
Naeve, Milo. Identifying American Furniture: Colonial to Contemporary. (Illus.). 102p. 1981. 11.95 (ISBN 0-910050-52-X). AASLH.
Nutting, Wallace. Wallace Nutting: Supreme Edition General Catalog. 1978. pap. 8.50 (ISBN 0-916838-09-9). Schiffer.
Oak Furniture Styles & Prices. rev. ed. 1980. pap. 7.95 (ISBN 0-87069-285-2). Wallace-Homestead.
Rodd, John. Repairing & Restoring Antique Furniture. 1976. 15.95 (ISBN 0-442-26970-6). Van Nos Reinhold.
Saunders, Richard. Collecting & Restoring Wicker Furniture. (Illus.). 1976. 7.95 (ISBN 0-517-52622-0). Crown.
Swedberg, Robert & Swedberg, Harriett. Victorian Furniture Styles & Prices, Bk. II. (Illus.). pap. 9.95 (ISBN 0-87069-327-1). Wallace-Homestead.
Symonds, Robert W., ed. Ornamental Designs of Chippendale. (Illus.). 1949. 9.50 (ISBN 0-85458-578-8). Transatlantic.
Thompson, Frances. The Complete Wicker Book. (Illus.). 1978. softbound 7.95 (ISBN 0-87069-211-9). Wallace-Homestead.
Thonet Co. Thonet Bentwood & Other Furniture: The 1904 Illustrated Catalogue & Supplements. (Illus.). 154p. 1980. pap. 8.95 (ISBN 0-486-24024-X). Dover.
Voss, Thomas M. Antique American Country Furniture: A Field Guide. LC 77-15898. (Illus.). 1978. 9.95 (ISBN 0-397-01219-5); pap. 6.95 (ISBN 0-397-01267-5). Lippincott.

FURNITURE–DESIGN

see Furniture Design

FURNITURE–DICTIONARIES

Antique Collectors' Club. Pictorial Dictionary of British Nineteenth Century Furniture Design. 583p. 1980. 69.50 (ISBN 0-902028-47-2). Antique Collect.
Aronson, Joseph. Encyclopedia of Furniture. rev. ed. (Illus.). (YA) (gr. 9 up). 1965. 11.95 (ISBN 0-517-03735-1). Crown.
Barber, E. A. & Lockwood, L. V. The Ceramic, Furniture & Silver Collectors' Glossary. (Architecture & Decorative Art Ser.). 1976. pap. 6.95 (ISBN 0-306-80049-7). Da Capo.
Filbee, Marjorie. The Connoisseur Dictionary of Country Furniture. new ed. (Illus.). 1977. 12.95 (ISBN 0-900305-17-7). Hearst Bks.
Gloag, John. A Short Dictionary of Furniture. 1976. pap. 14.95 (ISBN 0-04-749009-8). Allen Unwin.
Hoffman, Emanuel. Fairchild's Dictionary of Home Furnishings: Furniture, Accessories, Curtains & Draperies, Fabrics, Floor Coverings. new ed. Buck, Babs F. & Small, Verna, eds. LC 70-180155. (Illus.). 384p. 1974. lib. bdg. 25.00 (ISBN 0-87005-106-7). Fairchild.
Jay, E. Pictorial Dictionary of Nineteeth Century Furniture. (Illus.). 1980. 69.50 (ISBN 0-902028-47-2). Apollo.
Lockwood, Luke V. Furniture Collector's Glossary. LC 67-27460. (Architecture & Decorative Art Ser). 1967. Repr. of 1940 ed. lib. bdg. 12.50 (ISBN 0-306-70968-6). Da Capo.

FURNITURE–EXHIBITIONS

Barbour, Frederick K. & Barbour, Margaret R. Frederick K. & Margaret R. Barbour's Furniture Collection. (Illus.). 1963. 7.50 (ISBN 0-940748-14-2); pap. 5.00x (ISBN 0-940748-15-0); supplement 3.00 (ISBN 0-940748-16-9). Conn Hist Soc.
Dauterman, Carl C. & Watson, F. J. Wrightsman Collection, 2 vols. Incl. Vol. 3. Furniture, Snuff Boxes, Silver; Vol. 4. Porcelain. LC 66-10181. (Wrightsman Collection Ser). (Illus.). 865p. 1970. 65.00 set (ISBN 0-87099-105-1, Pub. by Metro Mus Art). NYGS.
Delehanty, Suzanne & Pincus-Witten, Robert. Improbable Furniture. (Illus.). 48p. 1977. pap. 7.00 (ISBN 0-88454-022-7). U of Pa Contemp Art.
Drexler, Arthur. Charles Eames: Furniture from the Design Collection. LC 73-76672. (Illus.). 56p. 1973. pap. 4.50 (ISBN 0-87070-314-5). Museum Mod Art.
Glaeser, Ludwig. Mies Van der Rohe: Furniture & Drawings. LC 76-24509. (Illus.). 1977. pap. 6.95 (ISBN 0-87070-555-5). Museum Mod Art.
Ott, Joseph K. John Brown House Loan Exhibition of Rhode Island Furniture. (Illus.). 1965. pap. 10.00 (ISBN 0-685-67652-8). RI Hist Soc.
Seymour, George D. George Dudley Seymour's Furniture Collection. (Illus.). 1958. 4.00x (ISBN 0-940748-19-3). Conn Hist Soc.

FURNITURE–HISTORY

Baroni, Daniele. The Furniture of Gerrit Thomas Rietveld. LC 77-17883. 1978. 16.95 (ISBN 0-8120-5201-3). Barron.
Battersby, Martin, et al. The History of Furniture. LC 76-7256. (Illus.). 1976. 29.95 (ISBN 0-688-03083-1). Morrow.
Clouston, R. S. English Furniture & Furniture Makers of the Eighteenth Century. (Illus.). 1977. Repr. of 1906 ed. 29.00 (ISBN 0-686-57965-8). Charles River Bks.
Denker, Bert & Denker, Ellen. The Rocking Chair Book. (Illus.). 1979. pap. 7.95 (ISBN 0-8317-7418-5, Mayflower Bks). Smith Pubs.
Early Country Furniture. (Americana Books Ser.). (Illus.). 1970. 1.50 (ISBN 0-911410-25-2). Applied Arts.
Fales, Dean A., Jr. American Painted Furniture Sixteen Sixty to Eighteen Eighty. (Illus.). 1979. pap. 13.95 (ISBN 0-525-47549-4). Dutton.
Fitzgerald, Oscar P. Three Centuries of American Furniture. (Illus.). 320p. 1981. 34.95 (ISBN 0-13-920371-0); pap. 16.95 (ISBN 0-13-920363-X). P-H.
Gandy, Charles & Zimmerman-Stidham, Susan. Contemporary Classics: Furniture of the Masters. (Architectural Record Ser.). (Illus.). 160p. 1981. 19.75 (ISBN 0-07-022760-8, P&RB). McGraw.
Gusler, Wallace B. Furniture of Williamsburg & Eastern Virginia, 1710-1790. LC 78-27282. (Illus.). 195p. 1979. 24.00 (ISBN 0-917046-05-6). VA Mus Fine Arts.
Hummel, Charles F. A Winterthur Guide to American Chippendale Furniture: Middle Atlantic & Southern Colonies. (Winterthur Ser.). (Illus.). 1976. 6.95 (ISBN 0-517-52783-9). Crown.
Killen, Geoffrey P. Ancient Egyptian Furniture, Vol. I (C.4000-1300 B.C.) (Illus.). 1980. 44.00x (ISBN 0-85668-095-8, Pub. by Aris & Phillips). Intl Schol Bk Serv.
Lucie-Smith, Edward. Furniture: A Concise History. (World of Art Ser.). (Illus.). 1979. 17.95 (ISBN 0-19-520145-0); pap. 9.95 (ISBN 0-19-520146-9). Oxford U Pr.
Madigan, Mary Jean S., intro. by. Eastlake-Influenced American Furniture, 1870-1890. LC 73-90034. (Illus.). 68p. 1974. pap. 5.00 (ISBN 0-87100-043-1, Pub. by Hudson River Mus). Pub Ctr Cult Res.
Peterson, Harold L. Picture Book of American Interiors: From Colonial Times to the Late Victorians. (Encore Edition). (Illus.). 1979. pap. 4.95 (ISBN 0-684-16918-5, SL861, ScribT). Scribner.
Quimby, Ian M., ed. American Furniture & Its Makers. LC 64-7642. (Winterthur Portfolio: No. 13). 1979. 20.00 (ISBN 0-226-92139-5). U of Chicago Pr.
Schiffer, Margaret B. Furniture & It's Makers of Chester County Pennsylvania. (Illus.). 434p. 1978. 35.00 (ISBN 0-916838-05-6). Schiffer.
Schwartz, Marvin D., et al. Furniture of John Henry Belter & the Rococo Revival. 1981. 24.95 (ISBN 0-525-93170-8). Dutton.
Sheldon, George W., ed. Artistic Country Seats, 2 vols, Vols. I & II. LC 78-17476. (Architecture & Decorative Arts: 1978). (Illus.). 1978. Repr. of 1887 ed. Set. lib. bdg. 125.00 (ISBN 0-306-70829-9); lib. bdg. 70.00 ea. Vol. I (ISBN 0-306-77598-0). Vol. II (ISBN 0-306-77599-9). Da Capo.
Synge, Lanto. Antique Furniture. LC 77-13369. (Arco Color Ser.). (Illus.). 1978. lib. bdg. 8.95 (ISBN 0-668-04471-3); pap. 5.95 (ISBN 0-668-04482-9). Arco.
Tracy, Berry. Nineteenth-Century America: Furniture & Other Decorative Arts. LC 77-109965. (Illus.). 272p. 1973. pap. 6.95 (ISBN 0-87099-005-5, Pub. by Metro Mus Art). NYGS.
Wilk, Christopher. Thonet: One Hundred Fifty Years of Furniture. (Furniture & Design Ser.). 1980. 18.95 (ISBN 0-8120-5384-2). Barron.

FURNITURE–MODELS

Daniele, Joseph W. Building Colonial Furnishings, Miniatures, & Folk Art. LC 76-17006. (Illus.). 256p. 1976. 17.95 (ISBN 0-8117-0451-3). Stackpole.
Hodges, Lewis H. Building Antique Doll House Furniture from Scratch. (Orig.). 1980. 14.95 (ISBN 0-8306-9946-5); pap. 9.95 (ISBN 0-8306-1240-8, 1240). TAB Bks.
Johnson, Audrey. Furnishing Dolls' Houses. LC 72-75079. (Illus.). 284p. 1972. 23.00 (ISBN 0-8231-3029-0). Branford.
Pipe, Ann K. Mastercrafting Miniature Rooms & Furniture: Techniques for the Serious Beginner. 200p. 1979. 18.95 (ISBN 0-442-26557-3). Van Nos Reinhold.
--Reproducing Furniture in Miniature. LC 79-50986. (Illus.). 1979. pap. 5.95 (ISBN 0-8092-7149-4). Contemp Bks.
Schiffer, Herbert & Schiffer, Peter. Miniature Antique Furniture. (Illus.). 288p. 1972. 20.00 (ISBN 0-87098-049-1). Livingston.
Williams, Guy R. Making a Miniature House. (Illus.). 1964. 9.50x (ISBN 0-19-273090-8). Oxford U Pr.
Worrell, Estelle A. Doll House Book. (Illus.). (gr. 7 up). 1964. 9.95 (ISBN 0-442-09550-3). Van Nos Reinhold.

FURNITURE–REPAIRING

see also Furniture Finishing

Albers, Vernon M. The Repair & Reupholstering of Old Furniture. LC 69-13029. 1969. 7.95 (ISBN 0-498-06911-7). A S Barnes.

--The Repair & Reupholstering of Old Furniture. LC 69-13029. (Large Type Editions Ser.). (Illus.). 160p. 1975. 7.95 (ISBN 0-498-01597-1). A S Barnes.

Alth, Max & Alth, Charlotte. The Furniture Buyer's Handbook: How to Buy, Arrange, Maintain & Repair Furniture. (Illus.). 1980. 14.95 (ISBN 0-8027-0636-3); pap. 9.95 (ISBN 0-8027-7155-6). Walker & Co.

Berger, Robert. All About Antiquing & Restoring Furniture. 1974. pap. 5.95 (ISBN 0-8015-0138-5, Hawthorn). Dutton.

Blandford, Percy. Do-It-Yourselfer's Guide to Furniture Repair & Refinishing. (Illus.). 1977. 9.95 (ISBN 0-8306-7894-8); pap. 5.95 (ISBN 0-8306-6894-2, 894). TAB Bks.

Brann, Donald R. How to Repair, Refinish & Reupholster Furniture-Caning Simplified. rev. ed. LC 66-27694. 1976. lib. bdg. 5.95 (ISBN 0-87733-023-9); pap. 3.00 (ISBN 0-87733-623-7). Easi-Bild.

Cox, Dorothy. Modern Upholstery. (Illus.). 152p. 1980. pap. 11.75x (ISBN 0-7135-1599-6, LTB). Sportshelf.

Editors of Time-Life Books. Repairing Furniture. (Home Repair & Improvement). (Illus.). 128p. 1981. 10.95 (ISBN 0-8094-2438-X). Time-Life.

Egge, Ruth S. Recycled with Flair: How to Remodel Old Furniture & Flea Market Finds. (Illus.). 1980. 10.95 (ISBN 0-698-11024-2); pap. 5.95 (ISBN 0-698-11031-5). Coward.

Family Handyman Magazine Editors. The Complete Book of Furniture Repair & Refinishing. rev. ed. 1981. 17.95 (ISBN 0-684-16839-1, ScribT). Scribner.

Farwell, William. Easy Does It Furniture Restoration: The Vermont Way. LC 70-113905. (Illus.). 1962. pap. 2.50 (ISBN 0-8048-0156-8). C E Tuttle.

Freeman, Larry. How to Restore Antiques. LC 60-13416. 1960. pap. 3.50 (ISBN 0-87282-049-1). Century Hse.

Grime, Kitty. Illustrated Guide to Furniture Repair & Restoration. LC 80-10795. (Illus.). 156p. 1980. lib. bdg. 17.95 (ISBN 0-668-04936-7, 4936-7). Arco.

Grotz, George. Furniture Doctor. LC 62-7640. 7.95 (ISBN 0-385-01444-9). Doubleday.

Hayward, Charles. Antique Furniture Repairs. LC 76-5223. (Illus.). 128p. 1977. 7.95 (ISBN 0-684-14720-3, ScribT). Scribner.

Hilts, Len & Hilts, Kay. Furniture Repair & Restoration. (Illus.). 144p. 1982. 17.95 (ISBN 0-932944-51-5); pap. text ed. 6.95 (ISBN 0-932944-52-3). CRC Pr.

Johnson, Edwin. Restoring Antique Furniture. LC 81-50987. (Illus.). 160p. 1981. 12.95 (ISBN 0-8069-5430-2); lib. bdg. 11.69 (ISBN 0-8069-5431-0); pap. 6.95 (ISBN 0-8069-8998-X). Sterling.

Johnson, Lorraine. How to Restore, & Repair Almost Everything. LC 77-8135. 1977. pap. 7.95 (ISBN 0-02-080560-8, Collier). Macmillan.

Jones, Peter. Fixing Furniture. Machtiger, B., ed. LC 79-13915. (Home Environment "Help" Bks). (Illus.). 1979. pap. 4.95 (ISBN 0-88421-067-7). New Century.

Jones, Thomas H. Furniture Fix & Finish Guide. (Illus.). 272p. 1980. 13.95 (ISBN 0-8359-2227-8). Reston.

Mackercher, V. M. The Woodworker's Furniture Construction - Repair Bible. (Illus.). 1979. 14.95 (ISBN 0-8306-9713-6); pap. 8.95 (ISBN 0-8306-1134-7, 1134). TAB Bks.

Marshall, Mel. How to Repair, Reupholster & Refinish Furniture. LC 79-4706. (Popular Science Bk.). (Illus.). 1979. 13.95 (ISBN 0-06-013035-0, HarpT). Har-Row.

Meyers, L. Donald & Demske, Richard. Furniture Repair & Refinishing. (Illus.). 1978. text ed. 14.95 (ISBN 0-87909-273-4); pap. 6.95 (ISBN 0-87909-290-4). Reston.

Nunn, Richard V. & Nunn, Beverly J. Furniture Repair & Refinishing. LC 75-2876. (Family Guidebooks Ser.). (Illus.). 96p. 1975. pap. 2.95 (ISBN 0-8487-0378-2). Oxmoor Hse.

Palmer, Frederick. Practical Upholstering: The Complete Guide to Authentic Renovation of Late 19th & Early 20th Century Furniture. LC 80-51766. (Illus.). 288p. 1980. 19.95 (ISBN 0-8128-2753-8). Stein & Day.

Perry, L. Day. Seat Weaving: A Manual for Furniture Fixers. (Illus.). 1977. pap. 2.95 (ISBN 0-684-15270-3, SL741, ScribT). Scribner.

Rowland, Tom. Restoring & Renovating Antique Furniture. 176p. 1980. pap. 5.95 (ISBN 0-442-21945-8). Van Nos Reinhold.

Rudman, Jack. Foreman Furniture Maintainer. (Career Examination Ser.: C-2023). (Cloth bdg. avail. on request). pap. 8.00 (ISBN 0-8373-2023-2). Natl Learning.

--Furniture Maintainer. (Career Examination Ser.: C-1059). (Cloth bdg. avail. on request). pap. 8.00 (ISBN 0-8373-1059-8). Natl Learning.

--Furniture Maintainer's Helper. (Career Examination Ser.: C-282). (Cloth bdg. avail. on request). pap. 8.00 (ISBN 0-8373-0282-X). Natl Learning.

Saunders, Richard. Collecting & Restoring Wicker Furniture. (Illus.). 1976. 7.95 (ISBN 0-517-52622-0). Crown.

Taubes, Frederic. Restoring & Preserving Antiques. (Illus.). 160p. 1976. pap. 7.95 (ISBN 0-8230-4544-7). Watson-Guptill.

Tierney, William F. Modern Upholstering Methods. (gr. 9 up). 1965. text ed. 14.00 (ISBN 0-87345-482-0). McKnight.

FURNITURE-RESTORATION

see Furniture-Repairing; Furniture Finishing

FURNITURE-CANADA

Shea, John G. Antique Country Furniture of North America, & Details of Its Construction. 228p. 1980. pap. 9.95 (ISBN 0-442-25156-4). Van Nos Reinhold.

Webster, Donald B. English-Canadian Furniture of the Georgian Period. (Illus.). 1979. 27.50 (ISBN 0-07-082980-2). McGraw.

FURNITURE-CHINA

Beurdeley, Michel. Chinese Furniture. Watson, Katherine, tr. LC 78-84654. (Illus.). 1980. 60.00 (ISBN 0-87011-387-9). Kodansha.

Ecke, Gustav. Chinese Domestic Furniture. LC 62-21540. (Illus.). 1962. boxed 59.50 (ISBN 0-8048-0098-7). C E Tuttle.

Kates, George. Chinese Household Furniture. (Illus.). 1948. pap. 3.50 (ISBN 0-486-20958-X). Dover.

Kates, George N. Chinese Household Furniture. (Illus.). 8.00 (ISBN 0-8446-2351-2). Peter Smith.

FURNITURE-EUROPE

Huth, Hans. Roentgen Furniture: Abraham & David Roentgen, European Cabinet Makers. (Illus.). 260p. 1974. 100.00x (ISBN 0-85667-003-0, Pub. by Sotheby Parke Bernet England). Biblio Dist.

Margon, Lester. Masterpieces of European Furniture Thirteen Hundred to Eighteen Forty. 1968. 16.50 (ISBN 0-8038-0151-3). Hastings.

Payne, Christopher. The Price Guide to Decorative Nineteenth Century European Furniture. (Price Guide Ser.). (Illus.). 550p. 1981. 59.50 (ISBN 0-902028-91-X). Antique Collect.

Thorne, Mrs. James W. European Rooms in Miniature. 6th ed. (Illus.). 62p. 1948. pap. 2.50 (ISBN 0-86559-002-8). Art Inst Chi.

FURNITURE-FRANCE

De Fusco, Renato. Le Corbusier, Designer--Furniture, 1929. LC 77-81368. 1977. 12.95 (ISBN 0-8120-5148-3). Barron.

Grotz, George. The Current Antique Furniture Style & Price Guide. LC 77-27673. 1979. 9.95 (ISBN 0-385-13165-8, Dolp). Doubleday.

Szabolcsi, Hedvig. French Furniture in Hungary. (Illus.). 1964. 3.75x (ISBN 0-8002-1433-1). Intl Pubns Serv.

Viollet-Le-Duc, Eugene E. Dictionnaire Raisonne Du Mobilier Francais De L'epoque Carlovingienne a la Renaissance, 6 Vols. 2nd ed. LC 76-153606. (Illus.). Repr. of 1875 ed. Set. lib. bdg. 345.00 (ISBN 0-404-09750-2); lib. bdg. 57.50 ea. Vol. 1 (ISBN 0-404-09751-0). Vol. 2 (ISBN 0-404-09752-9). Vol. 3 (ISBN 0-404-09753-7). Vol. 4 (ISBN 0-404-09754-5). Vol. 5 (ISBN 0-404-09755-3). Vol. 6 (ISBN 0-404-09756-1). AMS Pr.

FURNITURE-GREAT BRITAIN

Agius, Pauline. British Furniture: 1880-1915. (Illus.). 195p. 1977. 39.50 (ISBN 0-902028-76-6). Antique Collect.

Andrews, J. Price Guide to Victorian, Edwardian & Nineteen Twenty Furniture. (Illus.). 1980. 39.50 (ISBN 0-902028-89-8). Apollo.

--Price Guide to Victorian Furniture. (Illus.). 1973. 21.50 (ISBN 0-902028-18-9). Apollo.

Antique Collectors' Club. Pictorial Dictionary of British Nineteenth Century Furniture Design. 583p. 1980. 69.50 (ISBN 0-902028-47-2). Antique Collect.

Brackett, Oliver. English Furniture. 79p. 1980. Repr. lib. bdg. 15.00 (ISBN 0-89760-042-8). Telegraph Bks.

Cescinsky, H. English Furniture from Gothic to Sheraton. (Illus.). 17.50 (ISBN 0-8446-1829-2). Peter Smith.

Cescinsky, Herbert. English Furniture: From Gothic to Sheraton. (Illus.). 1968. pap. 10.00 (ISBN 0-486-21929-1). Dover.

--Gentle Art of Faking Furniture. LC 65-12295. (Illus.). 1967. pap. 7.95 (ISBN 0-486-21862-7). Dover.

Chinnery, V. Oak Furniture, the British Tradition. (Illus.). 1979. 69.50 (ISBN 0-902028-61-8). Apollo.

Chinnery, Victor. Oak Furniture, the British Tradition. (Illus.). 580p. 1979. 69.50 (ISBN 0-902028-61-8). Antique Collect.

Clouston, Kate W. The Chippendale Period in English Furniture. (Illus.). 1976. Repr. 25.00x (ISBN 0-7158-1127-4). Charles River Bks.

Clouston, R. S. English Furniture & Furniture Makers of the Eighteenth Century. (Illus.). 1977. Repr. of 1906 ed. 29.00 (ISBN 0-686-57965-8). Charles River Bks.

Dean, Margery. English Antique Furniture 1450-1850. 2nd ed. LC 78-670090. (Illus.). 1976. pap. 5.00x (ISBN 0-85036-020-X). Intl Pubns Serv.

Dunsworth, Charles E. A Treasury of Old & Historical American & British Furniture. (Illus.). 1979. deluxe ed. 41.55 (ISBN 0-930582-33-0). Gloucester Art.

Fiske, Willard M. The Fully Illustrated Scientific Book of British Furniture. (Illus.). 151p. 1981. 69.75 (ISBN 0-86650-012-X). Gloucester Art.

Gilbert, Christopher. Late Georgian & Regency Furniture. (Country Life Collector's Guide). 4.95 (ISBN 0-600-43575-X). Transatlantic.

Grotz, George. The Current Antique Furniture Style & Price Guide. LC 77-27673. 1979. 9.95 (ISBN 0-385-13165-8, Dolp). Doubleday.

Heal, Ambrose. The London Furniture Makers, 1660-1840. LC 72-87434. (Illus.). 320p. 1973. pap. 6.00 (ISBN 0-486-22903-3). Dover.

Joy, Edward. Pictorial Dictionary of British Nineteenth Century Furniture Designs. (Illus.). 578p. 1980. 59.50 (ISBN 0-686-65051-4). Hacker.

Joy, Edward T. English Furniture Eighteen Hundred to Eighteen Fifty-One. (Illus.). 318p. 1977. 60.00 (ISBN 0-85667-031-6, Pub. by Sotheby Parke Bernet England). Biblio Dist.

Learoyd, Stan. Guide to English Antique Furniture: Construction & Decoration 1500-1910. 128p. 1981. 12.95 (ISBN 0-442-25952-2). Van Nos Reinhold.

Negus, Arthur. Going for a Song: An Expert's Informal Guide to English Antiques. Robertson, Max, ed. LC 72-163886. (Illus.). 1972. 6.95 (ISBN 0-8008-3290-6). Taplinger.

Sheraton, Thomas. Cabinet Maker & Upholsterer's Drawing Book. (Illus.). 352p. 1972. pap. 7.95 (ISBN 0-486-22255-1). Dover.

Sigworth, Oliver. Four Styles of a Decade, 1740-1750. LC 60-15544. (Illus.). 1960. pap. 3.00 (ISBN 0-87104-078-6). NY Pub Lib.

Steer, Francis W., ed. Farm & Cottage Inventories of Mid - Essex, 1635 to 1749. (Illus.). 305p. 1969. 22.50x (ISBN 0-8476-1376-3). Rowman.

Symonds, R. W. English Furniture from Charles II - George II. (Illus.). 269p. 1981. 89.50 (ISBN 0-902028-95-2). Antique Collect.

Toller, Jane. English Country Furniture. LC 73-46. (Illus.). 200p. 1973. 8.95 (ISBN 0-498-01366-9). A S Barnes.

Webster, Donald B. English-Canadian Furniture of the Georgian Period. (Illus.). 1979. 27.50 (ISBN 0-07-082980-2). McGraw.

Wills, Geoffrey. Craftsmen & Cabinet-Makers of Classic English Furniture. 136p. (Orig.). 1974. 13.50 (ISBN 0-85152-941-0). Herman Pub.

--English Furniture Seventeen Sixty to Nineteen Hundred. (Illus.). 1980. 17.95 (ISBN 0-8069-9220-4, Pub by Guinness Superlatives England). Sterling.

FURNITURE-HUNGARY

Csillery, Klara K. Hungarian Village Furniture. 1972. 4.25x (ISBN 0-8002-0828-5). Intl Pubns Serv.

Szabolcsi, Hedvig. French Furniture in Hungary. (Illus.). 1964. 3.75x (ISBN 0-8002-1433-1). Intl Pubns Serv.

FURNITURE-UNITED STATES

Baird, Henry C. Victorian Gothic & Renaissance Revival Furniture. (The Athenaeum Library of Nineteenth Century America). (Illus.). 1977. Repr. of 1868 ed. text ed. 20.00 (ISBN 0-89257-019-9). Am Life Foun.

Baltimore Painted Furniture: 1800-1840. LC 72-77869. (Illus.). 1972. pap. 8.50 (ISBN 0-912298-32-4). Baltimore Mus.

Bishop, Robert. How to Know American Antique Furniture. 1973. pap. 8.50 (ISBN 0-525-47337-8). Dutton.

Blanchard, Roberta R. How to Restore & Decorate Chairs in Early American Styles. Orig. Title: How to Restore & Decorate Chairs. (Illus.). 128p. 1981. pap. price not set (ISBN 0-486-24177-7). Dover.

Burton, E. Milby. Charleston Furniture, 1700-1825. 2nd ed. LC 73-120917. Orig. Title: Contributions from the Charleston Museum: XII. (Illus.). 1970. lib. bdg. 19.50 (ISBN 0-87249-198-6). U of SC Pr.

Cathers, David M. Furniture of the American Arts & Crafts Movement: Stickley & Roycroft Mission Oak. 1981. 9.95 (ISBN 0-453-00397-4, H397). NAL.

Davidson, Marshall. The Bantam Illustrated Guide to Early American Furniture. 432p. 1980. 7.95 (ISBN 0-553-01222-3). Bantam.

Dunsworth, Charles E. A Treasury of Old & Historical American & British Furniture. (Illus.). 1979. deluxe ed. 41.55 (ISBN 0-930582-33-0). Gloucester Art.

Early Country Furniture. (Americana Books Ser.). (Illus.). 1970. 1.50 (ISBN 0-911410-25-2). Applied Arts.

Fairbanks, Jonathan & Bates, Elizabeth B. American Furniture Sixteen Twenty to the Present. (Illus.). 576p. 1981. 50.00 (ISBN 0-399-90096-9). Marek.

Fales, Dean A., Jr. American Painted Furniture Sixteen Sixty to Eighteen Eighty. (Illus.). 1979. pap. 13.95 (ISBN 0-525-47549-4). Dutton.

--American Painted Furniture, 1660-1880. LC 75-186361. (Illus.). 1972. 45.00 (ISBN 0-525-05387-5). Hennessey.

Felt, Joseph B. Customs of New England. 1967. Repr. of 1853 ed. 19.00 (ISBN 0-8337-1105-9). B Franklin.

Fitzgerald, Oscar P. Three Centuries of American Furniture. (Illus.). 320p. 1981. 34.95 (ISBN 0-13-920371-0); pap. 16.95 (ISBN 0-13-920363-X). P-H.

Forman, H. Chandlee. Old Buildings, Gardens & Furniture in Tidewater, Maryland. LC 67-17538. (Illus.). 1967. 12.50 (ISBN 0-87033-075-6, Pub. by Tidewater). Cornell Maritime.

Gilbert, Christopher. The Life & Work of Thomas Chippendale, 2 vols. (Illus.). 1979. case 100.00 (ISBN 0-02-543250-8). Vol. 1 (ISBN 0-02-543420-9). Vol. 2 (ISBN 0-02-543430-6). Macmillan.

Green, Henry D. Furniture of the Georgia Piedmont Before Eighteen Thirty. Farnham, Katherine G., ed. LC 76-20949. (Illus.). 144p. (Orig.). pap. 5.00 (ISBN 0-939802-10-4). High Mus Art.

Greenlaw, Barry A. New England Furniture at Williamsburg. LC 73-90536. (Decorative Arts Ser). (Illus., Orig.). 1974. pap. 5.95 (ISBN 0-87935-019-9). Williamsburg.

--New England Furniture at Williamsburg. abr. ed. LC 74-18017. (Decorative Arts Ser). (Illus.). 20p. 1974. pap. 0.25 (ISBN 0-87935-022-9). Williamsburg.

--New England Furniture at Williamsburg. LC 73-90536. 1975. 10.00x (ISBN 0-8139-0549-4, Williamsburg Decorative Arts Ser.). U Pr of Va.

Grotz, George. New Antiques. rev. ed. LC 73-78710. 1970. 7.95 (ISBN 0-385-01980-7). Doubleday.

Gusler, Wallace. Furniture of Eastern Virginia. LC 78-3499. (Illus.). 1978. pap. 2.00x (ISBN 0-917046-04-8). VA Mus Fine Arts.

Gusler, Wallace B. Furniture of Williamsburg & Eastern Virginia, 1710-1790. LC 78-27282. (Illus.). 195p. 1979. 24.00 (ISBN 0-917046-05-6). VA Mus Fine Arts.

Hagerty, Francis. Make Your Own Antiques. (Illus., Orig.). 1975. pap. 5.95 (ISBN 0-316-33783-8). Little.

Handberg, Ejner. Shop Drawings of Shaker Furniture & Woodenware, Vol. 1. LC 73-83797. 96p. 1973. pap. 4.95 (ISBN 0-912944-09-9). Berkshire Traveller.

Hanks, David. Innovative Furniture in America: From 1800 to the Present. (Illus.). 250p. 1981. text ed. 30.00 (ISBN 0-8180-0450-9). Horizon.

Hazen. Encyclopedia of E. A. Trades. 1970. 10.00 (ISBN 0-87282-073-4). Century Hse.

Hummel, Charles F. A Winterthur Guide to American Chippendale Furniture: Middle Atlantic & Southern Colonies. (Winterthur Ser.). (Illus.). 1976. 6.95 (ISBN 0-517-52783-9). Crown.

Kane, Patricia E. Three Hundred Years of American Seating Furniture. Chairs & Beds from the Mabel Brady Garvan & Other Collections at Yale University. LC 75-9097. 1976. 29.95 (ISBN 0-8212-0678-8, 844225). NYGS.

Kettell, Russell H. Pine Furniture of Early New England. 1929. 15.00 (ISBN 0-486-20145-7). Dover.

Kettell, Russell H., ed. Early American Rooms Sixteen Fifty-Sixteen Fifty-Eight. (Illus.). 1966. pap. 6.95 (ISBN 0-486-21633-0). Dover.

Kirk, John T. Connecticut Furniture, Seventeenth & Eighteenth Centuries. (Illus.). 1967. pap. 10.00x (ISBN 0-686-00357-8). Wadsworth Atheneum.

--Early American Furniture. LC 71-111232. (Illus.). 1970. pap. 7.95 (ISBN 0-394-70646-3). Knopf.

Kovel, Ralph & Kovel, Terry. American Country Furniture: 1780-1875. (Illus.). 1965. 10.00 (ISBN 0-517-09737-0). Crown.

Louie, Elaine. The Manhattan Home Furnishings Shopping Guide. 1979. pap. 5.95 (ISBN 0-02-080730-9, Collier). Macmillan.

Madigan, Mary Jean S., intro. by. Eastlake-Influenced American Furniture, 1870-1890. LC 73-90034. (Illus.). 68p. 1974. pap. 5.00 (ISBN 0-87100-043-1, Pub. by Hudson River Mus). Pub Ctr Cult Res.

Margon, Lester. Construction of American Furniture Treasures. (Illus.). 168p. 1975. pap. 5.00 (ISBN 0-486-23056-2). Dover.

--Construction of American Furniture Treasures. (Illus.). 9.50 (ISBN 0-8446-5220-2). Peter Smith.

--More American Furniture Treasures. 1971. 16.50 (ISBN 0-8038-0163-7). Hastings.

--More American Furniture Treasures. 15.00 (ISBN 0-8038-0163-7). Architectural.
Marlow, A. W. The Early American Furniture Maker's Manual. (Illus.). 160p. 1973. 12.95 (ISBN 0-02-579810-3). Macmillan.
Marsh, Moreton. Easy Expert in American Antiques: Knowing, Finding, Buying & Restoring Early American Furniture. rev. ed. LC 78-9050. Orig. Title: The Easy Expert in Collecting & Restoring American Antiques. 1978. 12.95 (ISBN 0-397-01287-X); pap. 7.95 (ISBN 0-397-01288-8). Har-Row.
Meader, Robert F. Illustrated Guide to Shaker Furniture. pap. 5.00 (ISBN 0-486-22819-3). Dover.
Miller, Edgar G., Jr. American Antique Furniture, 2 vols. (Illus.). Set. 32.50 (ISBN 0-8446-2589-2). Peter Smith.
--American Antique Furniture, 2 Vols. (Illus.). 1966. pap. 8.95 ea.; Vol. 1. pap. (ISBN 0-486-21599-7); Vol. 2. pap. (ISBN 0-486-21600-4). Dover.
Morningstar, Connie. Early Utah Furniture. (Illus.). 93p. 1976. 9.95 (ISBN 0-87421-087-9). Utah St U Pr.
Morse, John D., ed. Country Cabinetwork & Simple City Furniture. LC 77-114194. (Winterthur Conference Report 1969). (Illus.). 1970. 4.50 (ISBN 0-8139-0298-3, Pub. by Winterthur Museum). U Pr of Va.
Naeve, Milo. Identifying American Furniture: Colonial to Contemporary. LC 81-3524. (Illus.). 102p. Date not set. cancelled (ISBN 0-910050-52-X). AASLH.
Noyes, Eliot F. Organic Design in Home Furnishings. LC 70-86424. (Museum of Modern Art Publications in Reprint Ser). (Illus.). 1970. Repr. of 1941 ed. 14.00 (ISBN 0-405-01540-2). Arno.
Nutting, Wallace. Furniture of the Pilgrim Century, 2 Vols. (Illus.). Set. 20.00 (ISBN 0-8446-2672-4). Peter Smith.
--Furniture of the Pilgrim Century, 2 Vols. (Illus.). 1965. pap. 5.00 ea.; Vol. 1. pap. (ISBN 0-486-21470-2); Vol. 2. pap. (ISBN 0-486-21471-0). Dover.
--Furniture Treasury, 3 Vols. (Illus.). Vols. 1 & 2 In 1. 29.95 (ISBN 0-02-590980-0); Vol. 3. 24.95 (ISBN 0-02-591040-X). Macmillan.
O'Neill, James M. Early American Furniture. (gr. 7 up). 1963. text ed. 14.00 (ISBN 0-87345-045-0). McKnight.
Ormsbee, Thomas Hamilton. Early American Furniture Makers. LC 70-174089. 183p. 1975. Repr. of 1930 ed. 24.00 (ISBN 0-8103-4086-0). Gale.
Osburn, Burl N. & Osburn, Bernice B. Measured Drawings of Early American Furniture. LC 74-79936. (Illus.). 96p. 1975. pap. 3.50 (ISBN 0-486-23057-0). Dover.
Ott, Joseph K. John Brown House Loan Exhibition of Rhode Island Furniture. (Illus.). 1965. pap. 10.00 (ISBN 0-685-67652-8). RI Hist Soc.
Peterson, Harold L. Picture Book of American Interiors: From Colonial Times to the Late Victorians. (Encore Edition). (Illus.). 1979. pap. 4.95 (ISBN 0-684-16918-5, SL861, ScribT). Scribner.
Plain & Elegant, Rich & Common: Documented New Hampshire Furniture, 1750-1850. LC 79-13568. (Illus.). 153p. 1979. pap. 10.00 (ISBN 0-915916-09-6). U Pr of New Eng.
Quimby, Ian M., ed. American Furniture & Its Makers. LC 64-7642. (Winterthur Portfolio: No. 13). 1979. 20.00 (ISBN 0-226-92139-5). U of Chicago Pr.
Rogers, Meyric R. American Interior Design: The Traditions & Development of Domestic Design from Colonial Times to the Present. LC 75-22838. (America in Two Centuries Ser). (Illus.). 1976. Repr. of 1947 ed. 23.00x (ISBN 0-405-07709-2). Arno.
Sack, Albert. Fine Points of Furniture: Early America. 1950. 12.95 (ISBN 0-517-00148-9). Crown.
Salomonsky, Verna C. Masterpieces of Furniture. (Illus.). 11.50 (ISBN 0-8446-2856-5). Peter Smith.
--Masterpieces of Furniture in Photographs & Measured Drawings. rev. ed. (Illus.). 1953. pap. 5.00 (ISBN 0-486-21381-1). Dover.
Santore, Charles. The Windsor Style in America: A Pictorial Study of the History & Regional Characteristics of the Most Popular Furniture Form of 18th Century America, 1730-1830. Voss, Thomas M., ed. (Illus.). 204p. 1981. 22.50 (ISBN 0-89471-136-9); lib. bdg. 42.90 (ISBN 0-89471-137-7). Running Pr.
Schiffer, Margaret B. Furniture & It's Makers of Chester County Pennsylvania. (Illus.). 434p. 1978. 35.00 (ISBN 0-916838-05-6). Schiffer.
Schwartz, Marvin D. American Furniture of the Colonial Period. LC 76-18763. (Illus.). 1976. 6.95 (ISBN 0-87099-149-3). Metro Mus Art.
Shackleton, Robert & Shackleton, Elizabeth. Quest of the Colonial. LC 72-99075. (Illus.). 1970. Repr. of 1907 ed. 24.00 (ISBN 0-8103-3574-3). Gale.
Shea, John C. The Pennsylvania Dutch & Their Furniture. 240p. 1980. 19.95 (ISBN 0-442-27546-3). Van Nos Reinhold.
Shea, John G. American Shakers & Their Furniture. 1971. 17.95 (ISBN 0-442-27541-2). Van Nos Reinhold.
--Antique Country Furniture of North America, & Details of Its Construction. 228p. 1980. pap. 9.95 (ISBN 0-442-25156-4). Van Nos Reinhold.
Snyder, John J., Jr., ed. Philadelphia Furniture & Its Makers. LC 75-10932. 160p. 1975. 12.95x (ISBN 0-87663-250-9); pap. 7.95 (ISBN 0-87663-921-X). Universe.
Taylor, Lonn & Warren, David B. Texas Furniture: The Cabinetmakers & Their Work, 1840-1880. LC 75-20391. (Illus.). 399p. 1975. 40.00 (ISBN 0-292-73801-3). U of Tex Pr.
Thorne, Mrs. James W. American Rooms in Miniature. 7th ed. (Illus.). 74p. 1941. pap. 2.50 (ISBN 0-86559-001-X). Art Inst Chi.
Tinkham, Sandra S., ed. Catalog of Furniture & Decorative Accessories. (Index of American Design Ser.: Pt. 6). (Orig.). 1979. pap. 30.00x (ISBN 0-914146-73-4); incl. color microfiche 575.00x (ISBN 0-914146-72-6). Somerset Hse.
Tracy, Berry. Nineteenth-Century America: Furniture & Other Decorative Arts. LC 77-109965. (Illus.). 272p. 1973. pap. 6.95 (ISBN 0-87099-005-5, Pub. by Metro Mus Art). NYGS.
Tracy, Berry B. Federal Furniture & Decorative Arts of Boscobel. Black, Mary, ed. (Illus.). 168p. 1981. 40.00 (ISBN 0-8109-0917-0). Abrams.
Trent, Robert, ed. Pilgrim Century Furniture: An Historical Survey. LC 76-5095. (Antiques Magazine Library). (Illus.). 168p. 1976. 12.95x (ISBN 0-87663-239-8); pap. 7.95 (ISBN 0-87663-946-5). Universe.
Voss, Thomas M. Antique American Country Furniture: A Field Guide. LC 77-15898. (Illus.). 1978. 9.95 (ISBN 0-397-01219-5); pap. 6.95 (ISBN 0-397-01267-5). Lippincott.
Waring, Janet. Early American Stencil Decorations. LC 68-20904. (Illus.). 1968. 3.95 (ISBN 0-87282-094-7). Century Hse.
--Early American Stencils on Walls & Furniture. 147p. 1937. pap. 6.95 (ISBN 0-486-21906-2). Dover.
Williams, H. Lionel. Country Furniture of Early America. LC 76-42137. (Illus.). 1978. pap. 7.95 (ISBN 0-498-02045-2). A S Barnes.

FURNITURE, BUILT-IN
see Built-In Furniture

FURNITURE, SHAKER

Andrews, Edward D. & Andrews, F. Shaker Furniture: The Craftmanship of an American Communal Sect. (Illus.). 9.00 (ISBN 0-8446-1537-4). Peter Smith.
Andrews, Edward D. & Andrews, Faith. Religion In Wood: A Book of Shaker Furniture. LC 66-12722. (Illus.). 128p. 1966. 7.95x (ISBN 0-253-17360-4). Ind U Pr.
--Shaker Furniture: The Craftsmanship of an American Communal Sect. (Illus.). pap. 4.00 (ISBN 0-486-20679-3). Dover.
Handberg, Ejner. Measured Drawings of Shaker Furniture & Woodenware. LC 80-67765. (Illus.). 86p. (Orig.). 1980. pap. 5.95 (ISBN 0-912944-63-3). Berkshire Traveller.
--Shop Drawings of Shaker Furniture & Woodenware, Vol. 2. LC 73-83797. 1975. pap. 4.95 (ISBN 0-912944-29-3). Berkshire Traveller.
Kassay, John. The Book of Shaker Furniture. LC 79-4017. (Illus.). 1980. 40.00 (ISBN 0-87023-275-4). U of Mass Pr.
Meader, Robert F. Illustrated Guide to Shaker Furniture. 10.00 (ISBN 0-8446-4585-0). Peter Smith.
Moser, Thomas. How to Build Shaker Furniture. LC 76-46809. (Illus.). 224p. 1980. pap. 7.95 (ISBN 0-8069-8392-2). Sterling.
--How to Build Shaker Furniture. LC 76-46809. (Illus.). 1979. 14.95 (ISBN 0-8069-8394-9); PLB 12.49 (ISBN 0-8069-8395-7). Sterling.
Raycraft, Don & Raycraft, Carol. Shaker: A Collector's Source Book. (Illus.). pap. 12.95 (ISBN 0-87069-306-9). Wallace-Homestead.
Rubin, Cynthia & Rubin, Jerome. Shaker Miniature Furniture. 1979. pap. 7.95 (ISBN 0-442-27150-6). Van Nos Reinhold.
Shea, John G. American Shakers & Their Furniture. 1971. 17.95 (ISBN 0-442-27541-2). Van Nos Reinhold.

FURNITURE BUILDING
see Furniture Making

FURNITURE DESIGN

Alison, Filippo. Charles Rennie Mackintosh As a Designer of Chairs. LC 77-89120. 1978. 14.95 (ISBN 0-8120-5169-6). Barron.
Billcliffe, Roger. Charles Rennie Mackintosh: The Complete Furniture, Furniture Drawings, & Interior Designs. LC 78-72303. (Illus.). 1979. 60.00 (ISBN 0-8008-1773-7). Taplinger.
Chaffee, John. Designing & Making Fine Furniture. (Illus.). 1978. pap. 7.95 (ISBN 0-89104-095-1). A & W Pubs.
--Designing & Making Fine Furniture. 1978. 14.95 (ISBN 0-89104-096-X). A & W Pubs.
Design Council, ed. Street Furniture. 192p. 1979. pap. 32.50x (ISBN 0-85072-082-6, Pub. by Design Council England). Intl Schol Bk Serv.
Edwards, Ralph. Hepplewhite Furniture Designs. 1972. 16.50 (ISBN 0-685-52079-X). Transatlantic.
Fastnedge, R. Shearer Furniture Designs. 1966. 8.95 (ISBN 0-685-52092-7). Transatlantic.
Gandy, Charles & Zimmerman-Stidham, Susan. Contemporary Classics: Furniture of the Masters. (Architectural Record Ser.). (Illus.). 160p. 1981. 19.75 (ISBN 0-07-022760-8, P&RB). McGraw.
Godwin, E. W. Art Furniture. Stansky, Peter & Shewan, Rodney, eds. Incl. Artistic Conservatories. Adams, Maurice. LC 76-18322. (Aesthetic Movement & the Arts & Crafts Movement Ser.: Vol. 14). 1978. Repr. of 1880 ed. lib. bdg. 44.00x (ISBN 0-8240-2463-X). Garland Pub.
Handberg, Ejner. Shop Drawings of Shaker Furniture & Woodenware, Vol. 1. LC 73-83797. 96p. 1973. pap. 4.95 (ISBN 0-912944-09-9). Berkshire Traveller.
Hayward, Charles H. Antique Furniture Designs. (Illus.). 1980. 12.95 (ISBN 0-684-16302-0, ScribT). Scribner.
Kettless, Alonzo W. Designs for Wood: How to Plan & Create Your Own Furniture. LC 77-87177. (Illus.). 1978. 12.95 (ISBN 0-684-15541-9, ScribT). Scribner.
Makinson, Randell L. Greene & Greene: Furniture & Related Designs. LC 76-57792. (Illus.). 1978. 27.95 (ISBN 0-87905-060-8). Peregrine Smith.
Oates, Phyllis. The Story of Western Furniture. LC 81-47246. (Icon Editions Ser.). (Illus.). 256p. 1981. 20.00 (ISBN 0-06-436350-3, HarpT). Har-Row.
Page, Marian. Furniture Designed by Architects. (Illus.). 1980. 25.00 (ISBN 0-8230-7180-4, Whitney Lib). Watson-Guptill.
Schremp, William. Designer Furniture Anyone Can Make. 1973. pap. 3.95 (ISBN 0-671-21644-9, Fireside). S&S.
Sheraton, Thomas. Cabinet Maker & Upholsterer's Drawing Book. (Illus.). 352p. 1972. pap. 7.95 (ISBN 0-486-22255-1). Dover.
Stickley, Gustav. Craftsman Homes: Architecture & Furnishings of the American Arts & Crafts Movement. LC 78-73519. (Illus.). 1979. pap. 6.00 (ISBN 0-486-23791-5). Dover.

FURNITURE FINISHING

Berger, Robert. All About Antiquing & Restoring Furniture. 1974. pap. 5.95 (ISBN 0-8015-0138-5, Hawthorn). Dutton.
Blandford, Percy. Do-It-Yourselfer's Guide to Furniture Repair & Refinishing. (Illus.). 1977. 9.95 (ISBN 0-8306-7894-8); pap. 5.95 (ISBN 0-8306-6894-2, 894). TAB Bks.
Brumbaugh, James E. Wood Furniture: Finishing, Refinishing, Repairing. LC 73-91640. (Illus.). 352p. 1974. 9.95 (ISBN 0-672-23216-2). Audel.
Creel, Herrlee G. Sinism: Study of the Evolution of the Chinese World View. LC 74-2904. (China Studies: from Confucius to Mao Ser). 127p. 1975. Repr. of 1929 ed. 16.00 (ISBN 0-88355-165-9). Hyperion Conn.
Editors of Time-Life Books. Repairing Furniture. (Home Repair & Improvement). (Illus.). 128p. 1981. 10.95 (ISBN 0-8094-2438-X). Time-Life.
Egge, Ruth S. Recycled with Flair: How to Remodel Old Furniture & Flea Market Finds. (Illus.). 1980. 10.95 (ISBN 0-698-11024-2); pap. 5.95 (ISBN 0-698-11031-5). Coward.
Family Handyman Magazine Editors. The Complete Book of Furniture Repair & Refinishing. rev. ed. 1981. 17.95 (ISBN 0-684-16839-1, ScribT). Scribner.
Fischman, Walter. Furniture Finishing. LC 78-55663. (Illus.). 1978. 15.00 (ISBN 0-672-52349-3). Bobbs.
Gladstone, Bernard. Complete Guide to Furniture Finishing & Refinishing. 1981. 10.95 (ISBN 0-671-25603-3, Fireside); pap. 6.95 (ISBN 0-671-25604-1). S&S.
Grotz, George. The Fun of Refinishing Furniture. LC 78-22809. 1979. pap. 5.95 (ISBN 0-385-14916-6). Doubleday.
--Instant Furniture Refinishing & Other Crafty Practices. LC 66-12826. 1966. pap. 2.95 (ISBN 0-385-03628-0, Dolp). Doubleday.
--Staining & Finishing Unfinished Furniture & Other Naked Woods. LC 68-25596. 1968. pap. 2.95 (ISBN 0-385-01906-8, Dolp). Doubleday.
Guide to Furniture Refinishing & Antiquing. (McGraw-Hill Paperbacks Home Improvement Ser.). (Illus.). 112p. 1980. pap. 3.95 (ISBN 0-07-045973-8). McGraw.
Higgins, Afred. Common-Sense Guide to Refinishing Antiques. rev. ed. LC 76-8913. (Funk & W Bk.). (Illus.). 288p. 1976. 11.95 (ISBN 0-308-10252-5). T y Crowell.
Johnson, Lorraine. How to Restore, & Repair Almost Everything. LC 77-8135. 1977. pap. 7.95 (ISBN 0-02-080560-8, Collier). Macmillan.
Jones, Thomas H. Furniture Fix & Finish Guide. (Illus.). 272p. 1980. 13.95 (ISBN 0-8359-2227-8). Reston.
Joyner, Nina G. Furniture Refinishing at Home. rev. ed. (Creative Crafts Ser.). (Illus.). 160p. 1975. 11.95 (ISBN 0-8019-6144-0); pap. 6.95 (ISBN 0-8019-6145-9). Chilton.
Kuhn, H. W. How to Refinish Furniture. (Illus.). 160p. 1973. 9.00x (ISBN 0-7182-0944-3). Intl Pubns Serv.
Kuhn, W. H. Refinishing Furniture. LC 64-15182. (Illus.). 1963. lib. bdg. 5.95 (ISBN 0-668-01195-5). Arco.
--Refinishing Furniture. LC 64-15182. (Illus.). 1978. pap. 2.95 (ISBN 0-668-04367-9). Arco.
Linsley, Leslie. Fabulous Furniture Decorations: How to Create Designer Pieces from Unfinished Furniture. LC 77-13106. (Illus.). 1978. 14.95 (ISBN 0-690-01698-0). T Y Crowell.
Mackercher, V. M. The Woodworker's Furniture Construction - Repair Bible. (Illus.). 1979. 14.95 (ISBN 0-8306-9713-6); pap. 8.95 (ISBN 0-8306-1134-7, 1134). TAB Bks.
Maguire. Simple Furniture Making & Refinishing. 1977. 16.95 (ISBN 0-87909-765-5). Reston.
Marshall, Mel. How to Repair, Reupholster & Refinish Furniture. LC 79-4706. (Popular Science Bk.). (Illus.). 1979. 13.95 (ISBN 0-06-013035-0, HarpT). Har-Row.
Mason, Billy. A Furniture Stripping Business for the Small Man. 1975. pap. text ed. 5.00 (ISBN 0-686-20798-X). Kelso.
Meyers, L. Donald & Demske, Richard. Furniture Repair & Refinishing. (Illus.). 1978. text ed. 14.95 (ISBN 0-87909-273-4); pap. 6.95 (ISBN 0-87909-290-4). Reston.
Nunn, Richard V. & Nunn, Beverly J. Furniture Repair & Refinishing. LC 75-2876. (Family Guidebooks Ser.). (Illus.). 96p. 1975. pap. 2.95 (ISBN 0-8487-0378-2). Oxmoor Hse.
Rodd, John. Repairing & Restoring Antique Furniture. 1976. 15.95 (ISBN 0-442-26970-6). Van Nos Reinhold.
Savage, Jessie D. Professional Furniture Refinishing for the Amateur. rev. ed. LC 79-20720. (Illus.). 1980. pap. 4.50 (ISBN 0-668-04834-4). Arco.
--Professional Furniture Refinishing for the Amateur. LC 74-20414. (Illus.). 208p. 1975. 9.95 (ISBN 0-06-013774-6, HarpT). Har-Row.
Sunset Editors. Furniture Finishing & Refinishing. 2nd ed. LC 77-72512. (Illus.). 80p. 1977. pap. 3.95 (ISBN 0-376-01164-5, Sunset Bks.). Sunset-Lane.
Swedburg, Robert & Swedburg, Harriet. Off Your Rocker: A Complete Guide to Refinishing Furniture. 1975. softbound 3.95 (ISBN 0-87069-126-0). Wallace-Homestead.

FURNITURE INDUSTRY AND TRADE

Fairchild Market Research Division. Household Furniture & Bedding. (Fact Files Ser). 1978. pap. 10.00 (ISBN 0-87005-222-5). Fairchild.
Glossop, R. H. Method Study & the Furniture Industry. LC 75-112711. 1970. 21.00 (ISBN 0-08-015653-3). Pergamon.
Hornor, William M., Jr. Blue Book of Philadelphia Furniture. rev. ed. LC 77-73905. (Illus.). 1977. Repr. of 1935 ed. 75.00x (ISBN 0-918712-00-9). Highland Hse.
Mason, Billy. A Furniture Stripping Business for the Small Man. 1975. pap. text ed. 5.00 (ISBN 0-686-20798-X). Kelso.
Oliver, J. L. The Development & Structure of the Furniture Industry. 1966. 13.75 (ISBN 0-08-011460-1). Pergamon.
Slom, Stanley H. How to Sell Furniture. 3rd ed. LC 70-105380. 1970. 6.95 (ISBN 0-87005-088-5). Fairchild.
--Profitable Furniture Retailing for the Home Furnishings Markets. LC 67-14641. 1967. text ed. 7.95 (ISBN 0-87005-055-9). Fairchild.
Taylor, Lonn & Warren, David B. Texas Furniture: The Cabinetmakers & Their Work, 1840-1880. LC 75-20391. (Illus.). 399p. 1975. 40.00 (ISBN 0-292-73801-3). U of Tex Pr.

FURNITURE MAKING
see also Cabinet-Work; Furniture-Repairing; Furniture; Upholstery

Albers, Vernon M. Advanced Furniture Construction. LC 78-37822. (Illus.). 128p. 1972. 7.95 (ISBN 0-498-01110-0). A S Barnes.
--Amateur Furniture Construction. LC 75-88248. (Illus.). 1970. large type 7.95 (ISBN 0-498-01599-8). A S Barnes.
Alexander, John D., Jr. Make a Chair from a Tree: An Introduction to Working Green Wood. LC 78-58222. (Illus.). 128p. 1978. pap. write for info. (ISBN 0-918804-01-9, Dist. by Van Nostrand Reinhold). Taunton.
Bard, Rachel. Successful Wood Book: Selection & Use, Fastening & Finishing. LC 78-15547. 1978. 13.95 (ISBN 0-912336-73-0); pap. 6.95 (ISBN 0-912336-74-9). Structures Pub.
Bausert, John. Complete Book of Wicker & Cane Furniture Making. LC 75-36148. (Illus.). 1976. pap. 6.95 (ISBN 0-8069-8240-3). Sterling.

Blandford, Percy W. Sixty-Six Children's Furniture Projects. (Illus.). 1979. 14.95 (ISBN 0-8306-9769-1); pap. 9.95 (ISBN 0-8306-1188-6, 1188). TAB Bks.

Brann, Donald R. How to Build Bars. rev. ed. LC 67-15263. 1976. lib. bdg. 5.95 (ISBN 0-87733-090-5). Easi-Bild.

--How to Build Kitchen Cabinets, Room Dividers & Cabinet Furniture. rev. ed. LC 65-27708. 1978. lib. bdg. 5.95 (ISBN 0-87733-058-1); pap. 3.50 (ISBN 0-87733-658-X). Easi-Bild.

Brown, Raymond D. How to Design & Build Your Own Furniture. (Illus.). 272p. (Orig.). 1980. 14.95 (ISBN 0-8306-9734-9); pap. 7.95 (ISBN 0-8306-1180-0, 1180). TAB Bks.

Butler, David F. Simplified Furniture Design & Construction. LC 74-88253. (Illus.). 1970. 6.95 (ISBN 0-498-07345-9). A S Barnes.

Castle, Wendell & Edman, David. Wendell Castle Book of Wood Lamination. 192p. 1980. 18.95 (ISBN 0-442-21478-2). Van Nos Reinhold.

Chaffee, John. Designing & Making Fine Furniture. (Illus.). 1978. pap. 7.95 (ISBN 0-89104-095-1). A & W Pubs.

--Designing & Making Fine Furniture. 1978. 14.95 (ISBN 0-89104-096-X). A & W Pubs.

D'Addario, Joseph D. Build It: Out of Sight Sewing Center. 1972. pap. 3.95 (ISBN 0-686-01898-2). Classic Furn Kits.

Dal Fabbro, Mario. Upholstered Furniture: Design & Construction. LC 69-13602. (Illus.). 1969. 36.50 (ISBN 0-07-015180-6, P&RB). McGraw.

Daniele, Joseph W. Building Early American Furniture. LC 74-10953. (Illus.). 256p. 1974. 19.95 (ISBN 0-686-77039-0). Stackpole.

Douglass, J. Harvey. Projects in Wood Furniture. rev. ed. LC 67-21721. (Illus.). (gr. 7 up). 1967. text ed. 14.00 (ISBN 0-87345-027-2). McKnight.

Educational Research Council of America. Furniture Maker. rev. ed. Ferris, Theodore N. & Marchak, John P., eds. (Real People at Work Ser: C). (Illus.). 1976. pap. text ed. 2.25 (ISBN 0-89247-021-6). Changing Times.

Endacott, G. W. Woodworking & Furniture Making. (Drake Home Craftman Ser.). (Illus.). 1976. pap. 5.95 (ISBN 0-8069-8804-5). Sterling.

Family Handyman Staff. The Early American Furniture-Making Handbook. LC 72-38945. (Illus.). 160p. 1972. 14.95 (ISBN 0-684-12869-1, ScribT). Scribner.

Feirer & Hutchings. Advanced Woodwork & Furniture Making. rev. ed. (gr. 9-12). 1982. text ed. 18.60 (ISBN 0-87002-341-1). Bennett IL.

--Advanced Woodwork & Furniture Making. 1978. text ed. 17.28 (ISBN 0-87002-205-9); student guide 3.96 (ISBN 0-87002-269-5); visual masters 14.40 (ISBN 0-87002-148-6); tchr's. guide 2.52 (ISBN 0-87002-348-9). Bennett IL.

Feirer, John & Hutchings, Gilbert R. Advanced Woodwork & Furniture-Making. 4th. rev ed. (Illus.). 1978. 25.95 (ISBN 0-684-15728-4, ScribT). Scribner.

Gottshall, Franklin H. Masterpiece Furniture Making. LC 79-12. (Illus.). 224p. 1979. 24.95 (ISBN 0-8117-0974-4). Stackpole.

--Reproducing Antique Furniture: Construction-Hardware-Finishing. LC 76-147339. (Arts & Crafts Ser). (Illus.). 1971. 14.95 (ISBN 0-517-54308-7, K0889X). Crown.

Hayward, Charles H. Practical Woodwork. (Illus.). 192p. 1978. pap. 5.95 (ISBN 0-8069-8582-8). Sterling.

Hayward, Helena & Kirkham, Pat. William & John Linnel: 18th Century London Furniture-Makers, 2 vols. LC 80-51404. (Illus.). 400p. 1980. slipcased 125.00 (ISBN 0-8478-0325-2). Rizzoli Intl.

Hoard, F. & Marlow, Andrew. Good Furniture You Can Make Yourself. 1972. pap. 5.95 (ISBN 0-02-080290-0, Collier). Macmillan.

How to Build Antique Furniture. Repr. 4.95 (ISBN 0-912092-46-7). Educator Bks.

Howard, Paul. Easy to Make Wooden Furniture for Children. 176p. 1981. 12.95 (ISBN 0-920510-51-5, Pub. by Personal Lib); pap. 8.95 (ISBN 0-920510-10-8). Everest Hse.

Huth, Hans. Roentgen Furniture: Abraham & David Roentgen, European Cabinet Makers. (Illus.). 260p. 1974. 100.00x (ISBN 0-85667-003-0, Pub. by Sotheby Parke Bernet England). Biblio Dist.

Johnston, David. The Craft of Furniture Making. (Illus.). 1980. 12.95 (ISBN 0-684-16301-2, ScribT). Scribner.

Jones, Michael O. The Hand Made Object & Its Maker. LC 73-93055. (Illus.). 288p. 1975. 20.00 (ISBN 0-520-02697-7). U of Cal Pr.

Joyce, Ernest. Encyclopedia of Furniture Making. LC 76-49087. (Illus.). 1979. 17.50 (ISBN 0-8069-8302-7); PLB 14.99 (ISBN 0-8069-8303-5). Sterling.

Kettless, Alonzo W. Designs for Wood: How to Plan & Create Your Own Furniture. LC 77-87177. (Illus.). 1978. 12.95 (ISBN 0-684-15541-9, ScribT). Scribner.

King, Lis. Furniture: How to Make -Do, Make Over, Make Your Own. LC 76-16409. (Illus.). 1976. pap. 4.95 (ISBN 0-8069-8356-6). Sterling.

Margon, Lester. Construction of American Furniture Treasures. (Illus.). 9.50 (ISBN 0-8446-5220-2). Peter Smith.

Marlow, A. W. Classic Furniture Projects. (Illus.). 1979. pap. 7.95 (ISBN 0-8128-6034-9). Stein & Day.

Mitgutsch, Ali. From Tree to Table. LC 81-672. (Carolrhoda Start to Finish Bks.). Orig. Title: Vom Baum Zum Tisch. (Illus.). 24p. (ps-3). 1981. PLB 5.95 (ISBN 0-87614-165-3, AACR1). Carolrhoda Bks.

Moser, Thomas. How to Build Shaker Furniture. LC 76-46809. (Illus.). 224p. 1980. pap. 7.95 (ISBN 0-8069-8392-2). Sterling.

Palmer, Bruce. Making Children's Furniture & Play Structures. LC 75-8813. (Parents & Children Together Ser.). (Illus.). 160p. 1974. 8.95 (ISBN 0-911104-24-0); pap. 3.95 (ISBN 0-911104-25-9). Workman Pub.

Proper, Churchill. Furniture & Accessories. new ed. LC 76-185671. (Handicraft Ser.: No. 3). (Illus.). 32p. (Orig.). (gr. 7-12). 1971. lib. bdg. 2.45 incl. catalog cards (ISBN 0-686-01112-0); pap. 1.25 vinyl laminated covers (ISBN 0-87157-403-9). SamHar Pr.

Rubin, Cynthia & Rubin, Jerome. Mission Furniture: Making It, Decorating with It, Its History & Place in the Antique Market. LC 79-24376. (Illus.). 160p. (Orig.). 1980. pap. 8.95 (ISBN 0-87701-169-9). Chronicle Bks.

Scharff, Robert. Furniture You Can Make. 1981. 7.95 (ISBN 0-8359-2243-X). Reston.

Schmultzhart, Berthold. The Handmade Furniture Book. (Illus.). 144p. 1981. 13.95 (ISBN 0-13-383638-X); pap. 5.95 (ISBN 0-13-383620-7). P-H.

Schremp, William. Designer Furniture Anyone Can Make. 1973. pap. 3.95 (ISBN 0-671-21644-9, Fireside). S&S.

Shea, John G. Colonial Furniture Making for Everybody. 1964. pap. 9.95 (ISBN 0-442-27545-5). Van Nos Reinhold.

Stamberg, Peter S. Instant Furniture. 1976. 12.95 (ISBN 0-442-27935-3); pap. 8.95 (ISBN 0-442-27934-5). Van Nos Reinhold.

Stephenson, Sue H. Rustic Furniture. 1979. 15.95 (ISBN 0-442-27974-4). Van Nos Reinhold.

Sunset Editors. Furniture: Easy-to-Make. LC 76-46661. (Illus.). 80p. 1977. pap. 3.95 (ISBN 0-376-01175-0, Sunset Bks). Sunset-Lane.

--Tables & Chairs: Easy to Make. LC 75-26492. (Illus.). 80p. 1976. pap. 3.95 (ISBN 0-376-01653-1, Sunset Bks.). Sunset-Lane.

Taylor, V. J. How to Build Period Country Furniture. LC 79-3731. (Illus.). 1980. 14.95 (ISBN 0-8128-2696-5); pap. 7.95 (ISBN 0-8128-6047-0). Stein & Day.

Taylor, Victor J. Constructing Modern Furniture. LC 79-91383. (Home Craftsman Bk.). (Illus.). 144p. 1980. pap. 5.95 (ISBN 0-8069-8888-6). Sterling.

Treves, Ralph. Early American Furniture You Can Build. LC 76-5410. (Illus.). 1965. lib. bdg. 4.95 (ISBN 0-668-01215-3); pap. 2.95 (ISBN 0-668-04004-1). Arco.

Trigg, John & Field, David. Fashioning Furniture: Beautiful Designs That Will Save Money. LC 74-19758. (Leisuretime Ser.). (Illus.). 96p. 1975. bds. 5.95 (ISBN 0-668-03695-8). Arco.

Waring, Janet. Early American Stencils on Walls & Furniture. (Illus.). 12.50 (ISBN 0-685-22719-7). Peter Smith.

Windsor, H. H. Mission Furniture: How to Make It. LC 76-16111. (Illus.). 100p. 1976. pap. 6.50 (ISBN 0-87905-064-0). Peregrine Smith.

Zakas, Spiros, et al. More Furniture in Twenty-Four Hours. LC 78-3989. (Illus.). 1978. 10.95 (ISBN 0-312-54803-6); pap. 5.95 (ISBN 0-312-54804-4). St Martin.

Zegel, Jon M. Fast Furniture: The Zegel System. LC 77-29110. (Illus.). 1978. lib. bdg. 12.90 (ISBN 0-89471-029-X); pap. 5.95 (ISBN 0-89471-028-1). Running Pr.

FURNITURE MAKING–AMATEURS' MANUALS

Adams, Florence. Make Your Own Baby Furniture. LC 80-10495. (Illus.). 224p. 1980. pap. 9.95 (ISBN 0-87131-320-0). M Evans.

Better Homes & Gardens Books Editors. Better Homes & Gardens Outdoor Projects You Can Build. (Illus.). 1977. 5.95 (ISBN 0-696-00135-7). Meredith Corp.

Better Homes & Gardens Editors. Better Homes & Gardens Furniture Projects You Can Build. (Illus.). 1977. 5.95 (ISBN 0-696-00245-0). Meredith Corp.

Blandford, Percy. How to Make Early American & Colonial Furniture. (Illus.). 1979. 14.95 (ISBN 0-8306-9843-4); pap. 7.95 (ISBN 0-8306-1114-2, 1114). TAB Bks.

Brann, Donald. How to Build Colonial Furniture. LC 74-24602. 1976. lib. bdg. 6.95 (ISBN 0-87733-061-1); pap. 5.95 (ISBN 0-87733-761-6). Easi-Bild.

Brann, Donald R. How to Build Collectors' Display Cases. LC 78-57773. (Illus.). 194p. 1979. pap. 6.95 (ISBN 0-87733-792-6). Easi-Bild.

--How to Build Outdoor Furniture. LC 76-14045. 1978. pap. 5.95 (ISBN 0-87733-754-3). Easi-Bild.

Buckley, Larry. Easy-to-Make Slotted Furniture. (Illus.). 52p. (Orig.). 1980. pap. 2.25 (ISBN 0-486-23983-7). Dover.

Cohen, Maurice. Making Children' Furniture with Hand Tools. LC 77-88951. (Illus.). 1978. pap. 5.95 (ISBN 0-8069-8490-2, 023100). Sterling.

Dal Fabbro, Mario. How to Build Modern Furniture. 3rd ed. 1976. 11.95 (ISBN 0-07-015185-7, P&RB). McGraw.

Dunbar, Michael. Windsor Chairmaking. (Illus.). 160p. 1976. 9.95 (ISBN 0-8038-8077-4). Hastings.

Gottshall, F. H. How to Make Colonial Furniture. 1971. 8.95 (ISBN 0-685-01122-4, 80266). Glencoe.

Gottshall, Franklin H. How to Make Colonial Furniture. LC 79-20825. 1980. 15.95 (ISBN 0-02-544840-4). Macmillan.

Hagerty, Francis. Make Your Own Antiques. (Illus., Orig.). 1975. pap. 5.95 (ISBN 0-316-33783-8). Little.

Hennessey, James & Papanek, Victor. Nomadic Furniture One. LC 72-342. 1973. pap. 5.95 (ISBN 0-394-70228-X). Pantheon.

Hodges, Lewis H. Sixty Six Weekend Wood Furniture Projects. (Illus.). 1977. 10.95 (ISBN 0-8306-7974-X); pap. 6.95 (ISBN 0-8306-6974-4, 974). TAB Bks.

Isaacs, Ken. How to Build Your Own Living Structures. (Illus.). 144p. 1974. 9.95 (ISBN 0-517-50562-2); spiral bound 4.95 (ISBN 0-517-50559-2). Crown.

Johnston, David. The Craft of Furniture Making. 1979. 19.95 (ISBN 0-7134-1546-0, Pub. by Batsford England). David & Charles.

Kramer, Jack. Fold-Away Furniture. (Illus.). 1978. pap. 4.95 (ISBN 0-346-12341-0). Cornerstone.

LaBarge, L. Crate Craft: Easy-to-Make Furniture & Accessories You Can Build Quickly & Inexpensively. LC 76-9185. (Illus.). 1976. pap. 5.95 (ISBN 0-88421-053-7). New Century.

Laplante, Jerry C. Plastic Furniture for the Home Craftsman. LC 77-87474. (Illus.). 1978. pap. 5.95 (ISBN 0-8069-8566-6). Sterling.

Maguire. Simple Furniture Making & Refinishing. 1977. 16.95 (ISBN 0-87909-765-5). Reston.

Makepeace, John, et al. The Art of Making Furniture. LC 80-52623. (Illus.). 192p. 1981. 21.95 (ISBN 0-8069-5426-4); lib. bdg. 18.39 (ISBN 0-8069-5427-2). Sterling.

Marlow, A. W. Classic Furniture Projects. LC 76-54800. (Illus.). 1977. 12.95 (ISBN 0-8128-2184-X). Stein & Day.

--The Early American Furniture Maker's Manual. (Illus.). 160p. 1973. 12.95 (ISBN 0-02-579810-3). Macmillan.

--Fine Furniture. LC 55-13928. 1977. pap. 8.95 (ISBN 0-8128-2250-1). Stein & Day.

Martensson, Alf. The Book of Furniture Making. 1980. 15.00 (ISBN 0-312-08973-2). St Martin.

Meilach, Dona Z. & Meilach, Melvin. Creating Modern Furniture: Trends, Techniques, Appreciation. (Arts & Crafts Ser.). (Illus.). 328p. 1975. 12.95 (ISBN 0-517-51609-8); pap. 6.95 (ISBN 0-517-52461-9). Crown.

Ouimet, Ronald P. Contemporary Furniture Plans: 114 Projects You Can Build Yourself. LC 81-8811. (Illus.). 160p. (Orig.). 1981. pap. text ed. 7.95 (ISBN 0-8069-7546-6). Sterling.

Peterson, Franklynn. The Build-It-Yourself Furniture Catalog. LC 76-6567. 1977 (ISBN 0-685-93582-5, Reward). pap. 4.95 (ISBN 0-13-085902-8). P-H.

Popular Mechanics Co. Mission Furniture: How to Make It. (Illus.). vii, 342p. pap. 5.00 (ISBN 0-486-23966-7). Dover.

Schremp, William E. Designer Furniture Anyone Can Make. 1972. 7.95 (ISBN 0-671-21283-4); pap. 3.95 (ISBN 0-671-21644-9). S&S.

Stiles, David. Easy-to-Make Children's Furniture. (Illus.). 1980. 7.95 (ISBN 0-394-73871-3). Pantheon.

Stramberg, Peter. Build Your Own Furniture. 1981. pap. 8.95 (ISBN 0-345-29553-6). Ballantine.

Sunset Editors. Outdoor Furniture. LC 78-70271. (Illus.). 80p. 1979. pap. 3.95 (ISBN 0-376-01382-6, Sunset Bks.). Sunset-Lane.

Wyke, Anne V. The Craft of Soft Furnishing. 1978. 7.95 (ISBN 0-09-131670-7, Pub. by Hutchinson); pap. 3.95 (ISBN 0-09-131671-5). Merrimack Bk Serv.

Zakas, Spiros. Furniture in Twenty-Four Hours. 1976. pap. 6.95 (ISBN 0-02-082900-0, Collier). Macmillan.

FURNITURE WORKERS

see Cabinet-Workers

FURNIVALL, FREDERICK JAMES, 1825-1910

English Miscellany: Presented to Dr. Furnival in Honor of His 75th Birthday. LC 70-178531. Repr. of 1901 ed. 27.50 (ISBN 0-404-56548-4). AMS Pr.

FURRIERY

see Fur Garments

FURS (CLOTHING)

see Fur Garments

FURTWANGLER, WILHELM, 1886-1954

Gillis, Daniel. Furtwangler & America. (Illus.). 1970. 5.00 (ISBN 0-87141-031-1). Manyland.

--Furtwangler in America. LC 75-125028. (Illus.). 1980. Repr. of 1971 ed. 7.95 (ISBN 0-87867-079-3). Ramparts.

FURUSETH, ANDREW, 1854-1938

Weintraub, Hyman. Andrew Furuseth: Emancipator of the Seamen. Scott, Franklyn D., ed. LC 78-15860. (Scandinavians in America Ser.). 1979. Repr. of 1959 ed. lib. bdg. 20.00x (ISBN 0-405-11664-0). Arno.

Weintraub, Hyman G. Andrew Furuseth, Emancipator of the Seamen. (Institute of Industrial Relations, UC Berkeley). 1959. 24.00x (ISBN 0-520-01322-0). U of Cal Pr.

FURY (JET FIGHTER PLANES)

see Sabre (Jet Fighter Planes)

FURY (SHIP)

Parry, William E. Journal of a Second Voyage for the Discovery of a Northwest Passage from the Atlantic to the Pacific. Repr. of 1824 ed. lib. bdg. 34.00x (ISBN 0-8371-1448-9, PASV). Greenwood.

FUSAIN (ART)

see Charcoal-Drawing

FUSARIUM

Nelson, P. E., et al. Fusarium: Diseases, Biology, & Taxonomy. LC 81-47175. (Illus.). 560p. 1981. 39.50x (ISBN 0-271-00293-X). Pa St U Pr.

Palti, Josef. Toxigenic Fusaria, Their Distribution & Significance As Causes of Disease in Animal & Man. (Acta Phytomedica Ser.: Vol. 6). (Illus.). 112p. (Orig.). 1978. pap. text ed. 24.00 (ISBN 3-489-60326-5). Parey Sci Pubs.

Tousson, T. A. & Nelson, Paul E. A Pictorial Guide to the Identification of Fusarium Species. 2nd ed. LC 76-2027. (Illus.). 1976. pap. 7.95x (ISBN 0-271-01225-0). Pa St U Pr.

FUSED SALTS

Braunstein, J., et al. Advances in Molten Salt Chemistry, 3 vols. Incl. Vol. 1. 284p. 1971. 32.50 (ISBN 0-306-39701-3); Vol. 2. 259p. 1973. 32.50 (ISBN 0-306-39702-1); Vol. 3. 458p. 1975. 45.00 (ISBN 0-306-39703-X). LC 78-131884 (Plenum Pr). Plenum Pub.

Charlot, G. & Tremillon, B. Chemical Reactions in Solvents & Melts. 1969. 79.00 (ISBN 0-08-012678-2). Pergamon.

Inman, Douglas & Lovering, David G., eds. Ionic Liquids. 445p. 1981. 49.50 (ISBN 0-306-40412-5, Plenum Pr). Plenum Pub.

Janz, George J. Molten Salts Handbook. 1967. 78.00 (ISBN 0-12-380445-0). Acad Pr.

Lumsden, J. Thermodynamics of Molten-Salt Mixtures. 1966. 56.00 (ISBN 0-12-460150-2). Acad Pr.

Plambeck, J. A. Encyclopedia of Electrochemistry of the Elements, Vol. 10: Fused Salt Systems. 75.00 (ISBN 0-8247-2510-7). Dekker.

Plambeck, James. Fused Salt Systems. (Encyclopedia of Electrochemistry of the Elements: Vol. 10). 1976. 88.00 (ISBN 0-8247-2510-7). Dekker.

Status & Prospects of Thermal Breeders & Their Effect on Fuel Utilization. (Technical Reports Ser.: No. 195). 146p. 1980. pap. 22.00 (ISBN 92-0-155079-0, IDC195, IAEA). Unipub.

FUSELI, HENRY, 1741-1825

Fussli. (I Classici Dell'arte). (Illus.). 1977. pap. 9.95 (ISBN 0-8478-5150-8). Rizzoli Intl.

Schiff, Gert & Hofmann, Werner. Henry Fuseli 1741-1825. (Tate Gallery Art Ser.). (Illus.). 1977. pap. 8.95 (ISBN 0-8120-0852-9). Barron.

FUSION

BCC Staff, ed. Fusion Energy, E-030: Technical, Economic Implications. 1978. 675.00 (ISBN 0-89336-142-9). BCC.

CIAMDA Eighty: An Index to the Literature on Atomic & Molecular Collision Data Relevant to Fusion Research. 498p. 1980. pap. 31.25 (ISBN 92-0-039080-3, ISP550, IAEA). Unipub.

Commission of the European Communities, Luxembourg. Fusion Technology Nineteen Seventy-Eight: Proceedings, 2 vols. LC 79-40553. (Commission of the European Communities: Eur 6215). (Illus.). 1979. Set. pap. 235.00 (ISBN 0-08-023439-9). Pergamon.

--Fusion Technology: Proceedings of the 11th Symposium, Oxford, England, Sept. 15-19, 1980, 2 vols. (Illus.). 1000p. 1981. Set. 150.00 (ISBN 0-08-025697-X). Pergamon.

Dolan, Thomas J. Fusion Research, 2 vols. LC 80-18383. 1000p. Set. 100.01 (ISBN 0-08-025565-5); Vol. I. pap. 25.01 (ISBN 0-08-025566-3); Vol. II. pap. 25.01 (ISBN 0-08-025567-1). Pergamon.

Fusion Energy Foundation. Fusion Energy: The Ultimate Energy Source. (Fusion Energy Foundation Science Book Ser.). 1981. pap. 7.00 (ISBN 0-686-30566-3); pap. text ed. 7.00 (ISBN 0-686-30567-1). New Benjamin.

--The World Must Go Nuclear. (Fusion Energy Foundation Science Book Ser.). (Orig.). 1981. pap. 7.00 (ISBN 0-686-30568-X); pap. text ed. 7.00 (ISBN 0-686-30569-8). New Benjamin.
Kammash, Terry. Fusion Reactor Physics: Principles & Technology. LC 74-14430. 1977. 36.00 (ISBN 0-250-40076-6). Ann Arbor Science.
Teller, Edward, ed. Fusion: Magnetic Confinement, Vol. 1. 1981. Pt. A. write for info. (ISBN 0-12-685201-4); Pt. B. write for info. (ISBN 0-12-685241-3). Acad Pr.
Wharton, C. & Sindoni, E., eds. Course in Diagnostics for Fusion Experiments: Proceedings of the Commission of the European Communities, Varenna, Italy, 1978. (Commission of the European Communities, EUR, 6123). (Illus.). 1979. pap. 110.00 (ISBN 0-08-023429-1). Pergamon.

FUSION OF CORPORATIONS
see Consolidation and Merger of Corporations

FUSION REACTIONS, CONTROLLED
see Controlled Fusion

FUSULINIDAE
Petocz, Ronald G. Biostratigraphy & Lower Permian Fusulinidae of the Upper Delta River Area, East-Central Alaska Range. LC 76-111437. (Special Paper: No. 130). (Illus., Orig.). 1970. pap. 5.25x (ISBN 0-8137-2130-X). Geol Soc.
White, M. P. Some Texas Fusulinidae. (Illus.). 106p. 1932. 0.75 (ISBN 0-686-29352-5, BULL 3211). Bur Econ Geology.

FUTILITY
see Frustration

FUTUNA LANGUAGE
see also Polynesian Languages

FUTURE ESTATES
see Future Interests

FUTURE FARMERS OF AMERICA
Brewer, Robert S. & Curtis, Don B. Winning FFA Speeches. LC 76-8592. 1976. pap. 7.50x (ISBN 0-8134-1806-2, 1806). Interstate.

FUTURE INTERESTS
Conboy, William A., ed. The Challenge of the Future: Visions & Versions. LC 80-621213. 162p. (Orig.). 1979. pap. text ed. 6.95 (ISBN 0-936352-03-5, B277). U of KS Ind Stud Div.
Halbach, Edward C. & Scoles, Eugene F. Cases & Materials on Future Interests. 1977. pap. text ed. 9.95 (ISBN 0-316-33840-0). Little.
Partridge, Ernest, ed. Responsibilities to Future Generations: Environmental Ethics. LC 80-84401. 306p. 1981. 17.95 (ISBN 0-87975-153-3); pap. text ed. 9.95 (ISBN 0-87975-142-8). Prometheus Bks.
Powers, Mark J. & Vogel, David J. Inside the Financial Futures Markets. LC 80-23157. 320p. 1981. 19.95 (ISBN 0-471-08136-1). Ronald Pr.
Waggoner, Lawrence W. Future Interests in a Nutshell. LC 80-20195. (Nutshell Ser.). 399p. 1980. pap. 6.95 (ISBN 0-8299-2105-2). West Pub.

FUTURE LIFE
see also Children–Death and Future State; Eschatology; Eternity; Future Punishment; Immortality; Resurrection; Soul; Spiritualism
Alger, William R. Destiny of the Soul: Critical History of the Doctrine of a Future Life, 2 Vols. 10th ed. LC 68-19263. 1968. Repr. of 1880 ed. Set. lib. bdg. 43.25x (ISBN 0-8371-0003-8, ALDS). Greenwood.
Badham, Paul. Christian Beliefs About Life After Death. LC 75-43224. (Library of Philosophy & Religion Ser). 1976. text ed. 22.50x (ISBN 0-06-490280-3). B&N.
Barker, A. Trevor, ed. Mahatma Letters to A. P. Sinnett. 3rd ed. 1972. 7.50 (ISBN 0-8356-7013-9). Theos Pub Hse.
Battle, Dennis M. Life After Death? LC 81-65426. (Illus.). 52p. 1981. pap. 2.00 (ISBN 0-933464-13-4). D M Battle Pubns.
Baxter, Richard. Dying Thoughts: The Christian's Hope for the Life Hereafter. (Summit Bks). 1976. pap. 1.45 (ISBN 0-8010-0601-5). Baker Bk.
Benson, Elizabeth P., ed. Death & the Afterlife in Pre-Columbian America: A Conference at Dumbarton Oaks, October 27, 1973. LC 74-22694. (Illus.). 196p. 1975. 15.00x (ISBN 0-88402-062-2, Ctr Pre-Columbian). Dumbarton Oaks.
Bowers, Laverne E. Sterile. 1981. 6.95 (ISBN 0-533-04732-3). Vantage.
Brown, Theo. The Fate of the Dead: A Study in Folk-Eschatology in the West Country After the Reformation. (Folklore Society Mistletoe Ser.). 118p. 1979. 24.50x (ISBN 0-8476-6214-4). Rowman.
Budge, Ernest A. Egyptian Ideas of the Future Life. LC 73-18839. Repr. of 1899 ed. 14.00 (ISBN 0-404-11330-3). AMS Pr.
Burgess, Anthony. Nineteen-Eighty Five. LC 78-9583. 1978. 8.95 (ISBN 0-316-11651-3). Little.
Burton, Theodore M. God's Greatest Gift. LC 76-25324. 1976. 6.95 (ISBN 0-87747-617-9). Deseret Bk.
Cayce, Edgar & Cayce, Hugh L. God's Other Door & the Continuity of Life. 1976. pap. 1.95 (ISBN 0-87604-007-5). ARE Pr.
Conger, Wilda L. & Cushman, Elizabeth. Forever Is Now. 1964. pap. 4.95 (ISBN 0-8158-0077-0). Chris Mass.
Cooke, Grace & Cooke, Ivan. The Return of Arthur Conan Doyle. (Illus.). 1963. 12.95 (ISBN 0-85487-037-7). De Vorss.
Cornish, Edward, ed. The Information Society of Tomorrow. 1981. 5.95 (ISBN 0-930242-14-9). World Future.
Cournand, Andre & Levy, Maurice. Shaping the Future: Gaston Berger & the Concept of Prospective. LC 72-78388. (Current Topics of Contemporary Thought Ser.). 314p. 1973. 44.00x (ISBN 0-677-12550-X). Gordon.
Cribb, C. C. From Now till Eternity. LC 76-21571. 7.95 (ISBN 0-932046-00-2). Manhattan Ltd NC.
--The Horrified & the Glorified. LC 77-70214. pap. 1.95 (ISBN 0-932046-05-3). Manhattan Ltd NC.
Crookall, R. Supreme Adventure: Analyses of Psychic. Communications. rev. ed. 288p. 1975. 13.95 (ISBN 0-227-67606-8). Attic Pr.
Crowther, Duane S. Vida Eterna. DeHoyos, R., tr. from Eng. LC 81-80953. 390p. (Span.). 1981. 11.95 (ISBN 0-88290-185-0, 4802). Horizon Utah.
Daughters of St. Paul. Choose Your Tomorrow. 1975. pap. 1.95 (ISBN 0-8198-0488-6). Dghtrs St Paul.
Deal, William S. After Death, What? 1977. 1.75 (ISBN 0-686-19329-6). Deal Pubns.
Dehejia, Vidya. Living & Dying: An Inquiry into the Enigma of Death & After-Life. 1979. 8.95 (ISBN 0-7069-0815-5, Pub. by Vikas India). Advent NY.
DeWolf, L. Harold. Eternal Life: Why We Believe. LC 79-21670. 1980. pap. 5.95 (ISBN 0-664-24288-X). Westminster.
Do, Richard E. Tell Them I Am Coming. 1980. pap. 4.95 (ISBN 0-8007-5045-4, Power Bks). Revell.
Draper, William C. Personal Immortality or Nothingness? 1979. 5.95 (ISBN 0-533-04102-3). Vantage.
Ducasse, C. J. Paranormal Phenomena, Science, & Life After Death. LC 79-76282. (Parapsychological Monographs No. 8). 1969. pap. 2.25 (ISBN 0-912328-12-6). Parapsych Foun.
Ebon, Martin. The Evidence for Life After Death. (Orig.). 1977. pap. 1.50 (ISBN 0-451-07543-9, W7543, Sig). NAL.
Edwards, Don. Death - the Doorway to the Future. Graves, Martha J., ed. LC 77-73537. 1977. 5.00 (ISBN 0-918566-11-8); pap. 1.95 (ISBN 0-918566-00-2). Excelsior.
Edwards, Don, pseud. End - A New Beginning. Graves, Martha, ed. LC 77-78583. 1979. 8.00 (ISBN 0-918566-10-X); pap. 5.00 (ISBN 0-918566-03-7). Excelsior.
Ellis, Hilda R. Road to Hel: A Study of the Conception of the Dead in Old Norse Literature. LC 68-23286. (Illus.). 1968. Repr. of 1943 ed. lib. bdg. 15.00 (ISBN 0-8371-0070-4, ELRH). Greenwood.
Feather, Frank, ed. Through the Eighties: Thinking Globally, Acting Locally. 1980. 12.50 (ISBN 0-930242-11-4). World Future.
Fechner, Gustav T. On Life After Death. Wernekke, Hugo, tr. 134p. 1906. 9.95 (ISBN 0-87548-031-4). Open Court.
Fortman, Edmund J. Everlasting Life After Death. LC 76-41186. 1977. 6.95 (ISBN 0-8189-0333-3). Alba.
Friedman, Henry. Time Twins: A Nonsupernatural Concept of Survival After Death. 84p. (Orig.). 1981. pap. 4.50 (ISBN 0-9605876-0-8). B Hilltop Pr.
Greg, William R. Enigmas of Life. LC 72-323. (Essay Index Reprint Ser.). Repr. of 1879 ed. 19.00 (ISBN 0-8369-2794-X). Arno.
Gunn, Rodger S. Worlds Without End. 1974. pap. 2.00 (ISBN 0-89036-036-7). Hawkes Pub Inc.
Harner, Philip B. Everlasting Life in Biblical Thought. 1981. 6.95 (ISBN 0-8062-1611-5). Carlton.
Hellwig, Monika K. What Are They Saying About Death & Christian Hope? LC 78-61726. 1978. pap. 2.45 (ISBN 0-8091-2165-4). Paulist Pr.
Hembree, Ron. Ensayo Para el Cielo. 186p. (Span.). 1979. pap. 2.00 (ISBN 0-8297-0646-1). Life Pubs Intl.
--Rehearsal for Heaven. 1977. 4.95 (ISBN 0-8010-4187-2). Baker Bk.
Hendriksen, William. Bible on the Life Hereafter. (Direction Books). 1971. pap. 3.45 (ISBN 0-8010-4189-9). Baker Bk.
Hick, John H. Death & Eternal Life. LC 76-9965. 496p. 1980. pap. text ed. 9.95 (ISBN 0-06-063904-0, RD 332, HarpR). Har-Row.
Hodgkinson, Frank C. After Our Pilgrimage. LC 75-140962. 1971. pap. 1.50 (ISBN 0-8170-0513-7). Judson.
Holzer, Hans. There Is an Afterlife: A Scientific Evaluation. (Orig.). 1979. pap. 2.25 (ISBN 0-686-71741-4). Woodhill.
Horgan, Paul. Memories of the Future. 216p. 1966. 4.95 (ISBN 0-374-20756-9). FS&G.
Howells, William Dean, et al. In After Days: Thoughts on Future Life. Kastenaum, Robert, ed. LC 76-19576. (Death & Dying Ser.). (Illus.). 1977. Repr. of 1910 ed. lib. bdg. 18.00x (ISBN 0-405-09574-0). Arno.
Hudson, Thomas. A Scientific Demonstration of the Future Life. 1979. pap. 2.50 (ISBN 0-89083-464-4). Zebra.
Hughes, Ray H. The Order of Future Events. 1970. pap. 2.35 (ISBN 0-87148-650-4). Pathway Pr.
Hyslop, James H. Psychical Research & the Nature of Life After Death. (Illus.). 124p. 1980. deluxe ed. 66.35 (ISBN 0-89920-017-6). Am Inst Psych.
Johnson, Caesar, compiled by. You Can See Forever. (Illus.). 1977. boxed 4.95 (ISBN 0-8378-1792-7). Gibson.
Johnstone, Parker L. Life, Death, & Hereafter. LC 76-21518. 1976. 5.95 (ISBN 0-917802-00-4). Theoscience Found.
Kelsey, Morton. Afterlife: The Other Side of Dying. LC 79-90225. 324p. 1979. 10.95 (ISBN 0-8091-0296-X). Paulist Pr.
Kimball, Spencer W. Tragedy or Destiny. 1977. pap. 0.95 (ISBN 0-87747-652-7). Deseret Bk.
Kingslake, Brian. Aqueduct Papers. 1970. 4.95 (ISBN 0-8158-0239-0). Chris Mass.
Kirk, Joseph E. Death, Resurrection, Immortality. 1977. 4.00 (ISBN 0-910424-66-7). Concordant.
--Death, Resurrection, Immortality. 1977. pap. text ed. 2.00 (ISBN 0-910424-67-5). Concordant.
La Perchia, Alex. A Spiritual Guide to Eternal Life. LC 77-75258. 1977. 6.00 (ISBN 0-8022-2203-X). Philos Lib.
Lewis, Hywel D. Persons & Life After Death. LC 77-22635. (Library of Philosophy & Religion Ser). 1978. text ed. 23.50x (ISBN 0-06-494262-7). B&N.
Lindaman, Edward B. Thinking in the Future Tense. LC 77-91270. 1978. 5.95 (ISBN 0-8054-5591-4). Broadman.
Lindsay, Gordon. Forty Things You Have Always Wanted to Know About Death & the Hereafter. (Sorcery & Spirit World Ser.). 0.95 (ISBN 0-89985-096-0). Christ Nations.
--Life After Death. (Sorcery & Spirit World Ser.). 1.95 (ISBN 0-89985-083-9). Christ Nations.
--Paradise-Abode of the Righteous Dead. (Sorcery & Spirit World Ser.). 1.25 (ISBN 0-89985-085-5). Christ Nations.
--Scenes Beyond the Grave. (Sorcery & Spirit World Ser.). 2.95 (ISBN 0-89985-091-X). Christ Nations.
Loehr, Franklin. Diary After Death. 1976. pap. 1.50 (ISBN 0-89129-057-5). Jove Pubns.
Lummis, Charles F. My Friend Will. 1972. 3.00 (ISBN 0-87516-161-8). De Vorss.
Maeterlinck, Maurice. Light Beyond. facsimile ed. De Mattos, A. T., tr. LC 70-37844. (Essay Index Reprint Ser). Repr. of 1917 ed. 18.00 (ISBN 0-8369-2607-2). Arno.
Maloney, George A. The Everlasting Now. LC 79-57550. 224p. (Orig.). 1980. pap. 3.95 (ISBN 0-87793-201-8). Ave Maria.
Malz, Betty. My Glimpse of Eternity. LC 77-22671. 1977. 6.95 (ISBN 0-912376-20-1). Chosen Bks Pub.
Mann, Stella T. Beyond the Darkness. 1972. pap. 2.95 (ISBN 0-87516-054-9). De Vorss.
Meek, George W. After We Die, What Then? LC 79-90909. (Life's Energy Fields Ser.: Vol. 3). (Illus., Orig.). 1980. 10.50 (ISBN 0-935436-00-6); pap. 6.75 (ISBN 0-935436-01-4). Metascience.
Meyer, Howard & Donnelly, William J. Transition (So-Called Death) Before-During-After. 70p. 1972. pap. 2.25 (ISBN 0-917200-13-6). ESPress.
Montgomery, Mary. Death: End of the Beginning. (Infinity Ser.: No. 10). 1972. text ed. 2.50 (ISBN 0-03-004081-7, 245); tchr's. guide by Marian Nesset 1.15 (ISBN 0-03-004086-8, 246). Winston Pr.
Moore, Marvin. Where Is Bobby Now? (Flame Ser.). 1976. pap. 0.95 (ISBN 0-8127-0106-2). Review & Herald.
Newlove, Donald. Eternal Life. Date not set. pap. 4.95 (ISBN 0-686-74204-4, 46458). Avon.
Nikhilananda, Swami. Man in Search of Immortality. LC 68-101793. 112p. 4.95 (ISBN 0-911206-12-4). Ramakrishna.
Norman, Ruth E. Your Encounter with Life, Death & Immortality. (Illus.). 1978. pap. 2.00 (ISBN 0-932642-43-8). Unarius.
Osis, Karlis & Haraldsson, Erlendur. At the Hour of Death. 1980. pap. 3.95 (ISBN 0-380-01802-0, 49486, Discus). Avon.
Otis, George. Millennium Man. 8.95 (ISBN 0-686-31704-1); pap. 4.95 (ISBN 0-89728-043-1, 615644). Omega Pubns OR.
Pache, Rene. The Future Life. 1979. pap. 7.95 (ISBN 0-8024-2900-9). Moody.
Palms, Roger C. Seu Futuro Esta Na Maos...Deus. Date not set. 1.30 (ISBN 0-686-76438-2). Life Pubs Intl.
Penelhum, Terence. Survival & Disembodied Existence. (Studies in Philosophical Psychology). 1970. text ed. 10.00x (ISBN 0-391-00054-3); pap. text ed. 5.75x (ISBN 0-391-01751-9). Humanities.
The Philosophy of Life & the Philosophy of Death: Considerations & Anticipations of the Future Universe & of Man's Existence in It. 2nd ed. (Illus.). 1977. 27.25 (ISBN 0-89266-058-9). Am Classical Coll Pr.
Pratney, Winkie. Star Wars, Star Trek. 1978. pap. 1.75 (ISBN 0-89728-057-1, 693400). Omega Pubns OR.
Quadrupani, R. P. Light & Peace. LC 79-67860. 193p. 1980. pap. 3.00 (ISBN 0-89555-133-0). Tan Bks Pubs.
Ra, Bo Yin. The Book on Life Beyond. Reichenbach, B. A., tr. from Ger. LC 78-51633. 1978. pap. 3.50 (ISBN 0-915034-02-6). Kober Pr.
Randolph, P. B. After Death: The Immortality of Man. 1970. 5.95 (ISBN 0-686-05801-1). Philos Pub.
Rice, Max M. Your Rewards in Heaven. LC 80-68885. 160p. 1981. pap. 3.95 (ISBN 0-89636-063-6). Accent Bks.
Riggle, H. M. Beyond the Tomb. 288p. 4.00 (ISBN 0-686-29100-X). Faith Pub Hse.
Rogo, D. Scott. Man Does Survive Death. 1977. pap. 3.95 (ISBN 0-8065-0582-6). Citadel Pr.
Salter, W. H. Zoar: Or the Evidence of Psychical Research Concerning Survival. LC 75-7399. (Perspectives in Psychical Research Ser.). 1975. Repr. of 1961 ed. 13.00x (ISBN 0-405-07048-9). Arno.
Saltmarsh, H. F. Evidence of Personal Survival from Cross Correspondences. LC 75-7400. (Perspectives in Psychical Research Ser.). 1975. Repr. of 1938 ed. 12.00x (ISBN 0-405-07049-7). Arno.
Sandberg, Anne. Seeing the Invisible. 1977. pap. 3.95 (ISBN 0-88270-246-7). Logos.
Segraves, Kelly L. When You're Dead, You're Dead. 1980. pap. 2.95 (ISBN 0-89293-023-3). Beta Bk.
Seu Futuro Esta Nas Maos De Deus. 1980. pap. 1.30 (ISBN 0-686-69354-X). Life Pubs Intl.
Seymour, Richard. The Gift of God. pap. 1.50 (ISBN 0-686-12746-3). Grace Pub Co.
Shank, Robert. God's Tomorrow: The Life Beyond Death. (Orig.). 1975. pap. 1.95 (ISBN 0-911620-03-6). Westcott.
Shell, Joy. The Ministry of Angels. 1977. pap. 3.95 (ISBN 0-8065-0586-9). Citadel Pr.
Sherman, Harold. You Live After Death. 1979. pap. 1.75 (ISBN 0-449-13798-6, GM). Fawcett.
Spraggett, Allen. The Case for Immortality. 1975. pap. 1.50 (ISBN 0-451-06373-2, W6373, Sig). NAL.
Steiner, Rudolf. Life Between Death & Rebirth. Querido, R. M., tr. from Ger. LC 68-57429. 308p. (Orig.). 1975. pap. 7.95 (ISBN 0-910142-62-9). Anthroposophic.
Strauss, Lehman. Life After Death. 1979. pap. 1.95 (ISBN 0-89107-055-9). Good News.
Studer, Gerald C. After Death, What? LC 75-38074. 160p. 1976. pap. 1.95 (ISBN 0-8361-1792-1); student activity bk. 1.25 (ISBN 0-8361-1866-9). Herald Pr.
Stulman, J. & Laszlo, E. Emergent Man. new ed. LC 72-188124. (World Institute Creative Findings Ser.). 196p. 1973. 26.50x (ISBN 0-677-14930-1). Gordon.
Swedenborg, Emanuel. Heaven & Hell. LC 77-93044. trade ed. 8.25 (ISBN 0-87785-067-4); student ed 6.50 (ISBN 0-87785-066-6); pap. 1.95 (ISBN 0-87785-153-0). Swedenborg.
Van Dorn, Charles H. Six Things Everyone Should Know. 201p. 1980. 7.95 (ISBN 0-533-03707-7). Vantage.
Weldon, John & Levitt, Zola. Is There Life After Death? 1980. pap. 2.25 (ISBN 0-89081-232-2). Harvest Hse.
West, Steven & Tyburn-Lombard, Donald. What Happens After Death? (Illus.). 1977. 5.95 (ISBN 0-89519-001-X). AMW.
What Kind of World Are We Leaving Our Children? 1979. pap. 14.50 (ISBN 92-3-101623-7, U891, UNESCO). Unipub.
Whittiker, Adolphus. The Psychology of Spirit-Intercourse & the Conditions for Sex After Death. (Illus.). 137p. 1981. 73.85 (ISBN 0-89920-031-1). Am Inst Psych.
Winter, David. Hereafter: What Happens After Death? LC 72-94097. (Illus.). 96p. 1972. pap. 1.75 (ISBN 0-87788-341-6). Shaw Pubs.
Yangley, Ed. Mankind & the Hereafter. 1980. 7.95 (ISBN 0-533-04303-4). Vantage.
Zodhiates, Spiros. Life After Death!? Zodhiates, Spiros, tr. from Greek. Orig. Title: What Happens After Death? (Illus.). 1977. pap. 1.75 (ISBN 0-89957-525-0). AMG Pubs.

FUTURE LIFE–BIBLIOGRAPHY
Alger, William R. Destiny of the Soul: Critical History of the Doctrine of a Future Life, 2 Vols. 10th ed. LC 68-19263. 1968. Repr. of 1880 ed. Set. lib. bdg. 43.25x (ISBN 0-8371-0003-8, ALDS). Greenwood.
FUTURE LIFE–CASE STUDIES
Beard, Paul. Living on: How Consciousness Continues & Evolves After Death. 212p. 1981. 12.95 (ISBN 0-8264-0036-1); pap. 5.95 (ISBN 0-8264-0037-X). Continuum.
Moody, Raymond A., Jr. Life After Life. 176p. 1981. 7.95 (ISBN 0-89176-037-7); pap. 4.95 (ISBN 0-89176-036-9). Mockingbird Bks.
Rawlings, Maurice. Beyond Death's Door. 1979. Repr. pap. 2.25 (ISBN 0-553-14879-6). Bantam.
Ritchie, George G. & Sherrill, Elizabeth. Return from Tomorrow. 128p. 1981. pap. 2.50 (ISBN 0-8007-8412-X, Spire Bks). Revell.
FUTURE PUNISHMENT
see also Future Life; Hell; Purgatory; Universalism
Bunyan, John. Groans of a Lost Soul. LC 68-6571. 1967. pap. 3.25 (ISBN 0-685-19830-8). Reiner.
Pink, Arthur W. Eternal Punishment. pap. 0.75 (ISBN 0-685-00734-0). Reiner.
Rowell, Geoffrey. Hell & the Victorians: A Study of the 19th-Century Theological Controversies Concerning Eternal Punishment & the Future Life. 249p. 1974. 33.00x (ISBN 0-19-826638-3). Oxford U Pr.
FUTURE TIME PERSPECTIVE
see Time Perspective
FUTURES
see Commodity Exchanges; Short Selling; Speculation
FUTURISM
Arab-Ogly, E. In the Forecaster's Maze. 224p. 1975. 2.60 (ISBN 0-8285-0236-6, Pub. by Progress Pubs Russia). Imported Pubns.
Ciba Foundation, ed. The Future As an Academic Discipline. (Ciba Foundation Symposium Ser: No. 36). 240p. 1975. 20.50 (ISBN 0-444-15184-2, Excerpta Medica); pap. 13.50 (ISBN 0-444-15203-2). Elsevier.
Fitch, Robert M. & Svengalis, Cordell M. Futures Unlimited: Teaching About Worlds to Come. LC 79-52124. (Bulletin Ser.: No. 1). 86p. (Orig.). 1979. pap. 6.95 (ISBN 0-87986-023-5). Coun Soc Studies.
Freeman, Christopher & Jahoda, Marie, eds. World Futures: The Great Debate. LC 78-57544. 1978. 30.00x (ISBN 0-87663-328-9). Universe.
Fuller, R. Buckminster. Operating Manual for Spaceship Earth. 1977. pap. 3.95 (ISBN 0-525-47433-1). Dutton.
Graham, Robert K. The Future of Man. rev. ed. LC 74-112341. (Illus.). 101p. Date not set. pap. 3.50 (ISBN 0-939794-00-4). Foun Adv Man.
Hawrylyshyn, Bohdan. Road Maps to the Future: Towards More Effective Societies. (Illus.). 193p. 31.00 (ISBN 0-08-026115-9); pap. 11.00 (ISBN 0-08-026114-0). Pergamon.
Heilbroner, Robert L. The Future As History: The Historic Currents of Our Time & the Direction in Which They Are Taking America. 9.00 (ISBN 0-8446-5854-5). Peter Smith.
Kauffman, Draper L., Jr. Futurism & Future Studies. 60p. 1976. pap. 2.75 (ISBN 0-686-63687-2, 1803-6-06). NEA.
Kosolapov, V. Mankind & the Year Two Thousand. 236p. 1976. 3.00 (ISBN 0-8285-0243-9, Pub. by Progress Pubs Russia). Imported Pubns.
Peccei, Aurelio. One Hundred Pages for the Future. (Illus.). 150p. 1981. 17.50 (ISBN 0-08-028110-9); pap. 8.50 (ISBN 0-08-028117-6). Pergamon.
Pulliam, John P. & Bowman, Jim R. Educational Futurism: In Pursuance of Survival. 164p. 1975. pap. 3.95x (ISBN 0-8061-1299-9). U of Okla Pr.
Roman, Robert. Survival 21: Futurology for the 21st Century. 7.50 (ISBN 0-912314-00-1). Academy Pr-Santa.
Theobald, Robert. An Alternative Future for America's Third Century. LC 76-3135. 266p. 1976. pap. 5.95x (ISBN 0-8040-0725-X). Swallow.
FUTURISM (ART)
see also Action in Art; Letter Pictures; Post-Impressionism (Art)
Andreoli-De Villers, Jean-Pierre. Futurism & the Arts: A Bibliography, 1959-1973. LC 74-79005. 1975. 25.00x (ISBN 0-8020-2120-4). U of Toronto Pr.
Clough, Rosa. Futurism: The Story of a Modern Art Movement, a New Appraisal. LC 71-90487. Repr. of 1961 ed. lib. bdg. 17.50x (ISBN 0-8371-2166-3, CLFU). Greenwood.
Kozloff, Max. Cubism-Futurism. (Icon Editions). (Illus.). 256p. 1975. pap. 5.95 (ISBN 0-06-430059-5, IN-59, HarpT). Har-Row.
Nash, J. Cubism, Futurism & Constructivism. LC 77-76770. (Modern Movements in Art Ser.). 1978. pap. 1.95 (ISBN 0-8120-0881-2). Barron.
Pike, Christopher, ed. The Futurists, the Formalists & the Marxist Critique. Andrew, Joe & Pike, Christopher, trs. from Rus. 265p. 1979. text ed. 20.00x (ISBN 0-906133-14-9). Humanities.
Taylor, Christiana J. Futurism: Politics, Painting & Performance. Foster, Stephen, ed. (Studies in Fine Arts: The Avant-Garde, No. 8). 1980. 23.95 (ISBN 0-8357-1062-9, Pub. by UMI Res Pr). Univ Microfilms.
Taylor, Joshua C. Futurism. LC 61-11271. (Illus.). 154p. 1961. 6.50 (ISBN 0-87070-326-9, Pub. by Museum Mod Art). NYGS.
Tisdall, Caroline & Bozzola, Angelo. Futurism. LC 77-76819. (World of Art Ser.). (Illus.). 1978. 17.95 (ISBN 0-19-519983-9); pap. 9.95 (ISBN 0-19-519980-4). Oxford U Pr.
Walden, Herwarth. Einblick in Kunst: Expressionismus, Futurismus, Kubismus. (Foundations of Modern Art: No. 3). (Illus., Ger.). 1974. pap. 22.00x (ISBN 0-89032-001-2). Wittenborn.
FYOTI LANGUAGE
see Congo Language

G

GABLE, CLARK, 1901-1960
Essoe, Gabe. Films of Clark Gable. (Illus.). 1970. 12.00 (ISBN 0-8065-0011-5); pap. 6.95 (ISBN 0-8065-0273-8). Citadel Pr.
Scagnetti, Jack. The Life & Loves of Gable. LC 75-43842. (Illus.). 160p. 1976. 12.95 (ISBN 0-8246-0205-6). Jonathan David.
Tornabene, Lyn. Long Live the King: A Biography of Clark Gable. LC 76-43227. (Illus.). 1977. 10.95 (ISBN 0-399-11863-2). Putnam.
Williams, Chester. Gable. LC 68-54388. (Illus.). 1968. 6.95 (ISBN 0-8303-0059-7). Fleet.
--Gable. (Signet Film Ser). 1975. pap. 1.25 (ISBN 0-451-06304-X, Y6304, Sig). NAL.
GABO, NAUM, ORIGINALLY NAUM PEVSNER
Gabo, Naum. Gabo: Constructions, Structure, Paintings, Drawings & Engravings. LC 58-1904. 193p. 1957. Repr. 29.00 (ISBN 0-403-04073-6). Somerset Pub.
GABON
Carpenter, Allan & Hughes, James. Gabon. LC 76-6465. (Enchantment of Africa Ser.). (Illus.). (gr. 5 up). 1977. PLB 10.60 (ISBN 0-516-04563-6). Childrens.
Fernandez, James W. Bwiti: An Ethnography of the Religious Imagination in Africa. LC 81-47125. (Illus.). 708p. 1982. 70.00x (ISBN 0-691-09390-3); pap. 19.50x (ISBN 0-691-10122-1). Princeton U Pr.
Gardinier, David E. Historical Dictionary of Gabon. LC 81-5290. (African Historical Dictionaries Ser.: No. 30). 284p. 1981. 15.00 (ISBN 0-8108-1435-8). Scarecrow.
Remy, Mylene. Le Gabon Aujourd'hui. (Illus.). 1977. 21.95x (ISBN 2-85258-068-3). Intl Learn Syst.
Temy, Mylane. Gabon Today. 264p. 1979. 14.95 (ISBN 2-8525-8069-1, Pub. by J A Editions France). Hippocrene Bks.
Weinstein, Brian. Gabon: Nation-Building on the Ogooue. (Illus.). 1967. 17.00x (ISBN 0-262-23023-2). MIT Pr.
GABRIEL RICHARD, FATHER
Maxwell, Charles H. Adventures of Gabriel in His Search for God. 1933. Repr. 12.50 (ISBN 0-8274-1821-3). R West.
GADDANG (PHILIPPINE PEOPLE)
see also Ethnology–Philippine Islands
GADE (AFRICAN TRIBE)
see also Ethnology–Nigeria
GADGETS
see Implements, Utensils, etc.
GADSDEN PURCHASE
Griggs, et al. The Mexican Experience in Arizona: An Original Anthology. Cortes, Carlos E., ed. & intro. by. LC 76-5566. (Chicano Heritage Ser.). (Illus.). 1976. 16.00x (ISBN 0-405-09539-2). Arno.
GADSDEN TREATY, 1853
Garber, Paul M. The Gadsden Treaty. 1959. 8.00 (ISBN 0-8446-1195-6). Peter Smith.
GAEKWAD DYNASTY
Chavda, V. K. Gaekwad & the British: A Study of Their Problems, 1800-1920. 1966. 7.00x (ISBN 0-8426-1203-3). Verry.
GAELIC BALLADS AND SONGS
Campbell, John L. Highland Songs of the Forty-Five. LC 75-173105. Repr. of 1933 ed. 21.00 (ISBN 0-405-08338-6, Blom Pubns). Arno.
GAELIC FOLK-LORE
see Folk-Lore, Gaelic
GAELIC LANGUAGE
see also Celtic Languages; Irish Language; Manx Language
Aitken, A. J., et al, eds. A Dictionary of the Older Scottish Tongue: From the Twelfth Century to the End of the Seventeeth, Part XXIX. 1977. lib. bdg. 16.00x (ISBN 0-226-11720-0). U of Chicago Pr.
Blackie, John S. The Language & Literature of the Scottish Highlands. 1979. Repr. of 1876 ed. lib. bdg. 40.00 (ISBN 0-8495-0402-3). Arden Lib.
Calder. A Gaelic Grammar. 352p. 16.50x (ISBN 0-686-27678-7). Colton Bk.
Donovan, John A. Gaelic Names for Celtic Dogs. LC 78-56243. (Other Dog Bks.). (Illus.). 1980. 9.95 (ISBN 0-87714-067-7). Denlingers.
Dorian, Nancy. Language Death: The Life Cycle of a Scottish Gaelic Dialect. 1980. text ed. 25.00x (ISBN 0-8122-7785-6); pap. text ed. 11.95x (ISBN 0-8122-1111-1). U of Pa Pr.
Dunn, Charles W. Highland Settler: A Portrait of the Scottish Gael in Nova Scotia. LC 53-7025. 1953. pap. 5.95 (ISBN 0-8020-6094-3). U of Toronto Pr.
Dwelly. Illustrated Gaelic-English Dictionary. 8th ed. (Illus.). 35.00x (ISBN 0-686-00868-5). Colton Bk.
Gaelic-Speaking Children in the Highland Schools. (Scottish Council for Research in Education Ser.: No. 47). 1916. 2.75x (ISBN 0-8426-1264-5). Verry.
Green, David. The Irish Language: Great Languages. 1980. text ed. write for info. (ISBN 0-391-01135-9). Humanities.
Healy, Timothy. Basic Manx, Irish & Scottish Gaelic. 1977. pap. text ed. 9.25x (ISBN 90-6296-021-9). Humanities.
MacAlpine. Gaelic - English Pronouncing Dictionary. 12.50x (ISBN 0-686-01305-0). Colton Bk.
MacAlpine & Mackenzie. Gaelic - English, English - Gaelic (Pronouncing) Dictionary. 22.50x (ISBN 0-686-01306-9). Colton Bk.
Mackay, Charles. Dictionary of Lowland Scotch. LC 68-17998. 1968. Repr. of 1888 ed. 30.00 (ISBN 0-8103-3284-1). Gale.
--The Poetry & Humor of the Scottish Language. Repr. of 1882 ed. 45.00 (ISBN 0-686-19892-1). Ridgeway Bks.
--The Poetry & Humour of the Scottish Language. Repr. of 1882 ed. 45.00 (ISBN 0-686-18782-2). Scholars Ref Lib.
Mackechnie, John. Gaelic Without Groans. 3rd ed. 1974. pap. text ed. 4.50x (ISBN 0-05-002862-6). Longman.
MacKinnon, Kenneth. Language, Education & Social Processes in a Gaelic Communtiy. (Direct Editions Ser.). (Orig.). 1977. pap. 10.95 (ISBN 0-7100-8466-8). Routledge & Kegan.
Mackinnon, Roderick. Teach Yourself Gaelic. (Teach Yourself Ser.). 1972. pap. 4.95 (ISBN 0-679-10217-5). McKay.
Maclaren, J. Gaelic Self Taught. 4th ed. 8.50x (ISBN 0-686-00865-0). Colton Bk.
MacLennan, Malcolm. Gaelic Dictionary--Gaelic-English; English-Gaelic. 632p. 1980. 45.00 (ISBN 0-08-025713-5); pap. 22.00 (ISBN 0-08-025712-7). Pergamon.
O'Donaill. Foclair Gaeilge Bearla (Irish-English Dictionary) 30.00x (ISBN 0-686-28280-9). Colton Bk.
Pinkerton, John, ed. Scotish Poems, 3 vols. LC 70-144531. Repr. of 1792 ed. Set. 60.00 (ISBN 0-404-08680-2); 20.00 ea. AMS Pr.
Smith, George G. Specimens of Middle Scots. LC 70-144582. Repr. of 1902 ed. 34.00 (ISBN 0-404-08692-6). AMS Pr.
Warrack, Alexander. Chambers Scots Dictionary. Repr. of 1911 ed. 14.95 (ISBN 0-550-11801-2, Pub. by Two Continents). Hippocrene Bks.
GAELIC LITERATURE
see also Irish Literature (Collections)
Mackechnie, John, compiled by. Catalogue of Gaelic Manuscripts in Selected Libraries in Great Britain & Ireland, 2 vols. 1973. Set. 230.00 (ISBN 0-8161-0832-3). G K Hall.
MacLeod, Donald J. Twentieth Century Publications in Scottish Gaelic. 232p. 1981. 27.00x (ISBN 0-7073-0266-8, Pub. by Scottish Academic Pr Scotland). Columbia U Pr.
GAELIC LITERATURE–HISTORY AND CRITICISM
Cameron, Alexander. Reliquiae Celticae, 2 vols. MacBain, Alexander & Kennedy, John K., eds. LC 78-72621. (Celtic Language & Literature: Goidelic & Brythonic). Repr. of 1894 ed. Set. 84.50 (ISBN 0-404-17543-0). AMS Pr.
Hyde, Douglas. The Story of Early Gaelic Literature. LC 77-94587. 1978. Repr. of 1895 ed. lib. bdg. 20.00 (ISBN 0-89341-182-5). Longwood Pr.
Jordan, John, ed. The Pleasures of Gaelic Literature. 1977. pap. 4.25 (ISBN 0-85342-492-6). Irish Bk Ctr.
MacNeill, Nigel. The Literature of the Highlanders. Campbell, John M., ed. LC 78-72636. (Celtic Language & Literature: Goidelic & Brythonic). Repr. of 1929 ed. 44.50 (ISBN 0-404-17567-8). AMS Pr.
Nutt, Alfred T. Critical Study of Gaelic Literature Indispensable for the History of the Gaelic Race. LC 78-102861. (Research & Source Works Ser.: No. 204). 1971. Repr. of 1904 ed. 11.00 (ISBN 0-8337-2593-9). B Franklin.
O'Conor, Norreys J. Battles & Enchantments Retold from Early Gaelic Literature. facsimile ed. LC 71-124247. (Select Bibliographies Reprint Ser). Repr. of 1922 ed. 12.00 (ISBN 0-8369-5435-1). Arno.
GAELIC LITERATURE–TRANSLATIONS INTO ENGLISH
Campbell, John F. Popular Tales of the West Highlands, 4 Vols. LC 67-23921. 1969. Repr. of 1890 ed. 100.00 (ISBN 0-8103-3458-5). Gale.
Thomson, R. L., ed. John Carswell's Gaelic Translation of the Book of the Common Order. 1970. 15.00x (ISBN 0-7073-0035-5, Pub. by Scottish Academic Pr Scotland). Columbia U Pr.
GAELIC PHILOLOGY
Blackie, John S. The Language & Literature of the Scottish Highlands. LC 73-3441. 1973. lib. bdg. 20.00 (ISBN 0-8414-1776-8). Folcroft.
Cameron, Alexander. Reliquiae Celticae, 2 vols. MacBain, Alexander & Kennedy, John K., eds. LC 78-72621. (Celtic Language & Literature: Goidelic & Brythonic). Repr. of 1894 ed. Set. 84.50 (ISBN 0-404-17543-0). AMS Pr.
GAELIC POETRY–TRANSLATIONS INTO ENGLISH
Dixon, William M. Edinburgh Book of Scottish Verse, 1300-1900. Dixon, W. Macneile, ed. LC 76-164841. Repr. of 1910 ed. 52.50 (ISBN 0-404-08632-2). AMS Pr.
Merriman, Brian. The Midnight Court & the Adventures of a Luckless Fellow. LC 74-14678. 1926. 10.00 (ISBN 0-8414-8852-5). Folcroft.
Thomson, Derick. An Introduction to Gaelic Poetry. LC 73-86601. 319p. 1974. 10.00 (ISBN 0-312-42735-2). St Martin.
GAELIC TALES
see Tales, Gaelic
GAELS
see Celts
GAG, WANDA HAZEL, 1893-1946
Duin, Nancy E. Wanda Gag, Author & Illustrator of Childrens Books. Rahmas, D. Steve, ed. (Outstanding Personalities Ser.: No. 57). 32p. 1972. lib. bdg. 2.95 incl. catalog cards (ISBN 0-87157-546-9); pap. 1.50 vinyl laminated covers (ISBN 0-87157-046-7). SamHar Pr.
GAGAKU
Garfias, Robert. Gagaku: The Music & Dances of the Japanese Imperial Household. (Illus.). 1959. pap. 3.95 (ISBN 0-87830-540-8). Theatre Arts.
GAGARIN, YURI ALEKSEEVICH, 1934-1968
Golovanov, Y. Our Gagarin. 329p. 1978. 25.50 (ISBN 0-8285-1556-5, Pub. by Progress Pubs Russia). Imported Pubns.
Sharpe, Mitchell R. Yuri Gagarin: First Man in Space. LC 74-75841. (Heroes of Space Ser). (Illus.). (gr. 7 up). 1969. 4.95 (ISBN 0-87397-203-1). Strode.
GAGE, THOMAS, 1603-1656
Thompson, J. Eric. Thomas Gage's Travels in the New World. LC 81-2948. (Illus.). x, 379p. 1981. Repr. of 1958 ed. lib. bdg. 41.00x (ISBN 0-313-23015-3, THTN). Greenwood.
GAGE, THOMAS, 1721-1787
Alden, John R. General Gage in America. LC 77-90459. Repr. of 1948 ed. lib. bdg. 15.00 (ISBN 0-8371-2264-3, ALGG). Greenwood.
French, Allen. General Gage's Informers: New Material Upon Lexington & Concord, Benjamin Thompson As Loyalist & the Treachery of Benjamin Church, Jr. LC 68-54420. (Illus.). 1968. Repr. of 1932 ed. lib. bdg. 14.25x (ISBN 0-8371-0431-9, FRGI). Greenwood.
GAGER, WILLIAM, fl. 1580-1619
Rainolds, John. The Overthrow of Stage-Plays. 206p. Repr. of 1599 ed. 21.00 (ISBN 0-384-49510-9). Johnson Repr.
GAGES
see also Pressure-Gages; Strain Gages
Gage Blanks: B47.1-1974. 118p. 1975. pap. text ed. 20.00 (ISBN 0-685-54473-7, M00082). ASME.
Kennedy, C. W. & Andrews, D. E., eds. Inspection & Gaging. 5th rev. ed. (Illus.). 598p. 1977. 18.00 (ISBN 0-8311-1119-4). Indus Pr.
Ryder, G. H. Jigs, Fixtures, Tools & Gauges. 6th ed. Orig. Title: Jigs, Tools & Fixtures. (Illus.). 176p. 1973. text ed. 12.75x (ISBN 0-291-39432-9). Scholium Intl.
Urban, P., ed. Facts & Prospects of Gauge Theories: Proceedings of the XVII Internationale Universitaetswochen Fuer Kernphysik 1978 der Karl-Franzens-Universitaet Graz at Schladming (Steiermark, Austria) Feb. 21-March 3, 1978. (Acta Physica Austriaca: Supplementum 19). 1979. 122.80 (ISBN 0-387-81514-7). Springer-Verlag.

GAGING
Practical Applications of Neutron Radiography & Gaging. 1976. 25.50 (ISBN 0-686-52061-0, 04-586000-22). ASTM.
Roth, Edward S., ed. Gaging: Practical Design & Application. LC 80-53424. (Manufacturing Update Ser.). (Illus.). 289p. 1981. 29.00 (ISBN 0-87263-064-1). SME.
Urban, P., ed. Facts & Prospects of Gauge Theories: Proceedings of the XVII Internationale Universitaetswochen Fuer Kernphysik 1978 der Karl-Franzens-Universitaet Graz at Schladming (Steiermark, Austria) Feb. 21-March 3, 1978. (Acta Physica Austriaca: Supplementum 19). 1979. 122.80 (ISBN 0-387-81514-7). Springer-Verlag.
GAINE, HUGH, 1726 or 7-1807
Lorenz, Alfred L. Hugh Gaine: A Colonial Printer-Editor's Odyssey to Loyalism. LC 72-75335. (New Horizons in Journalism Ser.). 205p. 1972. 6.95x (ISBN 0-8093-0588-7). S Ill U Pr.
GAINES, WILLIAM M.
Jacobs, Frank. The Mad World of William M. Gaines. 1973. 7.95 (ISBN 0-8184-0054-4). Lyle Stuart.
GAINESVILLE, TEXAS-HISTORY
Acheson, Sam & O'Connell, Julie, eds. George Washington Diamond's Account of the Great Hanging at Gainesville, 1862. 1963. 5.00 (ISBN 0-87611-000-6); pap. 3.50 (ISBN 0-87611-001-4). Tex St Hist Assn.
Barrett, Thomas. Great Hanging at Gainesville. 1961. pap. 3.50 (ISBN 0-87611-004-9). Tex St Hist Assn.
GAINSBOROUGH, THOMAS, 1727-1788
Hayes, John. Drawings of Thomas Gainsborough, 2 Vols. LC 78-140108. (Paul Mellon Centre Studies). (Illus.). 1971. Set. 75.00x (ISBN 0-300-01425-2). Yale U Pr.
--Gainsborough As Printmaker. LC 79-179473. (Illus.). 136p. 1972. 35.00x (ISBN 0-300-01561-5). Yale U Pr.
Leonard, Jonathan N. World of Gainsborough. (Library of Art). (Illus.). 1969. 15.95 (ISBN 0-8094-0253-X). Time-Life.
--World of Gainsborough. LC 73-84574. (Library of Art Ser.). (Illus.). (gr. 6 up). 1969. 12.96 (ISBN 0-8094-0282-3, Pub. by Time-Life). Silver.
Lindsay, Jack. Thomas Gainsborough: His Life & Art. LC 80-54397. (Illus.). 248p. 1981. 25.00 (ISBN 0-87663-352-1). Universe.
Worman, Isabelle. Thomas Gainsborough. 1979. 16.00 (ISBN 0-900963-69-7, Pub. by Terence Dalton England). State Mutual Bk.
GAITHER, ALONZO
Curry, George E. Jake Gaither: America's Most Famous Black Coach. LC 76-50580. (Illus.). 1977. 7.95 (ISBN 0-396-07381-6). Dodd.
GAITSKILL, HUGH, 1906-1963
Williams, Philip M. Hugh Gaitskell: A Political Biography. (Illus.). 1979. 47.50x (ISBN 0-389-20032-8). B&N.
GALA LANGUAGE
see Bangala Language
GALACTOSEMIA
Gould, Barry K., et al. Galactorrhea. (Illus.). 128p. 1974. 13.75 (ISBN 0-398-02978-4). C C Thomas.
Hsia, David Yi-Yung. Galactosemia. (Illus.). 336p. 1969. photocopy ed. spiral 32.50 (ISBN 0-398-00879-5). C C Thomas.
GALAPAGOS ISLANDS
Beebe, William. The Arcturus Adventure. LC 80-8409. (Nature Library Ser.). 450p. 1981. pap. 5.95 (ISBN 0-06-090846-7, CN 846, CN). Har-Row.
De Roy Moore, Tui. Galapagos: Islands Lost in Time. LC 80-5360. (Illus.). 144p. 1980. 25.00 (ISBN 0-670-33361-1, Studio). Viking Pr.
McBirney, Alexander R. & Williams, Howel. Geology & Petrology of the Galapagos Islands. LC 79-98018. (Memoir: No. 118). (Illus., Orig.). 1970. 12.00x (ISBN 0-8137-1118-5). Geol Soc.
Selsam, Millicent E. Land of the Giant Tortoise: The Story of the Galapagos. LC 77-4897. (Illus.). 64p. (gr. 1-5). 1977. 7.95 (ISBN 0-590-07416-4, Four Winds). Schol Bk Serv.
Thornton, Ian. Darwin's Islands: A Natural History of the Galapagos. (Illus.). 8.95 (ISBN 0-385-07488-3). Natural Hist.
GALATIANS
see also Celts
Boatman, Don E. & Boles, Kenny. Galatians. rev. ed. LC 70-1141. (The Bible Study Textbook Ser.). (Illus.). 1976. 11.50 (ISBN 0-89900-039-8). College Pr Pub.
GALAXIES
see also Magellanic Clouds; Milky Way
Atanasijevi'c, I. Selected Exercises in Galactic Astronomy. (Astrophysics & Space Science Library: No.26). 144p. 1971. lib. bdg. 21.00 (ISBN 90-277-0198-9, Pub. by Reidel Holland). Kluwer Boston.
Baade, Walter. Evolution of Stars & Galaxies. Payne-Gaposchkin, Cecilia, ed. LC 75-24679. (Paperback Ser: No. 284). 352p. 1975. pap. 6.95 (ISBN 0-262-52033-8). MIT Pr.
Burton, W. B. The Large Scale Characteristics of the Galaxy. (International Astronomical Union: No. 84). 1979. lib. bdg. 73.50 (ISBN 90-277-1029-5, Pub. by Reidel Holland); pap. 37.00 (ISBN 90-277-1030-9, Pub. by Reidel Holland). Kluwer Boston.
Chiu Hone-Yeel & Muriel, Amador. Galactic Astronomy, Vols. 1 & 2. 1970. Vol. 1. 73.25x (ISBN 0-677-13750-8); Vol. 2. 63.75x (ISBN 0-677-13760-5); Set. 123.25 (ISBN 0-677-13770-2). Gordon.
Cornell University, Summer Seminar, 1965. Relativity Theory & Astrophysics: Galactic Structures. Ehlers, J., ed. 1974. Repr. 21.20 (ISBN 0-8218-1109-6, LAM-9). Am Math.
De Vaucouleurs, Gerard & De Vaucouleurs, Antoinette. Reference Catalogue of Bright Galaxies. 276p. 1964. 25.00x (ISBN 0-292-73348-8). U of Tex Pr.
De Vaucouleurs, Gerard, et al. Second Reference Catalogue of Bright Galaxies. LC 75-44009. (Illus.). 404p. 1976. text ed. 50.00x (ISBN 0-292-75509-0). U of Tex Pr.
European Astronomical Meeting, 1st, Athens, 1972. Galaxies & Relativistic Astrophysics: Proceedings, Vol. 3. Hadjidemetriou, J. & Barbanis, B., eds. LC 73-10665. (Illus.). 240p. 1973. 77.90 (ISBN 0-387-06416-8). Springer-Verlag.
Evans, David S., ed. Photometry, Kinematics & Dynamics of Galaxies. LC 79-56195. (Illus.). xi, 492p. (Orig.). 1979. pap. 16.00 (ISBN 0-9603796-0-6). U of Tex Dept Astron.
Fall, S. M. & Lynden-Bell, D., eds. The Structure & Evolution of Normal Galaxies. LC 80-42026. (Illus.). 280p. 1981. 29.95 (ISBN 0-521-23907-9). Cambridge U Pr.
Ferris, Timothy. Galaxies. LC 80-13139. (Illus.). 200p. 1980. 75.00 (ISBN 0-87156-273-1). Sierra.
Field, George B., et al. The Redshift Controversy. (Frontiers in Physics Ser.: No. 39). (Illus.). 1973. text ed. 26.50 (ISBN 0-8053-2512-3, Adv Bk Prog); pap. text ed. 14.50 (ISBN 0-8053-2513-1). Benjamin-Cummings.
Gribbin, John. Galaxy Formation: A Personal View. LC 75-31706. 1976. 27.95 (ISBN 0-470-32775-8). Halsted Pr.
Haynes, R. F., et al. A Compendium of Radio Measurements of Bright Galaxies. 1977. pap. 4.50x (ISBN 0-643-00144-1, Pub. by CSIRO). Intl Schol Bk Serv.
--Compendium of Radio Measurements of Bright Galaxies. 200p. 1981. 25.00x (ISBN 0-643-00144-1, Pub. by CSIRO Australia). State Mutual Bk.
Hazard, C. & Mitton, S., eds. Active Galactic Nuclei. LC 78-67426. 1979. 38.50 (ISBN 0-521-22494-2). Cambridge U Pr.
Hodge, Paul W. Atlas of the Andromeda Galaxy. (Illus.). 80p. 1981. 50.00 (ISBN 0-295-95795-6). U of Wash Pr.
I. A. U. Symposium No. 58, Canberra, Australia, 12-15 August 1973. The Formation & Dynamics of Galaxies: Proceedings. Shakeshaft, J. R., ed. LC 74-76476. (Symposium of the International Astronomical Union: No. 58). 1974. lib. bdg. 71.00 (ISBN 90-277-0460-0, Pub. by Reidel Holland); pap. text ed. 53.000 (ISBN 90-277-0461-9, Pub. by Reidel Holland). Kluwer Boston.
IAU Symposium; No. 44, Upsala, Sweden, August 10-14, 1970. External Galaxies & Quasi-Stellar Objects: Proceedings. Evans, D. S., ed. LC 77-154736. (IAU Symposia: No. 44). 549p. 1972. lib. bdg. 53.00 (ISBN 90-277-0199-7, Pub. by Reidel Holland). Kluwer Boston.
Inglis, Stuart J. Planets, Stars, & Galaxies. 4th ed. LC 75-31542. 352p. 1976. pap. text ed. 22.50 (ISBN 0-471-42738-1). Wiley.
International Astronomical Union Symposium, 44th, Uppsala, Sweden, 1970. External Galaxies & Quasi-Stellar Objects: Proceedings. Evans, D. S., ed. LC 77-154736. (Illus.). 549p. 1972. 42.50 (ISBN 0-387-91092-1). Springer-Verlag.
International School of Astrophysics, 2nd, Italy, June-July 1974 & Setti, G. Structure & Evolution of Galaxies. LC 75-22261. (NATO Advanced Study Institute Ser: No. C-21). viii, 334p. 1975. lib. bdg. 42.00 (ISBN 90-277-0325-6, Pub. by Reidel Holland). Kluwer Boston.
Jones, Kenneth G., ed. Webb Society Deep-Sky Observer's Handbook: Vol. 4, Galaxies. LC 77-359099. 296p. 1981. pap. 15.95x (ISBN 0-89490-050-1). Enslow Pubs.
Kaufmann, William J., III. Galaxies & Quasars. LC 79-10570. (Illus.). 1979. text ed. 17.95x (ISBN 0-7167-1133-8); pap. text ed. 8.95x (ISBN 0-7167-1134-6). W H Freeman.
Knight, David C. Galaxies, Islands in Space. (Illus.). (gr. 4-6). 1979. 6.50 (ISBN 0-688-22180-7); PLB 6.24 (ISBN 0-688-32180-1). Morrow.
Lequeux, James. Physique et Evolution Des Galaxies. LC 66-28070. (Cours & Documents de Mathematiques & de Physique Ser.). (Orig., Fr.). 1967. 49.50x (ISBN 0-677-50110-2). Gordon.
--Structure & Evolution of Galaxies. (Documents on Modern Physics Ser.). 1969. 45.75x (ISBN 0-677-30110-3). Gordon.
Lynds, Beverly T., ed. Dark Nebulae, Globules, & Protostars. LC 73-152040. (Illus.). 158p. 1971. 7.50x (ISBN 0-8165-0300-1). U of Ariz Pr.
Mitton, Simon. Exploring the Galaxies. LC 76-42913. (Encore Edition). (Illus.). 1978. pap. 1.95 (ISBN 0-684-16912-6, ScribT). Scribner.
NATO Advanced Study Institution, Athens, Greece, September 8-19, 1969. Structure & Evolution of the Galaxy: Proceedings. Mavaridis, L. N., ed. LC 77-135107. (Astrophysics & Space Science Library: No.22). 312p. 1971. lib. bdg. 42.00 (ISBN 90-277-0177-6, Pub. by Reidel Holland). Kluwer Boston.
Pacholczyk, A. G. Radio Galaxies: Radiation Transfer, Dynamics, Stability & Evolution of a Synchroton Plasmon. LC 76-27283. 1977. 42.00 (ISBN 0-08-021031-7). Pergamon.
Ronan, Colin. Discovery of the Galaxies. (Jackdaw Ser: No. S2). (Illus.). 1969. - 6.95 (ISBN 0-670-27414-3, Grossman). Viking Pr.
Shapley, Harlow. Galaxies. 3rd ed. Hodge, Paul W., rev. by. LC 77-169859. (Books on Astronomy Ser). (Illus.). 223p. 1972. 14.00x (ISBN 0-674-34051-5); pap. 5.95 (ISBN 0-674-34052-3). Harvard U Pr.
Symposium of the International Astronomical Union, No. 77. Structure & Properties of Nearby Galaxies: Proceedings. Berkhuijsen, Elly M. & Wielebinski, Richard, eds. 1978. lib. bdg. 39.50 (ISBN 90-277-0874-6, Pub. by Reidel Holland); pap. text ed. 26.00 (ISBN 90-277-0875-4). Kluwer Boston.
Tayler, R. J. & Everest, A. S. Galaxies: Structure & Evolution. LC 78-52248. (Wykeham Science Ser.: No. 49). 1979. 21.00x (ISBN 0-8448-1356-7). Crane-Russak Co.
Westerlund, Bengt E., ed. Stars & Star Systems. (Astrophysics & Space Science Library: No. 75). 1979. lib. bdg. 34.00 (ISBN 90-277-0983-1, Pub. by Reidel Holland). Kluwer Boston.
Woltjer, Lodewijk, ed. Galaxies & the Universe: Lectures. LC 68-20445. (Vetlesen Symposium, 1966). (Illus.). 1968. 15.00x (ISBN 0-231-03110-6). Columbia U Pr.
GALAXY (MILKY WAY)
see Milky Way
GALBRAITH, JOHN KENNETH, 1908-
Friedman, Milton. From Galbraith to Economic Freedom. (Institute of Economic Affairs Occasional Papers: No. 49). 1977. pap. 4.25 (ISBN 0-255-36089-4). Transatlantic.
Galbraith, John K. A Life in Our Times: Memoirs. 576p. 1981. 16.95 (ISBN 0-395-30509-8); spec. ed. 50.00 (ISBN 0-395-31135-7). HM.
Gambs, John S. John Kenneth Galbraith. (World Leaders Ser.: No. 37). 1975. lib. bdg. 9.95 (ISBN 0-8057-3681-6). Twayne.
--John Kenneth Galbraith. LC 74-24885. 200p. 1975. pap. 4.95 (ISBN 0-312-44380-3). St Martin.
Hession, Charles. Galbraith & His Critics. 1972. pap. 1.50 (ISBN 0-451-61174-8, MW1174, Ment). NAL.
Munro, C. Lynn. The Galbraithian Vision: The Cultural Criticism of John Kenneth Galbraith. 236p. 1977. pap. text ed. 9.50 (ISBN 0-8191-0255-5). U Pr of Amer.
Musgrave, Gerald L., ed. The Galbraith Viewpoint in Perspective: Critical Commentary on "The Age of Uncertainty" Television Series. LC 77-92085. (Hoover Special Project Ser). 1978. pap. 4.95 (ISBN 0-8179-4212-2). Hoover Inst Pr.
Pratson, Frederick. Perspectives on Galbraith: Conversations & Opinions. LC 78-8975. 1978. 14.95 (ISBN 0-8436-0748-3). CBI Pub.
Sharpe, Myron E. John Kenneth Galbraith & the Lower Economics. 2nd ed. LC 74-21267. 1974. 8.95 (ISBN 0-87332-040-9). M E Sharpe.
GALE, RICHARD M., 1932-
Bowley, Marian. Studies in the History of Economic Theory Before 1870. 1973. text ed. 19.50x (ISBN 0-391-00321-6). Humanities.
GALE, ZONA, 1874-1938
Simonson, Harold P. Zona Gale. (Twayne's United States Authors Ser). 1962. pap. 3.45 (ISBN 0-8084-0338-9, T18, Twayne). Coll & U Pr.
GALENUS
Durling, R. J., ed. Galenus Latinus I. (Ars Medica: Vol. 6). 1976. text ed. 91.75x (ISBN 3-11-005759-X). De Gruyter.
Temkin, Owsei. Galenism: Rise & Decline of a Medical Philosophy. LC 72-12411. (History of Science Ser.). (Illus.). 240p. 1973. 22.50x (ISBN 0-8014-0774-5). Cornell U Pr.
GALES
see Storms; Winds
GALIANI, FERDINANDO, 1728-1787
Gaudemet, Eugene. L' Abbe Galiani (1728-1787) et la Question du Commerce des Bles a la Fin du Regne de Louis XV. LC 72-87294. 233p. 1972. Repr. of 1899 ed. lib. bdg. 24.00 (ISBN 0-8337-1294-2). B Franklin.
GALICIA, SPAIN-DESCRIPTION AND TRAVEL
Buechler, Hans & Buechler, Judith-Maria. Carmen: The Autobiography of a Spanish Galician Peasant Woman. 256p. 1981. text ed. 16.95x (ISBN 0-87073-880-1); pap. text ed. 8.95x (ISBN 0-87073-846-1). Schenkman.
Carnarvon, Henry J. Portugal & Galicia: Review of the Social & Political State of the Basque Provinces. 3rd ed. LC 77-87712. Repr. of 1848 ed. 27.50 (ISBN 0-404-16578-8). AMS Pr.
Castroviego, Jose M. Rias Bajas of Galicia. (Spanish Guide Ser). (Illus.). 1959. 4.50x (ISBN 0-8002-1923-6). Intl Pubns Serv.
GALILEE
Freyne, Sean V. Galilee from Alexander the Great to Hadrian, 323 B. C. E. to 135 C. E. 27.50 (ISBN 0-89453-099-2). M. Glazier.
GALILEO (GALILEO GALILEI), 1564-1642
Brophy, James & Paolucci, Henry, eds. The Achievement of Galileo. 1962. 7.50x (ISBN 0-8084-0388-5); pap. 2.45 (ISBN 0-8084-0389-3). Coll & U Pr.
Butts, Robert E. & Pitt, Joseph C., eds. New Perspectives on Galileo. (Western Ontario Ser: No. 14). 1978. lib. bdg. 39.50 (ISBN 90-277-0859-2, Pub. by Reidel Holland); pap. 15.80 (ISBN 90-277-0891-6). Kluwer Boston.
Campanella, Thomas. The Defense of Galileo. LC 74-26254. (History, Philosophy & Sociology of Science Ser). 1975. Repr. 10.00 (ISBN 0-405-06582-5). Arno.
Cobb, Vicki. Truth on Trial: The Story of Galileo Galilei. LC 79-237. (Science Discovery Ser.). (Illus.). (gr. 3-7). 1979. PLB 5.99 (ISBN 0-698-30709-7). Coward.
Drake, Stillman. Galileo. (Pastmasters Ser.). 1981. 7.95 (ISBN 0-8090-4850-7); pap. 2.95 (ISBN 0-8090-1416-5). Hill & Wang.
--Galileo at Work: His Scientific Biography. LC 78-5239. xxiv, 536p. 1981. pap. 9.95 (ISBN 0-226-16227-3). U of Chicago Pr.
--Galileo at Work: His Scientific Biography. LC 78-5239. (Illus.). 1978. 25.00x (ISBN 0-226-16226-5). U of Chicago Pr.
--Galileo Studies: Personality, Tradition, & Revolution. LC 73-124427. 1970. 8.50x (ISBN 0-472-08283-3). U of Mich Pr.
Duhem, Pierre. To Save the Pheonomena: An Essay on the Idea of Physical Theory from Plato to Galileo. Dolan, Edmund & Maschler, Chaninah, trs. LC 71-77978. 1969. 8.00x (ISBN 0-226-16920-0). U of Chicago Pr.
Fahie, J. J. Galileo: His Life & Work. (Illus.). Repr. of 1903 ed. lib. bdg. 28.50x (ISBN 0-697-00003-6). Irvington.
Galilei, Galileo. Dialogue Concerning the Two Chief World Systems-Ptolemaic & Copernican. 2nd rev. ed. Drake, Stillman, tr. 1967. 28.50x (ISBN 0-520-00449-3); pap. 8.95x (ISBN 0-520-00450-7, CAL66). U of Cal Pr.
--Galileo Galilei: Operations of the Geometric & Military Compass. Drake, Stillman, tr. from Ital. & intro. by. LC 78-2433. (Illus.). 1978. pap. text ed. 5.95 (ISBN 0-87474-383-4). Smithsonian.
Galileo. (MacDonald Educational Ser.). (Illus., Arabic.). 3.50 (ISBN 0-686-53094-2). Intl Bk Ctr.
Galileo. Discoveries & Opinions of Galileo. LC 57-6305. 1957. pap. 3.95 (ISBN 0-385-09239-3, A94, Anch). Doubleday.
Gebler, Karl Von. Galileo Galilei & the Roman Curia from Authentic Sources. Sturge, Jane, tr. LC 76-1124. 1977. Repr. of 1897 ed. lib. bdg. 25.00x (ISBN 0-915172-11-9). Richwood Pub.
Golino, Carlo L., ed. Galileo Reappraised. LC 66-15485. (UCLA Center for Medieval & Renaissance Studies). 1966. 17.00x (ISBN 0-520-00490-6). U of Cal Pr.
Koyre, Alexandre. Galileo Studies. Mepham, J., tr. (European Philosophy & the Human Sciences Ser.). 1978. text ed. 46.25x (ISBN 0-391-00760-2). Humanities.
Langford, Jerome J. Galileo, Science & the Church. rev. ed. 1971. pap. 4.95x (ISBN 0-472-06173-9, 173, AA). U of Mich Pr.
Lijegren, Sten B. Studies in Milton. LC 67-30816. (Studies in Milton, No. 22). 1969. Repr. of 1918 ed. lib. bdg. 23.95 (ISBN 0-8383-0718-3). Haskell.
Liljegren, Sten B. Studies in Milton. 1918. lib. bdg. 6.75 (ISBN 0-8414-5707-7). Folcroft.
Morphet. Galileo & Copernican Astronomy: A Scientific World View Defined. (Siscon Ser.). 1977. 3.95 (ISBN 0-408-71303-8). Butterworth.
Rosen, Sidney. Galileo & the Magic Numbers. (Illus.). (gr. 7 up). 1958. 6.95 (ISBN 0-316-75704-7). Little.
Santillana, Giorgio. The Crime of Galileo. LC 55-7400. (Midway Reprint Ser). (Illus.). xvi, 339p. 1955. pap. 10.00x (ISBN 0-226-73481-1). U of Chicago Pr.
Shapere, David. Galileo: A Philosophical Study. LC 73-92023. 1974. pap. 2.95 (ISBN 0-226-75007-8, P594, Phoen). U of Chicago Pr.
Wallace, William A. Galileo's Early Notebooks. LC 77-89766. 1977. text ed. 14.95x (ISBN 0-268-00998-8). U of Notre Dame Pr.

GALILEO (GALILEO GALILEI), 1564-1642–DRAMA
Brecht, Bertolt. Galileo. Bentley, Eric, ed. Laughton, Charles, tr. from German. (Orig.). (YA) (gr. 9 up). 1966. pap. 1.95 (ISBN 0-394-17112-8, B120, BC). Grove.
Shea, William R. Galileo's Intellectual Revolution: Middle Period, 1610-1632. 216p. 1977. pap. 8.95 (ISBN 0-685-56651-X, Sci Hist). N Watson.
GALIUM
Dempster, Lauramay T. The Genus Galium (Rubiaceae) in Mexico & Central America. (Publications in Botany: No. 73). 1978. pap. 8.00x (ISBN 0-520-09578-2). U of Cal Pr.
Institute of Physics. Gallium Arsenide. (Institute of Physics Conference Ser.: No. 3). 1967. 24.50 (ISBN 0-9960028-2-0, Pub. by Inst Physics England). Heyden.
--Gallium Arsenide. (Institute of Physics Conference Ser.: No. 7). 1969. 45.00 (ISBN 0-9960028-6-3, Pub. by Inst Physics England). Heyden.
--Gallium Arsenide & Related Compounds. (Institute of Physics Conference Ser.: No. 9). 1971. 45.00 (ISBN 0-9960028-8-X, Pub. by Inst Physics England). Heyden.
GALL
see Bile
GALL-BLADDER
Berk, Robert N. & Clemett, Arthur R. Radiology of the Gallbladder & Bile Ducts. LC 76-54037. (Saunders Monographs in Clinical Radiology Ser.: Vol. 12). (Illus.). 1977. text ed. 30.00 (ISBN 0-7216-1702-6). Saunders.
Felson, Benjamin, ed. Roentgenology of the Gallbladder & Biliary Tract. (Seminars in Roentgenology Reprint). (Illus.). 160p. 1976. Repr. 25.75 (ISBN 0-8089-0999-1). Grune.
Hatfield, Philip M. & Wise, Robert E. Radiology of the Gallbladder & Bile Ducts. LC 76-3460. 276p. 1976. 31.00 (ISBN 0-686-74091-2). Krieger.
Hermann, R. E. Manual of Surgery of the Gallbladder, Bile Ducts, & Exocrine Pancreas. (Comprehensive Manuals of Surgical Specialties). (Illus.). 1979. 88.70 (ISBN 0-387-90351-8). Springer-Verlag.
Levine, Talya. Chronic Cholecystitis: Its Pathology & the Role of Vascular Factors in Its Pathogenesis. LC 75-6842. 1975. 37.95 (ISBN 0-470-53122-3). Halsted Pr.
Schein, Clarence J. Postcholecystectomy Syndromes. (Illus.). 1978. text ed. 32.50 (ISBN 0-06-142337-8, Harper Medical). Harper Row.
Smith & Sherlock. Surgery of the Gall Bladder & Bile Ducts. 2nd ed. 1981. 79.95 (ISBN 0-407-00118-2). Butterworth.
GALL-BLADDER–CALCULI
see Calculi, Biliary
GALL-DUCTS
see Biliary Tract
GALL-FLIES AND GALL-GNATS
see also Galls (Botany)
GALL-STONES
see Calculi, Biliary
GALLA PLACIDIA, 388-450
Nagl, Maria A. Galla Placidia. pap. 5.50 (ISBN 0-384-40815-X). Johnson Repr.
Oost, Stewart I. Galla Placidia Augusta: A Biographical Essay. LC 68-25090. (Illus.). 1968. 16.50x (ISBN 0-226-63050-1). U of Chicago Pr.
GALLANTY-SHOWS
see Shadow Pantomimes and Plays
GALLAS
Huntingford, G. W. Galla of Ethiopia: The Kingdoms of Kafa & Janjero. 1969. 11.50x (ISBN 0-8002-1441-2). Intl Pubns Serv.
Lewis, Herbert S. Galla Monarchy: Jimma Abba Jifar, Ethiopia, 1830-1932. (Illus.). 168p. 1965. 17.50x (ISBN 0-299-03690-1). U of Wis Pr.
Paulitschke, Philipp V. Ethnographie Nordost-Afrikas, 2 Vols. Repr. of 1893 ed. Set. 46.00 (ISBN 0-384-45233-7). Johnson Repr.
Prins, Adriaan H. East African Age-Class Systems: An Inquiry into the Social Order of Galla, Kipsigis & Kikuyu. LC 72-106785. (Illus.). Repr. of 1953 ed. 10.00x (ISBN 0-8371-3538-9). Greenwood.
GALLATIN, ALBERT, 1761-1849
Adams, Henry. Albert Gallatin. LC 80-25555. (American Statesmen Ser.). 695p. 1981. pap. 8.95 (ISBN 0-87754-194-9). Chelsea Hse.
--Life of Albert Gallatin. 12.50 (ISBN 0-8446-1006-2). Peter Smith.
Stevens, John A. Albert Gallatin. Morse, John T., Jr., ed. LC 74-128977. (American Statesmen: No. 13). Repr. of 1898 ed. 23.50 (ISBN 0-404-50863-4). AMS Pr.
Walters, Raymond, Jr. Albert Gallatin: Jeffersonian Financier & Diplomat. LC 57-8267. 1969. pap. 6.95 (ISBN 0-8229-5210-6). U of Pittsburgh Pr.
GALLEGO, FERNANDO, 1440-1507
Quinn, R. M. Fernando Gallego & the Retablo of Ciudad Rodrigo. LC 60-15915. (Illus., Span. & Eng.). 1961. 2.00 (ISBN 0-8165-0034-7). U of Ariz Pr.
GALLERIES (ART)
see Art Museums
GALLICANISM
see also Conciliar Theory
Neale, J. M. & Forbes, G. H. The Ancient Liturgies of the Gallican Church. LC 71-131030. Repr. of 1855 ed. 26.00 (ISBN 0-404-04655-X). AMS Pr.
GALLIER, JAMES
Gallier, James. Autobiography of James Gallier, Architect. LC 69-13715. (Architecture & Decorative Art Ser.). 1973. Repr. of 1864 ed. lib. bdg. 25.00 (ISBN 0-306-71247-4). Da Capo.
GALLIFORMES
see also Pheasants; Turkeys
Bent, Arthur C. Life Histories of North American Gallinaceous Birds. (Illus.). 12.50 (ISBN 0-8446-1635-4). Peter Smith.
--Life Histories of North American Gallinaceous Birds. (Illus.). 1932. pap. 8.00 (ISBN 0-486-21028-6). Dover.
GALLINAE
see Galliformes
GALLIPOLI CAMPAIGN, 1915
see European War, 1914-1918–Campaigns
GALLIPOLIS, OHIO–HISTORY
Belote, Theodore T. Scioto Speculation & the French Settlement at Gallipolis. LC 75-146138. (Research & Source Works Ser.: No. 717). 1971. Repr. of 1907 ed. lib. bdg. 18.50 (ISBN 0-8337-0221-1). B Franklin.
GALLIUM
Johnston, Gerald. Atlas of Gallium - 67 Scintigraphy: A New Method of Radioisotope Diagnosis. LC 73-18375. 223p. 1974. 29.50 (ISBN 0-306-30769-3, Plenum Pr). Plenum Pub.
GALLIUM ARSENIDE
Gallium Arsenide & Related Compounds: 1972. (Institute of Physics Conference Ser.: No. 17). 1972. 49.00 (ISBN 0-9960029-6-0, Pub. by Inst Physics England). Heyden.
Gallium Arsenide & Related Compounds: 1974. (Institute of Physics Conference Ser.: No. 24). 1974. 60.00 (ISBN 0-9960030-3-7, Pub. by Inst Physics England). Heyden.
Gallium Arsenide & Related Compounds: Edinburgh 1976. (Institute of Physics Conference Ser.: No. 33A). 1977. 67.50 (ISBN 0-9960031-2-6, Pub. by Inst Physics England). Heyden.
Gallium Arsenide & Related Compounds: St. Louis 1976. (Institute of Physics Conference Ser.: No. 33B). 1977. 67.50 (ISBN 0-9960031-3-4, Pub. by Inst Physics England). Heyden.
Gallium Arsenide & Related Compounds 1978: St. Louis. (Institute of Physics Conference Ser.: No. 45). 1979. 80.00 (ISBN 0-9960032-5-8, Pub. by Inst Physics England). Heyden.
GALLOWAY, JOSEPH, 1731-1803
Boyd, Julian P. Anglo-American Union: Joseph Galloway's Plans to Preserve the British Empire, 1774-1788. LC 76-120233. 1970. Repr. lib. bdg. 14.00x (ISBN 0-374-90900-8). Octagon.
Newcomb, Benjamin H. Franklin & Galloway: A Political Partnership. LC 72-75205. 360p. 1972. 25.00x (ISBN 0-300-01506-2). Yale U Pr.
GALLS (BOTANY)
see also Insects, Injurious and Beneficial
Russo, Ronald A. Plant Galls of the California Region. (Illus.). 1979. pap. 5.95 (ISBN 0-910286-71-X). Boxwood.
GALOIS THEORY
see also Modular Fields
Artin, Emil. Galois Theory. (Mathematical Lectures Ser.: No. 2). (Orig.). 1966. pap. 2.75 (ISBN 0-268-00108-1). U of Notre Dame Pr.
Buhler, J. P. Icosahedral Galois Representations. (Lecture Notes in Mathematics Ser.: Vol. 654). 1978. pap. 9.20 (ISBN 0-387-08844-X). Springer-Verlag.
Chase, S. U., et al. Galois Theory & Cohomology of Commutative Rings. LC 52-42839. (Memoirs: No. 52). 1978. pap. 7.60 (ISBN 0-8218-1252-1, MEMO-52). Am Math.
Chase, U. & Sweedler, M. E. Hopf Algebras & Galois Theory Two. LC 75-84143. (Lecture Notes in Mathematics: Vol. 97). (Orig.). 1969. pap. 10.70 (ISBN 0-387-04616-X). Springer-Verlag.
Gaal, Lisl. Classical Galois Theory. 3rd ed. LC 73-649. viii, 248p. 1979. text ed. 9.95 (ISBN 0-8284-1268-5). Chelsea Pub.
Haberland, K. Galois Cohomology of Algebraic Number Fields. 1978. 30.75 (ISBN 0-685-87204-1). Adler.
Kaplansky, Irving. Fields & Rings. rev. 2nd ed. LC 72-78251. (Chicago Lectures in Mathematics Ser). 224p. 1972. text ed. 10.00x (ISBN 0-226-42450-2); pap. text ed. 8.00x (ISBN 0-226-42451-0). U of Chicago Pr.
Lang, S. & Trotter, H. F. Frobenius Distributions in GL-Two Extensions. (Lecture Notes in Mathematics: Vol. 504). 274p. 1976. pap. 13.80 (ISBN 0-387-07550-X). Springer-Verlag.
Magid, A. R. Separable Galois Theory of Commutative Rings. (Pure & Applied Mathematics Ser: Vol. 27). 1974. 16.75 (ISBN 0-8247-6163-4). Dekker.
Postnikov, M. M. Fundamentals of Galois Thoery. (Russian Tracts on the Physical Sciences Ser). 1964. 45.25x (ISBN 0-677-20440-X). Gordon.
Stewart, I. Galois Theory. (Mathematics Ser.). 226p. 1973. pap. text ed. 14.95x (ISBN 0-412-10800-3, Pub. by Chapman & Hall England). Methuen Inc.
Winter, D. J. The Structure of Fields. LC 73-21824. (Graduate Texts in Mathematics Ser.: Vol. 16). (Illus.). 320p. 1974. 20.80 (ISBN 0-387-90074-8). Springer-Verlag.
GALSWORTHY, JOHN, 1867-1933
Aiyar, R. Sadasiva. Introduction to Galsworthy's Plays. LC 73-9722. 1925. lib. bdg. 12.50 (ISBN 0-8414-2856-5). Folcroft.
Barker, Dudley. Man of Principle: A Biography of John Galsworthy. LC 69-17943. 1970. pap. 4.95 (ISBN 0-8128-1297-2). Stein & Day.
Bellamy, William. The Novels of Wells, Bennett & Galsworthy 1890-1910. 1971. 19.95x (ISBN 0-7100-7002-0). Routledge & Kegan.
Chevrillon, Andre. Three Studies in English Literature, Kipling, Galsworthy & Shakespeare. LC 67-27585. Repr. of 1923 ed. 11.00 (ISBN 0-8046-0077-5). Kennikat.
Coats, R. H. John Galsworthy As a Dramatic Artist. LC 76-22510. Repr. of 1926 ed. lib. bdg. 25.00 (ISBN 0-8414-3580-4). Folcroft.
Croman, Natalie. John Galsworthy: A Study in Continuity & Contrast. LC 72-194104. 1933. lib. bdg. 10.00 (ISBN 0-8414-2416-0). Folcroft.
DuPont, V. John Galsworthy: The Dramatic Artist. LC 76-43253. 1942. lib. bdg. 20.00 (ISBN 0-8414-3812-9). Folcroft.
Fabes, Gilbert H. John Galsworthy: His First Editions. LC 73-10489. 1973. Repr. of 1932 ed. lib. bdg. 12.50 (ISBN 0-8414-1972-8). Folcroft.
--John Galsworthy: His First Editions. 1978. Repr. of 1932 ed. lib. bdg. 15.00 (ISBN 0-8495-1614-5). Arden Lib.
--John Galsworthy: His First Editions, Points & Values. 59p. 1980. Repr. of 1932 ed. lib. bdg. 15.00 (ISBN 0-89987-254-9). Darby Bks.
Gindin, James. The English Climate: An Excursion into a Biography of John Galsworthy. LC 79-98060. (Illus.). 1979. lib. bdg. 12.00x (ISBN 0-472-08349-X, 08349). U of Mich Pr.
Guyot, Edouard. John Galsworthy. 1973. Repr. of 1933 ed. 30.00 (ISBN 0-8274-0388-7). R West.
--John Galsworthy. 1978. Repr. of 1932 ed. lib. bdg. 45.00 (ISBN 0-8495-1934-9). Arden Lib.
Huang, John. Shaw & Galsworthy. LC 76-23312. 1932. lib. bdg. 10.00 (ISBN 0-8414-4812-4). Folcroft.
John Galsworth: An Appreciation. 1978. Repr. of 1926 ed. lib. bdg. 8.50 (ISBN 0-8274-3994-6). R West.
John Galsworthy: An Appreciation Together with a Bibliography. LC 76-52434. 1977. lib. bdg. 8.50 (ISBN 0-8414-2950-2). Folcroft.
Kaye-Smith, Sheila. John Galsworthy. LC 72-4609. (English Biography Ser., No. 31). 1972. Repr. of 1916 ed. lib. bdg. 29.95 (ISBN 0-8383-1611-5). Haskell.
Kroner, Johanna. The Technik Des Realistischen Dramas Bei Ibsen und Galsworthy. Repr. of 1935 ed. pap. 6.00 (ISBN 0-384-30490-7). Johnson Repr.
Manot, H. V. Bibliography of John Galsworthy. 1979. 42.50 (ISBN 0-685-62769-1, 091156-52.3). Porter.
Marrot, Harold V. Bibliography of the Works of John Galsworthy. 1928. 20.50 (ISBN 0-8337-2246-8). B Franklin.
--Bibliography of the Works of John Galsworthy. LC 72-12686. 1928. lib. bdg. 14.00 (ISBN 0-8414-0956-0). Folcroft.
--The Bibliography of the Works of John Galsworthy. 1978. Repr. of 1928 ed. lib. bdg. 35.00 (ISBN 0-8495-3739-8). Arden Lib.
Marrott, Harold V. Life & Letters of John Galsworthy. LC 78-128060. Repr. of 1936 ed. 29.50x (ISBN 0-678-02759-5). Kelley.
Mikhail, E. H., ed. John Galsworthy the Dramatist: A Bibliography of Criticism. LC 75-183299. 1971. 7.50x (ISBN 0-87875-009-6). Whitston Pub.
Ould, Hermon. John Galsworthy. 244p. 1980. Repr. of 1934 ed. lib. bdg. 25.00 (ISBN 0-8495-4218-9). Arden Lib.
--John Galsworthy. LC 74-18420. 1974. Repr. of 1934 ed. lib. bdg. 20.00 (ISBN 0-8414-6515-0). Folcroft.
Schalit, Leon. John Galsworthy. LC 74-133285. (English Literature Ser., No. 33). 1970. Repr. of 1927 ed. lib. bdg. 52.95 (ISBN 0-8383-1184-9). Haskell.
--John Galsworthy: A Survey. LC 73-14574. 1974. Repr. of 1929 ed. lib. bdg. 12.75 (ISBN 0-8414-7633-0). Folcroft.
Schmitz, Wilhelmine. Der Mensch und Die Gesellschaft Im Werke John Galsworthys. Repr. of 1936 ed. pap. 13.50 (ISBN 0-384-54150-X). Johnson Repr.
Shukla, S. Social & Moral Ideas in the Plays of Galsworthy. (Salzburg Studies in English Literature: 48). 263p. 1979. text ed. 25.00x (ISBN 0-391-01780-2). Humanities.
Smit, J. Henry. Short Stories of John Galsworthy. LC 68-877. (Studies in Fiction, No. 34). 1969. Repr. lib. bdg. 49.95 (ISBN 0-8383-0681-0). Haskell.
Stevens, Earl E. & Stevens, H. Ray, eds. John Galsworthy: An Annotated Bibliography of Writings About Him. LC 78-60456. (An Annotated Secondary Bibliography Series of English Literature in Transition, 1880-1920). 484p. 1980. 30.00x (ISBN 0-87580-073-4). N Ill U Pr.
Takahashi, Genji. Studies in the Works of John Galsworthy: With Special Reference to His Visions of Love & Beauty. 3rd ed. LC 72-179826. 500p. 1973. 30.00x (ISBN 0-8002-2032-3). Intl Pubns Serv.
GALT, JOHN, 1779-1839
Aldrich, Ruth I. John Galt. (English Authors Ser.: No. 231). 1978. lib. bdg. 12.50 (ISBN 0-8057-6657-X). Twayne.
Gordon, Ian. John Galt. 1978. 12.50x (ISBN 0-7073-0218-8, Pub. by Scottish Academic Pr Scotland). Columbia U Pr.
Gordon, Ian A. John Galt: The Life of a Writer. LC 72-97778. (Illus.). 1973. 12.50x (ISBN 0-8020-1941-2). U of Toronto Pr.
GALTON, FRANCIS, SIR, 1822-1911
Darwin, Francis. Rustic Sounds & Other Studies in Literature & Natural History. facs. ed. LC 69-17572. (Essay Index Reprint Ser). 1917. 15.00 (ISBN 0-8369-0069-3). Arno.
Forrest, D. W. Francis Galton: The Life & Work of a Victorian Genius. LC 74-5819. (Illus.). 280p. 1974. 14.95 (ISBN 0-8008-2682-5). Taplinger.
GALUTH
see Jews–Diaspora
GALVANIC BATTERIES
see Electric Batteries
GALVANIC CORROSION
see Electrolytic Corrosion
GALVANISM
see Electricity
GALVANIZING
see also Metals–Pickling; Tin Plate
International Galvanizing Conference Madrid 1976. Intergalva 76: Proceedings. Zinc Development Assoc., London, ed. (Illus.). 272p. (Orig.). 1978. pap. 32.50x (ISBN 0-8002-2228-8). Intl Pubns Serv.
GALVANOMAGNETIC EFFECTS
see also Hall Effect
Weiss, H. Structure & Application of Galvanomagnetic Devices. 1969. 60.00 (ISBN 0-08-012597-2). Pergamon.
GALVANOMETER
see also Electric Measurements
GALVANOPLASTY
see Electrometallurgy; Electroplating
GALVANOSURGERY
see Electrosurgery
GALVESTON, TEXAS
The Decline of Galveston Bay. 127p. 1974. pap. 4.00 (ISBN 0-89164-010-X). Conservation Foun.
Hayes, Charles W. Galveston: History of the Island & the City. (Illus.). slipcased 37.50 (ISBN 0-685-83960-5, Pub. by Jenkins Garrett Press). Jenkins.
Lewis, Carroll. Treasures of Galveston Bay. (Illus.). 1967. 8.95 (ISBN 0-87244-052-4). Texian.
Mason, Herbert M., Jr. Death from the Sea: Our Greatest Natural Disaster, the Galveston Hurricane of 1900. (Illus.). 1972. 7.95 (ISBN 0-8037-1824-1). Dial.
Weems, John E. A Weekend in September. LC 79-7415. (Illus.). 192p. 1980. Repr. of 1957 ed. 10.95 (ISBN 0-89096-097-6). Tex A&M Univ Pr.
GALVEZ, BERNARDO DE, 1746-1786
Caughey, John W. Bernardo De Galvez in Louisiana: 1776-1783. 2nd ed. LC 72-86562. (Illus.). 304p. 1972. Repr. of 1934 ed. 20.00 (ISBN 0-911116-78-8). Pelican.
De Galvez, Bernardo. Diario. 52p. 1966. pap. 5.00 (ISBN 0-686-70401-0). South Pass Pr.
Woodward, Ralph L., Jr., ed. Tribute to Don Bernardo De Galvez. LC 80-116160. (Illus.). xxviii, 148p. 1979. 14.95x (ISBN 0-917860-04-7). Historic New Orleans.
GALVEZ, JOSE DE, 1729-1787
Priestley, Herbert I. Jose De Galvez, Visitor General of New Spain 1765-1771. LC 78-10953. (Perspectives in Latin American History: No. 1). (Illus.). Repr. of 1916 ed. lib. bdg. 25.00x (ISBN 0-87991-605-2). Porcupine Pr.
GAMA, VASCO DA, 1469-1524
Correa, Gaspar. Three Voyages of Vasco Da Gama. 1964. 23.50 (ISBN 0-8337-3364-8). B Franklin.

Hart, Henry H. Sea Road to the Indies: An Account of the Voyages & Exploits of the Portuguese Navigators, Together with the Life & Times of Dom Vasco De Gama, Capitao-Mor, Viceroy of India & Count of Vidigueira. LC 70-135246. (Illus.). 1971. Repr. of 1950 ed. lib. bdg. 14.00x (ISBN 0-8371-5165-1, HARO). Greenwood.

Knight, David. Vasco Da Gama. new ed. LC 78-18057. (Illus.). 48p. (gr. 4-7). 1979. PLB 5.89 (ISBN 0-89375-175-8); pap. 1.75 (ISBN 0-89375-167-7). Troll Assocs.

Sanderlin, George. Eastward to India: Vasco Da Gama's Voyage. LC 65-20247. (Illus.). (gr. 5 up). 1965. PLB 10.89 (ISBN 0-06-025171-9, HarpJ). Har-Row.

GAMBETTA, LEON MICHEL, 1838-1882

Bury, J. P. Gambetta & the National Defense. LC 70-80531. 1970. Repr. of 1936 ed. 23.50 (ISBN 0-86527-077-5). Fertig.

Bury, John P. Gambetta - the National Defence: A Republican Dictatorship in France. LC 77-114490. (Illus.). 1971. Repr. of 1936 ed. lib. bdg. 15.25x (ISBN 0-8371-4818-9, BUGN). Greenwood.

GAMBIA

Archer, Francis Bisset. Gambia Colony & Protectorate: An Official Handbook. 342p. 1967. Repr. of 1906 ed. 28.00x (ISBN 0-7146-1139-5, F Cass Co). Biblio Dist.

Gailey, Harry A. Historical Dictionary of the Gambia. LC 75-5882. (African Historical Dictionaries Ser.: No. 4). 180p. 1975. 10.00 (ISBN 0-8108-0810-2). Scarecrow.

Gamble, David P. A General Bibliography of the Gambia, up to 31 December 1977. Sperling, Louise J., ed. 1979. lib. bdg. 45.00 (ISBN 0-8161-8177-2). G K Hall.

Gray, John M. History of Gambia. 508p. 1966. 32.50x (ISBN 0-7146-1668-0, F Cass Co). Biblio Dist.

Reeve, Henry F. Gambia, Its History. LC 75-79275. (Illus.). Repr. of 1912 ed. 23.25x (ISBN 0-8371-1449-7, Pub. by Negro U Pr). Greenwood.

Wright, Donald R., ed. Oral Tradition from the Gambia: Vol. II: Family Elders. LC 79-14855. (Papers in International Studies: Africa: No. 38). 1980. pap. 12.00 (ISBN 0-89680-084-9). Ohio U Ctr Intl.

GAMBIA RIVER

Gailey, Harry A. A History of the Gambia. rev. ed. 256p. 1980. text ed. 28.50x (ISBN 0-8290-0350-9); pap. text ed. 16.95x (ISBN 0-8290-0351-7). Irvington.

Jobson, Richard. The Golden Trade, or a Discovery of the River Gambra & the Golden Trade of the Aethiopians. LC 68-54651. (English Experience Ser.: No. 56). 166p. 1968. Repr. of 1623 ed. 21.00 (ISBN 90-221-0056-1). Walter J Johnson.

Reeve, Henry F. Gambia, Its History. LC 75-79275. (Illus.). Repr. of 1912 ed. 23.25x (ISBN 0-8371-1449-7, Pub. by Negro U Pr). Greenwood.

GAMBLING

see also Blackjack (Game); Book-Making (Betting); Cards; Cardsharping; Dice; Horse Race Betting; Lotteries; Probabilities; Roulette; Speculation

According to Gambling Times. . .the Rules of Gambling Games. (Illus.). 1982. pap. text ed. 2.95 (ISBN 0-89746-011-1). Gambling Times.

Ainslie, Tom. How to Gamble in a Casino: The Most Fun at the Least Risk. LC 78-31610. (Tome Ainslie-Winner's Circle Bk). (Illus.). 1979. 9.95 (ISBN 0-688-03460-8). Morrow.

Allen, Martin. Taking the Edge. 64p. (Orig.). 1981. pap. 2.95 (ISBN 0-89650-931-1). Gamblers.

Andersen, Ian. Turning the Tables on Las Vegas. LC 76-12005. (Illus.). 224p. 1976. 10.00 (ISBN 0-8149-0776-8). Vanguard.

--Turning the Tables on Las Vegas. 1978. pap. 2.50 (ISBN 0-394-72509-3, Vin). Random.

Berger, A. J. & Bruning, Nancy. Lady Luck's Companion: How to Play. How to Enjoy. How to Bet. How to Win. LC 79-1693. (Illus.). 1979. 14.95 (ISBN 0-06-014696-6, HarpT). Har-Row.

Bergler, Edmund. Psychology of Gambling. 1970. text ed. 17.50 (ISBN 0-8236-5570-9); pap. text ed. 4.95 (ISBN 0-8236-8255-2, 025570). Intl Univs Pr.

Blakey, George, ed. The Gambler's Companion. LC 78-27529. (Illus.). 1979. 10.00 (ISBN 0-448-22071-7). Paddington.

Bruns, Bernie P. Compulsive Gambler. 1973. 6.95 (ISBN 0-8184-0021-8). Lyle Stuart.

Caillois, Roger. Man, Play, & Games. Barash, Meyer, tr. from Fr. LC 79-12684. 1979. pap. 5.50 (ISBN 0-8052-0636-1). Schocken.

Canfield, Richard A. Blackjack Your Way to Riches. (Illus.). 1979. Repr. 10.00 (ISBN 0-8184-0273-3). Lyle Stuart.

Carone, Pasquale M., et al. Addictive Disorder Update: Alcoholism, Drug Abuse, Gambling. 1981. 19.95 (ISBN 0-89885-034-7). Human Sci Pr.

Carroll, David. Playboy's Illustrated Treasury of Gambling. (Illus.). 1977. 19.95 (ISBN 0-517-53050-3). Crown.

Casino Management. 384p. 1981. 75.00 (ISBN 0-8184-0311-X). Lyle Stuart.

Casurella, Frank. How Race Fans Lose Millions. LC 73-76623. 1974. pap. 3.25 (ISBN 0-914878-00-X). Charlotte Pubs.

Chaplin, Stephen. How to Pick Winners of a Baseball Game. pap. 2.95 (ISBN 0-685-38434-9). Wehman.

Charles, R. H. Gambling & Betting: Their Origin & Their Relation to Morality & to Religion. 3rd ed. 92p. 1928. text ed. 3.95 (ISBN 0-567-22066-4). Attic Pr.

Coleman, Ron. Lady Luck Ain't No Lady. (Gambler's Book Shelf). 64p. 1975. pap. 2.95 (ISBN 0-911996-46-X). Gamblers.

Collver, Donald L. Scientific Blackjack & Complete Casino Guide. LC 66-23116. (Illus.). 1967. pap. 1.95 (ISBN 0-668-02420-8). Arco.

Comstock, Anthony. Traps for the Young. Bremner, Robert H., ed. LC 67-17306. (The John Harvard Library). (Illus.). 1967. 15.00x (ISBN 0-674-90555-5). Harvard U Pr.

Cook, Fred J. A Two-Dollar Bet Means Murder. LC 72-854. 248p. 1972. Repr. of 1961 ed. lib. bdg. 15.00x (ISBN 0-8371-5927-X, COTD). Greenwood.

Culin, Stewart. Gambling Games of the Chinese in America. 1965. pap. 1.25 (ISBN 0-911996-03-6). Gamblers.

Dash, Norman. Win with Great Betting Systems. 186p. pap. 2.25 (ISBN 0-89343-042-0, Pub by Ermine). Hippocrene Bks.

De Ketchiva, Paul. Confessions of a Croupier. 1978. lib. bdg. 59.95 (ISBN 0-8490-1663-0). Gordon Pr.

Devereux, Edward C., Jr. Gambling & the Social Structure: A Sociological Study of Lotteries & Horse Racing in Contemporary America, 2 vols. Zuckerman, Harriet & Merton, Robert K., eds. LC 79-8993. (Dissertations on Sociology). 1980. Set. lib. bdg. 90.00x (ISBN 0-405-12964-5). Arno.

Devol, George H. Forty Years a Gambler on the Mississippi. 1892. 9.50 (ISBN 0-384-11595-0). Johnson Repr.

Dorgan, H. M. Horse Racing: The Method. 3.95 (ISBN 0-685-22041-9). Wehman.

Downes, D. M., et al. Gambling, Work & Leisure: A Study Across Three Areas. (International Library of Sociology). 1976. 25.00 (ISBN 0-7100-7708-4). Routledge & Kegan.

Druley, Ray M. You Can't Beat the System Without a System: How to Win in Atlantic City & Las Vegas. (Illus.). 58p. (Orig.). 1981. pap. 10.00 (ISBN 0-939836-01-7). Potomac Ent.

Drzazga, John. Wheels of Fortune. (Illus.). 376p. 1963. ed. spiral bdg. 32.50photocopy (ISBN 0-398-00477-3). C C Thomas.

Dubins, Lester E. & Savage, Leonard J. Inequalities for Stochastic Processes. LC 75-25001. 288p. 1976. pap. 4.00 (ISBN 0-486-63283-0). Dover.

Eadington, William R. Gambling & Society: Interdisciplinary Studies on the Subject of Gambling. (Illus.). 488p. 1976. 45.75 (ISBN 0-398-03459-1). C C Thomas.

Epstein, Richard A. The Theory of Gambling & Statistical Logic. rev. ed. 1977. 33.50 (ISBN 0-12-240760-1). Acad Pr.

Erdnase, Samuel R. Expert at the Card Table. 1946. pap. 1.95 (ISBN 0-685-19474-4). Powner.

Feinman, Jeffrey. Casino Gambling. LC 80-28722. 160p. (Orig.). 1981. pap. 2.95 (ISBN 0-668-05172-8, 5172). Arco.

Fleming, Alice. Something for Nothing: A History of Gambling. LC 77-86341. (Illus.). (gr. 5 up). 1978. 7.95 (ISBN 0-440-08036-3); PLB 7.45 (ISBN 0-440-08037-1). Delacorte.

Fried, Elliot & Enriquez, Helen. The Weekend Gambler's Guide to Las Vegas. (Weekend Gambler's Ser.). (Illus.). 1980. 10.95 (ISBN 0-935232-01-X); pap. 6.95 (ISBN 0-935232-02-8). Deep River Pr.

Friedman, A. J. Basketball: Picking Winners Against the Spread. 64p. (Orig.). 1978. pap. 2.95 (ISBN 0-89650-620-7, Gambler's Book Shelf). Gamblers.

--Football: Picking Winners Against the Spread. 64p. (Orig.). 1980. pap. 2.95 (ISBN 0-89650-703-3). Gamblers.

Friedman, Bill. Casino Games. (Golden Guide Ser). 160p. 1973. pap. 1.95 (ISBN 0-307-24358-3, Golden Pr). Western Pub.

Gaines, Milt. The Tote Board Is Alive and Well. 182p. (Orig.). 1981. pap. 9.95 (ISBN 0-89650-943-5). Gamblers.

Gambling Greats. 1982. pap. text ed. 2.95 (ISBN 0-89746-001-4). Gambling Times.

Gambling Times Complete Guide to Atlantic City. (Illus.). 1982. pap. text ed. 2.95 (ISBN 0-89746-003-0). Gambling Times.

Gambling Times Complete Guide to Las Vegas. (Gambling Times Complete Guide Ser.). (Illus.). 1983. pap. text ed. 2.95 (ISBN 0-685-44092-3). Gambling Times.

Gambling Times Complete Guide to Reno, Lake Tahoe. (Gambling Times Complete Guide to Ser.). (Illus.). 1983. pap. text ed. 2.95 (ISBN 0-89746-005-7). Gambling Times.

Gambling Times Guide to Gambling Junkets. (Illus.). 1983. pap. text ed. 2.95 (ISBN 0-89746-006-5). Gambling Times.

Gambling Times Guide to Harness Race Tracks. (Illus.). 1982. pap. text ed. 2.95 (ISBN 0-89746-002-2). Gambling Times.

Gambling Times Guide to Legal Off-Track Betting Establishments. 1983. pap. text ed. 2.95 (ISBN 0-89746-007-3). Gambling Times.

Gambling Times Guide to Quarter Horse, Appaloosa & Fair Racing. (Illus.). 1983. pap. text ed. 2.95 (ISBN 0-89746-008-1). Gambling Times.

Gambling Times Guide to Thoroughbred Race Tracks. 1983. pap. 2.95 (ISBN 0-89746-009-X). Gambling Times.

Gambling Times Magazine Staff, compiled by. Winning Answers. (Illus., Orig.). 1982. pap. text ed. 2.95 (ISBN 0-89746-019-7). Gambling Times.

Gambling Times on Blackjack. (Gambling Times on Gambling Games Ser.). 1982. pap. text ed. 2.95 (ISBN 0-89746-014-6). Gambling Times.

Gambling Times on Craps. (Gambling Times on Gambling Games Ser.). 1981. pap. text ed. 2.95 (ISBN 0-89746-013-8). Gambling Times.

Gambling Times on Jai Alai. (Illus.). 1980. pap. text ed. 2.95 (ISBN 0-89746-010-3). Gambling Times.

Gambling Times on Poker. (Gambling Times on Gambling Games Ser.). (Illus.). 1981. pap. text ed. 2.95 (ISBN 0-89746-015-4). Gambling Times.

Gambling Times on Roulette. (Gambling Times on Gambling Games Ser.). (Illus.). 1982. pap. text ed. 2.95 (ISBN 0-89746-017-0). Gambling Times.

Gardner, Jack I. Gambling: A Guide to Information Sources. LC 79-23797. (Sports, Games, & Pastimes Information Guide Ser.: Vol. 8). 1980. 36.00 (ISBN 0-8103-1229-8). Gale.

Gibson, Walter B. Bunko Book. (Gambler's Book Shelf). 64p. 1976. pap. 2.95 (ISBN 0-911966-56-0). Gamblers.

--Carnival Gaffs. (Gambler's Book Shelf). 64p. 1976. pap. 2.95 (ISBN 0-911996-66-4). Gamblers.

Graham, Virginia L. & Tulcea, C. Ionescu. A Book on Casino Gambling: Written by a Mathematician and a Computer Expert. 2nd ed. 1978. pap. 6.95 (ISBN 0-442-25829-1). Van Nos Reinhold.

--Casino Gambling. 1980. pap. 2.50 (ISBN 0-671-83187-9). PB.

Green, Jonathan H. Gambling Exposed, a Full Exposition of the Various Arts, Mysteries, Miseries of Gambling. LC 78-172603. (Criminology, Law Enforcement, & Social Problems Ser.: No. 193). (Illus., With intro. & index added). 1973. Repr. of 1857 ed. 15.00 (ISBN 0-87585-193-2). Patterson Smith.

Greenblat, Cathy. Gaming-Simulation: Rationale Designs & Applications. rev. ed. 250p. 1981. pap. write for info. (ISBN 0-8039-1675-2); pap. write for info. (ISBN 0-8039-1713-9). Sage.

Guild, Leo. World's Greatest Winning Systems. rev. ed. (Orig.). 1966. pap. 2.00 (ISBN 0-87067-614-8, BH614). Holloway.

Halliday, Jon & Fuller, Peter, eds. The Psychology of Gambling. 300p. 1975. pap. 4.25 (ISBN 0-06-090418-6, CN418, CN). Har-Row.

--The Psychology of Gambling. 6.75 (ISBN 0-8446-5197-4). Peter Smith.

Hamilton, Ross. Greyhound Betting for Profit. 64p. 1980. pap. 2.95 (ISBN 0-89650-725-4). Gamblers.

Haskins, Jim. Gambling: Who Really Wins? (First Bks.). (Illus.). (gr. 4 up). 1979. PLB 6.90 (ISBN 0-531-02942-5). Watts.

Herman, Robert D. Gamblers & Gambling. (Illus.). 1976. 16.95 (ISBN 0-669-00963-6). Lexington Bks.

Hutchens, John K., ed. The Gambler's Bedside Book. LC 74-20212. 1977. 12.95 (ISBN 0-8008-3123-3). Taplinger.

Hyde, Margaret O. Addictions. 1978. 7.95 (ISBN 0-07-031645-7, GB). McGraw.

Jasper, Jim. Sports Betting: A Computer Expert's Winning Secrets. LC 79-16383. 1979. 10.95 (ISBN 0-312-75330-6). St Martin.

Jenkins, John H. Audubon & Other Capers: Confessions of a Texas Bookmaker. LC 76-2347. (Illus.). 1976. 12.50 (ISBN 0-8363-0139-0). Jenkins.

Kavanagh. How You Can Beat the Races. pap. 3.00 (ISBN 0-87980-267-7). Wilshire.

King, Rufus. Gambling & Organized Crime. 1969. 6.00 (ISBN 0-8183-0171-6). Pub Aff Pr.

Knowles, Ruth S. The Greatest Gamblers: The Epic of American Oil Exploration. 2d ed. LC 78-21382. (Illus.). 1979. 10.95 (ISBN 0-8061-1513-0). U of Okla Pr.

Kornblum, Allan N. The Moral Hazards: Police Strategies for Honesty & Ethical Behavior. LC 75-34614. 224p. 1976. 22.95 (ISBN 0-669-00378-6). Lexington Bks.

Lake, Frederick. The Historical, Statistical & Scientific Guide on How to Make Money in Gambling Casinos with the Rules for Winning at Roulette & Faro. (Illus.). 1979. 49.75 (ISBN 0-89266-145-3). Am Classical Coll Pr.

Lake, Henry B. How to Win at Atlantic City, Las Vegas & Caribbean Gaming. Chase, Nan E., ed. (Illus.). 50p. (Orig.). 1981. pap. 3.50x programmed bk (ISBN 0-938512-01-3). Brigadoon.

Lee, Mike. Betting the Bases. 64p. pap. 2.95 (ISBN 0-89650-623-1). Gamblers.

Lemmel, Maurice. Gambling Nevada Style. LC 64-16205. pap. 2.95 (ISBN 0-385-07257-0, C476, Dolp). Doubleday.

Lester, David. Gambling Today. 160p. 1979. text ed. 13.75 (ISBN 0-398-03952-6). C C Thomas.

McClure, Wayne. Keno Winning Ways. 219p. 1979. text ed. 11.95 (ISBN 0-89650-778-5); pap. 6.95 (ISBN 0-89650-779-3). Gamblers.

McQuaid, Clement. Gambler's Digest. 2nd ed. LC 73-122378. (Illus.). 320p. (Orig.). 1981. pap. 10.95 (ISBN 0-910676-24-0, 7126). DBI.

Mahl, Huey. Average Purse Tables. (Gambler's Book Shelf). 64p. 1976. pap. 2.95 (ISBN 0-89650-564-2). Gamblers.

--Crossbet Two. (Gambler's Book Shelf). 64p. 1975. pap. 2.95 (ISBN 0-911996-51-6). Gamblers.

--The Race Is Pace. (Gambler's Book Shelf). 64p. 1975. pap. 2.95 (ISBN 0-911996-50-8). Gamblers.

Mahon, Gigi. The Company That Bought the Boardwalk: A Reporter's Story of Resorts International. LC 80-5302. 288p. 1981. 10.95 (ISBN 0-394-50978-1). Random.

Maines, Kenneth. Easy Money, Racing Secrets from las Vegas. 1974. 10.00 (ISBN 0-685-57205-6). Byzantine Pr.

Master Key Systems & Run up. (Gambler's Book Shelf). 56p. 1977. pap. 2.95 (ISBN 0-911996-84-2). Gamblers.

Mendelsohn, Martin. Castaways, One Hundred Thousand Dollar Nineteen Seventy-Nine Pro Football Handicapping Championship. 64p. (Orig.). 1980. pap. 2.95 (ISBN 0-89650-644-4). Gamblers.

Moody, Robert. Las Vegas-Sensibly! 1975. 6.95 (ISBN 0-686-15476-2). HamanD Pub.

Moore, Robin. Compulsion: The True Story of an Addictive Gambler. LC 78-20028. 384p. 1981. 15.95 (ISBN 0-385-13322-7). Doubleday.

Moore, William G., Sr. Moore's Parapsychology of Gambling - Craps & 21's. 1981. pap. text ed. 1.99 (ISBN 0-934488-05-3). Williams Ent.

New York, Kings Country, Grand Jury. A Presentment Concerning the Enforcement of the City of New York of the Laws Against Gambling by the Grand Jury for the Additional Extraordinary Special & Trial Term. facsimile ed. LC 73-3844. (Criminal Justice in America Ser.). 1974. Repr. of 1942 ed. 12.00x (ISBN 0-405-06148-X). Arno.

Nolan, Walter I. Facts of Keno. 1970. pap. 1.50 (ISBN 0-89650-021-7). Gamblers.

--Facts of Slots. 1970. pap. 1.50 (ISBN 0-89650-023-3). Gamblers.

Peddie, James. Racing for Gold: Or, Incidents in the Life of a Turf Commissioner with Examples of the Most Successful Systems of Speculating on the Turf & in Games of Chance. 1979. Repr. of 1891 ed. lib. bdg. 50.00 (ISBN 0-8495-4333-9). Arden Lib.

Petersen, William J. What You Should Know About Gambling. LC 74-75984. 128p. 1974. pap. 1.50 (ISBN 0-87983-081-6). Keats.

Peterson, Virgil W. Gambling: Should It Be Legalized? (American Lecture Public Protection). 128p. 1951. photocopy ed. spiral 12.75 (ISBN 0-398-04393-0). C C Thomas.

Petrakis, Harry M. Nick the Greek. LC 77-80909. 1979. 10.00 (ISBN 0-385-04909-9). Doubleday.

Quinn, John P. Gambling & Gambling Devices. (Illus.). 308p. 1979. pap. 8.95 (ISBN 0-89650-712-2). Gamblers.

--Gambling & Gambling Devices. LC 69-14942. (Criminology, Law Enforcement, & Social Problems Ser.: No. 48). (Illus.). 1969. Repr. of 1912 ed. 12.00 (ISBN 0-87585-048-0). Patterson Smith.

Reese, Terence. Winning at Casino Gambling. 1979. pap. 1.95 (ISBN 0-451-09640-1, J9640, Sig). NAL.

Rouge Et Noir. Gambling World. LC 68-22047. 1968. Repr. of 1898 ed. 24.00 (ISBN 0-8103-3551-4). Gale.

Scammon, Richard. The Odds: On Virtually Everything. 1980. 12.95 (ISBN 0-399-12483-7). Putnam.

Scarne, John. Scarne's Complete Guide to Gambling. (Illus.). 900p. 1974. 19.95 (ISBN 0-671-21734-8). S&S.

--Scarne's Guide to Casino Gambling. 1978. 13.95 (ISBN 0-671-24219-9). S&S.

Scharff, Robert. The Las Vegas Experts' Guide. abr. ed. 96p. 1970. pap. 1.25 (ISBN 0-911996-33-8). Gamblers.

Schneider, Maxine. Jackpot: To the Casino by Bus. (Gambler's Bookshelf). (Illus.). 80p. 1977. pap. 2.95 (ISBN 0-911996-77-X). Gamblers.

Scientific Betting. pap. 1.95 (ISBN 0-685-19497-3). Powner.

Shampaign, Charles E. Handbook on Percentages. (Gamblers Book Shelf). 1965. pap. 2.95 (ISBN 0-911996-02-8). Gamblers.

Silberstang, Edwin. How to Gamble & Win. 1980. pap. 2.95 (ISBN 0-346-12451-4). Cornerstone.

--Playboy's Guide to Casino Gambling: Craps, Blackjack, Roulette, & Baccarat. LC 80-7727. (Playboy's Lifestyles Library). (Illus.). 512p. 1980. 15.95 (ISBN 0-87223-618-8, Dist. by Har-Row). Playboy.

--The Winner's Guide to Casino Gambling. 1981. pap. 6.95 (ISBN 0-452-25286-5, Z5286, Plume). NAL.

--The Winner's Guide to Casino Gambling. LC 79-19848. 320p. 1980. 12.95 (ISBN 0-03-053481-X). HR&W.

Silverstone, Sidney. A Player's Guide to Casino Games. LC 80-84947. (Illus.). 155p. (Orig.). 1981. pap. 7.95 (ISBN 0-448-12249-9). G&D.

Sklansky, David. Sklansky on Poker Theory. rev. ed. 168p. 1980. pap. 5.95 (ISBN 0-89650-918-4). Gamblers.

Skolnick. House of Cards: Legalization & Control of Casino Gambling. (Orig.). 1981. pap. text ed. 8.95 (ISBN 0-316-79708-1). Little.

Skolnick, Jerome. House of Cards: Legalization & Control of Casino Gambling. LC 78-16991. 1978. 13.95 (ISBN 0-316-79699-9). Little.

Smith, Brian. Pineapple Hold 'Em. (Gambler's Book Shelf). 64p. 1979. pap. 2.95 (ISBN 0-89650-827-7). Gamblers.

Spanier, David. Pocket Guide to Gambling. 1980. 5.95 (ISBN 0-671-25515-0). S&S.

Steinmetz, Andrew. Gaming Table: Its Votaries & Victims, in All Times & Countries, Especially in England & in France, 2 Vols. LC 69-16247. (Criminology, Law Enforcement, & Social Problems Ser.: No. 96). 1969. Repr. of 1870 ed. Set. 40.00 (ISBN 0-87585-096-0). Patterson Smith.

Stuart, Lyle. Casino Gambling for the Winner. rev. ed. 208p. 1980. 20.00 (ISBN 0-8184-0299-7). Lyle Stuart.

Sturgeon, Kelso. Guide to Sports Betting. 1976. pap. 1.95 (ISBN 0-451-06901-3, J6901, Sig). NAL.

Sullivan, Donald. Winning by Computer. (Illus., Orig.). 1982. pap. text ed. 2.95 (ISBN 0-89746-018-9). Gambling Times.

Sutton, Irv. Gambling Know-How. 64p. (Orig.). 1980. pap. 2.95 (ISBN 0-89650-716-5). Gamblers.

Task Force on Legalized Gambling. Easy Money. LC 74-21880. Repr. of 1974 ed. pap. 5.00 (ISBN 0-527-02853-3). Kraus Repr.

Times Mirrow Press, ed. Gamblers Anonymous. new, rev., 3rd ed. 240p. 73. 5.95 (ISBN 0-686-05752-X). Gamblers Anon.

Tolerico, Jim. Fill Your Pockets in Atlantic City. 1978. pap. 5.00 (ISBN 0-89502-026-2). FEB.

Tredd, William E. Dice Games New & Old. (Oleander Games & Pastimes Ser.: Vol. 3). (Illus.). 64p. 1981. 9.95 (ISBN 0-906672-00-7); pap. 4.75 (ISBN 0-906672-01-5). Oleander Pr.

Tulcea, C. I. A Book on Casino Craps, Other Dice Games & Gambling Systems. 160p. 1980. 12.95 (ISBN 0-442-26713-4); pap. 8.95 (ISBN 0-442-25725-2). Van Nos Reinhold.

Villiod, Eugene. How They Cheat You at Cards. Barnhart, Russell, tr. from Fr. (Illus.). 192p. 1979. pap. 4.95 (ISBN 0-89650-750-5). Gamblers.

--Stealing Machine. Barnhart, Russell T., tr. LC 76-1271. 221p. 1975. 9.50 (ISBN 0-911996-99-0); pap. 4.50 (ISBN 0-686-67194-5). Gamblers.

Wallace, Frank R. An Obituary for the Public Professional Poker Player. 1978. pap. 9.95 (ISBN 0-911752-24-2). I & O Pub.

--Poker Odds. 16p. 1968. Repr. pap. 0.60 (ISBN 0-911996-34-6). Gamblers.

Wallace, Robert. The Gamblers. Time-Life Books, ed. (The Old West). (Illus.). 1979. 14.95 (ISBN 0-8094-2308-1). Time-Life.

--The Gamblers. LC 78-12281. (The Old West Ser.). (Illus.). 1978. lib. bdg. 12.96 (ISBN 0-686-51078-X). Silver.

Wiley, Dean. Money Management in the Casino. (Gambler's Book Shelf). 56p. pap. 2.95 (ISBN 0-911996-84-2). Gamblers.

--Understanding Gambling Systems. (Gambler's Book Shelf). 64p. 1975. pap. 2.95 (ISBN 0-911996-54-0). Gamblers.

Will & Finck, San Francisco, Cal., 1896 Gambler's Cheating Equipment Catalog Reprint. (Illus.). 16p. 1977. pap. 1.50 (ISBN 0-930478-00-2). Badger Bks.

Wilson, Allan N. Casino Gambler's Guide. rev & enl. ed. LC 71-127841. (Illus.). 1970. 12.95 (ISBN 0-06-014674-5, HarpT). Har-Row.

Winning Systems. 1978. pap. text ed. 2.00 (ISBN 0-89746-000-6). Gambling Times.

World's Greatest Gambling Systems. pap. 1.50 (ISBN 0-685-36861-0). Borden.

GAMBLING–GREAT BRITAIN

Ashton, John. History of Gambling in England. 1969. Repr. of 1899 ed. 15.00 (ISBN 0-8337-0099-5). B Franklin.

--History of Gambling in England. LC 69-14910. (Criminology, Law Enforcement, & Social Problems Ser.: No. 73). 1969. Repr. of 1898 ed. 10.00 (ISBN 0-87585-073-1). Patterson Smith.

--History of Gambling in England. LC 68-21520. 1968. Repr. of 1899 ed. 19.00 (ISBN 0-8103-3501-8). Gale.

Betting & Gambling. 60p. 1981. 120.00x (ISBN 0-686-71950-6, Pub. by Euromonitor). State Mutual Bk.

Herman, Robert D. Gamblers & Gambling. (Illus.). 1976. 16.95 (ISBN 0-669-00963-6). Lexington Bks.

GAMBLING PROBLEM (MATHEMATICS)

see Games of Chance (Mathematics)

GAME AND GAME-BIRDS

see also Animal Introduction; Cookery (Meat); Decoys (Hunting); Dogs–Training; Falconry; Fowling; Game-Laws; Game Protection; Hunting; Shooting; Shore Birds; Sports; Trapping; Water-Birds; Waterfowl;

also Particular Animals and Birds, e.g. Deer, Grouse, Rabbits, Woodcock

Anderson, Luther A. Hunting the Uplands with Rifle & Shotgun. (Illus.). 1977. 12.95 (ISBN 0-87691-191-2). Winchester Pr.

Atkinson, Herbert. Cockfighting & Game Fowl. 1981. 60.00x (ISBN 0-904558-23-1, Pub. by Saiga Pub). State Mutual Bk.

Billmeyer, Patricia. The Encyclopedia of Wild Game & Fish Cleaning & Cooking. LC 79-54388. 128p. pap. 3.95 (ISBN 0-9606262-0-4). Yesnaby Pubs.

Blair, Gerry. Predator Caller's Companion. 280p. 1981. 13.95 (ISBN 0-87691-336-2). Winchester Pr.

Brakefield, Tom. The Sportsman's Complete Book of Trophy & Meat Care. LC 75-17712. (Illus.). 224p. 1975. 8.95 (ISBN 0-8117-1685-6). Stackpole.

Bucher, Ruth & Gelb, Norman. The Book of Hunting. LC 77-5031. (Illus.). 1977. 60.00 (ISBN 0-448-22185-3). Paddington.

Burk, Bruce. Game Bird Carving. LC 72-79365. (Illus.). 1972. 19.95 (ISBN 0-87691-080-0). Winchester Pr.

Colby, C. B. Big Game: Animals of the Americas, Africa & Asia. (Illus.). (gr. 4-7). 1967. PLB 5.29 (ISBN 0-698-30024-6). Coward.

Dalrymple, Bryon. How to Call Wildlife. LC 74-33568. (Funk & W Bk.). (Illus.). 192p. 1975. 8.95 (ISBN 0-308-10208-8); (TYC-T). T Y Crowell.

Dickey, Charley. Charley Dickey's Dove Hunting. LC 75-12121. (Family Guidebooks Ser). (Illus.). 112p. 1976. pap. 2.95 (ISBN 0-8487-0385-5). Oxmoor Hse.

Elliott, Charles. Care of Game Meat & Trophies. LC 74-33570. (Funk & W Bk.). (Illus.). 160p. 1975. 7.50 (ISBN 0-308-10206-1); pap. 4.50 (ISBN 0-308-10207-X, TYC-T). T Y Crowell.

Gage, Rex. Game Shooting with Rex Gage. (Illus.). 1977. pap. 5.00x (ISBN 0-85242-592-9). Intl Pubns Serv.

Gooch, Bob. Conveys & Singles. LC 78-75306. (Illus.). 192p. 1980. 10.95 (ISBN 0-498-02342-7). A S Barnes.

Hagerbaumer, David. Selected American Game Birds. LC 74-137773. 1972. 30.00 (ISBN 0-87004-213-0). Caxton.

McCristal, Vic. Top End Safari. 14.95x (ISBN 0-392-05008-0, ABC). Sportshelf.

Oldham, J. The West of England Flying Tumbler. 1981. 25.00x (ISBN 0-904558-90-8, Pub. by Saiga Pub). State Mutual Bk.

Pettinger, Martin. Sporting Birds. 1981. 60.00x (ISBN 0-904558-52-5, Pub. by Saiga Pub). State Mutual Bk.

Poultry & Game Birds. (Illus.). 144p. 1982. pap. 8.95 plastic bdg. (ISBN 0-911658-29-7). Yankee Bks.

Scheid, D. Raising Game Birds. 1974. 2.50 (ISBN 0-684-14027-6, SL559, ScribT). Scribner.

Scott, P. A Coloured Key to the Wildfowl of the World. rev. ed. (Illus.). 1972. 15.00 (ISBN 0-685-12001-5). Heinman.

Scott, Peter. A Coloured Key to the Wildfowl of the World. rev. ed. (Illus.). 95p. 1972. 11.50x (ISBN 0-85493-013-2). Intl Pubns Serv.

Sherwood, Morgan. Big Game in Alaska. LC 81-3005. (Yale Western Americana Ser.: No. 33). (Illus.). 224p. 1981. 27.50x (ISBN 0-300-02625-0). Yale U Pr.

Smith, Guy N. Gamekeeping & Shooting for Amateurs. 1981. 30.00x (ISBN 0-904558-17-7, Pub. by Saiga Pub). State Mutual Bk.

--Hill Shooting & Upland Gamekeeping. 1981. 40.00x (ISBN 0-904558-41-X, Pub. by Saiga Pub). State Mutual Bk.

--Rating & Rabbiting for Amateur Gamekeepers. 1981. 25.00x (ISBN 0-904558-64-9, Pub. by Saiga Pub). State Mutual Bk.

Transactions of XIII International Congress of Game Biologists, Atlanta, Georgia, March 11-15. Proceedings. 538p. 1977. pap. 10.00 (ISBN 0-933564-04-X). Wildlife Soc.

GAME AND GAME-BIRDS–AFRICA

Robins, Eric. Secret Eden: Africa's Enchanted Wilderness. (Illus.). 128p. 1981. 25.00 (ISBN 0-241-10423-8, Pub. by Hamish Hamilton England). David & Charles.

GAME AND GAME-BIRDS–MEXICO

Tinker, Ben. Mexican Wilderness & Wildlife. LC 77-14030. (Illus.). 143p. 1978. 9.95 (ISBN 0-292-75037-4). U of Tex Pr.

GAME AND GAME-BIRDS–NEW ZEALAND

Poole, A. L. Wild Animals in New Zealand. LC 76-597144. (Illus.). 1969. 16.50 (ISBN 0-589-00411-5, Pub. by Reed Books Australia). C E Tuttle.

GAME AND GAME-BIRDS–NORTH AMERICA

Dalrymple, Byron. North American Game Animals. (Illus.). 1978. 14.95 (ISBN 0-517-53486-X). Crown.

Elman, Robert. Hunting America's Game Animals & Birds. (Illus.). 384p. 1980. 12.95 (ISBN 0-87691-172-6). Winchester Pr.

Jaques, Florence P. Geese Fly High. (Illus.). 1964. Repr. of 1939 ed. 8.95 (ISBN 0-8166-0311-1). U of Minn Pr.

Johnsgard, Paul A. North American Game Birds of Upland & Shoreline. LC 74-15274. (Illus.). xxx, 229p. 1975. pap. 7.95 (ISBN 0-8032-5811-9, BB 597, Bison). U of Nebr Pr.

Knap, Jerome, ed. All About Wildfowling in America. 1976. 11.95 (ISBN 0-87691-177-7). Winchester Pr.

Leopold, A. Starker & Darling, F. Fraser. Wildlife in Alaska, an Ecological Reconnaissance. LC 72-6927. 129p. 1973. Repr. of 1953 ed. lib. bdg. 15.00x (ISBN 0-8371-6509-1, LEWI). Greenwood.

Leopold, A. Starker, et al. North American Game Birds & Mammals. (Illus.). 224p. 1981. 19.95 (ISBN 0-684-17270-4, ScribT). Scribner.

Nesbitt, W. H. & Wright, Philip L., eds. Records of North American Big Game. 8th ed. (Records of North American Big Game). (Illus.). xii, 412p. 1981. 29.50 (ISBN 0-940864-00-2). Boone & Crockett.

Phillips, John C. American Game Mammals & Birds, a Catalogue of Books: Sport, Natural History, & Conservation, 1582-1925. Sterling, Keir B., ed. LC 77-83129. (Biologists & Their World Ser.). (Illus.). 1978. Repr. of 1930 ed. lib. bdg. 37.00x (ISBN 0-405-10744-7). Arno.

Rue, Leonard L., III. Complete Guide to Game Animals: A Field Book of North American Species. rev. ed. LC 80-8779. (Outdoor Life Bks.). (Illus.). 638p. 1981. 15.95 (ISBN 0-442-27796-2). Van Nos Reinhold.

Sanderson, Glen C., ed. Management of Migratory Shore & Upland Game Birds in North America. LC 79-23802. (Illus.). xiv, 358p. 1980. pap. 10.95 (ISBN 0-8032-9117-5, BB 725, Bison). U of Nebr Pr.

Tinsley, Russell, ed. All About Small Game Hunting in America. 1976. 11.95 (ISBN 0-87691-222-6). Winchester Pr.

Walsh, Harry M. The Outlaw Gunner. LC 71-180856. (Illus.). 1971. 12.50 (ISBN 0-87033-162-0, Pub. by Tidewater). Cornell Maritime.

Walsh, Roy E. Gunning the Chesapeake. LC 60-15800. (Illus.). 1960. 10.00 (ISBN 0-87033-028-4, Pub. by Tidewater). Cornell Maritime.

Zim, Herbert S. & Sprunt, Alexander, 4th. Gamebirds. (Golden Guide Ser). (gr. 9 up). 1961. PLB 10.38 (ISBN 0-307-63513-9, Golden Pr). Western Pub.

GAME-LAWS

see also Poaching

Hornaday, William T. Our Vanishing Wildlife: Its Extermination & Preservation. LC 77-125748. (American Environmental Studies). 1970. Repr. of 1913 ed. 18.00 (ISBN 0-405-02674-9). Arno.

--Thirty Years War for Wild Life. LC 71-125768. (American Environmental Studies). 1970. Repr. of 1931 ed. 14.00 (ISBN 0-405-02675-7). Arno.

Lund, Thomas A. American Wildlife Law. LC 78-68829. 1980. 12.95 (ISBN 0-520-03883-5). U of Cal Pr.

Munsche, P. B. Gentlemen & Poachers: The English Game Laws 1671-1831. LC 81-6168. (Illus.). 232p. Date not set. price not set (ISBN 0-521-23284-8). Cambridge U Pr.

Walsh, Harry M. The Outlaw Gunner. LC 71-180856. (Illus.). 1971. 12.50 (ISBN 0-87033-162-0, Pub. by Tidewater). Cornell Maritime.

GAME MANAGEMENT

see Wildlife Management

GAME PROTECTION

see also Birds, Protection of; Game-Laws

Coles, C. L. Game Conservation in a Changing Countryside. Date not set. 12.50 (ISBN 0-273-40133-5, SpS). Sportshelf.

Grinnell, George B. & Sheldon, Charles, eds. Hunting & Conservation. LC 71-125741. (American Environmental Studies). 1970. Repr. of 1925 ed. 25.00 (ISBN 0-405-02666-8). Arno.

Heiss, U. Askania-Nova: Animal Paradise in Russia. 8.75 (ISBN 0-370-01338-7). Transatlantic.

Hornaday, William T. Thirty Years War for Wild Life. LC 71-125768. (American Environmental Studies). 1970. Repr. of 1931 ed. 14.00 (ISBN 0-405-02675-7). Arno.

Rudman, Jack. Game Warden. (Career Examination Ser.: C-2012). (Cloth bdg. avail. on request). pap. 8.00 (ISBN 0-8373-2012-7). Natl Learning.

Spottiswoode, J. Moorland Gamekeeper. LC 77-74356. 1977. 7.50 (ISBN 0-7153-7384-6). David & Charles.

Steele, Melba. Cowboy, Game Warden & Longhorns. 104p. 1981. 6.95 (ISBN 0-686-72645-6). Dorrance.

Tillet, Paul. Doe Day: The Antlerless Deer Controversy in New Jersey. 1963. pap. 3.25 (ISBN 0-8135-0419-8). Rutgers U Pr.

Torbert, Floyd J. Park Rangers & Game Wardens the World Over. LC 68-26100. (Government Service the Whole World Over Ser). (Illus.). (gr. 4-6). 1968. 5.95g (ISBN 0-8038-5696-2). Hastings.

Wildlife Utilization & Game Ranching. (IUCN Occasional Paper: No. 17). (Illus.). 1978. pap. 9.50 (ISBN 2-88032-018-6, IUCN 69, IUCN). Unipub.

Wilkins, John. The Autobiography of an English Gamekeeper. 1976. 20.00 (ISBN 0-86023-025-2). State Mutual Bk.

GAME PROTECTION–AFRICA

Robins, Eric. Secret Eden: Africa's Enchanted Wilderness. (Illus.). 128p. 1981. 25.00 (ISBN 0-241-10423-8, Pub. by Hamish Hamilton England). David & Charles.

GAME ROOMS

see Recreation Rooms

GAME THEORY

see also Decision-Making; Games of Chance (Mathematics); Games of Strategy (Mathematics); Statistical Decision

Aizerman, M. A., et al. Sixteen Papers on Differential & Difference Equations, Functional Analysis, Games & Control. LC 51-5559. (Translations Ser.: No. 2, Vol. 87). 1970. 30.80 (ISBN 0-8218-1787-6, TRANS 2-87). Am Math.

Aubin, J. P. Mathematical Methods of Game & Economic Theory. (Studies in Mathematics & Its Applications: Vol. 4). 1979. 109.75 (ISBN 0-444-85184-4, North-Holland). Elsevier.

Aubin, Jean-Pierre. Applied Abstract Analysis. LC 77-2382. (Pure & Applied Mathematics, a W-I Ser. of Texts, Monographs & Tracts). 263p. 1977. 38.50 (ISBN 0-471-02146-6, Pub. by Wiley-Interscience). Wiley.

Bacharach, Michael. Economics & the Theory of Games. LC 76-27665. 1977. lib. bdg. 23.50x (ISBN 0-89158-704-7). Westview.

Bailey, Norman & Feder, Stuart. Operational Conflict Analysis. 1973. 7.00 (ISBN 0-8183-0145-7). Pub Aff Pr.

Bartos, Otomar J. Simple Models of Group Behavior. LC 67-21498. (Illus.). 345p. 1967. 22.50x (ISBN 0-231-02894-6); pap. 10.00x (ISBN 0-231-02893-8). Columbia U Pr.

Bell, Robert. Having It Your Way: The Strategy of Settling Everyday Conflicts. (Illus.). 1977. 8.95 (ISBN 0-393-01164-X). Norton.

Bell, Robert & Coplans, John. Decisions, Decisions: Game Theory & You. (Illus.). 160p. 1976. 7.95 (ISBN 0-393-01121-6). Norton.

Berne, Eric. Games People Play. 1978. pap. 2.75 (ISBN 0-345-29477-7). Ballantine.

Borch, Karl H. Economics of Uncertainty. LC 68-10503. (Studies in Mathematical Economics: Vol. 2). 1968. 22.50 (ISBN 0-691-04124-5). Princeton U Pr.

Brams, Steven J. Game Theory & Politics. LC 74-15370. (Illus.). 1975. pap. text ed. 9.95 (ISBN 0-02-904550-9). Free Pr.

CISM (International Center for Mechanical Sciences) Dept. of Automation & Information, 1973. Cooperative & Non-Cooperative Many Players Differential Games. Lietmann, G., ed. (CISM International Centre for Mechanical Sciences Ser.: No. 190). (Illus.). 77p. 1975. pap. 9.20 (ISBN 0-387-81275-X). Springer-Verlag.

Collatz, L. & Wetterling, W. Optimization Problems. Hadsack, P. R., tr. from Ger. (Applied Mathematical Sciences Ser.: Vol. 17). (Illus.). 370p. (Orig.). 1975. pap. text ed. 18.40 (ISBN 0-387-90143-4). Springer-Verlag.

Conway, John. On Numbers & Games. (London Mathematical Society Monographs). 1976. 27.00 (ISBN 0-12-186350-6). Acad Pr.

Davis, Morton D. Game Theory: A Nontechnical Introduction. LC 79-94295. 1973. pap. 4.95x (ISBN 0-465-09510-0, TB-5011). Basic.

Fararo, Thomas J. Mathematical Sociology: An Introduction to Fundamentals. LC 78-2379. 830p. 1978. Repr. of 1973 ed. lib. bdg. 33.50 (ISBN 0-88275-664-8). Krieger.

Friedman, James W. Oligopoly & the Theory of Games. (Advanced Textbooks in Economics Ser.: Vol. 8). 1977. 29.00 (ISBN 0-7204-0505-X, North-Holland). Elsevier.

Gale, David. Theory of Linear Economic Models. 1960. 27.50 (ISBN 0-07-022728-4, P&RB). McGraw.

Gamson, William A., ed. SIMSOC (Simulated Society) 3rd ed. LC 77-84285. 1978. pap. text ed. 7.95 (ISBN 0-02-911170-6). Free Pr.

Gibbs, G. C., ed. Academic Gaming & Simulation in Education & Training. LC 76-354655. 64p. 1975. pap. 5.00x (ISBN 0-85038-121-5). Intl Pubns Serv.

Glaser, Barney G. Experts Versus Laymen: A Study of the Patsy and the Subcontractor. 1976. Repr. text ed. 12.95 (ISBN 0-87855-217-0). Transaction Bks.

Goffman, Erving. Strategic Interaction. LC 74-92857. (Conduct & Communication Ser). 1971. 14.00x (ISBN 0-8122-7607-8); pap. 4.95x (ISBN 0-8122-1011-5, Pa Paperbks). U of Pa Pr.

Hajek, Otomar. Pursuit Games: An Introduction to the Theory & Applications of Differential Games of Pursuit & Evasion. (Mathematics in Science & Engineering Ser.). 1975. 25.50 (ISBN 0-12-317260-8). Acad Pr.

Hamburger, Henry. Games As Models of Social Phenomena. LC 78-23267. (Illus.). 1979. text ed. 18.95x (ISBN 0-7167-1011-0); pap. text ed. 8.95x (ISBN 0-7167-1010-2). W H Freeman.

Harsanyi, John C. Essays on Ethics, Social Behavior, & Scientific Explanation. LC 76-21093. (Theory & Decision Library Ser.: No. 12). 1976. lib. bdg. 50.00 (ISBN 90-277-0677-8, Pub. by Reidel Holland). Kluwer Boston.

Hartnett, William E., ed. Foundations of Coding Theory. LC 74-30030. (Episteme: No. 1). 216p. 1975. lib. bdg. 39.50 (ISBN 90-277-0536-4, Pub. by Reidel Holand). Kluwer Boston.

Hehn, R. & Moeschlin, O., eds. Mathematical Economics & Game Theory: Essays in Honor of Oskar Morgenstern. LC 76-30791. (Lecture Notes in Economics & Mathematical Systems: Vol. 141). 1977. pap. 28.70 (ISBN 0-387-08063-5). Springer-Verlag.

Isaacs, Rufus. Differential Games. 2nd ed. LC 73-92141. 424p. 1975. Repr. of 1965 ed. 21.50 (ISBN 0-88275-153-0). Krieger.

Jones, A. J. Game Theory: Mathematical Models of Conflict. LC 79-40972. (Mathematics & Its Applications Ser.). 309p. 1980. 49.95x (ISBN 0-470-26870-0). Halsted Pr.

Kuhn, Harold W. Contributions to the Theory of Games. Tucker, A. W., ed. (Annals of Mathematics Studies: Nos. 24). (Orig.). 1950-53. Vol. 1. pap. 20.00 (ISBN 0-691-07934-X). Princeton U Pr.

Kummer, B. Spiele Auf Graphen. (Internationale Schriftenreihe zur numerischen Mathematik: No. 44). 88p. (Ger.). 1980. pap. 18.50 (ISBN 3-7643-1077-4). Birkhauser.

Leach, J., et al, eds. Science, Decision & Value. LC 72-77877. (Western Ontario Ser: Vol. 1). 213p. 1973. lib. bdg. 30.00 (ISBN 90-277-0239-X, Pub. by Reidel Holland); pap. text ed. 14.50 (ISBN 90-277-0327-2). Kluwer Boston.

Leech, J. W. & Newman, D. J. How to Use Groups. 133p. 1969. pap. text ed. 10.95x (ISBN 0-412-20660-9, Pub. by Chapman & Hall England). Methuen Inc.

Leitmann, George, ed. Multicriteria Decision Making & Differential Games. (Mathematical Concepts & Methods in Science & Engineering Ser.: Vol. 3). 461p. 1976. 35.00 (ISBN 0-306-30920-3, Plenum Pr). Plenum Pub.

Luce, Robert D. & Raiffa, H. Games & Decisions: Introduction & Critical Survey. LC 57-12295. 1957. 29.50 (ISBN 0-471-55341-7). Wiley.

Neumann, John Von & Morgenstern, Oscar. Theory of Games & Economic Behavior. LC 53-4426. 664p. 1980. pap. 11.95 (ISBN 0-691-00362-9). Princeton U Pr.

Ordeshook, Peter C., ed. Game Theory & Political Science. LC 78-53028. (Studies in Game Theory & Mathematical Economics). 1978. 32.50x (ISBN 0-8147-6156-9). NYU Pr.

Parthasarathy, T. Selection Theorems & Their Applications. LC 72-78192. (Lecture Notes in Mathematics: Vol. 263). 108p. 1972. pap. 6.30 (ISBN 0-387-05818-4). Springer-Verlag.

Parthasarathy, T. & Raghavan, T. E. Some Topics in Two-Person Games. (Modern Analytic & Computational Methods in Science & Mathematics: No. 22). 1971. 26.50 (ISBN 0-444-00059-3, North Holland). Elsevier.

Rapaport, Anatol, ed. Game Theory As Theory of Conflict Resolution. LC 73-91434. (Theory & Decision Library: No. 2). 289p. 1974. lib. bdg. 44.00 (ISBN 90-277-0424-4, Pub. by Reidel Holland); pap. 29.00 (ISBN 90-277-0489-9, Pub. by Reidel Holland). Kluwer Boston.

Rapoport, A., et al. Coalition Formation by Sophisticated Players. (Lecture Notes in Economics & Mathematical Systems: Vol. 169). 1979. pap. 10.30 (ISBN 0-387-09249-8). Springer-Verlag.

Rapoport, Anatol. Two-Person Game Theory: The Essential Ideas. (Ann Arbor Science Library Ser). (Orig.). 1966. pap. 4.95 (ISBN 0-472-05015-X, 515, AA). U of Mich Pr.

Rapoport, Anatol & Chammah, Albert M. Prisoner's Dilemma. LC 65-11462. (Illus.). 1965. 7.50 (ISBN 0-472-75602-8). U of Mich Pr.

Rogers, C. A., et al, eds. Analytic Sets. LC 80-40647. (London Mathematical Society Symposia). 1981. 105.50 (ISBN 0-12-593150-6). Acad Pr.

Rosenmuller, J. Extreme Games & Their Solutions. LC 77-6655. (Lecture Notes in Economics & Mathematical Systems Ser: Vol. 145). 1977. pap. 10.10 (ISBN 0-387-08244-1). Springer-Verlag.

Sho-Kwan, Chow, et al. Sixteen Papers on Topology & One on Game Theory. LC 51-5559. (Translations Ser.: No. 2, Vol. 38). 1964. 24.40 (ISBN 0-8218-1738-8, TRANS 2-38). Am Math.

Shubik, Martin. The Uses & Methods of Gaming. LC 75-8275. 224p. 1975. 14.95 (ISBN 0-444-99007-0). Elsevier.

Shubik, Martin & Levitan, Richard. Market Structure & Behavior. LC 79-27108. (Illus.). 267p. 1980. text ed. 18.50x (ISBN 0-674-55026-9). Harvard U Pr.

Shubik, Martin, ed. Game Theory & Related Approaches to Social Behavior. LC 74-26575. 402p. 1975. Repr. of 1964 ed. 19.50 (ISBN 0-88275-229-4). Krieger.

Society for Academic Gaming & Simulation in Education & Training. Perspectives on Academic Gaming & Simulations Six: Games & Simulations - the Real & the Ideal. 220p. 1981. 32.00x (ISBN 0-85038-422-2). Nichols Pub.

Suppes, Patrick & Atkinson, Richard C. Markov Learning Models for Multiperson Interactions. 1960. 15.00x (ISBN 0-8047-0038-9). Stanford U Pr.

Symposium on Game Theory & Related Topics, Hagen & Bonn, Sept. 1978. Game Theory & Related Topics: Proceedings. Moeschlin, O. & Pallaschke, D., eds. 1979. 53.75 (ISBN 0-444-85342-1, North Holland). Elsevier.

Telser, Lester G. Competition, Collusion, & Game Theory. LC 70-141426. (Treatises in Modern Economics Ser). 1971. 19.95x (ISBN 0-202-06043-8). Beresford Bk Serv.

--Economic Theory & the Core. LC 77-21151. (Illus.). 1978. 36.00x (ISBN 0-226-79191-2). U of Chicago Pr.

Thie, Paul R. An Introduction to Linear Programming & Game Theory. LC 78-15328. 335p. 1979. text ed. 23.95 (ISBN 0-471-04248-X); tchr's. manual avail. (ISBN 0-471-04267-6). Wiley.

Ventsel, E. A. Elementos De la Teoria De los Juegos. 70p. (Span.). 1977. pap. 1.30 (ISBN 0-8285-1451-8, Pub. by Mir Pubs Russia). Imported Pubns.

Ventzel, Elena S. Lectures on Game Theory. (Russian Tracts on the Physical Sciences Ser). (Illus.). 1961. 18.75x (ISBN 0-677-20420-5). Gordon.

Vorob'Ev, N. N. Game Theory: Lectures for Economists & Systems. LC 77-1430. (Applications of Mathematics: Vol. 7). 1977. 20.40 (ISBN 0-387-90238-4). Springer-Verlag.

Williams, Thomas G. Game Playing with a Digital Computer. LC 73-118117. 126p. 19.00 (ISBN 0-686-01992-X). Mgmt Info Serv.

Zauberman, Alfred. Differential Games & Other Game-Theoretic Topics in Soviet Literature: A Survey. LC 75-665. 227p. 1975. 17.50x (ISBN 0-8147-9653-2). NYU Pr.

GAME WARDENS

see Game Protection

GAMES

see also Amusements; Ball Games; Bible Games and Puzzles; Board Games; Cards; Children's Parties; Dancing–Children's Dances; Games for Travelers; Geographical Recreations; Indoor Games; Jack Games; Kindergarten; Mathematical Recreations; Olympic Games; Play; Play-Party; Puzzles; Schools–Exercises and Recreations; Singing Games; Sports;

also specific games, e.g. Baseball, Contract Bridge, Tennis

Ahl, David. More Basic Computer Games. LC 78-74958. (Illus.). 1979. pap. 7.95 (ISBN 0-916688-09-7). Creative Comp.

Ainslie, Tom. Ainslie's Complete Hoyle. LC 74-32023. 544p. 1975. 15.95 (ISBN 0-671-21967-7); pap. 7.95 (ISBN 0-671-24779-4). S&S.

Allen, Edith B. Get in the Game. (Paperback Program Ser). (Orig.). 1971. pap. 1.95 (ISBN 0-8010-0014-9). Baker Bk.

Allen, Layman. Equations: Game of Creative Mathematics. 12.00 (ISBN 0-911624-38-4); tchrs' manual 1.75 (ISBN 0-911624-11-2). Wffn Proof.

--WFF: Beginner's Game of Modern Logic. 2.50 (ISBN 0-911624-01-5). Wffn Proof.

--Wffn Proof: Game of Modern Logic. 15.00 (ISBN 0-911624-36-8). Wffn Proof.

Allen, Layman, et al. Queries & Theories: Game of Science & Language. 15.00 (ISBN 0-911624-42-2). Wffn Proof.

Allen, Layman E., et al. On-Sets: Game of Set Theory. 12.00 (ISBN 0-911624-37-6). Wffn Proof.

Anastasio, Dina. Conversation Kickers. 1979. pap. 1.50 (ISBN 0-8431-0656-5). Price Stern.

Anderson, Doris. Encyclopedia of Games. 1968. pap. 3.95 (ISBN 0-310-20082-2). Zondervan.

Anderson, Ken & Carlson, Morry. Games for All Occasions. pap. 2.50 (ISBN 0-310-20152-7). Zondervan.

Arnold, Henri & Lee, Bob. Jumble--That Scrambled Word Game, No. 13. (Orig.). 1978. pap. 1.50 (ISBN 0-451-09831-5, W9831, Sig). NAL.

--Jumble: That Scrambled Word Game, No. 14. (Orig.). 1979. pap. 1.25 (ISBN 0-451-08910-3, Y8910, Sig). NAL.

Ault, Leslie. The Official Mastermind Handbook. 1976. pap. 1.50 (ISBN 0-451-07921-3, W7921, Sig). NAL.

Avedon, Elliott M. & Sutton-Smith, Brian. The Study of Games. LC 79-21194. 544p. 1979. Repr. of 1971 ed. lib. bdg. 22.50 (ISBN 0-89874-045-2). Krieger.

Beall, Pamela & Nipp, Susan. Wee Sing & Play. (Illus.). 64p. (Orig.). 1981. pap. 2.25 (ISBN 0-8431-0391-4). Price Stern.

Beaver, Edmund. Travel Games. (gr. 4 up). pap. 0.50 (ISBN 0-910208-01-8). Beavers.

Bentley, William G. Indoor & Outdoor Games. LC 66-28925. 1966. pap. 3.95 (ISBN 0-8224-3910-7). Pitman Learning.

Beram, Sandy. Games on the Go. LC 79-12412. (Illus.). 1979. pap. 5.95 (ISBN 0-02-028150-1, Collier). Macmillan.

Bieri, Arthur P. Action Games. LC 72-80025. 1972. pap. 3.95 (ISBN 0-8224-0060-X). Pitman Learning.

Big Book of Pencil Games. (Doubleday Activity Bks). (Illus.). (gr. 3-7). 1971. 1.95 (ISBN 0-385-04739-8). Doubleday.

Bike, Skate & Skateboard Games. (Kids Paperback Ser.). (Illus.). 1977. PLB 7.62 (ISBN 0-307-62353-X, Golden Pr); pap. 1.95 (ISBN 0-307-12353-7). Western Pub.

Blake, Kathleen. Play, Games, & Sport: The Literary Works of Lewis Carroll. LC 73-21362. (Illus.). 240p. 1974. 15.00x (ISBN 0-8014-0834-2). Cornell U Pr.

Board of Cooperative Education Services, Nassau County. Two Hundred Ways to Help Children Learn While You're at It. 1976. 12.95 (ISBN 0-87909-845-7). Reston.

Bohn, Henry G., ed. Hand-Book of Games. LC 73-84610. 1969. Repr. of 1850 ed. 24.00 (ISBN 0-8103-3570-0). Gale.

Boorman, Scott A. Protracted Game: A Wei-Ch'i Interpretation of Maoist Revolutionary Strategy. LC 70-83039. 1969. 14.95 (ISBN 0-19-500490-6). Oxford U Pr.

Boy Scouts Of America. Games for Cub Scouts. (Illus.). 96p. 1963. pap. 1.25x (ISBN 0-8395-3844-8, 3844). BSA.

Boyd, Neva L. Handbook of Recreational Games. LC 75-13385. 128p. 1975. pap. 2.50 (ISBN 0-486-23204-2). Dover.

--Hospital & Bedside Games. (Illus.). 72p. 1945. 3.95 (ISBN 0-912222-03-4, R532712). FitzSimons.

Brady, Maxine. The Monopoly Book. (Illus.). (gr. 7 up). 1976. pap. 3.95 (ISBN 0-679-14401-3). McKay.

Brandreth, Gyles. Game a Day Book. LC 79-91386. (Illus.). 192p. (gr. 2-12). 1980. 6.95 (ISBN 0-8069-4610-5); PLB 7.49 (ISBN 0-8069-4611-3). Sterling.

--Games for Trains, Planes, & Rainy Days. 1975. 7.95 (ISBN 0-685-52093-5). Pagurian.

--Home Entertainment for All the Family. LC 76-50266. (Illus.). 1977. pap. 5.95 (ISBN 0-8289-0298-4). Greene.

Brewster, Paul G., ed. Children's Games & Rhymes. LC 75-35063. (Studies in Play & Games: Vol. 1). 1976. Repr. 12.00x (ISBN 0-405-07914-1). Arno.

Bright, Greg. The Hole Maze Book. LC 79-1882. 1979. pap. 3.50 (ISBN 0-394-73754-7). Pantheon.

Bronstein, David. Two Hundred Open Games. (Illus.). 256p. 1975. 11.95 (ISBN 0-02-516500-3). Macmillan.

Brooke, Maxey. Coin Games & Puzzles. Orig. Title: Fun for the Money. 96p. 1973. pap. 1.50 (ISBN 0-486-22893-2). Dover.

Brown, Marice C. Amen, Brother Ben: A Mississippi Collection of Children's Rhymes. LC 78-32017. 1979. pap. text ed. 5.00 (ISBN 0-87805-094-9). U Pr of Miss.

Bruce, S. & Hart, Carol. Waiting Games. 320p. (Orig.). (YA) 1981. pap. 2.50 (ISBN 0-380-79012-2, Flare). Avon.

Buist, Charlotte A. & Schulman, Jerome L. Toys & Games for Educationally Handicapped Children. 240p. 1976. pap. 18.75 (ISBN 0-398-00250-9). C C Thomas.

Burleson, Donald R. Four Dimensional Tic-Tac-Toe. LC 70-172372. 1971. 4.95 (ISBN 0-912092-38-6). Educator Bks.

Buytendijk, Jacobus J. Wesen und Sinn Des Spiels: The Essence & Meaning of Games. LC 75-35064. (Studies in Play & Games). (Illus., German Text.). 1976. Repr. 12.00x (ISBN 0-405-07915-X). Arno.

Caillois, Roger. Jeux et Sports. (Methodique Ser.). 1848p. 49.95 (ISBN 0-686-56444-8). French & Eur.

Cardoza, Peter. Third Whole Kids Catalog. (Whole Kids Catalogs). 256p. (Orig.). 1981. pap. text ed. 8.95 (ISBN 0-553-01333-5). Bantam.

Carlson, Elliot. Learning Through Games. 1969. 6.00 (ISBN 0-8183-0178-3). Pub Aff Pr.

Cervantes De Salazar, Francisco. Life in the Imperial & Loyal City of Mexico in New Spain. Shepard, Minnie L., tr. LC 79-100224. Repr. of 1953 ed. lib. bdg. 15.00x (ISBN 0-8371-3033-6, CELM). Greenwood.

The Charlie Brown Xmas Activity Book. (Illus.). 96p. (gr. 2-6). 1979. pap. 1.25 (ISBN 0-448-16753-0). G&D.

Chase, Richard. Singing Games & Playparty Games. (Illus.). 3.75 (ISBN 0-8446-4721-7). Peter Smith.

Cole, Marion & Cole, Olivia H. Things to Make & Do for Easter. LC 78-12457. (Things to Make & Do Ser.). (Illus.). (gr. k-3). 1979. PLB 8.40 (ISBN 0-531-01463-0). Watts.

Conaway, Judith. Great Outdoor Games from Trash & Other Things. LC 77-7785. (Games & Activities Ser.). (Illus.). (gr. k-4). 1977. PLB 10.65 (ISBN 0-8172-0950-6). Raintree Pubs.

Cratty, Bryant J. Learning About Human Behavior: Through Active Games. (Illus.). 210p. 1975. ref. ed. o.p. 11.95 (ISBN 0-13-527473-7); pap. text ed. 8.95 (ISBN 0-13-527465-6). P-H.

Cuddon, J. A. The International Dictionary of Sports & Games. LC 79-20983. (Illus.). 800p. 1980. 29.95 (ISBN 0-8052-3733-X). Schocken.

Culin, Stewart. Chess & Playing-Cards. LC 75-35065. (Studies in Play & Games). (Illus.). 1976. Repr. 23.00x (ISBN 0-405-07916-8). Arno.

Daiken, Leslie. Children's Games Throughout the Year. LC 75-35067. (Studies in Play & Games). (Illus.). 1976. Repr. 17.00x (ISBN 0-405-07918-4). Arno.

Depew, Arthur M. Game Book. (Game & Party Books). 1977. pap. 5.95 (ISBN 0-8010-2877-9). Baker Bk.

Diagram Group. How to Hold a Crocodile & Hundreds of Other Practical Tips, Fascinating Facts, Quizzes, Gamees & Past Times. 1981. pap. 7.95 (ISBN 0-345-29577-3). Ballantine.

Donaldson, Judith E. Doodles, Diddles, Puzzles, Quizzies & Fun Stuff, Vol. 2. (Illus.). 144p. (Orig.). (YA) 1981. pap. 2.25 (ISBN 0-939942-00-3). Larkspur.

Donnelly, R. H., et al. Active Games & Contests. 2nd ed. 672p. 1958. 19.50 (ISBN 0-471-07088-2). Wiley.

Donnelly, R. J., et al. Active Games & Contests. 2nd ed. (Illus.). (gr. 7 up). 1958. 19.50 (ISBN 0-471-07088-2). Ronald Pr.

Dorwart, Harold L. Configurations: Number Puzzles & Patterns for All Ages. 7.00 (ISBN 0-911624-32-5). Wffn Proof.

Edmundson, Joseph. Games & Activities. 8.50x (ISBN 0-392-07339-0, LTB). Sportshelf.

Erickson, Alan. Bar Games, Bets & Challenges. (Orig.). 1981. pap. 1.95 (ISBN 0-446-90648-4). Warner Bks.

Erskine, Jim. Fold a Banana: & 146 Other Things to Do When You're Bored. (Illus.). 1978. pap. 5.95 (ISBN 0-517-53503-3, Dist. by Crown). Potter.

Evans, Larry. Gnomes Games. (Illus.). 64p. 1980. pap. 4.50 (ISBN 0-89844-020-3). Troubador Pr.

Falkener, Edward. Games Ancient & Oriental & How to Play Them. (Illus.). 1892. pap. 4.00 (ISBN 0-486-20739-0). Dover.

Featherman, Buzz. The Fun & Fantasy Book. new ed. (Illus.). cancelled (ISBN 0-932238-03-3). Word Shop.

Ferretti, Fred. The Great American Book of Sidewalk, Stoop, Dirt, Curb & Alley Games. LC 75-7291. (Illus.). 240p. (Orig.). (gr. 3 up). 1975. pap. 3.95 (ISBN 0-911104-59-3). Workman Pub.

FitzSimons, Ruth M. & Murphy, Albert T. Let's Play Hide & Seek. 7.50 (ISBN 0-686-11822-7); includes manual (ISBN 0-686-11823-5). Expression.

Fixx, James. More Games for the Super-Intelligent. 1977. pap. 2.50 (ISBN 0-445-04114-5). Popular Lib.

Fixx, James F. Games for the Superintelligent. LC 73-180074. 120p. 1972. 5.95 (ISBN 0-385-05768-7). Doubleday.

Fleming, June. Games (& More!) for Backpackers. LC 79-12631. (Illus.). 1979. pap. 4.50 (ISBN 0-918480-11-6). Victoria Hse.
Fletcher, Judy. Games. (A Nice Place to Live Ser.). pap. 1.95 (ISBN 0-570-07756-7, 12-2715). Concordia.
Folding Frenzy. 6p. 1981. pap. 4.95 (ISBN 0-517-54593-4, Harmony). Crown.
Ford, Robert. Children's Rhymes, Children's Games, Children's Songs & Stories. 59.95 (ISBN 0-87968-852-1). Gordon Pr.
Frederick, Filis. Design & Sell Toys, Games & Crafts. LC 76-55417. 1977. 12.50 (ISBN 0-8019-6223-4). Chilton.
Froh, Alfred & King, Margaret. Games for Young People. 1943. pap. 1.50 (ISBN 0-8066-0080-2, 10-2515). Augsburg.
Fun & Play All the Way. (Doubleday Activity Books). (Illus.). (gr. k-3). 1971. 1.49 (ISBN 0-385-01202-0). Doubleday.
Gallagher, Nora. Parlor Games. LC 79-17882. (Illus.). 1979. pap. 4.95 (ISBN 0-201-03084-5). A-W.
Gallagher, Rachel. Games in the Street. LC 75-34443. (Illus.). 112p. 1976. 7.95 (ISBN 0-590-17311-1, Four Winds). Schol Bk Serv.
Galleli, Gene. Activity Mind-Set Guide. 1977. 1.00 (ISBN 0-914634-53-4, 7722). DOK Pubs.
Gamec, Hazel S. The Disappearing ABC Game Book. (Illus.). 12p. write for info. (ISBN 0-938042-02-5). Printek.
--Looking Out of the Window. (Illus.). 12p. 1980. write for info. (ISBN 0-938042-01-7). Printek.
--The Magic Pencil Counting Book. (Illus.). 12p. 1980. write for info. (ISBN 0-938042-00-9). Printek.
Garden, Nancy. The Kid's Code & Cipher Book. LC 80-10434. (Illus.). 176p. (gr. 5 up). 1981. 10.95 (ISBN 0-03-053856-4); pap. 4.95 (ISBN 0-03-059267-4). HR&W.
Gardner, D. E. The Children's Play Centre. LC 76-108764. 1970. Repr. of 1937 ed. 7.50 (ISBN 0-87586-019-2). Agathon.
Gault, C. & Gault, G. Harlem Globetrotters Funniest Games. (ps-3). pap. 0.95 (ISBN 0-590-03000-0, Schol Pap). Schol Bk Serv.
Gee, John. Hidden Pictures: Favorites by John Gee. (Handbooks Ser.). (Illus.). 32p. (Orig.). (gr. 1-6). 1981. pap. 1.95 (ISBN 0-87534-230-2). Highlights.
Gibbons, Gail. Things to Make & Do for Columbus Day. (Things to Make & Do Ser.). (Illus.). (gr. 1-3). 1977. PLB 8.40 s&l (ISBN 0-531-01274-3). Watts.
Gibbs, G. I. Handbook of Games & Simulation Exercises. LC 73-88425. 226p. 1974. 15.00x (ISBN 0-8039-0333-2). Sage.
Greene, Lorne & Allen, Robert. Propaganda Game. 12.00 (ISBN 0-911624-39-2). Wffn Proof.
Greenman, Robert. The Rap Book. 1979. pap. 1.50 (ISBN 0-8431-0658-1). Price Stern.
Gregg, Elizabeth & Boston Children's Medical Center Staff. What to Do When There's Nothing to Do. 1970. pap. 1.50 (ISBN 0-440-39471-6). Dell.
Guiasu, S. & Malitza, M. Coalition & Connection in Games. 1980. text ed. 33.00 (ISBN 0-08-023033-4). Pergamon.
Hagstrom, Julie. Traveling Games for Babies: A Handbook of Games for Infants to Five-Year-Olds. (Illus.). 96p. 1981. pap. 4.95 (ISBN 0-89104-203-2). A & W Pubs.
Hagstrom, Julie & Morrill, Joan. Games Babies Play & More Games Babies Play. 1981. pap. 2.95 (ISBN 0-671-83628-5). PB.
Halperin, Ed, et al. Symbol Simons. 64p. (gr. 3-7). 1979. pap. 1.95 (ISBN 0-671-33060-8). Wanderer Bks.
Halperin, Edwin, et al. Symbol Simons: A New Type of Word Game & Puzzle. (Illus., Orig.). (gr. 5 up). 1979. pap. 1.95 (ISBN 0-671-33060-8). S&S.
Harbin, E. O. Old-Fashion Fun & Games. (Games & Party Books). 1978. pap. 3.45 (ISBN 0-8010-4184-8). Baker Bk.
Harbin, Elvin O. Fun Encyclopedia. (Illus.). (gr. 4 up). 1940. 8.95 (ISBN 0-687-13714-4). Abingdon.
Hardt, Elaine. Four Minute Fun for Parent & Child. LC 79-90463. 1978. pap. 2.95 (ISBN 0-932960-02-2). Horizons.
Hart, Harold H., compiled by. Grab a Pencil. 320p. 1980. pap. 4.95 (ISBN 0-89104-194-X). A & W Pubs.
Hertzano, Ephraim. The Official Rummikub Book: Including Rules, Strategy & Tactics for Winning. LC 77-93321. (Illus.). 1978. 6.95 (ISBN 0-8069-4944-9); lib. bdg. 6.69 (ISBN 0-8069-4945-7); pap. 2.95 (ISBN 0-8069-4946-5). Sterling.
Highlights Editors. Hidden Pictures & Other Challengers. (Handbooks Ser.). (Illus.). 32p. (Orig.). (gr. 1-6). 1981. pap. 1.95 (ISBN 0-87534-227-2). Highlights.
--Hidden Pictures & Other Fun. (Handbooks Ser.). (Illus.). 32p. (Orig.). (gr. 1-6). 1981. pap. 1.95 (ISBN 0-87534-178-0). Highlights.
--Hidden Pictures & Other Puzzlers. (Handbooks Ser.). (Illus.). 32p. (Orig.). (gr. 1-6). 1981. pap. 1.95 (ISBN 0-87534-180-2). Highlights.
--Hidden Pictures with Picture Clues & Other Games. (Handbooks Ser.). (Illus.). 32p. (Orig.). (gr. 1-6). 1981. pap. 1.95 (ISBN 0-87534-226-4). Highlights.
Hindman, Darwin A. Kick-the-Can & Over 800 Other Active Games & Sports. LC 77-14156. 1978. pap. 3.95 (ISBN 0-13-515163-5, Reward). P-H.
Hitz, Dimi. The Book of Moving Pictures. 1979. 4.95 (ISBN 0-394-84097-6); PLB 5.99 (ISBN 0-394-94097-0). Pantheon.
Hohenstein, Mary, compiled by. Games. 160p. (Orig.). 1980. pap. 5.95 (ISBN 0-87123-191-3, 210191). Bethany Hse.
Home Video Tape-Disc Guide: Movies & Entertainment. 1980. pap. 12.95 (ISBN 0-452-25255-5, 25255, Plume). NAL.
Howard, Vernon. One Hundred Games for Boys & Girls. 120p. 1974. pap. 2.50 (ISBN 0-310-26302-6). Zondervan.
Hoyle, Edmund. Hoyle's Games. 20th. rev ed. 1967. Repr. of 1950 ed. 14.00 (ISBN 0-7100-1566-6). Routledge & Kegan.
Humphrey, J. H. & Sullivan, Dorothy D. Teaching Slow Learners Through Active Games. 192p. 1973. 12.75 (ISBN 0-398-00886-8). C C Thomas.
Hunt, S. E. Games & Sports the World Around. 3rd ed. 271p. 1964. 13.95 (ISBN 0-471-07096-3). Wiley.
Hunt, Sarah E. Games & Sports the World Around. 3rd ed. (Illus.). (gr. 9-12). 1964. 13.95 (ISBN 0-471-07096-3). Ronald Pr.
Inn Games. 1976. pap. 2.50 (ISBN 0-8277-4878-7). British Bk Ctr.
International Council on Health, Physical Education & Recreation. ICHPER Book of Worldwide Games & Dances. (Illus.). 1967. pap. 7.00x (ISBN 0-685-05090-4, 245-07144). AAHPERD.
Ireson, Barbara. Your Book of Party Games. (Illus.). (gr. 7 up). 1969. 6.25 (ISBN 0-571-08449-4). Transatlantic.
Israel, Richard J. Jewish Identity Games: A How to Do It Book. LC 78-55201. 1978. 3.95 (ISBN 0-9603058-1-5). B'nai B'rith-Hillel.
Kaplan, Sandra, et al. The Big Book of Independent Study Games & Activities. LC 76-21556. (Big Book Ser.). (Illus.). 70p. 1976. spiral bdg. 16.95 (ISBN 0-87620-122-2). Goodyear.
Kate Greenaway's Book of Games. 4.75 (ISBN 0-686-08935-9, 18025). Merrimack.
Keeler, Ronald F. Games for Children: For Indoors & Outdoors. (Games & Party Books). 64p. 1982. pap. price not set (ISBN 0-8010-5437-0). Baker Bk.
Kohl, Marguerite & Young, Frederica. Games for Children. 1963. pap. 2.95 (ISBN 0-346-12348-8). Cornerstone.
--Games for Grownups. 1962. pap. 3.95 (ISBN 0-346-12281-3). Cornerstone.
Koziakin, Vladimir. A-Maze-Ing Facts. 128p. (Orig.). 1981. pap. 1.75 (ISBN 0-448-17309-3, Tempo). Ace Bks.
--Mystery Mazes. 128p. 1974. pap. 0.95 (ISBN 0-685-39097-7, 5734, Tempo). Ace Bks.
Latchaw, Marjorie. Pocket Guide of Movement Activities for the Elementary School. 2nd ed. 1970. pap. 11.95 (ISBN 0-13-684852-4). P-H.
Lee, Stan. Mighty Marvel Superheroes Fun Book. 1976. 2.95 (ISBN 0-671-22310-0, 22310). S&S.
--Mighty Marvel Superheroes Fun Book, No. 4. (Illus.). (gr. 3 up). 1979. pap. 2.95 (ISBN 0-671-24389-6, Fireside). S&S.
Levmore, Saul & Cook, Elizabeth E. Super Strategies: Games & Puzzles for Strategy Training. (Illus.). 168p. 1981. 10.95 (ISBN 0-385-17165-X). Doubleday.
Lewis. Games & Parties. (gr. 4 up). 1968. pap. 0.60 (ISBN 0-8049-2727-8, NF2). Airmont.
Lewis, Edward. Be a Winner. (Gamblers Book Shelf). 160p. 1979. pap. 2.95 (ISBN 0-89650-530-8). Gamblers.
Lombardy, Dana, ed. The Gamesmaster Catalog. (Illus., Orig.). 1980. pap. 6.95 (ISBN 0-933168-02-0). Boynton & Assoc.
Love, Brian. Great Board Games. 1979. 14.95 (ISBN 0-02-575570-6). Macmillan.
Lovinger, Sophie L. Learning Disabilities & Games. LC 78-24619. (Illus.). 1979. text ed. 15.95x (ISBN 0-88229-353-2); pap. 8.95x (ISBN 0-88229-652-3). Nelson-Hall.
Luschen, Gunther. The Cross-Cultural Analysis of Sport & Games. 1970. pap. 5.00x (ISBN 0-87563-038-3). Stipes.
McDonald, John. Strategy in Poker, Business & War. (Illus.). 1963. pap. 2.95 (ISBN 0-393-00225-X, Norton Lib). Norton.
McGovern, Ann. Ghostly Fun. (gr. 4-6). 1971. pap. 1.25 (ISBN 0-590-04448-6, Schol Pap). Schol Bk Serv.
Maclagen, Robert C., compiled by. Games & Diversions of Argyleshire. LC 75-34848. (Studies in Play & Games). (Illus.). 1976. Repr. 17.00x (ISBN 0-405-07927-3). Arno.
McToots, Rudi & Dreadnaught Group. The Kids Book of Games for Cars, Trains & Planes. 1980. pap. 4.95 (ISBN 0-553-01230-4). Bantam.
McWhirter, Norris & Pallas, Norvin. Guinness Game Book. LC 77-93311. (Illus.). (gr. 3 up). 1978. 5.95 (ISBN 0-8069-0122-5); PLB 5.89 (ISBN 0-8069-0123-3). Sterling.
Manchester, Richard B. Mammoth Book of Fun & Games. (Mammoth Bks). (Illus.). 512p. (Orig.). 1979. pap. 8.95 (ISBN 0-89104-162-1). A & W Pubs.
--The Second Mammoth Book of Fun & Games. LC 79-1213. (Illus.). 512p. 1980. pap. 8.95 (ISBN 0-89104-170-2). A & W Pubs.
Maskelyne, John N. Sharps & Flats: A Complete Revelation of the Secrets of Cheating at Games of Chance & Skill. 368p. 1972. pap. 6.95 (ISBN 0-89650-912-5). Gamblers.
Mason, Bernard S. & Mitchell, Elmer D. Party Games. 1962. pap. 2.95 (ISBN 0-06-463216-4, EH 216, EH). Har-Row.
Mauldon, Elizabeth & Redfern, H. B. Games Teaching: A Heuristic Approach for the Primary School. LC 74-416942. (Illus.). 1969. 7.00x (ISBN 0-7121-0706-1). Intl Pubns Serv.
Mayne, Lynn. Fabric Games. 1978. 12.95 (ISBN 0-395-27084-7); pap. 6.95 (ISBN 0-395-27209-2). HM.
Meyer, Jerome. The Big Book of Family Games. (Illus.). 208p. 1980. pap. 4.95 (ISBN 0-8015-0624-7, Hawthorn). Dutton.
Middleton, Thomas H., ed. Double-Crostics by Fans, No. 5. 1969. pap. 2.95 (ISBN 0-671-20405-X). S&S.
Millen, Nina. Children's Festivals from Many Lands. 1964. pap. 4.95 (ISBN 0-377-44501-0). Friend Pr.
--Children's Games from Many Lands. 1965. pap. 5.95 (ISBN 0-377-45011-1). Friend Pr.
Minter, James F. Pencil Pastimes, No. 9. 128p. 1981. pap. 2.50 (ISBN 0-89104-172-9). A & W Pubs.
Morehead, et al, eds. Hoyles Rules of Games. (RL 7). 1973. pap. 2.50 (ISBN 0-451-09001-2, E9701, Sig). NAL.
Moscow, Alvin. Collision Course. LC 81-47698. (Illus.). 352p. 1981. Repr. of 1959 ed. 12.95 (ISBN 0-448-12019-4). G&D.
Mott, Mrs. Hamilton, ed. Home Games & Parties. 1979. Repr. of 1891 ed. lib. bdg. 15.00 (ISBN 0-8492-6820-6). R West.
Mueting, Donald & Hawkins, Robert. Pinball Reference Guide. (Orig.). 1979. pap. 7.95 (ISBN 0-934422-19-2). Mead Co.
Mullin, Richard. Christmas Party Games. (Standard Ideas Ser.). 1978. pap. 1.75 (ISBN 0-87239-216-3, 2817). Standard Pub.
Muncy, Patricia T. Complete Book of Illustrated K-3 Alphabet Games & Activities. 1979. 14.95x (ISBN 0-87628-230-3). Ctr Appl Res.
New Games Foundation. More New Games Book. Fluegelman, Andrew, ed. LC 80-2559. (Illus.). 192p. 1981. pap. 6.95 (ISBN 0-385-17514-0, Dolp). Doubleday.
--The New Games Book. Fluegelman, Andrew, ed. 6.95 (ISBN 0-385-12516-X, Dolp). Doubleday.
Norback, Craig. The Fabulous Puzzle & Game Book. (Orig.). Date not set. pap. price not set (ISBN 0-440-52484-9). Dell.
Obermair, Gilbert. Matchstick Puzzles, Tricks & Games. LC 77-79510. (Illus.). (gr. 4 up). 1977. 5.95 (ISBN 0-8069-4564-8); PLB 5.89 (ISBN 0-8069-4565-6). Sterling.
Official Rules of Sports & Games. (Illus.). 1979. text ed. 25.00x (ISBN 0-392-05669-0, SpS). Sportshelf.
One Hundred Learning Games. (Doubleday Activity Bk). (Illus.). (gr. 1-3). 1970. 1.95 (ISBN 0-385-03792-9). Doubleday.
Orlick, Terry. The Cooperative Sports & Games Book: Challenge Without Competition. LC 77-88771. 1978. 10.00 (ISBN 0-394-42215-5); pap. 5.95 (ISBN 0-394-73494-7). Pantheon.
Palmer, Nicholas. Best of Board Wargaming. Date not set. 16.95 (ISBN 0-88254-525-6). Hippocrene Bks.
Pask, Gordon, et al. Calculator Saturnalia. LC 80-5489. 256p. 1981. pap. 5.95 (ISBN 0-394-74528-0, Vin). Random.
The Peanuts Giant Funtime Activity Book. (gr. 2-4). 1981. pap. 3.95 (ISBN 0-448-15498-6). G&D.
Playbook for Small Fry. (Doubleday Activity Bks.). (Illus.). (ps-1). 1.49 (ISBN 0-385-03748-1). Doubleday.
Plumb, Beatrice. Master Banquet & Party Book. (Game & Party Bks.). pap. 3.50 (ISBN 0-8010-6986-6). Baker Bk.
Polin, Robert & Rain, Michael. Pinball Wizardry: The Theory & Practice of the Art & Science of Pinball. LC 79-9323. (Illus.). 1979. pap. 4.95 (ISBN 0-13-676221-2). P-H.
Poynter, Dan. Toobee Players' Handook: The Amazing Flying Can. new ed. LC 80-20529. (Illus.). 52p. (Orig.). 1981. pap. 4.95 (ISBN 0-915516-25-X). Para Pub.
Pritchard, David, ed. Modern Board Games. (Illus.). 1976. pasteboard covers 10.00 (ISBN 0-86002-059-2). Hippocrene Bks.
Razzi, Jim. Encyclopedia Brown Puzzle & Game Books. (gr. 4-8). 1980. pap. 1.25 (ISBN 0-686-57991-7). Bantam.
--Encyclopedia Brown's Fourth Book of Games & Puzzles. 64p. (gr. 4-6). 1981. pap. 1.50 (ISBN 0-553-15110-X). Bantam.
--Encyclopedia Brown's Second Book of Puzzles & Games. 1.50 (ISBN 0-553-15099-5). Bantam.
--Encyclopedia Brown's Third Book of Games & Puzzles. 64p. (Orig.). (gr. 4-6). 1981. pap. 1.50 (ISBN 0-553-15077-4). Bantam.
Reeves, Robert. Make-It-Yourself Games Book. (Illus.). (gr. 9 up). 1964. 6.95 (ISBN 0-87523-152-7). Emerson.
Reinfeld, Fred. The Immortal Games of Capablanca. (Illus.). 252p. 1974. pap. 4.95 (ISBN 0-02-029690-8, Collier). Macmillan.
Rice, Wayne, et al. Fun-N-Games. 1977. pap. 4.95 (ISBN 0-310-35001-8). Zondervan.
Richardson, Hazel A. Games for the Elementary School Grades. 2nd ed. 1951. spiral bdg. 9.95x (ISBN 0-8087-1805-3). Burgess.
Roberts, Glyn C., et al. Social Science of Play, Games & Sport: Learning Experiences. 103p. 1979. pap. text ed. 9.95x (ISBN 0-931250-13-7). Human Kinetics.
Roberts, Jim. Star Force One Take Along Game. (gr. 3 up). 1980. pap. 3.95 (ISBN 0-671-95649-3). Wanderer Bks.
Rockwell, Anne. Games (& How to Play Them) LC 72-10936. (Illus.). (gr. 1 up). 1973. 9.95 (ISBN 0-690-32159-7, TYC-J); PLB 9.79 (ISBN 0-690-32160-0). Har-Row.
Roth, Walter. Games, Sports & Amusements. LC 75-35076. (Studies in Play & Games). (Illus.). 1976. Repr. 10.00x (ISBN 0-405-07926-5). Arno.
Sackson, Sid. Beyond Solitaire: Six Challenging New Games for One to Play with Pens & Pencils. LC 76-8666. (Illus.). 1976. pap. 2.95 (ISBN 0-394-83304-X). Pantheon.
--Calculate: Use Your Calculators & Your Wits in Six Challenging Pencil Games for Two or More Players. LC 78-31510. 1979. 2.95 (ISBN 0-394-84222-7). Pantheon.
Sanoff, Henry. Design Games: Playing for Keeps with Personal & Environmental Design Decisions. LC 79-10792. (Illus.). 111p. 1979. pap. 4.95 (ISBN 0-913232-63-7). W Kaufmann.
Scarne, John. Scarne's Encyclopedia of Games. LC 72-79691. (Illus.). 448p. 1973. 20.00 (ISBN 0-06-013813-0, HarpT). Har-Row.
Schaupp, Jack. Creating & Playing Games with Students. (Orig.). 1981. pap. 4.95 (ISBN 0-687-09809-2). Abingdon.
Seaman, Rosie. Through Their Looking Glass. LC 79-89647. (Illus.). 50p. (ps). 1979. pap. text ed. 5.95 (ISBN 0-913916-84-6, IP 84-6). Incentive Pubns.
Segal, Zev & Ayalon, Ofra. Getting Along: Games for Couple Compatibility. (Illus.). 128p. (Orig.). 1981. pap. 6.95 (ISBN 0-448-16169-9). G&D.
Sergeant, Philip W. The Unknown Morphy. 1973. pap. 1.75 (ISBN 0-486-22952-1). Dover.
Sharp, Evelyn. Thinking Is Child's Play. 1970. pap. 1.95 (ISBN 0-380-01580-3, 41103, Discus). Avon.
Sharp, Richard. The Best Games People Play. (Illus.). 14.95x (ISBN 0-8464-0188-6); pap. 7.95x (ISBN 0-8464-0194-0). Beekman Pubs.
Shepard, Mary & Shepard, Ray. Vegetable Soup Activities. 96p. 1975. text ed. 6.95 (ISBN 0-590-07443-1, Citation); pap. text ed. 2.25 (ISBN 0-590-09603-6). Schol Bk Serv.
Shepherd, Walter. The Big Book of Mazes & Labyrinths. LC 72-97817. 112p. (Orig.). 1973. pap. 2.25 (ISBN 0-486-22951-3). Dover.
Shortz, Will. Brain Games. 1979. pap. 4.95 (ISBN 0-671-24719-0, Fireside). S&S.
Smith, Thomas M., ed. Look It up in Hoyle. rev. ed. (Illus.). 1969. pap. 2.50 (ISBN 0-668-01779-1). Arco.
The Snoopy Xmas Activity Book. (Illus.). 96p. (gr. 2-6). 1979. pap. 1.25 (ISBN 0-448-16756-5). G&D.
SPI Editorial Staff. Wargame Design. 1981. pap. 9.95 (ISBN 0-88254-583-3). Hippocrene Bks.
Sports & Pastimes. 1981. pap. 6.00x (ISBN 0-904654-10-9, Pub. by Brit Lib England). State Mutual Bk.
Squire, Norman. How to Win at Roulette. 222p. 1972. pap. 2.95 (ISBN 0-89650-535-9). Gamblers.
Stein, Lincoln D. Family Games. (Illus.). 1979. pap. 9.95 (ISBN 0-02-029930-3, Collier). Macmillan.
--Family Games. (Illus.). 1979. 19.95 (ISBN 0-02-613750-X). Macmillan.
Stella, Jacques. Games & Pastimes of Childhood. Appelbaum, Stanley, tr. (Illus.). 5.50 (ISBN 0-8446-4608-3). Peter Smith.

Sternlict, Manny & Hurwitz, Abraham. Games Children Play: Instructive & Creative Play Activities for the Mentally Retarded & Developmentally Disabled Child. 128p. 1980. 12.95 (ISBN 0-442-25857-7). Van Nos Reinhold.

Stranks, Susan. Family Fun: Things to Make, Do & Play. LC 78-71829. (Illus.). 1979. 11.95 (ISBN 0-8120-5319-2). Barron.

Stuart, Sally E. The All-Occasion Game Book. LC 81-50350. (Illus.). 64p. (Orig.). 1981. pap. 2.95 (ISBN 0-87239-444-1, 2798). Standard Pub.

Sullivan, Donald. Winning by Computer. (Illus., Orig.). 1982. pap. text ed. 2.95 (ISBN 0-89746-018-9). Gambling Times.

Summers, George J. Mind Teasers: Logic Puzzles & Games of Deduction. LC 77-79511. (Illus.). (gr. 6 up). 1977. 6.95 (ISBN 0-8069-4566-4); PLB 6.69 (ISBN 0-8069-4567-2). Sterling.

Super Colossal Book of Puzzles, Games & Tricks. Date not set. pap. 6.95 (ISBN 0-553-01164-2). Bantam.

Sutton-Smith, Brian, ed. Studies in Play & Games, 21 vols. 1976. Set. 356.00x (ISBN 0-405-07912-5). Arno.

Things to Do While Traveling. (Elephant Bks.). 160p. (ps-3). 1973. pap. 1.25 (ISBN 0-448-02910-3). G&D.

Tolbert, Jim & Tolbert, Candace. Tilt: The Pinball Book. LC 78-52769. (Illus.). 1978. pap. 5.95 (ISBN 0-916870-14-6). Creative Arts Bk.

Toys & Games. (Ladybird Stories Ser.). (Illus., Arabic.). 2.50x (ISBN 0-86685-241-7). Intl Bk Ctr.

Trapunski, Edward. Special When Lit: A Visual & Anecdotal History of Pinball. 1979. 6.95 (ISBN 0-385-12251-9, Dolp). Doubleday.

Treasured Polish Folk Rhythms, Songs & Games. 1976. 5.95 (ISBN 0-685-84287-8). Polanie.

Tuckett, Neil & Tuckett, Guin. Just for Fun. (Orig.). 1965. pap. 1.95 (ISBN 0-8272-1702-1). Bethany Pr.

U. S. Children's Bureau. Handbook for Recreation. rev. 1959 ed. LC 74-174126. (Children's Bureau Publication Ser.: No. 231). (Illus.). x, 148p. 1975. Repr. of 1960 ed. 20.00 (ISBN 0-8103-4001-1). Gale.

Van Ryzin, Lani. Sidewalk Games. LC 77-28327. (Games & Activities Ser.). (Illus.). (gr. k-3). 1978. PLB 10.65 (ISBN 0-8172-1166-7). Raintree Pubs.

Vixen, Richard M. The Game of Orgy. LC 77-93805. (Illus.). 1978. pap. 1.95 (ISBN 0-930182-04-9). Avant-Garde OR.

Wackerbarth, Marjorie & Graham, Lillian S. Games for All Ages. (Direction Bks). (Orig.). 1973. pap. 3.45 (ISBN 0-8010-9536-0). Baker Bk.

Wade, Mildred. Games for Fun. LC 77-76616. 1977. pap. 3.95 (ISBN 0-8054-7513-3). Broadman.

Wallace, Frank R. Neo-Tech II. (Neo-Tech Discovery Ser.: Vol. 2). 480p. 1981. pap. 200.00x (ISBN 0-911752-35-8). I & O Pub.

Wasley, John. Games for Two. (Illus.). 224p. 1981. pap. 9.95 (ISBN 0-906071-26-7). Proteus Pub NY.

Weinstein, Matt & Goodman, Joel. Playfair: Everybody's Guide to Noncompetitive Play. LC 80-12591. (Orig.). 1980. pap. 8.95 (ISBN 0-915166-50-X). Impact Pubs Cal.

Wells, Herbert G. Floor Games. LC 75-35084. (Studies in Play & Games). (Illus.). 1976. Repr. 10.00x (ISBN 0-405-07932-X). Arno.

White, Suzanne. Suzanne White's Book of Chinese Chance. 384p. 1977. pap. 2.50 (ISBN 0-449-24194-7, Crest). Fawcett.

Whyte, Malcolm, ed. Pyramid Puzzles. (Illus.). 40p. (Orig.). (gr. 1-12). 1979. pap. 2.25 (ISBN 0-89844-003-3). Troubador Pr.

Wilson, Peter. Forty Games for Frivolous People. (Illus.). 1979. pap. 3.95 (ISBN 0-8256-3154-8, Quick Fox). Music Sales.

Wiswell, Phil. I Hate Charades & Forty-Nine Other New Games. LC 80-54341. (Illus.). 128p. 1981. 5.95 (ISBN 0-8069-4582-6); lib. bdg. 6.69 (ISBN 0-8069-4583-4). Sterling.

Yeatman, E. F. & Hall, Maud R. On the Green: Village Games. LC 72-7004. 1972. lib. bdg. 5.00 (ISBN 0-88305-800-6). Norwood Edns.

Youth for Christ-Campus Life. One Hundred & Twenty Five Crowdbreakers. Merrill, Dean & Baumann, Clayton, eds. LC 73-88094. (Orig.). (gr. 9-12). 1974. pap. 1.75 (ISBN 0-8307-0249-0, 50-099-01). Regal.

Zaks, Rodnay. Six Thousand Five Hundred & Two Games. (Illus.). 1980. pap. 12.95 (ISBN 0-89588-022-9, 0402). Sybex.

Zechlin, Katharina. Making Games in Wood. LC 80-54353. (Illus.). 80p. 1981. pap. 6.95 (ISBN 0-8069-8996-3). Sterling.

GAMES–BIBLIOGRAPHY

Hargrave, Catherine P. History of Playing Cards & a Bibliography of Cards & Gaming. (Illus.). 13.50 (ISBN 0-8446-2205-2). Peter Smith.

--History of Playing Cards & a Bibliography of Cards & Gaming. (Illus.). pap. 7.95 (ISBN 0-486-21544-X). Dover.

Jessel, Frederic & Horr, Norton T. Bibliographies of Works on Playing Cards & Gaming. Incl. Bibliography of Works in English on Playing Cards & Gaming. Jessel, Frederic. Repr. of 1905 ed; Bibliography of Card Games & of the History of Playing Cards. Horr, Norton T. Repr. of 1892 ed. LC 77-129310. (Criminology, Law Enforcement, & Social Problems Ser., No. 132). 1972. 20.00 (ISBN 0-87585-132-0). Patterson Smith.

GAMES–COMPUTER PROGRAMS

Ahl, David H., ed. Basic Computer Games: Trs-80, Vol. II. LC 78-50028. (Illus.). 208p. (Orig.). 1980. pap. 6.95 (ISBN 0-916688-19-4). Creative Comp.

Sagan, Hans. Beat the Odds: Microcomputer Simulations of Casino Games. 192p. 1980. pap. 8.70 (ISBN 0-8104-5181-6). Hayden.

Sage, Edwin R. Fun & Games with the Computer. 250p. 1975. pap. text ed. 9.95 (ISBN 0-87567-075-X). Entelek.

GAMES–DICTIONARIES

Gibbs, G. I. Dictionary of Gaming, Modelling & Simulation. LC 78-59784. 159p. 1978. 17.50x (ISBN 0-8039-1085-1). Sage.

GAMES–ENCYCLOPEDIAS

Arlott, John, ed. The Oxford Companion to World Sports & Games. (Illus.). 1024p. 1975. 35.00 (ISBN 0-19-211538-3). Oxford U Pr.

Diagram Group. The Official World Encyclopedia of Sports & Games: The Rules, Techniques of Play & Equipment for Over 400 Sports & 1000 Games. LC 79-10380. (Illus.). 1979. 15.95 (ISBN 0-448-22202-7). Paddington.

Gibson, Walter B. Hoyle's Modern Encyclopedia of Card Games, Rules of All the Basic Games & Popular Variations. LC 73-163085. 408p. 1974. pap. 5.95 (ISBN 0-385-07680-0, Dolp). Doubleday.

Silberstang, Edwin. Playboy's Book of Games. rev. ed. LC 79-4893. (Playboy's Lifestyles Library). (Illus.). 1979. pap. 8.95 (ISBN 0-87223-546-7, Dist. by Har-Row). Wideview Bks.

GAMES–HISTORY

Beaver, Patrick. Victorian Parlor Games. LC 78-12396. (Illus.). 1979. 7.95 (ISBN 0-525-66608-7). Elsevier-Nelson.

Bett, Henry. Games of Children, Their Origin & History. LC 68-31218. 1968. Repr. of 1929 ed. 19.00 (ISBN 0-8103-3473-9). Gale.

Kaye, Marvin. The Story of Monopoly, Silly Putty, Bingo Twister, Frisbee, Scrabble, Etcetera. LC 72-95990. 1977. 9.95 (ISBN 0-8128-2247-1); pap. 2.95 (ISBN 0-8128-2254-4). Stein & Day.

Loeper, John J. The Shop on High Street: Toys & Games of Early America. LC 77-24737. (Illus.). (gr. 3-6). 1978. 7.95 (ISBN 0-689-30622-9). Atheneum.

Opie, Iona & Opie, Peter. Children's Games in Street & Playground. (Illus.). 1969. 38.00 (ISBN 0-19-827210-3). Oxford U Pr.

Strutt, Joseph. Sports & Pastimes of the People of England: Including Rural & Domestic Recreations. LC 67-23901. (Social History Reference Series). (Illus.). 1968. Repr. of 1903 ed. 22.00 (ISBN 0-8103-3260-4). Gale.

GAMES–JUVENILE LITERATURE

Adler, David A. Hanukkah Fun Book: Puzzles, Riddles, Magic & More. LC 76-47459. (Illus.). (gr. 3-7). 1976. pap. 1.95 (ISBN 0-88482-754-2, Bonim Bks). Hebrew Pub.

--Passover Fun Book: Puzzles, Riddles, Magic & More. (Bonim Fun-to-Do Bk.). (Illus.). (gr. k-5). 1978. saddlewire bdg. 1.95 (ISBN 0-88482-759-3, Bonim Bks). Hebrew Pub.

Barry, Sheila A. Super-Colossal Book of Puzzles, Tricks & Games. LC 77-93325. (Illus.). (gr. 4 up). 1978. 17.95 (ISBN 0-8069-4580-X); PLB 15.99 (ISBN 0-8069-4581-8); pap. 9.95 (ISBN 0-686-77346-2). Sterling.

Benarde, Anita. Games from Many Lands. LC 71-86975. (Illus.). 64p. (gr. 3-7). 1971. PLB 7.95 (ISBN 0-87460-147-9). Lion Bks.

Board of Cooperative Education Services, Nassau County. Two Hundred Ways to Help Children Learn While You're at It. 1976. 12.95 (ISBN 0-87909-845-7). Reston.

Burnett, Millie. Melody Movement & Language: A Teacher's Guide of Music in Game Form for the Pre-School & Primary Grades. LC 73-80728. tchr's guide 5.00 (ISBN 0-88247-236-4). R & E Res Assoc.

Buskin, David. Outdoor Games. (Illus.). (gr. k-4). 1966. PLB 7.95 (ISBN 0-87460-090-1). Lion Bks.

Butler, William V. The Young Detective's Handbook. (Illus.). (gr. 3-7). 1981. 7.95 (ISBN 0-316-23422-2, Pub. by Atlantic Pr). Little.

Cobb, Vicki. How to Really Fool Yourself: Illusions for All Your Senses. LC 79-9620. (Illus.). 160p. (gr. 5 up). 1981. 8.95 (ISBN 0-397-31906-1, JBL-J); PLB 8.79 (ISBN 0-397-31907-X); pap. 4.95 (ISBN 0-397-31908-8). Har-Row.

Cole, Marion & Cole, Olivia H. Things to Make & Do for Easter. LC 78-12457. (Things to Make & Do Ser.). (Illus.). (gr. k-3). 1979. PLB 8.40 (ISBN 0-531-01463-0). Watts.

Conaway, Judith. Great Indoor Games from Trash & Other Things. LC 77-7383. (Games & Activities Ser.). (Illus.). (gr. k-4). 1977. PLB 10.65 (ISBN 0-8172-0952-2). Raintree Pubs.

D'Amato, Alex & D'Amato, Janet. Galaxy Games. LC 80-700. (Activity Bks.). (Illus.). 128p. (gr. 3-6). 1981. pap. 2.95 (ISBN 0-385-15434-8). Doubleday.

Debnam, Betty. The Mini Page Mighty Funny Party Book. (Alligator Original Paperback). (Illus.). (gr. 1-6). 1979. pap. 5.95 (ISBN 0-8362-4208-4). Andrews & McMeel.

Di Noto, Andrea. Anytime, Anywhere, Anybody Games. (A Golden Activity Bk.). (Illus.). 48p. (gr. 4-7). 1977. (Golden Pr); pap. 1.95 (ISBN 0-307-12351-0). Western Pub.

Estrada, Billie. How to Play Hopscotch: A Game Created by Children. (Illus.). 48p. (Orig.). (gr. k-6). 1974. pap. 4.25 (ISBN 0-9690490-0-5). B Estrada.

Fahrion, Muriel, illus. Strawberry Shortcake's Make-&-Do Book (A Strawberry Shortcake Book) (Illus.). 64p. (ps-3). 1980. pap. 2.95 (ISBN 0-394-84573-0). Random.

Fulton, Eleanor & Smith, Pat. Let's Slice the Ice. (Illus.). (gr. 3 up). 1978. pap. 5.00 (ISBN 0-918812-03-8); pap. text ed. 5.50 (ISBN 0-918812-02-X). Magnamusic.

Geromme, B. D. Forty-Eight Games to Make & Play for the Primary School. 1976. 14.00x (ISBN 0-8002-0807-2). Intl Pubns Serv.

Gibbons, Gail. Things to Make & Do for Columbus Day. (Things to Make & Do Ser.). (Illus.). (gr. 1-3). 1977. PLB 8.40 s&l (ISBN 0-531-01274-3). Watts.

Glovach, L. Little Witch's Book of Games. 1979. pap. 1.95 (ISBN 0-13-537886-9). P-H.

Harbin, Elvin O. Fun Encyclopedia. (Illus.). (gr. 4 up). 1940. 8.95 (ISBN 0-687-13714-4). Abingdon.

Hedges, Sid. Games for Children While Traveling. 80p. (gr. 1 up). 1975. pap. 1.25 (ISBN 0-448-11919-6). G&D.

Hobbie, Holly. Holly Hobbie's Jumbo Activity Book. (Illus.). (gr. 1-5). 1980. 3.95 (ISBN 0-525-69526-5, Gingerbread). Dutton.

Holbrook, David. Children's Games. LC 58-33275. 1979. 4.95 (ISBN 0-900406-09-7, Pub. by G Fraser). Intl Schol Bk Serv.

Kenney, Maureen, ed. Circle Round the Zero: Play Chants & Singing Games of City Children. (Illus.). 1975. pap. 6.95 (ISBN 0-918812-08-9). Magnamusic.

Leonard, Tom B. & Riddell, Mark. The Giant Book of Fun. (Activity Bks.). (Illus.). 256p. (gr. 3-6). 1981. pap. 3.95 (ISBN 0-385-15949-8). Doubleday.

Leverich, Kathleen & Cricket Magazine Editors. Cricket's Expeditions: Outdoor & Indoor Activities. LC 77-3231. (Illus.). (gr. 1-6). 1977. (BYR); PLB 3.99 (ISBN 0-394-93543-8). Random.

Levine, Caroline A. Snow Fun. (Easy-Read Activity Bks.). (Illus.). 32p. (gr. 1-3). 1981. lib. bdg. 8.90 (ISBN 0-531-04311-8). Watts.

The Lucy Xmas Activity Book. (Illus.). 96p. (gr. 2-6). 1979. pap. 1.25 (ISBN 0-448-16754-9). G&D.

Maar, Leonard & Maar, Nancy. Out of Sight Games: New & Exciting Action Games for Kids. LC 78-22339. (Illus.). 64p. (gr. 4-6). 1981. 7.95a (ISBN 0-385-14398-2); PLB (ISBN 0-385-14399-0). Doubleday.

McLenighan, Valjean. International Games. LC 77-28069. (Games & Activities Ser.). (Illus.). (gr. k-3). 1978. PLB 10.65 (ISBN 0-8172-1162-4). Raintree Pubs.

Nash, Bruce. The Star Trek Make-a-Game Book. (Star Trek: the Motion Picture Ser.). (Illus.). (gr. 4 up). 1979. pap. 6.95 (ISBN 0-671-95552-7). Wanderer Bks.

The Peanuts Xmas Activity Book. (Illus.). 96p. (gr. 2-6). 1979. pap. 1.25 (ISBN 0-448-16755-7). G&D.

Phillips, Louis. The World by Sevens: A/Kid's Book of Lists. (Illus.). 96p. (gr. 4 up). 1981. lib. bdg. 8.90 (ISBN 0-531-02883-6). Watts.

Razzi, Jim. Encyclopedia Brown's First Book of Puzzles & Games. 1.25 (ISBN 0-553-15058-8). Bantam.

Roberts, Alasdair. Out to Play: The Middle Years of Childhood. 175p. 1980. 22.50 (ISBN 0-08-025719-4); pap. 13.50 (ISBN 0-08-025718-6). Pergamon.

Robison, Nancy. Games to Play in the Pool. LC 79-24105. (Illus.). (gr. 1-5). 1980. 8.95 (ISBN 0-688-41926-7); PLB 8.59 (ISBN 0-688-51926-1). Lothrop.

Rockwell, Anne. Games (& How to Play Them) LC 72-10936. (Illus.). (gr. 1 up). 1973. 9.95 (ISBN 0-690-32159-7, TYC-J); PLB 9.79 (ISBN 0-690-32160-0). Har-Row.

Schoenfeld, Dianne D. Games Kids Like. 1974. loose-leaf text 15.00 (ISBN 0-88450-750-5, 2124-B). Communication Skill.

--More Games Kids Like. 1975. loose-leaf text 15.00 (ISBN 0-88450-751-3, 2125-B). Communication Skill.

Schumacher, Craig. Frisbee Fun. (Creative Games, Projects & Activities Ser.). (Illus.). 40p. (gr. 4-8). 1979. PLB 5.95 (ISBN 0-87191-674-6); pap. 2.95 (ISBN 0-89812-046-2). Creative Ed.

Shissler, Barbara. Sports & Games in Art. LC 65-29038. (Fine Art Books). (Illus.). (gr. 5-11). 1966. PLB 4.95 (ISBN 0-8225-0161-9). Lerner Pubns.

Stonerod, David. Friendly Games to Make & Learn. (Illus., Orig.). (gr. 3-9). 1976. pap. 4.95 (ISBN 0-918932-20-3). Activity Resources.

Summers, George J. Mind Teasers: Logic Puzzles & Games of Deductions. LC 77-79511. (Illus.). 1979. pap. 2.95 (ISBN 0-8069-8846-0). Sterling.

Thacher, Alida. Games for All Seasons. LC 77-19235. (Games & Activities Ser.). (Illus.). (gr. k-3). 1978. PLB 10.65 (ISBN 0-8172-1164-0). Raintree Pubs.

Thomson, Neil & Thomson, Ruth. Fairground Games to Make & Play. LC 77-23593. (Illus.). 48p. (gr. 3-6). 1978. 5.95 (ISBN 0-397-31770-0, JBL-J). Har-Row.

Zechlin, Katharina. Games You Can Build Yourself. LC 74-82327. (Illus.). 64p. (gr. 6 up). 1975. 9.95 (ISBN 0-8069-5308-X); PLB 9.29 (ISBN 0-8069-5309-8). Sterling.

Zubrowski, Bernie. A Children's Museum Activity Book: Milk Carton Blocks. LC 78-27215. (Children's Museum Bks.). (Illus.). (gr. 5-7). 1979. 6.95g (ISBN 0-316-98884-7); pap. 3.95 (ISBN 0-316-98885-5). Little.

GAMES, BRITISH

Douglas, Norman. London Street Games. 2nd rev. & enl. ed. (Folklore & Society Ser). 1969. Repr. of 1931 ed. pap. 9.50 (ISBN 0-384-12445-3). Johnson Repr.

--London Street Games. 2nd ed. LC 68-31089. 1968. Repr. of 1931 ed. 19.00 (ISBN 0-8103-3477-1). Gale.

Finn, Patrick T. Pub Games of England. (Oleander Games & Pastimes Ser.: Vol. 5). (Illus.). 156p. 1981. 18.95 (ISBN 0-900891-66-1); pap. 13.50 (ISBN 0-900891-67-X). Oleander Pr.

Gomme, Alice B. Traditional Games of England, Scotland & Ireland, 2 Vols. Set. 12.00 (ISBN 0-8446-2138-2). Peter Smith.

Opie, Iona & Opie, Peter. Children's Games in Street & Playground. (Illus.). 1969. 38.00 (ISBN 0-19-827210-3). Oxford U Pr.

Wheeler, Joyce. Better Netball. (Better Ser.). (Illus.). 1977. text ed. 15.95x (ISBN 0-7182-0151-5, SpS). Sportshelf.

GAMES, CHINESE

Culin, Stewart. Chinese Games with Dice & Dominoes. (Illus.). Repr. of 1893 ed. pap. 6.00 (ISBN 0-8466-6017-2, SJU17). Shorey.

--Gambling Games of the Chinese in America. 1965. pap. 1.25 (ISBN 0-911996-03-6). Gamblers.

GAMES, FLORAL

see Floral Games

GAMES, GREEK AND ROMAN

see also Secular Games

Murrell, John. Athletics, Sports & Games. (Greek & Roman Topics Ser.). 1975. pap. text ed. 3.95x (ISBN 0-04-930006-7). Allen Unwin.

GAMES, MAORI

Andersen, Johannes C. Maori String Figures. LC 75-35223. Repr. of 1927 ed. 27.50 (ISBN 0-404-14402-0). AMS Pr.

GAMES, OLYMPIC

see Olympic Games

GAMES, ORIENTAL

Falkener, Edward. Games Ancient & Oriental & How to Play Them. (Illus.). 1892. pap. 4.00 (ISBN 0-486-20739-0). Dover.

--Games Ancient & Oriental & How to Play Them. (Illus.). 8.00 (ISBN 0-8446-4543-5). Peter Smith.

Oriental Board Games. 1977. pap. 2.50 (ISBN 0-8277-4952-X). British Bk Ctr.

GAMES, PRIMITIVE

see also Indians–Games

Caillois, Roger. Man, Play, & Games. Barash, Meyer, tr. from Fr. LC 79-12684. 1979. pap. 5.50 (ISBN 0-8052-0636-1). Schocken.

Sutton-Smith, Brian, photos by. A Children's Game Anthology: Studies in Folklore & Anthropology. LC 75-35080. (Studies in Play & Games). (Illus.). 1976. Repr. 28.00x (ISBN 0-405-07928-1). Arno.

GAMES, PSYCHIC

see Psychic Games

GAMES, RHYTHMIC

see Games with Music

GAMES, SECULAR

see Secular Games

GAMES, THEORY OF

see Game Theory

GAMES FOR TRAVELERS

Beaver, Edmund. Travel Games. (gr. 4 up). pap. 0.50 (ISBN 0-910208-01-8). Beavers.

Brandreth, Gyles. Games for Rains, Planes, & Trains. LC 75-43595. 1976. 7.95 (ISBN 0-8289-0266-6). Greene.

Brown, George H. Travel Games: Vol. 3, Sports. Donaldson, Judith E., ed. (Illus.). 36p. Date not set. Repr. of 1977 ed. pap. text ed. 1.50 (ISBN 0-939942-07-0). Larkspur.

Donaldson, Judith E. Travel Games: Vol. 2, Five to Ten Years. Brown, George H., ed. (Illus.). 36p. (gr. k-5). Date not set. pap. text ed. 1.50 (ISBN 0-939942-06-2). Larkspur.

Donaldson, Judith E. & Brown, George H. Travel Games: Vol. 1, Family. (Illus.). 36p. (Orig.). Date not set. Repr. of 1976 ed. pap. text ed. 1.50 (ISBN 0-939942-05-4). Larkspur.

Latta, Richard. Games for Travel. (Illus.). 48p. (Orig.). 1976. pap. 1.50 (ISBN 0-8431-0406-6). Price Stern.

--Games for Travel, No. 4. 48p. 1981. pap. 1.75 (ISBN 0-8431-0242-X). Price Stern.

Miller, A. M. For Children on Wheels. 118p. 1980. 10.00x (ISBN 0-902628-49-6, Pub. by RAC). State Mutual Bk.

Simons, Howard. Simons' List Book. LC 77-1845. 1977. pap. 5.95 (ISBN 0-671-22605-3). S&S.

Wade, T. E., Jr. Fun for the Road. (gr. k-8). 1978. pap. 0.95 (ISBN 0-930192-04-4). Gazelle Pubns.

GAMES IN ART

Shissler, Barbara. Sports & Games in Art. LC 65-29038. (Fine Art Books). (Illus.). (gr. 5-11). 1966. PLB 4.95 (ISBN 0-8225-0161-9). Lerner Pubns.

GAMES OF CHANCE

see Gambling

GAMES OF CHANCE (MATHEMATICS)

see also Monte Carlo Method

Cooke, William P. Winning Parimutuel Wagering. LC 72-87534. 76p. 1973. pap. text ed. 3.95 (ISBN 0-686-05571-3). Le Voyageur.

Crowe & Bowen. With Tails We Win. (Illus.). 1954. pap. 2.00 (ISBN 0-9600102-5-4). Shields WI.

David, Florence N. Games, Gods & Gambling: The Origins & History of Probability & Statistical Ideas from the Earliest Times to the Newtonian Era. (Illus.). 1962. pap. 14.25 (ISBN 0-02-843710-1). Hafner.

De Moivre, Abraham. Doctrine of Chances: Including Treatise on Annuities. 3rd ed. LC 66-23756. 1967. 15.95 (ISBN 0-8284-0200-0). Chelsea Pub.

De Montmort, R. Essay D'analyse Sur les Jeux De Hazard. LC 79-1226. (Illus.). 463p. (Fr). 1980. Repr. of 1714 ed. text ed. 39.50 (ISBN 0-8284-0307-4). Chelsea Pub.

Dubins, Lester E. & Savage, Leonard J. Inequalities for Stochastic Processes. LC 75-25001. 288p. 1976. pap. 4.00 (ISBN 0-486-63283-0). Dover.

Eigen, Manfred & Winkler, Ruthild. Laws of the Game: How the Principles of Nature Govern Chance. LC 79-3494. (Illus.). 384p. 1981. 17.95 (ISBN 0-394-41806-9). Knopf.

Epstein, Richard A. The Theory of Gambling & Statistical Logic. rev. ed. 1977. 33.50 (ISBN 0-12-240760-1). Acad Pr.

Landa, Henry C. Gambling Probabilities. (Illus.). 1979. pap. 4.00 (ISBN 0-931974-05-4). FICOA.

Scammon, Richard. The Odds: On Virtually Everything. 1980. 12.95 (ISBN 0-399-12483-7). Putnam.

Sobol, I. M. Metodo De Montecarlo. 78p. (Span.). 1976. pap. 1.25 (ISBN 0-8285-1689-8, Pub. by Mir Pubs Russia). Imported Pubns.

Wilson, Allan N. Casino Gambler's Guide. rev & enl. ed. LC 71-127841. (Illus.). 1970. 12.95 (ISBN 0-06-014674-5, HarpT). Har-Row.

GAMES OF STRATEGY (MATHEMATICS)

see also Management Games

Braithwaite, Richard B. Theory of Games As a Tool for the Moral Philosopher. 1955. 15.50 (ISBN 0-521-04307-7). Cambridge U Pr.

Danskin, J. M. Theory of Max-Min, & Its Application to Weapons Allocation Problems. (Econometrics & Operation Research: Vol. 5). (Illus.). 1967. 24.10 (ISBN 0-387-03943-0). Springer-Verlag.

Harsanyi, J. C. Bargaining Equilibrium in Games & Social Situations. LC 75-39370. (Illus.). 352p. 1977. 47.50 (ISBN 0-521-20886-6). Cambridge U Pr.

Kaufmann, A. Graphs, Dynamic Programming & Finite Games. (Mathematics in Science & Engineering Ser.: Vol. 36). 1967. 50.00 (ISBN 0-12-402356-8). Acad Pr.

Schelling, Thomas C. Strategy of Conflict. LC 60-11560. (Illus.). 1960. 15.00x (ISBN 0-674-84030-5); pap. text ed. 6.95x (ISBN 0-674-84031-3). Harvard U Pr.

Swingle, Paul G., ed. Structure of Conflict. (Social Psychology Ser). 1970. 37.50 (ISBN 0-12-679160-0). Acad Pr.

Williams, John D. Compleat Strategyst. rev. ed. 1965. 16.75 (ISBN 0-07-070396-5, P&RB). McGraw.

GAMES WITH MUSIC

see also Singing Games

Athey, Margaret & Hotchkiss, Gwen. A Galaxy of Games for the Music Class. 1975. 11.95 (ISBN 0-13-346064-9, Parker). P-H.

Bley, Edgar S. Best Singing Games for Children of All Ages. rev. ed. LC 57-1014. (Illus.). (gr. k-6). 1959. 8.95 (ISBN 0-8069-4450-1); PLB 8.29 (ISBN 0-8069-4451-X). Sterling.

Burnett, Millie. Melody Movement & Language: A Teacher's Guide of Music in Game Form for the Pre-School & Primary Grades. LC 73-80728. tchr's guide 5.00 (ISBN 0-88247-236-4). R & E Res Assoc.

Ginglend, David R. & Stiles, Winifred E. Music Activities for Retarded Children. (Illus., Orig.). 1965. pap. 7.95 (ISBN 0-687-27309-9). Abingdon.

Newell, William W. Games & Songs of American Children. (Illus.). 6.75 (ISBN 0-8446-2648-1). Peter Smith.

--Games & Songs of American Children. 2nd ed. 1903. pap. 4.50 (ISBN 0-486-20354-9). Dover.

Poulsson, Emilie. Finger Plays for Nursery & Kindergarten. LC 74-165397. (Illus.). (ps-k). 1971. pap. 2.00 (ISBN 0-486-22588-7). Dover.

Ward, David. Sing a Rainbow: Musical Activities with Mentally Handicapped Children. (Illus.). 64p. (Orig.). 1979. pap. text ed. 8.95x (ISBN 0-19-317416-2). Oxford U Pr.

Winn, Marie, ed. What Shall We Do & Allee Galloo: Playsongs & Singing Games for Young Children. LC 72-85039. (Illus.). (ps). PLB 8.79 (ISBN 0-06-026537-X, HarpJ). Har-Row.

Writers Program. New Mexico. The Spanish-American Song & Game Book. LC 73-3642. Repr. of 1942 ed. 18.50 (ISBN 0-404-57941-8). AMS Pr.

GAMES WITH RATIONAL PAY-OFF (MATHEMATICS)

see Games of Strategy (Mathematics)

GAMING

see Gambling

GAMMA FUNCTIONS

see Functions, Gamma

GAMMA GLOBULIN

see also Hypergammaglobulinemia; Immunoglobulins

Grubb, R. & Samuelsson, G. Human Anti-Human Gammaglobulins: Their Specificity & Function. 240p. 1971. 42.00 (ISBN 0-08-016451-X). Pergamon.

Shugar, D. & Franek, F., eds. Gammaglobulins, Structure & Biosynthesis. 1969. 39.00 (ISBN 0-12-640850-5). Acad Pr.

GAMMA RAY SPECTROMETRY

Adams, F. & Dams, R. Applied Gamma-Ray Spectrometry. 2nd rev. ed. LC 79-114847. 1970. text ed. 92.00 (ISBN 0-08-006888-X). Pergamon.

Erdtmann, Gerhard & Soyka, W. The Gamma Rays of the Radionuclides: Tables for Applied Gamma Ray Spectrometry. (Topical Presentations in Nuclear Chemistry Ser.: Vol. 7). 1979. 141.20 (ISBN 0-89573-022-7). Verlag Chemie.

IAU Symposium, No. 37, Rome, Italy, May 8-18, 1969. Non-Solar X-Gamma-Ray Astronomy: Proceedings. Gratton, L., ed. LC 73-83561. (IAU Symposia). 425p. 1970. lib. bdg. 45.00 (ISBN 90-277-0160-1, Puub. by Reidel Holland). Kluwer Boston.

Kogan, R. M. Gamma Spectrometry of Natural Environments & Formations: Theory of the Method & Application to Geology & Geophysics. 348p. 1971. 35.00x (ISBN 0-7065-1059-3, Pub. by IPST). Intl Schol Bk Serv.

Morinaga, H. & Yamazaki, T. In-Beam Gamma-Ray Spectroscopy. 1977. 73.25 (ISBN 0-444-10569-7, North-Holland). Elsevier.

Neutron Capture Gamma-Ray Spectroscopy. (Illus., Orig.). 1969. pap. 47.25 (ISBN 92-0-130369-6, ISP235, IAEA). Unipub.

Radioisotope X-Ray Fluorescence Spectrometry. (Technical Reports: No. 115). (Illus., Orig.). 1970. pap. 9.50 (ISBN 92-0-165170-8, IDC115, IAEA). Unipub.

Shafroth, Stephen, ed. Scintillation Spectroscopy of Gamma Radiation, Vol. 1. 1967. 67.25x (ISBN 0-677-11070-7). Gordon.

GAMMA RAYS

see also Gamma Ray Spectrometry

Chupp, E. L. Gamma Ray Astronomy: Nuclear Transition Region. LC 76-21711. (Geophysics & Astrophysics Monographs: No. 14). 1976. lib. bdg. 55.00 (ISBN 90-277-0695-6, Pub. by Reidel Holland); pap. 26.00 (ISBN 90-277-0696-4, Pub. by Reidel Holland). Kluwer Boston.

COSPAR, Twenty-Second Plenary Meeting, Bangalore, India, 1979. Non-Solar Gamma-Rays: Proceedings. Cowsik, R. & Wills, R. D., eds. 254p. 1980. 50.00 (ISBN 0-08-024440-8). Pergamon.

Gamma-Ray Surveys in Uranium Exploration. (Technical Reports Ser.: No. 186). 1979. pap. 14.00 (ISBN 92-0-145079-6, IDC186, IAEA). Unipub.

Gill, R. D. Gamma-Ray Angular Correlations. 1975. 39.50 (ISBN 0-12-283850-5). Acad Pr.

Ginzburg, Vitaly L. Important Elementary Processes in Cosmic Ray Astrophysics & in Gamma & X-Ray. (Topics in Astrophysics & Space Physics Ser.). 1969. 31.50 (ISBN 0-677-01980-7). Gordon.

Goldstein, Herbert. Fundamental Aspects of Reactor Shielding. Repr. of 1959 ed. 22.50 (ISBN 0-384-19100-2). Johnson Repr.

International Astronomical Union Symposium, 37th, Rome, 1969. Non-Solar X & Gamma Ray Astronomy - Rome, Italy: Proceedings. Gratton, L., ed. LC 78-131545. (Illus.). 1970. 27.90 (ISBN 0-387-91037-9). Springer-Verlag.

Kaye, G., et al. Tables of Co-efficients for the Analysis of Triple Angular Correlations of Gamma-Rays from Aligned Nuclei. 1969. 42.00 (ISBN 0-08-012260-4). Pergamon.

Leipunskii, O. I., et al. The Propagation of Gamma Quanta in Matter. 1965. 37.00 (ISBN 0-08-010553-X); pap. 22.00 (ISBN 0-08-013564-1). Pergamon.

Lithium-Drifted Germanium Detectors. 1966. pap. 13.00 (ISBN 92-0-031066-4, ISP132, IAEA). Unipub.

Measurement of Absorbed Dose of Neutrons & Mixtures of Neutrons & Gamma - Rays. (NCRP Reports Ser.: No. 25). 1961. 6.00 (ISBN 0-913392-08-1). NCRP Pubns.

Medical X - Ray & Gamma - Ray Protection for Energies up to Ten MeV: Equipment Design & Use. (NCRP Reports Ser.: No. 33). 1968. 7.00 (ISBN 0-913392-15-4). NCRP Pubns.

Mezhiborskaya, Kh. B. Photoneutron Method of Determining Beryllium. LC 61-18758. 30p. 1962. 17.50 (ISBN 0-306-10568-3, Consultants). Plenum Pub.

Mingle, J. O. The Invariant Imbedding Theory of Nuclear Transport. LC 73-187686. (Modern Analytic & Computational Methods in Science & Mathematics Ser.: No. 39). 144p. 1973. 24.95 (ISBN 0-444-00123-9, North Holland). Elsevier.

Specification of Gamm - Ray Brachytherapy Sources. (NCEBP Reports Ser.: No. 41). 1974. 7.00 (ISBN 0-913392-23-5). NCRP Pubns.

Ziegler, Charles A., ed. Applications of Low-Energy X & Gamma Rays. LC 78-141897. (Illus.). 476p. 1971. 83.75x (ISBN 0-677-14640-X). Gordon.

--Applications of Low-Energy X & Gamma Rays. LC 78-141897. (Illus.). 476p. 1971. 83.75x (ISBN 0-677-14640-X). Gordon.

GAMMA RAYS-INDUSTRIAL APPLICATIONS

see also Radiography, Industrial

GAMOV, GEORGE, 1904-1968

Reines, Frederick, ed. Cosmology, Fusion & Other Matters: A Memorial to George Gamow. LC 77-159018. (Illus.). 336p. 1972. 15.00x (ISBN 0-87081-025-1). Colo Assoc.

GANDA

see Baganda

GANDA LANGUAGE

Snoxall, R. A., ed. Luganda-English Dictionary. 1967. 13.00x (ISBN 0-19-864406-X). Oxford U Pr.

GANDAVYUHA

Fontein, J. Pilgrimage of Sudhana. 1967. text ed. 49.50x (ISBN 90-2796-387-8). Mouton.

GANDHI, INDIRA (NEHRU), 1917-

B. N. Pande for Festschrift Committee, ed. The Spirit of India, 2 vols. (Indira Gandhi Festschrift Ser.). (Illus.). 1976. lib. bdg. 100.00x set (ISBN 0-685-68908-5). Vol. 1 (ISBN 0-210-40560-0). Vol. 2 (ISBN 0-210-40561-9). Asia.

Bhushan, Prashant. The Case That Shook India. LC 77-907825. 1978. 10.00x (ISBN 0-7069-0594-6). Intl Pubns Serv.

Carras, Mary C. Indira Gandhi in the Crucible of Leadership. LC 78-19598. 256p. 1980. pap. 5.95 (ISBN 0-8070-0243-7, BP-607). Beacon Pr.

--Indira Gandhi in the Crucible of Leadership. LC 78-19598. 1979. 13.95 (ISBN 0-8070-0242-9). Beacon Pr.

Christman, Henry M., ed. Indira Gandhi Speaks on Democracy, Socialism & Third World Non-Alignment. LC 72-6611. 160p. 1975. 8.95 (ISBN 0-8008-4180-8). Taplinger.

Church, Carol B. Indira Gandhi: Rose of India. Bender, David L. & McCuen, Gary E., eds. (Focus on Famous Women Ser). (gr. 3-9). 1976. 6.95 (ISBN 0-912616-43-1); read-along cassette 9.95 (ISBN 0-89908-242-4). Greenhaven.

Kapur, Jagga. What Price Perjury: Facts of the Shah Commission (India) 1978. text ed. 13.50x (ISBN 0-8426-1085-5). Verry.

Khosla, G. D. Indira Gandhi. LC 74-900843. (Illus.). 152p. 1974. 15.00x (ISBN 0-8002-0037-3). Intl Pubns Serv.

Masani, Z. Indira Gandhi: A Biography. 1976. 10.95 (ISBN 0-690-00169-X). Brown Bk.

Mashruwala, K. G. Gandhi & Marx. 119p. (Orig.). 1981. pap. 1.50 (ISBN 0-934676-30-5). Greenlf Bks.

Mehta, Ved. The New India. 1978. 10.00 (ISBN 0-670-50735-0). Viking Pr.

Modgal, H. M., et al, eds. Indira Gandhi: A Select Bibliography. LC 76-903277. 1976. 15.00x (ISBN 0-8002-0208-2). Intl Pubns Serv.

Moraes, Dom. Indira Gandhi. 340p. 1980. 14.95 (ISBN 0-316-58191-7). Little.

Pandit, C. S. End of an Era: Rise & Fall of Indira Gandhi. 1977. 8.00x (ISBN 0-8364-0091-7). South Asia Bks.

Sahgal, Nayantara. Indira Gandhi's Emergence & Style. LC 78-54439. 1978. 13.95 (ISBN 0-89089-090-0). Carolina Acad Pr.

Sarin, L. N. Indira Gandhi: A Political Biography. LC 73-907579. 128p. 1974. 6.00x (ISBN 0-8002-0061-6). Intl Pubns Serv.

Sethi, J. D. Gandhi Today. 2nd ed. 1979. text ed. 20.00 (ISBN 0-7069-0831-7, Pub. by Vikas India). Advent NY.

--Gandhi Today. LC 77-88664. 1978. 14.00 (ISBN 0-89089-088-9). Carolina Acad Pr.

Singh, Khushwant. Indira Gandhi Returns. 1980. 10.00x (ISBN 0-8364-0655-9, Pub. by Vision India). South Asia Bks.

Tahtinen, Unto. The Core of Gandhi's Philosophy. 1979. 9.50x (ISBN 0-8364-0516-1). South Asia Bks.

Thakur, Janardhan. Indira Gandhi & Her Power Game. 165p. 1980. text ed. 10.50x (ISBN 0-7069-0985-2, Pub. by Vikas India). Advent NY.

Vasudev, Uma. Two Faces of Indira Gandhi. 208p. 1977. 8.50x (ISBN 0-686-63736-4). Intl Pubns Serv.

Willcoxen, Harriett. First Lady of India: The Story of Indira Ghandi. LC 69-10999. (gr. 7-8). 1969. 5.95 (ISBN 0-385-08954-6). Doubleday.

GANDHI, MOHANDAS KARAMCHAND, 1869-1948

Alexander, Horace. Gandhi Remembered. LC 71-84674. (Orig.). 1969. pap. 0.70x (ISBN 0-87574-165-7). Pendle Hill.

--Gandhi Through Western Eyes. 9.00x (ISBN 0-210-22554-8). Asia.

Amritananda Das. Foundations of Gandhian Economics. LC 79-17126. 1979. 14.95x (ISBN 0-312-30005-0). St Martin.

Ashe, Geoffrey. Gandhi. LC 68-17318. 1969. pap. 7.95 (ISBN 0-8128-1231-X). Stein & Day.

Bandyopadhyaya, J. Mao Tse-Tung & Gandhi. 1973. 6.00x (ISBN 0-8188-1184-6). Paragon.

Bandyopadhyaya, Jayantanuja. Mao Tse-Tung & Gandhi: Perspectives on Social Transformation. 156p. 1973. 6.50x (ISBN 0-8002-1698-9). Intl Pubns Serv.

Barker, A. Trevor, compiled by. The Mahatma Letters to A. P. Sinnett. facsimile of 1926, 2nd ed. LC 75-10574. 1975. 10.00 (ISBN 0-911500-20-0); pap. 5.95 (ISBN 0-911500-21-9). Theos U Pr.

Bhattacharya, Bhabani. Mahatma Gandhi. (Indian Writers Ser.: Vol. 14). 236p. 1977. 10.00 (ISBN 0-86578-003-X). Ind-US Inc.

Biswas, S. C., ed. Gandhi: Theory & Practice, Social Impact & Contemporary Relevance. (Indian Institute of Advanced Study: No. 11). 1969. 22.00x (ISBN 0-8002-1446-3). Intl Pubns Serv.

Bondurant, Joan V. Conquest of Violence: The Gandhian Philosophy of Conflict. rev. ed. LC 65-23153. (gr. 9 up). 1965. 18.50x (ISBN 0-520-00143-5); pap. 4.95x (ISBN 0-520-00145-1, CAMPUS243). U of Cal Pr.

Brown, Judith M. Gandhi & Civil Disobedience. LC 76-10407. (Illus.). 1977. 39.50 (ISBN 0-521-21279-0). Cambridge U Pr.

--Gandhi's Rise to Power: Indian Politics 1915-1922. LC 71-171674. (Cambridge South Asian Studies: No. 11). (Illus.). 460p. 1972. 35.00 (ISBN 0-521-08353-2); pap. 9.95x (ISBN 0-521-09873-4). Cambridge U Pr.

Chatfield, Charles, ed. Americanization of Gandhi. LC 79-147747. (Library of War & Peace, Documentary Anthologies). 1976. lib. bdg. 38.00 (ISBN 0-8240-0446-9). Garland Pub.

Chaudhuri, Haridas & Frank, Leonard R. Mahatma Gandhi. (Orig.). 1969. pap. 1.00 (ISBN 0-89744-993-2, Pub. by Cultural Integration). Auromere.

Chaudhury, P. C. Gandhi's First Struggle in India. 2nd ed. 1963. bds. 2.75x (ISBN 0-8426-1200-9). Verry.

Coolidge, Olivia. Gandhi. (Illus.). (gr. 7 up). 1971. 7.95 (ISBN 0-395-12573-1). HM.

Dalal, C. B., compiled by. Gandhi Nineteen Fifteen to Nineteen Forty-Eight: A Detailed Chronology. 210p. 1971. 10.00x (ISBN 0-8426-0285-2). Verry.

Dandavate, M. Marx & Gandhi. 1979. text ed. 6.00x (ISBN 0-8426-1627-6). Verry.

Datta, Dhirendra M. Philosophy of Mahatma Gandhi. 168p. 1953. pap. 5.45 (ISBN 0-299-01014-7). U of Wis Pr.

De Jong, Constance & Glass, Philip. Satyagraha: M. K. Gandhi in South Africa, 1893-1914. (Illus., Orig.). 1980. pap. 5.00 (ISBN 0-918746-04-3). Standard Edns.

Devanesen, Chandran D. Making of the Mahatma. (Illus.). 445p. 1969. 10.50x (ISBN 0-8002-1688-1). Intl Pubns Serv.

Devanesen, Chandran D. S. The Making of the Mahatma. 1969. 13.50 (ISBN 0-8046-8808-7). Kennikat.
Diwaker, R. R., et al. Mohandas Karamchand Gandhi: A Bibliography. LC 75-901382. 1974. 18.00x (ISBN 0-8364-0490-4, Orient Longman). South Asia Bks.
Doctor, Adi H. Sarvodaya: A Political & Economic Study. 1968. 7.25x (ISBN 0-210-22653-6). Asia.
Dutt, Vishnu. Gandhi, Nehru & the Challenge. 1979. 14.00x (ISBN 0-8364-0322-3). South Asia Bks.
Easwaran, Eknath. Gandhi the Man. LC 77-25976. 1978. 10.50 (ISBN 0-915132-13-3); pap. 6.95 (ISBN 0-915132-14-1). Nilgiri Pr.
Erikson, Erik H. Gandhi's Truth: On the Origins of Militant Nonviolence. 1969. 10.00 (ISBN 0-393-01049-X, Norton Lib); pap. 5.95 (ISBN 0-393-00741-3). Norton.
Fischer, Louis. Gandhi. pap. 1.75 (ISBN 0-451-61623-5, ME1623, Ment). NAL.
--Gandhi & Stalin: Two Signs at the World's Crossroads. 1979. Repr. of 1948 ed. lib. bdg. 20.00 (ISBN 0-8495-1642-0). Arden Lib.
Fulop-Miller, Rene. Lenin & Gandhi. Flint, F. S. & Tait, D. F., trs. from Ger. LC 72-7057. (Select Bibliographies Reprint Ser.). 1972. Repr. of 1927 ed. 21.00 (ISBN 0-8369-6932-4). Arno.
--Lenin & Ghandi. LC 79-147617. (Library of War & Peace: Non-Resistance & Non-Violence). lib. bdg. 38.00 (ISBN 0-8240-0374-8). Garland Pub.
Gandhi, M. K. Autobiography. 2nd ed. 1979. Repr. of 1940 ed. 10.00 (ISBN 0-685-11994-7). Heinman.
--Satyagraha in South Africa. Desai, V. G., tr. from Gujarati. 1979. pap. 4.00 (ISBN 0-934676-03-8). Greenlf Bks.
Gandhi, Mahatma. All Men Are Brothers: Life & Thoughts of Mahatma Gandhi As Told in His Own Words. 186p. pap. 4.95 (ISBN 0-8164-9237-9). Continuum.
Gandhi, Mohandas K. Autobiography: The Story of My Experiments with Truth. 1957. pap. 7.95 (ISBN 0-8070-5981-1, BP35). Beacon Pr.
--Collected Works: Vols. 1-77. LC 58-36286. 1958-1979. Set. 10.00x ea. (ISBN 0-8002-0138-8). Intl Pubns Serv.
--Gandhi Reader: A Source Book of His Life & Writings. Jack, Homer, ed. LC 71-133812. 1970. Repr. of 1956 ed. 34.00 (ISBN 0-404-03540-X). AMS Pr.
--Gandhi's Autobiography. 1948. 6.00 (ISBN 0-8183-0223-2). Pub Aff Pr.
Gauba, K. L. The Assassination of Mahatma Gandhi. 1969. pap. 3.50 (ISBN 0-88253-140-9). Ind-US Inc.
Ghosh, P. C. Mahatma Gandhi As I Saw Him. 1968. 6.50x (ISBN 0-8426-1270-X). Verry.
Ghosh, Tapan. Gandhi Murder Trial. 330p. 1975. 16.00x (ISBN 0-210-27043-8). Asia.
Green, Martin. The Challenge of the Mahatmas. LC 77-20427. 1978. 11.95 (ISBN 0-465-00904-2). Basic.
Gregg, Richard B. Psychology & Strategy of Gandhi's Nonviolent Resistance. LC 76-147619. (Library of War & Peace; Non-Resis. & N3n-Vio.). lib. bdg. 38.00 (ISBN 0-8240-0376-4). Garland Pub.
Hunt, James D. Gandhi in London. 1978. 20.00x (ISBN 0-8364-0244-8). South Asia Bks.
Indian Ministry Of Information & Broadcasting, eds. Mahatma Gandhi: His Life in Pictures. rev. ed. LC 68-13808. (Illus.). 1968. 9.00x (ISBN 0-8002-0927-3). Intl Pubns Serv.
Iyer, Raghavan. Moral & Political Thought of Mahatma Gandhi. 400p. 1973. 17.95 (ISBN 0-19-501692-0). Oxford U Pr.
Iyer, Raghavan N. The Moral & Political Thought of Mahatma Gandhi. LC 72-96613. 1978. pap. 6.95 (ISBN 0-19-502357-9, GB527, GB). Oxford U Pr.
Joshi, P. S. The Tyranny of Colour: A Study of the Indian Problem in South Africa. LC 72-89266. 344p. 1973. Repr. of 1942 ed. 17.50 (ISBN 0-8046-1754-6). Kennikat.
Karunakaran, K. P. New Perspectives on Gandhi. LC 78-914687. (Indian Institute of Advanced Study Monographs). 115p. 1969. 6.00x (ISBN 0-8002-0938-9). Intl Pubns Serv.
Kaushik, P. D. Congress Ideology & Programme. 1964. 7.50x (ISBN 0-8188-1064-5). Paragon.
Keer, Dhananjay. Mahatma Gandhi: Political Saint & Unarmed Prophet. LC 73-903462. 819p. 1974. 17.00x (ISBN 0-8002-0925-7). Intl Pubns Serv.
Linton, George & Hanson, V. Reader's Guide to the Mahatma Letters. 4.95 (ISBN 0-8356-7481-9). Theos Pub Hse.
McLaughlin, Elizabeth T. Ruskin & Gandhi. LC 72-3260. 202p. 1974. 14.50 (ISBN 0-8387-1086-7). Bucknell U Pr.
Mahadevan, T. K. Dvija: A Prophet Unheard (Gandhi) 1977. 8.00x (ISBN 0-8364-0094-1). South Asia Bks.
--Gandhi My Refrain: Controversial Essays, 1950-1972. 223p. 1973. 11.25x (ISBN 0-8002-1445-5). Intl Pubns Serv.
Mahadevan, T. K., ed. Truth & Nonviolence: A Unesco Symposium on Gandhi. 1970. 10.00 (ISBN 0-8046-8816-8). Kennikat.
Mahadevan, T. M., ed. The Relevance of Mahatma Gandhi to the World of Thought. 192p. 1969. 5.00x (ISBN 0-8002-1914-7). Intl Pubns Serv.
Malhotra, S. L. Gandhi: An Experiment with Communal Politics. LC 75-903635. 1975. 10.00x (ISBN 0-88386-192-5). South Asia Bks.
Mehta, Ved. Mahatma Gandhi & His Apostles. 1977. pap. 3.95 (ISBN 0-14-004571-6). Penguin.
Merriam, Allen H. Gandhi & Jinnah. 1980. 16.00x (ISBN 0-8364-0039-9). South Asia Bks.
Misra, D. K. Gandhi & Social Order. LC 72-907964. 128p. 1974. 9.50x (ISBN 0-8002-1443-9). Intl Pubns Serv.
Muzumdar, H. T. Mahatma Gandhi: A Prophetic Voice. 210p. bds. 2.75x (ISBN 0-8426-1383-8). Verry.
Nanda, B. R. Mahatma Gandhi: Shapers of History. LC 65-22230. (YA) 1965. pap. text ed. 3.95 (ISBN 0-8120-0069-2). Barron.
Nanda, B. R., et al. Gandhi & Nehru. 76p. 1979. pap. text ed. 4.50x (ISBN 0-19-561148-9). Oxford U Pr.
Narayan, Shriman. India Needs(Mahatma) Gandhi. 156p. 1976. text ed. 7.50x (ISBN 0-8426-0870-2). Verry.
Nehru, Jawaharlal. Mahatma Gandhi. 1976. pap. 4.50 (ISBN 0-210-22542-4). Asia.
Polak, H. S., et al. Mahatma Gandhi. 1966. pap. 3.00 (ISBN 0-88253-170-0). Ind-US Inc.
Power, Paul F., ed. The Meanings of Gandhi. (Illus.). 1971. 10.00x (ISBN 0-8248-0104-0, Eastwest Ctr). U Pr of Hawaii.
Prasad, Rajendra. At the Feet of Mahatma Gandhi. LC 79-156204. 1971. Repr. of 1961 ed. lib. bdg. 16.75x (ISBN 0-8371-6154-1, PRMG). Greenwood.
--At the Feet of Mahatma Gandhi. LC 79-156204. 1971. Repr. of 1961 ed. lib. bdg. 16.75x (ISBN 0-8371-6154-1, PRMG). Greenwood.
Radhakrishnan, Sarvepalli, ed. Mahatma Gandhi, One Hundred Years. LC 68-16459. 1968. 6.00x (ISBN 0-8002-0924-9). Intl Pubns Serv.
Radharkrishnan, S., et al, eds. Mahatma Gandhi One Hundred Years. 1968. 12.50 (ISBN 0-8046-8821-4). Kennikat.
Ramachandran, G. & Mahadevan, T. K., eds. Gandhi: His Relevance for Our Times. 1971. pap. 2.95 (ISBN 0-912018-10-0). World Without War.
--Quest for Gandhi. 1970. 5.50x (ISBN 0-8426-0070-1). Verry.
Rao, K. L. Mahatma Gandhi & Comparative Religion. 1979. 15.00x (ISBN 0-89684-034-4). South Asia Bks.
Rao, K. L. Seshagiri. Mahatma Gandhi & Comparative Religion. 1978. 11.50 (ISBN 0-89684-034-4, Pub. by Motilal Banarsidass India). Orient Bk Dist.
Rau, M. C. Gandhi & Nehru. 1967. 4.50x (ISBN 0-8188-1116-1). Paragon.
Rolland, Romain. Gandhi et Romain Rolland. 1973. 14.95 (ISBN 0-686-55252-0). French & Eur.
--Mahatma Gandhi. (Library of War & Peace; Non-Resis. & Non-Vio.). lib. bdg. 38.00 (ISBN 0-8240-0498-1). Garland Pub.
--Mahatma Gandhi: The Man Who Became One with the Universal Being. 1977. Repr. of 1924 ed. 20.00 (ISBN 0-8274-4303-X). R West.
Roy-Chaudhury, P. C. Gandhi & His Contemporaries. 336p. 1972. 11.25x (ISBN 0-8002-1442-0). Intl Pubns Serv.
Rudolph, Lloyd I. & Rudolph, Susanne H. Modernity of Tradition: Political Development in India. LC 67-25527. 1967. 12.50x (ISBN 0-226-73134-0). U of Chicago Pr.
Rungachary, Santha. Pilgrim Centenary: A Remembrance. LC 73-904628. (Illus.). 317p. 1973. 11.25x (ISBN 0-8002-1800-0). Intl Pubns Serv.
Satyaprakash. Gandhiana, 1962-76: A Bibliography. 1977. 12.50 (ISBN 0-88386-977-2). South Asia Bks.
Saxena, K. S., ed. Gandhi Centenary Papers, 4 vols. LC 72-901588. 1971. Set. 30.00x (ISBN 0-8002-1444-7). Intl Pubns Serv.
Sharp, Gene. Gandhi As a Political Strategist: With Essays on Ethics & Politics. LC 79-84497. 384p. 1979. 14.95 (ISBN 0-87558-090-4); pap. 7.95 (ISBN 0-87558-092-0). Porter Sargent.
--Gandhi Wields the Weapon of Moral Power. bds. 4.00x (ISBN 0-8426-1525-3). Verry.
Shirer, William. Gandhi: A Memoir. 1981. 6.95 (ISBN 0-671-25080-9, Touchstone). S&S.
Shirer, William L. Ghandhi: A Memoir. 1981. pap. 4.95 (ISBN 0-671-25080-9, Touchstone Bks). S&S.
Shiridharani, Krishnalal. War Without Violence. LC 79-147633. (Library of War & Peace; Non-Resis. & Non-Vio.). lib. bdg. 38.00 (ISBN 0-8240-0409-4). Garland Pub.
Tendulkar, Dinanath G. Mahatma, Life of Mohandas Karamchand Gandhi, 8 Vols. rev. ed. 1960-63. Set. pap. 60.00x (ISBN 0-8426-1567-9). Verry.
Wolfenstein, E. Victor. Revolutionary Personality: Lenin, Trotsky, Gandhi. (Center of International Studies Ser.). 1971. 24.00 (ISBN 0-691-08611-7); pap. 8.95 (ISBN 0-691-02450-2, 251). Princeton U Pr.
Yapp, Malcolm. Gandhi. Killingray, Margaret & O'Connor, Edmund, eds. (World History Ser.). (Illus.). 32p. (gr. 10). 1980. Repr. of 1977 ed. lib. bdg. 5.95 (ISBN 0-89908-128-2); pap. text ed. 1.95 (ISBN 0-89908-103-7). Greenhaven.

GANDHI, MOHANDAS KARAMCHAND, 1869-1948–FICTION

Narayan, R. K. Waiting for the Mahatma. vii, 241p. 1955. 6.00 (ISBN 0-87013-012-9). Mich St U Pr.

GANDHI, MOHANDAS KARAMCHAND, 1869-1948–JUVENILE LITERATURE

Freitas, F. Bapu. (Nehru Library for Children). (Illus.). (gr. 1-9). 1979. Pt. I. pap. 1.50 (ISBN 0-89744-173-7); Pt. II. pap. 1.50 (ISBN 0-89744-174-5). Auromere.
Jacob, Helen P. Garland for Gandhi. LC 68-21993. (Illus.). (gr. 2-5). 1968. 5.95 (ISBN 0-87466-046-7). Parnassus.
Joshi, Uma. Stories from Bapu's Life. (Nehru Library for Children). (Illus.). (gr. 1-9). 1979. pap. 1.50 (ISBN 0-89744-180-X). Auromere.
Montgomery, Elizabeth R. Gandhi: Peaceful Fighter. LC 75-116039. (Century Biographies Ser.). (Illus.). (gr. 4-8). 1970. PLB 4.28 (ISBN 0-8116-4751-X). Garrard.
Rawding, F. W. Gandhi. LC 79-11008. (Cambridge Introduction to the History of Mankind Topic Book). (Illus.). (gr. 6). 1980. pap. 3.95 (ISBN 0-521-20715-0). Cambridge U Pr.
--Gandhi & the Struggle for India's Independence. (Cambridge Topic Bks.). (Illus.). 52p. (gr. 6 up). 1981. PLB 5.95 (ISBN 0-8225-1225-4). Lerner Pubns.
Shankar, R. Story of Gandhi. (Illus.). (gr. 3-10). 1979. 3.50 (ISBN 0-89744-166-4). Auromere.

GANGES RIVER

Darian, Steven G. The Ganges in Myth & History. LC 77-21374. 1978. text ed. 9.95x (ISBN 0-8248-0509-7). U Pr of Hawaii.
Douglas, Gina. The Ganges. LC 78-62983. (Rivers of the World Ser.). (Illus.). 1978. lib. bdg. 7.95 (ISBN 0-686-51134-4). Silver.
Sivaramamurti, C. Ganga. (Illus.). 1977. 12.50 (ISBN 0-88386-960-8). South Asia Bks.

GANGLIA, BASAL

see Basal Ganglia

GANGLIA, NERVOUS

see Nerves; Nervous System, Sympathetic

GANGRENE

see also Necrosis

Reid. A Surgeon's Management of Gangrene. 1978. 34.50 (ISBN 0-8391-1297-1). Univ Park.

GANGS

Bloch, Herbert A. & Niederhoffer, Arthur. The Gang: A Study in Adolescent Behavior. LC 76-6517. 1976. Repr. of 1958 ed. lib. bdg. 15.75x (ISBN 0-8371-8865-2, BLTG). Greenwood.
Cloward, Richard A. & Ohlin, Lloyd E. Delinquency & Opportunity: A Theory of Delinquent Gangs. LC 60-10892. 1966. 17.95 (ISBN 0-02-905600-4); pap. text ed. 5.95 (ISBN 0-02-905590-3). Free Pr.
Green, Janet. The Six. (gr. 6 up). 1978. cancelled (ISBN 0-8038-6753-0). Hastings.
Haskins, James. Street Gangs: Yesterday & Today. (Illus.). 192p. (gr. 7 up). 1974. PLB 8.95 (ISBN 0-8038-2662-1). Hastings.
--Street Gangs: Yesterday & Today. (Illus.). (gr. 6 up). 1977. pap. 4.95 (ISBN 0-8038-6740-9). Hastings.
Hoenig, Gary. Reaper: The Inside Story of a Gang Leader. LC 73-22673. 192p. 1975. 6.95 (ISBN 0-672-51896-1). Bobbs.
Keiser, Lincoln. The Vicelords: Warriors of the Streets, Fieldwork Edition. LC 75-16442. 1979. pap. text ed. 6.95 (ISBN 0-03-045396-8, HoltC). HR&W.
Krisberg, Barry A. The Gang & the Community. LC 75-5364. 1975. soft bdg. 9.00 (ISBN 0-88247-343-3). R & E Res Assoc.
McCoy, Duke. How to Start & Run Your Own Motorcycle Gang. 1981. pap. 7.95 (ISBN 0-686-30639-2). Loompanics.
McLean, Gordon. Terror in the Streets. LC 77-74159. (Illus.). 1977. pap. 2.95 (ISBN 0-87123-558-7, 200558). Bethany Hse.
Moore, Joan, et al. Homeboys: Gangs, Drugs & Prison in the Barrios of Los Angeles. LC 78-11808. (Illus.). 1979. 19.50x (ISBN 0-87722-121-9); pap. 8.95 (ISBN 0-87722-114-6). Temple U Pr.
Short, James F., Jr. & Strodtbeck, Frank L. Group Process & Gang Delinquency. LC 65-14434. 1965. 10.50x (ISBN 0-226-75464-2). U of Chicago Pr.
Thrasher, Frederic M. Gang: A Study of One Thousand Three Hundred Thirteen Gangs in Chicago. abr. ed. Short, James F., Jr., ed. LC 63-20899. 1963. 14.00x (ISBN 0-226-79929-8). U of Chicago Pr.
--Gang: A Study of One Thousand Three Hundred Thirteen Gangs in Chicago. abr ed. Short, James F., Jr., ed. LC 63-20899. (Orig.). 1963. pap. 7.00x (ISBN 0-226-79930-1). U of Chicago Pr.
Whyte, William F. Street Corner Society: The Social Structure of an Italian Slum. rev. ed. LC 55-5152. (Illus.). 1955. 15.00x (ISBN 0-226-89538-6); pap. 4.95x (ISBN 0-226-89539-4). U of Chicago Pr.

GANGSTERS

see Gangs

GANIVET, ANGEL, 1865-1898

Mellado de Hunter, Elena. El Estoicismo De Angel Ganivet. (UPREX, E. Literarios: No. 10). pap. 1.85 (ISBN 0-8477-0010-0). U of PR Pr.

GANNETS

Nelson, Bryan. The Gannet. LC 78-57690. (Illus.). 1978. 25.00 (ISBN 0-931130-01-8). Buteo.
Nelson, J. Bryan. The Sulidae: Gannets & Boobies. (Illus.). 1978. text ed. 105.00x (ISBN 0-19-714104-8). Oxford U Pr.

GANNETT, DEBORAH (SAMPSON) 1760-1827

Mann, Herman. The Female Review: Life of Deborah Sampson, the Female Soldier in the War of the Revolution. LC 72-2603. (American Women Ser: Images & Realities). 276p. 1972. Repr. of 1866 ed. 14.00 (ISBN 0-405-04476-3). Arno.

GANSEVOORT FAMILY

Kenney, Alice P. Gansevoorts of Albany: Dutch Patricians in the Upper Hudson Valley. LC 69-16981. (New York State Studies). (Illus.). 1969. 9.75 (ISBN 0-8156-2137-X). Syracuse U Pr.

GANZHEIT (PHILOSOPHY)

see Whole and Parts (Philosophy)

GAOLS

see Prisons

GARAGES

see also Automobile Parking; Automobiles–Service Stations

Brann, Donald R. How to Build a Two Car Garage, Lean-to Porch Cabana. LC 65-27707. 1979. pap. 5.95 (ISBN 0-87733-663-6). Easi-Bild.
--How to Build a Two Car Garage with Apartment Above. new ed. LC 76-29213. 1977. pap. 5.95 (ISBN 0-87733-763-2). Easi-Bild.
Crouse, William H. Automotive Service Business: Operation & Management. 1972. pap. text ed. 10.95 (ISBN 0-07-014605-5, G). McGraw.
Nulsen, David R. How to Build Patios, Porches, Carports & Storage Sheds for Mobile Homes. 1973. 3.95 (ISBN 0-87593-036-0). Trail-R.
Repair Garages. (Eighty-Ninety Ser). 1973. pap. 2.00 (ISBN 0-685-58141-1, 88B). Natl Fire Prot.
Rudman, Jack. Garageman-Driver (U.S.P.S.) (Career Examination Ser.: C-1757). (Cloth bdg. avail. on request). 1976. pap. 8.00 (ISBN 0-8373-1757-6). Natl Learning.
Russell, James E. Garages & Carports. Horowitz, Shirley M., ed. LC 81-66548. (Illus.). 160p. (Orig.). 1981. 17.95 (ISBN 0-932944-31-0); pap. 6.95 (ISBN 0-932944-32-9). Creative Homeowner.
Scharff, Robert. How to Build Your Garage, or Carport. LC 80-5207. (Popular Science Skill Bks.). (Illus.). 192p. (Orig.). 1980. pap. 4.95 (ISBN 0-06-090822-X, CN 822, CN). Har-Row.

GARAGIOLA, JOE

Garagiola, Joe. Baseball Is a Funny Game. 1980. pap. 1.95 (ISBN 0-553-13737-9). Bantam.

GARBAGE

see Refuse and Refuse Disposal

GARBO, GRETA, 1905-

Conway, Michael, et al. Films of Greta Garbo. (Illus.). 1968. pap. 7.95 (ISBN 0-8065-0148-0, C280). Citadel Pr.
Talbot, Toby. Dear Greta Garbo. (gr. 5-9). 1978. 6.95 (ISBN 0-399-20613-2). Putnam.
Walker, Alexander. Garbo. LC 80-12717. (Illus.). 192p. 1980. 19.95 (ISBN 0-02-622950-1). Macmillan.

GARCIA LORCA, FEDERICO, 1899-1936

Adams, Mildred. Garcia Lorca: Playwright & Poet. LC 77-77561. 1977. 8.95 (ISBN 0-8076-0873-4). Braziller.
Allen, Rupert C. Psyche & Symbol in the Theater of Federico Garcia Lorca: Perlimplin, Yerma, Blood Wedding. LC 74-7285. 234p. 1974. 12.50x (ISBN 0-292-76418-9). U of Tex Pr.
Babin, Maria T. Estudios Lorquianos. LC 76-1827. (Coleccion Mente y Palabra). 480p. (Span.). 1976. 7.50 (ISBN 0-8477-0528-5); pap. 6.25 (ISBN 0-8477-0529-3). U of PR Pr.

Barea, Arturo. Lorca: The Poet & His People. LC 72-92121. xv, 176p. 1973. Repr. of 1949 ed. lib. bdg. 10.00x (ISBN 0-8154-0447-6). Cooper Sq.
Campbell, Roy. Lorca: An Appreciation of His Poetry. LC 76-137665. (Studies in Poetry, No. 38). 1971. Repr. of 1952 ed. lib. bdg. 26.95 (ISBN 0-8383-1226-8). Haskell.
Cobb, Carl W. Federico Garcia Lorca. (World Authors Ser.: Spain: No. 23). 1968. lib. bdg. 9.95 (ISBN 0-8057-2544-X). Twayne.
Colecchia, Francesca. Garcia Lorca: An Annotated Bibliography of Criticism. LC 78-68301. (Reference Library of Humanities Ser.). 1979. lib. bdg. 34.00 (ISBN 0-8240-9800-5). Garland Pub.
Colecchia, Francesca, ed. Garcia Lorca: An Annotated Primary Bibliography. 1981. lib. bdg. 30.00 (ISBN 0-8240-9496-4). Garland Pub.
Craige, Betty Jean. Lorca's "Poet in New York". The Fall into Consciousness. LC 76-24339. (Studies in Romance Languages: No. 15). 112p. 1977. 10.50x (ISBN 0-8131-1349-0). U Pr of Ky.
Duran, Manuel, ed. Lorca, a Collection of Critical Essays. LC 76-49925. 1977. Repr. of 1962 ed. lib. bdg. 15.00x (ISBN 0-8371-9065-7, DULO). Greenwood.
Gibson, Ian. The Death of Lorca. LC 72-95426. 1973. 10.00 (ISBN 0-87955-306-5). O'Hara.
Higginbotham, Virginia. The Comic Spirit of Federico Garcia Lorca. 199p. 1976. 12.00x (ISBN 0-292-71033-X). U of Tex Pr.
Honig, Edwin. Garcia Lorca. rev. ed. 239p. 1980. Repr. of 1963 ed. lib. bdg. 15.50x (ISBN 0-374-93937-3). Octagon.
Laurenti, Joseph L. & Siracusa, Joseph. Federico Garcia Lorca y Su Mundo: Ensayo De una Bibliografia General. LC 74-2252. (Author Bibliographies Ser.: No. 15). 1974. 11.00 (ISBN 0-8108-0713-0). Scarecrow.
Pollin, Alice M. & Smith, Philip H., eds. A Concordance to the Plays & Poems Federico Garcia Lorca. LC 73-20817. (Concordances Ser.). 1200p. 1975. 42.50x (ISBN 0-8014-0808-3). Cornell U Pr.
Stanton, Edward F. The Tragic Myth: Lorca & Cante Jondo. LC 77-84067. (Studies in Romance Languages: No. 20). 152p. 1978. 13.00x (ISBN 0-8131-1378-4). U Pr of Ky.
Young, Howard T. Victorious Expression: A Study of Four Contemporary Spanish Poets, Unamuno, Machado, Jimenez, & Lorca. 1964. pap. 6.95x (ISBN 0-299-03144-6). U of Wis Pr.

GARCILASO DE LA VEGA, ca. 1539-1616
Castanien, Donald G. El Inca Carcilaso De la Vega. (World Authors Ser.: Peru: No. 61). lib. bdg. 10.95 (ISBN 0-8057-2928-3). Twayne.
Gicovate, Bernard. Garcilaso de la Vega. LC 74-28304. (World Authors Ser.: Spain: No. 349). 1975. lib. bdg. 12.50 (ISBN 0-8057-2342-0). Twayne.
Sarmiento, Edward, compiled by. Concordancias de las Obras Poeticas en Castellano de Garcilaso de la Vega. (Sp). 1970. 12.50 (ISBN 0-8142-0012-5). Ohio St U Pr.
Varner, John G. El Inca: The Life & Times of Garcilaso de la Vega. LC 68-55059. (Texas Pan American Ser). (Illus.). 431p. 1968. 22.50x (ISBN 0-292-78375-2). U of Tex Pr.

GARDEN APARTMENTS
see also Apartment Houses

GARDEN ARCHITECTURE
see Architecture, Domestic; Landscape Gardening

GARDEN CITIES
see also Housing
Howard, Ebenezer. Garden Cities of To-Morrow. (Illus.). 1965. pap. 4.95 (ISBN 0-262-58002-0). MIT Pr.
Smythe, William E. City Homes on Country Lanes: Philosophy & Practice of the Home-in-a-Garden. LC 73-2912. (Metropolitan America Ser.). (Illus.). 332p. 1974. 16.00x (ISBN 0-405-05425-4). Arno.
Stein, Clarence S. Toward New Towns for America. (Illus.). 1966. pap. 7.95x (ISBN 0-262-69009-8). MIT Pr.

GARDEN CITIES–GREAT BRITAIN
MacFadyen, Dugald. Sir Ebenezer Howard & the Town Planning Movement. 1970. 16.00x (ISBN 0-262-13066-1). MIT Pr.

GARDEN FARMING
see Truck Farming

GARDEN FERTILIZERS
see also Compost
Lloyd, Gordon B. Don't Call It "Dirt"! Improving Your Garden Soil. (Illus.). 128p. 1976. 6.95 (ISBN 0-916302-12-1); pap. 3.95 (ISBN 0-916302-02-4). Bookworm Pub.
Maddox, Harry. Your Garden Soil. (Illus.). 223p. 1975. 14.95 (ISBN 0-7153-6661-0). David & Charles.
Sinnes, A. Cort. All About Fertilizers, Soils & Water. Ortho Books Editorial Staff, ed. LC 79-52992. (Illus.). 112p. 1980. pap. 4.95 (ISBN 0-917102-80-0). Ortho.

GARDEN LIGHTING
Crockett, James U. & Murphy, Wendy B. Gardening Under Lights. (The Time-Life Encyclopedia of Gardening Ser.). (Illus.). 1978. lib. bdg. 11.96 (ISBN 0-686-51060-7). Silver.

GARDEN ORNAMENTS AND FURNITURE
see also Garden Lighting; Sun-Dials
Orcutt, Georgia. Successful Planters. LC 77-86465. (A Successful Book). (Illus.). 1977. 12.00 (ISBN 0-912336-48-X); pap. 4.95 (ISBN 0-912336-49-8). Structures Pub.
Sunset Editors. Garden Pools, Fountains & Waterfalls. 2nd ed. LC 73-89588. (Illus.). 80p. 1974. pap. 3.95 (ISBN 0-376-01224-2, Sunset Bks.). Sunset-Lane.
--Outdoor Furniture. LC 78-70271. (Illus.). 80p. 1979. pap. 3.95 (ISBN 0-376-01382-6, Sunset Bks.). Sunset-Lane.

GARDEN PESTS
see also Insects, Injurious and Beneficial; Plant Diseases
Biological Control of Plant Pests. 1.95 (ISBN 0-686-21131-6). Bklyn Botanic.
Cooper, W. E. ABC of Garden Pests & Diseases. (Illus.). 7.50x (ISBN 0-686-63609-0, LTB). Sportshelf.
Crockett, James U. & Cravens, Richard. Pests & Diseases. (The Time-Life Encyclopedia of Gardening Ser.). (Illus.). 1977. lib. bdg. 11.97 (ISBN 0-686-51062-3). Silver.
Dahl, Mogen & Thygesen, Thyge B. Garden Pests & Diseases of Flowers & Shrubs. Toms, A. M., ed. LC 78-8701. (Illus.). 224p. 1974. 6.95 (ISBN 0-02-619400-7). Macmillan.
Time-Life Books Editors, ed. Pest & Diseases. (Encyclopedia of Gardening Ser.). (Illus.). 1978. 12.95 (ISBN 0-8094-2566-1). Time-Life.
Westcott, Cynthia. The Gardener's Bug Book. LC 72-89822. 720p. 1973. 15.95 (ISBN 0-385-01525-9). Doubleday.

GARDEN POOLS
see Water Gardens

GARDEN WALKS
Russell, James E. Walks, Walls & Fences. Auer, Marilyn M., ed. LC 81-65752. (Illus., Orig.). 1981. 17.95 (ISBN 0-932944-35-3); pap. 6.95 (ISBN 0-932944-36-1). Creative Homeowner.

GARDENING
Here are entered general works. For works dealing with gardening in specific countries see the geographic subdivisions which follow. Works dealing with specific areas of the United states, e.g. Southern States are entered under the subdivision United States.
see also Aquatic Plants; Artificial Light Gardening; Bulbs; Climbing Plants; Container Gardening; Floriculture; Flower Gardening; Forcing (Plants); Fruit-Culture; Fungi in Agriculture; Garden Pests; Gardens; Grafting; Greenhouses; Grounds Maintenance; Herbs; Horticulture; Horticulturists; House Plants; Insects, Injurious and Beneficial; Landscape Gardening; Mulching; Nurseries (Horticulture); Organic Gardening; Plant Propagation; Plants, Ornamental; Plants, Potted; Pruning; Seaside Gardening; Topiary Work; Truck Farming; Vegetable Gardening; Weeds; Window-Gardening
Aaron, Jan. Plantworks: Indoor Gardening Made Easy. LC 74-21357. 208p. 1981. 14.95 (ISBN 0-8303-0146-1). Fleet.
Abraham, George. Green Thumb Book of Fruit & Vegetable Gardening. LC 78-85000. (Illus.). 1969. 11.95 (ISBN 0-13-365189-4). P-H.
Abraham, George & Abraham, Katy. Green Thumb Garden Handbook. rev & expanded ed. LC 77-22279. 1977. 14.95 (ISBN 0-13-365114-2). P-H.
Advanced Wiring. LC 78-1105. (Home Repair & Improvement Ser.). (Illus.). 1978. lib. bdg. 11.97 (ISBN 0-686-51034-8). Silver.
Allen, Oliver E. Shade Gardens. Time-Life Books, ed. LC 79-10953. (The Encyclopedia of Gardening). (Illus.). 1979. 12.95 (ISBN 0-8094-2645-5). Time-Life.
--Winter Gardens. Time-Life Books, ed. (The Encyclopedia of Gardening Ser.). (Illus.). 1980. 12.95 (ISBN 0-8094-3208-0). Time-Life.
Bailey, Leo L. A Step-by-Step Guide to Landscaping & Gardening. LC 74-84421. 1974. 10.00 (ISBN 0-682-48084-3, Banner). Exposition.
Bailey, Ralph, ed. House & Garden's Gardener's Day Book. LC 65-21771. (Illus.). 448p. 1965. 7.50 (ISBN 0-87131-008-2). M Evans.
Bailey, Ralph S. & McDonald, Elvin, eds. Good Housekeeping Basic Gardening Techniques. new ed. LC 74-79036. (Illus.). 320p. 1974. 10.95 (ISBN 0-87851-201-2). Hearst Bks.
Baker, Jerry. One-to-One Plant Problem Solver. 1979. pap. 1.75 (ISBN 0-89437-051-0). Baronet.
Bartholomew, Mel. Square Foot Gardening: A New Way to Garden in Less Space with Less Work. Halpin, Anne, ed. (Illus.). 288p. 1981. 13.95 (ISBN 0-87857-340-2); pap. 9.95 (ISBN 0-87857-341-0). Rodale Pr Inc.
Bartrum, Douglas. Foliage Plants for Your Garden. 4.50x (ISBN 0-392-06787-0, LTB). Sportshelf.
Beard, James B. & DiPaola, Joseph M. Introduction to Turfgrass Science & Culture Laboratory Exercises. 1979. pap. text ed. 10.95x (ISBN 0-8087-2894-6). Burgess.
Been, Margaret L. Wilderness & Gardens: An American Lady's Prospect. (Illus.). 1974. pap. 5.00 (ISBN 0-87423-011-X). Westburg.
Berrisford, Judith. Gardening on Chalk, Lime & Clay. 212p. 1979. 14.95 (ISBN 0-571-10952-7, Pub. by Faber & Faber); pap. 6.95 (ISBN 0-571-11129-7). Merrimack Bk Serv.
--The Weekend Garden. (Illus.). 160p. 1978. 14.95 (ISBN 0-571-11229-3, Pub. by Faber & Faber); pap. 7.95 (ISBN 0-571-11230-7). Merrimack Bk Serv.
Better Homes & Gardens Books Editors. Better Homes & Gardens Complete Guide to Gardening. (Illus.). 1979. 19.95 (ISBN 0-696-00041-5). Meredith Corp.
Better Homes & Gardens Books Editors, ed. Better Homes & Gardens Easiest Plants You Can Grow. (Illus.). 1978. 5.95 (ISBN 0-696-00365-1). Meredith Corp.
Betts, Edwin M. & Perkins, Hazlehurst B. Thomas Jefferson's Flower Garden at Monticello. rev. ed. 2nd ed. LC 78-150354. (Illus.). 96p. 1971. pap. 2.50x (ISBN 0-8139-0330-0). U Pr of Va.
Betts, Edwin M., ed. Thomas Jefferson's Garden Book. (Memoirs Ser.: Vol. 22). (Illus.). 1944. 12.00 (ISBN 0-87169-022-5). Am Philos.
Birdseye, Clarence & Birdseye, Eleanor G. Growing Woodland Plants. (Illus.). 6.75 (ISBN 0-8446-4510-9). Peter Smith.
Bisgrove, Richard. Your Problem Garden. 1980. 19.95 (ISBN 0-7134-1184-8, Pub. by Batsford England). David & Charles.
Bloom, Alan. Moisture Gardening. (Illus.). 128p. 1966. 7.95 (ISBN 0-571-06904-5, Pub. by Faber & Faber). Merrimack Bk Serv.
Boddy, Frederick A. Ground Cover & Other Ways to Weed-Free Gardens. LC 74-78251. (Illus.). 176p. 1974. 13.50 (ISBN 0-7153-6575-4). David & Charles.
Boland, Bridget. Gardener's Magic & Other Old Wives Lore. (Illus.). 64p. 1977. 5.95 (ISBN 0-374-16034-1). FS&G.
Boland, Bridget & Boland, Maureen. Old Wives' Lore for Gardeners. (Illus.). 1977. 6.95 (ISBN 0-374-22586-9); pap. 3.95 (ISBN 0-374-51639-1). FS&G.
Brenizer, Sherman. Hydro-Story, Hydroponic Gardening at Home. 1977. pap. 4.95 (ISBN 0-917316-13-4). Nolo Pr.
Briscoe, Alan. Home Garden Hints. 1975. pap. 1.95 (ISBN 0-88290-049-8). Horizon Utah.
Bristow, Alec. The Easy Garden. LC 78-65630. (Illus.). 1979. 11.95 (ISBN 0-690-01802-9); pap. 5.95 (ISBN 0-690-01822-3, TYC-T). T Y Crowell.
Brooks, A. E. Australian Native Plants for Home Gardens. 6th rev. ed. (Illus.). 1979. 13.95x (ISBN 0-85091-091-9, Pub. by Lothian). Intl Schol Bk Serv.
Broughton, Jacqueline P. Garden Flowers to Color. (Illus.). 32p. (ps-2). 1972. pap. 1.25 (ISBN 0-913456-51-9). Interbk Inc.
Brown, Dennis, ed. The Complete Indoor Gardener. rev. ed. LC 79-4799. (Illus.). 1979. 17.95 (ISBN 0-394-50748-7); pap. 8.95 (ISBN 0-394-73813-6). Random.
Brown, Edmund R. & Very, Alice. How to Use Peat Moss. (Orig.). 1953. pap. 0.50 (ISBN 0-8283-1162-5). Branden.
Brown, George E. Shade Plants for Garden & Woodland. (Illus.). 240p. 1980. 27.00 (ISBN 0-571-10377-4, Pub. by Faber & Faber). Merrimack Bk Serv.
Brown, R. H. Gardening Complete. (Illus.). 550p. 1968. 13.50 (ISBN 0-571-08332-3, Pub. by Faber & Faber). Merrimack Bk Serv.
Bryan, John & Castle, Coralie. Edible Ornamental Garden. LC 73-91941. (Illus.). 192p. (Orig.). 1974. pap. 4.95 (ISBN 0-686-76998-8). One Hund One Prods.
Bubel, Nancy. The Adventurous Gardener. LC 78-74251. (Illus.). 1979. 15.00 (ISBN 0-87923-275-7); pap. 7.95 (ISBN 0-87923-276-5). Godine.
--The Seed Starter's Handbook. LC 77-25332. 1978. 12.95 (ISBN 0-87857-209-0). Rodale Pr Inc.
Burlingame, Alice W. Hoe for Health. (Illus.). 1974. 10.50x (ISBN 0-686-10006-9). Garden Consul.
Carleton, R. Milton. Vegetables for Today's Gardens. pap. 2.00 (ISBN 0-87980-226-X). Wilshire.
Carr, David. The Beginners Guide to Good Gardening. (Illus.). 243p. 1980. 14.95 (ISBN 0-7137-0934-0, Pub. by Blandford Pr England). Sterling.
--The Gardener's Handbook, 2 bks. Incl. Vol. 1. Broad-Leaved Trees. (Illus.). 144p. 24.00 (ISBN 0-7134-1306-9); Vol. 2. Conifers. (Illus.). 144p. 24.00 (ISBN 0-7134-1307-7). (Illus.). 1980 (Pub. by Batsford England). David & Charles.
Casey, Lydian. Outdoor Gardening. LC 74-11890. (Early Craft Bks.). (Illus.). 32p. (gr. 1-4). 1975. PLB 3.95 (ISBN 0-8225-0864-8). Lerner Pubns.
Chancellor, R. J. Garden Weeds & Their Control. 93p. 1981. 24.00x (ISBN 0-909605-21-1, Pub. by Richmond Pub England). State Mutual Bk.
Chaplin, Mary. Gardening for the Physically Handicapped & Elderly. 1978. 14.95 (ISBN 0-7134-1081-7). David & Charles.
Chatto, Beth. The Dry Garden. (Illus.). 176p. 1979. 13.95x (ISBN 0-460-04317-X, Pub. by J. M. Dent England). Biblio Dist.
Clarkson, Rosetta E. The Golden Age of Herbs & Herbalists. (Illus.). 352p. 1972. pap. 5.00 (ISBN 0-486-22869-X). Dover.
Coe, Mary Lee. Growing with Community Gardening. (Illus., Orig.). 1978. 8.95 (ISBN 0-914378-36-8); pap. 6.95 (ISBN 0-914378-22-8). Countryman.
Colegrave, D. & D. R. Colegrave Seeds Ltd. The Colegrave Manual of Bedding Plants: Grower Manual. 1980. pap. 7.95 (ISBN 0-89955-213-7, Pub. by Grower Books England). Intl Schol Bk Serv.
The Complete Family Flower & Garden Book. (Illus.). 520p. 1981. 8.95 (ISBN 0-686-31186-8, 2541). Playmore & Prestige.
Coniferes ornementaux de nos jardins. new ed. (Collection "Flore"). (Illus.). 145p. (Fr.). 1972. 11.50x (ISBN 2-03-074701-7). Larousse.
Connell, Charles. Aphrodisiacs in Your Garden. LC 66-17666. (Illus.). 1966. 3.50 (ISBN 0-8008-0275-6). Taplinger.
Conners, Faith R. Garden Minder. new ed. 1975. pap. 1.95 (ISBN 0-686-12116-3). S O S Pubns.
Cook, E. T. The Century Book of Gardening. 610p. 1980. Repr. lib. bdg. 100.00 (ISBN 0-8495-0793-6). Arden Lib.
Coon, Nelson. Gardening for Fragrance: Indoors & Out. (Illus., Orig.). 1970. 5.95 (ISBN 0-8208-0068-6). Hearthside.
Cooper, W. E. ABC of Gardening. (Illus.). 7.50x (ISBN 0-392-06739-0, LTB). Sportshelf.
Courtright, Gordon. Trees & Shrubs for Western Gardens. LC 79-65785. (Illus.). 1979. 43.00 (ISBN 0-917304-13-6, Pub. by Timber Pr). Intl Schol Bk Serv.
Creative Ideas in Garden Design. 1.95 (ISBN 0-686-21144-8). Bklyn Botanic.
Crockett, James. Crockett's Victory Garden. (Illus.). 1977. 17.50 (ISBN 0-316-16120-9); pap. 12.95 (ISBN 0-316-16121-7). Little.
Crockett, James U. Crockett's Tool Shed. LC 79-18080. (Illus.). 1979. 15.00 (ISBN 0-316-16129-2); pap. 9.95 (ISBN 0-316-16130-6). Little.
Crockett, James U. & Allen, Oliver E. Shade Gardens. (The Time-Life Encyclopedia of Gardening Ser.). (Illus.). 1979. lib. bdg. 11.97 (ISBN 0-8094-2646-3); kivar bdg. 8.95 (ISBN 0-8094-2647-1). Silver.
Crockett, James U. & Prendergast, C. Easy Gardens. (The Time-Life Encyclopedia of Gardening Ser.). (Illus.). 1979. lib. bdg. 11.97 (ISBN 0-686-51065-8). Silver.
Crockett, James U. & Tanner, Ogden. Garden Construction. (The Time-Life Encyclopedia of Gardening Ser.). (Illus.). 1978. lib. bdg. 11.96 (ISBN 0-686-51059-3). Silver.
Crosby, Kate & Wood, Denis. Grow It & Cook It. (Illus.). 375p. 1975. 15.95 (ISBN 0-571-10571-8, Pub. by Faber & Faber). Merrimack Bk Serv.
Darlington, Jeanie. Grow Your Own. pap. 1.75 (ISBN 0-394-71520-9, V-520, Vin). Random.
Dawson, Oliver. Herbaceous Border. (Illus.). 144p. 1973. 4.95 (ISBN 0-7153-6211-9). David & Charles.
Dietz, Marjorie, ed. The Complete Guide to Successful Gardening. LC 78-23734. (Illus.). 1979. 14.95 (ISBN 0-8317-1625-8, Mayflower Bks). Smith Pubs.
Dietz, Marjorie J., ed. Ten Thousand Garden Questions Answered by Twenty Experts. LC 73-17596. (Illus.). 1400p. 1974. 12.95 (ISBN 0-385-08743-8). Doubleday.
Dingwall, Robert J. The Garden Answers. LC 77-93696. (Illus.). 1978. pap. 6.95 (ISBN 0-87445-001-2). Cadillac.
Dolowich, Madeline. The Kitchen Gardener: How to Recycle Your Leftovers to Grow Fruits & Vegetables Inside Your House. LC 81-3826. 192p. 1981. pap. 5.95 (ISBN 0-8253-0070-3). Beaufort Bks NY.
Doscher, Paul, et al. Intensive Gardening Round the Year. (Illus.). 224p. 1981. pap. 15.00 (ISBN 0-8289-0399-9). Greene.
Dougherty, Betty. Green Gardener: How an Amateur Created a Wild Garden. LC 74-81054. 1975. 5.95 (ISBN 0-7153-6498-7). David & Charles.
Downing, Andrew J. Rural Essays. Curtis, George W., ed. LC 69-13713. (Architecture & Decorative Art Ser). 640p. 1978. Repr. of 1854 ed. lib. bdg. 39.50 (ISBN 0-306-71035-8). Da Capo.
Dudley, Stuart. Taking the Ache Out of Gardening. 8.50x (ISBN 0-392-04862-0, SpS). Sportshelf.

Dworkin, Floss & Dworkin, Stan. The Apartment Gardener. 1979. pap. 4.95 (ISBN 0-452-25203-2, Z5203, Plume). NAL.
Eaton, Jerome A. & Calkins, Carroll C. How to Garden. LC 78-13121. (Illus.). 1979. 12.50 (ISBN 0-394-49383-4); pap. 6.95 (ISBN 0-394-73531-5). Knopf.
Elementary Science Study. Microgardening. 2nd ed. 1975. tchr's. guide 12.88 (ISBN 0-07-018583-2, W). McGraw.
Ellwanger, George H. The Garden's Story: Or, Pleasures & Trials of an Amateur Gardner. 1979. Repr. of 1898 ed. lib. bdg. 20.00 (ISBN 0-8495-1331-6). Arden Lib.
Emberton, Sybil C. A Year in the Shrub Garden. (Illus.). 264p. 1972. 8.95 (ISBN 0-571-09382-5, Pub. by Faber & Faber). Merrimack Bk Serv.
The Environment & the Home Gardener. 1977. 1.95 (ISBN 0-686-22154-0). Bklyn Botanic.
Evans, Mary. Garden Books, Old & New. LC 71-162512. 1971. Repr. of 1926 ed. 19.00 (ISBN 0-8103-3743-6). Gale.
Family Handyman Editors. Outdoor Projects for Home & Garden. (Illus.). 1979. pap. 8.95 (ISBN 0-8306-1116-9, 1116). TAB Bks.
Fatigati, Evelyn. Garden on Greenway Street. LC 77-2609. (Illus.). (gr. 5 up). 1977. 6.95 (ISBN 0-87857-166-3). Rodale Pr Inc.
Faust, Joan L., ed. The New York Times Garden Book. 1977. pap. 5.95 (ISBN 0-685-75024-8, 345-25682-4-495). Ballantine.
Faust, Joan L. & Oldenburg, Lisa, eds. The New York Times Book of Indoor & Outdoor Gardening Questions. LC 74-24293. (Illus.). 192p. 1975. 7.95 (ISBN 0-8129-0538-5). Times Bks.
Felice, Raymond. Successful Landscaping. LC 77-16624. (Illus.). 1978. 13.95 (ISBN 0-912336-55-2); pap. 6.95 (ISBN 0-912336-56-0). Structures Pub.
Fell, Derek. Annuals, Perennials, & Bulbs. 144p. (Orig.). 1982. pap. 7.95 (ISBN 0-88453-037-X). Countryside Bks.
Fenten, D. X. The Weekend Gardener. 1976. pap. 1.50 (ISBN 0-451-06953-6, W6953, Sig). NAL.
Firth, Grace. A Natural Year. 1973. 6.95 (ISBN 0-671-21205-2). S&S.
Fish, D. T. Popular Gardening, 4 vols. 1974. lib. bdg. 600.00 (ISBN 0-685-51357-2). Revisionist Pr.
Fish, Margery. A Flower for Every Day. 208p. 1981. pap. 9.95 (ISBN 0-571-11738-4, Pub. by Faber & Faber). Merrimack Bk Serv.
--Ground Cover Plants. (Illus.). 144p. 1980. pap. 7.95 (ISBN 0-571-11463-6, Pub. by Faber & Faber). Merrimack Bk Serv.
--We Made a Garden. (Illus.). 120p. 1970. 11.95 (ISBN 0-7153-4876-0). David & Charles.
Foster, Lee. Backyard Farming. LC 81-4449. (Urban Life Practical Solutions to the Challenges of the 80's Ser.). 96p. (Orig.). 1981. pap. 4.95 (ISBN 0-87701-224-5). Chronicle Bks.
Fox, Helen M. Gardening with Herbs for Flavor & Fragrance. (Illus.). 1972. pap. 3.75 (ISBN 0-486-22540-2). Dover.
Freese, Paul. Small Gardens for Small Spaces. McGourty, Frederick, ed. 1977. 1.95 (ISBN 0-686-22911-8). Bklyn Botanic.
Fundamentals of Gardening. 1977. pap. 3.98 ea.; pap. midwest-north ed. (ISBN 0-917102-20-7); pap. northeast ed. (ISBN 0-917102-21-5); pap. south ed. (ISBN 0-917102-22-3). Ortho.
Garden Construction Know-How. 1977. pap. 4.95 (ISBN 0-917102-69-X). Ortho.
Garden Structures. 1.95 (ISBN 0-686-21140-5). Bklyn Botanic.
Gardening Guide. 1.95 (ISBN 0-686-21171-5). Bklyn Botanic.
A Gardening Handbook. 1979. pap. text ed. 11.00x (ISBN 0-685-50327-5). State Mutual Bk.
Gardening in the Shade. 1.95 (ISBN 0-686-21155-3). Bklyn Botanic.
Gardening Without Pests. 1979. 1.95 (ISBN 0-686-27086-X). Bklyn Botanic.
Garland, Madge. The Small Garden in the City. LC 74-76646. (Illus.). 136p. 1974. 12.50 (ISBN 0-8076-0752-5). Braziller.
Garrison, Juanita B. Piedmont Garden: How to Grow by the Calendar. LC 80-23218. 1981. pap. text ed. 4.95 mechanical (ISBN 0-87249-403-9). U of SC Pr.
Genders, Roy. Home-Grown Food: A Guide for Town Gardeners. (Illus.). 1977. 11.50 (ISBN 0-7181-1473-6). Transatlantic.
--Pears Encyclopedia of Gardening: Flowers, Trees & Shrubs, Vol. 1. 1972. 9.95 (ISBN 0-7207-0249-6, Pub. by Michael Joseph). Merrimack Bk Serv.
--Pears Encyclopedia of Gardening: Fruits & Vegetables, Vol. 2. 1973. 9.95 (ISBN 0-7207-0537-1, Pub. by Michael Joseph). Merrimack Bk Serv.
--Wild Life in the Garden. (Illus.). 258p. 1977. 11.95 (ISBN 0-571-10307-3, Pub. by Faber & Faber). Merrimack Bk Serv.
Gibbons, Brian. Growplan Gardening Guide. (Illus.). 180p. 1979. 8.95 (ISBN 0-7153-7697-7). David & Charles.
Globus, Diane. Digging It: How to Grow Things Naturally. (Illus.). 256p. 1973. 5.75 (ISBN 0-8037-2002-5). Dial.
Gorer, Richard. Growing Plants from Seed. (Illus.). 144p. 1978. 12.95 (ISBN 0-571-11148-3, Pub. by Faber & Faber); pap. 6.95 (ISBN 0-571-11149-1). Merrimack Bk Serv.
Greenhouse Handbook for the Amateur. 1.95 (ISBN 0-686-21137-5). Bklyn Botanic.
Gribble, McPhee. Gardening: How to Grow Things. (Practical Puffins Ser.). (gr. 6 up). 1976. pap. 1.50 (ISBN 0-14-049143-0, Puffin). Penguin.
Gross, Sue A. & Gross, Sidney A. The Early Spring Garden Book. 1975. pap. 2.50 (ISBN 0-917234-05-7). Kitchen Harvest.
Grow Your Own: Successful Gardening Encyclopedia, 5 vols. 1980. 34.95 (ISBN 0-87475-722-3). Stuttman.
Guest, C. Z. & McDonald, Elvin. C.Z. & Elvin's Week-by-Week Garden Guide. LC 80-67097. (Illus.). 180p. (Orig.). 1980. pap. 5.95 (ISBN 0-87754-137-X). Chelsea Hse.
Hackett, Brian. Planting Design. (Illus.). 1979. 16.95 (ISBN 0-07-025402-8, P&RB). McGraw.
Halpin, Anne, ed. Gourmet Gardening. (Illus.). 256p. 1981. pap. 9.95 (ISBN 0-87857-349-6). Rodale Pr Inc.
Halpin, Anne M., ed. Rodale's Encyclopedia of Indoor Gardening. (Illus.). 912p. 1980. 29.95 (ISBN 0-87857-319-4). Rodale Pr Inc.
Harris, Cyril. Trees & Shrubs in the Modern Garden. 192p. 1975. 12.95 (ISBN 0-7207-0855-9, Pub. by Michael Joseph). Merrimack Bk Serv.
Harshbarger, Gretchen F. McCall's Garden Book. 1968. 12.95 (ISBN 0-671-45887-6). S&S.
--McCall's Garden Book. 1977. pap. 6.95 (ISBN 0-671-22773-4, Fireside). S&S.
Hawthorne, R. Dawson's Practical Lawncraft. (Illus.). 313p. 1977. 24.95x (ISBN 0-8464-1085-0). Beekman Pubs.
Hay, Roy & Ground, Roger, eds. Practical Gardening Encyclopedia. 1977. 19.95 (ISBN 0-442-22887-2). Van Nos Reinhold.
Hazlitt, W. C. Gleanings in Old Garden Literature. 59.95 (ISBN 0-8490-0238-9). Gordon Pr.
Hazlitt, William C. Gleanings in Old Garden Literature. LC 68-21773. 1968. Repr. of 1887 ed. 19.00 (ISBN 0-8103-3509-3). Gale.
Hedrick, U. P. Fruits for the Home Garden. (Illus.). 224p. 1973. pap. 3.50 (ISBN 0-486-22944-0). Dover.
Hellyer, A. G. The Amateur Gardener. 1973. 15.00 (ISBN 0-600-30082-X). Transatlantic.
Hellyer, A. G., rev. by. Sanders' Encyclopedia of Gardening. 1972. 16.00 (ISBN 0-600-44110-5). Transatlantic.
Hellyer, Arthur & Kalmbacher, George. The Color Guide to American Gardening. (Illus.). 192p. 1974. 7.98 (ISBN 0-517-51494-X). Crown.
Hennebo, D. & Hoffman, A. Geschichte der deutschen Gartenkunst, 3 vols. (Illus.). 930p. 1980. Repr. of 1962 ed. Set. lib. bdg. 187.00x (ISBN 3-87429-176-6). Lubrecht & Cramer.
Heriteau, Jacqueline. Easy Gardening Projects. 1975. pap. 1.50 (ISBN 0-445-03059-3). Popular Lib.
--Hurry up & Grow Plants & Gardens. 1979. pap. 1.95 (ISBN 0-445-04413-6). Popular Lib.
--Small Fruit & Vegetable Gardens. 192p. 1975. pap. 1.50 (ISBN 0-445-03062-3). Popular Lib.
Hessayon, D. G. Be Your Own Gardening Expert. 36p. 1977. pap. 1.95 (ISBN 0-8119-0355-9). Fell.
Hill, Lewis. Successful Cold Climate Gardening. 1981. 14.95 (ISBN 0-8289-0421-9); pap. 9.95 (ISBN 0-8289-0422-7). Greene.
Hill, Thomas. The Art of Gardening. LC 79-84117. (English Experience Ser.: No. 936). 276p. 1979. Repr. of 1608 ed. lib. bdg. 26.00 (ISBN 0-686-71070-3). Walter J Johnson.
Hills, Lawrence D. Down to Earth Gardening. (Illus.). 304p. (Orig.). 1975. pap. 6.50 (ISBN 0-571-10868-7, Pub. by Faber & Faber). Merrimack Bk Serv.
--Grow Your Own Fruit & Vegetables. 1974. 14.00 (ISBN 0-571-04830-7). Transatlantic.
--Grow Your Own Fruit & Vegetables. 328p. 1979. pap. 6.95 (ISBN 0-571-11366-4, Pub. by Faber & Faber). Merrimack Bk Serv.
Hodge, Peggy H. Tropical Gardening: A Handbook for the Home Gardener. LC 74-130417. (Illus.). 1970. 12.50 (ISBN 0-8048-0925-9). C E Tuttle.
Hollingsworth, Buckner. Gardening on Main Street. 1968. 9.50 (ISBN 0-8135-0578-X). Rutgers U Pr.
Hostage, Jacqueline. Jackie's Indoor-Outdoor Gardening Charts. (Illus.). 128p. (Orig.). 1982. pap. 5.95 plastic comb bdg. (ISBN 0-932620-07-8). Betterway Pubns.
House & Garden. House & Garden's Twenty Six Easy Little Gardens. (Handbook Ser.). (Illus.). 1979. pap. 8.95 (ISBN 0-14-046390-9). Penguin.
Hughes, Spike. The Art of Coarse Gardening or the Care & Feeding of Slugs. 1968. 5.95 (ISBN 0-09-088710-7, Pub. by Hutchinson). Merrimack Bk Serv.
Huxley, Anthony. An Illustrated History of Gardening. LC 78-5961. (Illus.). 1978. 24.95 (ISBN 0-448-22424-0). Paddington.
Jackson, Mary H. How Does Your Garden Grow? (Illus.). 64p. 1980. 4.95 (ISBN 0-517-54027-4); ten copy pre-pack 49.50 (ISBN 0-517-54118-1). Potter.
--How Does Your Garden Grow? 5.00 (ISBN 0-685-57223-4). Mary Inc.
Jankowiak, James. The Prosperous Gardener. Breslow, Lori, ed. LC 77-18089. 1978. 8.95 (ISBN 0-87857-204-X). Rodale Pr Inc.
Jobb, Jamie. The Complete Book of Community Gardening. LC 78-23840. (Illus.). 1979. 14.95 (ISBN 0-688-03409-8); pap. 7.95 (ISBN 0-688-08409-5). Morrow.
Johnson, Hugh. The Principles of Gardening. 1979. 29.95 (ISBN 0-671-24273-3). S&S.
Johnston, Marliss. The Whole Garden Catalog. (Illus.). 1980. lib. bdg. 17.50 (ISBN 0-933474-13-X, Gabriel Bks); pap. 12.95 (ISBN 0-933474-17-2, Gabriel Bks). Minn Scholarly.
--The Whole Garden Catalog: Everything Under the Sun for Those Who Like to Garden. (Illus.). 210p. 1981. pap. 12.95 (ISBN 0-933474-17-2). Gabriel Bks.
Kains, E. G. The Original Victory Garden Book. LC 77-21121. 1978. 8.95 (ISBN 0-8128-2429-6); pap. 3.95 (ISBN 0-8128-2428-8). Stein & Day.
Karolevitz, Robert. Everything's Green but My Thumb. LC 70-184510. (Illus.). 1971. 5.95 (ISBN 0-87970-124-2). North Plains.
Kelway, Christine. Gardening on Sandy Soil in North Temperate Areas. Orig. Title: Gardening on Sand. (Illus.). 144p. 1975. pap. 2.95 (ISBN 0-486-23199-2). Dover.
--Gardening on Sandy Soil in North Temperate Areas. (Illus.). 6.00 (ISBN 0-8446-5209-1). Peter Smith.
Kerr, Don. The New England Vegetable Garden. (Illus.). 240p. (Orig.). 1980. pap. 7.95 (ISBN 0-933614-03-9). Peregrine Pr.
King, Eleanor A. Bible Plants for American Gardens. LC 75-3646. (Illus.). 224p. 1975. pap. 3.50 (ISBN 0-486-23188-7). Dover.
Kingsley-Lewis, John. The Garden Diary. 220p. (Orig.). 1982. pap. 6.95 (ISBN 0-933474-31-8). Gabriel Bks.
Knight, Charles W. Secrets of Green Thumb Gardening. LC 64-17301. (gr. 9 up). 1964. 6.95 (ISBN 0-8119-0154-8). Fell.
Kramer, Jack. Complete Book of Gardening. (Illus.). 384p. Date not set. 29.95 (ISBN 0-686-30961-8). Everest Hse.
--Easy Plants for Difficult Places. LC 74-82401. (Illus.). 1975. 6.95 (ISBN 0-8027-0468-9). Walker & Co.
--Gardening in Small Spaces. (Illus.). 1980. pap. 7.95 (ISBN 0-89586-033-3). H P Bks.
--Gardens for All Seasons. (Illus.). 220p. 1981. 45.00 (ISBN 0-8109-0951-0). Abrams.
--The Old-Fashioned Cutting Garden: Growing Flowers for Pleasure & Profit. (Illus.). 1979. 8.95 (ISBN 0-02-566620-7). Macmillan.
--Once-a-Week Indoor Gardening Guide. (Orig.). pap. 1.75 (ISBN 0-515-04475-X). Jove Pubns.
--One Thousand Beautiful Garden Plants & How to Grow Them. LC 76-984. (Illus.). 1979. pap. 6.95 (ISBN 0-688-08025-1). Morrow.
--Victorian Gardens: How to Plan, Plant, & Enjoy Nineteenth Century Beauty Today. LC 80-8342. (Illus.). 160p. Date not set. 14.95 (ISBN 0-06-250480-0, HarpR); pap. 9.95 (ISBN 0-06-250481-9). Har-Row.
--Your Trellis Garden: How to Build It, How to Grow It, How to Show It. (Orig.). 1976. pap. 3.95 (ISBN 0-346-12218-X). Cornerstone.
Kulla, Patricia S. Make Your Summer Garden Last All Year. LC 75-8460. (Illus.). 8.95 (ISBN 0-915336-01-4); pap. 4.95 (ISBN 0-915336-10-3). Lyceum Bks.
Landscape Planning for Small Gardens. pap. 7.50x (ISBN 0-392-06854-0, ABC). Sportshelf.
Langer, Richard. Grow It. 1973. pap. 4.95 (ISBN 0-380-01234-0, 33688). Avon.
Langer, Richard W. After Dinner Gardening Book. 1971. pap. 1.95 (ISBN 0-02-009770-0, Collier). Macmillan.
Langham, Derald G. Circle Gardening. 1978. pap. 5.95 (ISBN 0-8159-5215-5). Devin.
Langhans, Robert W., ed. A Growth Chamber Manual: Environmental Control for Plants. LC 77-90906. (Illus.). 240p. 1978. 22.50x (ISBN 0-8014-1169-6). Comstock.
Lawrence, Elizabeth. Gardens in Winter. 1973. 5.00 (ISBN 0-685-00419-8). Claitors.
Lawrence, Martin, compiled by. The Homesteader's Handbook. (Illus.). 1979. pap. 7.95 (ISBN 0-8317-4532-0, Mayflower Bks). Smith Pubs.
Lecomte, Solange. What Lives in the Garden. (Rejoice Ser.). (ps). pap. 0.35 (ISBN 0-8091-6519-8). Paulist Pr.
Leighton, Ann. Early American Gardens: For "Meate & Medicine". (Illus.). 1970. 14.95 (ISBN 0-395-07907-1). HM.
Levitan, Lois. Improve Your Gardening with Backyard Research. (Illus.). 1980. 12.95 (ISBN 0-87857-306-2); pap. 6.95 (ISBN 0-87857-267-8). Rodale Pr Inc.
Lewis, W. H. Tackle Your New Garden This Way. 11.75x (ISBN 0-392-06773-0, LTB). Sportshelf.
Lloyd, Gordon B. Don't Call It "Dirt"! Improving Your Garden Soil. (Illus.). 128p. 1976. 6.95 (ISBN 0-916302-12-1); pap. 3.95 (ISBN 0-916302-02-4). Bookworm Pub.
Loewer, Peter. The Indoor Water Gardener's How-to Handbook. 1.98 (ISBN 0-517-31428-2). Bonanza.
MacCaskey, Michael R. Award-Winning Small-Space Gardens. Ortho Books Editorial Staff, ed. LC 79-52991. (Illus.). 112p. 1980. pap. 4.95 (ISBN 0-917102-81-9). Ortho.
McDonald, Elvin. Easy Gardens. 1981. 8.95 (ISBN 0-916752-20-8). Green Hill.
--Easy Gardens. 1981. 8.95 (ISBN 0-916752-20-8). Caroline Hse.
--Making Your Lawn & Garden Grow. 1981. 5.95 (ISBN 0-916752-07-0). Caroline Hse.
Macmillan. The Gardener's Diary. (Illus.). 340p. 1976. 6.98 (ISBN 0-02-578290-8). Macmillan.
Manning, Laurence. The How & Why of Better Gardening. 1980. pap. 4.95 (ISBN 0-442-22567-9). Van Nos Reinhold.
Marshall Cavendish Editorial Board. Gardening Is Easy - When You Know How. LC 74-76265. (gr. 2-9). 4.95 (ISBN 0-668-03482-3). Arco.
Melady, John H. Home Owners' Complete Garden Handbook. (Illus.). 1960. 4.95 (ISBN 0-448-01578-1, MSP). G&D.
Menage, Ronald H. Greenhouse Gardening. 1977. pap. 2.95 (ISBN 0-14-046241-4). Penguin.
Minar, William M. Greenhouse Gardening in the South. LC 76-1685. (Illus.). 96p. 1976. pap. 3.95 (ISBN 0-88415-327-4). Pacesetter Pr.
Minnich, Jerry. The Earthworm Book: How to Raise & Use Earthworms for Your Farm & Garden. LC 77-13405. 1977. 12.95 (ISBN 0-87857-193-0). Rodale Pr Inc.
Mitchell, Henry. The Essential Earthman: Henry Mitchell on Gardening. LC 81-47011. (Illus.). 256p. 1981. 12.95 (ISBN 0-253-17436-8). Ind U Pr.
Mittleider, Jacob R. Gardening by the Foot. LC 80-84564. 150p. 1981. pap. 6.95 (ISBN 0-88290-175-3, 4026). Horizon Utah.
Moncure, Jane B. See My Garden Grow. LC 76-4512. (Illus.). (ps-3). 1976. 6.45 (ISBN 0-913778-38-9). Childs World.
Moon, Doug. Gardening for People. LC 74-84449. (Illus.). 266p. (Orig.). 1975. pap. 6.00 (ISBN 0-912528-10-9). John Muir.
Moore, Larry. Larry Moore's Basic Twenty by Thirty Backyard Garden Guide. (Illus., Orig.). 1979. pap. 4.95 (ISBN 0-8362-2300-4). Andrews & McMeel.
Morris, Francesca. Making Your Lawn & Garden Grow: A Melnor Guide to Indoor and Outdoor Gardening. McDonald, Elvin, ed. LC 76-48843. (Illus.). 1977. 5.95 (ISBN 0-916752-07-0). Dorison Hse.
Muirhead, Desmond. Palms. LC 60-16856. (Illus., Orig.). 1961. 5.95 (ISBN 0-912762-07-1); pap. 2.50 (ISBN 0-912762-06-3). King.
Mumford, Edwin. The Second Flight of the Starfire. 1972. 4.00 (ISBN 0-682-47462-2). Exposition.
Murphy, Louise. My Garden: A Journal for Gardening Around the Year. LC 79-29650. (Illus.). (gr. 1-7). 1980. 8.95 (ISBN 0-684-16486-8). Scribner.
Natural Gardening. 1.95 (ISBN 0-686-21169-3). Bklyn Botanic.
Neese, Harvey C. Home Gardening: Practical & Simple. 1978. write for info (ISBN 0-686-23016-7). N & N Resources.
Nehrling, Arno & Nehrling, Irene. Easy Gardening with Drought - Resistant Plants. LC 75-17124. (Illus.). 320p. 1975. pap. 3.50 (ISBN 0-486-23230-1). Dover.
Newcomb, Duane G. The Postage Stamp Garden Book: How to Grow All the Food You Can Eat in Very Little Space. LC 74-23021. (Illus.). 150p. 1975. 7.95 (ISBN 0-87477-034-3); pap. 4.95 (ISBN 0-87477-035-1). J P Tarcher.
Nichols, Beverley. The Gift of a Garden; or, Some Flowers Remembered. Incl. Down the Garden Path; A Thatched Roof; A Village in the Valley. (Illus.). 344p. 1972. 7.50 (ISBN 0-396-06575-9). Dodd.
Nigh, Edward & Stark Research Associates. The Formula Book 3. new ed. (Formula Bks). (Illus.). 1978. 12.00 (ISBN 0-8362-2202-4); pap. 5.95 (ISBN 0-8362-2205-9). Andrews & McMeel.
Noble, Mary. Garden in Florida. 2nd rev. ed. (Illus.). 120p. 1975. pap. 3.95 (ISBN 0-913928-05-4). McQuerry-Orchid.

--You Can Grow Phalaenopsis Orchids. (Illus.). 148p. 1971. pap. 6.50 (ISBN 0-913928-03-8). McQuerry-Orchid.
O'Connor, John. Grow Your Own. rev. ed. 239p. 1978. 28.00 (ISBN 0-7156-1009-0, Pub. by Duckworth England); pap. 13.50 (ISBN 0-7156-1293-X, Pub. by Duckworth England). Biblio Dist.
Oddo, Sandra & Wolfe, Dolores. Growing Food in Solar Greenhouses: A Month by Month Guide to Raising Vegetables, Fruit, & Herbs Under Glass. LC 80-70556. (Illus.). 192p. 1981. pap. 9.95 (ISBN 0-385-17602-3, Dolp). Doubleday.
The Old Farmer's Almanac Gardener's Companion. (Illus.). 144p. 1982. pap. 1.50 (ISBN 0-686-76244-4). Yankee Bks.
Olszowy, Damon R. Horticulture for the Disabled & Disadvantaged. 240p. 1978. 17.50 (ISBN 0-398-03691-8). C C Thomas.
Oravetz, Jules, Sr. Gardening & Landscaping: Lawns, Vegetables, Flowers, Trees, & Shrubs. LC 74-28650. 1975. 9.95 (ISBN 0-672-23229-4, 23229). Audel.
Orcutt, Georgia, ed. The Old Farmer's Almanac Gardener's Companion, 1979. (Illus., Annual). 1979. pap. 1.50 (ISBN 0-911658-96-3). Yankee Bks.
Organic Gardening & Farming Staff & Editors. The Calendar of Organic Gardening: A Guidebook to Successful Gardening Through the Year. LC 73-2280. (Illus.). 1973. 7.95 (ISBN 0-87857-067-5). Rodale Pr Inc.
Organic Gardening Editors. Getting the Most from Your Garden. (Illus.). 1980. 15.95 (ISBN 0-87857-291-0). Rodale Pr Inc.
Owen, Millie. A Cook's Guide to Growing Herbs, Greens, & Aromatics. LC 77-20368. 1978. pap. 6.95 (ISBN 0-394-73454-8). Knopf.
Pacey, Arnold, compiled by. Gardening for Better Nutrition. (Illus.). 64p. (Orig.). 1980. pap. 3.50 (ISBN 0-903031-50-7, Pub. by Intermediate Tech England). Intermediate Tech.
Perper, Hazel. Citrus Seed Grower's Indoor How-to Book. LC 73-179694. (Illus.). 1971. 4.50 (ISBN 0-396-06434-5). Dodd.
Peterson, George. The Most Ridiculous Book on Gardening Ever. 1981. 6.95 (ISBN 0-533-04590-8). Vantage.
Peterson, Roger T., et al. Gardening with Wildlife. Bourne, Russell & MacConomy, Alma D., eds. LC 74-82797. (Illus.). 192p. 1974. 12.95g (ISBN 0-912186-15-1). Natl Wildlife.
Philbrick, Helen & Gregg, Richard B. Companion Plants. rev. ed. 1966. pap. 4.95 (ISBN 0-8159-5210-4). Devin.
Philbrick, John & Philbrick, Helen. Gardening for Health & Nutrition. LC 79-3595. 96p. 1980. pap. 3.95 (ISBN 0-06-066535-1, RD 402). Har-Row.
Pierot, Suzanne W. What Can I Grow in the Shade? (Illus.). 1977. 10.95 (ISBN 0-87140-627-6). Liveright.
Powell, Thomas & Powell, Betty. The Avant Gardener: A Handbook & Sourcebook of All That's New & Useful in Gardening. LC 74-34599. 320p. 1975. pap. 6.95 (ISBN 0-395-20506-9). HM.
Reynolds, Bruford S. Money Saving Recipes Through Sprouting & Gardening. pap. 4.95 (ISBN 0-89036-134-7). Hawkes Pub Inc.
Riker, Tom. City & Suburban Gardens: Frontyards, Backyards, Terraces, Rooftops & Window Boxes. LC 76-58532. (Illus.). 1977. 12.95 (ISBN 0-13-134544-3). P-H.
Riker, Tom & Rottenberg, Harvey. Food Gardens, Indoors, Outdoors, & Under Glass. LC 75-27155. (Illus.). 320p. 1975. pap. 6.95 (ISBN 0-688-07963-6). Morrow.
Riker, Tom, et al. The Gardener's Catalogue. LC 74-17429. 320p. 1974. pap. 6.95 (ISBN 0-688-05327-0). Morrow.
Riotte, Louise. Carrots Love Tomatoes: Secrets of Companion Planting for Successful Gardening. (Illus.). 160p. 1976. 6.95 (ISBN 0-88266-065-9); pap. 5.95 (ISBN 0-88266-064-0). Garden Way Pub.
--Success with Small Food Gardens. (Illus.). 1977. 8.95 (ISBN 0-88266-100-0); pap. 5.95 (ISBN 0-88266-099-3). Garden Way Pub.
Robertson, Josephine. Garden Meditations. LC 77-23316. (Illus.). 1977. 5.95 (ISBN 0-687-14000-5). Abingdon.
Robinette, Gary O. Roofscape. LC 76-57856. 1977. pap. 20.00 (ISBN 0-918436-02-8). Environ Des VA.
Robinson, Charles N. British Tar in Fact & Fiction. LC 68-26601. (Illus.). 1968. Repr. of 1909 ed. 24.00 (ISBN 0-8103-3514-X). Gale.
Robinson, William. The Wild Garden. (Illus.). 340p. 1978. 14.95 (ISBN 0-85967-439-8, Pub. by Scolar Pr England). Biblio Dist.
Rockwell & Grayson. Rockwell's Complete Guide to Successful Gardening. 1971. pap. 3.95 (ISBN 0-451-09743-2, E9743, Sig). NAL.
Rothery, Agnes E. Joyful Gardener. facs. ed. LC 77-99647. (Essay Index Reprint Ser). 1949. 17.00 (ISBN 0-8369-2128-3). Arno.
Sackville-West, V. V. Sackville-West's Garden Book. LC 68-8261. 1979. 8.95 (ISBN 0-689-10969-5). Atheneum.
Sanders, T. W. & Macself, A. J. Encyclopedia of Gardening. 1974. lib. bdg. 79.95 (ISBN 0-685-51359-9). Revisionist Pr.
Schmidt, Marjorie G. Growing California Native Plants. LC 78-62845. 400p. 1980. 15.95 (ISBN 0-520-03761-8). U of Cal Pr.
Schuler, Stanley. How to Grow Almost Everything. LC 65-13249. (Illus.). 256p. 1965. 6.95 (ISBN 0-87131-061-9); pap. 4.95 (ISBN 0-87131-257-3). M Evans.
Schumann, Donna N. Living with Plants: A Guide to the Practical Application of Botany. (Illus.). 328p. (Orig.). 1980. pap. 14.45 (ISBN 0-916422-20-8). Mad River.
Scymor, John. The Gardeners Delight. 1979. 5.95 (ISBN 0-517-53805-9). Crown.
Seymour, John. The Self-Sufficient Gardener: A Complete Guide to Growing & Preserving All Your Own Food. LC 78-19223. 1979. pap. 9.95 (ISBN 0-385-14671-X, Dolp). Doubleday.
Seymour, John & Seymour, Sally. The Fat of the Land: Family Farming on Five Acres. LC 74-26782. (Illus.). 1975. 6.95 (ISBN 0-8052-3579-5). Schocken.
Shaudys, Phyllis V. Gourmet Gardening: A Monthly Herbal Primer for Gardeners Who Love to Cook. (Illus.). 72p. (Orig.). 1979. pap. 4.00 (ISBN 0-935238-01-8). Pine Row.
Sherman, Ed. How to Build a Bigger Hydroponic Garden. 1978. pap. 3.95 (ISBN 0-917316-18-5). Nolo Pr.
Shewell-Cooper, W. E. Complete Vegetable Grower. 288p. 1973. pap. 5.50 (ISBN 0-571-04797-1, Pub. by Faber & Faber). Merrimack Bk Serv.
Short Hills Garden Club. Down to Earth Gardening. encore ed. LC 76-44611. 1976. pap. 2.95 (ISBN 0-684-16375-6, SL685, ScribT). Scribner.
Sinnes, A. Cort. All About Fertilizers, Soils & Water. Ortho Books Editorial Staff, ed. LC 79-52992. (Illus.). 112p. 1980. pap. 4.95 (ISBN 0-917102-80-0). Ortho.
Skelsey, Alice. Farming in a Flowerpot. rev. ed. LC 75-7289. (Illus.). 1975. pap. 2.75 (ISBN 0-911104-56-9). Workman Pub.
Skelsey, Alice & Huckaby, Gloria. Growing up Green. LC 74-156268. (Parents & Children Together Ser.). (Illus.). 224p. (gr. 3 up). 1973. 8.95 (ISBN 0-911104-22-4); pap. 4.95 (ISBN 0-911104-23-2). Workman Pub.
Smith, Joanna. Farm Your Garden. (Illus.). 1977. 14.95x (ISBN 0-8464-0405-2). Beekman Pubs.
Smyser, Carol A. Nature's Design: A Practical Guide to Natural Landscaping. (Illus.). 416p. 1982. 19.95 (ISBN 0-87857-343-7). Rodale Pr Inc.
Solomon, Steve. The Complete Guide to Organic Gardening West of the Cascades. 175p. 1981. pap. 9.95 (ISBN 0-914718-58-4). Pacific Search.
Southern Living Gardening Staff & Floyd, John A., Jr. Southern Living Garden Guide. LC 80-84409. (Illus.). 224p. 1981. 17.95 (ISBN 0-8487-0518-1). Oxmoor Hse.
Staff of Ortho Books, ed. Gardening with Color. LC 77-89690. (Illus.). 1978. pap. 4.95 (ISBN 0-917102-58-4). Ortho.
Stark, Norman, et al. The Formula Book One, Two, & Three Slipcased Gift Pack. (Formula Ser.). (Illus.). 1979. pap. 17.85 (ISBN 0-8362-2208-3). Andrews & McMeel.
Stevenson, Violet. Gifts from Your Garden. (Illus.). 182p. 1974. 12.00x (ISBN 0-460-07892-5). Intl Pubns Serv.
Stout, Ruth. Gardening Without Work. 1974. pap. 1.95 (ISBN 0-346-12158-2). Cornerstone.
--How to Have a Green Thumb Without an Aching Back. 1955. 5.50 (ISBN 0-682-40095-5, Banner). Exposition.
--How to Have a Green Thumb Without an Aching Back. 160p. 1968. pap. 3.50 (ISBN 0-346-12126-4). Cornerstone.
Stout, Ruth & Clemence, Richard. The Ruth Stout No-Work Garden Book. LC 70-152102. (Illus.). 1971. 7.95 (ISBN 0-87857-000-4). Rodale Pr Inc.
Sunset Editors. Basic Gardening: Introduction to. 3rd ed. LC 80-53478. (Illus.). 160p. 1981. pap. 5.95 (ISBN 0-376-03075-5, Sunset Bks). Sunset-Lane.
--Desert Gardening. LC 67-27445. (Illus.). 96p. 1967. pap. 2.95 (ISBN 0-376-03132-8, Sunset Bks). Sunset-Lane.
--Garden Color: Annuals & Perennials. LC 80-53479. (Illus.). 96p. 1981. pap. 3.95 (ISBN 0-376-03154-9, Sunset Bks). Sunset-Lane.
--Landscaping & Garden Remodeling. LC 77-82872. (Illus.). 80p. 1978. pap. 3.95 (ISBN 0-376-03455-6, Sunset Bks). Sunset-Lane.
--Small-Space Gardens. LC 77-82874. (Illus.). 80p. 1978. pap. 3.95 (ISBN 0-376-03702-4, Sunset Bks). Sunset-Lane.
--Western Garden Book: Sunset New. 4th ed. LC 78-70266. (Illus.). 512p. 1979. pap. 11.95 (ISBN 0-376-03889-6, Sunset Bks). Sunset-Lane.
Surcouf, Lorraine. Growing a Green Thumb. 1976. pap. text ed. 2.25 (ISBN 0-8120-0736-0). Barron.
Swain, William G. The Commonsense of Gardening. (Illus.). 414p. 1976. 13.95 (ISBN 0-7181-1382-9, Pub. by Michael Joseph). Merrimack Bk Serv.
Taylor, Jean. Planting for Pleasure. 1973. 5.95 (ISBN 0-09-118300-6, Pub. by Hutchinson); pap. 2.95 (ISBN 0-09-118301-4). Merrimack Bk Serv.
Time-Life Books, ed. Greenhouse Gardening. (The Encyclopedia of Gardening). (Illus.). 1977. 12.95 (ISBN 0-8094-2562-9). Time-Life.
Time-Life Books & Time Life Books Editors, eds. Gardening Under Lights. (The Encyclopedia of Gardening Ser.). (Illus.). 1978. 12.95 (ISBN 0-8094-2570-X). Time-Life.
Time Life Books Editors. The Time-Life Gardening Yearbook. (Encyclopedia of Gardening Ser.). (Illus.). 1978. 12.95 (ISBN 0-685-86572-X). Time-Life.
Time-Life Gardening Yearbook. (Best-Selling Single Titles Ser.). (Illus.). lib. bdg. 11.97 (ISBN 0-686-51033-X). Silver.
Tonge, Peter. The Good Green Garden. LC 79-66555. 1979. pap. 4.95 (ISBN 0-88448-013-5). Harpswell Pr.
Trelease, W. Plant Materials of Decorative Gardening: The Woody Plants. 5th rev. ed. 5.50 (ISBN 0-8446-3085-3). Peter Smith.
Tresemer, David. The Scythe Book: Mowing Hay, Cutting Weeds & Harvesting Small Grains with Hand Tools. (Illus.). 1981. pap. 6.95 (ISBN 0-938670-00-X). Greene.
Twelve Months Harvest. (Illus.). 1977. pap. 4.95 (ISBN 0-917102-12-6). Ortho.
Van Dersal, William R. Why Does Your Garden Grow? The Facts of Plant Life. LC 76-50830. (Illus.). 1977. 8.95 (ISBN 0-8129-0680-2). Times Bks.
Wahlfeldt, Bette G. Successful Sandy Soil Gardening. (Illus.). 1979. cancelled (ISBN 0-8306-9816-7); pap. 4.95 (ISBN 0-8306-1068-5, 1068). TAB Bks.
Walkden, Brian. Aids to Better Gardening. LC 73-176185. 3.95 (ISBN 0-7153-5341-1). David & Charles.
Walls, Ian G. & Horsburgh, A. S. Making Your Garden Pay: Profit from Garden & Nursery. 6.95 (ISBN 0-7153-6365-4). David & Charles.
Warner, Charles D. My Summer in a Garden. LC 70-131855. 1970. Repr. of 1889 ed. 8.00 (ISBN 0-403-00742-9). Scholarly.
--My Summer in a Garden. LC 76-127896. Repr. of 1871 ed. 9.00 (ISBN 0-404-06839-1). AMS Pr.
Watkins, John V. & Wolfe, Herbert S. Your Florida Garden. 5th ed. LC 68-23403. 382p. 1968. 9.95 (ISBN 0-8130-0233-8). U Presses Fla.
Wearne, Robert A., ed. Community Gardening. 1979. 1.95 (ISBN 0-686-24748-5). Bklyn Botanic.
The Weekend Gardener. LC 77-20470. (Illus.). 1978. pap. 6.95 (ISBN 0-8329-0212-8). New Century.
Weintz, Todd. The Gardener's Three Year Note Book. rev ed. LC 75-15199. (Illus.). 1977. comb bdg. 7.95 (ISBN 0-8397-2354-7). Eriksson.
Weston, Marybeth L. Decorating with Plants: A House & Garden Book. LC 77-16138. 1979. pap. 6.95 (ISBN 0-394-73465-3). Pantheon.
White, Katherine S. Onward & Upward in the Garden. White, E. B., ed. 384p. 1979. 12.95 (ISBN 0-374-22654-7); pap. 6.95 (ISBN 0-374-51629-4). FS&G.
Whitehead, George. Growing for Showing. (Illus.). 176p. 1981. pap. 7.95 (ISBN 0-571-11706-6, Pub. by Faber & Faber). Merrimack Bk Serv.
--Growing for Showing. (Illus.). 176p. 1978. 9.95 (ISBN 0-571-11206-4, Pub. by Faber & Faber). Merrimack Bk Serv.
Whitman, John. Starting from Scratch: A Guide to Indoor Gardening. (Illus.). 1978. pap. 1.95 (ISBN 0-451-08024-6, J8024, Sig). NAL.
Wiberg, Hugh. Vegetable Gardening for Beginners. pap. 2.00 (ISBN 0-87980-169-7). Wilshire.
Wickham, Cynthia. The Indoor Garden: The House Plant Lover's Complete Companion. LC 77-62. (Illus.). 1977. 17.50 (ISBN 0-89104-073-0). A & W Pubs.
Wilder, Louise B. The Fragrant Garden: A Book About Sweet Scented Flowers & Leaves. LC 73-76306. 379p. 1974. Repr. of 1936 ed. 5.00 (ISBN 0-486-23071-6). Dover.
Williams, George S. Greenhouse Flowers & Bedding Plants for Agribusiness Studies. LC 74-24772. xiv, 282p. 1975. 9.65 (ISBN 0-8134-1671-X, 1671). Interstate.
Williams, T. Jeff. How to Select, Use & Maintain Garden Equipment. ORTHO Books Editorial Staff, ed. LC 80-85221. (Illus.). 96p. (Orig.). 1982. pap. 5.95 (ISBN 0-917102-94-0). Ortho.
Wills, Keith. Cultivating Rough Ground. LC 80-52326. (Illus.). 1980. pap. 5.95 (ISBN 0-8069-8952-1). Sterling.
Wilson, Charles L. The Gardener's Hint Book. LC 76-26893. (Illus.). 1978. 12.95 (ISBN 0-8246-0210-2). Jonathan David.
Wilson, Helen Van Pelt. Color for Your Winter Yard & Garden: With Flowers, Berries, Birds, & Trees. (Illus.). 1979. pap. 7.95 (ISBN 0-684-15515-X, SL 768, ScribT). Scribner.
Witham-Fogg, H. G. Creating a Luxury Garden. 1975. 7.95 (ISBN 0-7028-1052-5). Herman Pub.
Wright, D. Macer, compiled by. The Countryman Gardening Book. (Countryman Books). 4.95 (ISBN 0-7153-6307-7). David & Charles.
Wright, Michael, ed. Complete Book of Gardening. 1980. pap. 9.95 (ISBN 0-446-87239-3). Warner Bks.
--The Complete Book of Gardening. 1979. 20.00 (ISBN 0-397-01292-6). Lippincott.
Wyman, Donald. The Saturday Morning Gardener: A Guide to Once-a-Week Maintenance. rev. ed. LC 73-11833. (Illus.). 256p. 1974. 7.95 (ISBN 0-02-632100-9). Macmillan.
Yarborough, Elizabeth O. A Walk in the Garden. 1977. 4.50 (ISBN 0-533-03156-7). Vantage.
Younger, Mab. Practical Garden Design. (Illus.). 72p. 1978. 14.50 (ISBN 0-589-50063-5, Pub. by Reed Books Australia). C E Tuttle.

GARDENING–BIBLIOGRAPHY

Falge, Pat & Leggett, Arnold. The Complete Garden. LC 75-7451. (Finder's Guide Ser.: No. 8). (Illus.). 318p. 1975. pap. 3.95 (ISBN 0-914400-11-8). Oliver Pr.
Hazlitt, William C. Gleanings in Old Garden Literature. LC 68-21773. 1968. Repr. of 1887 ed. 19.00 (ISBN 0-8103-3509-3). Gale.
Massachusetts Horticultural Society, Boston. Dictionary Catalog of the Library of the Massachusetts Horticultural Society, 3 Vols. 1963. Set. lib. bdg. 195.00 (ISBN 0-8161-0648-7). G K Hall.
Robinson, Charles N. British Tar in Fact & Fiction. LC 68-26601. (Illus.). 1968. Repr. of 1909 ed. 24.00 (ISBN 0-8103-3514-X). Gale.

GARDENING–DICTIONARIES

Bailey, Liberty H. Standard Cyclopedia of Horticulture, 3 Vols. (Illus.). 1935. Set. 65.00 (ISBN 0-686-57562-8); 22.00 ea. Macmillan.
Chittenden, F. J. & Synge, P. M., eds. Dictionary of Gardening: A Practical & Scientific Encyclopedia of Horticulture, 4 Vols. 2nd ed. 1956. 275.00x (ISBN 0-19-869106-8). Oxford U Pr.
Coutanceau, Maurice. Encyclopedie Des Jardins. new ed. 556p. (Fr.). 1973. 45.00 (ISBN 0-686-57141-X, M-6198). French & Eur.
Encyclopedie Du Jardinage. 512p. (Fr.). 1972. 27.50 (ISBN 0-686-57150-9, M-6208). French & Eur.
Jahn, H. Herder - Lexikon Pflanzen. 256p. (Ger.). 1975. pap. 15.95 (ISBN 3-451-17370-0, M-7448, Pub. by Herder). French & Eur.
Larousse And Co. Nouvelle Encyclopedie des jardins. (Illus., Fr.). 34.75x (ISBN 0-685-13906-9). Larousse.
Miller, P. The Gardener's Dictionary. 1969. Repr. of 1754 ed. 80.00 (ISBN 3-7682-0613-0). Lubrecht & Cramer.
Neues Grosses Gartenlexikon. (Ger.). 1973. 32.00 (ISBN 3-517-00442-1, M-7567, Pub. by Suedwest). French & Eur.
Synge, Patrick M., ed. Dictionary of Gardening - Supplement. 1969. 74.00x (ISBN 0-19-869116-5). Oxford U Pr.
Taylor, Norman, ed. Encyclopedia of Gardening. rev. ed. (Illus.). 1961. 27.95 (ISBN 0-395-08237-4). HM.
Vilmorin, Roger de. L' Encyclopedie Des Fleurs et Des Jardins, 3 vols. 2000p. (Fr.). 1975. Set. 95.00 (ISBN 0-686-57140-1, M-6197). French & Eur.
Whitehead, Stanley B. Everyman's Encyclopedia of Gardening. LC 75-497346. (Illus.). 600p. 1970. 10.00x (ISBN 0-460-03021-3). Intl Pubns Serv.
Wyman, Donald. Wyman's Gardening Encyclopedia. rev. & expanded ed. 1977. 29.95 (ISBN 0-02-632060-6, 63206). Macmillan.

GARDENING–EARLY WORKS TO 1800

Browne, Thomas. Hydriotaphia, Urne-Buriall, or, a Discourse of the Sepulchrall Urnes Lately Found in Norfolk. Together with the Garden of Cyrus, or the Quincunciall Lozenge, or Network Plantations of the Ancients, Artificially, Naturally Mystically Considered. Kastenbaum, Robert, ed. LC 76-19562. (Death & Dying Ser.). 1977. Repr. of 1927 ed. lib. bdg. 12.00x (ISBN 0-405-09558-9). Arno.
The Expert Gardener: A Treatise Containing Certaine Necessary, Secret, & Ordinary Knowledges in Grafting. LC 74-80178. (English Experience Ser.: No. 659). (Illus.). 54p. 1974. Repr. of 1640 ed. 6.00 (ISBN 90-221-0659-4). Walter J Johnson.
Strabo, Walahfrid. Hortulus. Lawrence, G., ed. Payne, R., tr. (Botanical Library). (Illus., Eng. & Lat.). 1966. 16.00x (ISBN 0-913196-09-6). Hunt Inst Botanical.

GARDENING–EXAMINATIONS, QUESTIONS, ETC.

Rudman, Jack. Foreman of Gardeners. (Career Examination Ser.: C-268). (Cloth bdg. avail. on request). pap. 8.00 (ISBN 0-8373-0268-4). Natl Learning.

--Gardener. (Career Examination Ser.: C-297). (Cloth bdg. avail. on request). pap. 8.00 (ISBN 0-8373-0297-8). Natl Learning.

GARDENING–FERTILIZERS AND MANURES

see Garden Fertilizers

GARDENING–JUVENILE LITERATURE

Barrett, Patricia & Dalton, Rosemary. The Kid's Garden Book. LC 74-17230. (Illus.). 192p. (Orig.). (gr. 1-6). 1974. pap. 4.95 (ISBN 0-911954-32-5). Nitty Gritty.

Boy Scouts Of America. Gardening. LC 19-600. (Illus.). 48p. (gr. 6-12). 1976. pap. 0.70x (ISBN 0-8395-3240-7, 3240). BSA.

Brown, Marc. Your First Garden Book. (Illus.). (gr. 1 up). 1981. 8.95 (ISBN 0-316-11217-8, Pub. by Atlantic Pr); pap. 4.95 (ISBN 0-316-11215-1). Little.

Creative Editors. How to Have Fun with a Vegetable Garden. LC 74-12297. (Creative Craft Bks.). (Illus.). 32p. (gr. 2-6). 1974. PLB 5.95 (ISBN 0-87191-363-1). Creative Ed.

Creative Educational Society Editors. How to Have Fun with an Indoor Garden. LC 73-18258. (Creative Craft Bks.). (Illus.). 32p. (gr. 2-5). 1973. PLB 5.95 (ISBN 0-87191-297-X). Creative Ed.

Crockett, James U. Crockett's Indoor Garden. LC 78-8939. 1978. 17.50 (ISBN 0-316-16124-1); pap. 12.95 (ISBN 0-316-16126-8). Little.

Crockett, James V., et al. Greenhouse Gardening. LC 76-51513. (Time-Life Encyclopedia of Gardening). (Illus.). (gr. 6 up). 1977. PLB 11.97 (ISBN 0-8094-2563-7, Pub by Time-Life). Silver.

Cutler, Katherine. Growing a Garden Indoors or Out. LC 73-4936. (Illus.). 128p. (gr. 4 up). 1973. PLB 7.44 (ISBN 0-688-31365-5). Lothrop.

Dunks, Thom & Dunks, Patty. Gardening with Children. LC 76-20871. (Illus.). 1977. pap. 4.95 (ISBN 0-917332-01-6). Harvest Pr.

Fujikawa, Gyo. Let's Grow a Garden. (Fujikawa Board Books). (Illus.). (gr. k-3). 1978. 3.50 (ISBN 0-448-14613-4). G&D.

Guidetti, Geri. A Seneca Garden. (Illus.). 26p. (Orig.). (gr. 2-8). 1981. pap. 3.95 (ISBN 0-938928-00-7). KMG Pubns OR.

Heath, Jennifer R. A Child's Gardening Primer. (Illus.). (gr. 1-4). 1978. pap. 3.50 (ISBN 0-686-23047-7). Calico Papers.

Jobb, Jamie. My Garden Companion. LC 76-57675. (Illus.). (gr. 4 up). 1977. 9.95 (ISBN 0-684-15018-2, ScribJ); pap. 4.95 (ISBN 0-684-15019-0, SL703, ScribJ). Scribner.

--My Garden Companion: A Complete Guide for the Beginner. LC 76-57675. (Sierra Club-Scribner Juvenile Ser.). (Illus.). (gr. 4 up). 1977. 9.95 (ISBN 0-684-15018-2); pap. 4.95 (ISBN 0-684-15019-0). Sierra.

Kains, M. G. Gardening for Young People. LC 77-16775. 1978. 8.95 (ISBN 0-8128-2438-5); pap. 4.95 (ISBN 0-8128-2440-7). Stein & Day.

McGee, Myra. Willie's Garden. LC 77-2892. (gr. 5 up). 1977. 4.95 (ISBN 0-87857-174-4). Rodale Pr Inc.

Mandry, Kathy. How to Grow a Jelly Glass Farm. LC 74-150. (Illus.). 40p. (ps-3). 1974. PLB 5.99 (ISBN 0-394-92928-4). Pantheon.

My Mother & I Are Growing Strong. Orig. Title: Mi Mama y Yo Nos Hacemos Fuertes. (gr. k-6). pap. 2.00 (ISBN 0-686-74722-4). Crossing Pr.

Nelson, Alix R. Raggedy Ann & Andy's Green Thumb Book. LC 73-22685. (Illus.). 160p. (YA) 1975. 7.95 (ISBN 0-672-51928-3). Bobbs.

Paul, Aileen & DeLulio, John. Kids Outdoor Gardening. LC 77-80907. (gr. 3-7). 1978. 5.95a (ISBN 0-385-12757-X); PLB (ISBN 0-385-12758-8). Doubleday.

Riedman, Sarah R. Gardening Without Soil. LC 78-13088. (First Bks.). (Illus.). (gr. 4-6). 1979. PLB 6.90 s&l (ISBN 0-531-02256-0). Watts.

Sholinsky, Jane. Growing Plants from Fruits & Vegetables. (Illus.). (gr. k-3). 1975. pap. 1.25 (ISBN 0-590-09847-0, Schol Pap). Schol Bk Serv.

Siegel, Alice & McLoone, Margo. The Herb & Spice Book for Kids. LC 77-26712. (Illus.). 1978. 6.95 (ISBN 0-03-041681-7). HR&W.

Springstubb, Tricia. Growing Things. 228p. (gr. 6). 1981. 8.95 (ISBN 0-686-69141-5, Pub. by Atlantic). Little.

Sweningson, Sally. Indoor Gardening. LC 74-33528. (Early Craft Bks.). (Illus.). 32p. (gr. 1-4). 1975. PLB 3.95g (ISBN 0-8225-0871-0). Lerner Pubns.

Swenson, Allan A. My Own Herb Garden. (Children's Collection Ser.). (Illus.). 72p. 1976. 8.95 (ISBN 0-87857-129-9). Rodale Pr Inc.

Walsh, Anne B. A Gardening Book: Indoors & Outdoors. LC 75-28272. (Illus.). 112p. (gr. 4-7). 1976. 6.95 (ISBN 0-689-50042-4, McElderry Bk). Atheneum.

Wanhala, Julie M. You Can Grow Tomatoes. LC 78-6684. (Illus.). (gr. 3-7). 1979. PLB 7.95 (ISBN 0-516-07637-X, Elk Grove Bks). Childrens.

Wickers, David & Tuey, John. How to Make Things Grow. (gr. 4-6). 1975. pap. 1.25 (ISBN 0-590-10136-6, Schol Pap). Schol Bk Serv.

GARDENING–AFRICA, SOUTH

D'Ewes, D. R. Guide to Gardening in South Africa. (Illus.). 104p. 1975. pap. 9.00x (ISBN 0-86977-060-8). Verry.

GARDENING–AUSTRALIA

Lindsay, Pax. The Australian Gardner's Guide to Pruning Trees & Shrubs. (Illus.). 1979. pap. 5.25 (ISBN 0-589-07178-5, Pub. by Reed Books Australia). C E Tuttle.

Lord, Ernest E. Shrubs & Trees for Australians Gardens. (Illus.). 1979. 30.95x (ISBN 0-85091-104-4, Pub. by Lothian). Intl Schol Bk Serv.

GARDENING–CARIBBEAN AREA

Smiley, Nixon. Tropical Planting & Gardening for South Florida & the West Indies. LC 61-9185. (Illus.). 1960. pap. 5.95 (ISBN 0-87024-008-0). U of Miami Pr.

GARDENING–GREAT BRITAIN

Berrisford, Judith. Backyards & Tiny Gardens. 160p. 1977 (Pub. by Faber & Faber). pap. 5.95 (ISBN 0-571-10837-7). Merrimack Bk Serv.

Eyler, Ellen C. Early English Gardens & Garden Books. LC 63-15259. (Folger Guides to the Age of Shakespeare). 1963. pap. 3.95 (ISBN 0-918016-30-4). Folger Bks.

Gorer, Richard. The Growth of Gardens. 584p. 1978. 17.50 (ISBN 0-571-10757-5, Pub. by Faber & Faber). Merrimack Bk Serv.

Hadfield, Miles. A History of British Gardening. 3rd ed. (Illus.). 1979. text ed. 26.00x (ISBN 0-7195-3644-8). Humanities.

Hadfield, Miles, et al, eds. British Gardeners: A Biographical Dictionary. 233p. 1980. 60.00x (ISBN 0-302-00541-2, Pub. by Wright Pub Scotland). State Mutual Bk.

Rockley, Alicia A. History of Gardening in England. LC 68-21522. 1969. Repr. of 1896 ed. 22.00 (ISBN 0-8103-3845-9). Gale.

Tait, A. A. The Landscape Garden in Scotland. 300p. 1980. 31.00x (ISBN 0-85224-372-3, Pub. by Edinburgh U Pr Scotland). Columbia U Pr.

Wilson, Ron. The Hedgerow Book. LC 78-75251. 1979. 17.95 (ISBN 0-7153-7728-0). David & Charles.

GARDENING–JAPAN

Bring, Mitchell & Wayembergh, Josse. Design & Meaning in Japanese Gardens. (Illus.). Date not set. price not set (ISBN 0-07-007825-4). McGraw.

Crockett, James U. & Murphy, Wendy B. Japanese Gardens. (The Time-Life Encyclopedia of Gardening Ser.). (Illus.). 1979. lib. bdg. 11.97 (ISBN 0-686-66220-2); kivar bdg. 8.95 (ISBN 0-686-66221-0). Silver.

Japanese Gardens & Miniature Landscapes. 1.95 (ISBN 0-686-21133-2). Bklyn Botanic.

Seike, Kiyoshi & Kudo, Masanobu. A Japanese Touch for Your Garden. LC 79-66238. (Illus.). 80p. 1980. 14.95 (ISBN 0-87011-391-7). Kodansha.

GARDENING–UNITED STATES

Arp, Gerald. Tropical Gardening Along the Gulf Coast. LC 78-53815. (Illus.). 96p. 1978. pap. 3.95 (ISBN 0-88415-883-7). Pacesetter Pr.

Bush-Brown, James & Bush-Brown, Louise. America's Garden Book. rev. ed. New York Botanical Garden, ed. (Illus.). 1980. 22.50 (ISBN 0-684-16270-9, ScribT). Scribner.

Caterson, Lucile P. Handbook of Florida Flowers. (Orig.). pap. 1.95 (ISBN 0-8200-0405-7). Great Outdoors.

Clay, Horace F. & Hubbard, James C. Tropical Exotics. LC 77-7363. (Hawaii Garden Ser: No. 1). (Illus.). 1977. 35.00 (ISBN 0-8248-0465-1). U Pr of Hawaii.

Cowen, Claudine L. The Virginia Gardener's Calendar 1980. LC 79-12693. 1979. pap. 5.95 (ISBN 0-8139-0823-X). U Pr of Va.

Doolittle, Rosalie & Tiedebohl, Harriet. Southwest Gardening. rev. ed. LC 52-11535. (Illus.). 222p. 1967. pap. 6.95 (ISBN 0-8263-0027-8). U of NM Pr.

Favretti, Rudy & Favretti, Joy. For Every House a Garden: A Guide for Reproducing Period Gardens. LC 76-51128. (Illus.). 1977. pap. 4.95 (ISBN 0-87106-080-9). Globe Pequot.

Feinman, Jeffrey. U.S. Gardening Catalog. 1979. 14.95 (ISBN 0-671-24026-9); pap. 6.95 (ISBN 0-671-24861-8). S&S.

Florance, Chris. Carolina Home Gardener. LC 75-23480. 146p. 1976. 4.95 (ISBN 0-8078-1258-7). U of NC Pr.

Hazeltine, Cheryl & Filvaroff, Joan. The Central Texas Gardener. LC 79-7409. (Illus.). 242p. 1980. 12.50 (ISBN 0-89096-078-X); pap. 7.95 (ISBN 0-89096-086-0). Tex A&M Univ Pr.

Heutte, Frederic. Fred Heutte's Gardening in the Temperate Zone. LC 77-11096. (Illus.). 1977. 9.95 (ISBN 0-915442-35-3). Donning Co.

Hill, Lewis. Fruits & Berries for the Home Garden. (Illus.). 224p. (Orig.). 1980. pap. 6.95 (ISBN 0-88266-168-X). Garden Way Pub.

Kell, J. Carroll. Southern Landscape & Garden Design. LC 80-473. (Illus.). 116p. 1980. pap. 3.95 (ISBN 0-88415-811-X). Pacesetter Pr.

Kelly, George W. Rocky Mountain Horticulture. 3rd ed. (Illus.). 1967. pap. 7.50 (ISBN 0-87108-014-1). Pruett.

Kruckeberg, Arthur. Gardening with Natives: An Illustrated Guide to Growing Plants of Ornamental Value Native to the Pacific Northwest. (Illus.). 1982. price not set. U of Wash Pr.

Lawrence, Elizabeth. A Southern Garden: A Handbook for the Middle South. rev. ed. LC 67-30978. (Illus.). 1967. 10.00 (ISBN 0-8078-1057-6). U of NC Pr.

McEachern, George R. Growing Fruits, Berries & Nuts in the South. LC 77-99266. (Illus.). 96p. 1978. pap. 3.95 (ISBN 0-88415-299-5). Pacesetter Pr.

McGourty, Frederick, Jr., ed. American Gardens: A Traveler's Guide. (Illus.). 1977. pap. 1.95 (ISBN 0-686-21107-3). Bklyn Botanic.

M'Mahon, Bernard. The American Gardener's Calendar: Adapted to the Climates & Seasons of the United States. 1977. Repr. of 1806 ed. 25.00 (ISBN 0-913728-25-X). Theophrastus.

Noel Hume, Audrey. Archaeology & the Colonial Gardener. LC 73-80008. (Archaeological Ser: No. 7). (Illus.). 96p. (Orig.). 1974. pap. 2.25 (ISBN 0-87935-012-1). Williamsburg.

Nunn, William L., et al. A Minnesota Gardener's Companion. LC 81-2480. (Illus.). 1981. pap. 7.50 (ISBN 0-932272-05-3). Minneapolis Star.

Perry, Mac. Florida Lawn & Garden Care. (Illus.). 1977. cancelled (ISBN 0-912458-98-4). E A Seemann.

--Mac Perry's Florida Lawn & Garden Care. 1980. pap. 7.95 (ISBN 0-916224-57-0). Banyan Bks.

Pettingill, Amos. The White-Flower-Farm Garden Book. 1977. pap. 6.95 (ISBN 0-316-70400-8). Little.

Piscatagua Gardening Club, compiled by. Gardening from the Merrimack to the Kennebec: A Personal Approach to Growing Flowers, Herbs, Fruits & Vegetables. rev. ed. LC 78-9726. 1978. pap. 6.95 (ISBN 0-917890-11-6). Heritage Bk.

Reynolds, Bruford S. How to Survive with Sprouting. 112p. 1970. pap. 3.50 (ISBN 0-89036-028-6). Hawkes Pub Inc.

River Oaks Garden Club, ed. Garden Book for Houston & the Gulf Coast. LC 75-5316. (Illus.). 191p. (Includes planting calendar). 1975. 8.95 (ISBN 0-88415-350-9). Pacesetter Pr.

Roberts, Pasco. Florida Gardening Book. LC 62-52630. (Orig.). pap. 3.95 (ISBN 0-8200-0402-2). Great Outdoors.

Rockwell, Frederick F. & Grayson, Esther C. Rockwells' Complete Guide to Successful Gardening. LC 64-13854. 1965. 12.50 (ISBN 0-385-02453-3). Doubleday.

Ross, Alison. Gardening with Children. (Illus.). 200p. 14.95 (ISBN 0-571-11564-0, Pub. by Faber & Faber). Merrimack Bk Serv.

Schuler, Stanley. Gardens Are for Eating. 1971. 9.95 (ISBN 0-02-607410-9). Macmillan.

Smiley, Nixon. Florida Gardening Month by Month. LC 78-125661. (Illus.). 1980. pap. 7.95 (ISBN 0-87024-302-0). U of Miami Pr.

--Tropical Planting & Gardening for South Florida & the West Indies. LC 61-9185. (Illus.). 1960. pap. 5.95 (ISBN 0-87024-008-0). U of Miami Pr.

Snyder, Leon C. Gardening in the Upper Midwest. LC 77-8650. (Illus.). 1980. pap. 6.95 (ISBN 0-8166-0959-4). U of Minn Pr.

--Gardening in the Upper Midwest. LC 77-8650. (Illus.). 1978. 12.50 (ISBN 0-8166-0833-4). U of Minn Pr.

--Trees & Shrubs for Northern Gardens. LC 79-27179. (Illus.). 1980. 17.95 (ISBN 0-8166-0943-8). U of Minn Pr.

Squibb, Robert. The Gardener's Calendar for South Carolina, Georgia, & North Carolina. LC 79-5191. (Brown Thrasher Bks.). 188p. 1980. Repr. of 1787 ed. 9.95 (ISBN 0-8203-0497-2). U of Ga Pr.

Webster, Bob. The South Texas Garden Book. 140p. (Orig.). 1980. pap. 10.95 (ISBN 0-931722-03-9). Corona Pub.

Willis, A. R. The Pacific Gardener. LC 75-35434. (Illus.). 150p. 1976. pap. 5.95 (ISBN 0-87564-620-4). Superior Pub.

GARDENS

see also Botanical Gardens; Garden Ornaments and Furniture; Garden Walks; Rock Gardens; Water Gardens

Althea. How Does Your Garden Grow. (ps-2). 1979. pap. 1.75 available in 5 pk (ISBN 0-85122-178-5, Pub. by Dinosaur Pubns). Merrimack Bk Serv.

Bowles, Edward A. My Garden in Spring. LC 78-178004. (Illus.). 1971. Repr. of 1914 ed. 12.50 (ISBN 0-685-61145-0). Theophrastus.

Burgess, Lorraine M. Garden Art: The Personal Pursuit of Artistic Refinements, Inventive Concepts, Old Follies, & New Conceits for the Home Gardener. (Illus.). 192p. 1981. 25.00 (ISBN 0-8027-0665-7). Walker & Co.

Certaine Excellent Knots & Mazes, for Plots of Gardens. LC 73-6148. (English Experience Ser.: No. 611). 1973. Repr. of 1623 ed. 5.00 (ISBN 90-221-0611-X). Walter J Johnson.

Clarkson, Rosetta E. The Golden Age of Herbs & Herbalists. (Illus.). 352p. 1972. pap. 5.00 (ISBN 0-486-22869-X). Dover.

Earle, Alice M. Old Time Gardens, Newly Set Forth. LC 68-31219. (Illus.). 1968. Repr. of 1901 ed. 22.00 (ISBN 0-8103-3429-1). Gale.

Encyclopedie Des Jardins et Maisons De Compagne. 500p. (Fr.). 27.50 (ISBN 0-686-57142-8, M-6199). French & Eur.

Favretti, Rudy J. & Favretti, Joy P. Landscapes & Gardens for Historic Buildings: A Handbook for Reproducing & Creating Authentic Landscape Settings. LC 78-17200. (Illus.). 1979. pap. 10.00 (ISBN 0-910050-34-1). AASLH.

Fuller, Henry B. Gardens of This World. 59.95 (ISBN 0-8490-0210-9). Gordon Pr.

Gothein, Marie-Luise. A History of Garden Art, 2 vols. LC 67-4274. (Illus.). 1979. Set. lib. bdg. 120.00 (ISBN 0-87817-008-1). Hacker.

Grant, John & Grant, Carol. Garden Design Illustrated. LC 54-12725. (Illus.). 172p. 1978. pap. 10.95 (ISBN 0-295-95608-9). U of Wash Pr.

Gunther, R. W., ed. Early British Botanists & Their Gardens. Repr. of 1922 ed. 18.00 (ISBN 0-527-36850-4). Kraus Repr.

Harris, John. A Garden Alphabet. (Octopus Bk.). (Illus.). 1979. 14.95 (ISBN 0-7064-1082-3, Mayflower Bks). Smith Pubs.

Harrison, S. G. Garden Shrubs & Trees. 9.75x (ISBN 0-392-06725-0, LTB). Sportshelf.

Hunter, Margaret K. & Hunter, Edgar H. The Indoor Garden: Design, Construction & Furnishing. LC 77-20942. 1978. 27.00 (ISBN 0-471-03016-3, Pub. by Wiley-Interscience). Wiley.

Huxley, Anthony. Financial Times Book of Garden Design. 9.50 (ISBN 0-7153-6777-3). David & Charles.

Johnson, Heather & Worl, Barbara. Garden Open Today: Heritage Rose Garden Tours 1982-1983. (Illus.). 85p. (Orig.). 1981. pap. 5.00 (ISBN 0-936736-04-6). Sweetbrier.

King, Ronald. Quest for Paradise: A History of the World's Gardens. LC 78-10812. (Illus.). 1979. 24.95 (ISBN 0-8317-7281-6, Mayflower Bks); pre-Jan. 1980 19.95 (ISBN 0-686-25732-4). Smith Pubs.

Langdon, E. Pioneer Gardens. (Winston Mine Editions). 1972. 7.95 (ISBN 0-685-33407-4); pap. 3.95 (ISBN 0-685-33408-2). HR&W.

Lehrman, Jonas. Earthly Paradise: Garden & Courtyard in Islam. LC 80-53153. (Illus.). 240p. 1981. 55.00 (ISBN 0-520-04363-4); prepub. 45.00 pre-Dec (ISBN 0-686-72560-3). U of Cal Pr.

Lewis, Richard. In a Spring Garden. LC 65-23965. (Illus.). 32p. (gr. k-3). 1976. pap. 1.75 (ISBN 0-8037-4033-6, Pied Piper). Dial.

Midgley, Kenneth. Garden Design. (Illus.). 224p. 1977. 12.95 (ISBN 0-7207-0982-2, Pub. by Michael Joseph). Merrimack Bk Serv.

Miniature Gardens. 1.95 (ISBN 0-686-21152-9). Bklyn Botanic.

More, Daphne. Ideas for Interesting Gardens. 1974. 5.95 (ISBN 0-7153-6445-6). David & Charles.

Moynihan, Elizabeth B. Paradise As a Garden: In Persia & Mughal India. (Illus.). 1979. 19.95 (ISBN 0-8076-0931-5); pap. 9.95 (ISBN 0-8076-0933-1). Braziller.

Nichols, R. Spanish & Portuguese Gardens. 1976. 59.95 (ISBN 0-8490-2646-6). Gordon Pr.

Phillips, C. E. Design of Small Gardens. (Illus.). 1969. 9.00x (ISBN 0-434-43654-2). Intl Pubns Serv.

Plants & Gardens, in Persian, Mughanl & Turkish Art. 1981. pap. 6.00x (ISBN 0-904654-27-3, Pub. by Brit Lib England). State Mutual Bk.

Proudley, Brian & Proudley, Valerie. Garden Flowers in Colors. (Illus.). 236p. 1980. pap. 6.95 (ISBN 0-7137-1120-5, Pub. by Blandford Pr England). Sterling.

Rohde, Eleanour S. Garden-Craft in the Bible, & Other Essays. facs. ed. LC 67-26775. (Essay Index Reprint Ser). 1927. 18.00 (ISBN 0-8369-0829-5). Arno.

Sanders, Rhea. The Fire Gardens of Maylandia. 1980. 10.00 (ISBN 0-937684-10-4). Tradd St Pr.

Scott, Frank J. Victorian Gardens: The Art of Beautifying Suburban Home Grounds, a Victorian Guidebook of 1870. (Library of Victorian Culture). (Illus.). 1977. pap. text ed. 8.00 (ISBN 0-89257-023-7). Am Life Foun.

Singleton, Esther. Shakespeare Garden. LC 75-176028. (Illus.). Repr. of 1933 ed. 15.00 (ISBN 0-404-06096-X). AMS Pr.
Soper, Tony. Wildlife Begins at Home. LC 75-10700. 1975. 11.95 (ISBN 0-7153-7111-8). David & Charles.
Strong, Patience. The Glory of the Garden. 6.95x (ISBN 0-392-06806-0, LTB). Sportshelf.
Sunset Editors. Garden & Patio Building Book. LC 69-13278. (Illus.). 96p. 1969. pap. 3.95 (ISBN 0-376-01213-7, Sunset Bks.). Sunset-Lane.
Tanner, Ogden. Garden Construction. Time-Life Books, ed. (The Time-Life Encyclopdia of Gardening). (Illus.). 1978. 12.95 (ISBN 0-8094-2583-1). Time-Life.
Thacker, Christopher. The History of Gardens. 1979. 35.00 (ISBN 0-520-03736-7). U of Cal Pr.
Thompson. Descanso Gardens: Its History & Camellias. pap. 1.00 (ISBN 0-685-27805-0). Borden.
Van Ravenswaay, Charles. A Nineteenth-Century Garden. LC 77-70471. (Illus.). 1977. pap. 5.95 (ISBN 0-87663-976-7, Main Street). Universe.
Weaver, Lawrence. House & Gardens of Edwin Lutyens. (Illus.). 344p. 1981. 49.50 (ISBN 0-902028-98-7). Antique Collect.
Whitehead, Stanley B. The Observer's Book of Flowering Trees & Shrubs for Your Garden. (The Observer Bks). (Illus.). 1979. 3.95 (ISBN 0-684-16029-3, ScribT). Scribner.
Wilber, Donald N. & MacDougall, Elisabeth B. Persian Gardens & Garden Pavilions. 2nd ed. LC 78-13801. (Illus.). 1979. 15.00x (ISBN 0-88402-082-7, Ctr Landscape Arch). Dumbarton Oaks.

GARDENS–POETRY

Wood, Denis, compiled by. Poets in the Garden. (Illus.). 127p. 1979. 15.00 (ISBN 0-7195-3562-X). Transatlantic.

GARDENS–CHINA

Chambers, William. Designs of Chinese Buildings, Furniture, Dresses, Machines & Utensils. LC 68-17156. (Illus.). 1968. Repr. of 1757 ed. 50.00 (ISBN 0-405-08348-3, Blom Pubns). Arno.
Chinese Garden of Serenity. 1959. 2.95 (ISBN 0-442-82170-0). Peter Pauper.
Keswick, Maggie. The Chinese Garden. LC 78-57898. (Illus.). 1978. 40.00 (ISBN 0-8478-0193-4). Rizzoli Intl.
Soochow Gardens. 1980. 85.00 (ISBN 0-8351-0696-9). China Bks.

GARDENS–EUROPE

Bridgeman, Harriet & Drury, Elizabeth. Visiting the Gardens of Europe: A Guide to One Thousand Two Hundred Lovely Gardens Open to the Public. 1979. pap. 9.95 (ISBN 0-525-04700-X). Dutton.
Comito, Terry. The Idea of the Garden in the Renaissance. 1978. 19.00 (ISBN 0-8135-0841-X). Rutgers U Pr.
Von Erdberg, Eleanor. Chinese Influence on European Garden Structures. (Illus.). 1936. 75.00x (ISBN 0-686-51351-7). Elliots Bks.

GARDENS–FRANCE

Adams, William H. The French Garden, Fifteen-Hundred-Eighteen-Hundred. LC 78-24655. (Illus.). 1979. 19.95 (ISBN 0-8076-0918-8); pap. 9.95 (ISBN 0-8076-0919-6). Braziller.
Wiebenson, Dora. The Picturesque Garden in France. LC 77-22704. (Illus.). 1978. text ed. 40.00 (ISBN 0-691-03930-5). Princeton U Pr.

GARDENS–GREAT BRITAIN

Anthony, John. The Gardens of Britain, Six: Derbyshire, Leicestershire, Lincolnshire, Northamptonshire & Nottinghamshire. 1979. 24.00 (ISBN 0-7134-1745-5, Pub. by Batsford England). David & Charles.
Batey, Mavis. Oxford Gardens. 1981. 50.00x (ISBN 0-86127-002-9, Pub. by Avebury Pub England). State Mutual Bk.
Bisgrove, Richard. The Gardens of Britain, Three: Berkshire, Oxfordshire, Buckinghamshire, Bedfordshire, Hertfordshire. 1978. 24.00 (ISBN 0-7134-1178-3, Pub. by Batsford England). David & Charles.
British Tourist Authority. Discovering Gardens in Britain. (Illus.). 80p. 1981. pap. 2.95 (ISBN 0-85263-456-0, Pub. by Auto Assn-British Tourist Authority England). Merrimack Bk Serv.
Cecil, Mrs. Evelyn. London Parks & Gardens. 1981. Repr. of 1907 ed. lib. bdg. 75.00 (ISBN 0-8495-0759-6). Arden Lib.
Clark, H. F. The English Landscape Garden. (Illus.). 128p. 1980. text ed. 16.50x (ISBN 0-904387-38-0). Humanities.
Crisp, Frank. Mediaeval Gardens. LC 67-4273. (Illus.). 1979. lib. bdg. 75.00 (ISBN 0-87817-007-3). Hacker.
Eastwood, Dorothea. The Story of Our Gardens. LC 75-602. 1979. 4.95x (ISBN 0-900406-04-6, Pub. by G Fraser). Intl Schol Bk Serv.
--Story of Our Gardens. (Illus.). 1968. Repr. of 1958 ed. 4.50 (ISBN 0-900406-04-6). Dufour.
Evans, William. Law for Gardens & Small Estates. 197p. 1975. 7.95 (ISBN 0-7153-6738-2). David & Charles.
Eyler, Ellen C. Early English Gardens & Garden Books. LC 63-15259. (Folger Guides to the Age of Shakespeare). 1963. pap. 3.95 (ISBN 0-918016-30-4). Folger Bks.
Farrer, Reginald. In a Yorkshire Garden. LC 73-87457. (Illus.). 1973. Repr. of 1909 ed. 12.50 (ISBN 0-685-61147-7). Theophrastus.
Findhorn Community. The Findhorn Garden. LC 75-6335. (A Lindisfarne Book). (Illus.). 192p. (YA) 1975. 12.95 (ISBN 0-06-011249-2, HarpT). Har-Row.
Fleming, Laurence & Gore, Alan. The English Garden. (Illus.). 256p. 1981. 24.95 (ISBN 0-7181-1816-2, Pub. by Michael Joseph). Merrimack Bk Serv.
Hellyer, Arthur. Shell Guide to Gardens. LC 77-316964. (Illus.). 1977. 10.00x (ISBN 0-434-32627-5). Intl Pubns Serv.
Historic Houses, Castles & Gardens in Great Britain & Ireland, 1976. 1976. pap. 3.00x (ISBN 0-8277-0351-1). British Bk Ctr.
Hole, S. Reynolds. Our Gardens. 1979. Repr. of 1899 ed. lib. bdg. 20.00 (ISBN 0-8495-2282-X). Arden Lib.
Hunt, John D. & Willis, Peter, eds. The Genius of the Place: The English Landscape Garden, 1620-1820. LC 75-25073. (Illus.). 480p. 1976. 25.00 (ISBN 0-06-014669-9, HarpT). Har-Row.
Hunt, John Dixon. The Figure in the Landscape: Poetry, Painting, & Gardening during the Eighteenth Century. LC 76-17227. (Illus.). 288p. 1977. 19.50x (ISBN 0-8018-1795-1). Johns Hopkins.
Lees-Milne, Alvilde & Verey, Rosemary, eds. The Englishwoman's Garden. (Illus.). 160p. 1980. 24.95 (ISBN 0-7011-2395-8, Pub. by Chatto Bodley Jonathan). Merrimack Bk Serv.
Lemmon, Kenneth. The Gardens of Britain, Five: Yorkshire & Humberside. 1979. 24.00 (ISBN 0-7134-1743-9, Pub. by Batsford England). David & Charles.
Loewenfeld, Claire & Back, Philippa. Britain's Wild Larder. (Illus.). 192p. 1980. 19.95 (ISBN 0-7153-7971-2). David & Charles.
Macgregor, Jessie. Gardens of Celebrities & Celebrated Gardens in & Around London. 1979. Repr. of 1918 ed. lib. bdg. 20.00 (ISBN 0-8492-1743-1). R West.
MacLean, Theresa. Medieval English Gardens. LC 79-56277. (Illus.). 288p. 1981. 25.00 (ISBN 0-670-46482-1). Viking Pr.
Patterson, Allen. The Gardens of Britain, Two: Dorset, Hampshire and the Isle of Wight. 1978. 24.00 (ISBN 0-7134-0992-4, Pub. by Batsford England). David & Charles.
Phillips, C. E. & Barber, Peter N. The Rothschild Rhododendrons: A Record of the Gardens at Exbury. (Illus.). 1980. 65.00 (ISBN 0-02-597440-8). Macmillan.
Singleton, Esther. The Shakespeare Garden: With Numerous Illustrations from Photographs & Reproductions of Old Wood Cuts. LC 74-8203. 1974. Repr. of 1922 ed. 26.00 (ISBN 0-8103-4048-8). Gale.
Strong, Roy. The Rennaissance Garden in England. 1979. 24.95 (ISBN 0-500-01209-1). Thames Hudson.
Synge, Patrick M. The Gardens of Britain, One: Devon & Cornwall. 1977. 24.00 (ISBN 0-7134-0927-4, Pub. by Batsford England). David & Charles.
Taylor, Gladys. Old London Gardens. 1978. 9.95 (ISBN 0-86025-806-8). State Mutual Bk.
Thelwell, Norman. A Plank Bridge by a Pool. (Encore Edition). (Illus.). 1979. 3.95 (ISBN 0-684-16695-X, ScribT). Scribner.
Thomas, Graham S. Great Gardens of Britain. (Illus.). 1979. 19.95 (ISBN 0-8317-3974-6, Mayflower Bks). Smith Pubs.
Verney, Peter. The Gardens of Scotland. 1976. 19.95 (ISBN 0-7134-3170-9, Pub. by Batsford England). David & Charles.
Wright, Tom. The Gardens of Britain, Four: Kent, Sussex & Surrey. 1978. 24.00 (ISBN 0-7134-1281-X, Pub. by Batsford England). David & Charles.
Wroth, Warwick. The London Pleasure Gardens of the Eighteenth Century. (Anchon Bks. on Popular Entertainment Ser.). (Illus.). 1979. Repr. of 1896 ed. 19.50 (ISBN 0-208-01768-2, Archon). Shoe String.

GARDENS–IRELAND

Historic Houses, Castles & Gardens in Great Britain & Ireland, 1976. 1976. pap. 3.00x (ISBN 0-8277-0351-1). British Bk Ctr.
Malins, Edward & Bowe, Patrick. Irish Gardens & Demesnes from Eighteen Hundred Thirty. LC 80-51500. (Illus.). 192p. 1980. 35.00 (ISBN 0-8478-0342-2). Rizzoli Intl.

GARDENS–JAPAN

Engel, David H. Japanese Gardens for Today: A Practical Handbook. LC 59-8191. (Illus.). 1959. 35.00 (ISBN 0-8048-0301-3). C E Tuttle.
Hayakawa, Masao. The Garden Art of Japan. LC 72-92257. (Heibonsha Survey of Japanese Art Ser). (Illus.). 1973. 17.50 (ISBN 0-8348-1014-X). Weatherhill.
Holborn, Mark. The Ocean in the Sand: Japan-from Landscape to Garden. LC 78-58223. (Illus.). 1978. pap. 6.95 (ISBN 0-394-73628-1). Shambhala Pubns.
Itoh, Teiji. The Imperial Gardens of Japan. LC 75-117174. (Illus.). 1970. 85.00 (ISBN 0-8348-1507-9). Weatherhill.
--Space & Illusion in the Japanese Garden. (Illus.). 232p. 1980. pap. 9.95 (ISBN 0-8348-1522-2, Pub. by John Weatherhill Inc Japan). C E Tuttle.
Kanto, Shigemori. The Japanese Courtyard Garden: Landscape for Small Spaces. (Illus.). 238p. 1981. 150.00 (ISBN 0-8348-0164-7, Pub. by John Weatherhill Inc Tokyo). C E Tuttle.
Kuck, Loraine. The World of the Japanese Garden: From Chinese Origins to Modern Landscape Art. LC 68-26951. (Illus.). 416p. 1980. 37.50 (ISBN 0-8348-0029-2, Pub. by John Weatherhill Inc Japan). C E Tuttle.
Kuck, Lorraine. The World of the Japanese Garden. LC 68-26951. (Illus.). 414p. 1968. 37.50 (ISBN 0-8348-0029-2). Weatherhill.
Murphy, Wendy. Japanese Gardens. Time-Life Books, ed. (The Encyclopedia of Gardening Ser.). (Illus.). 1980. 12.95 (ISBN 0-8094-3204-8). Time-Life.
Saito, Katsuo. Japanese Gardens. (Illus.). 60p. 1980. pap. 4.50 (ISBN 0-89955-104-1, Pub. by Shufunotomo Japan). Intl Schol Bk Serv.
Schaarschmidt-Richter, Irmtraud & Mori, Osamu. Japanese Gardens. Seligman, Janet, tr. from Ger. LC 79-87439. 1979. 70.00 (ISBN 0-688-03538-8). Morrow.
Shigemori, Kanto. The Japanese Courtyard Garden. (Illus.). 238p. 1981. 125.00 (ISBN 0-686-76610-5). Weatherhill.
Treib, Marc & Herman, Ron. A Guide to the Gardens of Kyoto. 216p. 1980. pap. text ed. 9.95 (ISBN 0-89955-312-5, Pub. by Shufunotomo Japan). Intl Schol Bk Serv.
Valavanis, William N. Japanese Five-Needle Pine: Nature-Gardens-Bonsai-Taxonomy. new ed. Symmes, Edwin C., Jr., tr. LC 76-5780. (The Encyclopedia of Classical Bonsai Art: Vol. 2). (Illus.). 68p. 1976. lib. bdg. 15.00 (ISBN 0-916352-05-6); pap. text ed. 9.95 (ISBN 0-916352-04-8). Symmes Syst.

GARDENS–MEXICO

O'Gorman, Patricia W. Patios & Gardens of Mexico. (Illus.). 1979. 22.95 (ISBN 0-8038-0210-2). Hastings.
--Patios & Gardens of Mexico. (Illus.). 1979. 22.95 (ISBN 0-8038-0210-2). Architectural.

GARDENS–UNITED STATES

Briggs, Loutrel W. Charleston Gardens. LC 51-70. (Illus.). 1951. 19.50 (ISBN 0-87249-025-4). U of SC Pr.
Colonial Williamsburg Foundation Staff. Gardens of Williamsburg. LC 70-140635. (Illus., Orig.). 1970. pap. 2.95 (ISBN 0-910412-89-8). Williamsburg.
Forman, H. Chandlee. Old Buildings, Gardens & Furniture in Tidewater, Maryland. LC 67-17538. (Illus.). 1967. 12.50 (ISBN 0-87033-075-6, Pub. by Tidewater). Cornell Maritime.
Gleasner, Bill & Gleasner, Diana. Hawaiian Gardens: Photographed on Kauai. LC 77-73322. (Illus.). 1978. pap. 4.00 (ISBN 0-932596-01-0, Pub. by Oriental). Intl Schol Bk Serv.
Graydon, Nell S. South Carolina Gardens. LC 73-77103. 20.00 (ISBN 0-685-30850-2). Beaufort.
House & Garden. House & Garden's Twenty Six Easy Little Gardens. (Handbook Ser.). (Illus.). 1979. pap. 8.95 (ISBN 0-14-046390-9). Penguin.
King, Eleanor A. Bible Plants for American Gardens. (Illus.). 6.75 (ISBN 0-8446-5211-3). Peter Smith.
LeBlanc, Joyce Y. Pelican Guide to Gardens of Louisiana. (Pelican Guide Ser.). (Illus.). 64p. 1974. pap. 2.95 (ISBN 0-88289-003-4). Pelican.
Leighton, Ann. American Gardens in the Eighteenth Century: "for Use or for Delight". 1976. 17.50 (ISBN 0-395-24764-0). HM.
McFadden, Dorothy L. Oriental Gardens in America: A Visitor's Guide. LC 75-46014. 1976. 15.95 (ISBN 0-913264-21-0). Douglas-West.
McMillan, Mary L. & Jones, Ruth D. Beautiful North Carolina & the World of Flowers. LC 79-91037. (Illus.). 1979. 9.95 (ISBN 0-87716-110-0, Pub. by Moore Pub Co). F Apple.
Noel Hume, Audrey. Archaeology & the Colonial Gardener. LC 73-80008. (Archaeological Ser: No. 7). (Illus.). 96p. (Orig.). 1974. pap. 2.25 (ISBN 0-87935-012-1). Williamsburg.
Payne, Rolce R. An Illustrated & Annotated Guide to New England Gardens Open to the Public. LC 78-66191. (Godine Guides: No. II). (Illus.). 1979. 17.50x (ISBN 0-87923-271-4); pap. 8.50 (ISBN 0-87923-272-2). Godine.
Shaffer, E. T. Carolina Gardens. (Illus.). 1963. 15.00 (ISBN 0-8159-5200-7). Devin.
Smith, J. Robert & Smith, Beatrice S. A Prairie Garden: Seventy Plants You Can Grow in Town or Country. 128p. 1980. 22.50 (ISBN 0-299-08300-4); pap. 9.95 (ISBN 0-299-08304-7). U of Wis Pr.
Williams, Dorothy H. Historic Virginia Gardens: Preservations by the Garden Club of Virginia. LC 74-19422. (Illus.). 320p. 1975. 20.00x (ISBN 0-8139-0604-0). U Pr of Va.

GARDENS, MINIATURE

see also Bonkei

Crockett, James U. & Perl, Philip. Miniatures & Bonsai. (The Time-Life Encyclopedia of Gardening Ser.). (Illus.). 1979. lib. bdg. 11.96 (ISBN 0-686-51066-6). Silver.
Hillier, Florence B. Basic Guide to Flower Arranging. (Illus.). 296p. 1974. 16.95 (ISBN 0-07-028907-7, P&RB). McGraw.
Japanese Gardens & Miniature Landscapes. 1.95 (ISBN 0-686-21133-2). Bklyn Botanic.
Kawamoto, Toshio. Saikei: Living Landscapes in Miniature. LC 67-26311. (Illus.). 132p. 1980. pap. 8.95 (ISBN 0-87011-418-2). Kodansha.
Lavine, Sigmund A. Wonders of Terrariums. LC 77-6493. (Wonders Ser.). (Illus.). (gr. 5 up). 1977. PLB 5.95 (ISBN 0-396-07488-X). Dodd.
Lewis, Glenn. Terrariums: The World of Nature Under Glass. LC 73-84642. (Illus.). 112p. 1973. 15.95 (ISBN 0-87294-053-5). Country Beautiful.
McDonald, Elvin. Little Plants for Small Spaces. 1974. pap. 1.50 (ISBN 0-445-03035-6). Popular Lib.
--Little Plants for Small Spaces. LC 75-15794. (Illus.). 192p. 1975. 8.95 (ISBN 0-87131-195-X). M Evans.
Perl, Philip. Miniatures & Bonsai. Time-Life Books, ed. LC 78-20889. (Encyclopedia of Gardening Ser.). (Illus.). 1979. 12.95 (ISBN 0-8094-2641-2). Time-Life.

GARDENS IN ART AND LITERATURE

Giamatti, A. Bartlett. Earthly Paradise & the Renaissance Epic. 1966. 23.00x (ISBN 0-691-06030-4); pap. 6.50 (ISBN 0-691-01292-X). Princeton U Pr.
Watson, Paul F. The Garden of Love in Tuscan Art & the Early Renaissance. LC 75-33476. 242p. 1979. 27.50 (ISBN 0-87982-019-5). Art Alliance.

GARDINER, ALFRED GEORGE, 1865-1946

Koss, Stephen. Fleet Street Radical: A. G. Gardiner & the Daily News. 352p. 1973. 19.50 (ISBN 0-208-01312-1, Archon). Shoe String.

GARDINER, SAMUEL RAWSON, 1829-1902

Shaw, William A. Bibliography of the Historical Works of Dr. Creighton, Dr. Stubbs, Dr. S. R. Gardiner, & the Late Lord Acton. 1969. 17.50 (ISBN 0-8337-3242-0). B Franklin.

GARDINER, STEPHEN, 1483-1555

Donaldson, P. S., ed. A Machiavellian Treatise by Stephen Gardiner. LC 74-12963. (Studies in the History & Theory of Politics). 204p. 1976. 37.50 (ISBN 0-521-20593-X). Cambridge U Pr.
Muller, James A. Stephen Gardiner & the Tudor Reaction. LC 69-16755. 1969. Repr. lib. bdg. 20.00x (ISBN 0-374-96004-6). Octagon.

GARDINER, WILLIAM, 1531-1597

Hotson, Leslie. Shakespeare Versus Shallow. LC 74-95430. (Studies in Shakespeare, No. 24). 1970. Repr. of 1931 ed. lib. bdg. 39.95 (ISBN 0-8383-0981-X). Haskell.
--Shakespeare Versus Shallow. LC 74-109652. (Select Bibliographies Reprint Ser). 1931. 22.00 (ISBN 0-8369-5261-8). Arno.

GARDINER FAMILY

Hotson, Leslie. Shakespeare Versus Shallow. LC 74-95430. (Studies in Shakespeare, No. 24). 1970. Repr. of 1931 ed. lib. bdg. 39.95 (ISBN 0-8383-0981-X). Haskell.
--Shakespeare Versus Shallow. LC 74-109652. (Select Bibliographies Reprint Ser). 1931. 22.00 (ISBN 0-8369-5261-8). Arno.

GARDNER, ERLE STANLEY, 1889-1970

Hughes, Dorothy B. Erle Stanley Gardner: The Case of the Real Perry Mason. 1978. 15.00 (ISBN 0-688-03282-6). Morrow.
Mundell, E. H. Erle Stanley Gardner: A Checklist. LC 70-97619. (Serif Ser.: No. 6). 1969. 6.50x (ISBN 0-87338-034-7). Kent St U Pr.

GARDNER, ISABELLA (STEWART) 1840-1924

Carter, Morris. Isabella Stewart Gardner & Fenway Court. 3rd ed. (Illus.). 1972. Repr. of 1925 ed. 8.00 (ISBN 0-914660-07-1). I S Gardner Mus.

GARDNER, JOHN

Renwick, Joyce & Smith, Howard. John Gardner: An Interview. (New London Interviews). 1980. signed ltd. ed. 10.00 (ISBN 0-89683-027-6); pap. 3.95 (ISBN 0-89683-026-8). New London Pr.

GARFIELD, JAMES ABRAM, PRES. U. S., 1831-1881

Bates, Richard O. The Gentleman from Ohio: A Biography of James A. Garfield. LC 72-90712. 1973. 12.95 (ISBN 0-87716-039-2, Pub. by Moore Pub Co). F Apple.

Doenecke, Justus D. The Presidencies of James A. Garfield & Chester A. Arthur. LC 80-18957. (The American Presidency Ser.). 232p. 1981. 15.00x (ISBN 0-7006-0208-9). Regents Pr KS.

Leech, Margaret & Brown, Harry J. The Garfield Orbit: The Life of President James A. Garfield. LC 76-5140. (Illus.). 1978. 15.00 (ISBN 0-06-012551-9, HarpT). Har-Row.

Norris, James D. & Shaffer, Arthur H., eds. Politics & Patronage in the Gilded Age: The Correspondence of James A. Garfield & Charles E. Henry. LC 70-629850. (Illus.). 1970. 15.00 (ISBN 0-87020-107-7). State Hist Soc Wis.

Peskin, Allan. Garfield. LC 77-15630. 1978. 20.00x (ISBN 0-87338-210-2). Kent St U Pr.

Williams, Frederick D. & Brown, Harry J., eds. Diary of James A. Garfield: Vol. 1, 1848-1871, Vol. 2, 1872-1874, 2 Vols. 1967. Set. 30.00x (ISBN 0-87013-111-7). Mich St U Pr.

Williams, Frederick D & Brown, Harry J., eds. The Diary of James A. Garfield, Vol. 3: 1875-1877. 600p. 22.50x (ISBN 0-87013-169-9). Mich St U Pr.

GARFIELD, JOHN

Gelman, Howard. The Films of John Garfield. (Illus.). 256p. 1975. 14.00 (ISBN 0-8065-0490-0). Citadel Pr.

--The Films of John Garfield. 1977. pap. 6.95 (ISBN 0-8065-0620-2). Citadel Pr.

Swindell, Larry. Body & Soul: The Story of John Garfield. LC 74-31470. 320p. 1975. 8.95 (ISBN 0-688-02907-8). Morrow.

GARFIELD COUNTY, COLORADO-HISTORY

Urquhart, Lena M. Cold Snows of Carbonate. (Illus.). 1967. pap. 1.00 (ISBN 0-87315-004-X). Golden Bell.

GARIBALDI, GIUSEPPE, 1807-1882

Abba, Giuseppe C. The Diary of One of Garibaldi's Thousand. Vincent, E. R., tr. from Ital. LC 80-24181. (Oxford Library of Italian Classics). (Illus.). xxi, 166p. 1981. Repr. of 1962 ed. lib. bdg. 18.75x (ISBN 0-313-22446-3, ABDO). Greenwood.

Delzell, Charles F., ed. The Unification of Italy, 1859-1861, Cavour, Mazzini, or Garibaldi? LC 76-15352. (European Problem Studies Ser.). 126p. 1976. pap. text ed. 5.50 (ISBN 0-88275-658-3). Krieger.

De Polnay, Peter. Garibaldi: The Legend & the Man. LC 75-22641. (Illus.). 234p. 1976. Repr. of 1960 ed. lib. bdg. 15.75x (ISBN 0-8371-8361-8, DEGA). Greenwood.

Hibbert, Christopher. Garibaldi & His Enemies. 1970. pap. 3.95 (ISBN 0-452-25031-5, Z5031, Plume). NAL.

Larg, David. Giuseppe Garibaldi: A Biography. LC 73-112811. 1970. Repr. of 1934 ed. 14.50 (ISBN 0-8046-1078-9). Kennikat.

Rudman, Harry. Italian Nationalism & English Letters. LC 72-182707. Repr. of 1940 ed. 17.50 (ISBN 0-404-05450-1). AMS Pr.

Tames, Richard. Garibaldi & the Risorgimento. (Jackdaw Ser: No. 74). (Illus.). 1970. 6.95 (ISBN 0-670-33551-7, Grossman). Viking Pr.

Trevelyan, George M. Garibaldi & the Thousand. lib. bdg. 30.00 (ISBN 0-8414-8406-6). Folcroft.

--Garibaldi & the Thousand. LC 75-41274. Repr. of 1909 ed. 32.50 (ISBN 0-404-14729-1). AMS Pr.

--Garibaldi's Defence of the Roman Republic, 1848-9. LC 76-156214. (Illus.). 1971. Repr. of 1912 ed. lib. bdg. 21.25x (ISBN 0-8371-6165-7, TRGD). Greenwood.

Viotti, Andrea. Garibaldi: The Revolutionary & His Men. (Illus.). 224p. 1980. 22.50 (ISBN 0-7137-0942-1, Pub. by Blandford Pr England). Sterling.

GARIBALDI, GIUSEPPE, 1807-1882-JUVENILE LITERATURE

Baker, Nina B. Garibaldi. (Illus.). (gr. 7-9). 1944. 6.95 (ISBN 0-8149-0264-2). Vanguard.

Trease, Geoffrey. Follow My Black Plume. LC 63-13784. (gr. 6-10). 6.95 (ISBN 0-8149-0426-2). Vanguard.

GARLAND, HAMLIN, 1860-1940

Ahnebrink, Lars. Beginnings of Naturalism in American Fiction, 1891-1903. LC 61-13093. 1961. Repr. of 1950 ed. 18.50 (ISBN 0-8462-0105-4). Russell.

Bryer, Jackson, et al. Hamlin Garland & the Critics: An Annotated Bibliography. LC 75-183300. v, 280p. 1973. 12.50x (ISBN 0-87875-020-7). Whitston Pub.

Gish, Robert. Hamlin Garland: The Far West. LC 76-45134. (Western Writers Ser.: No. 24). 1976. pap. 2.00 (ISBN 0-88430-023-4). Boise St Univ.

Pizer, Donald. Hamlin Garland's Early Work & Career. LC 69-17842. 1969. Repr. of 1960 ed. 9.00 (ISBN 0-8462-1329-X). Russell.

GARLAND, JUDY, 1922-1969

Baxter, Brian. The Films of Judy Garland. Castell, David, ed. (The Films of...Ser.). (Illus.). (gr. 7-12). 1978. Repr. of 1974 ed. PLB 5.95 (ISBN 0-912616-81-4). Greenhaven.

DiOrio, Al, Jr. Little Girl Lost: The Life & Hard Times of Judy Garland. (Illus.). 256p. 1975. pap. 1.50 (ISBN 0-532-15155-0). Woodhill.

Epstein, Ed & Morella, Joe. Judy: The Films of Judy Garland. 1970. 8.95 (ISBN 0-685-03373-2); pap. 6.95 (ISBN 0-8065-0206-1, 0206-1). Citadel Pr.

Finch, Christopher. Rainbow: The Stormy Life of Judy Garland. LC 74-5632. (Illus.). 256p. 1975. pap. 4.95 (ISBN 0-448-11731-2, MSP); pap. 7.95 (ISBN 0-448-12142-5). G&D.

GARLIC

Airola, Paavo. The Miracle of Garlic. 2.00 (ISBN 0-686-29852-7). Cancer Bk Hse.

Harris, Lloyd J. The Book of Garlic. 3rd rev. ed. (Illus.). 1980. pap. 8.95 (ISBN 0-915572-29-X). Panjandrum.

GARMENT CUTTING

see also Dressmaking-Pattern Design

Burda, ed. Whitework & Cutwork. (Burda Bks.). Date not set. 3.00x (ISBN 0-686-64667-3, B803). Toggitt.

Croonborg, Frederick T. The Blue Book of Men's Tailoring. 1977. 15.95 (ISBN 0-442-21763-3). Van Nos Reinhold.

Fernald, Mary & Shenton, Eileen. Costume Design & Making. 2nd ed. LC 67-14505. (Illus.). 1967. 14.95 (ISBN 0-87830-021-X). Theatre Arts.

Hillhouse, Marion S. & Mansfield, E. A. Dress Design: Draping & Flat Pattern Making. LC 48-7554. 1948. text ed. 19.50 (ISBN 0-395-04627-0, 3-25310). HM.

Minott, Jan. Fitting Commercial Patterns: The Minott Method. LC 77-87335. 1978. spiral bdg. 11.95x (ISBN 0-8087-3907-7). Burgess.

Oblander, Ruth. Slacks for Perfect Fit: Sew-Fit Method. LC 81-50280. (Illus.). 64p. 1981. pap. 3.04 (ISBN 0-933956-07-X); tchrs. ed. 3.04 (ISBN 0-686-31776-9). Sew-Fit.

GARMENT WORKERS

see Clothing Workers

GARNET, HENRY HIGHLAND, 1815-1882

Schor, Joel A. Henry Highland Garnet: A Voice of Black Radicalism in the 19th Century. LC 76-8746. (Contributions in American History Ser: No. 54). (Illus.). 256p. 1977. lib. bdg. 15.95x (ISBN 0-8371-8937-3, SHG/). Greenwood.

GARNETT, EDWARD, 1868-1937

Bates, Herbert E. Edward Garnett. LC 74-8320. 1974. Repr. of 1950 ed. lib. bdg. 12.50 (ISBN 0-8414-4505-2). Folcroft.

Hudson, W. H. Letters from W. H. Hudson to Edward Garnett. 1925. 30.00 (ISBN 0-932062-87-3). Sharon Hill.

GARNIER, ROBERT, 1544-1590

Garnier, Robert. Two Tragedies: Hippolyte and Marc Antoine. Hill, Christine M. & Morrison, Mary G., eds. (Renaissance Ser). 181p. 1975. text ed. 23.50x (ISBN 0-485-13809-3, Athlone Pr); pap. text ed. 13.00x (ISBN 0-485-12809-8). Humanities.

Jondorf, Gillian. Robert Garnier & the Themes of Political Tragedy. LC 69-11027. 1969. 36.00 (ISBN 0-521-07386-3). Cambridge U Pr.

Wieringa, L. La Troade de Robert Garnier. 1970. 10.70x (ISBN 90-232-0817-X, Pub by Van Gorcum). Intl Schol Bk Serv.

Witherspoon, Alexander M. Influence of Robert Garnier on Elizabethan Drama. LC 68-15697. 1967. Repr. of 1924 ed. 6.50 (ISBN 0-87753-046-7). Phaeton.

--Influence of Robert Garnier on Elizabethan Drama. (Yale Studies in English Ser.: No. 65). 1968. Repr. of 1924 ed. 15.00 (ISBN 0-208-00650-8, Archon). Shoe String.

GARNIER, TONY

Wiebenson, Dora. Tony Garnier: The Cite Industrielle. LC 79-78051. (Planning & Cities Ser). (Illus.). 1969. 7.95 (ISBN 0-8076-0515-8). Braziller.

GARNISHES IN COOKERY

see Cookery (Garnishes)

GARNISHMENT

see Attachment and Garnishment

GARRETT, EILEEN JEANETTE (LYTTLE), 1893-

Garrett, Eileen J. My Life As a Search for the Meaning of Mediumship. LC 75-7380. (Perspectives in Psychical Research Ser.). 1975. Repr. of 1939 ed. 15.00x (ISBN 0-405-07030-6). Arno.

GARRETT, PATRICK FLOYD, 1850-1908

Metz, Leon C. Pat Garrett: The Story of a Western Lawmen. (Illus.). 305p. 1974. 14.95 (ISBN 0-8061-1067-8). U of Okla Pr.

Scanland, John M. Life of Pat F. Garrett. (Wild & Woolly West Ser., No. 17). (Illus.). 1970. 7.00 (ISBN 0-910584-18-4); pap. 1.50 (ISBN 0-910584-76-1). Filter.

GARRETT COUNTY, MARYLAND-HISTORY

Scharf, John T. History of Western Maryland: Including Biographical Sketches of Their Representative Men, 2 Vols. LC 68-26127. (Illus.). 1968. Repr. of 1882 ed. Set. 85.00 (ISBN 0-8063-7965-0). Regional.

Streaker, Margaret M. Taming the Savage River. 1968. 5.25 (ISBN 0-87012-032-8). McClain.

GARRICK, DAVID, 1717-1779

Barton, Margaret. Garrick. LC 78-612. (Illus.). 312p. 1978. Repr. of 1949 ed. lib. bdg. 24.50x (ISBN 0-313-20270-2, BAGAR). Greenwood.

Berkowitz, Gerald M. David Garrick: A Reference Guide. (Scholarly Reference Publications). 1980. lib. bdg. 34.00 (ISBN 0-8161-8136-5). G K Hall.

Burnim, Kalman A. David Garrick: Director. LC 72-11834. (Arcturus Books Paperbacks). 250p. 1973. pap. 6.95 (ISBN 0-8093-0625-5). S Ill U Pr.

David Garrick, Seventeen Seventeen - Seventeen Seventy-Nine. 1981. pap. 9.00x (ISBN 0-904654-40-0, Pub. by Brit Lib England). State Mutual Bk.

Davies, Thomas. Memoirs of the Life of David Garrick, 2 vols. Jones, Stephen, ed. LC 73-82825. 1808. Set. 40.00 (ISBN 0-405-08438-2); 20.00 ea. Vol. 1 (ISBN 0-405-08439-0). Vol. 2 (ISBN 0-405-08440-4). Arno.

England, Martha W. Garrick & Stratford. LC 62-17403. (Illus., Orig.). 1962. pap. 5.00 (ISBN 0-87104-084-0). NY Pub Lib.

--Garrick's Jubilee. LC 64-17109. 1964. 6.25 (ISBN 0-8142-0046-X). Ohio St U Pr.

Hedgcock, Frank A. David Garrick & His French Friends. LC 70-81976. (Illus.). 1912. 22.00 (ISBN 0-405-08610-5, Blom Pubns). Arno.

Knight, Joseph. David Garrick. LC 74-91904. 1894. 17.00 (ISBN 0-405-08711-X, Blom Pubns). Arno.

Murphy, Arthur. Life of Garrick, 2 Vols. in 1. LC 76-84521. 1801. 30.00 (ISBN 0-405-08811-6, Pub. by Blom). Arno.

Parsons, Mrs. Clement. Garrick & His Circle. 417p. 1980. Repr. lib. bdg. 50.00 (ISBN 0-8495-4367-3). Arden Lib.

Parsons, Florence M. Garrick & His Circle. LC 78-82837. (Illus.). 1906. 20.00 (ISBN 0-405-08836-1, Pub. by Blom). Arno.

Pedicord, Harry W. Theatrical Public in the Time of Garrick. LC 53-12030. (Arcturus Books Paperbacks). 281p. 1966. lib. bdg. 7.00x (ISBN 0-8093-0221-7); pap. 2.65 (ISBN 0-8093-0222-5). S Ill U Pr.

Price, Cecil. Theatre in the Age of Garrick. (Drama & Theatre Studies). (Illus.). 212p. 1973. 16.50x (ISBN 0-87471-151-7). Rowman.

Reynolds, Joshua. Johnson & Garrick. LC 74-5045. 1927. Repr. lib. bdg. 10.00 (ISBN 0-8414-7293-9). Folcroft.

Stein, Elizabeth P. David Garrick, Dramatist. 315p. 1980. Repr. of 1937 ed. lib. bdg. 40.00 (ISBN 0-89760-827-5). Telegraph Bks.

--David Garrick, Dramatist. LC 67-23859. 1937. 18.00 (ISBN 0-405-08994-5, Pub. by Blom). Arno.

--David Garrick, Dramatist. (MLA Revolving Fund Ser.: No. 7). 1938. pap. 20.00 (ISBN 0-527-86100-6). Kraus Repr.

Stone, George W., Jr. The Journal of David Garrick. 1979. Repr. of 1939 ed. lib. bdg. 20.00 (ISBN 0-8495-5033-5). Arden Lib.

Stone, George W., Jr. & Kahrl, George M. David Garrick: A Critical Biography. LC 79-9476. (Illus.). 791p. 1979. 60.00x (ISBN 0-8093-0931-9). S Ill U Pr.

GARRISON, JAMES, 1921-

James, Rosemary & Wardlaw, Jack. Plot or Politics: The Garrison Case & Its Cast. (Illus.). 1967. pap. 2.95 (ISBN 0-911116-11-7). Pelican.

GARRISON, WILLIAM LLOYD, 1805-1879

Chapman, John J. William Lloyd Garrison. (American Newspapermen 1790-1933 Ser.). 1974. Repr. 17.50x (ISBN 0-8464-0027-8). Beekman Pubs.

Chapman, John Jay. William Lloyd Garrison. 1913. 15.00 (ISBN 0-8414-3016-0). Folcroft.

Chertkov, Vladimir. Short Biography of William Lloyd Garrison. LC 78-111569. Repr. of 1904 ed. 10.50x (ISBN 0-8371-4590-2). Greenwood.

Crosby, Ernest. Garrison the Non-Resistant. LC 72-137534. (Peace Movement in America Ser). 141p. 1972. Repr. of 1905 ed. lib. bdg. 9.95x (ISBN 0-89198-062-8). Ozer.

Fredrickson, George, ed. William Lloyd Garrison. (Great Lives Observed Ser). 1969. 8.95 (ISBN 0-13-346858-5, Spec); pap. 1.95 (ISBN 0-13-346841-0, Spec). P-H.

Garrison, Wendell P. William Lloyd Garrison, 1805-1879. LC 79-88431. 1885-1889. Repr. 63.00x (ISBN 0-8371-2479-4). Greenwood.

Garrison, Wendell P. & Garrison, Francis J. William Lloyd Garrison, Eighteen Hundred Five to Eighteen Seventy-Nine, 4 Vols. LC 71-82191. (Anti-Slavery Crusade in America Ser). 1969. Repr. of 1885 ed. Set. 74.00 (ISBN 0-405-00629-2); 20.00 ea. Vol. 1 (ISBN 0-405-00671-3). Vol. 2 (ISBN 0-405-00672-1). Vol. 3 (ISBN 0-405-00673-X). Vol. 4 (ISBN 0-405-00674-8). Arno.

Garrison, William L. William Lloyd Garrison on Non-Resistance. LC 73-10286. (American History & Americana Ser., No. 47). 1973. Repr. lib. bdg. 49.95 (ISBN 0-8383-1717-0). Haskell.

Grimke, Archibald H. William Lloyd Garrison, the Abolitionist. LC 73-168207. Repr. of 1891 ed. 12.50 (ISBN 0-404-00057-6). AMS Pr.

--William Lloyd Garrison, the Abolitionist. LC 75-92746. Repr. of 1891 ed. 15.00x (ISBN 0-8371-2190-6). Greenwood.

Johnson, Oliver. W. L. Garrison & His Times. facs. ed. LC 74-89400. (Black Heritage Library Collection Ser). 1881. 17.00 (ISBN 0-8369-8613-X). Arno.

--William Lloyd Garrison & His Times. pap. 3.95 (ISBN 0-685-16800-X, N310P). Mnemosyne.

Merrill, Walter M. Against Wind & Tide: A Biography of William Lloyd Garrison. LC 63-10871. (Illus.). 1963. 20.00x (ISBN 0-674-00950-9). Harvard U Pr.

--The Letters of William Lloyd Garrison: Vol. V, Let the Oppressed Go Free. LC 79-55430. 1979. 12 fiches 20.00 (ISBN 0-8357-0565-X, IS-00096, Pub. by Hist Soc PA). Univ Microfilms.

Merrill, Walter M., ed. Let the Oppressed Go Free, Eighteen Sixty-One to Eighteen Sixty-Seven. LC 75-133210. (Letters of William Lloyd Garrison Ser.: Vol. V). (Illus.). 1979. 37.50x (ISBN 0-674-52665-1, Belknap Pr). Harvard U Pr.

Nye, Russel B. William Lloyd Garrison & the Humanitarian Reformers. (Library of American Biography). 215p. 1969. pap. 4.95 (ISBN 0-316-61736-9). Little.

Villard, Fanny G., ed. William Lloyd Garrison on Nonresistance Together with a Personal Sketch by His Daughter and a Tribute by Leo Tolstoi. LC 74-137556. (Peace Movement in America Ser). xii, 79p. 1972. Repr. of 1924 ed. lib. bdg. 7.75x (ISBN 0-89198-087-3). Ozer.

Wolf, Charlotte. Garrison Community: A Study of an Overseas American Military Colony. LC 70-81523. (Contributions in Sociology Ser.: No. 2). 1969. lib. bdg. 15.50 (ISBN 0-8371-1853-0, WOG/). Greenwood.

GARVEY, MARCUS, 1887-1940

Burkett, Randall K. Garveyism As a Religious Movement: The Institutionalization of a Black Civil Religion. LC 78-15728. (ATLA Monograph Ser.: No. 13). 1978. 13.50 (ISBN 0-8108-1163-4). Scarecrow.

Burkett, Randall K., ed. Black Redemption: Churchmen Speak for the Garvey Movement. LC 77-81332. 1978. 17.50x (ISBN 0-87722-116-2). Temple U Pr.

Clarke, John H., ed. Marcus Garvey & the Vision of Africa. 1974. pap. 3.95 (ISBN 0-394-71888-7, Vin). Random.

Cronon, E. D., ed. Marcus Garvey. 1973. 6.95 (ISBN 0-13-556068-3). Brown Bk.

Cronon, E. David. Black Moses: The Story of Marcus Garvey & the Universal Negro Improvement Association. 2nd ed. (Illus.). 302p. 1969. pap. 7.95 (ISBN 0-299-01214-X). U of Wis Pr.

Davis, Lenwood G. & Sims, Janet L., eds. Marcus Garvey: An Annotated Bibliography. LC 80-653. xvi, 200p. 1980. lib. bdg. 22.50 (ISBN 0-313-22131-6, DMG/). Greenwood.

Essien-Udom, E. U. & Garvey, Amy, eds. More Philosophy & Opinions of Marcus Garvey: Previously Published Papers, Vol. 3. (Illus.). 248p. 1977. 22.50x (ISBN 0-7146-1751-2, F Cass Co); pap. 8.95x (ISBN 0-7146-4027-1). Biblio Dist.

Garvey, A. J. Garvey & Garveyism. 1970. pap. 2.95 (ISBN 0-02-032670-X, Collier). Macmillan.

Garvey, Amy J. Garvey & Garveyism. 1976. Repr. of 1970 ed. lib. bdg. 17.00x (ISBN 0-374-93015-5). Octagon.

Garvey, Amy J., ed. Philosophy & Opinions of Marcus Garvey; or, Africa for the Africans, 2 vols. in 1. 2nd rev. ed. (Illus.). 412p. 1977. 29.50x (ISBN 0-7146-1143-3, F Cass Co); pap. 12.50x (ISBN 0-7146-2120-X). Biblio Dist.

Maglangbayan, Shawna. Garvey, Lumumba, Malcolm: Black Nationalist-Separatists. 1972. 4.95 (ISBN 0-88378-022-4); pap. 2.95 (ISBN 0-88378-079-8). Third World.

Martin, Tony. Race First: The Ideological & Organizational Struggles of Marcus Garvey & the Universal Negro Improvement Assoc. LC 75-16968. (Contributions in Afro-American & African Studies: No. 19). 448p. 1976. lib. bdg. 18.50 (ISBN 0-8371-8280-8, MMG/). Greenwood.

Nembhard, Len S. The Trials & Triumphs of Marcus Garvey. LC 76-51869. 1978. lib. bdg. 22.00 (ISBN 0-527-66570-3). Kraus Repr.

Tolbert, Emory J. UNIA & Black Los Angeles: Ideology & Community in the American Garvey Movement. Hill, Robert A., ed. LC 80-18054. (Afro-American Culture & Society Monograph: No. 3). (Illus.). 138p. 1980. 13.95x (ISBN 0-934934-04-5); pap. 8.95x (ISBN 0-934934-05-3). Ctr Afro-Am Stud.

GARY, ELBERT HENRY, 1846-1927

Tarbell, Ida M. Life of Elbert H. Gary: The Story of Steel. Repr. of 1925 ed. lib. bdg. 19.75x (ISBN 0-8371-0675-3, TAEG). Greenwood.

GARY, INDIANA

Greer, Edward. Big Steel: Black Politics & Corporate Power in Gary, Indiana. LC 79-13178. 287p. 1981. 16.50 (ISBN 0-85345-490-6); pap. 6.50 (ISBN 0-85345-490-6). Monthly Rev.

GAS

see also Acetylene; Coal-Tar Products; Gas Manufacture and Works; Gases; Mineral Oils; Petroleum

Davis, Jerome A. High-Cost Oil & Gas Resources. 266p. 1981. 40.00x (ISBN 0-85664-588-5, Pub. by Croom Helm LTD England). Biblio Dist.

Hunt, V. Daniel. The Gasohol Handbook. (Illus.). 450p. 1981. 27.50 (ISBN 0-8311-1137-2). Indus Pr.

McGowan, J. W. & John, P. K. Gaseous Electronics. 132p. 1975. pap. 24.50 (ISBN 0-444-10777-0, North-Holland). Elsevier.

Medard, L. Gas Encyclopedia. 1976. 219.50 (ISBN 0-444-41492-4). Elsevier.

Seglin, Len, ed. Methanation of Synthesis Gas. LC 75-33967. (Advances in Chemistry Ser.: No. 146). 1975. 23.00 (ISBN 0-8412-0244-3). Am Chemical.

United Nations Institute for Training & Research. International Conference on the Future Supply of Nature-Made Petroleum & Gas: Proceedings. 1977. text ed. 76.00 (ISBN 0-08-021734-6); pap. text ed. 51.00 (ISBN 0-08-021735-4). Pergamon.

GAS-ANALYSIS

see Gases-Analysis

GAS, BOTTLED

see Liquefied Petroleum Gas

GAS, NATURAL

see also Boring; Gas Industry; Liquefied Natural Gas; Liquefied Petroleum Gas; Oil Fields

Breed, Alice G. The Change in Social Welfare from Deregulation: The Case of the Natural Gas Industry. LC 78-22683. (Energy in the American Economy Ser.). (Illus.). 1979. lib. bdg. 14.00x (ISBN 0-405-11986-0). Arno.

Brown, Keith C., ed. Regulation of the Natural Gas Producing Industry. LC 71-186502. (Resources for the Future Ser.). (Illus.). 271p. 1972. pap. 10.00x (ISBN 0-8018-1383-2). Johns Hopkins.

Callow, Clive. Power from the Sea: The Search for North Sea Oil & Gas. 190p. 1973. text ed. 12.00x (ISBN 0-575-01475-X). Verry.

Challa, Krishna. Investment & Returns in Exploration & the Impact on the Supply of Oil & Natural Gas Reserves. Bruchey, Stuart, ed. LC 78-22667. (Energy in the American Economy Ser.). (Illus.). 1979. lib. bdg. 14.00x (ISBN 0-405-11971-2). Arno.

Committee on Gas Production Opportunities. Potential for Increasing Production of Natural Gas from Existing Fields in the Near Term. 1978. pap. 6.25 (ISBN 0-309-02784-5). Natl Acad Pr.

Consumers Power Company. Fundamentals of Natural Gas. LC 74-100858. (Supervision Ser). 1970. pap. text ed. 10.95 (ISBN 0-201-01180-8). A-W.

Effect of Leaking Natural Gas on Soil & Vegetation in Urban Areas. (Agricultural Research Reports Ser.: 778). 1972. pap. 14.00 (ISBN 90-220-0401-5, PUDOC). Unipub.

Epple, Dennis. Petroleum Discoveries & Government Policy: An Econometric Study of Supply. LC 75-25626. 128p. 1975. text ed. 22.00 (ISBN 0-88410-420-6). Ballinger Pub.

Ffooks, Roger. Natural Gas by Sea: The Development of a New Technology. 234p. 1980. 45.00x (ISBN 0-85614-054-6). Nichols Pub.

Foster Associates. Energy Prices, 1960-73. LC 74-9503. (Ford Foundation Energy Policy Project Ser.). 280p. 1974. text ed. 25.00 (ISBN 0-88410-327-7); pap. text ed. 15.00 (ISBN 0-88410-330-7). Ballinger Pub.

Hawkins, Clark A. The Field Price Regulation of Natural Gas. LC 70-79582. ix, 268p. 1969. 12.00 (ISBN 0-8130-0427-6). U Presses Fla.

Hepple, Peter, ed. Outlook for Natural Gas: A Quality Fuel. LC 73-661. 268p. 1973. 32.95 (ISBN 0-470-37303-2). Halsted Pr.

Hooley, Richard W. Financing the Natural Gas Industry. LC 68-59256. (Columbia University. Studies in the Social Sciences: No. 602). Repr. of 1961 ed. 18.50 (ISBN 0-404-51602-5). AMS Pr.

Ikoku, Chi. Natural Gas Engineering. 776p. 1980. 49.00 (ISBN 0-87814-141-3). Pennwell Pub.

Kash, Don E., et al. Energy Under the Ocean: A Technology Assessment. LC 73-8374. (Illus.). 350p. 1973. pap. 9.95x (ISBN 0-8061-1145-3). U of Okla Pr.

Katz, D. L. Handbook of Natural Gas Engineering. 1959. 64.50 (ISBN 0-07-033384-X, P&RB). McGraw.

Klein, George D. Sandstone Depositional Models for Exploration for Fossil Fuels. LC 80-69772. (Illus.). 1975. text ed. 24.95x (ISBN 0-686-77016-1, CEPCO); pap. 18.95x (ISBN 0-8087-2978-0, CEPCO). Burgess.

Lawrence, Anthony G. Pricing & Planning in the U. S. Natural Gas Industry: An Econometric & Programming Study. Bruchey, Stuart, ed. LC 78-22693. (Energy in the American Economy Ser.). (Illus.). 1979. lib. bdg. 15.00x (ISBN 0-405-11996-8). Arno.

Lom, W. L. & Williams, A. F. Substitute Natural Gas: Manufacture & Properties. 1976. 49.95 (ISBN 0-470-15018-1). Halsted Pr.

Lovejoy, Wallace F. & Homan, Paul T. Methods of Estimating Reserves of Crude Oil, Natural Gas, & Natural Gas Liquids. (Resources for the Future Ser). 183p. (Orig.). 1965. pap. 4.00x (ISBN 0-8018-0398-5). Johns Hopkins.

MacAvoy, Paul W. Price Formation in Natural Gas Fields. LC 76-43984. (Yale Studies in Economics Ser.: No. 14). (Illus.). 1976. Repr. of 1962 ed. lib. bdg. 23.50 (ISBN 0-8371-8981-0, MAPF). Greenwood.

MacAvoy, Paul W. & Pindyck, Robert S. Price Controls & the Natural Gas Shortage. LC 75-10769. 1975. pap. 4.25 (ISBN 0-8447-3161-7). Am Enterprise.

Mangan, Frank. Pipeliners. LC 77-73481. (Illus.). 1977. 20.00 (ISBN 0-930208-06-4, Pub. by Guynes Press). Mangan Bks.

Mansvelt-Beck, Frederick W. & Wiig, Karl M. The Economics of Offshore Oil & Gas Supplies. LC 76-54558. (Illus.). 176p. 1977. 17.95 (ISBN 0-669-01306-4). Lexington Bks.

Marcus, Kenneth K. The National Government & the Natural Gas Industry, 1946-56: A Study in the Making of a National Policy. Bruchey, Stuart, ed. LC 78-22697. (Energy in the American Economy Ser.). (Illus.). 1979. lib. bdg. 72.00x (ISBN 0-405-12000-1). Arno.

Mead, Walter J., et al. Transporting Natural Gas from the Arctic: The Alternative Systems. LC 77-85373. 1977. pap. 5.25 (ISBN 0-8447-3270-2). Am Enterprise.

Moring, Frederick & Oliver, Joseph. Natural Gas Incremental Pricing: A Basic Guide. 1980. pap. 25.00 (ISBN 0-917386-30-2). Exec Ent.

Natural Gas Processing & Utilisation: Proceedings, No. 44, Dublin, April 1976. 420p. 1981. 160.00x (ISBN 0-85295-011-X, Pub. by Inst Chem Eng England). State Mutual Bk.

Netschert, Bruce C. The Future Supply of Oil & Gas: A Study of the Availability of Crude Oil, Natural Gas, & Natural Gas Liquids in the United States in the Period Through 1975. LC 77-23269. (Resources for the Future, Inc.). 1977. Repr. of 1958 ed. lib. bdg. 15.00 (ISBN 0-8371-9473-3, NEOG). Greenwood.

Neuner, Edward J. The Natural Gas Industry: Monopoly & Competition in the Field Markets. 1960. 16.95x (ISBN 0-8061-0463-5). U of Okla Pr.

Oil & Natural Gas Resources of Canada 1976: Oil Sands & Heavy Oils - the Prospects, 2 vols. 1978. pap. 5.50 set (ISBN 0-685-89403-7, 97, SSC); Vol. 1. pap. (ISBN 0-660-00859-9); Vol. 2. pap. (ISBN 0-685-89404-5). Unipub.

Page, John. Man Hour Cost Estimating Manual for Pipelines & Marine Structures. 1977. 25.00x (ISBN 0-87201-157-7). Gulf Pub.

Pierce, Richard J., Jr. Natural Gas Regulation Handbook. 1980. pap. 25.00 (ISBN 0-917386-29-9). Exec Ent.

Polanyi, George. What Price North Sea Gas. (Institute of Economic Affairs, Hobart Papers Ser.: No. 38). pap. 2.50 (ISBN 0-255-69556-X). Transatlantic.

Pritchard, R., et al. Handbook of Industrial Gas Utilization: Engineering Principles & Practices. 1977. text ed. 42.50x (ISBN 0-442-26635-9). Van Nos Reinhold.

Redford, Emmette S., ed. Public Administration & Policy Formation: Studies in Oil, Gas, Banking, River Development, & Corporate Investigations. Repr. of 1956 ed. lib. bdg. 15.00x (ISBN 0-8371-2497-2, REPA). Greenwood.

Satriana, M. Unconventional Natural Gas: Resources, Potential & Technology. LC 80-15215. (Energy Technology Review: No. 56). 358p. (Orig.). 1980. 42.00 (ISBN 0-8155-0808-5). Noyes.

Sichel, Werner. Public Utility Rate Making in an Energy Conscious Environment. 1979. lib. bdg. 23.25x (ISBN 0-89158-180-4). Westview.

Spann, Robert M. The Supply of Natural Resources: The Case of Oil & Natural Gas. Bruchey, Stuart, ed. LC 78-22748. (Energy in the American Economy Ser.). (Illus.). 1979. lib. bdg. 10.00x (ISBN 0-405-12013-3). Arno.

Spooner, Robert D. Response of Natural Gas & Crude Oil Exploration & Discovery to Economic Incentives. Bruchey, Stuart, ed. LC 78-22749. (Energy in the American Economy Ser.). (Illus.). 1979. lib. bdg. 18.00x (ISBN 0-405-12014-1). Arno.

Starratt, Patricia E. The Natural Gas Shortage & the Congress. LC 74-29378. 1975. pap. 4.25 (ISBN 0-8447-3148-X). Am Enterprise.

Stern, Jonathan P. Soviet Natural Gas Development to Nineteen Ninety: The Implications for the CMEA & the West. LC 79-2705. 208p. 1980. 21.95x (ISBN 0-669-03233-6). Lexington Bks.

Tenneco Oil Company. Operators Handbook. 217p. 1961. 11.95x (ISBN 0-87201-643-9). Gulf Pub.

The Arab Petroleum Research Center, Paris. Arab Oil & Gas Directory 1979-80. 5th ed. LC 75-646597. (Illus.). 415p. 1979. 150.00x (ISBN 0-8002-2231-8). Intl Pubns Serv.

Tiratsoo, E. N. Natural Gas. 3rd ed. 360p. 1980. 49.95 (ISBN 0-87201-578-5). Gulf Pub.

--Natural Gas: A Study. LC 67-28865. 386p. 1967. 35.00 (ISBN 0-306-30317-5, Plenum Pr). Plenum Pub.

Tissot, B. Petroleum Formation & Occurrence: A New Approach to Oil & Gas Exploration. (Illus.). 1978. 39.50 (ISBN 0-387-08698-6). Springer-Verlag.

United Nations Economic Commission for Europe. Gas Situation in the EEC Region Around the Year 1990. (European Committee for Economic Perspectives: Vol. 18). 1979. 69.00 (ISBN 0-08-024465-3). Pergamon.

U. S. Dept. of the Interior. Hearings Before the Secretary of the Interior on Leasing of Oil Lands & Natural-Gas Wells in Indian Territory & Territory of Oklahoma: May 8, 24, 25 & 29, & June 7, & 19, 1906. LC 72-2841. (Use & Abuse of America's Natural Resources Ser). 92p. 1972. Repr. of 1906 ed. 10.00 (ISBN 0-405-04509-3). Arno.

World Natural Gas - Two Thousand. 232p. Date not set. 150.00 (ISBN 0-686-76143-X). Barrows Co.

GAS, NATURAL-JUVENILE LITERATURE

Kraft, Betsy H. Oil & Natural Gas. (First Bks). (Illus.). (gr. 4 up). 1978. PLB 6.90 (ISBN 0-531-01411-8). Watts.

Ridpath, Ian, ed. Man & Materials: Gas. LC 74-10540. (Illus.). 32p. (gr. 4 up). 1975. PLB 4.95 (ISBN 0-201-09031-7, 9031, A-W Childrens). A-W.

GAS, NATURAL-LAW AND LEGISLATION

see also Oil and Gas Leases

Federal Oil & Gas Corporation Proposals. (Legislative Analyses). 96p. 1974. pap. 3.75 (ISBN 0-8447-0165-3). Am Enterprise.

Gault, John C. Public Utility Regulation of an Exhaustible Resource: The Case of Natural Gas. LC 78-75016. (Outstanding Dissertations in Economics). 1980. lib. bdg. 31.00 (ISBN 0-8240-4051-1). Garland Pub.

Helms, Robert B. Natural Gas Regulation: An Evaluation of Fpc Price Controls. LC 74-84019. (Orig.). 1974. pap. 4.25 (ISBN 0-8447-3136-6). Am Enterprise.

Mosburg, Lewis G., Jr., ed. Oklahoma Title Practice. LC 77-93066. 1977. 25.50 (ISBN 0-89419-015-6). Inst Energy.

Murphy, Blakely M., ed. Conservation of Oil & Gas: A Legal History, 1948. LC 72-2858. (Use & Abuse of America's Natural Resources Ser). 776p. 1972. Repr. of 1949 ed. 39.00 (ISBN 0-405-04522-0). Arno.

Natural Gas Deregulation Legislation. 1973. pap. 3.75 (ISBN 0-8447-0160-2). Am Enterprise.

Oil & Gas Law, 3 Vols. 1954-59. 60.00x (ISBN 0-8377-0925-3). Rothman.

Sander, Elizabeth. The Regulation of Natural Gas: Policy & Politics, 1938-1978. 208p. 1981. 18.95 (ISBN 0-87722-221-5). Temple U Pr.

Swan, Peter N. Ocean Oil & Gas Drilling & the Law. LC 79-15500. 1979. lib. bdg. 45.00 (ISBN 0-379-20664-1). Oceana.

GAS, NATURAL-TAXATION

Russell, Milton & Toenjes, Laurence. Natural Gas Producer Regulation & Taxation. LC 78-635475. 79p. 1971. pap. 4.75 (ISBN 0-87744-108-1). Mich St U Busn.

Simon, Simon M. Economic Legislation of Taxation: A Case Study of Depletion in Oil & Gas. Bruchey, Stuart, ed. LC 78-22709. (Energy in the American Economy Ser.). (Illus.). 1979. lib. bdg. 18.00x (ISBN 0-405-12011-7). Arno.

GAS AND OIL ENGINES

see also Diesel Motor; Jet Propulsion; Motor-Boats; Wankel Engine

Ayres, Robert U. & McKenna, Richard P. Alternatives to the Internal Combustion Engine: Impacts on Environmental Quality. LC 74-181555. (Resources for the Future Ser). 340p. 1972. 22.50x (ISBN 0-8018-1369-7). Johns Hopkins.

Benson, Rowland S. & Whitehouse, N. D. Internal Combustion Engines, 2 vols. LC 79-40359. (Thermodynamics & Fluid Mechanics for Mechanical Engineers). (Illus.). 1979. Set. 68.00 (ISBN 0-08-022717-1); Vol. 1. pap. 15.75 (ISBN 0-08-022718-X); Vol. 2. pap. 15.75 (ISBN 0-08-022720-1). Pergamon.

Blackmore, D. R. & Thomas, A. Fuel Economy of the Gasoline Engine. LC 77-3916. 1977. 27.95 (ISBN 0-470-99132-1). Halsted Pr.

Business Communications Staff. Oil & Gas Filled Equipment & Supplies: E-045. 1982. 950.00 (ISBN 0-89336-295-6). BCC.

Critser, James R., Jr. Air Pollution Control: Internal Combustion Engines - Exhaust Treatment 1976. (Ser. 4IC-76). 1977. 95.00 (ISBN 0-914428-40-3). Lexington Data.

Crouse, William H. Small Engines: Operation & Maintenance. (Automotive Technology Ser). (Illus.). 448p. 1973. pap. text ed. 12.95 (ISBN 0-07-014691-8, G); wkbk. 5.95 (ISBN 0-07-014692-6). McGraw.

Crouse, William H. & Anglin, Donald L. Pocket Automotive Dictionary, with Metric Conversion Table. new ed. (Automotive Technology Ser). 1976. pap. text ed. 4.25 (ISBN 0-07-014752-3, G). McGraw.

--Small Engine Mechanics. 2nd ed. LC 79-4658. (Illus.). 1979. pap. text ed. write for info. (ISBN 0-07-014795-7, G); instructor's planning guide 2.50 (ISBN 0-07-014797-3); wkbk. avail. (ISBN 0-07-014796-5). McGraw.

Cummins, C. Lyle, Jr. Internal Fire: The Internal Combustion Engine, 1673-1900. LC 75-40701. (Illus.). 1976. 20.00x (ISBN 0-917308-01-8). Carnot Pr.

Dempsey, Paul. How to Repair Small Gasoline Engines. 2nd ed. LC 76-45056. 1976. 12.95 (ISBN 0-8306-6917-5); pap. 9.95 (ISBN 0-8306-5917-X, 917). TAB Bks.

Drake, George. Repair & Maintenance of Small Gasoline Engines. (Illus.). 1978. pap. 6.95 (ISBN 0-87909-735-3). Reston.

--Small Gas Engines: Maintenance, Troubleshooting & Repair. 500p. 1981. text ed. 16.95 (ISBN 0-8359-7014-0); pap. text ed. 7.95 (ISBN 0-8359-7013-2); soln. manual avail. (ISBN 0-8359-7015-9). Reston.

Goring, Loris. The Care & Repair of Marine Gasoline Engines. LC 80-84623. (Illus.). 146p. 1981. 15.00 (ISBN 0-87742-139-0). Intl Marine.

Gray, J. A. & Barrow, R. W. Small Gas Engines. 357p. 1976. 17.95 (ISBN 0-13-813121-X); pap. text ed. 12.95 (ISBN 0-13-813113-9). P-H.

Kates, Edgar J. & Luck, William E. Diesel & High Compression Gas Engines. 3rd ed. (Illus.). 1974. 17.00 (ISBN 0-8269-0203-0). Am Technical.

Lewis, Alexander D. Gas Power Dynamics. LC 77-15095. 544p. 1978. Repr. of 1962 ed. lib. bdg. 29.00 (ISBN 0-88275-629-X). Krieger.

Lichty, Lester. Combustion Engine Processes. 7th ed. (Mechanical Engineering Ser.). 1967. text ed. 25.50 (ISBN 0-07-037720-0, C); solutions manual 1.95 (ISBN 0-07-037721-9). McGraw.

Lucke, Charles E. & Woodward, S. M. The Use of Alcohol & Gasoline in Farm Engines. (Illus.). 100p. 1980. pap. 6.00 (ISBN 0-936222-04-2). Rutan Pub.

MacDonald, K. L. Small Gasoline Engines Student's Workbook. 2nd ed. 1973. pap. 2.95 (ISBN 0-672-97632-3). Bobbs.

Mason, L. C. Building Mastiff: A Four Cylinder Petrol Engine. (Illus.). 139p. 1975. pap. 10.00x (ISBN 0-85242-429-9). Intl Pubns Serv.

--Model Four Stroke Petrol Engines. (Illus.). 116p. 1976. pap. 10.00x (ISBN 0-85242-431-0). Intl Pubns Serv.

Multicylinder Test Sequences for Evaluating Engine Oils, Pt. I: Sequence ID. (Special Technical Publications Ser.). 111p. 1980. soft cover 13.00x (ISBN 0-686-76072-7, 315H, 04-315080-12); looseleaf 16.00x (ISBN 0-686-76073-5, 315H, 04-315081-12). ASTM.

Multicylinder Test Sequences for Evaluating Engine Oils, Pt. II: Sequence IIID. (Special Technical Publications Ser.). 115p. 1980. soft cover 13.00x (ISBN 0-686-76074-3, 315H, 04-315090-12); 16.00 (ISBN 0-686-76075-1, 315H, 04-315091-12). ASTM.

Peterson, Franklyn, ed. Handbook of Landmower Repair. rev. ed. LC 77-92313. (Illus.). 1978. pap. 5.95 (ISBN 0-8015-3256-6, Hawthorn). Dutton.

Pipe, Ted. Gas Engine Manual. 2nd ed. LC 76-45883. 1977. 9.95 (ISBN 0-672-23245-6). Audel.

Potter, Philip J. Power Plant Theory & Design. 2nd ed. (Illus.). 1959. 28.95 (ISBN 0-8260-7205-4). Wiley.

Ranney, M. W. Fuel Additives for Internal Combustion Engines--Recent Developments. LC 78-57662. (Chemical Technology Review Ser. No. 112, Energy Technology Review Ser. No. 30). 1978. 39.00 (ISBN 0-8155-0709-7). Noyes.

Rogowski, Augustus R. Elements of Internal Combustion Engines. (Illus.). 1953. text ed. 24.00 (ISBN 0-07-053575-2, C). McGraw.

Roth, Alfred C. Small Gas Engines. LC 78-8279. (Illus.). 1978. text ed. 10.64 (ISBN 0-87006-251-4). Goodheart.

Rudman, Jack. Small Engine Repair. (Occupational Competency Examination Ser.: OCE-32). (Cloth bdg. avail. on request). pap. 9.95 (ISBN 0-8373-5732-2). Natl Learning.

Schilling, A. Automobile Engine Lubrication. (Illus.). 480p. 1972. text ed. 50.00x (ISBN 0-900645-00-8). Scholium Intl.

Shear Stability of Multigrade Crankcase Oil. 1973. pap. 7.75 (ISBN 0-8031-0090-6, DS49). ASTM.

Sitkei, Gyorgy. Heat Transfer & Thermal Loading in Internal Combustion Engines. LC 75-303894. 268p. 1975. 20.00x (ISBN 963-05-0097-3). Intl Pubns Serv.

Stephenson, George E. Small Gasoline Engines. LC 76-51117. 1978. pap. text ed. 6.80 (ISBN 0-8273-1026-9); instructor's guide 1.60 (ISBN 0-8273-1027-7). Delmar.

Taylor, Charles F. The Internal-Combustion Engine in Theory & Practice, Vol. 1: Thermodynamics, Fluid Flow, Performance. 2nd ed. 1967. pap. text ed. 15.00x (ISBN 0-262-70015-8). MIT Pr.

--The Internal-Combustion Engine in Theory & Practice, Vol. 2: Combustion, Fuels, Materials, Design. 1968. 50.00x (ISBN 0-262-20013-9); pap. 17.50x (ISBN 0-262-70016-6). MIT Pr.

Weissler, Paul. Small Gas Engines: How to Repair & Maintain Them. LC 75-13334. (A Popular Science Bk). (Illus.). 288p. 1975. 12.95 (ISBN 0-06-014564-1, HarpT). Har-Row.

Zinner, K. A. Supercharging of Internal Combustion Engines. (Illus.). 290p. 1981. pap. 32.40 (ISBN 0-387-08544-0). Springer-Verlag.

GAS AND OIL ENGINES–CARBURETORS
see Carburetors

GAS AND OIL LEASES
see Oil and Gas Leases

GAS APPLIANCES
see also Gas Flow

Meyerink, George. Appliance Service Handbook. (Illus.). 464p. 1973. ref. ed. 21.95x (ISBN 0-13-038844-0). P-H.

National Fuel Gas Code. (Fifty Ser.). Orig. Title: Installation of Gas Appliances & Gas Piping. 146p. 1974. pap. 3.00 (ISBN 0-685-46069-X, 54). Natl Fire Prot.

GAS AS FUEL
see also Liquefied Petroleum Gas

Price, Elizabeth C. & Cheremisinoff, Paul N. Biogas Production & Utilization. LC 79-56113. (Illus.). 1981. 29.95 (ISBN 0-250-40334-X). Ann Arbor Science.

Ridpath, Ian, ed. Man & Materials: Gas. LC 74-10540. (Illus.). 32p. (gr. 4 up). 1975. PLB 4.95 (ISBN 0-201-09031-7, 9031, A-W Childrens). A-W.

GAS BEARINGS
see Gas-Lubricated Bearings

GAS CHROMATOGRAPHY

Ambrose, D. Gas Chromatography. 227p. 1962. 16.50 (ISBN 0-442-20362-4, Pub. by Van Nos Reinhold). Krieger.

Analysis of Drugs & Metabolites by Gas Chromatography - Mass Spectrometry: Natural, Pyrolytic & Metabolic Products of Tobacco & Marijuana, Vol. 7. 1980. 69.50 (ISBN 0-8247-6861-2). Dekker.

Baiulescu, G. E. & Ilie, A. V. Stationary Phases in Gas Chromatography. 1975. text ed. 55.00 (ISBN 0-08-018075-2). Pergamon.

Berezkin, V. G. & Tatarinskii, V. S. Gas-Chromatographic Analysis of Trace Impurities. LC 72-94824. 177p. 1973. 35.00 (ISBN 0-306-10879-8, Consultants). Plenum Pub.

Berezkin, Viktor G. Analytical Reaction Gas Chromatography. LC 68-21473. (Illus.). 193p. 1968. 29.50 (ISBN 0-306-30338-8, Plenum Pr). Plenum Pub.

Berezkin, Viktor G., et al. Gas Chromatography of Polymers. LC 77-23184. (Journal of Chromatography Library: Vol. 10). 1977. 50.25 (ISBN 0-444-41514-9). Elsevier.

Brenner, N., ed. International Gas Chromatography Symposium, Third. 1962. 79.00 (ISBN 0-12-131650-5). Acad Pr.

Budde, William L. & Eichelberger, James W., eds. Organics Analysis Using Gas Chromatography-Mass Spectrometry: A Techniques & Procedures Manual. LC 79-88484. (Illus.). 1979. 24.00 (ISBN 0-250-40318-8). Ann Arbor Science.

Calculation of Physical Properties of Petroleum Products from Gas Chromatographic Analysis. 1975. pap. 10.75 (ISBN 0-686-51994-9, 04-577000-39). ASTM.

Coates, Donald R., ed. Gas Chromatography. 1958. 55.00 (ISBN 0-12-177350-7). Acad Pr.

Conder, John R. & Young, Colin L. Physiochemical Measurements by Gas Chromatography. LC 78-9899. 1979. 104.72 (ISBN 0-471-99674-2, Pub. by Wiley-Interscience). Wiley.

Dickes, G. J. & Nicholas, P. V. Gas Chromatrography in Food Analysis. 1976. 54.95 (ISBN 0-408-70781-X). Butterworth.

Domsky, I. & Perry, J., eds. Recent Advances in Gas Chromatography. 1971. 44.50 (ISBN 0-8247-1146-7). Dekker.

Drucker, D. B. Microbiological Applications of Gas Chromatography. LC 80-40447. 300p. Date not set. 99.50 (ISBN 0-521-22365-2). Cambridge U Pr.

Eik-Nes, K. B. & Horning, E. C. Gas Phase Chromatography of Steroids. LC 68-18620. (Monographs on Endocrinology: Vol. 2). (Illus.). 1968. 24.90 (ISBN 0-387-04277-6). Springer-Verlag.

Ettre, L. S. Open Tubular Columns in Gas Chromatography. LC 65-13583. 164p. 1965. 25.00 (ISBN 0-306-30188-1, Plenum Pr). Plenum Pub.

Ettre, Leslie & McFadden, William, eds. Ancillary Techniques of Gas Chromatography. LC 78-9476. (Chemical Analysis Ser.). 408p. 1978. Repr. of 1969 ed. lib. bdg. 24.50 (ISBN 0-88275-705-9). Krieger.

Federal Institute for Biology in Agriculture & Forestry, Institute for Plant Protection Agent Research, Berlin-Dahlem & Ebing, Winifried. Gaschromatographic der Pflanzenschutzmittel: Tabellarische Literaturreferate, 5 vols. new ed. (Ger.). Vol. II, 1972. 15.00 (ISBN 0-913106-10-0); Vol. III. 15.00 (ISBN 0-913106-11-9); Vol. IV. 15.00 (ISBN 0-913106-12-7); Vol. V, 1975. 15.00 (ISBN 0-913106-13-5). PolyScience.

Fowler, L., ed. Gas Chromatography. 1963. 42.00 (ISBN 0-12-263150-1). Acad Pr.

Gas Chromatographic Data Compilation: First Supplement. 1971. 40.00 (ISBN 0-8031-0021-3, 10-025011-39). ASTM.

Gas Chromatographic Headspace Analysis. 136p. Date not set. 19.00 (ISBN 0-686-76119-7, 13-112000-39). ASTM.

Goodman, Stephen I. & Markey, Sanford P., eds. Diagnosis of Organic Acidemias by Gas Chromatography-Mass Spectrometry. LC 81-8228. (Laboratory & Research Methods in Biology & Medicine Ser.: Vol. 6). 148p. 1981. 28.00 (ISBN 0-8451-1655-X). A R Liss.

Grob, Robert L., ed. Modern Practice of Gas Chromatography. LC 77-779. 654p. 1977. 37.50x (ISBN 0-471-01564-4, Pub. by Wiley-Interscience). Wiley.

Gudzinowicz, B. J. Analysis of Drugs & Metabolites by Gas Chromatography - Mass Spectometry: Antipsychotic, Antiemetic & Antidepressant Drugs, Vol. 3. 1977. 37.75 (ISBN 0-8247-6586-9). Dekker.

--Gas Chromatographic Analysis of Drugs & Pesticides. (Chromatographic Science Ser: Vol. 2). 1967. 79.50 (ISBN 0-8247-1255-2). Dekker.

Gudzinowicz, B. J., et al. Fundamentals of Integrated Gc-Ms, Pt. II: Mass Spectrometry. (Chromatographic Science Ser.: Vol. 7). 1976. 49.50 (ISBN 0-8247-6430-7). Dekker.

--Fundamentals of Integrated Gc-Ms, Pt. III: The Integrated Gc-Ms Analytical System. (Chromotographic Science Ser.: Vol. 7). 1977. 77.50 (ISBN 0-8247-6431-5). Dekker.

--Fundamentals of Integrated Gc-Ms, Pt.1: Gas Chromatograpghy. (Chromatographic Ser: Vol. 7). Orig. Title: Fundamentals of Integrated Gc-Ms-Gas Chromatography. 1976. 52.50 (ISBN 0-8247-6365-3). Dekker.

Gudzinowicz, Michael J. & Gudzinowicz, Benjamin J. The Analysis of Drugs & Related Compounds by GC-MS: Vol. 1; Respiratory Gases, Volatile Anesthetics, Ethyl Alcohol, & Related Toxicological Materials. 1977. 32.50 (ISBN 0-8247-6576-1). Dekker.

Hachenberg, H. Industrial Gas Chromatographic Trace Analysis. 1973. 30.00 (ISBN 0-85501-079-7). Heyden.

Hachenberg, H. & Schmidt, A. P. Gas Chromatographic Head Space Analysis. 1977. 33.00 (ISBN 0-85501-205-6). Heyden.

Haken, J. K. Gas Chromatography of Coating Materials. 352p. 1974. 49.50 (ISBN 0-8247-6123-5). Dekker.

Harris, W. E. Programmed Temperature Gas Chromatography. 305p. 1966. 16.25 (ISBN 0-471-35270-5, Pub. by Wiley). Krieger.

Industrial Gas Chromatographic Trace Analysis. 226p. Date not set. 22.00 (ISBN 0-686-76114-6, 13-105000-39). ASTM.

International Symposium, 3rd, Amsterdam, Sept. 1976. Analytical Pryolysis: Proceedings. Jones, C. E. & Cramers, C. A., eds. 1977. 53.75 (ISBN 0-444-41558-0). Elsevier.

Jennings. Applications of Glass Capilary Gas Chromatography. (Chromotographic Science Ser.: Vol. 14). 1981. 69.50 (ISBN 0-8247-1223-4). Dekker.

--Applications of Glass Capillary Gas Chromatography. (Chromatographic Science Ser.: Vol 15). 648p. 1981. write for info. Dekker.

Jennings, Walter, ed. Gas Chromatography with Glass Capillary Columns. 2nd ed. LC 79-8851. 1980. 25.00 (ISBN 0-12-384360-X). Acad Pr.

Jones, R. A. Introduction to Gas-Liquid Chromatography. 1970. 32.00 (ISBN 0-12-389850-1). Acad Pr.

Kaiser, Rudolf. Gas-Phase Chromatography, 2 vols. Incl. Vol. 1. Gas Chromatography. 207p (ISBN 0-306-35021-1); Vol. 2. Capillary Chromatography. 130p (ISBN 0-306-35022-X). 1963. 14.95 ea. (Plenum Pr). Plenum Pub.

Keulemans, A. I. Gas Chromatography. 2nd ed. 256p. 1959. 12.50 (ISBN 0-442-15239-6, Pub. by Van Nos Reinhold). Krieger.

Kiselev, A. V. & Yashin, Ya I. Gas-Adsorption Chromatography. LC 69-12531. 250p. 1969. 34.50 (ISBN 0-306-30370-1, Plenum Pr). Plenum Pub.

Kolb, B. Applied Headspace Gas Chromatography. 200p. 1980. 31.50 (ISBN 0-85501-488-1). Heyden.

Kroman, Henry S. & Bender, Sheldon R., eds. Theory & Application of Gas Chromatography in Industry & Medicine. (Illus.). 320p. 1968. 64.75 (ISBN 0-8089-0248-2). Grune.

Laub, Richard J. & Pecsok, Robert L. Physiochemical Applications of Gas Chromatography. LC 78-5493. 300p. 1978. 37.95 (ISBN 0-471-51838-7, Pub. by Wiley-Interscience). Wiley.

Lipsett, Mortimer, ed. Gas Chromatography of Steroids in Biological Fluids. LC 65-25243. 315p. 1965. 34.50 (ISBN 0-306-30204-7, Plenum Pr). Plenum Pub.

McFadden, W. H. Techniques of Combined Gas Chromatography - Mass Spectrometry: Applications in Organic Analysis. LC 73-6916. 463p. 1973. 34.00 (ISBN 0-471-58388-X, Pub. by Wiley-Interscience). Wiley.

McNair. Gas Chromatography: A Practical Introduction. 1976. write for info. (ISBN 0-685-83147-7). Elsevier.

McReynolds, W. O. Gas Chromatographic Retention Data. 1966. 40.00 (ISBN 0-912474-01-7). Preston Pubns.

Mitruka, Brij M. Gas Chromatographic Applications in Microbiology & Medicine. LC 74-18002. 492p. 1975. 55.50 (ISBN 0-471-61183-2). Krieger.

Noebels, H. J., ed. Gas Chromatography. 1961. 55.00 (ISBN 0-12-520450-7). Acad Pr.

Novak, Josef. Quantitative Analysis by Gas Chromatography. (Chromatographic Science Ser.: Vol. 5). 224p. 1975. 29.75 (ISBN 0-8247-6311-4). Dekker.

Perry, J. A. Introduction to Analytical Gas Chromatography: History, Principles, & Practice. 1981. 29.75 (ISBN 0-8247-1537-3). Dekker.

Polvani, Filippo, et al, eds. Meeting on Gas Chromatographic Determination of Hormonal Steroids. LC 68-19262. (Illus.). 1968. 50.00 (ISBN 0-12-561240-0). Acad Pr.

Preston, S. T. & Pankratz, Ronald. A Guide to the Analysis of Pesticides by Gas Chromatography. 1981. spiral plastic bdg. 25.00 (ISBN 0-913106-15-1). PolyScience.

--A Guide to the Analysis of Thioalcohols & Thioethers: (Mercaptans & Alkyl Sulfides) rev. ed. 1981. spiral plastic bdg. 25.00 (ISBN 0-913106-16-X). PolyScience.

Preston, S. T., Jr. A Guide to Selected Liquid Phases and Absorbents Used in Gas Chromatography. 1969. spiral bdg 20.00 (ISBN 0-913106-00-3). PolyScience.

--A Guide to the Analysis of Amines by Gas Chromatography. 2nd rev. ed. 1973. spiral bdg 25.00 (ISBN 0-913106-01-1). PolyScience.

--A Guide to the Analysis of Fatty Acids and Their Esters by Gas Chromatography. 1971. spiral bdg 25.00 (ISBN 0-913106-08-9). PolyScience.

--A Guide to the Analysis of Hydro-Carbons by Gas Chromatography. 2nd ed. 1976. spiral bdg 30.00 (ISBN 0-913106-02-X). PolyScience.

--A Guide to the Analysis of Phenols by Gas Chromatography. 1978. spiral bdg 25.00 (ISBN 0-913106-04-6). PolyScience.

Preston, S. T., Jr. & Pankratz, Ronald. A Guide to the Analysis of Alcohols by Gas Chromatography. 2nd ed. 1976. 25.00 (ISBN 0-913106-06-2). PolyScience.

--A Guide to the Analysis of Ketones by Gas Chromatography. 2nd rev. ed. 1975. spiral 25.00 (ISBN 0-913106-07-0). PolyScience.

Purnell, Howard. Progress in Gas Chromatography, Vol. 6. 392p. 1968. 22.50 (ISBN 0-470-70238-9, Pub. by Wiley). Krieger.

Scholler, R. & Jayle, M. F. Gas Chromatography of Hormonal Steroids. 1968..118.75 (ISBN 0-677-13280-8). Gordon.

Sevcik, J. Detectors in Gas Chromatography. (Journal of Chromatography Library: Vol. 4). 1976. 34.25 (ISBN 0-444-99857-8). Elsevier.

Signeur, Austin V. Guide to Gas Chromatography Literature, 3 vols. Incl. Vol. 1. 351p. 1964. 75.00 (ISBN 0-306-68201-X); Vol. 2. 379p. 1967. 75.00 (ISBN 0-306-68202-8); Vol. 3. 1089p. 1974. 95.00 (ISBN 0-306-68203-6). LC 64-20743. IFI Plenum.

Struppe, H. G., ed. Aspects in Gas Chromatography: Berlin 1968. 313p. 1971. 20.00 (ISBN 0-912474-05-X). Preston Pubns.

Szymanski, H. A. & Mattick, L. R. Lectures on Gas Chromatography, Vol. 3. LC 61-15520. 227p. 1967. 32.50 (ISBN 0-306-30289-6, Plenum Pr). Plenum Pub.

Szymanski, Herman A., ed. Biomedical Applications of Gas Chromatography, 2 vols. Incl. Vol. 1. 324p. 1964. 37.50 (ISBN 0-306-37581-8); Vol. 2. 198p. 1968. 32.50 (ISBN 0-306-37582-6). LC 64-13147 (Plenum Pr). Plenum Pub.

Tsuji, ed. GLC & HPLC: Determination of Therapeutic Agents, Vol. 9. (Chromatographic Science Ser.: Pt. III). 1979. 55.00 (ISBN 0-8247-6693-8). Dekker.

Tsuji, K. & Morozowich, W., eds. GLC & HPLC Determination of Therapeutic Agents, Vol. 9. (Chromatographic Science Ser.: Pt. II). 1978. 59.50 (ISBN 0-8247-6664-4). Dekker.

Tsuji, Kiyoshi & Morozowich, Walter, eds. GLC & HPLC: Determination of Therapeutic Agents, Vol. 9. (Chromatographic Science Ser.: Pt. I). 1978. 55.00 (ISBN 0-8247-6641-5). Dekker.

Weissberger, Arnold & Schupp, Orion E., eds. Techniques of Organic Chemistry: Gas Chromotography, Vol. 13. 437p. 1968. 36.50 (ISBN 0-470-93263-5). Krieger.

Zlatkis, A., ed. Advances in Chromatography, 1969. 1969. 15.00 (ISBN 0-912474-04-1). Preston Pubns.

--Advances in Gas Chromatography, 1967. 1967. 8.00 (ISBN 0-912474-03-3). Preston Pubns.

Zlatkis, A. & Ettre, L. S., eds. Advances in Gas Chromatography, 1965. 1965. 6.00 (ISBN 0-912474-02-5). Preston Pubns.

Zlatkis, Albert & Pretorius, Victor, eds. Preparative Gas Chromatography. 402p. (Orig.). 1971. 28.25 (ISBN 0-471-98384-5). Krieger.

GAS COMPANIES

Lawson, Thomas. Frenzied Finance. LC 72-78767. 1905. Repr. 22.00 (ISBN 0-403-02011-5). Somerset Pub.

Lawson, Thomas W. Frenzied Finance. Vol. 1: The Crime of Amalgamated. LC 68-28640. Repr. lib. bdg. 29.50x (ISBN 0-8371-0531-5, LAFF). Greenwood.

GAS COOLED REACTORS

Advanced & High-Temperature Gas-Cooled Reactors. (Illus., Orig.). 1968. pap. 57.00 (ISBN 92-0-050768-9, ISP197, IAEA). Unipub.

Fickeisen, D. H. & Schneider, M. J., eds. Gas Bubble Disease: Proceedings. LC 75-619327. 123p. 1967. pap. 6.00 (ISBN 0-686-75708-4); microfiche 3.00 (ISBN 0-686-75709-2). DOE.

Gas Cooled Reactor Technology: A Bibliography. (DOE Technical Information Center Ser.). 393p. 1978. write for info. DOE.

Gas-Cooled Reactors with Emphasis on Advanced Systems, Vol. 1. 1976. pap. 42.25 (ISBN 92-0-050076-5, ISP407-1, IAEA). Unipub.

IAEA-NEA Symposium, Julich, Oct. 13-17, 1975. Gas-Cooled Reactors with Emphasis on Advanced Systems Vol. 2, 1976: Proceedings. (Proceedings Ser.). (Illus., Orig.). 1976. pap. 53.75 (ISBN 92-0-050176-1, ISP407-2, IAEA). Unipub.

Proposed Section XI, Division 2, Rules for Inspection & Testing of Components of Gas-Cooled Plants. 1977. pap. text ed. 32.00 (ISBN 0-685-86876-1, E00122). ASME.

GAS DISTRIBUTION
see also Gases, Compressed

ASME Guide for Gas Transmission & Distribution Piping System: Includes All Addenda Issued up to the Publication of the 1983 Edition. 1980. pap. 125.00 (ISBN 0-685-67491-6, AX3080). ASME.

Kellogg, Orson. Every Pilot's Guide to Fuel Economy. 1980. pap. 4.95 (ISBN 0-911721-64-9, Pub. by Taxlogs Unltd). Aviation.

GAS DYNAMICS
see also Aerodynamics; Gas Flow; Jets–Fluid Dynamics

Becker, Ernst. Gas Dynamics. 1969. 51.00 (ISBN 0-12-084450-8). Acad Pr.

Benedict, Robert P. & Carlucci, Nicola A. Handbook of Specific Losses in Flow Systems. LC 65-25129. 193p. 1966. 32.50 (ISBN 0-306-65122-X). IFI Plenum.

Benedict, Robert P. & Steltz, W. G. Handbook of Generalized Gas Dynamics. LC 65-25128. 243p. 1966. 52.50 (ISBN 0-306-65118-1). IFI Plenum.

Bond, J. W., Jr., et al. Atomic Theory of Gas Dynamics. 1965. 19.50 (ISBN 0-201-00633-2, Adv Bk Prog). A-W.

Burgers, J. M. Flow Equations for Composite Gases. (Applied Mathematics & Mechanics Ser.: Vol. 11). 1969. 55.00 (ISBN 0-12-143250-5). Acad Pr.

CISM (International Center for Mechanical Sciences) Introduction to Gasdynamics of Explosions. Oppenheim, A. K., ed. (CISM Pubns. Ser.: No. 48). (Illus.). 220p. 1970. pap. 23.80 (ISBN 0-387-81083-8). Springer-Verlag.

--Lectures on Radiating Gasdynamics: General Equations & Boundary Conditions. Ferrari, C., ed. (CISM Pubns. Ser.: No. 146). (Illus.). 83p. 1975. pap. 12.40 (ISBN 0-387-81204-0). Springer-Verlag.

CISM (International Center for Mechanical Sciences), Dept. of Hydro & Gas Dynamics, 1970. Shock Waves in Real Gases. Bazhenova, T. V., ed. (CISM International Center for Mechanical Sciences Ser.: No. 37). (Illus.). 78p. 1974. pap. 12.40 (ISBN 3-211-81219-9). Springer-Verlag.

Davies, Donald G. & Barnes, Charles D., eds. Regulation of Ventilation & Gas Exchange. (Research Topics in Physiology). 1978. 32.50 (ISBN 0-12-204650-1). Acad Pr.

Dosanjh, Darshan S., ed. Modern Optical Methods in Gas Dynamic Research. LC 75-155352. 295p. 1971. 35.00 (ISBN 0-306-30537-2, Plenum Pr). Plenum Pub.
Goodman, Frank O & Wachman, Harold Y. Dynamics of Gas-Surface Scattering. 1976. 55.00 (ISBN 0-12-290450-8). Acad Pr.
John, James E. Gas Dynamics. 1969. text ed. 27.95 (ISBN 0-205-02262-6, 3222624). Allyn.
Karamcheti, K., ed. Rarefield Gas Dynamics. 1974. 51.50 (ISBN 0-12-398150-6). Acad Pr.
Klinzing, George E. Gas-Solid Transport. (Chemical Engineering Ser.). (Illus.). 358p. 1981. text ed. 28.50 (ISBN 0-07-035047-7, C). McGraw.
Kogan, M. N. Rarefied Gas Dynamics. LC 69-12532. 515p. 1969. 52.50 (ISBN 0-306-30361-2, Plenum Pr). Plenum Pub.
Kondratiev, V. N. & Nikitin, E. E. Gas-Phase Reactions: Kinetics & Mechanisms. (Illus.). 250p. 1980. 63.80 (ISBN 0-387-09956-5). Springer-Verlag.
Liepmann, Hans W. & Roshko, A. Elements of Gasdynamics. LC 56-9823. 1957. text ed. 31.95x (ISBN 0-471-53460-9). Wiley.
Loh, W. H. Modern Developments in Gas Dynamics. LC 69-14561. 386p. 1969. 42.50 (ISBN 0-306-30377-9, Plenum Pr). Plenum Pub.
Losev, S. A. Gasdynamic Laser. (Springer Series in Chemical Physics: Vol. 12). (Illus.). 300p. 1981. 42.00 (ISBN 0-387-10503-4). Springer-Verlag.
Napolitano, L. G. & Belotserkovsky, O. M. Computational Gasdynamics. (International Centre for Mechanical Sciences, Courses & Lectures: Vol. 40). (Illus.). pap. 40.80 (ISBN 0-387-81428-0). Springer-Verlag.
Niyogi, Pradip. Inviscid Gasdynamics. 1977. 14.00x (ISBN 0-333-90184-3). South Asia Bks.
Openheim, A. K., ed. Gasdynamics of Explosions & Reactive Systems: Proceedings of the Sixth International Colloquium Held in Stockholm, Sweden, 22-26 August 1977. (Illus.). 782p. 1980. 100.00 (ISBN 0-08-025442-X). Pergamon.
Oswatitsch. Contributions to the Development of Gas Dynamics. 1980. 85.00 (ISBN 0-9940012-9-0, Pub. by Vieweg & Sohn Germany). Heyden.
Predvoditelev, A. S., ed. Physics of Heat Exchange & Gas Dynamics. LC 62-12858. 99p. 1963. 25.00 (ISBN 0-306-10574-8, Consultants). Plenum Pub.
Robertson, A. J. Catalysis of Gas Reactions by Metals. (Illus.). 1970. 13.20 (ISBN 0-387-91031-X). Springer-Verlag.
Schatzman, Evry & Biermann, Ludwig. Cosmic Gas Dynamics. LC 73-16025. 291p. 1974. 23.00 (ISBN 0-471-75720-9, Pub. by Wiley). Krieger.
Steklov Institute of Mathematics, Academy of Sciences, U S S R, No. 87. Unsteady Motions of Compressible Media with Blast Waves: Proceedings. Sedov, Leond I., ed. 1967. 30.80 (ISBN 0-8218-1887-2, STEKLO-87). Am Math.
Steklov Institute of Mathematics, No. 122. Difference Methods of Solving Problems of Mathematical Physics. 2: Proceedings. Janenko, N. N., ed. LC 75-20006. 99p. 1975. 33.60 (ISBN 0-8218-3022-8, STEKLO-122). Am Math.
Symposium on Cosmical Gas Dynamics,6th, et al. Interstellar Gas Dynamics: Proceedings. Habing, H. J., ed. LC 78-124849. (IAU Symposia: No.39). 388p. 1970. lib. bdg. 42.00 (ISBN 90-277-0172-5, Pub. by Reidel Holland). Kluwer Boston.
Thompson, P. A. Compressible Fluid Dynamics. (Control Systems Engineering Ser.). 1971. text ed. 26.50 (ISBN 0-07-064405-5, C). McGraw.
Vincenti, W. G. & Kruger, C. H. Introduction to Physical Gas Dynamics. LC 75-5806. 556p. 1975. Repr. of 1965 ed. 29.50 (ISBN 0-88275-309-6). Krieger.
Wegener, P., ed. Molecular Beams & Low Density Gasdynamics. (Gasdynamics Ser.: Vol. 4). 1974. 47.75 (ISBN 0-8247-6199-5). Dekker.
Zucker, R. Fundamentals of Gas Dynamics. 1977. 29.95x (ISBN 0-916460-12-6, Pub by Matrix). Intl Schol Bk Serv.
Zucrow, Maurice J. & Hoffman, Joe D. Gas Dynamics, 2 vols. LC 76-6855. 768p. Vol. 1. text ed. 47.95 (ISBN 0-471-98440-X); Vol. 2. text ed. 44.95 (ISBN 0-471-01806-6). Wiley.

GAS ENGINES
see Gas and Oil Engines

GAS EQUIPMENT AND APPLIANCES
see Gas Appliances

GAS-FITTING
see also Pipe-Fitting; Plumbing

GAS FLOW
see also Air Flow; Gas-Lubricated Bearings
Bird, G. A. Molecular Gas Dynamics. (Oxford Engineering & Science Ser.). 1976. text ed. 74.00x (ISBN 0-19-856120-2). Oxford U Pr.
Chambre, Paul L. & Schaaf, Samuel A. Flow of Rarefied Gases. (Aeronautical Paperbacks Ser.: Vol. 8). (Orig.). pap. 8.00 (ISBN 0-691-07964-1). Princeton U Pr.
Dallman, John C. Investigation of Separated Flow Model in Annular Gas-Liquid Two-Phase Flows. LC 78-75007. (Outstanding Dissertations on Energy Ser.). 1979. lib. bdg. 20.00 (ISBN 0-8240-3988-2). Garland Pub.
Rhodes, E. & Scott, D. E., eds. Cocurrent Gas-Liquid Flow. LC 76-80084. 698p. 1969. 57.50 (ISBN 0-306-30404-X, Plenum Pr). Plenum Pub.
Sellin, R. H. Flow in Channels. 1970. 34.75x (ISBN 0-677-61650-3). Gordon.

GAS INDUSTRY
Here are entered general works on industries based on natural or manufactured gas.
see also Gas, Natural; Gas Appliances; Gas Manufacture and Works;
also other headings beginning with the word Gas
Allain, Louis J. Capital Investment Models of the Oil & Gas Industry: A Systems Approach. Bruchey, Stuart, ed. LC 78-22654. (Energy in the American Economy Ser.). (Illus.). 1979. lib. bdg. 36.00x (ISBN 0-405-11959-3). Arno.
Arab Petroleum Research Center. Arab Oil and Gas Directory: 1979-80. 450p. 1980. 143.00x (ISBN 0-686-64697-5, Pub. by Graham & Trotman England). State Mutual Bk.
Booth, Norman. Industrial Gases. LC 72-10293. 1973. pap. text ed. 9.25 (ISBN 0-08-016860-4). Pergamon.
Brown, Keith C., ed. Regulation of the Natural Gas Producing Industry. LC 71-186502. (Resources for the Future Ser.). (Illus.). 271p. 1972. pap. 10.00x (ISBN 0-8018-1383-2). Johns Hopkins.
California-Alaska Oil & Gas Review for 1969. 1970. 30.00 (ISBN 0-686-28269-8). Munger Oil.
California-Alaska Oil & Gas Review for 1971. 30.00 (ISBN 0-686-28270-1). Munger Oil.
California-Alaska Oil & Gas Review for 1972. 30.00 (ISBN 0-686-28271-X). Munger Oil.
California-Alaska Oil & Gas Review for 1973. 1974. 30.00 (ISBN 0-686-28272-8). Munger Oil.
California-Alaska Oil & Gas Review 1975. 1976. 30.00 (ISBN 0-686-28273-6). Munger Oil.
California Gas & Oil Exploration: 1963 Annual. 1964. 30.00 (ISBN 0-686-28263-9). Munger Oil.
California Oil & Gas Exploration: 1960 Edition. 1961. 30.00 (ISBN 0-686-28261-2). Munger Oil.
California Oil & Gas Exploration: 1962 Annual. 1963. 30.00 (ISBN 0-686-28262-0). Munger Oil.
California Oil & Gas Exploration: 1964 Annual. 1965. 30.00 (ISBN 0-686-28264-7). Munger Oil.
California Oil & Gas Exploration: 1965 Annual. 1966. 30.00 (ISBN 0-686-28265-5). Munger Oil.
California Oil & Gas Exploration: 1966 Annual. 1967. 30.00 (ISBN 0-686-28266-3). Munger Oil.
California Oil & Gas Exploration: 1967 Annual. 1968. 30.00 (ISBN 0-686-28267-1). Munger Oil.
California Oil & Gas Exploration: 1968 Annual. 1969. 30.00 (ISBN 0-686-28268-X). Munger Oil.
Campbell, Robert W. Trends in the Soviet Oil & Gas Industry. LC 76-15940. (Resources for the Future Ser). (Illus.). 144p. 1977. 12.00x (ISBN 0-8018-1870-2). Johns Hopkins.
Commission of the European Communities. New Technologies for Exploration & Exploitation of Oil & Gas Resources, Vol. 1. 800p. 1979. 55.00x (ISBN 0-86010-158-4, Pub. by Graham & Trotman England). State Mutual Bk.
Commisssion of the European Communities. Oil & Gas Multilingual Glossary. 500p. 1979. 44.00x (ISBN 0-86010-170-3, Pub. by Graham & Trotman England). State Mutual Bk.
Gas Directory & Who's Who 1979. (Benn Directories Ser.). 1979. 42.50 (ISBN 0-686-52400-4, Pub by Benn Pubns). Nichols Pub.
Gas Marketing Pocket Book 1979. (Benn Directories Ser.). 1978. 7.50 (ISBN 0-510-49666-0, Pub by Benn Pubns). Nichols Pub.
Harris, D. J., et al. Coal, Gas & Electricity Industries. (Reviews of United Kingdom Statistical Sources Ser.: Vol. XI). 1979. 55.00 (ISBN 0-08-022461-X). Pergamon.
Honti, G. D. The Nitrogen Industry. 1976. 85.00x (ISBN 963-05-0228-3). Intl Pubns Serv.
International Gas Union, compiled by. Supplement to Elsevier's Dictionary of the Gas Industry: Polygot. LC 61-8851. 216p. 1973. 29.50 (ISBN 0-444-07588-7). Elsevier.
Kohl, Arthur L. & Riesenfeld, Fred C. Gas Purification. 3rd ed. (Illus.). 825p. 1979. 39.95x (ISBN 0-87201-313-8). Gulf Pub.
Lawrence, Anthony G. Pricing & Planning in the U. S. Natural Gas Industry: An Econometric & Programming Study. Bruchey, Stuart, ed. LC 78-22693. (Energy in the American Economy Ser.). (Illus.). 1979. lib. bdg. 15.00x (ISBN 0-405-11996-8). Arno.
Mosburg, Lewis G., Jr., ed. Financing Oil & Gas Ventures: 1977 Update. 1977. 37.00 (ISBN 0-89419-011-3). Inst Energy.
Nineteen Seventy Seven California Oil & Gas Review. 1978. 30.00 (ISBN 0-686-16192-0). Munger Oil.
Oil & Gas Statistics Annual 1978 to 1979. 557p. (Orig.). 1981. pap. 32.50x (ISBN 92-64-02182-5). OECD.
Persch, Fritz. Petroleum & Natural Gas Dictionary: German-English & English-German. LC 72-565819. 671p. 1970. 45.00x (ISBN 0-8002-1330-0). Intl Pubns Serv.
Shell UK Exploration & Production Ltd. Winning Supply & Service Business in Offshore Oil & Gas Markets. 112p. 1976. 77.00x (ISBN 0-86010-025-1, Pub. by Graham & Trotman England). State Mutual Bk.
Starratt, Patricia E. The Natural Gas Shortage & the Congress. LC 74-29378. 1975. pap. 4.25 (ISBN 0-8447-3148-X). Am Enterprise.
State & Federal Exploratory Wells & Core Holes Drilled off the West Coast of Continental U.S.A. Prior to 1974. 1975. 40.00 (ISBN 0-686-28277-9). Munger Oil.
United Nations Economic Commission for Europe, Commission on Gas, Minsk, USSR, 1977. The Gas Industry & the Environment: Proceedings. 1978. text ed. 51.00 (ISBN 0-08-022412-1). Pergamon.
Wedemeyer, Karl E. Interstate Natural Gas Supply & Intrastate Market Behavior. Bruchey, Stuart, ed. LC 78-22714. (Energy in the American Economy Ser.). (Illus.). 1979. lib. bdg. 12.00x (ISBN 0-405-12024-9). Arno.
Whitehead, Harry, compiled by. An A-Z of Offshore Oil & Gas. (Illus.). 339p. 1976. 37.50x (ISBN 0-87201-051-1). Gulf Pub.

GAS LEASES
see Oil and Gas Leases

GAS LIGHTING
see also Acetylene; Gas Manufacture and Works; Lighting

GAS LIQUID CHROMATOGRAPHY
see Gas Chromatography

GAS-LUBRICATED BEARINGS
Constantinescu, V. N. Gas Lubrication: Translated from the Rumanian. Wehe, Robert L., ed. Technica, Scripta, tr. LC 78-93540. 630p. 1969. pap. 19.50 (ISBN 0-685-06526-X, G00015). ASME.
Gas Bearing Symposium. 4th ed. 1969. text ed. 29.00 (ISBN 0-686-63954-5, Dist. by Air Science Co.). BHRA Fluid.
Gross, William & Matsch, Lee A. Fluid Film Lubrication. Vohr, John H. & Wildman, Manfred, eds. LC 80-36889. 773p. 1980. 38.50 (ISBN 0-471-08357-7, Pub. by Wiley-Interscience). Wiley.
International Gas Bearings Symposium, 5th. Proceedings. 1969. lib. bdg. 29.00 (ISBN 0-686-71063-0). BHRA Fluid.
International Gas Bearings Symposium, 2nd. Proceedings. 1965. 26.00 (ISBN 0-686-71064-9). BHRA Fluid.
Seventh International Gas Bearing Symposium. Proceedings. 1977. pap. 52.00 (ISBN 0-900983-57-4, Dist. by Air Science Co.). BHRA Fluid.
Sixth International Gas Bearing Symposium. Proceedings. 1974. pap. 52.00 (ISBN 0-900983-36-1, Dist. by Air Science Co.). BHRA Fluid.
Stout, K., ed. Papers Presented at the Eight International Gas Bearing Symposium. (Illus.). 325p. 1981. pap. 60.00 (ISBN 0-906085-54-3). BHRA Fluid.

GAS MANUFACTURE AND WORKS
see also Coal Gasification; Gas Companies; Gas Industry
American Gas Association. Gas Engineers Handbook. Segeler, C. George, ed. LC 65-17328. (Illus.). 1550p. 1965. 63.00 (ISBN 0-8311-3011-3). Indus Pr.
Berger, Bill & Anderson, Ken. Gas Handling & Field Processing. (Plant Operations Training Ser.: Vol. 3). 162p. 20.00 (ISBN 0-87814-111-1). Pennwell Pub.
Booth, Norman. Industrial Gases. LC 72-10293. 1973. pap. text ed. 9.25 (ISBN 0-08-016860-4). Pergamon.
International Gas Union, ed. Elsevier's Dictionary of the Gas Industry, 2 vols. (Polyglot). 1961. 73.25 (ISBN 0-444-40757-X); pap. 24.50 supplement (ISBN 0-444-40758-8). Elsevier.
IP International Conference. A Guide to North Sea Oil & Gas Technology. 1978. casebound 24.50 (ISBN 0-85501-316-8). Heyden.
Schora, Frank C., Jr., ed. Fuel Gasification. LC 87-31495. (Advances in Chemistry Ser: No. 69). 1967. 23.50 (ISBN 0-8412-0070-X). Am Chemical.

GAS-PIPES
see also Electrolytic Corrosion
American Society of Civil Engineers, compiled by. An Overview of the Alaska Highway Gas Pipeline. 136p. 1978. pap. text ed. 11.00 (ISBN 0-87262-130-8). Am Soc Civil Eng.
ASME Guide for Gas Transmission & Distribution Piping System: Includes All Addenda Issued up to the Publication of the 1983 Edition. 1980. pap. 125.00 (ISBN 0-685-67491-6, AX3080). ASME.
National Fuel Gas Code. (Fifty Ser.). Orig. Title: Installation of Gas Appliances & Gas Piping. 146p. 1974. pap. 3.00 (ISBN 0-685-46069-X, 54). Natl Fire Prot.

GAS-PRODUCERS
see also Coal Gasification; Gas and Oil Engines; Gas Manufacture and Works
De Renzo, D. Energy from Bioconversion of Waste Materials. LC 77-71660. (Energy Technology Review Ser. No. 11: Pollution Technology Review No. 33). (Illus.). 1977. 32.00 (ISBN 0-8155-0656-2). Noyes.
Stafford, D. A., et al. Methane Production from Waste Organic Matter. LC 78-31274. 1980. 79.95 (ISBN 0-8493-5223-1). CRC Pr.
Wise, Donald L., ed. Fuel Gas Production from Biomass, 2 vols. 1981. Vol. I, 288 Pgs. 76.95 (ISBN 0-8493-5990-2); Vol. II, 272 Pgs. 74.95 (ISBN 0-8493-5991-0). CRC Pr.

GAS STATIONS
see Automobiles–Service Stations

GAS TUBES
see also Diodes

GAS-TURBINES
see also Automotive Gas Turbines
CIMAC: Tenth International Conference on Combustion Engines; Discussions Only. 1973. text ed. 65.00 (ISBN 0-685-38859-X, H00085); pap. text ed. 20.00 (ISBN 0-685-38860-3). ASME.
Cohen, H., et al. Gas Turbine Theory. 337p. 1972. 32.95 (ISBN 0-686-30860-3). Halsted Pr.
Coutsouradis, D., et al, eds. High Temperature Alloys for Gas Turbines. (Illus.). 1978. text ed. 91.00x (ISBN 0-85334-815-4, Pub. by Applied Science). Burgess-Intl Ideas.
Erickson, V. L. & Julien, H. L., eds. Gas Turbine Heat Transfer: 1978. 1978. 18.00 (ISBN 0-685-66801-0, H00125). ASME.
Harman, R. T. Gas Turbine Engineering: Applications Cycles & Characteristics. LC 80-21003. 270p. 1981. 29.95 (ISBN 0-470-27065-9). Halsted Pr.
Hart, A. B. & Cutler, A. J., eds. Deposition & Corrosion in Gas Turbines. LC 73-8187. 425p. 1973. 65.95 (ISBN 0-470-35639-1). Halsted Pr.
Lefebvre, Arthur H., ed. Gas Turbine Combustor Design Problems. LC 79-22350. 431p. 1979. text ed. 51.75 (ISBN 0-89116-177-5). Hemisphere Pub.
Manual on Requirements, Handling & Quality Control of Gas Turbine Fuel. 1973. 20.00 (ISBN 0-686-52068-8, 04-531000-12). ASTM.
Sawyer's Gas Turbine Engineering Handbook, 2 vols. Date not set. Set. 28.50 (ISBN 0-686-31374-7). Diesel Pubns.
Stationary Combustion Engines & Gas Turbines. (Thirty Ser). 1970. pap. 2.00 (ISBN 0-685-58106-3, 37). Natl Fire Prot.
Stodola, A. Steam & Gas Turbines, 2 vols. 6th ed. 40.00 (ISBN 0-8446-1424-6). Peter Smith.
Whittle, Frank. Gas Turbine Aero-Thermodynamics: With Special Reference to Aircraft Propulsion. LC 80-41372. 240p. 1981. 32.00 (ISBN 0-08-026719-X); pap. 18.00 (ISBN 0-08-026718-1). Pergamon.
Woodward, John B. Marine Gas Turbines. LC 74-31383. (Ocean Engineering Ser). 390p. 1975. 39.50 (ISBN 0-471-95962-6, Pub. by Wiley-Interscience). Wiley.

GAS-TURBINES, AIRCRAFT
see Airplanes–Turbojet Engines

GAS WELDING
see Oxyacetylene Welding and Cutting

GAS WELL DRILLING
Cozzolino, John M. Management of Oil & Gas Exploration Risk. LC 77-84169. (Business Risk Analysis Ser.). 1977. 47.50 (ISBN 0-9601408-1-6). Cozzolino Assocs.

GAS WELLS
Donohue, David A. & Ertekan, Turgay. Gaswell Testing. LC 81-80726. (Illus.). 192p. 1981. text ed. 29.50 (ISBN 0-934634-10-6); pap. text ed. 19.50 (ISBN 0-934634-12-2). Intl Human Res.

GASCOIGNE, GEORGE, 1542-1577
Gascoigne, George. George Gascoigne's a Hundredth Sundrie Flowres. Repr. of 1942 ed. 23.50 (ISBN 0-403-04077-9). Somerset Pub.
--The Steele Glas & The Complainte of Phylomene: A Critical Edition with Introduction. Wallace, William I., ed. (Salzburg Studies in English Literature, Elizabethan & Renaissance Studies Ser.: No. 24). 240p. 1975. pap. text ed. 25.00x (ISBN 0-391-01382-3). Humanities.
Johnson, Ronald C. George Gascoigne. (English Authors Ser.: No. 133). lib. bdg. 10.95 (ISBN 0-8057-1212-7). Twayne.

Prouty, Charles T. George Gascoigne. LC 65-19620. 1942. 16.00 (ISBN 0-405-08867-1, Pub. by Blom). Arno.
Schelling, Felix E. Life & Writings of George Gascoigne. LC 67-27852. 1967. Repr. of 1893 ed. 6.00 (ISBN 0-8462-1010-X). Russell.
--Life & Writings of George Gascoigne Including Three New Poems. LC 76-22614. Repr. of 1893 ed. lib. bdg. 7.50 (ISBN 0-8414-7735-3). Folcroft.
Ward, Bernard. A Hundreth Sundrie Flowres: From the Original Edition of 1573. rev. 2nd ed. Miller, Ruth L., ed. LC 74-31163. (Illus.). 1975. 15.00 (ISBN 0-8046-1880-1). Kennikat.

GASDYNAMICS
see Gas Dynamics

GASEOUS PLASMA
see Plasma (Ionized Gases)

GASES
see also Bubbles; Combustion Gases; Osmosis; Pneumatics
also Specific gases, e.g. Acetyelene, Helium, Hydrogen, Nitrogen, Oxygen

Ausloos, Pierre J., ed. Ion-Molecule Reactions in the Gas Phase. LC 66-28609. (Advances in Chemistry Ser: No. 58). 1966. 26.00 (ISBN 0-8412-0059-9). Am Chemical.
Bird, R. B., et al. Fundamental Physics of Gases. Donaldson, C. D., ed. (Princeton Aeronautical Paperbacks Ser.: Vol. 7). 1961. pap. 10.00 (ISBN 0-691-07968-4). Princeton U Pr.
Bretsznajder, S. Prediction of Transport and Other Physical Properties of Fluids. 424p. 1971. text ed. 46.00 (ISBN 0-08-013412-2). Pergamon.
Christophorou, Loucas G., ed. Gaseous Dielectrics II: Proceedings of the Second International Symposium on Gaseous Dielectrics, Knoxville, Tenn., U.S.A., March 9-13, 1980. 506p. 1980. 25.00 (ISBN 0-08-025978-2). Pergamon.
Cohen, I. Bernard, ed. Laws of Gases. LC 80-2099. (Development of Science Ser.). (Illus.). 1981. lib. bdg. 35.00x (ISBN 0-405-13864-4). Arno.
Cullis, C. F. & Firth, J. G., eds. Detection & Measurement of Hazardous Gases. 1981. text ed. 35.00x (ISBN 0-435-71030-3). Heinemann Ed.
Dymond, J. H. & Smith, E. B. The Second Virial Coefficients of Pure Gases & Mixtures: A Critical Compilation. (Oxford Science Research Papers Ser.). (Illus.). 534p. 1980. pap. text ed. 69.00x (ISBN 0-19-855361-7). Oxford U Pr.
Elementary Science Study. Gases & Airs. 1975. tchr's. guide 10.20 (ISBN 0-07-018519-0, W). McGraw.
Fast, Johan D. Interaction of Metals & Gases, Vol. 1. Thermodynamics & Phase Relations. 1965. 49.50 (ISBN 0-12-249801-1). Acad Pr.
Gerrard, W. Solubility of Gases & Liquids...a Graphic Approach. (Illus.). 275p. 1976. 45.00 (ISBN 0-306-30866-5, Plenum Pr). Plenum Pub.
Gruschka, H. & Wecken, F. Gasdynamic Theory of Detonation: Combustion Science & Technology. 1971. 42.25 (ISBN 0-677-03370-2). Gordon.
Gugan, Keith. Unconfined Vapor Cloud Explosions. 250p. 1979. 29.95x (ISBN 0-87201-887-3). Gulf Pub.
Hirschfelder, Joseph O., et al. Molecular Theory of Gases & Liquids. LC 54-7621. 1964. 75.00 (ISBN 0-471-40065-3, Pub. by Wiley-Interscience). Wiley.
Holub, Robert & Vonka, Petr. The Chemical Equilibrium of Gaseous Systems. LC 75-34393. 1976. PLB 47.50 (ISBN 90-277-0556-9, Pub. by Reidel Holland). Kluwer Boston.
Howatson, A. M. An Introduction to Gas Discharges. 2nd ed. 261p. 1976. text ed. 32.00 (ISBN 0-08-020575-5); pap. text ed. 10.75 (ISBN 0-08-020574-7). Pergamon.
International Conference on the Control of Sulphur & Other Gaseous Emissions, 3rd, University of Salford, 1979. The Control of Sulphur & Other Gaseous Emmisions: Proceedings, No. 57. 460p. 1981. 80.00x (ISBN 0-85295-117-5, Pub. by Inst Chem Eng England). State Mutual Bk.
International Gas Research Conference, 1st, 1980. Proceedings. LC 80-83454. 1016p. 1980. 43.50 (ISBN 0-86587-085-3). Gov Insts.
Kerr, J. Alistair, ed. Vols. I & II, Vol. I & II. 1981. Vol. I, 576p. 79.95 (ISBN 0-8493-0375-3); Vol. II 256p. 49.95 (ISBN 0-8493-0376-1). CRC Pr.
Krypton Eighty - Five in the Atmosphere: Accumulation, Biological Significance, & Control Technology. (NCRP Reports Ser.: No. 44). 1975. 8.00 (ISBN 0-913392-26-X). NCRP Pubns.
Lind, Samuel C., et al. Radiation Chemistry of Gases. LC 61-11887. (ACS Monograph: No. 151). 1961. 30.00 (ISBN 0-8412-0351-2). Am Chemical.
Millikan, Robert, et al. Mechanics, Molecular Physics, Heat, & Sound. (Illus.). 1965. pap. 4.95x (ISBN 0-262-63001-X). MIT Pr.
Noakes, G. R., ed. Sources of Physics Teaching: Gravity. Liquids. Gases, Vol. 5. 1970. pap. text ed. 12.95x (ISBN 0-85066-040-8). Intl Ideas.
Powals, Richard J. & Zaner, Lorin J., eds. Sampling Time Estimating Manual. LC 74-81584. 60p. 1974. pap. 10.00 (ISBN 0-87762-137-3). Technomic.
Saakyan, G. S. Equilibrium Configurations of Degenerate Gaseous Masses. Hall, C. F., tr. from Rus. LC 74-13583. 294p. 1974. 58.95 (ISBN 0-470-74805-2). Halsted Pr.
Saltsburg, Howard, et al, eds. Fundamentals of Gas-Surface Interactions: Proceedings. 1967. 56.00 (ISBN 0-12-616950-0). Acad Pr.
Schneider, G. M., et al, eds. Extraction with Supercritical Gases. 1980. 48.80 (ISBN 3-527-25854-X). Verlag Chemie.
Setser, D. W., ed. Reactive Intermediates in the Gas Phase: Generation & Monitoring. LC 79-51698. 1979. 42.50 (ISBN 0-12-637450-3). Acad Pr.
Smith, Ian W. Kinetics & Dynamics of Elementary Gas Reactions. LC 79-40533. (Illus.). 1980. 72.95 (ISBN 0-408-70790-9). Butterworth.
Specialty Gases. 1981. 950.00 (ISBN 0-89336-307-3, C-036). BCC.
Steklov Institute of Mathematics, Academy of Sciences, U S S R, No. 119 & Korobeinikov, V. P. Problems in the Theory of Point Explosion in Gases: Proceedings. 311p. 1976. 58.00 (ISBN 0-8218-3019-8, STEKLO-119). Am Math.
Storch, O. Industrial Separators for Gas Cleaning. LC 78-10916. (Chemical Engineering Monographs: Vol. 6). 388p. 1979. 70.75 (ISBN 0-444-99808-X). Elsevier.
Strauss, Werner. Industrial Gas Cleaning. 2nd, rev. ed. LC 74-8066. 632p. 1976. text ed. 82.00 (ISBN 0-08-017004-8); pap. 29.50 (ISBN 0-08-019933-X). Pergamon.
Symposium on Heavy Gas, Frankfurt-Main, September 3-4, 1979. Heavy Gas & Risk Assessment: Proceedings. Hartwig, Sylvius, ed. 355p. 1980. lib. bdg. 37.00 (ISBN 90-277-1108-9, Pub. by Reidel Holland). Kluwer Boston.
Thompson, Richard L. Equilibrium States on Thin Energy Shells. LC 74-14723. (Memoirs: No. 150). 110p. 1974. pap. 8.80 (ISBN 0-8218-1850-3, MEMO-150). Am Math.

GASES-ABSORPTION AND ADSORPTION

Arkharov, V. I., ed. Surface Interactions Between Metals & Gases. LC 65-23067. 163p. 1966. 35.00 (ISBN 0-306-10738-4, Consultants). Plenum Pub.
Danckwerts, P. V. Gas Liquid Reactions. 1970. text ed. 19.95 (ISBN 0-07-015287-X, C). McGraw.
Touloukian, Y. S. & Ho, C. Y. Thermal Accommodation & Adsorption Coefficients of Gases, Vol. II-1. 1st ed. (McGraw-Hill-CINDAS Data Ser. on Material Properties). 448p. (Orig.). 1981. 42.50 (ISBN 0-07-065031-4). McGraw.

GASES-ANALYSIS

Bochkova, O. P. & Shreyder, E. Y. Spectroscopic Analysis of Gaseous Mixtures. 1966. 54.00 (ISBN 0-12-109450-2). Acad Pr.
Hill, D. W. & Powell, T. Non-Dispersive Infrared Gas Analysis in Science, Medicine & Industry. LC 68-56425. 222p. 1968. 32.50 (ISBN 0-306-30374-4, Plenum Pr). Plenum Pub.
Meek, J. M. & Craggs, J. D. Electrical Breakdown of Gases. 878p. 1978. 153.50 (ISBN 0-471-99553-3). Wiley.
Touloukian, Y. S. & Ho, C. Y. Thermal Accommodation & Adsorption Coefficients of Gases, Vol. II-1. 1st ed. (McGraw-Hill-CINDAS Data Ser. on Material Properties). 448p. (Orig.). 1981. 42.50 (ISBN 0-07-065031-4). McGraw.

GASES-DIFFUSION
see Diffusion

GASES-IONIZATION
see Ionization of Gases

GASES-LIQUEFACTION
see also Hydrogen; Liquefied Natural Gas; Liquefied Petroleum Gas; Liquid Helium; Liquid Hydrogen; Low Temperature Research

Liquid Gas Carrier Register 1980. LC 75-644549. (Illus.). 143p. 1980. 100.00x (ISBN 0-8002-2461-2). Intl Pubns Serv.
Touloukian, Y. S. & Ho, C. Y. Properties of Nonmetallic Fluid Elements, Vol. III. (M-H-CINDAS Data Series on Material Properties). 224p. 1981. text ed. 33.50 (ISBN 0-07-065033-0). McGraw.
United Nations Economic Commission for Europe, Geneva, Switzerland. Oils & Gases from Coal: A Review of the State-of-the-Art in Europe & North America Based on the Work of the Symposium on the Gasification & Liquefaction of Coal Held Under the Auspices of the UNECE, Katowice, Poland. 23-27 April 1979. (ECE Seminars & Symposia Ser.). (Illus.). 316p. 1980. 59.00 (ISBN 0-08-025678-3). Pergamon.

GASES-SPECTRA

Murcray, David G., ed. Handbook of High Resolution Infrared Laboratory Spectra of Gases of Atmospheric Interest. 288p. 1981. 49.95 (ISBN 0-8493-2950-7). CRC Pr.
Weber, A. Raman Spectroscopy of Gases & Liquids. (Topics in Current Physics Ser.: Vol. 11). (Illus.). 1979. 31.00 (ISBN 0-387-09036-3). Springer-Verlag.

GASES-VISCOSITY
see Viscosity

GASES-TABLES, CALCULATIONS, ETC.

Canjar, Lawrence & Manning, Francis. Thermodynamic Properties & Reduced Correlations for Gases. (Illus.). 222p. 1967. 19.95x (ISBN 0-87201-867-9); pap. text ed. 4.95x (ISBN 0-87201-868-7). Gulf Pub.
Keenan, Joseph H., et al. Gas Tables: Thermodynamic Properties of Air Products of Combustion & Component Gases Compressible Flow Functions Including Those of Ascher H. Shapiro & Gilbert M. Edelman. 2nd ed. LC 79-15098. 217p. 1980. 27.95 (ISBN 0-471-02207-1, Pub. by Wiley-Interscience). Wiley.
Vargaftik, N. B. Tables on the Thermophysical Properties of Liquids & Gases: In Normal & Dissociated States. 2nd ed. LC 75-14260. (Advances in Thermal Engineering Ser.). 758p. 1975. 49.50 (ISBN 0-470-90310-4). Halsted Pr.

GASES-THERAPEUTIC USE

Grant, W. J. Medical Gases--Their Properties & Uses. (Illus.). 1978. pap. 17.95 (ISBN 0-8151-3875-X). Year Bk Med.

GASES-THERAPEUTIC USE-PROGRAMMED INSTRUCTION

Seedor, Marie M. Therapy with Oxygen & Other Gases: A Programmed Unit in Fundamentals of Nursing. rev. ed. (Nursing Education Monograph Ser, No. 10). (Illus.). 1971. pap. 7.25 (ISBN 0-397-54056-6, Pub. by Columbia U Pr). Lippincott.

GASES, ASPHYXIATING AND POISONOUS
see also Asphyxia; Carbon Dioxide; Carbon Monoxide; Chemical Warfare; Mine Gases

American Welding Society. The Welding Environment. new ed. LC 72-95119. (Illus.). 160p. (Orig.). 1973. pap. text ed. 20.00 (ISBN 0-87171-103-6). Am Welding.
Thain, William. Monitoring Toxic Gases in the Atmosphere. 1980. 25.00 (ISBN 0-08-023810-6). Pergamon.
Winternitz, Milton C. Collected Studies of the Pathology of War Gas Poisoning. (Illus.). 1920. 75.00x (ISBN 0-685-69885-8). Elliots Bks.

GASES, COMPRESSED
see also Liquefied Petroleum Gas

Compressed Gas Association. Handbook of Compressed Gases. 2nd ed. 1981. text ed. 44.50 (ISBN 0-442-25419-9). Van Nos Reinhold.

GASES, ELECTRIC DISCHARGES THROUGH
see Electric Discharges through Gases

GASES, FLOW OF
see Gas Flow

GASES, IONIZATION OF
see Ionization of Gases

GASES, IONIZED
see also Air, Ionized; Ion Flow Dynamics; Magneto-Ionic Theory; Plasma (Ionized Gases)

Mitchner, M. & Kruger, Charles H. Partially Ionized Gases. 518p. 1973. 34.50 (ISBN 0-685-91057-1, Pub. by Wiley). Krieger.

GASES, KINETIC THEORY OF

Al'pert, Y. L., et al. Space Physics with Artificial Satellites. LC 64-23253. 240p. 1965. 42.50 (ISBN 0-306-10727-9, Consultants). Plenum Pub.
Brittin, Wesley E., et al, eds. Boulder Lecture Notes in Theoretical Physics, 1966: Vol. 9-C, Kinetic Theory. (Orig.). 147.00x (ISBN 0-677-11620-9). Gordon.
Brush, S. G. The Kind of Motion We Call Heat: A History of the Kinetic Theory of Gases in the Nineteenth Century, 2 bks. 1976. Bk. 1. 24.75 (ISBN 0-7204-0370-7, North-Holland); Bk. 2. 59.75 (ISBN 0-7204-0482-7); Set. 75.00 (ISBN 0-686-67836-2). Elsevier.
Cercignani, Carlo. Mathematical Methods in Kinetic Theory. LC 69-15832. (Illus.). 227p. 1969. 29.50 (ISBN 0-306-30386-8, Plenum Pr). Plenum Pub.
Chapman, S. & Cowling, T. G. Mathematical Theory of Non-Uniform Gases. 3rd ed. LC 70-77285. (Illus.). 1970. 47.95 (ISBN 0-521-07577-7). Cambridge U Pr.
Dushman, S. & Lafferty, J. M. Scientific Foundations of Vacuum Technique. 2nd ed. LC 61-17361. 1962. 59.00 (ISBN 0-471-22803-6, Pub. by Wiley-Interscience). Wiley.
Ferziger, J. H. & Kaper, H. G. Mathematical Theory of Transport Processes in Gases. 1972. 63.50 (ISBN 0-444-10352-X, North-Holland). Elsevier.
Gatignol, T. Theorie Cinetique des Gaz a Repartition Descrete De Vitesses. 206p. 1975. pap. 14.70 (ISBN 0-387-07156-3). Springer-Verlag.
Heer, C. V. Statistical Mechanics, Kinetic, Theory & Stochastic Process. 1972. 24.95 (ISBN 0-12-336550-3). Acad Pr.
Johnston, Harold S. Gas Phase Reaction Rate Theory. 362p. 1966. 27.50 (ISBN 0-8260-4805-6, Pub. by Wiley-Interscience). Wiley.
Liboff, Richard L. Introduction to the Theory of Kinetic Equations. corr. ed. LC 76-30383. (Illus.). 410p. 1979. Repr. of 1969 ed. lib. bdg. 20.50 (ISBN 0-88275-496-3). Krieger.
Nozdrev, V. F. Application of Ultrasonics in Molecular Physics. (Russian Monographs Ser). (Illus.). 1963. 104.00 (ISBN 0-677-20360-8). Gordon.
Resibois, P. & De Leener, M. F. Classical Kinetic Theory of Fluids. LC 76-58852. 1977. 42.50 (ISBN 0-471-71694-4, Pub. by Wiley-Interscience). Wiley.
Sears, Francis W. & Salinger, Gerhard L. Thermodynamics, the Kinetic Theory of Gases & Statistical Mechanics. 3rd ed. 464p. 1975. text ed. 23.95 (ISBN 0-201-06894-X). A-W.
Tabor, D. Gases, Liquids & Solids. 2nd ed. LC 78-26451. (Illus.). 1980. 57.50 (ISBN 0-521-22383-0); pap. 15.95 (ISBN 0-521-29466-5). Cambridge U Pr.
Truesdell, C. & Muncaster, R. G. Fundamentals of Maxwell's Kinetic Theory of a Simple Monatomic Gas: Treated As a Branch of Rational Mechanics. (Pure & Applied Mathematics Ser.). 1979. 62.00 (ISBN 0-12-701350-4). Acad Pr.
Wu, T. Kinetic Equations of Gases & Plasmas. 1966. 16.50 (ISBN 0-201-08750-2, Adv Bk Prog). A-W.

GASES, PHOTOIONIZATION OF
see Photoionization of Gases

GASES, RARE
see also Argon; Helium; Radon

Asimov, Isaac. Noble Gases. LC 66-13510. (Science & Discovery Ser). (gr. 9 up). 1966. 11.00x (ISBN 0-465-05129-4). Basic.
Clever, H. L. Helium & Neon: Gas Solubilities. (Solubility Data Ser.: Vol. 1). 1979. 100.00 (ISBN 0-08-022351-6). Pergamon.
--Krypton, Xenon, & Radon: Gas Solubilities. (Solubility Data Ser.: Vol. 2). 1979. 100.00 (ISBN 0-08-022352-4). Pergamon.
Guttman, Viktor. Main Group Elements - Group 7 & Noble Gases. (Mtp International Review of Science-Inorganic Chemistry Ser. 1: Vol. 3). (Illus.). 24.50, index vol. 12.50 (ISBN 0-8391-1006-5). Univ Park.
Hawkins, Donald T., et al, eds. Noble Gas Compounds, a Bibliography 1962-1976. 1978. 45.00 (ISBN 0-306-65171-8). IFI Plenum.
Hyman, Herbert H., ed. Noble Gas Compounds. LC 63-20907. 1963. 15.00x (ISBN 0-226-36540-9). U of Chicago Pr.
Inert Gas Systems for Oil Tankers. 52p. 1981. pap. 15.75 (ISBN 9-2801-1110-8, IMCO 64, IMCO). Unipub.
Klein, M. L. & Venables, J. A., eds. Rare Gas Solids, Vol. 1. 1976. 99.00 (ISBN 0-12-413501-3). Acad Pr.
--Rare Gas Solids, Vol. 2. 1977. 81.00 (ISBN 0-12-413502-1). Acad Pr.
Macdonald, A. G. & Wann, K. T. Physiological Aspects of Anaesthetics & Inert Gases. 1978. 51.50 (ISBN 0-12-464150-4). Acad Pr.
Marine Publications Intl. Ltd., ed. Inert Gas System Manual. 1981. 100.00x (ISBN 0-686-75502-2, Pub. by Marine Pubns Intl England). State Mutual Bk.
Smith, B. L. & Webb, J. P. The Inert Gases: Model Systems for Science. (Wykeham Science Ser: No. 16). 1971. 9.95x (ISBN 0-8448-1118-1). Crane Russak Co.

GASES AT HIGH TEMPERATURES

Cambel, Ali B., et al. Real Gases. 1963. 30.00 (ISBN 0-12-155950-5). Acad Pr.
Fox, Robert. Caloric Theory of Gases from Lavoisier to Regnault. (Illus.). 1971. 32.00x (ISBN 0-19-858131-9). Oxford U Pr.
Shuler, Kurt E., ed. Ionization in High Temperature Gases. (Progress in Astronautics & Aeronautics: Vol. 12). 1963. 14.00 (ISBN 0-12-535112-7). Acad Pr.
Zel'Dovich, Ya B., et al. Physics of Shock Waves & High Temperature Hydrodynamic Phenomena, 2 Vols. Vol. 1 1966. 55.50 (ISBN 0-12-778701-1); Vol. 2 1967. 55.50 (ISBN 0-12-778702-X); Set. 91.00 (ISBN 0-686-76856-6). Acad Pr.

GASES IN METALS

Arkharov, V. I., ed. Surface Interactions Between Metals & Gases. LC 65-23067. 163p. 1966. 35.00 (ISBN 0-306-10738-4, Consultants). Plenum Pub.
Fast, Johan D. Interaction of Metals & Gases, Vol. 1. Thermodynamics & Phase Relations. 1965. 49.50 (ISBN 0-12-249801-1). Acad Pr.
Gulaev, B. B., ed. Gases in Cast Metals. LC 65-15007. 257p. 1965. 45.00 (ISBN 0-306-10726-0, Consultants). Plenum Pub.

Meinick, Laben M., et al, eds. Determination of Gaseous Elements in Metals. (Chemical Analysis Ser.: Vol. 40). 752p. (Orig.). 1974. 51.25 (ISBN 0-471-59328-1). Krieger.
Roberts, M. W. Chemistry of the Metal-Gas Interface. McKee, C. S., ed. (Monographs on the Physics & Chemistry of Materials). (Illus.). 1979. 69.00x (ISBN 0-19-851339-9). Oxford U Pr.

GASES IN MINES
see Mine Gases

GASES IN THE BLOOD
see Blood Gases

GASIFICATION OF COAL
see Coal Gasification

GASKELL, ELIZABETH CLEGHORN (STEVENSON), 1810-1865
Beer, Patricia. Reader, I Married Him: A Study of the Women Characters of Jane Austen, Charlotte Bronte, Elizabeth Gaskell & George Eliot. 1979. pap. 3.95 (ISBN 0-06-464034-5, BN4034, B&N). Har-Row.
Chadwick, Esther A. Mrs. Gaskell. 1973. 25.00 (ISBN 0-8274-0084-5). R West.
Chapple, J. A. & Sharps, J. G. Elizabeth Gaskell: A Portrait in Letters. 160p. 1981. 42.00x (ISBN 0-686-73058-5, Pub. by Manchester U Pr England). State Mutual Bk.
Craik, W. A. Elizabeth Gaskell & the English Provincial Novel. 1975. pap. 4.95x (ISBN 0-416-82640-7). Methuen Inc.
Duthie, Enid L. The Themes of Elizabeth Gaskell. 217p. 1980. 29.50x (ISBN 0-8476-6224-1). Rowman.
Easson, Angus. Elizabeth Gaskell. 1979. 22.00x (ISBN 0-7100-0099-5). Routledge & Kegan.
French, Yvonne. Mrs. Gaskell. 1979. Repr. of 1949 ed. lib. bdg. 15.00 (ISBN 0-8482-3959-8). Norwood Edns.
Ganz, Margaret. Elizabeth Gaskell. (The Artist in Conflict). 9.95 (ISBN 0-685-60123-4, Pub by Twayne). Cyrco Pr.
--Elizabeth Gaskell: The Artist in Conflict. LC 68-24279. 313p. 1969. text ed. 22.50x (ISBN 0-8290-0169-7). Irvington.
Gaskell, E. The Letters of Mrs. Gaskell. 1036p. 1966. 59.00x (ISBN 0-7190-0127-7, Pub. by Manchester U Pr England). State Mutual Bk.
Gerin, Winifred. Elizabeth Gaskell. (Ser. K). (Illus.). 352p. 1976. pap. 9.95 (ISBN 0-19-281296-3). Oxford U Pr.
--Elizabeth Gaskell: A Biography. 1976. 24.95x (ISBN 0-19-812070-2). Oxford U Pr.
Hopkins, A. B. Elizabeth Gaskell: Her Life & Work. LC 71-120631. 1970. Repr. lib. bdg. 24.00x (ISBN 0-374-93940-3). Octagon.
Lane, Margaret. Bronte Story. LC 75-108394. (Illus.). 1971. Repr. of 1953 ed. lib. bdg. 16.00x (ISBN 0-8371-3817-5, LABS). Greenwood.
Martin, Hazel T. Petticoat Rebels. LC 67-19629. 1968. 3.95 (ISBN 0-87037-021-9). Helios.
Payne, George A. Mrs. Gaskell: A Brief Biography. LC 76-9117. 1976. Repr. of 1929 ed. lib. bdg. 12.50 (ISBN 0-8414-6749-8). Folcroft.
--Mrs. Gaskell & Knutsford. 1973. Repr. of 1900 ed. 17.50 (ISBN 0-8274-0992-3). R West.
Pollard, Arthur. Mrs. Gaskell: Novelist & Biographer. LC 66-6073. (Illus.). 1965. 12.50x (ISBN 0-674-57750-7). Harvard U Pr.
Rubenius, Aina. The Woman Question in Mrs. Gaskell's Life & Works. LC 72-90568. viii, 396p. 1973. Repr. of 1950 ed. 22.00 (ISBN 0-8462-1717-1). Russell.
Sanders, Gerald D. Elizabeth Gaskell. 1971. Repr. of 1929 ed. 12.00 (ISBN 0-403-00711-9). Scholarly.
--Elizabeth Gaskell. LC 71-139938. (With bibl. by Clark S. Northup). 1971. Repr. of 1929 ed. 13.00 (ISBN 0-8462-1544-6). Russell.
Sharps, J. G. Mrs. Gaskell's Observation & Invention: The Fiction of Elizabeth Gaskell. 728p. 1970. 29.95x (ISBN 0-8464-0655-1). Beekman Pubs.
Shrivastava, K. C. Mrs. Gaskell As Novelist. (Salzburg Studies in English Literature: Romantic Reassessment Ser.: No. 70). 1977. pap. text ed. 25.00x (ISBN 0-391-01523-0). Humanities.
Whitehill, Jane. Letters to Mrs. Gaskell & Charles Eliot Norton. LC 73-14667. 1932. lib. bdg. 20.00 (ISBN 0-8414-9450-9). Folcroft.
Whitfield, A. Stanton. Mrs. Gaskell: Her Life & Work. LC 73-14820. 1929. lib. bdg. 25.00 (ISBN 0-8414-9462-2). Folcroft.

GASKELL, ELIZABETH CLEGHORN (STEVENSON), 1810-1865-BIBLIOGRAPHY
Sanders, Gerald D. Elizabeth Gaskell. 1971. Repr. of 1929 ed. 12.00 (ISBN 0-403-00711-9). Scholarly.
Selig, Robert L. Elizabeth Gaskell: A Reference Guide. (Reference Publications Ser.). 1977. lib. bdg. 30.00 (ISBN 0-8161-7813-5). G K Hall.
Welch, Jeffrey E. Elizabeth Gaskell: An Annotated Bibliography, 1929-1975. LC 75-42874. (Reference Library of the Humanities Ser.: Vol. 50). 1977. lib. bdg. 21.50 (ISBN 0-8240-9950-8). Garland Pub.

GASOLINE
see also Airplanes–Fuel
Allvine, Fred C. & Patterson, James M. Competition, Ltd.: The Marketing of Gasoline. LC 70-180491. (Illus.). 352p. 1972. 15.00x (ISBN 0-253-31390-2). Ind U Pr.
Effect of Automotive Emission Requirements on Gasoline Characteristics. 1971. pap. 9.50 (ISBN 0-8031-0004-3, 04-487000-12). ASTM.
Fleming, Harold M. Gasoline Prices & Competition. LC 65-26736. 1966. 20.00x (ISBN 0-89197-187-4). Irvington.
Hopkins, Robert A. Living Without Gasoline. LC 76-19477. 1979. 10.95 (ISBN 0-917240-06-5). Am Metric.
McGillivray, Robert G. Automobile Gasoline Conservation. (An Institute Paper). 67p. 1976. pap. 3.00 (ISBN 0-87766-162-6, 14100). Urban Inst.
Murizi, Alex & Kelly, Thom. Prices & Consumer Information: The Benefits from Posting Retail Gasoline Prices. 1978. pap. 4.25 (ISBN 0-8447-3295-8). Am Enterprise.
Scardino, Vince, et al. Impact of the FEA-EPA Fuel Economy Information Program: Final Report. 1976. pap. 11.80x (ISBN 0-89011-488-9, ECR-112). Abt Assoc.
--Impact of the FEA-EPA Fuel Economy Information Program: Summary. 1976. pap. 1.90x (ISBN 0-89011-487-0, ECR-111). Abt Assoc.
Tenneco Oil Company. Operators Handbook. 217p. 1961. 11.95x (ISBN 0-87201-643-9). Gulf Pub.

GASOLINE ENGINES
see Gas and Oil Engines

GASOLINE STATIONS
see Automobiles–Service Stations

GASP (COMPUTER PROGRAM LANGUAGE)
Horn, Carin & Poirot, James. Computer Literacy: Problem-Solving with Computers. (Illus.). 300p. (Orig.). (gr. 7 up). 1981. pap. 13.95 (ISBN 0-88408-133-8). Sterling Swift.
Pritsker, A. Alan. The Gasp IV Simulation Language. LC 74-3281. 416p. 1974. 31.00 (ISBN 0-471-70045-2, Pub. by Wiley-Interscience). Wiley.
Pritzker, Alan B. & Young, Robert E. Simulation with Gasp PL I: A PL I Based Continuous Discrete Simulation Language. LC 75-23182. 335p. 1975. 26.50 (ISBN 0-471-70046-0, Pub. by Wiley-Interscience). Wiley.
Prutsker, A., et al. Simulation with Gasp Two: A Fortran Based Simulation Language. (Automatic Computation Ser). 1969. pap. text ed. 16.95 (ISBN 0-13-810424-7). P-H.

GASPARD, LEON, 1882-1964
Waters, Frank. Leon Gaspard. rev. 2nd ed. (Illus.). 170p. 1981. Repr. of 1964 ed. price not set (ISBN 0-937634-02-6). Fenn Gall Pub.

GASPE, DISTRICT, QUEBEC-DESCRIPTION AND TRAVEL
Le Clercq, Chretien. New Relation of Gaspesia: With the Customs & Religion of the Gaspesian Indian. Ganong, William F., ed. LC 68-28600. 1968. Repr. of 1910 ed. lib. bdg. 33.75x (ISBN 0-8371-5044-2, LERG). Greenwood.

GASPERI, ALCIDE DE, 1881-1954
Carrillo, Elisa. Alcide DeGasperi: The Long Apprenticeship. 1965. 7.95x (ISBN 0-268-00001-8). U of Notre Dame Pr.

GASQUET, FRANCIS AIDAN, CARDINAL, 1846-1929
Chase, Don. A Road Past His Door: Gasquet. (Illus.). 1973. velo-bind 2.25 (ISBN 0-918634-30-X). D M Chase.

GASSENDI, PIERRE, 1592-1655
Detel, Wolfgang. Scientia Rerum Nature Occultarum Methodologische Studien Zur Physik Pierre Gassendis. (Quellen und Studien Zur Philosophie: Vol. 14). 1978. 52.00x (ISBN 3-11-007320-X). De Gruyter.
Mandon, L. Etude Sur le Syntagma Philosophicum De Gassendi. LC 74-105933. 1970. Repr. of 1858 ed. text ed. 20.50 (ISBN 0-8337-2198-4). B Franklin.
Pfaff, Rudolph F. Die Unterschiede Zwischen der Naturphilosophie Descartes und Derjenigen Gassendis und der Gegensatz Beider Philosophen Ueberhaupt. 1964. 18.00 (ISBN 0-8337-2732-X). B Franklin.
Thomas, P. Felix. Philosophie De Gassendi. 1889. lib. bdg. 23.50 (ISBN 0-8337-3514-4). B Franklin.

GASTEROMYCETES
see also Puffballs
Burk, W. R. A Bibliography of North American Gasteromycetes I: Phalales. 200p. 1981. pap. text ed. 20.00x (ISBN 3-7682-1262-9). Lubrecht & Cramer.
Coker, William C. & Couch, John N. The Gasteromycetes of Eastern United States & Canada. Bd. with The Gasteromycetes of Ohio. Johnson, Minne M. (Illus.). 7.50 (ISBN 0-8446-5017-X). Peter Smith.
--The Gasteromycetes of the Eastern United States & Canada. LC 73-91490. (Illus.). 447p. 1974. pap. 6.95 (ISBN 0-486-23033-3). Dover.
Johnson, Minnie M. The Gasteromycetae of Ohio: Puffballs, Bird's Nest Fungi & Stinkhorns. 1929. 1.50 (ISBN 0-686-30296-6). Ohio Bio Survey.

GASTEROPODA
see also Opisthobranchiata; Snails
Cameron, R. A. & Redfern, Margaret. British Land Snails: Mollusca: Gastropoda: Keys & Notes for the Identification of the Species. (Synopses of the British Fauna Ser.). 1976. 8.00 (ISBN 0-12-157050-9). Acad Pr.
Farmer, Wesley M. Sea-Slug Gastropods. (Illus.). 177p. (Orig.). 1980. pap. 10.00 (ISBN 0-937772-00-3). Farmer Ent.
Fretter, V. & Peake, J., eds. Pulmonates: Functonal Anatomy & Physiology, Vol. 1. 1975. 64.50 (ISBN 0-12-267501-0). Acad Pr.
Graham, Alistair. British Prosobranch & Other Operculate Gastropod Molluscs. (Synopses of the British Fauna: No. 2). 1972. 8.00 (ISBN 0-12-294850-5). Acad Pr.
Hubendick, Bengt. Fresh Water Gastropods of Sierra Leone. (Acta Regiae Societatis Scientiarum et Litterarum Gothoburgensis, Zoological: No. 11). (Illus., Orig.). 1977. pap. text ed. 3.75x (ISBN 91-85252-07-7). Humanities.
Keen, A. Myra & Doty, Charlotte L. Annotated Check List of the Gastropods of Cape Arago, Oregon. (Studies in Zoology Ser.: No. 3). 1942. pap. 2.50 (ISBN 0-87071-103-2). Oreg St U Pr.
Macan, T. T. A Key to the British Fresh - & Brackish - Water Gastropods. 4th ed. 1977. 11.00x (ISBN 0-900386-30-4, Pub. by Freshwater Bio). State Mutual Bk.
Thompson, Fred G. Aquatic Snails of the Family Hydrobiidae of Peninsular Florida. LC 68-9707. 1968. 9.00 (ISBN 0-8130-0273-7). U Presses Fla.
Welch, D'Alte A. Distribution of Variation of Achatinella Mustelina Mighels in the Waianae Mountains, Oahu. Repr. of 1938 ed. pap. 15.00 (ISBN 0-527-02260-8). Kraus Repr.

GASTON, A. G.
Gaston, A. G. Green Power: The Successful Way of A. G. Gaston. (Illus.). 1977. Repr. of 1968 ed. 8.95x (ISBN 0-916624-09-9). TSU Pr.
--Green Power: The Successful Way of A. G. Gaston. (Illus.). 1978. pap. 2.95x (ISBN 0-916624-10-2). TSU Pr.

GASTON 3RD PHOEBUS, COUNT OF FOIX, 1331-1391
Madden, D. H. Chapter of Mediaeval History. LC 74-91048. 1969. Repr. of 1924 ed. 15.00 (ISBN 0-8046-0658-7). Kennikat.

GASTRIC DISEASES
see Stomach–Diseases

GASTRIC JUICE
see also Pepsin
Beaumont, William. Experiments & Observations of the Gastric Jucie & the Physiology of Digestion. 1976. Repr. of 1833 ed. 28.00 (ISBN 0-403-06490-2, Regency). Scholarly.
Kasbekar, Dinkar K., et al, eds. Gastric Hydrogen Ion Secretion. (Nutrition & Clinical Nutrition Ser.: Vol. 3). 1976. 49.75 (ISBN 0-8247-6432-3). Dekker.
Shnitka, T. K., ed. Gastric Secretions - Mechanism & Control. 1967. 75.00 (ISBN 0-08-012412-7). Pergamon.

GASTRIC MUCOSA
Harmon, John. Basic Mechanisms of Gastrointestinal Mucosal Cell Injury & Protection. (Illus.). 380p. 1981. lib. bdg. 19.50 (ISBN 0-683-03892-3). Williams & Wilkins.
Kasbekar, Dinkar K., et al, eds. Gastric Hydrogen Ion Secretion. (Nutrition & Clinical Nutrition Ser.: Vol. 3). 1976. 49.75 (ISBN 0-8247-6432-3). Dekker.

GASTRITIS
see Stomach–Diseases

GASTROENTEROLOGY
see also Intestines; Stomach
Anderson, Neil V., ed. Veterinary Gastroenterology. LC 79-20234. (Illus.). 720p. 1980. text ed. 65.00 (ISBN 0-8121-0632-6). Lea & Febiger.
Asquith, Peter. Immunology of the Gastrointestinal Tract. (Illus.). 1979. text ed. 69.00 (ISBN 0-443-01589-9). Churchill.
Banks, Peter A. Pancreatitis. LC 78-11341. (Topics in Gastroenterology Ser.). (Illus.). 236p. 1979. 22.50 (ISBN 0-306-40116-9, Plenum Pr). Plenum Pub.
Barany, Franz R. & Torsoli, Aldo, eds. Gastrointestinal Emergencies: First International Symposium on Gastrointestinal Emergencies, Stockholm, 1975 - Proceedings. 1977. text ed. 51.00 (ISBN 0-08-020494-5). Pergamon.
Baron, J. H. & Moody, F., eds. Gastroenterology: Foregut, Vol. 1. (Butterworth International Medical Reviews). 1981. text ed. 29.95 (ISBN 0-407-02287-2). Butterworth.
Bockus, Henry L., ed. Gastroenterology, Vol. 1. 3rd ed. LC 73-91276. (Illus.). 1170p. 1974. text ed. 50.00 (ISBN 0-7216-1773-5). Saunders.
--Gastroenterology, Vol. 2. 3rd ed. LC 73-91276. (Illus.). 1976. text ed. 50.00 (ISBN 0-7216-1774-3). Saunders.
--Gastroenterology, Vol. 3. LC 73-91276. (Illus.). 1976. text ed. 50.00 (ISBN 0-7216-1775-1). Saunders.
--Gastroenterology, Vol. 4. LC 73-91276. (Illus.). 1976. text ed. 40.00 (ISBN 0-7216-1776-X). Saunders.
Bonfils, S., et al, eds. Hormonal Receptors in Digestive Tract Physiology. (INSERM Symposium: No. 3). 1977. 58.75 (ISBN 0-7204-0618-8, North-Holland). Elsevier.
Bouchier, I. A. Gastroenterology. 2nd ed. (Concise Medical Textbook Ser.). (Illus.). 1978. pap. text ed. 14.50 (ISBN 0-02-857300-5). Macmillan.
Bouchier, Ian A., ed. Recent Advances in Gastroenterology, No. 4. (Illus.). 352p. 1980. text ed. 45.00x (ISBN 0-443-01748-4). Churchill.
--Recent Advances in Gastroenterology, No. 3. LC 76-21318. (Recent Advances Ser.). (Illus.). 1977. text ed. 39.00 (ISBN 0-443-01319-5). Churchill.
Boyce, H. Worth, Jr. & Palmer, Eddy D. Techniques of Clinical Gastroenterology. (Illus.). 508p. 1975. 36.25 (ISBN 0-398-03182-7). C C Thomas.
Brooks, Frank P. Control of Gastrointestinal Function: An Introduction to the Physiology of the Gastrointestinal Tract. (Illus.). 1970. pap. text ed. 8.50x (ISBN 0-02-315090-4). Macmillan.
Brooks, Frank P., ed. Gastrointestinal Pathophysiology. 2nd ed. (Pathophysiology Ser.). 1978. text ed. 18.95x (ISBN 0-19-502330-7); pap. text ed. 11.95x (ISBN 0-19-502331-5). Oxford U Pr.
Caspary, Wolfgang F., ed. Sucralfate: A New Therapeutic Concept. (Illus.). 133p. 1981. pap. text ed. price not set (ISBN 0-8067-0341-5). Urban & S.
Cook, G. C. Tropical Gastroenterology. (Illus.). 464p. 1980. text ed. 59.50x (ISBN 0-19-261228-X). Oxford U Pr.
Crane, R. Gastrointestinal Physiology, Vol. III. 1979. 34.50 (ISBN 0-8391-1069-3). Univ Park.
Demling, L. & Ottenjanm, R., eds. Gastrointestinal Motility: International Symposium, July 1969. 1971. 17.50 (ISBN 0-12-209050-0). Acad Pr.
Dodge, J. A. Topics in Paediatric Gastroenterology. (Illus.). 1976. pap. text ed. 20.00x (ISBN 0-272-79375-2). State Mutual Bk.
Dodge, J. A., ed. Topics in Pediatric Gastroenterology. (Illus.). 1976. pap. text ed. 27.95x (ISBN 0-8464-0931-3). Beekman Pubs.
Duthie, H. L. & Wormsley, K. G. Scientific Basis of Gastroenterology. (Illus.). 1979. text ed. 49.00 (ISBN 0-443-01772-7). Churchill.
Duthrie, H. Gastrointestinal Motility. 1978. 39.50 (ISBN 0-8391-1268-8). Univ Park.
The Epidemiology & Control of Gastrointestinal Parasites of Sheep in Australia. 153p. pap. 11.00 (ISBN 0-643-00301-0, CO21, CSIRO). Unipub.
Fielding, L. P., ed. Gastrointestinal Mucosal Blood Flow. (Illus.). 248p. 1980. text ed. 40.00 (ISBN 0-443-02119-8). Churchill.
Floch, Martin H. Nutrition & Diet Therapy in Gastrointestinal Diseases. (Topics in Gastroenterology Ser.). 390p. 1981. 35.00 (ISBN 0-306-40508-3, Plenum Pr). Plenum Pub.
Fruehmorgen, P. & Claasen, M. Endoscopy & Biopsy in Gastroenterology. (Illus.). 256p. 1980. pap. 15.00 (ISBN 0-387-09645-0). Springer-Verlag.
Gastroenterological Symposium, 3rd. The Sphincter of Oddi: Proceedings. Delmont, J., ed. (Illus.). 1977. 37.25 (ISBN 3-8055-2623-7). S Karger.
Gillespie, Iain E. & Thomson, Thomas J. Gastroenterology: An Integrated Course. 2nd ed. 1977. pap. 12.50 (ISBN 0-443-01457-4). Churchill.
Gitnick, G. L. Current Gastroenterology, Vol. 1. 463p. 1980. 40.00 (ISBN 0-471-09536-2, Pub. by Wiley Med). Wiley.
Gitnick, Gary L., ed. Current Gastroenterology, Vol. 1. (Current Ser). (Illus.). 464p. 1980. 40.00 (ISBN 0-471-09536-2, Pub. by Wiley Med). Wiley.
--Current Gastroenterology & Hepatology. (Illus.). 510p. 1979. 45.00 (ISBN 0-471-09479-X, Pub. by Wiley Med). Wiley.
Given, Barbara A. & Simmons, Sandra J. Gastroenterology in Clinical Nursing. 3rd ed. LC 79-13048. (Illus.). 1979. pap. text ed. 17.95 (ISBN 0-8016-1855-X). Mosby.
Glass, George B., ed. Gastrointestinal Hormones. (Comprehensive Endocrinology Ser.). 1028p. 1980. text ed. 92.00 (ISBN 0-89004-395-7). Raven.
--Progress in Gastroenterology, Vols. I-II. LC 68-11924. (Illus.). 1968. Vol. 1, 1968 528pps. 81.00 (ISBN 0-8089-0149-4); Vol. II, 1970 544pps. 81.00 (ISBN 0-8089-0150-8). Grune.

--Progress in Gastroenterology, Vol. III. 1072p. 1977. 98.75 (ISBN 0-8089-1025-6). Grune.
Gryboski, Joyce. Gastrointestinal Problems in the Infant. LC 74-21012. (Mpcp Ser.: Vol. 13). (Illus.). 811p. 1975. text ed. 32.00 (ISBN 0-7216-4323-X). Saunders.
Harmon, John. Basic Mechanisms of Gastrointestinal Mucosal Cell Injury & Protection. (Illus.). 380p. 1981. lib. bdg. 19.50 (ISBN 0-683-03892-3). Williams & Wilkins.
Harries, J. T. Essentials of Paediatric Gastroenterology. LC 77-4440. (Illus.). 1978. text ed. 40.00 (ISBN 0-443-01645-3). Churchill.
Hill, Rolla B. The Gastrointestinal Tract. LC 77-1466. 242p. 1977. 21.00 (ISBN 0-683-04005-7). Krieger.
Immunology of the Gut. (Ciba Foundation Symposium Ser: No. 46). 1977. 34.25 (ISBN 90-219-4052-3, Excerpta Medica). Elsevier.
Kirsner, Joseph B. Inflammatory Bowel Disease. 2nd ed. Shorter, Roy G., ed. LC 79-8884. (Illus.). 693p. 1980. text ed. 74.00 (ISBN 0-8121-0698-9). Lea & Febiger.
Koretz, Ronald L., ed. Practical Gastroenterology: Family Practice Today: a Comprehensive Postgraduate Library. 276p. 1982. 24.00 (ISBN 0-471-09513-3, Pub. by Wiley Med). Wiley.
Langman, M. J. Concise Textbook of Gastroenterolgy. (Illus.). 212p. 1973. pap. text ed. 9.50 (ISBN 0-443-01024-2). Churchill.
Liebman, William. Pediatric Gastroenterology Case Studies. 1980. pap. 18.50 (ISBN 0-87488-084-X). Med Exam.
Lifshitz. Clinical Disorders in Pediatric Gastroenterology & Nutrition. (Pediatrics Ser.: Vol. 1). 464p. 1980. 44.50 (ISBN 0-8247-6954-6). Dekker.
Maratka, Z. & Ottenjann, R., eds. Inflammation in Gut: Esophagitis, Duodenitis, Segmental Colitis. (Bibliotheca Gastroenterologica: No. 9). (Illus.). 1970. pap. 35.50 (ISBN 3-8055-0043-2). S Karger.
Najarian, John S. & Delaney, John P., eds. Surgery of the Gastrointestinal Tract. LC 73-89912. (Illus.). 1974. 32.50 (ISBN 0-8151-6330-4, Pub. by Symposia Special). Year Bk Med.
Okolicsanyi, L. Familial Hyperbilirubinemia: Proceedings of the Workshop on Familial Disorders of Hepatic Bilirubin Metabolism Held in Venice, Italy 23rd-24th May 1980. LC 80-41457. 263p. 1981. 45.00 (ISBN 0-471-27927-7, Pub. by Wiley-Interscience). Wiley.
Op Den Orth, J. Odo. The Standard Biphasic-Contrast Examination of the Stomach & Duodenum. 1979. lib. bdg. 56.50 (ISBN 90-247-2159-8, Pub. by Martinus Nijhoff Netherlands). Kluwer Boston.
Palmer, Eddy D. Practical Points in Gastroenterology. 3rd. ed. LC 80-17916. 1980. 14.50 (ISBN 0-87488-733-X). Med Exam.
Performing G. I. Procedures. LC 81-965. (Nursing Photobook Ser.). (Illus.). 1981. 12.95 (ISBN 0-916730-31-X). Intermed Comm.
Pfeiffer, Carl J., et al. Gasfro-Intestinal Ultrastructure: An Atlas of Scanning & Transmission Electron Micrographs. 1974. 63.00 (ISBN 0-12-553750-6). Acad Pr.
Picazo, J. Glucagon in Gastroenterology. 146p. text ed. 13.95 (ISBN 0-8391-1375-7). Univ Park.
Powell, L. W. & Piper, D. W., eds. Fundamentals of Gastroenterology. 2nd ed. LC 77-21250. 1978. pap. 14.95 (ISBN 0-8391-1184-3). Univ Park.
--Fundamentals of Gastroenterology: With Self-Assessment Workbook. 3rd ed. (Illus.). 222p. 1980. pap. text ed. 17.50x incl. wkbk. (ISBN 0-909337-26-8); wkbk. avail. ADIS Pr.
Read, A. E. Modern Trends in Gastroenterology, Vol. 5. 1975. 44.95 (ISBN 0-407-00034-8). Butterworth.
Read, Alan E., et al. Basic Gastroenterology. 3rd ed. (Illus.). 568p. 1981. pap. text ed. 39.50 (ISBN 0-7236-0551-3). Wright-PSG.
Roy, et al. Pediatric Clinical Gastroenterology. 2nd ed. LC 75-22272. (Illus.). 1975. 41.50 (ISBN 0-8016-4613-8). Mosby.
Rozen, P., et al, eds. Gastrointestinal Cancer: Advances in Basic Sciences. (Frontiers of Gastrointestinal Research: Vol. 4). (Illus.). 1979. 57.00 (ISBN 3-8055-2903-1). S Karger.
--Gastrointestinal Cancer: Advances in Diagnostics Techniques & Therapy. (Frontiers of Gastrointestinal Research: Vol. 5). (Illus.). 1979. 57.00 (ISBN 3-8055-2905-8). S Karger.
Schapiro, Melvin & Kuritsky, Joel. The Gastroenterology Assistant: A Laboratory Manual. (Illus.). 112p. 1972. photocopy ed. spiral 11.75 (ISBN 0-398-02618-1). C C Thomas.
--The Gastroenterology Assistant: A Laboratory Manual. 2nd ed. LC 81-50268. (Illus.). 150p. 1981. 22.50x (ISBN 0-9605718-3-3). Valley Presbyterian.
Schiller, K. F. & Salmon, P. R. Modern Topics in Gastrointestinal Endoscopy. (Illus.). 1977. 27.50 (ISBN 0-8151-7557-4). Year Bk Med.
Sernka, Thomas & Jacobson, Eugene. Gastrointestinal Physiology: The Essentials. 1979. pap. 11.95 (ISBN 0-683-07720-1). Williams & Wilkins.
Sircus, Wilfred & Smith, Adam N. Scientific Foundations of Gastroenterology. LC 80-5260. (Illus.). 650p. 1980. 90.00 (ISBN 0-7216-8319-3). Saunders.
Sleisenger, Marvin H. & Fordtran, John S. Gastrointestinal Disease: Pathophysiology, Diagnosis, Management. 2nd ed. LC 77-2104. (Illus.). 1978. text ed. 70.00 (ISBN 0-7216-8362-2). Saunders.
Sodeman, William A., Jr. & Saladin, Thomas A. Gastroenterology Specialty Board Review. 1977. spiral bdg. 16.50 (ISBN 0-87488-316-4). Med Exam.
Spiro, Howard M. Clinical Gastroenterology. 2nd ed. (Illus.). 1977. text ed. 54.00x (ISBN 0-02-415260-9). Macmillan.
Tavares, Phyllis C. Organizing & Managing a Gastroenterology Department. (Illus.). 148p. 1981. 24.75 (ISBN 0-398-04119-9). C C Thomas.
Van der Reis, L., ed. Immune Disorders. (Frontiers of Gastrointestinal Research: Vol. 1). 200p. 1975. 58.75 (ISBN 3-8055-1751-3). S Karger.
Varro. Current Views in Gastroenterology, 2 vols. 1979. Vol. 1. 55.00 (ISBN 0-9960015-3-0, Pub. by Kaido Hungary); Vol. 2. 44.00 (ISBN 0-686-28202-7). Heyden.
Walker & Smith. Practical Approach to Gastroenterology & Procedures in Childhood. (Postgraduate Pediatric Ser.). 1981. text ed. write for info. (ISBN 0-407-00204-9). Butterworth.
Winawer, Sidney J., et al, eds. Colorectal Cancer: Prevention, Epidemiology, & Screening. (Progress in Cancer Research & Therapy). 432p. 1980. 47.50 (ISBN 0-89004-447-3). Raven.
Winick, Myron. Nutrition & Gastroenterology. LC 80-16169. (Current Concepts in Nutrition Ser.: Vol. 9). 221p. 1980. 37.00 (ISBN 0-471-08173-6, Pub. by Wiley Interscience). Wiley.
Wright, Ralph. Immunology of Gastrointestinal & Liver Disease. (Current Topics in Immunology Ser.: Vol. 8). (Illus., Orig.). 1979. pap. 13.95 (ISBN 0-8151-9367-X). Year Bk Med.
Wruble, Lawrence D., et al, eds. Gastroenterology. 3rd ed. Lewis, Myron & Levinson, Michael. (Medical Examination Review Book: Vol.22). 1977. spiral bdg. 16.50 (ISBN 0-87488-141-2). Med Exam.
Yardley & Goldman. Mucosal Biopsies in Gastroenterology. Date not set. text ed. write for info. (ISBN 0-443-08059-3). Churchill.

GASTROINTESTINAL HEMORRHAGE

Balint, John A, et al. Gastrointestinal Bleeding: Diagnosis & Management. LC 77-4423. (Clinical Gastroenterology Monographs). 101p. 1977. 23.95 (ISBN 0-471-04607-8, Pub. by Wiley Medical). Wiley.
Dykes, P. W. & Keighley, M. R., eds. Gastrointestinal Haemorrhage. (Illus.). 500p. 1981. text ed. 79.50 (ISBN 0-7236-0584-X). Wright-PSG.
Fiddian-Green, Richard & Turcotte, Jeremiah, eds. Gastrointestinal Hemorrhage. LC 80-11318. 1980. 44.50 (ISBN 0-8089-1267-4). Grune.
Matsumoto, Teruo. Current Management of Acute Gastrointestinal Hemorrhage. (Illus.). 272p. 1977. 25.00 (ISBN 0-398-03582-2). C C Thomas.
Palmer, Eddy D. Upper Gastrointestinal Hemorrhage. (Illus.). 420p. 1970. photocopy ed. spiral 39.75 (ISBN 0-398-01443-4). C C Thomas.
Papp, John P., ed. Endoscopic Control of Gastrointestinal Hemorrhage. 224p. 1981. 64.95 (ISBN 0-8493-6295-4). CRC Pr.
Thompson, James C., ed. Gastrointestinal Hormones: A Symposium. LC 75-3573. (Illus.). 680p. 1975. 27.50x (ISBN 0-292-72704-6). U of Tex Pr.

GASTROINTESTINAL TRACT

see Alimentary Canal

GASTROMYCETES

see Gasteromycetes

GASTRONOMY

see also Cookery; Dinners and Dining; Food; Menus; Stomach-Surgery

Arnott, Margaret L., ed. Gastronomy: The Anthropology of Food & Food Habits. (World Anthropology Ser). (Illus.). 1976. 27.00x (ISBN 0-202-90025-8). Beresford Bk Serv.
Bartrum, Douglas. Gourmet's Garden. (Illus.). 1964. 7.50x (ISBN 0-8002-0893-5). Intl Pubns Serv.
Beard, James. Delights & Prejudices. LC 80-24560. (Illus.). 1964. 6.95 (ISBN 0-689-00007-3, 66); pap. 7.95 (ISBN 0-689-70605-7). Atheneum.
Brame, Luise. Seattle's Gastronomic Shopper. (Illus.). 179p. (Orig.). 1981. pap. 6.95 (ISBN 0-932998-02-X). Reynard Hse.
Brillat-Savarin. The Physiology of Taste. Fisher, M. F., tr. LC 78-7199. 1978. pap. 4.95 (ISBN 0-15-671770-0, Harv). HarBraceJ.
Brillat-Savarin, Jean A. Physiology of Taste. Fisher, M. F., tr. (Illus.). 1971. 15.00 (ISBN 0-394-47343-4). Knopf.
Courtine, Robert J. Feasts of a Militant Gastronome. Guicharnaud, June & Kamman, Madeleine, trs. from Fr. LC 74-8826. (Illus.). 320p. 1974. 10.95 (ISBN 0-688-00296-X). Morrow.
Courtine, Robert J., ed. Nouveau Larousse Gastronomique. 1104p. (Fr.). 1968. 79.50 (ISBN 0-686-57062-6, M-6433). French & Eur.
Down, Edith. What's to Eat. 1981. text ed. 11.96 (ISBN 0-87002-333-0). Bennett IL.
Dumas, Alexandre. Histoire de la Cuisine. (Illus.). 176p. 1967. 5.95 (ISBN 0-686-55819-7). French & Eur.
Edwards, S. Too Much Is Not Enough: An Insider's Answer to Compulsive Eating. 1981. 10.95 (ISBN 0-07-019032-1). McGraw.
Ellwanger, G. H. The Pleasures of the Table. 59.95 (ISBN 0-8490-0843-3). Gordon Pr.
Ellwanger, George. Pleasures of the Table. LC 70-82031. 1969. Repr. of 1902 ed. 24.00 (ISBN 0-8103-3560-3). Gale.
Fisher, M. F. The Art of Eating. 1976. pap. 6.95 (ISBN 0-394-71399-0, Vin). Random.
George, Wilma. Eating in Eight Languages. LC 67-16287. 1974. pap. 1.95 (ISBN 0-8128-1050-3). Stein & Day.
Gopnik, Adam & Huberman, Jack. Voila Careme! The Gastronomic Adventures of History's Greatest Chef. 1980. pap. 4.95 (ISBN 0-312-85098-0). St Martin.
Hackwood, F. W. Good Cheer: The Romance of Food & Feasting. 59.95 (ISBN 0-8490-0249-4). Gordon Pr.
Henisch, Bridget Ann. Fast and Feast: Food in Medieval Society. LC 76-15677. (Illus.). 1977. 15.95 (ISBN 0-271-01230-7). Pa St U Pr.
Lapidus, Dorothy F. The Scrutable Feast: A Guide to Eating Authentically in Chinese Restaurants. 1977. pap. 6.95 (ISBN 0-396-07448-0). Dodd.
Magida, Phylis. Eating, Drinking, & Thinking: A Gourmet Perspective. LC 73-86024. 184p. 1973. 16.95 (ISBN 0-911012-91-5). Nelson-Hall.
Mathiot, G. Nouveau Larousse gastronomique. (Illus., Fr.). 79.75x (ISBN 0-685-14004-0, 3905). Larousse.
Point, Fernand. Ma Gastronomie. Kulla, Frank & Kulla, Patricia S., trs. LC 74-25591. (Illus.). 14.95 (ISBN 0-915336-00-6). Lyceum Bks.
Simon, Andre L. & Howe, Robin. Dictionary of Gastronomy. 2nd ed. LC 78-16260. (Illus.). 400p. 1979. 25.00 (ISBN 0-87951-081-1). Overlook Pr.
Timbrell, Tilly. The Winemaker's Dining Book. 1973. pap. 4.50 (ISBN 0-8277-2215-X). British Bk Ctr.
Trillin, Calvin. Alice, Let's Eat: Further Adventures of a Happy Eater. LC 79-11070. 1979. pap. 1.95 (ISBN 0-394-74171-4, Vin). Random.
--American Fried: Adventures of a Happy Eater. LC 79-11065. 1979. pap. 1.95 (ISBN 0-394-74172-2, Vin). Random.

GASTRONOMY–BIBLIOGRAPHY

Bitting, Katherine G. Gastronomic Bibliography. LC 71-168559. (Illus.). 1971. Repr. of 1939 ed. 41.00 (ISBN 0-8103-3758-4). Gale.
--Gastronomic Bibliography. LC 71-168559. (Illus.). 1971. Repr. of 1939 ed. 41.00 (ISBN 0-8103-3758-4). Gale.
Feret, Barbara L. Gastronomical & Culinary Literature: A Survey & Analysis of Historically-Oriented Collections in the U. S. A. LC 78-32098. 1979. lib. bdg. 10.00 (ISBN 0-8108-1204-5). Scarecrow.
Simon, Andre L. Bibliotheca Gastronomica, a Catalogue of Books & Documents on Gastronomy. (Illus.). xiv, 196p. 1978. Repr. of 1953 ed. 65.00 (ISBN 0-900470-85-2). Oak Knoll.
Vicaire, Georges. Bibliographie Gastronomique. (Illus.). xx, 483p. (Fr.). 1978. Repr. of 1890 ed. 65.00 (ISBN 0-900470-86-0). Oak Knoll.

GASTROPODA

see Gasteropoda

GASTROSCOPE AND GASTROSCOPY

Oshima, H., et al. Gastrokamera- und Roentgendiagnostik: Ein Atlas der kombinierten Magenuntersuchung mit histologischer Dokumentation. new ed. (Illus.). xii, 140p. 1972. 116.50x (ISBN 3-11-001687-7). De Gruyter.
Papp, John P., ed. Endoscopic Control of Gastrointestinal Hemorrhage. 224p. 1981. 64.95 (ISBN 0-8493-6295-4). CRC Pr.

GASTROSTOMY

see Stomach-Surgery

GATES

Brann, Donald R. How to Build Fences, Gates and Outdoor Projects. LC 74-28771. (Orig.). 1975. pap. 3.50 (ISBN 0-87733-607-5). Easi-Bild.
Edwards, Ifor. Davies Brothers Gatesmiths. (Illus.). 111p. 1980. pap. 9.50 (ISBN 0-905171-22-5, Pub. by Welsh Art Council Wales). Intl Schol Bk Serv.
Martin, George A. Fences, Gates & Bridges. Date not set. 6.95 (ISBN 0-686-26689-7). Dairy Goat.
--Fences, Gates & Bridges: A Practical Manual. LC 74-19255. (Illus.). 196p. 1974. 7.95 (ISBN 0-8289-0240-2). Greene.
Schuler, Stanley. How to Build Fences, Gates & Walls. (Illus.). 256p. 1976. 13.50 (ISBN 0-02-607370-6). Macmillan.
Sunset Editors. Fences & Gates. 4th ed. LC 81-81379. (Illus.). 96p. 1981. pap. 4.95 (ISBN 0-376-01105-X, Sunset Bks.). Sunset-Lane.
--Fences & Gates. 4th ed. LC 81-81379. (Illus.). 96p. 1981. pap. 4.95 (ISBN 0-376-01105-X, Sunset Bks). Sunset-Lane.
--Fences & Gates. 4th ed. LC 81-81379. (Illus.). 96p. 1981. pap. 4.95 (ISBN 0-376-01105-X, Sunset Bks). Sunset-Lane.

GATES, HORATIO, 1728-1806

Gregory, James & Dunnings, Thomas, eds. The Horatio Gates Papers, Seventeen Twenty-Six to Eighteen Twenty-Eight: A Guide to the Microfilm Edition. 212p. 1979. 9.75 (ISBN 0-667-00539-0). Microfilming Corp.
Nelson, Paul D. Horatio Gates: A Biography. LC 74-27191. (Illus.). 352p. 1976. 20.00x (ISBN 0-8071-0159-1). La State U Pr.
Patterson, Samuel W. Horatio Gates: Defender of American Liberties. LC 41-10193. Repr. of 1941 ed. 10.50 (ISBN 0-404-04917-6). AMS Pr.

GATES, JOHN WARNE, 1855-1911

Wendt, Lloyd & Kogan, Herman. Bet a Million! the Story of John W. Gates. Bruchey, Stuart, ed. LC 80-1349. (Railroads Ser.). (Illus.). 1981. Repr. of 1948 ed. lib. bdg. 30.00x (ISBN 0-405-13821-0). Arno.

GATLING GUNS

Johnson, F. Roy & Stephenson, Frank, Jr. The Gatling Gun & Flying Machine of Richard & Henry Gatling. (Illus.). 1979. 9.50 (ISBN 0-930230-37-X). Johnson NC.
Wahl, Paul & Toppel, Donald R. The Gatling Gun. LC 64-16612. (Illus.). 1978. pap. 5.95 (ISBN 0-668-04514-0, 4514). Arco.

GATT

see Contracting Parties to the General Agreement on Tariffs and Trade

GATTI-CASAZZA, GIULIO, 1869-1940

Gatti-Casazza, Giulio. Memories of the Opera. Taubman, Howard, ed. LC 71-183334. (Illus.). 326p. 1973. Repr. of 1941 ed. 25.00 (ISBN 0-8443-0022-5). Vienna Hse.

GAUCHOS

see also Cowboys

Nichols, Madaline W. Gaucho: Cattle Hunter, Cavalryman, Ideal of Romance. LC 68-58423. 1968. Repr. of 1942 ed. 7.50 (ISBN 0-87752-077-1). Gordian.
Riviere, Peter. The Forgotten Frontier: Ranchers of Northern Brazil. Spindler, George & Spindler, Louise, eds. (Case Studies in Cultural Anthropology). 144p. pap. text ed. 6.95x (ISBN 0-8290-0312-6). Irvington.
Tinker, Edward L. The Horsemen of the Americas & the Literature They Inspired. (Illus.). 168p. 1967. 25.00 (ISBN 0-292-73657-6). U of Tex Pr.

GAUCHOS–POETRY

Hernandez, Jose. The Gaucho Martin Fierro: New English Translation. Carrino, Frank G. & Carlos, Alberto J., trs. from Span. LC 74-17300. 96p. (Orig.). 1974. pap. 4.95 (ISBN 0-87395-284-7). State U NY Pr.

GAUDI Y CORNET, ANTONIO, 1852-1926

Collins, George R. Antonio Gaudi. LC 60-6078. (Masters of World Architecture Ser). 7.95 (ISBN 0-8076-0107-1). Braziller.
Dalisi, Riccardo. Gaudi: Furniture & Objects. LC 80-11463. 1980. 16.95 (ISBN 0-8120-5356-7). Barron.
Dunster, David, intro. by. Gaudi Architecture. LC 79-64340. (Architectural Monographs Ser.). (Illus.). 1980. pap. 13.95 (ISBN 0-8478-0229-9). Rizzoli Intl.
Martinell, Cesar. Gaudi: His Life, His Theories, His Work. Collins, George R., ed. Rohrer, Judith, tr. from Sp. LC 74-109. 500p. 1975. 55.00 (ISBN 0-262-13072-6). MIT Pr.
Mower, David. Gaudi. 1981. 27.00x (ISBN 0-905368-08-8, Pub. by Jupiter England). State Mutual Bk.
--Gaudi. (Illus.). 1977. 15.95 (ISBN 0-8467-0248-7, Pub. by Two Continents); pap. 9.95 (ISBN 0-8467-0247-9). Hippocrene Bks.
Sterner. Gaudi: The Architecture in Barcelona, Antoni. (Pocket Art Ser.). 1982. pap. 3.50 (ISBN 0-8120-2293-9). Barron.
Sterner, Gabriele. Antoni Gaudi: Architecture in Barcelona. (Pocket Art Ser.). (Illus.). 1982. pap. 3.50 (ISBN 0-8120-2293-9). Barron.

GAUDIER-BRZESKA, HENRI, 1891-1915

Harris, Frank. Contemporary Portraits. (Third Ser.). Repr. of 1920 ed. lib. bdg. 15.00 (ISBN 0-8371-2577-4, HACO). Greenwood.

Pound, Ezra. Gaudier-Brzeska: A Memoir. LC 78-107490. 1970. pap. 3.95 (ISBN 0-8112-0527-4, NDP372). New Directions.

GAUGES

see Gages

GAUGING

see Gaging

GAUGUIN, PAUL, 1848-1903

Daws, Gavan. A Dream of Islands. (Illus.). 1980. 14.95 (ISBN 0-393-01293-X). Norton.

Fezzi, Elda. Gauguin, 2 vols. Piper, David, ed. Brill, Susan & Carrol, Jane, trs. LC 80-66200. (Every Painting Ser.). (Illus.). 96p. 1980. Vol. 1, 96 Pgs. pap. 5.95 (ISBN 0-8478-0313-9); Vol. II, 96 Pgs. pap. 5.95 (ISBN 0-8478-0314-7). Rizzoli Intl.

Field, Richard S. Paul Gauguin: Monotypes. LC 73-77306. (Illus.). 148p. 1973. pap. 6.95 (ISBN 0-87633-011-1). Phila Mus Art.

--Paul Gauguin: The Paintings of the First Voyage to Tahiti. LC 76-23617. (Outstanding Dissertations in the Fine Arts Ser.). 1977. lib. bdg. 63.00 (ISBN 0-8240-2688-8). Garland Pub.

Gauguin. (The Painter & the Man Ser.). 1978. 59.95 (ISBN 0-8120-5117-3). Barron.

Gauguin, Paul. Drawings of Gauguin. Longstreet, Stephen, ed. (Master Draughtsman Ser.). (Illus., Orig.). treasure trove bdg. 6.47x (ISBN 0-685-07255-X); pap. 2.95 (ISBN 0-685-07256-8). Borden.

--Gauguin. Marchiore, Giuseppe, ed. (Art Library Ser.: Vol. 11). (Illus., Orig.). 1968. pap. 3.50 (ISBN 0-448-00460-7). G&D.

--Gauguin: L'Oeuvre Grave. rev. ed. Guerin, Marcel, ed. (Illus.). 272p. (Fr.). 1980. 100.00 (ISBN 0-915346-37-0). A Wofsy Fine Arts.

Goldwater, Robert. Gauguin. (Library of Great Painters Ser). (Illus.). 1957. 40.00 (ISBN 0-8109-0137-4). Abrams.

Gray, Christopher. Sculpture & Ceramics of Paul Gaugin. LC 79-91819. (Illus.). 330p. 1980. Repr. of 1963 ed. lib. bdg. 75.00 (ISBN 0-87817-263-7). Hacker.

Hind, Charles L. Post Impressionists. LC 75-102244. (Select Bibliographies Reprint Ser). 1911. 19.50 (ISBN 0-8369-5129-8). Arno.

Kantor-Gukovskaya, Asia. Gauguin. (Illus.). 1978. pap. 4.95 (ISBN 0-8109-2153-7). Abrams.

Raboff, Ernest. Paul Gauguin. LC 73-75360. 36p. (gr. 3-7). 1975. 6.95a (ISBN 0-385-05012-7); PLB (ISBN 0-385-06994-4). Doubleday.

Werner, Alfred. Paul Gauguin. (Color Slide Program of the Great Masters). (Illus.). 1967. 17.95 (ISBN 0-07-069441-9, P&RB). McGraw.

GAUL

Anderson, Paul L. For Freedom & for Gaul. 1931. 10.00 (ISBN 0-686-20090-X). Quality Lib.

GAUL–HISTORY

Caesar. Commentarii, 2 Vols. Du Pontet, R. L., ed. (O. C. T). 1900-1901. Vol. 1. 14.95x (ISBN 0-19-814602-7); Vol. 2. 14.95x (ISBN 0-19-814603-5). Oxford U Pr.

--Gallic War, Bk. 4. Gould, H. E. & Whitley, J. L., eds. (Modern School Classics Ser.). 1952. 3.50 (ISBN 0-312-31535-X). St Martin.

Caesar, Caius Julius. Egypt Books of Caius Julius Caesar Conteyning His Martiall Exploytes in Gallia. Goldinge, Arthur, tr. LC 68-54623. (English Experience Ser.: No. 36). 1968. Repr. of 1565 ed. 42.00 (ISBN 90-221-0036-7). Walter J Johnson.

Caesar, Julius. The Battle for Gaul. Wiseman, Anne & Wiseman, Peter, trs. from Lat. LC 79-54955. Orig. Title: De bello Gallico. (Illus.). 216p. 1980. 17.95 (ISBN 0-87923-306-0). Godine.

--Caesar's Gallic War. Pearl, Joseph, tr. from Latin. (Orig.). (gr. 10 up). 1962. 5.50 (ISBN 0-8120-5014-2); pap. text ed. 3.95 (ISBN 0-8120-0037-4). Barron.

--The Conquest of Gaul. Handford, S. A., tr. (Classics Ser). 1951. pap. 2.95 (ISBN 0-14-044021-6). Penguin.

--Gallic War. (Loeb Classical Library: No. 72). 11.00x (ISBN 0-674-99080-3). Harvard U Pr.

Cambridge School Classics Project Foundation Course. The Gauls. (Roman World Ser.). (Illus.). 1978. 1.50x (ISBN 0-521-21599-4). Cambridge U Pr.

Chilver, Guy E. Cisalpine Gaul: Social & Economic History from 49 B.C. to the Death of Trajan. LC 75-7308. (Roman History Ser.). (Illus.). 1975. Repr. 16.00x (ISBN 0-405-07190-6). Arno.

Funck-Brentano, Frantz. Earliest Times. LC 77-168074. (National History of France: No. 1). Repr. of 1927 ed. 30.00 (ISBN 0-404-50791-3). AMS Pr.

Hatt, Jean-Jacques. Celts & Gallo-Romans. Hogarth, James, tr. from Fr. (Archaeologia Mundi Ser.). (Illus.). 334p. 1970. 29.50 (ISBN 0-88254-139-0). Hippocrene Bks.

Holmes, Thomas R. Caesar's Conquest of Gaul. rev. 2nd ed. LC 78-137242. (BCL Ser.). Repr. of 1911 ed. 49.50 (ISBN 0-404-03317-2). AMS Pr.

James, Edward. The Merovingian Archaeology of South-West Gaul. 1977. 60.00x (ISBN 0-904531-71-6, Pub. by BAR). State Mutual Bk.

Moreau, Joseph. Dictionnaire De Geographie Historique De la Gaule et De la France. 426p. (Fr.). 1972. pap. 37.50 (ISBN 0-686-56815-X, M-6593). French & Eur.

Pirenne, Henri. Mohammed & Charlemagne. (B & N Paperback Ser.). (Orig.). 1968. pap. 5.95x (ISBN 0-06-480687-1, 444). B&N.

Trollope, Anthony. Selected Works of Anthony Trollop Ser. Hall, N. John, ed. LC 80-1890. (Selected Works of Anthony Trollopeser Ser.). 1981. Repr. of 1870 ed. lib. bdg. 22.00 (ISBN 0-405-14157-2). Arno.

GAUL–HISTORY–FICTION

Anderson, Paul L. With the Eagles. LC 57-9447. (Illus.). (gr. 7-11). 1929. 8.50x (ISBN 0-8196-0100-4). Biblo.

Wells, Reuben F. With Caesar's Legions. LC 60-16709. (Illus.). (gr. 7-11). 1951. 8.50x (ISBN 0-8196-0110-1). Biblo.

GAUL–JUVENILE LITERATURE

Lamprey, Louise. Children of Ancient Gaul. LC 60-16708. (Illus.). (gr. 7-11). 8.50x (ISBN 0-8196-0109-8). Biblo.

Whitehead, Albert C. Standard Bearer: A Story of Army Life in the Time of Caesar. (Illus.). (gr. 7-11). 1943. 8.50x (ISBN 0-8196-0116-0). Biblo.

GAULISH LANGUAGE

Whatmough, Joshua. Dialects of Ancient Gaul. LC 69-12739. 1970. text ed. 40.00x (ISBN 0-674-20280-5). Harvard U Pr.

GAULLE, CHARLES DE, PRES. FRANCE, 1890-1970

Cotteret & Moreau. Recherches sur le Vocabulaire du General de Gaulle: Analyse Statistique des Allocutions Radiodiffusees (1958-1965) 23.75 (ISBN 0-685-33949-1). French & Eur.

De Gaulle, Charles. Charles De Gaulle Memoirs of Hope: Renewal & Endeavor. 1972. 10.00 (ISBN 0-671-21118-8). S&S.

De Menil, Lois P. Who Speaks for Europe: The Case of De Gaulle. LC 77-77137. 1978. 12.50x (ISBN 0-312-87025-6). St Martin.

DePorte, Anton W. DeGaulle's Foreign Policy: 1944-1946. LC 67-29624. 1968. 16.50x (ISBN 0-674-19550-7). Harvard U Pr.

Dictionnaire Commente de l'oeuvre de General de Gaulle. 880p. (Fr.). 1975. 30.00 (ISBN 0-686-56811-7, M-6589). French & Eur.

Epstein, Sam & Epstein, Beryl. Charles De Gaulle: Defender of France. LC 72-6254. (Century Biographies Ser.). (Illus.). (gr. 4-8). 1973. PLB 4.28 (ISBN 0-8116-4756-0). Garrard.

Fish, Hamilton. Lafayette in America During & After the Revolutionary War: And Other Essays on Franco-American Relations. 1977. 6.95 (ISBN 0-533-02314-9). Vantage.

Furniss, E. S. De Gaulle & the French Army: A Crisis in Civil Military Relations. (Twentieth Century Fund Ser.). Repr. of 1964 ed. 5.00 (ISBN 0-527-02818-5). Kraus Repr.

Furniss, Edgar S., Jr. France, Troubled Ally. LC 74-2667. 512p. 1974. Repr. of 1960 ed. lib. bdg. 23.50x (ISBN 0-8371-7421-X, FUFR). Greenwood.

Gladwyn, Hubert M. Europe After De Gaulle. Crozier, Brian, ed. LC 70-86972. (World Realities Ser). (Orig.). 1969. 4.95 (ISBN 0-8008-2520-9). Taplinger.

Isenberg, Irwin, ed. France Under De Gaulle. (Reference Shelf Ser: Vol. 39, No. 1). 1967. 6.25 (ISBN 0-8242-0094-2). Wilson.

Kulski, Wladyslaw W. De Gaulle & the World: The Foreign Policy of the Fifth French Republic. LC 66-28137. 1966. 14.95x (ISBN 0-8156-0052-6). Syracuse U Pr.

Mauriac, Francois. De Gaulle. (Fr.). 1964. 14.50 (ISBN 0-685-11076-1). French & Eur.

--Mort du General de Gaulle. 1972. 9.95 (ISBN 0-686-55482-5). French & Eur.

Mengin, Robert. No Laurels for De Gaulle. Allen, Jay, tr. from Fr. LC 78-179734. (Biography Index Reprint Ser). Repr. of 1966 ed. 20.50 (ISBN 0-8369-8102-2). Arno.

--No Laurels for De Gaulle. Allen, Jay, tr. from Fr. LC 78-179734. (Biography Index Reprint Ser). Repr. of 1966 ed. 20.50 (ISBN 0-8369-8102-2). Arno.

Serfaty, Simon. France, DeGaulle, & Europe: The Policy of the Fourth & Fifth Republics Toward the Continent. LC 68-15453. 176p. 1968. 12.00x (ISBN 0-8018-0584-8). Johns Hopkins.

Sulzberger, C. L. The Test: De Gaulle & Algeria. LC 74-6097. 228p. 1974. Repr. of 1962 ed. lib. bdg. 15.00x (ISBN 0-8371-7492-9, SUTT). Greenwood.

Thomson, David. Two Frenchmen. LC 75-8806. 255p. 1975. Repr. of 1951 ed. lib. bdg. 14.50x (ISBN 0-8371-8115-1, THTWF). Greenwood.

Tournoux, Jean-Raymond. Sons of France: Petain & De Gaulle. Coburn, Oliver, tr. (Illus.). 1966. 5.95 (ISBN 0-670-65797-2). Viking Pr.

Werth, Alexander. The De Gaulle Revolution. LC 75-31477. 404p. 1976. Repr. of 1960 ed. lib. bdg. 22.75x (ISBN 0-8371-8508-4, WEDG). Greenwood.

White, Dorothy S. Seeds of Discord: De Gaulle, Free France, & the Allies. LC 64-16922. (Illus.). 1964. 14.95x (ISBN 0-8156-0038-0). Syracuse U Pr.

Williams, Philip M. & Harrison, Martin. De Gaulle's Republic. LC 78-23520. 1979. Repr. of 1960 ed. lib. bdg. 20.50x (ISBN 0-313-21085-3, WIDG). Greenwood.

Willis, F. Roy, ed. DeGaulle: Anachronism, Realist or Prophet? LC 77-12659. (European Problem Studies Ser.). 1978. pap. text ed. 5.50 (ISBN 0-88275-616-8). Krieger.

GAULS

see also Celts

GAUSS, KARL FRIEDRICH, 1777-1855

Buehler, W. K. Gauss: A Biographical Study. (Illus.). 208p. 1981. 16.80 (ISBN 0-387-10662-6). Springer-Verlag.

GAUSSIAN NOISE

see Random Noise Theory

GAUSSIAN QUADRATURE FORMULAS

Drygas, H. Coordinate-Free Approach to Gauss-Markov Estimation. LC 78-147405. (Lecture Notes in Operations Research & Mathematical Systems: Vol. 40). 1970. pap. 10.70 (ISBN 0-387-05326-3). Springer-Verlag.

Dym, H. & McKean, Henry P. Gaussian Processes: Complex Function Theory & the Inverse Spectral Method. (Probability & Mathematical Statistics Ser.). 1976. 50.50 (ISBN 0-12-226460-6). Acad Pr.

Steklov Institute of Mathematics, Academy of Sciences, U S S R, No. 108, 1968 & Rozanov, I. A. Infinite-Dimensional Gaussian Distributions: Proceedings. 1971. 24.40 (ISBN 0-8218-3008-2, STEKLO-108). Am Math.

GAUTAMA BUDDHA

Brewster, Earl H., compiled by. The Life of Gotama Buddha (Compiled Exclusively from the Pali Canon) LC 78-72380. Repr. of 1926 ed. 27.50 (ISBN 0-404-17229-6). AMS Pr.

Byles, Marie B. Footprints of Gautama the Buddha. LC 68-5855. (Illus.). 1967. pap. 1.75 (ISBN 0-8356-0399-7, Quest). Theos Pub Hse.

Carus, Paul. The Gospel of Buddha. 275p. 1972. pap. 3.65 (ISBN 0-912358-33-5). Omen Pr.

--The Gospel of Buddha. 59.95 (ISBN 0-8490-0252-4). Gordon Pr.

Csoma, Sandor K. The Life & Teachings of Buddha. LC 78-72399. Repr. of 1957 ed. 21.50 (ISBN 0-404-17258-X). AMS Pr.

Davids, Carolina A. Gotama, the Man. LC 78-72409. Repr. of 1928 ed. 25.00 (ISBN 0-404-17273-3). AMS Pr.

Davids, Rhys, intro. by. Stories of the Buddha. LC 78-72444. Repr. of 1929 ed. 30.00 (ISBN 0-404-17316-0). AMS Pr.

Davids, Thomas W. Buddhism: Being a Sketch of the Life & Teachings of Guatama, the Buddha. LC 78-72417. Repr. of 1877 ed. 28.00 (ISBN 0-404-17278-4). AMS Pr.

Foucher, Alfred C. The Life of the Buddha. Boas, Simone B., tr. LC 72-6195. 272p. 1972. Repr. of 1963 ed. lib. bdg. 20.00x (ISBN 0-8371-6476-1, FOLB). Greenwood.

Gautama. Gautama: The Nyaya Philosophy. Junankar, N. S., tr. from Sanskrit. 1978. 25.50 (ISBN 0-89684-002-6, Pub. by Motilal Banarsidass India). Orient Bk Dist.

Herold, A. Ferdinand. Life of Buddha: According to the Legend of Ancient India. LC 55-12748. 1954. pap. 5.95 (ISBN 0-8048-0382-X). C E Tuttle.

Holmes, Edmond. The Creed of Buddha. LC 72-9918. 260p. 1973. Repr. of 1957 ed. lib. bdg. 18.50x (ISBN 0-8371-6606-3, HOCB). Greenwood.

Ikeda, Daisaku. The Living Buddha: An Interpretive Biography. LC 75-40446. (Illus.). 164p. 1975. 7.95 (ISBN 0-8348-0117-5). Weatherhill.

Krom, N. J., ed. The Life of Buddha on the Stupa of Barabudur, According to the Lalitavistara-Text. LC 78-72460. Repr. of 1926 ed. 30.00 (ISBN 0-404-17328-4). AMS Pr.

Marshall, George N. Buddha: The Quest for Serenity. LC 78-53787. (Illus.). 1979. 11.95 (ISBN 0-8070-1346-3); pap. 4.95 (ISBN 0-8070-1347-1, BP580). Beacon Pr.

--Buddha: The Quest for Serenity. LC 78-53787. (Illus.). 1979. 11.95 (ISBN 0-8070-1346-3); pap. 4.95 (ISBN 0-8070-1347-1, BP580). Beacon Pr.

Nakamura, Hajime. Gotama Buddha. LC 77-8589. 1977. 8.95x (ISBN 0-914910-05-1); pap. 5.95x (ISBN 0-914910-06-X). Buddhist Bks.

Oldenberg, Hermann. Buddha: His Life, His Doctrine & His Order. 59.95 (ISBN 0-87968-800-9). Gordon Pr.

Parrinder, Geoffrey. The Wisdom of the Early Buddhists. LC 77-7945. (New Directions Wisdon Ser.). 1977. 7.50 (ISBN 0-8112-0666-1); pap. 2.95 (ISBN 0-8112-0667-X, NDP444). New Directions.

Pye, Michael. The Buddha. (Illus.). 158p. 1979. 18.00x (ISBN 0-7156-1302-2, 152, Pub. by Duckworth England); pap. 8.95x (ISBN 0-7156-1387-1, 153, Pub. by Duckworth England). Biblio Dist.

Saunders, Kenneth J. Gotama Buddha: A Biography. LC 78-70119. Repr. of 1922 ed. 18.00 (ISBN 0-404-17376-4). AMS Pr.

Serage, Nancy. Prince Who Gave up a Throne: A Story of the Buddha. LC 66-10064. (Illus.). (gr. 3-7). 1966. 8.95 (ISBN 0-690-65566-5, TYC-J). Har-Row.

Swearer, Donald K. Wat Haripunjaya: A Study of the Royal Temple of the Buddha's Relic, Lamphun, Thailand. LC 75-33802. (American Academy of Religion. Studies in Religion). 1976. pap. 7.50 (ISBN 0-89130-052-X, 010010). Scholars Pr Ca.

Syama-Sankara, Hara C. Buddha & His Sayings. LC 78-70128. Repr. of 1914 ed. 18.00 (ISBN 0-404-17387-X). AMS Pr.

Trungpa, Chogyam. Journey Without Goal: The Tantric Wisdom of the Buddha. 180p. (Orig.). 1981. pap. 7.95 (ISBN 0-87773-755-X). Great Eastern.

GAUTIER, THEOPHILE, 1811-1872

Cazelles, Brigitte. La Faiblesse Chez Gautier De Coinci. (Stanford French & Italian Studies: No. 14). (Fr.). 1978. pap. 20.00 (ISBN 0-915838-27-3). Anma Libri.

Du Camp, Maxime. Theophile Gautier. Gordon, J. E., tr. LC 74-153268. 1971. Repr. of 1893 ed. 12.50 (ISBN 0-8046-1564-0). Kennikat.

--Theophile Gautier. Gordon, J. E., tr. (Select Bibliographies Reprint Ser.). Repr. of 1893 ed. 16.00 (ISBN 0-8369-5732-6). Arno.

--Theophile Gautier. Gordon, J. E., tr. 1883. 25.00 (ISBN 0-8274-3592-4). R West.

--Theophile Gautier. 1893. 30.00 (ISBN 0-8495-6280-5). Arden Lib.

Grant, Richard B. Theophile Gautier. LC 75-4819. (World Authors Ser.: France: No. 362). 1975. lib. bdg. 10.95 (ISBN 0-8057-6213-2). Twayne.

Palache, J. G. Gautier & the Romantics. 35.00 (ISBN 0-8490-0212-5). Gordon Pr.

Palache, John G. Gautier & the Romantics. 186p. 1980. Repr. of 1927 ed. lib. bdg. 20.00 (ISBN 0-8495-4397-5). Arden Lib.

--Gautier & the Romantics. 1927. 20.00 (ISBN 0-8274-2393-4). R West.

--Gautier & the Romantics. 1979. Repr. of 1927 ed. lib. bdg. 20.00 (ISBN 0-8414-6821-4). Folcroft.

Smith, Albert B. Ideal & Reality in the Fictional Narratives of Theophile Gautier. LC 79-81256. (U of Fla. Humanities Monographs: No. 30). 1969. pap. 2.75 (ISBN 0-8130-0269-9). U Presses Fla.

--Theopile Gautier & the Fantastic. LC 76-56455. (Romance Monographs: No. 23). 1977. 15.00x (ISBN 84-399-6137-5). Romance.

Tennant, P. E. Theophile Gautier. (Athlone French Poets Ser). 150p. 1975. text ed. 24.75x (ISBN 0-485-14604-5, Athlone Pr); pap. text ed. 11.75x (ISBN 0-485-12204-9, Athlone Pr). Humanities.

GAUTIER DE CHATILLON, fl. 1170-1180

Willis, Raymond S., Jr. Relationship of the Spanish Libro De Alexandre to the Alexandreis of Gautier De Chatillon. (Elliott Monographs: Vol. 31). 1934. pap. 7.00 (ISBN 0-527-02634-4). Kraus Repr.

GAUTIER LE LEU, 13TH CENTURY

Livingston, C. H. Jongleur Gauthier le Leu: Etude Sur les Fabliaux. 1951. pap. 22.00 (ISBN 0-527-01122-3). Kraus Repr.

GAVESTON, PIERS, d. 1312

Dodge, Walter P. Piers Gaveston: A Chapter of Early Constitutional History. LC 74-173161. (Illus.). Repr. of 1899 ed. 15.00 (ISBN 0-405-08451-X, Blom Pubns). Arno.

GAVIIFORMES

see Loons

GAWAIN AND THE GREEN KNIGHT

Andrew, Malcolm. The Gawain-Poet: An Annotated Bibliography, 1839-1977. LC 78-68243. (Garland Reference Library of the Humanities: No. 129). 1980. lib. bdg. 25.00 (ISBN 0-8240-9815-3). Garland Pub.

Brewer, Elisabeth, tr. from Fr. From Cuchulainn to Gawain: Sources & Analogues of Sir Gawain & the Green Knight. 101p. 1973. pap. 6.00x (ISBN 0-87471-444-3). Rowman.

Burrow, J. A. A Reading of Sir Gawain & the Green Knight. 1978. pap. 7.95 (ISBN 0-7100-8695-4). Routledge & Kegan.

Chapman, Coolidge O. An Index of Names in Pearl, Purity, Patience & Gawain. LC 77-29259. 1978. Repr. of 1951 ed. lib. bdg. 15.00x (ISBN 0-313-20213-3, CHIN). Greenwood.

Gardner, John C. Sir Gawain & the Green Knight Notes. (Orig.). pap. 1.95 (ISBN 0-8220-0515-8). Cliffs.

Howard, Donald R. & Zacher, Christian K., eds. Critical Studies of Sir Gawain & the Green Knight. LC 68-12297. (Illus.). 1968. Repr. of 1968 ed. 4.95x (ISBN 0-268-00064-6). U of Notre Dame Pr.

Madden, Frederic. Syr Gawayne. 59.95 (ISBN 0-8490-1171-X). Gordon Pr.
Spearing, A. C. Gawain-Poet. LC 72-112476. 1971. 42.00 (ISBN 0-521-07851-2); pap. 10.95x (ISBN 0-521-29119-4). Cambridge U Pr.
Stone, Brian, tr. Sir Gawain & the Green Knight. (Classics Ser.). 1959. pap. 2.25 (ISBN 0-14-044092-5). Penguin.

GAY, EDWIN FRANCIS, 1867-1946

Heaton, Herbert. Scholar in Action, Edwin F. Gay. LC 68-9543. (Illus.). 1968. Repr. of 1952 ed. lib. bdg. 15.00 (ISBN 0-8371-0101-8, HEEG). Greenwood.

GAY, JOHN, 1685-1732

Armens, Sven M. John Gay, Social Critic. 1966. lib. bdg. 16.00x (ISBN 0-374-90285-2). Octagon.
Dobree, Bonamy. William Congreve: A Conversation Between Swift & Gay. LC 73-12881. 1929. lib. bdg. 6.00 (ISBN 0-8414-3675-4). Folcroft.
Gale, Steven. Monarch Notes on Gay: The Begger's Opera. pap. 1.50 (ISBN 0-671-00938-9). Monarch Pr.
Gay, Phoebe F. John Gay: His Place in the Eighteenth Century. 1973. Repr. of 1938 ed. 16.50 (ISBN 0-8274-0398-4). R West.
Gaye, Phoebe F. John Gay. LC 79-39401. (Select Bibliographies Reprint Series). 1972. Repr. of 1938 ed. 21.00 (ISBN 0-8369-9906-1). Arno.
--John Gay. LC 79-39401. (Select Bibliographies Reprint Series). 1972. Repr. of 1938 ed. 21.00 (ISBN 0-8369-9906-1). Arno.
Guerinot, Joseph V. & Jilg, Rodney. Contexts One: The Beggar's Opera. (Contexts Ser.). 188p. (Orig.). 1976. 15.00 (ISBN 0-208-01488-8, Archon). Shoe String.
Herbert, Alan P. Mr. Gay's London. LC 75-25258. (Illus.). 136p. 1975. Repr. of 1948 ed. lib. bdg. 13.50x (ISBN 0-8371-4805-7, HEGL). Greenwood.
Irving, William H. John Gay's London, Illustrated from the Poetry of the Time. (Illus.). 1968. Repr. of 1928 ed. 25.00 (ISBN 0-208-00618-4, Archon). Shoe String.
Kidson, Frank. Beggar's Opera: It's Predecessors & Successors. (Music - Practice & Theory Ser). 1969. Repr. of 1922 ed. 11.00 (ISBN 0-384-29395-6). Johnson Repr.
Klein, Julie T. John Gay: An Annotated Checklist of Criticism. LC 72-97234. xiii, 98p. 1973. 7.50x (ISBN 0-87875-041-X). Whitston Pub.
Melville, Lewis S. Life & Letters of John Gay. LC 72-194432. 1921. lib. bdg. 20.00 (ISBN 0-8414-6612-2). Folcroft.
Pearce, Charles E. Polly Peachum: The Story of Lavinia Fenton - "the Beggar's Opera". LC 68-21222. (Illus.). 1968. Repr. of 1913 ed. 20.00 (ISBN 0-405-08846-9). Arno.
Plessow, Max. Geschichte der Fabeldichtung in England Bis Zu John Gay (1762) Repr. of 1906 ed. 44.50 (ISBN 0-384-46821-7); pap. 41.50 (ISBN 0-384-46820-9). Johnson Repr.
--Geschichte der Fabeldichtung in England Bis Zu John Gay. 1973. Repr. of 1906 ed. lib. bdg. 28.50 (ISBN 0-8274-1377-7). R West.
Schultz, William E. Gay's Beggar's Opera: Its Content, History & Influence. LC 66-24756. 1967. Repr. of 1923 ed. 10.00 (ISBN 0-8462-0834-2). Russell.
--Gay's Beggar's Opera: Its Content, History & Influence. 1923. 9.50x (ISBN 0-686-51391-6). Elliots Bks.

GAY LIB

see Gay Liberation Movement

GAY LIBERATION MOVEMENT

Adair, Casey & Adair, Nancy. Word Is Out. 1978. 14.95 (ISBN 0-440-09888-2). Delacorte.
Brown, Howard. Familiar Faces, Hidden Lives: The Story of Homosexual Men in America Today. LC 77-3423. 1977. pap. 2.95 (ISBN 0-15-630120-2, Harv). HarBraceJ.
Crew, Louie, ed. The Gay Academic. LC 75-37780. 1978. 15.00 (ISBN 0-88280-036-1). ETC Pubns.
Dyer, Richard, et al. Gays & Film. 2nd ed. (BFI Ser.). (Illus., Orig.). 1981. pap. 6.95 (ISBN 0-85170-106-X). NY Zoetrope.
Gay, A. Nolder. The View from the Closet: Essays on Gay Life & Liberation, 1973-1977. LC 78-105579. 1978. pap. 3.00 (ISBN 0-9601570-0-X). Union Park.
Grahn, Judy. Edward the Dyke. 66p. pap. 3.00 (ISBN 0-686-74710-0). Crossing Pr.
Jay, Karla & Young, Allen. Lavender Culture. (Orig.). 1979. pap. 2.50 (ISBN 0-515-04462-8). Jove Pubns.
Kelly, George A. The Political Struggle of Active Homosexuals to Gain Social Acceptance. 106p. 1975. pap. 1.50 (ISBN 0-8199-0365-5). Franciscan Herald.
Lauritsen, John & Thorstad, David. The Early Homosexual Rights Movement (1864-1935) 96p. pap. 2.75 (ISBN 0-87810-027-X). Crossing Pr.
--Early Homosexual Rights Movement (1864-1935) LC 74-79104. (Illus.). 96p. (Orig.). 1974. 6.95 (ISBN 0-87810-527-1); pap. 2.75 (ISBN 0-87810-027-X). Times Change.
Mattachine Society. The Mattachine Review, 5 vols. LC 75-12336. (Homosexuality). 1975. Repr. Set. 200.00x (ISBN 0-405-07373-9). Arno.
Mendola, Mary. The Mendola Report: A New Look at Gay Couples. 288p. 1980. 12.95 (ISBN 0-517-54139-4). Crown.
Michaels, Kevin. The Gay Book of Etiquette. 80p. (Orig.). 1981. pap. 4.95 (ISBN 0-939020-75-0). MLP Ent.
Sagarin, Edward. Structure & Ideology in an Association of Deviants. LC 75-12346. (Homosexuality). 1975. Repr. 22.00x (ISBN 0-405-07402-6). Arno.
Steakley, James D. The Homosexual Emancipation Movement in Germany. LC 75-13728. (Homosexuality). (Illus.). 1975. 12.00x (ISBN 0-405-07366-6). Arno.
The Stone Wall: An Autobiography. LC 75-12307. (Homosexuality). 1975. Repr. of 1930 ed. 12.00x (ISBN 0-405-07404-2). Arno.
Tobin, Kay & Wicker, Randy. The Gay Crusaders. LC 75-12349. (Homosexuality). (Illus.). 1975. Repr. 12.00x (ISBN 0-405-07374-7). Arno.

GAYAL

Simoons, Frederick J. & Simoons, Elizabeth S. Ceremonial Ox of India: The Mithan in Nature, Culture, & History. LC 68-9023. (Illus.). 340p. 1968. 27.50x (ISBN 0-299-04980-9). U of Wis Pr.

GAYLEY, CHARLES MILLS, 1858-1932

Gayley, Charles M. The Charles Mill Gayley Anniversary Papers: 1889-1919. 1922. Repr. 11.75 (ISBN 0-8274-2042-0). R West.

GAYNOR, WILLIAM JAY, 1849-1913

Pink, Louis H. Gaynor, the Tammany Mayor Who Swallowed the Tiger: Lawyer, Judge, Philosopher. facsimile ed. LC 77-124251. (Select Bibliographies Reprint Ser.). Repr. of 1931 ed. 16.00 (ISBN 0-8369-5439-4). Arno.

GAZA-HISTORY

Downey, Glanville. Gaza in the Early Sixth Century. (Centers of Civilization Ser.: No. 8). (Illus.). 1963. 5.95 (ISBN 0-8061-0564-X). U of Okla Pr.
Meyer, Martin A. History of the City of Gaza from the Earliest Times to the Present. LC 7-29749. (Columbia University. Oriental Studies: No. 5). Repr. of 1907 ed. 18.25 (ISBN 0-404-50495-7). AMS Pr.

GAZETTEERS

see Geography-Dictionaries

GEARING

see also Automobiles-Steering Gear; Automobiles-Transmission Devices; Mechanical Movements

Broersma, G. Design of Gears. 194p. 1967. 50.00x (ISBN 0-85950-055-1, Pub. by Stam Pr England). State Mutual Bk.
--Manufacture & Testing of Gears. 192p. 1969. 50.00x (ISBN 0-85950-060-8, Pub. by Stam Pr England). State Mutual Bk.
Chironis, Nicholas P., ed. Gear Design & Application. 1967. 31.00 (ISBN 0-07-010787-4, P&RB). McGraw.
Dowson, Duncan & Higginson, Gordon R. Elasto-Hydrodynamics Lubrication: SI Edition. 2nd ed. 1977. 30.00 (ISBN 0-08-021303-0); pap. 14.00 (ISBN 0-08-021302-2). Pergamon.
Dudley, Darle W., ed. Gear Handbook: The Design, Manufacture & Application of Gears. (Illus.). 1962. 52.50 (ISBN 0-07-017902-6, P&RB). McGraw.
Evans, Martin. Model Locomotive Valve Gears. (Illus.). 98p. 1973. pap. 5.00x (ISBN 0-85242-162-1). Intl Pubns Serv.
Khiralla, T. W. On the Geometry of External Involute Spur Gears. LC 76-49243. (Illus.). 1976. 25.00 (ISBN 0-9601752-1-0). T W Khiralla.
Marshall, Alfred W. Gear Wheels & Gear Cutting. 92p. 6.50x (ISBN 0-85344-126-X). Intl Pubns Serv.
Michalec, George W. Precision Gearing: Theory & Practice. LC 66-21045. 1966. 51.50 (ISBN 0-471-60142-X, Pub. by Wiley-Interscience). Wiley.
Roy, G. J. Steam Turbines & Gearing: Questions & Answers. (Marine Engineering Ser.). 96p. 1975. pap. 9.50x (ISBN 0-540-07338-5). Sheridan.
Schmelcher, T. Low Voltage Switchgear. 1976. 28.50 (ISBN 0-85501-249-8). Heyden.
Shannon, J. F. Marine Gearing. (Marine Engineering Design & Installation Ser.). (Illus.). 1978. pap. 19.50 (ISBN 0-900976-67-5, Pub. by Inst Marine Eng). Intl Schol Bk Serv.
Shtipelman, Boris A. Design & Manufacture of Hypoid Gears. LC 78-8591. 1978. 51.00 (ISBN 0-471-03648-X, Pub. by Wiley-Interscience). Wiley.
Tourret. Performance & Testing of Gear Oils & Transmission Fluids. 1981. 90.00 (ISBN 0-85501-326-5). Heyden.
Tuplin, William A. Involute Gear Geometry. 10.50 (ISBN 0-8044-4939-2). Ungar.
Wade, Harlan. Los Engranes. Contreras, Mamie M., tr. from Eng. LC 78-26614. (A Book About Ser.). Orig. Title: Gears. (Illus., Sp.). (gr. k-3). 1979. PLB 7.95 (ISBN 0-8172-1486-0). Raintree Pubs.
--Les Engrenages. Potvin, Claude & Potvin, Rose-Ella, trs. from Eng. (A Book About Ser.). Orig. Title: Gears. (Illus., Fr.). (gr. k-3). 1979. PLB 7.95 (ISBN 0-8172-1461-5). Raintree Pubs.
--Gears. rev. ed. LC 78-21312. (A Book About Ser.). (Illus.). (gr. k-3). 1979. PLB 7.95 (ISBN 0-8172-1535-2). Raintree Pubs.

GEARS

see Gearing

GED TESTS

see General Educational Development Tests

GEESE

see also Brent-Goose; Canada Goose

Bartlett, Jen & Bartlett, Des. The Flight of the Snowgeese. LC 75-12752. (Illus.). 256p. 1975. 8.95 (ISBN 0-8128-1825-3). Stein & Day.
Batty, J. Domesticated Ducks & Geese. 1981. 40.00x (ISBN 0-904558-33-9, Pub. by Saiga Pub). State Mutual Bk.
Fegely, Thomas D. Wonders of Geese & Swans. LC 75-38360. (Wonder Ser.). (Illus.). (gr. 4 up). 1976. 5.95 (ISBN 0-396-07307-7). Dodd.
Hanson, Harold C. & Jones, Robert L. The Biogeochemistry of Blue, Snow, & Ross' Geese. LC 76-46617. (Illus.). 298p. 1976. 15.00x (ISBN 0-8093-0751-0). S Ill U Pr.
Jaques, Florence P. Geese Fly High. (Illus.). 1964. Repr. of 1939 ed. 8.95 (ISBN 0-8166-0311-1). U of Minn Pr.
Johnsgard, Paul A. Song of the North Wind: A Story of the Snow Goose. LC 79-13939. (Illus.). xii, 150p. 1979. 10.95x (ISBN 0-8032-2556-3); pap. 3.75 (ISBN 0-8032-7552-8, BB 719, Bison). U of Nebr Pr.
Kear, Janet & Berger, A. J. The Hawaiian Goose: An Experiment in Conservation. LC 79-55057. (Illus.). 160p. 1980. 30.00 (ISBN 0-931130-04-2). Buteo.
Kortright, E. H. Ducks, Geese & Swans of North America. rev. ed. Bellrose, Frank C., rev. by. LC 75-33962. (Illus.). 568p. 1981. 24.95 (ISBN 0-8117-0535-8). Stackpole.
Lorenz, Konrad. The Year of the Greylag Goose. Wolff, Helen, ed. Martin, Robert, tr. LC 79-1834. (Helen & Kurt Wolff Bk.). 1979. 25.00 (ISBN 0-15-199737-3). HarBraceJ.
Ogilvie, M. A. Wild Geese. LC 77-94181. (Illus.). 1978. 25.00 (ISBN 0-931130-00-X). Buteo.
Owen, Myrfyn. Wild Geese of the World. (Illus.). 236p. 1981. 45.00 (ISBN 0-686-77712-3, Pub. by Batsford England). David & Charles.
Romashko, Sandra D. Wild Ducks & Geese of North America. LC 77-81167. (Illus.). 1978. pap. 2.95 (ISBN 0-89317-018-6). Windward Pub.
Saiga Editors. Ducks & Geese. 1981. 10.00x (ISBN 0-86230-008-8, Pub. by Saiga Pub). State Mutual Bk.
Soames, Barbra. Keeping Domestic Geese. (Illus.). 128p. 1980. 13.95 (ISBN 0-7137-1070-5, Pub. by Blandford Pr England). Sterling.
Walters, John & Parker, Michael. Keeping Ducks, Geese & Turkeys. (Gardening Farming Ser.). 128p. 1976. 8.95 (ISBN 0-7207-0932-6, Pub. by Michael Joseph). Merrimack Bk Serv.

GEEZ LANGUAGE

see Ethiopic Language

GEHRIG, LOU, 1903-1941

Gehrig, Eleanor & Durso, Joe. My Luke & I. LC 75-44457. (Illus.). 224p. 1976. 7.95 (ISBN 0-690-01109-1). T Y Crowell.
Luce, Willard & Luce, Celia. Lou Gehrig: Iron Man of Baseball. LC 78-103956. (Americans All Ser). (Illus.). (gr. 3-6). 1970. PLB 6.48 (ISBN 0-8116-4559-2). Garrard.
Rubin, Robert. Lou Gehrig: Courageous Star. LC 78-31604. (Sports Shelf Ser.). (Illus.). (gr. 5 up). 1979. PLB 6.29 (ISBN 0-399-61135-5). Putnam.

GEISHAS

Crihfield, Liza. Ko-Uta: Little Songs of the Geisha World. LC 78-66085. (Illus.). 1979. 8.50 (ISBN 0-8048-1292-6). C E Tuttle.

GEISSMAR, BERTA, 1892-1949

Geissmar, Berta. Two Worlds of Music. LC 74-28326. Orig. Title: The Baton & the Jackboot. (Illus.). 327p. 1975. Repr. of 1946 ed. lib. bdg. 27.50 (ISBN 0-306-70664-4). Da Capo.

GEKRI (AFRICAN PEOPLE)

see also Ethnology-Nigeria

Moore, William A. History of Itsekiri. 2nd rev ed. 224p. 1970. 25.00x (ISBN 0-7146-1701-6, F Cass Co). Biblio Dist.

GEL PERMEATION CHROMATOGRAPHY

Altgelt, Klaus & Segal, Leon, eds. Gel Permeation Chromatography. 1971. 57.50 (ISBN 0-8247-1006-1). Dekker.
Bibliography on Liquid Exclusion Chromatography (Gel Permeation Chromatography) 1974. pap. 9.00 (ISBN 0-686-51996-5, 10-040000-39); pap. 9.50 1972-75 suppl. (ISBN 0-686-51997-3, 10-040010-39-). ASTM.
Dawkins. Gel Permeation Chromatography of Polymers. 1978. write for info. (ISBN 0-685-84732-2). Elsevier.
Determann, H. Gel Chromatography: Gel Filtration, Gel Permeation, Molecular Sieves-a Laboratory Handbook. Gross, E. & Harkin, J. M., trs. LC 68-59064. (Illus.). 1969. 22.20 (ISBN 0-387-04450-7). Springer-Verlag.
Fischer, L. Introduction to Gel Chromatography. (Lab Techiques in Biochemistry & Molecular Biology Vol. 1, Pt. 2). 1969. pap. 19.00 (ISBN 0-444-10197-7, North-Holland). Elsevier.
Kremmer, T. & Boross, L. Gel Chromatography. LC 77-24994. 299p. 1980. 62.75 (ISBN 0-471-99548-7, Pub. by Wiley-Interscience). Wiley.

GELASIUS 1ST, SAINT, POPE, d. 496

Moreton, Bernard. The Eighth-Century Gelasian Sacramentary: A Study in Tradition. (Oxford Theological Monographs). 1976. 45.00x (ISBN 0-19-826710-X). Oxford U Pr.

GELATIN

see also Cookery (Gelatin)

Cooper Madlener, Judith. The Sea Vegetable Gelatin Cookbook. LC 80-29228. (Illus., Orig.). 1981. pap. 7.95 (ISBN 0-912800-76-3). Woodbridge Pr.
Symposium on Photographic Gelatin - 2nd, Trinity College, Cambridge, 1970. Photographic Gelatin: Proceedings. Cox, R. J., ed. 1972. 48.50 (ISBN 0-12-194450-6). Acad Pr.
Veis, Arthur. Macromolecular Chemistry of Gelatin. (Molecular Biology: Vol. 5). 1964. 55.50 (ISBN 0-12-715450-7). Acad Pr.

GELEE, CLAUDE, CALLED CLAUDE LORRAIN, 1600-1682

Cotte, Sabine. Claude Lorrain. LC 76-137220. (Great Draughtsmen Ser). (Illus.). 1971. 7.95 (ISBN 0-8076-0594-8). Braziller.
Gelee, Glaude Lorrain. Drawings of Lorrain. Roethlisberger, Marcel, ed. (Master Draughtsman Ser). (Illus., Orig.). treasure trove bdg. 6.47x (ISBN 0-685-07273-8); pap. 2.95 (ISBN 0-685-07274-6). Borden.
Lorrain. (Artists Ser). (Illus.). 1977. pap. 5.95 (ISBN 0-8120-0818-9). Barron.
Manwaring, Elizabeth W. Italian Landscape in Eighteenth Century England. LC 66-10419. (Illus.). 1965. Repr. of 1925 ed. 10.00 (ISBN 0-8462-0705-2). Russell.
Manwaring, Elizabeth Wheeler. Italian Landscape in Eighteenth Century England. (Illus.). 243p. 1965. Repr. 25.00x (ISBN 0-7146-2069-6, F Cass Co). Biblio Dist.
Roethlisberger, Marcel. Claude Lorrain: The Drawings, 2 vols., boxed. Incl. Vol. 1. Catalogue (ISBN 0-520-01458-8); Vol. 2. Plates (ISBN 0-520-01805-2). LC 66-24050. (Studies in the History of Art: No. 8). (Illus.). 1969. 85.00x ea. U of Cal Pr.
Rothlisberger, Marcel. Claude Lorrain: The Paintings: Critical Catalogue & Illustrations, 2 vols. LC 79-83839. (Illus.). 1979. Repr. of 1961 ed. Set. lib. bdg. 100.00 (ISBN 0-87817-244-0). Hacker.

GELLER, URI

Collins, Jim. The Strange Story of Uri Geller. LC 77-24501. (Myth, Magic & Superstition Ser.). (Illus.). (gr. 4-5). 1977. PLB 10.65 (ISBN 0-8172-1037-7). Raintree Pubs.
Ebon, Martin, ed. The Amazing Uri Geller. (Orig.). 1975. pap. 1.50 (ISBN 0-451-06475-5, W6475, Sig). NAL.
Geller, Uri. Uri Geller: My Story. (Illus.). 272p. 1976. pap. 1.95 (ISBN 0-446-89025-1). Warner Bks.

GELLERT, CHRISTIAN FURCHTEFOTT, 1715-1764

Coym, Johannes. Gellerts Lustspiele. 1899. 14.00 (ISBN 0-384-09980-7); pap. 11.00 (ISBN 0-384-09981-5). Johnson Repr.

GELLIUS, AULUS

Yoder, Edward. Position of Possessive & Demonstrative Adjectives in the Noctes Atticae of Aulus Gellius. 1928. pap. 6.00 (ISBN 0-527-00748-X). Kraus Repr.

GELS

see Colloids

GEM CUTTING

Baxter, William T. Jewelry, Gem Cutting & Metalcraft. 3rd ed. 1950. 10.00 (ISBN 0-07-004149-0, GB). McGraw.
Cox, Jack R. & Gems And Minerals Staff. Gem Cutters Handbook, Specialized Gem Cutting. (Illus.). 1970. pap. 2.50 (ISBN 0-910652-13-9). Gembooks.
Dake, Henry C. Art of Gem Cutting. 6th ed. pap. 2.50 (ISBN 0-910652-07-4). Gembooks.
Geldart, Graham. Hand Lapidary Craft. LC 79-56446. (Illus.). 144p. 1980. 24.00 (ISBN 0-7134-1536-3, Pub. by Batsford England). David & Charles.
Gray, J. M. James & William Tassie: A Biographical & Critical Sketch. 25.00 (ISBN 0-685-53307-7). ARS Ceramica.
Gray, John M. James & William Tassie: Jem Cutters. 25.00 (ISBN 0-87556-607-3). Saifer.

Hunt, Henry. Lapidary Carving for Creative Jewelry. LC 80-67509. (Illus.). 144p. (Orig.). 1981. 17.95 (ISBN 0-937764-01-9); pap. 12.95 (ISBN 0-937764-02-7). Desert Pr.
Long, Frank W. Creative Lapidary: Materials, Tools, Techniques, Design. 1976. 14.95 (ISBN 0-442-24887-3). Van Nos Reinhold.
Perry, Nance & Perry, Ron. Practical Gemcutting. (Illus.). 96p. (Orig.). 1980. pap. 13.50 (ISBN 0-589-50192-5, Pub. by Reed Bks Australia). C E Tuttle.
--Practical Gemcutting: A Guide to Shaping & Polishing Gemstones. LC 81-10833. (Illus.). 96p. 1982. 11.95 (ISBN 0-668-05359-3, 5359). Arco.
Scarfe, Herbert. Advanced Lapidary Techniques. 1979. 27.00 (ISBN 0-7134-0398-5, Pub. by Batsford England). David & Charles.
Shore, Eric. Lapidary for Pleasure & Profit. LC 77-25058. (Illus.). 1978. 7.95 (ISBN 0-668-04533-7, 4533). Arco.
Soukup, E. J. Facet Cutters Handbook. 2nd ed. pap. 2.50 (ISBN 0-910652-06-6). Gembooks.
Sperisen, Francis J. Art of the Lapidary. rev. ed. 1961. 9.95 (ISBN 0-685-07609-1, 80712). Glencoe.
Sweetman, Leonard. Cabochon Gems Today. 72p. 1971. pap. 3.00 (ISBN 0-685-26766-0). L Sweetman.
Vargas, Glenn & Vargas, Martha. Diagrams for Faceting. LC 75-21404. (Illus.). 190p. 1975. 15.00 (ISBN 0-917646-02-9). Glenn Vargas.
Vargas, Glenn E. & Vargas, Martha D. Faceting for Amateurs. 2nd ed. LC 76-57449. (Illus.). 1977. 20.00 (ISBN 0-917646-01-0). Glenn Vargas.
Walter, Martin. Gem Cutting Is Easy. (Arts & Crafts Ser.). (Illus.). 96p. 1972. pap. 4.95 (ISBN 0-517-50020-5). Crown.
--Gemstone Carving. LC 76-27650. 1977. pap. 6.95 (ISBN 0-8019-6193-9). Chilton.
Wertz, Ed & Wertz, Leola. Handbook of Gemstone Carving. pap. 2.50 (ISBN 0-910652-10-4). Gembooks.

GEMATRIA
see also Cabala

GEMMATION (BOTANY)
see Plants–Reproduction

GEMS
Here are entered books on engraved stones and jewels, interesting from the point of view of antiquities or art. Works on mineralogical interest are entered under Precious Stones.
see also Cameos; Crown Jewels; Glyptics; Jewelry; Scarabs
Anderson, B. W. Gem Testing. 9th rev. ed. 1980. 29.95 (ISBN 0-408-00440-1). Butterworth.
--Gemstones for Everyman. (Illus.). 384p. 1976. 25.00 (ISBN 0-442-20360-8). Van Nos Reinhold.
Ash, Douglas. Dictionary of British Antique Glass. (Illus.). 210p. 1976. 14.00 (ISBN 0-7207-0837-0). Transatlantic.
Boardman, John & Vollenweider, Marie-Louise. Catalogue of the Engraved Gems & Finger Rings in the Ashmoleaw Museum, Vol. I: Greek & Etruscan. (Illus.). 1978. 79.00 (ISBN 0-19-813195-X). Oxford U Pr.
Coates, Donald R., ed. Glacial Gemorphology: Binghampton Symposia in Geomorphology. (International Ser.: No. 5). (Illus.). 304p. 1981. text ed. 20.00x (ISBN 0-04-551045-8). Allen Unwin.
Cooper, Lyn & Cooper, Ray. New Zealand Gemstones. (Illus.). 125p. 1966. 8.95 (ISBN 0-589-00256-2, Pub. by Reed Books Australia). C E Tuttle.
Curran, Mona. Treasury of Jewels & Gems. (Illus.). 1962. 9.95 (ISBN 0-87523-139-X). Emerson.
Delbrueck, Richard. Antike Porphyrwerke. (Studien zur spaetantiken Kunstgeschichte, Vol. 6). (Illus.). xxx, 246p. Repr. of 1932 ed. text ed. write for info. (ISBN 3-11-005702-6). De Gruyter.
Desautels, Paul E. The Gem Collection. new ed. LC 79-16475. (The Treasures in the Smithsonian Ser.: No. 1). (Illus.). 77p. 1980. 12.50 (ISBN 0-87474-360-5); pap. 6.95 (ISBN 0-87474-361-3). Smithsonian.
Ferguson, Robert W. Artistry in Cabochons. (Illus.). 64p. 1976. pap. 2.00 (ISBN 0-910652-21-X). Gembooks.
Fletcher, Edward. Rock & Gem Polishing. (Illus.). 1973. 4.95 (ISBN 0-7137-0617-1, Pub by Blandford Pr England). Sterling.
Fobes, Harriet K. Mystic Gems. 1977. 59.95 (ISBN 0-8490-2315-7). Gordon Pr.
Gems & Mineral Magazine Staff & Cox, Jack R. A Gem Cutter's Handbook - Plastic & Gemstones. (Illus.). 20p. 1974. pap. 1.00 (ISBN 0-910652-20-1). Gembooks.
Gill, Joseph O. Gill's Index to Journals, Articles, & Books Relating to Gems & Jewelry. 1978. 24.50 (ISBN 0-87311-009-9). Gemological.
James, Bill. Collecting Australian Gemstones. 17.50x (ISBN 0-392-02593-0, ABC). Sportshelf.
Jones, Lowell. Diary of a Gems Merchant. (Illus.). 1978. write for info. (ISBN 0-9602074-0-6). L Jones.
King, C. W. Antique Gems & Rings, 2 vols. 1977. 250.00 (ISBN 0-8490-1440-9). Gordon Pr.
King, G. W. Handbook of Engraved Gems. 1977. lib. bdg. 199.00 (ISBN 0-8490-1931-1). Gordon Pr.
Kunz, G. F. Gems & Precious Stones of North America. 2nd ed. (Illus., New intro. by Edward Olsen). Repr. 10.00 (ISBN 0-8446-2414-4). Peter Smith.
Kunz, George F. Curious Lore of Precious Stones. 1970. pap. 5.95 (ISBN 0-486-22227-6). Dover.
Macintosh, E. K. Guide to the Rocks, Minerals & Gemstones of Southern Africa. (Illus.). 1976. limp bdg. 11.00x (ISBN 0-86977-062-4). Verry.
Morisawa, Marie, ed. Fluvial Gemorphology: Binghamton Symposia in Geomorphology. (International Ser.: No. 4). 304p. 1981. Repr. of 1973 ed. text ed. 20.00x (ISBN 0-04-551046-6). Allen Unwin.
Pandit, M. P., ed. Gems from the Tantras, 2nd Series. 1971. 3.95 (ISBN 0-89744-103-6, Pub. by Ganesh & Co. India). Auromere.
Pavitt, William T. & Pavitt, Kate. Book of Talismans, Amulets & Zodiacal Gems. LC 72-157497. (Tower Bks). (Illus.). 1971. Repr. of 1914 ed. 30.00 (ISBN 0-8103-3901-3). Gale.
Pearl, Richard M. Colorado Gem Trails & Mineral Guide. rev., 3rd ed. LC 75-132587. (Illus.). 223p. 1972. 12.95 (ISBN 0-8040-0052-2, SB). Swallow.
Pownall, Glen. Jewellery & Gem Craft. (Creative Leisure Ser.). (Illus.). 84p. 1974. 7.50x (ISBN 0-85467-018-1). Intl Pubns Serv.
Preston, Ralph N. Oregon Gold & Gem Maps. (Illus.). 1977. pap. 4.95 (ISBN 0-8323-0309-7). Binford.
Read. Beginner's Guide to Gemmology. 9.95 (ISBN 0-686-27953-0). Butterworth.
St. Maur, Suzan & Streep, Norbert. The Jewelry Book. (Illus.). 198p. 1981. 9.95 (ISBN 0-312-44230-0). St Martin.
Sidney, Philip. A Cabinet of Gems: Cut & Polished by Sir Philip Sidney, Now for the More Radiance. Presented Without Their Setting by George Macdonald. 1892. Repr. 25.00 (ISBN 0-8274-1992-9). R West.
Sinkankas, John. Van Nostrand's Standard Catalog of Gems. LC 63-19369. 1968. pap. 9.95 (ISBN 0-442-27621-4). Van Nos Reinhold.
Smith, G. F. Gem Stones & Their Distinctive Characters. 1977. lib. bdg. 75.00 (ISBN 0-8490-1877-3). Gordon Pr.
Speckels, Milton J. Complete Guide to Micromounts. 96p. pap. 2.00 (ISBN 0-910652-04-X). Gembooks.
Streeter, Edwin M. Precious Stones & Gems. 1977. 79.95 (ISBN 0-8490-2466-8). Gordon Pr.
Weinstein, Michael. Precious & Semi-Precious Stones. 1977. 75.00 (ISBN 0-8490-2465-X). Gordon Pr.
--World of Jewel Stones. (Illus.). 1958. 22.50 (ISBN 0-911378-29-4). Sheridan.
Zucker, Benjamin. How to Buy & Sell Gems: Everyone's Guide to Rubies, Sapphires, Emeralds & Diamonds. 160p. 1980. 12.95 (ISBN 0-8129-0903-8). Times Bks.
--How to Invest in Gems: Everyone's Guide to Buying Rubies, Sapphires, Emeralds, & Diamonds. LC 75-36261. (Illus.). 192p. 1976. 12.95 (ISBN 0-8129-0606-3). Times Bks.

GEMS–JUVENILE LITERATURE
Pearl, Richard M. Wonders of Gems. (Illus.). (gr. 3-7). 1963. PLB 5.95 (ISBN 0-396-06403-5). Dodd.

GEMS, ARTIFICIAL
see Precious Stones, Artificial

GEMS (COMPUTER PROGRAM LANGUAGE)
see SIMSCRIPT (Computer Program Language)

GEMS (IN RELIGION, FOLK-LORE, ETC.)
Carley, Ken. Gems & Stones: Scientific Properties & Aspects of Twenty Two- a Comparative Study Based Upon the Edgar Cayce Psychic Readings. rev. ed. 1979. pap. 2.95 (ISBN 0-87604-110-1). ARE Pr.
Evans, Joan. Magical Jewels of the Middle Ages & the Renaissance Particularly in England. LC 75-26288. (Illus.). 288p. 1976. pap. 3.00 (ISBN 0-486-23367-7). Dover.
Finch, Elizabeth. The Psychic Values of Gemstones. LC 78-59205. 1979. pap. 3.00 (ISBN 0-89861-018-4). Esoteric Pubns.
Jones, William. History & Mystery of Precious Stones. LC 68-22031. 1968. Repr. of 1880 ed. 22.00 (ISBN 0-8103-3450-X). Gale.
Kunz, G. F. The Curious Lore of Precious Stones. (Illus.). 11.50 (ISBN 0-8446-0173-X). Peter Smith.
Kunz, George F. Curious Lore of Precious Stones. 1970. pap. 5.95 (ISBN 0-486-22227-6). Dover.
Lorusso, Julia & Glick, Joel. Healing Stoned: The Therapeutic Use of Gems & Minerals. 3rd ed. 1979. pap. 6.95 (ISBN 0-914732-05-6). Bro Life Bks.
Perkins, Percy H., Jr. Gemstones of the Bible. 2nd ed. (Illus.). 150p. 1980. pap. 11.95 (ISBN 0-9603090-1-2). P H Perkins.
Richardson, Wallace G. & Huett, Lenora. The Spiritual Value of Gem Stones. LC 79-54728. 168p. 1980. pap. 5.95 (ISBN 0-87516-383-1). De Vorss.
Swinburne, Laurence & Swinburne, Irene. The Deadly Diamonds. LC 77-10764. (Great Unsolved Mysteries Ser.). (Illus.). (gr. 4-5). 1977. PLB 10.65 (ISBN 0-8172-1064-4). Raintree Pubs.

GEMSTONE COLLECTING
see Mineralogy–Collectors and Collecting

GEMSTONES
see Precious Stones

GENEALOGICAL RESEARCH
see Genealogy

GENEALOGY
see also Bible–Genealogy; Biography; Court Records; Heraldry; Kings and Rulers–Genealogy; Land Grants; Pensions, Military; Registers of Births, Deaths, Marriages, etc.; Royal Descent, Families of; Wills
also names of families, e.g. Adams Family; and names of places with or without the subdivision Genealogy, e.g. United States - Genealogy
American Genealogical Research Institute Staff. How to Trace Your Family Tree. LC 73-88881. 200p. 1975. pap. 2.95 (ISBN 0-385-09885-5, Dolp). Doubleday.
Ames, Agnes H. Ames Ancestry: Europe to Maine. LC 79-91992. (Illus., Orig.). 1979. 20.00x (ISBN 0-9603714-1-9); pap. 15.00x (ISBN 0-9603714-2-7). C & H Pub.
Arbit Books, ed. Toledoteinu: Finding Your Own Roots. Tarachow, Mike, tr. (Illus.). 1978. pap. text ed. 1.95 (ISBN 0-930038-10-X). Arbit.
Arthur, William. An Etymological Dictionary of Family Christian Names. 59.95 (ISBN 0-8490-0135-8). Gordon Pr.
Ashton, Rick J., et al. Genealogy Beginner's Manual. 28p. 1977. pap. 1.50 (ISBN 0-685-41896-0). Newberry.
Ballonoff, Paul A., ed. Genealogical Mathematics. 311p. 1975. pap. text ed. 43.50x (ISBN 90-2797-901-4). Mouton.
Barber, Henry. British Family Names. 59.95 (ISBN 0-87968-791-6). Gordon Pr.
Baring-Gould, S. Family Names & Their Story. 59.95 (ISBN 0-8490-0152-8). Gordon Pr.
Barrow, Geoffrey. Genealogist's Guide. 1977. text ed. 12.50 (ISBN 0-8389-3203-7). ALA.
Barton, H. Arnold. The Search for Ancestors: A Swedish-American Family Saga. LC 78-15537. (Illus.). 189p. 1979. 11.95 (ISBN 0-8093-0893-2). S Ill U Pr.
Beard, Timothy F. & Demong, Denise. How to Find Your Family Roots. 1978. 24.95 (ISBN 0-07-004210-1, GB). McGraw.
Bell, James B. Family History Record Book. 1980. pap. 7.95 (ISBN 0-8166-0972-1). U of Minn Pr.
Bliss, Grace, compiled by. A Bliss Genealogy. 1979. 10.00 (ISBN 0-87164-096-1). William-F.
Bouressa, LaVonne J. Genealogy My Way. LC 77-95808. 1977. 8.95 (ISBN 0-686-77095-1). Genealogy Res.
Boy Scouts of America. Genealogy. LC 19-600. (Illus.). 32p. (gr. 6-12). 1973. pap. 0.70x (ISBN 0-8395-3383-7, 3383). BSA.
Bradley, Edward J. The Child & Family Genealogy Reporting System. 2nd ed. 1981. 9.95 (ISBN 0-935202-01-3). Child & Family Ent.
Braun, Johannes. Shenandoah Valley Family Data 1799-1813. Wust, Klaus, ed. & tr. from Ger. 1978. pap. 7.75 (ISBN 0-917968-05-0). Shenandoah Hist.
Crowther, Duane S. Family Ancestral Record: Adult Genealogy Starter Kit. LC 78-52113. 1981. 5.50 (ISBN 0-88290-088-9). Horizon Utah.
--My Family Heritage: Youth Genealogy Starter Kit. LC 78-52120. 1981. 5.50 (ISBN 0-88290-087-0). Horizon Utah.
Currer-Briggs, Noel. The Carters of Virginia: Their English Ancestry. 120p. 1979. 23.75x (ISBN 0-8476-2403-X). Rowman.
D'Angerville, Count, ed. Living Descendants of Blood Royal in America: World Nobility & Peerage, Vols 3 & 4. (Illus.). 1142p. 1970. 45.00x ea.; Vol. 4. Intl Pubns Serv.
Danky, James P., ed. Genealogical Research: An Introduction to the Resources of the State Historical Society of Wisconsin. LC 79-15148. 1979. pap. 2.00 (ISBN 0-87020-180-8). State Hist Soc Wis.
Discovering Your Family Tree. rev. ed. 64p. 1980. pap. 2.95 (ISBN 0-85263-404-8, Pub. by B T A). Merrimack Bk Serv.
Dixon, Janice T. & Flack, Dora D. Preserving Your Past: A Painless Guide to Writing Your Autobiography & Family History. LC 76-56278. 1977. 8.95 (ISBN 0-385-12817-7). Doubleday.
Doane, Gilbert H. & Bell, James B. Searching for Your Ancestors: The How & Why of Geneaology. 5th ed. 1980. 10.95 (ISBN 0-8166-0934-9). U of Minn Pr.
Durye, Pierre. Genealogy: An Introduction to Continental Concepts. Clough, Wilson O., tr. from Fr. LC 77-82714. 1977. pap. 7.50 (ISBN 0-686-10226-6). Polyanthos.
Eakle, Arlene H. & Gunn, L. Ray. Descriptive Inventory of the New York Collection. (Finding Aids to the Microfilmed Manuscript Collection of the Genealogical Society of Utah). (Orig.). 1980. pap. 20.00x (ISBN 0-87480-170-2). U of Utah Pr.
Eakle, Arlene H. & Weber, Georgia L. How to Prove Your Family Tree. (How-to Ser). (gr. 8-12). 1978. pap. text ed. 4.00x (ISBN 0-686-10808-6). Genealog Inst.
Egle, William H. Notes & Queries. Historical, Biographical & Genealogical Relating Chiefly to Interior Pennsylvania, 12 vols. LC 70-114834. 1970. Repr. of 1893 ed. Set. lib. bdg. 166.50 (ISBN 0-8063-0403-0). Genealog Pub.
Epstein, Ellen R. & Mendelsohn, Rona. Record & Remember. LC 78-1411. 1978. pap. 2.95 (ISBN 0-671-18356-7). Monarch Pr.
Fay, Loren V. New York Genealogical Research Secrets. 50p. 1979. pap. 5.00 (ISBN 0-686-27875-5). L V Fay.
Gambrill, Georgia. Genealogical Material & Local Histories in the St. Louis Public Library. 1966. first suppl., 1971 2.00 (ISBN 0-937322-01-6). St Louis Pub Lib.
Gibbs, Richard W. & Gibbs, Marcia G., eds. Family History Is Fun. 1978. 16.95 (ISBN 0-932924-00-X). Gibbs Pub NH.
--Family History Is Fun. 1978. 16.95 (ISBN 0-932924-00-X). Gibbs Pub NH.
Greenlaw, Lucy H. The Genealogical Advertiser. LC 73-23032. 194p. 1974. 25.00 (ISBN 0-8063-0610-6). Genealog Pub.
Greenwood, Val D. Researcher's Guide to American Genealogy. 1973. 22.50 (ISBN 0-8063-0560-6, ScribT). Scribner.
Groene, Bertram H. Tracing Your Civil War Ancestor. LC 73-77903. (Illus.). 1981. 8.95 (ISBN 0-89587-026-6). Blair.
Haines, Herbert. Manual of Monumental Brasses, 2 vols. in 1. LC 75-160448. 1970. Repr. of 1861 ed. 25.00 (ISBN 0-8063-0483-9). Genealog Pub.
Harding, Margery, compiled by. George Rogers Clark & His Men: Military Records, 1778-1784. LC 80-82439. 225p. 1981. 25.00 (ISBN 0-916968-09-X). Kentucky Hist.
Heimberg, Marilyn M. Discover Your Roots: A New, Easy Guide for Tracing Your Family Tree. LC 77-77291. (Illus.). 1977. pap. 3.95 (ISBN 0-918880-00-9). Comm Creat.
Helmbold, F. Wilbur. Tracing Your Ancestry: A Step-by-Step Guide to Researching Your Family History. LC 76-14109. (Illus.). 1976. 9.95 (ISBN 0-8487-0415-0); logbook o.p. 3.95 (ISBN 0-8487-0414-2). Oxmoor Hse.
--Tracing Your Ancestry Logbook. LC 76-14113. (Illus.). 256p. 1978. pap. 4.95 (ISBN 0-8487-0414-2). Oxmoor Hse.
--Tracing Your Ancestry: Step-by-Step Guide to Researching Your Family History. LC 76-14109. (Illus.). 1978. pap. 4.95 (ISBN 0-8487-0486-X). Oxmoor Hse.
Herrman, H. E. I Am the Son of Adam (How Do You Like Them Apples?) 1980. 6.50 (ISBN 0-533-04313-1). Vantage.
Hilts, Len. How to Find Your Own Roots. 1978. 3.95 (ISBN 0-346-12313-5). Cornerstone.
Hines, Benjamin M. Hines & Allied Families. LC 80-67479. 360p. 1981. 25.00 (ISBN 0-8059-2748-4). Dorrance.
Hopkins, Garland E. Your Family Tree. 1949. pap. 2.50 (ISBN 0-685-09026-4). Dietz.
Ironmonger, Elizabeth. Three Courageous Women & Their Kin: A Pescud Family Genealogy. LC 65-5363. 278p. 1965. 25.00x (ISBN 0-685-65070-7). Va Bk.
Jacobus, Donald L. Genealogy As Pastime & Profession. 2nd ed. LC 68-22955. 1978. 7.50 (ISBN 0-8063-0188-0). Genealog Pub.
Jaussi, Laureen & Chaston, Gloria. Fundamentals of Genealogical Research. 7.95 (ISBN 0-87747-647-0). Deseret Bk.
Jensen, C. Russell. Preliminary Survey of the French Collection. (Finding Aids to the Microfilmed Manuscript Collection of the Genealogical Society of Utah). (Orig.). 1981. pap. 25.00x (ISBN 0-87480-171-0). U of Utah Pr.
Johnson, Keith A. & Saintly, Malcolm R. Genealogical Research Directory 1981: Australasian Edition. 151p. 1981. pap. text ed. 9.95 (ISBN 0-908120-41-9, Pub. by Lib Australian Hist). Bks Australia.
Jones, Vincent L., et al. Family History for Fun & Profit. LC 72-75075. 1972. pap. 10.00 (ISBN 0-686-18976-0); pap. text ed. 10.00 (ISBN 0-686-18977-9); tchrs.ed. 10.00 (ISBN 0-686-18978-7). Genealog Inst.
Jordan, David S. & Kimball, Sarah L. Your Family Tree, Being a Glance at Scientific Aspects of Genealogy. LC 67-28625. 1979. Repr. of 1929 ed. 15.00 (ISBN 0-8063-0199-6). Genealog Pub.

Kranzler, David. My Jewish Roots: A Practical Guide to Tracing & Recording Your Genealogy & Family History. (Illus.). 1979. pap. 7.95 (ISBN 0-87203-074-1). Hermon.

Krause, Claire S. Genealogy: Your Past Revisited. Smith, Linda H., ed. 1980. pap. 3.95 (ISBN 0-936386-08-8). Creative Learning.

Kyvig, David & Marty, Myron A. Your Family History: A Handbook for Research & Writing. LC 77-86030. 1978. pap. text ed. 3.95x (ISBN 0-88295-774-0). Harlan Davidson.

Lee, Helen B. Bourne Genealogy. LC 73-175810. (Illus.). 1972. 5.00 (ISBN 0-87106-113-9). Globe Pequot.

--Joy Supplement, Two: Descendants of Thomas Joy, Pt.2. LC 76-45277. (Illus.). 1980. pap. 2.50 (ISBN 0-87106-075-2). Globe Pequot.

Lewis, Nancy, ed. My Roots Be Coming Back. (Illus.). 24p. 1973. pap. 3.50x (ISBN 0-89062-034-2, Pub. by Touchstone). Pub Ctr Cult Res.

Lichtman, Allan J. Your Family History: How to Use Oral History Family Archives, & Public Documents to Discover Your Heritage. LC 77-76582. 1978. pap. 3.95 (ISBN 0-394-72332-5, Vin). Random.

Linder, Bill R. How to Trace Your Family History: A Basic Guide to Genealogy. LC 78-57418. 1978. 6.95 (ISBN 0-89696-022-6). Everest Hse.

Ljungstedt, Milnor, ed. County Court Notebook & Ancestral Proofs & Probabilities. LC 77-173265. 788p. 1972. Repr. of 1931 ed. 30.00 (ISBN 0-8063-0505-3). Genealog Pub.

McNaughton, Arnold. The Book of Kings: A Royal Genealogy, 3 vols. LC 72-77538. 1000p. 1973. 125.00 (ISBN 0-8129-0280-7). Times Bks.

Mander, Meda. Tracing Your Ancestors. LC 75-42597. (Illus.). 1976. 11.95 (ISBN 0-7153-7022-7). David & Charles.

Michael, Prudence G. Don't Cry "Timber"! Genealogical Research Guide. 7th ed. LC 78-20129. 1981. pap. 4.95 postpaid (ISBN 0-9600932-1-4). P G Michael.

Milner, Anita C. Newspaper Genealogical Column Directory. 1979. 8.00 (ISBN 0-917890-16-7). Heritage Bk.

Moriarty, Daniel P. How to Publish a Worldwide Family-Name Newsletter. 1979. pap. 5.00 (ISBN 0-933968-02-7). D Moriarty.

Moss, Mary W. A Profile of the Dixon Family. (Illus.). 1980. pap. 4.50 (ISBN 0-682-49572-7). Exposition.

Ostler, Carolyn H. Collecting People: Your Ancestors & Mine. (gr. 6 up). 1981. 10.00x (ISBN 0-686-08736-4). Genealog Inst.

Peskett, Hugh. Discover Your Ancestors: A Quest for Your Roots. LC 77-25264. (Illus.). 1978. lib. bdg. 6.95 (ISBN 0-668-04529-9); pap. 2.95 (ISBN 0-668-04531-0). Arco.

Philips, George O. Philips Family Record 1978. (Illus.). 520p. (Orig.). 1979. pap. 17.50 (ISBN 0-940846-00-4). Hastings Bks.

Phillimore, W. P. How to Write the History of a Family: A Guide for the Genealogist. LC 70-179653. (Illus.). viii, 206p. 1972. Repr. of 1876 ed. 24.00 (ISBN 0-8103-3117-9). Gale.

Photograph Analysis. (Illus.). 1976. pap. 5.50x (ISBN 0-686-17533-6). Genealog Inst.

Pine, Leslie G. American Origins: Sources for Genealogical Research and Records Abroad. LC 67-30524. 1980. Repr. of 1960 ed. 15.00 (ISBN 0-686-66318-7). Genealog Pub.

--Genealogist's Encyclopedia. (Illus.). 1970. pap. 4.95 (ISBN 0-02-081160-8, Collier). Macmillan.

Playle, Ron. How You Can Trace Your Family Roots. (Illus., Orig.). 1977. pap. 4.95 (ISBN 0-89511-005-9). R & D Serv.

Popejoy, Charles L. The Popejoy Family in America 1700-1976. (Illus.). 26.00 (ISBN 0-686-10983-X). Popejoy.

Poteet, David. How to Trace Your Family Tree. 2nd ed. LC 79-84344. (Illus.). 157p. 1979. pap. 3.50 (ISBN 0-89877-002-5). Jeremy Bks.

--How to Trace Your Family Tree. LC 79-84344. 1979. pap. 3.50 (ISBN 0-87123-209-X, 210209). Bethany Hse.

Prud'Homme, Luclie & Christensen, Fern, eds. The Natchitoches Cemeteries: Transcriptions of Gravestones from the 18th, 19th, & 20th Centuries. LC 77-85632. 1978. pap. 17.50x (ISBN 0-686-09339-9). Polyanthos.

Richman, Carol. Lekachmacher Family. LC 76-23409. (Illus.). 1976. 8.95 (ISBN 0-914842-14-5). Madrona Pubs.

Round, Horace. Family Origins & Other Studies: Edited with a Memoir & Bibliography by William Price. (Genealogy Ser.: No. 4). 303p. 1971. Repr. of 1930 ed. 35.00x (ISBN 0-7130-0025-2, Pub. by Woburn Pr England). Biblio Dist.

Round, John H. Family Origins & Other Studies. Page, William, ed. LC 79-124474. 1970. Repr. of 1930 ed. 15.00 (ISBN 0-8063-0424-3). Genealog Pub.

Rye, Walter. Records & Record Searching. LC 68-30663. 1969. Repr. of 1897 ed. 22.00 (ISBN 0-8103-3133-0). Gale.

--Records & Record Searching (in England) A Guide to the Genealogist & Topographer. 2nd ed. LC 72-80643. 1969. Repr. of 1897 ed. 15.00 (ISBN 0-8063-0303-4). Genealog Pub.

Ryerson, Albert W. The Ryerson Genealogy: Genealogy & History of the Knickerbocker Families of Ryerson, Ryerse, Ryerss, Also Adriane & Martense Families All Descendants of Martin & Adriane Reyersz (Reyerszen) of Amsterdam, Holland. Holman, Alfred L., ed. 85.00x (ISBN 0-685-88555-0). Elliots Bks.

Scott, Kenneth & Stryker-Rodda, Kenn. Buried Genealogical Data. LC 77-82335. 1977. 15.00 (ISBN 0-8063-0782-X). Genealog Pub.

Skalka, Lois M. Tracing, Charting & Writing Your Family History. LC 75-15954. 1975. pap. 2.50 (ISBN 0-87576-052-X). Pilot Bks.

Smith, Leonard H., Jr. Rooting Your Family Tree: The First Fourteen, Pt. 1. LC 77-95196. (Illus.). 1977. 9.95 (ISBN 0-932022-11-1). L H Smith.

Stetson, Oscar F. The Art of Ancestor Hunting. 1975. 18.50 (ISBN 0-8044-5890-1, Pub by Stephen Daye Pr). Ungar.

Stevens, Cj, ed. Holloways of the South. 1978. 45.00x (ISBN 0-686-09338-0). Polyanthos.

Stevenson, Noel C. Genealogical Evidence: A Guide to the Standard of Proof Relating to Pedigrees, Ancestry, Heirship & Family History. LC 79-53622. (Orig.). 1979. pap. 14.80 (ISBN 0-89412-036-0). Aegean Park Pr.

--Search & Research. 4.95 (ISBN 0-87747-660-8). Deseret Bk.

Stevenson, Noel C., ed. The Genealogical Reader. LC 58-10649. 1978. pap. 12.50x (ISBN 0-686-09337-2). Polyanthos.

Stewart, J. How to Obtain U. S. Gov't Assistance in Family History Research. LC 81-66731. (Illus.). 108p. (Orig.). 1982. pap. 9.95 (ISBN 0-939774-00-3, AHS-00). Ancestral Hist.

Stoddard, Francis R. The Truth About the Pilgrims. LC 73-7218. 1976. Repr. of 1952 ed. 10.00 (ISBN 0-8063-0561-4). Genealog Pub.

Stryker-Rodda, Harriet. How to Climb Your Family Tree: Genealogy for Beginners. LC 77-24667. (YA) 1977. pap. 3.95 (ISBN 0-397-01243-8). Lippincott.

Towle, Laird C. Genealogical Periodical Annual Index Vol. 15, 1976. 1978. 10.00 (ISBN 0-917890-10-8). Heritage Bk.

Towle, Laird C., ed. Genealogical Periodical Annual Index: 1974, Vol. 13. 1976. pap. text ed. 6.00 (ISBN 0-917890-00-0). Heritage Bk.

Unett, John. Making a Pedigree. LC 75-141813. 1971. Repr. of 1961 ed. 10.00 (ISBN 0-8063-0464-2). Genealog Pub.

Von Redlich, Marcellus D. Pedigrees of Some of the Emperor Charlemagne's Descendants, Vol. I. LC 71-39170. 320p. Repr. of 1941 ed. 17.50 (ISBN 0-8063-0494-4). Genealog Pub.

Wagner, Anthony. Pedigree & Progress: Essays in the Genealogical Interpretation of History. 333p. 1975. 35.00x (ISBN 0-87471-782-5). Rowman.

Watkins, M. S. Ancestor Hunting. 1969. 15.00 (ISBN 0-685-08142-7). Claitors.

Watts, Dorothy C. The Tyree Tree with Angle, Byrd, Cook, Dillion & Woody Branches. LC 78-103547. (Illus.). 1978. 21.00 (ISBN 0-9603402-0-3). D C Watts.

Westin, Jeane E. Finding Your Roots: How Every American Can Trace His Ancestors. LC 76-62675. 1977. 8.95 (ISBN 0-87477-060-2). J P Tarcher.

Whitmore, William H. Family Tree Ancestral Tablets. 1955. pap. 7.75 (ISBN 0-8048-0684-5). C E Tuttle.

Whitmore, William H., ed. The Heraldic Journal: Recording the Armorial Bearings & Genealogies of American Families. LC 77-39169. (Illus.). 1972. Repr. of 1868 ed. 25.00 (ISBN 0-8063-0493-6). Genealog Pub.

Wiggam, Albert E. The Fruit of the Family Tree. 1924. lib. bdg. 20.00 (ISBN 0-8414-9131-3). Folcroft.

Williams, Ethel W. Know Your Ancestors: A Guide to Genealogical Research. LC 60-15252. 1960. bds. 8.50 (ISBN 0-8048-0344-7). C E Tuttle.

York, Courtney. How to Grow Your Family Tree. 120p. 1974. pap. 6.50 (ISBN 0-916660-19-2). Hse of York.

GENEALOGY–BIBLIOGRAPHY

Cappon, Lester J. American Genealogical Periodicals: A Bibliography with a Chronological Finding-List. LC 61-18771. 1964. pap. 4.00 (ISBN 0-87104-000-X). NY Pub Lib.

Filby, P. William, ed. Passenger & Immigration Lists Index: A Reference Guide to Published Lists of About 500,000 Passengers Who Arrived in America in the Seventeenth, Eighteenth & Nineteenth Centuries, 3 vols. 1981. Set. 225.00 (ISBN 0-8103-1099-6). Gale.

Gatfield, George. Guide to Printed Books & Manuscripts Relating to English & Foreign Heraldry & Genealogy. 1966. Repr. of 1892 ed. 30.00 (ISBN 0-8103-3121-7). Gale.

Genealogies in the Library of Congress: Supplement 1972-1976. LC 74-187078. 1977. 25.00 (ISBN 0-910946-19-1). Magna Carta Bk.

Gordon, Maurice B., et al. Book of the Descendants of Doctor Benjamin Lee & Dorothy Gordon. LC 73-169910. 1972. 8.50 (ISBN 0-911566-11-2). Ventnor.

Kaminkow, Marion J., ed. A Complement to Genealogies in the Library of Congress: A Bibliography. LC 80-85390. 1118p. 1981. 83.50 (ISBN 0-910946-24-8). Magna Carta Bk.

Lancour, Harold & Wolfe, Richard J., eds. Bibliography of Ship Passenger Lists, Fifteen Thirty-Eight to Eighteen Twenty-Five: A Guide to Published Lists of Early Immigrants to North America. 3rd ed. rev ed. LC 63-18141. 1978. 10.00 (ISBN 0-87104-023-9). NY Pub Lib.

Mayhew, Catherine M. Genealogical Periodical Annual Index, 1977, Vol. 16. Towle, Laird C., ed. 1979. 12.50 (ISBN 0-917890-17-5). Heritage Bk.

--Genealogical Periodical Annual Index: 1978, Vol. 17, Vol.17. Towle, Laird C., ed. xii, 167p. 1980. 12.50 (ISBN 0-917890-23-X). Heritage Bk.

Parker, J. Carlyle, ed. Library Service for Genealogists. LC 80-26032. (The Gale Genealogy & Local History Ser.: Vol. 15). 285p. 1981. 36.00 (ISBN 0-8103-1489-4). Gale.

Schreiner-Yantis, Netti, ed. Genealogical & Local History Books in Print. LC 75-4225. 1000p. 20.00 (ISBN 0-686-30194-3); pap. 15.00 (ISBN 0-89157-031-4). GBIP.

Sperry, Kip. Index to Genealogical Periodical Literature, 1960-1977. LC 79-9407. (Gale Genealogy & Local History Ser.: Vol. 9). 1979. 36.00 (ISBN 0-8103-1403-7). Gale.

Sperry, Kip, ed. Survey of American Genealogical Periodicals & Periodical Indexes. LC 78-55033. (Genealogy & Local History Ser.: Vol. 3). 1978. 36.00 (ISBN 0-8103-1401-0). Gale.

Towle, Laird C. Genealogical Periodical Annual Index: 1975, Vol. 14. 1977. pap. text ed. 7.50 (ISBN 0-917890-01-9). Heritage Bk.

GENEALOGY–JUVENILE LITERATURE

Barnes, Kathleen & Pearce, Virginia. You & Yours. (Illus.). 41p. (Orig.). (gr. 3-6). 1980. pap. 2.95 (ISBN 0-87747-823-6). Deseret Bk.

Chorzempa, Rosemary A. My Family Tree Workbook: Genealogy for Beginners. 64p. 1981. pap. price not set (ISBN 0-486-24229-3). Dover.

Frankel, Julie & Scheier, Michael. Digging for My Roots. (gr. 7 up). 1977. pap. 1.25 (ISBN 0-590-11840-4, Schol Pap). Schol Bk Serv.

Gilfond, Henry. Genealogy: How to Find Your Roots. (Impact Bks.). (Illus.). (gr. 7 up). 1978. PLB 7.45 s&l (ISBN 0-531-01455-X). Watts.

Henriod, Lorraine. Ancestor Hunting. LC 79-10767. (Illus.). 64p. (gr. 3-5). 1979. PLB 7.29 (ISBN 0-671-32998-7). Messner.

Hilton, Suzanne. Who Do You Think You Are? Digging for Your Family Roots. LC 75-40274. (Illus.). (gr. 7 up). 1976. 9.95 (ISBN 0-664-32587-4). Westminster.

Wubben, Pamela G. Genealogy for Children. 65p. (ps-7). 1981. pap. 7.95 (ISBN 0-935442-03-0). One Percent.

GENEALOGY–RESEARCH

see Genealogy

GENEALOGY–SOURCES

Fernow, Berthold. The Records of New Amsterdam: From 1653 to 1674 Anno Domini, 7 vols. LC 76-1195. (Illus.). 1976. Repr. of 1897 ed. 125.00 set (ISBN 0-8063-0715-3). Genealog Pub.

Smith, Clifford N. & Smith, Anna P. Encyclopedia of German-American Genealogical Research. LC 75-28205. 260p. 1976. 45.00 (ISBN 0-8352-0831-1). Bowker.

GENERAL ACTIVITY SIMULATION PROGRAM

see also GASP (Computer Program Language)

GENERAL AGREEMENT ON TARIFFS AND TRADE

see Contracting Parties to the General Agreement on Tariffs and Trade

GENERAL CONFERENCE MENNONITE CHURCH

Kauffman, J. Howard & Harder, Leland. Anabaptists Four Centuries Later. 400p. 1975. 9.95x (ISBN 0-8361-1136-2); pap. 6.95x (ISBN 0-8361-1137-0). Herald Pr.

GENERAL DYNAMICS B-58

see B-Fifty-Eight Bomber

GENERAL EDUCATION

see Education, Humanistic

GENERAL EDUCATIONAL DEVELOPMENT TESTS

see also High School Equivalency Examination

Bauernfeind, Robert H. School Testing Programs. (Guidance Monograph). 1968. pap. 2.40 (ISBN 0-395-09927-7, 9-78826). HM.

Farley, Eugene J., et al. High School Certification Through the General Educational Development Tests. (Adult Basic Education Ser). (RL 7-8). 1967. pap. text ed. 4.36 (ISBN 0-03-068510-9). HR&W.

Guercio, E., et al. Arco GED Series: Teacher's Manual. (GED Preparation Ser.). 128p. (Orig.). 1975. pap. 2.50 (ISBN 0-668-03692-3). Arco.

--General Mathematical Ability: Preparation & Review for the Mathematics Part of the High School Equivalency Diploma Test. LC 74-19738. (GED Preparation Ser.). 160p. (Orig.). 1975. lib. bdg. 7.00 (ISBN 0-668-03841-1); pap. 6.00 (ISBN 0-668-03689-3). Arco.

--Reading Interpretation in Social Sciences, Natural Sciences, & Literature: Preparation & Review for the Reading Parts of the High School Equivalency Diploma Test. LC 74-19739. (GED Preparation Ser.). 224p. (Orig.). 1975. lib. bdg. 7.00 (ISBN 0-668-03843-8); pap. 5.00 (ISBN 0-668-03690-7). Arco.

Rudman, Jack. Test of General Educational Development (GED) (Admission Test Ser.: ATS-61). 14.95 (ISBN 0-8373-5161-8); pap. 9.95 (ISBN 0-8373-5061-1). Natl Learning.

Turner, David R. High School Entrance & Scholarship Tests. 6th ed. (gr. 8-9). 1967. lib. bdg. 5.50 o. p. (ISBN 0-668-01392-3); pap. 5.00 (ISBN 0-668-00666-8). Arco.

GENERAL ELECTRIC COMPANY

Boulware, Lemuel R. Truth About Boulwarism: Trying to Do Right Voluntarily. LC 77-91413. 194p. 1969. 7.50 (ISBN 0-87179-010-6); pap. 2.85 (ISBN 0-87179-108-0). BNA.

Cox, James A. A Century of Light. LC 78-19204. (Illus.). 1979. Set. 17.50 (ISBN 0-87502-062-3). Benjamin Co.

General Electric Company. Professional Management in General Electric, 4 vols. Incl. Vol. 1. General Electric's Growth. Repr. of 1953 ed; Vol. 2. General Electric's Organization. Repr. of 1955 ed; Vol. 3. The Work of a Professional Manager. Repr. of 1954 ed; Vol. 4. The Work of a Functional Individual Contributor. Repr. of 1959 ed. (Management History Ser.: No. 76). (Illus.). 1200p. 1975. Set. 87.50 (ISBN 0-87960-113-2). Hive Pub.

Greenwood, Ronald G. Managerial Decentralization: A Study of the General Electric Philosophy. rev. 2nd. ed. (Hive Management History Ser.: No. 89). (Illus.). 225p. 1981. lib. bdg. price not set (ISBN 0-87960-123-X); pap. text ed. price not set (ISBN 0-87960-124-8). Hive Pub.

Loth, David. Swope of G. E. The Story of Gerard Swope & General Electric in American Business. LC 75-41769. (Companies & Men: Business Enterprises in America). 1976. Repr. of 1958 ed. 22.00x (ISBN 0-405-08084-0). Arno.

National Planning Association. The General Electric Company in Brazil. Bruchey, Stuart & Bruchey, Eleanor, eds. LC 76-5021. (American Business Abroad Ser.). (Illus.). 1976. Repr. of 1961 ed. 12.00x (ISBN 0-405-09288-1). Arno.

GENERAL EQUILIBRIUM (ECONOMICS)

see Equilibrium (Economics)

GENERAL JUDGMENT

see Judgment Day

GENERAL MOTORS CORPORATION

Chandler, Alfred D., ed. Managerial Innovation at General Motors: An Original Anthology. LC 79-7524. (History of Management Thought & Practice Ser.). 1980. lib. bdg. 14.00x (ISBN 0-405-12309-4). Arno.

Chandler, Alfred D., Jr. & Salsbury, Stephen. Pierre S. Dupont & the Making of the Modern Corporation. LC 78-123920. (Illus.). 1971. 20.00 (ISBN 0-06-010701-4, HarpT). Harrow.

Cray, Ed. Chrome Colossus: General Motors & Its Times. (Illus.). 548p. 1980. 14.95 (ISBN 0-07-013493-6). McGraw.

Curtice, Harlow H. & Finney, Frederick M. Development & Growth of the General Motors Corporation: An Economic Analysis, 1908-1955. 1979. 8.95 (ISBN 0-89421-006-8). Challenge Pr.

El-Messidi, Kathy G. The Bargain: The Story Behind the Thirty Year Honeymoon of GM & UAW. LC 78-26325. 1979. 10.00 (ISBN 0-8424-0120-2). Nellen Pub.

Jackson, Richard A., ed. The Multinational Corporation & Social Policy: Special Reference to General Motors in South Africa. LC 73-18872. (Special Studies). 1974. pap. 2.50 (ISBN 0-685-99394-9). Coun Rel & Intl.

Johnson, Thomas H. System & Profits: Early Management Accounting at Dupont & General Motors. original anthology ed. Brief, Richard P., ed. LC 80-1458. (Dimensions of Accounting Theory & Practice Ser.). 1981. lib. bdg. 25.00x (ISBN 0-405-13481-9). Arno.

Seltzer, Lawrence H. Financial History of the American Automobile Industry. LC 77-128076. Repr. of 1928 ed. lib. bdg. 17.50x (ISBN 0-678-03554-7). Kelley.

Sloan, Alfred P., Jr. Adventures of a White-Collar Man. facs. ed. Sparkes, Boyden, ed. LC 74-126258. (Select Bibliographies Reprint Ser). 1941. 17.00 (ISBN 0-8369-5485-8). Arno.

--My Years with General Motors. LC 64-11306. 560p. 1972. pap. 5.95 (ISBN 0-385-04235-3, Anch.). Doubleday.
Whiteside, Thomas. The Investigation of Ralph Nader. LC 72-79452. Orig. Title: Ralph Nader. 1972. 7.95 (ISBN 0-87795-034-2). Arbor Hse.
Wright, J. Patrick. On a Clear Day You Can See General Motors. 304p. 1980. pap. 2.95 (ISBN 0-380-51722-1, 51722). Avon.

GENERAL MOTORS CORPORATION SIT-DOWN STRIKE, 1936-1937
Fine, Sidney. Sit-Down: The General Motors Strike of 1936-1937. LC 73-83455. 1969. 16.95x (ISBN 0-472-32948-0). U of Mich Pr.

GENERAL PACT FOR RENUNCIATION OF WAR, PARIS, AUGUST 27, 1928
see Renunciation of War Treaty, Paris, Aug. 27, 1928

GENERAL PRACTICE (MEDICINE)
see Family Medicine

GENERAL PROBLEM SOLVER (COMPUTER PROGRAM)
see GPS (Computer Program Language)

GENERAL PROPERTY TAX
see Property Tax

GENERAL SEMANTICS
Barfield, Owen. The Rediscovery of Meaning & Other Essays. LC 76-41479. 1977. 15.00x (ISBN 0-8195-5006-X, Pub. by Wesleyan U Pr). Columbia U Pr.
Cerminara, Gina. Insights for the Age of Aquarius. LC 76-6173. 314p. 1976. pap. 5.75 (ISBN 0-8356-0483-7, Quest). Theos Pub Hse.
Chisholm, Francis P. Introductory Lectures on General Semantics. 1971. Repr. of 1944 ed. 5.00x (ISBN 0-910780-05-6). Inst Gen Semantics.
Conference on Research Designs in General Semantics, 1st, Pennsylvania State University. Proceedings. new ed. Johnson, Kenneth G., ed. 298p. 1975. 52.75x (ISBN 0-677-14370-2). Gordon.
Glorfeld, Louis E. Short Unit on General Semantics. LC 69-17339. 125p. 1969. pap. text ed. 3.95x (ISBN 0-02-474210-4, 47421). Macmillan.
Gorman, Margaret. General Semantics & Contemporary Thomism. LC 62-9136. 1962. pap. 2.95x (ISBN 0-8032-5075-4, BB 146, Bison). U of Nebr Pr.
Hayakawa, S. I. & Dresser, William, eds. Dimensions of Meaning. LC 68-24164. (Composition & Rhetoric Ser). (Orig.). 1970. pap. 2.95 (ISBN 0-672-60902-9, CR16). Bobbs.
Hayakawa, Samuel I. Symbol, Status, & Personality. LC 63-1772. 1966. pap. 3.25 (ISBN 0-15-687611-6, HB110, Harv). HarBraceJ.
Korzybski, Alfred. General Semantics Bulletin: Official Annual Journal of the Institute of General Semantics. Pula, Robert, ed. 20.00 (ISBN 0-910780-00-5). Inst Gen Semantics.
--Manhood of Humanity. 2nd ed. 326p. 1950. 9.00x (ISBN 0-937298-00-X). Inst Gen Semantics.
--Science & Sanity: An Introduction to Non-Aristotelian Systems & General Semantics. 4th ed. LC 58-6260. 806p. 1958. 19.50x (ISBN 0-937298-01-8). Inst Gen Semantics.
Lee, Irving, ed. Language of Wisdom & Folly. 3rd ed. LC 67-30831. 1977. pap. text ed. 5.50x (ISBN 0-918970-00-8). Intl Gen Semantics.
Lee, Irving J. Language Habits in Human Affairs: An Introduction to General Semantics. LC 78-31179. (Illus.). 1979. Repr. of 1941 ed. lib. bdg. 20.50x (ISBN 0-313-20962-6, LELH). Greenwood.
Morain, Mary, ed. Classroom Exercises in General Semantics. LC 80-80100. 1980. pap. 5.50x (ISBN 0-918970-26-1). Intl Gen Semantics.
Rapoport, Anatol. Science & the Goals of Man: A Study in Semantic Orientation. LC 70-138126. 1971. Repr. of 1950 ed. lib. bdg. 14.00x (ISBN 0-8371-4142-7, RASG). Greenwood.
Reiser, Oliver. Integration of Human Knowledge. (Extending Horizons Ser). (Illus.). 1958. 8.00 (ISBN 0-87558-031-9). Porter Sargent.
Steinberg, D. D. & Jakobovits, L. A. Semantics: An Interdisciplinary Reader in Philosophy, Linguistics & Psychology. LC 78-123675. (Illus.). 1971. 49.50 (ISBN 0-521-07822-9); pap. 14.95x (ISBN 0-521-20499-2). Cambridge U Pr.

GENERAL SLOCUM (STEAMBOAT)
Rust, Claude. The Burning of the General Slocum. (Illus.). 160p. (YA) 1981. 11.00 (ISBN 0-525-66715-6, 01068-320). Elsevier-Nelson.

GENERAL STAFFS
see Armies–Staffs

GENERAL STORES
Educational Research Council of America. General Store Owner. rev. ed. Ferris, Theodore N. & Marchak, John P., eds. (Real People at Work Ser: E). (Illus.). 1976. pap. text ed. 2.25 (ISBN 0-89247-032-1). Changing Times.
Elspeth. Country Store. 1975. pap. 2.50 (ISBN 0-87588-105-X). Hobby Hse.
Priamo, Carol. The General Store. (Illus.). 1978. 15.95 (ISBN 0-07-082780-X, GB). McGraw.

GENERAL STRIKE
see also Strikes and Lockouts

GENERAL STRIKE, GREAT BRITAIN, 1926
Arnot, Robert P. General Strike, May Nineteen Twenty-Six: Its Origin & History. LC 67-20085. Repr. of 1926 ed. 13.50x (ISBN 0-678-00254-1). Kelley.
Hughes, Michael, ed. Cartoons from the General Strike. LC 68-24687. (Illus.). 1968. 8.50x (ISBN 0-678-07770-3). Kelley.
Skelley, Jeffrey, ed. The General Strike 1926. 1976. text ed. 15.75x (ISBN 0-85315-337-X). Humanities.
Tames, Richard. General Strike. (Jackdaw Ser: No. 105). (Illus.). 1972. 6.95 (ISBN 0-670-33632-7, Grossman). Viking Pr.

GENERAL WARRANTS
see Warrants (Law)

GENERALIZED FUNCTIONS
see Distributions, Theory of (Functional Analysis)

GENERALIZED SPACES
see Spaces, Generalized

GENERALS
see also Marshals; Military Biography
Albert, Don E. General Wesley Merritt. LC 80-13126. (Illus.). 1979. 15.00 (ISBN 0-686-26105-4); deluxe ed. 40.00 (ISBN 0-686-26106-2). Presidial.
--General Wesley Merritt. LC 80-13126. (Illus.). 1979. 15.00 (ISBN 0-686-26105-4); deluxe ed. 40.00 (ISBN 0-686-26106-2). Presidial.
Alderman, Clifford L. Royal Opposition: The British Generals in the American Revolution. LC 73-119122. (Illus.). (gr. 7-12). 1970. 7.95 (ISBN 0-02-700240-3, CCPr). Macmillan.
Ashley, Maurice. General Monck. (Illus.). 316p. 1977. 20.00x (ISBN 0-87471-934-8). Rowman.
Bailey, John W. Pacifying the Plains: General Alfred Terry & the Decline of the Sioux, 1866-1890. LC 78-19300. (Contributions in Military History: No. 17). 1979. lib. bdg. 18.95 (ISBN 0-313-20625-2, BAT/). Greenwood.
Biggs, Bradley. Gavin. (Illus.). 182p. 1980. 17.50 (ISBN 0-208-01748-8, Archon). Shoe String.
Billias, George A., ed. George Washington's Generals. LC 79-28195. (Illus.). 327p. 1980. Repr. of 1964 ed. lib. bdg. 25.00x (ISBN 0-313-22280-0, BIGW). Greenwood.
Brett-Smith, Richard. Hitler's Generals. LC 77-85481. (Illus.). 1978. Repr. 12.95 (ISBN 0-89141-044-9). Presidio Pr.
Brown, Richard C. Social Attitudes of American Generals, Eighteen Ninety-Eight to Nineteen Forty. Kohn, Richard H., ed. LC 78-22413. (American Military Experience Ser.). 1979. lib. bdg. 25.00x (ISBN 0-405-11887-2). Arno.
Burlingame, Roger. General Billy Mitchell: Champion of Air Defense. LC 77-26823. (They Made America Ser.). (Illus.). 1978. Repr. of 1952 ed. lib. bdg. 20.00x (ISBN 0-313-20170-6, BUGM). Greenwood.
Connelly, Thomas L. The Marble Man: Robert E. Lee & His Image in American Society. LC 76-41778. 1978. pap. 7.95 (ISBN 0-8071-0474-4). La State U Pr.
Croizier, Ralph C. Koxinga & Chinese Nationalism: History, Myth & the Hero. (East Asian Monographs Ser: No. 66). 150p. 1977. pap. 9.00x (ISBN 0-674-50566-2). Harvard U Pr.
Davidson, Homer K. Black Jack Davidson: Life of General John W. Davidson. 1974. 15.50 (ISBN 0-87062-109-2). A H Clark.
Deweerd, Harvey A. Great Soldiers of the Two World Wars. facs. ed. LC 69-18926. (Essay Index Reprint Ser). 1941. 21.25 (ISBN 0-8369-1032-X). Arno.
Dixon, Norman F. On the Psychology of Military Incompetence. LC 76-9336. 1976. 12.50x (ISBN 0-465-05253-3). Basic.
Everest, Allan S. Moses Hazen & the Canadian Refugees in the American Revolution. LC 76-54260. 1976. 12.95 (ISBN 0-8156-0129-8). Syracuse U Pr.
Ferrero, Guglielmo. The Life of Caesar. Zimmern, A. E., tr. LC 77-9520. 1977. Repr. of 1933 ed. lib. bdg. 33.75x (ISBN 0-8371-9090-8, FELC). Greenwood.
Goebel, Dorothy B. & Goebel, Julius. Generals in the White House. facsimile ed. LC 78-134082. (Essay Index Reprint Ser). Repr. of 1945 ed. 18.00 (ISBN 0-8369-2501-7). Arno.
Hattaway, Herman. General Stephen D. Lee. LC 75-42612. (Illus.). 1976. 12.50x (ISBN 0-87805-071-X). U Pr of Miss.
Haupt, Herman. Reminiscences of General Herman Haupt. LC 80-1314. (Railroads Ser.). (Illus.). 1981. Repr. of 1901 ed. lib. bdg. 30.00x (ISBN 0-405-13786-9). Arno.
Howell, Roger, Jr. Cromwell. (Library of World Biography). 1977. 8.95 (ISBN 0-316-37581-0). Little.
Hudleston, Francis J. Warriors in Undress. facsimile ed. LC 73-93346. (Essay Index Reprint Ser). 1926. 17.00 (ISBN 0-8369-1298-5). Arno.
Humble, Richard. Hitler's Generals. (YA) 1981. pap. 2.25 (ISBN 0-89083-788-0). Zebra.
Humphreys, David. An Essay on the Life of the Honorable Major-General Israel Putnam. Repr. Of 1788 Ed. Bd. with A Genuine & Correct Account of the Captivity, Sufferings & Deliverance of Mrs. Jemima Howe. Howe, Jemima. Repr. of 1792 ed; The Affecting History of Mrs. Howe. Repr. of 1815 ed. LC 75-7040. (Indian Captivities Ser.: Vol. 19). 1977. lib. bdg. 44.00 (ISBN 0-8240-1643-2). Garland Pub.
Jackson, Harvey H. Lachlan McIntosh & the Politics of Revolutionary Georgia. LC 78-8995. 256p. 1979. 16.00 (ISBN 0-8203-0459-X). U of Ga Pr.
Johnston, Charles H. Famous Generals of the Great War. LC 74-93349. (Essay Index Reprints - Famous Leaders Ser.). 1919. 22.00 (ISBN 0-8369-1667-0). Arno.
Kieffer, Chester L. Maligned General: Thomas S. Jesup. LC 77-73552. (Illus.). 1979. 16.95 (ISBN 0-89141-027-9). Presidio Pr.
Kinchen, Oscar A. General Bennett H. Young. 1981. 8.95 (ISBN 0-8158-0404-0). Chris Mass.
Korngold, Ralph. Citizen Toussaint. LC 78-21026. 1979. Repr. of 1965 ed. lib. bdg. 22.50x (ISBN 0-313-20794-1, KOCT). Greenwood.
Lewin, Ronald. Slim: The Standardbearer-a Biography of Field-Marshall the Viscount Slim. (Illus.). 1976. 22.50 (ISBN 0-208-01637-6, Archon). Shoe String.
Liddell-Hart, B. A Greater Than Napoleon, Scipio Africanus. LC 75-156735. 281p. 1927. 15.00x (ISBN 0-8196-0269-8). Biblo.
Liddell Hart, Basil H. Reputations Ten Years After. facs. ed. LC 68-8478. (Essay Index Reprint Ser). (Illus.). 1968. Repr. of 1928 ed. 18.00 (ISBN 0-8369-0619-5). Arno.
--Sherman: Soldier, Realist, American. LC 78-536. 1978. Repr. of 1958 ed. lib. bdg. 33.75x (ISBN 0-313-20288-5, LHSH). Greenwood.
Longacre, Edward G. The Man Behind the Guns: A Biography of General Henry Jackson Hunt, Commander of Artillery, Army of the Potomac. LC 76-10885. (Illus.). 1977. 15.00 (ISBN 0-498-01656-0). A S Barnes.
Macartney, Clarence E. Grant & His Generals. facs. ed. LC 75-142660. (Essay Index Reprint Ser). 1953. 20.00 (ISBN 0-8369-2171-2). Arno.
MacDougall, William L. American Revolutionary: A Biography of General Alexander McDougall. LC 76-15324. (Contributions in American History: No. 57). (Illus.). 1977. lib. bdg. 15.00 (ISBN 0-8371-9035-5, MAR/). Greenwood.
Nag Raj, T. R. & Kendrick, Bryce. A Monograph of Chalara & Allied Generals. 200p. 1975. text ed. 14.95 (ISBN 0-88920-027-0, Pub. by Laurier U Pr Canada). Humanities.
Pinkowski, Edward. Pills, Pen & Politics: The Story of General Leon Jastremski. LC 74-29094. (Illus.). 188p. 1974. 6.95 (ISBN 0-9600814-1-0). Cptn Stanislaus.
Roddy, Lee. Robert E. Lee: Christian General & Gentleman. LC 77-7520. (Sowers Ser.). (Illus.). (gr. 3-6). 1977. pap. 4.25 (ISBN 0-915134-40-3). Mott Media.
Schultz, Duane. Hero of Bataan: The Story of General Wainwright. (Illus.). 512p. 1981. 19.95 (ISBN 0-312-85407-2). St Martin.
Shelley, Mary V. Dr. Ed: The Story of General Edward Hand. LC 78-10331. (Illus.). (gr. 4-7). 1978. 5.75 (ISBN 0-915010-24-0). Sutter House.
Siddiqui, A. H. Muslim Generals. pap. 3.50 (ISBN 0-686-18314-2). Kazi Pubns.
Simonds, Frank H. They Won the War. facs. ed. LC 68-58813. (Essay Index Reprint Ser). 1931. 12.00 (ISBN 0-8369-0126-6). Arno.
Smyth, John. Leadership in Battle 1914-1918. LC 75-20132. (Illus.). 191p. 1976. 12.50 (ISBN 0-88254-365-2). Hippocrene Bks.
Stafford, G. M. General Leroy A. Stafford. 1969. 15.00 (ISBN 0-685-00426-0). Claitors.
Taylor, Telford. Sword & Swastika: Generals & Nazis in Third Reich. 416p. 1972. pap. 2.95 (ISBN 0-8129-6098-X, QP304). Times Bks.
Von Mellenthin, F. W. German Generals of World War II: As I Saw Them. (Illus.). 1977. 12.95 (ISBN 0-8061-1406-1). U of Okla Pr.
Warner, Ezra J. Generals in Gray: Lives of the Confederate Commanders. LC 58-7551. (Illus.). 1959. 20.00 (ISBN 0-8071-0823-5). La State U Pr.
Westmoreland, W. C. A Soldier Reports. 1980. pap. 3.75 (ISBN 0-440-10025-9). Dell.
Westrate, E. V. Those Fatal Generals. LC 68-16300. 1968. Repr. of 1936 ed. 12.50 (ISBN 0-8046-0497-5). Kennikat.
Whitney, Courtney. MacArthur: His Rendezvous with History. LC 77-2965. 1977. Repr. of 1956 ed. lib. bdg. 36.75 (ISBN 0-8371-9564-0, WHMA). Greenwood.
Williams, T. Harry. Lincoln & His Generals. 1967. pap. 3.45 (ISBN 0-394-70362-6, Vin). Random.

GENERALS–CORRESPONDENCE, REMINISCENCES, ETC.
Grant, Ulysses S. Personal Memoirs. abr. ed. 9.50 (ISBN 0-8446-0657-X). Peter Smith.
Hitchcock, Ethan A. Fifty Years in Camp & Field: Diary of Major General Ethan Allan Hitchcock, U. S. A. facsimile ed. Croffut, W. A., ed. LC 78-169764. (Select Bibliographies Reprint Ser). Repr. of 1909 ed. 26.00 (ISBN 0-8369-5984-1). Arno.
Howard, Oliver O. My Life & Experiences Among Our Hostile Indians. LC 76-87436. (The American Scente Ser.). Repr. of 1907 ed. lib. bdg. 37.50 (ISBN 0-306-71506-6). Da Capo.
Lejeune, John A. Reminiscences. (Illus.). 488p. Date not set. Repr. 8.95 (ISBN 0-686-30999-5). MCA.
Napoleon First. Correspondance De Napoleon Ier, Supplement: Lettres Curieuses Omises Par le Comite De Publication, Rectifications. LC 77-173013. 1975. Repr. of 1887 ed. 20.00 (ISBN 0-404-07148-1). AMS Pr.
Pickett, George E. Soldier of the South: General Pickett's War Letters to His Wife. facsimile ed. Inman, Arthur C., ed. LC 78-160986. (Select Bibliographies Reprint Ser). Repr. of 1928 ed. 16.00 (ISBN 0-8369-5854-3). Arno.
Sheridan, Philip H. Personal Memories of P. H. Sheridan, General, 2 vols. LC 72-78831. 1902. Repr. 80.00 (ISBN 0-403-02023-9). Somerset Pub.
Verdy Du Vernois, Julius A. With the Royal Headquarters in 1870 to 1871. LC 72-131853. 263p. 1897. Repr. 16.00 (ISBN 0-403-00740-2). Scholarly.
Waldersee, Alfred H. A Field-Marshal's Memoirs: From the Diary, Correspondence, & Reminiscences of Alfred Count Von Waldersee. (Illus.). 1978. Repr. of 1924 ed. lib. bdg. 23.50 (ISBN 0-8371-5326-3, WAFM). Greenwood.

GENERATION
see Reproduction

GENERATION, SPONTANEOUS
see Spontaneous Generation

GENERATION GAP
see Conflict of Generations

GENERATIVE GRAMMAR
Ambrose-Grillet, Jeanne. Glossary of Transformational Grammar. LC 78-1819. 1978. pap. text ed. 7.95 (ISBN 0-88377-099-7). Newbury Hse.
Anderson, John M. Grammar of Case: Towards a Localistic Theory. LC 71-145602. (Studies in Linguistics Ser: No. 4). (Illus.). 1971. 35.00 (ISBN 0-521-08035-5); pap. 11.95 (ISBN 0-521-29057-0). Cambridge U Pr.
Baker, C. L. Introduction to Generative-Transformational Syntax. 1977. text ed. 19.95 (ISBN 0-13-484410-6). P-H.
Birnbaum, Henrik. Problems of Typological & Genetic Linguistics Viewed in a Generative Framework. LC 70-123298. (Janua Linguarum, Ser. Minor: No. 106). (Orig.). 1970. pap. text ed. 17.50x (ISBN 90-2791-541-5). Mouton.
Bliese, Loren. A Generative Grammar of Afar. (SIL Publications on Linguistics Ser.). 306p. 1981. 10.00 (ISBN 0-88312-083-6); microfiche 2.80 (ISBN 0-88312-483-1). Summer Inst Ling.
Bolinger, Dwight. Meaning & Form. LC 76-44857. (English Language Ser.). 1977. text ed. 18.95x (ISBN 0-582-55103-X); pap. text ed. 11.50x (ISBN 0-582-29104-6). Longman.
Bornstein, Diane. Introduction to Transformational Grammar. (Illus.). 1977. text ed. 13.95 (ISBN 0-87626-430-5); pap. 8.95 (ISBN 0-87626-429-1). Winthrop.
Botha, Rudolf B. Methodological Status of Grammatical Argumentation. LC 79-126050. (Janua Linguarum Ser.Maior: No. 105). (Orig.). 1970. pap. text ed. 12.95x (ISBN 90-2790-714-5). Mouton.
Botha, Rudolf P. Function of the Lexicon in Transformational Generative Grammar. (Janua Linguarum, Ser. Major: No. 38). 1968. text ed. 44.10x (ISBN 90-2790-688-2). Mouton.
--The Justification of Linguistic Hypotheses. (Janua Linguarum Ser.Maior: No. 84). 1973. text ed. 57.65x (ISBN 90-2792-542-9). Mouton.
Chomsky, Noam. Cartesian Linguistics: A Chapter in the History of Rationalist Thought. 1966. text ed. 22.50 scp (ISBN 0-06-041275-5, HarpC). Har-Row.
--Essays on Form & Interpretation. (Studies in Linguistic Analysis). 1977. 14.95 (ISBN 0-7204-8615-7, North-Holland). Elsevier.
--The Logical Structure of Linguistic Theory. LC 75-26985. (Illus.). 573p. 1975. 35.00 (ISBN 0-306-30760-X, Plenum Pr). Plenum Pub.
--Topics in the Theory of Generative Grammar. (Janua Linguarum, Ser. Minor: No. 56). (Orig.). 1978. pap. text ed. 12.50x (ISBN 90-279-3122-4). Mouton.

Dell, F. Generative Phonology. LC 79-14139. (Illus.). 1980. 42.50 (ISBN 0-521-22484-5); pap. 9.95x (ISBN 0-521-29519-X). Cambridge U Pr.
Dillon, George L. Language Processing & the Reading of Literature: Toward a Model of Comprehension. LC 77-9861. 240p. 1978. 12.50x (ISBN 0-253-33195-1). Ind U Pr.
Fauconnier, Gilles. Theoretical Implications of Some Global Phenomena in Syntax. Hankamer, Jorge, ed. LC 78-66574. (Outstanding Dissertations in Linguistics Ser.). 1979. lib. bdg. 33.00 (ISBN 0-8240-9687-8). Garland Pub.
Fiengo, Robert. Surface Structure: The Interface of Autonomous Components. LC 80-14680. (Language & Thought Ser.). 1980. text ed. 22.50x (ISBN 0-674-85725-9). Harvard U Pr.
Fodor, J. A., et al. The Psychology of Language. (Illus.). 512p. 1974. text ed. 22.00 (ISBN 0-07-021412-3, C). McGraw.
Fodor, Janet D. Semantics: Theories of Meaning in Generative Grammar. (Language & Thought Ser.). 240p. 1980. pap. 7.95x (ISBN 0-674-80134-2). Harvard U Pr.
Fowler, Roger. Understanding Language: An Introduction to Linguistics. 1974. 12.50x (ISBN 0-7100-7755-6); pap. 7.95 (ISBN 0-7100-7756-4). Routledge & Kegan.
Friedman, J., et al. A Computer Model of Transformational Grammar. (Mathematical Linguistics & Automatic Language Processing: No. 9). 1971. 22.50 (ISBN 0-444-00084-4). Elsevier.
Gleitman, Lila & Gleitman, Henry. Phrase & Paraphrase: Some Innovative Uses of Language. (Illus.). 1971. 14.95x (ISBN 0-393-04333-9). Norton.
Goldsmith, John A. Autosegmental Phonology. Hankamer, Jorge, ed. LC 78-67735. (Outstanding Dissertations in Linguistics Ser.). 1979. lib. bdg. 22.00 (ISBN 0-8240-9673-8). Garland Pub.
Grinder, J. T. & Elgin, S. H. Guide to Transformational Grammar: History, Theory, Practice. LC 72-79088. 1973. text ed. 11.95 (ISBN 0-03-080126-5, HoltC). HR&W.
Hagege, Claude. Critical Reflections on Transformational Grammar. rev. ed. Makkai, Valerie B., tr. from Fr. Orig. Title: La Grammaire Generative: Reflexions Critiques. 1981. pap. 12.00 (ISBN 0-933104-09-X). Jupiter Pr.
Haiman, John. Targets & Syntactic Change. LC 73-87535. (Janua Linguarum, Ser. Minor: No. 186). 156p. (Orig.). 1974. pap. text ed. 22.00x (ISBN 90-2792-703-0). Mouton.
Hockett, Charles F. Language, Mathematics, & Linguistics. (Janua Linguarum, Ser. Minor: No. 60). (Illus.). 1967. pap. text ed. 28.75x (ISBN 0-686-22442-6). Mouton.
Huddleston, Rodney. An Introduction to English Transformational Syntax. (English Language Ser.). (Illus.). 304p. 1975. text ed. 19.95x (ISBN 0-582-55061-0); pap. text ed. 14.50x (ISBN 0-582-55062-9). Longman.
Hurford, J. R. The Linguistic Theory of Numerals. LC 74-25652. (Studies in Linguistics: No. 16). 260p. 1975. 42.50 (ISBN 0-521-20735-5). Cambridge U Pr.
Jackendoff, Ray S. Semantic Interpretation in Generative Grammar. (Studies in Linguistics). 384p. 1972. 28.00x (ISBN 0-262-10013-4); pap. 9.95x (ISBN 0-262-60007-2). MIT Pr.
Jacobson, B. Transformational-Generative Grammar. (North Holland Linguistic Ser.: Vol. 17). 1978. 29.50 (ISBN 0-444-85240-9, North Holland). Elsevier.
Johnson, C. Douglas. Formal Aspects of Phonological Description. LC 79-190146. (Linguistic Analysis Monographs Ser: No. 3). (Illus.). 125p. (Orig.). 1972. pap. text ed. 20.75x (ISBN 90-2792-217-9). Mouton.
Katz, J. J. Propositional Structure & Illocutionary Force: A Study of the Contribution of Sentence Meaning to Speech Arts. 1977. pap. text ed. 26.95 scp (ISBN 0-690-00883-X, HarpC). Har-Row.
Kiefer, F. & Ruwet, N. Generative Grammar in Europe. LC 76-179893. (Foundations of Language Supplementary Ser: No. 13). 690p. 1973. lib. bdg. 84.00 (ISBN 90-277-0218-7, Pub. by Reidel Holland). Kluwer Boston.
Linell, Per. Psychological Reality in Phonology. LC 78-67429. (Cambridge Studies in Linguistics: No. 25). (Illus.). 1979. 44.50 (ISBN 0-521-22234-6). Cambridge U Pr.
Matthews, P. H. Generative Grammar & Linguistic Competence. (Illus.). 1979. text ed. 18.95x (ISBN 0-04-410002-7). Allen Unwin.
Neijt, Anneke. Gapping: A Contribution to Sentence Grammar. (Studies in Generative Grammar). 218p. 1979. text ed. 20.00x (ISBN 90-70176-12-2). Humanities.
Nida, Eugene A. Componential Analysis of Meaning. (Approaches to Semiotics Ser.). (Illus.). 272p. 1975. pap. text ed. 32.25x (ISBN 90-2793-137-2). Mouton.
Nilsen, Don L. Toward a Semantic Specification of Deep Case. (Janua Linguarum, Ser. Minor: No. 152). 52p. (Orig.). 1972. text ed. 11.25x (ISBN 90-2792-318-3). Mouton.
Perlmutter, David M. Deep & Surface Constraints in Syntax. LC 77-153956. 1971. pap. text ed. 12.95x (ISBN 0-03-084010-4). Irvington.
Pike, Kenneth L. Language in Relation to a Unified Theory of the Structure of Human Behavior. (Janua Linguarum, Ser. Major: No. 24). 1967. text ed. 105.50x (ISBN 90-2791-869-4). Mouton.
Russell, W. Keith, et al. Linguistics & Deaf Children: Transformational Syntax & Its Applications. LC 76-11696. (Illus.). 1976. pap. text ed. 7.95 (ISBN 0-88200-072-1, C2115). Alexander Graham.
Sanders, Gerald A. Equational Grammar. LC 72-86886. (Janua Linguarum, Ser. Minor: No. 108). (Illus.). 187p. (Orig.). 1972. pap. text ed. 22.00x (ISBN 90-2792-219-5). Mouton.
Schnitzer, Marc L. Generative Phonology: Evidence from Phonology. new ed. (Penn State Studies: No. 34). 1972. pap. text ed. 3.50 (ISBN 0-271-00517-3). Pa St U Pr.
Sgall, Petr, et al. Functional Approach to Syntax. (Mathematical Linguistics & Automatic Language Processing Ser.: No. 7). 1969. 14.00 (ISBN 0-444-00045-3, North Holland). Elsevier.
Stockwell, Robert P. Foundations of Syntactic Theory. LC 76-8021. (Foundations of Modern Linguistics Ser.). 1977. 14.95 (ISBN 0-13-329987-2); pap. text ed. 10.95 (ISBN 0-13-329979-1); wkbk. 5.95 (ISBN 0-13-965202-7). P-H.
Wasow, T. Anaphora in Generative Grammar. (Studies in Generative Linguistic Analysis: No. 2). 1980. text ed. 44.25x (ISBN 90-6439-162-9). Humanities.

GENERATIVE ORGANS
see also Change of Sex; Genito-Urinary Organs; Orgasm; Reproduction
Cavanagh, Dennis, et al. Septic Shock in Obstetrics & Gynecology, Vol. 11. LC 76-50147. (Illus.). 1977. text ed. 14.50 (ISBN 0-7216-2455-3). Saunders.
Follett, B. K. & Follett, D. E. Biological Clocks in Seasonal Reproductive Systems. LC 81-4614. 320p. 1981. 49.95 (ISBN 0-470-27175-2). Halsted Pr.
Hafez, E. S. & Blandau, R. J., eds. Mammalian Oviduct: Comparative Biology & Methodology. LC 68-29936. (Illus.). 1969. 27.50x (ISBN 0-226-31201-1). U of Chicago Pr.
International Seminar on Reproductive Physiology & Sexual Endocrinology, 3rd, Brussels, 1970. Basic Actions of Sex Steroids on Target Organs: Proceedings. Hubinont, P. O., et al, eds. 1971. 34.25 (ISBN 3-8055-1156-6). S Karger.
Korting. Practical Dermatology of the Genital Region. 1981. text ed. write for info. (ISBN 0-7216-5498-3). Saunders.
Linell, Per. Psychological Reality in Phonology. LC 78-67429. (Cambridge Studies in Linguistics: No. 25). (Illus.). 1979. 44.50 (ISBN 0-521-22234-6). Cambridge U Pr.
McKerns, Kenneth W., ed. The Gonads. 792p. 1969. 60.00 (ISBN 0-306-50050-7, Plenum Pr). Plenum Pub.
Tuxen, S. L., ed. Taxonomist's Glossary of Genitalia in Insects. 1970. text ed. 27.50 (ISBN 0-934454-76-0). Lubrecht & Cramer.
Van Wagenen, Gertrude & Simpson, Miriam E. Embryology of the Ovary & Testis: Homo Sapiens & Macaca Mulatta. (Illus.). 1965. 40.00x (ISBN 0-300-01005-2). Yale U Pr.

GENERATIVE ORGANS–ABNORMITIES AND DEFORMITIES
International Conference on Morphogenesis & Malformation, Lake Wilderness, Washington, 3rd, July 1976. Morphogenesis & Malformation of the Genital System: Proceedings. Blandau, Richard J. & Bergsma, Daniel, eds. LC 77-535. (Birth Defects Original Article Ser.: Vol. 13, No. 2). 174p. 1977. 21.00x (ISBN 0-8451-1009-8). A R Liss.
Money, John, ed. Sex Errors of the Body: Dilemmas, Education, Counseling. LC 68-15447. 145p. 1968. 10.00x (ISBN 0-8018-0467-1). Johns Hopkins.
Rashad, M. Nabil & Morton, W. R. Selected Topics on Genital Anomalies & Related Subjects. (Illus.). 952p. 1969. photocopy ed. spiral 94.75 (ISBN 0-398-01551-1). C C Thomas.

GENERATIVE ORGANS–DISEASES
Beard, George M. Sexual Neurasthenia, Its Hygiene, Causes, Symptoms & Treatment with a Chapter on Diet for the Nervous. 5th ed. Rockwell, A. D., ed. LC 76-180553. (Medicine & Society in America Ser). 312p. 1972. Repr. of 1898 ed. 15.00 (ISBN 0-405-03933-6). Arno.
Cotchin, E. & Marchant, J. Animal Tumors of the Female Reproductive Tract. 1977. 14.60 (ISBN 0-387-90209-0). Springer Verlag.
Einhorn, Lawrence H., ed. Testicular Tumors: Management & Treatment. LC 79-89999. (Cancer Management Series: Vol. 3). (Illus.). 224p. 1980. 38.00 (ISBN 0-89352-078-0). Masson Pub.
Graber & Graber. Gynecological Oncology. 406p. 1982. cancelled (ISBN 0-683-03749-8, Williams & Wilkins). Krieger.
Hafez, E. S., ed. Techniques of Human Andrology. (Human Reproductive Medicine: Vol 1). 1977. 68.50 (ISBN 0-7204-0614-5, North-Holland). Elsevier.
Jackson, James C. The Sexual Organism: Its Healthful Management. LC 73-20632. (Sex, Marriage & Society Ser.). 296p. 1974. Repr. of 1861 ed. 17.00x (ISBN 0-405-05807-1). Arno.
Ledger, William J. Infection in the Female. LC 76-21705. (Illus.). 240p. 1977. text ed. 12.00 (ISBN 0-8121-0560-5). Lea & Febiger.
Nasemann, Theodor. Viral Diseases of the Skin, Mucous Membranes & Genitals: Clinical Features, Differential Diagnosis & Therapy, with Basic Principles of Virology. Frosch, Peter J., tr. LC 75-25271. (Illus.). 1977. text ed. 29.95 (ISBN 0-7216-6655-8). Saunders.
Paulsen, C. Alvin, ed. Estrogen Assays in Clinical Medicine: Basis & Methodology. LC 65-14842. (Illus.). 416p. 1965. 15.00 (ISBN 0-295-73775-1). U of Wash Pr.
Quilligan, Edward J. Current Therapy in Obstetrics & Gynecology. LC 79-65461. (Illus.). 224p. 1980. text ed. 22.50 (ISBN 0-7216-7414-3). Saunders.
Robertson, Jack R. Genitourinary Problems in Women. (Amer. Lec. in Gynecology & Obstetrics Ser.). (Illus.). 168p. 1978. 21.75 (ISBN 0-398-03668-3). C C Thomas.
Yates, Robert & Gordon, Mildred. Male Reproductive System: Fine Structure Analysis by Scanning & Transmission Electron Microscopy. LC 77-71435. (Illus.). 214p. 1977. 47.75x (ISBN 0-89352-004-7). Masson Pub.

GENERATIVE ORGANS–SURGERY
see also Sterilization (Birth Control)
Copenhaver, Edward H. Surgery of the Vulva & Vagina: A Practical Guide. (Illus.). 100p. 1981. text ed. write for info. (ISBN 0-7216-2718-8). Saunders.
Horton, Charles E., ed. Plastic & Reconstructive Surgery of the Genital Area. (Illus.). 1973. 65.00 (ISBN 0-316-37381-8). Little.
Lipshultz, L. I., et al, eds. Surgery of the Male Reproductive Tract. (Clinics in Andrology Ser.: No. 2). (Illus.). 275p. 1980. lib. bdg. 71.00 (ISBN 90-247-2315-9, Pub. by Martinus Nijhoff Netherlands). Kluwer Boston.

GENERATIVE ORGANS, FEMALE
see also Gynecology; Obstetrics; also names of individual organs
Black, M. & English, M., eds. Physical Science Techniques in Obstetrics & Gynecology. (Illus.). 1977. 39.50 (ISBN 0-8391-1145-2). Univ Park.
Cohen, Melvin R. Laparoscopy, Culdoscopy & Gynecography: Technique & Atlas. LC 72-126452. (Major Problems in Obstetrics & Gynecology: Vol. 1). (Illus.). 1970. 15.00 (ISBN 0-7216-2650-5). Saunders.
Dallenbach-Hellweg, G., ed. Functional Morphologic Changes in Female Sex Organs Induced by Exogenous Hormones. (Illus.). 220p. 1980. 32.00 (ISBN 0-387-09885-2). Springer-Verlag.
Ferenczy, Alex & Richart, Ralph M. Female Reproductive System: Dynamics of Scanning & Transmission Electron Microscopy. LC 73-17486. 401p. 1974. 74.95 (ISBN 0-471-25730-3, Pub. by Wiley-Medical). Wiley.
Gibbs, Ronald S. Antibiotic Therapy in Obstetrics & Gynecology. LC 80-23095. 215p. 1981. 16.95 (ISBN 0-471-06003-8, Pub. by Wiley Med). Wiley.
Graber & Graber. Gynecological Oncology. 406p. 1982. cancelled (ISBN 0-683-03749-8, Williams & Wilkins). Krieger.
Gusberg, S. B. & Frick, H. C. Corscaden's Gynecologic Cancer. 4th ed. LC 76-40489. 638p. 1977. Repr. of 1970 ed. 29.00 (ISBN 0-88275-466-1). Krieger.
Histological Typing of Female Genital Tract Tumours. (World Health Organization: International Histological Classification of Tumours Ser.). (Illus.). 1975. 66.00 (ISBN 0-89189-113-7, 70-0-013-20); incl. slides 160.50 (ISBN 92-4-176013-3, 70-0-013-00). Am Soc Clinical.
Hudson, C. N. The Female Reproductive System. (Penguin Library of Nursing Ser.). (Illus.). 1978. pap. text ed. 6.25 (ISBN 0-443-01609-7). Churchill.
Ludwig, H. & Metzger, H. The Human Female Reproductive Tract: A Scanning Electron Microscopic Atlas. (Illus.). 1976. 79.60 (ISBN 0-387-07675-1). Springer-Verlag.
Meudt, R. & Hinselmann, M. Ultrasonoscopic (Real Time) Differential Diagnosis in Obstetrics & Gynecology. 2nd ed. LC 78-9759. (Illus.). 1978. 56.70 (ISBN 0-387-08839-3). Springer-Verlag.
Morrow, C. Paul & Townsend, Duane E. Synopsis of Gynecologic Oncology. LC 80-22384. (Clinical Monographs in Obstetrics & Gynecology). 500p. 1981. 32.00 (ISBN 0-471-06504-8, Pub. by Wiley-Med). Wiley.
Plentl, Albert A. & Friedman, Emanuel A. Lymphatic System of the Female Genitalia. LC 70-158402. (Major Problems in Obstetrics & Gynecology Ser.: Vol. 2). (Illus.). 1971. 17.50 (ISBN 0-7216-7266-3). Saunders.
Quilligan, Edward J. Current Therapy in Obstetrics & Gynecology. LC 79-65461. (Illus.). 224p. 1980. text ed. 22.50 (ISBN 0-7216-7414-3). Saunders.
Richter, K., et al. Pneumo-Pelvigraphy: Examination of the Female Genital Organs by a Radiological Method. (Illus.). 122p. 1974. 41.00 (ISBN 0-685-50593-6). Adler.
Riotton, C. & Christopherson, William. Cytology of the Female Genital Tract. (World Health Organization: International Histological Classification of Tumours Ser.). (Illus.). 1977. 66.00 (ISBN 0-89189-108-0, 70-0-008-20); incl. slides 160.50 (ISBN 0-89189-109-9, 70-0-008-00). Am Soc Clinical.
Robertson, Jack R. Genitourinary Problems in Women. (Amer. Lec. in Gynecology & Obstetrics Ser.). (Illus.). 168p. 1978. 21.75 (ISBN 0-398-03668-3). C C Thomas.
Rutledge, Felix, et al. Gynecologic Oncology. LC 75-30951. 272p. 1976. 37.50 (ISBN 0-471-74720-3, Pub. by Wiley Medical). Wiley.
Stevens, G. Melvin. The Female Reproductive System. (Atlas of Tumor Radiology Ser.). (Illus.). 1971. 45.00 (ISBN 0-8151-8240-6). Year Bk Med.

GENERATIVE ORGANS, MALE
see also names of individual organs
Brandes, David, ed. Male Accessory Sex Organs: Structure & Function in Mammals. 1974. 68.50 (ISBN 0-12-125650-2). Acad Pr.
Hafez, E. S., ed. Techniques of Human Andrology. (Human Reproductive Medicine: Vol 1). 1977. 68.50 (ISBN 0-7204-0614-5, North-Holland). Elsevier.
Hafez, E. S. & Spring-Mills, Elinor, eds. Accessory Glands of the Male Reproductive Tract. LC 79-89654. (Perspectives in Human Reproduction Ser.: Vol. 6). (Illus.). 1979. 34.00 (ISBN 0-250-40268-8). Ann Arbor Science.
International Symposium of the "Gesellschaft Zur Bekampfung De Krebskran Kheiten Nordrhein-West-Falen E. V.", 7th, Dusseldorf, Oct. 1975. Tumors of the Male Genital System. Grundmann, E. & Vahlensuck, W., eds. (Recent Results in Cancer Research Ser.: Vol. 60). 1977. 38.20 (ISBN 0-387-08029-5). Springer-Verlag.
Kelami, Alpay. Atlas of Operative Andrology: Selected Operations on Male Genitalia & Their Accessory Glands. 202p. 1980. 99.50 (ISBN 3-11-008180-6). De Gruyter.
Lipshultz, L. I., et al, eds. Surgery of the Male Reproductive Tract. (Clinics in Andrology Ser.: No. 2). (Illus.). 275p. 1980. lib. bdg. 71.00 (ISBN 90-247-2315-9, Pub. by Martinus Nijhoff Netherlands). Kluwer Boston.
Mann, T. & Lutwak-Mann, C. Male Reproductive Function & Semen. (Illus.). 498p. 1981. 88.50 (ISBN 0-387-10383-X). Springer-Verlag.
Newsam, J. E. & Petrie, J. J. Urology & Renal Medicine. 2nd ed. LC 75-308046. (Illus.). 288p. 1975. pap. text ed. 9.00 (ISBN 0-443-01158-3). Churchill.
Noyes, John H. Male Continence, 4 vols in 1. Incl. Dixon & His Copyists, a Criticism of the Accounts of the Oneida Community in "New America," "Spiritual Wives," & Kindred Publications. 2nd ed; Essay on Scientific Propagation; Salvation from Sin, the End of Christian Faith. LC 72-2975. Repr. of 1876 ed. 16.50 (ISBN 0-404-10739-7). AMS Pr.
Roen, Philip R. Male Sexual Health. (Illus.). 1974. 7.95 (ISBN 0-688-00223-4). Morrow.
Yates, Robert & Gordon, Mildred. Male Reproductive System: Fine Structure Analysis by Scanning & Transmission Electron Microscopy. LC 77-71435. (Illus.). 214p. 1977. 47.75x (ISBN 0-89352-004-7). Masson Pub.

GENERATORS, ELECTRIC
see Dynamos

GENERATORS, MAGNETOHYDRODYNAMIC
see Magnetohydrodynamic Generators

GENERATORS, PULSE
see Pulse Generators

GENES
see Heredity

GENESEE RIVER AND VALLEY
Cowan, Helen I. Charles Williamson. LC 68-55516. Repr. of 1941 ed. 19.50x (ISBN 0-678-00862-0). Kelley.
Imlay, Gilbert. Topographical Description of the Western Territory of North America. 3rd ed. 1797. 15.50 (ISBN 0-384-25685-6). Johnson Repr.
--Topographical Description of the Western Territory of North America. 3rd ed. LC 68-55739. (Illus.). Repr. of 1797 ed. 15.00x (ISBN 0-678-00541-9). Kelley.

McNall, Neil A. An Agricultural History of the Genesee Valley, 1790-1860. LC 75-25260. (Illus.). 1976. Repr. of 1952 ed. lib. bdg. 17.75x (ISBN 0-8371-8396-0, MCGV). Greenwood.
O'Reilly, Henry. Notices of Sullivan's Campaign. LC 73-120889. (American Bicentennial Ser). 1970. Repr. of 1842 ed. 12.50 (ISBN 0-8046-1282-X). Kennikat.
Platt, John A. Whispers from Old Genesee & Echoes of the Salmon River. (Illus.). 184p. 1975. 12.00 (ISBN 0-87770-143-1). Ye Galleon.
Seaver, James E. Narrative of the Life of Mrs. Mary Jemison. 7.00 (ISBN 0-8446-2899-9). Peter Smith.

GENESIS (MIDDLE HIGH GERMAN POEM)

Weller, Alfred. Die Fruhmittelhochdeutsche Wiener Genesis. Repr. of 1914 ed. 21.50 (ISBN 0-384-66731-7); pap. 18.50 (ISBN 0-384-66730-9). Johnson Repr.

GENET, EDMOND CHARLES, 1763-1834

Ammon, Harry. The Genet Mission. (Essays in American History Ser.). 208p. 1973. 6.95x (ISBN 0-393-05475-6); pap. text ed. 3.95x (ISBN 0-393-09420-0). Norton.
Brown, Walt, Jr., ed. An American for Lafayette: The Diaries of E. C. C. Genet, Lafayette Escadrille. (Illus.). 1981. write for info. (ISBN 0-8139-0893-0). U Pr of Va.
Genet, E. C. An American for Lafayette: The Diaries of E. C. C. Genet, Lafayette Escadrille. Brown, Walt, Jr., ed. 227p. 1981. price not set (ISBN 0-8139-0893-0). U Pr of Va.
Minnigerode, Meade. Lives & Times. LC 76-121490. (Essay Index Reprint Ser). 1925. 16.00 (ISBN 0-8369-1765-0). Arno.

GENET, JEAN, 1910-

Cetta, Lewis T. Profane Play, Ritual & Jean Genet. new ed. LC 73-10651. (Studies in the Humanities: No. 2). 120p. 1974. 8.95x (ISBN 0-8173-7313-6). U of Ala Pr.
Choukri, Mohamed. Jean Genet in Tangier. LC 73-86613. 1974. 5.95 (ISBN 0-912946-08-3). Ecco Pr.
Driver, Tom F. Jean Genet. LC 66-26003. (Essays on Modern Writers Ser.: No. 20). (Orig.). 1966. pap. 2.00 (ISBN 0-231-02942-X). Columbia U Pr.
Grossvogel, David I. The Blasphemers: The Theatre of Brecht, Ionesco, Beckett, Genet. 1965. pap. 3.95 (ISBN 0-8014-9006-5, CP6). Cornell U Pr.
Knapp, Bettina L. Jean Genet. LC 74-80080. (Griffin Authors Ser). 172p. 1975. pap. 4.95 (ISBN 0-312-44100-2). St Martin.
MacMahon. The Imagination of Jean Genet. 18.50 (ISBN 0-685-34133-X). French & Eur.
McMahon, Joseph H. The Imagination of Jean Genet. LC 80-16963. (Yale Romanic Studies: 2nd Ser., No. 10). viii, 273p. 1980. Repr. of 1963 ed. lib. bdg. 22.50x (ISBN 0-313-22430-7, MCIM). Greenwood.
Naish, Camille. A Genetic Approach to Structures in the Work of Jean Genet. LC 78-7059. (Harvard Studies in Romance Languages: No. 34). 1978. 9.00x (ISBN 0-674-34581-9). Harvard U Pr.
Sartre, Jean-Paul. Saint Genet. pap. 4.95 (ISBN 0-452-25153-2, Z5153, Plume). NAL.
--Saint Genet, Comedien et Martyr. 1952. pap. 15.95 (ISBN 0-685-11552-6). French & Eur.
Thody, Philip. Jean Genet: A Critical Appraisal. LC 69-17942. 1970. pap. 5.95 (ISBN 0-8128-1296-4). Stein & Day.

GENET, LOUIS, 1884-

Konkel, Sr. Mary H. Rene Fernandat, Poet & Critic. LC 71-128928. (CarL Ser.: No. 45). Repr. of 1952 ed. 22.00 (ISBN 0-404-50345-4). AMS Pr.

GENETIC CODE

Asimov, Isaac. Genetic Code. pap. 1.50 (ISBN 0-451-61659-6, MW1659, Ment). NAL.
Cold Spring Harbor Symposia on Quantitative Biology: The Genetic Code, Vol. 31. LC 34-8174. (Illus.). 784p. 1967. 30.00 (ISBN 0-87969-030-5). Cold Spring Harbor.
Laborit, Henri. Decoding the Human Message. LC 76-53312. 1977. text ed. 17.95x (ISBN 0-312-19022-0). St Martin.
Nierlich, Donald P., et al, eds. Molecular Mechanisms in the Control of Gene Expression, Vol. 5. 1976. 41.50 (ISBN 0-12-518550-2). Acad Pr.
Nishimura, S., ed. Coding. (Selected Papers in Biochemistry Ser.: Vol. 3). 1971. 19.50 (ISBN 0-8391-0613-0). Univ Park.
Silverstein, Alvin & Silverstein, Virginia. Code of Life. LC 77-175558. (Illus.). (gr. 5-9). 1972. 6.95 (ISBN 0-689-30038-7). Atheneum.
Ycas, M. The Biological Code. Neuberger, A. & Tatum, E. L., eds. (Frontiers of Biology Ser.: Vol. 12). 1969. 49.00 (ISBN 0-444-10325-2, North-Holland). Elsevier.

GENETIC COUNSELING

Atkinson, Gary M. & Moraczewski, Albert S. Genetic Counseling, the Church & the Law. LC 79-92084. xvii, 259p. (Orig.). 1980. pap. 9.95 (ISBN 0-935372-06-7). Pope John Ctr.
Berg, J. M. Genetic Counseling in Relation to Mental Retardation. 1971. pap. 6.25 (ISBN 0-08-016315-7). Pergamon.
Birth Defects Converence, 1978, San Francisco. Risk, Communication, & Decision Making in Genetic Counseling: Proceedings, Annual Review of Birth Defects, 1978, Pt. C. Epstein, Charles J., et al, eds. LC 79-5120. (Birth Defects: Original Article Ser.: Vol. XV, No. 5C). 392p. 1979. 36.00x (ISBN 0-8451-1030-6). A R Liss.
Capron, Alexander M., et al, eds. Genetic Counseling: Fact, Values & Norms. LC 79-1736. (Alan R. Liss Ser.: Vol. 15, No. 2). 1979. write for info. (ISBN 0-8451-1025-X). March of Dimes.
--Genetic Counseling: Facts, Values, & Norms. LC 79-1736. (Birth Defects Original Article Ser.: Vol. 15, No. 2). 346p. 1979. 34.00 (ISBN 0-8451-1025-X). A R Liss.
Epstein, Charles J., ed. Risk, Communication, & Decision Making in Genetic Counseling. LC 79-5120. (Alan R. Liss Ser.: Vol. 15, No. 5c). 1979. 36.00 (ISBN 0-8451-1030-6). March of Dimes.
Fuhrmann, W. & Vogel, F. Genetic Counseling. (Heidelberg Science Library: Vol. 10). (Illus.). 160p. 1976. pap. text ed. 9.80 (ISBN 0-387-90151-5). Springer-Verlag.
Harper, Peter S. Practical Genetic Counseling. 296p. 1981. text ed. 29.50 (ISBN 0-8391-1669-1). Univ Park.
Hendin, David & Marks, Joan. The Genetic Connection: How to Protect Your Family Against Genetic Disease. LC 77-10820. 1978. 8.95 (ISBN 0-688-03265-6). Morrow.
Hsia, Y. Edward, et al, eds. Counseling in Genetics. LC 79-3038. 372p. 1979. 34.00 (ISBN 0-8451-0205-2). A R Liss.
Kelly, P. T. Dealing with Dilemma: A Manual for Genetic Counselors. (Heidelberg Science Library Ser.). 1977. soft cover 9.60 (ISBN 3-540-90237-6). Springer-Verlag.
Kelly, Thaddeus E. Clinical Genetics & Genetics Counseling. (Illus.). 400p. 1980. 29.50 (ISBN 0-8151-5011-3). Year Bk Med.
Kessler, Seymour, ed. Genetic Counseling: Psychological Dimensions. LC 78-87879. 1979. 22.50 (ISBN 0-12-405650-4). Acad Pr.
Lubs, Herbert & Cruz, Felix de la, eds. Genetic Counseling. LC 76-52601. 616p. 1977. 37.50 (ISBN 0-89004-150-4). Raven.
Lynch, Henry T. Dynamic Genetic Counseling for Clinicians. (Illus.). 368p. 1969. photocopy ed. spiral 35.75 (ISBN 0-398-01172-9). C C Thomas.
Motulsky, Arno G., et al. Genetic Counseling. 256p. 1974. text ed. 21.50x (ISBN 0-8422-7150-3). Irvington.
Murphy, E. A. & Chase, G. A. Principles of Genetic Counseling. (Illus.). 1975. 27.95 (ISBN 0-8151-6239-1). Year Bk Med.
Reilly, Philip. Genetics, Law, & Social Policy. 1977. 15.00x (ISBN 0-674-34657-2). Harvard U Pr.
Stevenson, Alan C., et al. Genetic Counseling. 2nd ed. (Illus.). 1977. 18.00 (ISBN 0-397-58203-X). Lippincott.

GENETIC ENGINEERING

see also Cloning

Alberts, Bruce & Fox, C. Fred, eds. Mechanistic Studies of DNA Replication & Genetic Recombination. (ICN-UCLA Symposia on Molecular & Cellular Biology Ser.: Vol. XIX). 1980. 48.00 (ISBN 0-12-048850-7). Acad Pr.
Blank, Robert H. The Political Implications of Human Genetic Technology. (Special Studies in Science, Technology, & Public Policy). 209p. (Orig.). 1981. lib. bdg. 25.25x (ISBN 0-89158-975-9); pap. text ed. 12.00x (ISBN 0-86531-193-5). Westview.
Cooke, Robert. Improving on Nature: The Brave New World of Genetic Engineering. 1978. pap. 3.95 (ISBN 0-8129-6292-3). Times Bks.
Cripps, Yvonne M. Controlling Technology: Genetic Engineering & the Law. 170p. 1980. 21.95 (ISBN 0-03-056806-4). Praeger.
Garland, P. B. & Williamson, R., eds. Biochemistry of Genetic Engineering. (Symposia Ser.: No. 44). 145p. 1981. 27.50x (ISBN 0-904498-08-5, Pub. by Biochemical England). State Mutual Bk.
Glover, D. M. Genetic Engineering. (Outline Studies in Biology Ser.). 1980. pap. 5.95x (ISBN 0-412-16170-2, Pub. by Chapman & Hall). Methuen Inc.
Gupta, Akshey K. Genetics & Wheat Improvement. 268p. 1981. 80.00x (ISBN 0-686-76640-7, Pub. by Oxford & IBH India). State Mutual Bk.
Langone, John. Human Engineering: Marvel or Menace? (gr. 7 up). 1978. 6.95 (ISBN 0-316-51427-6). Little.
Rains, Donald W., et al, eds. Genetic Engineering of Osmoregulation: Impact of Plant Productivity for Food, Chemicals & Energy. (Basic Life Sciences Ser.: Vol. 14). 395p. 1980. 39.50 (ISBN 0-306-40454-0, Plenum Pr). Plenum Pub.
Rotter, Jerome I., et al, eds. The Genetics & Heterogeneity of Common Gastrointestinal Disorders. 1980. 35.00 (ISBN 0-12-598760-9). Acad Pr.
Santos, M. A. Genetics & Man's Future: Legal, Social, & Moral Implications of Genetic Engineering. (Illus.). 176p. 1981. 16.75 (ISBN 0-398-04533-X). C C Thomas.
Setlow, J. K. & Hollaender, A., eds. Genetic Engineering: Principles & Methods, Vol. 3. 346p. 1981. 39.50 (ISBN 0-306-40729-9, Plenum Pr). Plenum Pub.
Setlow, Jane K. & Hollaender, Alexander, eds. Genetic Engineering: Principles & Methods, Vol. 2. 298p. 1980. 32.50 (ISBN 0-306-40447-8, Plenum Pr). Plenum Pub.
Skamene, Emil, ed. Genetic Control of Natural Resistance to Infection & Malignancy. (Perspectives in Immunology Ser.). 1980. 33.00 (ISBN 0-12-647680-2). Acad Pr.
Subtelny, Stephen & Sussex, Ian M., eds. The Clonal Basis of Development. (Thirty Sixth Symposia of the Society for Developmental Biology Ser.). 1979. 29.50 (ISBN 0-12-612982-7). Acad Pr.
Williamson, R., ed. Genetic Engineering, Vol. 2. 1981. pap. price not set (ISBN 0-12-270302-2). Acad Pr.
Williamson, Robert, ed. Genetic Engineering, Vol. 1. 1981. 24.00 (ISBN 0-12-270301-4). Acad Pr.

GENETIC PSYCHOLOGY

Here are entered works on the evolutionary psychology of man in terms of origin and development, whether in the individual or in the species. Works on the psychological development of the individual from infancy to old age are entered under Developmental Psychology.
see also Age (Psychology); Culture Conflict; Emotional Maturity; Intelligence Levels; Maturation (Psychology); Sociobiology

Baldwin, James M. Development & Evolution: Including Psychophysical Evolution, Evolution by Orthoplasy & the Theory of Genetic Modes. LC 75-3022. (Philosophy in America Ser.). Repr. of 1902 ed. 28.50 (ISBN 0-404-59017-9). AMS Pr.
--Genetic Theory of Reality. LC 75-3024. (Philosophy in America Ser.). Repr. of 1915 ed. 24.50 (ISBN 0-404-59019-5). AMS Pr.
Bannister, D., ed. New Perspectives in Personal Construct Theory. 1977. 44.00 (ISBN 0-12-077940-4). Acad Pr.
Cold Spring Harbor Symposia on Quantitative Biology: Population Genetics, Vol. 20. LC 34-8174. (Illus.). 362p. 1956. 30.00 (ISBN 0-87969-019-4). Cold Spring Harbor.
Conrad, Herbert S., ed. Studies in Human Development: Selections from the Publications & Adresses of Harold Ellis Jones. (Century Psychology Ser.). (Illus.). 1966. 28.00x (ISBN 0-89197-581-0). Irvington.
Crow, James F. & Denniston, Carter. Genetic Distance. LC 74-23683. 195p. 1974. 32.50 (ISBN 0-306-30827-4, Plenum Pr). Plenum Pub.
Eysenck, H. J. The Inequality of Man. 1975. 10.95 (ISBN 0-912736-16-X). EDITS Pubs.
Fishbein, Harold. Evolution, Development & Children's Learning. Siegal, Alex, ed. LC 75-13478. (Goodyear Development Psychology Ser.). 320p. 1976. text ed. 14.95 (ISBN 0-87620-282-2). Goodyear.
Gary, A. L. & Glover, John A. Eye Color, Sex, & Children's Behavior. LC 76-3642. 208p. 1976. 15.95x (ISBN 0-88229-213-7). Nelson-Hall.
Griffin, Donald R. The Question of Animal Awareness: Evolutionary Continuity of Mental Experience. LC 76-18492. 1976. 8.95 (ISBN 0-87470-020-5). Rockefeller.
Havighurst, Robert J. Developmental Tasks & Education. 3rd ed. 1979. pap. text ed. 6.95x (ISBN 0-582-28112-1). Longman.
Heard, Gerald. Five Ages of Man. LC 63-22142. 1960. 8.50 (ISBN 0-517-52775-8). Crown.
Hobhouse, L. T. Mind in Evolution. Repr. of 1915 ed. 30.00 (ISBN 0-89987-057-0). Darby Bks.
Holtzman, Wayne H., ed. Introductory Psychology in Depth: Biological Topics. 1978. pap. text ed. 7.95 scp (ISBN 0-06-168414-7, HarpC). Har-Row.
Jennings, H. S. The Biological Basis of Human Nature. 1977. Repr. of 1930 ed. lib. bdg. 30.00 (ISBN 0-8414-5407-8). Folcroft.
Kaplan, Arnold R. Genetic Factors in Schizophrenia. (Illus.). 724p. 1972. pap. 68.50 (ISBN 0-398-02327-1). C C Thomas.
Kirkpatrick, Edwin A. Genetic Psychology. Repr. of 1909 ed. 25.00 (ISBN 0-89987-063-5). Darby Bks.
Langer, Jonas. Theories of Development. LC 69-13564. 1969. text ed. 13.95 (ISBN 0-03-073870-9, HoltC). HR&W.
Looft, William R. Developmental Psychology: A Book of Readings. LC 72-87737. 1972. pap. text ed. 7.95 (ISBN 0-03-089113-2, HoltC). HR&W.
Lorenz, Konrad. Evolution & Modification of Behavior. LC 65-24436. 1967. pap. 2.75 (ISBN 0-226-49333-4, P534, Phoen). U of Chicago Pr.
Michel, George & Moore, Celia L. Biological Perspectives in Developmental Psychology. Rebelsky, Freda & Dorman, Lynn, eds. LC 77-26003. (Psychology Lifespan Ser.). 1978. pap. text ed. 6.95 (ISBN 0-8185-0260-6). Brooks-Cole.
Milunsky, Aubrey. Prevention of Genetic Disease & Mental Retardation. LC 74-21015. (Illus.). 450p. 1975. 29.00 (ISBN 0-7216-6395-8). Saunders.
Munn, Norman L. The Growth of Human Behavior. 3rd ed. 512p. 1974. text ed. 20.95 (ISBN 0-395-17017-6). HM.
Nash, John. Developmental Psychology: A Psychobiological Approach. 2nd ed. LC 77-27813. (Illus.). 1978. ref. ed. 19.95 (ISBN 0-13-208272-1). P-H.
Patten, C. J., ed. The Passing of the Phantoms: A Study of Evolutionary Psychology & Morals. 95p. 1980. Repr. of 1924 ed. lib. bdg. 17.50 (ISBN 0-8495-4370-3). Arden Lib.
Pearce, Jane & Newton, Saul. Conditions of Human Growth. 1969. 6.95 (ISBN 0-685-08130-3); pap. 4.95 (ISBN 0-8065-0177-4). Citadel Pr.
Piaget, Jean. The Principles of Genetic Epistemology. Mays, Wolfe, tr. from Fr. LC 72-76915. 1972. text ed. 12.00x (ISBN 0-465-06319-5). Basic.
Pikunas, Justin. Human Development: An Emergent Science. 3rd ed. (Illus.). 1976. text ed. 15.95 (ISBN 0-07-050015-0, C); instructor's manual 3.95 (ISBN 0-07-050026-6). McGraw.
Pyschology, Evolution & Sex: A Study of the Mechanism of Evolution Based on a Comprehensive View of Biology. 176p. 1956. pap. 15.75 (ISBN 0-398-01224-5). C C Thomas.
Stanley, Hiram M. Studies in the Evolutionary Psychology of Feeling. 1977. Repr. of 1895 ed. lib. bdg. 35.00 (ISBN 0-8482-2502-3). Norwood Edns.
Symons, Donald. The Evolution of Human Sexuality. 1979. 17.95 (ISBN 0-19-502535-0). Oxford U Pr.
Wilson, Edward O. On Human Nature. LC 78-17675. 1978. 12.50 (ISBN 0-674-63441-1). Harvard U Pr.

GENETIC SURGERY

see Genetic Engineering

GENETICS

see also Adaptation (Biology); Bacterial Genetics; Behavior Genetics; Biology; Chemical Genetics; Chromosomes; Cytogenetics; Developmental Genetics; Epigenesis; Evolution; Genetic Psychology; Heredity; Human Genetics; Linkage (Genetics); Molecular Genetics; Mosaicism; Mutation (Biology); Natural Selection; Origin of Species; Population Genetics; Variation (Biology)

Applewhite, Steven R., et al, eds. Genetic Screening & Counseling: a Multidisciplinary Perspective: Proceedings. (Illus.). 260p. 1981. pap. 19.50 (ISBN 0-398-04080-X). C C Thomas.
Ashburner, M. & Wright, T. R., eds. The Genetics & Biology of Drosphila, Vol. 2D. LC 79-19614. 1980. 124.50 (ISBN 0-12-064943-8). Acad Pr.
Ashburner, M., et al, eds. The Genetics of Drosphila, Vol. 3, Pt. A. Carson, H. L. 1981. price not set (ISBN 0-12-064945-4). Acad Pr.
Auerbach, Charlotte. Notes for Introductory Courses in Genetics. rev. ed. 1965. pap. 0.95 (ISBN 0-910824-02-9). Kallman.
Avers, Charlotte G. Genetics. (Illus.). 659p. 1980. text ed. 21.95 (ISBN 0-442-26233-7). D Van Nostrand.
Ayala, Francisco & Kiger, John. Modern Genetics. 1980. 21.95 (ISBN 0-8053-0312-X). Benjamin-Cummings.
--Modern Genetics. 1980. 21.95 (ISBN 0-8053-0312-X). Benjamin-Cummings.
--Solutions Manual for Modern Genetics. 1980. pap. 3.95 (ISBN 0-8053-0313-8, 800F00). Benjamin Cummings.
Balakrishman, V., et al. Genetic Diversity Among Australian Aborigines. (AIAS Research & Regional Ser.: No. 3). (Illus.). 1975. pap. text ed. 7.00x (ISBN 0-85575-043-X). Humanities.
Bartsocas, Christos S. & Papadatos, Constantine J., eds. The Management of Genetic Disorders: Proceedings. LC 79-5298. (Progress in Clinical & Biological Research Ser.: Vol. 34). 430p. 1979. 32.00x (ISBN 0-8451-0034-3). A R Liss.
Batchelor, Bruce G. Practical Approach to Pattern Classification. LC 74-1614. 240p. 1974. 29.50 (ISBN 0-306-30796-0, Plenum Pr). Plenum Pub.

Bateson. Problems of Genetics. LC 79-15467. 1979. text ed. 25.00x (ISBN 0-300-02435-5); pap. 6.95 (ISBN 0-300-02436-3, Y-350). Yale U Pr.

Beadle, George W. Genetics & Modern Biology. LC 63-21535. (Memoirs Ser.: Vol. 57). (Illus.). 1963. 3.00 (ISBN 0-87169-057-8). Am Philos.

Beale, Geoffrey. Extranuclear Genetics. 142p. pap. text ed. 19.50 (ISBN 0-8391-1368-4). Univ Park.

Beers, Roland F., Jr. & Bassett, Edward G., eds. Recombinant Molecules: Impact on Science & Society. LC 77-5276. (Miles International Symposium Ser: 10th). 1977. 49.00 (ISBN 0-89004-131-8). Raven.

Bergsma, Daniel. Cancer & Genetics. (Alan R. Liss, Inc. Ser.: Vol 12. No. 1). 1976. 20.00 (ISBN 0-686-18077-1). March of Dimes.

Bergsma, Daniel, ed. Genetic Effects on Aging. (Alan R. Liss Ser.: Vol. 14, No. 1). 1978. 50.00 (ISBN 0-686-10130-8). March of Dimes.

--Genetics & Cytogenetics. (Symposia Ser.: Vol. 10, No. 9). 12.95 (ISBN 0-686-10016-6). March of Dimes.

--Trends in Teaching Genetics. (Alan R. Liss Ser.: Vol. 13, No. 6). 1977. 48.00 (ISBN 0-686-23125-2). March of Dimes.

Bergsma, Daniel, et al, eds. Trends & Teaching in Clinical Genetics. LC 77-24643. (Birth Defects Original Article Ser.: Vol. 13, No. 6). 200p. 1977. 19.00 (ISBN 0-8451-1015-2). A R Liss.

Berry, R. J. Genetics. (Teach Yourself Ser.). 1973. pap. 2.95 (ISBN 0-679-10397-X). McKay.

Biass-Ducroux, Francoise. Glossary of Genetics. 1970. 58.75 (ISBN 0-444-40712-X). Elsevier.

Bishop, J. A. & Cook, L. M., eds. Genetic Consequences of Man Made Change. LC 81-66391. 1981. price not set (ISBN 0-12-101620-X). Acad Pr.

Bodmer, W. F. & Cavalli-Sforza, L. L. Genetics, Evolution, & Man. LC 75-33990. (Illus.). 1976. 23.95x (ISBN 0-7167-0573-7). W H Freeman.

Bodmer, W. F., compiled by. Genetics of the Cell Surface. LC 79-670277. (Proceedings of the Royal Society). 1978. text ed. 25.00x (ISBN 0-85403-101-4). Scholium Intl.

Bogart, Ralph, ed. Genetics Lectures, Vol. 1. LC 73-87943. (Illus., Orig.). 1969. pap. 8.00 (ISBN 0-87071-431-7). Oreg St U Pr.

--Genetics Lectures, Vol. 2. LC 73-87943. 1971. pap. 8.00 (ISBN 0-87071-432-5). Oreg St U Pr.

--Genetics Lectures, Vol. 3. LC 73-87943. 1974. pap. 8.00 (ISBN 0-87071-433-3). Oreg St U Pr.

--Genetics Lectures, Vol. 4. LC 73-87943. (Illus.). 300p. (Orig.). 1975. pap. 12.00 (ISBN 0-87071-434-1). Oreg St U Pr.

--Genetics Lectures, Vol. 5. LC 73-87943. (Illus.). 1978. pap. text ed. 12.00 (ISBN 0-87071-435-X). Oreg St U Pr.

Boorman, Scott A. & Levitt, Paul R. The Genetics of Altruism. LC 79-52792. 1980. 29.50 (ISBN 0-12-115650-8). Acad Pr.

Bornstein, Jerry & Bornstein, Sandy. What Is Genetics? LC 79-15170. (Illus.). 192p. (gr. 10-12). 1979. PLB 8.29 (ISBN 0-671-32952-9). Messner.

Brody, Erness B. & Brody, Nathan, eds. Intelligence: Nature, Determinants, & Consequences. 1976. 24.00 (ISBN 0-12-134250-6). Acad Pr.

Brusick, David. Principles of Genetic Toxicology. 300p. 1980. 25.00 (ISBN 0-306-40414-1, Plenum Pr). Plenum Pub.

Brussard, Peter F., ed. Ecological Genetics: The Interface. LC 78-27196. (Proceedings in Life Sciences). (Illus.). 1979. 23.90 (ISBN 0-387-90378-X). Springer-Verlag.

Bryson, Vernon & Vogel, Henry J., eds. Evolving Genes & Proteins: A Symposium. 1965. 63.00 (ISBN 0-12-138250-8). Acad Pr.

Buckley, John J., Jr., ed. Genetics Now: Ethical Issues in Genetic Research. LC 78-57577. 1978. pap. text ed. 9.50 (ISBN 0-8191-0528-7). U Pr of Amer.

Bulmer, M. G. The Mathematical Theory of Quantitative Genetics. (Illus.). 220p. 1980. 74.00 (ISBN 0-19-857530-0). Oxford U Pr.

Burgio, G. R., et al, eds. Triscomy, Twenty-One: An International Symposium. (Human Genetics Supplementa Ser.: Vol. 2). (Illus.). 265p. 1981. pap. 25.70 (ISBN 0-387-10653-7). Springer-Verlag.

Burns, George W. The Science of Genetics. 4th ed. (Illus.). 1980. text ed. 21.95 (ISBN 0-02-317140-5). Macmillan.

Cannon, H. Graham. Lamarck & Modern Genetics. LC 75-10211. 152p. 1975. Repr. of 1959 ed. lib. bdg. 16.50x (ISBN 0-8371-8173-9, CALA). Greenwood.

Carney, Thomas P. Instant Evolution: We'd Better Get Good at It. LC 79-17835. 1981. pap. text ed. 6.95 (ISBN 0-268-01146-X, NDP-256). U of Notre Dame Pr.

--Instant Evolution: We'd Better Get Good at It. LC 79-17835. 1980. text ed. 13.95x (ISBN 0-268-01145-1). U of Notre Dame Pr.

Caspari, E. W. & Ravin, A. W., eds. Genetic Organization, Vol. 1. 1969. 64.00 (ISBN 0-12-163301-2); by subscription 64.00 (ISBN 0-686-76854-X). Acad Pr.

Catcheside, D. G. The Genetics of Recombination. LC 77-16201. (Genetics - Principles & Perspectives). 1978. pap. 15.95 (ISBN 0-8391-1196-7). Univ Park.

Chai Chen Kang. Genetic Evolution. LC 75-27898. (Illus.). 1976. text ed. 22.00x (ISBN 0-226-10066-9). U of Chicago Pr.

Chakrabarty, A. M. Genetic Engineering. (Uniscience Ser.). 208p. 1978. 59.95 (ISBN 0-8493-5259-2). CRC Pr.

Chase, Allen. The Legacy of Malthus: The Social Costs of the New Scientific Racism. 1977. 20.00 (ISBN 0-394-48045-7). Knopf.

Ciba Foundation. Human Genetics: Possibilities & Realities. LC 79-10949. (Ciba Foundation Symposium Ser.: No. 66). 1979. 51.25 (ISBN 0-444-90064-0, Excerpta Medica). Elsevier.

Cleton, F. J & Simons, J. W., eds. Genetic Origins of Tumor Cells. (Developments in Oncology Ser.: Vol. 1). xv, 125p. 1980. lib. bdg. 26.00 (ISBN 90-247-2272-1, Pub. by Martinus Nijhoff Netherlands). Kluwer Boston.

Cold Spring Harbor Symposia on Quantitative Biology: Exchange of Genetic Material, Vol. 23. LC 34-8174. (Illus.). 449p. 1959. 30.00 (ISBN 0-87969-022-4). Cold Spring Harbor.

Cold Spring Harbor Symposia on Quantitative Biology: Genetics & 20th Century Darwinism. LC 34-8174. (Illus.). 334p. 1960. 30.00 (ISBN 0-87969-023-2). Cold Spring Harbor.

Cold Spring Harbor Symposia on Quantitative Biology: Transcription of Genetic Material, Vol. 35. LC 34-8174. (Illus.). 909p. 1971. 35.00 (ISBN 0-87969-034-8). Cold Spring Harbor.

Colwell, Rita R., ed. The Role of Culture Collections in the Era of Molecular Biology: Proceedings of the 50th Anniversary Symposium of the American Type, Culture Collection. LC 76-4273. (American Type Culture Collection Ser.). 1976. 12.00 (ISBN 0-914826-08-5). Am Soc Microbio.

Conference on European & Regional Gene Banks Izmir, Turkey, April 1972 & Hawkes, J. G. European & Regional Gene Banks: Proceedings. (Illus.). 107p. 1974. pap. 8.00 (ISBN 90-220-0554-2, Pub. by PUDOC). Unipub.

Conference on Recombinant DNA, Committee on Genetic Experimentation (COGENE) & the Royal Society of London, Wye College, Kent, UK, April, 1979. Recombinant DNA & Genetic Experimentation: Proceedings. Morgan, Joan & Whelan, W. J., eds. LC 79-40962. (Illus.). 334p. 1979. 61.00 (ISBN 0-08-024427-0). Pergamon.

Conklin, Marie E. Genetic & Biochemical Aspects of the Development of Datura. Wolsky, A., ed. (Monographs in Developmental Biology: Vol. 12). (Illus.). 170p. 1976. 45.00 (ISBN 3-8055-2307-6). S Karger.

Cooke, Robert. Improving on Nature: The Brave New World of Genetic Engineering. LC 76-50815. 1977. 12.50 (ISBN 0-8129-0667-5). Times Bks.

Corwin, Harry O. & Jenkins, John B. Conceptual Foundation of Genetics: Selected Readings. LC 75-26092. (Illus.). 448p. 1976. pap. text ed. 11.50 (ISBN 0-395-24064-6). HM.

Cottle, Thomas J. Like Fathers, Like Sons: Portraits of Intimacy & Strain. 300p. 1981. 14.95 (ISBN 0-89391-054-6); pap. 8.95 (ISBN 0-89391-087-2). Ablex Pub.

Cove, D. J. Genetics. LC 75-160089. (Illus.). 1972. 35.50 (ISBN 0-521-08255-2); pap. text ed. 10.95x (ISBN 0-521-09663-4). Cambridge U Pr.

Crawford, M. H. & Workman, P. L., eds. Methods & Theories of Anthropological Genetics. LC 72-94660. (School of American Research, Advanced Seminar Ser.). 509p. 1973. 20.00x (ISBN 0-8263-0274-2). U of NM Pr.

Creed, Robert, ed. Ecological Genetics & Evolution: Essays in Honor of E. B. Ford. 391p. 1971. 32.50 (ISBN 0-306-50020-5, Plenum Pr). Plenum Pub.

Crow, James F. Genetic Notes. 7th ed. LC 75-16798. 1976. pap. text ed. 9.95x (ISBN 0-8087-0360-9). Burgess.

Crow, James F. & Denniston, Carter. Genetic Distance. LC 74-23683. 195p. 1974. 32.50 (ISBN 0-306-30827-4, Plenum Pr). Plenum Pub.

Darlington, C. D. Teaching Genetics. 1965. 7.50 (ISBN 0-8022-0340-X). Philos Lib.

Davern, Cedric I., intro. by. Genetics: Readings from Scientific American. LC 80-25208. (Illus.). 1981. text ed. 19.95x (ISBN 0-7167-1200-8); pap. text ed. 9.95x (ISBN 0-7167-1201-6). W H Freeman.

Dawkins, Richard. The Selfish Gene. 1976. 12.95 (ISBN 0-19-857519-X). Oxford U Pr.

Day, Peter R. Genetics of Host-Parasite Interaction. LC 73-17054. (Illus.). 1974. text ed. 23.95x (ISBN 0-7167-0844-2). W H Freeman.

Dean, D. H., et al, eds. Gene Structure & Expression. LC 80-17606. (Ohio State University Biosciences Colloquia: No. 6). (Illus.). 369p. 1980. 22.50x (ISBN 0-8142-0321-3). Ohio St U Pr.

De Garay, Alfonso L., et al, eds. Genetic & Anthropological Studies of Olympic Athletes. 1974. 28.00 (ISBN 0-12-208650-3). Acad Pr.

Demerec, M., ed. Advances in Genetics. Incl. Vol. 1. 1947 (ISBN 0-12-017601-7); Vol. 2. 1948 (ISBN 0-12-017602-5); Vol. 3. 1950 (ISBN 0-12-017603-3); Vol. 4. 1951 (ISBN 0-12-017604-1); Vol. 5. 1953 (ISBN 0-12-017605-X); Vol. 6. 1954 (ISBN 0-12-017606-8); Vol. 7. 1955 (ISBN 0-12-017607-6); Vol. 8. 1956 (ISBN 0-12-017608-4); Vol. 9. 1958 (ISBN 0-12-017609-2); Vol. 10. Caspari, E. W. & Thoday, J. M., eds. 1961 (ISBN 0-12-017610-6); Vol. 11. 1962 (ISBN 0-12-017611-4); Vol. 12. 1964 (ISBN 0-12-017612-2); Vol. 13. 1965 (ISBN 0-12-017613-0); Vol. 14. Caspari, E. W., ed. 1968 (ISBN 0-12-017614-9); Vol. 15. Caspari, E. W., ed. 1970 (ISBN 0-12-017615-7); Vol. 16. Caspari, E. W., ed. 1971 (ISBN 0-12-017616-5); Vol. 17. The Genetics of Tribolium & Related Species. 1973. 48.50 (ISBN 0-12-017617-3); Vol. 18. 1976. 52.50 (ISBN 0-12-017618-1); Vol. 19. 1977. 55.00 (ISBN 0-12-017619-X); Suppl. 1. The Genetics of Tribolium & Related Species. Sokoloff, Alexander. 1966. 38.00 (ISBN 0-12-017661-0). Vols. 1-16. 55.00 ea. Acad Pr.

--Advances in Genetics, Vol. 20. 1979. 50.50 (ISBN 0-12-017620-3). Acad Pr.

Desnick, Robert J., ed. Enzyme Therapy in Genetic Diseases: Part 2. LC 79-48026. (Alan R. Liss Ser.: Vol. 16, No. 1). 1980. 64.00 (ISBN 0-686-29474-2). March of Dimes.

Dillon, L. S. The Genetic Mechanism & the Origin of Life. LC 78-4478. (Illus.). 573p. 1978. 39.50 (ISBN 0-306-31090-2, Plenum Pr). Plenum Pub.

Druger, Marvin. Individualized Biology, Vol.14: Genetics - Script. (Life Sciences Ser.). 74p. 1976. pap. 1.95 (ISBN 0-201-01387-8). A-W.

Dubinin, N. & Gubarev, V. El Hijo De la Vida. 263p. (Span.). 1972. 3.10 (ISBN 0-8285-1465-8, Pub. by Mir Pubs Russia). Imported Pubns.

Dubinin, N. P. & Gol'dfarb, D. M., eds. Molecular Mechanisms of Genetic Processes. Mercado, A., tr. from Rus. LC 74-30205. 373p. 1975. 64.95 (ISBN 0-470-22330-8). Halsted Pr.

Eigen, M. & Schuster, P. The Hypercycle: A Principle of Natural Self-Organization. 1979. 10.30 (ISBN 0-387-09293-5). Springer-Verlag.

Elandt-Johnson, Regina C. Probability Models & Statistical Methods in Genetics. LC 75-140177. (Ser. in Probability & Mathematical Statistics). 1971. 51.00 (ISBN 0-471-23490-7, Pub. by Wiley-Interscience). Wiley.

Elseth, Gerald & Baumgardner, Kandy. Population Biology. (Illus.). 512p. 1980. text ed. 24.95 (ISBN 0-442-26235-3). Van Nos Reinhold.

Emery, Alen E. & Miller, James R., eds. Registers for the Detection & Prevention of Genetic Disease: Proceedings. LC 76-25940. (Illus.). 1976. 21.50 (ISBN 0-8151-3114-3, Pub. by Symposia Special). Year Bk Med.

Engdahl, Sylvia L. & Roberson, Rick. Tool for Tomorrow: New Knowledge About Genes. LC 78-13777. (Illus.). (gr. 5 up). 1979. 6.95 (ISBN 0-689-30679-2). Atheneum.

Evans, H. J., et al, eds. Edinburgh Conference, 1979: International Workshop on Human Gene Mapping, 5th, July 1979. (Human Gene Mapping Ser.: No. 5). (Illus.). vi, 236p. 1980. pap. 39.00 (ISBN 3-8055-0649-X). S Karger.

Facklam, Howard & Facklam, Margery. From Cell to Clone: The Story of Genetic Engineering. LC 79-87515. (gr. 7 up). 1979. 8.95 (ISBN 0-15-230262-X, HJ). HarBraceJ.

Falconer, D. S. Introduction to Quantitative Genetics. 2nd ed. (Illus.). 1981. pap. text ed. 25.00x (ISBN 0-582-44195-1). Longman.

Falconer, Douglas S. Introduction to Quantitative Genetics. (Illus.). 1960. 22.50 (ISBN 0-8260-2990-6). Wiley.

Farnsworth, M. W. Genetics. 1978. text ed. 26.50 scp (ISBN 0-06-042003-0, HarpC). Har-Row.

Feldman, M. Basic Principles of Genetics. (Biocore Ser: Unit 7). 1974. 15.00 (ISBN 0-07-005337-5, C). McGraw.

Festing, Michael F. Inbred Strains in Biomedical Research. 1980. text ed. 49.50x (ISBN 0-19-520111-6). Oxford U Pr.

Fincham, J. R., et al. Fungal Genetics. 4th ed. LC 78-65463. (Botanical Monographs). 1979. 62.50x (ISBN 0-520-03818-5). U of Cal Pr.

Fincham, J. R. S. Genetic Complementation. (Microbial & Molecular Biology Ser.: No. 3). 1966. 17.50 (ISBN 0-8053-2550-6, Adv Bk Prog). Benjamin-Cummings.

Ford, E. B. Ecological Genetics. 4th ed. 442p. 1979. text ed. 29.95x (ISBN 0-412-14130-2, Pub. by Chapman & Hall England). Methuen Inc.

--Genetics for Medical Students. 7th ed. LC 73-13385. (Illus.). 240p. 1973. text ed. 12.95x (ISBN 0-412-10950-6, Pub. by Chapman & Hall England). Methuen Inc.

--Understanding Genetics. LC 79-63132. (Illus.). 1979. text ed. 15.00x (ISBN 0-87663-728-4, Pica Pr). Universe.

Fraenkel-Conrat, H. & Wagner, R. R., eds. Comprehensive Virology, Vol. 10: Regulation & Genetics - Viral Gene Expression & Integeration. (Illus.). 496p. 1977. 39.50 (ISBN 0-306-35150-1, Plenum Pr). Plenum Pub.

--Comprehensive Virology, Vol. 11, Regulation & Genetics - Plant Viruses. LC 77-7908. (Illus.). 348p. 1977. 29.50 (ISBN 0-306-35151-X, Plenum Pr). Plenum Pub.

Frankel, Edward. DNA: The Ladder of Life. 2nd ed. (Illus.). (gr. 7 up). 1978. 8.95 (ISBN 0-07-021883-8, GB). McGraw.

Friedman. Infection, Immunity & Genetics. 1978. 16.50 (ISBN 0-8391-1292-0). Univ Park.

Fristrom, James W. & Spieth, Philip T. Principles of Genetics. LC 80-65757. (Illus.). 687p. 1980. text ed. 21.95x (ISBN 0-913462-05-5). Chiron Pr.

Gardner, Eldon J. & Snustad, D. Peter. Principles of Genetics. 6th ed. LC 80-12114. 688p. 1981. text ed. 24.95 (ISBN 0-471-04412-1). Wiley.

Gedda, Luigi & Brenci, Gianni. Chronogenetics: The Inheritance of Biological Time. (Illus.). 232p. 1978. 27.75 (ISBN 0-398-03641-1). C C Thomas.

Genetic Engineering: Its Applications & Limitations. 169p. 1975. pap. 15.00 (ISBN 0-89192-060-9, Pub. by Gottlieb Dutteiler Institute). Interbk Inc.

Genetica y la Revolucion En las Ciencias Biologicas. rev. ed. (Serie De Biologia: No. 1). (Span.). 1975. pap. 1.25 (ISBN 0-8270-6045-9). OAS.

Genetics for Blood Bankers. 118p. 1980. 20.00 (ISBN 0-914404-59-8). Am Assn Blood.

Giblett, Eloise R. Genetic Markers in Human Blood. (Illus.). 1969. 22.75 (ISBN 0-632-05290-2, Blackwell). Mosby.

Gibson, J. B. & Oakeshoff, J. G., eds. Genetic Studies of Drosophila Populations. 267p. (Orig.). 1981. pap. text ed. 15.95 (ISBN 0-686-30658-9, 0069, Pub. by ANUP Australia). Bks Australia.

Glass, Robert E. Gene Function: E. coli & Its Heritable Elements. 450p. 1980. 60.00x (ISBN 0-686-69929-7, Pub. by Croom Helm England). State Mutual Bk.

Glover, S. W. & Hopwood, D. A., eds. Genetics As a Tool in Microbiology. (Society for General Microbiology Symposium: No. 31). (Illus.). 450p. 1981. text ed. 65.00 (ISBN 0-521-23748-3). Cambridge U Pr.

Goldberger, Robert F., ed. Biological Regulation & Development, Vol. 1: Gene Expression. LC 78-21893. 576p. 1978. 39.50 (ISBN 0-306-40098-7, Plenum Pr). Plenum Pub.

Goldstein, Philip. Genetics Is Easy. rev. ed. (Illus.). (gr. 9 up). 8.05 (ISBN 0-8313-1539-3). Lantern.

Gooch, Stan. The Secret Life of Humans. 1981. 18.95x (ISBN 0-460-04527-X, Pub. by J M Dent England). Biblio Dist.

Goodenough, Ursula. Genetics. LC 77-26245. 840p. 1978. text ed. 25.95 (ISBN 0-03-019716-3, HoltC). HR&W.

Gottesman, Irving I. & Shields, James. Schizophrenia & Genetics. (Personality & Psychopathology Ser.: Vol. 13). 1972. 44.50 (ISBN 0-12-293450-4). Acad Pr.

Grant, Verne. The Origin of Adaptations. LC 63-11695. (Illus.). 606p. 1963. 27.50x (ISBN 0-231-02529-7); pap. 12.50x (ISBN 0-231-08648-2). Columbia U Pr.

Green, Earl L. Genetics Probability in Animal Breeding Experiments. (Illus.). 256p. 1981. text ed. 36.95x (ISBN 0-19-520159-0). Oxford U Pr.

Greenblatt, Augusta & Greenblatt, I. J. Your Genes & Your Destiny. LC 78-55655. 1978. 8.95 (ISBN 0-672-52302-7). Bobbs.

Grell, Rhoda F., ed. Mechanisms in Recombination. LC 74-20987. 450p. 1974. 35.00 (ISBN 0-306-30823-1, Plenum Pr). Plenum Pub.

Gurdon, J. B. Control of Gene Expression in Animal Development. LC 74-76589. 1974. pap. 5.95x (ISBN 0-674-16977-8). Harvard U Pr.

Harrison, David. Problems in Genetics: With Notes & Examples. (Biology Ser). 1970. pap. text ed. 3.25 (ISBN 0-201-02881-6). A-W.

Harsanyi, Zsolt & Hutton, Richard. Genetic Prophecy: Beyond the Double Helix -- Genes That Predict the Future. 294p. 1981. 14.95 (ISBN 0-89256-163-7). Rawson Wade.

Hecht, Max K. & Steere, William C., eds. Essays in Evolution & Genetics in Honor of Theodosius Dobzhansky: A Supplement to Evolutionary Biology. LC 74-105428. 594p. 1970. 37.50 (ISBN 0-306-50034-5, Plenum Pr). Plenum Pub.

Hendin, David & Marks, Joan. Genetic Connection. 1979. pap. 1.95 (ISBN 0-451-08558-2, J8558, Sig). NAL.

Herskowitz, Irwin H. The Elements of Genetics. 20.95 (ISBN 0-02-353950-X). Macmillan.

--Principles of Genetics. 2nd ed. 672p. 1977. 22.95 (ISBN 0-02-353930-5). Macmillan.

Hexter, W. & Yost, H. T. The Science of Genetics. (Illus.). 592p. 1976. 21.95 (ISBN 0-13-794750-X). P-H.

Hoagland, Mahlon B. The Roots of Life: A Layman's Guide to Genes, Evolution & the Ways of Cells. 1979. pap. 2.75 (ISBN 0-380-48041-7, 48041, Discus). Avon.

Howard, H. W. Genetics of the Potato: Solanum Tuberosum. LC 73-130343. (Illus.). 1970. 10.30 (ISBN 0-387-91030-1). Springer-Verlag.

Hsu, T. C. Human & Mammalian Cytogenetics: A Historical Perspective. (Heidelberg Science Library Ser.). (Illus.). 1979. pap. 12.40 (ISBN 0-387-90364-X). Springer-Verlag.

Hutt, Frederick B. Animal Genetics. 2nd ed. 544p. 1982. text ed. 23.95 (ISBN 0-471-08497-2). Wiley.

--Animal Genetics. (Illus.). 1964. 25.50 (ISBN 0-471-06787-3). Wiley.

--Genetics for Dog Breeders. LC 79-15169. (Illus.). 1979. text ed. 17.95x (ISBN 0-7167-1069-2). W H Freeman.

Huxley, Julian S. Heredity, East & West: Lysenko & World Science. LC 49-50254. 1969. Repr. of 1949 ed. 13.00 (ISBN 0-527-43810-3). Kraus Repr.

ICN-UCLA Symposia on Molecular & Cellular Biology. Eukaryotic Genetics Systems. Wilcox, Gary, et al, eds. 1977. 30.00 (ISBN 0-12-751550-X). Acad Pr.

Ingram, Vernon M. Hemoglobins in Genetics & Evolution. LC 63-10416. (Biology Ser.). (Illus.). 1963. 15.00x (ISBN 0-231-02585-8). Columbia U Pr.

Islam, A. S. Fundamentals of Genetics. 2nd ed. 520p. 1981. text ed. 27.50x (ISBN 0-7069-1238-1, Pub. by Vikas India). Advent NY.

Jackson, Laird G. & Schimke, R. Neil. Clinical Genetics: A Sourcebook for Physicians. LC 78-24414. 1979. 49.50 (ISBN 0-471-01943-7, Pub. by Wiley Medical). Wiley.

Jacob, Francois & Wollman, E. Sexuality & the Genetics of Bacteria. rev. ed. 1961. 53.50 (ISBN 0-12-379450-1). Acad Pr.

Jacob, Francoise. The Logic of Life: A History of Heredity. LC 73-18010. 1974. 10.00 (ISBN 0-394-47246-2). Pantheon.

Jacquard, A. The Genetic Structure of Populations. Charlesworth, B. & Charlesworth, D., trs. from Fr. LC 73-80868. (Biomathematics Ser.: Vol. 5). (Illus.). xviii, 569p. 1974. text ed. 15.50 (ISBN 0-387-06329-3). Springer-Verlag.

Jameson, D. L., ed. Evolutionary Genetics. (Benchmark Papers in Genetics: Vol. 8). 1977. 40.50 (ISBN 0-12-786755-4). Acad Pr.

Jenkins, John B. Genetics. 2nd ed. LC 78-69608. (Illus.). 1979. text ed. 21.95 (ISBN 0-395-26502-9); inst. manual 0.65 (ISBN 0-395-26501-0). HM.

Jude, Albert C. Cat Genetics. new ed. (Illus.). 1977. 7.95 (ISBN 0-87666-172-X, AP4600). TFH Pubns.

Karp, Laurence E. Genetic Engineering: Threat or Promise? LC 76-3497. (Illus.). 320p. 1976. 18.95x (ISBN 0-88229-261-7); pap. 9.95x (ISBN 0-88229-460-1). Nelson-Hall.

Keith, C. Gregory. Genetics & Ophthalmology. (Genetics in Medicine & Surgery Ser). (Illus.). 1978. text ed. 30.00 (ISBN 0-443-01323-3). Churchill.

Kempthorne, Oscar. Introduction to Genetic Statistics. 1957. facsimile ed 23.90x (ISBN 0-8138-2375-7). Iowa St U Pr.

Kenney, F. T., et al. Gene Expression & Its Regulation. LC 72-90334. (Basic Life Sciences Ser.: Vol. 1). 557p. 1973. 37.50 (ISBN 0-306-36501-4, Plenum Pr). Plenum Pub.

Kent, P. W., ed. New Approaches to Genetics. 1978. 28.00 (ISBN 0-85362-169-1, Oriel). Routledge & Kegan.

Kety, Seymour S., ed. Genetics of Neurological & Psychiatric Disorders. (Association for Research in Nervous & Mental Disease (ARNMD Research Publications). 1981. text ed. write for info. (ISBN 0-89004-626-3). Raven.

Kilbey, B. J., et al, eds. Handbook of Mutagenicity Test Procedures. 1977. 79.00 (ISBN 0-444-41338-3, North Holland). Elsevier.

King, James C. The Biology of Race. rev. ed. LC 81-1345. (Illus.). 220p. 1981. 15.95 (ISBN 0-520-04223-9). U of Cal Pr.

King, Robert C. Genetics. 2nd ed. (Illus.). 1965. 19.95x (ISBN 0-19-500932-0). Oxford U Pr.

King, Robert C., ed. Handbook of Genetics. Incl. Vol. 1. Bacteria, Bacteriophages, & Fungi. LC 74-8867. (Illus.). 676p. 49.50 (ISBN 0-306-37611-3); Vol. 2. Plants, Plant Viruses, & Protists. LC 74-23531. (Illus.). 631p. 1974. 49.50 (ISBN 0-306-37612-1); Vol. 3, Invertebrates of Genetic Interest. 874p. 1975. 49.50 (ISBN 0-306-37613-X); Vol. 4, Vertebrates of Genetic Interest. 669p. 1975. 49.50 (ISBN 0-306-37614-8); Vol. 5. Molecular Genetics. 667p. 1976. 49.50 (ISBN 0-306-37615-6). (Illus., Plenum Pr). Plenum Pub.

Kirk, R. L. The Distribution of Genetic Markers in Australian Aborigines. (AIAS Human Biology Ser.: No. 1). (Illus.). 1965. pap. text ed. 4.25x (ISBN 0-85575-099-5). Humanities.

Koger, Marvin, et al, eds. Crossbreeding Beef Cattle: Series II. LC 73-8847. 500p. 1973. 17.50 (ISBN 0-8130-0364-4). U Presses Fla.

Kohn, Alexander & Shatkay, Adam, eds. Control of Gene Expression. LC 74-3157. (Advances in Experimental Medicine & Biology Ser.: Vol. 44). 440p. 1974. 39.50 (ISBN 0-306-39044-2, Plenum Pr). Plenum Pub.

Kolodny, Gerald M. Eukaryotic Gene Regulation, 2 vols. 1981. vol. 1, 192 pgs. 59.95 (ISBN 0-8493-5225-8); vol. 2, 240 pgs. 59.95 (ISBN 0-8493-5226-6). CRC Pr.

Kormondy, Edward J. Introduction to Genetics: A Program for Self-Instruction. LC 79-13356. 270p. 1979. pap. 9.95 (ISBN 0-88275-992-2). Krieger.

Korochkin, L. I. Gene Interactions in Development. (Monographs on Theoretical & Applied Genetics: Vol. 4). (Illus.). 340p. 1980. 59.80 (ISBN 0-387-10112-8). Springer-Verlag.

Kushev, V. V. Mechanisms of Genetic Recombination. LC 73-83989. (Studies in Soviet Science-Life Sciences). (Illus.). 253p. 1974. 30.00 (ISBN 0-306-10891-7, Consultants). Plenum Pub.

Kuspira, John & Walker, G. W. Genetics: Questions & Problems. 1973. pap. text ed. 17.95 (ISBN 0-07-035672-6, C). McGraw.

Lande, Rivian & Knox, Marlys. Concepts of Genetics. (Orig.). Date not set. 5.95 (ISBN 0-8087-3826-7). Burgess.

Lappe, Marc. Genetic Politics. 1979. 9.95 (ISBN 0-671-22546-4). S&S.

Lerner, I. M. & Donald, H. P. Modern Developments in Animal Breeding. 1966. 47.00 (ISBN 0-12-444350-8). Acad Pr.

Lerner, I. Michael. The Genetic Basis of Selection. LC 73-19295. (Illus.). 298p. 1974. Repr. of 1958 ed. lib. bdg. 20.25x (ISBN 0-8371-7315-9, LEGB). Greenwood.

Levine, Louis. Biology of the Gene. 3rd ed. LC 80-10730. (Illus.). 1980. pap. text ed. 17.95 (ISBN 0-8016-2988-8). Mosby.

Levine, Robert P. Genetics. 2nd ed. LC 68-20101. (Modern Biology Ser). 1968. pap. text ed. 10.50 (ISBN 0-03-068975-9, HoltC). HR&W.

Lewin, Benjamin. Gene Expression, Vol. 3: Plasmids & Phages. LC 73-14382. 1977. 43.50 (ISBN 0-471-53170-7, Pub. by Wiley-Interscience); pap. 22.95 (ISBN 0-471-02715-4). Wiley.

Lewis, E. B. Genetics & Evolution: Selected Papers of A. H. Sturtevant. LC 61-17422. (Illus.). 1961. 25.95x (ISBN 0-7167-0611-3). W H Freeman.

Lipkin, Mack, Jr. & Rowley, Peter T. Genetic Responsibility: On Choosing Our Children's Genes. LC 74-12149. 176p. 1974. 22.50 (ISBN 0-306-30813-4, Plenum Pr). Plenum Pub.

Lovtrup, Soren. Epigenetics: A Treatise on Theoretical Biology. LC 72-5719. 550p. 1974. 83.50 (ISBN 0-471-54900-2, Pub. by Wiley-Interscience). Wiley.

Luce, Thomas G. Genetics with a Computer. 1977. pap. text ed. 14.95 (ISBN 0-87567-076-8). Entelek.

Luchnik, N. Why I'm Like Dad. 264p. 1971. 3.75 (ISBN 0-8285-0840-2, Pub. by Mir Pubs Russia). Imported Pubns.

Lucy, J. A., et al. Mammalian Cell Hybridization, II. (Illus.). 220p. 1973. text ed. 25.50x (ISBN 0-8422-7102-3). Irvington.

Lygre, David. Life Manipulation: From Test Tube Babies to Aging. 1979. 9.95 (ISBN 0-8027-0632-0). Walker & Co.

Lynch, Henry T. Genetics & Breast Cancer. 256p. 1981. text ed. 23.50 (ISBN 0-442-24919-5). Van Nos Reinhold.

Mackean, D. J. Introduction to Genetics. 3rd ed. 1978. pap. text ed. 8.95 (ISBN 0-7195-3346-5). Transatlantic.

McKinnell, Robert G. Cloning: Nuclear Transplantation in Amphibia. LC 78-3195. (Illus.). 1978. 25.00x (ISBN 0-8166-0831-8). U of Minn Pr.

Maclean, N. Control of Gene Expression. 1976. 33.50 (ISBN 0-12-464950-5). Acad Pr.

McNiel, N. A. & Magill, Clint. Genetics. 2nd ed. 1977. pap. text ed. 8.95x (ISBN 0-89641-004-8). American Pr.

Maragos, George D., ed. Seminar on Human Genetics. (Paediatrician: Vol. 6, No. 6). (Illus.). 1978. 18.75 (ISBN 3-8055-2909-0). S Karger.

Mariner, James L. An Introduction to Genetics & Evolution. (Illus.). (gr. 10-12). 1977. pap. text ed. 4.25 (ISBN 0-88334-092-5). Ind Sch Pr.

Massarik, Fred & Kaback, Michael M. Genetic Disease Control: A Social Psychological Approach. LC 80-28219. (Sage Library of Social Research: Vol. 116). (Illus.). 168p. 1981. 20.00 (ISBN 0-8039-1054-1); pap. 9.95 (ISBN 0-8039-1055-X). Sage.

Mather, K. & Jinks, J. L. Introduction to Biomedical Genetics. LC 77-76809. 1978. 22.50x (ISBN 0-8014-1123-8). Cornell U Pr.

May, Julian. Do You Have Your Father's Nose. Publication Associates, ed. LC 70-84734. (Illus.). (gr. 2-4). 1969. PLB 6.95 (ISBN 0-87191-036-5). Creative Ed.

Mays, Laura. Genetics: A Molecular Approach. 1981. text ed. 19.95 (ISBN 0-02-378320-6). Macmillan.

Medvedev, Zhores A. The Rise & Fall of T. D. Lysenko. Lerner, I. Michael, tr. LC 79-77519. 284p. 1969. 16.00x (ISBN 0-231-03183-1). Columbia U Pr.

Meier, Hans. Experimental Pharmacogenetics: Physiopathology of Heredity & Pharmacologic Responses. 1963. 38.50 (ISBN 0-12-488450-4). Acad Pr.

Mendel Centennial Symposium - Fort Collins - 1965. Heritage from Mendel. Brink, R. Alexander & Styles, E. Derek, eds. (Illus., Orig.). 1967. 27.50 (ISBN 0-299-04270-7); pap. 10.95 (ISBN 0-299-04274-X). U of Wis Pr.

Merrell, David J. Ecological Genetics. (Illus.). 570p. 1981. 25.00x (ISBN 0-8166-1019-3). U of Minn Pr.

--An Introduction to Genetics. 750p. 1975. text ed. 17.95x (ISBN 0-393-09247-X). Norton.

Mielke, James H. & Crawford, Michael H., eds. Current Developments in Anthropological Genetics: Vol. 1, Theory & Methods, Vol. 1. 450p. 1980. 45.00 (ISBN 0-306-40390-0, Plenum Pr). Plenum Pub.

Milunsky, Aubrey. Know Your Genes. 1978. pap. 1.95 (ISBN 0-380-40899-6, 40899). Avon.

Milunsky, Aubrey & Annas, George J. Genetics & the Law. LC 75-38569. 532p. 1976. 27.50 (ISBN 0-306-30906-8, Plenum Pr). Plenum Pub.

Milunsky, Aubrey & Annas, George J., eds. Genetics & the Law, II. (Illus.). 474p. 1980. 29.50 (ISBN 0-306-40388-9, Plenum Pr). Plenum Pub.

Moe, Martin A., Jr. Project Phoenix: A Concept for Future Existence. 96p. (Orig.). 1981. pap. 4.50 (ISBN 0-939960-00-1). Norns Pub Co.

Monod, Jacques. Chance & Necessity. 1972. pap. 2.45 (ISBN 0-394-71825-9, Vin). Random.

Moore, John A. Heredity & Development. rev. 2nd ed. (Illus.). 1972. pap. text ed. 5.95x (ISBN 0-19-501478-2). Oxford U Pr.

Morgan, Thomas H. Embryology & Genetics. LC 74-12886. (Illus.). 258p. 1975. Repr. of 1934 ed. lib. bdg. 16.50x (ISBN 0-8371-7772-3, MOEG). Greenwood.

--The Mechanism of Mendelian Heredity. 1972. Repr. of 1915 ed. 31.00 (ISBN 0-384-40136-8). Johnson Repr.

Morton, N. E. Outline of Genetic Epidemiology. (Illus.). x, 250p. 1981. pap. 25.75 (ISBN 3-8055-2269-X). S Karger.

Morton, Newton E., ed. A Genetics Program Library. 69p. 1969. 6.00x (ISBN 0-87022-522-7). U Pr of Hawaii.

Motulsky, A. G., et al, eds. Human Genetic Variation in Response to Medical & Environmental Agents: Pharmacogenetics & Ecogenetics. (Human Genetics: Supplement 1). (Illus.). 1979. pap. 22.00 (ISBN 0-387-09175-0). Springer-Verlag.

Mourant, A. E., et al. The Genetics of the Jews. (Research Monographs on Human Population Biology). (Illus.). 1978. text ed. 39.50x (ISBN 0-19-857522-X). Oxford U Pr.

Muller, Hermann J. The Modern Concept of Nature. Carlson, Elof A., ed. LC 74-170884. (Illus.). 200p. 1973. 19.50 (ISBN 0-87395-096-8); microfiche 19.50 (ISBN 0-87395-196-4). State U NY Pr.

Myers, Oval, et al. An Approach to Problem Solving in Genetics. 1976. pap. text ed. 5.00x (ISBN 0-87563-107-X). Stipes.

Neel, James V. & Schull, William J. Human Heredity. LC 54-12698. (Midway Reprint Ser). (Illus.). viii, 362p. 1975. pap. 13.00x (ISBN 0-226-57057-6). U of Chicago Pr.

New Haven Conference, International Workshop on Human Gene Mapping, 1st. Proceedings. Bergsma, Daniel, ed. (Symposia Ser.: Vol. 10, No. 3). 13.50 (ISBN 0-686-10020-4). March of Dimes.

New York Academy of Sciences, Nov. 28-30, 1979. Genetic Variation of Viruses, Vol. 354. Palese, Peter & Roizman, Bernard, eds. LC 80-25770. (Annals of the New York Academy of Sciences). 507p. 1980. 97.00x (ISBN 0-89766-097-8); pap. 97.00x (ISBN 0-89766-098-6). NY Acad Sci.

Newman, Horatio H., ed. Evolution, Genetics & Eugenics. LC 32-26475. (Illus.). 1969. Repr. of 1932 ed. lib. bdg. 24.50x (ISBN 0-8371-1880-8, NEEV). Greenwood.

Novitski, Edward. Human Genetics. 2nd ed. 1982. 19.95 (ISBN 0-686-75032-2). Macmillan.

--Human Genetics. (Illus.). 1977. text ed. 19.95 (ISBN 0-02-388550-5). Macmillan.

Nyhan, W. L. Genetic & Malformation Syndromes in Clinical Medicine. (Illus.). 1976. 69.50 (ISBN 0-8151-6486-6). Year Bk Med.

Old, R. W. & Primrose, S. B. Principles of Gene Manipulation: An Introduction to Genetic Engineering. LC 79-6740. (Studies in Microbiology: Vol. 2). 1980. 35.00x (ISBN 0-520-04143-7); pap. 12.75x (ISBN 0-520-04151-8). U of Cal Pr.

Olson, David F. Stone Grinding & Polishing. LC 73-83453. (Little Craft Book Ser.). (Illus.). 48p. (gr. 7 up). 1973. 5.95 (ISBN 0-8069-5286-5); PLB 6.69 (ISBN 0-8069-5287-3). Sterling.

Oosthuizen, G. C., et al, eds. Genetics & Society. 208p. 1980. text ed. 28.00x (ISBN 0-19-570185-2). Oxford U Pr.

Ormond, John K., et al. Genetics & the Urologist. (Illus.). 112p. 1972. photocopy ed. spiral 14.75 (ISBN 0-398-02372-7). C C Thomas.

An Overview: Genetic Resources, 1980. (UNEP Ser.: No. 5). 132p. 1980. pap. 12.00 (ISBN 0-686-70041-4, UNEP 034, UNEP). Unipub.

Pai, Anna C. Foundations of Genetics: A Science for Society. (Illus.). 320p. 1974. text ed. 18.95 (ISBN 0-07-048093-1, C); pap. text ed. 14.95 (ISBN 0-07-048092-3). McGraw.

Pai, Anna C. & Marcue-Roberts, Helen. Genetics: Its Concepts & Implications. (Illus.). 736p. 1981. text ed. 24.95 (ISBN 0-13-351007-7). P-H.

Patt, Donald I. & Patt, Gail R. An Introduction to Modern Genetics. LC 74-12803. (Life Sciences Ser.). (Illus.). 384p. 1975. text ed. 19.95 (ISBN 0-201-05743-3); sol. manual 2.50 (ISBN 0-201-05742-5). A-W.

Paulsen, F. R. Plant Mutations & Radiations: Genetics for the Layman. 1960. 5.00 (ISBN 0-911268-25-1). Rogers Bk.

Pedder, I. J. & Wynne, E. G. Genetics: A Basic Guide. 183p. 1974. pap. text ed. 5.95x (ISBN 0-393-09267-4). Norton.

Pieraut-Le Bonniec, Gilberte. Le Raisonnement Modal: Etude Genetique. (Connaissance et Language Ser.: No. 2). 288p. (Fr.). 1975. pap. text ed. 39.00x (ISBN 90-2797-516-7). Mouton.

Pollak, Edward, et al, eds. Proceedings of the International Conference on Quantitative Genetics. 1977. text ed. 19.95x (ISBN 0-8138-1895-8). Iowa St U Pr.

Pontecorvo, G. Trends in Genetic Analysis. LC 58-8805. (Columbia Biological Ser.: No. 18). 1958. 19.00x (ISBN 0-231-02268-9). Columbia U Pr.

Ramot, Bracha, ed. Genetic Polymorphisms & Diseases in Man. 1974. 33.00 (ISBN 0-12-577140-1). Acad Pr.

Ravin, Arnold W. Evolution of Genetics. (Illus., Orig.). 1965. 29.50 (ISBN 0-12-583450-0); pap. 13.00 (ISBN 0-12-583456-X). Acad Pr.

Redei, George P. Genetics. 1982. text ed. 23.95 (ISBN 0-02-398850-9). Macmillan.

Rees, Hubert & Jones, Robert N. Chromosome Genetics. LC 77-16211. (Genetics - Principles & Perspectives). 1978. pap. 14.95 (ISBN 0-8391-1195-9). Univ Park.

Riccardi, Vincent M. The Genetic Approach to Human Disease. (Illus.). 1977. text ed. 16.95x (ISBN 0-19-502175-4); pap. text ed. 9.95x (ISBN 0-19-502176-2). Oxford U Pr.

Robinson, Roy. Lepidoptera Genetics. 1971. 64.00 (ISBN 0-08-006659-3). Pergamon.

Roman, Herschel L., et al, eds. Annual Review of Genetics, Vol. 6. LC 67-29891. (Illus.). 1972. text ed. 17.00 (ISBN 0-8243-1206-6). Annual Reviews.

--Annual Review of Genetics, Vol. 7. LC 67-29891. (Illus.). 1973. text ed. 17.00 (ISBN 0-8243-1207-4). Annual Reviews.

--Annual Review of Genetics, Vol. 9. LC 67-29891. (Illus.). 1975. text ed. 17.00 (ISBN 0-8243-1209-0). Annual Reviews.

--Annual Review of Genetics, Vol. 10. LC 67-29891. (Illus.). 1976. text ed. 17.00 (ISBN 0-8243-1210-4). Annual Reviews.

--Annual Review of Genetics, Vol. 11. LC 67-29891. (Illus.). 1977. text ed. 17.00 (ISBN 0-8243-1211-2). Annual Reviews.

--Annual Review of Genetics, Vol. 12. LC 67-29891. (Illus.). 1978. text ed. 17.00 (ISBN 0-8243-1212-0). Annual Reviews.

--Annual Review of Genetics, Vol. 13. LC 67-29891. (Illus.). 1979. text ed. 17.00 (ISBN 0-8243-1213-9). Annual Reviews.
--Annual Review of Genetics, Vol. 14. LC 67-29891. (Illus.). 1980. text ed. 20.00 (ISBN 0-8243-1214-7). Annual Reviews.
--Annual Review of Genetics, Vol. 15. LC 67-29891. (Illus.). 500p. text ed. 20.00 (ISBN 0-8243-1215-5). Annual Reviews.
--Annual Review of Genetics, Vol. 8. LC 67-29891. (Illus.). 1974. text ed. 17.00 (ISBN 0-8243-1208-2). Annual Reviews.
Rothwell, Norman V. Understanding Genetics. 2nd ed. (Illus.). text ed. 21.95x (ISBN 0-19-502440-0). Oxford U Pr.
Rubenstein, et al, eds. Molecular Genetic Modification of Eucaryotes. 1977. 18.00 (ISBN 0-12-601150-8). Acad Pr.
Sadick, Tamah L. & Pueschal, Siegfried M., eds. Genetic Diseases & Developmental Disabilities: Aspects of Detection & Prevention. (AAAS Selected Symposium: No. 33). 1979. lib. bdg. 16.00x (ISBN 0-89158-367-X). Westview.
Sager, Ruth. Cytoplasmic Genes & Organelles. 1972. 29.50 (ISBN 0-12-614650-0). Acad Pr.
Samal, Babrubahan. Transcription of the Eukaryotic Genome, Vol. 2. Horrobin, D. F., ed. LC 80-482436. (Annual Research Reviews Ser.). 237p. 1980. 30.00 (ISBN 0-88831-071-4). Eden Med Res.
Scandalios, John G., ed. Physiological Genetics. (Physiological Ecology Ser.). 1979. 27.00 (ISBN 0-12-620980-4). Acad Pr.
Schroer, Michael M. Englisches Handwoertbuch in Genetischer Darstellung, 3 vols. LC 37-1148. 1937-70. Set. 90.00x (ISBN 3-533-02446-6). Intl Pubns Serv.
Schulman, Joseph D. & Simpson, Joe L., eds. Genetic Diseases in Pregnancy: Maternal Effects & Fetal Outcome. 1981. 49.00 (ISBN 0-12-630940-X). Acad Pr.
Schultz, J. & Whelan, W. J., eds. Genetic Manipulation As It Affects the Cancer Problem. 1977. 26.00 (ISBN 0-12-632755-6). Acad Pr.
Scott, Walter A., et al, eds. Mobilization & Reassembly of Genetic Information: Vol. 17 of the Miami Winter Symposia. LC 80-18845. 1980. 35.00 (ISBN 0-12-633360-2). Acad Pr.
Searle, Anthony G. Comparative Genetics of Coat Colour in Mammals. 1968. 46.50 (ISBN 0-12-633450-1). Acad Pr.
Sercarz, Eli, ed. Regulatory Genetics of the Immune System. 1977. 43.50 (ISBN 0-12-637160-1). Acad Pr.
Serra, J. A., ed. Modern Genetics, 3 vols. 1965-68. Vol. 1. 72.00 (ISBN 0-12-637201-2); Vol. 2. 81.00 (ISBN 0-12-637202-0); Vol. 3. 98.00 (ISBN 0-12-637203-9). Acad Pr.
Setlow, Jane K. & Hollaender, Alexander, eds. Genetic Engineering: Principles & Methods, Vol. 1. 277p. 1979. 29.50 (ISBN 0-306-40154-1, Plenum Pr). Plenum Pub.
Sheppard, P. M., ed. Practical Genetics. LC 73-9709. 337p. 1973. text ed. 49.95 (ISBN 0-470-78360-5). Halsted Pr.
Shine, Ian B. & Wrobel, Sylvia. Thomas Hunt Morgan: Pioneer of Genetics. LC 76-9519. (Kentucky Bicentennial Bookshelf Ser.). (Illus.). 176p. 1976. 6.95 (ISBN 0-8131-0219-7). U Pr of Ky.
--Thomas Hunt Morgan: Pioneer of Genetics. LC 76-40551. (Illus.). 188p. 1976. 9.50 (ISBN 0-8131-0095-X). U Pr of Ky.
Silvers, W. K. The Coat Color of Mice: A Model for Mammalian Gene Action & Interaction. (Illus.). 1979. 31.30 (ISBN 0-387-90367-4). Springer-Verlag.
Silverstein, Alvin & Silverstein, Virginia B. The Genetics Explosion. LC 79-22651. (Illus.). 160p. (gr. 7 up). 1980. 8.95 (ISBN 0-590-07517-9, Four Winds). Schol Bk Serv.
Simon, Edward H. & Grossfield, Joseph. The Challenge of Genetics: Problems Designed to Enlighten & Challenge Students of Genetics. LC 77-133895. (Biology Ser). 1971. pap. 5.95 (ISBN 0-201-07008-1). A-W.
Smith, Harold. Evolution of Genetic Systems: Brookhaven Symposium in Biology, No. 23. LC 74-181433. 600p. 1972. 70.00x (ISBN 0-677-12230-6). Gordon.
Smith, Michael H. & Joule, James, eds. Mammalian Population Genetics. LC 80-24667. 1981. 25.00 (ISBN 0-8203-0547-2). U of Ga Pr.
Sokatch, John R. Basic Bacteriology & Genetics. (Illus.). 1976. pap. 14.95 (ISBN 0-8151-8051-9). Year Bk Med.
Sokoloff, A. The Biology of Tribolium with Special Emphasis on Genetic Effects, Vol. 1. (Illus.). 1972. 52.50x (ISBN 0-19-857353-7). Oxford U Pr.
Sorsby, A. Clinical Genetics. 2nd ed. 1973. 77.95 (ISBN 0-407-13651-7). Butterworth.
Srb, Adrian M., ed. Genes, Enzymes, & Populations. LC 73-15867. (Basic Life Sciences Ser.: Vol. 2). (Illus.). 359p. 1973. 37.50 (ISBN 0-306-36502-2, Plenum Pr). Plenum Pub.
Srivastava, Probodh K. Basic Genetics for Health Professionals. LC 78-13310. (Illus.). 210p. 1979. 18.00 (ISBN 0-88416-233-8). Wright-PSG.
Stahl, Franklin W. Genetic Recombination: Thinking About It in Phage & Fungi. LC 79-13378. (Biology Ser.). (Illus.). 1979. text ed. 28.95x (ISBN 0-7167-1037-4). W H Freeman.
--Mechanics of Inheritance. 2nd ed. Suskind, Sigmund & Hartman, Philip, eds. LC 69-19870. (Foundations of Modern Genetics Ser). 1969. pap. 10.95 ref. ed. (ISBN 0-13-571042-1). P-H.
Stansfield, William D. Genetics. (Schaum Outline Ser). 1969. pap. 5.95 (ISBN 0-07-060842-3, SP). McGraw.
Stebbins, G. Ledyard. Basis of Progressive Evolution. LC 69-16216. (Orig.). 1969. pap. 5.50x (ISBN 0-8078-4038-6). U of NC Pr.
Stern, Curt & Sherwood, Eva R., eds. The Origin of Genetics: A Mendel Source Book. LC 66-27948. (Illus.). 1966. pap. text ed. 8.95x (ISBN 0-7167-0655-5). W H Freeman.
Stine, Gerald J. Biosocial Genetics: Human Heredity & Social Issues. (Illus.). 1977. 19.95 (ISBN 0-02-416490-9). Macmillan.
Straub, W., ed. Current Genetic, Clinical & Morphological Problems. (Developments in Ophthalmology: Vol. 3). (Illus.). vi, 218p. 1981. pap. 94.00 (ISBN 3-8055-2000-X). S Karger.
Strickberger, Monroe W. Genetics. 2nd ed. (Illus.). 880p. 1976. text ed. 22.95 (ISBN 0-02-418090-4). Macmillan.
Sturtevant, Alfred H. & Beadle, George W. Introduction to Genetics. (Illus.). 1939. pap. 4.50 (ISBN 0-486-60306-7). Dover.
Subtelny, Stephen & Abbott, Ursula K., eds. Levels of Genetic Control in Development. LC 81-1952. (Symposiums of the Society for Developmental Biology: 39th). 272p. 1981. 32.00 (ISBN 0-8451-1500-6). A R Liss.
Suzuki, David T. & Griffiths, A. J. An Introduction to Genetic Analysis. LC 75-29480. (Illus.). 1976. 20.95x (ISBN 0-7167-0574-5); answers to problems 0.75 (ISBN 0-7167-0362-9). W H Freeman.
Suzuki, David T. & Griffiths, Anthony J. F. Introduction to Genetic Analysis. 2nd ed. LC 80-24522. (Illus.). 1981. text ed. 22.95x (ISBN 0-7167-1263-6); instrs.' guide avail.; solutions manual avail. W H Freeman.
Symposium in Honor of the Jackson Laboratory's Fiftieth Anniversary, Bar Harbor, Maine, July 1979. Mammalian Genetics & Cancer: Proceedings. Russell, Elizabeth S., ed. LC 80-27531. 1981. 42.00x (ISBN 0-8451-0045-9). A R Liss.
Szekely, Maria. From DNA to Protein: The Transfer of Genetic Information. LC 79-11894. 284p. 1981. pap. 18.95 (ISBN 0-470-27155-8). Halsted Pr.
--From DNA to Protein: The Transfer of Genetic Information. LC 79-11894. 1980. 39.95x (ISBN 0-470-26687-2). Halsted Pr.
--Gene Structure & Organization. 1981. pap. 6.50x (ISBN 0-412-22840-8, Pub. by Chapman & Hall). Methuen Inc.
Tamarin. Principles of Genetics. 608p. 1981. text ed. 21.95 (ISBN 0-87872-281-5). Duxbury Pr.
Tamarin, Robert. Principles of Genetics. 726p. 1981. text ed. write for info (ISBN 0-87150-756-0, 40N 4411). Grant Pr.
Temtamy, Samia & McKusick, Victor, eds. Genetics of Hand Malformations. (Alan R. Liss Inc. Ser.: Vol. 14, No. 3). 1978. 90.00 (ISBN 0-686-26119-4). March of Dimes.
Thompson, James N. & Thoday, J. M., eds. Quantitative Genetic Variation. LC 79-9917. 1979. 26.00 (ISBN 0-12-688850-7). Acad Pr.
Thompson, James S. & Thompson, Margaret W. Genetics in Medicine. 3rd ed. LC 78-64726. (Illus.). 396p. 1980. text ed. 16.00 (ISBN 0-7216-8857-8). Saunders.
Timmis, K. N. & Puhler, A., eds. Plasmids of Medical Environmental & Commercial Importance. (Developments in Genetics Ser.: Vol. 1). 494p. 1979. 63.50 (ISBN 0-444-80161-8, North Holland). Elsevier.
Tobach, Ethel & Proshansky, Harold M., eds. Genetic Destiny: Scientific Controversy & Social Conflict. LC 76-5964. (AMS Studies in Modern Society). 21.50 (ISBN 0-404-10130-5). AMS Pr.
Tobach, Ethel & Rosoff, Betty, eds. Genetic Determinism & Children. (Genes & Gender Ser.: No. 3). 176p. (Orig.). 1980. pap. text ed. 7.95 (ISBN 0-87752-221-9). Gordian.
Toeplitz, Otto. The Calculus: A Genetic Approach. Kothe, Gottfried, ed. Lange, Louise, tr. LC 63-9731. 206p. Date not set. pap. price not set (ISBN 0-226-80667-7). U of Chicago Pr.
Truman, D. E. The Biochemistry of Cytodifferentiation. LC 73-21785. 122p. 1974. text ed. 15.95 (ISBN 0-470-89190-4). Halsted Pr.
Tsafrir, J. Soussi. Light-Eyed Negroes & the Klein-Waardenburg Syndrome. (Illus.). 150p. 1974. text ed. 27.50x (ISBN 0-333-14072-9). Verry.
Van Brink, J. M. & Vorontsov, N. N., eds. Animal Genetics & Evolution: Selected Papers. (Illus.). 393p. 1980. lib. bdg. 99.00 (ISBN 90-6193-602-0, Pub. by Junk Pubs Netherlands). Kluwer Boston.
Van der Awevera, Johan, ed. The Semantics of Determiners. 309p. text ed. 34.50 (ISBN 0-8391-4138-6). Univ Park.
Van Peenen, Hubert J. Biochemical Genetics. (Illus.). 352p. 1966. photocopy ed. spiral 34.50 (ISBN 0-398-01971-1). C C Thomas.
Voeller, Bruce R., ed. The Chromosome Theory of Inheritance. LC 68-19963. 229p. 1968. pap. 12.50 (ISBN 0-306-50080-9, Plenum Pr). Plenum Pub.
Von Blum, Ruth C., et al. Mendelian Genetics: A Problem-Solving Approach. (gr. 11-12). 1979. pap. text ed. 6.95x (ISBN 0-933694-00-8). COMPress.
Von Der Pahle, Alejo. Genetica. 1979. text ed. 6.00 (ISBN 0-06-319200-4, IntlDept). Har-Row.
Waddington, Conrad H. Principles of Development & Differentiation. (Illus., Orig.). 1966. pap. text ed. 5.95x (ISBN 0-02-423630-6). Macmillan.
Wagner, R. P. Genetics & Metabolism. 2nd ed. 673p. 1964. 18.52 (ISBN 0-471-91412-6, Pub. by Wiley). Krieger.
Wagner, Robert P., ed. Genes & Proteins. LC 75-8851. (Benchmark Papers in Genetics Ser: Vol. 2). 395p. 1975. 47.00 (ISBN 0-12-787710-X). Acad Pr.
Walcher, Dwain N., et al, eds. Mutations: Biology & Society. Barnett, Henry L. & Kretchmer, Norman. LC 78-63411. (Illus.). 432p. 1978. 31.50x (ISBN 0-89352-020-9). Masson Pub.
Wallace, Bruce. Chromosomes, Giant Molecules, & Evolution. (Illus.). 1966. 5.00x (ISBN 0-393-06343-7); pap. 3.95x (ISBN 0-393-09677-7, NortonC). Norton.
Wallace, Bruce & Srb, Adrian M. Adaption. LC 77-18812. (Foundations of Modern Biology Ser.). 1978. Repr. of 1964 ed. lib. bdg. 15.50x (ISBN 0-313-20212-5, WAAD). Greenwood.
Wallace, Robert A. The Genesis Factor. LC 79-65876. 1979. 9.95 (ISBN 0-688-03536-1). Morrow.
Watson, Jack E. Introductory Genetics: A Laboratory Textbook. 2nd ed. 1976. pap. text ed. 8.95 (ISBN 0-8403-0838-8). Kendall-Hunt.
Watson, James D. & Tooze, John. The DNA Story: A Documentary History of Gene Cloning. LC 81-3299. (Illus.). 1981. text ed. 17.95x (ISBN 0-7167-1292-X). W H Freeman.
Went, L. N., et al. Early Diagnosis & Prevention of Genetic Diseases. 1975. lib. bdg. 29.50 (ISBN 90-6021-237-1, Pub. by Leiden Univ. Holland). Kluwer Boston.
Westerveld, A. & Marin, G. Mammalian Cell Hybridization I. (Illus.). 220p. 1973. text ed. 25.50x (ISBN 0-8422-7096-5). Irvington.
Whitehouse, H. L. Towards an Understanding of the Mechanism of Heredity. 3rd ed. LC 73-82629. 513p. 1973. text ed. 21.50 (ISBN 0-312-81130-6); pap. 10.95 (ISBN 0-312-81095-4). St Martin.
Winchester, A. M. Genetics: A Survey of the Principles of Heredity. 5th ed. LC 76-14001. (Illus.). 1977. text ed. 18.95 (ISBN 0-395-24557-5); inst. manual & solutions 1.75 (ISBN 0-395-24559-1); twenty transparencies 7.75 (ISBN 0-395-24560-5). HM.
--Human Genetics. 3rd ed. 1979. pap. text ed. 8.95 (ISBN 0-675-08314-1). Merrill.
Woods, R. A. Biochemical Genetics. 2nd ed. LC 79-41695. (Outline Studies in Biology). 80p. 1980. pap. 5.95 (ISBN 0-412-22400-3, 6340, Pub. by Chapman & Hall England). Methuen Inc.
Wourms, John P., et al. Genetic Studies of Fish, Vol. 2. LC 74-516. 179p. 1974. text ed. 22.50x (ISBN 0-8422-7207-0). Irvington.
Wright, J. & Pal, R. Genetics of Insect Vectors of Disease. 1968. 97.75 (ISBN 0-444-40654-9). Elsevier.
Wright, James E., et al. Genetic Studies of Fish, Vol. 1. Ridgway, George J. & Morrison, William J., eds. LC 74-516. 172p. 1974. text ed. 22.50x (ISBN 0-8422-7177-5). Irvington.
Wright, Sewall. Evolution & the Genetics of Populations, 4 vols. Incl. Vol. I. Genetic & Biometric Foundations. 1968. 28.00x (ISBN 0-226-91049-0); Vol. II. Theorie of Gene Frequencies. 1969. 31.00x (ISBN 0-226-91050-4); Vol. 3. Experimental Results & Evolutionary Deductions. 1977. 37.50x (ISBN 0-226-91051-2); Vol. 4. Variability Within & Among Natural Populations. 1978. 37.50x (ISBN 0-226-91052-0). LC 67-25533. U of Chicago Pr.

GENETICS–DICTIONARIES

Biass-Ducroux, Francoise. Glossary of Genetics. 1970. 58.75 (ISBN 0-444-40712-X). Elsevier.
Rieger, R., et al. Glossary & Genetics & Cytogenetics. 4th rev. ed. LC 76-16183. (Illus.). 1976. soft cover 14.80 (ISBN 3-540-07668-9). Springer-Verlag.

GENETICS–LABORATORY MANUALS

Gardner, Elton J. & Mertens, Thomas R. Genetics Laboratory Investigations. 7th ed. 1980. 9.95x (ISBN 0-8087-0786-8). Burgess.
St. Lawrence, Patricia, et al. The Experimental Geneticist: An Introductory Laboratory Manual. (Illus.). 1974. pap. 7.95x (ISBN 0-7167-0588-5); lab separates 0.60 ea. (ISBN 0-685-39560-X); instr's guide avail. W H Freeman.
Stine, Gerald J. Laboratory Experiments in Genetics. (Illus.). 256p. 1973. pap. text ed. 9.95 (ISBN 0-02-417520-X). Macmillan.
Strickberger, M. W. Experiments in Genetics with Drosophila. LC 62-16158. 144p. 1962. pap. 14.95x (ISBN 0-471-83373-8). Wiley.
Winchester, A. M. Laboratory Manual: Genetics. 3rd ed. 145p. 1979. write for info. wire coil (ISBN 0-697-04677-X). Wm C Brown.

GENETICS–MATHEMATICAL MODELS

Ballonoff, Paul A., ed. Genetics & Social Structure: Mathematical Structuralism in Population Genetics & Social Theory. LC 73-20412. (Benchmark Papers in Genetics Ser). 520p. 1974. 40.50 (ISBN 0-12-786125-4). Acad Pr.
English, Darrel S., et al. Genetic & Reproductive Engineering. LC 73-22048. 1974. 29.75x (ISBN 0-8422-5157-X); pap. text ed. 9.50x (ISBN 0-8422-0383-4). Irvington.

GENETICS–PROGRAMMED INSTRUCTION

Baldwin, Roger E. Genetics. LC 73-5765. (Wiley Self-Teaching Guides). 296p. 1973. pap. text ed. 6.95 (ISBN 0-471-04588-8). Wiley.
Duran, John C. Exercises in Genetics. (EMI Programed Biology Ser). (Orig.). (gr. 9-12). 1969. pap. 2.50x (ISBN 0-88462-022-0, 304-22). Ed Methods.
Tribe, Michael A., et al. Case Studies in Genetics. LC 77-75778. (Basic Biology Course Ser.: Bk. 12). (Illus.). 1977. 29.95 (ISBN 0-521-21373-8); pap. 11.95x (ISBN 0-521-21372-X). Cambridge U Pr.

GENEVA

Bozeman, Adda B. Regional Conflicts Around Geneva. LC 49-10185. (Augustana College Library Ser.: No. 20). 1949. 7.00 (ISBN 0-910182-15-9). Augustana Coll.
Monter, E. William. Calvin's Geneva. LC 74-30258. (New Dimensions in History Historical Cities Ser). 266p. 1975. Repr. of 1967 ed. 10.50 (ISBN 0-88275-227-8). Krieger.

GENEVA, LAKE

Gribble, Francis. Lake Geneva & Its Literary Landmarks. 1978. Repr. of 1901 ed. lib. bdg. 25.00 (ISBN 0-8495-1918-7). Arden Lib.
--Lake Geneva & Its Literary Landmarks. 1901. Repr. 30.00 (ISBN 0-8274-2793-X). R West.

GENEVA AWARD

see Alabama Claims

GENGHIS KHAN

see Jenghis Khan, 1162-1227

GENITO-URINARY ORGANS

see also Generative Organs

Beller, F. K. & Schumacher, G. F. B., eds. The Biology of the Fluids of the Femal Genital Tract. 464p. 1979. 45.00 (ISBN 0-444-00362-2, North Holland). Elsevier.
Bergsma, Daniel, ed. Morphogenesis & Malformation of the Genital System, Vol. 13, No. 2. LC 77-535. (Alan R. Liss, Inc. Ser.). 1977. 18.00 (ISBN 0-686-20483-2). March of Dimes.
Bulmer, David. Functional Anatomy of the Urogenital System. (Illus.). 184p. 1974. pap. text ed. 16.95x (ISBN 0-8464-0444-3). Beekman Pubs.
--The Functional Anatomy of the Urogenital System. 1974. pap. text ed. 11.00x (ISBN 0-272-00124-4). State Mutual Bk.
Johannessen, Jans V. Electron Microscopy in Human Medicine: Vol. 9, Urogenital System & Breast. (Illus.). 396p. 1980. text ed. 74.00 (ISBN 0-07-032508-1, HP). McGraw.
Johnson, Thomas H. Genitourinary Radiology Case Studies. 1980. pap. 16.75 (ISBN 0-87488-090-4). Med Exam.
Rosenfield, Arthur T., ed. Genitourinary Ultrasonography. (Clinics in Diagnostic Ultrasound Ser.: Vol. 2). (Illus.). 1979. text ed. 20.50 (ISBN 0-443-08043-7). Churchill.
Strage, Mark. The Durable Fig Leaf: A Historical, Cultural, Medical, Social, Literary, & Iconographic Account of Man's Relations with His Penis. 1979. 14.95 (ISBN 0-688-03582-5); pap. 7.95 (ISBN 0-688-08582-2, Quill). Morrow.

GENITO-URINARY ORGANS–DISEASES

see also Gynecology; Urinary Organs–Diseases; Urine–Analysis and Pathology

Blaustein, A., ed. Pathology of the Female Genital Tract. 1976. 61.70 (ISBN 0-387-90180-9). Springer-Verlag.

Crawford, E. David & Borden, Thomas A. Genitourinary Cancer Surgery. (Illus.). 750p. Date not set. price not set (ISBN 0-8121-0812-4). Lea & Febiger.
Harrison, J. Hartwell, et al, eds. Campbells Urology. 4th ed. LC 75-44604. (Illus.). 1978. Vol. I. 55.00 (ISBN 0-7216-4540-2). Saunders.
Howe, Joseph W. Excessive Venery, Masturbation & Continence. LC 73-20629. (Sex, Marriage & Society Ser.). 298p. 1974. Repr. 17.00x (ISBN 0-405-05805-5). Arno.
Javadpour, Nasser. Recent Advances in Urologic Cancer. (International Perspective of Urology Ser.). (Illus.). 238p. 1981. lib. bdg. 25.00 (ISBN 0-683-04357-9). Williams & Wilkins.
Johnson, Douglas E. & Samuels, Melvin L., eds. Cancer of the Genitourinary Tract. LC 79-2070. 338p. 1979. text ed. 34.50 (ISBN 0-89004-383-3). Raven.
Murphy, Gerald P. & Mittelman, Arnold. Chemotherapy of Urogenital Tumors. (Illus.). 288p. 1975. 32.75 (ISBN 0-398-03319-6). C C Thomas.
Olsson, O. Roentgen Diagnosis of the Urogenital System. LC 73-14486. (Encyclopedia of Medical Radiology Ser., Vol. 13, Pt. 1). (Illus.). 690p. 1974. 221.30 (ISBN 0-387-06514-8). Springer-Verlag.
Pavone-Macaluso, M., et al, eds. Bladder Tumors & Other Topics in Urological Oncology. LC 79-20614. (Ettore Majorana International Science Ser., Life Sciences: Vol. I). 544p. 1980. 59.50 (ISBN 0-306-40308-0, Plenum Pr). Plenum Pub.
Westenfelder, M., ed. Malformations of the External Genitalia. (Monographs in Paediatrics: Vol. 12). (Illus.). xiii, 112p. 1981. pap. 38.50 (ISBN 3-8055-1509-X). S Karger.

GENITO-URINARY ORGANS–SURGERY

American Association of Genito-Urinary Surgeons, Vol. 71. 1980. pap. 33.00 (ISBN 0-683-00110-8). Williams & Wilkins.
Crawford, E. David & Borden, Thomas A. Genitourinary Cancer Surgery. (Illus.). 750p. Date not set. price not set (ISBN 0-8121-0812-4). Lea & Febiger.
Flocks, R. H. & Culp, David A. Surgical Urology: A Handbook of Operative Surgery. 4th ed. (Illus.). 575p. 1974. 38.95 (ISBN 0-8151-3262-X). Year Bk Med.
Kasirsky, Gilbert. Vasectomy, Manhood & Sex. LC 76-189307. (Illus.). 128p. 1972. text ed. 8.50 (ISBN 0-8261-1390-7). Springer Pub.
Libertino & Zinman. Pediatric & Adult Reconstructive Urologic Surgery. 1977. 46.00 (ISBN 0-683-04978-X). Williams & Wilkins.
McDougal, W. Scott. Traumatic Injuries of the Genitourinary System. (Illus.). 148p. 1980. 26.95 (ISBN 0-683-05768-5, 5768-5). Williams & Wilkins.
Mayor, Georges & Zingg, Ernst J. Urologic Surgery: Diagnois, Techniques Postoperative Treatment. 1976. 152.50 (ISBN 0-471-01408-7, Pub. by Wiley Medical). Wiley.
Smith, Robert B. & Skinner, Donald G., eds. Complications of Urologic Surgery: Prevention & Management. LC 75-25276. (Illus.). 1976. text ed. 40.00 (ISBN 0-7216-8418-1). Saunders.
Van De Velde, T. A. Ideal Marriage: Its Physiology & Technique. 400p. 1975. pap. 2.25 (ISBN 0-345-25841-X). Ballantine.
Williams, D. I. Urology. (Operative Surgery Ser.). 1977. 119.00 (ISBN 0-407-00612-5). Butterworth.

GENIUS

see also Creation (Literary, Artistic, etc.); Creative Ability; Gifted Children

Barlow, Fred. Mental Prodigies. LC 70-88982. Repr. of 1951 ed. lib. bdg. 15.75x (ISBN 0-8371-2092-6, BAMP). Greenwood.
Becker, George. The Mad Genius Controversy: A Study in the Sociology of Deviance. LC 78-875. (Sociological Observations: Vol. 5). 162p. 1978. pap. write for info. (ISBN 0-8039-0985-3); pap. price not set (ISBN 0-8039-0986-1). Sage.
Clarke, Edwin L. American Men of Letters: Their Nature & Nurture. LC 76-76714. (Columbia University Studies in the Social Sciences: No. 168). Repr. of 1916 ed. 8.50 (ISBN 0-404-51168-6). AMS Pr.
Cox, Catharine M. The Early Mental Traits of Three Hundred Geniuses. (Genetic Studies of Genius Ser). 1926. 32.50x (ISBN 0-8047-0010-9). Stanford U Pr.
Duff, William. Critical Observations on the Writings of the Most Celebrated Original Geniuses in Poetry (1770) LC 73-9526. 400p. 1973. Repr. lib. bdg. 39.00x (ISBN 0-8201-1119-8). Schol Facsimiles.
Eissler, K. R. Talent & Genius: The Fictitious Case of Tausk Contra Freud. LC 70-162813. 388p. 1971. 12.95 (ISBN 0-8129-0222-X). Times Bks.
Ellis, Havelock. A Study of British Genius. 1978. Repr. of 1926 ed. lib. bdg. 30.00 (ISBN 0-8495-1319-7). Arden Lib.
Galton, Francis. Hereditary Genius: An Inquiry into Its Laws & Consequences. 10.00 (ISBN 0-8446-2108-0). Peter Smith.
Gemant, Andrew. The Nature of the Genius. 216p. 1961. ed. spiral bdg. 18.75photocopy (ISBN 0-398-02546-0). C C Thomas.
Giles, Henry. Illustrations of Genius (Cervantes, Wordsworth, Burns, De Quincey) 1854. Repr. 35.00 (ISBN 0-8274-2555-4). R West.
--Illustrations of Genius, in Some of Its Relations to Culture & Society. 1979. Repr. of 1854 ed. lib. bdg. 35.00 (ISBN 0-8414-4599-0). Folcroft.
Ginzberg, Eli. Talent & Performance. LC 64-7534. 265p. 1964. 17.50x (ISBN 0-231-02766-4). Columbia U Pr.
Grosswirth, M. & Salny, A. The Mensa Genius Book. 1981. pap. 5.95 (ISBN 0-201-05959-2). A-W.
Hayware, Frank H. Professionalism & Originality. LC 73-14156. (Perspectives in Social Inquiry Ser.). 278p. 1974. Repr. 15.00x (ISBN 0-405-05502-1). Arno.
Hock, Alfred. Reason & Genius: Studies in Their Origin. LC 70-138150. 1971. Repr. of 1960 ed. lib. bdg. 15.00 (ISBN 0-8371-5607-6, HORG). Greenwood.
Jacobson, Arthur C. Genius: Some Revaluations. LC 76-105797. 1970. Repr. of 1926 ed. 12.00 (ISBN 0-8046-1358-3). Kennikat.
Kenmare, Dallas. The Nature of Genius. LC 76-158740. (Illus.). 180p. 1972. Repr. of 1960 ed. lib. bdg. 15.00x (ISBN 0-8371-6179-7, KENG). Greenwood.
--The Nature of Genius. 1960. 22.50 (ISBN 0-8274-3876-1). R West.
Kingsmill, Hugh, pseud. The English Genius. LC 73-105799. Repr. of 1939 ed. 13.50 (ISBN 0-8046-1359-1). Kennikat.
Larned, Josephus N. Study of Greatness in Men. facsimile ed. LC 73-156677. (Essay Index Reprint Ser). Repr. of 1911 ed. 18.00 (ISBN 0-8369-2557-2). Arno.
Marks, Jeanette. Genius & Disaster: Studies in Drugs & Genius. LC 68-26299. 1968. Repr. of 1926 ed. 12.00 (ISBN 0-8046-0301-4). Kennikat.
Nisbett, J. F. The Insanity of Genius. LC 72-8931. 1972. Repr. of 1900 ed. lib. bdg. 30.00 (ISBN 0-8414-0433-X). Folcroft.
Nitzsche, Jane C. The Genius Figure in Antiquity & the Middle Ages. LC 74-17206. 201p. 1975. 15.00x (ISBN 0-231-03852-6). Columbia U Pr.
Rothenberg, Albert & Hausman, Carl R. The Creativity Question. LC 75-30132. 1976. 16.75 (ISBN 0-8223-0353-1); pap. 9.75 (ISBN 0-8223-0354-X). Duke.
Sharpe, William. A Dissertation Upon Genius. LC 72-13112. (Hist. of Psych. Ser.). 168p. 1973. Repr. of 1755 ed. lib. bdg. 22.00x (ISBN 0-8201-1110-4). Schol Facsimiles.
Stern, Aaron. The Joy of Learning. LC 76-15510. (Illus.). 320p. 1977. 14.50 (ISBN 0-916560-01-5). Renaissance Pubs.
--The Making of a Genius. LC 70-181866. 171p. 1971. 11.95 (ISBN 0-916560-02-3). Renaissance Pubs.
Terman, Lewis M. Genius & Stupidity: A Study. LC 74-21430. (Classics in Child Development Ser). 70p. 1975. 9.00x (ISBN 0-405-06479-9). Arno.
Terman, Lewis M. & Oden, Melita H. The Gifted Child Grows up: Twenty-Five Years' Follow-up of a Superior Group. (Genetic Studies of Genius Ser.). 1947. 20.00x (ISBN 0-8047-0012-5). Stanford U Pr.
Terman, Lewis M., et al. Mental & Physical Traits of a Thousand Gifted Children. rev. ed. (Genetic Studies of Genius Ser). 1926. 29.50x (ISBN 0-8047-0009-5). Stanford U Pr.
Villard, Sebastian C. The Forces Which Contribute to Make Man a Genius & a Hero of Mankind. (Illus.). 157p. 1981. 59.65 (ISBN 0-89266-320-0). Am Classical Coll Pr.

GENIUS AND INSANITY

see Genius

GENIZAH

Ginzberg, L. & Davidson, I. Genizah Studies in Memory of Solomon Schechter, 3 vols. Incl. Vol. 1. Midrash & Haggadah. Ginzberg, L. 1969. Repr. of 1928 ed. 10.00 (ISBN 0-87203-015-6); Vol. 2. Geonic & Early Karaitic Halakah. Ginzberg, L. Repr. of 1929 ed. 11.50 (ISBN 0-87203-016-4); Vol. 3. Liturgical & Secular Poetry. Davidson, I. Repr. of 1928 ed. 7.50 (ISBN 0-87203-017-2). LC 73-76172. Set. 25.00 (ISBN 0-87203-093-8). Hermon.
Gottheil, Richard J., ed. Fragments from the Cairo Genizah in the Freer Collection. Repr. of 1927 ed. 31.00 (ISBN 0-384-38813-2). Johnson Repr.

GENOA

Byrne, E. H. Genoese Shipping in the Twelfth & Thirteenth Centuries. 1930. 18.00 (ISBN 0-527-01682-9). Kraus Repr.
Kedar, Benjamin Z. Merchants in Crisis: Genoese & Venetian Men of Affairs & the Fourteen-Century Depression. LC 75-43320. (Economic History Ser.). 1976. 22.50x (ISBN 0-300-01941-6). Yale U Pr.
Metcalf, Paul. Genoa: A Telling of Wonders. 1965. 10.00 (ISBN 0-912330-01-5, Dist. by Gnomon Pr); pap. 5.00 (ISBN 0-912330-17-1). Jargon Soc.
Miluck, Michael & Miluck, Nancy, eds. The Genoa-Carson Valley Book, 1981-82, Vol. III, 1981-1982 Issue. rev. ed. (Illus.). 96p. 1981. pap. 3.00 (ISBN 0-9606382-1-0). Dragon Ent.
Rubens, Peter P. Palazzi Di Genova, 2 vols in 1. LC 68-21226. (Illus.). 1968. Repr. of 1622 ed. 60.00 (ISBN 0-405-08901-5). Arno.

GENOCIDE

see also Holocaust, Jewish (1939-1945)

Baum, Rainer C. The Holocaust & the German Elite: Genocide & National Suicide, in Germany 1871 to 1945. 1981. 25.00x (ISBN 0-8476-6970-X). Rowman.
Chaim, B. Holocaust Now: Comparative Study of German, Russian, British, French, Chinese, Japanese, Italian, Cambodian, Vietnamese, Israeli, Arab, Cuban, Iranian, African & American Atrocities, 2 vols. (Illus.). 1980. Set. lib. bdg. 79.95 (ISBN 0-686-59684-6). Revisionist Pr.
Horowitz, Irving L. Taking Lives: Genocide & State Power. 3rd ed. LC 79-66341. 230p. 1981. pap. 9.95 (ISBN 0-87855-882-9). Transaction Bk.
Martin, James J. Raphael Lemkin & the Invention of Genocide. 1981. lib. bdg. 59.95 (ISBN 0-686-73485-8). Revisionist Pr.
Neilson, Francis. The Crime of Genocide: A Revisionist Viewpoint. (Revisionist Historiography Ser.). 1979. lib. bdg. 39.95 (ISBN 0-685-96616-X). Revisionist Pr.
Rassinier, Paul. Debunking the Genocide Myth. 441p. Date not set. 15.50 (ISBN 0-911038-24-8); pap. 8.00 (ISBN 0-911038-58-2). Inst Hist Rev.
--Debunking the Genocide Myth. LC 78-53090. 1978. 15.50 (ISBN 0-911038-24-8, Dist. by Inst Hist Rev); pap. 8.00 (ISBN 0-911038-58-2). Noontide.
Ternon, Yves. Armenians: History of a Genocide. LC 80-19499. 1981. write for info. (ISBN 0-88206-038-4). Caravan Bks.
Weisbord, Robert G. Genocide? Birth Control & the Black American. LC 75-13531. 219p. 1975. lib. bdg. 15.00 (ISBN 0-8371-8084-8, WBC). Greenwood.

GENRE (LITERATURE)

see Literary Form

GENRE PAINTING

see also Narrative Painting

Dutch Genre Painting. pap. text ed. 4.95 (ISBN 0-8277-7221-1). British Bk Ctr.
Hills, Patricia. The Genre Painting of Eastman Johnson: The Sources & Development of His Styles & Themes. LC 76-23627. (Outstanding Dissertations in the Fine Arts - American). (Illus.). 1977. Repr. of 1973 ed. lib. bdg. 48.00 (ISBN 0-8240-2697-7). Garland Pub.
R. W. Norton Art Gallery. Louisiana Landscape & Genre Paintings of the 19th Century. LC 81-50951. (Illus.). 48p. 1981. pap. 5.75x (ISBN 0-913060-19-4). Norton.
Schatborn, Peter & Van Hasselt, Carlos. Dutch Genre Drawings. LC 72-86013. (Illus.). 162p. (Orig.). 1972. pap. 7.50 (ISBN 0-686-70485-1). Intl Exhibit Foun.
Supka, Magdolna B. Genre Painting in the Hungarian National Gallery. (Illus.). 175p. 1974. 7.50x (ISBN 963-13-4360-X). Intl Pubns Serv.
Yamane, Yuzo. Momoyama Genre Painting. Shields, John, tr. from Japanese. LC 72-92099. (Heibonsha Survey of Japanese Art Ser). (Illus.). 176p. 1973. 17.50 (ISBN 0-8348-1012-3). Weatherhill.

GENTIANS

Bartlett, Mary. Gentians. (Illus.). 144p. 1981. text ed. 20.00 (ISBN 0-87663-363-7). Universe.
Wilkie. Gentians. LC 76-46559. (Illus.). 1977. Repr. of 1950 ed. 12.50 (ISBN 0-913728-19-5). Theophrastus.

GENTILE, GIOVANNI, 1875-1944

Brown, Merle E. Neo-Idealistic Aesthetics: Croce-Gentile-Collingwood. LC 65-20757. 1966. 12.95x (ISBN 0-8143-1274-8). Wayne St U Pr.
Holmes, Roger W. The Idealism of Giovanni Gentile. LC 78-63683. (Studies in Fascism: Ideology & Practice). Repr. of 1937 ed. 24.50 (ISBN 0-404-16948-1). AMS Pr.
Romanell, Patrick. Croce Versus Gentile: A Dialogue on Contemporary Italian Philosophy. LC 78-63709. (Studies in Fascism: Ideology & Practice). Repr. of 1947 ed. 12.50 (ISBN 0-404-16979-1). AMS Pr.
Smith, William A. Giovanni Gentile on the Existence of God. LC 70-111087. (Philosophical Questions Ser: No. 7). 1970. text ed. 10.00x (ISBN 0-391-00413-1). Humanities.
--Giovanni Gentile on the Existence of God. Matczak, S. A., ed. & intro. by. LC 70-111087. (Philosophical Questions Ser.: No. 7). 1970. 12.95 (ISBN 0-912116-04-8). Learned Pubns.

GENTOO LANGUAGE

see Telugu Language

GENTZ, FRIEDRICH VON, 1764-1832

Mann, Golo. Secretary of Europe: The Life of Friedrich Gentz, Enemy of Napoleon. 1970. Repr. of 1946 ed. 20.00 (ISBN 0-208-00957-4, Archon). Shoe String.
Reiff, Paul F. Friedrich Gentz, an Opponent of the French Revolution & Napoleon. Repr. of 1912 ed. 9.50 (ISBN 0-384-50210-5). Johnson Repr.
Sweet, Paul R. Friedrich Von Gentz, Defender of the Old Order. Repr. of 1941 ed. lib. bdg. 14.25x (ISBN 0-8371-2560-X, SWFG). Greenwood.

GEOBOTANY

see Phytogeography

GEOCHEMICAL PROSPECTING

Foldvari, Maria V. Theory & Practice of Regional Geochemical Exploration. 1978. 26.50 (ISBN 0-9960009-3-3, Pub. by Kaido Hungary). Heyden.
Siegel, Frederic R. Applied Geochemistry. LC 74-13486. 384p. 1974. 29.95 (ISBN 0-471-79095-8, Pub. by Wiley-Interscience). Wiley.
Sittig, Marshall, ed. Geophysical & Geochemical Techniques for Exploration of Hydrocarbons & Minerals. LC 79-24469. (Energy Technology Review Ser.: No. 52). (Illus.). 1980. 40.00 (ISBN 0-8155-0782-8). Noyes.
Tissot, B. Petroleum Formation & Occurrence: A New Approach to Oil & Gas Exploration. (Illus.). 1978. 39.50 (ISBN 0-387-08698-6). Springer-Verlag.

GEOCHEMISTRY

see also Chemical Oceanography; Geochemical Prospecting; Geothermal Resources; Mineralogical Chemistry; Mineralogy, Determinative; Rocks–Analysis

Abelson, Philip H., ed. Researches in Geochemistry, Vol. 2. 678p. 1967. 38.50 (ISBN 0-471-00167-8). Krieger.
Adler, Isidore. X-Ray Emission Spectrography in Geology. (Methods in Geochemistry & Geophysics: Vol. 4). 1966. 46.50 (ISBN 0-444-40004-4). Elsevier.
Ahrens, L. H. Origin & Distribution of the Elements. 1979. text ed. 115.00 (ISBN 0-08-022947-6). Pergamon.
Allegre, C. J. & Michard, G. Introduction to Geochemistry. Varney, R. N., tr. from Fr. LC 74-83871. (Geophysics & Astrophysics Monographs: No. 10). 1974. lib. bdg. 31.50 (ISBN 90-277-0497-X, Pub. by Reidel Holland); pap. text ed. 18.50 (ISBN 90-277-0498-8, Pub. by Reidel Holland). Kluwer Boston.
American Geological Institute. Geokhimiya Translations Nineteen Sixty-Nine: A Supplement to Geochemistry International, Vol. 6. LC 74-645947. 706p. (Orig., Rus.). 1980. pap. 35.00 (ISBN 0-913312-39-8). Am Geol.
--Geokhimiya Translations 1964: A Supplement to Geochemistry International, Vol. 1. 1973. 35.00 (ISBN 0-913312-24-X). Am Geol.
--Geokhimiya Translations 1965: A Supplement to Geochemistry International, Vol. 2. 1974. 50.00 (ISBN 0-913312-25-8). Am Geol.
--Geokhimiya Translations 1966: A Supplement to Geochemistry International, Vol. 3. 1975. 50.00 (ISBN 0-913312-26-6). Am Geol.
--Geokhimiya Translations 1967: A Supplement to Geochemistry International, Vol. 4. 1977. 30.00 (ISBN 0-913312-27-4). Am Geol.
--Geokhimiya Translations 1968: A Supplement to Geochemistry International. LC 74-645947. (Vol. 5). 1979. pap. 35.00 (ISBN 0-913312-11-8). Am Geol.
Applied Geochemistry Research Group. The Wolfson Geochemical Atlas of England & Wales. (Illus.). 1978. 129.00x (ISBN 0-19-891113-0). Oxford U Pr.
Berner, R. A. Principles of Chemical Sedimentology. 1971. 25.00 (ISBN 0-07-004928-9, C). McGraw.
Beus, A. A. Geochemistry of the Lithosphere. 1976. 10.00 (ISBN 0-8285-1817-3, Pub. by Mir Pubs Russia). Imported Pubns.
Beus, A. A. & Grigorian, S. V. Geochemical Exploration Methods for Mineral Deposits. Levinson, A. A., ed. Teteruk-Schneider, Rita, tr. LC 77-75045. (Illus.). 1977. 32.00x (ISBN 0-915834-03-0). Applied Pub.
Bowie, S. H. & Webb, J. S. Environmental Geochemistry & Health. (Royal Society Ser.). (Illus.). 216p. 1980. Repr. of 1979 ed. text ed. 63.00x (ISBN 0-85403-114-6, Pub. by Royal Society London). Scholium Intl.
Broecker, W. S. & Oversby, V. M. Chemical Equilibria in the Earth. LC 79-109246. (Illus.). 1970. text ed. 19.95 (ISBN 0-07-007997-8, C). McGraw.
Brown, G. C. & Mussett, A. E. The Inaccessible Earth. (Illus.). 272p. 1981. text ed. 41.00x (ISBN 0-04-550027-4); pap. text ed. 22.50x (ISBN 0-04-550028-2). Allen Unwin.
Brownlow, Arthur H. Geochemistry. (Illus.). 1979. text ed. 25.95 (ISBN 0-13-351064-6). P-H.

Cannon, Helen L. & Hopps, Howard C., eds. Environmental Geochemistry in Health & Disease. LC 78-111440. (Memoir: No. 123). (Illus.). viii, 230p. 1971. 19.00x (ISBN 0-8137-1123-1). Geol Soc.

Chayes, Felix. Ratio Correlation: A Manual for Students of Petrology & Geochemistry. LC 71-146110. 1971. text ed. 6.00x (ISBN 0-226-10218-1); pap. text ed. 2.25x (ISBN 0-226-10220-3). U of Chicago Pr.

Cherdyntsev, V. V. Abundance of Chemical Elements. rev. ed. Nichiporuk, Walter, tr. LC 61-11892. (Illus.). 1961. 12.00x (ISBN 0-226-10339-0). U of Chicago Pr.

Committee on Env. Geochem., National Research Council. Geochemistry & the Environment: Distribution of Trace Elements Related to the Occurrence of Certain Cancers, Cardiovascular Diseases, & Urolithiasis, Vol. III. (Geochemistry & the Environment Ser.). 1978. pap. text ed. 14.00x (ISBN 0-309-02795-0). Natl Acad Pr.

Douglas, A G. & Maxwell, J. R., eds. Advances in Organic Geochemistry 1979: Proceedings of the 9th International Meeting on Organic Geochemistry Held at Newcastle-Upon-Tyne, England, Sept. 1979. LC 80-41078. (International Ser. in Earth Sciences: Vol. 36). (Illus.). 750p. 1981. 160.00 (ISBN 0-08-024017-8). Pergamon.

Eglinton, G. & Murphy, Sr. M. T., eds. Organic Geochemistry: Methods & Results. LC 70-107318. (Illus.). 1969. 98.60 (ISBN 0-387-04669-0). Springer-Verlag.

Ellis, A. J. & Mahon, W. A., eds. Chemistry & Geothermal Systems. 1977. 46.50 (ISBN 0-12-237450-9). Acad Pr.

Energlyn, L. & Brealey, L. Analytical Geochemistry. LC 76-103358. (Methods in Geochemistry & Geophysics Ser.: No. 5). (Illus.). 441p. 1971. 70.75 (ISBN 0-444-40826-6). Elsevier.

Ernst, W. Geochemical Facies Analysis. (Methods in Geochemistry & Geophysics Ser: Vol. 11). 1970. 39.00 (ISBN 0-444-40847-9). Elsevier.

Ernst, W. G. Earth Materials. (gr. 10 up). 1969. pap. text ed. 8.95 (ISBN 0-13-222604-9). P-H.

Fairbridge, R., ed. Encyclopedia of Geochemistry & Environmental Sciences. LC 75-152326. (Encyclopedia of Earth Sciences Ser: Vol. IVA). 1972. 94.50 (ISBN 0-12-786460-1). Acad Pr.

Foeldvari-Vogl, Maria. Theory & Practice of Regional Geochemical Exploration. 1978. 25.00x (ISBN 963-05-1442-7). Intl Pubns Serv.

Fortescue, J. A. Environmental Geochemistry: A Holistic Approach. (Ecological Studies: Vol. 35). (Illus.). 347p. 1980. text ed. 34.80 (ISBN 0-387-90454-9). Springer-Verlag.

Fyfe, W. S., et al. Fluids in the Earth's Crust: Their Significance in Metamorphic, Tectonic, & Chemical Transport Process. (Developments in Geochemistry Ser: No. 1). 1978. 49.75 (ISBN 0-444-41636-6). Elsevier.

Garrels, Robert M., et al. Chemical Cycles & the Global Environment: Assessing Human Influences. 222p. 1975. pap. 6.50 (ISBN 0-913232-29-7). W Kaufmann.

Geochemistry of Water in Relation to Cardiovascular Disease. 1979. pap. 10.75 (ISBN 0-309-02884-1). Natl Acad Pr.

Golubev, V. S. & Garibyants, A. A. Heterogeneous Processes of Geochemical Migration. LC 73-140829. 145p. 1971. 27.50 (ISBN 0-306-10860-7, Consultants). Plenum Pub.

Hay, Richard L. Zeolites & Zeolitic Reactions in Sedimentary Rocks. LC 66-22146. (Special Paper: No. 85). (Illus., Orig.). 1966. pap. 7.25x (ISBN 0-8137-2085-0). Geol Soc.

Hobson, G. D., ed. Advances in Organic Geochemistry, 1969: Proceedings. 1970. 82.00 (ISBN 0-08-012758-4). Pergamon.

Hoefs, J. Stable Isotope Geochemistry. rev. ed. (Minerals & Rocks Ser.: Vol. 9). (Illus.). 180p. 1980. 32.00 (ISBN 0-387-09917-4). Springer-Verlag.

Hofmann, A. W., et al. Geochemical Transport & Kinetics. 1974. 27.00 (ISBN 0-87279-644-2, 634). Carnegie Inst.

Holland, Heinrich D. The Chemistry of the Atmosphere & Oceans. LC 77-28176. 1978. 34.00 (ISBN 0-471-03509-2, Pub. by Wiley-Interscience). Wiley.

Introduccion a la Geoquimica. (Serie De Quimica: No. 8). (Span.). 1972. pap. 1.00 (ISBN 0-8270-6360-1). OAS.

Jensen, M. L. & Bateman, A. M. Economic Mineral Deposits. 3rd rev. ed. LC 78-9852. 593p. 1981. text ed. 25.95 (ISBN 0-471-09043-3). Wiley.

Josephs, Melvin J. & Sanders, Howard J. Chemistry & the Environment. LC 67-30718. 1967. 6.75 (ISBN 0-8412-0103-X). Am Chemical.

Krauskopf, Konrad B. Introduction to Geochemistry. (Illus.). 1967. text ed. 23.00 (ISBN 0-07-035443-X, C). McGraw.

--Introduction to Geochemistry. 2nd ed. (International Earth & Planetary Sciences Ser.). (Illus.). 1979. text ed. 24.00 (ISBN 0-07-035447-2, C). McGraw.

Krumbein, Wolfgang E., ed. Environmental Biogeochemistry & Geomicrobiology, 3 vols. LC 77-84416. 1978. Vol. 1. 30.00 (ISBN 0-250-40218-1); Vol. 2. 30.00 (ISBN 0-250-40218-1); Vol. 3. 30.00 (ISBN 0-250-40220-3). Ann Arbor Science.

Lerman, A. Geochemical Processes: Water & Sediment Environments. LC 78-15039. 1979. 38.00 (ISBN 0-471-03263-8, Pub. by Wiley-Interscience). Wiley.

Levinson, A. A. Introduction to Exploration Geochemistry. 2nd ed. LC 79-54677. (Illus.). 1980. 50.00x (ISBN 0-915834-04-9); student ed. 25.00 (ISBN 0-686-65934-1). Applied Pub.

Manghnani, Merli H. High Pressure Research: Applications to Geophysics. 1977. 48.50 (ISBN 0-12-468750-4). Acad Pr.

Manskaya, S. M. & Drozdova, T. V. Geochemistry of Organic Substances. 1968. 60.00 (ISBN 0-08-012404-6). Pergamon.

Marshall, C. Edmund. The Physical Chemistry & Mineralogy of Soils: Soils in Place, Vol. II. LC 64-20074. 1977. 34.50 (ISBN 0-471-02957-2, Pub. by Wiley-Interscience). Wiley.

Mason, Brian. Handbook of Elemental Abundances in Meteorites: Reviews in Cosmochemistry & Allied Subjects. LC 71-148927. (Illus.). 564p. 1971. 117.25 (ISBN 0-677-14950-6). Gordon.

--Principles of Geochemistry. 3rd ed. LC 66-26752. 1966. 26.95 (ISBN 0-471-57521-6). Wiley.

Mason, Brian & Moore, Carleton B. Principles of Geochemistry. 4th ed. 352p. 1981. text ed. price not set (ISBN 0-471-57522-4). Wiley.

Mineralogical Society Geochemistry Group, November 1 & 2, 1978. The Evidence of Chemical Heterogeneity in the Earth's Mantle. Bailey, D. K., et al, eds. (Illus.). 357p. 1980. text ed. 100.00x (ISBN 0-85403-144-8, Pub. by Royal Soc London). Scholium Intl.

Mueller, R. F. & Saxena, S. K. Chemical Petrology: With Applications to the Terrestinal Planets & Meteorites. LC 76-26049. (Illus.). 1977. 37.80 (ISBN 0-387-90196-5). Springer-Verlag.

National Research Council, U. S. National Committee for Geochemistry. Geochemistry & the Environment: The Relation of Selected Trace Elements to Health & Disease, Vol. 1. LC 74-13309. (Illus.). ix, 113p. 1974. pap. 10.00 (ISBN 0-309-02223-1). Natl Acad Pr.

Nriagu, J. O., ed. The Biogeochemistry of Lead in the Environment. (Topics in Environmental Health Ser.: Vol. 1A). 1978. 80.50 (ISBN 0-444-41599-8, TEH 1:A, Biomedical Pr). Elsevier.

Nuclear Techniques in Geochemistry & Geophysics: Proceedings. (Illus.). 271p. 1976. pap. 27.75 (ISBN 92-0-041076-6, ISP425, IAEA). Unipub.

Parasnis, D. S. Mining Geophysics. 2nd ed. (Methods in Geochemistry & Geophysics Ser.). 395p. 1973. 19.95 (ISBN 0-444-41077-5). Elsevier.

Perel'Man, A. I. Geochemistry of Epigenesis. LC 65-25241. (Monographs in Geoscience Ser.). (Illus.). 266p. 1967. 32.50 (ISBN 0-306-30293-4, Plenum Pr). Plenum Pub.

Review of Research on Modern Problems in Geochemistry. (Earth Sciences Ser.: No. 16). 290p. 1980. pap. 35.50 (ISBN 92-3-101577-X, U-998, UNESCO). Unipub.

Ringwood, A. E. Origin of the Earth & Moon. (Illus.). 1979. 25.95 (ISBN 0-387-90369-0). Springer-Verlag.

Robertson, Eugene. The Nature of the Solid Earth. (International Ser. in the Earth & Planetary Sciences). (Illus.). 544p. 1971. text ed. 26.00 (ISBN 0-07-053165-X, C). McGraw.

Rodionov, Dmitrii A. Distribution Functions of the Element & Mineral Contents of Igneous Rocks. LC 64-23246. 80p. 1965. 25.00 (ISBN 0-306-10728-7, Consultants). Plenum Pub.

Rose, Arthur, et al. Geochemistry in Mineral Exploration. 2nd ed. 1980. pap. 30.00 (ISBN 0-12-596252-5). Acad Pr.

Rosler, H. J. & Lange, H. Geochemical Tables. LC 79-132143. 1973. 63.50 (ISBN 0-444-40894-0). Elsevier.

Saxena, S. K. & Bhattacharji, S., eds. Energetics of Geological Processes. LC 76-30859. 1977. 36.30 (ISBN 3-540-08119-4). Springer-Verlag.

Siegel, Frederic R. Applied Geochemistry. LC 74-13486. 384p. 1974. 29.95 (ISBN 0-471-79095-8, Pub. by Wiley-Interscience). Wiley.

Smales, A. A. & Wager, L. R. Methods in Geochemistry. 471p. 1960. 23.50 (ISBN 0-470-79893-9, Pub. by Wiley). Krieger.

Strens, R. G., ed. The Physics & Chemistry of Minerals & Rocks. LC 75-6930. 697p. 1975. 121.75 (ISBN 0-471-83368-1, Pub by Wiley-Interscience). Wiley.

Stumm, Werner, ed. Global Chemical Cycles & Their Alterations by Man. (Physical & Chemical Sciences Research Reports: No. 2). 1977. lib. bdg. 22.00 (ISBN 0-910000-06-9). Dahlem.

Swain, Frederick M. Non-Marine Organic Geochemistry. (Cambridge Earth Science Ser). (Illus.). 1970. 83.50 (ISBN 0-521-07757-5). Cambridge U Pr.

Tugarinov, A. I., ed. Recent Contributions to Geochemistry & Analytical Chemistry. Slutzkin, D., tr. from Rus. LC 74-8165. 694p. 1976. 87.95 (ISBN 0-470-89228-5). Halsted Pr.

U. S. National Committee for Geochemistry. Geochemistry & the Environment: The Relation of Other Selected Trace Elements to Health & Disease, Vol. II. 1977. pap. 12.00 (ISBN 0-309-02548-6). Natl Acad Pr.

U.S. National Committee for Geochemistry, Div. of Earth Sciences. Orientations in Geochemistry. (Illus.). 152p. 1974. pap. 8.00 (ISBN 0-309-02147-2). Natl Acad Pr.

Vernadsky, W. I. Problems of Biogeochemistry, Vol. 2. (Connecticut Academy of Arts & Sciences Transaction: Vol. 35). 1944. 7.50 (ISBN 0-208-00808-X). Shoe String.

Wainerdi, Richard E. & Uken, Ernst A., eds. Modern Methods of Geochemical Analysis. LC 75-157148. (Monographs in Geoscience Ser.). 397p. 1971. 32.50 (ISBN 0-306-30474-0, Plenum Pr). Plenum Pub.

Walker, James C. Evolution of the Atmosphere. 1978. 16.95 (ISBN 0-02-854390-4). Macmillan.

Waples, Douglas. Organic Geochemistry for Exploration Geologists. LC 80-70001. 144p. 1981. text ed. 21.95x (ISBN 0-8087-2961-6, Feffer & Simons); pap. text ed. 17.95x (ISBN 0-8087-2980-2, Feffer & Simons). Burgess.

Wedepohl, K. H., et al, eds. Handbook of Geochemistry, Vol. 2, Pt. 4. LC 78-85402. (Illus.). vi, 898p. 1975. loose-leaf 155.00 (ISBN 0-387-06879-1). Springer-Verlag.

--Handbook of Geochemistry, Vol. 2, Pt. 5. (Illus.). 1979. loose leaf binder 438.40 (ISBN 0-387-09022-3). Springer-Verlag.

Zajic, J. E. Microbial Biogeochemistry. 1969. 37.50 (ISBN 0-12-775350-8). Acad Pr.

GEOCHRONOLOGY

see Geological Time

GEODESY

see also Area Measurement; Astronautics in Geodesy; Astronomy, Spherical and Practical; Geography, Mathematical; Gravity; Isostasy; Least Squares; Longitude; Surveying

Bomford, G. Geodesy. 4th ed. 840p. 1980. 139.00x (ISBN 0-19-851946-X). Oxford U Pr.

Eberlein, Patrick. Geodesics & Ends in Certain Surfaces Without Conjugate Points. LC 77-28627. (Memoirs Ser.: No. 199). 1978. 11.60 (ISBN 0-8218-2199-7, MEMO-199). Am Math.

Ewing, C. E. & Mitchell, M. M. Introduction to Geodesy. 1970. text ed. 22.95 (ISBN 0-444-00055-0, North Holland). Elsevier.

Halmos, F. & Somogyi, J., eds. Optimization of Design & Computation of Control Networks. (Illus.). 733p. (Eng., Fr., & Ger.). 1979. 72.50x (ISBN 963-05-1716-7). Intl Pubns Serv.

Hirvonen, R. A. Adjustment by Least Squares in Geodesy & Photogrammetry. LC 71-158408. 261p. 15.50 (ISBN 0-8044-4397-1). Ungar.

Japan-United States Seminar on Minimal Submanifolds, Including Geodesics, Tokyo, 1977. Minimal Submanifolds & Geodesics: Proceedings. Obata, M., ed. 1979. 58.75 (ISBN 0-444-85327-8, North Holland). Elsevier.

Klingenberg. Lectures on Closed Geodesics. LC 77-13147. (Grundlehren der Mathematischen Wissenschaften: Vol. 230). 1978. 34.50 (ISBN 0-387-08393-6). Springer-Verlag.

Moritz, Helmut. Advanced Physical Geodesy. 516p. 1980. 57.00x (ISBN 0-85626-195-5, Pub. by Abacus Pr England). Intl Schol Bk Serv.

Robbins, A. R., et al. Satellite Doppler Tracking & Its Geodetic Applications. (Royal Society Ser.). (Illus.). 196p. 1980. Repr. of 1980 ed. text ed. 54.00x (ISBN 0-85403-128-6, Pub. by Royal Society London). Scholium Intl.

Rudman, Jack. Geodesist. (Career Examination Ser.: C-300). (Cloth bdg. avail. on request). pap. 10.00 (ISBN 0-8373-0300-1). Natl Learning.

Tengstrom, Erik & Teleki, George, eds. Refractional Influences in Astrometry & Geodesy. (International Astronomical Union Symposium: No. 89). 1979. lib. bdg. 50.00 (ISBN 90-277-1037-6); pap. 26.50 (ISBN 90-277-1038-4, Pub. by Reidel Holland). Kluwer Boston.

Torge, Wolfgang. Geodesy: An Introduction. Jekeli, Christopher J., tr. from Ger. 254p. 1980. 26.75 (ISBN 3-11-007232-7). De Gruyter.

GEODIMETER

Saastamoinen, J. J., ed. Surveyor's Guide to Electromagnetic Distance Measurement. LC 68-79061. 1969. 12.50x (ISBN 0-8020-1623-5). U of Toronto Pr.

GEODYNAMICS

see also Earthquakes; Metamorphism (Geology); Rock Mechanics

Bolt, B. A., et al. Geological Hazards. LC 74-32049. (Illus.). 450p. 1977. 22.90 (ISBN 0-387-90254-6). Springer-Verlag.

Carey, W. S. The Expanding Earth. (Developments in Geotectonics Ser.: No. 10). 1976. 48.00 (ISBN 0-444-41485-1). Elsevier.

Drake, Charles L. Geodynamics: Progress & Prospects. 1976. pap. 7.50 (ISBN 0-87590-203-0). Am Geophysical.

Love, A. E. Some Problems of Geodynamics. 5.50 (ISBN 0-8446-2488-8). Peter Smith.

NATO Advanced Study Institute,University of Iceland,Reykjavik,Iceland,July1-7,1974. Geodynamics of Iceland & the North Atlantic Area: Proceedings. Kristjansson, L., ed. LC 74-27848. (NATO Advanced Study Institute Ser: No.C11). 323p. 1974. lib. bdg. 39.50 (ISBN 90-277-0505-4, Pub. by Reidel Holland). Kluwer Boston.

NATO Study Institute, Reyrjavik, Iceland, August 11-20, 1974 & Thoft-Christensen, P. Continuum Mechanics Aspects of Geodynamics & Rock Fracture Mechanics: Proceedings. LC 74-34161. (NATO Advanced Study Institutes: No. C12). 273p. 1974. 34.00 (ISBN 90-277-0504-6, Pub. by Reidel Holland). Kluwer Boston.

Penck, Walther. Morphological Analysis of Land Forms: A Contribution to Physical Geology. Czech, Hella & Boswell, Katharine Cumming, trs. from Ger. Orig. Title: Die Morphologische Analyse. 443p. 1972. Repr. of 1953 ed. 21.75 (ISBN 0-02-850130-6). Hafner.

Saxena, S. K. & Bhattacharji, S., eds. Energetics of Geological Processes. LC 76-30859. 1977. 36.30 (ISBN 3-540-08119-4). Springer-Verlag.

Scheidegger, Adrien E. Principles of Geodynamics. 2nd ed. (Illus.). 1963. 44.90 (ISBN 0-387-03054-9). Springer-Verlag.

Shimer, John A. This Sculptured Earth: The Landscape of America. LC 59-10628. (Illus.). 1959. 22.50x (ISBN 0-231-02331-6). Columbia U Pr.

U. S. Program for the Geodynamics Project: Scope & Objectives. 1973. pap. 4.50 (ISBN 0-309-02211-8). Natl Acad Pr.

Uyeda, S., et al, eds. Geodynamics of the Western Pacific. (Advances in Earth & Planetary Sciences Ser.: Pt. 6). 592p. 1980. 49.50x (ISBN 0-89955-315-X, Pub. by JSSP Japan). Intl Schol Bk Serv.

Van Bemmelen, W. Geodynamic Models. (Developments in Geotectonics: Vol. 2). 1972. 46.50 (ISBN 0-444-40967-X). Elsevier.

GEO-ELECTRIC PROSPECTING

see Electric Prospecting

GEOFFREY OF MONMOUTH, C.1100-1154

Leckie, R. William, Jr. The Passage of Dominion: Geoffrey of Monmouth & the Periodization of Insular History in the Twelfth Century. 184p. 1981. 20.00x (ISBN 0-8020-5495-1). U of Toronto Pr.

GEOGNOSY

see Geology

GEOGRAPHERS

Ahmad, N. Muslim Contribution to Geography. pap. 4.95 (ISBN 0-686-18450-5). Kazi Pubns.

Association of Pacific Coast Geographers. Yearbooks of the Association of Pacific Coast Geographers, Vol. 1-42. Incl. Vols. 1-19. 1935 - 1957. pap. 5.00 ea.; Vol. 20-27. 1958 - 1965. pap. 5.00 ea.; Vols. 28, 29, 31. 1966 - 1967, 1969. pap. 5.00 ea; Vol. 30, 1968. 8.00 (ISBN 0-87071-230-6); Vols. 32-42. 1970 - 1980. pap. 7.00 ea.. LC 37-13376. Oreg St U Pr.

Dickinson, Robert E. Regional Concept: The Anglo-American Leaders. 1976. 26.75x (ISBN 0-7100-8272-X). Routledge & Kegan.

Dunbar, Gary S. Elisee Reclus: Historian of Nature. (Illus.). 1978. 15.00 (ISBN 0-208-01746-1, Archon). Shoe String.

Evans, Ifor M. & Lawrence, Heather. Christopher Saxton: Elizabethan Map-Maker, Vol. 6. (Cartographica Ser.). xvi, 186p. 1979. 45.00x (ISBN 0-901869-06-6, Pub. by Holland Pr England). W G Arader.

Freeman, T. W. & Pinchemel, Philippe, eds. Geographers: Biobibliographical Studies, Vol. 2. (Illus.). 1978. pap. 28.25 (ISBN 0-7201-0710-5, Pub. by Mansell England). Merrimack Bk Serv.

--Geographers: Biobibliographical Studies, Vol. 4. 168p. 1981. pap. text ed. 36.80 (ISBN 0-7201-1584-1, Pub. by Mansell England). Merrimack Bk Serv.

Freeman, T. W., et al, eds. Geographers: Biobibliographical Studies, Vol. 3. (Illus.). 1980. pap. 28.25 (ISBN 0-7201-0927-2, Pub. by Mansell England). Merrimack Bk Serv.

James, Preston E. & Martin, Geoffrey J. The Association of American Geographers: The First Seventy Five Years. LC 78-74887. (Illus.). 1979. 12.00 (ISBN 0-89291-134-4). Assn Am Geographers.

James, Preston E. & Jones, Clarence F., eds. American Geography: Inventory & Prospect. (Illus.). 1954. 15.00x (ISBN 0-8156-2013-6). Syracuse U Pr.

Kennedy, J. Gerald. The Astonished Traveler: William Darby Frontier Geographer & Man of Letters. LC 81-3711. 256p. 1981. text ed. 22.50x (ISBN 0-8071-0886-3). La State U Pr.

Martin, Geoffrey. The Life & Thought of Isaiah Bowman. (Illus.). 272p. 1980. 22.50 (ISBN 0-208-01844-1, Archon). Shoe String.

Ortroy, F. Van. Bio Bibliographie De Gemma Frisius. 1920. text ed. 20.00x (ISBN 9-06041-050-5). Humanities.

Taylor, Eva G. Late Tudor & Early Stuart Geography, 1583-1650. 1968. lib. bdg. 20.50x (ISBN 0-374-97809-3). Octagon.

--Tudor Geography, 1485-1583. 1968. lib. bdg. 18.00x (ISBN 0-374-97847-6). Octagon.

GEOGRAPHICAL ATLASES
see Atlases

GEOGRAPHICAL BOUNDARIES
see Boundaries

GEOGRAPHICAL DICTIONARIES
see Geography–Dictionaries

GEOGRAPHICAL DISTRIBUTION OF ANIMALS
see Zoogeography

GEOGRAPHICAL DISTRIBUTION OF ANIMALS AND PLANTS
see also Forest Ecology; Phytogeography; Zoogeography;
also subdivisions Geographical Distribution or Migration under names of organisms, e.g. Fishes–Geographical Distribution; Birds–Migration

Biology Colloquium, 37th, Oregon State University, 1976. Historical Biogeography, Plate Tectonics, & the Changing Environment: Proceedings. Gray, Jane & Boucot, Arthur J., eds. LC 78-31376. (Illus.). 512p. 1979. 59.75 (ISBN 0-87071-176-8). Oreg St U Pr.

A Classification of the Biogeographical Provinces of the World. (Illus.). 1975. pap. 7.50x (ISBN 2-88032-033-X, IUCN31, IUCN). Unipub.

Cox, Barry C., et al. Biogeography: An Ecological & Evolutionary Approach. 3rd ed. LC 79-22636. 1980. pap. text ed. 21.95x (ISBN 0-470-26893-X). Halsted Pr.

Dansereau, P. Biogeography: An Ecological Perspective. (Illus.). 1957. 24.00 (ISBN 0-8260-2330-4, Pub. by Wiley-Interscience). Wiley.

Donkin, R. A. Manna: An Historical Geography. (Biogeographica Ser.: No. 17). (Illus.). vii, 160p. 1980. lib. bdg. 47.50 (ISBN 90-6193-218-1, Pub. by Junk Pubs Netherlands). Kluwer Boston.

Grinnell, Joseph. An Account of the Mammals & Birds of the Lower Colorado Valley, with Especial Reference to the Distributional Problems Presented. Sterling, Keir B., ed. LC 77-81116. (Biologists & Their World Ser.). (Illus.). 1978. Repr. of 1914 ed. lib. bdg. 16.00x (ISBN 0-405-10708-0). Arno.

Heckman, Charles W. Rice Field Ecology in Northeastern Thailand. (Monographiae Biologicae: Vol. 34). (Illus.). 1979. lib. bdg. 38.00 (ISBN 90-6193-086-3, Pub. by Junk Pubs Netherlands). Kluwer Boston.

Hopkins, David M., ed. The Bering Land Bridge. (Illus.). 1967. 20.00x (ISBN 0-8047-0272-1). Stanford U Pr.

Hudson, John C. Geographical Diffusion Theory: Studies in Geography. (No. 19). 1972. pap. 4.95x (ISBN 0-8101-0398-2). Northwestern U Pr.

Jungbluth, Jurgen H. Der Tiergeographicshe Undokologische Beitrag Zur Okologischen Landschaftsforschung. (Biogeographica: No. 13). 1978. lib. bdg. 55.00 (ISBN 90-6193-214-9, Pub. by Junk Pubs Netherlands). Kluwer Boston.

Loffler, H., ed. Neusiedlersee: The Limnology of a Shallow Lake in Central Europe. (Monographiae Biologicae Ser.: No. 37). (Illus.). x, 559p. 1980. lib. bdg. 103.00 (ISBN 90-6193-089-8, Pub. by Junk Pubs Netherlands). Kluwer Boston.

Lowe, Charles H., Jr., ed. The Vertebrates of Arizona: With Major Section on Arizona Habitats. LC 63-11981. 1964. pap. 5.95x (ISBN 0-8165-0348-6). U of Ariz Pr.

MacArthur, Roger H. & Wilson, Edward O. Theory of Island Biogeography. (Monographs in Population Biology: Vol. 1). (Illus.). 1967. 15.00 (ISBN 0-691-08049-6); pap. 6.50 (ISBN 0-691-08050-X). Princeton U Pr.

Morafka, David J. A Biogeographical Analysis of the Chihuahuan Desert Through Its Herpetofauna. (Biogeographica: No. 9). (Illus.). 1977. lib. bdg. 50.00 (ISBN 90-6193-210-6, Pub. by Junk Pubs Netherlands). Kluwer Boston.

Muller, P. & Rathjens, C., eds. Landscape Ecology: In Honor of Prof. Dr. J. Schmithusen. (Biogeographica: No. 16). 1980. lib. bdg. 53.00 (ISBN 90-6193-217-3, Pub. by Junk Pubs Netherlands). Kluwer Boston.

Muller, Paul, ed. Ecosystem Research in South America. (Biogeographica Ser: Vol. 8). 1977. lib. bdg. 24.00 (ISBN 90-6193-209-2, Pub. by Junk Pubs. Netherlands). Kluwer Boston.

Neill, Wilfred T. Geography of Life. LC 68-8877. (Illus.). 48p. 1969. 22.50x (ISBN 0-231-02876-8). Columbia U Pr.

Nelson, Gareth & Platnick, Norman I. Systematics & Biogeography: Cladistics & Vicariance. LC 80-20828. (Illus.). 592p. 1981. 35.00x (ISBN 0-231-04574-3). Columbia U Pr.

Nelson, Gareth & Rosen, Donn E., eds. Vicariance Biogeography: A Critique. LC 80-15351. (Illus.). 616p. 1981. 35.00x (ISBN 0-231-04808-4). Columbia U Pr.

Pears, Nigel V. Basic Biogeography. LC 77-8108. (Illus.). 1977. pap. text ed. 12.95x (ISBN 0-582-48401-4). Longman.

Q A S General Secretariat, Dept. of Echnological & Scientific Affairs. Biogeografia de America Latina. 2nd ed. (Biologia: No. 13). (Illus.). 122p. (Span.). 1980. pap. 2.00 (ISBN 0-8270-1233-0). OAS.

Rushforth, Samuel R. & Tidwell, William. Plants & Man. 1971. spiral bdg. 9.95x (ISBN 0-8087-1831-2). Burgess.

Selections from the Literature of American Biogeography. LC 73-17844. (Natural Sciences in America Ser.). (Illus.). 512p. 1974. 26.00x (ISBN 0-405-05766-0). Arno.

Tivy, Joy. Biogeography: A Study of Plants in the Ecosphere. (Illus.). 1977. pap. text ed. 8.00x (ISBN 0-05-003122-8). Longman.

Wallace, Alfred R. Island Life. 3rd, rev. ed. LC 72-1667. Repr. of 1911 ed. 34.50 (ISBN 0-404-08183-5). AMS Pr.

Werger, M. J. A., ed. Biogrography & Ecology of Southern Africa, 2 vols. (Monographiae Biologicae: No. 31). 1977. lib. bdg. 192.00 set (ISBN 90-6193-083-9, Pub. by Junk Pubs Netherlands). Kluwer Boston.

GEOGRAPHICAL DISTRIBUTION OF DISEASES
see Medical Geography

GEOGRAPHICAL DISTRIBUTION OF MAN
see Anthropo-Geography; Ethnology; Man–Migrations

GEOGRAPHICAL DISTRIBUTION OF PLANTS
see Phytogeography

GEOGRAPHICAL DISTRIBUTION OF PLANTS AND ANIMALS
see Geographical Distribution of Animals and Plants

GEOGRAPHICAL MYTHS

Adams, Henry C. Wonder Book of Travellers' Tales. (Black & Gold Lib). (Illus.). 6.95 (ISBN 0-87140-998-4). Liveright.

Cohen, Daniel. Mysterious Places. LC 77-75787. (Illus.). 1969. 5.95 (ISBN 0-396-05892-2). Dodd.

Higginson, Thomas W. Tales of the Enchanted Islands of the Atlantic. LC 76-9894. (Children's Literature Reprint Ser). (Illus.). (gr. 6-7). 1976. Repr. of 1898 ed. 17.50x (ISBN 0-8486-0203-X). Core Collection.

Johnstone, Robert. The Lost World Does It Exist? 1978. text ed. 13.00x (ISBN 0-901072-75-3). Humanities.

Thule Press Editors, ed. Icelandic Folktales, Vol. 1. 1981. pap. 4.95 (ISBN 0-906191-71-8, Pub. by Findhorn-Thule Scotland). Hydra Bk.

--Icelandic Folktales, Vol. 2. 1981. pap. 4.95 (ISBN 0-906191-72-6, Pub. by Findhorn-Thule Scotland). Hydra Bk.

--Icelandic Folktales, Vol. 3. 1981. pap. 4.95 (ISBN 0-906191-73-4, Pub. by Findhorn-Thule Scotland). Hydra Bk.

GEOGRAPHICAL NAMES
see Names, Geographical

GEOGRAPHICAL PATHOLOGY
see Medical Geography

GEOGRAPHICAL POSITIONS
see also Geography, Mathematical; Longitude

GEOGRAPHICAL RECREATIONS

Brandreth, Gyles. Pears Round the World Quiz Book. (Illus.). 1979. pap. 7.95 (ISBN 0-7207-1110-X). Transatlantic.

Hunt, Sarah E. Games & Sports the World Around. 3rd ed. (Illus.). (gr. 9-12). 1964. 13.95 (ISBN 0-471-07096-3). Ronald Pr.

GEOGRAPHICAL RESEARCH

Amedeo, Douglas & Golledge, Reginald G. Introduction to Scientific Reasoning in Geography. LC 75-1411. 437p. 1975. text ed. 29.95 (ISBN 0-471-02537-2). Wiley.

American Geographical Society Library-New York. Research Catalogue of the American Geographical Society: First Supplement, 2 pts. Incl. Pt. 1. Regional Catalogue, 2 vols. 1972. lib. bdg. 250.00 (ISBN 0-8161-0999-0); Pt. 2. Topical Catalogue, 2 vols. 1974. lib. bdg. 255.00 (ISBN 0-8161-1083-2). G K Hall.

Association of Pacific Coast Geographers. Yearbook 40, 1978. LC 37-13376. (Illus.). pap. text ed. 7.00 (ISBN 0-87071-240-3). Oreg St U Pr.

Brown, E. H., ed. Geography Yesterday & Tomorrow. 312p. 1980. 29.95x (ISBN 0-19-874096-4). Oxford U Pr.

De Blij, H. J. Earth: A Topical Geography. 2nd ed. LC 79-18051. 1980. text ed. 24.95 (ISBN 0-471-05169-1). Wiley.

Haring, Lloyd & Lounsbury, John F. Introduction to Scientific Geographic Research. 2nd ed. 144p. 1975. pap. text ed. write for info. (ISBN 0-697-05255-9). Wm C Brown.

Indian Council of Social Science Research, New Delhi. A Survey of Research in Geography. (ICSSR Research Survey Ser). 397p. 1974. 11.25x (ISBN 0-8002-2042-0). Intl Pubns Serv.

McConnell, Harold & Yaseen, David W., eds. Models of Spatial Variation. LC 75-149933. (Perspectives in Geography Ser Vol. 1). (Illus.). 131p. 1971. 15.00x (ISBN 0-87580-024-6). N Ill U Pr.

Mikesell, Marvin W., ed. Geographers Abroad: Essays on the Problems & Prospects of Research in Foreign Areas. LC 73-87829. (Research Papers Ser.: No. 152). 296p. 1973. pap. 8.00 (ISBN 0-89065-059-4). U Chicago Dept Geog.

Science in Geography Series, 4 vols. Incl. Vol 1. Developments in Geographical Method. Fitzgerald, Brain P. (Illus.). 88p. pap. text ed. 5.95x (ISBN 0-19-913065-5); Vol 2. Data Collection. Daugherty, Richard. (Illus.). 70p. pap. text ed. 5.95x (ISBN 0-19-913066-3); Vol 3. Data Description & Presentation. Davis, Peter. (Illus.). 120p. pap. text ed. 5.95x (ISBN 0-19-913067-1); Vol 4. Data Use & Interpretation. McCullagh, Patrick. (Illus.). 120p. pap. text ed. 5.95x (ISBN 0-19-913068-X). 1974. Oxford U Pr.

U. S. Geographical Surveys. Report Upon United States Geographical Surveys West of the 100th Meridian: Incl. Supplement, 7 vols. (Illus.). 1875-89. Repr. 75.00 ea.; Vol. 1. (ISBN 0-404-11181-5); Vol. 2. (ISBN 0-404-11182-3); Vol. 3. (ISBN 0-404-11183-1); Vol. 4. (ISBN 0-404-11184-X); Vol. 5. (ISBN 0-404-11185-8); Vol. 6. (ISBN 0-404-11186-6); Vol. 7. (ISBN 0-404-11187-4); Set. 500.00 (ISBN 0-404-11180-7). AMS Pr.

Verstappen, H. T., ed. Aerospace Observation Techniques. 100p. 1975. pap. text ed. 24.00 (ISBN 0-08-019665-9). Pergamon.

Wright, John K. Aids to Geographical Research: Bibliographies, Periodicals, Atlases, Gazeteers & Other Reference Books. rev. ed. LC 73-106702. 1971. Repr. of 1947 ed. lib. bdg. 14.75x (ISBN 0-8371-3384-X, WRGR). Greenwood.

Yue-Man Yeung. National Development Policy & Urban Transformation in Singapore: A Study of Public Housing & the Marketing System. LC 73-79884. (Research Papers Ser.: No. 149). 204p. 1973. pap. 8.00 (ISBN 0-89065-056-X). U Chicago Dept Geog.

GEOGRAPHY
see also Anthropo-Geography; Atlases; Boundaries; Classical Geography; Discoveries (In Geography); Ecclesiastical Geography; Ethnology; Geographers; Geographical Research; Man-Influence of Environment; Maps; Medical Geography; Physical Geography; Voyages and Travels
also subdivision Description and Travel under names of countries, e.g. France–Description and Travel; and subdivision Description, Geography under names of countries of antiquity, e.g. Greece–Description, Geography; and subdivision Maps under names of places, e.g. France–Maps

AAG Consulting Services Panel. Suggestions for Self-Evaluation of Geography Programs. 1974. pap. 1.00 (ISBN 0-89291-141-7). Assn Am Geographers.

Abler, Ronald, et al. Spatial Organization: The Geographer's View of the World. LC 71-123081. (Geography Ser). (Illus.). 1971. text ed. 23.95 (ISBN 0-13-824086-8). P-H.

Abu al-Fida. Geographie d'Aboulfeda, 2 vols. in 3. Reinaud, M. & Guyard, S., trs. from Arabic. 1128p. (Fr.). 1981. Repr. of 1883 ed. lib. bdg. 180.00x (ISBN 0-89241-181-3). Caratzas Bros.

Ajaegbu, H. I. & Faniran, A. A New Approach to Practical Work in Geography. 2nd ed. 1973. text ed. 12.95x (ISBN 0-435-95041-X). Heinemann Ed.

Annual Meeting, AAG, 1970. Proceedings, Vol. 2. pap. 2.00 (ISBN 0-89291-101-8). Assn Am Geographers.

Annual Meeting, AAG, 1971. Proceedings, Vol. 3. pap. 3.00 (ISBN 0-89291-102-6). Assn Am Geographers.

Annual Meeting, AAG, 1972. Proceedings, Vol. 4. pap. 3.00 (ISBN 0-89291-103-4). Assn Am Geographers.

Annual Meeting, AAG, 1974. Proceedings, Vol. 6. pap. 5.00 (ISBN 0-89291-105-0). Assn Am Geographers.

Annual Meeting, AAG, 1975. Proceedings, Vol. 7. pap. 6.00 (ISBN 0-89291-106-9). Assn Am Geographers.

Annual Meeting of AAG. Proceedings, Vol. 8. Conzen, Michael, ed. LC 70-90414. 188p. 1976. pap. 6.00 (ISBN 0-89291-108-5). Assn Am Geographers.

Anuchin, V. A. Theoretical Problems of Geography. Fuchs, Roland J. & Demko, George J., eds. Shabad, Steven, tr. LC 77-8437. 1977. 16.00x (ISBN 0-8142-0221-7). Ohio St U Pr.

Archer, J. E. & Dalton, T. H. Fieldwork in Geography. 1970. 25.00 (ISBN 0-7134-2101-0, Pub. by Batsford England). David & Charles.

Association of Pacific Coast Geographers. Yearbook of the Association of Pacific Coast Geographers: 1935-1978, 40 vols. write for info. (ISBN 0-685-85651-8). Oreg St U Pr.

--Yearbook 37, 1975. (Illus.). 144p. pap. 7.00 (ISBN 0-686-65495-1). Oreg St U Pr.

--Yearbook 38, 1976. LC 37-13376. (Illus.). pap. 7.00 (ISBN 0-87071-238-1). Oreg St U Pr.

--Yearbook 39, 1977. LC 37-13376. (Illus.). pap. text ed. 7.00 (ISBN 0-87071-239-X). Oreg St U Pr.

--Yearbook 41, 1979. Monahan, Robert, ed. LC 37-13376. (Illus.). 180p. 1981. pap. 7.00 (ISBN 0-87071-241-1). Oreg St U Pr.

--Yearbook 42, 1980. Scott, James, ed. LC 37-13376. (Illus.). 172p. 1981. pap. 7.00 (ISBN 0-87071-242-X). Oreg St U Pr.

Banner, F. T., et al, eds. The North-West European Shelf Seas. LC 78-14524. (Elsevier Oceanography Ser.: Vol. 24A). 300p. 1979. 68.50 (ISBN 0-444-41693-5). Elsevier.

Bedard, Charles. Regime Juridique Des Grands Lacs De l'Amerique Du Nord et Du Saint-Laurent. 1966. 12.50x (ISBN 2-7637-6107-0, Pub. by Laval). Intl Schol Bk Serv.

Berry, Brian J. Essays on the Science of Geography: Reflections on a Revolution. 1980. 18.50 (ISBN 0-88410-428-1). Ballinger Pub.

Berry, Brian J., ed. The Nature of Change in Geographical Ideas. LC 75-39294. (Perspectives in Geography Ser.: Vol. 3). (Illus.). 167p. 1979. 17.50 (ISBN 0-87580-063-7); pap. 7.50 (ISBN 0-87580-525-6, 210P). N Ill U Pr.

Berry, Wendell. Farming: A Hand Book. LC 71-118828. 1971. pap. 2.95 (ISBN 0-15-630171-7, HB194, Harv). HarBraceJ.

Board, Christopher & Chorley, Richard J., eds. Progress in Geography, Vol. 8. LC 75-37304. 240p. 1976. 25.00 (ISBN 0-312-65065-5). St Martin.

Board, Christopher, et al, eds. Progress in Geography, Vols. 1-5. LC 74-94756. (International Reviews of Current Research Ser.). 1970. 22.50 ea. Vol. 1 (ISBN 0-312-64820-0). Vol. 2 (ISBN 0-312-64855-3). Vol. 3 (ISBN 0-312-64890-1). Vol. 4 (ISBN 0-312-64925-8). Vol. 5 (ISBN 0-312-64960-6). St Martin.

--Progress in Geography, Vol. 6. LC 74-94756. (Progress in Geography Ser). 320p. 1975. 25.00 (ISBN 0-312-64995-9). St Martin.

--Progress in Geography, Vol. 7. LC 74-22664. 320p. 1975. 25.00 (ISBN 0-312-65030-2). St Martin.

--Progress in Geography, Vol. 9. LC 76-14514. 1976. 25.00x (ISBN 0-312-65100-7). St Martin.

Bowen, D. Q. Inqua Field Guides, 16 vols. Incl. Vol. 1. East Anglia. West, R. G., ed; Vol. 2. The English Midlands. Shotton, F. W., ed; Vol. 3. The Isle of Man: Lancashire Coast & Lake District. Tooley, M. J., ed; Vol. 4. South East England & the Thames Valley. Shepherd-Thorn, E. R. & Wymer, J. J., eds.; Vol. 5. Yorkshire & Lincolnshire. Catt, J. A., ed; Vol. 6. South West England. Mottershead, D. N., ed; Vol. 7. Wales & the Cheshire Shropshire Lowland. Bowen, D. Q., ed; Vol. 8. Mid & North Wales. Watson, E., ed; Vol. 9. The Northern Highlands of Scotland. Clapperton, C. M., ed; Vol. 10. The Scottish Highlands. Sissons, J. B., ed; Vol. 11. Western Scotland I. Price, R. J., ed; Vol. 12. Western Scotland II. Dickson, J. H., ed; Vol. 13. South East Ireland. Huddart, D., ed; Vol. 14. South & Southwest Ireland. Lewis, C. A., ed; Vol. 15. Western Ireland. Finch, T; Vol. 16. Southern Shores of the North Sea. Paepe, R., ed. 1980. Set. pap. text ed. 112.00 (ISBN 0-686-64925-7, Pub. by GEO Abstracts England); pap. text ed. 8.00 ea. State Mutual Bk.

Bradshaw, Michael J., et al. The Earth's Changing Surface. LC 77-25024. 1978. pap. text ed. 20.95 (ISBN 0-470-99365-0). Halsted Pr.

Brunhes Delamarre, Mariel J., et al. Geographie Regionale, 2 vols. (Methodique Ser.). Vol. 1. 69.95 (ISBN 0-686-56439-1); Vol. 2. write for info. French & Eur.

Buchanan, Ronald H. The World of Man. (Geographies: An Intermediate Ser.). (Illus.). 1977. pap. text ed. 7.95x (ISBN 0-582-35151-0). Longman.

Buttimer, Anne. Values in Geography. LC 74-76634. (CCG Resource Papers Ser.: No. 24). (Illus.). 1974. pap. text ed. 4.00 (ISBN 0-89291-071-2). Assn Am Geographers.
Carpenter, Nathanael. Geography Delineated Forth in Two Books. LC 76-57369. (English Experience Ser.: No. 787). 1977. Repr. of 1625 ed. lib. bdg. 58.00 (ISBN 90-221-0787-6). Walter J Johnson.
Catamog: Concepts & Techniques in Modern Geography, 24 vols. Incl. Vol. 1. Introduction to Markov Chain Analysis. Callins, L; Vol. 2. Distance Decay in Spatial Interactions. Taylor, P. J; Vol. 3. Understanding Canonical Correlation Analysis. Clark, D; Vol. 4. Some Theoretical & Applied Aspects of Spatial Interaction Shopping Models. Openshaw, S; Vol. 5. An Introduction to Trend Surface: Analysis. Unwin, D; Vol. 6. Classification in Geography. Johnson, R. J; Vol. 7. An Introduction to Factor Analysis. Goddard, J. B. & Kirby, A.; Vol. 8. Principal Components Analysis. Daultrey, S; Vol. 9. Causal Interferences from Dichotomous Variables. Davidson, N; Vol. 10. Introduction to the Use of Logit Models in Geography. Wrigley, N; Vol. 11. Linear Programming: Elementary Geographical Applications of the Transportation Problem. Hay, A; Vol. 12. An Introduction to Quadrat Analysis. 2nd ed. Thomas, R. W; Vol. 13. An Introduction to Time-Geography. Thrift, N. J; Vol. 14. An Introduction to Graph Theoretical Methods in Geography. Tinkler, K. J; Linear Regression in Geography. Ferguson, R; Vol. 16. Probability Surface Mapping: An Introduction with Examples & FORTRAN Programs. Wrigley, N; Vol. 17. Sampling Methods for Geographical Research. Dixon, C. & Leach, B.; Vol. 18. Questionaires & Interviews in Geographical Research. Dixon, C. & Leach, B.; Vol. 19. Analysis of Frequency Distributions. Gardiner, Y. & Gardiner, G.; Vol. 20. Anlaysis of Covariance & Comparison of Regression Lines. Silk, J; Vol. 21. An Introduction to the Use of Simulataneous Equation Regression Analysis in Geography. Todd, D; Vol. 22. Transfer Function Modelling: Relationship Between Time Series Variables. Lai, Pong-Wai; Vol. 23. Stochastic Processes in One Dimensional Series: An Introduction. Richards, K. S; Vol. 24. Linear Programming: The Simplex Method with Geographical Applications. Killen, James E. 1980. Set. pap. text ed. 168.00x (ISBN 0-686-64924-9, Pub. by GEO Abstracts England); pap. text ed. 8.00x ea. State Mutual Bk.
Chatterjee, S. P. An Introductory Regional Geography. 170p. 1981. 10.00x (ISBN 0-86125-704-9, Pub. by Orient Longman India). State Mutual Bk.
--An Introductory Regional Geography: India. 64p. 1981. 10.00x (ISBN 0-86125-620-4, Pub. by Orient Longman India). State Mutual Bk.
Chorley, Richard J., ed. Integrated Models in Geography. Haggett, Peter. 1969. pap. 10.95x (ISBN 0-416-29840-0). Methuen Inc.
Chorley, Richard J. & Haggett, Peter, eds. Models in Geography. 1967. 77.00x (ISBN 0-416-29020-5). Methuen Inc.
Clout, Hugh D. Rural Geography. 1972. 18.00 (ISBN 0-08-017041-2); pap. 9.95 (ISBN 0-08-017042-0). Pergamon.
Coates, B. E., et al. Geography & Inequality. (Illus.). 1977. text ed. 37.50x (ISBN 0-19-874069-7); pap. text ed. 9.95x (ISBN 0-19-874070-0). Oxford U Pr.
Cohen, Chester G. Shtetl Finder. 1980. pap. 8.25 (ISBN 0-9605586-0-8). Periday.
Cole. USSR Geography. 1981. text ed. write for info. Butterworth.
Cole, J. P. Geography of World Affairs. 1959. 6.50 (ISBN 0-686-17720-7). Quest Edns.
Computer Handling of Geographical Data: An Examination of Selected Geographic Information Systems. (Natural Resources Research). (Illus.). 1976. pap. 17.50 (ISBN 92-3-101340-8, U97, UNESCO). Unipub.
Cooke, R. V. & Johnson, J. H. Trends in Geography: An Introductory Survey. 1969. 13.75 (ISBN 0-08-006675-5); pap. 6.25 (ISBN 0-08-006674-7). Pergamon.
Cuningham, William. The Cosmographical Glasse, Conteinyng the Principles of Cosmographie, Etc. LC 68-54632. (English Experience Ser.: No. 44). 1968. Repr. of 1559 ed. 49.00 (ISBN 90-221-0044-8). Walter J Johnson.
Dacey, Michael F., et al. Christaller Central Place Structures. (Studies in Geography: No. 22). 1977. 4.95x (ISBN 0-8101-0466-0). Northwestern U Pr.
Dawson, John A. & Unwin, David J. Computing for Geographers. LC 75-37400. 1976. 16.95x (ISBN 0-8448-0871-7). Crane-Russak Co.
De Cardonda, Nicolas. Geographic & Hydrographic Descriptions, Sixteen Thirty-Two. Mathes, Michael, ed. & tr. (Baja California Travels Ser.: No. 35). 1974. 18.00 (ISBN 0-87093-235-7). Dawsons.
Dickinson, Robert E. & Howarth, O. J. R. The Making of Geography. LC 75-38379. 1976. Repr. of 1933 ed. lib. bdg. 18.75x (ISBN 0-8371-8669-2, DIMG). Greenwood.
Doerr, Arthur H. & Guernsey, Lee. Principles of Geography: Physical & Cultural. rev. ed. LC 74-32106. (gr. 9up). 1975. pap. text ed. 4.50 (ISBN 0-8120-0629-1). Barron.
Dohrs, Fred E. & Sommers, Lawrence M. World Regional Geography: A Problem Approach. LC 76-3748. (Illus.). 1976. pap. text ed. 13.95 (ISBN 0-8299-0089-6). West Pub.
Douglas, Edward M. Boundaries, Areas, Geographic Centers & Altitudes in the U. S. 1981. Repr. lib. bdg. 29.00 (ISBN 0-403-00575-2). Scholarly.
Dutton, Geoffrey, ed. Harvard Papers on Geographic Information Systems, 8 vols. 1979. Set. text ed. 150.00 (ISBN 0-201-03920-6). A-W.
Ebdon, David. Statistics in Geography: A Practical Approach. 195p. 1977. (Pub. by Basil Blackwell); pap. 12.95x (ISBN 0-631-10131-4). Biblio Dist.
Egli, Johann J. Nomina Geographica. 2nd ed. LC 71-173707. (Research & Source Works Ser.: No. 837). 1971. Repr. of 1893 ed. lib. bdg. 57.50 (ISBN 0-8337-1026-5). B Franklin.
Eliot-Hurst, M. E. Transportation Geography: Comments & Readings. 1973. pap. 15.95 (ISBN 0-07-019190-5, C). McGraw.
English, Paul W. World Regional Geography: A Question of Place. 1977. text ed. 22.50 scp (ISBN 0-06-167401-X, HarpC); inst. manual avail. (ISBN 0-06-167410-9). Har-Row.
English, Paul W. & Mayfield, Robert C., eds. Man, Space & Environment: Concepts in Contemporary Human Geography. (Orig.). 1972. text ed. 9.95x (ISBN 0-19-501441-3). Oxford U Pr.
Enyedi, Gyorgy & Meszaros, Julia, eds. Development of Settlement Systems. (Studies in Geography in Hungary: 15). (Illus.). 265p. 1980. 27.50x (ISBN 963-05-1898-8). Intl Pubns Serv.
Fielding, Gordon J. Programmed Case Studies in Geography. 299p. 1974. pap. text ed. 8.95 scp (ISBN 0-06-042052-9, HarpC). Har-Row.
Fisher, William W. GEO Cepts 1. rev. ed. Charbonneau, Louis, ed. (GEO Cepts Program). (Illus.). (gr. 5 up). 1977. student wkbk. 4.95x (ISBN 0-87453-111-X). Denoyer.
--GEO Cepts 1. rev. ed. Charbonneau, Louis, ed. (GEO Cepts Program). (Illus.). 1977. tchr's ed. 17.00 (ISBN 0-87453-112-8). Denoyer.
Fleure, H. J. An Introduction to Geography. 1978. Repr. of 1929 ed. lib. bdg. 12.50 (ISBN 0-8492-0895-5). R West.
Frazier, John W., ed. Applied Geography: Selected Perspectives. (Illus.). 352p. 1982. 21.95 (ISBN 0-13-040451-9). P-H.
Freeman, T. W. The Geographer's Craft. 216p. 1967. 24.00x (ISBN 0-7190-0055-6, Pub. by Manchester U Pr England). State Mutual Bk.
--A History of Modern British Geography. LC 79-41477. (Illus.). 258p. 1980. text ed. 33.00x (ISBN 0-582-30030-4). Longman.
Fuson, Robert. Fundamental Place-Name Geography. 5th ed. 160p. 1981. pap. text ed. write for info. (ISBN 0-697-05207-9). Wm C Brown.
Fuson, Robert H. Introduction to World Geography: Regions & Cultures. LC 75-46351. 1978. pap. 8.95 (ISBN 0-8403-1413-2). Kendall-Hunt.
Gale, Stephen & Olsson, Gunnar, eds. Philosophy in Geography. (Theory & Decision Library: No. 20). 1979. lib. bdg. 40.00 (ISBN 9-0277-0948-3, Pub. by Reidel Holland). Kluwer Boston.
Geographical Handbook. pap. 3.50 (ISBN 0-528-21101-3). Rand.
Geography. 1981. text ed. 20.95 (ISBN 0-06-318186-X, Pub. by Har-Row Ltd England); pap. text ed. 12.95 (ISBN 0-06-318187-8). Har-Row.
Gerasimov, I. P., ed. Global Geography-76, 12 vols. Incl. Vol. 1. Geomorphology & Paleography. pap. text ed. 25.00 (ISBN 0-08-023141-1); Vol. 2. Climatology, Hydrology, Glaciology. pap. text ed. 25.00 (ISBN 0-08-023142-X); Vol. 3. Geography of the Ocean. pap. text ed. 15.00 (ISBN 0-08-023143-8); Vol. 4. Biogeography & Soil Geography. pap. text ed. 15.00 (ISBN 0-08-023144-6); Vol. 5. General Physical Geography. pap. text ed. 15.00 (ISBN 0-08-023145-4); Vol. 6. General Economic Geography. pap. text ed. 25.00 (ISBN 0-08-023146-2); Vol. 7. Geography of Population. pap. text ed. 25.00 (ISBN 0-08-023147-0); Vol. 8. Regional Geography. pap. text ed. 25.00 (ISBN 0-08-023148-9); Vol. 9. Historical Geography. pap. text ed. 15.00 (ISBN 0-08-023149-7); Vol. 10. Geographical Education, Geographical Literature & Dissemination of Geographical Knowledge. pap. text ed. 15.00 (ISBN 0-08-023150-0); Vol. 11. General Problems of Geography & Geosystems Modelling. pap. text ed. 15.00 (ISBN 0-08-023151-9); Vol. 12. Additional Volume Including Author Index. pap. text ed. 25.00 (ISBN 0-08-023152-7). LC 78-40224. 1978. pap. text ed. 200.00 set (ISBN 0-686-67353-0). Pergamon.
Getis, A. & Boots, B. Models of Spatial Processes. LC 75-17118. (Cambridge Geographical Studies Ser.: No.8). 1978. 29.95x (ISBN 0-521-20983-8). Cambridge U Pr.
Gold, John R. An Introduction to Behavioural Geography. 1980. 45.00x (ISBN 0-19-823233-0); pap. 11.95x (ISBN 0-19-823234-9). Oxford U Pr.
Gourou, Pierre. The Tropical World. 5th ed. Beaver, S. H., tr. from Fr. (Georgraphies for Advanced Study Ser.). (Illus.). 192p. 1980. pap. text ed. 11.95x (ISBN 0-582-30012-6). Longman.
Gregory, Derek. Ideology, Science & Human Geography. 1979. 16.95x (ISBN 0-312-40477-8). St Martin.
Gregory, K. J. & Ravenhill, W. L., eds. Exeter Essays in Geography. 256p. 1971. 35.00x (ISBN 0-900771-24-0, Pub. by Exeter Univ England). State Mutual Bk.
Haining, Robert. Specification & Estimation Problems in Models of Spatial Dependence. (Studies in Geography: No. 24). 1977. pap. 4.95x (ISBN 0-8101-0521-7). Northwestern U Pr.
Hamelin, Louis-Edmond. Geographie Difficile. (Fr). 1967. pap. 1.50x (ISBN 2-7637-6356-1, Pub. by Laval). Intl Schol Bk Serv.
--Pour la Documentation Geographique - Une Classification Autonome, Polyvalente Et Integree. (Groupe D'Etude De Choronymie et De Terminologie Geographique). (Fr). 1969. pap. 2.50x (ISBN 2-7637-6454-1, Pub. by Laval). Intl Schol Bk Serv.
Hamilton, F. E., ed. Proceedings of the First British-Soviet Geographical Seminar. (Illus.). 152p. 1981. 35.00 (ISBN 0-08-025795-X). Pergamon.
Hammond, R. & McCullagh, P. S. Quantitative Techniques in Geography. 2nd ed. 1978. 19.95x (ISBN 0-19-874066-2); pap. 13.95x (ISBN 0-19-874067-0). Oxford U Pr.
Hardy, A. V. The British Isles. 2nd ed. (Geography of the British Isles Ser.). (Illus.). 160p. Date not set. pap. price not set (ISBN 0-521-22258-3). Cambridge U Pr.
Harper, Robert A. & Schmudde, Theodore H. Between Two Worlds: An Introduction to Geography. 2nd ed. LC 77-76418. (Illus.). 1977. text ed. 21.50 (ISBN 0-395-25164-8); inst. manual 0.90 (ISBN 0-395-25165-6). HM.
Harris & Forbes. Land That Waited. (Illus.). 25.00x (ISBN 0-392-03615-0, ABC). Sportshelf.
Hart, John F. The Look of the Land. LC 74-20995. (Foundations of Cultural Geography Ser.). (Illus.). 224p. 1975. text ed. 11.95 ref. ed. (ISBN 0-13-540534-3); pap. text ed. 6.95 (ISBN 0-13-540526-2). P-H.
Hartshorne, Richard. The Nature of Geography. pap. 4.95x (ISBN 0-89291-087-9). Assn Am Geographers.
--Perspective on the Nature of Geography. LC 59-7032. (Monograph: No. 1). 4.95 (ISBN 0-89291-080-1). Assn Am Geographers.
Harvard University Library. Geography & Anthropology. (Widener Library Shelflist Ser.: No. 60). 1977. 30.00x (ISBN 0-674-34855-9). Harvard U Pr.
Harvey, David. Explanation in Geography. 1970. 17.95 (ISBN 0-312-27755-5). St Martin.
Heylyn, Peter. Microcosmus, or a Little Description of the Great World. LC 74-28863. (English Experience Ser.: No. 743). 1975. Repr. of 1621 ed. 31.00 (ISBN 90-221-0743-4). Walter J Johnson.
Hine, Al & Alcorn, John. Where in the World Do You Live. LC 62-7728. (Illus.). 40p. (gr. 1-3). 1962. 4.50 (ISBN 0-15-295605-0, HJ). HarBraceJ.
Hock, Tan K. & Brown, Ewen D. Geographical Interpretation Through Photographs (& Interpretation of Statistics) 1972. pap. text ed. 4.95x (ISBN 0-04-910048-3). Allen Unwin.
Holly, Brian P. & Harvey, Milton E. Themes in Geographic Thought. 224p. 1980. write for info. St Martin.
Honeybone, R. C. & Long, I. L. World Geography. 1972. pap. text ed. 9.50x (ISBN 0-435-34428-5). Heinemann Ed.
Hornbeck, David, Jr. & Kane, Phillip S., eds. Program Abstracts 1981. LC 79-63374. 250p. (Orig.). 1981. pap. text ed. 3.00 (ISBN 0-89291-153-0). Assn Am Geographers.
Hoy, Don R. Essentials of Geography & Development: Concepts & Processes. (Illus.). 1980. text ed. 19.95 (ISBN 0-02-357510-7). Macmillan.
--Essentials of Geography & Development: Student Supplement. (Illus.). 1980. pap. text ed. 6.95 (ISBN 0-02-357530-1). Macmillan.
--Geography & Development: A World Regional Approach. (Illus.). 1978. 18.95 (ISBN 0-686-67733-1). Macmillan.
--An Introduction to World Regional Geography: Rich Nations. (Illus.). 1977. text ed. 14.95 (ISBN 0-686-67724-2). Macmillan.
Hoyle, Brian S. Spatial Aspects of Development. LC 73-2785. 372p. 1974. 40.25 (ISBN 0-471-41753-X). Wiley.
Hutchins, Ross E. Hidden Valley of the Smokies: With a Naturalist in the Great Smoky Mountains. LC 74-160863. 1971. 6.50 (ISBN 0-396-06382-9). Dodd.
Igu Commission on Quantitative Geography, Meeting, 1972. Proceedings. Yeates, Maurice, ed. 190p. 1974. pap. 7.00 (ISBN 0-7735-0168-1). McGill-Queens U Pr.
International Geographical Congress, 22nd, Canada. International Geography 1972: Papers, 2 vols. Adams, W. Peter & Helleiner, Frederick M., eds. Set. 100.00x (ISBN 0-8020-3298-2). U of Toronto Pr.
International Geographical Congress, 21st, India, 1968 & Symposium on Land Use in Developing Countries, Aligarh, Nov. 1968. Proceedings. (Illus.). 299p. 1972. pap. 17.50x (ISBN 0-8002-1863-9). Intl Pubns Serv.
Irving, R. M. Readings in Canadian Geography: Canadian Studies. 2nd ed. (Winston Mine Editions). 1972. text ed. 6.04 (ISBN 0-685-26938-8, HoltC). HR&W.
Israel, S., et al. World Geography Today. 1976. text ed. 15.76 (ISBN 0-03-089521-9); tchr's resource bk. 3.44 (ISBN 0-03-089550-2). HR&W.
Ives, Jack D., ed. Geocology of the Front Range: A Study of Alpine & Subalpine Environments. (INSTAAR Studies in High Altitude Geoecology). (Illus.). 484p. 1980. lib. bdg. 26.25x (ISBN 0-89158-993-7). Westview.
Jackson, Richard H. & Hudman, Lloyd E. World Regional Geography: Issues for Today. 550p. 1982. text ed. 23.95 (ISBN 0-471-06214-6). Wiley.
James, Henry. Portraits of Places. LC 72-3300. (Essay Index Reprint Ser.). Repr. of 1883 ed. 19.50 (ISBN 0-8369-2910-1). Arno.
James, Preston E. & Webb, Kempton. One World Divided: A Geographer Looks at the Modern World. 3rd ed. LC 79-12136. 1980. text ed. 23.95 (ISBN 0-471-02687-5). Wiley.
Johnson, B. L. Pakistan. LC 79-10749. 1980. text ed. 19.95x (ISBN 0-435-35484-1). Heinemann Ed.
Johnston, R. J. Geography & Geographers: Anglo-American Human Geography Since 1945. LC 79-90464. 232p. 1980. 38.95x (ISBN 0-470-26881-6). Halsted Pr.
--Multivariate Statistical Analysis in Geography: A Primer of the General Linear Model. (Illus.). 1980. pap. text ed. 11.95x (ISBN 0-582-30034-7). Longman.
Juillard, E., ed. Recent Orientations of Regional Analysis in French Geography. 1976. pap. text ed. 28.00 (ISBN 0-08-019970-4). Pergamon.
Kendall, Henry M., et al. Introduction to Geography. 5th ed. (Illus.). 1976. text ed. 20.95 (ISBN 0-15-542152-2, HC); test item file with behavioral objectives avail. (ISBN 0-15-542153-0). HarBraceJ.
Kilchenman, A., ed. Quantitative & Theoretical Geography. 100p. 1975. pap. text ed. 24.00 (ISBN 0-08-019680-2). Pergamon.
Kromm, David E. World Regional Geography. (Illus.). 510p. 1981. text ed. 24.00 (ISBN 0-03-057781-0, HoltC). HR&W.
Lanegran, David & Palm, Risa. An Invitation to Geography. (Geography Ser.). (Illus.). 1977. pap. text ed. 8.95 (ISBN 0-07-036216-5, C). McGraw.
Lasalle, C. Clef de la Geographie Universelle, Montrant les Racines Linguistiques et Geographiques de la Toponymie Primitive. (Fr.). 1887. text ed. 13.25x (ISBN 90-6041-033-5). Humanities.
Ley, David & Samuels, Marwyn S., eds. Humanistic Geography: Prospects & Problems. LC 78-52408. (Illus.). 1978. text ed. 14.95x (ISBN 0-88425-013-X). Maaroufa Pr.

Linton, Ralph, ed. Most of the World: The Peoples of Africa, Latin America & the East Today. Repr. of 1949 ed. lib. bdg. 37.50x (ISBN 0-8371-3806-X, LIMW). Greenwood.

Lounsbury, John F. & Aldrich, Frank T. Introduction to Geographic Field Methods & Techniques. 1979. pap. text ed. 12.95 (ISBN 0-675-08304-4). Merrill.

Luther, Edward T. Our Restless Earth: The Geologic Regions of Tennessee. LC 77-21433. (Tennessee Three Star Bks. Ser.). (Illus.). 1977. lib. bdg. 8.50x (ISBN 0-87049-293-4); pap. 3.50 (ISBN 0-87049-230-6). U of Tenn Pr.

Maczuley, J. V. Lands of Contrast. 13.50x (ISBN 0-392-03629-0, ABC). Sportshelf.

Mandal, R. B. & Sinha, V. N., eds. Recent Trends & Concepts in Geography, 3 vols. Incl. Vol. 1. 1980 (ISBN 0-391-01820-5); Vol. 2. 1980 (ISBN 0-391-01821-3); Vol. 3. 1980 (ISBN 0-391-01822-1). text ed. 27.75x ea. Humanities.

Manson, Gary A. & Ridd, Merrill K. New Perspectives on Geographic Education: Putting Theory into Practice. LC 77-82146. 1977. pap. text ed. 7.95 (ISBN 0-8403-1782-4). Kendall-Hunt.

Mather, Paul M. Computers in Geography: A Practical Approach. (Illus.). 124p. 1976. bds. 21.95x (ISBN 0-631-16870-2, Pub. by Basil Blackwell). Biblio Dist.

Matthews, John A. Quantitative & Statistical Approaches to Geography: A Practical Manual. (Pergamon Oxford Geographies). 1981. 35.00 (ISBN 0-08-024296-0). Pergamon.

Mead, Margaret. World Enough: Rethinking the Future. (Illus.). 1976. 19.95 (ISBN 0-316-56470-2). Little.

Meinig, Donald, ed. On Geography: Selected Writings of Preston E. James. LC 77-170097. (Geographical Ser.: No. 3). (Illus.). 1971. 14.00x (ISBN 0-8156-0084-4). Syracuse U Pr.

--On Geography: Selected Writings of Preston E. James. LC 77-170097. (Geographical Ser.: No. 3). (Illus.). 1971. 14.00x (ISBN 0-8156-0084-4). Syracuse U Pr.

Meinig, Donald W. On the Margins of the Good Earth. LC 62-7266. (Monograph: No. 2). 3.95 (ISBN 0-89291-081-X). Assn Am Geographers.

Melanges Geographiques Canadiens Offerts a Raoul Blanchard. (Fr). 1959. pap. 9.25x (ISBN 2-7637-0069-1, Pub. by Laval). Intl Schol Bk Serv.

Meyer, Iain & Huggett, Richard. Geography Theory in Practice: Book Three. 1981. pap. text ed. 12.95 (ISBN 0-06-318164-9, IntlDept). Har-Row.

--Geography Theory in Practice: Book Two. 1980. pap. text ed. 13.10 (ISBN 0-06-318166-5, IntlDept). Har-Row.

Minshull, Roger. The Changing Nature of Geography. 1970. pap. text ed. 7.25x (ISBN 0-09-102711-X, Hutchinson U Lib). Humanities.

Mitchell, Bruce. Geography & Resource Analysis. (Illus.). 1979. text ed. 36.00x (ISBN 0-582-48732-3); pap. text ed. 18.00x (ISBN 0-582-48733-1). Longman.

Moreau, Daniel, ed. L' Allemagne. new ed. (Collection monde et voyages). (Illus.). 159p. (Fr.). 1973. 21.00x (ISBN 2-03-053104-9). Larousse.

--L' Angleterre. new ed. (Collection monde et voyages). (Illus.). 159p. (Fr.). 1973. 21.00x (ISBN 2-03-053109-X, 3893). Larousse.

--Les Antilles. (Collection monde et voyages). 159p. (Fr.). 1973. 21.00x (ISBN 2-03-053114-6, 4088). Larousse.

--Le Canada. new ed. (Collection monde et voyages). 159p. (Fr.). 1973. 18.95x (ISBN 2-03-053118-9). Larousse.

--L' Espagne. (Collection monde et voyages). (Illus.). 159p. (Fr.). 1973. 21.00x (ISBN 2-03-053101-4). Larousse.

--Les Etats Unis. (Collection monde et voyages). (Illus.). 159p. (Fr.). 1973. 21.00x (ISBN 2-03-053106-5, 3895). Larousse.

--La France. new ed. (Collection monde et voyages). (Illus.). 159p. (Fr.). 1973. 21.00x (ISBN 2-03-053107-3, 3896). Larousse.

--La Grece. new ed. (Collection monde et voyages). 159p. (Fr.). 1973. 21.00x (ISBN 2-03-053105-7, 3897). Larousse.

--L' Inde. (Collection monde et voyages). 159p. (Fr.). 1973. 21.00x (ISBN 2-03-053119-7). Larousse.

--L' Israel. (Collection monde et voyages). 159p. (Fr.). 1973. 21.00x (ISBN 2-03-053120-0). Larousse.

--L' Italie. (Collection monde et voyages). (Illus.). 159p. (Fr.). 1973. 21.00x (ISBN 2-03-053102-2, 3898). Larousse.

--Le Japon. new ed. (Collection monde et voyages). 159p. (Fr.). 1973. 21.00 (ISBN 2-03-053115-4, 2720). Larousse.

--Le Maroc. new ed. (Collection monde et voyages). (Illus.). 159p. (Fr.). 1973. 21.00x (ISBN 2-03-053111-1). Larousse.

--Le Mexique. new ed. (Collection monde et voyages). (Illus.). 159p. (Fr.). 1973. 21.00x (ISBN 2-03-053108-1, 3900). Larousse.

--Le Portugal. new ed. (Collection monde et voyages). (Illus.). 159p. (Fr.). 1973. 21.00x (ISBN 2-03-053113-8). Larousse.

--La Russie. new ed. (Collection monde et voyages). (Illus.). 159p. (Fr.). 1973. 21.00 (ISBN 2-03-053112-X, 3902). Larousse.

--La Scandinavie. new ed. (Collecion monde et voyages). 159p. (Fr.). 1973. 21.00 (ISBN 2-03-053116-2, 5164). Larousse.

--La Suisse. new ed. (Collection monde et voyages). (Illus.). 159p. (Fr.). 1973. 21.00 (ISBN 2-03-053103-0). Larousse.

--La Tunisie. new ed. (Collection monde et voyages). 159p. (Fr.). 1973. 18.95 (ISBN 0-88332-129-7). Larousse.

--La Turquie. new ed. (Collection monde et voyages). (Illus.). 159p. (Fr.). 1973. 21.00 (ISBN 2-03-053110-3). Larousse.

Mott, Pearle G. History of Davis & Canaan Valley. 1972. 15.00 (ISBN 0-87012-117-0). McClain.

Natoli, Salvatore J., ed. Careers in Geography. 3rd. rev. ed. LC 74-77075. (Illus.). 1976. 0.50 (ISBN 0-89291-121-2). Assn Am Geographers.

Navas, Gerardo, ed. Geography & Planning, No. 1. 1977. pap. text ed. 3.50 (ISBN 0-8477-2433-6). U of PR Pr.

Norwine, Jim & Anderson, Thomas D. Geography As Human Ecology? LC 80-8148. 70p. 1980. pap. text ed. 5.75 (ISBN 0-8191-1249-6). U Pr of Amer.

Nunn, G. E. The Geographical Conceptions of Columbus. 1973. lib. bdg. 11.50x (ISBN 0-374-96126-3). Octagon.

Odell, P. R. & Van Der Knapp, Bert. Economic Geography of Western Europe. 1980. write for info. (ISBN 0-06-318087-1, IntlDept). Har-Row.

Parkes, Don & Thrift, Nigel. Times, Spaces & Places: A Chronogeographic Perspective. 1980. 71.25 (ISBN 0-471-27616-2, Pub. by Wiley-Interscience). Wiley.

Peet, Richard, ed. Radical Geography: Alternative Viewpoints on Contemporary Social Issues. LC 76-55222. (Maaroufa Press Geography Ser.). (Illus.). 1977. pap. 7.95x (ISBN 0-88425-006-7). Maaroufa Pr.

Pemble, William. A Briefe Introduction to Geography. LC 77-7420. (English Experience Ser.: No. 883). 1977. Repr. of 1630 ed. lib. bdg. 7.00 (ISBN 90-221-0883-X). Walter J Johnson.

Peterson, Willis. Glory of Nature's Form. Shangle, Robert D., ed. LC 79-12418. (Illus.). 160p. 1979. 27.50 (ISBN 0-89802-001-8). Beautiful Am.

Pilbeam, Alan. Local Projects in 'A' Level Geography. (Illus.). 128p. (Orig.). 1980. pap. 6.95 (ISBN 0-04-910068-8). Allen Unwin.

Pitty, A. F. Geography & Soil Properties. 1979. pap. 13.95x (ISBN 0-416-71540-0). Methuen Inc.

Pocock, Douglas C., ed. Humanistic Geography & Literature: Essays on the Experience of Place. 224p. 1981. 27.00x (ISBN 0-389-20158-8). B&N.

Pounds & Taylor. World Geography. 7th ed. (gr. 9-12). 1967. text ed. 7.12 (ISBN 0-538-08810-9); study guide & projects 2.00 (ISBN 0-538-08811-7); tests 0.36 (ISBN 0-685-04822-5). SW Pub.

--World Geography. 8th ed. 1974. text ed. 9.96 (ISBN 0-538-08820-6, H82). SW Pub.

Roth, Cecil. A History of the Marranos. LC 74-10149. 448p. 1974. pap. 5.50 (ISBN 0-8052-0463-6). Schocken.

Rowles, Graham D. Prisoners of Space? Exploring the Geographical Experience of Older People. (Replica Edition Ser.). 216p. 1980. pap. text ed. 10.00x (ISBN 0-86531-072-6). Westview.

Rudman, Jack. Geography. (Undergraduate Program Field Test Ser.: UPFT-10). (Cloth bdg. avail. on request). pap. 9.95 (ISBN 0-8373-6010-2). Natl Learning.

Salter, Christopher & Lloyd, William. Landscape in Literature. Natoli, Salvatore J., ed. LC 76-29268. (Resource Papers for College Geography Ser.). 1977. pap. text ed. 4.00 (ISBN 0-89291-118-2). Assn Am Geographers.

Schmithuesen, Josef. Allgemeine Geosynergetik: Einfuehrung indie Landschaftskunde. (Lehrbuch der Allgemeinen Geographie, Vol. 12). (Ger.). 1976. 50.00x (ISBN 3-11-001635-4). De Gruyter.

Schwind, Martin. Allgemeine Staatengeographie. (Lehrbuch der Allgemeinen Geographie, Vol. 8). (Illus.). xxii, 585p. 1972. 58.25x (ISBN 3-11-001634-6). De Gruyter.

Shapiro, William, ed. Lands & Peoples, 6 vols. LC 80-84474. (Illus.). 1981. write for info. (ISBN 0-7172-8008-X). Grolier Ed Corp.

Sharp, William. Literary Geography. 1973. lib. bdg. 25.00 (ISBN 0-8414-8104-0). Folcroft.

Showers, Victor. World Facts & Figures: A Unique, Authoritative Collection of Comparative Information About Cities, Countries, & Geographic Features of the World. LC 78-14041. 1979. 27.00 (ISBN 0-471-04941-7, Pub. by Wiley-Interscience). Wiley.

Sollie, Finn, et al. The Challenge of New Territories. 1974. pap. 12.00x (ISBN 8-200-02334-6, Dist. by Columbia U Pr). Universitet.

The South, A Vade Mecum: Atlanta Annual Meeting Field Trip Guide, 1973. pap. 1.00 (ISBN 0-89291-098-4). Assn Am Geographers.

Spencer, J. E. & Thomas, W. L. Introducing Cultural Geography. 2nd ed. LC 77-20230. 1978. text ed. 20.95x (ISBN 0-471-81631-0). Wiley.

Spencer, J. E. & Thomas, William L. Cultural Geography. LC 67-28950. 591p. 1969. 19.00 (ISBN 0-471-81550-0, Pub. by Wiley). Krieger.

Sreniawski, R. W., ed. Readings in Geography. LC 72-86201. 320p. 1972. text ed. 34.50x (ISBN 0-8422-5031-X). Irvington.

Stamp, Elsa C. A First Geography of the Indian Sub-Continent. 1981. 10.00x (ISBN 0-86125-828-2, Pub. by Orient Longman India). State Mutual Bk.

--First Steps in World Geography. 136p. 1981. 10.00x (ISBN 0-86125-825-8, Pub. by Orient Longman India). State Mutual Bk.

Stamp, Laurence D. & Wooldridge, Sidney W. London Essays in Geography. facs. ed. LC 76-80399. (Essay Index Reprint Ser). 1951. 21.25 (ISBN 0-8369-1050-8). Arno.

Stanford, Quentin H. & Moran, Warren. Geography: A Study of Its Physical Elements. (Illus.). 1978. text ed. 12.95x (ISBN 0-19-540282-0). Oxford U Pr.

Statham, Ian & Finlayson, Brian. Hillslope Analysis. LC 80-40564. (Sources & Methods in Geography Ser.). 176p. 1980. pap. text ed. 8.95 (ISBN 0-408-10622-0). Butterworth.

Steel, R. W. & Prothero, R. M., eds. Geographies & the Tropics: Liverpool Essays. 1964. text ed. 8.00x (ISBN 0-391-01981-3). Humanities.

Steila, Donald, et al. Earth & Man: a Systematic Geography. LC 80-19689. 448p. 1981. text ed. 23.95 (ISBN 0-471-04221-8). Wiley.

Strahler, Arthur N. & Strahler, Alan H. Modern Physical Geography. LC 77-20242. 502p. 1978. text ed. 25.95x (ISBN 0-471-01871-6); tapes avail. (ISBN 0-471-04093-2); study guide 4.95x (ISBN 0-471-04310-9). Wiley.

Taaffe, Robert N. & Odland, John. Geographical Horizons. LC 77-80460. 1978. pap. text ed. 13.95 (ISBN 0-8403-1781-6). Kendall-Hunt.

Taylor, Peter J. Quantitative Methods in Geography: An Introduction to Spatial Analysis. LC 75-26097. (Illus.). 384p. 1977. text ed. 19.95 (ISBN 0-395-18699-4). HM.

Tietze, W., ed. Northern Frontier Problems. 100p. 1975. pap. text ed. 24.00 (ISBN 0-08-019675-6). Pergamon.

Truran, H. C. A Practical Guide to Statistical Maps & Diagrams. 1975. pap. text ed. 5.95x (ISBN 0-435-34895-7). Heinemann Ed.

Ullman, Edward L. Geography as Spatial Interaction. Boyce, Ronald R., ed. LC 79-6759. 252p. 1980. 16.50 (ISBN 0-295-95711-5). U of Wash Pr.

Vincentius, Bellovacensis. Hier Begynneth the Table of the Rubrices of This Presente Volume Namde the Myrrour of the Worlde or Thymage of the Same. Caxton, William, tr. from Fr. LC 79-84143. (English Experience Ser.: No. 960). 204p. (Eng.). 1979. Repr. of 1481 ed. lib. bdg. 30.00 (ISBN 90-221-0960-7). Walter J Johnson.

Walter, H. Vegetation of the Earth. 2nd ed. (Heidelberg Science Library). (Illus.). 1979. pap. 15.80 (ISBN 0-387-90404-2). Springer-Verlag.

Warman, Henry J. Geography: Backgrounds, Techniques & Prospects for Teachers. LC 54-2858. 164p. 1954. pap. 1.00 (ISBN 0-914206-01-X). Clark U Pr.

Weiland, Robert, et al. Geography in Living, Bk. I. (Social Studies in Living Ser. - Secondary Level). (Illus.). 1977. wkbk. spiral bound 5.95x (ISBN 0-87108-190-3). Pruett.

Wheeler, J., et al. Regional Geography of the World. 3rd ed. LC 69-17774. 1975. text ed. 23.95 (ISBN 0-03-089952-4, HoltC). HR&W.

White, Gilbert F., ed. Natural Hazards: Local, National, Global. (Illus.). 600p. 1974. pap. text ed. 9.95x (ISBN 0-19-501757-9). Oxford U Pr.

Wilson, A. G. Geography & the Environment: Systems Analytical Methods. LC 80-41696. 304p. 1981. 40.00 (ISBN 0-471-27956-0, Pub. by Wiley-Interscience); pap. 20.00 (ISBN 0-471-27957-9, Pub. by Wiley-Interscience). Wiley.

Wooldridge, Sidney W. Geographer As Scientist: Essays on the Scope & Nature of Geography. LC 69-14158. 1969. Repr. of 1956 ed. lib. bdg. 14.50x (ISBN 0-8371-0763-6, WOGS). Greenwood.

Wraight, A. Joseph. Our Dynamic World: A Survey in Modern Geography. 1972. 8.00 (ISBN 0-685-26749-0). U Pr of Wash.

Wrigley, Neil & Bennett, Robert J., eds. Quantitative Geography in Britain: Retrospect & Prospect. 448p. 1981. write for info. (ISBN 0-7100-0731-0). Routledge & Kegan.

Zimolzak, Chester & Stansfield, Charles. The Human Landscape: Geography & Culture. 1979. text ed. 21.95 (ISBN 0-675-08290-0); instructor's manual 3.95 (ISBN 0-685-96155-9). Merrill.

GEOGRAPHY–ATLASES

see Atlases

GEOGRAPHY–BIBLIOGRAPHY

American Geographical Society Library New York. Research Catalogue of the American Geographical Society, 15 Vols. (Illus.). 1962. Set. 1395.00 (ISBN 0-8161-0628-2). G K Hall.

Atkinson, Geoffroy. Litterature geographique francaise de la Renaissance, 2 vols. in 1. LC 68-7028. (Bibliography & Reference Ser.: No. 213). (Illus.). 1968. Repr. of 1927 ed. with supplement 45.50 (ISBN 0-8337-0113-4). B Franklin.

Bom, Gd. Bijdrage Tot Eene Geschiedenis van Het Geslacht Van Keulen Als Boekhandelaars, Uitgevers, Kaart-En Instrumentmakers: Een Cartobibliographie. (Dutch.). 1885. pap. text ed. 12.25x (ISBN 90-6041-005-X). Humanities.

Brunet, Roger, ed. Bibliographie Geographique Internationale, 1977: International Geographical Bibliography, 1977, Vol. 82. 752p. (Fr.). 1979. Set, 5 Fasciculae. pap. 67.50x (ISBN 0-8002-2218-0). Intl Pubns Serv.

Directory of the AAG. 1978. pap. 6.00 (ISBN 0-89291-107-7). Assn Am Geographers.

Freeman, T. W., et al, eds. Geographers Biobibliographical Studies, Vol. 1. (Illus.). 1977. pap. 28.25 (ISBN 0-7201-0637-0, Pub. by Mansell England). Merrimack Bk Serv.

--Geographers: Biobibliographical Studies, Vol. 3. (Illus.). 1980. pap. 28.25 (ISBN 0-7201-0927-2, Pub. by Mansell England). Merrimack Bk Serv.

Goddard. Information Sources in Geographical Science. (Butterworths Guides to Information Sources Ser.). 1982. text ed. write for info. (ISBN 0-408-10690-5). Butterworth.

Hall, Robert B. Japanese Geography: A Guide to Japanese Reference & Research Materials. LC 78-5578. (Univ of Michigan Center for Japanese Studies Biblio.: No. 6). 128p. 1978. Repr. of 1956 ed. lib. bdg. 21.75x (ISBN 0-313-20434-9, HAJG). Greenwood.

Harris, Chauncy D. Bibliography of Geography, Part I: Introduction to General Aids. LC 76-1910. (Research Papers Ser: No. 179). 288p. 1976. pap. 8.00 (ISBN 0-89065-086-1). U Chicago Dept.

--Guide to Geographical Bibliographies & Reference Works on Russian or in the Soviet Union. LC 74-84784. (Research Papers Ser.: No. 164). 496p. 1975. 8.00 (ISBN 0-89065-071-3). U Chicago Dept Geog.

Harris, Chauncy D. & Fellmann, Jerome D. International List of Geographical Serials. rev., 3rd ed. LC 80-16392. (Research Papers: No. 193). 457p. 1980. pap. 8.00 (ISBN 0-89065-100-0). U Chicago Dept Geog.

Hoggart, Keith. Geography & Local Administration: A Bibliography. (Public Administration Ser.: Bibliography P-530). 84p. 1980. pap. 9.00 (ISBN 0-686-29051-8). Vance Biblios.

Kish, George. Bibliography of International Geographical Congresses, Eighteen Seventy-One to Nineteen Seventy-Six. (Reference Bks.). 1979. lib. bdg. 32.50 (ISBN 0-8161-8226-4). G K Hall.

Kish, George, ed. A Source Book in Geography. LC 77-25972. (Source Bks. in the History of the Sciences). 1978. 30.00x (ISBN 0-674-82270-6). Harvard U Pr.

L'Union Geographique Internationale, ed. Bibliographie Geographique Internationale: International Geographical Bibliography, Vol. 81. LC 25-1167. 1977. 72.50x (ISBN 2-222-01965-6). Intl Pubns Serv.

Margerie, De E. Catalogue des Bibliographies Geologiques. (Fr.). 1896. pap. text ed. 40.00x (ISBN 90-6041-040-8). Humanities.

A Matter of Degree, a Directory of Geography Courses 1979-1980. 1980. pap. 2.95x (ISBN 0-686-27384-2, Pub. by GEO Abstracts England). State Mutual Bk.

Taylor, Eva G. Late Tudor & Early Stuart Geography, 1583-1650. 1968. lib. bdg. 20.50x (ISBN 0-374-97809-3). Octagon.

--Tudor Geography, 1485-1583. 1968. lib. bdg. 18.00x (ISBN 0-374-97847-6). Octagon.

Van Balen, John. Geography & Earth Science Publications, 2 vols. Incl. 1968-1972 (ISBN 0-87650-090-4); 1973-1975 (ISBN 0-87650-091-2). LC 78-52361. 50.00 set (ISBN 0-685-38823-9); 27.50 ea. Pierian.

Wasserman, Paul, et al, eds. Encyclopedia of Geographic Information Sources. 3rd ed. LC 78-55032. 1978. 58.00 (ISBN 0-8103-0374-4). Gale.

GEOGRAPHY–DICTIONARIES

Blois, John T. Michigan Gazetteer, 1838. 418p. 1979. 18.25 (ISBN 0-686-27820-8). Bookmark.

Brommer, ed. Lexique Anglais-Francais des Termes Appartenant Aux Techniques En Usage a I.G.N, Pt.2. 122p. (Fr. & Eng., English-French Lexicon of Terms Pertaining to Techniques Used at I.G.N). 1958. pap. 7.95 (ISBN 0-686-56778-1, M-6356). French & Eur.
Cooper, S. A. Concise International Dictionary of Mechanical Geography. 6.00 (ISBN 0-685-28348-8). Philos Lib.
De Mello, Fernando, ed. The International Geographic Encyclopedia & Atlas. 1024p. 1979. text ed. 55.00x (ISBN 3-11008-137-7). De Gruyter.
Deschamps, Pierre. Dictionnaire de Geographie Ancienne et Moderne. 2nd ed. 1008p. (Fr.). 1965. 85.00 (ISBN 0-686-56814-1, M-6592). French & Eur.
De Sola, Ralph. Worldwide What & Where: Geographic Glossary & Traveller's Guide. LC 74-82038. 720p. 1975. text ed. 15.75 (ISBN 0-87436-147-8). ABC-Clio.
Dey, Nundo Lal. The Geographical Dictionary of Ancient & Mediaeval India. LC 42-31336. (Illus.). 272p. 1971. Repr. of 1927 ed. 19.50x (ISBN 0-8002-1453-6). Intl Pubns Serv.
Dictionnaire Historique, Georgraphique et Biographique de Maine et Loire, 3 vols. 896p. (Fr.). 1978. Set. 115.00 (ISBN 0-686-56739-0, M-6463). French & Eur.
Egli, Jakob. Etymologisch Geographisches Lexikon. (Ger.). 1970. 62.50 (ISBN 3-500-21620-X, M-7371, Pub. by Saendig-Walluf). French & Eur.
Enciclopedia Geografica, 10 vols. 5500p. (Espn.). 1976. Set. 340.00 (ISBN 84-01-60601-2, S-50964). French & Eur.
Enciclopedia Geografica Juvenil, 13 vols. 1280p. (Espn.). 1974. Set. pap. 91.00 (ISBN 84-201-0410-8, S-50477). French & Eur.
Falconer, Lee N., compiled by. A Gazeteer of the Hyborian World of Conan. LC 77-79065. 1977. 4.95 (ISBN 0-916732-01-0). Starmont Hse.
Fischer, Eric & Elliott, Francis E. A German & English Glossary of Geographical Terms. LC 76-20474. (American Geographical Society Library Ser: No. 5). 111p. 1976. Repr. of 1950 ed. lib. bdg. 15.00x (ISBN 0-8371-8994-2, ELGG). Greenwood.
Forster, Klaus. Pronouncing Dictionary of English-Place Names. 308p. 1981. 30.00 (ISBN 0-7100-0756-6). Routledge & Kegan.
Garzanti. Encyclopedie Geographique. (Fr.). 1969. 25.00 (ISBN 0-686-57154-1, M-6213). French & Eur.
George, Pierre. Dictionnaire de la Geographie. 2nd ed. 460p. (Fr.). 1974. 47.50 (ISBN 0-686-57193-2, M-6267). French & Eur.
Graesse, Johann G. Orbis Latinus: Lexikon lateinischer geographischer Namen des Mittelalters und der Neuzeit, 3 vols. new ed. Plechl, Helmut, ed. 1800p. (Latin & Ger.). 1970. 275.00x (ISBN 3-7814-0087-5). Intl Pubns Serv.
The International Geographic Encyclopedia & Atlas. 1979. 24.95 (ISBN 0-395-27170-3). HM.
Klein, Johannes. Diccionario Rioduero: Paises De la Tierra. 296p. (Espn.). 1978. leatherette 15.75 (ISBN 84-220-0876-9, S-50165). French & Eur.
Klein, M. Herder - Lexikon Geographie. 238p. (Ger.). 1975. pap. 15.95 (ISBN 3-451-16451-5, M-7456, Pub. by Herder). French & Eur.
Klein, Margit & Klein, Johannes. Diccionario Rioduero: Geografia. 2nd ed. (Espn.). 1977. leatherette 9.95 (ISBN 84-220-0670-7, S-50173). French & Eur.
Knox, Alexander. Glossary of Geographical & Topographical Terms. LC 68-30592. 1968. Repr. of 1904 ed. 19.00 (ISBN 0-8103-3236-1). Gale.
Lock, Muriel. Geography & Cartography: A Reference Handbook. 3rd ed. (Guides to Subject Literature Ser.). (Orig.). 1976. 37.50 (ISBN 0-208-01522-1, Linnet). Shoe String.
Lowe, Joseph D., compiled by. Catalog of the Official Gazetteers of China in the University of Washington. LC 70-476883. 79p. 1966. 15.00x (ISBN 0-8002-1241-X). Intl Pubns Serv.
Merriam-Webster Editorial Staff. Webster's New Geographical Dictionary. rev. ed. (Illus.). 1568p. 1977. 14.95 (ISBN 0-87779-446-4). Merriam.
Monkhouse, F. J. Diccionario De Terminos Geograficos. 560p. (Espn.). 1978. 48.00 (ISBN 84-281-0386-0, S-50017). French & Eur.
Moore, W. C. Diccionario de Geografia. 158p. (Espn.). 1972. 11.95 (ISBN 84-237-0340-1, S-50246). French & Eur.
Moore, W. G. A Dictionary of Geography: Definitions & Explanations of Terms Used in Physical Geography. LC 77-94144. (Illus.). 1978. text ed. 18.50x (ISBN 0-06-494934-6). B&N.
Morse, Jedidiah. American Gazetteer, 1797. 629p. 1979. 21.70 (ISBN 0-686-27821-6). Bookmark.
Paxton, John, ed. The Stateman's Year-Book, 1976-1977. LC 4-3776. 1976. 19.95 (ISBN 0-312-76055-8). St Martin.
--Statesman's Yearbook World Gazetteer. LC 74-16097. 1975. 15.00 (ISBN 0-312-76125-2). St Martin.
Rand McNally Green Guide. 1974. pap. 15.00 (ISBN 0-528-21060-2). Rand.
Room, Adrian, compiled by. Place-Name Changes Since Nineteen Hundred: A World Gazetteer. LC 79-4300. 1979. 11.00 (ISBN 0-8108-1210-X). Scarecrow.
Sachs, Moshe Y. Worldmark Encyclopedia of the Nations, 5 vols. 5th ed. 1976. Set. 99.50 (ISBN 0-471-74833-1, Pub. by Wiley-Interscience). Wiley.
Seltzer, Leon E., ed. Columbia-Lippincott Gazetteer of the World, with 1961 Supplement. LC 62-4711. 1952. 135.00x (ISBN 0-231-01559-3). Columbia U Pr.
Stamp, Dudley & Clark, Audrey N. A Glossary of Geographical Terms. 3rd ed. 1979. text ed. 37.50x (ISBN 0-582-35258-4). Longman.
Stein, Henri. Dictionnaire Topographique de la France. Hubert, J., ed. 738p. (Fr.). 1954. pap. 25.00 (ISBN 0-686-57226-2, M-6525). French & Eur.
Thuillier. Lexique Anglais-Francais des Termes Appartenant Aux Technques En Usage I.G.N, 2 vols, Pt. 1. 464p. (Fr. -Eng., English_French Lexicon of Terms Pertaining to Techniques Used at I.G.N.). 1958. pap. 14.95 (ISBN 0-686-56781-1, M-6357). French & Eur.
Turner, T. G. Gazetter of St. Joseph Valley for 1867. (Illus.). 1978. Repr. of 1867 ed. 6.00 (ISBN 0-912382-24-4). Black Letter.
Wasserman, Paul, et al, eds. Encyclopedia of Geographic Information Sources. 3rd ed. LC 78-55032. 1978. 58.00 (ISBN 0-8103-0374-4). Gale.

GEOGRAPHY–EARLY WORKS
see Classical Geography; Geography, Ancient; Geography–15th-16th Centuries; Geography, Medieval

GEOGRAPHY–EXAMINATIONS, QUESTIONS, ETC.
Anthony, James T., et al. Basic Geography: A Manual of Exercises. 1975. pap. 3.25 (ISBN 0-910042-16-0). Allegheny.
Rudman, Jack. Geography. (Graduate Record Examination Ser.: GRE-7). (Cloth bdg. avail. on request). 9.95 (ISBN 0-8373-5207-X). Natl Learning.

GEOGRAPHY–GAMES
see Geographical Recreations

GEOGRAPHY–GAZETTEERS
see Geography–Dictionaries

GEOGRAPHY–HISTORY
see also Discoveries (In Geography); Geographical Myths; Geography, Ancient; Geography, Medieval; Maps, Early
Beazley, Charles. The Dawn of Modern Geography: A History of Exploration Geographical Science. 1976. Repr. of 1906 ed. 86.00 (ISBN 0-403-06495-3, Regency). Scholarly.
Beazley, Charles R. Dawn of Modern Geography, 3 vols. (Illus.). 45.00 (ISBN 0-8446-1063-1). Peter Smith.
Certaine Brief & Necessarie Rules of Geographie. LC 76-57402. (English Experience Ser.: No. 818). 1977. Repr. of 1573 ed. lib. bdg. 3.50 (ISBN 90-221-0818-X). Walter J Johnson.
Dickinson, Robert E. Regional Concept: The Anglo-American Leaders. 1976. 26.75x (ISBN 0-7100-8272-X). Routledge & Kegan.
Fischer, Eric, et al. Question of Place. 2nd ed. 1969. 27.50 (ISBN 0-87948-004-1). Beatty.
Geerz, F. Geschichte der Geographischen Vermessungen und der Landkarten Nordalbingiens. 1859. text ed. 16.00x (ISBN 9-06041-023-8). Humanities.
James, Preston E. & Martin, Geoffrey J. All Possible Worlds, a History of Geographical Ideas. 2nd ed. LC 80-25021. 508p. 1981. text ed. 23.95 (ISBN 0-471-06121-2). Wiley.
Keane, J. The Evolution of Geography. (Illus.). 1976. Repr. of 1899 ed. text ed. 30.25x (ISBN 90-6041-112-9). Humanities.
Morgan, Michael & Briggs, D., eds. Historical Sources in Geography. (Sources & Methods in Geography Ser.). 1979. pap. 6.95 (ISBN 0-408-10609-3). Butterworth.
Stoddart, D. R., ed. Geography, Ideology & Social Concern. (Illus.). 256p. 1981. 26.50x (ISBN 0-389-20207-X). B&N.
Survey of Research in Geography, Nineteen Sixty-Nine to Nineteen Seventy-Two (India) 1979. 12.50x (ISBN 0-8364-0524-2). South Asia Bks.
Taylor, Eva G. Late Tudor & Early Stuart Geography, 1583-1650. 1968. lib. bdg. 20.50x (ISBN 0-374-97809-3). Octagon.
--Tudor Geography, 1485-1583. 1968. lib. bdg. 18.00x (ISBN 0-374-97847-6). Octagon.

GEOGRAPHY–JUVENILE LITERATURE
Adler, Peggy. Geography Puzzles. (Illus.). (gr. 4-6). 1979. PLB 6.90 s&l (ISBN 0-531-02867-4). Watts.
Clayton, Robert. Mexico, Central America & the West Indies. LC 71-119588. (Finding Out About Geography Ser). (Illus.). (gr. 3-6). 1971. PLB 6.89 (ISBN 0-381-99849-5, A48900, JD-J). Har-Row.
Evans, F. C. A First Geography of the West Indies. (gr. 5 up). 1974. 5.95x (ISBN 0-521-20112-8). Cambridge U Pr.
Hine, Al & Alcorn, John. Where in the World Do You Live. LC 62-7728. (Illus.). 40p. (gr. 1-3). 1962. 4.50 (ISBN 0-15-295605-0, HJ). HarBraceJ.
MacDonald Countries, 8 bks. Incl. Canada. Harris, Jeanette. LC 77-70185 (ISBN 0-382-06110-1); Egypt. Von Haag, Michael. LC 77-70186 (ISBN 0-382-06112-8); India. Taalyarkhan, Natasha. LC 77-70187 (ISBN 0-382-06113-6); Mexico. Howard, John. LC 77-70189 (ISBN 0-382-06114-4); Nigeria. Synge, Richard. LC 77-70190 (ISBN 0-382-06115-2); Turkey. Hotham, David. LC 77-70192 (ISBN 0-382-06116-0); Netherlands. Huggett, Frank E. LC 77-70193 (ISBN 0-382-06117-9); Belgium & Luxembourg. Marey, Jean & Marey, George. LC 77-70194 (ISBN 0-382-06118-7). (gr. 6 up). 1977. lib. bdg. 7.95 (ISBN 0-686-57952-6). Silver.
Stavrianos, Leften S., et al. A Global History of Man. (gr. 9-12). 1974. text ed. 17.40 (ISBN 0-205-03815-8, 7838158); tchrs'. guide 4.40 (ISBN 0-205-03816-6, 7838166); tests & dup. masters 44.00 (ISBN 0-205-02467-X, 782467X). Allyn.

GEOGRAPHY–MATHEMATICAL MODELS
Wilson, A. G. Catastrophe Theory & Bifurcation: Applications to Urban & Regional Geography. (Illus.). 400p. 1981. 40.00x (ISBN 0-520-04370-7). U of Cal Pr.

GEOGRAPHY–METHODOLOGY
Beaujeu-Garnier, J. Methods & Perspectives in Geography. Bray, Jennifer, tr. from French. LC 75-23484. (Illus.). 144p. 1976. text ed. 11.95x (ISBN 0-582-48069-8). Longman.
Brewer, J. Gordon. The Literature of Geography: A Guide to Its Organisation & Use. 2nd ed. (Guide to Subject Literature Ser.). 1978. 19.50 (ISBN 0-208-01683-X, Linnet). Shoe String.
Estes, John E. & Senger, Leslie W. Remote Sensing: Techniques for Environmental Analysis. LC 73-8601. 1974. 19.95 (ISBN 0-471-24595-X). Wiley.
Freeman, T. W. The Writing of Geography. 100p. 1971. 15.00x (ISBN 0-7190-0454-3, Pub. by Manchester U Pr England). State Mutual Bk.
Gregory, S. Statistical Methods & the Geographer. 4th ed. LC 77-7025. (Geographies for Advanced Study Ser). (Illus.). 1978. pap. text ed. 11.95x (ISBN 0-582-48186-4). Longman.
Hartshorne, Richard. The Nature of Geography: A Critical Survey of Current Thought in the Light of the Past. LC 76-48691. (Annals of the Association of American Geographers). 1977. Repr. of 1949 ed. lib. bdg. 38.75 (ISBN 0-8371-9328-1, HANG). Greenwood.
Huggett, Richard. Systems Analysis in Geography. (Contemporary Problems in Geography Ser.). (Illus.). 218p. 1980. text ed. 33.00x (ISBN 0-19-874081-6); pap. text ed. 12.95x (ISBN 0-19-874082-4). Oxford U Pr.
International Geographical Union European Regional Conference, Budapest, August 11-14, 1971. Regional Studies, Methods & Analyses: Proceedings. Bencze, Imre, ed. (Illus.). 416p. 1974. 32.50x (ISBN 963-05-0417-0). Intl Pubns Serv.
Sreniawski, R. W., ed. Readings in Geography. LC 72-86201. 320p. 1972. text ed. 34.50x (ISBN 0-8422-5031-X). Irvington.

GEOGRAPHY–MISCELLANEA
Harris, Chauncy D. Annotated World List of Selected Current Geographical Serials. rev., 4th ed. LC 80-17561. (Research Papers: No. 194). 165p. 1980. pap. 8.00 (ISBN 0-89065-101-9). U Chicago Dept Geog.
Wood, C. M., et al. The Geography of Pollution: A Study of Greater Manchester. 150p. 1974. 27.00x (ISBN 0-7190-0564-7, Pub. by Manchester U Pr England). State Mutual Bk.

GEOGRAPHY–MODELS
Thomas, R. W. & Huggett, R. J. Modelling in Geography. 1980. text ed. 21.50 (ISBN 0-06-318060-X, IntlDept); pap. text ed. 17.25 (ISBN 0-06-318171-1). Har-Row.
--Modelling in Geography: A Mathematical Approach. 338p. 1980. 27.50x (ISBN 0-389-20049-2); pap. 17.00x (ISBN 0-389-20050-6). B&N.

GEOGRAPHY–PICTORIAL WORKS
see also Views
America: An Aerial View. Date not set. 5.95 (ISBN 0-517-25701-7). Aerial Photo.

GEOGRAPHY–READERS
see Readers–Geography

GEOGRAPHY–RESEARCH
see Geographical Research

GEORGRAPHY–STATISTICS
see Geography–Tables, Etc.

GEOGRAPHY–STUDY AND TEACHING
see also Area Studies; Geographical Recreations
African Geography for Schools. (Source Bks on Curricula & Methods). (Illus.). 309p. 1975. 28.25 (ISBN 92-3-101019-0, U7, UNESCO). Unipub.
Bailey, Patrick. Teaching Geography. (Teaching Ser.). (Illus.). 261p. 1975. 17.95 (ISBN 0-7153-6860-5). David & Charles.
Ball, John M., et al. The Social Sciences & Geographic Education: A Reader. LC 73-140549. 329p. 1971. pap. 11.50 (ISBN 0-471-04631-0, Pub. by Wiley). Krieger.
Broek, Jan O., et al. The Study & Teaching of Geography. 2nd ed. (Social Science Seminar, Secondary Education Ser.: No. C28). 120p. 1980. pap. text ed. 6.95 (ISBN 0-675-08163-7). Merrill.
Brown, E. H., ed. Geography Yesterday & Tomorrow. 312p. 1980. 29.95x (ISBN 0-19-874096-4). Oxford U Pr.
Dunlop, Stewart, ed. Place & People: A Guide to Modern Geography Teaching. 1976. text ed. 8.95x (ISBN 0-435-34697-0). Heinemann Ed.
Fink, L. Dee. Listening to the Learner: An Exploratory Study of Personal Meaning in College Geography Courses. LC 77-15501. (Research Papers: No. 184). (Illus.). 1977. pap. 8.00 (ISBN 0-89065-091-8). U Chicago Dept Geog.
Freeman, T. W., et al, eds. Geographers: Biobibliographical Studies, Vol. 3. (Illus.). 1980. pap. 28.25 (ISBN 0-7201-0927-2, Pub. by Mansell England). Merrimack Bk Serv.
Fuchs, Roland J. & Street, John M., eds. Geography in Asian Universities. 525p. 1975. pap. 7.00x (ISBN 0-8248-0376-0). U Pr of Hawaii.
Graves, Norman. Curriculum Planning in Geography. 1979. text ed. 29.95x (ISBN 0-435-35313-6); pap. text ed. 10.50x (ISBN 0-435-35312-8). Heinemann Ed.
Graves, Norman J. Geography in Education. 1975. text ed. 21.95 (ISBN 0-435-35310-1); pap. text ed. 9.95 (ISBN 0-435-35311-X). Heinemann Ed.
Hall, David. Geography & the Geography Teacher. (Unwin Education Books: Teaching Today Ser.). 1976. pap. text ed. 11.50x (ISBN 0-04-371044-1). Allen Unwin.
Hudson, Fred S. North America. (Advanced Level Geography Ser.). (Illus.). 462p. 1974. pap. 11.25x (ISBN 0-7121-1408-4). Intl Pubns Serv.
James, Preston E. & Jones, Clarence F., eds. American Geography: Inventory & Prospect. (Illus.). 1954. 15.00x (ISBN 0-8156-2013-6). Syracuse U Pr.
Jay, L. J. Geography Teaching with a Little Latitude. (Classroom Close-Ups Ser.: No. 7). (Illus.). 160p. 1981. text ed. 19.95x (ISBN 0-04-371077-8); pap. text ed. 8.95x (ISBN 0-04-371078-6). Allen Unwin.
Kiuchi, Shinzo, ed. Geography in Japan. (Illus.). 1976. 52.50x (ISBN 0-86008-159-1, Pub. by U of Tokyo Pr). Intl Schol Bk Serv.
Marchant, E. C., ed. Teaching of Geography at School Level. LC 74-29462. (Education in Europe Ser). (Orig.). 1971. pap. 9.50x (ISBN 0-245-50434-6). Intl Pubns Serv.
Masterton, Thomas & Salmon, Raymond. The Principles of Objective Testing in Geography. 1974. text ed. 11.95x (ISBN 0-435-35700-X). Heinemann Ed.
Mulloy, Teresa, ed. Guide to Graduate Departments of Geography in the United States & Canada, 1979-1980. 12th ed. LC 68-59269. 1979. pap. text ed. 6.00 (ISBN 0-89291-135-2). Assn Am Geographers.
Mulloy, Teresa A., ed. Guide to Graduate Departments of Geography in the United States & Canada, 1981-1982. 14th ed. LC 68-59269. 320p. 1981. pap. 8.00 (ISBN 0-89291-156-5). Assn Am Geographers.
--Guide to Graduate Departments of Geography in the United States & Canada, 1980-1981. 13th ed. LC 68-59269. 1980. pap. 6.00 (ISBN 0-89291-152-2). Assn Am Geographers.
Our World Cut-Outs - Junior Geographic Workbooks. (Illus.). 16p. (YA) 1.00 (ISBN 0-685-27303-2). Stewart.
Panel on Geography in the Two-Year Colleges. Geography in the Two-Year Colleges: No. 10. LC 73-133905. 1970. pap. 1.00 (ISBN 0-89291-038-0). Assn Am Geographers.
Reeder, Edwin H. A Method of Directing Children's Study of Geography. LC 73-177184. (Columbia University. Teachers College. Contributions to Education: No. 193). Repr. of 1925 ed. 17.50 (ISBN 0-404-55193-9). AMS Pr.
Stoddard, R. H. Planning College Geography Facilities. LC 73-83739. (General Ser.: No. 12). 1973. pap. 1.00 (ISBN 0-89291-043-7). Assn Am Geographers.
Thralls, Zoe A. Teaching of Geography. LC 58-6701. (Illus.). 1958. 18.50x (ISBN 0-89197-442-3); pap. text ed. 6.95x (ISBN 0-89197-443-1). Irvington.

Tricart, J. Teaching of Geography at University Level. LC 74-194640. (Education in Europe Ser). (Orig.). 1969. pap. 7.50x (ISBN 0-245-59753-0). Intl Pubns Serv.

UNESCO Source Book for Geography Teaching. 1965. 7.50 (ISBN 92-3-100584-7, UNESCO). Unipub.

White, C. Langdon, et al. Essentials of College Geography. LC 58-6374. (Illus.). 1958. text ed. 18.95x (ISBN 0-89197-553-5); pap. text ed. 8.95x (ISBN 0-89197-752-X). Irvington.

Williams, Michael, ed. Geography & the Integrated Curriculum. 1976. text ed. 21.95x (ISBN 0-435-35730-1); pap. text ed. 12.95x (ISBN 0-435-35731-X). Heinemann Ed.

GEOGRAPHY-TABLES, ETC.

see also Distances-Tables, Etc.

Clark, Isobel. Practical Geostatistics. 1979. 24.80x (ISBN 0-85334-843-X). Intl Ideas.

Silk, John. Statistical Concepts in Geography. (Illus.). 1979. text ed. 22.50x (ISBN 0-04-910065-3); pap. text ed. 9.95x (ISBN 0-04-910066-1). Allen Unwin.

GEOGRAPHY-TERMINOLOGY

see also Names, Geographical

Swayne, James C. A Concise Glossary of Geographical Terms. LC 76-3717. 164p. 1976. Repr. of 1968 ed. lib. bdg. 15.00x (ISBN 0-8371-8785-0, SWCG). Greenwood.

GEOGRAPHY-TEXTBOOKS

Boyce, Ronald R. Geographic Perspectives on Global Problems: An Introduction to Geography. 500p. 1982. text ed. 22.95 (ISBN 0-471-09336-X). Wiley.

De Blij, Harm J. Geography: Regions & Concepts. 3rd ed. LC 80-17961. 583p. 1981. text ed. 25.95 (ISBN 0-471-08015-2). study guide 10.95 (ISBN 0-471-07882-4). Wiley.

Doerr, Arthur H. & Guernsey, Lee. Principles of Geography: Physical & Cultural. rev. ed. LC 74-32106. (gr. 9up). 1975. pap. text ed. 4.50 (ISBN 0-8120-0629-1). Barron.

Drummond. The Western Hemisphere. (Our World Today Ser.). (gr. 5-8). 1978. text ed. 15.80 (ISBN 0-205-05856-6, 7758561); tchr's guide 9.60 (ISBN 0-205-05857-4, 77857X). Allyn.

Getis, Arthur, et al. Geography. 1981. text ed. 19.95x (ISBN 0-686-72533-6); student study guide 6.95 (ISBN 0-02-431580-X). Macmillan.

Haggett, Peter. Geography: A Modern Synthesis. 3rd ed. 1979. text ed. 22.95 scp (ISBN 0-06-042578-4, HarpC); scp study guide 8.50 (ISBN 0-06-042728-0); instructor's manual avail. (ISBN 0-06-362561-X). Har-Row.

Hoyt, Joseph B. Man & the Earth. 3rd ed. (Illus.). 512p. 1973. text ed. 21.95 (ISBN 0-13-550947-5). P-H.

Kariel, Herbert G. & Kariel, Patricia E. Explorations in Social Geography. LC 71-173959. 1972. text ed. 15.95 (ISBN 0-201-03634-7). A-W.

Knowles, R. North America in Maps: Topographical Map Studies of Canada & the USA. (Illus.). 1976. pap. text ed. 12.95x (ISBN 0-582-31017-2). Longman.

Lenglet Du Fresnoy, Nicolas. Geography of Children. (Early Childrens Books). 1969. Repr. of 1737 ed. 12.50 (ISBN 0-384-32280-8). Johnson Repr.

Meyer, Iain & Huggett, Richard. Geography, Bk. 1. 1979. pap. text ed. 9.50 (ISBN 0-06-318096-0, IntlDept). Har-Row.

Morris, John W. World Geography. 3rd ed. (Illus.). 672p. 1972. text ed. 21.00 (ISBN 0-07-043138-8, C); instructor's manual 3.95 (ISBN 0-07-043142-6); study guide 5.95 (ISBN 0-07-061120-3). McGraw.

Russell, Richard, et al. Culture Worlds. 2nd, rev. ed. (Illus.). 1969. text ed. 13.95x (ISBN 0-02-404800-3). Macmillan.

Stamp, Dudley. The World: A General Geography. 19th ed. Clarke, Audrey, ed. (Illus.). 1978. pap. text ed. 11.95x (ISBN 0-582-33055-6). Longman.

Trewartha, Glenn T., et al. Elements of Geography. 5th ed. 1967. text ed. 18.95 (ISBN 0-07-065155-8, C). McGraw.

Witthuhn, Burton O., et al. Discovery in Geography. LC 75-44923. 1976. pap. text ed. 3.95 (ISBN 0-8403-1396-9). Kendall-Hunt.

GEOGRAPHY-VIEWS

see Views

GEOGRAPHY-TO 400 A.D.

see Geography, Ancient

GEOGRAPHY-400-1400

see Geography, Medieval

GEOGRAPHY-15TH-16TH CENTURIES

Abbot, George. A Briefe Description of the Whole Worlde. LC 78-25701. (English Experience Ser.: No. 213). 68p. Repr. of 1599 ed. 9.50 (ISBN 90-221-0213-0). Walter J Johnson.

Botero, Giovanni. The Traveller's Breviant, or an Historical Description of the Most Famous Kingdomes. LC 72-175. (English Experience Ser.: No. 143). 180p. 1969. Repr. of 1601 ed. 21.00 (ISBN 90-221-0143-6). Walter J Johnson.

GEOGRAPHY, AERIAL

Here are entered works on the effect of aviation on geography, as well as works on geographical factors in aeronautics.

see also Aeronautics, Commercial

Monkhouse, F. J. Landscape from the Air. 2nd ed. LC 70-134621. (Illus.). 1971. text ed. 5.75x (ISBN 0-521-08000-2). Cambridge U Pr.

GEOGRAPHY, AGRICULTURAL

see Agricultural Geography

GEOGRAPHY, ANCIENT

Here are entered works on the geography of the ancient world in general. Works confined to the geography of Greece and Rome are entered under Classical Geography.

see also Cities and Towns, Ancient; also subdivision Description, Geography under names of countries of antiquity

Bunbury, E. H. A History of Ancient Geography: Among the Greeks & Romans from the Earliest Ages till the Fall of the Roman Empire, 2 vols. (Illus.). 1979. Repr. of 1879 ed. Set. text ed. 185.25x (ISBN 90-7026-511-7). Humanities.

Burton, Harry E. Discovery of the Ancient World. facsimile ed. LC 75-102228. (Select Bibliographies Reprint Ser). 1932. 17.00 (ISBN 0-8369-5113-1). Arno.

Cuntz, Otto. Die Geographie Des Ptolemaeus: Galliae, Germania, Raetia, Noricum, Pannoniae, Illyricum, Italia. LC 75-7310. (Roman History Ser.). 1975. Repr. 14.00x (ISBN 0-405-07192-2). Arno.

Dey, Nundo Lal. The Geographical Dictionary of Ancient & Mediaeval India. LC 42-31336. (Illus.). 272p. 1971. Repr. of 1927 ed. 19.50x (ISBN 0-8002-1453-6). Intl Pubns Serv.

Geyer, Paul, ed. Itinera Hierosolymitana, Saeculi 3-8. (Corpus Scriptorum Ecclesiasticorum Latinorum Ser: Vol. 39). Repr. of 1898 ed. pap. 33.00 (ISBN 0-384-18270-4). Johnson Repr.

Gupta, P. Geography in Ancient Indian Inscriptions, up to 650 A. D. (Illus.). 350p. 1973. text ed. 17.00x (ISBN 0-391-00498-0). Humanities.

Kennedy, E. S. Commentary Upon Biruni's Kitab Tahdid Al-Amakin: An 11th Century Treatise on Mathematical Geography. 1974. 16.95x (ISBN 0-8156-6042-1, Am U Beirut). Syracuse U Pr.

McEvedy, Colin. The Penguin Atlas of Ancient History. (Maps). (YA) (gr. 9 up). 1967. pap. 5.95 (ISBN 0-14-070832-4). Penguin.

Muir, Ramsey. Medieval & Modern: Including Ancient & Classical, 6th Ed. & Medieval & Modern, 11th Ed. Ancient, Medieval & Modern. 10th ed. Fullard, Harold & Treharne, R. E., eds. (Illus.). 1964. Repr. of 1911 ed. 19.50x (ISBN 0-06-495016-6). B&N.

Palmer, R. R., ed. Historical Atlas of the World. 1965. pap. text ed. 3.95 (ISBN 0-528-83081-3). Rand.

Ptolemy, Claudius. Geography of Claudius Ptolemy. Stevenson, Edward L., ed. LC 70-174287. Repr. of 1932 ed. 245.00 (ISBN 0-404-05148-0). AMS Pr.

Sabin, Francis E. Classical Associations of Places in Italy. 1921. 45.00 (ISBN 0-8274-3977-6). R West.

Strabo. Geography, 8 vols. Incl. Vol. 1. Bks. 1-2 (ISBN 0-674-99055-2); Vol. 2. Bks. 3-5 (ISBN 0-674-99056-0); Vol. 3. Bks. 6-7 (ISBN 0-674-99201-6); Vol. 4. Bks. 8-9 (ISBN 0-674-99216-4); Vol. 5. Bks. 10-12 (ISBN 0-674-99233-4); Vol. 6. Bks. 13-14 (ISBN 0-674-99246-6); Vol. 7. Bks. 15-16 (ISBN 0-674-99266-0); Vol. 8. Bk. 17. & General Index (ISBN 0-674-99295-4). (Loeb Classical Library: No. 49-50, 182, 196, 211, 223, 241, 267). 11.00x ea. Harvard U Pr.

Thomson, J. Oliver. History of Ancient Geography. LC 64-23024. 1948. 15.00x (ISBN 0-8196-0143-8). Biblo.

Tozer, Henry F. History of Ancient Geography. 2nd ed. LC 54-13396. 1897. 15.00x (ISBN 0-8196-0138-1). Biblo.

West, R. G. The Pre-Glacial Pleistocene of the Norfolk & Suffolk Coasts. LC 77-90191. (Illus.). 1980. 95.00 (ISBN 0-521-21962-0). Cambridge U Pr.

GEOGRAPHY, ANCIENT-MAPS

McEvedy, Colin & McEvedy, Sarah. The Classical World. LC 75-653786. (The Atlas of World History Ser.). (Illus.). 64p. (gr. 6-12). 1974. 9.95 (ISBN 0-02-765550-4, 76555, CCPr). Macmillan.

GEOGRAPHY, BIBLICAL

see Bible-Geography

GEOGRAPHY, CLASSICAL

see Classical Geography

GEOGRAPHY, COMMERCIAL

Davies, Ross L. Marketing Geography with Special Reference to Retailing. 300p. 1977. pap. text ed. 14.95x (ISBN 0-416-70700-9, Pub. by Chapman & Hall England). Methuen Inc.

Dawson, John A. Retail Geography. 248p. 1980. 32.95 (ISBN 0-470-27014-4, Pub. by Hlasted Pr). Wiley.

Staff of World Bank. World Tables: 1980. LC 79-3649. (World Bank Occasional Paper Ser.). (Illus.). 480p. 1980. text ed. 27.50x (ISBN 0-8018-2389-7); pap. text ed. 10.95x (ISBN 0-8018-2390-0). Johns Hopkins.

Stamp, L., et al, eds. Chisholm's Handbook of Commercial Geography. 20th ed. (Illus.). 1016p. 1980. text ed. 70.00x (ISBN 0-582-30015-0). Longman.

GEOGRAPHY, ECCLESIASTICAL

see Ecclesiastical Geography

GEOGRAPHY, ECONOMIC

see also Agricultural Geography; Geography, Commercial; also subdivision Economic Conditions under names of countries

Alexander, John W. & Gibson, L. Economic Geography. 2nd ed. 1979. 21.95 (ISBN 0-13-225151-5). P-H.

Berry, Brian J. L. & Conkling, Edgar C. Geography of Economic Systems. ref. ed. 544p. 1976. 22.85 (ISBN 0-13-351296-7); wkbk. study guide 5.50 (ISBN 0-13-351338-6). P-H.

Boesler, K. A. Geography & Capital. 1975. pap. text ed. 28.00 (ISBN 0-08-019712-4). Pergamon.

Boyce, Ronald R. The Bases of Economic Geography. 2nd ed. LC 77-21382. 1978. text ed. 22.95 (ISBN 0-03-019496-2, HoltC). HR&W.

Butler, Joseph H. Economic Geography: Spatial & Environmental Aspects of Economic Activity. LC 80-14542. 402p. 1980. 26.95 (ISBN 0-471-12681-0). Wiley.

Chatterjee, S. P. Elements of Economic Geography. 128p. 1981. 15.00x (ISBN 0-86131-091-8, Pub. by Orient Longman India). State Mutual Bk.

Cherry, William. Economic Geography. 1975. text ed. write for info. (ISBN 0-88429-008-5). Collegiate Pub.

Coats, B. E. & Tawstron, E. M. Regional Variations in Britain: Studies in Economic & Social Geography. 1972. 40.00 (ISBN 0-7134-2103-7, Pub. by Batsford England). David & Charles.

Conkling, Edgar C. & Yeates, Maurice H. Man's Economic Environment. (Geography Ser.). 1976. text ed. 17.50 (ISBN 0-07-012408-6, C). McGraw.

Demko, George J. & Fuchs, Roland J., eds. Geographical Perspectives in the Soviet Union: A Selection of Readings. Demko, George J. & Fuchs, Roland J., trs. LC 74-9853. (Illus.). 1974. 30.00x (ISBN 0-8142-0196-2). Ohio St U Pr.

DeSouza, Anthony & Foust, Brady. World Space-Economy. 1979. text ed. 21.95 (ISBN 0-675-08292-7) (ISBN 0-685-96154-0). Merrill.

Dicken, Peter & Lloyd, Peter. Modern Western Society. 1981. text ed. 31.50 (ISBN 0-06-318030-8, IntlDept); pap. text ed. 16.95 (ISBN 0-06-318048-0). Har-Row.

Earney, Fillmore C. Researcher's Guide to Iron Ore: An Annotated Bibliography on the Economic Geography of Iron Ore. LC 74-76986. 1974. lib. bdg. 50.00 (ISBN 0-87287-095-2). Libs Unl.

Eyre, S. R. The Real Wealth of Nations. LC 77-93019. 1978. 25.00x (ISBN 0-312-66525-3). St Martin.

Foust. The Economic Landscape: A Theoretical Introduction. (Geography Ser.). 1978. text ed. 20.95 (ISBN 0-675-08432-6). Merrill.

Ginsburg, Norton, ed. Essays on Geography & Economic Development. LC 60-2105. (Research Papers Ser.: No. 62). 196p. 1960. pap. 8.00 (ISBN 0-89065-003-9). U Chicago Dept Geog.

Guest, Arthur. Man & Landscape. 2nd ed. 1978. text ed. 10.50x (ISBN 0-435-35355-1). Heinemann Ed.

Haggett, P. Locational Analysis in Human Geography. (Illus.). 1965. 17.95 (ISBN 0-312-49420-3). St Martin.

Haggett, Peter, et al. Locational Analysis in Human Geography, 2 vols. 2nd ed. LC 77-8967. 1977. Set. 80.95 (ISBN 0-470-99207-7); Vol. 1, Locational Models. pap. 16.95 (ISBN 0-470-99208-5); Vol. 2, Locational Methods. pap. 21.95 (ISBN 0-470-99209-3). Halsted Pr.

Hodder, B. K. & Lee, R. K. Economic Geography. LC 74-77770. (Field of Geography Ser.). 224p. 1974. 12.95x (ISBN 0-312-23310-8). St Martin.

Hull, O. Geography of Production. 1967. 17.95 (ISBN 0-312-32235-6). St Martin.

King, Grace E., ed. Conflict & Harmony: A Source-Book of Man in His Environment. 450p. 1972. 15.95x (ISBN 0-8464-0274-2). Beekman Pubs.

Lloyd, Peter & Dicken, Peter. Location in Space. 2nd ed. 1977. text ed. 23.65 (ISBN 0-06-318058-8, IntlDept); pap. text ed. 19.80 (ISBN 0-06-318059-6). Har-Row.

Lloyd, Peter E. & Dicken, Peter. Location in Space: A Theoretical Approach to Economic Geography. 2nd ed. 1977. text ed. 22.95 scp (ISBN 0-06-044048-1, HarpC). Har-Row.

McCarty, Harold H. Geographic Basis of American Economic Life. LC 79-109297. (Illus.). 1971. Repr. of 1940 ed. lib. bdg. 28.50x (ISBN 0-8371-3840-X, MCAE). Greenwood.

Maksakovsky, V., ed. The Economic Geography of the World. (Illus.). 1978. 10.00 (ISBN 0-8285-0002-9, Pub. by Progress Pubs Russia). Imported Pubns.

Medvedkov, Yuri, ed. Regional Systems: IGU Congress, Moscow, 1976, Proceedings, Pt. 2. 1977. pap. text ed. 19.50 (ISBN 0-08-021323-5). Pergamon.

Molle, W., et al. Regional Disparity & Economic Development in the European Community. LC 79-91668. 428p. 1980. text ed. 37.50 (ISBN 0-916672-50-6). Allanheld.

O'Connor, A. M. An Economic Geography of East Africa. (Advanced Economic Geography Ser.). 1971. lib. bdg. 25.25x (ISBN 0-7135-1626-7). Westview.

O'Sullivan, Patrick. Geographical Economics. LC 80-39881. 199p. 1981. 24.95 (ISBN 0-470-27122-1). Halsted Pr.

Peattie, Roderick. Geography in Human Destiny. LC 74-113294. 1970. Repr. of 1940 ed. 14.00 (ISBN 0-8046-1327-3). Kennikat.

Perpillou, Aime V. Human Geography. 2d ed. LC 76-55302. (Geographies for Advanced Study Ser.). (Illus.). 1977. text ed. 21.00x (ISBN 0-582-48571-1); pap. text ed. 15.95x (ISBN 0-582-48572-X). Longman.

Phillips, A. D. & Turton, B. J., eds. Environment, Man & Economic Change: Essays Presented to S.H. Beaver. (Illus.). 500p. 1975. text ed. 42.00x (ISBN 0-582-50114-8). Longman.

Pounds, Norman J. Introduction to Economic Geography. (Illus.). 1952. 10.95 (ISBN 0-7195-1114-3). Dufour.

Saushkin, Y. G. Economic Geography: Theory & Methods. 312p. 1980. 8.00 (ISBN 0-8285-1721-5, Pub. by Progress Pubs Russia). Imported Pubns.

Spidchenko, B. Economic Geography of the World: A Popular Outline. 189p. 1975. 12.95x (ISBN 0-8464-0350-1). Beekman Pubs.

Staff of World Bank. World Tables: 1980. LC 79-3649. (World Bank Occasional Paper Ser.). (Illus.). 480p. 1980. text ed. 27.50x (ISBN 0-8018-2389-7); pap. text ed. 10.95x (ISBN 0-8018-2390-0). Johns Hopkins.

Thoman, Richard S. & Corbin, Peter. The Geography of Economic Activity. rev. 3rd ed. LC 74-5756. (Illus.). 528p. 1974. text ed. 19.95 (ISBN 0-07-064207-9, C); instructor's manual 2.95 (ISBN 0-07-029635-9). McGraw.

Tietze, W., ed. Settlement: The Most Important Productive Medium of Economic Man. 92p. 1975. pap. text ed. 24.00 (ISBN 0-08-019671-3). Pergamon.

Turnock, David. An Economic Geography of Romania. (Advanced Economic Geography Ser.). 1974. lib. bdg. 29.75x (ISBN 0-7135-1628-3). Westview.

Vinge, Clarence L. & Vinge, Ada. Economic Geography. 368p. 1966. 10.00x (ISBN 0-87471-741-8). Rowman.

Watts, H. D. The Branch Plant Economy: A Study of External Control. (Topics in Applied Geography Ser.). (Illus.). 128p. (Orig.). 1981. pap. text ed. 10.95x (ISBN 0-582-30028-2). Longman.

Wheeler, James O. & Muller, Peter O. Economic Geography. LC 80-21536. 450p. 1981. text ed. 25.95 (ISBN 0-471-93760-6). Wiley.

Whitbeck, Ray H. & Thomas, Olive J. Geographic Factor. LC 73-113303. 1970. Repr. of 1932 ed. 16.50 (ISBN 0-8046-1331-1). Kennikat.

Whitbeck, Ray H. & Williams, Frank E. Economic Geography of South America. 3rd ed. LC 72-100189. (Illus.). 1971. Repr. of 1940 ed. lib. bdg. 22.00x (ISBN 0-8371-3871-X, WHEG). Greenwood.

White, H. P. & Gleave, M. B. An Economic Geography of West Africa. (Advanced Economic Geography Ser.). 1971. pap. text ed. 17.75x (ISBN 0-7135-1721-2). Westview.

Wilbanks, Thomas J. Location & Well Being: An Introduction to Economic Geography. 1980. text ed. 20.50 scp (ISBN 0-06-167404-4, HarpC). Har-Row.

Wise, M. J. & Rawstron, E. M. R. O. Buchanan & Economic Geography. (Advanced Edonoic Geography Ser.). 1973. lib. bdg. 20.00x (ISBN 0-7135-1766-2). Westview.

Yeates, Maurice. An Introduction to Quantitative Analysis in Human Geography. (Illus.). 288p. 1973. pap. text ed. 13.95 (ISBN 0-07-072251-X, C). McGraw.

Yeates, Maurice Y. Introduction to Quantitative Analysis in Economic Geography. 1968. pap. 6.95 (ISBN 0-07-072259-5, C). McGraw.

GEOGRAPHY, ECONOMIC-MAPS

Cartographic Dept. of the Clarendon Pr. Oxford Economic Atlas of the World. 4th ed. (Illus.). 248p. 1972. 35.00 (ISBN 0-19-894106-4); pap. 9.95x (ISBN 0-19-894107-2). Oxford U Pr.

Ginsburg, Norton. Atlas of Economic Development. LC 61-5610. (Illus.). 1961. 11.00x (ISBN 0-226-29678-4). U of Chicago Pr.

GEOGRAPHY, HISTORICAL

see also Classical Geography; Ecclesiastical Geography; Geography, Ancient; Geography, Medieval;

also names of countries, regions, etc., or subdivision Historical Geography, or Description, Geography under names of countries, regions, etc.

Adams, I. H. Agrarian Landscape Terms: A Glossary for Historical Geography. (Special Publication of the Institute of British Geographers: No. 9). 1980. 23.00 (ISBN 0-12-044180-2). Acad Pr.

Brugsch, H. Geographische Inschriften Altagyptischer Denkmaler. (Ger.). 1860. text ed. 131.50x (ISBN 90-6041-089-0). Humanities.

Charlesworth, Andrew. Social Portrait in a Rural Society. (Historical Geography Research Ser.). 1980. pap. 3.50x (ISBN 0-686-27387-7, Pub. by GEO Abstracts England). State Mutual Bk.

Dall, W. H. History, Geography, Resources, Vol. 2. Repr. of 1902 ed. 35.00 (ISBN 0-527-38162-4). Kraus Repr.

East, W. Gordon. Geography Behind History. (Illus.). 1967. pap. 4.95 (ISBN 0-393-00419-8, Norton Lib). Norton.

Freeman, E. A. & Bury, J. B. The Historical Geography of Europe. 612p. 1974. 12.50 (ISBN 0-89005-045-7). Ares.

Gallois, L. Les Geographes Allenmands de la Renaissance. (Illus., Fr.). 1890. pap. text ed. 21.25x (ISBN 90-6041-022-X). Humanities.

Harley, J. B. Aordinance Survey & Landuse Mapping. (Historical Geography Research Ser.). 1980. pap. 3.50x (ISBN 0-686-65841-8, Pub. by GEO Abstracts England). State Mutual Bk.

Hegel, Georg W. The Geographical Basis of History. Rittenhouse, George A., ed. (The Most Meaningful Classics in World Culture Ser.). (Illus.). 1979. 49.75 (ISBN 0-89266-198-4). Am Classical Coll Pr.

Hill, M. N., ed. The Sea: Vol. 3 the Earth Beneath the Sea; History. LC 80-248. 980p. 1981. Repr. of 1963 ed. lib. bdg. write for info. (ISBN 0-89874-099-1). Krieger.

Kain, Roger & Prince, Hugh. The Tithe Surveys of England & Wales. (Studies in Historical Geography). (Illus.). Date not set. cancelled (ISBN 0-208-01726-7, Archon). Shoe String.

Kraus, A. Versuch Einer Geschichte der Handels- und Wirtschafts-Eographie. (Ger.). 1905. text ed. 7.00x (ISBN 90-6041-032-7). Humanities.

Mellor. Geography of Two Germanies. 1978. 20.40 (ISBN 0-06-318066-9, IntlDept). Har-Row.

Mintz, Leigh W. Historical Geology: The Science of a Dynamic Earth. 3rd ed. (Illus.). 576p. 1981. text ed. 22.95 (ISBN 0-675-08028-2); tchr's ed. 3.95 (ISBN 0-686-69492-9). Merrill.

Neubauer, A. La Geographie Du Talmud, 2 pts. Incl. Pt. 1. The Geography of Palestine; Pt. 2. The Geography of Adjacent & Foreign Countries. (Fr.). 1868. pap. text ed. 26.00x (ISBN 90-6041-048-3). Humanities.

Newcomb, Robert M. Planning the Past: Historical Landscape Resources & Recreation. (Studies in Historical Geography). (Illus.). 1979. 17.50 (ISBN 0-208-01728-3, Archon). Shoe String.

Norlind, A. Die Geogaphische Entwicklung des Rheindeltas Bis Um das Jahr 1500. (Illus., Ger.). 1912. text ed. 18.00x (ISBN 90-6041-077-7). Humanities.

Partsch, J. Die Darstellung Europa's in Dem Geographischen Werke des Agrippa. (Orig., Fr.). 1875. pap. text ed. 8.50x (ISBN 90-6041-151-X). Humanities.

Penrose, Boies. Travel & Discovery in the Renaissance, 1420-1620. LC 55-2546. 1962. pap. text ed. 4.95x (ISBN 0-689-70153-5, 10). Atheneum.

Pounds, N. J. An Historical Geography of Europe, 450 Bc-1330 AD. 1973. 59.50 (ISBN 0-521-08563-2); pap. 22.95x (ISBN 0-521-29126-7). Cambridge U Pr.

Powell, Joseph M. Mirrors of the New World: Images & Image - Makers in the Settlement Process. (Studies in Historical Geography Ser.). (Illus.). 1978. 17.50 (ISBN 0-208-01654-6, Archon). Shoe String.

Ramsay, W. M. The Historical Geography of Asia Minor. 495p. 1972. Repr. of 1890 ed. lib. bdg. 23.75x (ISBN 0-8154-0446-8). Cooper Sq.

Reed, M. A. Mapping the Landscape: Studies in the Interpretation of Historical Documents. 1982. 80.00x (ISBN 0-86127-307-9, Pub. by Avebury Pub England). State Mutual Bk.

Smith, Clifford T. An Historical Geography of Western Europe Before 1800. rev. ed. (Geographies for Advances Study Ser.). (Illus.). 1978. pap. text ed. 21.00x (ISBN 0-582-48986-5). Longman.

Wright, John K. The Geographical Lore of the Time of the Crusades. 59.95 (ISBN 0-8490-0217-6). Gordon Pr.

GEOGRAPHY, HISTORICAL–MAPS

Bahat, Dan. Historical Atlas of Jerusalem. 1978. 6.95 (ISBN 0-930038-05-3). Arbit.

Barraclough, Geoffrey, ed. The Times Atlas of World History. 1979. 70.00 (ISBN 0-8437-1125-6). Hammond Inc.

Bjorklund, Oddvar, et al. Historical Atlas of the World. LC 64-26. (Illus.). 1972. pap. 13.95x (ISBN 0-06-490435-0). B&N.

Chambers Atlas of World History. 136p. 1980. 25.00x (ISBN 0-550-14001-8, Pub. by W & R Chambers Scotland). State Mutual Bk.

Chambers Historical Atlas of the World. 1971. 4.50x (ISBN 0-8277-0513-1). British Bk Ctr.

Denuce, J. Oud-Nederlandsche Kaartmakers in Betrekking Met Plantijn, 2 vols. (Illus., Dutch.). 1913. Set. pap. text ed. 42.25x (ISBN 90-6041-009-2). Humanities.

Droeber, W. Kartographie Beiden Naturvolkern. (Illus., Ger.). 1903. pap. text ed. 6.00x (ISBN 90-6041-013-0). Humanities.

Duncan, T. Bentley. Atlantic Islands: Madeira, the Azores, & the Cape Verdes in Seventeenth Century Commerce & Navigation. LC 72-80157. (Studies in the History of Discoveries Ser). (Illus.). 320p. 1972. 12.50x (ISBN 0-226-17001-2). U of Chicago Pr.

Hammond Incorporated Editors. Atlas of World History. 5.95 (ISBN 0-8437-1130-2). Hammond Inc.

--Historical Atlas. (gr. 6-12). pap. 3.50x (ISBN 0-8437-7460-6). Hammond Inc.

Karpinski, L. C. Maps of Famous Cartographers Depicting North America: An Historical Atlas of the Great Lakes & Michigan, with Bibliography of the Printed Maps of Michigan to 1880. 2nd ed. (Illus.). 1977. text ed. 82.75x (ISBN 90-6041-109-9). Humanities.

Littell, Franklin H. Macmillan Atlas History of Christianity. LC 75-22113. (Illus.). 163p. 1976. 21.95 (ISBN 0-02-573140-8, 57314). Macmillan.

McEvedy, Colin. Penguin Atlas of Medieval History. (Orig., Maps). (YA) (gr. 9 up). 1968. pap. 4.95 (ISBN 0-14-070822-7). Penguin.

--Penguin Atlas of Modern History to 1815. (Orig., Maps). 1973. pap. 4.95 (ISBN 0-14-070841-3). Penguin.

Moore, R. I., ed. Historical Atlas of the World. (Illus.). 192p. 1981. 29.95 (ISBN 0-528-83124-0). Rand.

Muir, Ramsey. Medieval & Modern: Including Ancient & Classical, 6th Ed. & Medieval & Modern, 11th Ed. Ancient, Medieval & Modern. 10th ed. Fullard, Harold & Treharne, R. E., eds. (Illus.). 1964. Repr. of 1911 ed. 19.50x (ISBN 0-06-495016-6). B&N.

Rand McNally Historical Atlas of the World. (Illus.). 192p. 1981. 29.95 (ISBN 0-686-75349-6). Rand.

Sellman, R. R. Outline Atlas of World History. LC 78-120089. (Illus.). 1970. text ed. 7.95 (ISBN 0-312-59150-0, O86510). St Martin.

Shepherd, William R. Shepherd's Historical Atlas. 9th rev. ed. (Illus.). (gr. 7 up). 1976. 28.50x (ISBN 0-06-013846-7). B&N.

Toynbee, Arnold J. & Myers, Edward D. A Study of History: Historical Atlas & Gazetter. 1959. Vol. 11. 36.00x (ISBN 0-19-215223-8). Oxford U Pr.

Walker, Henry P. & Bufkin, Don. Historical Atlas of Arizona. LC 78-58086. (Illus.). 1979. 14.95 (ISBN 0-8061-1489-4); pap. 7.95 (ISBN 0-8061-1490-8). U of Okla Pr.

GEOGRAPHY, LINGUISTIC

see Linguistic Geography

GEOGRAPHY, MATHEMATICAL

see also Cartography; Geodesy; Longitude; Map-Projection; Nautical Astronomy; Surveying; Surveys

Cliff, A. D., et al. Elements of Spatial Structure. LC 74-12973. (Geographical Studies: No. 6). (Illus.). 206p. 1974. 37.50 (ISBN 0-521-20689-8). Cambridge U Pr.

Theakstone, W. & Harrison, C. Analysis of Geographical Data. 1970. pap. text ed. 6.95x (ISBN 0-435-34691-1). Heinemann Ed.

GEOGRAPHY, MEDICAL

see Medical Geography

GEOGRAPHY, MEDIEVAL

Bevan, W. L. & Phillot, H. W. Mediaeval Geography. 1969. Repr. of 1873 ed. text ed. 24.75x (ISBN 90-6041-075-0). Humanities.

Dey, Nundo Lal. The Geographical Dictionary of Ancient & Mediaeval India. LC 42-31336. (Illus.). 272p. 1971. Repr. of 1927 ed. 19.50x (ISBN 0-8002-1453-6). Intl Pubns Serv.

Fischer, T. Sammlung Mittelalterlicher Weltkarten Italienischen Ursprungs. 1886. text ed. 10.00x (ISBN 9-06041-020-3). Humanities.

Kimble, George H. Geography in the Middle Ages. LC 68-10930. (Illus.). 1968. Repr. of 1938 ed. 11.50 (ISBN 0-8462-1107-6). Russell.

Lelewel, J. Geographie Du Moven Age. 1857. text ed. 108.00x (ISBN 9-06041-035-1). Humanities.

Munster, Sebastian. Cosmography. (Science & Medicine Ser.). 1969. Repr. of 1550 ed. lib. bdg. 200.00 (ISBN 0-306-71816-2). Da Capo.

Schiltberger, J. Reisen in Europa, Asia und Afrika Von 1394 Bis 1427: Nach der Heidelberger Handschrift Herausgeben und Erlautert Von K. F. Neumann. (Ger.). 1859. pap. text ed. 14.00x (ISBN 90-6041-121-8). Humanities.

GEOGRAPHY, PHYSICAL

see Physical Geography

GEOGRAPHY, POLITICAL

see also Boundaries; Cities and Towns; Geopolitics; Territory, National

Boateng, E. A. A Political Geography of Africa. LC 77-80828. 1978. 37.95 (ISBN 0-521-21764-4); pap. 12.95x (ISBN 0-521-29269-7). Cambridge U Pr.

Burnett, Alan D. & Taylor, Peter J. Political Studies from Spatial Perspectives: Anglo-American Essays on Political Geography. LC 80-41384. 1981. write for info. (ISBN 0-471-27909-9, Pub. by Wiley-Interscience); pap. write for info. (ISBN 0-471-27910-2). Wiley.

Cole, J. P. Geography of World Affairs. 5th ed. (Illus.). 1979. pap. 5.95 (ISBN 0-14-020548-9, Pelican). Penguin.

Cox, Kevin R. Location & Public Problems: A Political Geography of the Contemporary World. LC 78-71125. (Illus.). 1979. text ed. 14.95x (ISBN 0-88425-015-6). Maaroufa Pr.

Fox, Edward W. History in Geographic Perspective: The Other France. LC 79-140754. (Illus.). 1972. pap. 2.45x (ISBN 0-393-00650-6, Norton Lib). Norton.

Glassner, Martin I. & Deblij, Harm J. Systematic Political Geography. 3rd ed. LC 79-26750. 537p. 1980. text ed. 29.95 (ISBN 0-471-05228-0). Wiley.

Gottmann, Jean. The Significance of Territory. LC 72-87807. (Page-Barbour Lecture Ser). (Illus.). 195p. 1973. 9.95x (ISBN 0-8139-0413-7). U Pr of Va.

Johnston, R. J. Political, Electoral, & Spatial Systems. (Contemporary Problems in Geography Ser.). (Illus.). 1979. 32.50x (ISBN 0-19-874071-9); pap. 11.95x (ISBN 0-19-874072-7). Oxford U Pr.

Kasperson, Roger K. & Minghi, Julian V., eds. Structure of Political Geography. LC 76-75051. 1969. 24.95x (ISBN 0-202-10031-6). Aldine Pub.

Maksakovsky, V., ed. The Economic Geography of the World. (Illus.). 1978. 10.00 (ISBN 0-8285-0002-9, Pub. by Progress Pubs Russia). Imported Pubns.

Muir, Richard. Modern Political Geography. 262p. 1975. 21.95 (ISBN 0-470-62356-X); pap. 16.95 (ISBN 0-470-99194-1). Halsted Pr.

Muir, Richard & Paddison, Ronan. Politics, Geography & Behavior. 1981. 27.50x (ISBN 0-416-31330-2); pap. 12.95x (ISBN 0-416-31340-X). Methuen Inc.

Muir, Richard & Paddison, Ronan, eds. Politics, Geography & Behavior. (Illus.). 196p. 1980. lib. bdg. cancelled (ISBN 0-86531-058-0). Westview.

Norris, Robert E. & Haring, L. Lloyd. Political Geography. (Geography Ser.). 328p. 1980. text ed. 24.95 (ISBN 0-675-08223-4). Merrill.

Paxton, John, ed. Statesman's Year-Book World Gazetteer. 2nd ed. (Illus.). 800p. 1980. 25.00x (ISBN 0-312-76126-0). St. Martin.

Pounds, Norman J. Political Geography. 2nd ed. (Geography Ser.). (Illus.). 448p. 1972. text ed. 21.00 (ISBN 0-07-050566-7, C). McGraw.

Prescott, J. R. Political Geography. 1972. 14.95 (ISBN 0-312-62300-3). St. Martin.

--Political Geography of the Oceans. LC 74-31813. 247p. 1975. 21.95 (ISBN 0-470-69672-9). Halsted Pr.

Soja, E. W. The Political Organization of Space. LC 70-135471. (CCG Resource Papers Ser.: No. 8). (Illus.). 1971. pap. text ed. 4.00 (ISBN 0-89291-055-0). Assn Am Geographers.

Sprout, Harold H. & Sprout, Margaret. The Ecological Perspective on Human Affairs, with Special Reference to International Politics. LC 78-27759. 1979. Repr. of 1965 ed. lib. bdg. 18.75x (ISBN 0-313-20914-6, SPEP). Greenwood.

Taylor, Griffith. Environment & Nation: Geographical Factors in the Cultural & Political History of Europe. LC 37-22776. (Illus.). 1936. 45.00x (ISBN 0-8020-7046-9). U of Toronto Pr.

Weigert, Hans W., et al. Principles of Political Geography. LC 56-9859. (Illus.). 1951. 36.50x (ISBN 0-89197-552-7). Irvington.

GEOGRAPHY, SOCIAL

see Anthropo-Geography

GEOGRAPHY, URBAN

see Cities and Towns

GEOGRAPHY AND AVIATION

see Geography, Aerial

GEOGRAPHY AND RELIGION

see Religion and Geography

GEOID

see Earth–Figure

GEOLOGICAL CHEMISTRY

see Geochemistry

GEOLOGICAL EROSION

see Erosion

GEOLOGICAL MAPS

see Geology–Maps

GEOLOGICAL MODELING

Chatterji, M. & Rompuy, P. Van, eds. Environment Regional Science & Interregional Modeling. 1976. pap. 12.70 (ISBN 0-387-07693-X). Springer-Verlag.

GEOLOGICAL OCEANOGRAPHY

see Submarine Geology

GEOLOGICAL PHYSICS

see Geophysics

GEOLOGICAL RESEARCH

see also Mohole Project

Carnegie Institution of Washington Year Book, Vol. 77. (Illus.). 1978. 16.50 (ISBN 0-87279-650-7). Carnegie Inst.

Chikishev, A. G., ed. Landscape Indicators. LC 72-88886. (Illus.). 165p. 1973. 35.00 (ISBN 0-306-10875-5, Consultants). Plenum Pub.

Finch, R. C., et al. Lab Studies in Physical Geology. 276p. 1980. 10.95x (ISBN 0-89459-112-6). Hunter NC.

Grabau, Amadeus W. Rhythm of the Ages. LC 78-15615. 620p. 1978. Repr. of 1940 ed. lib. bdg. 39.50 (ISBN 0-88275-694-X). Krieger.

Hisdal, Vidar, et al. Geological & Geophysical Research in Svalbard & on Jan Mayen. (Norsk Polarinstitutt Skrifter Ser.: No. 172). 181p. 1981. pap. 24.00 (ISBN 0-686-73227-8). Universitet.

Koefoed, O. The Application of the Kernel Function in Interpreting Geoelectrical Resistivity Measurements. Kunetz, G. & Sazov, S., eds. LC 70-390720. (Geoexploration Monographs: No. 2). (Illus.). 1968. 26.50x (ISBN 0-8002-0224-4). Intl Pubns Serv.

GEOLOGICAL SOCIETY OF AMERICA

Geological Society of America, ed. Memorials, 1975 Decedents, Vol. 7. LC 73-76887. (Illus.). 1977. pap. 8.00x (ISBN 0-8137-8075-6). Geol Soc.

--Memorials: 1976 Decedents, Vol. 8. LC 73-76887. (Illus.). pap. 9.00x (ISBN 0-8137-8076-4). Geol Soc.

Memorials: 1973 Decedents, Vol. 5. LC 73-76887. (Illus.). 1977. 8.00x (ISBN 0-8137-8073-X). Geol Soc.

GEOLOGICAL SOCIETY OF LONDON

Woodward, Horace B. The History of the Geological Society of London. Albritton, Claude C., Jr., ed. LC 77-6551. (History of Geology Ser.). (Illus.). 1978. Repr. of 1907 ed. lib. bdg. 25.00x (ISBN 0-405-10466-9). Arno.

GEOLOGICAL TIME

see also Earth–Age; Paleoclimatology; Radioactive Dating

Berry, William B. Growth of a Prehistoric Time Scale, Based on Organic Evolution. LC 68-14224. (Illus.). 1968. pap. 6.95x (ISBN 0-7167-0237-1). W H Freeman.

Bickford, M. E. & Mose, D. G. Geochronology of Precambrian Rocks in the St. Francois Mountains. LC 75-25345. (Special Paper: No. 165). (Illus.). 1975. pap. 7.00x (ISBN 0-8137-2165-2). Geol Soc.

Committee On Nuclear Sciences. Geochronology of North America. 1965. pap. 7.00 (ISBN 0-309-01276-7). Natl Acad Pr.

Croll, James. Stellar Evolution & Its Relation to Geological Time. LC 78-166616. 1893. Repr. 33.00 (ISBN 0-403-01459-X). Scholarly.

Eicher, Don L. Geologic Time. 2nd ed. (Foundations of Earth Sciences Ser.). (Illus.). 160p. 1976. pap. 8.95 (ISBN 0-13-352484-1). P-H.

Faul, Henry. Ages of Rocks, Planets & Stars. 1966. pap. text ed. 6.95 (ISBN 0-07-020070-X, C). McGraw.

Goldich, Samuel S., et al. Precambrian Geology & Geochronology of Minnesota. LC 61-8016. (Bulletin: No. 41). (Illus.). 1961. 4.00x (ISBN 0-8166-0224-7). Minn Geol Survey.

Hamilton, E. I. Applied Geochronology. 1965. 42.00 (ISBN 0-12-321450-5). Acad Pr.

Hurley, Patrick M. How Old Is the Earth? LC 78-25843. (Illus.). 1979. Repr. of 1959 ed. lib. bdg. 15.75x (ISBN 0-313-20776-3, HUHO). Greenwood.

Klemm, D. D. & Schneider, H. J., eds. Time- & Strata- Bound Ore Deposits. (Illus.). 1978. 49.70 (ISBN 0-387-08502-5). Springer-Verlag.

Nations, D. The Record of Geologic Time: A Vicarious Trip. (McGraw-Hill Concepts in Introductory Geology). (Illus.). 80p. 1975. text ed. 7.95x (ISBN 0-07-012326-8, C); slides 50.00 (ISBN 0-07-074427-0). McGraw.

Thornes, John & Brunsden, Denys. Geomorphology & Time. LC 76-30862. 208p. 1977. text ed. 15.95x (ISBN 0-416-80080-7, Pub. by Chapman & Hall England). Methuen Inc.

York, D. & Farquhar, R. M. The Earth's Age & Geochronology. 1972. pap. 14.50 (ISBN 0-08-016387-4). Pergamon.

Zeuner, Frederic E. Dating the Past: An Introduction to Geochronology. 4th ed. (Illus.). 1970. Repr. of 1946 ed. 24.75 (ISBN 0-02-855790-5). Hafner.

GEOLOGISTS

Clarke, John M. James Hall of Albany: Geologist & Palaeontologist, 1811-1898. Albritton, Claude C., ed. LC 77-6511. (History of Geology Ser.). (Illus.). Repr. of 1923 ed. lib. bdg. 35.00x (ISBN 0-405-10435-9). Arno.

Fenton, Carroll L. & Fenton, Mildred. Story of the Great Geologists. facs. ed. LC 73-84306. (Essay Index Reprint Ser.). 1945. 20.00 (ISBN 0-8369-1130-X). Arno.

Fodor, R. V. What Does a Geologist Do? LC 77-6483. (Illus.). (gr. 5 up). 1977. 5.95 (ISBN 0-396-07481-2). Dodd.

Joralemon, Ira B. Adventure Beacons. Joralemon, Peter, ed. LC 76-19746. (Illus.). 1976. 16.50x (ISBN 0-89520-041-4). Soc Mining Eng.

McCornack, Ellen C., ed. Thomas Condon: Pioneer Geologist of Oregon. (Illus.). 1928. 10.00 (ISBN 0-87071-331-0). Oreg St U Pr.

Memorials: 1969 Decedents, Vol. 1. LC 73-76887. (Illus., Orig.). 1973. pap. 4.00x (ISBN 0-8137-8069-1). Geol Soc.

Memorials: 1970 Decedents, Vol. 2. LC 73-76887. (Illus., Orig.). 1973. pap. 4.00x (ISBN 0-8137-8070-5). Geol Soc.

Memorials: 1971 Decedents, Vol. 3. LC 73-76887. (Illus., Orig.). 1974. pap. 6.00x (ISBN 0-8137-8071-3). Geol Soc.

Memorials: 1972 Decedents, Vol. 4. LC 73-76887. (Illus.). 1975. pap. 7.50x (ISBN 0-8137-8072-1). Geol Soc.

Merrill, George P. First One Hundred Years of American Geology. (Illus.). 1969. Repr. of 1924 ed. 32.75 (ISBN 0-02-849180-7). Hafner.

Merrill, George P. & Albritton, Claude C., eds. Contributions to a History of American State Geological & Natural History Surveys. LC 77-6529. (History of Geology Ser.). (Illus.). 1978. Repr. of 1920 ed. lib. bdg. 37.50 (ISBN 0-405-10450-2). Arno.

Phillips, John. Memoirs of William Smith. Albritton, Claude C., Jr., ed. LC 77-6535. (History of Geology Ser.). (Illus.). 1978. Repr. of 1844 ed. lib. bdg. 12.00x (ISBN 0-405-10455-3). Arno.

Shor, Elizabeth N. Fossils & Flies: The Life of a Compleat Scientist, Samuel Wendell Williston 1851-1918. LC 77-145503. (Illus.). 1971. 14.95x (ISBN 0-8061-0949-1). U of Okla Pr.

Woodward, Horace B. The History of the Geological Society of London. Albritton, Claude C., Jr., ed. LC 77-6551. (History of Geology Ser.). (Illus.). 1978. Repr. of 1907 ed. lib. bdg. 25.00x (ISBN 0-405-10466-9). Arno.

GEOLOGY

see also Aerial Photography in Geology; Caves; Continents; Coral Reefs and Islands; Creation; Crystallography; Deluge; Earth; Earthquakes; Erosion; Geophysics; Glaciers; Hydrogeology; Mineralogy; Mountains; Natural History; Nuclear Geophysics; Oceanography; Ore-Deposits; Paleoclimatology; Paleography; Paleontology; Petroleum-Geology; Petrology; Physical Geography; Rocks; Sand; Sedimentation and Deposition; Speleology; Submarine Geology; Volcanism; Volcanoes; Weathering

Adams, William M., ed. Engineering Geology Case Histories: Engineering Seismology - the Works of Man, No. 8. LC 58-2632. (Illus., Orig.). 1970. pap. 4.50x (ISBN 0-8137-4008-8). Geol Soc.

Agassiz, Louis. Geological Sketches. 1976. Repr. of 1866 ed. 22.00 (ISBN 0-403-05821-X, Regency). Scholarly.

Ager, D. V. Introducing Geology. 2nd ed. (Illus.). 256p. 1975. (Pub. by Faber & Faber); pap. 8.95 (ISBN 0-571-04858-7). Merrimack Bk Serv.

AGI-NAS-NRC. Geology & Earth Sciences Sourcebook. 1970. pap. text ed. 8.68 (ISBN 0-03-068550-8). HR&W.

Allen, John R. Physical Geology. (Introducing Geology Ser.). 1975. pap. text ed. 9.95x (ISBN 0-04-550022-3). Allen Unwin.

Allison, Ira S & Palmer, Donald F. Geology: The Science of a Changing Earth. 7th, rev. ed. (Illus.). 1980. text ed. 17.95x (ISBN 0-07-001123-0); pap. text ed. 15.95x (ISBN 0-07-001121-4); instr's manual 4.95x (ISBN 0-07-001122-2). McGraw.

Allison, Ira S., et al. Geology: The Science of a Changing Earth. 6th ed. (Illus.). 448p. 1974. text ed. 16.95 (ISBN 0-07-001118-4, C); pap. text ed. 14.95 (ISBN 0-07-001119-2); instructor's manual 2.95 (ISBN 0-07-001120-6). McGraw.

Alt, David & Hyndman, Donald. Rocks, Ice, & Water. LC 73-78910. (Roadside Geology Ser.). (Illus.). 104p. 1973. pap. 5.95 (ISBN 0-87842-041-X). Mountain Pr.

American Geological Institute. Geology: Science & Profession. 1976. pap. 1.00 (ISBN 0-913312-19-3). Am Geol.

Bakewell, Robert. An Introduction to Geology. Albritton, Claude C., Jr., ed. LC 77-6508. (History of Geology Ser.). 1978. Repr. lib. bdg. 30.00x (ISBN 0-405-10431-6). Arno.

Beck, A. E. Physical Principles of Exploration Methods. LC 81-80411. 256p. 1981. 39.95 (ISBN 0-470-27124-8); pap. 18.95 (ISBN 0-470-27128-0). Halsted Pr.

Ben-Menahem, A. & Singh, S. Seismic Waves & Sources. (Illus.). 1000p. 1980. 90.00 (ISBN 0-387-90506-5). Springer-Verlag.

Bennison, G. M. Introduction to Geological Structures & Maps: Metric. 3rd ed. (Illus.). 1975. pap. text ed. 9.95x (ISBN 0-7131-2513-6). Intl Ideas.

Bishop, Tom. Gold: The Way to Roadside Riches. 1971. pap. 2.95 (ISBN 0-933472-31-5). Johnson Bks.

Bloom, A. L. Surface of the Earth. (gr. 10 up). pap. text ed. 8.95 (ISBN 0-13-877944-9). P-H.

Blyth, F. G. & De Freitas, M. H. A Geology for Engineers. 6th ed. 1974. pap. 24.50x (ISBN 0-8448-0612-9). Crane-Russak Co.

Boyer, R. E. Field Guide to Rock Weathering. (Earth Science Curriculum Project Pamphlet Ser). 1971. pap. 3.20 (ISBN 0-395-02615-6, 2-14601). HM.

Boyer, Robert E. & Snyder, P. B. Geology Fact Book. LC 75-138627. (Fact Books). (Illus.). (gr. 7 up). 1972. PLB 5.95 (ISBN 0-8331-1700-9). Hubbard Sci.

Bradshaw, Michael J., et al. The Earth's Changing Surface. LC 77-25024. 1978. pap. text ed. 20.95 (ISBN 0-470-99365-0). Halsted Pr.

Brown, George D., Jr. & Ladd, George T. The Earth: Man's Geologic Environment. new ed. (Physical Science Ser.). 1976. pap. text ed. 7.95 (ISBN 0-675-08578-0); cassettes & filmstrips 230.00 (ISBN 0-675-08577-2); 2-4 sets 145.00, 5-9 sets 95.00 (ISBN 0-686-67316-6). Merrill.

Buckland, William. Geology & Mineralogy Considered with Reference to Natural Theology, 2 vols. Gould, Stephen J., ed. LC 79-8326. (The History of Paleontology Ser.). (Illus.). 1980. Repr. of 1836 ed. Set. lib. bdg. 60.00x (ISBN 0-405-12706-5); lib. bdg. 30.00x ea. Vol. 1 (ISBN 0-405-12707-3). Vol. 2 (ISBN 0-405-12708-1). Arno.

Cain, J. Allan & Tyna, Eugene J. Geology: A Synopsis: Pt. 1, Physical Geology. (Orig.). 1980. pap. text ed. 7.95 (ISBN 0-8403-2162-7). Kendall-Hunt.

Campbell, Angus S. Geology & History of Turkey. 1971. 42.50x (ISBN 0-8002-1456-0). Intl Pubns Serv.

Carozzi, Albert V. Microscopic Sedimentary Petrography. LC 60-6447. 498p. 1972. Repr. of 1960 ed. 24.50 (ISBN 0-88275-061-5). Krieger.

Casey, R. & Rawson, P. F. The Boreal Lower Cretaceous Geological Journal Special Issue, No. 5. (Liverpool Geological Society & the Manchester Geological Association). 448p. 1973. 53.75 (ISBN 0-471-27752-5, Pub. by Wiley-Interscience). Wiley.

Cathles, Lawrence M. The Viscosity of the Earth's Mantle. LC 74-16162. (Illus.). 400p. 1975. 35.00 (ISBN 0-691-08140-9). Princeton U Pr.

Cattermole, Peter. World of Geology. (Illus.). 1971. 6.95 (ISBN 0-584-10328-X). Transatlantic.

Cayeux, Lucien. Past & Present Causes in Geology. Carozzi, A. V., ed. & tr. 1971. Repr. of 1941 ed. 19.25 (ISBN 0-02-842670-3). Hafner.

Cazeau, Charles J. & Siemankowski, Francis T. Physical Geology Laboratory Manual. 2nd ed. 1977. wire coil bdg. 8.95 (ISBN 0-8403-0506-0). Kendall-Hunt.

Cazeau, Charles J., et al. Physical Geology: Principles, Processes, & Problems. (Illus.). 518p. 1976. text ed. 24.50 scp (ISBN 0-06-041209-7, HarpC); instructor's manual avail. (ISBN 0-06-361160-0); study guide scp 8.95 (ISBN 0-06-041208-9). Har-Row.

Chapin, C. E. & Elston, W. E., eds. Ash Flow Tuffs. LC 79-53022. (Special Paper: No. 180). (Illus.). 1979. pap. 38.00x (ISBN 0-8137-2180-6). Geol Soc.

Clairaut, Alexis-Claude. Theorie De la Figure De la Terre, Tiree Des Principes De L'hydrostatique. Repr. of 1743 ed. 90.00 (ISBN 0-8287-0199-7). Clearwater Pub.

Clark, Harold W. Fossils, Flood & Fire. (Illus.). 1968. 7.95 (ISBN 0-911080-16-3). Outdoor Pict.

Clark, Sydney P., Jr., ed. Handbook of Physical Constants. rev. ed. LC 66-19814. (Memoir: No. 97). (Illus.). 1966. 7.00x (ISBN 0-8137-1097-9). Geol Soc.

Clarke, E. D. Elements of Geology for Australian Students. 4th ed. 1967. 13.50x (ISBN 0-85564-028-6, Pub by U of W Austral Pr). Intl Schol Bk Serv.

Cleaveland, Parker. An Elementary Treatise on Mineralogy & Geology. Albritton, Claude C., Jr., ed. LC 77-6513. (History of Geology Ser.). (Illus.). 1978. Repr. of 1816 ed. lib. bdg. 40.00 (ISBN 0-405-10436-7). Arno.

Coates, Donald R. Environmental Geology. LC 80-21272. 731p. 1981. text ed. 21.95 (ISBN 0-471-06379-7). Wiley.

Coleman, R. G. Ophiolites: Ancient Oceanic Lithosphere. (Minerals & Rocks Ser.: Vol. 12). (Illus.). 1977. 39.80 (ISBN 0-387-08276-X). Springer-Verlag.

Compton, Robert R. Interpreting the Earth. 1977. text ed. 19.95 (ISBN 0-15-541547-6, HC); instructor's manual avail. (ISBN 0-15-541548-4); slides avail. (ISBN 0-685-80197-7). HarBraceJ.

Content, C. S. A Geologist's Sketch Book. 56p. 1977. pap. text ed. 8.75 (ISBN 0-87262-089-1). Am Soc Civil Eng.

Corliss, William R. Strange Life: A Sourcebook on the Mysteries of Organic Nature. LC 75-6128. (Strange Life Ser.: Vol. B1). (Illus.). 275p. 1975. 8.95x (ISBN 0-9600712-8-8). Sourcebook.

--Strange Planet: A Sourcebook of Unusual Geological Facts. LC 74-26226. (Strange Planet Ser.: Vol. E2). 1978. 8.95x (ISBN 0-915554-04-6). Sourcebook.

--Strange Planet: A Sourcebook of Unusual Geological Facts, Vol. E1. LC 74-26226. (Illus.). 283p. 1975. 8.95x (ISBN 0-9600712-3-7). Sourcebook.

--Unknown Earth: A Handbook of Geological Enigmas. LC 80-50159. (Illus.). 839p. 1980. 19.95 (ISBN 0-915554-06-2). Sourcebook.

Costa, John E. & Baker, Victor R. Surficial Geology Building with the Earth. 608p. 1981. text ed. 24.95 (ISBN 0-471-03229-8). Wiley.

Craig, G. Y. & Duff, D., eds. The Geology of the Lothians & Southeast Scotland. 1976. 12.50x (ISBN 0-7073-0106-8, Pub. by Scottish Academic Pr Scotland). Columbia U Pr.

Crittenden, Max D., Jr., et al, eds. Cordilleran Metamorphic Core Complexes. Davis, George H. & Coney, Peter J. (Memoir: No. 153). 1980. 27.00x (ISBN 0-8137-1153-3). Geol Soc.

Cuvier, Georges. Essay on the Theory of the Earth: Mineralogical Notes, & an Account of Cuvier's Geological Discoveries. Albritton, Claude C., Jr., ed. Kerr, Robert, tr. LC 77-6517. (History of Geology Ser.). (Illus.). 1978. Repr. of 1817 ed. lib. bdg. 24.00 (ISBN 0-405-10439-1). Arno.

Daly, Reginald. Earth's Most Challenging Mysteries. 1972. pap. 6.95 (ISBN 0-934532-30-3). Presby & Reformed.

Daly, Reginald A. Our Mobile Earth. LC 80-2889. (BCL Ser.: I & II). (Illus.). Repr. of 1926 ed. 47.50 (ISBN 0-404-18066-3). AMS Pr.

Dapples, Edward C. Basic Geology for Science & Engineering. LC 59-5880. 620p. 1973. Repr. of 1959 ed. 19.50 (ISBN 0-88275-106-9). Krieger.

Darwin, Charles. Journal of Researches into the Natural History & Geology of the Countries Visited During the Voyage of H. M. S. "Beagle" Round the World, Under the Command of Capt. Fitz Roy, R. A. 1977. Repr. of 1892 ed. lib. bdg. 25.00 (ISBN 0-8482-0544-8). Norwood Edns.

--Voyage of the Beagle. LC 62-2990. 1962. 3.95 (ISBN 0-385-02767-2, Anchor). Natural Hist.

Darwin, Charles R. Journal of Researches into the Geology & Natural History of the Various Countries Visited by H. M. S. Beagle Under the Command of Captain Fitzroy, R. N. from 1832 to 1836. (Illus.). 636p. 1969. Repr. of 1839 ed. 65.00x (ISBN 0-8002-1621-0). Intl Pubns Serv.

Davis, Stanley, et al. Geology: Our Physical Environment. 1975. text ed. 17.50 (ISBN 0-07-015680-8, C); instructor's manual 3.95 (ISBN 0-07-015681-6). McGraw.

Dennison, John H. Analysis of Geologic Structures. (Illus.). 1968. text ed. 12.95x (ISBN 0-393-09801-X, NortonC). Norton.

Dietrich, Richard V. & Skinner, Brian J. Rocks & Rock Minerals. LC 79-1211. 1979. text ed. 17.50 (ISBN 0-471-02934-3). Wiley.

Donath, F. A., et al, eds. Annual Review of Earth & Planetary Sciences, Vol. 2. LC 72-82137. (Illus.). 1974. text ed. 17.00 (ISBN 0-8243-2002-6). Annual Reviews.

Donnelly, Thomas W., ed. Earth Sciences: Problems & Progress in Current Research. LC 63-20901. 1963. 9.00x (ISBN 0-226-15656-7). U of Chicago Pr.

Dorr, John A., Jr. & Eschman, Donald F. Geology of Michigan. LC 69-17351. (Illus.). 1970. 19.95x (ISBN 0-472-08280-9). U of Mich Pr.

Dreghorn, William. Geology Explained: In the Forest of Dean & the Wye Valley. 1968. pap. 2.50 (ISBN 0-7153-4263-0). David & Charles.

Eastern Kentucky University, Dept. of Geology. Principles of Physical Geology Laboratory Manual. 80p. 1980. pap. text ed. 5.50 (ISBN 0-8403-2285-2). Kendall-Hunt.

Elder, John. The Bowels of the Earth. (Illus.). 1978. 19.95x (ISBN 0-19-854412-X); pap. 6.95 (ISBN 0-19-854413-8). Oxford U Pr.

Emerson, B. K., et al. Geology & Paleontology. Repr. of 1904 ed. 28.00 (ISBN 0-527-38164-0). Kraus Repr.

Emmons, Ebenezer. American Geology: Statement of the Principles of the Science, with Full Illustrations of the Characteristic American Fossils, 2 vols. in one. LC 73-17818. (Natural Sciences in America Ser.). (Illus.). 544p. 1974. Repr. 28.00x (ISBN 0-405-05734-2). Arno.

Emmons, R. C. The Universal Stage. LC 43-16915. (Memoir: No. 8). (Illus.). 1943. 7.50x (ISBN 0-8137-1008-1). Geol Soc.

Ernst, W. G. Earth Materials. (gr. 10 up). 1969. pap. text ed. 8.95 (ISBN 0-13-222604-9). P-H.

Evans, I. O. Observer's Book of Geology. (Observer Bks.). (Illus.). 1977. 3.95 (ISBN 0-684-15221-5, ScribT). Scribner.

Eveland, H. E. & Tennissen, A. C. Physical Geology Laboratory Manual. 3rd ed. 96p. 1979. pap. text ed. 7.95 (ISBN 0-8403-2061-2). Kendall-Hunt.

Fenner, Peter, ed. Quantitative Geology. LC 72-190171. (Special Paper: No. 146). (Illus.). viii, 80p. (Orig.). 1972. pap. 7.00x (ISBN 0-8137-2146-6). Geol Soc.

Fenton, Carroll Lane & Fenton, Mildred Adams. Rock Book. LC 40-36728. 1970. 12.95 (ISBN 0-385-06840-9). Doubleday.

Fichter, Lynn S. & Farmer, George T., Jr. Earth Materials & Earth Processes: An Introduction. 2nd ed. 1977. spiral bdg. 10.95x (ISBN 0-8087-0633-0). Burgess.

Flint, Richard F. & Skinner, Brian J. Physical Geology. 2nd ed. LC 76-23206. 1977. text ed. 24.95x (ISBN 0-471-26442-3); study guide 7.50 (ISBN 0-471-02593-3). Wiley.

Foster, Robert J. General Geology. 3rd ed. (Physical Science Ser.). 1978. text ed. 23.95 (ISBN 0-675-08440-7); study guide 7.95 (ISBN 0-675-08447-4). Merrill.

--Geology. 4th ed. (Physics & Physical Science Ser.). 192p. 1980. pap. text ed. 7.95 (ISBN 0-675-08183-1). Merrill.

--Physical Geology. 3rd ed. (Science Ser.). 1979. text ed. 21.95 (ISBN 0-675-08312-5); study guide avail. Merrill.

Frakes, L. A. Climates Throughout Geologic Time. 304p. 1979. 58.75 (ISBN 0-444-41729-X, North Holland). Elsevier.

Fraser, Donald, ed. Thermodynamics in Geology. (Nato Adv. Study Inst. Ser. C: No. 30). 1977. lib. bdg. 50.00 (ISBN 90-277-0794-4, Pub. by Reidel Holland); pap. 16.00 (ISBN 90-277-0834-7). Kluwer Boston.

Freeman, T. Field Guide to Layered Rocks. (Earth Science Curriculum Project Pamphlet Ser). 1971. pap. 3.20 (ISBN 0-395-02617-2). HM.

Froelich, et al. Complex Studies on Variations of the Secular Behavior in the Earth's Mantle. (Illus.). 145p. 1973. 40.00 (ISBN 0-685-39165-5). Adler.

Geiger, A. F. & Hatheway, Allen W., eds. Engineering Geology for Geologists. LC 78-64413. 1978. pap. 15.00 (ISBN 0-913312-06-1). Am Geol.

Geological Society Of America. Ten-Year Index to Vols. 41-50 of Geological Society of America Bulletin. LC 1-23380. (Orig.). 1941. pap. 6.00x (ISBN 0-8137-9041-7). Geol Soc.

--Ten-Year Index to Vols. 71-80 of Geological Society of America Bulletin. LC 1-23380. (Orig.). 1971. pap. 13.00x (ISBN 0-8137-9071-9). Geol Soc.

Geological Society of America, ed. Memorials: Nineteen Seventy-Seven Decedents. LC 73-76887. (Vol. 9). (Illus.). 1979. pap. 9.00x (ISBN 0-8137-8077-2). Geol Soc.

Gillispie, Charles C. Genesis & Geology: A Study in the Relations of Scientific Thought, Natural Theology, & Social Opinion in Great Britain, 1790-1850. 1959. lib. bdg. 10.50x (ISBN 0-88307-107-X). Gannon.

Gilluly, James, et al. Principles of Geology. 4th ed. LC 74-23076. (Geology Ser.). (Illus.). 1975. text ed. 21.95x (ISBN 0-7167-0269-X). W H Freeman.

Gobbett, D. J. & Hutchinson, C. S. Geology of the Mulny Peninsula. 438p. 1973. 84.50x (ISBN 0-471-30850-1, Pub. by Wiley-Interscience). Wiley.

Goguel, Jean. Geologie, 2 vols. (Methodique Ser.). 53.95 ea. French & Eur.

Gorshkov, G. & Yakushova, A. Physical Geology. 690p. 1977. 12.00 (ISBN 0-8285-1616-2, Pub. by Mir Pubs Russia). Imported Pubns.

--Physical Geology. Gurevich, A., tr. (Russian Monographs Ser.). 1969. 98.50x (ISBN 0-677-20790-5). Gordon.

Gorshkov, G. S. Volcanism & the Upper Mantle: Investigations in the Kurile Island Arc. LC 69-12530. (Monographs in Geoscience Ser.). 385p. 1970. 39.50 (ISBN 0-306-30407-4, Plenum Pr). Plenum Pub.

Gorshkov, George & Yakushova, Alexandra. Physical Geology. (Illus.). 596p. 1975. text ed. 17.50x (ISBN 0-8464-0718-3). Beekman Pubs.

Greenough, George B. A Critical Examination of the First Principles of Geology. Albritton, Claude C., Jr., ed. LC 77-6520. (History of Geology Ser.). 1978. Repr. of 1819 ed. lib. bdg. 20.00x (ISBN 0-405-10442-1). Arno.

Guest, John. Planetary Geology. 208p. 1980. 21.95x (ISBN 0-470-26887-5). Halsted Pr.
Gupta, A. & Yagi, K. Petrology & Genesis of Leucite-Bearing Rocks. (Minerals & Rocks Ser.: Vol. 14). (Illus.). 250p. 1980. 39.00 (ISBN 0-387-09864-X). Springer-Verlag.
Habberjam, G. M. Apparent Resistivity Observations & the Use of Square Array Techniques. (Geoexploration Monographs, I-9). (Illus.). 1979. lib. bdg. 43.65 (ISBN 3-443-13013-5). Lubrecht & Cramer.
Hamblin, Kenneth W. The Earth's Dynamic Systems: A Textbook of Physical Geology. 3rd ed. (Illus.). 544p. 1981. pap. text ed. price not set (ISBN 0-8087-3172-6). Burgess.
Hamblin, W. Kenneth & Howard, James D. Exercises in Physical Geology. 5th ed. 1980. pap. 10.95x (ISBN 0-8087-3154-8). Burgess.
Handbuch der Regionalen Geologie, Nos. 1-30. 1910-44. pap. 300.00 (ISBN 0-384-21285-9). Johnson Repr.
Hansen, E. Strain Facies. LC 72-89551. (Minerals, Rocks & Inorganic Materials Ser.: Vol. 2). (Illus.). 1970. 30.80 (ISBN 0-387-05204-6). Springer-Verlag.
Harbert, John C., ed. Cisternography & Hydrocephalus: A Symposium. (Illus.). 670p. 1972. 58.75 (ISBN 0-398-02308-5). C C Thomas.
Hardy, H. Reginald, Jr. First Conference on Acoustic Emission (Microseismic Activity) in Geologic Structures & Materials. new ed. (Illus.). 500p. 1977. text ed. 40.00x (ISBN 0-87849-017-5). Trans Tech.
Hatheway, Allen W. & McClure, Cole R., eds. Reviews in Engineering Geology, Vol. 4: Geology in the Siting of Nuclear Power Plants. LC 62-51690. (Illus.). 1979. 41.00x (ISBN 0-8137-4104-1). Geol Soc.
Heckman, Carol, et al, eds. GeoRef Thesaurus & Guide to Indexing. 2nd ed. LC 78-65083. 1978. pap. 35.00 (ISBN 0-913312-07-X) (ISBN 0-913312-40-1). Am Geol.
Heirtzler, J. R., ed. Indian Ocean Geology & Biostratigraphy. LC 77-88320. (Special Publication Ser.). 1978. 19.00 (ISBN 0-87590-208-1, SP0019). Am Geophysical.
Holmes, Arthur & Holmes, Doris L. Holmes Principles of Physical Geology. 3rd ed. 1978. 30.95 (ISBN 0-471-07251-6). Halsted Pr.
Horowitz, A. S. & Potter, P. E. Introductory Petrography of Fossils. LC 73-142385. (Illus.). 1971. 53.30 (ISBN 0-387-05275-5). Springer-Verlag.
Howard, Arthur D. & Remson, Irwin. Geology in Environmental Planning. (Illus.). 1977. text ed. 17.95 (ISBN 0-07-030510-2, C). McGraw.
Hutton, James. Theory of the Earth. 1960. Repr. of 1795 ed. 72.50 (ISBN 3-7682-0025-6). Lubrecht & Cramer.
Huxley, Thomas H. Discourses Biological & Geological. 1896. 12.00 (ISBN 0-8274-4221-1). R West.
Johnson, Arvid M. Physical Processes in Geology. LC 70-119373. 1970. text ed. 19.00x (ISBN 0-87735-319-0). Freeman C.
Joreskog, K. G., et al. Geological Factor Analysis. (Methods in Geomathematics: Vol. 1). 1976. 39.00 (ISBN 0-444-41367-7). Elsevier.
Judson, S., et al. Physical Geology. (Illus.). 592p. 1976. text ed. 21.95 (ISBN 0-13-669655-4); study guide 5.95 (ISBN 0-13-669630-9). P-H.
Keller, Edward. Environmental Geology. 2nd ed. 1979. text ed. 21.95 (ISBN 0-675-08296-X). Merrill.
Kelly, A., et al, eds. Creep of Engineering Materials & of the Earth. (Philosophical Transactions of the Royal Society). (Illus.). 1978. 57.50x (ISBN 0-85403-099-9). Scholium Intl.
Khan, M. A. & Matthews, B. Global Geology. LC 75-38616. (Wykeham Science Ser.: No. 41). 1976. 8.60x (ISBN 0-8448-1168-8). Crane Russak Co.
Kiersch, George A. & Cleaves, Arthur B., eds. Engineering Geology Case Histories: Some Legal Aspects of Geology in Engineering Practice, No. 7. LC 58-2632. (Illus., Orig.). 1969. pap. 4.50x (ISBN 0-8137-4007-X). Geol Soc.
Kingma, Jacobus. The Geological Structure of New Zealand. 407p. 1974. 73.50 (ISBN 0-471-47900-4, Pub. by Wiley). Krieger.
Kirwan, Richard. Geological Essays. Albritton, Claude C., ed. LC 77-6523. (History of Geology Ser.). Repr. lib. bdg. 30.00 (ISBN 0-405-10444-8). Arno.
Kitts, David B. The Structure of Geology. LC 77-7395. 1977. pap. 8.95 (ISBN 0-87074-162-4). SMU Press.
Knill, J. L., ed. Industrial Geology. (Illus.). 1979. 29.95x (ISBN 0-19-854520-7). Oxford U Pr.
Kolisko, Eugen. Geology. 1979. pap. 3.95x (ISBN 0-906492-01-7, Pub. by Kolisko Archives). St George Bk Serv.
Kopp, Otto C. An Introduction to Physical Geology. 3rd ed. (Illus.). 144p. 1980. 6.95x (ISBN 0-89459-103-7). Hunter NC.
Krauskopf, Konrad B. The Third Planet: An Invitation to Geology. LC 74-77823. (Illus.). 528p. 1974. text ed. 15.00x (ISBN 0-87735-359-X); pap. text ed. 9.75x (ISBN 0-87735-360-3). Freeman C.
Krynine, Dimitri P. & Judd, William R. Principles of Engineering Geology & Geotechnics. (Soil Mechanics & Foundations Library). (Illus.). 1957. text ed. 24.00 (ISBN 0-07-035560-6, C). McGraw.
Kuznetsov, S. I., ed. Geologic Activity of Microorganisms. LC 62-12850. 112p. 1962. 30.00 (ISBN 0-306-10537-3, Consultants). Plenum Pub.
Ladd, George T. & Snyder, P. B., eds. Selected Films on Geology. LC 78-52018. 1978. pap. 3.00 (ISBN 0-913312-04-5). Am Geol.
Lamarck, Jean B. Hydrogeology. Carozzi, Albert V., tr. from Fr. LC 64-12253. (Illus.). 1964. 10.00 (ISBN 0-252-72468-2). U of Ill Pr.
Laporte, Leo F. Ancient Environments. 2nd ed. (Foundations of the Earth Ser.). (Illus.). 1979. ref. 12.95 (ISBN 0-13-036392-8); pap. 8.95 ref. (ISBN 0-13-036384-7). P-H.
Larsen, Leonard H., et al, eds. Igneous & Metamorphic Geology: A Volume in Honor of Arie Poldervaart. LC 68-55355. (Memoir: No. 115). (Illus.). 1969. 30.00x (ISBN 0-8137-1115-0). Geol Soc.
Leet, Lewis D. & Leet, Florence J., eds. World of Geology. 1961. pap. 2.95 (ISBN 0-07-037016-8, SP). McGraw.
LeRoy, L. W. & LeRoy, D. O., eds. Subsurface Geology in Peroleum, Mining, Construction. 4th ed. LC 76-51265. 1977. 35.00 (ISBN 0-918062-00-4). Colo Sch Mines.
Levin, Harold. Contemporary Physical Geology. (Illus.). 608p. 1981. text ed. 23.95 (ISBN 0-03-057803-5, HoltC); study guide 9.95 (ISBN 0-03-057784-5). HR&W.
Long, Leon E. Geology. (Illus.). 544p. 1974. text ed. 18.50 (ISBN 0-07-038672-2, C); instructors' manual 2.95 (ISBN 0-07-038673-0). McGraw.
Low-Flow, Low-Permeability Measurements in Largely Impermeable Rocks. 1979. 16.00x (ISBN 92-64-01955-3). OECD.
Lowman, Paul D., Jr. The Third Planet. LC 77-128348. 1972. 40.00x (ISBN 0-8139-0577-X). U Pr of Va.
Ludman, Allan, et al. Physical Geology. (Illus.). 576p. 1982. text ed. 23.95 (ISBN 0-07-011510-9); price not set instructor's manual (ISBN 0-07-011511-7). McGraw.
Lyell, Charles. Principles in Geology, 3 vols. (Illus.). 1970. Repr. of 1833 ed. Set. text ed. 130.00 (ISBN 3-7682-0685-8). Lubrecht & Cramer.
--Principles of Geology: Being an Attempt to Explain the Former Changes of the Earth's Surface by Reference to Causes Now in Operation, 3 Vols. 1970. Repr. of 1830 ed. Set. 100.00 (ISBN 0-384-34524-7). Johnson Repr.
Mabbutt, J. A. Desert Landforms. 1977. 20.00x (ISBN 0-262-13131-5). MIT Pr.
McAlester, A. Earth: An Introduction to the Geological & Geophysical Sciences. 1973. 21.95 (ISBN 0-13-222422-4); instr. res. bk. 1.95 (ISBN 0-13-222695-2); study guide 3.95 (ISBN 0-13-222380-5). P-H.
McAlester, A. Lee & Hay, Edward A. Physical Geology: Principles & Perspectives. (Illus.). 448p. 1975. 19.95 (ISBN 0-13-669523-X); study guide 4.25 (ISBN 0-13-669531-0). P-H.
McDougall, D. J. Thermoluminescence of Geological Materials. 1968. 101.50 (ISBN 0-12-483350-0). Acad Pr.
MacGregor, A. R. Fife & Angus Geology. 1974. 15.00x (ISBN 0-7073-0054-1, Pub. by Scottish Academic Pr Scotland). Columbia U Pr.
McLean, Adam & Gribble, Colin. Geology for Civil Engineers. (Illus.). 1979. text ed. 30.00x (ISBN 0-04-624002-0); pap. text ed. 14.95x (ISBN 0-685-94492-1). Allen Unwin.
McLeod, G. C. Georges Bank: Past, Present, & Future. (Special Studies on Natural Resources & Energy Management). 225p. 1981. lib. bdg. 23.25x (ISBN 0-86531-199-4). Westview.
McQuillin, R. & Ardus, D. A. Exploring the Geology of Shelf Seas. 234p. 1977. 24.00x (ISBN 0-86010-070-7, Pub. by Graham & Trotman England). State Mutual Bk.
Mahadeuan, C. Mahadevan Volume: A Collection of Geological Papers in Commeration of the Sixty-First Birthday of Pr. C. Mahadevan. Krishman, M. S., ed. (Illus.). 1961. 5.00 (ISBN 0-934454-59-0). Lubrecht & Cramer.
Mallory, Bob F. & Cargo, David M. Physical Geology. new ed. (Illus.). 1979. text ed. 16.95 (ISBN 0-07-039795-3, C); instructor's manual 3.95 (ISBN 0-07-039796-1). McGraw.
Manual of Applied Geology for Engineers. 414p. 1980. pap. 75.00x (ISBN 0-7277-0038-3, Pub. by Telford England). State Mutual Bk.
Mason, Shirley L. Source Book in Geology, Fourteen Hundred to Nineteen Hundred. Mather, Kirtley F., ed. (Source Books in the History of the Sciences Ser). (Illus.). 1970. text ed. 35.00x (ISBN 0-674-82277-3). Harvard U Pr.
Mathewson, Christopher C. Engineering Geology. (Illus.). 416p. 1981. text ed. 24.95 (ISBN 0-675-08032-0). Merrill.
Memorials: 1973 Decedents, Vol. 5. LC 73-76887. (Illus.). 1977. 8.00x (ISBN 0-8137-8073-X). Geol Soc.
Menard, H. W. Geology, Resources & Society: An Introduction to Earth Science. LC 73-17151. (Geology Ser.). (Illus.). 1974. text ed. 21.95x (ISBN 0-7167-0260-6); instructor's guide avail. W H Freeman.
Merriam, D. Random Processes in Geology. LC 75-6848. 19.70 (ISBN 0-387-07277-2). Springer Verlag.
Mitchell-Thome, Raoul C. Geology of the South Atlantic Islands. (Beitraege zur regionalen Geologie der Erde: Vol. 10). (Illus.). 366p. 1970. lib. bdg. 90.05x (ISBN 3-443-11010-X, Pub by Gebrueder Borntraeger Germany). Lubrecht & Cramer.
Morey, G. B. & Hanson, Gilbert N., eds. Selected Studies of Archean Gneisses & Lower Proterozoic Rocks: Southern Canadian Shield. LC 80-67113. (Special Paper Ser.: No. 182). (Illus., Orig.). 1980. pap. 26.00x (ISBN 0-8137-2182-2). Geol Soc.
Murray, J. W. Guide to Classification in Geology. LC 80-41094. (Geology Ser.). 120p. 1981. 19.95 (ISBN 0-470-27090-X). Halsted Pr.
Murray, John. A Comparative View of the Huttonian & Neptunian Systems of Geology: In Answer to the Illustrations of the Huttonian Theory of the Earth. Albritton, Claude C., Jr., ed. LC 77-6533. (History of Geology Ser.). 1978. Repr. of 1802 ed. lib. bdg. 18.00 (ISBN 0-405-10453-7). Arno.
Northeastern Women's Geoscientists Conference, First. Women in Geology: Proceedings. Halsey, S. D., et al, eds. LC 76-21580. (Illus.). 1976. pap. 2.00 (ISBN 0-915492-02-4). Ash Lad Pr.
Page, Lou W. Geology. 1973. pap. text ed. 6.44 (ISBN 0-201-05653-4, Sch Div); tchr's manual 2.84 (ISBN 0-201-05654-2). A-W.
Paige, Sidney, ed. Application of Geology to Engineering Practice: Berkey Volume. LC 51-5562. (Illus.). 1950. 12.00x (ISBN 0-8137-4301-X). Geol Soc.
Palaeontological Association Symposium, Birmingham, Sept. 1974. The Ordovician System: Proceedings. Bassett, M. G., ed. 1976. pap. text ed. 60.00x (ISBN 0-7083-0582-2). Verry.
Pearl, Richard M. Turquoise. 1976. pap. 1.35 (ISBN 0-686-17441-0). Earth Science.
Peters, William C. Exploration & Mining Geology. LC 77-14006. 1978. text ed. 33.95 (ISBN 0-471-68261-6). Wiley.
Phillips, William. An Outline of Mineralogy & Geology: Intended for the Use of Those Who May Desire to Become Acquainted with the Elements of Those Sciences. Albritton, Claude C., Jr., ed. LC 77-6536. (History of Geology Ser.). (Illus.). 1978. Repr. of 1816 ed. lib. bdg. 12.00x (ISBN 0-405-10456-1). Arno.
Playfair, John. Illustrations of the Huttonian Theory of the Earth. 8.50 (ISBN 0-8446-2746-1). Peter Smith.
--Illustrations of the Huttonian Theory of the Earth. 1956. pap. 5.00 (ISBN 0-486-61168-X). Dover.
Press, Frank & Siever, Raymond. Earth. 2nd ed. LC 77-25209. (Illus.). 1978. text ed. 22.95x (ISBN 0-7167-0289-4); instr' guide avail. W H Freeman.
Putnam, William C. Geology. 3rd ed. 1978. 21.95x (ISBN 0-19-502285-8). Oxford U Pr.
Rahm, D. A. Slides for Geology: Study Guide. 1971. text ed. 3.95 (ISBN 0-07-075217-6, C); 450.00 (ISBN 0-07-075215-X). McGraw.
Rapp, George, Jr. & Vondra, Carl F., eds. Hominid States: Their Geologic Setting. (AAAS Selected Symposium: No. 63). 327p. 1981. lib. bdg. 26.50 (ISBN 0-86531-262-1). Westview.
Raspe, Rudolf E. Introduction to the Natural History of the Terrestrial Sphere. facsimile ed. 1970. 26.50 (ISBN 0-02-850840-8). Hafner.
Ray, John. Three Physico-Theological Discourses: Primitive Chaos, & Creation of the World, the General Deluge, Its Causes & Effects. Albritton, Claude C., Jr., ed. LC 77-6538. (History of Geology Ser.). 1978. Repr. of 1713 ed. lib. bdg. 25.00x (ISBN 0-405-10457-X). Arno.
Ray, Santosh. A Textbook of Geology. 480p. 1981. 25.00x (ISBN 0-86125-280-2, Pub. by Orient Longman India). State Mutual Bk.
Read, H. H. & Watson, Janet. Introduction & Geology, 2 vols. Incl. Vol. 1. Principles. 2nd ed. LC 76-50637. 1977. 30.95 (ISBN 0-470-99031-7); Vol. 2, 2 pts. LC 75-501. 1975; Pt. 1. Early Stages of Earth History. 221p. 21.95 (ISBN 0-470-71165-5); Pt. 2. Later Stages of Earth History. 371p. 24.95 (ISBN 0-470-71166-3). Halsted Pr.
Reaser, Donald F., ed. Basic Geology. 1978. 26.00 (ISBN 0-89419-017-2). Inst Energy.
Reeves, C. C., Jr. Caliche-Origin Classification, Morphology & Uses. LC 76-2234. 1976. text ed. 39.95x (ISBN 0-686-16733-3). Estacado Bks.
Reyer, Eduard. Questions on Geologic Principles. Keller, Allen, et al, trs. LC 79-89374. (Microform Publication: No. 9). (Illus.). 1979. 4.00x (ISBN 0-8137-6009-7). Geol Soc.
Rhodes & Stone. The Language of the Earth. 350p. 1981. text ed. 35.00 (ISBN 0-08-025981-2); pap. text ed. 17.50 (ISBN 0-08-025980-4). Pergamon.
Rhodes, Frank H. Geology. (Golden Guide Ser). (Illus.). (gr. 9 up). 1971. PLB 10.38 (ISBN 0-307-63549-X, Golden Pr); pap. 1.95 (ISBN 0-307-24349-4). Western Pub.
--Geology. (Golden Guide Ser). (Illus.). (gr. 9 up). 1971. PLB 10.38 (ISBN 0-307-63549-X, Golden Pr); pap. 1.95 (ISBN 0-307-24349-4). Western Pub.
Riban, David M. Introduction to Physical Science. (Illus.). 656p. 1981. text ed. 21.95 (ISBN 0-07-052140-9, C); instr's manual 4.95 (ISBN 0-07-052141-7). McGraw.
Rigby, J. Keith. Field Guide: Southern Colorado Plateau. LC 75-32499. (Geology Field Guide Ser.). (Illus.). 1977. pap. text ed. 6.95 (ISBN 0-8403-1314-4). Kendall-Hunt.
Roberts, John L. Introduction to Geological Structures. 1978. pap. text ed. 15.00 (ISBN 0-08-020920-3). Pergamon.
Ross, C. A., ed. Paleobiogeography. LC 76-12969. (Benchmark Papers in Geology Ser.: Vol. 31). 1976. 49.50 (ISBN 0-12-787365-1). Acad Pr.
Rudman, Jack. Geology. (Undergraduate Program Field Test Ser.: UPFT-11). (Cloth bdg. avail. on request). pap. 9.95 (ISBN 0-8373-6011-0). Natl Learning.
Rutten, M. G. The Origin of Life. LC 73-118255. (Illus.). 440p. 1969. 75.75 (ISBN 0-444-40887-8). Elsevier.
Salop, L. J. Precambrian of the Northern Hemisphere. (Developments in Paleontology & Stratigraphy: Vol. 3). 1977. 75.75 (ISBN 0-444-41510-6). Elsevier.
Sanders, John E. Principles of Physical Geology. 624p. 1981. text ed. 22.95 (ISBN 0-471-08424-7). Wiley.
Schultz, John R. & Cleaves, A. B. Geology in Engineering. LC 55-7317. 1955. text ed. 32.95x (ISBN 0-471-76461-2). Wiley.
Schwartz, Maurice L., ed. Barrier Islands. LC 73-12838. (Benchmark Papers in Geology Ser.). 464p. 1973. text ed. 50.00 (ISBN 0-12-787447-X). Acad Pr.
Shelton, John S. Geology Illustrated. LC 66-16380. (Illus.). 1966. text ed. 24.95x (ISBN 0-7167-0229-0). W H Freeman.
Shrock, Robert. Geology at MIT: 1865-1965. LC 77-71235. (Illus.). 1977. 25.00x (ISBN 0-262-19161-X). MIT Pr.
Siegfried, Robert & Dott, Robert H., Jr., eds. Humphry Davy's Lectures on Geology, Eighteen Hundred & Five. LC 79-5022. 192p. 1980. 17.50 (ISBN 0-299-08030-7). U of Wis Pr.
Silver, Burr A. Geology & Modern Problems. 1976. pap. text ed. 6.95 (ISBN 0-8403-1673-9). Kendall-Hunt.
Site Selection Factors for Repositories of Solid High-Level & Alpha Bearing Wastes in Geological Formations. (Illus.). 1978. pap. 9.75 (ISBN 92-0-125177-7, IDC177, IAEA). Unipub.
Squyres, Coy H., ed. Geology of Italy, 2 vols. 1975. Set. 135.00x (ISBN 0-8002-1458-7). Intl Pubns Serv.
Steinhart, J. S. & Smith, T. J., eds. The Earth Beneath the Continents. LC 66-62581. (Geophysical Monograph Ser.: Vol. 10). 1966. 16.50 (ISBN 0-87590-010-0). Am Geophysical.
Stirrup, M. N. Geology: The Science of the Earth. LC 78-73233. (Illus.). 1980. pap. 11.95 (ISBN 0-521-22567-1). Cambridge U Pr.
Stokes, William L. Essentials of Earth History: An Introduction to Historical Geology. 3rd ed. (Illus.). 512p. 1973. ref. ed. 22.95 (ISBN 0-13-285932-7). P-H.
Stokes, William L., et al. Introduction to Geology: Physical & Historical. 2nd ed. LC 77-21570. 1978. text ed. 22.95 (ISBN 0-13-484352-5). P-H.
Strahler, Arthur N. Physical Geology. 640p. 1981. text ed. 24.95 scp (ISBN 0-06-046462-3, HarpC). Har-Row.
--Principles of Physical Geology. (Illus.). 1977. text ed. 22.95 scp (ISBN 0-06-046457-7, HarpC); instructor's manual free (ISBN 0-06-366459-3). Har-Row.

Tank, Ronald W., ed. Focus on Environmental Geology: A Collection of Case Histories & Readings from Original Sources. 2nd ed. (Illus.). 544p. 1976. pap. text ed. 8.95x (ISBN 0-19-501968-7). Oxford U Pr.
Thurber, Walter A., et al. Geology. (Exploring Earth Science Program Ser.). (gr. 7-12). 1976. pap. text ed. 4.96 (ISBN 0-205-04741-6, 6947417). Allyn.
Tricart, J. The Landforms of the Humid Tropics, Forests, & Savannas. 1973. 21.50 (ISBN 0-312-46550-5). St Martin.
Turekian, Karl K., ed. Late Cenozoic Glacial Ages. LC 70-140540. (Silliman Lectures Ser). (Illus.). 1971. 42.50x (ISBN 0-300-01420-1). Yale U Pr.
Uhlig, H., ed. System & Theory of Geosciences, 2 pts. 103p. 1975. Vol. 1. pap. text ed. 24.00 (ISBN 0-08-019664-0); Vol. 7, Pt. 1. pap. text ed. 24.00 (ISBN 0-08-019670-5). Pergamon.
Uyeda, Seiya. The New View of the Earth: Moving Continents & Moving Oceans. Ohnuki, Masako, tr. LC 77-9900. (Geology Ser.). (Illus.). 1978. text ed. 19.95x (ISBN 0-7167-0283-5); pap. text ed. 9.95x (ISBN 0-7167-0282-7). W H Freeman.
Velikovsky, Immanuel. Earth in Upheaval. LC 55-11339. 1955. 8.95 (ISBN 0-385-04113-6). Doubleday.
--Earth in Upheavel. 1980. pap. 2.75 (ISBN 0-671-83454-1). PB.
Visser, W. A., ed. Geological Nomenclature. 568p. 1980. lib. bdg. 95.00 (ISBN 90-247-2403-1, Pub. by Martinus Nijhoff Netherlands). Kluwer Boston.
Vuke, Susan. Processes of the Earth's Surface. 96p. 1980. lab manual 6.95 (ISBN 0-686-70709-5). Mountain Pr.
Warren, Erasmus. Geologia: Discourse Concerning the Earth Before the Deluge, Wherein the Form & Properties Ascribed to It. LC 77-6546. (History of Geology Ser.). (Illus.). 1978. Repr. of 1690 ed. lib. bdg. 25.00x (ISBN 0-405-10470-7). Arno.
Watkins, et al. Our Geological Environment. LC 74-21018. (Illus.). 400p. 1975. pap. text ed. 13.95 (ISBN 0-7216-9133-1). HR&W.
Weber, Jon N., ed. Geochemistry of Germanium. LC 73-12621. (Benchmark Papers in Geology Ser). 480p. 1974. text ed. 54.00 (ISBN 0-12-787740-1). Acad Pr.
Whitehurst, John. An Inquiry into the Original State & Formation of the Earth: Deduced from Facts & the Laws of Nature. 2nd rev. ed. Albritton, Claude C., Jr., ed. LC 77-6548. (History of Geology Ser.). 1978. Repr. of 1786 ed. lib. bdg. 20.00x (ISBN 0-405-10465-0). Arno.
Whitten, E. H. Timothy, ed. Quantitative Studies in the Geological Sciences. LC 74-15932. (Memoir: No. 142). (Illus.). 1975. 31.00x (ISBN 0-8137-1142-8). Geol Soc.
Wood, B. J. & Fraser, D. G. Elementary Thermodynamics for Geologists. (Illus.). 1976. pap. text ed. 14.95x (ISBN 0-19-859927-7). Oxford U Pr.
Woodward, John. An Essay Toward a Natural History of the Earth, & Terrestrial Bodies Especially Minerals of the Sea, Rivers, & Springs: An Account of the Universal Deluge & of the Effects That It Had Upon the Earth. Albritton, Claude C., Jr., ed. LC 77-7406. (History of Geology Ser.). 1978. Repr. of 1695 ed. lib. bdg. 20.00 (ISBN 0-405-10468-5). Arno.
Wyllie, Peter J. The Way the Earth Works: An Introduction to the New Global Geology & Its Revolutionary Development. LC 75-23197. 296p. 1976. pap. text ed. 12.95 (ISBN 0-471-96896-X). Wiley.
Young, Keith. Geology: The Paradox of Earth & Man. 416p. 1975. text ed. 20.50 (ISBN 0-395-05561-X); instructor's manual 1.25 (ISBN 0-395-18267-0). HM.
Young, Keith, et al. Environmental Geology. 515p. 1970. 10.00 (ISBN 0-913312-37-1). Am Geol.
Zumberge, James H. & Nelson, Clemens A. Elements of Geology. 3rd ed. LC 79-180247. 544p. 1972. text ed. 22.95x (ISBN 0-471-98673-9). Wiley.
--Elements of Physical Geology. LC 75-26843. 432p. 1976. text ed. 22.95x (ISBN 0-471-98674-7). Wiley.
Zumberge, James H. & Rutford, Robert H. Laboratory Manual for Physical Geology. 5th ed. 200p. 1979. write for info. wire coil (ISBN 0-697-05037-8); instrs.' manual avail. (ISBN 0-685-91871-8). Wm C Brown.

GEOLOGY-BIBLIOGRAPHY

Agasiz, Jean L. Bibliographia Zoologiae Et Geologiae, 4 Vols. (Sources of Science Ser.: No. 20). Set. 231.00 (ISBN 0-384-00404-0). Johnson Repr.
Agassiz, Louis. Bibliographis Zoologia et Geologia: A General Catalogue of All Books, Tracfs & Memoirs on Zoology & Geology. Strickalnd, Hugh E., ed. 1976. Repr. of 1848 ed. 149.00 (ISBN 0-403-05818-X, Regency). Scholarly.
Chronic, John & Chronic, Halka. Bibliography of Theses in Geology: Nineteen Fifty-Eight to Nineteen Sixty-Three. 268p. 1965. 15.00 (ISBN 0-913312-30-4). Am Geol.
Editerral Editor's Handbook. 1980. pap. 10.51 (ISBN 0-686-27381-8, Pub. by GEO Abstracts England). State Mutual Bk.
Geological Society of America. Ten-Year Index to Volumes Sixty-One to Seventy of Geological Society of America Bulletin. LC 1-23380. 1962. 10.50x (ISBN 0-8137-9061-1). Geol Soc.
Goodman, G. T. & Bray, S. An Annotated Bibliography of Ecological Aspects of the Reclamation of Derelict & Disturbed Land. (Bibliography Ser.). 351p. 1980. 14.95x (ISBN 0-902246-52-6, Pub. by GEO Abstracts England). State Mutual Bk.
Harvard University Museum of Comparative Zoology. Catalogue of the Library of the Museum of Comparative Zoology, First Supplement. 1976. lib. bdg. 120.00 (ISBN 0-8161-0811-0). G K Hall.
Kasbeer, Tina. Bibliography of Continental Drift & Plate Tectonics, Vol. 2. LC 72-81724. (Special Paper: No. 164). 1975. pap. 13.00x (ISBN 0-8137-2164-4). Geol Soc.
Northrop, Stuart A. University of New Mexico Contributions in Geology, 1898-1964. LC 66-14777. (Geology Ser.: No. 7). 1966. pap. 2.00x (ISBN 0-8263-0117-7). U of NM Pr.
Richards, Horace G. & Shapiro, Earl A. Annotated Bibliography of Quaternary Shorelines: Third Supplement (1974-1977) (Bibliography Ser.). 245p. 1980. 21.00x (ISBN 0-86094-025-X, Pub. by GEO Abstracts England). State Mutual Bk.
U. S. Department of the Interior - U. S. Geological Survey, Washington, D. C. Catalog of the United States Geological Survey Library, 25 vols. 1964. Set. lib. bdg. 2375.00 (ISBN 0-8161-0712-2). G K Hall.
U. S. Department of the Interior - U. S. Geological Survey, Washington D. C. Catalog of the United States Geological Survey Library - Supplement 1, 11 vols. 1972. Set. 1155.00 (ISBN 0-8161-0876-5). G K Hall.
U. S. Department of the Interior.Washington D.C. Catalog of the United States Geological Survey 3rd Suppl, 6 vols. 1976. lib. bdg. 630.00 (ISBN 0-8161-0051-9). G K Hall.
Wallace, Harriet E., ed. Union List of Geologic Field Trip Guidebooks of North America. 3rd ed. LC 78-52012. 1978. pap. 20.00 (ISBN 0-913312-05-3). Am Geol.
Ward, Dederick C. & O'Callaghan, T. C. Bibliography of Theses in Geology: Nineteen Sixty-Five to Nineteen Sixty-Six. 255p. 1969. 8.00 (ISBN 0-913312-36-3). Am Geol.
Ward, Dederick C., et al. Geologic Reference Sources: A Subject & Regional Bibliography of Publications & Maps in the Geological Sciences. 2nd ed. LC 81-4770. 590p. 1981. 30.00 (ISBN 0-8108-1428-5). Scarecrow.
Whitaker, C. R. A Bibliography of Pediments. (Bibliography Ser.). 95p. 1980. pap. 3.50x (ISBN 0-686-27380-X, Pub. by GEO Abstracts England). State Mutual Bk.

GEOLOGY-DATA PROCESSING

Chen, C. H., ed. Computer-Aided Seismic Analysis & Discrimination. (Methods in Geochemistry & Geophysics Ser: Vol. 13). 1978. 37.00 (ISBN 0-444-41681-1). Elsevier.
Claerbout, Jon F. Fundamentals of Geophysical Data Processing: With Applications to Petroleum Prospecting. (International Ser. in the Earth & Planetary Sciences). 1976. text ed. 23.95 (ISBN 0-07-011117-0, C). McGraw.
Cutbill, J. L. Data Processing in Biology & Geology. (Systematics Association: Special Vol. 3). 1971. 55.00 (ISBN 0-12-199750-2). Acad Pr.
Davis, John C. Statistics & Data Analysis in Geology. LC 72-6792. (Illus.). 550p. 1973. 34.95 (ISBN 0-471-19895-1). Wiley.
Fu, K. S. Applications of Pattern Recognition. 304p. 1981. 84.95 (ISBN 0-8493-5729-2). CRC Pr.
Harbaugh, John W. & Bonham-Carter, Graeme. Computer Simulation in Geology. 590p. 1981. Repr. of 1970 ed. lib. bdg. write for info. (ISBN 0-89874-125-4). Krieger.
Loudon, T. V. Computer Methods in Geology. 1979. 46.50 (ISBN 0-12-456950-1). Acad Pr.
Merriam, D. F., ed. Capture, Management & Display of Geological Data: With Special Emphasis on Energy & Mineral Resources. LC 76-56893. 1977. pap. text ed. 41.25 (ISBN 0-08-021422-3). Pergamon.
--Computer Assisted Instruction in Geology: Proceedings of the 4th Geochautauqua, Syracuse University, 1975. 1976. pap. text ed. 41.25 (ISBN 0-08-021040-6). Pergamon.
--Geostatistics: A Colloquium. LC 71-142040. (Computer Applications in the Earth Sciences Ser.). 177p. 1970. 22.50 (ISBN 0-306-30519-4, Plenum Pr). Plenum Pub.

GEOLOGY-DICTIONARIES

American Geological Institute. Dictionary of Geological Terms. rev. ed. LC 73-9004. 600p. 1976. pap. 4.50 (ISBN 0-385-08452-8, Anch). Doubleday.
Bates, Robert L. & Jackson, Julia A., eds. Glossary of Geology. LC 79-57360. 749p. 1980. 60.00 (ISBN 0-913312-15-0). Am Geol.
Cagnacci-Schwicker, Angelo. Dictionnaire International de Metallurgie, Mineralogie, Geologie et Industries Extractives, 2 vols. 1530p. (Fr.). 1969. Set. 95.00 (ISBN 0-686-56933-4, M-6054). French & Eur.
Cailleux, E. Elements de Geologie En Six Langues. 191p. (Fr., Ger., Rus., Span. & Eng., Elements of Geology in Six Languages). 1965. pap. 19.95 (ISBN 0-686-56735-8, M-6055). French & Eur.
Challinor, John. A Dictionary of Geology. 5th ed. 1978. text ed. 14.95x (ISBN 0-19-520063-2). Oxford U Pr.
Chesnel De La Charbouclais, L. P. Dictionnaire de Geologie... et Dictionnaire de Chronologie Universelle par M. Champagnac, Vol. 50. Migne, J. P., ed. (Encyclopedie Theologique Ser.). 728p. (Fr.). Date not set. Repr. of 1849 ed. lib. bdg. 192.50x (ISBN 0-89241-253-4). Caratzas Bros.
Diccionario Rioduero: Geologia y Mineralogia. 2nd ed. (Espn.). 1978. leatherette 9.95 (ISBN 0-686-57363-3). French & Eur.
Entwicklungsgeschichte der Erde Mit Einem ABC der Geologie, 2 vols. 800p. (Ger.). 1970. Set. 22.50 (ISBN 3-7684-6026-6, M-7363, Pub. by W. Dausien). French & Eur.
Fairbridge, Rhodes W., ed. Encyclopedia of World Regional Geology: Part I: Western Hemisphere Including Australia & Antarctica, Pt. 1. LC 75-1406. (Encyclopedia of Earth Sciences Ser: Vol. 8A). 1975. 55.00 (ISBN 0-12-786461-X). Acad Pr.
Gagnacci-Schwicker, A. & Schwicker. International Dictionary of Metallurgy, Mineralogy, Geology and the Mining and Oil Industries. 1530p. (Eng., Fr., Ger. & It.). 1970. 88.00 (ISBN 3-7625-0751-1, M-7482, Pub. by Bauverlag). French & Eur.
Heckman, Carol, et al, eds. GeoRef Thesaurus & Guide to Indexing. 2nd ed. LC 78-65083. 1978. pap. 35.00 (ISBN 0-913312-07-X) (ISBN 0-913312-40-1). Am Geol.
Klein, J. Herder - Lexikon Geologie und Mineralogie. 238p. (Ger.). 1975. 15.95 (ISBN 3-451-16452-3, M-7457, Pub. by Herder). French & Eur.
Lexique Stratigraphique International. (Fr.-Eng.). pap. 37.50 (ISBN 0-686-57018-9, M-6369). French & Eur.
Murawski, H. Geologisches Woerterbuch. 7th ed. (Ger.). 1977. pap. 10.95 (ISBN 3-432-84107-8, M-7418, Pub. by DTV). French & Eur.
Murawski, Hans. Geologisches Woerterbuch. (Ger.). 1972. pap. 10.95 (ISBN 0-686-56476-6, 7419, Pub. by DTV). French & Eur.
Novitzky, Alejandro. Diccionario Minero-Metalurgico-Geologico-Mineralogico-Petrografico y de Petroleo: English-Spanish-French-German-Russian. 2nd ed. 376p. 1960. indice alfabetico 30.00 (ISBN 0-8002-0155-8). Intl Pubns Serv.
Riley, Sharon J., ed. GeoRef Thesaurus & Guide to Indexing. 3rd ed. 456p. 1981. 45.00 (ISBN 0-913312-53-3). Am Geol.
Rosenfeld, V. Kleines Fachwoerterbuch Geologie. 197p. (Ger.). 1966. 14.50 (ISBN 3-443-39048-X, M-7500, Pub. by Borntaeger). French & Eur.
Thompson, Reginald C. A Dictionary of Assyrian Chemistry & Geology. LC 78-72768. (Ancient Mesopotamian Texts & Studies). Repr. of 1936 ed. 24.50 (ISBN 0-404-18222-4). AMS Pr.
Watznauer, A. Woerterbuch Geowissenschaften, Vol. 2. (Ger. -Eng., German-English Dictionary of Geo-Sciences). 1973. 45.00 (ISBN 3-87144-140-6, M-6916). French & Eur.
Whitten & Brooks. Dictionary of Geology. (Reference Ser.). 1973. pap. 4.95 (ISBN 0-14-051049-4). Penguin.
Wilmarth, Mary G. Lexicon of Geologic Names in the U. S, 2 Vols. 1968. Repr. of 1938 ed. 175.00 (ISBN 0-403-00128-5). Scholarly.
Woerterbuch Fuer Metallurgie, Mineralogie, Geologie, Bergbau und die Oelindustrie. (Eng. , Fr. , Ger. & It., Dictionary of Metallurgy, Mineralogy, Geology, Mining and Oil Industry). 1970. 88.00 (ISBN 3-7625-0751-1, M-6912). French & Eur.
Wyllie, R. J. & Argall, George O., Jr., eds. World Mining Glossary of Mining, Processing & Geological Terms. LC 74-20169. (A World Mining Book). 432p. 1975. 47.50 (ISBN 0-87930-031-0). Miller Freeman.
Zylka, T. Geological Dictionary. 1493p. 1980. 90.00x (ISBN 0-569-07698-6, Pub. by Collet's). State Mutual Bk.

GEOLOGY-EXAMINATIONS, QUESTIONS, ETC.

Dolgoff, Anatole. Geology: Advanced Test for the G. R. E. rev. ed. LC 67-18360. (Orig.). 1967. pap. 3.95 (ISBN 0-668-01071-1). Arco.
Rudman, Jack. Earth Science & General Science - Sr. H.S. (Teachers License Examination Ser.: T-14). (Cloth bdg. avail. on request). pap. 10.00 (ISBN 0-8373-8014-6). Natl Learning.
--Geologist. (Career Examination Ser.: C-301). (Cloth bdg. avail. on request). pap. 8.00 (ISBN 0-8373-0301-X). Natl Learning.
--Geology. (College Level Examination Ser.: CLEP-15). (Cloth bdg. avail. on request). pap. 9.95 (ISBN 0-8373-5207-X). Natl Learning.
--Geology. (College Proficiency Examination Ser.: CPEP-13). (Cloth bdg. avail. on request). pap. 9.95 (ISBN 0-8373-5413-7). Natl Learning.
--Geology. (Graduate Record Examination Ser.: GRE-8). (Cloth bdg. avail. on request). pap. 9.95 (ISBN 0-8373-5208-8). Natl Learning.
--Junior Geologist. (Career Examination Ser.: C-414). (Cloth bdg. avail. on request). pap. 8.00 (ISBN 0-8373-0414-8). Natl Learning.
--Senior Geologist. (Career Examination Ser.: C-1006). (Cloth bdg. avail. on request). pap. 10.00 (ISBN 0-8373-1006-7). Natl Learning.
Savage, E. Lynn & Biren, Helen A. Putnam's Geology: Study Guide. 208p. (Orig.). 1978. pap. text ed. 7.95x (ISBN 0-19-502385-4). Oxford U Pr.

GEOLOGY-FIELD WORK

Bates, Denis E. & Kirkaldy, John F. Field Geology in Color. LC 76-56417. (Arco Color Books Ser.). (Illus.). 1977. 7.95 (ISBN 0-668-04208-7, 4208). Arco.
Bonney, Orrin H. & Bonney, Lorraine. Field Book. Incl. Teton Range & Gros Ventre Range: Climbing Routes & Back Country. rev., 2nd ed. LC 76-189201. (Wyoming Booklet: No. 2). 263p (ISBN 0-8040-0578-8); Yellowstone Park: Absaroka Range. rev. 2nd ed. LC 70-189202. 162p (ISBN 0-8040-0579-6); Big Horn Range. LC 72-132589. (Wyoming Booklet: No. 5). 172p (ISBN 0-8040-0536-2). (Illus.). 1977. pap. 7.95 ea. (SB). Swallow.
Compton, R. R. Manual of Field Geology. LC 61-17357. 1962. 22.50x (ISBN 0-471-16698-7). Wiley.
Feldmann, Rodney M. & Heimlich, Richard A. Geology Field Guide: The Black Hills. 208p. (Orig.). 1980. pap. 8.95 (ISBN 0-8403-2193-7). Kendall-Hunt.
Feldmann, Rodney M., et al. Field Guide: Southern Great Lakes. LC 77-75770. (Geology Field Guide Ser). (Illus.). 1977. pap. text ed. 7.95 (ISBN 0-8403-1730-1). Kendall-Hunt.
Kiersch, George A., et al, eds. Engineering Geology Case Histories, Nos. 6-10 In One Volume. LC 74-77141. (Illus.). 1974. 20.00x (ISBN 0-8137-4202-1). Geol Soc.
Lahee, Frederick H. Field Geology. 6th ed. 1961. text ed. 24.00 (ISBN 0-07-035808-7, C). McGraw.
Lozo, Frank E., ed. Woodbine & Adjacent Strata of the Waco Area of Central Texas: A Symposium. LC 52-10665. (Fondreu Science Ser.: No. 4). (Illus.). 1951. 15.00 (ISBN 0-87074-091-1); pap. 12.50 (ISBN 0-87074-092-X). SMU Press.
Moseley, Frank. Methods in Field Geology. (Illus.). 1981. text ed. 29.95x (ISBN 0-7167-1293-8); pap. text ed. 14.95x (ISBN 0-7167-1294-6). W H Freeman.
Simpson, I. M. Fieldwork in Geology. (Introducing Geology Ser.). (Illus.). 1977. pap. text ed. 5.50x (ISBN 0-04-550025-8). Allen Unwin.
Suchman, J. Richard. Idea Book for Geological Inquiry. 96p. (gr. 5-8). 1981. pap. 10.00 wkbk. (ISBN 0-89824-024-7). Trillium Pr.
Weiss, L. E. The Minor Structures of Deformed Rocks: A Photographic Atlas. LC 72-79582. (Illus.). 440p. 1972. 36.10 (ISBN 0-387-05828-1). Springer-Verlag.

GEOLOGY-GRAPHIC METHODS

McCammon, R. B., ed. Concepts in Geostatistics. LC 74-23669. (Illus.). xvi, 184p. 1975. pap. 14.50 (ISBN 0-387-06892-9). Springer-Verlag.
Reeves, Robert G., ed. Manual of Remote Sensing, 2 vols. Incl. Vol. 1. Theory, Principles & Techniques; Vol. 2. Photographic Interpretation & Applications. LC 75-7552. (Illus.). 1975. member 32.50 (ISBN 0-686-23107-4); non-member 45.00 (ISBN 0-686-23108-2). ASP.

GEOLOGY-HISTORY

Albritton, Claude C., ed. History of Geology Series, 37 vols. (Illus.). 1978. lib. bdg. 952.00set (ISBN 0-405-10429-4). Arno.
Alexander, Nancy. Father of Texas Geology: Robert T. Hill. LC 76-2621. (Bicentenial Series in American Studies: No. 4). (Illus.). 1976. 12.50 (ISBN 0-87074-152-7). SMU Press.

Alexandrov, Eugene, ed. Geological Bulletins, 5 bks. Incl. No. 1. Metallogenic Provinces & Metallogenic Epochs. Bilibin, Yu. A. 1968. pap. 1.00 (ISBN 0-930146-00-X); No. 2. Distribution & Preservation of Pollen in Sediments in the Western Part of the Pacific Ocean. Koreneva, Ye. V. 1968. pap. 1.00 (ISBN 0-930146-01-8); No. 3. Symposium on the New York City Group of Formations. 1969. pap. 3.00 (ISBN 0-930146-02-6); No. 4. Essays on Metallogeny. Smirnov, V. I., ed. 1971. pap. 2.00 (ISBN 0-930146-03-4); No. 5. Transactions of the Fifth Caribbean Geological Conference. Mattson, Peter H., ed. 1971. pap. 5.00 (ISBN 0-930146-04-2). Queens Coll Pr.

Fenton, Carroll L. & Fenton, Mildred. Story of the Great Geologists. facs. ed. LC 73-84306. (Essay Index Reprint Ser.). 1945. 20.00 (ISBN 0-8369-1130-X). Arno.

Hagood, Allen. Dinosaur: The Story Behind the Scenery. LC 75-157460. (Illus.). 1972. 7.95 (ISBN 0-916122-35-2); pap. 2.50 (ISBN 0-916122-10-7). KC Pubns.

Hall, D. History of the Earth Sciences During the Scientific & Industrial Revolution with Special Emphasis on Physical Geosciences. 1976. 34.25 (ISBN 0-444-41440-1). Elsevier.

Holmes, Arthur. The Age of the Earth. 80p. 1981. Repr. of 1927 ed. lib. bdg. 15.00 (ISBN 0-89987-369-3). Darby Bks.

Jameson, Robert. The Wernerian Theory of the Neptunian Origin of Rocks: A Facsimile Reprint of Elements of Geognosy, 1808. White, George W., ed. LC 75-43364. (Contributions to the History of Geology Ser.). (Illus.). 1976. Repr. of 1808 ed. 27.50 (ISBN 0-02-847160-1). Hafner.

Leveson, David J. Geology & the Human Environment. (Illus.). 1980. text ed. 18.95x (ISBN 0-19-502578-4). Oxford U Pr.

Merrill, George P. First One Hundred Years of American Geology. (Illus.). 1969. Repr. of 1924 ed. 32.75 (ISBN 0-02-849180-7). Hafner.

Moore, Ruth. Earth We Live On. 2nd ed. (Illus.). (YA) 1971. 13.95 (ISBN 0-394-46968-2). Knopf.

Schneer, Cecil J., ed. Two Hundred Years of Geology in America: Proceedings of the New Hampshire Bicentennial Conference. LC 78-63149. (Illus.). 401p. 1979. text ed. 22.50x (ISBN 0-87451-160-7). U Pr of New Eng.

Seeley, H. G. The Story of the Earth in Past Ages. 1979. Repr. of 1904 ed. lib. bdg. 25.00 (ISBN 0-8495-4912-4). Arden Lib.

Shackley, M. L. Rocks & Man. LC 76-52809. (Illus.). 1977. 16.95 (ISBN 0-312-68799-0). St Martin.

Sidar, Jean. George Hamell Cook: A Life in Agriculture & Geology, 1818-1889. 1976. 13.00 (ISBN 0-8135-0827-4). Rutgers U Pr.

Skinner, Brian J., ed. Earth's History, Structure, & Materials. LC 80-21698. (The Earth & Its Inhabitants: Selected Readings from American Scientist Ser.). (Illus.). 183p. (Orig.). 1980. pap. 8.95 (ISBN 0-913232-89-0). W Kaufmann.

Tynan, Eugene J. & Cain, J. Allen. Geology: A Synopsis Part 2 Historical Geology. LC 79-92086. 192p. 1981. pap. text ed. 8.95 (ISBN 0-8403-2306-9). Kendall-Hunt.

Von Zittel, K. A. Geschichte der Geologie und Paleontologie. 1889. 41.50 (ISBN 0-384-71020-4). Johnson Repr.

--History of Geology & Paleontology. Olgivie-Gordon, Maria M., tr. 1962. Repr. of 1901 ed. 25.00 (ISBN 3-7682-7100-5). Lubrecht & Cramer.

Wells, John W. Early Investigations of the Devonian System in New York, 1656-1836. LC 64-1862. (Special Paper: No. 74). (Illus., Orig.). 1963. pap. 5.00x (ISBN 0-8137-2074-5). Geol Soc.

Woodward, Horace B. History of Geology. LC 75-41298. (Illus.). Repr. of 1911 ed. 15.00 (ISBN 0-404-14707-0). AMS Pr.

--History of Geology. Albritton, Claude C., Jr., ed. LC 77-6550. (History of Geology Ser.). (Illus.). 1978. Repr. of 1911 ed. lib. bdg. 15.00x (ISBN 0-405-10467-7). Arno.

GEOLOGY–JUVENILE LITERATURE

Ames, Gerald & Wyler, Rose. Earth's Story. LC 66-30640. (Creative Science Ser). (gr. 4-9). 1967. PLB 7.95 (ISBN 0-87191-012-8). Creative Ed.

Blackbeer. Student Earth Scientist Explores the Geologic Past. LC 76-2565. (Student Scientist Ser.). (gr. 7 up). 1976. PLB 7.97 (ISBN 0-8239-0353-2). Rosen Pr.

Boy Scouts Of America. Geology. LC 19-600. (Illus.). 88p. (gr. 6-12). 1953. pap. 0.70x (ISBN 0-8395-3284-9, 3284). BSA.

Cartner, William. Fun with Geology. (Learning with Fun Ser.). (Illus.). (gr. 5 up). 1971. 12.50x (ISBN 0-7182-0076-4, SpS). Sportshelf.

Creative Editors. Geology of the Earth. LC 74-140639. (Our Changing Environment Ser). (Illus.). (gr. 4-9). 1971. PLB 6.95 (ISBN 0-87191-072-1). Creative Ed.

Elementary Science Study. Geo Blocks. 1975. tchr's guide 4.80 (ISBN 0-07-018520-4, W). McGraw.

--Rocks & Charts. 1975. tchr's guide 5.04 (ISBN 0-07-018527-1, W). McGraw.

Fodor, R. V. What Does a Geologist Do? LC 77-6483. (Illus.). (gr. 5 up). 1977. 5.95 (ISBN 0-396-07481-2). Dodd.

Harris, Stanley E., Jr., et al. Exploring the Land & Rocks of Southern Illinois: A Geological Guide. LC 76-51382. (Illus.). 256p. 1977. 11.85x (ISBN 0-8093-0740-5); pap. 5.95 (ISBN 0-8093-0769-3). S Ill U Pr.

McFall, Christie. Underwater Continent. LC 75-11851. (Illus.). 160p. (gr. 7 up). 1975. PLB 5.95 (ISBN 0-396-07175-9). Dodd.

McNulty, Faith. How to Dig a Hole to the Other Side of the World. LC 78-22479. (Illus.). (ps-3). 1979. 8.95 (ISBN 0-06-024147-0, HarpJ); PLB 8.79 (ISBN 0-06-024148-9). Har-Row.

Reed, W. Maxwell. Earth for Sam. rev. ed. Brandwein, Paul F., ed. LC 59-12825. (Illus.). (gr. 7 up). 1960. 7.95 (ISBN 0-15-224665-7, HJ). HarBraceJ.

Spizzirri Publishing Co. Staff. Paleozoic Life: An Educational Coloring Book. Spizzirri, Linda, ed. (Illus.). 32p. (gr. 1-8). 1981. pap. 1.25 (ISBN 0-86545-024-2). Spizzirri.

White, Anne T. All About Rocks & Minerals. (Allabout Ser: No. 12). (Illus.). (gr. 4-6). 1963. PLB 5.39 (ISBN 0-394-90212-2, BYR). Random.

Wyckoff, Jerome. The Story of Geology: Our Changing Earth Through the Ages. (Illus.). 1976. PLB 13.77 (ISBN 0-307-67750-8, Golden Pr). Western Pub.

Zim, Herbert S. What's Inside the Earth. (Illus.). (gr. 1 up). 1953. PLB 6.96 (ISBN 0-688-31475-9). Morrow.

GEOLOGY–LABORATORY MANUALS

Barksdale, Julian D., et al. Laboratory Manual for Elementary Geology. 2nd ed. (Illus., Orig.). 1969. pap. text ed. 3.95x (ISBN 0-87015-175-4). Pacific Bks.

Brice, James C., et al. Laboratory Studies in Geology, 25 studies. 1962-66. loose-leaf 0.60 ea. W H Freeman.

Dallmeyer, R. David. Physical Geology Laboratory Text & Manual: A Guide for the Study of Earth. 2nd ed. 1978. wire coil bdg. 9.95 (ISBN 0-8403-1231-8). Kendall-Hunt.

Fichter, Lynn S. & Poche, David J. Ancient Environments & the Interpretation of Geologic History. 1979. pap. 10.95x spiral bdg. (ISBN 0-8087-0669-1). Burgess.

Finch, R. C., et al. Lab Studies in Physical Geology. 276p. 1980. 10.95x (ISBN 0-89459-112-6). Hunter NC.

Gilbert, C. M. & Christensen, M. N. Physical Geology Laboratory Course. 2nd ed. 1967. 8.95 (ISBN 0-07-023206-7, C); instructor's manual 2.95 (ISBN 0-07-023209-1). McGraw.

Goldstein, Frederic. Physical Geology Laboratory Manual. 1976. spiral bdg. 4.95 (ISBN 0-88252-049-0). Paladin Hse.

Landes, Kenneth K. Plane Table Manual for Geologists. 1951. 1.50x (ISBN 0-685-21796-5). Wahr.

Metz, Robert, et al. Geology Laboratory Manual: Geology from New Jersey. LC 79-65477. (Illus.). 1979. 7.80 (ISBN 0-934434-00-X). RA Corp.

Tomikel, John. Historical Geology Lab Manual. 1970. pap. text ed. 3.50 (ISBN 0-910042-05-5). Allegheny.

GEOLOGY–MAPS

Allum, J. A. Photogeology & Regional Mapping. 1966. 21.00 (ISBN 0-08-012033-4); pap. 9.75 (ISBN 0-08-012032-6). Pergamon.

Barnes, J. W. Basic Geological Mapping. 128p. 1981. 12.95 (ISBN 0-470-27250-3). Halsted Pr.

Bennison, G. M. Introduction to Geological Structures & Maps: Metric. 3rd ed. (Illus.). 1975. pap. text ed. 9.95x (ISBN 0-7131-2513-6). Intl Ideas.

Bhattacharya, D. S. & Bagchi, T. S. Elements of Geological Map-Reading & Interpretation. 78p. 1981. 10.00x (ISBN 0-86125-433-3, Pub. by Orient Longman India). State Mutual Bk.

Blyth, F. G. Geological Maps & Their Interpretation. (Illus.). 1965. pap. 5.95 (ISBN 0-312-32340-9). St Martin.

Derry, Duncan. Concise World Atlas of Geology & Mineral Deposits: Non-Metallic Minerals, Metallic Minerals & Energy Minerals. LC 80-675233. 110p. 1980. 68.95 (ISBN 0-470-26996-0). Halsted Pr.

Engineering Geological Maps: A Guide to Their Preparation. (Earth Science Ser.: No. 15). (Illus.). 79p. 1976. pap. 14.50 (ISBN 0-685-66204-7, U222, UNESCO). Unipub.

Miller, Victor C. Photogeology. (International Ser. in Earth & Planetary Sciences). (Illus.). 1961. text ed. 27.00 (ISBN 0-07-042170-6, C). McGraw.

Moseley, Frank. Advanced Geological Map Interpretation. LC 79-11243. 1979. pap. 12.95x (ISBN 0-470-26708-9). Halsted Pr.

Platt, John. Selected Exercises Upon Geological Maps. 1974. pap. text ed. 3.25x (ISBN 0-04-550021-5). Allen Unwin.

--A Series of Elementary Exercises Upon Geological Maps. 1974. pap. text ed. 3.25x (ISBN 0-04-550019-3). Allen Unwin.

Platt, John & Challinor, John. Simple Geological Structures. 1974. pap. text ed. 4.95x (ISBN 0-04-550020-7). Allen Unwin.

Simpson, B. Geological Maps. 1968. 13.75 (ISBN 0-08-012781-9); pap. 6.25 (ISBN 0-08-012780-0). Pergamon.

Thomas, J. A. An Introduction to Geological Maps. 2nd rev ed. (Illus.). 1977. pap. text ed. 4.95x (ISBN 0-04-550018-5). Allen Unwin.

Wright, H. E., et al. Geology of the Cloquet Quadrangle, Carlton County, Minnesota. LC 71-653807. (Geologic Map Ser: No. 3). (Illus.). 1970. pap. text ed. 2.50x (ISBN 0-8166-0590-4). Minn Geol Survey.

GEOLOGY–MATHEMATICAL MODELS

Buerger, M. J. Numerical Structure Factor Tables. LC 41-23792. (Special Paper: No. 33). (Illus.). 1941. 5.75x (ISBN 0-8137-2033-8). Geol Soc.

Cubitt, J. M., ed. Mathematical Models in the Earth Sciences: Proceedings of the 7th Geochautauqua, Syracuse University, Oct. 1978. 90p. 1980. pap. 41.25 (ISBN 0-08-025305-9). Pergamon.

Fenner, Peter, ed. Quantitative Geology. LC 72-190171. (Special Paper: No. 146). (Illus.). viii, 80p. (Orig.). 1972. pap. 7.00x (ISBN 0-8137-2146-6). Geol Soc.

Merriam, D. F., ed. Recent Advances in Geomathematics: An International Symposium. 1978. text ed. 45.00 (ISBN 0-08-022095-9). Pergamon.

Romanova, Mariya A. & Sarmanov, O. V., eds. Topics in Mathematical Geology. LC 69-12516. 282p. 1970. 45.00 (ISBN 0-306-10832-1, Consultants). Plenum Pub.

Vistelius, Andrew B. Studies in Mathematical Geology. LC 65-25266. 294p. 1967. 45.00 (ISBN 0-306-10782-1, Consultants). Plenum Pub.

GEOLOGY–MOON

see Lunar Geology

GEOLOGY–OUTLINES, SYLLABI, ETC.

Pearl, Richard M. Geology. 4th rev. ed. 1975. pap. 4.95 (ISBN 0-06-460160-9, CO 160, Cos). Har-Row.

Spear, Steven G. Physical Geology Study Guide. 1977. wire coil bdg. 4.50 (ISBN 0-88252-068-7). Paladin Hse.

GEOLOGY–PERIODICALS

Annual Summary of Information on Natural Disasters, 1972, No. 7. 106p. (Orig.). 1974. pap. 5.25 (ISBN 0-685-50559-6, U28, UNESCO). Unipub.

Geological Society of America. Ten-Year Index to Volumes Eighty-One to Ninety of Geological Society of America. LC 1-23380. 1980. pap. 10.00x (ISBN 0-8137-9081-6). Geol Soc.

--Ten-Year Index to Volumes Eighty-One to Ninety of Geological Society of America. LC 1-23380. 1980. pap. 10.00x (ISBN 0-8137-9081-6). Geol Soc.

--Ten-Year Index to Volumes Sixty-One to Seventy of Geological Society of America Bulletin. LC 1-23380. 1962. 10.50x (ISBN 0-8137-9061-1). Geol Soc.

Rona, Peter A., ed. Mid-Atlantic Ridge, Part 1 & 2. LC 76-47736. (Microform Publication: No. 5). (Illus.). 1976. 9.00x (ISBN 0-685-88399-X). Geol Soc.

GEOLOGY–RESEARCH

see Geological Research

GEOLOGY–STATISTICAL METHODS

Davis, John C. Statistics & Data Analysis in Geology. LC 72-6792. (Illus.). 550p. 1973. 34.95 (ISBN 0-471-19895-1). Wiley.

Koch, George S., Jr. & Link, Richard F. Statistical Analysis of Geological Data, 2 vols. bound as 1. Date not set. 18.00 (ISBN 0-8446-5782-4). Peter Smith.

--Statistical Analysis of Geological Data. 850p. 1981. pap. 12.50 (ISBN 0-486-64040-X). Dover.

Merriam, D. F., ed. Geostatistics: A Colloquium. LC 71-142040. (Computer Applications in the Earth Sciences Ser.). 177p. 1970. 22.50 (ISBN 0-306-30519-4, Plenum Pr). Plenum Pub.

Mousset-Jones, Pierre F. Geostatistics. 180p. 1980. 15.50 (ISBN 0-07-043568-5). McGraw.

Vistelius, Andrew B. Studies in Mathematical Geology. LC 65-25266. 294p. 1967. 45.00 (ISBN 0-306-10782-1, Consultants). Plenum Pub.

GEOLOGY–STATISTICS

American Geological Institute. Geological Data Sheets. 1975. 10.00 (ISBN 0-913312-28-2). Am Geol.

Clark, Isobel. Practical Geostatistics. (Illus.). 1979. 28.50x (ISBN 0-85334-843-X, Pub. by Applied Science). Burgess-Intl Ideas.

Geological Survey of Norway, No. 334, Bulletin 43. 1978. pap. 12.00x (ISBN 82-00-31368-9). Universitet.

Geological Survey of Norway, No. 348, Bulletin 49. 150p. 1979. pap. 21.00x (ISBN 82-003-1382-4). Universitet.

Geological Survey of Norway, No. 350, Bulletin 50. 1979. pap. 21.00x (ISBN 82-00-31385-9). Universitet.

Geological Survey of Norway, No. 351,bulletin 51. 100p. 1980. pap. 21.00x (ISBN 82-003-1386-7). Universitet.

Journel, A. G. & Huijbregts, Ch. J. Mining Geostatistics. 600p. 1981. pap. 31.00 (ISBN 0-12-391056-0). Acad Pr.

Krige, D. G. Lognormal: De Wijsian Geostatistics for Ore Evaluation. 50p. 1980. 18.50x (ISBN 0-620-03006-2, Pub. by Mining Journal England). State Mutual Bk.

Owen, Alan. Geological Survey, No. 338, Bulletin 46. pap. 12.00x (ISBN 82-003-1632-7). Universitet.

Whitaker, John & McDonald, H. Geological Guide, Steinsfjord, Ringerike. 1977. 10.50x (ISBN 82-00-05013-0). Universitet.

GEOLOGY–STUDY AND TEACHING

Grabau, Amadeus W. Rhythm of the Ages. LC 78-15615. 620p. 1978. Repr. of 1940 ed. lib. bdg. 39.50 (ISBN 0-88275-694-X). Krieger.

Tomikel, John. Trends in American Geological Education During the Critical Years 1954-1969. LC 72-183704. 1972. 5.00 (ISBN 0-910042-08-X); pap. 2.50 (ISBN 0-910042-11-X). Allegheny.

GEOLOGY–VOCATIONAL GUIDANCE

see Geology As a Profession

GEOLOGY–AFRICA

Baker, B. H., et al. Geology of the Eastern Rift System of Africa. LC 76-178774. (Special Paper: No. 136). (Illus.). vi, 68p. (Orig.). 1972. pap. 6.25x (ISBN 0-8137-2136-9). Geol Soc.

Berry, W. B. N. & Boucot, A. J. Correlation of the African Silurian Rocks. LC 73-76886. (Special Paper: No. 147). (Illus.). 80p. (Orig.). 1973. pap. 6.75x (ISBN 0-8137-2147-4). Geol Soc.

Buckle, Colin. Landforms in Africa. (Illus.). 1977. pap. text ed. 10.95x (ISBN 0-582-60334-X). Longman.

Clark, John D. The Prehistoric Cultures of the Horn of Africa. LC 70-159173. xix, 385p. 1971. Repr. of 1954 ed. lib. bdg. 20.00x (ISBN 0-374-91657-8). Octagon.

--Stone Age Cultures of Northern Rhodesia, with Particular Reference to the Cultural & Climatic Succession in the Zambezi Valley & Its Tributaries. LC 78-111570. (Illus.). Repr. of 1950 ed. 21.50x (ISBN 0-8371-4595-3, Pub. by Negro U Pr). Greenwood.

Clifford, T. N. & Gass, I. G., eds. African Magmatism & Tectonics. (Illus.). 1970. 35.75 (ISBN 0-02-842990-7). Hafner.

Clifford, Tom N. Damaran Episode in the Upper Proterozoic-Lower Paleozoic Structural History of Southern Africa. LC 67-16337. (Special Paper: No. 92). (Illus., Orig.). 1967. pap. 6.00x (ISBN 0-8137-2092-3). Geol Soc.

Cosgriff, John W. Lower Triassic Temnospondyli of Tasmania. LC 73-87235. (Special Paper: No. 149). (Illus., Orig.). 1974. pap. 11.00x (ISBN 0-8137-2149-0). Geol Soc.

Evolution & Mineralization of the Arabian-Nubian Shield: Proceedings of a Symposium Convened by Ahmed M. Al-Shanti, Jeddah, Saudi Arabia, 6-16 Feb. 1978, Vol. 3. (Illus.). 120p. 1980. 34.00 (ISBN 0-08-024479-3); pap. 15.00 (ISBN 0-08-024480-7). Pergamon.

Gregory, John W. Great Rift Valley. (Illus.). 422p. 1968. Repr. of 1896 ed. 32.50x (ISBN 0-7146-1812-8, F Cass Co). Biblio Dist.

--The Rift Valleys & Geology of East Africa. LC 76-44726. Repr. of 1921 ed. 47.50 (ISBN 0-404-15863-3). AMS Pr.

Holland, C. H. Lower Palaeozoic Rocks of the World: With Essays on Lower Palaeozoic Rocks of the World. LC 80-41688. (Electrochemical Data Ser.). 1981. price not set (ISBN 0-471-27945-5, Pub. by Wiley-Interscience). Wiley.

GEOLOGY–ALASKA

Burk, C. A. Geology of the Alaska Peninsula: Island Arc & Continental Margin, 3 pts. LC 66-19334. (Memoir: No. 99). (Illus.). 1965. Set. 23.00x (ISBN 0-8137-1099-5); Pt. 1. 10.50x, text (ISBN 0-685-31555-X); Pt. 2. 9.00x, geologic map (ISBN 0-685-31556-8); 3.50x, tectonic map (ISBN 0-685-31557-6). Geol Soc.

Capps. Alaska Peninsula & Aleutian Islands. facsimile ed. (Geology Ser). (Illus.). 14p. Repr. of 1934 ed. pap. 3.50 (ISBN 0-8466-8003-3, SJG3). Shorey.

Clark, David L. Stratigraphy & Glacial-Marine Sediments of the Amerasian Basin,Central Arctic Ocean. LC 80-65270. (Special Paper Ser.: No. 181). (Illus., Orig.). 1980. pap. 13.00x (ISBN 0-8137-2181-4). Geol Soc.

Hopkins, David M., ed. The Bering Land Bridge. (Illus.). 1967. 20.00x (ISBN 0-8047-0272-1). Stanford U Pr.

Irvine, T. N. Petrology of the Duke Island Ultramafic Complex, Southeastern Alaska. LC 73-87233. (Memoir: No. 138). (Illus.). 1974. 30.00x (ISBN 0-8137-1138-X). Geol Soc.

Paige, S., et al. Reconaissance of the Point Barrow Region, Alaska. facs. ed. (Illus.). 56p. pap. 6.50 (ISBN 0-8466-8004-1, SJG4). Shorey.

Sharma, G. D. The Alaskan Shelf. (Illus.). 1979. 31.30 (ISBN 0-387-90397-6). Springer-Verlag.

GEOLOGY–ALPS

Oxburgh, E. R. The Geology of the Eastern Alps. 152p. 1968. 6.00 (ISBN 0-913312-33-9). Am Geol.

GEOLOGY–ANTARCTIC REGIONS

Adie, Raymond, ed. Antarctic Geology & Geophysics. (Illus.). 876p. 1973. 50.00x (ISBN 8-200-02253-6, Dist. by Columbia U Pr). Universitet.

Scott, Robert F. Voyage of the Discovery, 2 Vols. LC 68-55218. (Illus.). 1969. Repr. of 1905 ed. Set. lib. bdg. 57.00x (ISBN 0-8371-1334-2, SCDI). Greenwood.

Scott, Robert S. Voyage of the 'Discovery' (Illus.). 1951. 15.00 (ISBN 0-685-20649-1). Transatlantic.

GEOLOGY–ARCTIC REGIONS

Forbes, R. B., ed. Contributions to the Geology of the Bering Sea Basin & Adjacent Regions. LC 73-87232. (Special Paper: No. 151). (Illus.). 1975. pap. 19.00x (ISBN 0-8137-2151-2). Geol Soc.

Herman, Y., ed. Marine Geology & Oceanography of the Arctic Seas. LC 73-22236. (Illus.). 416p. 1974. 43.90 (ISBN 0-387-06628-4). Springer-Verlag.

Maupertuis, Pierre-Louis Moreau De. La Figure De la Terre Determinee Par les Observations Faites Par Ordre Du Roy Au Cercle Polaire. Repr. of 1738 ed. 61.00 (ISBN 0-8287-0593-3). Clearwater Pub.

GEOLOGY–ASIA

Argand, Emile. Tectonics of Asia. Carozzi, Albert V., ed. LC 76-14288. 1977. 20.85 (ISBN 0-02-840390-8). Hafner.

Geology & Paleontology of Southeast Asia, Vol. 14. 1975. 41.00x (ISBN 0-86008-125-7, Pub. by U of Tokyo Pr). Intl Schol Bk Serv.

Geology & Paleontology of Southeast Asia, Vol. 15. 1975. 41.00x (ISBN 0-86008-137-0, Pub. by U of Tokyo Pr). Intl Schol Bk Serv.

Geology & Paleontology of Southeast Asia, Vol. 16. 1976. 36.00x (ISBN 0-86008-154-0, Pub. by U of Tokyo Pr). Intl Schol Bk Serv.

Kobayashi, T. & Hashimoto, W., eds. Geology & Palaeontology of Southeast Asia, Vol. 17. (Illus.). 1977. 41.00x (ISBN 0-86008-175-3, Pub by U of Tokyo Pr). Intl Schol Bk Serv.

Kobayashi, T., et al. Geology & Palaeontology of Southeast Asia, Vol. 19. (Illus.). 1978. 52.00x (ISBN 0-86008-202-4, Pub. by U of Tokyo Pr). Intl Schol Bk Serv.

--Geology & Palaneontology of Southeast Asia, Vol. XXI. 381p. 1980. 52.00x (ISBN 0-86008-263-6, Pub. by U of Tokyo Pr Japan). Intl Schol Bk Serv.

Kobayashi, T., et al, eds. Geology & Palaeontology of Southeast Asia, Vol. 18. (Illus.). 1977. 41.00x (ISBN 0-86008-177-X, Pub. by U of Tokyo Pr). Intl Schol Bk Serv.

Kobayashi, Teiichi & Toriyama, Ryuzo, eds. Geology & Palaeontology of Southeast Asia, Vol. 13. (Illus.). 184p. 1974. 38.00x (ISBN 0-86008-099-4, Pub. by U of Tokyo Pr). Intl Schol Bk Serv.

--Geology & Paleontology of Southeast Asia. Incl. Vol. 1. 290p. 1964; Vol. 2. 360p. 1966. 18.00x (ISBN 0-86008-010-2); Vol. 3. 290p. 1967. 18.00x (ISBN 0-86008-011-0); Vol. 4. 370p. 1968. 26.00x (ISBN 0-86008-012-9); Vol. 5. 320p. 1968. 38.00x (ISBN 0-86008-013-7); Vol. 6. 480p. 1969. 41.00x (ISBN 0-86008-014-5); Vol. 7. 330p. 1969. 36.00x (ISBN 0-86008-015-3); Vol. 8. 452p. 1970. 36.00x (ISBN 0-86008-016-1); Vol. 9. 248p. 1971. 36.00x (ISBN 0-86008-017-X); Vol. 10. 498p. 1972. 40.00x (ISBN 0-86008-018-8); Vol. 11. 248p. 1973. 38.00x (ISBN 0-86008-019-6); Vol. 12. 366p. 1973. 40.00x (ISBN 0-86008-020-X). Pub by U of Tokyo Pr). Intl Schol Bk Serv.

Kobayashi, Teiichi, et al, eds. Geology & Palaeontology of Southeast Asia, Vol. 22. (Illus.). 200p. 1981. 49.50x (ISBN 0-86008-278-4, Pub. by U of Tokyo Japan). Columbia U Pr.

Kobayshi, Terichi. Geology & Palaeontology of Southeast Asia, Vol. I. new ed. (Illus.). 289p. 1974. 17.00x (ISBN 0-86008-009-9, Pub. by U of Tokyo Pr). Intl Schol Bk Serv.

Movius, Hallam L. Early Man & Pleistoçene Stratigraphy in Southern & Eastern Asia. (Illus.). 1944. pap. 14.00 (ISBN 0-527-01249-1). Kraus Repr.

Philippson, Alfred. Kleinasien. Repr. of 1915 ed. pap. 25.50 (ISBN 0-384-46300-2). Johnson Repr.

GEOLOGY–AUSTRALIA

Brown, D. S. W., et al. The Geological Evolution of Australia & New Zealand. 1968. 26.00 (ISBN 0-08-012278-7); pap. 14.50 (ISBN 0-08-012277-9). Pergamon.

Lands of the Alligator Rivers Area, Northern Territory. (Land Research Ser.: No. 38). 171p. 1976. pap. 13.50 (ISBN 0-643-00208-1, CO19, CSIRO). Unipub.

Stevens, N. C. A Guidebook to Field Geology in SE Queensland. 1973. 9.95x (ISBN 0-7022-0798-5). U of Queensland Pr.

Talent, J. A., et al. Correlation of the Silurian Rocks of Australia. LC 74-75784. (Special Paper: No. 150). (Illus., Orig.). 1975. pap. 16.50x (ISBN 0-8137-2150-4). Geol Soc.

GEOLOGY–BRAZIL

McNeil, Mary. Brazil's Uranium-Thorium Deposits, Geology, Reserves, Potential: A World Mining Report. LC 79-87816. (Illus.). 1979. pap. 95.00 (ISBN 0-87930-119-8). Miller Freeman.

GEOLOGY–BURMA

Chhibber, Harbans L. The Geology of Burma. LC 77-87011. Repr. of 1934 ed. 38.50 (ISBN 0-404-16803-5). AMS Pr.

Krishnan, M. S. Geology of India & Burma. 5th ed. (Illus.). 1968. 12.50x (ISBN 0-8002-1457-9). Intl Pubns Serv.

GEOLOGY–CALIFORNIA

Howard, Arthur D. Geological History of Middle California. LC 78-57299. (California Natural History Guide: No. 43). (Illus.). 1979. 14.95x (ISBN 0-520-03707-3); pap. 3.95 (ISBN 0-520-03874-6). U of Cal Pr.

Johnson, A. M. Styles of Folding: Mechanics & Mechanisms of Folding of Natural Elastic Materials. (Developments in Geotectonics). 1977. 66.00 (ISBN 0-444-41496-7). Elsevier.

Norris, R. M. & Webb, R. W. Geology of California. 379p. 1976. 24.95 (ISBN 0-471-61566-8). Wiley.

Oakeshott, Gordon B. California's Changing Landscapes. 2nd ed. (Illus.). 1978. pap. text ed. 14.95 (ISBN 0-07-047584-9, C). McGraw.

GEOLOGY–CANADA

Boucot, A. J., ed. Geology of the Arisaig Area, Antigonish County, Nova Scotia. LC 72-82614. (Special Paper: No. 139). (Illus., Orig.). 1974. pap. 13.00x (ISBN 0-8137-2139-3). Geol Soc.

Enos, Paul. Cloridorme Formation, Middle Ordovician Flysch, Northern Gaspe Peninsula, Quebec. LC 76-81692. (Special Paper: No. 117). (Illus., Orig.). 1969. pap. 3.25x (ISBN 0-8137-2117-2). Geol Soc.

Geology & Economic Minerals of Canada, 2 pts. (Illus.). 1978. pap. 28.00 set (ISBN 0-660-00553-0, SSC 96, SSC). Unipub.

Gill, James E. The Proterozoic in Canada. LC 58-21139. (Illus.). x, 191p. 1957. 17.50x (ISBN 0-8020-7015-9). U of Toronto Pr.

Hind, Henry Y. Narrative of the Canadian Red River Exploring Expedition of 1857, & of the Assiniboine & Saskatchewan Exploring Expedition of 1858, 2 Vols. LC 68-55195. (Illus.). 1968. Repr. of 1860 ed. Set. lib. bdg. 35.00x (ISBN 0-8371-3896-5, HIRR). Greenwood.

Palliser, John. Exploration - British North America: Papers, 2 Vols. LC 68-55211. (Illus.). 1968. Repr. of 1860 ed. lib. bdg. 18.75x (ISBN 0-8371-1430-6, PABN). Greenwood.

Sloss, L. L. Lithofacies Maps: An Atlas of the U.S. & Southern Canada. 108p. 1960. 9.50 (ISBN 0-471-79860-6, Pub. by Wiley). Krieger.

Teichert, Curt. A Tillite Occurrence on the Canadian Shield, Vol.| LC 76-21824. (Thule Expedition, 5th, 1921-1924: No. 6). Repr. of 1937 ed. 20.00 (ISBN 0-404-58306-7). AMS Pr.

Tesmer, Irving H., ed. Colossal Cataract: The Geological History of Niagara Falls. LC 80-26858. (Illus.). 210p. 1981. text ed. 34.00x (ISBN 0-87395-522-6, TECC); pap. text ed. 9.95x (ISBN 0-87395-523-4, TECC-P). State U NY Pr.

Ward, Dederick C., ed. Bibliography of Theses in Geology, United States & Canada Nineteen Sixty-Seven to Nineteen Seventy. LC 73-78974. (Special Paper: No. 143). 442p. (Orig.). 1973. pap. 17.00x (ISBN 0-8137-2143-1). Geol Soc.

Zaslow, Morris. Reading the Rocks: The Story of the Geological Survey of Canada, 1842-1972. (Illus.). 1975. uSA 20.00x (ISBN 0-7705-1303-4). NYU Pr.

GEOLOGY–CARIBBEAN AREA

Bowin, Carl. The Caribbean: Gravity Field & Plate Tectonics. LC 76-16261. (Special Paper: No. 169). (Illus.). 1976. pap. 12.00x (ISBN 0-8137-2169-5). Geol Soc.

Donnelly, Thomas W., ed. Caribbean Geophysical, Tectonic & Petrologic Studies. LC 74-165441. (Memoir: No. 130). (Illus.). 1971. 20.25x (ISBN 0-8137-1130-4). Geol Soc.

Hess, H. H., ed. Caribbean Geological Investigations. LC 66-22403. (Memoir: No. 98). (Illus.). 1966. 20.00x (ISBN 0-8137-1098-7). Geol Soc.

Khudoley, K. M. & Meyerhoff, A. A. Paleogeography & Geological History of the Greater Antilles. LC 77-129999. (Memoir: No. 129). (Illus.). 1971. 17.00x (ISBN 0-8137-1129-0). Geol Soc.

Kinghor, Marion. Bibliography of Jamaican Geology. (Bibliography Ser.). 150p. 1980. 6.90x (ISBN 0-686-27379-6, Pub. by GEO Abstracts England). State Mutual Bk.

Land, Lynton S. & Mackenzie, Fred T. Field Guide to Bermuda Geology. (Bermuda Biological Station Special Pubn.: No. 4). (Illus.). 35p. 1970. pap. 3.00 (ISBN 0-917642-04-X). Bermuda Bio.

Mattson, Peter H., ed. West Indies Island Arcs. (Benchmark Papers in Geology Ser.: Vol. 33). 1977. 51.50 (ISBN 0-12-787060-1). Acad Pr.

Mitchell-Thome, Raoul C. The Geology of the South Atlantic Islands. LC 76-572524. (Illus.). 370p. 1970. pap. text ed. 100.00x (ISBN 3-443-11012-6). Intl Pubns Serv.

Moore, Hilary B. Ecological Guide to Bermuda Inshore Water. (Bermuda Biological Station Special Pubn.: No. 5). (Illus.). ii, 42p. pap. 3.00 (ISBN 0-917642-05-8). Bermuda Bio.

Woodring, Wendell. Geology of the Republic of Haiti. lib. bdg. 69.95 (ISBN 0-8490-1882-X). Gordon Pr.

GEOLOGY–EGYPT

Butzer, Karl W. & Hansen, Carl L. Desert & River in Nubia: Geomorphology & Prehistoric Environments at the Aswan Reservoir. LC 67-20761. (Illus.). 1968. 35.00 (ISBN 0-299-04770-9); Set Of 15 Maps. 20.00x (ISBN 0-685-20706-4). U of Wis Pr.

Sandford, Kenneth S. & Arkell, W. J. Paleolithic Man & the Nile-Faiyum Divide, Vol. 1. LC 30-8240. (Illus.). 1930. 20.00 (ISBN 0-226-62104-9, OIP10). U of Chicago Pr.

GEOLOGY–EUROPE

Ager, D. V. & Brook, M. Europe from Crust to Core. LC 76-40096. 202p. 1977. 42.00 (ISBN 0-471-99420-0, Pub. by Wiley-Interscience). Wiley.

Ager, Derek V. The Geology of Europe. LC 80-40318. 535p. 1980. 44.95x (ISBN 0-470-26990-1). Halsted Pr.

Alvarez, Walter. Geology & History of Sicily. (Illus.). 291p. 1970. 32.50x (ISBN 0-8002-0824-2). Intl Pubns Serv.

Anderson, J. G. The Structure of Western Europe. 1978. text ed. 30.00 (ISBN 0-08-022045-2); pap. text ed. 14.00 (ISBN 0-08-022046-0). Pergamon.

Bailey, E. B. Tectonic Essays, Mainly Alpine. 1935. 39.50x (ISBN 0-19-854368-9). Oxford U Pr.

Brinkman, Roland. Geologic Evolution of Europe. 2nd rev. ed. Sanders, John E., tr. (Illus.). 1969. 15.25 (ISBN 0-02-841940-5). Hafner.

Burchfiel, B. C. Geology of Romania. LC 75-32832. (Special Paper: No. 158). (Illus., Orig.). 1976. pap. 12.75x (ISBN 0-8137-2158-X). Geol Soc.

Godwin, H. Fenland: Its Ancient Past & Uncertain Future. LC 77-8824. (Illus.). 1978. 32.50 (ISBN 0-521-21768-7). Cambridge U Pr.

Lemoine, M. Geological Atlas of Alpine Europe: Alpine Europe, Vol. 1. 1978. 170.75 (ISBN 0-444-41518-1). Elsevier.

Naylor, D. & Mounteney, N. Geology of the North West European Continental Shelf: The West British Shelf, Vol. 1. 162p. 1975. 20.00x (ISBN 0-86010-009-X, Pub. by Graham & Trotman England). State Mutual Bk.

Naylor, David. Geology of the Northwest European Continental Shelf: The West British Shelf, Vol. 1. LC 75-329129. 1975. 27.50x (ISBN 0-86010-009-X). Intl Pubns Serv.

Pegrum, R. M., et al. Geology of the North-West European Continental Shelf: The North Sea, Vol. 2. 1975. 32.50x (ISBN 0-86010-013-8). Intl Pubns Serv.

Pomerol, Charles, et al. Geology of France. (Illus.). 256p. 1980. 25.00x (ISBN 2-225-67001-3). Masson Pub.

Rutten, M. G. The Geology of Western Europe. 1970. 53.75 (ISBN 0-444-40710-3). Elsevier.

Scrope, George P. The Geology & Extinct Volcanos of the Central France. 2nd rev. ed. Albritton, Claude C., Jr., ed. LC 77-6540. (History of Geology Ser.). (Illus.). 1978. Repr. of 1858 ed. lib. bdg. 20.00 (ISBN 0-405-10459-6). Arno.

West, R. G. The Pre-Glacial Pleistocene of the Norfolk & Suffolk Coasts. LC 77-90191. (Illus.). 1980. 95.00 (ISBN 0-521-21962-0). Cambridge U Pr.

GEOLOGY–GREAT BRITAIN

Anderson, E. M. The Dynamics of Faulting. 2nd rev ed. LC 72-188368. (Illus.). 1972. Repr. of 1952 ed. 13.75 (ISBN 0-02-840310-X). Hafner.

Anderson, J. G. & Owen, T. R. The Structure of the British Isles. 2nd ed. LC 80-41075. (Illus.). 242p. 1980. 30.00 (ISBN 0-08-023998-6); pap. 14.50 (ISBN 0-08-023997-8). Pergamon.

Anderton, R., et al. A Dynamic Stratigraphy of the British Isles. (Illus.). 1979. text ed. 35.00x (ISBN 0-04-551027-X); pap. text ed. 19.95x (ISBN 0-04-551028-8). Allen Unwin.

Arkell, W. J. Jurassic System in Great Britain. (Illus.). 1970. 38.50x (ISBN 0-19-854371-9). Oxford U Pr.

Bate, R. H. & Robinson, E. A Stratigraphical Index of British Ostracada: Geological Journal Special Issue, No. 8. (Liverpool Geological Society & the Manchester Geological Association). 538p. 1980. 139.50 (ISBN 0-471-27755-X, Pub. by Wiley-Interscience). Wiley.

Bowes, D. R. & Leake, B. E. Crustal Evolution in Northwestern Britain & Adjacent Regions: Geological Journal Special Issue, No. 10. (Liverpool Geological Society & the Manchester Geological Association). 508p. 1980. 107.25 (ISBN 0-471-27757-6, Pub. by Wiley-Interscience). Wiley.

Brumhead, Derek. Geology Explained in the Yorkshire Dales & on the Yorkshire Coast. LC 78-660964. 1979. 17.95 (ISBN 0-7153-7703-5). David & Charles.

Campbell, John B. The Upper Palaeolithic of Britain: A Study of Man & Nature in the Late Ice Age, Vols. I & II. (Illus.). 1978. 79.00 set (ISBN 0-19-813188-7). Oxford U Pr.

Challinor, John & Bates, Dennis E. B. Geology Explained in North Wales. (Geology Explained Ser.). (Illus.). 1973. 5.50 (ISBN 0-7153-5942-8). David & Charles.

Conybeare, W. D. & Phillips, William. Outlines of the Geology of England & Wales: General Principles of That Sciences, & Comparative Views of the Structure of Foreign Countries. Albritton, Claude C., Jr., ed. LC 77-6516. (History of Geology Ser.). 1978. Repr. of 1822 ed. lib. bdg. 28.00x (ISBN 0-405-10438-3). Arno.

Cope, F. Wolverson. Geology Explained in the Peak District. LC 75-31321. (Geology Explained Ser.). (Illus.). 176p. 1976. 6.50 (ISBN 0-7153-6945-8). David & Charles.

Dreghorn, William. Geology Explained in the Severn Vale & Cotswolds. (Illus.). 192p. 1974. 14.95 (ISBN 0-7153-4102-2). David & Charles.

Ford, Trevor D. Limestone & Caves of the Peak District. 469p. 1980. 34.50x (ISBN 0-86094-005-5, Pub. by GEO Abstracts England); pap. 26.45x (ISBN 0-86094-004-7, Pub. by GEO Abstracts England). State Mutual Bk.

Hollis, G. E. Man's Influence on the Hydrological Cycle in the United Kingdom. 300p. 1980. 24.75x (ISBN 0-86094-024-1); pap. 19.55x (ISBN 0-86094-018-7, Pub. by GEO Abstracts England). State Mutual Bk.

Kidson, C. & Tooley, M. J. The Quaternary History of the Irish Sea: Geological Journal Special Issue, No. 7. (Liverpool Geological Society & the Manchester Geological Association). 356p. 1980. 71.50 (ISBN 0-471-27754-1, Pub. by Wiley-Interscience). Wiley.

Lovell, J. P. The British Isles Through Geological Time: A Northward Drift. (Illus.). 1977. pap. text ed. 6.95x (ISBN 0-04-554003-9). Allen Unwin.

Manten, A. A. Silurian Reefs of Gotland. (Developments in Sedimentology: Vol. 13). 1971. 83.00 (ISBN 0-444-40706-5). Elsevier.

Middlemiss, F. A. British Stratigraphy. (Introducing Geology Ser.). 1975. pap. text ed. 5.95x (ISBN 0-04-550023-1). Allen Unwin.

Miller, Hugh. The Old Red Sandstone, or New Walks in an Old Field. Albritton, Claude C., Jr., ed. LC 77-6531. (History of Geology Ser.). (Illus.). 1978. Repr. of 1851 ed. lib. bdg. 25.00x (ISBN 0-405-10451-0). Arno.

Owen, T. R. The Geological Evolution of the British Isles. 1976. text ed. 29.00 (ISBN 0-08-020461-9); pap. text ed. 11.95 (ISBN 0-08-020460-0). Pergamon.

--Geology Explained in South Wales. (Geology Explained Ser.). (Illus.). 1973. 14.95 (ISBN 0-7153-5860-X). David & Charles.

Parkins, John W. Geology Explained in Dorset. LC 76-54070. (Geology Explained Ser.). (Illus.). 1977. 8.95 (ISBN 0-7153-7319-6). David & Charles.

Perkins, John. Geology Explained: Dartmoor & the Tamar Valley. (Geology Explained Ser). 1972. 10.50 (ISBN 0-7153-5516-3). David & Charles.

Perkins, John W. Geology Explained in South & East Devon. (Geology Explained Ser.). (Illus.). 192p. 1971. 2.95 (ISBN 0-7153-5304-7). David & Charles.

Porter, Roy. The Making of Geology: Earth Science in Britain, 1660-1815. LC 76-56220. 1977. 35.50 (ISBN 0-521-21521-8). Cambridge U Pr.

Prosser, Robert. Geology Explained in the Lake District. (Geology Explained Ser.). 1977. 14.95 (ISBN 0-7153-7397-8). David & Charles.

Roberts, B. The Geology of Snowdonia & Llyn: An Outline & Field Guide. (Illus.). 1979. flexi 37.50 (ISBN 0-686-25752-9, Pub. by A Hilger England). Heyden.

Shotton, F. W., ed. British Quaternary Studies: Recent Advances. (Illus.). 1977. 49.50x (ISBN 0-19-854414-6). Oxford U Pr.

Wood, Alan, ed. Pre-Cambrian & Lower Palaeozoic Rocks of Wales: Symposium Report from the Univ. College of Wales. 1969. 22.50x (ISBN 0-900768-12-6). Verry.

Ziegler, A. M., et al. Correlation of the Silurian Rocks of the British Isles. LC 74-83052. (Special Paper: No. 154). (Illus., Orig.). 1974. pap. 17.75x (ISBN 0-8137-2154-7). Geol Soc.

GEOLOGY-HAWAII

Hinds, N. E. Geology of Kauai & Niihau. Repr. of 1930 ed. pap. 12.00 (ISBN 0-527-02177-6). Kraus Repr.

Macdonald, Gordon A. & Abbott, Agatin T. Volcanoes in the Sea: The Geology of Hawaii. (Illus.). 1970. 20.00 (ISBN 0-87022-495-6). U Pr of Hawaii.

Stearns, Harold T. Geology of the State of Hawaii. 2nd ed. (Illus.). 1981. 18.95 (ISBN 0-87015-234-3). Pacific Bks.

--Road Guide to Points of Geologic Interest in the Hawaiian Islands. 2nd ed. LC 78-17111. (Illus.). 1978. pap. 3.95 (ISBN 0-87015-228-9). Pacific Bks.

Wentworth, C. K. Geology of Lanai. Repr. of 1925 ed. pap. 7.00 (ISBN 0-527-02127-X). Kraus Repr.

--Pyroclastic Geology of Oahu. Repr. of 1926 ed. pap. 12.00 (ISBN 0-527-02133-4). Kraus Repr.

GEOLOGY-HIMALAYA MOUNTAINS

Gansser, Augusto. Geology of the Himalayas. LC 64-8902. (De Sitter Regional Geology Ser). 1964. 100.00x (ISBN 0-470-29055-2, Pub. by Wiley-Interscience). Wiley.

GEOLOGY-INDIA

Crawford, John J. History of the Indian Archipelago, 3 vols. (Illus.). 1967. Repr. 145.00x (ISBN 0-7146-1157-3, F Cass Co). Biblio Dist.

Dey, A. K. Geology of India. (India - Land & People Ser). (Illus.). 1968. 4.00x (ISBN 0-8426-1237-8). Verry.

Gondwana Stratigraphy. (Earth Sciences Ser., No. 2). (Illus., Orig.). 1969. pap. 28.25 (ISBN 92-3-000770-6, U267, UNESCO). Unipub.

Indian Geological Index Nineteen Seventy-One. 1978. 12.50x (ISBN 0-89955-286-2, Pub. by Intl Bk Dist). Intl Schol Bk Serv.

Indian Geological Index Nineteen Seventy-Two. 1978. 12.50x (ISBN 0-89955-287-0, Pub. by Intl Bk Dist). Intl Schol Bk Serv.

Indian Geological Index, Vol. Three: 1973. 1978. 14.00x (ISBN 0-89955-288-9, Pub. by Intl Bk Dist). Intl Schol Bk Serv.

Krishnan, M. S. Geology of India & Burma. 5th ed. (Illus.). 1968. 12.50x (ISBN 0-8002-1457-9). Intl Pubns Serv.

GEOLOGY-IRELAND

Holland, C. H. A Geology of Ireland. LC 81-6425. 316p. 1981. 49.95 (ISBN 0-470-27247-3). Halsted Pr.

Holland, Charles H., ed. Geology of Ireland. 400p. 1981. 40.00x (ISBN 0-7073-0269-2, Pub. by Scottish Academic Pr). Columbia U Pr.

GEOLOGY-JAPAN

Takai, Fuyuji, et al. Geology of Japan. 1964. 38.50x (ISBN 0-520-01249-6). U of Cal Pr.

GEOLOGY-LATIN AMERICA

McBirney, Alexander R. & Williams, Howel. Geology & Petrology of the Galapagos Islands. LC 79-98018. (Memoir: No. 118). (Illus., Orig.). 1970. 12.00x (ISBN 0-8137-1118-5). Geol Soc.

Weyl, Richard. Geology of Central America. 2nd ed. (Beitraege Zur Regionalen Geologie der Erde: Vol. 15). (Illus.). 371p. 1980. lib. bdg. 74.00 (ISBN 3-443-11015-0). Lubrecht & Cramer.

Williams, Howell, et al. Geologic Reconnaissance of Southeastern Guatemala. (U. C. Publ. in Geological Sciences: Vol. 50). 1964. pap. 7.50x (ISBN 0-520-09150-7). U of Cal Pr.

GEOLOGY-MEDITERRANEAN AREA

Vita-Finzi, Claudio. Mediterranean Valleys: Geological Change in Historical Times. LC 69-10341. (Illus.). 1969. 32.50 (ISBN 0-521-07355-3). Cambridge U Pr.

GEOLOGY-MEXICO

Baker, Charles L. Geologic Reconnaissance in the Eastern Cordillera of Mexico. LC 70-111438. (Special Paper: No. 131). (Illus.). x, 106p. (Orig.). 1971. pap. 6.00x (ISBN 0-8137-2131-8). Geol Soc.

Perkins, Bob F. Biostratigraphic Studies in the Comanche (Cretaceous) Series of Northern Mexico & Texas. LC 62-4272. (Memoir: No. 83). (Illus.). 1960. 13.00x (ISBN 0-8137-1083-9). Geol Soc.

Suplemento a la Segunda Edicion Del Diccionario Pornua De Historia, Biografia y Geografia de Mexico. 496p. (Span.). 17.50 (ISBN 0-686-56693-9, S-12280). French & Eur.

GEOLOGY-NEAR EAST

Brinkmann, R. Geology of Turkey. 1976. 46.50 (ISBN 0-444-99833-0). Elsevier.

Butzer, Karl W. Quarternary Stratigraphy & Climate in the Near East. 1958. pap. 15.50 (ISBN 0-384-06790-5). Johnson Repr.

Holland, C. H. Lower Palaeozoic Rocks of the World: With Essays on Lower Palaeozoic Rocks of the World. LC 80-41688. (Electrochemical Data Ser.). 1981. price not set (ISBN 0-471-27945-5, Pub. by Wiley-Interscience). Wiley.

Thompson, Reginald C. A Dictionary of Assyrian Chemistry & Geology. LC 78-72768. (Ancient Mesopotamian Texts & Studies). Repr. of 1936 ed. 24.50 (ISBN 0-404-18222-4). AMS Pr.

GEOLOGY-NEW ZEALAND

Brown, D. S. W., et al. The Geological Evolution of Australia & New Zealand. 1968. 26.00 (ISBN 0-08-012278-7); pap. 14.50 (ISBN 0-08-012277-9). Pergamon.

Marshall, P. New Zealand & Adjacent Islands. pap. 9.50 (ISBN 0-384-35470-X). Johnson Repr.

GEOLOGY-NEWFOUNDLAND

Kay, Marshall. Dunnage Melange & Subduction of the Protacadic Ocean, Northeast Newfoundland. LC 76-11901. (Special Paper: No. 175). (Illus.). 1976. pap. 8.00x (ISBN 0-8137-2175-X). Geol Soc.

GEOLOGY-NORTH AMERICA

Albritton, Claude C., ed. Charles Lyell on North American Geology: An Original Anthology. LC 77-6524. (History of Geology Ser.). (Illus.). 1978. lib. bdg. 38.00 (ISBN 0-405-10446-4). Arno.

Asano, Shuzo, ed. Structure of the Transition Zone. (Advances in Earth & Planetary Sciences Ser.: No. 8). 184p. 1980. lib. bdg. 26.50 (ISBN 90-277-1149-6, Pub. by D. Reidel). Kluwer Boston.

Berry, W. B. & Boucot, A. J. Correlation of the North American Silurian Rocks. LC 77-98012. (Special Paper: No. 102). (Illus., Orig.). 1970. pap. 15.00x (ISBN 0-8137-2102-4). Geol Soc.

Committee On Nuclear Sciences. Geochronology of North America. 1965. pap. 7.00 (ISBN 0-309-01276-7). Natl Acad Pr.

Darton, Nelson H. Catalogue & Index of Contributions to North American Geology: 1732-1891. Cohen, I. Bernard, ed. LC 79-7958. (Three Centuries of Science in America Ser.). 1980. Repr. of 1896 ed. lib. bdg. 75.00x (ISBN 0-405-12539-9). Arno.

Halbouty, Michel T. Salt Domes, Gulf Region, United States & Mexico. 2nd ed. 584p. 1979. 59.95 (ISBN 0-87201-803-2). Gulf Pub.

Hamblin, W. Kenneth. Atlas of Stereoscopic Aerial Photographs & Landsat Imagery of North America. LC 79-91239. (Illus.). 208p. (Orig.). 1980. 16.95 (ISBN 0-935698-00-0). Tasa Pub Co.

Hough, Jack L. Geology of the Great Lakes. LC 58-6995. (Illus.). 1958. 19.95 (ISBN 0-252-72441-0). U of Ill Pr.

Kay, Marshall & Colbert, E. H., eds. Stratigraphy & Life History. LC 64-20072. 736p. 1965. 27.50 (ISBN 0-471-46105-9). Wiley.

King, Philip B. Tectonics of Middle North America: Middle North America East of the Cordilleran Systems. (Illus.). 1969. Repr. 17.50 (ISBN 0-02-847920-3). Hafner.

King, Phillip B. The Evolution of North America. rev. ed. LC 77-71987. (Illus.). 1977. text ed. 32.50 (ISBN 0-691-08195-6); pap. text ed. 9.50 (ISBN 0-691-02359-X). Princeton U Pr.

Marcou, Jules, Jr. Jules Marcou on the Taconic System in North America: An Original Anthology. Albritton, Claude C., ed. LC 77-6527. (History of Geology Ser.). (Illus.). 1978. lib. bdg. 45.00x (ISBN 0-405-10448-0). Arno.

Petersen, Morris S., et al. Historical Geology of North America. 2nd ed. 225p. 1980. pap. text ed. write for info. (ISBN 0-697-05062-9). Wm C Brown.

Pewe, Troy L. & Updike, Randall G. San Francisco Peaks: A Guidebook to the Geology. 2nd ed. (MNA Special Publication Ser.: No. 12). 1976. pap. 2.50 (ISBN 0-89734-010-8). Mus Northern Ariz.

Roeder, Dietrich H. Rocky Mountains: Der Geologische Aufbau Des Kanadischen Felsengebirges. (Illus.). 1967. 52.80 (ISBN 3-443-11005-3). Lubrecht & Cramer.

Schoepf, J. D. Geology of Eastern North America. White, G. W., ed. Spieker, E. M., tr. from Ger. LC 78-183010. (History of Geology Ser.: Vol. 8). 1973. 24.00 (ISBN 0-02-851840-3). Hafner.

Schuchert, C. Atlas of Paleogeographic Maps of North America. 177p. 1955. pap. 10.50 (ISBN 0-471-76395-0, Pub. by Wiley). Krieger.

Stearn, Colin W., et al. Geological Evolution of North America. 3rd ed. LC 78-8124. 566p. 1979. text ed. 26.95x (ISBN 0-471-07252-4). Wiley.

Swain, F. M., ed. Stratigraphic Micropaleontology of Atlantic Basin & Borderlands. (Developments in Paleontology & Stratigraphy). 1977. 66.00 (ISBN 0-444-41554-8). Elsevier.

Titley, Spencer & Hicks, Carol, eds. Geology of the Porphyry Copper Deposits: Southwestern North America. LC 66-14229. (Illus.). 1966. 19.50x (ISBN 0-8165-0037-1). U of Ariz Pr.

GEOLOGY-NORTH SEA REGION

Fourteenth Inter-University Geological Congress. Geology & Shelf Seas: Proceedings. Donovan, D. T., ed. 1968. 11.75 (ISBN 0-934454-43-4). Lubrecht & Cramer.

GEOLOGY-NORWAY

Fortey, R. A. The Ordovician Trilobites of the Spitsbergen. (Norsk Polarinstitutt Skrifter: Vol. 171). (Illus.). 163p. 1980. pap. 19.00x (ISBN 82-00-29189-8). Universitet.

Gabrielson, R. Geological Survey of Norway, No. 355, Bulletin 53. 64p. 1980. pap. 14.00x (ISBN 82-00-31391-3). Universitet.

Geological Survey of Norway, No. 334, Bulletin 43. 1978. pap. 12.00x (ISBN 82-00-31368-9). Universitet.

Geological Survey of Norway, No. 348, Bulletin 49. 150p. 1979. pap. 21.00x (ISBN 82-003-1382-4). Universitet.

Geological Survey of Norway, No. 350, Bulletin 50. 1979. pap. 21.00x (ISBN 82-00-31385-9). Universitet.

Geological Survey of Norway, No. 351,bulletin 51. 100p. 1980. pap. 21.00x (ISBN 82-003-1386-7). Universitet.

Geological Survey of Norway, No. 363, Bulletin 60. (Illus.). 80p. 1981. pap. 16.00x (ISBN 82-00-31432-4). Universitet.

Geological Survey of Norway, No. 365, Bulletin 61. 64p. 1981. pap. 15.00x (ISBN 82-00-31432-4). Universitet.

Gjelle, S, et al. Geological Survey of Norway. (No. 343, Bulletin 48). pap. 16.00x (ISBN 82-00-31377-8, Dist. by Columbia U Pr.). Universitet.

Guezou, J & Nilsen, O. Geological Survey of Norway. (No. 340, Bulletin 47). 1979. pap. 19.00x (ISBN 82-00-31373-5, Dist. by Columbia U Pr.). Universitet.

Hisdal, Vidar, et al. Geological & Geophysical Research in Svalbard & on Jan Mayen. (Norsk Polarinstitutt Skrifter Ser.: No. 172). 181p. 1981. pap. 24.00 (ISBN 0-686-73227-8). Universitet.

Kollong, S. Geological Survey of Norway, No. 354, Bulletin 52. 150p. 1980. pap. 20.00x (ISBN 8-2003-1390-5). Universitet.

Lock, B. E., et al. The Geology of Edgeoya & Barentsoya: Svalbard. (Norsk Polarinstitutt Skrifter: Vol. 168). (Illus.). 64p. 1980. pap. text ed. 7.50x (ISBN 0-686-69913-0). Universitet.

Rowell, Unni H. Geological Survey of Norway, No. 361, Bulletin 58. 1981. pap. 12.00x (ISBN 82-00-31430-8). Universitet.

Stanton. Geological Survey of Norway, No. 360, Bulletin 57. (Illus.). 200p. 1981. pap. 24.00x (ISBN 82-00-31397-2). Universitet.

Sturt, B. A., et al. Geological Survey of Norway, No. 358, Bulletin 55. (Illus.). 60p. 1981. pap. 16.00x (ISBN 0-686-69761-8). Universitet.

Tedahl, C. O. Geological Survey of Norway, No. 356, Bulletin 54. 200p. 1980. pap. 22.00x (ISBN 82-003-1392-1). Universitet.

Tull, James F. Geology & Structure of Vestvagoey, Lofoten, North Norway. (Geological Survey of Norway Ser: No. 333, Bulletin 42). 1978. pap. 12.00x (ISBN 82-00-31367-0, Dist. by Columbia U Pr). Universitet.

Vidal, G. Geological Survey of Norway, No. 362, Bulletin 59. (Illus.). 64p. 1981. pap. 14.00x (ISBN 82-00-31431-6). Universitet.

Whitaker, John & McDonald, H. Geological Guide, Steinsfjord, Ringerike. 1977. 10.50x (ISBN 82-00-05013-0). Universitet.

Wielens, J. B., et al. Geological Survey of Norway, No. 359, Bulletin 56. (Illus.). 60p. 1981. pap. 14.00x (ISBN 0-686-69762-6). Universitet.

Winsnes, Thore S., ed. The Geological Development of Svalbard During the Precambrian, Lower Palaeozoic, & Devonian. (Norsk Polarinstitutt Skrifter: Vol. 167). (Illus.). 323p. 1980. pap. 30.00x (ISBN 82-90307-03-9). Universitet.

GEOLOGY-PACIFIC AREA

Chubb, L. J. Geology of Galapagos, Cocos & Easter Islands. Repr. of 1933 ed. pap. 7.00 (ISBN 0-527-02216-0). Kraus Repr.

--Geology of the Marquesas Islands. Repr. of 1930 ed. pap. 8.00 (ISBN 0-527-02174-1). Kraus Repr.

Hamilton, Edwin L. Sunken Islands of the Mid-Pacific Mountains. LC 56-2333. (Memoir: No. 64). (Illus.). 1956. 8.00x (ISBN 0-8137-1064-2). Geol Soc.

Hays, James D., ed. Geological Investigations of the North Pacific. LC 75-111442. (Memoir: No. 126). (Illus.). 1970. 19.75x (ISBN 0-8137-1126-6). Geol Soc.

Hoffmeister, J. E., et al. Geology of Eua, Tonga. Repr. of 1932 ed. pap. 12.00 (ISBN 0-527-02202-0). Kraus Repr.

Knopoff, L., et al, eds. The Crust & Upper Mantle of the Pacific Area. LC 68-61439. (Geophysical Monograph Ser.: Vol. 12). 1968. 24.00 (ISBN 0-87590-012-7). Am Geophysical.

Ladd, H. S. & Hoffmeister, J. E. Geology of Lau, Fiji. Repr. of 1945 ed. pap. 48.00 (ISBN 0-527-02289-6). Kraus Repr.

--Geology of Vitilevu Fiji. Repr. of 1934 ed. pap. 22.00 (ISBN 0-527-02225-X). Kraus Repr.

McKee, Bates. Cascadia: The Geologic Evolution of the Pacific Northwest. (Illus.). 416p. 1972. pap. text ed. 15.95 (ISBN 0-07-045133-8, C). McGraw.

Marshall, P. Geology of Mangaia. Repr. of 1927 ed. pap. 5.00 (ISBN 0-527-02139-3). Kraus Repr.

--Geology of Rarotonga & Atiu. Repr. of 1930 ed. pap. 8.00 (ISBN 0-527-02178-4). Kraus Repr.

Palmer, Harold S. Geology of Kaula, Nihoa, Necker & Gardner Islands & French Frigates Shoal. Repr. of 1927 ed. pap. 5.00 (ISBN 0-527-02138-5). Kraus Repr.

Stark, J. T. & Howland, A. L. Geology of Borabora Society Islands. 1941. pap. 6.00 (ISBN 0-527-02277-2). Kraus Repr.

Williams, H. Geology of Tahiti, Moorea, & Maiao. Repr. of 1933 ed. pap. 9.00 (ISBN 0-527-02211-X). Kraus Repr.

GEOLOGY-RUSSIA

Klein, Richard G. Ice-Age Hunters of the Ukraine. LC 73-77443. (Prehistoric Archaeology & Ecology Ser). 1973. 9.00x (ISBN 0-226-43945-3); pap. text ed. 4.50x (ISBN 0-226-43946-1). U of Chicago Pr.

Nalivkin, D. V. Geology of the U.S.S.R. Rast, Nicholas, tr. LC 72-97781. (Illus.). 1973. 85.00x (ISBN 0-8020-1984-6). U of Toronto Pr.

GEOLOGY-SCANDINAVIA

In Situ Heating Experiments in Geological Formations, Ludvika, Sweden, September. 1978. 1979. 16.50x (ISBN 92-64-01872-7). OECD.

GEOLOGY-SOUTH AMERICA

Delaney, Patrick J. Geology & Geomorphology of the Coastal Plain of Rio Grande Do Sul, Brazil & Northern Uruguay. LC 66-64637. (Coastal Studies: Vol. 15). (Illus.). 1966. pap. 4.00x (ISBN 0-8071-0428-0). La State U Pr.

--Quaternary Geologic History of the Coastal Plain of Rio Grande Do Sul, Brazil. LC 63-22269. (Coastal Studies: Vol. 7). (Illus.). 1964. pap. 4.00x (ISBN 0-8071-0429-9). La State U Pr.

Hartt, Fred. Geology & Physical Geography of Brazil: Scientific Results of a Journey in Brazil by Louis Agassiz & His Companions. LC 74-23607. 670p. 1975. Repr. of 1870 ed. 29.50 (ISBN 0-88275-244-8). Krieger.

GEOLOGY-UNITED STATES

Here are entered works on the geology of the United States as a whole, together with works on individual states or specific areas.

Adkins, W. S. & Arick, M. B. Geology of Bell County, Texas. (Illus.). 92p. 1930. 1.00 (ISBN 0-686-29346-0, BULL 3016). Bur Econ Geology.

Alexander, Nancy. Father of Texas Geology: Robert T. Hill. LC 76-2621. (Bicentenial Series in American Studies: No. 4). (Illus.). 1976. 12.50 (ISBN 0-87074-152-7). SMU Press.

Alt, David & Hyndman, Donald. Roadside Geology of Oregon. LC 77-2581. (Roadside Geology Ser.). (Illus.). 268p. 1978. pap. 7.95 (ISBN 0-87842-063-0). Mountain Pr.

American Geological Institute. Directory of the Geologic Division, U. S. Geological Survey. (Illus.). 144p. 1980. pap. 6.00 (ISBN 0-913312-45-2). Am Geol.

Association of American Geologists & Naturalists at Philadelphia, 1840 & 1841. Proceedings. Albritton, Claude C., ed. LC 77-6507. (History of Geology Ser.). Repr. of 1843 ed. lib. bdg. 35.00x (ISBN 0-405-10430-8). Arno.

Baker, Frank C. Life of the Pleistocene or Glacial Period. LC 74-80996. (BCL Ser. I). 1969. Repr. of 1920 ed. 37.50 (ISBN 0-404-00449-0). AMS Pr.

Baldwin, Ewart M. Geology of Oregon. 3rd ed. LC 76-4346. (Illus.). 1981. perfect bdg. 11.95 (ISBN 0-8403-2321-2). Kendall-Hunt.

Barnes, F. A. Canyon Country Geology for the Layman & Rockhound. new ed. LC 77-95050. (Illus.). 1978. pap. 3.95 (ISBN 0-915272-17-2). Wasatch Pubs.

Barnes, V. E. & Schofield, D. A. Potential Low-Grade Iron Ore & Hydraulic-Fracturing Sand in Cambrian Sandstones, Northwestern Llano Region, Texas. (Illus.). 58p. 1964. 2.00 (ISBN 0-686-29335-5, RI 53). Bur Econ Geology.

Barnes, V. E., et al. Geology of the Llano Region & Austin Area. rev. ed. 154p. 1976. Repr. of 1972 ed. 2.00 (ISBN 0-686-29321-5, GB 13). Bur Econ Geology.

Bassett, Allen M. & O'Dunn, Shannon. General Geology of the Western United States: A Laboratory Manual. rev. ed. (Illus.). 176p. 1980. pap. text ed. 11.95 (ISBN 0-917962-67-2). Peek Pubns.

Becker, Herman F. Oligocene Plants from the Upper Ruby River Basin, Southwest Montana. LC 61-2377. (Memoir: No. 82). (Illus.). 1961. 10.75x (ISBN 0-8137-1082-0). Geol Soc.

Bernard, H. A., et al. Recent Sediments of Southeast Texas-A Field Guide to the Brazos Alluvial & Deltaic Plains & the Galveston Barrier Island Complex. 132p. 1970. Repr. 6.00 (ISBN 0-686-29319-3, GB 11). Bur Econ Geology.

Bezy, John V. A Guide to the Desert Geology of the Lake Mead National Recreation Area. new ed. Jackson, Earl, ed. LC 78-56673. (Popular Ser.: No. 24). (Illus., Orig.). 1979. pap. 1.75x (ISBN 0-911408-51-7). SW Pks Mnmts.

Bickford, M. E. & Mose, D. G. Geochronology of Precambrian Rocks in the St. Francois Mountains. LC 75-25345. (Special Paper: No. 165). (Illus.). 1975. pap. 7.00x (ISBN 0-8137-2165-2). Geol Soc.

Blackwelder, E. United States of North America. 1912. 25.50 (ISBN 0-384-04645-2). Johnson Repr.

Bowen, Zeddie P. Brachiopoda of the Keyser Limestone (Silurian-Devonian) of Maryland & Adjacent Areas. LC 66-29257. (Memoir: No. 102). (Illus.). 1967. 8.50x (ISBN 0-8137-1102-9). Geol Soc.

Brand, J. P. Cretaceous of Llano Estacado of Texas. (Illus.). 59p. 1953. 0.70 (ISBN 0-686-29330-4, RI 20). Bur Econ Geology.

Briggs, Garrett, ed. Carboniferous of the Southeastern United States. LC 73-87234. (Special Paper: No. 148). (Illus., Orig.). 1974. pap. 10.00x (ISBN 0-8137-2148-2). Geol Soc.

Brown, L. F., et al. Pennsylvanian Depositional Systems in North-Central Texas: A Guide for Interpreting Terrigenous Clastic Facies in a Cratonic Basin. (Illus.). 122p. 1973. Repr. 3.50 (ISBN 0-686-29322-3, GB 14). Bur Econ Geology.

Brown, T. E., et al. Field Excursions, East Texas: Clay, Glauconite, Ironstone Deposits. (Illus.). 48p. 1969. 1.00 (ISBN 0-686-29317-7, GB 9). Bur Econ Geology.

Bullard, F. M. The Geology of Grayson County, Texas. (Illus.). 72p. 1931. 0.50 (ISBN 0-686-29350-9, BULL 3125). Bur Econ Geology.

Cady, John W. Magnetic & Gravity Anomalies in the Great Valley & Western Sierra Nevada Metamorphic Belt, California. LC 75-19540. (Special Paper: No. 168). (Illus.). 1975. pap. 9.00x (ISBN 0-8137-2168-7). Geol Soc.

Cady, Wallace M. Regional Tectonic Synthesis of Northwestern New England & Adjacent Quebec. LC 77-98020. (Memoir: No. 120). (Illus.). 1969. 14.00x (ISBN 0-8137-1120-7). Geol Soc.

Carter, George F. Pleistocene Man at San Diego. LC 77-74811. Repr. of 1957 ed. 37.00 (ISBN 0-404-14885-9). AMS Pr.

Caughey, C. A. Depositional Systems in the Paluxy Formation (Lower Cretaceous) Northeast Texas-Oil, Gas, & Ground-Water Resources. (Illus.). 59p. 1977. 2.00 (ISBN 0-686-29327-4, GC 77-8). Bur Econ Geology.

Chadwick, George H. Rocks of Greene County. 1973. pap. 2.00 (ISBN 0-685-40640-7). Hope Farm.

Chamberlain, Barbara B. These Fragile Outposts. 352p. 1981. pap. 9.95 (ISBN 0-940160-12-9). Parnassus Imprints.

Chapman, Carleton A. Geology of Acadia National Park. LC 73-107079. (Illus.). 1970. 6.95 (ISBN 0-87638-012-7); pap. 4.95 (ISBN 0-85699-010-8). Chatham Pr.

Cooper, William S. Coastal Dunes of California. LC 67-29290. (Memoir: No. 104). (Illus.). 1967. 11.00x (ISBN 0-8137-1104-5). Geol Soc.

--Coastal Sand Dunes of Oregon & Washington. LC 38-3503. (Memoir: No. 72). (Illus.). 1958. 10.00x (ISBN 0-8137-1072-3). Geol Soc.

Curtis, Bruce M., ed. Cenozoic History of the Southern Rocky Mountains. LC 74-30892. (Memoir: No. 144). (Illus.). 1975. 25.00x (ISBN 0-8137-1144-4). Geol Soc.

Dietrich, J. W. & Lonsdale, J. T. Mineral Resources of the Colorado River Industrial Development Association Area. (Illus.). 84p. 1958. 1.50 (ISBN 0-686-29332-0, RI 37). Bur Econ Geology.

Dietrich, Richard V. Geology & Virginia. LC 76-110752. (Illus.). 1971. 13.95x (ISBN 0-8139-0289-4). U Pr of Va.

Dorr, John A., Jr., et al. Deformation & Deposition Between a Foreland Uplift & an Impinging Thrust Belt: Hoback Basin Wyoming. LC 77-70022. (Special Papers: No. 177). (Illus.). 1977. pap. 10.00x (ISBN 0-8137-2177-6). Geol Soc.

Dutton, S. P., et al. Geology & Geohydrology of the Palo Duro Basin, Texas Panhandle: A Report on the Progress of Nuclear Waste Isolation Feasibility Studies 1978. (Illus.). 99p. 1979. 2.50 (ISBN 0-686-29328-2, GC 79-1). Bur Econ Geology.

Eargle, D. H., et al. Uranium Geology & Mines, South Texas. (Illus.). 59p. 1971. 1.75 (ISBN 0-686-29320-7, GB 12). Bur Econ Geology.

Eckel, Edwin B., ed. Nevada Test Site. LC 68-56611. (Memoir: No. 110). (Illus.). 1968. 11.00x (ISBN 0-8137-1110-X). Geol Soc.

Edmund, Rudolph W. Structural Geology & Physiography of the Northern End of the Teton Range, Wyoming. LC 52-3353. (Augustana College Library Ser.: No. 23). 1951. pap. 3.50 (ISBN 0-910182-18-3). Augustana Coll.

Ekman, Leonard C. Scenic Geology of the Pacific Northwest. 2nd. ed. LC 61-13278. (Illus.). 1970. 8.95 (ISBN 0-8323-0130-2). Binford.

Ellison, S. P., Jr. Sulfur in Texas. (Illus.). 1971. 2.00 (ISBN 0-686-29324-X, HB 2). Bur Econ Geology.

Emmons, Ebenezer. American Geology: Statement of the Principles of the Science, with Full Illustrations of the Characteristic American Fossils, 2 vols. in one. LC 73-17818. (Natural Sciences in America Ser.). (Illus.). 544p. 1974. Repr. 28.00x (ISBN 0-405-05734-2). Arno.

Evans, T. J. Bituminous Coal in Texas. (Illus.). 65p. 1974. 2.00 (ISBN 0-686-29325-8, HB 4). Bur Econ Geology.

Feldmann, Rodney M. & Heimlich, Richard A. Geology Field Guide: The Black Hills. 208p. (Orig.). 1980. pap. 8.95 (ISBN 0-8403-2193-7). Kendall-Hunt.

Fisher, W. L. Rock & Mineral Resources of East Texas. (Illus.). 439p. 1965. 5.00 (ISBN 0-686-29336-3, RI 54). Bur Econ Geology.

Fisher, W. L. & McGowen, J. H. Depositional Systems in the Wilcox Group of Texas & Their Relationship to Occurrence of Oil & Gas. 125p. 1967. Repr. 1.00 (ISBN 0-686-29326-6, GC 67-4). Bur Econ Geology.

Fisher, W. L. & Rodda, P. U. Lower Cretaceous Sands of Texas: Stratigraphy & Resources. (Illus.). 116p. 1967. 1.75 (ISBN 0-686-29340-1, RI 59). Bur Econ Geology.

Folk, R. L., et al. Field Excursion, Central Texas: Tertiary Bentonites of Central Texas. 53p. 1973. Repr. of 1961 ed. 1.25 (ISBN 0-686-29312-6, GB 3). Bur Econ Geology.

Frey, Robert W., ed. Excursions in Southeastern Geology: Field Trip Guidebooks, 2 vols. Incl. Vol. I. Field Trips-1-13. pap. 25.00 (ISBN 0-913312-48-7); Vol. II. Field Trips-14-23. pap. 25.00 (ISBN 0-913312-49-5). (Illus., Orig.). 1980. Set. pap. 40.00 (ISBN 0-913312-50-9). Am Geol.

Galenson, Walter, ed. Incomes Policy: What Can We Learn from Europe? LC 72-619695. (Pierce Ser.: No. 3). 1973. 7.50 (ISBN 0-87546-048-8). NY Sch Indus Rel.

Galloway, W. E., et al. South Texas Uranium Province, Geologic Perspective. (Illus.). 81p. 1979. 3.00 (ISBN 0-686-29323-1, GB 18). Bur Econ Geology.

Gastil, R. Gordon, et al. Reconnaissance Geology of the State of Baja California. LC 74-83806. (Memoir: No. 140). (Illus.). 1975. 25.00x (ISBN 0-8137-1140-1); pap. 21.00x (ISBN 0-685-56041-4). Geol Soc.

Gilbert, Grove K. Report of the Geology of the Henry Mountains: U.S. Geographical & Geological Survey of the Rocky Mounntain Region. Albritton, Claude C., Jr., ed. LC 77-6519. (History of Geology Ser.). (Illus.). 1978. Repr. of 1877 ed. lib. bdg. 15.00x (ISBN 0-405-10441-3). Arno.

Gilluly, James. Volcanism, Tectonism, & Plutonism in the Western United States. LC 65-15799. (Special Paper: No. 80). (Illus., Orig.). 1965. pap. 4.00x (ISBN 0-8137-2080-X). Geol Soc.

Girard, R. M. Texas Rocks & Minerals: An Amateur's Guide. (Illus.). 109p. 1964. Repr. 2.00 (ISBN 0-686-29314-2, GB 6). Bur Econ Geology.

Goldich, Samuel S., et al. Precambrian Geology & Geochronology of Minnesota. LC 61-8016. (Bulletin: No. 41). (Illus.). 1961. 4.00x (ISBN 0-8166-0224-7). Minn Geol Survey.

Graces, R. W., Jr. Geology of Hood Spring Quadrangle, Brewster County, Texas. (Illus.). 51p. 1954. 2.25 (ISBN 0-686-29331-2, RI 21). Bur Econ Geology.

Grant, Richard E. Faunas & Stratigraphy of the Snowy Range Formation (Upper Cambrian) in Southwestern Montana & Northwestern Wyoming. LC 65-26558. (Memoir: No. 96). (Illus.). 1965. 13.50x (ISBN 0-8137-1096-0). Geol Soc.

Green, John C. Stratigraphy & Structure of the Boundary Mountain Anticlinorium in the Errol Quadrangle, New Hampshire-Maine. LC 64-25378. (Special Paper: No. 77). (Illus., Orig.). 1964. pap. 5.75x (ISBN 0-8137-2077-X). Geol Soc.

Grout, Frank F. & Wolff, J. Fred. Geology of the Cuyuna District, Minnesota: A Progress Report. LC 55-9000. (Bulletin: No. 36). (Illus.). 1955. 3.00x (ISBN 0-8166-0106-2). Minn Geol Survey.

Gundersen, James N. & Schwartz, George M. Geology of the Metamorphosed Biwabik Iron Formation, Eastern Mesabi District, Minnesota. LC 62-9302. (Bulletin: No. 43). 1962. 4.25x (ISBN 0-8166-0274-3). Minn Geol Survey.

Hamblin, W. Kenneth, et al. Roadside Geology of U. S. Interstate 80 Between Salt Lake City & San Francisco. 53p. 1975. pap. 3.00 (ISBN 0-913312-43-6). Am Geol.

Harris, Ann G. Geology of National Parks. 2nd ed. LC 74-25041. (Illus.). 1977. pap. text ed. 12.95 (ISBN 0-8403-1092-7). Kendall-Hunt.

Hatfield, Craig B. Stratigraphy & Paleoecology of the Saluda Formation (Cincinnatian) in Indiana, Ohio & Kentucky. LC 68-23102. (Special Paper: No. 95). (Illus., Orig.). 1968. pap. 2.50x (ISBN 0-8137-2095-8). Geol Soc.

Heckel, Philip H. Nature, Origin, & Significance of the Tully Limestone. LC 72-82612. (Special Paper: No. 138). (Illus.). 160p. (Orig.). 1973. pap. 11.00x (ISBN 0-8137-2138-5). Geol Soc.

Henderson, G. G. Geology of Tom Green County. (Illus.). 116p. 1928. 0.50 (ISBN 0-686-29345-2, BULL 2807). Bur Econ Geology.

Henry, C. D. & Gluck, J. K. A Preliminary Assessment of the Geological Setting, Hydrology, & Geochemistry of the Hueco Tanks Geothermal Area, Texas & New Mexico. (Geological Circular Ser.: No. 81-1). (Illus.). 49p. 1981. write for info. U of Tex Econ Geology.

Hill, Mary. Geology of the Sierra Nevada. LC 73-93053. (California Natural History Guides Ser.). (Illus.). 1975. 14.95x (ISBN 0-520-02801-5); pap. 5.95 (ISBN 0-520-02698-5). U of Cal Pr.

Hoffmeister, J. Edward. Land from the Sea: The Geologic Story of South Florida. LC 73-20120. (Illus.). 128p. 1974. 9.95 (ISBN 0-87024-268-7). U of Miami Pr.

Horberg, Leland. The Structural Geology & Physiography of the Teton Pass Area, Wyoming. LC 39-7044. (Augustana College Library Ser.: No. 16). 1938. pap. 3.50 (ISBN 0-910182-11-6). Augustana Coll.

Hunt, Charles B. Death Valley: Geology, Ecology, Archaeology. LC 74-2460. 256p. 1975. 14.95 (ISBN 0-520-02460-5); CAL 315. pap. 7.95 (ISBN 0-520-03013-3). U of Cal Pr.

Johnson, A. M. Styles of Folding: Mechanics & Mechanisms of Folding of Natural Elastic Materials. (Developments in Geotectonics). 1977. 66.00 (ISBN 0-444-41496-7). Elsevier.

Johnson, Douglas W. Stream Sculpture on the Atlantic Slope: A Study in the Evolution of Appalachian Rivers. (Illus.). 1967. Repr. of 1931 ed. 14.25 (ISBN 0-02-847250-0). Hafner.

Kerr, Paul F., et al. Marysvale, Utah, Uranium Area. LC 57-59324. (Special Paper: No. 64). (Illus.). 1957. 13.00x (ISBN 0-8137-2064-8). Geol Soc.

King, P. B. The Geology of the Glass Mountains, Texas: Part I, Descriptive Geology. (Illus.). 167p. 1930. 2.50 (ISBN 0-686-29348-7, BULL 3038). Bur Econ Geology.

King, P. B. & Flawn, P. T. Geology & Mineral Deposits of Pre-Cambrian Rocks of the Van Horn Area, Texas. (Illus.). 218p. 1953. 5.75 (ISBN 0-686-29357-6, PUB 5301). Bur Econ Geology.

King, R. E. The Geology of the Glass Mountains, Texas: Part Ii, Faunal Summary & Correlation of the Permian Formations with Description of Brachiopoda. (Illus.). 146p. 1930. 2.50 (ISBN 0-686-29349-5, BULL 3042). Bur Econ Geology.

Lallemant, Hans G. Structure of the Canyon Mountain (Oregon) Ophiolite Its Implication for Sea-Floor Spreading. LC 75-41702. (Special Paper: No. 173), (Illus., Orig.). 1976. pap. 7.00x (ISBN 0-8137-2173-3). Geol Soc.

Larkin, Robert P., et al. Geology Field Guide: The Southern Rocky Mountains. 176p. (Orig.). 1980. pap. text ed. 9.95 (ISBN 0-8403-2207-0). Kendall-Hunt.

La Rocque, Aurele. Molluscan Faunas of the Flagstaff Formation of Central Utah. LC 60-2798. (Memoir: No. 78). (Illus., Orig.). 1960. 6.00x (ISBN 0-8137-1078-2). Geol Soc.

Lindgren, Waldemar. The Tertiary Gravels of the Sierra Nevada of California. LC 78-56519. (Illus.). 1978. 24.95 (ISBN 0-89632-006-5). Del Oeste.

Literary & Philosophical Society of New York, May, 1814 & Clinton, Dewitt. An Introductory Discourse: Proceedings. Albritton, Claude C., ed. LC 77-6515. (History of Geology Ser.). 1978. Repr. of 1815 ed. lib. bdg. 12.00x (ISBN 0-405-10437-5). Arno.

Lobeck, Armin K. Airways of America. LC 78-113287. 1970. Repr. of 1933 ed. 18.50 (ISBN 0-8046-1323-0). Kennikat.

Lozo, Frank E., ed. Woodbine & Adjacent Strata of the Waco Area of Central Texas: A Symposium. LC 52-10665. (Fondreu Science Ser.: No. 4). (Illus.). 1951. 15.00 (ISBN 0-87074-091-1); pap. 12.50 (ISBN 0-87074-092-X). SMU Press.

Lyell, Charles B. Second Visit to North America, 2 Vols. 1855. Set. 49.00 (ISBN 0-403-00357-1). Scholarly.

Lyons, Paul C. & Brownlow, Arthur, eds. Studies in New England Geology: A Memoir in Honor of C. Wroe Wolfe. LC 75-30494. (Memoir: No. 146). (Illus.). 1976. 29.75x (ISBN 0-8137-1146-0). Geol Soc.

McGowen, J. H. & Brewton, J. L. Historical Changes & Related Coastal Processes, Gulf & Mainland Shorelines, Matagorda Bay Area, Texas. (Illus.). 72p. 1975. 6.00 (ISBN 0-686-29363-0). Bur Econ Geology.

McGowen, J. H., et al. Geochemistry of Bottom Sediments, Matagorda Bay System, Texas. (Illus.). 64p. 1979. 1.50 (ISBN 0-686-29329-0, GC 79-2). Bur Econ Geology.

McKee, Edwin D., et al. History of the Redwall Limestone of Northern Arizona. LC 79-79040. (Memoir: No. 114). (Illus.). 1969. 25.00x (ISBN 0-8137-1114-2). Geol Soc.

Maclure, W. Observations on the Geology of the United States of America. Repr. of 1966 ed. text ed. 14.50 (ISBN 0-934454-67-1). Lubrecht & Cramer.

Matthes, Francois E. The Incomparable Valley: A Geologic Interpretation of the Yosemite. Fryxell, Fritiof, ed. (Illus.). 1950. pap. 6.95 (ISBN 0-520-00827-8). U of Cal Pr.

Matthews, W. H. The Geologic Story of Longhorn Cavern. 50p. 1963. 1.00 (ISBN 0-686-29313-4, GB 4). Bur Econ Geology.

--The Geologic Story of Palo Duro Canyon. (Illus.). 51p. 1969. 1.00 (ISBN 0-686-29316-9, GB 8). Bur Econ Geology.

--Texas Fossils: An Amateur Collector's Handbook. (Illus.). 123p. 1960. Repr. 1.00 (ISBN 0-686-29311-8, GB 2). Bur Econ Geology.

Matthews, William H., III. A Guide to the National Parks, Their Landscape - Geology. 1968. 6.95 (ISBN 0-385-06298-2). Natural Hist.

Maxwell, R. A. Mineral Resources of South Texas: Region Served Through the Port of Corpus Christi. (Illus.). 140p. 1962. 3.50 (ISBN 0-686-29333-9, RI 43). Bur Econ Geology.

Merrill, George P. First One Hundred Years of American Geology. (Illus.). 1969. Repr. of 1924 ed. 32.75 (ISBN 0-02-849180-7). Hafner.

Merrill, George P. & Albritton, Claude C., eds. Contributions to a History of American State Geological & Natural History Surveys. LC 77-6529. (History of Geology Ser.). (Illus.). 1978. Repr. of 1920 ed. lib. bdg. 37.50 (ISBN 0-405-10450-2). Arno.

Myers, D. A., et al. Geology of the Late Paleozoic Horseshoe Atoll in West Texas. (Illus.). 113p. 1956. 2.00 (ISBN 0-686-29360-6, PUB 5607). Bur Econ Geology.

Nash, J. P., et al. Road Building Materials in Texas. (Illus.). 159p. 1918. 0.50 (ISBN 0-686-29341-X, BULL 1839). Bur Econ Geology.

Nations, Dale & Stump, Edmund. Geology of Arizona. 208p. 1981. pap. text ed. 9.95 (ISBN 0-8403-2475-8). Kendall-Hunt.

Nelson, Vincent E. The Structural Geology of the Cache Creek Area, Gros Ventre Mountains, Wyoming. LC 43-15519. (Augustana College Library Ser.: No. 18). 1942. pap. 3.00 (ISBN 0-910182-13-2). Augustana Coll.

Palmer, Arthur N. A Geological Guide to Mammoth Cave National Park. (Speleologia Ser.). (Illus.). 1981. write for info. (ISBN 0-914264-27-3); pap. write for info. (ISBN 0-914264-28-1). Zephyrus Pr.

Patton, L. T. The Geology of Potter County. (Illus.). 180p. 1923. 0.50 (ISBN 0-686-29343-6, BULL 2330). Bur Econ Geology.

--The Geology of Stonewall County, Texas. (Illus.). 77p. 1930. 0.50 (ISBN 0-686-29347-9, BULL 3027). Bur Econ Geology.

Paull, Rachel K. & Paull, Richard A. Geology of Wisconsin & Upper Michigan: Including Parts of Adjacent States. LC 76-27036. (Illus.). 1977. pap. text ed. 9.95 (ISBN 0-8403-1596-1). Kendall-Hunt.

Perkins, Bob F. Biostratigraphic Studies in the Comanche (Cretaceous) Series of Northern Mexico & Texas. LC 62-4272. (Memoir: No. 83). (Illus.). 1960. 13.00x (ISBN 0-8137-1083-9). Geol Soc.

Pessagno, Emile A., Jr. Upper Cretaceous Stratigraphy of the Western Gulf Coast Area of Mexico, Texas & Arkansas. LC 70-76285. (Memoir: No. 111). (Illus.). 1969. 12.00x (ISBN 0-8137-1111-8). Geol Soc.

Pestana, Harold R. Bibliography of Congressional Geology. LC 79-175939. 1972. 24.75 (ISBN 0-02-850220-5). Hafner.

Platinum & Black Sand in Washington. facs. ed. (Geology Ser.). 17p. Repr. of 1928 ed. pap. 3.50 (ISBN 0-8466-8001-7, SJG1). Shorey.

Plummer, F. B. & Sargent, E. C. Underground Waters & Subsurface Temperatures of the Woodbine Sand in Northeast Texas. (Illus.). 178p. 1931. 1.00 (ISBN 0-686-29351-7, BULL 3138). Bur Econ Geology.
Reed, L. C. & Longnecker, O. M., Jr. The Geology of Hemphill County, Texas. (Illus.). 98p. 1932. 0.50 (ISBN 0-686-31764-5, BULL 3231). Bur Econ Geology.
Reid, Rolland R., et al. Precambrian Geology of North Snowy Block, Beartooth Mountains, Montana. LC 74-28529. (Special Paper: No. 157). (Illus.). 1975. pap. 16.00x (ISBN 0-8137-2157-1). Geol Soc.
Ross, Charles A. Standard Wolfcampian Series (Permian), Glass Mountains, Texas. LC 63-4964. (Memoir: No. 88). (Orig.). 1963. 17.50x (ISBN 0-8137-1088-X). Geol Soc.
Saunders, Bruce W. Upper Mississippian Ammonoids from Arkansas & Oklahoma. LC 72-89465. (Special Paper: No. 145). (Illus.). 80p. (Orig.). 1973. pap. 6.50x (ISBN 0-8137-2145-8). Geol Soc.
Schnable, Jon E. & Goodell, H. Grant. Pleistocene-Recent Stratigraphy, Evolution, & Development of the Apalachicola Coast, Florida. LC 68-26497. (Special Paper: No. 112). (Illus., Orig.). 1968. pap. 3.75x (ISBN 0-8137-2112-1). Geol Soc.
Schneer, Cecil J., ed. Two Hundred Years of Geology in America: Proceedings of the New Hampshire Bicentennial Conference. LC 78-63149. (Illus.). 401p. 1979. text ed. 22.50x (ISBN 0-87451-160-7). U Pr of New Eng.
Schneider, Allan F. Pleistocene Geology of the Randall Region, Central Minnesota. LC 61-63788. (Bulletin: No. 40). 1961. 4.25x (ISBN 0-8166-0244-1). Minn Geol Survey.
Schoepf, J. D. Geology of Eastern North America. White, G. W., ed. Spieker, E. M., tr. from Ger. LC 78-183010. (History of Geology Ser.: Vol. 8). 1973. 24.00 (ISBN 0-02-851840-3). Hafner.
Scholten, Robert & Ramspott, L. D. Tectonic Mechanisms Indicated by Structural Framework of Central Beaverhead Range, Idaho - Montana. LC 68-8595. (Special Paper: No. 104). (Illus., Orig.). 1968. pap. 5.75x (ISBN 0-8137-2104-0). Geol Soc.
Schumm, Stanley A. & Bradley, William C., eds. United States Contributions to Quaternary Research. LC 71-90050. (Special Paper: No. 123). (Illus., Orig.). 1969. pap. 14.00x (ISBN 0-8137-2123-7). Geol Soc.
Sellards, E. H., et al. The Geology of Texas: Vol.I, Stratigraphy. (Illus.). 1007p. 1978. Repr. of 1932 ed. 8.00 (ISBN 0-686-29353-3, BULL 3232). Bur Econ Geology.
Shimer, John A. This Sculptured Earth: The Landscape of America. LC 59-10628. (Illus.). 1959. 22.50x (ISBN 0-231-02331-6). Columbia U Pr.
Sibley, J. A. Geology of Baton Rouge & Environs. 1972. 12.50 (ISBN 0-685-08218-0); pap. 12.50 (ISBN 0-685-08219-9). Claitors.
Sidar, Jean. George Hamell Cook: A Life in Agriculture & Geology, 1818-1889. 1976. 13.00 (ISBN 0-8135-0827-4). Rutgers U Pr.
Silberling, N. J. Age Relationships of the Golconda Thrust Fault, Sonoma Range, North-Central Nevada. LC 74-31780. (Special Paper: No. 163). (Illus.). 1975. pap. 9.00x (ISBN 0-8137-2163-6). Geol Soc.
Silberling, N. J. & Roberts, Ralph J. Pre-Tertiary Stratigraphy & Structure of Northwestern Nevada. LC 63-1926. (Special Paper: No. 72). (Illus., Orig.). 1962. pap. 3.00x (ISBN 0-8137-2072-9). Geol Soc.
Sims, P. K. & Morey, G. B., eds. Geology of Minnesota. LC 73-62334. 1972. pap. 12.00 (ISBN 0-934938-00-8). Minn Geol Survey.
Slaughter, B. H., et al. The Hill-Shuler Local Faunas of the Upper Trinity River, Dallas & Denton Counties, Texas. (Illus.). 75p. 1962. 2.50 (ISBN 0-686-29334-7, RI 48). Bur Econ Geology.
Slaughter, M. & Earley, J. W. Mineralogy & Geological Significance of the Mowry Bentonites, Wyoming. LC 65-22397. (Special Paper: No. 83). (Illus., Orig.). 1965. pap. 6.00x (ISBN 0-8137-2083-4). Geol Soc.
Sloss, L. L. Lithofacies Maps: An Atlas of the U.S. & Southern Canada. 108p. 1960. 9.50 (ISBN 0-471-79860-6, Pub. by Wiley). Krieger.
Stenzel, H. B. The Geology of Henrys Chapel Quadrangle, Northeastern Cherokee County, Texas. (Illus.). 119p. 1953. 3.50 (ISBN 0-686-29358-4, PUB 5305). Bur Econ Geology.
Stewart, Anne & Roquitte, Ruth. The Land of Sky-Blue Waters. LC 78-9039. (Minnesota Adventures Ser.). (Illus.). (gr. 4-6). 1978. pap. text ed. 3.95 (ISBN 0-87518-161-9). Dillon.
--Minnesota Adventures Teacher's Guide. (Minnesota Adventures Ser.). 1979. pap. 6.95 (ISBN 0-87518-164-3). Dillon.
Stone, J. E. Surficial Geology of the New Brighton Quadrangle, Minnesota. LC 68-22771. (Geologic Map Series: No. 2). 1966. 1.75x (ISBN 0-8166-0376-6). Minn Geol Survey.
Strahler, Arthur N. Geologist's View of Cape Cod. LC 66-24306. 1966. 3.95 (ISBN 0-385-07177-9). Natural Hist.
Stringfield, V. T. & LeGrand, H. E. Hydrology of Limestone Terranes in the Coastal Plain of the Southeastern United States. LC 66-30771. (Special Paper: No. 93). (Illus., Orig.). 1966. pap. 3.00x (ISBN 0-8137-2093-1). Geol Soc.
Stumm, Erwin C. Silurian & Devonian Corals of the Falls of the Ohio. LC 64-8208. (Memoir: No. 93). (Illus.). 1964. 15.75x (ISBN 0-8137-1093-6). Geol Soc.
Subitzky, Seymour & Gill, Harold E., eds. Geology of Selected Areas in New Jersey & Eastern Pennsylvania & Guidebook of Excursions. 1969. 25.00 (ISBN 0-8135-0606-9). Rutgers U Pr.
Swenson, Frank A. Geology of the Northwest Flank of the Gros Ventre Mountains, Wyoming. LC 50-5669. (Augustana College Library Ser.: No. 21). 1949. pap. 3.50 (ISBN 0-910182-16-7). Augustana Coll.
Thom, Bruce G. Coastal & Fluvial Landforms: Horry & Marion Counties, South Carolina. LC 67-27549. (Coastal Studies, Vol. 19). (Illus.). 1967. pap. 4.00x (ISBN 0-8071-0811-1). La State U Pr.
Thompson, Robert W. Tidal Flat Sedimentation on the Colorado River Delta, Northwestern Gulf of California. LC 68-23892. (Memoir: No. 107). (Illus.). 1968. 12.00x (ISBN 0-8137-1107-X). Geol Soc.
Tomassy, Marie J. Geologie Pratique De la Louisiane: Practical Geology of Louisiana. LC 77-6542. (History of Geology Ser.). (Illus.). Repr. of 1860 ed. lib. bdg. 25.00 (ISBN 0-405-10461-8). Arno.
U. S. Department of the Interior - U. S. Geological Survey, Washington, D. C. Catalog of the United States Geological Survey Library, 25 vols. 1964. Set. lib. bdg. 2375.00 (ISBN 0-8161-0712-2). G K Hall.
Van Diver, Bradford B. Rocks & Routes of the North Country, New York. LC 76-46243. (Illus.). 1976. pap. text ed. 6.95 (ISBN 0-685-83503-0). Van Diver.
--Upstate New York. (Geology Field Guide Ser.). (Illus.). 288p. 1980. pap. text ed. 10.95 (ISBN 0-8403-2214-3). Kendall-Hunt.
Von Engeln, Oscar D. Finger Lakes Region: Its Origin & Nature. (Illus.). 1961. 11.95 (ISBN 0-8014-0437-1). Cornell U Pr.
Walton, A. W. & Henry, C. D., eds. Cenozoic Geology of the Trans-Pecos Volcanic Field of Texas. 202p. 1979. 4.00 (ISBN 0-686-31763-7, GB 19). Bur Econ Geology.
Ward, Dederick C., ed. Bibliography of Theses in Geology, United States & Canada Nineteen Sixty-Seven to Nineteen Seventy. LC 73-78974. (Special Paper: No. 143). 442p. (Orig.). 1973. pap. 17.00x (ISBN 0-8137-2143-1). Geol Soc.
Weaver, Charles E. Eocene & Paleocene Deposits at Martinez, California. LC 53-9284. (Publications in Geology: No. 7). (Illus.). 102p. 1953. pap. 10.00 (ISBN 0-295-73772-7). U of Wash Pr.
--Geology of Cretaceous (Gualala Group) & Teritiary Formations along the Pacific Coast between Point Arena & Fort Ross, California. LC 44-5269. (Publications in Geology: No. 6). (Illus.). 1944. pap. 7.50 (ISBN 0-295-73795-6). U of Wash Pr.
Weiss, M. P., et al. American Upper Ordovician Standard, Vol. VII: The Stratigraphy & Petrology of the Cynthiana & Eden Formations of the Ohio Valley. LC 65-19022. (Special Paper: No. 81). (Orig.). 1965. pap. 4.00x (ISBN 0-8137-2081-8). Geol Soc.
White, George W. Essays on History of Geology: An Original Anthology. Albritton, Claude C., Jr., ed. LC 77-6547. (History of Geology Ser.). (Illus.). 1978. lib. bdg. 30.00 (ISBN 0-405-10464-2). Arno.
Wiese, B. R. & White, W. A. Padre Island National Seashore-a Guide to the Geology, Natural Environments, & History of a Texas Barrier Island. 94p. 1981. 4.00 (ISBN 0-686-31762-9, GB 17). Bur Econ Geology.
Winters, Stephen S. Supai Formation (Permian) of Eastern Arizona. LC 63-20183. (Memoir: No. 89). (Illus.). 1963. 8.50x (ISBN 0-8137-1089-8). Geol Soc.
Winton, W. M. & Adkins, W. S. The Geology of Tarrant County. (Illus.). 122p. 1919. 0.50 (ISBN 0-686-29342-8, BULL 1931). Bur Econ Geology.
Wolfe, P. E. The Geology & Landscapes of New Jersey. LC 77-73871. (Illus.). 1977. 22.50x (ISBN 0-8448-1101-7). Crane-Russak Co.
Woodburne, Michael O. Cenozoic Stratigraphy of the Transverse Ranges & Adjacent Areas, Southern California. LC 75-2953. (Special Paper: No. 162). (Illus.). 1975. pap. 11.00x (ISBN 0-8137-2162-8). Geol Soc.
Wright, H. E., et al. Geology of the Cloquet Quadrangle, Carlton County, Minnesota. LC 71-653807. (Geologic Map Ser: No. 3). (Illus.). 1970. pap. text ed. 2.50x (ISBN 0-8166-0590-4). Minn Geol Survey.
Wright, Herbert E. & Frey, D. G., eds. The Quaternary of the United States. (Illus.). 1965. 55.00x (ISBN 0-691-08021-6). Princeton U Pr.
Young, Keith. Texas Mojsisovicziinae (Ammonoidea) & the Zonation of the Fredericksburg. LC 66-27014. (Memoir: No. 100). (Illus.). 1966. 8.75x (ISBN 0-8137-1100-2). Geol Soc.
Zen, E-An. The Taconide Zone & the Taconic Orogeny of the Western Part of the Northern Appalachian Orogen. LC 70-184513. (Special Paper: No. 135). (Illus.). vii, 72p. (Orig.). 1972. pap. 6.00x (ISBN 0-8137-2135-0). Geol Soc.
--Time & Space Relationships of the Taconic Allochthon & Autochthon. LC 67-24203. (Special Paper: No. 97). (Illus.). 1967. pap. 7.50x (ISBN 0-8137-2097-4). Geol Soc.

GEOLOGY, CHEMICAL

see Geochemistry; Mineralogical Chemistry; Mineralogy, Determinative; Rocks–Analysis

GEOLOGY, DYNAMIC

see Geodynamics

GEOLOGY, ECONOMIC

see also Coal; Engineering Geology; Gas, Natural; Mineral Oils; Mines and Mineral Resources; Mining Geology; Ores; Petroleum; Petroleum–Geology; Quarries and Quarrying; Soils; also other geological products, e.g. Asbesto-Graphite, Quartz

Bates, Robert L. Geology of the Industrial Rocks & Minerals. LC 69-15364. (Illus.). 1969. pap. 5.50 (ISBN 0-486-62213-4). Dover.
Baumann, Ludwig. Introduction to Ore Deposits. LC 74-26527. 163p. 1976. 21.95 (ISBN 0-470-05937-0). Halsted Pr.
Bischoff & Piper, eds. Marine Geology & Oceanography of the Pacific Manganese Nodule Province. (Marine Science Ser.: Vol. 9). 1979. 49.50 (ISBN 0-306-40187-8, Plenum Pr). Plenum Pub.
Butt, C. R. & Wilding, I. G., eds. Geochemical Exploration 1976. (Developments in Economic Geology). 1977. 50.75 (ISBN 0-444-41653-6). Elsevier.
Geochemical Exploration 1974: Proceedings. Elliot, I. & Fletcher, N. K., eds. LC 74-21855. (Developmens in Economic Geology Ser: Vol. 1). 720p. 1975. 95.25 (ISBN 0-444-41280-8). Elsevier.
Given, P. H. & Cohen, A. D. Interdisciplinary Studies of Peat & Coal Origins. LC 77-71662. (Microform Publication: No. 7). (Illus.). 1977. 4.00x (ISBN 0-8137-6007-0). Geol Soc.
Kesler, S. E. Our Finite Resources. 1975. 5.95 (ISBN 0-07-034245-8, C). McGraw.
Knill, J. L., ed. Industrial Geology. (Illus.). 1979. 29.95x (ISBN 0-19-854520-7). Oxford U Pr.
Riley, Charles M. Our Mineral Resources: An Elementary Textbook in Economic Geology. 4th ed. LC 76-57669. (Illus.). 348p. 1977. Repr. of 1967 ed. lib. bdg. 15.00 (ISBN 0-88275-530-7). Krieger.
Tarling, D. H. Economic Geology & Geotectonics. LC 81-673. 213p. 1981. 54.95 (ISBN 0-470-27145-0). Halsted Pr.

GEOLOGY, HISTORICAL

see Geology, Stratigraphic; Paleontology

GEOLOGY, LUNAR

see Lunar Geology

GEOLOGY, STRATIGRAPHIC

see also Borings; Flysch; Glacial Epoch; Oil Well Logging; Paleontology; Paleontology, Stratigraphic

Ager, D. V. Nature of the Stratigraphical Record. 2nd ed. LC 80-22559. 136p. 1981. 17.95 (ISBN 0-470-27052-7). Halsted Pr.
Bandy, Orville L., ed. Radiometric Dating & Paleontologic Zonation. LC 78-98015. (Special Paper: No. 124). (Illus., Orig.). 1970. pap. 7.75x (ISBN 0-8137-2124-5). Geol Soc.
Berry, W. B., et al, eds. Correlation of the Southeast Asian & Near Eastern Silurian Rocks. LC 72-82611. (Special Paper: No. 137). (Illus.). 66p. (Orig.). 1972. pap. 6.00x (ISBN 0-8137-2137-7). Geol Soc.
Brinkman, Roland. Geologic Evolution of Europe. 2nd rev. ed. Sanders, John E., tr. (Illus.). 1969. 15.25 (ISBN 0-02-841940-5). Hafner.
Brown, D. S. W., et al. The Geological Evolution of Australia & New Zealand. 1968. 26.00 (ISBN 0-08-012278-7); pap. 14.50 (ISBN 0-08-012277-9). Pergamon.
Dessalines, Charles V. Cours Elementaire de Paleontologie et de Geologie Stratigraphiques: Beginning Course in Paleontology & Stratigraphic Geology, 2 vols. in three. Gould, Stephen J., ed. LC 79-8339. (The History of Paleontology Ser.). (Illus., Fr.). 1980. Repr. of 1849 ed. Set. lib. bdg. 85.00x (ISBN 0-405-12725-1). Vol. 1 (ISBN 0-405-12726-X). Vol. 2 (ISBN 0-405-12727-8). Arno.
Douglas, Ian. Humid Landforms. (Illus.). 1977. text ed. 16.00x (ISBN 0-262-04054-9). Mit Pr.
Dunbar, Carl O. & Waage, Karl M. Historical Geology. 3rd ed. LC 72-89681. (Illus.). 1969. text ed. 25.95 (ISBN 0-471-22507-X). Wiley.
Englund, Kenneth J., et al. Proposed Pennsylvanian System Stratotype. West Virginia & Virginia. LC 78-74893. (AGI Selected Guidebook Ser.: No. 1). 1979. pap. 20.00 (ISBN 0-913312-08-8). Am Geol.
Gentile, Richard J. Influence of Structural Movement on Sedimentation During the Pennsylvania Period in Western Missouri. LC 74-4528. 1968. 4.50 (ISBN 0-8262-7619-9). U of Mo Pr.
Gondwana Stratigraphy. (Earth Sciences Ser., No. 2). (Illus., Orig.). 1969. pap. 28.25 (ISBN 92-3-000770-6, U267, UNESCO). Unipub.
Hallam, A. Facies Interpretation & the Stratigraphic Record. LC 80-24276. (Illus.). 1981. text ed. 27.95x (ISBN 0-7167-1291-1). W H Freeman.
Heirtzler, J. R., ed. Indian Ocean Geology & Biostratigraphy. LC 77-88320. (Special Publication Ser.). 1978. 19.00 (ISBN 0-87590-208-1, SP0019). Am Geophysical.
Huber, G. C. & Raese, Jon W. Stratigraphy & Uranium Deposits, Lisbon Valley District, San Juan County, Utah. (CSM Quarterly Ser.: Vol. 75, No. 2). (Illus.). 100p. (Orig.). 1980. pap. 10.00x (ISBN 0-686-63163-3). Colo Sch Mines.
International Subcommission on Stratigraphic Classification. International Stratigraphic Guide: A Guide to Stratigraphic Classification, Terminology, & Procedure. LC 75-33086. 1976. 15.50 (ISBN 0-471-36743-5, Pub. by Wiley-Interscience). Wiley.
Kay, Marshall & Colbert, E. H., eds. Stratigraphy & Life History. LC 64-20072. 736p. 1965. 27.50 (ISBN 0-471-46105-9). Wiley.
Keller, Fred, et al. Introduction to Historical Geology. (Illus.). 1979. lab manual 6.95x (ISBN 0-89459-040-5). Hunter NC.
Klemm, D. D. & Schneider, H. J., eds. Time- & Strata- Bound Ore Deposits. (Illus.). 1978. 49.70 (ISBN 0-387-08502-5). Springer-Verlag.
Krumbein, William C. & Sloss, L. L. Stratigraphy & Sedimentation. 2nd ed. LC 61-11422. 1963. 27.95x (ISBN 0-7167-0219-3). W H Freeman.
Langway, Chester C., Jr. Stratigraphic Analysis of a Deep Ice Core from Greenland. LC 75-111434. (Special Paper: No. 125). (Illus., Orig.). 1970. pap. 7.25x (ISBN 0-8137-2125-3). Geol Soc.
Levorsen, Arville I. Stratigraphic Type Oil Fields, 2 vols. 1976. lib. bdg. 250.00 (ISBN 0-8490-2694-6). Gordon Pr.
Lind, Aulis O. Coastal Landforms of Cat Island, Bahamas: A Study of Holocene Accretionary Topography & Sea Level Change. LC 76-77892. (Research Papers Ser.: No. 122). 156p. 1969. pap. 8.00 (ISBN 0-89065-029-2). U Chicago Dept Geog.
Matter, Albert & Tucker, Maurice E., eds. Modern & Ancient Lake Sediments. (International Association of Sedimentologists & the Societas Internationalis Limnologiae Symposium Proceding Ser.). 290p. 1979. 38.95 (ISBN 0-470-26571-X). Halsted Pr.
Matthews, Robley K. Dynamic Stratigraphy: An Introduction to Sedimentation & Stratigraphy. 1974. 22.95 (ISBN 0-13-222273-6). P-H.
Merriam, D. F., ed. Computer Assisted Instruction in Geology: Proceedings of the 4th Geochautauqua, Syracuse University, 1975. 1976. pap. text ed. 41.25 (ISBN 0-08-021040-6). Pergamon.
--Quantitative Stratigraphic Correlation: Proceedings of the 6th Geochautauqua, Syracuse University, October 1977. (Illus.). 112p. 1979. pap. 41.25 (ISBN 0-08-023979-X). Pergamon.
Middlemiss, F. A. British Stratigraphy. (Introducing Geology Ser.). 1975. pap. text ed. 5.95x (ISBN 0-04-550023-1). Allen Unwin.
Miller, Hugh. The Old Red Sandstone, or New Walks in an Old Field. Albritton, Claude C., Jr., ed. LC 77-6531. (History of Geology Ser.). (Illus.). 1978. Repr. of 1851 ed. lib. bdg. 25.00x (ISBN 0-405-10451-0). Arno.
Page, Lincoln R., ed. Contributions to the Stratigraphy of New England. LC 76-9220. (Memoir: No. 148). (Illus.). 1976. 30.00x (ISBN 0-8137-1148-7). Geol Soc.
Pearson, Ronald. Climate & Evolution. 1979. 41.00 (ISBN 0-12-548250-7). Acad Pr.
Poort, Jon M. Historical Geology: Interpretations & Applications. 3rd ed. 1980. pap. text ed. 10.95x (ISBN 0-8087-3303-6). Burgess.
Purser, B. H., ed. The Persian Gulf. LC 72-97023. (Illus.). viii, 471p. 1973. 35.00 (ISBN 0-387-06156-8). Springer-Verlag.
Quarternary Stratigraphy Symposium, 1975. Quarternary Stratigraphy of North America: Proceedings. Mahaney, W. C., ed. 1976. 54.00 (ISBN 0-12-787045-8). Acad Pr.
Rayner, D. Stratigraphy of the British Isles. 2nd ed. LC 79-8523. (Illus.). 400p. Date not set. 59.50 (ISBN 0-521-23452-2); pap. price not set (ISBN 0-521-29961-6). Cambridge U Pr.

Saito, Tsunemasa & Burckle, Lloyd H., eds. Late Neogene Epoch Boundaries. (Special Publications Ser.: No. 1). 1975. 25.00 (ISBN 0-913424-07-2). Am Mus Natl Hist.
Stratigraphic Correlation Between Sedimentary Basins of the ESCAP Region: Vol. VII, Atlas of Stratigraphy II. (Mineral Resources Development Ser.: No. 46). 108p. 1980. pap. 9.00 (ISBN 0-686-72369-4, UN80/2F2, UN). Unipub.
Swain, F. M., ed. Stratigraphic Micropaleontology of Atlantic Basin & Borderlands. (Developments in Paleontology & Stratigraphy). 1977. 66.00 (ISBN 0-444-41554-8). Elsevier.
Sweet, Walter C. & Bergstrom, Stig M., eds. Symposium on Conodont Biostratigraphy. LC 79-111443. (Memoir: No. 127). (Illus.). 1970. 19.50x (ISBN 0-8137-1127-4). Geol Soc.
Van Houten, Franklyn B., ed. Ancient Continental Deposits. (Bench Mark Papers in Geology Ser.). 1977. 44.50 (ISBN 0-12-787650-2). Acad Pr.
Van Landingham, S. L. Paleoecology & Microfloristics of Miocene Diatomites from the Otis Basin-Juntura Region of Harney & Malheur Counties, Oregon. (Illus.). 1967. pap. 20.00 (ISBN 3-7682-5426-7). Lubrecht & Cramer.
Wolf, K. H., ed. Handbook of Strata-Bound & Stratiform Ore Deposits, Vols. 1-4. Incl. Vol. 1. Classifications & Historical Studies (ISBN 0-444-41401-0); Vol. 2. Geochemical Studies (ISBN 0-444-41402-9); Vol. 3. Supergene & Surficial Ore Deposits: Textures & Fabrics (ISBN 0-444-41403-7); Vol. 4. Tectonics & Metamorphism (ISBN 0-444-41404-5). 1976. 444.00 (ISBN 0-686-57861-9); Vols. 1-4. 241.50 (ISBN 0-685-74759-X); 66.00 ea. Elsevier.

GEOLOGY, STRATIGRAPHIC–ARCHAEAN

McCall, G. J., ed. The Archean: Search for the Beginning. LC 76-11015. 1977. 59.00 (ISBN 0-12-787025-3). Acad Pr.

GEOLOGY, STRATIGRAPHIC–CALEDONIAN

see Geology, Stratigraphic–Paleozoic

GEOLOGY, STRATIGRAPHIC–CAMBRIAN

Cook, P. J. & Shergold, J. H., eds. Proterozoic-Cambrian Phosphorites. 1979. pap. text ed. 8.95 (ISBN 0-7081-1159-9, 0522, Pub. by ANUP Australia). Bks Australia.
Vugrinovich, R. G. Precambrian Geochronology of North America: An Annotated Bibliography,1951-1977. LC 80-68063. (Microform Publication: No. 11). 1980. 4.00x (ISBN 0-8137-6011-9). Geol Soc.

GEOLOGY, STRATIGRAPHIC–CARBONIFEROUS

see also Geology, Stratigraphic–Mississippian

Beus, Stanley S. & Rawson, Richard R., eds. Carboniferous Stratigraphy in the Grand Canyon Country, Northern Arizona & Southern Nevada. LC 78-74894. (AGI Selected Guidebook Ser.: No. 2). 1979. pap. 20.00 (ISBN 0-913312-09-6). Am Geol.
Cameron, Barry, ed. Carboniferous Basins of Southeastern New England. LC 79-51602. 1979. pap. 10.00 (ISBN 0-913312-14-2). Am Geol.
Dutro, J. Thomas, Jr., ed. Carboniferous of the Northern Rocky Mountains. LC 78-74895. (AGI Selected Guidebook Ser.: No. 3). 1979. pap. 12.00 (ISBN 0-913312-10-X). Am Geol.
Muir-Wood, Helen M. Malayan Lower Carboniferous Fossils & Their Bearing on the Visean Palaeogeography of Asia. (Illus.). 118p. 1948. 12.50x (ISBN 0-565-00374-7, Pub. by Brit Mus Nat Hist England). Sabbot-Natural Hist Bks.

GEOLOGY, STRATIGRAPHIC–CENOZOIC

see also Geology, Stratigraphic–Quaternary; Geology, Stratigraphic–Tertiary

Armentrout, John M., ed. Pacific Northwest Cenozoic Biostratigraphy. LC 80-82937. (Special Paper: No. 184). (Illus., Orig.). 1981. pap. 25.00 (ISBN 0-8137-2184-9). Geol Soc.
Carnegie Institution Of Washington. Studies on Cenozoic Vertebrates of Western America. Repr. of 1938 ed. pap. 23.00 (ISBN 0-685-02176-9). Johnson Repr.
Curtis, Bruce M., ed. Cenozoic History of the Southern Rocky Mountains. LC 74-30892. (Memoir: No. 144). (Illus.). 1975. 25.00x (ISBN 0-8137-1144-4). Geol Soc.
Frost, Stanley H. & Langenheim, Ralph L., Jr. Cenozoic Reef Biofacies: Tertiary Larger Foraminifera & Scleractinian Corals from Chiapas, Mexico. LC 72-7513. (Illus.). 399p. 1975. 50.00 (ISBN 0-87580-027-0). N Ill U Pr.
Pomerol, C. Cenozoic Era. 280p. 1981. 74.95 (ISBN 0-470-27140-X). Halsted Pr.
Smith, Robert B. & Eaton, Gordon P., eds. Cenozoic Tectonics & Regional Geophysics of Western Cordillera. LC 78-55296. (Memoir Ser.: No. 152). (Illus.). 1978. 55.00x (ISBN 0-8137-1152-5). Geol Soc.
Turekian, Karl K., ed. Late Cenozoic Glacial Ages. LC 70-140540. (Silliman Lectures Ser). (Illus.). 1971. 42.50x (ISBN 0-300-01420-1). Yale U Pr.
Woodburne, Michael O. Cenozoic Stratigraphy of the Transverse Ranges & Adjacent Areas, Southern California. LC 75-2953. (Special Paper: No. 162). (Illus.). 1975. pap. 11.00x (ISBN 0-8137-2162-8). Geol Soc.

GEOLOGY, STRATIGRAPHIC–CRETACEOUS

Kauffman, Erle G., et al. Stratigraphic, Paleontologic, & Paleoenvironmental Analysis of the Upper Cretaceous Rocks of Cimarr County, Northwestern Oklahoma. LC 76-47800. (Memoir Ser.: No. 149). (Illus.). 1977. 19.00x (ISBN 0-8137-1149-5). Geol Soc.
Pessagno, Emile A., Jr. Radiolarian Zonation & Stratigraphy of the Upper Cretaceous Portion of the Great Valley Sequence, California Coast Ranges. LC 76-34621. (Special Publication Ser.: No. 2). 96p. 1976. pap. text ed. 20.00 (ISBN 0-913424-09-9). Am Mus Natl Hist.
--Upper Cretaceous Stratigraphy of the Western Gulf Coast Area of Mexico, Texas & Arkansas. LC 70-76285. (Memoir: No. 111). (Illus.). 1969. 12.00x (ISBN 0-8137-1111-8). Geol Soc.
Reyment, R. A. & Bengston, P., eds. Aspects of Mid-Cretaceous Regional Geology. 1981. 72.00 (ISBN 0-12-587040-X). Acad Pr.
Saul, LouElla. The North Pacific Cretaceous Trigoniid Genus Yaadia. (Publications in Geological Science Ser.: Vol. 119). 1978. pap. 12.00x (ISBN 0-520-09582-0). U of Cal Pr.

GEOLOGY, STRATIGRAPHIC–DEVONIAN

Heckel, Philip H. Nature, Origin, & Significance of the Tully Limestone. LC 72-82612. (Special Paper: No. 138). (Illus.). 160p. (Orig.). 1973. pap. 11.00x (ISBN 0-8137-2138-5). Geol Soc.
Matti, Jonathan C., et al. Silurian & Lower Devonian Basin & Basin-Slope Limestones, Copenhagen Canyon, Nevada. LC 74-19734. (Special Paper: No. 159). (Illus., Orig.). 1975. pap. 9.00x (ISBN 0-8137-2159-8). Geol Soc.
Wells, John W. Early Investigations of the Devonian System in New York, 1656-1836. LC 64-1862. (Special Paper: No. 74). (Illus., Orig.). 1963. pap. 5.00x (ISBN 0-8137-2074-5). Geol Soc.

GEOLOGY, STRATIGRAPHIC–EOCENE

Weaver, Charles E. Eocene & Paleocene Deposits at Martinez, California. LC 53-9284. (Publications in Geology: No. 7). (Illus.). 102p. 1953. pap. 10.00 (ISBN 0-295-73772-7). U of Wash Pr.

GEOLOGY, STRATIGRAPHIC–JURASSIC

Arkell, W. J. Jurassic System in Great Britain. (Illus.). 1970. 38.50x (ISBN 0-19-854371-9). Oxford U Pr.
Hallam, A. Jurassic Environments. LC 74-80359. (Earth Science Ser.). (Illus.). 260p. 1975. 47.50 (ISBN 0-521-20555-7). Cambridge U Pr.

GEOLOGY, STRATIGRAPHIC–MESOZOIC

see also Geology, Stratigraphic–Cretaceous; Geology, Stratigraphic–Jurassic; Geology, Stratigraphic–Triassic

Bjaerke, Tor & Manum, Svein B. Mesozoic Palynology of Svalbard. (Norsk Polarinstitutt Skrifter: No. 165). (Illus.). 1978. pap. 8.00x (ISBN 82-00-29719-5, Dist. by Columbia U Pr). Universitet.
Hayami, Itaru & Kase, Tomoki. Systematic Survey of the Paleozoic & Mesozoic Gastropoda & Paleozoic Bivalvia from Japan. 1978. 29.00x (ISBN 0-86008-198-2, Pub. by U of Tokyo Pr). Intl Schol Bk Serv.
Hsu, Kenneth J. Paleocenography of the Mesozoic Alpine-Tethys. LC 75-32124. (Special Paper: No. 170). (Illus., Orig.). 1976. pap. 7.00x (ISBN 0-8137-2170-9). Geol Soc.
Klein, George D., ed. Late Paleozoic & Mesozoic Continental Sedimentation: Northeastern North America. LC 68-8808. (Special Paper: No. 106). (Illus., Orig.). 1968. pap. 13.50x (ISBN 0-8137-2106-7). Geol Soc.
Moullade, M. & Nairn, A. E., eds. The Phanerozoic Geology of the World: The Mesozoic, Vol. II,pt. A. 1978. 88.00 (ISBN 0-444-41671-4). Elsevier.
Silberling, N. J. & Roberts, Ralph J. Pre-Tertiary Stratigraphy & Structure of Northwestern Nevada. LC 63-1926. (Special Paper: No. 72). (Illus., Orig.). 1962. pap. 3.00x (ISBN 0-8137-2072-9). Geol Soc.

GEOLOGY, STRATIGRAPHIC–MISSISSIPPIAN

Griffin, James B. The Fort & Ancient Aspect. (Anthropological Papers: No. 28). (Illus.). 1966. pap. 6.00x (ISBN 0-932206-28-X). U Mich Mus Anthro.

GEOLOGY, STRATIGRAPHIC–ORDOVICIAN

Fortey, R. A. The Ordovician Trilobites of Spitsbergen I. Olenidae. (Norsk Polarinstitutt Ser: No. 162). 1974. 16.00x (ISBN 8-200-29180-4, Dist. by Columbia U Pr). Universitet.
Hatfield, Craig B. Stratigraphy & Paleoecology of the Saluda Formation (Cincinnatian) in Indiana, Ohio & Kentucky. LC 68-23102. (Special Paper: No. 95). (Illus., Orig.). 1968. pap. 2.50x (ISBN 0-8137-2095-8). Geol Soc.
Palaeontological Association Symposium, Birmingham, Sept. 1974. The Ordovician System: Proceedings. Bassett, M. G., ed. 1976. pap. text ed. 60.00x (ISBN 0-7083-0582-2). Verry.
Weiss, M. P., et al. American Upper Ordovician Standard, Vol. VII: The Stratigraphy & Petrology of the Cynthiana & Eden Formations of the Ohio Valley. LC 65-19022. (Special Paper: No. 81). (Orig.). 1965. pap. 4.00x (ISBN 0-8137-2081-8). Geol Soc.

GEOLOGY, STRATIGRAPHIC–PALEOCENE

Weaver, Charles E. Eocene & Paleocene Deposits at Martinez, California. LC 53-9284. (Publications in Geology: No. 7). (Illus.). 102p. 1953. pap. 10.00 (ISBN 0-295-73772-7). U of Wash Pr.

GEOLOGY, STRATIGRAPHIC–PALEOZOIC

see also Geology, Stratigraphic–Cambrian; Geology, Stratigraphic–Carboniferous; Geology, Stratigraphic–Devonian; Geology, Stratigraphic–Ordovician; Geology, Stratigraphic–Permian; Geology, Stratigraphic–Silurian

Campbell, John B. The Upper Palaeolithic of Britain: A Study of Man & Nature in the Late Ice Age, Vols. I & II. (Illus.). 1978. 79.00 set (ISBN 0-19-813188-7). Oxford U Pr.
Clifford, Tom N. Damaran Episode in the Upper Proterozoic-Lower Paleozoic Structural History of Southern Africa. LC 67-16337. (Special Paper: No. 92). (Illus., Orig.). 1967. pap. 6.00x (ISBN 0-8137-2092-3). Geol Soc.
Holland, C. H. Lower Palaeozoic Rocks of the World: With Essays on Lower Palaeozoic Rocks of the World. LC 80-41688. (Electrochemical Data Ser.). 1981. price not set (ISBN 0-471-27945-5, Pub. by Wiley-Interscience). Wiley.
Klein, George D., ed. Late Paleozoic & Mesozoic Continental Sedimentation: Northeastern North America. LC 68-8808. (Special Paper: No. 106). (Illus., Orig.). 1968. pap. 13.50x (ISBN 0-8137-2106-7). Geol Soc.
McBride, Earle F. & Thomson, Alan. Caballos Novaculite, Marathon Region, Texas. LC 74-98014. (Special Paper: No. 122). (Illus., Orig.). 1970. pap. 5.75x (ISBN 0-8137-2122-9). Geol Soc.
Owen, T. R., ed. Upper Palaeozoic & Post-Palaeozoic Rocks of Wales. 373p. 1974. text ed. 37.50x (ISBN 0-7083-0555-5). Verry.
Silberling, N. J. & Roberts, Ralph J. Pre-Tertiary Stratigraphy & Structure of Northwestern Nevada. LC 63-1926. (Special Paper: No. 72). (Illus., Orig.). 1962. pap. 3.00x (ISBN 0-8137-2072-9). Geol Soc.
Webster, G. D. Bibliography & Index of Paleozoic Crinoids, Nineteen Sixty-Nine to Nineteen Seventy-Three. LC 77-76475. (Microform Publication: No. 8). 1977. 4.50x (ISBN 0-8137-6008-9). Geol Soc.
Wood, Alan, ed. Pre-Cambrian & Lower Palaeozoic Rocks of Wales: Symposium Report from the Univ. College of Wales. 1969. 22.50x (ISBN 0-900768-12-6). Verry.
Zen, E-An. The Taconide Zone & the Taconic Orogeny of the Western Part of the Northern Appalachian Orogen. LC 70-184513. (Special Paper: No. 135). (Illus.). vii, 72p. (Orig.). 1972. pap. 6.00x (ISBN 0-8137-2135-0). Geol Soc.
Zharkov, M. A. History of Paleozoic Salt Accumulation. (Illus.). 308p. 1981. 39.50 (ISBN 0-387-10614-6). Springer-Verlag.

GEOLOGY, STRATIGRAPHIC–PERMIAN

Falke, Horst, ed. The Continental Permian in West, Central, & South Europe. (Nato Mathematical & Physical Sciences Ser.: No. 22). 1976. lib. bdg. 53.00 (ISBN 90-277-0664-6, Pub. by Reidel Holland). Kluwer Boston.

GEOLOGY, STRATIGRAPHIC–PLEISTOCENE

Baker, Frank C. Life of the Pleistocene or Glacial Period. LC 74-80996. (BCL Ser. I). 1969. Repr. of 1920 ed. 37.50 (ISBN 0-404-00449-0). AMS Pr.
Black, R. F., et al, eds. The Wisconsinan Stage. LC 72-89466. (Memoir: No. 136). (Illus.). 224p. 1973. 20.25x (ISBN 0-8137-1136-3). Geol Soc.
Butzer, Karl. Environment & Archeology: An Ecological Approach to Prehistory. 2nd ed. LC 74-115938. (Illus.). 1971. 29.95x (ISBN 0-202-33023-0). Aldine Pub.
Butzer, Karl W. & Isaac, Glynn Ll., eds. After the Australopithecines: Stratigraphy, Ecology, & Culture Change in the Middle Pleistocene. (World Anthropology Ser.). 984p. 1975. 67.50 (ISBN 0-202-90002-9). Beresford Bk Serv.
Carnegie Institution Of Washington. Papers Concerning the Palaeontology of the Pleistocene of California & the Tertiary of Oregon. Repr. of 1925 ed. pap. 15.50 (ISBN 0-685-02123-8). Johnson Repr.
--Studies of the Pleistocene Palaeobotany of California. Repr. of 1934 ed. pap. 23.00 (ISBN 0-685-02051-7). Johnson Repr.
Carter, George F. Pleistocene Man at San Diego. LC 77-74811. Repr. of 1957 ed. 37.00 (ISBN 0-404-14885-9). AMS Pr.
Coleman, Arthur P. The Last Million Years: A History of the Pleistocene in North America. LC 75-41062. (BCL Ser.: Ii). Repr. of 1941 ed. 21.50 (ISBN 0-404-14656-2). AMS Pr.
Daly, Reginald A. The Changing World of the Ice Age. 1963. Repr. of 1934 ed. 21.75 (ISBN 0-02-843500-1). Hafner.
Gray, J. M. & Lowe, J. J., eds. Studies in the Scottish Lateglacial Environment. 1977. text ed. 30.00 (ISBN 0-08-020498-8). Pergamon.
Hume, Gary W. The Ladizian: An Industry of the Asian Chopper-Chopping Tool Complex in Iranian Baluchistan. (Illus.). 355p. 1976. 12.00 (ISBN 0-8059-2091-9). Dorrance.
Movius, Hallam L. Early Man & Pleistocene Stratigraphy in Southern & Eastern Asia. (Illus.). 1944. pap. 14.00 (ISBN 0-527-01249-1). Kraus Repr.
Reynolds, S. H. The Pleistocene Mustelidae. Repr. of 1912 ed. pap. 13.00 (ISBN 0-384-50426-4). Johnson Repr.
Sandford, Kenneth S. & Arkell, W. J. Paleolithic Man & the Nile-Faiyum Divide, Vol. 1. LC 30-8240. (Illus.). 1930. 20.00 (ISBN 0-226-62104-9, OIP10). U of Chicago Pr.
Schneider, Allan F. Pleistocene Geology of the Randall Region, Central Minnesota. LC 61-63788. (Bulletin: No. 40). 1961. 4.25x (ISBN 0-8166-0244-1). Minn Geol Survey.
Schultz, Gerald E. Geology & Paleontology of a Late Pleistocene Basin in Southwest Kansas. LC 68-8133. (Special Paper: No. 105). (Illus., Orig.). 1969. pap. 4.00x (ISBN 0-8137-2105-9). Geol Soc.
Vigdorchik, Michael & Ives, Jack. Arctic Pleistocene History & the Development of Submarine Permafrost. LC 79-13561. (Westview Special Studies in Earth Science). 286p. 1980. lib. bdg. 38.75x (ISBN 0-89158-658-X). Westview.
West, R. G. Pleistocene Geology & Biology. 2nd ed. LC 76-28353. (Illus.). 1977. pap. text ed. 18.95x (ISBN 0-582-44620-1). Longman.
Williams, Howell & Curtis, G. H. The Sutter Buttes of California: A Study of Plio-Pleistocene Volcanism. (Library Reprint Ser.: No. 97). 1979. Repr. of 1977 ed. 12.95x (ISBN 0-520-03808-8). U of Cal Pr.

GEOLOGY, STRATIGRAPHIC–PLIOCENE

Sandford, Kenneth S. & Arkell, W. J. Paleolithic Man & the Nile-Faiyum Divide, Vol. 1. LC 30-8240. (Illus.). 1930. 20.00 (ISBN 0-226-62104-9, OIP10). U of Chicago Pr.

GEOLOGY, STRATIGRAPHIC–PRE-CAMBRIAN

see also Geology, Stratigraphic–Archaean

Bickford, M. E. & Mose, D. G. Geochronology of Precambrian Rocks in the St. Francois Mountains. LC 75-25345. (Special Paper: No. 165). (Illus.). 1975. pap. 7.00x (ISBN 0-8137-2165-2). Geol Soc.
Doe, Bruce R. & Smith, D. K., eds. Studies in Mineralogy & Precambrian Geology: A Volume in Honor of John W. Gruner. LC 70-190173. (Memoir: No. 135). (Illus.). viii, 304p. 1972. 22.25x (ISBN 0-8137-1135-5). Geol Soc.
French, Bevan M. Progressive Contact Metamorphism of the Biwabik Iron-Formation, Mesabi Range, Minnesota. LC 68-66592. (Bulletin: No. 45). (Illus.). 1968. 4.50x (ISBN 0-8166-0478-9). Minn Geol Survey.
Genesis of Precambrian Iron & Manganese Deposits. LC 73-79858. (Earth Sciences Ser., No. 9). (Illus.). 382p. (Orig.). 1973. 48.50 (ISBN 92-3-001108-8, U261, UNESCO). Unipub.
Gill, James E. The Proterozoic in Canada. LC 58-21139. (Illus.). x, 191p. 1957. 17.50x (ISBN 0-8020-7015-9). U of Toronto Pr.
Goldich, Samuel S., et al. Precambrian Geology & Geochronology of Minnesota. LC 61-8016. (Bulletin: No. 41). (Illus.). 1961. 4.00x (ISBN 0-8166-0224-7). Minn Geol Survey.
Gundersen, James N. & Schwartz, George M. Geology of the Metamorphosed Biwabik Iron Formation, Eastern Mesabi District, Minnesota. LC 62-9302. (Bulletin: No. 43). 1962. 4.25x (ISBN 0-8166-0274-3). Minn Geol Survey.
Killeen, P. G. & Heier, K. S. Radioelement Distribution & Heat Production in Precambrian Granitic Rocks, Southern Norway. 1975. pap. 11.00x (ISBN 8-200-01463-0, Dist. by Columbia U Pr). Universitet.
Reid, Rolland R., et al. Precambrian Geology of North Snowy Block, Beartooth Mountains, Montana. LC 74-28529. (Special Paper: No. 157). (Illus.). 1975. pap. 16.00x (ISBN 0-8137-2157-1). Geol Soc.
Salop, L. J. Precambrian of the Northern Hemisphere. (Developments in Paleontology & Stratigraphy: Vol. 3). 1977. 75.75 (ISBN 0-444-41510-6). Elsevier.
Vidal, Gonzalo. Late Precambrian Microfossils from the Visingso Beds in Southern Sweden. (Fossils & Strata: No.9). 1976. pap. text ed. 18.00x (ISBN 8-200-09418-9, Dist. by Columbia U Pr). Universitet.

Wood, Alan, ed. Pre-Cambrian & Lower Palaeozoic Rocks of Wales: Symposium Report from the Univ. College of Wales. 1969. 22.50x (ISBN 0-900768-12-6). Verry.

GEOLOGY, STRATIGRAPHIC–QUATERNARY

see also Geology, Stratigraphic–Pleistocene

Al-Sayari, S. S. & Zoetl, J. G., eds. Quaternary Period in Saudi Arabia One. (Illus.). 1978. 56.70 (ISBN 0-387-81448-5). Springer-Verlag.

Bowen, D. Q. Quaternary Geology. (Illus.). 224p. 1978. 45.00 (ISBN 0-08-020601-8); pap. 14.00 (ISBN 0-08-020409-0). Pergamon.

Butzer, Karl W. Quarternary Stratigraphy & Climate in the Near East. 1958. pap. 15.50 (ISBN 0-384-06790-5). Johnson Repr.

Cline, R. M. & Hays, J. D., eds. Investigation of Late Quaternary Paleoceanography & Paleoclimatology. LC 75-40899. (Memoir: No. 145). (Illus.). 1976. 30.00x (ISBN 0-8137-1145-2). Geol Soc.

Delaney, Patrick J. Quaternary Geologic History of the Coastal Plain of Rio Grande Do Sul, Brazil. LC 63-22269. (Coastal Studies: Vol. 7). (Illus.). 1964. pap. 4.00x (ISBN 0-8071-0429-9). La State U Pr.

Enos, Paul & Perkins, R. D. Quaternary Sedimentation in South Florida. LC 76-44123. (Memoir: No. 147). (Illus.). 1977. 34.00x (ISBN 0-8137-1147-9). Geol Soc.

Flint, Richard F. Glacial & Quaternary Geology. LC 74-141198. (Illus.). 1971. 38.50 (ISBN 0-471-26435-0). Wiley.

Goudie, Andrew. Environmental Change. (Contemporary Problems in Geography Ser.). (Illus.). 1977. 29.95x (ISBN 0-19-874073-5); pap. 9.50x (ISBN 0-19-874074-3). Oxford U Pr.

Hanihara, Kazuro & Sakaguchi, Yutaka, eds. Paleolithic Site of the Douara Cave & Paleography of Palmyra Basin in Syria, Pt. 1: Stratigraphy & Paleogeography in the Late Quarternary. 1978. 31.00x (ISBN 0-86008-209-1, Pub. by U of Tokyo Pr). Intl Schol Bk Serv.

Hulten, E. Outline of the History of the Arctic & Boreal Biota During the Quaternary Period. (Illus.). 1972. Repr. of 1937 ed. 32.00 (ISBN 3-7682-0006-X). Lubrecht & Cramer.

Neale, J. & Flenley, J., eds. The Quaternary in Britain: Essays Reviews & Original Work on the Quarternary Published in Honour of Lewis Penny on His Retirement. (Illus.). 278p. 1981. 40.00 (ISBN 0-08-026254-6). Pergamon.

Quaternary Era, 2 vols. 80.00x (ISBN 0-312-65905-9). St Martin.

Ruhe, Robert V. Quaternary Landscapes in Iowa. facsimile ed. LC 69-14312. (Illus.). 1969. 10.65x (ISBN 0-8138-2440-0). Iowa St U Pr.

Schnable, Jon E. & Goodell, H. Grant. Pleistocene-Recent Stratigraphy, Evolution, & Development of the Apalachicola Coast, Florida. LC 68-26497. (Special Paper: No. 112). (Illus., Orig.). 1968. pap. 3.75x (ISBN 0-8137-2112-1). Geol Soc.

Schumm, Stanley A. & Bradley, William C., eds. United States Contributions to Quaternary Research. LC 71-90050. (Special Paper: No. 123). (Illus., Orig.). 1969. pap. 14.00x (ISBN 0-8137-2123-7). Geol Soc.

Shotton, F. W., ed. British Quaternary Studies: Recent Advances. (Illus.). 1977. 49.50x (ISBN 0-19-854414-6). Oxford U Pr.

Wright, H. E., Jr. & Frey, David G., eds. International Studies on the Quaternary. LC 65-27703. (Special Paper: No. 84). (Illus.). 1965. pap. 20.00x (ISBN 0-8137-2084-2). Geol Soc.

Wright, Herbert E. & Frey, D. G., eds. The Quaternary of the United States. (Illus.). 1965. 55.00x (ISBN 0-691-08021-6). Princeton U Pr.

Wynne-Edwards, Hugh R. Terracy: Reconciliation with the Earth. (Illus.). Date not set. text ed. 12.00x (ISBN 0-87735-031-0). Freeman C.

GEOLOGY, STRATIGRAPHIC–SILURIAN

Bassett, Michael G. & Cocks, Leonard R. A Review of Silvrian Brachiopods from Gotland. (Fossils & Strata Ser: No. 3). 1974. 10.50x (ISBN 8-200-09349-2, Dist. by Columbia U Pr). Universitet.

Berry, W. B. & Boucot, A. J. Correlation of the North American Silurian Rocks. LC 77-98012. (Special Paper: No. 102). (Illus., Orig.). 1970. pap. 15.00x (ISBN 0-8137-2102-4). Geol Soc.

Berry, W. B. & Boucot, A. J., eds. Correlation of the South American Silurian Rocks. LC 74-184514. (Special Paper: No. 133). (Illus.). xii, 60p. (Orig.). 1972. pap. 6.00x (ISBN 0-8137-2133-4). Geol Soc.

Berry, W. B., et al, eds. Correlation of the Southeast Asian & Near Eastern Silurian Rocks. LC 72-82611. (Special Paper: No. 137). (Illus.). 66p. (Orig.). 1972. pap. 6.00x (ISBN 0-8137-2137-7). Geol Soc.

Helfrich, Charles T. Silurian Conodonts from Wills Mountain Anticline, Virginia, West Virginia, & Maryland. LC 74-28984. (Special Paper: No. 161). (Illus., Orig.). 1975. pap. 12.50x (ISBN 0-8137-2161-X). Geol Soc.

Larsson, Kent. Silurian Tentaculitids from Gotland & Scania. (Fossils & Strata Ser.: No. 11). 1979. pap. 35.00x (ISBN 82-00-09483-9, Dist. by Columbia U Pr.). Universitet.

Laufeld, Sven. Silurian Chitinozoa from Gotland. (Fossils & Strata Ser: No. 5). 1974. pap. 25.00x (ISBN 8-200-09358-1, Dist. by Columbia U Pr). Universitet.

Matti, Jonathan C., et al. Silurian & Lower Devonian Basin & Basin-Slope Limestones, Copenhagen Canyon, Nevada. LC 74-19734. (Special Paper: No. 159). (Illus., Orig.). 1975. pap. 9.00x (ISBN 0-8137-2159-8). Geol Soc.

Talent, J. A., et al. Correlation of the Silurian Rocks of Australia. LC 74-75784. (Special Paper: No. 150). (Illus., Orig.). 1975. pap. 16.50x (ISBN 0-8137-2150-4). Geol Soc.

GEOLOGY, STRATIGRAPHIC–TERTIARY

see also Geology, Stratigraphic–Eocene; Geology, Stratigraphic–Paleocene; Geology, Stratigraphic–Pliocene

Oaks, Robert Q., Jr. & DuBar, Jules R., eds. Post-Miocene Stratigraphy Central & Southern Atlantic Coastal Plain. 275p. 1974. 13.00 (ISBN 0-87421-065-8). Utah St U Pr.

Paleopedology & Stratigraphy on the Condrusian Peneplain: Belguim. (Agricultural Research Reports Ser.: 766). 1972. pap. 9.00 (ISBN 90-220-0377-9, PUDOC). Unipub.

Weaver, Charles E. Tertiary Stratigraphy of Western Washington & Northwestern Oregon. (Publications in Geology: No. 4). 266p. 1937. pap. 12.50 (ISBN 0-295-73962-2). U of Wash Pr.

GEOLOGY, STRATIGRAPHIC–TRIASSIC

Nichols, K. M. & Silberling, N. J. Stratigraphy & Depositional History of the Star Peak Group (Triassic) Northwestern Nevada. LC 77-89753. (Special Paper: No. 178). (Illus.). 1977. pap. 7.75x (ISBN 0-8137-2178-4). Geol Soc.

GEOLOGY, STRUCTURAL

see also Faults (Geology); Folds (Geology); Geomorphology; Mountains; Plate Tectonics

American Society of Civil Engineers, compiled by. Terzaghi Lectures. 432p. 1974. pap. text ed. 25.00 (ISBN 0-87262-060-3). Am Soc Civil Eng.

Bailey, E. B. Tectonic Essays, Mainly Alpine. 1935. 39.50x (ISBN 0-19-854368-9). Oxford U Pr.

Belousov, V. V. Geotectonics. (Illus.). 330p. 1981. 29.80 (ISBN 0-387-09173-4). Springer-Verlag.

Bernard, Raymond. The Hollow Earth. (Illus.). 1976. pap. 3.95 (ISBN 0-8065-0546-X). Citadel Pr.

Berner, Robert A. Early Diagenesis: A Theoretical Approach. LC 80-7510. (Princeton Series in Geochemistry: No. 1). (Illus.). 256p. 1980. 25.00x (ISBN 0-691-08258-8); pap. 9.50 (ISBN 0-691-08260-X). Princeton U Pr.

Billings, Marland P. Structural Geology. 3rd ed. (Illus.). 1972. 26.95 (ISBN 0-13-853846-8). P-H.

Carreras, J., et al. Shear Zones in Rocks: Papers Presented at the International Conference Held at the University of Barcelona, May 1979. 200p. 1980. pap. 40.00 (ISBN 0-08-026244-9). Pergamon.

Cermak, V. & Rybach, L., eds. Terrestrial Heat Flow in Europe. (Illus.). 1979. 51.50 (ISBN 0-387-09440-7). Springer-Verlag.

Clark, Sydney P. Structure of the Earth. (Foundations of Earth Science Ser). 1971. pap. text ed. 8.95 (ISBN 0-13-854646-0). P-H.

De Jong, Kees A. & Scholten, Robert, eds. Gravity & Tectonics. LC 73-1580. (Illus.). 502p. 1973. 53.50 (ISBN 0-471-20305-X, Pub. by Wiley-Interscience). Wiley.

Delaney, Patrick J. Geology & Geomorphology of the Coastal Plain of Rio Grande Do Sul, Brazil & Northern Uruguay. LC 66-64637. (Coastal Studies: Vol. 15). (Illus.). 1966. pap. 4.00x (ISBN 0-8071-0428-0). La State U Pr.

Dennis, John G. Structural Geology. 532p. 1972. 29.50 (ISBN 0-8260-2615-X). Wiley.

De Sitter, Lamoraal U. Structural Geology. 2nd ed. (International Earth & Planetary Sciences Ser). 1964. text ed. 24.95 (ISBN 0-07-016573-4, C). McGraw.

Dorr, John A., Jr., et al. Deformation & Deposition Between a Foreland Uplift & an Impinging Thrust Belt: Hoback Basin Wyoming. LC 77-70022. (Special Papers: No. 177). (Illus.). 1977. pap. 10.00x (ISBN 0-8137-2177-6). Geol Soc.

Ernst, W. G., ed. The Geotectonic Development of California, Vol. 1. (Illus.). 720p. 1981. text ed. 33.95 (ISBN 0-13-353938-5). P-H.

Geddes, James D. Large Ground Movements & Structures. LC 78-19092. 1978. 71.95 (ISBN 0-470-26460-8). Halsted Pr.

Goguel, Jean. Tectonics. Thalmann, H. E., tr. LC 62-7477. (Geology Ser.). (Illus.). 1962. 29.95x (ISBN 0-7167-0217-7). W H Freeman.

Hills, E. S. Elements of Structural Geology. 2nd ed. (Illus.). 502p. 1972. pap. 19.95x (ISBN 0-412-20750-8, Pub. by Chapman & Hall England). Methuen Inc.

Hobbs, B. E., et al. An Outline of Structural Geology. LC 75-20393. 512p. 1976. text ed. 25.95 (ISBN 0-471-40156-0). Wiley.

Johnson, Helgi & Smith, Bennett L., eds. The Megatectonics of Continents & Oceans. LC 69-13555. 1970. 20.00x (ISBN 0-8135-0625-5). Rutgers U Pr.

Jones, Michael. Finland, Daughter of the Sea. (Studies in Historical Geography). (Illus.). 1977. 19.50 (ISBN 0-208-01623-6, Archon). Shoe String.

King, Philip B. Tectonics of Middle North America: Middle North America East of the Cordilleran Systems. (Illus.). 1969. Repr. 17.50 (ISBN 0-02-847920-3). Hafner.

Lidiak, Edward D. & Zietz, Isidore. Interpretation of Aeromagnetic Anomalies Between Latitudes 37n & 38n in Eastern & Central United States. LC 76-12278. (Special Paper: No. 167). (Illus., Orig.). 1976. 8.75x (ISBN 0-8137-2167-9). Geol Soc.

Lobeck, A. K. Geomorphology. (Illus.). 1939. text ed. 23.50 (ISBN 0-07-038210-7, C). McGraw.

Lyons, Mark S. Interpretation of Planar Structure in Drill-Hole Core. LC 64-25035. (Special Paper: No. 78). (Illus.). 1964. pap. 5.50x (ISBN 0-8137-2078-8). Geol Soc.

Mainwaring, William L. Exploring Oregon's Central & Southern Cascades. LC 79-64841. (Illus.). 1979. pap. 7.95 (ISBN 0-918832-02-0). Westridge.

Neumann, Else-Ragnhild & Ramberg, Ivar B., eds. Petrology & Geochemistry of Continental Rifts. (Nato Advanced Study Institute Ser. C: No. 36). 1978. lib. bdg. 42.00 (ISBN 90-277-0866-5, Pub. by Reidel Holland). Kluwer Boston.

Platt, John & Challinor, John. Simple Geological Structures. 1974. pap. text ed. 4.95x (ISBN 0-04-550020-7). Allen Unwin.

Price, N. J. Fault & Joint Development in Brittle & Semi-Brittle Rock. 1966. 23.00 (ISBN 0-08-011275-7); pap. 10.75 (ISBN 0-08-011274-9). Pergamon.

Psuty, Norbert P. Geomorphology of Beach Ridges in Tabasco, Mexico. LC 67-63070. (Coastal Studies, Vol. 18). (Illus.). 1967. pap. 4.00x (ISBN 0-8071-0706-9). La State U Pr.

Ragan, Donal M. Structural Geology: An Introduction to Geometrical Techniques. 2nd ed. LC 73-3335. (Illus.). 288p. 1973. pap. text ed. 17.95 (ISBN 0-471-70481-4). Wiley.

Ramberg, Ivar B. & Neumann, Else-Ragnhild, eds. Tectonics & Geophysics of Continental Rifts. (NATO Advanced Study Institute Ser.: No. 37). 1978. lib. bdg. 42.00 (ISBN 90-277-0867-3, Pub. by Reidel Holland). Kluwer Boston.

Robertson, Eugene. The Nature of the Solid Earth. (International Ser. in the Earth & Planetary Sciences). (Illus.). 544p. 1971. text ed. 26.00 (ISBN 0-07-053165-X, C). McGraw.

Schweickert, Richard A. Shallow-Level Plutonic Complexes in the Eastern Sierra Nevada, California, & Their Tectonic Implications. LC 76-11570. (Special Paper: No. 176). (Illus.). 1976. pap. 7.50x (ISBN 0-8137-2176-8). Geol Soc.

Sheinmann, Yu. M. Tectonics & the Formation of Magmas. LC 70-136981. 173p. 1971. 30.00 (ISBN 0-306-10859-3, Consultants). Plenum Pub.

Sommerville, Paul. Dictionary of Geotechnics. 1981. text ed. price not set. Butterworth.

Spencer, Edgar W. Introduction to the Structure of the Earth. 2nd ed. 1977. text ed. 23.00 (ISBN 0-07-060197-6, C). McGraw.

Tarling, D. H. Economic Geology & Geotectonics. LC 81-673. 213p. 1981. 54.95 (ISBN 0-470-27145-0). Halsted Pr.

Tatsch, J. H. The Earth's Tectonosphere: Its Past Development & Present Behavior. 2nd ed. LC 74-78917. (Illus.). 468p. 1977. text ed. 30.00 (ISBN 0-912890-03-7). Tatsch.

Thornbury, William D. Principles of Geomorphology. 2nd ed. LC 68-8323. 594p. 1969. 28.95x (ISBN 0-471-86197-9). Wiley.

Turner, Francis J. & Weiss, Lionel. Structural Analysis of Metamorphic Tectonites. (International Series in the Earth & Planetary Sciences). 1963. text ed. 27.50 (ISBN 0-07-065574-X, C). McGraw.

Whitten, C. A., et al, eds. Recent Crustal Movement, 1977. (Developments in Geotectonics: Vol. 13). 1979. 78.00 (ISBN 0-444-41783-4). Elsevier.

GEOLOGY, SUBMARINE

see Submarine Geology

GEOLOGY AND RELIGION

see Religion and Science

GEOLOGY AS A PROFESSION

American Geological Institute. Geology: Science & Profession. 1976. pap. 1.00 (ISBN 0-913312-19-3). Am Geol.

Goldreich, Gloria & Goldreich, Esther. What Can She Be? A Geologist. LC 76-10316. (What Can She Be? Ser.). (Illus.). 48p. (gr. 1-5). 1976. 7.20 (ISBN 0-688-51767-6). Lothrop.

Snelgrove, Alfred K. Opportunities in Geology & Geological Engineering. LC 72-111531. (gr. 8 up). 1970. pap. 1.25 (ISBN 0-8442-6474-1). Natl Textbk.

GEOMAGNETISM

see Magnetism, Terrestrial

GEOMANCY

see also Divination

Bascom, William. Ifa Divination: Communication Between Gods & Men in West Africa. LC 69-10349. (Illus.). 604p. 1969. 35.00x (ISBN 0-253-32890-X). Ind U Pr.

Haines, Steven. Secrets of the Earth. (A Study of Geomancy). pap. cancelled (ISBN 0-915070-06-5). Leaves of Grass.

Jaulin, Robert. La Geomancie: Analyse Formelle. (Cahiers De L'homme, Nouvelle Ser.: No. 4). 1966. pap. 19.50x (ISBN 90-2796-063-1). Mouton.

Ouellette, Raymond. Psychic Magic. LC 74-78491. (Illus.). 343p. 1974. 12.95 (ISBN 0-936450-00-2). Aero Pr.

Pennick, Nigel. The Ancient Science of Geomancy: Man in Harmony with the Earth. (Illus.). 1979. 16.95 (ISBN 0-500-05032-5). Thames Hudson.

Skinner, Stephen. Terrestrial Astrology: Divination by Geomancy. (Illus.). 352p. 1980. 39.50 (ISBN 0-7100-0553-9). Routledge & Kegan.

Von Hartmann, Frank. The Techniques of Astrological Geomancy. (Illus.). 137p. 1981. 47.85 (ISBN 0-89920-019-2). Am Inst Psych.

GEOMETRICAL DRAWING

see also Design; Geometry, Descriptive; Graphic Methods; Mechanical Drawing; Perspective; Projection

Agarwal, D. D., et al. Geometrical Drawing. 1981. text ed. 10.50x (ISBN 0-7069-0802-3, Pub. by Vikas India). Advent NY.

Beard, Robert S. Patterns in Space. 1973. pap. text ed. 11.95 (ISBN 0-88488-015-X). Creative Pubns.

Bradley, Amos D. The Geometry of Repeating Design & Geometry of Design for High Schools. LC 72-176586. (Columbia University. Teachers College. Contributions to Education: No. 549). Repr. of 1933 ed. 17.50 (ISBN 0-404-55549-7). AMS Pr.

Critchlow, Keith. Order in Space: A Design Source Book. LC 73-120105. (Illus.). 1970. spiral bdg. 9.95 (ISBN 0-670-52830-7, Studio). Viking Pr.

Horemis, Spyros. Optical & Geometric Patterns & Designs. 1970. pap. 5.00 (ISBN 0-486-22214-4). Dover.

Hornung, Clarence P. Handbook of Designs & Devices. 2nd ed. (Illus.). 1946. pap. 3.50 (ISBN 0-486-20125-2). Dover.

Larcher, Jean. Geometrical Designs & Optical Art. LC 74-79464. (Pictorical Archive Ser.). (Illus.). 80p. 1974. 4.00 (ISBN 0-486-23100-3). Dover.

Lindgren, Harry. Recreational Problems in Geometric Dissections & How to Solve Them. Orig. Title: Geometric Dissections with Puzzles & Solutions. (Illus.). 184p. 1972. pap. 3.50 (ISBN 0-486-22878-9). Dover.

Macmahon, Horace. Stereogram Book of Contours. LC 74-188860. 32p. (gr. 1 up). 1972. pap. 3.00 plastic comb bdg. (ISBN 0-8331-1705-X). Hubbard Sci.

Madsen, David A. Geometric Dimensioning & Tolerancing. 128p. 1981. pap. 5.28 (ISBN 0-87006-231-X). Goodheart.

Slade, Richard. Geometrical Patterns. (Illus.). (gr. 4 up). 1970. 5.95 (ISBN 0-571-08793-0). Transatlantic.

Williams, Robert. The Geometric Foundation of Natural Structure: A Source Book of Design. LC 78-74118. (Illus.). 1979. pap. 6.00 (ISBN 0-486-23729-X). Dover.

Wolchonok, Louis. Art of Three Dimensional Design: How to Create Space Figures. LC 34-9269. 1969. pap. 4.50 (ISBN 0-486-22201-2). Dover.

GEOMETRICAL MODELS

see also Polyhedra–Models

Lyng, Merwin J. Dancing Curves: A Dynamic Demonstration of Geometric Principles. LC 78-2781. (Illus.). 1978. pap. 5.00x (ISBN 0-87353-124-8). NCTM.

Schattschneider, Doris & Walker, Wallace. M.C. Escher Kaleidocycles. (Illus.). 1977. pap. 8.95 (ISBN 0-345-25686-7). Ballantine.

GEOMETRICAL OPTICS

see Optics, Geometrical

GEOMETRY

see also Angle; Complexes; Congruences (Geometry); Curves; Geometrical Drawing; Hyperspace; Ratio and Proportion; Sphere; Surfaces; Topology; Transformations (Mathematics); Trigonometry

Abbot, W. Practical Geometry & Engineering Graphics. 8th ed. (Illus.). 1971. pap. text ed. 16.50x (ISBN 0-216-89450-6). Intl Ideas.

Abbott, P. Geometry. (Teach Yourself Ser.). 1973. pap. 6.95 (ISBN 0-679-10398-8). McKay.

Abelson, Harold & DiSessa, Andrea. Turtle Geometry: The Computer As a Medium for Exploring Mathematics. (Illus.). 416p. 1981. text ed. 20.00x (ISBN 0-262-01063-1). MIT Pr.

Abramov, L. M., et al. Fourteen Papers on Logic, Algebra, Complex Variables & Topology. LC 51-5559. (Translations Ser.: No. 2, Vol. 48). 1965. 26.80 (ISBN 0-8218-1748-5, TRANS 2-48). Am Math.

Algebra Lineal e Geometria Euclidiana. (Serie De Matematica: No. 6). (Port.). 1969. pap. 1.00 (ISBN 0-8270-6245-1). OAS.

Allendorfer, Carl B. Principles of Arithmetic & Geometry: For Elementary Teachers. 1971. text ed. 19.95 (ISBN 0-02-301860-7, 30186). Macmillan.

Anjaneyulu, M. S. Elements of Modern Pure Geometry. 6.50x (ISBN 0-210-26948-0). Asia.

Ashley, John P. & Harvey, E. R. Modern Geometry: Complete Course. Maier, Eugene, ed. (Mathematics for Individualized Instruction Ser). (Orig., Prog. Bk.). 1970. pap. text ed. 10.95x (ISBN 0-02-473490-X, 47349); dupl. masters 10.95x (ISBN 0-02-473400-4, 47340). Macmillan.

Atteia, M., et al. Nonlinear Problems of Analysis in Geometry & Mechanics. (Research Notes in Mathematics: No. 46). 203p. (Orig.). 1981. pap. text ed. 21.95 (ISBN 0-273-08493-3). Pitman Pub MA.

Baker, Henry F. Principles of Geometry, 6 vols. Incl. Vol. 1. Foundations. ix, 195p. 11.00 (ISBN 0-8044-4066-2); Vol. 2. Plane Geometry, Conics, Circles, Non-Euclidian Geometry. xix, 229p. 12.00 (ISBN 0-8044-4067-0); Vol. 3. Solid Geometry, Quadrics, Cubic Curves in Space, Cubic Surfaces. xv, 243p. 12.00 (ISBN 0-8044-4068-9); Vol. 4. Higher Geometry. 274p. 13.00 (ISBN 0-8044-4069-7); Vol. 5. Analytical Principles of the Theory of Curves. ix, 247p. 14.50 (ISBN 0-8044-4070-0); Vol. 6. Algebraic Surfaces. x, 308p. 13.00 (ISBN 0-8044-4071-9). LC 59-14676. Set. (ISBN 0-8044-4065-4). Ungar.

Barr, M. Autonomous Categories. (Lecture Notes in Mathematics: Vol. 752). 1979. pap. 9.50 (ISBN 0-387-09563-2). Springer-Verlag.

Bates, Virginia H. Geometry Now. (Illus.). 1978. pap. text ed. 9.95 (ISBN 0-89529-049-9). Avery Pub.

Baues, Hans J. Geometry of Loop Spaces & the Cobar Construction. LC 80-12430. (Memoirs of the American Mathematical Society Ser.). 1980. 7.60 (ISBN 0-8218-2230-6, MEMO-230). Am Math.

Beem. The Lorentzian Distance Function & Global Lorentzian Geometry. (Lecture Notes in Pure & Applied Mathematics Ser.: Vol. 67). 1981. 45.00 (ISBN 0-8247-1369-9). Dekker.

Beem & Ehrlich. Global Lorentzian Geometry. (Pure & Applied Mathematics Ser.: Vol. 67). 472p. 1981. 45.00 (ISBN 0-8247-1369-9). Dekker.

Behr, Marlyn J. & Jungst, Dale. Fundamentals of Elementary Mathematics Geometry. 326p. 1972. 17.95 (ISBN 0-12-084740-X); answer suppl. 3.00 (ISBN 0-12-084746-9). Acad Pr.

Bierberbach, L. Theorie der Geometrishen Konstruktionen. (Mathematische Rehihe Ser.: No. 13). (Illus.). 162p. (Ger.). 1952. 20.50 (ISBN 3-7643-0030-2). Birkhauser.

Bila, Dennis, et al. Geometry & Measurement. LC 76-19445. 1976. 5.95x (ISBN 0-87901-059-2). H S Worth.

Birkhoff, George D. & Beatley, R. Basic Geometry. 3rd ed. LC 59-7308. (gr. 9-12). 1959. text ed. 12.00 (ISBN 0-8284-0120-9); tchr's manual 2.50 (ISBN 0-8284-0034-2); answer bk. 1.50 (ISBN 0-8284-0162-4). Chelsea Pub.

Blaschke, W. Einfuhrung in Die Goemetrie der Waben. (Elemente der Mathematik Vom Hoeheren Standpunkt Aus: Vol. 4). 108p. (Ger.). 1955. pap. 14.50 (ISBN 3-7643-0033-7). Birkhauser.

--Projektive Geometrie. 3rd ed. (Mathematische Reihe Ser.: No. 17). (Illus.). 197p. 1954. 20.50 (ISBN 3-7643-0032-9). Birkhauser.

Bloom, D. M. Linear Algebra & Geometry. LC 77-26666. 1979. 41.50 (ISBN 0-521-21959-0); pap. 21.95x (ISBN 0-521-29324-3). Cambridge U Pr.

Blumenthal, Leonard M. A Modern View of Geometry. (Illus.). 1980. pap. text ed. 4.00 (ISBN 0-486-63962-2). Dover.

Blumenthal, Leonard M. & Menger, Karl. Studies in Geometry. LC 74-75624. (Illus.). 1970. text ed. 25.95x (ISBN 0-7167-0437-4). W H Freeman.

Brumfiel, Charles & Vance, Irvin. Algebra & Geometry for Teachers. LC 70-93983. (Mathematics Ser). 1970. text ed. 16.95 (ISBN 0-201-00667-7); instr's manual 1.25 (ISBN 0-201-00668-5). A-W.

Brunes, Tons. The Secrets of Ancient Geometry, 2 vols. 1967. Set. text ed. 87.50x (ISBN 0-391-01117-0). Humanities.

Bruni, James V. Experiencing Geometry. 1977. text ed. 15.95x (ISBN 0-534-00422-9). Wadsworth Pub.

Burckhardt, J. J. Die Bewegungsgruppen der Kristallographie. rev. 2nd ed. (Mineralogisch-Geotechnische Reihe Ser.: No. 2). 209p. (Ger.). 1966. 38.50 (ISBN 3-7643-0058-2). Birkhauser.

Burk, Raymond W. Selected Papers in Geometry. Date not set. pap. price not set (ISBN 0-88385-204-7). Math Assn.

Butzer, P. L., et al, eds. Linear Operators & Approximation, 2 vols. (International Ser. of Numerical Mathematics: Nos. 20 & 25). 1973. Vol. 1, 506p. 62.00 (ISBN 3-7643-0590-8); Vol. 2, 608p.,1975. 60.50 (ISBN 3-7643-0760-9). Birkhauser.

Byrnes. Partial Differential Equations & Geometry, Vol. 48. (Lecture Notes in Pure & Applied Math Ser.). 1979. 35.00 (ISBN 0-8247-6775-6). Dekker.

Carus, Paul. The Foundations of Mathematics: A Contribution to the Philosophy of Geometry. LC 75-3104. Repr. of 1908 ed. 18.00 (ISBN 0-404-59101-9). AMS Pr.

Ceitin, G. S., et al. Fourteen Papers on Logic, Geometry, Topology, & Algebra. LC 72-2350. (Translations Ser.: No. 2, Vol. 100). 1972. 42.00 (ISBN 0-8218-3050-3, TRANS 2-100). Am Math.

Cesaro, Ernesto. Vorlesungen Ueber Natuerliche Geometrie. (Bibliotheca Mathematica Teubneriana Ser: No. 36). (Ger). 1969. Repr. of 1921 ed. 27.00 (ISBN 0-384-08090-1). Johnson Repr.

Chakerian, Don, et al. Geometry: A Guided Inquiry. LC 71-179132. 1972. text ed. 18.50 (ISBN 0-395-13148-0, 3-53528); tchrs. ed. 19.95 (ISBN 0-395-13149-9, 3-53529); sample test questions 1.90 (ISBN 0-395-18003-1, 3-53531); solution key pap. 4.55 (ISBN 0-685-02024-X, 3-53530). HM.

Coxeter, H. S. Introduction to Geometry. 2nd ed. LC 72-93909. 1969. 31.95 (ISBN 0-471-18283-4). Wiley.

--Twisted Honeycombs. LC 75-145638. (CBMS Regional Conference Series in Mathematics: Vol. 4). iv, 47p. 1970. 7.40 (ISBN 0-8218-1653-5, CBMS-4). Am Math.

--Unvergangliche Geometrie. (Science & Civilization Ser.: No. 17). (Illus.). 552p. (Ger.). 1963. 48.50 (ISBN 3-7643-0071-X). Birkhauser.

Coxeter, H. S. & Greiter, S. L. Geometry Revisited. LC 67-20607. (New Mathematical Library: No.19). 1975. pap. 6.50 (ISBN 0-88385-619-0). Math Assn.

Crouch, R., et al. Preparatory Mathematics for Elementary Teachers. 595p. 1965. text ed. 13.50x (ISBN 0-471-18913-8, Pub. by Wiley). Krieger.

Dembowski, P. Finite Geometries. (Ergebnisse Er Mathematik und Ihrer Grenzgebiete: Vol. 44). 1977. 39.00 (ISBN 0-387-08310-3). Springer-Verlag.

Descartes, Rene. The Geometry of Rene Descartes. Smith, David E. & Latham, Marcia L., trs. from Fr. & Lat. LC 54-3995. 1954. lib. bdg. 10.50 (ISBN 0-88307-649-7). Gannon.

Dodson, C. T. & Poston, T. Tensor Geometry. (Surveys & References Ser.). 620p. (Orig.). 1979. pap. text ed. 24.95 (ISBN 0-686-31212-0). Pitman Pub MA.

Dorwart, Harold L. The Geometry of Incidence. pap. 4.00 (ISBN 0-911624-34-1). Wffn Proof.

Edwards, Myrtle. First Course in Geometry: A Modern Textbook for the High School. 1965. text ed. 7.50 (ISBN 0-682-43014-5, University). Exposition.

Efimov, N. V. Higher Geometry. 1980. 11.00 (ISBN 0-8285-1903-X, Pub. by Mir Pubs Russia). Imported Pubns.

Erhart, E. Polynomes Arithmetiques et Methode des Polyedres en Combinatoire. (International Series of Numerical Mathematics: No. 35). 169p. (Ger.). 1977. pap. 24.00 (ISBN 3-7643-0872-9). Birkhauser.

Eves, Howard. Survey of Geometry. rev. ed. 1972. text ed. 26.95x (ISBN 0-205-03226-5, 5632269). Allyn.

Faux, I. D. & Pratt, M. J. Computational Geometry for Designing & Manufacture. LC 78-40637. 329p. 1980. pap. 24.95 (ISBN 0-470-27069-1). Halsted Pr.

Feldman, Bernard. Basic Geometry. 1977. pap. 5.95x (ISBN 0-534-00510-1). Wadsworth Pub.

Fetisov, A. Proof in Geometry. 62p. 1978. pap. 1.75 (ISBN 0-8285-0742-2, Pub. by Mir Pubs Russia). Imported Pubns.

Fisher, Robert C. & Ziebur, Allen D. Integrated Algebra, Trigonometry & Analytic Geometry. 4th ed. (Illus.). 560p. 1982. 18.95 (ISBN 0-13-468967-4). P-H.

Flegg, H. Graham. From Geometry to Topology. LC 74-78155. 150p. 1974. 15.50x (ISBN 0-8448-0364-2). Crane-Russak Co.

Fomenko, V. T., et al. Twelve Papers on Functional Analysis & Geometry. LC 51-5559. (Translations Ser.: No. 2, Vol. 85). 1969. 28.80 (ISBN 0-8218-1785-X, TRANS 2-85). Am Math.

Foster, Lowell W. Geo-Metrics: The Metric Application of Geometric Tolerancing. (Illus.). 300p. 1974. 14.95 (ISBN 0-201-01989-2); pocket guide 9.95 (ISBN 0-201-01987-6). A-W.

Fueter, R. Analytische Geometrie der Ebene und Des Raumes. (Mathematische Reihe Ser.: No. 2). 180p. (Ger.). 1945. 18.50 (ISBN 3-7643-0130-9). Birkhauser.

Gattegno, Caleb. Geoboard Geometry. 1971. pap. 1.10 (ISBN 0-87825-020-4). Ed Solutions.

The Geometry of Metric & Linear Spaces: Proceedings. (Lecture Notes in Mathematics: Vol. 490). x, 244p. 1976. pap. 13.10 (ISBN 0-387-07417-1). Springer-Verlag.

Gillespie, R. J. Molecular Geometry. 1972. pap. 7.95x (ISBN 0-442-02697-8). Van Nos Reinhold.

Glenn, John. Children Learning Geometry. 1979. text ed. 15.50 (ISBN 0-06-318118-5, IntlDept); pap. text ed. 7.25 (ISBN 0-06-318119-3). Har-Row.

Grantham, Donald J. Geometry for Science & Technology. LC 76-40924. 121p. 1976. pap. text ed. 5.95x (ISBN 0-915668-28-9). G S E Pubns.

Grenander, U. Pattern Analysis: Lectures in Pattern Theory II. (Applied Mathematical Sciences Ser.: Vol. 24). (Illus.). 1978. pap. 21.70 (ISBN 0-387-90310-0). Springer-Verlag.

Guggenheimer, Henrich W. Applicable Geometry. LC 76-40007. 214p. 1977. pap. text ed. 13.50 (ISBN 0-88275-368-1). Krieger.

Haack, W. Elementare Differentialgeometrie. (Mathematische Reihe Ser.: No. 20). 242p. (Ger.). 1955. 26.00 (ISBN 3-7643-0158-9). Birkhauser.

Haag, Vincent H., et al. Elementary Geometry. 1970. text ed. 14.95 (ISBN 0-201-02658-9); instructor's manual 2.00 (ISBN 0-201-02659-7). A-W.

Hackworth, Robert D. & Howland, Joseph. Introductory College Mathematics: Geometric Measures. LC 75-23627. (Illus.). 70p. 1976. pap. text ed. 2.95 (ISBN 0-7216-4420-1). HR&W.

--Introductory College Mathematics: Geometry. LC 75-23619. 72p. 1976. pap. text ed. 2.95 (ISBN 0-7216-4412-0). HR&W.

Hadwiger, H. Altes und Neues Uber Konvexe Korper. (Elemente der Mathematik Vom Hoeheren Standpunkt Aus: Vol. 3). 116p. (Ger.). 1955. pap. 14.50 (ISBN 3-7643-0160-0). Birkhauser.

Harding, E. F. & Kendall, D. G., eds. Stochastic Geometry. LC 72-8603. (Ser. in Probability & Mathematical Statistics). 416p. 1974. 61.50 (ISBN 0-471-35141-5). Wiley.

Hargittai, M. & Hargittai, I. The Molecular Geometries of Coordination Compounds in the Vapour Phase. 1977. 36.00 (ISBN 0-444-99832-2). Elsevier.

Hawley, Newton & Suppes, Patrick. Key to Geometry Series, 8 bks. Gearheart, George & Rasmussen, Peter, eds. Incl. Bk. 1. Lines & Segments. 56p. pap. 1.15 (ISBN 0-913684-71-6); Bk. 2. Circles. 56p. pap. 1.15 (ISBN 0-913684-72-4); Bk. 3. Constructions. 56p. pap. 1.15 (ISBN 0-913684-73-2); Bk. 4. Perpendiculars. 56p. pap. 1.15 (ISBN 0-913684-74-0); Bk. 5. Squares & Rectangles. 56p. pap. 1.15 (ISBN 0-913684-75-9); Bk. 6. Angles. 56p. pap. 1.15 (ISBN 0-913684-76-7); Bk. 7. Perpendiculars & Parallels, Chords & Tangents, Circles. 154p. pap. 3.45 (ISBN 0-913684-77-5); Bk. 8. Triangles, Parallel Lines, Similar Polygons. 139p. pap. 3.45 (ISBN 0-913684-78-3). (gr. 4 up). 1980. pap. Key Curr Project.

Hermann, Robert. Cartanian Geometry, Nonlinear Waves, & Control Theory, Pt. B. Ackerman, Michael, tr. (Interdisciplinary Mathematics Ser.: Vol. 21). 585p. 1980. text ed. 60.00 (ISBN 0-915692-29-5, QA649.H46). Math Sci Pr.

--Cartanian Geometry, Nonlinear Waves, & Control Theory, Pt. A. (Interdisciplinary Mathematics Ser.: No. 20). 1979. pap. 50.00 (ISBN 0-915692-27-9). Math Sci Pr.

Herrmann, H. Ubungen zur Projektiven Geometrie. (Mathematische Reihe Ser.: No. 18). (Illus.). 168p. (Ger.). 1952. 16.50 (ISBN 3-7643-0170-8). Birkhauser.

Hilbert, David & Cohn-Vossen, Stephan. Geometry & the Imagination. LC 52-2894. (gr. 9 up). 1952. text ed. 14.95 (ISBN 0-8284-0087-3). Chelsea Pub.

Hobson, Ernest, et al. Squaring the Circle & Other Monographs, 4 vols. in 1. Incl. Squaring the Circle. Hobson, Ernest W; Ruler & Compasses. Hudson, Hilde P; Non-Differentiable Functions. Singh, A. N; How to Draw a Straight Line. Kempe, A. B. LC 58-21472. 9.95 (ISBN 0-8284-0095-4). Chelsea Pub.

--Squaring the Circle & Other Monographs, 4 vols. in 1. Incl. Squaring the Circle. Hobson, Ernest W; Ruler & Compasses. Hudson, Hilde P; Non-Differentiable Functions. Singh, A. N; How to Draw a Straight Line. Kempe, A. B. LC 58-21472. 9.95 (ISBN 0-8284-0095-4). Chelsea Pub.

Hoffer, Alan R. Geometry. (gr. 10-12). 1979. text ed. 15.04 (ISBN 0-201-02958-8, Sch Div); tchr's ed. 18.64 (ISBN 0-201-02959-6); solutions man. 13.60 (ISBN 0-201-02960-X); test booklet 12.12 (ISBN 0-201-02961-8). A-W.

Holiday, Ensor. Altair Design 4. LC 77-17417. (gr. 1 up). 1978. pap. 3.95 (ISBN 0-394-83794-0). Pantheon.

Hsiang, W., et al, eds. The Chern Symposium Nineteen Seventy Nine. (Illus.). 259p. 1981. 29.50 (ISBN 0-387-90537-5). Springer-Verlag.

Hunt, K. H. Kinematic Geometry of Mechanisms. (Engineering Science Ser.). (Illus.). 1979. 89.00x (ISBN 0-19-856124-5). Oxford U Pr.

Integral Geometry & Geometric Probability. (Encyclopedia of Mathematics & Its Applications: Vol. 1). 1976. pap. text ed. 21.50 (ISBN 0-201-13500-0, Adv Bk Prog). Benjamin Cummings.

Jablonski, Sergeiv. Diskrete Mathematik und Mathematische Fragen der Kybernetik. (Mathematische Reihe Ser.: No. 71). 260p. (Ger.). 1979. 39.80 (ISBN 3-7643-1071-5). Birkhauser.

Jacobs, Harold R. Geometry. LC 73-20024. (Illus.). 1974. text ed. 12.95 (ISBN 0-7167-0456-0); tchr's guide 6.95x (ISBN 0-7167-0460-9); test masters 4.95x (ISBN 0-7167-0459-5); transparency masters 45.00x (ISBN 0-7167-0458-7). W H Freeman.

Jeger, M. & Jeger, M. Einfuhrung in Die Vektorielle Geometrie und Lineare Algebra Fur Ingenieure und Naturwissenschafter. 252p. (Ger.). 1967. 33.00 (ISBN 3-7643-0198-8). Birkhauser.

Jones, Burton W. Elementary Concepts of Mathematics. 3rd ed. (Illus.). 1970. text ed. 13.95 (ISBN 0-02-361230-4). Macmillan.

Keedy, Mervin & Bittinger, Marvin. Functions & Basic Geometry. rev. ed. (Algebra, a Modern Introduction Ser.). (gr. 7-9). 1980. pap. text ed. write for info. A-W.

Kelly, Paul J. & Weiss, Max L. Geometry & Convexity: A Study in Mathematical Methods. LC 78-21919. (Pure & Applied Mathematics: Texts, Monographs & Tracts). 261p. 1979. 29.50 (ISBN 0-471-04637-X, Pub. by Wiley-Interscience). Wiley.

Kinney, L. B., et al. General Mathematics: A Problem Solving Approach, Bks. 1-2. (gr. 9-12). 1967-1968. text ed. 11.96 ea. (HoltE). Bk. 1 (ISBN 0-03-053100-4). Bk. 2 (ISBN 0-03-053110-1). annot. tchrs' ed. 5.64 ea. HR&W.

Klein, Felix. Vorlesungen Ueber Hoehere Geometrie. 3rd ed. LC 51-3040. 1976. text ed. 17.50 (ISBN 0-8284-0065-2). Chelsea Pub.

Kluge, Eike-Henner, tr. from Ger. Gottlob Frege on the Foundations of Geometry & Formal Theories of Arithmetic. LC 74-140533. 1971. 15.00x (ISBN 0-300-01393-0). Yale U Pr.

Kogan, B. Yu. The Applications of Mechanics to Geometry. LC 73-89789. (Popular Lectures in Mathematics Ser). 66p. 1975. pap. text ed. 4.50x (ISBN 0-226-45016-3). U of Chicago Pr.

Kutepov, A. Problems in Geometry. 208p. 1975. write for info. (Pub. by Mir Pubs Russia). Imported Pubns.

Lawlor, Robert. Sacred Geometry: Philosophy & Practice. Purce, Jill, ed. LC 81-67703. (The Illustrated Library of Sacred Imagination Ser.). (Illus.). 96p. 1982. 19.95 (ISBN 0-8245-0062-8); pap. 9.95 (ISBN 0-8245-0067-9). Crossroad NY.

Learning Achievement Corporation. Geometry & Design & Maintenance: Ratio, Proportion, Reading Graphs & Data. Zak, Therese A., ed. (MATCH Ser.). (Illus.). 128p. 1981. text ed. 5.28 (ISBN 0-07-037115-6, G). McGraw.

Lekkerkerker, C. G. Geometry of Numbers. (Bibliotheca Mathematica: Vol. 8). 1970. 68.50 (ISBN 0-444-10229-9, North-Holland). Elsevier.

Levi, Howard. Topics in Geometry. LC 75-19477. 112p. 1975. Repr. of 1968 ed. 5.50 (ISBN 0-88275-280-4). Krieger.

Lingenberg, Rolf. Metric Planes & Metric Vector Spaces. LC 78-21906. (Pure & Applied Mathematics: Texts, Monographs & Tracts). 1979. 29.95 (ISBN 0-471-04901-8, Pub. by Wiley-Interscience). Wiley.

Locher-Ernst, L. Einfuhrung in Die Freie Geometrie Ebener Kurven. (Elemente der Mathematik Vom Hoeheren Standpunkt Aus: Vol. 1). 85p. (Ger.). 1952. pap. 12.00 (ISBN 3-7643-0252-6). Birkhauser.

Lueneburg, H., ed. Translation Planes. 256p. 1980. 29.80 (ISBN 0-387-09614-0). Springer-Verlag.

Luneburg, H. Kombinatorik. (Elemente der Mathematik Vom Hoeheren Standpunkt Aus Ser.: Band 6). 108p. (Ger.). 1971. pap. 16.00 (ISBN 3-7643-0548-7). Birkhauser.

MacLane, Saunders. Selected Papers: Saunders MacLane. Kaplansky, I., ed. LC 79-10105. 1979. 31.30 (ISBN 0-387-90394-1). Springer-Verlag.

McLeod, Robin J. & Wachspress, Eugene L., eds. Frontiers of Applied Geometry: Proceedings of a Symposium, Las Cruces, New Mexico, 1980. 128p. 1981. pap. 23.40 (ISBN 0-08-026487-5). Pergamon.

Mandelbrot, Benoit B. Fractals: Form, Chance, & Dimension. LC 76-57947. (Mathematics Ser.). (Illus.). 1977. text ed. 22.95x (ISBN 0-7167-0473-0). W H Freeman.

Martin, Clyde & Hermann, Robert, eds. The Nineteen Seventy Six Ames Research Center (NASA) Conference on Geometric Control Theory. (Lie Groups: History, Frontiers &Applications: Vol. 7). 1977. pap. 36.00 (ISBN 0-915692-21-X). Math Sci Pr.

Math Review. pocket ed. 150p. (gr. 7-12). 1982. pap. text ed. 2.50 (ISBN 0-8120-2198-3). Barron.

May, J. P. The Geometry of Iterated Loop Spaces. LC 72-85090. (Lecture Notes in Mathematics: Vol. 271). ix, 175p. 1972. pap. 7.00 (ISBN 0-387-05904-0). Springer-Verlag.

Michael, W. Ortskurvengeometrie in der Komplexen Zahlenebene. (Illus.). 96p. (Ger.). 1950. 13.50 (ISBN 3-7643-0266-6). Birkhauser.

Miller, Leslie H. College Geometry. LC 57-5574. (Century Mathematics Ser.). (Illus.). 1957. text ed. 14.95x (ISBN 0-89197-088-6). Irvington.

Moise, Edwin E. Elementary Geometry from an Advanced Standpoint. 2nd ed. LC 73-2347. 1974. text ed. 17.95 (ISBN 0-201-04793-4). A-W.

Nagano, Tadashi. Homotopy Invariants in Differential Geometry. LC 52-42839. (Memoirs: No. 100). 1970. pap. 6.40 (ISBN 0-8218-1800-7, MEMO-100). Am Math.

National Council of Teachers of Mathematics. Geometry in the Mathematics Curriculum: 36th Yearbook. LC 73-16458. 1973. 16.90 (ISBN 0-87353-016-0). NCTM.

Nevanlinna, R. Raum, Zeit und Relativitat. (Science & Civilization Ser.: No. 19). (Illus.). 229p. (Ger.). 1964. 25.50 (ISBN 3-7643-0277-1). Birkhauser.

Nevanlinna, R. & Kustaanheimo, P. Grundlagen der Geometrie. rev. 2nd ed. (Mathematische Reihe Ser.: No. 43). 136p. (Ger.). 1977. 25.50 (ISBN 3-7643-0958-X). Birkhauser.

Nielsen, Kaj L. Mathematics for Practical Use. (Orig.). 1962. pap. 3.50 (ISBN 0-06-463212-1, EH 212, EH). Har-Row.

Orr, Leonard. Babaji. 1980. pap. 10.00 (ISBN 0-686-27683-3). L Orr.

Osserman, Robert & Weinstein, Alan, eds. Geometry of the LaPlace Operator. (Proceedings of Symposia in Pure Mathematics Ser.: Vol. 36). 1980. 20.40 (ISBN 0-8218-1439-7). Am Math.

Pedoe, Dan. Geometry & the Liberal Arts. LC 77-24023. (Illus.). 1978. 10.95 (ISBN 0-312-32370-0). St Martin.

Pogorelov, A. V. Hilbert's Fourth Problem. (Scripa Series in Mathematics). 97p. 1979. 16.00x (ISBN 0-470-26735-6). Halsted Pr.

Polya, G. & Szego, G. Problems & Theorems in Analysis II: Theory of Functions, Zeros, Polynomials, Determinants, Numger Theory, Geometry. Billigheimer, C. E., tr. (Illus.). 1977. pap. text ed. 18.90 (ISBN 0-387-90291-0). Springer-Verlag.

Porteous, I. R. Topological Geometry. 2nd ed. LC 79-41611. 1981. 59.50 (ISBN 0-521-23160-4); pap. 22.50 (ISBN 0-521-29839-3). Cambridge U Pr.

Posamentier, Alfred S., et al. Geometry: Its Elements & Structure. 2nd ed. 624p. (gr. 10). 1977. text ed. 12.56 (ISBN 0-07-050551-9, W); tchr's ed. 14.00 (ISBN 0-07-050552-7); tchr's manual 7.20 (ISBN 0-07-050554-3); tests 2.64 (ISBN 0-07-050553-5). McGraw.

Precalculus: Algebra, Trigonometry & Geometry. 1981. text ed. 17.95x (ISBN 0-02-379440-2). Macmillan.

Prenowitz, W. & Jantosciak, J. The Theory of Join Spaces: A Contemporary Approach to Convex Sets & Linear Geometry. (Undergraduate Texts in Mathematics). (Illus.). 1979. 20.80 (ISBN 0-387-90340-2). Springer-Verlag.

Rees, Paul K. Analytic Geometry. 3rd ed. 1970. text ed. 17.95 (ISBN 0-13-034264-5); ans. suppl. 0.50 (ISBN 0-13-034272-6). P-H.

Ringenberg, Lawrence A. College Geometry. LC 77-2631. (Illus.). 320p. 1977. Repr. of 1968 ed. lib. bdg. 13.50 (ISBN 0-88275-545-5). Krieger.

Row, T. S. Geometric Exercises in Paper Folding. rev. ed. Berman, W. W. & Smith, D. E., eds. (Illus.). 4.25 (ISBN 0-8446-2840-9). Peter Smith.

Row, T. Sundara. Geometric Exercises in Paper Folding. (Illus.). pap. 2.25 (ISBN 0-486-21594-6). Dover.

Rucker, Rudolf v. B. Geometry, Relativity & the Fourth Dimension. LC 76-22240. 1977. lib. bdg. 9.50x (ISBN 0-88307-584-9). Gannon.

Runion, Garth E. & Lockwood, James R. Deductive Systems. LC 78-17827. (Illus.). 1978. pap. 4.00x (ISBN 0-87353-129-9). NCTM.

Scherk, P., ed. Foundations of Geometry: Selected Proceedings of a Conference. LC 75-42127. 1976. 15.00x (ISBN 0-8020-2216-2). U of Toronto Pr.

Schmidt, H. J. Axiomatic Characterization of Physical Geometry. (Lecture Notes in Physics: Vol. 111). 163p. 1980. pap. 12.40 (ISBN 0-387-09719-8). Springer-Verlag.

Schools Council Sixth Form Mathematics Projects. Mathematics Applicable: Geometry from Coordinates. 1975. pap. text ed. 5.50x (ISBN 0-435-51697-3). Heinemann Ed.

Schutz, B. Geometrical Methods of Mathematical Physics. LC 80-40211. (Illus.). 300p. 1980. 39.95 (ISBN 0-521-23271-6); pap. 16.95 (ISBN 0-521-29887-3). Cambridge U Pr.

Schwerdtfeger, Hans. Geometry of Complex Numbers. LC 79-52529. 1980. pap. text ed. 4.00 (ISBN 0-486-63830-8). Dover.

Slaby, S. M. Fundamentals of Three-Dimensional Geometry. 2nd ed. 1976. 22.95x (ISBN 0-471-79621-2); wkbk. 10.95x (ISBN 0-471-79622-0). Wiley.

Smith, Vincent E., tr. Saint Thomas & the Object of Geometry. (Aquinas Lecture). 1953. 6.95 (ISBN 0-87462-118-6). Marquette.

Spitzbart, Abraham. Analytic Geometry. 1969. text ed. 15.95x (ISBN 0-673-05389-X). Scott F.

Stasheff, J. H-Spaces from a Homotopy Point of View. LC 71-134651. (Lecture Notes in Mathematics: Vol. 161). 1970. pap. 8.20 (ISBN 0-387-04940-1). Springer-Verlag.

Steiner, Jacob. Gesammelte Werke, 2 Vols. 2nd ed. LC 76-113151. (Ger). 1971. text ed. 49.50 set (ISBN 0-8284-0233-7). Chelsea Pub.

Stiefel, E. Lehrbuch der Darstellenden Geometrie. 3rd ed. (Mathematische Reihe Ser.: No. 6). 177p. (Ger.). 1971. 28.00 (ISBN 3-7643-0368-9). Birkhauser.

Stokes, William T. Gems of Geometry. rev. ed. (Illus.). 1978. pap. text ed. 5.95 (ISBN 0-914534-02-5). Stokes.

Sulanke, R. & Wintgen, P. Differentialgeometrie und Faserbundel. (Mathematische Reihe Ser.: No. 48). 299p. (Ger.). 1972. 38.80 (ISBN 3-7643-0646-7). Birkhauser.

Thomas, Brian. Geometry in Pictorial Composition. (Illus.). 1971. 10.00x (ISBN 0-85362-052-0, Oriel). Routledge & Kegan.

Uspenskii, V. A. Pascal's Triangle. McLarnan, Timothy & Sookne, David J., trs. from Rus. LC 73-90941. (Popular Lectures in Mathematics Ser). 42p. 1975. pap. text ed. 3.50x (ISBN 0-226-84316-5). U of Chicago Pr.

Vaisman. Foundations of Three Dimensional Euclidean Geometry. (Lecture Notes in Pure & Applied Mathematics Ser.: Vol. 56). 1980. 35.00 (ISBN 0-8247-6901-5). Dekker.

Verdina, Joseph. Geometry. new ed. (Mathematics Ser). (Illus.). 400p. 1975. text ed. 17.95x (ISBN 0-675-08738-4); instructor's manual 3.95 (ISBN 0-685-50986-9). Merrill.

Weyl, H. Symmetrie. (Science & Civilization Ser.: No. 11). (Illus.). 160p. 1956. 20.50 (ISBN 3-7643-0413-8). Birkhauser.

Wilson, Grace, et al. Geometry for Architects. 2nd ed. (Illus.). 1975. spiral bdg. 9.80x (ISBN 0-87563-092-8). Stipes.

Yaglam, I. M. Geometric Transformations II: (New Mathematical Library) LC 67-20607. 1968. pap. 6.50 (ISBN 0-88385-621-2). Math Assn.

Young, John W. Projective Geometry. (Carus Monograph: No. 4). 185p. 1930. 12.50 (ISBN 0-88385-004-4). Math Assn.

Zlot, William, et al. Elementary Geometry. LC 78-25633. 1979. pap. 6.50 (ISBN 0-88275-820-9). Krieger.

Zuckerman, Martin M. Geometry: A Straight Forward Approach. 1979. pap. text ed. 6.95x (ISBN 0-89582-020-X). Morton Pub.

GEOMETRY-CURIOSA AND MISCELLANY

Berloquin, Pierre. One Hundred Geometric Games. LC 75-40458. (gr. 7 up). 1976. 6.95 (ISBN 0-684-14611-8, ScribT). Scribner.

Lindgren, Harry. Recreational Problems in Geometric Dissections & How to Solve Them. Orig. Title: Geometric Dissections with Puzzles & Solutions. (Illus.). 184p. 1972. pap. 3.50 (ISBN 0-486-22878-9). Dover.

GEOMETRY-EARLY WORKS TO 1800

see also Mathematics, Greek

Babington, John. A Short Treatise of Geometrie. LC 76-25837. (English Experience Ser.: No. 296). 200p. Repr. of 1635 ed. 35.00 (ISBN 90-221-0296-3). Walter J Johnson.

Bibiena, Ferdinando G. Da. Architettura Civile. LC 68-57184. (Illus., It). 1969. 50.00 (ISBN 0-405-08268-1, Blom Pubns). Arno.

Descartes, Rene. La Geometrie. Smith, David E. & Latham, Marcia L., trs. from Fr. & Lat. (Illus.). xiii, 246p. 1952. 14.00 (ISBN 0-87548-168-X). Open Court.

--La Geometrie. (Illus.). 96p. 5.95 (ISBN 0-686-55671-2). French & Eur.

Euclid. The Elements, 3 Vols. Heath, Thomas L., ed. 1926. pap. 6.00 ea; Vol 1. pap. (ISBN 0-486-60088-2); Vol 2. pap. (ISBN 0-486-60089-0); Vol 3. pap. (ISBN 0-486-60090-4). Dover.

--Elements. Todhunter, Isaac, ed. 1957. 12.95x (ISBN 0-460-00891-9, Evman). Biblio Dist.

Milhaud, Gaston. Les Philosophes-Geometres de la Grece: Platon & Ses & Predecesseurs. facsimile ed. LC 75-13280. (History of Ideas in Ancient Greece Ser.). (Fr.). 1976. Repr. of 1900 ed. 22.00x (ISBN 0-405-07323-2). Arno.

Record, Robert. The Path-Way to Knowledg, Containing the First Principles of Geometrie. LC 74-80206. (English Experience Ser.: No. 687). 1974. Repr. of 1551 ed. 18.50 (ISBN 90-221-0687-X). Walter J Johnson.

Shelby, Lon R., ed. & tr. from Ger. Gothic Design Techniques: The Fifteenth-Century Design Booklets of Mathes Roriczer & Hanns Schmuttermayer. LC 77-2598. (Illus.). 192p. 1977. 15.00x (ISBN 0-8093-0810-X). S Ill U Pr.

Swetz, Frank & Kao, T. I. Was Pythagoras Chinese? An Examination of Right Triangle Theory in Ancient China. LC 76-41806. (Penn State Studies: No. 40). (Illus.). 1977. pap. 3.95 (ISBN 0-271-01238-2). Pa St U Pr.

Tannery, Paul. La Geometrie Grecque: Comment Son Histoire Nous Est Parvenue & E Que Nous En Savons. facsimile ed. LC 75-13296. (History of Ideas in Ancient Greece Ser.). (Fr.). 1976. Repr. of 1887 ed. 11.00x (ISBN 0-405-07340-2). Arno.

Universae Geometriae Mixtaeque Mathematicae Synopsis, et Bini Refractionum Demonstratarum Tractatus. Repr. of 1644 ed. 160.00 (ISBN 0-8287-1429-0). Clearwater Pub.

GEOMETRY-FAMOUS PROBLEMS

see Geometry-Problems, Famous

GEOMETRY-FOUNDATIONS

see also Axioms; Geometry, Non-Euclidean; Hyperspace; Parallels (Geometry)

Adler, Claire F. Modern Geometry. 2nd ed. 1967. text ed. 15.95 (ISBN 0-07-000421-8, C); teachers' manual 2.95 (ISBN 0-07-000419-6). McGraw.

Buseman, Herbert H. Metric Methods in Finsler Spaces. (Annals of Mathematics Studies: No. 8). 1942. pap. 12.00 (ISBN 0-527-02724-3). Kraus Repr.

Gemignani, Michael C. Axiomatic Geometry. LC 76-129519. (Mathematics Ser). 1971. text ed. 10.95 (ISBN 0-201-02336-9). A-W.

Haag, Vincent H., et al. Elementary Geometry. 1970. text ed. 14.95 (ISBN 0-201-02658-9); instructor's manual 2.00 (ISBN 0-201-02659-7). A-W.

Keedy, Mervin L. & Nelson, Charles W. Geometry: A Modern Introduction. 2nd ed. LC 79-178267. 1973. text ed. 13.95 (ISBN 0-201-03673-8). A-W.

Levi, Howard. Foundations of Geometry & Trignometry. 2nd ed. LC 74-23743. 360p. 1975. Repr. of 1956 ed. 16.00 (ISBN 0-88275-239-1). Krieger.

Nicod, Jean. Geometry & Induction: Containing Geometry in the Sensible World & the Logical Problem of Induction. Bell, J. & Wood, M., trs. LC 70-107149. 1970. 16.00x (ISBN 0-520-01689-0). U of Cal Pr.

Prenowitz, Walter & Jordan, M. Basic Concepts of Geometry. (Illus.). 1965. text ed. 27.95 (ISBN 0-471-00451-0). Wiley.

Robinson, Gilbert De B. Foundations of Geometry. 4th ed. 1959. 12.50x (ISBN 0-8020-1103-9). U of Toronto Pr.

Wren, Frank L. Basic Mathematical Concepts. 2nd ed. (Illus.). 608p. 1973. text ed. 15.95 (ISBN 0-07-071907-1, C); instructor's manual 1.50 (ISBN 0-07-071911-X); practice book 6.50 (ISBN 0-07-071910-1); ans. 1.50 (ISBN 0-07-071909-8). McGraw.

Wylie, Clarence R., Jr. Foundations of Geometry. (Illus.). 1964. text ed. 17.95 (ISBN 0-07-072191-2, C). McGraw.

GEOMETRY-HISTORY

Allman, George J. Greek Geometry from Thales to Euclid. facsimile ed. LC 75-13250. (History of Ideas in Ancient Greece Ser.). 1976. Repr. of 1889 ed. 16.00x (ISBN 0-405-07287-2). Arno.

Gray, Jeremy. Ideas of Space: Euclidean, Non-Euclidean & Relativistic. (Illus.). 1980. 49.50x (ISBN 0-19-853352-7). Oxford U Pr.

Ingraham, Mark H. Charles Sumner Slichter: The Golden Vector. LC 79-176412. 330p. 1972. 17.50 (ISBN 0-299-06060-8). U of Wis Pr.

Ivins, William M., Jr. Art & Geometry. 1946. pap. 2.50 (ISBN 0-486-20941-5). Dover.

Knorr, W. R. The Evolution of the Euclidean Elements: A Study of the Theory of Incommensurable Magnitudes & Its Significance for Early Greek Geometry. LC 75-12831. (Synthese Historical Library: No. 15). 372p. 1975. 66.00 (ISBN 90-277-0509-7, Pub. by Reidel Holland). Kluwer Boston.

Saraswatiamma, T. A. Geometry in Ancient & Medieval India. 1978. 13.95 (ISBN 0-89684-020-4, Pub. by Motilal Banarsidass India). Orient Bk Dist.

Tisdall, Fitzgerald. A Theory of the Origins & Development of the Heroic Hexameter. 1889. 25.00 (ISBN 0-8274-3982-2). R West.

Victor, Stephen K. Practical Geometry in the High Middle Ages: "Artis cuiuslibet consummatio & the "Pratike de geometrie". LC 78-73170. (Memoirs Ser.: Vol. 134). 1979. 8.00 (ISBN 0-87169-134-5). Am Philos.

GEOMETRY-JUVENILE LITERATURE

Bezuszka, Stanley, et al. Tessellations: The Geometry of Patterns. (gr. 4-12). 1977. wkbk. 8.50 (ISBN 0-88488-080-X). Creative Pubns.

Brownlee, Juanita. Tangram Geometry in Metric. (Illus., Orig.). (gr. 5-10). 1976. pap. 4.95 (ISBN 0-918932-43-2, 0140701407). Activity Resources.

Charosh, Mannis. Straight Lines, Parallel Lines, Perpendicular Lines. LC 76-106569. (Young Math Ser). (Illus.). (gr. 1-4). 1970. 7.95 (ISBN 0-690-77992-5, TYC-J); PLB 8.79 (ISBN 0-690-77993-3). Har-Row.

Cooney, Thomas J., et al. Geometry. 1982. text ed. price not set (ISBN 0-201-00974-9, Sch Div); price not set tchr's manual (ISBN 0-201-00975-7). A-W.

Diggins, Julia E. String, Straightedge & Shadow: The Story of Geometry. (Illus.). (gr. 4-9). 1965. 7.95 (ISBN 0-670-67858-9). Viking Pr.

Froman, Robert. Angles Are Easy As Pie. LC 75-6608. (Young Math Ser). (Illus.). 40p. (gr. k-3). 1976. PLB 8.79 (ISBN 0-690-00916-X, TYC-J). Har-Row.

Jenkins, Lee, et al. Geoblocks & Geojackets. (gr. 3-10). 1976. 5.99 (ISBN 0-918932-22-X). Activity Resources.

Luce, Marnie. Points, Lines, & Planes. LC 68-56704. (Math Concept Bks). (gr. 3-6). 1969. PLB 3.95 (ISBN 0-8225-0575-4). Lerner Pubns.

Phillips, Jo. Exploring Triangles: Paper-Folding Geometry. LC 74-14862. (Young Math Ser.). (Illus.). 40p. (gr. k-3). 1975. PLB 8.79 (ISBN 0-690-00645-4, TYC-J). Har-Row.

Ruchlis, Hy & Milgrom, Harry. Math Projects: Mathematical Shapes. (Illus., Orig.). (gr. 4-9). 1968. pap. 2.50 (ISBN 0-87594-015-3, 3030). Book-Lab.

GEOMETRY-PROBLEMS, EXERCISES, ETC.

see also Pythagorean Proposition

Bezuszka, Stanley, et al. Applications of Geometric Series. (Motivated Math Project Activity Bks.). 46p. (Orig.). (gr. 10-12). 1976. pap. text ed. 2.00 (ISBN 0-917916-14-X). Boston Coll Math.

Brunelle, Wallace & O'Neill, Robert. Constructional Geometry. Gray, Allan W., ed. 1972. pap. text ed. 8.25 (ISBN 0-89420-077-1, 350299); cassette recordings 107.95 (ISBN 0-89420-201-4, 350300). Natl Book.

Dobrovolny, J. S., et al. Problems in Engineering Drawing & Geometry, Series 12, 13, 15, 16, 21. 1964. pap. 5.20x ea. Stipes.

Dressler, Isidore. Geometry Review Guide. (gr. 10-12). 1973. pap. text ed. 5.42 (ISBN 0-87720-215-X). AMSCO Sch.

Hoelscher, Randolph P., et al. Problems in Engineering Geometry Series 1, 2, & 3. pap. 5.20x ea. Stipes.

Kespohl, Ruth C. Geometry Problems My Students Have Written. 1979. pap. 5.80 (ISBN 0-87353-142-6). NCTM.

Research & Education Association Staff. The Geometry Problem Solver: A Supplement to Any Class Text. LC 77-70336. (Illus.). 1977. pap. text ed. 16.85 (ISBN 0-87891-510-9). Res & Educ.

Schick, W. L., et al. Problems in Geometry for Architects, 2 pts. pap. 5.20x ea. Stipes.

Seymour, Dale & Schadler, Reuben. Creative Constructions. rev. ed. (Illus.). 62p. (gr. 5-12). 1974. wkbk. 4.95 (ISBN 0-88488-007-9). Creative Pubns.

Stallings, Pat. Puzzling Your Way into Geometry. new ed. (Illus.). (gr. 9-12). 1978. pap. text ed. 4.95 (ISBN 0-918932-52-1). Activity Resources.

GEOMETRY-PROBLEMS, FAMOUS

Ball, W. Rouse. Mathematical Recreations & Essays. rev. ed. 1960. 12.95 (ISBN 0-02-506430-4); pap. 1.95 (ISBN 0-02-091480-6). Macmillan.

Ball, Walter W. & Coxeter, H. S. Mathematical Recreations & Essays. 12th ed. LC 72-186276. 446p. 1974. pap. 7.50 (ISBN 0-8020-6138-9). U of Toronto Pr.

Klein, Felix. Famous Problems of Elementary Geometry & Other Monographs, 4 vols. in 1. Incl. From Determinant to Tensor. Sheppard, William F; Introduction to Combinatory Analysis. MacMahon, Percy A; Fermat's Last Theorem. Mordell, Louis J; Famous Problems of Elementary Geometry. Klein, Felix. (gr. 9 up). 1956. 9.95 (ISBN 0-8284-0108-X). Chelsea Pub.

GEOMETRY–PROGRAMMED INSTRUCTION

Ashley, John P. & Harvey, E. R. Modern Geometry: Complete Course. Maier, Eugene, ed. (Mathematics for Individualized Instruction Ser). (Orig., Prog. Bk.). 1970. pap. text ed. 10.95x (ISBN 0-02-473490-X, 47349); dupl. masters 10.95x (ISBN 0-02-473400-4, 47340). Macmillan.

GEOMETRY–STUDY AND TEACHING

Bouwsma, Ward D. Geometry for Teachers. (Illus.). 288p. 1972. text ed. 14.95 (ISBN 0-02-312870-4, 31287). Macmillan.

Brydegaard, Marguerite & Inskeep, James E., Jr., eds. Readings in Geometry from the Arithmetic Teacher. LC 74-138809. 1970. pap. 3.60 (ISBN 0-87353-086-1). NCTM.

Coleman, Robert. The Development of Informal Geometry. LC 78-176696. (Columbia University. Teachers College. Contributions to Education: No. 865). Repr. of 1942 ed. 17.50 (ISBN 0-404-55865-8). AMS Pr.

Collier, C. Patrick. Geometry for Teachers. LC 75-25017. (Illus.). 352p. 1976. text ed. 17.50 (ISBN 0-395-20661-8). solutions manual 1.90 (ISBN 0-395-24219-3). HM.

Dressler, Isidore. Geometry. (Orig.). (gr. 10-12). 1973. text ed. 12.58 (ISBN 0-87720-235-4); pap. text ed. 8.33 (ISBN 0-87720-234-6). AMSCO Sch.

Drooyan, Irving & Wooton, William. Elementary Algebra with Geometry. LC 75-35736. 334p. 1976. text ed. 19.95 (ISBN 0-471-22245-3). Wiley.

Elliott, H. A., et al. Geometry in the Classroom. (Winston Mine Editions). 1968. text ed. 5.01 (ISBN 0-685-26945-0, HoltC). HR&W.

Gillespie, N. J. Mira Activities for Junior High Geometry. 1973. pap. 4.75 wkbk. (ISBN 0-88488-017-6). Creative Pubns.

Lange, Muriel W. Geometry in Modules A-D, Bks. 1-4. (gr. 10-12). 1975. pap. text ed. 4.24 ea. (Sch Div); No. 1. pap. text ed. (ISBN 0-201-04125-1); No. 2. pap. text ed. 4.24 (ISBN 0-201-04126-X); No. 3. pap. text ed. 4.24 (ISBN 0-201-04127-8); No. 4. pap. text ed. 4.24 (ISBN 0-201-04128-6); tchr's commentary 12.44 (ISBN 0-201-04129-4). A-W.

Leblanc, John F., et al. Mathematics Methods Program: Awareness Geometry. 40p. 1976. pap. text ed. 2.95 (ISBN 0-201-14614-2); instructor's manual 1.50 (ISBN 0-201-14615-0). A-W.

O'Daffer, P. & Clemens, S. Geometry: An Investigative Approach. new ed. (Grades 10-11). 1976. pap. text ed. 19.25 (ISBN 0-201-05420-5, Sch Div); tchrs. ed. 5.80 (ISBN 0-201-05421-3); wkbk. 2.75 (ISBN 0-201-05422-1). A-W.

Perry, Winona M. A Study in the Psychology of Learning in Geometry. LC 72-177149. (Columbia University. Teachers College. Contributions to Education: No. 179). Repr. of 1925 ed. 17.50 (ISBN 0-404-55179-3). AMS Pr.

Smith, David E. The Teaching of Geometry. (Educational Ser.). 1911. Repr. 15.00 (ISBN 0-685-43643-8). Norwood Edns.

Stamper, Alva W. A History of the Teaching of Elementary Geometry. LC 70-177746. (Columbia University. Teachers College. Contributions to Education: No. 23). Repr. of 1909 ed. 17.50 (ISBN 0-404-55023-1). AMS Pr.

University of Oregon. Geometry & Visualization. 1977. 36.95 (ISBN 0-88488-091-5). Creative Pubns.

Walter, Marion I. Boxes, Squares, & Other Things: A Teacher's Guide for a Unit in Informal Geometry. LC 71-111259. 88p. 1970. 2.50 (ISBN 0-87353-024-1). NCTM.

Young, Grace C. & Young, William H. Beginner's Book of Geometry. LC 76-114211. Orig. Title: First Book of Geometry. (gr. 1-5). 1970. Repr. of 1905 ed. text ed. 9.50 (ISBN 0-8284-0231-0). Chelsea Pub.

Young, John E. & Bush, Grace A. Geometry for Elementary Teachers. LC 77-155559. 300p. 1971. text ed. 17.95x (ISBN 0-8162-9984-6); instr's manual 2.50 (ISBN 0-686-76946-5, 0-8162-9994). Holden-Day.

GEOMETRY, AFFINE

Nagata, M. Polynomial Rings & Affine Spaces. LC 78-8264. (Conference Board of the Mathematical Sciences Ser.: No. 37). 1980. Repr. of 1978 ed. 8.40 (ISBN 0-8218-1687-X, CBMS 37). Am Math.

Northcott, D. G. Affine Sets & Affine Groups. LC 79-41595. (London Mathematical Society Lecture Note Ser.: No. 39). 1980. pap. 26.95x (ISBN 0-521-22909-X). Cambridge U Pr.

Ostrom, T. G. Finite Translation Planes. LC 73-139732. (Lecture Notes in Mathematics: Vol. 158). 1970. pap. 8.20 (ISBN 0-387-05186-4). Springer-Verlag.

Snapper, Ernst & Troyer, Robert J. Metric Affine Geometry. 435p. 1971. text ed. 20.95 (ISBN 0-12-653650-3). Acad Pr.

Yale, Paul B. Geometry & Symmetry. LC 67-28042. 1968. 17.95x (ISBN 0-8162-9964-1). Holden-Day.

GEOMETRY, ALGEBRAIC

see also Algebraic Spaces; Curves, Algebraic; Geometry, Analytic; Global Analysis (Mathematics); Surfaces; Surfaces, Algebraic; Topology; Transformations (Mathematics)

Abhyankar, S. Ramification Theoretic Methods in Algebraic Geometry. (Annals of Mathematics Studies Ser.: No. 43). (Orig.). 1959. 10.00 (ISBN 0-691-08023-2, AM43). Princeton U Pr.

--Resolution of Singularities of Embedded Algebraic Surfaces. (Pure & Applied Mathematics Ser). 1966. 48.00 (ISBN 0-12-041956-4). Acad Pr.

Abhyankar, S. S., et al. Algebraic Geometry: Papers Presented at the Bombay Colloquium. (Tata Institute of Fundamental Research Studies in Mathematics Ser). 1969. 15.50x (ISBN 0-19-617607-7). Oxford U Pr.

Altmann, A. & Kleiman, S. Introduction to Grothendieck Duality Theory. LC 77-132180. (Lecture Notes in Mathematics: Vol. 146). 1970. pap. 8.20 (ISBN 0-387-04935-5). Springer-Verlag.

Andrianov, A. N., et al. Thirteen Papers on Group Theory, Algebraic Geometry & Algebraic Topology. LC 51-5559. (Translations Ser.: No. 2, Vol. 66). 1968. 30.00 (ISBN 0-8218-1766-3, TRANS 2-66). Am Math.

Artin, E. Geometric Algebra: Pure & Applied Mathematics. (A Wiley-Interscience Ser. of Texts, Monographs & Tracts). 214p. 1957. 50.50 (ISBN 0-470-03432-7, Pub. by Wiley-Interscience). Wiley.

Artin, Michael & Mumford, David, eds. Contributions to Algebraic Geometry in Honor of Oscar Zariski. 1979. text ed. 25.00 (ISBN 0-8018-2307-2). Johns Hopkins.

Brumfield, Gregory W. Partially Ordered Rings & Semi-Algebraic Geometry. (London Mathematical Society Lecture Note Ser.: No. 37). 1980. pap. 23.95x (ISBN 0-521-22845-X). Cambridge U Pr.

Carmo, M. Do, ed. Geometry & Topology. (Lecture Notes in Mathematics: Vol. 597). 1977. 30.30 (ISBN 0-387-08345-6). Springer-Verlag.

Cernikov, S. N., et al. Twelve Papers on Algebra, Algebraic Geometry & Topology. LC 51-5559. (Translations Ser.: No. 2, Vol. 84). 1969. 30.80 (ISBN 0-8218-1784-1, TRANS 2-84). Am Math.

Conn, Jack F. Non-Abelian Minimal Closed Ideals of Transitive Lie Algebras. LC 79-5479. (Mathematical Notes Ser.: 25). 216p. 1980. pap. 7.50x (ISBN 0-691-08251-0). Princeton U Pr.

Fulton, William. Algebraic Curves: An Introduction to Algebraic Geometry. (Math Lecture Notes Ser.: No. 30). 1974. (Adv Bk Prog); pap. 13.50 (ISBN 0-8053-3082-8, Adv Bk Prog). Benjamin-Cummings.

Geometrical Topology Conference, Park City, Utah, Feb. 19-22, 1974. Geometric Topology: Proceedings. Glaser, L. C. & Rushing, T. B., eds. LC 74-34326. (Lecture Notes in Mathematics: Vol. 438). x, 459p. 1975. pap. 20.30 (ISBN 0-387-07137-7). Springer-Verlag.

Griffiths, Phillip. Topics in Algebraic & Analytic Geometry. LC 74-2968. (Mathematical Notes Ser.: No. 13). 227p. 1974. 14.00x (ISBN 0-691-08151-4). Princeton U Pr.

--Topics in Algebraic & Analytic Geometry. LC 74-2968. (Mathematical Notes Ser.: No. 13). 227p. 1974. 14.00x (ISBN 0-691-08151-4). Princeton U Pr.

Griffiths, Phillip & Harris, Joseph. Principles of Algebraic Geometry. LC 78-6993. (Wiley-Interscience Ser. of Texts, Monographs & Tracts, Pure & Applied Mathematics). 813p. 1978. 54.50x (ISBN 0-471-32792-1, Pub. by Wiley-Interscience). Wiley.

Groups with Steinberg Relations & Coordinization of Polygonal Geometries. LC 77-4192. (Memoirs: No. 185). 1977. 11.60 (ISBN 0-8218-2185-7, MEMO-185). Am Math.

Gruenberg, K. W. Linear Geometry. 2nd ed. LC 76-27693. (Graduate Texts in Mathematics). (Illus.). 1977. 18.50 (ISBN 0-387-90227-9). Springer-Verlag.

Hartshorne, R. Algebraic Geometry. (Graduate Texts in Mathematics: Vol. 52). (Illus.). 1977. 24.80 (ISBN 0-387-90244-9). Springer-Verlag.

--Ample Subvarieties of Algebraic Varieties. (Lecture Notes in Mathematics: Vol. 156). 1970. pap. 11.20 (ISBN 0-387-05184-8). Springer-Verlag.

Hermann, Robert. Linear Systems Theory and Introductory Algebraic Geometry. (Interdisciplinary Mathematics Ser: No. 8). 282p. 1974. 24.00 (ISBN 0-915692-07-4). Math Sci Pr.

Hirzebruch, F. Topological Methods in Algebraic Geometry. Schwarzberger, R. L., tr. from German. (Grundlehren der Mathematischen Wissenschaften: Vol. 131). (2nd corrected printing of the 3rd enlarged ed.). 1978. 36.90 (ISBN 0-387-03525-7). Springer-Verlag.

Iitaka, S. Algebraic Geometry: Introduction to Birational Geometry of Algebraic Varieties. (Graduate Texts in Mathematics Ser.: Vol. 76). 304p. 1981. 35.00 (ISBN 0-387-90546-4). Springer-Verlag.

International Conference, Sonderforschungsbereich Theoretische Mathematik,University of Bonn, July 1976. Modular Functions of One Variable: Proceedings, No. 6. Serre, J. P. & Zagier, D. B., eds. (Lecture Notes in Mathematics: Vol. 627). 1977. pap. 18.30 (ISBN 0-387-08530-0). Springer-Verlag.

Jun-Ichi-Igusa, ed. Algebraic Geometry. LC 77-4603. (Centennial Lectures Ser). 1977. text ed. 12.00x (ISBN 0-8018-2021-9). Johns Hopkins.

Kompaniec, V. P., et al. Fourteen Papers on Algebra, Topology, Algebraic & Differential Geometry. LC 51-5559. (Translations Ser.: No. 2, Vol. 73). 1968. 29.60 (ISBN 0-8218-1773-6, TRANS 2-73). Am Math.

Lang, Serge A. Introduction to Algebraic Geometry. 3rd ed. 1958. 16.50 (ISBN 0-201-04164-2, Adv Bk Prog). A-W.

Lawvere, F. W., ed. Toposes, Algebraic Geometry & Logic. LC 72-86101. (Lecture Notes in Mathematics: Vol. 274). 189p. 1972. pap. 7.00 (ISBN 0-387-05920-2). Springer-Verlag.

Leblanc, John F., et al. Mathematics-Methods Program: Transformational Geometry. (Mathematics Ser.). (Illus.). 132p. 1976. pap. text ed. 3.50 (ISBN 0-201-14616-9); instr's manual 1.50 (ISBN 0-201-14617-7). A-W.

Lefschetz, Solomon. Selected Papers. LC 73-113137. 1971. text ed. 27.50 (ISBN 0-8284-0234-5). Chelsea Pub.

Libgober, A. & Wagreich, P., eds. Algebraic Geometry: Proceedings. (Lecture Notes in Mathematics Ser.: Vol. 862). 281p. 1981. pap. 16.80 (ISBN 0-387-10833-5). Springer-Verlag.

Lonsted, K., ed. Algebraic Geometry: Proceedings: Summer Meeting, Copenhagen, August 7-12, 1978. (Lecture Notes in Mathematics: Vol. 732). 1979. pap. 33.50 (ISBN 0-387-09527-6). Springer-Verlag.

McDonald, Bernard. Geometric Algebra & Local Rings. (Monographs in Pure & Applied Math: Vol. 36). 1976. 39.75 (ISBN 0-8247-6528-1). Dekker.

Manin, Ju. I., et al. Seven Papers on Algebra, Algebraic Geometry & Algebraic Topology. LC 51-5559. (Translations Ser.: No. 2, Vol. 63). 1967. 30.80 (ISBN 0-8218-1763-9, TRANS 2-63). Am Math.

Mansfield, Larry E. Linear Algebra with Geometric Applications. (Pure & Applied Mathematics Ser.: Vol. 34). 1976. 17.50 (ISBN 0-8247-6321-1). Dekker.

Milgram, R. J., ed. Algebraic & Geometric Topology, 2 pts. LC 78-14304. (Proceedings of Symposia in Pure Mathematics: Vol. 32). 1980. Repr. of 1978 ed. Set. 38.00 (ISBN 0-8218-1432-X, PSPUM 32.1); 22.40 (ISBN 0-686-77332-2, 32.2); 22.40 (ISBN 0-8218-1433-8). Am Math.

Milnor, John W. Singular Points of Complex Hypersurfaces. (Annals of Mathematics Studies: No. 61). 1969. pap. 10.50 (ISBN 0-691-08065-8). Princeton U Pr.

Moise, E. E. Geometric Topology in Dimensions 2 & 3. LC 76-49892. (Graduate Texts in Mathematics: Vol. 47). 1977. 26.20 (ISBN 0-387-90220-1). Springer-Verlag.

Mumford, D. Algebraic Geometry I: Complex Projective Varieties, I. (Grundlehren der Mathematischen Wissenschaften: Vol. 221). (Illus.). 186p. 1981. 19.70 (ISBN 0-387-07603-4). Springer-Verlag.

--Algebraic Geometry I: Complex Projective Varieties. (Grundlehren der Mathematischen Wissenschaften: Vol. 221). 1976. 19.70 (ISBN 0-387-07603-4). Springer-Verlag.

Olson, L. D., ed. Algebraic Geometry: Proceedings, Tromso Symposium, June 27-July 8,1977. (Lecture Notes in Mathematics: Vol. 687). 1979. pap. 14.40 (ISBN 0-387-08954-3). Springer-Verlag.

Pham, F. Singularities des Systemes Differentiels de Gauss-Manin. (Progress in Mathematics Ser.: No. 2). 340p. (Fr.). 1979. pap. 18.00 (ISBN 3-7643-3002-3). Birkhauser.

Pognoli, A. Institutiones Mathematicae: Algebraic Geometry & Nash Functions, Vol. III. 1981. 11.50 (ISBN 0-12-363603-5). Acad Pr.

Popp, H., ed. Moduli Theory & Classification Theory of Algebraic Varieties. (Lecture Notes in Mathematics: Vol 620). 1978. pap. 10.70 (ISBN 0-387-08522-X). Springer-Verlag.

Poston, T. & Woodcock, A. E. A Geometrical Study of the Elementary Catastrophes. LC 73-22575. (Lectures Notes in Mathematics: Vol. 373). (Illus.). v, 257p. 1974. pap. 14.60 (ISBN 0-387-06681-0). Springer-Verlag.

Segre, Beniamino. Some Properties of Differentiable Varieties & Transformations: With Special Reference to the Analytic & Algebraic Cases. 2nd ed. LC 72-137498. (Ergebnisse der Mathematik und Ihrer Grenzgebiete: Vol. 13). 1971. pap. 29.00 (ISBN 0-387-05085-X). Springer-Verlag.

Severi, Francesco. Vorlesungen Uber Algebraische Geometrie. (Bibliotheca Mathematica Teubneriana Ser: No. 32). (Ger). Repr. of 1921 ed. 31.00 (ISBN 0-384-54945-4). Johnson Repr.

Shafarevich, I. R. Basic Algebraic Geometry. LC 77-6425. (Springer Study Edition). 1977. pap. 24.00 (ISBN 0-387-08264-6). Springer-Verlag.

Slodowy, P. Simple Singularities & Simple Algebraic Groups. (Lecture Notes in Mathematics: Vol. 815). 175p. 1980. pap. 11.80 (ISBN 0-387-10026-1). Springer-Verlag.

Snyder, Virgil, et al. Selected Topics in Algebraic Geometry, 2 Vols in 1. 2nd ed. LC 78-113149. 1970. text ed. 13.95 (ISBN 0-8284-0189-6). Chelsea Pub.

Strange, Jerry D. & Rice, Bernard J. Analytical Geometry & Calculus: With Technical Applications. 462p. 1970. text ed. 21.95 (ISBN 0-471-83190-5). Wiley.

Symposia in Pure Mathematics, Humboldt State University, Arcata, Calif., July 29-August 16, 1974. Algebraic Geometry-Arcata 1974: Proceedings, Vol. 29. Hartstone, Robin, ed. LC 75-9530. 1979. Repr. of 1979 ed. with corrections 39.60 (ISBN 0-8218-1429-X, PSPUM-29). Am Math.

Toelke, J., ed. Cotributions to Geometry: Proceedings of the Geometry-Symposium Seigen 1978. Willis, J. 404p. 1979. softcover 49.00 (ISBN 3-7643-1048-0). Birkhauser.

Walker, R. J. Algebraic Curves. LC 78-11956. 1979. pap. 9.80 (ISBN 0-387-90361-5). Springer-Verlag.

Weil, Andre. Foundations of Algebraic Geometry. rev. ed. LC 62-7794. (Colloquium Pbns. Ser.: Vol. 29). 1978. Repr. of 1962 ed. 24.80 (ISBN 0-8218-1029-4, COLL-29). Am Math.

Zariski, O. Algebraic Surfaces. 2nd ed. LC 70-148144. (Ergebnisse der Mathematik & Ihrer Grenzgebiete: Vol. 61). 1971. 32.70 (ISBN 0-387-05335-2). Springer-Verlag.

GEOMETRY, ANALYTIC

see also Conic Sections; Curves; Surfaces

Adams, Lovincy J. & White, Paul A. Analytic Geometry & Calculus. 2nd ed. 1968. text ed. 15.95x (ISBN 0-19-500812-X). Oxford U Pr.

Andree, Richard V. Introduction to Calculus with Analytical Geometry. 1962. 16.95 (ISBN 0-07-001780-8, C). McGraw.

Anton, Howard. Calculus: With Analytic Geometry. brief edition ed. LC 81-50266. 854p. 1981. text ed. 23.95 (ISBN 0-471-09443-9). Wiley.

--Calculus with Analytic Geometry. LC 79-11469. 1980. 30.95 (ISBN 0-471-03248-4); solution manual avail. (ISBN 0-471-04498-9). Wiley.

Blaschke, W. Analytische Geometrie. 2nd ed. (Mathematics Reihe Ser.: No. 16). 190p. (Ger.). 1954. 20.50 (ISBN 3-7643-0031-0). Birkhauser.

Bohuslov, Ronald L. Analytic Geometry: A Precalculus Approach. (Illus.). 1970. text ed. 15.95 (ISBN 0-02-311810-5, 31181). Macmillan.

Borsuk, Karol. Multidimensional Analytic Geometry. 1969. 19.25 (ISBN 0-02-841690-2). Hafner.

Brink, Raymond W. Analytic Geometry. rev. ed. (Century Mathematics Ser.). 1935. text ed. 24.50x (ISBN 0-89197-025-8). Irvington.

Burdette, A. C. An Introduction to Analytic Geometry & Calculus. rev. ed. 1973. text ed. 19.95 (ISBN 0-12-142252-6). Acad Pr.

Campbell, Howard E. & Dierker, Paul F. Calculus with Analytic Geometry. 2nd ed. 1978. text ed. write for info. (ISBN 0-87150-244-5, PWS 1981). Prindle.

Carico, Charles C. & Drooyan, Irving. Analytic Geometry. LC 79-21633. 310p. 1980. 18.95 (ISBN 0-471-06435-1); student supplement avail. (ISBN 0-471-06378-9). Wiley.

Chasen, Sylvan H. Geometric Principles & Procedures for Computer Graphic Applications. LC 78-7998. (Illus.). 1978. 23.95 (ISBN 0-13-352559-7). P-H.

Clebsch, Rudolph F., tr. Vorlesungen Ueber Geometrie Mit Besonderer Benutzung der Vortrage Von Clebsch, 2 Vols. in 3 Pts. (Bibliotheca Mathematica Teubneriana Ser. 43-44). (Ger). 1969. Repr. Set. 107.00 (ISBN 0-384-09295-0). Johnson Repr.

Coble, A. B. Algebraic Geometry & Theta Functions. LC 30-12679. (Colloquium Pbns. Ser.: Vol. 10). 1961. Repr. of 1929 ed. 18.80 (ISBN 0-8218-1010-3, COLL-10). Am Math.
Crowell, Richard H. & Slesnick, William E. Calculus with Analytic Geometry. (Illus.). 1968. 17.95x (ISBN 0-393-09782-X). Norton.
Dadourian, H. M. Introduction to Analytic Geometry & the Calculus. 256p. 1981. Repr. of 1949 ed. lib. bdg. 12.50 (ISBN 0-89874-267-6). Krieger.
Descartes, Rene. La Geometrie. Smith, David E. & Latham, Marcia L., trs. from Fr. & Lat. (Illus.). xiii, 246p. 1952. 14.00 (ISBN 0-87548-168-X). Open Court.
--La Geometrie. (Illus.). 96p. 5.95 (ISBN 0-686-55671-2). French & Eur.
--Geometry. Smith & Latham, trs. 7.00 (ISBN 0-8446-1972-8). Peter Smith.
--Geometry. (Eng. & Fr.). 1925. pap. 3.50 (ISBN 0-486-60068-8). Dover.
Duraipandian, P. Textbook of Analytical Geometry. pap. 3.75x (ISBN 0-210-27192-2). Asia.
Edwards, C. H. & Penney, David E. Calculus & Analytic Geometry. 1120p. 1982. 31.95 (ISBN 0-13-111609-6). P-H.
Espacios Vectoriales y Geometria Analitica. rev. ed. (Serie De Matematica: No. 2). (Span.). 1974. pap. 1.00 (ISBN 0-8270-1096-6). OAS.
Fischer, G. Analytische Geometrie. (Mathematik Grundkurs Ser.). 199p. (Ger.). 1978. pap. 8.50 (ISBN 3-528-07235-0). Birkhauser.
--Complex Analytic Geometry. (Lecture Notes in Mathematics: Vol. 538). 1976. soft cover 12.70 (ISBN 0-387-07857-6). Springer-Verlag.
Fisher, Robert C. & Ziebur, Allen D. Calculus & Analytic Geometry. 3rd ed. (Illus.). 784p. 1975. text ed. 29.95 (ISBN 0-13-112227-4). P-H.
Flanders, H. & Price, J. Calculus with Analytic Geometry. 1041p. 1978. text ed. 26.95 (ISBN 0-12-259672-2); instr's. manual 3.00 (ISBN 0-12-259673-0). Acad Pr.
Fleming, Daniel J. & Kaput, James J. Calculus with Analytic Geometry. 1979. text ed. 28.50 scp (ISBN 0-06-382672-0, HarpC); scp study guide 8.50 (ISBN 0-06-382581-3); solutions manual avail. (ISBN 0-06-382580-5); instructor's manual avail. (ISBN 0-06-372860-5). Har-Row.
Fraleigh, John B. Calculus with Analytic Geometry. LC 79-18693. (Illus.). 1980. text ed. 26.95 (ISBN 0-201-03041-1). A-W.
Fuller, Gordon. Analytic Geometry. 5th ed. LC 78-55820. 1979. text ed. 14.95 (ISBN 0-201-02414-4); ans bk. 13.95 (ISBN 0-201-02415-2). A-W.
Gillett, Philip. Calculus & Analytic Geometry. 928p. 1981. text ed. 29.95 (ISBN 0-669-00641-6); solutions guide, vol. 1 6.95 (ISBN 0-669-00642-4); solutions guide vol. 2 6.95 (ISBN 0-669-03212-3); solutions guide vol. 3 6.95 (ISBN 0-669-03213-1). Heath.
Gondin, William R. & Sohmer, Bernard. Intermediate Algebra & Analytic Geometry Made Simple. 1959. pap. 3.50 (ISBN 0-385-00437-0, Made). Doubleday.
Goodman, A. W. Analytic Geometry & the Calculus. 4th ed. (Illus.). 1980. text ed. 28.95 (ISBN 0-02-344960-8). Macmillan.
--Analytic Geometry & the Calculus: Student Study Guide, 2 vols. 4th ed. (Illus.). 1980. pap. text ed. 7.95 ea. Vol. I (ISBN 0-02-344970-5). Vol. II (ISBN 0-02-344980-2). Macmillan.
Goodman, Adolph W. Modern Calculus with Analytic Geometry, 2 Vols. 1967. Vol. 2. text ed. 14.95x (ISBN 0-02-344920-9, 34492). Macmillan.
Griffiths, Phillip. Topics in Algebraic & Analytic Geometry. LC 74-2968. (Mathematical Notes Ser.: No. 13). 227p. 1974. 14.00x (ISBN 0-691-08151-4). Princeton U Pr.
--Topics in Algebraic & Analytic Geometry. LC 74-2968. (Mathematical Notes Ser.: No. 13). 227p. 1974. 14.00x (ISBN 0-691-08151-4). Princeton U Pr.
Gunning, Robert C. Lectures on Complex Analytic Varieties: Finite Analytic Mappings. LC 74-2969. (Mathematical Notes Ser.: No. 14). 170p. 1974. 12.00 (ISBN 0-691-08150-6). Princeton U Pr.
Johnson, Richard E., et al. Calculus with Analytic Geometry. 6th ed. 1978. text ed. 28.95x (ISBN 0-205-05917-1); tchr's man. 5.95 (ISBN 0-205-05918-X); study guide 8.50 (ISBN 0-205-05919-8). Allyn.
--Calculus with Analytic Geometry. 6th ed. 1978. text ed. 28.95x (ISBN 0-205-05917-1); tchr's man. 5.95 (ISBN 0-205-05918-X); study guide 8.50 (ISBN 0-205-05919-8). Allyn.
Kindle, Joseph H. Analytic Geometry. (Orig.). 1950. pap. 3.95 (ISBN 0-07-034575-9, SP). McGraw.
Kletenik, D. Problems in Analytic Geometry. MIR Publishers, tr. from Rus. (Illus.). 298p. 1975. text ed. 14.00x (ISBN 0-8464-0757-4). Beekman Pubs.
Kuiper, N. H. Linear Algebra & Geometry. 2nd rev. ed. 1965. 29.50 (ISBN 0-444-10226-4, North-Holland). Elsevier.
Larson, Roland E. & Hostetler, Robert P. Calculus with Analytic Geometry. 1979. text ed. 29.95 (ISBN 0-669-01301-3); solution manuals 6.95 ea. Vol. 1 (ISBN 0-669-03187-9). Vol. 2 (ISBN 0-669-03188-7). Vol. 3 (ISBN 0-669-03189-5). differential equations suppl. 1.95 (ISBN 0-669-03204-2); student manual 7.95 (ISBN 0-669-01705-1); appendix d 1.95 (ISBN 0-669-03190-9); instructor's manual to adopters 1.95 (ISBN 0-669-01302-1). Heath.
Leithold, Louis. The Calculus with Analytic Geometry, 2 vols. in 1. 4th ed. 1140p. 1980. Set. text ed. 28.95 scp (ISBN 0-686-72760-6, HarpC). Har-Row.
--The Calculus with Analytic Geometry: Functions of One Variable, Plane Analytic Geometry & Infinite Series, Vol. I. 819p. 1980. text ed. 18.95 scp (ISBN 0-06-043936-X, HarpC). Har-Row.
--The Calculus with Analytic Geometry: Infinite Series, Vectors, & Functions of Several Variables, No. 2. 4th. ed. 410p. 1980. text ed. 18.95 (ISBN 0-06-043937-8, HarpC). Har-Row.
Longley, W. R., et al. Analytic Geometry & Calculus. 1960. 24.95x (ISBN 0-471-00344-1). Wiley.
Middlemiss, Ross R., et al. Analytic Geometry. 3rd ed. LC 68-15472. 1968. text ed. 14.95 (ISBN 0-07-041896-9, C); instructor's manual 5.95 (ISBN 0-07-041897-7). McGraw.
Minnick, John H. Outline for the Study of the Calculus with Analytic Geometry, 3 vols. 1981. Vol. 1, 416 Pp. scp 8.50 (ISBN 0-06-044543-2, HarpC); Vol. 2, 340 Pp. pap. 7.50 scp (ISBN 0-06-044544-0); Vol. 3, 230 Pp. pap. 7.50 scp (ISBN 0-06-044545-9). Har-Row.
Niles, Nathan & Haborak, George. Calculus with Analytic Geometry. (Illus.). 640p. 1982. 21.95 (ISBN 0-13-112011-5). P-H.
Niles, Nathan O. & Haborak, George E. Calculus with Analytic Geometry. 1971. text ed. 19.95 (ISBN 0-13-112086-7). P-H.
Oakley, Cletus O. Analytic Geometry. (Illus., Orig.). 1957. pap. 3.95 (ISBN 0-06-460068-8, CO 68, COS). Har-Row.
Olmsted, John M. Calculus with Analytic Geometry, Vol. 1. LC 66-11169. (Century Mathematics Ser.). (Illus.). 1966. 26.50x (ISBN 0-89197-061-4). Irvington.
Pedoe, Daniel. A Geometric Introduction to Linear Algebra. 2nd ed. LC 72-78369. xi, 224p. 1976. text ed. 8.95 (ISBN 0-8284-0286-8). Chelsea Pub.
Person, R. V. Calculus with Analytic Geometry. LC 69-19016. 1970. text ed. 27.95 (ISBN 0-03-075430-5, HoltC). HR&W.
Pogorelov, A. V. Analytic Geometry. 240p. 1980. pap. 4.40 (ISBN 0-8285-1714-2, Pub. by Mir Pubs Russia). Imported Pubns.
Preston, Gerald C. & Lovaglia, Anthony R. Modern Analytic Geometry. 1971. text ed. 20.95 scp (ISBN 0-06-045256-0, HarpC); solutions manual avail. (ISBN 0-06-365250-1). Har-Row.
Protter, Murray H. & Morrey, Charles B., Jr. Analytic Geometry. 2nd ed. (Illus.). 432p. 1975. text ed. 14.95 (ISBN 0-201-05997-5). A-W.
--Calculus with Analytic Geometry: A First Course. 3rd ed. LC 76-12801. (Mathematics Ser.). 1977. text ed. 20.95 (ISBN 0-201-06037-X). A-W.
--Calculus with Analytic Geometry: A Second Course. LC 70-153066. (Mathematics Ser). 1971. text ed. 21.95 (ISBN 0-201-06021-3). A-W.
--College Calculus with Analytic Geometry. 3rd ed. LC 76-12800. (Mathematics Ser.). 1977. text ed. 25.95 (ISBN 0-201-06030-2). A-W.
Purcell, Edwin J. Analytic Geometry. LC 58-5609. (Century Mathematics Ser.). (Illus.). 1958. 34.00x (ISBN 0-89197-605-1). Irvington.
--Calculus with Analytic Geometry. 3rd ed. LC 77-7977. (Illus.). 1978. 29.95 (ISBN 0-13-112052-2); Solutions Manual by Patterson 4.95 (ISBN 0-13-112037-9); pap. text ed. 1.00 linear algebra suppl. (ISBN 0-13-112029-8). P-H.
Rees, Paul K. & Sparks, Fred W. Algebra, Trigonometry & Analytic Geometry. 2nd ed. (Illus.). 512p. 1975. text ed. 15.50 (ISBN 0-07-051720-7, C); instructor's manual 3.50 (ISBN 0-07-051719-3). McGraw.
--Calculus with Analytic Geometry. LC 68-17508. (Illus.). 1969. text ed. 20.95 (ISBN 0-07-051675-8, C); instructor's manual 2.95 (ISBN 0-07-051674-X). McGraw.
Resnikoff, H. L. & Wells, R. O., Jr., eds. Complex Analysis, 1972, Vol. 1: Geometry of Singularities. (Rice University Studies: Vol. 59, No. 1). 162p. 1973. pap. 3.25x (ISBN 0-89263-215-1). Rice Univ.
--Complex Analysis, 1972, Vol. 2: Analysis on Singularities. (Rice University Studies: Vol. 59, No. 2). 163p. 1973. pap. 3.25x (ISBN 0-89263-216-X). Rice Univ.
Riddle, Douglas F. Analytic Geometry with Vectors. 2nd ed. 1978. 19.95x (ISBN 0-534-00485-7). Wadsworth Pub.
--Calculus & Analytic Geometry. 3rd ed. 1979. text ed. 31.95x (ISBN 0-534-00626-4). Wadsworth Pub.
Roberts, A. Wayne. Introductory Calculus: Second Edition with Analytic Geometry & Linear Algebra. 1972. text ed. 20.95 (ISBN 0-12-589756-1); answer bk 3.00 (ISBN 0-12-589758-8). Acad Pr.
Rodi, Stephen. Solutions Manual to Accompany Swokowski's Calculus with Analytic Geometry, Vol. II. 2nd ed. 448p. 1981. pap. text ed. write for info. (33L 2191). Prindle.
Rodin, Burt. Calculus with Analytic Geometry. 1969. ref. ed. 29.95 (ISBN 0-13-112060-3). P-H.
Rudman, Jack. Calculus with Analytical Geometry. (College Level Examination Ser.: CLEP-43). (Cloth bdg. avail. on request). 1977. pap. 9.95 (ISBN 0-8373-5393-9). Natl Learning.
Schachter, H. Calculus & Analytic Geometry. 1972. text ed. 18.95 (ISBN 0-07-055056-5, G); ans. 2.00 (ISBN 0-07-055057-3). McGraw.
Schock, A. Clyde & Warshaw, Bernard. Analytic Geometry & an Introduction to Calculus. 2nd ed. 1965. 13.32 (ISBN 0-13-034512-1). P-H.
Selby, Peter H. Geometry & Trigonometry for Calculus. LC 74-23936. (Self-Teaching Guides Ser). 352p. 1975. pap. text ed. 6.95x (ISBN 0-471-77558-4). Wiley.
Shanks, M. E. Calculus, Analytic Geometry, Elementary Functions. 1973. text ed. 23.95 (ISBN 0-03-091492-2, HoltC). HR&W.
Shenk, Al. Calculus & Analytic Geometry. LC 76-17206. (Illus.). 1977. text ed. 24.95 (ISBN 0-87620-142-7); answer book free (ISBN 0-685-75089-2); solutions manual 7.95 (ISBN 0-87620-144-3); transparency masters free (ISBN 0-685-75090-6); instructor's manual free (ISBN 0-685-75091-4). Goodyear.
Shenk, Norman A. Calculus & Analytic Geometry. 2nd ed. (Illus.). 1979. 24.95 (ISBN 0-87620-195-8). Goodyear.
Simon, Arthur B. Algebra & Trigonometry with Analytic Geometry. LC 78-23409. (Mathematical Sciences Ser.). (Illus.). 1979. text ed. 18.95x (ISBN 0-7167-1016-1); solutions manual avail. W H Freeman.
Smith, William K. Analytic Geometry. (Illus.). 320p. 1972. text ed. 11.25x (ISBN 0-685-26689-3). Macmillan.
--Calculus with Analytic Geometry. (Illus.). 1969. text ed. 14.95x (ISBN 0-02-412900-3). Macmillan.
Spitzbart, Abraham. Calculus with Analytic Geometry. 768p. 1975. text ed. 17.95x (ISBN 0-673-07907-4). Scott F.
Steen, Frederick H. & Ballou, D. H. Analytic Geometry. 3rd ed. 1963. text ed. 18.95x (ISBN 0-471-00570-3). Wiley.
Stein, Sherman K. Calculus & Analytic Geometry. 3rd ed. (Illus.). 1977. text ed. 21.50 (ISBN 0-07-061008-8, C); instructor's manual 4.50 (ISBN 0-07-061009-6); solutions manual 8.95 (ISBN 0-07-061114-9). McGraw.
Swokowski, Earl W. Algebra & Trigonometry with Analytic Geometry. 5th ed. LC 80-29056. (The Swokowski Ser.). 544p. 1981. text ed. write for info. (ISBN 0-87150-310-7, 33L 2471). Prindle.
--Calculus with Analytic Geometry. 2nd ed. (Illus.). 1979. text ed. write for info. (ISBN 0-87150-268-2, PWS 2181). Prindle.
--Elements of Calculus with Analytic Geometry. (Illus.). 636p. text ed. 15.00 (ISBN 0-87150-504-5); tchr's manual 6.00 (ISBN 0-87150-507-X); calculator wkb. 4.00 (ISBN 0-686-64031-4); test bank 5.00 (ISBN 0-686-64032-2); solutiions man. 15.00 (ISBN 0-87150-508-8). Prindle.
Swokowski, Earl W. & Bronikowski, Thomas A. Student Supplement to Accompany Calculus with Analytic Geometry, 2 vols. 1979. Vol. 1. pap. text ed. write for info. (ISBN 0-87150-277-1, PWS 2183); Vol. 2. write for info. (ISBN 0-87150-278-X, WS 2186). Prindle.
Swokowski, Earl W. & Dobyns, Roy A. Programmed Guide to Calculus & Analytic Geometry. 1979. pap. text ed. write for info. (ISBN 0-87150-279-8, PWS 2185). Prindle.
Thomas, George. Elements of Calculus & Analytic Geometry. 4th ed. Date not set. text ed. 20.80 (ISBN 0-201-07664-0, Sch Div); price not set tchrs. commentary (ISBN 0-201-07665-9); solutions manual 22.40 (ISBN 0-201-07666-7); self study manual 7.12 (ISBN 0-201-07667-5). A-W.
Thomas, George B., Jr. Elements of Calculus & Analytic Geometry. 3rd ed. (gr. 11-12). 1976. text ed. 20.80 (ISBN 0-201-07549-0, Sch Div). A-W.
Thomas, George B., Jr. & Finney, Ross L. Calculus & Analytic Geometry. 5th ed. LC 78-55832. (Illus.). 1979. Combined Ed. text ed. 27.95 (ISBN 0-201-07540-7); Pt. 1. student suppl. & self-study manual avail. 20.95 (ISBN 0-201-07541-5); Pt. 2. 20.95 (ISBN 0-201-07542-3). A-W.
Tierney, John A. Calculus & Analytic Geometry. 4th ed. 1979. text ed. 28.95x (ISBN 0-205-06454-X); instr's man. avail. (ISBN 0-205-06455-8); solutions man. avail. (ISBN 0-205-06456-6); self-test supplement 8.50 (ISBN 0-205-06457-4). Allyn.
Wade, Thomas L. & Taylor, Howard E. Contemporary Analytic Geometry. LC 79-22955. 338p. 1980. Repr. of 1969 ed. lib. bdg. 17.50 (ISBN 0-89874-034-7). Krieger.
Washington, Allyn J. Solutions Manual to Technical Calculus with Analytical Geometry. 2nd ed. 1980. 3.95 (ISBN 0-8053-9533-4). Benjamin Cummings.
--Technical Calculus with Analytical Geometry. 2nd ed. 1979. 18.95 (ISBN 0-8053-9519-9); instr's guide 3.95 (ISBN 0-8053-9533-4). Benjamin-Cummings.
Wong, Yung-Chow. Isoclinic N-Planes in Euclidean 2n-Space, Clifford Parallels in Elliptic(2n-1) Space & the Hurwitz Matrix Equations. LC 52-42839. (Memoirs: No. 41). 1971. pap. 8.80 (ISBN 0-8218-1241-6, MEMO-41). Am Math.
Yefimov, N. Brief Course in Analytical Geometry. (Illus.). 1965. 12.95x (ISBN 0-8464-1080-X). Beekman Pubs.

GEOMETRY, ANALYTIC–PLANE

Carico, Charles. Analytic Geometry in R Squared. 1974. 4.95x (ISBN 0-534-00360-5). Wadsworth Pub.
Durfee, W. H. Calculus & Analytic Geometry. 1971. text ed. 22.00 (ISBN 0-07-018378-3, C); solutions manual 2.95 (ISBN 0-07-018379-1). McGraw.
Flanders, Harley, et al. A First Course in Calculus with Analytic Geometry. 1973. 19.95 (ISBN 0-12-259657-9); instrs' manual 3.00 (ISBN 0-12-259658-7). Acad Pr.
Graham, Walter W. & Rowan, William H. Plane Analytic Geometry. (Quality Paperback: No. 47). (Orig.). 1968. pap. 3.50 (ISBN 0-8226-0047-1). Littlefield.
Salmon, George. Conic Sections. 6th ed. LC 55-3390. 9.95 (ISBN 0-8284-0099-7); pap. 4.95 (ISBN 0-8284-0098-9). Chelsea Pub.
Scott, Charlotte A. Projective Methods in Plane Analytical Geometry. 3rd ed. LC 49-4920. 9.95 (ISBN 0-8284-0146-2). Chelsea Pub.

GEOMETRY, ANALYTIC–SOLID

Carico, Charles. Analytic Geometry in R Cubed. 1974. 4.95x (ISBN 0-534-00376-1). Wadsworth Pub.
Olmsted, John M. Solid Analytic Geometry. (Century Mathematics Ser.). 1947. text ed. 28.50x (ISBN 0-89197-417-2); pap. text ed. 16.50x (ISBN 0-89197-942-5). Irvington.
Salmon, George. Analytic Geometry of Three Dimensions, Vol. II. LC 56-13057. 1979. text ed. 12.00 (ISBN 0-8284-0196-9). Chelsea Pub.

GEOMETRY, DESCRIPTIVE

see also Engineering Graphics; Perspective; Projection

Earle, James H. Descriptive Geometry. 2nd ed. LC 76-55640. (Illus.). 384p. 1978. text ed. 17.95 (ISBN 0-201-01776-8). A-W.
Gordon, V. O. A Course in Descriptive Geometry. 1980. 10.00 (ISBN 0-8285-1870-X, Pub. by Mir Russia). Imported Pubns.
Guillemin, Victor & Sternberg, Shlomo. Geometric Asymptotics. LC 77-8210. (Mathematical Surveys Ser.: No. 14). 1977. 49.60 (ISBN 0-8218-1514-8, SURV-14). Am Math.
Hawk, M. C. Descriptive Geometry. (Orig.). 1962. pap. 3.95 (ISBN 0-07-027290-5, SP). McGraw.
Lobandiyevsky, P. & Krylov, K. Descriptive Geometry. 383p. 1974. 4.90 (ISBN 0-8285-0712-0, Pub. by Mir Pubs Russia). Imported Pubns.
Moschovakis, Y. N. Descriptive Set Theory. (Studies in Logic & the Foundations of Mathematics: Vol. 100). 640p. 1979. 73.25 (ISBN 0-444-85305-7, North Holland). Elsevier.
Pare, E. G., et al. Descriptive Geometry. 4th ed. (gr. 12). 1971. text ed. 17.95 (ISBN 0-02-391310-X); wkshts. ser. A 9.95 (ISBN 0-02-390890-4). Macmillan.
--Descriptive Geometry: Metric. 5th ed. 1977. 20.95 (ISBN 0-02-390880-7, 39088). Macmillan.
--Descriptive Geometry-Metric. 6th ed. 1982. text ed. 19.95 (ISBN 0-02-390930-7). Macmillan.
Slaby, Steve M. Engineering Descriptive Geometry. (Orig.). 1969. pap. 4.95 (ISBN 0-06-460101-3, CO 101, COS). Har-Row.

Wellman, B. Leighton. Technical Descriptive Geometry. 2nd ed. 1957. text ed. 17.50 (ISBN 0-07-069234-3, C); problem layouts 10.95 (ISBN 0-07-069237-8); solutions manual 3.95 (ISBN 0-07-069233-5). McGraw.

Whitehead, A. N. The Axioms of Descriptive Geometry. (Cambridge Tracts in Mathematics & Mathematical Physics Ser: No. 5). 1971. Repr. of 1907 ed. 7.50 (ISBN 0-02-854710-1). Hafner.

GEOMETRY, DESCRIPTIVE–PROBLEMS, EXERCISES, ETC.

Earle, J. H., et al. Design & Descriptive Geometry Problems 1. (Orig.). 1967. pap. text ed. 6.95 (ISBN 0-201-01633-8); tchrs' ed. 1.50 (ISBN 0-201-01635-4). A-W.

Gordon, V. O. & Ivanov, Y. A. Worked Problems in Descriptive Geometry. 332p. 1979. 8.70 (ISBN 0-8285-1536-0, Pub. by Mir Pubs Russia). Imported Pubns.

Pare, E. G., et al. Descriptive Geometry Worksheets. 5th ed. (A). 1982. text ed. 9.95 (ISBN 0-686-75024-1). Macmillan.

Warner, Frank M. & McNeary, M. Applied Descriptive Geometry. 5th ed. (Illus.). 1959. text ed. 13.95 (ISBN 0-07-068298-4, C); solutions manual 1.50 (ISBN 0-07-068296-8). McGraw.

GEOMETRY, DIFFERENTIAL

see also Calculus of Tensors; Congruences (Geometry); Convex Bodies; Convex Domains; Coordinates; Curves; Differential Forms; Differential Topology; Geometry, Riemannian; Hyperspace; Riemannian Manifolds; Spaces, Generalized; Surfaces; Transformations (Mathematics)

Abraham, Ralph & Marsden, Jerrold E. Foundations of Mechanics: A Mathematical Exposition of Classical Mechanics with an Introduction to the Qualitative Theory of Dynamical Systems & Applications to the Three-Body Problem. 2nd rev. & enl. ed. 1978. 46.50 (ISBN 0-8053-0102-X, Adv Bk Prog). Benjamin-Cummings.

Aleksandrov, A. D. & Zalgaller, V. A. Intrinsic Geometry of Surfaces. LC 66-30492. (Translations of Mathematical Monographs: Vol. 15). 1967. 26.80 (ISBN 0-8218-1565-2, MMONO-15). Am Math.

Ancikov, A. M., et al. Seventeen Papers on Topology & Differential Geometry. LC 51-5559. (Translations Ser.: No. 2, Vol. 92). 1970. 29.60 (ISBN 0-8218-1792-2, TRANS 2-92). Am Math.

Artzy, R. & Vaisman, I., eds. Geometry & Differential Geometry. (Lecture Notes in Mathematics: Vol. 792). 443p. 1980. pap. 24.50 (ISBN 0-387-09976-X). Springer-Verlag.

Atkin, E. The Metric Theory of Banach Manifolds. LC 78-14728. (Lecture Notes in Mathematics: Vol. 662). 1978. pap. 15.60 (ISBN 0-387-08915-2). Springer-Verlag.

Bieberbach, Ludwig. Differentialgeometrie. (Bibliothecha Mathematica Teubneriana Ser: No. 35). (Ger). 1969. 15.50 (ISBN 0-384-04240-6). Johnson Repr.

Blaschke, Wilhelm. Differentialgeometrie, 2 Vols. in 1. LC 62-11596. (Ger). 24.95 (ISBN 0-8284-0202-7). Chelsea Pub.

Bleuler, K. & Reetz, A., eds. Differential Geometrical Methods in Mathematical Physics. LC 76-30859. (Lecture Notes in Mathematics Ser: Vol. 570). 1977. pap. 24.60 (ISBN 0-387-08068-6). Springer-Verlag.

Bleuler, K., et al, eds. Differential Geometrical Methods in Mathematical Physics II: Proceedings, University of Bonn, July 13-16, 1977. (Lecture Notes in Mathematics Ser.: Vol. 676). 1979. pap. 31.80 (ISBN 0-387-08935-7). Springer-Verlag.

Bloom, F. Modern Differential Geometric Techniques in the Theory of Continuous Distributions of Dislocations. Dold, A. & Eckmann, B., eds. (Lecture Notes in Mathematics: Vol. 733). 1979. pap. 13.10 (ISBN 0-387-09528-4). Springer-Verlag.

Busemann, H. Recent Synthetic Differential Geometry. LC 13-120381. (Ergebnisse der Mathematik und Ihrer Grenzgebiete: Vol. 54). 1970. 22.20 (ISBN 0-387-04810-3). Springer-Verlag.

Busemann, Herbert. Geometry of Geodesics. (Pure and Applied Mathematics: Vol. 6). 1955. 47.00 (ISBN 0-12-148350-9). Acad Pr.

Cahen, M. & Flato, M., eds. Differential Geometry & Relativity. new ed. (Mathematical Physics & Applied Mathematics Ser: No. 3). 1976. lib. bdg. 42.00 (ISBN 90-277-0745-6, Pub. by Reidel Holland). Kluwer Boston.

Calenko, M. S., et al. Twenty-Two Papers on Algebra, Number Theory, & Differential Geometry. LC 51-5559. (Translations Ser.: No. 2, Vol. 37). 1964. 28.80 (ISBN 0-8218-1737-X, TRANS 2-37). Am Math.

Chern, S. S., ed. Studies in Global Geometry & Analysis. LC 67-16033. (MAA Studies: No. 4). 197p. 1967. 12.50 (ISBN 0-88385-104-0). Math Assn.

Colloquium Held at Dijon, June 17-22, 1974, et al. Differential Topology & Geometry: Proceedings. Joubert, G. P. & Moussu, R. P., eds. LC 75-25927. (Lecture Notes in Mathematics: Vol. 484). ix, 287p. 1975. pap. 14.70 (ISBN 0-387-07405-8). Springer-Verlag.

Do Carmo, Manfredo. Differential Geometry of Curves & Surfaces. 1976. 27.95 (ISBN 0-13-212589-7). P-H.

Dodson, C. T. & Poston, T. Tensor Geometry: The Geometric Viewpoint & Its Uses. new ed. (Illus.). 1979. pap. cancelled (ISBN 0-8224-1040-0). Pitman Learning.

Doebner, H. D., ed. Differential Geometric Methods in Mathematical Physics: Proceedings. (Lecture Notes in Physics Ser.: Vol. 139). 329p. 1981. pap. 20.00 (ISBN 0-387-10578-6). Springer-Verlag.

Eberlein, Patrick. Surfaces of Nonpositive Curvature. LC 79-15112. 90p. 1979. 8.00 (ISBN 0-8218-2218-7). Am Math.

Efimov, N. V., et al. Differential Geometry & Calculus of Variations. (Translations, Ser.: No. 1 Vol. 6). 1962. 26.00 (ISBN 0-8218-1606-3, TRANS 1-6). Am Math.

Eisenhart, L. P. Non-Riemannian Geometry. LC 28-28413. (Colloquium Pbns. Ser.: Vol. 8). 1972. Repr. of 1922 ed. 24.80 (ISBN 0-8218-1008-1, COLL-8). Am Math.

Eisenhart, Luther P. Introduction to Differential Geometry. rev. ed. (Mathematical Ser.: Vol. 3). 1947. 22.00 (ISBN 0-691-07983-8). Princeton U Pr.

Ferus, D., et al, eds. Global Differential Geometry & Global Analysis: Proceedings. (Lecture Notes in Mathematics: Vol. 838). 299p. 1981. pap. 19.50 (ISBN 0-387-10285-X). Springer-Verlag.

Fowler, R. H. The Elementry Differential Geometry of Plane Curves. 2nd ed. (Cambridge Tracts in Mathematics & Mathematical Physics Ser.: No. 20). 1964. Repr. of 1929 ed. 8.75 (ISBN 0-02-844830-8). Hafner.

Garcia, P. L., et al, eds. Differential Geometrical Methods in Mathematical Physics: Proceedings. (Lecture Notes in Mathematics: Vol. 836). 538p. 1981. 29.50 (ISBN 0-387-10275-2). Springer-Verlag.

Goetz, Abraham. Introduction to Differential Geometry. (Intermediate Mathematics Ser). 1970. text ed. 18.95 (ISBN 0-201-02431-4). A-W.

Guggenheimer, Heinrich. Differential Geometry. pap. text ed. 6.00 (ISBN 0-486-63433-7). Dover.

Hermann, Robert. Diffferential Geometry and the Calculus of Variations. 2nd ed. LC 68-14664. (Intermath Ser.: No. 17). 1977. 42.00 (ISBN 0-915692-24-4). Math Sci Pr.

--Gauge Fields, & Cartan-Enresmann Connections: Part a. LC 75-12199. (Interdisciplinary Mathematics: No. 10). 500p. 1975. 35.00 (ISBN 0-915692-09-0). Math Sci Pr.

--Geometric Structure of Systems Control Theory & Physics: Part B. LC 74-30856. (Interdisciplinary Mathematics Ser.: No. 11). 1976. 40.00 (ISBN 0-915692-14-7). Math Sci Pr.

--Geometry, Physics & Systems. (Pure & Applied Mathematics Ser: Vol. 18). 320p. 1973. 34.75 (ISBN 0-8247-6052-2). Dekker.

--Quantum & Fermion Differential Geometry, Pt. A. (Interdisciplinary Mathematics Ser.: No. 16). 1977. 18.00 (ISBN 0-915692-22-8). Math Sci Pr.

Hilbert, David & Cohn-Vossen, Stephan. Geometry & the Imagination. LC 52-2894. (gr. 9 up). 1952. text ed. 14.95 (ISBN 0-8284-0087-3). Chelsea Pub.

Hsiung, Chuan-Chih. A First Course in Differential Geometry. LC 80-22112. (Pure & Applied Mathematics Ser.). 343p. 1981. 29.95 (ISBN 0-471-07953-7, Pub. by Wiley-Interscience). Wiley.

Hurt, Norman & Hermann, R. Quantum Statistical Mechanics & Lie Group Harmonic Analysis, Pt. A. (Lie Groups; History, Frontiers & Applications: Vol. X). 1980. text ed. 30.00 (ISBN 0-915692-30-9, QC174.8.H87). Math Sci Pr.

Kamber, F. & Tondeur, P. Flat Manifolds. LC 68-55623. (Lecture Notes in Mathematics: Vol. 67). 1968. pap. 10.70 (ISBN 0-387-04237-7). Springer-Verlag.

Kenner, Hugh. Geodesic Math & How to Use It. LC 74-27292. 150p. 1976. 15.95x (ISBN 0-520-02924-0); pap. 5.95 (ISBN 0-520-03054-0, CAL 323). U of Cal Pr.

Klingenberg, W. A Course in Differential Geometry. Hoffman, D., tr. from Ger. LC 77-4475. (Graduate Texts in Mathematics: Vol. 51). 1978. pap. text ed. 19.60 (ISBN 0-387-90255-4). Springer-Verlag.

Kobayashi, S. Transformation Groups in Differential Geometry. LC 72-80361. (Ergebnisse der Mathematik und Ihrer Grenzgebiete: Vol. 70). 182p. 1972. 22.80 (ISBN 0-387-05848-6). Springer-Verlag.

Kobayashi, Shoshichi & Nomizu, K. Foundations of Differential Geometry, 2 pts. LC 63-19209. (Pure & Applied Mathematics Ser.: Vol. 15). 329p. 1963. Pt. 1. 38.50 (ISBN 0-470-49647-9); Pt. 2. 42.00 (ISBN 0-470-49648-7, Pub. by Wiley-Interscience). Wiley.

Kompaniec, V. P., et al. Fourteen Papers on Algebra, Topology, Algebraic & Differential Geometry. LC 51-5559. (Translations Ser.: No. 2, Vol. 73). 1968. 29.60 (ISBN 0-8218-1773-6, TRANS 2-73). Am Math.

Kreyszig, Erwin. Introduction to Differential Geometry & Riemannian Geometry. LC 68-108147. 1968. 17.50x (ISBN 0-8020-1501-8). U of Toronto Pr.

Lane, Ernest P. Metric Differential Geometry of Curves & Surfaces. LC 40-12579. (Illus.). 1940. 8.00x (ISBN 0-226-46861-5). U of Chicago Pr.

Laugwitz, D. Differential & Riemannian Geometry. Steinhardt, F., tr. 1965. 38.50 (ISBN 0-12-437750-5). Acad Pr.

Lipschutz, Martin. Differential Geometry. (Schaum's Outline Ser). 1969. pap. 4.95 (ISBN 0-07-037985-8, SP). McGraw.

Matsushima, Yozo. Holomorphic Vector Fields on Compact Kaehler Manifolds. LC 77-145641. (CBMS Regional Conference Series in Mathematics: No. 7). 1971. 7.40 (ISBN 0-8218-1656-X, CBMS-7). Am Math.

Millman, Richard S. & Parker, George D. Elements of Differential Geometry. LC 76-28497. (Illus.). 1977. 20.95 (ISBN 0-13-264143-7). P-H.

Milnor, John W. Morse Theory. (Annals of Mathematics Studies: Vol. 51). (Orig.). 1963. pap. 14.00 (ISBN 0-691-08008-9). Princeton U Pr.

NATO Advanced Study Institute, 1973. Geometric Methods in System Theory: Proceedings. Mayne, D. Q. & Brockett, R. W., eds. LC 73-91206. (NATO Advanced Study Institutes: No. C-3). 1973. lib. bdg. 39.50 (ISBN 90-277-0415-5, Pub. by Reidel Holland). Kluwer Boston.

Niemark, Ju. I. & Fufaev, N. A. Dynamics of Nonholonomic Systems. LC 72-3274. (Translations of Mathematical Monographs: No. 33). 1972. 78.40 (ISBN 0-8218-1583-0, MMONO-33). Am Math.

O'Neill, Barrett. Elementary Differential Geometry. 1966. text ed. 20.95 (ISBN 0-12-526750-9); answer bklt. 3.00 (ISBN 0-12-526756-8). Acad Pr.

Pogorelov, A. V. Extrinsic Geometry of Convex Surfaces. 2nd ed. (Illus.). 680p. 1972. 47.50x (ISBN 0-7065-1261-8, Pub. by IPST). Intl Schol Bk Serv.

Poor, Walter A. Differential Geometric Structures. (Illus.). 320p. 1981. text ed. 39.95 (ISBN 0-07-050435-0, C). McGraw.

Poston, T. & Woodcock, A. E. A Geometrical Study of the Elementary Catastrophes. LC 73-22575. (Lectures Notes in Mathematics: Vol. 373). (Illus.). v, 257p. 1974. pap. 14.60 (ISBN 0-387-06681-0). Springer-Verlag.

Rauzy, G., ed. Repartition Modulo 1. LC 75-20300. (Lecture Notes in Mathematics: Vol. 475). 258p. 1975. pap. 14.70 (ISBN 0-387-07388-4). Springer-Verlag.

Regional Conference on Relativity, Univ. of Pittsburgh, July 13-17, 1970. Methods of Local & Global Differential Geometry in General Relativity: Proceedings. Farnsworth, D., et al, eds. LC 72-75728. (Lecture Notes in Physics: Vol. 14). 194p. 1972. pap. 10.70 (ISBN 0-387-05793-5). Springer-Verlag.

Romanov, V. G. Integral Geometry & Inverse Problems for Hyperbolic Equations. (Springer Tracts in Natural Philosophy: Vol. 26). (Illus.). 152p. 1974. 34.20 (ISBN 0-387-06429-X). Springer-Verlag.

Schwartz, Jacob T. Differential Geometry & Topology. (Notes on Mathematics & Its Applications Ser). 1968. 37.50- (ISBN 0-677-01510-0). Gordon.

Singer, I. M. & Thorpe, J. A. Lecture Notes on Elementary Topology & Geometry. LC 76-26137. (Undergraduate Texts in Mathematics). 1976. 17.60 (ISBN 0-387-90202-3). Springer-Verlag.

Spivak, Michael. A Comprehensive Introduction to Differential Geometry, 5 vols. 2nd ed. LC 78-71771. (Illus.). 1979. Set. text ed. 87.50 (ISBN 0-914098-83-7); Vols. 1-2 Set. text ed. 31.25 (ISBN 0-914098-81-0); Vols. 3-5 Set. text ed. 62.50 (ISBN 0-914098-82-9); Vol. 1. pap. text ed. 12.50x (ISBN 0-914098-79-9); Vol. 2. pap. text ed. 10.00x (ISBN 0-914098-80-2). Publish or Perish.

Steklov Institute of Mathematics, Academy of Sciences, U S S R, No. 76. Two-Dimensional Manifolds of Bounded Curvature: Proceedings. Aleksandrov, A. D. & Zalgaller, V. A., eds. 1967. 36.00 (ISBN 0-8218-1876-7, STEKLO-76). Am Math.

Stoker, James. Differential Geometry. (Pure & Applied Mathematics Ser.). 404p. 1969. 37.50 (ISBN 0-471-82825-4, Pub. by Wiley-Interscience). Wiley.

Symposia in Pure Mathematics - Stanford, Calif., 1973. Differential Geometry, Pts 1-2: Vol. 27, 2 parts. Chern, S. S. & Osserman, R., eds. LC 75-6593. 1975. Set. 92.80 (ISBN 0-685-55822-3, PSPUM-27); Pt. 1. 52.00 (ISBN 0-8218-0247-X, PSPUM-27.1); Pt. 2. 52.00 (ISBN 0-8218-0248-8, PSPUM-27.2). Am Math.

Symposia in Pure Mathematics-Tempe, Ariz.-1960. Differential Geometry: Proceedings, Vol. 3. Allendoerfer, C. B., ed. LC 50-1183. 1961. 23.60 (ISBN 0-8218-1403-6, PSPUM-3). Am Math.

Thomas, Tracy Y. Concepts from Tensor Analysis & Differential Geometry. 2nd ed. (Mathematics in Science & Engineering: Vol. 1). 1965. 31.50 (ISBN 0-12-688462-5). Acad Pr.

Thorpe, J. Elementary Topics in Differential Geometry. (Undergraduate Texts in Mathematics). (Illus.). 1979. pap. 17.60 (ISBN 0-387-90357-7). Springer-Verlag.

Vaisman, Izu. Cohomology & Differential Forms. (Pure & Applied Mathematics Ser.: Vol. 21). 294p. 1973. 36.50 (ISBN 0-8247-6009-3). Dekker.

Willmore, T. J. Introduction to Differential Geometry. (Illus.). 1959. 19.50x (ISBN 0-19-853125-7). Oxford U Pr.

Yano, K. & Bochner, S. Curvature & Betti Numbers. 1953. pap. 9.00 (ISBN 0-527-02748-0). Kraus Repr.

GEOMETRY, DIFFERENTIAL–PROJECTIVE

Wilczynski, E. J. Projective Differential Geometry. LC 61-17959. 9.95 (ISBN 0-8284-0155-1). Chelsea Pub.

GEOMETRY, ENUMERATIVE

see also Curves; Surfaces

GEOMETRY, HYPERBOLIC

Balaban, T. On the Mixed Problem for a Hyperbolic Equation. LC 52-42839. (Memoirs: No. 112). 1971. 7.20 (ISBN 0-8218-1812-0, MEMO-112). Am Math.

Kelly, P. & Matthews, G. The Non-Euclidean Hyperbolic Plane. (Universitexts Ser.). (Illus.). 350p. 1981. pap. 24.00 (ISBN 0-387-90552-9). Springer-Verlag.

Smogovzhevsky, A. Lobachevskian Geometry. 71p. 1976. pap. 1.25 (ISBN 0-8285-0729-5, Pub. by Mir Pubs Russia). Imported Pubns.

GEOMETRY, INFINITESIMAL

see also Calculus; Calculus of Tensors

GEOMETRY, MODERN

see also Geometry, Affine; Geometry, Projective

Adler, Claire F. Modern Geometry. 2nd ed. 1967. text ed. 15.95 (ISBN 0-07-000421-8, C); teachers' manual 2.95 (ISBN 0-07-000419-6). McGraw.

Smart, James R. Modern Geometries. 2nd ed. Wisner, Robert J., ed. LC 77-15784. (Contemporary Undergraduate Mathematics). (Illus.). 1978. text ed. 18.95 (ISBN 0-8185-0265-7); inst. manual upon adoption of text free (ISBN 0-685-86623-8). Brooks-Cole.

GEOMETRY, MODERN-PLANE

Artzy, Rafael. Linear Geometry. 1965. 13.50 (ISBN 0-201-00362-7, Adv Bk Prog). A-W.

GEOMETRY, NON-EUCLIDEAN

see also Geometry-Foundations; Geometry, Hyperbolic; Geometry, Riemannian; Hyperspace; Parallels (Geometry); Screws, Theory of; Spaces, Generalized

Ball, W. Rouse, et al, eds. String Figures & Other Monographs, 4 vols. in 1. Incl. String Figures. Ball, W. R; History of the Slide Rule. Cajori, F; Non Euclidean Geometry. Carslaw, Horatio S; Methods Geometrical Construction. Petersen, Julius. LC 59-11780. 12.95 (ISBN 0-8284-0130-6). Chelsea Pub.

Boehm, J. & Hertel, E. Polyedergeometrie in n-dimensionalen Raeumen konstanter Kruemmung. (LMW-MA Ser.: No. 70). 288p. 1980. 45.00 (ISBN 3-7643-1160-6). Birkhauser.

Bonola, Roberto. Non-Euclidean Geometry. Carslaw, H. S., ed. 1954. pap. 5.50 (ISBN 0-486-60027-0). Dover.

--Non-Euclidean Geometry: A Critical & Historical Study of Its Development. LC 55-14932. lib. bdg. 13.50x (ISBN 0-88307-028-6). Gannon.

Coxeter, H. S. Non-Euclidean Geometry. 5th ed. 1965. 20.00x (ISBN 0-8020-1068-7). U of Toronto Pr.

Engel, Friederich & Stackel, Paul. Urkunden Zur Geschichte Der Nichteuklidischen Geometrie, 2 Vols. (Ger). Repr. of 1913 ed. Set. 62.00 (ISBN 0-384-63370-6). Johnson Repr.

Greenberg, Marvin J. Euclidean & Non-Euclidean Geometries: Development & History. 2nd ed. LC 79-19348. (Illus.). 1980. text ed. 19.95x (ISBN 0-7167-1103-6); instrs. manual & answer book avail. W H Freeman.

Hess, Adrien L. Four-Dimensional Geometry: Introduction. Smith, Seaton E. & Backman, Carl A., eds. LC 77-4310. 1977. pap. 2.15 (ISBN 0-87353-118-3). NCTM.

Kelly, P. & Matthews, G. The Non-Euclidean Hyperbolic Plane. (Universitexts Ser.). (Illus.). 350p. 1981. pap. 24.00 (ISBN 0-387-90552-9). Springer-Verlag.

Klein, Felix. Nicht-Euklidische Geometrie. LC 59-10281. (Ger). 13.95 (ISBN 0-8284-0129-2). Chelsea Pub.
Magnus, Wilhelm. Noneuclidian Tesselations & Their Groups. 1974. 30.00 (ISBN 0-12-465450-9). Acad Pr.
Rucker, Rudolf V. Geometry, Relativity & the Fourth Dimension. LC 76-22240. (Illus.). 1977. pap. text ed. 2.75 (ISBN 0-486-23400-2). Dover.
Sommerville, Duncan Y. Bibliography of Non-Euclidean Geometry. 2nd ed. LC 72-113150. 1960. text ed. 18.50 (ISBN 0-8284-0175-6). Chelsea Pub.
Yaglom, I. M. A Simple Noneuclidean Geometry & Its Physical Basis. (Heidelberg Science Library). (Illus.). 1979. pap. 20.80 (ISBN 0-387-90332-1). Springer-Verlag.

GEOMETRY, PLANE

see also Area Measurement; Circle; Conic Sections; Geometry, Analytic–Plane; Geometry, Modern–Plane; Triangle

Baker, H. F. Introduction to Plane Geometry. LC 70-141879. 1971. text ed. 14.95 (ISBN 0-8284-0247-7). Chelsea Pub.
Ball, W. Rouse, et al, eds. String Figures & Other Monographs, 4 vols. in 1. Incl. String Figures. Ball, W. R; History of the Slide Rule. Cajori, F; Non Euclidean Geometry. Carslaw, Horatio S; Methods Geometrical Construction. Petersen, Julius. LC 59-11780. 12.95 (ISBN 0-8284-0130-6). Chelsea Pub.
Birkhoff, George D. & Beatley, R. Basic Geometry. 3rd ed. LC 59-7308. (gr. 9-12). 1959. text ed. 12.00 (ISBN 0-8284-0120-9); tchr's manual 2.50 (ISBN 0-8284-0034-2); answer bk. 1.50 (ISBN 0-8284-0162-4). Chelsea Pub.
Bronstein, E. Lines & Half Planes. (Finite Math Text Ser.). write for info. (ISBN 0-685-84473-0). J W Wills.
Gomes Teixeira, Francisco. Traite Des Courbes Speciales Remarquables Planes et Gauches, 3 vols. 2nd ed. LC 73-113153. 1337p. (Fr.). 1972. text ed. 49.50 set (ISBN 0-8284-0255-8). Chelsea Pub.
Hemmerling, Edwin M. Fundamentals of College Geometry. 2nd ed. (Illus.). 1970. text ed. 21.95x (ISBN 0-471-37034-7). Wiley.
Horblit, Marcus & Nielsen, Kaj L. Plane Geometry Problems with Solutions. (Orig.). 1947. pap. 3.95 (ISBN 0-06-460063-7, CO 63, COS). Har-Row.
Pickett, Hale C. An Analysis of Proofs & Solutions of Exercises Used in Plane Geometry Tests. LC 78-177153. (Columbia University. Teachers College. Contributions to Education: No. 747). Repr. of 1938 ed. 17.50 (ISBN 0-404-55747-3). AMS Pr.
Pritulenko, P. V. Plane Figures & Sections: How to Construct Them Given Specific Conditions. 1980. 7.00 (ISBN 0-8285-1778-9, Pub. by Mir Pubs Russia). Imported Pubns.
Rich, Barnett. Plane Geometry. (Orig.). 1963. pap. 4.95 (ISBN 0-07-052245-6, SP). McGraw.
Scherk, P. & Lingenberg, R. Rudiments of Plane Affine Geometry. LC 75-11075. (Mathematical Expositions Ser.). 1975. 12.50x (ISBN 0-8020-2151-4). U of Toronto Pr.
Selby, Peter H. Geometry & Trigonometry for Calculus. LC 74-23936. (Self-Teaching Guides Ser). 352p. 1975. pap. text ed. 6.95x (ISBN 0-471-77558-4). Wiley.
Touton, Frank C. Solving Geometric Originals. LC 76-177698. (Columbia University. Teachers College. Contributions to Education: No. 146). Repr. of 1924 ed. 17.50 (ISBN 0-404-55146-7). AMS Pr.

GEOMETRY, PROJECTIVE

Ayres, Frank, Jr. Projective Geometry. (Schaum's Outline Ser). (Orig.). 1967. pap. 4.95 (ISBN 0-07-002657-2, SP). McGraw.
Baer, Reinhold. Linear Algebra & Projective Geometry. (Pure and Applied Mathematics Ser.: Vol. 2). 1952. 39.50 (ISBN 0-12-072250-X). Acad Pr.
Coxeter, H. S. Projective Geometry. 2nd ed. LC 73-86992. 1974. 12.50x (ISBN 0-8020-2104-2). U of Toronto Pr.
Deaux, Roland. Introduction to the Geometry of Complex Numbers. Eves, Howard, tr. LC 56-13198. 1956. 8.00 (ISBN 0-8044-4176-6). Ungar.
Grunbaum, B. Arrangements & Spreads. LC 71-38926. (CBMS Regional Conference Series in Mathematics: No. 10). 1980. Repr. of 1974 ed. 8.60 (ISBN 0-8218-1659-4, CBMS-10). Am Math.
Hartshorne, Robin. Foundations of Projective Geometry. (Math Lecture Notes Ser.: No. 10). 1967. pap. 11.50 (ISBN 0-8053-3757-1, Adv Bk Prog). Benjamin-Cummings.
Heyting, A. Axiomatic Projective Geometry. (Bibliotheca Mathematics Ser.: Vol. 5). 1963. 10.75 (ISBN 0-444-10212-4, North-Holland). Elsevier.
Horadam, A. F. A Guide to Undergraduate Projective Geometry. LC 71-110243. 1970. 27.00 (ISBN 0-08-017479-5). Pergamon.
Hughes, D. R. & Piper, F. C. Projective Planes. LC 72-75719. (Graduate Texts in Mathematics: Vol. 6). (Illus.). 1973. text ed. 25.00 (ISBN 0-387-90043-8); pap. text ed. 16.20 (ISBN 0-387-90044-6). Springer-Verlag.
Karteszi, F. Introduction to Finite Geometries. (North Holland Texts in Advanced Mathematics: Vol. 2). 1976. 46.50 (ISBN 0-444-10855-6, North-Holland). Elsevier.
Mihalek, R. J. Projective Geometry & Algebraic Structures. 1972. text ed. 18.95 (ISBN 0-12-495550-9). Acad Pr.
Okonek, Christian, et al. Vector Bundles on Complex Projective Spaces. (Progress in Mathematics Ser.: No. 3). 396p. 1980. pap. text ed. 20.00 (ISBN 3-7643-3000-7). Birkhauser.
Pickert, G. Projektive Ebenen. 2nd ed. LC 75-9953. (Die Grundlehren der Mathematischen Wissenschaften: Vol. 80). (Illus.). 371p. 1975. 57.90 (ISBN 0-387-07280-2). Springer-Verlag.
Room, Thomas G. & Kirkpatrick, P. B. Miniquaternion Geometry. LC 79-123347. (Tracts in Mathematics: No. 60). 1971. 28.95 (ISBN 0-521-07926-8). Cambridge U Pr.
Schreier, Otto & Sperner, Emanuel. Projective Geometry of N Dimensions. 11.95 (ISBN 0-8284-0126-8). Chelsea Pub.
Steiner, Jacob. Gesammelte Werke, 2 Vols. 2nd ed. LC 76-113151. (Ger). 1971. text ed. 49.50 set (ISBN 0-8284-0233-7). Chelsea Pub.
Stevenson, Frederick W. Projective Planes. LC 72-156824. (Illus.). 1972. text ed. 26.95x (ISBN 0-7167-0443-9); teacher's manual avail. W H Freeman.
Tyrrell, J. A. & Semple, J. G. Generalized Clifford Parallelism. LC 74-134625. (Tracts in Mathematics Ser.: No. 61). 1971. 23.95 (ISBN 0-521-08042-8). Cambridge U Pr.
Vajda, S. Patterns & Configurations in Finite Spaces. LC 68-6261. (Griffin's Statistical Monographs & Courses: Vol. 21). (Illus.). 1967. pap. 9.75 (ISBN 0-02-854060-3). Hafner.
Von Neumann, John. Continuous Geometry. (Mathematical Ser.: Vol. 25). 1960. 22.00x (ISBN 0-691-07928-5). Princeton U Pr.
Whitehead, A. N. The Axioms of Projective Geometry. (Cambridge Tracts in Mathematics & Mathematical Physics Ser: No. 4). 1971. Repr. of 1906 ed. 7.50 (ISBN 0-02-854720-9). Hafner.
Yale, Paul B. Geometry & Symmetry. LC 67-28042. 1968. 17.95x (ISBN 0-8162-9964-1). Holden-Day.

GEOMETRY, PROJECTIVE DIFFERENTIAL

see Geometry, Differential–Projective

GEOMETRY, RIEMANNIAN

Bender, William. The Scale Coordinate & Its Geometry: The Quantization of Riemannian Geometry. LC 76-9498. 1975. text ed. 10.00 (ISBN 0-682-48567-5, University). Exposition.
Blair, D. E. Contact Manifold in Riemannian Geometry. (Lecture Notes in Mathematics Ser: Vol. 509). 1976. pap. 9.90 (ISBN 0-387-07626-3). Springer-Verlag.
Cheeger, J. & Ebin, D. G. Comparison Theorems in Riemannian Geometry. LC 74-83725. (Mathematical Library: Vol. 9). 174p. 1975. 29.50 (ISBN 0-444-10764-9, North-Holland). Elsevier.
Eisenhart, Luther P. Riemannian Geometry. rev. ed. 1950. 19.00 (ISBN 0-691-08026-7). Princeton U Pr.
Kreyszig, Erwin. Introduction to Differential Geometry & Riemannian Geometry. LC 68-108147. 1968. 17.50x (ISBN 0-8020-1501-8). U of Toronto Pr.
Laugwitz, D. Differential & Riemannian Geometry. Steinhardt, F., tr. 1965. 38.50 (ISBN 0-12-437750-5). Acad Pr.

GEOMETRY, SOLID

see also Crystallography; Cube; Geometry, Analytic–Solid; Polyhedra; Sphere; Surfaces

Bassetti, Fred & Ruchlis, Hy. Math Projects: Polyhedral Shapes. (Illus., Orig.). (gr. 4-9). 1968. pap. 2.50 (ISBN 0-87594-016-1, 3040). Book-Lab.
Cohn, P. M. Solid Geometry. (Library of Mathematics). 1968. pap. 3.00 (ISBN 0-7100-6343-1). Routledge & Kegan.
Court, Nathan A. Modern Pure Solid Geometry. 2nd ed. LC 64-18134. 1979. text ed. 14.95 (ISBN 0-8284-0147-0). Chelsea Pub.
Hilbert, David & Cohn-Vossen, Stephan. Geometry & the Imagination. LC 52-2894. (gr. 9 up). 1952. text ed. 14.95 (ISBN 0-8284-0087-3). Chelsea Pub.
Wheeler, David. Presenting the Gattegno Prisms & Cubes. 1974. pap. 1.25 (ISBN 0-87825-029-8). Ed Solutions.
Zameeruddin, Qazi & Khanna, V. K. Solid Geometry. 1977. 15.00 (ISBN 0-7069-0560-1, Pub. by Vikas India). Advent NY.

GEOMETRY CONCEPT

Brunelle, Wallace & O'Neill, Robert. Constructional Geometry. Gray, Allan W., ed. 1972. pap. text ed. 8.25 (ISBN 0-89420-077-1, 350299); cassette recordings 107.95 (ISBN 0-89420-201-4, 350300). Natl Book.
Piaget, Jean, et al. Child's Conception of Geometry. Lunzer, E. A., tr. LC 60-7177. (Illus.). 1960. 13.95x (ISBN 0-465-01078-4). Basic.
--The Child's Conception of Geometry. Lunzer, E. A., tr. 432p. 1981. pap. 8.95 (ISBN 0-393-00057-5). Norton.

GEOMETRY OF NUMBERS

see also Numbers, Theory of

Cassels, J. W. Introduction to the Geometry of Numbers. 2nd ed. LC 75-154801. (Grundlehren der Mathematischen Wissenschaften: Vol. 99). (Illus.). 1971. 44.70 (ISBN 0-387-02397-6). Springer-Verlag.

GEOMETRY OF PATHS

see Spaces, Generalized

GEOMORPHOLOGY

see also Erosion; Landforms; Physical Geography; Volcanism

Ahmad, Enayat. Coastal Geomorphology of India. (Illus.). 222p. 1973. text ed. 7.50x (ISBN 0-391-00632-0). Humanities.
Andrews, John T. A Geomorphical Study of Post-Glacial Uplift: With Particular Reference to Arctic Canada. (Special Publication of the Institute of British Geographers: No. 2). 1980. 23.00 (ISBN 0-12-058580-4). Acad Pr.
Bird, J. Brian. The Physiography of Arctic Canada: With Special Reference to the Area South of Parry Channel. LC 67-16232. (Illus.). 384p. 1967. 25.00x (ISBN 0-8018-0072-2). Johns Hopkins.
Birkeland, Peter W. Pedology, Weathering & Geomorphological Research. (Illus.). 304p. 1974. text ed. 15.95x (ISBN 0-19-501730-7). Oxford U Pr.
Bloom, A. L. Surface of the Earth. (gr. 10 up). pap. text ed. 8.95 (ISBN 0-13-877944-9). P-H.
Bloom, Arthur L. Geomorphology: A Systematic Analysis of Late Cenozoic Landforms. LC 77-25816. (Illus.). 1978. ref. ed. 26.50 (ISBN 0-13-353086-8). P-H.
Brown, E. H. & Waters, R. S., eds. Progress in Geomorphology: Papers in Honour of David L. Linton. (Special Publication of the Institute of British Geographers: No. 7). 1980. 23.00 (ISBN 0-12-137780-6). Acad Pr.
Brunsden, Denys & Doornkamp, John, eds. The Unquiet Landscape. LC 74-8404. (Illus.). 176p. 1975. 17.50x (ISBN 0-253-36171-0). Ind U Pr.
Brunsden, Denys, et al, eds. The Unquiet Landscape. LC 77-15583. (The Geographical Magazine Ser.). 1978. Repr. of 1972 ed. 19.95 (ISBN 0-470-99345-6). Halsted Pr.
Butzer, Karl W. Geomorphology from the Earth. (Meinig Ser.). (Illus.). 512p. 1976. text ed. 26.50 scp (ISBN 0-06-041097-3, HarpC). Har-Row.
Carson, M. A. & Kirkby, M. J. Hillslope Form & Process. (Cambridge Geographical Studies). 49.50 (ISBN 0-521-08234-X). Cambridge U Pr.
Chapman, L. J. & Putnam, D. F. Physiography of Southern Ontario. 2nd ed. LC 66-6736. (Illus.). 1966. 25.00x (ISBN 0-8020-1944-7); pap. 7.50 (ISBN 0-8020-6071-4); maps 10.00x (ISBN 0-8020-2107-7). U of Toronto Pr.
Chikishev, A. G., ed. Landscape Indicators. LC 72-88886. (Illus.). 165p. 1973. 35.00 (ISBN 0-306-10875-5, Consultants). Plenum Pub.
Chorley, R. J., et al. History of the Study of Landforms; or, the Development of Geomorphology, Vol. 2: The Life & Work of William Morris Davis. 874p. 1973. 65.00x (ISBN 0-416-26890-0). Methuen Inc.
Coates, Donald, ed. Coastal Geomorphology. (Binghamton Symposia in Geomorphology International Ser.: No. 3). (Illus.). 416p. 1980. text ed. 20.00x (ISBN 0-04-551038-5). Allen Unwin.
Coates, Donald R., ed. Environmental Geomorphology & Landscape Conservation, 3 vols. Incl. Vol. 1. Prior to 1900. 1972. 50.00 (ISBN 0-12-786241-2); Vol. 2. Urban Areas. 464p. 1974. 50.00 (ISBN 0-12-786242-0); Vol. 3. Non-Urban Regions. 496p. 1973. 50.00 (ISBN 0-12-786243-9). LC 72-77882. (Benchmark Papers in Geology Ser.). (Illus.). Acad Pr.
--Geomorphology & Engineering. (Binghamton Symposia in Geomorphology: International Ser.: No. 7). (Illus.). 384p. 1980. text ed. 30.00x (ISBN 0-04-551040-7). Allen Unwin.
--Urban Geomorphology. LC 76-4242. (Special Paper: No. 174). (Illus., Orig.). 1976. pap. 15.00x (ISBN 0-8137-2174-1). Geol Soc.
Coates, Donald R. & Vitek, John D., eds. Thresholds in Geomorphology. (Binghamton Symposia in Geomorphology Ser.: Vol. 9). (Illus.). 512p. (Orig.). 1980. text ed. 35.00x (ISBN 0-04-551033-4). Allen Unwin.
Cooke, Ronald U. & Doornkamp, John C. Geomorphology in Environmental Management: An Introduction. (Illus.). 348p. 1974. text ed. 29.50x (ISBN 0-19-874020-4); pap. text ed. 16.50x (ISBN 0-19-874021-2). Oxford U Pr.
Cooke, Ronald U. & Warren, Andrew. Geomorphology in Deserts. 1974. 27.50x (ISBN 0-520-02280-7). U of Cal Pr.
Cullingford, R. A., et al. Timescales in Geomorphology. LC 79-40517. 1980. 85.75 (ISBN 0-471-27600-6, Pub. by Wiley-Interscience). Wiley.
Davies, Gordon L. The Earth in Decay: A History of British Geomorphology 1578-1878. LC 75-99798. 1969. lib. bdg. 15.00 (ISBN 0-685-52436-1). N Watson.
Delaney, Patrick J. Geology & Geomorphology of the Coastal Plain of Rio Grande Do Sul, Brazil & Northern Uruguay. LC 66-64637. (Coastal Studies: Vol. 15). (Illus.). 1966. pap. 4.00x (ISBN 0-8071-0428-0). La State U Pr.
Derbyshire, E., et al. Geomorphological Processes. LC 79-5285. (Studies in Physical Geography Ser.). 312p. 1980. lib. bdg. 31.25x (ISBN 0-89158-695-4, Pub. by Dawson Pub); pap. text ed. 13.50x (ISBN 0-89158-864-7). Westview.
Derbyshire, Edward, ed. Geomorphology & Climate. LC 75-4523. 514p. 1976. 89.75 (ISBN 0-471-20954-6, Pub. by Wiley-Interscience). Wiley.
Doehring, D. Geomorphology of Arid Regions. (Geomorphology Symposium: 8th). 1977. 10.00 (ISBN 0-686-10459-5). Pubns Geomorphology.
Doehring, Donald O., ed. Geomorphology in Arid Regions. (Binghamton Symposia in Geomorphology: International Ser.: No. 8). (Illus.). 276p. 1980. text ed. 20.00x (ISBN 0-04-551041-5). Allen Unwin.
Easterbrook, Don J. Principles of Geomorphology. LC 69-13207. (Illus.). 1969. text ed. 23.00 (ISBN 0-07-018780-0, C). McGraw.
Embleton, C. & King, C. A. Glacial & Periglacial Morphology, 2 vols. 2nd ed. Incl. Vol. 1. Glacial Geomorphology. LC 75-14188. pap. 21.95 (ISBN 0-470-23893-3); Vol. 2. Periglacial Geomorphology. LC 75-14187. pap. 15.95 (ISBN 0-470-23895-X). 1975. Halsted Pr.
Embleton, Clifford & Thornes, John, eds. Process in Geomorphology. LC 79-18747. 436p. 1979. 52.95x (ISBN 0-470-26807-7); pap. 22.95x (ISBN 0-470-26808-5). Halsted Pr.
Embleton, Clifford, et al, eds. Geomorphology: Present Problems & Future Prospects. (Illus.). 1978. text ed. 37.50x (ISBN 0-19-874078-6). Oxford U Pr.
Fairbridge, R., ed. Encyclopedia of Geomorphology. LC 68-58342. (Encyclopedia of Earth Sciences Ser: Vol. III). 1968. 78.00x (ISBN 0-12-786459-8). Acad Pr.
Garner, H. F. Origin of Landscapes: A Synthesis of Geomorphology. (Illus.). 656p. 1974. text ed. 20.95x (ISBN 0-19-501764-1). Oxford U Pr.
Geomorphological Map of Papua New Guinea. (Land Research Ser.: No. 33). (Illus.). 23p. 1979. 13.50 (ISBN 0-643-00092-5, CO17, CSIRO). Unipub.
Gladfelter, Bruce G. Meseta & Campina Landforms in Central Spain. LC 75-133028. (Research Papers Ser.: No. 130). (Illus., Orig.). 1971. pap. 8.00 (ISBN 0-89065-037-3, 130). U Chicago Dept Geog.
Gouldie, Andrew, ed. Geomorphological Techniques. (Illus.). 320p. 1981. text ed. 60.00x (ISBN 0-04-551042-3); pap. text ed. 29.95x (ISBN 0-04-551043-1). Allen Unwin.
Hails, John R., ed. Applied Geomorphology. 1977. 48.00 (ISBN 0-444-41317-0). Elsevier.
Helgren, David M. Rivers of Diamonds: An Alluvial History of the Lower Vaal Basin, South Africa. LC 79-17790. (Research Papers Ser.: No. 185). (Illus.). 388p. 1979. pap. 8.00 (ISBN 0-89065-092-6). U Chicago Dept Geog.
Hettner, Alfred. The Surface Features of the Land: Problems & Methods of Geomorphology. Tilley, Phillip, tr. from Ger. LC 73-175940. 1972. 18.50 (ISBN 0-02-845970-9). Hafner.
Hurlbut, Cornelius S., Jr. & Switzer, George S. Geomology. LC 78-13262. 1979. 29.50 (ISBN 0-471-42224-X, Pub. by Wiley-Interscience). Wiley.
Jackson, Roscoe G., II & Day, T. J. Mass Wasting, Nineteen Seventy-Five. (Guelph Geomorphology Ser.). 202p. 1980. 10.35x (ISBN 0-902246-58-5, Pub. by GEO Abstracts England). State Mutual Bk.
--Research in Fluvial Systems Nineteen Seventy-Seven. (Guelph Geomorphology Ser.). 214p. 1980. 11.50x (ISBN 0-86094-013-6, Pub. by GEO Abstracts England). State Mutual Bk.
--Research in Polar & Alpine Geomorphology, 1973. 206p. 1980. 11.50x (ISBN 0-902246-22-4, Pub. by GEO Abstracts England). State Mutual Bk.
--Research Methods in Pleistocene Geomorphology, 1971. (Guelph Geomorphology Ser.). 285p. 1980. 13.80x (ISBN 0-902246-17-8, Pub. by GEO Abstracts England). State Mutual Bk.

King, Cuchlaine, ed. Landforms & Geomorphology: Concepts & History. LC 76-3489. (Benchmark Papers in Geology Ser.: Vol. 28). 400p. 1976. 51.00 (ISBN 0-12-786845-3). Acad Pr.
King, Lester C. South African Scenery, a Textbook of Geomorphology. 3rd rev. ed. (Illus.). 1967. 15.25 (ISBN 0-02-847900-9). Hafner.
Leopold, Luna B., et al. Fluvial Processes in Geomorphology. LC 64-10919. (Geology Ser.). (Illus.). 1964. 27.95x (ISBN 0-7167-0221-5). W H Freeman.
Lobeck, A. K. Geomorphology. (Illus.). 1939. text ed. 23.50 (ISBN 0-07-038210-7, C). McGraw.
Loffler, E. Explanatory Notes to the Geomorphological Map of Papua New Guinea. (Land Pesearch Ser.: No. 33). (Illus.). 19p. 1977. pap. 7.25x (ISBN 0-643-00092-5, Pub. by CSIRO). Intl Schol Bk Serv.
McCullagh, Patrick. Modern Concepts in Geomorphology. (Science in Geography Ser.). (Illus.). 128p. (Orig.). 1978. pap. text ed. 7.95x (ISBN 0-19-913236-4). Oxford U Pr.
McFarlane, J. M. Laterite & Landscape. 1977. 26.50 (ISBN 0-12-484450-2). Acad Pr.
Michael, Henry N., ed. Archaeology & Geomorphology of Northern Asia: Selected Works. LC 65-1456. (Illus.). 1964. pap. 12.50x (ISBN 0-8020-3127-7). U of Toronto Pr.
Morisawa, Marie. Geomorphology Laboratory Manual with Report Forms. LC 76-13456. 1976. pap. text ed. 13.95x (ISBN 0-471-01847-3). Wiley.
Morisawa, W. Streams: Their Dynamics & Morphology. LC 68-12267. 1968. pap. text ed. 8.95 (ISBN 0-07-043123-X, C). McGraw.
Pitty, Alistair F. Introduction to Geomorphology. 1971. pap. 18.95x (ISBN 0-416-29760-9). Methuen Inc.
Rai, Rajkumar. The Geomorphology of Sonar Basin. 1980. pap. text ed. 14.50x (ISBN 0-391-01835-3). Humanities.
Rice, R. J. Fundamentals of Geomorphology. (Illus.). 1977. text ed. 32.00x (ISBN 0-582-48429-4); pap. text ed. 18.95x (ISBN 0-582-48430-8). Longman.
Ritchot, Gilles. Essais de Geomorphologie Structurale. (Travaus Du Departement De Geographie De L'universite Laval: No. 3). (Illus.). xix, 388p. (Fr.). 1975. pap. 24.00x (ISBN 2-7637-6742-7, Pub. by Laval). Intl Schol Bk Serv.
Ritter, Dale F. Process Geomorphology. 600p. 1978. text ed. write for info. (ISBN 0-697-05035-1). Wm C Brown.
Robbins, R. G., ed. Lands of the Ramu - Madang Area, Papua New Guinea. (Land Research Ser.: No. 37). (Illus.). 1977. pap. 7.25x (ISBN 0-643-00175-1, Pub. by CSIRO). Intl Schol Bk Serv.
Ruhe, Robert. Geomorphology. 1975. text ed. 20.95 (ISBN 0-395-18553-X). HM.
Ruhe, Robert V. Quaternary Landscapes in Iowa. facsimile ed. LC 69-14312. (Illus.). 1969. 10.65x (ISBN 0-8138-2440-0). Iowa St U Pr.
Scheidegger, Adrian E. Theoretical Geomorphology. 2nd ed. LC 70-110153. (Illus.). 1970. 69.10 (ISBN 0-387-05005-1). Springer-Verlag.
Schwartz, Maurice L., ed. Spits & Bars. LC 72-88983. (Benchmark Papers in Geology Ser). 1973. text ed. 50.00 (ISBN 0-12-787448-8). Acad Pr.
Sissons, J. B. Evolution of Scotland's Scenery. (Illus.). 1967. 19.50 (ISBN 0-208-00163-8, Archon). Shoe String.
Small, R. J. The Study of Landforms. 2nd ed. LC 77-71427. 1978. 57.50 (ISBN 0-521-21634-6); pap. 23.95x (ISBN 0-521-29238-7). Cambridge U Pr.
Snead, Rodman E. World Atlas of Geomorphic Features. LC 77-28009. 320p. 1980. 39.50 (ISBN 0-88275-272-3). Krieger.
Steers, J. A., ed. Applied Coastal Geomorphology. 1st u.s. ed. 1971. 17.50x (ISBN 0-262-19088-5). MIT Pr.
Steers, J. Alfred. Coastal Features of England & Wales: Eight Essays. (Illus.). 240p. 1981. 35.00 (ISBN 0-900891-70-X). Oleander Pr.
Thomas, Michael F. Tropical Geomorphology: A Study of Weathering & Land Form Development in Warm Climates. LC 73-13428. 1976. pap. 14.95 (ISBN 0-470-98939-4). Halsted Pr.
Thornes, John & Brunsden, Denys. Geomorphology & Time. LC 76-30862. 208p. 1977. text ed. 15.95x (ISBN 0-416-80080-7, Pub. by Chapman & Hall England). Methuen Inc.
Tricart, J. Structural Geomorphology. Beaver, S. & Derbyshire, E., trs. from Fr. LC 73-86130. (Geographies for Advanced Study). Orig. Title: Geomorphologie Structural. (Illus.). 320p. 1974. text ed. 16.95x (ISBN 0-582-48462-6). Longman.
Tricart, J. & Cailleux. An Introduction to Climatic Geomorphology. 1973. 21.50 (ISBN 0-312-42630-5). St Martin.
Twidale, C. R. Analysis of Landforms: An Introduction to Geomorphology. 572p. 1976. 34.95 (ISBN 0-471-89465-6, Pub. by Wiley-Interscience). Wiley.
Verstappen, H. Remote Sensing in Geomorphology. 1977. 53.75 (ISBN 0-444-41086-4). Elsevier.
Vocabulaire Franco-Anglo-Allemand De Geomorphologie. (Fr., Eng. & Ger.). 1970. pap. 14.95 (ISBN 0-686-57278-5, F-136940). French & Eur.
Weyman, Darrell & Weyman, Valerie. Landscape Processes: An Introduction to Geomorphology. (Processes in Physical Geography Ser). (Illus.). 1977. pap. text ed. 6.95x (ISBN 0-04-551026-1). Allen Unwin.

GEOPHAGY
see Pica (Pathology)

GEOPHYSICAL INSTRUMENTS
see also Meteorological Instruments

GEOPHYSICAL OBSERVATORIES
see also Meteorological Stations

GEOPHYSICAL PROSPECTING
see Prospecting–Geophysical Methods

GEOPHYSICAL RESEARCH

Cassinis, R., ed. The Solution of the Inverse Problem in Geophysical Interpretation. 380p. 1981. 45.00 (ISBN 0-306-40735-3, Plenum Pr). Plenum Pub.
Fitch, A. A., ed. Developments in Geophysical Exploration Methods- Two. (Developments Ser.). (Illus.). 234p. 1981. text ed. 36.00 (ISBN 0-85334-930-4, Pub. by Applied Sci England). J K Burgess.
Geophysics Research Board & Division Of Earth Sciences. Solid-Earth Geophysics: Survey & Outlook. 1964. pap. 5.00 (ISBN 0-309-01231-7). Natl Acad Pr.
Geophysics Research Board, National Research Council. Geophysical Predictions. LC 78-8147. (Studies in Geophysics Ser.). 1978. pap. text ed. 12.75 (ISBN 0-309-02741-1). Natl Acad Pr.
Gronlie, Gisle. Geophysical Studies in the Norwegian-Greenland Sea. (Norsk Polarinstitutt Skrifter: Vol. 170). (Illus.). 117p. 1980. pap. 10.00 (ISBN 82-90307-05-5). Universitet.
Persen, L. N. Rock Dynamics & Geophysical Exploration. LC 74-21865. (Developments in Geotechnical Engineering: Vol. 8). 276p. 1975. 53.75 (ISBN 0-444-41284-0). Elsevier.
Peser, John, ed. Agronomy Science in Action. 1981. free copy avail. (ISBN 0-89118-059-1). Am Soc Agron.
Silvia, M. T. & Robinson, E. A. Deconvolution of Geophysical Time Series in the Exploration of Oil & Natural Gas. (Developments in Petroleum Science Ser.: Vol. 10). 1979. 54.75 (ISBN 0-444-41679-X). Elsevier.

GEOPHYSICS
see also Astronautics in Geophysics; Atmospheric Electricity; Auroras; Continents; Earth Movements; Earth Tides; Geodynamics; Geology; Geophysical Research; Magnetism; Magnetohydrodynamics; Meteorology; Nuclear Geophysics; Oceanography; Plate Tectonics; Prospecting–Geophysical Methods; Radiative Transfer; Seismology; Van Allen Radiation Belts

Adam, A. Geoelectric & Geothermal Studies. 1976. 55.00x (ISBN 963-05-0887-7). Intl Pubns Serv.
Akasofu, Syun-Ichi & Chapman, Sidney. Solar-Terrestrial Physics. (International Ser. of Monographs on Physics). (Illus.). 1000p. 1972. 112.00x (ISBN 0-19-851262-7). Oxford U Pr.
American Meteorological Society - Boston. Cumulated Bibliography & Index to Meteorological & Geoastrophysical Abstracts: 1950-1969. 1972. Author Sequence, 5 Vols. 1340.00 (ISBN 0-685-01570-X). Dec. Class, 4 Vols (ISBN 0-8161-0183-3). G K Hall.
--Cumulated Bibliography & Index to Meteorological & Geoastrophysical Abstracts, 1950-1969: Author Sequence, 5 vols. 1972. 800.00 (ISBN 0-8161-0942-7). G K Hall.
Annals of the International Geophysical Year. Vols. 1-20, 1973. pap. text ed. 690.00 (ISBN 0-08-019913-5); Vols. 1-24. pap. text ed. 830.00 (ISBN 0-08-019911-9); Vols. 21-22 Separately, 1974. pap. text ed. 360.00 (ISBN 0-08-018913-X); Vols. 23-48, 1975. pap. text ed. 750.00 (ISBN 0-08-019914-3). Single Vols. 2, 5. pap. text ed. 28.00 ea. Pergamon.
Athay, R. G. Radiation Transport in Spectral Lines. LC 72-188002. (Geophysics & Astrophysics Monographs: No. 1). 266p. 1972. lib. bdg. 39.50 (ISBN 90-277-0228-4, Pub. by Reidel Holland); pap. 21.50 (ISBN 90-277-0241-1, Pub. by Reidel Holland). Kluwer Boston.
Augustithis, S. S. Atlas of the Textural Patterns of Basic & Ultrabasic Rocks & Their Genetic Significance. 1979. 150.00x (ISBN 3-11-006571-1). De Gruyter.
Baguelin, F., et al. The Pressuremeter & Foundation Engineering. (Rock & Soil Mechanics Ser.). (Illus.). 1978. 58.00x (ISBN 0-87849-019-1). Trans Tech.
Baranov, W. Potential Fields & Their Transformations in Applied Geophysics. Nostrand, van R. & Saxov, S., eds. (Geoexploration Monographs 1: No. 6). (Illus.). 1975. 50.00x (ISBN 3-443-13008-9). Intl Pubns Serv.
Bath, M. Spectral Analysis in Geophysics. (Development in Solid Earth Geophysics: Vol. 7). 208p. 1974. 88.00 (ISBN 0-444-41222-0). Elsevier.
Beck, A. E. Physical Principles of Exploration Methods. LC 81-80411. 256p. 1981. 39.95 (ISBN 0-470-27124-8); pap. 18.95 (ISBN 0-470-27128-0). Halsted Pr.
Beynon, Granville, ed. Solar-Terrestrial Physics: Proceedings of an International Symposium, Innsbruck, Austria, 1978. (Illus.). 240p. 1979. pap. 43.00 (ISBN 0-08-025054-8). Pergamon.
Bowhill, S. A., ed. Review Papers: International Solar-Terrestrial Physics Symposium, Sao-Paolo, June, 1974. 212p. 1976. pap. 55.00 (ISBN 0-08-019959-3). Pergamon.
Bruzek, Anton & Durrant, Christopher J., eds. Illustrated Glossary for Solar & Solar-Terrestrial Physics. (Astrophysics & Space Science Library: No. 69). 1977. lib. bdg. 34.00 (ISBN 90-277-0825-8, Pub. by Reidel Holland). Kluwer Boston.
Cermak, V. & Rybach, L., eds. Terrestrial Heat Flow in Europe. (Illus.). 1979. 51.50 (ISBN 0-387-09440-7). Springer-Verlag.
Clark, Sydney P. Structure of the Earth. (Foundations of Earth Science Ser.). 1971. pap. text ed. 8.95 (ISBN 0-13-854646-0). P-H.
Cook, A. H. The Physics of the Earth & the Planets. LC 72-12261. 316p. 1973. text ed. 38.95 (ISBN 0-470-16910-9). Halsted Pr.
Coulson, Kinsell L. Solar & Terrestrial Radiation. 1975. 35.75 (ISBN 0-12-192950-7). Acad Pr.
Dohr, Gerhard. Applied Geophysics: Introduction to Geophysical Prospecting. 2nd ed. LC 80-28695. (Geology of Petroleum Ser.). 256p. 1981. pap. 21.95 (ISBN 0-470-99102-X). Halsted Pr.
Duxbury, A. The Earth & Its Oceans. LC 73-131202. (Earth Science Ser.). 1971. 19.95 (ISBN 0-201-01616-8). A-W.
Egeland, Alv, et al, eds. Cosmical Geophysics. (Illus.). 360p. 1973. 33.50x (ISBN 8-200-02256-0, Dist. by Columbia U Pr). Universitet.
Eskinazi, S. Fluid Mechanics & Thermodynamics of Our Environment. 1975. 48.50 (ISBN 0-12-242540-5); lib ed 54.00 (ISBN 0-12-242541-3); microfiche 40.50 (ISBN 0-12-242542-1). Acad Pr.
Fitch, A. A., ed. Developments in Geophysical Exploration Methods, Vol. 1. (Illus.). 1979. 51.80x (ISBN 0-85334-835-9, Pub. by Applied Science). Burgess-Intl Ideas.
Flugge, S. Encyclopedia of Physics, Vol. 49, Pt. 5: Geophysics 3, Pt. 5. LC 56-2942. (Illus.). 420p. (Eng, Fr, & Ger.). 1976. 116.90 (ISBN 0-387-07512-7). Springer-Verlag.
Garland, George D. Introduction to Geophysics: Mantle, Core & Crust. 2nd ed. LC 78-54516. (Illus.). 1979. text ed. 20.00 (ISBN 0-7216-4026-5). HR&W.
Geophysics in the Americas: A Symposium of the Geophysics Commission of the Pan American Inst. of Geography & History Ottawa, Canada, Sept. 76. (Illus.). 1978. pap. 18.50 (ISBN 0-660-00702-9, SSC 102, SSC). Unipub.
Geophysics Research Board. Impact of Technology on Geophysics. xii, 121p. 1979. pap. 10.25 (ISBN 0-309-02887-6). Natl Acad Pr.
Geophysics Study Committee. Estuaries, Geophysics, & the Environment. LC 77-82812. (Studies in Geophysics). (Illus.). 1977. pap. text ed. 8.50 (ISBN 0-309-02629-6). Natl Acad Pr.
Goguel, Jean. Geophysique. (Methodique Ser.). 1336p. 53.95 (ISBN 0-686-56430-8). French & Eur.
Gordon, C. W. & Canuto, V. Handbook of Astronomy, Astrophysics, & Geophysics, Vol. I. 1978. 81.50x (ISBN 0-677-16100-X). Gordon.
Grant, F. S. & West, G. F. Interpretation Theory in Applied Geophysics. (Illus.). 1965. text ed. 29.00 (ISBN 0-07-024100-7, C). McGraw.
Griffiths, D. H. & King, R. F. Applied Geophysics for Geologists & Engineers: The Elements of Geophysical Prospecting. 2nd ed. (Illus.). 224p. 1981. 30.00 (ISBN 0-08-022071-1); pap. 14.50 (ISBN 0-08-022072-X). Pergamon.
Gy, P. M. Sampling of Particulate Materials. LC 79-16075. (Developments in Geomathematics Ser.: Vol. 4). 432p. 1979. 63.50 (ISBN 0-444-41826-1). Elsevier.
Habberjam, G. M. Apparent Restivity Observations & the Use of Square Array Techniques. (Geoexploration Monographs: No. 9). (Illus.). 1979. 55.00x (ISBN 3-443-13013-5). Intl Pubns Serv.
Hardy, H. Reginald & Leighton, Frederick W. Proceedings of the Second Conference on Acoustic Emission: Microseismic Activity in Geologic Structures & Materials. (Rock & Soil Mechanics Ser.). (Illus.). 500p. 1980. 45.00x (ISBN 0-87849-032-9). Trans Tech.
Hart, P. J., ed. The Earth's Crust & Upper Mantle. LC 75-600572. (Geophysical Monograph Ser.: Vol. 13). 1969. pap. 5.00 (ISBN 0-87590-000-3). Am Geophysical.
Howell, Benjamin F., Jr. Introduction to Geophysics. rev. ed. LC 77-814. (International Ser. in the Earth & Planetary Sciences). (Illus.). 412p. 1978. Repr. of 1959 ed. lib. bdg. 18.00 (ISBN 0-88275-540-4). Krieger.
Jacobs, John A., et al. Physics & Geology. 2nd ed. (International Ser. in the Earth & Planetary Sciences). (Illus.). 448p. 1974. text ed. 26.00 (ISBN 0-07-032148-5, C). McGraw.
Johnson, Francis S., ed. Satellite Environment Handbook. rev. ed. (Illus.). 1965. 10.00x (ISBN 0-8047-0090-7). Stanford U Pr.
Josephs, Melvin J. & Sanders, Howard J. Chemistry & the Environment. LC 67-30718. 1967. 6.75 (ISBN 0-8412-0103-X). Am Chemical.
King, J. W. & Newman, W. S. Solar Terrestrial Physics. 1967. 62.00 (ISBN 0-12-407850-8). Acad Pr.
Kovacs, William D. & Holtz, Robert D. An Introduction to Geotechnical Engineering. (Illus.). 720p. 1981. text ed. 28.95 (ISBN 0-13-484394-0). P-H.
Kulhanek, O. Introduction to Digital Filtering in Geophysics. (Developments in Solid Earth Geophysics Ser.: No. 8). 1976. 41.50 (ISBN 0-444-41331-6). Elsevier.
Landsberg, H. E., ed. Advances in Geophysics, 19 vols. Incl. Vol. 1. 1952 (ISBN 0-12-018801-5); Vol. 2. 1955 (ISBN 0-12-018802-3); Vol. 3. 1956 (ISBN 0-12-018803-1); Vol. 4. Landsberg, H. E. & Van Mieghen, J., eds. 1958 (ISBN 0-12-018804-X); Vol. 5. 1958 (ISBN 0-12-018805-8); Vol. 6. Atmospheric Diffusion & Air Pollution: Proceedings. Frenkiel, F. N. & Sheppard, P. A., eds. 1959 (ISBN 0-12-018806-6); Vol. 7. 1961 (ISBN 0-12-018807-4); Vol. 8. 1961 (ISBN 0-12-018808-2); Vol. 9. 1962 (ISBN 0-12-018809-0); Vol. 10. 1964 (ISBN 0-12-018810-4); Vol. 11. 1965 (ISBN 0-12-018811-2); Vol. 12. 1967 (ISBN 0-12-018812-0); Vol. 13. 1969 (ISBN 0-12-018813-9); Vol. 14. 1970 (ISBN 0-12-018814-7); Vol. 15. 1971 (ISBN 0-12-018815-5); Suppl. 1. Biometeorological Methods. Munn, R. E. 1966. 30.50 (ISBN 0-12-018861-9); Vol. 16. 1973 (ISBN 0-12-018816-3); Vol. 17. 1974 (ISBN 0-12-018817-1); Vol. 18A. 1974. 33.00 (ISBN 0-12-018818-X); Vol. 19. 1976. 48.00 (ISBN 0-12-018819-8). Vols. 1-17. 60.00 ea. Acad Pr.
Lee, W. H. & Steward, S. W. Advances in Geophysics, Supplement 2: Principles & Applications of Microearthquake Networks. LC 80-70588. 1981. price not set (ISBN 0-12-018862-7). Acad Pr.
Lobeck, Armin K. Things Maps Don't Tell Us: Adventure into Map Interpretation. (Illus.). 1956. 10.95 (ISBN 0-02-573790-2). Macmillan.
McAlester, A. Earth: An Introduction to the Geological & Geophysical Sciences. 1973. 21.95 (ISBN 0-13-222422-4); instr. res. bk. 1.95 (ISBN 0-13-222695-2); study guide 3.95 (ISBN 0-13-222380-5). P-H.
Manghnani, Merli H. High Pressure Research: Applications to Geophysics. 1977. 48.50 (ISBN 0-12-468750-4). Acad Pr.
Mitchell, R. L., ed. Agronomy: Science Problems, Serving People. 1981. free copy avail. (ISBN 0-89118-060-5). Am Soc Agron.
Odishaw, H. & Ruttenberg, S., eds. Geophysics & the IGY. LC 58-60035. (Geophysical Monograph Ser.: Vol. 2). 1958. 8.00 (ISBN 0-87590-002-X). Am Geophysical.
Paoletti, A., ed. Physics of Magnetic Garnets. (Enrico Fermi International Summer School of Physics Ser.: Course 70, 1977). 1978. 73.25 (ISBN 0-444-85200-X, North Holland). Elsevier.
Parasnis, D. S. Mining Geophysics. 2nd ed. (Methods in Geochemistry & Geophysics Ser.). 395p. 1973. 19.95 (ISBN 0-444-41077-5). Elsevier.
Pedlosky, J. Geophysical Fluid Dynamics. (Illus.). 1979. 39.80 (ISBN 0-387-90368-2). Springer-Verlag.
Pirson, S. J. Geologic Well Log Analysis. 2nd ed. (Illus.). 385p. 1978. 19.95x (ISBN 0-87201-901-2). Gulf Pub.
Polshkov, M. K., ed. Exploration Geophysics, Vols. 47-51. Incl. Vol. 47. 154p. 1968. 32.50 (ISBN 0-306-18647-0); Vol. 48. 194p. 1968. 32.50 (ISBN 0-306-18648-9); Vol. 49. 154p. 1969. 32.50 (ISBN 0-306-18649-7); Vol. 50. 162p. 1969. 32.50 (ISBN 0-306-18650-0); Vol. 51. 151p. 1969. 35.00 (ISBN 0-306-18651-9). LC 68-18539 (Consultants). Plenum Pub.

--Exploration Geophysics, Vols. 47-51. Incl. Vol. 47. 154p. 1968. 32.50 (ISBN 0-306-18647-0); Vol. 48. 194p. 1968. 32.50 (ISBN 0-306-18648-9); Vol. 49. 154p. 1969. 32.50 (ISBN 0-306-18649-7); Vol. 50. 162p. 1969. 32.50 (ISBN 0-306-18650-0); Vol. 51. 151p. 1969. 35.00 (ISBN 0-306-18651-9). LC 68-18539 (Consultants). Plenum Pub.

Pruppacher, ed. Middle Atmosphere. (Contributions to Current Research in Geophysics Ser.: No. 9). 661p. 1980. pap. text ed. 98.00 (ISBN 3-7643-1123-1). Birkhauser.

Reid, William H., ed. Mathematical Problems in the Geophysical Sciences I: Geophysical Fluid Dynamics. LC 62-21481. (Lectures in Applied Mathematics Ser.). 1971. 41.20 (ISBN 0-8218-1113-4, LAM-13). Am Math.

--Mathematical Problems in the Gephysical Sciences II: Inverse Problems, Dynamo Theory & Tides. LC 62-21481. (Lectures in Applied Mathematics Ser.: Vol. 14). 1971. 39.60 (ISBN 0-8218-1114-2, LAM-14). Am Math.

Riazuddin, ed. Physics & Contemporary Needs, Vol. 2. 528p. 1978. 49.50 (ISBN 0-306-40011-1, Plenum Pr). Plenum Pub.

Roberts, P. H. & Soward, A. M., eds. Rotating Fluids in Geophysics. 1979. 51.50 (ISBN 0-12-589650-6). Acad Pr.

Robertson, Eugene. The Nature of the Solid Earth. (International Ser. in the Earth & Planetary Sciences). (Illus.). 544p. 1971. text ed. 26.00 (ISBN 0-07-053165-X, C). McGraw.

Robinson, Enders A. & Treitel, Sven. Geophysical Signal Analysis. (Signal Processing Ser.). (Illus.). 1980. text ed. 36.00 (ISBN 0-13-352658-5). P-H.

Rudman, Jack. Geophysicist. (Career Examination Ser.: C-302). (Cloth bdg. avail. on request). pap. 10.00 (ISBN 0-8373-0302-8). Natl Learning.

Runcorn, S. K., ed. Palaeogeophysics. 1970. 82.50 (ISBN 0-12-602750-1). Acad Pr.

Rybach, Ladislaus & Stegena, Lajos, eds. Geothermics & Geothermal Energy. (Contributions to Current Research in Geophysics Ser.: Vol. 7). 1979. text ed. 65.00x (ISBN 3-7643-1062-6). Renouf.

Saltzman, Barry. Advances in Geophysics, Vol. 23. 1981. price not set (ISBN 0-12-018823-6); price not set lib. ed. (ISBN 0-12-018882-1); price not set microfiche (ISBN 0-12-018883-X). Acad Pr.

Saltzman, Barry, ed. Advances in Geophysics, Vol. 21. LC 52-12266. (Serial Publication). 1979. 48.50 (ISBN 0-12-018821-X); lib. ed. 59.00 (ISBN 0-12-018878-3); microfiche 31.50 (ISBN 0-12-018879-1). Acad Pr.

Salztman, Barry, ed. Advances in Geophysics, Vol. 20. 42.00 (ISBN 0-12-018820-1); lib. ed. 47.50 (ISBN 0-12-018876-7); microfiche 27.00 (ISBN 0-12-018877-5). Acad Pr.

Scheidegger, A. Foundations of Geophysics. 1976. pap. text ed. 29.50 (ISBN 0-444-41389-8). Elsevier.

Schindler, Karl, ed. Cosmic Plasma Physics. LC 78-188924. 369p. 1972. 37.50 (ISBN 0-306-30582-8, Plenum Pr). Plenum Pub.

Seeger, C. Ronald. Problems for Exploration Geophysics. LC 78-62263. 1978. pap. text ed. 4.25 (ISBN 0-8191-0573-2). U Pr of Amer.

Sharma, P. Geophysical Methods in Geology. (Methods in Geochemistry & Geophysics). 1976. pap. text ed. 22.50 (ISBN 0-444-41383-9, North Holland). Elsevier.

Shaw, Richard P., ed. Computing Methods in Geophysical Mechanics-AMD, Vol. 25. 208p. 1977. pap. text ed. 22.00 (ISBN 0-685-86858-3, I00113). ASME.

Sheriff, Robert E. A First Course in Geophysical Exploration & Interpretation. LC 78-70766. (Illus.). 313p. 1978. text ed. 28.00 (ISBN 0-934634-02-5). Intl Human Res.

Smith, Robert B. & Eaton, Gordon P., eds. Cenozoic Tectonics & Regional Geophysics of Western Cordillera. LC 78-55296. (Memoir Ser.: No. 152). (Illus.). 1978. 55.00x (ISBN 0-8137-1152-5). Geol Soc.

Spar, J. Earth, Sea & Air: A Survey of the Geophysical Sciences. 2nd ed. (gr. 9-12). 1965. pap. 8.50 (ISBN 0-201-07093-6). A-W.

Specialist Symposium on Geophysical Fluid Dynamics, European Geophysical Society, Fourth Meeting, Munich September, 1977. Proceedings. Davies, P. A. & Roberts, P. H., eds. 156p. 1978. 23.25 (ISBN 0-677-40115-9). Gordon.

Spencer, Edgar. Dynamics of the Earth: An Introduction to Physical Geology. 1972. text ed. 22.95 scp (ISBN 0-690-24844-X, HarpC). Har-Row.

Spilhaus, Athelstan. Satellite of the Sun: The Science of the Earth & Its Surroundings. LC 58-10605. (Illus.). 1964. pap. 1.25 (ISBN 0-689-70186-1, 57). Atheneum.

Stacey, Frank D. Physics of the Earth. 2nd ed. LC 76-41891. 414p. 1977. text ed. 29.95 (ISBN 0-471-81956-5). Wiley.

Sumner, J. S. Principles of Induced Polarization for Geophysical Exploration. (Developments in Economic Geology: No. 5). 1976. 44.00 (ISBN 0-444-41481-9). Elsevier.

Sutton, George H., et al, eds. The Geophysics of the Pacific Ocean Basin & Its Margin. LC 75-38816. (Geophysical Monograph Ser.: Vol. 19). (Illus.). 1976. 15.00 (ISBN 0-87590-019-4). Am Geophysical.

Symposium on Fundamental Problems in Turbulence & Their Relation to Geophysics. Turbulence in Geophysics. Frenkiel, F. N., ed. LC 62-60082. (Hard cover edition of July 1962, Vol. 67, No. 8, Journal of Geophysical Research). 5.00 (ISBN 0-87590-200-6). Am Geophysical.

Tatsch, J. H. The Earth's Tectonosphere: Its Past Development & Present Behavior. 2nd ed. LC 74-78917. (Illus.). 468p. 1977. text ed. 30.00 (ISBN 0-912890-03-7). Tatsch.

--Geothermal Deposits: Origin, Evolution, & Present Characteristics. LC 75-9303. (Illus.). 292p. 1976. text ed. 84.00 (ISBN 0-912890-10-X). Tatsch.

Telford, W. M., et al. Applied Geophysics. LC 74-16992. (Illus.). 700p. 1975. 95.50 (ISBN 0-521-20670-7); pap. 29.95x (ISBN 0-521-29146-1). Cambridge U Pr.

Tucker, R. H., et al. Global Geophysics. 1970. 19.50 (ISBN 0-444-19648-X). Elsevier.

U. S. Dept. of Energy. Solar, Geothermal, Electric & Storage Systems Program Summary Document. 475p. 1979. pap. 29.95 (ISBN 0-89934-053-9, H031-PP). Solar Energy Info.

Vinnichenko, N. K., et al. Turbulence in the Free Atmosphere. 2nd ed. (Illus.). 325p. 1980. 49.50 (ISBN 0-306-10959-X, Consultants). Plenum Pub.

Von Schwind, J. Geophysical Fluid Dynamics for Oceanographers. 1980. 29.95 (ISBN 0-13-352591-0). P-H.

Webster, Gary. Wonders of Earth. LC 67-13770. 1967. 3.50 (ISBN 0-685-42654-8, Pub. by Sheed). Guild Bks.

Weinstock, Harold & Overton, William C., Jr., eds. SQUID Applications to Geophysics. (Illus.). 1981. write for info. (ISBN 0-931830-18-4). Soc Exploration.

Wesson, Paul S. Cosmology & Geophysics. LC 78-10133. (Monographs on Astronomical Subjects). (Illus.). 1979. 24.95 (ISBN 0-19-520123-X). Oxford U Pr.

Wyss, Max, ed. Stress in the Earth. (Contributions to Current Research in Geophysics Ser.: Vol. 3). 1977. text ed. 80.00x (ISBN 3-7643-0952-0). Renouf.

GEOPHYSICS–BIBLIOGRAPHY

Tompkins, Dorothy C. Power from the Earth: Geothermal Energy. LC 72-8628. (Public Policy Bibliographies: No. 3). (Orig.). 1972. pap. 2.50x (ISBN 0-87772-165-3). Inst Gov Stud Berk.

GEOPHYSICS–DICTIONARIES

Runcorn, S. K., ed. International Dictionary of Geophysics, 2 vols. 1968. Set. 300.00 (ISBN 0-08-011834-8). Pergamon.

GEOPHYSICS–INTERNATIONAL COOPERATION

see also International Years of the Quiet Sun, 1964-1965

Pendleton, J. W., ed. Agronomy in Today's Society. 1981. write for info. (ISBN 0-89118-053-2). Am Soc Agron.

GEOPHYSICS–JUVENILE LITERATURE

Lauber, Patricia. This Restless Earth. (gr. 5-6). 1970. PLB 5.99 (ISBN 0-394-90802-3, BYR). Random.

GEOPOLITICS

see also Anthropo-Geography; Boundaries; Demography; Territory, National; World Politics

Clout, Hugh. Franco-Belgian Border Region. (Problem Regions of Europe Ser.). (Illus.). 1976. pap. text ed. 7.95x (ISBN 0-19-913182-1). Oxford U Pr.

Cohen, Saul B. Geography & Politics in a World Divided. 2nd ed. (Illus.). 400p. 1973. pap. text ed. 6.95x (ISBN 0-19-501695-5). Oxford U Pr.

Crone, G. R. Background to Political Geography. LC 69-14376. (Illus.). 1970. 8.95 (ISBN 0-8023-1202-0). Dufour.

Dorpalen, Andreas. World of General Haushofer: Geopolitics in Action. LC 66-21393. 1942. Repr. 12.50 (ISBN 0-8046-0112-7). Kennikat.

Gottmann, Jean. The Significance of Territory. LC 72-87807. (Page-Barbour Lecture Ser). (Illus.). 195p. 1973. 9.95x (ISBN 0-8139-0413-7). U Pr of Va.

Gyorgy, Andrew. Geopolitics, the New German Science. 14.00 (ISBN 0-384-20585-2); pap. 9.00 (ISBN 0-685-13435-0). Johnson Repr.

Koury, Enver M. Oil & Geopolitics in the Persian Gulf Area: A Center of Power. LC 73-85565. 96p. 1973. pap. 5.00 (ISBN 0-934484-03-1). Inst Mid East & North Africa.

Lowe, James T. Geopolitics & War: Mackinder's Philosophy of Power. LC 81-40029. (Illus.). 732p. (Orig.). 1981. lib. bdg. 28.50 (ISBN 0-8191-1542-8); pap. text ed. 19.75 (ISBN 0-8191-1543-6). U Pr of Amer.

Mattern, Johannes. Geopolitik Doctrine of Self-Sufficiency & Empire. LC 78-64186. (Johns Hopkins University. Studies in the Social Sciences. Sixtieth Ser. 1942: 2). Repr. of 1942 ed. 16.00 (ISBN 0-404-61293-8). AMS Pr.

Prescott, J. R. The Geography of State Policies. 1968. text ed. 6.00x (ISBN 0-09-088860-X, Hutchinson U Lib). Humanities.

Prescott, J. R., et al. Frontiers of Asia & Southeast Asia. (Illus.). 1977. pap. 13.50x (ISBN 0-522-84116-3, Pub. by Melbourne U Pr). Intl Schol Bk Serv.

Spykman, Nicholas J. Geography of the Peace. Nicholl, H. R., ed. (Illus.). 1969. Repr. of 1944 ed. 12.50 (ISBN 0-208-00654-0, Archon). Shoe String.

Strausz-Hupe, Robert. Geopolitics: The Struggle for Space & Power. LC 72-4303. (World Affairs Ser.: National & International Viewpoints). 290p. 1972. Repr. of 1942 ed. 14.00 (ISBN 0-405-04601-4). Arno.

Szuprowicz, Bohdan O. How to Avoid Strategic Material Shortages Dealing with Cartels, Embargoes & Supply Distributions. LC 80-24431. 312p. 1981. 19.95 (ISBN 0-471-07843-3, Pub. by Wiley-Interscience). Wiley.

Walters, Robert E. Sea Power & the Nuclear Fallacy: A Reevaluation of Global Strategy. LC 75-15754. 214p. 1975. Repr. of 1974 ed. 22.50x (ISBN 0-8419-0214-3). Holmes & Meier.

Weigert, Hans W. Generals & Geographers: The Twilight of Geopolitics. LC 70-167434. (Essay Index Reprint Ser.). Repr. of 1942 ed. 18.00 (ISBN 0-8369-2728-1). Arno.

Whitney, Joseph. China: Area, Administration & Nation Building. LC 75-104876. (Research Papers Ser.: No. 123). 198p. 1970. pap. 8.00 (ISBN 0-89065-030-6). U Chicago Dept Geog.

Whittlesey, Derwent S. The Earth & the State: A Study of Political Geography. LC 72-4308. (World Affairs Ser.: National & International Viewpoints). (Illus.). 636p. 1972. Repr. of 1939 ed. 30.00 (ISBN 0-405-04597-2). Arno.

GEORGE, KING OF BOHEMIA, 1420-1471

see Jiri Z Podebrad, King of Bohemia, 1420-1471

GEORGE 1ST, KING OF GREAT BRITAIN, 1660-1727

Hatton, Ragnhild. George the First, Elector & King. LC 77-15058. (Illus.). 1978. 20.00 (ISBN 0-674-34935-0). Harvard U Pr.

Imbert-Terry, Henry M. Constitutional King: George the First. LC 77-153223. (Illus.). 1971. Repr. of 1927 ed. 14.00 (ISBN 0-8046-1533-0). Kennikat.

Murray, John J. George First, the Baltic & Whig Split of 1717: A Study in Diplomacy & Propaganda. LC 68-54009. 1969. 11.50x (ISBN 0-226-55380-9). U of Chicago Pr.

Thornton, Percy M. Brunswick Accession. LC 75-118506. 1971. Repr. of 1887 ed. 12.50 (ISBN 0-8046-1254-4). Kennikat.

Wolfgang, Michael. England Under George I: The Beginnings of the Hanoverian Dynasty. LC 81-6495. (Studies in Modern History). viii, 406p. 1981. Repr. of 1936 ed. lib. bdg. 29.75x (ISBN 0-313-23040-4, MIEG). Greenwood.

GEORGE 2ND, KING OF GREAT BRITAIN, 1683-1760

Hervey, John. Some Materials Towards Memoirs of the Reign of King George Second, 3 Vols. Sedgwick, Romney, ed. LC 79-119102. Repr. of 1931 ed. Set. 80.00 (ISBN 0-404-03300-8). AMS Pr.

GEORGE 3RD, KING OF GREAT BRITAIN, 1738-1820

Barnes, Donald G. George Third & William Pitt, 1783-1806. 1965. lib. bdg. 25.00x (ISBN 0-374-90399-9). Octagon.

Brooke, John. King George III. (Illus.). 640p. 1974. pap. 4.95 (ISBN 0-586-03944-9, Pub. by Granada England). Academy Chi Ltd.

Fortescue, J., ed. The Correspondence of George III,1760-1783, 6 vols. 1967. 350.00x set (ISBN 0-7146-1108-5, F Cass Co). Biblio Dist.

George III. Letters from George III to Lord Bute, 1756 to 1766. Sedgwick, Romney, ed. LC 81-4155. (Studies in Modern History). lxviii, 277p. 1981. Repr. of 1939 ed. lib. bdg. 29.50x (ISBN 0-313-23039-0, SELG). Greenwood.

George Third. Later Correspondence of George Third, 5 vols. Aspinall, A., ed. Incl. Vol. 1. 1783-1793 (ISBN 0-521-04066-3); Vol. 2. 1793-1797 (ISBN 0-521-04067-1); Vol. 3. 1798-1801 (ISBN 0-521-04068-X); Vol. 4. 1802-1807 (ISBN 0-521-06918-1); Vol. 5. 1807-1810, with Index to Vols. 1-5 (ISBN 0-521-07451-7). LC 61-52516. 700p. 120.00 ea. Cambridge U Pr.

Jesse, J. Heneage. Memoirs of the Life & Reign of King George the Third, 3 vols. 1978. Repr. of 1867 ed. lib. bdg. 100.00 (ISBN 0-8414-5288-1). Folcroft.

McKelvey, James L. George Third & Lord Bute: The Leicester House Years. LC 72-96682. 160p. 1973. 9.75 (ISBN 0-8223-0292-6). Duke.

Mumby, F. A. George Third & the American Revolution. Repr. of 1924 ed. 22.00 (ISBN 0-527-65850-2). Kraus Repr.

GEORGE 4TH, KING OF GREAT BRITAIN, 1762-1830

Aldington, Richard. Four English Portraits: Eighteen Hundred & One to Eighteen Fifty-One. LC 79-51232. (Essay Index in Reprint Ser.). (Illus.). Date not set. Repr. of 1948 ed. 19.75x (ISBN 0-8486-3033-5). Core Collection.

Richardson, Joanna. The Disastrous Marriage: A Study of George IV & Caroline of Brunswick. LC 75-31823. (Illus.). 255p. 1976. Repr. of 1960 ed. lib. bdg. 16.50x (ISBN 0-8371-8439-8, RIDM). Greenwood.

Wilkins, W. H. Mrs. Fitzherbert & George IV. (Illus.). 476p. 1980. Repr. lib. bdg. 45.00 (ISBN 0-8492-8819-3). R West.

GEORGE 5TH, KING OF GREAT BRITAIN, 1865-1936

McElwee, William L. Britain's Locust Years: Nineteen Eighteen to Nineteen Forty. LC 78-25900. 1979. Repr. of 1962 ed. lib. bdg. 22.00x (ISBN 0-313-21162-0, MCBL). Greenwood.

GEORGE, SAINT, d. 303

Budge, Ernest A., tr. George of Lydda, the Patron Saint of England. LC 77-87668. (Luzac's Semitic Texts & Translations: No. 20). (Illus., Eng. & Ethiopic.). Repr. of 1930 ed. 55.00 (ISBN 0-404-11348-6). AMS Pr.

GEORGE, HENRY, 1839-1897

Andelson, Robert V. Critics of Henry George. 424p. 1979. 15.00 (ISBN 0-8386-2350-6). Schalkenbach.

Auchmuty, A. C., ed. Economics & Philosophy of Henry George. 109p. 1980. pap. 1.00 (ISBN 0-911312-23-4). Schalkenbach.

Barker, Charles A. Henry George. LC 74-12949. (Illus.). 696p. 1974. Repr. of 1955 ed. lib. bdg. 33.00x (ISBN 0-8371-7775-8, BAHG). Greenwood.

Davidson, J. Morrison. Concerning Four Precursors of Henry George & the Single Tax & Also the Land Gospel According to Winstanley the Digger. LC 77-115317. 1971. Repr. of 1899 ed. 10.00 (ISBN 0-8046-1108-4). Kennikat.

De Mille, Anna G. Henry George, Citizen of the World. Shoemaker, Don C., ed. LC 79-138218. (Illus.). 276p. 1972. Repr. of 1950 ed. lib. bdg. 22.75x (ISBN 0-8371-5575-4, DEHG). Greenwood.

Geiger, George R. The Philosophy of Henry George. LC 75-317. (The Radical Tradition in America Ser.). 603p. 1975. Repr. of 1933 ed. 32.50 (ISBN 0-88355-220-5). Hyperion Conn.

George, Henry, Jr. Henry George. LC 80-27958. (American Men & Women of Letters Ser.). Orig. Title: The Life of Henry George. 640p. 1981. pap. 10.95 (ISBN 0-87754-164-7). Chelsea Hse.

--The Life of Henry George. 634p. 1960. 5.00 (ISBN 0-911312-24-2). Schalkenbach.

Holmes, John H. Henry George. 59.95 (ISBN 0-8490-0294-X). Gordon Pr.

Lawrence, Elwood P. Henry George in the British Isles. 203p. 1957. 5.00 (ISBN 0-911312-25-0). Schalkenbach.

--Henry George in the British Isles. vi, 203p. 1957. 5.00 (ISBN 0-87013-029-3). Mich St U Pr.

Moran, James. Henry George: Printer, Bookseller, Stationer, & Bookbinder. (Illus.). 69p. 1980. 15.50 (ISBN 0-913720-17-8). Sandstone.

Oser, Jacob. Henry George. (World Leaders Ser.). 1974. lib. bdg. 9.95 (ISBN 0-8057-3682-4). Twayne.

Post, Louis F. An Account of the George-Hewitt Mayoralty Campaign in the Municipal Election of 1886. LC 75-341. (The Radical Tradition in America Ser). 202p. 1975. Repr. of 1886 ed. 17.50 (ISBN 0-88355-244-2). Hyperion Conn.

--The Prophet of San Francisco Henry George. 59.95 (ISBN 0-8490-0901-4). Gordon Pr.

Post, Louis F. & Leubuscher, Fred C. Henry George's Eighteen Hundred Eighty-Six Campaign. 193p. 1961. pap. 1.00 (ISBN 0-911312-21-8). Schalkenbach.

Rather, Lois. Henry George: Printer to Author. (Illus.). 1978. ltd. ed. 20.00 (ISBN 0-686-22963-0). Rather Pr.

Rose, Edward J. Henry George. (Twayne's United States Authors Ser). 1968. pap. 3.45 (ISBN 0-8084-0003-7, T128, Twayne). Coll & U Pr.

Teilhac, Ernest. Pioneers of American Economic Thought in the Nineteenth Century. Johnson, Edgar A., tr. LC 66-27162. 1967. Repr. of 1936 ed. 8.00 (ISBN 0-8462-0998-5). Russell.

GEORGE, STEFAN ANTON, 1868-1933

George, Stefan. The Works of Stefan George. 2nd ed. Marx, Olga & Morwitz, Ernst, trs. (Studies in the Germanic Languages & Literatures Ser.: No. 78). 427p. 1974. 22.00x (ISBN 0-8078-8078-7). U of NC Pr.

Goldsmith, Ulrich K. Stefan George. LC 78-110601. (Columbia Essays on Modern Writers Ser.). 48p. 1970. pap. 2.00 (ISBN 0-231-03204-8). Columbia U Pr.

Hobohm, Freya. Bedeutung Franzoesischer Dichter in Werk und Weltbild Stefan Georges. 1931. pap. 8.00 (ISBN 0-384-23720-7). Johnson Repr.
Viereck, Peter. Dream & Responsibility: Tension Between Poetry & Society. facsimile of 1953 ed. 1972. 3.00 (ISBN 0-87419-045-2). U Pr of Wash.

GEORGE, LAKE

DeCosta, Benjamin F. The Fight at Diamond Island, Lake George. 1977. Repr. 19.00 (ISBN 0-403-08069-X). Scholarly.
Van De Water, Frederick F. Lake Champlain & Lake George. LC 79-83478. (Empire State Historical Publications Ser: No. 68). 1969. Repr. of 1946 ed. 12.00 (ISBN 0-87198-068-1). Friedman.

GEORGETOWN COUNTY, SOUTH CAROLINA

Holcomb, Brent. Marriage & Death Notices from the Pendleton (S. C.) Messenger Eighteen Hundred & Seven to Eighteen Fifty-One. 123p. 1977. 17.50 (ISBN 0-89308-049-7). Southern Hist Pr.
--Marriage, Death & Estate Notices from Georgetown, S. C. Newspapers, Seventeen Ninety-One to Eighteen Sixty-One. 250p. 1978. 25.00 (ISBN 0-89308-150-7). Southern Hist Pr.
--Old Camden District, South Carolina Wills & Administrations Seventeen Eighty-One to Seventeen Eighty-Seven. 120p. 1978. 25.00 (ISBN 0-89308-050-0). Southern Hist Pr.
Rogers, George C., Jr. History of Georgetown County, South Carolina. LC 70-95260. 1970. 19.50x (ISBN 0-87249-143-9). U of SC Pr.

GEORGETOWN UNIVERSITY

Barron's Profile of Georgetown University. (College Profiles Ser.). 1978. pap. text ed. 2.50 (ISBN 0-8120-1044-2). Barron.

GEORGIA

see also Names of specific cities, counties, etc in Georgia

Blicksilver, Jack & Bowdoin, Mary H. Impact of Georgia Ports Upon the Economy of the State. LC 60-62989. (Research Monograph: No. 15). 1960. spiral bdg. 5.00 (ISBN 0-88406-032-2). Ga St U Busn Pub.
Bonner, James C. Georgia's Last Frontier: The Development of Carroll County. LC 77-156040. 238p. 1971. 12.50 (ISBN 0-8203-0303-8). U of Ga Pr.
--Milledgeville: Georgia's Antebellum Capital. LC 76-28923. 336p. 1978. 15.95 (ISBN 0-8203-0424-7). U of Ga Pr.
Bowdoin, Mary H. Georgia's Railway Freight Patterns: An Analysis of Composition & Routes, 1949-1955. LC 56-63614. (Research Monograph: No. 5). 1958. spiral bdg. 5.00 (ISBN 0-88406-026-8). Ga St U Busn Pub.
Candler, Allen D. & Evans, Clement A., eds. Georgia, Comprising Sketches of Counties, Towns, Events, Institutions, & Persons, Arranged in Cyclopedic Form, 4 vols. LC 72-187379. (Illus.). 1972. Repr. of 1906 ed. 32.50 ea. Vol. 1 (ISBN 0-87152-071-0). Vol. 2 (ISBN 0-87152-072-9). Vol. 3 (ISBN 0-87152-073-7). Vol. 4 (ISBN 0-87152-074-5). Set. 130.00 (ISBN 0-87152-302-7). Reprint.
Carpenter, Allan. Georgia. new ed. LC 79-12095. (New Enchantment of America State Bks.). (Illus.). (gr. 4 up). 1979. PLB 10.60 (ISBN 0-516-04110-X). Childrens.
Dittmer, John. Black Georgia in the Progressive Era, 1900-1920. LC 77-24249. (Blacks in the New World Ser.). 251p. 1980. pap. 5.95 (ISBN 0-252-00813-8). U of Ill Pr.
--Black Georgia in the Progressive Era, 1900-1920. LC 77-24249. (Blacks in the New World Ser). 1977. 15.95 (ISBN 0-252-00306-3). U of Ill Pr.
Georgia. 28.00 (ISBN 0-89770-086-4). Curriculum Info Ctr.
Gordon, Georgia Y. Between Two Georgia Rivers. 1981. 6.00 (ISBN 0-8062-1726-X). Carlton.
Johnson, Amanda. Georgia As Colony & State. LC 38-24161. 1970. Repr. of 1938 ed. cloth over boards 25.00 (ISBN 0-87797-013-0). Cherokee.
Krakow, Kenneth K. Georgia Place Names. 1975. 12.50 (ISBN 0-915430-00-2); pap. 8.00 (ISBN 0-915430-01-0). Winship Pr.
Longstreet, Augustus B. Georgia Scenes. 214p. 1971. Repr. of 1847 ed. bds. 5.00 (ISBN 0-87797-016-5). Cherokee.
Lucas, Silas E. Some Georgia County Records, Vol. 3. 400p. 1978. 35.00 (ISBN 0-89308-058-6). Southern Hist Pr.
Lucas, Silas E., Jr. Some Georgia County Records, Vol. 1. 432p. 1981. Repr. of 1977 ed. 35.00 (ISBN 0-89308-044-6). Southern Hist Pr.
--Some Georgia County Records, Vol. 2. 400p. 1981. Repr. of 1977 ed. 35.00 (ISBN 0-89308-057-8). Southern Hist Pr.
McKenzie, Barbara. Flannery O'Connor's Georgia. LC 80-10936. (Illus.). 132p. 1980. 24.95 (ISBN 0-8203-0517-0); pap. 12.50 (ISBN 0-8203-0518-9). U of Ga Pr.
Sherwood, Adiel. Gazetteer of Georgia. 4th ed. LC 70-111454. 1970. Repr. of 1860 ed. buckram over bds 20.00 (ISBN 0-87797-010-6). Cherokee.
State Industrial Directories Corp. Georgia State Industrial Directory, 1978. (State Industrial Directory Ser.). 1979. 30.00 (ISBN 0-916112-98-5). State Indus Dir.
White, George. Statistics of the State of Georgia. LC 71-187392. 701p. 1972. Repr. of 1849 ed. 27.00 (ISBN 0-87152-087-7). Reprint.

GEORGIA–BIBLIOGRAPHY

Rowland, Arthur R. & Dorsey, James E. Bibliography of the Writings on Georgia History, Nineteen Hundred to Nineteen Seventy. LC 77-21733. 1978. 30.00 (ISBN 0-87152-254-3). Reprint.

GEORGIA–DESCRIPTION AND TRAVEL

Borns, Steven. People of Plains, Ga. (Illus.). 1978. pap. 7.95 (ISBN 0-07-006535-7, SP). McGraw.
Carter, Hugh & Anderson, Richard. Plains Coloring Book. 1977. 1.00 (ISBN 0-918544-04-1). Wimmer Bks.
Federal Writers Project, Georgia. Augusta. LC 73-3606. (American Guide Ser.). Repr. of 1938 ed. 12.50 (ISBN 0-404-57910-8). AMS Pr.
Georgia: A Guide to Its Towns & Country-Side. LC 72-84467. 1940. 54.00 (ISBN 0-403-02162-6). Somerset Pub.
Harper, Francis & Presley, Delma E. Okefinokee Album. LC 80-14220. (Illus.). 240p. 1981. 14.95 (ISBN 0-8203-0530-8). U of Ga Pr.
Homan, Timothy. The Hiking Trails of North Georgia. 240p. 1980. 5.95 (ISBN 0-931948-11-8). Peachtree Pubs.
Kahn, E. J., Jr. Georgia from Rabun Gap to Tybee Light. LC 78-58083. 1978. 5.95 (ISBN 0-87797-045-9). Cherokee.
Klenbort, Daniel & Klenbort, Marcia. The Road to Plains: A Guide to Plains & Nearby Places of Interest in SW Georgia. 1977. pap. 2.00 (ISBN 0-686-21384-X). Avery Pr.
Kwilecki, Paul. Understandings: Photographs of Decatur County, Georgia. Harris, Alex, ed. LC 81-2958. (Illus.). 128p. 1981. 24.95 (ISBN 0-8078-1486-5). U of NC Pr.
Lewis, Paul M. Beautiful Georgia. Shangle, Robert D., ed. LC 78-7895. 72p. 1978. 14.95 (ISBN 0-915796-42-2); pap. 7.95 (ISBN 0-915796-41-4). Beautiful Am.
Lovell, Caroline C. Golden Isles of Georgia. 1970. Repr. of 1932 ed. cloth over bds 12.00 (ISBN 0-87797-012-2). Cherokee.
Martin, Harold H. Harold Martin Remembers a Place in the Mountains. Schaffer, Lee & Elliott, Helen L., eds. LC 79-67094. (Illus.). 1979. 10.95 (ISBN 0-931948-03-7). Peachtree Pubs.
Matschat, Cecile H. Suwannee River: Strange Green Land. LC 79-5190. (Brown Thrasher Bks.). (Illus.). 295p. 1980. 17.50x (ISBN 0-8203-0508-1); pap. 5.95x (ISBN 0-8203-0496-4). U of Ga Pr.
Montgomery, Robert & Barnwell, John. Most Delightful Golden Islands. LC 77-76733. 1969. Repr. of 1717 ed. cloth over bds 5.00 (ISBN 0-87797-007-6). Cherokee.
Price, Eugenia. St. Simons Memoir: The Personal Story of Finding the Island & Writing the St. Simons Trilogy of Novels. (Illus.). 1978. 10.00 (ISBN 0-397-01216-0). Har-Row.
Russell, Francis. The Okefenokee Swamp. LC 73-78582. (American Wilderness Ser). (Illus.). (gr. 6 up). 1973. lib. bdg. 11.97 (ISBN 0-8094-1181-4, Pub. by Time-Life). Silver.
Sehlinger, Bob & Otey, Don. A Canoeing & Kayaking Guide to the Streams of Georgia. (Illus.). Date not set. cancelled (ISBN 0-89732-005-0). Thomas Pr.
--Northern Georgia Canoeing. (Illus.). 1980. pap. 9.95 (ISBN 0-89732-005-0). Thomas Pr.
--Southern Georgia Canoeing. (Illus.). 1980. 9.95 (ISBN 0-89732-007-7). Thomas Pr.
Smith, Susan H. Where, When & How in Atlanta. Nicholson, Diana M., ed. (A Marmac Guide Ser.). 224p. (Orig.). 1981. pap. 8.50 (ISBN 0-939944-00-6). Marmac Pub.
Steed, Hal. Georgia: Unfinished State. 1976. Repr. 10.00 (ISBN 0-87797-014-9). Cherokee.
Valentine, James, photos by. Georgia. LC 77-76964. (Belding Imprint Ser.). (Illus.). 192p. (Text by Charles Wharton). 1977. 29.50 (ISBN 0-912856-35-1). Graphic Arts Ctr.
Wilcox, Herbert. Georgia Scribe: Selected Columns. LC 74-82935. 1974. bds. 7.00 (ISBN 0-87797-029-7). Cherokee.
Wood, Virginia S., ed. St. Simons Island, Georgia Brunswick & Vicinity: Description & History Written by William W Hazzard 1825. (Illus.). 1974. pap. 2.50 plus UPS (ISBN 0-915184-08-7, Pub. by Oak Hill). Channing Bks.

GEORGIA–GENEALOGY

Biographical Souvenir of the States of Georgia & Florida, Containing Biographical Sketches of the Representative Public & Many Early Settled Families in These States. LC 75-44662. (Illus.). 1976. Repr. of 1889 ed. 40.00 (ISBN 0-89308-040-3). Southern Hist Pr.
Brunson, Marion B. Our Bailey & Staggers History & Genealogy. 1980. 10.00 (ISBN 0-916620-51-4). Portals Pr.
Cain, Andrew W. History of Lumpkin County for the First Hundred Years, 1832-1932. LC 78-12902. 1978. Repr. of 1932 ed. 22.50 (ISBN 0-87152-277-2). Reprint.
Clements, J. B. History of Irwin County. LC 78-13229. 1978. Repr. of 1932 ed. 25.00 (ISBN 0-87152-278-0). Reprint.
Cobb, Mrs. Wilton P. History of Dodge County. LC 79-11196. (Illus.). 1979. Repr. of 1932 ed. 15.00 (ISBN 0-87152-293-4). Reprint.
Cook, Anna M. History of Baldwin County Georgia. LC 78-13226. 1978. Repr. of 1925 ed. 22.50 (ISBN 0-87152-279-9). Reprint.
Cooper, Walter G. Official History of Fulton County. LC 78-12918. 1978. Repr. of 1934 ed. 35.00 (ISBN 0-87152-280-2). Reprint.
Covington, W. A. History of Colquitt County. LC 80-13117. (Illus.). 424p. 1980. Repr. of 1937 ed. 25.00 (ISBN 0-87152-318-3). Reprint.
--History of Colquitt County. LC 80-13117. (Illus.). 424p. 1980. Repr. of 1937 ed. 25.00 (ISBN 0-87152-318-3). Reprint.
D.A.R.Thronateeska Chapter, compiled by. History & Reminiscences of Dougherty County Georgia. LC 78-12903. 1978. Repr. of 1924 ed. 20.00 (ISBN 0-87152-282-9). Reprint.
Davidson, Victor. History of Wilkinson County. LC 78-12919. 1978. Repr. of 1930 ed. 25.00 (ISBN 0-87152-283-7). Reprint.
Davis, Robert S., Jr. & Lucas, Silas E., Jr. The Families of Burke County, Georgia, 1755 to 1855: A Census. (Illus.). 750p. 1981. 37.50 (ISBN 0-686-75594-4). Southern Hist.
Dorsey, James E. Footprints Along the Hoopee: A History of Emanuel County, 1812-1900. LC 78-12908. 1978. 15.00 (ISBN 0-87152-291-8). Reprint.
Fleming, W. P. Crisp County, Georgia: Historical Sketches, Vol. 1. LC 80-13477. (Illus.). 288p. 1980. Repr. of 1932 ed. 20.00 (ISBN 0-87152-319-1). Reprint.
Georgia Genealogical Gems. LC 81-81357. 190p. pap. 13.50x perfect bd. (ISBN 0-915156-48-2, SP 48). Natl. Genealogical.
Georgia Historical Society. Index to United States Census of Georgia for 1820. 2nd ed. LC 79-90052. 1969. 12.50 (ISBN 0-8063-0156-2). Genealog Pub.
Gnann, Pearl R. & Lebay, Mrs. Charles. Georgia Salzburgers & Allied Families. 1979. Repr. of 1956 ed. 25.00 (ISBN 0-89308-012-8). Southern Hist Pr.
Gwinnett County, Georgia, Families 1818-1968. LC 80-52845. 662p. 1980. 30.00 (ISBN 0-87797-053-X). Cherokee.
Hays, Louise F. History of Macon County Georgia. LC 79-11202. (Illus.). 1979. Repr. of 1933 ed. 30.00 (ISBN 0-87152-294-2). Reprint.
History of Lowndes County Georgia, 1825-1941. LC 78-12915. 1978. Repr. of 1942 ed. 20.00 (ISBN 0-87152-281-0). Reprint.
Houston, Martha L. Marriages of Hancock County, Georgia, 1806 to 1850. LC 76-39658. (Reprinted with Land Lottery List of Hancock County, Georgia, 1806). 1977. Repr. 10.00 (ISBN 0-8063-0749-8). Genealog Pub.
Huxford, Folks. The History of Brooks County Georgia. LC 78-13225. 1978. Repr. of 1948 ed. 25.00 (ISBN 0-87152-284-5). Reprint.
Jackson, Ronald V. & Teeples, Gary R. Georgia Census Index 1820. LC 77-85909. (Illus.). lib. bdg. 26.00 (ISBN 0-89593-028-5). Accelerated Index.
--Georgia Census Index 1830. LC 77-85908. (Illus.). lib. bdg. 29.00 (ISBN 0-89593-029-3). Accelerated Index.
--Georgia Census Index 1840. LC 77-85914. (Illus.). lib. bdg. 50.00 (ISBN 0-89593-030-7). Accelerated Index.
--Georgia Census Index 1850. LC 77-85913. (Illus.). lib. bdg. 62.00 (ISBN 0-89593-031-5). Accelerated Index.
Johnston, Elizabeth L. Recollections of a Georgia Loyalist. Eaton, Arthur W., ed. LC 76-187388. (Illus.). 224p. 1972. Repr. of 1901 ed. 16.50 (ISBN 0-87152-083-4). Reprint.
Lucas, Silas E., Jr. Master Index to the Georgia Genealogical: Vols. 1-46, 1961-1972. 1973. 50.00 (ISBN 0-89308-018-7). Southern Hist Pr.
Lucas, Silas E., Jr. & Wilson, Caroline P. Records of Effingham County, Georgia. 1976. 25.00 (ISBN 0-89308-019-5). Southern Hist Pr.
McCall, Mrs. Howard H. Roster of Revolutionary Soldiers in Georgia & Other States, Vol. 2. LC 68-9361. 1968. 12.50 (ISBN 0-8063-0220-8). Genealog Pub.
--Roster of Revolutionary Soldiers in Georgia, Vol. 1. LC 68-9361. 1968. Repr. of 1941 ed. 15.00 (ISBN 0-8063-0219-4). Genealog Pub.
--Roster of Revolutionary Soldiers in Georgia, Vol. 3. LC 68-9361. 1969. 18.50 (ISBN 0-8063-0221-6). Genealog Pub.
McQueen, Alex S. History of Charlton County. LC 78-12909. 1978. Repr. of 1932 ed. 15.00 (ISBN 0-87152-286-1). Reprint.
Mann, Floris P. History of Telfair County from 1812 to 1949. LC 78-13175. 1978. Repr. of 1949 ed. 15.00 (ISBN 0-87152-285-3). Reprint.
Mitchell, Lizzie R. History of Pike County, Georgia, 1822-1932. LC 80-23352. x, 162p. 1980. Repr. 15.00 (ISBN 0-87152-345-0). Reprint.
Pate, John B. History of Turner County. LC 79-10025. (Illus.). 1979. Repr. of 1933 ed. 15.00 (ISBN 0-87152-295-0). Reprint.
Register, Alvaretta K. Index to the Eighteen Thirty Census of Georgia. LC 73-22267. 1974. 25.00 (ISBN 0-8063-0609-2). Genealog Pub.
Rice, Thaddeus B. & Williams, Carolyn W. History of Greene County Georgia Seventeen Eighty-Six to Eighteen Eighty-Six. LC 79-21459. (Illus.). 1979. Repr. of 1961 ed. 25.00 (ISBN 0-87152-299-3). Reprint.
Rigsby, Lewis W. Historic Georgia Families. LC 69-17128. 1969. Repr. of 1925 ed. 18.50 (ISBN 0-8063-0298-4). Genealog Pub.
Rogers, N. K. History of Chattahoochee County, Georgia. LC 75-44667. (Illus.). 1976. Repr. of 1933 ed. 20.00 (ISBN 0-89308-032-2). Southern Hist Pr.
Smith, Sarah Q. Early Georgia Wills & Settlements of Estates: Wilkes County. LC 76-25331. 1976. 5.00 (ISBN 0-8063-0735-8). Genealog Pub.
Stacy, James. History & Published Records of the Midway Congregational Church, Liberty County, Georgia. LC 79-22013. (Illus.). 1979. 27.50 (ISBN 0-87152-298-5). Reprint.
Tate, Luke E. History of Pickens County. LC 78-13223. 1978. Repr. of 1935 ed. 15.00 (ISBN 0-87152-287-X). Reprint.
Thomas, Mrs. Z. V. History of Jefferson County. LC 78-13224. 1978. Repr. of 1927 ed. 12.50 (ISBN 0-87152-289-6). Reprint.
Ward, Warren P. Ward's History of Coffee County. LC 78-13236. 1978. Repr. of 1930 ed. 17.50 (ISBN 0-87152-290-X). Reprint.

GEORGIA–HISTORY

Anderson, Mary S., et al. Georgia: A Pageant of Years. LC 74-2201. (Illus.). 316p. 1974. Repr. of 1933 ed. 16.50 (ISBN 0-87152-166-0). Reprint.
Avalov, Zurab D. The Independence of Georgia in International Politics, 1918-1920. LC 79-2890. 286p. 1981. Repr. of 1940 ed. 23.50 (ISBN 0-8305-0059-6). Hyperion Conn.
Avery, Isaac W. History of the State of Georgia from 1850-1881. LC 75-161709. Repr. of 1881 ed. 49.50 (ISBN 0-404-04571-5). AMS Pr.
Bolton, Herbert E. & Ross, Mary. Debatable Land: A Sketch of the Anglo-Spanish Contest for the Georgia Country. LC 68-25029. (Illus.). 1968. Repr. of 1925 ed. 7.00 (ISBN 0-8462-1141-6). Russell.
Bonner, James C. Georgia. LC 65-25494. (Orig.). 1965. pap. 2.95 (ISBN 0-8077-1095-4). Tchrs Coll.
Bonner, James C. & Roberts, Lucien E., eds. Studies in Georgia History & Government. LC 74-2315. 298p. 1974. Repr. of 1940 ed. 18.50 (ISBN 0-87152-167-9). Reprint.
Brooks, Robert P. Georgia Studies, Selected Writings of Robert Preston Brooks. facs. ed. LC 69-17565. (Essay Index Reprint Ser). 1952. 16.50 (ISBN 0-8369-1025-7). Arno.
--History of Georgia. LC 79-187378. (Illus.). 462p. 1972. Repr. of 1913 ed. 20.00 (ISBN 0-87152-070-2). Reprint.
Brown, Ira L. Georgia Colony. LC 73-95174. (Forge of Freedom Ser). (Illus.). (gr. 5-8). 1970. 8.95 (ISBN 0-02-714900-5, CCPr). Macmillan.
Bryan, T. Conn. Confederate Georgia. LC 53-7145. 229p. 1953. 12.50 (ISBN 0-8203-0040-3). U of Ga Pr.
Cain, Andrew W. History of Lumpkin County for the First Hundred Years, 1832-1932. LC 78-12902. 1978. Repr. of 1932 ed. 22.50 (ISBN 0-87152-277-2). Reprint.
Campbell, Archibald. Journal of an Expedition Against the Rebels of Georgia in North America Under the Orders of Archibald Campbell, Esquire, Lieut. Colonel of His Majesty's 71 Regiment, 1778. 1980. 25.00 (ISBN 0-937044-07-5); pap. 15.00 (ISBN 0-937044-08-3). Richmond Cty Hist Soc.
Capps, Clifford S. & Burney, Eugenia. Colonial Georgia. LC 73-181674. (Colonial History Books). (Illus.). (gr. 5 up). 1972. 7.95 (ISBN 0-525-67112-9). Elsevier-Nelson.
Cashin, Edward J. & Robertson, Heard. Augusta & the American Revolution: Events in the Georgia Back Country, 1773-1783. LC 74-28968. (Illus.). 1975. pap. 7.00 (ISBN 0-686-15798-2). Richmond Cty Hist Soc.
Church, Leslie F. Oglethorpe: A Study of Philanthropy in England & Georgia. 1932. 15.00x (ISBN 0-8401-0391-3). Allenson-Breckinridge.

Clarke, E. Y. Illustrated History of Atlanta. (Illus.). 1971. Repr. 5.00 (ISBN 0-87797-015-7). Cherokee.

Clements, J. B. History of Irwin County. LC 78-13229. 1978. Repr. of 1932 ed. 25.00 (ISBN 0-87152-278-0). Reprint.

Cobb, Mrs. Wilton P. History of Dodge County. LC 79-11196. (Illus.). 1979. Repr. of 1932 ed. 15.00 (ISBN 0-87152-293-4). Reprint.

Coleman, Kenneth. American Revolution in Georgia, 1763-1789. LC 58-59848. 352p. 1958. 15.00 (ISBN 0-8203-0015-2). U of Ga Pr.

--Colonial Georgia: A History. (A History of the American Colonies Ser.). 1976. lib. bdg. 25.00 (ISBN 0-527-18712-7). Kraus Intl.

--Georgia History in Outline. rev. ed. LC 78-14087. 142p. 1978. pap. text ed. 4.00x (ISBN 0-8203-0467-0). U of Ga Pr.

--A History of Georgia. LC 77-73640. (Illus.). 445p. 1977. 15.00 (ISBN 0-8203-0427-1); text ed. 12.50 (ISBN 0-8203-0433-6). U of Ga Pr.

Coleman, Kenneth & Ready, Milton, eds. Colonial Records of the State of Georgia: Original Papers of Governor Wright, President Habersham, & Others, 1764-1782, Vol. 28, Pt. II. LC 79-14348. 444p. 1979. 20.00 (ISBN 0-8203-0481-6). U of Ga Pr.

--The Colonial Records of the State of Georgia, Vol. 27. LC 74-30679. 350p. 1978. 20.00 (ISBN 0-8203-0423-9). U of Ga Pr.

--The Colonial Records of the State of Georgia, Vol. 28, Pt 1. LC 74-30679. 496p. 1976. 20.00x (ISBN 0-8203-0379-8). U of Ga Pr.

Cook, Anna M. History of Baldwin County Georgia. LC 78-13226. 1978. Repr. of 1925 ed. 22.50 (ISBN 0-87152-279-9). Reprint.

Cooper, Walter G. Official History of Fulton County. LC 78-12918. 1978. Repr. of 1934 ed. 35.00 (ISBN 0-87152-280-2). Reprint.

Coulter, E. Merton. Georgia: A Short History. 2nd rev. ed. 537p. 1960. 12.50 (ISBN 0-8078-0786-9). U of NC Pr.

Coulter, E. Merton & Saye, Albert B., eds. A List of the Early Settlers of Georgia. LC 49-10242. 111p. 1949. 8.00 (ISBN 0-8203-0119-1). U of Ga Pr.

Covington, W. A. History of Colquitt County. LC 80-13117. (Illus.). 424p. 1980. Repr. of 1937 ed. 25.00 (ISBN 0-87152-318-3). Reprint.

--History of Colquitt County. LC 80-13117. (Illus.). 424p. 1980. Repr. of 1937 ed. 25.00 (ISBN 0-87152-318-3). Reprint.

D.A.R.Thronateeska Chapter, compiled by. History & Reminiscences of Dougherty County Georgia. LC 78-12903. 1978. Repr. of 1924 ed. 20.00 (ISBN 0-87152-282-9). Reprint.

Daughters Of The American Revolution - Georgia. Historical Collections of the Joseph Habersham Chapter, Vol. 1. Peel, Mrs. William L., ed. LC 67-26474. 1967. Repr. of 1902 ed. 17.50 (ISBN 0-8063-0088-4). Genealog Pub.

--Historical Collections of the Joseph Habersham Chapter, Vol. 2. Peel, Mrs. William L., ed. LC 67-26474. 1968. Repr. of 1902 ed. 25.00 (ISBN 0-8063-0089-2). Genealog Pub.

--Historical Collections of the Joseph Habersham Chapter, Vol. 3. Peel, Mrs. William, ed. LC 67-26474. 1968. Repr. of 1910 ed. 15.00 (ISBN 0-8063-0090-6). Genealog Pub.

Davidson, Grace G. Early Records of Georgia (the Earliest Records of Wilkes County, Georgia, 2 vols. (Illus.). 1967. Repr. of 1933 ed. 35.00 (ISBN 0-89308-006-3). Southern Hist Pr.

--Historical Collections of the Georgia Chapters, Daughters of the American Revolution: Records of Elbert County, Georgia, Vol. 3. 1968. Repr. of 1930 ed. 20.00 (ISBN 0-89308-008-X). Southern Hist Pr.

Davidson, Victor. History of Wilkinson County. LC 78-12919. 1978. Repr. of 1930 ed. 25.00 (ISBN 0-87152-283-7). Reprint.

Davis, Harold E. The Fledgling Province: Social & Cultural Life in Colonial Georgia 1733-1776. LC 76-2570. (Institute of Early American History & Culture Ser.). (Illus.). 1976. 21.00x (ISBN 0-8078-1267-6). U of NC Pr.

Davis, Robert S., Jr. Georgia Citizens & Soldiers of the American Revolution. 350p. 1979. 30.00 (ISBN 0-89308-169-8). Southern Hist Pr.

--Research in Georgia: With a Special Emphasis Upon the Georgia Department of Archives & History. (Illus.). 268p. 1981. 25.00 (ISBN 0-89308-199-X); pap. 20.00 (ISBN 0-686-75593-6). Southern Hist.

--The Wilkes County Papers, Seventeen Seventy-Three to Eighteen Thirty-Three. 338p. 1979. 35.00 (ISBN 0-89308-170-1). Southern Hist Pr.

Davis, Robert S., Jr. & Lucas, Silas E., Jr., eds. Georgia's Loose Land Lottery Papers & Oaths, Eighteen Hundred & Five to Nineteen Fourteen. 338p. 1979. 22.50 (ISBN 0-89308-156-6). Southern Hist Pr.

Dorsey, James E. Footprints Along the Hoopee: A History of Emanuel County, 1812-1900. LC 78-12908. 1978. 15.00 (ISBN 0-87152-291-8). Reprint.

Drayton, John. Memoirs of the American Revolution, 2 Vols. Decker, Peter, ed. LC 77-76244. (Eyewitness Accounts of the American Revolution Ser., No. 2). 1969. Repr. of 1821 ed. Set. 34.00 (ISBN 0-405-01149-0); 17.00 ea. Vol. 1 (ISBN 0-405-01150-4). Vol. 2 (ISBN 0-405-01151-2). Arno.

Ettinger, Amos A. James Edward Oglethorpe, Imperial Idealist. (Illus.). 1968. Repr. of 1936 ed. 19.50 (ISBN 0-208-00664-8, Archon). Shoe String.

Evans, Lawton B. A History of Georgia for Use in Schools. LC 70-187381. (Illus.). 426p. 1972. Repr. of 1908 ed. 22.50 (ISBN 0-87152-076-1). Reprint.

Fancher, Betsy. Lost Legacy of Georgia's Golden Isles. LC 78-12511. (Illus.). 1979. Repr. of 1971 ed. 15.00 (ISBN 0-89783-000-8). Larlin Corp.

Faulk, Mrs. Hugh L. & Jones, Billy W. The History of Twiggs County, Georgia. (Illus.). 1970. Repr. of 1960 ed. 15.00 (ISBN 0-89308-009-8). Southern Hist Pr.

Fewell, Laura R. Aunt Quimby's Reminiscenses of Georgia. LC 74-187382. 117p. 1972. Repr. of 1871 ed. 12.50 (ISBN 0-87152-077-X). Reprint.

Fleming, W. P. Crisp County, Georgia: Historical Sketches, Vol. 1. LC 80-13477. (Illus.). 288p. 1980. Repr. of 1932 ed. 20.00 (ISBN 0-87152-319-1). Reprint.

Fradin, Dennis. Georgia: In Words & Pictures. (Young People's Stories of Our States Ser.). (Illus.). 48p. (gr. 2-5). 1981. PLB 9.25 (ISBN 0-516-03910-5). Childrens.

Gamble, Thomas, Jr. Bethesda, an Historical Sketch of Whitefield's House of Mercy in Georgia, & of the Union Society, His Associate & Successor in Philanthropy. LC 78-187383. (Illus.). 150p. 1972. Repr. of 1902 ed. 13.50 (ISBN 0-87152-078-8). Reprint.

Georgia Chapters, D. A. R. The Historical Collections Georgia Chapters, D. A. R. Old Bible Records & Land Lotteries, Vol. 4. 1969. Repr. of 1932 ed. 20.00 (ISBN 0-89308-011-X). Southern Hist Pr.

--Historical Collections of the Georgia Chapters, Daughters of the American Revolution, Vol. 1. 1968. Repr. of 1926 ed. 20.00 (ISBN 0-89308-010-1). Southern Hist Pr.

Georgia Colony. Colonial Records of the State of Georgia 1732-1782, 26 vols. in 28 pts. Candler, Allen D., ed. LC 70-138087. Repr. of 1916 ed. Set. 1330.00 (ISBN 0-404-07260-7); 47.50 ea. AMS Pr.

Georgia General Assembly. Confederate Records of the State of Georgia, 1860-1868, 6 Vols. Candler, Allen D., ed. LC 78-155622. Repr. of 1911 ed. Set. 290.00 (ISBN 0-404-07290-9); 58.00 ea. AMS Pr.

--Revolutionary Records of the State of Georgia, 1769-1784, 3 Vols. Candler, Allen D., ed. LC 72-965. Repr. of 1908 ed. Set. 142.50 (ISBN 0-404-07300-X); 47.50 ea. Vol. 1 (ISBN 0-404-07301-8). Vol. 2 (ISBN 0-404-07302-6). Vol. 3 (ISBN 0-404-07303-4). AMS Pr.

Gilmer, George R. Sketches of Some of the First Settlers of Upper Georgia. rev. ed. LC 65-25481. (Illus.). 1970. Repr. of 1926 ed. 20.00 (ISBN 0-8063-0384-0). Genealog Pub.

Goff, John H. Placenames of Georgia: Essays of John H. Goff. Utley, Francis L. & Hemperley, Marion R., eds. LC 73-88366. (Illus.). 534p. 1975. 18.50 (ISBN 0-8203-0342-9). U of Ga Pr.

Greene, Jack P. Quest for Power: The Lower Houses of Assembly in the Southern Royal Colonies, 1689-1776. 1972. pap. 3.95x (ISBN 0-393-00591-7, Norton Lib). Norton.

Harden, William. History of Savannah & South Georgia. LC 72-97929. 1969. Repr. of 1913 ed. buckram over bds 25.00 (ISBN 0-87797-009-2). Cherokee.

Harris, Joel C. Stories of Georgia. rev. ed. LC 72-187387. (Illus.). 315p. 1972. Repr. of 1896 ed. 16.50 (ISBN 0-87152-082-6). Reprint.

--Stories of Georgia. LC 73-174943. 1975. Repr. of 1896 ed. 22.00 (ISBN 0-8103-4082-8). Gale.

Hart, Bertha S. The Official History of Laurens County, Georgia, 1807-1941. LC 78-58066. 1978. cloth over bds 25.00 (ISBN 0-87797-042-4). Cherokee.

Hays, Louise F. History of Macon County Georgia. LC 79-11202. (Illus.). 1979. Repr. of 1933 ed. 30.00 (ISBN 0-87152-294-2). Reprint.

Hewatt, Alexander. An Historical Account of the Rise & Progress of the Colonies of South Carolina & Georgia, 2 Vols. LC 62-5133. 1962. Repr. of 1779 ed. 17.50 ea. Vol. 1 (ISBN 0-87152-008-7). Vol. 2 (ISBN 0-87152-009-5). Set. 35.00 (ISBN 0-87152-303-5). Reprint.

Hill, Louis B. Joseph E. Brown & the Confederacy. LC 70-138612. 360p. 1973. Repr. of 1939 ed. lib. bdg. 18.75x (ISBN 0-8371-5722-6, HIJB). Greenwood.

Historical Collections of the Georgia Chapters, Daughters of the American Revolution: Records of Richmond County, Georgia. Formerly St. Paul's Parish, Vol. 2. (Illus.). 1968. Repr. of 1927 ed. 20.00 (ISBN 0-89308-007-1). Southern Hist Pr.

History of Lowndes County Georgia, 1825-1941. LC 78-12915. 1978. Repr. of 1942 ed. 20.00 (ISBN 0-87152-281-0). Reprint.

History of Peach County, Georgia. LC 72-91463. 1972. cloth over bds 15.00 (ISBN 0-87797-023-8). Cherokee.

History of the Baptist Denomination in Georgia with Biographical Compendum & Portrait Gallery of Baptist Ministers & Georgia Baptists. (Illus.). 614p. 1976. Repr. of 1881 ed. 30.00 (ISBN 0-89308-038-1). Southern Hist Pr.

Holmes, James. Dr. Bullie's Notes: Reminiscences of Early Georgia & of Philadelphia & New Haven in the 1800s. Presley, Delma E., ed. LC 76-14370. (Illus.). 10.00 (ISBN 0-87797-038-6). Cherokee.

Hull, Barbara S. St. Simons: Enchanted Island. LC 80-80048. (Illus.). 136p. 1980. 7.95 (ISBN 0-87797-049-1). Cherokee.

Huxford, Folks. The History of Brooks County Georgia. LC 78-13225. 1978. Repr. of 1948 ed. 25.00 (ISBN 0-87152-284-5). Reprint.

Index to the Headright & Bounty Grants in Georgia from 1756-1909. 1970. 35.00 (ISBN 0-89308-017-9). Southern Hist Pr.

Ingram, C. Fred, ed. Beadland to Barrow: A History of Barrow County, Georgia from the Earliest Days to the Present. LC 78-58072. 1978. 25.00 (ISBN 0-87797-043-2). Cherokee.

Jackson, Harvey H., et al. Georgia's Signers & the Declaration of Independence. LC 81-67795. (Illus.). 100p. 1981. 8.95 (ISBN 0-87797-080-7). Cherokee.

Jenkins, Charles F. Button Gwinnett: Signer of the Declaration of Independence. LC 74-2194. (Illus.). 338p. 1974. Repr. of 1926 ed. 15.00 (ISBN 0-87152-171-7). Reprint.

Jones, Charles C. Monumental Remains of Georgia: Part First. LC 73-12510. 119p. 1973. Repr. of 1861 ed. 12.00 (ISBN 0-527-46690-5). Kraus Repr.

Jones, Charles C., Jr. Antiquities of the Southern Indians Particularly of the Georgia Tribes. LC 72-5001. (Harvard University. Peabody Museum of Archaeology & Ethnology, Antiquities of the New World: No. 6). (Illus.). Repr. of 1873 ed. 43.50 (ISBN 0-404-57306-1). AMS Pr.

--Biographical Sketches of the Delegates from Georgia to the Continental Congress. LC 74-187390. 221p. 1972. Repr. of 1891 ed. 16.50 (ISBN 0-87152-085-0). Reprint.

--The Dead Towns of Georgia. Bd. with Itinerant Observations in America. Kimber, Edward. (Collections of the Georgia Historical Society: Vol. 4). (Illus.). 338p. 1974. Repr. of 1878 ed. 16.50 (ISBN 0-87152-172-5). Reprint.

--History of Georgia, 2 Vols. LC 65-5051. (Illus.). 1965. Repr. of 1883 ed. Set. 40.00 (ISBN 0-87152-304-3); 20.00 ea. Vol. 1 (ISBN 0-87152-024-9). Vol. 2 (ISBN 0-87152-025-7). Reprint.

Jones, Frank S. History of Decatur County Georgia. LC 80-17698. 480p. 1980. Repr. of 1971 ed. 25.00 (ISBN 0-87152-336-1). Reprint.

Jones, Jacqueline. Soldiers of Light & Love: Northern Teachers & Georgia Blacks, 1865-1873. LC 79-27129. (Fred W. Morrison Ser. in Southern Studies). xiii, 273p. 1980. 17.50x (ISBN 0-8078-1435-0). U of NC Pr.

Jones, Mary G. & Reynolds, Lily. Coweta County (GA.) Chronicles. (Illus.). 1975. Repr. of 1928 ed. 35.00 (ISBN 0-89308-016-0). Southern Hist Pr.

Kelso, William M. Captain Jones's Wormslow: A Historical, Archaeological, & Architectural Study of an Eighteenth-Century Plantation Site Near Savannah, Georgia. LC 78-2288. (Wormsloe Foundations Publications Ser.: No. 13). (Illus.). 208p. 1979. 20.00x (ISBN 0-8203-0447-6). U of Ga Pr.

Killion, Ronald G. & Waller, Charles T. Georgia & the Revolution. LC 74-30922. 1975. bds. 10.00 (ISBN 0-87797-030-0). Cherokee.

Knight, Lucian L. Georgia's Roster of the Revolution. LC 67-24375. 1967. Repr. of 1920 ed. 22.50 (ISBN 0-8063-0204-6). Genealog Pub.

Longstreet, A. B. Georgia Scenes: Characters, Incidents, Etc. in the First Half Century of the Republic. 7.00 (ISBN 0-8446-0777-0). Peter Smith.

Lumpkin, Wilson. Removal of the Cherokee Indians from Georgia, 2 vols. in 1. LC 76-123200. Repr. of 1907 ed. lib. bdg. 27.50x (ISBN 0-678-00710-1). Kelley.

McCain, James R. Georgia As a Proprietary Proprietary Province: The Execution of a Trust. LC 78-187391. 357p. 1972. Repr. of 1917 ed. 15.00 (ISBN 0-87152-086-9). Reprint.

McCall, Hugh. History of Georgia. LC 79-75932. 1969. Repr. of 1909 ed. buckram over bds 30.00 (ISBN 0-87797-006-8). Cherokee.

McIntosh, Lachlan. Lachlan McIntosh Papers in the University of Georgia Libraries. Hawes, Lilla M., ed. LC 68-22842. 141p. 1968. pap. 5.00x (ISBN 0-8203-0110-8). U of Ga Pr.

McLendon, Samuel G. History of the Public Domain of Georgia. LC 74-2134. (Illus.). 200p. 1974. Repr. of 1924 ed. 15.00 (ISBN 0-87152-174-1). Reprint.

McMichael, Lois, compiled by. History of Butts County, Georgia 1825-1976. LC 78-58078. 1978. 35.00 (ISBN 0-87797-044-0). Cherokee.

McQueen, Alex S. History of Charlton County. LC 78-12909. 1978. Repr. of 1932 ed. 15.00 (ISBN 0-87152-286-1). Reprint.

Mann, Floris P. History of Telfair County from 1812 to 1949. LC 78-13175. 1978. Repr. of 1949 ed. 15.00 (ISBN 0-87152-285-3). Reprint.

Martin, Harold. William Berry Hartsfield, Mayor of Atlanta. LC 78-1550. 248p. 1978. 10.00 (ISBN 0-8203-0445-X). U of Ga Pr.

Martin, Harold H. Georgia. (The States & the Nation Ser.). (Illus.). 1977. 12.95 (ISBN 0-393-05606-6). Norton.

Mays, Lois B. Settlers of the Okefenokee. 208p. 1975. 6.95x (ISBN 0-9601606-0-4). Okefenokee Pr.

Mitchell, Frances L. Georgia Land & People. LC 74-2192. 526p. 1974. Repr. of 1900 ed. 22.50 (ISBN 0-87152-175-X). Reprint.

Mitchell, Lizzie R. History of Pike County, Georgia, 1822-1932. LC 80-23352. x, 162p. 1980. Repr. 15.00 (ISBN 0-87152-345-0). Reprint.

Montgomery, Robert & Barnwell, John. Most Delightful Golden Islands. LC 77-76733. 1969. Repr. of 1717 ed. cloth over bds 5.00 (ISBN 0-87797-007-6). Cherokee.

Myers, Robert M., ed. The Children of Pride: A True Story of Georgia & the Civil War. LC 79-998344. 1728p. 1972. 35.00x (ISBN 0-300-01214-4). Yale U Pr.

--Edge of the Sword. (Children of Pride Ser.: Vol. 3). 1977. pap. 1.95 (ISBN 0-445-04052-1). Popular Lib.

--The Finger of Providence. (The Children of Pride Ser: Vol. 2). 1977. pap. 1.95 (ISBN 0-445-08614-9). Popular Lib.

--A Georgian at Princeton. LC 75-33772. 416p. 1976. 12.95 (ISBN 0-15-135105-8). HarBraceJ.

--The God of Battle. (Children of Pride Ser: Vol. IV). 1977. pap. 1.95 (ISBN 0-445-04093-9). Popular Lib.

--Many Mansions. (The Children of Pride Ser: Vol. 1). 1977. pap. 1.95 (ISBN 0-445-08592-4). Popular Lib.

Narrative of the Tragical Death of Mr. Darius Barber, & His Seven Children, Who Were Inhumanly Butchered by the Indians... to Which Is Added an Account of the Captivity & Sufferings of Mrs. Barber, Repr. Of 1816 Ed. Incl. Shocking Murder by the Savage! of Mr. Darius Barber's Family in Georgia; Narrative of the Captivity & Sufferings of Mrs. Hannah Lewis, & Her 3 Children, Who Were Taken Prisoners by the Indians. Repr. of 1817 ed; Narrative of the Captivity & Providential Escape of Mrs. Lewis. Repr. of 1833 ed; Narrative of James Van Horne: On the Plains of Michigan. Repr. of 1817 ed; The Indian Captive: Or a Narrative of the Captivity & Sufferings of Zadock Steele... to Which Is Prefixed an Account of the Burning of Royalton. Repr. of 1818 ed. LC 75-7058. (Indian Captivities Ser.: Vol. 36). 1976. lib. bdg. 44.00 (ISBN 0-8240-1660-2). Garland Pub.

Northen, William J., ed. Men of Mark in Georgia: A Complete & Elaborate History of the State from Its Settlement to the Present Time, Vols. 1-7. Incl. Vol. 1. 25.00 (ISBN 0-87152-176-8); Vol. 2. 25.00 (ISBN 0-87152-177-6); Vol. 3. 25.00 (ISBN 0-87152-178-4); Vol. 4. 25.00 (ISBN 0-87152-179-2); Vol. 5. 25.00 (ISBN 0-87152-180-6); Vol. 6. 25.00 (ISBN 0-87152-181-4); Vol. 7. 25.00 (ISBN 0-87152-182-2). LC 74-2193. (Illus.). 3952p. 1974. Repr. of 1906 ed. Set. 175.00 (ISBN 0-87152-331-0). Reprint.

Pate, John B. History of Turner County. LC 79-10025. (Illus.). 1979. Repr. of 1933 ed. 15.00 (ISBN 0-87152-295-0). Reprint.

Peel, Mrs. William L. Historical Collections of the Joseph Habersham Chapter, Daughters of the American Revolution, Vol. 3. (Illus.). 1968. Repr. of 1910 ed. 17.50 (ISBN 0-89308-030-6). Southern Hist Pr.

Pendleton, Louis. In the Okefenokee: A Story of War Time and the Great Georgia Swamp. LC 72-1558. (Black Heritage Library Collection Ser.). Repr. of 1895 ed. 14.50 (ISBN 0-8369-9047-1). Arno.

Ready, Milton L. The Castle Builders: Georgia's Economy Under the Trustees, 1732-1754. LC 77-14750. (Dissertations in American Economic History Ser.). 1978. 31.00 (ISBN 0-405-11053-7). Arno.
Reese, Trevor R. Colonial Georgia: A Study in British Imperial Policy in the Eighteenth Century. LC 63-17349. 172p. 1963. 10.00 (ISBN 0-8203-0035-7). U of Ga Pr.
Reeve, Jewell B. Climb the Hills of Gordon. 304p. 1979. Repr. of 1962 ed. 15.00 (ISBN 0-89308-128-0). Southern Hist Pr.
Rice, Thaddeus B. & Williams, Carolyn W. History of Greene County Georgia Seventeen Eighty-Six to Eighteen Eighty-Six. LC 79-21459. (Illus.). 1979. Repr. of 1961 ed. 25.00 (ISBN 0-87152-299-3). Reprint.
Saye, Albert B. New Viewpoints in Georgia History. LC 44-3340. 256p. 1943. 9.50 (ISBN 0-8203-0132-9). U of Ga Pr.
Sears, Joan N. The First One Hundred Years of Town Planning in Georgia. LC 78-74091. (Illus.). 1979. 15.00 (ISBN 0-87797-046-7). Cherokee.
Shelton, Jane T. Pines & Pioneers: A History of Lowndes County, Georgia, 1825-1900. LC 75-42290. 1976. cloth over bds 10.00 (ISBN 0-87797-034-3). Cherokee.
Shryock, Richard H. Georgia & the Union in 1850. LC 72-182715. Repr. of 1926 ed. 27.00 (ISBN 0-404-05989-9). AMS Pr.
Simpson, John E. Georgia History: A Bibliography. LC 76-15642. 1976. 18.00 (ISBN 0-8108-0960-5). Scarecrow.
Smeal, Lee. Georgia Historical & Biographical Index. LC 78-53692. (Illus.). Date not set. lib. bdg. price not set (ISBN 0-89593-177-X). Accelerated Index.
Smith, George G. Story of Georgia & the Georgia People, 1732-1860. LC 68-9359. (Illus.). 1968. Repr. of 1901 ed. 25.00 (ISBN 0-8063-0317-4). Genealog Pub.
Smith, James F. The Eighteen Thirty-Two (Cherokee) Land Lottery. (Illus.). 1978. Repr. of 1838 ed. 22.50 (ISBN 0-89308-033-0). Southern Hist Pr.
Spalding, Phinizy. Oglethorpe in America. LC 76-8092. 1977. lib. bdg. 12.50 (ISBN 0-226-76846-5). U of Chicago Pr.
Stacy, James. History & Published Records of the Midway Congregational Church, Liberty County, Georgia. LC 79-22013. (Illus.). 1979. 27.50 (ISBN 0-87152-298-5). Reprint.
Swindler, William F. & Frech, Mary, eds. Chronology & Documentary Handbook of the State of Georgia. LC 73-499. (gr. 9-12). 1973. PLB 8.50 (ISBN 0-379-16135-4). Oceana.
Tailfer, Patrick, et al. A True & Historical Narrative of the Colony of Georgia in America. facsimile ed. LC 74-168522. (Black Heritage Library Collection). Repr. of 1741 ed. 10.75 (ISBN 0-8369-8874-4). Arno.
Tate, Luke E. History of Pickens County. LC 78-13223. 1978. Repr. of 1935 ed. 15.00 (ISBN 0-87152-287-X). Reprint.
Temple, Sarah B. The First Hundred Years: A Short History of Cobb County, in Georgia. 5th ed. LC 80-80671. 901p. 1979. Repr. of 1935 ed. 25.00 (ISBN 0-87797-050-5). Cherokee.
Thomas, Mrs. Z. V. History of Jefferson County. LC 78-13224. 1978. Repr. of 1927 ed. 12.50 (ISBN 0-87152-289-6). Reprint.
Thompson, C. Mildred. Reconstruction in Georgia. 418p. 1971. Repr. of 1915 ed. cloth over bds 15.00 (ISBN 0-87797-017-3). Cherokee.
Tift, Nelson. The Condition of Affairs in Georgia. facsimile ed. LC 73-164397. (Black Heritage Library Collection). Repr. of 1869 ed. 17.25 (ISBN 0-8369-8856-6). Arno.
Urlsperger, Samuel. Detailed Report on the Salzburger Emigrants Who Settled in America: Vol. 2, 1734-1735. Jones, George F., ed. Lacher, Hermann J., tr. LC 67-27137. (Wormsloe Foundation Publications Ser: No. 10). 253p. 1969. 12.00x (ISBN 0-8203-0238-4). U of Ga Pr.
Vance, Mary. Historical Society Architectural Publications: Georgia, Hawaii, Idaho, Illinois & Indiana. (Architecture Ser.: Bibliography A-157). 54p. 1980. pap. 6.00 (ISBN 0-686-26906-3). Vance Biblios.
Vanstory, Burnette. Georgia's Land of the Golden Isles. LC 56-13004. (Illus.). 225p. 1981. 15.00 (ISBN 0-8203-0557-X); pap. 8.95 (ISBN 0-8203-0558-8). U of Ga Pr.
--Georgia's Land of the Golden Isles. rev. ed. LC 56-13004. 225p. 1970. 8.95 (ISBN 0-8203-0081-0). U of Ga Pr.
Ver Steeg, Clarence L. Origins of a Southern Mosaic: Studies of Early Carolina & Georgia. LC 74-18587. (Mercer University Lamar Memorial Lectures Ser: No. 17). 167p. 1975. 9.95x (ISBN 0-8203-0365-8). U of Ga Pr.
Ward, Warren P. Ward's History of Coffee County. LC 78-13236. 1978. Repr. of 1930 ed. 17.50 (ISBN 0-87152-290-X). Reprint.
White, George. Historical Collections of Georgia. 3rd ed. Bd. with Name Index. Dutton, Alpha C. (Illus.). Repr. of 1920 ed. LC 68-9358. 1969. Repr. of 1855 ed. 30.00 (ISBN 0-8063-0376-X). Genealog Pub.
--Statistics of the State of Georgia. LC 71-187392. 701p. 1972. Repr. of 1849 ed. 27.00 (ISBN 0-87152-087-7). Reprint.
Whitson, Skip, compiled by. Georgia One Hundred Years Ago. (Sun Historical Ser). (Illus., Orig.). 1976. pap. 3.50 (ISBN 0-89540-025-1, SB025). Sun Pub.
Wilcox, Herbert. Georgia Scribe: Selected Columns. LC 74-82935. 1974. bds. 7.00 (ISBN 0-87797-029-7). Cherokee.
Williford, William B. The Glory of Covington (Georgia) LC 72-96820. 320p. 1973. bds. 12.00 (ISBN 0-87797-024-6). Cherokee.
Wilson, Caroline P. Annals of Georgia, 2 vols. in 1, Vols. 1 & 2. 1969. Repr. of 1928 ed. 20.00 (ISBN 0-89308-035-7). Southern Hist Pr.
Wood, Virginia S., ed. McIntosh County Academy, McIntosh County, Georgia: Minutes of the Commissioners 1820-1875 Account Book of Students, 1821-1834. (Illus.). xxvii, 257p. 1973. pap. 13.95 plus UPS (ISBN 0-915184-07-9, Pub. by Oak Hill). Channing Bks.
Woolley, Edwin C. Reconstruction of Georgia. LC 74-120211. (Columbia University. Studies in the Social Sciences: No. 36). Repr. of 1901 ed. 14.50 (ISBN 0-404-51036-1). AMS Pr.

GEORGIA–HISTORY–FICTION

Oertel, Theodore E. Jack Sutherland: A Tale of Bloody Marsh. LC 74-2401. (Illus.). 346p. 1974. Repr. of 1926 ed. 16.50 (ISBN 0-87152-183-0). Reprint.

GEORGIA–POLITICS AND GOVERNMENT

Abbot, W. W. The Royal Governors of Georgia, 1754-1775. LC 59-9568. (Institute of Early American History & Culture Ser.). 1959. 13.50x (ISBN 0-8078-0758-3). U of NC Pr.
Arnett, Alex M. Populist Movement in Georgia: A View of the Agrarian Crusade in the Light of Solid-South Politics. LC 74-158272. (Columbia University Studies in the Social Sciences: No. 235). Repr. of 1922 ed. 20.00 (ISBN 0-404-51235-6). AMS Pr.
Bartley, Numan V. From Thurmond to Wallace: Political Tendencies in Georgia 1948-1968. LC 75-11753. (Illus.). 176p. 1970. 11.50x (ISBN 0-8018-1170-8); pap. 3.50x (ISBN 0-8018-1555-X). Johns Hopkins.
Bonner, James C. & Roberts, Lucien E., eds. Studies in Georgia History & Government. LC 74-2315. 298p. 1974. Repr. of 1940 ed. 18.50 (ISBN 0-87152-167-9). Reprint.
Brooks, Robert P. Agrarian Revolution in Georgia, 1865-1912. LC 73-129939. Repr. of 1914 ed. 10.00x (ISBN 0-8371-1603-1, Pub. by Negro U Pr). Greenwood.
Chanin, Leah F. Reference Guide to Georgia Legal History & Legal Research. 175p. 1980. 20.00 (ISBN 0-87215-315-0). Michie-Bobbs.
Coleman, Kenneth & Ready, Milton, eds. The Colonial Records of the State of Georgia, Vol. 27. LC 74-30679. 350p. 1978. 20.00 (ISBN 0-8203-0423-9). U of Ga Pr.
Cushing, John D., compiled by. The First Laws of the State of Georgia, 2 vols. (Earliest Laws of the Original Thirteen States Ser.). 1981. 49.00 ea. Set (ISBN 0-89453-218-9). M Glazier.
Greene, Jack P. The Quest for Power: The Lower Houses of Assembly in the Southern Royal Colonies 1689-1776. (Institute of Early American History & Culture Ser.). 1963. 24.50x (ISBN 0-8078-0900-4). U of NC Pr.
Hepburn, Lawrence R. State Government in Georgia. 200p. (Orig.). (gr. 8-12). 1981. pap. text ed. 9.95 (ISBN 0-89854-067-4). U of GA Inst Govt.
Hepburn, Mary A. County Government in Georgia. 2nd ed. 128p. (gr. 8 up). 1981. pap. text ed. 7.95 (ISBN 0-89854-075-5). U of GA Inst Govt.
--Making Your Vote Count: Registration, Campaigns, & Elections in Georgia. 100p. 1976. spiral bdg. 5.00 (ISBN 0-89854-023-2). U of GA Inst Govt.
Hepburn, Mary A., et al. City Government in Georgia. LC 79-24128. 150p. (Orig.). (gr. 8-12). 1980. pap. 7.95 (ISBN 0-89854-052-6). U of GA Inst Govt.
Hughes, Melvin C. County Government in Georgia. LC 74-15165. (Illus.). 197p. 1975. Repr. of 1944 ed. lib. bdg. 15.00x (ISBN 0-8371-7805-3, HUCGG). Greenwood.
Jackson, Edwin L. Handbook for Georgia Legislators. 8th ed. 220p. 1980. pap. 10.00x (ISBN 0-89854-069-0). U of GA Inst Govt.
Jackson, Harvey H. Lachlan McIntosh & the Politics of Revolutionary Georgia. LC 78-8995. 256p. 1979. 16.00 (ISBN 0-8203-0459-X). U of Ga Pr.
Johnson, Michael P. Toward a Patriarchal Republic: The Secession of Georgia. LC 77-3029. 1977. 17.50 (ISBN 0-8071-0270-9). La State U Pr.
Kundell, James E. Litter Abatement Measures. 74p. 1979. spiral bdg. 5.00 (ISBN 0-89854-062-3). U of GA Inst Govt.
McVay, Kipling L. & Stubbs, Robert S. Governmental Ethics & Conflicts of Interest in Georgia. 227p. 1980. 22.50 (ISBN 0-87215-304-5); 1981 suppl. 7.50 (ISBN 0-87215-396-7). Michie-Bobbs.
Martin, Harold. William Berry Hartsfield, Mayor of Atlanta. LC 78-1550. 248p. 1978. 10.00 (ISBN 0-8203-0445-X). U of Ga Pr.
Mellichamp, Josephine. Senators from Georgia. LC 75-32113. 1976. 12.95 (ISBN 0-87397-082-9). Strode.
Nathans, Elizabeth S. Losing the Peace: Georgia Republicans & Reconstruction, 1865-1871. LC 68-8942. (Illus.). 1968. 17.50x (ISBN 0-8071-0627-5). La State U Pr.
Parks, Joseph H. Joseph E. Brown of Georgia. LC 74-27192. 1976. 40.00x (ISBN 0-8071-0189-3). La State U Pr.
Pearce, Haywood J. Benjamin A. Hill, Secession & Reconstruction. LC 70-97434. Repr. of 1928 ed. 14.50x (ISBN 0-8371-2727-0, Pub. by Negro U Pr). Greenwood.
Phillips, U. B. Correspondence of Robert Toombs, Alexander H. Stephens, & Howell Cobb. LC 68-54846. (American Scene Ser). 1970. Repr. of 1911 ed. lib. bdg. 79.50 (ISBN 0-306-71191-5). Da Capo.
Phillips, Ulrich B. Georgia & State Rights. LC 67-30578. (Illus.). 1968. 9.00x (ISBN 0-87338-068-1); pap. 4.00x (ISBN 0-87338-069-X). Kent St U Pr.
Pound, Merritt B. & Saye, Albert B. Handbook on the Constitutions of the United States & Georgia. rev. ed. LC 46-27121. 184p. 1975. pap. 2.00x (ISBN 0-8203-0216-3). U of Ga Pr.
Ready, Milton L. The Castle Builders: Georgia's Economy Under the Trustees, 1732-1754. LC 77-14750. (Dissertations in American Economic History Ser.). 1978. 31.00 (ISBN 0-405-11053-7). Arno.
Roberts, Derrell C. Joseph E. Brown & the Politics of Reconstruction. LC 78-92657. (Southern Historical Ser: Vol. 16). 256p. 1973. 10.95x (ISBN 0-8173-5222-8). U of Ala Pr.
Sentell, R. Perry. The Law of Municipal Tort Liability in Georgia. 3rd ed. LC 79-24276. 184p. 1980. pap. text ed. 15.00x (ISBN 0-89854-053-4). U of GA Inst Govt.
Sentell, R. Perry, Jr. Studies in Georgia Local Government Law. 3rd ed. 1977. 40.00 (ISBN 0-87215-189-1). Michie-Bobbs.
Stubbs, Robert E. Powers & Limits of State Government in Georgia. 660p. 1980. 50.00 (ISBN 0-89854-058-5). U of GA Inst Govt.
Ware, Ethel K. Constitutional History of Georgia. (Columbia University. Studies in the Social Sciences: No. 528). Repr. of 1947 ed. 12.50 (ISBN 0-404-51528-2). AMS Pr.
Weeks, J. Devereux. Handbook for Georgia Tax Commissioners. 2nd ed. LC 80-2. 80p. 1980. spiral bdg. 7.50 (ISBN 0-89854-056-9). U of GA Inst Govt.
Weeks, J. Devereux & Elmore, John F. Handbook for Georgia County Commissioners. LC 78-621230. 240p. 1978. pap. 10.00 (ISBN 0-89854-002-X). U of GA Inst Govt.

GEORGIA–PUBLIC LANDS

Lucas, Silas E., Jr. The Eighteen Hundred Seven Land Lottery of Georgia. (Illus.). 1968. 17.50 (ISBN 0-89308-020-9). Southern Hist Pr.
Smith, James F. Cherokee Land Lottery of Georgia, 1832. LC 67-28624. (Illus.). 1969. Repr. of 1838 ed. 20.00 (ISBN 0-8063-0318-2). Genealog Pub.
--The Eighteen Thirty-Two (Cherokee) Land Lottery. (Illus.). 1978. Repr. of 1838 ed. 22.50 (ISBN 0-89308-033-0). Southern Hist Pr.
Wood, Virginia S. & Wood, Ralph V., eds. Georgia Land Lottery, 1805. LC 65-691. xxi, 393p. 1964. pap. 20.00 plus UPS (ISBN 0-915184-06-0, Pub. by Oak Hill). Channing Bks.

GEORGIA–SOCIAL LIFE AND CUSTOMS

Borns, Steven. People of Plains, Ga. (Illus.). 1978. pap. 7.95 (ISBN 0-07-006535-7, SP). McGraw.
Fradin, Dennis. Georgia: In Words & Pictures. (Young People's Stories of Our States Ser.). (Illus.). 48p. (gr. 2-5). 1981. PLB 9.25 (ISBN 0-516-03910-5). Childrens.
Grout, Phil. A Spell in Plains. LC 78-2230. (Illus.). 1978. 19.95 (ISBN 0-916144-17-8); pap. 9.95 (ISBN 0-916144-18-6). Stemmer Hse.
Kemble, Frances A. Journal of a Residence on a Georgian Plantation in 1838-1839. LC 78-99386. 1969. Repr. of 1864 ed. lib. bdg. 14.75 (ISBN 0-8411-0057-8). Metro Bks.
Leigh, Frances B. Ten Years on a Georgia Plantation Since the War. LC 74-76857. Repr. of 1883 ed. 15.50x (ISBN 0-8371-1177-3). Greenwood.
Mitchell, George. I'm Somebody Important: Young Black Voices from Rural Georgia. LC 72-75489. (Illus.). 288p. 1973. 12.95 (ISBN 0-252-00268-7). U of Ill Pr.
Reeve, Jewell B. Climb the Hills of Gordon. 304p. 1979. Repr. of 1962 ed. 15.00 (ISBN 0-89308-128-0). Southern Hist Pr.
Steed, Hal. Georgia: Unfinished State. 1976. Repr. 10.00 (ISBN 0-87797-014-9). Cherokee.

GEORGIA (TRANSCAUCASIA)

Allen, W. E. A History of the Georgian People. 1978. lib. bdg. 75.00 (ISBN 0-8490-1998-2). Gordon Pr.
Lang, David M. A Modern History of Soviet Georgia. LC 75-11426. (Illus.). 298p. 1975. Repr. of 1962 ed. lib. bdg. 18.00x (ISBN 0-8371-8183-6, LASG). Greenwood.
Pitskhelauri, Georgi Z. The Long-Living of Soviet Georgia. Lesnoff-Caravaglia, Gari, ed. & tr. 1981. 14.95 (ISBN 0-89885-073-8). Human Sci Pr.

GEORGIA, UNIVERSITY OF

Brooks, Robert P. University of Georgia Under Sixteen Administrations 1785-1955. LC 56-7979. 260p. 1956. 15.00 (ISBN 0-8203-0195-7). U of Ga Pr.
Coulter, E. Merton. College Life in the Old South. LC 51-7109. 320p. 1951. 12.50 (ISBN 0-8203-0034-9). U of Ga Pr.
Hynds, Ernest C. Antebellum Athens & Clarke County Georgia. LC 73-81626. (Illus.). 208p. 1974. 10.00 (ISBN 0-8203-0341-0). U of Ga Pr.
Stegeman, John F. Ghosts of Herty Field: Early Days on a Southern Gridiron. LC 66-27606. 147p. 1966. 9.95 (ISBN 0-8203-0085-3). U of Ga Pr.

GEORGIA INFANTRY, 1861-1865

Austin, Aurelia. Georgia Boys with "Stonewall" Jackson. LC 57-31515. 99p. 1967. pap. 4.75 (ISBN 0-8203-0073-X). U of Ga Pr.

GEORGIAN TALES

see Tales, Georgian

GEOSCIENCE

see Earth Sciences; Geology–Graphic Methods

GEOTECHNIQUE

see Marine Geotechnique; Rock Mechanics; Soil Mechanics

GEOTECTONICS

see Geology, Structural

GEOTHERMAL RESOURCES

see also Springs

Adam. Geoelectric & Geothermal Studies. 1976. 55.00 (ISBN 0-9960004-2-9, Pub. by Kaido Hungary). Heyden.
Anderson, David N. & Lund, John. Direct Utilization of Geothermal Energy: A Layman's Guide, No. 8. (Special Report Ser.). (Illus.). 100p. (Orig.). pap. 8.00 (ISBN 0-934412-08-1). Geothermal.
Anderson, David N. & Axtell, L. H., eds. Compendium of First Day Papers Presented at the First Conference of the Geothermal Resources Council, El Centro, California, February 1972. (Special Report: No. 2). (Illus.). 77p. (Orig.). 1972. pap. 5.00 (ISBN 0-934412-02-2). Geothermal.
Anderson, David N. & Hall, Beverly A., eds. Geothermal Exploration in the First Quarter Century. (Special Report: No. 3). (Illus.). 200p. 1973. 12.00 (ISBN 0-934412-00-6); pap. 10.00 (ISBN 0-934412-03-0). Geothermal.
Anderson, David N. & Lund, John W., eds. Direct Utilization of Geothermal Energy: A Technical Handbook. (Special Report: No. 7). (Illus.). 251p. 1979. pap. 10.00 (ISBN 0-934412-07-3). Geothermal.
Armstead, H. C. Geothermal Energy: It's Past, Present & Future Contributions to the Energy Needs of Man. LC 78-2545. 1978. text ed. 35.00x (ISBN 0-419-11240-5, Pub. by E & FN Spon England). Methuen Inc.
Barbier, E., ed. Cerro Prieto Geothermal Field: Prodeedings of the First Symposium Held at San Diego, California, Sept. 1978. (Illus.). 300p. 1981. 77.00 (ISBN 0-08-026241-4). Pergamon.
Bowen, Robert. Geothermal Resources. LC 79-41547. 243p. 1980. 64.95x (ISBN 0-470-26917-0). Halsted Pr.
Butler, Edgar. An Industry Survey of the Need for a Federal Grant-Assisted Geothermal Demonstration Power Plant. (Illus.). 36p. 1978. pap. 3.50 (ISBN 0-934412-75-8). Geothermal.
Butler, Edgar W. & Pick, James B. Geothermal Energy Development: Problems & Prospects in the Imperial Valley of California. 305p. 1982. text ed. price not set (ISBN 0-306-40772-8, Plenum Pr). Plenum Pub.
Carlson, Rodger D. The Economics of Geothermal Power in California. Bruchey, Stuart, ed. LC 78-22666. (Energy in the American Economy Ser.). (Illus.). 1979. lib. bdg. 14.00x (ISBN 0-405-11970-4). Arno.
Cheremisinoff, Paul N. & Morrisi, Angelo C. Geothermal Energy Technology Assessment. LC 75-43009. (Illus.). 183p. 1976. pap. 20.00x (ISBN 0-87762-185-3). Technomic.
Collie, M. J., ed. Geothermal Energy: Recent Developments. LC 78-61893. (Energy Technology Review: No. 32). (Illus.). 1979. 40.00 (ISBN 0-8155-0727-5). Noyes.

Committee on Nuclear & Alternative Energy Systems, National Research Council. Geothermal Resources & Technology in the U. S. 1979. pap. text ed. 5.50 (ISBN 0-309-02874-4). Natl Acad Pr.
Edmunds, Stahrl & Rose, Adam. Geothermal Energy & Regional Development. 1979. 31.95 (ISBN 0-03-053316-3). Praeger.
Edwards, Lyman, et al, eds. Geothermal Energy Exploration & Engineering. (Illus.). 320p. 1981. 39.95x (ISBN 0-87201-322-7). Gulf Pub.
Elder, John. Geothermal Systems. LC 80-49663. 1981. 49.50 (ISBN 0-12-236450-3). Acad Pr.
Expanding the Geothermal Frontier. (Transactions Ser.: Vol. 3). (Illus.). 808p. 1979. text ed. 25.00 (ISBN 0-934412-53-7). Geothermal.
Geothermal Energy: A Novelty Becomes Resource. (Transactions: Vol. 2). (Illus.). 748p. 1980. Repr. of 1978 ed. 27.50 (ISBN 0-934412-52-9). Geothermal.
Geothermal Resources Council, ed. Commercial Uses of Geothermal Heat. (Special Report: No. 9). (Illus.). 143p. 1980. pap. 3.50 (ISBN 0-934412-09-X). Geothermal.
--A Conference on the Commercialization of Geothermal Resources, November 28-30, 1978, San Diego, California. (Illus.). 77p. (Orig.). 1978. pap. 7.50 (ISBN 0-934412-76-6). Geothermal.
--Geothermal: State of the Art. (Transactions Ser.: Vol. 1). (Illus.). 310p. 1979. Repr. of 1977 ed. 15.00 (ISBN 0-934412-51-0). Geothermal.
--Proceedings: State-Federal Geothermal Regulatory Interface Workshop, November 17-18, 1976, Asilomar, California. 79p. (Orig.). 1977. pap. 3.50 (ISBN 0-934412-73-1). Geothermal.
Geothermal Resources: Exploration & Exploitation. (ERDA Technical Information Center Ser.). write for info. DOE.
Gilbreth, Terry J. Governing Geothermal Steam: Intergovernmental Relations & Energy Policy. Bruchey, Stuart, ed. LC 78-22685. (Energy in the American Economy Ser.). 1979. lib. bdg. 22.00x (ISBN 0-405-11988-7). Arno.
Goldin, Augusta. Geothermal Energy: A Hot Prospect. LC 80-8800. (Illus.). (gr. 7 up). 1981. 10.95 (ISBN 0-15-230662-5, HJ). HarBraceJ.
Goodman, Louis J. & Love, Ralph N., eds. Geothermal Energy Projects: Planning & Management. (Policy Studies). 1980. 33.00 (ISBN 0-08-025095-5). Pergamon.
Griffin, O. M., ed. Ocean Thermal Energy Conversion: OED, Vol. 5. 1978. 18.00 (ISBN 0-685-66808-8, G00139). ASME.
Hoffer, Jerry M. Geothermal Exploration of Western Trans-Pecos Texas. (Science Ser.: No. 6). 1979. 3.00 (ISBN 0-87404-060-4). Tex Western.
K G R A Special Bulletin 1979. (Bulletin: Vol. 8, No. 3). (Illus.). 25p. 1979. pap. 2.50 (ISBN 0-934412-41-3). Geothermal.
Kappelmeyer, O. & Haenel, R. Geothermics with Special Reference to Application. Rosenbach, O. & Morelli, C., eds. LC 74-170842. (Geoexploration Monographs 1: No. 4). (Illus.). 1974. 58.00x (ISBN 3-443-13006-2). Intl Pubns Serv.
Lauber, Patricia. Tapping Earth's Heat. LC 78-6283. (Good Earth Ser.). (Illus.). (gr. 2-6). 1978. PLB 6.57 (ISBN 0-8116-6110-5). Garrard.
Milora, Stanley L. & Tester, Jefferson W. Geothermal Energy As a Source of Electric Power: Thermodynamics & Economic Design Criteria. LC 76-7008. 190p. 1976. text ed. 22.50x (ISBN 0-262-13123-4). MIT Pr.
Nasr, Louise H. Geothermal Loan Guaranty Program & Its Impact on Exploration & Development. 1979. 10.00 (ISBN 0-918062-05-5). Colo Sch Mines.
Rinehart, J. S. Geysers & Geothermal Energy. (Illus.). 223p. 1980. 19.80 (ISBN 0-387-90489-1). Springer-Verlag.
Rybach, L. & Muffler, L. J., eds. Geothermal Systems: Principles & Case Histories. LC 80-40290. 359p. 1981. 61.95 (ISBN 0-471-27811-4, Pub. by Wiley-Interscience). Wiley.
Rybach, Ladislaus & Stegena, Lajos, eds. Geothermics & Geothermal Energy. (Contributions to Current Research in Geophysics: No. 7). (Illus.). 341p. 1979. 58.80 (ISBN 3-7643-1062-6). Birkhauser.
--Geothermics & Geothermal Energy. (Contributions to Current Research in Geophysics Ser.: Vol. 7). 1979. text ed. 65.00x (ISBN 3-7643-1062-6). Renouf.
Schultz, Robert J., et al, eds. Geothermal: Energy for the Eighties. (Transactions: Vol. 4). (Illus.). 835p. 1980. 28.00 (ISBN 0-934412-54-5). Geothermal.
Strub, A. S. & Ungemach, P., eds. Advances in European Geothermal Research. 1096p. 1980. lib. bdg. 63.00 (ISBN 90-277-1138-0, Pub. by Reidel Holland). Kluwer Boston.
Training Needs in Geothermal Energy: Report of the Workshop. 51p. 1980. pap. 5.00 (ISBN 0-686-61498-4, TUNU 004, UNU). Unipub.
Wagner, Sharon C. State Taxation of Geothermal Resources Compared with State Taxation of Other Energy Minerals. (Special Report: No. 4). (Illus.). 86p. (Orig.). 1979. pap. 6.00 (ISBN 0-934412-04-9). Geothermal.
Wharton, James C. Geothermal Resource Development: Laws & Regulation. 1980. 22.00 (ISBN 0-89499-013-6). Bks Business.
Yates, Madeleine. Earth Power: The Story of Geothermal Energy. LC 79-25155. (Illus.). 64p. (gr. 4-7). 1980. 7.95g (ISBN 0-687-11450-0). Abingdon.

GERANIUMS

Shellard, Alan. Geraniums for Home & Garden. (Illus.). 200p. 1981. 24.00 (ISBN 0-7153-8124-5). David & Charles.
Stackhouse, Shirley. Australian House & Garden Book of Geraniums. pap. 7.50x (ISBN 0-392-06899-0, ABC). Sportshelf.

GERARD DE NERVAL, GERARD LABRUNIE, KNOWN AS, 1808-1855

Rinsler, Norma. Gerard de Nerval. 1973. text ed. 21.00x (ISBN 0-485-14601-0, Athlone Pr); pap. text ed. 8.75x (ISBN 0-485-12706-7, Athlone Pr). Humanities.
Sowerby, Benn. The Disinherited: The Life of Gerard de Nerval, 1808-1855. LC 73-20700. (Illus.). 182p. 1974. 12.50x (ISBN 0-8147-7757-0). NYU Pr.
Villas, James. Gerard de Nerval: A Critical Bibliography, 1900 to 1967. LC 68-63296. (Illus.). 1968. 10.00x (ISBN 0-8262-7814-0). U of Mo Pr.

GERARD DE NEVERS (PROSE ROMANCE)

Lowe, Lawrence F. Gerard De Nevers, a Study of the Prose Version of the Roman De la Violette. (Elliott Monographs: Vol. 13). 1923. pap. 5.00 (ISBN 0-527-02616-6). Kraus Repr.

GERBILS

Dobrin, Arnold. Jillions of Gerbils. LC 72-11502. (Fun-To-Read Bk.). (Illus.). (gr. 1-4). 1973. PLB 6.67 (ISBN 0-688-50051-X). Lothrop.
Hasenau, James J. Gerbils: How to Buy, Breed, Raise & Train. LC 75-34899. (Illus.). 96p. 1975. pap. 1.95 (ISBN 0-668-03919-1). Arco.
Henrie. Gerbils. (gr. 2-5). 1980. PLB 6.45 (ISBN 0-531-04121-2, E40). Watts.
How to Raise & Train Gerbils. pap. 2.00 (ISBN 0-87666-195-9, M524). TFH Pubns.
LeRoi, David. Fancy Mice, Rats & Gerbils. new ed. (Pets of Today Ser.). (Illus.). (gr. 5 up). 1976. 6.00x (ISBN 0-7182-0401-8, SpS). Sportshelf.
Paradise, Paul. Gerbils. (Illus.). 96p. 1980. 2.95 (ISBN 0-87666-927-5, KW-037). TFH Pubns.
Robinson, David. Encyclopedia of Gerbils. 224p. 1980. 9.95 (ISBN 0-87666-915-1, H-974). TFH Pubns.
--Exhibition & Pet Hamsters & Gerbils. 1981. 30.00x (ISBN 0-904558-39-8, Pub. by Saiga Pub). State Mutual Bk.
Saiga Editors. Gerbil Keeping. 1981. 10.00x (ISBN 0-86230-002-9, Pub. by Saiga Pub). State Mutual Bk.
Silverstein, Alvin & Silverstein, Virginia B. Gerbils. LC 75-34390. (gr. 3-6). 1976. 8.95 (ISBN 0-397-31660-7); pap. 3.95 (ISBN 0-397-31661-5). Lippincott.

GERIATRIC NURSING

Agate, John. Geriatrics for Nurses & Social Workers. (Illus.). 1972. pap. 22.95x (ISBN 0-433-00204-2). Intl Ideas.
Bollinger, Rick L. Communication Management of the Geriatric Patient. 1977. pap. 1.95x (ISBN 0-8134-1940-9, 1940). Interstate.
Brickner, Phillip W. Care of the Nursing-Home Patient. 1971. text ed. 14.95 (ISBN 0-02-314500-5, 31450). Macmillan.
Burns, E. M. & Isaacs, Bernard. Geriatric Nursing. (Modern Practical Nursing Ser.: No. 13). (Illus.). 1973. pap. 9.95x (ISBN 0-433-12540-3). Intl Ideas.
Burnside, Irene M. Nursing & the Aged. 2nd ed. (Illus.). 736p. 1980. text ed. 17.95 (ISBN 0-07-009211-7, HP). McGraw.
--Nursing & the Aged. 1976. 16.95 (ISBN 0-07-009209-5, HP); instr's manual 3.00 (ISBN 0-07-042705-4). McGraw.
--Psychosocial Nursing Care of the Aged. 2nd ed. (Illus.). 1980. pap. text ed. 8.95 (ISBN 0-07-009210-9). McGraw.
Carm, Sr. Joseph-Mary O. Complete Manual of Geriatric Nursing. 1971. 8.50 (ISBN 0-685-03850-5, N2001). Impress Hse.
Carnevali, Doris L., ed. Nursing Management for the Elderly. Patrick, Maxine. LC 79-4461. 1979. text ed. 21.75x (ISBN 0-397-54229-1, JBL-Med-Nursing). Har-Row.
Conahan, Judith M. Helping Your Elderly Patients: A Guide for Nursing Assistants. LC 75-40507. (Illus.). 128p. 1976. pap. 3.95 (ISBN 0-913292-29-X). Tiresias Pr.
Dunlop, Burton D. The Growth of Nursing Home Care. LC 78-14715. 1979. 18.95 (ISBN 0-669-02704-9). Lexington Bks.
Eliopolous, Charlotte. Geriatric Nursing. 1980. pap. text ed. 16.25 (ISBN 0-06-318132-0, IntlDept). Har-Row.
Falconer, Mary W., et al. Aging Patients: A Guide for Their Care. LC 76-26943. 1976. text ed. 16.50 (ISBN 0-8261-1970-0); pap. text ed. 8.95 (ISBN 0-8261-1971-9). Springer Pub.
Flaherty, Maureen O. The Care of the Elderly Person: A Guide for the Licensed Practical Nurse. 3rd. ed. LC 80-11236. (Illus.). 1980. pap. text ed. 10.45 (ISBN 0-8016-3706-6). Mosby.
Foundaton of the American College of Nursing Home Administrators. State Licensure Requirements for Nursing Home Administrators. 2nd ed. 1979. 15.00 (ISBN 0-686-64025-X). Panel Pubs.
Glasscote, R. M., et al. Old Folks at Home: A Field Study of Nursing & Board-&-Care Facilities. 148p. 1976. 8.00 (ISBN 0-685-76789-2, P222-0). Am Psychiatric.
Good, Shirley R. & Rodgers, Susan S. Analysis for Action: Nursing Care of the Elderly. (Illus.). 1980. pap. text ed. 11.95 (ISBN 0-13-032623-2). P-H.
Gunter, Laurie M. & Estes, Carmen A. Education for Gerontic Nursing. LC 78-10472. (Teaching of Nursing Ser.: Vol. 5). 1979. pap. text ed. 14.50 (ISBN 0-8261-2451-8). Springer Pub.
Gunter, Laurie M. & Ryan, Joanne E. Self-Assessment of Current Knnowledge in Geriatric Nursing. 1976. spiral bdg. 9.50 (ISBN 0-87488-295-8). Med Exam.
Hanebuth, Lorna, et al. Nursing Assistants & the Long-Term Health Care Facility. (Illus.). 1977. pap. text ed. 11.95x (ISBN 0-06-141090-X, Harper Medical). Har-Row.
Hirschberg, Gerald G., et al. Rehabilitation: A Manual for the Care of the Elderly & Disabled. 2nd ed. LC 76-40316. 492p. 1976. text ed. 17.95 (ISBN 0-397-54190-2, JBL-Med-Nursing). Har-Row.
Hodkinson, M. A. Nursing the Elderly. 1966. 18.00 (ISBN 0-08-011987-5); pap. 7.00 (ISBN 0-686-66515-5). Pergamon.
Hogstel, Mildred O. Nursing Care of the Older Adult. LC 80-22985. 587p. 1981. 17.95 (ISBN 0-471-06022-4, Pub. by Wiley Med). Wiley.
Meiners, Mark P. Nursing Home Costs - Nineteen Seventy-Two United States: August 1973-April 1974 National Nursing Home Survey. Stevenson, Taoria, ed. (Ser. 13: No.39). 1978. pap. text ed. 1.75 (ISBN 0-8406-0136-0). Natl Ctr Health Stats.
Mezey, Mathy D., et al. Health Assessment of the Older Individual. LC 79-24685. 1980. text ed. 16.95 (ISBN 0-8261-2900-5); pap. text ed. 10.95 (ISBN 0-8261-2901-3). Springer Pub.
O'Brien. The Care of the Elderly Person: A Guide for the Licensed Practical Nurse. 2nd ed. LC 74-20864. 1975. pap. text ed. 7.95 (ISBN 0-8016-3695-7). Mosby.
O'Connor, Andrea B., ed. Nursing: The Older Adult. LC 78-140954. (Contemporary Nursing Ser.). 242p. 1978. pap. text ed. 7.95 (ISBN 0-937126-21-7). Am Journal Nurse.
Pearson, Linda J. & Kotthoff, M. Ernestine. Geriatric Clinical Protocols. LC 79-12888. 1979. pap. text ed. 18.50 (ISBN 0-397-54270-4, JBL-Med-Nursing). Har-Row.
Reinhardt, Adina M. & Quinn, Mildred D. Current Practice in Gerontological Nursing, Vol. I. LC 78-31424. (Current Practice Ser.). 1979. text ed. 12.50 (ISBN 0-8016-4122-5); pap. text ed. 10.50 (ISBN 0-8016-4113-6). Mosby.
Shipp, Audrey, ed. Profile of Chronic Illness in Nursing Homes: United States, August 1973-April 1974, Ser. 13, No. 29. 1977. pap. 1.95 (ISBN 0-8406-0968-X). Natl Ctr Health Stats.
Standards of Gerontological Nursing Practice. rev. ed. 1976. pap. 1.00 (ISBN 0-686-21449-8). ANA.
Stilewell, Edna, ed. Readings in Gerontological Nursing. LC 80-51967. 1980. pap. 16.50 (ISBN 0-913590-70-3). C B Slack.
Stolten, Jane H. The Geriatric Aide. (Illus.). 1973. pap. 9.95 (ISBN 0-316-81741-4). Little.
Stryker, R. How to Reduce Employee Turnover in Nursing Homes. 1981. 21.75 (ISBN 0-398-04510-0). C C Thomas.
Weber, Helen I. Nursing Care of the Elderly. (Illus.). 240p. 1980. text ed. 13.95 (ISBN 0-8359-5035-2); pap. 11.95 (ISBN 0-8359-5034-4). Reston.
Weiner, Marcella B., et al. Working with the Aged. (Illus.). 1978. pap. 10.95 ref. ed. (ISBN 0-13-967570-1). P-H.
Wells, Thelma. Problems in Geriatric Nursing Care: A Study of Nurses' Problems in Care of Old People in Hospital. (Illus.). 1980. pap. 13.50 (ISBN 0-443-01939-8). Churchill.
Welter, Paul R. The Nursing Home: A Caring Community-Staff Manual. 96p. 1981. pap. 2.95 (ISBN 0-8170-0935-3). Judson.
--The Nursing Home: A Caring Community-Trainers' Manual. 176p. 1981. pap. 9.95 (ISBN 0-8170-0934-5). Judson.
Wolanin, Mary O. & Phillips, Linda R. Confusion: Prevention & Care. LC 80-18508. (Illus.). 415p. 1980. pap. text ed. 18.95 (ISBN 0-8016-5629-X). Mosby.
Yurick, Ann G., et al. The Aged Person & the Nursing Process. (Illus.). 550p. 1980. text ed. 17.95 (ISBN 0-8385-0082-X). ACC.

GERIATRIC PHARMACOLOGY

see Geriatrics–Formulae, Receipts, Prescriptions

GERIATRIC PSYCHIATRY

Barbagallo-Sangiorgi, G. & Exton-Smith, A. N., eds. The Aging Brain: Neurological & Mental Disturbances. (Ettore Majorana International Science Series-Life Sciences: Vol. 5). 393p. 1981. 42.50 (ISBN 0-306-40625-X, Plenum Pr). Plenum Pub.
Bellak, Leopold & Karasu, T., eds. Geriatric Psychiatry: A Handbook for Psychiatrists & Primary Care Physicians. LC 76-26287. (Illus.). 320p. 1976. 31.25 (ISBN 0-8089-0967-3). Grune.
Berezin, Martin A. & Cath, Stanley H., eds. Geriatric Psychiatry: Grief, Loss, & Emotional Disorders in the Aging Process. LC 65-25512. 1967. text ed. 20.00 (ISBN 0-8236-2120-0). Intl Univs Pr.
Brink, Terry L. Geriatric Psychotherapy. LC 78-26232. 1979. pap. text ed. 12.95 (ISBN 0-87705-344-8); pap. text ed. 9.95 (ISBN 0-87705-346-4). Human Sci Pr.
Busse, Ewald W. & Pfeiffer, Eric. Mental Illness in Later Life. 301p. 1973. casebound 12.00 (ISBN 0-685-38355-5, P188-1); pap. 9.00 (ISBN 0-685-38356-3, 188). Am Psychiatric.
Busse, Ewald W. & Blazer, Dan G., eds. Handbook of Geriatric Psychiatry. 560p. 1980. text ed. 34.50 (ISBN 0-442-20896-0). Van Nos Reinhold.
Butler, Robert N. & Lewis, Myrna I. Aging & Mental Health: Positive Psychosocial Approaches. 2nd ed. LC 76-27684. (Illus.). 1977. pap. text ed. 13.95 (ISBN 0-8016-0921-6). Mosby.
Fann, William E. & Maddox, George L. Drug Issues in Geropsychiatry. 122p. 1974. pap. 9.50 (ISBN 0-683-03002-7). Krieger.
Frankfather, Dwight. The Aged in the Community: Managing Senility & Deviance. LC 77-8327. (Praeger Special Studies). 1977. text ed. 22.95 (ISBN 0-03-021936-1); pap. 9.95 (ISBN 0-03-021931-0). Praeger.
Gallagher, Dolores & Thompson, Larry W., eds. Depression in the Elderly: A Behavioral Treatment Manual. LC 81-66766. 159p. 1981. pap. 8.50 (ISBN 0-88474-125-7). USC Andrus Geron.
GAP Committee on Aging. Aged & Community Mental Health: A Guide to Program Development, Vol. 8. LC 72-200268. (Report No. 81). 1971. pap. 2.00 (ISBN 0-87318-113-1, Pub. by Adv Psychiatry). Mental Health.
--Psychiatry & the Aged: An Introductory Approach, Vol. 5. LC 62-2872. (Report No. 59A). 1965. pap. 2.00 (ISBN 0-87318-111-5, Pub. by Adv Psychiatry). Mental Health.
--The Right to Die: Decision & Decision Makers, Vol. 8. LC 64-138. (Symposium No. 12). 1973. pap. 4.00 (ISBN 0-87318-123-9, Pub. by Adv Psychiatry). Mental Health.
--Toward a Public Policy on Mental Health Care of the Elderly, Vol. 7. LC 62-2872. (Report No. 79). 1970. pap. 2.00 (ISBN 0-87318-110-7, Pub. by Adv Psychiatry). Mental Health.
Gershon, S. & Raskin, A., eds. Genesis & Treatment of Psychologic Disorders in the Elderly: Aging, Vol. 2. LC 75-14573. 288p. 1975. 27.00 (ISBN 0-89004-004-4). Raven.
Glasscote, R. M., et al. Creative Mental Health Services for the Elderly. 189p. 1977. 10.00 (ISBN 0-685-86111-2). Am Psychiatric.
Glen, A. I. & Whalley, L. J. Alzheimer's Disease: Early Recognition of Potentially Reversible Deficits. (Symposium Ser.). (Illus.). 1980. text ed. 40.00 (ISBN 0-443-02080-9). Churchill.
Horton, Arthur M., Jr., ed. Mental Health Interventions for the Aging: Psychotherapeutic Treatment Approaches. 320p. 1981. 24.95 (ISBN 0-89789-007-8). J F Bergin.
Hussian, Richard A. Geriatric Psychology. 256p. 1981. text ed. 19.95 (ISBN 0-442-21916-4). Van Nos Reinhold.
Isaacs, A. D. & Post, F. Studies in Geriatric Psychiatry. LC 77-9990. 1978. 43.75 (ISBN 0-471-99550-9, Pub. by Wiley-Interscience). Wiley.
Kaplan, Oscar J. & Stein, Leon, eds. Mental Disorders in Later Life. LC 79-8673. (Growing Old Ser.). (Illus.). 1980. Repr. of 1945 ed. lib. bdg. 42.00x (ISBN 0-405-12789-8). Arno.
Levin, Sidney & Kahana, Ralph J., eds. Psychodynamic Studies on Aging: Creativity, Reminiscing & Dying. LC 67-27427. 1967. text ed. 20.00 (ISBN 0-8236-5640-3). Intl Univs Pr.
Lowenthal, Marjorie F. Lives in Distress: The Paths of the Elderly to the Psychiatric Ward. Stein, Leon, ed. LC 79-8675. (Growing Old Ser.). 1980. Repr. of 1964 ed. lib. bdg. 22.00x (ISBN 0-405-12791-X). Arno.

Lowenthal, Marjorie F. & Berkman, Paul L. Aging & Mental Disorder in San Francisco: A Social Psychiatric Study. LC 67-13168. (Social & Behavioral Science Ser.). 1967. 18.95x (ISBN 0-87589-001-6). Jossey-Bass.
Pearce, John & Miller, Edgar. Clinical Aspects of Dementia. (Illus.). 1973. text ed. 14.95 (ISBN 0-02-858870-3). Macmillan.
Pitt, Brice M. Psychogeriatrics: An Introduction to the Pyschiatry of Old Age. 192p. 1974. pap. text ed. 8.75 (ISBN 0-443-01190-7). Churchill.
Rudman, Jack. Mental Health Geriatric Consultant. (Career Examination Ser.: C-1582). (Cloth bdg. avail. on request). pap. 12.00 (ISBN 0-8373-1582-4). Natl Learning.
Sargent, S. Stansfeld. Nontradtional Therapy & Counseling with the Aging. LC 80-11303. 256p. 1980. 19.95 (ISBN 0-8261-2800-9); pap. 12.95 (ISBN 0-8261-2801-7). Springer Pub.
Thomas, Evelyn A. The Ladder up: Life After Retirement. LC 79-92188. (Illus.). 92p. 1980. 5.95 (ISBN 0-930626-05-2). Psych & Consul Assocs.
Verwoerdt, Adrian. Clinical Geropsychiatry. 353p. 1981. lib. bdg. 37.00 (ISBN 0-683-08592-1). Williams & Wilkins.

GERIATRICS

see also Aged-Care and Hygiene; Aged-Medical Care

Adams, George. Essentials of Geriatric Medicine. 1978. pap. text ed. 7.95x (ISBN 0-19-261216-6). Oxford U Pr.
Amann, Anton, ed. Open Care for the Elderly in Seven European Countries: A Pilot Study in the Possibilities & Limits of Care. LC 80-40816. 238p. 1980. 36.00 (ISBN 0-08-025215-X). Pergamon.
Anderson, W. Ferguson & Judge, T. G., eds. Geriatric Medicine. 1974. 46.50 (ISBN 0-12-057250-8). Acad Pr.
Andrews, J. & Von Hahn, H. P., eds. Geriatrics for Everyday Practice. (Illus.). viii, 220p. 1981. pap. 23.50 (ISBN 3-8055-1803-X). S Karger.
Baumhover, Lorin S. & Jones, Joan D., eds. Handbook of American Aging Programs. LC 76-28641. 1977. lib. bdg. 17.50x (ISBN 0-8371-9287-0, BAA/). Greenwood.
Bayles, Michael D., ed. Medical Treatment of the Dying: Moral Issues. 180p. 1981. pap. 8.95 (ISBN 0-87073-366-4). Schenkman.
Bell, Bill D. Contemporary Social Gerontology: Significant Developments in the Field of Aging. (Illus.). 480p. 1976. 36.25 (ISBN 0-398-03464-8). C C Thomas.
Berghorn, Forrest J., et al. Dynamics of Aging: Original Essays on the Process & Experience of Growing Old. 542p. 1980. lib. bdg. 33.75x (ISBN 0-89158-781-0); pap. text ed. 13.50x (ISBN 0-89158-782-9). Westview.
Brocklehurst, J. C., ed. Geriatric Care in Advanced Societies. (Illus.). 200p. 1976. 24.50 (ISBN 0-8391-0834-6). Univ Park.
--Textbook of Geriatric Medicine & Gerontology. 2nd ed. (Illus.). 1978. text ed. 89.00 (ISBN 0-443-01579-1). Churchill.
Brocklehurst, John C. & Hanley, Thomas. Geriatric Medicine for Students. LC 76-8473. (Livingstone Medical Texts Ser.). (Illus.). 1976. pap. text ed. 9.75 (ISBN 0-443-01470-1). Churchill.
Brown, Mollie, ed. Readings in Gerontology. 2nd ed. LC 77-14088. (Illus.). 1978. pap. text ed. 8.00 (ISBN 0-8016-0734-5). Mosby.
Brown, Warren J. A Doctor's Advice to Folks Over Fifty. 23p. 1976. pap. 1.00x (ISBN 0-912522-60-7). Aero-Medical.
Bustad, Leo K. Animals, Aging, & the Aged. (Wesley W. Spink Lectures in Comparative Medicine Ser.). (Illus.). 224p. 1981. 19.50x (ISBN 0-8166-0966-7). U of Minn Pr.
Cabot, Natalie H. You Can't Count on Dying. Stein, Leon, ed. LC 79-8662. (Growing Old Ser.). 1980. Repr. of 1961 ed. lib. bdg. 22.00x (ISBN 0-405-12779-0). Arno.
Caird, F. I. & Exton-Smith, A. N., eds. Metabolic & Nutritional Disorders in the Elderly. (Illus.). 336p. 1980. pap. 28.95 (ISBN 0-8151-1405-2). Year Bk Med.
Caldwell, Esther & Hegner, Barbara. Geriatrics: A Study of Maturity. 3rd ed. LC 79-55313. (Practical Nursing Ser.). (Illus.). 288p. 1981. pap. text ed. 8.80 (ISBN 0-8273-1935-5); instr's. guide 1.50 (ISBN 0-8273-1934-7). Delmar.
Canstatt, Carl. Die Krankheiten des Hoheren Alters unt Ihre Heilung, 2 vols. in one. Kastenbaum, Robert, ed. LC 78-22187. (Aging & Old Age Ser.). (Illus., Ger.). 1979. Repr. of 1839 ed. lib. bdg. 42.00x (ISBN 0-405-11805-8). Arno.
Carlin, Joseph M. Nutrition Education for the Elderly: The Technique. (Serving the Elderly Ser.: Pt. 4). 1978. pap. text ed. 3.00 (ISBN 0-89634-009-0, 046). New England Geron.
Carlisle, Anthony. An Essay on the Disorders of Old Age, & on the Means for Prolonging Human Life. Kastenbaum, Robert, ed. LC 78-22183. (Aging & Old Age Ser.). 1979. Repr. of 1818 ed. lib. bdg. 10.00x (ISBN 0-405-11802-3). Arno.
Charcot, Jean M. Clinical Lectures on Senile & Chronic Diseases. Kastenbaum, Robert, ed. Tuke, William S., tr. LC 78-22189. (Aging & Old Age Ser.). 1979. Repr. of 1881 ed. lib. bdg. 20.00x (ISBN 0-405-11807-4). Arno.
Coakley, Davis. Acute Geriatric Medicine. 290p. 1981. pap. 27.50 (ISBN 0-88416-354-7). Wright-PSG.
Coakley, Davis, ed. Acute Geriatric Medicine. 256p. 1980. 30.00 (ISBN 0-686-69916-5, Pub. by Croom Helm England). State Mutual Bk.
Colonial Penn Group, Inc. Perspectives on Aging. (Colonial Penn Lecture Ser.). Date not set. price not set professional ref. (ISBN 0-88410-734-5). Ballinger Pub.
Conrad, Kenneth & Bressler, Rubin. Drug Therapy for the Elderly. LC 81-38398. (Illus.). 480p. 1981. pap. text ed. 25.00 (ISBN 0-8016-0782-5). Mosby.
Cowdry, E. V. & Kastenbaum, Robert, eds. Problems of Aging: Biological & Medical Aspects. LC 78-22196. (Aging & Old Age Ser.). (Illus.). 1979. Repr. of 1939 ed. lib. bdg. 46.00x (ISBN 0-405-11813-9). Arno.
Crandall, Richard C. Gerontology: A Behavioral Science Approach. LC 79-25622. (Sociology Ser.). (Illus.). 1980. text ed. 16.95 (ISBN 0-201-01252-9). A-W.
Crepeau, Betty. New Title Activities Programming Recreation: An Activities Handbook-the Technique. (Serving the Elderly Ser.: Pt. 5). 1980. pap. text ed. 7.50 (ISBN 0-89634-010-4, 047). New England Geron.
Day, George E. A Practical Treatise on the Domestic Management & Most Important Diseases of Advanced Life. Kastenbaum, Robert, ed. LC 78-22198. (Aging & Old Age Ser.). 1979. Repr. of 1849 ed. lib. bdg. 15.00x (ISBN 0-405-11815-5). Arno.
Devas, M., ed. Geriatric Orthopaedics. 1977. 32.00 (ISBN 0-12-213750-7). Acad Pr.
Dilman, Vladimir M. Law of Deviation of Homeostasis & Diseases of Aging. LC 79-21456. (Illus.). 480p. 1981. 39.50 (ISBN 0-88416-250-8). Wright-PSG.
Dunbar, Robert E. & Segall, Harold F. A Doctor Discusses Learning to Cope with Arthritis Rheumatism & Gout. (Illus., Orig.). 1973. pap. 2.50 (ISBN 0-685-35675-2). Budlong.
Ebaugh, Franklin G., Jr. Management of Common Problems in Geriatric Medicine. 1981. 29.95 (ISBN 0-201-04076-X, Med-Nurse). A-W.
Eisdorfer, C. & Fann, W. E., eds. Psychopharmacology & Aging. LC 73-9995. (Advances in Behavioral Biology Ser.: Vol. 6). 253p. 1973. 22.50 (ISBN 0-306-37906-6, Plenum Pr). Plenum Pub.
Eisdorfer, Carl & Starr, Bernard, eds. Annual Review of Gerontology & Geriatrics. (Illus.). 416p. 1980. text ed. 25.50 (ISBN 0-8261-3080-1). Springer Pub.
Eisdorfer, Carl, et al. Annual Review of Gerontology & Geriatrics, Vol. 2. 1981. text ed. price not set (ISBN 0-8261-3081-X). Springer Pub.
Elkowitz, Edward B. Geriatric Medicine for the Primary Care Practitioner. 1981. text ed. write for info. (ISBN 0-8261-3230-8); pap. text ed. write for info. (ISBN 0-8261-3231-6). Springer Pub.
Epstein. Learning to Care for the Aged. 1977. text ed. 12.95 (ISBN 0-87909-442-7); pap. 10.95 (ISBN 0-87909-441-9). Reston.
Exton-Smith, A. N. Geriatrics. 344p. text ed. 24.50 (ISBN 0-8391-1456-7). Univ Park.
Exton-Smith, A. N. & Evans, J. G. Care of the Elderly: Meeting the Challenge of Dependency. 324p. 1977. 33.50 (ISBN 0-8089-1055-8). Grune.
Falconer, Mary W., et al. Aging Patients: A Guide for Their Care. LC 76-26943. 1976. text ed. 16.50 (ISBN 0-8261-1970-0); pap. text ed. 8.95 (ISBN 0-8261-1971-9). Springer Pub.
Floyer, John. Medicina Gerocomica. Kastenbaum, Robert, ed. LC 78-22199. (Aging & Old Age Ser.). 1979. Repr. of 1724 ed. lib. bdg. 12.00x (ISBN 0-405-11838-4). Arno.
Focus: Aging 1978-79. (Annual Editions Ser.). (Illus.). 1978. pap. text ed. 5.75 (ISBN 0-87967-206-4). Dushkin Pub.
Frolkis, V. V. & Bezrukov, V. V. Aging of the Central Nervous System. (Interdisciplinary Topics in Gerontology: Vol. 16). (Illus.). 1979. pap. 39.75 (ISBN 3-8055-2995-3). S Karger.
Gilbert, Jeanne G. The Paraprofessional & the Elderly. LC 77-90125. 1977. 18.00x (ISBN 0-916592-22-7). Panel Pubs.
Gilmore, A. J., et al, eds. Medicine & Social Science. (Aging - a Challenge to Science & Society Ser.: Vol. 2). (Illus.). 350p. 1981. 59.50 (ISBN 0-19-261255-7). Oxford U Pr.
Gitman, L. & Woodford-Williams, E., eds. Research, Training & Practice in Clinical Medicine of Aging. (Interdisciplinary Topics in Gerontology: Vol. 5). 1970. 21.00 (ISBN 3-8055-0505-1). S Karger.
Greenblatt, Robert B. Geriatric Endocrinology. LC 75-43196. (Aging Ser.: Vol. 5). 256p. 1978. 24.50 (ISBN 0-89004-112-1). Raven.
Gruman, Gerald J. & Kastenbaum, Robert, eds. Roots of Modern Gerontology & Geriatrics: An Original Anthology. LC 78-22184. (Aging & Old Age Ser.). 1979. lib. bdg. 25.00x (ISBN 0-405-11801-5). Arno.
Hahn, H. P., ed. Practical Geriatrics. (Illus.). 448p. 1975. 37.75 (ISBN 3-8055-1768-8). S Karger.
Hall, Granville S. Senescence, the Last Half of Life. LC 73-169385. (Family in America Ser). 530p. 1972. Repr. of 1923 ed. 26.00 (ISBN 0-405-03860-7). Arno.
Hartford, Margaret E. Older American Volunteer Program: Action Curriculum. 1973. pap. 5.00 (ISBN 0-89634-015-5, 054). New England Geron.
Haug, Marie. Elderly Patients & Their Doctors. 1981. text ed. write for info. (ISBN 0-8261-3570-6). Springer Pub.
Hayes, D. K., ed. International Conference on Chronobiology, 13th. new ed. LC 79-5118. (Illus.). 1979. lib. bdg. 50.00 (ISBN 0-89500-022-9). Sci Pr.
Helfand, Arthur E. Clinical Podogeriatrics. (Illus.). 362p. 1981. 33.00 (ISBN 0-686-77760-3, 3951-2). Williams & Wilkins.
Hess, Beth B. & Markson, Elizabeth W. Aging & Old Age: An Introduction to Social Gerontology. (Illus.). 1980. text ed. 16.95 (ISBN 0-02-354100-8). Macmillan.
Hess, Patricia & Day, Candra. Understanding the Aging Patient. LC 77-2596. 1977. 13.95 (ISBN 0-87618-733-5). R J Brady.
Hirschfield, Ira S. & Lambert, Theresa N. Audio Visual Aids: Uses & Resources in Gerontology. LC 78-59262. 1978. pap. 4.50 (ISBN 0-88474-047-1). USC Andrus Geron.
Hodkinson, H. M. An Outline of Geriatrics. 1975. 11.50 (ISBN 0-12-351450-9). Acad Pr.
Hodkinson, Malcolm. An Outline of Geriatrics. 1981. price not set (ISBN 0-8089-1397-2). Grune.
Holmes, Monica B. & Holmes, Douglas, eds. Handbook for Human Services for Older People. LC 78-27668. 1979. text ed. 24.95 (ISBN 0-87705-381-2). Human Sci Pr.
International Association Of Gerontology - 5th Congress. Medical & Clinical Aspects of Aging, Proceedings, Vol. 4. Blumenthal, H. T., ed. (Aging Around the World Ser.). 1962. 30.00x (ISBN 0-231-08952-X). Columbia U Pr.
Issacs, Bernard, ed. Recent Advances in Geriatric Medicine, No. 1. LC 77-30316. (Recent Advances in Geriatric Medicine Ser.). (Illus.). 1978. text ed. 25.00x (ISBN 0-443-01519-8). Churchill.
Joseph, N. R. Physical Chemistry of Aging. (Interdisciplinary Topics in Gerontology: Vol. 8). 1971. 25.25 (ISBN 3-8055-1084-5). S Karger.
Kahn, Samuel. Essays on Longevity. LC 74-76592. 200p. 1974. 10.00 (ISBN 0-8022-2146-7). Philos Lib.
Kane, Robert L., et al. Geriatrics in the United States: Manpower Projections & Training Considerations. LC 80-8840. (Illus.). 208p. 1981. 19.95 (ISBN 0-669-04386-9). Lexington Bks.
Kastenbaum, Robert & Kastenaum, Robert, eds. The Care of the Aged, the Dying, & the Dead. 2nd ed. LC 76-19596. (Death & Dying Ser.). 1977. Repr. of 1950 ed. lib. bdg. 10.00x (ISBN 0-405-09590-2). Arno.
Katzman, Robert, et al, eds. Alzheimer's Disease: Senile Dementia & Related Disorders. (Aging Ser.: Vol. 7). 703p. 1978. text ed. 53.00 (ISBN 0-89004-225-X). Raven.
Kay, Marguerite, et al, eds. Aging, Immunity & Arthritic Diseases. (Aging Ser.: Vol. 13). 275p. 1980. text ed. 27.00 (ISBN 0-89004-382-5). Raven.
Koff, T. Long-Term Care: An Approach to Serving the Frail Elderly. 1982. 12.95 (ISBN 0-686-75375-5); pap. 7.95 (ISBN 0-686-75376-3). Winthrop.
Kugler, Hans J. Dr. Kugler's Seven Keys to a Longer Life. LC 77-8755. 8.95 (ISBN 0-8128-2634-5). Stein & Day.
Landreth, Garry L. & Berg, Robert C. Counseling the Elderly: For Professional Helpers Who Work with the Aged. (Illus.). 532p. 1980. 26.75 (ISBN 0-398-04058-3); pap. 19.75 (ISBN 0-398-04059-1). C C Thomas.
LBJ School of Public Affairs. Meal System for the Elderly: Conventional Food in Novel Form. LC 76-620081. (Policy Research Project Report Ser.: No. 16). 1977. 3.50 (ISBN 0-89940-609-2). LBJ Sch Public Affairs.
Levenson, Alvin J. & Tollett, Susan M., eds. Multidisciplinary Assessment of the Geriatric Patient. 1981. text ed. write for info. (ISBN 0-89004-492-9). Raven.
Lewis, Sandra C. The Mature Years: A Geriatric Occupational Therapy Text. LC 78-4341. 1979. pap. 14.00x (ISBN 0-913590-57-6). C B Slack.
Liang, Daniel S. Facts About Aging. 120p. 1973. pap. 6.75 (ISBN 0-398-02727-7). C C Thomas.
Libow, Leslie S. & Sherman. The Core of Geriatric Medicine: A Guide for Students & Practitioners. LC 80-24704. (Illus.). 354p. 1980. text ed. 22.95 (ISBN 0-8016-3096-7). Mosby.
Lowy, Louis. Social Policies & Programs on Aging. LC 78-55355. 1980. 21.95x (ISBN 0-669-02342-6). Lexington Bks.
Lucas, Carol. Recreation in Gerontology. (Illus.). 192p. 1964. photocopy ed. spiral 14.50 (ISBN 0-398-01158-3). C C Thomas.
Mackay, I. R., ed. Multidisciplinary Gerontology: A Structure for Research in Gerontology in a Developed Country. (Interdisciplinary Topics in Gerontology: Vol. 11). (Illus.). 1977. 36.75 (ISBN 3-8055-2679-2). S Karger.
Malinchak, Alan A. Crime & Gerontology. (Ser. in Criminal Justice). (Illus.). 1980. text ed. 15.95 (ISBN 0-13-192815-5); pap. text ed. 13.95 (ISBN 0-13-192807-4). P-H.
Martineau, Janis A. Public Information Manual for Human Services: The Technique. (Serving the Elderly Ser.: Pt. 3). 1978. pap. 3.00 (ISBN 0-89634-004-X, 045). New England Geron.
Miller, Michael B. Current Issues in Clinical Geriatrics. LC 77-95435. 1979. casebound 13.50 (ISBN 0-913292-22-2). Tiresias Pr.
Morgan, Robert F. Interventions in Applied Gerontology. 256p. 1981. pap. text ed. 12.95 (ISBN 0-8403-2481-2). Kendall-Hunt.
Mummah, Hazel & Smith, Marsella. The Geriatric Assistant. (Illus.). 320p. 1980. pap. text ed. 11.95 (ISBN 0-07-044015-8, HP). McGraw.
Munnichs, Joep M., et al. Dependency or Interdependency in Old Age. 1976. lib. bdg. 26.00 (ISBN 9-0247-1895-3, Pub. by Martinus Nijhoff Netherlands). Kluwer Boston.
Nahemow, Lucille & Pousada, Lidia. Geriatric Diagnostics: A Case Studies Approach. Date not set. price not set (ISBN 0-8261-3670-2). Springer Pub.
Nascher, Ignatz L. Geriatrics: The Diseases of Old Age & Their Treatment. Kastenbaum, Robert, ed. LC 78-22212. (Aging & Old Age Ser.). (Illus.). 1979. Repr. of 1914 ed. lib. bdg. 32.00 (ISBN 0-405-11825-2). Arno.
O'Hara-Devereaux, Mary, et al, eds. Eldercare: A Practical Guide to Clinical Geriatrics. (Illus.). 400p. 1981. 22.00 (ISBN 0-8089-1285-2). Grune.
Paillat, P. M. & Bunch, M. E., eds. Age, Work & Automation. (Interdisciplinary Topics in Gerontology: Vol. 6). (Semmering 1966). 1970. 18.00 (ISBN 3-8055-0507-8). S Karger.
Palmore, Erdman, ed. International Handbook on Aging: Contemporary Developments & Research. LC 78-73802. (Illus.). xviii, 529p. 1980. lib. bdg. 35.00 (ISBN 0-313-20890-5, PIH/). Greenwood.
Peterson, David A. & Bolton, Christopher R. Gerontology Instruction in Higher Education. LC 79-22748. (Springer Ser. on Adulthood & Aging: Vol. 6). 1980. text ed. 16.95 (ISBN 0-8261-2860-2). Springer Pub.
Peterson, James A., ed. Journeys' End: A Discussion Guide. 1976. pap. text ed. 2.50 (ISBN 0-88474-030-7). U of S Cal Pr.
Place, Linna F., et al. Aging & the Aged: An Annotated Bibliography & Research Guide. (Westview Guides to Library Research). 175p. 1980. lib. bdg. 17.50x (ISBN 0-89158-934-1). Westview.
Rai, G. S. Databook on Geriatrics. 217p. text ed. 19.95 (ISBN 0-8391-4109-2). Univ Park.
Reichel, William. Clinical Aspects of Aging. (Illus.). 533p. 1978. 39.95 (ISBN 0-683-07198-X). Williams & Wilkins.
Reichel, William & Schechter, Mal, eds. The Geriatric Patient. (Illus.). 1978. 18.95x (ISBN 0-913800-09-0). HP Pub Co.
Robbins, Alan S., et al. Geriatric Medicine: An Education Resource Guide. 448p. 1981. prof. ref. 32.50x (ISBN 0-88410-728-0). Ballinger Pub.
Rossman, Isadore, ed. Clinical Geriatrics. 2nd ed. LC 79-1274. 1979. text ed. 47.50x (ISBN 0-397-50411-X, JBL Med-Nursing). Har-Row.
Rudd, Jacob L. & Margolin, Reuben J. Maintenance Therapy for the Geriatric Patient. 308p. 1968. photocopy ed. spiral 29.75 (ISBN 0-398-01628-3). C C Thomas.
Rudd, T. N. Human Relations in Old Age. 1969. 7.50x (ISBN 0-571-08151-7). Intl Pubns Serv.
Schow, Ronald L., et al, eds. Communication Disorders of the Aged. 1978. pap. 16.95 (ISBN 0-8391-1237-8). Univ Park.
Schwartz, Arthur N. & Peterson, James A. Introduction to Gerontology. LC 78-21890. 1979. text ed. 16.95 (ISBN 0-03-019506-3, HoltC). HR&W.
Seltzer, Mildred, et al. Gerontology in Higher Education. 1978. text ed. 25.00x (ISBN 0-534-00582-9). Wadsworth Pub.
Sheldon, J. H. Social Medicine of Old Age: Report of an Inquiry in Wolverhampton. LC 79-8688. (Growing Old Ser.). 1980. Repr. of 1948 ed. lib. bdg. 19.00 (ISBN 0-405-12804-5). Arno.

Sherwood, Sylvia & Mor, Vincent. The Hidden Patient. Date not set. price not set prof. reference (ISBN 0-88410-722-1). Ballinger Pub.

Shock, Nathan W. Classified Bibliography of Gerontology & Geriatrics: Supplement Two, 1956-1961. 1963. 25.00x (ISBN 0-8047-0412-0). Stanford U Pr.

Shock, Nathan W. & Stein, Leon, eds. Perspectives in Experimental Gerontology. LC 79-8689. (Illus.). 1980. Repr. of 1966 ed. lib. bdg. 32.00x (ISBN 0-405-12805-3). Arno.

Slade, Walter R., Jr., ed. Geriatric Neurology: Selected Topics. LC 81-66942. (Illus.). 350p. 1981. write for info. (ISBN 0-87993-164-7). Futura Pub.

Smith, I. M., et al, eds. Medical Care for the Elderly: Acute & Chronic Care. LC 80-26495. 276p. 1981. text ed. 30.00 (ISBN 0-89335-143-1). SP Med & Sci Bks.

Somers, Anne R. & Fabian, Dorothy R. The Geriatric Imperative: An Introduction to Gerontology & Clinical Geriatrics. (Illus.). 320p. 1981. pap. 16.50 (ISBN 0-8385-3130-X). ACC.

Steinberg, Franz U., ed. Cowdry's Care of the Geriatric Patient. rev. 5th ed. LC 75-37566. 1976. 38.50 (ISBN 0-8016-4773-8). Mosby.

Sterns, Harvey L., et al. Gerontology in Higher Education: Developing Institutional & Community Strength. new ed. 1979. text ed. 25.00x (ISBN 0-534-00708-2). Wadsworth Pub.

Stewart, Andrew. Live to Ninety & Stay Young. 1980. 15.00x (ISBN 0-85032-030-5, Pub. by Daniel Con England). State Mutual Bk.

Stonecypher, D. D., Jr. Getting Older & Staying Young. 352p. 1974. 8.95 (ISBN 0-393-01102-X). Norton.

Trowbridge House, Inc, ed. Geriatric Aide: A Career to Take Pride in. 1972. pap. 285.00 with 27 cassette tapes (ISBN 0-7216-9837-9); booklet only 10.00 (ISBN 0-7216-9845-X). Saunders.

U. S. Department of Health, Education & Welfare-Public Health Service. Working with Older People. Stein, Leon, ed. LC 79-8669. (Growing Old Ser.). 1980. Repr. of 1970 ed. lib. bdg. 12.00x (ISBN 0-405-12784-7). Arno.

Villaverde, Manuel M. & Macmillan, C. Wright. Ailments of Aging: From Symptom to Treatment. 816p. 1980. text ed. 34.50 (ISBN 0-442-25108-4). Van Nos Reinhold.

Von Dorotka Bagnell, Prisca, ed. Gerontology & Geriatrics Collections. (Special Collections Ser.: Vol. 1, No. 3). 176p. 1981. 24.95 (ISBN 0-917724-53-4, B53). Haworth Pr.

Von Hahn, H. P., ed. Gerontology One: Experimental Studies Reprinted Selected Top Articles Published 1976-1978. (Karger Highlights, Gerontology Ser.). (Illus.). 1979. pap. 9.00 (ISBN 3-8055-3008-0). S Karger.

Vowles, K. D. Surgical Problems in the Aged. (Illus.). 1979. 27.50 (ISBN 0-8151-9032-8). Year Bk Med.

Wear, Robert. Preserving Independence Through Fitness Programs for the Elderly: The Technique. (Serving the Elderly Ser.: Pt. 2). 1978. pap. 5.00 (ISBN 0-89634-001-5, 044). New England Geron.

Weaver, David C., et al. The Map Abstract of Mortality Factors Affecting the Elderly: Alabama, 1979. LC 79-14064. (Map Abstract Ser.: No. 6). 112p. 1979. pap. text ed. 7.75 (ISBN 0-8173-0016-3). U of Ala Pr.

WHO Expert Committee. Geneva, 1973. Planning & Organization of Geriatric Services: Report. (Technical Report Ser.: No. 548). (Also avail. in French & Spanish). 1974. pap. 2.00 (ISBN 92-4-120548-2). World Health.

Williams, Idris. The Care of the Elderly in the Community. 235p. 1979. 32.00x (ISBN 0-85664-789-6, Pub. by Croom Helm Ltd England). Biblio Dist.

Wolff, Kurt. Emotional Rehabilitation of the Geriatric Patient. 248p. 1970. 16.75 (ISBN 0-398-02111-2). C C Thomas.

Wolk, Robert L. & Wolk, Rochelle. The Gerontological Apperception Test. 1971. 24.95 (ISBN 0-87705-040-6). Human Sci Pr.

Zarit, Steven H. & Woods, Anita M. Brain Disorders in the Elderly: A Selected Bibliography. LC 79-63569. (Technical Bibliographies on Aging Ser.). 1979. pap. text ed. 3.00 (ISBN 0-88474-089-7). USC Andrus Geron.

GERIATRICS–FORMULAE, RECEIPTS, PRESCRIPTIONS

Crooks, J. Drugs & the Elderly. 304p. text ed. 49.50 (ISBN 0-8391-1438-9). Univ Park.

Jarvik, L. F., et al, eds. Clinical Pharmacology & the Aged Patient. (Aging Ser.). 264p. 1981. 28.50 (ISBN 0-89004-340-X, 349). Raven.

Lamy, Peter P. Prescribing for the Elderly. LC 78-55289. (Illus.). 744p. 1980. 39.50 (ISBN 0-88416-208-7). Wright-PSG.

Levenson, Alvin, ed. The Neuropsychiatric Side Effects of Drugs in the Elderly. LC 78-55806. (Aging Ser.: Vol. 9). 252p. 1979. 24.00 (ISBN 0-89004-285-3). Raven.

Nandy, K., ed. Geriatric Psychopharmacology. (Developments in Neurology: Vol. 3). 400p. 40.00 (ISBN 0-444-00339-8, North Holland). Elsevier.

Peterson, David M., et al. Drugs & the Elderly: Social & Pharmacological Issues. (Illus.). 280p. 1979. 26.25 (ISBN 0-398-03758-2). C C Thomas.

GERICAULT, JEAN LOUIS ANDRE THEODORE, 1791-1824

Berger, Klaus. Gericault & His Work. LC 76-39815. (Illus.). 1978. Repr. of 1955 ed. lib. bdg. 30.00 (ISBN 0-87817-198-3). Hacker.

Clement, Charles. Gericault: Etude Biographique et Critique, Averc Le Catalogue Raisonne De L'Oeuvre Du Maitre. rev ed. LC 73-83834. (Graphic Art Ser.). (Illus.). 550p. (Fr.). 1974. Repr. of 1879 ed. lib. bdg. 65.00 (ISBN 0-306-70643-1). Da Capo.

Gericault. (I Classici Dell'arte). (Illus.). 1978. pap. 9.95 (ISBN 0-8478-5186-9). Rizzoli Intl.

GERM CELLS

see also Oogenesis; Ovum; Spermatozoa

Austin, C. R. & Short, R. V., eds. Germ Cells & Fertilization. LC 73-174261. (Reproduction in Mammals Ser.: Bk. 1). (Illus.). 1972. 24.50 (ISBN 0-521-08408-3); pap. 6.50x (ISBN 0-521-09690-1). Cambridge U Pr.

Nieuwkoop, P. D. & Sutasurya, L. A. Primordial Germ Cells in the Chordates. LC 78-18101. (Developmental & Cell Biology Ser.: No. 7). (Illus.). 1979. 34.50 (ISBN 0-521-22303-2). Cambridge U Pr.

GERM FREE LIFE

see Germfree Life

GERM THEORY

see Life-Origin; Spontaneous Generation

GERM THEORY OF DISEASE

see also Air-Microbiology; Bacteria, Pathogenic; Bacteriology; Diseases–Causes and Theories of Causation

McLaren, Anne. Germ Cells & Soma: A New Look at Old Problem. LC 81-2971. (Silliman Lectures: No. 5). (Illus.). 128p. 1981. text ed. 15.00 (ISBN 0-300-02694-3). Yale U Pr.

Mosak, Harold H. & Phillips, Karen. Demons, Germs & Values. (AAI Monograph: No. 3). 23p. (Orig.). 1980. pap. text ed. 2.00x (ISBN 0-918560-25-X). Adler.

GERM WARFARE

see Biological Warfare

GERMACRANE

Sorm, Frantisek & Dolejs, Ladislaw. Guaianolides & Germacranolides. LC 66-16515. 1966. 20.00x (ISBN 0-8162-8261-7). Holden-Day.

GERMAINE COUSIN, SAINT, 1579-1601

Cantoni, Louise. St. Germaine. rev. ed. (gr. 4-8). 1973. 1.75 (ISBN 0-8198-0262-X). Dghtrs St Paul.

GERMAN-AMERICAN LITERATURE

see also Literature, Comparative–American and German

Heckert, Charles W. German-American Diary. 1980. 15.00 (ISBN 0-87012-327-0). McClain.

Kamman, William F. Socialism in German American Literature. LC 75-328. (The Radical Tradition in America Ser.). 124p. 1975. Repr. of 1917 ed. 14.50 (ISBN 0-88355-232-9). Hyperion Conn.

Schweitzer, Christoph E., ed. Francis Daniel Pastorius, Deliciae Hortenses or Garden Recreations: A Critical Edition. (Studies in German Literature, Linguistics & Culture: Vol. 2). (Illus.). 150p. 1982. 14.95x (ISBN 0-938100-06-8). Camden Hse.

Tolzmann, Don H. German-American Literature. LC 77-21596. 1977. 17.00 (ISBN 0-8108-1069-7). Scarecrow.

GERMAN-AMERICAN LITERATURE–BIBLIOGRAPHY

Seidensticker, O. First Century of German Printing in America, 1728-1830. 1893. 26.00 (ISBN 0-527-81100-9). Kraus Repr.

GERMAN-AMERICAN NEWSPAPERS

Wittke, K. The German Language Press in America. LC 72-5535. (American History & Americana Ser., No. 47). 1972. Repr. of 1953 ed. lib. bdg. 45.95 (ISBN 0-8383-1604-2). Haskell.

GERMAN ARCHITECTURE

see Architecture–Germany

GERMAN ART

see Art, German

GERMAN AUTHORS

see Authors, German

GERMAN BALLADS AND SONGS

see also Folk-Songs, German; Songs, German

Broicher, D. German Lyrics & Ballads Done into English Verse. 59.95 (ISBN 0-8490-0229-X). Gordon Pr.

GERMAN DRAMA (COLLECTIONS)

Here are entered collections of dramas in German. For translations into English, see subdivision Translations into English.

Bruford, Walter H. Theatre, Drama, & Audience in Goethe's Germany. LC 73-10579. 388p. 1974. Repr. of 1950 ed. lib. bdg. 26.25x (ISBN 0-8371-7016-8, BRTD). Greenwood.

Campbell, T. Moody, ed. German Plays of the Nineteenth Century. (Ger). 1930. 32.50x (ISBN 0-89197-188-2); pap. text ed. 18.50x (ISBN 0-89197-771-6). Irvington.

Cohn, Albert. Shakespeare in Germany in the Sixteenth & Seventeenth Centuries. LC 75-166208. (Studies in Shakespeare, No. 24). 1971. Repr. of 1865 ed. lib. bdg. 58.95 (ISBN 0-8383-1330-2). Haskell.

Foulkes, A. Peter & Lohner, Edgar, eds. Deutsche Drama Von Kleist Bis Hauptmann. LC 76-185793. 680p. 1973. text ed. 21.80 (ISBN 0-395-12742-4). HM.

Lohner, Edgar & Hannum, H. G. Modern German Drama. LC 66-3026. 1966. text ed. 21.30 (ISBN 0-395-04808-7, 3-33585). HM.

Raabe, Paul. Era of German Expressionism. 1980. 25.00 (ISBN 0-7145-0698-2); pap. 8.95 (ISBN 0-7145-0699-0). Riverrun NY.

Spectaculum: Fuenf Moderne Theaterstuecke und Materialien, Vol. 32. 300p. (Ger.). 1980. text ed. 13.00 (ISBN 0-686-64762-9, 3518-9101, Pub. by Suhrkamp Verlag Germany). Suhrkamp.

Steinhauer, Harry, ed. Das Deutsche Drama, Vol. 2. 1939. 6.95x (ISBN 0-393-09435-9, NortonC). Norton.

GERMAN DRAMA–BIBLIOGRAPHY

Binger, Norman. Bibliography of German Plays on Microcards. 1970. 18.50 (ISBN 0-208-00891-8). Shoe String.

GERMAN DRAMA–HISTORY AND CRITICISM

Bacon, Thomas I. Martin Luther & the Drama. (Amsterdamer Pulkationen Zur Sprache und Literature: No. 25). 1976. text ed. 14.25x (ISBN 90-6203-359-8). Humanities.

Baerg, G. The Supernatural in the Modern German Drama. 59.95 (ISBN 0-8490-1160-4). Gordon Pr.

Bauland, Peter. Hooded Eagle: Modern German Drama on the New York Stage. LC 67-31564. 1968. 15.95x (ISBN 0-8156-2119-1). Syracuse U Pr.

Benjamin, Walter. The Origin of German Tragic Drama. 1978. 19.00 (ISBN 0-902308-13-0, Pub by NLB). Schocken.

Bennett, Benjamin. Modern Drama & German Classicism: Renaissance from Lessing to Brecht. LC 79-14644. (Illus.). 1979. 19.50x (ISBN 0-8014-1189-0). Cornell U Pr.

Brecht, Bertolt. Der Ozeanflug, Die Horatier und Die Kuriater, Die Massnahme. (Edition Suhrkamp: Bd. 222). 112p. (Ger.). pap. text ed. 3.90 (ISBN 3-518-10222-2, Pub. by Suhrkamp Verlag Germany). Suhrkamp.

Collins, R. S. The Artist in Modern German Drama, 1885-1939. 59.95 (ISBN 0-87968-663-4). Gordon Pr.

Diebold, Bernhard. Anarchie Im Drama: Einfuhrung Von Klaus Kilian, 1972. 1972. Repr. of 1928 ed. 34.50 (ISBN 0-384-11735-X). Johnson Repr.

Garvin, Wilhelma C. Development of the Comic Figure in German Drama. LC 72-119091. (Studies in Comparative Literature, No. 35). 1970. Repr. of 1923 ed. lib. bdg. 22.95 (ISBN 0-8383-1087-7). Haskell.

Heins, O. Johann Rist und das Niederdeutsche Drama des siebzehnten Jahrhunderts. 1930. pap. 15.00 (ISBN 0-384-22110-6). Johnson Repr.

Helmrich, Elsie W. History of the Chorus in the German Drama. LC 12-32085. (Columbia University. Germanic Studies, Old Series: No. 15). Repr. of 1912 ed. 11.50 (ISBN 0-404-50415-9). AMS Pr.

Hill, Claude & Ley, Ralph. Drama of German Expressionism: A German-English Bibliography. LC 70-181905. (North Carolina. University. Studies in the Germanic Languages & Literatures: No. 28). Repr. of 1960 ed. 18.50 (ISBN 0-404-50928-2). AMS Pr.

Hoffmeister, Donna L. The Theater of Confinement: Language & Survival in the Milieu Plays of Marieluise Fleisser & Franz Xaver Kroetz. (Studies in German Literature, Linguistics & Culture: Vol. 11). (Illus.). 190p. 1982. 16.95x (ISBN 0-938100-12-2). Camden Hse.

Houston, Gertrude C. The Evolution of the Historical Drama in Germany. LC 72-2023. (Studies in German Literature, No. 13). 1972. Repr. of 1920 ed. lib. bdg. 29.95 (ISBN 0-8383-1470-8). Haskell.

Huettich, H. G. Theater in the Planned Society: Contemporary Drama in the German Democratic Republic in Its Historical, Political & Cultural Context. (Studies in the Germanic Languages & Literatures). 1978. 12.50x (ISBN 0-8078-8088-4). U of NC Pr.

Huish, Ian. Horvath: A Study. 105p. 1980. 11.50x (ISBN 0-8476-6269-1). Rowman.

Innes, C. D. Erwin Piscator's Political Theatre: The Development of Modern German Drama. LC 72-183223. (Illus.). 256p. 1972. 42.50 (ISBN 0-521-08456-3); pap. 10.50x (ISBN 0-521-29196-8). Cambridge U Pr.

Innes, Christopher. Modern German Drama: A Study in Form. LC 78-26597. 1979. 56.00 (ISBN 0-521-22576-0); pap. 13.95 (ISBN 0-521-29560-2). Cambridge U Pr.

Kaufmann, Friedrich W. German Dramatists of the Nineteenth Century. LC 70-173527. 1972. Repr. of 1940 ed. 16.00 (ISBN 0-8462-1620-5). Russell.

--German Dramatists of the Nineteenth Century. LC 72-108641. (Essay Index Reprint Ser). 1940. 16.00 (ISBN 0-8369-1578-X). Arno.

Kistler, Mark O. Drama of the Storm & Stress. LC 70-99550. (World Authors Ser.). 1969. lib. bdg. 12.95x (ISBN 0-8057-2268-8). Irvington.

Klenze, Camillo Von. From Goethe to Hauptmann: Studies in a Changing Culture. LC 66-23519. 1926. 10.50x (ISBN 0-8196-0178-0). Biblo.

Mauermann, Siegfried. Die Buhnenanweisungen Im Deutschen Drama Bis 1700. 21.50 (ISBN 0-384-35925-6); pap. 18.50 (ISBN 0-685-27601-5). Johnson Repr.

Michael, Wolfgang. Das Deutsche Drama Des Mittelalters. (Grundriss der germanischen Philologie, 20). 304p. 1971. 60.00x (ISBN 3-11-003310-0). De Gruyter.

Osborne, John. Naturalist Drama in Germany. 185p. 1971. 12.50x (ISBN 0-87471-027-8). Rowman.

Ritchie, J. M. German Expressionist Drama. (World Author Ser.: No. 421). 1977. lib. bdg. 9.95 (ISBN 0-8057-6261-2). Twayne.

Roessler, Erwin W. Soliloquy in German Drama. LC 15-5583. (Columbia University. Germanic Studies, Old Ser.: No. 19). Repr. of 1915 ed. 19.00 (ISBN 0-404-50419-1). AMS Pr.

Shaw, Leroy R. Playwright & Historical Change: Dramatic Strategies in Brecht, Hauptmann, Kaiser, & Wedekind. LC 75-106042. 194p. 1970. 17.50x (ISBN 0-299-05500-0). U of Wis Pr.

Sinden, Margaret. Gerhart Hauptmann: The Prose Plays. LC 73-93629. x, 238p. 1975. Repr. of 1957 ed. 18.00 (ISBN 0-8462-1785-6). Russell.

Stachel, Paul. Seneca und das Deutsche Renaissancedrama. Repr. of 1907 ed. 29.00 (ISBN 0-384-57401-7); pap. 26.00 (ISBN 0-384-57400-9). Johnson Repr.

Stork, Uwe. Der Sprachliche Rhythmus in Den Buhnenstucken John Millington Synges. (Salzburg Studies in Elizabethan Literature: Poetic Drama: No. 55). 1980. pap. text ed. 25.00x (ISBN 0-391-01876-0). Humanities.

Whitton, Kenneth S. The Theatre of Friedrich Durrenmatt. (Illus.). 200p. 1978. text ed. 20.75x (ISBN 0-391-01694-6). Humanities.

Witkowski, Georg. German Drama of the Nineteenth Century. LC 68-20230. 1968. Repr. of 1909 ed. 15.00 (ISBN 0-405-09101-X). Arno.

GERMAN DRAMA–TRANSLATIONS INTO ENGLISH

Corrigan, Robert W., ed. Masterpieces of the Modern German Theater. Incl. Woyzeck. Buechner, Georg; Maria Magdalena. Hebbel, Christian F; Weavers. Hauptmann, Gerhart; Marquis of Keith. Wedekind, Frank; Caucasian Chalk Circle. Brecht, Bertolt. 1967. pap. 1.95 (ISBN 0-02-012180-6, Collier). Macmillan.

Wellwarth, George E., ed. German Drama Between the Wars: An Anthology of Plays. 1974. pap. 4.95 (ISBN 0-525-47322-X). Dutton.

GERMAN DRAWINGS

see Drawings, German

GERMAN ESSAYS

Herder, Johann G. Herders Werke, 10 vols. LC 75-41133. Repr. of 1894 ed. 300.00 set (ISBN 0-404-14940-5). AMS Pr.

GERMAN FICTION

Here are entered collections of German fiction in German. For translations into English see subdivision Translations into English.

see also Short Stories, German

Hewett-Thayer, H. W. The Modern German Novel. 59.95 (ISBN 0-8490-0648-1). Gordon Pr.

Roseler, Robert & Duckert, Audrey, eds. Moderne Deutsche Erzaehler. 3rd ed. 1960. 7.95x (ISBN 0-393-09536-3, NortonC). Norton.

GERMAN FICTION–HISTORY AND CRITICISM

Bennett, E. K. History of the German Novelle. rev. ed. Waidson, H. M., rev. by. (Orig.). 1961. 47.50 (ISBN 0-521-04152-X); pap. 11.50 (ISBN 0-521-09152-7). Cambridge U Pr.

Bettex, Albert W. German Novel of to-Day: A Guide to Contemporary Fiction in Germany, to the Novels of the Emigrants & to Those of German-Speaking Swiss Writers. facsimile ed. LC 77-99655. (Select Bibliographies Reprint Ser). 1939. 11.00 (ISBN 0-8369-5084-4). Arno.

Boa, Elizabeth & Reid, J. H. Critical Strategies: German Fiction in the Twentieth Century. 224p. 1972. 10.00x (ISBN 0-7735-0174-6); pap. 5.00 (ISBN 0-7735-0175-4). McGill-Queens U Pr.

Botheroyd, Paul F. Ich und Er: First & Third-Person Self-Reference & Problems of Identity in Three Contemporary German-Language Novels. (De Proprietatibus Litterarum Series Practica: No.67). 143p. (Orig.). 1976. pap. text ed. 28.25x (ISBN 90-2793-214-X). Mouton.

Bramsted, Ernest. Aristocracy & the Middle-Classes in Germany: Social Types in German Literature, 1830-1900. rev. ed. 1964. 12.50x (ISBN 0-226-07106-5). U of Chicago Pr.

--Aristocracy & the Middle-Classes in Germany: Social Types in German Literature, 1830-1900. rev. ed. LC 64-15031. (Orig.). 1964. pap. 2.95 (ISBN 0-226-07107-3, P163, Phoen). U of Chicago Pr.

Graham, Ilse. Heinrich von Kleist Word into Flesh: A Poet's Quest for the Symbol. 1977. 42.50x (ISBN 3-11-007165-7). De Gruyter.

Hatfield, Henry. Crisis & Continuity in Modern German Fiction: Ten Essays. LC 70-87019. 1969. 17.50x (ISBN 0-8014-0523-8). Cornell U Pr.

Heitner, Robert R., ed. The Contemporary Novel in German: A Symposium. (Dept of Germanic Languages Pubns.). 1967. 10.00x (ISBN 0-292-73670-3). U of Tex Pr.

Hewett-Thayer, Harvey W. Modern German Novel: A Series of Studies & Appreciations. facs. ed. LC 67-23232. (Essay Index Reprint Ser). 1924. 16.00 (ISBN 0-8369-0537-7). Arno.

Hornaday, Clifford L. Nature in the German Novel of the Late Eighteenth Century. LC 40-31490. (Columbia University. Germanic Studies, New Ser.: No. 10). Repr. of 1940 ed. 19.00 (ISBN 0-404-50460-4). AMS Pr.

Kornchen, Hans. Zesens Romane. Repr. of 1912 ed. 14.00 (ISBN 0-384-30036-7); pap. 11.00 (ISBN 0-384-30035-9). Johnson Repr.

Neuburger, Paul. Die Verseinlage in der Prosadichtung der Romantik. 29.00 (ISBN 0-384-41121-5); pap. 26.00 (ISBN 0-384-41120-7). Johnson Repr.

Noth, Ernst E. Contemporary German Novel. 1961. pap. 1.95 (ISBN 0-87462-422-3). Marquette.

Pfeiler, William K. War & the German Mind. LC 41-21951. Repr. of 1941 ed. 19.50 (ISBN 0-404-05028-X). AMS Pr.

Rosenfeld, Hans F. Mittelhochdeutsche Novellenstudien. Repr. of 1927 ed. 44.50 (ISBN 0-384-51991-1); pap. 41.50 (ISBN 0-384-51990-3). Johnson Repr.

Steinhauer, Harry, tr. Twelve German Novellas. 1977. 28.50x (ISBN 0-520-03504-6); pap. 9.95x (ISBN 0-520-03002-8). U of Cal Pr.

Straub, Veronika. Entstehung und Entwicklung Des Fruneuhoch Deutschen Prosaromans: Studien Zur Prosaauflosung "Wilhelm Von Osterreich". (Amsterdamer Publikationen Zur Sprache und Literatur: Vol. 16). 158p. (Ger.). 1976. pap. text ed. 16.00x (ISBN 90-6203-487-X). Humanities.

Swales, M. The German Novelle. 1977. 17.50 (ISBN 0-691-06331-1). Princeton U Pr.

Wagener, Hans. The German Baroque Novel. (World Authors Ser.: Germany: No. 229). lib. bdg. 10.95 (ISBN 0-8057-2356-0). Twayne.

Wagman, Frederick H. Magic & Natural Science in German Baroque Literature. LC 42-9041. (Coulmbia University. Germanic Studies, New Ser.: No. 13). Repr. of 1942 ed. 19.00 (ISBN 0-404-50463-9). AMS Pr.

GERMAN FICTION-TRANSLATIONS INTO ENGLISH

Bruckner, Christine. The Time of the Leonids. Comjean, Marlies I., tr. from Ger. Orig. Title: Die Zeit Von Den Leoniden. 160p. 13.95 (ISBN 0-89182-040-X). Charles River Bks.

Herrmann, Elizabeth R. & Spitz, Edna H., eds. German Women Writers of the Twentieth Century. LC 78-40139. 1978. text ed. 25.00 (ISBN 0-08-021827-X); pap. text ed. 14.00 (ISBN 0-08-021828-8). Pergamon.

GERMAN FOLK-LORE

see Folk-Lore, German

GERMAN FOLK-SONGS

see Folk-Songs, German

GERMAN HEBREW

see Yiddish Language

GERMAN HYMNS

see Hymns, German

GERMAN IMPRINTS

Deutsches Buecherverzeichnis, 22 Vols. 1915-43. Set. 3320.00 (ISBN 0-384-11585-3); pap. 175.00 ea.; Set. pap. 2200.00 (ISBN 0-384-11586-1). Johnson Repr.

Guide to German & Trade Mark Publications. 1981. pap. 9.00x (ISBN 0-902914-47-2, Pub. by Brit Lib England). State Mutual Bk.

Hinrich's Buecherkatalog. Fuenfjahrs-Katalog der Im Deutschen Buchhandel Erschienenen Buecher, Zeitschriften, Landkarten, Etc, 3 Vols. in 1. 1851-1912. 135.00 (ISBN 0-384-23310-4); pap. 130.00 (ISBN 0-685-92801-2). Johnson Repr.

Mary, Geo T., ed. Literature on Africa - Afrika Schrifttum: Bibliography of Scholarly Publications on Africa South of the Sahara in the German Language, 2 vols. 1001p. (Ger.). 1966. Vol. 1. 22.50x (ISBN 3-515-00115-8); Vol. 2. 17.50x (ISBN 3-515-00116-6). Intl Pubns Serv.

Proctor, Robert. Index to German Books in the British Museum, 1500-1520. 35.00x (ISBN 0-87556-243-4). Saifer.

GERMAN LANGUAGE

see also Low German Language

Adorno, Theodor. The Jargon of Authenticity. Tarnowski, Knut & Will, Frederic, trs. from Ger. LC 27-96701. 160p. 1973. text ed. 9.95x (ISBN 0-8101-0407-5). Northwestern U Pr.

Anderson, Robert, et al, eds. Semasia: Beitrage Zur Germanisch-Romanischen Sprachforschung, Band 2. (Orig., Ger.). 1975. pap. text ed. 40.00x (ISBN 0-391-02045-5). Humanities.

--Semasia: Beitrage Zue Germanisch Romanischen Sprachforschung, Band III. 1976. pap. text ed. 22.00x (ISBN 0-391-02044-7). Humanities.

Apelt, H. P. Reading Knowledge in German for Art Historians & Archaeologists: An English-German Course in Art History & Archaeology. 1975. pap. 10.95 (ISBN 3-503-00799-7). Adler.

Arnoldson, Torild W. Parts of the Body in Older Germanic & Scandinavian. LC 71-158274. (Chicago. University. Germanic Studies: No. 2). Repr. of 1915 ed. 20.00 (ISBN 0-404-50282-2). AMS Pr.

Auf Deutsch, Bitte. Vols. 1-3. text ed. 7.95 ea.; tapebks. vols. 1 & 2 5.95 ea.; readers vols. 1 & 2 6.95 ea.; cassette sets vols. 1 & 2 115.00 ea.; tape sets vols. 1 & 2 225.00 ea. Inst Mod Lang.

Bauer, Heinrich. Vollstaendige Grammatik der neuhochdeutschen Sprache, 5 vols. 1967. Repr. of 1833 ed. Set. 361.50x (ISBN 3-11-000365-1). De Gruyter.

Bormann, Dennis R. & Leinfellner, Elisabeth. Adam Muller's Twelve Lectures on Rhetoric: A Translation with a Critical Essay. LC 78-50020. 1978. 20.75 (ISBN 0-8357-0297-9, SS-00059). Univ Microfilms.

Bulthaupt, Fritz. Milstater Genesis und Exodus: Eine Grammatisch-Stillistische Ist Untersuchung. (Ger.). 15.50 (ISBN 0-384-06341-1); pap. 13.00 (ISBN 0-685-02228-5). Johnson Repr.

Christie, F. M. Graded German Comprehension. 1968. pap. text ed. 3.00x (ISBN 0-435-38160-1). Heinemann Ed.

Cox, Richard G. Singer's Manual of German & French Diction. 1970. pap. text ed. 6.95 (ISBN 0-02-870650-1). Schirmer Bks.

Deutsch X 3. Incl. Gespraechsbuch II "Meine Meinung". (Illus.). 1978. pap. text ed. 4.30x (ISBN 3-468-49656-7); Glossar III, Einsprachig Deutsch. pap. text ed. 2.10x (ISBN 3-468-49711-3); Lehrerheft III. pap. text ed. 2.10x (ISBN 3-468-49706-7); Leseheft III, "Aktuell und interessant". Die wichtigsten Staedte in den deutsch sprachigen Laendern. (Illus.). pap. text ed. 3.75x (ISBN 3-468-49761-X); Loesungsheft III. pap. text ed. 2.10x (ISBN 3-468-49741-5); Sprachlabor-Cassetten II mit Sprechuebungen. price not set cassettes (ISBN 0-685-60100-5); Sprachlabor-Tonbaender II mit Sprechuebungen. price not set tapes (ISBN 0-685-60101-3); Sprechuebungen II. pap. text ed. price not set (ISBN 3-468-49646-X); Text-Cassette II mit ausgewaehlten Lektionstexten. cassette 10.90x (ISBN 3-468-84741-6); Uebungsbuch III. pap. text ed. 3.20x (ISBN 3-468-49751-2). 1978. M S Rosenberg.

Dictionnaire De Two Hundred One Verbes Allemandes. Date not set. 6.95 (ISBN 0-8120-2118-5). Barron.

Dornseiff, Franz. Der Deutsche Wortschatz nach Sachgruppen. 7th ed. (Ger). 1970. 36.25x (ISBN 3-11-000287-6). De Gruyter.

DuVal, F. Alan, et al. Moderne Deutsche Sprachlehre. 3rd ed. 672p. 1980. text ed. 17.95 (ISBN 0-394-32345-9); wkbk. 6.95 (ISBN 0-394-32406-4); tapes 250.00 (ISBN 0-394-32407-2); individualized instruction program 5.95 (ISBN 0-394-32434-X). Random.

Foltin, L. B. Aus Nah und Fern. 2nd ed. 1963. pap. text ed. 7.70 (ISBN 0-395-04464-2). HM.

Gamillscheg, Ernst. Romania Germanica: Sprach- und Siedlungsgeschichte der Germanen auf dem Boden des alten Roemerreiches. Incl. Vol. 1. Zu den aeltesten Beruehrungen zwischen Roemern und Germanen: Die Franken. rev. 2nd ed. (Illus.). xvi, 474p. 1970. 73.00x (ISBN 3-11-002680-5). (Ger.). De Gruyter.

Gaters. Die Lettische Sprache & Ihre Dialekte. 1977. 37.75x (ISBN 90-279-3126-7). Mouton.

Gilbert, Glenn G. Linguistic Atlas of Texas German. 155p. 1972. 125.00x (ISBN 0-292-70088-1). U of Tex Pr.

Goetze, Alfred. Fruehneuhochdeutsches Glossar. 7th ed. (Kleine Texte, No. 101). (Ger). 1971. Repr. of 1967 ed. bds. 12.50x (ISBN 3-11-003527-8). De Gruyter.

Griesbach, Heinz. Deutsch X 3. Incl. Gespraechsbuch I mit Uebungen, "Unterwegs". (Illus.). 1975. pap. text ed. 4.30x (ISBN 3-468-49556-0); Glossary I, German-English. 1974. pap. text ed. 2.10x (ISBN 3-468-49511-0); Glossary II, German-English. 1976. pap. text ed. 2.65x (ISBN 3-468-49611-7); Lehretheft I. (Illus.). 1974. pap. text ed. 2.10x (ISBN 3-468-49506-4); Lehrerheft II. 1976. pap. text ed. 2.10x (ISBN 3-468-49606-0); Lernbuch I. Horn, Herbert, illus. 1974. pap. text ed. 4.85x (ISBN 3-468-49501-3); Lernbuch II. Horn, Herbert, illus. 1975. pap. text ed. 4.85x (ISBN 3-468-49601-X); Lernbuch III. (Illus.). 1977. pap. text ed. 4.85x (ISBN 3-468-49701-6); Leseheft I mit Uebungen, "Aktuell und interessant". (Illus.). 1975. pap. text ed. 3.75x (ISBN 3-468-49561-7); Leseheft II mit Uebungen, "Aktuell und interessant". Die Laender der Bundesrepublik Deutschland. (Illus.). 1977. pap. text ed. 3.75x (ISBN 3-468-49661-3); Loesungsheft I. 1974. pap. text ed. 2.10x (ISBN 3-468-49541-2); Loesungsheft II. 1976. pap. text ed. 2.65x (ISBN 3-468-49641-9); Sprachlabor-Cassetten, Saemtliche Sprechuebungen, Doppelspur Mitnachsprechpausen, 10 Casetten. 1974. pap. text ed. 136.80x (ISBN 3-468-84722-X); Sprachlabor-Tonbaender saemtliche Sprechuebungen, Vollspur mit Nachsprechpausen, 10 Tonbaender. 1974. pap. text ed. 239.40x (ISBN 3-468-84726-2); Sprechuebungem I - Textheft. 1974. pap. text ed. 3.75x (ISBN 3-468-49546-3). M S Rosenberg.

Haiman, John. Targets & Syntactic Change. LC 73-87535. (Janua Linguarum, Ser. Minor: No. 186). 156p. (Orig.). 1974. pap. text ed. 22.00x (ISBN 90-2792-703-0). Mouton.

Hartmann, Peter. Dimensionierugg Als Wissenschaftliche Teilaufgabe in der Textlinguistik. (PDR Press Publication in Textual Linguistic Ser.: 1). 1975. pap. text ed. 1.50x (ISBN 9-0316-0015-6). Humanities.

Herbst, Thomas, et al. Grimm's Grandchildren: Current Topics in German Linguistics. (Longman Linguistics Library). (Illus.). 1980. text ed. 27.00x (ISBN 0-582-55487-X); pap. text ed. 15.95x (ISBN 0-582-55489-6). Longman.

Hubmann-Uhlich, Inge. Colloquial German. rev. ed. (Colloquial Ser.). 1980. pap. 7.50 (ISBN 0-7100-8032-8). Routledge & Kegan.

Keller, R. E. The German Language. 7th rev. ed. (Great Language Ser). 1978. text ed. 45.00x (ISBN 0-391-00732-7). Humanities.

Kelling, H. W. & Folsom, M. H. Wie Man's Sagt und Schreibt. LC 79-140659. 1972. pap. text ed. 8.95 (ISBN 0-03-086741-X, HoltC). HR&W.

Kraft, Wolfgang S. Deutsch: Aktuell 1. LC 78-11445. 1979. 9.50 (ISBN 0-88436-539-5); pap. 6.50 (ISBN 0-88436-537-9). EMC.

Kuhn, Hans. Kleine Schriften: Aufsaetze und Rezensionen aus den Gebieten der Germanischen und Nordischen Sprach-, Literatur-und Kulturgeschichte, Vol. 1. Hofmann, Dietrich, et al, eds. (Ger). 1969. 69.50x (ISBN 3-11-000244-2). De Gruyter.

--Kleine Schriften: Aufsaetze und Rezensionen aus den Gebieten der Germanischen und Nordischen Sprach-, Literatur-und Kulturgeschichte, Vol. 3. Hoffman, Dietrich, ed. LC 71-431553. viii, 511p. (Ger.). 1972. 99.75x (ISBN 3-11-004109-X). De Gruyter.

Kurz, Paul K. On Modern German Literature, Vol. I. McCarthy, Sr. Mary F., tr. LC 73-96419. Orig. Title: Uber Moderne Literatur. 249p. 1970. 17.50x (ISBN 0-8173-8000-0). U of Ala Pr.

Lederer, H., et al. Fortschritt Deutsch: Intermediate German. LC 75-26754. 1976. pap. text ed. 15.95 (ISBN 0-03-014936-3, HoltC). HR&W.

Logan, Gerald E. Deutsch: Kernstufe. LC 75-45475. 1976. text ed. 8.95 (ISBN 0-88377-013-X); tchrs' manual 5.95 (ISBN 0-88377-014-8). Newbury Hse.

Loram, Ian & Phelps, Leland, eds. Aus Unserer Zeit. 3rd. ed. LC 78-141590. 423p. (Ger.). 1972. pap. text ed. 8.95x (ISBN 0-393-09389-1). Norton.

Lunt, Peter. Udo Fahrt Nach Koln. LC 73-20464. (Ger). 1971. pap. text ed. 7.84 (ISBN 0-395-11058-0, 2-34500). HM.

MacDonald, Ian. Get to Know Germany. 1975. pap. text ed. 5.00x (ISBN 0-435-38560-7). Heinemann Ed.

Mayer, Hartwig. Old High German Glosses. LC 73-89849. 1974. 15.00x (ISBN 0-8020-2116-6). U of Toronto Pr.

Moeller, Jack & Liedloff, Helmut. Deutsch Heute: Grundstufe. 2nd ed. LC 78-52718. (Illus.). 1979. text ed. 17.15 (ISBN 0-395-27175-4); inst. annot. ed. 18.25 (ISBN 0-395-27174-6); wkbk. 5.50 (ISBN 0-395-27173-8); recordings 114.68 (ISBN 0-395-27171-1). HM.

Mueller, H. Deutsch-Zweites Buch. rev. ed. 1972. 6.95 (ISBN 0-02-823090-6). Glencoe.

Neckel, Gustav. Uber Die Altgermanischen Relativsatze. (Ger). 14.00 (ISBN 0-384-41045-6); pap. 11.00 (ISBN 0-685-02114-9). Johnson Repr.

Neuse, Erna K. Deutsch Fur Anfanger. LC 77-135899. (Orig., Ger.). 1971. text ed. 14.95 (ISBN 0-13-203356-9); audiotape 150.00 (ISBN 0-13-203372-0). P-H.

Polenz, Peter Von. Geschichte der Deutschen Sprache. (Sammlung Goeschen 2206). 1978. 5.45x (ISBN 3-11-007525-3). De Gruyter.

Pollard, Cecil V. The Key to German Translation. 1963. 11.50x (ISBN 0-88408-007-2). Univ Co-Op Soc.

La Pratique de l'Allemand. (Assimil Ser.). 11.95 (ISBN 0-685-36084-9). French & Eur.

Prawer, S. S., et al, eds. Essays in German Language, Culture & Society. 244p. 1969. 50.00x (ISBN 0-85457-036-5, Pub. by Inst Germanic Stud England). State Mutual Bk.

Prokosch, E. The Sounds & History of the German Language. 1979. Repr. of 1916 ed. lib. bdg. 30.00 (ISBN 0-685-95067-0). Arden Lib.

Rechtschaffen, Bernard, et al. Literatur Fuer Den Detschunterricht: Erste Stufe (Elementary) (Ger). 1964. pap. text ed. 2.95x (ISBN 0-442-22061-8). Van Nos Reinhold.

--Literatur Fuer Den Detschunterricht: Zweite Stufe (Elementary-Intermediate) (Ger). 1964. pap. text ed. 2.95x (ISBN 0-442-22062-6). Van Nos Reinhold.

Rudman, Jack. German. (Undergraduate Program Field Test Ser.: UPFT-12). (Cloth bdg. avail. on request). pap. 9.95 (ISBN 0-8373-6012-9). Natl Learning.

Rundle, Stanley. Cracking the Language Code: German. 1974. 19.95 (ISBN 0-87243-052-9, Pub. by Octavo Pr). Templegate.

Russon, A. & Russon, L. J. German Vocabulary in Context. 1977. pap. text ed. 2.50x (ISBN 0-582-36167-2). Longman.

Scaglione, Aldo. The Theory of German Word Order from the Renaissance to the Present. LC 80-16619. 275p. 1981. 22.50x (ISBN 0-8166-0980-2); pap. 9.95 (ISBN 0-8166-0983-7). U of Minn Pr.

Schenker, Walter. Die Sprache Huldrych Zwinglis Im Kontrast Zur Sprache Luthers. (Studia Linguistica Germanica: Vol. 14). (Illus.). 1977. 86.00x (ISBN 3-11-006605-X). De Gruyter.

Schmalzbauer, G. & Von Seuffert, T. Ich Spreche Deutsch. 1971. ref. ed. 11.95 (ISBN 0-13-449090-8). P-H.

Schwabe, Henry O. Semantic Development of Words for "Eating" & "Drinking" in Germanic. LC 70-173195. (Chicago. University. Linguistic Studies in Germanic: No. 1). Repr. of 1915 ed. 14.00 (ISBN 0-404-50281-4). AMS Pr.

Schwerin, Kurt. A Bibliography of German. (Language Legal Monograph Ser.). 383p. 1977. text ed. 58.00 (ISBN 3-7940-7037-2, Pub. by K G Saur). Gale.

Senner, Wayne M. & Schuback, Gertrude B. Geschichten Zur Unterhaltung. 178p. 1980. pap. text ed. 7.95 (ISBN 0-394-32377-7). Random.

Sonderegger, Stefan. Grundzuege deutscher Sprachgeschichte: Band 1. 1979. text ed. 52.00x (ISBN 3-11-003570-7). De Gruyter.

Stern, A. Z. & Reif, Joseph A., eds. Useful Expressions in German. (Useful Expressions Ser.). 64p. (Orig.). 1980. pap. 2.00 (ISBN 0-86628-007-3). Ridgefield Pub.

Strutz, Henry. One Thousand & One Pitfalls in German. 140p. (gr. 11-12). 1981. pap. text ed. 4.95 (ISBN 0-8120-0590-2). Barron.

Trier, Jost. Aufsatze und Vortrage Zur Wortfeldtheorie. (Janua Linguarum, Series Monor: No. 174). 1973. 34.50x (ISBN 0-686-21794-2). Mouton.

Two Hundred & One Verbos Alemanes. Date not set. 6.95 (ISBN 0-8120-2119-3). Barron.

Vail, Van Horn & Sparks, Kimberly. Modern German. 2nd ed. (Illus.). 1978. text ed. 16.95 (ISBN 0-15-561316-2, HC); tapes 300.00 (ISBN 0-15-561317-0); cassettes 125.00 (ISBN 0-15-561318-9). HarBraceJ.

Weiss, Edda. Deutsch: Entdecken Wir Es! Saslow, Joan, ed. (Illus., Ger., Pupil's ed.). (gr. 9). 1980. text ed. 13.12 (ISBN 0-07-069211-4); tchrs.' ed. 14.00 (ISBN 0-07-069212-2); wkbk. 3.96 (ISBN 0-07-069213-0); tests 52.00 (ISBN 0-07-069214-9); filmstrips 108.00 (ISBN 0-07-097813-1); tapes 344.00 (ISBN 0-07-097811-5); cassettes 296.00 (ISBN 0-07-097812-3). McGraw.

Wiesinger, Peter. Phonetisch-Phonologische Untersuchungen zur Vokalentwicklung in den deutschen Dialekten. Incl. Vol. 1. Die Langvokale im Hochdeutschen. (Illus.). xxx, 423p (ISBN 3-11-001895-0); Vol. 2. Die Diphtonge im Hochdeutschen. (Illus.). viii, 361p (ISBN 3-11-001896-9). (Studia Linguistica Germanica: Zweiter Deutscher Sprachatlas, Gesamtdarstellungen Volkalismus, Vols. 1 & 2). (Ger.). 1970. Set. 97.50x (ISBN 0-685-24226-9). De Gruyter.

Wilson, Eric. Es Geht Weiter. 1977. pap. text ed. 11.95 scp (ISBN 0-06-047145-X, HarpC). Har-Row.

GERMAN LANGUAGE–OLD HIGH GERMAN, 750-1050

Bergmann, Rolf. Verzeichnis der althochdeutschen und altsaechsischen Glossenhandschriften: Mit Bibliographie der Glosseneditionen, der Handschriftenbeschreibungen und der Dialektbestimmungen. LC 72-76056. (Ambieten Zur Fruehmittelalterforschung Ser: Vol. 6). (Ger.). 1973. 40.00x (ISBN 3-11-003713-0). De Gruyter.

Dickhoff, Emil. Das Zweigliedrige Wort-Asyndeton in der Alteren Deutschen Sprache. 1906. 21.50 (ISBN 0-384-11720-1); pap. 18.50 (ISBN 0-685-92810-1). Johnson Repr.

Diels, Paul. Die Stellung Des Verbums in der Alteren Althoch-Deutschen Prosa. 1906. 21.50 (ISBN 0-384-11745-7); pap. 18.50 (ISBN 0-384-11746-5). Johnson Repr.

Green, Dennis H. Carolingian Lord. 1965. 90.00 (ISBN 0-521-05138-X). Cambridge U Pr.

Haessler, Luise. Old High German Biteilen & Biskerien. 1935. pap. 6.00 (ISBN 0-527-00765-X). Kraus Repr.

Moulton, William G. Swiss German Dialect & Romance Patois. 1941. pap. 6.00 (ISBN 0-527-00780-3). Kraus Repr.

Newman, John. Old High German Reader. 158p. (Orig.). 1981. pap. text ed. 7.50x (ISBN 0-89894-012-5). Advocate Pub Group.

Raven, F. A. Die Schwachen Verben Des Althochdeutschen, 2 Vols. LC 64-23934. (Alabama Linguistic & Philological Ser., Vols. 4 & 5). 1964. vol. 1 23.30 (ISBN 0-8173-0800-8); Vol. 2. 24.60 (ISBN 0-8173-0801-6). U of Ala Pr.

Rosen, Harold. Old High German Preposition Compounds in Relation to Their Latin Originals. 1934. pap. 6.00 (ISBN 0-527-00762-5). Kraus Repr.

Sievers, Paul. Die Accente in Althochdeutschen und Altsachsischen Handschriften. Repr. of 1909 ed. 14.00 (ISBN 0-384-55360-5); pap. 11.00 (ISBN 0-685-13334-6). Johnson Repr.

GERMAN LANGUAGE–MIDDLE HIGH GERMAN, 1050-1500

Asher, John A. Short Descriptive Grammar of Middle High German. 1967. pap. 8.95x (ISBN 0-19-647410-8). Oxford U Pr.

Boot, Christine. Cassiodorus' Historia Tripartita in Stainreuter's German Translation. (Amsterdamer Publikationen Zur Sprache und Literatur: Nos.29-30). 1977. pap. text ed. 84.00 (ISBN 90-6203-139-0). Humanities.

Burger, Harald. Zeit und Ewigkeit: Studien zum Wortschatz der Geistlichen Texte des Alt-und Fruehmittelhochdeutschen. LC 74-174177. (Studia Linguistica Germanica: Vol. 6). 1972. 45.00x (ISBN 3-11-003995-8). De Gruyter.

Cutting, Starr W. Der Conjunctiv Bei Hartmann Von Aue. LC 76-173037. (Chicago. University. Germanic Studies: No. 1). Repr. of 1894 ed. 14.00 (ISBN 0-404-50271-7). AMS Pr.

Endres, Marion. Word Field & Word Content in Middle High German. (Goeppinger Arbeiten Zur Germanistik: Vol. 47). 387p. 1971. pap. 19.50x (ISBN 3-87452-084-6). Intl Pubns Serv.

Fahrner, R. Wortsinn und Wortschoepfung Bei Meister Eckehart. Repr. of 1929 ed. pap. 7.00 (ISBN 0-384-15090-X). Johnson Repr.

Loetscher, Andreas. Semantische Strukturen im Bereich der alt und mittelhochdeutschen Schallwoerter. (Quellen und Forschungen zur Sprach - und Kulturgeschichte der germanischen Voelker, N. F. 53). 1973. 33.75x (ISBN 3-11-003870-6). De Gruyter.

Wahnschaffe, Friedrich. Die Syntaktische Bedeutung Des Mittelhochdeutschen Enjambements. Repr. of 1919 ed. 21.50 (ISBN 0-384-65491-6); pap. 18.50 (ISBN 0-384-65490-8). Johnson Repr.

Wolf, Leo. Der Groteske und Hyperbolische Stil Des Mittelhochdeutschen Volksepos. (Ger). Repr. of 1877 ed. 14.00 (ISBN 0-384-69045-9); pap. 11.00 (ISBN 0-685-02157-2). Johnson Repr.

GERMAN LANGUAGE–MIDDLE HIGH GERMAN, 1050-1500–GRAMMAR

Herchenback, Hugo. Praesens Historicum Im Mittelhochdeutschen. Repr. of 1911 ed. 14.00 (ISBN 0-384-22460-1); pap. 11.00 (ISBN 0-685-02261-7). Johnson Repr.

GERMAN LANGUAGE–MIDDLE HIGH GERMAN, 1050-1500–READERS

Walshe, M. O. A Middle High German Reader: With Grammar, Notes & Glossary. 232p. 1974. pap. text ed. 8.95x (ISBN 0-686-77056-0). Oxford U Pr.

GERMAN LANGUAGE–MIDDLE HIGH GERMAN, 1050-1500–TEXTS

Benedictus, Saint Middle High German Translations of the Regula Sancti Benedicti. Selmer, Carl, ed. & intro. by. 1933. 19.00 (ISBN 0-527-01689-6). Kraus Repr.

GERMAN LANGUAGE–COMPOSITION AND EXERCISES

Diller, Edward & Wishard, Armin, eds. Spiel und Sprache. (Illus., Orig.). 1971. pap. text ed. 4.95x (ISBN 0-393-09545-2). Norton.

Ellert & Ellert. German A, 5 bks. (gr. 8-12). 1972. pap. text ed. 7.00 each (ISBN 0-686-57754-X). Learning Line.

--German B, 3 bks. (gr. 8-12). 1972. pap. text ed. 7.00 each (ISBN 0-8449-1423-1). Learning Line.

Evans, M. Blakemore, et al. Shorter College German. 3rd ed. LC 56-5843. (Illus.). 1956. text ed. 12.95x (ISBN 0-89197-403-2); pap. text ed. 6.95x (ISBN 0-89197-404-0). Irvington.

Feix, I. & Schlant, E. Gesprache, Diskussionen, Aufsatze. (Ger). 1969. pap. text ed. 11.95 (ISBN 0-03-080020-X, HoltC). HR&W.

Greenfield, Eric V. German Grammar. 3rd ed. (Orig., Ger.). 1968. pap. 4.95 (ISBN 0-06-460034-3, CO 34, COS). Har-Row.

Knust, H. Texte und Ubungen: Intermediate Readings & Exercises. 1977. pap. 9.95 (ISBN 0-13-903526-5). P-H.

Lloyd, Albert L. & Schmitt, Albert R. Deutsch Und Deutschland Heute. (Illus., Ger.). 1967. text ed. 13.95x (ISBN 0-442-23325-6); tapes 90.00 (ISBN 0-442-23327-2). Van Nos Reinhold.

--Ubungsbuch Fuer Deutsch und Deutschland Heute. (Ger). 1967. pap. text ed. 2.50x (ISBN 0-442-23326-4); tapes 15.00 (ISBN 0-442-23328-0). Van Nos Reinhold.

Rognebakke, Myrtle & Driessle, Hannelore. Warum Nicht Auf Deutsch, Vol. 2. 1969. 7.24 (ISBN 0-685-07674-1, 82691); tchr's ed. 8.80 (ISBN 0-685-07675-X). Glencoe.

Sevin, Dieter H. & Sevin, Ingrid A. Zur Diskussion: A Modern Approach to German Conversation. 2nd ed. 1979. pap. text ed. 14.95 scp (ISBN 0-06-045915-8, HarpC). Har-Row.

Vail, Van Horn & Sparks, Kimberly. Der Weg Zum Lesen. 2nd ed. 1974. pap. text ed. 9.95 (ISBN 0-15-595152-1, HC); tapes 100.00 (ISBN 0-15-595153-X). HarBraceJ.

Von Hofe, Harold & Eppert, Franz. Arbeits-und Ubungsbuch. 1971. pap. text ed. 5.95x (ISBN 0-684-12598-6, ScribC). Scribner.

Wells, Sydney W. Teach Yourself More German. (Teach Yourself Ser.). pap. 4.95 (ISBN 0-679-10190-X). McKay.

Wishard, Armin & Diller, Edward. Noch Einmal Spiel & Sprache. new ed. 1974. pap. text ed. 3.95x (ISBN 0-393-09328-X). Norton.

GERMAN LANGUAGE–CONVERSATION AND PHRASE BOOKS

see also German Language–Self-Instruction; German Language–Textbooks for Children

Adrienne. Der Gimmick, Gesprochenes Deutsch. 1977. pap. 4.95 (ISBN 0-393-04480-7). Norton.

Blanks, Harvey. The Golden Road Record Collector's Guide. Date not set. 15.00x (ISBN 0-392-07471-0, ABC). Sportshelf.

Bluske, Margaret K. & Walther, Elizabeth K. Das Erste Jahr. 4th ed. (Illus.). 1980. text ed. 16.95 scp (ISBN 0-06-040788-3, HarpC); Programmed Assignment Bk. scp 8.50 (ISBN 0-06-040795-6); instructor's manual free (ISBN 0-06-360784-0); scp tapes 275.00 (ISBN 0-06-047490-4). Har-Row.

Bonar, Lore S., et al. Say It in Another Language: Phrases in Spanish, French, Japanese, Swahili, & German. (YA) 1976. pap. text ed. 2.50 pkg. of 20 (ISBN 0-88441-414-0, 26-814). GS.

Bonnell, Peter & Sedwick, Frank. Conversation in German: Points of Departure. 3rd ed. (Orig.). 1981. pap. text ed. write for info. (ISBN 0-442-24466-5). D Van Nostrand.

--Conversation in German: Points of Departure. 2nd ed. 1976. pap. text ed. 6.95x (ISBN 0-442-20726-3). Van Nos Reinhold.

--German for Careers: Conversational Perspectives. (Orig.). 1980. pap. text ed. 8.95 (ISBN 0-442-20563-5). D Van Nostrand.

Clausing, Gerhard & Mueller, Klaus I. An Individualized Instruction Program in Basic German. 2nd ed. 1975. pap. text ed. 5.50x (ISBN 0-686-72045-8). Random.

Crean, John E., et al. Deutsche Sprach und Landeskunde. Incl. Ratyck, Joanna. wkbk. 6.95 (ISBN 0-394-32649-0); Crean, John E. lab manual 6.95 (ISBN 0-394-32650-4). 608p. 1981. text ed. 18.95 (ISBN 0-394-32648-2). Random.

Ellison, Al. Ellison's German Menu Reader. 1977. 2.95 (ISBN 0-930580-03-6). Ellison Ent.

Feld, Ellen. Zielsprache Deutsch: Deutsch. Feld, Von Nardroff, ed. 1981. text ed. 18.95x (ISBN 0-02-336810-1). Macmillan.

Funke, Erich. Gesprochenes Deutsch. LC 53-6356. 1947. text ed. 16.50x (ISBN 0-89197-505-5). Irvington.

Gekker, Cathrine O. Practical German for the Tourist. 1976. stitched 3.00 (ISBN 0-686-00543-0). Huffman Pr.

German in Twenty Lessons. rev. ed. (Cortina Method Language Ser). (Illus.). 6.95 (ISBN 0-385-00074-X). Doubleday.

German Review. pocket ed. 150p. (gr. 7-12). 1982. pap. text ed. 2.50 (ISBN 0-8120-2195-9). Barron.

Germany-Hugo Phrase Book. (Hugo's Language Courses Ser.: No. 561). 1970. pap. 1.50 (ISBN 0-8226-0561-9). Littlefield.

Goedsche, C. R. Sag's Auf Deutsch: A First Book for German Conversation. (Illus., Ger.). (gr. 10 up). 1979. pap. text ed. 6.95x (ISBN 0-8290-0026-7). Irvington.

Hamilton. Teach Yourself German Phrase Book. (Teach Yourself Ser.). pap. 2.95 (ISBN 0-679-10176-4). McKay.

Hamlyn German Phrase Book. pap. 2.95 (ISBN 0-600-34052-X, 8145). Larousse.

Holloway Staff. German. (Harper Phrase Books for the Traveler Ser.). (Orig.). 1977. pap. 1.00 (ISBN 0-8467-0310-6, Pub. by Two Continents). Hippocrene Bks.

Hughes, Charles A. Grosset's German Phrase Book & Dictionary for Travelers. 1971. pap. 2.95 (ISBN 0-448-00652-9). G&D.

Jackson, Eugene & Geiger, Adolph. German Made Simple. LC 65-10615. pap. 3.50 (ISBN 0-385-00129-0, Made). Doubleday.

Jespersen, Robert C. & Peters, George F. Using German. 1980. text ed. 17.50 scp (ISBN 0-06-043315-9, HarpC); instructor's manual free (ISBN 0-06-363329-9); scp tapes 275.00 (ISBN 0-06-047491-2); scp workbook 7.50 (ISBN 0-06-043316-7). Har-Row.

Joseph, Gerda. Follett Instant German Conversation Guide. (Illus., Orig.). 1966. 2.50 (ISBN 0-695-84197-1). New Century.

Juncker. Junckers German-English Phrase Book. Seiffhart, Arthur, ed. 1968. 1.75 (ISBN 0-685-06569-3). Assoc Bk.

Kahn, Lothar & Hook, Donald D. Conversational German One. 2nd ed. 1976. text ed. 11.95 (ISBN 0-442-22913-5); tapes 95.00 (ISBN 0-442-22914-3); cassettes 59.95 (ISBN 0-442-22917-8). D Van Nostrand.

Korner, Bruno. Fluency Drills in German. Date not set. pap. 5.95x (ISBN 0-392-08376-0, SpS). Sportshelf.

Kraft, Wolfgang S. Deutsch: Aktuell 2. LC 79-12315. (Illus.). 1980. 9.95 (ISBN 0-88436-542-5); pap. 6.95 (ISBN 0-88436-540-9, GEA 132021). EMC.

Kreplin, Dietrich. Guten Tag Instructor's Handbook. Von Faber, Helm, ed. 1975. Repr. 4.50x (ISBN 0-8354-2500-2). Intl Film.

Listen & Learn German. (Listen & Learn Ser.). 1981. Incl. 3 Cassettes & Manual. 14.95 (ISBN 0-486-99901-7). Dover.

Living German: Cassette Edition. 1969. 14.95, with 2 cassettes plus dictionary & manual (ISBN 0-517-00898-X). Crown.

Logan, Gerald E. German Conversational Practice. 1974. pap. text ed. 4.95 students bk (ISBN 0-88377-012-1); tchr's bk 5.95 (ISBN 0-88377-015-6). Newbury Hse.

Luedtke, Helmut, ed. Kommunikationstheoretische Grundlagen des Sprachwandels. (Grundlagen der Kommunikation). 280p. 1979. text ed. 58.00x (ISBN 3-11-007271-8). De Gruyter.

Madrigal, Margarita & Halpert, Inge. See It & Say It in German. (Orig.). pap. 1.75 (ISBN 0-451-09096-9, E9096, Sig). NAL.

Madrigal, Margarita & Meyer, Ursula. Madrigal's Magic Key to German. LC 66-20943. 1966. 8.95 (ISBN 0-385-03638-8). Doubleday.

Mathieu, Gustave & Stern, Guy. Listen & Learn German. 3.50 (ISBN 0-486-20878-8); with records 12.95 (ISBN 0-486-98878-3). Dover.

--Say It in German. (Orig.). 1957. pap. 1.25 (ISBN 0-486-20804-4). Dover.

Mathieu, M. M & Stern, Guy. Say It in German. LC 59-10440. 1957. lib. bdg. 8.50x (ISBN 0-88307-564-4). Gannon.

Meier, Regula S. & Ramsey, Donna. Guten Tag Study Worksheets. (Illus.). 1978. wkbk. 3.00x (ISBN 0-8354-2501-0). Intl Film.

Mueller, Hugo. Deutsch, Erstes Buch. (gr. 9-12). 1958-69. student tests 2.95 (ISBN 0-685-22893-2, 82298); tchrs' key to student tests 1.50 (ISBN 0-685-22894-0, 82302); 17 tapes 150.00 (ISBN 0-685-22896-7, 82306, 82348). wall charts 126.00 (ISBN 0-686-66599-6, 82612). Glencoe.

--Deutsch-Erstes Buch, 2 pts. Incl. Pt. 1. 1960-68. tchrs' key 1.50 (ISBN 0-685-22897-5, 82318); tchrs' manual 2.95 (ISBN 0-685-22898-3, 82300); wkbk. 1.95 (ISBN 0-685-22899-1, 82328, 82320, 82322); Pt. 2. 1967-69. 5.95 (ISBN 0-685-22900-9, 82324); tchrs' key 2.95 (ISBN 0-685-22901-7, 82326); wkbk. 1.95 (ISBN 0-685-22902-5, 82360); tapes 120.00 (ISBN 0-685-22903-3, 82330). (gr. 9-12). 1968. Glencoe.

--Deutsch-Zweites Buch. rev ed. 1963-69. tchr's key 1.95 (ISBN 0-685-22890-8, 82310); wkbk. 1.95 (ISBN 0-685-22891-6, 32308); tapes 150.00 (ISBN 0-685-22892-4, 82360, 82370, 82312). Glencoe.

Norman, Jill & Hitchin, Ute. German Phrase Book. (Orig., Bilingual). 1968. pap. 2.95 (ISBN 0-14-002697-5). Penguin.

Politzer, Robert L. Speaking German. LC 69-10287. 1969. text ed. 10.95 (ISBN 0-13-825794-9). P-H.

R. D. Cortina Company. Conversational German in Twenty Lessons. 360p. 1980. pap. 4.95 (ISBN 0-06-463602-X, EH 602). Har-Row.

Rehder, Helmut, et al. Deutsch: Denken, Wissen und Kennen. (German Basic Courses: Level 4). (gr. 11-12). 1966. text ed. 10.98 (ISBN 0-03-051785-0). HR&W.

Rogers, R. M. & Watkins, Arthur R. German Through Conversational Patterns. 3rd ed. (Illus.). 525p. 1981. text ed. 17.50 scp (ISBN 0-06-045551-9, HarpC); instructor's manual avail. (ISBN 0-06-365522-5); wkbk. scp 8.50 (ISBN 0-06-045554-3); tapes 250.00 (ISBN 0-06-047498-X). Har-Row.

Sager, Juan. German Structure Drills. Date not set. 14.95x (ISBN 0-392-08460-0, SpS). Sportshelf.

Schmidt, W. German. 660p. 1980. 10.00x (ISBN 0-569-05867-8, Pub. by Collet's). State Mutual Bk.

Siebs. Deutsche Aussprache: Reine und gemaessigte Hochlautung mit Aussprachewoerterbuch. 19th rev. ed. (Ger). 1969. 24.00x (ISBN 3-11-000325-2). De Gruyter.

Watson, H. W. & McGuinn, S. German in the Office. pap. text ed. 4.50x (ISBN 0-582-35256-8). Longman.

Young, Alex. Goals at Goodison. Date not set. 12.50x (ISBN 0-392-15084-0, SpS). Sportshelf.

GERMAN LANGUAGE–DIALECTS

Kauffmann, Friedrich. Geschichte der Schwaebischen Mundart im Mittelalter und in der Neuzeit: Mit Textproben und einer Geschichte der Schriftsprache in Schwaben. xxxvi, 355p. 1978. Repr. of 1890 ed. 70.00x (ISBN 3-11-003348-8). De Gruyter.

Moulton, William G. Swiss German Dialect & Romance Patois. 1941. pap. 6.00 (ISBN 0-527-00780-3). Kraus Repr.

Planta, Robert Von. Grammatik der Oskisch-Umbrischen Dialekte, 2 vols. 1973. Repr. of 1897 ed. 153.00 (ISBN 3-11-004563-X). De Gruyter.

Siebenbuergisch-Saechsisches Woerterbuch, 3 vols. Incl. Vol. 1 (a-c) 851p. 1924. 61.00x (ISBN 3-11-009500-9); Vol 2 (d-f) 548p. 1911-25. 35.50x (ISBN 3-11-009501-7); Vol 3 (g). 355p. 1971. 42.25x (ISBN 3-11-003707-6). De Gruyter.

Steinitz, Wolfgang. Ostjakologische Arbeiten: Band 1: Stjakische Volksdichtung und Erzahlungen Aus Zwel Dialekten Texte; Fur Die Neuherausgabe Wissenschaftliche Bearbeitet Von Gert Saver. (Janua Linguarum Ser., Practice 013: No. 254). 468p. 1975. pap. text ed. 91.50x (ISBN 90-2793-271-9). Mouton.

GERMAN LANGUAGE–DICTIONARIES

Bertelsmann Lexikon, 10 vols. (Ger.). 1972-74. Set. 950.00 (ISBN 0-686-56596-7, M-7306, Pub. by Bertelsmann). French & Eur.

Brinkman, Karl-Heinz & Schmidt, Rudolf. Data Systems Dictionary: English-German & German-English. 1974. pap. 40.00x (ISBN 3-87097-095-2). Intl Learn Syst.

Cassells. German Concise Dictionary. 1977. 8.95 (ISBN 0-02-052265-7). Macmillan.

Daum, Edmund & Schenk, W. Deutsch-Russisches Woerterbuch. 15th ed. (Ger. -Rus.). 1976. 13.50 (ISBN 0-686-56602-5, M-7333, Pub. by Max Hueber). French & Eur.

Deutsches Woerterbuch. (Ger.). 1977. 7.50 (ISBN 3-411-01702-3, M-7338, Bibliogr. Institut). French & Eur.

Duden, R. Duden-Stilwoerterbuch. 5th rev. ed. (Der Grosse Duden: Vol. 2). 18.50 (ISBN 0-685-05215-X). Adler.

Duden, R., ed. Duden-Bedeutungswoerterbuch. (Der Grosse Duden: Vol. 10). 1971. 18.50 (ISBN 3-4110-0910-1). Adler.

--Duden-Bildwoerterbuch. 2nd ed. (Der Grosse Duden: Vol. 3). (Illus.). 18.50 (ISBN 3-4110-0913-6). Adler.

--Duden-Rechtschreibung. 16th rev. ed. (Der Grosse Duden: Vol. 1). 1971. 18.50 (ISBN 3-4110-0911-X). Adler.

Eichhoff, J. Woertatlas der Deutschen Umgangssprachen, Vol. 1. 106p. (Ger.). 1977. 55.00 (ISBN 3-7720-1337-6, M-7689, Pub. by A. Francke). French & Eur.
Follett World Wide Dictionaries: German. 1966. pap. 3.95 (ISBN 0-695-89687-3). New Century.
Frank, Irmgard. Althochdeutschen Glossen der Handschrift Leipzig Rep. II. 6. (Arbeiten zur Fruehmittelalterforschung, Vol. 7). 294p. 1973. 57.00x (ISBN 3-11-004370-X). De Gruyter.
Froundiian-Dirair. Armenisch-Deutsches Woerterbuch. (Arm. & Ger.). 1952. 45.00 (ISBN 3-486-41021-0, Pub. by Oldenbourg). French & Eur.
Goetze, Alfred & Mitzka, Walther, eds. Truebners Deutsches Woerterbuch, 8 Vols. (Ger). 1947-57. Set. 300.00x (ISBN 3-11-000319-8). De Gruyter.
Gotze, Alfred. Trubners Deutsches Woerterbuch, 8 vols. 4851p. (Ger.). 1939. Set. 283.00 (ISBN 3-11-000319-8, M-7671, Pub. by de Gruyter). French & Eur.
Der Grosse Brockhaus, 12 vols. 18th ed. (Ger.). 1977. Set. 995.00 (ISBN 3-7653-0039-X, M-7326, Pub. by Brockhaus). French & Eur.
Herstig, David. Deutsch-Hebraeisches Woerterbuch. (Ger. -Heb.). 1971. 17.50 (ISBN 3-19-006285-4, M-7330, Pub. by Max Hueber). French & Eur.
--Hebraeisch - Deutsches Woerterbuch. (Heb. & Ger.). 1971. 17.50 (ISBN 3-19-006289-7, M-7441, Pub. by Max Hueber). French & Eur.
Heyne, Moritz. Deutsches Woerterbuch, 3 vols. 2nd ed. (Ger.). 1970. Set. 195.00 (ISBN 3-7776-0053-9, M-7334, Pub. by Hirzel). French & Eur.
Hoops, Johannes. Reallexikon der Germanischen Altertumskunde. 2nd, rev., enl. ed. Incl. Vol. 1. Aachen-Bajuwaren. (Illus.). xxxiv, 627p. 117.00 (ISBN 3-11-004489-7); Vol. 2. Bake Billigkeit. 162.00 (ISBN 3-11-004762-4). 1976. De Gruyter.
Isaacs, Alan, ed. Multilingual Commercial Dictionary. 1980. 22.50 (ISBN 0-87196-425-2). Facts on File.
Keller, Howard H. German Root Lexicon. LC 72-85112. (Miami Linguistics Ser: No. 11). 128p. 1973. 12.95x (ISBN 0-87024-244-X). U of Miami Pr.
Killer, W. K. Illustrated Technical German for Builders. 4th ed. 183p. (Eng. & Ger.). 1977. 15.95 (ISBN 3-7625-0898-4, M-7468, Pub. by Bauverlag). French & Eur.
Klatt, Edmund, et al, eds. Langenscheidt's Taschenworterbuch. 6th ed. 1264p. 1970. 10.95 (ISBN 3-468-11121-5). Hippocrene Bks.
Koester, Rudolf. Ullstein Lexikon der Deutschen Sprache. (Ger.). 1969. 20.00 (ISBN 3-550-06016-5, M-7672, Pub. by Ullstein Verlag/VVA). French & Eur.
Lexikon 2000, Vol. 1. (Ger.). 1970. 86.00 (ISBN 3-8075-1001-X, M-7189, Pub. by Wissen). French & Eur.
Lexikon 2000, Vol. 2. (Ger.). 1970. 86.00 (ISBN 3-8075-1002-8, M-7188, Pub. by Wissen). French & Eur.
Lexikon 2000, Vol. 3. (Ger.). 1971. 86.00 (ISBN 3-8075-1003-6, M-7187, Pub. by Wissen). French & Eur.
Lexikon 2000, Vol. 4. (Ger.). 1971. 86.00 (ISBN 3-8075-1004-4, M-7186, Pub. by Wissen). French & Eur.
Lexikon 2000, Vol. 5. (Ger.). 1971. 86.00 (ISBN 3-8075-1005-2, M-7185, Pub. by Wissen). French & Eur.
Lexikon 2000, Vol. 6. (Ger.). 1971. 86.00 (ISBN 3-8075-1006-0, M-7184, Pub. by Wissen). French & Eur.
Lexikon 2000, Vol. 7. (Ger.). 1972. 86.00 (ISBN 3-8075-1007-9, M-7183, Pub. by Wissen). French & Eur.
Lexikon 2000, Vol. 8. (Ger.). 1972. 86.00 (ISBN 3-8075-1008-7, M-7182, Pub. by Wissen). French & Eur.
Lexikon 2000, Vol. 9. (Ger.). 1972. 86.00 (ISBN 3-8075-1009-5, M-7181, Pub. by Wissen). French & Eur.
Lexikon 2000, Vol. 10. (Ger.). 1972. 86.00 (ISBN 3-8075-1010-9, M-7180, Pub. by Wissen). French & Eur.
Lexikon 2000, Vol. 11. (Ger.). 1973. 86.00 (ISBN 3-8075-1011-7, M-7179, Pub. by Wissen). French & Eur.
Lexikon 2000, Vol. 12. (Ger.). 1973. 86.00 (ISBN 3-8075-1012-5, M-7178, Pub. by Wissen). French & Eur.
Lexikon 2000, Vol. 13. (Ger.). 1973. 86.00 (ISBN 3-8075-1013-3, M-7177, Pub. by Wissen). French & Eur.
Mackensen, Lutz. Deutsches Woerterbuch. (Ger.). 1977. 38.50 (ISBN 3-517-00637-8, M-7339, Pub. by Suedwest). French & Eur.
Meinel, Hans. A Course in Scientific German: German for Technicians & Scientists. 1981. 40.00x (ISBN 0-686-75664-9, Pub. by European Schoolbks England). State Mutual Bk.
Neue Brokhaus, 5 vols., 1 atlas. 4th ed. (Ger., Atlas included). 1968. 280.00 (ISBN 0-686-56634-3, M-7566, Pub. by Wiesbaden). French & Eur.
Neue Herder: Lexikon, 14 vols. (Ger.). 1968-73. 995.00 (ISBN 0-686-56635-1, M-7568, Pub. by Herder). French & Eur.
Paul, Hermann. Deutsches Woerterbuch. 7th ed. (Ger.). 1976. 29.95 (ISBN 3-484-10057-5, M-7335, Pub. by Max Niemeyer). French & Eur.
Servotte, Jozef V. Commercial & Financial Dictionary in Four Languages: French-Dutch-English-German. rev. 4th ed. Orig. Title: Dictionnaire Commercial et Financier en 4 Langues. 968p. 1972. 52.50x (ISBN 90-02-11109-6). Intl Pubns Serv.
Smith, Josefa J., et al, eds. Cortina-Grosset Basic German Dictionary. LC 73-18523. 384p. 1975. pap. 3.50 (ISBN 0-448-14029-2). G&D.
Strasak, Jaroslav. Technical German: A Textbook. LC 74-861534. 1969. 8.50x (ISBN 3-87097-041-3). Intl Pubns Serv.
Strutz. Five Hundred & One German Verbs: Written in Japanese. Date not set. pap. 4.25 (ISBN 0-8120-2182-7). Barron.
Taschenlexikon Elektronik, Funktechnik. 320p. (Ger.). 1974. 12.50 (ISBN 3-87144-176-7, M-7630, Pub. by Verlag Harri Deutsch). French & Eur.
Technik-Worterbuch: Chemie & Chemische Technik. 720p. 1980. vinyl 70.00x (ISBN 0-569-07861-X, Pub. by Collet's). State Mutual Bk.
Technik-Worterbuch: Elektronik, Elektrotechnik. 1980. 100.00x (ISBN 0-686-72091-1, Pub. by Collet's). State Mutual Bk.
Vest-Pocket German. pap. 2.95 (ISBN 0-8329-1533-5). New Century.
Wahrig, Gerhard. Deutsches Woerterbuch. 2nd ed. 1975. 30.95 (ISBN 3-570-01631-5, M-7336, Pub. by Bertelsmann Lexikon VVA). French & Eur.
Wahrig-Gerhard. Fremdwoerter Lexikon. (Ger.). 1976. 15.95 (ISBN 3-570-01631-5, M-7416, Pub. by Bertelsmann Lexikon VVA). French & Eur.
Wahrmud. New German-Arabic Dictionary, 3 vols. 1974. 80.00x (ISBN 0-86685-178-X). Intl Bk Ctr.
Wahrmund, Adolf. Handworterbuch der Neu-Arabischen und Deutschen Sprache, 3 vols. 1974. Set. text ed. 37.50x (ISBN 0-8426-0776-5). Verry.
Walde, Alois. Vergleichendes Woerterbuch der Indogermanischen Sprachen, 3 vols. Pokorny, Julius, ed. 1973. Repr. of 1932 ed. Set. 224.00x (ISBN 3-11-004556-7). De Gruyter.
Weber, Albert. Grammatiken und Woerterbuecher des Schweizer Deutschen. 2nd ed. 354p. (Ger.). 1968. 14.50 (ISBN 3-85865-029-3, M-7431, Pub. by Hans Rohr). French & Eur.
Weigand, Karl. Deutsches Woerterbuch, 2 vols. 6th ed. 1968. Set. 252.00x (ISBN 3-11-000383-X, M-7337). De Gruyter.
Wennrich, Peter. Anglo-American & German Abbreviations in Environmental Protection. 624p. 1979. 60.00 (ISBN 0-89664-096-5, Pub. by K G Saur). Gale.
Wiswall, F. L. Development of Admiralty, Jurisdiction & Practice Since 1800. LC 77-108113. (Illus.). 1971. 35.50 (ISBN 0-521-07751-6). Cambridge U Pr.
World-Wide German Dictionary. pap. 3.95 (ISBN 0-686-31300-3). New Century.

GERMAN LANGUAGE-DICTIONARIES-CHINESE

Piasek, Martin. Chinesisch-Deutsches Woerterbuch. 3rd ed. (Eng. -Ger.). 1975. 28.95 (ISBN 0-686-56599-1, 7320, Pub. by Max Heuber). French & Eur.
Rudenberg, Werner. Chinesisch-Deutsches Woerterbuch. 3rd ed. 821p. (Eng. -Ger.). 1963. 196.00x (ISBN 0-686-56600-9, M-7321). De Gruyter.
Wilhelm, Hellmut. German-Chinese Dictionary. 1976. Repr. of 1958 ed. 175.00 (ISBN 0-518-19006-4). Arno.

GERMAN LANGUAGE-DICTIONARIES-ENGLISH

Barker, M. L. & Homeyer, H., eds. The Pocket Oxford German Dictionary, 2 vols. in 1. Incl. Pt. 1. German-English. 3rd ed. 1975; Pt. 2. English-German. Carr, C. T., compiled by. 1975. pap. 5.95x (ISBN 0-19-864138-9). Oxford U Pr.
Beigel, Hugo G. Dictionary of Psychology & Related Fields. LC 74-115063. (Ger. & Eng.). 18.00 (ISBN 0-8044-0042-3). Ungar.
Bein, G. German-English Dictionary of International Transport. 232p. 1980. 15.00x (ISBN 0-569-05117-7, Pub. by Collet's). State Mutual Bk.
Bertelsmann Dictionary English-German, German-English. (Ger. & Eng.). 1975. 17.50 (ISBN 3-570-01438-X, M-7444, Pub. by Bertelsmann Lexikon/VVA). French & Eur.
Betteridge, Harold T. Cassell's German Dictionary: German-English English-German. rev. ed. LC 77-18452. 1978. plain 13.50 (ISBN 0-02-522920-6); indexed 14.95 (ISBN 0-02-522930-3). Macmillan.
Birdmann, G. English-German -- German-English Solid State Physics & Electronics Dictionary. 1103p. 1980. 100.00x (ISBN 0-569-07204-2, Pub. by Collet's). State Mutual Bk.
Briese, K. English-German Dictionary. 624p. 1980. 20.00x (ISBN 0-569-06892-4, Pub. by Collet's). State Mutual Bk.
Cassells. German-English Dictionary. 1978. standard 14.95 (ISBN 0-02-052292-4); index 16.95 (ISBN 0-02-052293-2). Macmillan.
Cassell's New Compact German Dictionary. 1981. pap. 2.95 (ISBN 0-440-31100-4, LE). Dell.
Clark, J. M., ed. German-English, English-German Gem Dictionary. (Gem Foreign Language Ser.). 1953. leatheroid 2.95 (ISBN 0-00-458619-0, G3). Collins Pubs.
Clark, J. M., et al. Putnam's Contemporary German Dictionary. (Putnam's Contemporary Foreign Language Dictionaries). 1973. 3.50 (ISBN 0-399-11145-X). Putnam.
Cortina. Cortina-Ace Basic German Dictionary. (Foreign Language Dictionary Ser.). 384p. 1981. pap. 2.50 (ISBN 0-441-05002-6). Ace Bks.
DeVries, Louis. German-English Technical & Engineering Dictionary. 2nd ed. 1966. 47.50 (ISBN 0-07-016631-5, P&RB). McGraw.
DeVries, Louis & Jacolev, Leon. German-English Science Dictionary. 4th ed. 1978. 16.50 (ISBN 0-07-016602-1, P&RB). McGraw.
Edgren, A. H. & Whitney, W. D. A Compendious German-English Dictionary. 75.00 (ISBN 0-87968-914-5). Gordon Pr.
Eggeling, H. F. Dictionary of Modern German Prose Usage. 1961. 29.00x (ISBN 0-19-864110-9). Oxford U Pr.
Eichborn, R. V. Dictionary of Economics, 2 vols. Incl. Vol. 1. (Eng. & Ger.) (ISBN 3-4301-2392-5). plastic bdg. (ISBN 3-9213-9200-4); Vol. 2. (Ger. & Eng.) (ISBN 3-4301-2393-3). plastic bdg. (ISBN 3-9213-9201-2). 1975. 107.50 ea.; plastic bdg. 59.85 ea. Adler.
Engeroff, K. & Lovelace-Kaeufer, C. English-German Dictionary of Idioms. 18.75 (ISBN 3-1900-6217-X). Adler.
English-German -- German-English Welding Engineering Dictionary. 396p. 1980. 75.00x (ISBN 0-569-05715-9, Pub. by Collet's). State Mutual Bk.
Ernst, R. Dictionary of Chemical Terms, 2 Vols. Vol. 1, Ger-Eng. 33.70 (ISBN 3-8709-7011-1); Vol. 2, Eng-Ger. 41.20 (ISBN 3-8709-7012-X). Adler.
Fischer, Eric & Elliott, Francis E. A German & English Glossary of Geographical Terms. LC 76-20474. (American Geographical Society Library Ser: No. 5). 111p. 1976. Repr. of 1950 ed. lib. bdg. 15.00x (ISBN 0-8371-8994-2, ELGG). Greenwood.
Follett Vest-Pocket Dictionaries: German. 344p. 1975. pap. 2.95 (ISBN 0-695-80608-4). Follett.
Freeman, Henry G. Dictionary of Metal-Cutting Machine Tools, 2 Vols. (Eng-Ger. & Ger-Eng.). 1965. 61.75 ea. (ISBN 3-7736-5095-7). Adler.
--Technical Pocket Dictionary, English-German - German-English, 2 vols. 2nd ed. 11.00 ea. Ger.-Eng (ISBN 3-1900-6212-9). Eng.-Ger (ISBN 3-1900-6213-7). Adler.
--Tool Dictionary. 2nd ed. (Ger-Eng. & Eng-Ger.). 1960. 78.00 (ISBN 3-7736-5052-3). Adler.
Freeman, Henry G., compiled by. DIN Definitions: German-English with an English-German Vocabulary. 2nd rev. ed. 55.00 (ISBN 3-4101-0804-1). Heinman.
German-English & English-German Dictionary. pap. 1.35 (ISBN 0-686-00471-X). Dennison.
Glucksman, Paul H., ed. World-Wide German Dictionary. 1978. pap. 2.50 (ISBN 0-449-30850-2, Prem). Fawcett.
Goedsche, C. R. & Spann, Meno. Deutsch Fuer Amerikaner. 4th ed. (Illus., Ger.). 1979. text ed. 15.95 (ISBN 0-442-22058-8); tapes 95.00 (ISBN 0-442-22064-2); cassettes 59.95 (ISBN 0-442-22067-7); wkbk 3.50x (ISBN 0-442-22059-6). D Van Nostrand.
Gunston, C. A. Deutsch-Englishes Glossarium. 1292p. (Ger. -Eng., German-English Glossary of Financial and Economic Terms). 1977. 69.50 (ISBN 3-7819-2014-3, 7328, Pub. by Fritz Knapp Verlag). French & Eur.
Gunston, C. A. & Corner, C. M. German-English Glossary of Financial & Commercial Terms. new ed. (Ger. & Eng.). 1977. 57.50 (ISBN 3-7819-2008-9). Adler.
Hamlyn German-English Dictionary. 1977. pap. 3.95 (ISBN 0-600-36564-6, 8088). Larousse.
Heinze, S. Dictionary of Insurance Terms, 2 Vols. (Ger-Eng. & Eng-Ger.). 12.00 ea. Ger.-Eng (ISBN 3-8709-7016-2). Eng.-Ger (ISBN 3-8709-7017-0). Adler.
Herland, Leo. Dictionary of Mathematical Sciences, 2 vols. Incl. Vol. 1. German-English. 2nd ed. xii, 320p (ISBN 0-8044-4393-9); Vol. 2. English-German. 320p (ISBN 0-8044-4394-7). LC 65-16622. 18.50 ea. Ungar.
Hoffmann, E. Dictionary for the Glass Industry: Fachwoerterbuch fuer die Glasindustrie, 2 Pts. (Pt, 1, Ger-Eng, Pt, 2, Eng-Ger). 1963. 26.60 (ISBN 0-387-03007-7). Springer-Verlag.
Hugo Pocket Dictionary: German-English, English-German. 622p. 1969. 3.50 (ISBN 0-8226-0504-X, 504). Littlefield.
Hyman, Charles J. German-English, English-German Astronautics Dictionary. LC 65-20216. 273p. 1968. 30.00 (ISBN 0-306-10748-1, Consultants). Plenum Pub.
--German-English, English-German Electronics Dictionary. LC 64-7757. 182p. 1965. 35.00 (ISBN 0-306-10710-4, Consultants). Plenum Pub.
Hyman, Charles J., ed. Dictionary of Physics & Allied Sciences: German-English. LC 77-6949. 1978. 30.00 (ISBN 0-8044-4433-1). Ungar.
Institute for Language Study. Vest Pocket German. LC 58-8920. (Illus.). 128p. (Ger.). 1979. pap. 1.95 (ISBN 0-06-464902-4, BN 4900, BN). Har-Row.
Jeans Pocket Dictionaries: German-English. 224p. (Orig.). 1981. pap. 1.95 (ISBN 0-8437-1726-2). Hammond Inc.
Jones, Trevor, ed. The Oxford Harrap Standard German-English Dictionary, 3 vols. Incl. Vol. 1. A-E. 1978. (ISBN 0-19-864129-X); Vol. 2. F-K. 1978. (ISBN 0-19-864130-3); Vol. 3. L-R. 1978. (ISBN 0-19-864131-1). 49.00 ea. Oxford U Pr.
Kahn, Lothar & Hook, Donald D. Intermediate Conversational German. 3rd ed. 1973. text ed. 11.95 (ISBN 0-442-22915-1); 18 tapes 80.00 (ISBN 0-442-22919-4). D Van Nostrand.
Keller, Howard H. A German Word Family Dictionary: Together with English Equivalents. LC 76-19988. 1978. 14.95 (ISBN 0-520-03291-8). U of Cal Pr.
Killer, W. K. Illustrated Technical German for Builders-Bautechnisches Englisch Im Bild. LC 76-467695. 1977. pap. 12.50x (ISBN 3-7625-0898-4). Intl Pubns Serv.
Klaften, E. B. & Allison, F. C. German-English, English-German Patent Terminological Dictionary. 1971. 50.00 (ISBN 0-685-12020-1). Heinman.
Klatt, Edmund, et al. Langenscheidt's Standard German Dictionary: German-English, English-German. Orig. Title: Standard German Dictionary. 1264p. 1974. 11.95 (ISBN 0-685-39723-8). Hippocrene Bks.
Kleiber, A. W. German-English, English-German Welding Engineering Dictionary. 35.00 (ISBN 0-685-00398-1). Heinman.
Kniepkamp, H. P. Legal Dictionary. (Eng-Ger. & Ger-Eng.). 26.00 (ISBN 3-7678-0013-6). Adler.
Koehler, Friedrich. Woerterbuch der Amerikanismen. 3rd ed. (Ger.). 1972. 25.00 (ISBN 3-500-25340-7, M-7044). French & Eur.
Kolthoff, Benedict. Glass Terminology: A German-English Glossary. (Illus.). 1967. 17.00 (ISBN 0-913942-03-0). Lang Serv.
Langenscheidt Editorial Staff. Langenscheidt's Comprehensive English-German Dictionary. 1134p. 1972. 42.50x (ISBN 3-468-02120-8). Hippocrene Bks.
Langenscheidt Staff, ed. Langenscheidt New Pocket German Dictionary: German-English, English-German. (Langenscheidt Pocket Dictionaries Ser.). 702p. 1970. 5.95 (ISBN 0-685-31330-1). Hippocrene Bks.
Langenscheidt's Universal German-English, English-German Dictionary. 35th ed. (Universal Dictionaries Ser.). 512p. (Eng. & Ger.). 2.95 (ISBN 3-468-18121-3). Hippocrene Bks.
Messinger, Heinz. Langenscheidt's Comprehensive English-German Dictionary. 1978. 27.50 (ISBN 0-684-15731-4, ScribT). Scribner.
Messinger, Heinz & Rudenberg, Werner. Langenscheidt's New College German Dictionary (German-English, English-German) 1400p. 1973. 16.95 (ISBN 0-685-30210-5); thumb indexed 18.95 (ISBN 0-685-30211-3). Hippocrene Bks.
Mosse, Walter M. Theological German Vocabulary. 1968. lib. bdg. 11.00x (ISBN 0-374-95966-8). Octagon.
Moulton, Jenni H., ed. The Random House Basic Dictionary German. 1981. pap. 1.50 (ISBN 0-345-29619-2). Ballantine.
Moulton, William & Moulton, Jenni K. German Vest Pocket Dictionary. 1960. pap. 2.95 (ISBN 0-394-40056-9). Random.
Mueller, Peter B. German-English-English-German: A Dictionary of Professional Terminology of Speech Pathology & Audiology. 64p. 1967. photocopy ed. spiral 6.75 (ISBN 0-398-01368-3). C C Thomas.

Muret-Sanders, German-English Dictionary. Incl. Vol. 2, A-K. 1014p; Vol. 2, L-Z. 1040p. 1975. 80.00x ea. Hippocrene Bks.

Patterson, A. M. German-English Dictionary for Chemists. 3rd ed. 1950. 23.50 (ISBN 0-471-66990-3, Pub. by Wiley-Interscience). Wiley.

Pfeffer, J. Alan. Grunddeutsch: Basic (Spoken) German Dictionary for Everyday Usage. LC 73-116147. (German Ser). (Ger). 1970. ref. ed. 9.95 (ISBN 0-13-367755-9). P-H.

Pheby, John. The Oxford-Duden Pictorial German-English Dictionary. The Dudenredaktion & German Section of Oxford Pr Dictionary Department, eds. (Illus.). 776p. 1980. text ed. 29.50x (ISBN 0-19-864135-4). Oxford U Pr.

Rechtschaffen, Bernard & Marck, Louis. Two Thousand & One German & English Idioms: 2001 Deutsche und Englische Idiome. Date not set. pap. 9.95 (ISBN 0-8120-0474-4). Barron.

Renner, et al. Economic Terminology German-English. 2nd ed. 1970. 27.50 (ISBN 3-1900-6201-3). Adler.

Sasse, H. C., et al. Cassell's Concise German-English English-German Dictionary. LC 77-7567. 1977. 6.95 (ISBN 0-02-522650-9). Macmillan.

Schoeffler, Weis. Woerterbuch der Englischen und Deutschen Sprache, Vol. 1. (Ger. -Eng., Dictionary of the English & German Language). pap. 17.95 (ISBN 3-12-518100-3, M-7015). French & Eur.

--Woerterbuch der Englischen und Deutschen Sprache, Vol. 2. (Ger. -Eng., Dictionary of the English & German Language). pap. 17.95 (ISBN 3-12-518200-X, M-7014). French & Eur.

Smith, Josefa J., et al, eds. Cortina-Grosset Basic German Dictionary. LC 73-18523. 384p. 1975. pap. 3.50 (ISBN 0-448-14029-2). G&D.

Springer, Otto. Langenscheidt's New Muret-Sanders German-English Encyclopedic Dictionary: Vol. 1 a-K, Pt. 2. 1014p. 1974. 80.00x (ISBN 3-468-01124-5). Hippocrene Bks.

Standke, Wolfgang, compiled by. Foundry Dictionary: German-English & English-German. 1971. 21.50x (ISBN 3-87260-002-8). Intl Pubns Serv.

Taylor, Ronald J. & Gottschalk, W. German-English Dictionary of Idioms. 27.50 (ISBN 3-19-006216-1). Adler.

Technik-Worterbuch: Optik & Optischer Geratebau. 432p. 1980. vinyl 70.00x (ISBN 0-686-72097-0, Pub. by Collet's). State Mutual Bk.

Traupman, John C. German English Dictionary. 764p. (Orig.). 1981. pap. 2.50 (ISBN 0-553-14155-4). Bantam.

Traupman, John C., ed. The Bantam New College German & English Dictionary. 768p. (Orig.). (gr. 7-12). 1981. pap. 2.50 (ISBN 0-553-14155-4). Bantam.

Unseld, D. W. Medical Dictionary. (Ger-Eng, Eng-Ger.). 1971. 31.50 (ISBN 3-8047-0415-8). Adler.

Wahrig, G. German-English Dictionary. 661p. 1980. 20.00x (ISBN 0-569-05717-5, Pub. by Collet's). State Mutual Bk.

Webel, A. A German-English Dictionary of Technical, Scientific & General Terms. 3rd ed. 1969. Repr. of 1952 ed. 37.50 (ISBN 0-7100-2258-1). Routledge & Kegan.

Wernicke, H. Dictionary of Electronics, Communications & Electrical Engineering, 2 Vols. new ed. Vol. 1. 36.00 ea. (ISBN 0-685-05199-4); Vol. 2. 32.50 ea. (ISBN 0-685-05200-1). Adler.

Wichmann, K. Pocket Dictionary of the German & English Languages. 1952. 12.00 (ISBN 0-7100-2290-5). Routledge & Kegan.

Wildhagen. Englisch-Deutsches, Deutsch-Englisches Woerterbuch, Vol. 2. 2nd ed. (English-German, German-English Dictionary). 1972. 72.00 (ISBN 3-87097-047-2, Brandstetter). French & Eur.

--Englisch-Deutsches, Deutsch-Englishes Woerterbuch, Vol. 1. 2nd ed. (English-German, German-English Dictionary). 1973. 52.00 (ISBN 3-87097-046-4, Pub. by Brandstetter). French & Eur.

Zotter, Josefa, ed. Cortina-Grosset Basic German Dictionary. 1977. pap. 2.95 (ISBN 0-448-14029-2). G&D.

GERMAN LANGUAGE–DICTIONARIES–FRENCH

Bertaux, Pierre. Franzosisch-Deutsches, Deutsch-Franzosisches Woerterbuch, Vol. 1. (Ger. & Fr.). 1966. 52.00 (ISBN 3-87097-000-6, 7411, Pub. by Brandstetter). French & Eur.

--Franzosisch-Deutsches, Deutsch-Franzosisches Woerterbuch, Vol. 2. (Ger. & Fr.). 1966. 52.00 (ISBN 3-87097-001-4, 7412, Pub. by Brandstetter). French & Eur.

Dubois, F. & Werny, P. Dictionnaire Francais-Allemand des Locutions. (Fr.-Ger.). 1976. 23.95 (ISBN 0-686-57124-X, M-6172). French & Eur.

Eckel, Denis & Manfred, Hofer. Dictionnaire Allemand-Francais et Francais-Allemand. 1324p. (Fr.-Ger.). 1970. 25.95 (ISBN 0-686-57131-2, M-6184). French & Eur.

Grappin, P. Dictionnaire moderne Larousse, francais-allemand et allemand-francais. (Fr. & Ger.). 39.95 (ISBN 2-03-020603-2, 3778). Larousse.

Knauer, Karl. Bertelsmann Woerterbuch Duetsch-Franzoesisch, Franzoesisch-Deutsch. 640p. (Ger. -Fr.). 1974. 17.50 (ISBN 3-570-01486-X, M-7307, Pub. by Bertelsmann Lexikon VVA). French & Eur.

Larousse And Co. Interprete Larousse, francais-allemand et allemand-francais. pap. 3.95 (ISBN 0-685-13946-8, 3782). Larousse.

--Larousse de poche, francais-allemand et allemand-francais. pap. 5.95 (ISBN 0-685-13959-X). Larousse.

Pinloche, A. & Jolivet, A. Dictionnaire bilingue Larousse, francais-allemand et allemand-francais. (Apollo). (Fr. & Ger.). 10.50 (ISBN 0-685-13853-4, 3779). Larousse.

Roepke, F. Deutsch-Franzosisches Glossarium. 588p. (Ger. -Fr.). 1966. 35.00 (ISBN 3-7819-2006-2, M-7329, Pub. by Fritz Knapp Verlag). French & Eur.

Rotteck, ed. Dictionnaire Allemand-Francais, Francais-Allemand. 980p. (Fr.-Ger.). 1970. pap. 7.50 (ISBN 0-686-57093-6, M-6115). French & Eur.

Weis, E. & Mattutat, H. Woerterbuch der Franzoesischen und Deutschen Sprache, Vol. 1. (Fr. -Ger.). 18.95 (ISBN 3-215-01824-1, M-7004). French & Eur.

--Woerterbuch der Franzoesischen und Deutschen Sprache, Vol. 2. (Ger. -Fr.). 18.95 (ISBN 3-215-01825-X, M-7003). French & Eur.

Weis, Erich & Mattutat, Heinrich. Dictionnaire Allemand-Francais. 570p. (Ger. & Fr.). 1977. 29.95 (ISBN 0-686-57259-9, M-6570). French & Eur.

--Dictionnaire Francais-Allemand et Allemand-Francais. 1022p. (Fr. & Ger.). 1977. 55.00 (ISBN 0-686-57260-2, M-6571). French & Eur.

GERMAN LANGUAGE–DICTIONARIES–ITALIAN

Woerterbuch der Italienischen und Deutschen Sprache, Vol. 1. (It. -Ger.). 1970. 225.00 (ISBN 3-87097-033-2, M-6992). French & Eur.

Woerterbuch der Italienischen und Deutschen Sprache, Vol. 2. (Ger. -It.). 1972. 225.00 (ISBN 3-87097-034-0, M-6991). French & Eur.

GERMAN LANGUAGE–DICTIONARIES–POLYGLOT

Hoyer-Kreuter. Technological Dictionary in Three Languages, 3 vols. Schlomann, Alfred, ed. Incl. Vol. 1. German-English-French; Vol. 2. English-German-French; Vol. 3. French-German-English. Set. 120.00 (ISBN 0-8044-0202-7). Ungar.

GERMAN LANGUAGE–DICTIONARIES–PORTUGUESE

Michaelis, H., ed. Portuguese-German, German-Portuguese Dictionary, 2 Vols. Set. 42.00 (ISBN 0-8044-0375-9); 21.00 ea. Vol. 1 (ISBN 0-8044-0376-7). Vol. 2 (ISBN 0-8044-0377-5). Ungar.

GERMAN LANGUAGE–DICTIONARIES–RUSSIAN

Cutsumbis, Michael N. A Bibliographic Guide to Materials on Greeks in the United States, 1890-1968. LC 74-130283. 100p. 1970. pap. text ed. 8.95x (ISBN 0-913256-02-1, Dist. by Ozer). Ctr Migration.

Daum, Edmund & Schenk, W. Russich-Deutsches Woerterbuch. 7th ed. 1976. 17.50 (ISBN 3-19-006219-6, M-7606, Pub. by Max Hueber). French & Eur.

Grischen, N. Deutsch-Russische Wirtschaftssprache. 480p. (Ger. -Rus.). 1969. 27.50 (ISBN 3-19-006207-2, M-7332, Pub. by M. Hueber). French & Eur.

GERMAN LANGUAGE–DICTIONARIES–SPANISH

Amador, E. F. Martinez. Diccionario Aleman-Espanol, Espanol-Aleman. 1616p. (Ale. -Espn.). 50.95 (ISBN 84-303-0117-8, S-12381). French & Eur.

Amador, E. M. Martinez. Diccionario Manual Aleman-Espanol, Spanisch-Deutsch. 17th ed. 936p. (Ale. -Espn.). 1977. 5.95 (ISBN 84-7183-002-7, S-50382). French & Eur.

--Diccionario Manual Amador Aleman-Espanol, Espanol-Aleman. 1400p. (Ale. -Espn.). 17.95 (ISBN 84-303-0118-6, S-50385). French & Eur.

Diccionario Cuyas: Spanish-German, German-Spanish. 5.50x (ISBN 0-686-00851-0). Colton Bk.

Diccionario Iter Aleman-Espanol, Espanol-Aleman. 512p. (Ale. -Espn.). 1977. pap. 5.95 (ISBN 84-303-0126-7, S-50376). French & Eur.

Diccionario Iter Aleman-Espanol, Espanol-Aleman. 512p. (Ale. -Espn.). 1977. leatherette 6.75 (ISBN 84-303-0127-5, S-50377). French & Eur.

Diccionario Lexicon, Aleman-Espanol, Espanol-Aleman. 400p. (Ale. -Espn.). 5.75 (ISBN 0-686-57343-9, S-31392). French & Eur.

Diccionario Universal Herder Aleman-Espanol, Espanol-Aleman. 4th ed. 388p. (Ale. -Espn.). 1977. leatherette 4.50 (ISBN 84-254-0782-6, S-50378). French & Eur.

Haensch, Gunther. Diccionario Moderno Herder Aleman-Espanol, Espanol-Aleman. 684p. (Ale. -Espn.). 1977. 16.75 (ISBN 84-254-0652-8, S-50379). French & Eur.

Lerche, Mario R. Deutsch-Spanisches Glossarium. 460p. (Ger. -Span.). 1967. 17.50 (ISBN 3-7819-2012-7, M-7347, Pub. by Fritz Knapp Verlag). French & Eur.

Mink, H. Diccionario Tecnico Aleman-Espanol, Espanol-Aleman, 2 vols. 3rd ed. 2530p. (Espn. -Ale.). 1978. Set. 120.00 (ISBN 84-254-0704-4, S-50189). French & Eur.

Muller. Diccionario Aleman-Espanol, Espanol-Aleman. 900p. (Ale. -Espn.). leatherette 12.25 (ISBN 84-303-0119-4, S-50384). French & Eur.

Muller, Hans. Diccionario Lexicon Aleman-Espanol, Espanol-Aleman. 384p. (Ale. -Espn.). 1977. pap. 4.50 (ISBN 84-303-0124-0, S-31392). French & Eur.

Ruiz Torres, Francisco. Diccionario Aleman-Espanol, Espanol-Aleman de Medicina. 2nd ed. 860p. (Ale. -Espn.). 1971. pap. 41.25 (ISBN 84-205-0010-0, S-50089). French & Eur.

Slaby, R. J. & Grossman, R., eds. Spanish & German Dictionary, 2 vols. Incl. Vol. 1. Spanish-German. 19.00 (ISBN 0-8044-0581-6); Vol. 2. German-Spanish. 28.00 (ISBN 0-8044-0582-4). 2172p. Set. 45.00 (ISBN 0-8044-0580-8). Ungar.

Slaby, Rudolf. Diccionario De las Lenguas Espanola y Alemana, 2 vols. 3rd ed. 2422p. (Ale. -Espn.). 1977. Set. 110.00 (ISBN 84-254-0694-3, S-50380). French & Eur.

--Woerterbuch der Deutschen und Spanischen Sprache, Vol. 1. 3rd ed. (Ger. -Span.). 1975. 76.00 (ISBN 3-87097-067-7, M-7024). French & Eur.

--Woerterbuch der Deutschen und Spanischen Sprache, Vol. 2. 2nd ed. (Ger. -Span.). 1973. 66.00 (ISBN 3-87097-040-5, M-7023). French & Eur.

GERMAN LANGUAGE–ETYMOLOGY

Duden, R., ed. Duden-Etymologie. (Der Grosse Duden: Vol. 7). 18.50 (ISBN 3-4110-0907-1). Adler.

Holmberg, Marta A. Studien Zu Den Verbalen Pseudokomposita Im Deutschen. (Goteborger Germanistische Forschungen: No. 14). 106p. (Orig.). 1976. pap. text ed. 8.75x (ISBN 91-7346-016-8). Humanities.

Kjell-Ake, Forsgren. Wortdefinition und Feldstruktur: Zum Problem der Kategorisierung un der Spachwissenschaft. (Goteborger Germanistiche Forschungen: No. 16). (Ger.). 1977. pap. text ed. 8.00x (ISBN 91-7346-038-9). Humanities.

Maurer, Friedrich & Rupp, Heinz, eds. Deutsche Wortgeschichte, Vol. 3. 3rd ed. (Grundriss der Germanischen Philologie: Vol. 17, Pt. 3). 1978. 48.00x (ISBN 3-11-003620-7). De Gruyter.

GERMAN LANGUAGE–EXAMINATIONS, QUESTIONS, ETC.

Goldberg, Mark. Graduate School Foreign Language Test: German. 3rd ed. (Orig.). 1968. pap. 3.95 (ISBN 0-668-01460-1). Arco.

Greiner, Vivian. German Achievement Test. LC 68-10500. (College Board Achievement Test Ser). (Orig.). 1968. pap. text ed. 1.45 (ISBN 0-668-01698-1). Arco.

Rudman, Jack. German. (Graduate-Record Examination Ser.: GRE-9). (Cloth bdg. avail. on request). pap. 9.95 (ISBN 0-8373-5209-6). Natl Learning.

--German. (National Teachers Examination Ser.: NT-32). (Cloth bdg. avail. on request). pap. 9.95 (ISBN 0-8373-8442-7). Natl Learning.

--German. (College Level Examination Ser.: CLEP-45). (Cloth bdg. avail. on request). 1976. pap. 9.95 (ISBN 0-8373-5345-9). Natl Learning.

--Graduate School Foreign Language Test (GSFLT) German. (Admission Test Ser.: ATS-28B). (Cloth bdg. avail. on request). pap. 9.95 (ISBN 0-8373-5028-X). Natl Learning.

GERMAN LANGUAGE–FIGURES OF SPEECH

Weydt, Harald, ed. Die Partikein der Deutschen Sprache. 1979. 105.00x (ISBN 3-11-007833-3). De Gruyter.

GERMAN LANGUAGE–FOREIGN WORDS AND PHRASES

Duden, R., ed. Duden-Fremdwoerterbuch. 2nd rev. ed. (Der Grosse Duden: Vol. 5). 18.50 (ISBN 3-4110-0915-2). Adler.

Kershaw, F. & Russon, S. German for Business Studies. 1971. pap. text ed. 4.00x (ISBN 0-582-36186-9). Longman.

GERMAN LANGUAGE–GLOSSARIES, VOCABULARIES, ETC.

Apelt, H. P. Reading Knowledge in German for Art Historians & Archaeologists: An English-German Course in Art History & Archaeology. 1975. pap. 10.95 (ISBN 3-503-00799-7). Adler.

Apelt, Mary L. & Apelt, Hans-Peter. Reading Knowledge in German for Art Historians & Archaeologists. (Ger. -Eng.). 1975. pap. 15.00x (ISBN 0-685-59066-6). Wittenborn.

Gunston, C. A. Deutsch-Englishes Glossarium. 1292p. (Ger. -Eng., German-English Glossary of Financial and Economic Terms). 1977. 69.50 (ISBN 3-7819-2014-3, 7328, Pub. by Fritz Knapp Verlag). French & Eur.

Haenger, Heinrich. Mittelhochdeutsche Glossare und Vokabulare in Schweizerischen Bibliotheken bis 1500. (Quellen und Forschungen zur Sprach-und Kulturgeschichte der Germanischen Voelker N. F. 44). 88p. 1972. 29.50 (ISBN 3-11-003542-1). De Gruyter.

Odwarka, Karl & Konig, Fritz. A Word Frequency Study of Basic German Textbooks. LC 77-18487. 1977. pap. 8.50 (ISBN 0-8357-0292-8, SS-00056). Univ Microfilms.

Roepke, F. Deutsch-Franzosisches Glossarium. 588p. (Ger. -Fr.). 1966. 35.00 (ISBN 3-7819-2006-2, M-7329, Pub. by Fritz Knapp Verlag). French & Eur.

Schmidt, Karl A. Easy Ways to Enlarge Your German Vocabulary. LC 73-92020. (Orig.). 1974. 3.75 (ISBN 0-486-23044-9). Dover.

Wadepuhl, Walter & Morgan, Bayard. Minimum Standard German Vocabulary. 1934. pap. text ed. 1.95x (ISBN 0-89197-549-7). Irvington.

Zahn, Hans E. Englisch - Deutsches Glossarium. 528p. (English - German Glossary). 1977. 78.50 (ISBN 3-7819-2013-5, M-7355, Pub. by Fritz Knapp Verlag). French & Eur.

GERMAN LANGUAGE–GRAMMAR

Babcock, Leland S. & Frey, Erich A. German & Germany in Review. (Illus.). 1972. text ed. 10.95x (ISBN 0-442-20470-1); 14 tapes 65.00x (ISBN 0-442-30471-4). Van Nos Reinhold.

Bergethon, K. Roald & Finger, Ellis. Grammar for Reading German, Form C. rev. ed. 1979. pap. text ed. 9.40 (ISBN 0-395-26085-X); instrs'. answer key 6.60 (ISBN 0-395-26084-1). HM.

Boor, Helmut De & Wisniewski, Roswitha. Mittelhochdeutsche Grammatik. 8th ed. (Sammlung Goeschen 2209). 1978. 5.45x (ISBN 3-11-007639-X). De Gruyter.

Borgert, U. H. & Nylan, A. C. German Reference Grammar. 296p. 1975. 30.00x (ISBN 0-424-00010-5, Pub. by Sydney U Pr); pap. 14.00x (ISBN 0-424-00011-3, Pub. by Sydney U Pr). Intl Schol Bk Serv.

Brugmann, Karl. Kurze Vergleichende Grammatik der Indogermanischen Sprachen. (Ger). 1969. Repr. of 1904 ed. 100.00x (ISBN 3-11-000179-9). De Gruyter.

Brugmann, Karl & Delbrueck, Berthold. Grundriss der Vergleichenden Grammatik der Indogermanischen Sprachen, 5 vols. (Ger). 1970. Repr. of 1893 ed. 576.00x (ISBN 3-11-000180-2). De Gruyter.

Conant, Jonathan B. Cochran's German Review Grammar. 3rd ed. LC 73-21535. 384p. 1974. text ed. 14.95 (ISBN 0-13-139501-7). P-H.

Condoyannis, George E. Scientific German. LC 77-16570. 174p. 1978. pap. 8.50 (ISBN 0-88275-644-3). Krieger.

Curme, G. O. A Grammar of the German Language. 1980. Repr. of 1905 ed. lib. bdg. 50.00 (ISBN 0-89760-112-2). Telegraph Bks.

Curme, George O. Grammar of the German Language. 2nd ed. 1952. 30.00 (ISBN 0-8044-0113-6). Ungar.

--A Grammar of the German Language, 2 vols. Set. 250.00 (ISBN 0-87968-213-2). Gordon Pr.

Drath, V. H. Was Wollen Die Deutschen: 21 Zeitgenossen. 1970. text ed. 8.95 (ISBN 0-02-330100-7). Macmillan.

Duden, R., ed. Duden-Grammatik. 2nd rev. ed. (Der Grosse Duden: Vol. 4). 18.50 (ISBN 3-4110-0914-4). Adler.

Duff, Charles & Freund, Richard. The Basis & Essentials of German. (Quality Paperback: No. 248). 117p. 1972. pap. 1.75 (ISBN 0-8226-0248-2). Littlefield.

Duff, Charles & Stamford, Paul. German for Beginners. 2nd rev. ed. 1960. pap. 3.95 (ISBN 0-06-463217-2, EH 217, EH). Har-Row.

Eggeling, H. F. Dictionary of Modern German Prose Usage. 1961. 29.00x (ISBN 0-19-864110-9). Oxford U Pr.

Evans, M. Blakemore, et al. Shorter College German. 3rd ed. LC 56-5843. (Illus.). 1956. text ed. 12.95x (ISBN 0-89197-403-2); pap. text ed. 6.95x (ISBN 0-89197-404-0). Irvington.

Flygt, Sten G. Review of German. 1959. 6.95x (ISBN 0-393-09526-6). Norton.

German in Twenty Lessons. rev. ed. (Cortina Method Language Ser). (Illus.). 6.95 (ISBN 0-385-00074-X). Doubleday.

German Verbs Simplified. (Hugo's Language Courses Ser.: No. 551). 1970. pap. 1.50 (ISBN 0-8226-0551-1). Littlefield.

Goedsche, C. R. & Spann, Meno. German Oral Practice: Student Manual. (Orig.). 1968. pap. text ed. 3.95x (ISBN 0-442-22024-3); tapes 65.00 (ISBN 0-442-22030-8). Van Nos Reinhold.

Greenfield, Eric V. German Grammar. 3rd ed. (Orig., Ger.). 1968. pap. 4.95 (ISBN 0-06-460034-3, CO 34, COS). Har-Row.

Gschossman, Elke. German Grammar. (Schaum Outline Ser.). 256p. 1975. pap. text ed. 3.95 (ISBN 0-07-025090-1, SP). McGraw.

Hammond, Robin. A German Reference Grammar. 250p. 1981. 10.50 (ISBN 0-19-912048-X). Oxford U Pr.

Held, Karl. Verbum Ohne Pronominales Subjekt in der Aelteren Deutschen Sprache. 1967. Repr. of 1903 ed. 14.00 (ISBN 0-384-22176-9); pap. 11.00 (ISBN 0-384-22175-0). Johnson Repr.

Johnson, Charles B. Harrap's New German Grammar. 1971. pap. text ed. 13.50x (ISBN 0-245-52989-6). Intl Ideas.

Kahn, Lothar & Hook, Donald D. Intermediate Conversational German. 3rd ed. 1973. text ed. 11.95 (ISBN 0-442-22915-1); 18 tapes 80.00 (ISBN 0-442-22919-4). D Van Nostrand.

Kind, Uwe & Meyer, Ursula. O Suzanne, Ja Konjugier Fur Mich! (gr. 7-12). 1980. pap. text ed. 4.25 (ISBN 0-88345-359-2); cassettes 25.00 (ISBN 0-686-66262-8). Regents Pub.

Konrad, Roselinde. Essentials of German Grammar in Review. 1977. pap. text ed. 8.50 scp (ISBN 0-06-043751-0, HarpC). Har-Row.

--Reviewing German Grammar & Building Vocabulary. LC 80-6238. 415p. 1981. pap. text ed. 18.75 (ISBN 0-8191-1605-X). U Pr of Amer.

Krohn, Dieter. Verbinhalt und Semantische Merkmale. (Goteborger Germanistische Forschungen: No. 13). 172p. (Ger.). 1976. pap. text ed. 10.00x (ISBN 91-7346-015-X). Humanities.

Law, Marie H. How to Read German. 1966. pap. 4.95x (ISBN 0-393-04144-1, NortonC). Norton.

Lederer, Herbert. Basic German: An Introduction. (gr. 11 up). 1966. text ed. 7.95x (ISBN 0-684-13672-4, ScribC); tapes avail. (ISBN 0-685-20281-X). Scribner.

Lederer, Herbert, et al, eds. Reference Grammar of the German Language. LC 69-17352. 1969. text ed. 15.95x (ISBN 0-684-41329-9, ScribC). Scribner.

Lloyd, Albert L. & Schmitt, Albert R. Deutsch Und Deutschland Heute. (Illus., Ger.). 1967. text ed. 13.95x (ISBN 0-442-23325-6); tapes 90.00 (ISBN 0-442-23327-2). Van Nos Reinhold.

--Ubungsbuch Fuer Deutsch und Deutschland Heute. (Ger). 1967. pap. text ed. 2.50x (ISBN 0-442-23326-4); tapes 15.00 (ISBN 0-442-23328-0). Van Nos Reinhold.

Logan, Gerald E. Deutsch: Zweite Stufe. LC 76-51773. 1977. text ed. 8.95 (ISBN 0-88377-063-6); tchrs' manual 3.95 (ISBN 0-88377-083-0). Newbury Hse.

Lohnes, Walter & Strothman, F. W. German: A Structural Approach. 2nd ed. (Illus.). 500p. 1973. text ed. 11.95x (ISBN 0-393-09345-X); tchr's ed. 3.95x (ISBN 0-393-09360-3); study guide 4.45x (ISBN 0-393-09352-2). Norton.

Lohnes, Walter F. & Strothmann, F. W. German: A Structural Approach. 3rd ed. 1980. text ed. 13.95x (ISBN 0-393-95059-X); tchrs'. manual avail. (ISBN 0-393-95068-9); study guide 4.95x (ISBN 0-393-95064-6). Norton.

Madrigal, Margarita & Meyer, Ursula. Madrigal's Magic Key to German. LC 66-20943. 1966. 8.95 (ISBN 0-385-03638-8). Doubleday.

Manton, J. D. Introduction to Theological German. 1973. pap. 2.95 (ISBN 0-8028-1514-6). Eerdmans.

Medges, G. A. Der? Die? Das? The Gender of German. LC 74-34516. 1975. text ed. 6.00 (ISBN 0-682-48189-0, University). Exposition.

Meyer, Ursula & Wolfson, Alice. Workbook in Everyday German. (gr. 9-10). 1976. pap. text ed. 3.95 (ISBN 0-88345-277-4). Regents Pub.

Moeller, Jack R., et al. Blickpunkt Deutschland. LC 76-190308. 416p. 1973. text ed. 16.76 (ISBN 0-395-13690-3, 2-37474); instr. ed. 16.52 (ISBN 0-395-14218-0, 2-37475); workbook 4.24 (ISBN 0-395-14212-1). HM.

Moritz, Karl P. ABC-Buch Kinderlogik, 2 vols. Guenther, Horst, ed. (Ger.). Repr. of 1793 ed. text ed. 50.70 (ISBN 3-458-04938-X, Pub. by Insel Verlag Germany). Suhrkamp.

Mueller, Hugo. Deutsch, Erstes Buch. (gr. 9-12). 1958-69. student tests 2.95 (ISBN 0-685-22893-2, 82298); tchrs' key to student tests 1.50 (ISBN 0-685-22894-0, 82302); 17 tapes 150.00 (ISBN 0-685-22896-7, 82306, 82348). wall charts 126.00 (ISBN 0-686-66599-6, 82612). Glencoe.

--Deutsch-Erstes Buch, 2 pts. Incl. Pt. 1. 1960-68. tchrs' key 1.50 (ISBN 0-685-22897-5, 82318); tchrs' manual 2.95 (ISBN 0-685-22898-3, 82300); wkbk. 1.95 (ISBN 0-685-22899-1, 82328, 82320, 82322); Pt. 2. 1967-69. 5.95 (ISBN 0-685-22900-9, 82324); tchrs' key 2.95 (ISBN 0-685-22901-7, 82326); wkbk. 1.95 (ISBN 0-685-22902-5, 82360); tapes 120.00 (ISBN 0-685-22903-3, 82330). (gr. 9-12). 1968. Glencoe.

--Deutsch-Zweites Buch. rev ed. 1963-69. tchr's key 1.95 (ISBN 0-685-22890-8, 82310); wkbk. 1.95 (ISBN 0-685-22891-6, 32308); tapes 150.00 (ISBN 0-685-22892-4, 82360, 82370, 82312). Glencoe.

Pfeffer, J., et al. Basic Spoken German Grammar. LC 73-8875. (Illus.). 384p. 1974. text ed. 14.95 (ISBN 0-13-061994-9); tapes o.p. 150.00 (ISBN 0-13-062182-X); wkbk. & guide to tapes 6.95 (ISBN 0-13-062000-9). P-H.

Pink, Heinz-Guenther. Communicate in German Instantly. (Illus., Orig., Prog. Bk.). 1973. pap. 4.95 (ISBN 0-915946-06-8); cassettes 4.95 (ISBN 0-685-28750-5). Pink Hse Pub.

Politzer, Robert L. Speaking German. LC 69-10287. 1969. text ed. 10.95 (ISBN 0-13-825794-9). P-H.

Reh, A. M. Continuing German: A Bridge to Literature. 1971. text ed. 15.95 (ISBN 0-07-051698-7, C); tchr's manual 3.95 (ISBN 0-07-051711-8); tapes 225.00 (ISBN 0-07-051699-5); demonstration tape o.p. 3.95 (ISBN 0-07-051712-6). McGraw.

Rehder, Helmut. Deutsch: Verstehen Und Sprechen. 1970. text ed. 13.28 (ISBN 0-03-082751-5, HoltC); tchr's ed. 7.60, 66.00 cards., 136.00 projectuals., 10.60 wkbk (ISBN 0-03-083005-2). HR&W.

Rehder, Helmut & Twaddell, H. German. rev. ed. (gr. 9-12). 1958. text ed. 7.95 (ISBN 0-03-016170-3); tapes s.p. 140.00 (ISBN 0-685-12256-5). HR&W.

Rogers, R. Max, et al. Scenes from German Drama: A Review Grammar & Reader. (Illus.). 1978. text ed. 15.50 scp (ISBN 0-06-045546-2, HarpC). Har-Row.

Rognebakke, M. & Driessle, H. Warum Nicht Auf Deutsch, Vol. 1. rev. ed. 1970. 7.24 (ISBN 0-685-65902-X); tchr's ed. 8.80 (ISBN 0-02-826960-8). Glencoe.

Roseler, Robert O. German in Review. 4th ed. (gr. 9-12). 1967. text ed. 9.95 (ISBN 0-03-061735-9, HoltC). HR&W.

Roseler, Robert O. & Reichard, Joseph R. German Grammar Workbook. 1956. pap. text ed. 2.95x (ISBN 0-89197-533-0). Irvington.

Sandberg, Bengt. Die Neutrale - (E) N Ableitung der Deutschen Gegenwartssprache: Zu Dem Aspekt der Lexikalisierung Beiden Verbalsubstantiven. (Goteberg Germanistische Forschungen: No. 15). (Ger.). 1976. pap. text ed. 20.00x (ISBN 91-7346-022-2). Humanities.

Schaeublin, Peter. Probleme des adnominalen Attributs in der deutschen Sprache der Gegenwart. LC 70-174176. (Studia Linguistica Germanica). 1972. 40.00x (ISBN 3-1100-3346-1). De Gruyter.

Schinnerer, Otto P. & Schinnerer-Tovey, B. Beginning German. rev. ed. (Illus.). 1956. text ed. 8.95x (ISBN 0-02-406890-X). Macmillan.

Schmidt, Gerard F. Hoer Gut Zu: A Beginning German Audio-Lingual Reader. 1964. text ed. 11.95x (ISBN 0-02-407700-3). Macmillan.

Sembdner, H. Die Berliner Abendblatter H. V Kleista: Ihre Quellen und Redaktion. viii, 402p. 1970. 50.00 (ISBN 90-272-0003-3). Benjamins North Am.

Sharp, Stanley L. & Strothmann. German Reading Grammar. rev. ed. 1955. text ed. 15.50 (ISBN 0-470-00554-8). Wiley.

Solle, Reinhold. Sprechbewegung und Sprachstruktur: Morphographisch-Strukturelle Ableitungs Herarchie Eines Modell-Universume der Sprechdewegung und Sprachstruktur. (Janua Linguarum, Ser. Maior: No. 94). 296p. (Orig.). 1975. text ed. 69.00x (ISBN 90-2793-297-2). Mouton.

Sparks, Kimberly & Van Horn, Vail. German in Review. 1967. text ed. 14.95 (ISBN 0-15-529590-X, HC); tapes 75.00 (ISBN 0-15-529591-8, HC). HarBraceJ.

Stern, Guy & Bleiler, Everett F. Essential German Grammar. (Orig.). 1963. pap. 1.75 (ISBN 0-486-20422-7). Dover.

--Essential German Grammar. LC 74-28533. 1961. lib. bdg. 8.50x (ISBN 0-88307-576-8). Gannon.

Strutz, Henry B. Two Hundred & One German Verbs Fully Conjugated in All the Tenses. LC 63-16872. (Orig.). 1964. pap. text ed. 2.95 (ISBN 0-8120-0210-5). Barron.

Tilton, Helga, ed. Deutsch Mit Emil. 1980. pap. text ed. 5.95x (ISBN 0-393-95111-1). Norton.

Von Hofe, H. Der. Anfang. 3rd ed. (Ger). 1968. text ed. 16.95 (ISBN 0-03-068775-6, HoltC) (ISBN 0-03-068785-3). HR&W.

Weimar, Karl S. & Hoffmeister, Werner G. Practice & Progress: A German Grammar for Review & Reference. 1970. text ed. 15.95x (ISBN 0-471-00619-X); tapes avail. (ISBN 0-471-00621-1). Wiley.

--Practice & Progress: A German Grammar for Review & Reference. 1970. text ed. 15.95x (ISBN 0-471-00619-X); tapes avail. (ISBN 0-471-00621-1). Wiley.

Wellek, Susanne. Lachen und Lernen. enl. ed. LC 60-9145. text ed. 8.50 (ISBN 0-8044-0796-7). Ungar.

Wells, G. A. & Rowley, B. A. Barron's Card Guide to German Grammar. 1963. pap. text ed. 1.75 (ISBN 0-8120-5044-4). Barron.

Werba, H. Basic Conversational German: An Approach to Terms of Order & Value. (gr. 9 up). 1969. text ed. 18.95 (ISBN 0-03-073400-2, HoltC). HR&W.

Wilmanns, Wilhelm. Deutsche Grammatik: Gotisch, Alt-, Mittel-, und Neuhochdeutsch. 3rd ed. (Ger). 1967. Repr. of 1930 ed. 224.00x (ISBN 3-11-000315-5). De Gruyter.

Wilson, Eric. Es Geht Weiter. 1977. pap. text ed. 11.95 scp (ISBN 0-06-047145-X, HarpC). Har-Row.

Wilson, P. G. Teach Yourself German Grammar. (Teach Yourself Ser.). pap. 3.95 (ISBN 0-679-10175-6). McKay.

Wuethrich, Hans U. Das Konsonantensystem der deutschen Hochsprache. (Studia Linguistica Germanica, Vol. 11). 203p. 1974. 38.25x (ISBN 3-11-004735-7). De Gruyter.

Zieglschmid, A. J. Zur Entwicklung der Perfektumschreibung im Deutschen. Repr. of 1929 ed. pap. 6.00 (ISBN 0-527-00752-8). Kraus Repr.

Zimmermann, Jon, et al. Contemporary German Life. new ed. (Illus.). 384p. 1975. text ed. 14.95 (ISBN 0-07-072835-6, C); instructor's manual 4.95 (ISBN 0-07-072836-4). McGraw.

GERMAN LANGUAGE–GRAMMAR, COMPARATIVE

Bellman, Guenter. Slavoteutonica: Lexikalische Untersuchungen Zum Slawisch-deutschen Sprachkontakt Im Ostmitteldeutschen. (Studia Linguistica Germanica Ser.: Vol. 4). (Illus.). 356p. 1971. 51.75x (ISBN 3-11-003344-5). De Gruyter.

Kufner, Herbert. Grammatical Structures of English & German. LC 62-19625. (Orig.). 1962. pap. 5.00x (ISBN 0-226-45678-1). U of Chicago Pr.

Moulton, William G. Sounds of English & German. LC 62-20024. (Orig.). 1962. pap. 5.50x (ISBN 0-226-54309-9). U of Chicago Pr.

Van Coetsem, Frans & Kufner, Herbert L., eds. Toward a Grammar of Proto-Germanic. 338p. 1973. 42.50x (ISBN 3-484-10160-1). Intl Pubns Serv.

GERMAN LANGUAGE–GRAMMAR, HISTORICAL

Bouma, Lowell. The Semantics of the Modal Auxiliaries in Contemporary German. (Janua Linguarum Ser. Practica: No. 146). 1973. pap. text ed. 28.25x (ISBN 90-279-2390-6). Mouton.

Kehrein, Joseph. Grammatik der Deutschen Sprache des 15. Bis 17. Jahrhunderts, 3 vols. 2nd ed. (Ger.). 1968. 88.00 set (ISBN 3-500-21970-5, 7430, Pub. by Saendig - Walluf). French & Eur.

Sonderegger, Stefan. Althochdeutsche Sprache & Literatur: Eine Einfuehrung in das aelteste Deutsch. Darstellung & Grammatik. (Sammlung Goeschen, Vol. 8005). 272p. 1974. 10.50x (ISBN 3-11-004559-1). De Gruyter.

GERMAN LANGUAGE–HISTORY

Anderson, Robert, ed. Semasia: Beitrage zur Germanisch-Romanischen Sprachforschung, Band 5. (Orig.). 1980. pap. text ed. 19.50x (ISBN 0-391-02047-1). Humanities.

Bahnick, Karen R. The Determination of Stages in the Historical Development of the Germanic Languages by Morphological Criteria: An Evaluation. (Janua Linguarum Ser. Practica: No. 139). 1973. pap. text ed. 40.75x (ISBN 90-2792-389-2). Mouton.

Blackall, Eric A. The Emergence of German As a Literary Language, 1700-1775. 2nd ed. LC 77-14702. 1978. 25.00x (ISBN 0-8014-1170-X). Cornell U Pr.

Bruder, Reinhold. Die Germanische Frau im Lichte der Runeninschriften und der antiken Historiographie. LC 73-75482. (Quellen und Forschungen Zur Sprach - und Kulturgeschichte der Germanischen Voelker N. F. 57 181). 192p. 1974. 55.00x (ISBN 3-11-004152-9). De Gruyter.

Chambers, W. Walker & Wilkie, John R. A Short History of the German Language. 1970. pap. 10.95x (ISBN 0-416-18220-8). Methuen Inc.

Dill, Marshall, Jr. Germany: A Modern History. rev. ed. LC 60-13891. (History of the Modern World Ser). (Illus.). 1970. 10.00x (ISBN 0-472-07101-7). U of Mich Pr.

Goetti, Ernst. Die Gotischen Bewegungsverben: Ein Bietrag Zur Erforschung Des Gotischen Wortschatzes Mit Einem Asblick Auf Wulfilas Uebersetungstechink. LC 73-88296. (Ger.). 1974. 53.50x (ISBN 3-11-004331-9). De Gruyter.

Gruenert, Horst. Sprache und Politik: Untersuchungen zum Sprachgebrauch der "Paulskirche". LC 74-80634. (Studia Linguistica Germanica Vol. 10). 1974. 45.00x (ISBN 3-11-003609-6). De Gruyter.

Munske, Horst H. Der Germanische Rechtswortschatz im Bereich der Missetaten, Philologische und sprachgeographische Untersuchungen Vol. 1: Die Terminologie der aelteren westgermanischen Rechtsquellen. LC 72-76055. (Studia Linguista Germanica, Vol. 8, 1). 335p. 1973. 48.75x (ISBN 3-11-003578-2). De Gruyter.

Pasley, Malcolm. Germany: A Companion to German Studies. 1976. pap. 19.95x (ISBN 0-416-83540-6). Methuen Inc.

Richardson, Peter N. German-Romance Contact: Name-Giving in Walser Settlements. LC 74-79043. (Amsterdamer Publikationen Zur Sprache und Literatur: No. 15). 372p. (Orig.). 1974. pap. text ed. 34.25x (ISBN 90-6203-221-4). Humanities.

Russ, Charles V. Historical German Phonology & Morphology. (History of the German Language Ser.). (Illus.). 1979. 28.50x (ISBN 0-19-815727-4). Oxford U Pr.

Waterman, John T. A History of the German Language. rev. ed. LC 66-13542. (Illus.). 280p. 1976. text ed. 18.50 (ISBN 0-295-95510-4). U of Wash Pr.

GERMAN LANGUAGE–IDIOMS, CORRECTIONS, ERRORS

Duden, R. Duden-Stilwoerterbuch. 5th rev. ed. (Der Grosse Duden: Vol. 2). 18.50 (ISBN 0-685-05215-X). Adler.

Duden, R., ed. Duden-Hauptschwierigkeiten der Deutschen Sprache. (Der Grosse Duden: Vol. 9). 18.50 (ISBN 3-4110-0919-5). Adler.

Engeroff, K. & Lovelace-Kaeufer, C. English-German Dictionary of Idioms. 18.75 (ISBN 3-1900-6217-X). Adler.

Jacobs, Noah J. Embarrassing Moments in German & How to Avoid Them. LC 56-7180. (gr. 11-12). 6.00 (ISBN 0-8044-0208-6); pap. 3.95 (ISBN 0-8044-6309-3). Ungar.

Rechtschaffen, Bernard & Marck, Louis. Two Thousand & One German & English Idioms: 2001 Deutsche und Englische Idiome. Date not set. pap. 9.95 (ISBN 0-8120-0474-4). Barron.

Schaeublin, Peter. Probleme des adnominalen Attributs in der deutschen Sprache der Gegenwart. LC 70-174176. (Studia Linguistica Germanica). 1972. 40.00x (ISBN 3-1100-3346-1). De Gruyter.

Taylor, Ronald J. & Gottschalk, W. German-English Dictionary of Idioms. 27.50 (ISBN 3-19-006216-1). Adler.

GERMAN LANGUAGE–ORTHOGRAPHY AND SPELLING

Duden, R., ed. Duden-Hauptschwierigkeiten der Deutschen Sprache. (Der Grosse Duden: Vol. 9). 18.50 (ISBN 3-4110-0919-5). Adler.

--Duden-Rechtschreibung. 16th rev. ed. (Der Grosse Duden: Vol. 1). 1971. 18.50 (ISBN 3-4110-0911-X). Adler.

GERMAN LANGUAGE–PHONETICS

Moulton, William G. Sounds of English & German. LC 62-20024. (Orig.). 1962. pap. 5.50x (ISBN 0-226-54309-9). U of Chicago Pr.

Veith, W. H. Intersystemare Phonologie: Exemplarisch an diastratisch-Diatopischen Differenzierungen im Deutschen. x, 310p. 1972. 53.00x (ISBN 3-11-004350-5). De Gruyter.

GERMAN LANGUAGE–PROGRAMMED INSTRUCTION

Berlitz, Charles. German Step by Step. LC 78-73611. 1979. 9.95 (ISBN 0-89696-027-7). Everest Hse.

Clausing, Gerhard & Mueller, Klaus I. An Individualized Instruction Program in Basic German. 3rd ed. 1980. pap. text ed. 5.95x (ISBN 0-394-32434-X, RanC). Random.

Foreign Service Institute. Programmatic German, 2 vols. (Ger.). 1978. Vol. 1. 9 audio cassettes incl. 115.00x (ISBN 0-88432-017-0, G140-G147); Vol. 2. 8 audio cassettes incl. 98.00x (ISBN 0-88432-018-9, G151-G158). J Norton Pubs.

FSI German: A Programmed Introduction. (Prog. Bk.). 1971. pap. 9.75x (ISBN 0-686-10720-9); 22 cassettes 132.00x (ISBN 0-686-10721-7). Intl Learn Syst.

Meinel, Hans. A Course in Scientific German. 248p. 1972. 15.00 (ISBN 3-1900-1103-6). Adler.

Rosenberg, Joseph. German: How to Speak & Write It. LC 63-358. 1962. lib. bdg. 11.50x (ISBN 0-88307-597-0). Gannon.

Ruplin, Ferdinand A. & Russell, John R. Basic German: A Programmed Course. 1969. pap. text ed. 3.95x (ISBN 0-89197-535-7); access pen 0.65 (ISBN 0-685-52726-3). Irvington.

Sandberg, Karl C. & Wende, John R. German for Reading: A Programmed Approach. 1973. pap. text ed. 14.95 (ISBN 0-13-354019-7). P-H.

GERMAN LANGUAGE–PRONUNCIATION

Duden, R., ed. Duden-Ausspracheworterbuch. (Der Grosse Duden: Vol. 6). 18.50 (ISBN 3-4110-0916-0). Adler.

Krech, Hans. Woerterbuch der Deutschen Aussprache. 2nd ed. 549p. 1967. 19.95 (ISBN 0-686-56643-2, M-7033). French & Eur.

GERMAN LANGUAGE–READERS

see also German Language–Textbooks for Children

Apsler, Alfred. Sie Kamen aus Deutschen Landen. (Orig., Ger.). 1962. pap. text ed. 3.95x (ISBN 0-89197-408-3). Irvington.

Blume, Bernhard & Schmidt, Henry J. German Literature: Texts & Contexts. 416p. 1973. text ed. 13.95 (ISBN 0-07-006187-4, C). McGraw.

Boeninger, Hildegard R. & Pietschmann, D., eds. Ich Lausche Dem Leben. (Orig., Ger.). 1963. pap. 6.95x (ISBN 0-393-09558-4, NortonC). Norton.

Boll, Heinrich. Nicht Nur Zur Weignachtszeit: Der Mann Mit Den Messern. Berger, Dorothea, ed. (Ger). 1959. pap. text ed. 2.25x (ISBN 0-442-22020-0). Van Nos Reinhold.

Brecht, Bertolt. Kalendergeschichten. Hoffman, Charles W., ed. (Ger). 1960. pap. 3.45x (ISBN 0-393-09552-5, NortonC). Norton.

Browning, Robert M., ed. Freude am Lesen: A German Reader. (Orig., Ger.). 1964. pap. text ed. 7.95x (ISBN 0-89197-180-7). Irvington.

Cherubim, Dieter, ed. Sprachwandel: Reader Zur diachronischen Sprachwissenschaft. (Grundlagen der Kommunikation). x, 362p. 1975. pap. 17.75x (ISBN 3-11-004330-0). De Gruyter.

Crossgrove, Hannelore & Crossgrove, William C. Graded German Reader. 2nd ed. 1978. pap. text ed. 8.95x (ISBN 0-669-01533-4). Heath.

Dilber, Edward. Meisterwerke der Deutschen Sprache. 1970. text ed. 7.50 (ISBN 0-685-55621-2, 30169). Phila Bk Co.

Diller, Edward & Wishard, Armin, eds. Spiel und Sprache. (Illus., Orig.). 1971. pap. text ed. 4.95x (ISBN 0-393-09545-2). Norton.

Drath, V. H. & Graf, O. Typisch Deutsch. rev. ed. (Ger). (gr. 10-12). 1969. text ed. 9.95 (ISBN 0-03-080005-6, HoltC). HR&W.

Durrenmatt, Friedrich. Der Besuch der Alten Dame. Ackermann, Paul K., ed. LC 60-3863. (Ger). (gr. 11-12). 1960. pap. text ed. 7.20 (ISBN 0-395-04089-2). HM.

--Physiker. Helbling, Robert E., ed. (Illus., Orig., Ger.). 1965. pap. 4.95x (ISBN 0-19-500908-8). Oxford U Pr.

--Der Richter und Sein Henker. Gillis, William & Neumaier, J. J., eds. 1964. pap. text ed. 6.95 (ISBN 0-395-04499-5). HM.

--Der Verdacht. Gillis, William, ed. (gr. 9-12). 1964. pap. text ed. 7.20 (ISBN 0-395-04500-2). HM.

Evans, M. Blakemore, et al. Shorter College German. 3rd ed. LC 56-5843. (Illus.). 1956. text ed. 12.95x (ISBN 0-89197-403-2); pap. text ed. 6.95x (ISBN 0-89197-404-0). Irvington.

Fabrizius, Peter. Lacht am Besten. Bell, Clair H., ed. LC 57-5200. (Illus., Ger.). 1957. text ed. 14.00x (ISBN 0-89197-262-5). Irvington.

Fleissner, Otto S. & Fleissner, E. M., eds. Kunst der Prosa. 1941. text ed. 14.00x (ISBN 0-89197-260-9); pap. text ed. 4.95x (ISBN 0-89197-261-7). Irvington.

Flygt, Sten G. Review of German. 1959. 6.95x (ISBN 0-393-09526-6). Norton.

Foltin, Lore B. & Heinen, Hubert, eds. Paths to German Poetry: An Introductory Anthology. (Orig., Ger.). 1969. pap. text ed. 11.50 scp (ISBN 0-06-042112-6, HarpC). Har-Row.

Frisch, Max. Biedermann und Die Brandstifter. Ackermann, Paul K., ed. (gr. 10-12). 1963. pap. text ed. 7.20 (ISBN 0-395-04090-6). HM.

--Homo Faber. Ackermann, Paul K., ed. LC 72-9379. 300p. (Orig.). 1973. pap. text ed. 8.05 (ISBN 0-395-14402-7). HM.

Gewehr, Wolf & Von Schmitt, Wolff A. Reading German in the Humanities. 1972. pap. text ed. 5.95x (ISBN 0-442-22456-7). Van Nos Reinhold.

--Reading German in the Social Sciences. 1972. pap. text ed. 5.95x (ISBN 0-442-22455-9). Van Nos Reinhold.

Glaettli, Walter. Vierte Kurve, a Graded Reader. (Orig.). 1962. pap. text ed. 2.95x (ISBN 0-442-22022-7). Van Nos Reinhold.

Goedsche, C. R. & Glaettli, Walter E. Cultural Graded Readers: Elementary Ser, 5 vols. Incl. Sutter (ISBN 0-442-22025-1); Steuben (ISBN 0-442-32026-4); Carl Schurz (ISBN 0-442-22027-8); Einstein (ISBN 0-442-22028-6). (Ger.). 1963. pap. text ed. 2.95x ea. Van Nos Reinhold.

Hill, Claude. Lesen Mit Gewinn: A Vocabulary-Building German Reader. 1972. pap. text ed. 11.50 scp (ISBN 0-06-042824-4, HarpC). Har-Row.

Huch, Ricarda. Der Letzte Sommer. Cunz, Dieter, ed. (Ger). 1963. pap. 2.95x (ISBN 0-393-09603-3, NortonC). Norton.

Kaestner, Erich. Kleine Grenzverkehr. LC 56-9989. 4.95 (ISBN 0-8044-0241-8); pap. 2.95 (ISBN 0-8044-6335-2). Ungar.

Kafka, Franz. Die Verwandlung. Hoover, Marjorie L., ed. (Ger). 1960. pap. 4.95x (ISBN 0-393-09533-9, NortonC). Norton.

Kastner, Erich. Emil und die Detektive. (Easy Readers, B). 1979. pap. 3.75 (ISBN 0-88436-297-3). EMC.

Kauf, Robert & McCluney, Daniel C. Proben Deutscher Prosa. 1970. text ed. 6.95x (ISBN 0-393-09911-3, NortonC); taped exercises 1.25x (ISBN 0-393-09934-2); free tchrs. ed. (ISBN 0-393-09985-7); 85.00tapes (ISBN 0-393-99117-2). Norton.

Keeton, Kenneth E., ed. Scherz und Ernst: A German Intermediate Oral Reader. LC 67-15832. (Orig., Ger.). 1967. pap. text ed. 5.95x (ISBN 0-89197-389-3). Irvington.

Kritsch, Erna & Schlimbach, Alice, eds. Moderne Erzahlungen Fur Die Unter - Und Mittelstufe. (Illus., Orig., Ger.). 1964. pap. text ed. 8.95 (ISBN 0-13-594291-8). P-H.

Kurz, Edmund P. & Ruhleder, Karl H., eds. Probleme Unserer Zeit. LC 72-130785. (Orig., Ger.). 1971. pap. text ed. 4.95x (ISBN 0-89197-359-1). Irvington.

Law, Marie H. How to Read German. 1966. pap. 4.95x (ISBN 0-393-04144-1, NortonC). Norton.

Lloyd, Albert L. & Schmitt, Albert R. Deutsch Und Deutschland Heute. (Illus., Ger.). 1967. text ed. 13.95x (ISBN 0-442-23325-6); tapes 90.00 (ISBN 0-442-23327-2). Van Nos Reinhold.

--Ubungsbuch Fuer Deutsch und Deutschland Heute. (Ger). 1967. pap. text ed. 2.50x (ISBN 0-442-23326-4); tapes 15.00 (ISBN 0-442-23328-0). Van Nos Reinhold.

Lohan, Robert. Living German Literature, Vol. 1. 4th ed. 12.00 (ISBN 0-8044-0326-0). Ungar.

Loram, Ian C. & Phelps, Leland R., eds. Querschnitt. (Orig., Ger.). 1962. pap. 6.95x (ISBN 0-393-09575-4, NortonC). Norton.

Martin, Hansborg. Kein Schnaps Fur Tamara. (Easy Readers, B). (Illus.). 1977. pap. text ed. 3.75 (ISBN 0-88436-282-5). EMC.

Meyer, Ursula & Wolfson, Alice. Abenteur in Deutschland. (Illus.). (gr. 9-12). 1976. pap. text ed. 3.50 (ISBN 0-88345-276-6). Regents Pub.

Mueller, Klaus A. & Hoppmann-Liecty, Susanne. Die Presse: A Reader & Workbook. 192p. 1976. pap. text ed. 8.95x (ISBN 0-669-92536-5). Heath.

Musil, Robert. Three Short Stories. Sacker, Hugh, ed. (Clarendon German Ser). 1970. pap. 7.95x (ISBN 0-19-832467-7). Oxford U Pr.

Neuse, Erna K., ed. Neue Deutsche Prosa. LC 68-30796. (Illus., Orig., Ger.). 1968. pap. text ed. 5.95x (ISBN 0-89197-315-X). Irvington.

Otten, Anna, ed. Mensch und Zeit: An Anthology of German Radio Plays. Incl. Knopfe. Aichinger, Ilse; Schildkrotenspiel. Von Der Vring, Georg; Verschlossene Tur. Von Hoerschelmann, Fred; Zinngeschrei. Eich, Gunter; Begegnung in Balkanexpress. Hildesheimer, Wolfgang; Nachtliches Gesprach Mit Einem Verachteten Menschen. Durrenmatt, Friedrich. LC 66-19203. (Illus., Orig., Ger.). 1966. pap. text ed. 5.95x (ISBN 0-89197-300-1); script 1.00x (ISBN 0-89197-301-X). Irvington.

Pfeffer, J. Alan. Kontexte. 1976. pap. 7.95x (ISBN 0-669-73940-5). Heath.

Phelps, Reginald H. & Stein, J. M. The German Heritage. 3rd ed. (gr. 9-12). 1970. text ed. 18.95 (ISBN 0-03-084162-3, HoltC). HR&W.

Rehder, Helmut & Twaddell, H. German. rev. ed. (gr. 9-12). 1958. text ed. 7.95 (ISBN 0-03-016170-3); tapes s.p. 140.00 (ISBN 0-685-12256-5). HR&W.

Rehder, Helmut, et al. Deutsch: Denken, Wissen und Kennen. (German Basic Courses: Level 4). (gr. 11-12). 1966. text ed. 10.98 (ISBN 0-03-051785-0). HR&W.

--Deutsch: Lesen und Denken. (German Basic Courses: Level 3). (gr. 10-12). 1964. text ed. 7.47 (ISBN 0-03-045340-2). HR&W.

Reinecker, Herbert. Der Kommissar Lasst Bitten. (Easy Readers, B). 1978. pap. text ed. 3.75 (ISBN 0-88436-291-4). EMC.

Remarque, Erich M. Drei Kameraden. Peebles, Waldo C., ed. 1957. pap. text ed. 5.95x (ISBN 0-442-22070-7). Van Nos Reinhold.

Richmond, Garland & Kirby, George. Auslese. (Illus., Ger.). 1968. pap. text ed. 12.95 (ISBN 0-07-052627-3, C). McGraw.

Rilke, Rainer M. Ewald Tragy. Halpert, Inge D., ed. LC 61-7867. (Orig., Ger.). 1961. pap. text ed. 2.95x (ISBN 0-89197-155-6). Irvington.

Rogers, R. Max, et al. Scenes from German Drama: A Review Grammar & Reader. (Illus.). 1978. text ed. 15.50 scp (ISBN 0-06-045546-2, HarpC). Har-Row.

Roseler, Robert & Duckert, Audrey, eds. Moderne Deutsche Erzaehler. 3rd ed. 1960. 7.95x (ISBN 0-393-09536-3, NortonC). Norton.

Salamon, George & Spielman, John P., Jr., eds. Quellen und Darstellungen: Aus Deutscher Geschichte. (Illus., Orig., Ger.). 1968. pap. 5.95x (ISBN 0-19-501044-2). Oxford U Pr.

Schaum, Konrad, ed. Deutsche Lyrik. (Orig., Ger.). 1963. pap. 2.95x (ISBN 0-393-09612-2, NortonC). Norton.

Schinnerer, Otto P. & Schinnerer-Tovey, B. Beginning German. rev. ed. (Illus.). 1956. text ed. 8.95x (ISBN 0-02-406890-X). Macmillan.

Schmidt, Gerard F. Hoer Gut Zu: A Beginning German Audio-Lingual Reader. 1964. text ed. 11.95x (ISBN 0-02-407700-3). Macmillan.

Sobel, Eli & Wagener, Hans, eds. Liebesspiele. (Orig.). 1970. pap. text ed. 3.95x (ISBN 0-19-501056-6). Oxford U Pr.

Spaethling, Robert & Weber, Eugene M., eds. Reader in German Literature. (Illus., Orig., Ger.). 1969. pap. text ed. 6.95x (ISBN 0-19-501060-4). Oxford U Pr.

Spann, Meno & Goedsche, Curt R. Deutsche Denker und Forscher. (Orig., Ger.). (gr. 10-12). 1967. pap. text ed. 8.50 (ISBN 0-13-204008-5). P-H.

Sparks, Kimberly & Reichmann, Edith. So ist es: A Contemporary Reader. (Illus.). 90p. 1972. pap. text ed. 6.95 (ISBN 0-15-581382-X, HC). HarBraceJ.

Steinhauer, Harry. Kulturlesebuch Fur Anfanger. 2nd ed. (Orig., Ger.). pap. text ed. 8.95 (ISBN 0-02-416850-5). Macmillan.

Tucholsky, Kurt. Eine Auswahl. Schwarz, Egon, ed. (Ger). 1963. pap. 1.25x (ISBN 0-393-09606-8, NortonC). Norton.

Vail, Van Horn & Sparks, Kimberly. Der Weg Zum Lesen. 2nd ed. 1974. pap. text ed. 9.95 (ISBN 0-15-595152-1, HC); tapes 100.00 (ISBN 0-15-595153-X). HarBraceJ.

Van D'Elden, Karl H. & Kirchow, Evelyn. Was Deutsche Lesen. 192p. (Orig., Ger.). 1973. text ed. 8.95 (ISBN 0-07-066935-X, C). McGraw.

Von Hofmannsthal, Hugo. Schwierige. Yates, W. E., ed. 1966. text ed. 7.50x (ISBN 0-521-05283-1). Cambridge U Pr.

Von Keyserling, Edward H. Abendliche Hauser. rev. ed. Hewitt, Theodore B., ed. (Illus., Ger.). 1961. pap. text ed. 3.95x (ISBN 0-89197-000-2). Irvington.

Waidson, H. M. German Short Stories, Vol. 1. 1900-1945, Vol. 2. 1945-1955, Vol. 3. 1955-1965. Vol. 1. text ed. 4.75x (ISBN 0-521-06717-0); Vol. 2. text ed. 5.25x (ISBN 0-521-06718-9); Vol. 3. text ed. 5.75x (ISBN 0-521-07180-1). Cambridge U Pr.

Wellek, Susanne. Lachen und Lernen. enl. ed. LC 60-9145. text ed. 8.50 (ISBN 0-8044-0796-7). Ungar.

Whitton, K. S. Advanced Nacherzahlungen. 1969. 4.10 (ISBN 0-08-013065-8); pap. 3.00 (ISBN 0-08-013064-X). Pergamon.

Wishard, Armin & Diller, Edward. Noch Einmal Spiel & Sprache. new ed. 1974. pap. text ed. 3.95x (ISBN 0-393-09328-X). Norton.

Zeydel, Edwin, ed. Graded German Reader for Beginners. 2nd ed. 1947. text ed. 9.95x (ISBN 0-89197-561-6); pap. text ed. 3.95x (ISBN 0-89197-562-4). Irvington.

Zobel, K. & Griffel, R. Kleine Deutsche Typologie. LC 69-11761. (gr. 10-12). 1970. pap. text ed. 8.95 (ISBN 0-03-069160-5, HoltC). HR&W.

GERMAN LANGUAGE–READERS (SCIENCE)

Gewehr, Wolf & Von Schmitt, Wolff A. Reading German in the Natural Sciences. 1972. pap. text ed. 5.95x (ISBN 0-442-22454-0). Van Nos Reinhold.

Richter, F. K., ed. German Readings in Science & Technology. 159p. 1948. 5.00 (ISBN 0-87532-153-4). Hendricks House.

GERMAN LANGUAGE–SELF-INSTRUCTION

see also German Language–Conversation and Phrase Books

Adams, J., et al. Teach Yourself German. (Teach Yourself Ser.). pap. 3.95 (ISBN 0-679-10174-8). McKay.

Adrienne. German in Thirty-Two Lessons. (Gimmick Ser.). 1979. 10.95 (ISBN 0-393-04527-7); pap. 5.95 (ISBN 0-393-04533-1). Norton.

Berger, Erich W. & Berger, Dorothea. New German Self-Taught. 396p. (Ger.). 1982. pap. text ed. 5.05 (ISBN 0-06-463615-1, EH 615, BN). Har-Row.

Berlitz Schools Of Languages. Self-Teacher: German. 1958. 8.95 (ISBN 0-448-01422-X). G&D.

Cherel, Albert O. Aleman Sin Esfuerzo. 11.95 (ISBN 0-685-10984-4); records 65.00 (ISBN 0-685-10985-2); of 3 cassettes 65.00 set (ISBN 0-685-10986-0). French & Eur.

--Alemao Sem Custo. 11.95 (ISBN 0-685-10987-9); records 65.00 (ISBN 0-685-10988-7); of 3 cassettes 65.00 set (ISBN 0-685-10989-5). French & Eur.

--Allemand Sans Peine. 11.95 (ISBN 0-685-10990-9). French & Eur.

--German Without Toil. 11.95 (ISBN 0-685-11213-6). French & Eur.

--Tedesco Senza Sforzo. 9.95 (ISBN 0-685-11582-8). French & Eur.

Condoyannis, George E. Scientific German. LC 77-16570. 174p. 1978. pap. 8.50 (ISBN 0-88275-644-3). Krieger.

Foreign Service Institute. Advanced German Course. 375p. 1980. plus 18 audio-cassettes 160.00x (ISBN 0-88432-043-X, G160). J Norton Pubs.

Frobenius, Lore. Ferner Als der Fernste Stern. 1968. pap. text ed. 3.00x (ISBN 0-435-38320-5). Heinemann Ed.

Jackson, Eugene & Geiger, Adolph. German Made Simple. LC 65-10615. pap. 3.50 (ISBN 0-385-00129-0, Made). Doubleday.

Martin, Genevieve A. & Bertram, Theodor. Living German. (YA) (gr. 6-12). 1956. 14.95, with 4 lp records conversation manual & dictionary (ISBN 0-517-00131-4). Crown.

Martin, Genevieve A. & Bertram, Theodore. Living German for Spanish-Speaking People. 14.95, with 4 lp records conversation manual & dictionary (ISBN 0-517-50822-2). Crown.

Rosenberg, Joseph. German: How to Speak & Write It. (Illus.). 1962. pap. 4.00 (ISBN 0-486-20271-2). Dover.

Stringer, L. Teach Yourself First German. (Teach Yourself Ser.). 1966. pap. 3.95 (ISBN 0-679-10171-3). McKay.

Wells, Sydney W. Teach Yourself More German. (Teach Yourself Ser.). pap. 4.95 (ISBN 0-679-10190-X). McKay.

GERMAN LANGUAGE–SLANG–DICTIONARIES

Juncker. Junckers Worterbuch German-American Slang. Seiffhart, Arthur, ed. 1968. 3.00 (ISBN 0-685-06570-7). Assoc Bk.

GERMAN LANGUAGE–SPOKEN GERMAN

Adrienne. Der Gimmick, Gesprochenes Deutsch. 1977. pap. 4.95 (ISBN 0-393-04480-7). Norton.

Dapper, Gertrude. German Names for German Dogs. LC 78-52184. (Other Dog Bks.). (Illus.). 1980. 9.95 (ISBN 0-87714-066-9). Denlingers.

Goeschel, Joachim. Strukturelle und instrumentalphonetische Untersuchungen zur gesprochenen Sprache. LC 72-76054. (Studia Linguistica Germanica Vol. 9). (Illus.). 1973. 51.00x (ISBN 3-11-003624-X). De Gruyter.

Hiller, Renatz. Spoken German. 1980. pap. text ed. 6.95x (ISBN 0-669-03022-8). Heath.

Krahe, Hans. Germanische Sprachwissenschaft, Vol. 2, Formenlehre. 7th ed. Meid, Wolfgang, ed. (Sammlung Goeschen, Vol. 780). (Ger). 1969. 6.25x (ISBN 3-1100-7640-3). De Gruyter.

Krahe, Hans & Meid, Wolfgang. Germanische Sprachwissenschaft, Vol. 1, Einleitung Und Lautlehre. 7th ed. (Sammlung Goeschen, Vol. 238). (Ger). 1969. 6.25x (ISBN 3-1100-7641-1). De Gruyter.

--Germanische Sprachwissenschaft, Vol. 3, Wortbildungslehre. (Sammlung Goeschen, Vols. 1218 & 1218A). (Ger). 1967. 6.25x (ISBN 3-11-006290-9). De Gruyter.

Waengler, Hans H. Atlas of German Speech Sounds. LC 73-30801. (Illus.). 53p. 1968. 15.00x (ISBN 0-8002-1220-7). Intl Pubns Serv.

GERMAN LANGUAGE–STUDY AND TEACHING

Behler, Ernst, et al. Studies in German in Memory of Robert L. Kahn. Eichner, Hans & Kahn, Lisa, eds. (Rice University Studies: Vol. 57, No. 4). 134p. 1971. pap. 3.25x (ISBN 0-89263-210-0). Rice Univ.

Berlitz, Charles. Passport to German. 1974. pap. 1.75 (ISBN 0-451-09444-1, E9444, Sig). NAL.

Bock, C. V. London German Studies One. 165p. 1980. 30.00x (ISBN 0-85457-095-0, Pub. by Inst Germanic Stud England). State Mutual Bk.

Bolesch, Herman O., et al. Guten Tag wie geht's: Bilder aus der Bundesrepublik Deutschland. (Illus.). 172p. 1972. 1.00 (ISBN 0-685-56863-6). Intl Film.

Braun, K., et al. Deutsch Als Fremdsprache: Ein Unterrichtswerk Fuer Auslaender. Incl. Pt. 1. Grundkurs. text ed. 9.25x lehrbuch (ISBN 3-12-554100-X); strukturuebungen und tests 7.55x (ISBN 3-12-554150-6); dialogische uebungen 8.20x (ISBN 3-12-554160-3); glossar deutsch-englisch 2.10x (ISBN 3-12-556110-8); sprechuebungen fuer das elektronische klassenzimmer, textband. 8.60x, 8 tonbaender, 9.5 cm/s, tapes, 405.00x (ISBN 3-12-554120-4); 4 schallplatten, lektion 1-19 des grundkurses, 17 cm, 33 1/3 rpm, records 16.95x (ISBN 3-12-554110-7); compact-cassette, lektion 1-19 des grundkurses 16.65x (ISBN 0-685-47448-8); 16 tonba 200.00x (ISBN 0-685-47449-6); Pt. 1B. Ergaenzungskurs. text ed. 9.25x lehrbuch (ISBN 3-12-554500-5); glossar deutsch-englisch 2.20x (ISBN 3-12-556510-3); schallplatten, records 16.65x (ISBN 0-685-47450-X); Pt. 2. Aufbaukurs. text ed. 9.25x lehrbuch (ISBN 3-12-554200-6); strukturuebungen und tests 7.25x (ISBN 0-686-66995-9); dialogische uebungen 8.60x (ISBN 0-686-66996-7); glossar deutsch-englisch 2.20x (ISBN 3-12-556210-4); 3 schallplatten, lektion 1-17 des aufbaukurses,17 cm, 33 1/3 rpm, records 16.65x (ISBN 3-12-554210-3); compact-cassette, lektion 1-17 des aufbaukurses 16.65x (ISBN 0-685-47451-8); 12 tonbaender, dialoge und hoer-sprechuebungen, 9.5 cm/s, tapes 221.00x (ISBN 3-12-990430-1). Schoenhof.

Brecht, Bertold. Brecht: Mutter Courage und Ihre Kinder. Sander, Volkmar, ed. (Illus., Ger.). (gr. 9-12). 1964. pap. text ed. 5.95x (ISBN 0-19-500835-9). Oxford U Pr.

Brown, James I. Efficient Reading Revised, Form A. pap. text ed. 9.95x 1972 ed. (ISBN 0-669-61036-4); pap. text ed. 9.95x 1962 ed. (ISBN 0-669-20370-X). Heath.

Clausing, Gerhard & Mueller, Klaus I. An Individualized Instruction Program in Basic German. 3rd ed. 1980. pap. text ed. 5.95x (ISBN 0-394-32434-X, RanC). Random.

Durrenmatt, Friedrich. Der Besuch der Alten Dame. Ackermann, Paul K., ed. LC 60-3863. (Ger). (gr. 11-12). 1960. pap. text ed. 7.20 (ISBN 0-395-04089-2). HM.

Feld, E. S., et al. Anfang und Fortschrift: An Introduction to German. 2nd ed. 1973. 11.95 (ISBN 0-685-42859-1); wkbk. 1.95 (ISBN 0-685-42860-5). Macmillan.

Frisch, Max. Biedermann und Die Brandstifter. Ackermann, Paul K., ed. (gr. 10-12). 1963. pap. text ed. 7.20 (ISBN 0-395-04090-6). HM.

Grebe, Paul, et al, eds. Deutscher Wortschatz - Deutsch eklart. (Illus.). 444p. 1971. 5.00x (ISBN 3-468-96100-6). Intl Film.

Grimm, Jacob & Grimm, Wilhelm. Deutsches Woerterbuch, 33 vols. 1973. Repr. 3150.00 (ISBN 0-685-30396-9). Adler.

Hammond, Robin T. Fortbildung in der deutschen Sprache. (Illus.). 210p. (Ger.). 1969. pap. text ed. 9.95x (ISBN 0-19-912003-X); Set. eight tapes 55.00x (ISBN 0-19-519704-6). Oxford U Pr.

Hepworth, J. B. & Rahde, H. F. Heiteres und Ernstes. 2nd ed. 1967. pap. text ed. 8.95 (ISBN 0-02-353700-0). Macmillan.

Hildebrandt, Reiner, ed. Summarium Heinrici, Vol. 1: Textkritische Ausgabe der ersten Fassung, Buch I-X. LC 73-75487. (Quellen und Forschungen Zur Sprach-und Kulturgeschichte der Germanischen Voelker N. F. 61). 1974. text ed. 110.00 (ISBN 3-11-003750-5). De Gruyter.

Instant German. pap. 2.50 (ISBN 0-686-31295-3). New Century.

Kahn, Robert L., ed. Studies in German in Memory of Andrew Louis. (Rice University Studies: Vol. 55, No. 3). 250p. 1969. pap. 3.25x (ISBN 0-89263-201-1). Rice Univ.

Kessler, Hermann. Deutsch Fuer Auslaender: Grundstufe. Incl. Pt. 1. Leichter Anfang (Lehrbuch) pap. text ed. 9.10x (ISBN 0-685-47452-6); Pt. 1a. Leichte Aufgaben (Arbeitsheft) pap. text ed. 4.55x (ISBN 0-685-47453-4); Part 1 & Part 1a in One Volume. text ed. 8.50x (ISBN 0-685-47454-2); Pt. 1b. Leichte Erzaelungen (Leseband) pap. text ed. 3.60x (ISBN 0-685-47455-0); Pt. 1c. Sprachlaboruebungen. 4.25x (ISBN 0-685-47456-9); Tonbaender fuer das Sprachlabor. 11 tapes, 9.5 cm/s 260.00x (ISBN 0-685-47457-7); Tonband mit Lehrbuchtexten. tape, 9.5 cm/s 29.25 (ISBN 0-685-47458-5). Schoenhof.

--Deutsch Fuer Auslaender: Mittelstufe. Incl. Pt. 2. Schneller Fortgang (Lehrbuch) pap. text ed. 9.10x (ISBN 0-685-47459-3); Pt. 2a. Kurze Uebungen (Arbeitsheft) 4.55x (ISBN 0-685-47460-7); Part 2 & Part 2a in One Volume. text ed. 8.50x (ISBN 0-685-47461-5); Pt. 2b. Kurze Geschichten (Leseband) pap. text ed. 3.60x (ISBN 0-685-47462-3); Pt. 2c. Sprachlaboruebungen. 4.25x (ISBN 0-685-47463-1); Tonbaender fuer das Sprachlabor. 10 tapes, 9.5 cm/s 260.00x (ISBN 0-685-47464-X); Tonband mit Lehrbuchtexten. tape 29.25x (ISBN 0-685-47465-8). Schoenhof.

--Deutsch Fuer Auslaender: Oberstufe. Incl. Pt. 3. Deutschlandkunde (Lehrbuch) pap. text ed. 11.70 (ISBN 0-685-47466-6); Pt. 3b. Moderne Dichtungen (Leseband) pap. text ed. 4.25x (ISBN 0-685-47467-4); tonband 29.25x, tape, 9.5 cm/s (ISBN 0-685-47468-2); Pt. 3d. Dichter unserer Zeit. pap. text ed. 4.25x (ISBN 0-685-47469-0); tonband 29.25x, tape, 9.5 cm/s (ISBN 0-685-47470-4). Schoenhof.

Kreitz, Helmut. Wir Lernen Deutsch: German for the First Year. 512p. 1974. text ed. 10.95x (ISBN 0-673-05276-1). Scott F.

Kurtz, John W. & Politzer, Heinz. German: A Comprehensive Course. rev. ed. 1966. tapes 135.00 (ISBN 0-393-99110-5). Norton.

Lohnes, Walter F. & Nollendorfs, Valters, eds. German Studies in the United States: Assessment & Outlook. LC 76-13346. 1976. 17.50 (ISBN 0-299-97009-4); pap. 7.50x (ISBN 0-299-97010-8). U of Wis Pr.

Maurer, Friedrich & Rupp, Heinz, eds. Deutsche Wortgeschichte, Vol. 2. 3rd rev. ed. (Grundriss der germanischen Philologie, Vol. 17 Pt. 2). vi, 698p. (Ger.). 1974. 84.50x (ISBN 3-11-003619-3). De Gruyter.

Meyer, Erika, et al. Elementary German. 3rd ed. 1975. text ed. 11.60 (ISBN 0-395-19866-6); tapes 99.25 (ISBN 0-395-19869-0); wkbk. 5.00 (ISBN 0-395-19868-2). HM.

Meyer, Ursula. German. (Blue Book Ser). pap. 1.25 (ISBN 0-671-18109-2). Monarch Pr.

National Association of Independent Schools. A Teacher's Notebook: German. 1973. pap. 3.25 (ISBN 0-934338-02-7). NAIS.

Politzer, Robert L. Active Review of German: A German Review Grammar. LC 71-126627. 240p. (Orig.). 1971. 12.95 (ISBN 0-686-75237-6). Krieger.

Rehder, Helmut, et al. Sprechen & Lesen. rev. ed. (German Basic Courses: Level 2). (Follows Verstehenund Sprechen). (gr. 8-12). 1971. text ed. 10.98 (ISBN 0-03-084939-X); tchr's. manual. pap. 6.78 (ISBN 0-03-084940-3); testing program 2.88 (ISBN 0-03-084942-X); exercise manual. pap. 3.87 (ISBN 0-03-084941-1); tapes 217.29 (ISBN 0-03-086287-6). HR&W.

--Zweite Stufe, Level 1. (Follows Erste Stufe, leads into Sprechen und Lesen). (gr. 7). 1970. pap. text ed. 6.57 (ISBN 0-03-084958-6); wkbk 1.68 (ISBN 0-03-085680-9); testing program. pap. 1.38 (ISBN 0-03-085681-7); tapes 153.39 (ISBN 0-03-085470-9). HR&W.

Reinert, Harry. German First Year. (gr. 7-12). 1971. wkbk. 6.42 (ISBN 0-87720-583-3). AMSCO Sch.

Rivers, Wilga, et al. A Practical Guide to the Teaching of German. 375p. 1975. pap. text ed. 7.95x (ISBN 0-19-501910-5). Oxford U Pr.

Schneider, R. Guten Tag: A German Language Course for Television. 1974. pap. text ed. 6.50x (ISBN 0-685-47484-4). Schoenhof.

Schneider, Rudolf & Kreplin, Dietrich. Guten Tag. 220p. 1968. text ed. 4.50x (ISBN 3-468-96701-2). Intl Film.

Schneider, Rudolf, et al. Guten Tag wie geht's. (Illus.). 302p. 1972. text ed. 6.75x (ISBN 3-468-96710-1). Intl Film.

Schulz, Dora & Griesbach, Heinz. Deutsche Sprachlehre Fuer Auslaender. Incl. Grundstufe in einem Band. pap. text ed. 7.80x (ISBN 0-685-47472-0); glossar deutsch-englisch 4.10x (ISBN 0-685-47473-9); leseheft 1, by roland hils. 3.25x (ISBN 0-685-47474-7); grammar german-english 4.55xschuelerheft.contrastive (ISBN 0-685-47475-5); Grundstufe. Ausgabe in zwei Baenden. pap. text ed. 4.00xGrundstufe 1. teil (ISBN 0-685-47476-3); pap. text ed. 7.15x grundstufe 2. teil (ISBN 0-685-47477-1); teaching supplement-phraseological glossary-key 5.20x (ISBN 0-685-47478-X); 2 tonbaender, aufnahme der lesetexte des buches und von uebungen, 9.5 cm/s, tapes 52.00x (ISBN 0-685-47479-8); Mittelstufe; Moderner Deutscher Sprachgebrauch.Ein Lehrgang Fuer Fortgeschrittene. pap. text ed. 12.25x (ISBN 0-685-47480-1); lehrerheft 4.90x (ISBN 0-685-47481-X); schuelerheft mit schluessel zuden uebungen 7.15x (ISBN 0-685-47482-8); 1 tonband, aufnahme von 28 lesetexten des lehrbuchs, 9.5 cm/s, tapes 31.20x (ISBN 0-685-47483-6). Schoenhof.

Spechtler, Franz V., ed. Geistlichen Lieder des Moenchs von Salzburg. (Quellen und Forschungen zur Sprach-und Kulturgeschichte der germanischen Voelker, N.F. 57). xii, 378p. 1973. 67.25x (ISBN 3-11-001847-0). De Gruyter.

Stegemann, Jelle. Aspekte der kontrastiven Syntax am Beispiel des Niederlaendischen und Deutschen. (Studia Linguistica Germanica). 201p. 1979. text ed. 34.25x (ISBN 3-11-008017-6). De Gruyter.

Thimm, Franz. German Without a Teacher. 0.75 (ISBN 0-685-02612-4, 00545211). Stein Pub.

Weiss, Edda. Deutsch: Entdecken Wir Es, Level 1. (Learning German the Modern Way). (Illus.). 368p. (gr. 9). 1972. text ed. 13.12 (ISBN 0-07-069075-8, W); tchr's. ed. 14.00 (ISBN 0-07-069076-6); wkbk. 3.96 (ISBN 0-07-069077-4); cassettes 312.00 (ISBN 0-07-097807-7); filmstrips 92.00 (ISBN 0-07-097801-8); tapes 324.00 (ISBN 0-07-097800-X); test pkg. 50.00 (ISBN 0-07-069078-2). McGraw.

--Deutsch: Erleben Wir Es, Level 2. LC 72-8377. (Learning German the Modern Way Ser.). (Illus.). 418p. (gr. 10-12). 1973. text ed. 13.32 (ISBN 0-07-069081-2, W); tchr's. ed. 14.52 (ISBN 0-07-069082-0); wkbk. 3.96 (ISBN 0-07-069083-9); cassettes 332.00 (ISBN 0-07-097808-5); filmstrips 92.00 (ISBN 0-07-097806-9); tapes 404.00 (ISBN 0-07-097805-0); test pkg. 60.00 (ISBN 0-07-069084-7). McGraw.

Zeydel, Edwin. A First Course in Written & Spoken German: A Review & Exercise Book. 2nd ed. 1948. text ed. 9.95x (ISBN 0-89197-559-4); pap. text ed. 3.95x (ISBN 0-89197-560-8). Irvington.

Zimmermann, Jon, et al. Contemporary German Life. new ed. (Illus.). 384p. 1975. text ed. 14.95 (ISBN 0-07-072835-6, C); instructor's manual 4.95 (ISBN 0-07-072836-4). McGraw.

GERMAN LANGUAGE–SYNONYMS AND ANTONYMS

Duden, R., ed. Duden-Synonymenwoerterbuch. (Der Grosse Duden: Vol. 8). 18.50 (ISBN 3-4110-0918-7). Adler.

Farrell, R. B. Dictionary of German Synonyms. 3rd ed. LC 75-36175. 1977. 45.00 (ISBN 0-521-21189-1); pap. 12.95 (ISBN 0-521-29068-6). Cambridge U Pr.

GERMAN LANGUAGE–SYNTAX

Heringer, Hans-Juergen. Deutsche Syntax. 2nd ed. (Sammlung Goeschen Vol. 5246). (Illus., Ger.). 1972. 5.45 (ISBN 3-11-004015-8). De Gruyter.

Sandig, Barbara. Stilistik: Sprachpragmatische Grundlegung der Stilbeschreibung. (Grundlagen der Kommunikation De Gruyter Studienbuch). 1978. 17.75x (ISBN 3-11-007374-9). De Gruyter.

GERMAN LANGUAGE–TEXTBOOKS FOR CHILDREN

Cooper, Lee. Fun with German. (Illus.). (gr. 3 up). 1965. 8.95 (ISBN 0-316-15588-8). Little.

Drath, Viola & Moeller, Jack. Noch Dazu. LC 79-64140. (Sequential German Readers Ser.: Bk. II). (gr. 9-12). 1979. pap. text ed. 3.80 (ISBN 0-395-27930-5). HM.

Hankins, Gail J. Two Hundred & Fifty Conjugated German Verbs. 264p. (Orig.). 1981. pap. 2.50 (ISBN 0-8092-5844-7). Contemp Bks.

Liedloff, Helmut. Ohne Muhe! LC 79-84596. (German Sequential Readers Ser.). (Illus.). (gr. 9-10). 1979. text ed. 2.60 (ISBN 0-395-27931-3). HM.

Rehder, Helmut, et al. Erste Stufe: Erste Stufe. (gr. 8). 1970. text ed. 6.15 (ISBN 0-03-084957-8); testing program 1.20 (ISBN 0-03-085683-3). HR&W.

Zimmer, Stefan. Die Satzstellung des Finiten Verbs im Tocharischen. (Janua Linguarum, Ser. Practica: No. 238). 108p. 1976. pap. text ed. 26.25x (ISBN 90-279-3461-4). Mouton.

GERMAN LANGUAGE–TEXTBOOKS FOR FOREIGNERS

see also German Language–Conversation and Phrase Books; German Language–Self-Instruction

Apelt, Mary L. & Apelt, H. P. Reading Knowledge in German: A Course for Art Historians & Archaeologists (1975) pap. 12.50 (ISBN 3-503-00799-7). Heinman.

Assimil. Assimil Language Courses: For Dutch Speaking People Who Want to Learn German - Duits Zonder Moeite. 12.95 (ISBN 0-686-56172-4); accompanying records & tapes 75.00 (ISBN 0-686-56173-2). French & Eur.

--Assimil Language Courses: For English Speaking People Who Want to Learn German - German Without Toil. 11.95 (ISBN 0-686-56142-2); accompanying records & tapes 75.00 (ISBN 0-686-56143-0). French & Eur.

--Assimil Language Courses: For Italian Speaking People Who Want to Learn German - Il Tedesco Senza Sforzo. 11.95 (ISBN 0-686-56158-9); accompanying records & tapes 75.00 (ISBN 0-686-56159-7). French & Eur.

--Assimil Language Courses: For Portuguese Speaking People Who Want to Learn German - Alemao Sem Custo. 11.95 (ISBN 0-686-56126-0); accompanying records & tapes 75.00 (ISBN 0-686-56127-9). French & Eur.

--Assimil Language Courses: For Spanish Speaking People Who Want to Learn German - El Aleman Sin Esfuerzo. 11.95 (ISBN 0-686-56118-X); accompanying records & tapes 75.00 (ISBN 0-686-56119-8). French & Eur.

--Assimil Language Courses: For Yugoslav Speaking People Who Want to Learn German - Nemacki Bez Muke. 12.95 (ISBN 0-686-56166-X); accompanying records & tapes 75.00 (ISBN 0-686-56167-8). French & Eur.

Assimil, ed. German Without Toil. 1957. 9.50x (ISBN 2-7005-0006-7); 3 cassettes 70.00x (ISBN 0-686-09282-1); 10 records 70.00x (ISBN 0-686-28535-2); book & records 79.00x (ISBN 0-686-28536-0). Intl Learn Syst.

Brown, Samuel A., et al. FSI German Basic Course, Units 1-12. 1976. pap. text ed. 10.00x (ISBN 0-686-10722-5); 25 cassettes 150.00x (ISBN 0-686-10723-3). Intl Learn Syst.

--FSI German Basic Course, Units 13-24. 1975. pap. text ed. 5.45x (ISBN 0-686-10724-1); 25 cassettes 150.00x (ISBN 0-686-10725-X). Intl Learn Syst.

Cherel, Albert O. Duits Zonder Moeite. 11.95 (ISBN 0-685-11150-4). French & Eur.

--Nemacki Bez Muke. 11.95 (ISBN 0-685-11417-1). French & Eur.

Condoyannis, George E. Scientific German. LC 77-16570. 174p. 1978. pap. 8.50 (ISBN 0-88275-644-3). Krieger.

Doring, P. F. Learn German for English Speakers. pap. 8.50 (ISBN 0-87557-027-5, 027-6). Saphrograph.

Eichinger, H., et al. German Once a Week, 2 bks. 130p. 1976. pap. 5.25x ea. (Pub. by Basil Blackwell). Bk. 1, 1977, Repr. Of 1963 (ISBN 0-631-96270-0). Bk. 2, 1976, Repr. Of 1965 (ISBN 0-631-96280-8). Biblio Dist.

Fehling, Fred L., et al. Elementary German. 3rd ed. 1971. text ed. 14.95x (ISBN 0-442-21543-6). 26 tapes 95.00 (ISBN 0-442-21544-4). Van Nos Reinhold.

German in Three Months. (Hugo's Language Courses Ser.: No. 524). 1969. pap. 3.50 (ISBN 0-8226-0524-4). Littlefield.

Goedsche, C. R. & Spann, Meno. Deutsch Fuer Amerikaner. 4th ed. (Illus., Ger.). 1979. text ed. 15.95 (ISBN 0-442-22058-8); tapes 95.00 (ISBN 0-442-22064-2); cassettes 59.95 (ISBN 0-442-22067-7); wkbk 3.50x (ISBN 0-442-22059-6). D Van Nostrand.

Habicht, Werner, ed. English & American Studies in German: Summaries of Theses & Monographs: a Supplement to Anglica. annual Incl. 1968 Vol. 101p. 1969. pap. 12.50x (ISBN 3-484-43001-X); 1969 Vol. 108p. 1970. pap. 12.50x (ISBN 3-484-43001-X); 1970 Vol. 139p. 1971. pap. 15.00x (ISBN 3-484-43002-8); 1971 Vol. 190p. 1972. pap. 20.00x (ISBN 3-484-43003-6); 1972 Vol. 1973. pap. 27.50x (ISBN 3-484-43004-4); 1973 Vol. 1974. pap. 27.50x (ISBN 0-686-66977-0); 1974 Vol. 199p. 1975. pap. 40.00x (ISBN 3-484-43006-0); 1976. 170p. 1977. pap. 40.00x (ISBN 3-484-43008-7); 1977 Vol. 1978. pap. 52.50x (ISBN 3-484-43009-5); 1978 Vol. 163p. 1979. pap. 40.00x (ISBN 3-484-43010-9). Intl Pubns Serv.

Hildebrandt, Lieselotte M. Deutsche Phonetik fur Amerikaner. LC 76-19168. 259p. (Sponsored by The Dept. of Modern & Classical Languages, University of North Dakota). 1976. pap. 18.25 (ISBN 0-8357-0178-6, SS-00009). Univ Microfilms.

Holschuh, Albrecht. Leutebuch. LC 77-76512. (Illus., Orig.). 1977. pap. text ed. 9.95 (ISBN 0-15-550601-3, HC). HarBraceJ.

Hye, Allen, ed. Modernes Deutschland in Brennpunkt: A Cultural Reader. 1978. pap. text ed. 7.95x (ISBN 0-393-09067-1). Norton.

Lloyd, Albert. Deutsch und Deutschland Heute. 2nd ed. 1981. text ed. write for info. (ISBN 0-442-24461-4). D Van Nostrand.

Logan, Gerald E. & Braswell, David. Hallo Deutschland! LC 78-660. 1978. pap. text ed. 4.95 (ISBN 0-88377-101-2). Newbury Hse.

Madrigal, Margarita & Meyer, Ursula. An Invitation to German. (Illus.). 1978. pap. 2.95 (ISBN 0-671-24234-2, Fireside). S&S.

Pfister, Guenter G. Andere Lander, Andere Sitten Teil 1. (Illus.). 227p. (Ger.). 1981. text ed. 12.80x (ISBN 0-87563-199-1). Stipes.

Reck, Hanne G. Deutsch Fur Studenten Spicher Sprache-Aleman Para Estudiantes De Habla Espanola. LC 78-18825. 1979. pap. text ed. 7.50 (ISBN 0-8477-3321-1). U of PR Pr.

Reinert, Harry. Review Text in German, First Year. (Orig.). (gr. 10-12). 1971. pap. text ed. 5.33 (ISBN 0-87720-581-7). AMSCO Sch.

Rey, Marilyn B. & Maloof, Katherine. Deutsch Macht Spass. (gr. 8-11). 1979. wkbk. 4.50 (ISBN 0-87720-582-5). AMSCO Sch.

Schulz, R., et al. Lesen, Lachen, Lernen. LC 78-51929. (Illus.). pap. 10.95 (ISBN 0-03-019026-6, HoltC). HR&W.

Thomas, Ursala & Twaddell, Freeman. Lesetoff Nach Wahl: Einfuhrung. LC 76-11321. 1977. pap. text ed. 5.00 (ISBN 0-299-07144-8); tchrs' manual 10.00 (ISBN 0-299-07154-5). U of Wis Pr.

Three Hundred & One German Verbs. Date not set. 2.95 (ISBN 0-686-75972-9, 2498). Barron.

Von Hofe, Harold & Schulz, Dora. Deutsche Sprachlehre Fur Amerikaner. 2nd ed. (Ger.). 1970. text ed. 13.95x (ISBN 0-684-41465-1, ScribT); pap. text ed. 4.65x (ISBN 0-684-41466-X, ScribT). Scribner.

Weiss, Edda. Deutsch: Erleben Wir Es! 2nd ed. Saslow, Joan, ed. LC 80-16484. (Illus.). 344p. (Ger.). (gr. 10). 1980. text ed. 14.64 (ISBN 0-07-069215-7, W); tchrs. ed. 15.96 (ISBN 0-07-069216-5); wkbk. 4.26 (ISBN 0-07-069217-3); tests 69.00 (ISBN 0-07-069218-1); tapes 404.00 (ISBN 0-07-097815-8); cassettes 381.80 (ISBN 0-07-097816-6); filmstrips 113.36 (ISBN 0-07-097817-4). McGraw.

GERMAN LITERATURE (COLLECTIONS)

Here are entered works in German. For translations into English see subdivision Translations into English.

see also German-American Literature

Barnstorff, H. German Literature in Translation, 1891-1939. 59.95 (ISBN 0-8490-0228-1). Gordon Pr.

Basis Jahrbuch: Jahrbuch Fuer Deutsche Gegenwartsliteratur, Bd. 10. (Suhrkamp Taschenbuecher: Bd. 589). 263p. (Orig., Ger.). 1980. pap. text ed. 6.50 (ISBN 3-518-37089-8, Pub. by Suhrkamp Verlag Germany). Suhrkamp.

Buchner, G. Danton's Tod & Woyzeck. Jacobs, M., ed. 220p. 1954. 9.00x (ISBN 0-7190-0456-X, Pub. by Manchester U Pr England). State Mutual Bk.

Busch, Johann G. Kleine Schriften Von der Handlung und Anderem Gemeinnuetzigem Inhalte. 1973. Repr. of 1772 ed. 38.50 (ISBN 0-384-06690-9). Johnson Repr.

Busch, Marie, tr. Selected Austrian Short Stories. facsimile ed. LC 70-37260. (Short Story Index Reprint Ser). Repr. of 1928 ed. 16.00 (ISBN 0-8369-4071-7). Arno.

Francke, Kuno, ed. German Classics, 20 Vols. Repr. of 1914 ed. Set. 695.00 (ISBN 0-404-02600-1); 34.75 ea. AMS Pr.

German Short Stories: Contemporary Authors, German & English. bilingual ed. 155p. (Eng. & Ger.). 1975. pap. 4.55 (ISBN 3-4230-9097-9). Adler.

Gibb, Elias. Ottoman Literature. 59.95 (ISBN 0-8490-0781-X). Gordon Pr.

Goethe, Johann W. Maximen und Reflexionen. (Insel-Biblitothek). 368p. 1980. leather ed. 46.80 (ISBN 3-458-04944-4, Pub. by Insel Verlag Germany); text ed. 20.80 (ISBN 3-458-04934-7). Suhrkamp.

Heine, Heinrich. Family Life of Heinrich Heine. Von Embden, Ludwig, ed. LC 76-133280. (Studies in German Literature, No. 13). 1970. Repr. of 1892 ed. lib. bdg. 54.95 (ISBN 0-8383-1179-2). Haskell.

Hentschel, Cedric. Byronic Teuton: Aspects of German Pessimism 1800-1933. LC 76-26688. 1940. lib. bdg. 20.00 (ISBN 0-8414-4927-9). Folcroft.

Jerschow, Peter. Das Wunderpferdchen. (It 490). (Orig., Ger.). 1980. pap. text ed. 6.50 (ISBN 3-458-32190-X, Pub. by Suhrkamp Verlag Germany). Suhrkamp.

Laube, Heinrich. Aurora: Eine Literarische Laube, Redaktion, 25 vols, Vol. 1. 1973. Repr. of 1829 ed. 30.00 (ISBN 0-384-02580-3). Johnson Repr.

Lie, Sophus. Gesammelte Abhandlungen, 7 vols. 1973. Repr. of 1922 ed. 375.50 (ISBN 0-384-32619-6). Johnson Repr.

Lindberg, John D., ed. Weise, Christian Samtliche Werke, Vol. 21: Gedichte II. (Ausgaben Deutscher Literatur Des XV Bis XVII). (Illus.). 1978. 200.00x (ISBN 3-11-006745-5). De Gruyter.

Loffler, Bertold. Die Sieben Zwerge Scheewittchens. (Insel Taschbuecher Fuer Kinder: It 489). 40p. (Ger.). pap. text ed. 4.55 (ISBN 3-458-32189-6, Pub. by Insel Verlag Germany). Suhrkamp.

Lohan, Robert. Living German Literature, Vol. 1. 4th ed. 12.00 (ISBN 0-8044-0326-0). Ungar.

Mueller-Schwefe, Hans-Ulrich. Von Nun an Neue Deutsche Erzaehler. (Edition Suhrkamp). 300p. (Orig.). 1980. pap. text ed. 5.20 (ISBN 3-518-11003-9, Pub. by Suhrkamp Verlag Germany). Suhrkamp.

Murer, Jos. Saemtliche Dramen, 2 vols. Adomatis, Hans-Joachim, et al, eds. LC 73-78235. (Ausgaben Deutscher Literatur des 15. bis 18. Jahrhunderts, Reihe Dramen 4). 1974. 299.00x (ISBN 3-11-003864-1). De Gruyter.

Otten, Anna, ed. Meistererzahlungen. (Orig., Ger.). 1969. pap. text ed. 8.95 (ISBN 0-13-574251-X). P-H.

Rosenwald, Henry M., ed. Age of Romanticism. (Living German Literature Ser: Vol. 3). 1959. 10.50 (ISBN 0-8044-0482-8). Ungar.

Vizkelity, Andras, ed. Wolfhart Spangenberg, Saemtliche Werke Vol. 3, Part 2: Tierdichtungen II. (Ausgaben Deutscher Literature Des XV. Bis XVIII. Jahrhunderts). 1978. 107.00x (ISBN 3-11-007465-6). De Gruyter.

Wells, Benjamin. Modern German Literature. 1973. lib. bdg. 25.00 (ISBN 0-8414-9690-0). Folcroft.

Willig, P. Lichtstreifen. 141p. 1973. pap. 5.75 (ISBN 0-08-016281-9); pap. text ed. 3.80 (ISBN 0-08-017826-X). Pergamon.

Winkworth, Catherine. Lyra Germanica. 69.95 (ISBN 0-87968-366-X). Gordon Pr.

Wireman, H. D. Gems of German Lyrics. 69.95 (ISBN 0-87968-362-7). Gordon Pr.

Yuill, H. German Narrative Prose, Vol. 2. 1966. 13.50 (ISBN 0-85496-022-8). Dufour.

GERMAN LITERATURE (SELECTIONS: EXTRACTS, ETC.)

Cohen, Mitchell, et al, eds. Berlin: Anthology of Writing from Berlin. LC 77-642342. (Rockbottom Ser.). (Illus.). 288p. (Orig.). 1981. 18.00 (ISBN 0-930012-23-2); pap. 8.50 (ISBN 0-930012-22-4). Mudborn.

Vizkelety, Andras & Tarnai, Andor, eds. Wolfhart Spangenberg, Samtliche Werke, Vol. 3, Pt. 1. (Ausgaben Deutscher Literatur). 1977. 107.00x (ISBN 3-11-006938-5). De Gruyter.

GERMAN LITERATURE–BIBLIOGRAPHY

Bruckner, J. A Bibliographical Catalogue of Seventeenth-Century German Books Published in Holland. (Anglica Germanica: No. 13). 1971. text ed. 95.30x (ISBN 0-686-20922-2). Mouton.

Cazden, Robert E. German Exile Literature in America, 1933-1950: A History of the Free German Press & Book Trade. 262p. 1970. 10.00 (ISBN 0-8389-3098-0). ALA.

Faulhaver, Uwe K. & Goff, Penrith B. A Reference Guide to German Literature. LC 78-83349. (Reference Library of Humanities Ser.). 1979. lib. bdg. 32.50 (ISBN 0-8240-9831-5). Garland Pub.

Geils, Peter & Gorzny, Willi, eds. Bibliography of German Language Publications Seventeen Hundred to Nineteen Hundred Ten, 160 vols. 500p. (Ger.). 1979-1982. text ed. 12800.00 (ISBN 3-598-30000-X). K G Saur.

--Bibliography of German-Language Publications, 1700 to 1910, 160 vols. 1981. Set. 13000.00 (Pub. by K G Saur); 100.00 ea. Gale.

German Baroque Literature: A Descriptive Catalogue of the Collection of Harold Jantz, 2 vols. LC 74-23640. 1974. 145.00 (ISBN 0-89235-006-7). Res Pubns Conn.

German Baroque Literature: Bibliography - Index to the Microform Edition of the Yale University Library Collection. LC 71-172288. 216p. 1971. 55.00 (ISBN 0-89235-007-5). Res Pubns Conn.

German Books in Print, Nineteen Eighty to Eighty-One: Authors-Titles-Keywords, 4 vols. 10th ed. Set. 250.00 (ISBN 3-7657-0862-3, Dist by Gale Research Co.). K G Saur.

German Books in Print, Nineteen Eighty to Eighty-One: ISBN Register. 637p. 1980. 95.00 (ISBN 3-7657-0986-7, Dist. by Gale Research Co.). K G Saur.

German Books in Print, Nineteen Eighty to Eighty-One: Subject Guide, 3 vols. 3rd ed. 1980. Set. 240.00 (ISBN 0-686-70170-4, Dist. by Gale Research Co.). K G Saur.

Harvard University Library. German Literature: Classification Schedule - Author & Title Listing, 2 vols. LC 73-82347. (Widener Library Shelflist: No. 49-50). 1975. Set. text ed. 75.00x (ISBN 0-674-35070-7). Harvard U Pr.

Heidtmann, Frank, et al, eds. German Photographic Literature, Eighteen Thirty-Nine to Nineteen Seventy-Eight: Theory, Technology, Visual. A Classified Bibliography of German-Language Photographic Publications. 690p. 1980. 85.00 (ISBN 3-598-10026-4, Dist. by Gale Research Co.). K G Saur.

Institute for Contemporary History, Munich. Catalog of the Library of the Institute for Contemporary History, First Supplement. 850p. 1973. lib. bdg. 130.00 alphabetical catalog (ISBN 0-8161-0920-6); lib. bdg. 245.00 subject catalog (2 vols.) (ISBN 0-8161-0179-5); lib. bdg. 115.00 biographical catalog & regional catalog (ISBN 0-8161-1075-1). G K Hall.

Kohlschmidt, Werner & Mohr, Werner, eds. Reallexikon der deutschen Literaturgeschichte, 3 vols. 2nd ed. Incl. Vol 1 A-K. 915p. 1958. 87.50x (ISBN 3-11-000294-9); Vol. 2 L-O. 847p. 1964. 87.50x (ISBN 3-11-000295-7); Vol. 3, Pt. 1. 1977. 111.00x (ISBN 3-110073-99-4). De Gruyter.

Lindner, Kurt. Bibliographie der Deutschen und der Niederlaendischen Jagdliteratur Von 1480 Bis 1850. (Illus.). 1977. 211.50x (ISBN 3-11-006640-8). De Gruyter.

Magill, C. P. German Literature. (Oxford Paperbacks University Ser.). 208p. 1974. pap. 4.95x (ISBN 0-19-888063-4). Oxford U Pr.

Nollen, John S. A Chronology of Practical Bibliography of Modern German Literature. LC 76-27531. 1976. Repr. of 1903 ed. lib. bdg. 20.00 (ISBN 0-89341-052-7). Longwood Pr.

Oberschelp, Reinhard. Bibliography of German Language Publications Nineteen Hundred Eleven to Nineteen Hundred Sixty-Five. 500p. 1976-1980. text ed. 12450.00 (ISBN 3-7940-5600-0). K G Saur.

Oberschelp, Reinhard, ed. Bibliography of German-Language Publications, 1911 to 1965, 150 vols. 1981. Set. 12500.00 (Pub. by K G Saur); 90.00 ea. Gale.

Rose, Ernst. A History of German Literature. LC 60-9405. (Gotham Library). (Orig.). 1960. 12.00x (ISBN 0-8147-0362-3); pap. 6.00x (ISBN 0-8147-0363-1). NYU Pr.

Sack, Peter, ed. German New Guinea: A Bibliography. 298p. 1980. pap. text ed. 19.95 (ISBN 0-686-29668-0, 0549). Bks Australia.

Schuder, Werner, ed. Kuerschners Deutscher Literatur-Kalender: Nekrolog 1936-1970. xvi, 871p. 1973. 136.51x (ISBN 3-11-004381-5). De Gruyter.

Spalek, J. Ernst Toller & His Critics. LC 72-12777. (Studies in German Literature, No. 13). 1972. Repr. of 1968 ed. lib. bdg. 58.95 (ISBN 0-8383-1591-7). Haskell.

Taylor, Archer. Problems in German Literary History of the Fifteenth & Sixteenth Centuries. 1939. pap. 13.00 (ISBN 0-527-89056-1). Kraus Repr.

Ungar, Frederick, ed. Handbook of Austrian Literature. LC 71-125969. 416p. 1973. 16.50 (ISBN 0-8044-2929-4). Ungar.

Vijfrinkel, E. Bibliographie Zu Dem Lymburgroman. (Beschreibende Bibliographien: Vol. 6). 90p. (Ger.). 1976. pap. text ed. 8.00x (ISBN 90-6203-118-8). Humanities.

Weiser, Frederick S. & Heaney, Howell J., eds. The Pennsylvania German Fraktur of the Free Library of Philadelphia: An Illustrated Catalogue, Vol. 1. Neff, Larry M., tr. from Ger. LC 76-13357. (Illus.). 250p. 1976. 30.00 (ISBN 0-911122-32-X). Penn German Soc.

--The Pennsylvania German Fraktur of the Free Library of Philadelphia: Illustrated Catalogue, Vol. 2. Neff, Larry M., tr. from Ger. LC 76-13357. (Illus.). 1977. 30.00 (ISBN 0-911122-33-8). Penn German Soc.

Weismann, Willi, compiled by. Index of German Language Picture Books Nineteen Forty-Five to Nineteen Seventy-Five. 1978. 43.00 (ISBN 0-89664-038-8). K G Saur.

GERMAN LITERATURE–DISCOGRAPHY

Chassard, Jean & Weil, Gonthier. Dictionnaire des Oeuvres et des Themes de la Litterature Allemande. (Fr.). 1973. pap. 8.95 (ISBN 0-686-56853-2, M-6631). French & Eur.

GERMAN LITERATURE–HISTORY AND CRITICISM

see also Young Germany

Agler-Beck, Gayle. Der Von Kurenberg: Edition, Notes, & Commentary. xix, 230p. 1978. 25.00 (ISBN 90-272-0964-2, GLLM 4). Benjamins North Am.

Anderson, Robert R. & Thomas, James C. Index Verborum Zum Ackermann Aus Bohmen: Ein Alphabetisch Angerordnetes Wortregister Zu Texgestaltungen Des Akdermanns Aus Bohmen Von Knieschek Bis Jungbluth. (Amsterdamer Publikationen Zur Sprache und Literatur: Nos. 8 & 9). 985p. (Ger.). 1976. pap. text ed. 76.00x (ISBN 90-6203-071-8). Humanities.

Anderson, Walter E. The German Enigma: The Elitist Tradition in German Literature. LC 79-66491. 225p. 1981. 9.95 (ISBN 0-533-04398-0). Vantage.

Bambeck, Manfred. Goettliche Komoedie und Exegese. viii, 253p. 1975. pap. 47.10x (ISBN 3-11-004874-4). De Gruyter.

Barth, Bruno. Liebe und Ehe Im Altfranzosischen Fabel und in der Mittelhochdeutschen Novelle. Repr. of 1910 ed. 21.50 (ISBN 0-384-03465-9); pap. 18.50 (ISBN 0-685-02215-3). Johnson Repr.

Batt, Max. The Treatment of Nature in German Literature from Guenther to Appearance of Goethe's Werther. 1976. Repr. of 1902 ed. 25.00 (ISBN 0-403-06419-8, Regency). Scholarly.

--The Treatment of Nature in German Literature from Guenther to Goethe's Werner. 1976. lib. bdg. 59.95 (ISBN 0-8490-2764-0). Gordon Pr.

Bekker, Hugo. Nibelungenlied: A Literary Analysis. LC 70-151357. 1971. 15.00x (ISBN 0-8020-5235-5). U of Toronto Pr.

Boening, John, ed. & intro. by. The Reception of Classical German Literature in England, 1760-1860: A Documentary History from Contemporary Periodicals, 10 vols. Incl. Vol. 1. General Introduction & Reviews from 1760 to 1813 (ISBN 0-8240-0990-8); Vol. 2. Reviews from 1813 to 1835 (ISBN 0-8240-0991-6); Vol. 3. Reviews from 1835 to 1860 (ISBN 0-8240-0992-4); Vol. 4. Authors from Bodmer to Klopstock (ISBN 0-8240-0993-2); Vol. 5. Authors from Lavater to Novalis (ISBN 0-8240-0994-0); Vol. 6. The Reception of Early German Romantics: Richter, the Brothers Schlegel, Tieck & Hoffmann (ISBN 0-8240-0995-9); Vol. 7. General Critical Articles on Goethe & Reviews Which Discuss Goethe & Schiller Together, Arranged in Order of Appearance (ISBN 0-8240-0996-7); Vol. 8. Reviews of Werther, Goethe's Early Works, His Poems & Faust (ISBN 0-8240-0997-5); Vol. 9. The Works of Goethe's Midcareer, Wilhelm Meister & Such Works As Dichtung und Wahrheit, Etc (ISBN 0-8240-0998-3); Vol. 10. The English Reception of Specific Works of Schiller, from the Early Plays to the Historical Works (ISBN 0-8240-0999-1). 1977. Set. lib. bdg. 110.00 each (ISBN 0-686-77265-2). Garland Pub.

Bostock, J. Knight. A Handbook on Old High German Literature. 2nd ed. King, K. C. & McLintock, D. R., eds. (Illus.). 1976. 59.00x (ISBN 0-19-815392-9). Oxford U Pr.

Bottiger, K. A. Literarische Zustande und Zeitgenossen. Repr. of 1838 ed. 61.50 (ISBN 0-384-05290-8). Johnson Repr.

Boyesen, Hjalmar H. Essays on German Literature. LC 74-37509. (Essay Index Reprint Ser.). Repr. of 1892 ed. 19.50 (ISBN 0-8369-2536-X). Arno.

Braasch, Theodor. Vollstaendiges Woerterbuch Zur Sogenannten Caedmonschen Genesis. 1933. 15.95 (ISBN 3-533-00946-7, M-7682, Pub. by Carl Winter). French & Eur.

Bridgewater, Patrick. Nietzsche in Anglosaxony: A Study of Nietzsche's Impact on English & American Literature. 250p. 1972. text ed. 10.50x (ISBN 0-7185-1104-2, Leicester). Humanities.

Brietzmann, Franz. Die Boese Frau in der Deutschen Literatur Des Mittelalters. 21.50 (ISBN 0-384-05766-7); pap. 18.50 (ISBN 0-384-05765-9). Johnson Repr.

Brockes, Barthold H. Herrn B. H. Brockes... Aus Dem Englischen Uebersetzte Jahreszeiten Des Herrn Thomson. 640p. 1972. Repr. of 1745 ed. 46.00 (ISBN 0-384-05910-4). Johnson Repr.

Buehne, Sheema Z., et al, eds. Helen Adolf Festschrift. LC 68-25894. 1968. 14.50 (ISBN 0-8044-2095-5). Ungar.

Burger, Harald. Jakob Bidermanns Belisarius: Edition und Versuch einer Deutung. (Quellen und Forschungen-zur Sprach-und Kulturgeschichte der Germanischen Voelker). (Ger). 1966. 42.50x (ISBN 3-11-000211-6). De Gruyter.

Campbell, I. R. Kudrun: A Critical Appreciation. LC 77-1721. (Anglica Germanica Ser.: No. 2). 1978. 55.00 (ISBN 0-521-21618-4). Cambridge U Pr.

Cox, Richard. Figures of Transformation: Rilke & the Example of Valery. 199p. 1981. 40.00x (ISBN 0-85457-092-6, Pub. by Inst Germanic Stud England). State Mutual Bk.

Cysarz, Herbert. Sein und Werden, Entwurf Eines Universaltheoretischen Spektrums: Mit Einer Einfuhrung, 1970. LC 70-108599. (Classics in Germanic Literatures and Philosophy Ser). 1970. Repr. of 1948 ed. 23.00 (ISBN 0-384-10525-4). Johnson Repr.

Daemmrich, Horst S. & Haenicke, Diether H., eds. The Challenge of German Literature. LC 75-131425. 1971. 13.95x (ISBN 0-8143-1435-X). Wayne St U Pr.

Daly, Peter M. & Lappe, Claus O. Text und Variantenkonkordanz zu Schillers "Kabale und Liebe". 1976. 243.50x (ISBN 3-11-002225-7). De Gruyter.

De Man. Allegories of Reading. LC 79-64075. 1979. 19.50x (ISBN 0-300-02322-7). Yale U Pr.

Deutsche Litteraturblatt: Herausgegeben Von Ludolf Weinbarg, Hamburg, 1840-42, Vol. 1. (Nos. 1-82 all published). 1972. Repr. of 1843 ed. pap. 41.00 (ISBN 0-384-11538-1). Johnson Repr.

Doebele-Fluegel, Verena. Motivgeschichtliche Untersuchung Zur Deutschen Literatur, Insbesondere Zur Deutschen Lyrik. 1977. 57.65x (ISBN 3-11-005909-6). De Gruyter.

Domandi, A. Deutsche Literatur Von Heute. 1974. pap. text ed. 14.95 (ISBN 0-03-005626-8, HoltC). HR&W.

Egert, Eugene. The Holy Spirit in German Literature Until the Twelfth Century. (Studies in German Literature: No. 13). 1973. text ed. 47.00x (ISBN 90-2792-410-4). Mouton.

Ellis, J. M. Narration in the German Novelle. LC 73-82460. (Anglica Germanica Ser.: No. 2). 232p. 1974. 45.00 (ISBN 0-521-20330-9). Cambridge U Pr.
--Narration in the German Novelle. LC 78-73602. (Anglica Germanica Ser.: No. 2). 1979. pap. 10.95x (ISBN 0-521-29592-0). Cambridge U Pr.
Elster, E., ed. Beitraege Zur Deutschen Literaturwissenschaft, Nos. 1-40 In 14 Vols. 1907-1931. Set. 390.00 (ISBN 0-384-03788-7). Johnson Repr.
Emrich, Wilhelm. Literary Revolution & Modern Society & Other Essays. LC 70-125963. 1971. 10.50 (ISBN 0-8044-2169-2, 2169-2). Ungar.
Engel, Eva L., ed. German Narrative Prose, Vol. 1. 13.50 (ISBN 0-85496-021-X). Dufour.
Fetzer, John F. & Wheatley, Colen, eds. Bibliographie der Buchrezensionen fur Deutsche Literatur (1973-1974) LC 77-289. 1977. 17.75 (ISBN 0-8357-0255-3, SS-00027). Univ Microfilms.
Fitzell, John. Hermit in German Literature: From Lessing to Eichendorff. LC 74-168033. (North Carolina. University. Studies in the Germanic Languages & Literatures: No. 30). Repr. of 1961 ed. 18.50 (ISBN 0-404-50930-4). AMS Pr.
Francke, Kuno. History of German Literature As Determined by Social Forces. 4th ed. LC 73-100524. Repr. of 1901 ed. 37.50 (ISBN 0-404-02545-5). AMS Pr.
--Personality in German Literature Before Luther. LC 72-141480. 221p. 1973. Repr. of 1916 ed. lib. bdg. 15.00x (ISBN 0-8371-5865-6, FRPG). Greenwood.
--Social Forces in German Literature. 59.95 (ISBN 0-8490-1064-0). Gordon Pr.
Frank, Armin P. Literaturwissenschaft Zwischen Extremen. (De Gruyter Studienbuch). 1977. 17.75x (ISBN 3-11-007025-1). De Gruyter.
Froeb, Herman. Ernst Koch's Prinz Rosa-Stramin: Ein Beitrag Zur Hessischen Literaturgeschichte. pap. 7.00 (ISBN 0-384-17029-3). Johnson Repr.
Garland, H. B. Concise Survey of German Literature. LC 78-137565. 1971. 8.95x (ISBN 0-87024-187-7). U of Miami Pr.
Garland, Henry & Garland, Mary, eds. The Oxford Companion to German Literature. 992p. 1976. 35.00 (ISBN 0-19-866115-0). Oxford U Pr.
German Studies. facsimile ed. LC 70-99696. (Essay Index Reprint Ser). 1938. 21.00 (ISBN 0-8369-1409-0). Arno.
Gostwick, J. & Gostwick, Harrison. Outlines of German Literature. 1973. Repr. of 1873 ed. 25.00 (ISBN 0-8274-0737-8). R West.
Grenville, Peter. Kurt Tucholsky: The Ironic Sentimentalist. (German Literature & Society Ser.: Vol. 1). 1980. pap. text ed. write for info. (ISBN 0-85496-074-0). Humanities.
Gross, David. The Writer & Society: Heinrich Mann & Literary Politics in Germany, 1890-1940. 316p. 1980. text ed. 15.00x (ISBN 0-391-00972-9). Humanities.
Gross, Ruth V. Plan & the Austrian Rebirth: A Journal of Literature, Art, & Culture. (Studies in German Literature, Linguistics, & Culture: Vol. 6). 170p. 1981. 21.00x (ISBN 0-938100-03-3). Camden Hse.
Gundolf, Friedrich. Caesar in der Deutschen Literatur. 14.00 (ISBN 0-384-20461-9); pap. 11.00 (ISBN 0-384-20460-0). Johnson Repr.
Haberland, Paul M. The Development of Comic Theory in Germany During the 18th Century. LC 72-18496. (Goeppinger Arbeiten Zur Germanistik: No. 37). 145p. 1971. pap. 10.00x (ISBN 0-8002-1254-1). Intl Pubns Serv.
Hammer, Carl, Jr., ed. Studies in German Literature. LC 63-9645. (University Studies, Humanities Ser.: Vol. 13). 1963. pap. 9.95x (ISBN 0-8071-0520-1). La State U Pr.
Hankamer, Paul. Deutsche Literaturgeschichte. LC 72-120563. Repr. of 1930 ed. 21.50 (ISBN 0-404-03095-5). AMS Pr.
Heller, Erich. The Artist's Journey into the Interior & Other Essays. LC 75-40222. 240p. 1976. pap. 4.50 (ISBN 0-15-607950-X, HB332, Harv). HarBraceJ.
Heller, Otto. Studies in Modern German Literature. 1973. lib. bdg. 9.50 (ISBN 0-8414-5037-4). Folcroft.
Hesson, Elizabeth C. Twentieth Century Odyssey: A Study of Heimito Von Doderer's "Die Damonen". (Studies in German Literature, Linguistics & Culture: Vol. 9). (Illus.). 220p. 1982. 18.95x (ISBN 0-938100-07-6). Camden Hse.
Hochdoerfer, Richard. Introductory Studies in German Literature. 1973. Repr. of 1904 ed. 20.00 (ISBN 0-8274-0252-X). R West.
Huffines, Marion L. Stricker & Wernher: A View of Chivalry & Peasantry in Germany in the Late Middle Ages. 1978. lib. bdg. 69.95 (ISBN 0-87968-570-0). Gordon Pr.
Hughes, Glyn T. Romantic German Literature. LC 79-12994. 1979. text ed. 26.50x (ISBN 0-8419-0521-5). Holmes & Meier.
Hutchinson, Peter. Literary Presentations of Divided Germany. LC 76-51414. (Anglica Germanica Ser.: No. 2). 1977. 28.50 (ISBN 0-521-21609-5). Cambridge U Pr.
Jennings, Lee B. Justinus Kerners Weg Nach Weinsberg 1809-1819: Die Entpolitisierung eines Romantikers. LC 80-69125. (Studies in German Literature, Linguistics & Culture: Vol. 3). (Illus.). 160p. 1981. 17.00x (ISBN 0-938100-00-9). Camden Hse.
Jones, George F. Honor in German Literature. LC 60-62591. (North Carolina University. Studies in the Germanic Languages & Literature: No. 25). Repr. of 1959 ed. 18.50 (ISBN 0-404-50925-8). AMS Pr.
Kahn, Ludwig W. Social Ideals in German Literature: Seventeen Seventy to Eighteen Thirty. 1979. Repr. of 1938 ed. lib. bdg. 25.00 (ISBN 0-8495-3049-0). Arden Lib.
Kanzog, Klaus. Edition und Engagement, 150 Jahre Editions-Geschichter der Werke und Briefe Heinrich Von Kleists, 2 vols. 1979. Set. 54.50 (ISBN 0-685-63520-1). Vol. 1 (ISBN 3-11-005978-9). Vol. 2 (ISBN 3-11-005979-7). De Gruyter.
Kayser, Rudolf. The Saints of Qumran: Stories & Essays on Jewish Themes. Zohn, Harry, ed. LC 76-20273. 188p. 1977. 14.50 (ISBN 0-8386-2024-8). Fairleigh Dickinson.
Kettler, Wilfried. Das Juengste Gericht Philologische Studienzu Den Wschatologie Vorstellungen in Den Alt-und Fruehmittel Hochdeutschen Denkmaelern. (Quellen und Forschungen Zur Sprach und Kulturgeschichte der Germanischen Voelker: Vol.70). 1977. 51.25x (ISBN 3-11-007345-5). De Gruyter.
Kienast, R. Johann Valentin Andreae und Die Vier Echten Rosenkreutzer-Schriften. (Ger). Repr. of 1926 ed. 21.50 (ISBN 0-384-29405-7); pap. 18.50 (ISBN 0-685-02276-5). Johnson Repr.
Klapper, Roxana M. The German Literary Influence on Shelley. (Salzburg Studies in English Literature, Romantic Reassessment: No. 42). 1974. pap. text ed. 25.00x (ISBN 0-391-01449-8). Humanities.
Klieneberger, H. R. The Novel in England & Germany. 254p. 1981. pap. text ed. 12.50x (ISBN 0-85496-079-1, Pub. by Wolff England). Humanities.
Kopp, W. LaMarr. German Literature in the United States, 1945-1960. (Studies in Comparative Literature Ser.: No. 42). 1968. 13.50x (ISBN 0-8078-7042-0). U of NC Pr.
Kostka, Edmund. Glimpses of Germanic-Slavic Relations from Pushkin to Heinrich Mann. LC 73-8303. 162p. 1974. 14.50 (ISBN 0-8387-1371-8). Bucknell U Pr.
Krispyn, Egbert. Anti-Nazi Writers in Exile. LC 77-9568. 200p. 1978. 15.00 (ISBN 0-8203-0430-1). U of Ga Pr.
--Style & Society in German Literary Expressionism. LC 64-63741. (U of Fla. Humanities Monographs: No. 15). 1964. pap. 2.25 (ISBN 0-8130-0136-6). U Presses Fla.
Kuerschners Deutscher Literaturkalender. 1978. 130.00x (ISBN 3-11-006952-0). De Gruyter.
Kuhn, Hans. Kleine Schriften, Vol. 2: Literaturgeschichte. Heldensage und Heldendichtung. Religions-und Sittengeschichte. Recht und Gesellschaft. Hoffmann, Dietrich, ed. viii, 542p. 1971. 79.50x (ISBN 3-11-006407-3). De Gruyter.
Kurz, Paul K. On Modern German Literature, Vol. 2. McCarthy, Sr. Mary F., tr. from Ger. LC 73-96419. 188p. 1971. 13.25x (ISBN 0-8173-8001-9). U of Ala Pr.
--On Modern German Literature, Vol. 3. McCarthy, Sr. Mary F., tr. from Ger. LC 73-96419. Orig. Title: Uber Moderne Literatur. 154p. 1973. 11.00x (ISBN 0-8173-8002-7). U of Ala Pr.
--On Modern German Literature, Vol. 4. McCarthy, Mary F., tr. from Ger. LC 73-96419. Orig. Title: Uber Moderne Literatur. 272p. 1977. 20.25x (ISBN 0-8173-8003-5). U of Ala Pr.
Legge, James G. Rhyme & Revolution in Germany: A Study in German History, Life, Literature & Character. LC 72-126646. Repr. of 1918 ed. 33.45 (ISBN 0-404-03947-2). AMS Pr.
Liptzin, Solomon. Germany's Stepchildren. facsimile ed. LC 75-167378. (Essay Index Reprint Ser). Repr. of 1944 ed. 22.00 (ISBN 0-8369-2462-2). Arno.
--Historical Survey of German Literature. LC 72-89407. (Illus.). xiii, 300p. 1972. Repr. of 1936 ed. lib. bdg. 12.50x (ISBN 0-8154-0441-7). Cooper Sq.
Madelung, A. Margaret. The Laxdoela Saga: Its Structural Patterns. (Studies in the Germanic Languages & Literatures Ser.: No. 74). 18.00x (ISBN 0-8078-8074-4). U of NC Pr.
Magill, C. P. German Literature. (Oxford Paperbacks University Ser.). 208p. 1974. pap. 4.95x (ISBN 0-19-888063-4). Oxford U Pr.
Martens, Wolfgang, ed. Der Patriot: Nach der Originalausgabe Hamburg, 1724-26, 4 vols. Incl. Vol. 1. Jahrgang 1724, Stueck 1-52. vi, 445p. 1969. 73.75x (ISBN 3-11-000360-0); Vol. 2. Jahrgang 1725, Stueck 53-104. iv, 428p. 1970. 75.75x (ISBN 3-11-000361-9); Vol. 3. Jahrgang 1726, Stueck 105-156. iv, 460p. 1970. 87.75x (ISBN 0-685-23149-6); Vol. 4. Kommentarband. (Ausgaben Deutscher Literatur des Xv Bis XViii Jahrhunderts). (Ger.). De Gruyter.
Maurer, Warren R. The Naturalist Image of German Literature: A Study of the German Naturalists - Appraisal of Their Literary Heritage. 269p. 1972. bds. 36.70 (ISBN 3-7705-0726-6). Adler.
Miller, Henry. Maurizius Forever. 82p. 8.50 (ISBN 0-686-74425-X). Porter.
Mueller, Rolf R. Festival & Fiction in Heinrich Wittenwiler's "Ring". A Study of the Narrative in Its Relation to the Traditional Topoi of Marriage, Folly, & Play. viii, 155p. 1977. 18.00 (ISBN 90-272-0963-4). Benjamins North Am.
Muller, Max, ed. Early German Classics from the Fourth to the Fifteenth Century. 1978. Repr. of 1858 ed. lib. bdg. 40.00 (ISBN 0-89760-526-8, Telegraph). Dynamic Learn Corp.
Murdoch, Brian. The Fall of Man in the Early Middle High German Biblical Epic: The Wiener Genesis, the Vorauer Genesis & the Anegenge. (Goeppinger Arbeiten Zur Germanistik Ser: No. 58). 262p. 1972. pap. 15.00x (ISBN 3-87452-119-2). Intl Pubns Serv.
Murner, Thomas. Deutsche Schriften mit den Holzschnitten der Erstdrucke. Schultz, Franz, ed. (Ger). Repr. of 1918 ed. 255.25x (ISBN 3-11-000276-0). De Gruyter.
Muschg, Adolph. Besprechungen. (Poly Ser.: No. 10). 148p. (Ger.). Date not set. 12.00 (ISBN 3-7643-1156-8). Birkhauser.
Norman, F., ed. Essays in German Literature. 166p. 1965. 50.00x (ISBN 0-85457-023-3, Pub. by Inst Germanic Stud England). State Mutual Bk.
Osterkamp, Ernst. Lucifer Stationen Eines Motivs. (Komparatistische Studien: Vol. 9). 1979. 49.00x (ISBN 3-11-007804-X). De Gruyter.
Parent, David J. Werner Bergengreun's Das Buch Rodenstein: A Detailed Analysis. 1974. pap. text ed. 27.50x (ISBN 90-2792-622-0). Mouton.
Pascal, R. The German Novel. 354p. 1956. 32.00x (ISBN 0-7190-0195-1, Pub. by Manchester U Pr England). State Mutual Bk.
Phelps, Leland R. & Alt, A. Tilo, eds. Creative Encounter: Festschrift for Herman Salinger. (Studies in the Germanic Languages & Literatures). 1978. 14.00x (ISBN 0-8078-8091-4). U of NC Pr.
Priest, George M. A Brief History of German Literature. 1973. Repr. of 1910 ed. 30.00 (ISBN 0-8274-1122-7). R West.
Prokosch, E. The Sounds & History of the German Language. 1979. Repr. of 1916 ed. lib. bdg. 30.00 (ISBN 0-685-95067-0). Arden Lib.
Purdie, Edna. The Story of Judith in German & English Literature. 1973. Repr. of 1927 ed. 45.00 (ISBN 0-8274-0982-6). R West.
Ranke, Kurt. Die Welt der Einfachen Formen: Studien Zur Motiv- Wort- und Quellen-Kunde. 1978. 82.00x (ISBN 3-11-007420-6). De Gruyter.
Ranke, Kurt, ed. Enzyklopaedie des Maerchens: Handwoerterbuch zur historischen und vergleichenden Erzaehlforschung, 12 vols, Vol. 1, Fasc. 1. 144p. 230.50x (ISBN 3-11-005805-7). De Gruyter.
Rede und Redeszene in der Deutschen Erzahlung Bis Wolfram Von Eschenbach. Repr. of 1909 ed. 14.00 (ISBN 0-384-54370-7); pap. 11.00 (ISBN 0-685-02059-2). Johnson Repr.
Reed, Eugene E. The Civilized Vs. Civilization: Primitivism in the Literature of German Pre-Romanticism. LC 76-56590. 1978. 3.50 (ISBN 0-89301-039-1). U Pr of Idaho.
Reiss, Hans. The Writer's Task from Nietzsche to Brecht. 221p. 1978. 21.50x (ISBN 0-87471-870-8). Rowman.
Richards, David B. Goerthe's Search for the Muse: Translation & Creativity. vi, 114p. 1979. 14.00 (ISBN 90-272-0967-7, GLLM 7). Benjamins North Am.
Ritchie, James M., ed. Periods in German Literature, Vol. 1. 1967. 15.95 (ISBN 0-85496-031-7); pap. 12.95 (ISBN 0-85496-032-5). Dufour.
--Periods in German Literature, Vol. 2. 1970. 15.95 (ISBN 0-85496-033-3). Dufour.
Robertson, John G. Essays & Addresses on Literature. facs. ed. LC 68-26471. (Essay Index Reprint Ser). 1968. Repr. of 1935 ed. 16.00 (ISBN 0-8369-0828-7). Arno.
--The Literature of Germany. Repr. 10.00 (ISBN 0-8274-2965-7). R West.
Robson-Scott, W. D., ed. Essays in German & Dutch Literature. 191p. 1973. 50.00x (ISBN 0-85457-051-9, Pub. by Inst Germanic Stud England). State Mutual Bk.
Rose, Ernst. A History of German Literature. LC 60-9405. (Gotham Library). (Orig.). 1960. 12.00x (ISBN 0-8147-0362-3); pap. 6.00x (ISBN 0-8147-0363-1). NYU Pr.
Rose, William. From Goethe to Byron: The Development of Weltschmerz in German Literature. 59.95 (ISBN 0-8490-0203-6). Gordon Pr.
Ruh, Kurt, et al, eds. Verfasserlexikon: Die Deutsche Literatur Des Mittelalters, 6 vols, Vol. 1, Fasc. 1. 2nd rev. ed. 1977. 42.25x (ISBN 3-11-006927-X). De Gruyter.
Sammons, Jeffrey L. Six Essays on the Young German Novel. 2nd ed. (Studies in the Germanic Languages & Literatures Ser.: No. 75). 184p. 1975. 14.00x (ISBN 0-8078-8075-2). U of NC Pr.
Samuel, Richard & Thomas, R. Hinton. Expressionism in German Life, Literature & the Theatre, 1910-24. 1971. Repr. 10.00x (ISBN 0-87556-308-2). Saifer.
Sauerland, Karol. Diltheys Erlebnisbegriff: Entstehung, Glanzzeit und Verkuemmerung eines literaturhistorischen Begriffs. 182p. 1972. 39.45x (ISBN 3-11-003599-5). De Gruyter.
Scherer, W. History of German Literature, 2 Vols. Muller, M., ed. LC 77-130265. (Studies in German Literature, No. 13). 1970. Repr. of 1906 ed. lib. bdg. 79.95 (ISBN 0-8383-1172-5). Haskell.
Scherer, W., et al. A History of German Literature: From the Accession of Frederick the Great to the Death of Goethe. Muller, F. M., ed. Conybeare, Mrs. F. C., tr. 335p. 1980. Repr. of 1981 ed. lib. bdg. 45.00 (ISBN 0-8495-4898-5). Arden Lib.
Scherer, Wilhelm. Geschichte der Deutschen Litteratur. LC 70-126675. Repr. of 1885 ed. 34.50 (ISBN 0-404-05587-7). AMS Pr.
--History of German Literature, 2 vols. 1973. Repr. of 1886 ed. Set. 50.00 (ISBN 0-8274-1375-0). R West.
Schmitt, Franz A. Stoff-und Motivgeschichte der Deutschen Literatur. 3rd ed. 1976. 61.00x (ISBN 3-11-006506-1). De Gruyter.
Schoolfield, George C. Figure of the Musician in German Literature. LC 56-63563. (North Carolina. University. Studies in the Germanic Languages & Literatures: No. 19). 18.50 (ISBN 0-404-50919-3). AMS Pr.
Schrader, Monika. Mimesis und Poiesis Poetologische Zum Bildungsroman. (Quellen und Forschungen zur Sprach-und Kulturgeschichte der germanischen). 367p. (Ger.). 1975. 44.70x (ISBN 3-11-005904-5). De Gruyter.
Sebastian, Brant. Tugent Spyl: Nach der Ausgabe des Magister Johann Winckel von Strassburg. Roloff, Hans G., ed. (Ausgaben Deutscher Literatur des 15 bis 18 Jahrh). (Ger). 1968. 30.00x (ISBN 3-11-000350-3). De Gruyter.
Selss, Albert M. A Critical Outline of the Literature of Germany. LC 73-39070. (Essay Index Reprint Ser.). Repr. of 1865 ed. 16.00 (ISBN 0-8369-2721-4). Arno.
Senner, William M. German Literature in Iceland. 1975. lib. bdg. 69.95 (ISBN 0-8490-0227-3). Gordon Pr.
Siefken, Hinrich & Robinson, Alan, eds. Erfahrung und Uberlieferung: Festschrift for C. P. Magill. 230p. 1975. text ed. 21.00x (ISBN 0-8426-0812-5). Verry.
Spaethling, Robert & Weber, Eugene, eds. Literature Eins. 2nd ed. 1979. pap. 5.95x (ISBN 0-393-95041-7). Norton.
Spalek, J. Ernst Toller & His Critics. LC 72-12777. (Studies in German Literature, No. 13). 1972. Repr. of 1968 ed. lib. bdg. 58.95 (ISBN 0-8383-1591-7). Haskell.
Speier, Hans. Force & Folly: Essays on Foreign Affairs & the History of Ideas. 1968. pap. 2.95x (ISBN 0-262-69025-X). MIT Pr.
Stael, de. De l'Allemagne, 5 vols. (Grands Escrivains de France). 350p. 1967. 15.95 ea. French & Eur.
--De l'Allemagne, Vol. 1. Balaye, Simone, ed. 1959. pap. 4.50 (ISBN 0-686-54923-6). French & Eur.
Stehmann, Wilhelm. Die Mittelhochdeutsche Vovelle Vom Studentenabrnteuer. (Ger). Repr. of 1909 ed. 21.50 (ISBN 0-384-57780-6); pap. 18.50 (ISBN 0-685-02171-8). Johnson Repr.
Stern, J. P. Idylls & Realities: Studies in Nineteenth-Century German Literature. LC 72-157095. 1971. 12.00 (ISBN 0-8044-2830-1). Ungar.
Stirk, S. D. The Prussian Spirit: A Survey of German Literature & Politics, 1914-1940. 59.95 (ISBN 0-8490-0912-X). Gordon Pr.
Strelka, Joseph P., et al, eds. Protest-Form-Tradition: Essays on German Exile Literature. LC 78-18190. 1979. 11.50x (ISBN 0-8173-8008-6). U of Ala Pr.

Studies in Honor of John Albrecht Walz. facs. ed. LC 68-29249. (Essay Index Reprint Ser). 1968. Repr. of 1941 ed. 15.00 (ISBN 0-8369-0915-1). Arno.

Swales, Martin. The German Bildungsroman from Weiland to Hesse. LC 77-855681. (Essays in Literature Ser). 1978. 15.00 (ISBN 0-691-06359-1). Princeton U Pr.

Taylor, Bayard. Studies in German Literature. 1979. Repr. of 1893 ed. lib. bdg. 30.00 (ISBN 0-8495-5139-0). Arden Lib.

Taylor, Baynard. Studies in German Literature. LC 72-1145. (Essay Index Reprint Ser.). Repr. of 1877 ed. 23.00 (ISBN 0-8369-2865-2). Arno.

Thomas, Calvin. History of German Literature. LC 72-103235. 1970. Repr. of 1909 ed. 14.50 (ISBN 0-8046-0871-7). Kennikat.

--A History of German Literature. 59.95 (ISBN 0-8490-0328-8). Gordon Pr.

--A History of German Literature. 1909. lib. bdg. 30.00 (ISBN 0-8482-9952-3). Norwood Edns.

Thomas, Helmuth. Untersuchungen Zur Ueberlieferung der Spruchdichtung Frauenlobs. Repr. of 1939 ed. 21.50 (ISBN 0-384-60172-3); pap. 18.50 (ISBN 0-685-02052-5). Johnson Repr.

Tiedemann, Ruediger. Fabels Reich: Zur Tradition und Zum Programm Romantischer Dichtungstheorie. (Komparatistische Studien: Vol. 8). 1978. 51.00x (ISBN 3-11-006958-X). De Gruyter.

Von Loen, Johann M. Gesammelte Kleine Schriften, 4 vols. Schneider, J. C. & Muller, J. B., eds. (Illus.). Repr. of 1752 ed. Set. 180.00 (ISBN 0-384-33788-0). Johnson Repr.

Weiss, Adelaide M. Merlin in German Literature. LC 73-140017. (Catholic University Studies in German Ser.: No. 3). Repr. of 1933 ed. 16.00 (ISBN 0-404-50223-7). AMS Pr.

Wentzlaff-Eggebert, Friedrich-Wilhelm. Belehrung und Verkuendigung: Schriften zur deutschen Literatur vom Mittelalter bis zur Neuzeit. Dick, Manfred & Kaiser, Gerhard, eds. 344p. 1975. 85.30x (ISBN 3-11-005714-X). De Gruyter.

Werner, Oscar H. Unmarried Mother in German Literature. LC 17-18727. (Columbia University. Germanic Studies, Old Ser.: No. 22). Repr. of 1917 ed. 15.00 (ISBN 0-404-50422-1). AMS Pr.

Wernicke, Christian. Christian Wernickes Epigramme. Repr. of 1909 ed. 52.50 (ISBN 0-384-66880-1); pap. 49.00 (ISBN 0-685-02150-5). Johnson Repr.

Wetzels, Walter D., ed. Myth & Reason: A Symposium. LC 72-3096. (Germanic Languages Symposium Ser). 206p. 1973. 9.95x (ISBN 0-292-75003-X). U of Tex Pr.

Whitcomb, Merrick. A Literary Source-Book of the German and Italian Renaissance. LC 73-307. 1973. lib. bdg. 25.00 (ISBN 0-8414-1431-9). Folcroft.

Wiegand, Herbert E. Studien zur Minne und Ehe in Wolframs Parzival und Hartmanns Artusepik. (Quellen und Forschungen Zur Sprach-und Kulturgeschichte der Germanischen Voelker, 49). 352p. (Ger.). 1972. 67.25x (ISBN 3-11-003672-X). De Gruyter.

Wildonie, Herrand V. The Tales & Songs of Herrand von Wildonie. Thomas, J. W., tr. LC 76-183354. (Studies in Germanic Languages and Literatures: No. 4). 88p. 1972. 7.25x (ISBN 0-8131-1267-2). U Pr of Ky.

Willoughby, Leonard A. Dante Gabriel Rossetti & German Literature. 1978. Repr. of 1912 ed. lib. bdg. 8.50 (ISBN 0-8482-6973-X). Norwood Edns.

Willson, A. Leslie, ed. Dimension: A Reader of German Literature Since 1968. 320p. (Orig.). 1981. pap. 9.95 (ISBN 0-8264-0042-6). Continuum.

Zeydel, Edwin H. Holy Roman Empire in German Literature. LC 19-1736. Repr. of 1918 ed. 17.50 (ISBN 0-404-50423-X). AMS Pr.

GERMAN LITERATURE–HISTORY AND CRITICISM–EARLY MODERN, 1500-1700

Baumgartner, M. On Dryden's Relation to Germany. (Studies in Dryden: No. 10). 1979. pap. text ed. 12.95 (ISBN 0-8383-0084-7). Haskell.

Elema, Hans. Literarisches Erfolg in Sechzig Jahren. 1973. 32.10x (ISBN 90-232-1058-1, Pub by Van Gorcum). Intl Schol Bk Serv.

Els, Gerhard. Kleine Schriften Zur Altdeutschen Weltlichen Dichtung. (Amsterdamer Publikationen Zur Sprache und Literature Ser.: No. 38). (Orig., Ger.). 1979. pap. text ed. 61.50x (ISBN 90-6203-418-7). Humanities.

Forster, Leonard. Kleine Schriften Zur Deutschen Literatur Im 17 Jahrhundert. (Beihefte Zum Daphnis Ser.: No. 1). 1978. pap. text ed. 29.00x (ISBN 90-6203-230-3). Humanities.

Francke, Kuno. Personality in German Literature Before Luther. LC 72-141480. 221p. 1973. Repr. of 1916 ed. lib. bdg. 15.00x (ISBN 0-8371-5865-6, FRPG). Greenwood.

Kayser, Wolfgang J. Klangmalerei Bei Harsdoerffer. 1932. 21.50 (ISBN 0-384-28831-6); pap. 18.50 (ISBN 0-384-28830-8). Johnson Repr.

King, K. C. Selected Essays on Medieval German Literature. Flood, J. L. & Hatts, A. T., eds. 219p. 1975. 50.00x (ISBN 0-85457-063-2, Pub. by Inst Germanic Stud England). State Mutual Bk.

Kunstmann, John G. Middle Ages, Reformation, Volkskunde. LC 60-62592. (North Carolina. University. Studies in the Germanic Languages & Literatures: No. 26). Repr. of 1959 ed. 18.50 (ISBN 0-404-50926-6). AMS Pr.

Meisser, Ulrich. Die Sprichwortersammlung Sebastian Franks Von 1541. (Amsterdamer Publikationen Zur Sprache und Literature Ser.: No. 14). (Orig., Ger.). 1974. pap. text ed. 32.00x (ISBN 90-6203-121-8). Humanities.

Pascal, Roy. German Literature in the Sixteenth & Seventeenth Centuries: Renaissance-Reformation-Baroque. LC 79-9993. 1979. Repr. of 1968 ed. lib. bdg. 22.75x (ISBN 0-313-21461-1, PAGL). Greenwood.

Pickering, F. P. Essays on Medieval German Literature & Iconography. LC 78-73815. (Anglica Germanica Ser.). (Illus.). 1980. 32.50 (ISBN 0-521-22627-9). Cambridge U Pr.

Schmitt, Wolfram. Deutsche Fachprosa des Mittelalters. Ausgewaehlte Texte. (Kleine Texte fuer Vorlesungen und Uebungen, 190). 120p. 1972. 9.25x (ISBN 3-11-003801-3). De Gruyter.

Stambaugh, Ria, ed. Teufelbuecher in Auswahl, Vol. 4. (Ausgaben Detuscher Literatur Des XV. Bix XVIII, Jahrhunderts). 1979. 134.00x (ISBN 3-11-007331-5). De Gruyter.

Wagman, Frederick H. Magic & Natural Science in German Baroque Literature. LC 42-9041. (Coulmbia University. Germanic Studies, New Ser.: No. 13). Repr. of 1942 ed. 19.00 (ISBN 0-404-50463-9). AMS Pr.

GERMAN LITERATURE–HISTORY AND CRITICISM–18TH CENTURY

Batt, Max. Treatment of Nature in German Literature from Gunther to the Appearance of Goethe's Werther. LC 72-91034. 1969. Repr. of 1902 ed. 9.50 (ISBN 0-8046-0644-7). Kennikat.

Blackall, Eric A. The Emergence of German As a Literary Language, 1700-1775. 2nd ed. LC 77-14702. 1978. 25.00x (ISBN 0-8014-1170-X). Cornell U Pr.

Bruford, Walter H. Germany in the Eighteenth Century. 1935. 38.50 (ISBN 0-521-04354-9); pap. 11.50x (ISBN 0-521-09259-0, 259). Cambridge U Pr.

Conger, Syndy M. Matthew G. Lewis, Charles Robert Maturin & the Germans: An Interpretative Study of the Influence of German Literature on Two Gothic Novels. Varma, Devendra P., ed. LC 79-8448. (Gothic Studies & Dissertations Ser.). 1980. Repr. of 1977 ed. lib. bdg. 28.00x (ISBN 0-405-12652-2). Arno.

Kahn, Ludwig W. Social Ideals in German Literature. LC 75-84876. Repr. of 1938 ed. 12.95 (ISBN 0-404-03626-0). AMS Pr.

Kastner, Abraham G. Gesammelte Poetische & Prosaische Schoenwissenschaftliche Werke, 4 pts. in 2 vols. 823p. Repr. of 1841 ed. 58.50 (ISBN 0-384-28437-X). Johnson Repr.

Kelly, John A. England & the Englishman in German Literature of the Eighteenth Century. LC 21-7048. (Columbia University. Germanic Studies, Old Ser.: No. 24). Repr. of 1921 ed. 17.50 (ISBN 0-404-50424-8). AMS Pr.

Kohlschmidt, Werner. A History of German Literature, 1760-1805. Hilton, Ian, tr. from Ger. LC 74-32062. 420p. 1975. text ed. 39.50x (ISBN 0-8419-0195-3). Holmes & Meier.

Lohan, Robert. Golden Age of German Literature. 2nd ed. (Living German Literature, Vol. 2). 12.00 (ISBN 0-8044-0327-9). Ungar.

Mollenhauer, Peter. Friedrich Nicolais Satiren: Ein Beitrag Zur Kulturgeschichte Des 18. Jahrhunderts. viii, 267p. 1977. 28.00 (ISBN 90-272-0962-6, GLLM 2). Benjamins North Am.

Montgomery, Marshall. Studies in the Age of Goethe. LC 77-9357. 1977. lib. bdg. 20.00 (ISBN 0-8414-6208-9). Folcroft.

Riley, Kastinger. Die Webliche Muse. Sechs Essays Uber Kunstlerisch Schaffende Frauen der Goethezeit. (Studies in German Literature, Linguistics, & Culture: Vol. 8). (Illus.). 300p. 1982. 25.00x (ISBN 0-938100-05-X). Camden Hse.

Roloff, Hans-Gert, et al, eds. Gottsched, Johann Christoph: Ausgewaehlte Werke, 2 pts, Vol. 8. Incl. Pt. 1. 1978. 143.00x (ISBN 3-110074-67-2); Pt. 2. 1978. 117.00x (ISBN 3-110074-66-4). De Gruyter.

Stewart, Gordon M. The Literary Contributions of Christoph Daniel Ebeling. 1978. pap. text ed. 25.75x (ISBN 90-6203-477-2). Humanities.

Wahl, Hans. Geschichte Des Teutschen Merkur. 21.50 (ISBN 0-384-65471-1); pap. 18.50 (ISBN 0-384-65470-3). Johnson Repr.

Ward, Albert. Book Production, Fiction, & the German Reading Public. 215p. (Eng. & Ger.). 1974. text ed. 26.00x (ISBN 0-19-818157-4). Oxford U Pr.

Wentzlaff-Eggebert, Friedrich-Wilhelm. Der Triumphierende und der Besiegte Tod in der Wort und Bildkunst Des Barock. (Illus.). 203p. (Ger.). 1975. 82.00x (ISBN 3-11-005821-9). De Gruyter.

Willoughby, Leonard A. Classical Age of German Literature, 1748-1805. LC 66-15438. 1966. Repr. of 1926 ed. 15.00 (ISBN 0-8462-0683-8). Russell.

GERMAN LITERATURE–HISTORY AND CRITICISM–19TH CENTURY

Artiss, David. Theodor Storm: Studies in Ambivalence. xix, 215p. 1978. 23.00 (ISBN 90-272-0965-0, GLLM 5). Benajamins North Am.

Bertaux, Felix. A Panorama of German Literature from 1871-1931. Traunstine, John J., tr. from Fr. LC 73-132940. 1971. Repr. of 1935 ed. lib. bdg. 13.50x (ISBN 0-8154-0354-2). Cooper Sq.

Boeschenstein, Hermann. German Literature in the Nineteenth Century. LC 70-76383. 1969. 14.95 (ISBN 0-312-32585-1). St Martin.

Bulmahn, Heinz. Adolf Glassbrenner: His Development from "Jungdeutscher" to "Vormarzler". x, 159p. 1978. 19.00 (ISBN 0-686-31497-2, GLLM 6). Benjamins North Am.

Butler, Clark. G. W. F. Hegel. (World Authors Ser.: Germany: No. 461). 1977. lib. bdg. 12.50 (ISBN 0-8057-6298-1). Twayne.

Christiansen, Heinz C. Fritz Reuter Gedenkschrift. (Amsterdamer Publikationen Zur Sprache und Literature: No. 18). (Illus.). 1976. pap. text ed. 20.00x (ISBN 90-6203-468-3). Humanities.

Dolmetsch, Christopher. The German Press of the Shenandoah Valley, 1789-1854. (Studies in German Literature, Linguistics, & Culture: Vol. 4). (Illus.). 180p. 1982. 19.00x (ISBN 0-938100-01-7). Camden Hse.

Fuerst, Norbert. Victorian Age of German Literature: Eight Essays. LC 65-23845. 1965. 14.95x (ISBN 0-271-73107-9). Pa St U Pr.

Furst, Lillian R. Counterparts: The Dynamics of Franco-German Literary Relationships, 1770-1895. LC 77-2407. 1977. text ed. 13.50x (ISBN 0-8143-1582-8). Wayne St U Pr.

Glaser, Hermann, ed. The German Mind of the Nineteenth Century: A Literary & Historical Anthology. 416p. 1981. 19.50 (ISBN 0-8264-0041-8); pap. 8.95 (ISBN 0-8264-0044-2). Continuum.

Gode, Alexander. Natural Science in German Romanticism. LC 70-168170. (Columbia University. Germanic Studies, New Ser.: No. 11). Repr. of 1941 ed. 19.00 (ISBN 0-404-50461-2). AMS Pr.

Hatfield, Henry. Clashing Myths in German Literature: From Heine to Rilke. LC 73-83964. 256p. 1974. text ed. 14.00x (ISBN 0-674-13375-7). Harvard U Pr.

Heller, Erich. The Disinherited Mind: Essays in Modern German Literature & Thought. enl. ed. LC 74-19104. 358p. 1975. pap. 4.50 (ISBN 0-15-626100-6, HB305, Harv). HarBraceJ.

Heller, Otto. Studies in Modern German Literature. facs. ed. LC 67-26748. (Essay Index Reprint Ser). 1905. 16.00 (ISBN 0-8369-0531-8). Arno.

Kahn, Ludwig W. Social Ideals in German Literature. LC 75-84876. Repr. of 1938 ed. 12.95 (ISBN 0-404-03626-0). AMS Pr.

Klenze, Camillo Von. From Goethe to Hauptmann: Studies in a Changing Culture. LC 66-23519. 1926. 10.50x (ISBN 0-8196-0178-0). Biblo.

Lessing, Otto E. Masters in Modern German Literature. facs. ed. LC 67-23239. (Essay Index Reprint Ser). 1912. 15.00 (ISBN 0-8369-0616-0). Arno.

Lohan, Robert. Golden Age of German Literature. 2nd ed. (Living German Literature, Vol. 2). 12.00 (ISBN 0-8044-0327-9). Ungar.

Menhennet, Alan. Romantic Movement. (The Literary History of Germany Ser.: Vol. 6). 276p. 1981. 28.50x (ISBN 0-389-20104-9). B&N.

Mews, Siegfried, ed. Studies in German Literature of the Nineteenth & Twentieth Centuries: Festschrift for Frederic E. Coenen. (Studies in Comparative Literature Ser.: No. 67). 1971. 15.00x (ISBN 0-8078-8067-1). U of NC Pr.

Montgomery, Marshall. Studies in the Age of Goethe. LC 77-9357. 1977. lib. bdg. 20.00 (ISBN 0-8414-6208-9). Folcroft.

Riley, Kastinger. Die Webliche Muse. Sechs Essays Uber Kunstlerisch Schaffende Frauen der Goethezeit. (Studies in German Literature, Linguistics, & Culture: Vol. 8). (Illus.). 300p. 1982. 25.00x (ISBN 0-938100-05-X). Camden Hse.

Silz, Walter. Realism & Reality. LC 78-27815. (North Carolina. University. Studies in the Germanic Languages & Literatures: No. 11). Repr. 18.50 (ISBN 0-404-50911-8). AMS Pr.

Stern, J. P. Idylls & Realities: Studies in Nineteenth-Century German Literature. LC 72-157095. 1971. 12.00 (ISBN 0-8044-2830-1). Ungar.

--Re-Interpretations: Seven Studies in Nineteenth Century German Literature. 370p. Date not set. price not set (ISBN 0-521-23983-4); pap. price not set (ISBN 0-521-28366-3). Cambridge U Pr.

Von Klenze, Camillo. From Goethe to Hauptmann. 1973. Repr. of 1926 ed. 8.50 (ISBN 0-8274-1374-2). R West.

GERMAN LITERATURE–HISTORY AND CRITICISM–20TH CENTURY

Bartram, Graham & Waine, Anthony, eds. Brecht in Perspective. (German Literature & Society: Vol. 2). 1980. text ed. write for info. (ISBN 0-85496-076-7). Humanities.

Bertaux, Felix. A Panorama of German Literature from 1871-1931. Traunstine, John J., tr. from Fr. LC 73-132940. 1971. Repr. of 1935 ed. lib. bdg. 13.50x (ISBN 0-8154-0354-2). Cooper Sq.

Bosmajian, Hamida. Metaphors of Evil: Contemporary German Literature & the Shadow of Nazism. LC 79-22758. (Illus.). 1979. 14.00x (ISBN 0-87745-093-5); pap. 8.75 (ISBN 0-87745-096-X). U of Iowa Pr.

Carnegy, Patrick. Faust As Musician: A Study of Thomas Mann's Novel 'Dr. Faustus' LC 73-78718. 192p. 1973. 9.25 (ISBN 0-8112-0515-0). New Directions.

Demetz, Peter. Postwar German Literature: A Critical Introduction. LC 73-114169. 1972. pap. 2.95 (ISBN 0-8052-0368-0). Schocken.

--Postwar German Literature: A Critical Introduction. LC 73-114169. 264p. 1970. text ed. 24.50x (ISBN 0-8290-0198-0). Irvington.

Flower, J. E., et al. Writers & Politics in Modern Britain, France, & Germany. LC 77-7595. 1977. text ed. 29.50x (ISBN 0-8419-0320-4). Holmes & Meier.

Furness, Raymond. Literary History of Germany: The Twentieth Century,1890-1945, Vol. 8. LC 77-10037. (Literary History of Germany Ser.). 1978. text ed. 23.50x (ISBN 0-06-492310-X). B&N.

Genno, Charles N. & Wetzel, Heinz, eds. The First World War in German Narrative Prose. LC 79-26625. 1980. 17.50x (ISBN 0-8020-5490-0). U of Toronto Pr.

Gray, Ronald D. German Tradition in Literature. LC 65-17206. 1966. 48.00 (ISBN 0-521-05133-9); pap. 17.50 (ISBN 0-521-29278-6). Cambridge U Pr.

Hatfield, Henry. Clashing Myths in German Literature: From Heine to Rilke. LC 73-83964. 256p. 1974. text ed. 14.00x (ISBN 0-674-13375-7). Harvard U Pr.

Heller, Erich. The Disinherited Mind: Essays in Modern German Literature & Thought. enl. ed. LC 74-19104. 358p. 1975. pap. 4.50 (ISBN 0-15-626100-6, HB305, Harv). HarBraceJ.

Hesse, Hermann. My Belief: Essays on Life & Art. Lindley, Denver, tr. from Ger. 384p. 1974. 8.95 (ISBN 0-374-21666-5); pap. 5.95 (ISBN 0-374-51109-8). FS&G.

Horst, Karl A. Quest of Twentieth Century German Literature. Thompson, Elizabeth, tr. LC 71-165017. 14.50 (ISBN 0-8044-0402-X). Ungar.

Krispyn, Egbert. Anti-Nazi Writers in Exile. LC 77-9568. 200p. 1978. 15.00 (ISBN 0-8203-0430-1). U of Ga Pr.

Liere, C. G. Van. George Hermann: Materialien Zar Kenntnis Seines Libens und Seines Werkes. (Amsterdamer Publikationen Zur Sprache und Literature: Vol. 17). (Ger.). 1976. pap. text ed. 16.00x (ISBN 90-6203-378-4). Humanities.

Mews, Siegfried, ed. Studies in German Literature of the Nineteenth & Twentieth Centuries: Festschrift for Frederic E. Coenen. (Studies in Comparative Literature Ser.: No. 67). 1971. 15.00x (ISBN 0-8078-8067-1). U of NC Pr.

Mileck, Joseph. Hermann Hesse: Life & Art. LC 76-48020. 1978. 16.95 (ISBN 0-520-03351-5); pap. 5.95 (ISBN 0-520-04152-6). U of Cal Pr.

Reichert, Herbert W. Friedrich Nietzsche's Impact on Modern German Literature. (Studies in Comparative Literature Ser.: No. 84). 1975. 10.50x (ISBN 0-8078-8084-1). U of NC Pr.

Rosenberg, Alfred. Kampf Um die Macht: Aufsatze Von 1921-1932, Herausgegeben Von Thilo Von Trotha. LC 77-180426. Repr. of 1938 ed. 40.00 (ISBN 0-404-56160-8). AMS Pr.

Runge, Edith A. Primitivism & Related Ideas in Sturm und Drang Literature. LC 73-180618. xii, 308p. 1972. Repr. of 1946 ed. 18.00 (ISBN 0-8462-1666-3). Russell.

Salamon, George. Arnold Zweig. LC 75-12736. (World Author Ser.: Germany: No. 361). 1975. lib. bdg. 12.50 (ISBN 0-8057-6212-4). Twayne.

Scheffauer, Herman G. New Vision in the German Arts. LC 74-118432. 1971. Repr. of 1924 ed. 13.50 (ISBN 0-8046-1131-9). Kennikat.

Sokel, Walter H. The Writer in Extremis: Expressionism in Twentieth-Century German Literature. 1959. 10.00x (ISBN 0-8047-0556-9). Stanford U Pr.

Stirk, S. D. Prussian Spirit: A Survey of German Literature & Politics 1914-1940. LC 68-8245. 1969. Repr. of 1941 ed. 12.00 (ISBN 0-8046-0447-9). Kennikat.

Subiotto, A. V. Gunther Grass: The Literature of Politics. (German Literature & Society Ser.: Vol. 3). 1980. pap. text ed. write for info. (ISBN 0-85496-076-7). Humanities.

Taylor, Ronald. Literature & Society in Germany, 1918-1945. (Studies in Contemporary Literature & Culture). 363p. 1980. 28.50x (ISBN 0-389-20036-0). B&N.

GERMAN LITERATURE–TRANSLATIONS FROM FOREIGN LITERATURE

Blassneck, Marce. Frankreich Als Vermittler Englisch-Deutscher Einflusse Im Siebzehnten und Achtzehnten Jahrhundert. 1934. pap. 10.00 (ISBN 0-384-04685-1). Johnson Repr.

Fang, Ilse M., ed. Chinesische Anthologie: Ubersetzungen Aus Dem Wen Hsuan, 2 Vols. Von Zach, Erwin, tr. LC 58-6581. (Harvard-Yenching Institute Studies: No. 18). 1958. Set. pap. 25.00x (ISBN 0-674-12650-5). Harvard U Pr.

GERMAN LITERATURE–TRANSLATIONS INTO ENGLISH

Francke, Kuno, ed. German Classics, 20 Vols. Repr. of 1914 ed. Set. 695.00 (ISBN 0-404-02600-1); 34.75 ea. AMS Pr.

Goethe, Johann W. von. Johann Wolfgang Von Goethe's Roman Elegies & Venetian Epigrams. Lind, L. R., tr. from Ger. LC 74-7172. xii, 228p. 1974. 11.00x (ISBN 0-7006-0125-2). Regents Pr KS.

Meyrink, Gustav & Busson, Paul. The Golem & "The Man Who Was Born Again". Two German Supernatural Novels. Bleiler, E. F., ed. (Illus.). 479p. (Orig.). 1976. pap. 4.50 (ISBN 0-486-23327-8). Dover.

O'Neill, Patrick. German Literature in English Translation: A Select Bibliography. 136p. 1981. 15.00x (ISBN 0-8020-2409-2). U of Toronto Pr.

Schmidt, Peter. The German Correspondent Vol. 1, No. 1-6, N. Y. 1820. 1970. Repr. of 1820 ed. 7.00 (ISBN 0-685-40306-8). R & E Res Assoc.

Stringham, Mary, ed. Orff-Schulwerk: Background & Commentary. 1976. pap. 2.50 (ISBN 0-918812-05-4). Magnamusic.

GERMAN LITERATURE–TRANSLATIONS INTO ENGLISH–BIBLIOGRAPHY

Kopp, W. LaMarr. German Literature in the United States, 1945-1960. (Studies in Comparative Literature Ser.: No. 42). 1968. 13.50x (ISBN 0-8078-7042-0). U of NC Pr.

Morgan, Bayard Q. A Critical Bibliography of German Literature in English Translation, 1481-1927. 2nd ed. LC 65-13549. 1965. Repr. of 1938 ed. 13.50 (ISBN 0-8108-0032-2). Scarecrow.

Smith, Murray F. Selected Bibliography of German Literature in English Translation, 1956-1960: A Second Supplement to Bayard Quincy Morgan's - A Critical Bibliography of German Literature in English Translation. LC 76-157727. 1972. 14.50 (ISBN 0-8108-0411-5). Scarecrow.

GERMAN LITERATURE–TRANSLATIONS INTO ENGLISH–HISTORY AND CRITICISM

Bartscht, Waltraud. Goethe's "Das Marchen". Translation and Analysis. LC 72-132826. (Studies in Germanic Langauges & Literatures: No. 3). 112p. 1972. 9.00x (ISBN 0-8131-1237-0). U Pr of Ky.

Stockley, Violet A. German Literature As Known in England, 1750-1830. LC 70-93073. 1969. Repr. of 1929 ed. 14.50 (ISBN 0-8046-0686-2). Kennikat.

GERMAN MEASLES

see Rubella

GERMAN MERCENARIES

see also United States–History–Revolution, 1775-1783–German Mercenaries

GERMAN MUSIC

see Music, German

GERMAN NATIONAL CHARACTERISTICS

see National Characteristics, German

GERMAN NATIONAL PEOPLE'S PARTY

Hertzman, Lewis. D N V P: The Right-Wing Opposition in the Weimar Republic, 1918-1924. LC 63-15846. 1964. 16.50x (ISBN 0-8032-0068-4). U of Nebr Pr.

GERMAN NEWSPAPERS

see also German-American Newspapers

GERMAN OCCUPATION OF DENMARK, 1940-1945

see Denmark–History

GERMAN OCCUPATION OF NETHERLANDS, 1940-1945

see Netherlands–History–German Occupation, 1940-1945

GERMAN PAINTING

see also Painting, German

GERMAN PAINTINGS

see also Paintings, German

GERMAN PERIODICALS

Estermann, Alfred, compiled by. Registerband (to Complete Collection of Zeitschriften Des Jungen Deutschland) 200p. Repr. of 1972 ed. 17.00 (ISBN 0-384-50046-3). Johnson Repr.

Mayer, S. L., ed. Signal: Hitler's Wartime Picture Magazine. LC 75-28749. 1976. 12.50 (ISBN 0-13-810051-9). P-H.

GERMAN PERIODICALS–BIBLIOGRAPHY–CATALOGS

Erdelyi, Gabor & Peterson, Agnes F. German Periodical Publications. LC 66-28530. (Bibliographical Ser.: No. 27). 1967. pap. 6.00 (ISBN 0-8179-2272-5). Hoover Inst Pr.

Staats Bibliotech Preussischer Kulturbesitz Berlin, ed. Union List of German Language Serials, 2 vols. 2512p. 1978. 269.00 (ISBN 3-5980-2801-6). K G Saur.

Staats Bibliothek Preussischer Kulturbesitz, ed. Union List of Serials in Libraries of W. Germany. 8th ed. 1351p. 1978. 160.25 (ISBN 3-7940-2801-5). K G Saur.

GERMAN PHILOLOGY

Catholic University Of America. Catholic University Studies in German, 19 Vols. Repr. of 1943 ed. Set. write for info. (ISBN 0-404-50220-2). AMS Pr.

Maurer, Friedrich & Rupp, Heinz, eds. Deutsche Wortgeschichte, Vol. 1. 3rd ed. LC 73-88302. (Grundriss der Germanischen Philologie, Vol. 17 Pt. 1). 581p. 1974. 79.50x (ISBN 3-11-003627-4). De Gruyter.

Schirmer, Alfred. Deutsche Wortkunde: Kulturgeschichte des Deutschen Wortschatzes. 6th enl. ed. Mitzka, Walther, ed. (Sammlung Goeschen, No. 929). (Ger). 1969. 3.25x (ISBN 3-11-006206-2). De Gruyter.

Schmitt, Ludwig E., ed. Kurzer Grundriss der germanischen Philologie bis 1500, Vol. 1, Sprachgeschichte. (Ger). 1970. 30.00x (ISBN 3-11-000260-4). De Gruyter.

--Kurzer Grundriss der germanischen Philologie bis 1500, Vol. 2, Literaturgeschichte. (Ger). 1971. 36.25x (ISBN 3-11-006468-5). De Gruyter.

GERMAN PHILOSOPHY

see Philosophy, German

GERMAN POETRY (COLLECTIONS)

Here are entered works in the German language. For translations into English see subdivision Translations into English.

Allen, Roy F. German Expressionist Poetry. (World Authors Ser.: No. 421). 1979. lib. bdg. 13.50 (ISBN 0-8057-6386-4). Twayne.

Bruns, Friedrich, ed. Lese der Deutschen Lyrik: Von Klopstock bis Rilke. (Orig., Ger.,). 1961. pap. text ed. 12.95x (ISBN 0-89197-274-9). Irvington.

Eitner, Robert. Das Deutsche Lied Des XV und XVI Jahrhunderts, 2 vols. in 1. LC 71-178529. Repr. of 1876 ed. 37.50 (ISBN 0-404-56542-5). AMS Pr.

Fleissner, Otto S. & Fleissner, E. M., eds. Kleine Anthologie Deutscher Lyrik. (Ger.). 1935. text ed. 12.95x (ISBN 0-89197-257-9); pap. text ed. 4.95x (ISBN 0-89197-258-7). Irvington.

Foltin, Lore B. & Heinen, Hubert, eds. Paths to German Poetry: An Introductory Anthology. (Orig., Ger.). 1969. pap. text ed. 11.50 scp (ISBN 0-06-042112-6, HarpC). Har-Row.

Forster, Leonard, ed. Penguin Book of German Verse. (Poets Ser.). (Orig., Ger., With Prose Tr). (YA) (gr. 9 up). 1966. pap. 4.95 (ISBN 0-14-042036-3). Penguin.

Friedman, Clarence W. Prefigurations in Meistergesang. LC 75-140020. (Catholic University of America Studies in German Ser.: No. 18). Repr. of 1943 ed. 17.00 (ISBN 0-404-50238-5). AMS Pr.

--Prefigurations in Meistergesang. LC 75-140020. (Catholic University of America Studies in German Ser.: No. 18). Repr. of 1943 ed. 17.00 (ISBN 0-404-50238-5). AMS Pr.

Hamburger, Michael, ed. East German Poetry: An Anthology. Levenson, Christopher, et al, trs. from Ger. (Translation Ser.). 1979. 12.95 (ISBN 0-85635-034-6, Pub. by Carcanet New Pr England). Persea Bks.

--German Poetry Nineteen Ten to Nineteen Seventy-Five. 533p. (Orig.). 22.50 (ISBN 0-85635-161-X, Pub. by Carcanet New Pr England). Persea Bks.

Kaufmann, Walter, ed. & tr. from Ger. Twenty-Five German Poets: A Bilingual Collection. 325p. 1975. 8.95x (ISBN 0-393-04405-X). Norton.

Macleod, Norman. German Lyric Poetry. 1930. 20.00 (ISBN 0-8274-2405-1). R West.

Munsterberg, Margarete, ed. A Harvest of German Verse. LC 78-57860. (Granger Poetry Library). 1978. Repr. of 1916 ed. 21.50x (ISBN 0-89609-098-1). Granger Bk.

Prawer, Siegbert, ed. Seventeen Modern German Poets. (Clarendon German Ser). 204p. 1971. pap. 7.95x (ISBN 0-19-832474-X). Oxford U Pr.

Rose, William. Modern German Poetry. Repr. of 1931 ed. 10.00 (ISBN 0-686-18771-7). Scholars Ref Lib.

Rus, Vladimir. Selections from German Poetry. LC 66-14177. (Illus.). (gr. 8 up). 1966. PLB 5.29 (ISBN 0-8178-3752-3). Harvey.

Salinger, Herman, ed. Twentieth-Century German Verse. facsimile ed. LC 68-57065. (Granger Index Reprint Ser). 1952. 12.00 (ISBN 0-8369-6042-4). Arno.

Schaum, Konrad, ed. Deutsche Lyrik. (Orig., Ger.). 1963. pap. 2.95x (ISBN 0-393-09612-2, NortonC). Norton.

Stahl, Ernest L., ed. Oxford Book of German Verse, Twelfth to Twentieth Century. 3rd ed. (Ger). 1967. 29.50 (ISBN 0-19-812132-6). Oxford U Pr.

Von Wiese, B., ed. Deutsche Gedichte: Von Den Anfaengen Bis Zur Gegenwart. (Ger). 1972. 10.95 (ISBN 0-685-20235-6). Schoenhof.

Weimar, Karl S., ed. Thirty-Six German Poems. LC 50-14279. 1950. pap. text ed. 4.75 (ISBN 0-395-05524-5, 3-59405). HM.

GERMAN POETRY–HISTORY AND CRITICISM

Anderson, Robert R., et al, eds. Wortindex und Reimregister Zum Sogennanten Heinrich Von Melk. (Indices Verborum Zum Aldeitschen Schriftum: No. 3). 1977. pap. text ed. 19.00x (ISBN 90-6203-429-2). Humanities.

Angress, R. K. The Early German Epigram: A Study in Baroque Poetry. LC 70-111501. (Studies in Germanic Languages & Literatures: No. 2). 136p. 1971. 9.00x (ISBN 0-8131-1231-1). U Pr of Ky.

Arens, Hans. Ulrichs Von Lichtenstein Frauendienst: Untersuchungen Uber Den Hofischen Sprachstil. (Ger). Repr. of 1939 ed. 14.00 (ISBN 0-384-01898-X); pap. 11.00 (ISBN 0-685-02208-0). Johnson Repr.

Arndt, Walter, ed. The Genius of Wilhelm Busch. LC 79-63545. (Illus.). 450p. 1981. 39.95 (ISBN 0-520-03897-5); pre-jan. 35.00 (ISBN 0-686-76226-6). U of Cal Pr.

Bartsch, Karl F. Untersuchungen Zur Jenaer Leiderhandschrift. Repr. of 1923 ed. 14.00 (ISBN 0-384-03490-X); pap. 11.00 (ISBN 0-685-02216-1). Johnson Repr.

Baumann, Cecilia C. Wilhelm Muller: The Poet of the Schubert Song Cycles. LC 80-12806. (Studies in German Literature). (Illus.). 208p. 1981. 17.50x (ISBN 0-271-00266-2). Pa St U Pr.

Baumgartner, M. On Dryden's Relation to Germany. (Studies in Dryden: No. 10). 1979. pap. text ed. 12.95 (ISBN 0-8383-0084-7). Haskell.

Bekker, Hugo. Friedrich Von Hausen: Inquiries into His Poetry. (Studies in Germanic Languages & Literatures: No. 87). 1977. 12.95x (ISBN 0-8078-8087-6). U of NC Pr.

Belgardt, Raimund. Romantische Poesie. (Ger). 1970. text ed. 40.00x (ISBN 90-2791-248-3). Mouton.

Bell, Clair H., tr. Peasant Life in Old German Epics. (Illus.). 1965. lib. bdg. 16.00x (ISBN 0-374-90551-7). Octagon.

Bernd, Clifford A. German Poetic Realism. (World Authors Ser.: No. 605). 1981. lib. bdg. 12.95 (ISBN 0-8057-6447-X). Twayne.

Bithell, J. & Yarmolinsky, D. Contemporary German Poetry. 59.95 (ISBN 0-87968-938-2). Gordon Pr.

Braun, Wilhelm A. Types of Weltschmerz in German Poetry. LC 5-33195. (Columbia University. Germanic Studies, Old Ser.: No. 6). Repr. of 1905 ed. 14.50 (ISBN 0-404-50406-X). AMS Pr.

Browning, Robert M. German Baroque Poetry, 1618-1723. LC 77-136959. 1971. 16.95x (ISBN 0-271-01146-7). Pa St U Pr.

--German Poetry in the Age of the Enlightenment: From Brockes to Klopstock. LC 77-26832. (Penn State Series in German Literature). 1978. text ed. 17.95x (ISBN 0-271-00541-6). Pa St U Pr.

Bruns, Friedrich. Modern Thought in the German Lyric Poets from Goethe to Dehmel. 59.95 (ISBN 0-8490-0654-6). Gordon Pr.

Capelle, Carl. Volistaendiges Woerterbuch Ueber die Gedichte des Homores und der Homeriden. 9th ed. 1968. 48.00 (ISBN 3-534-03408-2, M-7681, Pub. by Wissenschaftl Buchgesells). French & Eur.

De Capua, A. G. German Baroque Poetry: Interpretive Readings. LC 73-152521. 1973. 15.50 (ISBN 0-87395-084-4); microfiche 15.50 (ISBN 0-87395-184-0). State U NY Pr.

Flores, John. Poetry in East Germany: Adjustments, Visions & Provocations 1945-1970. LC 77-115368. (Germanic Studies Ser.: No. 5). 1971. 27.50x (ISBN 0-300-01339-6). Yale U Pr.

Gillespie, Gerald. German Baroque Poetry. LC 74-110363. (World Authors Ser.). 1971. lib. bdg. 12.95x (ISBN 0-8057-2360-9). Irvington.

Gloss, August. The Genius of the German Lyric. 1976. lib. bdg. 59.95 (ISBN 0-8490-1879-X). Gordon Pr.

Gray, R. German Poetry: A Guide to Free Appreciation. rev. ed. LC 75-20834. 120p. 1976. 27.50 (ISBN 0-521-20931-5); pap. 8.95x (ISBN 0-521-29000-7). Cambridge U Pr.

Grundlehner, Philip. The Lyrical Bridge: Essays from Holderlin to Benn. LC 76-46765. (Illus.). 177p. 1978. 14.50 (ISBN 0-8386-1792-1). Fairleigh Dickinson.

Gumpel, Liselotte. Concrete Poetry from East & West Germany: The Language of Exemplarism & Experimentalism. LC 74-43317. (Germanic Studies Ser.: No. 16). 1976. 20.00x (ISBN 0-300-01914-9). Yale U Pr.

Han Yu. Poetische Werke. Hightower, James R., ed. Von Zach, Erwin, tr. LC 52-5409. (Harvard-Yenching Institute Studies: No. 7). xi, 393p. 1952. 12.50x (ISBN 0-674-67860-5). Harvard U Pr.

Hofacker, Erich P. Christian Morgenstern. (World Authors Ser.: No. 508 (Germany)). 1978. 12.50 (ISBN 0-8057-6349-X). Twayne.

Hofrichter, Ruth. Three Poets & Reality. LC 78-86024. (Essay & General Literature Index Reprint Ser). 1969. Repr. of 1942 ed. 12.50 (ISBN 0-8046-0564-5). Kennikat.

Huebner, Arthur. Daniel, eine Deutschordensdichtung. Repr. of 1911 ed. 14.00 (ISBN 0-384-24810-1); pap. 11.00 (ISBN 0-685-02266-8). Johnson Repr.

Knortz, K. Representative German Poems. 59.95 (ISBN 0-8490-0946-4). Gordon Pr.

Korff, H. A. Die Dichtung Von Sturm und Drang Im Zusammenhange der Geistesgeschichte. (Ger). Repr. of 1928 ed. 15.50 (ISBN 0-384-30215-7). Johnson Repr.

Liptzin, Solomon. Lyric Pioneers of Modern Germany. LC 28-5277. Repr. of 1928 ed. 16.45 (ISBN 0-404-03995-2). AMS Pr.

Macleod, Norman. German Lyric Poetry. LC 74-164696. Repr. of 1930 ed. 16.00 (ISBN 0-404-04138-8). AMS Pr.

Muensterberg, M. A Harvest of German Verse. 59.95 (ISBN 0-8490-0284-2). Gordon Pr.

Murdoch, Brian G. Hans Folz & the Adam-Legends. (Amsterdamer Publikationen Zur Sprache und Literatur: No. 28). 1977. pap. text ed. 23.00x (ISBN 90-6203-479-9). Humanities.

Nalbantian, Suzanne. The Symbol of the Soul from Holderlin to Yeats: A Study in Metonymy. LC 76-25550. 151p. 1976. 17.50x (ISBN 0-231-04148-9). Columbia U Pr.

Neuburger, Paul. Die Verseinlage in der Prosadichtung der Romantik. 29.00 (ISBN 0-384-41121-5); pap. 26.00 (ISBN 0-384-41120-7). Johnson Repr.

Newton, Robert P. Form in the Menscheitsdammerung: A Study of Prosodic Elements & Style in German Expressionist Poetry. LC 77-147934. (De Proprietatibus Litterarum, Ser. Practica: No. 7). 270p. 1971. pap. text ed. 32.50x (ISBN 90-2791-767-1). Mouton.

Paetzel, Walther. Die Variationen in der Altgermanischen Alliterations Poesie. Repr. of 1913 ed. 21.50 (ISBN 0-384-44441-5); pap. 18.50 (ISBN 0-384-44440-7). Johnson Repr.

Peacock, P. The Great War in German Lyrical Poetry. 59.95 (ISBN 0-8490-0262-1). Gordon Pr.

Politica. Geschichte der Dichtungen Vom Besten Staate. (Ger.). 1892. text ed. 28.25x (ISBN 90-6090-021-9). Humanities.

Remy, A. F. The Influence of India & Persia on the Poetry of Germany. 1976. lib. bdg. 59.95 (ISBN 0-8490-2059-X). Gordon Pr.

Remy, Arthur F. Influence of India & Persia on the Poetry of Germany. LC 12-28753. (Columbia University. Germanic Studies, Old Series: No. 44). Repr. of 1901 ed. 14.50 (ISBN 0-404-50404-3). AMS Pr.

Rosenfeld, Hellmut. Deutsche Bildgedicht: Seine Antiken Vorbilder und Seine Entwicklung Bis Zur Gegenwart. Repr. of 1935 ed. 21.50 (ISBN 0-384-52010-3); pap. 18.50 (ISBN 0-384-51980-6). Johnson Repr.

Schroeder, M. J. Mary-Verse in "Meistergesang". (Catholic University Studies in German: No. 16). 1970. Repr. of 1942 ed. 23.50 (ISBN 0-404-50236-9). AMS Pr.

Stein, Jack M. Poem & Music in the German Lied from Gluck to Hugo Wolf. LC 70-152772. 1971. 12.50x (ISBN 0-674-67451-0). Harvard U Pr.

Stork, Uwe. Der Sprachliche Rhythmus in Den Buhnenstucken John Millington Synges. (Salzburg Studies in Elizabethan Literature: Poetic Drama: No. 55). 1980. pap. text ed. 25.00x (ISBN 0-391-01876-0). Humanities.

Taylor, Archer. Literary History of Meistergesang. 1937. pap. 8.00 (ISBN 0-527-89050-2). Kraus Repr.

Thomas, John W. Medieval German Lyric Verse in English Translation. LC 78-27834. (North Carolina. University. Studies in the Germanic Languages & Literatures: No. 60). Repr. of 1968 ed. 18.50 (ISBN 0-404-50953-3). AMS Pr.

Wentzlaff-Eggebert, Friedrich W. Das Problem Des Todes in der Deutschen Lyrik Des 17 Jahrhunderts. (Ger). 21.50 (ISBN 0-384-66760-0); pap. 18.50 (ISBN 0-685-02149-1). Johnson Repr.

Ziolkowski, Theodore. The Classical German Elegy, Seventeen Ninety-Five to Nineteen Fifty. LC 79-3236. (Illus.). 1980. 20.00x (ISBN 0-691-06430-X). Princeton U Pr.

GERMAN POETRY–MIDDLE HIGH GERMAN, 1050-1500–HISTORY AND CRITICISM

Goenner, M. E. Mary Verse of the Teutonic Knights. LC 72-140022. (Catholic University of America Studies in German: No. 19). Repr. of 1943 ed. 20.00 (ISBN 0-404-50239-3). AMS Pr.

Hatto, A. T. Essays on Medieval German & Other Poetry. LC 87-54325. (Anglica Germanica Ser.: No. 2). 416p. 1980. 65.00 (ISBN 0-521-22148-X). Cambridge U Pr.

Lofmark, Carl. The Authority of the Source in Middle High German Narrative Poetry. 153p. 1981. 30.00x (ISBN 0-85457-098-5, Pub. by Inst Germanic Stud England). State Mutual Bk.

Pickering, F. P. Literature & Art in the Middle Ages. LC 79-102698. (Illus.). 1970. 17.95x (ISBN 0-87024-152-4). U of Miami Pr.

Stange, Manfred. Reinmars Lyrik, Forschungskritik und Uberlegungen Zu Einem Neuen Verstandis Reinmars Des Alten. (Amsterdamer Publikationen Zur Sprache und Literatur: No. 32). 1977. pap. text ed. 20.25x (ISBN 90-6203-140-4). Humanities.

GERMAN POETRY–TRANSLATIONS INTO ENGLISH

Davis, E. Z. Translations of German Poetry in American Magazines. 59.95 (ISBN 0-8490-1227-9). Gordon Pr.

Davis, Edward Z. Translations of German Poetry in American Magazines, 1741-1810. LC 66-27663. 1966. Repr. of 1905 ed. 19.00 (ISBN 0-8103-3209-4). Gale.

Deutsch, Babette & Yarmolinsky, Avrahm, eds. Contemporary German Poetry. facs. ed. LC 77-76934. (Granger Index Reprint Ser). 1923. 15.00 (ISBN 0-8369-6010-6). Arno.

Eich, Gunter, et al. Four German Poets: Gunter Eich, Hilde Domin, Erich Fried, & Gunter Kunert. Stein, Agnes, ed. & tr. from Ger. LC 78-59474. (Contemporary Poets Ser.). 1980. 12.95 (ISBN 0-87376-034-4). Red Dust.

Flores, Angel, ed. Anthology of German Poetry from Holderlin to Rilke. 8.50 (ISBN 0-8446-1185-9). Peter Smith.

Forster, Leonard, ed. Penguin Book of German Verse. (Poets Ser.). (Orig., Ger., With Prose Tr). (YA) (gr. 9 up). 1966. pap. 4.95 (ISBN 0-14-042036-3). Penguin.

Gode, Alexander & Ungar, Frederick, eds. Anthology of German Poetry Through the Nineteenth Century. 2nd rev. ed. LC 73-163479. (Ger. & Eng.). 1963. 14.50 (ISBN 0-8044-2242-7); pap. 5.95 (ISBN 0-8044-6241-0). Ungar.

Holderlin, Friedrich & Morike, Eduard. Selected Poems of Friedrich Holderlin & Eduard Morike. Middleton, Christopher, tr. from Ger. LC 72-79570. (German Literary Classics in Translation Ser). 304p. 1973. pap. 3.75 (ISBN 0-226-34934-9, P487, Phoen). U of Chicago Pr.

Kaufmann, Walter, ed. & tr. from Ger. Twenty-Five German Poets: A Bilingual Collection. 325p. 1975. 8.95x (ISBN 0-393-04405-X). Norton.

Kaufmann, Walter, ed. Twenty-Five German Poets: A Bilingual Collection. 352p. 1976. pap. 3.95x (ISBN 0-393-00771-5). Norton.

Legge, James G. Rhyme & Revolution in Germany: A Study in German History, Life, Literature & Character. LC 72-126646. Repr. of 1918 ed. 33.45 (ISBN 0-404-03947-2). AMS Pr.

Macleod, Norman. German Lyric Poetry. LC 74-164696. Repr. of 1930 ed. 16.00 (ISBN 0-404-04138-8). AMS Pr.

Osers, Ewald, tr. Contemporary German Poetry. (Oleander Modern Poets Ser.). 1976. pap. 4.35 (ISBN 0-902675-69-9). Oleander Pr.

Rose, William. Modern German Poetry. 1931. lib. bdg. 8.50 (ISBN 0-8414-7475-3). Folcroft.

Rus, Vladimir. Selections from German Poetry. LC 66-14177. (Illus.). (gr. 8 up). 1966. PLB 5.29 (ISBN 0-8178-3752-3). Harvey.

Salinger, Herman, ed. Twentieth-Century German Verse. facsimile ed. LC 68-57065. (Granger Index Reprint Ser). 1952. 12.00 (ISBN 0-8369-6042-4). Arno.

Schoolfield, George C., ed. German Lyric of the Baroque in English Translation. LC 78-182711. (North Carolina. University. Studies in the Germanic Languages & Literatures: No. 29). 18.50 (ISBN 0-404-50929-0). AMS Pr.

Thomas, John W. German Verse from the Twelfth to the Twentieth Century in English Translation. LC 73-182726. (North Carolina. University. Studies in the Germanic Languages & Literatures: No. 44). Repr. of 1963 ed. 18.50 (ISBN 0-404-50944-4). AMS Pr.

Von Hardenburg, Georg F. Hymns to the Night. Higgins, Dick, tr. from Ger. 48p. 1978. signed cloth 8.00 (ISBN 0-914232-23-1); pap. 3.00 (ISBN 0-914232-22-3). Treacle.

GERMAN POLICE DOGS

see Dogs–Breeds–German Shepherd Dogs

GERMAN PORCELAIN

see Porcelain

GERMAN POTTERY

see Pottery, German

GERMAN PROPAGANDA

see Propaganda, German

GERMAN PROSE LITERATURE

Feix, I. & Schlant, E. Junge Deutsche Prosa. (Rinehart Editions). 1973. 6.95 (ISBN 0-03-080092-7). HR&W.

Rehfeld, W. German Narrative Prose, Vol. 3. 1967. 13.50 (ISBN 0-8023-1113-X). Dufour.

GERMAN REFORMED CHURCH (U. S.)

see Reformed Church in the United States

GERMAN RESISTANCE MOVEMENT

see Anti-Nazi Movement

GERMAN REUNIFICATION QUESTION (1949-)

see also Berlin Wall (1961-)

Planck, Charles R. The Changing Status of German Reunification in Western Diplomacy, 1955-1966. LC 67-22894. (Studies in International Affairs: No.4). 72p. (Orig.). 1967. pap. 1.45x (ISBN 0-8018-0534-1). Johns Hopkins.

Sowden, J. K. The German Question, 1945-1973. LC 75-21518. 400p. 1975. 29.95 (ISBN 0-312-32620-3). St Martin.

Vali, Ferenc A. The Quest for a United Germany. LC 79-123197. 296p. 1967. 20.00x (ISBN 0-8018-0644-5). Johns Hopkins.

Windsor, Philip. German Reunification. (International Relations Ser.). 1969. 14.95x (ISBN 0-8464-0451-6). Beekman Pubs.

GERMAN SATIRE

see Satire, German

GERMAN SCULPTURE

see Sculpture–Germany

GERMAN SHORT-HAIRED POINTERS

see also Dogs–Breeds–German Short-Haired Pointers

Migliorini, Mario. German Shorthaired Pointers. LC 72-3316. (Illus.). 96p. 1973. bds. 1.95 (ISBN 0-668-02687-1). Arco.

GERMAN SONGS

see Songs, German

GERMAN SOUTHWEST AFRICA

see Namibia

GERMAN TALES

see Tales, German

GERMAN UNIFICATION QUESTION (1949-)

see German Reunification Question (1949-)

GERMAN WIT AND HUMOR

Kahn, Lothar & Hook, Donald D. Stimmen Aus Deutschen Landen. (Ger). 1972. pap. text ed. 5.95x (ISBN 0-442-24209-3). Van Nos Reinhold.

Muller-Casenov, Hans, ed. Humour of Germany. 1978. Repr. of 1892 ed. lib. bdg. 30.00 (ISBN 0-8492-3949-4). R West.

GERMANIC CALENDAR

see Calendar, Germanic

GERMANIC CIVILIZATION

see Civilization, Germanic

GERMANIC ETHICS

see Ethics, Germanic

GERMANIC LANGUAGES

see also Anglo-Saxon Language; Danish Language; Dutch Language; English Language; Friesian Language; German Language; Germanic Philology; Gothic Language; Icelandic and Old Norse Languages; Low German Language; Norwegian Language; Scandinavian Languages; Swedish Language

Baskett, William D. Parts of the Body in the Later Germanic Dialects. LC 75-161725. (Chicago. University. Linguistic Studies in Germanic: No. 5). Repr. of 1920 ed. 16.00 (ISBN 0-404-50285-7). AMS Pr.

Chicago University. Linguistic Studies in Germanic, 5 vols. Repr. of 1920 ed. Set. 79.50 (ISBN 0-404-50280-6). AMS Pr.

Crosby, Donald H. & Schoolfield, George C., eds. Studies in the German Drama: A Festschrift in Honor of Walter Silz. (Studies in the Germanic Languages & Literatures Ser.: No. 76). 1974. 19.50x (ISBN 0-8078-8076-0). U of NC Pr.

Daviau, Donald G., ed. The Letters of Arthur Schnitzler to Herman Bahr. LC 77-8076. (Germanic Languages & Literatures Ser.: No. 89). 183p. 1978. 14.50x (ISBN 0-8078-8089-2). U of NC Pr.

Fischer, Frank. Die Lehnworter Des Altwestnordischen. 21.50 (ISBN 0-384-15710-6); pap. 18.50 (ISBN 0-685-02249-8). Johnson Repr.

Fullerton, Lee. Historical Germanic Verb Morphology. (Studia Linguistica Germanica: Vol. 13). 1977. 32.50x (ISBN 3-11-006940-7). De Gruyter.

Hildebrandt, B. F. Strukturelemente der Deutschen Gegenwartshochsprache: Phone und Phonaden. (Janua Linguarum Ser: No. 231). 1976. 18.75x (ISBN 90-2793-405-3). Mouton.

Hopper, Paul J. The Syntax of the Simple Sentence in Proto - Germanic. LC 72-94524. (Janua Linguarum, Series Practice, No. 143). 104p. (Orig.). 1975. pap. text ed. 27.50x (ISBN 90-2793-282-4). Mouton.

Ihrig, Roscoe M. Semantic Development of Words for Walk, Run in the Germanic Languages, No. 4. LC 71-170058. (Chicago. University. Linguistic Studies in Germanic). Repr. of 1916 ed. 18.00 (ISBN 0-404-50284-9). AMS Pr.

Jones, William J. Lexicon of French Borrowings in the German Vocabulary. (Studia Linguistica Germanica Ser.: No. 12). 1976. 79.50x (ISBN 3-11-004769-1). De Gruyter.

Keller, R. E. German Dialects Phonology & Morphology, with Selected Texts. 408p. 1961. 24.00x (ISBN 0-7190-0762-3, Pub. by Manchester U Pr England). State Mutual Bk.

Kiliaans Etymologicum Teutonicae Lingvae (Antverpiae 1599) Opnieuw Uitgegeven Met Een in Leiding Van De. F. Claes. (Monumenta Lexicographica Neerlandica Ser: Vol. 3, No. 2). 1974. 62.50x (ISBN 90-2792-617-4). Mouton.

Lehmann, Winfred P. Development of Germanic Verse Form. LC 70-131252. 1971. Repr. of 1956 ed. text ed. 9.00 (ISBN 0-87752-014-3). Gordian.

Meillet, Antoine. General Characteristics of the Germanic Languages. Dismukes, William P., tr. LC 79-81615. (Miami Linguistics Ser: No. 6). 1970. 9.95x (ISBN 0-87024-131-1). U of Miami Pr.

Meritt, Herbert D. Construction Apo Koinou in the Germanic Languages. LC 39-3031. (Stanford University. Stanford Studies in Language & Literature: Vol. 6, Pt. 2). Repr. of 1938 ed. 14.50 (ISBN 0-404-51811-7). AMS Pr.

Scherer, P. Germanic-Balto-Slavic Etyma. 1941. pap. 6.00 (ISBN 0-527-00778-1). Kraus Repr.

Schwabe, Henry O. Semantic Development of Words for "Eating" & "Drinking" in Germanic. LC 70-173195. (Chicago. University. Linguistic Studies in Germanic: No. 1). Repr. of 1915 ed. 14.00 (ISBN 0-404-50281-4). AMS Pr.

Seymour, Richard K. Bibliography of Word Formation in the Germanic Language. LC 68-18780. 1968. 17.75 (ISBN 0-8223-0153-9). Duke.

Small, George W. Germanic Case of Comparison. 1929. pap. 6.00 (ISBN 0-527-00808-7). Kraus Repr.

Thomsen, Vilhelm. On the Influence of Germanic Languages on Finnish & Lapp. LC 67-63427. (Uralic & Altaic Ser: Vol. 87). (Ger.). 1967. pap. text ed. 7.00x (ISBN 0-87750-035-5). Res Ctr Lang Semiotic.

Wagner, Reinhard. Die Syntax Des Superlativs Im Gotischen, Altniederdeutschen, Althochdeutschen, Fruemittelhochdeutsc Im Beowulf und in der Aelteren Edda. 14.00 (ISBN 0-384-65440-1); pap. 11.00 (ISBN 0-685-13614-0). Johnson Repr.

Wood, Francis A. Verner's Law in Gothic, & Reduplicating Verbs in Germanic. LC 73-173039. (Chicago University. Germanic Studies: No. 2). Repr. of 1895 ed. 11.00 (ISBN 0-404-50272-5). AMS Pr.

GERMANIC LEGENDS

see Legends, Germanic

GERMANIC MAGIC

see Magic, Germanic

GERMANIC MYTHOLOGY

see Mythology, Germanic

GERMANIC NAMES

see Names, Germanic

GERMANIC PHILOLOGY

see also English Philology; Friesian Philology; German Philology; Scandinavian Philology; also names of various languages and literatures which form the Germanic group

Brinkmann, Richard, et al, eds. Germanistik International. 1978. pap. 27.50x (ISBN 3-484-10305-1). Intl Pubns Serv.

Chicago University. Germanic Studies, 3 Vols. Repr. of 1897 ed. Set. 36.00 (ISBN 0-404-50270-9). AMS Pr.

Columbia University. Columbia University Germanic Studies, Old Ser, Vols. 1-35, 1900-1931, New Ser., Vols. 1-14, 1936-1941. Repr. of 1941 ed. Set. 864.50 (ISBN 0-404-50400-0). AMS Pr.

Fowkes & Sanders, eds. Studies in Germanic Languages & Literature. 1967. 4.75 (ISBN 0-685-05292-3). Adler.

German Studies. facsimile ed. LC 70-99696. (Essay Index Reprint Ser). 1938. 21.00 (ISBN 0-8369-1409-0). Arno.

Gummere, Francis B. Germanic Origins: A Study in Primitive Culture. 69.95 (ISBN 0-8490-0231-1). Gordon Pr.

Hatfield, James T., ed. Curme Volume of Linguistic Studies. 1930. pap. 12.00 (ISBN 0-527-00811-7). Kraus Repr.

Mincoff, Marco K. Die Bedeutungsentwicklung der, Ag 5. (Ger). 14.00 (ISBN 0-384-39020-X); pap. 11.00 (ISBN 0-685-02056-8). Johnson Repr.

North Carolina University. University of North Carolina Studies in the Germanic Language & Literatures, 52 vols. Repr. of 1949 ed. Set. 944.00 (ISBN 0-404-50900-2). AMS Pr.

Raven, Frithjof A., et al, eds. Germanic Studies in Honor of Edward Henry Sehrt: Presented by His Colleagues, Students, & Friends. LC 68-12422. (Miami Linguistics Ser: No. 1). (Illus.). 1968. 14.95x (ISBN 0-87024-078-1). U of Miami Pr.

Stearns, MacDonald, Jr. Crimean Gothic. (Studia Linguistica et Philologica: No. 6). 1978. pap. 20.00 (ISBN 0-915838-45-1). Anma Libri.

Studies in Honor of John Albrecht Walz. facs. ed. LC 68-29249. (Essay Index Reprint Ser). 1968. Repr. of 1941 ed. 15.00 (ISBN 0-8369-0915-1). Arno.

Von Raumer, Rudolf H. Geschichte der germanischen Philologie vorzugsweise in Deutschland. (Akademie der Wissenschaften, Muenich. Historische Kommission Ser: Geschichte der Wissenschaften in Deutschland. Neuere Zeit. 9. Bd.). xii, 743p. Repr. of 1870 ed. 25.00 (ISBN 0-384-49680-6). Johnson Repr.

GERMANIC TRIBES

see also Barbarian Invasions of Rome; Civilization, Germanic; Jutes; Saxons

Owen, Francis. The Germanic People. 1960. pap. 2.45 (ISBN 0-8084-0145-9, B36). Coll & U Pr.

Todd, Malcolm. The Barbarians. 1981. 24.00 (ISBN 0-7134-1669-6, Pub. by Batsford England). David & Charles.

GERMANIC TRIBES–RELIGION

see also Mythology, Germanic; Mythology, Norse

De La Saussaye, P. Chantepie. The Religion of the Teutons. LC 76-27519. 1976. Repr. of 1902 ed. lib. bdg. 50.00 (ISBN 0-89341-030-6). Longwood Pr.

Dumezil, Georges. Gods of the Ancient Northmen. Haugen, Einar, ed. & tr. (Study of Comparative Folklore & Mythology, No. 3). 1974. 21.50x (ISBN 0-520-02044-8); CAL 371. pap. 3.95 (ISBN 0-520-03507-0). U of Cal Pr.

Grimm, Jacob. Teutonic Mythology, 4 Vols. 4th ed. Stallybrass, James S., tr. Set. 50.00 (ISBN 0-8446-2168-4). Peter Smith.

GERMANIUM

Basov, N. G., ed. Microwave Studies of Exciton Condensation in Germanium. (P. N. Lebedev Physics Institute Ser.: Vol. 100). (Illus.). 1979. 35.00 (ISBN 0-306-10952-2, Consultants). Plenum Pub.

Brownridge, I. C. Lithium-Drifted Germanium Detectors: Their Fabrication & Use. LC 73-183565. 216p. 1972. 35.00 (ISBN 0-306-65180-7). IFI Plenum.

Davydov, V. I. Germanium. 1966. 83.75x (ISBN 0-677-20610-0). Gordon.

Glockling, Frank. Chemistry of Germanium. 1969. 37.00 (ISBN 0-12-286450-6). Acad Pr.

Johnson, V. A. Karl Lark-Horovitz, Pioneer in Solid State Physics. LC 77-91464. (Men of Physics Ser.). 1970. 22.00 (ISBN 0-08-006581-3); pap. 10.75 (ISBN 0-08-006580-5). Pergamon.

Samsonov, G. V. & Bondarev, V. N. Germanides. LC 70-79918. 155p. 1969. 35.00 (ISBN 0-306-10823-2, Consultant). Plenum Pub.

--Germanides. LC 70-125852. (Illus.). 1970. 22.50x (ISBN 0-685-19586-4). Primary.

Weber, Jon N., ed. Geochemistry of Germanium. LC 73-12621. (Benchmark Papers in Geology Ser). 480p. 1974. text ed. 54.00 (ISBN 0-12-787740-1). Acad Pr.

Wolfendale, E. Transistor Bias Tables, 2 vols. Incl. Vol. 1. Germanium; Vol. 2. Silicon. 5.75x ea. Transatlantic.

GERMANS

Bailey, George. Germans: The Biography of an Obsession. 1974. pap. 3.50 (ISBN 0-380-00140-3, 53918, Discus). Avon.

Cole, John W. & Wolf, Eric R. The Hidden Frontier: Ecology & Ethnicity in an Alpine Valley. (Studies in Social Discontinuity Ser.). 1974. 27.50 (ISBN 0-12-785132-1). Acad Pr.

Evans, Richard J. & Lee, W. R., eds. The German Family: Essays on the Social History of the Family in Nineteenth & Twentieth Century Germany. 302p. 1981. 27.50x (ISBN 0-389-20101-4). B&N.

Grimm, Hans. Answer of a German. 69.95 (ISBN 0-87968-642-1). Gordon Pr.

Leslie, S. The Celt & the World: A Study of the Relation of Celt & Teuton in History. 59.95 (ISBN 0-87968-822-X). Gordon Pr.

Loewenstein, Hubertus Z. Germans in History. LC 78-95395. Repr. of 1945 ed. 34.50 (ISBN 0-404-04008-X). AMS Pr.

Ludwig, Emil. The Germans: Double History of a Nation. LC 78-63688. (Studies in Fascism: Ideology & Practice). Repr. of 1942 ed. 27.50 (ISBN 0-404-16951-1). AMS Pr.

Von Hagen, Victor W. The Germanic People in America. LC 75-15970. (Illus.). 416p. 1976. 19.95 (ISBN 0-8061-1317-0). U of Okla Pr.

GERMANS IN AFRICA

Bridgman, Jon & Clarke, David E. German Africa: A Select Annotated Bibliography. LC 64-7917. (Bibliographical Ser.: No. 19). 120p. 1965. pap. 6.95 (ISBN 0-8179-2192-3). Hoover Inst Pr.

GERMANS IN AUSTRIA

Langsam, Walter C. Napoleonic Wars & German Nationalism in Austria. (Columbia University. Studies in the Social Sciences: No. 324). Repr. of 1930 ed. 20.00 (ISBN 0-404-51324-7). AMS Pr.

GERMANS IN EASTERN EUROPE

Spira, Thomas. German-Hungarian Relations & the Swabian Problem. (East European Monographs: No. 25). 1977. 18.50x (ISBN 0-914710-18-4). East Eur Quarterly.

GERMANS IN ENGLAND

Colvin, Ian D. Germans in England, 1066-1598. LC 73-118464. 1971. Repr. of 1915 ed. 13.50 (ISBN 0-8046-1213-7). Kennikat.

GERMANS IN RUSSIA

Keller, Conrad P. The German Colonies in South Russia, Eighteen Hundred Four to Nineteen Hundred Four, Vol. 1. 1980. 11.50 (ISBN 0-914222-04-X). Am Hist Soc Ger.

Koch, Fred C. The Volga Germans: In Russia & the Americas, 1763 to the Present. LC 76-41155. 1977. 16.50x (ISBN 0-271-01236-6). Pa St U Pr.

Long, James. The German-Russians: A Bibliography. LC 78-19071. 136p. 1978. text ed. 17.50 (ISBN 0-87436-282-2). ABC-Clio.

Stumpp, Karl. The Emigration from Germany to Russia in the Years 1763-1862. 1978. 21.00 (ISBN 0-914222-00-7). Am Hist Soc Ger.

--The German-Russians: Two Centuries of Pioneering. 1978. 12.50 (ISBN 0-914222-03-1). Am Hist Soc Ger.

Williams, Hattie P. The Czar's Germans. 1975. 9.45 (ISBN 0-914222-01-5). Am Hist Soc Ger.

GERMANS IN THE CZECHOSLOVAK REPUBLIC

Cohen, Gary B. The Politics of Ethnic Survival: Germans in Prague,Eighteen Sixty-One to Nineteen-Fourteen. LC 81-47119. (Illus.). 316p. 1981. 21.00x (ISBN 0-691-05332-4). Princeton U Pr.

Luza, Radomir. The Transfer of the Sudeten Germans: A Study of Czech-German Relations, 1933-1962. LC 64-12558. 336p. 1964. 12.00x (ISBN 0-8147-0269-4). NYU Pr.

Smelser, Ronald M. The Sudeten Problem, 1933-38: "Volkstumpolitik" & the Formulation of Nazi Foreign Policy. LC 74-5912. 296p. 1975. 20.00x (ISBN 0-8195-4077-3, Pub. by Wesleyan U Pr). Columbia U Pr.

GERMANS IN THE UNITED STATES

see also Pennsylvania Germans

Abernethy, Francis, et al. Texas & Germany: Crosscurrents. Wilson, Joseph, ed. (Rice University Studies: Vol. 63, No. 3). (Illus.). 139p. 1977. pap. 4.25x (ISBN 0-89263-233-X). Rice Univ.

Adams, Herbert B. The Germanic Origin of New England Towns. LC 78-63731. (Johns Hopkins University. Studies in the Social Sciences. First Ser. 1882-1883: 2). Repr. of 1882 ed. 11.50 (ISBN 0-404-61002-1). AMS Pr.

Bayor, Ronald H. Neighbors in Conflict: The Irish, Germans, Jews & Italians of New York City, 1929-1941. 2nd ed. LC 77-14260. 256p. 1980. pap. 5.95 (ISBN 0-8018-2370-6). Johns Hopkins.

--Neighbors in Conflict: The Irish, Germans, Jews, & Italians of New York City, 1929-1941. LC 77-14260. (Studies in Historical & Political Science, 96th Ser: No. 2). 1978. text ed. 16.00x o. p. (ISBN 0-8018-2024-3); pap. 5.95 (ISBN 0-8018-2370-6). Johns Hopkins.

Benjamin, Gilbert G. The Germans in Texas: A Study in Immigration. 155p. 1974. 12.95 (ISBN 0-8363-0128-5). Jenkins.

Bittinger, Lucy F. Germans in Colonial Times. LC 68-25064. (Illus.). 314p. 1968. Repr. of 1901 ed. 8.50 (ISBN 0-8462-1225-0). Russell.

Blum, Howard. Wanted! The Search for Nazis in America. LC 76-9689. 1977. 8.95 (ISBN 0-8129-0607-1). Times Bks.

Bruntz, George G. Children of the Volga. 128p. 1981. 6.95 (ISBN 0-8059-2763-8). Dorrance.

Chambers, Theodore F. Early Germans of New Jersey: Their History, Churches & Genealogies. LC 78-85697. (Illus.). 1969. Repr. of 1895 ed. 25.00 (ISBN 0-8063-0070-1). Genealog Pub.

Child, Clifton J. German-Americans in Politics, 1914-1917. LC 70-129394. (American Immigration Collection, Ser. 2). (Illus.). 1970. Repr. of 1939 ed. 8.50 (ISBN 0-405-00549-0). Arno.

Conzen, Kathleen N. Immigrant Milwaukee, 1836-1860. (Studies in Urban History). 1976. text ed. 16.50x (ISBN 0-674-44436-1). Harvard U Pr.

Cronau, Rudolf. German Achievements in America. 59.95 (ISBN 0-8490-0225-7). Gordon Pr.

--Three Centuries of German Life in America. 59.95 (ISBN 0-8490-1210-4). Gordon Pr.

Dobbert, Guido A. The Disintegration of an Immigrant Community: The Cincinnati Germans, 1870-1920. Cordasco, Francesco, ed. LC 80-853. (American Ethnic Groups Ser.). 1981. lib. bdg. 39.00x (ISBN 0-405-13416-9). Arno.

Dolan, Jay P. The Immigrant Church: New York's Irish & German Catholics, 1815-1865. LC 75-12552. 1975. text ed. 16.00x (ISBN 0-8018-1708-0); pap. 3.95x (ISBN 0-8018-2018-9). Johns Hopkins.

Duden, Gottfried. Report on a Journey to the Western States of North America & a Stay of Several Years Along the Missouri: During the Years 1824, '25, '26 & '27. Goodrich, James W., ed. Kellner, George H., et al, trs. from German. LC 79-3335. 400p. 1980. text ed. 22.00 (ISBN 0-8262-0295-0). U of Mo Pr.

Edmunds, Adeline, ed. The Loving Spice of Life. Rauscher, Gerhard, tr. LC 80-51973. (Illus.). 279p. 1980. 14.51 (ISBN 0-9605846-0-9); pap. 9.31 (ISBN 0-9605846-1-7). A Edmunds.

Egle, William H. Pennsylvania Genealogies: Chiefly Scotch-Irish & German. 2nd ed. LC 70-86807. 1969. Repr. of 1896 ed. lib. bdg. 25.00 (ISBN 0-8063-0102-3). Genealog Pub.

Faust, Albert. The German Element in the U. S, 2 vols. LC 78-145009. 1927. Repr. 69.00 (ISBN 0-403-00959-6). Scholarly.

Faust, Albert B. German Element in the United States, 2 Vols. LC 69-18773. (American Immigration Collection Ser., No. 1). (Illus.). 1969. Repr. of 1927 ed. Set. 37.50 (ISBN 0-686-66371-3); Vol. 1. 18.50 (ISBN 0-405-00520-2); Vol. 2. 19.00 (ISBN 0-405-00521-0). Arno.

Friesen, Gerhard K. & Schatzberg, Walter, eds. The German Contribution to the Building of the Americas: Studies in Honor of Karl J. R. Arndt. LC 76-50679. 1977. 20.00x (ISBN 0-87451-133-X). Clark U Pr.

Furer, Howard B. The Germans in America, 1607-1970: A Chronology & Factbook. LC 72-10087. (Ethnic Chronology Ser.: No. 8). 160p. 1973. lib. bdg. 8.50 (ISBN 0-379-00506-9). Oceana.

Gilbert, Glenn G., ed. The German Language in America: A Symposium. 231p. 1971. 12.50x (ISBN 0-292-70149-7). U of Tex Pr.

Glasco, Laurence A. Ethnicity & Social Structure: Irish, Germans & Native-Born of Buffalo, N.Y., 1850-1860. Cordasco, Francesco, ed. LC 80-859. (American Ethnic Groups Ser.). 1981. lib. bdg. 35.00x (ISBN 0-405-13422-3). Arno.

Gleason, Philip. Conservative Reformers: German-American Catholics & the Social Order. 1968. 14.95x (ISBN 0-268-00061-1). U of Notre Dame Pr.

Goyne, Minetta A., ed. Lone Star & Double Eagle: Civil War Letters of a German - Texas Family. Date not set. price not set (ISBN 0-912646-68-3). Tex Christian.

Gustorf, Frederick & Gustorf, Gisela. Uncorrupted Heart: Journal & Letters of Frederick Julius Gustorf 1800-1845. LC 70-93049. 1969. 10.00x (ISBN 0-8262-0079-6). U of Mo Pr.

Hale, Douglas. The Germans from Russia in Oklahoma. LC 79-20152. (Newcomers to a New Land Ser.). (Illus.). 96p. (Orig.). 1980. pap. 3.95 (ISBN 0-8061-1620-X). U of Okla Pr.

Hawgood, John A. Tragedy of German-America: The Germans in the United States of America During the Nineteenth Century and After. LC 71-129401. (American Immigration Collection, Ser. 2). 1970. Repr. of 1940 ed. 13.50 (ISBN 0-405-00554-7). Arno.

Heitman, Sidney, ed. Germans from Russia in Colorado. LC 78-16496. (WSSA Monograph). 1978. 14.75 (ISBN 0-8357-0351-7, IS-00056, Pub. by Western Social Science Association). Univ Microfilms.

Hobbie, Margaret, compiled by. Museums, Sites, & Collections of Germanic Culture in North America: An Annotated Directory of German Immigrant Culture in the United States & Canada. LC 79-6822. 184p. 1980. lib. bdg. 19.95 (ISBN 0-313-22060-3, HGC/). Greenwood.

Hofmeister, Rudolph. The Germans of Chicago. 1976. 10.80 (ISBN 0-87563-113-4). Stipes.

Iverson, Noel. Germania, U.S.A. Social Change in New Ulm, Minnesota. LC 66-22152. 1966. 7.50x (ISBN 0-8166-0413-4). U of Minn Pr.

Jordan, Gilbert J. German Texana. 164p. 1980. 9.95 (ISBN 0-89015-261-6). Eakin Pubns.

Jordan, Terry G. German Seed in Texas Soil: Immigrant Farmers in Nineteenth-Century Texas. (Illus.). 251p. 1966. pap. 5.95 (ISBN 0-292-72707-0). U of Tex Pr.

Justman, Dorothy E. German Colonists in Houston. (Illus.). 384p. (12 ancestral charts & 4 coats-of-arms). 1974. 15.00 (ISBN 0-89015-075-3). Eakin Pubns.

Keresztesi, Michael & Cocozzoli, Gary, eds. German American History & Life: A Guide to Information Sources. LC 79-24065. (Ethnic Studies Information Guide Ser.: Vol. 4). 1980. 36.00 (ISBN 0-8103-1459-2). Gale.

Knoche, Carl H. The German Immigrant Press in Milwaukee. Cordasco, Francesco, ed. LC 80-871. (American Ethnic Groups Ser.). 1981. lib. bdg. 29.00x (ISBN 0-405-13433-9). Arno.

Koch, Fred C. The Volga Germans: In Russia & the Americas, 1763 to the Present. LC 76-41155. 1977. 16.50x (ISBN 0-271-01236-6). Pa St U Pr.

Krueger, Max A. Second Fatherland: The Life & Fortunes of a German Immigrant. Sibley, Marilyn, intro. by. LC 76-17975. (Centennial Ser. of the Association of Former Students: No. 4). (Illus.). 186p. 1976. 11.95 (ISBN 0-89096-017-8). Tex A&M Univ Pr.

Kunz, Virginia B. Germans in America. LC 66-10147. (In America Bks.). (gr. 5-11). 1966. PLB 6.95g (ISBN 0-8225-0208-9). Lerner Pubns.

Kutak, Robert I. Story of a Bohemian-American Village: A Study of Social Persistence & Change. LC 70-129406. (American Immigration Collection, Ser. 2). 1970. Repr. of 1933 ed. 9.00 (ISBN 0-405-00559-8). Arno.

Learned, M. D., ed. Guide to Manuscript Materials Relating to American History in the German State Archives. 1912. pap. 20.00 (ISBN 0-527-00691-2). Kraus Repr.

Leuchs, Frederick A. Early German Theatre in New York, 1840-1872. LC 28-25875. (Columbia University. Germanic Studies, Old Series: No. 32). Repr. of 1928 ed. 18.50 (ISBN 0-404-50432-9). AMS Pr.

Lich, Glen E. & Reeves, Dona B., eds. German Culture in Texas. (Immigrant Heritage of American Ser.). 1980. lib. bdg. 16.00 (ISBN 0-8057-8415-2). Twayne.

Luebke, Frederick C. Bonds of Loyalty: German Americans & World War I. Rishchin, Moses, ed. LC 73-15097. (American Minorities Ser). (Illus.). 340p. (gr. 12). 1974. pap. 6.00 (ISBN 0-87580-514-0). N Ill U Pr.

--Immigrants & Politics: The Germans of Nebraska, 1880-1900. LC 69-15924. (Illus.). 1969. 14.95x (ISBN 0-8032-0107-9). U of Nebr Pr.

Luebke, Frederick C., ed. Ethnic Voters & the Election of Lincoln. LC 72-139370. xxxii, 226p. 1971. 16.50x (ISBN 0-8032-0796-4); pap. 3.25x (ISBN 0-8032-5738-4, BB 567, Bison). U of Nebr Pr.

Meynen, Emil. Bibliography on German Settlements in Colonial North America. LC 66-25870. 1966. Repr. of 1937 ed. 43.00 (ISBN 0-8103-3336-8). Gale.

Nau, John F. The German People of New Orleans: 1850-1900. 1975. pap. 4.95 (ISBN 0-88289-100-6). Pelican.

O'Connor, Richard. The German-Americans. LC 68-21880. (Illus.). 1968. 12.95 (ISBN 0-316-62654-6). Little.

Olson, Audrey L. St. Louis Germans, 1850-1920: The Nature of an Immigrant Community & Its Relation to the Assimilation Process. Cordasco, Fransecso, ed. LC 80-886. (American Ethnic Groups Ser.). 1981. lib. bdg. 35.00x (ISBN 0-405-13447-9). Arno.

Paule, Dorothea. The German Settlement at Anaheim: Thesis. LC 74-167576. 1974. Rep. of 1952 ed. soft bdg. 7.00 (ISBN 0-88247-293-3). R & E Res Assoc.

Reeves, Dona B. & Lich, Glen E., eds. Retrospect & Retrieval: The German Element in Review, Essays on Cultural Preservation. LC 78-26757. (Illus.). 1978. pap. 14.75 (ISBN 0-8357-0365-7, SS-00078). Univ Microfilms.

Rippley, La Vern. Of German Ways. LC 75-76194. (Heritage Bks.). (Illus.). 1970. 8.95 (ISBN 0-87518-013-2). Dillon.

Rippley, La Vern J. The German-Americans. LC 75-26917. (Immigrant Heritage of America Ser.). 1976. lib. bdg. 9.95 (ISBN 0-8057-8405-5). Twayne.

Rohrs, Richard C. The Germans in Oklahoma. LC 79-6715. (Newcomers to a New Land Ser.: Vol. 7). (Illus.). 96p. (Orig.). 1980. pap. 3.95 (ISBN 0-8061-1673-0). U of Okla Pr.

Rosengarten, Joseph G. The German Soldier in the Wars of the U. S. LC 70-167572. 10.00 (ISBN 0-88247-200-3). R & E Res Assoc.

Scheuerman, Richard & Trafzer, Clifford. The Volga Germans: Pioneers in the Pacific Northwest. LC 80-52314. (GEM Books-Historical Ser.). (Illus.). 240p. (Orig.). 1981. 18.95 (ISBN 0-89301-073-1). U Pr of Idaho.

Schrader, Frederick F. The Germans in the Making of America. LC 72-1249. (American History & Americana Ser., No. 47). 1972. Repr. of 1924 ed. lib. bdg. 34.95 (ISBN 0-8383-1432-5). Haskell.

Schuricht, Herrmann. The German Element in Virginia, 2 vols. in 1. LC 77-82334. 1977. 17.50 (ISBN 0-8063-0783-8). Genealog Pub.

Shultz, Edward T. First Settlements of Germans in Md. Gross, Ruth T., ed. LC 76-151613. 1976. pap. 5.00 (ISBN 0-9606946-0-9). R T Gross.

Smith, Clifford N. Emigrants from the Principality of Hessen-Hanau, Germany, 1741-1767. (German-American Genealogical Research Monographs: No. 6). 1979. pap. 8.00 (ISBN 0-915162-05-9). Westland Pubns.

--Emigration from the Siegkreis (Nordrhein-Westfalen, Germany) Mainly to the United States. (German-American Genealogical Research Monograph No. 10). 1980. pap. 10.00 (ISBN 0-915162-09-1). Westland Pubns.

--Mercenaries from Hessen-Hanau Who Remained in Canada & the United States After the American Revolution. (German-American Genealogical Research Monograph: No. 5). Orig. Title: Deserter-Immigrants of the American Revolution from Hessen-Hanau. 75p. (Orig.). 1976. pap. 10.00 (ISBN 0-915162-04-0). Westland Pubns.

Spalek, John M. Guide to the Archival Materials of the German-Speaking Emigration to the United States After 1933: Verzeichnis der Quellen und Materialien der Deutschspragen Emigration in den U. S. A. Seit 1933. LC 78-10847. 1979. 27.50x (ISBN 0-8139-0749-7). U Pr of Va.

Tolzmann, Don H. German Americana: A Bibliography. LC 74-28085. 1975. 18.00 (ISBN 0-8108-0784-X). Scarecrow.

Turrou, Leon G. Nazi Spy Conspiracy in America. LC 72-1433. (Select Bibliographies Reprint Ser.). 1972. Repr. of 1939 ed. 20.00 (ISBN 0-8369-6838-7). Arno.

Urlsperger, Samuel. Detailed Reports on the Salzburger Emigrants Who Settled in America, 1736, Vol. 3. Jones, George F. & Hahn, Marie, eds. LC 67-27137. xiv, 368p. 1972. 12.00 (ISBN 0-8203-0278-3). U of Ga Pr.

--Detailed Reports on the Salzburger Emigrants Who Settled in America, 1738, Vol. 5. Jones, George J. & Wilson, Renate, eds. LC 67-27137. (Wormsloe Foundation Publications: No. 14). 374p. 1980. 18.00 (ISBN 0-8203-0482-4). U of Ga Pr.

Vogeth, Lamberta. Germans in Los Angeles County, 1850-1909. 1968. Repr. of 1933 ed. 6.00 (ISBN 0-685-40307-6). R & E Res Assoc.

Von Herff, Ferdinand. The Regulated Emigration of the German Proletariat with Special Reference to Texas, a Translation. Finck, Arthur L., Jr., tr. from Ger. 1978. 10.00 (ISBN 0-911536-72-8). Trinity U Pr.

Wandel, Joseph. German Dimension of American History. LC 78-26050. 1979. 16.95x (ISBN 0-88229-147-5); pap. 8.95x (ISBN 0-88229-668-X). Nelson-Hall.

Weber, Samuel E. Charity School Movement in Colonial Pennsylvania. LC 78-89251. (American Education: Its Men, Institutions & Ideas Ser). 1969. Repr. of 1905 ed. 11.00 (ISBN 0-405-01489-9). Arno.

Weygandt, Cornelius. Red Hills. LC 71-83484. (Keystone State Historical Publications Ser: No. 7). (Illus.). 1969. Repr. of 1929 ed. 12.00 (ISBN 0-87198-507-1). Friedman.

Wilhelm, Hubert G. Organized German Settlement & Its Effects on the Frontier of South-Central Texas. Cordasco, Francesco, ed. LC 80-905. (American Ethnic Groups Ser.). (Illus.). 1981. lib. bdg. 25.00x (ISBN 0-405-13464-9). Arno.

Wirsing, Dale R. Builders, Brewers & Burghers: Germans of Washington State. LC 77-71316. 1977. pap. 5.00 (ISBN 0-917048-03-2, Pub. by Wash. St. American Revolution Bicentennial Commission). Wash St Hist Soc.

Wittke, Carl. Germans in America. LC 67-13193. 1967. pap. 2.95 (ISBN 0-8077-2344-4). Tchrs Coll.

Wittke, Carl F. Refugees of Revolution. Repr. of 1952 ed. lib. bdg. 18.25x (ISBN 0-8371-2988-5, WIRR). Greenwood.

Wust, Klaus. The Virginian Germans. LC 69-17334. Repr. of 1975 ed. 10.95x (ISBN 0-8139-0256-8). U Pr of Va.

Zeitlin, Richard H. Germans in Wisconsin. (Illus.). 1977. pap. 1.25 (ISBN 0-87020-173-5). State Hist Soc Wis.

Zucker, Adolf E., ed. The Forty-Eighters: Political Refugees of the Revolution of 1848. LC 66-27186. (Illus.). 1967. Repr. of 1950 ed. 8.50 (ISBN 0-8462-0859-8). Russell.

GERMANTOWN, PENNSYLVANIA-HISTORY

Pennypacker, Samuel W. Settlement of Germantown, Pennsylvania, & the Beginning of German Emigration to North America. LC 69-13248. (Illus.). 1969. Repr. of 1899 ed. 18.00 (ISBN 0-405-08847-7). Arno.

Wolf, Stephanie G. Urban Village: Population, Community, & Family Structure in Germantown, Pennsylvania, 1683-1800. LC 76-3025. 376p. 1980. 26.00 (ISBN 0-691-04632-8); pap. 6.95 (ISBN 0-691-00590-7). Princeton U Pr.

GERMANY

Here are entered works on Germany for the pre-1949 period, the Territories under Allied Occupation, and East Germany and West Germany, collectively, for the post-1949 period. see also Germany, East; Germany, West; also specific cities, areas, etc. in Germany

Barker, J. Ellis. Foundations of Germany. LC 70-110894. 1970. Repr. of 1916 ed. 12.50 (ISBN 0-8046-0877-6). Kennikat.

Cramb, J. A. Germany & England. 1914. 12.50 (ISBN 0-685-43882-1). Norwood Edns.

Lowie, Robert H. Toward Understanding Germany. (Midway Reprint Ser). xvi, 396p. 1975. pap. text ed. 11.00x (ISBN 0-226-49452-7). U of Chicago Pr.

Romantic Germany. (Panorama Bks.). (Illus., Eng. & Fr.). 3.95 (ISBN 0-685-11540-2). French & Eur.

Rose, J. H., et al. Germany in the Nineteenth Century: Five Lectures. Manchester Univ. Pubns. Historical Ser. No. 13. facs. ed. LC 67-30189. (Essay Index Reprint Ser). 1912. 13.00 (ISBN 0-8369-0471-0). Arno.

Seger, Gerhart H. Germany. rev. ed. LC 77-83909. (World Cultures Ser.). (Illus.). 188p. (gr. 6 up). 1978. text ed. 9.95 ea. 1-4 copies (ISBN 0-88296-180-2); text ed. 7.96 ea. 5 or more copies; tchrs'. guide 8.94 (ISBN 0-88296-369-4). Fideler.

Sinnhuber, K. A. Germany: Its Geography & Growth. 1972. 14.00 (ISBN 0-7195-1286-7). Transatlantic.

Sinnhuber, Karl A. Germany. 2nd ed. (Geography & Growth Ser). 1970. 12.50x (ISBN 0-7195-1286-7). Intl Pubns Serv.

Stael, de. De l'Allemagne, 5 vols. (Grands Escrivains de France). 350p. 1967. 15.95 ea. French & Eur.

--De l'Allemagne, Vol. 1. Balaye, Simone, ed. 1959. pap. 4.50 (ISBN 0-686-54923-6). French & Eur.

Tower, Charles. Germany of Today. lib. bdg. 15.00 (ISBN 0-8495-5330-X). Arden Lib.

--Germany of Today. buckram bdg. 9.50 (ISBN 0-686-17009-1). Quest Edns.

Wightman, Margaret. Faces of Germany: An Introduction to the German People. (Illus.). 1971. 14.95x (ISBN 0-245-50399-4). Intl Ideas.

GERMANY–AIR FORCE

Bekker, Cajus. The Luftwaffe War Diaries. Ziegler, Frank, tr. 608p. 1975. pap. 3.95 (ISBN 0-345-28799-1). Ballantine.

Davis, Brian L., ed. Luftwaffe Air Crews: Battle of Britain, 1940. LC 73-83744. (Key Uniform Guides). (Illus.). 48p. 1974. pap. 1.95 (ISBN 0-668-03364-9). Arco.

Germany's Luftwaffe in Sweden. Date not set. price not set (ISBN 0-914144-28-6). Monogram Aviation.

Green, William. Warplanes of the Third Reich. LC 68-29673. 1970. 12.50 (ISBN 0-385-05782-2). Doubleday.

Imrie, Alex. Pictorial History of the German Army Air Service: 1914-1918. 14.95 (ISBN 0-685-56067-8). Beachcomber Bks.

Jet Planes of the Third Reich. Date not set. price not set (ISBN 0-914144-27-8). Monogram Aviation.

MacKsey, Kenneth. Kesselring: The Making of the Luftwaffe. 1978. 27.00 (ISBN 0-7134-0862-6, Pub. by Batsford England). David & Charles.

Maloney, Edward T. Luftwaffe Aircraft & Aces. (Illus.). 1969. pap. 6.95 (ISBN 0-911721-74-6, Pub. by WW). Aviation.

Nielsen, Andreas. German Air Force General Staff. LC 68-22551. (German Air Force in World War 2 Series). (Charts). 1968. Repr. of 1959 ed. 15.00 (ISBN 0-405-00043-X). Arno.

Plocher, Hermann. German Air Force Versus Russia, Nineteen Forty-One. LC 68-22547. (German Air Force in World War 2 Series). (Illus.). 1968. Repr. of 1965 ed. 16.00 (ISBN 0-405-00044-8). Arno.

--German Air Force Versus Russia, Nineteen Forty-Two. LC 68-22548. (German Air Force in World War 2 Series). (Illus.). 1968. Repr. of 1966 ed. 21.00 (ISBN 0-405-00045-6). Arno.

--German Air Force Versus Russia, Nineteen Forty-Three. LC 68-22549. (German Air Force in World War 2 Series). (Illus.). 1968. Repr. of 1967 ed. 16.00 (ISBN 0-405-00046-4). Arno.

Suchenwirth, Richard. Command and Leadership in the German Air Force. LC 71-111598. (German Air Force in World War 2 Ser). Repr. of 1969 ed. 20.00 (ISBN 0-405-00051-0). Arno.

--Development of the German Air Force, Nineteen Nineteen to Nineteen Thirty-Nine. LC 78-111597. (German Air Force in World War 2 Ser). Repr. of 1968 ed. 17.00 (ISBN 0-405-00050-2). Arno.

--Historical Turning Points in the German Air Force War Effort. LC 68-22554. (German Air Force in World War 2 Series). 1968. Repr. of 1959 ed. 12.00 (ISBN 0-405-00048-0). Arno.

Van Ishoven, Armand. The Luftwaffe in the Battle of Britain. (Illus.). 160p. 1980. 19.95 (ISBN 0-684-16703-4, ScribT). Scribner.

West, Kenneth S. The Captive Luftwaffe. (Putnam Aeronautical Books). (Illus.). 160p. 1979. 13.95 (ISBN 0-370-30020-3, Pub. by Chatto Bodley Jonathan). Merrimack Bk Serv.

GERMANY–ANTIQUITIES

Boehringer, Christof. Zur Chronologie mittelhellenistischer Muenzserien 220-160 Vor Chr. (Antike Muenzen und Geschnittene Steine Ser.: Vol. 5). (Illus.). 240p. 1972. 111.00x (ISBN 3-11-001763-6). De Gruyter.

Haffner, A. Die Westliche Hunsrueck-Eifel-Kultur: Text-Vol. & Vol. with Plates. (Roemisch-Germanische Forschungen, Vol. 36). (Illus.). 1976. 519.25x (ISBN 3-11-004889-2). De Gruyter.

Meier-Arendt, W. Die Hinkelstein-Gruppe der Uebergang Vom Frueh-Zum Mittelneolithikum in Suedwestdeutschland: Text-Vol. & Vol. with Plates. (Roemisch-Germanische Forschungen: Vol. 35). (Illus.). x, 237p. 1975. 162.25x (ISBN 3-11-004758-6). De Gruyter.

GERMANY–ARMED FORCES

Cooper, Matthew. The German Army: Vol. 3 Decline & Fall. (World at War Ser.: No. 15). 1979. pap. 2.50 (ISBN 0-89083-493-8). Zebra.

Crow, Duncan, ed. Armored Fighting Vehicles of Germany. LC 78-3546. 1978. 15.95 (ISBN 0-668-04641-4, 4641). Arco.

Feist, Uwe. Deutsche Panzer Nineteen Seventeen to Nineteen Forty-Five. (Illus.). 1979. pap. 7.95 (ISBN 0-8168-5008-9). Aero.

Hicks, James E. German Weapons, Uniforms, Insignia, 1841-1918. 6.00 (ISBN 0-685-07321-1). Borden.

Mollo, Andrew. German Uniforms of World War Two. LC 76-6757. (Illus.). 1976. 17.50 (ISBN 0-88254-402-0). Hippocrene Bks.

GERMANY–ARMY

Bender, Roger J. & Odegard, Warren W. Uniforms, Organization & History of the Panzertruppe. (Illus.). 336p. 1980. 24.95 (ISBN 0-912138-18-1). Bender Pub CA.

Cooper, Matthew. The German Army: Vol. 2 Conquest 1933-1945. (World at War Ser.: No. 14). 1979. pap. 2.50 (ISBN 0-89083-485-7). Zebra.

--The German Army 1933-1945. 1978. 17.95 (ISBN 0-8128-2468-7). Stein & Day.

Davis, W. J. German Army Handbook, 1939-45. LC 73-86000. (Illus.). 176p. 1974. 7.95 (ISBN 0-668-03376-2). Arco.

Ellis, Chris. German Infantry & Assault Engineer Equipment 1939-1945. 1976. pap. 6.00x (ISBN 0-85242-456-6). Intl Pubns Serv.

Fried, John H. The Guilt of the German Army. LC 75-10823. Repr. of 1942 ed. 35.00 (ISBN 0-404-14493-4). AMS Pr.

The German Army: Vol. 1 Rebirth 1933-1945. (World at War Ser.: No. 13). 1979. pap. 2.50 (ISBN 0-89083-472-5). Zebra.

Guderian, Heinz. Panzer Leader. LC 79-19897. Repr. of 1952 ed. 15.00 (ISBN 0-89201-076-2). Zenger Pub.

A Handbook of the German Army in War January 1917. 125p. 1974. Repr. of 1917 ed. 12.00x (ISBN 0-8277-2728-3). British Bk Ctr.

Handbook of the German Army in War-January, 1917. (Illus.). 1976. Repr. 10.00x (ISBN 0-85409-863-1). Charles River Bks.

Lefferts, Charles. Uniforms of the American, British, French & German Armies in the War of the American Revolution, 1775-1783. rev. ed. LC 70-27396. (Illus.). 304p. 1971. Repr. of 1926 ed. 8.00 (ISBN 0-87364-232-5). Paladin Ent.

Necker, Wilhelm. The German Army of Today, 1943. (Illus.). 1976. Repr. 15.00x (ISBN 0-85409-896-8). Charles River Bks.

O'Neill, Robert J. German Army & the Nazi Party, 1933-39. (Illus.). 1967. 8.50 (ISBN 0-685-11957-2). Heineman.

GERMANY–BIBLIOGRAPHY

American Historical Association - Committee for the Study of War Documents. A Catalogue of Files & Microfilms of the German Foreign Ministry Archives, 1867-1920. LC 59-2654. Repr. of 1959 ed. 59.00 (ISBN 0-527-02150-4). Kraus Repr.

Estermann, Alfred, compiled by. Registerband (to Complete Collection of Zeitschriften Des Jungen Deutschland) 200p. Repr. of 1972 ed. 17.00 (ISBN 0-384-50046-3). Johnson Repr.

Merritt, Anna J. & Merritt, Richard L., eds. Politics, Economics, & Society in the Two Germanies, 1945-75: A Bibliography of English-Language Works. LC 77-26853. 1978. 12.00 (ISBN 0-252-00684-4). U of Ill Pr.

Richter, Paul E. Bibliotheca Geographica Germaniae. 1966. 51.50 (ISBN 0-8337-2993-4). B Franklin.

Walther, Philipp A. Systematisches Repertorium Ueber Die Schriften Saemmtlicher Historischer Gesellschaften Deutschlands. (Ger). 1969. Repr. of 1845 ed. 35.50 (ISBN 0-8337-3681-7). B Franklin.

GERMANY–BIOGRAPHY

Allgemeine Deutsche Biographie, 56 vols. Repr. of 1875 ed. 4570.00 set (ISBN 3-4280-0124-9). Adler.

Anderson, Margaret L. Windthorst: A Political Biography. 528p. 1981. 74.00x (ISBN 0-19-822578-4). Oxford U Pr.

Barraclough, Geoffrey, tr. Mediaeval Germany, 911-1250: Essays by German Historians, 2 vols. LC 75-41019. Repr. of 1938 ed. Set. 35.00 (ISBN 0-404-14800-X). AMS Pr.

Bosl, Karl. Biographisches Woerterbuch zur Deutschen Geschichte, 3 vols. 1st ed. (Ger.). 1973. Set. 375.00 (ISBN 3-7720-1082-2, M-7312, Pub. by Francke). French & Eur.

Charles, Elizabeth. Chronicles of the Schonberg-Cotta Family, 2 vols. in 1. LC 79-8251. Repr. of 1864 ed. 44.50 (ISBN 0-404-61818-9). AMS Pr.

Dombrowski, Eric. German Leaders of Yesterday & To-Day. facs. ed. LC 67-23206. (Essay Index Reprint Ser). 1920. 18.00 (ISBN 0-8369-0384-6). Arno.

Dutch, Oswald. The Errant Diplomat: The Life of Franz von Papen. LC 78-63665. (Studies in Fascism: Ideology & Practice). Repr. of 1940 ed. 26.00 (ISBN 0-404-16928-7). AMS Pr.

Eckert, Geroge. Wilhelm Liebknecht. 1973. 60.00x (ISBN 90-232-0858-7, Pub by Van Gorcum). Intl Schol Bk Serv.

Fest, Joachim C. The Face of the Third Reich: Portraits of the Nazi Leadership. Bullock, Michael, tr. LC 66-10412. 1977. pap. 5.95 (ISBN 0-394-73407-6). Pantheon.

Fromm, Hans & Grubmueller, Klaus, eds. Konrad von Fussesbrunnen: Die Kindheit Jesu. LC 72-94025. 220p. (Ger.). 1973. 69.50x (ISBN 3-11-003332-1). De Gruyter.

Genealogia Welforum. Eine Alte Genealogie der Welfen & Des Moenchs Von Weingarten. Grandaur, Georg, tr. 80p. pap. 5.50 (ISBN 0-384-14060-2). Johnson Repr.

Gilbert, G. M. The Psychology of Dictatorship: Based on an Examination of the Leaders of Nazi Germany. LC 79-15335. (Illus.). 1979. Repr. of 1950 ed. lib. bdg. 19.75x (ISBN 0-313-21975-3, GIPD). Greenwood.

Gluckel. The Memoirs of Gluckel of Hameln. Lowenthal, Marvin, tr. from Ger. LC 77-75290. 1977. pap. 6.95 (ISBN 0-8052-0572-1). Schocken.

Goethe, Katharina E. Goethe's Mother. LC 73-37695. (Women of Letters Ser.). Repr. of 1880 ed. 20.00 (ISBN 0-404-56752-5). AMS Pr.

Groeg, Otto J., ed. Who's Who in Germany, 2 vols. 7th ed. (Who's Who Ser.). 1600p. 1980. 147.00x (ISBN 3-921220-28-9, Pub. by Who's Who Germany). Standing Orders.

--Who's Who in Germany, 2 vols. 6th ed. (Who's Who Ser.). 1977. Set. 122.00x (ISBN 3-921220-11-4, Pub. by Who's Who-Book & Pub. GmbH). Standing Orders.

--Who's Who in Germany, 1980, 2 vols. 7th ed. LC 56-3621. 1500p. 1980. Set. 175.00 (ISBN 3-921220-28-9). Intl Pubns Serv.

Heiderich, Birgit. Mit Geschlossenen Augen: Ein Tagebuch. (Suhrkamp Taschenbuecher: No. 638). 144p. (Orig.). 1980. pap. text ed. 4.55 (ISBN 3-518-37138-X, Pub. by Suhrkamp Verlag Germany). Suhrkamp.

Heineman, John L. Hitler's First Foreign Minister: Constantin Freiherr von Neurath. LC 77-71061. 1980. 35.00x (ISBN 0-520-03442-2). U of Cal Pr.

Historische Kommission Dei der Bayerischen Akademie der Wissenschaften, ed. Neue Deutsche Biographie, 20 vols, Vols. 1-11. (Ger.). 1957-72. 100.00x ea., sold as set only (ISBN 3-428-00181-8). Intl Pubns Serv.

Hofacker, Erich P. Christian Morgenstern. (World Authors Ser.: No. 508 (Germany)). 1978. 12.50 (ISBN 0-8057-6349-X). Twayne.

Hohne, Heinz. Canaris. Brownjohn, J. Maxwell, tr. LC 78-56303. (Illus.). 1979. 15.95 (ISBN 0-385-08777-2). Doubleday.

Hoyt, Edwin P. Guerilla: The Story of Colonel von Lettow-Vorbeck & Germany's East African Empire. (Illus.). 256p. 1981. 14.95 (ISBN 0-02-555210-4). Macmillan.

Kurschner's Deutscher Gelehrten: Kalender 1976, 2 vols. 12th ed. 1976. Set. 188.50x (ISBN 3-11-004470-6). De Gruyter.

Leonhad, Wolfgang. Child of the Revolution. Woodhouse, C. M., tr. 1980. pap. 9.95 (ISBN 0-906133-26-2, Pub. by Ink Links England). Path Pr NY.

Luttger, Hans & Jeschek, Hans H., eds. Festschrift Fuer Eduard Dreher Zum. 1977. 148.50x (ISBN 3-11-005988-6). De Gruyter.

Masur, Gerhard. Das Ungewisse Herz: Berichte aus Berlin uber die Suche nach dem Freien. (Illus.). 1978. 18.00 (ISBN 0-918288-50-9, D15 M35 A38). Blenheim Pub.

Mueller, Gene. The Forgotten Marshal: Wilhelm Keitel. LC 79-64176. 1979. 16.95 (ISBN 0-87716-105-4, Pub. by Moore Pub Co). F Apple.

O'Connor, John T. Negotiator Out of Season: The Career of Wilhelm Egon von Furstenberg (1629-1704) LC 77-23872. 272p. 1978. 20.00x (ISBN 0-8203-0436-0). U of Ga Pr.

Parkinson, Roger. Clausewitz. LC 79-150602. (Illus.). 1979. pap. 5.95 (ISBN 0-8128-6021-7). Stein & Day.

Rilke, Rainer M. The Lay of Love & Death of Cornet Christopher Rilke. Phillips, Leslie & Schimanski, Stefan, trs. from Ger. 81p. 1981. Repr. of 1948 ed. lib. bdg. 20.00 (ISBN 0-89760-740-6). Telegraph Bks.

Ryder, Rowland. Ravenstein: Portrait of a German General. (Illus.). 1978. 14.95 (ISBN 0-241-89957-5). Hippocrene Bks.

Scheidemann, Philipp. Memoirs of a Social Democrat. Michell, J. E., tr. LC 78-63712. (Studies in Fascism: Ideology & Practice). 1977. Repr. of 1929 ed. 57.50 (ISBN 0-404-16930-9). AMS Pr.

Schuder, Werner, ed. Kueschners Deutscher Gelehrten-Kalender 1976, 2 vols. 1977. Set. 178.50x (ISBN 3-11-004470-6). De Gruyter.

Taylor, Telford. Sword & Swastika: Generals & Nazis in Third Reich. 416p. 1972. pap. 2.95 (ISBN 0-8129-6098-X, QP304). Times Bks.

Wagner, M. S. The Monster of Dusseldorf: The Life & Trial of Peter Kurten. 59.95 (ISBN 0-8490-0665-1). Gordon Pr.

Wer Ist Wer? 20th ed. LC 50-3718. 1979. 130.00x (ISBN 3-7950-2001-8). Intl Pubns Serv.

Whittle, Tyler. The Last Kaiser: A Biography of Wilhelm II, German Emperor & King of Prussia. LC 77-79047. 1977. 15.00 (ISBN 0-8129-0716-7). Times Bks.

Who's Who in Germany, 2 vols. deluxe ed. 165.00 set (ISBN 3-921220-29-7). Adler.

Wolfgang, Leonhard. Child of the Revolution. 2nd ed. Woodhouse, C. M., tr. from Ger. 448p. 1980. pap. text ed. 13.00x (ISBN 0-906133-26-2). Humanities.

GERMANY–CHURCH HISTORY

Bonifacius, Saint Winfrid. Briefe Des Heiligen Bonifatius. pap. 19.00 (ISBN 0-384-05025-5). Johnson Repr.

Entscheidungen in Kirchensachen Seit 1946, Vol. 13. 1978. 110.00x (ISBN 3-11-007625-X). De Gruyter.

Heyen, Franz Josef, ed. Germania Sacra: Die Bistuemer der Kirchenprovinz Trier: Das Erzbistum Trier, 1. das Stift St. Paulin Vor Trier. (Germania Sacra: Historisch-Statistische Beschreibung der Kirche Des Alten Reiches, N. F. 6). xiv, 855p. 1972. pap. 122.00 (ISBN 3-11-002273-7). De Gruyter.

Matheson, Peter. The Third Reich & the Christian Churches. LC 80-26767. 112p. (Orig.). 1981. pap. 5.95 (ISBN 0-8028-1873-0). Eerdmans.

Otto, Von St. Blasien. Die Chronik Des Otto Von St. Blasien. Kohl, Horst, tr. (Ger). Repr. of 1873 ed. pap. 8.00 (ISBN 0-384-43970-5). Johnson Repr.

Otto Bishop Of Freising. Der Chronik Des Bischofs Otto Von Freising, Sechstes und Siebentes Buch. Kohl, H., tr. (Ger). Repr. of 1939 ed. pap. 8.00 (ISBN 0-384-43965-9). Johnson Repr.

Schutz, Wilhelm W. Pens Under the Swastika. LC 70-118415. 1971. Repr. of 1946 ed. 10.00 (ISBN 0-8046-1192-0). Kennikat.

GERMANY–CIVILIZATION

Babcock, Leland S. & Frey, Erich A. German & Germany in Review. (Illus.). 1972. text ed. 10.95x (ISBN 0-442-20470-1); 14 tapes 65.00x (ISBN 0-442-30471-4). Van Nos Reinhold.

Borchardt, Frank L. German Antiquity in Renaissance Myth. LC 75-166484. 336p. 1972. 22.00x (ISBN 0-8018-1268-2). Johns Hopkins.

Chandler, Albert R. Rosenberg's Nazi Myth. LC 69-10073. 1969. Repr. of 1945 ed. lib. bdg. 15.00x (ISBN 0-8371-0038-0, CHNM). Greenwood.

Deutsche Revue: Herausgegeben Von Karl Gutzkow & Ludolf Weinbarg, No. 1. Bd. with Nos. 1 & 2. Deutsche Blatter Leben, Kunst Wissenschaft: Herausgegeben Von Karl Gutzkow. (Unpublished). Repr. of 1835 ed. (Unpublished). 1973. Repr. of 1835 ed. 19.00 (ISBN 0-384-11535-7); unbound 14.50 (ISBN 0-685-30624-0). Johnson Repr.

Engel, Johann J. Schriften, 12 vols. 4323p. 1801-06. Repr. 396.00 (ISBN 0-384-14361-X). Johnson Repr.

Ford, Ford M. Between Saint Denis & Saint George. LC 73-153640. (English Literature Ser., No. 33). 1971. Repr. lib. bdg. 38.95 (ISBN 0-8383-1244-6). Haskell.

Francke, Kuno. Glimpses of Modern German Culture. 1978. Repr. of 1898 ed. lib. bdg. 25.00 (ISBN 0-8492-4603-2). R West.

--History of German Literature As Determined by Social Forces. 4th ed. LC 73-100524. Repr. of 1901 ed. 37.50 (ISBN 0-404-02545-5). AMS Pr.

Gerstenberg, Heinrich W. Von. Vermischte Schriften, 3 vols. 1262p. Repr. of 1815 ed. 131.00 (ISBN 0-384-18220-8). Johnson Repr.

Janssen, Johannes. History of the German People at the Close of the Middle Ages, 17 Vols. LC 1-22270. Repr. of 1925 ed. Set. 552.50 (ISBN 0-404-03570-1); 32.50 ea. AMS Pr.

Kelling, H. W. Deutsche Kulturgeschichte. 1973. 18.50 (ISBN 0-03-085508-X, HoltC). HR&W.

Leibniz, Gottfried W. Leibnizens Nachgelassene Schriften: Physikalischen, Mechanischen und Technischen Inhalts. 1973. Repr. of 1906 ed. 19.50 (ISBN 0-384-32125-9). Johnson Repr.

Lowie, Robert H. The German People: A Social Portrait to 1914. 1972. lib. bdg. 13.00x (ISBN 0-374-95137-3). Octagon.

Peake, A. S., et al. Germany in the Nineteenth Century: Second Ser. Manchester Univ. Pubns. Historical Ser. No. 24. facs. ed. LC 67-30189. (Essay Index Reprint Ser). 1915. 13.00 (ISBN 0-8369-0472-9). Arno.

Prawer, S. S., et al, eds. Essays in German Language, Culture & Society. 244p. 1969. 50.00x (ISBN 0-85457-036-5, Pub. by Inst Germanic Stud England). State Mutual Bk.

Puckett, Hugh W. Germany's Women Go Forward. LC 30-8154. Repr. of 1930 ed. 19.50 (ISBN 0-404-05173-1). AMS Pr.

Reinhardt, Kurt F. Germany: Two Thousand Years, 2 Vols. rev. ed. LC 60-53139. Vol.1. 15.00 (ISBN 0-8044-1783-0); Vol.2. 15.00 (ISBN 0-8044-1784-9); Vol.1. pap. 6.95 (ISBN 0-8044-6692-0); Vol.2. pap. 6.50 (ISBN 0-8044-6693-9). Set. pap. 13.45 (ISBN 0-8044-6691-2). Ungar.

Veblen, Thorstein B. Imperial Germany. LC 63-23510. Repr. of 1939 ed. 17.50x (ISBN 0-678-00050-6). Kelley.

Vermeil, Edmond. Germany's Three Reichs. LC 68-9638. 1969. Repr. of 1944 ed. 28.50 (ISBN 0-86527-086-4). Fertig.

Wister, Owen. The Pentecost of Calamity. 148p. 1981. Repr. lib. bdg. 15.00 (ISBN 0-89984-509-6). Century Bookbindery.

GERMANY-COLONIES

Beer, George L. African Questions at the Paris Peace Conference. LC 73-79813. (Illus.). Repr. of 1923 ed. 28.00x (ISBN 0-8371-1469-1, Pub. by Negro U Pr). Greenwood.

Bixler, Raymond W. Anglo-German Imperialism in South Africa, 1880-1900. LC 77-155374. Repr. of 1932 ed. 12.00x (ISBN 0-8371-1271-0, Pub. by Negro U Pr). Greenwood.

Carlson, Andrew R. German Foreign Policy, 1890-1914 & Colonial Policy to 1914: A Handbook & Annotated Bibliography. 1970. 10.00 (ISBN 0-8108-0296-1). Scarecrow.

Fletcher, C. Brunsdon. Stevenson's Germany: The Case Against Germany in the Pacific. LC 78-111755. (American Imperialism: Viewpoints of United States Foreign Policy, 1898-1941). 1970. Repr. of 1920 ed. 12.00 (ISBN 0-405-02018-X). Arno.

Gann, L. H. & Duignan, Peter. The Rulers of German Africa, 1884-1914. LC 76-54100. (Illus.). 1977. 17.50x (ISBN 0-8047-0938-6). Stanford U Pr.

Great Britain Foreign Office Historical Section. German African Possessions, Late. LC 70-79815. (Illus.). Repr. of 1920 ed. 17.50x (ISBN 0-8371-1475-6, Pub. by Negro U Pr). Greenwood.

Henderson, W. O. Studies in German Colonial History. 150p. 1962. 24.00x (ISBN 0-7146-1674-5, F Cass Co). Biblio Dist.

Johannsen, G. Kurt & Kraft, H. H. Germany's Colonial Problem. LC 76-110910. 1970. Repr. of 1937 ed. 10.00 (ISBN 0-8046-0892-X). Kennikat.

Moses, John A. & Kennedy, Paul M. Germany in the Pacific & Far East: 1870-1914. 1977. 29.95x (ISBN 0-7022-1330-6). U of Queensland Pr.

Newton, Arthur P., ed. Sea Commonwealth, & Other Papers. Imperial Studies Ser. facs. ed. LC 68-22114. (Essay Index Reprint Ser). 1919. 11.75 (ISBN 0-8369-0742-6). Arno.

Oxford University, British Commonwealth Group. Germany's Colonial Demands. Bullock, A. L., ed. LC 75-8482. (Illus.). 274p. 1975. Repr. of 1939 ed. lib. bdg. 19.50x (ISBN 0-8371-8154-2, BUGC). Greenwood.

Rudin, Harry R. Germans in the Cameroons, Eighteen Eighty-Four to Nineteen Fourteen: A Case Study in Modern Imperialism. (Illus.). 1968. Repr. of 1938 ed. 22.50 (ISBN 0-208-00680-X, Archon). Shoe String.

Schmokel, Wolfe W. Dream of Empire: German Colonialism, 1919-1945. LC 80-15400. (Yale Historical Publications: Miscellany 78). xiv, 204p. 1980. Repr. of 1964 ed. lib. bdg. 22.50x (ISBN 0-313-22437-4, SCDE). Greenwood.

Schnee, Heinrich. German Colonization Past & Future: The Truth About the German Colonies. LC 77-110921. 1970. Repr. of 1926 ed. 10.50 (ISBN 0-8046-0903-9). Kennikat.

Smith, Woodruff D. The German Colonial Empire. LC 77-18155. 1978. 18.50x (ISBN 0-8078-1322-2). U of NC Pr.

Taylor, A. J. Germany's First Bid for Colonies, 1884-1885: A Move in Bismarck's European Policy. 1970. pap. 1.25x (ISBN 0-393-00530-5, Norton Lib). Norton.

--Germany's First Bid for Colonies, 1884-1885: A Move in Bismarck's European Policy. 1967. Repr. of 1938 ed. 13.50 (ISBN 0-208-00233-2, Archon). Shoe String.

Townsend, Mary E. Origins of Modern German Colonialism, 1871-1885. LC 74-2493. (Columbia University Studies in History, Economics, & Public Law). 205p. 1975. Repr. of 1921 ed. 19.75 (ISBN 0-86527-144-5). Fertig.

GERMANY-COMMERCE

Barnum, H. Gardiner. Market Centers & Hinterlands in Baden-Wuerttemburg. LC 65-28149. (Research Papers Ser.: No. 103). 172p. 1966. pap. 8.00 (ISBN 0-89065-013-6). U Chicago Dept Geog.

Bauder, Paul G. Directory of American Business in Germany. 7th ed. LC 78-482335. 1978. pap. 55.00x (ISBN 0-8002-1264-9). Intl Pubns Serv.

Deutschland Liefert-Germany Supplies 1981. 23rd ed. LC 57-18209. 2300p. (Span. , Ger. , Eng. & Fr.). 1981. 65.00x (ISBN 0-8002-2779-4). Intl Pubns Serv.

Deutschland Liefert-Germany Supplies 1981. 23rd ed. LC 57-18209. 2300p. 1981. 65.00 (ISBN 0-8002-2779-4). Intl Pubns Serv.

Forrester, David A. Schmalenbach & After: A Study of the Evolution of German Business Economics. 1978. 14.95x (ISBN 0-906161-00-2, Pub. by Strathclyde Convergencies). Intl Schol Bk Serv.

Gurland, A. R., et al. The Fate of Small Business in Nazi Germany. LC 74-12275. 160p. 1975. Repr. of 1943 ed. 17.50 (ISBN 0-86527-065-1). Fertig.

Mueller, Rudolf, et al. Doing Business in Germany. 174p. 1980. 33.00x (ISBN 0-7121-5487-6, Pub. by Macdonald & Evans). State Mutual Bk.

--Doing Business in Germany: A Legal Manual. 7th fully rev ed. LC 76-884451. 160p. 1972. 17.50x (ISBN 3-7819-0108-4). Intl Pubns Serv.

Reihlen, H., intro. by. Export Directory of German Industries, 1980. 27th ed. LC 57-16210. 1332p. (Orig.). 1980. pap. 55.00x (ISBN 0-8002-2695-X). Intl Pubns Serv.

Sailing Aktienfuehrer: Sailing Shares Guide, 1980. 73rd ed. LC 57-405999. 1062p. (Ger.). 1979. 50.00x (ISBN 3-8203-0025-2). Intl Pubns Serv.

Spoehr, Florence M. White Falcon: The House of Godeffroy & Its Commercial & Scientific Role in the Pacific. LC 63-18693. (Illus.). 1963. 7.95 (ISBN 0-87015-119-3). Pacific Bks.

Vogl, Frank. German Business After the Economic Miracle. LC 73-15142. 1973. 32.95 (ISBN 0-470-90970-6). Halsted Pr.

Who Supplies What? - Wer Liefert Was? For Import & Export. (Illus.). 1950p. (Eng. , Ger. , Fr. , Ital. , Span.). 1980. 75.00x (ISBN 0-8002-2451-5). Intl Pubns Serv.

GERMANY-CONSTITUTIONAL HISTORY

Dietze, Gottfried. Two Concepts of the Rule of Law. LC 73-5664. 118p. 1973. 5.00x (ISBN 0-913966-01-0). Liberty Fund.

Laufs, Adolf. Rechtsentwicklungen in Deutschland. 2nd ed. (De Gruyter Lehrbuch). 1978. 15.75x (ISBN 3-11-007563-6). De Gruyter.

GERMANY-COURT AND COURTIERS

William Second, Ex-Emperor of Germany. My Early Life. LC 71-137306. (Illus.). Repr. of 1926 ed. 26.50 (ISBN 0-404-06947-9). AMS Pr.

GERMANY-DESCRIPTION AND TRAVEL

Barba, Preston A. Cooper in Germany. 59.95 (ISBN 0-87968-944-7). Gordon Pr.

Dibdin, Thomas F. Bibliographical, Antiquarian, & Picturesque Tour in France & Germany, 3 Vols. 2nd ed. LC 76-111768. Repr. of 1829 ed. Set. 80.00 (ISBN 0-404-02130-1). AMS Pr.

Domville-Fife, C. This Is Germany. 59.95 (ISBN 0-8490-1195-7). Gordon Pr.

Einberg, Elizabeth. The Kennedys Abroad: Ann & Peter in Southern Germany. Date not set. 9.50 (ISBN 0-392-08619-0, SpS). Sportshelf.

Germany. 9th ed. (A Panorama in Color Ser.). (Illus.). 186p. 1972. 27.50x (ISBN 3-524-00039-8). Intl Pubns Serv.

Germany: Country, Cities, Villages, & People. (Illus.). 24.95 (ISBN 3-5240-0041-X). Adler.

Grzesinski, Albert C. Inside Germany. Lipschitz, Alexander S., tr. LC 79-180405. Repr. of 1939 ed. 27.00 (ISBN 0-404-56129-2). AMS Pr.

Hodgskin, Thomas. Travels in the North of Germany, 2 Vols. LC 68-55735. Repr. of 1820 ed. 45.00x (ISBN 0-678-00587-7). Kelley.

Kyngeston, Richard. Expeditions to Prussia & the Holy Land Made by Henry Earl of Derby. Smith, L. T., ed. 1965. Repr. of 1894 ed. 22.50 (ISBN 0-384-30775-2). Johnson Repr.

Lanier, Alison R. Update -- Germany. LC 80-83912. (Country Orientation Ser.). 1980. pap. text ed. 25.00x (ISBN 0-933662-40-8). Intercult Pr.

Marshall, Joseph. Travels Through Germany, Russia & Poland in the Years 1769 & 1770. LC 77-135821. (Eastern Europe Collection Ser). 1970. Repr. of 1772 ed. 12.00 (ISBN 0-405-02763-X). Arno.

Montaigne, Michel de & Dedeyan, Charles. Journal de Voyage en Italie. 520p. 1946. 13.50 (ISBN 0-686-54777-2). French & Eur.

Moreau, Daniel, ed. L' Allemagne. new ed. (Collection monde et voyages). (Illus.). 159p. (Fr.). 1973. 21.00x (ISBN 2-03-053104-9). Larousse.

Mueller-Alfeld, Theodor. Germany: The Federal Republic. LC 74-171363. (Illus.). 256p. 1974. 35.00x (ISBN 3-524-00593-4). Intl Pubns Serv.

Rippier, Joseph S., intro. by. Germany: Romantic & Modern. LC 68-97745. (Illus.). 132p. 1967. 12.50x (ISBN 3-524-00041-X). Intl Pubns Serv.

Rodnick, David. A Portrait of Two German Cities: Lubeck & Hamburg. LC 79-54321. 1980. 20.00x (ISBN 0-912570-06-7). Caprock Pr.

Schuster, H. J. Analyse und Bewertung Von Pflanzengesell-Schaften Im Noerdliche Frankenjura - ein Beitrag Zum Problem der Quantifizierung Unter-Schiedlich Anthropogen Beeinflusster Oekosystems. (Dissertationes Botanicae: No. 53). (Illus.). 482p. (Ger.). 1981. pap. text ed. 40.00x (ISBN 3-7682-1264-5). Lubrecht & Cramer.

Seger, Gerhart H. Germany. rev. ed. LC 77-83909. (World Cultures Ser.). (Illus.). 188p. (gr. 6 up). 1978. text ed. 9.95 ea. 1-4 copies (ISBN 0-88296-180-2); text ed. 7.96 ea. 5 or more copies; tchrs'. guide 8.94 (ISBN 0-88296-369-4). Fideler.

Shelley, Mary. Rambles in Germany & Italy in Eighteen Forty, Eighteen Forty-Two, & Eighteen Forty-Three, 2 vols. LC 75-26765. Repr. of 1844 ed. Set. lib. bdg. 75.00 (ISBN 0-8414-7826-0). Folcroft.

Siefert, Fritz. Das Lexikon der Deutschen Staedt und Gemeinden. (Ger.). 1973. 25.00 (ISBN 3-517-00453-7, M-7261). French & Eur.

Sitwell, Osbert. Discursions on Travel, Art & Life. 1925. lib. bdg. 14.75x (ISBN 0-8371-4336-5, SIDI). Greenwood.

Spender, Stephen. European Witness. LC 74-138186. 246p. 1972. Repr. of 1946 ed. lib. bdg. 15.00 (ISBN 0-8371-5643-2, SPEW). Greenwood.

--European Witness. LC 74-138186. 246p. 1972. Repr. of 1946 ed. lib. bdg. 15.00 (ISBN 0-8371-5643-2, SPEW). Greenwood.

Stambaugh, Ria, ed. Teufelbuecher in Auswahl, 5 vols. (Ausgaben Deutscher Literatur Des 15. bis 18. Jahrh). (Ger). Vol. 1, 1970. 104.25x (ISBN 3-11-006388-3); Vol. 2, 1972. 112.00x (ISBN 3-11-003924-9); Vol. 3, 1973. 141.00x (ISBN 3-11-004127-8). De Gruyter.

Sterling Editors, ed. East Germany: In Pictures. LC 77-79502. (Visual Geography Ser.). (Illus.). (gr. 4 up). 1977. PLB 4.99 (ISBN 0-8069-1217-0); pap. 2.95 (ISBN 0-8069-1216-2). Sterling.

Zimmern, Helen. The Hansa Towns. 1889. Repr. 15.00 (ISBN 0-685-43156-8). Norwood Edns.

GERMANY-DESCRIPTION AND TRAVEL-GUIDEBOOKS

Baedecker. The Baedecker Guide to Germany. (The Baedecker Travel Ser.). 320p. 1981. 19.95 (ISBN 0-13-055822-2); pap. 11.95 (ISBN 0-686-71977-8). P-H.

Bristow, Philip. Through the German Waterways. 168p. 1980. 15.00x (ISBN 0-245-51000-1, Pub. by Nautical England). State Mutual Bk.

Chester, Carole. Germany. LC 79-89186. (A Rand McNally Pocket Guide). (Illus., Orig.). 1980. pap. 3.95 (ISBN 0-528-84287-0). Rand.

Dollarwise Guide to Germany: 1980-81 Edition. 1981. pap. 4.95 (ISBN 0-671-25487-1). Frommer-Pasmantier.

Fodor's Budget Germany, 1981. 1981. pap. 4.95 (ISBN 0-679-00650-8). McKay.

Fodor's Germany, 1981. 1981. 12.95 (ISBN 0-679-00687-7); pap. 9.95 (ISBN 0-679-00688-5). McKay.

Kane, Robert S. The A to Z Travel Guides. 6.95 (ISBN 0-686-73303-7). Rand.

--Germany A to Z Guide. LC 79-88686. (Illus., Orig.). 1980. pap. 6.95 (ISBN 0-528-84331-1). Rand.

Michelin Guides & Maps. Michelin Red Guide to Germany. (Red Guide Ser.). 1981. 14.95 (ISBN 3-92-107801-6). Michelin.

Michelin Guides & Maps Dept. Michelin Green Guide to Germany. 4th ed. (Green Guide Ser.). (Avail. in Fr., Ger.). pap. 7.95 (ISBN 2-06-015030-2). Michelin.

Strutz, Herbert, intro. by. Beautiful Carinthla-Schoenes Kaernten. 7th ed. (Illus.). 80p. 1972. 7.50x (ISBN 3-524-00338-9). Intl Pubns Serv.

GERMANY-ECONOMIC CONDITIONS

Arndt, Helmut. Recht, Macht, und Wirtschaft. Bd. with The Quinine "Convention" of 1959-1962: A Case Study of an International Cartel. LC 71-359258. 209p. 1968. 22.50 (ISBN 3-428-01764-1). Intl Pubns Serv.

Balabkins, Nicholas. Germany Under Direct Controls: Economic Aspects of Industrial Disarmament, 1945-1948. 1964. 16.00 (ISBN 0-8135-0449-X). Rutgers U Pr.

Bohme, Helmut. An Introduction to the Social & Economic History of Germany. Lee, W. R., tr. from Ger. LC 78-18913. 1978. 22.50 (ISBN 0-312-43315-8). St Martin.

Bresciani-Turroni, Constantino. Economics of Inflation. Savers, Millicent E., tr. LC 68-6120. (Illus.). Repr. of 1937 ed. 19.50x (ISBN 0-678-06030-4). Kelley.

Bruck, Werner F. Social & Economic History of Germany from William the Second to Hitler, 1888-1938: A Comparative Study. LC 62-13828. 1962. Repr. of 1938 ed. 16.00 (ISBN 0-8462-0141-0). Russell.

Bruford, Walter H. Germany in the Eighteenth Century. 1935. 38.50 (ISBN 0-521-04354-9); pap. 11.50x (ISBN 0-521-09259-0, 259). Cambridge U Pr.

Chapman, Frank T. The Germanization of Europe: The Peace-War Prospects for the World. (Illus.). 146p. 1981. 63.45 (ISBN 0-930008-72-3). Inst Econ Pol.

Child, Frank C. Theory & Practice of Exchange in Germany. Wilkins, Mira, ed. LC 78-3904. (International Finance Ser.). 1978. Repr. of 1958 ed. lib. bdg. 17.00x (ISBN 0-405-11209-2). Arno.

Clapham, John H. Economic Development of France & Germany 1815-1914. 4th ed. 1935. 50.50 (ISBN 0-521-04664-5); pap. 15.95 (ISBN 0-521-09150-0, 150). Cambridge U Pr.

Danton, George H. Germany Ten Years After. facsimile ed. LC 79-150180. (Select Bibliographies Reprint Ser). Repr. of 1928 ed. 18.00 (ISBN 0-8369-5693-1). Arno.

DEVINDEX: Nineteen Seventy-Seven. 1979. pap. 10.00 (ISBN 0-88936-195-9, IDRC119, IDRC). Unipub.

Douglas, P. German Market Survey. 1977. 39.50x (ISBN 0-8464-0450-8). Beekman Pubs.

Engberg, Holger L. Mixed Banking & Economic Growth in Germany, 1850-1931. Bruchey, Stuart, ed. LC 80-2806. (Dissertations in European Economic History II). (Illus.). 1981. lib. bdg. 24.00x (ISBN 0-405-13990-X). Arno.

Erhard, Ludwig. Germany's Comeback in the World Market. Johnston, W. H., tr. LC 76-15289. (Illus.). 1976. Repr. of 1954 ed. lib. bdg. 16.75x (ISBN 0-8371-8948-9, ERGC). Greenwood.

Feldman, G. Iron & Steel in the German Inflation, 1916-1923. 1977. 37.50x (ISBN 0-691-04215-2). Princeton U Pr.

Flink, Salomon J. German Reichsbank & Economic Germany. LC 70-95097. Repr. of 1930 ed. lib. bdg. 15.00x (ISBN 0-8371-2542-1, FLGR). Greenwood.

Frowen, S. F., et al, eds. Monetary Policy & Economic Activity in West Germany. LC 77-2403. 1977. 58.95 (ISBN 0-470-99131-3). Halsted Pr.

Gellately, Robert. The Politics of Economic Despair: Shopkeepers & German Politics 1890-1914. LC 74-81024. (Sage Studies in 20th Century History: Vol. 1). 317p. 1974. 20.00x (ISBN 0-8039-9917-8). Sage.

Graham, Frank D. Exchange, Prices & Production in Hyper-Inflation: Germany, 1920-1923. LC 66-27086. 1967. Repr. of 1930 ed. 11.00 (ISBN 0-8462-1020-7). Russell.

Guillebaud, Claude W. Economic Recovery of Germany from 1933 to the Incorporation of Austria in March 1938. LC 72-180859. (Studies in Fascism, Ideology & Practice). Repr. of 1939 ed. 24.50 (ISBN 0-404-56135-7). AMS Pr.

Hamburger, Ludwig. How Nazi Germany Has Controlled Business. LC 78-63678. (Studies in Fascism: Ideology & Practice). Repr. of 1943 ed. 12.50 (ISBN 0-404-16939-2). AMS Pr.

Hamerow, Theodore S. Restoration, Revolution, Reaction: Economics & Politics in Germany, 1815-1871. 1958. 20.00x (ISBN 0-691-05146-1); pap. 6.95 (ISBN 0-691-00755-1). Princeton U Pr.

Harris, C. R. Germany's Foreign Indebtedness. Wilkins, Mira, ed. LC 78-3921. (International Finance Ser.). (Illus.). 1978. Repr. of 1935 ed. lib. bdg. 11.00x (ISBN 0-405-11224-6). Arno.

Hartrich, Edwin. The Fourth & Richest Reich. 1980. 12.95 (ISBN 0-02-548480-X). Macmillan.

Heyn, Udo. Private Banking & Industrialization: The Case of Frankfurt Am Main, 1825-1875. Bruchey, Stuart, ed. LC 80-2810. (Dissertations in European Economic History II). (Illus.). 1981. lib. bdg. 38.00x (ISBN 0-405-13994-2). Arno.

Kessler, Harry. Germany & Europe. LC 75-137950. (Economic Thought, History & Challenge Ser). 1971. Repr. of 1923 ed. 12.50 (ISBN 0-8046-1452-0). Kennikat.
Kitchen, Martin. The Political Economy of Germany, Eighteen Fifteen to Nineteen Fourteen. 1978. 20.95x (ISBN 0-7735-0501-6). McGill-Queens U Pr.
Kossler, Armin. Aktionsfeld Osmanisches Reich: Die Wirtschaftsinteressen des Deutschen Kaiserreiches in der Turkei 1871-1908 (Unter Besonderer Berucksichtigung Europaischer Literatur) Bruchey, Stuart, ed. LC 80-2814. (Dissertations in European Economic History II). (Illus.). 1981. lib. bdg. 38.00x (ISBN 0-405-13998-5). Arno.
Kuczynski, Jurgen. Germany: Economic & Labour Conditions Under Fascism. LC 68-30824. (Illus.). 1968. Repr. of 1945 ed. lib. bdg. 15.50x (ISBN 0-8371-0519-6, KUGE). Greenwood.
Meakin, W. The New Industrial Revolution. Wilkins, Mira, ed. LC 76-29998. (European Business Ser.). 1977. Repr. of 1928 ed. lib. bdg. 17.00x (ISBN 0-405-09756-5). Arno.
Mendershausen, Horst. Two Postwar Recoveries of the German Economy. LC 73-21101. (Contributions in Economic Analysis Ser.: No. 8). (Illus.). 130p. 1974. Repr. of 1955 ed. lib. bdg. 15.00 (ISBN 0-8371-6000-6, MEGE). Greenwood.
Milward, Alan S. The German Economy at War. 1965. text ed. 14.00x (ISBN 0-485-11075-X, Athlone Pr). Humanities.
Moulton, Harold G. Reparation Plan. Repr. of 1924 ed. lib. bdg. 14.50x (ISBN 0-8371-4290-3, MORP). Greenwood.
Nathan, Otto. Nazi Economic System: Germany's Mobilization for War. LC 78-102522. (Illus.). 1971. Repr. of 1944 ed. 18.50 (ISBN 0-8462-1501-2). Russell.
Neuburger, Hugh. German Banks & German Economic Growth from Unification to World War I. Bruchey, Stuart, ed. LC 77-77182. (Dissertations in European Economic History Ser.). 1977. lib. bdg. 15.00x (ISBN 0-405-10795-1). Arno.
Northrop, Mildred B. Control Policies of the Reichsbank, 1924-1933. LC 68-58613. (Columbia University. Studies in the Social Sciences: No. 436). Repr. of 1938 ed. 27.50 (ISBN 0-404-51436-7). AMS Pr.
Poole, Kenyon E. German Financial Policies, 1932-1939. 1977. lib. bdg. 59.95 (ISBN 0-8490-1884-6). Gordon Pr.
Quigley, Hugh & Clark, R. T. Republican Germany. LC 67-24592. (Illus.). 1968. Repr. of 1928 ed. 22.50 (ISBN 0-86527-166-6). Fertig.
Rettig, Rudi. Das Investitions und Finanzierungsverhalten Deutscher Grossunternehmen 1880-1911. Bruchey, Stuart, ed. LC 80-2827. (Dissertations in European Economic History II). 1981. lib. bdg. 29.00x (ISBN 0-405-14019-3). Arno.
Riesser, J. The German Great Banks & Their Concentration in Connection with the Economic Development of Germany. Wilkins, Mira, ed. LC 76-29741. (European Business Ser.). (Illus.). 1977. Repr. of 1911 ed. lib. bdg. 59.00x (ISBN 0-405-09758-1). Arno.
Rist, Ray C. Guestworkers in Germany: Prospects for Pluralism. LC 78-6282. (Praeger Special Studies). 1978. 27.95 (ISBN 0-03-040766-4). Praeger.
Roll, Erich. Spotlight on Germany. LC 70-180424. Repr. of 1933 ed. 18.50 (ISBN 0-404-56158-6). AMS Pr.
Schacht, Hjalmar H. The Stabilization of the Mark. Wilkins, Mira, ed. LC 78-3946. (International Finance Ser.). 1978. Repr. of 1927 ed. lib. bdg. 16.00x (ISBN 0-405-11246-7). Arno.
Schapiro, Jacob S. Social Reform & the Reformation. LC 74-127456. (Columbia University Studies in the Social Sciences: No. 90). 1970. Repr. of 1909 ed. 16.50 (ISBN 0-404-51090-6). AMS Pr.
Scheele, Godfrey. The Weimar Republic, Overture to the Third Reich. LC 75-25268. 360p. 1975. Repr. of 1946 ed. lib. bdg. 27.25x (ISBN 0-8371-8388-X, SCWR). Greenwood.
Schweitzer, Arthur. Big Business in the Third Reich. LC 63-62857. 752p. 1977. Repr. of 1964 ed. 27.50x (ISBN 0-253-10670-2). Ind U Pr.
Stolper, Gustav. German Economy, Eighteen Seventy to Nineteen Forty: Issues & Trends. LC 78-63722. (Studies in Fascism: Ideology & Practice). Repr. of 1940 ed. 26.00 (ISBN 0-404-16995-3). AMS Pr.
Tipton, Frank B., Jr. Regional Variations in the Economic Development of Germany During the Nineteenth Century. LC 76-6857. 288p. 1976. lib. bdg. 25.00x (ISBN 0-8195-4096-X, Pub. by Wesleyan U Pr). Columbia U Pr.
Vogl, Frank. German Business After the Economic Miracle. LC 73-15142. 1973. 32.95 (ISBN 0-470-90970-6). Halsted Pr.
Wallich, Henry C. Mainsprings of the German Revival. LC 76-25963. (Yale Studies in Economics: Vol. 5). 1976. Repr. of 1955 ed. lib. bdg. 28.75 (ISBN 0-8371-9017-7, WAMG). Greenwood.
Whale, Barrett. Joint Stock Banking in Germany. 369p. 1968. 29.50x (ISBN 0-7146-1259-6, F Cass Co). Biblio Dist.
Woolston, Maxine Y. Structure of the Nazi Economy. LC 68-10957. (Illus.). 1968. Repr. of 1941 ed. 10.00 (ISBN 0-8462-1088-6). Russell.

GERMANY–ECONOMIC POLICY

Anderson, Evelyn. Hammer or Anvil. LC 72-92773. 200p. 1973. Repr. of 1945 ed. 10.00 (ISBN 0-88211-043-8). S A Russell.
Backer, John H. Priming the German Economy. LC 70-142289. 1971. 12.75 (ISBN 0-8223-0243-8). Duke.
Barkin, Kenneth. Controversy Over German Industrialization, 1890-1902. LC 78-101359. 1970. 16.00x (ISBN 0-226-03712-6). U of Chicago Pr.
Bruck, Werner F. Social & Economic History of Germany from William the Second to Hitler, 1888-1938: A Comparative Study. LC 62-13828. 1962. Repr. of 1938 ed. 16.00 (ISBN 0-8462-0141-0). Russell.
Campbell, Colin D., ed. Wage-Price Controls in World War Two, United States & Germany. 1971. pap. 3.75 (ISBN 0-8447-1058-X). Am Enterprise.
Carroll, Berenice A. Design for Total War: Arms & Economics in the Third Reich. LC 68-15527. (Studies in European History: Vol. 17). 1968. text ed. 50.00x (ISBN 90-2790-299-2). Mouton.
Chamberlin, Waldo. Industrial Relations in Germany 1914-1939. LC 75-180664. Repr. of 1942 ed. 21.50 (ISBN 0-404-56400-3). AMS Pr.
Dawson, William H. Bismarck & State Socialism: An Exposition of the Social & Economic Legislation of Germany Since 1804. LC 79-106366. 1970. Repr. of 1890 ed. 8.00 (ISBN 0-403-00192-7). Scholarly.
Erhard, Ludwig. Prosperity Through Competition. Roberts, Edith T. & Wood, John B., trs. LC 75-27681. 260p. 1976. Repr. of 1958 ed. lib. bdg. 15.75x (ISBN 0-8371-8457-6, ERPC). Greenwood.
Goren, Simon L. & Forrester, Ian S., trs. The German Commercial Code As Amended to January 1, 1978. 1979. lib. bdg. 48.00 (ISBN 90-271-1559-1, Pub. by Kluwer Law Netherlands). Kluwer Boston.
Guillebaud, Claude W. Economic Recovery of Germany from 1933 to the Incorporation of Austria in March 1938. LC 72-180859. (Studies in Fascism, Ideology & Practice). Repr. of 1939 ed. 24.50 (ISBN 0-404-56135-7). AMS Pr.
Hardach, Karl. Political Economy of Germany in the Twentieth Century. LC 78-64754. 240p. 1980. 24.50x (ISBN 0-520-03809-6); pap. 5.95x (ISBN 0-520-04023-6). U of Cal Pr.
Hartrich, Edwin. The Fourth & Richest Reich. 1980. 12.95 (ISBN 0-02-548480-X). Macmillan.
Knott, Jack H. Managing the German Economy: Budgetary Politics in a Federal State. LC 80-8888. (Illus.). 240p. 1981. 22.95x (ISBN 0-669-04401-6). Lexington Bks.
Moulton, Harold G. & McGuire, Constantine E. Germany's Capacity to Pay: A Study of the Reparation Problem. 1971. Repr. of 1923 ed. 23.00 (ISBN 0-384-40239-9, S886). Johnson Repr.
Pfennigstorf, Werner, tr. from Ger. German Insurance Laws: Statutes & Regulations Concerning Insurance Supervision & Contracts, 1977 Supplement. 1977. pap. 3.00 (ISBN 0-910058-85-7). Am Bar Foun.
Veblen, Thorstein B. Imperial Germany. LC 63-23510. Repr. of 1939 ed. 17.50x (ISBN 0-678-00050-6). Kelley.

GERMANY–EMIGRATION AND IMMIGRATION

Diffenderffer, Frank R. The German Immigration into Pennsylvania Through the Port of Philadelphia from 1700 to 1775, & the Redemptioners. LC 77-77782. (Illus.). 1979. Repr. of 1900 ed. 15.00 (ISBN 0-8063-0776-5). Genealog Pub.
Inoki, Takenori. Aspects of German Peasant Emigration to the United States 1815-1914: A Reexamination of Some Behavioral Hypotheses in Migration Theory. Bruchey, Stuart, ed. LC 80-2812. (Dissertations in European Economic History II). (Illus.). 1981. lib. bdg. 25.00x (ISBN 0-405-13997-7). Arno.
Simmendinger, Ulrich. True & Authentic Register of Persons...Who in the Year 1709...Journeyed from Germany to America. 1978. pap. 3.00 (ISBN 0-8063-0313-1). Genealog Pub.
Smith, Clifford N. Nineteenth-Century Emigration of "Old Lutherans" from Eastern Germany (Mainly Pomerania & Lower Silesia) to Australia, Canada, & the United States. (German-American Genealogical Research Monograph: No. 7). 1979. pap. 12.50 (ISBN 0-915162-06-7). Westland Pubns.
Smith, Clifford Neal, tr. from Ger. Immigrants to America & Central Europe from Beihingen am Neckar, Baden-Wuerttemberg, Germany, No. 11. (German-American Genealogical Research). 49p. 1980. pap. 10.00 (ISBN 0-915162-10-5). Westland Pubns.
--Reconstructed Passenger Lists for 1850: Hamburg to Australia, Brazil, Canada, Chile & the United States, 4 pts. (German & Central European Emigration Ser.: No. 1). 79p. 1981. pap. 10.00 (ISBN 0-915162-50-4). Westland Pubns.
Walker, Mack. Germany & the Emigration, 1816-1885. LC 64-13431. (Historical Monographs Ser: No. 56). 1964. 15.00x (ISBN 0-674-35300-5). Harvard U Pr.
Young, George F. The Germans in Chile: Immigration & Colonization, 1849-1914. LC 73-92118. (Illus.). 234p. 1974. pap. text ed. 5.95x (ISBN 0-913256-14-5, Dist. by Ozer). Ctr Migration.

GERMANY–FOREIGN ECONOMIC RELATIONS

Holbik, Karel & Myers, Henry Allen. West German Foreign Aid, 1956-1966. LC 68-58498. 1968. 7.95x (ISBN 0-8419-8716-5, Pub. by Boston U Pr). Holmes & Meier.
Sutton, Antony C. Wall Street & the Rise of Hitler. LC 76-14011. (Orig.). 1976. 8.95 (ISBN 0-89245-004-5). Seventy Six.

GERMANY–FOREIGN OPINION

Browning, Christopher R. The Final Solution & the German Foreign Office. LC 78-8996. 1978. text ed. 28.00x (ISBN 0-8419-0403-0). Holmes & Meier.
Collier, Price. Germany & the Germans from an American Point of View. 1978. Repr. of 1913 ed. lib. bdg. 30.00 (ISBN 0-8414-0370-8). Folcroft.
Connors, Michael. Dealing in Hate: The Development of Anti-German Propaganda. 1981. lib. bdg. 59.95 (ISBN 0-686-73180-8). Revisionist Pr.
Gorgey, Laszlo C. Bonn's Eastern Policy, 1964-71: Evolution & Limitations. 192p. 1972. 17.50 (ISBN 0-208-01272-9, Archon). Shoe String.

GERMANY–FOREIGN RELATIONS

Arnold, Hans. Foriegn Cultural Policy: A Survey from a German Point of View. 1979. pap. 18.50 (ISBN 0-85496-210-7). Dufour.
Bloch, Kurt. German Interests & Policies in the Far East. LC 75-30098. (Institute of Pacific Relations). Repr. of 1939 ed. 11.50 (ISBN 0-404-59507-3). AMS Pr.
Bulow, Bernhard H. Imperial Germany. Lewenz, Marie A., tr. LC 78-12268. (Illus.). 1979. Repr. of 1914 ed. lib. bdg. 20.00x (ISBN 0-313-21176-0, BUIG). Greenwood.
Carlson, Andrew R. German Foreign Policy, 1890-1914 & Colonial Policy to 1914: A Handbook & Annotated Bibliography. 1970. 10.00 (ISBN 0-8108-0296-1). Scarecrow.
Carr, William. Arms, Autarky, & Agression. (Foundations of Modern History Ser.). 136p. 1973. 7.00 (ISBN 0-393-05486-1); pap. 3.95x (ISBN 0-393-09361-1). Norton.
Carroll, E. Malcolm. Germany & the Great Powers, 1866-1914: A Study in Public Opinion & Foreign Policy. 852p. 1975. Repr. of 1938 ed. lib. bdg. 45.00x (ISBN 0-374-91299-8). Octagon.
Doeker, Gunther. Federal Republic of Germany & German Democratic Republic in International Relations, Vols. 1-3. LC 79-1334. 1979. Set. lib. bdg. 135.00 (ISBN 0-379-20329-4). Oceana.
Drath, Viola & Schwab, George, eds. Germany in World Politics. (Cyrco Press Ser. on World & National Issues). 1979. 15.95 (ISBN 0-915326-13-2); pap. 9.95 (ISBN 0-915326-21-3). Cyrco Pr.
Fabian Society - London - International Research Section. Hitler's Route to Baghdad. facs. ed. LC 70-142624. (Essay Index Reprint Ser). 1939. 18.00 (ISBN 0-8369-2046-5). Arno.
Fischer, Fritz. Germany's Aims in the First World War. 1968. pap. 8.95x (ISBN 0-393-09798-6, NortonC). Norton.
Fuller, Joseph V. Bismarck's Diplomacy at Its Zenith. 1922. 27.50 (ISBN 0-86527-011-2). Fertig.
Geiss, Imanuel. German Foreign Policy, 1871-1914. (Orig.). 1976. pap. 18.00 (ISBN 0-7100-8303-3). Routledge & Kegan.
Goldston, Robert. The Life & Death of Nazi Germany. 1978. pap. 2.25 (ISBN 0-449-30830-8, Prem). Fawcett.
--Life & Death of Nazi Germany. LC 66-29906. (gr. 7 up). 7.95 (ISBN 0-672-50354-9). Bobbs.
Hale, Oron J. Germany & the Diplomatic Revolution: A Study in Diplomacy & the Press, 1904-1906. LC 74-120621. 1970. Repr. lib. bdg. 15.00x (ISBN 0-374-93378-2). Octagon.
Hiden, John. Germany & Europe, 1919-1939. LC 77-3299. 1978. text ed. 15.00x (ISBN 0-582-48489-8); pap. text ed. 9.50x (ISBN 0-582-48490-1). Longman.
Hildebrand, Klaus. The Foreign Policy of the Third Reich. LC 79-149942. 1974. 18.50x (ISBN 0-520-01965-2); pap. 6.50x (ISBN 0-520-02528-8). U of Cal Pr.
Hood, Miriam. Gunboat Diplomacy. LC 76-24618. 1977. 8.95 (ISBN 0-498-01946-2). A S Barnes.
Jacobson, Jon. Locarno Diplomacy: Germany & the West. LC 74-154998. 1972. 28.00 (ISBN 0-691-05190-9). Princeton U Pr.
Kent, George O., ed. A Catalog of Files & Microfilms of the German Foreign Ministry Archives, 1920-1945, Vol. 4. LC 69-19204. (Publications Ser.: No. 120). 982p. 1972. 35.00 (ISBN 0-8179-6201-8). Hoover Inst Pr.
Kim, Kie-Taek & Kaulins, Andis, eds. The Foreign Policies & Foreign Trade of the German Democratic Republic & the Korean Democratic People's Republic. (German Korea Studies Group Ser.). 144p. 1980. pap. 15.00 (ISBN 0-8188-0117-4, Pub. by German Korea Stud Germany). Paragon.
Kimmich, Christoph M. German Foreign Policy, Nineteen Eighteen to Nineteen Forty-Five: A Guide to Research & Research Materials. LC 80-53889. 293p. write for info. (ISBN 0-8420-2167-1). Scholarly Res.
Kraeche, Ennos E. Metternich's German Policy, Vol. 2, The Contest With Alexander, 1818-1848. Date not set. price not set (ISBN 0-691-05186-0). Princeton U Pr.
Lewin, Evans. The Germans & Africa. 1977. lib. bdg. 59.95 (ISBN 0-8490-1886-2). Gordon Pr.
Liang, Hsi-Huey. The Sino-German Connection: Alexander von Falckenhausen Between China & Germany. (Van Gorcum Historical Library: No. 94). (Illus.). 1978. pap. text ed. 23.75x (ISBN 90-232-1554-0). Humanities.
Lichtenberger, Henri. Third Reich. Pinson, Koppel S., tr. LC 73-102249. (Select Bibliographies Reprint Ser). 1937. 29.00 (ISBN 0-8369-5134-4). Arno.
Merkl, Peter H. German Foreign Policies, West & East: On the Threshold of a New European Era. LC 73-92506. (Studies in International & Comparative Politics: No. 3). (Illus.). 232p. 1974. text ed. 20.85 (ISBN 0-87436-133-8). ABC-Clio.
Mosse, W. E. European Powers & the German Question, 1848-1871. LC 74-76002. 1969. Repr. of 1958 ed. lib. bdg. 30.00x (ISBN 0-374-95928-5). Octagon.
Post, Gaines. The Civil-Military Fabric of Weimar Foreign Policy. LC 72-7799. 384p. 1973. 28.00x (ISBN 0-691-05211-5). Princeton U Pr.
Reece, B. Carroll. Peace Through Law. pap. 3.75 (ISBN 0-912806-21-4). Long Hse.
Rich, Norman. Friedrich Von Holstein: Politics & Diplomacy in the Era of Bismarck & Wilhelm. 1965. 130.00 (ISBN 0-521-06077-X). Cambridge U Pr.
--Hitler's War Aims: Ideology, the Nazi State, & the Course of Expansion. (Illus., Orig.). 1973. Vol. 1. 12.95x (ISBN 0-393-05454-3). Norton.
Rupieper, Herman J. The Cuno Government & Reparations, 1922-1923. (Studies in Contemporary History: No. 1). 1979. lib. bdg. 51.00 (ISBN 90-247-2114-8, Pub. by Martinus Nijhoff Netherlands). Kluwer Boston.
Saeter, Martin. The Federal Republic, Europe & the World: Perspectives in West Germany Foreign Policy. 120p. 1980. text ed. 15.00x (ISBN 82-00-05315-6). Universitet.
Schrecker, John E. Imperialism & Chinese Nationalism: Germany in Shantung. LC 73-129119. (East Asian Ser: No. 58). (Illus.). 1971. 17.50x (ISBN 0-674-44520-1). Harvard U Pr.
Seabury, Paul. The Wilhelmstrasse: A Study of German Diplomats Under the Nazi Regime. LC 76-2403. (Illus.). 217p. 1976. Repr. of 1954 ed. lib. bdg. 15.50x (ISBN 0-8371-8790-7, SEWI). Greenwood.
Sinanian, Sylva, et al, eds. Eastern Europe in the 1970's. LC 72-85944. (Special Studies in International Politics & Government). 1972. 29.50x (ISBN 0-275-28632-0); pap. text ed. 14.95x (ISBN 0-89197-740-6). Irvington.
Spira, Thomas. German-Hungarian Relations & the Swabian Problem. (East European Monographs: No. 25). 1977. 18.50x (ISBN 0-914710-18-4). East Eur Quarterly.
Taylor, A. J. Germany's First Bid for Colonies, 1884-1885: A Move in Bismarck's European Policy. 1970. pap. 1.25x (ISBN 0-393-00530-5, Norton Lib). Norton.
--Germany's First Bid for Colonies, 1884-1885: A Move in Bismarck's European Policy. 1967. Repr. of 1938 ed. 13.50 (ISBN 0-208-00233-2, Archon). Shoe String.

U. S. Dept. of State. Consultation Among the American Republics with Respect to the Argentine Situation. LC 76-29632. (Latin America in the 20th Century Ser.). 1976. Repr. of 1946 ed. lib. bdg. 15.00 (ISBN 0-306-70838-8). Da Capo.
Von Buelow, Bernhard H. Imperial Germany. LC 77-127900. Repr. of 1914 ed. 21.00 (ISBN 0-404-01228-0). AMS Pr.
--Memoirs of Prince Von Buelow, 4 Vols. LC 77-127900. Repr. of 1932 ed. Set. 115.00 (ISBN 0-404-01230-2). AMS Pr.
Waller, Bruce. Bismarck at the Crossroads: The Reorientation of German Foreign Policy After the Congress of Berlin 1878-1880. (University of London Historical Studies: No. 35). 273p. 1974. text ed. 32.50x (ISBN 0-485-13135-8, Athlone Pr). Humanities.
Weinberg, Gerhard L. The Foreign Policy of Hitler's Germany: Starting World War II, 1937-1939. LC 79-26406. 1980. 44.00x (ISBN 0-226-88511-9). U of Chicago Pr.
--The Foreign Policy of Hitler's Germany: 1933-1936. LC 70-124733. 1971. 22.00x (ISBN 0-226-88509-7). U of Chicago Pr.

GERMANY–FOREIGN RELATIONS–CZECHOSLOVAKIA

Braddick, Henderson B. Germany, Czechoslovakia, & the "Grand Alliance" in the May Crisis, 1938. (Monograph Ser. in World Affairs, Vol. 6: 1968-69 Ser., Pt. B). 4.00 (ISBN 0-87940-019-6). U of Denver Intl.
Campbell, F. Gregory. Confrontation in Central Europe: Weimar Germany & Czechoslovakia. LC 74-11618. (Midway Reprint). 1978. pap. text ed. 14.00x (ISBN 0-226-09252-6). U of Chicago Pr.

GERMANY–FOREIGN RELATIONS–FRANCE

Gooch, George P. Franco-German Relations, 1871-1914. LC 66-24694. 1967. Repr. of 1923 ed. 5.00 (ISBN 0-8462-0830-X). Russell.
Lehrs, Max. Geschichte und Kritischer Katalog Des Deutschen, Niederlandischen und Franzosischen Kupferstichs Im Xv. Jahrhundert, 10 vols. (Illus.). 4270p. 1969. Repr. 350.00 set (ISBN 0-442-81034-2). Hacker.
McDougall, Walter A. France's Rhineland Policy, 1914-1924: The Last Bid for a Balance of Power in Europe. LC 77-85550. 1978. 31.00 (ISBN 0-691-05268-9). Princeton U Pr.
Mitchell, Allan. Bismarck & the French Nation: 1848-1890. LC 72-167692. 1971. 24.50x (ISBN 0-672-53510-6). Irvington.
Pottinger, Evelyn A. Napoleon Third & the German Crisis, 1865-1866. LC 66-18253. (Historical Studies: No. 75). 1966. 12.50x (ISBN 0-674-60050-9). Harvard U Pr.
Reynaud, Louis. Influence Allemande En France Au Dix-Huitieme et Au Dix-Neuvieme Siecle. LC 78-168933. (Research & Source Works Ser.: No. 834). (Fr). 1971. Repr. of 1922 ed. lib. bdg. 26.50 (ISBN 0-8337-4338-4). B Franklin.

GERMANY–FOREIGN RELATIONS–GREAT BRITAIN

Anderson, Pauline R. Background of Anti-English Feeling in Germany, 1890-1902. LC 78-86268. 1969. Repr. of 1939 ed. lib. bdg. 24.00x (ISBN 0-374-90209-7). Octagon.
Aydelotte, William O. Bismarck & British Colonial Policy: The Problem of South West Africa, 1883-1885. LC 71-111563. 1937. Repr. of 1937 ed. 10.25x (ISBN 0-8371-4584-8, Pub. by Negro U Pr). Greenwood.
Gardiner, Samuel R., ed. Letters & Other Documents Illustrating the Relations Between England & Germany at the Commencement of the Thirty Years' War, 2 Vols. LC 70-168100. (Camden Society, London. Publications, First Ser.: Nos. 90 & 98). Repr. of 1868 ed. Set. 42.00 (ISBN 0-404-50211-3); 21.00 ea. Vol. 1 (ISBN 0-404-50190-7). Vol. 2 (ISBN 0-404-50198-2). AMS Pr.
Hale, O. J. Publicity & Diplomacy with Special Reference to England & Germany (1890-1914) 8.50 (ISBN 0-8446-1215-4). Peter Smith.
Henderson, Neville. Failure of a Mission: Berlin, 1937-1939. LC 75-41131. Repr. of 1940 ed. 15.50 (ISBN 0-404-14670-8). AMS Pr.
Mander, John. Our German Cousins: Anglo-German Relations in the 19th & 20th Centuries. 273p. 1975. 12.50 (ISBN 0-7195-2894-1). Transatlantic.
Middlemas, Keith. The Strategy of Appeasement: The British Government & Germany, 1937-1939. LC 73-182509. 1972. 15.00 (ISBN 0-8129-0241-6). Times Bks.
Newman, Simon K. March Nineteen Thirty-Nine: A Study in the Continuity of British Foreign Policy. 1976. 45.00x (ISBN 0-19-822532-6). Oxford U Pr.
Sontag, Raymond J. Germany & England: Background of Conflict, 1848-1894. 1969. pap. 3.95x (ISBN 0-393-00180-6, Norton Lib). Norton.
--Germany & England: Background of Conflict, 1848-1894. LC 64-15034. 1964. Repr. of 1938 ed. 10.00 (ISBN 0-8462-0467-3). Russell.
Wood, Bryce. Peaceful Change & the Colonial Problem. LC 70-76639. (Columbia University. Teachers College. Contributions to Education: No. 464). Repr. of 1940 ed. 15.00 (ISBN 0-404-51464-2). AMS Pr.

GERMANY–FOREIGN RELATIONS–ITALY

Toscano, Mario. Origins of the Pact of Steel. LC 67-24276. 464p. 1968. 25.00x (ISBN 0-8018-0635-6). Johns Hopkins.

GERMANY–FOREIGN RELATIONS–JAPAN

Boyd, Carl. The Extraordinary Envoy: General Hiroshi Oshima & Diplomacy in the Third Reich 1934-1939. LC 79-9600. 246p. 1980. text ed. 18.50 (ISBN 0-8191-0957-6); pap. text ed. 9.75 (ISBN 0-8191-0958-4). U Pr of Amer.
Morley, James W., ed. Deterrent Diplomacy, Japan, Germany, & the USSR, 1935-1940: Japans Road to the Pacific War. LC 75-25524. (Studies of the East Asian Institute Ser.). 363p. 1976. 20.00x (ISBN 0-231-08969-4). Columbia U Pr.
Presseisen, Ernst L. Germany & Japan: A Study in Totalitarian Diplomacy, 1933-1941. LC 68-57832. 1970. Repr. of 1958 ed. 25.00 (ISBN 0-86527-082-1). Fertig.

GERMANY–FOREIGN RELATIONS–MOROCCO

Barlow, Ima C. Agadir Crisis. 1971. Repr. of 1940 ed. 25.00 (ISBN 0-208-01023-8, Archon). Shoe String.
Williamson, Francis T. Germany & Morocco Before 1905. LC 78-64165. (Johns Hopkins University. Studies in the Social Sciences. Fifty-Fifth Ser. 1937: 1). Repr. of 1937 ed. 19.50 (ISBN 0-404-61275-X). AMS Pr.

GERMANY–FOREIGN RELATIONS–POLAND

Jedrzejewicz, Waclaw, ed. Diplomat in Berlin, 1933-1939: Papers & Memoirs of Jozef Lipski, Ambassador of Poland. LC 67-25871. (Illus.). 1968. 22.50x (ISBN 0-231-03070-3). Columbia U Pr.
Kulski, W. W. Germany & Poland: From War to Peaceful Relations. (Illus.). 358p. 1976. 22.50x (ISBN 0-8156-0118-2); pap. 9.95x (ISBN 0-8156-0122-0). Syracuse U Pr.
Lachs, Manfred. Polish-German Frontier. 80p. 1964. 2.00 (ISBN 0-686-30936-7). Polish Inst Arts.
Ortmayer, Louis. Conflict, Compromise, & Conciliation: West German-Polish Normalization, 1966-1976. (Monograph Ser. in World Affairs: Vol. 13, 1975-76, Pt. C). pap. 4.00 perfect bdg. (ISBN 0-87940-047-1). U of Denver Intl.
Przewieniecki, W. M. German-Polish Frontier. 166p. 1959. 4.50 (ISBN 0-686-30923-5). Polish Inst Arts.
Von Riekhoff, Harald. German-Polish Relations 1918-1933. LC 73-141999. 416p. 1971. 25.00x (ISBN 0-8018-1310-7). Johns Hopkins.
--German-Polish Relations 1918-1933. LC 73-141999. 416p. 1971. 25.00x (ISBN 0-8018-1310-7). Johns Hopkins.

GERMANY–FOREIGN RELATIONS–RUSSIA

Dallin, Alexander. German Rule in Russia 1941-1945. 2nd rev. ed. (A Study of Occupation Policies). 700p. lib. bdg. 35.00 (ISBN 0-86531-102-1). Westview.
Hilger, G. & Meyer, A. G. The Incompatible Allies: German-Soviet Rlations, 1918-1941. (Illus.). 1971. Repr. of 1953 ed. 18.00 (ISBN 0-02-846010-3). Hafner.
Ierace, Francis A. America & the Nazi-Soviet Pact. 1978. 6.95 (ISBN 0-533-03544-9). Vantage.
Kochan, Lionel. Russia & the Weimar Republic. LC 78-17679. 1978. Repr. of 1954 ed. lib. bdg. 18.75x (ISBN 0-313-20503-5, KORW). Greenwood.
Rosenbaum, Kurt. Community of Fate: German-Soviet Diplomatic Relations, 1922-1928. LC 65-18573. 1965. 16.95x (ISBN 0-8156-2079-9). Syracuse U Pr.
Sontag, Raymond J. & Beddie, James S., eds. Nazi-Soviet Relations, 1939-1941: Documents from Archives of German Foreign Office. LC 75-35371. (U.S. Government Documents Program Ser.). 362p. 1976. Repr. of 1948 ed. lib. bdg. 25.00x (ISBN 0-8371-8612-9, GENS). Greenwood.

GERMANY–FOREIGN RELATIONS–SPAIN

Weinberg, Gerhard L. Germany & the Soviet Union, 1939-1941. 218p. 1972. Repr. of 1954 ed. text ed. 15.50x (ISBN 90-0403-348-3). Humanities.

GERMANY–FOREIGN RELATIONS–TURKEY

Friedman, Isaiah. Germany, Turkey, & Zionism, 1897-1918. 1977. 52.50x (ISBN 0-19-822528-8). Oxford U Pr.
Weber, Frank G. The Evasive Neutral: Germany, Britain, & the Quest for a Turkish Alliance in the Second World War. LC 78-19641. 1979. text ed. 19.50x (ISBN 0-8262-0262-4). U of Mo Pr.

GERMANY–FOREIGN RELATIONS–UNITED STATES

Birnbaum, Karl E. Peace Moves & U-Boat Warfare: A Study of Imperial Germany's Policy Towards the United States, April 18, 1916 - January 9, 1917. (Illus.). 1970. Repr. of 1958 ed. 19.50 (ISBN 0-208-00908-6, Archon). Shoe String.
Gatzke, Hans W. Germany & the United States: A "Special Relationship?". (American Foreign Policy Library). (Illus.). 330p. 1980. 18.50 (ISBN 0-674-35326-9). Harvard U Pr.
Learned, M. D., ed. Guide to Manuscript Materials Relating to American History in the German State Archives. 1912. pap. 20.00 (ISBN 0-527-00691-2). Kraus Repr.
Offner, Arnold. American Appeasement: United States Foreign Policy & Germany, 1933-1938. 352p. 1976. pap. 3.95x (ISBN 0-393-00801-0, Norton Lib). Norton.
Offner, Arnold A. American Appeasement: United States Foreign Policy & Germany 1933-1938. LC 69-13767. 1969. 16.50x (ISBN 0-674-01840-0, Belknap Pr). Harvard U Pr.
Peterson, Edward N. The American Occupation of Germany: Retreat to Victory. LC 77-28965. 1978. 18.95x (ISBN 0-8143-1588-7). Wayne St U Pr.
Ryden, George H. The Foreign Policy of the United States in Relation to Samoa. xviii, 634p. 1975. Repr. of 1933 ed. lib. bdg. 30.00x (ISBN 0-374-97000-9). Octagon.
Trefousse, Hans L. Germany & American Neutrality, 1939-1941. 1969. lib. bdg. 13.50x (ISBN 0-374-97980-4). Octagon.
Trefousse, Hans L., ed. Germany & America: Essays on Problems of International Relations & Immigration. 270p. 1981. 23.00x (ISBN 0-930888-06-5). Brooklyn Coll Pr.
Wilson, Hugh R., Jr. A Career Diplomat, the Third Chapter: The Third Reich. LC 72-11747. (Illus.). 112p. 1973. Repr. lib. bdg. 15.00x (ISBN 0-8371-6702-7, WICD). Greenwood.

GERMANY–GEHEIME STAATSPOLIZEI

see Germany–Secret Police

GERMANY–HISTORICAL GEOGRAPHY

Hansen, C. P. Das Schleswig'sche Wattenmeer und Die Friesischen Inseln. (Illus., Ger.). 1865. text ed. 21.25x (ISBN 90-6041-115-3). Humanities.
Mellor. Geography of Two Germanies. 1978. 20.40 (ISBN 0-06-318066-9, IntlDept). Har-Row.
Mellor, Roy E. H. The Two Germanies: A Modern Geography. (Illus.). 1978. text ed. 22.50x (ISBN 0-06-494778-5); pap. 9.95x (ISBN 0-06-494779-3). B&N.
Quirin, H., et al, eds. Historischer Handatlas Von Brandenburg und Berlin. 1962-75. Fasc. 1-6. write for info. (ISBN 0-685-26079-8); Fasc. 7-36. write for info. (ISBN 0-685-26080-1); Fasc. 42-46. write for info. (ISBN 0-685-26081-X). De Gruyter.

GERMANY–HISTORY

Angell, James W. The Recovery of Germany. rev. ed. LC 75-138197. (Illus.). 442p. 1972. Repr. of 1932 ed. lib. bdg. 19.25x (ISBN 0-8371-5550-9, ANRG). Greenwood.
Atkinson, Christopher T. A History of Germany, 1715-1815. LC 70-114456. (Illus.). xx, 732p. Repr. of 1908 ed. lib. bdg. 34.25x (ISBN 0-8371-4807-3, ATHG). Greenwood.
Baring-Gould, Sabine. The Story of Germany. 1886. 40.00 (ISBN 0-685-43778-7). Norwood Edns.
Barraclough, Geoffrey. Factors in German History. LC 78-21483. (Illus.). 1979. Repr. of 1946 ed. lib. bdg. 18.75x (ISBN 0-313-21066-7, BAFG). Greenwood.
Conze, Werner. The Shaping of the German Nation: A Historical Analysis. Mellon, Neville, tr. LC 79-5140. 1979. 15.05 (ISBN 0-312-71623-0). St Martin.
Daenell, E. Bluetezeit der deutsche Hanse: Hansische Geschichte Von der Zweiten Haelfte des Xiv Bis Zum Letzten Viertel Des Xv Jahrhunderts, 2 vols. 1035p. 1973. Repr. of 1906 ed. Set. 135.30x (ISBN 3-11-004562-1). De Gruyter.
Dawson, William H. Germany Under the Treaty. (Select Bibliographies Reprint Ser). 1972. Repr. of 1933 ed. 18.25 (ISBN 0-8369-9958-4). Arno.
Detwiler, Donald S. Germany: A Short History. LC 76-4563. 288p. 1976. 14.95x (ISBN 0-8093-0491-0); pap. 7.95 (ISBN 0-8093-0768-5). S Ill U Pr.
Dill, Marshall, Jr. Germany: A Modern History. rev. ed. LC 60-13891. (History of the Modern World Ser). (Illus.). 1970. 10.00x (ISBN 0-472-07101-7). U of Mich Pr.
Dornberg, John. The Two Germanys. LC 73-15446. (Illus.). 288p. (gr. 7 up). 1974. 8.95 (ISBN 0-8037-8757-X). Dial.
Dorwart, Reinhold A. Administrative Reforms of Frederick William First of Prussia. LC 70-138221. 1971. Repr. of 1953 ed. lib. bdg. 14.75x (ISBN 0-8371-5578-9, DOAR). Greenwood.
Eidelberg, Shlomo, ed. Jews & the Crusaders: The Hebrew Chronicles of the First & Second Crusades. 1977. 17.50 (ISBN 0-299-07060-3). U of Wis Pr.
Ekkehardus. Die Chronik Des Ekkehard Von Aura. (Ger). pap. 8.00 (ISBN 0-384-14080-7). Johnson Repr.
Engel-Janosi, Friedrich. The Growth of German Historicism. LC 78-64195. (Johns Hopkins University. Studies in the Social Sciences. Sixty-Second Ser. 1944: 2). Repr. of 1944 ed. 15.00 (ISBN 0-404-61301-2). AMS Pr.
Epstein, Klaus. The Genesis of German Conservatism. 747p. 1975. 35.00x (ISBN 0-691-05121-6); pap. 18.50x (ISBN 0-691-10030-6). Princeton U Pr.
Feuchtwanger, E. J., ed. Upheaval & Continuity: A Century of German History. LC 73-17691. 1974. 10.95 (ISBN 0-8229-1113-2); pap. 4.95x (ISBN 0-685-39229-5). U of Pittsburgh Pr.
Foerster, Friedrich W. Europe & the German Question. LC 70-180399. Repr. of 1940 ed. 31.00 (ISBN 0-404-56123-3). AMS Pr.
Fuller, J. F. The First of the League Wars: Lessons & Omens. 59.95 (ISBN 0-8490-0172-2). Gordon Pr.
Gagliardo, John G. From Pariah to Patriot: The Changing Image of the German Peasant, 1770-1840. LC 72-80091. 352p. 1969. 19.00x (ISBN 0-8131-1187-0). U Pr of Ky.
Gamillscheg, Ernst. Romania Germanica: Sprach- und Siedlungsgeschichte der Germanen auf dem Boden des alten Roemerreiches. Incl. Vol. 1. Zu den aeltesten Beruehrungen zwischen Roemern und Germanen: Die Franken. rev. 2nd ed. (Illus.). xvi, 474p. 1970. 73.00x (ISBN 3-11-002680-5). (Ger.). De Gruyter.
Goering, Hermann. Germany Reborn. 1977. lib. bdg. 59.95 (ISBN 0-8490-1888-9). Gordon Pr.
Gooch, George P. Studies in German History. LC 70-75465. 1969. Repr. of 1948 ed. 14.00 (ISBN 0-8462-1337-0). Russell.
Haller, Johannes & Dannenbauer, Heinrich. Eintritt der Germanen in die Geschichte. 4th ed. (Sammlung Goeschen, No. 1117). (Ger). 1970. 3.25x (ISBN 3-11-002764-X). De Gruyter.
--Von den Staufern zu den Habsburgern: Aufloesung des Reiches und Emporkommen der Landesstaaten (1250 bis 1519) 3rd ed. (Sammlung Goeschen, No. 1077). (Ger). 1970. 3.25x (ISBN 3-11-002892-1). De Gruyter.
Headlam-Morley, James. Bismarck & the Foundation of the German Empire. LC 73-14447. (Heroes of the Nations Ser.). Repr. of 1899 ed. 30.00 (ISBN 0-404-58265-6). AMS Pr.
Hermannus, Contractus. Chronik Herimanns Von Reichenau. Repr. of 1892 ed. pap. 5.50 (ISBN 0-384-22475-X). Johnson Repr.
Hintze, Otto. The Historical Essays of Otto Hintze. Gilbert, Felix, ed. 1975. 25.00x (ISBN 0-19-501819-2); pap. 6.95x (ISBN 0-19-501883-4). Oxford U Pr.
Historia Diplomatica Friderici Secundi. Historia Diplomatica Friderici Secundi, 7 vols. in 12. Repr. of 1852 ed. 335.00 set (ISBN 0-404-56630-8); per vol. 28.00 (ISBN 0-404-56630-8). AMS Pr.
Holborn, Hajo. A History of Modern Germany, 3 vols. Incl. Vol. 1. The Reformation. 1959. 20.50 (ISBN 0-394-42878-1); Vol. 2. 1648-1840. 20.50 (ISBN 0-394-42879-X); Vol. 3. 1840-1945. 20.50 (ISBN 0-394-42877-3). Knopf.
--A History of Modern Germany, 3 vols. Incl. Vol. 1. The Reformation. 1959. text ed. 13.95 (ISBN 0-394-30276-1); Vol. 2. 1648-1840. text ed. 13.95 (ISBN 0-394-30277-X); Vol. 3. 1840-1945. text ed. 13.95 (ISBN 0-394-30278-8). (Illus., KnopfC). Knopf.
Kahler, Erich. The Germans. Kimber, Rita & Kimber, Robert, eds. 300p. 1974. 22.00 (ISBN 0-691-05222-0). Princeton U Pr.
Katzenstein, Peter. Disjoined Partners: Austria & Germany Since 1815. LC 74-30526. 1976. 24.50x (ISBN 0-520-02945-3). U of Cal Pr.
Kaufman, Theodore N. Germany Must Perish. 59.95 (ISBN 0-87968-294-9). Gordon Pr.
Keller, John. From the Kaiser to Willy Brandt: Social Democrats & German Foreign Policy 1870-1976. 12.50 (ISBN 0-87164-067-8). William-F.
Kohlrausch, Frederick. A History of Germany: From the Earliest Period to the Present Time. Haas, James D., tr. LC 76-145125. 487p. 1972. Repr. of 1864 ed. 24.00 (ISBN 0-403-01062-4). Scholarly.
Kohlrausch, Friedrich. History of Germany: From the Earliest Period to the Present Time. Haas, James D., tr. LC 72-124771. Repr. of 1864 ed. 22.50 (ISBN 0-404-03737-2). AMS Pr.
Kraus, Georg. Siebenburgische Chronik Des Schassburger Stadtschreibers, Georg Kraus 1608-1685, 2 vols. Repr. of 1864 ed. Vol. 3. pap. 19.00 (ISBN 0-384-30418-4); Vol. 4. pap. 42.00 (ISBN 0-685-02284-6). Johnson Repr.
Krispyn, Egbert. Anti-Nazi Writers in Exile. LC 77-9568. 200p. 1978. 15.00 (ISBN 0-8203-0430-1). U of Ga Pr.

Kurze, Dietrich, ed. Aus Theorie und Praxis der Geschichtswissenschaft: Festschrift fur Hans Herzfeld zum 80, Geburtstag. (Veroeffentlichungen der Historischen Kommission zu Berlin, Band 37). xii, 445p. (Ger.). 1972. 95.75x (ISBN 3-11-003813-7). De Gruyter.

Lambert, Von Hersfeld. Die Jahrbucher Des Lambert Von Hersfeld. (Ger). Repr. of 1892 ed. pap. 23.00 (ISBN 0-384-31103-2). Johnson Repr.

Legge, J. E. Rhyme & Revolution in Germany. 59.95 (ISBN 0-8490-0954-5). Gordon Pr.

Legge, James G. Rhyme & Revolution in Germany: A Study in German History, Life, Literature & Character. LC 72-126646. Repr. of 1918 ed. 33.45 (ISBN 0-404-03947-2). AMS Pr.

Lichtenberger, Henri. Germany & Its Evolution in Modern Times. Ludovici, A. M., tr. 1977. lib. bdg. 59.95 (ISBN 0-8490-1887-0). Gordon Pr.

Liddell Hart, B. H. The German Generals Talk. 1971. pap. 5.95 (ISBN 0-688-06012-9). Morrow.

Ludwig, Emil. The Germans: Double History of a Nation. LC 78-63688. (Studies in Fascism: Ideology & Practice). Repr. of 1942 ed. 27.50 (ISBN 0-404-16951-1). AMS Pr.

Luedtke, Gerhard, ed. Kuerschners Deutscher Literatur-Kalender Nekrolog 1901-1935. 976p. 1973. Repr. of 1936 ed. 77.25x (ISBN 3-11-004432-3). De Gruyter.

Maehl, William H. Germany in Western Civilization. LC 77-1394. 832p. 1979. 27.50x (ISBN 0-8173-5707-6). U of Ala Pr.

Mansfeld, Guenter. Die Fibeln der Heuneburg 1950-1970: Ein Beitrag zur Geschichte der Spaethallstattfibel Heuneburgstudien II. LC 72-75868. (Roemisch-Germanische Forschungen, Vol. 33). (Illus.). xii, 299p. 1973. 162.25x (ISBN 3-11-003769-6). De Gruyter.

Matthias Of Neuenburg. Die Chronik Des Mathias Von Neuenberg. (Ger). pap. 23.00 (ISBN 0-384-35883-7). Johnson Repr.

Meinecke, Friedrich. The Age of German Liberation, 1795-1815. Paret, Peter & Fischer, Helmut, trs. from Ger. LC 74-79767. Orig. Title: Das Zeitalter der Deutschen Erhebung. 1977. 24.00x (ISBN 0-520-02792-2); pap. 5.95x (ISBN 0-520-03454-6). U of Cal Pr.

Mosse, George L. The Nationalization of the Masses: Political Symbolism & Mass Movements in Germany, from the Napoleonic Wars Through the Third Reich. LC 74-11105. (Illus.). xiv, 272p. 1975. 25.00 (ISBN 0-86527-140-2). Fertig.

Nalaman, S. Die Konstituierung der Deutshen Arbeiter Bewegung 1862-1863. 1040p. (Ger.). 1975. 75.00x (ISBN 90-232-0939-7, Pub. by Van Gorcum). Intl Schol Bk Serv.

O'Connor, John T. Negotiator Out of Season: The Career of Wilhelm Egon von Furstenberg (1629-1704) LC 77-23872. 272p. 1978. 20.00x (ISBN 0-8203-0436-0). U of Ga Pr.

Pachter, Henry M. Modern Germany: A Social, Cultural, & Political History. (Illus.). 1979. lib. bdg. 29.75x (ISBN 0-89158-166-9). Westview.

Pasley, Malcolm. Germany: A Companion to German Studies. 1976. pap. 19.95x (ISBN 0-416-83540-6). Methuen Inc.

Perthes, Clemens T. Das Deutsche Staatssleban Vor der Revolution. Mayer, J. P., ed. LC 78-67375. (European Political Thought Ser.). (Ger.). 1979. lib. bdg. 22.00x (ISBN 0-405-11725-6). Arno.

Pinnow, Hermann. History of Germany. facsimile ed. Brailsford, Mabel R., tr. from Ger. LC 74-130563. (Select Bibliographies Reprint Ser). Repr. of 1933 ed. 21.00 (ISBN 0-8369-5536-6). Arno.

Presseisen, Ernst L. Amiens & Munich. (Comparisons in Appeasement). 1978. 31.50 (ISBN 90-247-2067-2, Pub. by Martinus Nijhoff Netherlands). Kluwer Boston.

Reinhardt, Kurt F. Germany: Two Thousand Years, 2 Vols. rev. ed. LC 60-53139. Vol.1. 15.00 (ISBN 0-8044-1783-0); Vol.2. 15.00 (ISBN 0-8044-1784-9); Vol.1. pap. 6.95 (ISBN 0-8044-6692-0); Vol.2. pap. 6.50 (ISBN 0-8044-6693-9). Set. pap. 13.45 (ISBN 0-8044-6691-2). Ungar.

Saffenreuther, Elfriede & Giegerich, Artur. The Giegerich Chronicle: A Geneological Study in the History & Folk Life of the Odenwald. LC 80-27990. 1981. 24.35 (ISBN 0-8357-0578-1, SS-00148). Univ Microfilms.

Sagarra, Eda. A Social History of Germany 1648-1914. LC 77-24201. 1978. text ed. 45.00x (ISBN 0-8419-0332-8). Holmes & Meier.

Schaber, Will, ed. AUFBAU (Reconstruction) LC 72-81086. (Illus.). 416p. (Ger.). 1972. 11.95 (ISBN 0-87951-001-3). Overlook Pr.

--Weinberg der Freiheit. Date not set. 12.00 (ISBN 0-8044-2763-1). Ungar.

Scharfe, Wolfgang. Abriss der Kartographie Brandenburgs 1771-1821. (Illus.). xii, 357p. 1972. 52.50x (ISBN 3-11-003898-6). De Gruyter.

Schultz, Alwin. Das Hofische Leben zur zeit der Minnesinger, 2 vols. LC 78-63509. (Illus.). Repr. of 1889 ed. Set. 97.50 (ISBN 0-404-17200-8). AMS Pr.

Shine, H. Carlyle's Unfinished History of Germany. LC 72-6243. (Studies in German Literature, No. 13). 1972. Repr. of 1956 ed. lib. bdg. 48.95 (ISBN 0-8383-1602-6). Haskell.

Sieg Heil. (Illus.). 1981. 14.95 (ISBN 0-918058-03-1). Authors Edn.

Sieg Heil! An Illustrated History of Germany from Bismark to Hitler. (Illus.). 1981. 14.95 (ISBN 0-918058-03-1). Authors Edn.

Sisson, Edgar & Creel, George. The Sisson Report on the German Bolshevik Conspiracy. 1980. lib. bdg. 59.95 (ISBN 0-8490-3097-8). Gordon Pr.

Smith, Clifford N. Nineteenth-Century Emigration from the Simmern Kreise (Hunsrueck), Rheinland-Pfalz, Germany, to Brazil, England, Russian Poland & the United States. (German-American Genealogical Research Monograph: No. 8). 80p. (Orig.). 1980. pap. 12.00 (ISBN 0-915162-07-5). Westland Pubns.

Snyder, Louis L. Roots of German Nationalism. LC 77-74437. (Illus.). 320p. 1978. 17.50x (ISBN 0-253-35026-3). Ind U Pr.

Taddey, Gerhard. Lexikon der Deutschen Geschichte. (Ger.). 1977. 99.50 (ISBN 3-520-81301-7, M-7263). French & Eur.

Taylor, Telford. Sword & Swastika: Generals & Nazis in Third Reich. 416p. 1972. pap. 2.95 (ISBN 0-8129-6098-X, QP304). Times Bks.

Tellenbach, Gerd. Konigtum & Stamme in der Werdezeit Des Deutschen Reiches. LC 80-2002. Repr. of 1939 ed. 18.50 (ISBN 0-404-18600-9). AMS Pr.

U. S. Dept. Of State. Historical Office: Documents of Germany 1944-61. 1971. Repr. of 1961 ed. 49.00 (ISBN 0-403-01774-2). Scholarly.

Uslar, Rafael Von. Westgermanische Bodenfunde Des Ersten Bis Dritten Jahrhunderts N. Ch. Aus Mittel-und Westdeutschland, 2 vols. (Illus.). 1978. 132.50x (ISBN 3-11-002250-8). De Gruyter.

Vermeil, Edmond. Germany's Three Reichs: Their History & Culture. Dickes, E. W., tr. 1978. Repr. of 1945 ed. lib. bdg. 25.00 (ISBN 0-8482-2822-7). Norwood Edns.

Vexler, Robert I. Germany: A Chronology & Fact Book. LC 73-7792. (World Chronology Ser.). 160p. 1973. lib. bdg. 8.50x (ISBN 0-379-16305-5). Oceana.

Vita Liutbirgae Virginis. Das Leben der Liutbirg. (Ger). Repr. of 1944 ed. pap. 5.50 (ISBN 0-384-64620-4). Johnson Repr.

Von Buelow, Bernhard H. Imperial Germany. LC 77-127900. Repr. of 1914 ed. 21.00 (ISBN 0-404-01228-0). AMS Pr.

Von Constanz, Bernold. Chronik Bernolds Von St. Blasien. Repr. of 1893 ed. pap. 8.00 (ISBN 0-384-04039-X). Johnson Repr.

Walker, Mack. German Home Towns: Community State, & General Estate, 1648-1871. LC 76-162540. (Illus.). 487p. 1971. 28.50x (ISBN 0-8014-0670-6). Cornell U Pr.

Wister, Owen. The Pentecost of Calamity. 148p. 1981. Repr. lib. bdg. 15.00 (ISBN 0-89984-509-6). Century Bookbindery.

GERMANY–HISTORY–HISTORIOGRAPHY

Fout, John C. German History & Civilization - 1806-1914: A Bibliography of Scholarly Periodical Literature. LC 74-10803. 1974. 15.00 (ISBN 0-8108-0742-4). Scarecrow.

Fredericq, Paul. The Study of History in Germany & France. LC 78-63795. (Johns Hopkins University. Studies in the Social Sciences. Eighth Ser. 1890: 5-6). Repr. of 1890 ed. 11.50 (ISBN 0-404-61060-9). AMS Pr.

Iggers, Georg G. The German Conception of History: The National Tradition of Historical Thought from Herder to the Present. LC 68-17147. 1968. 20.00x (ISBN 0-8195-3088-3, Pub. by Wesleyan U Pr). Columbia U Pr.

Von Wegele, Franz X. Geschichte der Deutschen Historiographie. 1885. 58.00 (ISBN 0-384-66430-X). Johnson Repr.

GERMANY–HISTORY–PHILOSOPHY

Calleo, D. The German Problem Reconsidered. LC 78-9683. 1978. 19.95 (ISBN 0-521-22309-1). Cambridge U Pr.

Flint, Robert. The Philosophy of History in France & Germany. 631p. 1971. Repr. of 1874 ed. 57.50x (ISBN 0-8002-1333-5). Intl Pubns Serv.

Moeller Van Den Bruck, Arthur. Germany's Third Empire. 1972. 22.50 (ISBN 0-86527-085-6). Fertig.

Weber, Max & Shils, Edward. Max Weber on Universities: The Power of the State & the Dignity of the Academic Calling in Imperial Germany. LC 73-94103. (Midway Reprints). 1977. pap. text ed. 3.50x (ISBN 0-226-87727-2). U of Chicago Pr.

GERMANY–HISTORY–SOURCES

Epstein, Fritz T. German Source Materials in American Libraries. 1958. pap. 1.95 (ISBN 0-87462-409-6). Marquette.

Hungarian Historical Research Society. Records, Notes, Reports Connected with the Removal to Germany in the Year 1945. LC 77-95243. 120p. 1980. pap. 6.50 (ISBN 0-935484-07-8). Universe Pub Co.

Kent, George O., ed. A Catalog of Files & Microfilms of the German Foreign Ministry Archives, 1920-1945, Vol. 4. LC 69-19204. (Publications Ser.: No. 120). 982p. 1972. 35.00 (ISBN 0-8179-6201-8). Hoover Inst Pr.

Lutz, Ralph H. Fall of the German Empire, 1914-1918, 2 Vols. 1969. lib. bdg. 50.00x (ISBN 0-374-95168-3). Octagon.

Otto of Freising. Deeds of Frederick Barbarossa. Mierow, Christopher, tr. 1966. pap. 7.45x (ISBN 0-393-09697-1, NortonC). Norton.

Sachsische Geschichten Auf Grund Des Textes der Scriptores Rerum Germanicarum. Hirsch, Paul, ed. 1931. pap. 19.00 (ISBN 0-384-68290-1). Johnson Repr.

Snyder, Louis L., ed. Documents of German History. LC 75-32435. 619p. 1976. Repr. of 1958 ed. lib. bdg. 33.00x (ISBN 0-8371-8493-2, SNDG). Greenwood.

Strauss, Gerald, ed. & tr. Manifestations of Discontent in Germany on the Eve of the Reformation: A Collection of Documents. LC 75-135014. 276p. 1971. 10.95x (ISBN 0-253-33670-8); pap. 4.50x (ISBN 0-253-33671-6). Ind U Pr.

Teutsch, Georg D., ed. Urkundenbuch Zur Geschichte Siebenburgens. lxxxiv, 204p. Repr. of 1857 ed. pap. 19.00 (ISBN 0-384-59870-6). Johnson Repr.

Vexler, Robert I. Germany: A Chronology & Fact Book. LC 73-7792. (World Chronology Ser.). 160p. 1973. lib. bdg. 8.50x (ISBN 0-379-16305-5). Oceana.

Wolfe, Robert, ed. Captured German & Related Records: A National Archives Conference. LC 74-82495. (National Archives Conferences Ser.: Vol. 3). (Illus.). xix, 279p. 1974. 17.00x (ISBN 0-8214-0172-6). Ohio U Pr.

GERMANY–HISTORY–TO 1517

Barraclough, Geoffrey, tr. Mediaeval Germany, 911-1250: Essays by German Historians, 2 vols. LC 75-41019. Repr. of 1938 ed. Set. 35.00 (ISBN 0-404-14800-X). AMS Pr.

Bax, E. Belfort. German Society at the Close of the Middle Ages. 1977. lib. bdg. 59.95 (ISBN 0-8490-1885-4). Gordon Pr.

--The Social Side of the Reformation in Germany, 3 vols. Incl. Vol. 1. German Society at the Close of the Middle Ages. LC 67-25997. 276p. Repr. of 1894 ed. lib. bdg. 12.50x (ISBN 0-678-00312-2); Vol. 2. The Peasants' War in Germany 1525-1526. LC 68-57371. 367p. Repr. of 1899 ed. lib. bdg. 9.25x (ISBN 0-678-00445-5); Vol. 3. The Rise & Fall of the Anapabtists. LC 75-101125. 407p. Repr. of 1903 ed. lib. bdg. 15.00x (ISBN 0-678-00593-1). lib. bdg. 37.50x set (ISBN 0-678-00772-1). Kelley.

Bayley, Charles C. The Formation of the German College of Electors in the Mid-Thirteenth Century. (Scholarly Reprint Ser.). 1980. 30.00x (ISBN 0-8020-7102-3). U of Toronto Pr.

Borchardt, Frank L. German Antiquity in Renaissance Myth. LC 75-166484. 336p. 1972. 22.00x (ISBN 0-8018-1268-2). Johns Hopkins.

Duggan, Lawrence G. Bishop & Chapter: The Governance of the Bishopric of Speyer to 1552. 1978. 22.00 (ISBN 0-8135-0857-6). Rutgers U Pr.

Fisher, Herbert A. Medieval Empire, 2 Vols. LC 72-95147. Repr. of 1898 ed. 34.50 (ISBN 0-404-02398-3). AMS Pr.

Fleckenstein, J. Early Medieval Germany. (A History of Germany: Vol. 1). 1978. 34.25 (ISBN 0-444-85134-8, North-Holland). Elsevier.

Freed, John B. The Friars & German Society in the Thirteenth Century. 1977. 14.00 (ISBN 0-910956-60-X). Medieval Acad.

Hampe, Karl. Germany Under the Salian & Hohenstaufen Emperors. rev. ed. Bennett, Ralph F., tr. from Ger. (Illus.). 306p. 1973. 19.50x (ISBN 0-87471-173-8). Rowman.

Helmold Priest Of Bosau. Chronicle of the Slavs. Tschan, Francis J., tr. 1967. lib. bdg. 17.00x (ISBN 0-374-98018-7). Octagon.

Henderson, Ernest F. History of Germany in the Middle Ages. LC 68-25240. (World History Ser., No. 48). 1969. Repr. of 1894 ed. lib. bdg. 39.95 (ISBN 0-8383-0954-2). Haskell.

Hill, Boyd H. Medieval Monarchy in Action: The German Empire from Henry I to Henry IV. (Historical Problems Studies & Documents). 1972. text ed. 18.95x (ISBN 0-04-943017-3); pap. text ed. 8.95x (ISBN 0-04-943018-1). Allen Unwin.

Huffines, Marion L. Chivalry & Peasantry in Germany of the Late Middle Ages. 1975. lib. bdg. 69.95 (ISBN 0-87968-570-0). Gordon Pr.

Kantorowicz, Ernst. Frederick the Second, 1194-1250. Lorimer, E. O., tr. LC 57-9408. (Illus.). 1957. 24.50 (ISBN 0-8044-1468-8). Ungar.

Kieckhefer, Richard. Repression of Heresy in Medieval Germany. LC 78-65112. (The Middle Ages Ser.). 1979. 16.00x (ISBN 0-8122-7758-9). U of Pa Pr.

Leuschner, J. Germany in the Late Middle Ages. (Europe in the Middle Ages: Selected Studies: Vol. 17). 250p. 1979. 36.75 (ISBN 0-444-85135-6, North Holland). Elsevier.

Reinke, Edgar C. The Dialogus of Andreas Meinhardi: A Utopian Description of Wittenberg & Its University, 1508. LC 76-14594. (Sponsored by The Committee on Creative Work & Research, Valparaiso Univ.). 1976. 29.00 (ISBN 0-8357-0176-X, SS-00007, Pub by University Microfilms International). Univ Microfilms.

Stubbs, William. Germany in the Early Middle Ages, 476-1250. 1908. 7.50 (ISBN 0-86527-083-X). Fertig.

--Germany in the Early Middle Ages, 476-1250. LC 73-38337. Repr. of 1908 ed. 16.50 (ISBN 0-404-06300-4). AMS Pr.

--Germany in the Later Middle Ages, 1200-1500. LC 77-149675. Repr. of 1908 ed. 16.50 (ISBN 0-404-06301-2). AMS Pr.

--Germany in the Later Middle Ages, 1200-1500. 1908. 7.50 (ISBN 0-86527-084-8). Fertig.

Wippo Presbyter. Leben Kaiser Konrad II: Nebst Auszugen Aus Den Jahrbuchern Von Sanct Gallen & der Schwabischen Weltchronik. (Ger). pap. 8.00 (ISBN 0-384-68730-X). Johnson Repr.

GERMANY–HISTORY–1517-1648

see also Peasants' War, 1524-1525; Thirty Years' War, 1618-1648

Bellardi, Werner. Die Geschichte der "Christlichen Gemeinschaft" in Strassburg: 1546-1550. Repr. of 1934 ed. 29.00 (ISBN 0-384-03849-2); pap. 23.00 (ISBN 0-384-03850-6). Johnson Repr.

Benecke, Gerhard. Germany in the Thirty Years War. LC 78-21443. (Illus.). 1979. 17.95x (ISBN 0-312-32626-2). St Martin.

Bireley, Robert. Religion & Politics in the Age of the Counterreformation: Emperor Ferdinand II, William Lamormaini, S.J., & the Formation of Imperial Policy. LC 80-27334. 400p. 1981. 28.00x (ISBN 0-8078-1470-9). U of NC Pr.

Duggan, Lawrence G. Bishop & Chapter: The Governance of the Bishopric of Speyer to 1552. 1978. 22.00 (ISBN 0-8135-0857-6). Rutgers U Pr.

Hatto, A. T. & Walshe, M. O., eds. Medieval German Studies for F. Norman. 302p. 1973. 50.00x (ISBN 0-85457-057-8, Pub. by Inst Germanic Stud England). State Mutual Bk.

Janssen, Johannes. History of the German People at the Close of the Middle Ages, 17 Vols. LC 1-22270. Repr. of 1925 ed. Set. 552.50 (ISBN 0-404-03570-1); 32.50 ea. AMS Pr.

Peacham, Henry. A Most True Relation of the Affaires of Cleve & Gulick, with the Articles of Peace Propounded at Santen. LC 72-6024. (English Experience Ser.: No. 549). (Illus.). 44p. 1973. Repr. of 1615 ed. 7.00 (ISBN 90-221-0549-0). Walter J Johnson.

Scribner, Bob & Benecke, Gerhard. German Peasant War Fifteen Twenty-Five: New Viewpoints. (Illus.). 1979. text ed. 22.50x (ISBN 0-04-900031-4); pap. text ed. 8.95x (ISBN 0-04-900032-2). Allen Unwin.

Strauss, Gerald. Nuremberg in the Sixteenth Century: City Politics & Life Between Middle Ages & Modern Times. LC 76-12379. (Illus.). 320p. 1976. 12.50x (ISBN 0-253-34149-3); pap. text ed. 5.95x (ISBN 0-253-34150-7). Ind U Pr.

Von Ranke, Leopold. Ferdinand I & Maximilian II of Austria. LC 74-153627. Repr. of 1853 ed. 14.50 (ISBN 0-404-09265-9). AMS Pr.

Wedgewood, Cicily V. Thirty Years War. 1962. text ed. 18.75x (ISBN 0-224-00690-8). Humanities.

GERMANY–HISTORY–18TH CENTURY

Reill, Peter H. The German Enlightenment & the Rise of Historicism. LC 73-87244. 318p. 1975. 32.50x (ISBN 0-520-02594-6). U of Cal Pr.

GERMANY–HISTORY–1789-1900

Here are entered works in the period between 1789 and 1900 either as a whole or in part, except those subdivisions immediately below. see also Austro-Prussian War, 1866; Schleswig-Holstein Question

Atkinson, Christopher T. A History of Germany, 1715-1815. LC 70-114456. (Illus.). xx, 732p. Repr. of 1908 ed. lib. bdg. 34.25x (ISBN 0-8371-4807-3, ATHG). Greenwood.

Busch, Moritz. Our Chancellor: Sketches for a Historical Picture, 2 Vols. facsimile ed. Beatty-Kingston, W., tr. LC 76-109615. (Select Bibliographies Reprint Ser). 1884. Set. 45.00 (ISBN 0-8369-5225-1). Arno.

Carr, William. A History of Germany Eighteen Fifteen to Nineteen Forty-Five. 2nd ed. LC 79-20108. (Illus.). 1979. 18.95x (ISBN 0-312-37871-8); pap. 9.95 (ISBN 0-312-37872-6). St Martin.

Craig, Gordon A. Germany, Eighteen Sixty-Six to Nineteen Forty-Five. (History of Modern Europe Ser.). 1980. pap. text ed. 10.95x (ISBN 0-19-502724-8). Oxford U Pr.
--Germany, Eighteen Sixty-Six to Nineteen Forty-Five. (Oxford History of Modern Europe Ser.). 1978. 22.50 (ISBN 0-19-822113-4). Oxford U Pr.
Diefendorf, Jeffry M. Businessmen & Politics in the Rhineland, 1789-1834. LC 79-3200. 1980. 22.50x (ISBN 0-691-05298-0). Princeton U Pr.
Engels, Frederick. Germany: Revolution & Counter-Revolution. rev. ed. LC 69-20353. (Orig.). 1969. pap. 1.95 (ISBN 0-7178-0077-6, NW). Intl Pub Co.
Engels, Friedrich. The German Revolutions. Incl. The Peasant War in Germany; Germany: Revolution & Counter-Revolution. LC 67-15314. 256p. 1967. pap. 2.95 (ISBN 0-226-20869-9, P256, Phoen). U of Chicago Pr.
--German Revolutions: The Peasant War in Germany. L., intro. by. Incl. Germany: Revolution & Counter-Revolution. LC 67-15314. 1967. 8.75x (ISBN 0-226-20868-0). U of Chicago Pr.
Farrar, L. L., Jr. Arrogance & Anxiety: The Ambivalence of German Power, 1848-1914. LC 81-10374. (Iowa Studies in History: Vol. 1). 231p. 1981. text ed. 15.00x (ISBN 0-87745-112-5). U of Iowa Pr.
Fest, Wilfried. Dictionary of German History 1806-1945. LC 78-54658. 1979. 18.50x (ISBN 0-312-20103-6). St Martin.
Gazley, John G. American Opinion of German Unification, 1848-1871. LC 77-130939. (Columbia University Social Science Studies Ser.: No. 267). 1970. Repr. of 1926 ed. 10.00 (ISBN 0-404-51267-4). AMS Pr.
Hamerow, Theodore S. Social Foundations of German Unification, 1858-1871. Incl. Vol. 1. Ideas & Institutions. 1969. 25.00x (ISBN 0-691-05174-7); pap. 7.95 (ISBN 0-691-00773-X); Vol. II. Struggles & Accomplishments. 1972. 25.00x (ISBN 0-691-05195-X). LC 75-75241. Princeton U Pr.
Henderson, W. O. The Rise of German Industrial Power, 1834-1914. LC 75-17293. 1976. 24.50x (ISBN 0-520-03073-7); pap. 6.95x (ISBN 0-520-03120-2). U of Cal Pr.
Hohenlohe-Schillingsfuerst, Chlodwig K. Memoirs of Prince Chlodwig of Hohenlohe-Schillingsfuerst, 2 Vols. LC 75-111765. Repr. of 1906 ed. 57.50 (ISBN 0-404-03305-9). AMS Pr.
Keating, John E. The Wreck of the Deutschland. LC 74-13638. 1963. Repr. lib. bdg. 15.00 (ISBN 0-8414-5510-4). Folcroft.
Lee, Lloyd E. The Politics of Harmony: Civil Service, & Social Reform in Baden, 1800-1850. LC 77-92569. 272p. 1980. 22.50 (ISBN 0-87413-143-X). U Delaware Pr.
Legge, James G. Rhyme & Revolution in Germany: A Study in German History, Life, Literature & Character. LC 72-126646. Repr. of 1918 ed. 33.45 (ISBN 0-404-03947-2). AMS Pr.
Morris, Warren B. The Road to Olmutz: The Political Career of Joseph Maria Von Radowitz. 1975. lib. bdg. 69.95 (ISBN 0-87700-230-4). Revisionist Pr.
Moses, John A. Germany, Eighteen Forty-Eight to Eighteen Seventy-Nine. (History Monographs). 1973. pap. text ed. 4.50x (ISBN 0-435-31620-6). Heinemann Ed.
Neilson, Francis. Bismarck's Relations with England. 1979. lib. bdg. 39.50 (ISBN 0-685-96611-9). Revisionist Pr.
Passant, Ernest J. Short History of Germany: Eighteen Fifteen - Nineteen Forty-Five. 1962. 32.95 (ISBN 0-521-05915-1); pap. 9.95x (ISBN 0-521-09173-X). Cambridge U Pr.
Pinson, Koppel S. Modern Germany. 2nd ed. 1966. text ed. 20.95 (ISBN 0-02-395420-5). Macmillan.
Sagarra, Eda. An Introduction to Nineteenth Century Germany. (Illus.). 300p. 1981. text ed. 21.00x (ISBN 0-582-35138-3); pap. text ed. 9.95x (ISBN 0-582-35137-5). Longman.
Sheehan, James J. German Liberalism in the Nineteenth Century. LC 77-25971. 1978. lib. bdg. 27.00x (ISBN 0-226-75207-0). U of Chicago Pr.
Stadelmann, Rudolph. The Social & Political History of the German 1848 Revolution. Chastain, James G., tr. from Ger. LC 74-27711. Orig. Title: Soziale und Politis Che Geschichet der Revolution Von 1848. xvi, 218p. 1975. 15.00x (ISBN 0-8214-0177-7). Ohio U Pr.
Stern, Fritz. Gold & Iron: Bismarck, Bleishroder, & the Building of the German Empire. LC 79-11462. (Illus.). 1979. pap. 7.95 (ISBN 0-394-74034-3, Vin). Random.
Von Poschinger, Margaret E. Life of the Emperor Frederick. LC 72-151599. Repr. of 1901 ed. 31.50 (ISBN 0-404-05089-1). AMS Pr.
Von Sybel, Heinrich. Founding of the German Empire by William 1, 7 Vols. Perrin, Marshall L., tr. LC 68-31005. (Illus.). 1968. Repr. of 1890 ed. Set. lib. bdg. 150.00x (ISBN 0-8371-0674-5, SYGE). Greenwood.
--Founding of the German Empire by William First, 7 Vols. 1890-98. Repr. Set. 140.00 (ISBN 0-685-20256-9); 21.50 ea. Scholarly.
Von Treitschke, Heinrich. History of Germany in the Nineteenth Century. LC 75-5072. (Classic European Historians Ser). xxx, 411p. 1975. lib. bdg. 16.00x (ISBN 0-226-81278-2). U of Chicago Pr.
Von Treitschke, Heinrich G. History of Germany in the 19th Century, 7 Vols. Repr. of 1919 ed. Set. 276.50 (ISBN 0-404-06610-0); 39.50 ea. AMS Pr.
Ward, Adolfus W. Germany, Eighteen Fifteen to Eighteen Ninety, 3 Vols. LC 75-41288. Repr. of 1918 ed. 78.50 set (ISBN 0-404-15090-X). AMS Pr.
Zucker, Adolf E., ed. The Forty-Eighters: Political Refugees of the Revolution of 1848. LC 66-27186. (Illus.). 1967. Repr. of 1950 ed. 8.50 (ISBN 0-8462-0859-8). Russell.

GERMANY–HISTORY–FRANCO-GERMAN WAR, 1870-1871

see Franco-German War, 1870-1871

GERMANY–HISTORY–1871-1918

Blackbourn, David. Class, Religion, & Local Politics: The Centre Party in Wurttemberg Before 1914. LC 80-11878. 288p. 1980. text ed. 30.00x (ISBN 0-300-02464-9). Yale U Pr.
Calkins, Kenneth R. Hugo Haase: Democrat & Revolutionary. LC 77-88657. 1979. 14.95 (ISBN 0-89089-075-7); pap. 7.95 (ISBN 0-89089-073-0). Carolina Acad Pr.
Calleo, D. The German Problem Reconsidered. LC 78-9683. 1978. 19.95 (ISBN 0-521-22309-1). Cambridge U Pr.
Calleo, David. The German Problem Reconsidered. LC 78-9683. 208p. 1980. pap. 6.95 (ISBN 0-521-29966-7). Cambridge U Pr.
Chickering, Roger. Imperial Germany & a World Without War: The Peace Movement & German Society, 1892-1914. LC 75-2983. 550p. 1975. 35.00 (ISBN 0-691-05228-X); pap. 13.50 (ISBN 0-691-10036-5). Princeton U Pr.
Der Bagdasarian, Nicholas. The Austro-German Rapprochement, 1870-1879: From the Battle of Sedan to the Dual Alliance. LC 74-199. 334p. 1976. 20.00 (ISBN 0-8386-1527-9). Fairleigh Dickinson.
Epstein, Klaus. Matthias Erzberger & the Dilemma of German Democracy. LC 75-80546. 1971. Repr. of 1959 ed. 27.50 (ISBN 0-86527-123-2). Fertig.
Evans, Richard J., ed. Society & Politics in Wilhelmine Germany. LC 77-14746. 1978. text ed. 22.50x (ISBN 0-06-492036-4). B&N.
Fishman, Sterling. The Struggle for the Mind of German Youth, 1890-1914. 1974. lib. bdg. 59.95 (ISBN 0-87700-229-0). Revisionist Pr.
Gay, Peter. Freud, Jews & Other Germans: Masters & Victims in Modernist Culture. LC 77-76834. 1979. pap. 4.95 (ISBN 0-19-502493-1, GB514, GB). Oxford U Pr.
Henderson, W. O. The Rise of German Industrial Power, 1834-1914. LC 75-17293. 1976. 24.50x (ISBN 0-520-03073-7); pap. 6.95x (ISBN 0-520-03120-2). U of Cal Pr.
Hohenlohe-Schillingsfuerst, Chlodwig K. Memoirs of Prince Chlodwig of Hohenlohe-Schillingsfuerst, 2 Vols. LC 75-111765. Repr. of 1906 ed. 57.50 (ISBN 0-404-03305-9). AMS Pr.
Kimmich, Christoph M. Germany & the League of Nations. LC 75-36400. 1976. lib. bdg. 17.50x (ISBN 0-226-43534-2). U of Chicago Pr.
Kitchen, Martin. The Political Economy of Germany, Eighteen Fifteen to Nineteen Fourteen. 1978. 20.95x (ISBN 0-7735-0501-6). McGill-Queens U Pr.
Kossler, Armin. Aktionsfeld Osmanisches Reich: Die Wirtschaftsinteressen des Deutschen Kaiserreiches in der Turkei 1871-1908 (Unter Besonderer Berucksichtigung Europaischer Literatur) Bruchey, Stuart, ed. LC 80-2814. (Dissertations in European Economic History II). (Illus.). 1981. lib. bdg. 38.00x (ISBN 0-405-13998-5). Arno.
Morrow, John H., Jr. Building German Airpower, Nineteen Nine to Nineteen Fourteen. LC 76-15287. (Illus.). 1976. 12.95x (ISBN 0-87049-196-2). U of Tenn Pr.
Pflanze, Otto, ed. The Unification of Germany, 1848-1871. LC 78-23470. (European Problem Studies). 128p. 1979. pap. 5.50 (ISBN 0-88275-803-9). Krieger.
Rohl, John. Germany Without Bismarck. LC 67-26960. 1967. 27.50x (ISBN 0-520-01086-8). U of Cal Pr.
Rosenberg, Arthur. Birth of the German Republic, 1871-1918. Morrow, Ian F., tr. LC 62-20319. 1962. Repr. of 1931 ed. 13.00 (ISBN 0-8462-0263-8). Russell.
Ross, Ronald J. Beleaguered Tower: The Dilemma of Political Catholicism in Wilhelmine Germany. LC 74-12568. 256p. 1976. text ed. 14.95x (ISBN 0-268-00547-8). U of Notre Dame Pr.
Ryder, A. J. Twentieth-Century Germany. 300p. 1972. 22.50x (ISBN 0-231-03692-2); pap. 10.00x (ISBN 0-231-08350-5). Columbia U Pr.
Silverman, Dan P. Reluctant Union: Alsace-Lorraine & Imperial Germany, 1871-1918. LC 73-180693. (Illus.). 272p. 16.50x (ISBN 0-271-01111-4). Pa St U Pr.
Snyder, Louis L. Basic History of Modern Germany. LC 80-12659. (ANVIL Ser.). 192p. 1980. pap. text ed. 4.95 (ISBN 0-89874-203-X). Krieger.
Steenson, Gary P. Not One Man! Not One Penny! German Social Democracy, 1863-1914. LC 80-54058. (Illus.). 336p. 1981. 19.95 (ISBN 0-8229-3440-X); pap. 8.95x (ISBN 0-8229-5329-3). U of Pittsburgh Pr.
Tampka, Jurgen. The Ruhr & Revolution: The Revolutionary Movement in the Rhenish-Westphalian Industrial Region 1912-1919. LC 78-52788. (Illus.). 1979. text ed. 17.95 (ISBN 0-7081-0745-1, 0521, Pub. by ANUP Australia). Bks Australia.
Waldersee, Alfred H. A Field-Marshal's Memoirs: From the Diary, Correspondence, & Reminiscences of Alfred Count Von Waldersee. (Illus.). 1978. Repr. of 1924 ed. lib. bdg. 23.50 (ISBN 0-8371-5326-3, WAFM). Greenwood.
Whittle, Tyler. The Last Kaiser: A Biography of Wilhelm II, German Emperor & King of Prussia. LC 77-79047. 1977. 15.00 (ISBN 0-8129-0716-7). Times Bks.
Wilke, Ekkehard-Teja P. Political Decadence in Imperial Germany: Personnel-Political Aspects of the German Government Crisis, 1894-97. LC 76-3591. (Illinois Studies in Social Sciences: No. 59). 1976. 14.00 (ISBN 0-252-00571-6). U of Ill Pr.
Willey, Thomas E. Back to Kant: The Revival of Kantianism in German Social & Historical Thought, 1860-1914. LC 77-29215. 1978. text ed. 17.95x (ISBN 0-8143-1590-9). Wayne St U Pr.
Wynne, Graeme C. If Germany Attacks: The Battle in Depth in the West. LC 72-84291. (West Point Military Library Ser). 1976. Repr. of 1940 ed. lib. bdg. 21.50x (ISBN 0-8371-5029-9, WYIG). Greenwood.

GERMANY–HISTORY–20TH CENTURY

Berghahn, Volker R. & Kitchen, Martin, eds. Germany in the Age of Total War. 266p. 1981. 25.00x (ISBN 0-389-20186-3). B&N.
Calleo, D. The German Problem Reconsidered. LC 78-9683. 1978. 19.95 (ISBN 0-521-22309-1). Cambridge U Pr.
Calleo, David. The German Problem Reconsidered. LC 78-9683. 208p. 1980. pap. 6.95 (ISBN 0-521-29966-7). Cambridge U Pr.
Carr, William. A History of Germany Eighteen Fifteen to Nineteen Forty-Five. 2nd ed. LC 79-20108. (Illus.). 1979. 18.95x (ISBN 0-312-37871-8); pap. 9.95 (ISBN 0-312-37872-6). St Martin.
Childs, David. Germany Since Nineteen Eighteen. LC 80-5321. 1980. 20.00 (ISBN 0-312-32628-9). St Martin.
Chotjewitz, Peter O. The Thirty Years Peace. Kimber, Robert & Kimber, Rita, trs. from Ger. LC 80-24472. 256p. 1981. 12.95 (ISBN 0-394-50182-9). Knopf.
Cochran, Michael H. Germany Not Guilty in 1914. LC 72-80274. 1972. 6.95 (ISBN 0-87926-009-2); pap. 2.50 (ISBN 0-87926-010-6). R Myles.
Craig, Gordon A. Germany, Eighteen Sixty-Six to Nineteen Forty-Five. (History of Modern Europe Ser.). 1980. pap. text ed. 10.95x (ISBN 0-19-502724-8). Oxford U Pr.
--Germany, Eighteen Sixty-Six to Nineteen Forty-Five. (Oxford History of Modern Europe Ser.). 1978. 22.50 (ISBN 0-19-822113-4). Oxford U Pr.
De Jonge, Alex. The Weimer Chronicle: Prelude to Hitler. LC 78-6952. (Illus.). 12.95 (ISBN 0-448-22188-8). Paddington.
Documents on German Foreign Policy: 1918-1945. (D Ser. Index). 1976. 175.00x (ISBN 0-912162-00-7). Open-Door.
Eyck, Erich. A History of the Weimar Republic, 2 vols. Hanson, Harlan P. & Waite, Robert G. L., trs. Incl. Vol. 1. From the Collapse of the Empire to Hindenburg's Election. 373p. 1962; Vol. 2. From the Locarno Conference to Hitler's Seizure of Power. 535p. 1963. 25.00x (ISBN 0-674-40351-7). LC 62-17219. Harvard U Pr.
Farrar, L. L., Jr. Arrogance & Anxiety: The Ambivalence of German Power, 1848-1914. LC 81-10374. (Iowa Studies in History: Vol. 1). 231p. 1981. text ed. 15.00x (ISBN 0-87745-112-5). U of Iowa Pr.
Fest, Wilfried. Dictionary of German History 1806-1945. LC 78-54658. 1979. 18.50x (ISBN 0-312-20103-6). St Martin.
Gordon, Harold J., Jr. Hitler & the Beer Hall Putsch. LC 73-166383. 632p. 1972. 37.50x (ISBN 0-691-05189-5); pap. 11.95 (ISBN 0-691-00775-6). Princeton U Pr.
Harms, John. The Ideological Illusion: Germany As the Scapegoat of Modern History. 75.00 (ISBN 0-685-26303-7). Revisionist Pr.
Harpprecht, Klaus. East German Rising, Seventeenth June 1953. Wheeler, Charles, tr. LC 78-14103. (Illus.). 1979. Repr. of 1957 ed. 18.50 (ISBN 0-88355-797-5). Hyperion Conn.
Heckart, Beverly. From Bassermann to Bebel: The Grand Bloc's Quest for Reform in the Kaiserreich, 1900-1914. 352p. 1975. 23.00x (ISBN 0-300-01747-2). Yale U Pr.
Hillgruber, Andreas. Germany & the Two World Wars. Kirby, William C., tr. LC 80-27036. 144p. 1981. text ed. 14.50x (ISBN 0-674-35321-8). Harvard U Pr.
Hye, Allen, ed. Modernes Deutschland in Brennpunkt: A Cultural Reader. 1978. pap. text ed. 7.95x (ISBN 0-393-09067-1). Norton.
Kessler, Harry. Walther Rathenau: His Life & Work. LC 68-9663. 1970. Repr. 9.00 (ISBN 0-86527-203-4). Fertig.
Kessler, Harry K. Walther Rathenau, His Life & Work. LC 70-181937. Repr. of 1930 ed. 9.00 (ISBN 0-404-03665-1). AMS Pr.
Lewis, Wyndham. Hitler, the Germans & the Jews, 5 vols. 1522p. 1973. Set. 600.00 (ISBN 0-8490-0366-0). Gordon Pr.
Luckau, Alma. The German Delegation at the Paris Peace Conference. LC 70-80569. 1971. Repr. 35.00 (ISBN 0-86527-078-3). Fertig.
Medlicott, W. N., ed. From Metternich to Hitler: Aspects of British & Foreign History, 1814-1939. 1963. 14.95x (ISBN 0-7100-1821-5). Routledge & Kegan.
Mosse, George L. The Crisis of German Ideology: Intellectual Origins of the Third Reich. LC 78-19126. vill, 373p. 1981. Repr. of 1964 ed. 27.50x (ISBN 0-86527-036-8). Fertig.
--The Crisis of Germany Ideology: Intellectual Origins of the Third Reich. 384p. 1981. Repr. of 1964 ed. pap. text ed. 7.95 (ISBN 0-8052-0669-8). Schocken.
Nurge, Ethel. Blue Light in the Village: Daily Life in a German Village in 1965-66. LC 77-10296. 1977. pap. 15.00 (ISBN 0-8357-0264-2, SS-00039). Univ Microfilms.
Passant, Ernest J. Short History of Germany: Eighteen Fifteen - Nineteen Forty-Five. 1962. 32.95 (ISBN 0-521-05915-1); pap. 9.95x (ISBN 0-521-09173-X). Cambridge U Pr.
Peck, Abraham J. Radicals & Reactionaries: The Crisis of Conservatism in Wilhelmine Germany. LC 78-62921. (Illus.). 1978. pap. text ed. 12.00 (ISBN 0-8191-0601-1). U Pr of Amer.
Peterson, Edward N. The American Occupation of Germany: Retreat to Victory. LC 77-28965. 1978. 18.95x (ISBN 0-8143-1588-7). Wayne St U Pr.
Pinson, Koppel S. Modern Germany. 2nd ed. 1966. text ed. 20.95 (ISBN 0-02-395420-5). Macmillan.
Poppel, Stephen M. Zionism in Germany 1897-1933: The Shaping of a Jewish Identity. LC 76-14284. 1977. 7.95 (ISBN 0-8276-0085-2, 395). Jewish Pubn.
Ryder, A. J. Twentieth-Century Germany. 300p. 1972. 22.50x (ISBN 0-231-03692-2); pap. 10.00x (ISBN 0-231-08350-5). Columbia U Pr.
Schoenberg, Hans W. Germans from the East: A Study of Their Migration, Resettlement, & Subsequent Group History Since 1945. (Studies in Social Life Ser: No. 15). (Illus.). 1970. 50.00x (ISBN 90-247-5044-X). Intl Pubns Serv.
Snyder, Louis L. Basic History of Modern Germany. LC 80-12659. (ANVIL Ser.). 192p. 1980. pap. text ed. 4.95 (ISBN 0-89874-203-X). Krieger.
Speier, Hans. From the Ashes of Disgrace: A Journal from Germany, 1945-1955. LC 80-21599. 328p. 1981. lib. bdg. 20.00x (ISBN 0-87023-135-9). U of Mass Pr.
Stachura, Peter D. Nazi Youth in the Weimar Republic. LC 74-14196. (Studies in International & Comparative Politics: No. 5). 301p. 1975. text ed. 21.50 (ISBN 0-87436-198-2); pap. text ed. 11.75 (ISBN 0-87436-199-0). ABC-Clio.
Sutton, Antony C. Wall Street & the Rise of Hitler. LC 76-14011. (Orig.). 1976. 8.95 (ISBN 0-89245-004-5). Seventy Six.
Taylor, Ronald. Literature & Society in Germany, 1918-1945. (Studies in Contemporary Literature & Culture). 363p. 1980. 28.50x (ISBN 0-389-20036-0). B&N.
Vogt, Hannah. Burden of Guilt: A Short History of Germany, 1914-1945. Strauss, H., tr. (Illus.). (gr. 9-12). 1964. pap. 5.95x (ISBN 0-19-501093-0). Oxford U Pr.
Von Papen, Franz. Memoirs. Connell, Brian, tr. LC 78-63703. (Studies in Fascism: Ideology & Practice). Repr. of 1953 ed. 37.50 (ISBN 0-404-16975-9). AMS Pr.

GERMANY–HISTORY–1918-1933

see also Anschluss Movement, 1918-1938

Bennett, Edward W. German Rearmament & the West, 1932-1933. LC 78-70277. 1979. 40.00 (ISBN 0-691-05269-7). Princeton U Pr.
Bullivant, Keith, ed. Culture & Society in the Weimar Republic. 205p. 1977. 19.50x (ISBN 0-8476-6012-5). Rowman.
Colton, Ethan T. Four Patterns of Revolution. facs. ed. LC 79-121456. (Essay Index Reprint Ser). 1935. 17.00 (ISBN 0-8369-1747-2). Arno.
De Jonge, Alex. The Weimar Chronicle: Prelude to Hitler. 1979. pap. 5.95 (ISBN 0-452-00515-9, F515, Mer). NAL.
Edwards, Tony. Hitler & Germany 1919-1939. (History Broadsheets Ser.). 1972. pap. text ed. 6.95x (ISBN 0-435-31175-1). Heinemann Ed.
Eyck, Erich. History of the Weimar Republic. LC 62-17219. 1970. Vol. 1. pap. text ed. 3.25x (ISBN 0-689-70218-3, 152A); Vol. 2. pap. text ed. 3.95x (ISBN 0-689-70219-1, 152B). Atheneum.
Fraenkel, Ernst. Military Occupation & the Rule of Law: Occupation Government in the Rhineland 1918-1923. (Institute of World Affairs Ser.). 279p. 1944. 20.00x (ISBN 0-8014-0140-2). Cornell U Pr.
Gangulee, N., ed. The Mind & Face of Nazi Germany: An Anthology. LC 78-63671. (Studies in Fascism: Ideology & Practice). 1979. Repr. of 1942 ed. 17.50 (ISBN 0-404-16528-1). AMS Pr.
German Army Handbook April 1918. LC 77-73456. (Illus.). 1977. 12.50 (ISBN 0-88254-437-3). Hippocrene Bks.
Goebbels, Joseph. My Part in Germany's Fight. Fiedler, Kurt, tr. from Ger. LC 76-27871. 1979. Repr. of 1935 ed. 23.50 (ISBN 0-86527-137-2). Fertig.
Grathwol, Robert P. Stresemann & the DNVP: Reconciliation or Revenge in German Foreign Policy, 1924-1928. (Illus.). 352p. 1980. 22.00x (ISBN 0-7006-0199-6). Regents Pr Ks.
Halperin, Samuel W. Germany Tried Democracy. 1965. pap. 6.95 (ISBN 0-393-00280-2, Norton Lib). Norton.
Herford, C. H. The Post-War Mind of Germany & Other European Studies. Repr. of 1927 ed. lib. bdg. 30.00 (ISBN 0-8414-5046-3). Folcroft.
Jarman, T. L. The Rise & Fall of Nazi Germany. LC 56-9548. 388p. 1956. cusa 19.50x (ISBN 0-8147-0217-1). NYU Pr.
Kahle, P. E. Bonn University in Pre-Nazi & Nazi Times, Nineteen Twenty Three - Nineteen Thirty Nine: Experiences of a German Professor. 1978. lib. bdg. 69.95 (ISBN 0-685-62292-4). Revisionist Pr.
Kochan, Lionel. Russia & the Weimar Republic. LC 78-17679. 1978. Repr. of 1954 ed. lib. bdg. 18.75x (ISBN 0-313-20503-5, KORW). Greenwood.
Levine-Meyer, Rosa. Levine the Spartacist. 1978. pap. 6.95 (ISBN 0-86033-062-1). Gordon-Cremonesi.
Liang, Hsi-huey. The Berlin Police Force in the Weimar Republic, 1918-1933. LC 74-85452. (Illus.). 1970. 24.00x (ISBN 0-520-01603-3). U of Cal Pr.
Lutz, Ralph H. German Revolution, Nineteen Eighteen to Nineteen Nineteen. LC 68-54283. (Stanford University. Stanford Studies in History, Economics, & Political Science: Vol. 1, Pt. 1). Repr. of 1922 ed. 17.45 (ISBN 0-404-50961-4). AMS Pr.
Lutz, Ralph H., ed. Causes of the German Collapse in 1918: Sections of the Officially Authorized Report of the Commission of the German Constituent Assembly & of the German Reichstag, 1919-1928. 1969. Repr. of 1934 ed. 19.50 (ISBN 0-208-00700-8, Archon). Shoe String.
Nelson, Keith L. Victors Divided: America & the Allies in Germany, 1918-1923. (Illus.). 424p. 1975. 32.50x (ISBN 0-520-02315-3). U of Cal Pr.
Nicholls, A. J. Weimar & the Rise of Hitler. 2nd ed. LC 79-10134. (The Making of the Twentieth Century Ser.). 1980. write for info. (ISBN 0-312-86066-8); pap. text ed. write for info. (ISBN 0-312-86067-6). St Martin.
Niewyk, Donald L. Socialist, Anti-Semite, & Jew: German Social Democracy Confronts the Problem of Anti-Semitism, 1918-1933. LC 79-137123. 1971. 17.50x (ISBN 0-8071-0531-7). La State U Pr.
Quigley, Hugh & Clark, R. J. Republican Germany: A Political & Economic Study, 1919-1928. 1976. lib. bdg. 69.95 (ISBN 0-8490-2518-4). Gordon Pr.
Quigley, Hugh & Clark, R. T. Republican Germany. LC 67-24592. (Illus.). 1968. Repr. of 1928 ed. 22.50 (ISBN 0-86527-166-6). Fertig.
Reissner, Larissa. Hamburg at the Barricades. Chappell, Richard, tr. from Rus. (Illus.). 228p. 1980. text ed. 12.00 (ISBN 0-904383-36-9). Pluto Pr.
Rudin, Harry R. Armistice 1918. (Illus.). 1967. Repr. of 1944 ed. 22.50 (ISBN 0-208-00280-4, Archon). Shoe String.
Ryder, A. J. German Revolution of Nineteen Eighteen. 1967. 41.95 (ISBN 0-521-06176-8). Cambridge U Pr.
Sidman, Charles F. The German Collapse in 1918. 141p. 1972. 5.00x (ISBN 0-87291-054-7). Coronado Pr.
Steinberg, Michael S. Sabers & Brown Shirts: The German Students' Path to National Socialism, 1918-1935. LC 77-2638. (Illus.). 1977. 19.00x (ISBN 0-226-77188-1). U of Chicago Pr.
Waite, Robert G. Vanguard of Nazism: The Free Corps Movement in Postwar Germany, 1918-1923. LC 52-5045. (Harvard Historical Studies Ser: No. 60). 1952. 16.50x (ISBN 0-674-93142-4). Harvard U Pr.
Waldman, Eric. Spartacist Uprising of Nineteen-Nineteen & the Crisis of the German Socialist Movement: A Study of Political Theory & Party Practice. 1958. 9.95 (ISBN 0-87462-430-4). Marquette.
Willett, John. Art & Politics in the Weimar Period: The New Sobriety, 1917-1933. (Illus.). 1980. pap. 8.95 (ISBN 0-394-73991-4). Pantheon.

GERMANY–HISTORY–1933-1945

see also Anschluss Movement, 1918-1938; Anti-Nazi Movement

Angolia, John R. For Fuhrer & Fatherland: Civil Awards of the Third Reich. 1978. 19.00 (ISBN 0-912138-16-5). Quaker.
Backer, John H. Priming the German Economy. LC 70-142289. 1971. 12.75 (ISBN 0-8223-0243-8). Duke.
Baynes, Helton G. Germany Possessed. LC 73-180389. (Studies in Fascism Ser.). Repr. of 1941 ed. 18.00 (ISBN 0-404-56106-3). AMS Pr.
Boyd, Carl. The Extraordinary Envoy: General Hiroshi Oshima & Diplomacy in the Third Reich 1934-1939. LC 79-9600. 246p. 1980. text ed. 18.50 (ISBN 0-8191-0957-6); pap. text ed. 9.75 (ISBN 0-8191-0958-4). U Pr of Amer.
Brennecke, Fritz, compiled by. The Nazi Primer: Offical Handbook for Schooling the Hitler Youth. Childs, Harwood L., tr. from Ger. LC 71-180391. Repr. of 1938 ed. 17.50 (ISBN 0-404-56107-1). AMS Pr.
Chuikov, V. The End of the Third Reich. 273p. 1978. 5.40 (ISBN 0-686-74577-9, Pub. by Progress Pubs Russia). Imported Pubns.
Cooper, Matthew. The German Army: Vol. 2 Conquest 1933-1945. (World at War Ser.: No. 14). 1979. pap. 2.50 (ISBN 0-89083-485-7). Zebra.
--The German Army: Vol. 3 Decline & Fall. (World at War Ser.: No. 15). 1979. pap. 2.50 (ISBN 0-89083-493-8). Zebra.
--The German Army 1933-1945. 1978. 17.95 (ISBN 0-8128-2468-7). Stein & Day.
Detwiler, Donald S., ed. World War Two German Military Studies, 10 pts. in 23 vols. Incl. Pt. 1. Introduction & Guide (ISBN 0-8240-4300-6); Pt. 2. The Extinct Series (European Theatre Interrogations, 2 pts. Pt. A (ISBN 0-8240-4301-4). Pt. B (ISBN 0-8240-4302-2); Pt. 3. Command Structure, 3 pts. Pt. A (ISBN 0-8240-4303-0). Pt. B (ISBN 0-8240-4304-9). Pt. C (ISBN 0-8240-4305-7); Pt. 4. The OKW (Oberkommando der Wehrmacht) War Diary Series, 5 pts. Pt. A (ISBN 0-8240-4306-5). Pt. B (ISBN 0-8240-4307-3). Pt. C (ISBN 0-8240-4308-1). Pt. D (ISBN 0-8240-4309-X). Pt. E (ISBN 0-8240-4310-3); Pt. 5. The Western Theatre (ISBN 0-8240-4311-1); Pt. 6. The Mediterranean Theatre, 2 pts. Pt. A (ISBN 0-8240-4312-X). Pt. B (ISBN 0-8240-4313-8); Pt. 7. The Eastern Theatre, 5 pts. Pt. A (ISBN 0-8240-4314-6). Pt. B (ISBN 0-8240-4315-4). Pt. C (ISBN 0-8240-4316-2). Pt. D (ISBN 0-8240-4317-0). Pt. E (ISBN 0-8240-4318-9); Pt. 8. Diplomacy, Strategy & Military Theory, 2 pts. Pt. A (ISBN 0-8240-4319-7). Pt. B (ISBN 0-8240-4320-0); Pt. 9. German Military Government (ISBN 0-8240-4321-9); Pt. 10. Special Topics, 2 pts. Pt. A (ISBN 0-8240-4322-7). Pt. B (ISBN 0-8240-4323-5). 1979. lib. bdg. 60.50 ea., vol. Garland Pub.
Edwards, Tony. Hitler & Germany 1919-1939. (History Broadsheets Ser.). 1972. pap. text ed. 6.95x (ISBN 0-435-31175-1). Heinemann Ed.
Fest, Joachim C. The Face of the Third Reich: Portraits of the Nazi Leadership. Bullock, Michael, tr. LC 66-10412. 1977. pap. 5.95 (ISBN 0-394-73407-6). Pantheon.
Gallin, Mary A. German Resistance to Hitler, Ethical & Religious Factors. 1969. pap. 8.95 (ISBN 0-8132-0261-2). Cath U Pr.
Gangulee, N., ed. The Mind & Face of Nazi Germany: An Anthology. LC 78-63671. (Studies in Fascism: Ideology & Practice). 1979. Repr. of 1942 ed. 17.50 (ISBN 0-404-16528-1). AMS Pr.
Garlinski, Jozef & Lisicki, Tadeus. Enigma War. 1980. 14.95 (ISBN 0-684-15866-3, ScribT). Scribner.
The German Army: Vol. 1 Rebirth 1933-1945. (World at War Ser.: No. 13). 1979. pap. 2.50 (ISBN 0-89083-472-5). Zebra.
Goldston, Robert. The Life & Death of Nazi Germany. 1978. pap. 2.25 (ISBN 0-449-30830-8, Prem). Fawcett.
Grunberger, Richard. The Twelve Year Reich. LC 69-16189. (Illus.). 1979. pap. 7.95 (ISBN 0-03-048226-7). HR&W.
Hartshorne, Edward Y. The German Universities & National Socialism. LC 78-63679. (Studies in Fascism: Ideology & Practice). Repr. of 1937 ed. 18.00 (ISBN 0-404-16943-0). AMS Pr.
Hehn, Paul N. The German Struggle Against the Yugoslav Guerrillas in World War II. (East European Monographs: No. 57). 1979. 10.00x (ISBN 0-914710-48-6). East Eur Quarterly.
Heineman, John L. Hitler's First Foreign Minister: Constantin Freiherr von Neurath. LC 77-71061. 1980. 35.00x (ISBN 0-520-03442-2). U of Cal Pr.
Heinz, Grete & Peterson, Agnes F., eds. NSDAP Hauptarchiv. LC 64-17344. (Bibliographical Ser.: No. 17). 175p. 1964. pap. 5.00 (ISBN 0-8179-2172-9). Hoover Inst Pr.
Henderson, Neville. Failure of a Mission: Berlin, 1937-1939. LC 75-41131. Repr. of 1940 ed. 15.50 (ISBN 0-404-14670-8). AMS Pr.
Hoffmann, Peter. History of German Resistance, Nineteen Thirty-Three to Nineteen Forty-Five. Barry, Richard, tr. from Ger. 1979. 27.50x (ISBN 0-262-08088-5); pap. 9.95 (ISBN 0-262-58038-1). MIT Pr.
Homze, Edward L. Arming the Luftwaffe: The Reich Air Ministry & the German Aircraft Industry, 1919-39. LC 75-38055. (Illus.). 1976. 14.95x (ISBN 0-8032-0872-3). U of Nebr Pr.
Hungarian Historical Research Society. Records, Notes, Reports Connected with the Removal to Germany in the Year 1945. LC 77-95243. 120p. 1980. pap. 6.50 (ISBN 0-935484-07-8). Universe Pub Co.
Irving, David. The War Path: Hitler's Germany. 1978. 14.95 (ISBN 0-670-74971-0). Viking Pr.
Kahle, P. E. Bonn University in Pre-Nazi & Nazi Times, Nineteen Twenty Three - Nineteen Thirty Nine: Experiences of a German Professor. 1978. lib. bdg. 69.95 (ISBN 0-685-62292-4). Revisionist Pr.
Kandel, Isaac L. The Making of Nazis. LC 76-104284. 143p. 1935. Repr. lib. bdg. 15.00x (ISBN 0-8371-3966-X, KAMN). Greenwood.
Katz, William L. An Album of Nazism. LC 78-12723. (Picture Album Ser.). (Illus.). (gr. 5 up). 1979. PLB 8.40 s&l (ISBN 0-531-01500-9). Watts.
Klotz, Helmut, ed. The Berlin Diaries: May 30, 1932 - January 30, 1933. LC 70-180408. Repr. of 1934 ed. 18.00 (ISBN 0-404-56132-2). AMS Pr.
Lang, Daniel. A Backward Look. 1979. 8.95 (ISBN 0-07-036239-4, GB). McGraw.
--A Backward Look: Germans Remember. (McGraw-Hill Paperbacks Ser.). (Illus.). 144p. (Orig.). 1981. pap. 4.95 (ISBN 0-07-036241-6). McGraw.
Leuner, H. D. When Compassion Was a Crime: Germany's Silent Heroes, 1933-1945. 1978. pap. 12.95 (ISBN 0-85496-138-0). Dufour.
Loewenstein, Karl. Hitler's Germany. LC 72-7104. (Select Bibliographies Reprint Ser.). 1972. Repr. of 1940 ed. 19.00 (ISBN 0-8369-6947-2). Arno.
Meinecke, Friedrich. German Catastrophe. 1963. pap. 3.95x (ISBN 0-8070-5667-7, BP160). Beacon Pr.
Mendelssohn Bartholdy, Albrecht. The War & German Society: The Testament of a Liberal. LC 78-63695. (Studies in Fascism: Ideology & Practice). Repr. of 1937 ed. 27.50 (ISBN 0-404-16956-2). AMS Pr.
Nathan, Otto. Nazi Economic System: Germany's Mobilization for War. LC 78-102522. (Illus.). 1971. Repr. of 1944 ed. 18.50 (ISBN 0-8462-1501-2). Russell.
Powell, E. Alexander. Long Roll on the Rhine: A Study of Hitler's Germany. 1976. 69.95 (ISBN 0-8490-2183-9). Gordon Pr.
Price, Alfred. Luftwaffe Handbook. (Encore Edition). (Illus.). 1977. 3.95 (ISBN 0-684-16691-7, ScribT). Scribner.
Santoro, Cesare. Hitler Germany. 75.00 (ISBN 0-8490-0365-2). Gordon Pr.
Schoenbaum, David. Hitler's Social Revolution: Class & Status in Nazi Germany 1933-1939. 352p. 1980. pap. 5.95 (ISBN 0-393-00993-9). Norton.
Schutz, Wilhelm W. Pens Under the Swastika. LC 70-118415. 1971. Repr. of 1946 ed. 10.00 (ISBN 0-8046-1192-0). Kennikat.
Schweitzer, Arthur. Big Business in the Third Reich. LC 63-62857. 752p. 1977. Repr. of 1964 ed. 27.50x (ISBN 0-253-10670-2). Ind U Pr.
Shirer, William L. The Berlin Diary: The Journal of a Foreign Correspondent, 1934-1941. 1979. pap. 5.95 (ISBN 0-14-005182-1). Penguin.
--The Rise & Fall of the Third Reich. 1981. pap. 9.95 (ISBN 0-671-42813-6, Touchstone Bks). S&S.
--The Rise & Fall of the Third Reich. 1978. pap. 3.95 (ISBN 0-449-23442-8, Crest). Fawcett.
--Rise & Fall of the Third Reich: A History of Nazi Germany. (gr. 9 up). 1960. 24.95 (ISBN 0-671-62420-2). S&S.
Snyder, Louis. Encyclopedia of the Third Reich. (Illus.). 1976. 26.50 (ISBN 0-07-059525-9, P&RB). McGraw.
Snyder, Louis L., ed. Hitler's Third Reich: A Documentary History. LC 81-9512. 640p. 1981. text ed. 33.95x (ISBN 0-88229-705-8); pap. text ed. 16.95x (ISBN 0-88229-793-7). Nelson-Hall.
Speer, Albert. Infiltration: The SS & German Armament. Neugrosschel, Joachim, tr. 604p. 1981. 15.95 (ISBN 0-02-612800-4). Macmillan.
--Inside the Third Reich. (Illus.). 624p. 1981. pap. 8.95 (ISBN 0-02-037500-X). Macmillan.
Stachura, Peter. The German Youth Movement. LC 80-14527. 1981. 22.50 (ISBN 0-312-32624-6). St Martin.
Steiner, John M. Power Politics & Social Change in National Socialist Germany: A Process of Escalation into Mass Destruction. (Issues in Contemporary Politics: No. 2). 1975. text ed. 42.50x (ISBN 90-2797-651-1). Mouton.
Steinert, Marlis G. Hitler's War and the Germans: Public Mood and Attitude During the Second World War. De Witt, Thomas E., tr. from Ger. LC 76-25618. 387p. 1977. 21.95x (ISBN 0-8214-0186-6); pap. 11.95x (ISBN 0-8214-0402-4). Ohio U Pr.
Stephenson, Jill. Women in Nazi Society. LC 75-25208. 223p. 1975. text ed. 20.00x (ISBN 0-06-496528-7). B&N.
Van Ishoven, Armand. The Luftwaffe in the Battle of Britain. (Illus.). 160p. 1980. 19.95 (ISBN 0-684-16703-4, ScribT). Scribner.
Vogt, Hannah. Burden of Guilt: A Short History of Germany, 1914-1945. Strauss, H., tr. (Illus.). (gr. 9-12). 1964. pap. 5.95x (ISBN 0-19-501093-0). Oxford U Pr.
Von Hassel, Ulrich. The Von Hassell Diaries, 1938-1944: The Story of the Forces Against Hitler Inside Germany. LC 78-63680. (Studies in Fascism: Ideology & Practice). Repr. of 1947 ed. 32.50 (ISBN 0-404-16944-9). AMS Pr.
Waite, R. Hitler & Nazi Germany. LC 65-19350. 1969. pap. text ed. 8.95 (ISBN 0-03-082797-3, HoltC). HR&W.
Weinberg, Gerhard L. The Foreign Policy of Hitler's Germany: Starting World War II, 1937-1939. LC 79-26406. 1980. 44.00x (ISBN 0-226-88511-9). U of Chicago Pr.
Wolf, Christa. A Model Childhood. Molinaro, Ursule & Rappolt, Hedwig, trs. from Ger. 416p. 1980. 17.50 (ISBN 0-374-21170-1). FS&G.
Zassenhaus, Hiltgunt. Walls: Resisting the Third Reich - One Woman's Story. LC 73-16443. 256p. 1974. 9.95 (ISBN 0-8070-6388-6); pap. 4.95 (ISBN 0-8070-6389-4, BP534); pap. 2.95 (ISBN 0-8070-6375-4, BP557). Beacon Pr.
Zeller, Eberhard. The Flame of Freedom: The German Struggle Against Hitler. LC 69-14861. 1969. 19.95x (ISBN 0-87024-102-8). U of Miami Pr.

GERMANY–HISTORY–1933-1945–FICTION

Forman, James. Horses of Anger. LC 67-15004. 224p. (gr. 7 up). 1967. 3.95 (ISBN 0-374-33333-5). FS&G.

GERMANY–HISTORY–1933-1945–UNDERGROUND LITERATURE

Mayer, S. L., ed. Signal: The Years of Retreat 1943-44. LC 79-84835. (Illus.). 1979. 14.95 (ISBN 0-13-810028-4). P-H.

GERMANY–HISTORY–ALLIED OCCUPATION, 1945-

see also Denazification; German Reunification Question (1949-)

App, Austin J. The Sudeten-German Tragedy. (Illus.). 84p. (Orig.). 1979. pap. 3.00x (ISBN 0-911038-66-3, Inst Hist Rev). Noontide.
Backer, John H. The Decision to Divide Germany: American Foreign Policy in Transition. LC 77-84614. 1978. 12.75 (ISBN 0-8223-0391-4). Duke.
Bailey, George. Germans: The Biography of an Obsession. 1974. pap. 3.50 (ISBN 0-380-00140-3, 53918, Discus). Avon.
Baring, Arnulf M. Uprising in East Germany: June 17, 1953. Onn, Gerald, tr. from Ger. LC 70-38284. 208p. 1972. Repr. of 1965 ed. 16.50x (ISBN 0-8014-0703-6). Cornell U Pr.
Bower, Tom. Pledge Betrayed: America & Britain & the Denazification of Post-War Germany. LC 81-43047. (Illus.). 432p. 1981. 17.95 (ISBN 0-385-17700-3). Doubleday.
Clay, Lucius D. Decision in Germany. LC 72-110045. Repr. of 1950 ed. lib. bdg. 21.50x (ISBN 0-8371-4427-2, CLDG). Greenwood.
Gimbel, John. The American Occupation of Germany: Politics & the Military, 1945-1949. LC 68-26778. 1968. 17.50x (ISBN 0-8047-0667-0). Stanford U Pr.
--A German Community Under American Occupation. 1961. 15.00x (ISBN 0-8047-0061-3). Stanford U Pr.

Gottlieb, Manuel. The German Peace Settlement & the Berlin Crisis. 275p. 1970. 14.95 (ISBN 0-87855-033-X). Transaction Bks.

Merritt, Anna J. & Merritt, Richard L., eds. Public Opinion in Occupied Germany: The OMGUS Surveys, 1945-1949. LC 74-94397. (Illus.). 1970. 15.00 (ISBN 0-252-00077-3). U of Ill Pr.

Moreton, N. Edwina. East Germany & the Warsaw Alliance: The Politics of Detente. (A Westview Replica Edition). 1978. lib. bdg. 25.75x (ISBN 0-89158-265-7). Westview.

Rodnick, David. Postwar Germans. 1948. 37.50x (ISBN 0-685-89773-7). Elliots Bks.

Settel, Arthur, ed. This Is Germany. facsimile ed. LC 70-156715. (Essay Index Reprint Ser). Repr. of 1950 ed. 23.00 (ISBN 0-8369-2427-4). Arno.

Sharp, Tony. The Wartime Alliance & the Zonal Division of Germany. (Illus.). 232p. 1975. 37.50x (ISBN 0-19-822521-0). Oxford U Pr.

Smith, Jean E., ed. The Papers of General Lucius D. Clay: Germany 1945-1949, 2 vols. LC 73-16536. 1216p. 1975. 40.00x (ISBN 0-253-34288-0). Ind U Pr.

U. S. Congress - Dept. of State Historical Office. Documents on Germany, Nineteen Forty-Four to Nineteen Sixty-One. LC 68-55113. (Illus.). 1968. Repr. of 1961 ed. lib. bdg. 30.75x (ISBN 0-8371-0696-6, DOGE). Greenwood.

Willis, F. Roy. The French in Germany, 1945-1949. 1962. 15.00x (ISBN 0-8047-0100-8). Stanford U Pr.

Zink, Harold. The United States in Germany 1944-1955. LC 74-9321. (Illus.). 374p. 1975. Repr. of 1957 ed. lib. bdg. 23.50x (ISBN 0-8371-7641-7, ZIUS). Greenwood.

GERMANY–HISTORY, MILITARY

Atkinson, Christopher T. A History of Germany, 1715-1815. LC 70-114456. (Illus.). xx, 732p. Repr. of 1908 ed. lib. bdg. 34.25x (ISBN 0-8371-4807-3, ATHG). Greenwood.

Bekker, Cajus. The Luftwaffe War Diaries. Ziegler, Frank, tr. 608p. 1975. pap. 3.95 (ISBN 0-345-28799-1). Ballantine.

Bender, Roger J. & Odegard, Warren W. Uniforms, Organization & History of the Panzertruppe. (Illus.). 336p. 1980. 24.95 (ISBN 0-912138-18-1). Bender Pub CA.

Benoist-Mechin, Jacques. History of the German Army Since the Armistice. 345p. 1979. Repr. of 1939 ed. 22.50 (ISBN 0-86527-094-5). Fertig.

Britton, Jack. German Medals & Decorations of World War II. LC 79-112464. (Illus.). 1976. pap. 2.50 (ISBN 0-912958-01-4). MCN Pr.

Burdick, Charles B. Germany's Military Strategy & Spain in World War Two. LC 68-26994. (Illus.). 1968. 13.95x (ISBN 0-8156-2122-1). Syracuse U Pr.

Chamberlain, Peter & Gander, Terry. Weapons of the Third Reich. LC 78-20293. 1979. 12.50 (ISBN 0-385-15090-3). Doubleday.

Cooper, Matthew. The German Army: Vol. 2 Conquest 1933-1945. (World at War Ser.: No. 14). 1979. pap. 2.50 (ISBN 0-89083-485-7). Zebra.

Duffy, Christopher. The Army of Frederick the Great. LC 74-80439. (Historic Armies & Navies Ser). (Illus.). 272p. 1974. 14.95 (ISBN 0-88254-277-X). Hippocrene Bks.

Dupuy, T. N. A Genius for War: Eighteen Seven to Nineteen Fourty-Five. LC 77-22263. 1977. 14.95 (ISBN 0-13-351114-6). P-H.

Fraenkel, Ernst. Military Occupation & the Rule of Law: Occupation Government in the Rhineland 1918-1923. (Institute of World Affairs Ser.). 279p. 1944. 20.00x (ISBN 0-8014-0140-2). Cornell U Pr.

Gatzke, Hans W. Germany's Drive to the West: (Drang Nach Weten) A Study of Germany's Western War Aims During the First World War. LC 78-6668. 1978. Repr. of 1967 ed. lib. bdg. 24.50x (ISBN 0-313-20507-8, GAGD). Greenwood.

--Stresemann & the Rearmament of Germany. 1969. pap. 2.65x (ISBN 0-393-00486-4, Norton Lib). Norton.

German Army Handbook April 1918. LC 77-73456. (Illus.). 1977. 12.50 (ISBN 0-88254-437-3). Hippocrene Bks.

The German Army: Vol. 1 Rebirth 1933-1945. (World at War Ser.: No. 13). 1979. pap. 2.50 (ISBN 0-89083-472-5). Zebra.

Gorlitz, Walter. History of the German General Staff, 1657-1945. Battershaw, Brian, tr. from Ger. LC 75-3867. (Illus.). 508p. 1975. Repr. of 1953 ed. lib. bdg. 33.00x (ISBN 0-8371-8092-9, GOGG). Greenwood.

Hancock, M. Donald. The Bundeswehr & the National Peoples Army: A Comparative Study of German Civil-Military Polity. (Monograph Ser. in World Affairs, Vol. 10: 1972-73 Ser., Pt. B). 4.90 (ISBN 0-87940-034-X). U of Denver Intl.

Hinsley, Francis H. Hitler's Strategy: The Naval Evidence. (Illus.). xii, 254p. 1981. Repr. of 1951 ed. lib. bdg. 19.50x (ISBN 0-87991-641-9). Porcupine Pr.

Hoyt, Edwin P. Guerilla: The Story of Colonel von Lettow-Vorbeck & Germany's East African Empire. (Illus.). 256p. 1981. 14.95 (ISBN 0-02-555210-4). Macmillan.

Humble, Richard. Hitler's Generals. (YA) 1981. pap. 2.25 (ISBN 0-89083-788-0). Zebra.

Kitchen, Martin. A Military History of Germany: From the Eighteenth Century to the Present Day. 1976. pap. 4.95 (ISBN 0-8065-0524-9). Citadel Pr.

--A Military History of Germany from the 18th Century to the Present Day. LC 74-17022. 392p. 1975. 12.50x (ISBN 0-253-33838-7). Ind U Pr.

Lloyd, Henry. History of the Late War in Germany Between the King of Prussia, & the Empress of Germany & Her Allies, 2 Vols. (Vol. 1, repr. of 1766 ed; vol. 2, repr. of 1781 ed.). Set. lib. bdg. 46.00x (ISBN 0-8371-5016-7, LLLW). Greenwood.

Malleson, George B. Battlefields of Germany, from the Outbreak of the Thirty-Years' War. Repr. of 1884 ed. lib. bdg. 16.00x (ISBN 0-8371-5017-5, MABG). Greenwood.

Pfannes, Charles E. & Salamone, Victor A. The Great Commanders of World War II. (The Germans Ser.: Vol. 1). (YA) 1981. pap. 2.75 (ISBN 0-89083-727-9). Zebra.

Ritter, Gerhard. The Sword & the Scepter: The Problem of Militarism in Germany. Norden, Heinz, tr. Incl. Vol. 1. The Prussian Tradition 1740-1890. 1969. 19.95x (ISBN 0-87024-127-3); Vol. 2. The European Powers & the Wilhelminian Empire, 1890-1914. 1970. 19.95x (ISBN 0-87024-128-1); Vol. 3. The Tragedy of Statesmanship: Bethmann Hollweg As War Chancellor (1914-1917) 1972. 19.95x (ISBN 0-87024-182-6); Vol. 4. The Reign of German Militarism & the Disaster of 1918. 1973. 19.95x (ISBN 0-87024-235-0). LC 68-31041. Set. 69.95x (ISBN 0-87024-297-0). U of Miami Pr.

Robinson, Douglas H. The Zeppelin in Combat: A History of the German Naval Airship Division, 1912-1918. LC 80-13791. (Illus.). 432p. 1980. Repr. of 1971 ed. 25.00 (ISBN 0-295-95752-2). U of Wash Pr.

Showalter, Dennis E. Railroads & Rifles: Soldiers, Technology & Unification of Germany. (Illus.). 267p. 1975. 17.50 (ISBN 0-208-01505-1, Archon). Shoe String.

Spielberger, Walter J. & Feist, Uwe. Panzerkampfwagen IV. LC 68-56381. (Illus.). 1968. pap. 4.95 (ISBN 0-8168-7109-4). Aero.

Taylor, Telford. Sword & Swastika: Generals & Nazis in Third Reich. 416p. 1972. pap. 2.95 (ISBN 0-8129-6098-X, QP304). Times Bks.

Van Creveld, Martin L. Hitler's Strategy 1940-1941: The Balkan Clue. LC 72-97885. (International Studies). (Illus.). 272p. 1973. 27.50 (ISBN 0-521-20143-8). Cambridge U Pr.

Wilkinson-Latham. Luftwaffe Airborne & Field Units. LC 73-83332. (Men-at-Arms Ser). (Illus.). 40p. 1973. pap. 7.95 (ISBN 0-88254-164-1). Hippocrene Bks.

Windrow, Martin. The Panzer Divisions. LC 73-83331. (Men-at-Arms Ser). (Illus.). 40p. 1973. pap. 7.95 (ISBN 0-88254-165-X). Hippocrene Bks.

--Waffen SS. LC 73-83334. (Men-at-Arms Ser). (Illus.). 40p. 1973. pap. 7.95 (ISBN 0-88254-169-2). Hippocrene Bks.

GERMANY–HISTORY, NAVAL

Bekker, Cajus. Hitler's Naval War. (YA) 1981. pap. 2.75 (ISBN 0-89083-759-7). Zebra.

Witthoeft, Hans. Lexikon der Deutschen Marinegeschichte. (Ger.). 1977. 35.00 (ISBN 3-7822-0144-2, M-7262). French & Eur.

GERMANY–INDUSTRY

Balabkins, Nicholas. Germany Under Direct Controls: Economic Aspects of Industrial Disarmament, 1945-1948. 1964. 16.00 (ISBN 0-8135-0449-X). Rutgers U Pr.

Barkin, Kenneth. Controversy Over German Industrialization, 1890-1902. LC 78-101359. 1970. 16.00x (ISBN 0-226-03712-6). U of Chicago Pr.

Dawson, William H. The German Workman: A Study in National Efficiency. LC 77-87732. Repr. of 1906 ed. 25.50 (ISBN 0-404-16505-2). AMS Pr.

Germany Supplies, (Deutschland Liefert) 23rd ed. LC 57-18209. (Illus.). 1981. 65.00x (ISBN 0-8002-2779-4). Intl Pubns Serv.

Kaelble, Hartmut. Berliner Unternehmer waehrend der fruehen Industrialisierung: Herkunft, sozialer Status und politischer Einfluss. (Veroeffentlichungen der Historischen Kommission zu Berlin 40). xii, 302p. (Ger.). 1972. 42.00x (ISBN 3-11-003873-0). De Gruyter.

Klein, Burton H. Germany's Economic Preparations for War. LC 59-7655. (Economic Studies: No. 109). 1959. 14.00x (ISBN 0-674-35350-1). Harvard U Pr.

Levy, Hermann. Industrial Germany. new ed. 245p. 1966. 29.50x (ISBN 0-7146-1336-3, F Cass Co). Biblio Dist.

Little, A. D. New Technology-Based Firms in the United Kingdom & the Federal Republic of Germany. LC 78-301104. (Illus.). 1977. pap. 50.00x (ISBN 0-905492-04-8). Intl Pubns Serv.

Peltzer, Martin & Treumann, Walter. Produzentenhaftpflicht in USA und Deutschland: Product Liability in Germany & the USA. 2nd ed. German American Chamber of Commerce, ed. Fischer-Theurer, Anette, tr. 54p. (Ger. & Eng.). 1981. pap. 15.00 (ISBN 0-86640-002-8). German Am Chamber.

Sailing Aktienfuehrer: Sailing Shares Guide, 1980. 73rd ed. LC 57-405999. 1062p. (Ger.). 1979. 50.00x (ISBN 3-8203-0025-2). Intl Pubns Serv.

GERMANY–INTELLECTUAL LIFE

Blanning, T. C. Reform & Revolution in Mainz, 1743-1803. (Studies in Early Modern History). 384p. 1974. 41.95 (ISBN 0-521-20418-6). Cambridge U Pr.

Browning, Robert M. German Poetry in the Age of the Enlightenment: From Brockes to Klopstock. LC 77-26832. (Penn State Series in German Literature). 1978. text ed. 17.95x (ISBN 0-271-00541-6). Pa St U Pr.

Danton, George H. Germany Ten Years After. facsimile ed. LC 79-150180. (Select Bibliographies Reprint Ser). Repr. of 1928 ed. 18.00 (ISBN 0-8369-5693-1). Arno.

Deak, Istvan. Weimar Germany's Left-Wing Intellectuals: A Political History of the Weltbuhne & Its Circle. LC 68-9271. (Illus.). 1968. 26.75x (ISBN 0-520-00309-8). U of Cal Pr.

Demiashkevich, Michael. The National Mind: English, French, German. 1979. Repr. of 1938 ed. lib. bdg. 45.00 (ISBN 0-8495-1104-6). Arden Lib.

Dippel, Horst. Germany & the American Revolution, 1770-1800: A Sociohistorical Investigation of Late Eighteenth-Century Political Thinking. Uhlendorf, Bernhard A., tr. LC 77-367. (Institute of Early American History & Culture Ser.). (Illus.). 1977. 24.50x (ISBN 0-8078-1301-X). U of NC Pr.

Gay, Peter. Freud, Jews & Other Germans: Masters & Victims in Modernist Culture. 1978. 15.95x (ISBN 0-19-502258-0). Oxford U Pr.

--Weimar Culture: The Outsider As Insider. 1970. pap. 4.95x (ISBN 0-06-131482-X, TB1482, Torch). Har-Row.

Krieger, Leonard. The German Idea of Freedom. 1973. pap. 3.75 (ISBN 0-226-45347-2, P495, Phoen). U of Chicago Pr.

Laqueur, Walter. Weimar: A Cultural History. LC 74-16605. (Illus.). 295p. 1976. 4.95 (ISBN 0-399-50346-3, Perigee). Putnam.

McDonald, William C. & Goebel, Ulrich. German Medieval Literary Patronage from Charlemagne to Maximilian the First: A Critical Commentary with Special Emphasis on Imperial Promotion of Literature. LC 73-82154. (Amsterdamer Publikationen Zur Sprache und Literatur: No. 10). 220p. (Orig.). 1973. pap. text ed. 23.00x (ISBN 90-6203-201-X). Humanities.

Mosse, George L. The Crisis of Germany Ideology: Intellectual Origins of the Third Reich. 384p. 1981. Repr. of 1964 ed. pap. text ed. 7.95 (ISBN 0-8052-0669-8). Schocken.

Spender, Stephen. European Witness. LC 74-138186. 246p. 1972. Repr. of 1946 ed. lib. bdg. 15.00 (ISBN 0-8371-5643-2, SPEW). Greenwood.

Stael, de. De l'Allemagne, 5 vols. (Grands Escrivains de France). 350p. 1967. 15.95 ea. French & Eur.

--De l'Allemagne, Vol. 1. Balaye, Simone, ed. 1959. pap. 4.50 (ISBN 0-686-54923-6). French & Eur.

Willey, Thomas E. Back to Kant: The Revival of Kantianism in German Social & Historical Thought, 1860-1914. LC 77-29215. 1978. text ed. 17.95x (ISBN 0-8143-1590-9). Wayne St U Pr.

GERMANY–JUVENILE LITERATURE

Norris, Grace. Young Germany. LC 69-18461. (Young Ser.). (Illus.). (gr. 3 up). 1969. PLB 3.95 (ISBN 0-396-05884-1). Dodd.

Singer, Julia. Impressions: A Trip to the German Democratic Republic. LC 78-11299. (Illus.). (gr. 4-6). 1979. 8.95 (ISBN 0-689-30696-2). Atheneum.

Wohlrabe, Raymond A. & Krusch, Werner E. Land & People of Germany. rev. ed. LC 75-37248. (Portraits of the Nations Ser.). (Illus.). (gr. 6 up). 1972. 8.95 (ISBN 0-397-31261-X). Lippincott.

GERMANY–MILITARY POLICY

Anton, Hans H. Studien Zu Den Klosterprivilegien der Paepste Im Fruehen Mittelalter Unter Besonderer Beruecksichti der Privilegierung Von St. Maurice D'agaune. (Beitraege Zur Geschichte und Quellenkunde Des Mittelalters Ser.: Vol. 4). 1975. pap. 47.00x (ISBN 3-11-004686-5). De Gruyter.

Carroll, Berenice A. Design for Total War: Arms & Economics in the Third Reich. LC 68-15527. (Studies in European History: Vol. 17). 1968. text ed. 50.00x (ISBN 90-2790-299-2). Mouton.

Feist, Uwe. Armor Series, Vol. 13. 52p. 1980. pap. 3.95 (ISBN 0-8168-2046-5). Aero.

Kelleher, Catherine M. Germany & the Politics of Nuclear Weapons. LC 75-16168. (Institute of War & Peace Studies). (Illus.). 372p. 1975. 20.00x (ISBN 0-231-03960-3). Columbia U Pr.

Klein, Burton H. Germany's Economic Preparations for War. LC 59-7655. (Economic Studies: No. 109). 1959. 14.00x (ISBN 0-674-35350-1). Harvard U Pr.

GERMANY–NAVY

Bekker, Cajus. The German Navy: Nineteen Thirty-Nine to Nineteen Forty-Five. (Illus.). 192p. 1975. 12.50 (ISBN 0-8037-3132-9). Dial.

Hansen, Hans J. Ships of the German Fleet, Eighteen Forty-Eight - Nineteen Forty-Five. LC 74-14197. (Illus.). 192p. 1975. 25.00 (ISBN 0-668-03648-6). Arco.

Herwig, Holger H. Luxury Fleet: The Imperial German Navy Eighteen Eighty-Eight to Nineteen Eighteen. (Illus.). 1980. text ed. 22.50x (ISBN 0-04-943023-8). Allen Unwin.

--Politics of Frustration: The United States in German Naval Planning, 1889-1941. 1976. 18.00 (ISBN 0-316-35890-8). Little.

Hurd, Archibald S. German Sea-Power, Its Rise, Progress, & Economic Basis. LC 71-110846. (Illus.). xv, 388p. Repr. of 1913 ed. lib. bdg. 16.75x (ISBN 0-8371-4513-9, HUGS). Greenwood.

Schmalenbach, Paul. German Raiders: A History of Auxiliary Cruisers of the German Navy 1895-1945. LC 78-71801. (Illus.). 144p. 1980. 16.95 (ISBN 0-87021-824-7). Naval Inst Pr.

GERMANY–POLITICS AND GOVERNMENT

Barker, J. Ellis. Foundations of Germany. LC 70-110894. 1970. Repr. of 1916 ed. 12.50 (ISBN 0-8046-0877-6). Kennikat.

Blachly, Frederick F. & Oatman, Miriam E. Government & Administration of Germany. (Brookings Institution Reprint Ser). Repr. of 1928 ed. lib. bdg. 34.50x (ISBN 0-697-00152-0). Irvington.

Bracher, Karl D. The German Dictatorship: The Origins, Structure, and Effects of National Socialism. Steinberg, Jean, tr. from German. LC 70-95662. Orig. Title: Die Deutsche Diktatur: Enstehung, Struktur, & Folgen Des Nationalsozialismus. 553p. 1972. pap. text ed. 8.95x (ISBN 0-686-70700-1). HR&W.

Brecht, Arnold. The Art & Technique of Administration in German Ministries. LC 70-138205. (Illus.). 191p. 1972. Repr. of 1940 ed. lib. bdg. 15.00x (ISBN 0-8371-5557-6, BRGM). Greenwood.

Cartright, Hilary. German Laws Relating to Inventions of Employees & Directives Issued Thereunder. 2nd ed. 1971. 5.00x (ISBN 0-8002-1276-2). Intl Pubns Serv.

Connerton, P. The Tragedy of Enlightenment. LC 79-16102. (Cambridge Studies in the History & Theory of Politics). 1980. 29.95 (ISBN 0-521-22842-5); pap. 7.95 (ISBN 0-521-29675-7). Cambridge U Pr.

Conradt, David P. The German Polity. LC 77-17711. (Comparative Studies of Political Life Ser.). 1978. text ed. 15.95x (ISBN 0-582-28034-6); pap. text ed. 10.95x (ISBN 0-582-28033-8). Longman.

Craig, Gordon A. From Bismarck to Alexander: Aspects of German Statecraft. LC 78-1080. (The Albert Shaw Lectures on Diplomatic History, 1958). 1979. Repr. of 1958 ed. lib. bdg. 16.75x (ISBN 0-313-21233-3, CRFB). Greenwood.

--Politics of the Prussian Army Sixteen Forty - Nineteen Forty-Five. 1964. pap. 7.95 (ISBN 0-19-500257-1, GB). Oxford U Pr.

Dahrendorf, Ralf. Society & Democracy in Germany. LC 79-15142. 1980. Repr. of 1969 ed. lib. bdg. 33.50x (ISBN 0-313-22027-1, DASO). Greenwood.

Dawson, William H. Social Insurance in Germany, 1883-1911. LC 78-32002. (Illus.). xi, 283p. Repr. of 1912 ed. lib. bdg. 21.25x (ISBN 0-8371-5446-4, DASI). Greenwood.

De Graziani, Vincenzo G. The Franco-German Coalition & the Emergence of a New International Superpower: Its Effects Upon the Future Course of History. (Illus.). 1979. deluxe ed. 55.75 (ISBN 0-930008-31-6). Inst Econ Pol.

Emerson, Rupert. State & Sovereignty in Modern Germany. LC 79-1626. 1981. Repr. of 1928 ed. 22.50 (ISBN 0-88355-931-5). Hyperion Conn.

Engel-Janosi, Friedrich. The Growth of German Historicism. LC 78-64195. (Johns Hopkins University. Studies in the Social Sciences. Sixty-Second Ser. 1944: 2). Repr. of 1944 ed. 15.00 (ISBN 0-404-61301-2). AMS Pr.

Forschungsgruppe Wahlen e.V., Mannheim. German Election Panel Study, 1976. LC 78-71175. 1978. codebook 22.00 (ISBN 0-89138-994-6). ICPSR.

Goodnow, Frank J., ed. Comparative Administrative Law: An Analysis of the Administrative Systems of the U. S., England, France & Germany. 1970. Repr. of 1893 ed. Set. text ed. 44.50 (ISBN 0-8337-1384-1). B Franklin.

Gottlieb, Fichte J. Addresses to the German Nation. Jones, R. F. & Turnbull, G. H., eds. LC 78-12431. 1979. Repr. of 1922 ed. lib. bdg. 20.00x (ISBN 0-313-21207-4, FIAG). Greenwood.

Hopwood, Robert F., ed. Germany: People & Politics. LC 68-134435. (Selections from History Today Ser.: No. 12). (Illus.). 1969. 3.95 (ISBN 0-05-001656-3). Dufour.

Howard, Burt E. German Empire. LC 74-95142. Repr. of 1906 ed. 28.50 (ISBN 0-404-03354-7). AMS Pr.

Jacobs, Dan N., et al. Comparative Politics: Introduction to the Politics of Britain, the United Kingdom, France, Germany, & the Soviet Union. 320p. 1982. pap. text ed. 9.95x (ISBN 0-934540-05-5). Chatham Hse Pubs.

King-Hall, Stephen & Ullmann, Richard K. German Parliaments: A Study of the Development of Representative Institutions in Germany. LC 78-20475. 1979. Repr. of 1954 ed. 16.50 (ISBN 0-88355-853-X). Hyperion Conn.

Kohn, Walter S. Governments & Politics of the German-Speaking Countries. LC 79-16859. 292p. 1980. text ed. 18.95x (ISBN 0-88229-262-5). Nelson-Hall.

Loewenstein, Hubertus Z. Germans in History. LC 78-95395. Repr. of 1945 ed. 34.50 (ISBN 0-404-04008-X). AMS Pr.

Marx, Karl & Engels, Friedrich. The German Ideology. 711p. 1976. 4.75 (ISBN 0-8285-0008-8, Pub. by Progress Pubs Russia). Imported Pubns.

Meinecke, Friedrich. Cosmopolitanism & the National State: Welburgertum Und Nationalstaat. Kimber, Robert B., tr. LC 65-17150. 1970. 25.00 (ISBN 0-691-05177-1). Princeton U Pr.

Pflanze, Otto. Bismarck & the Development of Germany, Vol. 1: The Period of Unification, 1815-1871. 1971. 28.00x (ISBN 0-691-05106-2); pap. 8.95 (ISBN 0-691-00765-9). Princeton U Pr.

Reece, B. Carroll. Peace Through Law. pap. 3.75 (ISBN 0-912806-21-4). Long Hse.

Reichard, Richard W. Crippled from Birth: German Social Democracy 1844-1870. (Illus.). 1969. 9.50 (ISBN 0-8138-0372-1). Iowa St U Pr.

Ritter, Gerhard. The Sword & the Scepter: The Problem of Militarism in Germany. Norden, Heinz, tr. Incl. Vol. 1. The Prussian Tradition 1740-1890. 1969. 19.95x (ISBN 0-87024-127-3); Vol. 2. The European Powers & the Wilhelminian Empire, 1890-1914. 1970. 19.95x (ISBN 0-87024-128-1); Vol. 3. The Tragedy of Statesmanship: Bethmann Hollweg As War Chancellor (1914-1917) 1972. 19.95x (ISBN 0-87024-182-6); Vol. 4. The Reign of German Militarism & the Disaster of 1918. 1973. 19.95x (ISBN 0-87024-235-0). LC 68-31041. Set. 69.95x (ISBN 0-87024-297-0). U of Miami Pr.

Schweigler, Gebhard L. National Consciousness in Divided Germany. LC 74-83959. (Sage Library of Social Research: Vol. 15). 1975. 20.00 (ISBN 0-8039-9932-1); pap. 9.95 (ISBN 0-8039-9931-3). Sage.

Seidl-Hohenveldern, Ignaz. The Austrian-German Arbitral Tribunal, Vol. 11. 1972. 10.00x (ISBN 0-8156-2159-0). U Pr of Va.

Thomas, R. Hinton. Liberalism, Nationalism & the German Intellectuals, 1822-1847. LC 75-11803. 148p. 1975. Repr. of 1951 ed. lib. bdg. 15.00x (ISBN 0-8371-8140-2, THLI). Greenwood.

Uexkuell, Juergen-Detlev. German Patent Law, Utility Model Law & Trademark Law. LC 70-431330. 1968. 7.50x (ISBN 3-452-18469-2). Intl Pubns Serv.

Vermeil, Edmond. Germany's Three Reichs. LC 68-9638. 1969. Repr. of 1944 ed. 28.50 (ISBN 0-86527-086-4). Fertig.

Von Beyme, Klaus, ed. German Political Studies, Vol. 1. LC 74-82535. 284p. 1974. 22.50x (ISBN 0-8039-9927-5). Sage.

--German Political Systems: Theory & Practice in the Two Germanies. LC 74-82535. (German Political Studies: Vol. 2). 234p. 1976. 22.50 (ISBN 0-8039-9963-1). Sage.

GERMANY-POLITICS AND GOVERNMENT-18TH CENTURY

Bruford, Walter H. Germany in the Eighteenth Century. 1935. 38.50 (ISBN 0-521-04354-9); pap. 11.50x (ISBN 0-521-09259-0, 259). Cambridge U Pr.

Fisher, Herbert. Studies in Napoleonic Statesmanship: Germany. LC 68-25230. (World History Ser., No. 48). 1969. Repr. of 1903 ed. lib. bdg. 54.95 (ISBN 0-8383-0939-9). Haskell.

Fisher, Herbert A. Studies in Napoleonic Statesmanship: Germany. LC 69-13897. Repr. of 1903 ed. lib. bdg. 18.75x (ISBN 0-8371-1302-4, FINS). Greenwood.

GERMANY-POLITICS AND GOVERNMENT-1789-1900

Aris, Reinhold. History of Political Thought in Germany, 1789-1815. 414p. 1965. Repr. 28.00x (ISBN 0-7156-1646-3, F Cass Co). Biblio Dist.

Dawson, William H. German Empire, Eighteen Sixty-Seven - Nineteen Fourteen, & the Unity Movement, 2 Vols. 1966. Repr. of 1919 ed. Set. 32.50 (ISBN 0-208-00025-9, Archon). Shoe String.

De Jonge, Alfred R. Gottfried Kinkel As Political & Social Thinker. LC 70-163695. (Columbia University. Germanic Studies, Old Ser.: No. 30). Repr. of 1926 ed. 21.00 (ISBN 0-404-50430-2). AMS Pr.

Diefendorf, Jeffry M. Businessmen & Politics in the Rhineland, 1789-1834. LC 79-3200. 1980. 22.50x (ISBN 0-691-05298-0). Princeton U Pr.

Fisher, Herbert. Studies in Napoleonic Statesmanship: Germany. LC 68-25230. (World History Ser., No. 48). 1969. Repr. of 1903 ed. lib. bdg. 54.95 (ISBN 0-8383-0939-9). Haskell.

Fisher, Herbert A. Studies in Napoleonic Statesmanship: Germany. LC 69-13897. Repr. of 1903 ed. lib. bdg. 18.75x (ISBN 0-8371-1302-4, FINS). Greenwood.

Guilland, Antoine. Modern Germany & Her Historians. Repr. of 1915 ed. lib. bdg. 15.25x (ISBN 0-8371-4506-6, GUMG). Greenwood.

Hamerow, Theodore S. Restoration, Revolution, Reaction: Economics & Politics in Germany, 1815-1871. 1958. 20.00x (ISBN 0-691-05146-1); pap. 6.95 (ISBN 0-691-00755-1). Princeton U Pr.

Hertz, Frederick. The German Public Mind, in the Nineteenth Century: A Social History of German Political Sentiments, Aspirations & Ideas. Eyck, Frank, ed. Northcott, Eric, tr. 422p. 1975. 22.50x (ISBN 0-87471-580-6). Rowman.

Mosse, W. E. European Powers & the German Question, 1848-1871. LC 74-76002. 1969. Repr. of 1958 ed. lib. bdg. 30.00x (ISBN 0-374-95928-5). Octagon.

Robertson, C. Grant. Bismarck. LC 68-9604. 1969. Repr. of 1918 ed. 29.50 (ISBN 0-86527-008-2). Fertig.

Simon, Walter M. The Failure of the Prussian Reform Movement, 1807-1819. LC 73-80591. 1971. Repr. 25.00 (ISBN 0-86527-062-7). Fertig.

Snell, John L. & Schmitt, Hans A. The Democratic Movement in Germany, 1789-1914. (James Sprunt Studies in History and Political Science: Vol. 55). 1976. 22.50x (ISBN 0-8078-1283-8). U of NC Pr.

Sontag, Raymond J. Germany & England: Background of Conflict, 1848-1894. 1969. pap. 3.95x (ISBN 0-393-00180-6, Norton Lib). Norton.

--Germany & England: Background of Conflict, 1848-1894. LC 64-15034. 1964. Repr. of 1938 ed. 10.00 (ISBN 0-8462-0467-3). Russell.

Von Sybel, Heinrich. Founding of the German Empire by William 1, 7 Vols. Perrin, Marshall L., tr. LC 68-31005. (Illus.). 1968. Repr. of 1890 ed. Set. lib. bdg. 150.00x (ISBN 0-8371-0674-5, SYGE). Greenwood.

--Founding of the German Empire by William First, 7 Vols. 1890-98. Repr. Set. 140.00 (ISBN 0-685-20256-9); 21.50 ea. Scholarly.

Werner, George S. Bavaria in the German Confederation, 1820-1848. 46p. 1977. 18.00 (ISBN 0-8386-1932-0). Fairleigh Dickinson.

Windell, George G. Catholic & German Unity, Eighteen Sixty-Six to Eighteen Seventy-One. LC 54-13011. 1954. 10.00x (ISBN 0-8166-0100-3). U of Minn Pr.

Zucker, Stanley. Ludwig Bamberger: German Liberal Politician & Social Critic,1823-1899. LC 74-17839. 1975. 16.95 (ISBN 0-8229-3298-9). U of Pittsburgh Pr.

GERMANY-POLITICS AND GOVERNMENT-1871-1918

Blackbourn, David. Class, Religion, & Local Politics: The Centre Party in Wurttemberg Before 1914. LC 80-11878. 288p. 1980. text ed. 30.00x (ISBN 0-300-02464-9). Yale U Pr.

Bulow, Bernhard H. Imperial Germany. Lewenz, Marie A., tr. LC 78-12268. (Illus.). 1979. Repr. of 1914 ed. lib. bdg. 20.00x (ISBN 0-313-21176-0, BUIG). Greenwood.

Cecil, Lamar. The German Diplomatic Service 1871-1914. 1976. text ed. 26.00 (ISBN 0-691-05235-2). Princeton U Pr.

Crothers, George D. German Elections of 1907. LC 68-58564. (Columbia University Studies in the Social Sciences: No. 479). Repr. of 1941 ed. 21.00 (ISBN 0-404-51479-0). AMS Pr.

Dawson, William H. German Empire, Eighteen Sixty-Seven - Nineteen Fourteen, & the Unity Movement, 2 Vols. 1966. Repr. of 1919 ed. Set. 32.50 (ISBN 0-208-00025-9, Archon). Shoe String.

Dronberger, Ilse. Political Thought of Max Weber: In Quest of Statesmanship. LC 70-133904. (Orig.). 1971. 24.00x (ISBN 0-89197-349-4); pap. text ed. 8.95x (ISBN 0-89197-350-8). Irvington.

Fischer, Fritz. War of Illusions: German Policies, 1911-1914. Jackson, Marion, tr. from German. 578p. 1975. 9.95x (ISBN 0-393-09161-9). Norton.

Guttsman, W. L. The German Social Democratic Party 1875-1933. (Illus.). 1981. text ed. 37.50x (ISBN 0-04-943024-6). Allen Unwin.

Haller, Johannes. Philip Eulenberg: the Kaiser's Friend, 2 vols. facsimile ed. Mayne, Ethel C., tr. LC 72-148883. (Select Bibliographies Reprint Ser). Repr. of 1930 ed. Set. 45.00 (ISBN 0-8369-5651-6). Arno.

Kitchen, Martin. The Silent Dictatorship: The Politics of the German High Command Under Hindenburg & Ludendorff, 1916-1918. LC 76-16055. 1976. text ed. 29.50x (ISBN 0-8419-0277-1). Holmes & Meier.

Knight, Maxwell E. The German Executive, 1890-1933. LC 78-80560. (Illus.). 52p. 1973. Repr. of 1952 ed. 13.75 (ISBN 0-86527-079-1). Fertig.

Lutz, Ralph H. Fall of the German Empire, 1914-1918, 2 Vols. 1969. lib. bdg. 50.00x (ISBN 0-374-95168-3). Octagon.

Mishark, John W. Road to Revolution, German Marxism & World War 1. 15.00 (ISBN 0-685-16805-0). Moira.

Rich, Norman. Friedrich Von Holstein: Politics & Diplomacy in the Era of Bismarck & Wilhelm. 1965. 130.00 (ISBN 0-521-06077-X). Cambridge U Pr.

Rohl, John. Germany Without Bismarck. LC 67-26960. 1967. 27.50x (ISBN 0-520-01086-8). U of Cal Pr.

Roth, Guenther. The Social Democrats in Imperial Germany: A Study in Working-Class Isolation & National Integration. Coser, Lewis A. & Powell, Walter W., eds. LC 79-7018. (Perennial Works in Sociology Ser.). 1979. Repr. of 1963 ed. lib. bdg. 23.00x (ISBN 0-405-12117-2). Arno.

Smith, Woodruff D. The German Colonial Empire. LC 77-18155. 1978. 18.50x (ISBN 0-8078-1322-2). U of NC Pr.

Snell, John L. & Schmitt, Hans A. The Democratic Movement in Germany, 1789-1914. (James Sprunt Studies in History and Political Science: Vol. 55). 1976. 22.50x (ISBN 0-8078-1283-8). U of NC Pr.

Von Bismarck, Otto. Kaiser Vs. Bismarck. Miall, Bernard, tr. LC 75-136405. Repr. of 1921 ed. 14.50 (ISBN 0-404-00869-0). AMS Pr.

Von Buelow, Bernhard H. Imperial Germany. LC 77-127900. Repr. of 1914 ed. 21.00 (ISBN 0-404-01228-0). AMS Pr.

White, Dan S. The Splintered Party: National Liberalism in Hessen & the Reich, 1867-1918. LC 75-23213. 445p. 1976. 15.00x (ISBN 0-674-83320-1). Harvard U Pr.

Zucker, Stanley. Ludwig Bamberger: German Liberal Politician & Social Critic,1823-1899. LC 74-17839. 1975. 16.95 (ISBN 0-8229-3298-9). U of Pittsburgh Pr.

GERMANY-POLITICS AND GOVERNMENT-20TH CENTURY

Berlau, A. Joseph. German Social Democratic Party, 1914-1921. LC 77-120228. 1970. Repr. lib. bdg. 19.00x (ISBN 0-374-90612-2). Octagon.

Bleuel, Hans P. Deutschlanfs Bekenner: German Men of Knowledge: the Professiate from the Rule of the Kaiser to the Rise of Hitler. Metzger, Walter P., ed. LC 76-55206. (The Academic Profession Ser.). (Illus., Ger.). 1977. Repr. of 1968 ed. lib. bdg. 14.00x (ISBN 0-405-10032-9). Arno.

Brecht, Arnold. Political Education of Arnold Brecht - An Autobiography: 1884-1970. LC 77-100994. 1970. 30.00x (ISBN 0-691-07527-1). Princeton U Pr.

Broszat, Martin. The Hitler State: The Foundation & Development of the Internal Structure of the Third Reich. Hiden, John, tr. from Ger. (Illus.). 400p. 1981. text ed. 24.00x (ISBN 0-582-49200-9); pap. text ed. 14.50x (ISBN 0-582-48997-0). Longman.

Burdick, Charles B. & Lutz, Ralph H., eds. The Political Institutions of the German Revolution, 1918-1919. LC 66-13464. (Publications Ser.: No. 40). 305p. 1966. 10.95 (ISBN 0-8179-1401-3). Hoover Inst Pr.

Glaser, Hermann. The Cultural Roots of National Socialism. Menze, Ernest A., tr. LC 77-89144. Orig. Title: Spiesser-ideologie. 289p. 1978. 15.00x (ISBN 0-292-71044-5). U of Tex Pr.

Graham, M. W., Jr. New Governments of Eastern Europe. LC 27-20024. (Illus.). 1969. Repr. of 1927 ed. 33.00 (ISBN 0-527-35250-0). Kraus Repr.

Hallowell, John H. The Decline of Liberalism As an Ideology. LC 75-80554. 1971. Repr. 19.50 (ISBN 0-86527-038-4). Fertig.

Hitler, Adolf. Mein Kampf. Manheim, Ralph, tr. 15.95 (ISBN 0-395-07801-6); pap. 8.95 (ISBN 0-686-57537-7). HM.

--Mein Kampf. 1962. pap. 8.95 (ISBN 0-395-08362-1, 13, SenEd). HM.

Mann, Thomas. Order of the Day. facs. ed. LC 79-80389. (Essay Index Reprint Ser). 1942. 16.75 (ISBN 0-8369-1060-5). Arno.

Mosse, George L. Germans & Jews: The Right, the Left, & the Search for a 'third Force' in Pre-Nazi Germany. LC 68-14552. 1970. 20.00 (ISBN 0-86527-081-3). Fertig.

Scheidemann, Philip. Making of New Germany, 2 Vols. facs. ed. Michell, J. E., tr. (Select Bibliographies Reprint Ser). 1929. Set. 42.00 (ISBN 0-8369-5615-X). Arno.

Schorske, Carl E. German Social Democracy, 1905-1917: The Development of the Great Schism. LC 71-81471. (Illus.). 1970. Repr. of 1955 ed. 18.00 (ISBN 0-8462-1379-6). Russell.

Snell, John L. Nazi Revolution: Hitler's Dictatorship & the German Nation. 2nd ed. Mitchell, Allan, rev. by. (Problems in European Civilization Ser). 1973. pap. text ed. 4.95x (ISBN 0-669-81752-X). Heath.

Stern, Fritz. The Failure of Liberalism: Essays on the Political Culture of Modern Germany. LC 75-22748. (Phoenix Ser). xliv, 244p. 1976. pap. 3.95 (ISBN 0-226-77316-7, P659, Phoen). U of Chicago Pr.

Stirk, S. D. Prussian Spirit: A Survey of German Literature & Politics 1914-1940. LC 68-8245. 1969. Repr. of 1941 ed. 12.00 (ISBN 0-8046-0447-9). Kennikat.

Stresemann, Gustav. Essays & Speeches on Various Subjects. facs. ed. Turner, C. R., tr. LC 68-26476. (Essay Index Reprint Ser). Orig. Title: Reden und Schriften. (Illus.). 1968. Repr. of 1930 ed. 18.00 (ISBN 0-8369-0909-7). Arno.

Ursachen Des Terrorismus in der Bundesrepublik Deutschland. (Sammlung Goeschen: Vol. 2806). 1978. 9.35x (ISBN 3-11-007702-7). De Gruyter.

Von Buelow, Bernhard H. Memoirs of Prince Von Buelow, 4 Vols. LC 77-127900. Repr. of 1932 ed. Set. 115.00 (ISBN 0-404-01230-2). AMS Pr.

Von Klemperer, Klemens. Germany's New Conservatism: Its History & Dilemma in the Twentieth Century. 1957. 19.00x (ISBN 0-691-05124-0); pap. 6.95 (ISBN 0-691-00753-5). Princeton U Pr.

GERMANY-POLITICS AND GOVERNMENT-1918-1933

Abraham, David. The Collapse of the Weimar Republic: Political Economy & Crisis. LC 80-8533. 550p. 1981. 30.00x (ISBN 0-691-05322-7); pap. 12.50x (ISBN 0-691-10118-3). Princeton U Pr.

Allen, William S. Nazi Seizure of Power: The Experience of a Single German Town, 1930-1935. (Illus.). 1965. pap. 6.95 (ISBN 0-531-06439-5). Watts.

Bennett, Edward W. Germany & the Diplomacy of the Financial Crisis, 1931. LC 62-13261. (Historical Monographs Ser: No. 50). 1962. 16.50x (ISBN 0-674-35250-5). Harvard U Pr.

Berghahn, V. R. Germany & the Approach of War in 1914. LC 73-86664. (Making of the Twentieth Century Ser). 256p. 1974. pap. text ed. 5.95 (ISBN 0-312-32480-4). St Martin.

Bolkosky, Sidney M. The Distorted Image: German Jewish Perceptions of Germans & Germany, 1918-1935. LC 75-8270. 224p. 1975. 13.95 (ISBN 0-444-99014-3). Elsevier.

Braunthal, Gerard. Socialist Labor & Politics in Weimar Germany: The General Federation of German Trade Unions. (Illus.). 1978. 20.00 (ISBN 0-208-01740-2, Archon). Shoe String.

Brecht, Arnold. Federalism & Regionalism in Germany: The Division of Prussia. LC 77-151541. (Illus.). xvi, 202p. 1971. Repr. of 1945 ed. 12.00 (ISBN 0-8462-1592-6). Russell.

Breitman, Richard. German Socialism & Weimar Democracy. LC 80-21412. 296p. 1981. 20.00x (ISBN 0-8078-1462-8). U of NC Pr.

Carsten, F. L. Reichswehr & Politics: Nineteen Eighteen to Nineteen Thirty-Three. 1974. pap. 7.95x (ISBN 0-520-02492-3). U of Cal Pr.

Carsten, Franz L. Reichswehr & Politics: Nineteen Eighteen to Nineteen Thirty-Three. 1966. 36.00x (ISBN 0-19-821457-X). Oxford U Pr.

Eksteins, Modris. The Limits of Reason: The German Democratic Press & the Collapse of Weimar Democracy. (Oxford Historical Monographs). 362p. 1975. 42.00x (ISBN 0-19-821862-1). Oxford U Pr.

Eley, Geoff. Reshaping the German Right: Radial Nationalism & Political Change After Bismarck. LC 79-20711. 1980. text ed. 30.00 (ISBN 0-300-02386-3). Yale U Pr.

Gay, Peter. Weimar Culture: The Outsider As Insider. 1970. pap. 4.95x (ISBN 0-06-131482-X, TB1482, Torch). Har-Row.

Guttsman, W. L. The German Social Democratic Party 1875-1933. (Illus.). 1981. text ed. 37.50x (ISBN 0-04-943024-6). Allen Unwin.
Haller, Johannes. Philip Eulenberg: the Kaiser's Friend, 2 vols. facsimile ed. Mayne, Ethel C., tr. LC 72-148883. (Select Bibliographies Reprint Ser). Repr. of 1930 ed. Set. 45.00 (ISBN 0-8369-5651-6). Arno.
Heneman, Harlow J. The Growth of Executive Power in Germany. LC 74-11935. 256p. 1975. Repr. of 1934 ed. lib. bdg. 15.75x (ISBN 0-8371-7721-9, HEEP). Greenwood.
Hertzman, Lewis. D N V P: The Right-Wing Opposition in the Weimar Republic, 1918-1924. LC 63-15846. 1964. 16.50x (ISBN 0-8032-0068-4). U of Nebr Pr.
Hitler, Adolph. Mein Kampf. Hurst & Blackett, trs. 12.00 (ISBN 0-913022-10-1). Angriff Pr.
--My New Order. De Roussy De Sales, Raoul, ed. LC 73-3444. 1008p. 1973. Repr. of 1941 ed. lib. bdg. 40.00x (ISBN 0-374-93918-7). Octagon.
Hunt, Richard N. German Social Democracy 1918-1933. 1972. pap. 3.45 (ISBN 0-8129-6117-X, QP306). Times Bks.
Jarman, T. L. The Rise & Fall of Nazi Germany. LC 56-9548. 388p. 1956. cusa 19.50x (ISBN 0-8147-0217-1). NYU Pr.
Kaufmann, Walter H. Monarchism in the Weimar Republic. rev ed. 1972. lib. bdg. 17.50x (ISBN 0-374-94527-6). Octagon.
Kessler, Harry. Germany & Europe. LC 75-137950. (Economic Thought, History & Challenge Ser). 1971. Repr. of 1923 ed. 12.50 (ISBN 0-8046-1452-0). Kennikat.
Koch, H. W. The Hitler Youth: Origins & Development Nineteen Twenty-Two to Nineteen Twenty-Four. (Illus.). 1975. 21.00 (ISBN 0-8464-0986-0). Beekman Pubs.
Lane, Barbara M. & Rupp, Leila J., trs. from Ger. Nazi Ideology before 1933: A Documentation. 208p. 1978. 12.95x (ISBN 0-292-75512-0). U of Tex Pr.
Laqueur, Walter. Weimar: A Cultural History. LC 74-16605. (Illus.). 295p. 1976. 4.95 (ISBN 0-399-50346-3, Perigee). Putnam.
Large, David C. The Politics of Law & Order: A History of the Bavarian Einwohnerwehr, 1918-1921. LC 79-54273. (Transactions Ser.: Vol. 70, Pt. 2). 1980. 8.00 (ISBN 0-87169-702-5). Am Philos.
Leopold, John A. Alfred Hugenberg: The Radical Nationalist Campaign Against the Weimar Republic. LC 77-4026. (Illus.). 1977. 25.00x (ISBN 0-300-02068-6). Yale U Pr.
Loewenstein, Karl. Max Weber's Political Ideas in the Perspective of Our Time. LC 66-16541. 1966. pap. 5.00x (ISBN 0-87023-009-3). U of Mass Pr.
Merkl, Peter H. Political Violence Under the Swastika: 581 Early Nazis. 1975. 47.50 (ISBN 0-691-07561-1); pap. 16.50 (ISBN 0-691-10028-4). Princeton U Pr.
Moeller Van Den Bruck, Arthur. Germany's Third Empire. 1972. 22.50 (ISBN 0-86527-085-6). Fertig.
Nicholls, A. J. Weimar & the Rise of Hitler. Thorne, Christopher, ed. LC 68-29506. (Making of the Twentieth Century Ser). (Illus., Orig.). 1969. pap. 5.95 (ISBN 0-312-86065-X, W15701). St Martin.
Pois, Robert A. Bourgeois Democrats of Weimar Germany. LC 76-3198. (Transactions Ser.: Vol. 66, Pt. 3). 1976. pap. 6.00 (ISBN 0-87169-664-9). Am Philos.
Roll, Erich. Spotlight on Germany. LC 70-180424. Repr. of 1933 ed. 18.50 (ISBN 0-404-56158-6). AMS Pr.
Scheele, Godfrey. The Weimar Republic, Overture to the Third Reich. LC 75-25268. 360p. 1975. Repr. of 1946 ed. lib. bdg. 27.25x (ISBN 0-8371-8388-X, SCWR). Greenwood.
Schmokel, Wolfe W. Dream of Empire: German Colonialism, 1919-1945. LC 80-15400. (Yale Historical Publications: Miscellany 78). xiv, 204p. 1980. Repr. of 1964 ed. lib. bdg. 22.50x (ISBN 0-313-22437-4, SCDE). Greenwood.
Snyder, Louis L., ed. Hitler's Third Reich: A Documentary History. LC 81-9512. 640p. 1981. text ed. 33.95x (ISBN 0-88229-705-8); pap. text ed. 16.95x (ISBN 0-88229-793-7). Nelson-Hall.
Thompson, Wayne C. In the Eye of the Storm: Kurt Riezler & the Crises of Modern Germany. LC 79-24251. (Illus.). 312p. 1980. text ed. 17.95x (ISBN 0-87745-094-3). U of Iowa Pr.
Thyssen, Fritz. I Paid Hitler. LC 71-153243. 1971. Repr. of 1941 ed. 14.00 (ISBN 0-8046-1553-5). Kennikat.
Trotsky, Leon. The Struggle Against Fascism in Germany. Breitman, George & Maisel, Merry, eds. LC 73-119532. 1970. 25.00 (ISBN 0-87348-135-6); pap. 6.95 (ISBN 0-87348-136-4). Path Pr NY.
Tucholsky, Kurt. Deutschland, Deutschland, uber alles: A Picture Book. Halley, Anne, tr. LC 77-181360. (Illus.). 256p. 1972. 12.50x (ISBN 0-87023-038-7). U of Mass Pr.
Turner, Henry A., Jr. Stresemann & the Politics of the Weimar Republic. LC 78-26856. 1979. Repr. of 1963 ed. lib. bdg. 22.50x (ISBN 0-313-20900-6, TUST). Greenwood.
Von Klemperer, Klemens. Germany's New Conservatism: Its History & Dilemma in the Twentieth Century. 1957. 19.00x (ISBN 0-691-05124-0); pap. 6.95 (ISBN 0-691-00753-5). Princeton U Pr.
Wright, Jonathan R. Above Parties: The Political Attitudes of the German Protestant Church Leadership 1918-1933. (Oxford Historical Monographs Ser.). 216p. 1974. 22.50x (ISBN 0-19-821856-7). Oxford U Pr.
Wurgaft, Lewis D. The Activists: Kurt Hiller & the Politics of Action on the German Left, 1914-1933. (Transactions Ser.: Vol. 67, Pt. 8). 1977. 12.00 (ISBN 0-87169-678-9). Am Philos.

GERMANY–POLITICS AND GOVERNMENT–1933-1945

Almond, Gabriel A., ed. Struggle for Democracy in Germany. LC 65-17874. 1965. Repr. of 1949 ed. 9.50 (ISBN 0-8462-0596-3). Russell.
Aycoberry, Pierre. The Nazi Question: An Essay on the Interpretations of National Socialism (1922-1975) Hurley, Robert, tr. 1981. 15.95 (ISBN 0-394-50948-X); pap. 6.95 (ISBN 0-394-74841-7). Pantheon.
Barron, L. Smythe. The Nazis in Africa: Lost Documents on the Third Reich, Vol. 3. 1978. 24.95 (ISBN 0-89712-076-0). Documentary Pubns.
Bayles, William D. Caesars in Goose Step. LC 68-2622. 1968. Repr. of 1940 ed. 12.50 (ISBN 0-8046-0021-X). Kennikat.
Beyerchen, Alan D. Scientists Under Hitler: Politics & the Physics Community in the Third Reich. LC 77-2167. (Illus.). 1977. 25.00x (ISBN 0-300-01830-4). Yale U Pr.
Brady, Robert A. The Spirit & Structure of German Fascism. LC 68-9629. 1970. Repr. of 1937 ed. 25.00 (ISBN 0-86527-189-5). Fertig.
Cargill, Morris. A Gallery of Nazis. (Illus.). 1978. 12.00 (ISBN 0-8184-0256-3). Lyle Stuart.
Carsten, Franz L. Reichswehr & Politics: Nineteen Eighteen to Nineteen Thirty-Three. 1966. 36.00x (ISBN 0-19-821457-X). Oxford U Pr.
Chadwick, H. Munro. The Heroic Age. LC 73-7696. (Illus.). 474p. 1974. Repr. of 1912 ed. lib. bdg. 25.00x (ISBN 0-8371-6939-9, CHHA). Greenwood.
Churchill, Winston S. While England Slept: A Survey of World Affairs 1932-8. facsimile ed. LC 76-165621. (Select Bibliographies Reprint Ser). Repr. of 1938 ed. 23.00 (ISBN 0-8369-5928-0). Arno.
Devaney, John. Hitler: Mad Dictator of World War II. LC 77-21057. (Illus.). (gr. 6-8). 1978. 8.95 (ISBN 0-399-20627-2). Putnam.
Dutch, Oswald, pseud. Hitler's Twelve Apostles. facsimile ed. LC 75-93333. (Essay Index Reprint Ser). 1940. 17.00 (ISBN 0-8369-1286-1). Arno.
Ebenstein, William. The Nazi State. 1973. lib. bdg. 20.00x (ISBN 0-374-92463-5). Octagon.
Germany Speaks. LC 70-180400. Repr. of 1938 ed. 28.00 (ISBN 0-404-56124-1). AMS Pr.
Goering, H. W. Political Testament of Hermann Goering. Blood-Ryan, H. W., tr. LC 71-180403. Repr. of 1939 ed. 21.00 (ISBN 0-404-56127-6). AMS Pr.
Goldston, Robert. The Life & Death of Nazi Germany. 1978. pap. 2.25 (ISBN 0-449-30830-8, Prem). Fawcett.
--Life & Death of Nazi Germany. LC 66-29906. (gr. 7 up). 7.95 (ISBN 0-672-50354-9). Bobbs.
Harriman, Helga H. Slovenia Under Nazi Occupation, Nineteen Forty-One to Nineteen Forty-Five. LC 76-151284. 94p. 1977. 6.00 (ISBN 0-686-28385-6). Studia Slovenica.
Heydecker, Joe & Leeb, Johannes. The Nuremberg Trail. LC 75-9111. 398p. 1975. Repr. of 1962 ed. lib. bdg. 24.25x (ISBN 0-8371-8131-3, HENT). Greenwood.
Hilberg, Raul. The Destruction of European Jews. LC 61-7931. 800p. 1979. pap. 9.50 (ISBN 0-06-090660-X, CN 660, CN). Har-Row.
Huxley, Julian S. Democracy Marches. LC 75-117813. (Essay Index Reprint Ser). 1941. 15.00 (ISBN 0-8369-1757-X). Arno.
Irving, David. Hitler's War. 1977. 17.50 (ISBN 0-670-37412-1). Viking Pr.
Lichtenberger, Henri. Third Reich. Pinson, Koppel S., tr. LC 73-102249. (Select Bibliographies Reprint Ser). 1937. 29.00 (ISBN 0-8369-5134-4). Arno.
Mosse, George L. The Crisis of German Ideology: Intellectual Origins of the Third Reich. LC 78-19126. viii, 373p. 1981. Repr. of 1964 ed. 27.50x (ISBN 0-86527-036-8). Fertig.
Nawyn, William. American Protestantism's Response to Germany's Jews & Refugees, 1933-1941. Berkhofer, Robert, ed. LC 81-7552. (Studies in American History & Culture: No. 30). 1981. write for info. (ISBN 0-8357-1208-7, Pub. by UMI Res Pr). Univ Microfilms.
Prittie, Terence. The Velvet Chancellors: A History of Post-War Germany. (Illus.). 286p. 1981. text ed. 24.50x (ISBN 0-8419-6750-4). Holmes & Meier.
Rauschning, Hermann. Men of Chaos. facsimile ed. LC 71-167405. (Essay Index Reprint Ser). Repr. of 1942 ed. 21.00 (ISBN 0-8369-2471-1). Arno.
Reitlinger, Gerald. SS: Alibi of a Nation. 1981. 17.50 (ISBN 0-13-839936-0). P-H.
Remak, Joachim, ed. Nazi Years: A Documentary History. LC 69-11359. 1969. pap. text ed. 3.95 (ISBN 0-13-610535-1, S195, Spec). P-H.
Ritter, Gerhard. German Resistance. facs. ed. Clark, R. T., tr. LC 74-124253. (Select Bibliographies Reprint Ser). 1958. 20.00 (ISBN 0-8369-5441-6). Arno.
Rubin, Arnold P. Evil That Men Do: The Story of the Nazis. LC 77-2272. 224p. (YA) (gr. 7 up). 1981. PLB 10.79 (ISBN 0-671-32852-2). Messner.
Schmokel, Wolfe W. Dream of Empire: German Colonialism, 1919-1945. LC 80-15400. (Yale Historical Publications: Miscellany 78). xiv, 204p. 1980. Repr. of 1964 ed. lib. bdg. 22.50x (ISBN 0-313-22437-4, SCDE). Greenwood.
Schuman, Frederick L. The Nazi Dictatorship: A Study in Social Pathology & the Politics of Fascism. Repr. of 1936 ed. 32.50 (ISBN 0-404-56403-8). AMS Pr.
Speer, Albert. Inside the Third Reich: Memoirs of Albert Speer. (Illus.). 1970. 24.95 (ISBN 0-02-612820-9). Macmillan.
Stachura, Peter, ed. The Shaping of the Nazi State. LC 77-10038. 1978. text ed. 20.00x (ISBN 0-06-496492-2). B&N.
Thyssen, Fritz. I Paid Hitler. LC 71-153243. 1971. Repr. of 1941 ed. 14.00 (ISBN 0-8046-1553-5). Kennikat.
Unger, A. L. The Totalitarian Party. LC 73-93786. (International Studies). 290p. 1974. 29.50 (ISBN 0-521-20427-5). Cambridge U Pr.
U. S. Chief of Counsel for the Prosecution of Axis Criminality, 11 vols. LC 70-180435. Repr. of 1948 ed. 57.00 ea.; Set. 620.00 (ISBN 0-404-56180-2). AMS Pr.
Von Hassel, Ulrich. The Von Hassell Diaries, 1938-1944. LC 74-110828. xiv, 400p. Repr. of 1947 ed. lib. bdg. 18.00x (ISBN 0-8371-3228-2, HADI). Greenwood.
Wahle, Kent O. W. Don't Forget, Don't Forgive, Don't Hate. 1981. 6.95 (ISBN 0-533-04495-2). Vantage.
Wolfe, Burton H. Hitler & the Nazis. (gr. 7 up). 1970. PLB 5.49 (ISBN 0-399-60261-5). Putnam.

GERMANY–POLITICS AND GOVERNMENT–1945-

see also Denazification

Almond, Gabriel A., ed. Struggle for Democracy in Germany. LC 65-17874. 1965. Repr. of 1949 ed. 9.50 (ISBN 0-8462-0596-3). Russell.
Baker, Kendall L., et al. Germany Transformed: Political Culture & the New Politics. LC 80-18244. (Illus.). 384p. 1981. text ed. 25.00 (ISBN 0-674-35315-3). Harvard U Pr.
Baylis, Thomas A. The Technical Intelligentsia & the East German Elite: Legitimacy & Social Change in Mature Communism. LC 72-95306. (Illus.). 1974. 24.50x (ISBN 0-520-02395-1). U of Cal Pr.
Dahrendorf, Ralf. Society & Democracy in Germany. 1979. pap. 6.95 (ISBN 0-393-00953-X). Norton.
Dulles, Eleanor L. One Germany or Two: The Struggle at the Heart of Europe. LC 70-96725. (Publications Ser.: No. 86). 1970. 10.95 (ISBN 0-8179-1861-2). Hoover Inst Pr.
Erdstein, Erich & Bean, Barbara. Inside the Fourth Reich. pap. 1.95 (ISBN 0-515-04897-6). Jove Pubns.
Fraenkel, Ernst. Dual State. LC 78-86276. 1969. Repr. of 1941 ed. lib. bdg. 14.00x (ISBN 0-374-92831-2). Octagon.
Kaase, Max & Von Beyme, Klaus, eds. Elections & Parties. LC 78-63119. (German Political Studies: Vol. 3). 322p. 1979. 22.50 (ISBN 0-8039-9888-0); pap. 12.50 (ISBN 0-8039-9889-9). Sage.
Kim, Youn-Soo. Korea & Germany: The Status & Future Prospects of Divided Nations. Bussen, Friedrich, ed. (Monograph of the German Korean-Studies Group: No. I). (Orig.). 1979. pap. text ed. 15.00x (ISBN 0-685-97140-6). Paragon.
Litchfield, Edward H., et al. Governing Postwar Germany, 2 Vols. LC 78-153226. 1971. Repr. of 1953 ed. Set. 35.00x (ISBN 0-8046-1536-5). Kennikat.
Poulantzas, Nicos. Fascism & Dictatorship. 1980. pap. 7.95. (ISBN 0-86091-716-9, Pub. by Verso). Schocken.
Richardson, James L. Germany & the Atlantic Alliance: The Interaction of Strategy & Politics. LC 66-13184. (Center for International Affairs Ser). 1966. 20.00x (ISBN 0-674-35200-9). Harvard U Pr.
Wallenberg, Hans. Report on Democratic Institutions in Germany. LC 78-27612. 1979. Repr. of 1956 ed. lib. bdg. 15.00 (ISBN 0-313-20917-0, WADI). Greenwood.

GERMANY–POPULATION

Knodel, John E. Decline of Fertility in Germany, 1871-1939. LC 72-9944. (Office of Population Research Ser). 320p. 1974. 22.50 (ISBN 0-691-09359-8). Princeton U Pr.
Koehl, Robert. R K F D V: German Resettlement & Population Policy, 1939-1945: A History of the Reich Commission for the Strengthening of Germandom. LC 57-8625. (Historical Monographs Ser: No. 31). 1957. 14.00x (ISBN 0-674-77326-8). Harvard U Pr.
Wild, Trevor. West Germany: A Geography of Its People. LC 79-55698. (Illus.). 1980. text ed. 22.50x (ISBN 0-06-497658-0). B&N.

GERMANY–RACE QUESTION

De Graziani, Vincenzo G. The Franco-German Coalition & the Emergence of a New International Superpower: Its Effects Upon the Future Course of History. (Illus.). 1979. deluxe ed. 55.75 (ISBN 0-930008-31-6). Inst Econ Pol.
Hillel, Marc & Henry, Clarissa. Of Pure Blood. LC 76-8505. 1977. 10.00 (ISBN 0-07-028895-X, GB). McGraw.
Komjathy, Anthony T. & Stockwell, Rebecca S. German Minorities & the Third Reich: Ethnic Germans of East Central Europe Between the Wars. LC 79-26520. 1980. text ed. 26.50x (ISBN 0-8419-0540-1). Holmes & Meier.
Tenenbaum, Joseph. Race & Reich: The Story of an Epoch. LC 76-8503. (Illus.). 1976. Repr. of 1956 ed. lib. bdg. 35.25x (ISBN 0-8371-8857-1, TERR). Greenwood.

GERMANY–RELATIONS (GENERAL) WITH FOREIGN COUNTRIES

Connors, Michael. Dealing in Hate. 40p. Date not set. pap. 2.50 (ISBN 0-911038-55-8). Inst Hist Rev.
Davis, Garold N. German Thought & Culture in England, 1700-1770. (Studies in Comparative Literature Ser.: No. 47). 1969. 10.50x (ISBN 0-8078-7047-1). U of NC Pr.
Farguharson, J. B. & Holt, S. C. Europe from Below: An Assessment of Franco-German Popular Contacts. LC 75-591. 224p. 1975. 19.95 (ISBN 0-312-26915-3). St Martin.
Haines, George. German Influence Upon English Education and Science, 1800-1866. LC 57-8607. (Connecticut College Monograph: No. 6). 1957. 3.50 (ISBN 0-686-11477-9). Conn Coll Bkshp.
Hammer, Carl, Jr., ed. Studies in German Literature. LC 63-9645. (University Studies, Humanities Ser.: Vol. 13). 1963. pap. 9.95x (ISBN 0-8071-0520-1). La State U Pr.
Schieber, Clara E. Transformation of American Sentiment Toward Germany, 1870-1914. LC 72-85006. xvi, 294p. 1973. Repr. of 1923 ed. 15.00 (ISBN 0-8462-1707-4). Russell.
Willis, F. Roy. France, Germany, & the New Europe, 1945-1967. rev. ed. 1968. 25.00x (ISBN 0-8047-0241-1). Stanford U Pr.

GERMANY–RELIGION

Arsen'ev, Nicolai S. We Beheld His Glory. Ewer, Mary A., tr. LC 76-113545. Repr. of 1936 ed. 18.00 (ISBN 0-404-00407-5). AMS Pr.
Chandler, Albert R. Rosenberg's Nazi Myth. LC 69-10073. 1969. Repr. of 1945 ed. lib. bdg. 15.00x (ISBN 0-8371-0038-0, CHNM). Greenwood.
Cochrane, Arthur C. The Church's Confession Under Hitler. 2nd ed. LC 76-57655. (Pittsburgh Reprint Ser.: No. 4). 1977. pap. text ed. 8.50 (ISBN 0-915138-28-X). Pickwick.
Duncan-Jones, Arthur S. Struggle for Religious Freedom in Germany. LC 72-136064. 1971. Repr. of 1938 ed. lib. bdg. 14.75x (ISBN 0-8371-5214-3, DURF). Greenwood.
Frey, Arthur. Cross & Swastika, the Ordeal of the German Church. McNab, J. Strathearn, tr. LC 78-63668. (Studies in Fascism: Ideology & Practice). Repr. of 1938 ed. 24.50 (ISBN 0-404-16526-5). AMS Pr.
Freytag, Justus & Ozaki, Kenji. Nominal Christianity: Studies of Church & People in Hamburg. (World Council of Churches Studies in Mission). 1970. pap. 3.50 (ISBN 0-377-82011-3). Friend Pr.
Herman, Stewart W. It's Your Souls We Want. LC 72-180406. Repr. of 1943 ed. 24.50 (ISBN 0-404-56130-6). AMS Pr.
Kieckhefer, Richard. Repression of Heresy in Medieval Germany. LC 78-65112. (The Middle Ages Ser.). 1979. 16.00x (ISBN 0-8122-7758-9). U of Pa Pr.
Krausen, Edgard. Germania Sacra, New Series II: Bistuemer der Kirchenprovinz Salzburg. 1977. 97.50x (ISBN 3-11-006826-5). De Gruyter.
Loader, Jamer A. Polar Structures in the Book of Qohelet. (Beihefte aur Zeitschrift fuer die alttestamentliche Wissenschaft). 150p. 1979. text ed. 34.50x (ISBN 3-11-007636-5). De Gruyter.

Power, Michael. Religion in the Reich. LC 78-63706. (Studies in Fascism: Ideology & Practice). 1979. Repr. of 1939 ed. 24.00 (ISBN 0-404-16976-7). AMS Pr.

Smith, Clifford N. Nineteenth-Century Emigration of "Old Lutherans" from Eastern Germany (Mainly Pomerania & Lower Silesia) to Australia, Canada, & the United States. (German-American Genealogical Research Monograph: No. 7). 1979. pap. 12.50 (ISBN 0-915162-06-7). Westland Pubns.

Theologica Germanica. 1981. 20.00x (ISBN 0-7224-0006-3, Pub. by Watkins England). State Mutual Bk.

Trillhaas, Wolfgang. Schleiermachers Predigt. 2nd ed. (Theologische Bibliothek Toepelmann, Vol. 28). 1975. 26.50x (ISBN 3-11-005739-5). De Gruyter.

Viehmeyer, L. Allen. Tumultuous Years - Schwenkfelder Chronicles Fifteen Eighty to Seventeen Fifty: The Reports of Martin John, Jr. & Balthazar Hoffmann. 157p. (Orig.). 1980. pap. write for info. (ISBN 0-935980-00-8). Schwenkfelder Lib.

Walther, Wilhelm. Deutsche Bibelubersetzung Des Mittelalters. (Ger). 1971. Repr. of 1892 ed. 40.00 (ISBN 0-403-00788-7). Scholarly.

GERMANY–SECRET POLICE

Aronson, Shlomo. The Beginnings of the Gestapo System. 80p. 1969. casebound 5.95 (ISBN 0-87855-203-0). Transaction Bks.

Cobler, Sebastian. A Policeman's Utopia: An Interview with the Director of the West German FBI, with an Essay by Hans Magnus Enzensberger. Taubes, Tonia & Wilkins, Sophie, trs. from Ger. (Orig.). 1981. pap. 4.95 (ISBN 0-89396-044-6). Urizen Bks.

Crankshaw, Edward. Gestapo: Instrument of Tyranny. LC 79-21687. Repr. of 1956 ed. 12.95 (ISBN 0-89201-086-X). Zenger Pub.

Elgey, Georgette. The Open Window. Underwood, James, tr. from Fr. (Illus.). 212p. 1974. 15.00x (ISBN 0-7130-0122-4, Pub. by Woburn Pr England). Biblio Dist.

Reitlinger, Gerald. SS: Alibi of a Nation. LC 79-21727. Repr. of 1957 ed. 19.50 (ISBN 0-89201-087-8). Zenger Pub.

Stieber, Wilhelm J. The Chancellor's Spy: The Revelations of the Chief of Bismarck's Secret Service. Van Heurck, Jan, tr. from German. LC 79-52090. Orig. Title: Spion Des Kanzlers. 272p. 1981. 17.50 (ISBN 0-394-50869-6, GP 839). Grove.

Sydnor, Charles W. Soldiers of Destruction: The SS Death's Head Division, LC 76-56688. 1977. text ed. 28.50 (ISBN 0-691-05255-7); pap. text ed. 9.95 (ISBN 0-691-10075-6). Princeton U Pr.

GERMANY–SOCIAL CONDITIONS

Adorno, Theodore. Positivist Dispute in German Sociology. 1981. pap. text ed. 17.50x (ISBN 0-435-82656-5). Heinemann Ed.

Bloch, Ernst, et al. Aesthetics & Politics. 1979. 19.25 (ISBN 0-902308-38-6, Pub. by NLB). Schocken.

Bohme, Helmut. An Introduction to the Social & Economic History of Germany. Lee, W. R., tr. from Ger. LC 78-18913. 1978. 22.50 (ISBN 0-312-43315-8). St Martin.

Bramsted, Ernest. Aristocracy & the Middle-Classes in Germany: Social Types in German Literature, 1830-1900. rev. ed. 1964. 12.50x (ISBN 0-226-07106-5). U of Chicago Pr.

--Aristocracy & the Middle-Classes in Germany: Social Types in German Literature, 1830-1900. rev. ed. LC 64-15031. (Orig.). 1964. pap. 2.95 (ISBN 0-226-07107-3, P163, Phoen). U of Chicago Pr.

Bruck, Werner F. Social & Economic History of Germany from William the Second to Hitler, 1888-1938: A Comparative Study. LC 62-13828. 1962. Repr. of 1938 ed. 16.00 (ISBN 0-8462-0141-0). Russell.

Cunningham, Charles. Germany Today & Tomorrow. LC 70-180396. Repr. of 1936 ed. 19.00 (ISBN 0-404-56117-9). AMS Pr.

Dahrendorf, Ralf. Society & Democracy in Germany. 1979. pap. 6.95 (ISBN 0-393-00953-X). Norton.

Danton, George H. Germany Ten Years After. facsimile ed. LC 79-150180. (Select Bibliographies Reprint Ser). Repr. of 1928 ed. 18.00 (ISBN 0-8369-5693-1). Arno.

DEVINDEX: Nineteen Seventy-Seven. 1979. pap. 10.00 (ISBN 0-88936-195-9, IDRC119, IDRC). Unipub.

Engels, Frederick. Peasant War in Germany. LC 66-21949. (Illus.). 1966. pap. 1.95 (ISBN 0-7178-0152-7). Intl Pub Co.

Engels, Friedrich. The German Revolutions. Incl. The Peasant War in Germany; Germany: Revolution & Counter-Revolution. LC 67-15314. 256p. 1967. pap. 2.95 (ISBN 0-226-20869-9, P256, Phoen). U of Chicago Pr.

--German Revolutions: The Peasant War in Germany. L., intro. by. Incl. Germany: Revolution & Counter-Revolution. LC 67-15314. 1967. 8.75x (ISBN 0-226-20868-0). U of Chicago Pr.

Guillebaud, C. W. The Social Policy of Nazi Germany. LC 71-80553. 1971. Repr. 16.50 (ISBN 0-86527-183-6). Fertig.

Koch, H. W. The Hitler Youth: Origins & Development Nineteen Twenty-Two to Nineteen Twenty-Four. (Illus.). 1975. 21.00 (ISBN 0-8464-0986-0). Beekman Pubs.

Krejci, Jaroslav. Social Structure in Divided Germany: A Contribution to the Comparative Analysis of Social Systems. LC 76-1338. 192p. 1976. 18.95 (ISBN 0-312-73535-9). St Martin.

Mayer, Milton. They Thought They Were Free: The Germans 1933-45. 2nd ed. LC 55-5137. 1966. pap. 5.95 (ISBN 0-226-51192-8, P222, Phoen). U of Chicago Pr.

Mayhew, Henry. German Life & Manners As Seen in Saxony at the Present Day, 2 vols. LC 77-87726. Repr. of 1864 ed. Set. 82.50 (ISBN 0-404-16520-6). AMS Pr.

Pascal, Roy. Social Basis of the German Reformation: Martin Luther & His Times. LC 68-30539. Repr. of 1933 ed. 15.000 (ISBN 0-678-00549-4). Kelley.

Rohr, Donald G. Origins of Social Liberalism in Germany. LC 63-20914. 1963. 8.50x (ISBN 0-226-72412-3). U of Chicago Pr.

Sagarra, Eda. A Social History of Germany 1648-1914. LC 77-24201. 1978. text ed. 45.00x (ISBN 0-8419-0332-8). Holmes & Meier.

Schaber, Will, ed. Weinberg der Freiheit. Date not set. 12.00 (ISBN 0-8044-2763-1). Ungar.

Schapiro, Jacob S. Social Reform & the Reformation. LC 74-127456. (Columbia University Studies in the Social Sciences: No. 90). 1970. Repr. of 1909 ed. 16.50 (ISBN 0-404-51090-6). AMS Pr.

Shanahan, William O. German Protestants Face the Social Question: The Conservative Phase, 1815-1871. 1954. 12.95x (ISBN 0-268-00110-3). U of Notre Dame Pr.

Willey, Thomas E. Back to Kant: The Revival of Kantianism in German Social & Historical Thought, 1860-1914. LC 77-29215. 1978. text ed. 17.95x (ISBN 0-8143-1590-9). Wayne St U Pr.

GERMANY–SOCIAL LIFE AND CUSTOMS

Andrews, Peter, ed. Christmas in Germany. LC 74-83569. (Round the World Christmas Program Ser.). (Illus.). 1974. 7.95 (ISBN 0-7166-2000-6). World Bk-Childcraft.

Bax, E. Belfort. The Social Side of the Reformation in Germany, 3 vols. Incl. Vol. 1. German Society at the Close of the Middle Ages. LC 67-25997. 276p. Repr. of 1894 ed. lib. bdg. 12.50x (ISBN 0-678-00312-2); Vol. 2. The Peasants' War in Germany 1525-1526. LC 68-57371. 367p. Repr. of 1899 ed. lib. bdg. 9.25x (ISBN 0-678-00445-5); Vol. 3. The Rise & Fall of the Anapabtists. LC 75-101125. 407p. Repr. of 1903 ed. lib. bdg. 15.00x (ISBN 0-678-00593-1). lib. bdg. 37.50x set (ISBN 0-678-00772-1). Kelley.

Bruford, Walter H. Germany in the Eighteenth Century. 1935. 38.50 (ISBN 0-521-04354-9); pap. 11.50x (ISBN 0-521-09259-0, 259). Cambridge U Pr.

Dahrendorf, Ralf. Society & Democracy in Germany. LC 79-15142. 1980. Repr. of 1969 ed. lib. bdg. 33.50x (ISBN 0-313-22027-1, DASO). Greenwood.

Dawson, William H. German Life in Town & Country. 1977. Repr. 35.00 (ISBN 0-403-08061-4). Scholarly.

Mayhew, Henry. German Life & Manners As Seen in Saxony at the Present Day, 2 vols. LC 77-87726. Repr. of 1864 ed. Set. 82.50 (ISBN 0-404-16520-6). AMS Pr.

Nurge, Ethel. Blue Light in the Village: Daily Life in a German Village in 1965-66. LC 77-10296. 1977. pap. 15.00 (ISBN 0-8357-0264-2, SS-00039). Univ Microfilms.

Prawer, S. S., et al, eds. Essays in German Language, Culture & Society. 244p. 1969. 50.00x (ISBN 0-85457-036-5, Pub. by Inst Germanic Stud England). State Mutual Bk.

Rippley, La Vern. Of German Ways. LC 75-76194. (Heritage Bks.). (Illus.). 1970. 8.95 (ISBN 0-87518-013-2). Dillon.

Rippley, Lavern. Of German Ways. (BN 4000 Ser.). 310p. 1980. pap. 4.95 (ISBN 0-06-464036-1). Har-Row.

Russ, Jennifer. Customs & Festivals in Germany. (Illus.). 1980. text ed. write for info. (ISBN 0-85496-365-0). Humanities.

Saffenreuther, Elfriede & Giegerich, Artur. The Giegerich Chronicle: A Geneological Study in the History & Folk Life of the Odenwald. LC 80-27990. 1981. 24.35 (ISBN 0-8357-0578-1, SS-00148). Univ Microfilms.

Schad, Susanne P. Empirical Social Research in Weimar-Germany. LC 72-93157. (International Social Science Council Publications Ser: No. 15). 155p. 1972. text ed. 25.00x (ISBN 90-2797-166-8). Mouton.

Spicker, Friedemann. Deutsche Wanderer -, Vagabunden - und Vagantenlyrik in Den Jahren 1910 Bis 1933. (Quellen und Forschungen Zur Sprachund Kulturgeschichte der Germanischen Voelker, N. F.). 1976. text ed. 61.00x (ISBN 3-11-004936-8). De Gruyter.

Tucholsky, Kurt. Deutschland, Deutschland, uber alles: A Picture Book. Halley, Anne, tr. LC 77-181360. (Illus.). 256p. 1972. 12.50x (ISBN 0-87023-038-7). U of Mass Pr.

GERMANY–STATISTICS

Central Statistical Board, ed. Statistical Pocketbook of the German Democratic Republic 1979. LC 63-47828. (Illus.). 144p. 1979. 5.00x (ISBN 0-8002-2245-8). Intl Pubns Serv.

GERMANY, DEMOCRATIC REPUBLIC OF

see Germany, East

GERMANY, EAST

Here are entered works on the present Democratic Republic, and works on the eastern part of the former jurisdiction, Germany.

Agee, Joel. Twelve Years: An American Boyhood in East Germany. 324p. 1981. 14.95 (ISBN 0-374-27958-6). FS&G.

Baring, Arnulf M. Uprising in East Germany: June 17, 1953. Onn, Gerald, tr. from Ger. LC 70-38284. 208p. 1972. Repr. of 1965 ed. 16.50x (ISBN 0-8014-0703-6). Cornell U Pr.

Cultural Policy in the German Democratic Republic. (Studies & Documents on Cultural Policies Ser.). (Illus.). 26p. 1976. pap. 4.00 (ISBN 92-3-101291-6, U120, UNESCO). Unipub.

Hanhardt, Arthur M., Jr. German Democratic Republic. LC 68-16842. (Integration & Community Building in Eastern Europe Ser: No. 1). (Illus.). 137p. (Orig.). 1968. 10.50x (ISBN 0-8018-0252-0); pap. 2.45x (ISBN 0-8018-0253-9, JHEE1). Johns Hopkins.

Harpprecht, Klaus. East German Rising, Seventeenth June 1953. Wheeler, Charles, tr. LC 78-14103. (Illus.). 1979. Repr. of 1957 ed. 18.50 (ISBN 0-88355-797-5). Hyperion Conn.

Herspring, Dale R. East German Civil-Military Relations: The Impact of Technology, 1949-1972. LC 73-11035. (Special Studies in International Politics & Government). 1973. 27.50x (ISBN 0-275-28753-X). Irvington.

Honecker, Erich. The GDR: Pillar of Peace & Socialism. 1979. text ed. 12.50 (ISBN 0-7178-0561-1); pap. 4.25 (ISBN 0-7178-0558-1). Intl Pub Co.

International Symposium on the German Democratic Republic, 6th. Studies in GDR Culture & Society: Proceedings. Gerber, Margy, et al, eds. LC 80-6255. 324p. (Orig.). 1981. lib. bdg. 23.50 (ISBN 0-8191-1735-8); pap. text ed. 12.75 (ISBN 0-8191-1736-6). U Pr of Amer.

Krisch, Henry. The German Democratic Republic: A Profile. (Nations of Contemporary Eastern Europe Ser.). 128p. 1982. lib. bdg. 16.50x (ISBN 0-89158-850-7). Westview.

Leptin, Gert & Melzer, Manfred. Economic Reform in East German Industry. Clarke, Roger A., tr. LC 77-30589. (Economic Reforms in East European Industry Ser.). (Illus.). 1979. 45.00x (ISBN 0-19-215346-3). Oxford U Pr.

Ludz, Peter C., ed. Changing Party Elite in East Germany. 1972. 19.95x (ISBN 0-262-12053-4). MIT Pr.

Mellor, Roy E. The Two Germanies: A Modern Geography. 1978. text ed. 15.70 (ISBN 0-06-318066-9, IntlDept, IntlDept). Har-Row.

Mellor, Roy E. H. The Two Germanies: A Modern Geography. (Illus.). 1978. text ed. 22.50x (ISBN 0-06-494778-5); pap. 9.95x (ISBN 0-06-494779-3). B&N.

Mensh, Elaine & Mensh, Harry. Behind the Scenes in Two Worlds: Life & Theatre in the German Democratic Republic & the U.S.A. LC 77-19314. 1978. 15.00 (ISBN 0-7178-0497-6); pap. 4.95 (ISBN 0-7178-0489-5). Intl Pub Co.

Nagel Staff. Nagel Guide to the German Democratic Republic. (Nagel Encyclopedia Guides). Date not set. cancelled (ISBN 0-88254-246-X). Hippocrene Bks.

Nettl, J. P. The Eastern Zone & Soviet Policy in Germany 1945-1950. 1977. Repr. of 1951 ed. lib. bdg. 19.00x (ISBN 0-374-96051-8). Octagon.

Schneider, Eberhard. The G. D. R. The History, Politics, Economy & Society of East Germany. 1978. 14.95x (ISBN 0-312-31491-4). St Martin.

Steele, Jonathan. Inside East Germany: The State That Came in from the Cold. 1977. 12.95 (ISBN 0-916354-73-3); pap. 4.95 (ISBN 0-916354-74-1). Urizen Bks.

Wettig, Gerhard. Community & Conflict in the Socialist Camp 1965-1972: The Soviet Union, the GDR, & the German Problem. LC 75-6048. 174p. 1975. 21.50 (ISBN 0-312-15295-7). St Martin.

Whetten, Lawrence L. Germany East & West: Conflicts, Collaboration & Confrontation. LC 79-3713. 244p. 1981. 17.50x (ISBN 0-8147-9193-X). NYU Pr.

GERMANY, EAST–ECONOMIC CONDITIONS

Ludz, Peter C. The German Democratic Republic from the Sixties to the Seventies: A Socio-Political Analysis. (Harvard University. Center for International Affairs. Occasional Papers in International Affairs: No. 26). Repr. of 1970 ed. 11.50 (ISBN 0-404-54626-9). AMS Pr.

GERMANY, EAST–FICTION

Tate, D. The East German Novel: Identity, Community & Continuity, 1945, 1980. 1982. 60.00x (ISBN 0-86127-211-0, Pub. by Avebury Pub England). State Mutual Bk.

GERMANY, EAST–POLITICS AND GOVERNMENT

Baring, Arnulf M. Uprising in East Germany: June 17, 1953. Onn, Gerald, tr. from Ger. LC 70-38284. 208p. 1972. Repr. of 1965 ed. 16.50x (ISBN 0-8014-0703-6). Cornell U Pr.

Croan, Melvin. East Germany: The Soviet Connection. LC 76-21138. (The Washington Papers: No. 36). 72p. 1976. 4.00x (ISBN 0-8039-0656-0). Sage.

Heidenheimer, A. & Kommers, D. P. Governments of Germany. 4th ed. 1975. pap. text ed. 9.50 scp (ISBN 0-690-00808-2, HarpC). Har-Row.

Ludz, Peter C. The German Democratic Republic from the Sixties to the Seventies: A Socio-Political Analysis. (Harvard University. Center for International Affairs. Occasional Papers in International Affairs: No. 26). Repr. of 1970 ed. 11.50 (ISBN 0-404-54626-9). AMS Pr.

Merritt, Anna J. & Merritt, Richard L., eds. Politics, Economics, & Society in the Two Germanies, 1945-75: A Bibliography of English-Language Works. LC 77-26853. 1978. 12.00 (ISBN 0-252-00684-4). U of Ill Pr.

Pittman, Magrit. Encounters in Democracy: A Journalists View of the G.D.R. (Orig.). 1981. pap. write for info. (ISBN 0-7178-0584-0). Intl Pub Co.

Roskin, Michael. Other Governments of Europe: Sweden, Spain, Italy, Yugoslavia, E. Germany. 1977. pap. text ed. 7.95 (ISBN 0-13-642959-9). P-H.

Sontheimer, Kurt & Bleek, Wilhelm. The Government & Politics of East Germany. LC 75-43485. 205p. 1976. 15.95 (ISBN 0-312-34125-3). St Martin.

Viney, Deryck, tr. The East German Army: The Second Power in the Warsaw Pact. rev. ed. (Illus.). 310p. 1981. text ed. 27.50x (ISBN 0-04-355012-6). Allen Unwin.

GERMANY, EASTERN

see Germany, East

GERMANY, FEDERAL REPUBLIC OF

see Germany, West

GERMANY, WEST

Here are entered works on the present Federal Republic, and works on the western part of the former jurisdiction, Germany.

Deutsch, Karl W. Arms Control & the Atlantic Alliance. 167p. 1967. text ed. 8.50 (ISBN 0-471-21140-0, Pub. by Wiley). Krieger.

Golay, John F. Founding of the Federal Republic of Germany. LC 57-11205. (Midway Reprint Ser). 300p. 1974. pap. 11.50x (ISBN 0-226-30083-8). U of Chicago Pr.

Kloss, Gunther. West Germany: An Introduction. LC 75-25564. 180p. 1976. text ed. 31.95 (ISBN 0-470-49357-7). Halsted Pr.

McGeehan, Robert. The German Rearmament Question: American Diplomacy & European Defense After World War Two. LC 79-146009. 295p. 1971. 17.50 (ISBN 0-252-00160-5). U of Ill Pr.

Mellor, Roy E. The Two Germanies: A Modern Geography. 1978. text ed. 15.70 (ISBN 0-06-318066-9, IntlDept, IntlDept). Har-Row.

Merritt, Anna J. & Merritt, Richard L., eds. Politics, Economics, & Society in the Two Germanies, 1945-75: A Bibliography of English-Language Works. LC 77-26853. 1978. 12.00 (ISBN 0-252-00684-4). U of Ill Pr.

Merritt, Richard L. & Merritt, Anna J. West Germany Enters the Seventies. LC 76-155347. (Headline Ser.: No. 205). (Illus.). 1971. pap. 2.00 (ISBN 0-87124-012-2). Foreign Policy.

Tilford, R. B. & Preece, R. J. Federal Germany: Social & Political Order. LC 79-75845. 1969. 7.75 (ISBN 0-8023-1219-5). Dufour.

Whetten, Lawrence L. Germany East & West: Conflicts, Collaboration & Confrontation. LC 79-3713. 244p. 1981. 17.50x (ISBN 0-8147-9193-X). NYU Pr.

Wild, Trevor. West Germany: A Geography of Its People. LC 79-55698. (Illus.). 1980. text ed. 22.50x (ISBN 0-06-497658-0). B&N.

GERMANY, WEST–COMMERCE

Wilhelms, Christian. Market & Marketing in the Federal Republic of Germany: A Manual for Exporters from Developing Countries. 1971. 10.00x (ISBN 3-87895-100-0). Intl Pubns Serv.

GERMANY, WEST–DESCRIPTION AND TRAVEL

Evans, Craig. On Foot Through Europe: A Trail Guide to West Germany. Whitney, Stephen, ed. (Illus.). 384p. 1980. lib. bdg. 10.95 (ISBN 0-933710-09-7); pap. 5.95 (ISBN 0-933710-08-9). Foot Trails.

--A Trail Guide to West Germany. Whitney, Stephen, ed. (On Foot Through Europe Ser.). (Illus.). 384p. 1980. lib. bdg. 10.95 (ISBN 0-933710-09-7); pap. 5.95 (ISBN 0-933710-08-9). Foot Trails.

Institute of Directors Guide to West Germany. pap. 1.95 (ISBN 0-8277-0483-6). British Bk Ctr.

Marsden, Walter. West Germany. 1978. 22.50 (ISBN 0-7134-1087-6). David & Charles.

Nagel Travel Guide to Germany (Federal Republic) 900p. 1974. 52.00 (ISBN 2-8263-0357-0). Hippocrene Bks.

GERMANY, WEST–ECONOMIC CONDITIONS

Arndt, Hans-Joachim. West Germany: Politics of Non-Planning. (National Planning Ser.: No. 8). (Orig.). 1966. pap. 3.95x (ISBN 0-8156-2094-2). Syracuse U Pr.

De Graziani, Vincenzo G. The Franco-German Coalition & the Emergence of a New International Superpower: Its Effects Upon the Future Course of History. (Illus.). 1979. deluxe ed. 55.75 (ISBN 0-930008-31-6). Inst Econ Pol.

Frowen, S. F., et al. Monetary Policy & Economic Activity in West Germany. LC 77-2403. 268p. 1977. 37.50 (ISBN 0-470-99131-3). Krieger.

Hallett, Graham. The Social Economy of West Germany. LC 73-85268. 160p. 1974. 17.95 (ISBN 0-312-73255-4). St Martin.

Johnson, Nevil & Cochrane, Allan. Economic Policy Making by Local Authorities in Britain & West Germany. (The New Local Government Ser.: No. 21). 212p. 1981. text ed. 37.50x (ISBN 0-04-352097-9). Allen Unwin.

Mellor, Roy E. H. The Two Germanies: A Modern Geography. (Illus.). 1978. text ed. 22.50x (ISBN 0-06-494778-5); pap. 9.95x (ISBN 0-06-494779-3). B&N.

Pohl, Reinhard, ed. Handbook of the Economy of the German Democratic Republic. Furtmuller, Lux, tr. from Ger. 366p. 1980. 40.00 (ISBN 0-566-00256-6). Bowker.

Reuss, Frederick G. Fiscal Policy for Growth Without Inflation: The German Experiment. (Goucher College Ser). 335p. 1963. 22.00x (ISBN 0-8018-0553-8). Johns Hopkins.

Saling's Share Guide: Saling Aktienfuehrer 1980. 73rd ed. 1062p. 1979. pap. 50.00x (ISBN 3-8203-0025-2). Intl Pubns Serv.

GERMANY, WEST–FOREIGN RELATIONS

Balabkins, Nicholas. West German Reparations to Israel. LC 70-152724. 1971. 25.00 (ISBN 0-8135-0691-3). Rutgers U Pr.

Deutsch, Karl W. & Edinger, Lewis J. Germany Rejoins the Powers: Mass Opinion Interest Groups & Elites in Contemporary German Foreign Policy. LC 73-4236. 320p. 1973. Repr. of 1959 ed. lib. bdg. 17.00x (ISBN 0-374-92137-7). Octagon.

Griffith, William E. The Ostpolitik of the Federal Republic of Germany. (MIT Studies in Communism, Revisionism, & Revolution Ser.). 1978. 22.50x (ISBN 0-262-07072-3). MIT Pr.

Hanrieder, Wolfram F., ed. West Germany's Foreign Policy: Nineteen Forty-Nine to Nineteen Seventy-Nine. (Special Study in West European Politics & Society). 1979. lib. bdg. 25.75 (ISBN 0-89158-579-6). Westview.

Kohl, Wilfied L. & Basevi, Giorgio. West Germany: A European Global Power. (Illus.). 1980. 17.95 (ISBN 0-669-03162-3). Lexington Bks.

Krippendorff, Ekkehart & Rittberger, Volker, eds. The Foreign Policy of West Germany: Formation & Contents. LC 80-40149. (German Political Studies: Vol. 4). (Illus.). 372p. 1980. 22.50 (ISBN 0-8039-9818-X); pap. 12.50 (ISBN 0-8039-9819-8). Sage.

Mahncke, Dieter. Nukleare Mitwirkung: Die Bundesrepublik Deutschland in der atlantischen Allianz 1954-1970. (Beitraege zur auswaertigen und internationalen Politik 6). xvi, 274p. 1972. 40.00x (ISBN 3-11-001820-9). De Gruyter.

Merkl, Peter H. German Foreign Policies, West & East: On the Threshold of a New European Era. LC 73-92506. (Studies in International & Comparative Politics: No. 3). (Illus.). 232p. 1974. text ed. 20.85 (ISBN 0-87436-133-8). ABC-Clio.

Morgan, Roger. West Germany's Foreign Policy Agenda. LC 78-56333. (The Washington Papers: No. 54). 80p. 1978. pap. 4.00 (ISBN 0-8039-1049-5). Sage.

Schulz, Eberhard, et al. Foreign Policy of the GDR. Stahnke, Arthur A., ed. Vale, Michel, tr. from Ger. Orig. Title: Drei Jahrzehnte Aussenpolitik der DDR. 320p. 1982. 25.00 (ISBN 0-87332-203-7). M E Sharpe.

Survey Research Center. Attitudes Toward American Foreign Policy: West Germany, 1962. 1973. codebook 8.00 (ISBN 0-89138-063-9). ICPSR.

Vogel, Rolf, ed. German Path to Israel. LC 70-88600. 1970. 14.95 (ISBN 0-8023-1229-2). Dufour.

GERMANY, WEST–HISTORY

Gottlieb, Manuel. The German Peace Settlement & the Berlin Crisis. 275p. 1970. 14.95 (ISBN 0-87855-033-X). Transaction Bks.

Pridham, Geoffrey. Christian Democracy in Western Germany. LC 77-9235. 1978. 22.50x (ISBN 0-312-13396-0). St Martin.

Slater, Phil. Origin & Significance of the Frankfurt School: A Marxist Perspective. (International Library of Sociology). 1976. 22.50x (ISBN 0-7100-8438-2). Routledge & Kegan.

GERMANY, WEST–JUVENILE LITERATURE

Fairclough, Chris. Take a Trip to West Germany. (Take a Trip to Ser.). (Illus.). 32p. (gr. 1-3). 1981. lib. bdg. 6.90 (ISBN 0-531-04320-7). Watts.

Kirby, George. Looking at Germany. LC 77-37629. (Looking at Other Countries Ser.). (Illus.). (gr. 4-6). 1972. 8.95 (ISBN 0-397-31337-3, JBL-J). Har-Row.

Morey, George. West Germany. LC 75-44866. (Macdonald Countries). (Illus.). (gr. 7 up). 1976. lib. bdg. 7.95 (ISBN 0-685-73288-6, Pub. by Macdonald Ed). Silver.

Sterling Publishing Company Editors. West Germany in Pictures. LC 67-16018. (Visual Geography Ser). (Illus., Orig.). (gr. 6 up). 1967. PLB 4.99 (ISBN 0-8069-1095-X); pap. 2.95 (ISBN 0-8069-1094-1). Sterling.

GERMANY, WEST–POLITICS AND GOVERNMENT

Ashkenasi, Abraham. Modern German Nationalism. LC 75-33702. 222p. 1976. 14.95 (ISBN 0-470-03492-0). Halsted Pr.

Asopa, D. N. Political System of West Germany: A Study in Party Politics & Parliamentary Process. 292p. 1974. 13.50x (ISBN 0-8002-1812-4). Intl Pubns Serv.

Baumert, Gerhard, et al. German Election Studies, 1961. Hildebrandt, Kai, tr. from Ger. 1975. codebk. 14.00 (ISBN 0-89138-122-8). ICPSR.

Berdes, George R. Up from Ashes: An American Journalist Reports from Germany. 1964. pap. 4.95 (ISBN 0-87462-426-6). Marquette.

Blair, Philip M. Federalism & Judicial Review in West Germany. 356p. 1981. 59.00 (ISBN 0-19-827427-0). Oxford U Pr.

Braunthal, Gerard. The Federation of German Industry in Politics. 409p. 1965. 29.50z (ISBN 0-8014-0052-X). Cornell U Pr.

--The West German Legislative Process: A Case Study of Two Transportation Bills. LC 74-37750. (Illus.). 312p. 1972. 27.50x (ISBN 0-8014-0695-1). Cornell U Pr.

Bunn, Ronald F. German Politics & the Spiegel Affair: A Case Study of the Bonn System. LC 68-21803. 1968. 17.50 (ISBN 0-8071-0335-7). La State U Pr.

Burkett, Tony. Parties & Elections in West Germany: The Search for Stability. LC 75-6051. 200p. 1975. 17.95 (ISBN 0-312-59745-2). St Martin.

Cerny, Karl H., ed. Germany at the Polls: The Bundestag Election of 1976. 1978. pap. 7.25 (ISBN 0-8447-3310-5). Am Enterprise.

Childs, David & Johnson, Jeffrey. West Germany: Politics & Society. 1980. write for info. (ISBN 0-312-86300-4). St Martin.

Edinger, Lewis J. Politics in West Germany. 2nd ed. (Ser. in Comparative Politics). 360p. 1977. pap. 9.95 (ISBN 0-316-21081-1). Little.

Erler, Fritz. Democracy in Germany. LC 65-16683. (Center for International Affairs Ser). 1965. 7.95x (ISBN 0-674-19700-3). Harvard U Pr.

Gimbel, John. The American Occupation of Germany: Politics & the Military, 1945-1949. LC 68-26778. 1968. 17.50x (ISBN 0-8047-0667-0). Stanford U Pr.

Grass, Gunter. Speak Out: Speeches, Open Letters, Commentaries. Manheim, Ralph, tr. LC 69-12035. (Helen & Kurt Wolff Bk). Orig. Title: Ueber das Selbstverstaendliche. 1969. 5.75 (ISBN 0-15-184704-5). HarBraceJ.

Hanrieder, Wolfram & Auton, Graeme P. Foreign Policies of West Germany, France, & Britian. 1980. pap. text ed. 9.95 (ISBN 0-13-326397-5). P-H.

Heidenheimer, A. & Kommers, D. P. Governments of Germany. 4th ed. 1975. pap. text ed. 9.50 scp (ISBN 0-690-00808-2, HarpC). Har-Row.

Hiscocks, Richard. The Adenauer Era. LC 75-35027. 312p. 1976. Repr. of 1966 ed. lib. bdg. 17.50x (ISBN 0-8371-8569-6, HIAE). Greenwood.

Johnson, Nevil. Government in the Federal Republic of Germany: The Executive at Work. LC 73-12759. 232p. 1974. text ed. 16.50 (ISBN 0-08-017699-2). Pergamon.

Kohl, Wilfied L. & Basevi, Giorgio. West Germany: A European Global Power. (Illus.). 1980. 17.95 (ISBN 0-669-03162-3). Lexington Bks.

Kommers, Donald P. Judicial Politics in West Germany: A Study of the Federal Constitutional Court. LC 72-98037. (Sage Ser. on Politics & the Legal Order Ser.: Vol. 5). 320p. 1976. 20.00 (ISBN 0-8039-0125-9). Sage.

Mayntz, Renate & Scharpf, Fritz W. Policy-Making in the German Federal Bureaucracy. LC 74-21862. 180p. 1975. 14.95 (ISBN 0-444-41272-7). Elsevier.

Mellor, Roy E. H. The Two Germanies: A Modern Geography. (Illus.). 1978. text ed. 22.50x (ISBN 0-06-494778-5); pap. 9.95x (ISBN 0-06-494779-3). B&N.

Mierheim, et al. Die Personelle Vermoegensverteilung in der Bundersrepublik Deutschland. 1979. write for info. (ISBN 3-11-007603-9). De Gruyter.

Nagle, John D. The National Democratic Party: Right-Radicalism in the Federal Republic of Germany. LC 78-101340. 1970. 24.00x (ISBN 0-520-01649-1). U of Cal Pr.

Noelle-Neumann, Elisabeth, ed. The Germans: Public Opinions Polls, 1967-1980. rev. ed. LC 81-1075. (Illus.). 552p. 1981. lib. bdg. 35.00 (ISBN 0-313-22490-0, NEG/). Greenwood.

Pollock, James K. Source Materials on the Government & Politics of Germany. 1964. 8.00x (ISBN 0-685-21805-8). Wahr.

Roberts, Geoffrey K. West German Politics. LC 77-185875. 206p. 1972. 10.95 (ISBN 0-8008-8151-6); pap. 5.95 (ISBN 0-8008-8152-4). Taplinger.

Smith, Gordon. Democracy in Western Germany: Parties & Politics in the Federal Republic. LC 79-13243. (Illus.). 1980. text ed. 19.50x (ISBN 0-8419-0522-3); pap. 10.95x (ISBN 0-8419-0528-2). Holmes & Meier.

Sontheimer, Kurt. Government & Politics of West Germany. 1972. text ed. 8.00x (ISBN 0-09-111130-7, Hutchinson U Lib). Humanities.

UNESCO Institut fuer Sozialwissenschaften. Social Bases of West German Politics, 1953. 1974. codebk. 10.00 (ISBN 0-89138-110-4). ICPSR.

Williams, Arthur. Broadcasting & Democracy in West Germany. LC 77-90539. (International & Comparative Broadcasting Ser.). 1978. 15.00x (ISBN 0-87722-111-1). Temple U Pr.

--Broadcasting & Democracy in West Germany. 1976. 19.95x (ISBN 0-8464-0218-1). Beekman Pubs.

GERMANY, WEST–SOCIAL CONDITIONS

Aptheker, Herbert. Early Years of the Republic, 1783-1793. LC 76-40213. (History of the American People: Vol. 3). (Orig.). 1976. pap. 2.75 (ISBN 0-7178-0471-2). Intl Pub Co.

Hallett, Graham. The Social Economy of West Germany. LC 73-85268. 160p. 1974. 17.95 (ISBN 0-312-73255-4). St Martin.

Hearnden, Arthur. Education, Culture & Politics in West Germany. King, Edmanuel J., ed. 153p. 1976. text ed. 21.00 (ISBN 0-08-019916-X); pap. text ed. 10.50 (ISBN 0-08-019915-1). Pergamon.

Hiscocks, Richard. The Adenauer Era. LC 75-35027. 312p. 1976. Repr. of 1966 ed. lib. bdg. 17.50x (ISBN 0-8371-8569-6, HIAE). Greenwood.

Mellor, Roy E. H. The Two Germanies: A Modern Geography. (Illus.). 1978. text ed. 22.50x (ISBN 0-06-494778-5); pap. 9.95x (ISBN 0-06-494779-3). B&N.

Pridham, Geoffrey. Christian Democracy in Western Germany. LC 77-9235. 1978. 22.50x (ISBN 0-312-13396-0). St Martin.

GERMANY, WESTERN

see Germany, West

GERMFREE LIFE

Coates, Marie E. Germ-Free Animal in Research. LC 68-24698. (Illus.). 1968. 46.00 (ISBN 0-12-177150-4). Acad Pr.

Heneghan, James B., ed. Germfree Research: Biological Effects of Gnotobiotic Environments. 1973. 54.50 (ISBN 0-12-340650-1). Acad Pr.

Luckey, Thomas D. Germfree Life & Gnotobiology. 1963. 63.50 (ISBN 0-12-458750-X). Acad Pr.

Mirand, E. A. & Back, N., eds. Germ Free Biology. LC 69-16518. (Advances in Experimental Medicine & Biology Ser.: Vol. 3). 423p. 1969. 42.50 (ISBN 0-306-39003-5, Plenum Pr). Plenum Pub.

Runkle, Robert S. & Phillips, G. Briggs. Microbial Contamination Control Facilities. (Illus.). 1969. 17.95x (ISBN 0-442-15625-1). Van Nos Reinhold.

GERMICIDES

see Disinfection and Disinfectants; Fungicides

GERMINATION

Bewley, D. & Black, M. Physiology & Biochemistry of Seeds in Relation to Germination Vol.1: Germination & Growter. LC 77-7953. (Illus.). 1978. 49.80 (ISBN 0-387-08274-3). Springer-Verlag.

Heslop-Harrison, J. Aspects of the Structure, Cytochemistry & Germination of the Pollen of Rye. LC 79-41655. 1980. 21.00 (ISBN 0-12-344950-2). Acad Pr.

Khan, A. A., ed. The Physiology & Biochemistry of Seed Dormancy & Germination. 1977. 79.00 (ISBN 0-7204-0643-9, North-Holland). Elsevier.

Knapp, Ruediger. Gegenseitige Beeinflussung und Temperatur-Wirkung bei tropischen und subtropischen Pflanzen: Bericht ueber neue experimentelle Untersuchungen an Nutzpflanzen und Arten der spontanen Vegetation. (Illus.). 1967. pap. 6.00 (ISBN 3-7682-0576-2). Lubrecht & Cramer.

Kuchalla, Susan. All About Seeds. LC 81-11480. (Now I Know Ser.). (Illus.). 32p. (gr. k-2). 1982. PLB 7.95 (ISBN 0-89375-658-X); pap. 1.25 (ISBN 0-89375-659-8). Troll Assocs.

Levinson, H. S., et al, eds. Sporulation & Germination. (Illus.). 1981. 24.00 (ISBN 0-914826-35-2). Am Soc Microby.

Mayer, A. M., et al. The Germination of Seeds. 2nd ed. Wareing, P. F. & Galston, A. W., eds. 160p. 1976. text ed. 30.00 (ISBN 0-08-018966-0); pap. text ed. 18.00 (ISBN 0-08-018965-2). Pergamon.

Rubenstein, Irwin, et al, eds. The Plant Seed: Development, Preservation & Germination. 1979. 23.50 (ISBN 0-12-602050-7). Acad Pr.

GERMS

see Bacteria; Bacteriology; Germ Theory of Disease; Micro-Organisms

GERONA, SPAIN (PROVINCE)–DESCRIPTION AND TRAVEL

Clyne, Douglas. Your Guide to the Costa Brava. 2nd ed. LC 65-6617. (Your Guide Ser). 1965. 5.25x (ISBN 0-8002-0790-4). Intl Pubns Serv.

Lujan, Nestor. Costa Brava. LC 66-4510. (Spanish Guide Ser). (Illus.). 1964. 4.50x (ISBN 0-8002-0727-0). Intl Pubns Serv.

GERONIMO, APACHE CHIEF, 1829-1909

Barrett, S. M. Geronimo's Story of His Life. 1981. Repr. lib. bdg. 29.00 (ISBN 0-686-71919-0). Scholarly.

Bloody Trail of Geronimo. 10.00 (ISBN 0-686-74359-8). Westernlore.

Davis, Britton. The Truth About Geronimo. Quaife, M. M., ed. LC 75-37958. (Illus.). xxx, 263p. 1976. 16.95x (ISBN 0-8032-0877-4); pap. 5.25 (ISBN 0-8032-5840-2, BB 622, Bison). U of Nebr Pr.

Debo, Angie. Geronimo: The Man, His Time, His Place. LC 76-13858. (The Civilization of the American Indian Ser: No.142). 1976. 15.95 (ISBN 0-8061-1333-2). U of Okla Pr.

Faulk, Odie B. Geronimo Campaign. LC 72-83042. (Illus.). 1969. 10.95 (ISBN 0-19-500544-9). Oxford U Pr.

Grant, Matthew G. Geronimo. LC 73-12203. 1974. PLB 5.95 (ISBN 0-87191-267-8). Creative Ed.

Syme, Ronald. Geronimo. LC 74-16337. (Illus.). 96p. (gr. 3-7). 1975. 7.25 (ISBN 0-688-22013-4); PLB 6.96 (ISBN 0-688-32013-9). Morrow.

GERONTOLOGY

see Aged; Geriatrics; Old Age

GERRY, ELBRIDGE, 1744-1814

Austin, James T. The Life of Elbridge Gerry, 2 Vols. LC 77-99470. (American Public Figures Ser). 1970. Repr. of 1828 ed. lib. bdg. 69.50 (ISBN 0-306-71841-3). Da Capo.

GERRYMANDER

see also Administrative and Political Divisions; Election Districts; Legislative Bodies; Representative Government and Representation

Griffith, Elmer C. The Rise & Development of the Gerrymander. LC 73-19149. (Politics & People Ser.). 124p. 1974. Repr. 7.00x (ISBN 0-405-05872-1). Arno.

GERSHWIN, GEORGE, 1898-1937

Armitage, Merle. George Gershwin, Man & Legend. facsimile ed. LC 75-117324. (Biography Index Reprint Ser). 1958. 24.00 (ISBN 0-8369-8016-6). Arno.

Bryant, Bernice. George Gershwin: Young Composer. (Childhood of Famous Americans Ser). (Illus.). (gr. 3-7). 3.95 (ISBN 0-672-50065-5). Bobbs.

Ewen, David. George Gershwin: His Journey to Greatness. LC 77-6821. (Illus.). 1977. Repr. of 1970 ed. lib. bdg. 25.00x (ISBN 0-8371-9663-9, EWGG). Greenwood.

Gerber, Irving. George Gershwin: the Music Man. 1979. Set Of 10. 6.75 (ISBN 0-87594-184-2). Book Lab.

Goldberg, Isaac. George Gershwin: A Study in American Music. LC 58-11627. (Illus.). 1958. pap. 5.95 (ISBN 0-8044-6195-3). Ungar.

Jablonski, Edward, intro. by. New York Times Gershwin Years in Song. LC 73-82478. 1973. spiral bdg. 14.95 (ISBN 0-8129-0368-4). Times Bks.

--The New York Times Gershwin Years in Song. LC 73-82478. (Illus.). 328p. 1976. pap. 8.95 (ISBN 0-8129-6267-2). Times Bks.

Kimball, Robert E. & Simon, Alfred E. The Gershwins. LC 73-80749. (Illus.). 1973. 25.00 (ISBN 0-689-10569-X). Atheneum.

Rosenberg, Deena. The Brothers Gershwin. (Illus.). 1979. 15.00 (ISBN 0-394-42875-7). Random.
Rushmore, Robert. Life of George Gershwin. (Illus.). (gr. 9 up). 1968. 6.95 (ISBN 0-02-777890-8, CCPr). Macmillan.
Schwartz, Charles. George Gershwin: A Selective Bibliography & Discography. LC 74-75913. (Bibliographies in American Music: No. 1). 1974. 8.50 (ISBN 0-911772-59-6). Info Coord.
--Gershwin, His Life & Music. (Paperbacks Ser.). 1979. pap. 7.95 (ISBN 0-306-80096-9). Da Capo.

GERSHWIN, IRA, 1896-
Jablonski, Edward, intro. by. The New York Times Gershwin Years in Song. LC 73-82478. (Illus.). 328p. 1976. pap. 8.95 (ISBN 0-8129-6267-2). Times Bks.
Kimball, Robert E. & Simon, Alfred E. The Gershwins. LC 73-80749. (Illus.). 1973. 25.00 (ISBN 0-689-10569-X). Atheneum.
Rosenberg, Deena. The Brothers Gershwin. (Illus.). 1979. 15.00 (ISBN 0-394-42875-7). Random.

GERSON, JOANNES, 1363-1429
Gerson, Joannes. The Ad Deum Vadit of Jean Gerson. Repr. of 1917 ed. 9.50 (ISBN 0-384-18210-0). Johnson Repr.
Schwab, Johann B. Johannes Gerson, Professor der Theologie und Kanzler De Universitat Paris, 2 Vols. 1967. Repr. of 1858 ed. Set. 57.50 (ISBN 0-8337-3181-5). B Franklin.
Yule, G. Udny. Statistical Study of Literary Vocabulary. 1968. Repr. of 1944 ed. 19.50 (ISBN 0-208-00689-3, Archon). Shoe String.

GESENIUS, FRIEDRICH HEINRICH WILHELM, 1786-1842
Miller, Edward F. Influence of Gesenius on Hebrew Lexicography. LC 28-3581. (Columbia University. Contributions to Oriental History & Philology: No. 11). Repr. of 1927 ed. 14.00 (ISBN 0-404-50541-4). AMS Pr.

GESTA FRANCORUM ET ALIORUM HIEROSOLYMITANORUM
Gavigan, John J. Syntax of the Gesta Francorum. 1943. pap. 6.00 (ISBN 0-527-00783-8). Kraus Repr.

GESTA ROMANORUM
Douce, Francis. Illustrations of Shakespeare & of Ancient Manners. LC 68-58465. (Research & Source Ser.: No. 329). (Illus.). 1969. Repr. of 1839 ed. 21.50 (ISBN 0-8337-0892-9). B Franklin.

GESTALT PSYCHOLOGY
see also Bender-Gestalt Test
Diack, Hunter. Reading & the Psychology of Perception. LC 77-138220. (Illus.). 155p. 1972. Repr. of 1960 ed. lib. bdg. 15.00x (ISBN 0-8371-5577-0, DIRP). Greenwood.
Dye, H. Allan & Hackney, Harold. Gestalt Approaches to Counseling. 1975. pap. 2.40 (ISBN 0-395-20041-5). HM.
Ellis, Willis D., ed. Source Book of Gestalt Psychology. 1967. text ed. 31.25x (ISBN 0-7100-6115-3). Humanities.
Feder, Bud & Ronall, Ruth E., eds. Beyond the Hot Seat: Gestalt Approaches to Group. LC 79-20648. 1980. 17.50 (ISBN 0-87630-205-3). Brunner-Mazel.
Hamlyn, D. W. Psychology of Perception: A Philosophical Examination of Gestalt Theory & Derivative Theories of Perception. (Studies in Philosophical Psychology). 1961. pap. text ed. 5.75x (ISBN 0-391-01104-9). Humanities.
Hartmann, George W. Gestalt Psychology: A Survey of Facts & Principles. LC 73-16649. (Illus.). 325p. 1974. Repr. of 1935 ed. lib. bdg. 25.00x (ISBN 0-8371-7213-6, HAGE). Greenwood.
Kanizsa, Gaetano. Organization in Vision: Essays on Gestalt Perception. LC 79-11857. (Praeger Special Studies Ser.). 288p. 1979. 29.95 (ISBN 0-03-049071-5). Praeger.
Kaplan, M. L., et al. The Structural Approach in Psychological Testing. LC 70-93755. 1970. 21.00 (ISBN 0-08-006867-7). Pergamon.
Katz, David. Gestalt Psychology: Its Nature & Significance. Tyson, Robert, tr. LC 79-12343. 1979. Repr. of 1950 ed. lib. bdg. 19.75x (ISBN 0-313-20896-4, KAGE). Greenwood.
Koffka, Kurt. Growth of the Mind. LC 80-50103. (Social Science Classics Ser.). 383p. 1980. text ed. 19.95 (ISBN 0-87855-360-6); pap. text ed. 7.95 (ISBN 0-87855-784-9). Transaction Bks.
--Principles of Gestalt Psychology. LC 35-7711. 1967. pap. 6.95 (ISBN 0-15-674460-0, H059, Hbgr). HarBraceJ.
Kohler, Wolfgang. Gestalt Psychology. 1980. pap. 4.95 (ISBN 0-452-00531-0, F531, Mer). NAL.
--Gestalt Psychology. new ed. LC 72-114375. 1970. pap. 5.95 (ISBN 0-87140-018-9). Liveright.
--Gestalt Psychology. 224p. 1974. pap. 1.50 (ISBN 0-451-61432-1, MW1432, Ment). NAL.
--Task of Gestalt Psychology. LC 69-17397. (Illus.). 1969. 14.50 (ISBN 0-691-08614-1); pap. write for info. (ISBN 0-691-02452-9). Princeton U Pr.
Lewin, Kurt. Dynamic Theory of Personality. 1955. pap. 3.95 (ISBN 0-07-037451-1, SP). McGraw.
--Principles of Topological Psychology. 1969. Repr. of 1936 ed. 27.00 (ISBN 0-384-32460-6). Johnson Repr.
Merleau-Ponty, Maurice. Structure of Behavior. 1963. pap. 4.95x (ISBN 0-8070-2987-4, BP266). Beacon Pr.
Passons, W. Gestalt Approaches in Counseling. LC 74-22223. 1975. pap. text ed. 9.95 (ISBN 0-03-089421-2, HoltC). HR&W.
Perls, Frederick, et al. Gestalt Therapy: Excitement & Growth in the Human Personality. 1954. 10.00 (ISBN 0-517-52764-2). Crown.
Rhyne, Janie. The Gestalt Art Experience. LC 73-84603. 1974. text ed. 17.95 (ISBN 0-8185-0102-2). Brooks-Cole.
Rosenfeld, Edward. The Gestalt Bibliography. LC 81-80961. 76p. (Orig.). 1981. pap. text ed. 6.00 (ISBN 0-939266-01-6). Gestalt Journal.
Scandura, M. N. Structural-Process Models of Complex Human Behavior, No. 26. (NATO Advanced Study Applied Science Ser.). 620p. 1978. 49.00x (ISBN 9-0286-0578-9). Sijthoff & Noordhoff.
Schutz, Albert L. Call Adonoi: Manual of Practical Cabalah & Gestalt Mysticism. Lowenkopf, Anne N., ed. LC 80-50264. 200p. (Orig.). 1980. 11.95 (ISBN 0-936596-01-5); pap. 8.95 (ISBN 0-936596-00-7). Quantal.
Tolor, Alexander & Schulberg, Herbert C. An Evaluation of the Bender-Gestalt Test. 256p. 1963. photocopy ed. spiral 24.75 (ISBN 0-398-01931-2). C C Thomas.
Wertheimer, Max. Productive Thinking. Wertheimer, Michael, ed. LC 77-25961. (Illus.). 1978. Repr. of 1959 ed. lib. bdg. 23.25 (ISBN 0-313-20077-7, WEPR). Greenwood.
Zakia, Richard D. Perception & Photography. LC 74-3402. (Illus.). 1979. 13.95 (ISBN 0-87992-016-5); pap. text ed. 6.95 (ISBN 0-87992-015-7). Light Impressions.

GESTALT TEST
see Bender-Gestalt Test

GESTALT THERAPY
Fagan, Joen & Shepherd, Irma L., eds. Gestalt Therapy Now. LC 69-20468. 1970. 9.95x (ISBN 0-8314-0023-4). Sci & Behavior.
--Gestalt Therapy Now: Theory, Techniques, Applications. 1971. pap. 5.95 (ISBN 0-06-090237-X, CN237, CN). Har-Row.
Greenwald, Jerry. Creative Intimacy. 1977. pap. 2.75 (ISBN 0-515-05971-4). Jove Pubns.
Hatcher, Chris & Himmelstein, Philip, eds. Handbook of Gestalt Therapy. LC 75-42544. 600p. 1976. 35.00x (ISBN 0-87668-239-5, 23952). Aronson.
Kempler, Walter. Principles of Gestalt Family Therapy. LC 74-26006. pap. 8.50 (ISBN 0-9600808-1-3). Kempler Inst.
Kogan, Jerry. Gestalt Therapy Resources. 3rd ed. 44p. 1980. pap. 5.00 (ISBN 0-930162-03-X). Transform Berkeley.
Latner, Joel. The Gestalt Therapy Book. LC 73-82442. 224p. 1974. 10.00 (ISBN 0-517-52762-6). Crown.
Lieblich, Amia. Tin Soldiers on Jerusalem Beach. LC 78-51810. 1978. 10.95 (ISBN 0-394-42738-6). Pantheon.
Marcus, Eric. Gestalt Therapy & Beyond. LC 79-50663. 1979. 9.95 (ISBN 0-916990-06-0). Meta Pubns.
Naranjo, Claudio. The Techniques of Gestalt Therapy. 1980. pap. 8.00 (ISBN 0-939266-00-8). Gestalt Journal.
Perls, Frederick, et al. Gestalt Therapy: Excitement & Growth in the Human Personality. 1954. 10.00 (ISBN 0-517-52764-2). Crown.
--Gestalt Therapy: Excitement and Growth in the Human Personality. 1977. pap. 3.95 (ISBN 0-553-14109-0). Bantam.
Perls, Frederick S. Gestalt Therapy Verbatim. Stevens, John O., ed. 1971. pap. 2.75 (ISBN 0-553-14201-1). Bantam.
--Gestalt Therapy Verbatim. LC 79-80835. 1969. 9.00 (ISBN 0-911226-02-8); pap. 5.50 (ISBN 0-911226-03-6). Real People.
Perls, Frederick S. & Van Dusen, Wilson. Gestalt Is. LC 74-25590. 1975. 9.00 (ISBN 0-911226-14-1); pap. 5.50 (ISBN 0-911226-15-X). Real People.
Perls, Fritz. The Gestalt Approach & Eye Witness to Therapy. 224p. 1976. pap. 2.95 (ISBN 0-553-13842-1, G13842-1). Bantam.
--The Gestalt Approach & Eyewitness to Therapy. 1973. 6.95 (ISBN 0-8314-0034-X). Sci & Behavior.
Polster, Irving & Polster, Miriam. Gestalt Therapy Integrated: Contours of Theory & Practice. LC 74-3424. 1974. pap. 3.95 (ISBN 0-394-71006-1, V-6, Vin). Random.
Schiffman, Muriel. Gestalt Self Therapy. LC 73-75228. 240p. (Orig.). 1980. pap. 4.95 (ISBN 0-914640-02-X, Pub. by Self Therapy Pr). Wingbow Pr.
Simkin, James. Gestalt Therapy Mini Lectures. LC 76-11344. 1976. pap. 4.95 (ISBN 0-89087-170-1). Celestial Arts.
Simkin, James S. Mini-Lectures in Gestalt Therapy. Levitsky, Abraham & Snyder, Mary A., eds. 1974. pap. 3.95 (ISBN 0-915104-01-6). Wordpress.
Smith, Edward W., ed. The Growing Edge of Gestalt Therapy. LC 75-43828. 1976. 17.50 (ISBN 0-87630-116-2). Brunner-Mazel.
Stephenson, F. Douglas. Gestalt Therapy Primer. LC 78-74056. 214p. 1978. 20.00 (ISBN 0-87668-355-3). Aronson.
--Gestalt Therapy Primer: Introductory Readings in Gestalt Therapy. (Illus.). 232p. 1975. pap. 22.75 (ISBN 0-398-03233-5). C C Thomas.
Thomas, Jesse J. The Youniverse: Gestalt Therapy, Non-Western Religions & the Present Age. LC 77-89164. (Illus.). 1978. 8.95 (ISBN 0-930626-00-1); pap. 3.95 (ISBN 0-930626-01-X). Psych & Consul Assocs.
Zinker, Joseph. Creative Process in Gestalt Therapy. (Giant Ser.). (Illus.). pap. 3.95 (ISBN 0-394-72567-0, V-567, Vin). Random.
--Creative Process in Gestalt Therapy. LC 76-49430. 1977. 17.50 (ISBN 0-87630-140-5). Brunner-Mazel.

GESTAPO
see Germany-Secret Police

GESTATION
see Pregnancy

GESTURE
see also Pantomime
Austin, Gilbert. Chironomia: Or, a Treatise on Rhetorical Delivery. Robb, Mary M. & Thonssen, Lester, eds. LC 66-17967. (Landmarks in Rhetoric & Public Address Ser). (Illus.). 658p. 1966. 12.50x (ISBN 0-8093-0229-2). S Ill U Pr.
Bauml, Betty J. & Bauml, Franz H. A Dictionary of Gestures. LC 75-3144. 1975. 12.00 (ISBN 0-8108-0863-3). Scarecrow.
Blake, William H. A Preliminary Study of the Interpretation of Bodily Expression. LC 75-176568. (Columbia University. Teachers College. Contributions to Education: No. 574). Repr. of 1933 ed. 17.50 (ISBN 0-404-55574-8). AMS Pr.
Bouissac, Paul. La Mesure Des Gestes: Prolegomenes a la Semiotique Gestuelle. (Approaches to Semiotics, Paperback Ser.: No. 3). 1973. pap. 42.35x (ISBN 90-279-2377-9). Mouton.
Bulwer, John. Chirologia, 2 vols. in 1. LC 75-147955. (Language, Man & Society Ser.). Repr. of 1644 ed. 27.00 (ISBN 0-404-08205-X). AMS Pr.
Critchley, Macdonald. Language of Gesture. LC 72-191591. 1939. lib. bdg. 17.00 (ISBN 0-8414-2414-4). Folcroft.
--Silent Language. 231p. 1975. 23.95 (ISBN 0-408-70634-1). Butterworth.
Efron, David. Gesture, Race, & Culture. Sebeok, Thomas A., ed. LC 78-165138. (Approaches to Semiotics Ser: Vol. 9). (Illus.). 226p. 1972. text ed. 50.00x (ISBN 90-2792-112-1). Mouton.
Feldman, Sandor S. Mannerisms of Speech & Gestures in Everyday Life. LC 59-6713. 1969. text ed. 20.00 (ISBN 0-8236-3100-1); pap. text ed. 5.95 (ISBN 0-8236-8144-0, 023100). Intl Univs Pr.
Gerstner-Hirzel, Arthur. Economy of Action & the Word in Shakespeare's Plays. LC 70-168111. Repr. of 1957 ed. 5.40 (ISBN 0-404-02715-6). AMS Pr.
La Meri. Gesture Language of the Hindu Dance. LC 63-23185. (Illus.). Repr. of 1941 ed. 22.00 (ISBN 0-405-08723-3, Pub. by Blom). Arno.
Morris, Desmond, et al. Gestures. LC 79-66248. 328p. 1980. pap. 7.95 (ISBN 0-8128-6054-3). Stein & Day.
--Gestures. LC 78-66248. (Illus.). 1979. 12.95 (ISBN 0-8128-2607-8). Stein & Day.
Siddons, Henry. Practical Illustrations of Rhetorical Gesture & Action. LC 67-18425. (Illus.). 1968. Repr. of 1822 ed. 25.00 (ISBN 0-405-08971-6). Arno.
Wolff, Charlotte. A Psychology of Gesture. 2nd ed. Tennant, Anne, tr. from Fr. LC 72-348. (Body Movement Ser). 268p. 1972. Repr. of 1948 ed. 15.00 (ISBN 0-405-03147-5). Arno.

GESTURE IN ART
Barasch, Moshe. Gestures of Despair in Medieval & Early Renaissance Art. LC 76-4601. 1976. 28.50x (ISBN 0-8147-1006-9). NYU Pr.
Brilliant, Richard. Gesture & Rank in Roman Art. (Connecticut Academy of Arts & Sciences Memoirs: No. 14). 1963. pap. 30.00 (ISBN 0-208-00639-7). Shoe String.

GESTURE IN LITERATURE
Josephs, Herbert. Diderot's Dialogue of Language & Gesture: 'Le Neveu De Rameau' LC 69-17522. 1970. 8.00 (ISBN 0-8142-0008-7). Ohio St U Pr.

GESTURE LANGUAGE
see Deaf-Means of Communication; Indians of North America-Sign Language

GESU
see Gisu (Bantu Tribe)

GESUALDO, CARLO, DON, 1560-1614
Gray, Cecil. Carlo Gesualdo, Prince of Venosa, Musician & Murderer. LC 76-104268. (Illus.). 1971. Repr. of 1926 ed. lib. bdg. 15.00x (ISBN 0-8371-3934-1, GRCG). Greenwood.
Watkins, Glenn. Gesualdo: The Man & His Music. LC 72-78154. Orig. Title: Don Carlo Gesualdo. (Illus.). 359p. 1974. 22.00x (ISBN 0-8078-1201-3). U of NC Pr.

GETTY (J. PAUL) MUSEUM
Fredericksen, Burton B. Catalogue of Paintings. (Illus.). 1972. pap. 5.95 (ISBN 0-89236-021-6). J P Getty Mus.
--Masterpieces of Painting in the J. Paul Getty Museum. LC 79-54099. (Illus.). 110p. 1980. write for info (ISBN 0-89236-028-3); pap. write for info (ISBN 0-89236-022-4). J P Getty Mus.
Frel, Jiri. The Getty Bronze. (Illus., Orig.). Date not set. pap. text ed. 1.50 (ISBN 0-89236-009-7). J P Getty Mus.
Frel, Jiri, ed. The J. Paul Getty Museum Journal: No. 5. (Illus.). 1977. pap. 8.95 (ISBN 0-89236-000-3). J P Getty Mus.
Lattimore, Helen, et al. The J. Paul Getty Museum. 1975. text ed. 9.95 (ISBN 0-89236-019-4). J P Getty Mus.
Morgan, Sandra, ed. The J. Paul Getty Museum Journal, No. 6-7. (Illus.). 1979. pap. write for info. (ISBN 0-89236-018-6). J P Getty Mus.

GETTYSBURG
Bandy, Ken & Freeland, Florencecompiled by. The Gettysburg Papers, 2 vols. 1978. Vol. 1, 1978. 17.50 (ISBN 0-89029-044-X); Vol. 2 1978. 22.50 (ISBN 0-685-47636-7); boxed set 45.00 (ISBN 0-686-67001-9). Pr of Morningside.
Edward Everett at Gettysburg. (Massachusetts Historical Society Picture Books Ser.). 1963. 2.00 (ISBN 0-686-21434-X). Mass Hist Soc.
Frassanito, William. Gettysburg: A Journey in Time. LC 74-10597. 1976. pap. 8.95 (ISBN 0-684-14696-7, ScribT). Scribner.
Nitchkey, Charles R. Gettysburg: Eighteen Sixty-Three & Today. (Illus.). 1979. 8.50 (ISBN 0-682-49495-X, Banner). Exposition.
Schildt, John W. Roads to Gettysburg. 1978. 18.00 (ISBN 0-87012-295-9). McClain.

GETTYSBURG, BATTLE OF, 1863
Army of the Potomac: Part 1. LC 76-41427. (Civil War Monographs). 1977. lib. bdg. 41.00 (ISBN 0-527-17550-1); pap. 35.00 (ISBN 0-527-17548-X). Kraus Repr.
Army of the Potomac: Part 2. LC 76-41428. (Civil War Monographs). 1977. lib. bdg. 34.00 (ISBN 0-527-17551-X); pap. 28.00 (ISBN 0-527-17552-8). Kraus Repr.
Barton, William E. Lincoln at Gettysburg: What He Intended to Say; What He Said; What He Was Reported to Have Said; What He Wished He Had Said. (Illus.). 8.00 (ISBN 0-8446-1059-3). Peter Smith.
Catton, Bruce. Gettysburg: The Final Fury. LC 73-11896. (Illus.). 128p. 1974. slip cased 10.00 (ISBN 0-385-02060-0). Doubleday.
Drake, Samuel A. Battle of Gettysburg, Eighteen Sixty-Three. 1977. Repr. 20.00 (ISBN 0-403-08394-X). Scholarly.
Fox, Charles K. Gettysburg. LC 69-14885. (Illus.). 1969. pap. 3.95 (ISBN 0-498-07446-3). A S Barnes.
Hassler, Warren W., Jr. Crisis at the Crossroads: The First Day at Gettysburg. LC 72-104930. 1970. 13.75 (ISBN 0-8173-5103-5). U of Ala Pr.
Hunt, Henry J. Three Days at Gettysburg. Jones, William R., ed. (Illus.). 1978. pap. 3.95 (ISBN 0-89646-036-3). Outbooks.
Kantor, MacKinlay. Gettysburg. (Landmark Ser.: No. 23). (Illus.). (gr. 7-9). 1952. PLB 5.99 (ISBN 0-394-90323-4, BYR). Random.
Longstreet, H. D. Lee & Longstreet at High Tide: Gettysburg in the Light of the Official Records. 1904. write for info. (ISBN 0-527-58200-X). Kraus Repr.
Young, Jesse B. The Battle of Gettysburg. (Illus.). 1975. Repr. 17.50 (ISBN 0-685-69611-1). Pr of Morningside.

GETTYSBURG ADDRESS
see Lincoln, Abraham, Pres. U. S., 1809-1865-Gettysburg Address

GETTYSBURG CAMPAIGN, 1863
see also Gettysburg, Battle Of, 1863
Coddington, Edwin B. The Gettysburg Campaign. 1979. Repr. 30.00 (ISBN 0-685-96114-1). Pr of Morningside.
Tucker, Glenn. High Tide at Gettysburg. rev. ed. 462p. 1974. Repr. of 1958 ed. 15.00 (ISBN 0-89029-016-4). Pr of Morningside.

GHALIB, 1796?-1869
Ghalib, Asadullah. Ghalib, Seventeen Ninety-Seven to Eighteen Sixty-Nine: Life & Letters, Vol. 1. Russell, Ralph & Islam, Khurshidul, eds. 1969. 20.00x (ISBN 0-674-35435-4). Harvard U Pr.
Saran, Saraswati. Mirza Ghalib: The Poet of Poets. 1976. 11.00x (ISBN 0-88386-813-X). South Asia Bks.

GHANA
see also Gold Coast

Agbodeka, Francis. Ghana in the Twentieth Century. LC 74-173372. 1972. 10.00x (ISBN 0-8002-0570-7). Intl Pubns Serv.
Assimeng, J. M., ed. Traditional Life, Culture and Literature in Ghana. (Africa in Transition Ser.). 200p. 1976. 17.50 (ISBN 0-914970-26-7). Conch Mag.
Beecham, John. Ashantee & the Gold Coast, Being a Sketch of the History, Social State & Superstitions of the Inhabitants of Those Countries, with a Notice of the State & Prospects of Christianity Among Them. LC 68-93641. (Landmarks in Anthropology). Repr. of 1841 ed. lib. bdg. 31.00 (ISBN 0-384-03755-0). Johnson Repr.
Collins, W. B. They Went to Bush. 231p. 6.00 (ISBN 0-685-26801-2). Univ Place.
Cultural Policy in Ghana. (Studies & Documents on Cultural Policies Ser.). (Illus.). 50p. 1976. pap. 5.00 (ISBN 92-3-101328-9, U121, UNESCO). Unipub.
Davidson, Basil. Ghana: An African Portrait. LC 75-13608. (Illus.). 144p. 1976. 30.00 (ISBN 0-912334-65-7); pap. 18.50 (ISBN 0-89381-009-6). Aperture.
Dickson, Kwamina B. & Benneth, George. New Geography of Ghana. (Illus.). 1977. pap. 8.50x (ISBN 0-582-60343-9). Intl Pubns Serv.
Dodds, Maggie, ed. Ghana Talks: Contemporary Views on Ghana's History, Music, Politics, Religions. LC 76-46239. (Illus., Orig.). 1976. 10.00x (ISBN 0-914478-35-4); pap. 6.00x (ISBN 0-914478-36-2). Three Continents.
Levtzion, Nehemia. Ancient Ghana & Mali. LC 79-27281. 1980. text ed. 21.50x (ISBN 0-8419-0431-6, Africana); pap. text ed. 9.75x (ISBN 0-8419-0432-4). Holmes & Meier.
MacDonald, George. Gold Coast Past & Present: A Short Description of the Country & Its People. LC 70-94483. (Illus.). Repr. of 1898 ed. 17.00x (ISBN 0-8371-2370-4, Pub. by Negro U Pr). Greenwood.
Perl, Lila. Ghana & Ivory Coast, Spotlight on West Africa. LC 74-23106. (Illus.). 160p. (gr. 5-9). 1975. 7.92 (ISBN 0-688-31833-9). Morrow.
Remy, Mylene. Ghana Today. 256p. 1979. 14.95 (ISBN 2-85258-045-4, Pub. by J A Editions France). Hippocrene Bks.
Report to the Government of Ghana on Conservation Management & Utilization of Ghana's Wildlife Resources. 1969. pap. 7.50x (ISBN 2-88032-043-7, IUCN59, IUCN). Unipub.
Schildkrout, Enid. People of the Zongo: The Transformation of Ethnic Identities in Ghana. LC 76-47188. (Cambridge Studies in Social Anthropology: No. 20). 1978. 27.50 (ISBN 0-521-21483-1). Cambridge U Pr.

GHANA–ANTIQUITIES

Shaw, Thurstan. Excavation at Dawu. (Illus.). 1961. 11.25x (ISBN 0-8002-0568-5). Intl Pubns Serv.

GHANA–BIBLIOGRAPHY

Aguolu, Christian C. Ghana in the Humanities & Social Sciences, 1900-71: A Bibliography. LC 73-9519. 1973. 16.50 (ISBN 0-8108-0635-5). Scarecrow.
Cardinall, Allan W. Bibliography of the Gold Coast. LC 74-109321. Repr. of 1932 ed. 20.50x (ISBN 0-8371-3587-7, Pub. by Negro U Pr). Greenwood.
Research Library on African Affairs, ed. Ghana National Bibliography 1975. LC 71-224085. 113p. (Orig.). 1977. pap. 10.00x (ISBN 0-8002-2350-0). Intl Pubns Serv.

GHANA–DESCRIPTION AND TRAVEL

Boateng, E. A. Geography of Ghana. 17.95 (ISBN 0-521-04272-0); pap. 8.95x (ISBN 0-521-04273-9). Cambridge U Pr.
Wright, Richard. Black Power: A Record of Reactions in a Land of Pathos. LC 73-13457. (Illus.). 358p. 1974. Repr. of 1954 ed. lib. bdg. 22.50x (ISBN 0-8371-7136-9, WRBP). Greenwood.

GHANA–ECONOMIC CONDITIONS

Antwi, Anthony K. Public Expenditures: The Impact of Distribution on Income - the Ghana Case. LC 78-63269. 1978. pap. text ed. 9.50 (ISBN 0-8191-0620-8). U Pr of Amer.
Atta, Jacob K. A Macroeconometric Model of a Developing Economy: Ghana (Simulations & Policy Analysis) LC 80-67178. 346p. (Orig.). 1981. pap. text ed. 12.50 (ISBN 0-8191-1504-5). U Pr of Amer.
Brever, Helmut. Estimation of Foreign Capital Requirements As a Guide to Economic Policy: The Case of Ghana for 1968-1972. LC 75-467141. 1969. 15.00x (ISBN 3-7769-0093-8). Intl Pubns Serv.
Ewusi, Kodwo. Economic Development Planning in Ghana. LC 73-82085. 1973. 6.00 (ISBN 0-682-47750-8, University). Exposition.
Foster, Philip & Zolberg, Aristide R., eds. Ghana & the Ivory Coast: Perspectives on Modernization. LC 70-159784. 1971. 12.50x (ISBN 0-226-25752-5). U of Chicago Pr.
Hart, David. The Volta River Project. 200p. 1980. 20.00x (ISBN 0-85224-366-9, Pub. by Edinburgh U Pr Scotland). Columbia U Pr.
Howard, Rhoda. Colonialism & Underdevelopment in Ghana. LC 78-5773. 1978. text ed. 29.50x (ISBN 0-8419-0387-5, Africana). Holmes & Meier.
Killick. Development Economics in Action: A Study of Economic Policies in Ghana. LC 77-74764. 1978. 17.95 (ISBN 0-312-19682-2). St Martin.
Leith, J. Clark. Foreign Trade Regimes & Economic Development: Ghana, Bk. 2. Bhagwati, Jagdish N. & Krueger, Anne O., eds. (Special Conference Ser.). 1975. 15.00 (ISBN 0-87014-502-9, Dist. by Columbia U Pr). Natl Bur Econ Res.
Milburn, Josephine F. British Business & Ghanaian Independence. LC 76-50681. (Illus.). 166p. 1977. text ed. 12.50x (ISBN 0-87451-138-0). U Pr of New Eng.
Okoso-Amaa, Kweku. Rice Marketing in Ghana: An Analysis of Government Intervention in Business. 1975. pap. text ed. 12.50x (ISBN 0-8419-9724-1). Holmes & Meier.
Steel, William F. Small-Scale Employment & Production in Developing Countries: Evidence from Ghana. LC 75-44940. (Special Studies). 1977. text ed. 25.95 (ISBN 0-275-56330-8). Praeger.

GHANA–FOREIGN RELATIONS

Aluko, Olajide, ed. Ghana & Nigeria 1957-1970: A Study in Inter-African Discord. LC 75-1614. (Illus.). 275p. 1976. text ed. 18.50x (ISBN 0-06-490163-7). B&N.
Dei-Anang, Michael. The Administration of Ghana's Foreign Relations 1957-65: A Personal Memoir. (Commonwealth Papers Ser: No. 17). 96p. 1975. pap. text ed. 10.50x (ISBN 0-485-17617-3, Athlone Pr). Humanities.
Howard, Rhoda. Colonialism & Underdevelopment in Ghana. LC 78-5773. 1978. text ed. 29.50x (ISBN 0-8419-0387-5, Africana). Holmes & Meier.
Thompson, W. Scott. Ghana's Foreign Policy, Nineteen Fifty-Seven - Nineteen Sixty-Six: Diplomacy, Ideology, & the New State. LC 68-56322. 1969. 30.00x (ISBN 0-691-03076-6). Princeton U Pr.

GHANA–HISTORY

Alexander, H. T. African Tightrope: My Two Years As Nkrumah's Chief of Staff. 1966. 7.50 (ISBN 0-685-56706-0). Univ Place.
Arhin, Kwame. West African Traders in Ghana in the Nineteenth & Twentieth Centuries. (Legon History Ser.). (Illus.). 1979. pap. text ed. 30.00x (ISBN 0-582-64650-2). Longman.
Austin, Dennis & Lucuham, Robin, eds. Politicians & Soldiers in Ghana, 1966-1972. 332p. 1975. 28.50x (ISBN 0-7146-3049-7, F Cass Co). Biblio Dist.
Boahen. Ghana: Evolution & Change in the 19th & 20th Centuries. 1979. pap. text ed. 5.50x (ISBN 0-582-60065-0). Longman.
Bourret, F. M. Ghana: The Road to Independence, 1919-1957. rev. ed. 1960. 12.50x (ISBN 0-8047-0400-7). Stanford U Pr.
Dunn, J. & Robertson, A. F. Independence & Opportunity: Political Change in Ahafo. LC 73-79303. (African Studies, No. 8). (Illus.). 420p. 1974. 36.00 (ISBN 0-521-20270-1). Cambridge U Pr.
Fitch, Bob & Oppenheimer, Mary. Ghana: End of an Illusion. LC 66-25601. (Orig.). 1966. pap. 2.95 (ISBN 0-85345-038-2, PB-0382). Monthly Rev.
James, C. L. R. Nkrumah & the Ghana Revolution. LC 77-73128. 288p. 1977. 12.95 (ISBN 0-88208-077-6). Lawrence Hill.
Kuklick, Henrika. The Imperial Bureaucrat: The Colonial Administrative Service in the Gold Coast,1920-1939. LC 79-2463. (Publications Ser.: No. 217). 256p. 1979. 11.95 (ISBN 0-8179-7171-8). Hoover Inst Pr.
Lewin, Thomas J. Asante Before the British: The Prempean Years, 1875-1900. LC 78-8003. (Illus.). 1978. 15.50x (ISBN 0-7006-0180-5). Regents Pr KS.
Mensah, Joseph A. Ghana: History & Traditional Customs of a Proud People. 1980. 12.50 (ISBN 0-682-49471-2, University). Exposition.
Nkrumah, Kwame. Africa Must Unite. LC 70-140209. 1970. 6.95 (ISBN 0-7178-0295-7); pap. 2.95 (ISBN 0-7178-0296-5). Intl Pub Co.
Pinkney, Robert. Ghana Under Military Rule, 1966-1969. (Studies in African History Ser.) 1976. pap. 4.95x (ISBN 0-416-75090-7). Methuen Inc.
Semak, Michael. Image 4: Ghana, If This Is the Time. (Illus.). 1969. 8.50 (ISBN 0-7735-0063-4). McGill-Queens U Pr.
Vogt, John. Portuguese Rule on the Gold Coast, 1469-1682. LC 77-18831. 288p. 1978. 19.50x (ISBN 0-8203-0443-3). U of Ga Pr.
Wilks, I. Asante in the Nineteenth Century. LC 74-77834. (African Studies: No. 13). (Illus.). 872p. 1975. 69.50 (ISBN 0-521-20463-1). Cambridge U Pr.

GHANA–JUVENILE LITERATURE

Sale, J. Kirk. The Land & People of Ghana. rev. ed. LC 74-377734. (Portraits of the Nations Ser.). (Illus.). (gr. 6 up). 1972. 8.95 (ISBN 0-397-31298-9, JBL-J). Har-Row.

GHANA–POLITICS AND GOVERNMENT

Aluko, Olajide, ed. Ghana & Nigeria 1957-1970: A Study in Inter-African Discord. LC 75-1614. (Illus.). 275p. 1976. text ed. 18.50x (ISBN 0-06-490163-7). B&N.
Apter, D. E. Ghana in Transition. 1972. pap. 8.95 (ISBN 0-691-02166-X). Princeton U Pr.
Austin, Dennis. Ghana Observed: Essays on the Politics of a West African Republic. LC 76-15398. 1976. text ed. 28.50x (ISBN 0-8419-0278-X, Africana). Holmes & Meier.
Austin, Dennis & Lucuham, Robin, eds. Politicians & Soldiers in Ghana, 1966-1972. 332p. 1975. 28.50x (ISBN 0-7146-3049-7, F Cass Co). Biblio Dist.
--Politicians & Soldiers in Ghana, 1966-1972. 332p. 1975. pap. 9.95x (ISBN 0-7146-4019-0, F Cass Co). Biblio Dist.
Chantler, Clyde. The Ghana Story. 216p. 1971. 12.00x (ISBN 0-8464-0452-4). Beekman Pubs.
Dunn, J. & Robertson, A. F. Independence & Opportunity: Political Change in Ahafo. LC 73-79303. (African Studies, No. 8). (Illus.). 420p. 1974. 36.00 (ISBN 0-521-20270-1). Cambridge U Pr.
Foster, Philip & Zolberg, Aristide R., eds. Ghana & the Ivory Coast: Perspectives on Modernization. LC 70-159784. 1971. 12.50x (ISBN 0-226-25752-5). U. of Chicago Pr.
Holm, John D., et al. A Comparative Study of Political Involvement in Three African States: Botswana, Ghana & Kenya. LC 78-14731. (Foreign & Comparative Studies-African Ser.: No. 30). 139p. 1978. pap. 6.50x (ISBN 0-915984-52-0). Syracuse U Foreign Comp.
Jarmon, Charles. The Nkrumah Regime: An Evaluation of the Role of Charismatic Authority. Nyang, Sulayman S., ed. (Third World Monograph Ser.). 24p. (Orig.). 1981. pap. 1.50x (ISBN 0-931494-05-2). Brunswick Pub.
Kay, Geoffrey, ed. Political Economy of Colonialism in Ghana: A Collection of Documents and Statistics, 1900-1960. Hymer, S. (Illus.). 1971. 47.50 (ISBN 0-521-07952-7). Cambridge U Pr.
Kesse-Adu, K. The Politics of Political Detention. (Illus.). 236p. 1971. pap. 5.00x (ISBN 0-8002-1817-5). Intl Pubns Serv.
Kimble, David. Political History of Ghana: The Rise of Gold Coast Nationalism, 1850-1928. 1963. 37.50x (ISBN 0-19-821623-8). Oxford U Pr.
Kwame Nkrumah. 1976. pap. text ed. 5.95x (ISBN 0-8277-4840-X). British Bk Ctr.
Ladouceur, Paul A. Chiefs & Politicians: Regionalism & Political Development in North Ghana. (Legon History Ser.). (Illus.). 1979. text ed. 40.00x (ISBN 0-582-64646-4). Longman.
Lefever, Ernest W. Spear & Scepter: Army, Police, & Politics in Tropical Africa. 1970. 11.95 (ISBN 0-8157-5200-8). Brookings.
Le Vine, Victor T. Political Corruption: The Ghana Case. LC 74-13629. (Publications Ser.: No. 138). 169p. 1975. 8.95 (ISBN 0-8179-1381-5). Hoover Inst Pr.
Newbury, Colin W. West African Commonwealth. LC 64-22875. (Commonwealth Studies Center: No. 22). 1964. 7.75 (ISBN 0-8223-0121-0). Duke.
Nkrumah, Kwame. Ghana: The Autobiography of Kwame Nkrumah. LC 70-148514. 1971. 7.50 (ISBN 0-7178-0293-0); pap. 3.25 (ISBN 0-7178-0294-9). Intl Pub Co.
Ocran, A. K. Politics of the Sword: A Personal Memoir on Military Involvement in Ghana & of Problems of Military Government. 167p. 1977. 16.50x (ISBN 0-8476-3101-X). Rowman.
Omari, T. Peter. Kwame Nkrumah: The Anatomy of an African Dictatorship. LC 74-103939. 1970. 23.50x (ISBN 0-8419-0036-1, Africana). Holmes & Meier.
Owusu, Maxwell. Uses & Abuses of Political Power: A Case Study of Continuity & Change in the Politics of Ghana. LC 73-121354. 1970. 15.00x (ISBN 0-226-64240-2). U of Chicago Pr.
Smock, David R. & Smock, Audrey C. The Politics of Pluralism: A Comparative Study of Lebanon and Ghana. LC 75-8278. 356p. 1975. 14.95 (ISBN 0-444-99008-9). Elsevier.
Staniland, Martin. The Lions of Dagbon. LC 74-16989. (African Studies: No. 16). (Illus.). 300p. 1975. 33.00 (ISBN 0-521-20682-0). Cambridge U Pr.
Uche, U. U. Contractual Obligations in Ghana & Nigeria. 300p. 1971. 29.50x (ISBN 0-7146-2611-2, F Cass Co). Biblio Dist.
Wight, Martin. The Gold Coast Legislative Council. Perham, Margery, ed. LC 74-14030. (Studies in Colonial Legislatures: Vol. 2). (Illus.). 285p. 1974. Repr. of 1947 ed. lib. bdg. 16.50x (ISBN 0-8371-7783-9, WIGC). Greenwood.
Woronoff, Jon. West African Wager: Houphouet Versus Nkrumah. LC 72-5155. 1972. 13.00 (ISBN 0-8108-0523-5). Scarecrow.

GHANA–RELIGION

Appiah-Kubi, Kofi. Man Cures, God Heals: Religion & Medical Practice Among the Akans of Ghana. (Illus.). 224p. 1981. text ed. 25.00 (ISBN 0-86598-011-X). Allanheld.
--Man Cures, God Heals: Traditional Medical Practice Among the Akans of Ghana. (Orig.). 1981. pap. 10.95 (ISBN 0-377-00114-7). Friend Pr.
Field, Margaret J. Religion & Medicine of the Ga People. LC 76-44718. 1977. Repr. of 1937 ed. 27.50 (ISBN 0-404-15923-0). AMS Pr.
Wyllie, Robert W. Spiritism in Ghana: A Study of New Religious Movements. Cherry, Conrad, ed. LC 79-20486. (Studies in Religion: No. 21). 139p. 13.50 (ISBN 0-89130-355-3); pap. 9.00 (ISBN 0-89130-356-1). Scholars Pr CA.

GHANA–SOCIAL CONDITIONS

Appiah-Kubi, Kofi. Man Cures, God Heals: Religion & Medical Practice Among the Akans of Ghana. (Illus.). 224p. 1981. text ed. 25.00 (ISBN 0-86598-011-X). Allanheld.
Chantler, Clyde. The Ghana Story. 216p. 1971. 12.00x (ISBN 0-8464-0452-4). Beekman Pubs.
Goody, Esther N. Contexts of Kinship an Essay in the Family Sociology of the Gonja of Northern Ghana. LC 72-78892. (Cambridge Studies in Social Anthropology: No. 7). (Illus.). 300p. 1973. 28.95 (ISBN 0-521-08583-7). Cambridge U Pr.
Goody, Jack, ed. Changing Social Structure in Ghana. (Illus.). 1975. pap. 11.25x (ISBN 0-85302-041-8). Intl Pubns Serv.
Harvey, William B. Law & Social Change in Ghana. 1966. 26.00 (ISBN 0-691-03033-2). Princeton U Pr.
Hill, Polly. The Occupations of Migrants in Ghana. (Anthropological Papers: No. 42). 1970. pap. 2.00x (ISBN 0-932206-40-9). U Mich Mus Anthro.
Pellow, Deborah. Women in Accra: Options for Autonomy. Kitchen, Cole, ed. LC 77-78740. (Illus.). 1977. 12.50 (ISBN 0-917256-03-4). Ref Pubns.
Wright, Richard. Black Power: A Record of Reactions in a Land of Pathos. LC 73-13457. (Illus.). 358p. 1974. Repr. of 1954 ed. lib. bdg. 22.50x (ISBN 0-8371-7136-9, WRBP). Greenwood.

GHANA–SOCIAL LIFE AND CUSTOMS

Cardinall, Allan W. In Ashanti & Beyond. LC 77-106868. (Illus.). Repr. of 1927 ed. 20.75x (ISBN 0-8371-3285-1, Pub. by Negro U Pr). Greenwood.
--In Ashanti & Beyond: The Record of a Resident Magistrate's Many Years in Tropical Africa. LC 27-24653. 1971. Repr. of 1927 ed. 25.50 (ISBN 0-384-07520-7). Johnson Repr.
Ellis, Alfred B. Tshi-Speaking Peoples of the Gold Coast of West Africa. 1964. 16.50 (ISBN 0-910216-02-9). Benin.
--Tshi-Speaking Peoples of the Gold Coast of West Africa. 1966. text ed. 14.75x (ISBN 90-6234-009-1). Humanities.
Grindal, Bruce. Growing up in Two Worlds: Education & Transition Among the Sisala of Northern Ghana. Spindler, George & Spindler, Louise, eds. (Case Studies in Education & Culture). 128p. pap. text ed. 6.95x (ISBN 0-8290-0318-5). Irvington.
Kilson, Marion. Kpele Lala: Ga Religious Songs & Symbols. LC 79-135188. 1971. pap. 12.50x (ISBN 0-674-50567-0). Harvard U Pr.
Mensah, Joseph A. Ghana: History & Traditional Customs of a Proud People. 1980. 12.50 (ISBN 0-682-49471-2, University). Exposition.
Osseo-Asare, Francislee. A New Land to Live in. LC 77-72527. 1977. pap. 3.95 (ISBN 0-87784-722-3). Inter-Varsity.

GHANAIAN TALES

see Tales, Ghanaian

GHANDI, MAHATMA

see Gandhi, Mohandas Karamchand, 1869-1948

GHAZALI, AL, 1058-1111

McCarthy, Richard J. Freedom & Fulfillment. Al-Ghazalio, tr. (International Studies & Translations Program--Arabic Literature Ser.). 1980. lib. bdg. 27.00 (ISBN 0-8057-8167-6). Twayne.

GHAZNEVIDS

Bosworth, Clifford. The Ghaznavids. (Arab Background Ser.). 1973. 16.00x (ISBN 0-86685-005-8). Intl Bk Ctr.
Bosworth, Clifford E. The Later Ghaznavids: Splendor & Decay, the Dynasty in Afganistan & Northern India. LC 77-7879. 196p. 1977. text ed. 17.50x (ISBN 0-231-04428-3). Columbia U Pr.

GHENT-HISTORY

Henry of Ghent: Summa Quaestionum Ordinarum. (Text Ser). 1953. Repr. of 1920 ed. Vol. 1. 20.00 (ISBN 0-686-11550-3); Vol. 2. 20.00 (ISBN 0-686-11551-1). Franciscan Inst.

GHENT, TREATY OF, 1814

Dangerfield, George. Era of Good Feelings. LC 51-14815. 1963. pap. 5.50 (ISBN 0-15-629000-6, H034, Hbgr). HarBraceJ.

Updyke, Frank A. The Diplomacy of the War of 1812. 8.50 (ISBN 0-8446-1455-6). Peter Smith.

GHIBERTI, LORENZO, 1378-1455

Krautheimer, R. Lorenzo Ghiberti. (Monographs in Art & Archaeology: No. 31). 1970. Repr. 65.00x (ISBN 0-691-03820-1). Princeton U Pr.

GHOORKAS

see Gurkhas

GHOSE, AUROBINDO, 1872-1950

Chaudhuri, Haridas. Being, Evolution & Immortality. rev. ed. LC 74-4821. Orig. Title: Philosophy of Integralism. 224p. 1974. pap. 2.75 (ISBN 0-8356-0449-7, Quest). Theos Pub Hse.

Donnelly, Morwenna. Founding the Life Devine: An Introduction to the Integral Yoga of Sri Aurobindo. LC 74-2430. 250p. 1976. pap. 3.95 (ISBN 0-913922-13-7). Dawn Horse Pr.

Keshavamurti. Sri Aurobindo: The Hope of Man. (Illus.). 1969. 8.25x (ISBN 0-8426-1331-5). Verry.

O'Connor, June. The Quest for Political & Spiritual Liberation: A Study in the Thought of Sri Aurobindo Ghose. LC 75-5249. 153p. 1976. 12.00 (ISBN 0-8386-1734-4). Fairleigh Dickinson.

Rishabhchand. In the Mother's Light, 2 pts. 1960. Pt. 1. pap. 1.75 (ISBN 0-685-24397-4); Pt. 2. pap. 1.25 (ISBN 0-685-24398-2). Assoc Bk.

Satprem. Sri Aurobindo, or the Adventure of Consciousness. Tehmi, tr. from Fr. LC 74-6770. (Lindisfarne Book). (Illus.). 400p. (YA) 1974. pap. 5.95 (ISBN 0-06-013773-8, TD-204, HarpT). Har-Row.

GHOST DANCE

Ghost Dancers in the West: The Sioux at Pine Ridge & Wounded Knee in 1891. 1976. pap. 1.00 (ISBN 0-916552-08-X). Acoma Bks.

Lesser, Alexander. Pawnee Ghost Dance Hand Game. LC 79-82340. (Columbia Univ. Contributions to Anthropology Ser.: Vol. 16). 1969. Repr. of 1933 ed. 21.00 (ISBN 0-404-50566-X). AMS Pr.

Mooney, James. Ghost-Dance Religion & the Sioux Outbreak of 1890. Wallace, Anthony F., ed. LC 64-24971. (Orig.). 1965. pap. 4.95 (ISBN 0-226-53517-7, P176, Phoen). U of Chicago Pr.

--Ghost Dance Religion: Shakers of Puget Sound - Extracts. facsimile ed. 27p. Repr. of 1896 ed. pap. 3.50 (ISBN 0-8466-0003-X, SJS3). Shorey.

Utley, Robert M. Last Days of the Sioux Nation. (Western Americana Ser.: No. 3). (Illus.). 1963. 25.00x (ISBN 0-300-01003-6); pap. 5.95x (ISBN 0-300-00245-9, YW15). Yale U Pr.

GHOST STORIES

see also Horror Tales

Arneson, D. J. The Most Famous Ghost of All & Other Ghost Stories. LC 78-14772. (Illus.). (gr. 5 up). 1978. pap. 2.50 (ISBN 0-671-32974-X). Wanderer Bks.

Arthur, Robert. Ghosts & More Ghosts. (Illus.). (gr. 5-8). 1963. PLB 6.99 (ISBN 0-394-91192-X, BYR). Random.

Bates, Arlo. The Intoxicated Ghost: And Other Stories, Vol 1. LC 72-4419. (Short Story Index Reprint Ser). Repr. of 1908 ed. 18.00 (ISBN 0-8369-4170-5). Arno.

Blackwood, Algernon. Best Ghost Stories. 7.50 (ISBN 0-8446-5006-4). Peter Smith.

Bleiler, E. F., ed. Five Victorian Ghost Novels. Incl. Uninhabited House. Riddell, Mrs. J. H; Amber Witch. Meinhold, W; Monsieur Maurice. Edwards, A; Phantom Lover. Lee, Vernon; Ghost of Guir House. Beale, C. W. LC 77-102771. (Illus.). 1971. pap. 4.95 (ISBN 0-486-22558-5). Dover.

Bleiler, Everett F. A Treasury of Victorian Ghost Stories. 320p. 1982. 16.95 (ISBN 0-684-17299-2, ScribT). Scribner.

Boyer, Dwight. Ghost Ships of the Great Lakes. LC 68-23094. (Illus.). 1968. 8.95 (ISBN 0-396-05783-7). Dodd.

Briggs, Julia. Night Visitors: The Rise & Fall of the English Ghost Story. 240p. 1977. 18.95 (ISBN 0-571-11113-0, Pub. by Faber & Faber). Merrimack Bk Serv.

Bright, Robert. Jorgito. LC 76-23789. (ps-k). 1977. PLB 5.95 (ISBN 0-385-12005-2). Doubleday.

Cannon, Timothy L. & Whitmore, Nancy F. Ghosts & Legends of Fredrick County. LC 79-64285. (Illus., Orig.). 1979. pap. 2.95 (ISBN 0-9602816-0-6). T L Cannon & N F Whitmore.

Carmer, Carl. Screaming Ghost & Other Stories. (Illus.). (gr. 7-11). 1956. PLB 4.99 (ISBN 0-394-91587-9). Knopf.

Cerf, Bennett, ed. Famous Ghost Stories. 1944. 3.95 (ISBN 0-394-60073-8, 73). Modern Lib.

--Famous Ghost Stories. 1956. pap. 2.45 (ISBN 0-394-70140-2, Vin, V140). Random.

Cerf, Bennett A. Famous Ghost Stories. Repr. lib. bdg. 18.55x (ISBN 0-88411-146-6). Amereon Ltd.

Chin Hao. Stories About Ghosts. Lin Lan, ed. (Tales from the Orient Ser.: No. 14). (Chinese.). 5.00 (ISBN 0-89986-238-1). E Langstaff.

Cohen, Daniel. The World's Most Famous Ghosts. (Illus.). (gr. 4-9). 1978. 5.95 (ISBN 0-396-07543-6). Dodd.

Curtin, Jeremiah. Tales of the Fairies & the Ghost-World. LC 75-152760. Repr. of 1895 ed. 14.00 (ISBN 0-405-08416-1, Blom Pubns). Arno.

Dickens, Charles, et al. Classic Ghost Stories. LC 74-12599. 330p. (Orig.). 1975. pap. 4.50 (ISBN 0-486-20735-8). Dover.

Furman, A. L., ed. Ghost Stories. (gr. 5-7). 1978. pap. 1.25 (ISBN 0-671-29922-0). Archway.

Furman, Abraham L., ed. More Teen-Age Ghost Stories. (gr. 6-10). 1963. PLB 6.19 (ISBN 0-8313-0052-3). Lantern.

--More Teen-Age Haunted Stories. (gr. 5-10). 1967. PLB 6.19 (ISBN 0-8313-0057-4). Lantern.

--Teen-Age Ghost Stories. (Illus.). (gr. 6-10). 1961. PLB 6.19 (ISBN 0-8313-0058-2). Lantern.

--Teen-Age Haunted Stories. (gr. 6-10). PLB 6.19 (ISBN 0-8313-0045-0). Lantern.

Gerrick, David J. Ohio's Ghostly Greats: An Anthology of Ohio Ghost Stories. 1973. pap. 4.95 (ISBN 0-916750-40-X). Dayton Labs.

Gordon, Giles, ed. Prevailing Spirits: A Book of Scottish Ghost Stories. 1979. 17.95 (ISBN 0-241-89403-4, Pub. by Hamish Hamilton England). David & Charles.

Graydon, Nell S. South Carolina Ghost Tales. 6.95 (ISBN 0-685-06834-X). Beaufort.

Haining, Peter, ed. The Ghost's Companion: A Haunting Anthology. LC 75-30227. 192p. 1976. 7.95 (ISBN 0-8008-3228-0). Taplinger.

Harden, John. Tar Heel Ghosts. 1954. 9.95 (ISBN 0-8078-0660-9); pap. 4.95 (ISBN 0-8078-4069-6). U of NC Pr.

Hitchcock, Alfred, ed. Alfred Hitchcock's Haunted Houseful. (Illus.). (gr. 4-9). 1961. 6.95 (ISBN 0-394-81224-7, BYR). Random.

Hoffman, Elizabeth P. Here a Ghost, There a Ghost. LC 78-2544. (Illus.). 96p. (gr. 4-6). 1978. PLB 7.29 (ISBN 0-671-32851-4). Messner.

Hoke, Helen. Terrors, Terrors, Terrors. (Terrific Triple Titles Ser.). (Illus.). (gr. 7 up). 1979. PLB 8.40 s&l (ISBN 0-531-04093-3). Watts.

Hone, Joseph, ed. Irish Ghost Stories. 1978. 17.95 (ISBN 0-241-89680-0, Pub. by Hamish Hamilton England). David & Charles.

James, Montague R. More Ghost Stories of an Antiquary. facsimile ed. LC 72-163031. (Short Story Index Reprint Ser.). Repr. of 1911 ed. 17.00 (ISBN 0-8369-3945-X). Arno.

Jeffrey, Adi-Kent T. Across the Land from Ghost to Ghost. LC 75-44194. 180p. (Orig.). 1975. pap. 1.50 (ISBN 0-915460-04-1). New Hope.

--Ghosts of the Revolution. (Orig.). 1976. pap. 1.50 (ISBN 0-915460-16-5). New Hope.

Johnson, F. Roy. Supernaturals Among Carolina Folk & Their Neighbors. (Illus.). 256p. (gr. 8-12). 1974. 8.50 (ISBN 0-930230-25-6). Johnson NC.

Kelley, Leo P., ed. The Supernatural in Fiction. (Patterns in Literary Art Ser.). 324p. (gr. 10-12). 1973. pap. text ed. 6.12 (ISBN 0-07-033497-8, W). McGraw.

Leach, Maria. Thing at the Foot of the Bed. LC 59-6658. (Illus.). (gr. 3-5). 1959. PLB 5.99 (ISBN 0-529-03545-6). Philomel.

--Whistle in the Graveyard: Folktales to Chill Your Bones. 128p. (gr. 4-6). 1974. 7.95 (ISBN 0-670-76245-8). Viking Pr.

Lines, Kathleen, ed. House of the Nighmare & Other Eerie Tales. LC 68-23749. 256p. (gr. 7 up). 1968. 5.95 (ISBN 0-374-33432-3). FS&G.

Ludlam, Harry. Restless Ghosts of Ladye Place & Other True Hauntings. LC 68-31250. 1968. 6.95 (ISBN 0-8008-6775-0). Taplinger.

MacManus, D. A. Between Two Worlds: True Ghost Stories of the British Isles. 1977. text ed. 11.25x (ISBN 0-900675-83-7). Humanities.

McSpadden, Joseph W., ed. Famous Ghost Stories. facsimile ed. LC 70-152949. (Short Story Index Reprint Ser.). Repr. of 1918 ed. 16.00 (ISBN 0-8369-3808-9). Arno.

--Famous Psychic & Ghost Stories, 2 vols. in 1. LC 73-77. (Short Story Index Reprint Ser.). Repr. of 1918 ed. 36.00 (ISBN 0-8369-4248-5). Arno.

Manley, Seon & Lewis, Gogo, eds. Masters of Shades & Shadows. LC 77-76255. (gr. k up). 1978. PLB 7.95 (ISBN 0-385-12744-8). Doubleday.

Morgan, Fred T. Ghost Tales of the Uwharries. LC 68-58501. (Illus.). (YA) 1980. 7.95 (ISBN 0-910244-52-9). Blair.

Musick, Ruth A. The Telltale Lilac Bush & Other West Virginia Ghost Tales. LC 64-14000. (Illus.). 208p. 1976. pap. 6.50 (ISBN 0-8131-0136-0). U Pr of Ky.

Onions, Oliver. The First Book of Ghost Stories: Widdershins. LC 77-20545. 1978. pap. 3.00 (ISBN 0-486-23608-0). Dover.

Otting, Rae. The Gray Ghosts of Gotham. (Illus.). (gr. 2-5). 1978. pap. 1.25 (ISBN 0-89508-059-1). Rainbow Bks.

Quiller-Couch, Arthur T. Old Fires & Profitable Ghosts: A Book of Stories. LC 72-10813. (Short Story Index Reprint Ser). 1973. Repr. of 1900 ed. 20.00 (ISBN 0-8369-4224-8). Arno.

Reinstedt, Randall A. Ghostly Tales & Mysterious Happenings of Old Monterey. LC 79-110356. (Illus.). 64p. 1977. pap. 3.95 (ISBN 0-933818-04-1). Ghost Town.

Riddell, Mrs. J. H. The Collected Ghost Stories of Mrs. J. H. Riddell. Bleiler, E. F., ed. (Illus.). 1977. pap. 5.00 (ISBN 0-486-23430-4). Dover.

Ridler, Anne. Best Ghost Stories. Repr. of 1945 ed. 20.00 (ISBN 0-89987-134-8). Darby Bks.

Roach, Marilynne K. Encounters with the Invisible World: Being Ten Tales of Ghosts, Witches, & the Devil Himself in New England. LC 76-22186. (Illus.). (gr. 5-9). 1977. 8.95 (ISBN 0-690-01277-2, TYC-J). Har-Row.

Roberts, Bruce & Roberts, Nancy. America's Most Haunted Places. LC 75-23188. 96p. (gr. 6-7). 1976. 6.95 (ISBN 0-385-09965-7). Doubleday.

Rolt, L. T. Sleep No More: Railway, Canal & Other Stories of the Supernatural. (Illus.). 162p. 1975. 11.00x (ISBN 0-85527-023-3). Intl Pubns Serv.

Seaman, Barrett & Moritz, Michael. Ghosts: A Treasury of Chilling Tales Old & New. LC 81-43044. 384p. 1981. 17.95 (ISBN 0-385-17180-3). Doubleday.

Sechrist, Elizabeth H., ed. Thirteen Ghostly Yarns. rev. ed. (Illus.). (gr. 3 up). 1963. PLB 7.97 (ISBN 0-8255-8171-0). Macrae.

Snow, Edward R. Ghost, Gales & Gold. LC 72-3936. (Illus.). 288p. 1972. 6.95 (ISBN 0-396-06658-5). Dodd.

Sullivan, Jack. Elegant Nightmares: The English Ghost Story from le Fanu to Blackwood. LC 77-92258. 155p. 1978. 12.95x (ISBN 0-8214-0374-5). Ohio U Pr.

Tomlinson, Dorothy, ed. Walk in Dread: Twelve Classic Eerie Tales. LC 72-2204. 285p. 1972. 6.95 (ISBN 0-8008-8037-4). Taplinger.

Tucker, George H. Virginia Supernatural Tales: Ghosts, Witches & Eerie Doings. LC 77-12746. (Illus.). 1977. pap. 4.95 (ISBN 0-915442-40-X). Donning Co.

Underwood, Peter, ed. Thirteen Famous Ghost Stories: Haunting Tales to Keep You from Your Sleep. 1977. pap. 2.25x (ISBN 0-460-01749-7, Evman). Biblio Dist.

Wilkins-Freeman, Mary E. Collected Ghost Stories. 1974. 7.95 (ISBN 0-87054-065-3). Arkham.

Windham, Kathryn T. Thirteen Tennessee Ghosts & Jeffrey. LC 76-45946. (Illus.). 1977. 7.95 (ISBN 0-87397-108-6). Strode.

GHOST TOWNS

see Cities and Towns, Ruined, Extinct, etc.

GHOSTS

see also Apparitions; Demonology; Hallucinations and Illusions; Hiding-Places (Secret Chambers, Etc.); Poltergeists; Psychical Research; Spiritualism; Superstition

Anderson, Jean. The Haunting of America: Ghost Stories from Our Past. LC 73-5864. (Illus.). 176p. (gr. 5 up). 1973. 6.95 (ISBN 0-395-17518-6). HM.

Aylesworth, Thomas G. Vampires & Other Ghosts. LC 76-392966. (Illus.). 128p. (gr. 6 up). 1972. PLB 7.95 (ISBN 0-201-00157-8, A-W Childrens). A-W.

Bangs, John K. Ghosts I Have Met. 1971. pap. 2.45 (ISBN 0-87877-005-4, P-5). Newcastle Pub.

Bardens, Dennis. Ghosts & Hauntings. LC 68-14553. (Illus.). 1968. 8.50 (ISBN 0-8008-3250-7). Taplinger.

Bell, Charles B. & Miller, Harriett P. A Mysterious Spirit: The Bell Witch of Tennessee. 1972. 10.00 (ISBN 0-918450-06-3); pap. 6.00 (ISBN 0-918450-13-6). C Elder.

Bennett, Ernest N. Apparitions & Haunted Houses: A Survey of Evidence. LC 76-164100. Repr. of 1939 ed. 26.00 (ISBN 0-8103-3752-5). Gale.

Briggs, Julia. Night Visitors: The Rise & Fall of the English Ghost Story. 240p. 1977. 18.95 (ISBN 0-571-11113-0, Pub. by Faber & Faber). Merrimack Bk Serv.

Clyne, Patricia E. Ghostly Animals of America. LC 77-6487. (Illus.). (gr. 5 up). 1977. 5.95 (ISBN 0-396-07465-0). Dodd.

Cohen, Daniel. Ghostly Animals. LC 76-23751. (gr. 4-7). 1977. PLB (ISBN 0-385-11568-7). Doubleday.

--In Search of Ghosts. LC 70-175312. (Illus.). (gr. 7 up). 1972. 5.95 (ISBN 0-396-06485-X). Dodd.

--Real Ghosts. (Illus.). (gr. 4 up). 1979. pap. 1.50 (ISBN 0-671-29908-5). Archway.

--Real Ghosts. LC 77-6502. (Illus.). (gr. 4-9). 1977. 5.95 (ISBN 0-396-07454-5). Dodd.

Day, James W. In Search of Ghosts. LC 71-95353. 1970. 4.95 (ISBN 0-8008-4192-1). Taplinger.

Eberhart, George M., compiled By. A Geo-Bibliography of Anomalies: Primary Access to Observations of UFOs, Ghosts, & Other Mysterious Phenomena. LC 79-6183. xl, 1114p. 1980. lib. bdg. 59.95 (ISBN 0-313-21337-2, EBA/). Greenwood.

Ebon, Martin, ed. True Experiences with Ghosts. Date not set. pap. 1.50 (ISBN 0-451-09622-3, W9622, Sig). NAL.

Flammarion, Camille. Haunted Houses. LC 76-159957. (Tower Bks). 1971. Repr. of 1924 ed. 24.00 (ISBN 0-8103-3911-0). Gale.

Fuller, Elizabeth. My Search for the Ghost of Flight 401. 1978. pap. 1.95 (ISBN 0-425-04011-9, Dist. by Putnam). Berkley Pub.

Gettings, Fred. Ghosts in Photographs: The Extraordinary Story of Spirit Photography. 1978. 10.95 (ISBN 0-517-52930-0). Crown.

Ghosts Legends of Wiltshire. 12.00 (ISBN 0-8277-7262-9). British Bk Ctr.

Green, A. Our Haunted Kingdom. 1975. pap. 2.25 (ISBN 0-531-06066-7, Fontana Pap). Watts.

Green, Andrew. Ghosts of the South East of England. LC 75-26364. (Illus.). 144p. 1976. 2.50 (ISBN 0-7153-7092-8). David & Charles.

Hallam, Jack. Ghosts' Who's Who. 1977. 7.95 (ISBN 0-7153-7452-4). David & Charles.

Harper, Charles G. Haunted Houses: Tales of the Supernatural with Some Account of Hereditary Curses & Family Legends. LC 79-164326. (Illus.). xvi, 283p. 1971. Repr. of 1907 ed. 28.00 (ISBN 0-8103-3928-5). Gale.

Harter, Walter. The Phantom Hand. LC 75-35955. (Illus.). 96p. (gr. 4up). 1976. 5.95 (ISBN 0-13-661843-X). P-H.

Hoffman, Elizabeth P. This House Is Haunted! LC 77-10981. (Myth, Magic & Superstition Ser.). (Illus.). (gr. 4-5). 1977. PLB 10.65 (ISBN 0-8172-1033-4). Raintree Pubs.

Hoke, Helen. Ghost & Ghastlies. (Illus.). 192p. (gr. 4-6). 1976. PLB 7.90 (ISBN 0-531-01210-7). Watts.

Holzer, Hans. Some of My Best Friends Are Ghosts. 1978. pap. 1.95 (ISBN 0-532-19203-6). Woodhill.

--Westghosts: The Psychic World of California. LC 77-88693. Orig. Title: Ghosts of the Golden West. xiv, 233p. 1980. pap. 5.95 (ISBN 0-8040-0759-4). Swallow.

--White House Ghosts. Orig. Title: Spirits (1976), Ghosts (1971) 1979. pap. 1.75 (ISBN 0-8439-0692-8, Leisure Bks). Nordon Pubns.

Hurwood, Bernhardt J., ed. Hag of the Dribble, & Other True Ghosts. LC 71-107014. 1971. 7.50 (ISBN 0-8008-3810-6). Taplinger.

Jeffrey, Adi-Kent T. Across the Land from Ghost to Ghost. LC 75-44194. 180p. (Orig.). 1975. pap. 1.50 (ISBN 0-915460-04-1). New Hope.

Jenkins, Alan C. World of Ghosts. (Illus.). 64p. 1978. 6.95 (ISBN 0-7011-5087-4, Pub. by Chatto Bodley Jonathan). Merrimack Bk Serv.

Kennaway, James. Household Ghosts. 188p. 1981. 30.00x (ISBN 0-906391-14-8, Pub. by Mainstream). State Mutual Bk.

Kettelkamp, Larry. Haunted Houses. (Illus.). (gr. 5-9). 1969. 7.25 (ISBN 0-688-21377-4); PLB 6.96 (ISBN 0-688-31377-9). Morrow.

Knight, David C. The Haunted Souvenir Warehouse. LC 77-76251. (gr. 3-7). 1978. PLB 5.95 (ISBN 0-385-12729-4). Doubleday.

Lang, Andrew. The Book of Dreams & Ghosts. LC 80-19690. 301p. 1980. Repr. of 1972 ed. lib. bdg. 9.95x (ISBN 0-89370-610-8). Borgo Pr.

--Book of Dreams & Ghosts. 1972. pap. 2.95 (ISBN 0-87877-010-0, P-10). Newcastle Pub.

--Book of Dreams & Ghosts. LC 71-108815. Repr. of 1897 ed. 10.00 (ISBN 0-404-03848-4). AMS Pr.

--Cock Lane & Common-Sense. LC 74-110572. Repr. of 1894 ed. 12.00 (ISBN 0-404-03846-8). AMS Pr.

Leadbeater, Charles W. Saved by a Ghost. LC 79-9981. 1979. pap. 5.50 (ISBN 0-8356-0526-4, Quest). Theos Pub Hse.

Legg, Rodney, et al. Ghosts of Dorset, Devon & Somerset. 117p. 25.00 (ISBN 0-686-75656-8, Pub. by Dorset). State Mutual Bk.

Lethbridge, T. C. Ghost & Ghoul. 1967. pap. 4.95 (ISBN 0-7100-6191-9). Routledge & Kegan.

Ludlam, Ed. B Y Harry. Elliott O'Donnell's Casebook of Ghosts. LC 73-84645. (Illus.). 1969. 8.95 (ISBN 0-8008-2385-0). Taplinger.

McBain, Ed. Ghosts. (Large Print Bks.). 1980. lib. bdg. 12.95 (ISBN 0-8161-3128-7). G K Hall.

McHugh, James N. Hantu Hantu: An Account of Ghost Belief in Modern Malaya. 2nd ed. LC 77-87031. (Illus.). Repr. of 1959 ed. 14.50 (ISBN 0-404-16839-6). AMS Pr.

McInnes, John. The Ghost Said Boo. LC 73-20392. (Easy Venture Ser.). (Illus.). (gr. k-1). 1974. PLB 6.09 (ISBN 0-686-74663-5). Garrard.

MacKenzie, Andrew, ed. A Gallery of Ghosts: An Anthology of Reported Experience. LC 73-2019. 160p. 1973. 7.95 (ISBN 0-8008-3122-5). Taplinger.

MacQueen-Pope, W. Ghosts & Greasepaint. 334p. 1980. Repr. lib. bdg. 30.00 (ISBN 0-8492-6753-6). R West.

Martin, Margaret R. Charleston Ghosts. LC 63-22508. (Illus.). 1963. 5.95 (ISBN 0-87249-091-2); pap. 2.25x (ISBN 0-87249-286-9). U of SC Pr.

May, Antoinette. Haunted Houses & Wandering Ghosts of California. LC 77-92799. (A California Living Book). (Illus.). 1978. pap. 7.95 (ISBN 0-89395-002-5). Cal Living Bks.

Maynard, Christopher. All About Ghosts. LC 77-17613. (The World of the Unknown). (Illus.). (gr. 4-5). 1978. PLB 6.95 (ISBN 0-88436-469-0). EMC.

Myers, Arthur. The Ghost Hunters. LC 80-19668. (Illus.). 160p. (gr. 7 up). 1980. PLB 9.29 (ISBN 0-671-33076-4). Messner.

Poole, Keith B. Ghosts of Wessex. (Ghosts Ser.). 1977. 4.50 (ISBN 0-7153-7287-4). David & Charles.

Reinstedt, Randall A. Incredible Ghosts of Old Monterey's Hotel Del Monte. (Illus.). 48p. pap. 2.95 (ISBN 0-933818-07-6). Ghost Town.

Richelson, Geraldine. Come Out, Come Out Whoever You Are! (Illus.). 32p. 1980. pap. 2.95 (ISBN 0-8252-1113-1); pap. text ed. 5.95 (ISBN 0-8252-1112-3). Quist.

Risedorf, Gwen. Ghosts & Ghouls. LC 77-14333. (Myth, Magic & Superstition Ser.). (Illus.). (gr. 4-5). 1977. PLB 10.65 (ISBN 0-8172-1038-5). Raintree Pubs.

Roberts, Bruce & Roberts, Nancy. Ghosts of the Carolinas. LC 62-21045. (Orig.). 5.95 (ISBN 0-87461-952-1); pap. 4.95 (ISBN 0-87461-953-X). McNally.

--Illustrated Guide to Ghosts & Mysterious Occurrences in the Old North State. LC 59-14157. (Orig.). 5.95 (ISBN 0-87461-954-8); pap. 4.50 (ISBN 0-87461-955-6). McNally.

Roberts, Nancy. Southern Ghosts. LC 77-82962. (Illus.). 1979. 6.95a (ISBN 0-385-12813-4); PLB (ISBN 0-385-12814-2). Doubleday.

Roberts, Nancy & Roberts, Bruce. Illustrated Guide to Ghosts. (Illus.). 6.95 (ISBN 0-87461-954-8); pap. 4.95 (ISBN 0-87461-955-6). McNally NC.

--This Haunted Land. 6.95 (ISBN 0-87461-956-4); pap. 4.95 (ISBN 0-87461-957-2). McNally NC.

Rogo, Scott D. Haunted House Handbook. write for info. Ace Bks.

Ronan, Margaret. The Dynamite Book of Ghosts & Haunted Houses. 96p. (Orig.). (gr. 3 up). 1980. pap. 1.50 (ISBN 0-590-30622-7, Schol Pap). Schol Bk Serv.

Scott, Beth & Norman, Michael. Haunted Wisconsin. LC 80-22151. (Illus.). 256p. (Orig.). 1980. pap. 9.95 (ISBN 0-88361-082-5). Stanton & Lee.

Sergeant, Philip W. Historic British Ghosts. (Illus.). 288p. 1975. Repr. of 1936 ed. 14.95x (ISBN 0-8464-0477-X). Beekman Pubs.

Simon, Seymour. Ghosts. LC 75-37520. (gr. 1-3). 1976. 7.95 (ISBN 0-397-31664-X); pap. 2.95 (ISBN 0-397-31665-8). Lippincott.

Sutton, Harry T. Ghost Hunters: The Inside Story of Haunted Places. 1978. pap. 3.50 (ISBN 0-7134-1729-3, Pub. by Batsford England). David & Charles.

Tabori, Paul & Underwood, Peter. The Ghosts of Borley: Annals of the Haunted Rectory. (Illus.). 1974. 4.95 (ISBN 0-7153-6118-X). David & Charles.

Taillepied, Noel. A Treatise of Ghosts. LC 71-162520. 1971. Repr. of 1933 ed. 22.00 (ISBN 0-8103-3741-X). Gale.

Taves, Isabella. True Ghost Stories. (Illus.). (gr. 5 up). 1978. PLB 6.90 s&l (ISBN 0-531-02225-0). Watts.

Thayer, Jane. Gus Was a Mexican Ghost. (Illus.). 32p. (ps-3). 1974. 7.75 (ISBN 0-688-20104-0); PLB 7.44 (ISBN 0-688-30104-5). Morrow.

Thurston, Herbert. Ghosts & Poltergeists. LC 77-9596. 1977. Repr. of 1953 ed. lib. bdg. 25.00 (ISBN 0-8414-8557-7). Folcroft.

Titler, Dale. Haunted Treasures. LC 76-10304. (Illus.). (gr. 5-8). 1976. PLB 5.95 (ISBN 0-13-384172-3). P-H.

Von Bober, Wolffgang. The Carver Effect: A Paranormal Experience. (Illus.). 224p. 1979. 11.95 (ISBN 0-8117-0329-0). Stackpole.

Weinberg, Alyce T. Spirits of Frederick. LC 79-54039. (Illus.). 73p. (Orig.). 1979. pap. 3.95x (ISBN 0-9604552-0-5). A T Weinberg.

Wells, Dean F. The Ghosts of Rowan Oak: William Faulkner's Ghost Stories for Children. LC 80-52628. (Illus.). 64p. 1980. 9.95 (ISBN 0-686-77580-5). Yoknapatawpha.

Westbie, Constance & Cameron, Harold. Night Stalks the Mansion. 1979. pap. 2.50 (ISBN 0-553-14960-1). Bantam.

Williams, Gurney. Ghosts & Poltergeists. (Illus.). (gr. 4-6). 1979. PLB 5.90 s&l (ISBN 0-531-02214-5). Watts.

Windham, Kathryn T. Jeffrey Introduces Thirteen More Southern Ghosts. LC 70-170663. (Illus.). (gr. 9 up). 1971. 7.95 (ISBN 0-87397-016-0). Strode.

--Thirteen Georgia Ghosts & Jeffrey. LC 73-87004. 1973. 7.95 (ISBN 0-87397-041-1). Strode.

Windham, Kathryn T. & Figh, Margaret G. Thirteen Alabama Ghosts & Jeffrey. LC 71-94443. 1969. 7.95 (ISBN 0-87397-008-X). Strode.

GHURKAS

see Gurkhas

GIACOMETTI, ALBERTO, 1901-1966

Giacometti, No. 65. (Derriere le Miroir Ser.). (Fr.). 1977. pap. 19.95 (ISBN 0-8120-0913-4). Barron.

Lord, James. A Giacometti Portrait. 1980. 10.95 (ISBN 0-374-16199-2); pap. 7.95 (ISBN 0-374-51573-5). FS&G.

GIANNINI, AMADEO PETER, 1870-1949

James, Marquis. Biography of a Bank: The Story of Bank of America N. T. & S. A. LC 77-109291. (Illus.). 1971. Repr. of 1954 ed. lib. bdg. 28.00x (ISBN 0-8371-3834-5, JABI). Greenwood.

GIANNUZZI'S SEMILUNAR BODIES

see Salivary Glands

GIANTS

Frankcom, G. & Musgrave, J. H. The Irish Giant. (Illus.). 128p. 1976. 15.50x (ISBN 0-7156-1021-X, Pub. by Duckworth England). Biblio Dist.

Goldstein, Sam. Goliath to Gog: A Gallery of Giants from Fable, Fact, Fiction & Folklore. (Odd Books for Odd Moments Ser.). (Illus.). 72p. (Orig.). 1980. pap. 3.95 (ISBN 0-938338-00-5). Winds World Pr.

Hoke. Giants, Giants, Giants. (gr. 7 up). 1980. PLB 8.40 (ISBN 0-531-04172-7, E41). Watts.

Naden, C. J. I Can Read About All Kinds of Giants. new ed. LC 78-65833. (Illus.). (gr. 2-4). 1979. pap. 1.25 (ISBN 0-89375-201-0). Troll Assocs.

Odor, Ruth S. Learning About Giants. (Learning About Ser.). (Illus.). (gr. 2-6). 1981. PLB 9.25 (ISBN 0-516-06534-3). Childrens.

Wallace, Daisy, ed. Giant Poems. LC 77-21038. (Illus.). (gr. k-3). 1978. PLB 5.95 (ISBN 0-8234-0326-2). Holiday.

Wood, Edward J. Giants & Dwarfs. LC 76-42260. 1976. Repr. of 1868 ed. lib. bdg. 45.00 (ISBN 0-8414-9609-9). Folcroft.

GIANTS (BASEBALL CLUB)

see San Francisco Baseball Club (National League, Giants)

GIBBERELLIN

Merritt, James H., ed. Gibberellins. LC 61-11135. (Advances in Chemistry Ser: No. 28). 1961. 11.25 (ISBN 0-8412-0029-7). Am Chemical.

GIBBON, EDWARD, 1737-1794

Blunden, Edmund. Edward Gibbon & His Age. 1978. Repr. of 1935 ed. lib. bdg. 7.50 (ISBN 0-8495-0448-1). Arden Lib.

Blunden, Edmund C. Edward Gibbon & His Age. LC 74-14702. 1974. Repr. of 1935 ed. lib. bdg. 7.50 (ISBN 0-8414-3287-2). Folcroft.

Bond, Harold L. The Literary Art of Edward Gibbon. LC 75-4977. 167p. 1975. Repr. of 1960 ed. lib. bdg. 15.00x (ISBN 0-8371-8050-3, BOLA). Greenwood.

Bowersock, Glen, et al, eds. Edward Gibbon & the Decline & Fall of the Roman Empire. 1977. 12.50 (ISBN 0-674-23940-7). Harvard U Pr.

Fuglum, Per. Edward Gibbon: His View of Life & Conception of History. LC 73-16350. 1953. lib. bdg. 22.50 (ISBN 0-8414-4166-9). Folcroft.

Gay, Peter. Style in History. LC 76-25490. (McGraw-Hill Paperbacks). 1976. pap. 3.95 (ISBN 0-07-023063-3, SP). McGraw.

Gibbon, Edward. Autobiography. (World's Classics, No. 139). 14.95 (ISBN 0-19-250139-9). Oxford U Pr.

Gibboniana, 17 vols. Incl. Vol. 1 (ISBN 0-8240-1338-7); Vol. 2 (ISBN 0-8240-1339-5); Vol. 3 (ISBN 0-8240-1340-9); Vol. 4 (ISBN 0-8240-1341-7); Vol. 5 (ISBN 0-8240-1342-5); Vol. 6 (ISBN 0-8240-1343-3); Vol. 7 (ISBN 0-8240-1344-1); Vol. 8 (ISBN 0-8240-1345-X); Vol. 9 (ISBN 0-8240-1346-8); Vols. 10 & 11. Set. lib. bdg. 76.00 (ISBN 0-8240-1347-6); Vol. 12 (ISBN 0-8240-1348-4); Vol. 13 (ISBN 0-8240-1349-2); Vol. 14 (ISBN 0-8240-1350-6); Vol. 15 (ISBN 0-8240-1351-4); Vol. 16 (ISBN 0-8240-1352-2); Vol. 17 (ISBN 0-8240-1353-0). (The Life & Times of Seven Major British Writers Ser). 1974. lib. bdg. 47.00 ea. Garland Pub.

Gossman, Lionel. The Empire Unpossess'd: An Essay on Gibbon's "Decline & Fall". LC 80-24008. (Illus.). 176p. 1981. 19.95 (ISBN 0-521-23453-0). Cambridge U Pr.

Groom, Bernard. The Autobiography of Edward Gibbon. 198p. 1980. Repr. of 1930 ed. lib. bdg. 15.00 (ISBN 0-89760-312-5, Telegraph). Dynamic Learn Corp.

Hitchcock, Thomas. Unhappy Loves of Men of Genius: Gibbon, Johnson, Goethe, Mozart & Irving. 1979. Repr. of 1892 ed. lib. bdg. 25.00 (ISBN 0-8492-5322-5). R West.

Jordan, David P. Gibbon & His Roman Empire. LC 78-141515. 1971. 17.50 (ISBN 0-252-00152-4). U of Ill Pr.

Joyce, Michael & Fuglum, Per. Edward Gibbon. 1953. Repr. 25.00 (ISBN 0-8274-3804-4). R West.

Keynes, Geoffrey, ed. Edward Gibbon's Library: A Catolgue. (Illus.). 288p. 1980. Repr. of 1940 ed. 30.00x (ISBN 0-906795-02-8). U Pr of Va.

McCloy, Shelby T. Gibbon's Antagonism to Christianity. 1933. 23.50 (ISBN 0-8337-2311-1). B Franklin.

Morison, J. C. Gibbon. Morley, John, ed. LC 68-58387. (English Men of Letters). Repr. of 1887 ed. lib. bdg. 12.50 (ISBN 0-404-51719-6). AMS Pr.

Morison, James C. Gibbon. 1979. Repr. of 1879 ed. lib. bdg. 15.00 (ISBN 0-8495-3842-4). Arden Lib.

--Gibbon. 1977. Repr. lib. bdg. 15.00 (ISBN 0-8492-1754-7). R West.

Mowat, R. B. Gibbon. 282p. 1980. Repr. of 1936 ed. lib. bdg. 30.00 (ISBN 0-8495-3827-0). Arden Lib.

--Gibbon. 1936. 30.00 (ISBN 0-8274-2407-8). R West.

Norton, Jane E. Bibliography of the Works of Edward Gibbon. 1940. 14.95 (ISBN 0-8337-2577-7). B Franklin.

Parkinson, R. N. Edward Gibbon. (English Authors Ser.: No. 159). 1973. lib. bdg. 10.95 (ISBN 0-8057-1218-6). Twayne.

Walpole, Spencer. Studies in Biography: Mr. Disraeli & Edward Gibbon. 1979. Repr. of 1907 ed. lib. bdg. 30.00 (ISBN 0-8492-2988-X). R West.

White, Lynn, Jr. The Transformation of the Roman World: Gibbon's Problem After Two Centuries. (UCLA Center for Medieval & Renaissance Studies). 1966. pap. 5.95x (ISBN 0-520-02491-5). U of Cal Pr.

Young, G. Gibbon. 59.95 (ISBN 0-8490-0234-6). Gordon Pr.

Young, G. M. Gibbon. 182p. 1980. Repr. of 1932 ed. lib. bdg. 25.00 (ISBN 0-8495-6125-6). Arden Lib.

GIBBONS, ORLANDO, 1583-1625

Fellowes, Edmund H. Orlando Gibbons & His Family: The Last of the Tudor School of Musicians. 2nd ed. (Illus.). 1970. Repr. of 1951 ed. 12.50 (ISBN 0-208-00848-9, Archon). Shoe String.

GIBBONS

Borea, Phyllis. Seymour, a Gibbon: About Apes & Other Animals & How You Can Help to Keep Them Alive. LC 73-75431. (Illus.). (gr. 4-7). 1973. PLB 5.25 (ISBN 0-689-30415-3, McElderry Bk). Atheneum.

Carpenter, Clarence R. A Field Study in Siam of the Behavior & Social Relations of the Gibbon. LC 76-44702. Repr. of 1941 ed. 26.00 (ISBN 0-404-15855-2). AMS Pr.

Hancock, Lyn. Gypsy in the Classroom. LC 79-92182. (Illus.). 1980. 9.95x (ISBN 0-89696-085-4). Everest Hse.

Rumbaught, Duane M., ed. Gibbon & Siamang: A Series of Volumes on the Lesser Apes, 4 vols. Incl. Vol. 1. Evolution, Ecology, Behavior & Captive Maintenance. 1972. 81.00 (ISBN 3-8055-1362-3); Vol. 2. Anatomy, Dentition, Taxonomy & Molecular Evolution & Behavior. 1973. 81.00 (ISBN 3-8055-1341-0); Vol. 3. Natural History, Social Behavior, Reproduction, Vocalizations, Prehension. 1974. 78.00 (ISBN 3-8055-1602-9); Vol. 4. Suspensory Behavior, Locomotion, & Other Behaviors of Captive Gibbons; Cognition. 1976. 140.75 (ISBN 3-8055-1658-4). (Illus.). Set. 380.25 (ISBN 3-8055-2308-4). S Karger.

GIBBONS FAMILY

Fellowes, Edmund H. Orlando Gibbons & His Family: The Last of the Tudor School of Musicians. 2nd ed. (Illus.). 1970. Repr. of 1951 ed. 12.50 (ISBN 0-208-00848-9, Archon). Shoe String.

GIBBS, JOSIAH WILLARD, 1839-1908

Crowther, James G. Famous American Men of Science. facs. ed. LC 69-18925. (Essay Index Reprint Ser). 1937. 25.00 (ISBN 0-8369-0040-5). Arno.

Donnan, Frederick G. & Haas, Arthur, eds. Commentary on the Scientific Writings of Josiah-Willard Gibbs: A Propos de la Publication Des Ses Memories Scientifiques, 3 vols. in 2. LC 79-7963. (Three Centuries of Science in America Ser.). 1980. Repr. of 1936 ed. Set. lib. bdg. 100.00x (ISBN 0-405-12544-5); lib. bdg. 50.00x ea. Vol. 1 (ISBN 0-405-12611-5). Vol. 2 (ISBN 0-405-12612-3). Arno.

Seeger, Raymond J. Josiah Willard Gibbs-American Physicist Par Excellance. (Men of Physics Ser.). 1975. 34.00 (ISBN 0-08-018013-2). Pergamon.

Wheeler, Lynde P. Josiah Willard Gibbs, the History of a Great Mind. (Illus.). 1970. Repr. of 1962 ed. 18.50 (ISBN 0-208-00826-8, Archon). Shoe String.

GIBRALTAR

Stamp, Maxwell. Gibraltar: British or Spanish? 256p. 1976. 65.00x (ISBN 0-904655-10-5). Intl Pubns Serv.

Truver, Scott G. The Strait of Gibraltar & the Mediterranean. (International Straits of the World Ser.: No. 4). 280p. 1980. 40.00x (ISBN 90-286-0709-9). Sijthoff & Noordhoff.

GIBRALTAR-HISTORY

McGuffie, T. H. The Seige of Gibraltar, 1779-1783. (Illus.). 1965. 8.50 (ISBN 0-8023-1074-5). Dufour.

GIBRAN, KAHLIL, 1883-1931

Bushrui. Gibran of Lebanon. 12.00x (ISBN 0-86685-008-2). Intl Bk Ctr.

Ghougassian, Joseph P. Kahlil Gibran: Wings of Thought. (Illus.). 235p. 1973. 7.50 (ISBN 0-685-30347-0). Philos Lib.

Gibran, Kahlil. Secrets of the Heart. 160p. 1973. pap. 1.25 (ISBN 0-451-07332-0, Y7332, Sig). NAL.

Hilu, Virginia, ed. Beloved Prophet: The Love Letters of Kahlil Gibran & Mary Haskell & Her Private Journal. 1972. 12.95 (ISBN 0-394-43298-3). Knopf.

Kahlil Gibran: Collection of His Famous Works. 25.00x (ISBN 0-86685-149-6). Intl Bk Ctr.

Sherfan, Andrew D. Kahlil Gibran: Nature of Love. LC 70-136015. 1971. 4.75 (ISBN 0-685-77557-7). Philos Lib.

Young, Barbara. This Man from Lebanon. (Illus.). (YA) 1950. 12.50 (ISBN 0-394-44848-0). Knopf.

GIBSON, ALTHEA, 1927-

Fago, John N. & Farr, Naunerle C. Jim Thorpe - Althea Gibson. (Pendulum Illustrated Biography Ser.). (Illus.). (gr. 4-12). 1979. text ed. 5.00 (ISBN 0-88301-372-X); pap. text ed. 1.95 (ISBN 0-88301-360-6); wkbk. 1.25 (ISBN 0-88301-384-3). Pendulum Pr.

Gibson, Althea. I Always Wanted to Be Somebody. (Illus.). 1958. PLB 8.79 (ISBN 0-06-011516-5, HarpT). Har-Row.

GIBSON, CHARLES DANA, 1867-1944

Gibson, Charles D. Gibson Girl & Her America. Gillon, Edmund V., ed. LC 68-28065. (Illus., Orig.). 1969. pap. 4.50 (ISBN 0-486-21986-0). Dover.

GIBSON, GEORGE RUTLEDGE, 1810-ca. 1885

Gibson, George R. Journal of a Soldier Under Kearny & Doniphan: 1846-47. Bieber, Ralph P., ed. LC 74-7159. (Southwest Historical Ser.: Vol. 3). (Illus.). 371p. Repr. of 1935 ed. lib. bdg. 20.00x (ISBN 0-87991-303-7). Porcupine Pr.

GIBSON, WALTER MURRAY

Adler, Jacob & Barrett, Gwynn W. The Diaries of Walter Murray Gibson, 1886-1887. LC 75-188977. (Illus.). 200p. 1973. 12.00 (ISBN 0-8248-0211-X). U Pr of Hawaii.

Bailey, Paul. Hawaii's Royal Prime Minister: The Life & Times of Walter Murray Gibson. new ed. (Illus.). 320p. 1980. 13.95 (ISBN 0-8038-3058-0). Hastings.

Daws, Gavan. A Dream of Islands. (Illus.). 1980. 14.95 (ISBN 0-393-01293-X). Norton.

GIBSON, WILLIAM, 1914-

Gibson, William. A Season in Heaven. LC 74-77624. 192p. 1974. 6.95 (ISBN 0-689-10615-7). Atheneum.

--Shakespeare's Game. LC 77-15912. 1978. 10.95 (ISBN 0-689-10877-X); pap. 5.95 (ISBN 0-689-70573-5, 241). Atheneum.

GIDE, ANDRE PAUL GUILLAUME, 1869-1951

Ames, V. M. Andre Gide. LC 47-11811. Repr. of 1947 ed. 18.00 (ISBN 0-527-02350-7). Kraus Repr.

Andre Gide, Eighteen Sixty Nine-Nineteen Fifty One. (YFS Ser.: No. 7). pap. 6.00 (ISBN 0-527-01715-9). Kraus Repr.

Arland, Marcel & Mouton, Jean, eds. Entretiens Sur Andre Gide: Decades Du Centre Culturel International De Cerisy-la-Salle. (Nouvelle Ser.: No. 3). 1967. pap. 20.50x (ISBN 90-2796-014-3). Mouton.

Bettinson, Christopher. Gide: A Study. 104p. 1977. 10.00x (ISBN 0-87471-936-4). Rowman.

Brennan, J. G. Three Philosophical Novelists. 1964. 9.95 (ISBN 0-02-514930-X). Macmillan.

Ciholas, Karin. Gide's Art of the Fugue: A Thematic Study of "les Faux-Monnayeurs". (Studies in the Romance Languages & Literatures: No. 153). 1974. pap. 10.50x (ISBN 0-8078-9153-3). U of NC Pr.

Claudel, Paul. Correspondance avec Andre Gide: 1899-1926. 1949. pap. 7.95 (ISBN 0-686-51967-1). French & Eur.

Cordle, Thomas. Andre Gide. (World Authors Ser.: France: No. 86). lib. bdg. 12.50 (ISBN 0-8057-2364-1). Twayne.

--Andre Gide. LC 74-80079. (Griffin Authors Ser). 183p. 1975. pap. 4.95 (ISBN 0-312-03640-X). St Martin.
Cunningham, Joyce I. & Wilson, W. D. A Concordance to Andre Gide's la Symphonie Pastorale. LC 78-19620. (Reference Library of the Humanities: Vol. 124). 1979. lib. bdg. 30.00 (ISBN 0-8240-9754-8). Garland Pub.
Davis, J. C. Gide: L'Immoraliste & La Porte Etroite. (Studies in French Literature). 1974. pap. text ed. 3.95x (ISBN 0-7131-5518-3). Dynamic Learn Corp.
Delay, Jean. Youth of Andre Gide. Guicharnaud, June, tr. LC 63-13060. 1963. 12.00x (ISBN 0-226-14207-8). U of Chicago Pr.
Doucet, Jacques. Cataloguede Fonds Speciauxde la Bibliotheque Litteraire Jacques Doucet (Paris, France) (Lettres a Andre Gide). 1972. 90.00 (ISBN 0-8161-0951-6). G K Hall.
Du Gard, Roger M. Notes on Andre Gide. Russell, John, tr. 1953. 15.00 (ISBN 0-8274-3049-3). R West.
Falk, Eugene H. Types of Thematic Structure. LC 67-16775. 1967. 12.00x (ISBN 0-226-23609-9). U of Chicago Pr.
Freedman, Ralph. Lyrical Novel: Studies in Hermann Hesse, Andre Gide, & Virginia Woolf. 1963. 19.00 (ISBN 0-691-06071-1); pap. 7.95 (ISBN 0-691-01267-9, 62). Princeton U Pr.
Gide, Andre & Gosse, Edmund. The Correspondence of Andre Gide & Edmund Gosse: 1904-1928. Brugmans, Linette F., ed. LC 77-22619. (New York University. Studies in Romance Languages & Literature: No. 2). 1977. Repr. of 1959 ed. lib. bdg. 17.50x (ISBN 0-8371-9736-8, GICO). Greenwood.
Gide, Andre, et al. Correspondance, 1897-1944, 2 vol, Vol. 1. 1976. 75.00 (ISBN 0-686-56067-1). French & Eur.
--Correspondance, 1891-1938. 351p. 1975. 35.00 (ISBN 0-686-56065-5). French & Eur.
Goulet, Alain. Caves du Vatican d'Andre Gide: Etude methodologigue. new ed. (La Collection themes et textes). 288p. (Orig., Fr.). 1972. pap. 4.95 (ISBN 2-03-035006-0, 2693). Larousse.
Guerard, Albert J. Andre Gide. rev. ed. LC 74-88805. 1969. 16.50x (ISBN 0-674-03525-9). Harvard U Pr.
Laidlaw, G. Norman. Elysian Encounter: Diderot & Gide. LC 63-19193. 1963. 12.95x (ISBN 0-8156-2054-3). Syracuse U Pr.
Lemaitre, George. Four French Novelists: Marcel Proust, Andre Gide, Jean Giraudoux, Paul Morand. LC 68-8201. (Essay & General Literature Reprint Ser). 1969. Repr. of 1938 ed. 15.00 (ISBN 0-8046-0267-0). Kennikat.
McLaren, James C. Theatre of Andre Gide: Evolution of a Moral Philosopher. LC 73-120645. 1970. Repr. lib. bdg. 10.00x (ISBN 0-374-95522-0). Octagon.
Mann, Klaus. Andre Gide & the Crisis of Modern Thought. 1978. lib. bdg. 16.50x (ISBN 0-374-95266-3). Octagon.
Martin du Gard, Roger. Notes sur Andre Gide. 156p. 1951. 3.95 (ISBN 0-686-55504-X). French & Eur.
Naville. Bibliographie des Ecrits d'Andre Gide Depuis 1891 Jusqu'a Sa Mort. 13.50 (ISBN 0-685-34162-3). French & Eur.
Naville, Arnold. Bibliographie des Ecrits d'Andre Gide De 1891 Jusqu'a 1949, 2 vols. in 1. 1971. Repr. of 1949 ed. lib. bdg. 22.50 (ISBN 0-8337-2503-3). B Franklin.
Neilson, Francis. Andre Gide: Individualist. 1979. lib. bdg. 39.95 (ISBN 0-685-96608-9). Revisionist Pr.
Nersoyan, H. J. Andre Gide: The Theism of an Atheist. LC 69-17717. 1969. 15.95x (ISBN 0-8156-2135-3). Syracuse U Pr.
O'Brien, Justin. Portrait of Andre Gide. 390p. 1976. Repr. of 1953 ed. lib. bdg. 22.50x (ISBN 0-374-96139-5). Octagon.
O'Neill, K. Andre Gide & the Roman D'adventure. (Australian Humanities Research Council Monograph: No. 15). 1969. pap. 5.00x (ISBN 0-424-05990-8, Pub by Sydney U Pr). Intl Schol Bk Serv.
Peters, Arthur K. Jean Cocteau & Andre Gide: An Abrasive Friendship. LC 73-185393. 1973. 30.00 (ISBN 0-8135-0709-X). Rutgers U Pr.
Pierre-Quint, Leon. Andre Gide. Richardson, Dorothy, tr. 1934. 30.00 (ISBN 0-8274-1865-5). R West.
Rossi, Vinio. Andre Gide. LC 68-54458. (Columbia Essays on Modern Writers Ser.: No. 35). (Orig.). 1968. pap. 2.00 (ISBN 0-231-02960-8). Columbia U Pr.
Schlumberger, Jean. Madeleine & Andre Gide. Akeroyd, Richard H., tr. (Illus.). 1980. 12.50 (ISBN 0-916620-45-X). Portals Pr.
Stoltzfus, Ben. Gide & Hemingway: Rebels Against God. (National University Pubns. Literary Criticism Ser.). 1978. 9.95 (ISBN 0-8046-9214-9). Kennikat.
--Gide's Eagles. LC 69-11502. (Crosscurrents-Modern Critiques Ser.). 201p. 1969. 7.95 (ISBN 0-8093-0347-7). S Ill U Pr.
Thomas, Lawrence. Andre Gide: The Ethic of the Artist. 1950. 30.00 (ISBN 0-8274-1866-3). R West.
Weinberg, Kurt. On Gide's Promethee: Private Myth & Public Mystification. LC 70-173760. (Princeton Essays in Literature Ser.). 144p. 1972. 14.50x (ISBN 0-691-06222-6). Princeton U Pr.

GIDEON, JUDGE OF ISRAEL

Andre, G. Gideon, Samson & Other Judges of Israel. (Let's Discuss It Ser.). pap. 0.95 (ISBN 0-686-13261-0); pap. 9.50 per doz. (ISBN 0-686-13262-9). Believers Bkshelf.
Keller, W. Phillip. Mighty Man of Valor. 1979. 6.95 (ISBN 0-8007-0997-7); pap. 4.95 (ISBN 0-8007-5072-1, Power Bks). Revell.
Lindsay, Gordon. Gideon & the Early Judges. (Old Testament Ser.). 1.25 (ISBN 0-89985-135-5). Christ Nations.

GIDEON, CLARENCE EARL

Lewis, Anthony. Clarence Earl Gideon & the Supreme Court. (Sundial Paperbks.). 1972. pap. 2.45 (ISBN 0-394-70807-5, VS7, Vin). Random.
--Gideon's Trumpet. 1964. pap. 2.50 (ISBN 0-394-70315-4, Vin). Random.

GIFFEN, ROBERT, SIR, 1837-1910

Bain, Francis W. Corner in Gold: Its History & Theory. LC 68-28615. 1968. Repr. of 1893 ed. lib. bdg. 15.00 (ISBN 0-8371-0292-8, BACG). Greenwood.

GIFFORD, WILLIAM, 1756-1826

Clark, Roy B. William Gifford, Tory Satirist, Critic & Editor. LC 66-27053. 1967. Repr. of 1930 ed. 9.00 (ISBN 0-8462-0872-5). Russell.
Dyce, Alexander. Remarks on Mister J. P. Collier's & Mister C. Knight's Editions of Shakespeare. LC 79-164815. Repr. of 1844 ed. 24.00 (ISBN 0-404-02230-8). AMS Pr.

GIFT-BOOKS (ANNUALS, ETC.)

Althea. Herb for Presents. (ps-2). 1979. pap. 1.45 avail. in 5 pk. (ISBN 0-85122-179-3, Pub. by Dinosaur Pubns). Merrimack Bk Serv.
Franklin, Linda C. Address Book. (Old Fashioned Keepbook). (Illus.). 128p. 1981. 14.95 (ISBN 0-934504-07-5). Tree Comm.
--A Baby Book for... (Old Fashioned Keepbook Ser.). 96p. 1980. 9.95 (ISBN 0-934504-03-2). Tree Comm.
--Wedding Notebook for the Bride. (Old Fashioned Keepbook Ser.). 128p. 1980. 9.95 (ISBN 0-934504-02-4). Tree Comm.
Gifts Annual Buyers Guide 1979. (Benn Directories Ser.). 1979. 20.00 (ISBN 0-686-52401-2, Pub by Benn Pubns). Nichols Pub.
Hammel, Faye. A Star Is Born. (Illus.). 1979. boxed ed. 5.95 (ISBN 0-89742-013-6, Dawne-Leigh). Celestial Arts.
Haugan, Randolph E., ed. Christmas: An American Annual of Christmas Literature & Art, Vol. 46. LC 32-30914. 1976. 8.95 (ISBN 0-8066-8948-X, 17-0113); pap. 4.75 (ISBN 0-8066-8947-1, 17-0112). Augsburg.
Hughes, Lynn, ed. Hares. (Illus.). 64p. 1981. 4.95 (ISBN 0-312-92284-1). Congdon & Lattes.
--Unicorns. (Illus.). 64p. 1981. 4.95 (ISBN 0-312-92865-3). Congdon & Lattes.
Hughs, Lynn, ed. Cats. (Illus.). 64p. 1981. 4.95 (ISBN 0-312-92087-3). Congdon & Lattes.
Martin, Robert J. My Graduation Year. 1977. PLB 9.95 (ISBN 0-8010-6021-4). Baker Bk.
Thompson, Ralph. American Literary Annuals & Gift Books, 1825-1865. 1967. Repr. of 1936 ed. 17.50 (ISBN 0-208-00400-9, Archon). Shoe String.

GIFT OF TONGUES

see Glossolalia

GIFT TAX

see Gifts–Taxation

GIFT WRAPPING

Cornell, Jane. The Art of Gift Wrapping. LC 80-14156. (The Warner Lifestyle Library). (Illus.). 1980. 13.95 (ISBN 0-446-51212-5); pap. 7.95 (ISBN 0-446-97474-9). Warner Bks.
Oka, Hideyuki. How to Wrap Five More Eggs: Traditional Japanese Packaging. LC 74-23690. (Illus.). 216p. 1975. 18.75 (ISBN 0-8348-0108-6). Weatherhill.
Wrapping Methods Manual. 90p. 1968. soft bdg. 5.50 (ISBN 0-685-44064-8, SM867). Natl Ret Merch.

GIFTED CHILDREN

see also Children as Actors; Children as Artists; Children As Authors; Children As Musicians; Talented Students

American Association for Gifted Children. The Gifted Child. Witty, Paul, ed. LC 79-148630. 338p. 1972. Repr. of 1951 ed. lib. bdg. 21.50x (ISBN 0-8371-6002-2, AAGC). Greenwood.
--On Being Gifted. LC 78-58622. 1979. 8.95 (ISBN 0-8027-0616-9); pap. 7.95 (ISBN 0-8027-7138-6). Walker & Co.
Barbe, Walter B. & Renzulli, Joseph S., eds. Psychology & Education of the Gifted. 3rd ed. 544p. 1981. text ed. 18.95x (ISBN 0-8290-0234-0). Irvington.
Brumbaugh, F. N., et al. Intellectually Gifted. Frampton, Merle E. & Gall, Elena D., eds. (Special Education Ser). 1956. pap. 1.00 (ISBN 0-87558-016-5). Porter Sargent.
Burks, Barbara S., et al. The Promise of Youth: Follow-up Studies of a Thousand Gifted Children. (Genetic Studies of Genius Ser). 1930. 27.50x (ISBN 0-8047-0011-7). Stanford U Pr.
Callahan, Carolyn M. Developing Creativity in the Gifted & Talented. LC 78-68115. 1978. pap. text ed. 5.00 (ISBN 0-86586-019-X). Coun Exc Child.
Conklin, Agnes M. Failure of Highly Intelligent Pupils: A Study of Their Behavior by Means of the Control Group. LC 76-176666. (Columbia University. Teachers College. Contributions to Education: No. 792). Repr. of 1940 ed. 17.50 (ISBN 0-404-55792-9). AMS Pr.
Counseling Your Gifted Child. (Ser. on Talented & Gifted Education). 1979. 2.95 (ISBN 0-89354-134-6). Northwest Regional.
Cox, Catharine M. The Early Mental Traits of Three Hundred Geniuses. (Genetic Studies of Genius Ser). 1926. 32.50x (ISBN 0-8047-0010-9). Stanford U Pr.
Dennis, Wayne & Dennis, Margaret W., eds. The Intellectually Gifted: An Overview. LC 76-41850. (Illus.). 352p. 1976. 38.00 (ISBN 0-8089-0962-2). Grune.
Fortna, Richard O. & Boston, Bruce O. Testing the Gifted Child: An Interpretation in Lay Language. LC 76-46730. 1976. pap. text ed. 3.75 (ISBN 0-86586-085-8). Coun Exc Child.
Gowan, John C. & Bruch, Catherine B. Academically Talented Student & Guidance. (Guidance Monograph). 1970. pap. 2.60 (ISBN 0-395-10850-0, 9-78853). HM.
Hayes, Leola G. Occupational & Vocational Interest for the Exceptional Individual. 150p. 1977. pap. text ed. 7.50 (ISBN 0-8191-0146-X). U Pr of Amer.
Hollingworth, Leta S. Children Above 180 Iq Stanford Binet: Origins & Development. LC 74-21417. (Classics in Child Development Ser). (Illus.). 356p. 1975. Repr. 22.00x (ISBN 0-405-06467-5). Arno.
--Gifted Children: Their Nature & Nurture. 1979. Repr. of 1926 ed. lib. bdg. 45.00 (ISBN 0-8492-5345-4). R West.
Kaplan, Sandra N. Activities for Gifted Children. (Illus.). Date not set. 11.95 (ISBN 0-685-59802-0); pap. 8.95 (ISBN 0-685-59803-9). Goodyear.
Kaufmann, Felice. Your Gifted Child & You. LC 76-21990. 1977. pap. text ed. 4.50 (ISBN 0-86586-096-3). Coun Exc Child.
Khatena, Joe. The Creatively Gifted Child: Suggestions for Parents & Teachers. 1978. 6.95 (ISBN 0-533-03240-7). Vantage.
Lamson, Edna E. A Study of Young Gifted Children in Senior High School. LC 73-176972. (Columbia University. Teachers College. Contributions to Education: No. 424). Repr. of 1930 ed. 17.50 (ISBN 0-404-55424-5). AMS Pr.
Laubenfels, Jean M. The Gifted Student: An Annotated Bibliography. (Contemporary Problems of Childhood: No. 1). 1977. lib. bdg. 15.00 (ISBN 0-8371-9760-0, LGC/). Greenwood.
Laycock, Frank. Gifted Children. 1979. pap. text ed. 8.95x (ISBN 0-673-15142-5). Scott F.
Mallis, Jackie. You & Your Gifted Child. 200p. (Orig.). 1981. pap. 11.95x (ISBN 0-86617-020-0). Multi Media TX.
Martinson, Ruth A. The Identification of the Gifted & Talented. LC 75-37392. 1975. pap. text ed. 6.35 (ISBN 0-86586-043-2). Coun Exc Child.
Moore, Margaret. A Study of Young High School Graduates. LC 74-177081. (Columbia University. Teachers College. Contributions to Education: No. 583). Repr. of 1933 ed. 17.50 (ISBN 0-404-55583-7). AMS Pr.
Nazzaro, Jean, ed. Exceptional Timetables: Historical Events Affecting the Handicapped & Gifted. 1977. pap. text ed. 5.00 (ISBN 0-86586-031-9). Coun Exc Child.
Revesz, Geza. Psychology of a Musical Prodigy. Repr. of 1925 ed. lib. bdg. 15.00x (ISBN 0-8371-4004-8, REMP). Greenwood.
Sattler, Jerome M. Assessement of Children's Intelligence & Special Abilities. 2nd ed. 850p. 1981. text ed. 24.95 (ISBN 0-205-07362-X, 7973624); tchrs ed. free (ISBN 0-205-07379-4, 7973799); write for info. study guide. Allyn.
Seagoe, May V. Terman & the Gifted. LC 75-19063. 271p. 1975. 12.50 (ISBN 0-913232-27-0). W Kaufmann.
Sellin, Don & Birch, Jack. Psycoeducational Development of Gifted & Talented Learners. 350p. 1981. text ed. write for info. (ISBN 0-89443-362-8). Aspen Systems.
Simmons, Rachel. A Study of a Group of Children of Exceptionally High Intelligence Quotient in Situations Partaking of the Nature of Suggestion. LC 71-177781. (Columbia University. Teachers College. Contributions to Education: No. 788). Repr. of 1940 ed. 17.50 (ISBN 0-404-55788-0). AMS Pr.
Terman, Lewis M. & Oden, Melita H. The Gifted Child Grows up: Twenty-Five Years' Follow-up of a Superior Group. (Genetic Studies of Genius Ser.). 1947. 20.00x (ISBN 0-8047-0012-5). Stanford U Pr.
--The Gifted Group at Mid-Life: Thiry-Five Years' Follow-up of the Superior Child. (Genetic Studies of Genius Ser). 1959. 12.50x (ISBN 0-8047-0013-3). Stanford U Pr.
Terman, Lewis M., et al. Mental & Physical Traits of a Thousand Gifted Children. rev. ed. (Genetic Studies of Genius Ser). 1926. 29.50x (ISBN 0-8047-0009-5). Stanford U Pr.
Torrance, E. Paul, ed. Discovery & Nurturance of Giftedness in the Culturally Different. 1977. pap. text ed. 6.50 (ISBN 0-86586-021-1). Coun Exc Child.
Vail, Priscilla L. The World of the Gifted Child. 1979. 10.95 (ISBN 0-8027-0611-8). Walker & Co.
Weeks, Thelma E. Slow Speech Development of a Bright Child. LC 73-23019. (Illus.). 1974. 17.95 (ISBN 0-669-91876-8). Lexington Bks.
Who Is Gifted? (Ser. on Talented & Gifted Education). 1979. 2.95 (ISBN 0-89354-133-8). Northwest Regional.
Willings, David. The Creatively Gifted: Recognising & Developing the Creative Personality. 184p. 30.00x (ISBN 0-85941-120-6, Pub. by Woodhead-Faulkner England). State Mutual Bk.
Ziv, Avner. Counselling the Intellectually Gifted Child. 1977. pap. text ed. 4.50x (ISBN 0-8077-8021-9). Tchrs Coll.

GIFTED CHILDREN–EDUCATION

Administering Policy for Talented & Gifted. (Ser. on Talented & Gifted Education). 1979. 2.95 (ISBN 0-89354-126-5). Northwest Regional.
American Association for Gifted Children. Reaching Out: Advocacy for the Gifted & Talented. Tannenbaum, Abraham J., ed. (Perspectives on Gifted & Talented Education Ser.). (Orig.). 1980. pap. text ed. 4.95x (ISBN 0-8077-2591-9). Tchrs Coll.
Bagley, Richard, et al. Identifying the Talented & Gifted. (Ser. on Talented & Gifted Education). (Illus., Orig.). 1979. 2.95 (ISBN 0-89354-125-7). Northwest Regional.
Baldwin, Alexinia Y., et al, eds. Educational Planning for the Gifted: Overcoming Cultural, Geographic, & Socioeconomic Barriers. LC 78-60442. 1978. pap. text ed. 5.25 (ISBN 0-86586-025-4). Coun Exc Child.
Barbe, Walter B. & Renzulli, Joseph S., eds. Psychology & Education of the Gifted. 3rd ed. 544p. 1981. text ed. 18.95x (ISBN 0-8290-0234-0). Irvington.
Baughman, M. Dale, ed. Challenging Talented Junior High School Youth. pap. text ed. 1.50x (ISBN 0-8134-0589-0, 589). Interstate.
Boston, Bruce O. Gifted & Talented: Developing Elementary & Secondary School Programs. LC 75-24853. 1975. pap. text ed. 4.15 (ISBN 0-86586-037-8). Coun Exc Child.
Boston, Bruce O., ed. The Sorcerer's Apprentice: A Case Study in the Role of the Mentor. LC 76-21101. 1976. pap. text ed. 2.75 (ISBN 0-86586-075-0). Coun Exc Child.
Callahan, Carolyn M. Developing Creativity in the Gifted & Talented. LC 78-68115. 1978. pap. text ed. 5.00 (ISBN 0-86586-019-X). Coun Exc Child.
Characteristics of Talented & Gifted Children. (Ser. on Talented & Gifted Education). 1979. 2.95 (ISBN 0-89354-132-X). Northwest Regional.
Cherry, Clare. Creative Art for the Developing Child: A Teacher's Handbook for Early Childhood Education. LC 72-81202. 1972. pap. 7.95 (ISBN 0-8224-1630-1). Pitman Learning.
Clendening, Corinne P. & Davies, Ruth A. Creating Programs for the Gifted. (Illus.). 500p. 1980. 24.95 (ISBN 0-8352-1265-3). Bowker.
Corrigan, Dean C. & Howey, Kenneth R., eds. Special Education in Transition: Concepts to Guide the Education of Experienced Teachers with Implications for PL 94-142. LC 80-68281. 208p. 1980. pap. 12.95 (ISBN 0-86586-109-9). Coun Exc Child.
Coy, Genevieve L. The Interests, Abilities & Achievements of a Special Class for Gifted Childred. LC 70-176675. (Columbia University. Teachers College. Contributions to Education: No. 131). Repr. of 1923 ed. 17.50 (ISBN 0-404-55131-9). AMS Pr.
Dransfield, John E. Administration of Enrichment to Superior Children in a Typical Classroom. LC 70-176730. (Columbia University. Teachers College. Contributions to Education: N0. 558). Repr. of 1933 ed. 17.50 (ISBN 0-404-55558-6). AMS Pr.
Epstein, Carol. The Gifted & Talented. 1979. pap. 11.95 (ISBN 0-87545-017-2). Natl Sch Pr.
Gallagher, James J. Teaching the Gifted Child. 2nd ed. 416p. 1975. text ed. 20.95 (ISBN 0-205-04689-4, 2246899). Allyn.

George, William C., et al, eds. Educating the Gifted: Acceleration & Enrichment. LC 79-7559. (Hyman Blumberg Symposium on Research in Early Childhood Education). 1980. pap. text ed. 4.95x (ISBN 0-8018-2266-1). Johns Hopkins.

The Gifted Preschool Child. (Talented & Gifted Education Ser.). 1979. 2.95 (ISBN 0-89354-131-1). Northwest Regional.

Ginsberg, Gina & Harrison, Charles. How to Help Your Gifted Child. 1977. pap. 4.95 (ISBN 0-671-18759-7). Monarch Pr.

Gowan, John C. & Demos, George D. The Education & Guidance of the Ablest. (Illus.). 528p. 1964. photocopy ed. spiral 45.50 (ISBN 0-398-00714-4). C C Thomas.

Gowan, John C., et al. The Guidance of Exceptional Children. 2nd ed. LC 70-185135. 1980. pap. text ed. 12.95x (ISBN 0-582-28169-5, Pub. by MacKay). Longman.

Grossi, John A. Model State Policy, Legislation & State Plan Toward the Education of Gifted & Talented Students: A Handbook for State & Local Districts. 224p. (Orig.). 1980. pap. 14.95 (ISBN 0-86586-101-3). Coun Exc Child.

Hagen, Elizabeth. Identification of the Gifted. Tannenbaum, Abraham J., ed. (Perspectives on Gifted & Talented Education Ser.). (Orig.). 1980. pap. text ed. 5.50x (ISBN 0-8077-2588-9). Tchrs Coll.

Haisley, Fay B. & Wilhelmi, George. Talented & Gifted Education Policy. (Ser. on Talented & Gifted Education). (Illus., Orig.). 1979. 2.95 (ISBN 0-89354-127-3). Northwest Regional.

Hall, Eleanor & Skinner, Nancy. Somewhere to Turn: Strategies for Parents of Gifted & Talented Children. Tannenbaum, Abraham J., ed. (Perspectives on Gifted & Talented Education Ser.). (Orig.). 1980. pap. text ed. 5.50x (ISBN 0-8077-2589-7). Tchrs Coll.

Hasazi, Susan E. Under One Cover: Implementing the Least Restrictive Environment Concept. LC 80-68096. 208p. 1980. pap. 11.25 (ISBN 0-86586-106-4). Coun Exc Child.

Hegeman, Kathryn T. Gifted Children in the Regular Classroom: The Complete Guide for Teachers & Administrators. (Illus.). 200p. 1980. tchrs' ed. 15.00 (ISBN 0-89824-014-X). Trillium Pr.

Hellmuth, Jerome, ed. Special Child in Century 21. LC 64-55973. 1964. 16.00x (ISBN 0-87562-008-6). Spec Child.

Heuer, Janet, et al. Magic Kits: Meaningful Activities for the Gifted in the Classroom Through Knowledge, Interests, Training & Stimulation. (Illus.). 53p. 1980. pap. 7.95 (ISBN 0-936386-11-8). Creative Learning.

Hildreth, Gertrude H., et al. Educating Gifted Children at Hunter College Elementary School. Repr. of 1952 ed. lib. bdg. 15.00 (ISBN 0-8371-3941-4, HIEG). Greenwood.

Hopkins, Lee B. & Shapiro, Annette F. Creative Activities for the Gifted Child. (Illus.). 1969. pap. 3.95 (ISBN 0-8224-1625-5). Pitman Learning.

Hopkinson, David. The Education of Gifted Children. (New Education Ser.). 179p. 1978. 17.50x (ISBN 0-7130-0156-9, Pub. by Woburn Pr England). Biblio Dist.

Jackson, David M. Curriculum Development for the Gifted. (Special Education Series). (Illus.). 1980. pap. text ed. 10.95 (ISBN 0-89568-188-9). Spec Learn Corp.

--Foundations of Gifted Education. (Special Education Series). (Illus.). 1980. pap. text ed. 10.95 (ISBN 0-89568-189-7). Spec Learn Corp.

Jordan, June B. & Grossi, John A., eds. An Administrator's Handbook on Designing Programs for the Gifted & Talented. LC 80-68984. 144p. 1980. pap. 9.75 (ISBN 0-86586-112-9). Coun Exc Child.

Kaplan, Sandra. Providing Programs for the Gifted & Talented: A Handbook. LC 75-37393. 1975. pap. text ed. 6.75 (ISBN 0-86586-068-8). Coun Exc Child.

Karnes, Frances A. & Collins, Emily C. Assessment in Gifted Education. (Illus.). 304p. 1981. 21.75 (ISBN 0-398-04172-5). C C Thomas.

--Handbook of Instructional Resources & References for Teaching the Gifted. 1980. text ed. 18.95 (ISBN 0-205-06823-5, 246823-9). Allyn.

Karnes, Frances A. & Peddicord, Herschel, Jr. Programs, Leaders, Consultants & Other Resources in Gifted & Talented Education. 360p. 1980. 29.75 (ISBN 0-398-04099-0). C C Thomas.

Kemnitz, T. M., et al. Management Systems for Gifted & Special Education Programs: A Manual for Cost-Effective Administration. LC 81-52540. 150p. (Orig.). 1981. pap. text ed. 25.00 (ISBN 0-686-76575-3). Trillium Pr.

Keyes, Fenton. Exploring Careers for the Gifted. (Careers in Depth Ser.). (Illus.). 160p. (gr. 7-12). 1981. lib. bdg. 5.97 (ISBN 0-8239-0533-0). Rosen Pr.

Khatena, Joe. The Creatively Gifted Child: Suggestions for Parents & Teachers. 1978. 6.95 (ISBN 0-533-03240-7). Vantage.

Lake, S., ed. Gifted Education. 1981. pap. 12.50 (ISBN 0-912700-93-9). Oryx Pr.

Lake, Sara, ed. Gifted Education. (Special Interest Resource Guides in Education Ser.). (Orig.). 1981. pap. 12.50x (ISBN 0-912700-93-9). Oryx Pr.

Lamkin, Jill S. Getting Started: Career Education Activities for Exceptional Students. 144p. 1980. pap. 5.50 (ISBN 0-86586-113-7). Coun Exc Child.

Lawless, Ruth F. A Guide for Educating a Gifted Child in Your Classroom. (gr. 1-12). 1976. 2.25 (ISBN 0-914634-35-6). DOK Pubs.

--Programs for Gifted, Creative, Talented Children (for Little or No Money) (Illus.). 1977. 2.95 (ISBN 0-914634-38-0). DOK Pubs.

Lewis, Christine L., et al. Gemini: Gifted Education Manual for Individualizing Networks of Instruction. 80p. 1980. tchrs' ed 15.00 (ISBN 0-89824-015-8). Trillium Pr.

--Pegasus: Providing Enrichment for the Gifted by Adapting Selected Units of Study. Cantor, Marjorie A., ed. 250p. 1980. tchr's ed. 15.00 (ISBN 0-89824-017-4). Trillium Pr.

Lindsey, Margaret. Training Teachers of the Gifted & Talented. Tannenbaum, Abraham J., ed. LC 80-11867. (Perspectives on Gifted & Talented Education Ser.). (Orig.). 1980. pap. text ed. 5.50x (ISBN 0-8077-2590-0). Tchrs Coll.

Maker, C. June. Providing Programs for the Gifted Handicapped. LC 77-70241. (Illus.). 1977. pap. text ed. 6.50 (ISBN 0-86586-069-6). Coun Exc Child.

Maker, June. Curiculum Development for the Gifted. 375p. 1981. text ed. write for info. (ISBN 0-89443-347-4). Aspen Systems.

Male, Robert A. & Perrone, Philip. The Development Education & Guidance of Talented Learners. 350p. 1981. text ed. write for info. (ISBN 0-89443-359-8). Aspen Systems.

Mallis, Jackie. Reaching for the Stars: A Minicourse for Education of Gifted Students, 10 bks. Incl. Bk. 1. Characteristics. Heinemann, Alison. 106p. pap. text ed. 27.00 (ISBN 0-86617-001-4); Bk. 2. Needs. Duke, Elizabeth. 70p. pap. text ed. 22.00 (ISBN 0-86617-002-2); Bk. 3. Underachieving Gifted. Heinemann, Alison. 50p. pap. text ed. 15.00 (ISBN 0-86617-003-0); Bk. 4. Handicapped Gifted. Alexander, Nancy. 62p. pap. text ed. 18.00 (ISBN 0-86617-004-9); Bk. 5. Disadvantaged Gifted. Duke, Elizabeth. 56p. pap. text ed. 17.00- (ISBN 0-86617-005-7); Bk. 6. Using Knowledge About Intelligence. 70p. pap. text ed. 22.00 (ISBN 0-86617-006-5); Bk. 7. Using Knowledge About Creativity. Heinemann, Alison. 57p. pap. text ed. 17.00 (ISBN 0-86617-007-3); Bk. 8. Enrichment. Gilman, Sharlene. 125p. pap. text ed. 31.00 (ISBN 0-86617-008-1); Bk. 9. Programs. Heinemann, Alison. 169p. pap. text ed. 39.00 (ISBN 0-86617-009-X); Bk. 10. Counseling for the Gifted. Heinemann, Alison. 167p. pap. text ed. 40.00 (ISBN 0-86617-010-3). 1979. Set. pap. text ed. 180.00x (ISBN 0-86617-000-6). Multi Media TX.

Mann, Lester & Sabatino, David A., eds. The Fourth Review of Special Education. (Illus.). 499p. 1980. 44.50 (ISBN 0-8089-1263-1). Grune.

Mass, Lynne. Kids Working with Kids. 48p. 1980. 10.00 (ISBN 0-89824-018-2). Trillium Pr.

Moore, L. P. Does This Mean My Kid's a Genius. 224p. 1981. 10.96 (ISBN 0-07-042960-X). McGraw.

Morgan, Harry M., et al. Elementary & Secondary Level Programs for the Gifted & Talented. Tannenbaum, Abraham J., ed. (Perspectives on Gifted & Talented Education Ser.). (Orig.). 1980. pap. text ed. 5.95x (ISBN 0-8077-2592-7). Tchrs Coll.

Muia, Joseph & Alexander, Patricia. Gifted Education: A Comprehensive Roadmap. 300p. 1981. text ed. price not set (ISBN 0-89443-383-0). Aspen Systems.

Nason, Leslie J. Academic Achievement of Gifted High School Students. LC 58-8969. 92p. 1958. text ed. 3.95 (ISBN 0-88474-015-3). U of S Cal Pr.

Newland, T. Ernest. Gifted in Socio-Educational Perspective. (Special Education Ser.). (Illus.). 448p. 1976. 19.95 (ISBN 0-13-356287-5). P-H.

Noller, Ruth, et al. It's a Gas to Be Gifted. (Illus.). 52p. (Orig.). 1979. pap. text ed. 2.95 (ISBN 0-914634-64-X, 7908). DOK Pubs.

Olgilvie, Eric & George, David. Living Things-Environmental Sciences: Curriculum Enrichment Units for the Gifted & Academically Talented. (Special Education Ser.). (Illus.). 1980. 59.00 (ISBN 0-89568-231-1). Spec Learn Corp.

Olgilvie, Eric & Smith, Ron. Discovering History-Humanities: Curriculum Enrichment Units for the Gifted & Academically Talented. (Special Education Ser.). (Illus.), 1980. 59.00 (ISBN 0-89568-230-3). Spec Learn Corp.

Olgilvie, Eric & Wood, Anthony. Making Changes-Mathematics: Curriculum Enrichment Units for the Gifted & Academically Talented. (Special Education Ser.). (Illus.). 1980. 59.00 (ISBN 0-89568-229-X). Spec Learn Corp.

Olgilvie, Eric, et al. Eskimo Carving-Arts: Curriculum Enrichment Units for the Gifted & Academically Talented. (Special Education Ser.). (Illus.). 1980. 59.00 (ISBN 0-89568-232-X). Spec Learn Corp.

Organizing a Parent Support Group for Talented & Gifted. (Ser. on Talented & Gifted Education). 1979. 2.95 (ISBN 0-89354-129-X). Northwest Regional.

Osdol, William R. & Shane, Don G. Introduction to Exceptional Children, 3rd ed. 496p. 1981. pap. text ed. write for info. (ISBN 0-697-06061-6); instr's. manual avail. (ISBN 0-697-06062-4). Wm C Brown.

Parenting Gifted Children. (Ser. on Talented & Gifted Education). 1979. 2.95 (ISBN 0-89354-128-1). Northwest Regional.

Passow, A. Harry, ed. The Education of the Gifted & Talented: Seventy-Eighth Yearbook of the Society for the Study of Education Yearbooks, Pt. I. LC 78-66031. 1979. lib. bdg. 14.00x (ISBN 0-226-60126-9). U of Chicago Pr.

Philadelphia Suburban School Study Council Group A. Improving Programs for the Gifted. LC 65-27076. 1965. pap. text ed. 3.00x (ISBN 0-8134-0852-0, 852). Interstate.

Polette, Nancy & Hamlin, Marjorie. Exploring Books with Gifted Children. LC 80-23721. 1980. lib. bdg. 17.50x (ISBN 0-87287-216-5). Libs Unl.

Povey, Robert. Educating the Gifted Child. 1980. text ed. 20.95 (ISBN 0-06-318133-9, IntlDept); pap. text ed. 10.50 (ISBN 0-06-318147-9). Har-Row.

--Educating the Gifted Child. 1980. text ed. 20.95 (ISBN 0-06-318133-9, IntlDept); pap. text ed. 10.50 (ISBN 0-06-318147-9). Har-Row.

Raph, Jane B., et al. Bright Underachievers. LC 66-25459. 1966. text ed. 11.50x (ISBN 0-8077-2021-6). Tchrs Coll.

Renzulli, Joseph S. The Enrichment Triad Model: A Guide for Developing Defensible Programs for the Gifted & Talented. (Illus.). 89p. 1977. pap. 7.95 (ISBN 0-936386-01-0). Creative Learning.

Renzulli, Joseph S. & Smith, Linda H. A Guidebook for Developing Individualized Educational Programs for Gifted & Talented Students. 51p. 1979. pap. 7.95 (ISBN 0-936386-13-4). Creative Learning.

--Learning Styles Inventory: A Measure of Student Preference for Instructional Techniques. 1978. pap. 6.95 (ISBN 0-936386-14-2). Creative Learning.

Renzulli, Joseph S. & Stoddard, Elizabeth P., eds. Under One Cover: Gifted & Talented Education in Perspective. LC 80-68284. 248p. 1980. pap. 11.25 (ISBN 0-86586-108-0). Coun Exc Child.

Renzulli, Joseph S., et al. Scales for Rating Behavioral Characteristics of Superior Students. 1977. pap. 6.95 (ISBN 0-936386-00-2). Creative Learning.

Rice, Joseph P. The Gifted: Developing Total Talent. (American Lecture Special Education). (Illus.). 352p. 1970. pap. 34.50 (ISBN 0-398-01584-8). C C Thomas.

Roedell, Wendy C., et al. Gifted Young Children. Tannenbaum, Abraham J., ed. LC 80-10707. (Perspectives on Gifted & Talented Education Ser.). (Orig.). 1980. pap. text ed. 6.50x (ISBN 0-8077-2587-0). Tchrs Coll.

Sanderlin, Owenita & Lundy, Ruthe R. Gifted Children: How to Identify & Teach Them. LC 79-50768. (Illus.). 1979. 10.95 (ISBN 0-498-02328-1). A S Barnes.

Sellin, Don & Birch, Jack. Educating Gifted & Talented Learners. LC 80-19565. 359p. 1980. text ed. 24.50 (ISBN 0-89443-295-8). Aspen Systems.

Shields, J. B. The Gifted Child. (Exploring Education Ser.). 1968. pap. text ed. 5.00x (ISBN 0-901225-42-8, NFER). Humanities.

Smilansky, Moshe & Nevo, David. The Gifted Disadvantaged: A Ten Year Longitudinal Study of Compensatory Education in Israel. 356p. 1980. 29.25 (ISBN 0-677-04400-3). Gordon.

Smith, Douglas K. Classroom Teacher & the Special Child. (Special Education Ser.). (Illus.). 224p. 1980. pap. text ed. 10.95 (ISBN 0-89568-187-0). Spec Learn Corp.

Stanley, Julian C., et al, eds. The Gifted & the Creative: A Fifty Year Perspective. LC 77-4790. (Hyman Blumberg Symposium Ser.: No. 6). (Illus.). 1978. pap. 4.95 (ISBN 0-8018-1975-X). Johns Hopkins.

--Mathematical Talent, Discovery, Description, & Development. LC 73-19342. (Illus.). 234p. 1974. 15.00x (ISBN 0-8018-1585-1); pap. 4.45x (ISBN 0-8018-1592-4). Johns Hopkins.

Student Record of Community Exploration. 1977. 2.25 (ISBN 0-89354-603-8). Northwest Regional.

Talented & Gifted School Programs. (Ser. on Talented & Gifted Education). 1979. 2.95 (ISBN 0-89354-130-3). Northwest Regional.

Tannenbaum, Abraham J. Perspectives on Gifted & Talented Education, 6 vols. (Orig.). Set. pap. text ed. 32.50x (ISBN 0-8077-2594-3). Tchrs Coll.

Torrance, E. P. Gifted Children in the Classroom. (Orig.). 1965. pap. text ed. 3.50x (ISBN 0-02-420950-3). Macmillan.

Torrance, E. Paul. Education & the Creative Potential. LC 63-63112. (Modern School Practices Ser: No. 5). 1963. 4.50x (ISBN 0-8166-0299-9); pap. 2.25x (ISBN 0-8166-0442-8, MP2). U of Minn Pr.

Vail, Priscilla L. The World of the Gifted Child. 1980. pap. 3.95 (ISBN 0-14-005546-0). Penguin.

Vogeli, Bruce R. Soviet Secondary Schools for the Mathematically Talented. LC 68-30961. 1968. pap. 3.40 (ISBN 0-87353-092-6). NCTM.

--Soviet Secondary Schools for the Mathematically Talented. LC 68-30961. 1968. pap. 3.40 (ISBN 0-87353-092-6). NCTM.

Whitmore. Giftedness, Conflict & Underachievement. 478p. 1980. text ed. 20.95 (ISBN 0-205-06870-7, 2468700). Allyn.

GIFTED CHILDREN-EDUCATION-DIRECTORIES

Baskin, Barbara & Harris, Karen. Books for the Gifted Child. LC 79-27431. 1980. 16.95 (ISBN 0-8352-1161-4). Bowker.

Freeman, Darlene & Stuart, Virginia. Resources for Gifted Children in the New York Area. LC 79-91434. 350p. (Orig.). 1980. pap. 10.00 (ISBN 0-89824-005-0). Trillium Pr.

GIFTS

see also Gift Wrapping

Cortazar, Mercedes. Astrogifts. LC 80-7665. (Illus.). 192p. (Orig.). 1980. pap. 5.95 (ISBN 0-06-090798-3, CN 798, CN). Har-Row.

Creekmore, Betsey B. Making Gifts from Oddments & Outdoor Materials. (Illus.). 1970. 8.95 (ISBN 0-8208-0069-4). Hearthside.

Dillon, Wilton. Gifts & Nations: The Obligation to Give, Receive & Repay. (New Babylon Studies in the Social Sciences: No. 5). (Illus., Orig.). 1968. pap. text ed. 8.90x (ISBN 0-686-22435-3). Mouton.

Encyclopedie Des Cadeaux. 500p. (Fr.). 27.50 (ISBN 0-686-57138-X, M-6193). French & Eur.

Hautzig, Esther. Let's Make More Presents: Easy & Inexpensive Gifts for Every Occasion. LC 72-92445. (How-to Bk.). (Illus.). 160p. (gr. 5 up). 1973. 8.95 (ISBN 0-02-743490-7). Macmillan.

Hulbert, Anne. Making Gifts. 1975. 14.95 (ISBN 0-7134-2948-8, Pub. by Batsford England). David & Charles.

King, Judith. The Greatest Gift Guide Ever. LC 79-65184. (Illus., Orig.). 1980. pap. 4.00 (ISBN 0-9602776-0-9). Variety Pr.

McCarthy, David S. Gifts That Never Wear Out. 96p. 1980. pap. 3.95 (ISBN 0-8170-0878-0). Judson.

McNair, Jim. Love & Gifts. LC 76-6555. 1976. 3.50 (ISBN 0-87123-328-2, 210328). Bethany Hse.

McPhee Gribble Publishers. Presents: Making Them to Match People. (Practical Puffins Ser.). (Illus.). 1978. pap. 1.50 (ISBN 0-14-049163-5, Puffin). Penguin.

Mauss, Marcel. Gift: Forms & Functions of Exchange in Archaic Societies. 1967. pap. 4.95 (ISBN 0-393-00378-7, Norton Lib). Norton.

Parr, Sarah, ed. Gifts to Make for Children. LC 76-15483. (Illus.). 72p. 1976. 5.95 (ISBN 0-87131-214-X). M Evans.

Purdy, Susan. Christmas Gifts Good Enough to Eat. (Holiday Cookbooks). (Illus.). 96p. (gr. 4 up). 1981. PLB 8.90 (ISBN 0-531-04314-2). Watts.

Rodway, Pamela. Gifts Galore: Gifts to Make for Everyone. LC 74-19758. (Leisuretime Ser.). (Illus.). 96p. 1975. bds. 5.95 (ISBN 0-668-03696-6). Arco.

Tournier, Paul. Meaning of Gifts. LC 63-19172. 1963. 4.25 (ISBN 0-8042-2124-3). John Knox.

--The Meaning of Gifts. LC 63-19122. 1976. pap. 1.25 (ISBN 0-8042-3604-6). John Knox.

Webb, David M. Gift. 26p. 1980. pap. 2.25 (ISBN 0-935054-02-2). Webb-Newcomb.

The Woman's Day Book of Gifts to Make. 1976. 9.95 (ISBN 0-671-22316-X). S&S.

GIFTS-TAXATION

see also Real Property and Taxation

Carter, Virginia L. & Garigan, Catherine S., eds. Planned Giving Ideas. 48p. 1980. pap. 9.50 (ISBN 0-89964-039-7). CASE.

Clark, John A. How to Save Time & Taxes in Handling Estates. 28.50 (ISBN 0-685-02518-7). Bender.

Commerce Clearing House. Federal Estate & Gift Taxes Explained, Including Estate Planning: 1981 Edition. 1980. 9.00 (ISBN 0-686-75917-6). Commerce.

Crumbley, D. Larry. A Practical Guide to Preparing a Federal Gift Tax Return. 5th ed. 1980. pap. text ed. 8.50 (ISBN 0-88450-058-6, 1705-B). Lawyers & Judges.

Federal Estate & Gift Taxes Code & Regulations As of April 1981. 8.50 (ISBN 0-686-75916-8). Commerce.

Federal Taxation of Estates, Gifts, & Trusts. 3rd ed. 645p. 1980. 55.00 (ISBN 0-686-28716-9, T118C). ALI-ABA.

Gerhart, Frederick J. The Gift Tax. LC 79-93253. 215p. 1980. text ed. 30.00 (ISBN 0-686-61027-X, D1-0150). PLI.

Jantscher, Gerald R. Trusts & Estate Taxation. (Studies of Government Finance). 11.95 (ISBN 0-8157-4576-1); pap. 4.95 (ISBN 0-8157-4575-3). Brookings.

Kahn, Douglas & Waggoner, Lawrence. Federal Taxation of Gifts, Trusts & Estates. 848p. 1977. text ed. 22.00 (ISBN 0-316-48199-8). Little.

Kahn, Douglas A. & Waggoner, Lawrence W. Federal Taxation of Gifts, Trusts & Estates. 1980. 1980 suppl. 6.95 (ISBN 0-316-48201-3). Little.

McNulty, John K. Federal Estate & Gift Taxation in a Nutshell. 2nd ed. LC 79-13469. (Nutshell Ser.). 488p. 1979. pap. text ed. 7.95 (ISBN 0-8299-2043-9). West Pub.

Moriarty, Charles P. Adopt Your Way to Inheritance & Gift Tax Savings. LC 80-23202. 160p. 1980. 12.95 (ISBN 0-916076-31-8). Writing.

Plutzer, Louis. Estate & Gift Tax Provisions. 4th ed. 1979. pap. 24.50 (ISBN 0-917126-07-6). Mason Pub.

Rabinowitz, Joel. Federal Estate & Gift Tax. 3rd ed. (Sum & Substance Ser.). 1979. 13.95 (ISBN 0-686-27112-2). Center Creative Ed.

Shoup, Carl S. Federal Estate & Gift Taxes. LC 79-26968. (Brookings Institution, National Committee on Government Finance, Studies of Government Finance). (Illus.). xvi, 253p. 1980. Repr. of 1966 ed. lib. bdg. 23.50x (ISBN 0-313-22292-4, SHFE). Greenwood.

Stephens, et al. Federal Estate & Gift Taxation Study Problems. 1978. 4.95 (ISBN 0-88262-248-X). Warren.

Stephens, Richard B., et al. Federal Estate & Gift Taxation. 4th. ed. 1978. 64.00 (ISBN 0-88262-221-8, 78-56834); pap. text ed. 21.75 (ISBN 0-88262-229-3). Warren.

Taylor, Bernard P. Guide to Creative Giving. 89p. (Orig.). 1980. pap. 4.95 (ISBN 0-916068-13-7). Groupwork Today.

Weinberger, Michael J. Estate & Gift Tax After Tax Reform. LC 77-78054. 1977. 25.00 (ISBN 0-685-85338-1, D1-0143). PLI.

GIFTS, SPIRITUAL

see also Fear of God; Glossolalia; Prophecy (Christianity)

Baldwin, Lindley. March of Faith: Samuel Morris. 1969. pap. 1.95 (ISBN 0-87123-360-6, 200360). Bethany Hse.

Bennett, Dennis & Bennett, Rita. The Holy Spirit & You: The Text Book of the Charismatic Renewal. LC 73-75963. 224p. 1971. pap. 4.95 (ISBN 0-912106-34-4). Logos.

Bernier, Paul, ed. Bread from Heaven. LC 77-74581. 182p. 1977. pap. 2.95 (ISBN 0-8091-2029-1). Paulist Pr.

Bittlinger, Arnold. Gifts & Graces. LC 68-28848. 1968. pap. 1.95 (ISBN 0-8028-1307-0). Eerdmans.

Brown, Dale W. Flamed by the Spirit. 1978. pap. 2.95 (ISBN 0-87178-277-4). Brethren.

Carter, Howard. Questions & Answers on Spiritual Gifts. 1976. pocket bk. 2.50 (ISBN 0-89274-007-8). Harrison Hse.

--Spiritual Gifts & Their Operation. 1968. pap. 1.50 (ISBN 0-88243-593-0, 02-0593). Gospel Pub.

Criswell, W. A. The Baptism, Filling & Gifts of the Holy Spirit. 192p. 1973. pap. 1.95 (ISBN 0-310-22752-6). Zondervan.

DePree, Gordon & DePree, Gladis. The Gift. (Illus.). 128p. 1976. padded cover & boxed 10.95 (ISBN 0-310-23650-9). Zondervan.

--The Gift. (Illus.). 1979. pap. 7.95 (ISBN 0-310-23651-7). Zondervan.

Edvarsen, Aril. Les Dons Spirituels. (French Bks.). (Fr.). 1979. 2.10 (ISBN 0-8297-0521-X). Life Pubs Intl.

Gangel, Kenneth. You & Your Spiritual Gifts. 1975. pap. 1.25 (ISBN 0-8024-9821-3). Moody.

Gee, Donald. Concerning Spiritual Gifts. rev. ed. 1972. pap. 2.50 (ISBN 0-88243-486-1, 02-0486). Gospel Pub.

--Spiritual Gifts in the Work of the Ministry Today. 1963. pap. 1.25 (ISBN 0-88243-592-2, 02-0592). Gospel Pub.

Griffiths, Michael. Grace-Gifts. 1980. pap. 2.65 (ISBN 0-8028-1810-2). Eerdmans.

Heyer, Robert, ed. Pentecostal Catholics. (New Catholic World Ser.). 1975. pap. 2.45 (ISBN 0-8091-1879-3). Paulist Pr.

Hodges, Melvin L. Spiritual Gifts. 1964. pap. 0.75 (ISBN 0-88243-743-7, 02-0743). Gospel Pub.

Horton, Harold. Los Dones Del Espiritu Santo. (Span.). 1981. 2.25 (ISBN 0-686-76362-9). Life Pubs Intl.

--Os Dons Do Espirito Santo. (Portuguese Bks.). 1979. 1.35 (ISBN 0-8297-0837-5). Life Pubs Intl.

--The Gifts of the Spirit. 208p. 1975. pap. 1.95 (ISBN 0-88243-504-3, 02-0504, Radiant Bks). Gospel Pub.

Horton, Stanley. Los Dones Del Espiritu Santo. Mercado, Benjamin, ed. 225p. (Span.). 1979. pap. 1.90 (ISBN 0-8297-0535-X). Life Pubs Intl.

Judisch, Douglas. An Evaluation of Claims to the Charismatic Gifts. (Baker Biblical Monographs). 1978. pap. 3.95 (ISBN 0-8010-5082-0). Baker Bk.

Kinghorn, Kenneth C. Gifts of the Spirit. LC 75-22268. 128p. 1976. pap. 3.25 (ISBN 0-687-14695-X). Abingdon.

Koch, Kurt E. Charismatic Gifts. 1975. pap. 2.95 (ISBN 0-8254-3023-2). Kregel.

Lindsay, Gordon. Gifts of the Spirit, 4 vols. 2.50 ea. Vol. 1 (ISBN 0-89985-195-9). Vol. 2 (ISBN 0-89985-196-7). Vol. 3 (ISBN 0-89985-197-5). Vol. 4 (ISBN 0-89985-199-1). Christ Nations.

Lutzer, Erwin W. You're Richer Than You Think! 1978. pap. 3.50 (ISBN 0-88207-777-5). Victor Bks.

MacGorman, J. W. The Gifts of the Spirit. LC 75-55191. 1980. pap. 2.95 (ISBN 0-8054-1385-5). Broadman.

McRae, William J. The Dynamics of Spiritual Gifts. 160p. 1976. pap. 1.95 (ISBN 0-310-29092-9). Zondervan.

Nee, Watchman. Full of Grace & Truth, Vol. II. Kaung, Stephen, tr. 1981. pap. 2.95 (ISBN 0-935008-51-9). Christian Fellow Pubs.

Neighbour, Ralph W. This Gift Is Mine. LC 73-93907. 1974. 3.25 (ISBN 0-8054-5223-0). Broadman.

O'Connor, Edward D., ed. Perspectives on Charismatic Renewal. 228p. 1976. 10.95x (ISBN 0-268-01516-3); pap. 3.95x (ISBN 0-268-01517-1). U of Notre Dame Pr.

Ogilvie, Lloyd J. You've Got Charisma. LC 75-14414. 176p. 1975. 6.95 (ISBN 0-687-47269-5). Abingdon.

O'Rourke, Edward. Gift of Gifts. LC 77-74580. 1977. pap. 1.95 (ISBN 0-8091-2025-9). Paulist Pr.

Sanders, J. Oswald. Holy Spirit & His Gifts. (Contemporary Evangelical Perspectives Ser). kivar 4.95 (ISBN 0-310-32481-5). Zondervan.

Thomas, Robert L. Understanding Spiritual Gifts. 1978. pap. 4.95 (ISBN 0-8024-9023-9). Moody.

Tollett, T. O., compiled by. Best Gifts. 1979. pap. 1.00 (ISBN 0-89114-062-X). Baptist Pub Hse.

Tuttle, Robert G., Jr. The Partakers: Holy Spirit Power for Persevering Christians. LC 74-9561. (Festival Books). 1977. pap. 1.25 (ISBN 0-687-30110-6). Abingdon.

Unger, Merrill F. The Baptism & Gifts of the Holy Spirit. 192p. 1974. pap. text ed. 3.95 (ISBN 0-8024-0467-7). Moody.

Weber, Max. Max Weber on Charisma & Institution Building. Eisenstadt, S. N., ed. LC 68-54202. (Heritage of Sociology Ser). (Orig.). 1968. 15.00x (ISBN 0-226-87722-1); pap. text ed. 7.00x (ISBN 0-226-87724-8). U of Chicago Pr.

Wilson, Bryan. The Noble Savages: An Essay on Charisma-the Rehabilitation of a Concept. LC 74-81444. (Quantum Bk Ser.). 1975. 14.95x (ISBN 0-520-02815-5). U of Cal Pr.

Yohn, Rick. Discover Your Spiritual Gift and Use It. 1975. pap. 2.95 (ISBN 0-8423-0668-4). Tyndale.

GIGLIO, GIOVANNI

Giglio, Giovanni. Triumph of Barabbas. Mosbacher, E., tr. LC 74-180401. Repr. of 1937 ed. 24.00 (ISBN 0-404-56125-X). AMS Pr.

GIKUYU LANGUAGE

see Kikuyu Language

GILA RIVER AND VALLEY

Corle, Edwin. Gila: River of the Southwest. LC 51-6152. (Illus.). 1964. pap. 4.50 (ISBN 0-8032-5040-1, BB 305, Bison). U of Nebr Pr.

Gladwin, Harold, et al. Excavations at Snaketown: Material Culture. LC 65-23304. 1965. 16.50x (ISBN 0-8165-0031-2). U of Ariz Pr.

GILBERT, CASS, 1859-1934

Thompson, Neil B. Minnesota's State Capitol: The Art & Politics of a Public Building. LC 74-4326. (Minnesota Historic Sites Pamphlet Ser.: No. 9). (Illus.). 100p. 1974. pap. 5.50 (ISBN 0-87351-085-3). Minn Hist.

GILBERT, HUMPHREY, SIR, 1539-1583

Gosling, William G. Life of Sir Humphrey Gilbert, England's First Empire Builder. LC 76-109737. Repr. of 1911 ed. lib. bdg. 15.25x (ISBN 0-8371-4227-X, GOHG). Greenwood.

Peckham, Sir George. A True Reporte of the Late Discoueries of the Newfound Landes. LC 78-25630. (English Experience Ser.: No. 341). 1971. Repr. of 1583 ed. 11.50 (ISBN 90-221-0341-2). Walter J Johnson.

Slafter, Carlos, ed. Sir Humfrey Gylberte & His Enterprise of Colonization in America. 1966. 24.00 (ISBN 0-8337-3286-2). B Franklin.

GILBERT, JOHN GIBBS, 1810-1889

Winter, William. Sketch of the Life of John Gilbert. 1968. Repr. of 1890 ed. 16.50 (ISBN 0-8337-3827-5). B Franklin.

GILBERT, WILLIAM SCHWENCK, SIR, 1836-1911

Ayre, Leslie. The Gilbert & Sullivan Companion. 496p. (RL 7). 1976. pap. 4.95 (ISBN 0-452-25124-9, Z5124, Plume). NAL.

Cellier, Francois & Bridgeman, Cunningham. Gilbert & Sullivan & Their Operas. LC 72-91479. (Illus.). 1914. 25.00 (ISBN 0-405-08346-7, Blom Pubns). Arno.

Dark, Sidney & Grey, Rowland. W. S. Gilbert, His Life & Letters. LC 71-164210. 1971. Repr. of 1923 ed. 22.00 (ISBN 0-8103-3789-4). Gale.

--W. S. Gilbert: His Life & Letters. LC 76-177509. (Illus.). Repr. of 1923 ed. 14.00 (ISBN 0-405-08430-7, Blom Pubns). Arno.

Dunn, George E. A Gilbert & Sullivan Dictionary. LC 72-10177. 1972. Repr. of 1936 ed. lib. bdg. 7.50 (ISBN 0-8414-0683-9). Folcroft.

Dunn, George E., ed. Gilbert & Sullivan Dictionary. LC 72-125070. (Music Ser). 1971. Repr. of 1936 ed. lib. bdg. 14.50 (ISBN 0-306-70007-7). Da Capo.

Godwin, A. H. Gilbert & Sullivan: A Critical Appreciation of the Savoy Operas. LC 68-26216. 1969. Repr. of 1926 ed. 12.50 (ISBN 0-8046-0170-4). Kennikat.

--Gilbert & Sullivan: A Critical Approach to the Savoy Operas. 1926. 20.00 (ISBN 0-8274-2408-6). R West.

Goldberg, Isaac. Sir William Gilbert. 59.95 (ISBN 0-8490-2610-5). Gordon Pr.

--Story of Gilbert & Sullivan. LC 76-113194. Repr. of 1928 ed. 20.00 (ISBN 0-404-02858-6). AMS Pr.

--Story of Gilbert & Sullivan. 59.95 (ISBN 0-8490-1134-5). Gordon Pr.

Jacobs, Arthur. Gilbert & Sullivan. LC 76-181191. 64p. 1951. Repr. 18.00 (ISBN 0-403-01596-0). Scholarly.

Jones, John Bush, ed. W. S. Gilbert: A Century of Scholarship & Commentary. LC 79-80066. 1970. 12.00x (ISBN 0-8147-0464-6). NYU Pr.

Kline, Peter. The Theatre Student: Gilbert & Sullivan Production. LC 74-170281. (Theatre Student Ser). (gr. 7 up). 1972. PLB 12.50 (ISBN 0-8239-0252-8). Rosen Pr.

Pearson, Hesketh. Gilbert: His Life & Strife. LC 78-3698. 1978. Repr. of 1957 ed. lib. bdg. 21.50x (ISBN 0-313-20364-4, PEGI). Greenwood.

Pearsons, H. Gilbert & Sullivan. lib. bdg. 15.00 (ISBN 0-685-95443-9). Scholarly.

Sutton, Max K. W. S. Gilbert. (English Authors Ser.: No. 178). 1975. lib. bdg. 10.95 (ISBN 0-8057-1217-8). Twayne.

Taylor, Ian. How to Produce Concert Versions of Gilbert & Sullivan. 1972. 12.95x (ISBN 0-8464-0494-X). Beekman Pubs.

GILBERT, WILLIAM SCHWENCK, SIR, 1836-1911-BIBLIOGRAPHY

Searle, Townley. A Bibliography of Sir William Schwenck Gilbert. (Illus.). 1967. Repr. of 1931 ed. 21.00 (ISBN 0-8337-3217-X). B Franklin.

GILBERT ISLANDS

Grimble, Rosemary. Migrations, Myths & Magic from the Gilbert Islands: Early Writings of Sir Arthur Grimble. (Illus.). 1972. 27.95 (ISBN 0-7100-7164-7). Routledge & Kegan.

Sabatier, Ernest. Astride the Equator. Nixon, Ursula, tr. 1978. 44.00x (ISBN 0-19-550520-4). Oxford U Pr.

GILBRETH, FRANK BUNKER, 1868-1924

Gilbreth, Frank B. & Carey, Ernestine G. Cheaper by the Dozen. rev. ed. LC 63-20411. (Illus.). 1963. 13.95 (ISBN 0-690-18632-0). T y Crowell.

Gilbreth, Lillian M. The Quest of the One Best Way. LC 73-1170. (Management History Ser.: No. 21). (Illus.). 65p. 1973. Repr. of 1928 ed. 10.00 (ISBN 0-87960-032-2). Hive Pub.

Yost, Edna. Frank & Lillian Gilbreth: Partners for Life. (Hive Management History Ser.: No. 88). (Illus.). 384p. 1981. lib. bdg. 22.50 (ISBN 0-87960-119-1); pap. 12.50 (ISBN 0-87960-121-3). Hive Pub.

GILBRETH, LILLIAN EVELYN (MOLLER), 1878-1972

Gilbreth, Frank B. & Carey, Ernestine G. Cheaper by the Dozen. rev. ed. LC 63-20411. (Illus.). 1963. 13.95 (ISBN 0-690-18632-0). T y Crowell.

Gilbreth, Frank B., Jr. & Carey, Ernestine G. Belles on Their Toes. LC 50-13907. (Illus.). 1950. 8.95 (ISBN 0-690-13023-6). T Y Crowell.

Yost, Edna. Frank & Lillian Gilbreth: Partners for Life. (Hive Management History Ser.: No. 88). (Illus.). 384p. 1981. lib. bdg. 22.50 (ISBN 0-87960-119-1); pap. 12.50 (ISBN 0-87960-121-3). Hive Pub.

GILCHRIST, MRS. ANNE (BURROWS) 1828-1885

Gilchrist, Anne. Anne Gilchrist: Her Life & Writings. 2nd ed. Gilchrist, Herbert H., ed. LC 74-148783. Repr. of 1887 ed. 27.00 (ISBN 0-404-02767-9). AMS Pr.

Gould, Elizabeth P. Anne Gilchrist & Walt Whitman. LC 73-444. 1972. Repr. of 1900 ed. lib. bdg. 15.00 (ISBN 0-8414-1506-4). Folcroft.

--Anne Gilchrist & Walt Whitman. 1979. Repr. of 1900 ed. lib. bdg. 15.00 (ISBN 0-8482-0907-9). Norwood Edns.

Whitman, Walt & Gilchrist, Anne. The Letters of Anne Gilchrist & Walt Whitman. Harned, Thomas B., ed. LC 72-6286. (Studies in Whitman, No. 28). (Illus.). 282p. 1972. Repr. of 1918 ed. lib. bdg. 36.95 (ISBN 0-8383-1630-1). Haskell.

GILD SOCIALISM

see also Syndicalism

Cole, G. D. Guild Socialism Restated. (Social Science Classics Ser.). 224p. 1980. text ed. 19.95 (ISBN 0-87855-386-X); pap. text ed. 6.95 (ISBN 0-87855-817-9). Transaction Bks.

Cole, George D. Self-Government in Industry. facsimile ed. LC 71-152979. (Select Bibliographies Reprint Ser). Repr. of 1918 ed. 19.00 (ISBN 0-8369-5731-8). Arno.

Wright, A. W. G. D. H. Cole & Socialist Democracy. 1979. 36.00x (ISBN 0-19-827421-1). Oxford U Pr.

GILDAS, 6TH CENTURY

Singer, Charles. From Magic to Science. 1960. 6.00 (ISBN 0-8446-2944-8). Peter Smith.

GILDER, RICHARD WATSON, 1844-1909

Smith, Herbert F. Richard Watson Gilder. LC 70-110705. (United States Authors Ser.). 1970. lib. bdg. 8.95x (ISBN 0-89197-923-9); pap. text ed. 4.95x (ISBN 0-8290-0012-7). Irvington.

GILDING

see also Electroplating; Metals-Coloring

Chambers, Donald L. How to Gold-Leaf Antiques & Other Art Objects. (Arts & Crafts Ser.). (Illus.). 96p. 1973. pap. 9.95 (ISBN 0-517-54217-X). Crown.

GILDS

see also Employers' Associations; Trade and Professional Associations; Trade-Unions

Barron, Caroline M. The Medieval Guildhall of London. 59p. 1975. text ed. 22.50x (ISBN 0-8426-0828-1). Verry.

Blanc, Hippolyte. Bibliographie des corporations ouvrieres avant 1789. LC 68-7209. (Bibliography & Reference Ser.: No. 201). 1968. Repr. of 1885 ed. 20.95 (ISBN 0-8337-0306-4). B Franklin.

Brentano, Lujo. On the History & Development of Gilds & the Origin of Trade Unions. 1969. Repr. of 1870 ed. 20.00 (ISBN 0-8337-0368-4). B Franklin.

Burgess, John S. Guilds of Peking. LC 77-127446. (Columbia Studies in the Social Sciences Ser.: No. 308). Repr. of 1928 ed. 16.00 (ISBN 0-404-51308-5). AMS Pr.

Camp, Charles W. The Artisan in Elizabethan Literature. LC 73-159171. 180p. 1972. Repr. of 1924 ed. lib. bdg. 14.00x (ISBN 0-374-91261-0). Octagon.

Fagniez, Gustave C. Etudes sur l'Industrie et la Classe Industrielle a Paris aux 13e et au 14e Siecle. LC 73-126393. (Research & Source Works: No. 566). (Fr). 1970. Repr. of 1877 ed. 32.50 (ISBN 0-8337-1096-6). B Franklin.

Franklin, Alfred L. Corporations Ouvrieres De Paris Du Douzieme Au Dix-Huitieme Siecle. LC 72-164481. (Research & Source Works Ser: No. 776). 1971. lib. bdg. 29.00 (ISBN 0-8337-1229-2). B Franklin.

Gross, Charles. Bibliography of British Municipal History, Including Gilds & Parliamentary Representation. 1897. 32.50 (ISBN 0-8337-1465-1). B Franklin.

Hibbert, F. Aidan. Influence & Development of English Gilds. LC 79-107907. Repr. of 1891 ed. 12.50x (ISBN 0-678-00630-X). Kelley.

Hsu, F. L. Iemoto: The Heart of Japan. LC 74-5352. 260p. 1975. text ed. 11.25 (ISBN 0-470-41755-2); pap. text ed. 7.95x (ISBN 0-470-41756-0). Halsted Pr.

Kramer, Stella. The English Craft Gilds. LC 70-153335. Repr. of 1927 ed. 17.50 (ISBN 0-404-03777-1). AMS Pr.

--English Craft Gilds & the Government: An Examination of the Accepted Theory Regarding the Decay of the Craft Guilds. LC 68-5666. (Columbia University, Studies in the Social Sciences Ser.: No. 61). Repr. of 1905 ed. 16.50 (ISBN 0-404-51061-2). AMS Pr.

Michwitz, Gunnar. Die Kartellfunktionen der Zunfte und Ihre Bedeutung bei der Entstehung des Zunftwesens: Eine Studie in Spatantiker und mittelalterlicher Wirtschaftsgeschichte. Finley, Moses, ed. LC 79-4993. (Ancient Economic History Ser.). (Ger.). 1980. Repr. of 1936 ed. lib. bdg. 20.00x (ISBN 0-405-12379-5). Arno.
Morse, Hosea B. Gilds of China. 2nd ed. LC 66-24733. 1967. Repr. of 1932 ed. 6.50 (ISBN 0-8462-0877-6). Russell.
Reddaway, T. F. & Walker, Lorna E. The Early History of the Goldsmiths' Company, 1327-1509: Including the Book of Ordinances, 1478-83. (Illus.). 378p. 1976. 21.50x (ISBN 0-87471-804-X). Rowman.
Renard, Georges. Guilds in the Middle Ages. Terry, Dorothy, tr. LC 68-55330. Repr. of 1918 ed. 12.50x (ISBN 0-678-00438-2). Kelley.
Saint-Leon, Etienne M. Histoire Des Corporation De Metiers: History of the Guilds. 3rd ed. LC 74-25781. (European Sociology Ser.). 876p. 1975. 50.00x (ISBN 0-405-06534-5). Arno.
Staley, Edgcumbe. Guilds of Florence. LC 67-12458. (Illus.). 1906. 30.00 (ISBN 0-405-08992-9, Pub. by Blom). Arno.
Unwin, G., ed. Guilds & Companies of London. 4th ed. (Illus.). 401p. 1963. 27.50x (ISBN 0-7146-1366-5, F Cass Co). Biblio Dist.

GILDS, ALTAR
see Altar Gilds

GILDS, NEIGHBORHOOD
see Social Settlements

GILES, SAINT, fl. 7TH CENTURY
Hewson, Anthony M. Giles of Rome and the Medieval Theory of Conception. (University of London Historical Ser: No. 38). 280p. 1975. text ed. 49.50x (ISBN 0-485-13138-2, Athlone Pr). Humanities.

GILES, WILLIAM BRANCH, 1762-1830
Anderson, Dice R. William Branch Giles: A Study in the Politics of Virginia & the Nation from 1790 to 1830. 1966. 8.50 (ISBN 0-8446-1028-3). Peter Smith.

GILFILLAN, GEORGE, 1813-1878
Shenstone, William. Poetical Works. LC 68-54436. (Illus.). 1968. Repr. of 1854 ed. lib. bdg. 14.25x (ISBN 0-8371-0655-9, SHWS). Greenwood.

GILGAMESH
Heidel, Alexander. Gilgamesh Epic & Old Testament Parallels. 2nd ed. LC 49-5734. 1963. 5.50 (ISBN 0-226-32398-6, P136, Phoen). U of Chicago Pr.
Konnyu, et al. Gilgamesh Illustrated. 170p. 1980. pap. 10.00 (ISBN 0-686-64331-3). Hungarian Rev.
Tigay, Jeffrey H. The Evolution of the Gilgamesh Epic. LC 81-51137. 272p. 1982. 25.00x (ISBN 0-8122-7805-4). U of Pa Pr.

GILL, ERIC, 1882-1940
Attwater, Donald, ed. Modern Christian Revolutionaries. facsimile ed. LC 76-156608. (Essay Index Reprint Ser). Repr. of 1947 ed. 23.00 (ISBN 0-8369-2304-9). Arno.
Brewer, Roy. Eric Gill: The Man Who Loved Letters. (Illus.). 86p. 1973. 16.50x (ISBN 0-87471-148-7). Rowman.
Heppenstall, Rayner. Four Absentees: Eric Gill, George Orwell, Dylan Thomas and J. Middleton Murry. 1979. Repr. of 1960 ed. lib. bdg. 30.00 (ISBN 0-8495-2277-3). Arden Lib.

GILLESPIE, DIZZIE, 1917-
Hay, J. Macdougall. Gillespie. 619p. 1914. Repr. 54.00 (ISBN 0-403-08927-1). Somerset Pub.
James, Michael. Dizzy Gillespie. pap. 3.95 (ISBN 0-498-04030-5, Prpta). A S Barnes.

GILLRAY, JAMES, 1757-1815
Gillray, James. The Satirical Etchings of James Gillray. Hill, Draper, ed. (Illus.). 10.00 (ISBN 0-8446-5579-1). Peter Smith.
Rickword, K. & Rickword, E. Gillray & Cruikshank. (Clarendon Biography Ser.). (Illus.). pap. cancelled (ISBN 0-912728-64-7). Newbury Bks.

GILMER, FRANCIS WALKER, 1790-1826
Trent, William P. English Culture in Virginia: A Study of the Gilmer Letters & an Account of the English Professors Obtained by Jefferson for the University of Virginia. Repr. of 1889 ed. pap. 12.50 (ISBN 0-685-30641-0). Johnson Repr.

GILPIN, WILLIAM, 1724-1804
Templeman, William D. Seventeen Twenty-Four to Eighteen Hundred & Four: 1724 to 1804. 336p. 1980. Repr. of 1939 ed. lib. bdg. 40.00 (ISBN 0-89987-805-9). Darby Bks.

GILPIN, WILLIAM, 1815-1894
Karnes, Thomas L. William Gilpin: Western Nationalist. (Illus.). 393p. 1970. 22.50x (ISBN 0-292-70003-2). U of Tex Pr.

GILPIN COUNTY, COLORADO–HISTORY
Axford, H. William. Gilpin County Gold: Peter McFarlane, 1848-1929 Mining Entrepreneur in Central City, Colorado. LC 76-115034. (Illus.). xii, 210p. 1976. 12.95 (ISBN 0-8040-0550-8, SB). Swallow.

GIMBALA LANGUAGE
see Congo Language

GIN RUMMY
see Rummy (Game)

GINGERBREAD
see Cake

GINGIVITIS
see Gums–Diseases

GINSBERG, ALLEN, 1926-
Burroughs, William S. Letters to Allen Ginsberg, 1953-1957. 210p. (Orig.). 1981. 17.95 (ISBN 0-916190-16-1); pap. 6.00 (ISBN 0-916190-17-X). Full Court NY.
Dowden, George & McGilvery, Laurence, eds. A Bibliography of Works by Allen Ginsberg. LC 78-128182. (Illus.). 343p. 1971. text ed. 17.50 (ISBN 0-87286-062-0). City Lights.
Gifford, Barry, ed. As Ever: The Collected Correspondence of Allen Ginsberg & Neal Cassady. LC 77-82182. 1977. 15.00 (ISBN 0-916870-09-X); pap. 5.95 (ISBN 0-916870-08-1). Creative Arts Bk.
Ginsberg, Allen. Journals: Early Fifties Early Sixties. Ball, Gordon, ed. & intro. by. LC 76-54581. (Illus.). 1977. pap. 6.95 (ISBN 0-394-17034-2, E704, Ever). Grove.
Kraus, Michelle. Allen Ginsberg: An Annotated Bibliography, 1699-1977. LC 79-27132. (Author Bibliographies Ser.: No. 46). 362p. 1980. 17.50 (ISBN 0-8108-1284-3). Scarecrow.
McBride, Dick. Cometh with Clouds, (Memory: Allen Ginsberg) 64p. 1981. 12.00x (ISBN 0-916156-54-0); pap. 4.50x (ISBN 0-916156-51-6). Cherry Valley.
Portuges, Paul. The Visionary Poetics of Allen Ginsberg. LC 78-6094. 1978. lib. bdg. 11.95 (ISBN 0-915520-17-6); pap. 5.95 (ISBN 0-915520-12-5). Ross-Erikson.
Tytell, John. Naked Angels: The Lives & Literature of the Beat Generation. LC 75-22206. 260p. 1976. 10.00 (ISBN 0-07-065723-8, GB). McGraw.

GINSENG
Dixon, Pamela. Ginseng. 102p. 1976. 16.00 (ISBN 0-7156-1006-6, Pub. by Duckworth England); pap. 4.50 (ISBN 0-7156-1007-4, Pub. by Duckworth England). Biblio Dist.
Hardacre, Val. Ginseng. 2nd ed. (Illus.). 1975. 14.95 (ISBN 0-913042-07-2). Holland Hse Pr.
Harding, A. R. Ginseng & Other Medicinal Plants. LC 72-87757. (Illus.). 320p. 1973. 7.50 (ISBN 0-88278-009-3); pap. 4.00 (ISBN 0-88278-007-7). Emporium Pubns.
--Ginseng & Other Medicinal Plants. rev. ed. 386p. 1972. pap. 4.00 (ISBN 0-936622-09-1, A399155). A R Harding Pub.
Harriman, Sarah. Book of Ginseng. (Health Ser.). (Orig.). 1973. pap. 1.75 (ISBN 0-515-05438-0, A2988). Jove Pubns.
Harris, Ben Charles. Ginseng: What It Is, What It Can Do for You. LC 78-59174. 1978. pap. 1.95 (ISBN 0-87983-179-0). Keats.
Hou, Joseph P. Ginseng: The Myth & Truth. 1979. 3.00 (ISBN 0-87980-367-3). Wilshire.
--The Myth & Truth About Ginseng. LC 77-74115. (Illus.). 1978. 9.95 (ISBN 0-498-02083-5). A S Barnes.
Kimmens, Andrew, ed. Tales of the Ginseng. LC 75-9888. (Illus.). 224p. 1975. pap. 3.95 (ISBN 0-688-07942-3). Morrow.

GIONG
see Moso (Tribe)

GIONO, JEAN, 1895-1970
Giono, Jean. Jean le Bleu. 288p. 1974. 3.95 (ISBN 0-686-53972-9). French & Eur.
Goodrich, Norma L. Giono: Master of Fictional Modes. LC 72-4041. 344p. 1973. 21.00 (ISBN 0-691-06239-0). Princeton U Pr.
Redfern, Walter D. Private World of Jean Giono. LC 67-20396. 1967. 12.75 (ISBN 0-8223-0144-X). Duke.

GIORGIONE, GIORGIO BARBARELLI, KNOWN AS, 1477-1511
Folon. Lettres a Giorgio. (Illus.). 1976. pap. 15.95 (ISBN 0-8120-0722-0, Alice Editions). Barron.
Stearns, Frank P. Four Great Venetians. facs. ed. LC 76-86786. (Essay Index Reprint Ser). 1901. 19.50 (ISBN 0-8369-1156-3). Arno.
Stokes, Adrian D. Art & Science: A Study of Alberti, Pierodella Francesca & Giorgione. LC 50-2168. 75p. 1949. Repr. 29.00 (ISBN 0-403-07226-3). Somerset Pub.

GIOTTO DI BONDONE, 1266?-1337
Cole, Bruce. Giotto: And Florentine Painting 1280-1375. LC 75-7632. (Icon Editions). (Illus.). 176p. 1976. 15.95 (ISBN 0-06-430900-2, HarpT). Har-Row.
--Giotto & Florentine Painting, 1280-1375. LC 75-7632. (Icon Editions). (Illus.). 1977. pap. 6.95 (ISBN 0-06-430071-4, IN71, HarpT). Har-Row.
Eimerl, Sarel. World of Giotto. (Library of Art). (Illus.). 1967. 15.95 (ISBN 0-8094-0239-4). Time-Life.
--World of Giotto. LC 67-23024. (Library of Art Ser.). (Illus.). (gr. 6 up). 1967. 12.96 (ISBN 0-8094-0268-8, Pub. by Time-Life). Silver.
Euler, Walter. Giotto Frescoes: The Scrouegni Chapel in Padua. LC 77-84768. (World in Color Ser.). (Illus.). 50p. 1976. 3.95 (ISBN 0-88254-390-3). Hippocrene Bks.
Lloyd, Christopher. Giotto. 1981. 45.00x (ISBN 0-906379-24-5, Pub. by Jupiter England). State Mutual Bk.
Meiss, Millard. Giotto & Assisi. (Illus.). 12.50 (ISBN 0-912158-42-5). Hennessey.
Ruskin, John. Giotto & His Works in Padua. LC 77-9344. 1977. Repr. of 1854 ed. lib. bdg. 25.00 (ISBN 0-89341-207-4). Longwood Pr.
Siren, Osvald. Giotto & Some of His Followers. Schenek, Frederick, tr. LC 75-189860. 1975. Repr. of 1917 ed. 75.00 (ISBN 0-87817-112-6). Hacker.
Smart, Alastair. The Assisi Problem & the Art of Giotto. LC 81-81724. (Illus.). 310p. 1981. Repr. of 1971 ed. lib. bdg. 85.00 (ISBN 0-87817-283-1). Hacker.
Stubblebine, James, ed. Giotto: The Arena Chapel Frescoes. LC 67-17689. (Critical Studies in Art History Ser). (Illus.). 1969. pap. text ed. 7.95x (ISBN 0-393-09858-3, NortonC). Norton.
Trachtenberg, Marvin. The Campanile of Florence Cathedral: Giotto's Tower. LC 70-124532. (Illus.). 458p. 1971. 45.00x (ISBN 0-8147-8151-9). NYU Pr.

GIOVANNI, NIKKI
A Poetic Equation: Conversations Between Nikki Giovanni & Margaret Walker. 1981. pap. 6.95 (ISBN 0-686-73608-7, 088-4). Howard U Pr.

GIOVANNI DA PIAN DEL CARPINE, ABP. OF ANTIVARI, d. 1252
Skelton, R. A., et al. Vinland Map & the Tartar Relation. (Illus.). 1965. 35.00x (ISBN 0-300-00959-3). Yale U Pr.
Viglione, August. The Idea of Christian Reform in Giovanni Dominici. 1978. pap. text ed. 7.75 (ISBN 0-8191-0475-2). U Pr of Amer.

GIPSIES
Acton, Thomas. Gypsy Politics & Social Change. 1974. 20.00x (ISBN 0-7100-7838-2). Routledge & Kegan.
Adams, Barbara, et al. Gypsies & Government Policy in England. 1975. text ed. 40.00x (ISBN 0-435-85080-6). Heinemann Ed.
Balazs, Janos. A Hungarian Gipsy Artist. (Illus.). 1977. 9.50x (ISBN 963-13-0168-0). Intl Pubns Serv.
Bercovici, Konrad. Singing Winds: Stories of Gypsy Life. LC 79-133814. (BCL Ser. I). 1970. Repr. of 1926 ed. 22.00 (ISBN 0-404-00787-2). AMS Pr.
--The Story of the Gypsies. LC 78-164051. (Illus.). xii, 294p. 1975. Repr. of 1928 ed. 24.00 (ISBN 0-8103-4042-9). Gale.
--The Story of the Gypsies. (Illus.). 1979. Repr. of 1929 ed. lib. bdg. 30.00 (ISBN 0-8414-9839-3). Folcroft.
Black, George F. Gypsy Bibliography. LC 74-149780. 1971. Repr. of 1914 ed. 22.00 (ISBN 0-8103-3708-8). Gale.
--A Gypsy Bibliography. LC 76-30594. 1977. Repr. of 1914 ed. lib. bdg. 45.00 (ISBN 0-8414-9946-2). Folcroft.
Block, Martin. Gypsies, Their Life & Their Customs. Kuczynski, Barbara & Taylor, Duncan, trs. LC 75-3451. (Illus.). Repr. of 1939 ed. 31.50 (ISBN 0-404-16886-8). AMS Pr.
Brown, Irving H. Nights & Days on the Gypsy Trail: Through Andalusia & Other Mediterranean Shores. LC 75-3452. (Illus.). Repr. of 1922 ed. 23.50 (ISBN 0-404-16885-X). AMS Pr.
Cohn, W. The Gypsies. 1973. pap. 5.95 (ISBN 0-201-11362-7, 11362). A-W.
Cohn, Werner. The Gypsies. 1973. pap. text ed. 5.95 (ISBN 0-8461-1362-7). Benjamin-Cummings.
Cuttriss, Frank. Romany Life: Experienced & Observed During Many Years of Friendly Intercourse with the Gypsies. LC 75-3453. (Illus.). Repr. of 1915 ed. 26.50 (ISBN 0-404-16887-6). AMS Pr.
Farre, Rowena. Gypsy Idyll: A Personal Experience Among the Romanies. LC 64-16254. (Illus.). 8.95 (ISBN 0-8149-0092-5). Vanguard.
Greenfeld, Howard. Gypsies. LC 77-23746. (Illus.). (gr. 6 up). 1977. 7.95 (ISBN 0-517-52842-8). Crown.
Groome, Francis H. In Gypsy Tents. LC 73-13616. (Folklore Ser). 15.00 (ISBN 0-88305-233-4). Norwood Edns.
Gropper, Rena C. Gypsies in the City: Culture Patterns & Survival. LC 70-161055. (Illus.). 235p. 1975. 9.95 (ISBN 0-87850-008-1); pap. 3.95x (ISBN 0-87850-009-X). Darwin Pr.
Harvey, Denis. The Gypsies: Waggon Time & After. (Illus.). 144p. 1980. 24.00 (ISBN 0-7134-1548-7, Pub. by Batsford England). David & Charles.
Jackson, Ward C. & Harvey, Denis E. English Gypsy Caravan. 1974. 16.95 (ISBN 0-7153-5680-1). David & Charles.
Kester, Paul. Tales of the Real Gypsy. LC 77-142004. 1971. Repr. of 1897 ed. 22.00 (ISBN 0-8103-3633-2). Gale.
Leland, Charles G. English Gypsies & Their Language. LC 68-22035. 1969. Repr. of 1874 ed. 26.00 (ISBN 0-8103-3883-1). Gale.
--The Gypsies. LC 75-3460. Repr. of 1882 ed. 27.00 (ISBN 0-404-16891-4). AMS Pr.
--Gypsy Sorcery & Fortune-Telling. (Illus.). 6.00 (ISBN 0-8446-0181-0). Peter Smith.
McCormick, Andrew. The Tinker-Gypsies. (Folklore Ser). 35.00 (ISBN 0-685-36489-5). Norwood Edns.
McDowell, Bart & National Geographic Society. Gypsies. LC 70-125339. (Special Publications Ser.). (Illus.). 1970. 6.95 (ISBN 0-87044-088-8). Natl Geog.
McLaughlin, John B. Gypsy Lifestyles. LC 80-7572. 128p. 1980. 14.95 (ISBN 0-669-03754-0). Lexington Bks.
MacRitchie, David. Scottish Gypsies Under the Stewarts. LC 75-3463. Repr. of 1894 ed. 14.50 (ISBN 0-404-16892-2). AMS Pr.
MacRitchie, David, ed. Accounts of the Gypsies of India. LC 75-3461. (Illus.). Repr. of 1886 ed. 24.00 (ISBN 0-404-16893-0). AMS Pr.
Nickels, George. The Gypsy Season. Date not set. 10.95 (ISBN 0-87949-187-6). Ashley Bks.
Petulengro, Gipsy. Romany Remedies & Recipes. 1972. pap. 2.25 (ISBN 0-87877-016-X, H-16). Newcastle Pub.
Puxon, Grattan. Rom: Europe's Gypsies. (Minority Rights Group: No. 14). 1973. pap. 2.50 (ISBN 0-89192-113-3). Interbk Inc.
Quintana, B. B. & Floyd, L. Que Guitano: Gypsies of Southern Spain. LC 77-159724. (Case Studies in Cultural Anthropology). 1972. pap. text ed. 5.95 (ISBN 0-03-086120-9, HoltC). HR&W.
Rehfisch, Farnham, ed. Gypsies, Tinkers, & Other Travellers. 1975. 48.00 (ISBN 0-12-585850-7). Acad Pr.
Smith, Hubert F. Tent Life with English Gypsies in Norway. 2nd ed. LC 75-3464. (Illus.). Repr. of 1874 ed. 39.00 (ISBN 0-404-16894-9). AMS Pr.
Sutherland, Anne. Gypsies: The Hidden Americans. LC 75-3762. 1975. Repr. 16.95 (ISBN 0-02-932200-6). Free Pr.
Trigg, Elwood B. Gypsy Demons & Divinities: The Magic & Religion of the Gypsies. 256p. 1974. 7.95 (ISBN 0-8065-0379-3). Citadel Pr.
Tyrner-Stastny, Gabrielle. The Gypsy in Northwest America. LC 77-78813. (Illus.). 1977. pap. 5.00 (ISBN 0-917048-06-7). Wash St Hist Soc.
Vesey-Fitzgerald, Brian. Gypsies of Britain. 272p. 1973. pap. 4.50 (ISBN 0-7153-7231-9). David & Charles.
Webb, Godfrey E. Gypsies, the Secret People. LC 73-1437. (Illus.). 189p. 1974. Repr. of 1960 ed. lib. bdg. 15.00 (ISBN 0-8371-6794-9, WEGY). Greenwood.
Wedeck, H. E. Dictionary of Gypsy Life & Lore. (Illus.). 530p. 1973. 20.00 (ISBN 0-8022-2094-0). Philos Lib.
White, Walter G. The Sea Gypsies of Malaya: An Account of the Nomadic Mawken Pople of the Mergui Archipelago. LC 77-87082. Repr. of 1922 ed. 34.50 (ISBN 0-404-16878-7). AMS Pr.
Wood, Manfri F. In the Life of a Romany Gypsy. Brune, J. A., ed. (Illus.). 1979. pap. 6.95 (ISBN 0-7100-0197-5). Routledge & Kegan.
Yoors, Jan. Gypsies. 1969. pap. 3.95 (ISBN 0-671-20342-8, Touchstone Bks). S&S.

GIPSIES–LANGUAGE
De Bairacli Levy, Juliette. Traveler's Joy. LC 78-61327. 1979. 8.95 (ISBN 0-87983-182-0); pap. 4.95 (ISBN 0-87983-183-9). Keats.
Jonson, Ben. Gypsies Metamorphosed. Cole, G., ed. (Modern Language Association of America Revolving Fund Ser). 1931. pap. 16.00 (ISBN 0-527-46750-2). Kraus Repr.
Smart, Bath C. & Crofton, H. T. Dialect of the English Gypsies. 2nd ed. LC 68-22050. 1968. Repr. of 1875 ed. 22.00 (ISBN 0-8103-3292-2). Gale.
Wood, Manfri F. In the Life of a Romany Gypsy. Brune, J. A., ed. (Illus.). 1979. pap. 6.95 (ISBN 0-7100-0197-5). Routledge & Kegan.

GIPSIES–STORIES
Ellner, Joseph, ed. Gipsy Pattern. facsimile ed. LC 75-101807. (Short Story Index Reprint Ser.). 1926. 16.00 (ISBN 0-8369-3195-5). Arno.

GIPSON, FREDERICK BENJAMIN, 1908-
Cox, Mike. Fred Gipson: Texas Storyteller. (Illus.). 256p. 1980. 15.00 (ISBN 0-88319-054-0). Shoal Creek Pub.

GIPSY MAGIC
see Magic, Gipsy

GIRAFFES
Brown, Louise C. Giraffes. LC 79-52037. (A Skylight Bk.). (Illus.). (gr. 2-5). 1980. 4.95 (ISBN 0-396-07730-7). Dodd.
Conklin, Gladys. Giraffe Lives in Africa. LC 75-151755. (Life-Cycle Bks). (Illus.). 48p. (gr. k-3). 1971. reinforced bdg. 4.50 (ISBN 0-8234-0190-1). Holiday.
--Giraffe Lives in Africa. LC 75-151755. (Life-Cycle Bks). (Illus.). 48p. (gr. k-3). 1971. reinforced bdg. 4.50 (ISBN 0-8234-0190-1). Holiday.

Cooke, Ann. Giraffes at Home. LC 79-158686. (A Let's-Read-&-Find-Out Science Bk.). (Illus.). (gr. k-3). 1972. 7.95 (ISBN 0-690-33082-0, TYC-J); PLB 8.79 (ISBN 0-690-33083-9). Har-Row.
Dagg, Anne I. & Foster, J. Bristol-the Giraffe: Its Biology, Behavior & Ecology. LC 80-21839. 210p. Date not set. Repr. of 1981 ed. price not set (ISBN 0-89874-275-7). Krieger.
Dagg, Anne I & Foster, J. Bristol. The Giraffe: Its Biology, Behavior, & Ecology. 210p. 1981. Repr. of 1976 ed. text ed. write for info. (ISBN 0-89874-275-7). Krieger.
Ellis, Julie. Savage Oaks. 1977. 10.00 (ISBN 0-671-22874-9). S&S.
Hopf, Alice L. Biography of a Giraffe. LC 76-52934. (Nature Biography Ser.). (Illus.). (gr. 2-5). 1978. PLB 6.59 (ISBN 0-399-61088-X). Putnam.
Kilpatrick, Cathy. Giraffes. LC 79-18959. (Animals of the World Ser.). (Illus.). (gr. 4-8). 1980. PLB 11.95 (ISBN 0-8172-1086-5). Raintree Pubs.
MacClintock, Dorcas & Ugo, Mochi. A Natural History of Giraffes. LC 72-9580. (gr. 5-9). 1973. 7.95 (ISBN 0-684-13239-7, ScribT). Scribner.
Rey, H. A. Cecily G. & the Nine Monkeys. (Illus.). (gr. 1-3). 1942. reinforced bdg. 7.95 (ISBN 0-395-18430-4). HM.
Schlein, Miriam. Giraffe: The Silent Giant. LC 76-7922. (Illus.). 64p. (gr. 2-5). 1976. 6.95 (ISBN 0-590-07421-0, Four Winds). Schol Bk Serv.

GIRARD NATIONAL BANK OF PHILADELPHIA

Adams, Donald R., Jr. Finance & Enterprise in Early America: A Study of Stephen Girard's Bank, 1812-1831. LC 77-20301. 1978. 17.00x (ISBN 0-8122-7736-8). U of Pa Pr.
Leach, Josiah G. The History of the Girard National Bank of Philadelphia, 1832-1902. LC 73-75577. (Illus.). 120p. Repr. of 1902 ed. lib. bdg. 15.00x (ISBN 0-8371-4617-8, LEGN). Greenwood.

GIRAUDOUX, JEAN, 1882-1944

Alberes. Esthetique et Morale chez Giradoux. 1957. 24.95 (ISBN 0-685-33933-5). French & Eur.
Celler, Morton M. Giraudoux et la Metaphore: Une Etude Des Images Dans Ses Romans. (De Proprietatibus Litterarum, Series Practica: No. 54). 1974. pap. 21.25x (ISBN 0-686-20927-3). Mouton.
Cohen, Robert. Giraudoux: Three Faces of Destiny. LC 68-29058. 1970. pap. 2.45 (ISBN 0-226-11248-9, P371, Phoen). U of Chicago Pr.
--Giraudoux: Three Faces of Destiny. LC 68-29058. 1968. 8.75x (ISBN 0-226-11247-0). U of Chicago Pr.
Giraudoux, Jean & Body, Jacques. Lettres. 290p. 1975. 35.00 (ISBN 0-686-54006-9). French & Eur.
Lemaitre, George. Four French Novelists: Marcel Proust, Andre Gide, Jean Giraudoux, Paul Morand. LC 68-8201. (Essay & General Literature Reprint Ser). 1969. Repr. of 1938 ed. 15.00 (ISBN 0-8046-0267-0). Kennikat.
Lewis, Roy. Giraudoux: La Guerre De Troie N'Aura Pas Lieu. (Studies in French Literature). 1973. pap. text ed. 3.95x (ISBN 0-7131-5528-0). Dynamic Learn Corp.
Mankin, Paul A. Precious Irony: The Theatre of Jean Giraudoux. LC 78-165146. (Studies in French Literature: No. 19). 195p. (Orig.). 1971. pap. text ed. 32.50x (ISBN 90-2791-918-6). Mouton.
Raymond, Agnes. Jean Giraudoux: The Theatre of Victory & Defeat. LC 65-26238. 1966. pap. 8.00x (ISBN 0-87023-013-1). U of Mass Pr.
Reilly, John H. Jean Giraudoux. (Twayne's World Authors Ser.). 1978. lib. bdg. 9.95 (ISBN 0-8057-6354-6). G K Hall.
--Jean Giraudoux. (World Authors Ser.: No. 513 (France)). 1978. 12.50 (ISBN 0-8057-6354-6). Twayne.
Zenon, Renee. Le Traitement Des Mythes Dans le Theatre De Jean Giraudoux. LC 80-5815. 148p. (Orig.). 1981. lib. bdg. 17.75 (ISBN 0-8191-1576-2); pap. text ed. 7.75 (ISBN 0-8191-1577-0). U Pr of Amer.

GIRDERS

see also Bridges; Building, Iron and Steel; Graphic Statics; Influence Lines; Roofs; Steel, Structural

Chen Wai-Fah & Atsuta, T. Theory of Beam Columns Vol 2: Space Behavior & Design. 1977. text ed. 45.50x (ISBN 0-07-010759-9, C). McGraw.
Donnell, Lloyd H. Beams, Plates & Shells. (Engineering Societies Monograph). 1976. text ed. 29.50 (ISBN 0-07-017593-4, C). McGraw.
Gorman, D. J. Free Vibration Analysis of Beams & Shafts. LC 74-20504. 448p. 1975. 38.50x (ISBN 0-471-31770-5, Pub. by Wiley-Interscience). Wiley.
Hetenyi, Miklos. Beams on Elastic Foundation: Theory with Applications in the Fields of Civil & Mechanical Engineering. (Illus.). 1946. 15.00x (ISBN 0-472-08445-3). U of Mich Pr.
Heyman, J. Beams & Framed Structures. 2nd ed. LC 74-2234. 160p. 1974. text ed. 18.75 (ISBN 0-08-017945-2); pap. text ed. 9.25 (ISBN 0-08-017946-0). Pergamon.
Kani, Gaspar. Analysis of Multistory Frames. Hyman, Charles J., tr. LC 57-6114. 1967. 8.50 (ISBN 0-8044-4486-2). Ungar.
Kristek, Vladimir. Theory of Box Girders. LC 78-8637. 371p. 1980. 40.50 (ISBN 0-471-99678-5, Pub. by Wiley-Interscience). Wiley.
White, G. W. Elementary Beam Theory & the Ship Girder. 124p. 1979. 15.00x (ISBN 0-540-07352-0). Sheridan.

GIRDERS–TABLES, CALCULATIONS, ETC.

Anger, Georg & Tramm, Karl. Deflection Ordinates for Single Span & Continuous Beams. Amerongen, C. V., tr. LC 65-20500. 1965. 10.50 (ISBN 0-8044-4056-5). Ungar.
Griffel, William. Beam Formulas. LC 68-31449. 1970. 15.00 (ISBN 0-8044-4338-6). Ungar.
Iyengar, K. T. & Ramu, S. Anantha. Design Tables for Beams on Elastic Foundations & Related Structural Problems. (Illus.). 1979. 38.90x (ISBN 0-85334-841-3, Pub. by Applied Science). Burgess-Intl Ideas.
Rogers, Paul. Tables & Formulas for Fixed End Moments of Members of Constant Moment of Inertia & for Simply Supported Beams. 2nd ed. LC 65-28016. 1965. 11.50 (ISBN 0-8044-4850-7). Ungar.
Woelfer, K. H. Elastically Supported Beams & Plates Cylindrical Shells. bilingual, 4th ed. (Illus.). 180p. 1978. plastic bdg. 55.00x (ISBN 3-7625-0778-3). Intl Pubns Serv.

GIRDERS, CONTINUOUS

see also Influence Lines

Baum, Gunter. Basic Values on Single Span Beams: Tables for Calculating Continuous Beams & Frame Constructions, Including Prestressed Beams. (Illus.). 1966. 21.70 (ISBN 0-387-03464-1). Springer-Verlag.
Hahn, J. Structural Analysis of Beams & Slabs. Amerongen, C. V., tr. LC 68-20516. 1967. 18.50 (ISBN 0-8044-4368-8). Ungar.
Vreden, Werner. Curved Continuous Beams for Highway Bridges. LC 68-9396. 1969. 11.00 (ISBN 0-8044-4975-9). Ungar.

GIRL SCOUTS OF THE U. S. A.

Bender, Sandra B., et al. Odyssey Outdoors. Feirman, Sylvia, ed. (Illus.). 28p. (gr. 8-12). 1974. pap. text ed. 0.75 (ISBN 0-88441-415-9, 26-201). GS.
Blueprints for Action. (gr. 1-7). 1973. pap. 0.85 (ISBN 0-88441-129-X, 19-987). GS.
Girl Scout Student Loan Exhibition Catalogue. (Illus.). 1977. Repr. of 1929 ed. 37.50x (ISBN 0-686-74501-9). Antique Classic.
Girl Scouts of the U. S. A. Every Girl Scout Camp an EQ Camp. (gr. 1-12). 1970. pap. 0.50 (ISBN 0-88441-014-5, 19-940). GS.
--To Guide a Girl Scout Troop. pap. 0.15 (ISBN 0-88441-024-2, 19-951). GS.
--Worlds to Explore Handbook for Brownie & Junior Girl Scouts. LC 20-700. (Illus.). (gr. 1-6). 1977. pap. text ed. 3.25 (ISBN 0-88441-316-0). GS.
Girl Scouts of the U. S. A. Program Department. Girl Scout Badges & Signs. (Illus.). 208p. (Orig.). (gr. 4-6). 1980. pap. text ed. 2.50 (ISBN 0-686-73735-0). GS.
Girl Scouts of the U.S. Daisy Low of the Girl Scouts: The Story of Juliette Gordon Low, Founder of the Girl Scouts of United States of America. 1954. pap. 0.25 (ISBN 0-88441-134-6, 19-991). GS.
Girl Scouts of the USA. Be an EQ Traveler. (gr. 1-8). 1971. pap. 0.15 (ISBN 0-88441-122-2, 19-966). GS.
--The Beginner's Cookbook. (gr. 1-6). 1972. pap. 0.95 (ISBN 0-88441-442-6, 26-114, Pub. by Dell). GS.
--Being Aware. (Illus., Orig.). 1971. pap. 0.50 (ISBN 0-88441-025-0, 19-974). GS.
--Feeding a Crowd. (gr. 4-12). 1973. pap. 0.35, 6 for 1.25 (ISBN 0-88441-125-7, 19-977). GS.
--Helping Leaders Help Girls Grow. 1972. 5.00 (ISBN 0-88441-320-9, 19-978). GS.
--Hola! Bienvenida a las Girl Scouts. (Span.). (gr. 1-8). 1971. pap. 0.25 ea., 10 for 2.00 (ISBN 0-88441-017-X, 19-964). GS.
--How Girls Can Help Their Country. (Facsimille of 1913 handbook). (gr. 4-12). 1972. pap. 0.50 (ISBN 0-88441-308-X, 20-200). GS.
--Partnership in Planning. 1972. pap. 0.25 ea., 10 for 2.25 (ISBN 0-88441-020-X, 19-970). GS.
--Sing Together: A Girl Scout Songbook. (Illus.). (gr. 1-12). 1973. 4.50 (ISBN 0-88441-309-8, 20-206). GS.
Girl Scouts of the U.S.A. Training About Girl Scouting. 1978. pap. 5.50 (ISBN 0-88441-431-0, 26-180). GS.
--Wide World of Girl Guiding & Girl Scouting. (Illus.). 88p. (gr. 1-6). 1980. pap. text ed. 3.95 (ISBN 0-88441-143-5, 19-713). GS.
Girl Scouts of the USA. Worlds to Explore Brownie & Junior Leaders Guide. LC 20-702. (Illus.). 1977. pap. 2.25 (ISBN 0-88441-318-7). GS.
--Worlds to Explore Junior Badges & Signs. LC 20-701. (Illus.). (gr. 1-6). 1977. pap. text ed. 1.00 (ISBN 0-88441-317-9). GS.
Girl Scouts of the U.S.A. You Make the Difference. (Illus.). 128p. (Orig.). (YA) (gr. 7-12). pap. text ed. 2.75 (ISBN 0-88441-329-2, 20-704). GS.
Girl Scouts of the U.S.A. Program Department. Girl Scout Badges & Signs: Leaders Guide. 1980. pap. text ed. 2.00 (ISBN 0-88441-327-6, 20-712). GS.
--Moreabouts for Brownie Girl Scout Leaders. (Illus.). 96p. 1980. pap. text ed. 3.00 (ISBN 0-88441-328-4, 20-703). GS.
Girl Scouts of the USA Program Department. Mundos a Explorar: Guia Para Lideres De Brownie y Junior Girl Scouts. Girl Scouts of the USA Training Department, tr. 48p. (Span.). (gr. 1-6). 1981. pap. 2.25 (ISBN 0-88441-332-2, 20-709). GS.
--Mundos a Explorar: Manual Para las Brownie y las Junior Girl Scouts. Girl Scouts of the USA Training Department, tr. 175p. (Orig., Span.). (gr. 1-6). Date not set. pap. 3.25 (ISBN 0-88441-331-4, 20-708). GS.
Girl Scouts of the U.S.A. Program Dept. Let's Make It Happen. (GS Catalogue: No. 20-815). (gr. 9-12). 2.50 (ISBN 0-88441-322-5). GS.
Girl Scouts of the U.S.A. Training Department. You Make the Difference: Leaders Guide. (Orig.). 1980. pap. text ed. 2.00 (ISBN 0-88441-330-6, 20-705). GS.
Munz, Elizabeth. Happily Appley. Filbey, Beverly, ed. (Illus.). 63p. 1975. pap. text ed. 1.00 (ISBN 0-88441-133-8, 19-995). GS.
School's Out. (gr. 1-12). 1972. pap. 0.60 (ISBN 0-88441-251-2, 19-967). GS.
World Association of Girl Guides & Girl Scouts. Basics of the World Association of Girl Guides & Girl Scouts. 1979. pap. text ed. 1.00 (ISBN 0-900827-28-9, 23-961). GS.
World Bureau of Girl Guides & Girl Scouts. Trefoil Round the World. (Illus.). (gr. 4-12). 1967. Repr. of 1977 ed. 4.50 (ISBN 0-900827-29-7, 23-962). GS.

GIRLS

see also Adolescent Girls; Children; Church Work with Children; Education of Women; Women; Young Women; Youth

Bowne, Eliza S. A Girl's Life Eighty Years Ago: Selection from the Letters of Eliza Southgate Bowne. LC 74-3933. (Women in America Ser). (Illus.). 280p. 1974. Repr. of 1888 ed. 17.00x (ISBN 0-405-06079-3). Arno.
Brown, John M. Morning Faces: A Book of Children & Parents. LC 78-167317. (Essay Index Reprint Ser.). (Illus.). Repr. of 1949 ed. 16.00 (ISBN 0-8369-2755-9). Arno.
Carlson, Dale. Girls Are Equal Too. LC 73-76333. (Illus.). 160p. (gr. 6-9). 1973. 9.95 (ISBN 0-689-30106-5). Atheneum.
Crow, Martha F. The American Country Girl. LC 74-3936. (Women in America Ser). (Illus.). 398p. 1974. Repr. of 1915 ed. 23.00x (ISBN 0-405-06083-1). Arno.
Fedder, Ruth. Girl Grows Up. 4th ed. (Illus.). (gr. 9 up). 1967. 5.95 (ISBN 0-07-020294-X, GB). McGraw.
Frank, Lawrence K., et al. Personality Development in Adolescent Girls. 1951. pap. 14.00 (ISBN 0-527-01552-0). Kraus Repr.
Lewis, Dio. Our Girls. LC 74-3958. (Women in America Ser). 388p. 1974. Repr. of 1871 ed. 23.00x (ISBN 0-405-06106-4). Arno.
Mead, Margaret. Coming of Age in Samoa. 8.00 (ISBN 0-8446-2571-X). Peter Smith.
Paul, Eden & Paul, Cedar, trs. A Young Girl's Diary. LC 77-91523. 1977. Repr. of 1921 ed. lib. bdg. 25.00 (ISBN 0-89341-467-0). Longwood Pr.
Shuttleworth, Frank K. Physical & Mental Growth of Girls & Boys Age Six to Nineteen in Relation to Age at Maximum Growth. 1939. pap. 16.00 (ISBN 0-527-01510-5). Kraus Repr.
--Sexual Maturation & the Physical Growth of Girls Age Six to Nineteen. 1937. pap. 14.00 (ISBN 0-527-01498-2). Kraus Repr.
--Sexual Maturation & the Skeletal Growth of Girls Age Six to Nineteen. 1938. pap. 4.00 (ISBN 0-527-01505-9). Kraus Repr.
Stuart, Dorothy M. The Girl Through the Ages. LC 70-89292. (Illus.). 264p. 1969. Repr. of 1933 ed. 19.00 (ISBN 0-8103-3581-6). Gale.
Sugarman, Daniel A. & Hochstein, Rolaine. Seventeen Guide to Knowing Yourself. (gr. 7-12). 1968. 9.95 (ISBN 0-02-615300-9). Macmillan.
Union College Character Research Project & Barber, Lucie W. Girls. (Illus.). 1979. pap. 1.00 (ISBN 0-915744-19-8). Character Res.
Woods, Robert A. & Kennedy, Albert J. Young Working Girls. 185p. 1974. Repr. of 1913 ed. lib. bdg. 20.00 (ISBN 0-87821-280-9). Milford Hse.

GIRLS–BIOGRAPHY

see also Biography–Juvenile Literature; Children–Biography; Children in the Bible

Darton, J. M. Famous Girls Who Have Become Illustrious Women: Forming Models for Imitation for the Young Women of England. facsimile ed. LC 79-38751. (Essay Index Reprint Ser). Repr. of 1864 ed. 19.00 (ISBN 0-8369-2644-7). Arno.
Ferris, Helen J., ed. Five Girls Who Dared. LC 77-107699. (Essay Index Reprint Ser.). Repr. of 1931 ed. 18.00 (ISBN 0-8369-2313-8). Arno.
Hausman, Suzanne, illus. Yes, Virginia. 4.95 (ISBN 0-685-86235-6). Phinmarc Bks.
Kirkland, Winifred M. & Kirkland, Frances. Girls Who Became Writers. facsimile ed. LC 78-152182. (Essay Index Reprint Ser). Repr. of 1933 ed. 12.00 (ISBN 0-8369-2234-4). Arno.
--Girls Who Made Good. facsimile ed. LC 71-152183. (Essay Index Reprint Ser). Repr. of 1930 ed. 11.00 (ISBN 0-8369-2235-2). Arno.

GIRLS–EDUCATION

see Education of Women

GIRLS–EMPLOYMENT

see Children–Employment; Coeducation; Education of Women; Youth–Employment

GIRLS–RELIGIOUS LIFE

Johnson, Lois. Just a Minute, Lord: Prayers for Girls. LC 73-78265. (Illus.). 96p. (Orig.). (gr. 5-8). 1973. pap. 2.50 (ISBN 0-8066-1329-7, 10-3605). Augsburg.
Kapp, Ardeth G. Miracles in Pinafores & Bluejeans. LC 77-4268. 81p. pap. 1.50 (ISBN 0-87747-741-8). Deseret Bk.
Thiele, Margaret. Girl Alive. LC 80-11623. (Orion Ser.). 1980. pap. 1.95 (ISBN 0-8127-0268-9). Review & Herald.
Wallis, Reginald. New Girl. (gr. 3-7). pap. 1.00 (ISBN 0-87213-911-5). Loizeaux.

GIRLS–SOCIETIES AND CLUBS

see also Gangs

Vance, Catherine S. The Girl Reserve Movement of the Young Women's Christian Association: An Analysis of the Educational Principles & Procedures Used Throughout Its History. LC 70-177683. (Columbia University. Teachers College. Contributions to Education: No. 730). Repr. of 1937 ed. 17.50 (ISBN 0-404-55730-9). AMS Pr.

GIRLS' BASKETBALL

see Basketball for Women

GIRLS' CLUBS

see Girls–Societies and Clubs

GIRLS IN THE BIBLE

see Children in the Bible

GIRONDISTS

Brace, Richard M. Bordeaux & the Gironde, 1789-1794. LC 68-10905. 1968. Repr. of 1947 ed. 10.00 (ISBN 0-8462-1072-X). Russell.
Lamartine, Alphonse M. Histoire Des Girondins, 8 Vols. 3rd ed. LC 70-171644. Repr. of 1848 ed. Set. 280.00 (ISBN 0-404-07330-1); 35.00 ea. AMS Pr.
Scherr, Marie. Charlotte Corday & Certain Men of the Revolutionary Torment. LC 79-100512. Repr. of 1929 ed. 22.50 (ISBN 0-404-05588-5). AMS Pr.
Sydenham, M. J. The Girondins. LC 72-4006. 252p. 1973. Repr. of 1961 ed. lib. bdg. 19.75x (ISBN 0-8371-6433-8, SYGI). Greenwood.

GISSING, GEORGE ROBERT, 1857-1903

Collie, Michael. The Alien Art: A Critical Study of George Gissing's Novels. 1978. 19.50 (ISBN 0-208-01731-3, Archon). Shoe String.
--George Gissing: A Biography. 1977. 17.50 (ISBN 0-208-01700-3, Archon). Shoe String.
Coustillas, Pierre, ed. Collected Articles on George Gissing. 186p. 1968. 24.00x (ISBN 0-7146-2054-8, F Cass Co). Biblio Dist.
Coustillas, Pierre & Partridge, Colin, eds. Gissing: The Critical Heritage. (Critical Heritage Ser.). 1972. 40.00 (ISBN 0-7100-7367-4). Routledge & Kegan.
Davis, Oswald H. George Gissing, a Study in Literary Leanings. LC 74-3007. 1966. lib. bdg. 15.00 (ISBN 0-8414-3729-7). Folcroft.
Gapp, Samuel V. George Gissing, Classicist. LC 72-189876. 1936. lib. bdg. 15.00 (ISBN 0-8414-1109-3). Folcroft.
Gissing, Ellen. Some Personal Recollections of George Gissing. 1929. lib. bdg. 5.00 (ISBN 0-8414-4652-0). Folcroft.
Gissing, George. Letters of George Gissing to Members of His Family. LC 77-130257. (English Literature Ser., No. 33). 1970. Repr. of 1927 ed. lib. bdg. 58.95 (ISBN 0-8383-1158-X). Haskell.
Gissing, George R. The Letters of George Gissing to Eduard Bertz: 1887-1903. Young, Arthur C., ed. LC 80-12936. xl, 337p. 1980. Repr. of 1961 ed. lib. bdg. 28.25x (ISBN 0-313-22454-4, GILE). Greenwood.
Goode, John. George Gissing: Idealogy & Fiction. (Barnes & Noble Critical Study Ser). 205p. 1979. text ed. 20.00x (ISBN 0-06-492488-2). B&N.
Gordon, John D. George Gissing, Eighteen Fifty-Seven to Nineteen Three: An Exhibition from the Berg Collection. 1978. Repr. of 1954 ed. lib. bdg. 8.50 (ISBN 0-8414-4615-6). Folcroft.

Korg, Jacob. George Gissing: A Critical Biography. LC 63-9938. (Illus.). 320p. 1963. 14.00 (ISBN 0-295-73798-0); pap. 6.95 (ISBN 0-295-95679-8). U of Wash Pr.
McCarthy, Desmond. Reviews of George Gissing. LC 74-20618. 1974. Repr. of 1938 ed. lib. bdg. 5.00 (ISBN 0-8414-5916-9). Folcroft.
McKay, Ruth C. George Gissing & His Critic, Frank Swinnerton. 111p. 1980. Repr. of 1933 ed. lib. bdg. 20.00 (ISBN 0-8495-3527-1). Arden Lib.
--George Gissing & His Critic Frank Swinnerton. LC 74-20774. 1974. Repr. of 1933 ed. lib. bdg. 8.00 (ISBN 0-8414-5929-0). Folcroft.
Michaux, Jean-Pierre, ed. George Gissing: Critical Essays. (Critical Studies). 214p. 1981. 25.00x (ISBN 0-389-20061-1). B&N.
Poole, Adrian. Gissing in Context. 231p. 1975. 20.00x (ISBN 0-87471-744-2). Rowman.
Spiers, John & Coustillas, Pierre. Rediscovery of George Gissing: A Reader's Guide. 1971. pap. text ed. 7.25x (ISBN 0-85353-067-X). Humanities.
Tindall, Gillian. The Born Exile: George Gissing. LC 74-6387. 296p. 1974. 10.00 (ISBN 0-15-113594-0). HarBraceJ.
Weber, Anton. George Gissing und Die Soziale Frage. pap. 18.50 (ISBN 0-384-66295-1). Johnson Repr.
Wolff, Joseph, compiled by. George Gissing: An Annotated Bibliography of Writings About Him. LC 73-15093. (Annotated Secondary Bibliography Series on English Literature in Transition, 1880-1920). 293p. 1974. 20.00 (ISBN 0-87580-038-6). N Ill U Pr.

GISSING, GEORGE ROBERT, 1857-1903–BIBLIOGRAPHY

Collie, Michael. George Gissing: A Biography. LC 75-22129. 192p. 1976. 20.00x (ISBN 0-8020-5330-0). U of Toronto Pr.

GISU (BANTU TRIBE)

Roscoe, John. Reports of the Mackie Ethnological Expedition to Central Africa, Pts. 2 & 3. Incl. Pt. 2. The Banyaakole; Pt. 3. The Bagesu. 1968. Repr. of 1923 ed. text ed. 16.00x (ISBN 0-576-59255-2). Humanities.

GIVE-AWAYS

see Free Material

GIVING, CHRISTIAN

see Stewardship, Christian

GIZA

Fisher, Clarence S. The Minor Cemetery at Giza. (Eckley B. Coxe Foundation Ser.: Vol. 1). (Illus.). 170p. 1924. 20.00 (ISBN 0-686-11902-9). Univ Mus of U PA.

GLACIAL EPOCH

see also Geology, Stratigraphic–Pleistocene

America's Ice Age Hunters. (Wonders of Learning Kits Ser.). (gr. 3-5). 1980. incl. cassette & tchrs. guide 23.50 (ISBN 0-686-74402-0, 04966). Natl Geog.
Ames, Gerald & Wyler, Rose. Story of the Ice Age. LC 56-6816. (Illus.). (gr. 3-7). 1956. PLB 6.89 (ISBN 0-06-020066-9, HarpJ). Har-Row.
Birman, Joseph H. Glacial Geology Across the Crest of the Sierra Nevada, California. LC 63-7471. (Special Paper: No. 75). (Illus., Orig.). 1964. pap. 8.75x (ISBN 0-8137-2075-3). Geol Soc.
Black, R. F., et al, eds. The Wisconsinan Stage. LC 72-89466. (Memoir: No. 136). (Illus.). 224p. 1973. 20.25x (ISBN 0-8137-1136-3). Geol Soc.
Cole, Joanna. Saber-Toothed Tiger & Other Ice-Age Mammals. (Illus.). (gr. 1-5). 1977. o.p. 8.25 (ISBN 0-688-22120-3); PLB 7.92 (ISBN 0-688-32120-8). Morrow.
Coleman, Arthur P. Ice Ages Recent & Ancient. LC 77-105678. (BCL Ser.: Ii). Repr. of 1926 ed. 24.50 (ISBN 0-404-01596-4). AMS Pr.
--The Last Million Years: A History of the Pleistocene in North America. LC 75-41062. (BCL Ser.: Ii). Repr. of 1941 ed. 21.50 (ISBN 0-404-14656-2). AMS Pr.
Daly, Reginald A. The Changing World of the Ice Age. 1963. Repr. of 1934 ed. 21.75 (ISBN 0-02-843500-1). Hafner.
Denton, G. H. & Hughes, T. J. The Last Great Ice Sheets. LC 79-27808. 484p. 1980. 95.00 (ISBN 0-471-06006-2, Pub. by Wiley-Interscience). Wiley.
Fodor, Ronald. Frozen Earth: Explaining the Ice Ages. LC 80-21588. (Illus.). 64p. (gr. 7-12). 1981. PLB 7.95 (ISBN 0-89490-036-6). Enslow Pubs.
Goldthwait, Richard P., ed. Till: A Symposium. LC 70-153422. (Illus.). 1972. 20.00x (ISBN 0-8142-0148-2). Ohio St U Pr.
Goudie, Andrew. Environmental Change. (Contemporary Problems in Geography Ser.). (Illus.). 1977. 29.95x (ISBN 0-19-874073-5); pap. 9.50x (ISBN 0-19-874074-3). Oxford U Pr.
Gray, J. M. & Lowe, J. J., eds. Studies in the Scottish Lateglacial Environment. 1977. text ed. 30.00 (ISBN 0-08-020498-8). Pergamon.
Hadingham, Evan. Secrets of the Ice Age. Winslow, Richard, ed. (Illus.). 1979. 14.95 (ISBN 0-8027-0624-X). Walker & Co.
Hambrey, M. J. & Harland, W. M. Earth's Pre-Pleistocene Glacial Record. LC 80-41613. (Illus.). 1000p. Date not set. price not set (ISBN 0-521-22860-3). Cambridge U Pr.
Holman, J. Allan & Gringhuis, Dirk. Mystery Mammals of the Ice Age-Great Lakes Region. LC 72-90919. (Illus.). 45p. (Orig.). (gr. 5-8). 1972. pap. 1.75 (ISBN 0-910726-74-4). Hillsdale Educ.
Hoyle, Fred. Ice: The Ultimate Human Catastrophe. (Illus.). 192p. 1981. 14.95 (ISBN 0-8264-0064-7). Continuum.
Imbrie, John & Imbrie, Katherine P. Ice Ages: Solving the Mystery. LC 78-13246. 1979. 15.95x (ISBN 0-89490-015-3). Enslow Pubs.
Lauber, Patricia. All About the Ice Age. (Allabout Ser.: No. 31). (Illus.). (gr. 5-9). 1959. PLB 5.39 (ISBN 0-394-90231-9). Random.
Lewis, Richard S. The Coming of the Ice Age. 1979. 10.00 (ISBN 0-399-12374-1). Putnam.
Lyell, Charles. Geological Evidence of the Antiquity of Man. 4th ed. LC 72-1728. (Illus.). Repr. of 1873 ed. 35.00 (ISBN 0-404-08138-X). AMS Pr.
Matsch, Charles L. North America & the Great Ice Age. new ed. (Earth Science Paperback Ser.). (Illus.). 1976. pap. text ed. 5.95 (ISBN 0-07-040935-8, C). McGraw.
Matthews, William H., 3rd. The Story of Glaciers & the Ice Age. LC 73-79452. (Story of Science Ser.). (Illus.). 128p. (gr. 5-12). 1974. PLB 7.29 (ISBN 0-8178-5142-9). Harvey.
Maynard, Christopher. Exploring the Great Ice Age. (Explorer Bks.). (Illus.). (gr. 3-5). 1979. 2.95 (ISBN 0-531-09128-7); PLB 6.90 s&l (ISBN 0-531-09113-9). Watts.
Patten, Donald W. Biblical Flood & the Ice Epoch. 1966. 9.00 (ISBN 0-8010-7012-0); pap. 7.50 (ISBN 0-8010-7013-9). Baker Bk.
Schultz, Gwen. Ice Age Lost. LC 73-13280. 1974. 10.00 (ISBN 0-385-05759-8, Pub. by Anchor Pr-Doubleday). Reading Gems.
Terra, Hellmut D. & Paterson, Thomas T. Studies on the Ice Age in India & Associated Human Cultures. LC 76-44795. (Carnegie Institution of Washington Publication: No. 493). Repr. of 1939 ed. 39.00 (ISBN 0-404-15881-1). AMS Pr.
Turekian, Karl K., ed. Late Cenozoic Glacial Ages. LC 70-140540. (Silliman Lectures Ser). (Illus.). 1971. 42.50x (ISBN 0-300-01420-1). Yale U Pr.
Von Engeln, Oscar D. Finger Lakes Region: Its Origin & Nature. (Illus.). 1961. 11.95 (ISBN 0-8014-0437-1). Cornell U Pr.
West, R. G. Pleistocene Geology & Biology. 2nd ed. LC 76-28353. (Illus.). 1977. pap. text ed. 18.95x (ISBN 0-582-44620-1). Longman.
Wright, A. E. & Moseley, F. Ice Ages: Ancient & Modern; Geological Journal Special Issue, No. 6. (Liverpool Geological Society & the Manchester Geological Association). 320p. 1980. 57.25 (ISBN 0-471-27753-3, Pub. by Wiley-Interscience). Wiley.

GLACIER BAY NATIONAL MONUMENT

Boehm, William D. Glacier Bay. LC 75-17886. (Illus.). 136p. 1975. pap. 9.95 album style (ISBN 0-88240-056-8). Alaska Northwest.
Muir, John. The Discovery of Glacier Bay (1879) Jones, William R., ed. (Illus.). 16p. 1978. Repr. of 1895 ed. pap. 2.00 (ISBN 0-89646-045-2). Outbooks.

GLACIER METAL COMPANY

Brown, Wilfred. Piecework Abandoned: The Effect of Wage Incentive Systems on Managerial Authority. (Glacier Project Ser.). 127p. 1962. 5.95x (ISBN 0-8093-0371-X). S Ill U Pr.

GLACIER NATIONAL PARK

Edwards, Gordon. A Climber's Guide to Glacier National Park. LC 76-15238. (Illus.). 155p. 1976. pap. 5.95 (ISBN 0-87842-064-9). Mountain Pr.
Hanna, Warren L. The Grizzlies of Glacier. LC 77-23004. (Illus.). 154p. 1978. pap. 5.95 (ISBN 0-87842-072-X). Mountain Pr.
Nelson, Dick & Nelson, Sharon. Easy Field Guide to Interesting Birds of Glacier National Park. (Illus.). 32p. (Orig.). (gr. 1-12). 1978. pap. 1.00 (ISBN 0-915030-17-9). Tecolote Pr.
--Easy Field Guide to Mammals of Glacier National Park. (Illus.). 32p. (Orig.). (gr. 1-12). 1978. pap. 1.00 (ISBN 0-915030-15-2). Tecolote Pr.
--Easy Field Guide to Trees of Glacier National Park. (Illus.). 32p. (Orig.). (gr. 1-12). 1978. pap. 1.00 (ISBN 0-915030-16-0). Tecolote Pr.
--Hiker's Guide to Glacier National Park. (Illus.). 112p. (Orig.). 1978. pap. 5.95 (ISBN 0-915030-24-1). Tecolote Pr.
--Short Hikes & Strolls in Glacier National Park. (Illus.). 48p. (Orig.). (gr. 7-12). 1978. pap. 2.95 (ISBN 0-915030-23-3). Tecolote Pr.
On, Danny & Sumner, David, photos by. Along the Trail: A Photographic Essay of Glacier National Park & the Northern Rockies. LC 79-53223. (Illus.). 1980. 20.00 (ISBN 0-913504-53-X); pap. 10.95 (ISBN 0-913504-54-8). Lowell Pr.
Radlauer, Ruth S. Glacier National Park. LC 76-48993. (Parks for People Ser). (Illus.). (gr. 3 up). 1977. 3.95 (ISBN 0-516-17491-6, Elk Grove Bks); PLB 10.00 (ISBN 0-516-07491-1). Childrens.
Schultz, J. W. Blackfeet Tales of Glacier National Park. 1977. lib. bdg. 69.95 (ISBN 0-8490-1514-6). Gordon Pr.

GLACIERS

see also Erosion

Agassiz, Louis. Studies on Glaciers. Carozzi, Albert V., tr. & ed. Bd. with Discourse of Neuchatel. (Illus.). 1967. 38.50 (ISBN 0-02-840200-6). Hafner.
American Geographical Society Library New York. Author, Title, Subject & Geographic Catalogs of the Glaciology Collection, Department of Exploration & Field Research, 3 vols. 1971. Set. 285.00 (ISBN 0-8161-0922-2). G K Hall.
Antarctic Glaciology in the International Hydrological Decade. (Technical Papers in Hydrology Ser). (Orig.). 1969. pap. 2.25 (ISBN 0-685-20805-2, U31, UNESCO). Unipub.
Balch, Edwin S. Glacieres or Freezing Caverns. Repr. of 1900 ed. 11.50 (ISBN 0-914264-32-X). Cave Bks TN.
Brown, Wilfred & Jaques, Elliot. Glacier Project Papers: Some Essays on Organization & Management from the Glacier Project Research. (Glacier Project Ser.). 285p. 1965. 7.95x (ISBN 0-8093-0373-6). S Ill U Pr.
Coleman, Arthur P. Ice Ages Recent & Ancient. LC 77-105678. (BCL Ser.: Ii). Repr. of 1926 ed. 24.50 (ISBN 0-404-01596-4). AMS Pr.
Combined Heat, Ice & Water Balances at Selected Glacier Basins. 1970. pap. 3.25 (ISBN 92-3-100855-2, U75, UNESCO). Unipub.
Embleton, C. & King, C. A. Glacial & Periglacial Morphology, 2 vols. 2nd ed. Incl. Vol. 1. Glacial Geomorphology. LC 75-14188. pap. 21.95 (ISBN 0-470-23893-3); Vol. 2. Periglacial Geomorphology. LC 75-14187. pap. 15.95 (ISBN 0-470-23895-X). 1975. Halsted Pr.
Fluctuations of Glaciers, 1965-1970, Vol. 2. (Illus.). 357p. (Orig.). 1974. pap. 22.75 (ISBN 92-3-101045-X, U252, UNESCO). Unipub.
Fluctuations of Glaciers 1970-1975, Vol. III. 1978. 44.75 (ISBN 92-3-101462-5, U848, UNESCO). Unipub.
Gilbert, G. K. Glaciers & Glaciation, Vol. 3. 1910. 28.00 (ISBN 0-527-38163-2). Kraus Repr.
Hamelin, Louis-Edmond & Cook, Frank A. Periglaciaire Par l'Image - Illustrated Glossary of Periglacial Phenomena. (Travaux et Documents De Centre D'etudes Nordiaues Ser.: No. 4). (Fr). 1967. 12.00x (ISBN 2-7637-6344-8, Pub. by Laval). Intl Schol Bk Serv.
Hanna, Warren. Montana's Many Splendored Glacier Land. LC 76-3614. (Illus.). 1976. pap. 5.95 (ISBN 0-87564-622-0). Superior Pub.
Hoole, R. Engineering Behaviour of Glacial Materials. 240p. 1980. pap. 21.85 (ISBN 0-686-27382-6, Pub. by GEO Abstracts England). State Mutual Bk.
Kasser, Peter. Fluctuations of Glaciers, 1959-1965, Vol. 1. (Illus.). 1967. pap. 8.25 (ISBN 92-3-100643-6, U251, UNESCO). Unipub.
King, C. A., ed. Periglacial Processes. LC 75-33696. (Benchmark Papers in Geology Ser.: Vol. 27). 1976. 56.00 (ISBN 0-12-786846-1). Acad Pr.
Lowe, J. J., et al, eds. Studies in the Lateglacial of North-West Europe: Including Papers Presented at a Symposium of the Quaternary Research Association Held at University College London, January 1979. (Illus.). 215p. 1980. 44.00 (ISBN 0-08-024001-1). Pergamon.
MacDowell, L. D. Alaska Glacier & Ice Fields. facs. ed. 18p. 1906. pap. 3.75 (ISBN 0-8466-0064-1, SJS64). Shorey.
Paterson, W. S. The Physics of Glaciers. 2nd ed. (Illus.). vii, 380p. 1981. 48.00 (ISBN 0-08-024005-4); pap. 17.50 (ISBN 0-08-024004-6). Pergamon.
Shumski, P. A. Principles of Structural Glaciology. Kraus, tr. (Illus.). 8.75 (ISBN 0-8446-2935-9). Peter Smith.
Sugden, D. E. & John, B. S. Glaciers & Landscape: A Geomorphological Approach. LC 76-11014. 1976. 21.95x (ISBN 0-470-15113-7). Halsted Pr.
Thorarinsson, Sigurdur. Glácier: Portrait of Vatnajokull. 1981. 16.50 (ISBN 0-906191-69-6, Pub. by Findhorn-Thule Scotland). Hydra Bk.
Washburn, A. Periglacial Processes & Environments. 1973. 25.00 (ISBN 0-312-60095-X). St Martin.
Washburn, A. L. Geocryology: A Survey of Periglacial Processes & Environments. LC 78-22026. 1980. 71.95x (ISBN 0-470-26582-5). Halsted Pr.

GLACIERS–JUVENILE LITERATURE

Lauber, Patricia. Icebergs & Glaciers. LC 61-9738. (Junior Science Ser.). (gr. 2-5). 1961. PLB 5.49 (ISBN 0-8116-6158-X). Garrard.
Nixon, Hershell H. & Nixon, Joan L. Glaciers: Nature's Frozen Rivers. LC 79-24655. (Skylight Ser.). (Illus.). (gr. 2-5). 1980. PLB 4.95 (ISBN 0-396-07802-8). Dodd.
Tangborn, Wendell V. Glaciers. LC 65-18702. (A Let's-Read-&-Find-Out Science Bk). (Illus.). (gr. k-3). 1965. (TYC-J); PLB 8.79 (ISBN 0-690-33119-3). Har-Row.

GLACIOLOGY

see Glaciers

GLADDEN, WASHINGTON, 1836-1918

Dorn, Jacob H. Washington Gladden: Prophet of the Social Gospel. LC 67-17173. (Illus.). 1968. 8.00 (ISBN 0-8142-0045-1). Ohio St U Pr.

GLADNESS

see Happiness

GLADSTONE, CATHERINE (GLYNNE) 1812-1900

Checkland, S. G. Gladstones: A Family Biography. LC 72-134611. 1971. 44.50 (ISBN 0-521-07966-7). Cambridge U Pr.
Slicer, Thomas R. From Poet to Premier: The Centennial Cycle, 1809-1909 - Poe, Lincoln, Holmes, Darwin, Tennyson, Gladstone. 1977. Repr. of 1909 ed. lib. bdg. 25.00 (ISBN 0-8495-4820-9). Arden Lib.

GLADSTONE, WILLIAM EWART, 1809-1898

Adelman, Paul. Gladstone, Disraeli & Later Victorian Politics. 1970. pap. text ed. 4.50x (ISBN 0-582-31409-7). Longman.
Archer, Thomas. William Ewart Gladstone & His Contemporaries: Fifty Years of Social & Political Progress, 4 vols. Repr. Set. 50.00 (ISBN 0-685-43663-2). Norwood Edns.
Chadwick, Owen. Acton & Gladstone. 1976. pap. text ed. 6.50x (ISBN 0-485-14122-1, Athlone Pr). Humanities.
Checkland, S. G. Gladstones: A Family Biography. LC 72-134611. 1971. 44.50 (ISBN 0-521-07966-7). Cambridge U Pr.
Drew, Mary. Acton, Gladstone & Others. facs. ed. LC 68-20294. (Essay Index Reprint Ser). 1924. 12.00 (ISBN 0-8369-0390-0). Arno.
--Acton, Gladstone & Others. LC 68-16292. 1968. Repr. of 1924 ed. 10.00 (ISBN 0-8046-0118-6). Kennikat.
Eversley, George J. Gladstone & Ireland: The Irish Policy of Parliament from 1850-1894. LC 74-114520. 1971. Repr. of 1912 ed. lib. bdg. 14.25x (ISBN 0-8371-4795-6, EVGI). Greenwood.
Eyck, Erich. Gladstone. Miall, Bernard, tr. LC 68-56055. Repr. of 1938 ed. 25.00x (ISBN 0-678-05045-7). Kelley.
Eyck, Erich & Miall, B., trs. Gladstone. new ed. 505p. 1966. 30.00x (ISBN 0-7146-1472-6, F Cass Co). Biblio Dist.
Feuchtwanger, E. J. Gladstone. LC 75-7712. (British Political Biography Ser.). 250p. 1975. 17.95 (ISBN 0-312-32760-9). St Martin.
Gladstone, William E. The Gladstone Diaries: Volumes V & VI, 1844-1868. Matthew, H. C., ed. (Gladstone Diaries Ser.). (Illus.). 1978. 174.00x set (ISBN 0-19-822445-1). Oxford U Pr.
--The Gladstone Diaries: 1840-1854, Vols. 3 & 4. Foot, M. R. & Foot, M. R., eds. (Illus.). 1450p. 1975. Set. 125.00x (ISBN 0-19-822425-7). Oxford U Pr.
Hammond, J. L. Gladstone & the Irish Nation. 2nd ed. 785p. 1964. 32.50x (ISBN 0-7146-1479-3, F Cass Co). Biblio Dist.
Hammond, John L. Gladstone & the Irish Nation. LC 74-9396. (Illus.). 768p. 1974. Repr. of 1938 ed. lib. bdg. 45.00x (ISBN 0-8371-7665-4, HAGI). Greenwood.
Jerrold, Walter. W. E. Gladstone: England's Great Commoner. 10.00 (ISBN 0-8414-5381-0). Folcroft.
Knaplund, Paul. Gladstone & Britain's Imperial Policy. 256p. 1966. 25.00x (ISBN 0-7146-1489-0, F Cass Co). Biblio Dist.
--Gladstone's Foreign Policy. 1970. Repr. of 1935 ed. 16.50 (ISBN 0-208-00243-X, Archon). Shoe String.
--Gladstone's Foreign Policy. 1970. Repr. of 1935 ed. 24.00x (ISBN 0-7146-1490-4, F Cass Co). Biblio Dist.
Medlicott, William N. Bismarck, Gladstone, & the Concert of Europe. Repr. of 1956 ed. lib. bdg. 15.00 (ISBN 0-8371-0567-6). Greenwood.
Morley, John. The Life of William Ewart Gladstone, 3 vols. LC 70-145193. 1966p. 1972. Repr. of 1903 ed. Set. 359.00 (ISBN 0-403-01117-5). Scholarly.
--Life of William Ewart Gladstone, 3 vols. 1911. Repr. Set. 75.00 (ISBN 0-8274-3864-8). R West.
Morley, John M. Life of William Ewart Gladstone, 3 Vols. LC 68-57630. (Illus.). 1969. Repr. of 1903 ed. Set. lib. bdg. 64.50x (ISBN 0-8371-0576-5, MOWG). Greenwood.
Palmerston, H. J. Gladstone & Palmerston: Being the Correspondence of Lord Palmerston with Mister Gladstone, 1851-1865. Guedalla, P., ed. & intro. by. Repr. of 1928 ed. 20.00 (ISBN 0-527-69340-5). Kraus Repr.
Seton-Watson, R. W. Disraeli, Gladstone & Eastern Question. 2nd ed. 590p. 1962. 28.50x (ISBN 0-7146-1513-7, F Cass Co). Biblio Dist.

Shannon, Richard. Gladstone & the Bulgarian Agitation, 1876. 2nd ed. xxviii, 308p. 1975. Repr. of 1963 ed. 19.50 (ISBN 0-208-01487-X, Archon). Shoe String.
Stansky, Peter. Gladstone: A Progress in Politics. 224p. 1981. pap. 4.95 (ISBN 0-393-00037-0). Norton.
--Gladstone: A Progress in Politics. LC 79-586. 1979. 9.95 (ISBN 0-316-81058-4). Little.
Vidler, Alec R. The Orb & the Cross: A Normative Study in the Relations of Church & State, with Reference to Gladstones Early Writings. 1945. text ed. 7.50x (ISBN 0-8401-2544-5). Allenson-Breckinridge.

GLAND OF INTERNAL SECRETION
see Endocrine Glands

GLANDS
see also Cystic Fibrosis; Endocrine Glands; Secretion;
also particular glands, e.g. Carotid Gland, Kidneys
Beermann, W., ed. Biochemical Differentiation in Insect Glands. LC 77-23423. (Results & Problems in Cell Differentiation: Vol. 8). (Illus.). 1977. 45.70 (ISBN 0-387-08286-7). Springer-Verlag.
Elgin, Kathleen. The Glands. LC 76-131148. (Human Body Ser). (Illus.). (gr. 4-6). 1971. PLB 4.90 (ISBN 0-531-01179-8). Watts.
Kapp, M. W. Glands, Our Invisible Guardians. 1977. 5.95 (ISBN 0-686-00385-3). AMORC.
Peaker, M. & Linzell, J. L. Salt Glands in Birds & Reptiles. LC 74-12966. (Physiological Society Monographs: No. 32). (Illus.). 296p. 1975. 53.50 (ISBN 0-521-20629-4). Cambridge U Pr.
Peterson, O. H. The Electrophysiology of Gland Cells. LC 80-40303. (Physiological Society Monographs: No. 36). 1981. 47.00 (ISBN 0-12-552150-2). Acad Pr.
Reiter, Russel J., ed. The Pineal Gland: Volume 1, Anatomy & Biochemistry. 288p. 1981. 74.95 (ISBN 0-8493-5714-4). CRC Pr.
Weart, Edith L. The Story of Your Glands. (Health Bks.). (Illus.). (gr. 4-7). 1962. PLB 6.59 (ISBN 0-698-30335-0). Coward.
Zurbruegg, R. P. Hypothalamic-Pituitary-Adrenocortical(HPA) Regulation: A Contribution to Its Assessment, Development, & Disorders in Infancy & Childhood with Special Reference to Plasma Cortisol Circadian Rhythm. (Monographs in Paediatrics: Vol. 7). (Illus.). 120p. 1975. 29.50 (ISBN 3-8055-2253-3). S Karger.

GLANDS, DUCTLESS
see Endocrine Glands

GLANDS, LACRIMAL
see Lacrimal Organs

GLANDS, MAMMARY
see Mammary Glands

GLANDS, SALIVARY
see Salivary Glands

GLANDULAR FEVER
see Mononucleosis

GLAONI, EL, T'HAMI, PASHA OF MARRAKESH
Friedlaender, Jonathan S. Patterns of Human Variation: The Demography, Genetics, & Phenetics of the Bougainville Islanders. LC 74-17858. (Illus.). 288p. 1975. text ed. 20.00x (ISBN 0-674-65855-8). Harvard U Pr.

GLASGOW, ELLEN ANDERSON GHOLSON, 1874-1945
Field, Louise. Ellen Glasgow: Novelist of the Old & New South. LC 74-11118. 1923. lib. bdg. 5.00 (ISBN 0-8414-4214-2). Folcroft.
Godbold, E. Stanly, Jr. Ellen Glasgow & the Woman Within. LC 71-165068. (Illus.). 344p. 1972. 22.50x (ISBN 0-8071-0040-4). La State U Pr.
Holman, C. Hugh. Three Modes of Modern Southern Fiction: Ellen Glasgow, William Faulkner, Thomas Wolfe. LC 66-19490. (Mercer University Lamar Lecture Ser: No. 9). 95p. 1966. 7.00x (ISBN 0-8203-0185-X). U of Ga Pr.
Inge, M. Thomas, ed. Ellen Glasgow: Centennial Essays. LC 75-15976. 1976. 9.75x (ISBN 0-8139-0620-2). U Pr of Va.
McDowell, Frederick P. Ellen Glasgow & the Ironic Art of Fiction. 304p. 1960. pap. 5.95 (ISBN 0-299-02114-9). U of Wis Pr.
Mann, Dorothea L. Ellen Glasgow: With Critical Essays & a Bibliography. LC 76-27975. 1928. lib. bdg. 5.00 (ISBN 0-8414-6112-0). Folcroft.
Raper, J. R. Without Shelter: The Early Career of Ellen Glasgow. LC 74-142337. (Southern Literary Studies). 1971. 20.00x (ISBN 0-8071-0904-5). La State U Pr.
Richards, Marion K. Ellen Glasgow's Development As a Novelist. LC 70-110957. (Studies in American Literature: No. 24). 1971. text ed. 32.50x (ISBN 90-2791-606-3). Mouton.
Rouse, Blair. Ellen Glasgow. (Twayne's United States Authors Ser). 1962. pap. 3.45 (ISBN 0-8084-0120-3, T26, Twayne). Coll & U Pr.
--Ellen Glasgow. LC 62-16821. (United States Authors Ser.). 1962. lib. bdg. 8.95x (ISBN 0-89197-745-7); pap. text ed. 2.95x (ISBN 0-8290-0010-0). Irvington.
Sherman, Stuart P., et al. Ellen Glasgow: Critical Essays. LC 77-13260. 1929. lib. bdg. 8.50 (ISBN 0-8414-7865-1). Folcroft.

GLASGOW, SCOTLAND
Annan, Thomas. Photographs of the Old Closes & Streets of Glasgow, 1868-1877. 9.00 (ISBN 0-8446-5550-3). Peter Smith.
--Photographs of the Old Closes & Streets of Glasgow, 1868-1877. (Eighteen Sixty-Eight to Eighteen Seventy-Seven). (Illus.). 96p. 1977. pap. 5.00 (ISBN 0-486-23442-8). Dover.
Cochrane, Andrew. Cochrane Correspondence Regarding the Affairs of Glasgow. Dennistoun, James, ed. LC 72-1034. (Maitland Club, Glasgow. Publications: No. 37). Repr. of 1836 ed. 20.00 (ISBN 0-404-53009-5). AMS Pr.
Dillon, John. Inventory of the Ornaments, Reliques, Jewels, Vestments, Books, Etc. Belonging to the Cathedral Church of Glasgow. LC 76-168150. (Maitland Club, Glasgow. Publications: No. 13). Repr. of 1831 ed. 15.00 (ISBN 0-404-52945-3). AMS Pr.
Glasgow. Index to a Private Collection of Notices Entitled Memorabilia of the City of Glasgow. (Maitland Club, Glasgow. Publications: No. 39). 1836. 10.00 (ISBN 0-404-53013-3). AMS Pr.
Jones's Directory of Glasgow-1789. 1978. Repr. of 1789 ed. text ed. 14.00x (ISBN 0-8277-5432-9). British Bk Ctr.
MacGeorge, Andrew. Old Glasgow: The Place & the People, from the Roman Occupation to the Eighteenth Century. (Illus.). 1977. Repr. of 1880 ed. 29.00x (ISBN 0-7158-1178-9). Charles River Bks.
Roxburgh, James M. School Board of Glasgow, 1873-1919. (Scottish Council for Research in Education Ser.: No. 63). 264p. 1971. 10.00x (ISBN 0-8426-1496-6). Verry.
Smith, John, ed. Burgh Records of the City of Glasgow. LC 71-168149. (Maitland Club, Glasgow. Publications: No. 16). Repr. of 1834 ed. 20.00 (ISBN 0-404-52952-6). AMS Pr.

GLASGOW, UNIVERSITY OF
Innes, Cosmos & Robertson, Joseph, eds. Munimenta Alme Universitatis Glasquensis 4 Vols. LC 79-168167. (Maitland Club, Glasgow. Publications: No. 72). Repr. of 1854 ed. Set. 170.00 (ISBN 0-404-53100-8). AMS Pr.
Thomson, William, ed. Deeds Instituting Bursaries, Scholarships & Other Foundations, in the College & University of Glasgow. LC 75-168166. (Maitland Club, Glasgow. Publications: No. 69). Repr. of 1850 ed. 32.50 (ISBN 0-404-53083-4). AMS Pr.

GLASPELL, SUSAN, 1882-1948
Waterman, Arthur E. Susan Glaspell. (Twayne's United States Authors Ser). 1966. pap. 3.45 (ISBN 0-8084-0288-9, T101, Twayne). Coll & U Pr.
--Susan Glaspell. LC 66-17062. (United States Authors Ser.). 1966. lib. bdg. 7.95x (ISBN 0-89197-958-1); pap. text ed. 2.95x (ISBN 0-8290-0016-X). Irvington.

GLASS, CARTER, 1858-1946
Smith, R. & Beasley, N. Carter Glass: A Biography. LC 72-172012. (FDR & the Era of the New Deal Ser). (Illus.). 520p. 1972. Repr. of 1939 ed. lib. bdg. 49.50 (ISBN 0-306-70392-0). Da Capo.
Smith, Rixey & Beasley, Norman. Carter Glass, a Biography. facs. ed. LC 72-124258. (Select Bibliographies Reprint Ser). 1939. 23.00 (ISBN 0-8369-5446-7). Arno.

GLASS, HUGH, 1780-1833
Myers, John M. The Saga of Hugh Glass: Pirate, Pawnee, & Mountain Man. LC 75-38613. viii, 237p. 1976. 15.95x (ISBN 0-8032-0867-7); pap. 3.25 (ISBN 0-8032-5834-8, BB 614, Bison). U of Nebr Pr.

GLASS
see also Glass Fibers; Glassware; Pyroceramics
Balta, P. & Balta, E. An Introduction to the Physical Chemistry of the Vitreous State. 1976. 42.50x (ISBN 0-85626-088-6, Pub. by Abacus Pr). Intl Schol Bk Serv.
Blair, Dorothy. A History of Glass in Japan. LC 72-94022. 1973. 60.00 (ISBN 0-87011-196-5). Corning.
Borisova, Z. U. Glassy Semiconductors. Adashko, J. George, tr. from Rus. 497p. 1981. text ed. 69.50 (ISBN 0-306-40609-8, Plenum Pr). Plenum Pub.
Cummings, Keith. The Technique of Glass Forming. (Illus.). 168p. 1980. 27.00 (ISBN 0-7134-1612-2, Pub. by Batsford England). David & Charles.
Curtis, Tony, ed. Glass. (Illus.). 1978. 3.95 (ISBN 0-902921-48-7). Apollo.
Darling, Sharon S. Chicago Ceramics & Glass. LC 79-91566. (Illus.). 240p. 1980. 25.00 (ISBN 0-913820-10-5). Chicago Hist.
Day, D. E. Glass Surfaces: Properties & Characterization. 1976. 73.25 (ISBN 0-444-11067-4, North-Holland). Elsevier.
--Relaxation Processes in Glass: Special Journal Issue. (Journal of Non-Crystalline Solids: Vol. 14). 1974. 66.00 (ISBN 0-444-10613-8, North-Holland). Elsevier.
Dinkel, Alvin L. Glass Cutting Techniques. (Illus., Orig.). 1978. pap. 2.00 (ISBN 0-916552-18-7). Acoma Bks.
Doremus, Robert H. Glass Science. LC 73-4713. (Science & Technology of Materials Ser). 349p. 1973. 40.00 (ISBN 0-471-21900-2, Pub. by Wiley-Interscience). Wiley.
Dubrova, Sara K. Vitreous Lithium Silicates: Their Properties & Field of Application. 46p. 1964. 20.00 (ISBN 0-306-10679-5, Consultants). Plenum Pub.
Duncan, Alastair. Leaded Glass: A Handbook of Techniques. (Illus.). 216p. 1976. 19.95 (ISBN 0-8230-2660-4). Watson-Guptill.
Emanuele, Concetta. Stems. 1970. 5.95 (ISBN 0-87069-147-3). Wallace-Homestead.
Frechette, V. D., et al. Surfaces & Interfaces of Glass & Ceramics. (Materials Science Research Ser.: Vol. 7). 548p. 1974. 45.00 (ISBN 0-306-38507-4, Plenum Pr). Plenum Pub.
Gedde, Walter. A Booke of Sundry Draughtes Principally for Glasiers: Whereunto Is Annexed How to Anniel in Glas, 4 pts. LC 78-26524. (English Experience Ser.: No. 316). (Illus.). 136p. 1971. Repr. of 1616 ed. Set. 21.00 (ISBN 90-221-0316-1). Walter J Johnson.
Gilman, J. J., ed. Metallic Glasses. (TN 693.m4m37). 1977. 58.00 (ISBN 0-87170-051-4). ASM.
Goldstein, Martin & Simha, Robert, eds. The Glass Transition & the Nature of the Glassy State, Vol. 279. (Annals of the New York Academy of Sciences). 246p. 1976. 26.00x (ISBN 0-89072-025-8). NY Acad Sci.
Herman, Herbert, ed. Treatise on Materials Science & Technology, Vol. 17: Glass 11. 1979. 54.00 (ISBN 0-12-341817-8). Acad Pr.
Hix, John. The Glass House. (Illus.). 208p. 1974. pap. 9.95 (ISBN 0-262-58044-6). MIT Pr.
Journal of Glass Studies, Vol. 22. (Illus.). 165p. 1980. 15.00x (ISBN 0-87290-022-3). Corning.
Matcham, Jonathan & Dreiser, Peter. The Techniques of Glass Engraving. LC 81-81041. (Illus.). 1981. 19.95 (ISBN 0-88332-267-6, 8195). Larousse.
Mazelev, L. Ya. Borate Glasses. LC 60-8719. 159p. 1960. 32.50 (ISBN 0-306-10511-X, Consultants). Plenum Pub.
Mazurin, O. V. Electrical Properties & the Structure of Glass. LC 58-44503. (The Structure of Glass Ser.: Vol. 4). 158p. 1966. 37.50 (ISBN 0-306-18304-8, Consultants). Plenum Pub.
Myuller, R. L. Solid State Chemistry. LC 65-26631. 256p. 1966. 42.50 (ISBN 0-306-10743-0, Consultants). Plenum Pub.
New Glass Review 1. (Illus.). 16p. pap. 25.00 (ISBN 0-87290-074-6). Corning.
Nord. Etching of Glass & Sandblasting. (Illus.). 80p. 1980. 6.95 (ISBN 0-935656-01-4, 101 B). Chrome Yellow.
Payton, Mary & Payton, Geoffrey. The Observer's Book of Glass. (Illus.). 1977. 2.95 (ISBN 0-684-14940-0, ScribT). Scribner.
Porai-Koshits, E. A., ed. Catalyzed Crystallization of Glass. LC 58-44503. (The Structure of Glass Ser.: Vol. 3). 208p. 1964. 37.50 (ISBN 0-306-18303-X, Consultants). Plenum Pub.
--Methods of Studying the Structure of Glass. LC 58-44503. (The Structure of Glass Ser.: Vol. 7). 240p. 1966. 37.50 (ISBN 0-306-18307-2, Consultants). Plenum Pub.
--Methods of Studying the Structure of Glass. LC 58-44503. (The Structure of Glass Ser.: Vol. 7). 240p. 1966. 37.50 (ISBN 0-306-18307-2, Consultants). Plenum Pub.
--Properties, Structure & Physical-Chemical Effects: Proceedings. LC 58-44503. (The Structure of Glass Ser.: Vol. 6). 240p. 1966. 37.50 (ISBN 0-306-18306-4, Consultants). Plenum Pub.
--The Structure of Glass Series, Vol. 1. LC 58-44503. 291p. 1958. 37.50 (ISBN 0-306-18301-3, Consultants). Plenum Pub.
--The Structure of Glass Series, Vol. 2. LC 58-44503. 480p. 1960. 45.00 (ISBN 0-306-18302-1, Consultants). Plenum Pub.
Pye, L. D., et al, eds. Borate Glasses: Structure, Properties, Applications. 1978. 54.50 (ISBN 0-306-40016-2, Plenum Pr). Plenum Pub.
--Introduction to Glass Science. LC 72-76933. 722p. 1972. 42.50 (ISBN 0-306-30596-8, Plenum Pr). Plenum Pub.
Reser, Margie, et al, eds. Symposium on Nucleation & Crystallization in Glasses & Melts. 15.00 (ISBN 0-916094-15-4). Am Ceramic.
Scholes, Samuel. Modern Glass Practice. 7th, rev. ed. Greene, Charles H., ed. LC 74-32219. (Illus.). 440p. 1975. 32.50 (ISBN 0-8436-0612-6). CBI Pub.
Shults, Eric. Glass, Mosaics, & Plastic. (Encore Edition). (Illus.). 1979. 3.95 (ISBN 0-684-16924-X, ScribT). Scribner.
Stennett-Wilson, Ronald. Modern Glass. 1975. 25.00 (ISBN 0-442-27958-2). Van Nos Reinhold.
Toropov, N. A. Structural Transformations in Glasses at High Temperatures. LC 58-44503. (The Structure of Glass Ser.: Vol. 5). 223p. 1965. 37.50 (ISBN 0-306-18305-6, Consultants). Plenum Pub.
Turner, D. P. Window Glass Design Guide. (Illus.). 1977. 15.00x (ISBN 0-89397-028-X). Nichols Pub.
Uhlmann, D. R. & Kreidl, N. J., eds. Glass: Science & Technology, Vol. 5, Elasticity & Strength in Glasses. 1980. 35.00 (ISBN 0-12-706705-1). Acad Pr.
Umbraco, Kitty & Umbraco, Russell. Iridescent Stretch Glass. 1972. pap. 5.95 (ISBN 0-685-57716-3). Borden.
Vogel, W. Structure & Crystallization of Glasses. 1971. 46.00 (ISBN 0-08-006998-3). Pergamon.
Von Saldern, Axel. Ancient & Byzantine Glass from Sardis. LC 79-27959. (Archaeological Exploration of Sardis Monograph: No. 6). (Illus.). 184p. 1981. text ed. 35.00 (ISBN 0-674-03303-5). Harvard U Pr.
Vose, Ruth H. Glass. (Collins Archaeology Ser.: No. 4). 1980. text ed. 33.75x (ISBN 0-00-211379-1, Pub. by Collins Sons England). Humanities.
Wong, Joe & Angell, C. Austin. Glass: Structure by Spectroscopy. 1976. 69.50 (ISBN 0-8247-6468-4). Dekker.
Zerwick, Chloe. A Short History of Glass. (Illus.). 95p. 1981. pap. 5.00 (ISBN 0-486-24158-0). Dover.
--A Short History of Glass. LC 79-57251. (Illus.). 96p. 1980. pap. 5.00 (ISBN 0-87290-072-X). Corning.

GLASS-BIBLIOGRAPHY
American Craft Council. Glass: A Bibliography. rev. ed. 14p. 1978. 3.70 (ISBN 0-88321-027-4). Am Craft.
Hench, Larry L. & McEldowney, B. A., eds. Bilbliograhy on Ceramics & Glass. LC 67-7492. 12.00 (ISBN 0-916094-17-0). Am Ceramic.

GLASS-COLLECTORS AND COLLECTING
see Glassware

GLASS-DICTIONARIES
Encyclopedia of New Carnival & Iridescent Glass. 1975. 15.95 (ISBN 0-685-55970-X). R M Presznick.
Kolthoff, Benedict. Glass Terminology: A German-English Glossary. (Illus.). 1967. 17.00 (ISBN 0-913942-03-0). Lang Serv.
Newman, Harold. An Illustrated Dictionary of Glass. (Illus.). 1978. 27.50 (ISBN 0-500-23262-8). Thames Hudson.

GLASS-JUVENILE LITERATURE
Mitgutsch, Ali. From Sand to Glass. LC 80-29572. (Carolrhoda Start to Finish Bks.). Orig. Title: Vom Sand Zum Glas. (Illus.). 24p. (ps-3). 1981. PLB 5.95 (ISBN 0-87614-162-9). Carolrhoda Bks.
Nord, Barry & Nord, Elaine. The Child's Book of Glass. (Illus.). 64p. (Orig.). (gr. 7-9). Date not set. pap. price not set (101E). Chrome Yellow.
Philippe, Joseph. Glass. (Q Books: Where Do Things Come from?). (Illus.). 28p. 1978. 3.95 (ISBN 0-8467-0442-0, Pub. by Two Continents). Hippocrene Bks.

GLASS-RESEARCH
see Glass Research

GLASS, COLORED
see also Glass Painting and Staining
Bamford, C. R. Colour Generation & Control in Glass. 1977. 44.00 (ISBN 0-444-41614-5). Elsevier.
Halliday, Sonia & Lushington, Laura. The Seasons in Stained Glass. (Illus.). 32p. 1981. 7.95 (ISBN 0-8028-3552-X). Eerdmans.
Middlemass, Keith. Continental Coloured Glass. (Illus.). 20.00 (ISBN 0-87556-263-9). Saifer.
Stout, Sandra. Depression Glass in Color. No. 1. plastic bdg. 6.95 (ISBN 0-87069-022-1); No. 2. plastic bdg. 6.95 (ISBN 0-87069-023-X). Wallace-Homestead.
Weatherman, Hazel M. Decorated Tumbler "PriceGuy". 128p. 1979. pap. 3.75 (ISBN 0-913074-13-6). Weatherman.

GLASS, CUT
see Cut Glass

GLASS, ORNAMENTAL
see also Glass, Colored; Glass Painting and Staining
Hartley, Julia M. & Cobb, Mary M. Early American Pattern Glass. LC 76-27580. (The States Ser.). (Illus.). 1976. pap. 7.50 (ISBN 0-912646-01-2). Tex Christian.
Landman, Hedy B. Selection IV: Glass from the Museum's Collection. LC 73-94132. (Illus.). 1974. 6.50 (ISBN 0-686-05873-9). Mus of Art RI.
Matheson, Susan B. Ancient Glass in the Yale University Art Gallery. 1980. write for info. (ISBN 0-89467-010-7). Yale Art Gallery.
Matthews, Robert T. Engraved Glass & Other Decorated Glass. LC 76-48555. (Illus.). 1978. soft bound 10.95 (ISBN 0-9601150-1-3). R T Matthews.

Miller, Robert W., ed. Wallace-Homestead Price Guide to Antiques & Pattern Glass. 7th ed. (Illus.). 592p. 1980. pap. 10.95 (ISBN 0-87069-305-0). Wallace-Homestead.
Rothenberg, Polly. Complete Book of Creative Glass Art. (Arts & Crafts Ser.). (Illus.). 228p. 1974. 9.95 (ISBN 0-517-51690-X); pap. 7.95 (ISBN 0-517-51691-8). Crown.
Traub, Jules S. The Glass of Desire Christian: Ghost for Galle. LC 78-73256. (Illus.). 1979. 39.50 (ISBN 0-932988-01-6). Art Glass Exchange.

GLASS, PRESSED
see Pressed Glass

GLASS, STAINED
see Glass Painting and Staining

GLASS BLOWING AND WORKING
see also Bottles

Barbour, R. Glassblowing for Laboratory Technicians. 2nd ed. 1978. text ed. 45.00 (ISBN 0-08-022155-6); pap. text ed. 14.00 (ISBN 0-08-022156-4). Pergamon.
Berlye, M. K. Encyclopedia of Working with Glass. LC 67-25903. 1968. 20.00 (ISBN 0-379-00274-4). Oceana.
Campana, D. M. Teacher of Firing China & Glass. (Illus.). 2.95 (ISBN 0-939608-02-2). Campana Art.
Carberry, Edward. Glassblowing: An Introduction to Artistic & Scientific Flameworking. rev. ed. LC 78-51569. (Illus.). 1980. 16.95 (ISBN 0-9601682-1-4). M G L S Pub.
Doyle, P. J., ed. Glass Making Today. (Illus.). 1979. 40.00x (ISBN 0-86108-047-5). Intl Pubns Serv.
Farrar, Estelle S. H. P. Sinclaire, Jr., Glassmaker, Vol. 1: The Years Before 1920. (Illus.). viii, 152p. 1974. pap. 10.95 (ISBN 0-686-09327-5). Farrar Bks.
Hammesfahr, James E. & Stong, Clair L. Creative Glass Blowing: Scientific & Ornamental. LC 68-14225. (Illus.). 1968. pap. text ed. 12.95x (ISBN 0-7167-0088-3). W H Freeman.
Isenberg, Anita & Isenberg, Seymour. Crafting in Glass: Molding, Fusing, Embellishing, Designing. LC 80-70386. (Illus.). 240p. 1981. 14.95 (ISBN 0-8019-6946-8); pap. 9.95 (ISBN 0-8019-6947-6). Chilton.
Katona, Imre. Beakers, Cups, Goblets. Halapy, Lily, tr. from Hungarian. (Illus.). 1978. 5.00x (ISBN 963-1302-86-5). Intl Pubns Serv.
Kulasiewicz, Frank. Glassblowing. LC 74-12446. (Illus.). 216p. 1974. 21.95 (ISBN 0-8230-2120-3). Watson-Guptill.
Littleton, Harvey. Glassblowing: A Search for Form. 136p. 1980. pap. 11.95 (ISBN 0-442-24341-3). Van Nos Reinhold.
Rudman, Jack. Glazier. (Career Examination Ser.: C-303). (Cloth bdg. avail. on request). pap. 6.00 (ISBN 0-8373-0303-6). Natl Learning.
Schuler, Frederic. Flameworking: Glassmaking for the Craftsman. LC 68-30863. (Illus.). 1968. 12.50 (ISBN 0-8019-5350-2). Chilton.
Schuler, Frederic W. & Schuler, Lilli. Glassforming: Glassmaking for the Craftsman. LC 71-135056. (Illus.). 1970. 12.50 (ISBN 0-8019-5558-0). Chilton.
Woodward, H. W. Art, Feat & Mystery: The Story of Thomas Webb & Sons, Glassmakers. 61p. 1978. 25.00x (ISBN 0-9506439-0-4, Pub. by Mark & Moody England). State Mutual Bk.

GLASS FIBERS
see also Glass Reinforced Plastics

Cheremisinoff, Nicholas P. & Cheremisinoff, Paul N., eds. Fiberglass-Reinforced Plastics Deskbook. LC 78-62293. 1978. 37.50 (ISBN 0-250-40245-9). Ann Arbor Science.
Loewenstein, K. L. The Manufacturing Technology of Continuous Glass Fibres. LC 72-97429. 300p. 1973. 49.00 (ISBN 0-444-41109-7). Elsevier.
Lubin, George. Handbook of Fiberglass & Advanced Plastics Composites. LC 75-1316. 912p. (Orig.). 1975. Repr. of 1969 ed. 44.00 (ISBN 0-88275-286-3). Krieger.
Mohr, J. Gilbert & Rowe, William P. Fiberglass. 1978. text ed. 24.50x (ISBN 0-442-25447-4). Van Nos Reinhold.
Steele, Gerald L. Fiber Glass. (Illus.). (gr. 11-12). 1962. text ed. 13.28 (ISBN 0-87345-174-0). McKnight.
Tiranti, John. Glass Fibre for Schools. (gr. 9-12). 1972. 8.95 (ISBN 0-85458-330-0); pap. 4.95 (ISBN 0-85458-340-8). Transatlantic.
Warring, Ronald H. New Glassfibre Book. 1971. 8.50x (ISBN 0-85242-666-6). Intl Pubns Serv.

GLASS FRUIT JARS

Schroeder, Bill. One Thousand Fruit Jars. (Illus.). 1978. pap. 4.95 (ISBN 0-89145-011-4). Collector Bks.
Toulouse, Julian H. Fruit Jars: A Collector's Manual with Prices. LC 73-77267. (Collector's Books Ser.). (Illus.). 8.95 (ISBN 0-8407-5615-1). Nelson.

GLASS MANUFACTURE
see also Glass Blowing and Working; Mirrors; Optical Instruments; Precious Stones, Artificial

Babcock, C. L. Silicate Glass Technology Methods. LC 76-30716. (Pure & Applied Optics Ser). 326p. 1977. 44.00 (ISBN 0-471-03965-9, Pub. by Wiley-Interscience). Wiley.
Barnett, George E. Chapters on Machinery & Labor. LC 68-25563. (Masterworks in Industrial Relations Ser.). 191p. 1969. Repr. of 1926 ed. 6.95x (ISBN 0-8093-0397-3). S Ill U Pr.
Blaser, Werner. Filigree Architecture: Metal & Glass Construction. (Illus.). 216p. (Eng. Fr. & Ger.). 1980. pap. 19.00 (ISBN 0-89192-298-9). Interbk Inc.
Corning Museum of Glass. A Survey of Glassmaking from Ancient Egypt to the Present. LC 77-15599. 1977. 2 color fiches incl. 28.50 (ISBN 0-226-68902-6, Chicago Visual Lib). U of Chicago Pr.
Davis, Pearce. Development of the American Glass Industry. LC 75-81456. (Illus.). 1970. Repr. of 1949 ed. 12.00 (ISBN 0-8462-1360-5). Russell.
Doremus, Robert H. Glass Science. LC 73-4713. (Science & Technology of Materials Ser). 349p. 1973. 40.00 (ISBN 0-471-21900-2, Pub. by Wiley-Interscience). Wiley.
Doyle, P. J., ed. Glass Making Today. (Illus.). 1979. 40.00x (ISBN 0-86108-047-5). Intl Pubns Serv.
Duffy, J. I., ed. Glass Technology: Developments Since 1978. LC 80-26045. (Chemical Tech. Rev. Ser.: 184). (Illus.). 323p. 1981. 48.00 (ISBN 0-8155-0838-7). Noyes.
European Glass Directory & Buyers' Guide, Nineteen Seventy-Nine. (Illus.). 548p. (Orig., Polyglot.). 1979. pap. 27.50x (ISBN 0-86108-050-5). Intl Pubns Serv.
Farrar, Estelle S. H. P. Sinclaire, Jr., Glassmaker, Vol. 2: The Manufacturing Years. (Illus.). 1975. pap. 11.75 (ISBN 0-686-10549-4). Farrar Bks.
Giegerich, W. & Trier, W., eds. Glass Machines: Construction & Operation of Machines for the Forming of Hot Glass. Kreidl, Norbert J., tr. LC 68-56941. (Illus.). 1969. 47.60 (ISBN 0-387-04493-0). Springer-Verlag.
Hoffmann, E. Fachwoerterbuch Fuer die Glasindustriel. 160p. (Ger. -Eng., Dictionary doe the Glass Industry). 1963. 36.00 (ISBN 3-540-03007-7, M-7396, Pub. by Springer). French & Eur.
Honeywell, Marie-Anne. Index Journal of Glass Studies, 1959-1973: Volumes 1-15. LC 59-12390. 1976. pap. 8.00 (ISBN 0-87290-061-4). Corning.
Hunter, Frederick W. Stiegel Glass. (Illus.). 1966. pap. 5.00 (ISBN 0-486-20128-7). Dover.
Isenberg, Anita & Isenberg, Seymour. Crafting in Glass: Molding, Fusing, Embellishing, Designing. LC 80-70386. (Illus.). 211p. 1981. 14.95 (ISBN 0-8019-6946-8); pap. 9.95 (ISBN 0-8019-6947-6). Chilton.
Jarves, Deming. Reminiscences of Glassmaking. 1968. Repr. of 1865 ed. 7.50 (ISBN 0-9600568-2-3). Weinstock.
Journal of Glass Studies. LC 59-12390. 1972-81. 15.00x ea. Vol. 14 (ISBN 0-87290-014-2). Vol. 15 (ISBN 0-87290-015-0). Vol. 16 (ISBN 0-87290-016-9). Vol. 17 (ISBN 0-87290-017-7). Vol. 18 (ISBN 0-87290-018-5). Vol. 19 (ISBN 0-87290-019-3). Vol. 20 (ISBN 0-87290-020-7). Vol. 21 (ISBN 0-87290-021-5). Corning.
Lee, Ruth W. Sandwich Glass. rev. ed. (Illus.). 25.00 (ISBN 0-910872-04-X). Lee Pubns.
--Sandwich Glass Handbook. (Illus.). 6.95 (ISBN 0-910872-05-8). Lee Pubns.
McConnell, Robert R. Modeling Glass Furnace, Refiner & Forehearth Design & Operation for Energy Efficiency & Improved Control. LC 78-75008. (Outstanding Dissertations on Energy Ser.). 1979. lib. bdg. 28.00 (ISBN 0-8240-3976-9). Garland Pub.
McKearin, Helen & McKearin, George S. American Glass. (Illus.). 1941. 22.50 (ISBN 0-517-00111-X). Crown.
Matson, F. B. & Rindone, G. E., eds. Advances in Glass Technology: Pt. 2, Historical Papers & Discussions of the Technical Papers. 410p. 1963. 49.50 (ISBN 0-306-37002-6, Plenum Pr). Plenum Pub.
Mitgutsch, Ali. From Sand to Glass. LC 80-29572. (Carolrhoda Start to Finish Bks.). Orig. Title: Vom Sand Zum Glas. (Illus.). 24p. (ps-3). 1981. PLB 5.95 (ISBN 0-87614-162-9). Carolrhoda Bks.
Mouly, R. J., ed. Automatic Control in Glass. LC 73-86352. 255p. 1973. pap. text ed. 20.00 (ISBN 0-87664-225-3). Instru Soc.
Reyntiens, Patrick. Technique of Stained Glass. (Illus.). 1967. 18.95 (ISBN 0-8230-5225-7). Watson-Guptill.
Rindone, G. E., ed. Advances in Glass Technology: Pt. 1, Technical Papers. LC 61-15176. 639p. 1962. 55.00 (ISBN 0-306-37001-8, Plenum Pr). Plenum Pub.
Scholes, Samuel. Modern Glass Practice. 7th, rev. ed. Greene, Charles H., ed. LC 74-32219. (Illus.). 440p. 1975. 32.50 (ISBN 0-8436-0612-6). CBI Pub.
Scoville, Warren C. Revolution in Glassmaking: Entrepreneurship & Technological Change in the American Industry, 1880-1920. LC 76-38264. (The Evolution of Capitalism Ser.). 440p. 1972. Repr. of 1948 ed. 22.00 (ISBN 0-405-04144-6). Arno.
Spillman, Jane S. Glassmaking: America's First Industry. LC 76-17354. (Illus.). 35p. 1976. pap. 1.40 (ISBN 0-87290-062-2). Corning.
Weatherman, H. M. Fostoria: Its First Fifty Years. (Illus.). 352p. 1972. 18.00 (ISBN 0-913074-02-0). Weatherman.

GLASS MANUFACTURE–FRANCE

Scott, Joan W. The Glassworkers of Carmaux. LC 73-83423. (Studies in Urban History). 256p. 1974. text ed. 12.50x (ISBN 0-674-35440-0); pap. 5.95x (ISBN 0-686-76999-6). Harvard U Pr.
Scoville, Warren C. Capitalism & French Glassmaking. Repr. of 1950 ed. pap. 12.50 (ISBN 0-384-54480-0). Johnson Repr.

GLASS MANUFACTURE–GREAT BRITAIN

Godfrey, Eleanor S. The Development of English Glassmaking, 1560-1640. LC 75-19021. 296p. 1976. 19.50x (ISBN 0-8078-1256-0). U of NC Pr.
Kenyon, G. H. Glass Industry of the Weald. LC 67-98056. (Illus.). 1967. 13.50x (ISBN 0-678-08036-4). Kelley.

GLASS PAINTING AND STAINING
see also Glass, Colored

Adam, Stephen. Decorative Stained Glass. (All Color Paperbacks Ser.). (Illus.). 88p. 1980. pap. 8.50 (ISBN 0-8478-0283-3). Rizzoli Intl.
Baker, John. English Stained Glass of the Medieval Period. (Illus.). 1979. pap. 8.95 (ISBN 0-500-27128-3). Thames Hudson.
Bonnie Doon Art Glass Co. Stained Glass Art. (Illus.). 130p. 1981. pap. 14.95 (ISBN 0-8256-3856-9, Hidden Hse). Music Sales.
Brady, Darlene & Serban, William, eds. Stained Glass: A Guide to Information Sources. LC 79-23712. (Art & Architecture Information Guide Ser.: Vol. 10). 1980. 36.00 (ISBN 0-8103-1445-2). Gale.
Caviness, Madeline H. The Early Stained Glass of Canterbury Cathedral: 1175-1220. (Illus.). 1978. text ed. 45.00 (ISBN 0-691-03927-5). Princeton U Pr.
Clarke, Brian. Architectural Stained Glass. LC 79-211. (Illus.). 1979. 29.50 (ISBN 0-07-011264-9, Architectural Rel Bks). McGraw.
Clow, Barbara & Clow, Gerry. Stained Glass: A Basic Manual. (The Crafts Ser.). 1976. pap. 4.95 (ISBN 0-316-14754-0). Little.
Divine, J. A. & Blachford, G. Stained Glass Craft. 115p. 1972. pap. 2.00 (ISBN 0-486-22812-6). Dover.
--Stained Glass Craft. (Illus.). 6.50 (ISBN 0-8446-4539-7). Peter Smith.
Duncan, Alistair. Tiffany Windows. 1980. 45.00 (ISBN 0-671-24951-7). S&S.
Duval, Jean-Jacques. Working with Stained Glass: Fundamental Techniques & Applications. LC 74-184975. (Funk & W Bk.). (Illus.). 144p. 1975. pap. 5.95 (ISBN 0-308-10153-7, F112). T Y Crowell.
Eden, Sydney. The Intelligent Understanding of Stained & Painted Glass. (Illus.). 131p. 1980. 49.85 (ISBN 0-930582-81-0). Gloucester Art.
Elskus, Albinas. Art of Painting on Glass. (Illus.). 152p. 1980. 17.95 (ISBN 0-684-16465-5, ScribT). Scribner.
Fox, Vincent. Stained Glass Bevel Making. (Illus.). 224p. 1981. pap. 7.95 (ISBN 0-8256-3858-5, Hidden Hse). Music Sales.
French, Jennifer. Glassworks: The Copper-Foil Technique of Stained Glass. (Illus.). 96p. 1974. pap. 7.95 (ISBN 0-442-22443-5). Van Nos Reinhold.
French, Jennnie. Design for Stained Glass. 1979. 18.95 (ISBN 0-442-22467-2). Van Nos Reinhold.
Frohbieter-Mueller, Jo. Stained Glass Miniature Village. 56p. 1981. pap. 3.95 (ISBN 0-8256-3836-4, Hidden Hse). Music Sales.
Gick, James E. Patterns for Stained Glass. (Illus.). 1977. pap. 3.00 (ISBN 0-918170-24-9). Gick.
Giorgi, Louis P. The Windows of Saint Justin Martyr. LC 80-67119. (Illus.). 128p. 1981. 25.00 (ISBN 0-87982-034-9). Art Alliance.
Halliday, Sonia & Lushington, Laura. Stained Glass. 1976. 39.95 (ISBN 0-517-52728-6). Crown.
Hill, Robert & Hill, Jill. Stained Glass: Music for the Eye. LC 79-65725. (Illus.). 108p. (Orig.). 1979. pap. 9.95 (ISBN 0-295-95699-2). U of Wash Pr.
Hollender, Gary. Stained Glass Patterns in Color. (Illus.). 96p. 1981. pap. 3.95 (ISBN 0-8256-3831-3, Hidden Hse). Music Sales.
--Stained Glass Patterns in Color. (Illus.). 1978. pap. 5.95 (ISBN 0-8256-3835-6, Hidden Hse). Music Sales.
Irimie, Cornel & Focsa, Marcela. Romanian Icons Painted on Glass. (Illus.). 1971. 75.00 (ISBN 0-393-04309-6). Norton.
Isenberg, Anita & Isenberg, Seymour. How to Work in Stained Glass. (Creative Crafts Ser.). (Illus.). 237p. 1972. 13.95 (ISBN 0-8019-5638-2); pap. 8.95 (ISBN 0-8019-5896-2). Chilton.
--Stained Glass: Advanced Techniques & Projects. (Illus.). 1976. 15.00 (ISBN 0-8019-6194-7). Chilton.
--Stained Glass Lamps: Construction & Design. (Creative Crafts Ser.). 272p. 1974. 14.50 (ISBN 0-8019-5839-3); pap. 8.95 (ISBN 0-8019-5840-7). Chilton.
Isenberg, Anita, et al. Stained Glass Painting: The Techniques of the Craft. LC 78-21826. (Chilton's Arts & Crafts Ser.). (Illus.). 1979. 14.95 (ISBN 0-8019-6650-7); pap. 9.95 (ISBN 0-8019-6651-5). Chilton.
Kramer, Jack. Painting on Glass. (Illus.). 1977. 12.95 (ISBN 0-442-20821-9). Van Nos Reinhold.
Kyle, Carolyn. Stained Glass Designs for Bevels. (Illus.). 130p. 1981. pap. 5.95 (ISBN 0-8256-3857-7, Hidden Hse). Music Sales.
--Stained Glass Frames for Plants & Mirrors. (Illus.). 32p. 1981. pap. 4.95 (ISBN 0-8256-3854-2, Hidden Hse). Music Sales.
Lee, Lawrence. The Appreciation of Stained Glass. (The Appreciation of the Arts Ser.: No.9). 1977. 18.50x (ISBN 0-19-211913-3). Oxford U Pr.
Lillich, Meredith P. The Stained Glass of Saint-Pere de Chartres. LC 77-13926. (Illus.). 1978. 40.00x (ISBN 0-8195-5023-X, Pub. by Wesleyan U Pr). Columbia U Pr.
Lips, Claude. Art & Stained Glass. LC 72-92255. 96p. 1973. pap. 5.95 (ISBN 0-385-08286-X). Doubleday.
Luciano. Stained Glass Calendar. (Illus.). 1981. pap. 6.95 (ISBN 0-8256-3860-7, Hidden Hse). Music Sales.
--Stained Glass Lamps & Terrariums. (Illus.). 112p. 1981. pap. 3.95 (ISBN 0-8256-3800-3, Hidden Hse). Music Sales.
--Stained Glass Window Art. (Illus.). 104p. 1981. pap. 6.95 (ISBN 0-8256-3802-X, Hidden Hse). Music Sales.
Luciano & Colson. Stained Glass Lamp Art. (Illus.). 144p. 1981. pap. 6.95 (ISBN 0-8256-3812-7, Hidden Hse). Music Sales.
Luciano & Malmstrom. Stained Glass for Plants. (Illus.). 64p. 1981. pap. 3.95 (ISBN 0-8256-3822-4, Hidden Hse). Music Sales.
--Stained Glass for Plants: Ten Planter & Terrarium Projects with Full-Size Patterns & Step-by-Step Instructions. 1977. pap. 3.95 (ISBN 0-8256-3822-4, Hidden Hse). Music Sales.
Luciano & Mayo, Gene. Stained Glass Home Studio Guide. (Illus.). 72p. 1981. pap. 4.95 (ISBN 0-8256-3844-5, Hidden Hse). Music Sales.
Luciano & Miller, Judy. Stained Glass Lamp Patterns. 88p. 1981. pap. 4.95 (ISBN 0-8256-3837-2, Hidden Hse). Music Sales.
McKee, Barbara W. Stained Glass Alphabet Pattern Book. 40p. 1981. pap. 4.95 (ISBN 0-8256-3834-8, Hidden Hse). Music Sales.
McKee, Barbara W., compiled by. Stained Glass Vistas. 80p. 1981. pap. 5.95 (ISBN 0-8256-3838-0, Hidden Hse). Music Sales.
Marks, Paul. Stained Glass Astrology & Tarot Card Designs. (Illus.). 64p. 1981. pap. 2.95 (ISBN 0-8256-3842-9, Hidden Hse). Music Sales.
Mendez, Pepe. Complete Course in Stained Glass. 1977. 6.95 (ISBN 0-672-23287-1). Bobbs.
Miller, Judy. Stained Glass Christmas Designs. (Illus.). 48p. 1981. pap. 3.95 (ISBN 0-8256-3859-3, Hidden Hse). Music Sales.
--Stained Glass Images. (Illus.). 120p. 1981. pap. 5.95 (ISBN 0-8256-3833-X, Hidden Hse). Music Sales.
--Stained Glass Images II. (Illus.). 112p. 1981. pap. 5.95 (ISBN 0-8256-3839-9, Hidden Hse). Music Sales.
Miller, Judy & Mayo, Gene. Stained Glass Window, Bk. 7. (Patterns for Beginners-Bks). (Illus.). 32p. 1981. pap. 4.95 (ISBN 0-8256-3852-6, Hidden Hse). Music Sales.
--Stained Glass Window, Bk. 8. (Patterns for Beginners). (Illus.). 32p. 1981. pap. 4.95 (ISBN 0-8256-3853-4, Hidden Hse). Music Sales.
Mollica, Peter. Stained Glass Primer, Vol. 1. 1971. pap. 3.95 (ISBN 0-9601306-1-6). Mollica Stained Glass.
--Stained Glass Primer, Vol. 2. rev ed. 1978. pap. 4.95 (ISBN 0-9601306-3-2). Mollica Stained Glass.
Nord, Barry & Nord, Elaine. Glass Etching-Pattern Book I: Fruit, Flowers, & Birds. (Illus.). 50p. (Orig.). 1980. pap. 3.95 (ISBN 0-935656-02-2, 101C). Chrome Yellow.
--Glass Etching-Pattern Book II: Wildlife, Alphabets, Geometrics. (Illus.). 50p. (Orig.). 1980. pap. 3.95 (ISBN 0-935656-03-0, 101D). Chrome Yellow.
O'Brien, Vincent. Techniques of Stained Glass: Leaded, Faceted, & Laminated Glass. (Illus.). 1977. 14.95 (ISBN 0-442-26259-0). Van Nos Reinhold.

Olson, K. B. Stained Glass Window, Bk. 1. (Patterns for Beginners). (Illus.). 64p. 1981. pap. 4.95 (ISBN 0-8256-3840-2, Hidden Hse). Music Sales.
--Stained Glass Window, Bk. 2. (Patterns for Beginners). (Illus.). 64p. 1981. pap. 4.95 (ISBN 0-8256-3841-0, Hidden Hse). Music Sales.
--Stained Glass Window, Bk. 3. (Patterns for Beginners). (Illus.). 64p. 1981. pap. 4.95 (ISBN 0-8256-3846-1, Hidden Hse). Music Sales.
--Stained Glass Window, Bk. 4. (Patterns for Beginners). 64p. 1981. pap. 4.95 (ISBN 0-8256-3847-X, Hidden Hse). Music Sales.
--Stained Glass Window, Bk. 5. (Patterns for Beginners). (Illus.). 64p. 1981. pap. 4.95 (ISBN 0-8256-3850-X, Hidden Hse). Music Sales.
--Stained Glass Window, Bk. 6. (Patterns for Beginners). 64p. 1981. pap. 4.95 (ISBN 0-8256-3851-8, Hidden Hse). Music Sales.
--Stained Glass Window Patterns for Beginners, Book I. (Illus.). 64p. 1980. pap. 4.95 (ISBN 0-8256-3840-2, Hidden Hse-Flash). Music Sales.
--Stained Glass Window Patterns for Beginners, Book II. (Illus.). 64p. 1980. pap. 4.95 (ISBN 0-8256-3841-0, Hidden Hse-Flash). Music Sales.
Osborne, June. Stained Glass in England. 224p. 1981. 60.00x (ISBN 0-584-97293-8, Pub. by Muller Ltd). State Mutual Bk.
Painting Bottles & Glasses. 1976. pap. 1.50 (ISBN 0-8277-5726-3). British Bk Ctr.
Peacham, Henry. The Art of Drawing with the Pen, & Limming with Water Colours. LC 71-25631. (English Experience Ser.: No. 230). 70p. 1970. Repr. of 1606 ed. 14.00 (ISBN 90-221-0230-0). Walter J Johnson.
Quagliata, Narcissus. Stained Glass from Mind to Light: An Inquiry into the Nature of the Medium. LC 76-10019. (Orig.). 1976. 25.00 (ISBN 0-916854-00-0). Mattole Pr.
Read, H. E. English Stained Glass. Repr. of 1926 ed. 48.00 (ISBN 0-527-74250-3). Kraus Repr.
Reyntiens, Patrick. Technique of Stained Glass. (Illus.). 1967. 18.95 (ISBN 0-8230-5225-7). Watson-Guptill.
Rigan, Otto B. New Glass. LC 76-22734. (Illus.). 128p. 1976. 14.95 (ISBN 0-913374-52-0). SF Bk Co.
Rothenberg, Polly. Creative Stained Glass. (Arts & Crafts Ser.). (Illus.). 96p. 1973. 7.95 (ISBN 0-517-50581-9); pap. 3.95 (ISBN 0-517-50582-7). Crown.
--Decorating Glass. (Illus.). 1976. 6.95 (ISBN 0-517-52391-4). Crown.
Schuler, Frederic W. & Schuler, Lilli. Glassforming: Glassmaking for the Craftsman. LC 71-135056. (Illus.). 1970. 12.50 (ISBN 0-8019-5558-0). Chilton.
Scobey, Joan. Stained Glass: Traditions & Techniques. (Illus.). 1979. 18.95 (ISBN 0-8037-7926-7); pap. 9.95 (ISBN 0-8037-4610-5). Dial.
Sewter, A. Charles. The Stained Glass of William Morris & His Circle: A Catalogue, Vol. 2. LC 72-91307. (Studies in British Art Ser.). 344p. 1975. 125.00 (ISBN 0-300-01836-3). Yale U Pr.
--The Stained Glass of William Morris & His Circle, Vol. 1. LC 72-91307. (Studies in British Art Ser.). (Illus.). 384p. 1974. 100.00x (ISBN 0-300-01471-6). Yale U Pr.
Sibbett, Ed. Easy-to-Make Stained Glass Lampshades. (Illus., Orig.). 1980. pap. 3.95 (ISBN 0-486-23997-7). Dover.
Sibbett, Ed, Jr. Art Deco Stained Glass Pattern Book. LC 77-77051. (Illus.). 1977. pap. 2.50 (ISBN 0-486-23550-5). Dover.
--Art Nouveau Stained Glass Pattern Book. LC 77-87497. (Pictorial Archives Ser.). (Illus.). 1978. pap. 2.75 (ISBN 0-486-23577-7). Dover.
--Contemporary Stained Glass Projects. LC 77-84743. (Illus.). 1978. pap. 2.75 (ISBN 0-486-23559-9). Dover.
--Easy-to-Make Stained Glass Lightcatchers: Sixty-Seven Designs for Small Ornaments, with Full-Size Templates. (Illus., Orig.). 1981. pap. 3.50 (ISBN 0-486-24081-9). Dover.
--Full-Size Stained Glass Templates: Sixteen Attractive & Easy Patterns. (Illus.). 1979. pap. 4.50 (ISBN 0-486-23744-3). Dover.
--Historic Styles Stained Glass Pattern Book. (Illus.). 64p. (Orig.). 1981. pap. price not set (ISBN 0-486-24176-9). Dover.
--New Glass Stained Glass Pattern Book. (Illus.). 64p. (Orig.). 1980. pap. 3.00 (ISBN 0-486-24029-0). Dover.
--Stained Glass Pattern Book: Eighty Eight Designs for Workable Projects. LC 76-15447. (Pictorial Archive Ser). (Illus., Orig.). 1976. pap. 2.75 (ISBN 0-486-23360-X). Dover.
--Stained Glass Pattern Book: 88 Designs for Workable Projects. 6.75 (ISBN 0-8446-5522-8). Peter Smith.
--Victorian Stained Glass Pattern Book: 96 Designs for Workable Projects. 1979. pap. 3.00 (ISBN 0-486-23811-3). Dover.
Sowers, Robert. The Language of Stained Glass. (Illus.). 220p. 1981. 24.95 (ISBN 0-917304-61-6, Pub. by Timber Pr). Intl Schol Bk Serv.
Stained Glass Window Patterns in Color. (Illus.). 32p. 1981. pap. 3.95 (ISBN 0-8256-3835-6, Hidden Hse). Music Sales.
Stephany, Konrad. Ludwig Schaffrath, Stained Glass & Mosaic. LC 77-79948. 1977. write for info. (ISBN 0-686-05497-0). C & R Loo.
Stillman, Peter. Stained Glass for the Amateur. new ed. Rahmas, D. Steve, ed. (Handicraft Ser.: No. 8). (Illus.). 32p. (Orig.). 1973. lib. bdg. 2.45 incl. catalog cards (ISBN 0-87157-908-1); pap. 1.25 vinyl laminated covers (ISBN 0-87157-408-X). SamHar Pr.
Theophilus. On Divers Arts: The Foremost Medieval Treatise on Painting, Glassmaking, & Metalwork. Hawthorne, John G. & Smith, Cyril S., trs. from Latin. (Illus.). 1979. pap. text ed. 5.00 (ISBN 0-486-23784-2). Dover.
Wallach, Joel. Patterns & Designs in Stained Glass. (Illus.). 1974. 3.95 (ISBN 0-934280-00-2). Glass Works.
--Patterns & Designs in Stained Glass, Bk. 2. (Illus.). 1976. pap. 3.95 (ISBN 0-934280-01-0). Glass Works.
--Patterns & Designs in Stained Glass, Bk. 3. (Illus.). 1978. pap. 3.95 (ISBN 0-934280-02-9). Glass Works.
Wallach, Joel L. Beginning Stained Glass Patterns, Bk. 1. (Illus.). 48p. (Orig.). 1980. pap. 4.95x (ISBN 0-934280-04-5). Glass Works.
--Beginning Stained Glass Patterns, Bk. 2. (Illus.). 48p. (Orig.). 1980. pap. 4.95x (ISBN 0-934280-05-3). Glass Works.
--First Project Stained Glass Patterns, Bk. 1. (Illus., Orig.). 1981. pap. 4.95x (ISBN 0-934280-06-1). Glass Works.
Walton, Mark. Stained Glass Advanced Window Techniques. (Illus.). 144p. 1981. pap. 6.95 (ISBN 0-8256-3824-0, Hidden Hse). Music Sales.
Walton Studios. Stained Glass Designs. 1978. pap. 4.95 (ISBN 0-8256-3823-2, Hidden Hse). Music Sales.
Weiner, Kay. Stained Glass Magic: Mix & Match Patterns & Projects. LC 78-21827. (Chilton's Arts & Crafts Ser.). (Illus.). 1979. pap. 8.95 (ISBN 0-8019-6726-0). Chilton.
Winterbotham, Ann V. Treasury of Traditional Stained Glass Designs. (Illus.). 80p. (Orig.). 1981. pap. 3.50 (ISBN 0-486-24084-3). Dover.
Wood, Paul W. Stained Glass Crafting. rev. ed. LC 67-27750. (Illus.). (gr. 10 up). 1971. 8.95 (ISBN 0-8069-5094-3); PLB 8.29 (ISBN 0-8069-5095-1). Sterling.
--Working with Stained Glass. LC 80-54350. (Illus.). 104p. 1981. 9.95 (ISBN 0-8069-5440-X); lib. bdg. 9.29 (ISBN 0-8069-5441-8); pap. 5.95 (ISBN 0-8069-8966-1). Sterling.
Woodforde, C. Stained Glass in Somerset. 18.00x (ISBN 0-87556-418-6). Saifer.
Zakin, Helen J. French Cistercian Grisaille Glass. LC 78-74385. (Outstanding Dissertations in the Fine Arts, Fourth Ser.). 1979. lib. bdg. 44.00 (ISBN 0-8240-3971-8). Garland Pub.

GLASS REINFORCED PLASTICS

see also Fiberglass Boats

Figg, Keith & Hayward, John. G R P Boat Construction. (Questions & Answers Ser.). (Illus.). 86p. (Orig.). 1979. pap. 7.50 (ISBN 0-408-00317-0). Transatlantic.
Hollaway, L. Glass Reinforced Plastics in Construction: Engineering Aspects. 228p. 1978. 36.95 (ISBN 0-470-99338-3). Halsted Pr.

GLASS RESEARCH

Duffy, J. I., ed. Glass Technology: Developments Since 1978. LC 80-26045. (Chemical Tech. Rev. Ser.: 184). (Illus.). 323p. 1981. 48.00 (ISBN 0-8155-0838-7). Noyes.
Persson, Rune. Flat Glass Technology. LC 72-83172. 177p. 1969. 17.50 (ISBN 0-306-30649-2, Plenum Pr). Plenum Pub.
Porai-Koshits, E. A. Phase-Separation Phenomena in Glasses. LC 58-44503. (The Structure of Glass Ser.: Vol. 8). 208p. 1973. 32.50 (ISBN 0-306-18308-0, Consultants). Plenum Pub.
Pye, L. D., et al, eds. Introduction to Glass Science. LC 72-76933. 722p. 1972. 42.50 (ISBN 0-306-30596-8, Plenum Pr). Plenum Pub.

GLASS TRADE

Doctorow, Donald. China & Glassware Merchandiser. 161p. soft bdg. 9.00 (ISBN 0-685-45923-3, M436). Natl Ret Merch.
Hoffmann, E. Fachwoerterbuch Fuer die Glasindustriel. 160p. (Ger.-Eng., Dictionary doe the Glass Industry). 1963. 36.00 (ISBN 3-540-03007-7, M-7396, Pub. by Springer). French & Eur.
Porai-Koshits, E. A., ed. Methods of Studying the Structure of Glass. LC 58-44503. (The Structure of Glass Ser.: Vol. 7). 240p. 1966. 37.50 (ISBN 0-306-18307-2, Consultants). Plenum Pub.
Scoville, Warren C. Capitalism & French Glassmaking. Repr. of 1950 ed. pap. 12.50 (ISBN 0-384-54480-0). Johnson Repr.

GLASSWARE

see also Bottles; Cut Glass; Paperweights; Pressed Glass; Salt Shakers

Ancient Glass at the Newark Museum. LC 76-47222. 1977. 15.95 (ISBN 0-932828-02-7); pap. 9.95 (ISBN 0-686-19145-5). Newark Mus.
Andre, Jean M. The Restorer's Handbook of Ceramics & Glass. 1976. 24.95 (ISBN 0-442-20363-2). Van Nos Reinhold.
Archer, Douglas & Archer, Margaret. Glass Candlesticks. (Illus.). 1979. pap. 8.95 (ISBN 0-89145-001-7). Collector Bks.
Arwas, Victor. Glass: Art Nouveau to Art Deco. LC 76-62548. (Illus.). 1978. 50.00 (ISBN 0-8478-0112-8). Rizzoli Intl.
--Lalique. LC 79-92368. (All Color Paperbacks Ser.). (Illus.). 88p. 1980. pap. 8.50 (ISBN 0-8478-0282-5). Rizzoli Intl.
Beard, Geoffrey. International Modern Glass. LC 78-56432. (Illus.). 1978. 30.00 (ISBN 0-684-15934-1, ScribT). Scribner.
Charleston, Robert. Masterpieces of Glass: A World History from the Corning Museum of Glass. (Illus.). 1980. 40.00 (ISBN 0-8109-1753-X). Abrams.
Clairmont, Christoph W. The Glass Vessels: Final Report Iv, Part V. LC 43-2669. 20.00 (ISBN 0-685-71743-7). J J Augustin.
Cole, Susan D. Richmond-Windows to the Past. LC 79-57178. (Illus.). 96p. (Orig.). 1980. pap. 6.95 (ISBN 0-936034-00-9). Wildcat Canyon.
Cosgrove, Maynard G. The Enamels of China & Japan. LC 72-7199. (Illus.). 248p. 1974. 10.00 (ISBN 0-396-06733-6). Dodd.
Davis, Frank. Early Eighteenth Century English Glass. (Country Life Collectors Guides Ser). 1972. 4.95 (ISBN 0-600-43601-2). Transatlantic.
Ettinghausen, Richard. Ancient Glass in the Freer Gallery of Art. (Illus.). 1962. pap. 1.50 (ISBN 0-934686-14-9). Freer.
Freeman, Larry G. Iridescent Glass. (Illus.). 1956. 6.50 (ISBN 0-87282-058-0). Century Hse.
Garner, Philippe. Emile Galle. LC 76-11257. (Illus.). 1979. pap. 19.95 (ISBN 0-8478-0227-2). Rizzoli Intl.
Glass from the Corning Museum of Glass: A Guide to the Collections. (Illus.). 99p. 1965. pap. 3.50x (ISBN 0-8139-0574-5). U Pr of Va.
Goldstein, Sidney M. Pre-Roman & Early Roman Glass in the Corning Museum of Glass. LC 78-70440. (Catalog Ser.). (Illus.). 1979. 40.00 (ISBN 0-87290-067-3). Corning.
Hartung, M. Carnival Pattern Series, 1-10. write for info. (ISBN 0-685-83490-5). Hartung.
Honeywell, Marie-Anne. Index Journal of Glass Studies, 1959-1973: Volumes 1-15. LC 59-12390. 1976. pap. 8.00 (ISBN 0-87290-061-4). Corning.
Jarves, Deming. Reminiscences of Glassmaking. 1968. Repr. of 1865 ed. 7.50 (ISBN 0-9600568-2-3). Weinstock.
Journal of Glass Studies, Vol. 23. (Illus.). 160p. 1981. 15.00x (ISBN 0-87290-023-1). Corning.
Klamkin, Marian. The Collector's Guide to Depression Glass. (Illus.). 288p. 1973. pap. 12.50 (ISBN 0-8015-1399-5, Hawthorn). Dutton.
Lee, Ruth W. Nineteenth Century Art Glass. (Illus.). Date not set. 7.95 (ISBN 0-910872-19-8). Lee Pubns.
--Price Guide to Pattern Glass. rev. ed. 8.95 (ISBN 0-910872-09-0). Lee Pubns.
--Sandwich Glass Handbook. (Illus.). 6.95 (ISBN 0-910872-05-8). Lee Pubns.
Lee, Ruth W. & Rose, James H. American Glass Cup Plates. (Illus.). 445p. 1971. 35.00 (ISBN 0-910872-18-X). Lee Pubns.
Logerberg, Ted & Logerberg, Vi. Collectible Glass, 4 bks. Incl. Bk. I; Bk. II; Bk. III. Durand Glass (ISBN 0-87069-234-8); Bk. IV. British Glass (ISBN 0-87069-235-6). (Illus.). 1978. ringbound 6.95 ea. Wallace-Homestead.
McClinton, Katherine M. An Introduction to Lalique Glass. (Illus.). 1978. 17.95 (ISBN 0-87069-238-0). Wallace-Homestead.
Malone, Lawrence A. How to Mend Your Treasured Porcelain, China, Glass & Pottery. (Illus.). 256p. 1975. 15.95 (ISBN 0-87909-344-7). Reston.
New Glass: A Worldwide Survey. LC 78-74015. 1979. Corning.
Noel Hume, Ivor. Glass in Colonial Williamsburg's Archaeological Collections. LC 79-84022. (Archaeological Ser: No. 1). (Illus., Orig.). 1969. pap. 2.25 (ISBN 0-910412-06-5). Williamsburg.
Owens, Richard. Carnival Glass Tumblers. (Illus.). 1978. 9.95 (ISBN 0-87069-217-8). Wallace-Homestead.
Padgett, Leonard. Pairpoint Glass. (Illus.). 1978. 29.95 (ISBN 0-87069-218-6). Wallace-Homestead.
Pearson, J. Michael. Encyclopedia of American Cut & Engraved Glass-Realistic Patterns, Vol. 2. LC 74-18615. (Illus.). 172p. 1977. 20.00 (ISBN 0-916528-03-0). J M Pearson.
Traub, Jules S. The Glass of Desire Christian: Ghost for Galle. LC 78-73256. (Illus.). 1979. 39.50 (ISBN 0-932988-01-6). Art Glass Exchange.
Vincent, Keith. Nailsea Glass. (Illus.). 112p. 1975. 7.50 (ISBN 0-7153-6807-9). David & Charles.
Von Saldern, Axel. Ancient Glass in the Museum of Fine Arts, Boston. LC 67-31751. (Illus.). 1968. pap. 2.95 (ISBN 0-87846-157-4). Mus Fine Arts Boston.
Weatherman, H. M. Colored Glassware of the Depression Era, Bk. 2. (Illus.). 400p. 1977. 25.00 (ISBN 0-913074-04-7). Weatherman.
Weatherman, Hazel. The Decorated Tumbler. (Illus.). 160p. 1978. pap. 15.00 (ISBN 0-913074-11-X). Weatherman.
Weatherman, Hazel M. Decorated Tumbler "PriceGuy". 128p. 1979. pap. 3.75 (ISBN 0-913074-13-6). Weatherman.
Wells, Susan. Mend Your Own China & Glass. (Illus.). 80p. 1976. 11.50 (ISBN 0-7135-1875-8); pap. 8.95 (ISBN 0-7135-1883-9). Transatlantic.

GLASSWARE–COLLECTORS AND COLLECTING

Archer, Margaret & Archer, Douglas. Glass Candlesticks II. (Illus.). 1978. pap. 8.95 (ISBN 0-89145-061-0). Collector Bks.
Belknap, E. McCamly. Milk Glass. (Illus.). 1949. 10.95 (ISBN 0-517-09740-0). Crown.
Cambridge Glass Identification & Value Guide. (Illus.). 1976. 14.95 (ISBN 0-89145-020-3). Collector Bks.
Conway, Darlyne. Depression Era Glass Handbook & Pricing Guide. LC 75-184288. 1971. 8.95 (ISBN 0-912092-41-6). Educator Bks.
Coppen-Gardner, Sylvia. A Background for Glass Collectors. (Illus.). 172p. 1976. 12.25 (ISBN 0-7207-0624-6). Transatlantic.
Corning Museum of Glass. Czechoslovakian Glass Thirteen Hundred & Fifty to Nineteen Eighty. LC 80-85452. (Illus.). 176p. 1981 (ISBN 0-87290-100-9). pap. 115.00 (ISBN 0-686-72142-X). Corning.
--New Glass: A Worldwide Survey. (Illus.). 286p. 1981. pap. 25.00 (ISBN 0-486-24156-4). Dover.
Edwards, Bill. Fenton Carnival Glass, the Early Years. (Illus.). 1981. 9.95 (ISBN 0-89145-161-7). Collector Bks.
--Imperial Carnival Glass. (Illus.). 1980. pap. 9.95 (ISBN 0-89145-138-2). Collector Bks.
--Standard Carnival Glass Price Guide. (Illus.). 1981. 3.95 (ISBN 0-89145-163-3). Collector Bks.
Encyclopedia of Victorian Colored Pattern Glass, Bk. 6, limited ed. 22.00 (ISBN 0-915410-15-X); pap. 16.95 (ISBN 0-915410-14-1). Antique Pubns.
Fauster, Carl U., ed. Libbey Glass, Since Eighteen Eighteen: Pictorial History & Collectors Guide. 1979. 30.00 (ISBN 0-686-25838-X). Len Beach Pr.
Field, Anne E. On the Trail of Stoddard Glass. 1975. pap. 4.95 (ISBN 0-87233-021-4). Bauhan.
Florence, Gene. The Collector's Encyclopedia of Depression Glass. 5th ed. (Illus.). 224p. 1981. 17.95 (ISBN 0-89145-180-3). Collector Bks.
--Kitchen Glassware of the Depression Years. (Illus.). 1981. 17.95 (ISBN 0-89145-170-6). Collector Bks.
Gardner, Paul F. Glass of Frederick Carder. 1976. 22.50 (ISBN 0-517-50440-5). Crown.
Grimmer, Elsa H. Wave Crest Ware: An Illustrated Guide to the Victorian World of C. F. Monroe. 1979. pap. 9.95 (ISBN 0-87069-279-8); price guide 1.50 (ISBN 0-87069-289-5). Wallace-Homestead.
Grover, Ray & Grover, Lee. Art Glass Nouveau. LC 67-10197. 1967. 49.50 (ISBN 0-8048-0032-4). C E Tuttle.
Hollingworth, June. Collecting Decanters. (The Christies International Collectors Ser.). (Illus.). 128p. 1980. 14.95 (ISBN 0-8317-2161-8, Mayflower Bks). Smith Pubs.
Imperial Glass Identification & Value Guide. (Illus.). 1978. 14.95 (ISBN 0-89145-074-2). Collector Bks.
Iness, Lowell, intro. by. M'kee & Bros. Victorian Glass: Five Complete Glass Catalogues from 1859 - 60, 71. (Illus.). 160p. 1981. pap. 5.00 (ISBN 0-486-24121-1). Dover.
Innes, Lowell. Pittsburgh Glass, 1797-1891: A History & Guide for Collectors. 1976. 30.00 (ISBN 0-395-20733-9). HM.
Investing in Georgian Glass. (Illus.). 12.50 (ISBN 0-87556-262-0). Saifer.
James, Margaret. Black Glass. 80p. 1981. pap. 5.95 (ISBN 0-89145-176-5). Collector Bks.
Kamm, Minnie W. Two Hundred Pattern Glass Pitchers. LC 68-5611. (Illus.). 1968. pap. 5.50x (ISBN 0-87282-082-3, 50531). Century Hse.
Klamkin, Marian. The Collector's Guide to Carnival Glass. 224p. 1976. 21.50 (ISBN 0-8015-1396-0, Hawthorn); pap. 9.95 (ISBN 0-8015-1397-9, Hawthorn). Dutton.

--The Collector's Guide to Depression Glass. (Illus.). 288p. 1973. pap. 12.50 (ISBN 0-8015-1399-5, Hawthorn). Dutton.
Lalique, Rene. Latique Glass: The Complete Illustrated Catalogue for 1932. (Illus.). 160p. 1981. pap. 8.95 (ISBN 0-486-24122-X). Dover.
Lee, Ruth W. Antique Fakes & Reproductions. rev. ed. (Illus.). 15.00 (ISBN 0-910872-07-4). Lee Pubns.
McCain, Mollie H. Standard Pattern Glass Price Guide. (Illus.). 1980. 5.95 (ISBN 0-89145-155-2). Collector Bks.
Manley, Cyril C. Decorative Victorian Glass. 128p. 1981. 24.95 (ISBN 0-442-25872-0). Van Nos Reinhold.
Metz, Alice. Early American Pattern Glass. (Illus.). 1978. pap. 14.95 (ISBN 0-89145-091-2). Collector Bks.
--Much More Early American Pattern Glass. (Illus.). 1978. pap. 14.95 (ISBN 0-89145-092-0). Collector Bks.
Old Pattern Glass: According to Heacock. pap. 9.95 (ISBN 0-915410-16-8). Antique Pubns.
Percy, Christopher V. The Glass of Lalique: A Collector's Guide. (Illus.). 1978. 30.00 (ISBN 0-684-15603-2, ScribT). Scribner.
Peterson, Arthur G. Four Hundred Trademarks on Glass. LC 68-12557. (Illus.). 52p. (Orig.). 1968. lib. bdg. 10.50 (ISBN 0-9605664-0-6); pap. 6.75 (ISBN 0-9605664-1-4). A G Peterson.
--Glass Patents & Patterns. LC 72-91628. (Illus.). 226p. 1973. lib. bdg. 15.50x (ISBN 0-9605664-2-2); pap. 11.75 (ISBN 0-9605664-3-0). A G Peterson.
--Glass Salt Shakers: One Thousand Patterns. LC 70-93972. (Illus.). 196p. 1970. lib. bdg. 12.75 (ISBN 0-9605664-4-9). A. G. Peterson.
Phillips, Phoebe. The Encyclopedia of Glass. (Herbert Michelman Bk.). (Illus.). 332p. 1981. 27.50 (ISBN 0-517-53792-3). Crown.
Revi, Albert C. American Art Nouveau Glass. LC 68-18778. (Illus.). 476p. 1981. Repr. 40.00 (ISBN 0-916838-40-4). Schiffer.
Revin, A. C. Nineteenth Century Glass. rev. ed. (Illus.). 302p. 1981. Repr. of 1959 ed. price not set. Schiffer.
Robertson, R. A. Chats on Old Glass. rev. ed. (Illus.). 5.50 (ISBN 0-8446-0879-3). Peter Smith.
Smith, Patricia. French Dolls, Vol. II. (Illus.). 1981. 9.95 (ISBN 0-89145-169-2). Collector Bks.
Stout, S. Price Guide to Depression Glass, No. 1. 1976. 1.50 (ISBN 0-87069-102-3). Wallace-Homestead.
--Price Guide to Depression Glass, No. 2. 1976. 1.50 (ISBN 0-87069-103-1). Wallace-Homestead.
Stout, Sandra M. Depression Glass Book Three in Colors. (Illus.). 6.95 (ISBN 0-87069-181-3); price guide 1.50 (ISBN 0-87069-182-1). Wallace-Homestead.
Suomen Lasi-Finnish Glass. 68p. 1980. pap. 5.95x (ISBN 0-904461-56-4, Pub. by Ceolfrith Pr England). Intl Schol Bk Serv.
Weatherman, H. M. Colored Glassware of the Depression Era 1970, Bk. 1. (Illus.). 240p. 1981. 12.00 (ISBN 0-913074-00-4). Weatherman.
Weatherman, Hazel M. Decorated Tumbler "PriceGuy". 128p. 1979. pap. 3.75 (ISBN 0-913074-13-6). Weatherman.
Webber, Norman W. Collecting Glass. LC 72-97035. (Illus.). 196p. 1973. 8.95 (ISBN 0-668-02952-8). Arco.
Weiss, Jeffrey. Cornerstone's Collector's Guide to Glass. 128p. 1981. 9.95 (ISBN 0-346-12534-0). Cornerstone.

GLASSWARE-DICTIONARIES

Krause, Gail. The Encyclopedia of Duncan Glass. 1976. 17.50 (ISBN 0-682-48527-6). Exposition.
Pearson, J. Michael. Encyclopedia of American Cut & Engraved Glass: Geometric Motifs, Vol. 3. LC 74-18615. (Illus.). 260p. 1978. 30.00 (ISBN 0-916528-05-7). J M Pearson.

GLASSWARE-PRICES

Cambridge Glass Identification & Value Guide. (Illus.). 1976. 14.95 (ISBN 0-89145-020-3). Collector Bks.
Evers, Jo. The Standard Cut Glass Value Guide. (Illus.). 1979. pap. 8.95 (ISBN 0-89145-002-5). Collector Bks.
House of Collectibles, Inc. Official Price Guide to Collectible Glassware. (Collector Ser.). (Illus.). 400p. 1980. pap. 9.95 (ISBN 0-87637-125-X, 125-0X). Hse of Collectibles.
Klamkin, Marian. The Carnival Glass Collector's Price Guide. LC 77-92365. (Illus., Orig.). 1978. pap. 5.95 (ISBN 0-8015-1094-5, Hawthorn). Dutton.
--The Depression Glass Collector's Price Guide. (Illus.). 96p. 1974. pap. 4.50 (ISBN 0-8015-2018-5, Hawthorn). Dutton.
Kovel, Ralph & Kovel, Terry. The Kovels' Illustrated Price Guide to Depression Glass & American Dinnerware. (Illus.). 256p. 1980. pap. 9.95 (ISBN 0-517-54023-1). Crown.
Lee, Ruth W. Current Values of Antique Glass. rev. ed. 8.95 (ISBN 0-910872-08-2). Lee Pubns.

GLASSWARE-CZECHOSLOVAKIA

Corning Musuem of Glass, ed. Czechoslovakian Glass, Thirteen Fifty - Nineteen Eighty. (Illus.). 176p. (Orig.). 1981. pap. 25.00 (ISBN 0-486-24237-4). Dover.

GLASSWARE-EUROPE

Blount, Henry & Blount, Berniece. French Cameo Glass. 25.00 (ISBN 0-87069-030-2). Wallace-Homestead.
Dermant, Janine B. The Art of French Glass, 1860-1914. Dermant, Janine Blocm, tr. LC 80-50853. Orig. Title: L' Art du Verre en France. (Illus.). 204p. (Fr.). 1980. 40.00 (ISBN 0-86565-000-4). Vendome.
Grover, Ray & Grover, Lee. Carved & Decorated European Art Glass. LC 71-94025. (Illus.). 1970. 55.00 (ISBN 0-8048-0707-8). C E Tuttle.

GLASSWARE-GREAT BRITAIN

Fleming, Arnold. Scottish & Jacobite Glass. (Illus.). 1977. Repr. of 1938 ed. 35.00x (ISBN 0-7158-1207-6). Charles River Bks.
Grover, Ray & Grover, Lee. English Cameo Glass. (Illus.). 1980. 50.00 (ISBN 0-517-53815-6). Crown.
Schnitzer, Barbara & Nicholls, R. Glass at the Fitzwilliam Museum. LC 77-27570. (Illus.). 1978. 42.50 (ISBN 0-521-22008-4); pap. 11.95 (ISBN 0-521-29335-9). Cambridge U Pr.
Thorpe, W. A. History of English & Irish Glass to 1969. 100.00x (ISBN 0-87556-334-1). Saifer.
Wills, Geoffrey. Victorian Glass. (Illus.). 1977. 24.00 (ISBN 0-7135-1949-5). Transatlantic.

GLASSWARE-IRELAND

Thorpe, W. A. History of English & Irish Glass to 1969. 100.00x (ISBN 0-87556-334-1). Saifer.
Warren, Phelps. Irish Glass: Waterford, Cork, Belfast in the Age of Exuberance. 2nd rev. ed. (Faber Monographs on Glass). (Illus.). 280p. 1981. 50.00 (ISBN 0-571-18028-0, Pub. Faber & Faber). Merrimack Bk Serv.

GLASSWARE-JAPAN

Blair, Dorothy. A History of Glass in Japan. LC 72-94022. (Illus.). 480p. 1973. 75.00 (ISBN 0-87011-196-5). Kodansha.
--A History of Glass in Japan. (Illus.). 479p. 1973. 60.00x (ISBN 0-87011-196-5, Corning Museum of Glass). U Pr of Va.
Fukai, Shinji. Persian Glass. LC 77-23736. (Illus.). 1977. 50.00 (ISBN 0-8348-1515-X). Weatherhill.

GLASSWARE-SPAIN

Frothingham, Alice W. Spanish Glass. (Illus.). 1964. 12.50 (ISBN 0-87535-127-1). Hispanic Soc.

GLASSWARE-UNITED STATES

Darling, Sharon S. Chicago Ceramics & Glass. LC 79-91566. (Illus.). 240p. 1980. 25.00 (ISBN 0-913820-10-5). Chicago Hist.
Edwards, Bill. Millersburg: The Queen of Carnival Glass. (Illus.). 1979. pap. 8.95 (ISBN 0-89145-073-4). Collector Bks.
--Northwood, King of Carnival Glass. (Illus.). 1978. pap. 8.95 (ISBN 0-89145-070-X). Collector Bks.
--Rarities in Carnival Glass. (Illus.). 1978. pap. 8.95 (ISBN 0-89145-075-0). Collector Bks.
Farrar, Estelle S. & Spillman, Jane S. The Complete Cut & Engraved Glass of Corning. (Illus.). 1978. 14.95 (ISBN 0-517-53432-0). Crown.
Florence, Gene. Pocket Guide to Depression Glass. 2nd ed. (Illus.). 1980. pap. 8.95 (ISBN 0-89145-148-X). Collector Bks.
Freeman, Larry. Grand Old American Bottles. LC 63-23066. 1964. 25.00 (ISBN 0-87282-045-9). Century Hse.
Freeman, Larry G. Iridescent Glass. (Illus.). 1956. 6.50 (ISBN 0-87282-058-0). Century Hse.
Hartley, Julia. Old American Glass: The Mills Collection at TCU. LC 75-10110. 1975. 3.00 (ISBN 0-912646-02-0). Tex Christian.
Heiges, George L. Henry William Stiegel & His Associates. LC 48-9287. 1976. pap. 5.00 (ISBN 0-915010-18-6). Sutter House.
Hunter, Frederick W. Stiegel Glass. (Illus.). 11.00 (ISBN 0-8446-2286-9). Peter Smith.
--Stiegel Glass. (Illus.). 1966. pap. 5.00 (ISBN 0-486-20128-7). Dover.
Kamm, M. W. & Wood. Encyclopedia of Pattern Glass, 2 Vols. LC 61-5439. 1961. Vol. 1. 40.00 set (ISBN 0-87282-080-7); Vol. 2. (ISBN 0-87282-081-5). Century Hse.
Kamm, Minnie W. Two Hundred Pattern Glass Pitchers. LC 68-5611. (Illus.). 1968. pap. 5.50x (ISBN 0-87282-082-3, 50531). Century Hse.
Koch, Robert. Louis C. Tiffany's Art Glass. (Illus.). 1977. 12.95 (ISBN 0-517-53068-6). Crown.
Lee, Ruth W. Antique Fakes & Reproductions. rev. ed. (Illus.). 15.00 (ISBN 0-910872-07-4). Lee Pubns.
--Current Values of Antique Glass. rev. ed 8.95 (ISBN 0-910872-08-2). Lee Pubns.
--Early American Pressed Glass. rev. ed. (Illus.). 25.00 (ISBN 0-910872-00-7). Lee Pubns.
--Handbook of Early American Pressed Glass Patterns. (Illus.). 6.95 (ISBN 0-910872-01-5). Lee Pubns.
--Sandwich Glass. rev. ed. (Illus.). 25.00 (ISBN 0-910872-04-X). Lee Pubns.
--Sandwich Glass Handbook. (Illus.). 6.95 (ISBN 0-910872-05-8). Lee Pubns.
--Victorian Glass. (Illus.). 25.00 (ISBN 0-910872-02-3). Lee Pubns.
--Victorian Glass Handbook. (Illus.). 6.95 (ISBN 0-910872-03-1). Lee Pubns.
Lee, Ruth W., ed. Boston & Sandwich Glass Co. Factory Catalogue. 6.95 (ISBN 0-910872-06-6). Lee Pubns.
Lehner, Lois. Ohio Pottery & Glass Marks & Manufacturers. 1977. 9.95 (ISBN 0-87069-168-6). Wallace-Homestead.
Lindsey, Bessie M. American Historical Glass. LC 67-11934. (Illus.). 570p. 1966. Repr. of 1948 ed. 27.50 (ISBN 0-8048-0009-X). C E Tuttle.
McKearin, Helen & McKearin, George S. American Glass. (Illus.). 1941. 22.50 (ISBN 0-517-00111-X). Crown.
Millard, S. T. Goblets, 2 vols. 1975. 5.95 ea. Vol. 1 (ISBN 0-87069-128-7). Vol. 2 (ISBN 0-87069-129-5). Wallace-Homestead.
Norton(R.W.) Art Gallery. American Silver & Pressed Glass. LC 67-24712. (Illus.). 1967. pap. 3.50x (ISBN 0-9600182-0-4). Norton Art.
Plaut, James. Steuben Glass: A Monograph. 3rd rev. ed. LC 72-78376. (Illus.). 111p. 1972. pap. 4.00 (ISBN 0-486-22892-4). Dover.
Plaut, James S. Steuben Glass. 3rd rev. ed. (Illus.). 10.00 (ISBN 0-8446-5838-3). Peter Smith.
Revi, Albert C. American Cut & Engraved Glass. LC 65-22016. (Collector's Books Ser.). 1965. 24.50 (ISBN 0-8407-4304-1). Nelson.
Spillman, Jane S. & Farrar, Estelle S. Cut & Engraved Glass of Corning, 1868-1940. LC 77-73626. 1977. pap. 5.00 (ISBN 0-87290-064-9). Corning.
Stout, Sandra. Depression Glass in Color. No. 1. plastic bdg. 6.95 (ISBN 0-87069-022-1); No. 2. plastic bdg. 6.95 (ISBN 0-87069-023-X). Wallace-Homestead.
Tinkham, Sandra S., ed. Catalog of Ceramics & Glass. (Index of American Design Ser.: Pt. 8). (Orig.). 1979. pap. 30.00x (ISBN 0-914146-77-7); incl. color microfiche 620.00x (ISBN 0-914146-76-9). Somerset Hse.

GLASTONBURY ABBEY

Coard, Peter. Portraits of Glastonbury & Wells. (Illus.). 9.95 (ISBN 0-906230-40-3, Pub. by Kingsmead Pr England). State Mutual Bk.
Mathias, Michael & Hector, Derek. Glastonbury: Mecca of the Westcountry. LC 78-51083. (Illus.). 1979. 10.50 (ISBN 0-7153-7798-1). David & Charles.

GLAUCOMA

see also Tonometry

Bellows, John G., ed. Glaucoma: Contemporary International Concepts. LC 79-88728. (Illus.). 448p. 1980. 54.50x (ISBN 0-89352-058-6). Masson Pub.
Chandler, Paul A. & Grant, W. Morton, eds. Glaucoma. 2nd ed. LC 79-11465. (Illus.). 381p. 1979. text ed. 26.00 (ISBN 0-8121-0660-1). Lea & Febiger.
Collins, R. & Van Der Werff, T. J. Mathematical Models of the Dynamics of the Human Eye. (Lecture Notes in Biomathematics: Vol. 34). 99p. 1980. pap. 9.80 (ISBN 0-387-09751-1). Springer-Verlag.
Crick, R. Pitts & Caldwell, A. D., eds. Glaucoma. LC 79-41342. (Royal Society of Medicine International Congress & Symposium Ser.: No. 21). 1980. 26.00 (ISBN 0-8089-1250-X). Grune.
Dausch, D. & Honegger, H. Timolol Ophthalmic Solution in the Treatment of Glaucoma. LC 78-72505. 1978. 3.00 (ISBN 0-911910-95-6). Merck-Sharp-Dohme.
Elliot, Robert H. A Treatise on Glaucoma. (Classic in Ophthalmology). (Illus.). 1979. Repr. of 1922 ed. lib. bdg. 34.00 (ISBN 0-88275-842-X). Krieger.
Ferrer, Olga M., ed. Symposium on Glaucoma. (Illus.). 296p. 1976. 28.50 (ISBN 0-398-03294-7). C C Thomas.
Gorin. Clinical Glaucoma. (Ophthalmology Ser.: Vol. 1). 1977. 45.00 (ISBN 0-8247-6456-0). Dekker.
Greve, E. L., ed. Symposium on Medical Therapy in Gloucoma. (Documenta Ophthalmologica Proceedings Ser.: Vol. 12). 1976. lib. bdg. 26.00 (ISBN 90-6193-152-5, Pub. by Junk Pubs Netherlands). Kluwer Boston.
Greve, Erik L., ed. Glaucoma Symposium Amsterdam: Diagnosis & Therapy. (Documenta Opthalmologica Proceedings Ser.: No. 22). 419p. 1980. lib. bdg. 92.00 (ISBN 90-6193-164-9, Pub. by Junk Pubs Netherlands). Kluwer Boston.
Halasa, Adnan H. The Basic Aspects of the Glaucomas. (Illus.). 244p. 1972. 19.75 (ISBN 0-398-02529-0). C C Thomas.
Halberg, G. Peter, ed. Glaucoma Update. LC 79-91968. (Illus.). 156p. (Orig.). 1979. pap. text ed. 14.00x (ISBN 0-935726-00-4). Inter-Optics Pubns.
International Glaucoma Symposium, Nara, Japan, May 7-11, 1978. Glaucoma Update: Proceedings. Krieglstein, G. K. & Leydecker, W., eds. LC 79-10747. (Illus.). 1979. pap. 31.50 (ISBN 0-387-09350-8). Springer-Verlag.
Josephson, Emanuel. Glaucoma & Its Medical Treatment with Cortin: Myopia Its Cause & Prevention. (Natural Health Ser.). 92p. (Orig.). 1937. pap. text ed. 6.95 (ISBN 0-686-29295-2, Pub. by Chedney). Alpine Ent.
Josephson, Emanuel M. Glaucoma & Its Medical Treatment with Cortin. 1979. write for info. (ISBN 0-685-96462-0). Revisionist Pr.
--Glaucoma & Its Medical Treatment with Cortin. 92p. 1976. 25.00 (ISBN 0-685-66408-2); pap. 15.00 (ISBN 0-685-66409-0). Chedney.
Kolker, Allan E. & Hetherington, John. Becker-Shaffer's Diagnosis & Therapy of the Glaucomas. 4th ed. LC 76-4591. (Illus.). 1976. 45.00 (ISBN 0-8016-2720-6). Mosby.
Krasnov, Mikhail M. Microsurgery of the Glaucomas. LC 78-26221. (Illus.). 1979. text ed. 36.00 (ISBN 0-8016-2743-5). Mosby.
Leychecker, Wolfgang & Crick, Ronald P. All About Glaucoma: Questions & Answers for People with Glaucoma. 80p. 1981. 14.95 (ISBN 0-571-11764-3, Pub. by Faber & Faber); pap. 5.95 (ISBN 0-571-11765-1, Pub. by Faber & Faber). Merrimack Bk Serv.
Lichter, Paul R. & Anderson, Douglas R., eds. Discussions on Glaucoma. 176p. 1977. 29.25 (ISBN 0-8089-1033-7). Grune.
Merte, H. J., ed. Genesis of Glaucoma. (Documenta Opthalmologica Proceedings Ser.: No. 16). 1978. lib. bdg. 53.00 (ISBN 9-06193-156-8, Pub. by Junk Pubs Netherlands). Kluwer Boston.
Nesterov, A., et al. Intraocular Pressure. 390p. 1978. 9.60 (ISBN 0-8285-0761-9, Pub. by Mir Pubs Russia). Imported Pubns.
New Orleans Academy of Ophthalmology. Symposium on Glaucoma. LC 81-2326. (Illus.). 486p. 1981. text ed. 57.95 (ISBN 0-8016-3667-1). Mosby.
Portney, Gerald L. Glaucoma Guidebook. LC 77-1568. (Illus.). 158p. 1977. text ed. 9.75 (ISBN 0-8121-0587-7). Lea & Febiger.
Rehak, S. & Paterson, G., eds. Recent Advances in Glaucoma: International Glaucoma Symposium, Prague, 1976. (Illus.). 1977. 45.70 (ISBN 0-387-07944-0). Springer-Verlag.
Spaeth, George L. The Pathogenesis of Nerve Damage in Glaucoma: The Contribution of Flurescein Angiography to the Diagnosis & Management of Glaucoma. 192p. 1977. 36.75 (ISBN 0-8089-1045-0). Grune.
Veirs, Everett R. So You Have Glaucoma. 2nd ed. LC 76-120304. (Illus.). 96p. 1970. 19.50 (ISBN 0-8089-0659-3). Grune.

GLAZES

Behrens, Richard. Ceramic Glazemaking. 3.95 (ISBN 0-934706-07-7). Prof Pubns Ohio.
--Glaze Projects. 3.95 (ISBN 0-934706-06-9). Prof Pubns Ohio.
Bellaire, Marc. Underglaze Decoration. 3.95 (ISBN 0-934706-01-8). Prof Pubns Ohio.
Cooper, Emanuel. The Potter's Book of Glaze Recipes. 1980. 15.95 (ISBN 0-684-16670-4, ScribT). Scribner.
Cooper, Emmanuel & Royle, Derek. Glazes for the Potter. (Illus.). 1979. 13.95 (ISBN 0-684-16021-8, ScribT). Scribner.
Grebanier, Joseph. Chinese Stoneware Glazes. (Illus.). 144p. 1975. 15.95 (ISBN 0-8230-0625-5). Watson-Guptill.
Green, David. A Handbook of Pottery Glazes. 1979. 17.50 (ISBN 0-8230-2181-5). Watson-Guptill.
--Pottery Glazes. new rev. ed. (Illus.). 144p. (YA) 1973. 14.50 (ISBN 0-8230-4217-0). Watson-Guptill.
Greenfield, Verni. Glazing Without a Gram Scale. LC 76-42076. 1976. pap. 2.99 (ISBN 0-935066-01-2). Keramos Bks.
Mason, Ralph. Native Clays & Glazes for Ceramists in the Western States. (Illus.). Date not set. pap. 7.95 (ISBN 0-917304-02-0, Pub by Timber Pr). Intl Schol Bk Serv.
Parmelee, C. W. Ceramic Glazes. 3rd ed. Harman, Cameron G., ed. LC 70-183371. 1973. 24.95 (ISBN 0-8436-0609-6). CBI Pub.
Sanders, Herbert H. Glazes for Special Effects. LC 74-6126. (Illus.). 152p. 1974. 18.95 (ISBN 0-8230-2134-3). Watson-Guptill.
Sealant Technology in Glazing Systems. 1977. pap. 9.50 (ISBN 0-686-51989-2, 04-638000-10). ASTM.
Starkey, Peter. Saltglaze. (Ceramic Skillbooks Ser.). (Illus.). 1979. 8.95 (ISBN 0-8230-4629-X). Watson-Guptill.
Troy, Jack. Salt-Glazed Ceramics. (Illus.). 1977. 19.50 (ISBN 0-8230-4630-3). Watson-Guptill.
Wood, Nigel. Oriental Glazes. (Illus.). 1978. 9.95 (ISBN 0-8230-3385-6). Watson-Guptill.

GLEBES
see Church Lands
GLEES, CATCHES, ROUNDS, ETC.
Barrett, William A. English Glee & Madrigal Writers. LC 77-75190. 1977. Repr. of 1877 ed. lib. bdg. 10.00 (ISBN 0-89341-089-6). Longwood Pr.
--English Glees & Part Songs. LC 77-75200. 1977. Repr. of 1886 ed. lib. bdg. 40.00 (ISBN 0-89341-104-3). Longwood Pr.
Cartledge, J. A., compiled by. List of Glees, Madrigals, Part-Songs, Etc. in the Henry Watson Music Library. LC 74-80247. (Bibliography & Reference Ser.: No. 362). 1970. Repr. of 1913 ed. lib. bdg. 24.50 (ISBN 0-8337-0483-4). B Franklin.
Hilton, John. Catch That Catch Can. LC 75-87492. (Music Ser). 1970. Repr. of 1652 ed. lib. bdg. 17.50 (ISBN 0-306-71498-1). Da Capo.
Langstaff, John, ed. Sweetly Sings the Donkey: Animal Rounds for Children to Sing or Play on Recorders. LC 76-9530. (Illus.). 32p. (gr. 3 up). 1976. 6.95 (ISBN 0-689-50063-7, McElderry Bk). Atheneum.
Mason, Lowell & Webb, George J. The Boston Glee Book. LC 76-52481. (Music Reprint Ser., 1977). 1977. Repr. of 1844 ed. lib. bdg. 27.50 (ISBN 0-306-70860-4). Da Capo.
National Council Authors. Collection of Catches, Canons & Glees, 4 vols. LC 72-128762. 1973. Set. 190.00 (ISBN 0-8420-0026-7). Scholarly Res Inc.
Taylor, Mary & Dyk, Carol. Book of Rounds. 1977. pap. 14.95 (ISBN 0-87690-182-8). Dutton.
GLEIG, GEORGE ROBERT, 1796-1888
Gleig, George R. The Campaigns of the British Army at Washington & New Orleans. 208p. 1972. Repr. of 1827 ed. 11.50x (ISBN 0-87471-023-5). Rowman.
GLEN CANYON, UTAH
Alps, Glen. Glen Alps Retrospective: The Collagraph Idea, Nineteen Fifty Six to Nineteen Eighty. Bellevue Art Museum, ed. LC 79-54958. (Illus.). pap. 4.95 (ISBN 0-295-95703-4). U of Wash Pr.
Cutler, Hugh C. Corn, Cucurbits & Cotton from Glen Canyon. (Glen Canyon Ser: No. 30). Repr. of 1966 ed. 26.00 (ISBN 0-404-60680-6). AMS Pr.
GLENCOE MASSACRE, 1692
Prebble, John. The Massacre at Glencoe. (Jackdaw Ser: No. 110). (Illus.). 1972. 6.95 (ISBN 0-670-46130-X, Grossman). Viking Pr.
GLENN, JOHN HERSCHEL, 1921-
Westman, Paul. John Glenn: Around the World in Ninety Minutes. LC 79-19515. (Taking Part Ser.). (Illus.). (gr. 3 up). 1980. PLB 6.95 (ISBN 0-87518-186-4). Dillon.
GLENN, JOHN HERSCHEL, 1921-- JUVENILE LITERATURE
Akens, David S. John Glenn: First American in Orbit. LC 78-75842. (Heroes of Space Ser). (Illus.). (gr. 7 up). 1969. 4.95 (ISBN 0-87397-200-7). Strode.
John Glenn. (gr. 1). 1974. pap. text ed. 2.80 (ISBN 0-205-03870-0, 8038708); tchrs'. guide 12.00 (ISBN 0-205-03866-2, 803866X). Allyn.
GLIAL CELLS
see Neuroglia
GLIDERS (AERONAUTICS)
see also Gliding and Soaring
Beeson, Colin R. The Glider Pilot War at Home & Overseas. (Orig.). 1978. pap. 25.00x (ISBN 0-89126-063-3). MA-AH Pub.
Coates, Andrew. Jane's World Sailplanes & Motorgliders. (Illus.). 1978. 12.95 (ISBN 0-87165-021-5, Zd Books). Ziff-Davis Pub.
Kaufmann, John. Flying Hand-Launched Gliders. LC 73-17236. (Illus.). 96p. (gr. 7 up). 1974. PLB 6.96 (ISBN 0-688-30108-8). Morrow.
Morrow, Linda & Morrow, Ray. Go Fly a Sailplane. LC 80-65995. (Illus.). 192p. 1981. 10.95 (ISBN 0-689-11080-4). Atheneum.
Perna, Albert F. Glider Gladiators of World War Two. LC 70-91840. (Illus.). 398p. 1970. 15.00 (ISBN 0-9600302-0-4). Podiatric Educ.
Piggott, Derek. Gliding: A Handbook on Soaring Flight. 4th ed. (Illus.). 270p. 1976. 20.00x (ISBN 0-06-495570-2). B&N.
Schroder, Jack E. How to Build & Fly Radio Control Gliders. Angle, Burr, ed. (Illus., Orig.). 1980. pap. 3.50 (ISBN 0-89024-549-5). Kalmbach.
Wills, Maralys. Manbirds: Hang Gliders & Hang Gliding. 320p. 1981. 17.95 (ISBN 0-13-551101-1). P-H.
GLIDING AND SOARING
see also Gliders (Aeronautics); Hang Gliding
Bowers, Pete. Modern Soaring Guide. 2nd ed. (Illus.). 1979. 9.95 (ISBN 0-8306-9781-0); pap. 6.95 (ISBN 0-8306-2257-8, 2257). TAB Bks.
Byars, Ed & Holbrook, Bill. Soaring Cross Country. new ed. LC 74-78637. (Illus.). 180p. 1974. 9.95 (ISBN 0-914600-00-1). Soaring Symposia.
Carrier, Rick. Fly: The Complete Book of Sky Sailing. new ed. LC 74-4221. (Illus.). 128p. 1975. pap. 6.95 (ISBN 0-07-010096-9, SP). McGraw.
Flying Magazine, ed. Sport Flying. LC 75-38672. (Encore Edition). (Illus.). 1976. 5.95 (ISBN 0-684-15942-2, ScribT). Scribner.
Handbook of Meteorological Forecasting for Soaring Flight. (Technical Note Ser.: No. 158). 1978. pap. 18.00 (ISBN 92-63-10495-6, W399, WMO). Unipub.
Joss, John, ed. Advanced Soaring. LC 74-18760. (Illus.). 1974. pap. 5.95 (ISBN 0-930514-03-3, Pub. by Soaring). Aviation.
--Soarsierra. (Illus.). 150p. 1976. 8.95 (ISBN 0-930514-05-X, Pub. by Soaring); pap. 5.95 (ISBN 0-930514-07-6). Aviation.
Knauff, Thomas. Glider Basics from First Flight to Solo. Northcut, Allan & Northcut, Debbie, eds. LC 80-81375. (Illus.). 155p. 1980. text ed. 12.95 (ISBN 0-9605676-0-7). Knauff.
Lincoln, Joseph C. Soaring on the Wind: A Photographic Essay on the Sport of Soaring. LC 72-79074. (Illus.). 112p. 1973. 15.00 (ISBN 0-87358-100-8). Northland.
Lincoln, Joseph C., ed. On Quiet Wings: A Soaring Anthology. LC 70-174993. (Illus.). 1972. 30.00 (ISBN 0-87358-082-6). Northland.
McKinnie, Charles M. Correspondence Course & Study Guide for Glider Pilots. spiral bdg. 12.60x (ISBN 0-685-84218-5, Pub. by Black Forest). Aviation.
Moffat, George B. Winning on the Wind: Championship Soaring Techniques, Sailplanes & History. LC 74-82783. (Illus.). 244p. 1974. pap. 5.95 (ISBN 0-930514-00-9, Pub. by Soaring). Aviation.
Piggott, Derek. Beginning Gliding: The Fundamentals of Soaring Flight. (Illus.). 1977. 22.50x (ISBN 0-06-495569-9). B&N.
--Going Solo: A Simple Guide to Soaring. (Illus.). 112p. 1978. pap. 8.95x (ISBN 0-06-495571-0). B&N.
--Understanding Gliding: The Principles of Soaring Flight. (Illus.). 1977. 22.50x (ISBN 0-06-495568-0). B&N.
Poynter, Dan. Manned Kiting: The Basic Handbook of Tow Launched Hang Gliding. 2nd ed. LC 74-20186. (Illus.). 1975. pap. 3.95 (ISBN 0-915516-04-7). Para Pub.
Richards, Norman. The Complete Beginner's Guide to Soaring & Hang Gliding. LC 74-18827. 144p. (gr. 6 up). 1976. 5.95 (ISBN 0-385-08318-1). Doubleday.
Schweizer Aircraft Corporation. Start Soaring. 1978. pap. 3.25x (ISBN 0-911721-75-4). Aviation.
Scull, Bill. Soaring Across Country. (Illus.). 192p. 1981. 17.95 (ISBN 0-7207-1153-3, Pub. by Michael Joseph). Merrimack Bk Serv.
Smith, Norman F. Gliding, Soaring, & Skysailing. LC 79-27680. (Illus.). 160p. (gr. 9 up). 1980. PLB 7.79 (ISBN 0-671-32981-2). Messner.
Stanton, David. Flying High: The Beginner's Guide to Daring Airsports. (Illus., Orig.). 1980. pap. 3.00 (ISBN 0-939468-01-8). Sportsbks.
Wallington, C. E. Meteorology for Glider Pilots. 3rd ed. (Illus.). 331p. 1980. 24.00 (ISBN 0-7195-3303-1). Transatlantic.
Wolters, Richard. The World of Silent Flight. LC 78-15822. (Illus.). 1979. 15.95 (ISBN 0-07-071561-0, GB). McGraw.
Wolters, Richard A. Art & Technique of Soaring. 1971. 14.95 (ISBN 0-07-071560-2, GB). McGraw.
GLOBAL ANALYSIS (MATHEMATICS)
see also Differential Topology; Functions of Complex Variables; Geometry, Algebraic
Clark, J., et al. Global Simulation Models: A Comparative Study. LC 74-32231. 135p. 1975. 26.75 (ISBN 0-471-15899-2, Pub. by Wiley-Interscience). Wiley.
Delves, L. M. & Freeman, T. L. Analysis of Global Expansion Methods: Weakly Asymtotically Diagonal Systems. (Computational Mathematics & Application Ser.). 1981. 49.00 (ISBN 0-12-208880-8). Acad Pr.
Ferus, D., et al, eds. Global Differential Geometry & Global Analysis: Proceedings. (Lecture Notes in Mathematics: Vol. 838). 299p. 1981. pap. 19.50 (ISBN 0-387-10285-X). Springer-Verlag.
Hamilton, R. S. Harmonic Maps of Manifolds with Boundary. (Lecture Notes in Mathematics Ser.: Vol. 471). 168p. 1975. pap. 10.90 (ISBN 0-387-07185-7). Springer-Verlag.
Kahn, Donald W. Introduction to Global Analysis: Pure & Applied Mathematics Ser. LC 79-8858. 1980. 34.50 (ISBN 0-12-394050-8). Acad Pr.
Morse, Marston. Global Variational Analysis: Weierstrass Integrals on a Riemannian Manifold. LC 76-836. (Mathematical Notes: No. 16). 264p. 1976. pap. 15.00x (ISBN 0-691-08181-6). Princeton U Pr.
Spencer, D. C. & Iyanaga, S., eds. Global Analysis: Papers in Honor of K. Kodaira. (Mathematical Ser: Vol. 29). (Published jointly with the University of Tokyo). 1970. 28.00x (ISBN 0-691-08077-1). Princeton U Pr.
GLOBAL SATELLITE COMMUNICATIONS SYSTEMS
see Artificial Satellites in Telecommunication
GLOBE THEATER
see Southwark, England-Globe Theatre
GLOBES
see also World Maps
Hodd, Thomas. Use of Both the Globes. LC 70-38111. (English Experience Ser.: No. 389). 54p. 1971. Repr. of 1592 ed. 16.00 (ISBN 90-221-0389-7). Walter J Johnson.
Hood, Thomas. Use of the Celestial Globe in Plans. LC 72-6007. (English Experience Ser.: No. 533). 96p. 1973. Repr. of 1590 ed. 21.00 (ISBN 90-221-0533-4). Walter J Johnson.
Moxon, Joseph. Tutor to Astronomy & Geography. 3rd rev., enl. ed. LC 68-56778. (Research & Source Works Ser.: No. 264). (Illus.). 1968. Repr. of 1674 ed. 24.50 (ISBN 0-8337-2478-9). B Franklin.
Stevenson, Edward L. Terrestrial & Celestial Globes: Their History & Construction, 2 vols. LC 21-18954. Repr. of 1921 ed. Set. 69.50 (ISBN 0-384-58127-7). Johnson Repr.
Using Maps & Globes. 1975. write for info. tchrs' guide (ISBN 0-87453-117-9). Denoyer.
Wright, Edward. The Description & Use of the Sphaere. LC 71-25883. (English Experience Ser.: No. 136). 104p. 1969. Repr. of 1613 ed. 14.00 (ISBN 90-221-0136-3). Walter J Johnson.
GLOBULAR PROTEINS
see Proteins
GLOBULIN
see also Gamma Globulin
Norgaard-Pederson. Human Alpha Feto-Protein. 1976. 6.95 (ISBN 0-8391-0987-3). Univ Park.
Poulik, M. D., ed. Beta Two-Microglobulin: Its Significance in Clinical Medicine. (Journal: Vox Sanguinis: Vol. 38, No. 6). (Illus.). 1980. soft cover 19.75 (ISBN 3-8055-1560-X). S Karger.
GLOMERULONEPHRITIS
Beregi, E. & Varga, I. Renal Biopsy in Glomerular Diseases. 1978. 34.50 (ISBN 0-9960012-1-2, Pub. by Kiado Hungary). Heyden.
Grundmann, E., ed. Glomerulonephritis. LC 59-49162. (Current Topics in Pathology: Vol. 61). 320p. 1976. 52.40 (ISBN 0-387-07442-2). Springer-Verlag.
Kincaid-Smith, P., et al. Progress in Glomerulonephritis. (Perspectives in Nephrology & Hypertension Ser.). 458p. 1979. 62.00 (ISBN 0-471-04424-5, Pub. by Wiley Med). Wiley.
Okabayashi, Atsushi & Kondo, Yoichiro. Masugi Nephritis & Its Immunopathologic Implications. LC 79-91335. (Illus.). 1980. 41.00 (ISBN 0-89640-039-5). Igaku-Shoin.
Samter, Max, ed. Immunological Diseases, 2 vols. 3rd ed. 1384p. 1978. Set. 85.00 (ISBN 0-686-66325-X). Vol. 1 (ISBN 0-316-76984-3). Vol. 2 (ISBN 0-316-76985-1). Little.
Symposium on Nephrology, 3rd, Hannover, June 1975. Glomerulonephritis: Proceedings. Sterzel, R. B., ed. (Contributions to Nephrology: Vol.2). (Illus.). 200p. 1976. 30.75 (ISBN 0-8055-2318-9). S Karger.
GLORIFICATION (THEOLOGY)
see Glory of God
GLORY, DIVINE
see Glory of God
GLORY OF GOD
see also Theophanies
DeHaan, M. R. Broken Things. 1977. pap. 1.95 (ISBN 0-310-23272-4). Zondervan.
The Foundations of Jewish Life: Three Studies. LC 73-2197. (The Jewish People; History, Religion, Literature Ser.). 29.00 (ISBN 0-405-05263-4). Arno.
Kuhlman, Kathryn. Vislumbres De Gloria. (Span.). Date not set. 2.00 (ISBN 0-686-76354-8). Life Pubs Intl.
Pentecost, J. Dwight. Glory of God. LC 78-57677. 1978. pap. 4.95 (ISBN 0-930014-24-3). Multnomah.
Smith, W. R. Glorifying God. rev. ed. (Way of Life Ser.: No. 134). 1979. 2.95 (ISBN 0-89112-134-X). Bibl Res Pr.
GLOSSOLALIA
see also Pentecostal Churches
Banks, William. Questions You Have Always Wanted to Ask About Tongues, but... (Illus.). 1979. pap. 2.25 (ISBN 0-89957-526-9). AMG Pubs.
Basham, Don. Handbook on Tongues, Interpretation & Prophecy. (Handbk. Ser.: No. 2). 1971. pap. 2.95 (ISBN 0-88368-004-1). Whitaker Hse.
Baxter, Ronald E. The Charismatic Gift of Tongues. 190p. 1981. pap. 5.95 (ISBN 0-8254-2225-6). Kregel.
Bouterse, Wesley. Scriptural Light on Speaking in Tongues. 1980. pap. 0.85 (ISBN 0-86544-010-7). Salvation Army.
Burgess, W. J. Glossolalia. 1979. pap. 1.00 (ISBN 0-89114-053-0). Baptist Pub Hse.
Christenson, Larry. Speaking in Tongues. LC 97-5595. 1968. pap. 2.25 (ISBN 0-87123-518-8, 200518). Bethany Hse.
Cutten, George B. Speaking with Tongues: Historically & Psychologically Considered. 1927. 27.50x (ISBN 0-685-69805-X). Elliots Bks.
Dillow, Jody. Speaking in Tongues. 160p. 1975. pap. 2.95 (ISBN 0-310-23702-5). Zondervan.
Ensley, Eddie. Sounds of Wonder: A Popular History of Speaking in Tongues in the Catholic Tradition. LC 77-70456. 1977. pap. 2.95 (ISBN 0-8091-2002-X). Paulist Pr.
Goodman, Felicitas D. Speaking in Tongues: A Cross-Cultural Study of Glossolalia. LC 70-182871. 224p. 1972. 12.50x (ISBN 0-226-30324-1). U of Chicago Pr.
--Speaking in Tongues: A Cross-Cultural Study of Glossolalia. LC 70-182871. xxii, 176p. 1974. pap. 3.95 (ISBN 0-226-30326-8, P605, Phoen). U of Chicago Pr.
Gromacki, Robert G. Modern Tongues Movement. pap. 3.95 (ISBN 0-8010-3708-5). Baker Bk.
--Modern Tongues Movement. 1967. 3.95 (ISBN 0-87552-304-8). Presby & Reformed.
Gustafson, Robert R. Authors of Confusion. pap. 1.45 (ISBN 0-686-12743-9). Grace Pub Co.
Harris, Ralph W. Spoken by the Spirit. LC 73-87106. 1973. pap. 1.25 (ISBN 0-88243-725-9, 02-0725). Gospel Pub.
Horton, Stanley M. Tongues & Prophecy. (Charismatic Bk). 1972. pap. 0.69 (ISBN 0-88243-917-0, 02-0917). Gospel Pub.
Humphreys, Fisher & Tolbert, Malcolm. Speaking in Tongues. LC 73-86749. 94p. (Orig.). 1973. pap. 3.00 (ISBN 0-914520-05-9). Insight Pr.
Kelsey, Morton. Tongue Speaking: The History & Meaning of the Charismatic Experience. 256p. 1981. pap. 8.95 (ISBN 0-8245-0073-3). Crossroad NY.
Koch, Kurt E. Strife of Tongues. LC 74-160689. 1966. pap. 1.25 (ISBN 0-8254-3001-1). Kregel.
Lightner, Robert P. Speaking in Tongues & Divine Healing. LC 65-5805. 1978. pap. 1.95 (ISBN 0-87227-059-9). Reg Baptist.
Martin, Ira J. Glossolalia, the Gift of Tongues. 75p. 1970. pap. 1.95 (ISBN 0-87148-352-1). Pathway Pr.
Mauro, Philip. Speaking in Tongues. 1978. pap. 0.50 (ISBN 0-685-36793-2). Reiner.
Meyer, Matthew. Speaking in Tongues. pap. 1.95 (ISBN 0-87178-809-8). Brethren.
Montague, George T. The Spirit & His Gifts. LC 74-77425. 72p. (Orig.). 1974. pap. 1.45 (ISBN 0-8091-1829-7, Deus). Paulist Pr.
Picirilli, Robert. What the Bible Says About Tongues. 1981. pap. 0.60 (ISBN 0-89265-071-0). Randall Hse.
Samarin, William J. Tongues of Men & Angels. 1972. 7.95 (ISBN 0-02-606820-6). Macmillan.
Sherrill, John. They Speak with Other Tongues. 1966. pap. 1.95 (ISBN 0-8007-8041-8, Spire). Revell.
Smith, Charles R. Tongues in Biblical Perspective. pap. 3.95 (ISBN 0-88469-005-9). BMH Bks.
Smolchuck, Fred. Tongues & Total Surrender. 1974. pap. 0.50 (ISBN 0-88243-823-9, 02-0823). Gospel Pub.
Speaking with Other Tongues. 53p. 0.85 (ISBN 0-87509-132-6). Chr Pubns.
Turner, William H. Pentecost & Tongues. pap. 3.50 (ISBN 0-911866-83-3). Advocate.
Unger, Merrill F. New Testament Teaching on Tongues. LC 70-165057. 1971. pap. 2.95 (ISBN 0-8254-3900-0). Kregel.
Welborn, Don. On the Subject of Tongues: From the New Testament. 56p. pap. 0.35 (ISBN 0-937396-48-6). Walterick Pubs.
Zeller, George W. God's Gift of Tongues: The Nature, Purpose, & Duration of Tongues As Taught in the Bible. LC 78-100. (Orig.). 1978. pap. 2.50 (ISBN 0-87213-985-9). Loizeaux.
Zodhiates, Spiros. Tongues!? (I Corinthians). (Illus.). 1974. pap. 2.95 (ISBN 0-89957-512-9). AMG Pubs.
GLOUCESTER, EARLS OF
Schmidt, Michael. My Brother Gloucester. 1976. 6.25 (ISBN 0-8023-1255-1). Dufour.
GLOUCESTER, ENGLAND
Brooks, Alfred M. Gloucester Recollected: A Familiar History. Garland, Joseph E., ed. (Illus.). 9.50 (ISBN 0-8446-5012-9). Peter Smith.
Finberg, H. P., ed. Gloucestershire Studies. 1957. text ed. 13.00x (ISBN 0-7185-1013-5, Leicester). Humanities.
Herbert, N. M., ed. A History of the County of Gloucester, Vol 7. (Victoria History of the Counties of England Ser.). (Illus.). 250p. 1981. 149.00x (ISBN 0-19-722755-4). Oxford U Pr.
Ryder, T. A. Portrait of Gloucestershire. LC 66-73378. (Portrait Bks.). (Illus.). 1966. 10.50x (ISBN 0-7091-3318-9). Intl Pubns Serv.
Verey, David. Gloucestershire: A Shell Guide. (Shell Guide Ser.). (Illus.). 1972. 7.95 (ISBN 0-571-04710-6, Pub. by Faber & Faber). Merrimack Bk Serv.

GLOUCESTER COUNTY, VIRGINIA
Ironmonger, Elizabeth. Hogg Family of York & Gloucester Counties, Va. LC 75-1275. 494p. 1968. 15.00 (ISBN 0-685-65072-3). Va Bk.
GLOVES
Beck, S. William. Gloves: Their Annals & Associations. LC 75-75801. 1969. Repr. of 1883 ed. 19.00 (ISBN 0-8103-3825-4). Gale.
Upitis, Lizbeth. Latvian Mittens: Traditional Designs & Techniques. 1981. 10.50 (ISBN 0-932394-04-3). Dos Tejedoras.
GLOW-LAMPS
see Electric Lamps
GLOXINIAS
Nitrogen, Salinity, Substrates & Growth of Gloxinia & Chrysanthemum. (Agricultural Research Reports Ser.: 739). 1970. pap. 9.75 (ISBN 90-220-0295-0, PUDOC). Unipub.
GLUCAGON
Andreani, Dominico, et al, eds. Current Views on Hypoglycemia & Glucagon: Proceedings. LC 79-41558. (Serono Symposia: No. 30). 1980. 65.00 (ISBN 0-12-058680-0). Acad Pr.
Foa, P. P. & Bajaj, J. S., eds. Glucagon. LC 77-13657. (Its Role in Physiology & Clinical Medicine). 1978. 31.60 (ISBN 0-387-90297-X). Springer-Verlag.
GLUCINIUM
see Beryllium
GLUCK, CHRISTOPH WILLIBALD, RITTER VON, 1714-1787
Berlioz, Hector. Gluck & His Operas. Evans, Edwin, tr. LC 73-7695. (Illus.). 167p. 1973. Repr. of 1915 ed. lib. bdg. 15.00 (ISBN 0-8371-6938-0, BEGO). Greenwood.
Cooper, Martin. Gluck. LC 74-181129. 293p. 1935. Repr. 20.00 (ISBN 0-403-01526-X). Scholarly.
Hopkinson, Cecil. Bibliography of the Printed Works of C.W. Von Gluck, 1714-1787. 2nd ed. (Illus.). 100p. 1967. 30.00x (ISBN 0-8450-7001-0). Broude.
Howard, Patricia. C. W. von Gluck: Orfeo. (Cambridge Opera Handbooks Ser.). (Illus.). 200p. Date not set. 22.50 (ISBN 0-521-22827-1); pap. 7.95 (ISBN 0-521-29664-1). Cambridge U Pr.
--Gluck & the Birth of Modern Opera. (Illus.). 1963. 8.95 (ISBN 0-312-32970-9). St Martin.
Newman, Ernest. Gluck & the Opera: A Study in Musical History. 1976. Repr. of 1967 ed. lib. bdg. 23.00x (ISBN 0-8371-8849-0, NEGO). Greenwood.
--Gluck & the Opera: A Study in Musical History. LC 76-43929. (Music & Theatre in France in the 17th & 18th Centuries). Repr. of 1895 ed. 18.00 (ISBN 0-404-60176-6). AMS Pr.
Prod'Homme, Jacques G. Gluck. LC 76-43934. (Music & Theatre in France in the 17th & 18th Centuries). (Fr.). Repr. of 1948 ed. 27.50 (ISBN 0-404-60185-5). AMS Pr.
GLUCOSE
see also Blood Sugar
Birch, G. G., et al, eds. Glucose Syrups & Related Carbohydrates. (Illus.). 1970. 18.00x (ISBN 0-444-20103-3, Pub. by Applied Science). Burgess-Intl Ideas.
Goltz, Ronald E. Glucose: Up or Down. (Illus.). 1978. 20.00 (ISBN 0-916750-23-X). Dayton Labs.
Recommended International Standard for Glucose Syrup. 1970. pap. 4.50 (ISBN 0-685-36301-5, F675, FAO). Unipub.
WHO Scientific Group, Geneva, 1966. Standardization of Procedures for the Study of Glucose-6-Phosphate Dehydrogenase: A Report. (Technical Report Ser: No. 366). 53p. (Eng, Fr, Rus, & Span.). 1967. pap. 2.00 (ISBN 92-4-120366-8). World Health.
GLUCOSE METABOLISM
Grote, E. H. CNS Control Mechanisms on Glucose Metabolism. (Acta Neurochirurgia Supplementum Ser.: No. 31). (Illus.). 160p. 1981. pap. 36.90 (ISBN 0-387-81619-4). Springer-Verlag.
Hollmann, Siegfried. Non-Glycolytic Pathways of Metabolism of Glucose. Touster, Oscar, tr. 1964. 32.50 (ISBN 0-12-352650-7). Acad Pr.
GLUCOSIDES
see also Glycosides; Oligosaccharides
GLUCURONIC ACID
Dutton, G. J. Glucuronidation of Drugs & Other Compounds. 288p. 1980. 69.95 (ISBN 0-8493-5295-9). CRC Pr.
Dutton, Geoffrey J., ed. Glucuronic Acid: Free & Combined Chemistry, Biochemistry, Pharmacology & Medicine. 1966. 78.00 (ISBN 0-12-225350-7). Acad Pr.
GLUE
see also Adhesives
Daniels, George. Glues, Adhesives & How to Use Them. LC 77-26475. (A Popular Science Skill Bk.). (Illus.). 1980. pap. 4.95 (ISBN 0-06-090722-3, CN 722, CN). Har-Row.
Scharff, Robert. Adhesives & Glues: How to Choose & Use Them. 1981. 9.95 (ISBN 0-8359-0157-2). Reston.
GLUMR EYJOLFSSON, CALLED VIGA GLUMR, 10TH CENTURY
Hollander, Lee M., tr. Viga-Glum's Saga & the Story of Ogmund Dytt. (International Studies & Translations Ser). lib. bdg. 8.95 (ISBN 0-8057-3381-7). Twayne.
GLUTAMIC ACID
Davidson, Neil. Neurotransmitter Amino Acids. 1976. 26.00 (ISBN 0-12-205950-6). Acad Pr.
Filer, L. J., Jr., et al, eds. Glutamic Acid: Advances in Biochemistry & Physiology. LC 78-56782. (Mario Negri Institute for Pharmacological Research Monographs). 416p. 1979. text ed. 38.00 (ISBN 0-89004-356-6). Raven.
Mora, Jaime & Palacios, Rafael, eds. Glutamine: Metabolism, Enzymology & Regulation. 1980. 28.00 (ISBN 0-12-506040-8). Acad Pr.
Santen, R. J. & Henderson, I. C., eds. A Comprehensive Guide to the Therapeutic Use of Aminoglutethimide. (Pharmanual Ser.: Vol. 2). (Illus.). vi, 162p. 1981. pap. 21.75 (ISBN 3-8055-2871-X). S Karger.
GLUTATHIONE
Colowick, Sidney P., et al, eds. Glutathione: A Symposium. 1954. 51.50 (ISBN 0-12-181876-4). Acad Pr.
Flohe, L., et al. Glutathione. 1974. 55.50 (ISBN 0-12-260750-3). Acad Pr.
Sies, H. & Wondel, A., eds. Functions of Glutathione in Liver & Kidney. (Proceedings in Life Sciences). (Illus.). 1979. 34.10 (ISBN 0-387-09127-0). Springer-Verlag.
GLUTEN-FREE DIET
Hills, Hilda C. Good Food: Gluten-Free. LC 75-10538. 1976. 7.95 (ISBN 0-87983-138-3); pap. 4.50 (ISBN 0-87983-103-0). Keats.
GLYCERIN
Ashworth, M. R. Analytical Methods for Glycerol. 1979. 56.00 (ISBN 0-12-065050-9). Acad Pr.
GLYCOGEN
see also Polysaccharides
Gregory, John D. & Jeanloz, Roger, eds. Glycoconjugate Research: Proceedings of the Fourth International Symposium on Glycoconjugates, Vol. 2. LC 79-15164. 1979. 37.50 (ISBN 0-12-301302-X). Acad Pr.
Lennarz, William J., ed. The Biochemistry of Glycoproteins & Proteoglycans. (Illus.). 395p. 1980. 35.00 (ISBN 0-306-40243-2, Plenum Pr). Plenum Pub.
GLYCOGEN METABOLISM
Whelan, W. J. & Whelan, W. J., eds. Control of Glycogen Metabolism. LC 68-31572. (Illus.). 1968. 36.00 (ISBN 0-12-745750-X). Acad Pr.
GLYCOSIDE METABOLISM
Varma, R. S. & Varma, R., eds. Glycosaminoglycans & Proteoglycans in Physiological & Pathological Processes of Body Systems. (Illus.). x, 470p. 1981. 178.50 (ISBN 3-8055-3440-X). S Karger.
GLYCOSIDES
see also Glycoside Metabolism
Bochkov, A. E. & Zaikov, G. E. Chemistry of the O-Glycosidic Bond: Formation & Cleavage. 1979. 45.00 (ISBN 0-08-022949-2). Pergamon.
Horowitz, Martin & Pigman, Ward, eds. Glycoconjugates: Mammalian Glycoproteins & Glycolipids, Vol. 1. LC 76-27445. 1977. 59.50 (ISBN 0-12-356101-9). Acad Pr.
International Symposium, Bonn, Germany, 27-29 Jan. 1977. Cardiac Glycosides. Bodem, G. & Benglor, H. J., eds. (Illus.). 1978. pap. 30.60 (ISBN 0-387-08692-7). Springer-Verlag.
Piras, Romano & Piras, Horatio G., eds. Biochemistry of the Glycosidic Linkage: An Integrated View, Proceedings. 1972. 47.00 (ISBN 0-12-557250-6). Acad Pr.
Varma, R. S. & Varma, R., eds. Glycosaminoglycans & Proteoglycans in Physiological & Pathological Processes of Body Systems. (Illus.). x, 470p. 1981. 178.50 (ISBN 3-8055-3440-X). S Karger.
GLYNDEBOURNE FESTIVAL OPERA COMPANY
Hughes, Spike. Glyndebourne: A History of the Festival Opera. LC 80-70705. (Illus.). 400p. 1981. 35.00 (ISBN 0-7153-7891-0). David & Charles.
GLYPTICS
see also Cameos; Gems; Intaglios; Medals; Netsukes; Plaques, Plaquettes; Seals (Numismatics)
Porada, Edith, ed. Ancient Art in Seals: Essays by Pierre Amiet, Nimet Ozguc, & John Boardman. LC 79-19462. (Illus.). 1980. 20.00x (ISBN 0-691-03951-8). Princeton U Pr.
GNEISENAU (BATTLESHIP)
Garrett, Richard. Scharnhorst & Gneisenau: The Elusive Sisters. 1978. 17.50 (ISBN 0-88254-467-5). Hippocrene Bks.
GNOMES
see Fairies
GNOMES (MAXIMS)
see Aphorisms and Apothegms; Maxims; Proverbs
GNOMIC POETRY
Williams, Blanche C. Gnomic Poetry in Anglo-Saxon. LC 14-9944. Repr. of 1914 ed. 17.00 (ISBN 0-404-06958-4). AMS Pr.
GNOMONICS
see Sun-Dials
GNOSTICISM
see also Mandaeans
Bloom, Harold. An American Gnosis. 160p. 1981. 9.95 (ISBN 0-8164-9307-3). Continuum.
Doellinger, Johann J. Beitrage Zur Sektengenchichte des Mittelalter, 2 vols in 1. LC 91-26634. (Social Science Ser). (Ger). 1970. Repr. of 1890 ed. Set. lib. bdg. 57.50 (ISBN 0-8337-0880-5). B Franklin.
Doresse, Jean. The Secret Books of the Egyptian Gnostics. LC 79-153316. Repr. of 1960 ed. 24.50 (ISBN 0-404-04646-0). AMS Pr.
Faye, Eugene De. Gnostiques et gnosticisme: Etude Critique Des Documents Du Gnosticisme Chretien Aux Deuxieme et Troisieme Siecles. LC 77-84699. Repr. of 1913 ed. 34.00 (ISBN 0-404-16106-5). AMS Pr.
Grant, Robert M., ed. Gnosticism: A Source Book of Heretical Writings from the Early Christian Period. LC 77-85274. Repr. of 1961 ed. 23.50 (ISBN 0-404-16108-1). AMS Pr.
Jonas, Hans. Gnostic Religion. 1963. pap. 5.95 (ISBN 0-8070-5799-1, BP259). Beacon Pr.
--Gnostic Religion: The Message of the Alien God & the Beginnings of Christianity. 2nd, rev. ed. 9.50 (ISBN 0-8446-2339-3). Peter Smith.
King, C. W. The Gnostics & Their Remains. LC 73-76092. (Illus.). 500p. Date not set. Repr. of 1887 ed. 19.50 (ISBN 0-913510-34-3). Wizards.
Kraeling, Carl H. Anthropos & Son of Man. LC 27-23162. (Columbia University. Oriental Studies: No. 25). Repr. of 1927 ed. 18.50 (ISBN 0-404-50515-5). AMS Pr.
Layton, Bentley. The Gnostic Treatise on Resurrection from Nag Hammadi. LC 79-18521. (Harvard Dissertations in Religion Ser.: No. 12). 1979. 12.00 (ISBN 0-89130-341-3, 020112); pap. 7.50 (ISBN 0-89130-342-1). Scholars Pr Ca.
MacGregor, Geddes. Gnosis. LC 78-64908. 1979. 10.75 (ISBN 0-8356-0522-1, Quest); pap. 5.50 (ISBN 0-8356-0520-5, Quest). Theos Pub Hse.
Mansel, Henry L. The Gnostic Heresies of the First & Second Centuries. Lightfoot, J. B., ed. LC 78-63170. (Heresies of the Early Christian & Medieval Era: Second Ser.). Repr. of 1875 ed. 26.50 (ISBN 0-404-16185-5). AMS Pr.
Norelli-Bachelet, Patrizia. The Gnostic Circle. 1978. pap. 7.95 (ISBN 0-87728-411-3). Weiser.
Pagels, Elaine. The Gnostic Gospels. LC 80-12341. 256p. 1981. pap. 2.95 (ISBN 0-394-74043-2, Vin). Random.
--The Gnostic Gospels. LC 79-4764. 1979. 10.00 (ISBN 0-394-50278-7). Random.
Perkins, Pheme. The Gnostic Dialogue. LC 80-81441. (Theological Inquiries Ser.). 256p. 1980. pap. 6.95 (ISBN 0-8091-2320-7). Paulist Pr.
Raschke, Carl A. The Interruption of Eternity: Modern Gnosticism & the Origins of the New Religious Consciousness. LC 79-16460. 1980. 18.95x (ISBN 0-88229-374-5). Nelson-Hall.
Voegelin, Eric. Science, Politics & Gnosticism. 2.95 (ISBN 0-89526-964-3). Regnery-Gateway.
Wilson, Robert M. The Gnostic Problem. LC 78-63175. (Heresies of the Early Christian & Medieval Era: Second Ser.). Repr. of 1958 ed. 23.50 (ISBN 0-404-16193-6). AMS Pr.
GNOTOBIOLOGY
see Germfree Life
GO (GAME)
Iwamoto, Kaoru. Go for Beginners. LC 76-45790. (Illus.). 1977. 7.95 (ISBN 0-394-41352-0); pap. 2.45 (ISBN 0-394-73331-2). Pantheon.
Kishikawa, Shigemi. Stepping Stones to Go. LC 65-13411. (Illus.). 1965. pap. 5.95 (ISBN 0-8048-0547-4). C E Tuttle.
Korschelt, O. Theory & Practice of Go. Leckie, George & King, Samuel P., trs. LC 65-22637. (Illus.). 1965. 7.95 (ISBN 0-8048-0572-5). C E Tuttle.
Kushi, Michio. The Book of Do-In: Exercise for Physical & Spiritual Development. (Illus.). 176p. (Orig.). 1979. pap. 10.95 (ISBN 0-87040-382-6). Japan Pubns.
Lasker, Edward. Go & Go Moku. (Illus.). 1960. pap. 3.50 (ISBN 0-486-20613-0). Dover.
Smith, Arthur. Game of Go. LC 56-12653. (Illus.). 1956. pap. 5.25 (ISBN 0-8048-0202-5). C E Tuttle.
GO-KART RACING
see Karting
GOA
Golden Goa. 1981. 26.00x (ISBN 0-8364-0763-6, Pub. by Marg India). South Asia Bks.
Mascarenhas, Telo. When the Mango Trees Blossomed. LC 76-901528. 1976. 10.00x (ISBN 0-8364-0491-2, Orient Longman). South Asia Bks.
Mezerik, Avrahm, ed. Goa: Indian Takeover. 15.00 (ISBN 0-685-40641-5, 70). Intl Review.
Richards, James. Discovering Goa. (Illus.). 128p. 1981. text ed. 17.95x (ISBN 0-7069-1287-X, Pub. by Vikas India). Advent NY.
GOA-HISTORY
De Souza, Teotonio. Medieval Goa. 309p. 1981. text ed. 18.00x (ISBN 0-391-02352-7, Pub. by Concept India). Humanities.
Saksena, R. N. Goa into the Main Stream. 1973. 6.00x (ISBN 0-8426-0604-1). Verry.
GOATS
Belanger, Jerry. Raising Milk Goats the Modern Way. LC 75-3493. (Illus.). 151p. 1975. pap. 4.95 (ISBN 0-88266-062-4). Garden Way Pub.
Bronson, Wilfrid S. Goats. LC 59-6029. (Illus.). (gr. 1-5). 1959. 5.50 (ISBN 0-15-231109-2, HJ). HarBraceJ.
Considine, Harvey & Trimberger, George W. Judging Techniques. Date not set. 15.95 (ISBN 0-686-26692-7). Dairy Goat.
Dairy Goats: Breeding-Feeding Management. Date not set. 1.75 (ISBN 0-686-26685-4). Dairy Goat.
Downing, Elizabeth. Keeping Goats. (Pelham Ser.). (Illus.). 128p. 1976. 8.95 (ISBN 0-7207-0883-4, Pub. by Michael Joseph). Merrimack Bk Serv.
Eberhardt, Jo. Good Beginnings with Dairy Goats. Date not set. 6.00 (ISBN 0-686-26687-0). Dairy Goat.
Ensminger, M. Eugene. Sheep & Wool Science. 4th ed. LC 73-79612. (gr. 9-12). 1970. text ed. 23.35 (ISBN 0-8134-1113-0). Interstate.
Gall, C., ed. Goat Production: Breeding & Management. LC 81-66393. 1981. price not set (ISBN 0-12-273980-9). Acad Pr.
Guss, Sam. Management & Diseases of Dairy Goats. Date not set. 14.95 (ISBN 0-686-26691-9). Dairy Goat.
Hall, Alice. Dairy Goats: Selecting, Fitting, Showing. LC 77-153203. (Illus.). 1975. pap. 3.50x (ISBN 0-932218-02-4). Hall Pr.
--The Pygmy(Goat) in America. (Illus.). 80p. (Orig.). 1982. pap. 5.00 (ISBN 0-932218-13-X). Hall Pr.
Herman, Harry A. Artificial Insemination of Dairy Goat. Date not set. 2.50 (ISBN 0-686-26684-6). Dairy Goat.
Jenkins, Marie M. Goats, Sheep, & How They Live. LC 77-20149. (Illus.). (gr. 5 up). 1978. 7.95 (ISBN 0-8234-0317-3). Holiday.
Lavine, Sigmund A. & Scuro, Vincent. Wonders of Goats. LC 79-6647. (Wonders Ser.). (Illus.). (gr. 4 up). 1980. 5.95 (ISBN 0-396-07816-8). Dodd.
Leach, C. E. The Goat Owners' Scrapbook. Date not set. 7.50 (ISBN 0-686-26682-X). Dairy Goat.
Leach, Corl A. Aids to Goatkeeping. Date not set. 10.00 (ISBN 0-686-26686-2). Dairy Goat.
Lee, Hollis. Goats, Rabbits & Chickens. (Country Home & Small Farm Guides Ser.). (Illus.). 1978. pap. 2.95 (ISBN 0-88453-006-X). Barrington.
Luisi, Billie. A Practical Guide to Small-Scale Goatkeeping. 1979. 8.95 (ISBN 0-87857-239-2). Rodale Pr Inc.
Mackenzie, David. Goat Husbandry. 4th ed. Laing, Jean, ed. (Illus.). 375p. 1981. 23.00 (ISBN 0-571-18024-8, Pub. by Faber & Faber); pap. 9.95 (ISBN 0-571-11322-2). Merrimack Bk Serv.
Nievergelt, B. Ibexes in an African Environment. (Ecological Studies Ser.: Vol. 40). (Illus.). 230p. 1981. 49.80 (ISBN 0-387-10592-1). Springer-Verlag.
Observations on the Goat. (Agricultural Studies: No. 80). 1974. pap. 12.25 (ISBN 0-685-48621-4, F303, FAO). Unipub.
Owen, Nancy L. The Illustrated Standard of the Dairy Goat. Date not set. 10.00 (ISBN 0-686-26679-X). Dairy Goat.
Pegler, H. S. The Book of the Goat. Date not set. 6.00 (ISBN 0-686-26688-9). Dairy Goat.
Reinhardt, Mrs. Robert M. & Hall, Alice G. Nubian History: America & Great Britain. LC 77-809029. (Illus.). 1978. pap. text ed. 5.00 (ISBN 0-932218-07-5). Hall Pr.
Rogers, Ferial & Minter, Phyllis V. Goats: Their Care & Breeding. (Illus.). 100p. 1980. 3.95 (ISBN 0-686-63088-2, 4948-0, Pub. by K & R Bks England). Arco.
Saiga Editors, ed. Goat Keeping. 1981. 10.00x (ISBN 0-86230-022-3, Pub. by Saiga Pub). State Mutual Bk.
Salmon, Jill. The Goatkeeper's Guide. LC 80-69354. (Illus.). 152p. 1981. 14.95 (ISBN 0-7153-8055-9). David & Charles.
--The Goatkeeper's Guide. Date not set. 10.95 (ISBN 0-686-26681-1). Dairy Goat.
Scott, Jack D. The Book of the Goat. (Illus.). (gr. 6-8). 1979. 8.95 (ISBN 0-399-20681-7). Putnam.
Sheep & Goat Breeding. (Better Farming Ser.: No. 12). 1979. pap. 6.00 (ISBN 92-5-100152-9, F70, FAO). Unipub.
Shields, Joan & Shields, Harry. The Modern Dairy Goat. Date not set. 5.00 (ISBN 0-686-26683-8). Dairy Goat.
Shields, John. Exhibition & Practical Goatkeeping. 1981. 30.00x (ISBN 0-904558-26-6, Pub. by Saiga Pub). State Mutual Bk.
GOBANG (GAME)
see Go (Game)

GOBBLEDYGOOK
see Languages, Mixed
GOBI
Hedin, Sven A. Across the Gobi Desert. Cant, H. J., tr. LC 68-23296. (Illus.). 1968. Repr. of 1931 ed. lib. bdg. 25.25x (ISBN 0-8371-0103-4, HEGD). Greenwood.
Perkins, John & American Museum of Natural History. To the Ends of the Earth: Four Expeditions to the Arctic, the Congo, the Gobi, & Siberia. (Illus.). Date not set. 25.00 (ISBN 0-394-50900-5). Pantheon.
GOBINEAU, JOSEPH ARTHUR, COMTE DE, 1816-1882
Rowbotham, Arnold H. The Literary World of Count De Gobineau. 1973. Repr. of 1929 ed. 40.00 (ISBN 0-8274-0936-2). R West.
Schemann, Ludwig. Gobineau: Eine Biographie & Alexis De Tocqueville, 3 vols. in two. Mayer, J. P., ed. LC 78-67384. (European Political Thought Ser.). (Illus.). 1979. Repr. of 1911 ed. Set. lib. bdg. 94.00x (ISBN 0-405-11734-5); lib. bdg. 47.00 ea. Vol. 1 (ISBN 0-405-11735-3). Vol. 2 (ISBN 0-405-11736-1). Arno.
Valette, Rebecca M. Arthur de Gobineau & the Short Story. (Studies in the Romance Languages & Literatures: No. 79). 1969. pap. 9.50x (ISBN 0-8078-9079-0). U of NC Pr.
GOBLET CELLS
see Exfoliative Cytology
GOBLINS
see Fairies
GOD
see also Agnosticism; Anthropomorphism; Atheism; Beatific Vision; Causation; Christianity; Creation; Deism; Fear of God; Free Thought; Glory of God; Holy Spirit; Jesus Christ; Metaphysics; Monotheism; Myth; Mythology; Natural Theology; Ontology; Pantheism; Providence and Government of God; Rationalism; Religion; Teleology; Theism; Theodicy; Theology; Trinities; Trinity; Trust in God
Adams, James E. Liberacion: El Evangelo de Dios. 1980. pap. 2.95 (ISBN 0-686-70961-6). Banner of Truth.
Adams, Jay E. Godliness Through Discipline. 1977. pap. 0.75 (ISBN 0-8010-0057-2). Baker Bk.
Adams, Walter E. Simplicity of God. 140p. (Orig.). 1980. pap. 3.50 (ISBN 0-937408-00-X). Gospel Pubns FL.
--Who Is God??? God Is Love!!! 115p. (Orig.). 1981. pap. 2.95 (ISBN 0-937408-02-6). Gospel Pubns Fl.
Adler, Mortimer J. How to Think About God: A Guide for the Twentieth-Century Pagan. 1980. 9,95 (ISBN 0-02-500540-5). Macmillan.
Alexander, S. Space, Time & Deity: The Gifford Lectures at Glasgow 1916-1918, 2 Vols. Set. 25.00 (ISBN 0-8446-1521-8). Peter Smith.
Allen, Grant. The Evolution of the Idea of God. 1977. lib. bdg. 59.95 (ISBN 0-8490-1796-3). Gordon Pr.
Allnutt, Frank. The Force of Star Wars. 1977. pap. 1.95 (ISBN 0-89728-030-X, 689135). Omega Pubns OR.
Allred, Gordon T. God the Father. 1979. 7.95 (ISBN 0-87747-746-9). Deseret Bk.
Ammerman, Thomas J. God, If You Exist, Prove It to Me. 1981. 6.95 (ISBN 0-8062-1595-X). Carlton.
Anderson, Robert. The Silence of God. LC 78-9528. (Sir Robert Anderson Library). 1978. pap. 3.50 (ISBN 0-8254-2128-4). Kregel.
Angeles, Peter, ed. Critiques of God. pap. 7.00 (ISBN 0-87980-349-5). Wilshire.
Angeles, Peter A. The Problem of God: A Short Introduction. rev. ed. LC 73-85469. (Skeptic's Bookshelf Ser.). 156p. 1981. pap. text ed. 8.95 (ISBN 0-675-08887-9). Prometheus Bks.
Anselm Of Canterbury. Anselm of Canterbury: Why God Became Man. Hopkins, Jasper & Richardson, Herbert, eds. 105p. 1980. soft cover 4.95x (ISBN 0-88946-009-4). E Mellen.
Arya, Usharbudh. God. LC 79-88824. 162p. (Orig.). 1979. pap. 4.95 (ISBN 0-89389-060-X). Himalayan Intl Inst.
Association for Research & Enlightenment, Inc. Virginia Beach, Va. Study Groups, et al, eds. Search for God, 2 Bks. 1942-1950. 3.95 ea. Bk. 1 (ISBN 0-87604-000-8). Bk. 2 (ISBN 0-87604-001-6). ARE Pr.
Battle, Edith K. Our Children Ask About God. 1944. pap. 0.25 (ISBN 0-687-29515-7). Abingdon.
Belleggia, Sr. Concetta. God & the Problem of Evil. 1980. 3.75 (ISBN 0-8198-3007-0); pap. 2.50 (ISBN 0-8198-3008-9). Dghtrs St Paul.
Berry, Roger L. God's World: His Story. 1981. pap. 14.30 (ISBN 0-87813-914-1). Christian Light.
--God's World-His Story. (Christian Day School Ser.). 1976. 10.60x (ISBN 0-87813-911-7). Christian Light.
Bertocci, Peter. Person God Is. (Muirhead Library of Philosophy). 1970. text ed. 11.50x (ISBN 0-391-00095-0). Humanities.
Bingham, Geoffrey. God & the Powers of Darkness. 64p. (Orig.). 1981. pap. 1.95 (ISBN 0-87784-844-0). Inter-Varsity.
Bonaventura, Saint The Mind's Road to God. Boas, George, tr. 1953. pap. 2.50 (ISBN 0-672-60195-8, LLA32). Bobbs.
Bowker, John. The Religious Imagination & the Sense of God. 1978. text ed. 24.95x (ISBN 0-19-826646-4). Oxford U Pr.
Bremyer, Jayne. Dear God, Am I Important? LC 76-2867. 1976. pap. 3.95 (ISBN 0-87680-856-9, 98079). Word Bks.
Brightman, Edgar S. The Problem of God. LC 75-3085. (Philosophy in America Ser.). Repr. of 1930 ed. 21.50 (ISBN 0-404-59084-5). AMS Pr.
Brightman, Edgare S. The Problem of God. 1979. Repr. of 1930 ed. lib. bdg. 30.00 (ISBN 0-8482-7365-6). Norwood Edns.
Brother Lawrence. God-Illuminated Cook: The Practice of the Presence of God. (East Ridge Press). (Illus.). 144p. 1980. pap. 3.95 (ISBN 0-686-30081-5, 02-5). Multimedia.
Brown, Cheever M. God As Mother: A Feminine Theology in India, an Historical & Theological Study of the Brahmavaivarta Purana. LC 74-76006. (God Ser.: No. 106). 1974. 15.00 (ISBN 0-89007-004-0). C Stark.
Brumback, Carl. God in Three Persons. 192p. 1959. pap. 3.75 (ISBN 0-87148-354-8). Pathway Pr.
Calvin, John. Concerning the Eternal Predestination of God. Reid, J. K., ed. 1961. 13.95 (ISBN 0-227-67438-3). Attic Pr.
Carretto, Carlo. God Who Comes. 1976. pap. 1.50 (ISBN 0-89129-062-1). Jove Pubns.
Centre, Michael. In Search of God-the Solar Connection. LC 78-73706. (Illus.). 1978. pap. 4.95x (ISBN 0-932876-01-3). Centre Ent.
Charnock, Stephen. Existence & Attributes of God, 2 vols. 24.95 (ISBN 0-8010-2437-4). Baker Bk.
Cheney, Lois A. God Is No Fool. (Orig.). pap. 1.50 (ISBN 0-89129-251-9). Jove Pubns.
--God Is No Fool: Ninety-Nine Acts of Communication with God. (Festival Bks.). 1977. pap. 1.50 (ISBN 0-687-15180-5). Abingdon.
Clemens, David A. God Encountered, Vol. 1. LC 79-52420. (Steps to Maturity Ser.). 1973. tchrs'. manual 15.95 (ISBN 0-86508-002-X); student's manual 13.95 (ISBN 0-86508-001-1); visuals packet 4.25 (ISBN 0-86508-007-0). BCM Inc.
Collins, James D. God in Modern Philosophy. LC 77-25963. 1978. Repr. of 1959 ed. lib. bdg. 34.00x (ISBN 0-313-20079-3, COGM). Greenwood.
Colquhoun, Frank. Hard Questions. LC 77-74848. 1979. pap. 3.95 (ISBN 0-87784-720-7). Inter-Varsity.
Compton, Arthur H. Man's Destiny in Eternity. LC 75-117821. (Essay Index Reprint Ser). 1949. 17.00 (ISBN 0-8369-1762-6). Arno.
Corlett, D. Shelby. God in the Present Tense. 176p. 1974. 1.95 (ISBN 0-8341-0248-X). Beacon Hill.
Davis, Elise M. The Answer Is God. (Spire Bks.). 272p. 1980. pap. 1.95 (ISBN 0-8007-8104-X). Revell.
--Answer Is God. 1975. pap. 1.25 (ISBN 0-89129-068-0, PV068). Jove Pubns.
Davis, Roy E. With God We Can. 1978. pap. 4.95 (ISBN 0-87707-211-6). CSA Pr.
DeLong, Russell V. So You Don't Believe in God? (Direction Bks). 1977. pap. 1.25 (ISBN 0-8010-2867-1). Baker Bk.
Diamond, Malcolm L. Contemporary Philosophy & Religious Thought: An Introduction to the Philosophy of Religion. new ed. 416p. 1974. (C); pap. text ed. 10.95 (ISBN 0-07-016720-6). McGraw.
Diamond, Malcolm L. & Litzenburg, Thomas V., Jr. The Logic of God: Theology & Verification. LC 74-32235. 562p. 1975. 17.95 (ISBN 0-672-60792-1). Bobbs.
Dieu Repond: Problemes-Hommes. Date not set. 2.00 (ISBN 0-686-76396-3). Life Pubs Intl.
Donceel, Joseph F. The Searching Mind: An Introduction to a Philosophy of God. LC 79-18166. 1979. text ed. 15.95x (ISBN 0-268-01700-X); pap. text ed. 6.95x (ISBN 0-268-01701-8). U of Notre Dame Pr.
Dugan, LeRoy. Help Yourself to a Healthier Mind. 96p. (Orig.). 1980. 4.95 (ISBN 0-87123-205-7, 210205). Bethany Hse.
Durrant, Michael. The Logical Status of God. LC 72-93886. (New Studies in the Philosophy of Religion). 132p. 1973. 14.95 (ISBN 0-312-49455-6). St Martin.
Erickson, Millard J., ed. Living God: Readings in Christian Theology. 1973. pap. 9.95 (ISBN 0-8010-3305-5). Baker Bk.
The Existence of God: Finally, Indisputable Proof. 190p. (Orig.). 1981. cancelled (ISBN 0-934894-38-8). Islamic Prods.
Exley, Richard D. El Otro Dios. (Span.). Date not set. 1.75 (ISBN 0-686-76328-9). Life Pubs Intl.
Faber, Frederick W. The Creator & Creature. LC 78-66301. 1978. pap. 7.50 (ISBN 0-89555-076-8). TAN Bks Pubs.
Ferntheil, Carol, ed. Garden of Cheer. (Illus.). 16p. (Orig.). 1979. pap. 0.85 (ISBN 0-87239-343-7, 7946). Standard Pub.
Ferre, Nels. The Christian Understanding of God. LC 78-12234. 1979. Repr. of 1951 ed. lib. bdg. 19.75x (ISBN 0-313-21183-3, FECU). Greenwood.
Frost, Robert. Our Heavenly Father. 1978. pap. 3.95 (ISBN 0-88270-266-1). Logos.
Gaither, Gloria. Because He Lives. 1977. 6.95 (ISBN 0-8007-0881-4). Revell.
Gee, Donald. Is It God? (Charismatic Bk). 1972. pap. 0.69 (ISBN 0-88243-916-2, 02-0916). Gospel Pub.
Gill, Jerry H. On Knowing God. 1981. pap. price not set (ISBN 0-664-24380-0). Westminster.
Goblet D'Alviella, Eugene F. Lectures on the Origin & Growth of the Conception of God As Illustrated by Anthropology & History. Wicksteed, P. H., tr. LC 77-27163. (Hibbert Lectures: 1887). Repr. of 1892 ed. 26.50 (ISBN 0-404-60409-9). AMS Pr.
Goldsmith, Joel S. Conscious Union with God. 1977. pap. text ed. 4.95 (ISBN 0-8065-0578-8). Citadel Pr.
Goulet, Yvonne. To Live God's Word. (Illus.). 1979. 8.95 (ISBN 0-88347-104-3). Thomas More.
Graham, Billy. Paz Con Dios. Muntz, Carrie, tr. from Eng. Orig. Title: Peace with God. 272p. 1980. pap. 3.25 (ISBN 0-311-43037-6). Casa Bautista.
Gray, Donald. Finding God Among Us. 2nd ed. LC 77-89322. 1977. pap. 3.95 (ISBN 0-88489-090-2). St Mary's.
Griffiths, Rees. God in Idea & Experience: The Apriori Elements of Religious Consciousness; an Epistemological Study. 316p. Repr. of 1931 ed. text ed. 5.95 (ISBN 0-567-02128-9). Attic Pr.
Guder, Eileen. The Naked I: Seeking God & Finding Identity. LC 73-144363. 1976. pap. 3.50 (ISBN 0-87680-855-0, 98072). Word Bks.
Guest, Dean. Discovering, the Word of God. 64p. (Orig.). 1980. Repr. pap. 1.95 (ISBN 0-89841-011-8). Zoe Pubns.
Hamilton, Elizabeth. I Stay in the Church. 1973. 5.95 (ISBN 0-85478-053-X). Attic Pr.
Hanson, R. P. C. Attractiveness of God: Essays in Christian Doctrine. 9.95 (ISBN 0-686-73880-2). John Knox.
Hartshorne, Charles. Divine Relativity: A Social Conception of God. new ed. 1964. 15.00x (ISBN 0-300-00539-3). Yale U Pr.
Hartshorne, Charles & Reese, William L. Philosophers Speak of God. LC 53-10041. (Midway Reprint Ser.). 1976. 14.00x (ISBN 0-226-31862-1). U of Chicago Pr.
Haughton, Rosemary. The Passionate God. LC 81-80049. 352p. 1981. pap. 11.95 (ISBN 0-8091-2383-5). Paulist Pr.
Heijke, Joseph. St. Augustine's Comments on Imago Dei. 3.00 (ISBN 0-686-23375-1). Classical Folia.
Henry, Carl F. God, Revelation & Authority: God Who Speaks & Shows, Vols. 3 & 4. 1979. 19.95 ea. Vol. 3 (ISBN 0-8499-0091-3). Vol. 4 (ISBN 0-8499-0126-X). Word Bks.
Herder, Johann G. God: Some Conversations. Burkhardt, Fredrick H., tr. from Ger. LC 62-20496. 1940. pap. text ed. 2.00x (ISBN 0-672-60352-7). Irvington.
Hess, Lee R. Me and You with God in View. 1978. pap. 3.95 (ISBN 0-89293-007-1). Beta Bk.
Hick, John. God & the Universe of Faiths. LC 73-88027. 224p. 1974. 19.95 (ISBN 0-312-33040-5). St Martin.
Hicks, Robert & Bewes, Richard. God. (Understanding Bible Truth Ser.). (Orig.). 1981. pap. 1.50 (ISBN 0-89840-024-4). Heres Life.
Hitchcook, Ruth. The Good Hand of Our God. LC 75-4177. 1975. 3.95 (ISBN 0-912692-65-0). Cook.
Hoeksema, Herman. God's Eternal God's Pleasure. LC 80-8081. 1980. 9.95 (ISBN 0-8254-2842-4). Kregel.
Hoeksema, Homer C. In the Beginning, God. 1975. pap. 1.00 (ISBN 0-8254-2823-8). Kregel.
Holt, Arthur E. This Nation Under God. 1939. 10.00 (ISBN 0-8414-5098-6). Folcroft.
Hopkins, Jasper. Nicholas of Cusa on God As Not-Other: A Translation & an Appraisal of "De Li Non Aliud". Hopkins, Jasper, tr. from Latin. 1979. text ed. 20.00x (ISBN 0-8166-0881-4). U of Minn Pr.
Houston, James. I Believe in the Creator. LC 79-13542. (I Believe Ser.). 1979. pap. 4.95 (ISBN 0-8028-1749-1). Eerdmans.
Howard, Leslie G. The Expansion of God. LC 81-4521. 464p. (Orig.). 1981. pap. 14.95 (ISBN 0-88344-121-7). Orbis Bks.
Humphreys, Fisher. The Almighty. 107p. pap. 1.95 (ISBN 0-89191-458-7, 94581). Cook.
Hutchinson, Roger. Works. 1842. 25.50 (ISBN 0-384-25120-X). Johnson Repr.
Ilon. The Supremacy of God. LC 80-66408. 1980. pap. 3.00 (ISBN 0-9600958-6-1). Birth Day.
Isaacs, Alan. Electrons & Gods. rev. ed. Date not set. cancelled (ISBN 0-89793-007-X). Hunter Hse.
Jansen, John F. Let Us Worship God. pap. 2.95 (ISBN 0-8042-9622-7). John Knox.
Jenkins, Daniel. Believing in God. (Layman's Theological Library). 1965. pap. 1.45 (ISBN 0-664-24004-6). Westminster.
Johann, Robert O. Pragmatic Meaning of God. (Aquinas Lecture). 1966. 6.95 (ISBN 0-87462-131-3). Marquette.
Johnson, Margaret. Por Que Senor? (Span.). Date not set. 2.25 (ISBN 0-686-76334-3). Life Pubs Intl.
Johnston, Russ. God Can Make It Happen. 144p. 1976. pap. 3.95 (ISBN 0-88207-741-4). Victor Bks.
Johnstone, Parker L. Is God a Separate Being? LC 76-706635. 1977. 5.95 (ISBN 0-917802-01-2). Theoscience Found.
Joyce, George H. Principles of Natural Theology. LC 79-170829. Repr. of 1923 ed. 37.45 (ISBN 0-404-03609-0). AMS Pr.
Junker. Knowing Where You Stand with God. LC 76-8560. pap. 2.95 (ISBN 0-8054-5241-9). Broadman.
Kahn, Lothar, ed. God: What People Have Said About Him. 320p. 1980. 9.95 (ISBN 0-8246-0251-X). Jonathan David.
Kantonen, T. A. Man in the Eyes of God. 1973. pap. 2.35 (ISBN 0-89536-421-2). CSS Pub.
Kaufman, Gordon D. God the Problem. LC 70-174543. 1972. 15.00x (ISBN 0-674-35525-3); pap. 4.95x (ISBN 0-674-35526-1). Harvard U Pr.
--The Theological Imagination: Constructing the Concept of God. 1981. pap. price not set (ISBN 0-664-24393-2). Westminster.
Kehoe, K. Theology of God: Sources. 1971. pap. 4.75 (ISBN 0-02-816670-1). Glencoe.
Kerr, William F., ed. God: What Is He Like. pap. 1.95 pocket bk. (ISBN 0-8423-1098-3). Tyndale.
Kesler, Jay & Stafford, Tim. Breakthrough! Questions for Youth About God. (Campus Life Bk.). 176p. (Orig.). 1981. pap. 4.95 (ISBN 0-310-43371-1). Zondervan.
Kline, Meredith G. Images of the Spirit. (Baker Biblical Monographs). (Orig.). 1980. pap. 6.95 (ISBN 0-8010-5416-8). Baker Bk.
Koch, Kurt E. God Among the Zulus. 334p. 1981. pap. 6.95 (ISBN 0-8254-3046-1). Kregel.
Konig, Adrio. Here Am I: A Believer's Reflection on God. 272p. (Orig.). 1981. pap. 8.95 (ISBN 0-686-75062-4). Eerdmans.
Kramer, William A. God's People. LC 75-16790. 1975. lib. bdg. 7.25 (ISBN 0-8100-0010-5, 06N552). Northwest Pub.
Krol, John C. God-the Cornerstone of Our Life. 1978. 5.50 (ISBN 0-8198-0531-9); pap. 3.95 (ISBN 0-8198-0532-7). Dghtrs St Paul.
Krol, Cardinal John. To Insure Peace Acknowledge God. 1978. 5.50 (ISBN 0-8198-0561-0); pap. 3.95 (ISBN 0-8198-0562-9). Dghtrs St Paul.
Kuhlman, Kathryn. Nothing Is Impossible with God. (Orig.). pap. 1.75 (ISBN 0-89129-084-2). Jove Pubns.
Laird, Carobeth. Encounter with an Angry God. 1977. pap. 2.25 (ISBN 0-345-28464-X). Ballantine.
Lampe, G. W. God As Spirit: The Bampton Lectures for 1976. 1978. 16.95 (ISBN 0-19-826644-8). Oxford U Pr.
Larimore, John. The Creator of This World & the Universe. LC 78-54161. 1979. 9.95 (ISBN 0-87949-115-9). Ashley Bks.
Lawrence. Practice of the Presence of God. 128p. 1981. pap. 6.95 (ISBN 0-87243-129-0). Templegate.
Lawrence, Brother. The Practice of the Presence of God. 96p. 1981. pap. 2.50 (ISBN 0-88368-105-6). Whitaker Hse.
Lee, Jung Y. The Theology of Change: A Christian Concept of God in an Eastern Perspective. LC 78-16745. 1979. pap. 5.95 (ISBN 0-88344-492-5). Orbis Bks.
Leuba, J. H. The Belief in God & Immortality, a Psychological, Anthropological & Statistical Study. LC 17-54. Repr. of 1916 ed. 18.00 (ISBN 0-527-56600-4). Kraus Repr.
Lewis, H. D. Our Experience of God. (Fount Religious Paperbacks Ser.). 1976. pap. 3.95 (ISBN 0-00-642151-2, FA2151). Collins Pubs.
Lilly, John C. Simulations of God. LC 75-1039. 1975. 9.95 (ISBN 0-671-21981-2). S&S.
Lloyd-Jones, D. Martyn. God's Ultimate Purpose. (Illus.). 10.95 (ISBN 0-8010-5591-1). Baker Bk.
Loomis, Farnsworth W. God Within. (Illus.). 1968. 5.95 (ISBN 0-8079-0122-9). October.
Lossky, Vladimir. In the Image & Likeness of God. LC 76-383878. 232p. 1974. pap. 6.95 (ISBN 0-913836-13-3). St Vladimirs.
--The Vision of God. 139p. 1963. 6.95 (ISBN 0-913836-19-2). St Vladimirs.
Loudy, Adlai. God's Eonian Purpose. text ed. 5.00 (ISBN 0-910424-56-X). Concordant.

Luijpen, William A. What Can You Say About God? Except God. LC 76-171103. 1971. pap. 1.95 (ISBN 0-8091-1713-4). Paulist Pr.
MacDonald, William. There's a Way Back to God. pap. 1.25 (ISBN 0-937396-42-7). Walterick Pubs.
McGinty, Park. Interpretation & Dionysos: Method in the Study of a God. (Religon & Reason Ser.: No. 16). 1978. 37.75x (ISBN 90-279-7844-1). Mouton.
Machen, J. Gresham. Christian Faith in the Modern World. 1967. pap. 3.95 (ISBN 0-8028-1120-5). Eerdmans.
Machlachlan, Lewis. God Face to Face. 1968. pap. 3.50 (ISBN 0-227-67728-5). Attic Pr.
MacIntosh, H. R. The Highway of God. (Scholar As Preacher Ser.). 263p. 1952. Repr. of 1931 ed. text ed. 7.75 (ISBN 0-567-04424-6). Attic Pr.
Maclean, Angus H. The Idea of God in Protestant Religious Education. LC 75-177033. (Columbia University. Teachers College. Contributions to Education: No. 410). Repr. of 1930 ed. 17.50 (ISBN 0-404-55410-5). AMS Pr.
McLean, George, ed. Traces of God in a Secular Culture. new ed. LC 73-3141. 401p. (Orig.). 1973. pap. 5.95 (ISBN 0-8189-0268-X). Alba.
MacMaster, Eve. God's Family. (Stories of God & His People: No. 1). (Illus.). 168p. (gr. 3 up). 1981. pap. 5.95 (ISBN 0-686-73514-5). Herald Pr.
McPherson, Thomas. The Argument from Design. LC 72-77774. (New Studies in the Philosophy of Religion). 96p. 1972. 12.95 (ISBN 0-312-04865-3). St Martin.
McTaggart, John. Some Dogmas of Religion. LC 7-7484. 1968. Repr. of 1906 ed. 14.00 (ISBN 0-527-60000-8). Kraus Repr.
Madden, Edward H., et al. The Idea of God: Philosophical Perspectives. (American Lecture Philosophy). 196p. 1968. photocopy ed. spiral 16.75 (ISBN 0-398-01190-7). C C Thomas.
Mangan, Celine. I Am with You: Biblical Experiences of God. 1.95 (ISBN 0-685-62266-5). M Glazier.
Marsh, F. E. Living God's Way. LC 80-8073. 224p. (Reprint of The Spiritual Life, 1830 ed.). 1981. pap. 4.95 (ISBN 0-8254-3233-2). Kregel.
Martin, Ralph. Hungry for God. 1976. pap. 1.50 (ISBN 0-89129-040-0). Jove Pubns.
Masterson, Patrick. Atheism & Alienation: A Study of the Philosophical Sources of Contemporary Atheism. LC 76-160424. 204p. 1971. 7.95x (ISBN 0-268-00452-8); pap. 2.95x (ISBN 0-268-00496-X). U of Notre Dame Pr.
Matczak, Sebastian A., ed. God in Contemporary Thought: A Philosophical Perspective. LC 75-31391. (Philosophical Questions Ser.: No. 10). 1977. 55.00x (ISBN 0-912116-12-9). Learned Pubns.
Mathias, Willis D. Ideas of God & Conduct. LC 71-177059. (Columbia University. Teachers College. Contributions to Education: No. 874). Repr. of 1943 ed. 17.50 (ISBN 0-404-55874-7). AMS Pr.
Mays, Benjamin E. Negro's God As Reflected in His Literature. LC 69-16578. (Illus.). Repr. of 1938 ed. 16.50x (ISBN 0-8371-1139-0, Pub. by Negro U Pr). Greenwood.
Mercado, Benjamin, ed. El Testimonio De Dios. Flores, Rhode, tr. 148p. (Span.). 1980. pap. 1.60 (ISBN 0-686-77612-7). Life Pubs Intl.
Moncure, Jane B. How Beautiful God's Gifts. Buerger, Jane, ed. (Illus.). 32p. 1980. 4.95 (ISBN 0-89565-172-6, 4923). Standard Pub.
Mooney, Christopher F., ed. Presence & Absence of God. LC 68-8748. 1969. 15.00 (ISBN 0-8232-0810-9). Fordham.
Mulford, Elisha. The Republic of God: An Institute of Theology. LC 75-3291. Repr. of 1881 ed. 18.00 (ISBN 0-404-59277-5). AMS Pr.
Muller, Olga E. Let There Be God. LC 66-23436. 1967. 3.00 (ISBN 0-8022-1169-0). Philos Lib.
Mullet, Rosa M. God's Marvelous Work, Bk. 2. 1981. write for info. (ISBN 0-686-25256-X); tchr's ed. avail. (ISBN 0-686-25257-8). Rod & Staff.
Murphree, Jon T. A Loving God & a Suffering World. 144p. (Orig.). 1981. pap. 3.95 (ISBN 0-87784-877-7). Inter-Varsity.
Murray, Andrew. Secret of Power from on High. (Secret Ser.). (Orig.). 1980. pap. 1.25 (ISBN 0-87508-392-7). Chr Lit.
Nee, T. S. Plan De Dios y los Vencedores. (Span.). Date not set. 5.00 (ISBN 0-686-76330-0). Life Pubs Intl.
--El Testimonio De Dios. (Span.). Date not set. 1.75 (ISBN 0-686-76343-2). Life Pubs Intl.
Nee, T. S. Watchman. Plano De Deus E Os Vencedores. Date not set. 1.20 (ISBN 0-686-76432-3). Life Pubs Intl.
--O Testemunho De Deus. Date not set. 1.20 (ISBN 0-686-76441-2). Life Pubs Intl.
Neill, Stephen. The Christians' God. 1980. 1.25 (ISBN 0-686-28774-6). Forward Movement.
Nicholas Of Cusa. The Vision of God. Gurney, Emma, tr. LC 60-9104. pap. 3.95 (ISBN 0-8044-6594-0). Ungar.
Nixon, Joan L. When God Listens. LC 75-56878. 1978. 4.95 (ISBN 0-87973-379-9); pap. 2.50 (ISBN 0-87973-359-4). Our Sunday Visitor.
Ochs, Robert. God Is More Present Than You Think. LC 70-174586. 64p. 1970. pap. 1.95 (ISBN 0-8091-1580-8). Paulist Pr.
Ogilvie, Lloyd J. Autobiography of God. LC 78-53355. 1981. pap. 5.95 (ISBN 0-8307-0791-3, 5415106). Regal.
Oman, John. Dialogue with God. 1950. pap. 4.95 (ISBN 0-227-67441-3). Attic Pr.
Otis, George. The God They Never Knew. 1978. pap. 3.95 (ISBN 0-89728-011-3, 678276). Omega Pubns OR.
--Thunder of His Power. 1978. 5.95 (ISBN 0-89728-012-1). Omega Pubns OR.
Ott, Heinrich. God. LC 73-5350. 128p. 1974. pap. 4.50 (ISBN 0-8042-0590-6). John Knox.
Packer, J. I. Knowing God. LC 73-81573. 1973. 9.95 (ISBN 0-87784-867-X); pap. 4.95 (ISBN 0-87784-770-3). Inter-Varsity.
Palms, Roger C. Seu Futuro Esta Na Maos...Deus. Date not set. 1.30 (ISBN 0-686-76438-2). Life Pubs Intl.
Pattison, A. Seth. Idea of God in the Light of Recent Philosophy: Gifford Lectures Delivered in the University of Aberdeen, 1912 & 1913. 2nd ed. rev. ed. Repr. of 1920 ed. 18.00 (ISBN 0-527-81500-4). Kraus Repr.
Pentecost, J. Dwight. Problemas Do Homen Resposta... Date not set. 1.60 (ISBN 0-686-76433-1). Life Pubs Intl.
Pettazzoni, Rattaele. The All Knowing God: Researches into the Early Religion & Cultlure. Bolle, Kees W., ed. LC 77-79150. (Mythology Ser.). (Illus.). 1978. Repr. of 1956 ed. lib. bdg. 30.00x (ISBN 0-405-10559-2). Arno.
Phillips, John B. Your God Is Too Small. 8.95 (ISBN 0-02-597410-6). Macmillan.
Pink, Arthur W. Gleanings in the Godhead. 256p. 10.95 (ISBN 0-8024-2977-7). Moody.
Le Plan De Dieu. Date not set. 14.00 (ISBN 0-686-76386-6). Life Pubs Intl.
Qamar, J. God's Existence & Contemporary Science. pap. 1.00 (ISBN 0-686-18452-1). Kazi Pubns.
Ramm, Bernard. The Devil, Seven Wormwoods, & God. LC 77-83302. 1977. 6.95 (ISBN 0-8499-0041-7). Word Bks.
Reichenbach, Bruce R. Cosmological Argument: A Reassessment. (Illus.). 160p. 1972. 14.50 (ISBN 0-398-02387-5). C C Thomas.
Rice, Richard. Openness of God. (Horizon Ser.). 96p. 1981. pap. write for info. (ISBN 0-8127-0303-0). Review & Herald.
Robertson, C. Alton. Is God Still Here: Q-Book No. 15. (Orig.). 1968. pap. 0.75 ea. (ISBN 0-377-86371-8). Friend Pr.
Robinson, John A. Exploration into God. LC 67-26529. 1967. 2.95 (ISBN 0-8047-0322-1). Stanford U Pr.
--The Human Face of God. LC 73-78. 1979. softcover 5.95 (ISBN 0-664-24241-3). Westminster.
Rodriguez, Roger. Senhor, Faze-Me Chorar! Date not set. 1.50 (ISBN 0-686-76439-0). Life Pubs Intl.
Rollins, Marion J. The God of the Old Testament in Relation to War. LC 72-176551. (Columbia University. Teachers College. Contributions to Education: No. 263). Repr. of 1927 ed. 17.50 (ISBN 0-404-55263-3). AMS Pr.
Rosenthal, Stanley. One God or Three? 1978. pap. text ed. 1.25 (ISBN 0-87508-464-8). Chr Lit.
Royce, Josiah. Conception of God. 1898. Repr. 32.00 (ISBN 0-403-00309-1). Scholarly.
Schillebeeckx, E. & Van Iersel, B., eds. A Personal God. (Concilium Ser.: Vol. 103). 1977. pap. 4.95 (ISBN 0-8245-0263-9). Crossroad NY.
Seek Ye First. pap. 1.25 (ISBN 0-937396-38-9). Walterick Pubs.
Shea, John. Stories of God: An Unauthorized Biography. 1978. pap. 5.95 (ISBN 0-88347-085-3). Thomas More.
Shoemaker, Samuel M. By the Power of God. 1977. Repr. 3.25 (ISBN 0-8499-2817-6, 2817-6). Word Bks.
Siltman, Ellie. God Talks to Me. 1980. pap. 4.95 (ISBN 0-88270-428-1). Logos.
Smith, Joyce M. A Rejoicing Heart. 1979. pap. 1.75 (ISBN 0-8423-5418-2). Tyndale.
Solovyev, Vladimir. God, Man & the Church. Attwater, Donald, tr. from Rus. 1975. 8.95 (ISBN 0-227-67690-4). Attic Pr.
Somervell, R. Ursula, compiled by. Thank God: An Anthology of Praise. 1964. pap. 1.00 (ISBN 0-227-67676-9). Attic Pr.
Spicer, Jack. Fifteen False Propositions About God. 1974. pap. 2.50 (ISBN 0-686-28709-6). Man-Root.
Staten, John C. Conscience & the Reality of God. (Religion & Reason Ser.). 1979. write for info. Mouton.
Staton, Knofel. How to Know the Will of God. LC 78-62707. 96p. (Orig.). 1979. pap. 1.95 (ISBN 0-87239-236-8, 40073). Standard Pub.
Steeman, T. What's Wrong with God. McNamee, Fantan, ed. (Synthesis Ser). pap. 0.65 (ISBN 0-8199-0391-4). Franciscan Herald.
Steeves, Paul. Getting to Know God. LC 73-81574. 120p. 1973. pap. 2.50 (ISBN 0-87784-357-0). Inter-Varsity.
Steiner, Robert A. The Truth Shall Make You Free: An Inquiry into the Legend of God. LC 80-80646. (Illus.). 56p. (Orig.). (gr. 6 up). 1980. pap. 2.95 (ISBN 0-9604044-0-6). Penseur Pr.
Steuer, Alexel D. & McClendon, James W., Jr., eds. Is God God? LC 81-1927. 288p. (Orig.). 1981. pap. 9.95 (ISBN 0-687-19703-1). Abingdon.
Swinburne, Richard. The Existence of God. 1979. 39.00x (ISBN 0-19-824611-0). Oxford U Pr.
Tchurmin, Avrhum Y. Meditations from an Exploration of the Ultimate Mysteries. LC 72-85932. 110p. 1972. 3.95 (ISBN 0-8158-0295-1). Chris Mass.
Thomas Aquinas, St. Summa Contra Gentiles, 4 bks. Incl. Bk. 1. God. Pegis, Anton C., tr. 317p. text ed. 11.95x (ISBN 0-268-01677-1); pap. 4.95x (ISBN 0-685-61134-5); Bk. 2. Creation. Anderson, James F., tr. 351p. text ed. 12.95x (ISBN 0-268-01679-8); pap. 4.45x (ISBN 0-268-01680-1); Bk. 3. Providence, 2 bks. in 1. Bourke, Vernon J., tr. 560p. text ed. 10.95x (ISBN 0-268-01681-X); pap. 4.95x (ISBN 0-268-01682-8); Bk. 4. Salvation. O'Neil, Charles J., tr. 360p. text ed. 12.95x (ISBN 0-268-01683-6); pap. 5.95x (ISBN 0-268-01684-4). LC 75-19883. 1975. U of Notre Dame Pr.
Thompson, Bert. Theistic Evolution. pap. 5.50 (ISBN 0-89315-300-1). Lambert Bk.
Tozer, A. W. La Busqueda De Dios. Bruchez, Dardo, tr. 130p. (Orig.). 1979. pap. 2.00 (ISBN 0-87509-162-8); pap. 1.50 mass mkt. (ISBN 0-87509-159-8). Chr Pubns.
Treash, Gordon. Der Einzig Mogliche Beweisgrund: The One Possible Basis for a Demonstration of the Existence of God. LC 77-86227. 1978. 20.00 (ISBN 0-913870-37-4). Abaris Bks.
Turner, J. E. The Revelation of Deity. Repr. of 1931 ed. 12.00 (ISBN 0-527-91170-4). Kraus Repr.
Vedder, E. P., Jr. The Man of God. (Let's Discuss It Ser.). pap. 0.95 (ISBN 0-686-13255-6); pap. 9.50 per doz. (ISBN 0-686-13256-4). Believers Bkshelf.
Verheijen, J. A. Het Hoogste Wezen Bij De Manggaraiers. Repr. of 1951 ed. 38.50 (ISBN 0-384-64290-X). Johnson Repr.
Vincent, M. O. God, Sex & You. (Trumpet Bks). 1976. pap. 1.75 (ISBN 0-87981-058-0). Holman.
Vinoi, Lawrence. God & Man: The Essential Knowledge Which Everyone, but Absolutely Everyone Ought to Possess About Human Nature & the Nature of God & How the Two Are Related. (Essential Knowledge Ser. Books). (Illus.). 1978. plastic spiral bdg. 24.75 (ISBN 0-89266-118-6). Am Classical Coll Pr.
Ward, Bob. Breakthrough. 1979. pap. 2.25 (ISBN 0-89337-009-6). Maranatha Hse.
Ward, Keith. The Concept of God. LC 74-82271. 256p. 1975. 19.95 (ISBN 0-312-15925-0). St Martin.
Warren, Thomas B. & Matson, Wallace I. Warren-Matson Debate on the Existence of God. LC 78-64546. 1979. 13.95 (ISBN 0-934916-41-1); pap. 9.95 (ISBN 0-934916-45-4). Natl Christian Pr.
Warren, Thomas B. & Flew, A. G. N., eds. Warren-Flew Debate on the Existence of God. 1977. 13.95 (ISBN 0-934916-40-3). Natl Christian Pr.
Watson, David. Is Anyone There? & Does It Really Matter? 108p. 1981. pap. 3.95 (ISBN 0-87788-395-5). Shaw Pubs.
Webb, Clement C. Divine Personality & Human Life: Being the Gifford Lectures Delivered in the University of Aberdeen in the Years 1918 & 1919, Second Course. facsimile ed. LC 77-37917. (Select Bibliographies Reprint Ser.). Repr. of 1920 ed. 19.00 (ISBN 0-8369-6754-2). Arno.
--God & Personality: Being the Gifford Lectures Delivered in the University of Aberdeen in the Years 1918 & 1919. facsimile ed. LC 76-164632. (Select Bibliographies Reprint Ser.). Repr. of 1919 ed. 18.00 (ISBN 0-8369-5916-7). Arno.
Whitworth, John McKelvie. God's Blueprints. 1975. 25.00x (ISBN 0-7100-8002-6). Routledge & Kegan.
Wilmont, Laurence. Whitehead & God: Prolegomena to Theological Reconstruction. 200p. 1979. text ed. 13.75 (ISBN 0-88920-070-X, Pub. by Laurier U Pr Canada). Humanities.
Wilson, Margery. God: Here & Now. 1978. pap. 4.95 (ISBN 0-87707-207-8). CSA Pr.
Yogananda, Paramahansa. Man's Eternal Quest. LC 75-17183. 484p. 1975. 7.95 (ISBN 0-87612-231-4). Self Realization.
Yohn, Rick. What Every Christian Should Know About God: A Study Manual. LC 76-20396. 1976. 2.95 (ISBN 0-89081-054-0). Harvest Hse.
Zubiri, Xavier. Nature, History, God. Fowler, Thomas B., Jr., tr. from Span. LC 80-1355. 441p. 1981. lib. bdg. 23.25 (ISBN 0-8191-1530-4); pap. text ed. 14.00 (ISBN 0-8191-1531-2). U Pr of Amer.

GOD–ANGER

see God–Wrath

GOD–ART

see also Gods in Art; Jesus Christ–Art

Nichols, Aidan. Theology & Symbol from Genesis to the Twentieth Century: Theology & Symbol from Genesis to the Twentieth Century. LC 80-81443. 192p. 1980. pap. 7.95 (ISBN 0-8091-2300-2). Paulist Pr.
Stucki, Margaret E. War on Light: The Destruction of the Image of God in Man Through Modern Art. 1975. 10.00 (ISBN 0-686-23419-7). Birds' Meadow Pub.

GOD–ATTRIBUTES

see also Providence and Government of God

Alleine, Richard. Heaven Opened. (Summit Books). 1978. pap. 3.95 (ISBN 0-8010-0136-6). Baker Bk.
Davidheiser, Bolton. To Be As God. pap. 1.50 (ISBN 0-87552-250-5). Presby & Reformed.
Derham, William. Physico-Theology: A Demonstration of the Being & Attributes of God, from His Works of Creation. Egerton, Frank N., 3rd, ed. LC 77-74212. (History of Ecology Ser.). 1978. Repr. of 1716 ed. lib. bdg. 28.00 (ISBN 0-405-10383-2). Arno.
Farnell, Lewis R. The Attributes of God. LC 77-27205. (Gifford Lectures: 1924-25). Repr. of 1925 ed. 24.00 (ISBN 0-404-60475-7). AMS Pr.
Frost, William P. Visions of the Divine. 1977. pap. text ed. 6.50 (ISBN 0-8191-0310-1). U Pr of Amer.
Henry, Carl F. God, Revelation & Authority: God Who Speaks & Shows, Vols. 3 & 4. 1979. 19.95 ea. Vol. 3 (ISBN 0-8499-0091-3). Vol. 4 (ISBN 0-8499-0126-X). Word Bks.
Knudsen, Harald. Gottesbeweise im Deutschen Idealismus: Die modaltheoretische Begruendung des Absoluten, dargestellt an Kant, Hegel und Weisse. (Theologische Bibliothek Toepelmann 23). vi, 280p. 1972. 40.00x (ISBN 3-11-003787-4). De Gruyter.
Maloney, George S. A Theology of Uncreated Energies of God. (Pere Marquette Lecture Ser.). 1978. 6.95 (ISBN 0-87462-516-5). Marquette.
Morich, Randy. How Does God Reward. 1979. pap. 2.25 (ISBN 0-89337-013-4). Maranatha Hse.
Ochs, Carol. Behind the Sex of God: Toward a New Consciousness - Transcending Matriarchy & Patriarchy. 1977. pap. 4.95 (ISBN 0-8070-1113-4, BP576). Beacon Pr.
Pike, Nelson. God & Timelessness. LC 74-100988. (Studies in Ethics & the Philosophy of Religion Ser). 1970. 7.00x (ISBN 0-8052-3332-6). Schocken.
Pink, A. W. Los Attributos De Dios. 2.95 (ISBN 0-686-12561-4). Banner of Truth.
Pink, Arthur W. Attributes of God. 1961. pap. 2.95 (ISBN 0-685-19823-5). Reiner.
Plantinga, Alvin. Does God Have a Nature? LC 80-6585. (Aquinas Lecture Ser.). 1980. 6.95 (ISBN 0-87462-145-3). Marquette.
Scharlemann, Robert P. The Being of God: Theology & the Experience of Truth. 224p. 1981. 14.95 (ISBN 0-8164-0494-1). Seabury.
Schillebeeckx, Edward & Metz, Johannes B. God As Father, Vol. 143. (Concilium 1981). 128p. (Orig.). 1981. pap. 6.95 (ISBN 0-8164-2310-5). Seabury.
Scragg, Walter R. Directions: A Look at the Paths of Life. LC 77-78101. (Horizon Ser.). 1977. pap. 4.50 (ISBN 0-8127-0136-4). Review & Herald.
Strauss, Lehman. First Person. LC 67-20931. 1967. 5.50 (ISBN 0-87213-815-1). Loizeaux.
Swain, Joseph R. What Does God Do All Day? 1977. 7.00 (ISBN 0-682-48919-0, Testament). Exposition.
Swinburne, Richard. The Coherence of Theism. (Clarendon Library of Logic & Philosophy). 1977. 39.00x (ISBN 0-19-824410-X). Oxford U Pr.
Synan, J. A. The Trinity, or the Tri-Personal Being of God. pap. 2.95 (ISBN 0-911866-00-0). Advocate.
Tozer, A. W. The Knowledge of the Holy. LC 75-12279. 128p. 1978. pap. 4.95 (ISBN 0-06-068412-7, RD 291, HarpR). Har-Row.
Walters, Julie & De Leu, Barbara. God Is Like: Three Parables for Little Children. (Illus.). 96p. 1974. pap. 1.65 (ISBN 0-87793-073-2). Ave Maria.
Webber, Robert E. God Still Speaks. 244p. 1980. 10.95 (ISBN 0-8407-5189-3). Nelson.
Williamson, Clark M. God Is Never Absent. 1977. pap. 2.50 (ISBN 0-8272-1230-5). Bethany Pr.

GOD–BIBLICAL TEACHING

Barrosse, Thomas J. God Exists. (Orig.). 1963. pap. 1.25x (ISBN 0-268-00111-1). U of Notre Dame Pr.

Bryson, Harold T. Portraits of God. LC 77-82401. 1978. 4.95 (ISBN 0-8054-5160-9). Broadman.

Crenshaw, James L. Hymnic Affirmation of Divine Justice. LC 75-22349. (Society of Biblical Literature. Dissertation Ser.). 180p. 1975. pap. 7.50 (ISBN 0-89130-016-3, 060124). Scholars Pr Ca.

De Dietrich, Suzanne. The Witnessing Community: The Biblical Record of God's Purpose. 1978. pap. 3.95 (ISBN 0-664-24199-9). Westminster.

Gray, John. The Biblical Doctrine of the Reign of God. 414p. Repr. of 1979 ed. text ed. 32.95x (ISBN 0-567-09300-X). Attic Pr.

Hamerton-Kelly, Robert. God the Father: Theology & Patriarchy in the Teaching of Jesus, No. 4. Brueggemann, Walter & Donahue, John R., eds. LC 78-54551. (Overtures to Biblical Theology Ser). 144p. 1979. pap. 5.95 (ISBN 0-8006-1528-X, 1-1528). Fortress.

Henry, Carl F. God, Revelation & Authority: God Who Speaks & Shows, 2 vols. Incl. Vol. 1 (ISBN 0-87680-477-6, 80477); Vol. 2 (ISBN 0-87680-485-7, 80485). LC 76-15936. 1976. 19.95 ea. Word Bks.

Hodges, Zane C. The Hungry Inherit: Whetting Your Appetite for God. new ed. LC 80-23676. (Illus.). 1980. pap. 5.95 (ISBN 0-930014-50-2). Multnomah.

McDowell, Josh. Evidence Growth Guide: Vol. 2, Uniqueness of the Bible. 80p. (Orig.). 1981. wkbk. 2.95 (ISBN 0-86605-019-1). Campus Crusade.

Parke-Taylor, G. H. Yahweh: The Divine Name in the Bible. 134p. 1975. text ed. 11.00 (ISBN 0-88920-014-9, Pub. by Laurier U Pr Canada). Humanities.

Spittler, Russell P. God the Father. (Radiant Life). 1976. pap. 1.25 (ISBN 0-88243-898-0, 02-0898, Radiant Bks); teacher's ed 2.50 (ISBN 0-88243-170-6, 32-0170). Gospel Pub.

Yohn, Rick. God's Answer to Life's Problems: A Study Manual. LC 76-17438. 1976. 2.95 (ISBN 0-89081-050-8). Harvest Hse.

GOD–COMPARATIVE STUDIES

Roberts, Brigham H. Mormon Doctrine of Deity: The Roberts-Van der Donckt Discussion. 296p. 1975. 8.50 (ISBN 0-88290-058-7). Horizon Utah.

GOD–FEAR

see Fear of God

GOD–GLORY

see Glory of God

GOD–HISTORY OF DOCTRINES

Durrant, Michael. Theology & Intelligibility. (Studies in Ethics & the Philosophy of Religion). (Illus.). 222p. 1973. 16.95x (ISBN 0-7100-7488-3). Routledge & Kegan.

Empson, William. Milton's God. LC 78-14409. 1978. Repr. of 1961 ed. lib. bdg. 19.50x (ISBN 0-313-21021-7, EMMG). Greenwood.

Fortman, Edmund J. Theology of God: Commentary. 1968. pap. text ed. 5.95 (ISBN 0-02-816650-7). Glencoe.

Hick, John H. Existence of God. 1964. pap. 3.95 (ISBN 0-02-085450-1). Macmillan.

Lossky, Vladimir. The Vision of God. 139p. 1963. 6.95 (ISBN 0-913836-19-2). St Vladimirs.

Macquarrie, John. New Directions in Theology Today. (New Directions in Philosophy Today: Vol. 3). 1967. pap. 2.85 (ISBN 0-664-24787-3). Westminster.

Murray, John C. Problem of God: Yesterday & Today. (St. Thomas More Lectures Ser.: No. 1). (Orig.). 1964. 12.50x (ISBN 0-300-00781-7); pap. 3.95x (ISBN 0-300-00171-1, Y138). Yale U Pr.

Patterson, Robert L. The Conception of God in the Philosophy of Thomas Aquinas. 508p. 1977. Repr. of 1935 ed. lib. bdg. 28.50 (ISBN 0-915172-27-5). Richwood Pub.

Rooney, E. Gene. God's Bill of Rights. 1980. 8.95 (ISBN 0-8062-1440-6). Carlton.

GOD–IMMANENCE

see Immanence of God

GOD–JUVENILE LITERATURE

Boyer, Linda. God Made Me. LC 81-50677. (A Happy Day Bk.). (Illus.). 24p. (Orig.). (ps-1). 1981. pap. 0.98 (ISBN 0-87239-464-6, 3597). Standard Pub.

Bragg, Joseph H., Jr. I Wonder About God's World. 1977. student bk. 0.90 (ISBN 0-687-18608-0); leader's guide 2.35 (ISBN 0-687-18607-2); resource packet 6.95 (ISBN 0-687-18609-9). Abingdon.

Cone, Molly. About God. (Shema Storybooks: No. 4). (Illus.). 64p. (gr. 1-2). 1973. pap. 5.00 (ISBN 0-8074-0126-9, 101084). UAHC.

Dean, Bessie. Aprendamos el Plan De Dios. Balderas, Eduardo, tr. from Eng. LC 80-82256. (Books for LDS Children Ser.). Orig. Title: Let's Learn God's Plan. (Illus.). 64p. (Orig., Span.). (gr. k-3). pap. text ed. 4.50 (ISBN 0-88290-135-4). Horizon Utah.

Dueland, Joy V. Filled up Full. 2nd ed. (Illus.). 32p. (gr. k-2). 1974. pap. 2.50g (ISBN 0-87510-100-3). Chr Science.

Fitch, Florence. Book About God. LC 53-6735. (Illus.). (gr. k-3). 1953. PLB 7.92 (ISBN 0-688-51253-4). Lothrop.

Gaither, Gloria. I Guess God Thought of Everything. LC 75-18616. (Especially for Children Ser.: Vol. 3). (Illus.). 32p. (ps-8). 1975. 4.50 (ISBN 0-914850-73-3). Impact Tenn.

Gerlinger, Lorena. God Has a Reason. (Illus.). 1976. 3.75 (ISBN 0-686-15469-X). L Gerlinger.

Gilbert, Sr. Marjorie. Come Little Christians. (Illus.). 64p. (Orig.). (ps-1). 1975. pap. 1.50 (ISBN 0-87973-376-4). Our Sunday Visitor.

--More Stories for Little Christians. (Illus.). 64p. (Orig.). (ps-1). 1975. pap. 1.50 (ISBN 0-87973-380-2). Our Sunday Visitor.

Goddard, Carrie Lou. Isn't It a Wonder! LC 75-15664. (Illus.). (gr. k-3). 1976. 7.95 (ISBN 0-687-19715-5). Abingdon.

God's Plan for Air. 16p. (ps-3). 1980. pap. 1.50 (ISBN 0-8024-3060-0). Moody.

God's Plan for Animals. 16p. (ps-3). Date not set. pap. 1.50 (ISBN 0-8024-3061-9). Moody.

God's Plan for Birds. 16p. (ps-3). 1980. pap. 1.50 (ISBN 0-8024-3062-7). Moody.

God's Plan for Insects. 16p. (ps-3). 1980. pap. 1.50 (ISBN 0-8024-3063-5). Moody.

God's Plan for Me. 16p. (ps-3). 1980. pap. 1.50 (ISBN 0-8024-3064-3). Moody.

God's Plan for Plants. 16p. (ps-3). 1980. pap. 1.50 (ISBN 0-8024-3065-1). Moody.

God's Plan for Seasons. 16p. (ps-3). 1980. pap. 1.50 (ISBN 0-8024-3067-8). Moody.

God's Plan for Seeds. 16p. (ps-3). 1980. pap. 1.50 (ISBN 0-8024-3068-6). Moody.

God's Plan for the Seashore. 16p. (ps-3). 1980. pap. 1.50 (ISBN 0-8024-3065-1). Moody.

Hein, Lucille E. Thank You, God. (Illus.). 32p. 1981. pap. 3.50 (ISBN 0-8170-0912-4). Judson.

--Walking in God's World. (Illus.). 32p. (Orig.). (ps). 1972. pap. 1.50 (ISBN 0-8170-0568-4). Judson.

Hutson, Joan. I Think...I Know: A Poster Book About God. (Illus.). 32p. (Orig.). (gr. 2-4). 1979. pap. 1.95 (ISBN 0-87793-186-0). Ave Maria.

Jones, Mary A. Tell Me About God. rev. ed. LC 67-15727. (ps-3). 1967. pap. 3.95 (ISBN 0-528-87656-2). Rand.

Larson, Nora E. The Alphabet of God. LC 81-66071. (Illus.). 56p. (Orig.). (gr. 1-4). 1981. pap. 3.25 (ISBN 0-87516-450-1). De Vorss.

LeBar, Mary. How God Gives Us Apples. (A Happy Day Book). (Illus.). 24p. (gr. k-5). 1979. 0.98 (ISBN 0-87239-357-7, 3627). Standard Pub.

--How God Gives Us Bread. (A Happy Day Book). (Illus.). 24p. (gr. k-5). 1979. 0.98 (ISBN 0-87239-359-3, 3629). Standard Pub.

--How God Gives Us Peanut Butter. (A Happy Day Book). (Illus.). 24p. (gr. k-5). 1979. 0.98 (ISBN 0-87239-356-9, 3626). Standard Pub.

Marxhausen, Joanne. Three in One: Picture of God. 48p. (gr. k-4). 1973. 6.95 (ISBN 0-570-03419-1, 56-1148). Concordia.

Metropolitan Philaret. On the Law of God: To the Young People of the Church. 1975. pap. 5.00 (ISBN 0-913026-76-X, Synaxis Pr). St Nectarios.

Moskin, Marietta. In Search of God. LC 79-10493. (Illus.). (gr. 5 up). 1979. 10.95 (ISBN 0-689-30719-5). Atheneum.

Murphy, Elspeth. Everybody, Shout Hallelujah! (David & I Talk to God Ser.). (Illus.). 24p. 1981. pap. 1.75 (ISBN 0-89191-369-6, 53694). Cook.

--Sometimes I Get Lonely. LC 80-70251. (David & I Talk to God Ser.). (Illus.). 24p. 1981. pap. 1.75 (ISBN 0-89191-367-X, 53678). Cook.

Peterson, Lorraine. If God Loves Me, Why Can't I Get My Locker Open? 192p. (Orig.). (gr. 6-12). 1980. pap. 3.95 (ISBN 0-87123-251-0, 210251). Bethany Hse.

Rabens, Neil W. No One but God. (gr. k-3). 1978. pap. 1.69 (ISBN 0-87239-178-7, 2312). Standard Pub.

Richards, Lawrence O. How I Can Experience God. (Answers for Youth Ser.). 1980. pap. 2.95 (ISBN 0-310-38991-7). Zondervan.

Spinelli, Jackaline. Where Is God? (Color Us Wonderful Ser.). (ps). 1971. pap. 0.35 (ISBN 0-8091-6520-1). Paulist Pr.

Swafford, Z. W. Knowing God. rev. ed. 32p. (gr. k-2). 1980. tchrs' ed. 2.00 (ISBN 0-89114-090-5). Baptist Pub Hse.

Watson, Elizabeth E. God Knows You. LC 81-50678. (A Happy Day Bk.). (Illus.). 24p. (Orig.). (ps-1). 1981. pap. 0.98 (ISBN 0-87239-463-8, 3596). Standard Pub.

--Where Are You, God? (Illus.). 1977. bds. 2.95 (ISBN 0-8054-4235-9). Broadman.

Wolcott, Carolyn M. I Can See What God Does. LC 69-16940. (Illus.). (gr. k-2). 1969. 4.95 (ISBN 0-687-18424-X). Abingdon.

Wolf, Ingrid. A B See God. (Illus.). 32p. (gr. 1-3). 1980. pap. 1.25 (ISBN 0-89622-128-8). Twenty-Third.

--Count on God. (Illus.). 32p. (gr. 1-3). 1980. pap. 1.25 (ISBN 0-89622-129-6). Twenty-Third.

Ziegler, Sandy. Friends. Buerger, Jane, ed. 112p. 1980. 5.95 (ISBN 0-89565-174-2, 4931). Standard Pub.

GOD–KNOWABLENESS

Arnold, Eberhard. The Inner Land, Vol. 3: The Experience of God. LC 75-9720. 1975. 3.95 (ISBN 0-87486-155-1). Plough.

Baba, Meher. God to Man & Man to God. Purdom, Charles, ed. 1975. pap. 3.95 (ISBN 0-913078-21-2). Sheriar Pr.

Barth, Karl. The Knowledge of God & the Service of God According to the Teaching of the Reformation: Recalling the Scottish Confession of 1560. LC 77-27187. (Gifford Lectures: 1937-38). Repr. of 1939 ed. 24.00 (ISBN 0-404-60495-1). AMS Pr.

Bryden, W. W. The Christian's Knowledge of God. 5.50 (ISBN 0-227-67434-0). Attic Pr.

Christensen, Chuck & Christensen, Winnie. How to Listen When God Speaks. LC 78-73294. 1979. pap. 1.75 (ISBN 0-87788-355-6). Shaw Pubs.

Deratany, Edward. When God Calls You. LC 76-6539. 192p. 1976. pap. 3.95 (ISBN 0-8407-5601-1). Nelson.

Dunne, John S. A Search for God in Time & Memory. LC 76-20165. 1977. text ed. 10.95x (ISBN 0-268-01689-5); pap. 3.95 (ISBN 0-268-01673-9). U of Notre Dame Pr.

Eddy, George S. Man Discovers God. facs. ed. LC 68-24849. (Essay Index Reprint Ser). 1968. Repr. of 1942 ed. 16.00 (ISBN 0-8369-0401-X). Arno.

Fitti, Charles J. Between God & Man. LC 78-50527. 48p. 1978. 6.75 (ISBN 0-8022-2225-0). Philos Lib.

Foster, Timothy. You & God: The Abba Relationship. 120p. 1980. pap. 2.95 (ISBN 0-88207-221-8). Victor Bks.

Giardini, Fabio. Loving Awareness of God's Presence in Prayer. LC 78-9654. 1978. 4.50 (ISBN 0-8189-0370-8). Alba.

Gilson, Etienne. God & Philosophy. (Powell Lectures Ser.). 1941. 15.00x (ISBN 0-300-00491-5); pap. 3.45x (ISBN 0-300-00097-9, Y8). Yale U Pr.

Golz, Lud. A Daily Guide to Knowing God. 1978. pap. 4.95 (ISBN 0-8423-0510-6). Tyndale.

Gwatkin, Henry M. The Knowledge of God & Its Historical Development, 2 vols. LC 77-27219. (Gifford Lectures: 1904-05). 1978. Repr. of 1906 ed. Set. 49.50 (ISBN 0-404-60490-0). AMS Pr.

Hartshorne, Charles. The Logic of Perfection & Other Essays in Neoclassical Metaphysics. LC 61-11286. 335p. 1972. pap. 6.95 (ISBN 0-87548-037-3). Open Court.

Hazelton, Roger. Knowing the Living God. LC 69-11679. (Orig.). 1969. pap. 1.50 (ISBN 0-8170-0417-3). Judson.

Hill, William J. Knowing the Unknown God. LC 70-145465. 1971. 12.00 (ISBN 0-8022-2049-5). Philos Lib.

Howard, David M. How Come, God? Reflections from Job About God & Puzzled Man. (Illus.). 1977. pap. 2.95 (ISBN 0-87981-075-0). Holman.

Humitz, R. Man Meets God. 1971. pap. 4.00 (ISBN 0-02-644500-X); tchr's manual 2.68 (ISBN 0-02-644520-4, 64452); tchr's ed. 6.16 (ISBN 0-02-644510-7). Benziger Pub Co.

McLelland, Joseph C. God the Anonymous. LC 76-27405. (Patristic Monograph Ser: No. 4). 1976. pap. 6.50 (ISBN 0-915646-03-X). Phila Patristic.

Maritain, Jacques. Approaches to God. O'Reilly, Peter, tr. from Fr. LC 78-16555. 1978. Repr. of 1954 ed. lib. bdg. 16.50x (ISBN 0-313-20606-6, MATG). Greenwood.

Morich, Randy. Communicating with God. 1979. pap. 1.65 (ISBN 0-89337-010-X). Maranatha Hse.

My Most Memorable Encounter with God. pap. 3.95 (ISBN 0-8423-4655-4). Tyndale.

Neville, Robert C. God the Creator: On the Transcendence & Presence of God. LC 68-13128. (Illus.). 1968. 12.50x (ISBN 0-226-57641-8). U of Chicago Pr.

O'Connor, William R. Natural Desire for God: Aquinas Lectures. 1948. 6.95 (ISBN 0-87462-113-5). Marquette.

Owen, H. P. Christian Knowledge of God. 1969. text ed. 37.75x (ISBN 0-485-11107-1, Athlone Pr). Humanities.

Packer, James I., pref. by. Knowing God: Study Guide. 1975. pap. 1.95 (ISBN 0-87784-413-5). Inter-Varsity.

Price, Eugenia. What Is God Like? 160p. 1973. 2.25 (ISBN 0-310-31362-7, 10587P). Zondervan.

Rahner, Karl. Spirit in the World. Lynch, William, tr. LC 67-29676. 1968. 13.50 (ISBN 0-8164-1122-0). Crossroad NY.

Roth, Robert J., ed. God Knowable & Unknowable. LC 77-188274. 269p. 1973. 20.00 (ISBN 0-8232-0920-2). Fordham.

Sangster, W. E. Can I Know God? (Sangter Sermon Library). pap. 2.95 (ISBN 0-8010-8058-4). Baker Bk.

Sproul, R. C. Objections Answered. LC 77-90579. 1978. pap. 3.50 (ISBN 0-8307-0584-8, 54-081-05). Regal.

Stevenson, Dwight E. Monday's God. new ed. 128p. (Orig.). 1976. pap. 1.25 (ISBN 0-8272-2309-9). Bethany Pr.

Synan, J. A. The Trinity, or the Tri-Personal Being of God. pap. 2.95 (ISBN 0-911866-00-0). Advocate.

Tozer, A. W. The Pursuit of God. pap. 2.00 (ISBN 0-8423-5110-8). Tyndale.

Tyrrell, Bernard J. Bernard Lonergan's Philosophy of God. LC 73-22205. 224p. 1974. text ed. 12.95x (ISBN 0-268-00540-0). U of Notre Dame Pr.

Wheeler, Gerald. Is God a Committee? (Flame Ser.). 48p. 1975. pap. text ed. 0.95 (ISBN 0-8127-0093-7). Review & Herald.

White, Ellen G. Can We Know God? (Uplook Ser.). 1970. pap. 0.75 (ISBN 0-8163-0067-4, 03035-3). Pacific Pr Pub Assn.

William of St. Thierry, Vol. 3: The Enigma of Faith. LC 74-4465. (Cistercian Fathers Ser.: No. 9). 1974. 7.95 (ISBN 0-87907-309-8). Cistercian Pubns.

GOD–LOVE

Here are entered works on God's love toward man. Works on the love and worship which man accords to God are entered under the heading God–Worship and Love.

Armstrong, Edward. Prayer & God's Infinate Power. 119p. pap. 0.45 (ISBN 0-87509-120-2). Chr Pubns.

Barbotin, Edmond. The Humanity of God. O'Connell, Matthew T., tr. from Fr. LC 76-304. 1976. 12.95x (ISBN 0-88344-184-5). Orbis Bks.

Bertocci, Peter A. The Goodness of God. LC 80-6094. (Illus.). 356p. (Orig.). 1981. lib. bdg. 20.75 (ISBN 0-8191-1636-X); pap. text ed. 12.25 (ISBN 0-8191-1637-8). U Pr of Amer.

Best, W. E. God Forgives Sinners. 1978. pap. 2.95 (ISBN 0-8010-0720-8). Baker Bk.

Bothwell, Sr. Mary. God Guides Us. (Christ Our Life Ser). (Illus.). (gr. 3). 1981. pap. text ed. 3.80 (ISBN 0-8294-0365-5); tchr's ed. 6.95 (ISBN 0-8294-0366-3). Loyola.

Buess, Bob. Favor, the Road to Success. 110p. 1980. pap. 1.25 (ISBN 0-934244-15-4, 317). Sweeter Than Honey.

Bussard, Paul. How to Get Ready to Sleep, How to Get Ready for Surgery, & How to Get Ready to Die: A Thanatology. 1978. 4.00 (ISBN 0-682-49107-1). Exposition.

Castro, Carol C. Welcoming God's Forgiveness. 120p. 1978. pap. text ed. 3.50 (ISBN 0-697-01681-1); leader's guide 4.50 (ISBN 0-697-01682-X); classroom tchr's guide .75 (ISBN 0-686-77605-4); adult resource book, pack/10,10.25 1.05 (ISBN 0-697-01685-4). Wm C Brown.

Charles, Feinberg. Zecharian: God Remembers. pap. 5.95 (ISBN 0-8423-8850-8). Tyndale.

Christenson, Evelyn. Gaining Through Losing. 1980. 8.95 (ISBN 0-88207-795-3); pap. 4.95 (ISBN 0-88207-344-3). Victor Bks.

Come Me Sacaras De Este Apuro, Senor? (Span.). 1979. pap. 1.75 (ISBN 0-8297-0553-8). Life Pubs Intl.

Cooper, Douglas. Living God's Love. LC 74-27171. (Redwood Ser.). 1975. pap. 3.95 (ISBN 0-8163-0176-X, 12523-7). Pacific Pr Pub Assn.

Culver, Robert. The Living God. 1978. pap. 3.95 (ISBN 0-88207-765-1). Victor Bks.

De La Touche, Louise-M. The Sacred Heart & the Priesthood. LC 79-90487. 1979. pap. 5.00 (ISBN 0-89555-128-4). TAN Bks Pubs.

Demaray, Donald E. & Brother Lawrence, eds. The Practice of the Presence of God. (Devotional Classics Ser). 64p. 1975. pap. 1.95 (ISBN 0-8010-2844-2). Baker Bk.

De Waters, Lillian. The Finished Kingdom. 5.95 (ISBN 0-686-05716-3). L De Waters.

--God & Oneself. pap. 3.00 (ISBN 0-686-05705-8). L De Waters.

--God Is All. pap. 0.95 (ISBN 0-686-05711-2). L De Waters.

Diemer, J. Nature & Miracle. 1977. pap. 1.95 (ISBN 0-88906-015-0). Wedge Pub.

Dobson, Theodore. Inner Healing: God's Great Assurance. LC 78-65129. 1978. pap. 3.95 (ISBN 0-8091-2161-1). Paulist Pr.

Douty, Norman. Loving Kindness of the Sovereign God. pap. 0.50 (ISBN 0-685-88383-3). Reiner.

Durland, Frances. Growing in God's Love. LC 80-66806. 1980. pap. 3.25 (ISBN 0-8054-5284-2). Broadman.

Farrell, Edward. The Father Is Very Fond of Me. 4.95 (ISBN 0-87193-029-3). Dimension Bks.

Finney, Charles G. God's Love for a Sinning World. LC 66-19200. (Charles G. Finney Memorial Library). 1975. pap. 2.50 (ISBN 0-8254-2620-0). Kregel.

Gee, Donald. God's Great Gift. (Charismatic Bk). 1972. pap. 0.69 (ISBN 0-88243-923-5, 02-0923). Gospel Pub.
God Loves His People. (Christ Our Life Ser.). (gr. 6). 1975. text ed. 3.80 (ISBN 0-8294-0237-3); tchrs. ed 5.95 (ISBN 0-8294-0238-1). Loyola.
The God Who Loves. (Faith & Life Ser.). 2.10 (ISBN 0-02-802360-9). Benziger Pub Co.
Guillet, Jacques. A God Who Speaks. LC 78-65898. 108p. 1979. pap. 4.95 (ISBN 0-8091-2195-6). Paulist Pr.
Haas, Lois J. Tell Me About God Kit: 12 Lessons, Vol. 1. (Tiny Steps of Faith Ser.). (ps). 1966. complete kit 10.95 (ISBN 0-86508-011-9); text only 2.50 (ISBN 0-86508-012-7); color & action book 0.90 (ISBN 0-86508-013-5). BCM Inc.
Hagin, Kenneth E. El Shaddai. 1980. pap. 1.25 (ISBN 0-89276-401-5). Hagin Ministries.
Hamilton, Elizabeth. Servants of Love. LC 76-5148. 1976. pap. 2.75 (ISBN 0-87973-680-1). Our Sunday Visitor.
Hastings, Gerald. Life, God & Man. 1980. cancelled (ISBN 0-87881-040-4). Mojave Bks.
Hayes, Norvel. The Unopened Gift. Date not set. 7.98 (ISBN 0-89841-002-9). Zoe Pubns.
Hick, John H. Evil & the God of Love. rev. ed. LC 76-62953. 1977. pap. 6.95 (ISBN 0-06-063902-4, RD219, HarpR). Har-Row.
Hughes, Hugh P. The Philanthropy of God: Described & Illustrated in a Series of Sermons. 1978. Repr. of 1892 ed. lib. bdg. 12.50 (ISBN 0-8482-4402-8). Norwood Edns.
Jones, E. Stanley. Como Nos Guia Dios? Borgeson, Paul, tr. 1977. pap. 0.25x (ISBN 0-8358-0363-5). Upper Room.
Knoche, Philip B. Has God Given You up. (Uplook Ser). 1970. pap. 0.75 (ISBN 0-8163-0257-X, 08165-3). Pacific Pr Pub Assn.
Koenig, John. Charismata: God's Gift for God's People. (Biblical Perspectives on Current Issues). 1978. softcover 4.95 (ISBN 0-664-24176-X). Westminster.
Landorf, Joyce. His Stubborn Love. pap. 2.95 (ISBN 0-310-27122-3). Zondervan.
Larsen, Norma C. His Everlasting Love: Stories of the Father's Help to His Children. LC 77-79752. 1977. 7.95 (ISBN 0-88290-083-8). Horizon Utah.
Larson, Bruce. The One & Only You. LC 73-91549. 1976. pap. 1.50 (ISBN 0-87680-870-4, 91012, Key Word Bks). Word Bks.
Lovasik, Lawrence G. God Loves Us All. (Saint Joseph Picture Bks.). (Illus.). flexible bdg. 0.95 (ISBN 0-686-14271-3, 282). Catholic Bk Pub.
Maloney, George. Inward Stillness. 4.95 (ISBN 0-87193-062-5). Dimension Bks.
Manning, Joseph F. The Miracle of Agape Love. 160p. 1977. pap. 1.95 (ISBN 0-88368-079-3). Whitaker Hse.
Marcum, Elvis. Outreach: God's Miracle Business. new ed. LC 75-10507. 154p. 1975. pap. 2.95 (ISBN 0-8054-5556-6). Broadman.
Mullet, Rosa M. God's Marvelous Work, Bk. 1. 1975. Repr. of 1980 ed. write to pub. for info. (ISBN 0-686-11149-4); tchrs. ed avail. (ISBN 0-686-11150-8). Rod & Staff.
Newlands, George. Theology of the Love of God. LC 80-22547. 224p. 1981. 12.50 (ISBN 0-8042-0726-7); pap. 6.95 (ISBN 0-8042-0727-5). John Knox.
O'Shea, Kevin. The Way of Tenderness. LC 78-61728. (Orig.). 1978. pap. 2.45 (ISBN 0-8091-2166-2). Paulist Pr.
Otis, George. The Ghost of Hagar. pap. 2.50 (ISBN 0-89728-033-4, 581116). Omega Pubns OR.
Peace, R. Learning to Love Ourselves. LC 68-12955. pap. 1.95 (ISBN 0-87784-453-4). Inter-Varsity.
Preston, Geoffrey. God's Way to Be Human. LC 78-65902. 112p. 1978. 4.95 (ISBN 0-8091-0280-3). Paulist Pr.
Rice, Helen S. Love. (Illus.). 128p. 1980. regular ed. 9.95 (ISBN 0-8007-1072-X); Keepsake ed. 11.95 (ISBN 0-8007-1073-8). Revell.
Seger, Doris L. Straight Arrows for God. 1976. pap. 3.95 (ISBN 0-8024-8359-3). Moody.
Sica, Joseph F. God So Loved the World. LC 81-40441. 120p. (Orig.). 1981. lib. bdg. 16.50 (ISBN 0-8191-1677-7); pap. text ed. 7.50 (ISBN 0-8191-1678-5). U Pr of Amer.
Simpson, A. B. The Love Life of Our Lord. pap. 2.50 (ISBN 0-87509-028-1). Chr Pubns.
Stroud, Marion. I Love God - & My Husband. 96p. 1976. pap. 2.50 (ISBN 0-88207-734-1). Victor Bks.
Sudanimm, A. Godianity. 1981. 6.95 (ISBN 0-533-04942-3). Vantage.
Tam, Stanley. Dios Es el Dueno De Mi Negocio. 212p. (Span.). 1979. pap. 1.85 (ISBN 0-8297-0939-8). Life Pubs Intl.
Tanksley, Perry. Love from the Living Bible. (Illus.). 1978. 6.95 (ISBN 0-8007-0965-9). Revell.
Thorndike, Ruth M. God's Everlasting Arms of Love. 1977. 6.50 (ISBN 0-682-48736-8). Exposition.
Tonn, Katie. Try God, You'll Like Him. (Uplook Ser.). 1975. pap. 0.75 (ISBN 0-8163-0178-6, 20340-6). Pacific Pr Pub Assn.
Warren, Thomas B. Our God: A "Sun & Shield" for Troubled Hearts. 1963. 4.95 (ISBN 0-934916-38-1). Natl Christian Pr.
Weber, Gerard P., et al. Grow in God's Love. 2nd ed. 1977. 2.64 (ISBN 0-02-658200-7); tchrs. ed. 8.00 (ISBN 0-02-658210-4); family handbook 1.00 (ISBN 0-02-658250-3). Benziger Pub Co.
--Growth in Love. 1976. pap. 2.28 (ISBN 0-02-658010-1); tchrs. ed 3.44 (ISBN 0-02-658020-9); parent ed. 1.76 (ISBN 0-02-658030-6). Benziger Pub Co.
Wenham, John W. The Goodness of God. LC 73-93141. 205p. 1974. pap. 4.50 (ISBN 0-87784-764-9). Inter-Varsity.
Wild, Robert. Who I Will Be: Is There Joy & Suffering in God? 5.95 (ISBN 0-87193-089-7). Dimension Bks.
Williams, Granville M. Joy in the Lord. LC 71-189764. 128p. (Orig.). 1972. pap. 2.00 (ISBN 0-88203-001-9). Parameter Pr.
Wyatt, Molly M. Sharing God's Love with Others. 1979. pap. 3.50 (ISBN 0-570-07795-8, 56-1333). Concordia.

GOD–MISCELLANEA

Carey, George. God Incarnate. LC 77-27690. 1978. pap. 1.95 (ISBN 0-87784-503-4). Inter-Varsity.
Duncan, James E., Jr. The Reason for Joy. LC 77-78470. 1978. 3.25 (ISBN 0-8054-5154-4). Broadman.
Green, Arthur & Holtz, Barry. Your Word Is Fire. LC 77-83589. (The Spiritual Masters Ser.). 144p. 1977. pap. 2.45 (ISBN 0-8091-2047-X). Paulist Pr.
Kendrick, Rosalyn. Does God Have a Body? 1979. pap. 3.95 (ISBN 0-8192-1257-1). Morehouse.
Otis, George. God, Money & You. 1975. pap. 1.50 (ISBN 0-89129-004-4). Jove Pubns.
Pitts, V. Peter, ed. Children's Pictures of God. LC 79-56298. (Illus.). (gr. 1-4). 1979. pap. 3.95 (ISBN 0-915744-20-1). Character Res.
Russell, A. J. God at Eventide. 1975. pap. 1.25 (ISBN 0-89129-069-9, PV069). Jove Pubns.
Vander Lugt, Herbert. God's Plan in All the Ages: The Kingdom & Redemption from Genesis to Revelation. 208p. 1980. pap. 4.95 (ISBN 0-310-42181-0). Zondervan.
Vincent, M. O. God, Sex & You. 1976. pap. 1.75 (ISBN 0-89129-191-1). Jove Pubns.

GOD–NAME

Jukes, Andrew. Names of God in Holy Scripture. LC 67-28843. 1976. pap. 4.95 (ISBN 0-8254-2958-7). Kregel.
Lockyer, Herbert. All the Divine Names & Titles in the Bible. 352p. 1975. 12.95 (ISBN 0-310-28040-0). Zondervan.
Stone, Nathan. Names of God. 1944. pap. 1.95 (ISBN 0-8024-5854-8). Moody.
Strauss, Lehman. First Person. LC 67-20931. 1967. 5.50 (ISBN 0-87213-815-1). Loizeaux.
William of St. Thierry, Vol. 3: The Enigma of Faith. LC 74-4465. (Cistercian Fathers Ser.: No. 9). 1974. 7.95 (ISBN 0-87907-309-8). Cistercian Pubns.

GOD–OMNIPOTENCE

Baxter, J. Sidlow. Does God Still Guide? pap. 4.95 (ISBN 0-310-20611-1). Zondervan.
Benson, Bob. Something's Going on Here. LC 76-29334. 1977. 5.95 (ISBN 0-914850-77-6); pap. 2.95 (ISBN 0-914850-93-8). Impact Tenn.
Coles, Elisha. God's Sovereignty. (Summit Bks). 1978. Repr. of 1831 ed. pap. 3.45 (ISBN 0-8010-2429-3). Baker Bk.
Crenshaw, James L. & Sandmel, Samuel. The Divine Helmsman: Studies on God's Control of Human Events. Date not set. 20.00x (ISBN 0-87068-700-X). Ktav.
Erb, Paul. El Alfa & la Omega. 1968. pap. 3.30x (ISBN 0-8361-1111-7). Herald Pr.
Hayes, Norvel. God's Power Through Laying on of Hands. 48p. 1977. pap. 1.50 (ISBN 0-917726-09-X). Hunter Bks.
Kenny, Anthony. The God of the Philosophers. 1979. 15.95x (ISBN 0-19-824594-7). Oxford U Pr.
Krakovsky, Levi. The Omnipotent Light Revealed: Wisdom of the Kabbalah. 4.00 (ISBN 0-686-13335-8). Yesod Pubs.
The Lord God Almighty Now Reigns on Earth As He Does in Heaven: By a Christian Messenger. 1978. 6.50 (ISBN 0-533-03593-7). Vantage.
Maleske, Herald. God Is Still in Control. 128p. (Orig.). 1982. pap. 2.95 (ISBN 0-937792-01-2). Nat Therapy.
Marosi, Esteban, ed. El Plan De Dios y los Vencedores. Flores, Rhode, tr. 112p. (Span.). 1980. pap. 1.40 (ISBN 0-8297-0605-4). Life Pubs Intl.
Pink, A. W. La Soberania De Dios. 3.50 (ISBN 0-686-12562-2). Banner of Truth.
--The Sovereignty of God. 1976. pap. 3.45 (ISBN 0-85151-133-3). Banner of Truth.
Pink, Arthur W. Sovereignty of God. (Summit Bks). 1977. pap. 3.95 (ISBN 0-8010-7016-3). Baker Bk.
Spurgeon, C. H. Immutability of God. 1977. pap. 0.50 (ISBN 0-686-23221-6). Pilgrim Pubns.
Urban, Linwood P. & Walton, Douglas, eds. The Power of God: Readings on Omnipotence & Evil. 1979. text ed. 10.95 (ISBN 0-19-502201-7); pap. text ed. 5.95 (ISBN 0-19-502202-5). Oxford U Pr.
Wilcox, L. D. Power from on High. 1.50 (ISBN 0-686-27776-7). Schmul Pub Co.
Wilkerson, Gwen. Par Sa Force. (French Bks.). (Fr.). 1979. 1.85 (ISBN 0-8297-0927-4). Life Pubs Intl.

GOD–PERMISSIVE WILL

see Theodicy

GOD–PROMISES

Achtemeier, Paul J. & Achtemeier, Elizabeth. The Old Testament Roots of Our Faith. LC 78-14659. 160p. 1979. pap. 4.50 (ISBN 0-8006-1348-1, 1-1348). Fortress.
Bale, John. Chief Promises of God. LC 70-133635. (Tudor Facsimile Texts. Old English Plays: No. 21). Repr. of 1908 ed. 31.50 (ISBN 0-404-53321-3). AMS Pr.
Baxter, J. Sidlow. His Part & Ours. pap. 3.95 (ISBN 0-310-20661-8). Zondervan.
Branson, Robert. God's Word in Man's Language. 83p. (Orig.). 1980. pap. 2.75 (ISBN 0-8341-0659-0). Beacon Hill.
Deffner, Donald. You Promised Me God. LC 12-2792. (Illus.). 1981. pap. 4.95 (ISBN 0-570-03827-8). Concordia.
Harold Shaw Publishers, ed. Promesas Personales De la Biblia. 107p. (Span.). 1981. pap. 1.95 (ISBN 0-87788-692-X). Shaw Pubs.
Johnson, Joseph S. Precious Promises. LC 76-8561. 96p. 1976. 6.50 (ISBN 0-8054-5146-3). Broadman.
Lawrence, John. Down to Earth: Laws of Harvest. pap. 3.95 (ISBN 0-8423-0673-0). Tyndale.
Lilly, Gene. God Is Calling His People to Forgiveness. 1977. pap. 2.25 (ISBN 0-917726-15-4). Hunter Bks.
Meyer, F. B. Secrets of Christian Living. (One Evening Christian Classic). 1979. pap. 1.95 (ISBN 0-89107-044-3). Good News.
Murphey, Cecil. But God Has Promised. LC 76-16283. 1976. pap. 2.95 (ISBN 0-88419-002-1). Creation Hse.
Nederhood, Joel. Promises, Promises, Promises. LC 79-18889. (Orig.). 1979. pap. text ed. 2.45 (ISBN 0-933140-09-6). Bd of Pubns CRC.
O'Brien, Bonnie Ball. Promises Kept. LC 77-80944. 1978. 5.95 (ISBN 0-8054-5588-4). Broadman.
Portillo, Carlos. God's Formula of Faith. 32p. 1977. pap. 1.00 (ISBN 0-89350-008-9). Fountain Pr.
El Testimonio De Dios. 1980. pap. 1.35 (ISBN 0-686-69355-8). Life Pubs Intl.

GOD–PROOF

Barth, Karl. Anselm: Fides Quaerens Intellectum. Robertson, Ian W., tr. from Ger. LC 76-10795. (Pittsburgh Reprint Ser.: No. 2). 1976. text ed. 5.00 (ISBN 0-915138-09-3). Pickwick.
Bonansea, Bernardino M. God & Atheism: A Philosophical Approach to the Problem of God. 1979. 15.00 (ISBN 0-8132-0549-2). Cath U Pr.
Buckley, Michael J. Motion & Motion's God: Thematic Variations in Aristotle, Cicero, Newton, & Hegel. LC 73-132234. 1971. 19.00 (ISBN 0-691-07124-1). Princeton U Pr.
Edwards, Jonathan. Faithful Narrative of Surprising Work of God. (Summit Bks). 1979. pap. 2.45 (ISBN 0-8010-3354-3). Baker Bk.
Fein, Jess. Godyssey: The True Story of a Young Man's Search for God & Proof of His Existence. LC 80-81677. (Illus.). 236p. (Orig.). 1980. pap. 7.95 (ISBN 0-9604366-0-X). J Fein.
Gilson, Etienne. God & Philosophy. (Powell Lectures Ser.). 1941. 15.00x (ISBN 0-300-00491-5); pap. 3.45x (ISBN 0-300-00097-9, Y8). Yale U Pr.
Hartshorne, Charles. Anselm's Discovery: A Re-Examination of the Ontological Proof for God's Existence. LC 65-20278. 333p. 1965. 17.50 (ISBN 0-87548-216-3); pap. 6.95 (ISBN 0-87548-217-1). Open Court.
--Man's Vision of God & the Logic of Theism. 1964. Repr. of 1941 ed. 19.50 (ISBN 0-208-00498-X, Archon). Shoe String.
Hayward, Alan. God Is. 224p. 1980. pap. 4.95 (ISBN 0-8407-5746-8). Nelson.
Hick, John H. Existence of God. 1964. pap. 3.95 (ISBN 0-02-085450-1). Macmillan.
Hick, John H. & McGill, Arthur C., eds. Many-Faced Argument: Recent Studies in the Ontological Argument for the Existence of God. (Orig.). 1967. 8.95 (ISBN 0-02-551360-5); pap. 11.95 (ISBN 0-02-085440-4). Macmillan.
Hosier, Helen K. How to Know When God Speaks. LC 79-84721. 160p. (Orig.). pap. 4.95 (ISBN 0-89081-197-0). Harvest Hse.
Kung, Hans. Does God Exist? An Answer for Today. Quinn, Edward, tr. LC 79-6576. 864p. 1980. 17.50 (ISBN 0-385-13592-0). Doubleday.
Laird, John. Theism & Cosmology. facs. ed. LC 74-84317. (Essay Index Reprint Ser). 1942. 19.50 (ISBN 0-8369-1147-4). Arno.
McLean, George F., ed. The Existence of God. LC 73-161203. (Proceedings of the American Catholic Philosophical Association: Vol. 46). 1972. pap. 8.00 (ISBN 0-918090-06-7). Am Cath Philo.
Philaretos, S. D. The Idea of Being. Orthodox Christian Educational Society, ed. Cummings, D., tr. from Hellenic. 287p. 1963. 3.00x (ISBN 0-938366-09-2). Orthodox Chr.
Plantinga, Alvin. God & Other Minds: A Study of the Rational Justification of Belief in God. LC 74-7639. (Contemporary Philosophy Ser). 277p. 1967. 18.50x (ISBN 0-8014-0338-3). Cornell U Pr.
Ross, Robert R. N. The Non-Existence of God: Linguistic Paradox in Tillich's Thought. LC 78-65486. (Toronto Studies in Theology: Vol. 1). xiv, 197p. 1978. soft cover 19.95x (ISBN 0-88946-905-9). E Mellen.
Rowe, William L. The Cosmological Argument. 284p. 1975. 18.50x (ISBN 0-691-07210-8). Princeton U Pr.
Smith, John E. Experience & God. LC 68-18566. 216p. 1974. pap. 4.95 (ISBN 0-19-501847-8, GB424, Gb). Oxford U Pr.
Stewart, David. God's Existence: Can Science Prove It? LC 76-49367. 1976. pap. 1.25 (ISBN 0-917952-00-6). Dwapara.

GOD–PROOF, EMPIRICAL

Buber, Martin. I & Thou. Kaufman, Walter, tr. LC 72-123845. 1970. 12.50 (ISBN 0-684-15575-3, ScribT); pap. 2.95 (ISBN 0-684-71725-5, SL243, ScribT). Scribner.
Klocker, Harry. God & the Empiricists. (Horizons in Philosophy Ser). 1968. pap. 1.95x (ISBN 0-02-819840-9, 81982). Glencoe.
Robertson, John & Robertson, Mary. How Come It's Taking Me So Long to Get Better? Discussion Guide. 1.00 (ISBN 0-8423-1509-8). Tyndale.

GOD–PROVIDENCE AND GOVERNMENT

see Providence and Government of God

GOD–WILL

Allen, Blaine. When God Says No. 168p. 1981. pap. 4.95 (ISBN 0-8407-5781-6). Nelson.
Boas, George. Vox Populi: Essays in the History of an Idea. LC 69-13538. (Seminars in the History of Ideas Ser: No. 1). (Illus.). 307p. 1969. 19.50x (ISBN 0-8018-1008-6); pap. 3.95x (ISBN 0-8018-1009-4). Johns Hopkins.
Bray, Gerald L. Holiness & the Will of God: Perspectives on the Theology of Tertullian. LC 79-5211. (New Foundations Theological Library). (Peter Toon & Ralph Martin series editors). 1980. 18.50 (ISBN 0-8042-3705-0). John Knox.
Coleman, Charles G., Jr. Divine Guidance: That Voice Behind You. LC 77-6796. 1977. pap. 2.50 (ISBN 0-87213-087-8). Loizeaux.
Copeland, Gloria. God's Will Is Prosperity. 2.95 (ISBN 0-89274-090-6, HH-090). Harrison Hse.
Devine, James. Find God's Will for You. LC 76-57035. (Orig.). 1977. pap. 3.95 (ISBN 0-8307-0527-9, 54-055-05). Regal.
Dieu Vent Que...Quatre Choses. (Fr.). Date not set. 14.50 (ISBN 0-686-76385-8). Life Pubs Intl.
Dobson, James. Dr. Dobson Fala Sobre Amor Ira, Culpa, Vontade De Deus. 192p. (Portugal.). 1980. pap. 1.80 (ISBN 0-8297-0674-7). Life Pubs Intl.
Elliot, Elisabeth. A Slow & Certain Light. LC 73-76252. 1976. pap. 2.25 (ISBN 0-87680-864-X, 91009, Key Word Bks). Word Bks.
Flynn, Leslie & Flynn, Bernice. God's Will: You Can Know It. 1979. pap. 3.50 (ISBN 0-88207-779-1). Victor Bks.
Henion, Huntington. Meet the Living. 1980. 4.75 (ISBN 0-8062-1471-6). Carlton.
Hook, Martha. A Woman's Workshop on Faith. 1977. 2.95 (ISBN 0-310-26231-3); study guide 1.95 (ISBN 0-310-26241-0). Zondervan.
Howard, J. Grant. Knowing God's Will - & Doing It. 128p. 1976. pap. 2.50 (ISBN 0-310-26282-8). Zondervan.
Katterjohn, Arthur & Fackler, Mark. Lord, When? LC 76-16284. 1976. pap. 1.50 (ISBN 0-88419-003-X). Creation Hse.
Lindsay, Gordon. How to Find the Perfect Will of God. 0.95 (ISBN 0-89985-003-0). Christ Nations.
Little, Paul. Affirming the Will of God. pap. 0.50 (ISBN 0-87784-139-X). Inter-Varsity.
Macarthur, John, Jr. Found: God's Will. Orig. Title: God's Will Is Not Lost. 1977. pap. 1.95 (ISBN 0-88207-503-9). Victor Bks.
Murphy, Cecil. Getting There from Here. 1981. 7.95 (ISBN 0-686-72230-2). Word Bks.
Murray, Andrew. Not My Will. 1977. pap. 2.50 (ISBN 0-310-29722-2). Zondervan.
--Secret of Power from on High. (Secret Ser.). (Orig.). 1980. pap. 1.25 (ISBN 0-87508-392-7). Chr Lit.

Otis, George. The Solution to Crisis America. pap. 1.50 (ISBN 0-89728-056-3, 669155). Bible Voice.

Quesnell, Quentin. His Word Endures. LC 72-13196. 126p. 1974. pap. 0.95 (ISBN 0-8189-1111-5, Pub. by Alba Bks). Alba.

Redpath, A. Getting to Know the Will of God. pap. 0.50 (ISBN 0-87784-107-1). Inter-Varsity.

Rosenthal, Joan. Lord Is My Strength. 1976. pap. 1.25 (ISBN 0-89129-086-9). Jove Pubns.

St. Alphonsus de Liguori. Uniformity with God's Will. 1977. pap. 0.75 (ISBN 0-89555-019-9, 188). TAN Bks Pubs.

Simpson, James & Story, Edward. Discerning God's Will. LC 79-14695. 1979. pap. 9.95 (ISBN 0-8407-5684-4). Nelson.

Smith, M. Blaine. Knowing God's Will. LC 78-24756. 1979. pap. 3.95 (ISBN 0-87784-610-3). Inter-Varsity.

Stark, Tom & Stark, Joan. Guidance & God's Will. (Fisherman Bible Study Guide Ser.). 1978. saddle stitch 2.25 (ISBN 0-87788-324-6). Shaw Pubs.

Weatherhead, Leslie. Will of God. 1976. pap. 1.25 (ISBN 0-89129-165-2). Jove Pubns.

Weatherhead, Leslie D. The Will of God. (Festival Books). 1976. pap. 1.25 (ISBN 0-687-45600-2). Abingdon.

Weiss, G. Christian. Perfect Will of God. 1950. pap. 1.50 (ISBN 0-8024-6468-8). Moody.

GOD-WILL, PERMISSIVE

see Theodicy

GOD-WISDOM

Allan, John. The Kingdom of God. pap. 2.50 (ISBN 0-87516-286-X). De Vorss.

Doyle, Alfreda. God Always Has an Answer. Date not set. 7.95 (ISBN 0-939476-22-3); pap. text ed. 5.95 (ISBN 0-939476-23-1). Bibliotheca.

Duff, Clarence W. God's Higher Ways. 1978. kivar 7.50 (ISBN 0-87552-257-2). Presby & Reformed.

Fortuna, James L., Jr. The Unsearchable Wisdom of God: A Study of Providence in Richardson's Pamela. LC 80-14919. (University of Florida Humanities Monograph: No. 49). vii, 130p. 1980. pap. 5.50 (ISBN 0-8130-0676-7). U Presses Fla.

Hayes, Norvel. The Unopened Gift. Date not set. 7.98 (ISBN 0-89841-002-9). Zoe Pubns.

Prabhavananda, Swami. Srimad Bhagavatam: The Wisdom of God. 1979. pap. 3.95 (ISBN 0-87481-490-1). Vedanta Pr.

Taylor, Jack R. God's Miraculous Plan of Economy. LC 75-27411. 168p. 1975. 6.95 (ISBN 0-8054-5565-5). Broadman.

Wright, Tom. Small Faith, Great God. 1979. 3.95 (ISBN 0-8007-1061-4). Revell.

GOD-WORSHIP AND LOVE

see also Bhakti; Fear of God

Barnhouse, Donald G. The Love Life. LC 72-94754. 1977. pap. 2.95 (ISBN 0-8307-0451-5, S270-1-29). Regal.

Bothwell, Sr. Mary D. We Worship. (Christ Our Life Ser.). (Illus.). (gr. 5). 1975. text ed. 3.80 (ISBN 0-8294-0235-7); tchrs. ed. 5.95 (ISBN 0-8294-0236-5). Loyola.

Breault, Joseph. Seeking Purity of Heart: The Gift of Ourselves to God. (Illus.). 96p. (Orig.). 1975. pap. 1.50 (ISBN 0-914544-07-1). Living Flame Pr.

Carothers, Merlin. Bringing Heaven into Hell. 1976. pap. 3.95 (ISBN 0-8007-0833-4). Revell.

Carson, Alex. Confidence in God in Times of Danger. pap. 2.75 (ISBN 0-685-88371-X). Reiner.

Coniaris, A. M. Making God Real in the Orthodox Christian Home. 1977. pap. 4.95 (ISBN 0-937032-07-7). Light&Life Pub Co MN.

De Robeck, Nesta. Praise the Lord. 1967. 4.50 (ISBN 0-8199-0086-9, L38643). Franciscan Herald.

Dettoni, Carol. Master of All. 1975. pap. 1.50 (ISBN 0-8423-4184-6). Tyndale.

God's Good News. pap. 1.25 (ISBN 0-937396-17-6). Walterick Pubs.

Godsey, John D. Preface to Bonhoeffer: The Man & Two of His Shorter Writings. LC 79-7378. 80p. 1979. pap. 2.95 (ISBN 0-8006-1367-8, 1-1367). Fortress.

Habig, Marion A. My God & My All. 1977. 2.95 (ISBN 0-685-77278-0). Franciscan Herald.

Houston, James. I Believe in the Creator. LC 79-13542. (I Believe Ser.). 1979. pap. 4.95 (ISBN 0-8028-1749-1). Eerdmans.

Huff, Sr. M. Cyria. Sonnet - Ne Me Mueve, Mi Dios - Its Theme in Spanish Tradition. LC 73-94177. (Catholic University of America Studies in Romance Languages & Literatures Ser: No. 33). Repr. of 1948 ed. 16.00 (ISBN 0-404-50333-0). AMS Pr.

Hunter, Frances. Praise the Lord Anyway. 1978. pap. 2.25 (ISBN 0-87162-131-2). Hunter Bks.

Lawrence, Bro. Practice of the Presence of God. Attwater, Donald, tr. 1974. 6.95 (ISBN 0-87243-129-0). Templegate.

Leavell, Landrum P. God's Spirit in You. LC 73-89526. 2.95 (ISBN 0-8054-8122-2). Broadman.

Levitt, Zola & McCall, Tom. Raptured. LC 75-15481. 1975. pap. 3.95 (ISBN 0-89081-014-1, 0141). Harvest Hse.

Lussier, Ernest. Adore the Lord: Adoration Viewed Through the Old Testament. LC 78-20783. 1979. 6.95 (ISBN 0-8189-0380-5). Alba.

--Jesus Christ Is Lord: Adoration Viewed Through the New Testament. LC 79-15581. 1980. 7.95 (ISBN 0-8189-0382-1). Alba.

MacDonald, William. God's Answers to Man's Questions. pap. 0.95 (ISBN 0-937396-16-8). Walterick Pubs.

Mann, Stella T. Change Your Life Through Faith & Work. 1971. pap. 2.95 (ISBN 0-87516-051-4). De Vorss.

Marshall, John F. By the Light of His Lamp. (Spirit & Life Ser). 1967. 2.00 (ISBN 0-686-11574-0). Franciscan Inst.

Miller, Sarah Walton. One Nation Under God. 32p. 1975. saddle wire 0.95 (ISBN 0-8054-9723-4). Broadman.

Nee, Watchman. Do All to the Glory of God. Kaung, Stephen, tr. (Basic Lesson Ser.: Vol. 5). 1974. 5.00 (ISBN 0-935008-03-9); pap. 3.75 (ISBN 0-935008-04-7). Christian Fellow Pubs.

Newmark, Lawrence T. How to Get All You Want from God. (A Human Development Library Book). (Illus.). 1979. 27.75 (ISBN 0-89266-200-X). Am Classical Coll Pr.

Ovies, Bob. New Lives: What Happened When Twenty-Two Ordinary People Encountered the Extraordinary Love of God. (Orig.). 1980. pap. 1.95 (ISBN 0-89283-077-8). Servant.

Peace, R. Learning to Love God. LC 68-12955. pap. 1.95 (ISBN 0-87784-452-6). Inter-Varsity.

Price, Frederick K. Thank God for Everything. pap. 0.60 mini-bk. (ISBN 0-89274-056-6). Harrison Hse.

Purdom, Charles, ed. God to Man & Man to God. 1975. 6.95 (ISBN 0-913078-27-1). Sheriar Pr.

Radford, Ruby L. Many Paths to God. LC 77-122431. (Illus.). 1970. 3.95 (ISBN 0-8356-0408-X, Quest). Theos Pub Hse.

Riffel, Herman. Voice of God. 1978. pap. 3.95 (ISBN 0-8423-7803-0). Tyndale.

St. Francis de Sales. Treatise on the Love of God, 2 vols. Ryan, John K., tr. LC 63-16638. 1974. Vol.1. pap. 3.50 (ISBN 0-89555-062-8, 166-1); Vol.2. pap. text ed. 3.50 (ISBN -089555-063-6); Set. pap. 7.00 (ISBN 0-89555-064-4). TAN Bks Pubs.

Salls, Betty R. Greatest of These-Love. pap. 1.75 (ISBN 0-686-12744-7). Grace Pub Co.

Schlink, M. Basilea. I Found the Key to the Heart of God. LC 75-23920. 416p. 1975. pap. 4.50 (ISBN 0-87123-239-1, 200239). Bethany Hse.

Schrotenboer, P. Man in God's World. 1977. pap. 1.00 (ISBN 0-88906-200-5). Wedge Pub.

Seeley, Robert R. The House of Israel--What It Really Is. 1978. 5.95 (ISBN 0-533-03462-0). Vantage.

Smith, Judy. What Does God Expect of Me. 1979. pap. 2.15 (ISBN 0-89536-371-2). CSS Pub.

Smith, W. Have You Considered Him? pap. 0.50 (ISBN 0-87784-108-X). Inter-Varsity.

Solov'ev, Vladimir. God, Man & the Church. LC 40-9276. 1937. text ed. 9.50x (ISBN 0-8401-2230-6). Allenson-Breckinridge.

Thompson, Virginia. Help Me Lord--I Hurt. LC 78-55505. (Illus., Orig.). 1978. pap. 2.25 (ISBN 0-89081-145-8, 1458). Harvest Hse.

Thou Shalt Call His Name. (Illus.). 102p. 1975. pap. 2.50 (ISBN 0-915952-00-9). Lord's Line.

Toner, Erwin J. Ways to God. (Illus.). 56p. (Orig.). 1970. pap. 1.00 (ISBN 0-913452-15-7). Jesuit Bks.

Tozer, Aiden W. Pursuit of God. 4.95 (ISBN 0-87509-191-1); pap. 2.75 (ISBN 0-87509-192-X); mass market 1.95 (ISBN 0-87509-223-3). Chr Pubns.

Trombley, Charles. How to Praise the Lord. (Orig.). 1976. pap. 2.50 (ISBN 0-89350-009-7). Fountain Pr.

Van Zeller, Hubert. Choice of God. 1973. pap. 3.95 (ISBN 0-87243-047-2). Templegate.

Vent-Qui-Pleure. Mon Coeur Te Cherche. Date not set. 2.25 (ISBN 0-686-76406-4). Life Pubs Intl.

Wainwright, Geoffrey. Doxology: The Praise of God in Worship, Doctrine, & Life. 1980. 24.95 (ISBN 0-19-520192-2). Oxford U Pr.

Weber, Gerard P., et al. Live in God's World. 2nd ed. (The Word Is Life Ser.). (gr. 1). 1977. 2.64 (ISBN 0-02-658100-0); tchrs. ed. 8.00 (ISBN 0-02-658110-8); family handbook 1.00 (ISBN 0-02-658150-7). Benziger Pub Co.

Weil, Simone. Waiting for God. pap. 4.95 (ISBN 0-06-090295-7, CN295, CN). Har-Row.

Wilkinson, Bruce. God Has No Grandchildren. 6.95 (ISBN 0-8423-1045-2). Tyndale.

Willimon, William H. The Gospel for the Person Who Has Everything. 1978. pap. 3.95 (ISBN 0-8170-0758-X). Judson.

Winter, Miriam T. God-with-Us: Resources for Prayer & Praise. LC 78-13616. 1979. pap. 5.95 (ISBN 0-687-15300-X). Abingdon.

Wolter, Allan B. Life in God's Love. 1958. pap. 1.75 (ISBN 0-8199-0059-1, L38375). Franciscan Herald.

GOD-WRATH

Mains, David. When God Gets Angry with a Nation. (Chapel Talks Ser.). 64p. 1.75 (ISBN 0-89191-263-0, 52639). Cook.

Vatai, Laszlo. Az Isten Szornyetege: Ady Iiraja. 2nd ed. LC 77-89126. (Hungarian.). 1977. 12.00 (ISBN 0-911050-45-0). Occidental.

GOD (BRAHMANISM)

see God (Hinduism)

GOD (EGYPTIAN RELIGION)

Lurker, Manfred. The Gods & Symbols of Ancient Egypt: An Illustrated Dictionary. Clayton, Peter A., rev. by. (Illus.). 144p. 1980. 16.95 (ISBN 0-500-11018-2, Quest). Thames Hudson.

GOD (GREEK RELIGION)

Caird, Edward. Evolution of Theology in the Greek Philosophers, the Gifford Lectures, 1900-1902, 2 Vols. 1968. 35.00 (ISBN 0-403-00116-1). Scholarly.

Hack, Roy K. God in Greek Philosophy to the Time of Socrates. 1970. Repr. of 1931 ed. lib. bdg. 12.50 (ISBN 0-8337-1514-3). B Franklin.

GOD (HINDUISM)

Bhaktivedanta, Swami A. C. Krsna: The Supreme Personality of Godhead, 3 vols. LC 74-118081. (Illus.). 1970. Set. pap. 6.95 (ISBN 0-912776-30-7); pap. 2.95 ea.; Vol. 1. pap. (ISBN 0-912776-31-5); Vol. 2. pap. (ISBN 0-912776-32-3); Vol. 3. pap. (ISBN 0-912776-33-1). Bhaktivedanta.

--Krsna: The Supreme Personality of Godhead, 3 vols. LC 74-118081. (Illus.). 1970. Set. 24.95 (ISBN 0-912776-60-9); 9.95 ea. Vol. 1 (ISBN 0-912776-57-9). Vol. 2 (ISBN 0-912776-58-7). Vol. 3 (ISBN 0-912776-59-5). Bhaktivedanta.

GOD (ISLAM)

Ali ibn Isma'il, A. H., et al. Al ibanah 'an usul addiyanah. Klein, W. C., tr. (American Oriental Ser.: Vol. 19). 1940. pap. 12.00 (ISBN 0-527-02693-X). Kraus Repr.

Friedlander, Ira. The Ninety-Nine Names of Allah. (Orig.). 1978. pap. 3.50 (ISBN 0-06-090621-9, CN 621, CN). Har-Row.

GOD (JUDAISM)

Katz, Steven T. Jewish Ideas & Concepts. LC 77-75285. 1978. 12.50 (ISBN 0-8052-3664-3). Schocken.

Marmorstein, Arthur. Doctrine of Merits in Old Rabbinic Literature & the Old Rabbinic Doctrine of God, 3 vols. in one. rev. ed. 1968. Repr. 35.00x (ISBN 0-87068-087-0). Ktav.

Phillips, Anthony. God B. C. 1977. text ed. 7.50x (ISBN 0-19-213959-2). Oxford U Pr.

GOD, FEAR OF

see Fear of God

GOD, GLORY OF

see Glory of God

GOD AND MAN, MYSTICAL UNION OF

see Mystical Union

GOD IN LITERATURE

Berryman, Charles. From Wilderness to Wasteland: The Trial of the Puritan God in the American Imagination. (National University Publications, Literary Criticism Ser.). 1979. 15.00 (ISBN 0-8046-9235-1). Kennikat.

Goldmann, Lucien. Hidden God. Thody, Philip, tr. (International Library of Philosophy & Scientific Method Ser.). 1976. text ed. 22.50x (ISBN 0-7100-3621-3). Humanities.

Miller, J. Hillis. The Disappearance of God: Five Nineteenth Century Writers. 392p. 1976. text ed. 18.50x (ISBN 0-674-21101-4). Harvard U Pr.

GOD IS DEAD THEOLOGY

see Death of God Theology

GOD TRANSCENDENCE

see Transcendence of God

GODARD, JEAN LUC, 1930-

Collet, Jean. Jean-Luc Godard. Vaughan, Ciba, tr. LC 77-93411. (Illus.). 1970. pap. 2.95 (ISBN 0-685-08726-3, L00028). Crown.

Kawin, Bruce F. Mindscreen: Bergman, Godard, & First-Person Film. LC 78-51161. (Illus.). 1978. 18.50 (ISBN 0-691-06365-6); pap. 5.95 (ISBN 0-691-01348-9). Princeton U Pr.

Kreidl, John. Jean-Luc Godard. (Theatrical Arts Ser.). 1980. lib. bdg. 12.95 (ISBN 0-8057-9270-8). Twayne.

Lesage, Julia. Jean-Luc Godard: A Guide to References & Resources. 1979. lib. bdg. 42.50 (ISBN 0-8161-7925-5). G K Hall.

MacCabe, Colin. Godard: Images, Sounds, Politics. LC 80-8592. (Illus.). 176p. 1981. 22.50x (ISBN 0-253-12384-4); pap. 9.95x (ISBN 0-253-21266-9). Ind U Pr.

Roud, Richard. Godard. LC 70-115456. (Cinema One Ser: No. 1). (Illus.). 192p. 1970. pap. 2.25x (ISBN 0-253-13201-0). Ind U Pr.

GODDEN, RUMER, 1907-

Simpson, Hassell A. Rumer Godden. (English Authors Ser.: No. 151). 1973. lib. bdg. 10.95 (ISBN 0-8057-1219-4). Twayne.

GODDESSES, MOTHER

see Mother-Goddesses

GODEFFROY (J.C.) UND SOHN

Spoehr, Florence M. White Falcon: The House of Godeffroy & Its Commercial & Scientific Role in the Pacific. LC 63-18693. (Illus.). 1963. 7.95 (ISBN 0-87015-119-3). Pacific Bks.

GODEFROY, MAXIMILIAN, fl. 1806-1824

Alexander, Robert L. The Architecture of Maximilian Godefroy. LC 74-6810. (Studies in Nineteenth-Century Architecture). (Illus.). 258p. 1975. 19.00x (ISBN 0-8018-1286-0). Johns Hopkins.

GODEL, KURT

see Goedel, Kurt

GODEL'S THEOREM

see Goedel's Theorem

GODFREY OF BOUILLON

Andressohn, John C. Ancestry & Life of Godfrey of Bouillon. LC 70-38379. (Biography Index Reprints - Social Science Ser.: No. 5). Repr. of 1947 ed. 13.50 (ISBN 0-8369-8114-6). Arno.

GODKIN, EDWIN LAWRENCE, 1831-1902

Armstrong, William M. E. L. Godkin: A Biography. LC 77-12918. 1978. 35.00 (ISBN 0-87395-371-1). State U NY Pr.

--E. L. Godkin & American Foreign Policy: 1865-1900. LC 77-9534. 1977. Repr. of 1957 ed. lib. bdg. 19.25x (ISBN 0-8371-9711-2, ARGA). Greenwood.

Armstrong, William M., ed. The Gilded Age Letters of E. L. Godkin. LC 74-6462. (Illus.). 1974. 39.00 (ISBN 0-87395-246-4); microfiche 39.00 (ISBN 0-87395-247-2). State U NY Pr.

GODOY ALCAYAGA, LUCILA, 1889-1957

Arce de Vazquez, Margot. Gabriela Mistral: The Poet & Her Work. Anderson, Helen Masso, tr. LC 64-16899. (Orig.). 1964. pap. 3.95x (ISBN 0-8147-0011-X). NYU Pr.

Gazarian-Gautier, Marie-Lise. Gabriela Mistral. 1974. 7.50 (ISBN 0-8199-0544-5). Franciscan Herald.

GODOY ALVAREZ DE FARIA RIOS SANCHEZ y ZARZOSA, MANUEL DE, PRINCIPE DE LA PAZ, 1767-1851

Chastenet, Jacques. Godoy: Master of Spain. Huntington, J. F., tr. LC 70-153205. 1971. Repr. of 1953 ed. 12.00 (ISBN 0-8046-1515-2). Kennikat.

GODS

see also Kings and Rulers (In Religion, Folk-Lore, etc.); Mother-Goddesses; Myth; Mythology; Religions

Apuleius. The Story of Cupid & Psyche As Related by Apuleius. Purser, Louis C., ed. (College Classical Ser.). cviii, 155p. 1981. pap. text ed. 12.00x (ISBN 0-89241-111-2). Caratzas Bros.

Blofeld, John. Bodhisattva of Compassion: The Mystical Tradition of Kuan Yin. LC 77-91352. (Illus.). 1978. pap. 3.95 (ISBN 0-394-73609-5). Shambhala Pubns.

Brockman, Chris. What About Gods? (Skeptic's Bookshelf Ser.). (Illus.). 1978. pap. 3.95 (ISBN 0-87975-106-1). Prometheus Bks.

Budge, Ernest A. Egyptian Ideas of the Future Life. LC 73-18839. Repr. of 1899 ed. 14.00 (ISBN 0-404-11330-3). AMS Pr.

Carlyon, Richard. A Guide to Gods & Goddesses. 398p. 1981. 17.50 (ISBN 0-8245-0070-9). Crossroad NY.

Clothey, Fred W. The Many Faces of Murukan: The History & Meaning of a South Indian God. (Religion & Society Ser.: No. 6). 1978. text ed. 42.25x (ISBN 90-2797-632-5). Mouton.

Davidson, H. R. Gods & Myths of Northern Europe. lib. bdg. 9.50x (ISBN 0-88307-333-1). Gannon.

Demarast, Arthur A. Viracocha: The Nature & Antiquity of the Andean High God. Condon, Lorna, ed. LC 81-80344. (Peabody Museum Monograph: No. 6). (Illus.). 102p. (Orig.). 1981. pap. text ed. 10.00 (ISBN 0-87365-906-6). Peabody Harvard.

Denning, Melita & Phillips, Osborne. The Llewellyn Practical Guide to Evocation of the Gods. 1982. 5.95 (ISBN 0-87542-187-3). Llewellyn Pub.

--Llewellyn Practical Guide to the Evocation of the Gods. 1981. 5.95 (ISBN 0-686-73839-X). Llewellyn Pubns.

Francis, Mother Mary. Strange Gods Before Me. 199p. 1976. pap. 4.95 (ISBN 0-8199-0599-2). Franciscan Herald.

Harnsberger, Caroline T. Gods & Heroes: A Quick Guide to the Occupations, Associations & Experiences of the Greek & Roman Gods & Heroes. LC 76-21470. 1977. 20.00x (ISBN 0-87875-125-4). Whitston Pub.

Haydon, A. Eustace. Biography of the Gods. LC 67-13617. 1967. pap. 5.95 (ISBN 0-8044-6257-7). Ungar.

Heschel, Abraham J. Man's Quest for God: Studies in Prayer & Symbolism. LC 54-10371. (Hudson River Edition Ser.). 1981. 15.00x (ISBN 0-684-16829-4, ScribT). Scribner.

Hillman, et al. Facing the Gods. Hillman, James, ed. 171p. (Orig.). 1980. pap. text ed. 8.50 (ISBN 0-88214-312-3). Spring Pubns.

Jayne, Walter A. The Healing Gods of Ancient Civilizations. LC 75-23728. Repr. of 1925 ed. 49.00 (ISBN 0-404-13286-3). AMS Pr.
Kalicz, Nandor. Clay Gods. 1970. 5.00x (ISBN 0-8002-0297-X). Intl Pubns Serv.
Love, Jeff. The Quantum Gods. 1979. pap. 7.95 (ISBN 0-87728-476-8). Weiser.
Monaghan, Patricia. The Book of Goddesses & Heroines. LC 80-29355. 288p. 1981. pap. 12.25 (ISBN 0-525-47664-4). Dutton.
Redfield, Bessie G., ed. Gods: A Dictionary of the Deities of All Lands Including Supernatural Beings, Mythical Heroes & Kings & Sacred Books of Religions. 1977. lib. bdg. 75.00 (ISBN 0-8490-1893-5). Gordon Pr.
Schwab, Gustav. Gods & Heroes. LC 47-873. 1977. pap. 6.95 (ISBN 0-394-73402-5). Pantheon.
Von Daniken, Eric. Signs of the Gods. (Illus.). 239p. 1980. 10.95 (ISBN 0-399-12559-0). Putnam.
Wildung, Dietrich. Egyptian Saints: Deification in Pharaonic Egypt. LC 76-15147. 1977. 25.00x (ISBN 0-8147-9169-7). NYU Pr.
Wohlstein, Herman. The Sky-God An-Anu: Head of the Mesopotamian Pantheon in Sumerian Akkadian Literature. Curt, E., ed. Attanasio, Salvator, tr. from Ger. LC 76-10388. 1976. 17.50 (ISBN 0-9601138-0-0). P A Stroock.

GODS IN ART
see also Idols and Images
Albricus. Allegoriae Poeticae, Repr. Of 1520 Ed. Incl. Theologia Mythologica. Pictorius, Georg. Repr. of 1532 ed; Apotheoseos Tam Exterarum Gentium Quam Romanorum Deorum. Pictorius, Georg. Repr. of 1558 ed. LC 75-27845. (Renaissance & the Gods Ser.: Vol. 4). (Illus.). 1976. lib. bdg. 73.00 (ISBN 0-8240-2053-7). Garland Pub.
Cartari, Vincenzo. Le Imagini...Degli Dei. LC 75-27855. (Renaissance & the Gods Ser.: Vol. 12). (Illus.). 1976. Repr. of 1571 ed. lib. bdg. 73.00 (ISBN 0-8240-2061-8). Garland Pub.
Henle, Jane. Greek Myths: A Vase Painter's Notebook. LC 72-75639. (Illus.). 256p. 1973. 12.50x (ISBN 0-253-32635-4); pap. 3.50x (ISBN 0-253-32636-2). Ind U Pr.
Pal, Pratapaditya. Bronzes of Kashmir. LC 75-902. (Illus.). 205p. 1975. lib. bdg. 40.00 (ISBN 0-87817-158-4). Hacker.
Seznec, Jean. The Survival of the Pagan Gods: The Mythological Tradition & Its Place in Renaissance Humanism & Art. Sessions, Barbara, tr. (Bollingen Ser.: Vol. 38). (Illus.). 108p. 1972. 22.50 (ISBN 0-691-09829-8); pap. 6.95 (ISBN 0-691-01783-2). Princeton U Pr.
Spence, Joseph. Polymetis. LC 75-27886. (Renaissance & the Gods Ser.: Vol. 41). (Illus.). 1976. Repr. of 1747 ed. lib. bdg. 73.00 (ISBN 0-8240-2090-1). Garland Pub.
Tempesta, Antonio. Metamorphoseon...Ovidianarum. LC 75-27861. (Renaissance & the Gods Ser.: Vol. 19). (Illus.). 1976. Repr. of 1606 ed. lib. bdg. 73.00 (ISBN 0-8240-2067-7). Garland Pub.
Valeriano Bolzani, Giovanni P. Hieroglyphica. LC 75-27864. (Renaissance & the Gods Ser.: Vol. 17). (Illus.). 1977. Repr. of 1602 ed. lib. bdg. 73.00 (ISBN 0-8240-2069-3). Garland Pub.
--Les Hieroglyphiques. Montlyard, I. de, tr. LC 75-27867. (Renaissance & the Gods Ser.: Vol. 23). (Illus., Fr.). 1977. Repr. of 1615 ed. lib. bdg. 73.00 (ISBN 0-8240-2072-3). Garland Pub.
Vermeule, Cornelius. Greek & Roman Sculpture in Gold & Silver. (Illus.). 1974. pap. 2.95 (ISBN 0-87846-081-0). Mus Fine Arts Boston.
Vermeule, Cornelius C. The Goddess Roma in the Art of the Roman Empire. (Illus.). 1974. 18.00 (ISBN 0-87846-152-3). Mus Fine Arts Boston.

GODS IN LITERATURE
see also God in Literature

GODUNOV, BORIS FYODOROVICH, 1552-1605
Graham, Stephen. Boris Godunof. (Illus.). 1970. Repr. of 1933 ed. 18.50 (ISBN 0-208-00969-8, Archon). Shoe String.
Platonov, Sergei F. Boris Godunov: Tsar of Russia. Pyles, L. Rex, tr. from Rus. LC 73-176467. (Russian Ser.: Vol. 10). (Illus.). 280p. 1973. 14.50 (ISBN 0-87569-024-6). Academic Intl.

GODWIN, MARY (WOLLSTONECRAFT) 1759-1797
see Wollstonecraft, Mary, 1759-1797

GODWIN, WILLIAM, 1756-1836
Brown, Ford K. The Life of William Godwin. LC 72-10170. 1974. Repr. of 1926 ed. lib. bdg. 25.00 (ISBN 0-8414-0641-3). Folcroft.
Clark, John P. The Philosophical Anarchism of William Godwin. LC 76-24291. 1977. 25.00 (ISBN 0-691-07217-5). Princeton U Pr.
Earle, O. The Reputation & Influence of William Godwin in America. 59.95 (ISBN 0-8490-0948-0). Gordon Pr.
Fleisher, D. William Godwin. 69.95 (ISBN 0-87968-276-0). Gordon Pr.
Fleisher, David. William Godwin: A Study in Liberalism. LC 73-1838. (Illus.). 154p. 1973. Repr. of 1951 ed. lib. bdg. 15.00x (ISBN 0-8371-6807-4, FLWG). Greenwood.
Godwin, William. Enquiry Concerning Political Justice. abr. ed. Carter, K. Codell, ed. 1971. pap. 9.95x (ISBN 0-19-871019-4). Oxford U Pr.
Grylls, Rosalie G. William Godwin & His Work. LC 74-13753. 1974. Repr. of 1953 ed. lib. bdg. 20.00 (ISBN 0-8414-4525-7). Folcroft.
--William Godwin & His World. 1978. Repr. of 1953 ed. lib. bdg. 30.00 (ISBN 0-8495-1930-6). Arden Lib.
Hughes, Dean T. Romance & Psychological Realism in William Godwin's Novels. Varma, Devendra P., ed. LC 79-8459. (Gothic Studies & Dissertations Ser.). 1980. lib. bdg. 17.00x (ISBN 0-405-12673-5). Arno.
Locke, Don. A Fantasy of Reason: The Life & Thought of William Godwin. (Illus.). 1980. 28.00 (ISBN 0-7100-0387-0). Routledge & Kegan.
Monro, D. H. Godwin's Moral Philosophy. LC 76-40456. 1953. lib. bdg. 20.00 (ISBN 0-8414-6083-3). Folcroft.
Monro, David H. Godwin's Moral Philosophy: An Interpretation of William Godwin. LC 78-5640. 1978. Repr. of 1953 ed. lib. bdg. 17.00x (ISBN 0-313-20451-9, MOGM). Greenwood.
Munoz, V. William Godwin: A Chronology. Johnson, W. Scott, tr. (Libertarian & Anarchist Chronology Ser.). 1979. lib. bdg. 59.95 (ISBN 0-8490-3026-9). Gordon Pr.
Paul, C. Kegan. William Godwin: His Friends & Contemporaries, 2 Vols. LC 73-115359. Repr. of 1876 ed. Set. 19.50 (ISBN 0-404-04941-9); 10.00 ea. Vol. 1 (ISBN 0-404-04942-7). Vol. 2 (ISBN 0-404-04943-5). AMS Pr.
Powers, Katherine R. The Influence of William Godwin on the Novels of Mary Shelley. Varma, Devendra P., ed. LC 79-7469. (Gothic Studies & Dissertations Ser.). 1980. lib. bdg. 17.00x (ISBN 0-405-12657-3). Arno.
Preu, James. The Dean & the Anarchist. LC 72-888. (Studies in Anarchy & Anarchism, No. 99). 124p. 1972. Repr. of 1959 ed. lib. bdg. 29.95 (ISBN 0-8383-1419-8). Haskell.
Robinson, Victor. William Godwin & Mary Wollstonecraft. 59.95 (ISBN 0-8490-1304-6). Gordon Pr.
--William Godwin & Mary Wollstonecraft: Lives of Great Altrurians. LC 78-31579. 1978. lib. bdg. 10.00 (ISBN 0-8414-7361-7). Folcroft.
Rodway, A. E., ed. Godwin & the Age of Transition. LC 76-52953. (English Literature Ser, No. 33). 1977. lib. bdg. 32.95 (ISBN 0-8383-2146-1). Haskell.
Rodway, Allan E. Godwin & the Age of Transition. LC 75-33700. 1975. Repr. of 1952 ed. lib. bdg. 25.00 (ISBN 0-8414-7249-1). Folcroft.
Scheuermann, Mona. The Novels of William Godwin & Those of His Contemporaries. Varma, Devendra P., ed. LC 79-8477. (Gothic Studies & Dissertations Ser.). 1980. lib. bdg. 25.00x (ISBN 0-405-12678-6). Arno.
Wardle, Ralph M., ed. Godwin & Mary: Letters of William Godwin & Mary Wollstonecraft. LC 76-13032. (Illus.). 1977. 9.50x (ISBN 0-8032-0901-0); pap. 2.65 (ISBN 0-8032-5852-6, BB 631, Bison). U of Nebr Pr.

GOEBBELS, JOSEPH, 1897-1945
Goebbels, Joseph. My Part in Germany's Fight. Fiedler, Kurt, tr. from Ger. LC 76-27871. 1979. Repr. of 1935 ed. 23.50 (ISBN 0-86527-137-2). Fertig.
Semmler, Rudolf. Goebbels, the Man Next to Hitler. LC 78-63716. (Studies in Fascism: Ideology & Practice). Repr. of 1947 ed. 22.50 (ISBN 0-404-16987-2). AMS Pr.
Trevor-Roper, Hugh, ed. Final Entries 1945: The Diaries of Joseph Goebbels. pap. 2.75 (ISBN 0-380-42408-8, 42408). Avon.
--The Final Entries, 1945: The Diaries of Joseph Goebbels. LC 78-6707. (Illus.). 1978. 14.95 (ISBN 0-399-12116-1). Putnam.

GOEBEL, WILLIAM, 1856-1900
Klotter, James C. William Goebel: The Politics of Wrath. LC 77-76335. (Kentucky Bicentennial Bookshelf Ser.). (Illus.). 152p. 1977. 6.95 (ISBN 0-8131-0240-5). U Pr of Ky.

GOECKINGK, LEOPOLD FRIEDRICH GUNTHER VON, 1748-1828
Kasch, F. Leopold F. G. Von Goeckingk. 1909. pap. 7.00 (ISBN 0-384-28720-4). Johnson Repr.

GOEDEL, KURT
Chihara, Charles S. Ontology & the Vicious-Circle Principle. LC 72-4569. 260p. 1973. 22.50x (ISBN 0-8014-0727-3). Cornell U Pr.

GOEDEL'S THEOREM
Davis, M., ed. The Undecidable: Basic Papers on Undecidable Propositions, Unsolvable Problems & Computable Functions. LC 65-3996. 1965. 15.00 (ISBN 0-911216-01-4). Raven.
Siefkes, D. Decidable Theories: Buechi's Monadic Second Order Successor Arithmetic. LC 70-111900. (Lecture Notes in Mathematics: Vol. 120). 1970. pap. 10.70 (ISBN 0-387-04909-6). Springer-Verlag.

GOERDELER, CARL FRIEDRICH, 1884-1944
Ritter, Gerhard. German Resistance. facs. ed. Clark, R. T., tr. LC 74-124253. (Select Bibliographies Reprint Ser). 1958. 20.00 (ISBN 0-8369-5441-6). Arno.

GOERING, HERMANN WILHELM, 1893-1946
Butler, Ewan & Young, Gordon. Marshall Without Glory. LC 78-63656. (Studies in Fascism: Ideology & Practice). Repr. of 1951 ed. 24.50 (ISBN 0-404-16915-5). AMS Pr.
Gritzbach, Erich. Hermann Goering -- the Man & His Work. Griffin, Gerald, tr. from Ger. (Illus.). 256p. pap. 5.00 (ISBN 0-686-30250-8). Hist Rev Pr.
--Hermann Goering: The Man & His Work. Griffin, Gerald, tr. LC 75-180404. Repr. of 1939 ed. 23.50 (ISBN 0-404-56128-4). AMS Pr.
Mosley, Leonard. Reich Marshal: A Biography of Hermann Goering. LC 73-20825. 480p. 1974. 12.50 (ISBN 0-385-04961-7). Doubleday.
Skipper, G. C. Goering & the Luftwaffe. LC 80-16947. (World at War Ser.). (Illus.). 48p. (gr. 3-8). 1980. PLB 8.65 (ISBN 0-516-04784-1); pap. 2.95 (ISBN 0-516-44784-X). Childrens.

GOERRES, JOHANN JOSEPH VON, 1776-1848
Schultz, Franz. Joseph Gorres Als Herausgeber. Repr. of 1902 ed. 21.50 (ISBN 0-384-54288-3); pap. 18.50 (ISBN 0-384-54295-6). Johnson Repr.

GOETHE, JOHANN WOLFGANG VON, 1749-1832
Andrews, William P. Goethe's Key to Faust. LC 67-27573. 1913. Repr. 7.50 (ISBN 0-8046-0012-0). Kennikat.
--Goethe's Key to Faust. 59.95 (ISBN 0-8490-0245-1). Gordon Pr.
Atkins, H. G. Johann Wolfgang Goethe. LC 74-9902. 1904. lib. bdg. 30.00 (ISBN 0-8414-2981-2). Folcroft.
Bahr, Ehrhard & Stewart, Walter K., eds. Internationales Verzeichnis der Goethe-Dissertationen, 1952-1976. LC 78-27790. 1978. pap. 12.75 (ISBN 0-8357-0367-3, SS-00079). Univ Microfilms.
Bielchowsky, Albert. Goethe, Sein Leben und Seine Werke, 2 vols. 1973. Repr. of 1910 ed. 75.00 set (ISBN 0-8274-1215-0). R West.
Bielschowsky, A. Life of Goethe, 3 Vols. LC 70-92935. (Studies in German Literature, No. 13). 1969. Repr. of 1905 ed. lib. bdg. 84.95 (ISBN 0-8383-1000-1). Haskell.
Bielschowsky, Albert. Life of Goethe, 3 Vols. Cooper, William A., tr. LC 73-113555. (BCL Ser. I). (Illus.). Repr. of 1908 ed. Set. 35.00 (ISBN 0-404-00870-4); 12.00 ea. Vol. 1 (ISBN 0-404-00871-2). Vol. 2 (ISBN 0-404-00872-0). Vol. 3 (ISBN 0-404-00873-9). AMS Pr.
Blackall, Eric A. Goethe & the Novel. LC 75-38426. 344p. 1976. 24.50x (ISBN 0-8014-0978-0). Cornell U Pr.
Blackie, John S. The Wisdom of Goethe. LC 74-1443. 1883. lib. bdg. 30.00 (ISBN 0-8414-9918-7). Folcroft.
Boyd, James. Goethe's Knowledge of English Literature. LC 72-6894. (Studies in German Literature, No. 13). 320p. 1972. Repr. of 1932 ed. lib. bdg. 39.95 (ISBN 0-8383-1637-9). Haskell.
Boynton, Henry W. World's Leading Poets. facs. ed. LC 68-8439. (Essay Index Reprint Ser). 1912. 18.00 (ISBN 0-8369-0238-6). Arno.
Brandes, George. Wolfgang Goethe, 2 vols. 1973. Repr. of 1925 ed. 45.00 set (ISBN 0-8274-0073-X). R West.
Braun, Frederick A. Margaret Fuller & Goethe. LC 72-195018. 1910. lib. bdg. 15.00 (ISBN 0-8414-2537-X). Folcroft.
Brown, Jane K. Goethe's Cyclical Narratives: Die Unterhaltungen Deutscher Ausgewanderten & Wilhelm Meisters Wanderjahre. (Studies in the Germanic Languages & Literatures: No. 82). 1975. 10.25x (ISBN 0-8078-8082-5). U of NC Pr.
Brown, P. H. The Youth of Goethe. LC 77-133283. (Studies in German Literature, No. 13). Repr. of 1913 ed. lib. bdg. 54.95 (ISBN 0-8383-1182-2). Haskell.
Brown, P. Hume. Life of Goethe, 2 Vols. LC 77-163114. (Studies in German Literature, No. 13). 1971. Repr. of 1920 ed. Set. lib. bdg. 79.95 (ISBN 0-8383-1307-8). Haskell.
Browning, Oscar. Goethe: His Life & Writings. LC 72-2126. (Studies in German Literature, No. 13). 1972. Repr. of 1892 ed. lib. bdg. 31.95 (ISBN 0-8383-1493-7). Haskell.
Burckhardt, Sigurd. The Drama of Language: Essays on Goethe & Kleist. LC 77-97492. 183p. 1970. 12.00x (ISBN 0-8018-1049-3). Johns Hopkins.
Butler, E. M. Byron & Goethe: Analysis of a Passion. 229p. 1980. Repr. lib. bdg. 25.00 (ISBN 0-8495-0626-3). Arden Lib.
--Goethe & Byron. LC 74-5069. 1949. lib. bdg. 6.00 (ISBN 0-8414-3110-8). Folcroft.
Calvert, George H. Coleridge, Shelley, Goethe. 1880. lib. bdg. 20.00 (ISBN 0-8414-1565-X). Folcroft.
--Coleridge, Shelley, Goethe. 1978. Repr. lib. bdg. 30.00 (ISBN 0-8495-0816-9). Arden Lib.
--Goethe: His Life & Works. 1872. 35.00 (ISBN 0-8274-2420-5). R West.
Carlson, Marvin A. Goethe & the Weimar Theatre. (Illus.). 1978. 22.50x (ISBN 0-8014-1118-1). Cornell U Pr.
Carre, Jean M. Goethe. Hard, Eleanor, tr. 1973. Repr. of 1929 ed. 20.00 (ISBN 0-8274-0082-9). R West.
Carus, Paul. Goethe: With Special Consideration of His Philosophy. 1973. Repr. of 1915 ed. 30.00 (ISBN 0-8274-0083-7). R West.
Cassirer, Ernst. Rousseau, Kant, & Goethe. 1970. 15.00 (ISBN 0-691-07168-3); pap. 4.95 (ISBN 0-691-01970-3). Princeton U Pr.
Cottrell, Alan P., ed. Goethe's Faust: Seven Essays. (Studies in Germanic Languages & Lit.: No. 86). 1976. 11.50x (ISBN 0-8078-8086-8). U of NC Pr.
Crawford, Mary C. Goethe & His Woman Friends. LC 72-1563. (Studies in German Literature, No. 13). (Illus.). 1972. Repr. of 1911 ed. lib. bdg. 72.95 (ISBN 0-8383-1448-1). Haskell.
Croce, Benedetto. Goethe. LC 78-103179. 1970. Repr. of 1923 ed. 11.50 (ISBN 0-8046-0816-4). Kennikat.
Davidson, Thomas. Philosophy of Goethe's Faust. LC 68-24963. (Studies in German Literature, No. 13). 1969. Repr. of 1906 ed. lib. bdg. 33.95 (ISBN 0-8383-0933-X). Haskell.
De Quincey, Thomas. Biographies of Shakespeare, Pope, Goethe, & Schiller. LC 75-164822. (Illus.). Repr. of 1862 ed. 24.50 (ISBN 0-404-02079-8). AMS Pr.
Dieckmann, Liselotte. Johann Wolfgang Goethe. (World Authors Ser.: Germany: No. 292). 1974. lib. bdg. 10.95 (ISBN 0-8057-2378-1). Twayne.
Duntzer, H. Life of Goethe, 2 vols. 250.00 (ISBN 0-8490-0531-0). Gordon Pr.
--Life of Goethe, 2 vols. 1973. 50.00 set (ISBN 0-8274-1366-1). R West.
Enright, Dennis J. Commentary on Goethe's Faust. 158p. 1980. Repr. of 1949 ed. lib. bdg. 20.00 (ISBN 0-8414-1916-7). Folcroft.
Era of Goethe Essays Presented to James Boyd. facs. ed. LC 68-20296. (Essay Index Reprint Ser). 1959. 13.50 (ISBN 0-8369-0418-4). Arno.
Ewen, Frederic. Prestige of Schiller in England, 1788-1859. Repr. of 1932 ed. 22.50 (ISBN 0-404-02364-9). AMS Pr.
Fahrner, R. Hoelderlins Begegnung Mit Goethe und Schiller. Repr. of 1925 ed. pap. 7.00 (ISBN 0-384-15080-2). Johnson Repr.
Fairley, Barker. A Study of Goethe. LC 76-56253. 1977. Repr. of 1947 ed. lib. bdg. 17.00x (ISBN 0-8371-9330-3, FASG). Greenwood.
Farrelly, D. L. Goethe & Inner Harmony: A Study of 'Schoene Seele' in the Apprenticeship of William Meister. 220p. 1973. 10.00x (ISBN 0-7165-2157-1, Pub. by Irish Academic Pr Ireland). Biblio Dist.
Fiedler, H. G. Textual Studies of Goethe's Faust. LC 73-20371. (Studies in Goethe, No. 61). 1974. lib. bdg. 49.95 (ISBN 0-8383-1809-6). Haskell.
Fiedler, Hermann G. Textual Studies of Goethe's Faust. 92p. 1980. Repr. of 1946 ed. lib. bdg. 15.00 (ISBN 0-8492-4705-5). R West.
Fischer-Lamberg, Hanna, ed. Der Junge Goethe, 5 vols. Incl. Vol. 1, August 1749-Marz 1770. 1963. 69.00x (ISBN 3-11-005119-2); Vol. 2, April 1770-Setember 1772. 1963. 48.00x (ISBN 0-685-85551-1); Vol. 3, Setember 1772-Dezember 1773. 1966. 57.70 (ISBN 3-11-005120-6); Vol. 4, Januar-Dezember 1774. 1968. 44.65 (ISBN 3-11-005122-2); Vol. 5, Januar-Oktober 1775. 1973. 77.00x (ISBN 3-11-004047-6). De Gruyter.
--Der Junge Goethe: Neu Bearbeitete Ausgabe in Fuenf Baenden. Registerband (Namen-, Werk-, und Sachregister zu Den Baenden I-V. viii, 116p. (Ger.). 1974. text ed. 38.75x (ISBN 3-11-004807-8). De Gruyter.
Freeman, Arnold. The Riddle of Goethe's Faust. LC 76-46931. 1976. Repr. of 1954 ed. lib. bdg. 10.00 (ISBN 0-8414-4151-0). Folcroft.
Fuchs, Albert. Goethe-Studien. (Kleinere Schriften zur Literatur und Geistesgeschichte). (Illus.). viii, 319p. (Ger.). 1968. 35.00x (ISBN 3-11-000239-6). De Gruyter.
Gearey, John. Goethes's Faust: The Making of Part I. LC 80-25826. 256p. 1981. 19.00x (ISBN 0-300-02571-8). Yale U Pr.
Goethe, Johann W. Goethe's Autobiography. 1949. 15.00 (ISBN 0-685-57341-9). Pub Aff Pr.
--Goethe's World View: Presented in His Reflections & Maxims. Ungar, Frederick, ed. Norden, Heinz, tr. LC 63-18513. pap. 4.50 (ISBN 0-8044-6192-9). Ungar.

Goethe, Johann W. Von. Faust. new ed. Hamlin, Cyrus, ed. Arndt, Walter, tr. from Ger. (Critical Edition Ser). 24p. 1976. pap. text ed. 5.45x (ISBN 0-393-09208-9). Norton.
--Goethe, the Lyricist. 2nd, rev. ed. LC 78-31302. (BCL Ser.: I). Repr. of 1955 ed. 18.50 (ISBN 0-404-50916-9). AMS Pr.
Goethe, Johann Wolfgang Von. The Autobiography of Johann Wolfgang Von Goethe, 2 vols. Oxenford, John, tr. from German. 1975. 10.00 ea. Vol. I (ISBN 0-226-30055-2). Vol.II (ISBN 0-226-30056-0). U of Chicago Pr.
Goethes Letzte Schweizer Reise. (Insel Taschenbuecher: No. 375). (Illus.). 438p. (Orig.). 1980. pap. text ed. 7.80 (ISBN 0-686-64714-9, Pub. by Insel Verlag Germany). Suhrkamp.
Gooch, G. P. Goethe: Some Makers of the Modern Spirit. Macmurray, John, ed. 1933. 8.50 (ISBN 0-8274-2421-3). R West.
Graham, Ilse. Goethe: Portrait of the Artist. LC 76-54974. 1977. 48.75x (ISBN 3-11-006928-8). De Gruyter.
Gray, Ronald D. Goethe: A Critical Introduction. (Orig.). 44.50 (ISBN 0-521-05134-7); pap. text ed. 14.50x (ISBN 0-521-09404-6). Cambridge U Pr.
--Goethe, the Alchemist: A Study of Alchemical Symbolism in Goethe's Literary & Scientific Works. LC 79-8612. Repr. of 1952 ed. 30.00 (ISBN 0-404-18476-6). AMS Pr.
Griggs, Edward H. Goethe's Faust: A Handbook of Ten Lectures. LC 76-42256. 1976. Repr. of 1906 ed. lib. bdg. 10.00 (ISBN 0-8414-4409-9). Folcroft.
Grimm, Herman. The Life & Times of Goethe. facsimile ed. LC 78-152986. (Select Bibliographies Reprint Ser). Repr. of 1880 ed. 26.00 (ISBN 0-8369-5738-5). Arno.
--The Life & Times of Goethe. 1880. 25.50 (ISBN 0-8274-2874-X). R West.
Grumach, Renate, ed. Goethe, Begegnungen und Gesprache: 1786-1792, Vol.3. 1977. 111.00x (ISBN 3-11-006836-2). De Gruyter.
Gundolf, Friedrich. Goethe. LC 79-170845. Repr. of 1930 ed. 44.50 (ISBN 0-404-02961-2). AMS Pr.
--Goethe. LC 79-170845. Repr. of 1930 ed. 44.50 (ISBN 0-404-02961-2). AMS Pr.
Haile, H. G. Artist in Chrysalis: A Biographical Study of Goethe in Italy. LC 72-92632. (Illus.). 120p. 1973. 14.50 (ISBN 0-252-00326-8). U of Ill Pr.
--Invitation to Goethe's Faust. LC 77-7461. (No. 21). 244p. 1978. 16.75x (ISBN 0-8173-7326-8). U of Ala Pr.
Hammer, Carl, Jr. Goethe & Rousseau: Resonances of the Mind. LC 72-91665. 232p. 1973. 12.00x (ISBN 0-8131-1289-3). U Pr of Ky.
Hammer, Carl, Jr., ed. Goethe After Two Centuries: A Series of Essays. LC 68-26257. 1969. Repr. of 1952 ed. 12.00 (ISBN 0-8046-0192-5). Kennikat.
Haskell, Juliana. Bayard Taylor's Translation of Goethe's Faust. LC 8-14930. (Columbia University. Germanic Studies. Old Series: No. 10). Repr. of 1908 ed. 11.50 (ISBN 0-404-50410-8). AMS Pr.
Haskell, Julianna. Bayard Taylor's Translation of Goethe's Faust. 1973. Repr. of 1908 ed. 11.00 (ISBN 0-8274-1367-X). R West.
Hatfield, Henry C. Goethe, a Critical Introduction. LC 64-24031. 1963. 14.00x (ISBN 0-674-35550-4). Harvard U Pr.
Hauhart, William F. Reception of Goethe's Faust in England in the First Half of the Nineteenth Century. LC 9-17319. (Columbia University. Germanic Studies, Old Series: No. 11). Repr. of 1909 ed. 11.50 (ISBN 0-404-50411-6). AMS Pr.
Heller, Erich. The Poet's Self & the Poem: Essays on Goethe, Nietzsche & Thomas Mann. 1976. text ed. 13.00x (ISBN 0-485-11164-0, Athlone Pr). Humanities.
Heller, Otto. Faust & Faustus: A Study of Goethe's Relation to Marlowe. LC 72-187841. 174p. 1972. Repr. of 1931 ed. lib. bdg. 11.00x (ISBN 0-8154-0412-3). Cooper Sq.
Herford, C. H. Goethe. 93p. 1981. Repr. lib. bdg. 10.00 (ISBN 0-89987-365-0). Darby Bks.
--Goethe. 1973. 10.00 (ISBN 0-8274-0040-3). R West.
Heun, Hans G. Satzbau in Der Prosa Des Jungen Goethe. 1930. 14.00 (ISBN 0-384-22781-3); pap. 11.00 (ISBN 0-384-22780-5). Johnson Repr.
Hiebel, Friedrich. Goethe's Message of Beauty in Our Twentieth Century World. 1979. 1.75 (ISBN 0-916786-37-4). St George Bk Serv.
Hitchcock, Thomas. Unhappy Loves of Men of Genius: Gibbon, Johnson, Goethe, Mozart & Irving. 1979. Repr. of 1892 ed. lib. bdg. 25.00 (ISBN 0-8492-5322-5). R West.
Howe, Susanne. Wilhelm Meister & His English Kinsmen. LC 30-1541. Repr. of 1930 ed. 17.00 (ISBN 0-404-03367-9). AMS Pr.
Hoyer, W. Goethe's Life in Pictures. (Illus.). 1963. 1.95 (ISBN 0-685-00761-8). Adler.
Hoyer, Walter. Goethe's Life in Pictures. (Illus.). 1969. 5.00 (ISBN 0-85496-063-5). Dufour.
Hungerford, Edward B. Shores of Darkness. 7.00 (ISBN 0-8446-2285-0). Peter Smith.
Jantz, Harold. The Form of Faust: The Work of Art & Its Intrinsic Structures. LC 78-1447. 1978. text ed. 14.00x (ISBN 0-8018-2080-4). Johns Hopkins.
--Goethe's Faust As a Renaissance Man: Parallels & Prototypes. LC 74-2251. 216p. 1974. Repr. of 1951 ed. 9.00 (ISBN 0-87752-174-3). Gordian.
--The Mothers in Faust: The Myth of Time & Creativity. LC 68-31017. (Illus.). 96p. 1969. 8.00x (ISBN 0-8018-0311-X). Johns Hopkins.
Kaufmann, Walter. Discovering the Mind, Vol. 1: Goethe, Kant, & Hegel. LC 79-18004. 1980. 14.95 (ISBN 0-07-033311-4). McGraw.
Klenze, Camillo Von. From Goethe to Hauptmann: Studies in a Changing Culture. LC 66-23519. 1926. 10.50x (ISBN 0-8196-0178-0). Biblo.
Knoblaugh, Von W., ed. The Early Life of Goethe. Oxenford, John, tr. 378p. 1981. Repr. of 1904 ed. lib. bdg. 35.00 (ISBN 0-89984-248-8). Century Bookbindery.
Kostovski, Ilya. Goethe & Dostoyevsky: Two Devils, Two Geniuses, a Study of the Demonic in Their Work. 1974. lib. bdg. 69.95 (ISBN 0-87700-215-0). Revisionist Pr.
Lamport, F. J. A Student's Guide to Goethe. 1971. pap. text ed. 5.00x (ISBN 0-435-37572-5). Heinemann Ed.
Lee, Meredith. Studies in Goethe's Lyric Cycles. (Studies in the Germanic Languages & Literatures). 1979. 14.50x (ISBN 0-8078-8093-0). U of NC Pr.
Lewes, George H. The Life of Goethe. 1979. Repr. of 1864 ed. lib. bdg. 30.00 (ISBN 0-8482-1627-X). Norwood Edns.
Ludwig, Emil. Goethe, the History of a Man: 1749-1832. 1928. 25.00 (ISBN 0-8274-2425-6). R West.
Lukacs, Georg. Goethe & His Age. Anchor, R., tr. from Ger. 1968. text ed. write for info. (ISBN 0-391-01982-1); pap. text ed. write for info. (ISBN 0-391-01983-X). Humanities.
--Goethe & His Age. Anchor, Robert, tr. from Ger. 1978. Repr. of 1968 ed. 22.50 (ISBN 0-86527-256-5). Fertig.
Mabie, Hamilton W. Backgrounds of Literature. LC 72-111846. (Essay Index Reprint Ser). 1904. 26.00 (ISBN 0-8369-1617-4). Arno.
Macintosh, W. Scott & Goethe. LC 71-113340. 1970. Repr. of 1925 ed. 12.00 (ISBN 0-8046-1026-6). Kennikat.
Mason, Eudo C. Goethe's Faust: Its Genesis & Purport. 1967. 24.00x (ISBN 0-520-00821-9). U of Cal Pr.
Masson, David. Essays Biographical & Critical: Chiefly on English Poets. 1856. lib. bdg. 50.00 (ISBN 0-8414-6491-X). Folcroft.
--Three Devils: Luther's, Milton's & Goethe's. LC 72-193946. 1874. lib. bdg. 17.50 (ISBN 0-8414-6495-2). Folcroft.
Mendelssohn-Bartholdy, F. Goethe & Mendelssohn. LC 70-122622. (Studies in German Literature, No. 13). 1970. Repr. of 1874 ed. lib. bdg. 49.95 (ISBN 0-8383-0902-X). Haskell.
Metchnikoff, Elias. Optimism & Pessimism in Goethe's Life. (Illus.). 113p. 1981. Repr. of 1908 ed. 41.85 (ISBN 0-89901-025-3). Found Class Reprints.
Milch, Robert J. Faust, Pts. 1 & 2, Notes. (Orig.). pap. 1.95 (ISBN 0-8220-0479-8). Cliffs.
Montgomery, Marshall. Studies in the Age of Goethe. LC 77-9357. 1977. lib. bdg. 20.00 (ISBN 0-8414-6208-9). Folcroft.
Montgomery, Paul. Monarch Notes on Goethe's Faust. (Orig.). pap. 1.75 (ISBN 0-671-00521-9). Monarch Pr.
Moore, Charles L. Incense & Iconoclasm. 343p. 1980. Repr. of 1915 ed. lib. bdg. 30.00 (ISBN 0-89987-573-4). Century Bookbindery.
Muller, Curt R. Die Geschichtlichen Voraussetzungen Des Symbolbegriffs in Goethes Kunstanschauung. 21.50 (ISBN 0-384-40390-5); pap. 18.50 (ISBN 0-685-13442-3). Johnson Repr.
Nevinson, Henry W. Goethe: Man & Poet. 69.95 (ISBN 0-8490-0244-3). Gordon Pr.
--Goethe: Man & Poet. facsimile ed. LC 77-164619. (Select Bibliographies Reprint Ser). Repr. of 1931 ed. 18.00 (ISBN 0-8369-5902-7). Arno.
Nisbet, H. B. Goethe & the Scientific Tradition. 83p. 1972. 35.00x (ISBN 0-85457-050-0, Pub. by Inst Germanic Stud England). State Mutual Bk.
Orrick, James. Matthew Arnold & Goethe. LC 70-179267. (Studies in Comparative Literature, No. 35). 1972. Repr. of 1928 ed. lib. bdg. 40.95 (ISBN 0-8383-1368-X). Haskell.
Orrick, James B. Matthew Arnold & Goethe. LC 72-194341. 1928. lib. bdg. 10.00 (ISBN 0-8414-9232-8). Folcroft.
Oxenford, John. Goethe's Boyhood Seventeen Hundred & Forty Nine to Seventeen Hundred & Sixtyfour: Being the First Five Books Forming Part One of Goethe's Autobiography. 1973. Repr. of 1888 ed. 25.00 (ISBN 0-8274-1012-3). R West.
Pinger, W. R. Laurence Sterne & Goethe. LC 72-196547. 1920. lib. bdg. 10.00 (ISBN 0-8414-9258-1). Folcroft.
Pyritz, Hans W. Goethe-Bibliographie, 2 vols. Incl. Vol. 1. Up to 1954. 856p. 1965. 90.00x (ISBN 3-533-01000-7); Vol. 2. 1955-1964. 347p. 1968. 45.00x (ISBN 0-685-28779-3). (Ger.). 1972. Intl Pubns Serv.
Reed, T. J. The Classical Centre: Goethe & Weimar Seventeen Seventy-Five to Eighteen Thirty-Two. LC 79-54252. (Literary History of Germany Ser.: Vol. 5). 1980. text ed. 28.50x (ISBN 0-06-495825-6). B&N.
Reik, Theodor. Fragment of a Great Confession. LC 73-2643. 497p. 1973. Repr. of 1965 ed. lib. bdg. 20.00x (ISBN 0-8371-6812-0, REGC). Greenwood.
Richards, David B. Goerthe's Search for the Muse: Translation & Creativity. vi, 114p. 1979. 14.00 (ISBN 90-272-0967-7, GLLM 7). Benjamins North Am.
Robertson, J. G. Goethe. 1973. Repr. of 1927 ed. 20.00 (ISBN 0-8274-0988-5). R West.
--Goethe. LC 74-16295. (Studies in Goethe, No. 61). 1974. lib. bdg. 51.95 (ISBN 0-8383-2036-8). Haskell.
--Goethe & the Twentieth Century. LC 72-3678. (Studies in German Literature, No. 13). 1972. Repr. of 1912 ed. lib. bdg. 32.95 (ISBN 0-8383-1581-X). Haskell.
--The Life & Work of Goethe. LC 72-8646. (Studies in German Literature, No. 13). 1973. Repr. of 1932 ed. lib. bdg. 43.95 (ISBN 0-8383-1671-9). Haskell.
Robertson, John G. Goethe & Byron. LC 77-23089. 1925. lib. bdg. 12.50 (ISBN 0-8414-7386-2). Folcroft.
--The Life & Work of Goethe, 1749-1832. facsimile ed. LC 79-179536. (Select Bibliographies Reprint Ser). Repr. of 1932 ed. 21.00 (ISBN 0-8369-6665-1). Arno.
--The Life & Work of Goethe 1749-1832. 1973. lib. bdg. 14.75 (ISBN 0-685-35442-3). Folcroft.
--Matthew Arnold & Goethe. 1925. lib. bdg. 12.50 (ISBN 0-8414-7461-3). Folcroft.
Robson-Scott, W. D. The Younger Goethe & the Visual Arts. (Angelica Germanica Ser.). 200p. 49.50 (ISBN 0-521-23321-6). Cambridge U Pr.
Rolland, Romain. Goethe & Beethoven. LC 67-13338. (Illus.). 1968. Repr. of 1931 ed. 15.00 (ISBN 0-405-08896-5, Blom Pubns). Arno.
Rueff, H. Zur Entstehungsgeschichte Von Goethes Torquato Tasso. Repr. of 1910 ed. pap. 7.00 (ISBN 0-384-52485-0). Johnson Repr.
Salm, Peter. The Poem As Plant: A Biological View of Goethe's Faust. LC 71-141461. (Illus.). 1971. 12.00 (ISBN 0-8295-0204-1). UPB.
Santayana, George. Three Philosophical Poets. LC 74-134467. 1971. Repr. of 1910 ed. lib. bdg. 11.00x (ISBN 0-8154-0361-5). Cooper Sq.
Schaeffer, Emil, ed. Goethes Aussere Erscheinung. (Illus.). 120p. 1980. text ed. 31.20 (ISBN 3-458-04925-8, Pub. by Insel Verlag Germany). Suhrkamp.
Seeley, John. Goethe. LC 76-130246. (Studies in German Literature, No. 13). 1970. Repr. of 1894 ed. lib. bdg. 48.95 (ISBN 0-8383-1136-9). Haskell.
Seeley, John R. Goethe. 1973. Repr. of 1894 ed. 20.00 (ISBN 0-8274-1807-8). R West.
Sime, James. Life of Johann Wolfgang Goethe. LC 77-160782. 1971. Repr. of 1888 ed. 12.00 (ISBN 0-8046-1614-0). Kennikat.
--Life of Johann Wolfgang Goethe. 1977. Repr. of 1888 ed. lib. bdg. 17.50 (ISBN 0-8492-2416-0). R West.
Snider, Denton J. Goethe's Faust: A Commentary, 2 vols. 1973. Repr. of 1886 ed. 65.00 (ISBN 0-8274-0458-1). R West.
Spalding, John L. Opportunity, & Other Essays & Addresses. facs. ed. LC 68-57339. (Essay Index Reprint Ser). 1900. 15.00 (ISBN 0-8369-0894-5). Arno.
Stawell, Florence M. Goethe & Faust, an Interpretation with Passages Newly Translated. LC 74-38845. (Studies in German Literature, No. 13). 291p. 1972. Repr. of 1928 ed. lib. bdg. 38.95 (ISBN 0-8383-1392-2). Haskell.
Steer, A. G., Jr. Goethe's Science in the Structure of the Wanderjahre. LC 78-9886. 256p. 1979. 18.00 (ISBN 0-8203-0454-9). U of Ga Pr.
Steer, Alfred G., Jr. Goethe's Social Philosophy As Revealed in "Campagne in Frankreich" & "Belagerlung Von Mainz". LC 55-62599. (North Carolina University. Studies in the Germanic Languages & Literatures: No. 15). Repr. of 1955 ed. 18.50 (ISBN 0-404-50915-0). AMS Pr.
Steiner, Rudolf. Goethe's Conception of the World. LC 72-6483. (Studies in German Literature, No. 13). 320p. 1972. Repr. of 1932 ed. lib. bdg. 49.95 (ISBN 0-8383-1618-2). Haskell.
--The Theory of Knowledge Implicit in Goethe's World Conception. 2nd ed. Wannamaker, Olin D., tr. from Ger. LC 70-76994. Orig. Title: Grundlinien Einer Erkenntnistheorie der Goetheschen Weltanschauung. 133p. 1978. 9.95 (ISBN 0-910142-94-7); pap. 5.95 (ISBN 0-910142-85-8). Anthroposophic.
Sternfeld, Frederick. Goethe & Music. (Music Reprint Ser.). 176p. 1979. Repr. of 1954 ed. 19.50 (ISBN 0-306-79515-9). Da Capo.
Stewart, Walter K. Time Structure in Drama, Goethe's Storm und Drgng Plays. (Amsterdamer Publikationen Zur Sprache und Literatur: No. 35). 1978. pap. text ed. 34.50x (ISBN 90-6203-682-1). Humanities.
Strich, Fritz. Goethe & World Literature. Sym, C. A., tr. from Ger. LC 71-138188. 1971. Repr. of 1949 ed. lib. bdg. 17.75x (ISBN 0-8371-5645-9, STGO). Greenwood.
--Goethe & World Literature. LC 75-159710. 1971. Repr. of 1949 ed. 15.00 (ISBN 0-8046-1648-5). Kennikat.
Thomas, Calvin. Goethe. 1973. Repr. of 1917 ed. 25.00 (ISBN 0-8274-0427-1). R West.
Trevelyan, Humphry. Goethe & the Greeks. LC 81-3908. 368p. Date not set. price not set (ISBN 0-521-24137-5); pap. price not set (ISBN 0-521-28471-6). Cambridge U Pr.
--Goethe & the Greeks. LC 72-5134. xvi, 321p. 1972. Repr. of 1941 ed. lib. bdg. 15.00x (ISBN 0-374-97994-4). Octagon.
Van Abbe, Derek. Goethe: New Perspectives on a Writer & His Time. 175p. 1974. 10.00 (ISBN 0-8387-1539-7). Bucknell U Pr.
Vietor, Karl. Goethe the Poet. Hadas, Moses, tr. LC 72-81482. 1970. Repr. of 1949 ed. 16.00 (ISBN 0-8462-1391-5). Russell.
Wadepuhl, Walter. Goethe's Interest in the New World. LC 72-10003. (Studies in German Literature, No. 13). 1973. Repr. of 1934 ed. lib. bdg. 29.95 (ISBN 0-8383-1684-0). Haskell.
Wahr, F. B. Emerson & Goethe. 59.95 (ISBN 0-8490-0104-8). Gordon Pr.
Wahr, Frederick B. Emerson & Goethe. 197p. 1980. Repr. of 1915 ed. lib. bdg. 25.00 (ISBN 0-8492-2979-0). R West.
--Emerson & Goethe. LC 72-8647. 1915. lib. bdg. 25.00 (ISBN 0-8414-0392-9). Folcroft.
Weinberg, Kurt. The Figure of Faust in Valery & Goethe. LC 75-30211. (Princeton Essays in Literature Ser.). 1976. 19.50 (ISBN 0-691-06304-4). Princeton U Pr.
White, Ann. Names & Nomenclature in Goethe's Faust. 176p. 1981. 40.00x (ISBN 0-85457-093-4, Pub. by Inst Germanic Stud England). State Mutual Bk.
Willoughby, L. A., ed. Papers About Goethe: Goethe & Wordsworth, Coleridge & His Contemporaries. Fairley, Barker. 1934. lib. bdg. 20.00 (ISBN 0-8414-9354-5). Folcroft.

GOETZ, KARL, 1875-1950

Kienast, Gunter W. The Medals of Karl Goetz. LC 67-21457. (Illus.). 284p. 1980. Repr. of 1967 ed. 38.00 (ISBN 0-686-30950-2). Artus Co.

GOFFMAN, ERVING

Ditton, Jason, ed. The View from Goffman. LC 79-25202. Date not set. 25.00x (ISBN 0-312-84598-7). St Martin.

GOGARTY, OLIVER ST. JOHN, 1878-1957

Carens, James F. Surpassing Wit: Oliver St. John Gogarty, His Poetry &His Prose. LC 78-12644. 304p. 1979. 17.50x (ISBN 0-231-04642-1). Columbia U Pr.
Jeffares, A. Norman. The Circus Animals: Essays on W. B. Yeats. LC 73-13824. 1970. 10.00x (ISBN 0-8047-0754-5). Stanford U Pr.
Lyons, J. B. Oliver St. John Gogarty. (Irish Writers Ser.). 89p. 1976. 4.50 (ISBN 0-8387-1359-9); pap. 1.95 (ISBN 0-8387-1397-1). Bucknell U Pr.
--Oliver St. John Gogarty: A Biography. 348p. 1981. text ed. 25.00x (ISBN 0-686-72929-3, 0-90547121, Pub. by Blackwater Ireland). Humanities.
O'Connor, Ulick. Times I've Seen. (Illus.). 1964. 10.00 (ISBN 0-8392-1119-8). Astor-Honor.

GOGH, VINCENT VAN

see Van Gogh, Vincent, 1853-1890

GOGOL, NIKOLAI VASILEVICH, 1809-1852

Debreczeny, Paul. Nikolay Gogol & His Contemporary Critics. LC 66-18702. (Transactions Ser.: Vol. 56, Pt. 3). 1966. pap. 1.00 (ISBN 0-87169-563-4). Am Philos.
Ehre, Milton, ed. The Theater of Nikolay Gogol. Gottschalk, Fruma, tr. from Rus. LC 79-23745. 1980. lib. bdg. 18.50x (ISBN 0-226-30064-1). U of Chicago Pr.
Fanger, Donald. The Creation of Nikolai Gogol. LC 79-14135. 1979. 16.50x (ISBN 0-674-17565-4). Harvard U Pr.
--Dostoevsky & Romantic Realism: A Study of Dostoevsky in Relation to Balzac, Dickens, Gogol. LC 65-13841. 1968. pap. 7.00x (ISBN 0-226-23747-8). U of Chicago Pr.

Gippius, V. V. Gogol. Maguire, R., tr. 1981. 17.50 (ISBN 0-88233-612-6). Ardis Pubs.
Gippius, Vasily. Gogol. LC 63-7522. (Slavic Reprint Ser.: No. 1). 246p. (Rus). 1963. pap. text ed. 6.00x (ISBN 0-87057-069-2, Pub. by Brown U Pr). U Pr of New Eng.
Karlinsky, Simon. The Sexual Labyrinth of Nikolai Gogol. 1976. 16.50x (ISBN 0-674-80281-0). Harvard U Pr.
Lavrin, Janko. Gogol. LC 72-2123. (Studies in European Literature, No. 56). 1972. Repr. of 1926 ed. lib. bdg. 34.95 (ISBN 0-8383-1473-2). Haskell.
Lindstrom, Thais S. Nikolay Gogol. (World Authors Ser.: Russia: No. 299). 1974. lib. bdg. 12.50 (ISBN 0-8057-2377-3). Twayne.
Little, T. E. The Fantasts: Studies of J. R. R. Tolkien, Lewis Carroll, Mervyn Peake, Nikolay Gogol & Kenneth Grahame. 1981. 50.00x (ISBN 0-86127-212-9, Pub. by Avebury Pub England). State Mutual Bk.
Maguire, Robert A., ed. Gogol from the Twentieth Century: Eleven Essays. LC 73-16750. 428p. 1974. 28.50 (ISBN 0-691-06268-4); pap. 8.95 (ISBN 0-691-01326-8). Princeton U Pr.
Meyer, Priscilla & Rudy, Stephen, eds. Dostoevsky & Gogol: Texts & Criticism. 1979. 17.50 (ISBN 0-88233-315-1); pap. 6.50 (ISBN 0-686-76827-2). Ardis Pubs.
Nabokov, Vladimir. Nikolai Gogol. LC 44-8135. 1961. pap. 4.95 (ISBN 0-8112-0120-1, NDP78). New Directions.
Rowe, William Woodin. Through Gogol's Looking Glass: Reverse Vision, False Focus & Precarious Logic. LC 75-21982. 201p. 1976. 12.50x (ISBN 0-8147-7366-4); pap. 5.95x (ISBN 0-8147-7377-X). NYU Pr.
Rozanov, Vasily. Dostoevsky & the Legend of the Grand Inquisitor. Roberts, Spencer E., tr. from Rus. LC 79-37754. 288p. 1972. 20.00x (ISBN 0-8014-0694-3). Cornell U Pr.
Setchkarev, Vsevolod. Gogol: His Life & Works. Kramer, Robert, tr. LC 65-19518. (Gotham Library). (Orig.). 1965. pap. 4.95x (ISBN 0-8147-0380-1). NYU Pr.
Slonimskii, Aleksandr L. Tekhnika Komicheskogo U Gogolia. LC 63-7523. (Slavic Reprint Ser., No. 2). 71p. (Rus.). 1963. pap. text ed. 3.50x (ISBN 0-87057-070-6, Pub. by Brown U Pr). U Pr of New Eng.
Sobel, Ruth. Gogol's Forgotten Book: Selected Passages & Its Contemporary Readers. LC 80-8292. 1981. lib. bdg. 19.50 (ISBN 0-8191-1630-0); pap. text ed. 10.50 (ISBN 0-8191-1631-9). U Pr of Amer.
Stromecky, O. The How of Gogol. Penot, D. & Heller, Hertha, trs. from Russian & Ukrainian. 1975. 5.00 (ISBN 0-933958-02-1). UAH Pr.
Trahan, Elizabeth, ed. Gogol's "Overcoat". An Anthology of Critical Essays. 1981. 15.00 (ISBN 0-88233-614-2). Ardis Pubs.
Zeldin, Jesse. Nikolai Gogol's Quest for Beauty: An Exploration into His Works. LC 78-2693. 1978. 13.50x (ISBN 0-7006-0173-2). Regents Pr KS.

GOGOLAK, PETE
Gogolak, Peter & Carter, Joseph. Nothing to Kick About: The Autobiography of a Modern Immigrant. LC 73-3904. (Illus.). 256p. 1973. 6.95 (ISBN 0-396-06820-0). Dodd.

GOHDES, CLARENCE LOUIS FRANK
Woodress, James L., ed. Essay Mostly on Periodical Publishing in America: A Collection in Honor of Clarence Gohdes. LC 72-96683. xiv, 224p. 1973. 9.50 (ISBN 0-8223-0281-0). Duke.

GOIDELIC LANGUAGES
see also Gaelic Language; Irish Language; Manx Language

GOING AWAY TO SCHOOL
see Residence and Education

GOITER
see also Cretinism
DeGroot, Leslie J. & Stanbury, John B. The Thyroid & Its Diseases. 4th ed. LC 73-17916. 840p. 1975. 51.95 (ISBN 0-471-20530-3). Krieger.
Delange, F. Endemic Goitre & Thyroid Function in Central Africa. Falkner, F., et al, eds. (Monographs in Pediatrics: Vol. 2). (Illus.). xvi, 160p. 1974. 44.50 (ISBN 3-8055-1687-8). S Karger.
Hamburger, Joel I. Nontoxic Goiter: Concept & Controversy. (Illus.). 232p. 1973. 14.50 (ISBN 0-398-02723-4). C C Thomas.
Lewis, Alan E. Graves' Disease. LC 80-15624. (Discussions in Patient Management Ser.). 1980. pap. 12.00 (ISBN 0-87488-870-0). Med Exam.
The Role of Cassava in the Etiology of Endemic Goitre & Cretinism. 182p. 1980. pap. 10.00 (ISBN 0-686-62998-1, IDRC-136, IDRC). Unipub.
Stanbury, John B. Endemic Goiter & Endemic Cretinism: Iodine Nutrition in Health. LC 79-22459. 1980. 45.50 (ISBN 0-471-05819-X, Pub. by Wiley Medical). Wiley.

GOITER, EXOPHTHALMIC
see Graves' Disease

GOKHALE, GOPAL KRISHNA, 1866-1914
Nanda, B. R. Gokhale: The Indian Moderates & the British Raj. LC 77-72129. (Illus.). 1977. text ed. 37.50 (ISBN 0-691-03115-0). Princeton U Pr.

GOLCONDA, INDIA
Palmer, Vance. Golconda. 296p. 1972. 15.00x (ISBN 0-7022-0789-6); pap. 7.95x (ISBN 0-7022-0790-X). U of Queensland Pr.
Richards, J. F. Mughal Administration in Golconda. (Illus.). 360p. 1975. 49.00x (ISBN 0-19-821561-4). Oxford U Pr.

GOLD
see also Alchemy; Coinage; Currency Question; Gold Mines and Mining; Gold Standard; Goldwork; Jewelry; Money; Quantity Theory of Money; Silver Question
Beach, Walter E. British International Gold Movements & Banking Policy, 1881-1913. LC 76-138201. (Illus.). xiv, 218p. Repr. of 1935 ed. lib. bdg. 15.50x (ISBN 0-8371-5554-1, BEBG). Greenwood.
Beckhardt, Israel. The Small Investor's Guide to Gold. 1979. pap. 2.95 (ISBN 0-532-23232-1). Woodhill.
Bleifuss, William. Gold: How and Where to Find It Yourself. LC 80-679. 1981. pap. 7.95 (ISBN 0-672-52661-1). Bobbs.
Branson, Oscar T. What You Need to Know About Your Gold & Silver. (Illus.). 56p. (Orig.). 1980. pap. 4.95 (ISBN 0-918080-44-4). Treasure Chest.
Cairnes, John E. Essays in Political Economy. LC 65-20923. Repr. of 1873 ed. 17.50x (ISBN 0-678-00105-7). Kelley.
Chevalier, Michel. On the Probable Fall in the Value of Gold. Cobden, Richard, ed. LC 68-28619. Repr. of 1859 ed. lib. bdg. 15.00x (ISBN 0-8371-0045-3, CHPF). Greenwood.
Cuse, Arthur. How to Make it in Gold & Not Get @#$! (Orig.). 1974. pap. 9.95 (ISBN 0-917474-02-3). Guideline Pub.
Doering, David & Doering, Susan. California Fractional Gold. (Illus.). 1980. lib. bdg. 60.00 (ISBN 0-686-64452-2). S J Durst.
Emmons, William H. Gold Deposits of the World: With a Section on Prospecting. LC 74-350. (Vol. 13). (Illus.). 562p. 1974. Repr. of 1937 ed. gold 33.00x (ISBN 0-405-05912-4). Arno.
Flueler, Niklaus & Speich, Sebastian, eds. Gold. (Illus.). 144p. 60.00 (ISBN 0-933516-26-6). Alpine Fine Arts.
Flumiani, Carlo M. The Nine Deceits & the Collapse of Gold. (Illus.). 1977. 49.75 (ISBN 0-89266-051-1). Am Classical Coll Pr.
Frankel, S. Herbert. Gold & International Equity Investment. (Institute of Economic Affairs, Hobart Papers Ser.: No. 45). (Orig.). pap. 2.50 (ISBN 0-255-69643-4). Transatlantic.
Gajda, George. Gold Refining. 2nd rev. ed. 1980. 18.25 (ISBN 0-686-17797-5). G Gajda.
Gayer, A. D., ed. Lessons of Monetary Experience: Essays in Honor of Irving Fisher. LC 70-86089. Repr. of 1937 ed. 19.50x (ISBN 0-678-00643-1). Kelley.
The Geochemistry of Gold & It's Deposits. (Geological Survey Bulletin: No. 280). 584p. 1980. pap. 83.50 (ISBN 0-660-01769-5, SSC 136, SSC). Unipub.
Gold: Historical & Economic Aspects, 18 vols. facsimile ed. 1974. Set. 435.00 (ISBN 0-405-05910-8). Arno.
Grimaudet, Francois & Von Humboldt, Alexander. Fluctuations of Gold Together with the Law of Payment. LC 75-157156. (Research & Source Works Ser.: No. 722). 1971. Repr. of 1900 ed. 18.50 (ISBN 0-8337-4622-7). B Franklin.
Hardy, Charles O. Is There Enough Gold? (Brookings Institution Reprint Ser). Repr. of 1936 ed. lib. bdg. 27.50x (ISBN 0-697-00157-1). Irvington.
Hinshaw, Randall, ed. Monetary Reform & the Price of Gold: Alternative Approaches. LC 67-24630. 176p. 1967. 12.50x (ISBN 0-8018-0274-1). Johns Hopkins.
Hobson, John A. Gold Prices & Wages. LC 68-55733. Repr. of 1913 ed. 13.50x (ISBN 0-678-00767-5). Kelley.
Keynes, John M. Essays in Persuasion. 1963. pap. 5.95 (ISBN 0-393-00190-3, Norton Lib). Norton.
Madden, John T. & Nadler, Marcus. International Money Markets. LC 68-23311. Repr. of 1935 ed. lib. bdg. 37.50 (ISBN 0-8371-0552-8, MAIM). Greenwood.
Merton, Henry A. Your Gold & Silver: An Easy Guide to Appraising Household Objects, Coins, Heirlooms & Jewelry. (Illus.). 96p. 1981. pap. 4.95 (ISBN 0-02-077410-9, Collier). Macmillan.
Miller, Roger L. & Manne, Henry G. Gold, Money & the Law. LC 75-20705. 160p. 1975. 12.95 (ISBN 0-202-06072-1). Beresford Bk Serv.
Mitchell, Wesley C. Gold, Prices & Wages Under the Greenback Standard. pap. 27.00 (ISBN 0-384-39220-2). Johnson Repr.
--Gold, Prices, & Wages Under the Greenback Standard. LC 66-21688. Repr. of 1908 ed. 25.00x (ISBN 0-678-00200-2). Kelley.
Mortensen, Michael H. Gold, Swiss Banks & the World Monetary Catastrophe. (Illus.). 1981. 49.65 (ISBN 0-930008-43-X). Inst Econ Pol.
Nelson, Robert N. How to Buy Gold for Thirty Percent Below Market: And How to Avoid Confiscation by the Government. Date not set. 45.00 (ISBN 0-940372-00-2). Berot Bk.
New International Monetary Developments & the Approaching Collapse in the Price of Gold. 1979. deluxe ed. 55.85 (ISBN 0-918968-29-1). Inst Econ Finan.
Preston, Ralph N. Oregon Gold & Gem Maps. (Illus.). 1977. pap. 4.95 (ISBN 0-8323-0309-7). Binford.
Puddephatt, R. J. The Chemistry of Gold. (Topics in Inorganic & General Chemistry: Vol. 16). 1978. 58.00 (ISBN 0-444-41624-2). Elsevier.
Rimmer, Robert H. Gold Lovers. 1974. pap. 1.25 (ISBN 0-451-06970-6, Y6970, Sig). NAL.
Rist, Charles. Triumph of Gold. Cortney, Philip, tr. Repr. of 1961 ed. lib. bdg. 15.00x (ISBN 0-8371-2296-1, RITQ). Greenwood.
Rosen, Lawrence R. When & How to Profit from Buying & Selling Gold. LC 74-29743. 206p. 1975. 14.95 (ISBN 0-87094-096-1). Dow Jones-Irwin.
Ruhe-Schoen, Janet. Pan for Gold on Your Next Vacation. LC 77-1378. 1978. pap. 2.50 (ISBN 0-87576-059-7). Pilot Bks.
Sarnoff, Paul. Trading in Gold. 1982. 14.95 (ISBN 0-671-41329-5). S&S.
--Trading in Gold. 144p. 1981. limeted professional ed. 22.50 (ISBN 0-89047-039-1). Herman Pub.
Sennholz, Hans F., ed. Gold Is Money. LC 74-15161. (Contributions in Economics & Economic History Ser.: No. 12). 1975. lib. bdg. 15.00 (ISBN 0-8371-7804-5, SGM/). Greenwood.
Sinclair, James E. & Schultz, Harry D. How You Can Profit from Gold. 1980. 14.95 (ISBN 0-87000-473-5). Arlington Hse.
Stirling, Patrick J. Australian & Californian Gold Discoveries & Their Probable Consequences. Repr. of 1853 ed. lib. bdg. 19.00x (ISBN 0-8371-0670-2, STGD). Greenwood.
Tatsch, J. H. Gold Deposits: Origin, Evolution, and Present Characteristics. LC 75-1947. (Illus.). 275p. 1975. text ed. 72.00 (ISBN 0-912890-07-X). Tatsch.
U. S. House of Representatives, Committee on Banking & Currency. Gold Panic Investigation. LC 74-363. (Vol. 3). 483p. 1974. Repr. of 1870 ed. 25.00x (ISBN 0-405-05923-X). Arno.
Waller, ed. And There's Gold Out There. (Illus.). 17.50x (ISBN 0-392-02108-0, ABC). Sportshelf.

GOLD–HISTORY
Bordet, Henri. L'Or et L'Argent En 1864. 62p. 1981. Repr. of 1864 ed. lib. bdg. 40.00 (ISBN 0-8287-1576-9). Clearwater Pub.
Buranelli, Vincent. Gold: An Illustrated History. Dembner, Red, ed. (Illus.). 1979. 30.00 (ISBN 0-8437-3136-2). Hammond Inc.
Center for Inter-American Relations & American Federation of Arts. El Dorado: The Gold of Ancient Columbia. LC 74-175969. (Illus.). 150p. 1980. pap. 14.95 (ISBN 0-295-95736-0). U of Wash Pr.
Cohen, Daniel. Gold: The Fascinating Study of the Noble Metal Through the Ages. LC 76-18067. (Illus.). 192p. (gr. 7 up). 1976. 6.95 (ISBN 0-87131-218-2). M Evans.
Einzig, Paul. The Destiny of Gold. LC 72-85830. 1972. 18.95 (ISBN 0-312-19565-6). St Martin.
Garrard, Timothy H. Akan Weights & the Gold Trade. LC 79-40718. (Legon History Ser.). (Illus.). 393p. 1980. text ed. 50.00x (ISBN 0-582-64631-6). Longman.
Hahn, Emily. Love of Gold. LC 80-7877. 224p. 1980. 10.95 (ISBN 0-690-01832-0). Har-Row.
Marx, Jenifer. The Magic of Gold. LC 76-53413. 1978. 10.95 (ISBN 0-385-11099-5). Doubleday.
Nolan, Tony. The Romantic World of Gold. Date not set. price not set (Pub. by Reed Books Australia). C E Tuttle.

GOLD–JUVENILE LITERATURE
Brindze, Ruth. Story of Gold. LC 55-11840. (Illus.). (gr. 4-8). 1954. 6.95 (ISBN 0-8149-0276-6). Vanguard.
O'Donnell, James J. Gold: The Noble Metal. LC 78-19167. 160p. (gr. 7 up). 1978. PLB 7.29 (ISBN 0-671-32877-8). Messner.

GOLD–STANDARDS OF FINENESS
see also Hall-Marks

GOLD–THERAPEUTIC USE
Block, Walter D. & Van Goor, Kornelius. Metabolism, Pharmacology & Therapeutic Uses of Gold Compounds. (American Lecture Dermatology). 80p. 1956. ed. spiral bdg. 9.75photocopy (ISBN 0-398-04212-8). C C Thomas.

GOLD ARTICLES
see Goldwork

GOLD COAST
see also Ghana
Ahuma, S. R. & Attoch. Gold Coast Nation & National Consciousness. 63p. 1971. Repr. of 1911 ed. 25.00x (ISBN 0-7146-1742-3, F Cass Co). Biblio Dist.
Claridge, W. W. History of Gold Coast & Ashanti, 2 vols. 2nd ed. 1964. 85.00x (ISBN 0-7146-1642-7, F Cass Co). Biblio Dist.
Crooks, J. J. Records Relating to the Gold Coast Settlements from 1750 to 1874. 576p. 1973. 36.00x (ISBN 0-7146-1647-8, F Cass Co). Biblio Dist.
Cruickshank, Bruce. Eighteen Years on the Gold Coast of Africa, 2 vols. 1966. 55.00x (ISBN 0-7146-1802-0, F Cass Co). Biblio Dist.
Ellis, Alfred B. History of the Gold Coast of West Africa. LC 77-75551. (Illus.). Repr. of 1893 ed. 14.50x (ISBN 0-8371-1126-9, Pub. by Negro U Pr). Greenwood.
Gildea, Roy Y. Nationalism & Indirect Rule in the Gold Coast: 1900-1950. 1975. pap. 2.00 (ISBN 0-87164-074-0). William-F.
Hayford, J. E. Gold Coast Native Institutions. 418p. 1970. Repr. of 1903 ed. 30.00x (ISBN 0-7146-1754-7, F Cass Co). Biblio Dist.
Holthouse, Hector. Gold Coast in Colour. LC 74-93148. (Colourful Australia Ser). (Illus.). 32p. 1973. 6.50x (ISBN 0-85179-130-1). Intl Pubns Serv.
Horton, Africanus B. Letters on the Political Condition of the Gold Coast Since the Exchange of Territory Between the English & Dutch Governments on January 1, 1868: Together with a Short Account of the Ashantee War 1862-1864 & the Awoonan War, 1866. 178p. 1970. Repr. of 1870 ed. 27.50x (ISBN 0-7146-1758-X, F Cass Co). Biblio Dist.
Kwame, Arhin, ed. The Papers of George Ekem Ferguson: A Fanti Official of the Government of the Gold Coast, 1890-1897. LC 75-321109. (African Social Research Documents: Vol. 7). 1974. pap. 13.50x (ISBN 0-8002-1780-2). Intl Pubns Serv.
Loyer, Godefroy. Relation du Voyage du Royaume d'Issigny, Cote d'Or, Pays de Guinee, en Afrique. (Bibliotheque Africaine Ser.). 318p. (Fr.). 1974. Repr. of 1714 ed. lib. bdg. 84.00x (ISBN 0-8287-0556-9, 72-2121). Clearwater Pub.
Meredith, Henry. Account of the Gold Coast of Africa. (Illus.). 264p. 1967. 27.50x (ISBN 0-7146-1039-9, F Cass Co). Biblio Dist.
Reynolds, Edward. Trade & Economic Change on the Gold Coast: 1807-1874. LC 74-77603. (Legon History Ser.). (Illus.). 210p. 1974. text ed. 12.00x (ISBN 0-582-64582-4). Longman.
Wight, Martin. The Gold Coast Legislative Council. Perham, Margery, ed. LC 74-14030. (Studies in Colonial Legislatures: Vol. 2). (Illus.). 285p. 1974. Repr. of 1947 ed. lib. bdg. 16.50x (ISBN 0-8371-7783-9, WIGC). Greenwood.

GOLD COINS
Durst, Lorraine S. & Durst, Sanford J. World Gold Coin Value Guide. LC 80-51832. 1980. softcover 9.00 (ISBN 0-686-64442-5); lib. bdg. 12.00 (ISBN 0-915262-54-1). S J Durst.
Durst, Sanford J. Contemporary World Gold Coins: Comprehensive Catalog. (Illus.). 128p. 1975. 10.00 (ISBN 0-915262-01-0). S J Durst.
Durst, Sanford J. & Ganz, David L. Encyclopedia of Values: U.S. Gold Coins. 1979. deluxe ed. 37.50 (ISBN 0-685-91294-9); lib. bdg. 29.50 (ISBN 0-915262-27-4). S J Durst.
Norweb, Emery M. English Gold Coins: Ancient to Modern Times. LC 68-9275. (Illus.). 96p. 1968. pap. text ed. 10.00x (ISBN 0-910386-44-7, Pub. by Cleveland Mus Art). Ind U Pr.

GOLD CURE
see Alcoholism–Treatment

GOLD MINES AND MINING
see also California–Gold Discoveries; Hydraulic Mining; Klondike Gold Fields; Prospecting
Allen, Joseph. Story of Superstition Mountain & the Lost Dutchman Gold Mine. (Orig.). 1971. pap. 2.25 (ISBN 0-671-83694-3). Archway.
Angier, Bradford. Looking for Gold. (Illus.). 224p. 1981. pap. 8.95 (ISBN 0-8117-2034-9). Stackpole.
Averill, Charles V., et al. Placer Mining for Gold in California. (Illus.). 357p. 1981. Repr. text ed. 24.95 (ISBN 0-89632-011-1). Del Oeste.
Bancroft, Caroline. Colorado's Lost Gold Mines & Buried Treasures. 1961. pap. 2.75 (ISBN 0-933472-16-1). Johnson Bks.
Black, Jack. Gold Locations of the United States. LC 77-92557. 176p. 1975. pap. 6.95 (ISBN 0-89632-000-6). Del Oeste.
Blue, Daniel. Thrilling Narrative of the Adventures, Sufferings & Starvation of Pike's Peak Gold Seekers on the Plains of the West in the Winter & Spring of 1859. 23p. 1968. Repr. of 1860 ed. pap. 2.50 (ISBN 0-87770-032-X). Ye Galleon.
Boericke, William F. Prospecting & Operating Small Gold Placers. 2nd ed. 1936. 18.00 (ISBN 0-471-08514-6, Pub. by Wiley-Interscience). Wiley.

Borthwick, J. D. Gold Hunters. LC 70-146785. 1971. Repr. of 1917 ed. 25.00 (ISBN 0-8103-3635-9). Gale.

Byers, William N. & Kellom, John H. Hand Book to the Gold Fields of Nebraska & Kansas. LC 72-9432. (The Far Western Frontier Ser.). (Illus.). 122p. 1973. Repr. of 1859 ed. 9.00 (ISBN 0-405-04963-3). Arno.

Campbell, Gilbert L. Wet Plates & Dry Gulches. LC 71-41602. (Wild & Woolly West Ser., No. 8). (Illus., Orig.). 1973. 7.00 (ISBN 0-910584-94-X); pap. 2.00 (ISBN 0-910584-11-7). Filter.

Carpenter, Kenneth E., ed. Gold Mining Company Prospect Uses: California, Alaska, Arizona, Colorado, Idaho, Utah, 2 pts. LC 74-365. (Vol. 6). (Illus.). 1974. gold 26.00 (ISBN 0-405-05926-4). Arno.

Cash, Joseph H. Working the Homestake. (Illus.). 150p. 1973. 5.95 (ISBN 0-8138-0755-7). Iowa St U Pr.

Chisholm, James. South Pass, 1868: James Chisholm's Journal of the Wyoming Gold Rush. Homsher, Lola M., ed. LC 60-12692. (Pioneer Heritage Ser: Vol. 3). (Illus.). vi, 245p. 1960. pap. 2.95 (ISBN 0-8032-5824-0, BB 606, Bison). U of Nebr Pr.

Conner, Daniel E. Confederate in the Colorado Gold Fields. Berthrong, Donald J. & Davenport, Odessa, eds. LC 70-88149. (Illus.). 1970. 12.95 (ISBN 0-8061-0891-6). U of Okla Pr.

Cornelius, Temple H. & Marshall, John B. Golden Treasures of the San Juan. LC 61-9435. 235p. 1961. pap. 5.95 (ISBN 0-8040-0636-9, SB). Swallow.

--Golden Treasures of the San Juan. LC 61-9435. 235p. 1961. pap. 5.95 (ISBN 0-8040-0636-9, SB). Swallow.

Emden, P. H. Randlords. 59.95 (ISBN 0-8490-0927-8). Gordon Pr.

Emmons, William H. Gold Deposits of the World: With a Section on Prospecting. LC 74-350. (Vol. 13). (Illus.). 562p. 1974. Repr. of 1937 ed. gold 33.00x (ISBN 0-405-05912-4). Arno.

Fahey, John. Ballyhoo Bonanza: Charles Sweeny & the Idaho Mines. LC 68-11046. (Illus.). 302p. 1971. 15.00 (ISBN 0-295-95129-X). U of Wash Pr.

Faulk, Terry R. Simple Methods of Mining Gold. 2nd ed. (Wild & Woolly West Ser. No. 10). (Illus., Orig.). 1981. 7.00 (ISBN 0-910584-97-4); pap. 1.50 (ISBN 0-910584-98-2). Filter.

Fielder, Mildred. The Treasure of Homestake Gold: The Story of Homestake Gold Mine. LC 70-113967. (Illus.). 478p. 1970. 7.95 (ISBN 0-87970-115-3). North Plains.

Fisher, Vardis & Holmes, Opal L. Gold Rushes & Mining Camps of the Early American West. LC 68-15028. (Illus.). 1968. 22.95 (ISBN 0-87004-043-X). Caxton.

Genta, Ellen G. Dig Your Own Gold. 1976. 4.95 (ISBN 0-89036-062-6). Hawkes Pub Inc.

Gerrick, David J. Gold Prospecting in Ohio. 84p. 1980. pap. 5.95 (ISBN 0-916750-25-6). Dayton Labs.

Gold Mines of the World. 1981. 52.10 (ISBN 0-686-30561-2). Minobras.

Gudde, Erwin G. California Gold Camps: A Geographical & Historical Dictionary of Camps, Towns, & Localities Where Gold Was Found & Mines, & of Wayside Stations & Trading Centers. Gudde, Elisabeth K., ed. LC 73-85788. (Illus.). 1975. 30.00 (ISBN 0-520-02572-5). U of Cal Pr.

Hafen, LeRoy & Hafen, Ann W. Reports from Colorado, 1859-65. (Illus.). 1961. 15.00 (ISBN 0-87062-040-1). A H Clark.

Hafen, Leroy R., ed. Colorado Gold Rush: Contemporary Letters & Reports 1858-1859. LC 74-7163. (Southwest Historical Ser.: Vol. 10). (Illus.). 386p. Repr. of 1941 ed. lib. bdg. 20.00x (ISBN 0-87991-306-1). Porcupine Pr.

Hill, Mary. Diving & Digging for Gold. rev ed. LC 73-22389. (Illus.). 48p. 1973. pap. 2.50 (ISBN 0-87961-005-0). Naturegraph.

Huntting, Marshall T. Gold in Washington. Repr. of 1955 ed. pap. 12.75 (ISBN 0-8466-6035-0, SJU35). Shorey.

An Illinois Gold Hunter in the Black Hills: The Diary of Jerry Bryan. 1960. pap. 2.00 (ISBN 0-912226-02-1). Ill St Hist. Soc.

Johnson, Maureen G. Placer Gold Deposits of Arizona. (Illus.). 103p. 1981. pap. 6.95 (ISBN 0-89632-009-X). Del Oeste.

--Placer Gold Deposits of Nevada. (Illus.). 118p. 1981. pap. 6.95 (ISBN 0-89632-010-3). Del Oeste.

--Placer Gold Deposits of New Mexico. (Illus.). 48p. 1980. pap. 4.95 (ISBN 0-89632-004-9). Del Oeste.

--Placer Gold Deposits of Utah. (Illus.). 32p. 1980. pap. 3.95 (ISBN 0-89632-007-3). Del Oeste.

Keane, Augustus H. Gold of Ophir, Whence Brought & by Whom. LC 76-88441. Repr. of 1901 ed. 12.75x (ISBN 0-8371-1725-9, Pub. by Negro U Pr). Greenwood.

Lagal, Roy. Gold Panning Is Easy. rev. ed. Nelson, Bettye, ed. LC 76-11382. (Guidebook Ser.). (Illus., Orig.). 1980. pap. 3.95 (ISBN 0-915920-39-5). Ram Pub.

Lapp, Rudolph M. Blacks in Gold Rush California. LC 76-30534. (Yale Western Americana Ser.: No. 13). (Illus.). 1977. 25.00x (ISBN 0-300-01988-2). Yale U Pr.

LeGaye, E. S. Gold: ABC's of Panning! new rev. 3rd ed. LC 74-128599. (Illus.). 1975. pap. 4.95 (ISBN 0-685-70348-7). Western Her Texas.

--Gold: ABC's of Panning! rev. 2nd ed. LC 74-128599. (Illus.). 1970. pap. 3.00 (ISBN 0-685-70349-5). Western Her Texas.

--Pan Your Own Gold. (Illus.). 42p. 1976. pap. 3.00 (ISBN 0-89351-031-9). Western Her Texas.

Miller, Tron. Gold Rocker Handbook. (Illus.). 1981. 7.00 (ISBN 0-686-71583-7). Exanimo Pr.

--Gold Rocker Handbook. 1980. pap. 4.00 (ISBN 0-89316-619-7); plastic bdg. 6.00 (ISBN 0-686-70739-7). Exanimo Pr.

Morrell, W. P. Gold Rushes. 2nd ed. LC 67-23287. (Illus.). 1968. 11.95 (ISBN 0-8023-1140-7). Dufour.

Neese, Harvey, ed. Gold Mining for Recreation. LC 81-3831. (Illus., Orig.). 1981. pap. 4.95 (ISBN 0-87701-182-6). Chronicle Bks.

Oliver, Herman. Gold & Cattle Country. 2nd ed. LC 61-13276. (Illus.). 1968. pap. 7.50 (ISBN 0-8323-0281-3). Binford.

Pallatz, Harold. The Gold Fields. (Illus., Orig.). 1977. pap. 1.50 (ISBN 0-685-82435-7). Ideal World.

--The Gold Towns. 1977. pap. 1.50 (ISBN 0-685-82436-5). Ideal World.

Parker, Morris B. White Oaks: Life in a New Mexico Gold Camp, 1880-1900. Sonnichsen, C. L., ed. LC 75-143274. (Southwest Chronicles). 1971. pap. 4.50 (ISBN 0-8165-0261-7). U of Ariz Pr.

Paul, Rodman W. California Gold: The Beginning of Mining in the Far West. LC 47-54111. (Illus.). 1965. pap. 3.95 (ISBN 0-8032-5149-1, BB 313, Bison). U of Nebr Pr.

Peters, Karl. Eladorado of the Ancients. LC 70-88445. (Illus.). Repr. of 1902 ed. 31.00x (ISBN 0-8371-1905-7, Pub. by Negro U Pr). Greenwood.

--King Solomon's Golden Ophir: A Research into the Most Ancient Gold Production in History. LC 74-88446. Repr. of 1899 ed. 11.00x (ISBN 0-8371-1835-2, Pub. by Negro U Pr). Greenwood.

Petralia, Joseph F. Gold! Gold! - a Beginners Handbook & Recreational Guide: How to Prospect for Gold. 2nd ed. (Illus.). 112p. (Orig.). 1981. 9.95 (ISBN 0-9605890-2-3); pap. 5.95 (ISBN 0-9605890-1-5). Sierra Trading.

--Gold! Gold! A Beginners' Handbook & Recreational Guide: How to Prospect for Gold. (Illus.). 110p. (Orig.). Date not set. pap. 5.95 (ISBN 0-88839-118-8, Pub. by Hancock Hse). Universe.

Potter, Miles. Oregon's Golden Years. LC 75-12292. 185p. 1976. pap. 9.95 (ISBN 0-87004-254-8). Caxton.

Poynter, Margaret. Gold Rush! The Yukon Stampede of 1898. LC 78-14503. (Illus.). (gr. 5 up). 1979. 7.95 (ISBN 0-689-30694-6). Atheneum.

Ransom, Jay E. The Gold Hunter's Field Book: How & Where to Find Gold in the United States & Canada. LC 74-20409. 1980. pap. 5.95 (ISBN 0-06-090775-4, CN 775, CN). Har-Row.

Reinhart, Herman F. The Golden Frontier: The Recollections of Herman Francis Reinhart, 1851-1869. Nunis, Doyce B., Jr., ed. (Personal Narratives of the West Ser.: No. 2). (Illus.). 381p. 1962. 14.95x (ISBN 0-292-73251-1). U of Tex Pr.

Roberts, Bruce. Carolina Goldrush: America's First. LC 70-165464. 4.50 (ISBN 0-87461-958-0). McNally.

Robertson, Walter J. Gold Panning for Profit. Jones, William R., ed. (Illus.). 32p. 1978. pap. 2.95 (ISBN 0-89646-035-5). Outbooks.

Rynerson, Fred. Exploring & Mining for Gems & Gold in the West. (Illus.). 184p. (gr. 4 up). 1970. 8.95 (ISBN 0-911010-61-0); pap. 4.95 (ISBN 0-911010-60-2). Naturegraph.

Santschi, R. J. Treasure Trails. (Doodlebug Edition Ser.). 1974. plastic bag 6.00 (ISBN 0-89316-612-X); pap. 4.00 (ISBN 0-89316-601-4). Exanimo Pr.

Stultz, Arthur L. Gold Rush Eighty, Vol. 1. (Getting Rich Ser.: No. 1). (Illus.). 300p. 1981. 17.00 (ISBN 0-9605958-0-5); lib. bdg. 20.00 (ISBN 0-9605958-2-1); pap. 10.00 (ISBN 0-9605958-1-3, GR-801). Ophir Intl.

Tanis, Norman, ed. Oregon Gulch Gold Mining Company of Butte County, California, 1852. (American Classics Facsimile Ser.: Pt. V). 1976. pap. 10.00 (ISBN 0-937048-04-6). CSUN.

Van Mueller, Karl. Gold Panner's Handbook. 1981. pap. 4.00 (ISBN 0-89316-621-9); plastic bdg 6.00 (ISBN 0-686-69464-3). Exanimo Pr.

Van Onselen, Charles. Chibaro: African Mine Labour in Southern Rhodesia 1900-1933. 326p. 1980. text ed. 16.95 (ISBN 0-902818-88-0). Pluto Pr.

Von Mueller, Karl. Gold Dredger's Handbook. 2nd ed. 1980. pap. 4.00 (ISBN 0-89316-609-X); plastic bdg. 6.00 (ISBN 0-89316-610-3). Exanimo Pr.

--Placer Miner's Manual, Vol. 1. 1980. pap. 5.00 (ISBN 0-89316-611-1); plastic bdg. 7.50 (ISBN 0-89316-612-X). Exanimo Pr.

--Placer Miner's Manual, Vol. 2. 1980. pap. 5.00 (ISBN 0-89316-613-8); plastic bdg 7.50 (ISBN 0-89316-614-6). Exanimo Pr.

--Placer Miner's Manual, Vol. 3. 1980. pap. 5.00 (ISBN 0-89316-615-4); plastic bdg. 7.50 (ISBN 0-89316-616-2). Exanimo Pr.

--Vibrating Gold Concentrators. 1980. pap. 4.00 (ISBN 0-89316-617-0); plastic bdg. 6.00 (ISBN 0-89316-618-9). Exanimo Pr.

Wagner, Jack R. Gold Mines of California. LC 79-115852. 1970. 20.00 (ISBN 0-8310-7002-1). Howell-North.

White, Helen M., ed. Ho! for the Gold Fields: Northern Overland Wagon Trains of the 1860s. LC 66-64828. (Illus.). 289p. 1966. 8.50 (ISBN 0-87351-030-5). Minn Hist.

Wilson, Helen. Gold Fever. (Illus.). 1979. pap. 7.25 (ISBN 0-913814-27-X). Nevada Pubns.

Wiltsee, Ernest A. The Pioneer Miner & the Pack Mule Express. LC 76-4134. (Illus.). 160p. 1976. Repr. 35.00x (ISBN 0-88000-084-8). Quarterman.

GOLD MINES AND MINING–JUVENILE LITERATURE

King, Joseph E. A Mine to Make a Mine: Financing the Colorado Mining Industry, 1859-1902. LC 76-51655. 240p. 1977. 13.75 (ISBN 0-89096-034-8). Tex A&M Univ Pr.

The Story of the Gold at Sutter's Mill. (Cornerstones of Freedom Ser.). (Illus.). (gr. 3-6). 1981. PLB 7.95 (ISBN 0-516-04617-9); pap. 2.50 (ISBN 0-516-44617-7). Childrens.

GOLD MINES AND MINING–AFRICA, SOUTH

Frankel, S. Herbert. Investment & the Return to Equity Capital in the South African Gold Mining Industry, 1887-1965: An International Comparison. LC 68-1574. (Illus.). 1967. 9.95x (ISBN 0-674-46550-4). Harvard U Pr.

Letcher, Owen. The Gold Mines of Southern Africa: The History Technology & Statistics of the Gold Industry. LC 74-353. (Vol. 18). (Illus.). 580p. 1974. Repr. 33.00x (ISBN 0-405-05915-9). Arno.

Nesbitt, Lewis M. Gold Fever, Vol. 11. LC 74-355. 214p. 1974. Repr. of 1936 ed. 13.00 (ISBN 0-405-05916-7). Arno.

Phillips, Lionel. All That Glittered: Selected Correspondence of Lionel Phillips, 1890-1924. Fraser, Maryna & Jeeves, Alan, eds. (Illus.). 444p. 1977. text ed. 31.00x (ISBN 0-19-570100-3). Oxford U Pr.

Reunert, Theodore. Diamonds & Gold in South Africa. LC 72-3916. (Black Heritage Library Collection Ser.). Repr. of 1893 ed. 29.50 (ISBN 0-8369-9106-0). Arno.

GOLD MINES AND MINING–ALASKA

Landru, H. C. The Blue Parka Man: Alaskan Gold Rush Bandit. LC 79-25575. (Illus.). 208p. 1980. 8.95 (ISBN 0-396-07821-4). Dodd.

May, Robin. The Gold Rushes. LC 78-58612. (Illus.). 1978. 10.95 (ISBN 0-88254-469-1). Hippocrene Bks.

Pierce, W. H. Thirteen Years of Travel & Exploration in Alaska: 1877-1889. De Armond, Robert N., ed. LC 77-2893. (Northern History Library). (Illus.). 1977. pap. 3.95 (ISBN 0-88240-076-2). Alaska Northwest.

GOLD MINES AND MINING–AUSTRALIA

Darbyshire, John. More Old Gold Towns of Victoria. LC 74-166664. (Colourful Australia Ser). (Illus.). 32p. 1970. 6.50x (ISBN 0-85179-391-6). Intl Pubns Serv.

--Old Gold Towns of New South Wales. LC 72-160553. (Colourful Australia Ser). (Illus.). 32p. 1973. 6.50x (ISBN 0-85179-270-7). Intl Pubns Serv.

Holthouse, Hector. River of Gold. (Illus.). 1968. 7.95 (ISBN 0-685-20620-3). Transatlantic.

Keesing, Nancy, ed. Gold Fever: The Australian Goldfields 1851-1890's. (Illus.). 1968. 15.00 (ISBN 0-685-20588-6). Transatlantic.

Korzelinski, Seweryn. Memoirs of Gold Digging in Australia. Robe, Stanley, tr. from Polish. (Illus.). 1980. 19.95x (ISBN 0-7022-1346-2). U of Queensland Pr.

Potts, E. Daniel. Young America & Australian Gold: Americans & the Gold Rush of the 1850's. 1974. 25.00x (ISBN 0-7022-0894-9). U of Queensland Pr.

Preshaw, G. O. Banking Under Difficulties: Life on the Goldfields of Victoria, New South Wales & New Zealand, Vol. 8. LC 74-357. (Gold Ser.). 179p. 1974. Repr. of 1888 ed. 14.00x (ISBN 0-405-05918-3). Arno.

GOLD MINES AND MINING–BRAZIL

Burton, Richard F. Explorations of the Highlands of Brazil, with a Full Account of the Gold & Diamond Mines. Incl. Canoeing Down Fifteen Hundred Miles of the Great River Sao Francisco, from Sabara to the Sea. LC 68-55181. (Illus.). 1968. Repr. of 1869 ed. Set. 2 Vols. lib. bdg. 32.75x (ISBN 0-8371-3793-4, BUHB). Greenwood.

GOLD MINES AND MINING–CANADA

Cariboo: The Newly Discovered Gold Fields of British Columbia. 1975. Repr. of 1862 ed. 8.00 (ISBN 0-87770-131-8). Ye Galleon.

Cornwallis, Kinahan. The New el Dorado; or, British Columbia. LC 72-9437. (The Far Western Frontier Ser.). (Illus.). 442p. 1973. Repr. of 1858 ed. 20.00 (ISBN 0-405-04967-6). Arno.

Elliot, Gordon R. Barkerville, Quesnel, & the Cariboo Gold Rush. LC 79-301801. (Illus.). 216p. 1980. pap. 7.95 (ISBN 0-295-95775-1, Pub. by Douglas & McIntyre Canada). U of Wash Pr.

GOLD MINES AND MINING–NEW GUINEA

O'Neill, Jack. Up from the South: A Prospector in New Guinea, Nineteen Thirty-One to Nineteen Thirty-Seven. Sinclair, James, ed. (Illus.). 224p. 1979. text ed. 23.50x (ISBN 0-19-550567-0). Oxford U Pr.

GOLD MINES AND MINING–RUSSIA

Littlepage, John D. & Bess, Demaree. In Search of Soviet Gold. LC 75-115558. (Russia Observed, Series I). 1970. Repr. of 1937 ed. 13.00 (ISBN 0-405-03044-4). Arno.

GOLD MINES AND MINING–SCOTLAND

Atkinson, Stephen. Discoverie & Historie of the Gold Mynes in Scotland. LC 77-38492. (Bannatyne Club, Edinburgh. Publications: No. 14). Repr. of 1825 ed. 24.50 (ISBN 0-404-52714-0). AMS Pr.

GOLD PLATE

see Plate

GOLD STANDARD

see also Bimetallism

Bloomfield, Arthur I. Monetary Policy Under the International Gold Standard. Wilkins, Mira, ed. LC 78-3899. (International Finance Ser.). 1978. Repr. of 1959 ed. lib. bdg. 10.00x (ISBN 0-405-11204-1). Arno.

Brown, William A., Jr. England & the New Gold Standard: 1919-1926. Wilkins, Mira, ed. LC 78-3901. (International Finance Ser.). (Illus.). 1978. Repr. of 1929 ed. lib. bdg. 21.00x (ISBN 0-405-11206-8). Arno.

--International Gold Standard Reinterpreted, 1914-1934, 2 Vols. Repr. of 1940 ed. 75.00 (ISBN 0-404-04645-2). AMS Pr.

Cassel, Gustav. Downfall of the Gold Standard. 262p. 1966. 24.00x (ISBN 0-7146-1213-8, F Cass Co). Biblio Dist.

Dalgaard, Bruce R. South Africa's Impact on Britain's Return to Gold, 1925. Bruchey, Stuart, ed. LC 80-2801. (Dissertations in European Economic History II). (Illus.). 1981. lib. bdg. 18.00x (ISBN 0-405-13985-3). Arno.

De Cecco, Marcello. Money & Empire: The International Gold Standard 1890-1914. 254p. 1975. 22.50x (ISBN 0-87471-625-X). Rowman.

Flumiani, C. M. The Gyrations of the Dollar & the Deceit of Gold. (Illus.). 1978. deluxe ed. 47.75 (ISBN 0-930008-16-2). Inst Econ Pol.

Graham, Frank D. & Whittlesey, Charles R. Golden Avalanche. Wilkins, Mira, ed. LC 78-3919. (International Finance Ser.). (Illus.). 1978. Repr. of 1939 ed. lib. bdg. 15.00x (ISBN 0-405-11222-X). Arno.

Gregory, Theodor E. The Gold Standard & Its Future. Wilkins, Mira, ed. LC 78-3920. (International Finance Ser.). (Illus.). 1978. Repr. of 1932 ed. lib. bdg. 11.00x (ISBN 0-405-11223-8). Arno.

Hawtrey, Ralph G. The Gold Standard in Theory & Practice. 5th ed. LC 79-18281. 1980. Repr. of 1947 ed. lib. bdg. 22.50x (ISBN 0-313-22104-9, HAGS). Greenwood.

Jastram, Roy W. The Golden Constant: The English & American Experience, 1560-1976. LC 77-15034. 1977. 24.95 (ISBN 0-471-02303-5, Pub. by Wiley-Interscience). Wiley.

Joseph, Jay, Jr. Can the Gold Standard Save Us? 1980. lib. bdg. 42.50 (ISBN 0-686-59403-7). Revisionist Pr.

Kemmerer, Edwin W. Gold & the Gold Standard. Wilkins, Mira, ed. LC 78-3927. (International Finance Ser.). 1978. Repr. of 1944 ed. lib. bdg. 15.00x (ISBN 0-405-11229-7). Arno.

League of Nations, Financial Committee, Gold Delegation. Report & Interim Report, 2 vols. in 1. Wilkins, Mira, ed. LC 78-3929. (International Finance Ser.). 1978. Repr. of 1930 ed. lib. bdg. 15.00x (ISBN 0-405-11232-7). Arno.

Matsukata, Masayoshi. Report on the Adoption of the Gold Standard in Japan. Wilkins, Mira, ed. LC 78-3937. (International Finance Ser.). (Illus.). 1978. Repr. of 1899 ed. lib. bdg. 27.00x (ISBN 0-405-11238-6). Arno.

Moggridge, D. E. British Monetary Policy, Nineteen Twenty-Four to Nineteen Thirty-One. LC 76-169576. (Department of Applied Economics Monographs: No. 21). 1972. 42.50 (ISBN 0-521-08225-0). Cambridge U Pr.

The Nine Deceits & the Collapse of Gold. 1976. 45.80 (ISBN 0-89266-076-7). Inst Econ Finan.

Parliamentary Debates, Great Britain. Report from the Select Committee on the High Price of Gold Bullion. Wilkins, Mira, ed. LC 78-3915. (International Finance Ser.). 1978. Repr. of 1812 ed. lib. bdg. 22.00x (ISBN 0-405-11219-X). Arno.

Pierson, Vernon C. The New Attempts at the Monetization of Gold & Their Meaning for the Future of the World. (Illus.). 127p. 1980. 59.85 (ISBN 0-918968-72-0). Inst Econ Finan.

Royal Institute Of International Affairs. International Gold Problem. (Social Economic History Ser). Repr. of 1931 ed. 15.50 (ISBN 0-384-52280-7). Johnson Repr.

Russell, William H. The Deceit of the Gold Standard & of Gold Monetization. (Illus.). 148p. 1982. 69.85 (ISBN 0-89266-324-3). Am Classical Coll Pr.

Silver, Gold & the Approaching Revolution in the International Monetary Order. 1976. 45.25 (ISBN 0-913314-42-0). Inst Econ Finan.

Skousen, Mark. The One Hundred Percent Gold Standard. 1977. 10.75 (ISBN 0-8191-0328-4). U Pr of Amer.

Snyder, Leslie. Why Gold? The One Sure Cure for Inflation & Economic Tyranny. LC 73-92853. 1974. 6.00 (ISBN 0-682-47884-9, University). Exposition.

Sutton, Antony C. The War on Gold. 1977. 9.95 (ISBN 0-89245-008-8). Seventy Six.

GOLD WORK

see Goldwork

GOLDEN EAGLE

Hamerstrom, Frances. An Eagle to the Sky. LC 78-12803. (Illus.). 1978. pap. 4.95 (ISBN 0-89594-016-7). Crossing Pr.

Olendorff, Richard. Golden Eagle Country. 1975. 15.00 (ISBN 0-394-48292-1). Knopf.

GOLDEN FLEECE

see Argonauts

GOLDEN GATE (STRAIT)

Cassady, Stephen. Spanning the Gate: Building the Golden Gate Bridge. LC 77-83284. (Illus.). 1979. 18.50 (ISBN 0-916290-06-9); pap. write for info. (ISBN 0-916290-07-7). Squarebooks.

GOLDEN HAMSTER

see Hamsters

GOLDEN RETRIEVERS

see Dogs–Breeds–Golden Retrievers

GOLDEN SECTION

Cook, Theodore A. The Curves of Life. 1979. pap. 5.95 (ISBN 0-486-23701-X). Dover.

GOLDFISH

Axelrod & Vorderwinkler. Goldfish and Koi in Your Home. (Illus.). 1970. 9.95 (ISBN 0-87666-075-8, H909). TFH Pubns.

Cooper, Kay. All About Goldfish As Pets. LC 76-26519. (Illus.). 64p. (gr. 3 up). 1976. PLB 6.97 (ISBN 0-671-32801-8). Messner.

Evans, Anthony. Goldfish. Foyle, Christina, ed. (Foyle's Handbks). 1973. 3.95 (ISBN 0-685-55819-3). Palmetto Pub.

Gannon, Robert. Start Right with Goldfish. (Orig.). pap. 2.00 (ISBN 0-87666-081-2, M504). TFH Pubns.

Hervey, George F. & Hems, Jack. The Goldfish. rev. ed. (Illus.). 284p. 1981. pap. 9.50 (ISBN 0-571-11611-6, Pub. by Faber & Faber). Merrimack Bk Serv.

Orme, Frank W. Fancy Goldfish Culture. 1981. 40.00x (ISBN 0-904558-63-0, Pub. by Saiga Pub). State Mutual Bk.

Paradise, Paul R., ed. Goldfish. (Illus.). 1979. 2.95 (ISBN 0-87666-511-3, KW-014). TFH Pubns.

Powers, Edwin B. The Goldfish (Carassius Carassius) As a Test Animal in the Study of Toxicity. Repr. of 1918 ed. pap. 6.00 (ISBN 0-384-47495-0). Johnson Repr.

Saiga Editors. Goldfish Keeping. 1981. 10.00x (ISBN 0-86230-020-7, Pub. by Saiga Pub). State Mutual Bk.

Stein, Sara B. How to Raise Goldfish & Guppies: A Child's Book of Pet Care. LC 76-8139. (Illus.). (ps-5). 1976. PLB 5.99 (ISBN 0-394-93225-0, BYR); pap. 3.95 (ISBN 0-394-83225-6). Random.

Wolburg, H. Axonal Transport, Degeneration, & Regeneration in the Visual System of the Goldfish. (Advances in Anatomy, Embryology & Cell Biology Ser.: Vol. 67). (Illus.). 100p. 1981. pap. 22.90 (ISBN 0-387-10336-8). Springer-Verlag.

Wong, Herbert & Vessel, Matthew. My Goldfish. Date not set. PLB 6.95 (ISBN 0-686-74808-5, 8720). A-W.

Zim, Herbert S. Goldfish. (Illus.). (gr. 3-7). 1947. PLB 6.48 (ISBN 0-688-31340-X). Morrow.

GOLDIE, GEORGE DASHWOOD TAUBMAN, SIR, 1846-1925

Muffett, D. J. Empire Builder Extraordinary Sir George Goldie: His Philosophy of Government & Empire. (Illus.). 1978. text ed. 22.75x (ISBN 0-904980-18-9). Humanities.

Wellington, Dorothy Violet. Sir George Goldie, Founder of Nigeria: A Memoir. Wilkins, Mira, ed. LC 76-29765. (European Business Ser.). (Illus.). 1977. Repr. of 1934 ed. lib. bdg. 13.00x (ISBN 0-405-09779-4). Arno.

GOLDING, WILLIAM GERALD, 1911-

Baker, James R. & Siegler, Arthur B., Jr., eds. Lord of the Flies: Text, Notes & Criticism. casebook ed. 1964. pap. text ed. 3.50 (ISBN 0-399-30002-3). Putnam.

Biles, Jack I. & Evans, Robert O., eds. William Golding: Some Critical Considerations. LC 77-73705. 296p. 1978. 18.00x (ISBN 0-8131-1362-8). U Pr of Ky.

Calandra, Denis M. Lord of the Flies Notes. (Orig.). pap. 1.95 (ISBN 0-8220-0754-1). Cliffs.

Dewsnap, Terence. Monarch Notes on Golding's the Inheritors & Free Fall. (Orig.). pap. 1.95 (ISBN 0-671-00893-5). Monarch Pr.

Dick, Bernard F. William Golding. (English Authors Ser.: No. 57). 1968. lib. bdg. 10.95 (ISBN 0-8057-1224-0). Twayne.

Johnston, Arnold. Of Earth & Darkness: The Novels of William Golding. LC 79-3332. 1980. text ed. 13.95x (ISBN 0-8262-0292-6). U of Mo Pr.

Monarch Notes on Golding's Lord of the Flies & Other Works. (Orig.). pap. 1.75 (ISBN 0-671-00616-9). Monarch Pr.

Stalhammar, Mall M. Imagery in Golding's the Spire. (Gothenburg Studies in English Ser.: No. 37). 1977. pap. text ed. 16.75x (ISBN 91-7346-030-3). Humanities.

Tiger, Virginia. William Golding: The Dark Fields of Discovery. 256p. 1978. pap. 7.95 (ISBN 0-7145-2595-2, Pub. by M Boyars). Merrimack Bk Serv.

--William Golding: The Dark Fields of Discovery. (Critical Appraisals Ser.). 240p. 1974. text ed. 15.00x (ISBN 0-7145-1012-2). Humanities.

Whitely, J. S. Golding: Lord of the Flies. (Studies in English Literature). 1970. pap. text ed. 3.95x (ISBN 0-7131-5504-3). Dynamic Learn Corp.

GOLDMAN, EMMA, 1869-1940

Ganguli, B. N. Emma Goldman: Portrait of a Rebel Woman. 1979. 6.00x (ISBN 0-8364-0452-1). South Asia Bks.

Goldman, Emma. Living My Life. abr. ed. Drinnon, Richard & Drinnon, Anna M., eds. 1977. pap. 6.95 (ISBN 0-452-00476-4, F476, Mer). NAL.

Goldman, Emma & Berkman, Alexander. Nowhere at Home: Letters from Exile of Emma Goldman & Alexander Berkman. Drinnon, Richard & Drinnon, Anna M., eds. LC 73-91346. 1977. 12.95x (ISBN 0-8052-3537-X); pap. 6.95 (ISBN 0-8052-0562-4). Schocken.

Rich, Andrea & Smith, Arthur L. Rhetoric of Revolution. LC 79-99291. 12.00 (ISBN 0-87716-010-4, Pub. by Moore Pub Co). F Apple.

GOLDONI, CARLO, 1707-1793

Dole, Nathan H. Teacher of Dante, & Other Studies in Italian Literature. facs. ed. LC 67-26733. (Essay Index Reprint Ser). 1908. 16.00 (ISBN 0-8369-0383-8). Arno.

Goldoni, Carlo. Memoirs of Carlo Goldoni. 1926. 35.00 (ISBN 0-932062-64-4). Sharon Hill.

--Memoirs of Carlo Goldoni. Drake, William A., ed. Black, John, tr. from Fr. LC 76-8013. 1976. Repr. of 1926 ed. lib. bdg. 27.75x (ISBN 0-8371-8871-7, GOME). Greenwood.

Kennard, Joseph. Goldoni & the Venice of His Times. 59.95 (ISBN 0-8490-0248-6). Gordon Pr.

Kennard, Joseph S. Goldoni & the Venice of His Times. LC 67-23852. Repr. of 1920 ed. 25.00 (ISBN 0-405-08691-1, Blom Pubns). Arno.

Luciani, Vincent, ed. Goldoni: Le Smanie per la Villeggiatura. 1961. pap. 2.95x (ISBN 0-913298-17-4). S F Vanni.

Riedt, Heinz. Carlo Goldoni. Molinaro, Ursule, tr. from Ger. LC 73-85411. (World Dramatists Ser). (Illus.). 160p. 1974. 10.95 (ISBN 0-8044-2729-1). Ungar.

GOLDSCHMIDT, RICHARD BENEDICT 1878-

Piternick, L. K., ed. Richard Goldschmidt: Controversial Geneticist & Creative Biologist. (Experientia Supplementa: No. 35). 154p. 1980. 14.50 (ISBN 3-7643-1093-6). Birkhauser.

GOLDSMITH, JOEL S., 1892-1964

Goldsmith, Joel S. Horizons of Consciousness: The Correspondence of Joel S. Goldsmith with Lorraine Sinkler. Sinkler, Lorraine, ed. LC 81-47436. 320p. 1981. 14.95 (ISBN 0-06-063151-1, HarpR). Har-Row.

GOLDSMITH, OLIVER, 1728-1774

Balderston, Katharine C. A Census of the Manuscripts of Oliver Goldsmith. 1978. Repr. lib. bdg. 12.50 (ISBN 0-8495-0375-2). Arden Lib.

--Collected Letters of Oliver Goldsmith. LC 75-42214. 1928. lib. bdg. 15.00 (ISBN 0-8414-3334-8). Folcroft.

Balderston, Katherine C. A Census of the Manuscripts of Oliver Goldsmith. LC 76-41731. 1976. lib. bdg. 15.00 (ISBN 0-8414-1789-X). Folcroft.

--The Collected Letters of Oliver Goldsmith. 189p. 1980. Repr. of 1928 ed. lib. bdg. 20.00 (ISBN 0-8492-3757-2). R West.

--The History & Sources of Percy's Memoir of Goldsmith, 1926. Bd. with Collected Letters. Goldsmith. 1928. 18.00 (ISBN 0-527-04700-7). Kraus Repr.

Black, William. Goldsmith. 1909. lib. bdg. 12.00 (ISBN 0-8414-1648-6). Folcroft.

--Goldsmith. Morley, John, ed. LC 68-58370. (English Men of Letters). Repr. of 1887 ed. lib. bdg. 12.50 (ISBN 0-404-51702-1). AMS Pr.

Cliff's Notes Editors. Vicar of Wakefield Notes. (Orig.). pap. 2.50 (ISBN 0-8220-1329-0). Cliffs.

Danziger, Marlies K. Oliver Goldsmith & Richard Brinsley Sheridan. LC 77-6946. (World Dramatists Ser.). 1978. 10.95 (ISBN 0-8044-2129-3). Ungar.

Dobson, Austin. Life of Oliver Goldsmith. 1973. Repr. of 1888 ed. 15.50 (ISBN 0-8274-1365-3). R West.

--Life of Oliver Goldsmith. LC 72-38350. (Select Bibliographies Reprint Ser.). Repr. of 1888 ed. 16.00 (ISBN 0-8369-6767-4). Arno.

An Exhibition in the Yale University Library of the Works of Oliver Goldsmith in Connection with the Bicentenary of His Birth. (Yale University Library). 1928. pap. 12.50x ltd. ed. (ISBN 0-686-51383-5). Elliots Bks.

Forster, John. The Life & Time of Oliver Goldsmith. 1973. Repr. of 1890 ed. 40.00 (ISBN 0-8274-1806-X). R West.

--The Life & Times of Oliver Goldsmith, 2 vols. 1979. Repr. of 1877 ed. Set. lib. bdg. 50.00 (ISBN 0-8495-1749-4). Arden Lib.

--The Life & Times of Oliver Goldsmith. LC 70-145020. (Literature Ser). (Illus.). 496p. 1972. Repr. of 1890 ed. 40.00 (ISBN 0-403-00967-7). Scholarly.

--Life of Oliver Goldsmith. abr. ed. Ingpen, Roger, ed. LC 78-98835. 1971. Repr. of 1903 ed. lib. bdg. 22.50x (ISBN 0-8371-3100-6, FOOG). Greenwood.

--Life of Oliver Goldsmith. abr. ed. Ingpen, Roger, ed. LC 78-98835. 1971. Repr. of 1903 ed. lib. bdg. 22.50x (ISBN 0-8371-3100-6, FOOG). Greenwood.

Freeman, John. Oliver Goldsmith. LC 74-5386. 1952. lib. bdg. 25.00 (ISBN 0-8414-4185-5). Folcroft.

Ginger, John. The Notable Man: The Life & Times of Oliver Goldsmith. (Illus.). 1978. 25.00 (ISBN 0-241-89626-6, Pub. by Hamish Hamilton England). David & Charles.

Goldsmith, Oliver. Essays on Goldsmith by Scott, Macaulay & Thackeray, & Selections from His Writings. Repr. of 1946 ed. 25.00 (ISBN 0-403-04056-6). Somerset Pub.

--She Stoops to Conquer. Lavin, J. A., ed. (New Mermaids Ser.). 1980. pap. 6.95x (ISBN 0-393-90046-0). Norton.

--The Vicar of Wakefield. Friedman, Arthur, ed. (Oxford English Novels Ser.). 250p. 1974. 16.50x (ISBN 0-19-255345-3). Oxford U Pr.

Gompertz, M. Helps to the Study of Goldsmith's The Traveller. 1973. Repr. of 1900 ed. 12.50 (ISBN 0-8274-0402-6). R West.

--Helps to the Study of Goldsmith's the Traveller. LC 77-21465. 1977. Repr. of 1900 ed. lib. bdg. 12.50 (ISBN 0-8414-4607-5). Folcroft.

Gwynn, Stephen. Oliver Goldsmith. LC 74-30338. (English Literature Ser., No. 33). 1974. lib. bdg. 41.95 (ISBN 0-8383-1843-6). Haskell.

--Oliver Goldsmith. LC 74-9728. 1935. lib. bdg. 15.75 (ISBN 0-8414-4511-7). Folcroft.

Hadow, G. E. & Wheeler, C. B. Essays on Goldsmith by Scott, Macaulay, and Thackeray. 1973. Repr. of 1918 ed. 30.00 (ISBN 0-8274-0390-9). R West.

Harp, Richard L. Thomas Percy's Life of Dr. Oliver Goldsmith: A Critical Edition. (Salzburg Studies in English Literature, Romantic Reassessment: No. 52). 1976. pap. text ed. 25.00x (ISBN 0-391-01398-X). Humanities.

Hogarth, William, illus. English Humorists of the Eighteenth Century: Sir Richard Steele, Joseph Addison, Laurence Sterne, Oliver Goldsmith. Repr. of 1906 ed. lib. bdg. 35.00 (ISBN 0-8492-0078-4). R West.

Hopkins, Robert H. The True Genius of Oliver Goldsmith. LC 69-15760. (Illus.). 250p. 1969. 16.00x (ISBN 0-8018-1016-7). Johns Hopkins.

Hudson, William H. Johnson & Goldsmith & Their Poetry. LC 75-120963. (Poetry & Life Ser.). Repr. of 1918 ed. 7.25 (ISBN 0-404-52515-6). AMS Pr.

--Johnson & Goldsmith & Their Poetry. LC 72-194976. 1918. lib. bdg. 7.50 (ISBN 0-8414-5192-3). Folcroft.

--Johnson & Goldsmith & Their Poetry. 1978. Repr. of 1918 ed. lib. bdg. 8.00 (ISBN 0-8495-2308-7). Arden Lib.

Irving, Washington. The Complete Works of Washington Irving-Oliver Goldsmith & the Biography & Poetical Remains of the Late Margaret Davidson: A Biography & Poetical Remains of the Late Margaret Miller Davidson. West, Elsie L., ed. (Critical Editions Ser.). 1978. lib. bdg. 25.00 (ISBN 0-8057-8521-3). Twayne.

--Oliver Goldsmith. LC 72-1507. (English Literature Ser., No. 33). 1972. Repr. of 1882 ed. lib. bdg. 43.95 (ISBN 0-8383-1446-5). Haskell.

Jackson, Robert W. Oliver Goldsmith: Essays Towards an Interpretation. (Biography Index Reprint Ser.). Repr. of 1951 ed. 9.25 (ISBN 0-8369-8199-5). Arno.

Jenks, Tudor. In the Days of Goldsmith. 1973. Repr. of 1907 ed. 30.00 (ISBN 0-8274-0020-9). R West.

Kent, Elizabeth. Goldsmith & His Booksellers. LC 77-3411. 1933. lib. bdg. 8.45 (ISBN 0-8414-5545-7). Folcroft.

Kent, Elizabeth E. Goldsmith & His Booksellers. LC 76-107925. (English Book Trade). Repr. of 1933 ed. lib. bdg. 8.00x (ISBN 0-678-00725-X). Kelley.

--Goldsmith & His Booksellers. 1978. Repr. of 1933 ed. lib. bdg. 12.50 (ISBN 0-8495-3017-2). Arden Lib.

King, Richard A. Oliver Goldsmith. LC 76-53568. 1976. Repr. of 1910 ed. lib. bdg. 30.00 (ISBN 0-8414-5534-1). Folcroft.

Krans, Horatio S. Oliver Goldsmith: A Critical Biography. 1918. lib. bdg. 10.00 (ISBN 0-8414-5605-4). Folcroft.

Life of Oliver Goldsmith: 1728-74. 1979. Repr. of 1888 ed. lib. bdg. 25.00 (ISBN 0-8492-0695-2). R West.

Macaulay, Lord. Bibliographies: Bunyan, Goldsmith, & Johnson, with Notes of His Connection with Edinburgh, and Extracts from His Letters & Speeches. 1979. Repr. of 1860 ed. lib. bdg. 25.00 (ISBN 0-8495-3513-1). Arden Lib.

Moore, Frank F. The Life of Oliver Goldsmith. 1973. Repr. of 1910 ed. 40.00 (ISBN 0-8274-1020-4). R West.

Morley, John. Goldsmith. 1887. Repr. 12.00 (ISBN 0-8274-2429-9). R West.

Paden, William D. & Hyder, Clyde K., eds. A Concordance to the Poems of Oliver Goldsmith. Repr. of 1940 ed. 19.00 (ISBN 0-403-04014-0). Somerset Pub.

Pitman, James H. Goldsmith's Animated Nature: A Study of Goldsmith. (Yale Studies in English Ser.: No. 66). 1972. Repr. of 1924 ed. 16.50 (ISBN 0-208-01135-8, Archon). Shoe String.

Prior, James. The Life of Oliver Goldsmith, 4 vols. 1609p. 1980. Repr. of 1837 ed. Set. lib. bdg. 100.00 (ISBN 0-8414-6823-0). Folcroft.

--The Life of Oliver Goldsmith, 2 vols. 1973. Repr. of 1837 ed. 75.00 (ISBN 0-8274-1000-X). R West.

Rousseau, G. S. Goldsmith: The Critical Heritage. (Critical Heritage Ser.). 412p. 1974. 30.00x (ISBN 0-7100-7720-3). Routledge & Kegan.

Scott, Temple. Oliver Goldsmith: Bibliographically & Biographically Considered. LC 74-2487. 1974. Repr. of 1928 ed. lib. bdg. 50.00 limited ed. (ISBN 0-8414-7738-8). Folcroft.

Sells, Arthur L. Les Sources Francaises De Goldsmith. 1979. Repr. of 1924 ed. lib. bdg. 75.00 (ISBN 0-8492-8087-7). R West.

Smith, H. J. Oliver Goldsmith's Citizen of the World. LC 70-91190. (Yale Studies in English Ser.: No. 71). 1970. Repr. of 1926 ed. 16.50 (ISBN 0-208-00911-6, Archon). Shoe String.

Swarbrick, A. P., ed. Oliver Goldsmith: His Reputation Re-Assessed. 1982. 60.00x (ISBN 0-86127-213-7, Pub. by Avebury Pub England). State Mutual Bk.

Wibberley, Leonard. The Good Natured-Man: A Life of Oliver Goldsmith. LC 79-89683. 1979. 9.95 (ISBN 0-688-03522-1). Morrow.

GOLDSMITHING

see Goldwork

GOLDWATER, BARRY MORRIS, 1909-

Cosman, Bernard. Five States for Goldwater: Continuity & Change in Southern Voting Patterns, 1920-1964. LC 66-17568. 1965. 8.95x (ISBN 0-8173-4712-7). U of Ala Pr.

Goldwater, Barry M. With No Apologies: The Personal & Political Memoirs of a U. S. Senator. 1980. pap. 2.95 (ISBN 0-425-04663-X). Berkley Pub.

--With No Apologies: The Personal & Political Memoirs of United States Senator Barry M. Goldwater. LC 79-16823. (Illus.). 1979. 12.95 (ISBN 0-688-03547-7). Morrow.

GOLDWORK

see also Gilding; Jewelry; Jewelry Making; Plate

Abbey, S. Goldsmith's & Silversmith's Handbook. 2nd rev. ed. (Illus.). 1968. 17.50 (ISBN 0-685-12021-X). Heinman.

Badcock, W. & Reynolds, J. A New Touch-Stone for Gold & Silver Wares. 390p. Repr. of 1679 ed. 10.00x (ISBN 0-686-28346-5, Pub. by Irish Academic Pr). Biblio Dist.

Barr, Elaine. George Wickes: Royal Goldsmith 1698 to 1761. LC 80-5472. (Illus.). 214p. 1980. 37.50 (ISBN 0-686-63412-8). Rizzoli Intl.
Braun, Joseph. Meisterwerke der deuschen Goldschmiedekunst der vongotischen Ziet. Freitag, Wolfgang M., ed. LC 78-50268. (Metalwork Ser.: Vol. 4). (Illus.). 1979. lib. bdg. 40.00 (ISBN 0-8240-3354-X). Garland Pub.
Bray, Warwick. Gold of Eldorado. 1979. pap. 12.50 (ISBN 0-8109-2224-X). Abrams.
Cellini, Benvenuto. Treatises of Benvenuto Cellini on Goldsmithing & Sculpture. Ashbee, C. R., tr. (Illus.). 10.00 (ISBN 0-8446-1828-4). Peter Smith.
--Treatises of Benvenuto Cellini on Goldsmithing & Sculpture. Ashbee, C. R., tr. (Illus.). 1966. pap. 5.00 (ISBN 0-486-21568-7). Dover.
Choate, Sharr & De May, Bonnie C. Creative Gold & Silversmithing: Jewelry, Decorative Metalcraft. (Arts & Crafts Ser). (Illus.). 1970. 11.95 (ISBN 0-517-54309-5, L00036); pap. 8.95 (ISBN 0-517-52413-9). Crown.
Connaissance des Arts Editors. Les Orfevres de Louis XIII a Charles X. (Illus.). 75.00 (ISBN 0-685-11470-8). French & Eur.
--Les Orfevres de Louis XIII a Charles X. (Illus.). 75.00 (ISBN 0-685-11470-8). French & Eur.
Davis, Ellen N. The Vapheio Cups & Aegean Gold & Silver Ware. LC 76-23609. (Outstanding Dissertations in the Fine Arts). (Illus.). 1977. Repr. of 1973 ed. lib. bdg. 63.00 (ISBN 0-8240-2681-0). Garland Pub.
Glover, Elizabeth. The Gold & Silver Wyre-Drawers. (Illus.). 91p. 1979. 47.50x (ISBN 0-8476-3144-3). Rowman.
Grimwade, Arthur. London Goldsmiths, 1697-1837. 730p. 1976. 108.00 (ISBN 0-571-10550-5, Pub. by Faber & Faber). Merrimack Bk Serv.
Grimwade, Arthur G. London Goldsmith's, Sixteen Ninety-Seven to Eighteen Thirty-Seven: Their Marks & Lives from the Original Registers at Goldsmiths' Hall & Other Sources. (Illus.). 728p. 1976. 97.50x (ISBN 0-87471-794-9). Rowman.
Hayward, J. F. Virtuoso Goldsmiths & the Triumph of Mannerism, 1540-1620. (Illus.). 796p. 1976. 145.00x (ISBN 0-85667-005-7, Pub. by Sotheby Parke Bernet England). Biblio Dist.
Jackson, Charles J. English Goldsmiths & Their Marks. 22.50 (ISBN 0-486-21206-8). Dover.
Kovacs, Eva. Romanesque Goldsmith's Art in Hungary. (Illus.). 154p. 1974. 5.00x (ISBN 963-13-4415-0). Intl Pubns Serv.
Le Corbeiller, Clare. Gold Boxes: The Wrightsman Collection. LC 77-23592. (Illus.). 1977. pap. 2.95 (ISBN 0-87099-166-3). Metro Mus Art.
Negbi, Ora. The Hoards of Goldwork from Tell el Ajjul. (Studies in Mediterranean Archaeology Ser.: No. XXV). (Illus.). 1970. pap. text ed. 14.00x (ISBN 0-391-01990-2). Humanities.
Reddaway, T. F. & Walker, Lorna E. The Early History of the Goldsmiths' Company, 1327-1509: Including the Book of Ordinances, 1478-83. (Illus.). 378p. 1976. 21.50x (ISBN 0-87471-804-X). Rowman.
Reid, F. H. & Goldie, W. Gold Plating Technology. 630p. 1980. 89.00x (ISBN 0-901150-02-9, Pub. by Electrochemical Scotland). State Mutual Bk.
Taylor, Joan J. Bronze Age Goldwork of the British Isles. LC 75-12160. (Gulbenkian Archaeological Ser.). (Illus.). 188p. 1981. 95.00 (ISBN 0-521-20802-5). Cambridge U Pr.
Texier, J. R. Dictionnaire d'orfevererie, de Gravure et de Ciselure Chretiennes. Migne, J. P., ed. (Troisieme et Derniere Encyclopedie Theologique Ser.: Vol. 27). 748p. (Fr.). Date not set. Repr. of 1857 ed. lib. bdg. 95.00x (ISBN 0-89241-307-7). Caratzas Bros.
Wigley, Thomas. The Art of the Goldsmith & Jeweler. 1977. lib. bdg. 75.00 (ISBN 0-8490-1455-7). Gordon Pr.
Willsberger, Johann. Gold. LC 76-9636. 180p. 1976. 24.95 (ISBN 0-385-12266-7). Doubleday.

GOLENIEWSKI, MICHAL, 1922-

Richards, Guy. Imperial Agent: The Goleniewski-Romanov Case. 1966. 7.95 (ISBN 0-8159-5804-8). Devin.

GOLF

see also Golf for Women; Putting (Golf); Swing (Golf)

Allan, Peter. Play the Best Courses. 1973. 12.95 (ISBN 0-09-116340-4, Pub. by Hutchinson). Merrimack Bk Serv.
Allen, Frank Kenyon, et al. Golfer's Bible. LC 68-11788. 1968. pap. 3.50 (ISBN 0-385-01402-3). Doubleday.
Alliss, Peter. The Shell Book of Golf. LC 81-65956. (Illus.). 224p. 1981. 27.00 (ISBN 0-7153-7988-7). David & Charles.
Alliss, Peter & Trevillion, Paul. Easier Golf. LC 72-116128. (Illus.). 1970. 6.95 (ISBN 0-498-07669-5). A S Barnes.
Alpert, Hollis, et al. How to Play Double Bogey Golf. LC 75-8288. (Illus.). 192p. 1975. 7.95 (ISBN 0-8129-0571-7). Times Bks.
Armour, Tommy. How to Play Your Best Golf All the Time. 1971. pap. 3.95 (ISBN 0-671-21150-1, Fireside). S&S.
Aultman, Dick & Golf Digest Editors. One Hundred & One Ways to Win at Golf. LC 80-66689. 248p. (Orig.). 1980. pap. 5.95 (ISBN 0-914178-40-7, 41417-8). Golf Digest.
Baker, Stephen. How to Play Golf in the Low 120's. 1977. 7.95 (ISBN 0-13-428169-1, Reward); pap. 4.95 (ISBN 0-13-428151-9). P-H.
Ballard, Jim & Quinn, Brennan. How to Perfect Your Golf Swing. LC 80-66691. (Illus.). 176p. (Orig.). 1981. 13.50 (ISBN 0-914178-38-5). Golf Digest.
Bartlett, Michael. The Golf Book. LC 80-67625. (Illus.). 1980. 22.95 (ISBN 0-87795-297-3) (ISBN 0-686-64654-1). Arbor Hse.
Bassler, Charles T. & Gibson, Nevin H. You Can Play Par Golf. large type ed. LC 66-13087. (Illus.). 102p. 1976. 6.95 (ISBN 0-498-01881-4). A S Barnes.
Bernardoni, Gus. Golf God's Way. LC 77-80414. 1978. 9.95 (ISBN 0-88419-144-3). Creation Hse.
Biddulph, Michael W. The Golf Shot. LC 79-19060. (Illus.). 116p. 1980. 10.95 (ISBN 0-393-01312-X). Norton.
Blake, Mindy. Golf: The Technique Barrier. (Illus.). 1979. 10.95 (ISBN 0-393-08825-1). Norton.
Boros, Julius. Swing Easy, Hit Hard. 192p. 1968. pap. 2.95 (ISBN 0-346-12305-4). Cornerstone.
Bowen, Bob & Clemence, B. J. Golf - Everyone. 154p. 1981. pap. text ed. 4.95x (ISBN 0-89459-098-7). Hunter Hse.
Brody, Steve. How to Break Ninety Before You Reach It: A Collection of Verse About Golf & Other Sports. 1980. pap. 4.95 (ISBN 0-88427-040-8). Caroline Hse.
Bruce, Ben & Davies, Evelyn. Beginning Golf. rev ed. 1968. pap. 3.95x (ISBN 0-534-00641-8). Wadsworth Pub.
Campbell, Bailey. Golf Lessons from Sam Snead. 1973. pap. 3.50 (ISBN 0-8015-3090-3, Hawthorn). Dutton.
Casper, B. & Barkow, Al. The Good Sense of Golf. 1980. 9.95 (ISBN 0-13-360511-6). P-H.
Charles, Bob. Lefthanded Golf with Bob Charles. (Illus.). 1965. 8.95 (ISBN 0-13-527200-9). P-H.
Cherellia, George. All About Hitting the Sweet Spot. 1976. pap. text ed. 3.80x (ISBN 0-87563-105-3). Stipes.
Chui, Edward F. Golf. 2nd ed. LC 72-91475. (Phys. Ed. Ser.). 1973. pap. text ed. 5.95 (ISBN 0-87620-356-X); instructor's manual avail. (ISBN 0-685-28770-X). Goodyear.
Clark, R. Golf: A Royal & Ancient Game. (Illus.). 1976. Repr. 25.00x (ISBN 0-7158-1116-9). Charles River Bks.
The Club Makers. 5.00 (ISBN 0-686-30841-7). US Golf Assn.
Consumer Guide Magazine Editors, ed. Consumer Guide---Complete Guide to Golfing Equipment. (Orig.). 1975. pap. 1.95 (ISBN 0-451-06668-5, J6668, Sig). NAL.
Cooley, Myra. Meet Me on the Green: Great Figures of the Old West. 1973. 4.50 (ISBN 0-87164-015-5). William-F.
Cousins, Geoffrey. Golf in Britain. 1975. 15.95 (ISBN 0-7100-8028-X). Routledge & Kegan.
Cross, Glenda. Friendly Fairways of Michigan. LC 78-54174. (Orig.). 1978. 4.95 (ISBN 0-686-12255-0). Friendly Fairways.
Daly, Glenn F. Easy Way of Doing Things. 1978, pap. 4.00 (ISBN 0-682-49177-2). Exposition.
Dante, Jim & Diegel, Leo. Nine Bad Shots of Golf & What to Do About Them. 186p. 1961. pap. 4.95 (ISBN 0-346-12327-5). Cornerstone.
Dante, Jim & Elliott, Len. Four Magic Moves of Winning Golf. 192p. 1963. pap. 3.95 (ISBN 0-346-12299-6). Cornerstone.
Davies, Peter. Davies' Dictionary of Golfing Terms. 1980. 13.95 (ISBN 0-671-24761-1). S&S.
Decisions on the Rules of Golf by the United States Golf Association(1956-1979, 2 vols. 25.00 (ISBN 0-686-30834-4). US Golf Assn.
De Monte, John R. The Kings James' Versions of the Games of Golfe. (Illus.). 82p. (Orig.). 1980. pap. 3.50 (ISBN 0-9605176-0-X). Raycol Prods.
Dey, Joseph C., compiled by. Golf Rules in Pictures. 96p. 3.95 (ISBN 0-686-30835-2). US Golf Assn.
Dey, Joseph C., Jr., ed. Golf Rules in Pictures. pap. 3.95 (ISBN 0-448-01360-6). G&D.
Diaz, Carroll. Golf: A Beginner's Guide. LC 73-93342. (Illus.). 87p. 1974. 12.95 (ISBN 0-87484-217-4); pap. 4.95 (ISBN 0-87484-216-6). Mayfield Pub.
Dobereiner. Glorious World of Golf. 9.95 (ISBN 0-448-14376-3, MSP). G&D.
Dobereiner, Peter. The World of Golf. LC 80-66010. 1981. 12.95 (ISBN 0-689-11094-4). Atheneum.
Emery, Fred. Colonel Bogey's Coloring Book for Golfers. (Illus.). 52p. (Orig.). 1981. pap. 6.95x (ISBN 0-932746-02-0). Today News.
Esquire Editors. Esquire World of Golf. 7.95 (ISBN 0-671-23010-7). Trident.
Evans, Webster. Encyclopedia of Golf. 2nd ed. LC 72-165470. (Illus.). 352p. 1973. 10.95 (ISBN 0-312-24850-4). St Martin.
Faulkner, Max & Scott, Tom. Play Championship Golf All Your Life. (Illus.). 136p. 1973. 10.00 (ISBN 0-7207-0256-9). Transatlantic.
Fishman, Lew & Golf Magazine Editors, eds. Golf Magazine's Shortcuts to Better Golf. LC 78-19559. (Illus.). 1979. 12.50 (ISBN 0-06-011273-5, HarpT). Har-Row.
Ford, Doug. Getting Started in Golf. 124p. 1964. pap. 2.50 (ISBN 0-346-12354-2). Cornerstone.
--Start Golf Young. LC 77-93324. (gr. 5 up). 1978. 7.95 (ISBN 0-8069-4126-X); PLB 7.49 (ISBN 0-8069-4127-8). Sterling.
Geiberger, Al & Dennis, Larry. Tempo (Golf's Master Key: How to Find It, How to Keep It) LC 79-52550. (Illus.). 160p. 1980. 9.95 (ISBN 0-914178-34-2). Golf Digest.
Gibb, Eileen, ed. Golfer's Handbook 1981. 78th ed. LC 51-18000. (Illus.). 694p. 1981. 35.00x (ISBN 0-8002-2815-4). Intl Pubns Serv.
Gladstone, Irving. Confessions of a Golf Duffer in Search of No Fault Insurance. LC 77-10114. 1977. 6.95 (ISBN 0-8119-0286-2). Fell.
Golf. new ed. (Know the Game Ser.). (Illus.). 1975. pap. 2.50 (ISBN 0-7158-0215-1). Charles River Bks.
Golf. LC 19-600. (Illus.). 72p. 1977. pap. 0.70x (ISBN 0-8395-3397-7, 3397). BSA.
Golf Digest Editors & Toski, Bob. Touch System for Better Golf. LC 70-162620. (Illus.). 1980. 6.95 (ISBN 0-671-25481-2). S&S.
Golf Digest Editors, ed. The Best of Golf Digest. 224p. 1975. 10.00 (ISBN 0-671-22167-1). S&S.
Golf Digest Magazine Editors. Instant Golf Lessons. LC 77-92907. (Instant Lesson Ser.). 225p. (Orig.). 1978. pap. 4.95 (ISBN 0-914178-16-4, 24167). Golf Digest.
Golf Magazine Editors, ed. Golf Magazine's Encyclopedia of Golf. rev. ed. LC 77-11818. (Illus.). 1979. 19.95 (ISBN 0-06-011552-1, HarpT). Har-Row.
Graham, Lou & Bibb, John. Mastering Golf. LC 77-91155. 1978. o. p. 9.95 (ISBN 0-8092-7763-8); pap. 6.95 (ISBN 0-8092-7761-1). Contemp Bks.
Green, Michael. The Art of Coarse Golf. 1967. 5.95 (ISBN 0-09-084730-X, Pub. by Hutchinson). Merrimack Bk Serv.
Grout, Jack & Aultman, Dick. Let Me Teach You Golf As I Taught Jack Nicklaus. LC 75-13515. (Illus.). 1977. 10.95 (ISBN 0-689-10688-2); pap. 6.95 (ISBN 0-689-70557-3). Atheneum.
Gunn, Harry E. & Stewart, Earl, Jr. Golf Begins at Forty. (Illus.). 1977. 5.95 (ISBN 0-8092-7283-0). Contemp Bks.
Hay, Alex. The Golf Manual. (Illus.). 192p. 1980. 19.95 (ISBN 0-571-11642-6, Pub. by Faber & Faber). Merrimack Bk Serv.
--The Mechanics of Golf. 1979. 9.95 (ISBN 0-312-52450-1). St Martin.
--Skills & Tactics of Golf. LC 79-18629. (Skills & Tactics Ser.). (Illus.). 152p. 1980. 9.95 (ISBN 0-668-04839-5). Arco.
Heise, Jack G. How You Can Play Better Golf with Self-Hypnosis. (Orig.). 1960. pap. 3.00 (ISBN 0-87980-073-9). Wilshire.
Henry Cotton Says Play Better Golf. 9.50x (ISBN 0-392-06918-0, SpS). Sportshelf.
Hexter, Paul L. You Can Play Golf Forever. 1979. 9.95 (ISBN 0-8092-7364-0); pap. 5.95 (ISBN 0-8092-7363-2). Contemp Bks.
Hill, Dave & Seitz, Nick. Teed off. LC 76-30769. (Illus.). 1977. 8.95 (ISBN 0-13-902247-3). P-H.
Hobbs, Michael, ed. Golf for the Connoisseur: A Golfing Anthology. (Illus.). 256p. 1980. 30.00 (ISBN 0-7134-1397-2, Pub. by Batsford England). David & Charles.
Hogan, Ben. Five Lessons: The Modern Fundamentals of Golf. 7.95 (ISBN 0-498-08046-3). A S Barnes.
--Modern Fundamentals of Golf. 128p. 1962. pap. 3.95 (ISBN 0-346-12326-7). Cornerstone.
--Power Golf. 1977. pap. 1.75 (ISBN 0-671-81222-X). PB.
Houghton, George. Golf Addict Visits the U. S. A. Date not set. pap. 5.00x (ISBN 0-392-09589-0, SpS). Sportshelf.
--Golf Addicts on Parade. Date not set. 10.00x (ISBN 0-392-08197-0, SpS). Sportshelf.
--Golf on My Pillow. pap. 5.00x (ISBN 0-392-05414-0, SpS). Sportshelf.
--How to Be a Golf Addict. 1972. 8.75 (ISBN 0-7207-0499-5). Transatlantic.
--More Confessions of a Golf Addict. Date not set. pap. 5.00x (ISBN 0-392-09575-0, SpS). Sportshelf.
Hudson, D. C. Your Book of Golf. (Your Book Ser.). (Illus.). 54p. 1967. 6.95 (ISBN 0-571-08123-1, Pub. by Faber & Faber). Merrimack Bk Serv.
Humphreys, Eric. The Dunlop Golfer's Companion. (Illus.). 1979. 15.00 (ISBN 0-903214-09-1, Pub. by Terence Dalton England). State Mutual Bk.
Hunter, Mac. Golf for Beginners. (Illus.). 96p. 1973. pap. 3.95 (ISBN 0-448-11538-7). G&D.
Jacobs, John & Aultman, Dick. Quick Cures for Weekend Golfers. (Illus.). 1979. 10.95 (ISBN 0-671-22658-4). S&S.
Jacobs, John & Bowden, Ken. Practical Golf. LC 76-189149. 288p. 1972. 11.50 (ISBN 0-8129-0274-2). Times Bks.
--Practical Golf. LC 76-189149. (Illus.). 192p. 1976. pap. 6.95 (ISBN 0-8129-6268-0). Times Bks.
Jennison, Keith & Pratt, William A. Year-Around Conditioning for Part-Time Golfers. LC 78-53836. (Illus.). 1979. 9.95 (ISBN 0-689-10875-3). Atheneum.
Johnson, Carol & Johnstone, Ann. Golf: A Positive Approach. LC 74-24619. 1975. pap. text ed. 6.75 (ISBN 0-201-03416-6). A-W.
Johnson, Dewayne J., et al. Golf. 61p. 1979. pap. text ed. 2.95x (ISBN 0-89641-027-7). American Pr.
Jones, Bob. Golf Odyssey. LC 73-80899. 8.95 (ISBN 0-912216-15-8). Angel Pr.
Jones, Rees L. & Rando, Guy L. Golf Course Developments. LC 73-86554. (Technical Bulletin Ser.: No. 70). (Illus.). 112p. 1974. pap. 12.00 (ISBN 0-87420-070-9). Urban Land.
Judd, H. Stanley. How to Play Golf the Easy Way: A Weekender's Guide to Successful Shotmaking. LC 79-3832. (Illus., Orig.). 1980. pap. 3.95 (ISBN 0-06-090766-5, CN 766, CN). Har-Row.
Keane, Christopher. The Tour. LC 73-90708. 300p. 1974. 25.00 (ISBN 0-8128-1667-6). Stein & Day.
Kelley, Homer. The Golfing Machine. rev. ed. LC 78-65234. (Illus.). 1980. text ed. 12.50 (ISBN 0-932890-04-0). Star System.
Kemp, Charles F. The World of Golf & the Game of Life. (Illus.). 1978. pap. 2.95 (ISBN 0-8272-4212-3). Bethany Pr.
Lardner, Rex. Downhill Lies & Other Falsehoods; or, How to Play Dirty Golf. (Illus.). 192p. 1973. pap. 3.95 (ISBN 0-8015-2198-X, Hawthorn). Dutton.
Laureti, Mario. Golf Inequities: All Putts Should Count One-Half Stroke. 1980. 7.95 (ISBN 0-8200-9908-2). Great Outdoors.
Lohren, Carl & Dennis, Larry. One Move to Better Golf. 1976. pap. 1.95 (ISBN 0-451-07027-5, J7027, Sig). NAL.
Longo, Peter. Simplified Golf: There's No Trick to It! De Mente, Boye, ed. (Illus.). 144p. (Orig.). 1980. pap. 9.95 (ISBN 0-914778-34-X). Phoenix Bks.
McCormack, Mark H. Dunhill Golf Yearbook 1980. 448p. 1980. 18.95 (ISBN 0-385-14942-5); pap. 10.95 (ISBN 0-385-14943-3). Doubleday.
--The Wonderful World of Professional Golf. LC 68-13716. (Illus.). 1973. 20.00 (ISBN 0-689-10550-9). Atheneum.
McCormick, Bill. The Complete Beginner's Guide to Golf. LC 73-78770. 144p. (gr. 5-9). 1974. PLB 4.95 (ISBN 0-385-05529-3). Doubleday.
McDougal. One Hundred & One Great Golf Jokes' & Stories. 1.95 (ISBN 0-8065-0326-2). Citadel Pr.
McDougal, Stan. The World's Greatest Golf Jokes. 1980. 9.95 (ISBN 0-686-65057-3). Lyle Stuart.
McGurn, Robert & Williams, S. A. Golf Power in Motion. 144p. 1969. pap. 1.95 (ISBN 0-346-12139-6). Cornerstone.
Mackey, Richard T. Golf, Learn Thru Auditory & Visual Cues. (Illus.). 1978. pap. text ed. 3.25 (ISBN 0-8403-1113-3). Kendall-Hunt.
MacLaren, Muir, compiled by. The Golfer's Bedside Book. (Illus.). 1976. 14.95 (ISBN 0-589-07204-8). C E Tuttle.
Metz, Richard. The Graduated Swing Method. (Illus.). 128p. 1981. 14.95 (ISBN 0-684-16868-5, ScribT). Scribner.
Morgan, John. Golf. (Sports Library). (Illus.). 1979. 12.95 (ISBN 0-8069-9116-X); pap. 6.95 (ISBN 0-8069-9118-6). Sterling.
--Golf. (EP Sports Books). (Illus.). 112p. 1976. 6.95 (ISBN 0-7158-0596-7). Charles River Bks.
Mulvoy, Mark. Sports Illustrated Golf. LC 80-8692. (Illus.). 192p. 1981. 8.95 (ISBN 0-06-014871-3, HarpT); pap. 5.95 (ISBN 0-06-090868-8, CN868). Har-Row.
Murdoch, Joseph S. & Seagle, Janet, eds. Golf: A Guide to Information Sources. LC 79-23270. (Sports, Games & Pastimes Information Guide Ser.: Vol. 7). 1979. 36.00 (ISBN 0-8103-1457-6). Gale.
Murphy, Michael. Golf in the Kingdom. 1973. pap. 3.95 (ISBN 0-440-53092-X, Delta). Dell.
Murray, Henry A. Golf Secret. (Illus.). 1954. 7.95 (ISBN 0-87523-093-8). Emerson.
--More Golf Secrets. (Illus.). 1954. 7.95 (ISBN 0-87523-099-7). Emerson.

Nance, Virginia L. & Davis, Elwood C. Golf. 4th ed. (Physical Education Activity Ser.). 96p. 1980. pap. text ed. write for info. (ISBN 0-697-07087-5). Wm C Brown.
National Golf Foundation-Athletic Institute. Golf. Bluth, Robert G., ed. LC 79-109498. (Sports Technique Ser.). (Illus.). 1977. 3.95 (ISBN 0-87670-007-5); pap. 1.95 (ISBN 0-685-65762-0). Athletic Inst.
New York Times. The Complete Book of Golf. LC 79-92319. (Sports Ser.). (Illus.). 224p. 1980. 14.95 (ISBN 0-672-52636-0). Bobbs.
Nicklaus, Jack. My Fifty-Five Ways to Lower Your Golf Score. 1964. 9.95 (ISBN 0-671-50505-X). S&S.
--Play Better Golf, Vol. II. (Orig.). 1981. pap. 2.95 (ISBN 0-671-83624-2). PB.
--Play Better Golf with Jack Nicklaus. (Orig.). (gr. 10-12). 1980. pap. 2.50 (ISBN 0-671-83522-X). PB.
Nicklaus, Jack & Bowden, Ken. Golf My Way. (Illus.). 1974. 13.95 (ISBN 0-671-21702-X). S&S.
--Jack Nicklaus' Lesson Tee. LC 76-46733. (Illus.). 160p. 1977. 10.95 (ISBN 0-914178-11-3). Golf Digest.
--Jack Nicklaus' Lesson Tee. (Illus.). 1978. pap. 5.95 (ISBN 0-671-24217-2, Fireside). S&S.
--Jack Nicklaus' Playing Lessons. LC 80-84953. (Illus.). 144p. 1981. 12.95 (ISBN 0-914178-42-3, 42901-9). Golf Digest.
Nicklaus, Jack & Wind, Herbert W. Greatest Game of All: My Life in Golf. 1969. 10.95 (ISBN 0-671-20215-4). S&S.
O'Byrne, Robert. Senior Golf. 1977. 10.95 (ISBN 0-87691-231-5). Winchester Pr.
Olson, Bill & Linkert, Lo. Beat the Links. LC 78-59843. (Sports Library). (Illus., Orig.). 1978. 8.95 (ISBN 0-89149-040-X); pap. 5.95 (ISBN 0-89149-039-6). Jolex.
Pennick, Frank. Frank Pennick's Choice of Golf Courses. 1977. pap. 9.75 (ISBN 0-7136-1659-8). Transatlantic.
PGA Tour. Official PGA Tour Media Guide Nineteen Eighty-One. 240p. 1981. pap. 5.95 (ISBN 0-89480-142-2). Workman Pub.
Player, Gary. Gary Player's Golf Clinic. LC 81-65104. (Illus.). 160p. 1981. pap. 6.95 (ISBN 0-910676-23-2, 6036). DBI.
Player, Gary & Sullivan, George. Gary Player's Golf Book for Young People. LC 79-55882. (Illus.). 112p. (gr. 7-12). 1980. 8.95 (ISBN 0-914178-35-0, 25483-9). Golf Digest.
Rankin, Judy. A Natural Way to Golf Power. 1977. pap. 2.95 (ISBN 0-346-12253-8). Cornerstone.
Ravielli, Anthony. What Is Golf? LC 75-38342. (gr. 4-8). 1976. 6.95 (ISBN 0-689-30518-4). Atheneum.
Record Book of USGA Championships & International Events: 1895 Through 1980, 2 vols. 7.50 (ISBN 0-686-30840-9). US Golf Assn.
The Rules of Golf: Case-Bound Edition. 5.00 (ISBN 0-686-30833-6). US Golf Assn.
Runyan, Paul & Aultman, Dick. The Short Way to Lower Scoring. LC 79-52549. (Illus.). 175p. 1980. 13.50 (ISBN 0-914178-27-X, 24921-5). Golf Digest.
Runyon, Paul. Paul Runyon's Book for Senior Golfers. (Illus.). 1963. 4.50 (ISBN 0-396-04758-0). Dodd.
Saunders, Vivien & Clark, Clive. The Young Golfer. (Illus.). 1978. 9.75 (ISBN 0-09-131730-4, Pub. by Hutchinson); pap. 4.75 (ISBN 0-09-131731-2). Merrimack Bk Serv.
Scott, Tom. Observer's Book of Golf. (Observer Bks.). (Illus.). 1977. 2.95 (ISBN 0-684-15212-6, ScribT). Scribner.
Seitz, Nick. Improve Your Game (and Learn About) the Superstars of Golf. 192p. Date not set. pap. cancelled (ISBN 0-346-12477-8). Cornerstone.
--Quick Tips from the CBS Golf Spot. LC 80-84950. (Illus.). 208p. 1981. pap. 6.95 (ISBN 0-914178-43-1, 42903-5). Golf Digest.
--Superstars of Golf. LC 77-92910. (Illus.). 192p. 1977. 10.95 (ISBN 0-914178-13-X, 22975). Golf Digest.
Shankland, Craig, et al. The Golfer's Stroke-Saving Handbook. (Illus.). 1979. pap. 2.50 (ISBN 0-451-08606-6, E8606, Sig). NAL.
--The Golfer's Stroke Saving Handbook. LC 77-20905. (Illus.). 1978. 12.95 (ISBN 0-316-78260-2). Little.
Shay, Arthur. Forty Common Errors in Golf & How to Correct Them. LC 77-23706. 1978. pap. 5.95 (ISBN 0-8092-7827-8). Contemp Bks.
Sheehan, Larry, ed. Great Golf Humor. LC 79-52547. (Illus.). 1979. 9.95x (ISBN 0-914178-31-8, 25166-X). Golf Digest.
--The Whole Golf Catalog. LC 78-20351. (Illus.). 1979. pap. 14.95 (ISBN 0-689-10979-2). Atheneum.
Simek, Thomas C. & O'Brien, Richard M. Total Golf: A Behavioral Approach to Lowering Your Score & Getting More Out of Your Game. LC 79-6086. (Illus.). 240p. 1981. 14.95 (ISBN 0-385-15404-6). Doubleday.
Smith, R. Craig. Enjoy Golf & Win: Mental Golf--Its Impact on Scoring & Enjoyment. LC 81-50344. 60p. (Orig.). 1981. pap. 6.95 (ISBN 0-686-31629-0). Wordsmith.
Snead, Sam. The Driver. 160p. 1965. pap. 3.95 (ISBN 0-346-12355-0). Cornerstone.
--Golf Begins at Forty. 1979. lib. bdg. 10.95 (ISBN 0-8161-6674-9, Large Print Bks). G K Hall.
--How to Hit a Golf Ball. 1940. pap. 1.95 (ISBN 0-385-00089-8). Doubleday.
Snead, Sam & Aultman, Dick. Golf Begins at Forty. (Illus.). 1978. 9.95 (ISBN 0-8037-2850-6). Dial.
Sports Illustrated. Golf Lessons from Great Pros. 1961. 9.95 (ISBN 0-13-359851-9). P-H.
Sports Illustrated Editors. Sports Illustrated Golf. rev. ed. LC 72-4143. (Illus.). (gr. 7-9). 1972. 5.95 (ISBN 0-397-00937-2); pap. 2.95 (ISBN 0-397-00938-0). Lippincott.
Stanley, Louis. Pelham Golf Year. (Illus.). 448p. 1981. 19.95 (ISBN 0-7207-1290-4, Pub. by Michael Joseph). Merrimack Bk Serv.
Stobbs, John. Anatomy of Golf: Technique & Tactic. (Illus.). 8.95 (ISBN 0-87523-135-7). Emerson.
--Tackle Golf. rev. ed. (Tackle Ser). (Illus.). 128p. 1976. pap. text ed. 6.95x (ISBN 0-09-123841-2, SpS). Sportshelf.
Toski, Bob & Aultman, Dick. Bob Toski's Complete Guide to Better Golf. LC 75-39958. (Illus.). 1980. pap. 8.95 (ISBN 0-689-70592-1). Atheneum.
--The Touch System for Better Golf. Golf Digest Magazine, ed. LC 70-161626. (Illus.). 128p. 1980. pap. 6.95 (ISBN 0-914178-36-9). Golf Digest.
Toski, Bob, et al. How to Become a Complete Golfer. LC 77-92909. (Illus.). 288p. 1978. 14.95 (ISBN 0-914178-15-6, 24169). Golf Digest.
Tremayne, Nicholas. Golf: How to Become a Champ. (Illus.). 1976. pap. 5.95 (ISBN 0-86002-129-7). Transatlantic.
Trevillion, Paul. Dead Heat. 12.50x (ISBN 0-392-05378-0, SpS). Sportshelf.
USGA Golf Handbook. 7.50 (ISBN 0-686-30839-5). US Golf Assn.
Van Evera, Maxine. Building Your Swing for Better Golf with Amy Alcott. LC 78-69645. (Illus.). 1980. 12.95 (ISBN 0-498-02141-6). A S Barnes.
Wagenvoord, James. Golf Diary. (Illus.). 160p. 1981. 6.95 (ISBN 0-312-33806-6). St Martin.
Walsh, Eleanor & Hardy, Merrill. Golf. 1980. pap. text ed. 5.95 (ISBN 0-87620-353-5). Goodyear.
Watson, Thomas S. & Hannigan, Frank. The Rules of Golf Explained & Illustrated. LC 79-4758. (Illus.). 1980. 12.95 (ISBN 0-394-50740-1); pap. 5.95 (ISBN 0-394-73908-6). Random.
Watson, Tom & Hanningan, Frank. The Rules of Golf Illustrated & Explained. 12.95 (ISBN 0-686-30836-0); pap. 5.95 (ISBN 0-686-30837-9). US Golf Assn.
Wilde, Larry. The Official Golfers Joke Book. 1977. pap. 1.95 (ISBN 0-523-41469-2). Pinnacle Bks.
Williams, Evan & Sheehan, Larry. You Can Hit the Golf Ball Farther. LC 79-50544. (Illus.). 127p. 1979. 9.95 (ISBN 0-914178-26-1, 24922); pap. 5.95 (ISBN 0-914178-29-6, 24964). Golf Digest.
Wind, Herbert W. Golf Quiz. LC 80-66690. (Illus.). 192p. (Orig.). 1980. pap. 8.95 (ISBN 0-914178-41-5, 41416-X). Golf Digest.
--The Story of American Golf: Its Champions & Its Championships. LC 72-602. (Illus.). 564p. 1972. Repr. of 1956 ed. lib. bdg. 24.75x (ISBN 0-8371-5991-1, WIAG). Greenwood.
Wiren, Gary. Golf. (Sport Ser). (Illus.). (gr. 10 up). 1971. pap. 3.95 ref. ed. (ISBN 0-13-358010-5). P-H.
Wise, Kris M. The Answers to Par Golf. LC 78-357. (Illus.). 1978. pap. 3.95 (ISBN 0-89543-010-X). Grossmont Pr.
Yogi, Count. Five Simple Steps to Perfect Golf. 1979. pap. 2.95 (ISBN 0-346-12379-8). Cornerstone.

GOLF–BIBLIOGRAPHY

Kennington, Don. Sourcebook of Golf. (Illus.). 240p. 1981. lib. bdg. 34.50x (ISBN 0-85365-584-7, Pub. by Lib Assn England). Oryx Pr.
Murdoch, Joseph, ed. Library of Golf 1743-1966: A Bibliography of Golf Books. LC 67-29083. (Illus.). 1968. 34.00 (ISBN 0-8103-0961-0). Gale.

GOLF–BIOGRAPHY

Argea, Angelo & Edmondson, Jolee. The Bear & I: The Story of the World's Most Famous Caddie. LC 79-63844. (Illus.). 1979. 7.95 (ISBN 0-689-10983-0). Atheneum.
Elliot, Len & Kelly, Barbara. Who's Who in Golf. 1976. 8.95 (ISBN 0-87000-225-2). Arlington Hse.
Hahn, James & Hahn, Lynn. Nancy Lopez: Golfing Pioneer. LC 78-13162. (Champions & Challengers II). (gr. 3-5). 1979. text ed. 5.95 (ISBN 0-88436-480-1); pap. text ed. 3.50 (ISBN 0-88436-481-X). EMC.
Hill, Dave & Seitz, Nick. Teed off. LC 76-30769. (Illus.). 1977. 8.95 (ISBN 0-13-902247-3). P-H.
Lopez, Nancy & Schwed, Peter. The Education of a Woman Golfer. 1979. 9.95 (ISBN 0-671-24756-5). S&S.
Robison, Nancy. Nancy Lopez: Wonder Woman of Golf. (Sports Stars Ser.). (Illus.). (gr. 2-6). 1979. PLB 7.95 (ISBN 0-516-04302-1); pap. 2.50 (ISBN 0-516-44302-X). Childrens.
Schumacher, Craig. Nancy Lopez. (Sports Superstars Ser.). (Illus.). (gr. 3-9). 1979. PLB 5.95 (ISBN 0-87191-694-0); pap. 2.95 (ISBN 0-89812-164-7). Creative Ed.
Van Riper, Guernsey, Jr. Golfing Greats: Two Top Pros. LC 74-16266. (Sports Library Ser). (Illus.). 96p. (gr. 3-6). 1975. PLB 6.48 (ISBN 0-8116-6669-7). Garrard.

GOLF–HISTORY

Cousins, Geoffrey. Lords of the Links: The Story of Professional Golf. (Illus.). 1978. 10.95 (ISBN 0-09-131560-3, Pub. by Hutchinson). Merrimack Bk Serv.
Cousins, Geoffrey & Scott, Tom. A Century of Opens. 1972. 10.00 (ISBN 0-584-10037-X). Transatlantic.
Evans, Webster. Rubs of the Green: Golf's Triumphs & Tragedies. (Illus.). 1970. 6.95 (ISBN 0-7207-0251-8). Transatlantic.
Gibson, Nevin. Golf's Greatest Shots by the World's Greatest Players. 160p. 1981. 9.95 (ISBN 0-89962-218-6). Todd & Honeywell.
McDonnell, Michael. Great Moments in Sport: Golf. (Illus.). 216p. 7.95 (ISBN 0-919364-61-6, ADON 3536). Pagurian.
Martin, Harry B. Fifty Years of American Golf. (Illus.). 1966. Repr. of 1936 ed. boxed 15.00 (ISBN 0-87266-020-6). Argosy.
Steel, Donald. Golf Facts & Feats. (Guinness Superlatives Ser.). (Illus.). 256p. 1980. 19.95 (ISBN 0-8069-9240-9, Pub. by Guinness Superlatives England). Sterling.
Taylor, Dawson. St. Andrews: Cradle of Golf. LC 74-16. (Illus.). 288p. 1976. 15.00 (ISBN 0-498-01442-8). A S Barnes.
Ward-Thomas, F. The Royal & Ancient. (Illus.). 200p. 1980. 14.95x (ISBN 0-7073-0260-9, Pub. by Scottish Academic Pr Scotland). Columbia U Pr.
Wilson, Mark & Bowden, Ken, eds. The Best of Henry Longhurst. LC 78-69793. 208p. 1978. 8.50 (ISBN 0-914178-22-9, 24574). Golf Digest.
Wind, Herbert W. The Story of American Golf. 3rd ed. 1975. 20.00 (ISBN 0-394-49020-7). Knopf.

GOLF–JUVENILE LITERATURE

Dypwick, Otis J. & Jacobs, Helen H. Golf, Swimming & Tennis. (Illus.). (gr. 4 up). 1962. PLB 7.95 (ISBN 0-87191-024-1). Creative Ed.
Ford, Doug. Start Golf Young. LC 77-93324. (gr. 5 up). 1978. 7.95 (ISBN 0-8069-4126-X); PLB 7.49 (ISBN 0-8069-4127-8). Sterling.
Golf Digest Editors. Better Golf. (Better Ser.). (Illus.). (gr. 7 up). 15.95x (ISBN 0-7182-0141-8, SpS). Sportshelf.
--Better Golf for Boys. LC 65-13512. (Illus.). (gr. 6 up). 1965. PLB 5.95 (ISBN 0-396-06589-9). Dodd.
Hasegawn, Sam. Johnny Miller. (Creative's Superstars Ser.). (Illus.). (gr. 3-9). 1975. PLB 5.95 (ISBN 0-87191-455-7). Creative Ed.
Hudson, D. C. Your Book of Golf. (gr. 7 up). 1969. 4.95 (ISBN 0-571-08123-1). Transatlantic.
Jacobs, Linda. Laura Baugh: Golf's Golden Girl. LC 74-31187. (Women Who Win Ser.: No. 2). 1974. lib. bdg. 5.95 (ISBN 0-88436-160-8); pap. 3.50 (ISBN 0-88436-161-6). EMC.
--Lee Elder: The Daring Dream. LC 75-45429. (Black American Athletes Ser.). (Illus.). 40p. (gr. 4-6). 1976. PLB 5.95 (ISBN 0-88436-267-1); pap. 3.50 (ISBN 0-88436-268-X). EMC.
May, Julian. The Masters. LC 75-8761. (Sports Classics Ser.). (Illus.). 48p. (gr. 4-12). 1975. PLB 8.95 (ISBN 0-87191-443-3). Creative Ed.
--The PGA Championship of Golf. LC 76-8464. (Sports Classics Ser.). (Illus.). (gr. 4-12). 1976. PLB 8.95 (ISBN 0-87191-524-3). Creative Ed.
--U. S. Open. LC 75-6959. (Sports Classics Ser.). (Illus.). 48p. (gr. 4-6). 1975. PLB 8.95 (ISBN 0-87191-445-X). Creative Ed.
O'Shea, Mary J. & Keely, John. Laura Baugh. LC 75-38826. (Sports Superstars Ser.). (Illus.). (gr. 3-9). 1976. PLB 5.95 (ISBN 0-87191-501-4). Creative Ed.
Robison, Nancy. Nancy Lopez: Wonder Woman of Golf. (Sports Stars Ser.). (Illus.). (gr. 2-6). 1979. PLB 7.95 (ISBN 0-516-04302-1); pap. 2.50 (ISBN 0-516-44302-X). Childrens.
Schumacher, Craig. Nancy Lopez. (Sports Superstars Ser.). (Illus.). (gr. 3-9). 1979. PLB 5.95 (ISBN 0-87191-694-0); pap. 2.95 (ISBN 0-89812-164-7). Creative Ed.

GOLF–PSYCHOLOGICAL ASPECTS

Gallwey, W. Timothy. The Inner Game of Golf. 1981. 12.95 (ISBN 0-394-50534-4). Random.
Kemp, Charles F. Smart Golf. new ed. LC 74-82856. (Illus.). 200p. (Orig.). 1974. pap. 3.85 (ISBN 0-87706-057-6). Branch Smith.
Rotella, Robert & Bunker, Linda. Mind Mastery for Winning Golf: Using Your Head to Reach Par & to Enjoy Playing. 160p. 1981. 12.95 (ISBN 0-13-583328-0); pap. 5.95 (ISBN 0-13-583310-8). P-H.
Taylor, Dawson. Inside Golf. LC 77-91177. 1978. pap. 5.95 (ISBN 0-8092-7803-0). Contemp Bks.
Wiren, Gary, et al. The New Golf Mind. 164p. 1981. pap. 4.95 (ISBN 0-346-12478-6). Cornerstone.

GOLF–STUDY AND TEACHING

Aultman, Dick & Golf Digest Editors. Square-to-Square Golf Swing. 1975. pap. 5.95 (ISBN 0-671-21947-2, Fireside). S&S.
Bernier, Robert. The Pro Golf Teaching Manual. pap. 2.95 (ISBN 0-89741-008-4). Roadrunner Tech.
Boomer, Percy. On Learning Golf. (Illus.). 1946. 8.95 (ISBN 0-394-41008-4). Knopf.
Boros, Julius. Swing Easy, Hit Hard. 192p. 1968. pap. 2.95 (ISBN 0-346-12305-4). Cornerstone.
Dante, Jim & Diegel, Leo. Nine Bad Shots of Golf & What to Do About Them. 186p. 1961. pap. 4.95 (ISBN 0-346-12327-5). Cornerstone.
Dante, Jim & Elliott, Len. Four Magic Moves of Winning Golf. 192p. 1963. pap. 3.95 (ISBN 0-346-12299-6). Cornerstone.
Golf Digest Editors. Better Golf. (Better Sports Ser.). (Illus.). 93p. 1974. 8.50x (ISBN 0-7182-0141-8). Intl Pubns Serv.
Hogan, Ben. Modern Fundamentals of Golf. 128p. 1962. pap. 3.95 (ISBN 0-346-12326-7). Cornerstone.
Jessop, J. C. Teach Yourself Golf. Date not set. 7.50x (ISBN 0-340-05286-4, SpS). Sportshelf.
Nicklaus, Jack. Golf My Way. 1976. pap. 6.95 (ISBN 0-671-22278-3, Fireside). S&S.
Redford, Ken & Tremayne, Nick. Success in Golf. (Success Sportbooks Ser.). (Illus.). 1977. 9.95 (ISBN 0-7195-2862-3). Transatlantic.
Trevillion, Paul. How to Improve Your Golf. LC 74-188016. (Illus.). 256p. 1974. pap. 1.95 (ISBN 0-02-029870-6, Collier). Macmillan.

GOLF COURSES

Alliss, Peter. The Shell Book of Golf. LC 81-65956. (Illus.). 224p. 1981. 27.00 (ISBN 0-7153-7988-7). David & Charles.
Cornish, Geoffrey S. & Whitten, Ronald F. The Golf Course. (Illus.). 320p. 1981. 35.00 (ISBN 0-8317-3947-9, Rutledge Pr). Smith Pubs.
Davis, William H., ed. Great Golf Courses of the World. LC 74-77084. (Illus.). 1974. 19.95 (ISBN 0-914178-06-7). Times Bks.
Green Section Staff. Building Golf Holes for Good Turf Management. 56p. 1.00 (ISBN 0-686-30838-7). US Golf Assn.
Heuer, Karla L. Golf Courses: A Guide to Analysis & Valuation. (Illus.). 1980. text ed. 15.00 (ISBN 0-911780-47-5). Am Inst Real Estate Appraisers.
Jenkins, Dan. Sports Illustrated the Best Eighteen Golf Holes in America. (Illus.). 1966. 15.00 (ISBN 0-440-08215-3). Delacorte.
Sobey, Edwin J. C. Complete Circuit Training Guide. LC 78-66002. (Illus.). 160p. 1980. pap. 4.95 (ISBN 0-89037-202-0). Anderson World.

GOLF FOR WOMEN

Edmondson, Jolee. The Woman Golfer's Catalogue. LC 79-65116. (Illus.). 1980. 18.95 (ISBN 0-8128-2685-X); pap. 10.95 (ISBN 0-8128-6041-1). Stein & Day.
O'Shea, Mary J. & Keely, John. Laura Baugh. LC 75-38826. (Sports Superstars Ser.). (Illus.). (gr. 3-9). 1976. PLB 5.95 (ISBN 0-87191-501-4). Creative Ed.
Saunders, Vivien. The Complete Woman Golfer. 1975. 14.95 (ISBN 0-09-124090-5, Pub. by Hutchinson). Merrimack Bk Serv.

GOLF-LINKS

see Golf Courses

GOLGI APPARATUS

Cook, G. M. The Golgi Apparatus. 2nd ed. Head, J. J., ed. LC 78-53328. (Carolina Biology Readers Ser.). 16p. (gr. 11-12). 1981. pap. text ed. 1.65 (ISBN 0-89278-277-3, 45-9677). Carolina Biological.
Golgi Centennial Symposium, September 1973. Golgi Centennial Symposium: Perspectives in Neurobiology. Santini, Maurizo, ed. LC 74-21985. 1975. 68.50 (ISBN 0-911216-80-4). Raven.
Whaley, W. G. The Golgi Apparatus. LC 75-20055. (Cell Biology Monographs: Vol. 2). (Illus.). 200p. 1975. 48.60 (ISBN 0-387-81315-2). Springer-Verlag.

GOLIARDS

Cambridge Songs. The Cambridge Songs, a Goliard's Song Book of the 11th Century. Breul, Karl, ed. LC 77-178517. Repr. of 1915 ed. 16.50 (ISBN 0-404-56529-8). AMS Pr.
Symonds, John A., ed. & tr. Wine, Women, & Song. LC 74-112944. Repr. of 1884 ed. 9.00 (ISBN 0-404-06319-5). AMS Pr.
Symonds, John A., ed. Wine, Women & Song: Medieval Latin Students' Songs. LC 66-26826. (The Medieval Library Ser.). Repr. of 1883 ed. 8.50x (ISBN 0-8154-0228-7). Cooper Sq.

Waddell, Helen. Wandering Scholars. 7th, rev. ed. 1968. Repr. of 1934 ed. 21.50x (ISBN 0-06-497280-1). B&N.
Whicher, George F., tr. The Goliard Poets: Medieval Latin Songs & Satires. LC 78-23583. 1979. Repr. of 1949 ed. lib. bdg. 21.00x (ISBN 0-313-21192-2, GOML). Greenwood.

GOMBROWICZ, WITOLD, 1904-
Gombrowicz, Witold. A Kind of Testament. Hamilton, Alastair, tr. LC 72-89199. 158p. 1973. 10.00x (ISBN 0-87722-051-4). Temple U Pr.
Thompson, Eva M. Witold Gombrowicz. (Twayne World Authors Ser.). 1979. lib. bdg. 12.95 (ISBN 0-8057-6351-1). G K Hall.
Thompson, Ewa M. Witold Gombrowicz. (World Authors Ser.: Poland: No. 510). 1979. lib. bdg. 14.50 (ISBN 0-8057-6351-1). Twayne.

GOMEZ, VICENTE
Clinton, Daniel J. Gomez, Tyrant of the Andes. LC 70-97833. Repr. of 1936 ed. lib. bdg. 14.75x (ISBN 0-8371-2698-3, CLG). Greenwood.

GOMEZ DE LA SERNA, RAMON, 1888-1963
Gardiol, Rita M. Ramon Gomez De la Serna. LC 74-13340. (World Authors Ser.: Spain: No. 338). 176p. 1974. lib. bdg. 10.95 (ISBN 0-8057-2379-X). Twayne.

GOMPERS, SAMUEL, 1850-1924
Babcock, Robert H. Gompers in Canada: A Study in American Continentalism Before the First World War. LC 74-78507. 1974. pap. 7.50 (ISBN 0-8020-6242-3). U of Toronto Pr.
Dick, William M. Labor & Socialism in America: The Gompers Era. LC 71-189555. (National University Publications). 1972. 15.00 (ISBN 0-8046-9005-7). Kennikat.
Grubbs, Frank L., Jr. Gompers & the Great War: Protecting Labor's Standards. LC 79-89867. 1980. 12.95 (ISBN 0-87716-111-9, Pub. by Moore Pub Co). F Apple.
--Struggle for Labor Loyalty: Gompers, the A F of L & the Pacifists, 1917-1920. LC 68-26691. (Illus.). 1968. 9.75 (ISBN 0-8223-0078-8). Duke.
Harvey, Rowland H. Samuel Gompers: Champion of the Toiling Masses. 1973. lib. bdg. 18.50x (ISBN 0-374-93730-3). Octagon.
Kurland, Gerald. Samuel Gompers: Founder of the American Labor Movement. Rahmas, D. Steve, ed. LC 72-190242. (Outstanding Personalities Ser: No. 24). 32p. (Orig.). (gr. 7-9). 1972. lib. bdg. 2.95 incl. catalog cards (ISBN 0-87157-524-8); pap. 1.50 vinyl laminated covers (ISBN 0-87157-024-6). SamHar Pr.
Larson, Simeon. Labor & Foreign Policy: Gompers, the A. F. of L. & the First World War, 1914-1918. LC 73-2898. 176p. 1975. 12.00 (ISBN 0-8386-1290-3). Fairleigh Dickinson.
Livesay, Harold. Samuel Gompers & Organized Labor in America. (Library of American Biography). 1978. 9.95 (ISBN 0-316-52873-0); pap. text ed. 4.95 (ISBN 0-316-52872-2). Little.
Thorne, Florence C. Samuel Gompers, American Statesman. Repr. of 1957 ed. lib. bdg. 15.00x (ISBN 0-8371-2293-7, THSG). Greenwood.

GOMPERS, SAMUEL, 1850-1924–FICTION
Hughes, Rupert. Giant Wakes. 3.00 (ISBN 0-685-07322-X). Borden.

GONADOTROPIN
Albert, A. Human Pituitary Gonadotropins: A Workshop Conference. (Illus.). 448p. 1961. ed. spiral bdg. 40.75photocopy (ISBN 0-398-00023-9). C C Thomas.
Franchimont, P. & Burger, H., eds. Human Growth Hormone & Gonadotrophins in Health & Disease. LC 73-86079. 494p. 1975. 78.00 (ISBN 0-444-10594-8, North-Holland). Elsevier.
Hearn, J. P., et al. Gonadotrophins: Current Research, 3 vols, Vol. 1. 1974. text ed. 21.50x (ISBN 0-8422-7204-6). Irvington.
McKerns, Kenneth W., ed. Structure & Function of the Gonadotropins. LC 78-12372. (Biochemical Endocrinology Ser.). (Illus.). 646p. 1978. 49.50 (ISBN 0-306-40097-9, Plenum Pr). Plenum Pub.
Moudgal, N. R. Gonadotropins & Gonadal Function. 1974. 39.50 (ISBN 0-12-508850-7). Acad Pr.
Ranadive, K. J., et al, eds. Gonadotrophins: Current Research, 3 vols, Vol. 3. 1974. text ed. 21.50x (ISBN 0-685-55782-0). Irvington.
Rosemberg, Eugenia, ed. Gonadotropin Therapy in Female Infertility. (International Congress Ser.: No. 266). 300p. 1973. 55.25 (ISBN 0-444-15028-5, Excerpta Medica). Elsevier.
--Gonadotropins Nineteen Sixty Eight: Proceedings of the Workshop Conference Held at Vista Hermosa, Mor., Mexico, June 24-26, 1968. LC 68-59129. (Illus.). 1968. text ed. 12.00x (ISBN 0-87672-004-1). Geron-X.
Saxena, Brij B., et al. Gonadotropins. LC 73-38948. 830p. 1972. 46.50 (ISBN 0-471-75570-2, Pub. by Wiley). Krieger.
Segal, Sheldon J., ed. Chorionic Gonadotropin. 485p. 1981. 42.50 (ISBN 0-306-40563-6, Plenum Pr). Plenum Pub.
Seidel, G. E., et al. Gonadotrophins: Current Research, 3 vols, Vol. 2. 1974. text ed. 21.50x (ISBN 0-8422-7205-4). Irvington.

GONCHAROV, IVAN ALEKSANDROVIC, 1812-1891
Chamot, Mary. Goncharova. 1981. 27.00x (ISBN 0-905368-52-5, Pub. by Jupiter England). State Mutual Bk.
Ehre, Milton. Oblomov & His Creator: The Life & Art of Ivan Goncharov. LC 72-5378. (Studies of the Russian Institute, Columbia University Ser). 375p. 1974. 22.00x (ISBN 0-691-06245-5). Princeton U Pr.
Lavrin, Janko. Goncharov. LC 68-27070. 1969. Repr. of 1954 ed. 6.50 (ISBN 0-8462-1203-X). Russell.
Lyngstad, Alexandra & Lyngstad, Sverre. Ivan Goncharov. (World Authors Ser.: Russia: No. 200). lib. bdg. 10.95 (ISBN 0-8057-2380-3). Twayne.

GONCOURT, EDMOND, AND JULES, DE
Goncourt, Jules D. & Goncourt, Edmond D. Pages from the Goncourt Journal. Baldick, Robert, tr. (Oxford Paperback Books). (Illus.). 456p. pap. text ed. 6.95x (ISBN 0-19-281250-5). Oxford U Pr.
Grant, Richard B. The Goncourt Brothers. (World Authors Ser.: France: No. 183). lib. bdg. 10.95 (ISBN 0-8057-2384-6). Twayne.

GONDS
see also Muria

GONDWANA (GEOLOGY)
see also Continental Drift

GONGORA Y ARGOTE, LUIS DE, 1561-1627
Beverley, John. Aspects of Gongora's "Soledades". iv, 139p. 1980. 19.00 (ISBN 90-272-1711-4, PUMRL 1). Benjamins North Am.
Woods, M. J. The Poet & the Natural World in the Age of Gongora. (Modern Languages & Literature Monographs). 1978. 37.50x (ISBN 0-19-815533-6). Oxford U Pr.

GONGU-HROLFS SAGA
Hartmann, Jacob W. Gongu-Hrolfssaga: A Study in Old Norse Philology. LC 12-20208. (Columbia University. Germanic Studies, Old Ser.: No. 14). Repr. of 1912 ed. 14.00 (ISBN 0-404-50414-0). AMS Pr.

GONIOSCOPY
Kimura, Ryozo. Color Atlas of Gonioscopy. (Illus.). 1973. 35.00 (ISBN 0-89640-037-9). Igaku-Shoin.

GONJA LANGUAGE
Painter, Colin. Gonja: A Phonological & Grammatical Study. (African Ser: Vol. 1). (Gonja). 1970. pap. text ed. 20.00x (ISBN 0-87750-139-4). Res Ctr Lang Semiotic.

GONZALES, NARCISO GENER, 1858-1903
Jones, Lewis Pinckney. Stormy Petrel: N. G. Gonzales and His State. LC 73-8792. 300p. 1973. 14.95x (ISBN 0-87249-253-2). U of SC Pr.

GONZALES, PANCHO
Morse, Charles & Morse, Ann. Pancho Gonzales. LC 74-1359. (Creative's Superstars Ser). 32p. 1974. 5.95 (ISBN 0-87191-341-0). Creative Ed.

GONZALES, RAMON, 1922-
Poggie, John J., Jr. Between Two Cultures: The Life of an American-Mexican. LC 72-84765. 1973. pap. 2.65x (ISBN 0-8165-0334-6). U of Ariz Pr.

GONZALEZ, ABRAHAM, 1864-1913
Beezley, William H. Insurgent Governor: Abraham Gonzalez & the Mexican Revolution in Chihuahua. LC 72-86257. (Illus.). xvi, 195p. 1973. 13.95x (ISBN 0-8032-0821-9). U of Nebr Pr.

GONZALEZ, JULIO, 1877-1942
Julio Gonzalez. (Tate Gallery Art Ser.). (Illus.). 1977. pap. 3.95 (ISBN 0-8120-0844-8). Barron.
Withers, Josephine. Julio Gonzalez: Sculpture in Iron. LC 76-26798. (Illus.). 1978. 40.00x (ISBN 0-8147-9171-9). NYU Pr.

GONZALO DE BERCEO, 13TH CENTURY
Fitz-Gerald, John D. Versification of the Cuaderna Via As Found in Berceo's Vida De Santo Domingo De Silos. LC 71-168035. (Columbia University. Studies in Romance Philology & Literature: No. 7). Repr. of 1905 ed. 15.00 (ISBN 0-404-50607-0). AMS Pr.
Goode, Teresa C. Gonzalo De Berceo. (Carl Ser.: No. 7). Repr. of 1933 ed. 16.00 (ISBN 0-404-50307-1). AMS Pr.
Keller, John E. Gonzalo de Berceo. (World Authors Ser.: Spain: No. 187). lib. bdg. 10.95 (ISBN 0-8057-2144-4). Twayne.
Perry, T. Anthony. Art & Meaning in Berceo's Vida De Santa Oria. (Romantic Studies, Second Ser.: No. 19). 1968. 18.50x (ISBN 0-300-00823-6). Yale U Pr.

GOOCHLAND COUNTY, VIRGINIA
Agee, Helene B. Facets of Goochland (Virginia) County's History. 1962. 5.95 (ISBN 0-685-47896-3). Dietz.

GOOD AND EVIL
see also Evil in Literature; Guilt; Providence and Government of God; Sin; Theodicy
Augustine, Saint On Free Choice of the Will. Benjamin, A. S. & Hackstaff, L. H., trs. LC 63-16932. (Orig.). 1964. pap. 4.95 (ISBN 0-672-60368-3, LLAS150). Bobbs.
Bacon, Francis. Essays & Colours of Good & Evil. LC 72-56. (Select Bibliographies Reprint Ser). 1972. Repr. of 1862 ed. 18.25 (ISBN 0-8369-9951-7). Arno.
Basham, Don. Deliver Us from Evil. 1972. pap. 4.95 (ISBN 0-912376-06-6) (ISBN 0-685-56346-4). Chosen Bks Pub.
Becker, Ernest. Escape from Evil. LC 75-12059. 1976. pap. 3.95 (ISBN 0-02-902340-8). Free Pr.
Brown, Stuart, ed. Reason & Religion. LC 77-3115. 1977. 22.50x (ISBN 0-8014-1025-8); pap. 7.95 (ISBN 0-8014-9166-5). Cornell U Pr.
Bunyan, John. The Holy War. (Summit Bks). 1977. pap. 3.95 (ISBN 0-8010-0714-3). Baker Bk.
Camus, Albert. Homme Revolte: Essai. (Coll. Soleil). 1951. 16.50 (ISBN 0-685-11234-9); pap. 4.95 (ISBN 0-686-66425-6). French & Eur.
--Rebel. 1954. 10.95 (ISBN 0-394-44232-6). Knopf.
--Rebel: An Essay on Man in Revolt. Bower, Anthony, tr. 1956. pap. 2.95 (ISBN 0-394-70030-9, V30, Vin). Random.
--Resistance, Rebellion, & Death. 1963. 3.95 (ISBN 0-394-60339-7, M339). Modern Lib.
Cioran, E. M. The New Gods. Howard, Richard, tr. LC 74-77939. 128p. 1974. 5.95 (ISBN 0-8129-0475-3). Times Bks.
Conn, Charles W. The Anatomy of Evil. LC 80-21103. 1981. 7.95 (ISBN 0-8007-1177-7). Revell.
Cuss, Gladys. Hidden Manna Revealed by the Comforter. 192p. 1981. 9.00 (ISBN 0-682-49768-1). Exposition.
Davis, Stephen T., ed. Encountering Evil: Live Options in Theodicy. LC 80-84647. 1981. pap. 7.95 (ISBN 0-8042-0517-5). John Knox.
Doob, Leonard W. Panorama of Evil: Insights from the Behavioral Sciences. LC 77-87964. (Contributions in Philosophy: No. 10). 1978. lib. bdg. 16.95 (ISBN 0-313-20030-0, DPE/). Greenwood.
Ewing, Alfred C. The Definition of Good. LC 78-59021. 1979. Repr. of 1947 ed. 18.50 (ISBN 0-88355-695-2). Hyperion Conn.
Faley, Ronald J. The Cup of Grief. LC 77-6839. 1977. pap. 4.95 (ISBN 0-8189-0352-X). Alba.
Feinberg, John S. Theologies & Evil. LC 79-66474. 1979. text ed. 14.50 (ISBN 0-8191-0838-3); pap. text ed. 9.00 (ISBN 0-8191-0839-1). U Pr of Amer.
Ferre, Nels F. Evil & the Christian Faith. facsimile ed. LC 71-134075. (Essay Index Reprints - Reason & the Christian Faith Ser.: Vol. 2). Repr. of 1947 ed. 16.00 (ISBN 0-8369-2393-6). Arno.
Fontenrose, Joseph. Python. 1959. 27.00x (ISBN 0-8196-0285-X). Biblo.
Fromm, Erich. The Heart of Man: Its Genius for Good & Evil. LC 64-18053. 1980. pap. 3.95 (ISBN 0-06-090119-5, CN 795, CN). Har-Row.
Galligan, Michael. God & Evil. LC 75-36172. 96p. 1976. pap. 1.95 (ISBN 0-8091-1925-0). Paulist Pr.
Geisler, Norman L. The Roots of Evil. (Christian Free University Curriculum Ser.). 1978. pap. 3.95 (ISBN 0-310-35751-9). Zondervan.
Goldberg, Gerald J. Fate of Innocence. 1965. pap. text ed. 7.50x (ISBN 0-13-308189-3). P-H.
Green, Michael. I Believe in Satan's Downfall. (I Believe Ser.). 256p. (Orig.). 1981. pap. 5.95 (ISBN 0-8028-1892-7). Eerdmans.
Hagerty, Cornelius. The Problem of Evil. LC 77-3022. 1978. 7.95 (ISBN 0-8158-0352-4). Chris Mass.
Harris, Errol E. & Litt, D. The Problem of Evil. LC 77-72325. (Aquinas Lecture Ser.). 1977. 6.95 (ISBN 0-87462-142-9). Marquette.
Herman, A. L. The Problem of Evil & Indian Thought. 1976. 12.50 (ISBN 0-8426-0991-1). Orient Bk Dist.
Hick, John H. Evil & the God of Love. rev. ed. LC 76-62953. 1977. pap. 6.95 (ISBN 0-06-063902-4, RD219, HarpR). Har-Row.
James, Henry, Sr. The Nature of Evil: Considered in a Letter to the Rev. Edward Beecher, D.D. LC 72-920. (The Selected Works of Henry James, Sr.: Vol. 6). Repr. of 1855 ed. 27.50 (ISBN 0-404-10086-4). AMS Pr.
Jenyns, Soame. A Free Enquiry into the Nature & Origin of Evil. 2nd ed. Wellek, Rene, ed. LC 75-11226. (British Philosophers & Theologians of the 17th & 18th Centuries: Vol. 28). 1976. Repr. of 1757 ed. lib. bdg. 42.00 (ISBN 0-8240-1780-3). Garland Pub.
Kelsey, Morton. Discernment: A Study in Ecstasy. LC 78-58958. 168p. 1978. pap. 4.95 (ISBN 0-8091-2157-3). Paulist Pr.
King, William. William King (Sixteen Fifty to Seventeen Twenty-Nine) LC 75-11228. (British Philosophers & Theologians of the 17th & 18th Centuries Ser.). 1978. lib. bdg. 42.00 (ISBN 0-8240-1782-X). Garland Pub.
Knoch, A. E. The Problem of Evil & the Judgments of God. 1976. pap. text ed. 3.00 (ISBN 0-910424-59-4). Concordant.
Lewis, C. S. Great Divorce. 1946. pap. 2.50 (ISBN 0-02-086780-8). Macmillan.
--Problem of Pain. 1943. 7.95 (ISBN 0-02-570910-0); pap. 2.95 (ISBN 0-02-086840-5). Macmillan.
Lord God of Truth Within. 1976. Repr. of 1940 ed. 12.00 (ISBN 0-911662-56-1). Yoga.
Lyman, Stanford. The Seven Deadly Sins. 1978. text ed. 15.95x (ISBN 0-312-71324-X); pap. text ed. 8.95x (ISBN 0-312-71325-8). St Martin.
Die Machte Des Guten und Bosen: Vorstellungen Um 12 und 13. (Miscellanea Mediaevalia: Vol.11). 1977. 117.00x (ISBN 3-11-007261-0). De Gruyter.
Madden, Edward H. & Hare, Peter H. Evil & the Concept of God. (American Lecture Philosophy). 152p. 1968. photocopy ed. spiral 12.75 (ISBN 0-398-01192-3). C C Thomas.
Maritain, Jacques. Saint Thomas & the Problem of Evil. (Aquinas Lecture). 1942. 6.95 (ISBN 0-87462-106-2). Marquette.
Mayakovsky, V. What Is Good & What Is Bad. 22p. 1979. pap. 1.10 (ISBN 0-8285-1624-3, Pub. by Progress Pubs Russia). Imported Pubns.
Murphy, Elspeth. Sometimes I'm Good, Sometimes I'm Bad. (David & I Talk to God Ser.). (Illus.). 24p. 1981. pap. 1.75 (ISBN 0-89191-368-8, 53686). Cook.
Nietzsche, Friedrich. Beyond Good & Evil: Prelude to a Philosophy for the Future. 4th ed. Zimmern, Helen, tr. 1923. text ed. 13.50x (ISBN 0-04-192020-1). Allen Unwin.
O'Flaherty, Wendy D. The Origins of Evil in Hindu Mythology. 1977. 20.00x (ISBN 0-520-03163-6); pap. 6.95 (ISBN 0-520-04098-8). U of Cal Pr.
Plantinga, Alvin. God, Freedom, & Evil. 1978. pap. 3.95 (ISBN 0-8028-1731-9). Eerdmans.
Pratney, Winkie. Star Wars, Star Trek. 1978. pap. 1.75 (ISBN 0-89728-057-1, 693400). Omega Pubns OR.
Rashdall, H. Theory of Good & Evil: A Treatise on Moral Philosophy, 2 Vols. in 1. 2nd ed. Repr. of 1924 ed. 30.00 (ISBN 0-527-73910-3). Kraus Repr.
Rice, Philip Blair. On the Knowledge of Good & Evil. LC 75-8968. 299p. 1975. Repr. of 1955 ed. lib. bdg. 16.00x (ISBN 0-8371-8124-0, RIGE). Greenwood.
Ricoeur, Paul. Symbolism of Evil. Buchanan, Emerson, tr. LC 67-11506. 1969. pap. 5.95 (ISBN 0-8070-1567-9, BP323). Beacon Pr.
Royce, Josiah. Studies of Good & Evil: A Series of Essays Upon Problems of Philosophy & of Life. 1964. Repr. of 1898 ed. 20.00 (ISBN 0-208-00555-2, Archon). Shoe String.
Salmon, Elizabeth G. Good in Existential Metaphysics. (Aquinas Lecture). 1952. 6.95 (ISBN 0-87462-117-8). Marquette.
Sanford, John A. Evil: The Shadow Side of Reality. 176p. 1981. 10.95 (ISBN 0-8245-0037-7). Crossroad NY.
Schilling, S. Paul. God & Human Anguish. LC 77-5857. 1977. 5.95 (ISBN 0-687-14909-6). Abingdon.
Schutze, Alfred. Enigma of Evil. 1978. pap. 9.50 (ISBN 0-903540-10-X, Pub by Floris Books). St George Bk Serv.
Schwartz, Richard B. Samuel Johnson & the Problem of Evil. LC 74-27314. 128p. 1975. 15.00 (ISBN 0-299-06790-4). U of Wis Pr.
Simon, Ulrich. A Theology of Auschwitz: The Christian Faith & the Problem of Evil. LC 78-71046. 1979. pap. 3.95 (ISBN 0-8042-0724-0). John Knox.
Smith, Donald. How to Cure Yourself of Positive Thinking. LC 77-70191. 1977. 7.95 (ISBN 0-912458-80-1). E A Seemann.
Steiner, Rudolf. The Deed of Christ & the Opposing Spiritual Powers Lucifer, Ahriman, Mephistopheles, Asuras. 2.75 (ISBN 0-919924-02-6). Anthroposophic.
--The Influences of Lucifer & Ahriman. Osmond, D. S., tr. from Ger. 1976. pap. 4.95 (ISBN 0-919924-00-X). Anthroposophic.
Sylvester, Hugh. Arguing with God. LC 76-186348. 128p. 1972. pap. 1.50 (ISBN 0-87784-350-3). Inter-Varsity.
Taylor, Richard. Good & Evil: A New Direction. 1970. 9.95 (ISBN 0-02-616690-9); pap. 1.95 (ISBN 0-02-089680-8). Macmillan.
Thompson, William I. Evil & World Order. (World Perspectives Ser.). 1977. pap. 4.95x (ISBN 0-06-131951-1, TB1951, Torch). Har-Row.
Tsanoff, R. A. Nature of Evil. Repr. of 1931 ed. 18.00 (ISBN 0-527-90980-7). Kraus Repr.
Von Wright, George H. Varieties of Goodness. 1963. text ed. 15.00x (ISBN 0-7100-3614-0). Humanities.

Zappulli, Cesare. The Power of Goodness. 1980. 3.00 (ISBN 0-8198-5800-5); pap. 2.00 (ISBN 0-8198-5801-3). Dghtrs St Paul.
Zimmer, Heinrich. King & the Corpse: Tales of the Soul's Conquest of Evil. Campbell, Joseph, ed. (Bollingen Ser.: Vol. 11). 1971. 21.50x (ISBN 0-691-09779-8); pap. 5.95 (ISBN 0-691-01776-X, 257). Princeton U Pr.

GOOD FRIDAY
Becker, Ralph. Lent, Good Friday & Easter. pap. 0.50 (ISBN 0-685-41825-1). Reiner.
Ferrell, Charles. A Service for Good Friday. 1971. 1.25 (ISBN 0-89536-081-0). CSS Pub.
Sayre, Francis B. To Stand in the Cross. (Lenten Bks). 1978. 5.95 (ISBN 0-8164-0380-5). Seabury.

GOOD SAMARITAN (PARABLE)
see Jesus Christ–Parables

GOOD-WILL (IN BUSINESS, ETC.)
Bicklecombe, Peter. Goodwill, the Wasted Asset. 175p. 1971. 19.95x (ISBN 0-8464-1103-2). Beekman Pubs.

GOOD WORKS (THEOLOGY)
see also Antinomianism; Corporal Works of Mercy; Justification; Reward (Theology)
El Bien Me Seguira! (Span.). pap. 1.60 (ISBN 0-8297-0925-8). Life Pubs Intl.
Rogers, Dale E. Angel Unaware. (Orig.). pap. 1.95 (ISBN 0-515-05325-2). Jove Pubns.

GOODMAN, BENNY, b. 1909
Baron, Stanley. Benny: King of Swing. LC 79-84693. 1979. 25.00 (ISBN 0-688-03502-7). Morrow.
Connor, D. Russell & Hicks, Warren W. B G on the Record: A Bio-Discography of Benny Goodman. rev. ed. LC 79-79599. (Illus.). 1969. 22.95 (ISBN 0-87000-059-4). Arlington Hse.

GOODMAN, GODFREY, BP. OF GLOUCESTER, 1583-1656
Soden, Geoffrey I. Godfrey Goodman, Bishop of Gloucester, 1583-1656. (Church Historical Society Ser.: No. 58). 1953. 16.00x (ISBN 0-8401-5058-X). Allenson-Breckinridge.

GOODNIGHT, CHARLES, 1836-1929
Haley, J. Evetts. Charles Goodnight: Cowman & Plainsman. (Illus.). 1979. Repr. of 1949 ed. 17.50 (ISBN 0-8061-0200-4). U of Okla Pr.

GOODRICH, SAMUEL GRISWOLD, 1793-1860
Roselle, Daniel. Samuel Griswold Goodrich, Creator of Peter Parley. LC 68-19534. 1968. 15.50 (ISBN 0-87395-033-X); microfiche 15.50 (ISBN 0-87395-133-6). State U Ny Pr.

GOODRICH, SAMUEL GRISWOLD, 1793-1860–BIBLIOGRAPHY
Goodrich, Samuel G. Recollections of a Lifetime, or Men & Things I Have Seen. LC 67-23886. 1967. Repr. of 1857 ed. 24.00 (ISBN 0-8103-3041-5). Gale.

GOODRICH FAMILY
Goodrich, Samuel G. Recollections of a Lifetime, or Men & Things I Have Seen. LC 67-23886. 1967. Repr. of 1857 ed. 24.00 (ISBN 0-8103-3041-5). Gale.

GOODSPEED, CHARLES, ELIOT, b. 1867
Goodspeed, Charles E. Yankee Bookseller. LC 73-15401. (Illus.). 325p. 1974. Repr. of 1937 ed. lib. bdg. 20.00x (ISBN 0-8371-7173-3, GOYB). Greenwood.

GOOLAGONG, EVONNE, 1951–JUVENILE LITERATURE
Herda, D. J. Free Spirit: Evonne Goolagong. LC 76-16197. (Sports Profiles Ser.). (Illus.). 48p. (gr. 4-11). 1976. PLB 9.30 (ISBN 0-8172-0146-7). Raintree Pubs.
Jacobs, Linda. Evonne Goolagong: Smiles & Smashes. LC 74-31267. (Women Who Win Ser.: No. 2). 1974. lib. bdg. 5.95 (ISBN 0-88436-158-6); pap. 3.50 (ISBN 0-88436-159-4). EMC.

GOOSE
see Geese

GOOSE SHOOTING
Adams, Chuck. The Digest Book of Duck & Goose Hunting. (The Sports & Leisure Library). (Illus.). 96p. 1979. pap. 2.95 (ISBN 0-695-81324-2). New Century.
Cadieux, Charles L. Goose Hunting. LC 79-19953. (Illus.). 1979. 14.00 (ISBN 0-913276-30-8). Stone Wall Pr.
Gard, Robert E. Wild Goose Country: Horicon Marsh to Horseshoe Island. LC 75-18194. (Illus.). 1975. 15.00 (ISBN 0-88361-039-6). Stanton & Lee.

GOPHERS
see Ground Squirrels

GORDIMER, NADINE
Haugh, Robert F. Nadine Gordimer. (World Authors Ser.: South Africa: No. 315). 1974. lib. bdg. 10.95 (ISBN 0-8057-2387-0). Twayne.

GORDIUS
May, Henry G. Contributions to the Life Histories of Gordius Robustus Leidy & Paragordius Varius: Leidy. (Illus.). Repr. of 1920 ed. 9.50 (ISBN 0-384-36060-2). Johnson Repr.

GORDON, AARON DAVID, 1856-1922
Rose, Herbert H. Life & Thought of A. D. Gordon. 1964. 3.50x (ISBN 0-8197-0176-9). Bloch.

GORDON, ADAM LINDSAY, 1833-1870
Hutton, Geoffrey. Adam Lindsay Gordon: The Man & the Myth. (Illus.). 216p. 1978. 18.95 (ISBN 0-571-10921-7, Pub. by Faber & Faber). Merrimack Bk Serv.

GORDON, BENJAMIN LEE, 1875-
Gordon, Benjamin L. New Judea: Jewish Life in Modern Palestine & Egypt. Davis, Moshe, ed. LC 77-70697. (America & the Holy Land Ser.). (Illus.). 1977. Repr. of 1919 ed. lib. bdg. 22.00x (ISBN 0-405-10251-8). Arno.

GORDON, CAROLINE, 1895-
Landess, Thomas H., ed. The Short Fiction of Caroline Gordon: A Symposium. 1972. 4.95 (ISBN 0-685-77627-1). U of Dallas Pr.
McDowell, Frederick P. Caroline Gordon. (Pamphlets on American Writers Ser: No. 59). (Orig.). 1966. pap. 1.25x (ISBN 0-8166-0404-5, MPAW59). U of Minn Pr.
Stuckey, W. J. Caroline Gordon. (U. S. Authors Ser.: No. 200). lib. bdg. 10.95 (ISBN 0-8057-0332-2). Twayne.

GORDON, CHARLES GEORGE, 1833-1885
Abdullah, Achmed & Pakenham, Thomas C. Dreamers of Empire. facs. ed. LC 68-57300. (Essay Index Reprint Ser). 1929. 16.00 (ISBN 0-8369-0099-5). Arno.
Charles, Elizabeth R. Three Martyrs of the Nineteenth Century. LC 73-77196. Repr. of 1886 ed. 15.00 (ISBN 0-8371-1296-6). Greenwood.
Crabites, Pierre. Gordon, the Sudan & Slavery. LC 72-88999. Repr. of 1933 ed. 15.25x (ISBN 0-8371-1764-X, Pub. by Negro U Pr). Greenwood.
Gordon, C. G. General Gordon's Private Diary & His Exploits in China; Amplified by Samuel Mossman. Repr. of 1885 ed. 24.00 (ISBN 0-527-34610-1). Kraus Repr.
Hake, A. Egmont. The Journals of Major-Gen. C. G. Gordon, C. B., at Kartoum. 1885. Repr. 20.00 (ISBN 0-685-43046-4). Norwood Edns.
Strachey, Lytton. Eminent Victorians. 7.50 (ISBN 0-8446-5836-7). Peter Smith.
--Eminent Victorians. 1969. pap. 4.50 (ISBN 0-15-628697-1, HPL40, HPL). HarBraceJ.
Tames, R. General Gordon. (Clarendon Biography Ser.). (Illus.). 1973. pap. 3.50 (ISBN 0-912728-65-5). Newbury Bks.
Tornch, Charles C. The Road to Khartoum: A Life of General Charles Gordon. (Illus.). 1979. 15.95 (ISBN 0-393-01237-9). Norton.

GORDON, LORD GEORGE, 1751-1793
Colson, Percy. Their Ruling Passions. facs. ed. LC 70-136645. (Biography Index Reprint Ser.). 1949. 19.00 (ISBN 0-8369-8040-9). Arno.

GORDON, WILLIAM A.
Gordon, William A. Writer & Critic: A Correspondence with Henry Miller. LC 68-15427. 1968. 8.95x (ISBN 0-8071-0513-9). La State U Pr.

GORDON FAMILY
Ree, Stephen. Gordon Ballads. LC 74-14557. 1975. Repr. of 1903 ed. lib. bdg. 7.50 (ISBN 0-88305-570-8). Norwood Edns.

GORDON RIOTS, 1780
Kazantzis, Judith. The Gordon Riots. (Jackdaw Ser: No. 48). (Illus.). 1967. 6.95 (ISBN 0-670-34670-5, Grossman). Viking Pr.

GORDON SETTER
see Dogs–Breeds–Gordon Setter

GOREY, EDWARD, 1925-
Gorey, Edward. Gorey Posters. 1979. pap. 8.95 (ISBN 0-8109-2179-0). Abrams.

GORGAS, JOSIAH, 1818-1925
Vandiver, Frank E. Ploughshares into Swords: Josiah Gorgas & Confederate Ordnance. 363p. 1977. pap. text ed. 14.50x (ISBN 0-292-76434-0). U of Tex Pr.

GORGAS, WILLIAM CRAWFORD, 1854-1920
Judson, Clara I. Soldier Doctor: The Story of William Gorgas. (Illus.). (gr. 4-9). 1942. reinforced bdg. 5.95 (ISBN 0-684-13470-5, ScribJ). Scribner.

GORGES, FERDINANDO, SIR, 1565-1647
Baxter, James P. Sir Ferdinando Gorges (1565-1647) & His Province of Maine, 3 vols. 1966. Set. 62.00 (ISBN 0-8337-0190-8). B Franklin.

GORILLAS
D'Aulaire, Emily & D'Aulaire, Ola. Chimps & Baboons. Bourne, Russell & Rifkin, Natalie S., eds. LC 74-80051. (Ranger Rick's Best Friends Ser.: No. 3). (Illus.). (gr. 1-6). 1974. 2.00 (ISBN 0-912186-14-3). Natl Wildlife.
Desmond, Adrian J. The Ape's Reflexion. 1979. 10.95 (ISBN 0-8037-0674-X, J Wade). Dial.
Dixson, Alan. The Natural History of the Gorilla. LC 81-57. 1981. 19.95 (ISBN 0-231-05318-5). Columbia U Pr.
Elting, Mary. Gorilla Mysteries. (Illus.). 64p. (gr. 1-9). 1981. 4.95 (ISBN 0-448-47488-3). G&D.
Fenner, Carol. Gorilla Gorilla. (gr. 2 up). 1973. (BYR); PLB 5.99 (ISBN 0-394-92069-4). Random.
Hamsa, Bobbie. Your Pet Gorilla. (Far-Fetched Pets Ser.). (Illus.). (ps-3). 1981. PLB 8.65 (ISBN 0-516-03365-4); pap. 2.95 (ISBN 0-516-43365-2). Childrens.
Hogan, Paula Z. The Gorilla. LC 79-13602. (Life Cycles). (Illus.). (gr. k-3). 1979. PLB 11.15 (ISBN 0-8172-1501-8). Raintree Pubs.
Jones, C. & Sabater Pi, J. Comparative Ecology of Gorilla & Pan Troglodytes in Rio Muni, West Africa. (Bibliotheca Primatologica: No. 13). 1971. pap. 15.00 (ISBN 3-8055-0293-1). S Karger.
Kevles, Bettyann. Thinking Gorillas: Testing & Teaching the Greatest Ape. LC 79-12782. (gr. 7 up). 1980. 10.95 (ISBN 0-525-41074-0). Dutton.
McDearmon, Kay. Gorillas. LC 78-11292. (Skylight Bks.). (Illus.). (gr. 3-5). 1979. 4.95 (ISBN 0-396-07645-9). Dodd.
Maple, Terry & Hoff, M. P. Gorilla Behavior. (VNR Primate Behavior & Development Ser.). 272p. 1981. text ed. price not set. Van Nos Reinhold.
Meyers, Susan. The Truth About Gorillas. LC 79-19393. 40p. (gr. 1-4). 1980. 7.95 (ISBN 0-525-41564-5, Smart Cat). Dutton.
Moody, Elizabeth. Patty Cake. LC 73-90185. (Illus.). 85p. 1974. 6.95 (ISBN 0-8129-0433-8). Times Bks.
Noell, Anna M. History of Noell's Ark Gorilla Show. Himber, David K., ed. (Illus.). 326p. 1980. 16.00 (ISBN 0-9602422-2-8). Noells Ark.
Patterson, Francine & Linden, Eugene. The Education of Koko. LC 81-1325. (Illus.). 240p. 1981. 15.95 (ISBN 0-03-046101-4). HR&W.
Schaller, George B. Mountain Gorilla: Ecology & Behavior. LC 63-11401. xviii, 432p. 1963. 20.00x (ISBN 0-226-73635-0). U of Chicago Pr.
--The Mountain Gorilla: Ecology & Behavior. LC 63-11401. (Illus.). 1976. pap. 9.00x (ISBN 0-226-73636-9, P684, Phoen). U of Chicago Pr.
--Year of the Gorilla. LC 64-13946. (Illus.). 1964. 15.00x (ISBN 0-226-73637-7); pap. 5.50 (ISBN 0-226-73638-5, P209, Phoen). U of Chicago Pr.
Schick, Alice. Kongo & Kumba. LC 73-15444. (Illus.). 96p. (gr. 3-6). 1974. 4.95 (ISBN 0-8037-4613-X); PLB 4.58 (ISBN 0-8037-4619-9). Dial.
Willoughby, David P. All About Gorillas. LC 76-50215. (Illus.). 1978. 19.95 (ISBN 0-498-01845-8). A S Barnes.

GORKHALI LANGUAGE
see Nepali Language

GORKHAS
see Gurkhas

GORKI, MAXIM, 1868-1936
Gorki, Maxim. Reminiscences of My Youth. 334p. 1980. Repr. of 1924 ed. lib. bdg. 25.00 (ISBN 0-8492-4961-9). R West.
--Reminiscences of My Youth. Dewey, Veronica, tr. 334p. 1979. lib. bdg. 20.00 (ISBN 0-89760-308-7, Telegraph). Dynamic Learn Corp.
Gorky, Maxim. Childhood. (Soviet Authors' Library). (Illus.). 232p. 1975. 11.95x (ISBN 0-8464-0242-4). Beekman Pubs.
--Letters. 199p. 1973. 3.75 (ISBN 0-8285-1085-7, Pub. by Progress Pubs Russia). Imported Pubns.
--My Apprenticeship. Wilks, Ronald, tr. (Classics Ser.). (Orig.). 1974. pap. 2.95 (ISBN 0-14-044291-X). Penguin.
--My Apprenticeship: My Universities. (Illus.). 485p. 1975. 16.00x (ISBN 0-8464-0660-8). Beekman Pubs.
--My Universities. Wilks, Ronald, tr. from Rus. (Classics Ser.). 1979. pap. 2.95 (ISBN 0-14-044302-9). Penguin.
Gourfinkel, Nina. Gorky. Feshbach, Ann, tr. LC 75-11423. (Illus.). 192p. 1975. Repr. of 1960 ed. lib. bdg. 16.00x (ISBN 0-8371-8190-9, GOGO). Greenwood.
Habermann, Gerhard. Maksim Gorki. Schlant, Ernestine, tr. LC 75-129114. (Modern Literature Ser.). 1971. 10.95 (ISBN 0-8044-2326-1); pap. 4.95 (ISBN 0-8044-6239-9). Ungar.
Hare, Richard. Maxim Gorky: Romantic Realist & Conservative Revolutionary. LC 78-3868. 1978. Repr. of 1962 ed. lib. bdg. 19.50x (ISBN 0-313-20365-2, HAMGO). Greenwood.
Kaun, Alexander S. Maxim Gorky & His Russia. LC 67-13330. 1968. Repr. of 1931 ed. 26.00 (ISBN 0-405-08686-5, Blom Pubns). Arno.
MIR Publishers, ed. Lenin & Gorky: Letters, Reminiscences, Articles. (Illus.). 429p. 1973. 19.95x (ISBN 0-8464-0555-5). Beekman Pubs.
Ostwald, Hans. Maxim Gorky. 1905. Repr. 20.00 (ISBN 0-8274-2695-X). R West.

GORKY, ARSHILE, 1904-1948
Jordan, Jim M. & Goldwater, Robert. The Paintings of Arshile Gorky: A Critical Catalogue. LC 79-2248. (Illus.). 480p. 1981. text ed. 75.00x (ISBN 0-8147-4160-6). NYU Pr.
Mooradian, Karlen. The Many Worlds of Arshile Gorky. LC 80-65868. (Illus.). 327p. (Orig.). 1981. 18.95 (ISBN 0-936684-01-1); pap. 9.95 (ISBN 0-936684-02-X). Gilgamesh Pr IL.
Rand, Harry. Arshile Gorky: The Implication of Symbols. LC 77-25046. (Illus.). 256p. 1981. text ed. 40.00 (ISBN 0-8390-0209-2). Allanheld & Schram.
Reiff, Robert F. A Stylistic Analysis of Arshile Gorky's Art from 1943-1948. LC 76-23679. (Outstanding Dissertations in the Fine Arts - American). (Illus.). 1977. Repr. of 1961 ed. lib. bdg. 52.00 (ISBN 0-8240-2719-1). Garland Pub.
Rosenberg, Harold. Arshile Gorky: The Man, the Times, the Idea. (Illus.). 144p. 1981. pap. 5.95 (ISBN 0-935296-20-4). Sheep Meadow.
Seitz, William C. Arshile Gorky. LC 75-169313. (Museum of Modern Art Publications in Reprint). (Illus.). 60p. 1972. Repr. of 1962 ed. 14.00 (ISBN 0-405-01571-2). Arno.
Shearer, Linda. Acquisition Priorities: Aspects of Postwar Painting in America. (Illus.). 1976. pap. 6.00 (ISBN 0-89207-005-6). S R Guggenheim.
Waldman, Diane. Arshile Gorky: A Retrospective. 1981. 45.00 (ISBN 0-8109-0976-6). Abrams.
--Arshile Gorky, Nineteen Four to Nineteen Forty-Eight: A Retrospective. LC 80-52992. (Illus.). 286p. 1981. cover museum catalogue 17.95soft (ISBN 0-89207-025-0). S R Guggenheim.

GORMAN, LAWRENCE, 1846-1917
Ives, Edward D. & Dorson, Edward, eds. Larry Gorman: The Man Who Made the Songs. LC 77-70601. (International Folklore Ser.). (Illus.). 1977. Repr. of 1964 ed. lib. bdg. 14.00x (ISBN 0-405-10100-7). Arno.

GOROSTIZA, JOSE, 1901-
Rubin, Mordecai S. Poetica Moderna: Muerte Sin Fin De Jose Gorostiza; Analisis y Comentario. LC 65-16385. 288p. 1966. 15.50x (ISBN 0-8173-7800-6). U of Ala Pr.

GORRES, JOHANN JOSEPH VON, 1776-1848
see Goerres, Johann Joseph Von, 1776-1848

GORTON, SAMUEL, 1592-1677
Winslow, Edward. Hypocrisie Unmasked by the True Relation of the Proceedings of the Governour & Company of Massachusetts Against Samuel Gorton. LC 68-57130. (Research & Source Works Ser.: No. 312). 1969. Repr. of 1916 ed. 19.00 (ISBN 0-8337-3820-8). B Franklin.

GOSCHEN, GEORGE JOACHIM, 1831-1907
Baxter, Robert D. Local Government & Taxation, & Mr. Goschen's Report. 1976. Repr. of 1874 ed. 25.00 (ISBN 0-403-06440-6, Regency). Scholarly.
Spinner, T. J., Jr. George Joachim Goschen: The Transformation of a Victorian Liberal. (Conference on British Studies Biographical Ser.). 268p. 1973. 39.00 (ISBN 0-521-20210-8). Cambridge U Pr.

GOSPEL, SOCIAL
see Social Gospel

GOSPEL AND LAW
see Law and Gospel

GOSPEL MUSIC
see also Spirituals (Songs)
Dixon, Robert M. Blues & Gospel Records, 1902-1942. 1977. Repr. 95.00 (ISBN 0-403-08268-4). Scholarly.
Gaither, Bill & Gaither, Gloria. God Can. (Especially for Children Ser.: Vol. 10). (Illus.). (ps-8). 1977. 4.50 (ISBN 0-914850-12-1). Impact Tenn.
--I'm a Promise. (Especially for Children Ser.: Vol. 8). (Illus.). 1977. 4.50 (ISBN 0-914850-10-5). Impact Tenn.
--Jesus, I Heard You Had a Big House, Vol. 7. (Especially for Children Ser.). (Illus.). (ps-8). 1977. 4.50 (ISBN 0-914850-09-1). Impact Tenn.
--Let All the Little Children Praise the Lord. (Especially for Children Ser.: Vol. 12). (Illus.). (ps-8). 1977. 4.50 (ISBN 0-914850-18-0). Impact Tenn.
--This Is the Day That the Lord Hath Made. (Especially for Children Ser.: Vol. 9). (ps-8). 1977. 4.50 (ISBN 0-914850-11-3). Impact Tenn.
Holm, Dallas & Lamb, Robert P. This Is My Story. 160p. (YA) 1981. mass paper 2.25 (ISBN 0-86608-007-4). Zondervan.
--This Is My Story. LC 80-81756. 150p. 1980. pap. 4.95 (ISBN 0-914850-96-2). Impact Tenn.
Jackson, Irene V., compiled by. Afro-American Religious Music: A Bibliography & a Catalogue of Gospel Music. LC 78-60527. (Illus.). 1979. lib. bdg. 19.95 (ISBN 0-313-20560-4, JGM/). Greenwood.
MacKenzie, Joy. That's Him. (Especially for Children Ser.: Vol. 11). (Illus.). 1977. 4.50 (ISBN 0-914850-13-X). Impact Tenn.
North, Gail & Anderson, Bob. Gospel Music Encyclopedia. LC 79-65072. (Illus.). 1979. 14.95 (ISBN 0-8069-0174-8); lib. bdg. 13.29 (ISBN 0-8069-0175-6). Sterling.

Ricks, George R. Some Aspects of the Religious Music of the United States Negro. Dorson, Richard M., ed. LC 77-70621. (International Folklore Ser.). 1977. Repr. of 1977 ed. lib. bdg. 27.00x (ISBN 0-405-10123-6). Arno.

Sallee, James. History of Evangelistic Hymnody. 1978. 6.95 (ISBN 0-8010-8111-4). Baker Bk.

Sankey, Ira D., et al. Gospel Hyms, 6 vols, No. 1-6. facsimile ed. LC 70-171076. (Earlier American Music Ser.: No. 5). 512p. 1972. Repr. of 1895 ed. lib. bdg. 25.00 (ISBN 0-306-77305-8). Da Capo.

Shinn, Duane & Hoffman, Diane. Evangelistic Embellishments: How to Make Hymns & Gospel Songs Come Alive. 1980. spiral bdg. 49.95 (ISBN 0-912732-49-0). Duane Shinn.

Sizer, Sandra S. Gospel Hymns & Social Religion: The Rhetoric of Nineteenth-Century Revivalism. Davis, Allen F., ed. LC 78-10165. (American Civilization Ser.). 1978. lib. bdg. 19.50x (ISBN 0-87722-142-1). Temple U Pr.

Warrick, Mancel & Hillsman, Joan R. The Progress of Gospel Music. 1977. 4.95 (ISBN 0-533-02152-9). Vantage.

Wells, Edmund E. Wells of Salvation. (Orig.). pap. 1.00 (ISBN 0-686-30400-4). WOS.

GOSSE, EDMUND WILLIAM, SIR, 1849-1928

Braybrooke, Patrick. Considerations of Edmund Gosse. Repr. 20.00 (ISBN 0-8274-2092-7). R West.

Charteris, Evan. The Life & Letters of Sir Edmund Gosse. LC 72-2097. (English Literature Ser., No. 33). 1972. Repr. of 1931 ed. lib. bdg. 66.95 (ISBN 0-8383-1456-2). Haskell.

Gide, Andre & Gosse, Edmund. The Correspondence of Andre Gide & Edmund Gosse: 1904-1928. Brugmans, Linette F., ed. LC 77-22619. (New York University. Studies in Romance Languages & Literature: No. 2). 1977. Repr. of 1959 ed. lib. bdg. 17.50x (ISBN 0-8371-9736-8, GICO). Greenwood.

Woolf, James D. Sir Edmond Gosse. (English Authors Ser.: No. 117). 12.50 (ISBN 0-8057-1232-1). Twayne.

--Sir Edmund Gosse. LC 79-125822. (English Authors Ser.). 1972. lib. bdg. 6.95x (ISBN 0-89197-937-9). Irvington.

GOSSE, PHILIP HENRY, 1810-1888

Gosse, Edmund. Father & Son. 1963. pap. 4.95 (ISBN 0-393-00195-4, Norton Lib). Norton.

GOTHIC ARCHITECTURE

see Architecture, Gothic

GOTHIC ART

see Art, Gothic

GOTHIC DECORATION AND ORNAMENT

see Decoration and Ornament, Gothic

GOTHIC LANGUAGE

Bennett, William H. An Introduction to the Gothic Language. 4th, rev. ed. Lehmann, Winfred P., ed. LC 79-87574. (Introductions to the Older Languages of Europe Ser.: No. 2). xvii, 190p. 1981. 18.50x (ISBN 0-87352-290-7). Modern Lang.

D'Alquen, Richard J. Gothic Ai & Av. LC 72-94440. (Janua Linguarum, Ser. Practica: No. 151). 182p. 1974. pap. text ed. 41.25x (ISBN 0-686-22578-3). Mouton.

Hempel, Heinrich. Gotisches Elementarbuch: Grammatik, Texte mit Uebersetzung und Erlaeuterungen. 4th ed. (Sammlung Goeschen, Nos. 79 & 79a). (Ger). 1966. 5.00x (ISBN 3-11-006077-9). De Gruyter.

MacAndrew, Elizabeth. The Gothic Tradition. LC 79-9447. 1980. 20.00x (ISBN 0-231-04674-X). Columbia U Pr.

Rice, Allan L. Gothic Prepositional Compounds in Their Relation to the Greek Originals. 1932. pap. 8.00 (ISBN 0-527-00757-9). Kraus Repr.

Skeireins. Gothic Commentary on the Gospel of John. Bennett, W. H., tr. 1960. pap. 9.00 (ISBN 0-527-83350-9). Kraus Repr.

Wood, Francis A. Verner's Law in Gothic, & Reduplicating Verbs in Germanic. LC 73-173039. (Chicago University. Germanic Studies: No. 2). Repr. of 1895 ed. 11.00 (ISBN 0-404-50272-5). AMS Pr.

Wright, Joseph. Grammar of the Gothic Language & the Gospel of St. Mark. 2nd ed. 1954. 24.95x (ISBN 0-19-811922-4). Oxford U Pr.

GOTHIC LITERATURE

Berenbaum, Linda B. The Gothic Imagination: Expansion in Gothic Literature & Art. LC 80-67035. (Illus.). 140p. 1981. 15.00 (ISBN 0-8386-3068-5). Fairleigh Dickinson.

Brauchli, Jakob. Der Englische Schauerroman um 1880 unter Berucksichtigung der unbekannten Bucher. Bleiler, E. F., ed. LC 78-60913. (The Fiction of Popular Culture Ser.: Vol. 2). 260p. 1979. lib. bdg. 26.00 (ISBN 0-8240-9666-5). Garland Pub.

Dorer, Nancy & Dorer, Frances. You Will Like It Here. (Orig.). 1979. pap. 1.95 (ISBN 0-532-23257-7). Woodhill.

Garrett, John. Gothic Strains & Bourgeois Sentiments in the Novels of Mrs. Ann Radcliffe & Her Imitations. Varma, Devendra P., ed. LC 79-8454. (Gothic Studies & Dissertations Ser.). 1980. lib. bdg. 40.00x (ISBN 0-405-12668-9). Arno.

Hess, Kamelle. Shadows of Fear. (Orig.). 1979. pap. 1.95 (ISBN 0-532-23251-8). Woodhill.

Platzner, Robert L. The Metaphysical Novel in England: The Romantic Phase. Varma, Devendra P., ed. LC 79-8468. (Gothic Studies & Dissertations Ser.). 1980. lib. bdg. 29.00x (ISBN 0-405-12656-5). Arno.

Radcliffe, Elsa J. Gothic Novels of the Twentieth Century: An Annotated Bibliography. LC 78-24357. 291p. 1979. lib. bdg. 13.00 (ISBN 0-8108-1190-1). Scarecrow.

Reddin, Chitra P. Forms of Evil in the Gothic Novel. Varma, Devendra P., ed. LC 79-8472. (Gothic Studies & Dissertations Ser.). 1980. lib. bdg. 28.00x (ISBN 0-405-12669-7). Arno.

Sedgwick, Eve K. The Coherence of Gothic Conventions. Varma, Devendra P., ed. LC 79-8462. (Gothic Studies & Dissertations Ser.). 1980. lib. bdg. 17.00x (ISBN 0-405-12650-6). Arno.

Skarda, Patricia L. & Jaffe, Nora C., eds. The Evil Image: Two Centuries of Gothic Short Fiction & Poetry. 1981. pap. 8.95 (ISBN 0-686-71368-0, F549, Mer). NAL.

Tarr, Sr. Mary. Catholicism in Gothic Fiction. Bleiler, E. F., ed. LC 78-60815. (The Fiction of Popular Culture Ser.: Vol. 16). 148p. 1979. lib. bdg. 15.00 (ISBN 0-8240-9652-5). Garland Pub.

Tracy, Ann B. The Gothic Novel, Seventeen Ninety to Eighteen Thirty: Plot Summaries & Index to Motifs. LC 79-4013. 224p. 1981. 14.00x (ISBN 0-8131-1397-0). U Pr of Ky.

Varma, Devendra P., ed. Gothic Studies & Dissertations Series, 34 bks. 1980. Set. lib. bdg. 829.00x (ISBN 0-405-12644-1). Arno.

GOTHIC PAINTING

see Painting, Gothic

GOTHIC SCULPTURE

see Sculpture, Gothic

GOTHS

see also Barbarian Invasions of Rome; Germanic Tribes

Bradley, Henry. The Goths. 376p. 1981. Repr. of 1903 ed. lib. bdg. 45.00 (ISBN 0-89987-099-6). Darby Bks.

Czarnecki, Jan. The Goths in Ancient Poland. LC 74-20750. 1975. 12.50x (ISBN 0-87024-264-4). U of Miami Pr.

Hodgin, T. Theodoric the Goth: Barbarian Champion of Civilization. 1977. lib. bdg. 59.95 (ISBN 0-8490-2739-X). Gordon Pr.

Jordanes. Jordanis Gotengeschichte Nebst Auszuegen Aus Seiner Roemischen Geschichte. Martens, Wilhelm, ed. Repr. of 1913 ed. pap. 8.00 (ISBN 0-384-27860-4). Johnson Repr.

Prokopius Of Caesarea. Gothenkrieg. Repr. of 1903 ed. pap. 31.00 (ISBN 0-384-48050-0). Johnson Repr.

Schutte, G. Our Forefathers: the Gothonic Nations: Manual of the Ethnography of the Gothic, German, Dutch, Anglo-Saxon, Frisian & Scandinavian Peoples, 2 vols. Young, J., tr. 1977. lib. bdg. 200.00 (ISBN 0-8490-2389-0). Gordon Pr.

Vasiliev, A. A. The Goths in the Crimea. 1978. lib. bdg. 59.95 (ISBN 0-8490-1897-8). Gordon Pr.

Vasiliev, Alexander A. Goths in Crimea. 1968. Repr. of 1936 ed. 12.50 (ISBN 0-910956-09-X). Medieval Acad.

GOTTFRIED VON STASSBURG, fl. 1210

Endres, Marion. Word Field & Word Content in Middle High German. (Goeppinger Arbeiten Zur Germanistik: Vol. 47). 387p. 1971. pap. 19.50x (ISBN 3-87452-084-6). Intl Pubns Serv.

Jackson, William T. Anatomy of Love: A Study of the Tristan of Gottfried Von Strassburg. LC 70-154859. 1971. 16.00x (ISBN 0-231-03504-7). Columbia U Pr.

GOTTSCHALK, LOUIS MOREAU, 1829-1869

Doyle, J. G. Louis Moreau Gottschalk. (Bibliographies in American Music). 1981. write for info. (ISBN 0-911772-66-9). Info Coord.

Gottschalk, Louis M. Piano Music of Louis Moreau Gottschalk: 26 Complete Pieces from Original Editions. Jackson, Richard, ed. & intro. by. 10.00 (ISBN 0-8446-4746-2). Peter Smith.

Loggins, Vernon. Where the Word Ends: The Life of Louis Moreau Gottschalk. LC 58-7553. 1958. 20.00x (ISBN 0-8071-0607-0); pap. 7.95 (ISBN 0-8071-0373-X). La State U Pr.

GOUBERVILLE, GILLES DE, 1521-1578

Fedden, Katharine. Manor Life in Old France: From the Journal of the Sire De Gouberville for the Years 1549-1562. LC 70-168013. Repr. of 1933 ed. 21.00 (ISBN 0-404-02374-6). AMS Pr.

GOUDRIAAN, JAN, 1893-

Harmon, Elmer M. Commodity Reserve Currency. LC 68-59258. (Columbia University Studies in the Social Sciences: No. 599). Repr. of 1959 ed. 15.00 (ISBN 0-404-51599-1). AMS Pr.

GOULD, JAY, 1836-1892

Grodinsky, Julius. Jay Gould: His Business Career, 1867-1892. Bruchey, Stuart, ed. LC 80-1312. (Railroads Ser.). (Illus.). 1981. Repr. of 1957 ed. lib. bdg. 55.00x (ISBN 0-405-13785-0). Arno.

O'Connor, Richard. Gould's Millions. LC 73-5271. (Illus.). 335p. 1973. Repr. of 1962 ed. lib. bdg. 16.50x (ISBN 0-8371-6875-9, OCGM). Greenwood.

Ogilvie, John S. Life & Death of Jay Gould & How He Made His Millions. Bruchey, Stuart, ed. LC 80-1336. (Railroads Ser.). (Illus.). 1981. Repr. of 1892 ed. lib. bdg. 18.00x (ISBN 0-405-13809-1). Arno.

GOURAGE LANGUAGE

see Gurage Language

GOURDS

Dodge, Ernest S. Hawaiian & Other Polynesian Gourds. 1978. 5.00 (ISBN 0-914916-34-3). Topgallant.

Heiser, Charles B. The Gourd Book. LC 78-21389. (Illus.). 1979. 14.95 (ISBN 0-8061-1524-6). U of Okla Pr.

Karel, Leonard. Dried Grasses, Grains, Gourds, Pods & Cones. LC 74-31178. (Illus.). 1975. 10.00 (ISBN 0-8108-0792-0). Scarecrow.

GOURMONT, REMY DE, 1858-1915

Aldington, Richard. Remy De Gourmont: A Modern Man of Letters. LC 74-28305. 1928. 10.00 (ISBN 0-8414-2855-7). Folcroft.

Burne, Glenn S. Remy De Gourmont: His Ideas & Influence in England & America. LC 63-14295. (Crosscurrents-Modern Critiques Ser.). 205p. 1963. 7.95 (ISBN 0-8093-0105-9). S Ill U Pr.

Jacob, Paul E. Remy de Gourmont. 176p. 1980. Repr. of 1931 ed. lib. bdg. 25.00 (ISBN 0-89984-260-7). Century Bookbindery.

GOUT

see also Arthritis

Copeman, W. S. C. A Short History of the Gout & the Rheumatic Diseases. LC 64-16012. 1964. 25.00x (ISBN 0-520-00267-9). U of Cal Pr.

Ellwanger, George H. Meditations of Gout. LC 68-29548. 270p. 1968. Repr. 3.85 (ISBN 0-8048-0400-1). C E Tuttle.

Gutta Podagrica: A Treatise of the Gout, Perused by P. H. Dr. in Physick. LC 72-25642. (English Experience Ser.: No. 319). 1971. Repr. of 1633 ed. 9.50 (ISBN 9-0221-0319-6). Walter J Johnson.

Katz, Jack L., et al. Gout I: Recent Studies. 200p. 1974. text ed. 21.50x (ISBN 0-8422-7191-0). Irvington.

Kelley, W. N. & Weiner, I. M., eds. Uric Acid. (Handbook of Experimental Pharmacology: Vol. 51). (Illus.). 1978. 184.30 (ISBN 0-387-08611-0). Springer-Verlag.

Schumacher, H. Ralph, Jr. Gout & Pseudogout. (Discussions in Patient Management Ser.). 1978. spiral 9.50 (ISBN 0-87488-888-3). Med Exam.

Watts, R. W. E., et al. Gout II: Recent Studies. 1974. 21.50x (ISBN 0-8422-7208-9). Irvington.

Wyngaarden, James B. & Kelley, William N. Gout & Hyperuricemia. LC 76-22595. (Illus.). 528p. 1976. 61.50 (ISBN 0-8089-0946-0). Grune.

GOVERNMENT

see Civics; Political Science;

also subdivision Politics and Government under names of countries, states, etc., e.g. United States–Politics and government; New York (state) State Politics and Government

GOVERNMENT, COMPARATIVE

see Comparative Government

GOVERNMENT, PRIMITIVE

Bloch, Maurice, ed. Political Language & Oratory in Traditional Society. 1975. 36.00 (ISBN 0-12-106850-1). Acad Pr.

Clastres, Pierre. Society Against the State. Hurley, Robert, tr. 1977. 12.95 (ISBN 0-916354-38-5). Urizen Bks.

Fortes, Meyer & Evans-Pritchard, E. E., eds. African Political Systems. (International African Institute Ser.). (Illus.). 1970. pap. 7.95x (ISBN 0-19-285040-7, OPB). Oxford U Pr.

Mair, Lucy. Primitive Government: A Study of Traditional Political Systems in Eastern Africa. rev. ed. LC 77-6963. 288p. 1978. 10.95x (ISBN 0-253-34603-7); pap. 3.95x (ISBN 0-253-34604-5). Ind U Pr.

Middleton, John & Tait, David, eds. Tribes Without Rulers: Studies in African Segmentary Systems. 1970. pap. text ed. 7.75x (ISBN 0-391-00090-X). Humanities.

Swartz, Marc J., et al, eds. Political Anthropology. LC 66-15210. 1966. 27.95x (ISBN 0-202-01026-0). Aldine Pub.

GOVERNMENT, RESISTANCE TO

see also Allegiance; Anomy; Civil War; Coups D'Etat; Insurgency; Revolutions

Alinsky, Saul D. Rules for Radicals. 224p. 1972. pap. 2.45 (ISBN 0-394-71736-8, V736, Vin). Random.

Bacciocco, Edward J., Jr. The New Left in America: Reform to Revolution 1956-1970. LC 73-75887. (Publications Ser.: No. 130). 300p. 1974. 10.95 (ISBN 0-8179-6301-4). Hoover Inst Pr.

Ballou, Adin. Christian Non-Resistance in All Its Important Bearings, Illustrated & Defended. Bd. with Non-Resistance. C. H.; Discourse on Christian Non-Resistance in Extreme Cases. Ballou, Adin; Christian Non-Resistance Defended (Against Rev. Henry Ward Beecher, in His Discourse on Ephesians Chapter 4, Verse 13) Ballou, Adin. LC 77-147697. (Library of War & Peace; Proposals for Peace: a History). lib. bdg. 38.00 (ISBN 0-8240-0225-3). Garland Pub.

Bedau, Hugo A., ed. Civil Disobedience: Theory & Practice. LC 69-27984. (Orig.). 1969. pap. 6.95 (ISBN 0-672-63514-3). Pegasus.

Berrigan, Daniel. Consequences, Truth and. LC 67-12794. 1967. pap. 1.45 (ISBN 0-02-083780-1). Macmillan.

Bickel, Alexander M. The Morality of Consent. LC 75-10988. 176p. 1975. 15.00x (ISBN 0-300-01911-4); pap. 4.95x (ISBN 0-300-02119-4). Yale U Pr.

Booth, Sally S. Seeds of Anger: Revolts in America, 1670-1771. 1977. 10.95 (ISBN 0-8038-6742-5). Hastings.

Bridenbaugh, Carl. Cities in Revolt: Urban Life in America, 1743-1776. (Illus.). 1970. pap. 6.95 (ISBN 0-19-501362-X, GB). Oxford U Pr.

Calvert, Peter. Study of Revolution. 1970. 29.50x (ISBN 0-19-827177-8). Oxford U Pr.

Christopherson, John. An Exhortation to All Menne to Take Hede & Beware of Rebellion. LC 73-6113. (English Experience Ser.: No. 580). 504p. 1973. Repr. of 1554 ed. 29.00 (ISBN 90-221-0580-6). Walter J Johnson.

Coffin, William S., Jr. & Leibman, Morris I. Civil Disobedience: Aid or Hindrance to Justice. 11.25 (ISBN 0-8447-2031-3). Am Enterprise.

Cohen, Carl. Civil Disobedience: Conscience, Tactics & the Law. LC 14-7897. 222p. 1971. 15.00x (ISBN 0-231-03470-9); pap. 5.00x (ISBN 0-231-08646-6). Columbia U Pr.

Cox, Archibald, et al. Civil Rights, the Constitution & the Courts. LC 67-20874. 1967. 5.50x (ISBN 0-674-13300-5). Harvard U Pr.

Crough, Colin. Student Revolt. 1971. 6.95 (ISBN 0-370-01320-4). Transatlantic.

Datta, K. K. Anti-British Plots & Movements Before 1857. 1970. 5.50x (ISBN 0-8426-0169-4). Verry.

Depugh, Robert. Can You Survive? Guidelines for Resistance to Tyranny for You & Your Family. 3.50 (ISBN 0-686-24163-0). Liberty Lobby.

Dick, James C. Violence & Oppression. LC 78-2235. 224p. 1979. 12.00x (ISBN 0-8203-0446-8). U of Ga Pr.

Douglas, William O. Points of Rebellion. 1970. 7.95 (ISBN 0-394-44068-4). Random.

--Points of Rebellion. LC 79-107197. 1970. pap. 1.95 (ISBN 0-394-70603-X, V603, Vin). Random.

Fromm, Erich. On Disobedience & Other Essays. LC 81-2260. 144p. 1981. 9.95 (ISBN 0-8164-0500-X). Seabury.

Gilbert, C. Hampton. Here Lies Duffy Baker. 1978. 8.00 (ISBN 0-682-49047-4). Exposition.

Goodman, Christopher. How Superior Powers Oght to Be Obeyed of Their Subjects. LC 70-38197. (English Experience Ser.: No. 460). 240p. 1972. Repr. of 1548 ed. 22.00 (ISBN 90-221-0460-5). Walter J Johnson.

Hamburger, Joseph. James Mill & the Art of Revolution. LC 77-8124. (Yale Studies in Political Science: No. 8). 1977. Repr. of 1963 ed. lib. bdg. 19.75x (ISBN 0-8371-9675-2, HAJM). Greenwood.

Harvey, Arthur. Theory & Practice of Civil Disobedience. 27p. 1961. pap. 1.00 (ISBN 0-934676-04-6). Greenlf Bks.

Heath, G. Louis. The Hot Campus: The Politics That Impede Change in the Technoversity. LC 73-8824. 1973. 13.50 (ISBN 0-8108-0648-7). Scarecrow.

Held, Virginia, et al, eds. Philosophy & Political Action. 288p. 1972. pap. text ed. 4.95x (ISBN 0-19-501503-7). Oxford U Pr.

Hosmer, William. Higher Law, in Its Relations to Civil Government, with Particular Reference to Slavery & the Fugitive Slave Law. LC 69-18993. (Illus.). Repr. of 1852 ed. 11.50x (ISBN 0-8371-0929-9, Pub. by Negro U Pr). Greenwood.

Houlton, Bob. The Activist's Handbook. 1975. pap. 1.95 (ISBN 0-09-910130-0, Pub. by Hutchinson). Merrimack Bk Serv.

Jacobs, Harold, ed. Weatherman. LC 75-132205. (Illus.). 519p. (Orig.). 1971. lib. bdg. 20.00 (ISBN 0-87867-001-7); pap. 3.45 (ISBN 0-671-20725-3). Ramparts.
Jaszi, Oscar & Lewis, John D. Against the Tyrant. 1957. 7.95 (ISBN 0-02-916250-5). Free Pr.
Kaiser, Leo, ed. The Seven Against Thebes. Thoreau, Henry D. LC 80-2522. (Emerson Society Quarterly No. Seventeen; Nineteen Fifty-Nine, 1-30). Repr. of 1959 ed. 14.00 (ISBN 0-404-19070-7). AMS Pr.
Kane, Frank. Voices of Dissent: Positive Good or Disruptive Evil? (gr. 10-12). 1970. pap. text ed. 5.28 (ISBN 0-13-943613-8). P-H.
Lakey, George. Manifesto for a Nonviolent Revolution. 1980. staple back bdg. 1.75 (ISBN 0-86571-004-X). New Soc Pubs.
Languet, Hubert. A Defense of Liberty Against Tyrants. 229p. 1972. Repr. of 1924 ed. lib. bdg. 18.00 (ISBN 0-8337-4213-2). B Franklin.
Lowenthal, Leo & Guterman, Norbert. Prophets of Deceit: A Study of the Techniques of the American Agitator. 2nd ed. LC 68-31291. (Pacific Books Paperbounds, PB-8). (Illus.). 1970. pap. 1.95 (ISBN 0-87015-182-7). Pacific Bks.
Madden, Edward H. Civil Disobedience & Moral Law in Nineteenth-Century American Philosophy. LC 68-11043. 222p. 1970. pap. 2.95 (ISBN 0-295-95070-6). U of Wash Pr.
Marsh, Alan. Protest & Political Consciousness. LC 77-8985. (Sage Library of Social Research: Vol. 49). (Illus.). 272p. 1977. 20.00 (ISBN 0-8039-0876-8); pap. 9.95x (ISBN 0-8039-0877-6). Sage.
Mayhew, Jonathan. A Discourse Concerning Unlimited Submission. Tanis, Norman E., ed. (American Classics Facsimile Ser.: Pt. III). 1976. pap. 10.00 (ISBN 0-937048-02-X). CSUN.
--Sermons. LC 76-83429. (Religion in America, Ser. 1). 1969. Repr. of 1749 ed. 14.00 (ISBN 0-405-00254-8). Arno.
Meyers, W. & Rinard, eds. Making Activism Work. 1972. 26.50x (ISBN 0-677-04650-2). Gordon.
Middleton, Lamar. Revolt, U. S. A. facs. ed. LC 68-29232. (Essay Index Reprint Ser). (Illus.). 1968. Repr. of 1938 ed. 15.50 (ISBN 0-8369-0708-6). Arno.
Muste, A. J. Of Holy Disobedience. 23p. 1952-1964. pap. 1.00 (ISBN 0-934676-09-7). Greenlf Bks.
Peoples Lawbook Collective & International Liberation School. Beat the Heat: A Radical Survival Handbook. LC 72-178225. (Illus.). 1973. 7.95 (ISBN 0-87867-025-4); pap. 2.95 (ISBN 0-87867-017-3). Ramparts.
Pirmell, Charles. The Trashing of America. 1975. 7.00 (ISBN 0-686-11117-6); pap. 3.50 (ISBN 0-686-11118-4). Kulchur Foun.
Regan, Richard J. Private Conscience & Public Law: The American Experience. LC 72-77602. 245p. 1972. 17.50 (ISBN 0-8232-0945-8). Fordham.
Russell, D. E. Rebellion, Revolution, and Armed Force: A Comparative Study of Fifteen Countries with Special Emphasis on Cuba and South Africa. 1974. 30.00 (ISBN 0-12-785745-1). Acad Pr.
Sibley, Mulford Q. Obligation to Disobey. LC 72-128194. (Special Studies Ser.). 1970. pap. 2.00 (ISBN 0-87641-209-6). Coun Rel & Intl.
Thoreau, Henry D. Civil Disobedience. Brown, Edmund R., ed. (International Pocket Library). pap. 2.00 (ISBN 0-686-77251-2). Branden.
--The Variorum Civil Disobedience. Harding, Walter, ed. 91p. text ed. 20.00x (ISBN 0-8290-0215-4); pap. text ed. 8.95x (ISBN 0-8290-0216-2). Irvington.
--The Variorum Civil Disobedience. 1978. 9.95 (ISBN 0-685-60151-X, Pub by Twayne). Cyrco Pr.
--Walden. Bd. with On the Duty of Civil Disobedience. 1962. pap. 1.95 (ISBN 0-02-054720-X, 05472, Collier). Macmillan.
--Walden. Sherman, Paul, ed. Bd. with Civil Disobedience. LC 60-16148. (YA) (gr. 9 up). 1960. pap. 3.95 (ISBN 0-395-05113-4, A14, RivEd, 3-47648). HM.
--Walden. Bd. with Civil Disobedience. (Classics Edition). pap. 1.25 (ISBN 0-06-080615-X, HC615, PL). Har-Row.
--Walden. Bd. with On Civil Disobedience. (Classics Ser). (gr. 10up). pap. 1.50 (ISBN 0-8049-0083-3, CL-83). Airmont.
--Walden & Civil Disobedience. Thomas, Owen, ed. (Critical Editions). (Annotated). (gr. 9-12). 1966. pap. text ed. 5.95x (ISBN 0-393-09665-3, Nortonc). Norton.
--Walden: On the Duty of Civil Disobedience. Pearson, Norman H., ed. (Rinehart Editions). 1948. pap. text ed. 5.95 (ISBN 0-03-009320-1, HoltC). HR&W.
Tolstoy, Leo. Law of Love & the Law of Violence. Tolstoy, Mary K., tr. LC 73-105433. 1970. pap. 1.75 (ISBN 0-03-085495-4). HR&W.
Urquhart, Clara, ed. A Matter of Life. LC 72-9052. 255p. 1973. Repr. of 1963 ed. lib. bdg. 15.00 (ISBN 0-8371-6561-X, URML). Greenwood.
Walter, Eugene V. Terror & Resistance: A Study of Political Violence. 1972. pap. 4.95 (ISBN 0-19-501562-2, Gb). Oxford U Pr.
Walzer, Michael. Obligations: Essays on Disobedience, War, & Citizenship. LC 70-111489. 1970. 12.50x (ISBN 0-674-63000-9). Harvard U Pr.
Weber, David R., ed. Civil Disobedience in America: A Documentary History. LC 77-90914. 1978. 22.50x (ISBN 0-8014-1005-3). Cornell U Pr.
Zinn, Howard. Disobedience & Democracy: Nine Fallacies on Law & Order. 1968. pap. 1.65 (ISBN 0-394-70483-5, Vin). Random.

GOVERNMENT ACCOUNTING
see Finance, Public–Accounting

GOVERNMENT AGENCIES
see Administrative Agencies

GOVERNMENT AIRCRAFT
see also Airplanes, Military

Albertazzie, Ralph & TerHorst, Jerald F. The Flying White House: The Story of Air Force One. LC 78-25556. (Illus.). 1979. 11.95 (ISBN 0-698-10930-9). Coward.
Juptner, Joseph. U. S. Civil Aircraft, Vol. 6. LC 62-15967. (Illus.). 1974. 14.95 (ISBN 0-8168-9170-2). Aero.

GOVERNMENT AIRPLANES
see Government Aircraft

GOVERNMENT AND BUSINESS
see Industry and State

GOVERNMENT AND FORESTRY
see Forest Policy; Forestry Law and Legislation

GOVERNMENT AND THE PRESS

Berdes, George R. Friendly Adversaries: The Press & Government. pap. 4.95 (ISBN 0-87462-427-4). Marquette.
Blanchard, Robert O., ed. Congress & the News Media. (Studies in Public Communication). 1974. 19.95 (ISBN 0-8038-1192-6); pap. text ed. 10.75x (ISBN 0-8038-1194-2). Hastings.
Cohen, Bernard C. Press & Foreign Policy. 1963. 18.00 (ISBN 0-691-07519-0). Princeton U Pr.
Cornwell, Elmer E., Jr. Presidential Leadership of Public Opinion. LC 78-11946. (Illus.). 1979. Repr. of 1965 ed. lib. bdg. 24.00x (ISBN 0-313-21076-4, COPL). Greenwood.
Cox, H. & Morgan, D. City Politics & the Press. LC 72-96678. (Illus.). 200p. 1973. 23.95 (ISBN 0-521-20162-4). Cambridge U Pr.
Dunn, Delmer D. Public Officials & the Press. (Political Science Ser). 1969. pap. 6.95 (ISBN 0-201-01565-X). A-W.
Elias, T. O., ed. Nigerian Press Law. 156p. 1969. 10.50x (ISBN 0-237-28989-X). Intl Pubns Serv.
Gerald, J. Edward. The Press & the Constitution, 1931-1947. 7.50 (ISBN 0-8446-0641-3). Peter Smith.
Hale, Oron J. Captive Press in the Third Reich. LC 64-12182. (Illus.). 368p. 1964. 23.00x (ISBN 0-691-05109-7); pap. 7.95 (ISBN 0-691-00770-5). Princeton U Pr.
Hsu Ting, Lee-Hsia. Government Control of the Press in Modern China, 1900-1949. LC 74-79850. (East Asian Monographs: No. 57). 299p. 1975. pap. text ed. 9.00x (ISBN 0-674-35820-1). Harvard U Pr.
Juergens, George. News from the White House: The Presidential-Press Relationship in the Progressive Era. LC 81-7634. 1981. lib. bdg. 25.00x (ISBN 0-226-41472-8). U of Chicago Pr.
Knappman, Edward W., ed. Government & the Media in Conflict: 1970-74. 204p. 1974. pap. 5.50x (ISBN 0-87196-356-6). Facts on File.
--Government & the Media in Conflict: 1970-1974. 1975. 19.95x (ISBN 0-87196-357-4). Facts on File.
Margach, James. The Abuse of Power: The War Between Downing Street & the Media from Lloyd George to James Callaghan. (Illus.). 1978. 15.95 (ISBN 0-491-02044-9). Transatlantic.
Markel, Lester. What You Don't Know Can Hurt You. 1972. 7.50 (ISBN 0-8183-0221-6). Pub Aff Pr.
Mass Media & American Politics. 320p. 1980. pap. 6.95 (ISBN 0-87187-181-5). Congr Quarterly.
Morgan, David. The Capitol Press Corps: Newsmen & the Governing of New York State. LC 77-84771. (Contributions in Political Science: No. 2). 1978. lib. bdg. 16.95 (ISBN 0-8371-9883-6, MCP/). Greenwood.
Paletz, David L. & Entman, Robert M. Media Power Politics. LC 80-1642. 1981. 16.95 (ISBN 0-02-923650-9). Free Pr.
Pollard, James E. The Presidents & the Press. LC 73-10262. xiii, 866p. 1973. Repr. of 1947 ed. lib. bdg. 45.00x (ISBN 0-374-96514-5). Octagon.
Porter, William E. Assault on the Media: The Nixon Years. LC 75-14898. 1976. 11.95 (ISBN 0-472-73520-9); pap. 6.50 (ISBN 0-472-06301-4). U of Mich Pr.
The Presidency & the Press. LC 76-620044. (Symposia Ser.). 1976. 3.50 (ISBN 0-89940-405-7). LBJ Sch Public Affairs.
Rivers, William. Adversaries: Politics & the Press. LC 75-101326. 1971. pap. 2.95 (ISBN 0-8070-6181-6, BP409). Beacon Pr.
Sigal, Leon V. Reporters & Officials: The Organization & Politics of New Making. LC 72-7014. (Illus.). 256p. 1973. 17.95 (ISBN 0-669-85035-7). Lexington Bks.
--Reporters & Officials: The Organization & Politics of Newsmaking. 1973. pap. text ed. 8.95x (ISBN 0-669-89276-9). Heath.
Smith, Anthony. The Geopolitics of Information: How Western Culture Dominates the World. 192p. 1980. 13.95 (ISBN 0-19-520208-2). Oxford U Pr.
Smith, Anthony, ed. Newspapers & Democracy. 320p. 1980. text ed. 25.00x (ISBN 0-262-19184-9). MIT Pr.
Smith, Culver H. The Press, Politics, & Patronage: The American Government's Use of Newspapers, 1789-1875. LC 75-26051. 351p. 1977. 22.50x (ISBN 0-8203-0404-2). U of Ga Pr.
Weaver, David H., et al, eds. Media Agenda Setting in a Presidential Election: Issues, Images & Interest. 238p. 1981. 24.95 (ISBN 0-03-059066-3). Praeger.
White, Graham J. FDR & the Press. LC 78-11423. 1979. 13.95 (ISBN 0-226-89512-2). U of Chicago Pr.
Wise, David. The Politics of Lying: Government Deception, Secrecy, & Power. LC 72-11414. 1973. 10.00 (ISBN 0-394-47932-7). Random.

GOVERNMENT ATTORNEYS
see also Attorneys-General; Government Litigation; Public Prosecutors

Horowitz, Donald L. The Jurocracy: Government Lawyers, Agency Programs, & Judicial Decisions. LC 76-27921. 1977. 16.95 (ISBN 0-669-00986-5). Lexington Bks.
Membership Division, Natl. District Attorneys Assn. National Directory. rev. ed. 1977. 25.00 (ISBN 0-686-00314-4). Natl Dist Atty.
Shriver, Harry C. The Government Lawyer: Essays on Men, Books, & the Law. LC 74-83402. (Illus.). 1975. 6.95 (ISBN 0-914932-01-2). Fox Hills.
Twentieth Century Fund. Task Force Report for a National News Council. A Free & Responsive Press. Balk, Alfred, ed. LC 72-97796. 96p. pap. 8.00 (ISBN 0-527-02812-6). Kraus Repr.

GOVERNMENT BUILDINGS
see Public Buildings

GOVERNMENT BUSINESS ENTERPRISES
see also Corporations, Government; Government Ownership; Government Trading; Municipal Ownership

Baldwin, John R. The Regulatory Agency & the Public Corporation: The Canadian Air Transport Industry. LC 75-8916. 256p. 1975. 19.50 (ISBN 0-88410-262-9). Ballinger Pub.
Bhalla, G. S. Financial Administration of Nationalised Industries in the United Kingdom & India. (Illus.). 392p. 1968. 13.75x (ISBN 0-8426-1159-2). Verry.
Dominguez, George S. Government Business Public Affairs Handbook: Practical Guide. 425p. 1981. 27.50 (ISBN 0-471-06421-1, Pub. by Wiley-Interscience). Wiley.
Friedmann, Wolfgang G. & Garner, J. F., eds. Government Enterprise. (A Comparative Study). 351p. 1971. 22.50x (ISBN 0-231-03448-2). Columbia U Pr.
Government Control of Energy. 1973. pap. 3.75 (ISBN 0-8447-1822-X). Am Enterprise.
Hamilton, Neil W. & Hamilton, Peter R. Governance of Public Enterprise: A Case Study of Urban Mass Transit. LC 80-5349. 1981. 18.95 (ISBN 0-686-77664-X). Lexington Bks.
Haskins & Sells. Revolving Funds & Business Enterprises of the Government, Exclusive of Lending Agencies. Repr. of 1949 ed. lib. bdg. 15.00 (ISBN 0-8371-3168-5, HARF). Greenwood.
Holtz, Herman R. One Hundred Billion Dollar Market: How to Do Business with the U. S. Government. (Illus.). 320p. 1980. 16.95 (ISBN 0-8144-5578-6). Am Mgmt.
Horn, Richard J., ed. Studies in the Management of Government Enterprise. (Social Dimensions of Economics Ser.: Vol. 1). 1981. lib. bdg. write for info. (ISBN 0-89838-052-9, Pub. by Martinus Nijhoff Netherlands). Kluwer Boston.
How to Get Started in Government Business. LC 79-54754. 1979. write for info. Danbury Pr.
Jewkes, John. Public & Private Enterprise. LC 66-12709. 1967. 4.50x (ISBN 0-226-39908-7). U of Chicago Pr.
Marglin, Stephen A. Public Investment Criteria. (Studies in Economic Development of India Ser.). 1967. pap. text ed. 4.95x (ISBN 0-04-332041-4). Allen Unwin.
Perera, M. H. Accounting for State Industrial & Commercial Enterprises in a Developing Country. Brief, Richard P., ed. LC 80-1516. (Dimensions of Accounting Theory & Practice Ser.). 1981. lib. bdg. 28.00x (ISBN 0-405-13495-9). Arno.
Pozen, Robert C. Legal Choices for State Enterprises in the Third World. LC 75-27045. 192p. 1976. 25.00x (ISBN 0-8147-6564-5). NYU Pr.
Robbins, Lord, et al. The Taming of Government: Micro-Macro Disciplines on Whithall & Town Hall. (Institute of Economic Affairs Readings Ser.: No. 21). (Orig.). 1979. 10.95 (ISBN 0-255-36125-4). Transatlantic.
Shepherd, William G., ed. Public Enterprise: Economic Analysis of Theory & Practice. LC 75-41926. (Illus.). 256p. 1976. 18.95 (ISBN 0-669-00477-4). Lexington Bks.
Tordoff, W. Administration in Zambia. 320p. 1981. 80.00x (ISBN 0-686-73055-0, Pub. by Manchester U Pr England). State Mutual Bk.
Turvey, Ralph & Christie, Herbert. Economic Analysis & Public Enterprises. 150p. 1971. 11.50x (ISBN 0-87471-068-5). Rowman.
U.S. Commission on Organization of the Executive Branch of the Government. Reorganization of Federal Business Enterprises. Repr. of 1949 ed. lib. bdg. 15.00 (ISBN 0-8371-2271-6, REFB). Greenwood.

GOVERNMENT BUSINESS ENTERPRISES–GREAT BRITAIN

Boyson, Rhodes, ed. Goodbye to Nationalization. pap. 3.50 (ISBN 0-902782-05-3). Transatlantic.
Pryke, Richard. Public Enterprise in Practice. LC 71-187569. 1972. 27.50 (ISBN 0-312-65450-2). St Martin.
Turvey, Ralph & Christie, Herbert. Economic Analysis & Public Enterprises. 150p. 1971. 11.50x (ISBN 0-87471-068-5). Rowman.

GOVERNMENT BUSINESS ENTERPRISES–INDIA

Bhalla, G. S. Financial Administration of Nationalised Industries in the United Kingdom & India. (Illus.). 392p. 1968. 13.75x (ISBN 0-8426-1159-2). Verry.
Jain, R. K. Management of State Enterprises in India. 1967. 12.00x (ISBN 0-8188-1054-8). Paragon.
Sinha, Jai B. Some Problems of Public Sector Organizations. LC 73-901014. (Illus.). 171p. 1974. 11.25x (ISBN 0-8002-1990-2). Intl Pubns Serv.

GOVERNMENT BUSINESS ENTERPRISES–ITALY

Posner, M. V. & Woolf, Stuart J. Italian Public Enterprises. LC 67-4204. 1967. 10.00x (ISBN 0-674-46951-8). Harvard U Pr.

GOVERNMENT CENTRALIZATION
see Decentralization in Government

GOVERNMENT COMPETITION
see also Government Business Enterprises

Lowi, Theodore J., ed. Private Life & Public Order. (Problems of Modern Government Ser). 1968. pap. 4.95x (ISBN 0-393-09727-7, NortonC). Norton.
Mills, Daniel Q. The Special Interest State. 208p. Date not set. 14.95 (ISBN 0-262-13168-4). MIT Pr.
Winter, Ralph K. Government & the Corporation. 1978. pap. 4.25 (ISBN 0-8447-3313-X). Am Enterprise.

GOVERNMENT CONTRACTS
see Public Contracts

GOVERNMENT CORPORATIONS
see Corporations, Government

GOVERNMENT DECENTRALIZATION
see Decentralization in Government

GOVERNMENT DOCUMENTS
see Government Publications

GOVERNMENT EMPLOYEE STRIKES
see Strikes and Lockouts–Civil Service

GOVERNMENT EMPLOYEES
see Civil Service

GOVERNMENT EXECUTIVES

Cleveland, Harlan. The Future Executive: A Guide for Tomorrow's Managers. LC 79-138715. 128p. 1972. 12.95 (ISBN 0-06-010817-7, HarpT). Har-Row.
Corson, John J. & Paul, R. Shale. Men Near the Top: Filling Key Posts in the Federal Service. (Committee for Economic Development Ser). (Illus.). 208p. 1966. 12.00x (ISBN 0-8018-0143-5); pap. 3.95x (ISBN 0-8018-0142-7). Johns Hopkins.
Heclo, Hugh. A Government of Strangers: Executive Politics in Washington. LC 76-51882. 1977. 17.95 (ISBN 0-8157-3536-7); pap. 7.95 (ISBN 0-8157-3535-9). Brookings.
Rachal, Patricia. Executive Reorganization in the Federal Government. 200p. 1981. 19.95 (ISBN 0-86569-089-8). Auburn Hse.
Rudman, Jack. County Executive. (Career Examination Ser.: C-1224). (Cloth bdg. avail on request). pap. 12.00 (ISBN 0-8373-1224-8). Natl Learning.
Shafritz, Jay M. Personal Management in Government: Politic & Process. (Political Science & Public Administration Ser.). 1978. 16.50 (ISBN 0-8247-6629-6). Dekker.

Silvan, Matthew. Lazarus, Come Out! The Story of My Life. Moran, Hugh, ed. Giannini, Vera, tr. from It. LC 80-82599. Orig. Title: Quella Violenza Di Dio. 224p. (Orig.). 1981. pap. 5.95 (ISBN 0-911782-36-2). New City.

Stanley, David T. The Higher Civil Service: An Evaluation of Federal Personnel Practices. 1964. 8.95 (ISBN 0-8157-8104-0). Brookings.

Stanley, David T., et al. Men Who Govern: A Biographical Profile of Federal Political Executives. 1967. 10.95 (ISBN 0-8157-8108-3). Brookings.

Warner, William L., et al. The American Federal Executive. LC 75-11487. 405p. 1975. Repr. of 1963 ed. lib. bdg. 21.25x (ISBN 0-8371-8207-7, WAAF). Greenwood.

GOVERNMENT EXECUTIVES–JAPAN

Kubota, Akira. Higher Civil Servants in Post-War Japan: Their Social Origins, Educational Background, & Career Patterns. LC 68-27405. 1969. 18.50 (ISBN 0-691-03073-1). Princeton U Pr.

GOVERNMENT EXECUTIVES–PERU

Hopkins, Jack W. Government Executive of Modern Peru. LC 67-64870. (Latin American Monographs: Ser. 2, No. 3). (Illus.). 1967. pap. 3.75 (ISBN 0-8130-0113-7). U Presses Fla.

GOVERNMENT EXPENDITURES

see Expenditures, Public

GOVERNMENT HOUSING

see Public Housing

GOVERNMENT IMMUNITY

see Government Liability

GOVERNMENT INFORMATION

see also Executive Privilege (Government Information); Government and the Press

Barker, Carol M. & Fox, Matthew H. Classified Files: The Yellowing Pages. LC 72-80587. 1974. pap. 6.00 (ISBN 0-527-02850-9). Kraus Repr.

Bureau Of The Census, ed. Government Dossier: An Inventory of Government Information About Individuals. LC 69-19367. 1968. Repr. of 1968 ed. 15.00 (ISBN 0-405-00015-4). Arno.

Cox, Arthur M. The Myths of National Security: The Peril of Secret Government. LC 75-5288. 256p. 1975. pap. 4.50 (ISBN 0-8070-0497-9, BP538). Beacon Pr.

Cross, Harold L. People's Right to Know. LC 75-170844. Repr. of 1953 ed. 25.00 (ISBN 0-404-01859-9). AMS Pr.

Flaherty, David H. Privacy & Government Databanks: An International Perspective. 1979. 37.00 (ISBN 0-7201-0930-2, Pub. by Mansell England). Merrimack Bk Serv.

Flaherty, David H., et al, eds. Privacy & Access to Government Data for Research: An International Bibliography. 1979. 33.00 (ISBN 0-7201-0920-5, Pub. by Mansell England). Merrimack Bk Serv.

Franck, Thomas M. & Weisband, Edward, eds. Secrecy & Foreign Policy. 1976. pap. text ed. 5.95x (ISBN 0-19-502120-7). Oxford U Pr.

Franklin, Justin D. & Bouchard, Robert F., eds. Guidebook to the Freedom of Information & Privacy Acts. LC 79-27406. 1980. 39.50 (ISBN 0-87632-310-7). Boardman.

Galnoor, Itzhak, ed. Government Secrecy in Democracies. (Orig.). 1977. pap. 5.95 (ISBN 0-06-090440-2, CN 440, CN). Har-Row.

Helm, Lewis, et al. Informing the People: A Public Information Handbook. (Longman Series in Public Communication). (Illus.). 512p. 1981. text ed. 27.95x (ISBN 0-582-28200-4). Longman.

Hernon, Peter. Microforms & Government Information. LC 81-4393. (Library Micrographics Management Ser.: No. 6). 1981. 28.95x (ISBN 0-913672-12-2). Microform Rev.

The Market for Government Data Bases Sold Through Commercial Firms. 1980. 950.00 (ISBN 0-686-28893-9, A829). Frost & Sullivan.

Morss, Elliott R. & Rich, Robert F. Government Information Management: A Counter-Report to the Commission on Federal Paperwork. (Westview Special Studies in Information Management). 225p. 1980. lib. bdg. 27.75x (ISBN 0-89158-596-6). Westview.

Rowat, Donald C., ed. Administrative Secrecy in Developed Countries. LC 78-16376. (International Institute of Administrative Sciences Ser.). 1979. 21.50x (ISBN 0-231-04596-4). Columbia U Pr.

Thurman, S. David. The Right of Access to Information from the Government. LC 73-7990. (Legal Almanac Ser.: No. 71). 128p. 1973. lib. bdg. 5.95 (ISBN 0-379-11085-7). Oceana.

Wise, David. The Politics of Lying: Government Deception, Secrecy, & Power. LC 72-11414. 1973. 10.00 (ISBN 0-394-47932-7). Random.

GOVERNMENT INFORMATION SERVICES

see Government Publicity

GOVERNMENT INSTITUTIONS

see Public Institutions

GOVERNMENT INVESTIGATIONS

see Governmental Investigations

GOVERNMENT JOBS

see Civil Service Positions

GOVERNMENT LAWYERS

see Government Attorneys

GOVERNMENT LENDING

see also Agricultural Credit

Benson, George C. & McClelland, Harold F. Consolidated Grants: A Means of Maintaining Fiscal Responsibility. 41p. 1961. pap. 3.75 (ISBN 0-8447-3030-0). Am Enterprise.

Glover, John D. Public Loans to Private Business. Bruchey, Stuart & Carosso, Vincent P., eds. LC 78-18961. (Small Business Enterprise in America Ser.). (Illus.). 1979. lib. bdg. 32.00x (ISBN 0-405-11465-6). Arno.

Schaevitz, Robert C. & Van, Elizabeth A. Handbook of Federal Assistance: Financing, Grants, Technical Aids. 48.50 (ISBN 0-88262-373-7, 80-50774). Warren.

GOVERNMENT LIABILITY

see also Tort Liability of Municipal Corporations; Tort Liability of School Districts; Liability for School Accidents

Early, Stephen T., Jr. & Knight, Barbara B. Responsible Government: American & British. LC 80-29601. 336p. 1981. text ed. 21.95 (ISBN 0-88229-658-2); pap. text ed. 10.95 (ISBN 0-88229-776-7). Nelson-Hall.

Hurwitz, Leon. The State As Defendant: Governmental Accountability & the Redress of Individual Grievances. LC 80-657. (Contributions in Political Science: No. 51). (Illus.). xv, 211p. 1981. lib. bdg. 27.50 (ISBN 0-313-21257-0, HSD/). Greenwood.

Jacobs, Clyde E. The Eleventh Amendment & Sovereign Immunity. LC 71-149959. (Contributions in American History: No. 19). 1972. lib. bdg. 15.00 (ISBN 0-8371-6058-8, JAE/). Greenwood.

Perez, Ramon A. Liability Risk Management for Local Governments. 1982. spiral bdg. 25.00 (ISBN 0-88406-148-5). GA St U Busn Pub.

Richland, W. Bernard. You Can Beat City Hall. LC 79-67640. 1980. 9.95 (ISBN 0-89256-125-4). Rawson Wade.

Street, H. Governmental Liability: A Comparative Study. xiii, 224p. 1975. Repr. of 1953 ed. 16.50 (ISBN 0-208-01484-5, Archon). Shoe String.

Turner, David R. Claim Examiner -- Investigator. 4th ed. LC 72-92669. (Orig.). 1971. pap. 8.00 (ISBN 0-668-00149-6). Arco.

GOVERNMENT LIABILITY (INTERNATIONAL LAW)

see also Claims; State Succession

Lillich, Richard B. International Claims: Postwar British Practice, Vol. 6. 1967. 10.00x (ISBN 0-8139-0850-7). U Pr of Va.

--International Claims: Their Adjudication by National Commissions, Vol. I. 1962. 10.00x (ISBN 0-8139-0834-5). U Pr of Va.

--International Claims: Their Preparation & Presentation, Vol. 2. 1962. 10.00x (ISBN 0-8139-0835-3). U Pr of Va.

Protocol to the Convention on Duties & Rights of States in the Event of Civil Strife. (Treaty Ser.: No. 7). (Eng., Span., Port & Fr.). 1959. pap. 1.00 (ISBN 0-8270-0300-5). OAS.

Silvanie, Haig. Responsibility of States for Acts of Unsuccessful Insurgent Governments. LC 68-58622. (Columbia University Studies in the Social Sciences: No. 457). 18.50 (ISBN 0-404-51457-X). AMS Pr.

Weston, Burns. International Claims: Postwar French Practice, Vol. 9. 1971. 10.00x (ISBN 0-8156-2153-1). U Pr of Va.

GOVERNMENT LIBRARIANS

Kortendick, James J. & Stone, Elizabeth W. Job Dimensions & Educational Needs in Librarianship. LC 70-157141. 510p. 1971. text ed. 15.00 (ISBN 0-8389-3126-X). ALA.

GOVERNMENT LIBRARIES

see Libraries, Governmental, Administrative, etc.

GOVERNMENT LITIGATION

Federal Judicial Center - Board Of Editors. Manual of Complex Litigation. LC 77-27536. 1978. looseleaf with 1978 rev. pages 40.00 (ISBN 0-87632-089-2). Boardman.

Gottlieb, Stephen E. Systematic Litigation Planning. LC 78-8522. 1978. 7.50 (ISBN 0-87179-282-6). BNA.

Halperin, Morton H. & Adler, Allan, eds. The Nineteen Eighty-Two Edition of Litigation Under the Federal Freedom of Information Act & Privacy Act. 400p. 1981. pap. 25.00 (ISBN 0-86566-023-9). Ctr Natl Security.

Manual for Complex Litigation with Amendments to June, 1977. 1978. pap. 6.00 (ISBN 0-685-39491-3). Commerce.

GOVERNMENT LOANS

see Government Lending

GOVERNMENT MISSIONS

see also Diplomatic and Consular Service; Economic Assistance; Technical Assistance

Williams, Justin. Japan's Political Revolution Under MacArthur: A Participant's Account. LC 78-5592. (Illus.). 352p. 1979. 16.50 (ISBN 0-8203-0452-2). U of Ga Pr.

GOVERNMENT-OWNED AIRCRAFT

see Government Aircraft

GOVERNMENT OWNERSHIP

see also Corporations, Government; Government Competition; Government Trading; Land, Nationalization of; Municipal Ownership; Railroads and State

Agrawal, H. N. A Portrait of Nationalised Banks. 334p. 1980. text ed. 18.00x (ISBN 0-391-02130-3). Humanities.

Bellamy, Edward. Edward Bellamy Speaks Again! LC 75-302. (The Radical Tradition in America Ser). (Illus.). 249p. 1975. Repr. of 1937 ed. 18.50 (ISBN 0-88355-207-8). Hyperion Conn.

Faundez, Julio & Picciotto, Sol, eds. The Nationalization of Multinationals in Peripheral Economies. 1979. text ed. 27.50x (ISBN 0-8419-5045-8). Holmes & Meier.

Government Television. 1975. 2.00, institutions 5.00 (ISBN 0-686-09557-X). Network Project.

Lane, David. The Socialist Industrial State: Towards a Political Sociology of State Socialism. 1977. pap. text ed. 7.95x (ISBN 0-04-320117-2). Allen Unwin.

Margolis, J. & Guitton, H., eds. Public Economics: An Analysis of Public Production & Consumption & Their Relations to the Private Sector. LC 70-84182. (International Economics Assn. Ser). 1969. 32.50 (ISBN 0-312-65415-4). St Martin.

Petras, James F., et al. The Nationalization of Venezuelan Oil. LC 77-7822. (Praeger Special Studies). 1977. text ed. 24.95 (ISBN 0-03-022656-2). Praeger.

Schmid, A. Allan. Property, Power & Public Choice: An Inquiry into Law & Economics. LC 78-5930. (Praeger Special Studies). 1978. 24.95 (ISBN 0-03-042956-0). Praeger.

Sloman, Martyn. Socialising Public Ownership. 1978. text ed. 20.00x (ISBN 0-333-22640-2). Humanities.

Vennard, E. Government in the Power Business. LC 68-13105. (Illus.). 1968. 16.95 (ISBN 0-07-067396-9, G). McGraw.

Winter, Ralph K. Government & the Corporation. 1978. pap. 4.25 (ISBN 0-8447-3313-X). Am Enterprise.

GOVERNMENT OWNERSHIP–FRANCE

Einaudi, Mario, et al. Nationalization in France & Italy. 270p. 1955. 15.00x (ISBN 0-8014-0116-X). Cornell U Pr.

GOVERNMENT OWNERSHIP–GREAT BRITAIN

Boyson, Rhodes, ed. Goodbye to Nationalization. pap. 3.50 (ISBN 0-902782-05-3). Transatlantic.

Hanson, Albert. Parliament & Public Ownership. LC 73-13326. 248p. 1974. Repr. of 1961 ed. lib. bdg. 15.00x (ISBN 0-8371-7124-5, HAPO). Greenwood.

Jenkins, Clive. Power at the Top: A Critical Survey of the Nationalized Industries. LC 75-45383. 292p. 1976. Repr. of 1959 ed. lib. bdg. 16.75x (ISBN 0-8371-8661-7, JEPT). Greenwood.

Kelf-Cohen, R. British Nationalization: Nineteen Forty-Five to Nineteen Seventy-Three. LC 73-86069. 1974. 19.95 (ISBN 0-312-10360-3). St Martin.

--Twenty Years of Nationalization: British Experience. LC 69-13689. 1969. 18.95 (ISBN 0-312-82460-2). St Martin.

Pryke, Richard. Public Enterprise in Practice. LC 71-187569. 1972. 27.50 (ISBN 0-312-65450-2). St Martin.

Spero, Sterling D. Labor Relations in British Nationalized Industry. LC 55-10746. 83p. 1955. 4.50x (ISBN 0-8147-0397-6). NYU Pr.

GOVERNMENT OWNERSHIP–ITALY

Einaudi, Mario, et al. Nationalization in France & Italy. 270p. 1955. 15.00x (ISBN 0-8014-0116-X). Cornell U Pr.

GOVERNMENT OWNERSHIP–JAPAN

Smith, Thomas C. Political Change & Industrial Development in Japan: Government Enterprise, 1868-1880. 1955. 10.00x (ISBN 0-8047-0469-4). Stanford U Pr.

GOVERNMENT OWNERSHIP OF RAILROADS

see Railroads and State

GOVERNMENT POSITIONS

see Civil Service Positions

GOVERNMENT PRICE REGULATION

see Price Regulation

GOVERNMENT PUBLICATIONS

see also Exchanges, Literary and Scientific; Government Publicity; Printing, Public;
also subdivision Government Publications under names of countries, states, counties, cities, etc., e.g. United States–Government Publications

Bibliographic Guide to Government Publications - Foreign: 1976. (Bibliographic Guides Ser.). 1977. lib. bdg. 115.00 (ISBN 0-8161-6827-X). G K Hall.

Bibliographic Guide to Government Publications-Foreign: 1975. 1976. lib. bdg. 100.00 (ISBN 0-8161-6815-6). G K Hall.

Cherns, J. J. Official Publishing, an Overview: An International Survey & Review of the Role, Organization & Principles of Official Publishing. LC 78-41157. (Guides to Official Publication Ser.: Vol. 3). 1979. 60.00 (ISBN 0-08-023340-6). Pergamon.

Childs, James B., ed. Government Document Bibliography in the United States & Elsewhere. 3rd ed. 1942. 8.00 (ISBN 0-384-08785-X). Johnson Repr.

Congressional Informaion Service, ed. Directory of Government Documents: Collections & Librarians. 3rd ed. Date not set. price not set. Cong Info.

Congressional Quarterly Staff, ed. Historic Documents of 1977, Vol. 6. 1978. 44.00 (ISBN 0-87187-126-2). Congr Quarterly.

Fry, B. N., ed. Government Publications. 1981. 100.00 (ISBN 0-08-028092-7). Pergamon.

Fry, Bernard M. & Hernon, Peter, eds. Government Publications: Key Papers. (Guides to Official Publications Ser.: Vol. 8). (Illus.). 684p. 1981. 100.00 (ISBN 0-08-025216-8). Pergamon.

Government Documents Round Table, ed. Directory of Govefnment Document Collections & Librarians. LC 78-5459. 1981. pap. text ed. 32.50 (ISBN 0-912380-49-7); prepub. 27.50 (ISBN 0-686-76843-4). Cong Info.

Gregory, Winifred, ed. List of the Serial Publications of Foreign Governments, 1815-1931. 1932. 78.00 (ISBN 0-527-57400-7). Kraus Repr.

Hasse, Adelaide R. Index of Economic Material in Documents of the States of the United States, 13 vols. 1907-1922. Set. 465.00 (ISBN 0-527-00708-0). Kraus Repr.

Hazelhurst, Cameron & Woodland, Christine, eds. A Guide to the Papers of British Cabinet Ministers, 1900-1951. (Royal Historical Society Ser.). 174p. 1974. pap. 10.75x (ISBN 0-8476-1348-8). Rowman.

Hernon, Peter. Use of Government Publications by Social Scientists. LC 79-16144. (Libraries & Librarianship Ser.). 1979. 17.50 (ISBN 0-89391-024-4). Ablex Pub.

Hernon, Peter, ed. Library Government Documents, First Annual Conference: Proceedings. 1981. 29.95x (ISBN 0-930466-37-3). Meckler Bks.

Ker, Anita M. Mexican Government Publications. 1976. lib. bdg. 59.95 (ISBN 0-8490-0615-5). Gordon Pr.

Morehead, Joe. Introduction to U. S. Public Documents. 2nd ed. LC 78-16866. (Library Science Text). (Illus.). 1978. lib. bdg. 22.50x (ISBN 0-87287-186-X); pap. text ed. 13.50x (ISBN 0-87287-190-8). Libs Unl.

Nakata, Yuri. From Press to People: Collecting & Using U. S. Government Publications. 1979. 15.00 (ISBN 0-8389-0264-2). ALA.

New York Public Library Research Libraries & Library of Congress. Bibliographic Guide to Government Publications: U. S.: 1979. 1979. 180.00 (ISBN 0-8161-6870-9). G K Hall.

Newsome, Walter L. New Guide to Popular Government Publications: For Libraries & Home Reference. LC 78-12412. 1978. lib. bdg. 20.00 (ISBN 0-87287-174-6). Libs Unl.

O'Hara, F. J. A Guide to Publications of the Executive Branch. LC 78-66368. 1979. 35.00 (ISBN 0-87650-072-6); pap. 17.50 (ISBN 0-87650-088-2). Pierian.

O'Hara, Frederic J., ed. Reader in Government Documents. LC 72-86633. (Reader Ser. in Library & Information Science). 1973. 18.00 (ISBN 0-910972-24-9). IHS-PDS.

Palic, Vladimir M. Government Publications. 1978. text ed. 37.00 (ISBN 0-08-021457-6). Pergamon.

Poore, Benjamin P. A Descriptive Catalogue of the Government Publications 9-5-1774 & 3-4 1881. LC 70-145240. 1392p. 1885. Repr. 75.00 (ISBN 0-403-01155-8). Scholarly.

Research Libraries of the New York Public Library & the Library of Congress. Bibliographic Guide to Government Publications - Foreign: 1980. (Library Catalogs-Bib. Guides Ser.). 1981. lib. bdg. 195.00 (ISBN 0-8161-6886-5). G K Hall.

Research Libraries of the New York Pulic Library & the Library of Congress. Bibliographic Guide to Government Publications-Foreign: 1978. (Library Catalogs-Bib. Guides). 1979. lib. bdg. 150.00 (ISBN 0-8161-6854-7). G K Hall.

Research Libraries of the New York Public Library & the Library of Congress. Bibliographic Guide to Government Publications-Foreign: 1979. (Library Catalogs-Bib. Guides). 1980. lib. bdg. 175.00 (ISBN 0-8161-6869-5). G K Hall.

Research Libraries of the New York Public Library. Catalog of Government Publications, Supplement 1974. 1976. lib. bdg. 200.00 (ISBN 0-8161-0060-8). G K Hall.

Rosiem, Barbara. Greater los Angeles Public Service to City, County, State Several Offices. 4th ed. 1978. 34.95 (ISBN 0-686-14609-3); pap. 29.95 (ISBN 0-686-14610-7). Public Serv Pubns.

Schorr, A. E. Government Documents in the Library Literature. 1976. 10.00 (ISBN 0-87650-071-8). Pierian.

Slade, Rod. Government Documents. Mignon, Edmund, ed. LC 81-66782. (Print Samples Ser.: Vol. 2). 130p. (Orig.). 1981. pap. 25.00 (ISBN 0-939920-02-6). Database Serv.

U. S. Library Of Congress. Guide to the Official Publications of Other American Republics: Washington, 1945-48, 2 Vols. Repr. of 1948 ed. Set. 75.00 (ISBN 0-384-63000-6). Johnson Repr.

United States Superintendent of Documents. Decennial Cumulative Index 1941-1950 to United States Government Publications Monthly Catalog, 2 Vols. LC 77-84611. 1972. Repr. of 1953 ed. 65.00 (ISBN 0-8103-3361-9). Gale.

GOVERNMENT PUBLICATIONS–CATALOGING

see Cataloging of Government Publications

GOVERNMENT PUBLICITY

see also Government and the Press; Government Publications; Radio Broadcasting

Englefield, Dermot. Parliament & Information. 176p. 1981. lib. bdg. 18.00x (ISBN 0-85365-570-7, Pub. by Lib Assn England); pap. text ed. 12.00x (ISBN 0-85365-993-1, Pub. by Lib Assn England). Oryx Pr.

Gilbert, William H., ed. Public Relations in Local Government. LC 75-29400. (Municipal Management Ser.). 1975. text ed. 24.00 (ISBN 0-87326-012-0). Intl City Mgt.

Helm, Lewis, et al. Informing the People: A Public Information Handbook. (Longman Series in Public Communication). (Illus.). 512p. 1981. text ed. 27.95x (ISBN 0-582-28200-4). Longman.

Lee, John, ed. Diplomatic Persuaders: New Role of the Mass Media in International Relations. (Government & Communications Ser). 205p. 1968. text ed. 10.75 (ISBN 0-471-52210-4, Pub. by Wiley). Krieger.

Mokwa, Michael & Permut, Steven, eds. Government Marketing: Theory & Practice. (Public & Nonprofit Sector Marketing Ser.). 400p. 1981. 31.95 (ISBN 0-03-058316-0). Praeger.

Rourke, Francis E. Secrecy & Publicity: Dilemmas of Democracy. 236p. 1961. pap. 2.95x (ISBN 0-8018-0565-1). Johns Hopkins.

Rudman, Jack. Public Information Specialist. (Career Examination Ser.: C-2103). (Cloth bdg. avail. on request). 1977. pap. 8.00 (ISBN 0-8373-2103-4). Natl Learning.

Thum & Thum. Persuasion & Propaganda in War & Peace. (Contemporary Concerns Ser.). (gr. 9-12). 1974. pap. text ed. 4.92 (ISBN 0-88343-620-5); tchrs'. manual 1.50 (ISBN 0-88343-621-3). McDougal-Littell.

GOVERNMENT PURCHASING

see also Eminent Domain; Public Contracts; Purchasing Agents

Agapos, A. Michael. Government-Industry & Defense: Economics & Administration. LC 74-15674. (Illus.). 226p. 1975. 15.95x (ISBN 0-8173-4604-X). U of Ala Pr.

Agreement on Government Procurement. 30p. 1980. pap. 2.50 (ISBN 0-686-63027-0, G133, GATT). Unipub.

Amihud, Yakov, ed. Bidding & Auctioning for Procurement & Allocation: Proceedings of a Conference at the Center for Applied Economics, New York University. LC 75-27104. 220p. 1976. 20.00x (ISBN 0-8147-0558-8). NYU Pr.

Arco Editorial Board. Buyer, Assistant Buyer, Purchase Inspector. 2nd ed. LC 74-20068. (Orig.). 1975. pap. 6.00 (ISBN 0-668-01366-4). Arco.

Gross, Harry. How to Do Business with the Government. 1979. pap. 2.50 (ISBN 0-87576-020-1). Pilot Bks.

Organization for Economic Cooperation & Development. Government Purchasing: Regulations & Procedures. 116p. 1976. 7.00x (ISBN 92-64-11491-2). OECD.

Page, Harry R. Public Purchasing & Materials Management. LC 79-2039. 528p. 1980. 32.95x (ISBN 0-669-03059-7). Lexington Bks.

Robertson, Jack. Selling to the Federal Government: A Guide for Business. 1978. 17.95 (ISBN 0-07-053170-6, P&RB). McGraw.

Rudman, Jack. Principal Purchase Inspector. (Career Examination Ser.: C-1747). (Cloth bdg. avail. on request). 1977. pap. 10.00 (ISBN 0-8373-1747-9). Natl Learning.

--Procurement Agent. (Career Examination Ser.: C-621). (Cloth bdg. avail. on request). pap. 8.00 (ISBN 0-8373-0621-3). Natl Learning.

--Procurement Supervisor. (Career Examination Ser.: C-2711). (Cloth bdg. avail. on request). 1980. pap. 12.00 (ISBN 0-8373-2711-3). Natl Learning.

--Purchasing Agent: Food. (Career Examination Ser.: C-2731). (Cloth bdg. avail. on request). 1980. pap. 10.00 (ISBN 0-8373-2731-8). Natl Learning.

--Purchasing Agent: Lumber. (Career Examination Ser.: C-2732). (Cloth bdg. avail. on request). 1980. pap. 10.00 (ISBN 0-8373-2732-6). Natl Learning.

--Purchasing Agent: Medical. (Career Examination Ser.: C-2733). (Cloth bdg. avail. on request). 1980. pap. 10.00 (ISBN 0-8373-2733-4). Natl Learning.

--Purchasing Agent: Printing. (Career Examination Ser.: C-2734). (Cloth bdg. avail. on request). 1980. pap. 10.00 (ISBN 0-8373-2734-2). Natl Learning.

Seldon, Robert. Life Cycle Costing: A Better Method for Government Procurement. (Westview Special Studies in Public Policy & Public Management). 1979. lib. bdg. 33.25x (ISBN 0-89158-277-0). Westview.

Singer, H. Halleck & Micken, Charles M. Law of Purchasing. LC 64-15589. 1964. pap. text ed. 3.95x (ISBN 0-8134-0024-4, 24). Interstate.

Thomas, Arthur G. Principles of Government Purchasing. (Brookings Institution Reprint Ser). Repr. of 1919 ed. lib. bdg. 24.50x (ISBN 0-697-00173-3). Irvington.

GOVERNMENT RECORDS

see Public Records

GOVERNMENT REGULATION OF COMMERCE

see Commercial Policy; Industrial Laws and Legislation; Industry and State; Interstate Commerce; Trade Regulation

GOVERNMENT REGULATION OF RAILROADS

see Interstate Commerce; Railroad Law; Railroads and State

GOVERNMENT RESPONSIBILITY

see Government Liability

GOVERNMENT SECRECY

see Executive Privilege (Government Information); Government Information

GOVERNMENT SPENDING POLICY

see also Expenditures, Public; Public Works; also subdivision Appropriations and Expenditures under names of countries (for descriptive and statistical works on government spending)

Anton, Thomas J., et al. Moving Money: An Empirical Analysis of Federal Expenditure Patterns. LC 80-21700. 288p. 1980. text ed. 22.50 (ISBN 0-89946-066-6). Oelgeschlager.

Askari, Hossein & Glover, Michael C. Military Expenditures & the Level of Economic Development. (Studies in International Business: No. 3). 1977. pap. 4.00 (ISBN 0-87755-272-X). U of Tex Busn Res.

Bahl, Roy, ed. Government Finance: Emerging Trends. LC 80-39559. (Urban Affairs Annual Reviews Ser.: Vol. 20). 300p. 1981. 20.00 (ISBN 0-8039-1564-0); pap. 9.95 (ISBN 0-8039-1565-9). Sage.

Beck, Morris. Government Spending: Trends & Issues. 156p. 1981. 19.95 (ISBN 0-03-058629-1). Praeger.

Blin, J. M. Patterns & Configurations in Economic Science: A Study of Social Decision Processes. LC 72-92525. 148p. 1973. lib. bdg. 26.00 (ISBN 90-277-0302-7, Pub. by Reidel Holland). Kluwer Boston.

Borcherding, Thomas E., ed. Budgets & Bureaucrats: The Sources of Government Growth. LC 75-30407. 1977. 16.75 (ISBN 0-8223-0352-3). Duke.

Bowen, Frank M. & Lee, Eugene C. Limiting State Spending: The Legislature or the Electorate. LC 79-10327. (Research Report: No. 79-4). 1979. pap. 5.00x (ISBN 0-87772-265-X). Inst Gov Stud Berk.

Burns, A. E. & Watson, D. S. Government Spending & Economic Expansion. LC 75-173452. (FDR & the Era of the New Deal Ser). 174p. 1972. Repr. of 1940 ed. lib. bdg. 20.00 (ISBN 0-306-70368-8). Da Capo.

Chamber of Commerce Staff. Consumer Attitudes Toward Government Taxation & Spending. LC 80-50208. 1981. pap. 5.00 1-9 copies (ISBN 0-686-72852-1, 6446); pap. 4.00 10-99 copies (ISBN 0-686-72853-X); pap. 3.50 100 copies or more (ISBN 0-686-72854-8). Chamber Comm US.

Clark, W. Edmund. Socialist Development & Public Investment in Tanzania, 1964-73. LC 77-8180. 1978. 30.00x (ISBN 0-8020-5376-9). U of Toronto Pr.

Committee for Economic Development. Improving Federal Program Performance. LC 70-173676. 86p. 1971. lib. bdg. 2.50 (ISBN 0-87186-743-5); pap. 1.50 (ISBN 0-87186-043-0). Comm Econ Dev.

Dilemmas of Government Expenditure. (Readings: No. 15). 1977. pap. 7.50 (ISBN 0-255-36081-9). Transatlantic.

Dorfman, Robert, ed. Measuring Benefits of Government Investments. LC 79-28577. (Brookings Institution, National Committee on Government Finance, Studies of Government Finance). (Illus.). xv, 429p. 1980. Repr. of 1965 ed. lib. bdg. 32.75x (ISBN 0-313-22307-6, DOMB). Greenwood.

Due, John F. & Friedlaender, Ann F. Government Finance: Economics of the Public Sector. 7th ed. 1981. 20.00x (ISBN 0-256-02492-8). Irwin.

Egle, Walter P. Economic Stabilization. (University of Cincinnati Ser.). 1952. 14.00 (ISBN 0-691-04123-7). Princeton U Pr.

Gramlich, Edward M. Benefit-Cost Analysis of Government Programs. (Illus.). 304p. 1981. text ed. 17.95 (ISBN 0-13-074757-2). P-H.

Harriss, C. L., ed. Government Spending & Landvalues. LC 72-9988. 262p. 1973. 21.50x (ISBN 0-299-06320-8). U of Wis Pr.

Heclo, Hugh & Wildavsky, Aaron. The Private Government of Public Money: Community & Policy in British Political Administration. LC 73-79474. 1974. 30.00x (ISBN 0-520-02497-4). U of Cal Pr.

Heilbroner, Robert L. & Bernstein, Peter L. Primer on Government Spending. 2nd ed. (Primer Economics Ser). 1970. pap. text ed. 3.95x (ISBN 0-394-30750-X, RanC). Random.

Henderson, William C. & Cameron, Helen. The Public Economy: An Introduction to Government Finance. 1969. text ed. 9.95 (ISBN 0-685-41968-1). Phila Bk Co.

Hubbard, Joshua C. Creation of Income by Taxation. Repr. of 1950 ed. lib. bdg. 15.00x (ISBN 0-8371-0110-7, HUCI). Greenwood.

Ippolito, Dennis S. Congressional Spending. (Illus.). 312p. 1982. pap. price not set (ISBN 0-8014-9230-0). Cornell U Pr.

Lambro, Donald. Fat City: How Washington Wastes Your Taxes. LC 79-92080. 336p. 1980. 12.95 (ISBN 0-89526-680-6). Regnery-Gateway.

Margolis, Julius, ed. Analysis of Public Output. (Conference Ser.: No. 23). 1970. text ed. 15.00x (ISBN 0-87014-220-8, Dist. by Columbia U Pr). Natl Bur Econ Res.

Mieszlowski, Peter & Oakland, William, eds. Fiscal Federalism & Grants-in-Aid. (Papers on Public Economics Ser.: Vol.1). 166p. (Orig.). 1979. pap. text ed. 10.00 (ISBN 0-87766-254-1, 26300). Urban Inst.

Pechman, Joseph A. Setting National Priorities: The 1978 Budget. 1977. 14.95 (ISBN 0-8157-6980-6); pap. 5.95 (ISBN 0-8157-6979-2). Brookings.

Proxmire, William. Uncle Sam: Last of the Bigtime Spenders. 1972. 6.95 (ISBN 0-671-21432-2). S&S.

Raskin, Marcus, ed. The Federal Budget & Social Reconstruction: The People & the State. LC 77-55935. (Orig.). 1978. pap. 7.95 (ISBN 0-87855-647-8). Transaction Bks.

Raskin, Marcus G., ed. The Federal Budget & Social Reconstruction. 470p. 1978. pap. 8.95 (ISBN 0-89758-000-1). Inst Policy Stud.

Samuels, Warren J. & Wade, Larry L., eds. Taxing & Spending Policy. LC 79-3689. (A Policy Studies Organization Book). 1980. 19.95 (ISBN 0-669-03469-X). Lexington Bks.

Schick, Allen. Congress & Money: Budgeting, Spending & Taxing. LC 80-53322. 600p. 1980. 27.50 (ISBN 0-87766-278-9); pap. 9.95 (ISBN 0-87766-294-0, 31800). Urban Inst.

Schultze, Charles L. The Public Use of Private Interest. 1977. 9.95 (ISBN 0-8157-7762-0); pap. 3.95 (ISBN 0-8157-7761-2). Brookings.

Scott, Claudia D. Forecasting Local Government Spending. 1972. 4.95 (ISBN 0-87766-023-9, 50010). Urban Inst.

Turnbull, A. B. Government Budgeting & PPBS: A Programmed Introduction. 1970. pap. 12.95 (ISBN 0-201-07615-2). A-W.

Wildavsky, Aaron. How to Limit Government Spending. 197p. 1980. 11.95 (ISBN 0-520-04227-1). U of Cal Pr.

Worthley, John A. & Ludwin, William G., eds. Zero-Base Budgeting in State & Local Government: Current Experiences & Cases. LC 79-10162. 1979. 20.95 (ISBN 0-03-049121-5). Praeger.

Wright, Maurice, ed. Public Spending Decisions: Growth & Restraint in the 1970's. (Illus.). 1980. text ed. 27.50x (ISBN 0-04-350056-0). Allen Unwin.

GOVERNMENT SUPPORT OF SCIENCE, LITERATURE, AND ART

see State Encouragement of Science, Literature, and Art

GOVERNMENT SURVEYS

see Surveys

GOVERNMENT TRADING

Kostecki, M. M. State Trading in International Markets: Theory & Practice of Industrialized & Developing Countries. 1981. 35.00x (ISBN 0-312-75693-3). St Martin.

GOVERNMENTAL INVESTIGATIONS

see also Criminal Investigation; Executive Privilege (Government Information); Legislative Hearings; Police

Barth, Alan. Government by Investigation. LC 71-122068. Repr. of 1955 ed. 13.50x (ISBN 0-678-03150-9). Kelley.

Bliss, Edward N. Defense Investigation. 336p. 1956. pap. 24.50 (ISBN 0-398-04209-8). C C Thomas.

Burton, Frank & Carlen, Pat. Official Discourse: On Discourse Analysis, Government Publications, Ideology & the State International Library of Sociology. (Illus.). 1979. 20.00x (ISBN 0-7100-0328-5). Routledge & Kegan.

Clokie, Hugh M. & Robinson, J. William. Royal Commissions of Inquiry: The Significance of Investigation in British Politics. LC 70-86274. 1969. Repr. of 1937 ed. lib. bdg. 13.00x (ISBN 0-374-91710-8). Octagon.

Dimock, Marshall E. Congressional Investigating Committees. LC 72-155626. Repr. of 1929 ed. 12.50 (ISBN 0-404-02134-4). AMS Pr.

Dorman, Michael. Witch Hunt. LC 75-32917. 192p. (gr. 7 up). 1976. 8.95 (ISBN 0-440-09689-8). Delacorte.

Eberling, Ernest J. Congressional Investigations: A Study of the Origin & Development of the Power of Congress to Investigate & Punish for Contempt. 1972. lib. bdg. 21.00x (ISBN 0-374-92465-1). Octagon.

Greene, Robert W. The Sting Man: The Inside Story of Abscam. (Illus.). 256p. 1981. 13.50 (ISBN 0-525-20985-9). Dutton.

--The Sting Man: The Inside Story of Abscam. (Illus.). 256p. 1981. 13.50 (ISBN 0-525-20985-9). Dutton.

Hatton, Henry, ed. Uncle Sam Is Watching You. 1971. 6.00 (ISBN 0-8183-0100-7). Pub Aff Pr.

Lipsky, Michael & Olson, David J. Commission Politics: The Processing of Racial Crisis in America. LC 74-20192. 500p. 1977. 14.95 (ISBN 0-87855-078-X). Transaction Bks.

McGeary, M. Nelson. Development of Congressional Investigative Power. 1966. lib. bdg. 12.00x (ISBN 0-374-95491-7). Octagon.

Marcy, Carl. Presidential Commissions. LC 72-8109. (Studies in American History & Government Ser.). 156p. 1973. Repr. of 1945 ed. lib. bdg. 19.50 (ISBN 0-306-70532-X). Da Capo.

Packer, Herbert L. Ex-Communist Witnesses: Four Studies in Fact Finding. 1962. 12.50x (ISBN 0-8047-0121-0). Stanford U Pr.

Popper, Frank. President's Commissions. LC 73-12304. 74p. 1973. Repr. of 1970 ed. pap. text ed. 5.00 (ISBN 0-527-71960-9). Kraus Repr.

Report of the Seventh Session of WMO Executive Committee Inter-Governmental Panel on the First GARP Global Experiments. (GARP Special Report Ser.). 132p. 1980. pap. 25.00 (ISBN 0-686-62175-1, W 458, WMO). Unipub.

Schlesinger, Arthur M., Jr. & Bruns, Roger, eds. Congress Investigates: A Documented History, Seventeen Ninety-Two to Nineteen Seventy-Four. abr. ed. LC 75-28106. 1975. 32.50 (ISBN 0-8352-0864-8, Pub by Chelsea Hse). Bowker.

--Congress Investigates: A Documented History, 1792-1974, 5 vols. 3560p. 1981. Set. pap. 85.00 (ISBN 0-87754-132-9, 3560). Chelsea Hse.

Wraith, R. E. & Lamb, G. B. Public Inquiries As an Instrument of Government. (Royal Institute of Public Administration). 1971. text ed. 42.50x (ISBN 0-04-351037-X). Allen Unwin.

GOVERNOR SHIRLEY'S WAR

see United States–History–King George's War, 1744-1748

GOVERNORS–UNITED STATES

Abbot, W. W. The Royal Governors of Georgia, 1754-1775. LC 59-9568. (Institute of Early American History & Culture Ser.). 1959. 13.50x (ISBN 0-8078-0758-3). U of NC Pr.

Almaraz, Felix D., Jr. Tragic Cavalier: Governor Manuel Salcedo of Texas, 1808-1813. 218p. 1981. pap. 6.95 (ISBN 0-292-78039-7). U of Tex Pr.

Broer, Jill S., et al. Governors of Tennessee, Seventeen Ninety to Eighteen Thirty-Five: I. Crawford, Charles W., ed. LC 79-129790. (The Tennessee Ser.: Vol. 3). (Illus.). 1979. 12.95 (ISBN 0-87870-075-7). Memphis St Univ.

Coffman, Tom. Catch a Wave: A Case Study of Hawaii's New Politics. rev. 2nd ed. LC 72-98011. 1973. pap. text ed. 3.95x (ISBN 0-8248-0270-5). U Pr of Hawaii.

Combs, Bert T. The Public Papers of Governor Bert T. Combs, 1959-1963. Robinson, George W. & Sexton, Robert F., eds. LC 78-58103. (The Public Papers of the Governors of Kentucky). 568p. 1980. 28.00x (ISBN 0-8131-0604-4). U Pr of Ky.

Goff, John S. George W. P. Hunt & His Arizona. LC 72-78585. (Illus.). 320p. 12.00 (ISBN 0-87026-038-3). Westernlore.

Haider, Donald H. When Governments Come to Washington: Governors, Mayors, & Intergovernmental Lobbying. LC 73-17643. (Illus.). 1974. 15.95 (ISBN 0-02-913370-X). Free Pr.

Hartley, Robert. Big Jim Thompson of Illinois. LC 79-19262. (Illus.). 1979. 9.95 (ISBN 0-528-81824-4). Rand.

Hinckley, Ted C. Alaskan John G. Brady: Missionary, Businessman, Judge, & Governor, 1878-1918. 300p. 1981. 20.00 (ISBN 0-8142-0336-1). Ohio St U Pr.

Johnson, Keen. The Public Papers of Governor Keen Johnson, Nineteen Thirty-Nine to Nineteen Forty-Three. Ogden, Frederic D. & Sexton, Robert F., eds. LC 79-57562. (The Public Papers of the Governors of Kentucky Ser.). 1981. 28.00x (ISBN 0-8131-0605-2). U Pr of Ky.
Johnson, Willis. The Year of the Longley. LC 78-70046. (Illus.). 1978. pap. 4.75 (ISBN 0-686-15970-5). Penobscot Bay.
Kallenbach, Joseph E. & Kallenbach, Jessamine S. American State Governors, 1776-1976: Electoral & Personal Data, 3 vols. LC 76-51519. 1977. lib. bdg. 40.00 ea. (ISBN 0-379-00665-0). Oceana.
Lipson, Leslie. American Governor from Figurehead to Leader. (Illus.). 1969. Repr. of 1939 ed. lib. bdg. 14.25x (ISBN 0-8371-0540-4, LIAG). Greenwood.
McIlwaine, H. R., ed. The Letters of Patrick Henry. LC 27-2700. (Official Letters of the Governors of the State Virginia Ser: Vol. 1). 1926. 7.50 (ISBN 0-88490-018-5). VA State Lib.
--The Letters of Thomas Jefferson. LC 27-2700. (Official Letters of the Governors of the State of Virginia Ser: Vol. 2). 1928. 7.50 (ISBN 0-88490-019-3). VA State Lib.
--The Letters of Thomas Nelson & Benjamin Harrison. LC 27-2700. (Official Letters of the Governors of Virginia Ser: Vol. 3). 1929. 7.50 (ISBN 0-88490-020-7). VA State Lib.
Macmillan, Margaret B. The War Governors in the American Revolution. 1943. 8.00 (ISBN 0-8446-1295-2). Peter Smith.
Merritt, Elizabeth. James Henry Hammond, 1807-1864. LC 78-64112. (Johns Hopkins University. Studies in the Social Sciences. Forty-First Ser. 1923: 4). Repr. of 1923 ed. 17.50 (ISBN 0-404-61227-X). AMS Pr.
Miller, Janice B. Juan Nepomuceno De Quesada: Governor of Spanish East Florida, 1790-1795. LC 81-40589. (Illus.). 196p. (Orig.). 1981. lib. bdg. 19.50 (ISBN 0-8191-1833-8); pap. text ed. 9.50 (ISBN 0-8191-1834-6). U Pr of Amer.
Morrison, Joseph L. Governor O. Max Gardner: A Power in North Carolina & New Deal Washington. LC 74-132253. (Illus.). 1971. 14.95 (ISBN 0-8078-1153-X). U of NC Pr.
Pack, Robert. Jerry Brown: The Philosopher-Prince. LC 77-16251. 1978. 10.00 (ISBN 0-8128-2437-7). Stein & Day.
Pierce, Walter M. Oregon Cattleman, Governor, Congressman: Memoirs & Times of Walter M. Pierce. Bone, Arthur H., ed. LC 80-81718. (Illus.). 528p. 1981. pap. 14.95 (ISBN 0-87595-098-1). Oreg Hist Soc.
Powell, William S., ed. The Correspondence of William Tryon & Other Selected Papers, Vol. I: 1758-1767. (Illus.). lvi, 664p. 1980. 25.00 (ISBN 0-86526-141-5). NC Archives.
Ramirez, Anthony. Romualdo Pacheco: Governor of California. LC 74-15571. (Illus.). (gr. 3-6). 1974. 3.50 (ISBN 0-911302-26-3). San Francisco Pr.
Ransone, Coleman B. Office of Governor in the United States. facs. ed. LC 78-130564. (Select Bibliographies Reprint Ser). 1956. 22.00 (ISBN 0-8369-5537-4). Arno.
Rohr, Charles J. The Governor of Maryland, a Constitutional Study. LC 78-64147. (Johns Hopkins University. Studies in the Social Sciences. Fiftieth Ser. 1932: 3). Repr. of 1932 ed. 21.00 (ISBN 0-404-61258-X). AMS Pr.
Sabato, Larry. Goodbye to Good-Time Charlie. LC 78-333. (Illus.). 1978. 21.95 (ISBN 0-669-02161-X). Lexington Bks.
Shaw, Bynum & Folk, Edgar E. W. W. Holden: A Political Biography. (Illus.). 288p. 1981. 14.95 (ISBN 0-89587-025-8). Blair.
Smith, Marion J. General William King. LC 79-67417. (Illus.). 182p. 1980. 11.95 (ISBN 0-89272-072-7). Down East.
Sobel, Robert, ed. Biographical Directory of the Governors of the United States, 1789-1978. LC 77-10435. 1978. 225.00x (ISBN 0-930466-00-4). Meckler Bks.
Steffen, Jerome O. William Clark: Jeffersonian Man on the Frontier. (Illus.). 1979. pap. 5.95 (ISBN 0-8061-1593-9). U of Okla Pr.
Sumners, Cecil L. Governors of Mississippi. (Governors of the State Ser.). (Illus.). 180p. 1980. 13.95 (ISBN 0-88289-237-1). Pelican.
TePaske, John J. Governorship of Spanish Florida, 1700-1763. LC 64-18659. 1964. 14.75 (ISBN 0-8223-0173-3). Duke.
Turner, Martha A. Richard Bennett Hubbard: An American Life. (Illus.). 208p. 1979. 15.00 (ISBN 0-88319-043-5). Shoal Creek Pub.
Wilson, Don W. Governor Charles Robinson of Kansas. LC 75-6875. (Illus.). 214p. 1975. 11.00x (ISBN 0-7006-0133-3). Regents Pr Ks.
Winthrop, John. Life & Letters of John Winthrop, 2 Vols. Winthrop, Robert C., ed. LC 72-152833. (American Public Figures Ser). 1971. Repr. of 1864 ed. Set. lib. bdg. 75.00 (ISBN 0-306-70147-2). Da Capo.

GOVERNORS (MACHINERY)
see also Electronic Control

GOVINDA SIMBA, 10TH GURU OF THE SIKHS, 1666-1708
Johar, S. S. Guru Gobind Singh: A Biography. 1967. 7.50x (ISBN 0-8426-1322-6). Verry.
Singh, Khushwant & Singh, Suneet V. Homage to Guru Gobind Singh. 1970. pap. 2.30 (ISBN 0-88253-088-7). Ind-US Inc.

GOWER, JOHN, 1325-1408
Dodd, William G. Courtly Love in Chaucer & Gower. 1958. 7.50 (ISBN 0-8446-1490-4). Peter Smith.
Fisher, John H. John Gower: Moral Philosopher & Friend of Chaucer. LC 64-21811. 1964. 12.00x (ISBN 0-8147-0149-3). NYU Pr.
Fox, George G. Medieval Sciences in the Works of John Gower. LC 65-21089. (Studies in Poetry, No. 38). 1969. Repr. of 1931 ed. lib. bdg. 49.95 (ISBN 0-8383-0553-9). Haskell.
Ker, William P. Essays on Medieval Literature. LC 72-10254. 1905. lib. bdg. 27.50 (ISBN 0-8414-0704-5). Folcroft.
Morley, Henry, ed. Confessio Amantis of John Gower. 446p. 1980. Repr. of 1889 ed. lib. bdg. 35.00 (ISBN 0-8492-6832-X). R West.
Peck, Russell A. Kingship & Common Profit in Gower's "Confessio Amantis". LC 78-8984. (Literary Structures Ser.). 232p. 1978. 13.95x (ISBN 0-8093-0801-0). S Ill U Pr.
Yeager, Robert F. John Gower Materials: A Bibliography Through Nineteen Seventy-Nine. 1981. lib. bdg. 25.00 (ISBN 0-8240-9351-8). Garland Pub.

GOWNS, COLLEGE
see Academic Costume

GOYA Y LUCIENTES, FRANCISCO JOSE DE, 1746-1828
Bihalji-Merin, Oto. Francisco Goya: Caprichos: Their Hidden Truth. Woods, John E., tr. LC 81-47300. (Illus.). 192p. 1981. 65.00 (ISBN 0-15-133463-3). HarBraceJ.
--Goya, Then & Now: Paintings, Portraits, Frescoes. Woods, John E., tr. (Illus.). 288p. 1981. price not set. HarBraceJ.
Biografia De Goya. (Span.). 7.95 (ISBN 84-241-5416-9). E Torres & Sons.
Du Gue Trapier, Elizabeth. Goya & His Sitters. (Illus.). 1964. 10.00 (ISBN 0-87535-101-8). Hispanic Soc.
Gassier, Pierre, ed. Life & Work of Francisco Goya. Wilson, Juliet. Lachenal, Francois, ed. (Illus.). 1971. 55.00 (ISBN 0-688-61054-4). Reynal.
Glendinning, Nigel. Goya & His Critics. LC 76-49697. 1977. 50.00x (ISBN 0-300-02011-2). Yale U Pr.
Goya. (Art Library Ser.: Vol. 6). pap. 3.50 (ISBN 0-448-00459-3). G&D.
Goya. Drawings of Goya. (Master Draughtsman Ser). treasure trove bdg. 6.47x (ISBN 0-685-07257-6); pap. 2.95 (ISBN 0-685-07258-4). Borden.
Gudiol, J. Goya. (Library of Great Painters Ser). 1965. 40.00 (ISBN 0-8109-0149-8). Abrams.
Halo, Selma. Goya: Los Disparates. (J. Paul Getty Museum Publications Ser.). (Illus., Orig.). 1976. pap. 7.50x (ISBN 0-912158-29-8, Pub. by Wash St U Pr). Hennessey.
Licht, Fred. Goya: The Origins of the Modern Temper in Art. LC 78-54740. (Illus.). 288p. 1979. 16.50x (ISBN 0-87663-294-0). Universe.
Mayer, August L. Francisco De Goya. LC 70-15338. Repr. of 1924 ed. 34.50 (ISBN 0-404-07954-7). AMS Pr.
Ortega Y Gasset, Jose. Velazquez Goya, the Dehumanization of Art & Other Essays. Brown, Alexis, tr. (Illus.). 142p. 1972. 17.50x (ISBN 0-393-04358-4). Norton.
Roderick, Samuel D. The Fully Colored Art Quaderno of the Best Paintings by Francisco Goya. (Illus.). 1979. deluxe ed. 17.50 (ISBN 0-930582-45-4). Gloucester Art.
Schickel, Richard. World of Goya. (Library of Art). (Illus.). 1968. 15.95 (ISBN 0-8094-0247-5). Time-Life.
--World of Goya. LC 68-56432. (Library of Art Ser.). (Illus.). (gr. 6 up). 1968. 12.96 (ISBN 0-8094-0276-9, Pub. by Time-Life). Silver.
Symmonds, Sarah. Goya. 1981. 27.00x (ISBN 0-905368-12-6, Pub. by Jupiter England). State Mutual Bk.
Symmons, Sarah. Goya. LC 77-77884. (Illus.). 1977. 15.95 (ISBN 0-8467-0354-8, Pub. by Two Continents); pap. 9.95 (ISBN 0-8467-0353-X). Hippocrene Bks.
Vallentin, Antonina. This I Saw: The Life & Times of Goya. Woods, Katherine W., tr. from Fr. LC 78-152612. (Illus.). 371p. Repr. of 1949 ed. lib. bdg. 17.75x (ISBN 0-8371-6047-2, VATI). Greenwood.
Virch, C. Francisco Goya. (Color Slide Program of the Great Masters). 1968. 17.95 (ISBN 0-07-067508-2, P&RB). McGraw.
Young, Eric. Francisco Goya. LC 77-95304. (Art for All Ser.). (Illus.). 1978. pap. 5.95 (ISBN 0-312-30319-X). St Martin.

GOYENS, WILLIAM, 1794-1856
Northouse, Cameron. William Goyen: A Descriptive Bibliography of First Printings of His Work. (First Printings Ser.). 60p. 1981. limited ed. 30.00 (ISBN 0-939722-06-2). Pressworks.
Phillips, Robert. William Goyen. (United States Authors Ser.: No. 329). 1979. lib. bdg. 12.50 (ISBN 0-8057-7269-3). Twayne.

GOYTISOLO, JUAN
Ortega, Jose. Alienacion y Agnesion En Juan Goytisolo En Senas De Identidad y Reivindicacion Del Conde Don Julian. 1973. 10.50 (ISBN 0-88303-012-8); pap. 7.50 (ISBN 0-685-73216-9). E Torres & Sons.
Romero, Hector R. La Evolucion Literaria De Juan Goytisolo. LC 78-74702. (Coleccion Polymita Ser.). 162p. (Span.). 1979. pap. 9.95 (ISBN 0-89729-222-7). Ediciones.

GOZO (MALTESE ISLAND)
Kininmonth, Christopher. The Travellers' Guide to Malta & Gozo. 3rd. ed. (Travellers' Guide Ser.). (Illus.). 230p. 1979. 7.95 (ISBN 0-224-01656-3, Pub. by Chatto Bodley Jonathan). Merrimack Bk Serv.

GOZZI, CARLO, CONTE, 1722-1806
Rusack, Hedwig H. Gozzi in Germany. LC 31-2392. (Columbia University. Germanic Studies, Old Ser.: No. 34). Repr. of 1930 ed. 19.00 (ISBN 0-404-50434-5). AMS Pr.

GPS (COMPUTER PROGRAM LANGUAGE)
Bobillier, P. A., et al. Simulation with Gpss & Gpssv. LC 75-40316. 1976. 27.50 (ISBN 0-13-810549-9). P-H.
Ernst, George W. & Newell, Allen. G P S: A Case Study in Generality & Problem Solving. (ACM Monograph Ser). 1969. 47.00 (ISBN 0-12-241050-5). Acad Pr.
Gordon, Geoffrey. The Application of GPSS Five to Discrete System Simulation. (Illus.). 336p. 1975. 24.95 (ISBN 0-13-039057-7). P-H.
Greenberg, Stanley. GPSS Primer. LC 79-27196. 344p. 1981. Repr. text ed. write for info. (ISBN 0-89874-075-4). Krieger.
Maisel, Herbert & Gnugnoli, Guiliano. Simulation of Discrete Stochastic Systems. LC 72-80761. (Illus.). 465p. 1972. 21.95 (ISBN 0-574-16133-3, 13-1565). SRA.
Schmidt, B. GPSS FORTRAN. LC 80-40968. (Computing Ser.). 523p. 1980. 39.00 (ISBN 0-471-27881-5, Pub. by Wiley-Interscience). Wiley.

GRABBE, CHRISTIAN DIETRICH, 1801-1836
Cowen, Roy C. Christian Dietrich Grabbe. (World Authors Ser.: Germany: No. 206). lib. bdg. 10.95 (ISBN 0-8057-2396-X). Twayne.

GRACCHUS, TIBERIUS SEMPRONIUS, 168 B.C.-133 B.C.
Bernstein, Alvin H. Tiberius Sempronius Gracchus: Tradition & Apostasy. 1978. 19.50x (ISBN 0-8014-1078-9). Cornell U Pr.

GRACE (THEOLOGY)
see also Covenants (Theology); Law and Gospel
Bansemer, Richard. Grace & the Grave. Date not set. price not set (ISBN 0-89536-506-5). CSS Pub.
Boff, Leonardo. Liberating Grace. Drury, John, tr. from Sp. LC 79-4206. 1979. pap. 8.95 (ISBN 0-88344-282-5). Orbis Bks.
Booth, Abrh. The Reign of Grace. 5.95 (ISBN 0-685-88390-6). Reiner.
Bunyan, John. Doctrine of Law & Grace Unfolded. 1974. pap. 2.95 (ISBN 0-685-52817-0). Reiner.
--Grace Abounding. 1959. pap. 1.50 (ISBN 0-8024-3293-X). Moody.
--Saved by Grace. pap. 2.25 (ISBN 0-685-88393-0). Reiner.
Chafer, Lewis S. Grace. pap. 6.95 (ISBN 0-310-22331-8). Zondervan.
Cheesman, John, et al. The Grace of God in the Gospel. 1976. pap. 2.45 (ISBN 0-85151-153-8). Banner of Truth.
Clarkson, Margaret. Grace Grows Best in Winter. large print ed. 208p. 1975. kivar 5.95 (ISBN 0-310-22467-5). Zondervan.
Cooke, Joseph R. Free for the Taking. 1975. 7.95 (ISBN 0-8007-0731-1). Revell.
Cote, Richard G. Universal Grace: Myth or Reality? LC 77-5570. 1977. 4.95 (ISBN 0-88344-521-2). Orbis Bks.
Custance, Arthur C. Sovereignty of Grace. 1979. 12.95 (ISBN 0-87552-160-6). Presby & Reformed.
Davey, James E. Riches of Grace. pap. 0.95 (ISBN 0-87509-127-X). Chr Pubns.
Ditmanson, Harold H. Grace in Experience & Theology. LC 77-22447. 1977. 9.95 (ISBN 0-8066-1598-2, 10-2881); pap. 6.95 (ISBN 0-8066-1587-7, 10-2880). Augsburg.
Drewery, Benjamin. Origen & the Doctrine of Grace. 1960. text ed. 12.00x (ISBN 0-8401-0579-7). Allenson-Breckinridge.
Flavel, John. Method of Grace. (Summit Bks). 1977. pap. 3.95 (ISBN 0-8010-3481-7). Baker Bk.
Grace of God. pap. 0.95 (ISBN 0-937396-18-4). Walterick Pubs.
Guardini, Romano. Freedom, Grace, & Destiny. Murray, John, tr. from Ger. LC 75-8786. 384p. 1975. Repr. of 1961 ed. lib. bdg. 14.50x (ISBN 0-8371-8111-9, GUFG). Greenwood.
Haight, Roger. The Experience & Language of Grace. LC 79-84403. 1979. pap. 4.95 (ISBN 0-8091-2200-6). Paulist Pr.
Hendriksen, William. The Covenant of Grace. 1978. pap. 1.95 (ISBN 0-8010-4196-1). Baker Bk.
Hong, Edna. The Gayety of Grace. LC 77-176484. 124p. 1979. pap. 3.95 (ISBN 0-8066-1775-6, 10-2541). Augsburg.
Hudson, Lofton R. Grace Is Not a Blue-Eyed Blonde. LC 68-21506. pap. 0.95 (ISBN 0-87680-909-3, 90009). Word Bks.
Jones, J. D. The Gospel of Grace. (Minister's Paperback Library). 284p. 1976. pap. 3.95 (ISBN 0-8010-5067-7). Baker Bk.
Jones, Michael, ed. Prayers & Graces. 1980. 6.75 (ISBN 0-903540-33-9, Pub. by Flores Books). St George Bk Serv.
Kapur, B. L. Hanuman Chalisa: The Descent of Grace. 130p. 1974. text ed. 7.50x (ISBN 0-8426-0727-7). Verry.
Moffatt, James. Grace in the New Testament. 419p. 1981. Repr. of 1931 ed. lib. bdg. 45.00 (ISBN 0-89984-339-5). Century Bookbindery.
Murray, Andrew. Secret of the Throne of Grace. (Secret Ser.). (Orig.). 1980. pap. 1.25 (ISBN 0-87508-393-5). Chr Lit.
Nee, Watchman. Full of Grace & Truth, Vol. II. Kaung, Stephen, tr. 1981. pap. 2.95 (ISBN 0-935008-51-9). Christian Fellow Pubs.
O'Donovan, L. J. A World of Grace. 1980. 14.95 (ISBN 0-8245-0404-6); pap. 7.95 (ISBN 0-8164-2006-8). Crossroad NY.
Pinnock, Clark H. Grace Unlimited. LC 75-22161. 272p. 1975. pap. 5.95 (ISBN 0-87123-185-9, 210185). Bethany Hse.
Riggle, H. M. The Two Works of Grace. 56p. pap. 0.40 (ISBN 0-686-29168-9); pap. 1.00 3 copies (ISBN 0-686-29169-7). Faith Pub Hse.
Segundo, Jean L. Grace & the Human Condition. Drury, John, tr. from Span. LC 72-85794. (A Theology for Artisans of a New Humanity Ser: Vol. 2). 196p. 1973. 7.95x (ISBN 0-88344-482-8); pap. 4.95x (ISBN 0-88344-488-7). Orbis Bks.
Spurgeon, C. H. Exposition of the Doctrines of Grace. 1.25 (ISBN 0-686-09096-9). Pilgrim Pubns.
--Grace. 1976. pap. 1.25 (ISBN 0-686-16843-7). Pilgrim Pubns.
Spurgeon, Charles H. All of Grace. pap. 1.95 (ISBN 0-8024-0001-9). Moody.
--All of Grace. (Summit Books). 1976. pap. text ed. 2.45 (ISBN 0-8010-8095-9). Baker Bk.
--Seven Wonders of Grace. (Summit Bks). 1978. 2.95 (ISBN 0-8010-8131-9). Baker Bk.
Sumner, Robert L. Saved by Grace...for Service. 1979. 8.95 (ISBN 0-87398-797-7, Pub. by Bibl Evang Pr). Sword of Lord.
Teasley, D. O. The Double Cure, or Redemption Twofold. 160p. pap. 1.50 large print (ISBN 0-686-29147-6). Faith Pub Hse.
Thomas, J. D. The Biblical Doctrine of Grace. LC 76-56472. (Way of Life Ser: No. 111). (Orig.). 1977. pap. 2.95 (ISBN 0-89112-111-0). Bibl Res Pr.
Tournier, Paul. Guilt & Grace. LC 62-7305. 1962. 8.95 (ISBN 0-06-068330-9, HarpR). Har-Row.
Van Til, Cornelius. Common Grace & the Gospel. pap. 3.50 (ISBN 0-87552-482-6). Presby & Reformed.
Vogel, Arthur A. The Gift of Grace. 1980. 1.50 (ISBN 0-686-28778-9). Forward Movement.
Woodson, Les. Divorce & the Gospel of Grace. 1979. pap. 4.95 (ISBN 0-8499-2852-4). Word Bks.

GRACE, GIFTS OF
see Gifts, Spiritual

GRACE AT MEALS
Simons, Thomas G. Blessings: A Reappraisal of Their Nature, Purpose, & Celebration. LC 80-54275. 1981. pap. 9.95 (ISBN 0-89390-025-7). Resource Pubns.
Tengbom, Mildred, compiled by. Table Prayers: New Prayers, Old Favorites, Songs, & Responses. LC 77-72451. 1977. pap. 2.95 (ISBN 0-8066-1594-X, 10-6185). Augsburg.
Tudor, Tasha. First Graces. LC 59-12017. (Illus.). (gr. k-3). 1955. 3.50 (ISBN 0-8098-1953-8). Walck.

GRACES, EXPECTIVE
see Benefices, Ecclesiastical

GRACIAN Y MORALES, BALTASAR, 1601-1658
Foster, Virginia R. Baltasar Gracian. (World Authors Ser.: Spain: No. 337). 1975. lib. bdg. 12.50 (ISBN 0-8057-2398-6). Twayne.
Romera-Navarro, M. Estudios sobre Gracian. (Hispanic Studies: No. 2). 152p. 1950. pap. 5.00x (ISBN 0-292-73213-9). U of Tex Pr.
Welles, Marcia L. Style & Structure in Gracian's el Criticon. (Studies in the Romance Languages & Literatures Ser: No. 166). 1976. pap. 13.00x (ISBN 0-8078-9166-5). U of NC Pr.

GRACKLES
see Blackbirds
GRADE LABELING
see Labels
GRADED SCHOOLS
see Ability Grouping in Education; Grading and Marking (Students)
GRADING
see also Labels; Specifications; Standardization; Testing

Doblin, F. Men's Garment Designing & Grading. rev. ed. (Illus.). Date not set. 25.00 (ISBN 0-686-30449-7). Master Design.

Newman, Isadore, et al. An Introduction to the Basic Concepts & Techniques of Measurement & Evaluation. 4th ed. 210p. 1976. pap. text ed. 5.00 (ISBN 0-917180-05-4). I Newman.

Price, Jeanne & Zamkoff, Bernard. Grading Techniques for Modern Design. LC 73-8403. (Illus.). 150p. 1973. 14.50 (ISBN 0-87005-102-4). Fairchild.

Schearer, William J. The Grading of Schools. (Educational Ser.). 1898. Repr. 6.50 (ISBN 0-685-43648-9). Norwood Edns.

GRADING AND MARKING (STUDENTS)
see also Ability Grouping in Education; School Credits

Ahmann & Glock. Evaluating Student Progress: Principles of Tests & Measurements. 6th ed. 540p. 1980. text ed. 19.95 (ISBN 0-205-06561-9, 246561-2); test manual (ISBN 0-205-06562-7, 246562-0). Allyn.

Akridge, Garth H. Pupil Progress Policies & Practices. LC 70-176505. (Columbia University. Teachers College. Contributions to Education: No. 691). Repr. of 1937 ed. 17.50 (ISBN 0-404-55691-4). AMS Pr.

Armstrong, David G. & Pinney, Robert H. Record Keeping for Individualized Instruction Programs. 64p. 1977. pap. 4.50 (ISBN 0-686-63696-1, 1601-7-06). NEA.

Association For Supervision And Curriculum Development. Evaluation As Feedback & Guide. LC 44-6213. 1967. pap. 6.50 (ISBN 0-87120-023-6, 610-17700). Assn Supervision.

Backhouse, John K. Pass or Fail? A Study of Pass Rates in the G. C. E. at the "O" Level. (General Ser.). (Illus.). 44p. 1974. pap. text ed. 6.25x (ISBN 0-85633-036-1, NFER). Humanities.

Baird, Leonard L. Using Self-Reports to Predict Student Performance. LC 76-4312. (Research Monographs: No. 7). 1976. pap. 5.00 (ISBN 0-87447-098-6, 251701). College Bd.

Bellanca, James A. Grading. 96p. 1977. pap. 5.75 (ISBN 0-686-63688-0, 1603-3-06). NEA.

Coleman, James S. & Karweit, Nancy L. Information Systems & Performance Measures in Schools. LC 72-79547. 152p. 1972. 15.95 (ISBN 0-87778-038-2). Educ Tech Pubns.

Colligan. The A Plus Guide to Good Grades. (gr. 7-12). 1980. pap. 1.50 (ISBN 0-590-30001-6, Schol Pap). Schol Bk Serv.

Connor, Ruth. The Scholastic Behavior of a Selected Group of Undergraduate Home Economics Students. LC 70-176667. (Columbia University. Teachers College. Contributions to Education: No. 497). Repr. of 1931 ed. 17.50 (ISBN 0-404-55497-0). AMS Pr.

Crafts, Kathy & Hauther, Brenda. The Student's Guide to Good Grades: Surviving the Undergraduate Jungle. LC 76-16671. 1976. pap. 2.45 (ISBN 0-394-17009-1, B405, BC); pre-pack of 12 26.95 (ISBN 0-394-17756-8). Grove.

--Success in College: The Student's Guide Ot Good Grades. rev. ed. 192p. (Orig.). 1981. pap. 3.95 (ISBN 0-394-17740-1, BC). Grove.

Gray, Jenny. Teacher's Survival Guide. 2nd ed. LC 73-83493. 1974. pap. 5.95 (ISBN 0-8224-6795-X). Pitman Learning.

Green, Kenneth A., et al. Better Grades in College with Less Effort. LC 70-134238. 176p. (Orig.). 1971. pap. 2.95 (ISBN 0-8120-0415-9). Barron.

Gronlund, Norman E. Improving Marking & Reporting in Classroom Instruction. (Illus.). 64p. 1974. text ed. 3.50 (ISBN 0-02-348140-4, 34814). Macmillan.

Hayman, John L., Jr. & Napier, Rodney W. Evaluation in the Schools: A Human Process for Renewal. LC 74-21960. (Basic Concepts in Educational Psychology Ser.). (Illus.). 1975. pap. text ed. 6.95 (ISBN 0-8185-0145-6). Brooks-Cole.

Keepes, Jillian M. & Rechter, Bernard. English & Its Assessment. 165p. 1973. pap. text ed. 8.50x (ISBN 0-85563-089-2). Verry.

Kelley, Truman L. Educational Guidance: Experimental Study in the Analysis & Prediction of Ability of High School Pupils. LC 70-176931. (Columbia University. Teachers College. Contributions to Education: No. 71). Repr. of 1914 ed. 17.50 (ISBN 0-404-55071-1). AMS Pr.

Kelly, F. J. Teacher's Marks: Their Variability & Standardization. LC 74-176932. (Columbia University. Teachers College. Contributions to Education: No. 66). Repr. of 1914 ed. 17.50 (ISBN 0-404-55066-5). AMS Pr.

Marshall, Max S. Teaching Without Grades. LC 68-56417. 1968. pap. 4.95 (ISBN 0-87071-317-5). Oreg St U Pr.

Milton, Ohmer & Edgerly, John W. The Testing & Grading of Students. 2nd ed. LC 77-73000. 1977. pap. 2.95 (ISBN 0-915390-14-0). Change Mag.

National Education Association. Evaluation & Reporting of Student Achievement. LC 74-10908. (What Research Says to the Teacher Ser.). Orig. Title: Evaluating & Reporting Pupil Progress. 1974. pap. 1.00 (ISBN 0-8106-1007-8). NEA.

Oman, Robert M. The Easy Way to Higher Grades. 40p. 1978. pap. 2.45 (ISBN 0-931660-01-7). R Oman Pubns.

Osgood, Judy. How to Beat the Grade Game. LC 78-53464. 1978. pap. 2.25 (ISBN 0-89516-040-4). Condor Pub Co.

Reed, Mary M. An Investigation of Practices in First Grade Admission & Promotion. LC 70-177183. (Columbia University. Teachers College. Contributions to Education: No. 290). Repr. of 1927 ed. 17.50 (ISBN 0-685-27470-5). AMS Pr.

Reeves, Floyd W., et al, eds. Instructional Problems in the University. LC 71-168086. Repr. of 1933 ed. 18.00 (ISBN 0-404-05236-3). AMS Pr.

Richard, J. A. Student's Guide to Better Grades. pap. 3.00 (ISBN 0-87980-152-2). Wilshire.

Rowntree, Derek. Assessing Students. 1980. pap. text ed. 11.50 (ISBN 0-06-318145-2, IntlDept). Har-Row.

Schwarzrock, Shirley & Wrenn, C. Gilbert. Grades, What's So Important About Them, Anyway? (Coping with Ser.). (Illus.). 33p. (gr. 7-12). pap. text ed. 1.30 (ISBN 0-913476-34-X). Am Guidance.

Simon, Sidney B. & Bellanca, James A., eds. Degrading the Grading Myths: A Primer of Alternatives to Grades & Marks. LC 76-20413. 1976. pap. 6.00 (ISBN 0-87120-080-5, 611-76082). Assn Supervision.

Smallwood, Mary L. An Historical Study of Examinations & Grading Systems in Early American Universities. 1935. pap. 15.50 (ISBN 0-384-56115-2). Johnson Repr.

Spence, Ralph B. The Improvement of College Marking Systems. LC 70-177751. (Columbia University. Teachers College. Contributions to Education: No. 252). Repr. of 1927 ed. 17.50 (ISBN 0-404-55252-8). AMS Pr.

Tyler, Henry T. Bearing of Certain Personality Factors Other Than Intelligence on Academic Success: Study of Tests Made at Teacher's College, Columbia University. LC 78-177693. (Columbia University. Teachers College. Contributions to Education: No. 468). Repr. of 1931 ed. 17.50 (ISBN 0-404-55468-7). AMS Pr.

York, L. Jean. Team Teaching Modules, 7 vols. Incl. Vol. 1. Philosophy & Background of Team Teaching. pap. 3.50x (ISBN 0-685-22706-5); Vol. 2. The Roles of the Professional & Paraprofessional in Team Teaching. pap. 3.50x (ISBN 0-685-22707-3); Vol. 3. Materials & Resources Needed for Team Teaching & Individualized Instruction. pap. 3.50x (ISBN 0-685-22708-1); Vol. 4. Grouping Children for Instruction in Team Teaching. pap. 3.50x (ISBN 0-685-22709-X); Vol. 5. Team Teaching As a Facilitator of the Nongraded School. pap. 3.50x (ISBN 0-685-22710-3); Vol. 6. Evaluation of Team Teaching & Children's Continuous Progress. pap. 3.50x (ISBN 0-685-22711-1); Vol. 7. Prerequisites for Good Planning Sessions in Team Teaching. pap. 3.50x (ISBN 0-685-22712-X). 1971. pap. 24.50x set (ISBN 0-685-22705-7). Leslie Pr.

GRADUATE WORK
see Universities and Colleges–Graduate Work
GRADUATED TAXATION
see Taxation, Progressive
GRADUATION SERMONS
see Baccalaureate Addresses
GRADY, HENRY WOODFIN, 1851-1889

Grady, Henry W. The Complete Orations & Speeches of Henry W. Grady. Shurter, Edwin, ed. 1976. lib. bdg. 59.95 (ISBN 0-8490-1657-6). Gordon Pr.

Harris, Joel C., ed. The Life of Henry W. Grady Including His Writings & Speeches. LC 70-39490. (American Biography Ser. 32). 650p. 1972. Repr. of 1890 ed. lib. bdg. 58.95 (ISBN 0-8383-1402-3). Haskell.

Nixon, Raymond B. Henry W. Grady, Spokesman of the New South. LC 68-27076. (Illus.). 1969. Repr. of 1943 ed. 12.00 (ISBN 0-8462-1289-7). Russell.

Terrell, Russell F. Henry W. Grady. (Amer. Newspapermen Ser.: 1790-1933). 1976. 14.50x (ISBN 0-8464-0006-5). Beekman Pubs.

--A Study of the Early Journalistic Writing of Henry W. Grady. (American Newspapermen 1790-1933 Ser.). 177p. 1974. Repr. of 1927 ed. 14.50x (ISBN 0-8464-0006-5). Beekman Pubs.

GRAEBNER, CLARK, 1943-

McPhee, John. Levels of the Game. 160p. 1969. 9.95 (ISBN 0-374-18568-9); pap. 4.95 (ISBN 0-374-51526-3). FS&G.

GRAEBNER, NORMAN A.

Zwelling, Shomer S. Expansion & Imperialism. LC 75-96840. (William P. Lyons Master's Essay Award Ser). 1970. 3.50 (ISBN 0-8294-0059-1). Loyola.

GRAFF, EVERETT DWIGHT, 1885-1964–LIBRARY

Storm, Colton, ed. Catalogue of the Everett D. Graff Collection of Western Americana. LC 66-20577. (Illus.). 1968. 37.50x (ISBN 0-226-77579-8). U of Chicago Pr.

GRAFFITI

Abel, Ernest L. & Buckley, Barbara E. The Handwriting on the Wall: Toward a Sociology & Psychology of Graffiti. LC 76-50408. (Contributions in Sociology: No. 27). 1977. lib. bdg. 14.50x (ISBN 0-8371-9475-X, AVJ/). Greenwood.

Artic-Waters, Edward, ed. Graffiti du jour: The Graffiti of Iowa. 52p. (Orig.). 1980. pap. 2.95 (ISBN 0-935954-09-0). Beacon Presse IA.

Beach, Mary, ed. Journal for the Protection of All Beings, No. 2. (Illus., Orig.). 1968. pap. 1.50 (ISBN 0-87286-023-X). City Lights.

Cesaretti, Gusmano. Street Writers: A Guided Tour of Chicano Graffiti. (Illus.). 1975. 10.00 (ISBN 0-918226-03-1); pap. 3.95 (ISBN 0-918226-01-5). Acrobat.

Edgerton, William F., ed. Medinet Habu Graffiti. LC 42-23005. (Oriental Institute Pubns. Ser: No. 36). (Illus.). 1937. 40.00x (ISBN 0-226-62133-2). U of Chicago Pr.

Lang, Mabel. Graffiti in the Athenian Agora. (Excavations of the Athenian Agora Picture Bks.: No. 14). (Illus.). 1974. pap. 1.50x (ISBN 0-87661-614-7). Am Sch Athens.

Pritchard, Violet. English Medieval Graffiti. 1967. 47.50 (ISBN 0-521-05998-4). Cambridge U Pr.

Shaw, Susanna. Women in the John. LC 78-53383. 1980. pap. 5.95 (ISBN 0-916870-27-8). Creative Arts Bk.

The Thinking Man's Graffiti. (Illus.). 184p. pap. 2.95 (ISBN 0-685-58406-2). Timco Intl.

GRAFT (IN POLITICS)
see Corruption (In Politics)
GRAFTING
see also Plant Propagation

Allen, Oliver. Pruning & Grafting. Time-Life Books, ed. (Encyclopedia of Gardening). (Illus.). 1979. 12.95 (ISBN 0-8094-2633-1). Time-Life.

The Expert Gardener: A Treatise Containing Certaine Necessary, Secret, & Ordinary Knowledges in Grafting. LC 74-80178. (English Experience Ser.: No. 659). (Illus.). 54p. 1974. Repr. of 1640 ed. 6.00 (ISBN 90-221-0659-4). Walter J Johnson.

Garner, Robert J. The Grafter's Handbook. 4th ed. (Illus.). 1979. 16.95 (ISBN 0-19-520133-7). Oxford U Pr.

Mascall, Leonard. A Booke of the Arte & Manner How to Plant & Graffe All Sortes of Trees. LC 74-80200. (English Experience Ser.: No. 679). 90p. 1974. Repr. of 1572 ed. 13.00 (ISBN 90-221-0679-9). Walter J Johnson.

GRAFTING OF SKIN
see Skin-Grafting
GRAFTON, AUGUSTUS HENRY FITZROY, 3RD DUKE OF, 1735-1811

Grafton, A. H. Autobiography & Political Correspondence. LC 5-875. Repr. of 1898 ed. 28.00 (ISBN 0-527-35150-4). Kraus Repr.

GRAFTON COUNTY, NEW HAMPSHIRE

Cawley, James & Cawley, Margaret. Tales of Old Grafton. LC 73-104. (Illus.). 160p. 1974. 6.95 (ISBN 0-498-01277-8); pap. 2.95 (ISBN 0-498-01389-8). A S Barnes.

GRAHAM, BENJAMIN, 1894-

Harmon, Elmer M. Commodity Reserve Currency. LC 68-59258. (Columbia University Studies in the Social Sciences: No. 599). Repr. of 1959 ed. 15.00 (ISBN 0-404-51599-1). AMS Pr.

GRAHAM, JAMES ROBERT GEORGE, SIR, BART, 1792-1861

Erickson, Arvel B. The Public Career of Sir James Graham. LC 74-382. 433p. 1974. Repr. of 1952 ed. lib. bdg. 20.00x (ISBN 0-8371-7383-3, ERJG). Greenwood.

GRAHAM, MARTHA

Armitage, Merle, ed. Martha Graham: The Early Years. LC 78-17608. (Da Capo Series in Dance). (Illus.). 1978. lib. bdg. 19.50 (ISBN 0-306-79504-3); pap. 5.95 (ISBN 0-306-80084-5). Da Capo.

Graham, Martha. The Notebooks of Martha Graham. LC 72-75416. (Illus.). 1973. 27.50 (ISBN 0-15-167265-2). HarBraceJ.

McDonagh, Don. Martha Graham. 384p. 1975. pap. 1.95 (ISBN 0-445-08358-1). Popular Lib.

Terry, Walter. Frontiers of Dance: The Life of Martha Graham. LC 75-9871. (Women of America Ser.). (Illus.). 160p. (gr. 5-9). 1975. 10.95 (ISBN 0-690-00920-8, TYC-J). Har-Row.

GRAHAM, WILLIAM FRANKLIN, 1918-

Adler, Bill, ed. Wit & Wisdom of Billy Graham. LC 80-65430. 256p. 1981. pap. 5.95 (ISBN 0-915684-61-6). Christian Herald.

Ashman, Chuck. The Gospel According to Billy. 1977. 8.95 (ISBN 0-8184-0251-2). Lyle Stuart.

Brown, Joan W., compiled by. Day-by-Day with Billy Graham. 1978. deluxe ed. 7.95 browncover (ISBN 0-89066-018-2); deluxe ed. 7.95 white cover (ISBN 0-89066-017-4). World Wide Pubs.

--Dia-Tras-Dia Con Billy Graham. Orig. Title: Day by Day with Billy Graham. 1978. 2.90 (ISBN 0-311-40039-6, Edit Mundo). Casa Bautista.

--Day-by-Day with Billy Graham. 1976. pap. 3.95 (ISBN 0-89066-000-X). World Wide Pubs.

Frady, Marshall. Billy Graham: A Biography of American Righteousness. LC 79-9947. 1979. 12.95 (ISBN 0-316-29130-7). Little.

Graham, Mrs. Billy. Our Christmas Story. 1976. pap. 2.95 (ISBN 0-89066-005-0). World Wide Pubs.

Graham, Ruth B. It's My Turn. 192p. 1981. 9.95 (ISBN 0-8007-1274-9). Revell.

Mitchell, Curtis. Billy Graham: Saint or Sinner. 1979. 10.95 (ISBN 0-8007-1048-7); pap. 2.95 (ISBN 0-8007-8387-5, Spire Bks). Revell.

Pollock, John. Billy Graham Biography. LC 66-194605. 1966. pap. 1.50 (ISBN 0-89066-028-X). World Wide Pubs.

--Billy Graham: Evangelist to the World. (Illus.). 1979. 10.00 (ISBN 0-06-066691-9, HarpR). Har-Row.

--Billy Graham-Evangelist to the World: An Authorized Biography. LC 79-62949. (Illus.). 352p. 1980. pap. 4.95 (ISBN 0-06-066692-7, RD 495). Har-Row.

Strober, Gerald S. Graham: A Day in Billy's Life. LC 77-598. (Spring 1977 Inspirational Ser.). 1977. 10.95 (ISBN 0-8161-6468-1, Large Print Books). G K Hall.

Westman, Paul. Billy Graham: Reaching Out to the World. (Taking Part Ser.). (Illus.). 48p. (gr. 3 up). 1981. PLB 6.95 (ISBN 0-87518-220-8). Dillon.

Wilson, Jean. Crusader for Christ (Billy Graham) (gr. 6-9). 1973. pap. 1.95 (ISBN 0-87508-602-0). Chr Lit.

GRAHAM-JONES, OLIVER

Graham-Jones, Oliver. First Catch Your Tiger. LC 72-8320. 1973. 7.95 (ISBN 0-8008-2739-2). Taplinger.

GRAHAME, KENNETH, 1859-1932

Chalmers, Patrick R. Kenneth Grahame: Life, Letters & Unpublished Work. LC 76-160747. (Illus.). 1971. Repr. of 1933 ed. 14.50 (ISBN 0-8046-1560-8). Kennikat.

Little, T. E. The Fantasts: Studies of J. R. R. Tolkien, Lewis Carroll, Mervyn Peake, Nikolay Gogol & Kenneth Grahame. 1981. 50.00x (ISBN 0-86127-212-9, Pub. by Avebury Pub England). State Mutual Bk.

GRAIL

Brown, Arthur C. Origin of the Grail Legend. LC 65-17878. 1966. Repr. of 1943 ed. 14.00 (ISBN 0-8462-0655-2). Russell.

Carter, Henry H. The Portuguese Book of Joseph of Arimathea. (Studies in the Romance Languages & Literatures: No. 71). 1968. pap. 19.00x (ISBN 0-8078-9071-5). U of NC Pr.

Evans, Sabastian, ed. High History of the Holy Grail. (Illus.). 395p. 1969. 12.95 (ISBN 0-227-67727-7). Attic Pr.

Fisher, Lizette A. Mystic Vision in the Grail Legend & in the Divine Comedy. LC 79-168029. Repr. of 1917 ed. 16.50 (ISBN 0-404-02389-4). AMS Pr.

Hall, Manly P. Orders of the Quest - the Holy Grail. 5.75 (ISBN 0-89314-533-5). Philos Res.

Heline, Corinne. Mysteries of the Holy Grail. pap. 3.95 (ISBN 0-87613-015-5). New Age.

Locke, Frederick W. Quest for the Holy Grail. LC 70-181948. (Stanford University. Stanford Studies in Language & Literature: No. 21). Repr. of 1960 ed. 17.50 (ISBN 0-404-51831-1). AMS Pr.

Loomis, Roger S. Wales & the Arthurian Legend. LC 77-6306. 1956. lib. bdg. 25.00 (ISBN 0-8414-5826-X). Folcroft.

Lovelich, Henry. The History of the Holy Grail, Pts. 1-5. Furnivall, F. J., ed. (EETS, ES Ser.: Nos. 20, 28). Repr. of 1875 ed. Pts. I & II. 25.00 (ISBN 0-527-00234-8); Pts. 3-5, 1877 - 1905. 21.00 (ISBN 0-527-00235-6). Kraus Repr.

Matarasso, P. M., tr. Quest of the Holy Grail. (Classics Ser.). 304p. 1969. pap. 2.95 (ISBN 0-14-044220-0). Penguin.

Newstead, Helaine. Bran the Blessed in Arthurian Romance. LC 40-4360. Repr. of 1939 ed. 14.50 (ISBN 0-404-04687-8). AMS Pr.

Nutt, Alfred. Studies on the Legend of the Holy Grail. LC 65-23219. Repr. of 1885 ed. 11.50x (ISBN 0-8154-0167-1). Cooper Sq.

Nutt, Alfred T. Legends of the Holy Grail. LC 78-139176. (Popular Studies in Mythology, Romance & Folklore: No. 14). Repr. of 1902 ed. 5.50 (ISBN 0-404-53514-3). AMS Pr.

Thomas, Edward E. Grail Yoga. (East Ridge Press). 128p. 1978. pap. 3.95 (ISBN 0-914896-28-8). Multimedia.

Waite, Arthur E. Hidden Church of the Holy Graal. 710p. 1975. Repr. of 1909 ed. 12.00 (ISBN 0-911662-54-5). Yoga.

Webb, James, ed. A Quest Anthology. LC 75-36916. (Occult Ser.). 1976. Repr. of 1976 ed. 35.00x (ISBN 0-405-07971-0). Arno.

Weston, Jessie. The Quest of the Holy Grail. LC 72-10823. (Arthurian Legend & Literature Ser., No. 1). 1973. Repr. of 1913 ed. lib. bdg. 49.95 (ISBN 0-8383-0642-X). Haskell.

Weston, Jessie L. From Ritual to Romance. McLaughlin, Mary M., tr. 7.50 (ISBN 0-8446-3162-0). Peter Smith.

--From Ritual to Romance. LC 57-3633. 1957. pap. 2.95 (ISBN 0-385-09334-9, A125, Anch). Doubleday.

GRAIN

see also Cereals As Food;
also names of the various cereal plants, e.g. Corn; Rye; Wheat

Adams, Ruth & Murray, Frank. Seeds, Grains, Nuts. 1.75 (ISBN 0-686-29844-6). Cancer Bk Hse.

Babakina, V. S., ed. Grain & Pulse Crops. 255p. 1981. 60.00x (ISBN 0-686-76641-5, Pub. by Oxford & IBH India). State Mutual Bk.

Bland, Brian F. Crop Production: Cereals & Legumes. 1971. 73.50 (ISBN 0-12-104050-X). Acad Pr.

Broekhuizen, S. & Thran, P., eds. Atlas of the Cereal Growing Areas in Europe. 1969. 107.50 (ISBN 0-444-40819-3). Elsevier.

Brooker, Donald B., et al. Drying Cereal Grains. (Illus.). 1974. text ed. 26.50 (ISBN 0-87055-161-2); pap. 19.50 (ISBN 0-87055-303-8). AVI.

Brown, Lester R. Increasing World Food Output. LC 75-26298. (World Food Supply Ser). (Illus.). 1976. Repr. of 1965 ed. 10.00x (ISBN 0-405-07770-X). Arno.

Bumgarner, Marlene A. Book of Whole Grains. (Illus.). 256p. 1976. pap. 5.95 (ISBN 0-312-09240-7). St Martin.

Bushuk, W. Rye: Production, Chemistry, & Technology. LC 76-29382. (AACC Monograph: No. V). 192p. 1976. text ed. 18.00 (ISBN 0-913250-11-2). Am Assn Cereal Chem.

Cereals: Better Farming Ser. (No. 15). 1979. pap. 4.50 (ISBN 92-5-100150-2, F72, FAO). Unipub.

Fenton, Carroll L. & Kitchen, Hermine B. Plants We Live On: The Story of Grains & Vegetables. rev. ed. LC 78-89322. (Illus.). (gr. 3-6). 1971. PLB 7.89 (ISBN 0-381-99819-3; A61600, JD-J). Har-Row.

Grain Production & Assimilate Utilizatíon of Wheat in Relation to Cultiver Characteristics, Climate Factors & Nitrogen Supply. (Agricultural Research Reports Ser.: No. 881). 1978. pap. 6.00 (ISBN 90-220-0682-4, PDC 133, PUDOC). Unipub.

Grossbard, E., ed. Straw Decay & Its Effect on Disposal & Utilization. LC 79-42841. 337p. 1979. 55.25x (ISBN 0-471-27694-4, Pub. by Wiley Interscience). Wiley.

High-Yielding Varieties of Grain. LC 75-26315. (World Food Supply Ser). (Illus.). 1976. 15.00x (ISBN 0-405-07800-5). Arno.

Hu, H., ed. The Nature & Behavior of Grain Boundaries. LC 72-81907. 440p. 1972. 42.50 (ISBN 0-306-30704-9, Plenum Pr). Plenum Pub.

IMCO Grain Rules. 35p. 1977. 7.00 (ISBN 0-686-70786-9, IMCO). Unipub.

Johnson, D. Gale & Gustafson, Robert L. Grain Yields & the American Food Supply. LC 62-18115. 1962. 6.50x (ISBN 0-226-40236-3). U of Chicago Pr.

Karel, Leonard. Dried Grasses, Grains, Gourds, Pods & Cones. LC 74-31178. (Illus.). 1975. 10.00 (ISBN 0-8108-0792-0). Scarecrow.

Kent, N. L. Technology of Cereals. 2nd ed. LC 75-6654. 320p. 1975. pap. text ed. 14.00 (ISBN 0-08-018177-5). Pergamon.

Knobel, Edward. Field Guide to the Grasses, Sedges & Rushes of the United States. LC 77-72531. (Illus.). 1977. pap. 2.00 (ISBN 0-486-23505-X). Dover.

Laidman, D. L. & Jones, R. G., eds. Recent Advances in the Biochemistry of Cereals. 1979. 56.00 (ISBN 0-12-433950-6). Acad Pr.

Leonard, Warren H. & Martin, John H. Cereal Crops. 1963. text ed. 20.95 (ISBN 0-02-369830-6). Macmillan.

Logsdon, Gene. Small Scale Grain Raising. LC 76-56102. 1977. 9.95 (ISBN 0-87857-134-5); pap. 7.95 (ISBN 0-87857-147-7). Rodale Pr Inc.

National Grain Policies 1975. (Illus.). 271p. 1976. pap. 28.00 (ISBN 92-5-100001-8, F296, FAO). Unipub.

Pomeranz, Y. Advances in Cereal Science & Technology, Vol. II. 463p. 1978. text ed. 32.50 (ISBN 0-913250-08-2). Am Assn Cereal Chem.

Pomeranz, Y., ed. Cereals Seventy-Eight: Better Nutrition for the World's Millions. LC 78-69838. 1978. lib. bdg. 10.00 (ISBN 0-913250-13-9). Am Assn Cereal Chem.

Report of the Twentieth Session of the Intergovernmental Group on Grains to the Committee on Commodity Problems. 30p. 1980. pap. 7.50 (ISBN 92-5-100919-8, F1953, FAO). Unipub.

Seed Protein Improvement in Cereals & Grain Legumes, 2 vols. 1979. pap. 53.75 (ISBN 92-0-010079-1, ISP496-1, IAEA); pap. 59.50 (ISBN 92-0-010179-8, ISP496-2, IAEA). Unipub.

Staniforth, A. R. Cereal Straw. (Illus.). 1980. 45.00x (ISBN 0-19-859466-6). Oxford U Pr.

Thran, P. & Brockhuizen, S., eds. Agro-Ecological Atlas of Cereal Growing in Europe. Incl. Vol. 1. Agro-Climatic Atlas of Europe. 1965. 98.00 (ISBN 0-444-40569-0). Elsevier.

Titow, J. Z. Winchester Yields: A Study in Medieval Agricultural Productivity. LC 72-171685. (Cambridge Studies in Economic History). 1972. 29.50 (ISBN 0-521-08349-4). Cambridge U Pr.

Turnbull, Roderick. Turnbull on Grain. LC 77-93122. 1978. 9.95 (ISBN 0-8134-2014-8, 2014). Interstate.

Wills, Walter J. Introduction to Grain Marketing. LC 74-155289. 155p. 1972. 11.65 (ISBN 0-8134-1299-4, 1299). Interstate.

GRAIN–BREEDING

see also Rice Breeding

Maximizing the Efficiency of Fertilizer Use by Grain Crops. (FAO Fertilizer Bulletin Ser.: No. 3). 30p. 1980. pap. 7.50 (ISBN 92-5-100954-6, F2131, FAO). Unipub.

Nuclear Techniques for Seed Protein Improvement. (Illus.). 442p. (Orig.). 1973. pap. 34.25 (ISBN 92-0-111073-1, ISP320, IAEA). Unipub.

GRAIN–DISEASES AND PESTS

Egerton, Frank N., 3rd, ed. Phytopathological Classics of the Eighteenth Century: An Originial Anthology. LC 77-74247. (History of Ecology Ser.). (Illus.). 1978. lib. bdg. 36.00x (ISBN 0-405-10416-2). Arno.

Graham, et al. A Compendium of Alfalfa Disease. LC 79-88555. (Compendium Ser.: 4). (Illus.). 1979. saddle stitched 9.00 (ISBN 0-89054-026-8). Am Phytopathol Soc.

Jenkyn, J. F. & Plumb, R. T. Strategies for the Control of Cereal Disease: Organized by the British Plant Pathologist, Vol. 2. (Federation of British Plant Pathologists Ser.: Vol. 9). 219p. 1981. 47.50 (ISBN 0-470-27049-7). Halsted Pr.

Shurtleff, M. C. Compendium of Corn Diseases. 2nd ed. LC 80-67517. (Compendium Ser.: No. 1). (Illus.). 124p. 1980. 11.00 (ISBN 0-89054-029-2). Am Phytopathol Soc.

GRAIN–JUVENILE LITERATURE

Brown, Elizabeth B. Grains: An Illustrated History with Recipes. LC 76-10223. (Illus.). (gr. 7 up). 1977. PLB 8.95 (ISBN 0-13-362269-X). P-H.

GRAIN–MILLING

see also Flour; Flour Mills; Milling Machinery

Association of Operative Millers. Cereal Miller's Handbook. 1963. 25.00 (ISBN 0-686-00364-0). AG Pr.

--Technical Bulletins: 1944-1974, Vol. 3. 1975. 25.00 (ISBN 0-686-00376-4). AG Pr.

--Technical Bulletins: 1944-1975, Vol. 4. 1977. 25.00 (ISBN 0-686-00375-6). AG Pr.

Moritz, L. A. Grain-Mills & Flour in Classical Antiquity. Finley, Moses, ed. LC 79-4994. (Ancient Economic History Ser.). (Illus.). 1980. Repr. of 1958 ed. lib. bdg. 21.00x (ISBN 0-405-12381-7). Arno.

GRAIN–STORAGE

Christensen, C. M. Storage of Cereal Grains & Their Products. LC 73-82902. (AACC Monographs: No. II). 568p. 1974. text ed. 32.50 (ISBN 0-913250-05-8). Am Assn Cereal Chem.

Christensen, Clyde M. & Kaufmann, Henry H. Grain Storage: The Role of Fungi in Quality Loss. LC 70-76174. (Illus.). 1969. 10.95x (ISBN 0-8166-0518-1). U of Minn Pr.

Gardner, Bruce. Optimal Stockpiling of Grain. LC 78-24768. 192p. 1979. 21.00 (ISBN 0-669-02829-0). Lexington Bks.

Harris, Kenton L. & Lindblad, Carl L., eds. Postharvest Grain Loss Assessment Methods Manual. LC 78-71322. 1978. lib. bdg. 13.00 (ISBN 0-913250-14-7, Dist. by Volunteers in Technical Assistance). Am Assn Cereal Chem.

Midwest Plan Service Engineers. Structures & Environment Handbook. 10th, rev. ed. Midwest Plan Service Staff, ed. LC 76-27983. (Illus.). 490p. 1980. pap. 12.00 (ISBN 0-686-68276-9, MWPS-1). Midwest Plan Serv.

Midwest Plan Service Personnel. Low Temperature & Solar Grain Drying Handbook. (Illus.). 86p. 1980. pap. 4.00 (ISBN 0-89373-048-3, MWPS-22). Midwest Plan Serv.

Smith, C. V. Meteorology & Grain Storage. (Technical Note Ser.: No. 101). (Illus., Orig.). 1970. pap. 10.00 (ISBN 0-685-22323-X, WMO). Unipub.

Storage of Food Grain: A Guide for Extension Workers. (Illus.). 33p. 1976. pap. 7.50 (ISBN 0-685-66340-X, F1206, FAO). Unipub.

Trezise, Philip H. Rebuilding Grain Reserves: Toward an International System. 1976. pap. 3.95 (ISBN 0-8157-8529-1). Brookings.

GRAIN ELEVATORS

Babb, Emerson M. Purdue Grain Elevator Management Game: Student Manual. 1979. Repr. of 1973 ed. 4.95 (ISBN 0-933836-06-6). Simtek.

Patton, Harold S. Grain Growers' Cooperation in Western Canada. LC 71-100529. Repr. of 1928 ed. 29.50 (ISBN 0-404-00630-2). AMS Pr.

GRAIN PESTS

see Grain–Diseases and Pests

GRAIN SORGHUM

see Sorghum

GRAIN TRADE

see also Wheat Trade

Ainsworth, Ralph M. Grain Trading As a Foundation for Total Futures Trading. (Illus.). 197p. 1980. 79.75 (ISBN 0-918968-74-7). Inst Econ Finan.

--Profitable Grain Trading. LC 80-53316. 256p. 1980. Repr. of 1933 ed. text ed. 25.00 (ISBN 0-934380-04-X). Traders Pr.

Clark, John G. The Grain Trade in the Old Northwest. LC 80-18227. (Illus.). xi, 324p. 1980. Repr. of 1966 ed. lib. bdg. 27.25x (ISBN 0-313-22419-6, CLGT). Greenwood.

Corn Quality in World Markets. Hill, Lowell D., ed. LC 74-24848. 270p. 1975. text ed. 9.75 (ISBN 0-8134-1698-1, 1698). Interstate.

Freivalds, John. Grain Trade: The Key to World Power & Human Survival. LC 76-10134. 1976. 10.95 (ISBN 0-685-70109-3). Stein & Day.

Gardner, Bruce. Optimal Stockpiling of Grain. LC 78-24768. 192p. 1979. 21.00 (ISBN 0-669-02829-0). Lexington Bks.

Gaudemet, Eugene. L' Abbe Galiani (1728-1787) et la Question du Commerce des Bles a la Fin du Regne de Louis-XV. LC 72-87294. 233p. 1972. Repr. of 1899 ed. lib. bdg. 24.00 (ISBN 0-8337-1294-2). B Franklin.

Gras, Norman S. Evolution of the English Corn Market from the Twelfth to the Eighteenth Century. LC 66-27087. 1967. Repr. of 1926 ed. 12.50 (ISBN 0-8462-0934-9). Russell.

Grennes, Thomas, et al. Economics of World Grain Trade. LC 77-13715. (Praeger Special Studies). 1978. 22.95 (ISBN 0-03-022836-0). Praeger.

Hoare, Peter R. Tracts on Our Present Money System & National Bankruptcy. LC 67-27467. Repr. of 1814 ed. 17.50x (ISBN 0-678-00574-5). Kelley.

Johnson, D. Gale. The Soviet Impact on World Grain Trade. LC 77-78146. 72p. 1977. 3.00 (ISBN 0-902594-30-3). Natl Planning.

Klingaman, David C. Colonial Virginia's Coastwise & Grain Trade. new ed. LC 75-2584. (Dissertations in American Economic History). (Illus.). 1975. 13.00x (ISBN 0-405-07204-X). Arno.

Lele, Uma J. Food Grain Marketing in India: Private Performance & Public Policy. LC 75-146111. (Illus.). 1971. 32.50x (ISBN 0-8014-0618-8). Cornell U Pr.

Morgan, Dan. Merchants of Grain. 1979. 14.95 (ISBN 0-670-47150-X). Viking Pr.

Morgan, Daniel. Merchants of Grain. 1980. pap. 3.95 (ISBN 0-14-005502-9). Penguin.

National Grain Policies. annual Incl. 1963. pap. 4.50 (ISBN 0-685-48309-6, F288); 1964. pap. 4.50 (ISBN 0-685-48310-X, F289); 1966. pap. 4.75 (ISBN 0-685-48311-8, F290); 1967. pap. 7.25 (ISBN 0-685-48312-6, F291); 1968. pap. 7.25 (ISBN 0-685-48313-4, F292); 1969. pap. 12.25 (ISBN 0-685-48314-2, F293); 1970 Supplement. pap. 6.75 (ISBN 0-685-48315-0, F294); 1972. pap. 9.25 (ISBN 0-685-48316-9, F295). (Orig., FAO). Unipub.

Patton, Harold S. Grain Growers' Cooperation in Western Canada. LC 71-100529. Repr. of 1928 ed. 29.50 (ISBN 0-404-00630-2). AMS Pr.

Schonberg, James. The Grain Trade, How It Works. 1956. text ed. 15.00 (ISBN 0-682-40084-X, University). Exposition.

--The Grain Trade, How It Works. 1956. text ed. 15.00 (ISBN 0-682-40084-X, University). Exposition.

The Stabilization of World Trade in Course Grains: A Consideration of the Underlying Economic Issues. (FAO Commodity Policy Studies: No. 14). (Orig.). 1963. pap. 10.00 (ISBN 0-685-09407-3, F439, FAO). Unipub.

Torrens, Robert. Essay on the External Corn Trade. new ed. LC 68-58037. Repr. of 1829 ed. 19.50x (ISBN 0-678-00751-9). Kelley.

Usher, Abbot P. The History of the Grain Trade in France, 1400-1710. LC 73-159234. 405p. 1973. Repr. of 1913 ed. lib. bdg. 22.50x (ISBN 0-374-98063-2). Octagon.

Wills, Walter J. Introduction to Grain Marketing. LC 74-155289. 155p. 1972. 11.65 (ISBN 0-8134-1299-4, 1299). Interstate.

World Grain Trade Statistics: Exports by Source & Destination. annual Incl. 1959-60. 1960. pap. 4.50 (ISBN 0-685-48253-7, F510); 1961-62. 1962. pap. 4.50 (ISBN 0-685-48254-5, F512); 1963-64. 1964. pap. 2.25 (ISBN 0-685-48255-3); 1964-65. 1966. pap. 4.75 (ISBN 0-685-48256-1, F514); 1965-66. 1967. pap. 4.50 (ISBN 0-685-48257-X, F513); 1966-67. 1968. pap. 4.50 (ISBN 0-685-48258-8, F510); 1968-69. 1970. pap. 4.50 (ISBN 0-685-48259-6, F518); 1969-70. 1971. pap. 6.25 (ISBN 0-685-48260-X, F519); 1970-71. 1972. pap. 7.50 (ISBN 0-685-48261-8, F520); 1971-72. 1973. pap. 6.75 (ISBN 0-685-48262-6, F521). (Orig.). (FAO). Unipub.

World Grain Trade Statistics: Exports by Source & Destination, 1972-73. 78p. (Orig.). 1974. pap. 9.25 (ISBN 0-685-51119-7, F522, FAO). Unipub.

World Grain Trade Statistics, 1973-1974: Exports by Source & Destination. (Illus.). 78p. 1975. pap. 9.00 (ISBN 0-685-54195-9, 523, FAO). Unipub.

GRAIN TRIBUTE (CHINA)

Hinton, Harold C. Grain Tribute System of China, Eighteen Forty-Five to Nineteen Eleven. rev. ed. LC 56-14273. (East Asian Monographs Ser: No. 2). 1956. 9.00x (ISBN 0-674-36025-7). Harvard U Pr.

Hoshi Ayao. The Ming Tribute Grain System. Elvin, Mark, tr. from Japanese. (Michigan Abstracts of Chinese & Japanese Works in Chinese History Ser.: No. 1). (Illus.). 112p. 1970. pap. 2.00 (ISBN 0-89264-901-1). U of Mich Ctr Chinese.

GRAINING

see also Painting, Industrial

GRAMMAR

see Grammar, Comparative and General;
also subdivision Grammar under names of languages, e.g. English Language–Grammar

GRAMMAR, COMPARATIVE AND GENERAL

see also Generative Grammar; Language and Languages; Phonemics

Abraham, Werner, ed. Valence Semantic Case & Grammatical Relations. xiv, 729p. 1978. 46.00 (ISBN 90-272096-2-6, SLCS1). Benjamins North Am.

Akmajian, Adrian. Aspects of the Grammar of Focus in English. Hankamer, Jorge, ed. LC 78-66534. (Outstanding Dissertations in Linguistics Ser.). 1979. lib. bdg. 37.50 (ISBN 0-8240-9691-6). Garland Pub.

Alarie, Julia & Conlon, Elizabeth. Green Thumb Grammar: Teaching Parts of Speech with Indoor Plants. (Illus.). 28p. (Orig.). (gr. 4-6). 1981. pap. text ed. 4.50 (ISBN 0-686-76454-4). Monkey Sisters.

Allen, James P. The Inflection of the Verb in the Pyramid Texts. (Bibliotheca Aegyptia: Vol. 2). 1981. write for info. (ISBN 0-89003-086-3); pap. write for info. (ISBN 0-89003-087-1). Undena Pubns.

Arndt, Walter W., et al, eds. Studies in Historical Linguistics in Honor of George Sherman Lane. (Studies in the Germanic Languages & Literatures Ser.: No. 58). 1967. 17.00x (ISBN 0-8078-8058-2). U of NC Pr.

Bacher, Wilhelm. Die Anfange der Hebraischen Grammatik (1895) Together with Die Hebraische Sprachwissenschaft Vom 10. Bis Zum 16. Jahrhundert (1892) xix, 235p. 1974. 39.00 (ISBN 90-272-0895-6, SIHOL 4); pap. 35.00 (ISBN 0-686-31496-4). Benjamins North Am.

Ballard, D. Lee, et al. More on the Deep & Surface Grammar of Interclausal Relations. (Language Data, Asian-Pacific Ser: No. 1). 61p. 1971. pap. 2.50 (ISBN 0-88312-201-4); microfiche 1.00 (ISBN 0-88312-301-0). Summer Inst Ling.

Ballmer, T. Logical Grammar. (North Holland Linguistic Ser.: Vol. 39). 1978. 42.75 (ISBN 0-444-85205-0, North Holland). Elsevier.

Bartholomew, Doris. A Manual for Practical Grammars. 44p. 1976. pap. 4.00x (ISBN 0-685-51606-7). Summer Inst Ling.

Bartlett, Barrie E. Beauzee's Grammaire Generale: Theory & Methodology. LC 74-81133. (Janua Linguarum Series Maior: No. 82). 202p. 1975. text ed. 45.00x (ISBN 90-2793-433-9). Mouton.

Beattie, James. Theory of Language, Pts. 1 & 2. LC 78-147953. Repr. of 1788 ed. 36.50 (ISBN 0-404-08201-7). AMS Pr.

Bell, A. & Hooper, J. B., eds. Syllables & Segments. (North Holland Linguistic Ser.: Vol. 40). 1978. 27.00 (ISBN 0-444-85241-7, North Holland). Elsevier.

Bohusch, Otmar. Lexikon der Grammatischen Terminologie. (Ger.). 1972. 19.95 (ISBN 3-403-00298-5, M-7254). French & Eur.

Botha, Rudolf P. The Justification of Linguistic Hypotheses. (Janua Linguarum Ser.Maior: No. 84). 1973. text ed. 57.65x (ISBN 90-2792-542-9). Mouton.
Bowers, John S. The Theory of Grammatical Relations. LC 80-21018. 304p. 1981. 24.50x (ISBN 0-8014-1079-7). Cornell U Pr.
Bresnan, Joan, ed. The Mental Representation of Grammatical Relations. (Cognitive Theory & Mental Representation Ser.: Vol. 1). 700p. 1981. text ed. 35.00x (ISBN 0-262-02158-7). MIT Pr.
Bursill-Hall, G. L. Speculative Grammars of the Middle Ages: The Doctrine of Partes Orationis of the Modistae. LC 70-151246. (Approaches to Semiotics Ser: No. 11). 424p. 1971. text ed. 70.00x (ISBN 90-2791-913-5). Mouton.
Cassidy, F. G. & Duckert, A. R. A Method for Collecting Dialect. (Publications of the American Dialect Society: No. 20). 96p. 1970. pap. 2.50x (ISBN 0-8173-0620-X). U of Ala Pr.
Chomsky, Noam. Essays on Form & Interpretation. (Studies in Linguistic Analysis). 1977. 14.95 (ISBN 0-7204-8615-7, North-Holland). Elsevier.
--The Logical Structure of Linguistic Theory. LC 75-26985. (Illus.). 573p. 1975. 35.00 (ISBN 0-306-30760-X, Plenum Pr). Plenum Pub.
Clifford, John E. Tense & Tense Logic. (Janua Linguarum, Ser. Minor: No. 215). 173p. (Orig.). 1975. pap. text ed. 28.75x (ISBN 90-2793-453-3). Mouton.
Collinson, William E. & Morris, A. V. Indication: A Study of Demonstratives, Articles & Other Indicators. 1937. pap. 6.00 (ISBN 0-527-00821-4). Kraus Repr.
Conference of Linguists. 12th. Valence, Semantic Case & Grammatical Relations. Workshop Studies: Proceedings. Abraham, Werner, ed. (Studies in Language Companion: No. 1). 1978. text ed. 55.00x (ISBN 0-391-01270-3). Humanities.
Cook, Walter A. Case Grammar: Development of the Matrix Model (1970-1976) LC 79-11067. 223p. 1979. pap. text ed. 7.95 (ISBN 0-87840-174-1). Georgetown U Pr.
Cowan, Marian M. Tzotzil Grammar. (Publications in Linguistics & Related Fields Ser.: No. 18). 119p. 1969. pap. 2.25x (ISBN 0-88312-020-8); microfiche 1.60 (ISBN 0-88312-420-3). Summer Inst Ling.
Davis, Marianna W. Transformational Grammar & Written Sentences. (Janua Linguarum Ser. Didactica: No. 2). 1973. pap. text ed. 16.25x (ISBN 90-2792-384-1). Mouton.
Davis, Philip W. Modern Theories of Language. (Illus.). 496p. 1973. 15.95 (ISBN 0-13-598987-6). P-H.
Davis, Steven & Mithun, Marianne, eds. Linguistics, Philosophy, & Montague Grammar. 354p. 1979. text ed. 19.95x (ISBN 0-292-74625-3). U of Tex Pr.
Dearborn, Benjamin. The Columbian Grammar. 59.95 (ISBN 0-87968-909-9). Gordon Pr.
Decker, Clarabelle D. Common-Sense English Grammar. 1980. Index. 5.00 (ISBN 0-682-49578-6). Exposition.
DeMaria, Robert. The Language of Grammar. LC 63-15677. 1973. 7.95 (ISBN 0-88427-008-4); pap. text ed. 5.95 (ISBN 0-88427-009-2, Dist. by Caroline House Pubs). North River.
Deszoe, Laslo. Studies on Syntactic Topology & Contrastive Grammar. (Janua Linguarum, Series Practica). 1979. pap. text ed. 27.75x (ISBN 90-279-3108-9). Mouton.
Earle, J. A Simple Grammar of English Now in Use. 1898. 12.50 (ISBN 0-8274-3414-6). R West.
Edwards, R., et al. Target Mechanics: Guides for Capitalization, Punctuation. 1976. tchr's. ed. 290.00 (ISBN 0-201-46622-8, Sch Div); target usage kit avail. (46600); dupe masters avail. A-W.
Elimelech, Baruch. A Tonal Grammar of Etsako. (Publications in Linguistics Ser.: Vol. 87). 1979. 11.50x (ISBN 0-520-09576-6). U of Cal Pr.
Ellis, Jeffrey. Towards a General Comparative Linguistics. (Janua Linguarum, Ser. Minor: No. 52). (Orig.). 1966. pap. text ed. 26.25x (ISBN 90-2790-584-3). Mouton.
Fenollosa, Ernest. Chinese Written Character As a Medium for Poetry. Pound, Ezra, ed. 1963. pap. 2.00 (ISBN 0-87286-014-0). City Lights.
Frantz, Donald G. Toward a Generative Grammar of Blackfoot. (Publications in Linguistics & Related Fields Ser.: No. 34). 151p. 1971. microfiche 1.60 (ISBN 0-88312-436-X). Summer Inst Ling.
Givon, Talmy. On Understanding Grammar. (Perspectives in Neurolinguistics & Psycholinguistics Ser.). 1979. 26.00 (ISBN 0-12-285450-0). Acad Pr.
Gould, Gerald. Groundwork: Exercises in Perceiving & Understanding Grammar. 1977. pap. text ed. 9.95 (ISBN 0-15-529695-7, HC). HarBraceJ.
Gray, B. Grammatical Foundations of Rhetoric. (Janua Linguarum Ser. Major: No. 51). 1977. 50.00 (ISBN 90-279-7915-4). Mouton.
Green, Georgia M. Semantics & Syntactic Regularity. LC 74-9947. 256p. 1974. 12.50x (ISBN 0-253-35160-X). Ind U Pr.
Greenbaum, S. Acceptability in Language. (Contributions to the Sociology of Langauge Ser.: No. 17). 1977. 17.75x (ISBN 90-279-7623-6). Mouton.
Gross, M. & Lentin, A. Introduction to Formal Grammars. Salkoff, M., tr. LC 76-98261. (Illus.). 1970. 26.30 (ISBN 0-387-04827-8). Springer-Verlag.
Harrison, Sheldon P. Mokilese Reference Grammar. LC 76-2687. (Pali Language Texts: Micronesia). 1976. pap. text ed. 14.50x (ISBN 0-8248-0412-0). U Pr of Hawaii.
Hatcher, A. G. Reflexive Verbs, Latin, Old French, Modern French. 1973. Repr. of 1942 ed. 15.50 (ISBN 0-384-21765-6). Johnson Repr.
Heatwole, O. W. A Comparative Practical Grammar of French, Spanish & Italian. 1977. 8.95x (ISBN 0-913298-39-5); pap. 6.50 (ISBN 0-913298-26-3). S F Vanni.
Hendricks, W. Grammars of Style & Styles of Grammar. (Studies in Theoretical Poetics: Vol. 3). 1976. pap. 24.50 (ISBN 0-444-11095-X, North-Holland). Elsevier.
Holisky, Dee A. Aspect & the Georgian Medieval Verbs. 1981. price not set (ISBN 0-88206-046-5). Caravan Bks.
Huang, Shuan-Fan. A Study of Adverbs. (Janua Linguarum, Ser. Minor: No. 213). 96p. (Orig.). 1975. pap. text ed. 17.00x (ISBN 90-2793-363-4). Mouton.
Hudson, J. The Core of Walmatjari Grammar. (AIAS New Ser.: No. 2). (Illus.). 1978. pap. text ed. 12.50x (ISBN 0-391-00971-0). Humanities.
Hunt, R. W. The History of Grammar in the Middle Ages. Bursell-Hall, G. L., ed. xxxvi, 214p. 1980. 25.00 (ISBN 90-272-0896-4, SIHOL 5). Benjamins North Am.
Hurford, J. R. The Linguistic Theory of Numerals. LC 74-25652. (Studies in Linguistics: No. 16). 260p. 1975. 42.50 (ISBN 0-521-20735-5). Cambridge U Pr.
Ibrahim, Muhammad H. Grammatical Gender. (Janua Linguarum Ser.: No. 166). 1973. pap. 17.00x (ISBN 0-686-21237-1). Mouton.
Jespersen, Otto. Philosophy of Grammar. (Illus.). 1965. pap. 7.95 (ISBN 0-393-00307-8, Norton Lib.). Norton.
--The Philosophy of Grammar. 1924. text ed. 25.00x (ISBN 0-04-400009-X). Allen Unwin.
Johnson, David E. Toward a Theory of Rationally Based Grammar. Hankamer, Jorge, ed. LC 78-66553. (Outstanding Dissertations in Linguistics Ser.). 1979. lib. bdg. 21.00 (ISBN 0-8240-9682-7). Garland Pub.
Johnson, Oscar E. Tense Significance As the Time of the Action. 1936. pap. 6.00 (ISBN 0-527-00767-6). Kraus Repr.
Kac, Michael B. Corepresentation of Grammatical Structure. LC 77-75632. 1978. 15.00x (ISBN 0-8166-0810-5). U of Minn Pr.
Karmiloff-Smith, A. A Functional Approach to Child Language. LC 78-15450. (Cambridge Studies in Linguistics: No. 24). (Illus.). 1979. 29.95 (ISBN 0-521-22416-0). Cambridge U Pr.
Katicic, Radoslav. Contribution to the General Theory of Comparative Linguistics. LC 77-110956. (Janua Linguarum, Ser. Minor: No. 83). (Orig.). 1970. pap. text ed. 20.00x (ISBN 0-686-22411-6). Mouton.
Kilbury, James. The Development of Morphophonemic Theory. viii, 155p. 1976. 19.00 (ISBN 90-272-0953-7, SIHOL 10). Benjamins No Rth Am.
Kolbe, F. W. Language-Study Based on Bantu. facs. ed. LC 78-154081. (Black Heritage Library Collection Ser). 1888. 12.75 (ISBN 0-8369-8792-6). Arno.
Kramsky, Jiri. The Article & the Concept of Definiteness in Language. (Janua Linguarum, Ser. Minor: No. 125). 1972. pap. text ed. 30.00x (ISBN 90-2792-119-9). Mouton.
--Word As a Linguistic Unit. LC 79-89794. (Janua Linguarum, Ser. Minor: No. 75). (Orig.). 1969. pap. text ed. 13.75x (ISBN 0-686-22423-X). Mouton.
Lehrberger, John. Functor Analysis of Natural Language. LC 74-82387. (Janua Linguarum, Ser. Minor: No. 197). 155p. 1974. pap. text ed. 27.50x (ISBN 90-2793-342-1). Mouton.
Leonard, Laurence B. Meaning in Child Language. LC 76-45665. 272p. 1976. 29.50 (ISBN 0-8089-0977-0). Grune.
Levin, Samuel R. The Semantics of Metaphor. LC 77-4550. (Illus.). 1977. text ed. 12.00x (ISBN 0-8018-1981-4). Johns Hopkins.
Lloyd, Albert L. Anatomy of the Verb: The Gothic Verb As a Model for a Unified Theory of Aspect, Actional Types, & Verbal Velocity. x, 351p. 1979. 32.00 (ISBN 90-272-3003-X, SLCS 4). Benjamins North Am.
Longacre, Robert E. Grammar Discovery Procedures: A Field Manual. (Janua Linguarum Ser. Minor: No. 33). (Orig.). 1964. pap. text ed. 17.00x (ISBN 90-2792-431-7). Mouton.
Loos, Eugene E. Phonology of Capanahua & Its Grammatical Basis. (Publications in Linguistics & Related Fields Ser.: No. 20). 233p. 1969. pap. 3.50x (ISBN 0-88312-022-4); microfiche 2.20 (ISBN 0-88312-422-X). Summer Inst Ling.
Lyons, J. Semantics One. LC 76-40838. (Illus.). 1977. 42.50 (ISBN 0-521-21473-4); pap. 11.95x (ISBN 0-521-29165-8). Cambridge U Pr.
Lyons, John. Introduction to Theoretical Linguistics. (Illus., Orig.). 1968. 49.50 (ISBN 0-521-05617-9); pap. text ed. 13.95x (ISBN 0-521-09510-7). Cambridge U Pr.
McDavid, Raven I. Dialects in Culture. 432p. 1979. 22.75x (ISBN 0-8173-0501-7). U of Ala Pr.
McMahon, W. E. Hans Reichenbach's Philosophy of Grammer. (Janua Linguarum Ser: No. 90). 284p. 1976. text ed. 64.00x (ISBN 90-2793-204-2). Mouton.
Matthews, P. H. Morphology: An Introduction to the Theory of Word-Structure. LC 73-91817. (Cambridge Textbooks in Linguistics Ser.). 256p. 1974. 37.50 (ISBN 0-521-20448-8); pap. 9.95x (ISBN 0-521-09856-4). Cambridge U Pr.
Merrifield, William R. Palantla Chinantec Grammar. 127p. 1968. pap. 1.50x (ISBN 0-88312-794-6); microfiche 1.60 (ISBN 0-88312-359-2). Summer Inst Ling.
Meyerstein, R. S. Reduction in Language. LC 73-92545. (Janua Linguarum, Ser. Minor: No. 53). 212p. (Orig.). 1974. pap. text ed. 32.50x (ISBN 0-686-22576-7). Mouton.
Nida, Eugene A. Morphology: The Descriptive Analysis of Words. 2nd ed. 1949. pap. 7.95x (ISBN 0-472-08684-7). U of Mich Pr.
Nilsen, Don L. Toward a Semantic Specification of Deep Case. (Janua Linguarum, Ser. Minor: No. 152). 52p. (Orig.). 1972. text ed. 11.25x (ISBN 90-2792-318-3). Mouton.
Padley, G. A. Grammatical Theory in Western Europe 1500-1700. LC 75-44573. 320p. 1976. 47.50 (ISBN 0-521-21079-8). Cambridge U Pr.
Paetow, L. J. The Arts Course at Medieval Universities with Special Reference to Grammar & Rhetoric. (Medieval Studies Ser.). Repr. of 1910 ed. lib. bdg. 24.50x (ISBN 0-697-00015-X). Irvington.
Panfilov, V. Z. Grammar & Logic. LC 68-15535. (Janua Linguarum, Ser. Minor: No. 63). (Orig.). 1968. pap. text ed. 17.50x (ISBN 90-2790-591-6). Mouton.
Parisi, D. & Antinucci, F. Essentials of Grammar. (Language, Thought & Culture Ser.). 1976. 20.00 (ISBN 0-12-544650-0). Acad Pr.
Peeke, Catherine. Preliminary Grammar of Auca. (Publications in Linguistics & Related Fields Ser.: No. 39). 1973. pap. 6.00x (ISBN 0-88312-041-0); microfiche 1.50 (ISBN 0-88312-441-6). Summer Inst Ling.
Pei, Mario A. Glossary of Linguistic Terminology. LC 66-21013. 299p. 1966. 20.00x (ISBN 0-231-03012-6). Columbia U Pr.
Pike, K. L. & Pike, E. G. Grammatical Analysis. rev. ed. (Publications in Linguistics & Related Fields Ser.: No. 51). 1981. pap. 15.00x (ISBN 0-88312-066-6); microfiche 4.00 (ISBN 0-686-67824-9). Summer Inst Ling.
Pike, Kenneth L. & Pike, Evelyn. Instructors Guide to Grammatical Analysis. 1977. instructor's guide 16.00x (ISBN 0-88312-910-8). Summer Inst Ling.
Pulgram, Ernst. Syllable, Word, Nexus, Cursus. (Janua Linguarum Ser: No. 81). 1970. pap. text ed. 18.75x (ISBN 90-2790-706-4). Mouton.
Pullum, Geoffrey K. Rule Interaction & the Organization of a Grammar. Hankamer, Jorge, ed. LC 78-64618. (Outstanding Dissertations in Linguistics Ser.). 1979. lib. bdg. 44.00 (ISBN 0-8240-9668-1). Garland Pub.
Robbins, Frank E. Quiotepec Chinantec Grammar. 150p. 1968. pap. 1.50x (ISBN 0-88312-799-7). Summer Inst Ling.
Robins, Robert H. Ancient & Mediaeval Grammatical Theory in Europe. LC 71-113296. (Classics Ser). 1971. Repr. of 1951 ed. 10.50 (ISBN 0-8046-1202-1). Kennikat.
Rosenberg, Sheldon, ed. Sentence Production: Developments in Research & Theory. LC 77-1754. 1977. 17.95 (ISBN 0-470-99114-3). Halsted Pr.
Ross, Gregory A. Grounds for Grammar. 1976. pap. text ed. 7.50 (ISBN 0-8191-0063-3). U Pr of Amer.
Schachter, J. Prolegomena to a Critical Grammar. Foulkes, P., tr. from Ger. LC 72-77879. (Vienna Circle Collection Ser: Vol. 2). Orig. Title: Prolegomena Zu Einer Kritischen Grammatik. 161p. 1973. lib. bdg. 29.00 (ISBN 90-277-0296-9, Pub. by Reidel Holland); pap. text ed. 16.00 (ISBN 90-277-0301-9, Pub. by Reidel Holland). Kluwer Boston.
Schank, R. C. Conceptual Information Processing. LC 74-84874. (Fundamental Studies in Computer Science: Vol. 3). 374p. 1975. 36.75 (ISBN 0-444-10773-8, North-Holland). Elsevier.
Starck, E. L. Grammar & Language. 1887. 12.50 (ISBN 0-8274-2434-5). R West.
Strong, Herbert A., et al. Introduction to the Study of the History of Language. LC 74-147995. Repr. of 1891 ed. 25.00 (ISBN 0-404-08238-6). AMS Pr.
Tanz, Christine. Studies in the Acquisition of Deictic Terms. LC 79-12272. (Cambridge Studies in Linguistics: No. 26). (Illus.). 1980. 32.50 (ISBN 0-521-22740-2). Cambridge U Pr.
Tripp, Raymond, Jr. & Johnson, William, Jr. The Ladder of Language: An Introductory Structural Grammar. 1973. write for info. Soc New Lang Study.
Turner, L. D. Notes on the Sounds & Vocabulary of Gullah. (Publications of the American Dialect Society: No. 3). 28p. 1945. pap. 2.50x (ISBN 0-8173-0603-X). U of Ala Pr.
Vestergaard, T. Prepositional Phrases & Prepositional Verbs: A Study in Grammatical Function. (Janua Linguarum, Ser. Minor: No. 161). 1977. 24.50x (ISBN 90-279-7616-3). Mouton.
Wilson, G. P. Instructions to Collectors of Dialect. (Publications of the American Dialect Society: No. 1). 1944. pap. 1.50x (ISBN 0-8173-0601-3). U of Ala Pr.
Wilson, Saul & Wilson, Frieberger. Nung Grammar. (SIL Publications in Linguistics Ser.). 150p. 1980. pap. 8.50x (ISBN 0-88312-081-X); microfiche 1.60 (ISBN 0-88312-481-5). Summer Inst Ling.
Wittgenstein, Ludwig. Philosophical Grammar. Kenny, A. J., tr. 1974. 32.50x (ISBN 0-520-02664-0); pap. 6.95 (ISBN 0-520-03725-1). U of Cal Pr.
Young, R. A. The Verb in Bena-Bena: Its Form & Function. v, 68p. 1971. pap. 1.85x (ISBN 0-88312-651-6). Summer Inst Ling.

GRAMMAR, COMPARATIVE AND GENERAL–PHONOLOGY

Arnason, K. Quantity in Historical Phonology. LC 79-41363. (Cambridge Studies in Linguistics: No. 30). (Illus.). 256p. 1980. 44.50 (ISBN 0-521-23040-3). Cambridge U Pr.
Augerot, James E. Romanian Phonology. 1974. 2.50 (ISBN 0-89301-010-3). U Pr of Idaho.
Dalgarno, George. Works of George Dalgarno of Aberdeen. Maitland, Thomas, ed. LC 74-165338. (Maitland Club, Glasgow. Publications: No. 29). Repr. of 1834 ed. 16.75 (ISBN 0-404-52987-9). AMS Pr.
Dell, F. Generative Phonology. LC 79-14139. (Illus.). 1980. 42.50 (ISBN 0-521-22484-5); pap. 9.95x (ISBN 0-521-29519-X). Cambridge U Pr.
Dinnsen, Daniel A., ed. Current Approaches to Phonological Theory. LC 78-3241. 352p. 1979. 22.50x (ISBN 0-253-31596-4). Ind U Pr.
Dressler, Wolfgang U. Morphonology: The Dynamics of Derivation. (Linguistica Extranea: Studia: No. 12). 250p. 13.50 (ISBN 0-89720-034-9); pap. 10.50 (ISBN 0-89720-035-7). Karoma.
Elson, Benjamin & Pickett, Velma. An Introduction to Morphology & Syntax. 167p. 1967. pap. 4.50 (ISBN 0-88312-901-9). Summer Inst Ling.
Fisiak, Jacek, ed. Recent Developments in Historical Phonology. (Trends in Linguistics Ser.). 1978. pap. text ed. 69.50x (ISBN 90-279-7706-2). Mouton.
Foley, James. Foundations of Theoretical Phonology. LC 76-27904. (Cambridge Studies in Linguistics Monographs: No. 2). 1977. 26.95 (ISBN 0-521-21466-1). Cambridge U Pr.
Goldsmith, John A. Autosegmental Phonology. Hankamer, Jorge, ed. LC 78-67735. (Outstanding Dissertations in Linguistics Ser.). 1979. lib. bdg. 22.00 (ISBN 0-8240-9673-8). Garland Pub.
Goyvaerts, D. Phonology of the Nineteen Eighties. (Story-Scientia Linguistics Ser.: No. 4). 1980. text ed. write for info. (ISBN 90-6439-150-5). Humanities.
Goyvaerts, Didier. Aspects of Post-SPE Phonology. (Illus.). 1979. pap. text ed. 33.50x (ISBN 0-391-01602-4). Humanities.
Grayshon, M. Towards a Social Grammar of Language. 1977. 15.50x (ISBN 90-279-7633-3). Mouton.
Grunwell, P. The Nature of Phonological Disability in Children. (Studies in Applied Linguistics). 256p. 1981. 31.00 (ISBN 0-12-305250-5). Acad Pr.
Hodson, Barbara W. The Assessment of Phonological Processes. (Illus.). 52p. pap. 24.95 (ISBN 0-8134-2123-3). Interstate.
Hyman, Larry M. Phonology: Theory & Analysis. LC 74-32172. 1975. pap. text ed. 13.95 (ISBN 0-03-012141-8, HoltC). HR&W.
Jakobson, Roman & Waugh, Linda R. The Sound Shape of Language. LC 78-19552. (Illus.). 352p. 1979. 17.50x (ISBN 0-253-16417-6). Ind U Pr.

Johnson, C. Douglas. Formal Aspects of Phonological Description. LC 79-190146. (Linguistic Analysis Monographs Ser: No. 3). (Illus.). 125p. (Orig.). 1972. pap. text ed. 20.75x (ISBN 90-2792-217-9). Mouton.

Kenstowicz, Michael & Kisseberth, Charles. Generative Phonology: Description & Theory. LC 79-319. 1979. 34.50 (ISBN 0-12-405160-X). Acad Pr.

Lehiste, Ilse. Suprasegmentals. 1970. 15.00x (ISBN 0-262-12023-2). MIT Pr.

Linell, Per. Psychological Reality in Phonology. LC 78-67429. (Cambridge Studies in Linguistics: No. 25). (Illus.). 1979. 44.50 (ISBN 0-521-22234-6). Cambridge U Pr.

Loos, Eugene, ed. Materiales Para Estudios Fonologicos, 2 vols. (Documentos Del Trabajo (Peru): No. 9). Set. pap. 17.50 (ISBN 0-88312-787-3); microfiche 4.00 (ISBN 0-88312-355-X). Summer Inst Ling.

McEarthron, Margaret. A Phonics Primer for Teens & Adults (for the Reading Helper) rev ed. Incl. Bk. 1. Helper's Instruction Book. 160p. pap. 9.95 (ISBN 0-9604388-1-5); Bk. 2. Student's Account Book. 120p. wkbk. 4.95 (ISBN 0-9604388-2-3). (Illus., Orig.). (gr. 4 up). 1980. Set. pap. 14.90 (ISBN 0-9604388-0-7). Reading Hse.

Makkai, Valerie B. Phonological Theory: Evolution & Current Practice. LC 76-138654. xii, 711p. 1978. pap. text ed. 15.00x (ISBN 0-933104-05-7). Jupiter Pr.

Markey, T. L., ed. & tr. from Swedish. On Dating Phonological Change: A Miscellany of Articles by Lennart Moberg, Axel Kock, and Ernst Wigforss. (Linguistica Extranea Ser.: Studia 1). 113p. 1978. lib. bdg. 8.25 (ISBN 0-89720-002-0); pap. 5.50 (ISBN 0-89720-000-4). Karoma.

Merrifield, William, et al. Laboratory Manual for Morphology & Syntax. 183p. 1965. pap. 7.00 (ISBN 0-88312-902-7). Summer Inst Ling.

Sapir, E. Notes on Chasta Costa Phonology & Morphology. (Anthropological Publications Ser.: Vol. 2-2). (Illus.). 1914. 2.00 (ISBN 0-686-24092-8). Univ Mus of U.

Saumjan, S. K. Problems of Theoretical Phonology. Vanek, Anthony L., tr. LC 68-17897. (Janua Linguarum Ser.: No. 41). (Orig.). 1968. pap. text ed. 30.00x (ISBN 90-2790-576-2). Mouton.

Schnitzer, Marc L. Generative Phonology: Evidence from Phonology. new ed. (Penn State Studies: No. 34). 1972. pap. text ed. 3.50 (ISBN 0-271-00517-3). Pa St U Pr.

Sloat, Clarence, et al. Introduction to Phonology. LC 77-23100. (Illus.). 1978. ref. 13.95 (ISBN 0-13-492207-7). P-H.

Sommerstein, Alan H. Modern Phonology. LC 77-12173. (Theoretical Linguistics Ser: Vol. 2). 1978. pap. 19.95 (ISBN 0-8391-1172-X). Univ Park.

Stampe, David. A Dissertation on Natural Phonology. Hankamer, Jorge, ed. LC 78-66538. (Outstanding Dissertations in Linguistics Ser.). 1979. lib. bdg. 16.50 (ISBN 0-8240-9674-6). Garland Pub.

Trubetzkoy, N. S. Principles of Phonology. Baltaxe, Christiane A., tr. LC 68-16112. 1969. 31.50x (ISBN 0-520-01535-5). U of Cal Pr.

Trubetzkoy, N. S., et al. Etudes Phonologiques Dediees a la Memoire De M. le Prince N. S. Trubetzkoy. LC 66-63491. (Alabama Linguistic & Philological Ser: No. 2). (Bilingual Fr, & Ger). 1964. 19.95x (ISBN 0-8173-0150-X). U of Ala Pr.

Wang, W. The Lexicon in Phonological Change. (Monographs on Linguistics Analysis: No. 5). 1977. 62.00 (ISBN 90-279-7814-X). Mouton.

Weidert, Alfons. Componential Analysis of Lushai Phonology. xiv, 139p. 1975. 23.00 (ISBN 90-272-0903-0, CIL T 2); pap. 19.00 (ISBN 0-686-31505-7). Benjamins North Am.

Weiner. Phonological Process Analysis. 1978. 21.95 (ISBN 0-8391-1300-5). Univ Park.

Zonneveld, Wim. A Formal Theory of Exceptions in Generative Phonology. (Illus.). 1978. pap. text ed. 23.00x (ISBN 0-685-92395-9). Humanities.

Zwirner, E. & Zwirner, K. Phonometrie, Teil 1. 3rd ed. Zwirner, E. & Ezawa, K., eds. (Illus.). vi, 218p. 1981. pap. 49.75 (ISBN 3-8055-2370-X). S Karger.

GRAMMAR, COMPARATIVE AND GENERAL–SYNTAX

Aissen, Judith. The Syntax of Causative Constructions. Hankamer, Jorge, ed. LC 78-66533. (Outstanding Dissertations in Linguistics Ser.). 1979. lib. bdg. 27.50 (ISBN 0-8240-9690-8). Garland Pub.

Akhmanova, Olga & Mikael'An, Galina. Theory of Syntax in Modern Linguistics. LC 69-13300. (Janua Linguarum, Ser. Minor: No. 68). (Orig.). 1969. pap. text ed. 24.70x (ISBN 90-2790-683-1). Mouton.

Baker, C. L. Introduction to Generative-Transformational Syntax. 1977. text ed. 19.95 (ISBN 0-13-484410-6). P-H.

Bartsch, R. Grammar of Adverbials. (Linguistics Ser.: Vol. 16). 1976. 49.00 (ISBN 0-444-10964-1, North-Holland). Elsevier.

Brown, E. K. & Miller, J. E. Syntax: A Linguistic Introduction to Sentence Structure. 394p. 1981. text ed. 33.75x (ISBN 0-09-138621-7, Hutchinson U Lib); pap. text ed. 15.50x (ISBN 0-09-138621-7). Humanities.

Chomsky, Noam. Aspects of the Theory of Syntax. 1965. 20.00x (ISBN 0-262-03011-X); pap. 4.95 (ISBN 0-262-53007-4). MIT Pr.

Contreras, H. A Theory of Word Order with Special Reference to Spanish. (Linguistics Ser.: Vol. 29). 1976. 24.50 (ISBN 0-7204-6210-X, North-Holland). Elsevier.

Elson, Benjamin & Pickett, Velma. An Introduction to Morphology & Syntax. 167p. 1967. pap. 4.50 (ISBN 0-88312-901-9). Summer Inst Ling.

Fauconnier, Gilles. Theoretical Implications of Some Global Phenomena in Syntax. Hankamer, Jorge, ed. LC 78-66574. (Outstanding Dissertations in Linguistics Ser.). 1979. lib. bdg. 33.00 (ISBN 0-8240-9687-8). Garland Pub.

Kimball, John P. & Tedesch, Philip, eds. Syntax & Semantics, Vol. 14: Tense & Aspect. 1981. 34.00 (ISBN 0-12-613514-2). Acad Pr.

Kimball, John P., et al. Syntax & Semantics, 13 vols. Incl. Vol. 1. Studies in Language. 260p. 1973. 35.00 (ISBN 0-12-785421-5); Vol. 2. 1973. 30.50 (ISBN 0-12-785422-3); Vol. 3. 1975. 35.00 (ISBN 0-12-785423-1); Vol. 4. 1975. 40.50 (ISBN 0-12-785424-X); Vol. 5. Japanese Generative Grammar. 1975. 52.00 (ISBN 0-12-785425-8); Vol. 6. 1976. 48.50 (ISBN 0-12-785426-6); Vol. 7. 1976. 34.50 (ISBN 0-12-613507-X); Vol. 8. 1976. 34.50 (ISBN 0-12-613508-8); Vol. 9. Pragmatics. 1978. 31.00 (ISBN 0-12-613509-6); Vol. 10. 1979. 43.50 (ISBN 0-12-613510-X); Vol. 11. Presupposition. 1979. 40.00 (ISBN 0-12-613511-8); Vol. 12. Discourse & Syntax. 1979. 49.50 (ISBN 0-12-613512-6); Vol. 13. Current Approaches to Syntax. 1980. 32.00 (ISBN 0-12-613513-4). Acad Pr.

Kuczaj, Stan A., ed. Language Development: Syntax & Semantics. (David Palermo Child Psychology Ser.). 528p. 1981. text ed. 29.95 (ISBN 0-89859-100-7). L Erlbaum Assocs.

Levin, Samuel R. Linguistic Structures in Poetry. (Janua Linguarum, Ser. Minor: No. 23). 1973. pap. text ed. 12.50x (ISBN 90-2790-678-5). Mouton.

Lightfoot, D. W. Principles of Diachronic Syntax. LC 78-54717. (Cambridge Studies in Linguistics Monograph: No. 23). (Illus.). 1979. 69.50 (ISBN 0-521-22082-3); pap. 17.50x (ISBN 0-521-29350-2). Cambridge U Pr.

Matthews, P. H. Syntax. LC 80-41664. (Cambridge Textbooks in Linguistics Ser.). (Illus.). 325p. Date not set. price not set (ISBN 0-521-22894-8); pap. price not set (ISBN 0-521-29709-5). Cambridge U Pr.

Melcuk, Igor A. Studies in Dependency Syntax. Roberge, Paul T., ed. Stern, Lev, tr. from Russian. (Linguistica Extranea: Studia 2). 172p. 1979. pap. 7.25 (ISBN 0-89720-001-2). Karoma.

Merrifield, William, et al. Laboratory Manual for Morphology & Syntax. 183p. 1965. pap. 7.00 (ISBN 0-88312-902-7). Summer Inst Ling.

Perlmutter, David M. Deep & Surface Constraints in Syntax. LC 77-153956. 1971. pap. text ed. 12.95x (ISBN 0-03-084010-4). Irvington.

Pike, Evelyn G. Coordination & Its Implications for Roots & Stems of Sentence & Clause. (PDR Press Publications in Taqmemics: No. 1). 1974. pap. text ed. 1.50x (ISBN 90-316-0025-3). Humanities.

Schlesinger, I. M. Production & Comprehension of Utterances. LC 77-3734. 1977. 14.95 (ISBN 0-470-99136-4). Halsted Pr.

Stockwell, Robert P. Foundations of Syntactic Theory. LC 76-8021. (Foundations of Modern Linguistics Ser.). 1977. 14.95 (ISBN 0-13-329987-2); pap. text ed. 10.95 (ISBN 0-13-329979-1); wkbk. 5.95 (ISBN 0-13-965202-7). P-H.

Wall, Carol. Predication: A Study of Its Development. LC 74-76119. (Illus.). 258p. 1974. pap. text ed. 26.25x (ISBN 90-2792-665-4). Mouton.

Zawadowski, Leo. Inductive Semantics & Syntax: Foundations of Empirical Linguistics. (Janua Linguarum Series Maior: No. 58). 316p. 1975. text ed. 66.00x (ISBN 90-2793-463-0). Mouton.

GRAMMAR, GENERATIVE

see Generative Grammar

GRAMMAR, TRANSFORMATIONAL

see Generative Grammar

GRAMMAR SCHOOLS

see Public Schools

GRAMOPHONE

see Phonograph

GRAMSCI, ANTONIO, 1891-1937

Boggs, Carl. Gramsci's Marxism. (Ideas in Progress Ser.). 148p. (Orig.). 1980. pap. 4.95 (ISBN 0-904383-03-2). Pluto Pr.

Buci-Glucksmann, Christine. Gramsci & the State. Fernbach, David, tr. from Fr. 485p. 1980. text ed. 36.50x (ISBN 0-85315-483-X). Humanities.

Cammett, John M. Antonio Gramsci & the Origins of Italian Communism. 1967. 15.00x (ISBN 0-8047-0141-5); pap. 5.95 (ISBN 0-8047-0142-3, SP91). Stanford U Pr.

Cavalcanti, Pedro & Piccone, Paul, eds. History, Philosophy & Culture in the Young Gramsci. LC 74-82995. 160p. (Orig.). 1975. 9.50 (ISBN 0-914386-07-7); pap. 3.95 (ISBN 0-914386-05-0). Telos Pr.

Clark, Martin. Antonio Gramsci & the Revolution That Failed. LC 76-49754. 1977. 25.00x (ISBN 0-300-02077-5). Yale U Pr.

Davidson, Alastair. Antonio Gramsci: Towards an Intellectual Bibliography. (International Library of Social & Political Thought). 1977. text ed. 19.50x (ISBN 0-391-00671-1). Humanities.

Davis, John A., ed. Gramsci & Italy's Passive Revolution. LC 79-53440. (Illus.). 1979. text ed. 27.50x (ISBN 0-06-491609-X). B&N.

Entwistle, Harold. Antonio Gramsci: Conservative Schooling for Radical Politics. (Routledge Education Bks.). 1979. 21.00 (ISBN 0-7100-0333-1); pap. 9.50 (ISBN 0-7100-0334-X). Routledge & Kegan.

Joll, James. Antonio Gramsci. (Modern Masters Ser.). 160p. 1978. 9.95 (ISBN 0-670-12942-9). Viking Pr.

--Antonio Gramsci. (Modern Masters Ser). 1978. pap. 3.95 (ISBN 0-14-004934-7). Penguin.

Mouffe, Chantal. Gramsci & Marxist Theory. 1979. 26.00x (ISBN 0-7100-0357-9); pap. 14.50 (ISBN 0-7100-0358-7). Routledge & Kegan.

Salamini, Leonardo. The Sociology of Political Praxis: An Introduction to Gramsci's Theory. 256p. 1981. price not set (ISBN 0-7100-0928-3). Routledge & Kegan.

Sassoon, Ann S. Gramsci's Politics. LC 79-47375. 272p. 1980. 25.00x (ISBN 0-312-34238-1). St Martin.

GRANADA (CITY)–DESCRIPTION

Handler, Andrew. Zirids of Granada. LC 75-143459. 1974. 11.95x (ISBN 0-87024-216-4). U of Miami Pr.

Peers, E. Allison. Granada. 1929. 12.50 (ISBN 0-685-72772-6). Norwood Edns.

Prieto-Moreno, Francisco. Granada. (Spanish Guide Ser). (Illus.). 1973. 4.50x (ISBN 0-8002-1465-X). Intl Pubns Serv.

GRANADA (KINGDOM)–HISTORY

Handler, Andrew. Zirids of Granada. LC 75-143459. 1974. 11.95x (ISBN 0-87024-216-4). U of Miami Pr.

Irving, Washington. Chronicle of the Conquest of Granada, 2 vols. 1980. Set. lib. bdg. 200.00 (ISBN 0-8490-3144-3). Gordon Pr.

--Chronicle of the Conquest of Granada, 2 Vols. LC 73-120558. Repr. of 1829 ed. Set. 21.50 (ISBN 0-404-03532-9). AMS Pr.

--Chronicle of the Conquest of Granada, 2 Vols. 1829. Set. 50.00 (ISBN 0-403-00122-6). Scholarly.

Markham, Clements. Conquest of New Granada. LC 76-130333. (Latin-American History & Culture Ser). 1971. Repr. of 1912 ed. 13.00 (ISBN 0-8046-1388-5). Kennikat.

GRAND ARMY OF THE REPUBLIC

Dearing, Mary R. Veterans in Politics. LC 74-9625. (Illus.). 523p. 1974. Repr. of 1952 ed. lib. bdg. 29.50x (ISBN 0-8371-7605-0, DEVP). Greenwood.

GRAND CANYON

Babbitt, Bruce. Grand Canyon: An Anthology. LC 78-58470. (Illus.). 276p. 1980. pap. 8.95 (ISBN 0-87358-275-6). Northland.

--Grand Canyon: An Anthology. LC 78-58470. (Illus.). 1978. 15.95 (ISBN 0-87358-180-6). Northland.

Beal, Merrill D. Grand Canyon: The Story Behind the Scenery. rev. ed. DenDooven, Gweneth R., ed. LC 75-14775. (Illus.). 1978. 7.95 (ISBN 0-916122-31-X); pap. 3.00 (ISBN 0-916122-06-9). KC Pubns.

Belknap, Bill & Belknap, Frances. Gunnar Widforss: Painter of the Grand Canyon. LC 69-94654. (Illus.). 1969. 14.50 (ISBN 0-87358-044-3). Northland.

Belknap, Buzz. Grand Canyon River Guide: Powell Centennial. LC 70-92769. (Illus.). 52p. 1969. waterproof 8.95 (ISBN 0-916370-01-1); pap. 5.95 (ISBN 0-916370-00-3). Westwater.

Berkowitz, Alan. A Guide to the Bright Angel Trail. 1979. pap. 1.00 (ISBN 0-938216-09-0). GCNHA.

--A Guide to the North Kaibab Trail. 1980. pap. 1.00 (ISBN 0-938216-10-4). GCNHA.

Beus, Stanley S. & Rawson, Richard R., eds. Carboniferous Stratigraphy in the Grand Canyon Country, Northern Arizona & Southern Nevada. LC 78-74894. (AGI Selected Guidebook Ser.: No. 2). 1979. pap. 20.00 (ISBN 0-913312-09-6). Am Geol.

Blaustein, John & Abbey, Edward. The Hidden Canyon: A River Journey. (Large Format Ser). (Illus.). 1977. pap. 11.95 (ISBN 0-14-004678-X). Penguin.

Breed, William, ed. Geology of the Grand Canyon. 2nd ed. Roat, Evelyn. (MNA Special Publication Ser.: No. 11). 1976. 5.00 (ISBN 0-89734-007-8). Mus Northern Ariz.

Butchart, Harvey. Grand Canyon Treks. rev. ed. (Illus.). 1976. 2.95 (ISBN 0-910856-38-9). La Siesta.

--Grand Canyon Treks II. 1976. 1.95 (ISBN 0-910856-61-3). La Siesta.

Common Wildflowers of the Grand Canyon. (Nature & Scenic Bks.). pap. 3.50 (ISBN 0-937512-00-1). Wheelwright UT.

Crampton, C. Gregory, ed. & intro. by. Sharlot Hall on the Arizona Strip. LC 74-76087. (Illus.). 112p. 1974. 7.50 (ISBN 0-87358-127-X). Northland.

Dutton, Clarence E. Tertiary History of the Grand Canyon District, 2 vols. LC 77-15074. (Illus.). 1977. Repr. of 1882 ed. 175.00 set (ISBN 0-87905-031-4). Peregrine Smith.

Euler, Robert & Tikalsky, Frank, eds. The Grand Canyon: Up Close & Personal. 1980. pap. 7.25 (ISBN 0-916552-10-1). Acoma Bks.

Fletcher, Colin. Man Who Walked Through Time. LC 67-18601. (Illus.). (YA) 1968. 12.95 (ISBN 0-394-43536-2). Knopf.

--The Man Who Walked Through Time. 1972. pap. 2.45 (ISBN 0-394-71852-6, V852, Vin). Random.

Fowler, Don D., ed. Photographed All the Best Scenery: Jack Hillers's Diary of the Powell Expeditions 1871-1875. LC 78-189755. (University of Utah Publications in the American West: Vol. 9). (Illus.). 1971. 20.00 (ISBN 0-87480-066-8). U of Utah Pr.

Geerlings, Paul F. Down the Grand Staircase: Grand Canyon's Living Adventure. (Illus.). 142p. (Orig.). 1980. pap. write for info. (ISBN 0-9604276-0-0). Grand Canyon.

Granger, Byrd H. Grand Canyon Place Names. 1960. pap. 1.95 (ISBN 0-8165-0538-1). U of Ariz Pr.

Heiniger, E. A. Grand Canyon. Osers, Edward, tr. from Ger. (Illus.). 1975. 30.00 (ISBN 0-88331-074-0). Luce.

Hughes, Donald. In the House of Stone & Light. LC 77-93502. 137p. 1978. pap. 7.50 (ISBN 0-938216-00-7). GCNHA.

Johnson, Paul C. Grand Canyon. LC 70-128693. (This Beautiful World Ser.: Vol. 23). (Illus., Orig.). 1971. pap. 4.95 (ISBN 0-87011-141-8). Kodansha.

Krutch, Joseph W. Grand Canyon. 1968. pap. 5.95 (ISBN 0-688-06013-7). Morrow.

--Grand Canyon: Today & All Its Yesterdays. (Illus.). 8.00 (ISBN 0-8446-2411-X). Peter Smith.

Loving, Nancy J. Along the Rim: A Road Guide to the South Rim of Grand Canyon. (Illus.). 56p. (Orig.). 1981. pap. 3.50 (ISBN 0-938216-13-9). GCNHA.

McAdams, Cliff. The Grand Canyon: Guide & Reference Book. (Illus.). 100p. (Orig.). 1981. pap. 5.95 (ISBN 0-87108-577-1). Pruett.

Mitchell, Roger. Grand Canyon Jeep Trails. (Jeep Trails Ser.). (Illus.). 1977. pap. 1.50 (ISBN 0-910856-65-6). La Siesta.

Morris, Larry A. Hiking the Grand Canyon & Havasupai. (Illus.). 96p. 1981. pap. 5.95 (ISBN 0-89404-053-7). Aztex.

Muir, John. Grand Canyon of the Colorado. Jones, William R., ed. (Illus.). 1981. pap. 2.00 (ISBN 0-89646-075-4). Outbooks.

Powell, John W. Canyons of the Colorado. (Illus.). 1964. Repr. of 1895 ed. 17.50 (ISBN 0-87266-026-5). Argosy.

--Exploration of the Colorado River & Its Canyons. Orig. Title: Canyons of the Colorado. (Illus.). 1895. pap. 5.00 (ISBN 0-486-20094-9). Dover.

--An Overland Trip to the Grand Canyon: Northern Arizona As Powell Saw It in 1870. LC 77-29657. (Wild & Woolly West Ser: No. 28). (Illus.). 40p. 1974. 7.00 (ISBN 0-910584-37-0); pap. 1.50 (ISBN 0-910584-84-2). Filter.

Redfern, Ron. Corridors of Time: 1,700,000,000 Years of Earth. 200p. 1980. 55.00 (ISBN 0-8129-0922-4). Times Bks.

Rusho, W. L. Powell's Canyon Voyage. LC 70-64908. (Wild & Woolly West Ser., No. 11). (Illus., Orig.). 1969. 7.00 (ISBN 0-910584-86-9); pap. 2.00 (ISBN 0-910584-12-5). Filter.

Schullery, Paul, ed. The Grand Canyon: Early Impressions. LC 80-66185. 130p. 1981. 15.00 (ISBN 0-87081-086-3); pap. 6.95 (ISBN 0-87081-087-1). Colo Assoc.

Schwartz, Douglas W., et al. Archaeology of the Grand Canyon: Unkar Delta. LC 80-21667. (Grand Canyon Archaeological Ser.: Vol. 2). (Illus.). 405p. (Orig.). 1981. pap. 10.95 (ISBN 0-933452-04-7). Schol Am Res.

--Archaeology of the Grand Canyon: The Walhalla Plateau. LC 81-5730. (Grand Canyon Archaeological Ser.: Vol. 3). (Illus.). 270p. (Orig.). 1981. pap. 9.95 (ISBN 0-933452-06-3). Schol Am Res.

--Archaeology of the Grand Canyon: The Bright Angel Site. LC 79-63535. (Grand Canyon Archaeological Ser: Vol. 1). (Orig.). 1979. pap. 4.95 (ISBN 0-933452-00-4). Schol Am Res.

Spamer, Earle E., et al. Bibliography of the Grand Canyon & the Lower Colorado River. 150p. (Orig.). 1981. pap. 10.00 (ISBN 0-938216-14-7). Grand Canyon.

--Bibliography of the Grand Canyon & the Lower Colorado River. 100p. (Orig.). 1981. pap. 10.00 (ISBN 0-938216-14-7). GCNHA.

Thybony, Scott. Guide to Inner Canyon Hiking: Grand Canyon National Park. rev. ed. (Illus.). pap. 1.75 (ISBN 0-938216-12-0). Grand Canyon.

Wallace, Robert. The Grand Canyon. (The American Wilderness Ser). (Illus.). 1972. 12.95 (ISBN 0-8094-1144-X). Time-Life.

--The Grand Canyon. LC 71-179463. (American Wilderness Ser). (Illus.). (gr. 6 up). 1972. lib. bdg. 11.97 (ISBN 0-8094-1145-8, Pub. by Time-Life). Silver.

Wampler, Joseph, et al. Havasua Canyon Home. (Illus.). 125p. 1981. 6.00 (ISBN 0-686-11222-9). J Wampler.

Young, John V. The Grand Canyon. LC 71-13482. (Wild Woolly West Ser., No. 13). (Illus., Orig.). 1969. 7.00 (ISBN 0-910584-71-0); pap. 1.50 (ISBN 0-910584-10-9). Filter.

GRAND CANYON-JUVENILE LITERATURE

Gamble, Felton O. Explore Grand Canyon. LC 77-161511. (Illus.). (gr. 3-11). 1971. pap. 1.00 (ISBN 0-87358-072-9). Northland.

Penzler, Otto. The Grand Canyon: Journey Through Time. new ed. LC 75-23413. (Illus.). 32p. (gr. 5-10). 1976. PLB 6.89 (ISBN 0-89375-007-7); pap. 2.50 (ISBN 0-89375-023-9). Troll Assocs.

Radlauer, Ruth S. Grand Canyon National Park. LC 76-58525. (Parks for People Ser.). (Illus.). (gr. 3 up). 1977. 3.95 (ISBN 0-516-17492-4, Elk Grove Bks); PLB 10.00 (ISBN 0-516-07492-X). Childrens.

GRAND COULEE DAM

Baljo, Wallace, Jr. Grand Coulee: A Story of the Columbia River from Molten Lavas & Ice to Grand Coulee Dam. rev. ed. Orig. Title: Grand Coulee from "Hell to Breakfast". (Illus.). 80p. (gr. 4-6). Date not set. pap. price not set (ISBN 0-9606084-0-0). Clipboard.

GRAND COUNTY, COLORADO

McGuire, Bill & Teed, Charles. Fruit Belt Route: The Railways of Grand Junction, Colorado. (Illus.). 52p. (Orig.). 1981. pap. 4.95 (ISBN 0-939646-00-5). Natl Rail Rio Grande.

GRAND JURY

Clark, Leroy D. The Grand Jury: The Use & Abuse of Power. LC 72-91377. 192p. 1975. 7.95 (ISBN 0-8129-0320-X); pap. 2.95 (ISBN 0-8129-6276-1). Times Bks.

Frankel, Marvin & Naftalis, Gary. The Grand Jury: An Institution on Trial. 1977. 8.95 (ISBN 0-8090-5092-7, AmCen); pap. 3.95 (ISBN 0-8090-0129-2). Hill & Wang.

Morrill, J. S. The Cheshire Grand Jury, 1625-1959: A Social & Administrative Study. (Occasional Papers in English Local History, Third Series: No. 1). (Illus., Orig.). 1976. pap. text ed. 6.75x (ISBN 0-7185-2031-9, Leicester). Humanities.

National Lawyers Guild. Representation of Witnesses Before Federal Grand Juries. LC 76-20443. 1976. looseleaf with 1979 rev. pages 55.00 (ISBN 0-87632-107-4). Boardman.

Somers, John. Security of Englishmen's Lives, or the Trust Power & Duty of Grand Juries. (Civil Liberties in American History Ser.). 1974. Repr. of 1681 ed. lib. bdg. 12.50 (ISBN 0-306-70604-0). Da Capo.

Younger, Richard D. People's Panel: The Grand Jury in the United States, 1634-1941. LC 63-12993. 271p. 1965. Repr. of 1963 ed. text ed. 12.50x (ISBN 0-87057-076-5). U Pr of New Eng.

GRAND NATIONAL (STEEPLE CHASE RACE)

Pye, J. K. A Grand National Commentary. (Illus.). 11.35 (ISBN 0-85131-121-0, Dist. by Sporting Book Center). J A Allen.

GRAND RAPIDS-HISTORY

Jennings, Carrie B. Fire Service of Grand Rapids. (Illus.). 80p. 1971. pap. 4.50 (ISBN 0-912382-08-2). Black Letter.

Lydens, Z. Z. A Look at Early Grand Rapids. LC 76-12083. 1976. pap. 3.95 (ISBN 0-8254-3115-8). Kregel.

Mapes, Lynn G. & Travis, Anthony. A Pictorial History of Grand Rapids. LC 75-8015. 1976. 14.95 (ISBN 0-8254-3213-8). Kregel.

Tuttle, Chas. R. History of Grand Rapids with Biographical Sketches. LC 73-93481. Orig. Title: History of Grand Rapids. (Illus.). 156p. 1974. pap. 5.00 (ISBN 0-912382-15-5). Black Letter.

GRAND TETON NATIONAL PARK

Adams, Ansel & Newhall, Nancy. The Tetons & the Yellowstone. (Illus.). 1970. pap. 7.95 (ISBN 0-8212-0726-1, 838004). NYGS.

Bach, Orville E., Jr. Hiking the Yellowstone Backcountry. LC 72-96121. (Totebook Ser.). (Illus.). 240p. 1973. pap. 7.95 (ISBN 0-87156-078-X). Sierra.

Bonney, Orrin H. & Bonney, Lorraine G. Bonney's Guide to Grand Teton National Park & Jackson's Hole. rev. ed. (Illus.). 1972. pap. 2.45 (ISBN 0-685-07190-1). Bonney.

Crandall, Hugh. Grand Teton: The Story Behind the Scenery. DenDooven, Gweneth R., ed. LC 78-57539. (Illus.). 1978. lib. bdg. 7.95 (ISBN 0-916122-47-6); pap. 3.00 (ISBN 0-916122-22-0). KC Pubns.

Grand Teton. (Animal Friends Ser.). pap. 1.50 (ISBN 0-915266-11-3). Awani Pr.

Huser, Verne & Belknap, Buzz. Snake River Guide: Grand Teton National Park. LC 72-86478. (Illus.). 72p. 1972. pap. 5.95 (ISBN 0-916370-02-X). Westwater.

Johnsgard, Paul A. Teton Wildlife: Sketches by a Naturalist. 1982. 16.95 (ISBN 0-87081-099-5); pap. 6.95 (ISBN 0-87081-125-8). Colo Assoc.

Lawrence, Paul. Hiking the Teton Backcountry. LC 73-79896. (Totebook Ser.). (Illus.). 160p. 1973. pap. 5.95 (ISBN 0-87156-092-5). Sierra.

Manning, Harvey. Wildlife in Yellowstone & Grand Teton National Parks. LC 77-3206. (Illus.). 32p. 1977. pap. 2.95 (ISBN 0-87564-626-3). Superior Pub.

Plants of Yellowstone & Grand Teton National Parks. (Nature & Scenic Bks.). pap. 5.95 (ISBN 0-685-90233-1). Wheelwright UT.

Radlauer, Ruth. Grand Teton National Park. LC 80-12257. (Parks for People Ser.). (Illus.). 48p. (gr. 3 up). 1980. PLB 10.00 (ISBN 0-516-07740-6). Childrens.

Shaw, Richard J. Field Guide to the Vascular Plants of Grand Teton National Park & Teton County, Wyoming. (Illus.). 300p. 1976. 7.00 (ISBN 0-87421-081-X). Utah St U Pr.

Wildflowers of Yellowstone & Grand Teton National Parks. (Nature & Scenic Bks.). pap. 3.50 (ISBN 0-937512-05-2). Wheelwright UT.

Wildlife of Yellowstone & Grand Teton National Parks. (Nature & Scenic Bks.). pap. 2.95 (ISBN 0-937512-06-0). Wheelwright UT.

GRAND VALLEY, ONTARIO-HISTORY-SOURCES

Johnston, Charles M. Valley of the Six Nations: A Collection of Documents on the Indian Lands of the Grand River. LC 65-1239. (Illus.). 1965. 17.50 (ISBN 0-8020-1339-2). U of Toronto Pr.

GRANDISON, OTHO DE, SIR, d. 1328

Clifford, Esther R. Knight of Great Renown. LC 60-14361. (Illus.). 1961. 15.00x (ISBN 0-226-11019-2). U of Chicago Pr.

GRANDPARENTS

Amstutz, Beverly. I Love My Foster Grandparents. (Illus.). 24p. (gr. k-7). 1981. pap. 2.50x (ISBN 0-937836-06-0). Precious Res.

Brandt, Catharine. God Bless Grandparents. LC 78-52189. (Illus.). 1978. pap. 3.50 (ISBN 0-8066-1658-X, 10-2559). Augsburg.

Carter, Lanie. Congratulations! You're Going to Be a Grandmother. LC 80-1345. 1980. PLB 5.95 (ISBN 0-916392-48-1); pap. 4.95 (ISBN 0-916392-53-8). Oak Tree Pubns.

Dodson, Fitzhugh & Ruben, Paula. How to Grandparent. LC 80-7849. 304p. 1981. 12.95 (ISBN 0-690-01874-6, HarpT). Har-Row.

Goode, Ruth. A Book for Grandmothers. (Paperbacks Ser.). 1977. pap. 3.95 (ISBN 0-07-023740-9, SP). McGraw.

Graves, Charles P. Grandma Moses. LC 69-14830. (Americans All Ser.). (Illus.). 96p. (gr. 4). 1969. PLB 6.48 (ISBN 0-8116-4553-3). Garrard.

Hazen, Barbara S., compiled by. Grandmother Equals Love. 1979. pap. 4.50 (ISBN 0-8378-5021-5). Gibson.

--You're One in a Millon, Grandpa! 1979. pap. 4.50 (ISBN 0-8378-5022-3). Gibson.

Hyde, Tracy E. The Single Grandmother. LC 73-88510. 250p. 1974. 14.95x (ISBN 0-88229-128-9). Nelson-Hall.

Kornhaber, Arthur & Woodward, Kenneth L. Grandparents - Grandchildren: The Vital Connection. LC 79-6083. (Illus.). 312p. 1981. 11.95 (ISBN 0-385-15577-8, Anchor Pr). Doubleday.

Kramer, Sydelle & Masur, Jenny, eds. Jewish Grandmothers. LC 75-5292. (Illus.). 256p. 1976. pap. 4.95 (ISBN 0-8070-5421-6, BP553). Beacon Pr.

Land, Betty E. The Art of Grandparentry. (Illus.). 200p. 1974. 4.95 (ISBN 0-685-50364-X); pap. 2.95 (ISBN 0-685-50365-8). Georgetown Pr.

Madden, Myron C. & Madden, Mary B. For Grandparents: Wonders & Worries. LC 80-12778. (Christian Care Books). 1980. pap. 5.95 (ISBN 0-664-24325-8). Westminster.

Morse, Charles & Morse, Ann. Let This Be a Day for Grandparents. LC 72-77716. (Illus.). 72p. (Orig.). 1972. pap. 2.50 (ISBN 0-88489-045-7). St Marys.

Nixon, Joan L. The Grandmother's Book. LC 78-13621. 1979. 5.95 (ISBN 0-687-15681-5). Abingdon.

Oda, Stephanie C., compiled by. A Grandmother Is for Loving. (Illus.). 1981. 4.95 (ISBN 0-8378-1710-2). Gibson.

Raynor, Dorka. Grandparents Around the World. Rubin, Caroline, ed. LC 76-57661. (Concept Books Ser.). (Illus.). (gr. k). 1977. 7.50g (ISBN 0-8075-3037-9). A Whitman.

Reay, Lee & Reay, Marjorie. Grandparenting Made Easy. LC 79-92769. (Illus.). 1980. pap. 3.50 (ISBN 0-934826-02-1). Meadow Lane.

Richardson, Arleta. Still More Stories from Grandma's Attic. (gr. 1-7). 1980. pap. 2.50 (ISBN 0-686-65608-3). Cook.

Shedd, Charles W. Grandparents: Then God Created Grandparents & It Was Very Good. LC 75-42892. (Illus.). 144p. 1976. 8.95 (ISBN 0-385-11067-7); pap. 5.95 (ISBN 0-385-13115-1). Doubleday.

Shedd, Charlie W. Grandparents. (Inspirational Bks). 1977. lib. bdg. 7.95 (ISBN 0-8161-6519-X, Large Print Bks). G K Hall.

--Grandparents: Then God Created Grandparents & It Was Very Good. LC 77-80913. (Illus.). 1978. pap. 5.95 (ISBN 0-385-13115-1, Galilee). Doubleday.

Sherudi, Edwina. Grandma Strikes Back. 172p. 1979. 9.95 (ISBN 0-8119-0316-8). Fell.

Shulkin, Sunny & Gollub, Wendy L. Grandparents & Grandchildren: A Whimsical, Joyful Sharing Book. (Illus., Orig.). 1979. pap. 4.95 (ISBN 0-934382-01-8). Progs & Pubns.

Storr, Catherine. Hugo & His Grandma. (Illus.). 24p. 1980. pap. 1.60 ea. (Pub. by Dinosaur Pubns); pap. in 5 pk. avail. (ISBN 0-85122-136-X). Merrimack Bk Serv.

Wagenvoord, James. A Grandparent's Book: Thoughts, Memories, & Hopes for a Grandchild. rev. ed. 12.95 (ISBN 0-89256-181-5). Rawson Wade.

GRANGE

see Patrons of Husbandry

GRANITE

Atherton, M. P. & Tarney, J., eds. Origin of Granite Batholiths, Geochemical Evidence. 152p. (Orig.). 1979. pap. text ed. 12.50 (ISBN 0-906812-00-3, Pub. by Shiva Pub England). Imprint Edns.

Didier, J. Granites & Their Enclaves. LC 76-179999. (Developments in Petrology Ser.: Vol. 3). 412p. 1973. 75.75 (ISBN 0-444-40974-2). Elsevier.

Gilluly, James, ed. Origin of Granite. LC 48-3945. (Memoir: No. 28). (Illus.). 1948. 7.00x (ISBN 0-8137-1028-6). Geol Soc.

Marmo, V. Granite Petrology & the Granite Problem. (Developments in Petrology Ser.: Vol. 2). 1971. 66.00 (ISBN 0-444-40852-5). Elsevier.

Symposium on the Granites of West Africa, Ivory Coast, Nigeria, Cameroon, 1965. Proceedings. 1968. 17.50 (ISBN 0-685-20791-9, U488, UNESCO). Unipub.

GRANITE CUTTERS

see Stone-Cutters

GRANITEVILLE COMPANY

Mitchell, Broadus. William Gregg, Factory Master of the Old South. 1966. lib. bdg. 16.50x (ISBN 0-374-95795-9). Octagon.

GRANODIORITE

see also Rocks, Igneous

GRANSON, OTON DE, d. 1397

Braddy, Haldeen. Chaucer & the French Poet Graunson. LC 68-16278. 1968. Repr. of 1947 ed. 9.50 (ISBN 0-8046-0039-2). Kennikat.

GRANT, CARY, 1904-

Deschner, Donald. The Films of Cary Grant. 288p. 1973. 12.00 (ISBN 0-8065-0376-9). Citadel Pr.

--The Films of Cary Grant. 288p. 1973. 12.00 (ISBN 0-8065-0376-9). Citadel Pr.

--The Films of Cary Grant. LC 73-84151. (Illus.). 288p. 1975. pap. 6.95 (ISBN 0-8065-0500-1). Citadel Pr.

Godfrey, Lionel. Cary Grant the Light Touch. (Illus.). 256p. 1981. 10.95 (ISBN 0-312-12309-4). St Martin.

Vermilye, Jerry. Cary Grant. LC 74-33232. (Film Stars Ser.). 5.95 (ISBN 0-88365-291-9). Brown Bk.

GRANT, CHARLES, 1746-1823

Embree, Ainslie T. Charles Grant & British Rule in India. LC 77-166029. (Columbia University Studies in the Social Sciences: No. 606). 10.00 (ISBN 0-404-51606-8). AMS Pr.

GRANT, ULYSSES SIMPSON, PRES. U. S., 1822-1885

Badeau, Adam. Grant in Peace: From Appomattox to Mount McGregor. LC 72-152971. (Select Bibliographies Reprint Ser.). 1972. Repr. of 1887 ed. 35.00 (ISBN 0-8369-5723-7). Arno.

Brooks, William E. Grant of Appomattox, a Study of the Man. LC 73-138577. (Illus.). 1971. Repr. of 1942 ed. lib. bdg. 14.75x (ISBN 0-8371-5776-5, BRGR). Greenwood.

Cadawallader, Sylvanus. Three Years with Grant: As Recalled by War Correspondent Sylvanus Cadwallader. Thomas, Benjamin P., ed. LC 80-21191. (Illus.). xiv, 361p. 1980. Repr. of 1955 ed. lib. bdg. 28.75x (ISBN 0-313-22576-1, CATY). Greenwood.

Catton, Bruce. Grant Moves South. (Illus.). 1960. 16.95 (ISBN 0-316-13207-1). Little.

--Grant Takes Command. LC 69-12632. 1969. 16.50 (ISBN 0-316-13210-1). Little.

Church, William C. Ulysses S. Grant & the Period of National Preservation & Reconstruction. LC 73-14437. (Heroes of the Nation Ser.). Repr. of 1897 ed. 30.00 (ISBN 0-404-58255-9). AMS Pr.

Conger, Arthur L. Rise of U. S. Grant. facs. ed. LC 74-137371. (Select Bibliographies Reprint Ser). (Illus.). 1931. 21.00 (ISBN 0-8369-5572-2). Arno.

Coolidge, Louis A. Ulysses S. Grant. Morse, John T., Jr., ed. LC 75-128953. (American Statesmen: No. 32). Repr. of 1917 ed. 29.00 (ISBN 0-404-50894-4). AMS Pr.

Dye, John S. History of the Plots & Crimes of the Great Conspiracy to Overthrow Liberty in America. facs. ed. LC 76-75508. (Select Bibliographies Reprint Ser). 1866. 25.00 (ISBN 0-8369-5006-2). Arno.

Eaton, John. Grant, Lincoln & the Freedman. LC 70-78763. (Illus.). Repr. of 1907 ed. 17.50x (ISBN 0-8371-1388-1, Pub. by Negro U Pr). Greenwood.

Fuller, J. F. The Generalship of Ulysses S. Grant. 1979. Repr. of 1929 ed. lib. bdg. 40.00 (ISBN 0-8495-1640-4). Arden Lib.

Fuller, John F. Generalship of Ulysses S. Grant. 2nd ed. LC 58-12720. (Indiana University Civil War Centennial Ser). (Illus.). 1968. Repr. of 1958 ed. 23.00 (ISBN 0-527-31750-0). Kraus Repr.

--Grant & Lee: A Study in Personality & Generalship. LC 57-10723. (Civil War Centennial Ser). (Illus.). 336p. 1957. 10.50x (ISBN 0-253-13400-5). Ind U Pr.

Grant, Matthew G. Ulysses S. Grant. LC 73-18213. 1974. PLB 5.95 (ISBN 0-87191-298-8). Creative Ed.

Grant, Ulysses S. The Papers of Ulysses S. Grant: Vol. 4 - January 8 to March 31, 1862. Simon, John Y. & Bridges, Roger D., eds. LC 67-10725. (Illus.). 558p. 1972. 22.50x (ISBN 0-8093-0507-0). S Ill U Pr.

--The Papers of Ulysses S. Grant: Vol. 5 - April 1 to August 31, 1862. Simon, John Y. & Alexander, Thomas G., eds. LC 67-10725. (Illus.). 488p. 1973. 30.00x (ISBN 0-8093-0636-0). S Ill U Pr.

--The Papers of Ulysses S. Grant: Vol. 6 - September 1 to December 8, 1862. Simon, John Y., ed. LC 67-10725. (Illus.). 516p. 1977. 30.00x (ISBN 0-8093-0694-8). S Ill U Pr.

--The Papers of Ulysses S. Grant, Vol. 7: December 9, 1862 to March 31, 1863. Simon, John Y., ed. LC 67-10725. (Illus.). 612p. 1979. 35.00x (ISBN 0-8093-0880-0). S Ill U Pr.

--The Papers of Ulysses S. Grant, Vol. 8: April 1 to July 6, 1863. Simon, John Y., ed. LC 67-10725. (Illus.). 634p. 1979. 35.00x (ISBN 0-8093-0884-3). S Ill U Pr.

Hesseltine, William B. Ulysses S. Grant: Politician. LC 57-12323. (American Classics Ser). 17.50 (ISBN 0-8044-1385-1). Ungar.

Lewis, Lloyd. Captain Sam Grant. 1950. 10.95 (ISBN 0-316-52332-1). Little.

Macartney, Clarence E. Grant & His Generals. facs. ed. LC 75-142660. (Essay Index Reprint Ser). 1953. 20.00 (ISBN 0-8369-2171-2). Arno.

McFeely, William S. Grant: A Biography. (Illus.). 1981. 19.95 (ISBN 0-393-01372-3). Norton.

Mantell, Martin E. Johnson, Grant, & the Politics of Reconstruction. LC 72-13452. 209p. 1973. 15.00x (ISBN 0-231-03507-1). Columbia U Pr.

Miers, Earl S. The Web of Victory: Grant at Vicksburg. LC 78-1838. (Illus.). 1978. Repr. of 1955 ed. lib. bdg. 25.75 (ISBN 0-313-20354-7, MIWV). Greenwood.

Moran, P. Ulysses S. Grant. Eighteen Twenty-One to Eighteen Fifty-Five: Chronology, Documents, Bibliographical Aids. LC 68-23568. (Presidential Chronology Ser). 1968. 8.00 (ISBN 0-379-12056-9). Oceana.

Nevins, Allan. Hamilton Fish: The Inner History of the Grant Administration, 2 Vols. LC 57-9967. (American Classics Ser.). (Illus.). 1957. 45.00 (ISBN 0-8044-1676-1). Ungar.

Pitkin, Thomas M. The Captain Departs: Ulysses S. Grant's Last Campaign. LC 73-4321. (Illus.). 185p. 1973. 10.95x (ISBN 0-8093-0637-9). S Ill U Pr.

Stewart, Ruth A. Richard T. Greener & Grant's Tomb. Date not set. Repr. price not set (ISBN 0-915992-08-6). Eastern Acorn.

Williams, Thomas H. McClellan, Sherman, & Grant. LC 76-29654. (Illus.). 1976. Repr. of 1962 ed. lib. bdg. 15.00x (ISBN 0-8371-9280-3, WIMS). Greenwood.

GRANTS

see Subsidies

GRANTS, LAND
see Land Grants
GRANTS-IN-AID
see also Economic Assistance, Domestic; Research Grants;
also subdivision Finance under particular subjects, e.g. Education–Finance
Alkin, Marvin C., et al. Conducting Evaluations: Three Perspectives. LC 80-52791. 60p. (Orig.). 1980. pap. 2.95 (ISBN 0-87954-036-2). Foundation Ctr.
Anderson, William. The Nation & the States, Rivals or Partners? LC 73-16640. 263p. 1974. Repr. of 1955 ed. lib. bdg. 15.00 (ISBN 0-8371-7210-1, ANNS). Greenwood.
Annual Register of Grant Support: 1979-80. 13th ed. LC 69-18307. 743p. 1979. 57.50 (ISBN 0-8379-1906-1, 031078). Marquis.
Bittermann, Henry J. State & Federal Grants-In-Aid. Repr. of 1938 ed. 31.00 (ISBN 0-384-04511-1). Johnson Repr.
Boulding, Kenneth E. & Wilson, Thomas F., eds. Redistribution Through the Financial System: The Grants Economics of Money & Credit. LC 78-18017. 1978. 32.95 (ISBN 0-03-045341-0). Praeger.
Break, George F. Intergovernmental Fiscal Relations in the United States. (Studies of Government Finance). 1967. 14.95 (ISBN 0-8157-1074-7); pap. 5.95 (ISBN 0-8157-1073-9). Brookings.
Cappalli, Richard B. Rights & Remedies Under Federal Grants. LC 79-12004. 414p. 1979. 25.00 (ISBN 0-87179-304-0). BNA.
Clark, Jane P. Rise of a New Federalism: Federal-State Cooperation in the United States. LC 65-18798. 1965. Repr. of 1938 ed. 8.50 (ISBN 0-8462-0662-5). Russell.
Coleman, William, et al, eds. A Casebook of Grant Proposals in the Humanities. 350p. 1981. 29.95 (ISBN 0-918212-45-6). Neal-Schuman.
Coleman, William E. Grants in the Humanities: A Scholar's Guide to Funding Sources. LC 79-25697. 1980. pap. 12.95x (ISBN 0-918212-21-9). Neal-Schuman.
Conrad, Daniel L. How to Get Federal Grants. 2nd ed. LC 79-53107. 1979. 47.50 (ISBN 0-916664-10-4). Public Management.
Conrad, Daniel L. & Research & Development Staff of the Institute for Fund Raising. The Grants Planner. LC 76-54604. 1976. 37.50 (ISBN 0-916664-02-3). Public Management.
Corry, Emmett. Grants for the Smaller Library: Sources of Funding & Proposal Writing Techniques for the Small & Medium-Sized Library. 230p. 1981. lib. bdg. 22.50x (ISBN 0-87287-262-9). Libs Unl.
Council of State Governments. Federal Grants-in-Aid. LC 77-74937. (American Federalism-the Urban Dimension). (Illus.). 1978. Repr. of 1949 ed. lib. bdg. 20.00x (ISBN 0-405-10484-7). Arno.
Darnbrough, Ann & Kinrade, Derek. Fund-Raising & Grant-Aid: A Practical & Legal Guide for Charities & Voluntary Organisations. 160p. 1980. 24.00x (ISBN 0-85941-075-7, Pub. by Woodhead-Faulkner England). State Mutual Bk.
Derthick, Martha. Influence of Federal Grants: Public Assistance in Massachusetts. LC 73-95919. (Joint Center for Urban Studies Publications Ser). 1970. 15.00x (ISBN 0-674-45425-1). Harvard U Pr.
Dommel, Paul R. The Politics of Revenue Sharing. LC 74-376. (Illus.). 224p. 1974. 10.00x (ISBN 0-253-34551-0). Ind U Pr.
Fogelson, Robert M., et al, eds. Federal Aid to the Cities: An Original Anthology. LC 77-74925. (American Federalism-the Urban Dimension). (Illus.). 1978. lib. bdg. 34.00x (ISBN 0-405-10481-2). Arno.
Foundation Center. COMSEARCH: Geographic. (COMSEARCH Printouts). (Orig.). 1980. write for info. (ISBN 0-87954-030-3); pap. write for info. (ISBN 0-87954-033-8). Foundation Ctr.
--COMSEARCH: Special Topics. (COMSEARCH Printouts). (Orig.). 1980. pap. 12.00 (ISBN 0-87954-031-1); microfiche 4.00 (ISBN 0-87954-034-6). Foundation Ctr.
--COMSEARCH: Subjects. (COMSEARCH Printouts). (Orig.). 1980. pap. 12.00 (ISBN 0-87954-029-X); microfiche 4.00 (ISBN 0-87954-032-X). Foundation Ctr.
--Foundation Center National Data Book, 2 vols. 4th ed. 846p. (Orig.). 1979. pap. 45.00 (ISBN 0-87954-027-3). Foundation Ctr.
--The Foundation Center National Data Book, 2 vols. 5th ed. LC 80-70715. 840p. (Orig.). 1981. pap. 45.00 (ISBN 0-87954-039-7). Foundation Ctr.
--Foundation Center Source Book Profiles, Series 4. Goldstein, Sherry E., ed. LC 77-79015. (Orig.). 1980. looseleaf bdg. 200.00 (ISBN 0-87954-037-0). Foundation Ctr.
--The Foundation Directory. 8th ed. 1981. 41.50 (ISBN 0-87954-041-9). Foundation Ctr.
--The Foundation Grants Index, 1979. Noe, Lee, et al, eds. LC 72-76018. 540p. (Orig.). 1980. pap. 27.00 (ISBN 0-87954-028-1). Foundation Ctr.
--Foundation Grants Index, 1980. LC 72-76018. 540p. (Orig.). 1981. pap. 30.00 (ISBN 0-87954-040-0). Foundation Ctr.
Gadney, Alan. Gadney's Guide to 1800 International Contests, Festivals & Grants in Film & Video, Photography, Tv-Radio Broadcasting, Writing, Poetry, Playwriting & Journalism. LC 77-89041. (Orig.). 1979. 22.95 (ISBN 0-930828-01-1); pap. 15.95 (ISBN 0-930828-00-3). Festival Pubns.
The Grantsmanship Workplan. 1974. 29.95 (ISBN 0-934752-07-9). Eckman Ctr.
Harbert, Anita S. Federal Grants-in-Aid: Maximizing Benefits to the States. LC 76-12854. 1976. text ed. 24.95 (ISBN 0-275-23370-7). Praeger.
Hillman, Howard. Art of Winning Corporate Grants. LC 79-64398. (Art of Winning Grants Ser.). 1980. 8.95 (ISBN 0-8149-0822-5). Vanguard.
Hillman, Howard & Abarbanel, Karin. The Art of Winning Foundation Grants. LC 75-387. 192p. 1975. 8.95 (ISBN 0-8149-0759-8). Vanguard.
Johnson, Richard R., ed. Directory of Evaluation Consultants. LC 80-67499. (Orig.). 1981. pap. 8.95 (ISBN 0-87954-035-4). Foundation Ctr.
Key, Valdimer O. Administration of Federal Grants to States. LC 38-27056. 1971. Repr. of 1937 ed. 23.00 (ISBN 0-384-29290-9, P520). Johnson Repr.
Kostelanetz, Richard. The Grants-Fix: Arts & Literary Funding in America. 225p. (Orig.). 1981. 14.95 (ISBN 0-915520-42-7); pap. 7.95 (ISBN 0-915520-43-5). Ross-Erikson.
Kurzig, Carol, et al, eds. Foundation Grants to Individuals. 2nd ed. LC 79-90273. 236p. 1979. pap. 15.00 (ISBN 0-87954-025-7). Foundation Ctr.
Kurzig, Carol M. Foundation Fundamentals: A Guide for Grantseekers. LC 80-67501. (Illus.). 148p. (Orig.). 1980. pap. 4.95 (ISBN 0-87954-026-5). Foundation Ctr.
Lauffer, Armand. Grantsmanship. LC 77-10013. (Sage Human Services Guides: Vol. 1). 120p. 1977. pap. 6.00 (ISBN 0-8039-0880-6). Sage.
Lee, Lawrence. The Grants Game: How to Get Free Money. 224p. 1981. 12.95 (ISBN 0-936602-18-X); pap. 8.95 (ISBN 0-936602-03-1). Harbor Pub CA.
Levi, Julian H. Municipal & Institutional Relations Within Boston. LC 64-10497. 1964. pap. 5.00x (ISBN 0-226-47410-0). U of Chicago Pr.
MacDonald, A. F. Federal Aid: A Study of the American Subsidy System. (American Federalism-the Urban Dimension). (Illus.). 1978. Repr. of 1928 ed. lib. bdg. 20.00x (ISBN 0-405-10494-4). Arno.
Martin, R. C. The Cities & the Federal System. LC 77-74949. (American Federalism-the Urban Dimension). 1978. Repr. of 1965 ed. lib. bdg. 15.00x (ISBN 0-405-10495-2). Arno.
Mieszlowski, Peter & Oakland, William, eds. Fiscal Federalism & Grants-in-Aid. (Papers on Public Economics Ser.: Vol.1). 166p. (Orig.). 1979. pap. text ed. 10.00 (ISBN 0-87766-254-1, 26300). Urban Inst.
National Directory of Grants & Aid to Individuals in the Arts, International. 4th ed. LC 70-112695. (Arts Patronage Ser.: No. 8). (Orig.). 1980. pap. 15.95 (ISBN 0-912072-09-1). Wash Intl Arts.
Ott, Tony W. Grant & Contract Funding Newsletters, Journals, Periodicals & Newspapers: An Annotated Buyer's & Researcher's Bibliography. 125p. 1980. 15.00 (ISBN 0-938606-00-X). Grant Admin.
--Grantsmanship & Proposal Development Publications: An Annotated Buyer's & Researcher's Bibliography. 125p. 1980. 15.00 (ISBN 0-938606-02-6). Grant Admin.
--Major Sources of Grant & Contract Program Information: An Annotated Buyer's & Researcher's Bibliography. 500p. 1980. 25.00 (ISBN 0-938606-03-4). Grant Admin.
Palley, Marion & Hale, George. Politics of Federal Grants. Woy, Jean, ed. (Congressional Quarterly Politics & Public Policy Ser.). 225p. (Orig.). 1981. pap. text ed. 7.50 (ISBN 0-87187-161-0). Congr Quarterly.
Public Management Institute. The Complete Grants Sourcebook for Higher Education. 1980. 79.50 (ISBN 0-8268-1245-7). ACE.
Public Management Institute Staff. Grant Strategies: The Four Steps to Funding. Date not set. price not set ring binder. Public Management.
--The Grant Writer's Handbook Nineteen Seventy-Nine to Nineteen Eighty. 2nd ed. LC 78-71777. 400p. 1980. 37.50 (ISBN 0-916664-18-X). Public Management.
Raising Money from Grants & Other Sources, 7 bks. 1978. 99.50 (ISBN 0-685-83456-5). Intl Wealth.
Reagan, Michael D. & Sanzone, John G. The New Federalism. 2nd ed. 208p. 1981. pap. text ed. 3.95x (ISBN 0-19-502772-8). Oxford U Pr.
Robinson, Peter S., ed. Foundation Guide for Religious Grant Seekers. LC 79-19006. (Scholars Press Handbooks in Humanities Ser.: No. 1). 1979. 9.00 (ISBN 0-89130-339-1, 001501); pap. 6.00 (ISBN 0-89130-340-5). Scholars Pr Ca.
Rudman, Jack. Grants Analyst. (Career Examination Ser.: C-2832). (Cloth bdg. avail. on request). 1980. pap. 10.00 (ISBN 0-8373-2832-2). Natl Learning.
--Grants Coordinator. (Career Examination Ser.: C-2797). (Cloth bdg. avail. on request). 1980. 12.00 (ISBN 0-8373-2797-0). Natl Learning.
--Manpower Grants Technician. (Career Examination Ser.: C-2822). (Cloth bdg. avail. on request). 1980. pap. 12.00 (ISBN 0-8373-2822-5). Natl Learning.
--Senior Grants Analyst. (Career Examination Ser.: C-2833). (Cloth bdg. avail. on request). 1980. pap. 10.00 (ISBN 0-8373-2833-0). Natl Learning.
--Supervising Grants Analyst. (Career Examination Ser.: C-2834). (Cloth bdg. avail. on request). 1980. pap. 14.00 (ISBN 0-8373-2834-9). Natl Learning.
Shapek, Raymond A. Managing Federalism: Evolution & Development of the Grants-in-Aid System. LC 80-65751. 360p. 1980. 17.95 (ISBN 0-930388-05-4). Comm Collaborators.
Sladek, Frea E. & Stein, Eugene L. Grant Budgeting & Finance: Getting the Most Out of Your Grant Dollar. 375p. 1981. 19.50 (ISBN 0-306-40607-1, Plenum Pr). Plenum Pub.
--Grant Budgeting & Finance: Getting the Most Out of Your Grant Dollar. 375p. 1981. 19.50 (ISBN 0-306-40607-1). Plenum Pub.
Smith, Craig & Skjei, Eric. Getting Grants. LC 78-20187. 1980. 12.95 (ISBN 0-06-014013-5, HarpT). Har-Row.
--Getting Grants: A Creative Guide to the Grants System: How to Find Funders, Write Convincing Proposals, & Make Your Grants Work. LC 78-20187. 288p. pap. 4.95 (ISBN 0-06-090834-3, CN 834, CN). Har-Row.
Spiva, Ulysses V. How to Get a Grant for Your Own Special Project. 73p. 1980. pap. text ed. 7.75 (ISBN 0-89917-301-2). TIS Inc.
Sulz, Harry. Grantwriting for Health Professionals. 1981. pap. write for info. (ISBN 0-316-82196-9). Little.
Turner, Roland. The Grants Register: Nineteen Seventy-Nine to Nineteen Eighty-One. 800p. 1979. 26.50 (ISBN 0-312-34406-6). St Martin.
U.S Advisory Commission on Intergovernmental Relations. The Role of Equalization in Federal Grants. LC 77-74926. (American Federalism-the Urban Dimension). (Illus.). 1978. Repr. of 1964 ed. lib. bdg. 15.00x (ISBN 0-405-10475-8). Arno.
U.S. Commission on Intergovernmental Relations. A Report to the President for Transmittal to the Congress. LC 77-74962. (American Federalism-the Urban Dimension). (Illus.). 1978. Repr. of 1955 ed. lib. bdg. 20.00x (ISBN 0-405-10505-3). Arno.
U.S. House Committee on Government Operations. Federal-State-Local Relations: Federal Grants-in Aid State & Local Officials, 2 vols. in 1. LC 77-74935. (American Federalism-the Urban Dimension). 1978. lib. bdg. 32.00 (ISBN 0-405-10482-0). Arno.
U.S. Senate Committee on Government Operations. Creative Federalism, 3 vols. in one. LC 77-74958. (American Federalism-the Urban Dimension). (Illus.). 1978. lib. bdg. 64.00x (ISBN 0-405-10501-0). Arno.
White, Virginia. Grants for the Arts. 275p. 1980. 19.50 (ISBN 0-306-40270-X, Plenum Pr). Plenum Pub.
Wilson, William K. & Wilson, Betty L., eds. Directory of Research Grants, 1981. 6th. ed. 368p. 1981. pap. 37.50 (ISBN 0-912700-92-0). Oryx Pr.
Wright, Deil S. Federal Grants-In-Aid: Perspectives & Alternatives. LC 68-9148. 1968. pap. 2.00 (ISBN 0-8447-3061-0). Am Enterprise.
GRANTS-IN-AID, INTERNATIONAL
see Economic Assistance; International Relief
GRANULAR CONJUNCTIVITIS
see Trachoma
GRANULAR LIDS
see Trachoma
GRANULAR MATERIALS
Broersma, G. Behavior of Granular Materials. 266p. 1972. 50.00x (ISBN 0-85950-045-4, Pub. by Stam Pr England). State Mutual Bk.
Litwiniszyn, J. Stochastic Methods in Mechanics of Granular Bodies. (CISM - International Centre for Mechanical Sciences, Courses & Lectures: Vol. 93). (Illus.). 93p. 1975. pap. 13.30 (ISBN 0-387-81310-1). Springer-Verlag.
Sherrington, P. J. & Oliver, R. Granulation: Monographs in Powder Science & Technology. 1980. 29.50 (ISBN 0-85501-177-7). Heyden.
GRANULOCYTES
see also Leucocytes
Byrne, Gerald E., Jr., et al. Granulocyte Identification. LC 78-720294. (Laboratory Learning Aids Ser.). (Illus.). 1977. text & slides 40.00 (ISBN 0-89189-062-9, 71-5-003-00). Am Soc Clinical.
Greenwalt, Tibor J. & Jamieson, G. A., eds. The Granulocyte: Function & Clinical Utilization; Proceedings of the American National Red Cross Eighth Annual Scienific Symposium, Washington, D. C., May 1976. LC 76-47960. (Progess in Clinical & Biological Research: Vol. 13). 322p. 1977. 35.00x (ISBN 0-8451-0013-0). A R Liss.
GRANULOMA BENIGNUM
see Sarcoidosis
GRANVILLE, JOHN CARTERET, EARL, 1690-1763
Williams, Basil. Carteret & Newcastle: A Contrast in Contemporaries. (Illus.). 240p. 1966. 25.00x (ISBN 0-7146-1524-2, F Cass Co). Biblio Dist.
GRANVILLE-BARKER, HARLEY GRANVILLE, 1877-1946
Purdom, Charles B. Harley Granville Barker Man of the Theatre, Dramatist & Scholar. LC 72-156205. (Illus.). 1971. Repr. of 1956 ed. lib. bdg. 17.25x (ISBN 0-8371-6155-X, PUGB). Greenwood.
GRAPES
see also Viticulture
Brandt, Johanna. The Grape Cure. 1.25 (ISBN 0-686-29874-8). Cancer Bk Hse.
Chazanof, William. Welch's Grape Juice. 1979. pap. 9.95x (ISBN 0-8156-2211-2). Syracuse U Pr.
Clarke, J. Harold. Growing Berries & Grapes at Home. (Illus.). 7.50 (ISBN 0-8446-5474-4). Peter Smith.
Flaherty, Donald L., et al, eds. Grape Pest Management. LC 80-70846. (Illus.). 312p. (Orig.). 1981. pap. 25.00x (ISBN 0-931876-44-3, 4105). Ag Sci Pubns.
Frazier, N. W., ed. Virus Diseases of Small Fruits & Grapevines. 1970. 7.50x (ISBN 0-931876-21-4, 4056). Ag Sci Pubns.
John Windle Publishing Co. Grapes & Grape Vines of California. (Illus.). 64p. 1981. Repr. of 1877 ed. 35.00 (ISBN 0-686-72889-0). HarBraceJ.
Lee, Hollis. Nuts, Berries & Grapes. (Country Home & Small Farm Guides Ser.). (Illus.). 1978. pap. 2.95 (ISBN 0-88453-009-4). Barrington.
Major Wine Grape Varieties of Australia. 61p. 1979. pap. 6.50 (ISBN 0-643-02517-0, CO12, CSIRO). Unipub.
Recommended International Standards for Grape Juice, Concentrated Grape Juice, & Sweetened Concentrated Labrusca Type Grape Juice Preserved Exclusively by Physical Means. (Codex Alimentarius Commission). 17p. 1978. pap. 4.50 (ISBN 0-685-87288-2, F579, FAO). Unipub.
Some Wine Grape Varieties for Australia. 50p. 1976. pap. 6.00 (ISBN 0-643-00180-8, CO09, CSIRO). Unipub.
Table Grapes & Refrigeration. 1978. pap. 13.75 (ISBN 0-685-66524-0, IIR14, IIR). Unipub.
GRAPES–VARIETIES
Kasimatis, A. N., et al. Wine Grape Varieties in the North Coast Counties of California. 1977. pap. 3.00x (ISBN 0-931876-22-2, 4069). Ag Sci Pubns.
--Wine Grape Varieties in the San Joaquin Valley. 1972. pap. 5.00x (ISBN 0-931876-23-0, 4009). Ag Sci Pubns.
Wagner, Philip M. Wine-Grower's Guide. rev ed. (Illus.). 1965. 10.95 (ISBN 0-394-40183-2). Knopf.
GRAPH THEORY
see also Bond Graphs; Four-Color Problem; Network Analysis (Planning)
Alavi, Y. & Lick, D. R., eds. Theory & Applications of Graphs: Proceedings, Michigan, May 11-15, 1976. (Lecture Notes in Mathematics: Vol. 642). 1978. pap. 27.00 (ISBN 0-387-08666-8). Springer-Verlag.
Balaban, A. T. Chemical Applications of Graph Theory. 1976. 46.50 (ISBN 0-12-076050-9). Acad Pr.
Barbut, M. Combinatorics, Graphs & Algebra by Centre De Mathematique Sociale, Ecole Deshautes Etudes En Sciences Sociales. (Methods & Models in the Social Sciences: No. 5). pap. 23.50x (ISBN 90-2797-511-6). Mouton.
Beineke, Lowell & Wilson, Robin, eds. Selected Topics in Graphs Theory. 1979. 72.00 (ISBN 0-12-086250-6). Acad Pr.
Bellman, Richard E., et al. Algorithms, Graphs & Computers. (Mathematics in Science & Engineering Ser.: Vol. 62). 1970. 38.00 (ISBN 0-12-084840-6). Acad Pr.
Berge, C. Graphs & Hypergraphs. 2nd rev. ed. LC 72-88288. (Mathematical Library: No. 6). (Illus.). 555p. 1976. 49.00 (ISBN 0-7204-0479-7, North-Holland). Elsevier.
Biggs, N. L. Algebraic Graph Theory. LC 73-86042. (Tracts in Mathematics Ser.: No. 67). (Illus.). 180p. 1974. 28.95x (ISBN 0-521-20335-X). Cambridge U Pr.

Bollabas, Bela. Extreme Graph Theory. (L. M. S. Monogrphs). 1978. 81.00 (ISBN 0-12-111750-2). Acad Pr.

Bollobas, B. Graph Theory: An Introductory Course. (Graduate Texts in Mathematics Ser.: Vol. 63). (Illus.). 1979. 17.60 (ISBN 0-387-90399-2). Springer-Verlag.

Bollobas, B., ed. Advances in Graph Theory. (Annals of Discrete Mathematics Ser: No. 3). 1978. 53.75 (ISBN 0-444-85075-9, North-Holland). Elsevier.

Bondy, J. A. & Murty, U. S. Graph Theory with Applications: U.S. Reprint. 1979. text ed. 21.50 (ISBN 0-444-19451-7, North Holland). Elsevier.

Bondy, J. A. & Murty, U. S., eds. Graph Theory & Related Topics. LC 78-27025. 1979. 43.00 (ISBN 0-12-114350-3). Acad Pr.

Brown, David R. AIGA Graphic Design. (AIGA Graphic Design U.S.A. Annual Ser.: No. 2). (Illus.). 432p. 1981. 40.00 (ISBN 0-8230-2144-0). Watson-Guptill.

Brown, William G., ed. Reviews in Graph Theory, 4 vols. 1980. Set. 200.00 (ISBN 0-8218-0214-3); Vol. 1. 68.00 (ISBN 0-8218-0210-0); Vol. 2. 68.00 (ISBN 0-8218-0211-9); Vol. 3. 68.00 (ISBN 0-8218-0212-7); Vol. 4. 40.00 (ISBN 0-8218-0213-5). Am Math.

Busacker, Robert G. & Saaty, T. Finite Graphs & Networks: An Introduction with Applications. (International Pure & Applied Mathematics Ser). 1965. text ed. 18.95 (ISBN 0-07-009305-9, C). McGraw.

Capital Conference on Graph Theory & Conbinatorics, George Washington University, June 18-22, 1973. Graphs & Combinatorics: Proceedings. Bari, R. A. & Harary, F., eds. LC 74-13955. (Lecture Notes in Mathematics: Vol. 406). viii, 355p. 1974. pap. 18.30 (ISBN 0-387-06854-6). Springer-Verlag.

Capobianco, M. & Molluzzo, J. C. Examples & Counter Examples in Graph Theory. 1978. 19.95 (ISBN 0-444-00255-3, North-Holland). Elsevier.

Chachra, V., et al. Applications of Graph Theory Algorithms. 1979. 22.95 (ISBN 0-444-00268-5, North Holland). Elsevier.

Chartrand, Gary, ed. & The Theory & Application of Graphs: Fourth International Conference, Western Michigan Univ., May 6-9, 1980. LC 80-27978. 500p. 1981. 30.00 (ISBN 0-471-08473-5, Pub. by Wiley-Interscience). Wiley.

Chen, W. K. Applied Graph Theory: Graphs & Electrical Networks. 2nd rev. ed. (North-Holland Ser. in Applied Mathematics & Mechanics: Vol. 13). 1976. text ed. 53.75 (ISBN 0-7204-2835-1, North-Holland); pap. text ed. 31.75 (ISBN 0-444-10871-8). Elsevier.

Conference on Graph Theory, Third, Ann Arbor. New Directions in the Theory of Graphs: Proceedings. Harary, Frank, ed. 1973. 34.00 (ISBN 0-12-324255-X). Acad Pr.

Conference On Graph Theory - Western Michigan University - Kalamazoo - 1968. Many Facets of Graph Theory: Proceedings. Chartrand, G. & Kapoor, S. F., eds. LC 70-101693. (Lecture Notes in Mathematics: Vol. 110). (Illus.). 1969. pap. 14.70 (ISBN 0-387-04629-1). Springer-Verlag.

Deo, Narsingh. Graph Theory with Applications to Engineering & Computer Science. 1974. 27.95 (ISBN 0-13-363473-6). P-H.

Dicks, W. Groups, Trees & Projective Modules. (Lecture Notes in Mathematics: Vol. 790). 127p. 1980. pap. 9.80 (ISBN 0-387-09974-3). Springer-Verlag.

Flores, Ivan. Data Structure & Management. 2nd ed. 1977. 24.95 (ISBN 0-13-197335-5). P-H.

Frank, Howard & Frisch, Ivan T. Communication, Transmission, & Transportation Networks. LC 78-119666. (Engineering Ser). 1971. text ed. 25.95 (ISBN 0-201-02081-5). A-W.

Frederique & Papy. Graph Games. LC 72-157647. (Young Math Ser). (Illus.). (gr. 1-4). 1971. PLB 7.89 (ISBN 0-690-34965-3, TYC-J). Har-Row.

Fulkerson, D. R., ed. Studies in Graph Theory, Pt. I. new ed. LC 75-24987. (MAA Studies in Mathematics: No. 11). 1976. 12.50 (ISBN 0-88385-111-3). Math Assn.

Golumbic, Martin C. Algorithmic Graph Theory & Perfect Graphs. LC 79-22956. (Computer Science & Applied Mathematics Ser.). 1980. 34.00 (ISBN 0-12-289260-7). Acad Pr.

Graham, Ronald L. Rudiments of Ramsey Theory. LC 80-29667. (CBMS Ser.: No. 45). Date not set. 6.60 (ISBN 0-8218-1696-9). Am Math.

Graovac, A., et al. Topological Approach to the Chemistry of Conjugated Molecules. (Lecture Notes in Chemistry: Vol. 4). 1977. pap. 10.70 (ISBN 0-387-08431-2). Springer-Verlag.

Graver, J. E. & Watkins, M. E. Combinatorics: With Emphasis on the Theory of Graphs. LC 77-1200. (Graduate Texts in Mathematics: Vol. 54). (Illus.). 1977. pap. text ed. 27.30 (ISBN 0-387-90245-7). Springer-Verlag.

Haggard, Gary. Excursions in Graph Theory. 211p. 1979. pap. 7.95 (ISBN 0-89101-040-8). U Maine Orono.

Harary, Frank. Graph Theory. 1969. text ed. 20.95 (ISBN 0-201-02787-9). A-W.

--Proof Techniques in Graph Theory. 1969. 49.50 (ISBN 0-12-324260-6). Acad Pr.

Harary, Frank & Palmer, Edgar M. Graphical Enumeration. 1973. 42.00 (ISBN 0-12-324245-2). Acad Pr.

Harary, Frank, et al, eds. Topics in Graph Theory. (Annals of the New York Academy of Sciences: Vol. 328). 206p. (Orig.). 1979. pap. 40.00x (ISBN 0-89766-028-5). NY Acad Sci.

Henley, Ernest J. & Williams, R. A. Graph Theory in Modern Engineering: Computer Aided Design, Optimization, Reliability Analysis. (Mathematics in Science & Engineering Ser.: Vol. 98). 1973. 37.50 (ISBN 0-12-340850-4). Acad Pr.

International Computation Centre. Theory of Graphs. 1967. 90.75 (ISBN 0-677-11780-9). Gordon.

Johnson, David E. & Johnson, Johnny R. Graph Theory: With Engineering Applications. 392p. 1972. 34.00x (ISBN 0-8260-4775-0, Pub. by Wiley-Interscience). Wiley.

Kaufmann, A. Graphs, Dynamic Programming & Finite Games. (Mathematics in Science & Engineering Ser.: Vol. 36). 1967. 50.00 (ISBN 0-12-402356-8). Acad Pr.

Koenig, Denes. Endlichen und Unendlichen Graphen. LC 51-3002. (Ger). 12.95 (ISBN 0-8284-0072-5). Chelsea Pub.

Lefschetz, S. Applications of Algebraictopology, Graphs & Networks: The Picard-Lefschetz Theory & Feynman Integrals. LC 75-6924. (Applied Mathematical Sciences Ser.: Vol. 16). (Illus.). 200p. 1975. pap. 13.10 (ISBN 0-387-90137-X). Springer-Verlag.

Malkevitch, Joseph & Meyer, Walter. Graphs, Models & Finite Mathematics. (Illus.). 480p. 1974. ref. ed. 19.95 (ISBN 0-13-363465-5). P-H.

Nakanishi, N. Graph Theory & Feynman Intervals. (Mathematics & Its Applications Ser.). 1971. 35.75x (ISBN 0-677-02950-0). Gordon.

New York City Graph Theory Conference, 1st, 1970. Recent Trends in Graph Theory: Proceedings. Capobianco, M., et al, eds. (Lecture Notes in Mathematics: Vol. 186). (Illus.). 1971. pap. 11.20 (ISBN 0-387-05386-7). Springer-Verlag.

Ore, Oystein. Theory of Graphs. LC 61-15687. (Colloquium Pbns. Ser.: Vol. 38). 1974. Repr. of 1962 ed. 23.20 (ISBN 0-8218-1038-3, COLL-38). Am Math.

Read, Ronald C., ed. Graph Theory & Computing. 1972. 49.50 (ISBN 0-12-583850-6). Acad Pr.

Roberts, Fred S. Graph Theory & Its Applications to Problems of Society. LC 78-6277. (CBMS-NSF Regional Conference Ser.: Vol. 29). (Illus., Orig.). 1978. pap. text ed. 11.50 (ISBN 0-89871-026-X). Soc Indus-Appl Math.

Roy, B. Modern Algebra & Graph Theory Applied to Management. LC 77-724. (Universitext). (Illus.). 1978. 24.70 (ISBN 0-387-08006-6). Springer-Verlag.

Saito, N. & Nishizoki, T., eds. Graph Theory & Algorithms: Proceedings. (Lecture Notes in Computer Sciences Ser.: Vol. 108). 216p. 1981. pap. 14.00 (ISBN 0-387-10704-5). Springer-Verlag.

Slepian, Paul. Mathematical Foundations of Network Analysis. LC 68-29708. (Springer Tracts in Natural Philosophy: Vol. 16). 1968. 29.90 (ISBN 0-387-04344-6). Springer-Verlag.

Steiglitz, Kenneth. An Introduction to Discrete Systems. LC 73-6820. 318p. 1974. text ed. 27.95x (ISBN 0-471-82097-0); solutions manual avail. (ISBN 0-471-82103-9). Wiley.

Trudeau, Richard J. Dots & Lines. rev. ed. LC 78-16894. (Illus.). 1978. 12.50x (ISBN 0-87338-223-4); pap. 6.50x (ISBN 0-87338-224-2). Kent St U Pr.

Weisfeiler, B., ed. On Construction & Identification of Graphs. (Lecture Notes in Mathematics Ser.: Vol. 558). 1976. soft cover 14.10 (ISBN 0-387-08051-1). Springer-Verlag.

Welsh, D. J. Matriod Theory. (London Mathematical Society Monograph Series). 1976. 68.50 (ISBN 0-12-744050-X). Acad Pr.

Wilson, R. J., ed. Graph Theory & Combinatorics. (Research Notes in Mathematics Ser.: No. 34). 148p. (Orig.). 1979. pap. text ed. 19.95 (ISBN 0-273-08435-6). Pitman Pub MA.

--Graph Theory & Combinatorics. (Research Notes in Mathematics Ser.). (Illus.). 1979. pap. cancelled (ISBN 0-8224-8435-8). Pitman Learning.

Wilson, Robin & Beineke, Lowell, eds. Applications of Graph Theory. LC 78-73892. 1980. 49.00 (ISBN 0-12-757840-4). Acad Pr.

GRAPHIC ARTS

see also Bookbinding; Commercial Art; Drawing; Engraving; Painting; Printing; Printing As a Graphic Art; Prints; Television Graphics

American Artists' Congress. Graphic Works of the American '30s. (Illus.). 1977. Repr. of 1936 ed. pap. 7.95 (ISBN 0-306-80078-0). Da Capo.

American Showcase of Photography, Illustration, & Graphic Design, Vol. IV. (Illus.). 400p. 1981. 39.95 (ISBN 0-8317-0323-7, Rutledge Pr) (ISBN 0-8317-0324-5). Smith Pubs.

Anno, Mitsumasa. The Unique World of Mitsumasa Anno: Selected Works 1968-1977. Morse, Samuel, tr. LC 80-12827. (Illus.). 64p. (gr. 7 up). 1980. 19.95 (ISBN 0-399-20743-0). Philomel.

Askeland, Jan. Norwegian Printmakers: A Hundred Years of Graphic Arts. Shaw, Pat, tr. from Norwegian. LC 79-305965. (Tokens of Norway Ser.). (Illus.). 55p. (Orig.). 1978. pap. 10.50x (ISBN 82-518-0688-7). Intl Pubns Serv.

The Association of Illustrators' Third Annual. (Illus.). 1979. 29.95 (ISBN 0-8317-4861-3, Mayflower Bks). Smith Pubs.

Ballinger, Raymond A. Art & Reproduction: Graphic Reproduction Techniques. (Illus.). 1977. pap. 10.95 (ISBN 0-442-20550-3); pap. 9.95 (ISBN 0-442-20551-1). Van Nos Reinhold.

--Layout & Graphic Design. 96p. 1980. pap. 9.95 (ISBN 0-442-20178-8). Van Nos Reinhold.

Baro, Gene. Graphicstudio U. S. F. An Experiment in Art & Education. LC 78-6796. (Illus.). 1978. pap. 8.95 (ISBN 0-87273-068-9). Bklyn Mus.

Barton, Linda & Benedict, Brad. Phonographics: The Album of Albums, Contemporary Album Cover Art Design. LC 77-92314. 1977. 19.95 (ISBN 0-02-507570-5). Macmillan.

Beakley, George C. Introduction to Engineering Graphics. (Illus.). 341p. 1975. pap. text ed. 15.95 (ISBN 0-02-307210-5, 30721). Macmillan.

Beakley, George C. & Autore, Donald D. Graphics for Design & Visualization: Problem Series B. 1975. pap. 11.95 (ISBN 0-02-307270-9, 30727). Macmillan.

Beardsley, Aubrey. Beardsley's Illustrations for le Morte d'Arthur. (Facsimile Dent Edition). Repr. of 1893 ed. 9.00 (ISBN 0-8446-4507-9). Peter Smith.

Berryman, Gregg. Notes on Graphic Design & Visual Communication. LC 80-15711. 48p. (Orig.). 1980. pap. 3.95 (ISBN 0-913232-86-6). W Kaufmann.

Biesele, Igildo. Graphic Design Education. (Illus.). 190p. 1981. 67.50 (ISBN 0-8038-2712-1, Visual Communication). Hastings.

Blechman, R. O. R. O. Blechman: Behind the Lines. LC 80-15191. (Illus.). 188p. 1980. 32.50 (ISBN 0-933920-07-5). Hudson Hills.

Booth-Clibborn, Edward & Baroni, Daniele. The Language of Graphics. (Illus.). 320p. 1980. 35.00 (ISBN 0-686-62695-8, 1252-X). Abrams.

Booth-Clibborn, Edward, ed. European Illustration Seventy-Nine to Eighty: The Sixth Annual of European Editorial, Book, Advertising, Television, Cinema, & Design Art. (Illus.). 1980. 50.00 (ISBN 0-8038-1956-0). Hastings.

Born, Ernst. Lexikon Fuer Die Graphische Industrie. 2nd ed. (Ger.). 68.00 (ISBN 3-87641-184-X, M-7201). French & Eur.

Bourcard, Gustave & Goodfriend, James. Felix Buhot Catalogue Descriptif De Son Oeuvre Grave. (Illus.). 1979. 75.00 (ISBN 0-931036-04-6). Martin Gordon.

Bowe, Nicola G. Harry Clarke: His Graphic Art. (Illus.). 120p. 1980. text ed. 39.00x (ISBN 0-85105-359-9, Dolmen Pr). Humanities.

Bradley, Will. Will Bradley: His Graphic Art. Hornung, Clarence & Wong, Roberta W., eds. (Illus.). pap. 5.00 (ISBN 0-486-20701-3). Dover.

Brandt, Bill. Shadow of Light. LC 76-52463. (Illus.). 1977. lib. bdg. 29.50 (ISBN 0-306-70858-2); pap. 14.50 (ISBN 0-306-80066-7). Da Capo.

Broekhuizen, Richard. Graphic Communications. 380p. 1979. text ed. 15.72 (ISBN 0-87345-246-1); study guide 3.96 (ISBN 0-87345-247-X); ans. key free (ISBN 0-87345-248-8). McKnight.

Brown, David R. A I G A Graphic Design USA, No. 2. (Illus.). 432p. 1981. 40.00 (ISBN 0-8230-2144-0). Watson-Guptill.

Bruyninckx, Jozef. Phototypography & Graphic Arts Dimension Control Photography. LC 74-115394. (Illus.). 150p. 1976. 14.80 (ISBN 0-911126-03-1). Perfect Graphic.

Camden, Kenneth. Graphical Work. Date not set. pap. 5.95x (ISBN 0-392-08412-0, ABC). Sportshelf.

Carlsen, D. & Tryon, V. Communication: Graphic Arts. 1976. 7.20 (ISBN 0-13-153197-2); pap. 5.80 (ISBN 0-13-153189-1). P-H.

Carlsen, Darvey. Graphic Arts. new ed. (gr. 7-12). 1977. text ed. 10.48 (ISBN 0-87002-177-X); tchr's guide free. Bennett IL.

Carter, Judith Q. & Carter, Richard D., eds. Herbert L. Fink: Graphic Artist. LC 80-39918. (Illus.). 168p. 1981. 29.95 (ISBN 0-8093-1016-3). S Ill U Pr.

Claus, R. James & Claus, Karen E. Street Graphics: A Perspective. (Illus.). 1975. 3.50 (ISBN 0-911380-37-X). Signs of Times.

Cleaver, James. History of Graphic Art. LC 73-95115. Repr. of 1963 ed. lib. bdg. 24.00x (ISBN 0-8371-2522-7, CLGA). Greenwood.

--A History of Graphic Art. (Illus.). 1977. Repr. of 1963 ed. 32.00x (ISBN 0-7158-1209-2). Charles River Bks.

Craig, James. Production for the Graphic Designer. (Illus.). 208p. 1974. 21.95 (ISBN 0-8230-4415-7). Watson-Guptill.

Cummings, Thomas S. Historic Annals of the National Academy of Design. LC 71-87503. (Library of American Art). 1969. Repr. of 1865 ed. 39.50 (ISBN 0-306-71411-6). Da Capo.

Dalley, Terence, ed. The Complete Guide to Illustration & Design: Techniques & Materials. LC 79-13326. (Illus.). Date not set. 19.95 (ISBN 0-8317-1612-6, Mayflower Bks). Smith Pubs.

Darracott, Joseph C., ed. The First World War in Posters. (Illus., Orig.). 1974. 9.95 (ISBN 0-486-23027-9); pap. 4.95 (ISBN 0-486-22979-3). Dover.

Dean, Roger, ed. The Album Cover Album. LC 77-71713. (Illus.). 1977. 25.00 (ISBN 0-89104-085-4); pap. 10.95 (ISBN 0-89104-074-9). A & W Pubs.

Delhaye, Jean. Art Deco-Posters & Graphics: Posters & Graphics. LC 77-74339. (Illus.). 1978. pap. 12.50 (ISBN 0-8478-0110-1). Rizzoli Intl.

De Montebello, Philippe & Fontein, Jan, eds. The Painterly Print: Monotypes from the Seventeenth to the Twentieth Century. LC 80-10441. (Illus.). 261p. 1980. 37.50 (ISBN 0-8478-5323-3). Rizzoli Intl.

Dennis, Erwin A. & Jenkins, John D. Comprehensive Graphic Arts. LC 72-92620. 1974. 20.95 (ISBN 0-672-97607-2); tchrs' manual, 1975 6.67 (ISBN 0-672-97609-9); student's manual, 1976 9.50 (ISBN 0-672-97608-0). Bobbs.

Detroit Institute Of Arts. The Graphic Art of Rolf Nesch. LC 74-8117. (Illus.). 1969. pap. 5.00 (ISBN 0-8143-1446-5). Wayne St U Pr.

Dezart, Louis. Drawing for Publication. (Illus.). 128p. 1981. 22.50x (ISBN 0-85139-185-0). Nichols Pub.

Dunthorne, Gordon. Flower & Fruit Prints of the Eighteenth & Early Nineteenth Centuries. LC 67-25443. (Graphic Art Ser). (Illus.). 1970. Repr. of 1938 ed. lib. bdg. 75.00 (ISBN 0-306-70958-9). Da Capo.

Eastman Kodak Company Staff. Graphic Design. (Exploring the World of Graphic Communications Ser.). (gr. 7-12). 1976. pap. text ed. 4.95 (ISBN 0-87985-170-8, GA-11-2). Eastman Kodak.

Ediciones Poligrafa (Barcelona) at Redfern Gallery (London) (Illus.). 69p. (Orig.). 1979. pap. 60.00x (ISBN 0-8150-0930-5). Wittenborn.

Educational Research Council of America. Graphic Artist. rev. ed. Ferris, Theodore N. & Marchak, John P., eds. (Real People at Work Ser: B). (Illus.). 1977. pap. text ed. 2.25 (ISBN 0-89247-013-5). Changing Times.

Environmental Communications. Big Art: Megamurals & Supergraphics. Teacher, Stuart, et al, eds. LC 77-14043. (Illus.). 1977. lib. bdg. 19.80 (ISBN 0-89471-007-9); pap. 7.95 (ISBN 0-89471-006-0). Running Pr.

Erte. LC 77-95013. (Illus.). 1978. pap. 8.50 (ISBN 0-8478-0164-0). Rizzoli Intl.

Field, Janet N., et al, eds. Graphic Arts Manual. LC 79-6549. (Illus.). 650p. 1980. lib. bdg. 65.00 (ISBN 0-405-12941-6). Arno.

The Fifty-Eighth Art Directors Annual. (Illus.). 1979. 29.95 (ISBN 0-916800-22-9). ADC Pubns.

Forseth, Kevin. Graphics for Architecture. 1979. pap. 9.95 (ISBN 0-442-26390-2). Van Nos Reinhold.

French, Thomas E. & Vierck, Charles J. Graphic Science & Design. 3rd ed. (Engineering Drawing Ser). 1970. text ed. 21.95 (ISBN 0-07-022301-7, C); problems 10.95 (ISBN 0-07-067443-4). McGraw.

Gabor, Mark. The Pin-up: A Modest History. LC 73-189116. (Illus.). 272p. 1973. pap. 6.95 (ISBN 0-87663-910-4). Universe.

Gatto, Joseph, et al. Exploring Visual Design. Brommer, Gerald F. & Horn, George F., eds. LC 78-55398. (Illus.). 1978. text ed. 14.50 (ISBN 0-87192-101-4). Davis Mass.

Geary, Ida. Plant Printing. (Illus.). 1978. pap. 3.50 (ISBN 0-912908-03-3). Tamal Land.

Gerry De La Ree, ed. Fifth Book of Virgil Finlay. (Illus.). 1979. 15.75 (ISBN 0-938192-02-7). De La Ree.

Glaser, Milton. Milton Glaser: Graphic Design. LC 73-79228. (Illus.). 240p. 1973. 60.00 (ISBN 0-87951-013-7). Overlook Pr.

Gluck, Felix, ed. Modern Publicity, Vol. 48. 1979. 42.50 (ISBN 0-02-857800-7). Macmillan.

Goodchild, Jon. By Design. 1979. pap. 12.95 (ISBN 0-8256-3122-X, Quick Fox). Music Sales.

Gos, Francois & Baldausky, Karen. Alpine Flower Designs for Artists & Craftsmen. (Illus.). 64p. (Orig.). 1980. pap. 4.00 (ISBN 0-486-23982-9). Dover.

Gottschall, Edward M. Graphic Communication Eighties' (Illus.). 200p. 1981. 19.95 (ISBN 0-13-363382-9). P-H.

Grannis, Chandler B. The Heritage of the Graphic Arts. LC 69-19210. (Illus.). 291p. 1972. 24.95 (ISBN 0-8352-0213-5). Bowker.

--The Heritage of the Graphic Arts. LC 69-19210. (Illus.). 291p. 1972. 24.95 (ISBN 0-8352-0213-5). Bowker.

Graphic Arts Green Book: 1981 Midwest Edition. 500p. 1981. pap. 50.00 (ISBN 0-910880-09-3). Lewis.

Graphic Design International. (Illus.). 1977. 67.50 (ISBN 0-8038-2689-3). Hastings.

Gray, Bill. More Studio Tips for Artists & Graphic Designers. 1978. pap. 5.95 (ISBN 0-442-22811-2). Van Nos Reinhold.

--Studio Tips for Artists & Graphic Designers. 1976. pap. 5.95 (ISBN 0-442-22819-8). Van Nos Reinhold.

Hamilton, Edward D. The Engraved Works, Seventeen Fifty-Five to Eighteen Twenty-Two. rev. ed. (Scripta Artis Monographia). (Illus.). 216p. 1973. pap. 15.00 (ISBN 0-8390-0126-6). Allanheld & Schram.

Harling, Robert, ed. Alphabet & Image: A Quarterly of Typography & Graphic Arts, 2 vols, Nos. 1-8. LC 75-138686. (Contemporary Art Ser.). (Illus.). Repr. of 1946 ed. Set. 80.00 (ISBN 0-405-00766-3). Arno.

Harter, Jim. Harter's Picture Archive for Collage & Illustration: Over 300 Nineteenth Century Cuts. 1978. pap. 5.00 (ISBN 0-486-23659-5). Dover.

Hartmann, Robert. Graphics for Designers. (Illus.). 1976. text ed. 10.50x (ISBN 0-8138-0760-3). Iowa St U Pr.

Hinwood, Tony. Graphics Ad Lib Number 1. 2nd ed. (Illus.). 1977. Repr. 39.50x (ISBN 0-8464-0455-9). Beekman Pubs.

Hipgnosis. Walk Away Rene. (Illus.). 1978. 25.00 (ISBN 0-89104-105-2); pap. 10.95 (ISBN 0-89104-104-4). A & W Pubs.

Hirth, Georg. Picture Book of the Graphic Arts: Thirty-Five Hundred Woodcuts, Etchings, & Engravings by the Masters 1500-1800, 6 Vols. Tanasescu, Elena, tr. LC 68-56472. (Illus.). 1969. Repr. of 1881 ed. Set. 250.00 (ISBN 0-405-08624-5, Blom Pubns); 50.00 ea. Vol. 1 (ISBN 0-405-08625-3). Vol. 2 (ISBN 0-405-08626-1). Vol. 3 (ISBN 0-405-08627-X). Vol. 4 (ISBN 0-405-08628-8). Vol. 5 (ISBN 0-405-08629-6). Vol. 6 (ISBN 0-405-08630-X). Arno.

Hornung, Clarence. Background Patterns, Textures & Tints. (Pictorial Archive Ser.). (Illus.). 112p. (Orig.). 1976. pap. 5.00 (ISBN 0-486-23260-3). Dover.

Hornung, Clarence P. & Johnson, Fridolf. Two Hundred Years of American Graphic Arts. (Illus.). 224p. 1976. 25.00 (ISBN 0-8076-0791-6). Braziller.

Hurlburt, Allen. Layout. (Illus.). 1977. 17.95 (ISBN 0-8230-2655-8). Watson-Guptill.

Institute of Graphic Designers. Graphic Design, San Francisco. LC 79-23535. (Illus.). 144p. 1980. 22.50 (ISBN 0-87701-160-5). Chronicle Bks.

Jakimowicz, Irena. Contemporary Polish Graphic Art. (Illus.). 1977. 35.00 (ISBN 0-685-80790-8). Heinman.

Johnson, Malcolm. David Claypool Johnston, American Graphic Humorist, 1798-1865. (Illus.). 1970. 4.00 (ISBN 0-89073-028-8); pap. 2.00 (ISBN 0-685-72185-X). Boston Public Lib.

Kagy, Frederick D. Graphic Arts. LC 78-5456. (Illus.). 1978. text ed. 5.20 (ISBN 0-87006-252-2). Goodheart.

Klinger, Max. Graphic Works of Max Klinger. (Illus.). 128p. 1977. pap. 5.00 (ISBN 0-486-23437-1). Dover.

Knowles, Alison. Gem Duck. (Illus.). 1978. pap. 10.00 (ISBN 0-914162-28-4). Printed Edns.

Kunst der Graphik: Renaissance in Italien, Sechszehnter Jahrhundert. (Kunst Der Graphik Ser). (Illus.). 1964. Repr. of 1966 ed. 6.50 (ISBN 0-405-00297-1). Arno.

Kunst der Graphik: Zwischen Renaissance und Barock, das Zeithalter Von Bruegel und Bellange. (Illus.). 1967. 7.75 (ISBN 0-405-00298-X). Arno.

Lambert, F. W. Graphics-Britain. 1972. 25.00 (ISBN 0-7137-0554-X). Transatlantic.

Laseau, Paul. Graphic Thinking for Architects & Designers. 224p. 1980. text ed. 18.95 (ISBN 0-442-26247-7); pap. text ed. 12.50 (ISBN 0-442-25698-1). Van Nos Reinhold.

Lem, Dean P. Graphics Master, No. 2. LC 76-41508. (Illus.). 113p. 1977. 47.50 (ISBN 0-914218-02-6). D Lem Assocs.

Lippard, Lucy, frwd. by. Kathe Kollwitz: Graphics, Posters, Drawings. (Illus.). 1981. 20.00 (ISBN 0-394-51948-5); pap. 12.95 (ISBN 0-394-74878-6). Pantheon.

Londenberg, K. Papier & Form: Paper & Form. (Illus., Ger.). 1972. pap. 25.00x (ISBN 0-685-41587-2). Museum Bks.

Los Angeles Unified School District. Graphic Arts. Vorndran, Richard A., ed. LC 77-73302. 128p. (gr. 7-9). 1978. pap. text ed. 4.40 (ISBN 0-02-820430-1). Glencoe.

Ludlow, Norman H., Jr. Clip Book Number Ten: Shapes, Frames & Borders. (Illus.). 1979. pap. text ed. 12.95x (ISBN 0-916706-16-8). N H Ludlow.

Ludman, Joan. Fairfield Porter, a Catalogue Raisonne of His Prints. Leerburger, Benedict A., ed. LC 81-4150. (Illus.). 160p. 1981. 24.50 (ISBN 0-938988-00-X). Highland NY.

Lundquist, Par. Color Graphics. (Illus.). 188p. 1980. 29.95 (ISBN 0-240-51046-1). Focal Pr.

McCay, Winsor. Dreams of the Rarebit Fiend. (Illus.). 80p. 1973. pap. 3.50 (ISBN 0-486-21347-1). Dover.

McKnight Staff Members & Miller, Wilbur R. Graphic Arts. LC 78-53390. (Basic Industrial Arts Ser.). (Illus.). 1978. 6.00 (ISBN 0-87345-795-1); softbound 4.48 (ISBN 0-87345-787-0). McKnight.

Meder, J. & Handbuck, Ein. Durer-Katalog. LC 75-87642. (Graphic Art Ser.: Vol. 12). (Illus.). 358p. 1971. Repr. of 1932 ed. lib. bdg. 59.50 (ISBN 0-306-71788-3). Da Capo.

Menten, Theodore. Ready-to-Use Banners. (Clip Art Ser.). (Illus.). 1979. pap. 2.50 (ISBN 0-486-23899-7). Dover.

Monthan, Doris. R. C. Gorman: The Lithographs. LC 78-58469. (Illus.). 1978. 35.00 (ISBN 0-87358-179-2). Northland.

Monza, Louis, illus. Graphic Work of Louis Monza. (Illus.). 60p. 1973. natural finish buckram 22.50 (ISBN 0-686-14552-6). Plantin Pr.

Mullen, Chris. Cigarette Pack Art. 1979. pap. 7.95 (ISBN 0-312-13842-3). St Martin.

Musuem, Victor & Musuem, Albert. Berthold Wolpe. (Illus.). 96p. 1981. 22.00 (ISBN 0-571-11655-8, Pub. by Faber & Faber). Merrimack Bk Serv.

Otto, Frei, et al, eds. IL Eight: Nets in Nature & Technics. (Illus., Orig., Eng. & Ger.). 1975. pap. 34.50x (ISBN 0-8150-0662-4). Wittenborn.

Phillips, Sandra. Matt Phillips: The Graphic Work. 1976. 6.00 (ISBN 0-686-24037-5). Bellevue Pr.

Pillsbury, Edmund P. & Richards, Louise E. The Graphic Art of Federico Barocci. 1978. pap. 6.00 (ISBN 0-89467-004-2). Yale Art Gallery.

Pitseolak. Pitseolak: Pictures Out of My Life. Eber, Dorothy, ed. LC 72-4111. (Illus.). 96p. 1979. pap. 6.95 (ISBN 0-295-95632-1). U of Wash Pr.

Revens, Lee, ed. The Graphic Work of Felicien Rops. (Illus.). 1975. 14.95 (ISBN 0-685-59185-9). L Amiel Pub.

Sawamura, Kaichi, intro. by. Graphic Arts Japan, 1980-81, Vol. 22. LC 64-43886. 178p. (Orig.). 1981. pap. 35.00x (ISBN 0-8002-2760-3). Intl Pubns Serv.

Schad, Tennyson & Shapiro, Ira, eds. American Showcase of Photography, Illustration, Graphic Design, TV, Film, & Video. 336p. 37.50 (ISBN 0-931144-06-X); pap. 25.00 (ISBN 0-931144-05-1). Am Showcase.

Schmid, Calvin F. & Schmid, Stanton E. Handbook of Graphic Presentation. 2nd ed. LC 78-13689. 1979. 18.50 (ISBN 0-471-04724-4, Pub. by Wiley-Interscience). Wiley.

Schmittel, Wolfgang. Process Visual: The Development of Corporate Visibility. (Illus.). 1978. 67.50 (ISBN 0-8038-5869-8). Hastings.

Silver, Gerald. Graphic Layout & Design. LC 80-65062. (Graphic Arts Ser.). 216p. 1981. pap. text ed. 10.40 (ISBN 0-8273-1374-8); instructor's guide 1.20 (ISBN 0-8273-1375-6). Delmar.

Singer, Hans W. Max Klingers Radierungen Stiche und Steindrucke. (Illus.). 1978. 75.00 (ISBN 0-931036-03-8). Martin Gordon.

The Sixieth Art Directors Annual. Solomon, Miriam L., ed. (Illus.). 688p. 1981. 34.95 (ISBN 0-937414-01-8). ADC Pubns.

Skal, David J., ed. Graphic Communications for the Performing Arts. LC 81-51181. (Illus.). 152p. (Orig.). 1981. pap. 12.95 (ISBN 0-930452-11-9). Theatre Comm.

Smith, C. Ray & Miho, James N. AIGA Graphic Design USA, No. 1. (The Annual of the American Institute of Graphic Arts). (Illus.). 432p. 1980. 40.00 (ISBN 0-8230-2148-3). Watson-Guptill.

Smith, Virginia. Alphagraphics. (Illus.). 1978. pap. 9.95 (ISBN 0-684-15978-3, ScribT). Scribner.

Sol LeWitt: Graphik 1970-1975. (Illus.). 96p. pap. 16.00 (ISBN 0-686-74781-X). Bklyn Mus.

Solo, Dan X. Special Effects & Topical Alphabets. 1978. pap. 3.50 (ISBN 0-486-23657-9). Dover.

Spear, Mary E. Practical Charting Techniques. 1969. 23.50 (ISBN 0-07-060010-4, P&RB). McGraw.

Spence, William P. & Vequist, David G. Graphic Reproduction. 1981. 32.50 (ISBN 0-684-16764-6, ScribT). Scribner.

Spurgeon, C. H. The Art of Illustration. 3.95 (ISBN 0-686-09090-X). Pilgrim Pubns.

Stevens, Peter S. A Handbook of Regular Patterns: An Introduction to Symmetry in Two Dimensions. (Illus.). 384p. 1981. 37.50 (ISBN 0-262-19188-1). MIT Pr.

Strauss, Victor. Graphic Arts Management. LC 73-84853. (Illus.). 340p. 1973. 24.75 (ISBN 0-914114-01-8). Bowker.

Swerdlow, R. Basic Book of Graphic Arts. (Illus.). 1979. 6.00 (ISBN 0-8269-2665-7). Am Technical.

--Introduction to Graphic Arts. (Illus.). 1979. 12.33 (ISBN 0-8269-2745-9). Am Technical.

Tait, Jack. Beyond Photography. (Illus.). 1977. 28.50 (ISBN 0-240-50822-X). Focal Pr.

Tanaka, Ikko, et al, eds. Illustration in Japan, Vol. 1. (Illus.). 260p. 1981. 49.50 (ISBN 0-87011-473-5). Kodansha.

Thorson, Victoria. Rodin Graphics: A Catalogue Raisonne of Drypoints & Book Illustrations. LC 75-16941. (Illus.). 1975. pap. 4.50 (ISBN 0-88401-007-4). Fine Arts Mus.

Tunick, David & Driver, Arthur. Italian Prints of the Eighteenth Century. (Illus.). 200p. 1981. pap. 8.00 (ISBN 0-9605298-0-2). Tunick Inc.

Turnbull, Arthur T. & Baird, Russell N. The Graphics of Communication: Typography, Layout, Design, Production. 4th ed. LC 79-19850. 398p. 1980. text ed. 17.95 (ISBN 0-03-021666-4, HoltC). HR&W.

Van Uchelen, Rod. Say It with Pictures: Graphic Communication with Illustration. 1979. 12.95 (ISBN 0-442-28642-2); pap. 7.95 (ISBN 0-442-28644-9). Van Nos Reinhold.

Vassos, John. Contempo, Phobia & Other Graphic Interpretations. LC 76-696. (Illus.). 115p. (Orig.). 1976. pap. 4.50 (ISBN 0-486-23338-3). Dover.

Veres, Peter & Patchen, Miriam. The Argument of Innocence: A Selection from the Arts of Kenneth Patchen. LC 75-9695. (Illus.). 96p. 1977. pap. 7.50 (ISBN 0-912020-39-3). Scrimshaw Calif.

Walker, John R. Graphic Arts Fundamentals. LC 79-24182. (Illus.). 320p. 1980. 12.80 (ISBN 0-87006-288-3); wkbk 3.20 (ISBN 0-87006-303-0). Goodheart.

Warford, H. Stanley. Design for Print Production. (Library of Printing Technology). (Illus.). 216p. 1972. 19.95 (ISBN 0-240-50741-X). Focal Pr.

Weiner, Douglas. Tibetan & Himalayan Woodblock Prints. (Illus., Orig.). 1974. pap. 6.00 (ISBN 0-486-22988-2). Dover.

Weitenkampf, Frank. American Graphic Art. new & enl. ed. LC 24-12503. (American Studies). Repr. of 1924 ed. 18.50 (ISBN 0-384-66645-0). Johnson Repr.

Wileman, Ralph E. Exercises in Visual Thinking. 1980. 14.95 (ISBN 0-8038-7212-7). Hastings.

Wofsy, Alan. Survey of Graphic Art: Prints & Illustrated Books from Six Centuries. 1974. 5.00 (ISBN 0-915346-21-4). A Wofsy Fine Arts.

Woodbine, Paul. Revisor. 1979. text ed. 7.00 (ISBN 0-916258-09-2, Colophon Bks). Woodbine-Volaphon.

GRAPHIC ARTS–BIBLIOGRAPHY

Graphic Arts Trade Journals Intl Inc. Export Graficas USA, 1981 to 1982. Humphrey, G. A. & Miura, Lydia, eds. (Illus.). 136p. (Orig.). 1981. pap. 15.00 (ISBN 0-910762-07-4). Graph Arts Trade.

Stokes, I. N. & Haskell, Daniel C. American Historical Prints: Early Views of American Cities, Etc., from the Phelps Stokes & Other Collections. LC 77-180284. (Illus.). 235p. 1974. Repr. of 1933 ed. 32.00 (ISBN 0-8103-3950-1). Gale.

GRAPHIC ARTS–DICTIONARIES

Comte, R. & Pernin, A. Lexique des Industries Graphiques. 128p. (Fr.). 1975. pap. 17.50 (ISBN 0-686-56959-8, M-6082). French & Eur.

Cooper, Al. World of Logotypes: Trademark Encyclopedia, Vol. 2. LC 75-29774. (Illus.). 1978. 24.50 (ISBN 0-910158-34-7). Art Dir.

Crawford, Tad & Kopelman, Arie. Selling Your Graphic Design & Illustration. 272p. 1981. 13.95 (ISBN 0-312-71252-9). St Martin.

Dictionary for the Graphic Arts: German-English, English-German. 1979. plastic bdg. 26.25 (ISBN 3-87641-158-0). Perfect Graphic.

Dictionary for the Graphic Arts in Six Languages: German-English-French-Spanish-Italian-Swedish. 1979. plastic bdg. 75.00 (ISBN 3-87641-192-0). Perfect Graphic.

Mintz, Patricia. Dictionary of Graphic Arts Terms: A Communication Tool for People Who Buy Type & Printing. 328p. 1981. text ed. 17.95 (ISBN 0-686-77460-4). Van Nos Reinhold.

Stevenson, George A. Graphic Arts Encyclopedia. 2nd ed. (Illus.). 1979. 29.95 (ISBN 0-07-061288-9). McGraw.

Thompson, Philip & Davenport, Peter, eds. Dictionary of Graphic Cliches. LC 79-2094. (Illus.). 1979. 30.00x (ISBN 0-312-20108-7). St Martin.

GRAPHIC ARTS–STUDY AND TEACHING

Nash, Ray, et al. Education in the Graphic Arts. 1969. 3.00 (ISBN 0-89073-025-3). Boston Public Lib.

Tettaton, Lonnie. Sign Painting & Graphics Course. LC 80-12135. (Illus.). 240p. 1981. 29.95 (ISBN 0-88229-478-4); pap. 15.95 (ISBN 0-88229-768-6). Nelson-Hall.

GRAPHIC ARTS–TECHNIQUE

Basic Color for the Graphic Arts. 1981. 6.00 (ISBN 0-87985-031-0, Q7). Eastman Kodak.

Brunner, Felix. Handbook of Graphic Reproduction Processes. Date not set. 67.50 (ISBN 0-686-76149-9). Hastings.

Capon, Robin. Introducing Graphic Techniques. 1979. 17.95 (ISBN 0-7134-2435-4, Pub. by Batsford England). David & Charles.

Craig, James. Designing with Type. rev. ed. Meyer, Susan, ed. (Illus.). 1980. 15.95 (ISBN 0-8230-1321-9). Watson-Guptill.

Croy, Peter. Graphic Design & Reproduction Techniques. rev. ed. (Visual Communication Bks.). 1972. 19.95 (ISBN 0-240-44872-3). Focal Pr.

Garrett, Lillian. Visual Design: A Problem Solving Approach. LC 75-12638. 216p. 1967. Repr. of 1966 ed. 13.50 (ISBN 0-88275-332-0). Krieger.

Gill, Bob. Forget All the Rules You Ever Learned About Graphic Design: Including the Ones in This Book. 168p. 1981. 22.50 (ISBN 0-686-69766-9). Watson-Guptill.

Graphic Arts Handbook. 30.00 (ISBN 0-87985-127-9, W24). Eastman Kodak.

Henton, Richard W. Quick-Sketch: A New Technique in Interior Design Graphics. 144p. 1980. pap. text ed. 8.95 (ISBN 0-8403-2233-X). Kendall-Hunt.

Hofmann, Armin. Graphic Design Manual: Principles & Practice. (Illus.). 1965. pap. 7.95 (ISBN 0-442-23469-4). Van Nos Reinhold.

Holland, D. K. Graphic Artists Guild Handbook. 4th ed. 144p. 1981. pap. 12.95 (ISBN 0-932102-03-4). Graphic Artists.

Kemper, Alfred M. Presentation Drawings by American Architects. LC 76-40891. 380p. 1977. 41.00 (ISBN 0-471-01369-2, Pub. by Wiley-Interscience). Wiley.

Porter, Tom & Greenstreet, Robert. Manual of Graphic Techniques. (Illus.). 1980. pap. 9.95 (ISBN 0-684-16504-X, ScribT). Scribner.

Satterthwaite, Les L. Graphics: Skills, Media & Materials, a Laboratory Mnaual. 3rd ed. (Illus.). 1977. pap. text ed. 7.95 (ISBN 0-8403-8009-7). Kendall-Hunt.

Spence. Graphic Reproductions. 1980. text ed. 22.64 (ISBN 0-87002-285-7); student guide 2.60 (ISBN 0-87002-319-5). Bennett IL.

Van Uchelen, Rod. Paste-up: Art Production for the New Art World. 1976. 14.95 (ISBN 0-442-29022-5); pap. 7.95 (ISBN 0-442-29021-7). Van Nos Reinhold.

Watson, Ernest W. & Watson, Aldren A. The Watson Drawing Book. 1981. pap. 9.95 (ISBN 0-442-20054-4). Van Nos Reinhold.

Wentink, S. & Koch, S. UV Curing in Screen Printing for Printed Circuits & the Graphic Arts. 1980. 92.00 (ISBN 0-936840-00-5). Tech Marketing.

White, Jan. The Graphic Idea Notebook. (Illus.). 1980. 14.50 (ISBN 0-8230-2149-1). Watson-Guptill.

GRAPHIC ARTS–YEARBOOKS

Cordy, Peter, ed. Creative Source: Third Annual 1982. 414p. 1981. 45.00 (ISBN 0-920986-02-1). Wilcord Pubns.

Graphic Arts Trade Journal Intl Inc. Export Grafics USA 1980-81. Humphrey, G. A. & Miura, Lydia, eds. (Illus.). 94p. (Orig.). 1980. pap. 15.00 (ISBN 0-910762-06-6). Graph Arts Trade.

Herdeg, Walter, ed. Graphis Annual: 1980-81. Date not set. 59.50 (ISBN 0-8038-2709-1). Hastings.

GRAPHIC DATA PROCESSING

see Computer Graphics

GRAPHIC DIFFERENTIATION

see Numerical Integration

GRAPHIC METHODS

see also Decision Logic Tables; Flow Charts; Flowgraphs; Graphic Statics; Line of Balance (Management); Nomography (Mathematics); Regge Trajectories;
also subdivision Graphic Methods under specific subjects, e.g. Statistics–Graphic Methods

Berge, C. Graphs & Hypergraphs. 2nd rev. ed. LC 72-88288. (Mathematical Library: No. 6). (Illus.). 555p. 1976. 49.00 (ISBN 0-7204-0479-7, North-Holland). Elsevier.

Biggs, Norman, et al. Graph Theory: Seventeen Thirty-Six to Nineteen Thirty-Six. (Illus.). 1976. 59.00x (ISBN 0-19-853901-0). Oxford U Pr.

Broekhuizen, Richard. Graphic Communications. 380p. 1979. text ed. 15.72 (ISBN 0-87345-246-1); study guide 3.96 (ISBN 0-87345-247-X); ans. key free (ISBN 0-87345-248-8). McKnight.
Cameron, P. J. & Van Lint, J. H. Graphs, Codes & Designs. (London Mathematical Society Lecture Notes Ser.: No. 43). 180p. 1980. 19.95x (ISBN 0-521-23141-8). Cambridge U Pr.
Cardamone, Tom. Chart & Graph Preparation Skills. 1981. 18.95 (ISBN 0-442-26284-1); pap. 9.95 (ISBN 0-442-26286-8). Van Nos Reinhold.
Carre, Bernard. Graphs & Networks. (Oxford Applied Mathematics & Computing Science Ser.). (Illus.). 1979. 55.00 (ISBN 0-19-859615-4); pap. 19.50x (ISBN 0-19-859622-7). Oxford U Pr.
Centre De Mathematique Sociale Ecole Des Hautes Etudes En Sciences Sociales. Combinatorics Graphs & Algebra. (Methods & Models in the Social Sciences: No. 5). (Illus., Orig.). 1976. text ed. 23.50x (ISBN 90-2797-511-6). Mouton.
Chartrand, Gary. Graphs As Mathematical Models. 1977. text ed. write for info. (ISBN 0-87150-236-4, PWS 1901). Prindle.
Coxeter, H. S., et al. Zero-Symmetric Graphs: Trivalent Graphical Regular Representations of Groups. LC 81-4604. 1981. 15.00 (ISBN 0-686-77441-8). Acad Pr.
Cvetlovic, Dragos, et al, eds. Spectra of Graphs: Theory & Applications. LC 79-50490. (Pure & Applied Mathematics Ser.). 1980. 51.50 (ISBN 0-12-195150-2). Acad Pr.
Dlab, Vlastimil & Ringel, Claus M. Indecomposable Representations of Graphs & Algebras. LC 76-18784. (Memoirs: No. 173). 1976. pap. 10.00 (ISBN 0-8218-1873-2, MEMO-173). Am Math.
Enrick, Norbert L. Handbook of Effective Graphic & Tabular Communication. LC 79-44833. 224p. 1980. 12.50 (ISBN 0-88275-914-0). Krieger.
Fitts, Gary. Module XI: Graphing Functions. Ablon, Leon J., ed. LC 76-62884. (Ser. in Mathematics Modules). 1977. pap. 4.95 (ISBN 0-8465-0265-8). Benjamin-Cummings.
Fritz, Lawrence W., pref. by. Analytical Plotter Symposium & Workshop: Proceedings. (Illus.). 1980. 17.50 (ISBN 0-937294-00-4). ASP.
Frost, Percival. Curve Tracing. 5th ed. LC 60-10348. 9.95 (ISBN 0-8284-0140-3). Chelsea Pub.
Fry, Edward B. Graphical Comprehension: How to Read & Make Graphs. (Illus.). 160p. (Orig.). (gr. 9-12). 1981. pap. text ed. 5.60x (ISBN 0-89061-240-4, 782). Jamestown Pubs.
Gelfand, I. M., et al. Functions & Graphs. (Pocket Mathematical Library Ser.). 1968. 18.75x (ISBN 0-677-20690-9). Gordon.
Grossman, I. & Magnus, W. Groups & Their Graphs. LC 64-8512. (New Mathematical Library: No. 14). 1975. pap. 6.50 (ISBN 0-88385-614-X). Math Assn.
Hackworth, Robert D. & Howland, Joseph. Introductory College Mathematics: Tables & Graphs. LC 75-23628. (Illus.). 62p. 1976. pap. text ed. 2.95 (ISBN 0-7216-4421-X). HR&W.
Hou, S. L., ed. Sixteenth Annual Fall Symposium on Business Graphics. LC 76-46764. 1976. pap. 14.00 (ISBN 0-89208-088-4). Soc Photo Sci & Eng.
Hypergraph Seminar, Ohio State University, 1972. Proceedings. Berge, C. & Ray-Chaudhuri, D., eds. (Lecture Notes in Mathematics: Vol. 411). x, 287p. 1974. pap. 15.20 (ISBN 0-387-06846-5). Springer-Verlag.
Kepler, Harold B. Basic Graphical Kinematics. 2nd ed. (Illus.). 384p. 1973. text ed. 17.95 (ISBN 0-07-034171-0, G); problems 4.95 (ISBN 0-07-034173-7); solutions for problems 3.00 (ISBN 0-07-034172-9); solutions manual 3.00 (ISBN 0-07-034174-5). McGraw.
Lassea, Paul. Graphic Problem Solving for Architects & Builders. LC 75-8607. 1975. 19.95 (ISBN 0-8436-0154-X); pap. 12.75 (ISBN 0-685-93090-4). CBI Pub.
Leblanc, John F., et al. Mathematics-Methods Program: Graphs, the Picturing of Information. (Mathematics Ser.). (Illus.). 160p. 1976. pap. text ed. 3.95 (ISBN 0-201-14622-3); instr's man. 1.50 (ISBN 0-201-14623-1). A-W.
Lefferts, Robert. Elements of Graphics: How to Prepare Charts & Graphs for Effective Reports. LC 80-8209. (Illus.). 192p. 1981. 12.95 (ISBN 0-06-012578-0, HarpT). Har-Row.
Levens, A. S. Graphical Methods in Research. rev ed. LC 75-15676. 256p. 1975. Repr. of 1965 ed. 12.50 (ISBN 0-88275-316-9). Krieger.
MacGregor, A. J. Graphics Simplified: How to Plan & Prepare Effective Charts, Graphs, Illustrations, & Other Visual Aids. LC 79-10358. (Orig.). 1979. pap. 2.95 (ISBN 0-8020-6363-2). U of Toronto Pr.
Maxwell, Lee M. & Reed, Myril B. The Theory of Graphs: A Basis for Network Theory. LC 77-106387. 181p. 1975. 16.00 (ISBN 0-08-016321-1). Pergamon.
Mulhearn, Henry J. Graphing, Charting Simplified. 1976. 6.00 (ISBN 0-87526-221-X). Gould.
Muller-Brockmann, Josef. Grid Systems in Graphic Design: A Visual Communications Manual. (Visual Communications Bks.). (Illus.). 176p. (Eng. & Ger.). 1981. 45.00 (ISBN 0-8038-2711-3). Hastings.
Ore, Oystein. Graphs & Their Use. LC 63-9345. (New Mathematical Library: No. 10). 1975. pap. 4.50 (ISBN 0-88385-610-7). Math Assn.
Picard, C. F. Graphs & Questionnaires. (Mathematical Studies Ser.: Vol. 32). 1978. 39.00 (ISBN 0-444-85239-5, North-Holland). Elsevier.
Robinson, D. F. & Foulds, L. R. Diagraphs: Theory & Technique. 271p. 1980. 38.50 (ISBN 0-677-05470-X). Gordon.
Rudman, Jack. Director of Graphics & Production. (Career Examination Ser.: C-1795). (Cloth bdg. avail. on request). pap. 10.00 (ISBN 0-8373-1795-9). Natl Learning.
Shilov, G. Plotting Graphs. 1978. pap. 1.25 (ISBN 0-8285-0736-8, Pub. by Mir Pubs Russia). Imported Pubns.
Swokowski, Earl W. Functions & Graphs. 3rd ed. 507p. 1980. write for info (ISBN 0-87150-283-6, 2221). Prindle.
Turner, David R. Graph, Chart & Table: Interpretation for Test-Takers. LC 80-14351. 224p. 1980. pap. 8.00 (ISBN 0-668-04817-4, 4817-4). Arco.
Typony. Etcetera: Graphic Devices. 176p. 1980. pap. 12.95 (ISBN 0-442-24456-8). Van Nos Reinhold.
Use of Graphs in Internal Reporting. (Accounting Practice Report: No. 13). 2.50 (ISBN 0-686-09800-5, 6128). Natl Assn Accts.

GRAPHIC STATICS

see also Bridges; Building, Iron and Steel; Girders; Girders, Continuous; Influence Lines; Mechanical Drawing; Nomography (Mathematics); Roofs; Strains and Stresses; Strength of Materials

Henneberg, L. E. Graphische Statik der Starren Systeme. (Bibliotheca Mathematica Teubneriana, Ser: No. 38). (Ger). 1969. Repr. of 1911 ed. 46.00 (ISBN 0-384-22325-7). Johnson Repr.
M. Roshan Ali Khan. A Textbook of Graphic Statics. (Illus.). 108p. 1973. pap. text ed. 4.00 (ISBN 0-210-22598-X). Asia.

GRAPHICS, COMPUTER

see Computer Graphics

GRAPHICS, ENGINEERING

see Engineering Graphics

GRAPHICS, TELEVISION

see Television Graphics

GRAPHITE

Blackman, L. C. Modern Aspects of Graphite Technology. 1970. 52.50 (ISBN 0-12-103350-3). Acad Pr.
McCreight, L. R., et al. Ceramic & Graphic Fibers & Whiskers: A Survey of Technology. (Refractory Materials Ser., Vol. 1). 1965. 47.00 (ISBN 0-12-482950-3). Acad Pr.
Mantell, Charles L. Carbon & Graphite Handbook. LC 78-21468. 548p. 1979. Repr. of 1968 ed. lib. bdg. 29.50 (ISBN 0-88275-796-2). Krieger.
Manufactured Carbon & Graphite Products. pap. 3.50 (ISBN 0-686-51992-2, 06-305001-00). ASTM.
Reynolds, W. N. Physical Properties of Graphite. (Illus.). 1968. text ed. 26.00x (ISBN 0-444-20012-6). Intl Ideas.
Sittig, Marshall. Carbon & Graphite Fibers: Manufacture & Applications. LC 80-16275. (Chemical Technology Review: No. 162). 422p. (Orig.). 1980. 54.00 (ISBN 0-8155-0806-9). Noyes.

GRAPHOLOGY

see also Drawing, Psychology Of

Bauml, Franz H., ed. Kudrun: Die Handschrift. (Ger). 1969. 58.00x (ISBN 3-11-000376-7). De Gruyter.
Bunker, M. N. Handwriting Analysis: The Science of Determining Personality by Graphoanalysis. 13.95 (ISBN 0-911012-68-0). Nelson-Hall.
--What Handwriting Tells You: About Yourself, Your Friends, & Famous People. 13.95 (ISBN 0-911012-02-8). Nelson-Hall.
Byrd, Anita. Handwriting Analysis. LC 81-3461. (Illus.). 160p. 1981. 8.95 (ISBN 0-668-05307-0); pap. 3.95 (ISBN 0-668-05311-9). Arco.
Casewit, Curtis. Graphology Handbook. (Illus.). 168p. (Orig.). 1980. pap. 6.95 (ISBN 0-914918-15-X). Para Res.
Colombe, Sainte. Grapho-Therapeutics. pap. 3.95 (ISBN 0-685-07323-8). Borden.
De Sainte Colombe, Paul. Grapho-Therapeutics: Pen & Pencil Therapy. 1966. pap. 8.95 (ISBN 0-87516-297-5). De Vorss.
Engel, Joel. Handwriting Analysis Self-Taught. (Illus.). 1980. 10.95 (ISBN 0-525-66687-7); pap. 6.95 (ISBN 0-525-66697-4). Elsevier-Nelson.
Falcon, Hal. How to Analyze Handwriting. 1971. 5.95 (ISBN 0-671-27079-6). Trident.
--How to Analyze Handwriting. 160p. 1964. pap. 1.95 (ISBN 0-346-12161-2). Cornerstone.
Frazer, Persifor. Bibliotics. LC 70-156017. (Illus.). Repr. of 1901 ed. 23.75 (ISBN 0-404-09117-2). AMS Pr.
French, William L. Your Handwriting & What It Means. LC 80-19831. 226p. 1980. Repr. of 1976 ed. lib. bdg. 9.95x (ISBN 0-89370-636-1). Borgo Pr.
Frith, Henry. Graphology: The Science of Handwriting. LC 80-80536. (Illus.). 128p. 1980. pap. 4.50 (ISBN 0-8334-1756-8). Steinerbks.
--Graphology: The Science of Handwriting. LC 80-80536. (Illus.). 128p. 1980. pap. 4.50 (ISBN 0-8334-1756-8). Steinerbks.
Gardner, Ruth. Graphology Student's Workbook. 2nd ed. (Illus.). 137p. 1975. 4.95 (ISBN 0-87542-250-0). Llewellyn Pubns.
Gologie, Ralph V. A Study in Symbolism: An Empirical Foundation of Graphology. LC 73-86368. 256p. 1973. pap. 5.95x (ISBN 0-915286-00-9). Unique Bks.
Green, Jane. You & Your Private I. LC 75-2320. (Illus.). 225p. 1975. pap. 4.95 (ISBN 0-87542-295-0). Llewellyn Pubns.
Hagan, W. E. Treatise on Disputed Handwriting & the Determination of Genuine from Forged Signatures. LC 76-38666. Repr. of 1894 ed. 23.00 (ISBN 0-404-09175-X). AMS Pr.
Handwriting: A Key to Personality. LC 52-7197. 1977. 12.95 (ISBN 0-394-42762-9). Pantheon.
Harper, Charles G. Haunted Houses: Tales of the Supernatural with Some Account of Hereditary Curses & Family Legends. LC 79-164326. (Illus.). xvi, 283p. 1971. Repr. of 1907 ed. 28.00 (ISBN 0-8103-3928-5). Gale.
Hartford, Huntington. You Are What You Write. LC 72-91262. 360p. 1973. 12.95 (ISBN 0-02-548500-8). Macmillan.
--You Are What You Write. (Illus.). 400p. 1976. pap. 4.95 (ISBN 0-02-080210-2, Collier). Macmillan.
Hearns, Rudolph S. Self-Portraits in Autographs. 1981. 7.95 (ISBN 0-8062-1550-X). Carlton.
Hill, Barbara. Graphology. LC 80-27752. (Illus.). 144p. 1981. 9.95 (ISBN 0-312-34444-9). St Martin.
Holder, Robert. You Can Analyze Your Own Handwriting. pap. 2.25 (ISBN 0-451-09642-8, E9642, Sig). NAL.
Holt, Arthur G. Handwriting in Psychological Interpretations. (Illus.). 276p. 1974. text ed. 21.75 (ISBN 0-398-00864-7). C C Thomas.
Hughes, Albert E. What Your Handwriting Reveals. 1978. 2.00 (ISBN 0-87980-365-7). Wilshire.
Jansen, Abraham. Validation of Graphological Judgements: An Experimental Study. LC 76-184573. (Psychological Studies, Ser. Major: No. 8). (Illus.). 189p. (Orig.). 1973. pap. text ed. 22.00x (ISBN 90-2797-267-2). Mouton.
Lester, David. The Psychological Basis of Handwriting Analysis: The Relationship of Handwriting to Personality & Psychopathology. LC 79-23957. 192p. 1981. text ed. 18.95x (ISBN 0-88229-533-0). Nelson-Hall.
LeVialle, Robert F. Thirty-Six Illustrated Handwriting Traits for the Supervisor & Manager (& the Employee) (Illus.). 1978. 6.95 (ISBN 0-8059-2540-6). Dorrance.
Lucas, DeWitt B. Handwriting & Character. 1956. 3.95 (ISBN 0-910140-09-X). Anthony.
--Handwriting & Character Analysis. 1959. flexible plastic bgd. 3.50 (ISBN 0-685-06560-X). Assoc Bk.
Mann, Peggy. The Telltale Line: The Secrets of Handwriting Analysis. LC 76-8436. (Illus.). 96p. (gr. 5 up). 1976. 8.95 (ISBN 0-02-762240-1, 76224). Macmillan.
Marley, John. Handwriting Analysis Made Easy. pap. 3.00 (ISBN 0-87980-045-3). Wilshire.
Mendel, Alfred O. Personality in Handwriting: A Handbook of American Graphology. 2nd ed. (Illus.). (gr. 9-12). text ed. 15.00 (ISBN 0-8044-5676-3, Pub. by Stephen Daye Pr). Ungar.
Meyer, Jerome S. The Handwriting Analyzer. 1974. pap. 4.95 (ISBN 0-671-21757-7, Fireside). S&S.
Myer, Oscar N. Language of Handwriting: And How to Read It. (Illus.). pap. 4.95 (ISBN 0-8044-6556-8, Pub. by Stephen Daye Pr). Ungar.
Olyanova, Nadya. Psychology of Handwriting. (Illus.). pap. 3.00 (ISBN 0-87980-128-X). Wilshire.
Robie, Joan H. What Your Handwriting Tells About You. LC 77-91726. 1978. 5.95 (ISBN 0-8054-6922-2). Broadman.
Rockwell, Frances. Graphology for Lovers. (Orig.). 1979. pap. 1.75 (ISBN 0-451-08854-9, E8854, Sig). NAL.
Ruiz, Mary & Amend, Karen S. The Complete Book of Handwriting Analysis. 1980. pap. 9.95 (ISBN 0-87877-050-X). Newcastle Pub.
Ruiz, Mary S. & Amend, Karen. The Complete Book of Handwriting Analysis. LC 80-8672. (Illus.). 196p. 1980. Repr. of 1980 ed. lib. bdg. 17.95 (ISBN 0-89370-650-7). Borgo Pr.
Saudek, Robert. Anonymous Letters. LC 75-38671. (Foundations of Criminal Justice Ser.). (Illus.). Repr. of 1933 ed. 14.00 (ISBN 0-404-09182-2). AMS Pr.
--Experiments with Handwriting. 1978. 29.50 (ISBN 0-935422-00-5). Bks for Profs.
--The Psychology of Handwriting. 1978. 27.50 (ISBN 0-935422-01-3). Bks for Profs.
Schweighofer, Fritz. Graphology & Psychoanalysis: The Handwriting of Sigmund Freud & His Circle. Ray, Susan, tr. from Ger. LC 79-19170. Orig. Title: Psychanalyse und Graphologie. 1979. text ed. 22.95 (ISBN 0-8261-2990-0). Springer Pub.
Singer, Eric. Manual of Graphology. 2nd ed. (Illus.). 244p. 1974. 28.00 (ISBN 0-7156-0415-5, Pub. by Duckworth England); pap. 13.50 (ISBN 0-7156-0784-7, Pub. by Duckworth England). Biblio Dist.
--Personality in Handwriting. 2nd ed. (Illus.). 120p. 1974. 28.00 (ISBN 0-7156-0786-3, Pub. by Duckworth England); pap. 13.50 (ISBN 0-7156-0785-5, Pub. by Duckworth England). Biblio Dist.
Solomon, Shirl. How to Really Know Yourself Through Your Handwriting. LC 72-8321. 1973. 7.95 (ISBN 0-8008-3966-8). Taplinger.
--Knowing Your Child Through His Handwriting & Drawing. (Illus.). 1978. 8.95 (ISBN 0-517-53287-5). Crown.
Sovik, Nils. Developmental Cybernetics of Handwriting & Graphic Behavior: An Experimental System Analysis of Writing Readiness & Instruction. 1975. pap. text ed. 30.00x (ISBN 8-200-01476-2, Dist. by Columbia U Pr). Universitet.
Whiting, Eldene & Blazi, Peter. Trait-Match: Discovering the Occupational Personality Through Handwriting Analysis. LC 77-83729. 1977. 10.00 (ISBN 0-914350-19-6). Vulcan Bks.
Williamson, Doris M. & Meenach, Antoinette E. Cross-Check System for Forgery & Question Document Examination. LC 81-1974. (Illus.). 136p. 1981. text ed. 21.95 (ISBN 0-88229-430-X). Nelson-Hall.
Wolff, Werner. Diagrams of the Unconscious - Handwriting & Personality in Measurement, Experiment & Analysis. LC 49-985. (Illus.). 438p. 1948. 43.50 (ISBN 0-8089-0542-2). Grune.
Wyland, Johanna L. Your Paths in Ink: Graphoanalysis & the Personality. (Illus.). 86p. 1980. 6.95 (ISBN 0-682-49604-9). Exposition.

GRAPHOLOGY–DICTIONARIES

Roman, Klara G. Encyclopedia of the Written Word: A Lexicon for Graphology & Other Aspects of Writing. Wolfson, Rose & Edwards, Maurice, eds. LC 68-12124. (gr. 11-12). 1968. text ed. 30.00 (ISBN 0-8044-3260-0). Ungar.

GRAPHOPHONE

see Phonograph

GRAPHS

see Graphic Methods

GRAPTOLITES

Bjerreskov, Merete. Llandoverian & Wenlockian Graptolites from Bornholm. (Fossils & Strata: No.8). 1975. pap. text ed. 25.00x (ISBN 8-200-09392-1, Dist. by Columbia U Pr). Universitet.
Braithwaite, Lee F. Graptolites from the Lower Ordovician Pogonip Group of Western Utah. LC 75-31373. (Special Paper: No. 166). (Illus., Orig.). 1976. pap. 9.75x (ISBN 0-8137-2166-0). Geol Soc.
Bulman, O. M. The Caradoc Balclatchie Graptolites from Limestones in Laggan Burn, Ayrshire, Pts. 1-3. (Illus.). 1945-47. Set. pap. 23.00 (ISBN 0-384-06325-X). Johnson Repr.
--The Dendroid Graptolites, Pts. 1-3. 1927-34. Set. pap. 19.00 (ISBN 0-384-06335-7). Johnson Repr.
Elles, Gertrude L. & Wood, Ethel M. British Graptolites. 1901-1918. Set. pap. 60.00 (ISBN 0-384-14155-2). Johnson Repr.

GRASLIN, J., 1727-1790

Desmars, J. Un Precurseur D'Adam Smith en France: J. J. L. Graslin (1727-1790) LC 77-159696. 257p. (Fr.). 1973. Repr. of 1900 ed. 20.50 (ISBN 0-8337-0840-6). B Franklin.

GRASS, GUNTER, 1927-

Cunliffe, W. Gordon. Gunter Grass. (World Authors Ser.: Germany: No. 65). 1969. lib. bdg. 10.95 (ISBN 0-8057-2400-1). Twayne.
Grass, Gunter. Inmarypraise. Middleton, Christopher, tr. from Ger. (A Helen & Kurt Wolff Bk.). (Illus.). 88p. 1974. 15.00 (ISBN 0-15-144406-4). HarBraceJ.
Hollington, Michael. Gunter Grass: The Writer in a Pluralist Society. LC 79-56840. 192p. 1980. 16.00 (ISBN 0-7145-2678-9, Pub. by M Boyars). Merrimack Bk Serv.

Reddick, John. The Danzig Trilogy of Gunter Grass: A Study of the Tin Drum, Cat & Mouse, & Dog Years. LC 74-11027. 290p. 1975. pap. 5.95 (ISBN 0-15-623829-2, HB285, Harv). HarBraceJ.

Simons, John. Monarch Notes on Gunter Grass' Tin Drum. pap. 1.50 (ISBN 0-671-00936-2). Monarch Pr.

Tank, Kurt L. Gunter Grass. Conway, John, tr. LC 68-31458. (Modern Literature Ser.). 1969. 10.95 (ISBN 0-8044-2863-8); pap. 4.95 (ISBN 0-8044-6892-3). Ungar.

GRASS, GUNTER, 1927--BIBLIOGRAPHY

Everett, George A., Jr. A Select Bibliography of Gunter Grass from 1956 to 1973, Including the Works, Editions, Translations & Critical Literature. LC 74-1420. 1974. 15.00 (ISBN 0-89102-041-1). B Franklin.

O'Neill, Patrick. Gunter Grass: A Bibliography 1955-75. LC 76-17278. 1976. 15.00x (ISBN 0-8020-5362-9). U of Toronto Pr.

GRASS PARAKEET

see Budgerigars

GRASS TETANY

Grunes, D. L. & Rendze, V. V., eds. Grass Tetany. (Illus.). 1981. 5.00 (ISBN 0-89118-056-7). Am Soc Agron.

GRASS VALLEY, CALIFORNIA

Morely, Jim & Foley, Doris, eds. Gold Cities: Grass Valley & Nevada City. 2nd ed. (Illus.). 96p. 1980. 9.95 (ISBN 0-8310-7136-2); pap. 3.50 (ISBN 0-8310-7135-4). Howell-North.

Morley, Jim & Foley, Doris. Gold Cities: Grass Valley & Nevada City. LC 65-18741. (Illus.). 1965. 9.95 (ISBN 0-8310-7048-X); pap. 3.50 (ISBN 0-8310-6004-2). Howell-North.

GRASSES

see also Forage Plants; Grasslands; Grazing; Pastures;

also names of grasses

An Analysis of Yields of Grasses in Mixed & Pure Stands. (Agricultural Research Reports Ser.: 714). 1968. pap. 6.50 (ISBN 0-686-51207-3, PUDOC). Unipub.

Arber, A. The Gramineae: A Study of Cereal, Bamboo & Grass. (Illus.). 1973. Repr. of 1934 ed. 40.00 (ISBN 3-7682-0276-3). Lubrecht & Cramer.

Beard, J. Turfgrass: Science & Culture. (Illus.). 1972. ref. ed. 24.95 (ISBN 0-13-933002-X). P-H.

Bews, John W. The World's Grasses: Their Differentiation, Distribution, Economics & Ecology. LC 72-84980. (Illus.). 408p. 1973. Repr. of 1929 ed. 18.00 (ISBN 0-8462-1678-7). Russell.

--The World's Grasses: Their Differention, Distribution, Economics. 1977. lib. bdg. 59.95 (ISBN 0-8490-2848-5). Gordon Pr.

Bor, N. L. Grasses of India, Burma & Ceylon: Excluding Bambuseae. (Illus.). 1973. Repr. of 1960 ed. 83.00 (ISBN 3-87429-043-3). Lubrecht & Cramer.

Brown, Lauren. Grasses: An Identification Guide. (Peterson Native Library). 1979. 9.95 (ISBN 0-395-27624-1). HM.

Butler, G. W. & Bailey, R. W., eds. Chemistry & Biochemistry of Herbage, 3 vols. Incl. Vol. 1. 1973. 97.50 (ISBN 0-12-148101-8); Vol. 2. 1974. 68.00 (ISBN 0-12-148102-6); Vol. 3. 1974. 47.00 (ISBN 0-12-148103-4). Acad Pr.

Chase, Agnes. First Book of Grasses: The Structure of Grasses Explained for Beginners. 3rd ed. LC 76-48919. (Illus.). 127p. 1977. text ed. 8.95x (ISBN 0-87474-307-9). Smithsonian.

Christiansen, Mogens S. Grasses, Sedges & Rushes in Color. (Illus.). 1979. 9.95 (ISBN 0-7137-0945-6, Pub. by Blandford Pr England). Sterling.

Clifford, H. T. & Watson, L. Identifying Grasses: Data, Methods & Illustrations. 1977. text ed. 35.00x (ISBN 0-7022-1312-8). U of Queensland Pr.

Crampton, Beecher. Grasses in California. (California Natural History Guides Ser.). (Illus., Orig.). 1974. 14.95x (ISBN 0-520-02739-6); pap. 3.95 (ISBN 0-520-02507-5). U of Cal Pr.

Gould, Frank W. Common Texas Grasses: An Illustrated Guide. LC 78-6368. (Natural History Ser.: No. 3). (Illus.). 280p. 1978. 10.95 (ISBN 0-89096-057-7); pap. 6.95 (ISBN 0-89096-058-5). Tex A&M Univ Pr.

--Grass Systematics. LC 68-25214. 1968. text ed. 24.00 (ISBN 0-07-023848-0, C). McGraw.

--The Grasses of Texas. LC 75-18688. (Illus.). 672p. 1975. 20.00 (ISBN 0-89096-005-4). Tex A&M Univ Pr.

--Grasses of the Southwestern United States. (Illus.). 1973. pap. 4.25x (ISBN 0-8165-0406-7). U of Ariz Pr.

Grounds, Roger. Ornamental Grasses. 216p. 1981. 16.95 (ISBN 0-442-24707-9). Van Nos Reinhold.

Hanson, A. A. & Juska, F. V., eds. Turfgrass Science. (Illus.). 1969. 12.50 (ISBN 0-89118-015-X). Am Soc Agron.

Harrington, H. D. How to Identify Grasses & Grasslike Plants. LC 76-17744. (Illus.). 142p. 1977. pap. 6.95x (ISBN 0-8040-0746-2). Swallow.

Hitchcock, A. S. Manual of Grasses of the United States, 2 vols. 2nd ed. (Illus.). 24.50 set (ISBN 0-8446-0309-0). Peter Smith.

--Manual of the Grasses of the United States, 2 Vols. 2nd ed. (Illus.). 1971. pap. 7.50 ea.; Vol. 1. pap. (ISBN 0-486-22717-0); Vol. 2. pap. (ISBN 0-486-22718-9). Dover.

Humphrey, Robert R. Arizona Range Grasses. LC 61-63166. 1970. pap. 3.50x (ISBN 0-8165-0254-4). U of Ariz Pr.

Judd, B. Ira. Handbook of Tropical Forage Grasses. 1979. lib. bdg. 14.50 (ISBN 0-8240-7050-X). Garland Pub.

Kahlenberg, Mary H. Book of Grass Crafts. (Illus.). 1981. pap. 12.95 (ISBN 0-525-47630-X). Dutton.

Karel, Leonard. Dried Grasses, Grains, Gourds, Pods & Cones. LC 74-31178. (Illus.). 1975. 10.00 (ISBN 0-8108-0792-0). Scarecrow.

Knobel, Edward. Field Guide to the Grasses, Sedges & Rushes of the United States. 6.00 (ISBN 0-8446-5593-7). Peter Smith.

--Field Guide to the Grasses, Sedges & Rushes of the United States. LC 77-72531. (Illus.). 1977. pap. 2.00 (ISBN 0-486-23505-X). Dover.

Knobloch, Irving W. A Check List of Crosses in the Gramineae. 1968. pap. 10.00 (ISBN 0-934454-22-1). Lubrecht & Cramer.

Koch, Stephen D. The Eragrostis Pectinacea-Pilosa Complex in North & Central America (Gramineae Erogrostoideae) LC 73-2454. (Biological Monographs Ser: No. 48). (Illus.). 86p. 1974. pap. 7.95 (ISBN 0-252-00389-6). U of Ill Pr.

Kucera, Clair L. Grasses of Missouri. LC 61-5880. (Illus.). 1961. 16.00x (ISBN 0-8262-0544-5). U of Mo Pr.

Kuelen, Van H. Simulation of Water Use & Herbage Growth in Arid Regions. 180p. 1981. 105.00x (ISBN 0-686-76664-4, Pub. by Oxford & IBH India). State Mutual Bk.

Lazarides, M. The Tropical Grasses of Southeast Asia: Excluding Bamboos. 350p. 1980. lib. bdg. 40.00 (ISBN 3-7682-1255-6). Lubrecht & Cramer.

Loewer, H. Peter. Growing & Decorating with Grasses: A Creative Approach. LC 76-53640. (Illus.). 1977. 14.95 (ISBN 0-8027-0562-6); pap. 6.95 (ISBN 0-8027-7112-2). Walker & Co.

Madison, John H. Practical Turfgrass Management. (Illus.). 1971. 24.95x (ISBN 0-442-15648-0). Van Nos Reinhold.

--Principles of Turfgrass Culture. (Illus.). 1971. 22.50x (ISBN 0-442-15647-2). Van Nos Reinhold.

Mohlenbrock, Robert H. Grasses: Bromus to Paspalum. LC 71-156793. (Illustrated Flora of Illinois Ser.). (Illus.). 352p. 1972. 22.95x (ISBN 0-8093-0520-8). S Ill U Pr.

--Grasses: Panicum to Danthonia. LC 73-6807. (Illustrated Flora of Illinois Ser). (Illus.). 398p. 1973. 22.95x (ISBN 0-8093-0521-6). S Ill U Pr.

Pohl, Richard W. How to Know the Grasses. 3rd ed. (Pictured Key Nature Ser.). 1978. text ed. write for info. (ISBN 0-697-04877-2); write for info. wire coil (ISBN 0-697-04876-4). Wm C Brown.

Rattray, J. M. Grass Cover of Africa. (FAO Agricultural Studies: No. 49). (Orig.). 1968. pap. 10.25 (ISBN 92-5-100386-6, FAO). Unipub.

Roberts, E. C., ed. Proceedings from the Second International Turfgrass Research Conference. (Illus.). 1974. 17.00 (ISBN 0-89118-007-9). Am Soc Agron.

Rotar, Peter P. Grasses of Hawaii. (Illus.). 1968. text ed. 16.00x (ISBN 0-87022-715-7). U Pr of Hawaii.

Schaffner, John H. The Grasses of Ohio. 1917. 1.50 (ISBN 0-686-30283-4). Ohio Bio Survey.

Shantz, Homer L. & Marbut, Curtis F. Vegetation & Soils of Africa. LC 70-170848. Repr. of 1923 ed. 19.00 (ISBN 0-404-05953-8). AMS Pr.

Sikula, Jaromir. Grasses. (Concise Guides Ser.). (Illus.). 1979. 7.95 (ISBN 0-600-34045-7). Transatlantic.

Smithsonian Institution, Washington, D. C. Index to Grass Species, 3 Vols. Chase, Agnes & Niles, Cornelia D., eds. 1963. Set. 270.00 (ISBN 0-8161-0445-X). G K Hall.

Sprague, Howard B. Turf Management Handbook. 2nd ed. LC 74-19656. 1976. 14.65 (ISBN 0-8134-1692-2). Interstate.

Sund, Robert. Bunch Grass. LC 70-94014. 88p. 1969. pap. 3.95 (ISBN 0-295-95005-6). U of Wash Pr.

Trinius, K. B. Species Graminum Iconibus et Descriptionbus Illustravit, 3 vols. in 1. (Illus.). 1970. Repr. of 1836 ed. 137.50 (ISBN 3-7682-0669-6). Lubrecht & Cramer.

Vengris, Jonas. Lawns -- Basic Factors, Construction & Maintenance of Fine Turf Areas. rev. ed. 10.00 (ISBN 0-913702-05-6). Thomson Pub CA.

Wilson, Charles M. Grass & People. Repr. of 1961 ed. lib. bdg. 15.00x (ISBN 0-8371-3160-X, WIGP). Greenwood.

Youngner, V. B. & McKell, C. M., eds. The Biology & Utilization of Grasses. (Physiological Ecology Ser.). 1972. 54.00 (ISBN 0-12-774750-8). Acad Pr.

GRASSES–DISEASES AND PESTS

Cummins, G. B. Rust Fungi of Cereals, Grasses & Bamboos. LC 75-147257. (Illus.). 1971. 39.80 (ISBN 0-387-05336-0). Springer-Verlag.

GRASSES–JUVENILE LITERATURE

Goldin, Augusta. Grass: The Everything, Everywhere Plant. LC 76-52502. (Illus.). 160p. (gr. 5 up). 7.95 (ISBN 0-525-66453-X). Elsevier-Nelson.

GRASSHOPPERS

see Locusts

GRASSLAND ECOLOGY

African Pastureland Ecology. (FAO Pasture & Fodder Crop Studies: No. 7). 203p. 1981. pap. 14.50 (ISBN 92-5-100873-6, F2099, FAO). Unipub.

Allen, Durward L. Life of Prairies & Plains. (Our Living World of Nature Ser). 1967. 9.95 (ISBN 0-07-001099-4, P&RB); by subscription 3.95 (ISBN 0-07-046005-1). McGraw.

Coupland, R. T., ed. Grassland Ecosystems of the World. LC 77-83990. (International Biological Programme Ser.: No. 18). 1979. 75.00 (ISBN 0-521-21867-5). Cambridge U Pr.

Estes, James R., et al. Grass & Grasslands: Systematics & Ecology. LC 81-40294. (Illus.). 400p. 1981. 25.00x (ISBN 0-8061-1776-1); pap. 12.50x (ISBN 0-8061-1778-8). U of Okla Pr.

French, N. R., ed. Perspectives in Grassland Ecology: Results & Applications of the US-IBP Grassland Biome Study. LC 78-13971. (Ecological Studies: Vol. 32). (Illus.). 1979. 28.10 (ISBN 0-387-90384-4). Springer-Verlag.

Gutierrez, Luis T. & Fey, Willard R. Ecosystem Succession: A General Hypothesis & a Test Model of a Grassland. (Illus.). 1980. text ed. 25.00x (ISBN 0-262-07075-8). MIT Pr.

Innis, G. S., ed. Grassland Simulation Model. LC 77-23016. (Ecological Studies: Vol. 26). (Illus.). 1977. 27.30 (ISBN 0-387-90269-4). Springer-Verlag.

Kowal, J. M. & Kassam, A. H. Agricultural Ecology of Savanna: A Study of West Africa. LC 77-30412. (Illus.). 1979. 74.00x (ISBN 0-19-859462-3). Oxford U Pr.

Numata, Makoto, ed. Ecology of Grasslands & Bamboolands in the World. 1980. lib. bdg. 53.00 (ISBN 90-6193-601-2, Pub. by Junk Pubs Netherlands). Kluwer Boston.

Parry, John & Butterworth, Bill. Grassland Management. (Illus.). 208p. 1981. 21.00x (ISBN 0-7198-2518-0). Intl Ideas.

Van Dyne, G. M. Grasslands, Systems Analysis & Man. Breymeyer, A. I., ed. LC 77-28249. (International Biological Programme Ser.: No. 19). 1980. 140.00 (ISBN 0-521-21872-1). Cambridge U Pr.

GRASSLANDS

see also Pampas; Prairies; Steppes

Adrian, Mary. Wildlife on the African Grasslands. LC 79-994. (Illus.). 64p. (gr. 4 up). 1979. PLB 6.97 (ISBN 0-671-32999-5). Messner.

Curry-Lindahl, Kai. Wildlife of the Prairies & Plains. LC 80-27927. (Illus.). 232p. 1981. 18.95 (ISBN 0-8109-1766-1). Abrams.

Hoogerkamp, M. Ley, Periodically Reseeded Grassland, or Permanent Grassland. (Agricultural Research Reports: No. 81). 35p. 1974. pap. 5.75 (ISBN 90-220-0500-3, Pub. by PUDOC). Unipub.

Horton, Catherine. A Closer Look at Grasslands. (Closer Look at Ser.). (Illus.). (gr. 4 up). 1979. PLB 6.90 s&l (ISBN 0-531-03411-9). Watts.

Krause, W., ed. Application of Vegetation Science to Grassland Husbandry. (Handbook of Vegetation Science: No. 13). (Illus.). 1977. lib. bdg. 79.00 (ISBN 90-6193-194-0, Pub. by Junk Pubs Netherlands). Kluwer Boston.

Management & the Use of Grasslands, Democratic Republic of the Congo. 152p. 1966. pap. 9.75 (ISBN 0-686-70623-4, F1918, FAO). Unipub.

Numata, M., ed. Ecological Studies in Japanese Grasslands. (Japan International Biological Program Synthetics Ser.: Vol. 13). 1975. pap. 32.50 (ISBN 0-86008-223-7, Pub. by U of Tokyo Pr). Intl Schol Bk Serv.

Parry, John & Butterworth, Bill. Grassland Mangement. 208p. 1981. 35.00x (ISBN 0-7198-2518-0, Pub. by Northwood Bks). State Mutual Bk.

The Role of Nitrogen in Intensive Grassland Production. 171p. 1981. pap. 30.00 (ISBN 90-220-0734-0, PDC 214, Pudoc). Unipub.

Scott, Geoffrey A. Grassland Development in the Gran Pajonal of Eastern Peru: A Study of Soil-Vegetation Nutrient Systems. LC 78-31729. (Hawaii Monographs in Geography: No. 1). 1979. pap. 14.75 (ISBN 0-8357-0369-X, IS-00070, University of Hawaii at Manoa, Department of Geography, Honolulu). Univ Microfilms.

Sprague, Howard B., ed. Grasslands of the United States: Their Economic & Ecological Importance. (Illus.). 375p. 1974. text ed. 8.50x (ISBN 0-8138-0745-X). Iowa St U Pr.

Staten, Hi W. Grasses & Grassland Farming. (Illus.). 6.50 (ISBN 0-8159-5609-6). Devin.

GRASSMAN'S THEORY OF EXTENSION

see Ausdehnungslehre

GRATEFUL DEAD

Gerould, Gordon H. The Grateful Dead. 177p. 1980. Repr. of 1908 ed. lib. bdg. 25.00 (ISBN 0-8492-4957-0). R West.

Harrison, Hank. The Dead. LC 79-56661. (Illus.). 336p. (Orig.). 1980. 14.95 (ISBN 0-89087-282-1); pap. 9.95 (ISBN 0-89087-300-3). Celestial Arts.

GRATEFULNESS

see Gratitude

GRATES

see Fireplaces; Furnaces

GRATITUDE

Hallinan, P. K. I'm Thankful Each Day. 24p. (gr. k-6). 1981. pap. 2.50 (ISBN 0-8249-8008-5). Ideals.

Nouwen, Henri J. From Resentment to Gratitude. (Synthesis Ser.). 1976. 0.65 (ISBN 0-685-77512-7). Franciscan Herald.

Rodenmayer, Robert N. Thanks Be to God. 1960. 3.50 (ISBN 0-227-67615-7). Attic Pr.

We Break Bread in Loving Thanksgiving. (gr. 5). 2.85 (ISBN 0-02-649450-7, 64945); tchr's manual 2.52 (ISBN 0-02-649460-4, 64946). Benziger Pub Co.

GRATTAN, HENRY, 1746-1820

Lecky, Wm. Edward. Leaders of Public Opinion in Ireland, 2 vols. LC 76-159800. (Europe 1815-1945 Ser.). 720p. 1973. Repr. of 1903 ed. Set. lib. bdg. 59.50 (ISBN 0-306-70574-5). Da Capo.

GRAVEL (PATHOLOGY)

see Calculi, Urinary

GRAVES, RICHARD, 1715-1804

Hill, Charles J. The Literary Career of Richard Graves: The Author of 'the Spiritual Quixote' 1934-1935. 1973. 30.00 (ISBN 0-8274-1412-9). R West.

GRAVES, ROBERT, 1895-

Canary, Robert H. Robert Graves. (English Authors Ser.: No. 279). 1980. lib. bdg. 8.95 (ISBN 0-8057-6720-7). Twayne.

Enright, D. J. Robert Graves & the Decline of Modernism. LC 74-12209. 1960. lib. bdg. 6.50 (ISBN 0-8414-3960-5). Folcroft.

Graves, Robert. Good-Bye to All That: An Autobiography. 446p. 1980. Repr. lib. bdg. 30.00 (ISBN 0-8492-4985-6). R West.

Keane, Patrick J. A Wild Civility: Interactions in the Poetry & Thought of Robert Graves. LC 79-5428. 1980. pap. 6.95 (ISBN 0-8262-0296-9). U of Mo Pr.

Kirkham, Michael. Poetry of Robert Graves. 1969. text ed. 15.00x (ISBN 0-485-11103-9, Athlone Pr). Humanities.

Mehoke, James S. Robert Graves: Peace-Weaver. (Studies in English Literature: No. 63). 168p. 1975. pap. text ed. 31.25x (ISBN 90-2793-194-1). Mouton.

Presley, John W. The Robert Graves Manuscripts & Letters at Southern Illinois University: An Inventory. LC 75-8383. vii, 261p. 1976. 18.00x (ISBN 0-87875-075-4). Whitston Pub.

Snipes, Katherine. Robert Graves. LC 78-20943. (Modern Literature Ser.). 1979. 13.50 (ISBN 0-8044-2825-5). Ungar.

Stade, George. Robert Graves. LC 67-16890. (Columbia Essays on Modern Writers Ser.: No. 25). (Orig.). 1967. pap. 2.00 (ISBN 0-231-02907-1). Columbia U Pr.

GRAVES

see Burial; Epitaphs; Funeral Rites and Ceremonies; Mounds; Sepulchral Monuments; Tombs

GRAVES' DISEASE

see also Goiter

Lewis, Alan E. Graves' Disease. LC 80-15624. (Discussions in Patient Management Ser.). 1980. pap. 12.00 (ISBN 0-87488-870-0). Med Exam.

GRAVESEND, RICHARD, BP. OF LONDON, d. 1303

Hale, William H. & Ellacombe, H. T., eds. Account of the Executors of Richard Bishop of London 1303, & of the Executors of Thomas Bishop of Exeter 1310. 1874. 22.50 (ISBN 0-384-20950-5). Johnson Repr.

GRAVESTONES

see Sepulchral Monuments

GRAVEYARDS

see Cemeteries

GRAVIMETRIC ANALYSIS

see Chemistry, Analytic–Quantitative

GRAVITATION
Here are entered theoretical works on the phenomenon of gravitation. Works relating to measurement of the intensity and direction of the earth's force of attraction are entered under the heading Gravity.
see also Ether (Of Space); Mass (Physics); Matter; Potential, Theory of; Relativity (Physics); Weightlessness

Airy, George B. & Cohen, I. Bernard, eds. Gravitation. LC 80-2113. (Development of Science Ser.). (Illus.). 1981. lib. bdg. 20.00x (ISBN 0-405-13833-4). Arno.
Benedikt, E. T., ed. Weightlessness: Physical Phenomena & Biological Effects. special vol ed. 1960. 15.00 (ISBN 0-87703-000-6). Am Astronaut.
Bergmann, Peter G. Riddle of Gravitation. LC 68-11537. 1968. lib. bdg. 20.00 (ISBN 0-684-15378-5, ScribT). Scribner.
Bergmann, Peter G. & De Sabbath, Venzo, eds. Cosmology & Gravitation: Spin, Torsion, Rotation, & Supergravity. (NATO Advances Study Institutres Ser. (Series B--Physics): Vol. 58). 560p. 1980. 65.00 (ISBN 0-306-40478-8, Plenum Pr). Plenum Pub.
Berry, M. Principles of Cosmology and Gravitation. LC 75-22559. (Illus.). 200p. 1976. 34.95 (ISBN 0-521-21061-5); pap. 11.95x (ISBN 0-521-29028-7). Cambridge U Pr.
Bertotti, B., ed. Experimental Gravitation. (Italian Physical Society: Course 56). 1974. 67.50 (ISBN 0-12-368856-6). Acad Pr.
Bowler, M. G. Gravitation & Relativity. 1976. text ed. 27.00 (ISBN 0-08-020567-4); pap. text ed. 14.50 (ISBN 0-08-020408-2). Pergamon.
Braginsky, V. B. & Manukin, A. B. Measurement of Weak Forces in Physics Experiments. Douglass, David H., ed. LC 76-22953. (Illus.). 1977. lib. bdg. 11.00x (ISBN 0-226-07070-0). U of Chicago Pr.
Branley, Franklyn M. Gravity Is a Mystery. LC 70-101922. (A Let's-Read-and-Find-Out Science Bk). (Illus.). (gr. k-3). 1970. 8.95 (ISBN 0-690-35071-6, TYC-J); PLB 8.79 (ISBN 0-690-35072-4). Har-Row.
Breuer, R. A. Gravitational Perturbation Theory & Synchrotron Radiation. (Lecture Notes in Physics: Vol.44). 210p. 1976. pap. 10.50 (ISBN 0-387-07530-5). Springer-Verlag.
Cohen, I. Bernard, ed. Gravitation, Heat & X-Rays. LC 80-2104. (Development of Science Ser.). (Illus.). 1981. lib. bdg. 35.00x (ISBN 0-405-13869-5). Arno.
Dal Cin, Mario, et al, eds. Fundamental Interactions at High Energy Three: Tracts in Mathematics & Natural Sciences, 5 vols. Incl. Vol. 1. Nonpolynomial Lagrangians Renormalization & Gravity. Salam, Abdus. 32.50x (ISBN 0-677-12050-8); Vol. 2. Broken Scale Variance & the Light Cone. Gell-Mann, M. & Wilson, K. 34.75x (ISBN 0-677-12060-5); Vol. 3. Invited Papers. Hamermesh, M. 34.75x (ISBN 0-677-12070-2); Vol. 4. Troubles in the External Field Problem for Invariant Wave Equations. Wightman, A. S. 23.75x (ISBN 0-677-12080-X); Vol. 5. Multiperipheral Dynamics. Chew, G. 23.75x (ISBN 0-677-12090-7). LC 79-85472. (Illus.). 648p. 1971. Set. 133.75x (ISBN 0-677-12100-8). Gordon.
Dicke, Robert H. Gravitation & the Universe. LC 78-107344. (Memoirs Ser.: Vol. 78). (Illus.). 1970. 3.00 (ISBN 0-87169-078-0). Am Philos.
Eddington, Arthur S. Space, Time & Gravitation. 26.50 (ISBN 0-521-04865-6). Cambridge U Pr.
Ehlers, J., ed. Isolated Gravitating Systems in General Relativity. 1979. 85.50 (ISBN 0-444-85329-4, North Holland). Elsevier.
Fock, V. A. The Theory of Space, Time & Gravitation. 2nd ed. 1964. 52.00 (ISBN 0-08-010061-9). Pergamon.
Halpern, Leopold, ed. On the Measurement of Cosmological Variations of the Gravitational Constant. LC 78-8350. (A Florida State Univ. Book Ser.). 1978. 14.50 (ISBN 0-8130-0610-4, IS-00053, Pub. by University Presses of Florida). Univ Microfilms.
Harrison, B. Kent, et al. Gravitation Theory & Gravitational Collapse. LC 65-17293. 1965. 11.00x (ISBN 0-226-31802-8). U of Chicago Pr.
Held, A., ed. General Relativity & Gravitation: One Hundred Years After the Birth of Albert Einstein, 2 vols. (Illus.). 1980. Set. 99.50 (ISBN 0-686-58609-3, Plenum Pr); 57.50 ea. Vol. 1 (ISBN 0-306-40265-3). Vol. 2 (ISBN 0-306-40266-1). Plenum Pub.
Hoyle, Fred & Narlikar, J. V. Action at a Distance in Physics & Cosmology. LC 74-4158. (Astronomy & Astrophysics Ser.). (Illus.). 1974. text ed. 31.95x (ISBN 0-7167-0346-7). W H Freeman.
IAU Symposium No. 64, Warsaw, Poland, 5-8 September 1973. Gravitational Radiation & Gravational Collapse: Proceedings. DeWitt-Morettè, Cecile, ed. LC 73-91436. (Symposium of the International Astronomical Union: No. 64). 226p. 1974. lib. bdg. 39.50 (ISBN 90-277-0435-X, Pub. by Reidel Holland); pap. 29.00 (ISBN 90-277-0436-8, Pub. by Reidel Holland). Kluwer Boston.
International Conference, 7th, Tel Aviv, June 23-28, 1974. General Relativity & Gravitation: Proceedings. Shaviv, G., ed. LC 75-33824. 1976. 54.95 (ISBN 0-470-77939-X). Halsted Pr.
Jordan, Pascual. The Expanding Earth. Beer, Arthur, ed. 224p. 1971. 34.00 (ISBN 0-08-015827-7). Pergamon.
Kramer, D., et al. Exact Solutions of Einstein's Field Equations. (Cambridge Monographs on Mathematical Physics). 400p. 1981. 72.00 (ISBN 0-521-23041-1). Cambridge U Pr.
Kuper, C. G. & Peres, A. Relativity & Gravitation. 336p. 1971. 73.25x (ISBN 0-677-14300-1). Gordon.
Larson, Dewey B. Beyond Newton. LC 63-22695. (Illus.). 1964. 5.00 (ISBN 0-913138-03-7). North Pacific.
Levy & Deser, eds. Recent Developments in Gravitation. (NATO Advanced Study Institutes Ser. B: Physics: Vol. 44). 1979. 69.50 (ISBN 0-306-40198-3, Plenum Pr). Plenum Pub.
Lightman, Alan P., et al. Problem Book in Relativity & Gravitation. 500p. 1975. 32.50 (ISBN 0-691-08160-3); pap. 10.50 (ISBN 0-691-08162-X). Princeton U Pr.
Maeterlinck, Maurice. Supreme Law. LC 75-86042. (Essay & General Literature Index Reprint Ser). 1969. Repr. of 1935 ed. 10.00 (ISBN 0-8046-0571-8). Kennikat.
Marlow, A. R. Quantum Theory & Gravitation. LC 79-277837. 1980. 18.50 (ISBN 0-12-473260-7). Acad Pr.
Mehra, J. Einstein, Hilbert & the Theory of Gravitation. LC 73-91833. 1974. pap. 10.00 (ISBN 90-277-0440-6, Pub. by Reidel Holland). Kluwer Boston.
Misner, Charles W., et al. Gravitation. LC 78-156043. (Physics Ser.). (Illus.). 1279p. 1973. pap. text ed. 38.95x (ISBN 0-7167-0344-0). W H Freeman.
Moller, C. Evidence for Gravitational Theories. (Italian Physical Society: Course 20). 1963. 49.50 (ISBN 0-12-368820-5). Acad Pr.
Murdeshwar, M. G. General Topology. LC 80-18434. 480p. 1981. 19.95 (ISBN 0-470-26916-2). Halsted Pr.
Ohanian, Hans C. Gravitation & Space Time. new ed. (Illus.). 400p. 1976. text ed. 19.95x (ISBN 0-393-09198-8). Norton.
Pisello, Daniel M. Gravitation, Electromagnetism & Quantized Charge: The Einstein Insight. LC 78-67493. 1979. 15.00 (ISBN 0-250-40286-6). Ann Arbor Science.
Sabbata, V. De & Weber, J., eds. Topics in Theoretical & Experimental Gravitation Physics. (NATO Advanced Study Institutes, B Ser.: Vol. 27). 354p. 1977. 37.50 (ISBN 0-306-35727-5, Plenum Pr). Plenum Pub.
Smarr, Larry. Sources of Gravitational Radiation. LC 79-50177. (Illus.). 1979. 24.95 (ISBN 0-521-22778-X). Cambridge U Pr.
Tornbohm, Hakan. A Paradigm Shift in Theories of Gravitation. (Studies in the Story of Science: No. 6). 1977. pap. text ed. 34.00x (ISBN 91-24-15683-3). Humanities.
Wald, Robert M. Space, Time & Gravity: The Theory of the Big Bang & Black Holes. LC 77-4038. (Illus.). 1977. 10.95 (ISBN 0-226-87030-8); pap. 3.95 (ISBN 0-226-87031-6). U of Chicago Pr.
Weinberg, Steven. Gravitation & Cosmology; Principles & Applications of the General Theory of Relativity. LC 78-37175. 750p. 1972. 37.50 (ISBN 0-471-92567-5). Wiley.
Will, Clifford E. Theory & Experiment in Gravitational Physics. LC 80-39642. (Illus.). 272p. Date not set. 75.00 (ISBN 0-521-23237-6). Cambridge U Pr.
Zeldovich, Ya. B. & Novikov, I. D. Relativistic Astrophysics: Stars & Relativity, Vol. I. Thorne, Kip & Arnett, W. David, eds. Arlock, Eli, tr. LC 77-128549. (Midway Reprint). 1978. pap. text ed. 18.00x (ISBN 0-226-97956-3). U of Chicago Pr.

GRAVITY

Applewhite, James. Following Gravity. LC 80-21578. 1981. 7.95x (ISBN 0-8139-0885-X). U Pr of Va.
Bowin, Carl. The Caribbean: Gravity Field & Plate Tectonics. LC 76-16261. (Special Paper: No. 169). (Illus.). 1976. pap. 12.00x (ISBN 0-8137-2169-5). Geol Soc.
Caputo, Michele. Gravity Field of the Earth: Classical & Modern Methods. (International Geophysics Ser.: Vol. 10). 1967. 38.00 (ISBN 0-12-159050-X). Acad Pr.
Constant, James N. Gravitational Action. LC 78-71229. 1978. 12.95 (ISBN 0-914330-16-0). Pioneer Pub Co.
Cook, A. H. & Saunders, V. T. Gravity & the Earth. (Wykeham Science Ser.: No. 6). 1969. 9.95x (ISBN 0-8448-1108-4). Crane Russak Co.
Davies, P. C. The Search for Gravity Waves. (Illus.). 160p. 1980. 13.95 (ISBN 0-521-23197-3). Cambridge U Pr.
De Jong, Kees A. & Scholten, Robert, eds. Gravity & Tectonics. LC 73-1580. (Illus.). 502p. 1973. 53.50 (ISBN 0-471-20305-X, Pub. by Wiley-Interscience). Wiley.
Dow, T. W. Reshape Newton's Laws. LC 64-19218. 1965. 5.00 (ISBN 0-910340-03-X). Celestial Pr.
Garland, G. D. Earth's Shape & Gravity. 1965. 21.00 (ISBN 0-08-010823-7); pap. 9.75 (ISBN 0-08-010822-9). Pergamon.
Goltz, Ronald E. G-Force & Man. (Illus.). 1978. 20.00 (ISBN 0-916750-22-1). Dayton Labs.
Gordon, Solon A. & Cohen, Melvin J., eds. Gravity & the Organism. LC 70-156302. 1971. 14.00x (ISBN 0-226-30447-7). U of Chicago Pr.
McCally, Michael, et al, eds. Hypodynamics & Hypogravics: The Physiology of Inactivity & Weightlessness. LC 68-18675. (Illus.). 1968. 52.50 (ISBN 0-12-482050-6). Acad Pr.
Noakes, G. R., ed. Sources of Physics Teaching: Gravity. Liquids. Gases, Vol. 5. 1970. pap. text ed. 12.95x (ISBN 0-85066-040-8). Intl Ideas.
Pick, M., et al. Theory of the Earth's Gravity Field. 1973. 85.50 (ISBN 0-444-40939-4). Elsevier.
Ramberg, Hans. Gravity, Deformation & the Earth's Crust: In Theory, Experiments & Geological Application. 2nd ed. 1981. 79.00 (ISBN 0-12-576860-5). Acad Pr.
Selsam, Millicent & Dewey, Kenneth. Up, Down & Around: The Force of Gravity. LC 76-23796. (gr. 1-3). 1977. 5.95a (ISBN 0-385-09863-4); PLB (ISBN 0-385-09865-0). Doubleday.
Tomoda, Yoshibumi, ed. Reference Book for Gravity, Magnetic & Bathymetric Data of the Pacific Ocean & Adjacent Seas 1963-1971. 100p. 1974. 13.50 (ISBN 0-86008-111-7, Pub. by U of Tokyo Pr). Intl Schol Bk Serv.
Wesson, Paul, ed. Gravity, Particles, & Astrophysics. (Astrophysics & Space Science Library Ser.: No. 79). 276p. 1980. lib. bdg. 34.00 (ISBN 90-277-1083-X, Pub. by Reidel). Kluwer Boston.

GRAVITY–JUVENILE LITERATURE

Branley, Franklyn M. Weight & Weightlessness. LC 70-132292. (Let's-Read-&-Find-Out Science Bk.). (Illus.). (gr. k-3). 1972. PLB 8.79 (ISBN 0-690-87329-8, TYC-J). Har-Row.
Engelbrektson, Sune. Gravity at Work & Play. (Illus.). 1963. 1.95 (ISBN 0-685-12257-3). HR&W.
Feravolo, Rocco V. Wonders of Gravity. LC 65-11945. (Wonders Ser.). (Illus.). (gr. 3-7). 1965. PLB 5.95 (ISBN 0-396-05105-7). Dodd.
Selsam, Millicent & Dewey, Kenneth. Up, Down & Around: The Force of Gravity. LC 76-23796. (gr. 1-3). 1977. 5.95a (ISBN 0-385-09863-4); PLB (ISBN 0-385-09865-0). Doubleday.

GRAVITY, SPECIFIC
see Specific Gravity

GRAVITY-FREE STATE, PHYSIOLOGICAL EFFECT OF
see Weightlessness

GRAY, ASA, 1810-1888

Dupree, A. Hunter. Asa Gray. LC 59-12967. (Illus.). 1968. pap. text ed. 3.95x (ISBN 0-689-70066-0, 132). Atheneum.
Gray, Asa. Letters of Asa Gray, 2 vols. Gray, Jane L., ed. LC 73-170952. 1973. Repr. of 1893 ed. Set. lib. bdg. 47.00 (ISBN 0-8337-1430-9). B Franklin.

GRAY, MARTIN

Duncan, David D. The Fragile Miracle of Martin Gray. LC 79-88970. (Illus.). 96p. 7.95 (ISBN 0-89659-073-9). Abbeville Pr.

GRAY, THOMAS, 1716-1771

Cecil, David. Poetry of Thomas Gray: A Lecture. Repr. of 1945 ed. lib. bdg. 5.00 (ISBN 0-685-25636-7). Folcroft.
--Two Quiet Lives, Dorothy Osborne & Thomas Gray. 182p. 1981. Repr. of 1949 ed. lib. bdg. 30.00 (ISBN 0-8495-0854-1). Arden Lib.
Cook, Albert S. A Concordance to English Poems of Thomas Gray. LC 74-8062. Repr. of 1908 ed. lib. bdg. 20.00 (ISBN 0-8414-3355-0). Folcroft.
--A Concordance to the English Poems of Thomas Gray. 10.00 (ISBN 0-8446-1124-7). Peter Smith.
Gosse, Edmund. Gray. 1902. Repr. 12.00 (ISBN 0-8274-2436-1). R West.
Gosse, Edmund W. Gray. Morley, John, ed. LC 68-58380. (English Men of Letters). Repr. of 1889 ed. 12.50 (ISBN 0-404-51712-9). AMS Pr.
Gray, Thomas. The Correspondence of Thomas Gray & William Mason. (Illus.). 1853. Repr. lib. bdg. 50.00 (ISBN 0-8414-4670-9). Folcroft.
--An Elegy Wrote in a Country Churchyard. facsimile ed. 74p. 1976. Repr. of 1751 ed. 13.95x (ISBN 0-85967-311-1, Pub. by Scolar Pr England). Biblio Dist.
--Gray & His Friends. Tovey, Duncan C., ed. 1890. Repr. lib. bdg. 20.00 (ISBN 0-8414-4672-5). Folcroft.
Hudson, William H. Gray & His Poetry. LC 72-120981. (Poetry & Life Ser.). Repr. of 1912 ed. 7.25 (ISBN 0-404-52513-X). AMS Pr.
--Gray & His Poetry. LC 76-41924. 1912. lib. bdg. 7.50 (ISBN 0-8414-4940-6). Folcroft.
Jones, William P. Thomas Gray, Scholar: The True Tragedy of an 18th Century Gentleman, with Two Youthful Notebooks from the Original Manuscripts in the Morgan Library. LC 65-17904. 1965. Repr. of 1937 ed. 7.50 (ISBN 0-8462-0643-9). Russell.
McDermott, F. William Penn, Thomas Gray & an Account of the Historical Associations of Stoke Poges. 1973. Repr. of 1930 ed. lib. bdg. 25.00 (ISBN 0-8414-6026-4). Folcroft.
Martin, Roger. Essai Sur Thomas Gray. 458p. 1980. Repr. of 1934 ed. lib. bdg. 100.00 (ISBN 0-89984-335-2). Century Bookbindery.
--Essai Sur Thomas Gray. LC 75-145165. 1971. Repr. of 1934 ed. 42.00 (ISBN 0-403-01093-4). Scholarly.
--Essai sur Thomas Gray. LC 74-14593. 1974. Repr. of 1934 ed. lib. bdg. 75.00 (ISBN 0-8414-6172-4). Folcroft.
Morley, John. Gray. 1889. Repr. 12.00 (ISBN 0-8274-2437-X). R West.
Northup, Clark S., compiled by. Bibliography of Thomas Gray. LC 75-102524. 1970. Repr. of 1917 ed. 11.50 (ISBN 0-8462-1165-3). Russell.
Occasional Memorandums: Being Extracts from a Journal for the Year 1767, Now First Printed from the Original Manuscript of Thomas Gray. 1979. Repr. of 1950 ed. lib. bdg. 8.50 (ISBN 0-8414-1742-3). Folcroft.
Roberts, Sydney C. Thomas Gray of Pembroke. LC 73-11384. Repr. of 1955 ed. lib. bdg. 8.50 (ISBN 0-8414-2593-0). Folcroft.
Sells, A. L. Thomas Gray: His Life & Works. (Illus.). 320p. 1980. text ed. 29.50x (ISBN 0-04-928043-0). Allen Unwin.
Starr, Herbert W. Elegy Written in a Country Churchyard - Thomas Gray. 1968. pap. text ed. 2.50x (ISBN 0-675-09563-8). Merrill.
--Gray, As a Literary Critic. LC 74-11433. 1974. Repr. of 1941 ed. lib. bdg. 20.00 (ISBN 0-8414-7786-8). Folcroft.

GRAY, THOMAS, 1716-1771–BIBLIOGRAPHY

Gray, Thomas. Correspondence of Thomas Gray, 3 vols. Toynbee, Paget & Whibley, Leonard, eds. 1935. 109.00x (ISBN 0-19-811335-8). Oxford U Pr.
Starr, Herbert W. Bibliography of Thomas Gray,, Nineteen Seventeen to Nineteen Fifty-One. LC 53-9728. 1969. Repr. of 1953 ed. 11.00 (ISBN 0-527-85720-3). Kraus Repr.

GRAY FRIARS
see Franciscans

GRAY MARKET
see Black Market

GRAY SNAPPER

Starck, Walter A., 2nd & Schroeder, Robert E. Investigations on the Gray Snapper. LC 70-125664. (Studies in Tropical Oceanography Ser: No. 10). 1971. 12.00x (ISBN 0-87024-181-8). U Miami Marine.

GRAZING
see also Forage Plants; Pastures; Stock-Ranges

Arnold, G. W. & Dudzinski, M. L. Ethology of Free Ranging Domestic Animals. (Developments in Animal & Veterinary Sciences Ser.: Vol. 2). 1979. 51.25 (ISBN 0-444-41700-1). Elsevier.
Calef, Wesley. Private Grazing & Public Lands. Bruchey, Stuart, ed. LC 78-56701. (Management of Public Land Law in the U. S. Ser.). 1979. Repr. of 1960 ed. lib. bdg. 22.00x (ISBN 0-405-11321-8). Arno.
Foss, Phillip O. Politics & Grass: The Administration of Grazing on the Public Domain. LC 75-90508. (Illus.). ix, 236p. Repr. of 1960 ed. lib. bdg. 15.00x (ISBN 0-8371-2136-1, FOPG). Greenwood.
Voigt, William, Jr. Public Grazing Lands: Use & Misuse by Industry & Government. LC 75-42250. (Illus.). 365p. 1976. 25.00 (ISBN 0-8135-0819-3). Rutgers U Pr.

GRAZZINI, ANTONIO FRANCESCO, CALLED IL LASCA, 1503-1584

Rodini, Robert J. Antonfrancesco Grazzini: Poet, Dramatist, & Novelliere 1503-1584. 258p. 1970. 25.00 (ISBN 0-299-05590-6). U of Wis Pr.

GREASE
see Lubrication and Lubricants; Oils and Fats

GREAT ATLANTIC AND PACIFIC TEA COMPANY

Adelman, Morris A. A & P: A Study in Price-Cost Behavior & Public Policy. LC 59-14733. (Economic Studies: No. 113). (Illus.). 1959. 25.00x (ISBN 0-674-00050-1). Harvard U Pr.

GREAT AWAKENING
Here are entered works dealing with the revival of religion that occurred in the American colonies in the 18th century.
see also Evangelical Revival
Gaustad, Edwin S. Great Awakening in New England. 192p. 1972. pap. 2.95 (ISBN 0-8129-6062-9, QP46). Times Bks.
--The Great Awakening in New England. 7.50 (ISBN 0-8446-1491-2). Peter Smith.
Gewehr, Wesley M. The Great Awakening in Virginia 1740-1790. 1930. 7.50 (ISBN 0-8446-1197-2). Peter Smith.
Heimert, Alan & Miller, Perry, eds. The Great Awakening: Documents Illustrating the Crisis & Its Consequences. LC 66-23537. 1967. 26.50x (ISBN 0-672-50977-6). Irvington.
Heimert, Alan E. & Miller, Perry, eds. Great Awakening: Documents Illustrating the Crisis & Its Consequences. LC 66-23537. (Orig.). 1967. pap. 9.95 (ISBN 0-672-60044-7, AHS34). Bobbs.
Maxson, Charles H. The Great Awakening in the Middle Colonies. 7.00 (ISBN 0-8446-1306-1). Peter Smith.
Rutman, Darrett B., ed. The Great Awakening: Event & Exegesis. 208p. 1977. pap. text ed. 5.75 (ISBN 0-88275-605-2). Krieger.
Whitefield, George. Journals of George Whitefield, 1737-1741. LC 73-81363. (Illus.). 1969. Repr. of 1905 ed. 52.00x (ISBN 0-8201-1069-8). Schol Facsimiles.

GREAT BARRIER REEF, AUSTRALIA
Ferrier, Lucy. Diving the Great Barrier Reef. new ed. LC 75-23411. (Illus.). 32p. (gr. 5-10). 1976. PLB 6.89 (ISBN 0-89375-005-0); pap. 2.50 (ISBN 0-89375-021-2). Troll Assocs.
Gillett, Keith. The Australian Great Barrier Reef in Colour. rev. ed. (Illus.). 96p. 1980. Repr. of 1968 ed. 11.95 (ISBN 0-589-50199-2, Pub. by Reed Books Australia). C E Tuttle.
McGregor, Craig. The Great Barrier Reef. (The World's Wild Places Ser). (Illus.). 1973. 12.95 (ISBN 0-8094-2006-6). Time-Life.
Maxwell, W. G. Atlas of the Great Barrier Reef. 1968. 83.00 (ISBN 0-444-40707-3). Elsevier.
Stoddart, D. R. & Yonge, Maurice, eds. The Northern Great Barrier Reaf. (Proceedings of the Royal Society). (Illus.). 364p. 1979. text ed. 95.75x (ISBN 0-85403-102-2, Pub. by Royal Soc London). Scholium Intl.

GREAT BASIN
Cline, Gloria G. Exploring the Great Basin. LC 63-8988. (American Exploration & Travel Ser.: Vol. 39). (Illus.). 254p. 1963. pap. 6.95 (ISBN 0-8061-1014-7). U of Okla Pr.
Cronquist, A., et al. Intermountain Flora: Vascular Plants of the Intermountain West, U.S.A. - the Monocotyledons, Vol. 6. LC 73-134298. 1977. 60.00x (ISBN 0-231-04120-9). Columbia U Pr.
Jennings, Jesse D. Prehistory of Utah & the Eastern Great Basin: A Review, 1968-1976. (University of Utah Anthropological Papers: No. 98). (Illus.). 1978. pap. 20.00x (ISBN 0-87480-121-4). U of Utah Pr.
Phillips, Fred M. Desert People & Mountain Men: Exploration of the Great Basin 1824-1865. (Illus.). 1977. 6.50 (ISBN 0-912494-24-7); pap. 3.95 (ISBN 0-912494-25-5). Chalfant Pr.
Sharrock, Floyd W. Prehistoric Occupation Patterns in Southwest Wyoming & Cultural Relationships with the Great Basin & Plains Culture Areas. (Utah Anthropological Papers: No. 77). Repr. of 1966 ed. 24.00 (ISBN 0-404-60677-6). AMS Pr.

GREAT BLUE HERON
Crowell, Marnie R. Great Blue. 1980. 10.95 (ISBN 0-8129-0905-4). Times Bks.

GREAT BRITAIN
see also Commonwealth of Nations; England; also names of cities, districts, and geographical areas in Great Britain
Area Studies, 2 pts. Incl. Pt. 1. United States of America, 60 vols. Set. 4626.00x (ISBN 0-686-01201-1); Pt. 2. China & Japan, 52 vols. Set. 4284.00x (ISBN 0-686-01202-X). (British Parliamentary Papers Ser.). 1971 (Pub. by Irish Academic Pr Ireland). Biblio Dist.
Barker, Ernest. Britain & the British People. LC 75-28660. (Illus.). 1978. Repr. of 1955 ed. lib. bdg. 17.75x (ISBN 0-8371-8483-5, BABB). Greenwood.
Bivand, Roger & Bivand, Ewa S. Britain: Continuity & Change. LC 80-40778. (Illus.). 196p. 1981. 7.95 (ISBN 0-08-025312-1). Pergamon.
British Parliamentary Papers Indexes, 2 pts. Incl. Pt. 1. General, 8 vols. Set. 756.00 (ISBN 0-686-01199-6); Pt. 2. East Indies, 1 vol. 61.00 (ISBN 0-686-01200-3). (British Parliamentary Papers Ser.). 1971 (Pub. by Irish Academic Pr Ireland). Biblio Dist.
Burton, Anthony. The David & Charles Book of Curious Britain. LC 81-67007. (Illus.). 304p. 1981. 19.95 (ISBN 0-7153-8083-4). David & Charles.
Carr, E. H. Britain. 1939. 10.00 (ISBN 0-685-43745-0). Norwood Edns.
Dixon, J. H. Whittingham Vale, Northumberland. (Folklore Ser.). Repr. 20.00 (ISBN 0-685-43674-8). Norwood Edns.
Edwards, L. A. Exchange & Mart: Selected Issues 1868 - 1948. (Illus.). 232p. 1970. 5.95 (ISBN 0-7153-5006-4). David & Charles.
Ershov. A. P. Ershov: The British Lectures. 1980. 17.00 (ISBN 0-85501-491-1). Heyden.
Fawcett, Charles B. Political Geography of the British Empire. LC 74-109731. Repr. of 1933 ed. lib. bdg. 19.25x (ISBN 0-8371-4221-0, FAPG). Greenwood.
Gill, Crispin, ed. Countryman's Britain. LC 76-20122. (Countryman Books). 1976. 17.95 (ISBN 0-7153-7284-X). David & Charles.
Hammond, Reginald. Britain. LC 77-437537. (Red Guide Ser.). (Illus.). 256p. 1969. 7.50x (ISBN 0-7063-1082-9). Intl Pubns Serv.
Hudson, William H. Afoot in England. 1973. lib. bdg. 25.00 (ISBN 0-8414-5185-0). Folcroft.
Hurstfield, Joel. Elizabethan Nation. 1967. lib. bdg. 11.50x (ISBN 0-88307-154-1). Gannon.
Irwin, John. Modern Britain: An Introduction. 1976. pap. text ed. 7.50x (ISBN 0-04-301080-6). Allen Unwin.
Lodge, Thomas & Greene, Robert. Looking-Glass for London & England. LC 71-133697. (Tudor Facsimile Texts. Old English Plays: No. 67). Repr. of 1914 ed. 31.50 (ISBN 0-404-53367-1). AMS Pr.
Mackinder, Hanford. Britain & the British Seas. LC 68-25248. (British History Ser., No. 30). 1969. Repr. of 1902 ed. lib. bdg. 49.95 (ISBN 0-8383-0212-2). Haskell.
MacKinder, Hanford J. Britain & the British Seas. Repr. of 1902 ed. lib. bdg. 15.75x (ISBN 0-8371-2754-8, MABR). Greenwood.
Marriott, John. This Realm of England. facsimile ed. LC 78-140368. (Select Bibliographies Reprint Ser). Repr. of 1938 ed. 19.50 (ISBN 0-8369-5611-7). Arno.
Marsden, W. E. North West England. 2nd ed. LC 78-67243. (Geography of the British Isles). 1979. pap. 5.95 (ISBN 0-521-22474-8). Cambridge U Pr.
Marx, Karl & Engels, Frederick. Articles on Britain. 466p. 1971. 15.95x (ISBN 0-8464-0153-3). Beekman Pubs.
Mosley, O. The Greater Britain. 59.95 (ISBN 0-8490-0263-X). Gordon Pr.
Rosebery, Archibald P. Miscellanies: Literary & Historical, 2 vols. facsimile ed. LC 71-152211. (Essay Index Reprint Ser). Repr. of 1921 ed. 39.00 (ISBN 0-8369-2253-0). Arno.
Skyvington, William. Great Britain Today. (Illus.). 240p. 1979. 14.95 (ISBN 2-8525-8109-4, Pub. by J A Editions France). Hippocrene Bks.
West, Kenyon. Cliveden. 1976. Repr. of 1903 ed. 4.50 (ISBN 0-89133-049-6). Preservation Pr.
Who Owns Whom: United Kingdom & the Republic of Ireland 1980-81, 2 vols. 23rd ed. LC 59-52911. 2200p. 1980. 190.00x (ISBN 0-8002-2418-3). Intl Pubns Serv.

GREAT BRITAIN–ADMIRALTY
Fox, Grace E. British Admirals & Chinese Pirates, 1832-1869. LC 73-873. (China Studies: from Confucius to Mao Ser.). (Illus.). xiv, 227p. 1973. Repr. of 1940 ed. 21.50 (ISBN 0-88355-068-7). Hyperion Conn.
Sainty, J. C., compiled by. Admiralty Officials Sixteen Sixty-Eighteen Seventy. (No. 4). 159p. 1975. text ed. 19.50x (ISBN 0-485-17144-9, Athlone Pr). Humanities.

GREAT BRITAIN–AIR MINISTRY
Reid, John P. Some of the Few: Airmen of the Battle of Britain. 1960. 5.00 (ISBN 0-913076-16-3). Beachcomber Bks.
Tanner, John, ed. RAF Airborne Forces Manual. LC 79-84780. (RAF Museum Ser.: Vol. 8). (Illus.). 1979. 29.95 (ISBN 0-88254-485-3). Hippocrene Bks.

GREAT BRITAIN–ANTIQUITIES
Addison, Sir William. The Old Roads of England. (Illus.). 144p. 1980. 27.00 (ISBN 0-7134-1714-5, Pub. by Batsford England). David & Charles.
Adkins, Lesley & Adkins, Roy A. A Thesaurus of British Archaeology. 320p. 1982. 27.50x (ISBN 0-389-20245-2). B&N.
The Archaeology of London. LC 74-83860. (Illus.). 1975. 9.95 (ISBN 0-8155-5033-2, NP). Noyes.
Arthur, Paul & Marsh, Geoff. Early Fine Wares in Roman Britain. 1978. 54.00x (ISBN 0-86054-041-3, Pub. by BAR). State Mutual Bk.
Ashbee, Paul. The Ancient British. 314p. 1980. 19.55 (ISBN 0-86094-015-2, Pub. by GEO Abstracts England); pap. 14.95 (ISBN 0-86094-014-4, Pub. by GEO Abstracts England). State Mutual Bk.
Barrett, John & Bradley, Richard, eds. Settlement & Society in the British Isles Bronze Age. 500p. 1980. 80.00x (ISBN 0-86054-108-8, Pub. by BAR). State Mutual Bk.
Birley, Robin. On Hadrian's Wall: Vindolanda: Roman Fort & Settlement. (Illus.). 1977. 22.50 (ISBN 0-500-39014-2). Thames Hudson.
Blackstone, Sir William. Tracts Chiefly Relating to the Antiquities & Laws of England. 3rd ed. Repr. of 1771 ed. lib. bdg. 30.00x (ISBN 0-87991-750-4). Porcupine Pr.
Bonanno, Anthony. Portraits & Other Heads on Roman Historical Relief up to the Age of Septimus Severus. 1976. 30.00x (ISBN 0-904531-38-4, Pub. by BAR). State Mutual Bk.
Bord, Janet & Bord, Colin. Mysterious Britain. (Illus.). 287p. 1981. pap. 5.95 (ISBN 0-586-08157-7, Pub. by Granada England). Academy Chi Ltd.
--Mysterious Britain. (Illus.). 1978. pap. text ed. 5.95x (ISBN 0-8464-0663-2). Beekman Pubs.
--The Secret Country. (Illus.). 247p. 1981. pap. 5.95 (ISBN 0-586-08267-0, Pub. by Granada England). Academy Chi Ltd.
--The Secret Country. 1977. 9.95 (ISBN 0-8027-0559-6). Walker & Co.
Branigan, Keith. Gatcombe: The Excavation & Study of Roman-British Villa Estate, 1967-1976. 1977. 30.00x (ISBN 0-904531-96-1, Pub. by BAR). State Mutual Bk.
Bronte, Patrick. Complete Transcript of the Leyland Manuscripts. Symington, J. Alex, ed. LC 72-193739. 1925. lib. bdg. 10.00 (ISBN 0-8414-2503-5). Folcroft.
Buckland, P. C. The Environmental Evidence from the Church Street Roman Sewer System. (Archaeology of York - the Past Environment of York Ser.: Vol. 14, Fas. 1). 44p. pap. text ed. 5.95 (ISBN 0-900312-41-6, Pub. by Coun Brit Archaeology). Humanities.
Burgess, Colin & Coombs, David, eds. Bronze -Age Hoards: Some Finds Old & New. 1979. 43.00x (ISBN 0-86054-054-5, Pub. by BAR). State Mutual Bk.
Burl. The Stone Circles of the British Isles. 1979. 35.00 (ISBN 0-300-01972-6); pap. 11.95 (ISBN 0-300-02398-7, Y-341). Yale U Pr.
Burl, Aubrey. Rings of Stone: The Prehistoric Stone Circles of Britain & Ireland. LC 79-17741. (Illus.). 280p. 1980. 19.95 (ISBN 0-89919-000-6). Ticknor & Fields.
Burn, A. R. Romans in Britain: An Anthology of Inscriptions. 2nd ed. LC 77-75795. (Illus.). 1969. 12.95x (ISBN 0-87249-142-0). U of SC Pr.
Carver, M. O., et al. Riverside Structures & a Well in Skeldergate & Buildings in Bishophill. (Archaeology of York the Colonia Ser.: Vol. 4). (Illus.). 55p. 1978. pap. text ed. 14.95 (ISBN 0-900312-59-9, Pub. by Coun Brit Archaeological). Humanities.
Chambers, Robert, ed. Book of Days: A Miscellany of Popular Antiquities in Connection with the Calendar, Including Anecdote, Biography & History, Curiosities of Literature, & Oddities of Human Life & Character, 2 Vols. LC 67-13009. (Illus.). 1967. Repr. of 1862 ed. 74.00 (ISBN 0-8103-3002-4). Gale.
Childe, V. Gordon. Prehistoric Communities of the British Isles. LC 72-82207. (Illus.). Repr. of 1940 ed. 19.00 (ISBN 0-405-08358-0, Blom Pubns). Arno.
Childe, Vere G. Prehistoric Communities of the British Isles. 2nd ed. LC 76-114498. (Illus.). 1971. Repr. of 1947 ed. lib. bdg. 15.75x (ISBN 0-8371-4732-8, CHPC). Greenwood.
Clark, John G. The Mesolithic Age in Britian. LC 76-44704. Repr. of 1932 ed. 24.00 (ISBN 0-404-15914-1). AMS Pr.
Clough, T. H. & Cummins, W. A., eds. Stone Axe Studies: Archaeological, Petrological, Experimental & Ethnographic. (CBA Research Report Ser.: No. 23). 137p. 1979. pap. text ed. 35.00 (ISBN 0-900312-63-7, Pub. by Coun Brit Archaeology). Humanities.
Collingwood, R. G. & Richmond, Ian. The Archaeology of Roman Britain. 2nd ed. 1969. 49.95x (ISBN 0-416-27580-X). Methuen Inc.
Cowie, Trevor G. Bronze Age Food Vessel Urns in Northern Britain. 1978. 28.00x (ISBN 0-86054-031-6, Pub. by BAR). State Mutual Bk.
Cunliffe, Barry. Hengistbury Head. (Illus.). 1978. 14.95 (ISBN 0-236-40125-4, Pub. by Paul Elek). Merrimack Bk Serv.
--Iron Age Communities in Britain. 2nd ed. (Archaeology of Britain Ser). (Illus.). 1978. 42.00 (ISBN 0-7100-8725-X). Routledge & Kegan.
--The Regni. (People of Roman Britain Ser.). 1973. text ed. 17.50x (ISBN 0-7156-0669-7). Humanities.
Dyer, James. Your Book of Prehistoric Britain. (Your Book Ser.). (Illus.). 80p. (gr. 5 up). 1974. 7.95 (ISBN 0-571-09883-5, Pub. by Faber & Faber). Merrimack Bk Serv.
Eames, Elizabeth S. Catalogue of Medieval Lead-Glazed Earthenware Tiles in the Department of Medieval & Later Antiquities, British Museum. 794p. 1981. 300.00x (ISBN 0-7141-1338-7, Pub. by Brit Mus Pubns England). State Mutual Bk.
Ehrenberg, Margaret R. Bronze-Age Spearheads from Berks., Bucks & Oxon. 1977. 10.00x (ISBN 0-904531-61-9, Pub. by BAR). State Mutual Bk.
Evans, J. G., et al, eds. The Effect of Man on the Landscape: The Highland Zone. (CBA Research Report Ser.: No. 11). 129p. 1975. pap. text ed. 22.50x (ISBN 0-900312-27-0, Pub. by Coun Brit Archaeology). Humanities.
Evans, John C. The Environment of Early Man in the British Isles. LC 74-29803. 256p. 1975. 24.50x (ISBN 0-520-02973-9). U of Cal Pr.
Farrell, Robert T. Bede & Anglo-Saxon England. 18.00x (ISBN 0-86054-005-7, Pub. by BAR). State Mutual Bk.
Fenwick, Valerie. The Gravenney Boat: A Tenth-Century Find from Kent. (National Maritime Museum, Greenwich, Archaeological Ser.: No. 3). 1978. 54.00x (ISBN 0-86054-030-8, Pub. by BAR). State Mutual Bk.
Forde-Johnston, J. Castles & Fortificaions of Britain & Ireland. (Illus.). 192p. 1977. 12.50x (ISBN 0-460-04195-9, J M Dent England). Biblio Dist.
--Hillforts of the Iron Age in England & Wales: A Survey of the Surface Evidence. (Illus.). 331p. 1976. 55.00x (ISBN 0-87471-802-3). Rowman.
--Prehistoric Britain & Ireland. 1976. 11.50 (ISBN 0-393-05605-8). Norton.
Foster, I. L. & Alcock, L., eds. Culture & Environment: Essays in Honor of Sir Cyril Fox. 1963. text ed. 24.25x (ISBN 0-7100-1387-6). Humanities.
Foster, Jennifer. Bronze Door Figurines in the Iron Age & Roman Britain. 1977. 10.00x (ISBN 0-904531-74-0, Pub. by BAR). State Mutual Bk.
Fowler, Peter J., ed. Recent Work in Rural Archaeology. (Illus.). 160p. 1975. 15.00x (ISBN 0-87471-596-2). Rowman.
Fowley, John. John Aubrey's Monumenta Britannica. 600p. 250.00x (ISBN 0-686-75655-X, Pub. by Dorset). State Mutual Bk.
Garrod, Dorothy A. The Upper Palaeolithic Age in Britain. LC 76-44722. Repr. of 1926 ed. 21.50 (ISBN 0-404-15926-5). AMS Pr.
Gentry, Anne P. Roman Military Stone-Built Granaries in Britain. 1976. 10.00x (ISBN 0-904531-45-7, Pub. by BAR). State Mutual Bk.
Gibson, Alex M. Bronze Age Pottery in the North-East of England. 1978. 25.00x (ISBN 0-86054-037-5, Pub. by BAR). State Mutual Bk.
Gomme, George L. Primitive Folk-Moots: Or, Open-Air Assemblies in Britain. LC 67-23899. 1968. Repr. of 1880 ed. 14.00 (ISBN 0-8103-3433-X). Gale.
Green, H. Stephen. The Flint Arrowheads of the British Isles: A Detailed Study Material from England & Wales with Comparanda from Scotland & Ireland. 469p. 1980. 75.00x (ISBN 0-86054-077-4, Pub. by BAR). State Mutual Bk.
Green, Miranda J. A Corpus of Cult Objects from the Military Areas of Roman Britain. 1978. 15.00x (ISBN 0-86054-032-4, Pub. by BAR). State Mutual Bk.
--A Corpus of Religious Materials from the Civilian Areas of Roman Britain. 1976. 25.00x (ISBN 0-904531-27-9, Pub. by BAR). State Mutual Bk.
Grinsell, Leslie V. Folklore of Prehistoric Sites in Britain. LC 76-8624. (Illus.). 304p. 1976. 12.00 (ISBN 0-7153-7241-6). David & Charles.
Hadingham, Evan. Circles & Standing Stones: An Illustrated Exploration of Magalith Mysteries of Early Britain. LC 74-82169. (Illus.). 24p. 1975. 12.50 (ISBN 0-8027-0463-8). Walker & Co.
Harding, D., ed. Hillforts: Later Prehistoric Earthworks in Britain & Ireland. 1976. 94.50 (ISBN 0-12-324750-0). Acad Pr.
Hassall, M. W. & Ireland, Robert, eds. De Rebus Bellicis, 2 pts. 1979. 54.00x (ISBN 0-86054-063-4, Pub. by BAR). State Mutual Bk.
Haverfield, Francis J. The Romanization of Roman Britain. LC 78-12798. (Illus.). 1979. Repr. of 1923 ed. lib. bdg. 15.00 (ISBN 0-313-21148-5, HARM). Greenwood.
Henig, Martin. A Corpus of Roman Engraved Gemstones from British Sites. 1981. 40.00x (ISBN 0-86054-039-1, Pub. by BAR). State Mutual Bk.
Hodgetts, J. Frederick. Olden England, 2 vols. 413p. 1981. Repr. of 1884 ed. Set. lib. bdg. 200.00 (ISBN 0-89987-364-2). Darby Bks.
Hogg, A. H. British Hill-Forts: An Index. 1979. 30.00x (ISBN 0-86054-046-4, Pub. by BAR). State Mutual Bk.
Jennings, Jesse D. Proceedings of the Sixth Plains Archeological Conference, 1948. (Utah Anthropological Papers: No. 11). Repr. of 1959 ed. 32.00 (ISBN 0-404-60611-3). AMS Pr.
Johnson, Walter. Folk-Memory: Or, the Continuity of British Archaeology. LC 71-173112. (Illus.). Repr. of 1908 ed. 18.75 (ISBN 0-405-08673-3, Blom Pubns). Arno.
Johnston, D. E., ed. The Saxon Shore. (CBA Research Report Ser.: No. 18). 92p. 1977. pap. text ed. 20.95x (ISBN 0-900312-43-2, Pub. by Coun Brit Archaeology). Humanities.

Jope, E. M. & Jacobsthal, P. Early Celtic Art in the British Isles, 2 vols. (Illus.). 392p. 1980. text ed. 99.00x (ISBN 0-19-817318-0). Oxford U Pr.
Kewley, Joyce. British Archaeology: An Introductory Booklist. 16p. 1976. pap. text ed. 2.95x (ISBN 0-900312-37-8, Pub. by Coun Brit Archaeology). Humanities.
Kiszely, Istvan. The Anthropology of the Lombards. 1979. 100.00x (ISBN 0-86054-061-8, Pub. by BAR). State Mutual Bk.
Leeds, E. Thurlow. Archaeology of the Anglo-Saxon Settlements. (Oxford Reprints Ser). (Illus.). 1913. 19.50x (ISBN 0-19-813161-5). Oxford U Pr.
Leland, John. Leland's Itinerary in England & Wales, 5 Vols. Smith, Lucy T., ed. LC 65-10026. (Centaur Classics Ser.). 1373p. 1964. boxed 75.00x (ISBN 0-8093-0168-7). S Ill U Pr.
Limbrey, Susan & Evans, J. G., eds. The Effect of Man on the Landscape: The Lowland Zone. (CBA Research Report: No. 21). 153p. 1978. pap. text ed. 29.95x (ISBN 0-900312-60-2, Pub. by Coun Brit Archaeology). Humanities.
MacGregor, Arthur. Finds from a Roman Sewer System & an Adjacent Building in Church Street. (Archaeology of York - Small Finds Ser.: Vol. 17, Fas. 1). 29p. 1976. pap. text ed. 4.25x (ISBN 0-900312-31-9, Pub. by Coun Brit Archaeology). Humanities.
--Roman Finds from Skeldergate & Bishophill. (Archaeology of York-Small Finds Ser.: Vol. 17). 66p. 1978. pap. text ed. 7.95x (ISBN 0-900312-72-6, Pub. by Coun Brit Archeology). Humanities.
Megaw, J. V. & Simpson, D. D., eds. Introduction to British Prehistory. 1979. text ed. 47.50x (ISBN 0-7185-1122-0, Leicester). Humanities.
Meller, Walter C. Old Times. LC 68-26592. (Illus.). 1968. Repr. of 1925 ed. 19.00 (ISBN 0-8103-3453-4). Gale.
Mercer, Roger. Beakers in Britain & Europe. 1977. 10.00x (ISBN 0-904531-83-X, Pub. by BAR). State Mutual Bk.
Mercer, Roger, ed. Farming Practices in Prehistoric Britain. 160p. 1981. 20.00x (ISBN 0-85224-414-2, Pub. by Edinburgh U Pr Scotland). Columbia U Pr.
Morris, Pat. Agricultural Buildings in Roman Britain. 1979. 30.00x (ISBN 0-86054-065-0, Pub. by BAR). State Mutual Bk.
Muir, Richard. Riddles in the British Landscape. (Illus.). 200p. 1981. 17.95 (ISBN 0-500-24108-2). Thames Hudson.
Nelson, John. The History of Islington: A Facsimile of the First Edition (1811) Together with 79 Additional Illustrations & an Introductio N by Julia Melvin. Melvin, Julia, ed. (Illus.). 417p. 1980. Repr. of 1811 ed. 80.00x (ISBN 0-85667-104-5, Pub. by Sotheby Parke Bernet England). Biblio Dist.
Nichols, John & Gough, Richard. Bibliotheca Topographica Britannica, 10 Vols. LC 70-138264. Repr. of 1800 ed. 660.00 (ISBN 0-404-04740-8). AMS Pr.
Pitt-Rivers, Augustus H. Excavations in Cranborne Chase: Near Rushmore, on the Borders of Dorset & Wilts: 1880-1896, 4 vols. LC 77-86426. Repr. of 1898 ed. 315.00 set (ISBN 0-404-16640-7). AMS Pr.
Prehistoric Society of East Anglia. Report on the Excavations at Grime's Graves: Weeting, Norfolk, March - May, 1914. Clarke, W. G., ed. LC 77-86437. Repr. of 1915 ed. 28.00 (ISBN 0-404-16676-8). AMS Pr.
Radford, C. A. & Swanton, M. J. Arthurian Sites in the West. 62p. 1975. pap. text ed. 3.25x (ISBN 0-85989-026-0, Pub. by U Exeter England). Humanities.
Rees, Sian E. Agricultural Implements in Prehistoric & Roman Britain. 1979. 90.00x (ISBN 0-86054-064-2, Pub. by BAR). State Mutual Bk.
Renfrew, Colin, ed. British Prehistory: A New Outline. LC 74-83800. (Illus.). 1975. 20.00 (ISBN 0-8155-5032-4, NP). Noyes.
Salway, Peter. Frontier People of Roman Britain. (Cambridge Classical Studies). 1965. 34.00 (ISBN 0-521-06187-3). Cambridge U Pr.
Sedgley, Jeffrey P. The Roman Milestones of Britain: Their Petrography & Probable Origins. 1975. 10.00x (ISBN 0-904531-20-1, Pub. by BAR). State Mutual Bk.
Shelton, Kathleen J. The Esquiline Treasure. 160p. 1981. 100.00x (ISBN 0-7141-1356-5, Pub. by Brit Mus Pubns England). State Mutual Bk.
Swanton, Michael. Exploring Early Britain. (Countryside Leisure Ser.). (Illus.). 1978. 9.95 (ISBN 0-7158-0472-3). Charles River Bks.
Taylor, Joan Du Plat & Cleere, Henry, eds. Roman Shipping & Trade: Britain & the Rhine Provinces. (CBA Research Report Ser.: No. 24). 86p. 1978. pap. text ed. 20.95x (ISBN 0-900312-62-9, Pub. by Coun Brit Archaeology). Humanities.
Taylor, Joan J. Bronze Age Goldwork of the British Isles. LC 75-12160. (Gulbenkian Archaeological Ser.). (Illus.). 188p. 1981. 95.00 (ISBN 0-521-20802-5). Cambridge U Pr.
Thom, A. Megalithic Remains in Britain & Brittany. (Illus.). 1979. 37.50x (ISBN 0-19-858156-4). Oxford U Pr.
Thomas, Charles. The Early Christian Archaeology of North Britian: Hunter Marshall Lectures Delivered at the University of Glasgow in Jan. & Feb. 1968. 270p. 1971. 15.95x (ISBN 0-19-214102-3). Oxford U Pr.
Tilley, Christopher Y. Post-Glacial Communities in the Cambridge Region: Some Theoretical Approaches to Settlement & Subsistence. 1979. 11.00x (ISBN 0-86054-053-7, Pub. by BAR). State Mutual Bk.
Todd, Malcolm. The Coritani. (Peoples of Roman Britain Ser.). 1973. text ed. 17.50x (ISBN 0-7156-0649-2). Humanities.
Wacher, John. Roman Britain. (Illus.). 286p. 1980. pap. 11.00x (ISBN 0-460-02212-1, Pub. by J M Dent England). Biblio Dist.
Ward, F. A. A Catalogue of European Scientific Instruments in the Department of Medieval & Later Antiquities of the British Museum. 176p. 1981. 150.00x (ISBN 0-7141-1345-X, Pub. by Brit Mus Pubns England). State Mutual Bk.
Ward, John. Roman Era in Britain. LC 79-118507. 1971. Repr. of 1911 ed. 13.00 (ISBN 0-8046-1255-2). Kennikat.
Whatmore, Arthur W. Insulae Britannicae. LC 72-118508. 1971. Repr. of 1913 ed. 15.00 (ISBN 0-8046-1256-0). Kennikat.
Wheeler, Robert E. M. Maiden Castle: Dorset. LC 77-86440. (Society of Antiquaries of London. Research Committe. Reports: No. 12). Repr. of 1943 ed. 56.50 (ISBN 0-404-16683-0). AMS Pr.
Wilson, Roger J. A Guide to the Roman Remains in Britain. 1981. 15.00x (ISBN 0-686-75469-7, Pub. by Constable Pubs). State Mutual Bk.
Wymer, John. Gazetter of Mesolithics Sites in England & Wales. 1980. pap. 27.60 (ISBN 0-900312-49-1, Pub. by GEO Abstracts England). State Mutual Bk.

GREAT BRITAIN–APPROPRIATIONS AND EXPENDITURES

Heclo, Hugh & Wildavsky, Aaron. The Private Government of Public Money: Community & Policy in British Political Administration. LC 73-79474. 1974. 30.00x (ISBN 0-520-02497-4). U of Cal Pr.

GREAT BRITAIN–ARMED FORCES

Adair, Robin. British Eighth Army. LC 73-83742. (Key Uniform Ser.). (Illus.). 48p. 1974. pap. 1.95 (ISBN 0-668-03363-0). Arco.
Chant, Chris. Armed Forces of the United Kingdom. LC 80-66428. (Illus.). 80p. 1980. 14.95 (ISBN 0-7153-8024-9). David & Charles.
Davis, Howard P. British Parachute Forces, 1940-45. LC 73-83741. (Key Uniform Guides). (Illus.). 48p. 1974. pap. 1.95 (ISBN 0-668-03362-2). Arco.
Funcken, Lilliane & Funcken, Fred. British Infantry Uniforms from Marlborough to Wellington. (Illus.). pap. 14.95x (ISBN 0-8464-0213-0). Beekman Pubs.
Geraghty, Tony. Inside the SAS. (Elite Unit Ser.: No. 2). (Illus.). 249p. 1981. 17.95 (ISBN 0-89839-039-7). Battery Pr.
Johnson, Franklyn. Defence by Ministry. LC 79-28587. 234p. 1980. text ed. 42.50x (ISBN 0-8419-0598-3). Holmes & Meier.
Lawford, James. Britain's Army in India. (Illus.). 1977. text ed. 22.50x (ISBN 0-04-954020-3). Allen Unwin.
Martin, Nancy. Search & Rescue: The Story of the Coast Guard Service. LC 74-81053. (David & Charles Children's Bks). (Illus.). 80p. (gr. 3-8). 1975. 5.95 (ISBN 0-7153-6501-0). David & Charles.
Owen, David L. Providence Their Guide: The Story of the Long Range Desert Group 1940-1945. (Elite Unit Ser.: No. 3). (Illus.). 238p. 1981. 19.50 (ISBN 0-89839-040-0). Battery Pr.
Tyler, R. A. Bloody Provost: An Account of the Provost Service of the British Army & the Early Years of the Corps of Royal Military Police. (Illus.). 246p. 1980. 23.75x (ISBN 0-8476-3166-4). Rowman.

GREAT BRITAIN–ARMED FORCES–MEDALS, BADGES, DECORATIONS, ETC.

Fraser, Edward & Gibbons, John. Soldier & Sailor Words & Phrases. LC 68-30635. 1968. Repr. of 1925 ed. 26.00 (ISBN 0-8103-3281-7). Gale.

GREAT BRITAIN–ARMY

see also Great Britain–History, Military

Barzilay, David. British Army in Ulster. (Illus.). 1976. Repr. of 1973 ed. 29.95x set (ISBN 0-8464-0209-2). Beekman Pubs.
Bayley, C. C. Mercenaries for the Crimea: The German, Swiss, & Italian Legions in British Service, 1854-1856. 1977. lib. bdg. 13.50x (ISBN 0-7735-0273-4). McGill-Queens U Pr.
Bond, Brian. British Military Policy Between the Two World Wars. 480p. 1980. 48.00x (ISBN 0-19-822464-8). Oxford U Pr.
Bowler, R. Arthur. Logistics & the Failure of the British Army in America, 1775-1783. 320p. 1975. 21.00 (ISBN 0-691-04630-1). Princeton U Pr.
Brett-James, Antony. Life in Wellington's Army. 1972. text ed. 13.50x (ISBN 0-04-940042-8). Allen Unwin.
Bruce, A. P. Annotated Bibliography of the British Army, Sixteen Sixty to Nineteen Fourteen. LC 75-23072. (Reference Library of Social Science: Vol. 14). 255p. 1975. lib. bdg. 28.00 (ISBN 0-8240-9988-5). Garland Pub.
Buckley, Rober N. Slaves in Red Coats: The British West India Regiments, 1795-1815. LC 78-16830. (Illus.). 1979. 19.50x (ISBN 0-300-02216-6). Yale U Pr.
Calver, William L. & Bolton, Reginald P. History Written with Pick & Shovel. LC 50-10740. (New York Historical Society). (Illus.). 1970. 8.00x (ISBN 0-685-73900-7). U Pr of Va.
Churchill, Winston S. My Early Life: A Roving Commission. (Illus.). 1930. lib. rep. ed. 17.00x (ISBN 0-684-15154-5, ScribT). Scribner.
Clammer, David. The Victorian Army in Photographs. LC 75-7908. (Illus.). 96p. 1975. 12.50 (ISBN 0-88254-352-0). Hippocrene Bks.
Cruickshank, C. G. Elizabeth's Army. 2nd ed. (Orig.). 1966. pap. 3.00x (ISBN 0-19-881148-9, OPB). Oxford U Pr.
Cunningham, Hugh. The Volunteer Force: A Social & Political History, 1859-1908. (Illus.). viii, 168p. 1975. 16.50 (ISBN 0-208-01569-8, Archon). Shoe String.
Dalton, Charles. English Army Lists & Commission Registers, 1661-1714, 6 Vols. in 3. 1960. Repr. of 1892 ed. Set. lib. bdg. 100.00 (ISBN 0-8063-0427-8). Genealog Pub.
Davies, Godfrey. Wellington & His Army. LC 74-8376. (Illus.). 154p. 1974. Repr. of 1954 ed. lib. bdg. 15.00x (ISBN 0-8371-7566-6, DAWA). Greenwood.
Fabb, John. Victorian & Edwardian Army from Old Photographs. 1975. 24.00 (ISBN 0-7134-2973-9). David & Charles.
Fortescue, John W. History of British Army from the Expedition to Egypt 1807, to the Battle of Coruna, January, 1809, Vol. 6. Repr. of 1910 ed. 27.50 (ISBN 0-404-02557-9). AMS Pr.
--History of British Army from the Fall of the Bastille to the Peace of Amiens, Pts. 1 & 2, Vol. 4. Repr. of 1915 ed. 47.50 (ISBN 0-404-02554-4). AMS Pr.
--History of British Army from the Fall of the Bastille to the Peace of Amiens: Supplementary Volume, Pt. 3, Vol. 4. Repr. of 1915 ed. 22.50 (ISBN 0-404-02555-2). AMS Pr.
--History of British Army from the Renewal of the War to the Evacuation of Rio De la Plata, Vol. 5. Repr. of 1910 ed. 27.50 (ISBN 0-404-02556-0). AMS Pr.
--History of British Army to the Close of the Seven Year's War, Vols. 1-2. Repr. of 1910 ed. 27.50 ea. Vol. 1 (ISBN 0-404-02551-X). Vol. 2 (ISBN 0-404-02552-8). AMS Pr.
--History of British Army to the Second Peace of Paris, Vol. 3. Repr. of 1911 ed. 27.50 (ISBN 0-404-02553-6). AMS Pr.
--History of British Army 1809-1810, Pt. 1., Vol. 7. Repr. of 1912 ed. 27.50 (ISBN 0-404-02558-7). AMS Pr.
--History of British Army 1809-1810: Supplementary Volume, Pt. 2, Vol. 7. (Illus.). Repr. of 1912 ed. 22.50 (ISBN 0-404-02559-5). AMS Pr.
--History of British Army 1811-1812, Pt. 1, Vol. 8. Repr. of 1917 ed. 27.50 (ISBN 0-404-02560-9). AMS Pr.
--History of British Army 1811-1812: Supplementary Volume, Pt. 2, Vol. 8. (Illus.). Repr. of 1917 ed. 22.50 (ISBN 0-404-02561-7). AMS Pr.
--History of British Army 1813-1815, Vols. 9-10. Repr. of 1920 ed. 27.50 ea. Vol. 9 (ISBN 0-404-02562-5). Vol. 10 (ISBN 0-404-02563-3). AMS Pr.
--History of British Army 1813-1815, Supplementary Volume, Pt. 2, Vol. 10. (Illus.). Repr. of 1920 ed. 22.50 (ISBN 0-404-02564-1). AMS Pr.
--History of British Army 1815-1838, Vol. 11. Repr. of 1923 ed. 27.50 (ISBN 0-404-02565-X). AMS Pr.
--History of British Army 1839-1852, Pt. 1, Vol. 12. Repr. of 1927 ed. 27.50 (ISBN 0-404-02566-8). AMS Pr.
--History of British Army 1839-1852: Supplementary Volume, Pt. 2, Vol. 12. (Illus.). Repr. of 1927 ed. 22.50 (ISBN 0-404-02567-6). AMS Pr.
--History of British Army 1852-1870, Pt. 1,vol. 13. Repr. of 1930 ed. 27.50 (ISBN 0-404-02568-4). AMS Pr.
--History of British Army 1852-1870: Supplementary Volume, Pt. 2, Vol. 13. (Illus.). Repr. of 1930 ed. 22.50 (ISBN 0-404-02569-2). AMS Pr.
--A History of the British Army, Vols. 1-13 & 6 Supplementary Vols. LC 70-116765. Repr. of 1930 ed. Set. 510.00 (ISBN 0-404-02550-1). AMS Pr.
Fraser, Edward & Gibbons, John. Soldier & Sailor Words & Phrases. LC 68-30635. 1968. Repr. of 1925 ed. 26.00 (ISBN 0-8103-3281-7). Gale.
Glover, Michael. Wellington's Army: In the Peninsula 1808-1814. LC 76-25238. (Historic Armies & Navies Ser). 1977. 14.95 (ISBN 0-88254-413-6). Hippocrene Bks.
Graham, John W. Conscription & Conscience: A History 1916-1919. LC 78-81509. Repr. of 1922 ed. 17.50x (ISBN 0-678-00507-9). Kelley.
Harries-Jenkins, Gwyn. The Army in Victorian Society. 1977. 17.50x (ISBN 0-8020-2263-4). U of Toronto Pr.
Haswell, Jock. The British Army: A Concise History. (Illus.). 1977. 14.50 (ISBN 0-500-01128-1). Thames Hudson.
Hawkes, Charles P. Authors-At-Arms. LC 70-107709. (Essay Index Reprint Ser). 1934. 17.00 (ISBN 0-8369-1511-9). Arno.
Hayter, Tony. The Army & the Crowd in Mid-Georgian England. 239p. 1979. 22.50x (ISBN 0-8476-6034-6). Rowman.
Kishlansky, Mark A. The Rise of the New Model Army. LC 79-4285. 1979. 21.50 (ISBN 0-521-22751-8). Cambridge U Pr.
Kitson, Frank. Bunch of Five. (Illus.). 320p. 1977. 14.95 (ISBN 0-571-11050-9, Pub. by Faber & Faber). Merrimack Bk Serv.
Robbe-Grillet, Alain. La Maison de Rendez-vous. Howard, Richard, tr. from Fr. 1966. pap. 1.95 (ISBN 0-394-17120-9, B143, BC). Grove.
Rogers, H. C. The British Army of the Eighteenth Century. LC 76-16779. (Illus.). 1977. 14.95 (ISBN 0-88254-418-7). Hippocrene Bks.
Rothstein, A. The Soldier's Strikes of Nineteen Nineteen. 1980. text ed. 27.00x (ISBN 0-333-27693-0). Humanities.
Shy, John. Toward Lexington: The Role of the British Army in the Coming of the American Revolution. 1965. 27.50x (ISBN 0-691-04570-4). Princeton U Pr.
Spiers, Edward M. The Arym & Society, 1815-1914. (Themes in British Social History Ser.). 336p. 1980. text ed. 25.00x (ISBN 0-582-48565-7). Longman.
Stanhope, Henry. The Soldiers: An Anatomy of the British Army. (Illus.). 372p. 1980. 30.00 (ISBN 0-241-10273-1, Pub. by Hamish Hamilton England). David & Charles.
Tylden, G. Horses & Saddlery of the British Army, 17th to 20th Century. (Illus.). 26.00x (ISBN 0-87556-339-2). Saifer.
Tylden, Major G. Horses & Saddlery of the British Army. (Illus.). 19.00 (ISBN 0-85131-083-4, Dist. by Sporting Book Center). J A Allen.

GREAT BRITAIN–ARMY–REGIMENTAL HISTORIES

Adams, W. H. Famous Regiments of the British Army. (Illus.). 1977. Repr. of 1864 ed. 17.50x (ISBN 0-7158-1029-4). Charles River Bks.
Adams, W. H. D. Famous Regiments of the British Army. (Illus.). 320p. 1975. Repr. of 1864 ed. 16.00x (ISBN 0-8464-0401-X). Beekman Pubs.
Houlding, J. A. Fit for Service: The Training of the British Army, 1715-1795. (Illus.). 488p. 1981. 74.00 (ISBN 0-19-822647-0). Oxford U Pr.
Lawford, James. Wellington's Peninsular Army. LC 73-83323. (Men-at-Arms Ser). (Illus.). 40p. 1973. pap. 7.95 (ISBN 0-88254-170-6). Hippocrene Bks.
Morris, Thomas. Napoleonic Wars. Selby, John, ed. (Military Memoirs Ser.). 1968. 15.00 (ISBN 0-208-00631-1, Archon). Shoe String.
Newman, P. R. Royalist Officers in England & Wales, 1642 to 1660: A Biographical Dictionary. LC 80-8594. 1981. lib. bdg. 90.00 (ISBN 0-8240-9503-0). Garland Pub.
Swinson. A Register of the Regiments & Corps of the British Army: The Ancestry of the Regiments & Corps of the Regular Establishment. 1972. lib. bdg. 17.50x (ISBN 0-85591-000-3). Intl Pubns Serv.

GREAT BRITAIN–ARMY–UNIFORMS

Lefferts, Charles. Uniforms of the American, British, French & German Armies in the War of the American Revolution, 1775-1783. rev. ed. LC 70-27396. (Illus.). 304p. 1971. Repr. of 1926 ed. 8.00 (ISBN 0-87364-232-5). Paladin Ent.
War Office. Dress Regulations for the Officers of the Army, 1900. LC 74-94949. (Illus.). 1970. Repr. 10.00 (ISBN 0-8048-0727-2). C E Tuttle.
Wilkinson-Latham, Robert & Wilkinson-Latham, Christopher. Cavalry Uniforms of Britain & the Commonwealth. (Color Ser.). (Illus.). 1969. 9.95 (ISBN 0-7137-0134-X, Pub by Blandford Pr England). Sterling.

--Infantry Uniforms of Britain & the Commonwealth in Color, 1855-1939. LC 79-95304. (World Uniforms in Color Ser). 1971. 8.90 (ISBN 0-02-628730-7). Macmillan.

GREAT BRITAIN–BARONETAGE

His Majesties Commission Touching the Creation of Baronets. LC 70-26416. (English Experience Ser.: No. 309). 1971. Repr. of 1611 ed. 8.00 (ISBN 90-221-0309-9). Walter J Johnson.

Montague-Smith, Patrick. Debrett's Peerage & Baronetage. new ed. (Illus.). 1978. 95.00 (ISBN 0-670-26234-X, Debrett's Peerage, Ltd.). Viking Pr.

Montaigne-Smith, Patrick, ed. Debrett's Peerage & Baronetage. LC 42-17925. 2336p. 1980. 112.50x (ISBN 0-905649-20-6). Intl Pubns Serv.

Pine, Leslie G. New Extinct Peerage, 1884-1971. LC 72-6707. (Illus.). 1973. 27.00 (ISBN 0-8063-0521-5). Genealog Pub.

GREAT BRITAIN–BIBLIOGRAPHY

Allibone, S. Austin. Critical Dictionary of English Literature & British & American Authors, 3 Vols. LC 67-295. 1965. Repr. of 1872 ed. Set. 145.00 (ISBN 0-8103-3017-2). Gale.

Anderson, I. G., ed. Current British Directories: A Guide to the Directories Published in Great Britain, Ireland, British Commonwealth & South Africa. 9th ed. 369p. 1979. 120.00 (ISBN 0-900246-31-6). Gale.

Anderson, John P. Book of British Topography: Classified Catalogue of Topographical Works in the Library of the British Museum Relating to Great Britain & Ireland. LC 77-113836. 1970. Repr. of 1881 ed. 20.00 (ISBN 0-8063-0401-4). Genealog Pub.

Bishop, William W. Checklist of American Copies of Short-Title Catalogue Books. 2nd ed. LC 68-54415. 1968. lib. bdg. 20.25x (ISBN 0-8371-0315-0, BICH). Greenwood.

Cust, Edward. Lives of the Warriors of the Civil Wars of France & England: Warriors of the Seventeenth Century, 2 vols. facsimile ed. LC 76-38737. (Essay Index Reprint Ser). Repr. of 1867 ed. 40.00 (ISBN 0-8369-2642-0). Arno.

Dictionary of National Biography, Concise Dictionary Pt. 1: From the Beginning to 1900. 1953. 49.95x (ISBN 0-19-865301-8). Oxford U Pr.

Dictionary of National Biography, Concise Dictionary Pt. 2: 1900-1950. 1961. 43.00x (ISBN 0-19-865302-6). Oxford U Pr.

Di Roma, Edward & Rosenthal, Joseph A., eds. Numerical Finding List of British Command Papers Published, 1833-1962. LC 70-137702. (New York Public Library Publications in Reprint Ser). 1971. Repr. of 1967 ed. 10.00 (ISBN 0-405-01748-0). Arno.

Erskine, Stuart R. King Edward Seventh & Some Other Figures. facs. ed. LC 67-22092. (Essay Index Reprint Ser). 1936. 16.00 (ISBN 0-8369-1331-0). Arno.

Kirk, John F. Supplement to Allibone's Critical Dictionary of English Literature & British & American Authors, 2 Vols. LC 67-296. 1965. Repr. of 1891 ed. 84.00 (ISBN 0-8103-3018-0). Gale.

Pemberton, J. E. British Official Publications. 2nd ed. LC 73-16231. 328p. 1974. text ed. 13.80 (ISBN 0-08-017797-2). Pergamon.

Ritcheson, Charles R. & Hargrave, O. T., eds. Current Research in British Studies by American & Canadian Scholars, 1968 Edition. LC 78-97803. 1969. pap. 4.00 (ISBN 0-87074-101-2). SMU Press.

Stevenson, Bruce, compiled by. Reader's Guide to Great Britain: A Bibliography. 558p. 1977. 32.50x (ISBN 0-8476-6171-7). Rowman.

Westergaard, John, et al, eds. Modern British Society: A Bibliography. LC 76-51508. 1978. 17.95x (ISBN 0-312-53775-1). St Martin.

Wing, Donald. Short-Title Catalogue of Books Printed in England, Scotland, Ireland, Wales, & British America & of English Books Printed in Other Countries, 1641-1700, Vol. 2. rev. 2nd ed. Crist, Timothy J., ed. LC 70-185211. 700p. 1981. 125.00x (ISBN 0-87352-045-9). Modern Lang.

Wing, Donald, compiled by. Short-Title Catalogue of Books Printed in England, Scotland, Ireland, Wales, & British America & of English Books Printed in Other Countries, 1641-1700, Vol. 1. 2nd rev & enl ed. 1972. 100.00x (ISBN 0-87352-044-0). Modern Lang.

GREAT BRITAIN–BIOGRAPHY

Abbott, Wilbur C. Adventures in Reputation. LC 69-16486. (Essay & General Literature Index Reprint Ser). 1969. Repr. of 1935 ed. 12.50 (ISBN 0-8046-0517-3). Kennikat.

--Conflicts with Oblivion. LC 68-8193. (Essay & General Literature Index Reprint Ser). 1969. Repr. of 1924 ed. 15.00 (ISBN 0-8046-0000-7). Kennikat.

Abercrombie, Lascelles, et al. Revaluations: Studies in Biography. LC 75-30773. (English Biography Ser., No. 31). 1975. lib. bdg. 49.95 (ISBN 0-8383-2106-2). Haskell.

Aldington, Richard. Four English Portraits: Eighteen Hundred & One to Eighteen Fifty-One. LC 79-51232. (Essay Index in Reprint Ser.). (Illus.). Date not set. Repr. of 1948 ed. 19.75x (ISBN 0-8486-3033-5). Core Collection.

Allison, Thomas. Pioneers of English Learning. 1978. lib. bdg. 20.00 (ISBN 0-8495-0104-0). Arden Lib.

Armin, Robert. Two Maids of Moreclacke. LC 77-133634. (Tudor Facsimile Texts. Old English Plays: No. 127). Repr. of 1913 ed. 31.50 (ISBN 0-404-53427-9). AMS Pr.

Askwith, Betty. The Lyttletons: A Family Chronicle of the Nineteenth Century. 1978. 12.95 (ISBN 0-7011-2109-2, Pub. by Chatto Bodley Jonathan). Merrimack Bk Serv.

Ayer, Jules A. Part of My Life. (Illus.). 320p. 1978. pap. 5.95 (ISBN 0-19-281245-9, GB). Oxford U Pr.

Bailey, Anthony. America, Lost & Found. 1981. 10.95 (ISBN 0-394-51088-7). Random.

Balston, Thomas. James Whatman, Father & Son. Bidwell, John, ed. LC 78-74386. (Nineteenth-Century Book Arts & Printing History Ser.: Vol. 1). (Illus.). 1979. lib. bdg. 22.00 (ISBN 0-8240-3875-4). Garland Pub.

Baring-Gould, S. The Vicar of Morwenstow: A Life of Robert Stephen Hawker. 1973. 20.00 (ISBN 0-8274-1426-9). R West.

Barman, Christian. The Man Who Built London Transport: A Biography of Frank Pick. 1979. 24.00 (ISBN 0-7153-7753-1). David & Charles.

Baylen, J. O. & Gossman, N. J. The Biographical Dictionary of Modern British Radicals Since 1770: 1770-1832, Vol. 1. 500p. 1979. text ed. 86.50x (ISBN 0-391-00914-1). Humanities.

Baylen, J. O. & Grossman, N. J. The Biographical Dictionary of Modern British Radicals Since 1770: 1833-1914, Vol.2. 1980. text ed. write for info. (ISBN 0-391-01058-1). Humanities.

Baylen, J. O. & Gossman, N. J., eds. The Biographical Dictionary of Modern British Radicals Since 1770: 1915-1970, Vol. 3. 1980. text ed. write for info. (ISBN 0-391-01059-X). Humanities.

Beals, Michael. Tragicall Historie of Alfred, Lord of Winslor. pap. 5.50 (ISBN 0-87164-046-5). William-F.

Bennett, Henry S. Six Medieval Men & Women. LC 55-14637. 1962. pap. text ed. 3.95x (ISBN 0-689-70009-1, 3). Atheneum.

Billington, Michael. How Tickled I Am: A Celebration of Ken Dodd. (Illus.). 11.95 (ISBN 0-241-89345-3, Pub. by Hamish Hamilton England). David & Charles.

Bingham, Madeleine. Peers & Plebs. 1978. pap. 6.95 (ISBN 0-04-920055-0). Allen Unwin.

Biographia Brittanica; or the Lives of the Most Emminent Persons Who Have Flourished in Great Britain & Ireland, 6 vols. in 7. Repr. of 1766 ed. Set. 850.00 (ISBN 3-4870-2460-8). Adler.

Biographia Brittanica; or, the Lives of the Most Emminent Persons Who Have Flourished in Great Britain & Ireland, 5 vols. 2nd ed. Repr. of 1793 ed. Set. 666.40 (ISBN 3-4870-5267-9). Adler.

Birkenhead, Frederick E. Contemporary Personalities. facsimile ed. LC 69-17562. (Essay Index Reprint Ser). 1924. 17.00 (ISBN 0-8369-0061-8). Arno.

--Points of View, 2 Vols. facsimile ed. LC 77-111815. (Essay Index Reprint Ser.). 1923. 33.00 (ISBN 0-8369-1594-1). Arno.

Bishop, Evelyn M. Blake's Hayley: The Life, Works, & Friendships of William Hayley. LC 72-5490. (Biography Index Reprint Ser). 1972. Repr. of 1951 ed. 27.75 (ISBN 0-8369-8133-2). Arno.

Blue Book Nineteen Seventy-Six: Leaders of the English-Speaking World, 2 vols. LC 73-13918. 1979. Set. 85.00 (ISBN 0-8103-0216-0). Gale.

Boase, Frederic. Modern English Biographies, 4 vols. lib. bdg. 100.00 set (ISBN 0-686-76990-2). Milford Hse.

--Modern English Biography, 6 vols. Set. 650.00 (ISBN 0-8490-0647-3). Gordon Pr.

Bond, Brian, ed. Chief of Staff: The Diaries of Lieutenant General Sir Henry Pownall, Vol. 1, 1933-40. (Illus.). xxxii, 381p. 1973. 23.50 (ISBN 0-208-01326-1, Archon). Shoe String.

Boston, L. M. Perverse & Foolish. LC 78-71593. 180p. 1979. 8.95 (ISBN 0-689-50136-6, McElderry Bk). Atheneum.

Bowditch, Vincent Y. Life & Correspondence of Henry Ingersoll Bowditch, 2 vols. LC 72-121501. (Select Bibliographies Reprint Ser.). 1972. Repr. of 1902 ed. Set. 40.00 (ISBN 0-8369-5459-9). Arno.

Bowen, Marjorie. Sundry Great Gentlemen. 359p. 1980. Repr. lib. bdg. 30.00 (ISBN 0-89984-056-6). Century Bookbindery.

Boyd, Elizabeth F. Bloomsbury Heritage: Their Mothers & Their Aunts. LC 76-422. (Illus.). 1976. 10.50 (ISBN 0-8008-0821-5). Taplinger.

Boyle, Andrew. Poor Dear Brendan. 11.95 (ISBN 0-09-120860-2, Pub. by Hutchinson). Merrimack Bk Serv.

Brendon, Piers. Eminent Edwardians. 1980. 10.95 (ISBN 0-395-29195-X). HM.

Bridges, Robert S. Three Friends. LC 75-3863. (Illus.). 243p. Repr. of 1932 ed. lib. bdg. 14.75x (ISBN 0-8371-8094-5, BRTFR). Greenwood.

Bridges, Thomas C. & Tiltman, Hubert H. Kings of Commerce. facs. ed. LC 68-8442. (Essay Index Reprint Ser). 1928. 16.00 (ISBN 0-8369-0102-9). Arno.

Briggs, Asa. Victorian People: A Reassessment of Persons & Themes, 1851-67. new rev. ed. LC 55-5118. (Chicago Collectors Editions Ser.). (Illus.). x, 314p. 1975. pap. 4.95 (ISBN 0-226-07488-9, P365, Phoen). U of Chicago Pr.

Brittain, Vera. Testament of Friendship. 12.95 (ISBN 0-87223-681-1); pap. 7.95 (ISBN 0-87223-680-3). Wideview Bks.

Brown, George M. Under Brinkie's Brae. 152p. 1981. 25.00x (ISBN 0-903065-29-0, Pub. by Wright Pub Scotland). State Mutual Bk.

Brown, John. Arthur H. Hallam. LC 73-1672. 1973. Repr. of 1862 ed. lib. bdg. 7.50 (ISBN 0-8414-1796-2). Folcroft.

Bruce, F. F. In Retrospect: Remembrance of Things Past. 272p. 1980. 13.95 (ISBN 0-8028-3537-6). Eerdmans.

Bryce, James B. Studies in Contemporary Biography. facsimile ed. LC 77-156619. (Essay Index Reprint Ser). Repr. of 1903 ed. 23.00 (ISBN 0-8369-2271-9). Arno.

Buchan, John. Some Eighteenth Century Byways. LC 72-13299. 1972. Repr. of 1908 ed. lib. bdg. 20.00 (ISBN 0-8414-1178-6). Folcroft.

Buckland, C. E. Dictionary of Indian Biography. LC 68-26350. (Reference Ser. No. 44). 1969. Repr. of 1906 ed. lib. bdg. 59.95 (ISBN 0-8383-0277-7). Haskell.

Buckland, Charles E. Dictionary of Indian Biography. LC 68-23140. 1968. Repr. of 1906 ed. 41.00 (ISBN 0-8103-3156-X). Gale.

--Dictionary of Indian Biography. LC 69-13845. Repr. of 1906 ed. lib. bdg. 21.00x (ISBN 0-8371-0331-2, BUIB). Greenwood.

Budge, Frances A. Thomas Ellwood & Other Worthies of the Olden Time. 1891. Repr. 20.00 (ISBN 0-8274-3609-2). R West.

Bullied, H. A. The Aspinall Era. 17.95x (ISBN 0-392-07597-0, SpS). Sportshelf.

Chalmers, A., ed. General Biographical Dictionary, 32 Vols. rev ed. 1812-1817. Set. 800.00 (ISBN 0-527-15900-X). Kraus Repr.

Chapman, Hester. Four Fine Gentlemen. LC 77-20589. (Illus.). 1978. 17.95x (ISBN 0-8032-1401-4). U of Nebr Pr.

Chapman, Hester W. Great Villiers: A Study of George Villiers, 2nd Duke of Buckingham, 1628-1687. 1949. Repr. 25.00 (ISBN 0-8274-2448-5). R West.

Child, Daphne. Charles Smythe: Pioneer, Premier & Administrator of Natal. (Illus.). 275p. 1973. 13.50x (ISBN 0-86977-030-6). Verry.

Churchill, Reginald C. He Served Human Liberty. 1978. lib. bdg. 10.00 (ISBN 0-8495-0738-3). Arden Lib.

Churchill, Winston S. Great Contemporaries. facsimile ed. LC 79-156630. (Essay Index Reprint Ser). Repr. of 1937 ed. 23.00 (ISBN 0-8369-2309-X). Arno.

--Great Contemporaries. LC 73-77128. 1974. Repr. of 1938 ed. 7.95x (ISBN 0-226-10630-6). U of Chicago Pr.

Clarke, M. L. Richard Porson: A Biographical Essay. 1978. Repr. of 1937 ed. lib. bdg. 20.00 (ISBN 0-8495-0828-2). Arden Lib.

Clay, Edith. Lady Blessington at Naples. 1979. 12.50 (ISBN 0-241-89975-3, Pub. by Hamish Hamilton England). David & Charles.

Clyne, Norval. The Romantic Scottish Ballads & the Lady Wardlaw Heresy. LC 74-13040. 1974. Repr. of 1859 ed. lib. bdg. 7.59 (ISBN 0-88305-119-2). Norwood Edns.

Cockerill, A. W. Sir Percy Sillitoe: The Biography of the Former Head of M-15. 223p. 1976. 8.95 (ISBN 0-491-01702-2). Transatlantic.

Cohen, J. M. Life of Ludwig Mond. 7.50 (ISBN 0-686-05399-0). British Am Bks.

Connell, John. W. E. Henley. LC 78-160750. 1971. Repr. of 1949 ed. 17.50 (ISBN 0-8046-1566-7). Kennikat.

Cope, Esther. The Life of a Public Man: Edward, First Baron Montague of Boughton. LC 79-54279. (Memoirs Ser.: Vol. 142). 1981. 9.50 (ISBN 0-87169-142-6). Am Philos.

Costigan, Giovanni. Makers of Modern England. 1967. 6.95 (ISBN 0-02-528430-4). Macmillan.

Courtney, Janet E. Adventurous Thirties: A Chapter in the Women's Movement. facs. ed. LC 67-26728. (Essay Index Reprint Ser). 1933. 16.00 (ISBN 0-8369-0341-2). Arno.

Courtney, William P. Eight Friends of the Great. LC 74-1376. 1973. Repr. of 1910 ed. lib. bdg. 20.00 (ISBN 0-8414-3546-4). Folcroft.

Coustillas, Pierre, ed. London & the Life of Literature in Late Victorian England: The Diary of George Gissing, Novelist. LC 77-72970. 617p. 1978. 40.00 (ISBN 0-8387-2145-1). Bucknell U Pr.

Cromer, Evelyn B. Political & Literary Essays: 2nd Series. facsimile ed. LC 73-108636. (Essay Index Reprint Ser). 1914. 18.00 (ISBN 0-8369-1564-X). Arno.

Crow, H. C. Memoirs of the Late Captain Hugh Crow of Liverpool. (Illus.). 316p. 1970. Repr. of 1830 ed. 35.00x (ISBN 0-7146-1801-2, F Cass Co). Biblio Dist.

Davenant, William. Gondibert. Gladish, David F., ed. 358p. 1971. 13.75x (ISBN 0-19-812420-1). Oxford U Pr.

Davidson, John M. Eminent English Liberals in & Out of Parliament. facsimile ed. LC 70-37521. (Essay Index Reprint Ser). Repr. of 1880 ed. 18.00 (ISBN 0-8369-2542-4). Arno.

Davies, Celia. Clean Clothes on Sunday. (Illus.). 1979. 12.00 (ISBN 0-900963-59-X, Pub. by Terence Dalton England). State Mutual Bk.

Davis, Celia. Far to Go. (Illus.). 1979. 12.00 (ISBN 0-686-26045-7, Pub. by Terence Dalton England). State Mutual Bk.

Davye, Arnold, et al. Lagonga: A History of the Marque. 1979. 21.00 (ISBN 0-7153-7695-0). David & Charles.

Dell, Penelope. Nettie & Sissie: A Biography of Ethel M. Dell & Her Sister Ella. (Illus.). 1978. 16.95 (ISBN 0-241-89663-0, Pub. by Hamish Hamilton England). David & Charles.

Derry, John W. Castlereagh. LC 75-29820. (British Political Biography Ser.). 250p. 1976. 18.95 (ISBN 0-312-12355-8). St Martin.

De Selincourt, Aubrey. Six Great Englishmen. 221p. 1980. lib. bdg. 20.00 (ISBN 0-8482-3652-1). Norwood Edns.

Dictionary of National Biography, Concise Dictionary Pt. 1: From the Beginning to 1900. 1953. 49.95x (ISBN 0-19-865301-8). Oxford U Pr.

Dictionary of National Biography, Concise Dictionary Pt. 2: 1900-1950. 1961. 43.00x (ISBN 0-19-865302-6). Oxford U Pr.

Dobree, Bonamy, ed. From Anne to Victoria: Essays by Various Hands. facs. ed. LC 67-30184. (Essay Index Reprint Ser). 1937. 25.00 (ISBN 0-8369-0378-1). Arno.

Dobson, Austin. Fielding. 210p. 1980. Repr. of 1902 ed. lib. bdg. 15.00 (ISBN 0-89987-153-4). Darby Bks.

Dodds, E. R. Missing Persons: An Autobiography. (Illus.). 1977. 16.95x (ISBN 0-19-812086-9). Oxford U Pr.

Donaldson, Augustas B. Five Great Oxford Leaders: Keble, Newman, Pusey, Liddon & Church. 1978. Repr. of 1900 ed. lib. bdg. 35.00 (ISBN 0-8495-1036-8). Arden Lib.

Donnelly, Peter, ed. Mrs. Milburn's Diaries: An English-Woman's Day-to-Day Reflections, 1935-45. LC 80-11442. (Illus.). 320p. 1980. 12.95 (ISBN 0-8052-3748-8). Schocken.

Duff, David. Hessian Tapestry: The Hesse Family & British Royalty. (Illus.). 1979. 28.00 (ISBN 0-7153-7838-4). David & Charles.

Duffy, Maureen. Inherit the Earth. (Illus.). 192p. 1980. 19.95 (ISBN 0-241-10205-7, Pub. by Hamish Hamilton England). David & Charles.

Duval, Claude. Pat on the Back: The Story of Pat Eddery. 1976. 8.95 (ISBN 0-09-126240-2, Pub. by Hutchinson). Merrimack Bk Serv.

Elias, Edith L. In Georgian Times: Short Character-Studies of the Great Figures of the Period. 1912. Repr. 25.00 (ISBN 0-8274-2561-9). R West.

Ellis, Havelock. A Study of British Genius. 1978. Repr. of 1926 ed. lib. bdg. 30.00 (ISBN 0-8495-1319-7). Arden Lib.

Elwin, Warwick, ed. Some Eighteenth Century Men of Letters, Vols. I & II. 1040p. 1980. Repr. of 1902 ed. Set. lib. bdg. 100.00 (ISBN 0-89987-203-4). Darby Bks.

Emden, Paul H. Regency Pageant. 295p. 1980. Repr. of 1936 ed. lib. bdg. 35.00 (ISBN 0-89987-204-2). Darby Bks.

Escott, Thomas H. Great Victorians: Memories & Personalities. 1916. lib. bdg. 30.00 (ISBN 0-8414-3943-5). Folcroft.

Evans, Joan. The Endless Web: John Dickinson & Co. Ltd., Eighteen Hundred & Four to Nineteen Fifty-Four. LC 78-2673. (Illus.). xvi, 273p. 1978. Repr. of 1955 ed. lib. bdg. 26.75x (ISBN 0-313-20361-X, EVEW). Greenwood.

Fane, Julian. Gentleman's Gentleman. 148p. 1981. 14.95 (ISBN 0-241-10434-3, Pub. by Hamish Hamilton England). David & Charles.

Feiling, Keith G. Sketches in Nineteenth Century Biography. LC 73-107698. (Essay Index Reprint Ser). 1930. 15.00 (ISBN 0-8369-1501-1). Arno.

Fitzgerald, Penelope. The Knox Brothers. LC 77-22621. (Illus.). 1978. 10.95 (ISBN 0-698-10860-4). Coward.

Foley, Winifred. As the Twig Is Bent: Sketches of a Bittersweet Life. LC 77-92766. 1978. 9.95 (ISBN 0-8008-0421-X). Taplinger.

Foss, Edward. Judges of England, 9 Vols. LC 76-168126. Repr. of 1864 ed. Set. 287.50 (ISBN 0-404-02580-3). AMS Pr.

Frankland, Noble. Prince Henry: Duke of Gloucester. (Illus.). 343p. 1980. 25.00x (ISBN 0-297-77705-X, Pub. by Weidenfeld & Nicolson England). Biblio Dist.

Freeman, Arthur. Elizabeth's Misfits. LC 74-2067. (Illus.). 1977. lib. bdg. 15.00x (ISBN 0-8240-1051-5). Garland Pub.
Fuller, Hester T. Three Freshwater Friends: Tennyson, Watts & Mrs. Cameron. 1933. Repr. 15.00 (ISBN 0-8274-3621-1). R West.
Fuller, Thomas. History of the Worthies of England, 3 Vols. Nuttall, P. Austin, ed. LC 76-168071. Repr. of 1840 ed. Set. 125.00 (ISBN 0-404-02680-X). AMS Pr.
Fussey, Joyce. Cows in the Corn. (Illus.). 1979. 10.95 (ISBN 0-236-40149-1, Pub. by Paul Elek). Merrimack Bk Serv.
Gardiner, Alfred G. Portraits & Portents. facsimile ed. LC 79-167344. (Essay Index Reprint Ser). Repr. of 1926 ed. 21.00 (ISBN 0-8369-2499-1). Arno.
Gardiner, Samuel R. Cromwell's Place in History. 1897. Repr. 15.00 (ISBN 0-685-43038-3). Norwood Edns.
Gebbett, Jean R. Henslaw of Hitcham. (Illus.). 1979. 16.00 (ISBN 0-900963-76-X, Pub. by Terence Dalton England). State Mutual Bk.
Gibbins, H. De B. English Social Reformers. 1978. Repr. of 1892 ed. lib. bdg. 20.00 (ISBN 0-8492-1045-3). R West.
Gittings, Robert. The Nature of Biography. LC 78-3136. (The Jessie & John Danz Lecture Ser.). 1978. 7.95 (ISBN 0-295-95604-6). U of Wash Pr.
Green, Michael. Squire Haggard's Journal. 1975. 5.95 (ISBN 0-09-123930-3, Pub. by Hutchinson). Merrimack Bk Serv.
Grugel, Lee E. George Jacob Holyoake: A Study in the Evolution of a Victorian Radical. LC 76-8241. 225p. 1975. lib. bdg. 15.00x (ISBN 0-87991-619-2). Porcupine Pr.
Hadfield, Charles & Skempton, A. W. William Jessop, Engineer. 1979. 28.00 (ISBN 0-7153-7603-9). David & Charles.
Ham, Randall E. The County & the Kingdom: Sir Herbert Croft & the Elizabethan State. 316p. 1977. pap. text ed. 11.75 (ISBN 0-8191-0260-1). U Pr of Amer.
Hardy, Forsyth. John Grierson: A Documentary Biography. LC 79-670273. (Illus.). 270p. 1979. 21.95 (ISBN 0-571-10331-6, Pub. by Faber & Faber). Merrimack Bk Serv.
Harmsworth, Cecil. Immortals at First Hand: Jane Austen, David Garrick, Edward Gibbon, Charles Lamb, Andrew Marvell, Sir Walter Scott: Famous People As Seen by Their Contemporaries. 1977. Repr. of 1933 ed. lib. bdg. 30.00 (ISBN 0-8495-2209-9). Arden Lib.
Hasted, Jane-Eliza. Unsuccessful Ladies. facs. ed. LC 73-148216. (Biography Index Reprint Ser.). 1950. 21.00 (ISBN 0-8369-8063-8). Arno.
Hawkins, Laetitia M. Gossip About Dr. Johnson & Others. LC 77-10159. 1977. Repr. of 1926 ed. lib. bdg. 25.00 (ISBN 0-8414-7876-7). Folcroft.
Hay, Carla H. James Burgh, Spokesman for Reform in Hanoverian England. LC 79-89204. 1979. pap. text ed. 9.00 (ISBN 0-8191-0800-6). U Pr of Amer.
Haydn, Joseph T. Book of Dignities, Containing Lists of the Official Personages of the British Empire from the Earliest Period to the Present Time...the Orders and Knighthood of the United Kingdom and India, Etc.....Continued to the Present Time...by Horace Ockerby. 3rd ed. LC 70-140398. 1970. Repr. of 1894 ed. 35.00 (ISBN 0-8063-0431-6). Genealog Pub.
Healey, Edna. Lady Unknown: The Life of Angela Burdett-Coutts. LC 78-5470. (Illus.). 1978. 12.50 (ISBN 0-698-10939-2). Coward.
Heath's Memoirs of the American War. facsimile ed. LC 76-119932. (Select Bibliographies Ser). Repr. of 1904 ed. 19.50 (ISBN 0-8369-5375-4). Arno.
Hedley, Olwen. Queen Charlotte. (Illus.). 371p. 1976. 15.00 (ISBN 0-7195-3104-7). Transatlantic.
Hellicar, Eileen. Prime Ministers of Britain. LC 77-85014. 1978. 7.50 (ISBN 0-7153-7486-9). David & Charles.
Herbert Of Cherbury, Edward. The Life of Edward, Lord Herbert of Cherbury. (Oxford English Memoirs and Travels Ser.). 1976. 17.50x (ISBN 0-19-255411-5). Oxford U Pr.
Hollis, Christopher. Dr. Johnson: 1707-1784. 203p. 1980. Repr. of 1928 ed. lib. bdg. 30.00 (ISBN 0-89987-357-X). Darby Bks.
Hone, Joseph. The Moores of Moore Hall. 1939. Repr. 40.00 (ISBN 0-8274-2760-3). R West.
Honeycombe, Gordon. Red Watch. (Illus.). 1976. 8.95 (ISBN 0-09-126310-7, Pub. by Hutchinson). Merrimack Bk Serv.
Howell, Michael & Ford, Peter. The True History of the Elephant Man. 1980. pap. 2.95 (ISBN 0-14-005622-X). Penguin.
Huch, Ronald K. The Radical Lord Radnor: The Public Life of Viscount Folkestone, Third Earl of Radnor, 1779-1869. (Minnesota Monographs in the Humanities: Vol. 10). 1977. 18.50x (ISBN 0-8166-0809-1). U of Minn Pr.
Hughes, M. V. London Home on the Eighteen Nineties. 1978. pap. 4.95 (ISBN 0-19-281257-2). Oxford U Pr.
Humphreys, Christmas. Both Sides of the Circle: The Autobiography of Christmas Humphreys. (Illus.). 1978. 18.95 (ISBN 0-04-921023-8). Allen Unwin.
Hyde, H. Montgomery. The Londonderrys: Portrait of a Noble Family. (Illus.). 1979. 30.00 (ISBN 0-241-10153-0, Pub. by Hamish Hamilton England). David & Charles.
Inge, William R., intro. by. Post Victorians. facsimile ed. LC 77-37791. (Essay Index Reprint Ser). Repr. of 1933 ed. 31.00 (ISBN 0-8369-2618-8). Arno.
Innes, Arthur D. Leading Figures in English History: Tudor & Stewart Period. facs. ed. LC 67-23233. (Essay Index Reprint Ser). 1931. 18.00 (ISBN 0-8369-0559-8). Arno.
Ivanovic, Vane. LX. LC 76-27414. (Illus.). 1977. 14.95 (ISBN 0-15-154797-1). HarBraceJ.
Jarman, A. H. Geoffrey of Monmouth. pap. 3.95 (ISBN 0-686-22373-X). British Am Bks.
Jenkins, Hugh. The Culture Gap: An Experience of Government & the Arts. 288p. 1981. 15.00 (ISBN 0-7145-2643-6, Pub. by M Boyars); pap. 9.95 (ISBN 0-7145-2742-4). Merrimack Bk Serv.
Jessup, Ronald. Man of Many Talents: An Informal Biography of James Douglas, 1753-1819. (Illus.). 310p. 1975. 23.50x (ISBN 0-8476-1282-1). Rowman.
Johnston, Harry H. The Story of My Life. 1923. 15.00 (ISBN 0-8495-6267-8). Arden Lib.
Jolly, W. P. Sir Oliver Lodge: Psychical Researcher & Scientist. LC 74-24803. 256p. 1975. 12.50 (ISBN 0-8386-1703-4). Fairleigh Dickinson.
Jones, Peter, et al. British Foreign Secretaries Since 1945. 1977. 9.50 (ISBN 0-7153-7381-1). David & Charles.
Joyce, Michael. My Friend H. John Cam Hobhouse, Baron Broughton of Broughton De Gyfford. 1979. lib. bdg. 30.00 (ISBN 0-89984-250-X). Century Bookbindery.
Judd, Gerrit Parmele. Members of Parliament, 1734-1832. LC 73-179572. vii, 389p. 1972. Repr. of 1955 ed. 21.50 (ISBN 0-208-01230-3, Archon). Shoe String.
Kenin, Richard. Return to Albion: Americans in England 1760-1940. LC 78-1033. (Illus.). 1979. 16.95 (ISBN 0-03-042861-0). HR&W.
Keppel, Sonia. The Sovereign Lady: A Life of Elizabeth, Third Lady Holland, with Her Family. (Illus.). 1978. 22.50 (ISBN 0-241-02299-1, Pub. by Hamish Hamilton England). David & Charles.
Kernan, Michael. The Violet Dots. LC 77-9449. 1978. 7.95 (ISBN 0-8076-0887-4). Braziller.
Kircher, Rudolf. Englander. facs. ed. Vesey, C., tr. LC 68-8476. (Essay Index Reprint Ser). 1928. 19.00 (ISBN 0-8369-0596-2). Arno.
Kirk-Greene, Anthony. A Biographical Dictionary of the British Colonial Governor: Volume I, Africa. LC 80-81949. 256p. 1980. 31.95 (ISBN 0-8179-2611-9). Hoover Inst Pr.
Knight, R. J., ed. Guide to the Manuscripts in the National Maritime Museum: The Personal Collections, Vol. 1. 1977. lib. bdg. 31.50 (ISBN 0-7201-0714-8, Pub. by Mansell England). Merrimack Bk Serv.
Kraus, Rene. Men Around Churchill. facs. ed. LC 79-142653. (Essay Index Reprint Ser). 1941. 19.00 (ISBN 0-8369-2056-2). Arno.
Laurence Urdang Associates. Lives of the Georgian Age: 1714-1837. Gould, William & Hanks, Patrick, eds. LC 77-2684. (Lives of the... Age Ser). (Illus.). 1978. 25.00x (ISBN 0-06-494332-1). B&N.
Lawton, Mary. The Queen of Cooks - & Some Kings: (the Story of Rosa Lewis) 1979. Repr. of 1925 ed. lib. bdg. 20.00 (ISBN 0-8495-3322-8). Arden Lib.
Lean, E. Tangye. Napoleonists: A Study in Political Disaffection, 1760-1960. 1970. 17.00x (ISBN 0-19-215184-3). Oxford U Pr.
Lee, Sidney. Great Englishmen of the Sixteenth Century. LC 77-128269. (Essay Index Reprint Ser). 1904. 19.50 (ISBN 0-8369-1885-1). Arno.
--Great Englishmen of the Sixteenth Century. Repr. 14.50 (ISBN 0-8274-2442-6). R West.
--Great Englishmen of the Sixteenth Century. 1977. Repr. of 1904 ed. lib. bdg. 25.00 (ISBN 0-8495-3213-2). Arden Lib.
Le Scrope, Richard. De controversia in Curia Militari inter Ricardum le Scrope et Robertum Grosvenor Milites, 2 vols. LC 78-63514. (Vol. 2, The Controversy between Sir Richard Scrope & Sir Robert Grosvenor, in the Court of Chivalry). Repr. of 1832 ed. 115.00 set (ISBN 0-404-17220-2). AMS Pr.
Lester, Malcom. Anthony Merry Redivivus: A Reappraisal of the British Minister to the United States, 1803-6. LC 77-20910. 1978. 13.95x (ISBN 0-8139-0750-0). U Pr of Va.
Lloyd, Christopher. Mr. Barrow of the Admiralty: A Life of Sir John Barrow. 224p. 1970. 14.50x (ISBN 0-8448-0048-1). Crane-Russak Co.
Loftis, John, ed. The Memoirs of Anne, Lady Halkett, & Ann, Lady Fanshawe. 1979. 37.50x (ISBN 0-19-812087-7). Oxford U Pr.
Long, Helen. Change into Uniform. (Illus.). 1979. 15.00 (ISBN 0-900963-91-3, Pub. by Terence Dalton England). State Mutual Bk.
Lowe, Roger. The Diary of Roger Lowe: Of Ashton-in-Makerfield, Lancashire, 1663-74. Sacse, William L., ed. 1978. Repr. of 1938 ed. lib. bdg. 30.00 (ISBN 0-8495-3231-0). Arden Lib.
McCarthy, Justin. Portraits of the Sixties. facsimile ed. LC 79-142661. (Essay Index Reprint Ser). Repr. of 1903 ed. 23.00 (ISBN 0-8369-2061-9). Arno.
McCurdy, Sylvia. Sylvia: A Victorian Childhood. 1979. 7.50 (ISBN 0-686-26046-5, Pub. by Terence Dalton England). State Mutual Bk.
MacDonagh, Oliver. The Inspector-General: Sir Jeremiah Fitzpatrick & the Politics of Social Reform 1783-1802. 336p. 1981. 49.00x (ISBN 0-85664-421-8, Pub. by Croom Helm Ltd England). Biblio Dist.
Macdonald, Hugh, ed. Portraits in Prose. LC 71-101830. (Biography Index Reprint Ser). 1946. 25.00 (ISBN 0-8369-8004-2). Arno.
Macdonald, J. Ramsay. Margaret Ethel Macdonald. 1978. Repr. of 1924 ed. lib. bdg. 15.00 (ISBN 0-8414-0072-5). Folcroft.
McFarlane, K. B. Lancastrian Kings & Lollard Knights. Highfield, J. R. & Harriss, G. L., eds. 268p. 1972. 37.50x (ISBN 0-19-822344-7). Oxford U Pr.
McMasters, S. Y. A Biographical Index to the History of England. 59.95 (ISBN 0-87968-752-5). Gordon Pr.
Mairet, Philip. Autobiographical & Other Papers. Sisson, C. H., ed. 288p. (Orig.). 1981. pap. 14.95 (ISBN 0-85635-326-4, Pub. by Carcanet New Pr England). Persea Bks.
Malpass, E. Deanne, pref. by. Personalities & Policies: Essays on English & European History. LC 76-43381. (Illus.). 1977. lib. bdg. 6.00 (ISBN 0-912646-39-X). Tex Christian.
Mansbridge, Albert. Fellow Men. LC 73-117329. (Biography Index Reprint Ser). 1948. 19.00 (ISBN 0-8369-8021-2). Arno.
Marsden, Philip. The Officers of the Commons 1363-1965. 5.95 (ISBN 0-686-05402-4). British Am Bks.
Martindale, Hilda. Some Victorian Portraits & Others. 106p. 1980. Repr. lib. bdg. 25.00 (ISBN 0-89984-332-8). Century Bookbindery.
--Some Victorian Portraits & Others. 1977. Repr. of 1948 ed. lib. bdg. 20.00 (ISBN 0-8414-6224-0). Folcroft.
Massingham, Harold J. & Massingham, Hugh, eds. Great Victorians. facsimile ed. LC 70-156692. (Essay Index Reprint Ser). Repr. of 1932 ed. 16.00 (ISBN 0-8369-2284-0). Arno.
Masson, Madeleine. Christine: A Search for Christine Granville. 1978. 17.50 (ISBN 0-241-89274-0, Pub. by Hamish Hamilton England). David & Charles.
Mathews, Ronald. English Messiahs. 1936. 30.00 (ISBN 0-8414-6455-3). Folcroft.
Meredith, George. Letters of George Meredith, 3 Vols. Cline, C. L., ed. 1970. 98.00x (ISBN 0-19-811473-7). Oxford U Pr.
Messman, Frank J. Richard Payne Knight: The Twilight of Virtuosity. 1974. text ed. 31.25x (ISBN 0-686-22564-3). Mouton.
Middleton, R. D. Dr. Routh. 1978. Repr. of 1938 ed. lib. bdg. 45.00 (ISBN 0-8495-3818-1). Arden Lib.
Millard, Joseph. Edgar Cayce, Man of Miracles. 224p. 20.00x (ISBN 0-85435-473-5, Pub. by Spearman England). State Mutual Bk.
Mitford, Jessica. Daughters & Rebels. LC 81-47450. 304p. 1981. pap. 6.95 (ISBN 0-03-059683-1). HR&W.
Morgan, Kenneth & Morgan, Jane. Portrait of a Progressive: The Political Career of Christopher, Viscount Addison. (Illus.). 352p. 1980. 42.00x (ISBN 0-19-822494-X). Oxford U Pr.
Morrill, Georgiana L., ed. Speculum Guidonis de Warewyke. (EETS, ES Ser.: No. 75). Repr. of 1898 ed. 16.00 (ISBN 0-527-00277-1). Kraus Repr.
Mosley, Diana M. A Life of Contrasts. LC 77-93053. 1978. 10.95 (ISBN 0-8129-0758-2). Times Bks.
Murray, Grace A. Personalities of the Eighteenth Century. LC 72-7299. Repr. of 1927 ed. lib. bdg. 22.50 (ISBN 0-8414-0316-3). Folcroft.
Murray, James A., ed. Thomas of Erceldoune. (EETS, OS Ser.: No. 61). Repr. of 1875 ed. 7.00 (ISBN 0-527-00055-8). Kraus Repr.
Myatt, Frederick. Peninsular General: Sir Thomas Picton, Seventeen Fifty-Eight to Eighteen Fifteen. LC 79-56256. (Illus.). 224p. 1980. 28.00 (ISBN 0-7153-7923-2). David & Charles.
Nagle, Elizabeth. Other Bentley Boys. 12.50 (ISBN 0-392-04098-0, SpS). Sportshelf.
Newbolt, Margaret, ed. The Later Life & Letters of Sir Henry Newbolt. 1979. Repr. of 1942 ed. lib. bdg. 30.00 (ISBN 0-8492-1976-0). R West.
Newman, Arnold. The Great British. LC 79-84891. (Illus.). 1979. 19.95 (ISBN 0-8212-0754-7, 326437). NYGS.
Nichols, John. Minor Lives: A Collection of Biographies. Hart, Edward L., ed. LC 73-131470. (Illus.). 1971. 20.00x (ISBN 0-674-57630-6). Harvard U Pr.
Nockolds, Harold. Rescue from Disaster: The Story of the RFD Group. LC 80-66422. (Illus.). 224p. (Orig.). 1980. 32.00 (ISBN 0-7153-7969-0). David & Charles.
Notestein, Wallace. English Folk. LC 72-99643. (Essay Index Reprint Ser). 1938. 25.00 (ISBN 0-8369-1475-9). Arno.
Oman, Charles W. Warwick the Kingmaker. facsimile ed. LC 79-137383. (Select Bibliographies Reprint Ser). Repr. of 1891 ed. 16.00 (ISBN 0-8369-5584-6). Arno.
Ormond, Richard. Early Victorian Portraits, 2 vol. (Illus.). 900p. 1980. Set. 160.00 (ISBN 0-312-22480-X). St Martin.
O'Sullivan, Timothy. Julian Hodge: A Biography. 160p. 1981. 24.95 (ISBN 0-7100-0592-X). Routledge & Kegan.
Palgrave, Mary E. Mary Rich, Countess of Warwick, 1625-1678. 1973. Repr. of 1901 ed. 25.004 (ISBN 0-8274-1419-6). R West.
Paston, George. Little Memoirs of the Nineteenth Century. 376p. 1980. Repr. of 1902 ed. lib. bdg. 25.00 (ISBN 0-89984-379-4). Century Bookbindery.
Peterson, W. S. Victorian Heretic: Mrs. Humphry Ward's Robert Elsmere. 288p. 1976. text ed. 9.25x (ISBN 0-7185-1147-6, Leicester). Humanities.
Phillips, Cecil E. Cromwell's Captains. facsimile ed. LC 73-37908. (Select Bibliographies Reprint Ser). Repr. of 1938 ed. 25.00 (ISBN 0-8369-6746-1). Arno.
Pielman, M. H. & Jerrold, Walter. Hugh Thomson, His Art, His Letters, His Humor & His Charm. 269p. 1980. Repr. of 1931 ed. lib. bdg. 125.00 (ISBN 0-89984-405-7). Century Bookbindery.
Pike, Royston E. Britain's Prime Ministers from Walpole to Wilson. (Illus.). 1970. 8.95 (ISBN 0-600-72032-2). Transatlantic.
Pinto, Vivian De Sola, ed. English Biography in the Seventeenth Century. facsimile ed. LC 72-101833. (Biography Index Reprint Ser). 1951. 18.00 (ISBN 0-8369-8007-7). Arno.
Pollitt, Ronald & Curry, Herbert F., eds. Portraits in British History. 1975. pap. text ed. 10.95x (ISBN 0-256-01679-8). Dorsey.
Ponsonby, Arthur. Henry Ponsonby, Queen Victoria's Private Secretary. 1943. 25.00 (ISBN 0-8274-2483-3). R West.
Porchey. Ermine Tales: More Memoirs of the Earl of Carnarvon. (Illus.). 158p. 1980. 14.50x (ISBN 0-297-77763-7, Pub. by Weidenfeld & Nicolson England). Biblio Dist.
--No Regrets: Memoirs of the Earl of Carnarvon. (Illus.). 227p. 1978. Repr. of 1976 ed. 17.00x (ISBN 0-297-77246-5, Pub. by Weidenfeld & Nicolson England). Biblio Dist.
Porter, McKenzie. Julie: The Royal Mistress. 1977. pap. 4.95 (ISBN 0-7715-9952-8). Vanguard.
Proctor, Dennis, ed. The Autobiography of G. Lowes Dickinson. (Illus.). 287p. 1973. 12.50x (ISBN 0-7156-0647-6, Pub. by Duckworth England). Biblio Dist.
Quennell, Peter. Four Portraits: Studies in the Eighteenth Century. Repr. of 1946 ed. lib. bdg. 20.00 (ISBN 0-8495-4425-4). Arden Lib.
--The Profane Virtues: Four Studies of the Eighteenth Century. LC 79-51246. (Essay Index in Reprint Ser.). (Illus.). Date not set. Repr. of 1945 ed. 23.75x (ISBN 0-8486-3045-9). Core Collection.
--The Profane Virtues: Four Studies of the Eighteenth Century. LC 78-11551. (Illus.). 1979. Repr. of 1945 ed. lib. bdg. 18.75x (ISBN 0-313-21039-X, QUPV). Greenwood.
Ralfe, James. The Naval Biography of Great Britain: Consisting of Historical Memoirs of Those Officers of the British Navy Who Distinguished Themselves During the Reign of His Majesty George III, 4 vols. LC 72-20833. (American Revolutionary Ser.). Repr. of 1828 ed. Set. lib. bdg. 140.00x (ISBN 0-8398-1773-8). Irvington.
Reel, Jerome V., Jr. Index to Biographies of Englishmen, 1000-1485: Found in Dissertations & Theses. LC 74-19807. 689p. 1975. lib. bdg. 37.00 (ISBN 0-8371-7846-0, RIB/). Greenwood.
Reid, B. L. The Lives of Roger Casement. LC 75-18184. (Illus.). 576p. 1976. 35.00x (ISBN 0-300-01801-0). Yale U Pr.
Reynolds, E. E. Margaret Roper: Eldest Daughter of St. Thomas More. 149p. 1981. Repr. of 1960 ed. lib. bdg. 35.00 (ISBN 0-89987-720-6). Darby Bks.
Richards, Denis. Portal of Hungerford: The Life of Marshal of the Royal Air Force Viscount Portal of Hungerford KG, GCB, OM, DSO, MC. (Illus.). 1978. text ed. 24.50x (ISBN 0-8419-6103-4). Holmes & Meier.

Richmond, Colin. John Hopton: A Fifteenth-Century Suffolk Gentleman. (Illus.). 280p. 1981. 37.50 (ISBN 0-521-23434-4). Cambridge U Pr.

Roche, Stanley. Foreigner: The Story of Grace Morton As Told to Stanley Roche. (Illus.). 216p. 1979. text ed. 18.95x (ISBN 0-19-558044-3). Oxford U Pr.

Rolph, C. H. London Particulars. 192p. 1980. 19.50x (ISBN 0-19-211755-6). Oxford U Pr.

Rosebery, Archibald P. Miscellanies: Literary & Historical, 2 vols. facsimile ed. LC 71-152211. (Essay Index Reprint Ser). Repr. of 1921 ed. 39.00 (ISBN 0-8369-2253-0). Arno.

Rosenbaum, Robert A. Earnest Victorians. LC 74-9043. (Illus.). 383p. 1974. Repr. of 1961 ed. lib. bdg. 19.50x (ISBN 0-8371-7607-7, ROEV). Greenwood.

Rowe, Violet A. Sir Henry Vane the Younger: A Study in Political & Administrative History. (Univ. of London on Historical Studies: No. 28). 1970. text ed. 15.25x (ISBN 0-485-13128-5, Athlone Pr). Humanities.

Rowse, A. L. A Cornish Childhood: Autobiography of a Cornishman. 1979. 10.95 (ISBN 0-517-53845-8). Potter.

Rowse, Alfred & Harrison, George. Queen Elizabeth & Her Subjects. LC 79-76913. (Essay Index Reprint Ser). 1935. 13.00 (ISBN 0-8369-1895-9). Arno.

Rubinstein, Hilary L. Captain Luckless: James First Duke of Hamilton, 1606-1649. (Illus.). 290p. 1976. 16.50x (ISBN 0-87471-806-6). Rowman.

Rupp, Ernest G. Six Makers of English Religion, Fifteen Hundred to Seventeen Hundred. (Essay Index Reprint Ser.). Repr. of 1957 ed. 14.75 (ISBN 0-518-10159-2). Arno.

Russell, George W. E. Portraits of the Seventies. LC 73-117834. (Essay Index Reprint Ser). 1916. 20.00 (ISBN 0-8369-1717-0). Arno.

Sachse, William L. Lord Somers: A Political Portrait. LC 75-885. 334p. 1975. 30.00x (ISBN 0-299-06890-0). U of Wis Pr.

Sackville-West, V. The Diary of the Lady Anne Clifford. 1979. Repr. of 1923 ed. lib. bdg. 20.00 (ISBN 0-8482-6394-4). Norwood Edns.

Saltonstall, William G. Lewis Perry of Exeter. LC 79-55586. (Illus.). 1980. 7.95 (ISBN 0-689-11056-1). Atheneum.

Sandford, Jeremy. Smiling David. LC 75-309907. (Illus.). 128p. 1979. 9.95 (ISBN 0-7145-1048-3, Pub. by M Boyars); pap. 5.95 (ISBN 0-7145-1049-1, Pub. by M Boyars). Merrimack Bk Serv.

Senior, Dorothy. Some Old English Worthies. 1973. lib. bdg. 22.50 (ISBN 0-8414-8128-8). Folcroft.

Shilton, Peter. Shilton in Goal. 1974. 5.95 (ISBN 0-09-121260-X, Pub. by Hutchinson); pap. 2.95 (ISBN 0-09-121261-8). Merrimack Bk Serv.

Simms, Norman T. William of Palerne. LC 72-14189. 1973. Repr. ltd. ed. 30.00 (ISBN 0-88305-612-7). Norwood Edns.

Skinner, B. G. Henry Francis Lyte: Brixham's Poet & Priest. 164p. 1974. 20.00x (ISBN 0-900771-92-5, Pub. by Exeter Univ England). State Mutual Bk.

Smith, George. Dictionary of National Biography, 22 vols. Stephen, Leslie & Lee, Sidney, eds. 1882-1953. suppl. 1. 1250.00x (ISBN 0-19-865101-5); suppl. 2. 89.00x (ISBN 0-19-865201-1); suppl. 3 89.00x (ISBN 0-19-865202-X); suppl. 4 65.00x (ISBN 0-19-865203-8); suppl. 5 89.00x (ISBN 0-19-865204-6); suppl. 6 89.00x (ISBN 0-19-865205-4). Oxford U Pr.

Smith-Dampier, Louis L. Who's Who in Boswell. 1935. lib. bdg. 14.95 (ISBN 0-8414-1594-3). Folcroft.

Smithers, Jack. The Early Life & Vicissitudes of Jack Smithers. LC 79-8079. Repr. of 1939 ed. 26.50 (ISBN 0-404-18388-3). AMS Pr.

Sprigge, S. Squire. The Life & Times of Thomas Wakley. LC 73-89696. 542p. 1974. Repr. of 1897 ed. 22.50 (ISBN 0-88275-134-4). Krieger.

Standish, Robert. The Prince of Storytellers: The Life of E. Phillips Oppenheim. 1979. Repr. of 1957 ed. lib. bdg. 25.00 (ISBN 0-8495-4913-2). Arden Lib.

Stauffer, Donald A. English Biography Before Seventeen Hundred. 392p. Repr. of 1930 ed. lib. bdg. 22.50x (ISBN 0-87991-065-8). Porcupine Pr.

Stebbins, Lucy. London Ladies. LC 52-6272. Repr. of 1952 ed. 16.50 (ISBN 0-404-06226-1). AMS Pr.

Stenton, Michael. Who's Who of British Members of Parliament: 1919-1945, Vol. 3. 1979. text ed. 86.50x (ISBN 0-391-00768-8). Humanities.

Stephen, Leslie. Studies of a Biographer, 4 vols. LC 78-128115. 1973. Repr. of 1898 ed. lib. bdg. 79.50 (ISBN 0-8337-3394-X). B Franklin.

Surtees, Virginia. Charlotte Canning - Lady-in-Waiting to Queen Victoria & Wife of the First Viceroy of India 1917-1861. (Illus.). 319p. 1976. 15.00 (ISBN 0-7195-3230-2). Transatlantic.

Sykes, Christopher S. The Visitor's Book: A Family Album. LC 78-53402. (Illus.). 1978. 25.00 (ISBN 0-399-12212-5). Putnam.

Symonds, Emily M. Little Memoirs of the Nineteenth Century. facs. ed. LC 70-86787. (Essay Index Reprint Ser). 1902. 19.00 (ISBN 0-8369-1197-0). Arno.

Symonds, J. A. Sir Philip Sidney. 59.95 (ISBN 0-8490-1055-1). Gordon Pr.

Tarkington, Booth. Some Old Portraits. LC 78-93382. (Essay Index Reprint Ser). 1939. 25.00 (ISBN 0-8369-1315-9). Arno.

Taylor, William C. Modern British Plutarch: Or, Lives of Men Distinguished in the Recent History of England for Their Talents, Virtues, or Achievements. LC 72-1264. (Essay Index Reprint Ser.). Repr. of 1846 ed. 21.00 (ISBN 0-8369-2866-0). Arno.

Thompson, Dorothy. Sophie's Son. (Illus.). 1979. 8.95 (ISBN 0-900963-16-6, Pub. by Terence Dalton England). State Mutual Bk.

Thompson, Edward R. Portraits of the New Century. LC 74-117853. (Essay Index Reprint Ser). 1928. 17.00 (ISBN 0-8369-1685-9). Arno.

--Portraits of the Nineties. LC 78-117854. (Essay Index Reprint Ser). 1921. 19.50 (ISBN 0-8369-1686-7). Arno.

--Uncensored Celebrities. LC 71-117855. (Essay Index Reprint Ser). 1919. 16.00 (ISBN 0-8369-1687-5). Arno.

Thomson, George M. The First Churchill: The Life of John, First Duke of Marlborough. LC 79-66008. (Illus.). 1980. 12.95 (ISBN 0-688-03556-6). Morrow.

Timpson, George F. Kings & Commoners. facs. ed. LC 70-80401. (Essay Index Reprint Ser). 1936. 15.50 (ISBN 0-8369-1051-6). Arno.

Tingsten, Herbert. Victoria & the Victorians. (Illus.). 1972. 15.00 (ISBN 0-440-09423-2, Sey Lawr). Delacorte.

Tobias, J. J. Prince of Fences: The Life & Crimes of Ikey Solomons. (Illus.). 178p. 1974. 18.00x (ISBN 0-85303-174-6, Pub. by Vallentine Mitchell England). Biblio Dist.

Toynbee, Arnold J. Acquaintances. 1967. 14.95 (ISBN 0-19-500189-3). Oxford U Pr.

Trevisick, Charles. My Home Is a Zoo. 1976. 8.95 (ISBN 0-09-127490-7, Pub. by Hutchinson). Merrimack Bk Serv.

Tschiffely, A. F. Don Roberto: Being an Account of R. B. Cunningham-Grahame. 35.00 (ISBN 0-8490-0057-2). Gordon Pr.

Tweedy, Maureen. A Label Around My Neck. (Illus.). 1979. 12.00 (ISBN 0-900963-66-2, Pub. by Terence Dalton England). State Mutual Bk.

University Of London - Institute Of Historical Research. Corrections & Additions to the Dictionary of National Biography Cumulated from the Bulletin of the Institute of Historical Research Covering the Years 1923-1963. 1966. lib. bdg. 75.00 (ISBN 0-8161-0723-8). G K Hall.

Ustinov, Nadia B. Klop & the Ustinov Family. (Illus.). 320p. 1973. Repr. 8.95 (ISBN 0-89388-108-2). Okpaku Communications.

Uya, Okon E. From Slavery to Public Service: Robert Small, Eighteen Thirty-Nine - Nineteen Fifteen. 192p. 1971 (ISBN 0-19-501291-7). pap. 3.95x (ISBN 0-19-501290-9). Oxford U Pr.

Valentine, Alan. The British Establishment Seventeen Sixty to Seventeen Eighty-Four: An Eighteenth Century Biographical Dictionary, 2 vols. LC 69-16734. 1976. Set. 30.00x (ISBN 0-8061-0877-0); pap. 15.00x (ISBN 0-8061-1378-2). U of Okla Pr.

Vaughan, Herbert M. From Anne to Victoria: Fourteen Biographical Studies Between 1702 & 1901. LC 66-25950. Repr. of 1931 ed. 11.00 (ISBN 0-8046-0478-9). Kennikat.

Wallas, Ada R. Before the Bluestockings. LC 77-20229. 1977. Repr. of 1929 ed. lib. bdg. 25.00 (ISBN 0-8414-9637-4). Folcroft.

Walpole, Spencer. Studies in Biography: Mr. Disraeli & Edward Gibbon. 1979. Repr. of 1907 ed. lib. bdg. 30.00 (ISBN 0-8492-2988-X). R West.

Ward, Wilfrid P. Ten Personal Studies. LC 73-107742. (Essay Index Reprint Ser). 1908. 19.00 (ISBN 0-8369-1584-4). Arno.

Watson, J. N. Captain General & Rebel Chief: The Life of James, Duke of Monmouth. (Illus.). 1979. text ed. 22.50x (ISBN 0-04-920058-5). Allen Unwin.

Whibley, Charles. Essays in Biography. facs. ed. LC 68-57343. (Essay Index Reprint Ser). 1913. 15.75 (ISBN 0-8369-0987-9). Arno.

White, De Vere. Tom Moore. 1979. 11.50 (ISBN 0-241-89622-3, Pub. by Hamish Hamilton England). David & Charles.

Who Was Who, Vol. VI. LC 20-14622. (Who Was Who Ser.). 1972. 62.00x (ISBN 0-312-87745-5). St Martin.

Who Was Who: Companion to Who's Who, 6 vols. Incl. Vol. 1. Eighteen Ninety-Seven to Nineteen-Fifteen. 4th ed. 790p. 1953 (ISBN 0-312-87570-3); Vol. 2. Nineteen-Sixteen to Nineteen Twenty-Eight. 3rd ed. 1160p. 1962 (ISBN 0-312-87605-X); Vol. 3. Nineteen Twenty-Nine to Nineteen-Forty. 1508p. 1941 (ISBN 0-312-87640-8); Vol. 4. Nineteen Forty-One to Nineteen Fifty. rev ed. 1278p. 1958 (ISBN 0-312-87675-0); Vol. 5. Nineteen Fifty-One to Nineteen-Sixty. 1206p. 1961 (ISBN 0-312-87710-2). 62.00 ea.; Set. 240.00x (ISBN 0-312-87535-5). St Martin.

Willcock, John. Sir Thomas Urquhart of Cromartie Knight. 1979. Repr. of 1899 ed. lib. bdg. 45.00 (ISBN 0-8495-5749-6). Arden Lib.

Williams, E. T. & Palmer, Helen M., eds. The Dictionary of National Biography, 1951-1960. 7th suppl ed. 1176p. 1971. 89.00x (ISBN 0-19-865206-2). Oxford U Pr.

Williams, Orio. Life & Letters of John Rickman: (Lamb's Friend the Census-Taker) Repr. 30.00 (ISBN 0-8274-2907-X). R West.

Williams, Robert F. Mephistophiles in England: Or, the Confessions of a Prime Minister, 3 vols. in 1. LC 79-8217. Repr. of 1835 ed. 44.50 (ISBN 0-404-62171-6). AMS Pr.

Williamson, Hugh R. The Arrow & the Sword. LC 79-8126. Repr. of 1955 ed. 24.00 (ISBN 0-404-18440-5). AMS Pr.

Winter, James. Robert Lowe. LC 75-43814. (Illus.). 340p. 1976. 22.50x (ISBN 0-8020-5323-8). U of Toronto Pr.

Wintle, Justin & Kenin, Richard, eds. The Dictionary of Biographical Quotation. LC 78-452. 1978. 25.00 (ISBN 0-394-50027-X). Knopf.

Wolfenden, John. Turning Points: The Memoirs of Lord Wolfenden. (Illus.). 1979. 9.50 (ISBN 0-370-10442-0, Pub. by Chatto Bodley Jonathan). Merrimack Bk Serv.

GREAT BRITAIN–CABINET OFFICE

Mackintosh, John P. British Cabinet. 3rd ed. 1981. pap. 15.95x (ISBN 0-416-31380-9). Methuen Inc.

Mosley, R. K. Story of the Cabinet Office. (Library of Political Studies). 1969. text ed. 6.00x (ISBN 0-7100-6600-7). Humanities.

GREAT BRITAIN–CENSUS

Great Britain, Census Office. Abstract of the Answers & Returns: The Census Report for 1801, 2 vols. LC 79-366591. Date not set. Repr. of 1802 ed. Set. lib. bdg. 90.00x (ISBN 0-678-05225-5). Vol. 1, Enumeration. Vol. 2, Parish Registers. Kelley.

Lawton, Richard, ed. The Census & Social Structure: An Interpretative Guide to Nineteenth-Century Censuses for England & Wales. 330p. 1978. 29.50x (ISBN 0-7146-2965-0, F Cass Co). Biblio Dist.

Spackman, William F. Analysis of the Occupations of the People. LC 68-58020. Repr. of 1847 ed. 17.50x (ISBN 0-678-00573-7). Kelley.

GREAT BRITAIN–CHARTERS, GRANTS, PRIVILEGES

Birch, Walter D., ed. Cartularium Saxonicum: A Collection of Charters Relating to Anglo-Saxon History, 3 vols. Repr. of 1893 ed. Set. with index. 192.50 (ISBN 0-384-04405-0); sep. index 14.00 (ISBN 0-685-13365-6). Johnson Repr.

Carlton, Charles. Descriptive Syntax of the Old English Charters. LC 73-102955. (Janua Linguarum Ser. Practica: No. 111). (Illus., Orig.). 1970. pap. text ed. 40.00x (ISBN 90-2790-744-7). Mouton.

Hart, C. R. The Early Charters of Northern England & the North Midlands. (Studies in Early English History Ser: No. 6). 424p. 1975. text ed. 36.50x (ISBN 0-7185-1131-X, Leicester). Humanities.

His Maiesties Gracious Grant & Privilege to William Braithwaite, for the Sole Printing & Publishing Musicke, His Way. LC 73-6105. (English Experience Ser.: No. 573). 1973. Repr. of 1636 ed. 3.50 (ISBN 90-221-0573-3). Walter J Johnson.

Hunter, Joseph, ed. Ecclesiastical Documents. 1840. 15.50 (ISBN 0-384-24935-3). Johnson Repr.

GREAT BRITAIN–CHURCH HISTORY

see also Celtic Church

Beda Venerabilis. The Ecclesiastical History of the English Nation: From the Coming of Julius Caesar into This Island in the Sixtieth Year Before the Incarnation of Christ, till the Year of Our Lord 731. 1976. Repr. of 1723 ed. 59.00 (ISBN 0-403-06515-1, Regency). Scholarly.

Bready, John W. England, Before & After Wesley: The Evangelical Revival & Social Reform. LC 72-139906. (Illus.). 463p. 1971. Repr. of 1938 ed. 17.00 (ISBN 0-8462-1533-0). Russell.

Bright, William. Chapters in Early English Church History. 3rd ed. 1897. 25.00 (ISBN 0-8337-4005-9). B Franklin.

Burke, Arthur M. Key to the Ancient Parish Registers of England & Wales. LC 62-6577. (Illus.). 1971. Repr. of 1908 ed. 10.00 (ISBN 0-8063-0445-6). Genealog Pub.

Cheney, C. R. Medieval Texts & Studies. 382p. 1973. 42.00x (ISBN 0-19-822399-4). Oxford U Pr.

Clark, Henry W. History of English Nonconformity from Wiclif to the Close of the 19th Century, 2 Vols. LC 65-18797. (Repr. of 1911, 1913 edns.). 1965. Set. 20.00 (ISBN 0-8462-0660-9). Russell.

Cox, J. Charles. Parish Registers of England. (Illus.). 290p. 1974. Repr. of 1910 ed. 14.50x (ISBN 0-87471-541-5). Rowman.

Creighton, Mandell. Historical Lectures & Addresses. facs. ed. Creighton, L., ed. LC 67-26730. (Essay Index Reprint Ser). 1904. 18.00 (ISBN 0-8369-0350-1). Arno.

Dodd, Charles. Dodd's Church History of England, 1500-1688, 5 Vols. Tierney, M. A., ed. LC 75-119152. Repr. of 1843 ed. Set. 170.00 (ISBN 0-404-02150-6); 34.00 ea. Vol. 1 (ISBN 0-404-02151-4). Vol. 2 (ISBN 0-404-02152-2). Vol. 3 (ISBN 0-404-02153-0). Vol. 4 (ISBN 0-404-02154-9). Vol. 5 (ISBN 0-404-02155-7). AMS Pr.

Faulkner, Harold U. Chartism & the Churches. LC 79-76712. (Columbia University. Studies in the Social Sciences: No. 173). Repr. of 1916 ed. 12.50 (ISBN 0-404-51173-2). AMS Pr.

--Chartism & the Churches: A Study in Democracy. 152p. 1970. Repr. of 1916 ed. 25.00x (ISBN 0-7146-1308-8, F Cass Co). Biblio Dist.

Gater, George H. & Hiorns, F. R. The Parish of St. Martin-in-the Fields: Trafalgar Square & Neighborhood, Pt. 3. LC 70-37852. (London County Council. Survey of London: No. 20). Repr. of 1940 ed. 74.50 (ISBN 0-404-51670-X). AMS Pr.

Harvey, John. Cathedrals of England & Wales. 1974. 38.00 (ISBN 0-7134-0616-X). David & Charles.

Moorman, John R. A History of the Church in England. 3rd rev ed. 485p. 1973. 24.95 (ISBN 0-8192-1282-2). Morehouse.

Nuttall, Geoffrey F. & Chadwick, O., eds. From Uniformity to Unity, 1662-1962. 1962. 20.00x (ISBN 0-8401-1746-9). Allenson-Breckinridge.

Schwartz, Hillel. Knaves, Fools, Madmen & That Subtile Effluvium: A Study of the Opposition to the French Prophets in England, 1706-1710. LC 78-1692. (U of Fla. Social Science Monographs: No. 62). 1978. pap. 5.50 (ISBN 0-8130-0505-1). U Presses Fla.

Stephens, William R., et al. History of the English Church, 8 vols. in 9. Repr. of 1910 ed. Set. 265.50 (ISBN 0-404-50750-6); 29.50 ea. AMS Pr.

Suffling, Ernest R. English Church Brasses from the 13th to the 17th Century, a Manual for Antiquaries, Archaeologists & Collectors. LC 73-126133. (Illus.). 1970. Repr. of 1910 ed. 20.00 (ISBN 0-8063-0437-5). Genealog Pub.

GREAT BRITAIN–CHURCH HISTORY–SOURCES

Foliot, G. The Letters & Charters of Gilbert Foliot. Morey, A. & Brooke, C. N., eds. 1967. 80.00 (ISBN 0-521-05765-5). Cambridge U Pr.

Gee, H. & Hardy, W. J. Documents Illustrative of English Church History. 1896. 22.00 (ISBN 0-527-33100-7). Kraus Repr.

Hunter, Joseph, ed. Ecclesiastical Documents. 1840. 15.50 (ISBN 0-384-24935-3). Johnson Repr.

Saltman, Avrom. Theobald Archbishop of Canterbury. LC 69-14068. 1969. Repr. of 1956 ed. lib. bdg. 23.00x (ISBN 0-8371-0643-5, SATH). Greenwood.

Tate, W. E. Parish Chest. 3rd ed. LC 67-28686. (Illus.). 1969. 41.00 (ISBN 0-521-06603-4). Cambridge U Pr.

Trinterud, Leonard J., ed. Elizabethan Puritanism. (Library of Protestant Thought). 1971. 16.95x (ISBN 0-19-501281-X). Oxford U Pr.

GREAT BRITAIN–CHURCH HISTORY–TO 843

Hunt, William. English Church from Its Foundation to the Norman Conquest, 597-1066. LC 2-21442. (History of the English Church: No. 1). Repr. of 1899 ed. 29.50 (ISBN 0-404-50751-4). AMS Pr.

Mayr-Harting, Henry. The Coming of Christianity to England. LC 74-169818. (Fabric of British History Ser). (Illus.). 300p. 1972. 12.50x (ISBN 0-8052-3436-5). Schocken.

Saklatvala, Beram. The Christian Island. LC 75-92561. (Illus.). 150p. 1970. 10.00 (ISBN 0-8386-7571-9). Fairleigh Dickinson.

GREAT BRITAIN–CHURCH HISTORY–ANGLO-SAXON PERIOD, 449-1066

Allison, Thomas. English Religious Life in the Eighth Century. LC 75-106708. Repr. of 1929 ed. lib. bdg. 15.00 (ISBN 0-8371-3438-2, ALRL). Greenwood.

--English Religious Life in the Eighth Century As Illustrated by Contemporary Letters. LC 70-136409. Repr. of 1929 ed. 9.00 (ISBN 0-404-00348-6). AMS Pr.

Beda. The History of the Church of Englande. (English Experience Ser.: No. 234). 382p. Repr. of 1565 ed. 55.00 (ISBN 90-221-0234-3). Walter J Johnson.

Bede. Historical Works, 2 Vols. (Loeb Classical Library: No. 246, 248). 11.00x ea. Vol. 1 (ISBN 0-674-99271-7). Vol. 2 (ISBN 0-674-99273-3). Harvard U Pr.

--History of the English Church & People. Sherley-Price, tr. (Classics Ser.). (Orig.). 1955. pap. 3.50 (ISBN 0-14-044042-9). Penguin.

Bede The Venerable. Ecclesiastical History of England. Giles, John A., ed. LC 78-136367. (Bohn's Antiquarian Lib.). (Illus.). Repr. of 1849 ed. 34.50 (ISBN 0-404-50001-3). AMS Pr.

--Ecclesiastical History of the English People. Colgrave, Bertram & Minors, R. A., eds. (Oxford Medieval Texts Ser). 1969. 59.00x (ISBN 0-19-822202-5). Oxford U Pr.

--Ecclesiastical History of the English Nation. Stevens, John, tr. 1973. 9.95x (ISBN 0-460-00479-4, Evman). Biblio Dist.

Dunleavy, Gareth W. Colum's Other Island: The Irish at Lindisfarne. (Illus.). 160p. 1960. 11.50x (ISBN 0-299-02120-3). U of Wis Pr.

Edwards, David L. Christian England: Its Story to the Reformation. (Illus.). 356p. 1981. 19.95 (ISBN 0-19-520229-5). Oxford U Pr.

Hugh The Chantor, pseud. The History of the Church of York, 1066-1127. Johnson, Charles, tr. from Lat. & intro. by. LC 80-2227. Repr. of 1961 ed. 34.50 (ISBN 0-404-18764-1). AMS Pr.

Levison, Wilhelm. England & the Continent in the Eighth Century. (Ford Lectures Ser). 1946. 32.50 (ISBN 0-19-821232-1). Oxford U Pr.

Mayr-Harting, Henry. The Coming of Christianity to England. LC 74-169818. (Fabric of British History Ser). (Illus.). 300p. 1972. 12.50x (ISBN 0-8052-3436-5). Schocken.

Soames, Henry. The Anglo-Saxon Church: Its History, Revenues & General Character. 4th ed. LC 80-2212. Repr. of 1856 ed. 39.50 (ISBN 0-404-18786-2). AMS Pr.

GREAT BRITAIN–CHURCH HISTORY–MEDIEVAL PERIOD, 1066-1485

Cantor, Norman F. Church, Kingship & Lay Investiture in England, 1089-1135. 1969. lib. bdg. 18.50x (ISBN 0-374-91273-4). Octagon.

Capes, William W. English Church in the Fourteenth & Fifteenth Centuries, 1272-1486. LC 2-21441. (History of the English Church: No. 3). Repr. of 1900 ed. 29.50 (ISBN 0-404-50753-0). AMS Pr.

Cheney, C. R. From Becket to Langton English Church Government, 1170 to 1212. 222p. 1956. 27.00x (ISBN 0-7190-0064-5, Pub. by Manchester U Pr England). State Mutual Bk.

Coulton, George G. Ten Medieval Studies. 7.75 (ISBN 0-8446-1132-8). Peter Smith.

Cutts, Edward L. Parish Priests & Their People in the Middle Ages in England. LC 74-107457. Repr. of 1898 ed. 32.50 (ISBN 0-404-01898-X). Ams Pr.

Edwards, David L. Christian England: Its Story to the Reformation. (Illus.). 356p. 1981. 19.95 (ISBN 0-19-520229-5). Oxford U Pr.

Gasquet, Francis A. Eve of the Reformation. LC 75-118522. 1971. Repr. of 1900 ed. 17.50 (ISBN 0-8046-1144-0). Kennikat.

Longchamp, Nigel. Mirror for Fools: Book of Burnel the Ass. Mozley, J. H., tr. 1963. pap. 1.95x (ISBN 0-268-00180-4). U of Notre Dame Pr.

Matthew, Donald. The Norman Monasteries & Their English Possessions. LC 78-26293. (Oxford Historical Ser.). 1979. Repr. of 1962 ed. lib. bdg. 18.75x (ISBN 0-313-20847-6, MANM). Greenwood.

Ordericus, Vitalis. Historiae Ecclesiasticae Libri Tredecim, 5 Vols. Le Prevost, A., ed. Repr. of 1838 ed. Set. 177.00 (ISBN 0-384-43511-4); Set. pap. 154.00 (ISBN 0-384-43512-2). Johnson Repr.

Owst, Gerald R. Preaching in Medieval England: An Introduction to Sermon Manuscripts of the Period c. 1350-1450. LC 65-18825. (Illus.). 1965. Repr. of 1926 ed. 9.50 (ISBN 0-8462-0667-6). Russell.

Smith, H. Maynard. Pre-Reformation England. LC 63-15182. 1963. Repr. of 1938 ed. 10.00 (ISBN 0-8462-0321-9). Russell.

Stephens, William R. English Church from the Norman Conquest to the Accession of Edward First, 1066-1272. LC 2-21443. (History of the English Church: No. 2). Repr. of 1901 ed. 29.50 (ISBN 0-404-50752-2). AMS Pr.

Trevelyan, George M. England in the Age of Wycliffe. 3rd ed. LC 78-178560. Repr. of 1900 ed. 28.50 (ISBN 0-404-56677-4). AMS Pr.

GREAT BRITAIN–CHURCH HISTORY–16TH CENTURY

see also Reformation–England

Child, Gilbert W. Church & State Under the Tudors. LC 72-183695. 452p. 1974. Repr. of 1890 ed. lib. bdg. 29.50 (ISBN 0-8337-4041-5). B Franklin.

Church of England. A Parte of a Register, Contayninge Sundrie Memorable Matters, Written by Diuers Godly & Learned in Our Time, Which Stande for the Reformation of Our Church. LC 72-5981. (English Experience Ser.: No. 509). 1973. Repr. of 1593 ed. 67.00 (ISBN 90-221-0509-1). Walter J Johnson.

Faulkner, Robert K. Richard Hooker & the Politics of a Christian England. LC 79-65776. 195p. 1981. 19.50x (ISBN 0-520-03993-9). U of Cal Pr.

Frere, W. H. The English Church in the Reigns of Elizabeth & James I: 1558-1625. 1977. lib. bdg. 59.95 (ISBN 0-8490-1773-4). Gordon Pr.

Frere, Walter H. English Church in the Reigns of Elizabeth & James First, 1558-1625. (History of the English Church: No. 5). Repr. of 1904 ed. 29.50 (ISBN 0-404-50755-7). AMS Pr.

Gairdner, James. English Church in the Sixteenth Century, from the Accession of Henry Eighth to the Death of Mary, 1509-1558. LC 72-168089. (History of the English Church: No. 4). Repr. of 1902 ed. 29.50 (ISBN 0-404-50754-9). AMS Pr.

Haugaard, William P. Elizabeth & the English Reformation. LC 68-23179. 1968. 49.50 (ISBN 0-521-07245-X). Cambridge U Pr.

Heal, Felicity & O'Day, Rosemary. Church & Society in England: Henry VIII to James I. 1977. 16.50 (ISBN 0-208-01649-X, Archon). Shoe String.

Jordan, W. K. The Development of Religious Toleration in England, 4 vols. Incl. Vol. 1. From the Beginning of the English Reformation to the Death of Queen Elizabeth (ISBN 0-8446-1251-0); Vol. 2. From the Accession of James One to the Convention of the Long Parliament (ISBN 0-8446-1252-9); Vol. 3. From the Convention of the Long Parliament to the Restoration (ISBN 0-8446-1253-7); Vol. 4. Attainment of the Theory & Accomodations in Thought & Institutiions (ISBN 0-8446-1254-5). 1932. 10.00 ea. Peter Smith.

Kreider, Alan. English Chantries: The Road to Dissolution. LC 78-12453. (Harvard Historical Studies: No. 97). 1979. 20.00x (ISBN 0-674-25560-7). Harvard U Pr.

Mutschmann, Heinrich & Wentersdorf, Karl. Shakespeare & Catholicism. LC 71-105107. 1970. Repr. of 1952 ed. 31.50 (ISBN 0-404-04547-2). AMS Pr.

Overton, John H. & Relton, Frederic. English Church from the Accession of George First to the End of the Eighteenth Century, 1714-1800. (History of the English Church: No. 7). Repr. of 1906 ed. 29.50 (ISBN 0-404-50757-3). AMS Pr.

Pierce, William. Historical Introduction to the Marprelate Tracts: A Chapter in the Evolution of Religious & Civil Liberty in England. 1908. 23.50 (ISBN 0-8337-2762-1). B Franklin.

Plummer, Alfred. English Church History: From the Death of Archbishop Parker to the Death of King Charles I. 1977. lib. bdg. 59.95 (ISBN 0-8490-1772-6). Gordon Pr.

Pollen, John H. English Catholics in the Reign of Queen Elizabeth: A Study of Their Politics, Civil Life & Government. 1971. Repr. of 1920 ed. lib. bdg. 24.50 (ISBN 0-8337-2798-2). B Franklin.

Porter, H. C., ed. Puritanism in Tudor England. LC 75-145532. (History in Depth Ser). 1971. 9.95x (ISBN 0-87249-222-2); pap. 4.95x (ISBN 0-87249-223-0). U of SC Pr.

Saint German, Christopher. A Treatise Concernynge the Division Betwene the Spiritualitie & Temporalitie. LC 72-6027. (English Experience Ser.: No. 453). 94p. 1972. Repr. of 1532 ed. 14.00 (ISBN 90-221-0453-2). Walter J Johnson.

Thompson, Craig R. The English Church in the Sixteenth Century. LC 79-65981. (Folger Guides to the Age of Shakespeare). 1979. pap. 3.95 (ISBN 0-918016-08-8). Folger Bks.

White, Helen C. Social Criticism in Popular Religious Literature of the Sixteenth Century. 1965. lib. bdg. 16.50x (ISBN 0-374-98455-7). Octagon.

GREAT BRITAIN–CHURCH HISTORY–17TH CENTURY

Cragg, Gerald R. Puritanism in the Period of the Great Persecution, 1660-1688. LC 76-143557. 1971. Repr. of 1957 ed. 16.00 (ISBN 0-8462-1578-0). Russell.

Frere, W. H. The English Church in the Reigns of Elizabeth & James I: 1558-1625. 1977. lib. bdg. 59.95 (ISBN 0-8490-1773-4). Gordon Pr.

Frere, Walter H. English Church in the Reigns of Elizabeth & James First, 1558-1625. (History of the English Church: No. 5). Repr. of 1904 ed. 29.50 (ISBN 0-404-50755-7). AMS Pr.

Green, I. M. The Re-Establishment of the Church of England, 1660-1663. (Oxford Historical Monographs). 1978. 33.00x (ISBN 0-19-821867-2). Oxford U Pr.

Haller, William. Liberty & Reformation in the Puritan Revolution. LC 54-6482. 410p. 1955. pap. 7.50x (ISBN 0-231-08547-8, 47). Columbia U Pr.

Havran, Martin J. The Catholics in Caroline England. 1962. 12.50x (ISBN 0-8047-0112-1). Stanford U Pr.

Jones, Rufus M. Mysticism & Democracy in the English Commonwealth. 1965. lib. bdg. 12.50x (ISBN 0-374-94313-3). Octagon.

Jordan, W. K. The Development of Religious Toleration in England, 4 vols. Incl. Vol. 1. From the Beginning of the English Reformation to the Death of Queen Elizabeth (ISBN 0-8446-1251-0); Vol. 2. From the Accession of James One to the Convention of the Long Parliament (ISBN 0-8446-1252-9); Vol. 3. From the Convention of the Long Parliament to the Restoration (ISBN 0-8446-1253-7); Vol. 4. Attainment of the Theory & Accomodations in Thought & Institutiions (ISBN 0-8446-1254-5). 1932. 10.00 ea. Peter Smith.

Miller, J. Popery & Politics in England, 1660-1688. LC 73-79306. (Illus.). 278p. 1973. 41.50 (ISBN 0-521-20236-1). Cambridge U Pr.

Overton, John H. & Relton, Frederic. English Church from the Accession of George First to the End of the Eighteenth Century, 1714-1800. (History of the English Church: No. 7). Repr. of 1906 ed. 29.50 (ISBN 0-404-50757-3). AMS Pr.

Plummer, Alfred. English Church History: From the Death of Archbishop Parker to the Death of King Charles I. 1977. lib. bdg. 59.95 (ISBN 0-8490-1772-6). Gordon Pr.

Schlatter, Richard B. Social Ideas of Religious Leaders, 1660-1688. LC 77-120663. 1970. Repr. lib. bdg. 14.50x (ISBN 0-374-97102-1). Octagon.

Shaw, William A. A History of the English Church During the Civil Wars & Under the Commonwealth, 1640-1660. LC 78-184708. 1974. Repr. of 1900 ed. lib. bdg. 57.50 (ISBN 0-8337-4389-9). B Franklin.

Sommerville, C. John. Popular Religion in Restoration England. LC 77-7618. (University of Florida Social Science Monographs: No. 59). 1977. pap. 4.50 (ISBN 0-8130-0564-7). U Presses Fla.

Ward, Nathaniel. Simple Cobler of Aggawam in America. Zall, Paul M., ed. LC 69-19107. 1969. 7.50x (ISBN 0-8032-0188-5). U of Nebr Pr.

Whiting, Charles E. Studies in English Puritanism from the Restoration to the Revolution 1660-1688. LC 68-56060. Repr. of 1931 ed. 20.00x (ISBN 0-678-05203-4). Kelley.

GREAT BRITAIN–CHURCH HISTORY–MODERN PERIOD, 1485-

Clark, Ruth. Strangers & Sojourners at Port Royal. 1972. lib. bdg. 20.00x (ISBN 0-374-91664-0). Octagon.

Flynn, John S. Influence of Puritanism. LC 72-102569. 1970. Repr. of 1920 ed. 12.75 (ISBN 0-8046-0729-X). Kennikat.

Hunt, John. Religious Thought in England from the Reformation to the End of the Last Century, 3 Vols. LC 72-153593. Repr. of 1873 ed. Set. 94.50 (ISBN 0-404-09480-5). Vol. 1 (ISBN 0-404-09481-3). Vol. 2 (ISBN 0-404-09482-1). Vol. 3 (ISBN 0-404-09483-X). AMS Pr.

Lee, Umphrey. Historical Backgrounds of Early Methodist Enthusiasm. LC 31-18047. (Columbia University. Studies in the Social Sciences: No. 339). Repr. of 1931 ed. 17.50 (ISBN 0-404-51339-5). AMS Pr.

Seaton, Alexander A. The Theory of Toleration Under the Later Stuarts. 1972. lib. bdg. 17.50x (ISBN 0-374-97233-8). Octagon.

GREAT BRITAIN–CHURCH HISTORY–18TH CENTURY

Clarke, Basil. The Building of the Eighteenth Century Church. (Illus.). 1963. text ed. 15.00x (ISBN 0-8401-0404-9). Allenson-Breckinridge.

Schwartz, Hillel. The French Prophets: The History of a Millenarian Group in Eighteenth-Century England. LC 78-65459. (Illus.). 1980. 31.50x (ISBN 0-520-03815-0). U of Cal Pr.

Sher, Richard B. Church, University, Enlightenment: The Moderate Literati of Edinburgh, 1720-1793. 1980. text ed. write for info. (ISBN 0-391-01208-8). Humanities.

GREAT BRITAIN–CHURCH HISTORY–19TH CENTURY

Bentley, James. Ritualism & Politics in Victorian Britain. (Oxford Theological Monographs). (Illus.). 1978. 32.50x (ISBN 0-19-826714-2). Oxford U Pr.

Elliott-Binns, L. Development of English Theology in the Later Nineteenth Century. LC 72-122411. 1971. Repr. of 1952 ed. 13.50 (ISBN 0-208-01045-9, Archon). Shoe String.

Machin, G. I. Politics and the Churches in Great Britain, 1832-1868. 1978. 62.00x (ISBN 0-19-826436-4). Oxford U Pr.

Newman, John H. The Letters & Diaries of John Henry Newman. Dessain, Charles S. & Gornall, Thomas, eds. Incl. Vol. 23. Defeat at Oxford-Defence at Rome, January to December 1867. 454p. 29.00x (ISBN 0-19-920040-8); Vol. 24. A Grammar of Ascent, January 1868 to December 1869. 444p. 29.00x (ISBN 0-19-920043-2); Vol. 25. The Vatican Council, January 1870 to December 1871. 518p. 38.50x (ISBN 0-19-920055-6); Vol. 26. Aftermaths, January 1872 to December 1873. 456p. 38.50x (ISBN 0-19-920056-4). 1973. Oxford U Pr.

Newsome, David H. Wilberforces & Henry Manning: The Parting of Friends. LC 67-2. (Illus.). 1966. 25.00x (ISBN 0-674-95280-4, Belknap Pr). Harvard U Pr.

Overton, John H. The English Church in the Nineteenth Century (1800-1833) (Victorian Age Ser). 1894. Repr. 35.00 (ISBN 0-685-43421-4). Norwood Edns.

GREAT BRITAIN–CIVILIZATION

Addison, William. Worthy Dr. Fuller. 1951. Repr. 13.50 (ISBN 0-8274-3772-2). R West.

Altholz, Josef L., ed. The Mind & Art of Victorian England. 1976. 19.50x (ISBN 0-8166-0772-9). U of Minn Pr.

Barnie, John. War in Medieval English Society: Social Values & the Hundred Years War 1337-99. LC 74-2687. 204p. 1974. 16.50x (ISBN 0-8014-0865-2). Cornell U Pr.

Bergonzi, Bernard. Reading the Thirties: Texts & Contexts. LC 78-4262. (Critical Essays in Modern Literature). 1978. 9.95 (ISBN 0-8229-1135-3). U of Pittsburgh Pr.

Bevington, Merle M. Saturday Review, Eighteen Fifty-Five to Eighteen Sixty-Eight: Representative Educated Opinion in Victorian England. LC 41-25970. Repr. of 1941 ed. 17.50 (ISBN 0-404-00795-3). AMS Pr.

Black, J. B. Reign of Elizabeth, Fifteen Fifty-Eight to Sixteen Three. 2nd ed. (Oxford History of England Ser.). 1959. 39.00x (ISBN 0-19-821701-3). Oxford U Pr.

Booker, Christopher. Neophiliacs. LC 76-112442. 1970. 8.95 (ISBN 0-87645-000-1). Gambit.

Branch, Newton, ed. This Britain. facsimile ed. LC 79-90612. (Essay Index Reprint Ser). 1951. 32.00 (ISBN 0-8369-1549-6). Arno.

Briggs, Asa. Victorian People: A Reassessment of Persons & Themes, 1851-67. new rev. ed. LC 55-5118. (Chicago Collectors Editions Ser.). (Illus.). x, 314p. 1975. pap. 4.95 (ISBN 0-226-07488-9, P365, Phoen). U of Chicago Pr.

Brinton, Clarence C. United States & Britain. LC 75-97340. Repr. of 1948 ed. lib. bdg. 15.00x (ISBN 0-8371-2964-8, BRUS). Greenwood.

British Life & Thought: An Illustrated Survey. facsimile ed. LC 76-128215. (Essay Index Reprint Ser.). Repr. of 1941 ed. 37.00 (ISBN 0-8369-2346-4). Arno.

Buckle, Henry T. History of Civilization in England, Vol. 1. 1919. Repr. 30.00 (ISBN 0-403-01773-4). Scholarly.

Burn, William L. Age of Equipoise. 1965. pap. 3.95x (ISBN 0-393-00319-1, Norton Lib). Norton.

Carr, Philip. English Are Like That. facs. ed. LC 70-142613. (Essay Index Reprint Ser). 1941. 18.00 (ISBN 0-8369-2041-4). Arno.

Chatterjee, S. K., ed. The Cultural Heritage of England, Vol. 5. 60.00x (ISBN 0-686-75617-7, Pub. by Ramakrishna Vedanta England). State Mutual Bk.

Clark, G. Kitson. Making of Victorian England. LC 62-51827. 1967. pap. text ed. 5.95x (ISBN 0-689-70049-0, 104). Atheneum.

Clemoes, Peter & Hughes, Kathleen, eds. England Before the Conquest. LC 76-154508. (Illus.). 1971. 53.95 (ISBN 0-521-08191-2). Cambridge U Pr.

Clifford, James L., ed. Man Versus Society in Eighteenth Century Britain. LC 68-12057. 1968. 22.95 (ISBN 0-521-04675-0). Cambridge U Pr.

Cochrane, Robert. The Treasury of British Eloquence. 1902. Repr. 50.00 (ISBN 0-8274-3644-0). R West.

Coleridge, Hartley. The Worthies of Yorkshire & Lancashire: Being Lives of the Most Distinguished Persons That Have Been Born in, or Connected with Those Provinces. 1836. 100.00 (ISBN 0-8274-3771-4). R West.

Coulton, G. G. Medieval Panorama: The English Scene from Conquest to Reformation. (Illus.). 816p. 1974. pap. 4.95 (ISBN 0-393-00708-1, Norton Lib). Norton.

Dodds, John W. Age of Paradox: A Biography of England, 1841-1851. LC 70-108390. Repr. of 1952 ed. lib. bdg. 26.25x (ISBN 0-8371-3813-2, DOAO). Greenwood.

Drabble, Margaret. For Queen & Country: Victorian England. LC 78-9782. (Illus.). (gr. 6 up). 1979. 8.95 (ISBN 0-395-28960-2, Clarion). HM.

Dunham, William H. & Pargellis, Stanley M. Complaint & Reform in England, 1436-1714. 1967. lib. bdg. 37.50x (ISBN 0-374-92413-9). Octagon.

Earle, Peter. The World of Defoe. LC 76-40310. 1977. 12.50 (ISBN 0-689-10772-2). Atheneum.
Einstein, Lewis D. Italian Renaissance in England. LC 77-143671. (Research & Source Works Ser.: No. 26). 1971. Repr. of 1903 ed. 26.50 (ISBN 0-8337-1027-3). B Franklin.
Ford, Ford M. Between Saint Denis & Saint George. LC 73-153640. (English Literature Ser., No. 33). 1971. Repr. lib. bdg. 38.95 (ISBN 0-8383-1244-6). Haskell.
Fox, David S. Mediterranean Heritage. (Illus.). 1978. 22.00x (ISBN 0-7100-8840-X). Routledge & Kegan.
Garlick & Macintyre. The Diary of Joseph Farington, R. A. LC 78-7056. 1979. text ed. 75.00x set (ISBN 0-300-02418-5). Vol. 4 (ISBN 0-300-02416-9). Vol. 5 (ISBN 0-300-02417-7). Yale U Pr.
Glassman, Bernard. Anti-Semitic Stereotypes Without Jews: Images of the Jews in England, 1290-1700. LC 75-16391. 218p. 1975. 13.95 (ISBN 0-8143-1545-3). Wayne St U Pr.
Goldring, Douglas. The Nineteen Twenties. LC 75-28131. 1975. Repr. of 1945 ed. lib. bdg. 20.00 (ISBN 0-8414-4548-6). Folcroft.
Green, Martin. Transatlantic Patterns: Cultural Comparisons of England with America. LC 74-78305. 1977. 11.95 (ISBN 0-465-08688-8). Basic.
Greene, Donald. Age of Exuberance: Backgrounds to Eighteenth Century Literature, 1660-1785. (Language & Literature Studies). (Orig.). 1967. pap. text ed. 3.95 (ISBN 0-394-30638-4, RanC). Random.
Heindel, Richard H. American Impact on Great Britain, 1898-1914. 1968. lib. bdg. 18.00x (ISBN 0-374-93800-8). Octagon.
Hilton, R. H. Peasants, Knights & Heretics. LC 76-1137. (Past & Present Publications Ser.). 320p. 1976. 34.50 (ISBN 0-521-21276-6). Cambridge U Pr.
Hindley, Geoffrey. England in the Age of Caxton. LC 79-4329. (Illus.). 1979. 17.95x (ISBN 0-685-94384-4). St Martin.
Houghton, Walter E. Victorian Frame of Mind, 1830-1870. 1963. pap. 7.95x (ISBN 0-300-00122-3, Y99). Yale U Pr.
Hughes, Ann, ed. Seventeenth-Century England: A Changing Culture, Vol. 1: Primary Sources. 1981. 28.50x (ISBN 0-389-20168-5). B&N.
Hynes, Samuel. Edwardian Turn of Mind. LC 68-12929. (Illus.). 1968. 28.00 (ISBN 0-691-06031-2); pap. 8.95 (ISBN 0-691-01302-0). Princeton U Pr.
Inge, William R. English Genius: A Survey of the English Achievement. facsimile ed. Lunn, Hugh K., ed. LC 73-167380. (Essay Index Reprint Ser). Repr. of 1938 ed. 18.00 (ISBN 0-8369-2435-5). Arno.
Knachel, Philip A., ed. Case of the Commonwealth of England, Stated, by Marchamont Nedham. (Documents Ser). 1978. 15.00x (ISBN 0-8139-0277-0). Folger Bks.
Larned, Josephus N., et al. English Leadership. LC 70-93353. (Essay Index Reprint Ser). 1918. 22.00 (ISBN 0-8369-1416-3). Arno.
Levine, George L., ed. Emergence of Victorian Consciousness. LC 66-24458. 1967. pap. text ed. 6.95 (ISBN 0-02-918890-3). Free Pr.
Lloyd, T. H. The English Wool Trade in the Middle Ages. LC 76-11086. (Illus.). 1977. 53.50 (ISBN 0-521-21239-1). Cambridge U Pr.
McCarthy, Justin. Portraits of the Sixties. facsimile ed. LC 79-142661. (Essay Index Reprint Ser). Repr. of 1903 ed. 23.00 (ISBN 0-8369-2061-9). Arno.
Massingham, H. J. Where Man Belongs (Austen, Shakespeare, Etc.) 1973. lib. bdg. 25.00 (ISBN 0-8414-6488-X). Folcroft.
Megaw, J. V. & Simpson, D. D., eds. Introduction to British Prehistory. 1979. text ed. 47.50x (ISBN 0-7185-1122-0, Leicester). Humanities.
Notestein, Wallace. English People on the Eve of Colonization: English People on the Eve of Colonization: Sixteen Hundred & Three to Sixteen Thirty. (New American Nation Ser.). (Illus.). pap. 6.50x (ISBN 0-06-133006-X, TB3006, Torch). Har-Row.
Owens, W. R., ed. Seventeenth-Century England: A Changing Culture, Vol. 2: Modern Studies. 352p. 1981. 28.50x (ISBN 0-389-20169-3). B&N.
Richmond, Hugh M. Puritans & Libertines: Anglo-French Literary Relations in the Reformation. 400p. 1981. 27.50x (ISBN 0-520-04179-8). U of Cal Pr.
Rowse, A. L. The Elizabethan Renaissance: The Life of the Society. (Illus.). 320p. 1972. lib. rep. ed. 20.00x (ISBN 0-684-15656-3, ScribT). Scribner.
Sampson, Anthony. The New Anatomy of Britain. LC 78-186150. 800p. 1973. pap. 10.95 (ISBN 0-8128-1583-1). Stein & Day.
Simon, Edith. The Anglo-Saxon Manner: The English Contribution to Civilization. 1972. 14.95x (ISBN 0-8464-0136-3). Beekman Pubs.
Smith, H. Maynard. Pre-Reformation England. LC 63-15182. 1963. Repr. of 1938 ed. 10.00 (ISBN 0-8462-0321-9). Russell.
Smith, Thomas. Discourse of the Commonwealth of This Realm of England. Dewar, Mary, ed. (Documents Ser). 1978. 15.00x (ISBN 0-8139-0277-0). Folger Bks.
Stephens, George R. Knowledge of Greek in England in the Middle Ages. LC 73-943. 1933. lib. bdg. 20.00 (ISBN 0-8414-2600-7). Folcroft.
Stone, Lawrence. Crisis of the Aristocracy, Fifteen Fifty-Eight to Sixteen Forty-One. abr. ed. (Illus.). 1967. pap. 6.95 (ISBN 0-19-500274-1, GB). Oxford U Pr.
--Crisis of the Aristocracy, 1558-1641. 1965. 49.00x (ISBN 0-19-821314-X). Oxford U Pr.
Sulloway, Alison G. Gerard Manley Hopkins & the Victorian Temper. 300p. 1972. 17.50x (ISBN 0-231-03645-0). Columbia U Pr.
Tillemans, T. King & Courtier: A Cultural Reconnaissance into an Age of Transition (Sir Thomas Wyatt, Etc.) LC 77-22071. 1977. Repr. of 1951 ed. lib. bdg. 10.00 (ISBN 0-8414-8603-4). Folcroft.
Traill, Henry D. & Mann, James S. Social England: A Record of the Progress of People in Religion, 6 Vols. LC 78-108550. 1902-1904. Set. 200.00 (ISBN 0-403-00269-9); 34.50 ea. Scholarly.
Warner, Marina. The Crack in the Teacup: Britain in the Twentieth Century. LC 78-27423. (Illus.). 160p. (gr. 6 up). 1979. 10.95 (ISBN 0-395-28972-6, Clarion). HM.
Weber, Conrad G. Studies in the English Outlook in the Period Between the World Wars. 1945. Repr. 25.00 (ISBN 0-8274-3543-6). R West.
Weymouth, Anthony, ed. English Spirit. facsimile ed. LC 70-167437. (Essay Index Reprint Ser). Repr. of 1942 ed. 15.00 (ISBN 0-8369-2677-3). Arno.
Wilkinson, Bertie. Later Middle Ages in England: 1216-1485. LC 73-78343. (History of England Ser.). 1977. pap. text ed. 11.50x (ISBN 0-582-48032-9). Longman.

GREAT BRITAIN–CLIMATE

Bowen, David. Britain's Weather: Its Workings, Lore & Forecasting. (Illus.). 310p. 1969. 14.50 (ISBN 0-7153-4717-9). David & Charles.
Chandler, T. J. The Climate of the British Isles. Gregory, S., ed. (Illus.). 1976. text ed. 24.00x (ISBN 0-582-48558-4). Longman.
Holford, Ingrid. British Weather Disasters. LC 76-20117. 1976. 6.50 (ISBN 0-7153-7276-9). David & Charles.

GREAT BRITAIN–COLONIAL OFFICE

Blakeley, Brian L. Colonial Office, Eighteen Sixty-Eight-Eighteen Ninety-Two. LC 71-161357. 1971. 14.75 (ISBN 0-8223-0252-7). Duke.
Foreign & Commonwealth Office, London. Catalogue of the Colonial Office Library: Third Supplement, 4 vols. 1979. Set. lib. bdg. 520.00 (ISBN 0-8161-0010-1). G K Hall.
Heussler, Robert. Yesterday's Rulers: The Making of the British Colonial Service. LC 63-8326. (Illus.). 1963. 14.95x (ISBN 0-8156-0029-1). Syracuse U Pr.
Kubicek, Robert V. The Administration of Imperialism: Joseph Chamberlain at the Colonial Office. LC 72-89874. 1969. 11.50 (ISBN 0-8223-0216-0). Duke.

GREAT BRITAIN–COLONIES

see also Commonwealth of Nations; Imperial Federation

Amery, Leopold S. The Forward View. facsimile ed. LC 75-179500. (Selected Bibliographies Reprint Ser). Repr. of 1935 ed. 22.00 (ISBN 0-8369-6629-5). Arno.
Beer, George L. British Colonial Policy. 8.75 (ISBN 0-8446-1065-8). Peter Smith.
Bell, J. Bowyer. On Revolt: Strategies of National Liberation. 368p. 1976. 15.00x (ISBN 0-674-63655-4). Harvard U Pr.
Bining, Arthur C. British Regulation of the Colonial Iron Industry. LC 68-55481. Repr. of 1933 ed. 12.50x (ISBN 0-678-00924-4). Kelley.
Black, Jeannette D., ed. Blathwayt Atlas, Vol. 1, The Maps. LC 78-654217. (Illus.). 1970. Set. text ed. 500.00x unbound boxed (ISBN 0-87057-125-7, Pub. by Brown U Pr). U Pr of New Eng.
Bollan, William. Coloniae Anglicanae Illustratae: Or, the Acquest of the Dominion.., Pt. 1. LC 75-31082. Repr. of 1762 ed. 14.00 (ISBN 0-404-13501-3). AMS Pr.
--A Succint View of the Origin of Our Colonies. LC 75-31084. 1976. Repr. of 1766 ed. 9.50 (ISBN 0-404-13503-X). AMS Pr.
Campbell, Persia C. Chinese Coolie Emigration to Countries Within the British Empire. LC 70-88402. Repr. of 1923 ed. 13.25x (ISBN 0-8371-1751-8, Pub. by Negro U Pr). Greenwood.
Cheng, Seymour C. Schemes for the Federation of the British Empire. LC 68-59048. (Columbia University Studies in the Social Sciences: No. 335). Repr. of 1931 ed. 24.50 (ISBN 0-404-51335-2). AMS Pr.
Colonies, 8 pts. Incl. Pt. 1. General, 37 vols. Set. 3114.00x (ISBN 0-686-01186-4); Pt. 2. Africa, 70 vols. Set. 5589.00x (ISBN 0-686-01187-2); Pt. 3. Australia, 34 vols. Set. 2349.00x (ISBN 0-686-01188-0); Pts. 4 & 5, 36 vols. Canada, 33 Vols. Set. 2313.00x (ISBN 0-686-01189-9); Canadian Boundary, 3 Vols. Set. 225.00x (ISBN 0-686-01190-2); Pt. 6. East India, 22 vols. Set. 2151.00x (ISBN 0-686-01191-0); Pt. 7. New Zealand, 17 vols. Set. 1467.00x (ISBN 0-686-01192-9); Pt. 8. West Indies, 10 vols. Set. 819.00x (ISBN 0-686-01193-7). (British Parliamentary Papers Ser.). 1971 (Pub. by Irish Academic Pr Ireland). Biblio Dist.
Colquhoun, Archibald R. Mastery of the Pacific. LC 70-111750. (American Imperialism: Viewpoints of United States Foreign Policy, 1898-1941). 1970. Repr. of 1904 ed. 20.00 (ISBN 0-405-02009-0). Arno.
Eden, Anthony. Days for Decision. LC 50-13062. 1969. Repr. of 1950 ed. 12.00 (ISBN 0-527-26300-1). Kraus Repr.
Fawcett, Charles B. Political Geography of the British Empire. LC 74-109731. Repr. of 1933 ed. lib. bdg. 19.25x (ISBN 0-8371-4221-0, FAPG). Greenwood.
Great Britain Foreign Office Historical Section. British Possessions, 2: The Congo. LC 70-79814. (Illus.). Repr. of 1920 ed. 18.50x (ISBN 0-8371-1474-8, Pub. by Negro U Pr). Greenwood.
Great Britain Parliament. Report of Select Committee on Aborigines, 2 Vols. (Official Blue-Book Reprint Series, Vol. 1: Pts. 1 & 2). 1966. Repr. 66.48x (ISBN 0-8426-1281-5). Verry.
Greene, Evarts B. & Harrington, Virginia. American Population Before Federal Census of 1790. 1932. 8.50 (ISBN 0-8446-1208-1). Peter Smith.
Hobson, John A. Imperialism. 1965. pap. 5.95 (ISBN 0-472-06103-8, 103, AA). U of Mich Pr.
Knowles, Lillian C. & Knowles, C. M. The Economic Development of the British Overseas Empire, 3 vols. Repr. of 1924 ed. lib. bdg. 67.50x (ISBN 0-678-01332-2). Kelley.
Kuczynski, Robert R. Demographic Survey of the British Colonial Empire, 3 Vols. LC 68-26540. Repr. of 1953 ed. Set. 95.00x (ISBN 0-678-00740-3). Kelley.
Louis, William R. Imperialism at Bay: The United States & the Decolonization of the British Empire, 1941-1945. 1978. 22.50x (ISBN 0-19-821125-2). Oxford U Pr.
Lugard, Lady A. Tropical Dependency. 32.50x (ISBN 0-686-11114-1, F Cass Co). Biblio Dist.
McIntyre, W. David. Imperial Frontier in the Tropics: Eighteen Sixty-Five to Eighteen Seventy-Five. 1969. 19.95 (ISBN 0-312-40985-0). St Martin.
Meek, Charles Kingsley. Land Law & Custom in the Colonies. 2nd ed. 337p. 1968. Repr. of 1949 ed. 28.50x (ISBN 0-7146-1698-2, F Cass Co). Biblio Dist.
Morgan, D. J. Developing British Colonial Resources Nineteen Forty-Five to Nineteen Fifty-One, Vol. 2. 1980. text ed. cancelled (ISBN 0-391-01685-7). Humanities.
--Guidance Towards Self-Government in British Colonies: 1941-1971, Vol. 5. (Official History of Colonial Development Ser.). 1980. text ed. cancelled (ISBN 0-391-01688-1). Humanities.
Morris-Jones, W. H. & Fischer, Georges, eds. Decolonisation & After: The British & French Experience. (Studies in Commonwealth Politics & History: No. 7). 369p. 1980. 29.50x (ISBN 0-7146-3095-0, F Cass Co). Biblio Dist.
Porter, Bernard. Critics of Empire: British Radical Attitudes Toward African Colonialism: 1895-1914. LC 68-20349. 1969. 19.95 (ISBN 0-312-17570-1). St Martin.
Porter, George R. Progress of the Nation. new ed. Hirst, F. W., ed. LC 77-85189. Repr. of 1912 ed. 25.00x (ISBN 0-678-00538-9). Kelley.
Scholes, Theophilius E. British Empire & Alliances, Or, Britain's Duty to Her Colonies & Subject Races. LC 70-109982. Repr. of 1899 ed. 20.00x (ISBN 0-8371-4139-7, Pub. by Negro U Pr). Greenwood.
Schuyler, Robert L. Fall of the Old Colonial System: A Study in British Free Trade, 1770-1870. 1966. Repr. of 1945 ed. 19.50 (ISBN 0-208-00254-5, Archon). Shoe String.
Thornton, A. P. For the File on Empire. 1969. 19.95 (ISBN 0-312-29785-8). St Martin.
Winch, Donald N. Classical Political Economy & Colonies. LC 66-662. (London School of Economics & Political Science Publications Ser). 1965. 10.00x (ISBN 0-674-13450-8). Harvard U Pr.
Winks, Robin W. British Imperialism: Gold, God, Glory. LC 63-14412. 1963. pap. text ed. 5.95 (ISBN 0-03-012260-0, HoltC). HR&W.

GREAT BRITAIN–COLONIES–ADMINISTRATION

Andrews, Charles M. Our Earliest Colonial Settlements: Their Diversities of Origin & Later Characteristics. (YA) (gr. 9-12). 1959. pap. 3.95 (ISBN 0-8014-9016-2, CP16). Cornell U Pr.
Beer, George L. British Colonial Policy. 8.75 (ISBN 0-8446-1065-8). Peter Smith.
--Origins of British Colonial System. 8.75 (ISBN 0-8446-1067-4). Peter Smith.
Bell, Sydney S. Colonial Administration of Great Britain. LC 74-114023. Repr. of 1859 ed. lib. bdg. 22.50x (ISBN 0-678-00639-3). Kelley.
Blakeley, Brian L. Colonial Office, Eighteen Sixty-Eight-Eighteen Ninety-Two. LC 71-161357. 1971. 14.75 (ISBN 0-8223-0252-7). Duke.
Booth, Sally S. Seeds of Anger: Revolts in America, 1670-1771. 1977. 10.95 (ISBN 0-8038-6742-5). Hastings.
Braibanti, Ralph J., ed. Asian Bureaucratic Systems Emergent from the British Imperial Tradition. LC 66-27487. (Commonwealth Studies Center: No. 28). 1966. 24.75 (ISBN 0-8223-0021-4). Duke.
Bruce, Charles. The Broad Stone of Empire: Problems of Crown Colony Administration, 2 vols. facsimile ed. LC 70-179507. (Select Bibliographies Reprint Ser.). Repr. of 1910 ed. Set. 62.00 (ISBN 0-8369-6636-8). Arno.
Burgh, James. Political Disquisitions, 3 Vols. LC 78-146144. (American Constitutional & Legal History Ser). 1971. Repr. of 1775 ed. lib. bdg. 135.00 (ISBN 0-306-70101-4). Da Capo.
Channing, Edward. Town & Country Government in the English Colonies of North America. LC 78-63749. (Johns Hopkins University. Studies in the Social Sciences. Second Ser. 1884: 10). Repr. of 1884 ed. 11.50 (ISBN 0-404-61018-8). AMS Pr.
Church, Archibald G. East Africa, a New Dominion: A Crucial Experiment in Tropical Development & Its Significance to the British Empire. LC 79-137229. Repr. of 1927 ed. 16.50x (ISBN 0-8371-3646-6, Pub. by Negro U Pr). Greenwood.
Cumpston, I. M., ed. The Growth of the British Commonwealth: 1880-1932. (Documents of Modern History Ser.). 192p. 1973. 15.95 (ISBN 0-312-35140-2). St Martin.
Dickerson, Oliver M. American Colonial Government, 1696-1765. LC 61-17198. (Illus.). 1962. Repr. of 1912 ed. 8.50 (ISBN 0-8462-0166-6). Russell.
Dixon, C. Willis. Colonial Administration of Sir Thomas Maitland. 1968. Repr. of 1939 ed. 24.00x (ISBN 0-7146-1469-6, F Cass Co). Biblio Dist.
Egerton, Hugh E. Origin & Growth of the English Colonies & Their System of Government. LC 77-89023. Repr. of 1903 ed. 12.75x (ISBN 0-8371-1900-6). Greenwood.
Elgin, James B. Letters & Journals. Walrond, Theodore, ed. LC 6-20542. 1969. Repr. of 1872 ed. 17.00 (ISBN 0-527-26750-3). Kraus Repr.
Evatt, Herbert V. King & His Dominion Governors. 2nd ed. 324p. 1967. 30.00x (ISBN 0-7146-1471-8, F Cass Co). Biblio Dist.
Froude, James A. English in the West Indies, or the Bow of Ulysses. LC 74-77200. (Illus.). Repr. of 1888 ed. 18.75x (ISBN 0-8371-1312-1, Pub. by Negro U Pr). Greenwood.
Gage, Thomas. Correspondence of General Thomas Gage: Reprint of 1931-33 Eds, 2 Vols. Carter, Clarence E., ed. LC 73-85914. 1969. Set. 37.50 (ISBN 0-208-00812-8, Archon). Shoe String.
Gailey, Harry A., Jr. The Road to Aba: A Study of British Administrative Policy in Eastern Nigeria. LC 77-11519. 1970. 12.00x (ISBN 0-8147-0461-1). NYU Pr.
Gann, Lewis H. Birth of a Plural Society: The Development of Northern Rhodesia Under the British South African Company. 1958. text ed. 18.00x (ISBN 0-391-00451-4). Humanities.
Greene, Evarts B. Provincial Governor in the English Colonies of North America. LC 66-24700. 1966. Repr. of 1898 ed. 8.50 (ISBN 0-8462-0779-6). Russell.
--The Provincial Governor in the English Colonies of North America. 8.50 (ISBN 0-8446-1209-X). Peter Smith.
Grey, H. G. Colonial Policy of Lord John Russell's Administration, 2 vols. in 1. LC 9-34540. Repr. of 1853 ed. 30.00 (ISBN 0-527-35900-9). Kraus Repr.
Hailey, William M. Native Administration in the British African Territories, 5 vols. LC 74-15047. Repr. of 1953 ed. Set. 110.00 (ISBN 0-404-12077-6). AMS Pr.
Hall, Michael G. Edward Randolph & the American Colonies, 1676-1703. 1969. pap. 4.25x (ISBN 0-393-00480-5, Norton Lib). Norton.
--Edward Randolph & the American Colonies, 1676-1703. (Institute of Early American History & Culture Ser.). 1960. 13.50x (ISBN 0-8078-0798-2). U of NC Pr.

Hancock, W. K. Survey of British Commonwealth Affairs, 2 vols. LC 76-56781. (Illus., Includes color map on microfiche). 1977. Repr. of 1937 ed. lib. bdg. 72.75x (ISBN 0-8371-9414-8, HABCA). Greenwood.
Heussler, Robert. British Tanganyika. LC 78-142291. 1971. 8.75 (ISBN 0-8223-0247-0). Duke.
Holmes, Brian, ed. Educational Policy & the Mission Schools: Case Studies from the British Empire. 1967. text ed. 16.75x (ISBN 0-7100-6002-5). Humanities.
Jennings, William I. The British Commonwealth of Nations. LC 78-14363. 1978. Repr. of 1961 ed. lib. bdg. 20.00x (ISBN 0-8371-9357-5, JEBC). Greenwood.
Kaye, Percy L. The Colonial Executive Prior to the Restoration. LC 78-63874. (Johns Hopkins University. Studies in the Social Sciences. Eighteenth Ser. 1900: 5-6). Repr. of 1900 ed. 11.50 (ISBN 0-404-61130-3). AMS Pr.
--English Colonial Administration Under Lord Clarendon, 1660-1667. LC 78-63908. (Johns Hopkins University. Studies in the Social Sciences. Twenty-Third Ser. 1905: 5-6). Repr. of 1905 ed. 17.50 (ISBN 0-404-61160-5). AMS Pr.
Kesner, Richard M. Economic Control & Colonial Development: Crown Colony Finincial Management in the Age of Joseph Chamberlain. LC 80-27173. (Contributions in Comparative Colonial Studies: No. 7). (Illus.). 228p. 1981. lib. bdg. 35.00 (ISBN 0-313-22898-1, KEC/). Greenwood.
Knaplund, Paul. James Stephen & the British Colonial System, 1813-1847. LC 74-7611. 315p. 1974. Repr. of 1953 ed. lib. bdg. 17.50x (ISBN 0-8371-7590-9, KNJS). Greenwood.
Labaree, Leonard W., ed. Royal Instructions to British Colonial Governors, 1670-1776, 2 Vols. 1967. lib. bdg. 27.50x (ISBN 0-374-94674-4). Octagon.
Lord, Eleanor L. Industrial Experiments in the British Colonies of North America. LC 68-56784. (Research & Source Works Ser: No. 273). (Illus.). 1969. Repr. of 1898 ed. 17.50 (ISBN 0-8337-2145-3). B Franklin.
Manning, Helen T. British Colonial Government After the American Revolution, 1782-1820. 1966. Repr. of 1933 ed. 25.00 (ISBN 0-208-00181-6, Archon). Shoe String.
Martin, Eveline C. British West African Settlements, 1750-1821, a Study in Local Administration. LC 79-109342. (Illus.). Repr. of 1927 ed. 12.00x (ISBN 0-8371-3612-1, Pub. by Negro U Pr). Greenwood.
Merivale, Herman. Lectures on Colonization & Colonies Delivered Before the University of Oxford in 1839, 1840, & 1841. 2nd ed. LC 67-25954. Repr. of 1861 ed. 19.50x (ISBN 0-678-00273-8). Kelley.
Mills, Lennox A. British Rule in Eastern Asia: A Study of Contemporary Government & Economic Development in British Malaya & Hong Kong. LC 76-83863. (Illus.). 1970. Repr. of 1942 ed. 17.50 (ISBN 0-8462-1415-6). Russell.
Morison, John L. The Eighth Earl of Elgin. LC 73-109798. (Illus.). 317p. Repr. of 1928 ed. lib. bdg. 14.75x (ISBN 0-8371-4289-X, MOEE). Greenwood.
Morton, Richard L. Struggle Against Tyranny & the Beginning of a New Era: Virginia, 1677-1699. (Illus.). 1957. pap. 1.95x (ISBN 0-8139-0133-2). U Pr of Va.
Padmore, George. Africa: Britain's Third Empire. LC 75-92754. Repr. of 1949 ed. 13.25x (ISBN 0-8371-2182-5, Pub. by Negro U Pr). Greenwood.
--How Britain Rules Africa. LC 79-92755. Repr. of 1936 ed. 18.75x (ISBN 0-8371-2176-0, Pub. by Negro U Pr). Greenwood.
Penson, Lillian M. Colonial Agents of the British West Indies: A Study in Colonial Administration, Mainly in the Eighteenth Century. 128p. 1971. Repr. of 1924 ed. 28.50x (ISBN 0-7146-1944-2, F Cass Co). Biblio Dist.
Pownall, T. Administration of the Colonies. LC 79-146155. (Era of the American Revolution Ser). 1971. Repr. of 1768 ed. lib. bdg. 39.50 (ISBN 0-306-70123-5). Da Capo.
Proudfoot, Mary M. Britain & the United States in the Caribbean: A Comparative Study in Methods of Development. LC 74-385. (Illus.). 1976. Repr. of 1954 ed. lib. bdg. 27.25x (ISBN 0-8371-7382-5, PRBR). Greenwood.
Silburn, P. A. Governance of Empire. LC 70-118502. 1971. Repr. of 1910 ed. 14.00 (ISBN 0-8046-1250-1). Kennikat.
Wainwright, Mary D., ed. Brothers in India. 1979. 22.00x (ISBN 0-8364-0510-2). South Asia Bks.
Wakefield, Edward G., ed. View of the Art of Colonization. LC 68-30548. Repr. of 1849 ed. 19.50x (ISBN 0-678-00561-3). Kelley.
Washburne, George A. Imperial Control of the Administration of Justice in the Thirteen American Colonies 1684-1776. LC 70-109920. (Columbia Univesity. Studies in the Social Sciences: No. 238). Repr. of 1923 ed. 17.50 (ISBN 0-404-51238-0). AMS Pr.
Webb, Stephen S. The Governors-General: The English Army & the Definition of the Empire 1569-1681. LC 78-8746. (Illus.). 1979. 22.50x (ISBN 0-8078-1331-1). U of NC Pr.
Worsfold, William B. South Africa: A Study in Colonial Administration & Development. LC 79-82087. (Illus.). Repr. of 1895 ed. 14.50x (ISBN 0-8371-1544-2). Greenwood.

GREAT BRITAIN–COLONIES–BIBLIOGRAPHY

Great Britain - Colonial Office, London. Catalogue of the Colonial Office Library, London, 15 vols. 1964. Set. 965.00 (ISBN 0-8161-0688-6); First Suppl. 1963-67. 130.00 (ISBN 0-8161-0729-7); Second Suppl. 1972. 2 Vols. 185.00 (ISBN 0-8161-0843-9). G K Hall.
Royal Commonwealth Society, London. Subject Catalogue of the Royal Commonwealth Society, 7 vols. 1971. Set. 615.00 (ISBN 0-8161-0885-4). G K Hall.
Winks, Robin W., ed. Historiography of the British Empire-Commonwealth. LC 66-15555. 1966. 22.75 (ISBN 0-8223-0193-8). Duke.

GREAT BRITAIN–COLONIES–EDUCATION

Murray, A. Victor. School in the Bush: A Critical Study of the Theory & Practice of Native Education in Africa. (Illus.). 454p. 1967. Repr. of 1929 ed. 32.50x (ISBN 0-7146-1704-0, F Cass Co). Biblio Dist.

GREAT BRITAIN–COLONIES–HISTORY

Andrews, K. R., et al, eds. Westward Enterprise: English Activites in Ireland, the Atlantic & America 1480-1650. LC 79-13801. 1979. 19.95x (ISBN 0-8143-1647-6). Wayne St U Pr.
Beer, George L. Origins of British Colonial System. 8.75 (ISBN 0-8446-1067-4). Peter Smith.
Blenman, Jonathan. Remarks on Several Acts of Parliament Relating More Especially to the Colonies Abroad. LC 70-141127. (Research Library of Colonial Americana). 1971. Repr. of 1742 ed. 13.00 (ISBN 0-405-03331-1). Arno.
Bolton, Geoffrey. Britian's Legacy Overseas. 176p. (Orig.). 1973. pap. 3.50x (ISBN 0-19-888076-6, OPB). Oxford U Pr.
Bowle, John. Charles I: A Biography. 1976. 12.50 (ISBN 0-316-10404-3). Little.
Carrington, Charles E. British Overseas. 2nd ed. LC 68-23176. (Illus.). 1968. 53.50 (ISBN 0-521-07174-7). Cambridge U Pr.
--An Exposition of Empire. LC 75-41051. (BCL Ser. II). Repr. of 1947 ed. 15.00 (ISBN 0-404-14650-3). AMS Pr.
Clark, Peter, et al, eds. English Commonwealth Fifteen Forty-Seven to Sixteen Forty: Essays in Politics & Society. LC 78-32060. (Illus.). 1979. text ed. 30.00x (ISBN 0-06-491171-3). B&N.
Coupland, Reginald. American Revolution & the British Empire. LC 65-18801. 1965. Repr. of 1930 ed. 7.50 (ISBN 0-8462-0601-3). Russell.
Egerton, Hugh E. A Short History of British Colonial Policy, 1606-1909. 9th ed. LC 74-15035. Repr. of 1932 ed. 42.50 (ISBN 0-404-12040-7). AMS Pr.
Fay, Charles R. Imperial Economy & Its Place in the Formation of Economic Doctrine. LC 74-29638. 151p. 1975. Repr. of 1934 ed. lib. bdg. 15.00x (ISBN 0-8371-8007-4, FAIE). Greenwood.
Graham, G. S. Tides of Empire: Discursions on the Expansion of Britain Overseas. 1972. 7.00 (ISBN 0-7735-0137-1). McGill-Queens U Pr.
Gunn, Hugh, ed. The British Empire, 12 vols. Incl. Vol. 1. Dominions & Dependencies of the British Empire. (Illus.). 20.00 (ISBN 0-404-54301-4); Vol. 2. The Story of the Empire. Lucas, C. 14.00 (ISBN 0-404-54302-2); Vol. 3. The Constitution, Administration & Laws of the Empire. Keith, A. B. 15.00 (ISBN 0-404-54303-0); Vol. 4. The Resources of the Empire & Their Development. Lewin, E. 15.00 (ISBN 0-404-54304-9); Vol. 5. Health Problems of the Empire, Past, Present & Future. Balfour, A. & Scott, H. H. 17.50 (ISBN 0-404-54305-7); Vol. 6. The Press & Communications of the Empire. Mills, J. S. 17.50 (ISBN 0-404-54306-5); Vol. 7. The Trade, Commerce... of the Empire. McLeod, C. C. 17.50 (ISBN 0-404-54307-3); Vol. 8. Makers of the Empire. Gunn, H. 17.50 (ISBN 0-404-54308-1); Vol. 9. The Native Races of the Empire. Lagden, G. 17.50 (ISBN 0-404-54309-X); Vol. 10. The Universities & Educational Systems of the British Empire. 17.50 (ISBN 0-404-54310-3); Vol. 11. The Literature of the Empire; the Art of the Empire. Salaman, E. & Longden, A. A. 17.50 (ISBN 0-404-54311-1); Vol. 12. Migration Within the Empire. Belcher, E. A. & Williamson, J. A. 17.50 (ISBN 0-404-54312-X). Repr. of 1924 ed. Set. 200.00 (ISBN 0-404-54300-6). AMS Pr.
Guttridge, George H. Colonial Policy of William III in America & West Indies. new ed. 190p. 1966. 24.00x (ISBN 0-7146-1478-5, F Cass Co). Biblio Dist.
Hall, W. P., et al. History of England & the Empire Commonwealth. 5th ed. 1971. text ed. 28.95 (ISBN 0-471-00225-9). Wiley.
Huttenback, Robert A. The British Imperial Experience. LC 75-31434. (Illus.). 225p. 1976. Repr. of 1966 ed. lib. bdg. 18.00x (ISBN 0-8371-8505-X, HUBI). Greenwood.
Johnson, Gerald W. British Empire: An American View of Its History from 1776 to 1945. (Illus.). (gr. 5 up). 1969. o.p. 7.75 (ISBN 0-688-21124-0); PLB 7.44 (ISBN 0-688-31124-5). Morrow.
Johnston, W. Ross. Great Britain Great Empire. (Scholars' Library). (Illus.). 207p. 1981. text ed. 37.50x (ISBN 0-7022-1576-7). U of Queensland Pr.
Kaye, Percy L. English Colonial Administration Under Lord Clarendon, 1660-1667. LC 78-63908. (Johns Hopkins University. Studies in the Social Sciences. Twenty-Third Ser. 1905: 5-6). Repr. of 1905 ed. 17.50 (ISBN 0-404-61160-5). AMS Pr.
Knaplund, Paul. Britain: Commonwealth & Empire, 1901-1955. LC 74-3744. (Illus.). 541p. 1974. Repr. of 1956 ed. lib. bdg. 32.50x (ISBN 0-8371-7467-8, KNBR). Greenwood.
--British Empire, Eighteen Fifteen to Nineteen Thirty. LC 68-9617. (Illus.). 1970. Repr. 29.50 (ISBN 0-86527-017-1). Fertig.
Labarge, Margaret W. Gascony, England's First Colony 1204-1453. (Illus.). 276p. 1980. 24.50x (ISBN 0-389-20142-1). B&N.
MacInnes, C. Malcolm. Bristol: Gateway of Empire. LC 68-23841. (Illus.). Repr. of 1939 ed. 17.50x (ISBN 0-678-05609-9). Kelley.
Marshall, Peter & Williams, Glyn, eds. The British Atlantic Empire Before the American Revolution. 130p. 1980. 25.00x (ISBN 0-7146-3158-2, F Cass Co). Biblio Dist.
Martin, R. M. History of the Colonies of the British Empire. (Illus.). 906p. 1967. Repr. of 1843 ed. 35.00x (ISBN 0-8464-0483-4). Beekman Pubs.
Morgan, D. J. The Official History of Colonial Development, 5 vols. Incl. Vol. 1. The Origins of British Aid Policy 1924-1945. 253p (ISBN 0-391-01684-9); Vol. 2. Developing British Colonial Resources 1945-1951. 398p (ISBN 0-391-01685-7); Vol. 3. Reassessment of British Aid Policy 1951-1965. 334p (ISBN 0-391-01686-5); Vol. 4. Changes in British Aid Policy 1951-1970. 275p (ISBN 0-391-01687-3); Vol. 5. Guidance Towards Self-Government on British Colonies 1941-1971. 382p (ISBN 0-391-01688-1). 1980. text ed. 37.50x ea. Humanities.
Morrell, W. P. British Colonial Policy in the Age of Peel and Russell. new ed. 554p. 1966. 29.50x (ISBN 0-7146-1504-8, F Cass Co). Biblio Dist.
Sioussant, St. George L. The English Statutes in Maryland. LC 78-63899. (Johns Hopkins University. Studies in the Social Sciences. Twenty-First Ser. 1903: 11-12). Repr. of 1903 ed. 18.00 (ISBN 0-404-61152-4). AMS Pr.
Tucker, Josiah. True Interest of Britain Set Forth in Regard to the Colonies & the Only Means of Living in Peace & Harmony with Them, Including Five Different Plans for Effecting This Desirable Event. LC 76-141126. (Research Library of Colonial Americana). 1971. Repr. of 1776 ed. 13.00 (ISBN 0-405-03337-0). Arno.
Whitney, Edson L. Government of the Colony of South Carolina. LC 78-63836. (Johns Hopkins University. Studies in the Social Sciences. Thirteenth Ser. 1895: 1-2). Repr. of 1895 ed. 11.50 (ISBN 0-404-61095-1). AMS Pr.
Williamson, J. A. Short History of British Expansion, 2 vols. Incl. Vol. 1. Old Colonial Empire. 3rd ed. 470p. 1969 (ISBN 0-312-71785-7); Vol. 2. Modern Empire & Commonwealth. 6th ed. 408p. 1967 (ISBN 0-312-71820-9). (Illus.). 15.95 (ISBN 0-685-23147-X). St Martin.
Williamson, James A. Great Britain & the Commonwealth. 3rd ed. 1965. text ed. 5.50x (ISBN 0-7136-0844-7). Humanities.
Woodcock, George. Who Killed the British Empire. LC 73-90173. 352p. 1974. 10.00 (ISBN 0-8129-0419-2). Times Bks.
Wright, Louis B. Religion & Empire. 1965. lib. bdg. 14.50x (ISBN 0-374-98816-1). Octagon.

GREAT BRITAIN–COLONIES–HISTORY–SOURCES

Keith, Arthur B. Speeches & Documents on the British Dominions, 1918-1931: From Self-Government to National Sovereignty. Keith, Arthur B., intro. by. LC 75-41159. Repr. of 1932 ed. 24.50 (ISBN 0-404-14561-2). AMS Pr.
Willer, Thomas F., compiled by. Southeast Asian References in the British Parliamentary Papers, 1801-1972-73: An Index. LC 77-620034. (Papers in International Studies: Southeast Asia: No. 48). 1977. pap. 8.50 (ISBN 0-89680-033-4). Ohio U Ctr Intl.

GREAT BRITAIN–COLONIES–AFRICA

Aronson, Theo. Royal Ambassadors: British Royalties in Southern Africa, 1860-1947. (Illus.). 144p. 1975. 14.00x (ISBN 0-8476-2392-0). Rowman.
Aydelotte, W. O. Bismarck & British Colonial Policy: The Problem of South West Africa, 1883-1885. LC 76-120225. 1970. Repr. lib. bdg. 14.00x (ISBN 0-374-90325-5). Octagon.
Aydelotte, William O. Bismarck & British Colonial Policy: The Problem of South West Africa, 1883-1885. 2nd & enl. ed. LC 73-113161. (Illus.). 1970. Repr. of 1937 ed. 13.50 (ISBN 0-8462-1249-8). Russell.
Bannister, Saxe. Humane Policy: Justice to the Aborigines. LC 71-75539. Repr. of 1830 ed. 21.50x (ISBN 0-8371-0993-0, Pub. by Negro U Pr). Greenwood.
Bixler, Raymond W. Anglo-German Imperialism in South Africa, 1880-1900. LC 77-155374. Repr. of 1932 ed. 12.00x (ISBN 0-8371-1271-0, Pub. by Negro U Pr). Greenwood.
British Africa. LC 77-88401. Repr. of 1901 ed. 23.75x (ISBN 0-8371-1836-0, Pub. by Negro U Pr). Greenwood.
Browne, John H. South Africa: A Glance at Current Conditions. LC 70-76494. Repr. 12.75x (ISBN 0-8371-1091-2). Greenwood.
Channock, Martin. Britain, Rhodesia & South Africa, 1900-1945: The Unconsummated Union. (Illus.). 289p. 1977. 27.50x (ISBN 0-7146-6001-9, F Cass Co). Biblio Dist.
Church, Archibald G. East Africa, a New Dominion: A Crucial Experiment in Tropical Development & Its Significance to the British Empire. LC 79-137229. Repr. of 1927 ed. 16.50x (ISBN 0-8371-3646-6, Pub. by Negro U Pr). Greenwood.
Crooks, J. J. Records Relating to the Gold Coast Settlements from 1750 to 1874. 576p. 1973. 36.00x (ISBN 0-7146-1647-8, F Cass Co). Biblio Dist.
Davies, K. G. Royal African Company. LC 57-6673. 1970. pap. 3.45 (ISBN 0-689-70239-6, NL24). Atheneum.
Dilley, Marjorie R. British Policy in Kenya Colony. 2nd ed. 300p. 1966. 24.00x (ISBN 0-7146-1655-9, F Cass Co). Biblio Dist.
Evans, Ifor L. British in Tropical Africa, an Historical Outline. LC 74-94476. (Illus.). Repr. of 1929 ed. 18.25x (ISBN 0-8371-2351-8, Pub. by Negro U Pr). Greenwood.
Evans, Maurice S. Black & White in Southeast Africa: A Study in Sociology. LC 78-78765. (Illus.). Repr. of 1911 ed. 15.50x (ISBN 0-8371-1390-3, Pub. by Negro U Pr). Greenwood.
George, Claude. Rise of British West Africa. new ed. 468p. 1968. 32.50x (ISBN 0-7146-1667-2, F Cass Co). Biblio Dist.
Hailey, William M. Native Administration in the British African Territories, 5 vols. LC 74-15047. Repr. of 1953 ed. Set. 110.00 (ISBN 0-404-12077-6). AMS Pr.
Hazzledine, George D. White Man in Nigeria. LC 74-78370. (Illus.). Repr. of 1904 ed. 14.50x (ISBN 0-8371-1338-5). Greenwood.
Johnston, Harry H. Britain Across the Seas: Africa, a History & Description of the British Empire in Africa. LC 78-78371. (Illus.). Repr. of 1910 ed. 41.00x (ISBN 0-8371-1344-X, Pub. by Negro U Pr). Greenwood.
Jones, E. Morse. Roll of the British Settlers in South Africa: Pt. 1. up to 1826. (Illus.). 1969. 12.00x (ISBN 0-8426-1325-0). Verry.
Lugard, Frederick J. Dual Mandate in British Tropical Africa. 1965. Repr. 32.50x (ISBN 0-7146-1690-7, F Cass Co). Biblio Dist.
--Rise of Our East African Empire: Early Efforts in Nyasaland Uganda, 2 vols. (Illus.). 1968. Repr. of 1893 ed. 87.50x set (ISBN 0-7146-1691-5, F Cass Co). Biblio Dist.
Macaulay, Kenneth. Colony of Sierra Leone Vindicated from the Misrepresentations of Mr. MacQueen of Glasgow. 127p. 1968. Repr. of 1827 ed. 25.00x (ISBN 0-7146-1831-4, F Cass Co). Biblio Dist.
Mackenzie, John. Austral Africa: Losing It or Ruling It, 2 Vols. LC 79-82060. (Illus.). Repr. of 1887 ed. 41.00x (ISBN 0-8371-4998-3, Pub. by Negro U Pr). Greenwood.
Martin, Eveline C. British West African Settlements, 1750-1821, a Study in Local Administration. LC 79-109342. (Illus.). Repr. of 1927 ed. 12.00x (ISBN 0-8371-3612-1, Pub. by Negro U Pr). Greenwood.
Murray, A. Victor. School in the Bush: A Critical Study of the Theory & Practice of Native Education in Africa. (Illus.). 454p. 1967. Repr. of 1929 ed. 32.50x (ISBN 0-7146-1704-0, F Cass Co). Biblio Dist.
Padmore, George. Africa: Britain's Third Empire. LC 75-92754. Repr. of 1949 ed. 13.25x (ISBN 0-8371-2182-5, Pub. by Negro U Pr). Greenwood.
--How Britain Rules Africa. LC 79-92755. Repr. of 1936 ed. 18.75x (ISBN 0-8371-2176-0, Pub. by Negro U Pr). Greenwood.

Perham, Margery F. The Colonial Reckoning: End of Imperial Rule in Africa in the Light of British Experience. LC 76-25998. 1976. Repr. of 1962 ed. lib. bdg. 18.75x (ISBN 0-8371-9016-9, PECR). Greenwood.

Rai, Kauleshwar. Indians & British Colonialism in East Africa, 1883-1939. 1979. 12.50x (ISBN 0-8364-0504-8). South Asia Bks.

Raphael, Lois A. Cape-To-Cairo Dream: A Study in British Imperialism. 1971. lib. bdg. 25.00x (ISBN 0-374-96714-8). Octagon.

Sanderson, Edgar. Great Britain in Modern Africa. LC 72-100276. Repr. of 1907 ed. 19.75x (ISBN 0-8371-2860-9, Pub. by Negro U Pr). Greenwood.

Smith, Robert S. The Lagos Consulate, 1851-1861. 1979. 26.75x (ISBN 0-520-03746-4). U of Cal Pr.

Tamuno, T. N. The Evolution of the Nigerian State: The Southern Phase, 1898-1914. (Ibadan History Ser.). (Illus.). 250p. 1972. text ed. 14.00x (ISBN 0-391-00232-5). Humanities.

Wallis, Charles B. Advance of Our West African Empire. LC 70-77215. (Illus.). Repr. of 1903 ed. 19.75x (ISBN 0-8371-1300-8, Pub. by Negro U Pr). Greenwood.

Worsfold, William B. South Africa: A Study in Colonial Administration & Development. LC 79-82087. (Illus.). Repr. of 1895 ed. 14.50x (ISBN 0-8371-1544-2). Greenwood.

GREAT BRITAIN–COLONIES–AMERICA

Alvord, Clarence W. Mississippi Valley in British Politics, 2 Vols. LC 59-6233. (Illus.). 1959. Repr. of 1916 ed. Set. 22.50 (ISBN 0-8462-0108-9). Russell.

Andrews, Charles M. Boston Merchants & the Non-Importation Movement. LC 67-18290. 1968. Repr. of 1918 ed. 6.50 (ISBN 0-8462-1058-4). Russell.

--Colonial Background of the American Revolution: Four Essays in American Colonial History. rev. ed. LC 31-2404. 1961. 20.00x (ISBN 0-300-00268-8); pap. 5.95x (ISBN 0-300-00004-9, Y44). Yale U Pr.

--Our Earliest Colonial Settlements: Their Diversities of Origin & Later Characteristics. (YA) (gr. 9-12). 1959. pap. 3.95 (ISBN 0-8014-9016-2, CP16). Cornell U Pr.

Barrow, Thomas C. Trade & Empire: The British Customs Service in Colonial America, 1660-1775. LC 67-11666. 1967. 16.50x (ISBN 0-674-89925-3). Harvard U Pr.

Beer, George L. The Commercial Policy of England Toward the American Colonies. 7.50 (ISBN 0-8446-1068-2). Peter Smith.

Bining, Arthur C. British Regulation of the Colonial Iron Industry. LC 68-55481. Repr. of 1933 ed. 12.50x (ISBN 0-678-00924-4). Kelley.

Bloch, Julius M., ed. An Account of Her Majesty's Revenue in the Province of New York, Seventeen Hundred & One to Seventeen Hundred & Nine. (Illus.). 1966. 25.00 (ISBN 0-8398-0059-2). Parnassus Imprints.

Bolton, Herbert E. & Marshall, Thomas M. The Colonization of North America, 1492-1783. (Illus.). 1971. Repr. of 1920 ed. 24.75 (ISBN 0-02-841590-6). Hafner.

Bolton, Herbert E. & Ross, Mary. Debatable Land: A Sketch of the Anglo-Spanish Contest for the Georgia Country. LC 68-25029. (Illus.). 1968. Repr. of 1925 ed. 7.00 (ISBN 0-8462-1141-6). Russell.

Boyd, Julian P. Anglo-American Union: Joseph Galloway's Plans to Preserve the British Empire, 1774-1788. LC 76-120233. 1970. Repr. lib. bdg. 14.00x (ISBN 0-374-90900-8). Octagon.

Brigham, Clarence S., ed. British Royal Proclamations Relating to America, 1603-1783. Repr. of 1911 ed. pap. 23.00 (ISBN 0-384-19815-5). Johnson Repr.

Brock, Leslie V. The Currency of the American Colonies, Seventeen Hundred to Seventeen Sixty-Four: A Study in Colonial Finance & Imperial Relations. LC 75-2576. (Dissertations in American Economic History). (Illus.). 1975. 43.00x (ISBN 0-405-07257-0). Arno.

Burke, Edmund. On the American Revolution. 2nd ed. Barkan, E. R., ed. 7.50 (ISBN 0-8446-0045-8). Peter Smith.

Burns, John F. Controversies Between Royal Governors & Their Assemblies in the Northern American Colonies. LC 68-15107. 1969. Repr. of 1923 ed. 12.50 (ISBN 0-8462-1229-3). Russell.

Channing, Edward. Town & Country Government in the English Colonies of North America. LC 78-63749. (Johns Hopkins University. Studies in the Social Sciences. Second Ser. 1884: 10). Repr. of 1884 ed. 11.50 (ISBN 0-404-61018-8). AMS Pr.

Christie, Ian R. Crisis of Empire: Great Britain & the American Colonies 1754-1783. (Foundations of Modern History Ser). 1966. pap. 2.95x (ISBN 0-393-09650-5, NortonC). Norton.

Dickinson, John. Letters from a Farmer in Pennsylvania to the Inhabitants of the British Colonies. LC 3-20873. 1903. 27.00 (ISBN 0-403-00186-2). Scholarly.

Durham, John G. Lord Durham's Report on the Affairs of British North America, 3 Vols. Lucas, C. P., ed. LC 73-117388. Repr. of 1912 ed. lib. bdg. 45.00x (ISBN 0-678-00647-4). Kelley.

Essays in Colonial History Presented to Charles McLean Andrews by His Students. facs. ed. LC 67-22094. (Essay Index Reprint Ser). 1931. 15.00 (ISBN 0-8369-0423-0). Arno.

Evans, Charles H., ed. Exports, Domestic & Foreign from the American Colonies to Great Britain, from 1697 to 1789. LC 75-22813. (America in Two Centuries Ser). 1976. Repr. of 1884 ed. 15.00x (ISBN 0-405-07683-5). Arno.

Gipson, Lawrence H. The British Empire Before the American Revolution, 15 vols. Incl. Vol. 1. The British Isles & the American Colonies: Great Britain & Ireland, 1748-1754. rev. ed. 1958 (ISBN 0-394-41784-4); Vol. 2. The British Isles & the American Colonies: The Southern Plantations, 1748-1754. rev. ed. 1960 (ISBN 0-394-41782-8); Vol. 3. The British Isles & the American Colonies: The Northern Plantations, 1748-1754. rev. ed. 1960 (ISBN 0-394-41783-6); Vol. 4. Zones of International Friction: North America, South of the Great Lakes Region, 1748-1754 (ISBN 0-394-45340-9); Vol. 4. Zones of International Friction: The Great Lakes Frontier, Canada, the West Indies, India, 1748-1754014vol. 5 (ISBN 0-394-45341-7); Vol. 6. The Great War for the Empire: The Years of Defeat, 1754-1757 (ISBN 0-394-42718-1); Vol. 7. The Great War for the Empire: The Victorious Years, 1758-1760 (ISBN 0-394-45057-4); Vol. 8. The Great War for the Empire: The Culmination, 1760-1763 (ISBN 0-394-42719-X); Vol. 9. The Triumphant Empire: The Triumphant Empire. 1956 (ISBN 0-394-44963-0); Vol. 10. The Triumphant Empire: Thunder-Clouds Gather in the West, 1763-1766. 1961 (ISBN 0-394-41785-2); Vol. 11. The Triumphant Empire: The Rumbling of the Coming Storm, 1766-1770. 1965 (ISBN 0-394-41791-7); Vol. 12. The Triumphant Empire: Britain Sails into the Storm, 1770-1776. 1965 (ISBN 0-394-41795-X); Vol. 13. The Triumphant Empire: The Empire Beyond the Storm, 1770-1776. 1967 (ISBN 0-394-41797-6); Vol. 14. A Bibliographical Guide to the History of the British Empire, 1748-1776. 1968 (ISBN 0-394-41686-4); Vol. 15. A Guide to Manuscripts Relating to the History of the British Empire, 1748-1776. 1970 (ISBN 0-394-41786-0). Vols. 2-7, 9, 11-15. 15.00 ea. Knopf.

Guttridge, George H. Colonial Policy of William III in America & West Indies. new ed. 190p. 1966. 24.00x (ISBN 0-7146-1478-5, F Cass Co). Biblio Dist.

Haffenden, Philip S. New England in the English Nation 1689-1713. 328p. 1974. text ed. 22.50x (ISBN 0-19-821124-4). Oxford U Pr.

Hagthorpe, John. Englands Exchequer, or, a Discourse of the Sea. LC 74-80181. (English Experience Ser.: No. 662). 50p. 1974. Repr. of 1625 ed. 6.00 (ISBN 90-221-0662-4). Walter J Johnson.

Hargreaves-Mawdsley, R., ed. Bristol & America: A Record of the First Settlers in the Colonies of North America, 1654-1685. LC 64-19762. 1978. Repr. of 1929 ed. 12.50 (ISBN 0-8063-0170-8). Genealog Pub.

Henretta, James A. Salutary Neglect: Colonial Administration Under the Duke of Newcastle. LC 70-166377. 388p. 1972. 26.00x (ISBN 0-691-05196-8). Princeton U Pr.

Kellogg, L. P. American Colonial Charter. LC 71-75291. (Era of the American Revolution Ser). 1971. Repr. of 1904 ed. lib. bdg. 14.50 (ISBN 0-306-71292-X). Da Capo.

Kinchen, Oscar A. Lord Russell's Canadian Policy: A Study in British Heritage & Colonial Freedom. (Perspectives in Canadian History Ser.: No. 8). v, 238p. lib. bdg. 16.50x (ISBN 0-87991-115-8). Porcupine Pr.

Lang, James. Conquest & Commerce: Spain & England in the Americas. 1975. 26.50 (ISBN 0-12-436450-0). Acad Pr.

Leslie, Kim C. Roots of America. 1981. 10.00x (ISBN 0-900801-38-7, Pub. by County Archivist England). State Mutual Bk.

Leslie, Kim C., ed. Roots of Aerica: A Anthology of Documents Relating to American History in the West Sussex Record Office. 114p. 1976. 20.00x (ISBN 0-686-75544-8, Pub. by W Sussex Rec off). State Mutual Bk.

Lonn, Ella. The Colonial Agents of the Southern Colonies. 1945. 7.75 (ISBN 0-8446-1286-3). Peter Smith.

Lounsbury, Ralph G. British Fishery at Newfoundland, 1634-1763. LC 69-19217. 1969. Repr. of 1934 ed. 25.00 (ISBN 0-208-00795-4, Archon). Shoe String.

McCormac, Eugene I. Colonial Opposition to Imperial Authority During the French & Indian War, Vol. 1. LC 73-172188. (Research & Source Works Ser.: No. 828). 1971. Repr. of 1911 ed. lib. bdg. 16.50 (ISBN 0-8337-2313-8). B Franklin.

Malone, Joseph J. Pine Trees & Politics. Bruchey, Stuart, ed. LC 78-53552. (Development of Public Land Law in the U. S. Ser.). 1979. Repr. of 1964 ed. lib. bdg. 15.00x (ISBN 0-405-11380-3). Arno.

Miller, John C. Origins of the American Revolution. (Illus.). 1959. 18.50x (ISBN 0-8047-0593-3); pap. 5.95 (ISBN 0-8047-0594-1, SP8). Stanford U Pr.

Mitchell, Harold P. Europe in the Caribbean. LC 73-75777. (Illus.). xi, 211p. 1973. Repr. of 1963 ed. lib. bdg. 10.00x (ISBN 0-8154-0479-4). Cooper Sq.

Mitchell, John. Contest in America Between Great Britain & France. 1965. Repr. of 1757 ed. 19.50 (ISBN 0-384-39210-5). Johnson Repr.

Mullett, Charles F. Fundamental Law & the American Revolution, 1760-1776. 1966. lib. bdg. 14.50x (ISBN 0-374-96023-2). Octagon.

Nettels, Curtis P. Money Supply of the American Colonies Before 1720. LC 64-22242. Repr. of 1934 ed. 15.00x (ISBN 0-678-00061-1). Kelley.

Oldmixon, John. British Empire in America, 2 vols. LC 68-56558. Repr. of 1741 ed. Set. 57.50x (ISBN 0-678-00524-9). Kelley.

Olson, Alison G. Anglo-American Politics Sixteen Sixty to Seventeen Seventy-Five: The Relationship Between Parties in England & Colonial America. 1973. 10.95 (ISBN 0-19-519748-8). Oxford U Pr.

Olson, Alison G. & Brown, Richard M., eds. Anglo-American Political Relations, 1675-1775. LC 73-108758. 1970. 20.00 (ISBN 0-8135-0624-7). Rutgers U Pr.

Osgood, Herbert L. American Colonies in the Eighteenth Century, 4 vols. 10.00 ea. (ISBN 0-8446-1334-7). Peter Smith.

--American Colonies in the Seventeenth Century, 3 vols. 10.00 ea. (ISBN 0-8446-1333-9). Peter Smith.

Postlethwayt, Malachy. Britain's Commercial Interest Explained & Improved, 2 Vols. LC 68-22376. Repr. of 1757 ed. Set. 45.00x (ISBN 0-678-00392-0). Kelley.

--Great Britain's True System. LC 67-18579. Repr. of 1757 ed. 25.00x (ISBN 0-678-00250-9). Kelley.

Pownall, T. Administration of the Colonies. LC 79-146155. (Era of the American Revolution Ser). 1971. Repr. of 1768 ed. lib. bdg. 39.50 (ISBN 0-306-70123-5). Da Capo.

Price, Jacob M. Capital & Credit in British Overseas Trade: The View from the Chesapeake 1770-1776. LC 80-13815. 233p. 1980. text ed. 18.50x (ISBN 0-674-09480-8). Harvard U Pr.

Reese, Trevor R. Colonial Georgia: A Study in British Imperial Policy in the Eighteenth Century. LC 63-17349. 172p. 1963. 10.00 (ISBN 0-8203-0035-7). U of Ga Pr.

Root, Winfred T. Relations of Pennsylvania with the British Government, 1696-1765. LC 71-99249. Repr. of 1912 ed. 28.50 (ISBN 0-404-00608-6). AMS Pr.

--Relations of Pennsylvania with the British Government, 1696-1765. 1912. 24.00 (ISBN 0-8337-3054-1). B Franklin.

Saye, Albert B., ed. Georgia's Charter of 1732. (Illus.). 63p. 1942. pap. 3.00x (ISBN 0-8203-0030-6). U of Ga Pr.

Sharp, Granville. Declaration of the People's Natural Right to a Share in the Legislature. LC 74-119046. (Era of the American Revolution Ser). 1971. Repr. of 1774 ed. lib. bdg. 27.50 (ISBN 0-306-71955-X). Da Capo.

Shy, John. Toward Lexington: The Role of the British Army in the Coming of the American Revolution. 1965. 27.50x (ISBN 0-691-04570-4). Princeton U Pr.

Sosin, Jack M. Agents & Merchants: British Colonial Policy & the Origins of the American Revolution, 1763-1775. LC 65-13913. (Illus.). 1965. 17.50x (ISBN 0-8032-0178-8). U of Nebr Pr.

Sutherland, Stella H. Population Distribution in Colonial America. LC 70-182725. Repr. of 1936 ed. 24.50 (ISBN 0-404-06306-3). AMS Pr.

Van Tyne, Claude H. Causes of the War of Independence. 8.50 (ISBN 0-8446-1459-9). Peter Smith.

Walton, G. M. & Shepherd, J. F. The Economic Rise of Early America. LC 78-13438. (Illus.). 1979. 26.95 (ISBN 0-521-22282-6); pap. 6.50x (ISBN 0-521-29433-9). Cambridge U Pr.

Wells, Robert V. The Population of the British Colonies in America Before 1776: A Survey of Census Data. LC 75-3483. 380p. 1975. 25.00x (ISBN 0-691-04616-6). Princeton U Pr.

Wickwire, Franklin B. British Subministers & Colonial America, 1763-1783. 1966. 16.50x (ISBN 0-691-04509-7). Princeton U Pr.

Wrong, George M. Canada & the American Revolution: The Disruption of the First British Empire. LC 68-31300. Repr. of 1935 ed. 17.50x (ISBN 0-8154-0261-9). Cooper Sq.

GREAT BRITAIN–COLONIES–ASIA

Chakravarty, Suhash. From Khyber to Oxus: A Study in Imperial Expansion. 1977. 14.00x (ISBN 0-88386-944-6, Orient Longman). South Asia Bks.

Hunter, F. M. Account of the British Settlement of Aden in Arabia. 232p. 1968. 28.50x (ISBN 0-7146-1986-8, F Cass Co). Biblio Dist.

Silcock, Thomas H. Commonwealth Economy in Southeast Asia. LC 59-7085. (Commonwealth Studies Center: No. 10). 1959. 16.75 (ISBN 0-8223-0154-7). Duke.

Willer, Thomas F., compiled by. Southeast Asian References in the British Parliamentary Papers, 1801-1972-73: An Index. LC 77-620034. (Papers in International Studies: Southeast Asia: No. 48). 1977. pap. 8.50 (ISBN 0-89680-033-4). Ohio U Ctr Intl.

GREAT BRITAIN–COLONIES–CYPRUS

Lee, Dwight E. Great Britain & the Cyprus Convention Policy of 1878. LC 35-2422. (Historical Studies: No. 38). (Illus.). 1934. 10.00x (ISBN 0-674-36100-8). Harvard U Pr.

GREAT BRITAIN–COLONIES–INDIA

Ambirajan, S. Classical Political Economy & British Policy in India. LC 76-21020. (South Asian Studies: No. 21). (Illus.). 1978. 44.50 (ISBN 0-521-21415-7). Cambridge U Pr.

Busch, Briton C. Britain, India, & the Arabs, 1914-1921. LC 71-132421. 1971. 29.50x (ISBN 0-520-01821-4). U of Cal Pr.

Dutt, Romesh C. The Economic History of India. Incl. Vol. 1. The Economic History of Early British Rule; Vol. 2. India in the Victorian Age. LC 79-80224. 1902-04. Repr. Set. 46.50 (ISBN 0-8337-0981-X). B Franklin.

East India Company Library. Catalogue of the Library of the Honorable East India Company, 2 Vols. 1969. Set. 43.50 (ISBN 0-8337-0494-X). B Franklin.

Lawford, James. Britain's Army in India. (Illus.). 1977. text ed. 22.50x (ISBN 0-04-954020-3). Allen Unwin.

Lyall, Alfred. The Rise & Expansion of the British Dominion in India. LC 67-24585. 1968. Repr. of 1894 ed. 25.00 (ISBN 0-86527-172-0). Fertig.

Sinha, D. P. Some Aspects of British Social & Administrative Policy in India: During the Administration of Lord Auckland. 1969. 12.50x (ISBN 0-8426-0144-9). Verry.

Tomlinson, B. R. Political Economy of the Raj, Nineteen Fourteen to Nineteen Forty-Seven: The Economics of Decolonization in India. (Cambridge Commonwealth Ser.). (Illus.). 1979. text ed. 37.50x (ISBN 0-333-22361-6). Humanities.

Walsh, Judith. Growing up in British India. 190p. 1981. text ed. 27.50x (ISBN 0-8419-0734-X). Holmes & Meier.

GREAT BRITAIN–COMMERCE

Anderson, Adam. Historical & Chronological Account of the Origin of Commerce, 4 vols. LC 67-20805. Repr. of 1801 ed. 150.00x (ISBN 0-678-00259-2). Kelley.

Anglo-American Trade Directory 1979-80. 63rd ed. LC 62-51858. 1979. 85.00x (ISBN 0-8002-2251-2). Intl Pubns Serv.

Anthony, Vivian. Britain's Overseas Trade. (Studies in British Economy Ser). 1976. pap. text ed. 4.00x (ISBN 0-435-84566-7). Heinemann Ed.

Ashley, Percy. Modern Tariff History: Germany, United States, France. LC 68-9645. 1970. Repr. of 1926 ed. 24.00 (ISBN 0-86527-131-3). Fertig.

Ashley, William J. An Introduction to English Economic History & Theory, 2 vols. in 1. Incl. Pt. 1. The Middle Ages. Repr. of 1888 ed; Pt. 2. The End of the Middle Ages. Repr. of 1893 ed. LC 65-26358. 27.50x (ISBN 0-678-00167-7). Kelley.

Atton, Henry & Holland, Henry H. King's Customs, 2 Vols. LC 67-21884. Repr. of 1908 ed. Set. 50.00x (ISBN 0-678-00272-X). Kelley.

Bailey, Frank E. British Policy & the Turkish Reform Movement: A Study in Anglo-Turkish Relations, 1826-1853. LC 74-80519. 1970. Repr. of 1942 ed. 24.50 (ISBN 0-86527-019-8). Fertig.

Berard, Victor. British Imperialism & Commercial Supremacy. LC 70-80613. 298p. 1973. Repr. of 1906 ed. 24.00 (ISBN 0-86527-018-X). Fertig.

Bolton, Edmund. The Cities Advocate: Whether Apprentiship Extinguisheth Gentry? LC 74-28834. (English Experience Ser.: No. 715). 1975. Repr. of 1629 ed. 7.00 (ISBN 90-221-0715-9). Walter J Johnson.

Bourne, H. R. English Merchants: Memoirs in Illustration of the Progress of British Commerce, 2 Vols. in 1. LC 14-5863. 1866. 42.00 (ISBN 0-527-10400-0). Kraus Repr.

Buck, Norman S. Development of the Organisation of Anglo-American Trade, 1800-1850. 1969. Repr. of 1925 ed. 15.00 (ISBN 0-208-00746-6, Archon). Shoe String.
--Development of the Organization of Anglo-American Trade, 1800-1850. LC 68-57590. (Illus.). 1969. Repr. of 1925 ed. lib. bdg. 15.00x (ISBN 0-8371-0329-0, BUAA). Greenwood.
Carl, George E. First Among Equals: Great Britain & Venezuela, 1810-1910. Robinson, David J., ed. LC 80-17481. (Dellplain Latin American Studies: No. 5). (Illus.). 188p. (Orig.). 1980. pap. 17.75 (ISBN 0-8357-0574-9, SS-00142, Pub. by Syracuse U Dept Geog). Univ Microfilms.
Carr, Cecil T., ed. Select Charters of Trading Companies A.D. 1530-1707. LC 76-130593. (Research & Source Works: No. 551). 1970. Repr. of 1913 ed. lib. bdg. 24.00 (ISBN 0-8337-0479-6). B Franklin.
Carus-Wilson, E. M., ed. & pref. by. The Overseas Trade of Bristol in the Later Middle Ages. (Illus.). 1967. Repr. of 1937 ed. lib. bdg. 12.50 (ISBN 0-678-08063-1). Kelley.
Cawston, George & Keane, A. H. Early Chartered Companies: A.D. 1296-1858. LC 68-57901. (Research & Source Works Ser.: No. 140). (Illus.). 1968. Repr. of 1896 ed. 22.50 (ISBN 0-8337-0506-7). B Franklin.
Chalmers, George. Considerations on Commerce, Bullion, & Coin, Circulation & Exchanges. LC 68-55502. Repr. of 1811 ed. 15.00x (ISBN 0-678-00431-5). Kelley.
--Estimate of the Comparative Strength of Great Britain. new ed. LC 67-29496. Repr. of 1794 ed. 19.50x (ISBN 0-678-00415-3). Kelley.
Chaloner, W. H. & Ratcliffe, Barrie M., eds. Trade & Transport: Essays in Economic History in Honour of T.S. Willan. 293p. 1977. 29.50x (ISBN 0-8476-6013-3). Rowman.
Chambers Commercial Guide to Lancashire, Cheshire & North Wales, 1975. 1975. lib. bdg. 12.50x (ISBN 0-8277-2847-6). British Bk Ctr.
Chambers Commercial Guide to South Wales & South West England, 1975. 1975. lib. bdg. 10.50x (ISBN 0-8277-2844-1). British Bk Ctr.
Cocks, Richard. Diary of Richard Cocks, Cape Merchant in the English Factory in Japan: 1615-1622, 2 Vols. Thompson, Edward M., ed. (Hakluyt Society. First Ser.: Nos. 66-67). 1965. Set. 59.00 (ISBN 0-8337-3518-7). B Franklin.
Coke, Roger. A Discourse of Trade. (History of English Economic Thought Ser). 1970. Repr. of 1670 ed. 12.50 (ISBN 0-384-09502-X). Johnson Repr.
Connell-Smith, Gordon. Forerunners of Drake. LC 75-7237. (Royal Empire Society Imperial Studies Ser). (Illus.). 264p. 1975. Repr. of 1954 ed. lib. bdg. 15.00x (ISBN 0-8371-8100-3, COFOD). Greenwood.
Cottrell, P. L. British Overseas Investment in the 19th Century. (Studies in Economic & Social History Ser.). (Illus.). 79p. 1975. pap. text ed. 3.00x (ISBN 0-333-13590-3). Humanities.
Cullen, L. M. Anglo-Irish Trade Sixteen Hundred Sixty to Eighteen Hundred. LC 68-56548. 1968. 15.00x (ISBN 0-678-06757-0). Kelley.
Cunningham, William. The Growth of English Industry & Commerce, 3 vols. in 2. Incl. Vol. 1. Early & Middle Ages. 5th ed; Vol. 2. Modern Times: the Mercantile System. 4th ed; Vol. 3. Modern Times: Laissez Faire. 4th ed. LC 66-21667. Repr. of 1907 ed. Set. 50.00x (ISBN 0-678-00288-6). Kelley.
--Growth of the English Industry & Commerce. 5th ed. 1968. Repr. 95.00x (ISBN 0-7146-1296-0, F Cass Co). Biblio Dist.
Davies, Peter N. Henry Tyrer: A Liverpool Shipping Agent & His Enterprise 1879-1979. 159p. 1979. 25.00x (ISBN 0-85664-966-X, Pub. by Croom Helm Ltd England). Biblio Dist.
Davis, Ralph. English Overseas Trade Fifteen Hundred to Seventeen Hundred. (Studies in Economic & Social History). 1973. pap. 1.50x (ISBN 0-333-14419-8). Humanities.
--The Industrial Revolution & British Overseas Trade. (Illus.). 1978. text ed. 20.50x (ISBN 0-391-00925-7, Leicester); pap. text ed. 9.75x (ISBN 0-391-00927-3). Humanities.
Decker, Mathew. An Essay on the Causes of the Decline of the Foreign Trade, Consequently of the Value of Lands of Britain, & on the Means to Restore Both. (History of English Economic Thought Ser). 1970. Repr. of 1744 ed. 15.50 (ISBN 0-384-11170-X). Johnson Repr.
Decker, Matthew. Essay on the Causes of the Decline of the Foreign Trade. 4th ed. LC 67-29502. Repr. of 1751 ed. 15.00x (ISBN 0-678-00864-7). Kelley.
Defoe, Daniel. Best of Defoe's Review. facs. ed. Payne, William L., ed. LC 73-128233. (Essay Index Reprint Ser). 1951. 19.50 (ISBN 0-8369-1873-8). Arno.
--Complete English Tradesman, 2 Vols. 2nd ed. LC 69-11241. Repr. of 1727 ed. 29.50x (ISBN 0-678-00579-6). Kelley.
--Plan of the English Commerce, 3 Pts. 2nd ed. LC 67-20365. Repr. of 1730 ed. 25.00x (ISBN 0-678-00316-5). Kelley.
De Malynes, Gerald. Center of the Circle of Commerce. LC 66-21687. Repr. of 1623 ed. 15.00x (ISBN 0-678-00296-7). Kelley.
De Malynes, Gerard. Maintenance of Free Trade. LC 73-115927. Repr. of 1622 ed. lib. bdg. 15.00x (ISBN 0-678-00644-X). Kelley.
Dulles, Foster R. Eastward Ho! LC 73-90632. (Essay Index Reprint Ser). 1931. 17.00 (ISBN 0-8369-1256-X). Arno.
Dunham, Arthur L. Anglo-French Treaty of Commerce of 1860 & the Progress of the Industrial Revolution in France. LC 75-151546. (Illus.). 1971. Repr. of 1930 ed. 18.00 (ISBN 0-8462-1580-2). Russell.
--Anglo-French Treaty of Commerce of 1860. LC 77-159180. 1971. Repr. of 1930 ed. lib. bdg. 20.00x (ISBN 0-374-92411-2). Octagon.
East India Company & English & Stevens, Henry. Dawn of British Trade to the East Indies. 1886. 29.00 (ISBN 0-8337-3405-9). B Franklin.
Fedorowicz, J. K. England's Baltic Trade in the Early Seventeenth Century. LC 78-67629. (Cambridge Studies in the Economic History). (Illus.). 1980. 42.50 (ISBN 0-521-22425-X). Cambridge U Pr.
Fraser, C. M. & Emsley, K. Tyneside. 1974. 3.50 (ISBN 0-7153-5764-6). David & Charles.
Gower Publications, ed. Business Atlas of Great Britain 1974. 1974. 35.00x (ISBN 0-8464-0223-8). Beekman Pubs.
Graham, Gerald S. Sea Power & British North America, 1783-1820: A Study in British Colonial Policy. LC 69-10101. 1969. Repr. of 1941 ed. lib. bdg. 17.25x (ISBN 0-8371-0453-X, GRBP). Greenwood.
Jack, Sybil M. Trade & Industry in Tudor & Stuart England. (Historical Problems - Studies & Documents). 1977. text ed. 29.95x (ISBN 0-04-942155-7); pap. text ed. 12.50x (ISBN 0-04-942156-5). Allen Unwin.
John, Wheeler. A Treatise of Commerce. Wilkins, Mira, ed. LC 76-29979. (European Business Ser.). 1977. Repr. of 1931 ed. lib. bdg. 28.00x (ISBN 0-405-09745-X). Arno.
Jordan Dataquest, ed. Britain's Top One Thousand Private Companies 1979. pap. text ed. 60.00 (ISBN 0-85938-096-3). State Mutual Bk.
Jordon Dataquest, ed. Britain's Top One Thousand Foreign Owned Companies 1979. pap. text ed. 65.00 (ISBN 0-686-25493-7). State Mutual Bk.
Kahn, Alfred E. Great Britain in the World Economy. (Social & Economic History Ser). 1969. Repr. of 1946 ed. 19.50 (ISBN 0-384-28480-9). Johnson Repr.
Kemp's Directory of Business & Trade in the British Isles. 1975. text ed. 60.00x (ISBN 0-8277-2842-5). British Bk Ctr.
Keymer, John. Original Papers Regarding Trade in England & Abroad. Prichard, F., ed. LC 67-29746. 1967. 7.50x (ISBN 0-678-00342-4). Kelley.
King, Charles, ed. British Merchant, Or, Commerce Preserved, 3 Vols. LC 67-29508. Repr. of 1721 ed. Set. 57.50x (ISBN 0-678-00356-4). Kelley.
Lawson, Murray B. Fur: A Study in English Mercantilism Seventeen Hundred to Seventeen Seventy-Five. (Illus.). Repr. of 1943 ed. lib. bdg. 13.50x (ISBN 0-87991-813-6). Porcupine Pr.
Lewenhak, Sheila. Merchant Adventures. (Jackdaw Ser: No. 45). 1970. 6.95 (ISBN 0-670-47125-9, Grossman). Viking Pr.
Lingelbach, William E. Merchant Adventurers of England, Their Laws & Ordinances with Other Documents. LC 71-172190. (Selected Essays in History, Economics & Social Science Ser: No. 315). 298p. 1972. Repr. of 1902 ed. lib. bdg. 26.50 (ISBN 0-8337-2111-9). B Franklin.
McCulloch, John R., ed. Select Collection of Scarce & Valuable Tracts on Commerce. LC 65-16985. Repr. of 1859 ed. 32.50x (ISBN 0-678-00146-4). Kelley.
Malynes, Gerard De. A Treatise of the Canker of Englands Common Wealth. LC 77-7412. (English Experience Ser.: No. 880). 1977. Repr. of 1601 ed. lib. bdg. 10.50 (ISBN 90-221-0880-5). Walter J Johnson.
Manchester, Alan K. British Preeminence in Brazil. 1964. lib. bdg. 20.00x (ISBN 0-374-95263-9). Octagon.
Misselden, Edward. Circle of Commerce. LC 66-21686. Repr. of 1623 ed. 15.00x (ISBN 0-678-00304-1). Kelley.
--The Circle of Commerce. or the Ballance of Trade, in Defence of Free Trade. LC 72-25886. (English Experience Ser.: No. 166). 1969. Repr. of 1623 ed. 20.00 (ISBN 90-221-0166-5). Walter J Johnson.
--Free Trade, or, the Means to Make Trade Flourish. LC 70-25644. (English Experience Ser.: No. 267). 136p. 1970. Repr. of 1622 ed. 16.00 (ISBN 90-221-0267-X). Walter J Johnson.
Morgan, Edward D., ed. Early Voyages & Travels to Russia & Persia, 2 vols. LC 68-6281. 1967. 63.00 (ISBN 0-8337-1836-3). B Franklin.
Mun, Thomas. Discourse of Trade. LC 68-30534. Repr. of 1621 ed. 10.00x (ISBN 0-678-00873-6). Kelley.
--A Discourse of Trade Unto the East Indies. LC 72-6257. (English Experience Ser.: No. 85). 58p. 1969. Repr. of 1621 ed. 11.50 (ISBN 90-221-0085-5). Walter J Johnson.
--England's Treasure by Forraign Trade. LC 74-370398. Repr. of 1664 ed. 10.00x (ISBN 0-678-06274-9). Kelley.
Page, William, ed. Commerce & Industry, 2 Vols in One. LC 67-19709. Repr. of 1919 ed. 30.00x (ISBN 0-678-00404-8). Kelley.
Paish, F. W. How the Economy Works & Other Essays. 1970. text ed. 17.00x (ISBN 0-333-11067-6). Humanities.
Parsons, Burke A. British Trade Cycles & American Bank Credit: Some Aspects of Economic Fluctuations in the United States, 1815-1840. Bruchey, Stuart, ed. LC 76-39839. (Nineteen Seventy-Seven Dissertations Ser.). (Illus.). 1977. lib. bdg. 25.00x (ISBN 0-405-09919-3). Arno.
Pigou, Arthur Cecil. Protective & Preferential Import Duties. 117p. 1968. Repr. of 1906 ed. 24.00x (ISBN 0-7146-1241-3, F Cass Co). Biblio Dist.
Platt, D. C. Latin America & British Trade: 1806-1914. (Merchant Adventurers). (Illus.). 1972. text ed. 11.25x (ISBN 0-7136-1309-2). Humanities.
Postlethwayt, Malachy. Britain's Commercial Interest Explained & Improved, 2 Vols. LC 68-22376. Repr. of 1757 ed. Set. 45.00x (ISBN 0-678-00392-0). Kelley.
--Universal Dictionary of Trade & Commerce, 2 Vols. 4th ed. LC 67-29516. Repr. of 1774 ed. Set. 185.00x (ISBN 0-678-00551-6). Kelley.
Pritchard, Earl H. Anglo-Chinese Relations During the Seventeenth & Eighteenth Centuries. LC 74-96190. 1969. Repr. lib. bdg. 15.00x (ISBN 0-374-96612-5). Octagon.
Puryear, Vernon J. International Economics & Diplomacy in the Near East: A Study of British Commercial Policy in the Levant, 1834-1853. (Illus.). 1969. Repr. of 1935 ed. 18.50 (ISBN 0-208-00699-0, Archon). Shoe String.
Redford, Arthur. Manchester Merchants & Foreign Trade, 2 vols. Incl. Vol. 1. 1794-1858. xii, 251p; Vol. 2. 1850-1939. 304p. Repr. of 1956 ed. LC 73-1675. 30.00x (ISBN 0-678-00750-0). Kelley.
Rees, Graham L. Britain's Commodity Markets. LC 72-185243. 1972. 12.50x (ISBN 0-236-31076-3). Intl Pubns Serv.
Reuber, G. L. Britain's Export Trade with Canada. LC 61-3841. 1960. 7.50x (ISBN 0-8020-3060-2). U of Toronto Pr.
Roberts, Lewes. The Marchants Mapp of Commerce. LC 74-80203. (English Experience Ser.: No. 689). 468p. 1974. Repr. of 1638 ed. 126.00 (ISBN 90-221-0689-6). Walter J Johnson.
Rostow, Walt W. British Trade Fluctuations, 1868-1896: Dissertations in European Economic History II. Bruchey, Stuart, ed. LC 80-2828. (Illus.). 1981. lib. bdg. 49.00x (ISBN 0-686-73124-7). Arno.
Rowland, Albert L. & Manhart, G. B. Studies in English Commerce & Exploration in the Reign of Elizabeth, 2 vols. in 1. (Research & Source Works Ser.: No. 213). 1968. Repr. of 1924 ed. 22.50 (ISBN 0-8337-3081-9). B Franklin.
SarDesai, D. R., ed. British Trade & Expansion in Southeast Asia, 1830-1914. 1977. 14.00x (ISBN 0-88386-988-8). South Asia Bks.
Schlote, Werner. British Overseas Trade from 1700 to the 1930's.-LC 75-40922. 181p. 1976. Repr. of 1952 ed. lib. bdg. 14.25x (ISBN 0-8371-8692-7, SCBO). Greenwood.
Sell's British Exporters, 1975. rev. ed. 1975. pap. 25.00x (ISBN 0-8277-2619-8). British Bk Ctr.
Sell's British Exporters 1980. LC 75-640255. (Illus.). 230p. (Orig.). 1980. pap. 32.50x (ISBN 0-85499-547-1). Intl Pubns Serv.
Sell's Directory of Products & Services, 1975. rev. ed. 1975. pap. 32.00x (ISBN 0-8277-2617-1). British Bk Ctr.
Sell's Publications Ltd. Staff, ed. Sell's British Exporters. 250p. 1981. 90.00x (ISBN 0-85499-548-X, Pub. by Sells Pubns England). State Mutual Bk.
Semmel, Bernard. Rise of Free Trade Imperialism. LC 71-112473. 1970. 41.50 (ISBN 0-521-07725-7). Cambridge U Pr.
Sheffield, John B. Observations on the Commerce of American States. new ed. LC 68-58014. Repr. of 1784 ed. 19.50x (ISBN 0-678-00612-1). Kelley.
Stevens, Henry. Dawn of British Trade to the East Indies. 331p. Repr. of 1967 ed. 27.50x (ISBN 0-7146-1105-0, F Cass Co). Biblio Dist.
Tawney, Richard H. Business & Politics Under James I: Lionel Cranfield As Merchant & Minister. LC 73-94147. (Illus.). xii, 325p. 1976. Repr. of 1958 ed. 20.00 (ISBN 0-8462-1790-2). Russell.
Thomas, Parakunnel J. Mercantilism & the East India Trade. LC 66-5362. Repr. of 1926 ed. 19.50x (ISBN 0-678-05197-6). Kelley.
Unwin, George, ed. Finance & Trade Under Edward III. Repr. of 1918 ed. 27.50x (ISBN 0-678-05199-2). Kelley.
Vanderlint, Jacob. Money Answers All Things. (History of English Economic Thought Ser). Repr. of 1734 ed. 38.50 (ISBN 0-384-63883-X). Johnson Repr.
--Money Answers All Things. 1970. Repr. of 1734 ed. 28.00x (ISBN 0-8464-0640-3). Beekman Pubs.
Wilbur, Marguerite K. East India Company & the British Empire in the Far East. LC 70-102555. (Illus.). 1970. Repr. of 1945 ed. 18.50 (ISBN 0-8462-1485-7). Russell.
Willan, Thomas S. Early History of the Russia Company, 1553-1603. LC 72-6021. (Illus.). 1956. 15.00x (ISBN 0-678-06770-8). Kelley.
--English Coasting Trade 1600-1750. LC 67-31863. Repr. of 1938 ed. 12.50x (ISBN 0-678-06771-6). Kelley.
--Studies in Elizabethan Foreign Trade. LC 74-878. 1959. 17.50x (ISBN 0-678-06772-4). Kelley.
Williamson, J. A. Short History of British Expansion, 2 vols. Incl. Vol. 1. Old Colonial Empire. 3rd ed. 470p. 1969 (ISBN 0-312-71785-7); Vol. 2. Modern Empire & Commonwealth. 6th ed. 408p. 1967 (ISBN 0-312-71820-9). (Illus.). 15.95 (ISBN 0-685-23147-X). St Martin.
Williamson, James A. Maritime Enterprise, 1485-1558. LC 74-159237. 1971. Repr. of 1913 ed. lib. bdg. 18.00x (ISBN 0-374-98634-7). Octagon.
--The Ocean in English History: Being the Ford Lectures. LC 78-12510. 1979. Repr. of 1941 ed. lib. bdg. 18.50x (ISBN 0-313-21157-4, WIOE). Greenwood.
Wilson, Charles Henry. Anglo-Dutch Commerce & Finance in the Eighteenth Century. Wilkins, Mira, ed. LC 76-29980. (European Business Ser.). (Illus.). 1977. Repr. of 1941 ed. lib. bdg. 16.00x (ISBN 0-405-09746-8). Arno.

GREAT BRITAIN-COMMERCIAL POLICY

Beer, George L. The Commercial Policy of England Toward the American Colonies. 7.50 (ISBN 0-8446-1068-2). Peter Smith.
Buchanan, David. Inquiry into the Taxation & Commercial Policy of Great Britain. Repr. of 1844 ed. 19.50x (ISBN 0-678-01018-8). Kelley.
Chalmers, Thomas. An Enquiry into the Extent & Stability of National Resources. Repr. of 1808 ed. 17.50x (ISBN 0-678-01030-7). Kelley.
Geale, R. G. International Commerce & Economic Theory. LC 68-30522. Repr. of 1925 ed. 13.50x (ISBN 0-678-01086-2). Kelley.
Gee, Joshua. Trade & Navigation of Great Britain Considered. 4th ed. LC 71-97977. Repr. of 1738 ed. 14.50x (ISBN 0-678-00576-1). Kelley.
Graham, Gerald S. British Policy & Canada, 1774-1791. LC 74-136532. (Imperial Studies: No. 4). 161p. 1974. Repr. of 1930 ed. lib. bdg. 15.00x (ISBN 0-8371-5453-7, GRPC). Greenwood.
--Sea Power & British North America, 1783-1820: A Study in British Colonial Policy. LC 69-10101. 1969. Repr. of 1941 ed. lib. bdg. 17.25x (ISBN 0-8371-0453-X, GRBP). Greenwood.
Hoskins, Halford L. British Routes to India. 1966. lib. bdg. 25.00x (ISBN 0-374-93971-3). Octagon.
LeVeen, E. Phillip. British Slave Trade Suppression Policies 1821-1865: Impact & Implications. Bruchey, Stuart, ed. LC 77-77179. (Dissertations in European Economic History Ser.). (Illus.). 1977. lib. bdg. 18.00x (ISBN 0-405-10792-7). Arno.
Mercantilist Views of Trade & Monopoly: Four Essays, 1645-1720. LC 77-38468. (The Evolution of Capitalism Ser.). 140p. 1972. Repr. 12.00 (ISBN 0-405-04127-6). Arno.
Mun, Thomas. England's Treasure by Forraign Trade. LC 74-370398. Repr. of 1664 ed. 10.00x (ISBN 0-678-06274-9). Kelley.
Postlethwayt, Malachy. Britain's Commercial Interest Explained & Improved, 2 Vols. LC 68-22376. Repr. of 1757 ed. Set. 45.00x (ISBN 0-678-00392-0). Kelley.
--Great Britain's True System. LC 67-18579. Repr. of 1757 ed. 25.00x (ISBN 0-678-00250-9). Kelley.
Schuyler, Robert L. Fall of the Old Colonial System: A Study in British Free Trade, 1770-1870. 1966. Repr. of 1945 ed. 19.50 (ISBN 0-208-00254-5, Archon). Shoe String.

Tucker, Josiah. The Elements of Commerce & the Theory of Taxes. (History of English Economic Thought Ser). 1970. Repr. of 1755 ed. 38.50 (ISBN 0-384-61903-7). Johnson Repr.

Wakefield, Edward G. England & America. LC 66-21699. Repr. of 1834 ed. 19.50x (ISBN 0-678-00236-3). Kelley.

GREAT BRITAIN–CONSTITUTION

Bonno, Gabriel D. La Constitution britannique devant l'opinion francaise de Montesquieu a Bonaparte. LC 71-157163. (Research & Source Work Ser.). 324p. (Fr.). 1972. Repr. of 1932 ed. 21.50 (ISBN 0-8337-3995-6). B Franklin.

Bromhead, Peter. Britain's Developing Constitution. LC 74-82270. 227p. 1974. 20.00 (ISBN 0-312-09905-3). St Martin.

Dartford, Gerald P. The British Constitution. 1978. pap. text ed. 2.75x (ISBN 0-88334-107-7). Ind Sch Pr.

De Lolme, J. L. & Machelon, Jean-Pierre. The Constitution of England & les Idees Politiques De J.L. De Lolme: 1741-1806, 2 vols. in one. Mayer, J. P., ed. LC 78-67366. (European Political Thought Ser.). (Eng. & Fr.). 1979. Repr. of 1807 ed. lib. bdg. 44.00x (ISBN 0-405-11714-0). Arno.

Low, Sidney. The British Constitution. 1928. 10.00 (ISBN 0-685-43865-1). Norwood Edns.

Robson, William A. Justice & Administrative Law: A Study of the British Constitution. 3rd ed. Repr. of 1951 ed. lib. bdg. 25.50x (ISBN 0-8371-3143-X, ROJU). Greenwood.

Tyrrell, Sir James. Bibliotheca Politica, 2 vols. Berkowitz, David S. & Thorne, Samuel E., eds. (English Legal History Ser.: Vol. 80). 1094p. 1979. 55.00 ea. (ISBN 0-8240-3067-2). Garland Pub.

GREAT BRITAIN–CONSTITUTIONAL HISTORY

see also Great Britain–Parliament

Ashley, Maurice. Magna Carta in the Seventeenth Century. LC 65-23456. (Illus., Orig.). 1965. pap. 1.95x (ISBN 0-8139-0014-X). U Pr of Va.

Bagehot, Walter. The English Constitution. LC 77-86594. (Classics of English Legal History in the Modern Era Ser.: Vol. 84). 1978. Repr. of 1867 ed. lib. bdg. 55.00 (ISBN 0-8240-3071-0). Garland Pub.

Baumer, Franklin L. Early Tudor Theory of Kingship. LC 66-13162. 1966. Repr. of 1940 ed. 8.50 (ISBN 0-8462-0715-X). Russell.

Cherry, George. Early English Liberalism. LC 62-19359. 325p. 1962. text ed. 24.50x (ISBN 0-8290-0167-0). Irvington.

Chrimes, Stanley B. English Constitutional History. 4th ed. 1967. pap. 3.50x (ISBN 0-19-500314-4). Oxford U Pr.

Davies, R. G. & Denton, J. H., eds. The English Parliament in the Middle Ages. LC 81-3423. (Middle Ages Ser.). 212p. 1981. 22.50x (ISBN 0-8122-7802-X). U of Pa Pr.

De Lolme, Jean L. The Rise & Progress of the English Constitution, Vol. 82. Berkowitz, David & Thorne, Samuel, eds. LC 77-86589. (Classics of English Legal History in the Modern Era). 1979. Repr. of 1838 ed. lib. bdg. 55.00 (ISBN 0-686-77117-6). Garland Pub.

Filmer, Sir Robert. A Disclosure Whether It May Be Lawful to Take Use for Money. Berkowitz, David S. & Thorne, Samuel E., eds. LC 77-89250. (Classics of English Legal History in the Modern Era Ser.: Vol. 79). 166p. 1979. lib. bdg. 40.00 (ISBN 0-8240-3179-2). Garland Pub.

Finley, M. I. The Ancestral Constitution. 1971. text ed. 3.25x (ISBN 0-521-08352-4). Cambridge U Pr.

Gneist, Rudolph. The History of the English Constitution, 2 vols. Ashworth, Philip A., tr. from Ger. 1980. Repr. of 1886 ed. Set. lib. bdg. 75.00x (ISBN 0-8377-0613-0). Rothman.

Hallam, Henry. Constitutional History of England, from the Accession of Henry VII to the Death of George II, Vol. 83. Berkowitz, David & Thorne, Samuel, eds. LC 77-86590. (Classics of English Legal History in the Modern Era Ser.: Vol. 21). 1979. lib. bdg. 40.00 (ISBN 0-8240-3070-2). Garland Pub.

Hanham, H. J., ed. Nineteenth Century Constitution, Eighteen Fifteen to Nineteen Fourteen. LC 69-11148. 1969. 44.50 (ISBN 0-521-07351-0); pap. 15.95x (ISBN 0-521-09560-3, 560). Cambridge U Pr.

Hargrave, Francis. Collectanea Juridica: Consisting of Tracts Relative to the Law & Constitution of England, 2 vols. 1981. Repr. of 1791 ed. lib. bdg. 75.00x (ISBN 0-8377-0632-7). Rothman.

Haskins, George L. The Statute of York & the Interest of the Commons. LC 77-4920. 1977. Repr. of 1935 ed. lib. bdg. 15.00 (ISBN 0-8371-9610-8, HASY); microfiche avail. (ISBN 0-8371-9612-4). Greenwood.

Howard, A. Dick. Magna Carta: Text & Commentary. LC 64-66214. (Illus.). 1978. pap. 1.95x (ISBN 0-8139-0121-9). U Pr of Va.

Jolliffe, John E. Constitutional History of Medieval England: From the English Settlement to 1485. 1967. pap. 8.95x (ISBN 0-393-00417-1, Norton Lib). Norton.

Judson, Margaret A. Crisis of the Constitution. 1964. lib. bdg. 24.00x (ISBN 0-374-94465-2). Octagon.

Keir, David L. Constitutional History of Modern Britain Since 1485. 1967. pap. 6.95x (ISBN 0-393-00405-8). Norton.

Knappen, Marshall M. Constitutional & Legal History of England. 607p. 1964. Repr. of 1942 ed. 17.50 (ISBN 0-208-01439-X, Archon). Shoe String.

Lyon, Bryce. A Constitutional & Legal History of Medieval England. 2nd ed. 1980. 16.95x (ISBN 0-393-95132-4). Norton.

McKechnie, William S. Magna Carta: A Commentary on the Great Charter of King John, with Historical Introduction. 2nd ed. 1914. 35.00 (ISBN 0-8337-2330-8). B. Franklin.

Maitland, Frederic W. Constitutional History of England. 1908. text ed. 59.95x (ISBN 0-521-05656-X); pap. text ed. 15.95x (ISBN 0-521-09137-3). Cambridge U Pr.

Marriott, John A. Crisis of English Liberty, a History of the Stuart Monarchy & the Puritan Revolution. Repr. of 1930 ed. lib. bdg. 18.75x (ISBN 0-8371-4272-5, MAEL). Greenwood.

Pike, Luke O. Constitutional History of the House of Lords. 1894. 24.50 (ISBN 0-8337-2770-2). B Franklin.

Pocock, J. G. Ancient Constitution & the Feudal Law: A Study of English Historical Thought in the 17th Century. 1967. pap. 3.95x (ISBN 0-393-00387-6, Norton Lib). Norton.

Stubbs, W. Historical Introductions to the Rolls Series. LC 68-25267. (British History Ser., No. 30). 1969. Repr. of 1902 ed. lib. bdg. 45.95 (ISBN 0-8383-0243-2). Haskell.

Stubbs, William & Cornford, James, eds. The Constitutional History of England. 2nd ed. LC 78-61574. (Classics of British Historical Literature Ser.). 1979. lib. bdg. 27.00x (ISBN 0-226-77834-7). U of Chicago Pr.

Thompson, Faith. First Century of Magna Carta: Why It Persisted As a Document. LC 66-27166. 1967. Repr. of 1925 ed. 7.50 (ISBN 0-8462-1033-9). Russell.

--Magna Carta: Its Role in the Making of the English Constitution, 1300-1629. LC 70-159233. x, 410p. 1971. Repr. of 1948 ed. lib. bdg. 20.00x (ISBN 0-374-97870-0). Octagon.

Weston, Corinne C. English Constitutional Theory & the House of Lords. LC 79-127441. (Columbia University Social Science Studies Ser.: No. 607). Repr. 17.50 (ISBN 0-404-51607-6). AMS Pr.

White, Albert B. Making of the English Constitution, 449-1485. 2nd rev. ed. LC 71-111772. Repr. of 1925 ed. 29.50 (ISBN 0-404-06929-0). AMS Pr.

GREAT BRITAIN–CONSTITUTIONAL HISTORY–SOURCES

Adams, George B. Select Documents of English Constitutional History. 1930. 40.00 (ISBN 0-685-43705-1). Norwood Edns.

De Lolme, Jean L. The Rise & Progress of the English Constitution, 2 vols. Berkowitz, David S. & Thorne, Samuel E., eds. LC 77-86589. (Classics of English Legal History in the Modern Era Ser.: Vol. 20). 1322p. 1979. lib. bdg. 80.00 (ISBN 0-686-77775-1). Garland Pub.

Elton, Geoffrey R. Tudor Constitution: Documents & Commentary. (Orig.). 1960. 47.00 (ISBN 0-521-04891-5); pap. 15.95x (ISBN 0-521-09120-9, 120). Cambridge U Pr.

Kenyon, John P. Stuart Constitution, Sixteen Hundred Three to Sixteen Eighty Eight: Documents & Commentary. (Orig.). 1966. 62.00 (ISBN 0-521-05884-8); pap. 17.95x (ISBN 0-521-09370-8). Cambridge U Pr.

Lodge, E. C. & Thornton, G. A. English Constitutional Documents, 1307-1485. 1972. lib. bdg. 20.00x (ISBN 0-374-95076-8). Octagon.

Pulton, Ferdinand. De Pace Regis et Regni. Berkowitz, David S. & Thorne, Samuel E., eds. LC 77-86638. (Classics of English Legal History in the Modern Era Ser.: Vol.29). 574p. 1979. lib. bdg. 40.00 (ISBN 0-8240-3078-8). Garland Pub.

Stephenson, Carl & Marcham, F. G. Sources of English Constitutional History, 2 vols. rev. ed. 1972. Vol. 1. pap. text ed. 16.95 scp (ISBN 0-06-044202-6, HarpC); Vol. 2. pap. text ed. 16.95 scp (ISBN 0-06-044203-4, HarpC). Har-Row.

Williams, E. N. Eighteenth-Century Constitution: Documents & Commentary. (English Constitutional History Ser). 47.95 (ISBN 0-521-06810-X); pap. 14.95x (ISBN 0-521-09123-3). Cambridge U Pr.

Wolfe, Don M., ed. Leveller Manifestoes of the Puritan Revolution. 1968. text ed. 15.00x (ISBN 0-391-00476-X). Humanities.

GREAT BRITAIN–CONSTITUTIONAL LAW

Bagehot, Walter. The English Constitution. (Orig.). (YA) (gr. 9-12). 1966. pap. 5.95 (ISBN 0-8014-9023-5, CP23). Cornell U Pr.

--English Constitution. (World's Classics Ser.). 1933. 10.95 (ISBN 0-19-250330-8). Oxford U Pr.

Bradley, A. W. & Wade, E. C. S., eds. Wade & Phillips Constitutional & Administrative Law. 9th ed. LC 77-5941. 1978. text ed. 34.00x (ISBN 0-582-48826-5); pap. text ed. 19.95x (ISBN 0-582-48827-3). Longman.

Chalmers, George. Opinions of Eminent Lawyers on Various Points of English Jurisprudence, Chiefly Concerning the Colonies, Fisheries & Commerce of Great Britain, 2 Vols. LC 70-173704. (Research & Source Works Ser.: No. 842). 1971. Repr. of 1814 ed. Set. 41.00 (ISBN 0-8337-0519-9). B Franklin.

Corwin, Edward S. Higher Law Background of American Constitutional Law. 101p. 1955. pap. 2.45 (ISBN 0-8014-9012-X, CP12). Cornell U Pr.

Elton, Geoffrey R. Tudor Constitution: Documents & Commentary. (Orig.). 1960. 47.00 (ISBN 0-521-04891-5); pap. 15.95x (ISBN 0-521-09120-9, 120). Cambridge U Pr.

Evatt, Herbert V. King & His Dominion Governors. 2nd ed. 324p. 1967. 30.00x (ISBN 0-7146-1471-8, F Cass Co). Biblio Dist.

Hayward, C. The Courtesan: The Part She Has Played in Classical & Modern Literature & in Life. Winick, Charles, ed. LC 78-60872. (Prostitution Ser.: Vol. 7). (Illus.). 492p. 1979. lib. bdg. 40.00 (ISBN 0-8240-9721-1). Garland Pub.

Jaconelli, Joseph. Enacting a Bill of Rights: The Legal Problems. 340p. 1980. text ed. 39.00x (ISBN 0-19-825351-6). Oxford U Pr.

Jennings, Ivor. British Constitution. 5th ed. (English Institution Ser). (Illus.). 1961. pap. 9.95x (ISBN 0-521-09136-5, 136). Cambridge U Pr.

McKechnie, William S. New Democracy & the Constitution. LC 71-118485. 1971. Repr. of 1912 ed. 12.50 (ISBN 0-8046-1234-X). Kennikat.

Smith, Thomas. De Republica Anglorum, the Maner of Government of England. LC 73-25629. (English Experience Ser.: No. 219). 120p. 1970. Repr. of 1583 ed. 16.00 (ISBN 90-221-0219-X). Walter J Johnson.

GREAT BRITAIN–COURT AND COURTIERS

see also Great Britain–Kings and Rulers

Akrigg, George P. Jacobean Pageant: The Court of King James First. LC 62-5508. (Illus.). 1967. pap. text ed. 6.95x (ISBN 0-689-70003-2, 103). Atheneum.

Auchincloss, Louis. Persons of Consequence: Queen Victoria & Her Circle. LC 78-26626. (Illus.). 1979. 17.95 (ISBN 0-394-50427-5). Random.

Cunningham, Peter. Extracts from the Accounts of the Revels at Court, in the Reigns of Queen Elizabeth & King James One. LC 74-127902. Repr. of 1842 ed. 21.50 (ISBN 0-404-01885-8). AMS Pr.

Dasent, Arthur I. Nell Gwyn Sixteen Fifty-Sixteen Eighty-Seven. LC 70-82824. 1924. 15.00 (ISBN 0-405-08432-3, Blom Pubns). Arno.

Dunlop, Ian. Palaces & Progresses of Elizabeth First. LC 72-107009. 1970. 10.00 (ISBN 0-8008-6209-0). Taplinger.

Esler, Anthony. Aspiring Mind of the Elizabethan Younger Generation. LC 66-26025. 1966. 12.75 (ISBN 0-8223-0054-0). Duke.

Fulford, Roger. Wicked Uncles: The Father of Queen Victoria - His Brothers. facs. ed. LC 68-8461. (Essay Index Reprint Ser). 1968. Repr. of 1933 ed. 17.00 (ISBN 0-8369-0466-4). Arno.

George Third. Later Correspondence of George Third, 5 vols. Aspinall, A., ed. Incl. Vol. 1. 1783-1793 (ISBN 0-521-04066-3); Vol. 2. 1793-1797 (ISBN 0-521-04067-1); Vol. 3. 1798-1801 (ISBN 0-521-04068-X); Vol. 4. 1802-1807 (ISBN 0-521-06918-1); Vol. 5. 1807-1810, with Index to Vols. 1-5 (ISBN 0-521-07451-7). LC 61-52516. 700p. 120.00 ea. Cambridge U Pr.

Graves, Thornton S. Court & the London Theatres During the Reign of Elizabeth. LC 72-194353. 1913. lib. bdg. 5.95 (ISBN 0-8414-4669-5). Folcroft.

--Court & the London Theatres During the Reign of Elizabeth. LC 66-27088. 1967. Repr. of 1913 ed. 6.00 (ISBN 0-8462-1021-5). Russell.

Hall, Hubert. Court Life Under the Plantagenets: Reign of Henry the Second. facsimile ed. LC 70-109627. (Select Bibliographies Reprint Ser). 1899. 20.00 (ISBN 0-8369-5236-7). Arno.

Linklater, Eric. Ben Jonson & King James. LC 74-168250. 1972. Repr. of 1931 ed. 15.00 (ISBN 0-8046-1689-2). Kennikat.

MacDonald, J. Ramsey. National Defence: A Study in Militarism. LC 70-147522. (Library of War & Peace; Labor, Socialism & War). lib. bdg. 38.00 (ISBN 0-8240-0310-1). Garland Pub.

Mathew, David. Jacobean Age. LC 72-118488. 1971. Repr. of 1938 ed. 16.50 (ISBN 0-8046-1237-4). Kennikat.

Nichols, John. Progresses & Public Processions of Queen Elizabeth, 3 Vols. LC 3-17051. Repr. of 1823 ed. 90.00 (ISBN 0-404-04770-X). AMS Pr.

--Progresses & Public Processions of Queen Elizabeth, 3 Vols. (Illus.). 1966. Repr. of 1823 ed. 115.00 (ISBN 0-8337-2532-7). B Franklin.

--Progresses & Public Processions of Queen Elizabeth, 3 Vols. LC 3-17051. (Illus.). 1968. Repr. of 1823 ed. Set. 90.00 (ISBN 0-527-67160-6). Kraus Repr.

--Progresses, Processions & Magnificent Festivities of King James First, His Royal Consort, Family & Court, 4 Vols. LC 3-29463. Repr. of 1828 ed. 108.00 (ISBN 0-404-04780-7). AMS Pr.

--Progresses, Processions & Magnificent Festivities of King James the First, His Royal Consort, Family & Court, 4 Vols. (Illus.). 1967. Repr. of 1828 ed. 140.00 (ISBN 0-8337-2537-8). B Franklin.

--Progresses, Processions & Magnificent Festivities of King James First, His Royal Consort, Family & Court, 4 Vols. LC 3-29463. (Illus.). 1968. Repr. of 1828 ed. Set. 108.00 (ISBN 0-527-67170-3). Kraus Repr.

Ogilvy, Mabell F. In Whig Society. LC 75-29167. 1975. Repr. of 1921 ed. lib. bdg. 30.00 (ISBN 0-8414-6145-7). Folcroft.

Paul, John E. Catherine of Aragon & Her Friends. LC 66-15774. 1966. 20.00 (ISBN 0-8232-0685-8). Fordham.

Pearce, Charles E. Polly Peachum: The Story of Lavinia Fenton - "the Beggar's Opera". LC 68-21222. (Illus.). 1968. Repr. of 1913 ed. 20.00 (ISBN 0-405-08846-9). Arno.

Ross, Williamson H. Sir Walter Raleigh. LC 78-17033. 1978. Repr. of 1951 ed. lib. bdg. 19.75x (ISBN 0-313-20577-9, ROSI). Greenwood.

Rowse, Alfred & Harrison, George. Queen Elizabeth & Her Subjects. LC 79-76913. (Essay Index Reprint Ser). 1935. 13.00 (ISBN 0-8369-1895-9). Arno.

Sherwood, Roy. The Court of Oliver Cromwell. 194p. 1977. 17.50x (ISBN 0-87471-874-0). Rowman.

Steele, Mary S. Plays & Masques at Court During the Reigns of Elizabeth, James & Charles, 1558-1642. LC 67-18296. 1968. Repr. of 1926 ed. 9.00 (ISBN 0-8462-1113-0). Russell.

Tillemans, T. King & Courtier: A Cultural Reconnaissance into an Age of Transition (Sir Thomas Wyatt, Etc.) LC 77-22071. 1977. Repr. of 1951 ed. lib. bdg. 10.00 (ISBN 0-8414-8603-4). Folcroft.

Tittler, Robert. Nicholas Bacon: The Making of a Tudor Statesman. LC 75-36976. (Illus.). 255p. 1976. 15.00x (ISBN 0-8214-0225-0). Ohio U Pr.

Wilson, Violet A. Society Women of Shakespeare's Time. LC 73-113370. 1970. Repr. of 1924 ed. 12.50 (ISBN 0-8046-1040-1). Kennikat.

GREAT BRITAIN–COURTS

Crompton, Richard. Star-Chamber Cases, Shewing What Causes Properly Belong to the Cognizance of That Court. LC 74-28842. (English Experience Ser.: No. 723). 1975. Repr. of 1630 ed. 6.00 (ISBN 90-221-0723-X). Walter J Johnson.

Duncan, G. I. High Court of Delegates. LC 73-138376. (Studies in English Legal History). 1971. 47.00 (ISBN 0-521-08024-X). Cambridge U Pr.

Fuller, Nicholas. The Argument of Master Nicholas Fuller, in the Case of Thomas Lad, & Richard Maunsell...Proved That the Ecclesiasticall Commissioners Have No Power...to Imprison...His Maiesties Subjects. LC 74-28857. (English Experience Ser.: No. 738). 1975. Repr. of 1607 ed. 3.50 (ISBN 90-221-0738-8). Walter J Johnson.

Hastings, Margaret. Court of Common Pleas in Fifteenth Century England: A Study of Legal Administration & Procedure. LC 75-143885. (Illus.). 1971. Repr. of 1947 ed. 19.50 (ISBN 0-208-01121-8, Archon). Shoe String.

Morrison, Fred L. Courts & the Political Process in England. LC 72-98041. (Sage Ser. on Politics & the Legal Order: Vol. 3). 320p. 1973. 20.00x (ISBN 0-8039-0126-7). Sage.

Ranger, C. Gray's Inn Journal. 1978. 50.00 (ISBN 0-379-20369-3). Oceana.

Reid, R. R. The King's Council in the North. 532p. 1975. Repr. of 1921 ed. 35.00x (ISBN 0-87471-710-8). Rowman.

Scofield, Cora L. Study of the Court of the Star Chamber Largely Based on Manuscripts in the British Museum & the Public Record Office. LC 68-58467. (Research & Source Works Ser.: No. 331). 1969. Repr. of 1900 ed. 19.00 (ISBN 0-8337-3201-3). B Franklin.

Stephen, H. State Trials Political & Social, 4 Vols. in 2. Repr. of 1902 ed. Set. 42.00 (ISBN 0-527-86300-9). Kraus Repr.

Wellesley, William L. A View of the Court of Chancery. 110p. 1980. Repr. of 1830 ed. lib. bdg. 15.00x (ISBN 0-8377-1303-X). Rothman.

GREAT BRITAIN–CUSTOMS AND EXCISE DEPARTMENT

Carson, Edward. The Ancient & Rightful Customs: A History of the English Customs Service. 1972. 19.50 (ISBN 0-208-01271-0, Archon). Shoe String.

GREAT BRITAIN–DEFENSES

Cairnes, John E. Political Essays. LC 66-22615. Repr. of 1873 ed. 17.50x (ISBN 0-678-00206-1). Kelley.

De Kadt, Emmanuel J. British Defence Policy & Nuclear War. 144p. 1964. 24.00x (ISBN 0-7146-1558-7, F Cass Co). Biblio Dist.

Freedman, Lawrence. Britain & Nuclear Weapons. 1981. text ed. 27.50x (ISBN 0-333-30494-2). Humanities.

Goldstein, Walter. Dilemma of British Defense: The Imbalance Between Commitments & Resources. LC 66-63556. (Orig.). 1966. pap. 1.50 (ISBN 0-8142-0054-0). Ohio St U Pr.

Hogg, A. H. Hill-Forts of Britain. 1979. 29.95x (ISBN 0-8464-0100-2). Beekman Pubs.

Kaldor, Mary, et al, eds. Democratic Socialism & the Cost of Defence: The Report & Papers of the Labour Party Defence Study Group. Smith, Dan & Vines, Steve. 566p. 1979. 45.00x (ISBN 0-85664-886-8, Pub. by Croom Helm Ltd England). Biblio Dist.

Lamb, R. G. Iron Age Promontory Forts in the Northern Isles. 114p. 1980. 24.00x (ISBN 0-86054-087-1, Pub. by BAR). State Mutual Bk.

MacDonald, J. Ramsey. National Defence: A Study in Militarism. LC 70-147522. (Library of War & Peace; Labor, Socialism & War). lib. bdg. 38.00 (ISBN 0-8240-0310-1). Garland Pub.

O'Neil, Bryan H. Castles & Cannon. LC 74-30843. (Illus.). 121p. 1975. Repr. of 1960 ed. lib. bdg. 15.00 (ISBN 0-8371-7933-5, ONCC). Greenwood.

Preston, Richard A. Canada & "Imperial Defense". A Study of the Origins of the British Commonwealth's Defense Organization, 1867-1919. LC 66-29550. (Commonwealth Studies Center Ser, No. 29). 1967. 19.75 (ISBN 0-8223-0138-5). Duke.

Rosecrance, Richard N. Defense of the Realm: British Strategy in the Nuclear Epoch. LC 67-26368. 1968. 20.00x (ISBN 0-231-03065-7). Columbia U Pr.

Shay, Robert P., Jr. British Rearmament in the Thirties: Politics & Profits. LC 76-45911. 1977. text ed. 23.50 (ISBN 0-691-05248-4). Princeton U Pr.

GREAT BRITAIN–DESCRIPTION AND TRAVEL

see also England–Description and Travel; Scotland–Description and Travel; Wales–Description and Travel

Adair, John. Cheriton, Sixteen Forty-Four. 1980. 24.00x (ISBN 0-900093-19-6, Pub. by Roundwood). State Mutual Bk.

Alderson, Frederick. Inland Resorts & Spas of Britain. (Illus.). 176p. 1973. 5.95 (ISBN 0-7153-6048-5). David & Charles.

Allen, Walter. The British Isles in Colour. 1965. 27.00 (ISBN 0-7134-0002-1, Pub. by Batsford England). David & Charles.

Allen, Walter & Maxwell, Francisintro. by. The British Isles in Colour. (Illus.). 1981. 18.95 (ISBN 0-393-01465-7). Norton.

Allen, Zachariah. The Practical Tourist; or, Sketches of the State of the Useful Arts, & of Society, Scenery in Great Britain, France & Holland, 2 vols. in 1. LC 73-38258. (The Evolution of Capitalism Ser.). 896p. 1972. Repr. of 1832 ed. 39.00 (ISBN 0-405-04111-X). Arno.

Anderson, J. R. The Oldest Road. 1977. 15.00 (ISBN 0-7045-0167-8). State Mutual Bk.

Anthony, John. The Gardens of Britain, Six: Derbyshire, Leicestershire, Lincolnshire, Northamptonshire & Nottinghamshire. 1979. 24.00 (ISBN 0-7134-1745-5, Pub. by Batsford England). David & Charles.

Armstrong, Patrick. Changing Landscape. (Illus.). 1979. 16.00 (ISBN 0-900963-53-0, Pub. by Terence Dalton England). State Mutual Bk.

Ashby, M. K. Changing English Village. 1980. 18.00x (ISBN 0-900093-35-8, Pub. by Roundwood). State Mutual Bk.

Automobile Association. AA Guesthouses & Inns in Britain. rev. ed. (Illus.). 264p. 1981. pap. 8.95 (ISBN 0-86145-042-6, Pub. by Auto Assn-British Tourist Authority England). Merrimack Bk Serv.

--AA Guesthouses, Farmhouses & Inns in Europe. rev. ed. (Illus.). 256p. 1981. pap. 9.75 (ISBN 0-686-31829-3, Pub. by Auto Assn-British Tourist Authority England). Merrimack Bk Serv.

--AA Hotels & Restaurants in Britain. rev. ed. (Illus.). 600p. 1981. pap. 12.95 (ISBN 0-86145-040-X, Pub. by Auto Assn-British Tourist Authority England). Merrimack Bk Serv.

--AA Self Catering in Britain. rev. ed. (Illus.). 272p. 1981. pap. 8.95 (ISBN 0-86145-043-4, Pub. by Auto Assn-British Tourist Authority England). Merrimack Bk Serv.

--AA Stately Homes, Museums, Castles & Gardens. rev. ed. (Illus.). 272p. 1981. pap. 8.95 (ISBN 0-86145-044-2, Pub. by Auto Assn-British Tourist Authority England). Merrimack Bk Serv.

--AA The Motorists' Atlas of Western Europe. (Illus.). Date not set. pap. 12.95 (ISBN 0-86145-029-9, Pub. by Auto Assn-British Tourist Authority England). Merrimack Bk Serv.

Automobile Association & British Tourist Authority. AA-BTA Where to Go in Britain. (Illus.). 224p. 1981. 18.95 (ISBN 0-86145-028-0, Pub. by Auto Assn-British Tourist Authority England). Merrimack Bk Serv.

--Britain: Four Countries, One Kingdom. (Illus.). 64p. 1981. pap. 3.50 3-copy minimum order (ISBN 0-85122-188-2, Pub. by Auto Assn-British Tourist Authority England). Merrimack Bk Serv.

Automobile Association - British Tourist Authority. AA Wildlife in Great Britain. (Illus.). 1979. 22.95 (ISBN 0-09-126390-5, Pub. by B T a). Merrimack Bk Serv.

Automobile Association of England. Illustrated Guide to Britain. 1979. 22.95 (ISBN 0-393-01227-1). Norton.

Barton, Stuart. Castles in Britain. 1973. 12.50 (ISBN 0-8277-2222-2). British Bk Ctr.

Beckinsale, Robert & Beckinsale, Monica. The English Heartland. (Illus.). 446p. 1980. 39.50x (ISBN 0-7156-1389-8, Pub. by Duckworth England). Biblio Dist.

Beddis, R. A. The Land & People of Britain. 3rd ed. LC 68-104459. (New Secondary Geographies Ser: Pt. 1). 160p. 1969. 3.75x (ISBN 0-340-07412-4). Intl Pubns Serv.

Beresford, M. W. & St. Joseph, J. K. Medieval England: An Aerial Survey. 2nd ed. LC 77-90200. (Cambridge Air Surveys). 1979. 29.95 (ISBN 0-521-21961-2). Cambridge U Pr.

Birch, Clive. Book of Chesham. 1977. 20.00x (ISBN 0-86023-014-7). State Mutual Bk.

Bird, Vivian. Bird's Eye View: The Midlands. 1980. 9.00x (ISBN 0-900093-36-6, Pub. by Roundwood); pap. 3.00x (ISBN 0-900093-04-8). State Mutual Bk.

--Straffordshire. 1974. 19.95 (ISBN 0-7134-2863-5, Pub. by Batsford England). David & Charles.

--Sunset Coasts. 1980. 9.00x (ISBN 0-900093-14-5, Pub. by Roundwood). State Mutual Bk.

Birnbaum, Stephen. Great Britain & Ireland Nineteen Eighty-Two. (The Get 'em & Go Travel Guide Ser.). 704p. 1981. pap. 10.95 (ISBN 0-395-31535-2). HM.

Bisgrove, Richard. The Gardens of Britain, Three: Berkshire, Oxfordshire, Buckinghamshire, Bedfordshire, Hertfordshire. 1978. 24.00 (ISBN 0-7134-1178-3, Pub. by Batsford England). David & Charles.

Bland, John. Odd & Unusual England. LC 75-307395. (Curiosities Ser.). (Illus.). 144p. 1974. 11.00x (ISBN 0-902875-61-2). Intl Pubns Serv.

Bloxham, Christine. The Book of Banbury. 1977. 20.00x (ISBN 0-86023-007-4). State Mutual Bk.

Brereton, William. Travels in Holland, the United Provinces, England, Scotland & Ireland. Repr. of 1844 ed. 17.00 (ISBN 0-384-05670-9). Johnson Repr.

The British Isles. 384p. 1981. 35.00 (ISBN 0-8317-0985-5, Rutledge Pr). Smith Pubs.

British Tourist Authority. Discovering Cathedrals. (Illus.). 80p. 1981. pap. 2.95 (ISBN 0-85263-472-2, Pub. by Auto Assn-British Tourist Authority England). Merrimack Bk Serv.

--Discovering English Customs & Traditions. (Illus.). 80p. 1981. pap. 2.95 (ISBN 0-686-31832-3, Pub. by Auto Assn-British Tourist Authority). Merrimack Bk Serv.

--Discovering Gardens in Britain. (Illus.). 80p. 1981. pap. 2.95 (ISBN 0-85263-456-0, Pub. by Auto Assn-British Tourist Authority England). Merrimack Bk Serv.

--Discovering Preserved Railways. (Illus.). 72p. 1981. pap. 2.95 (ISBN 0-85263-515-X, Pub. by Auto Assn-British Tourist Authority England). Merrimack Bk Serv.

--East Anglia. rev. ed. (Illus.). 114p. 1981. pap. 2.95 (ISBN 0-86143-044-1, Pub. by Auto Assn-British Tourist Authority England). Merrimack Bk Serv.

--East Midlands. rev. ed. (Illus.). 66p. 1981. pap. 2.95 (ISBN 0-86143-042-5, Pub. by Auto Assn-British Tourist Authority England). Merrimack Bk Serv.

--English Lakeland: Cumbria. rev. ed. (Illus.). 114p. 1981. pap. 2.95 (ISBN 0-86143-037-9, Pub. by Auto Assn-British Tourist Authority England). Merrimack Bk Serv.

Brown, William W. American Fugitive in Europe, Sketches of Places & People Abroad. LC 72-88424. Repr. of 1855 ed. 14.50x (ISBN 0-8371-1906-5, Pub. by Negro U Pr). Greenwood.

--Sketches of Places & People Abroad. facs. ed. LC 71-133149. (Black Heritage Library Collection Ser). 1854. 15.00 (ISBN 0-8369-8705-5). Arno.

Bryce, Iris. Canals Are My Home. (Illus.). 144p. 1979. 12.95 (ISBN 0-85937-171-9). Sheridan.

Bulfield, Anthony. The Icknield Way. (Illus.). 1979. 16.50x (ISBN 0-900963-43-3, Pub. by Terence Dalton England). State Mutual Bk.

Burke, John. Beautiful Britain. 1976. pap. 4.50 (ISBN 0-7134-3200-4, Pub. by Batsford England). David & Charles.

Burritt, Elihu. Walks in the Black Country & Its Green Borderland. 1980. 15.00x (ISBN 0-900093-48-X, Pub. by Roundwood). State Mutual Bk.

Burton, Anthony & Burton, Pip. Green Bag Travellers: Britain's First Tourists. (Illus.). 1979. 10.95 (ISBN 0-233-96761-3). Transatlantic.

Camden, William. Britannia, 4 vols. 2nd ed. LC 73-113571. (Illus.). Repr. of 1806 ed. Set. 145.00 (ISBN 0-404-01370-8). Vol. 1 (ISBN 0-404-01371-6). Vol. 2 (ISBN 0-404-01372-4). Vol. 3 (ISBN 0-404-01373-2). Vol. 4 (ISBN 0-404-01374-0). AMS Pr.

--Camden's Britannia. 1971. Repr. of 1695 ed. 92.50 (ISBN 0-384-07350-6). Johnson Repr.

--Remaines Concerning Britain. LC 77-113572. (Illus.). Repr. of 1657 ed. 46.50 (ISBN 0-404-01367-8). AMS Pr.

Canal & River Cruising. 1977. pap. 2.50 (ISBN 0-8277-5219-9). British Bk Ctr.

Carmichael, Alasdair. Kintyre. (Island Ser.). 1974. 16.95 (ISBN 0-7153-6317-4). David & Charles.

Chapman, Geoff & Young, Bob. Box Hill. (Illus., Orig.). 1979. pap. 7.95 (ISBN 0-9504143-1-X). Bradt Ent.

Clucas, Philip. A Journey Through England. (Illus.). 288p. 1980. cancelled (ISBN 0-8317-2803-5, Mayflower Bks). Smith Pubs.

Coard, Peter. Portraits of Glastonbury & Wells. (Illus.). 9.95 (ISBN 0-906230-40-3, Pub. by Kingsmead Pr England). State Mutual Bk.

Cobbett, William. Rural Rides. Martin, E. W., ed. 1958. Repr. 9.95x (ISBN 0-8464-0805-8). Beekman Pubs.

Coles, W. Crosbie & Owen, James G. Kingsley's Country: A Guide to Bideford & District. 1894. Repr. 20.00 (ISBN 0-8274-2652-6). R West.

Colourmaster. Day Outings. (Travel in England Ser.). (Illus.). 96p. 1975. 8.95 (ISBN 0-85936-004-0). Transatlantic.

--Southern England (Kent, Sussex, Hampshire, Isle of Wight) (Travel in England Ser.). (Illus.). 96p. 1975. 7.95 (ISBN 0-85933-007-9). Transatlantic.

--West Country (Cornwall, Devon, Dorset, Somerset) (Travel in England Ser.). (Illus.). 96p. 1975. 7.95 (ISBN 0-685-51761-6). Transatlantic.

Cooper, James F. Gleanings in Europe: Italy. (The Writings of James Fenimore Cooper Ser.). (Illus.). 377p. 1981. pap. text ed. 8.95x (ISBN 0-87395-460-2, COGI-P). State U NY Pr.

Country Inns: Britain. 1981. 5.95 (ISBN 0-89102-162-0). B Franklin.

Country Inns of Great Britain. 1979. pap. 4.95 (ISBN 0-89102-162-0). B Franklin.

Daiches, David & Flower, John. Literary Landscapes of the British Isles: A Narrative Atlas. LC 78-11446. (Illus.). 1979. 12.95 (ISBN 0-448-22205-1). Paddington.

Datches, David & Flower, John. Literary Landscapes of the British Isles: A Narrative Atlas. (Illus.). 288p. 1978. 14.95 (ISBN 0-87196-305-1). Facts on File.

Davies, Evan. The Book of Dulwich. 1977. 20.00x (ISBN 0-86023-003-1). State Mutual Bk.

Defoe, Daniel. Daniel Defoe's Tour Through Great Britain, 2 vols. 1968. Repr. of 1927 ed. 65.00x (ISBN 0-7146-1298-7, F Cass Co). Biblio Dist.

Delderfield, Eric R. Inns and Their Signs: Fact and Fiction. LC 75-10564. (Illus.). 96p. 1975. 11.95 (ISBN 0-7153-7112-6). David & Charles.

Dent, Alan. Preludes & Studies. LC 75-105778. 1970. Repr. of 1942 ed. 12.00 (ISBN 0-8046-0948-9). Kennikat.

Dodd, A. E. & Dodd, E. M. Peakland Roads & Trackways. 191p. 1980. 32.50x (ISBN 0-86190-004-9, Pub. by Moorland England). State Mutual Bk.

Douglas, John. A Walk Down Summer Lane. 1980. 12.00x (ISBN 0-900093-66-8, Pub. by Roundwood). State Mutual Bk.

Dunstan, Bob. The Book of Falmouth & Penryn. 1977. 20.00x (ISBN 0-86023-002-3). State Mutual Bk.

Dury, G. H. The British Isles. 5th ed. (Illus.). 365p. 1978. pap. 15.00x (ISBN 0-06-491836-X). B&N.

Eagle, Dorothy & Carnell, Hilary. The Oxford Literary Guide to the British Iles. (Illus.). 464p. 1980. pap. 8.95 (ISBN 0-19-285098-9, GB 617). Oxford U Pr.

Eastment, Winifred. Down at the Vicarage. 261p. 1967. 24.75x (ISBN 0-905858-08-5, Pub. by Egon England). State Mutual Bk.

Finden, William & Finden, Edward. Ports & Harbours of Great Britain. (Illus.). 1975. Repr. of 1836 ed. 19.00x (ISBN 0-8464-0738-8). Beekman Pubs.

Geikie, Archibald. Types of Scenery & Their Influence on Literature. LC 72-113335. 1970. Repr. of 1898 ed. 9.50 (ISBN 0-8046-0954-3). Kennikat.

Gill, Crispin. Countryman's Britain in Pictures. (Countryman Books). 1977. 5.95 (ISBN 0-7153-7450-8). David & Charles.

Gladwin, D. D. The Waterways of Britain: A Social Panorama. 1976. 22.50 (ISBN 0-7134-3159-8). David & Charles.

Graves, N. J. Geography of the British Isles. 4th ed. 1976. pap. text ed. 9.95x (ISBN 0-435-34275-4). Heinemann Ed.

Guillemin, Anne. The Kennedys Abroad: Ann & Peter in Brittany. Date not set. 9.50 (ISBN 0-392-15943-0, SpS). Sportshelf.

Hadfield, Charles. British Canals: An Illustrated History. 6th ed. LC 79-52377. (Illus.). 1979. 22.50 (ISBN 0-7153-7852-X). David & Charles.

Hanson, Harry. Canal People. LC 77-91714. (Illus.). 1978. 19.95 (ISBN 0-7153-7559-8). David & Charles.

Harvard Student Agencies. Let's Go, Britain & Ireland: The Budget Guide 1981 to 1982 Edition. (Illus.). 550p. 1981. pap. 5.95 (ISBN 0-525-93143-0). Dutton.

Hawkes, Jaquetta. A Land. LC 78-51961. 1978. 8.95 (ISBN 0-7153-7639-X). David & Charles.

Hawkins, Desmond. Avalon & Sedgemoor. (Illus.). 1973. 4.95 (ISBN 0-7153-6024-8). David & Charles.

Heath, Cyril. The Book of Hertford. 1977. 20.00x (ISBN 0-86023-005-8). State Mutual Bk.

Henderson, Ian T. Pictorial Souvenirs of Britain. LC 74-83321. (Illus.). 160p. 1975. 6.50 (ISBN 0-7153-6660-2). David & Charles.

Henderson, William O., ed. Industrial Britain Under the Regency. LC 67-30258. (Illus.). 1968. 19.50x (ISBN 0-678-05058-9). Kelley.

Hey, David. The Making of South Yorkshire. 160p. 1980. 28.75x (ISBN 0-903485-44-3, Pub. by Moorland England). State Mutual Bk.

Higden, Ranulphus. Descripcion of Britayne & Also Irlonde Taken Oute of Policronicon. LC 75-171738. (English Experience Ser.: No. 386). 60p. 1971. Repr. of 1480 ed. 7.00 (ISBN 90-221-0386-2). Walter J Johnson.

Hillaby, John. A Walk Through Britain. 1978. 7.95 (ISBN 0-395-07796-6); pap. 4.95 (ISBN 0-395-25016-1). HM.

Howells, W. D. Seven English Cities. 1979. Repr. of 1909 ed. lib. bdg. 20.00 (ISBN 0-8492-5327-6). R West.

Hudson, W. H. A Foot in England. 1978. Repr. of 1909 ed. lib. bdg. 30.00 (ISBN 0-8495-2252-8). Arden Lib.

Jebb, Miles. The Thomas Valley Heritage Walk. 1981. 15.00x (ISBN 0-09-463420-3, Pub. by Constable,Pubs). State Mutual Bk.

Jones, David, ed. The Shaping of Southern England. LC 80-40888. (Special Publications of the Institute of British Geographers: Vol.2). 1981. 35.50 (ISBN 0-12-388950-2). Acad Pr.

Jowitt, Dorothy. The Solent & Its Surroundings. (Illus.). 15.00x (ISBN 0-900963-88-3, Pub. by Terence Dalton England). State Mutual Bk.

Jusserand, Jean J. English Essays from a French Pen. LC 77-112488. Repr. of 1895 ed. 19.50 (ISBN 0-404-03624-4). AMS Pr.

Kissack, Keith. The River Wye. (Illus.). 1979. 14.95x (ISBN 0-900963-79-4, Pub. by Terence Dalton England). State Mutual Bk.

Langeren, Jacob Van. Direction for the English Traveller. LC 72-211. (English Experience Ser.: No. 197). 1969. Repr. of 1635 ed. 8.00 (ISBN 90-221-0197-5). Walter J Johnson.

Lanier, Alison R. Update -- Britain. LC 80-83917. (Country Orientation Ser.). 1980. pap. text ed. 25.00x (ISBN 0-933662-35-1). Intercult Pr.

LeHuray, C. P. Bailiwick of Guernsey. rev. ed. LC 74-522873. (The Queen's Channel Islands Ser.). (Illus.). 182p. 1969. 8.75x (ISBN 0-340-00959-4). Intl Pubns Serv.

Leland, John. Leland's Itinerary in England & Wales, 5 Vols. Smith, Lucy T., ed. LC 65-10026. (Centaur Classics Ser.). 1373p. 1964. boxed 75.00x (ISBN 0-8093-0168-7). S Ill U Pr.

Lemmon, Kenneth. The Gardens of Britain, Five: Yorkshire & Humberside. 1979. 24.00 (ISBN 0-7134-1743-9, Pub. by Batsford England). David & Charles.

Lewis, Roy H. The Book Browser's Guide: Britain's Secondhand & Antiquarian Bookshops. LC 75-10562. 224p. 1975. 14.95 (ISBN 0-7153-7038-3). David & Charles.

Liholiho, Alexander. Journal of Prince Alexander Liholiho: Voyages Made to the United States, England, & France in 1849-50. Adler, Jacob, ed. LC 67-27052. (Personal Diary, Photos, Index, Notes, 188p). 1967. 10.00 (ISBN 0-87022-009-8). U Pr of Hawaii.

Lockley, R. M. Britain in Colour. 1976. 11.95 (ISBN 0-7134-0016-1, Pub. by Batsford England). David & Charles.
Malster, Robert. Wherries & Waterways. (Illus.). 1979. 16.00 (ISBN 0-900963-30-1, Pub. by Terence Dalton England). State Mutual Bk.
Mason, E. J. Caves & Caving in Britain. (Illus.). 1977. 12.00 (ISBN 0-7091-6195-6). Transatlantic.
Matson, John A. Dear Osborne. (Illus.). 1978. 17.95 (ISBN 0-241-89870-6, Pub. by Hamish Hamilton England). David & Charles.
Maxwell, Francis. The British Isles in Colour. 18.95 (ISBN 0-393-01465-7). Norton.
Mead, Harry. Inside the North York Moors. 1978. 17.95 (ISBN 0-7153-7699-3). David & Charles.
Middleton, Tom. The Book of Maidenhead. 1977. 25.00x (ISBN 0-86023-006-6). State Mutual Bk.
Miller, George. Rambles Round the Edge Hills. 154p. 1980. 9.00x (ISBN 0-900093-27-7, Pub. by Roundwood). State Mutual Bk.
Millward, R. & Robinson, A. Upland Britain. LC 79-56047. (Illus.). 192p. 1980. 25.00 (ISBN 0-7153-7823-6). David & Charles.
Mitchell, Jean B. Great Britain: Geographical Essays. 1962. 48.00 (ISBN 0-521-05739-6); pap. 19.95x (ISBN 0-521-09986-2). Cambridge U Pr.
Moir, Esther. Discovery of Britain: The English Tourists, 1540-1840. 1964. text ed. 6.50x (ISBN 0-7100-1864-9). Humanities.
Monkhouse, F. J. & Hardy, A. V. The Man-Made Landscape. (Illus.). 96p. 1974. text ed. 5.75x (ISBN 0-521-20365-1). Cambridge U Pr.
Moreau, Daniel, ed. L' Angleterre. new ed. (Collection monde et voyages). (Illus.). 159p. (Fr.). 1973. 21.00x (ISBN 2-03-053109-X, 3893). Larousse.
Morley, Frank. Literary Britain: A Reader's Guide to Its Writers & Landmarks. LC 78-2147. (Illus.). 482p. 1980. 19.95 (ISBN 0-06-013056-3, HarpT). Har-Row.
Muir, Richard. The English Village. (Illus.). 208p. 1980. 19.95 (ISBN 0-500-24106-6). Thames Hudson.
Mukasa, Ham. Uganda's Katikiro in England. facs. ed. Millar, Ernest, tr. LC 74-152926. (Black Heritage Library Collection Ser). 1904. 18.25 (ISBN 0-8369-8770-5). Arno.
Munro, Ian S. Island of Bute. (Islands Ser). (Illus.). 208p. 1973. 16.95 (ISBN 0-7153-6081-7). David & Charles.
Nicolson, Adam. Long Walks in England, Scotland, & Wales. (Illus.). 1981. 15.95 (ISBN 0-517-54509-8, Harmony). Crown.
Nucius, Nicander. Second Book of the Travels of Nicander Nucius, of Corcyra. Cramer, J. A., tr. (Camden Society, London. Publications, First Ser.: No. 17). Repr. of 1841 ed. 14.00 (ISBN 0-404-50117-6). AMS Pr.
--The Second Book of the Travels of Nicander Nucius of Corcyra. Repr. of 1841 ed. 15.50 (ISBN 0-384-42240-3). Johnson Repr.
Oldale, Adrienne & Oldale, Peter. Navigating Britain's Coastline: Portland to Dover. LC 80-68901. (Illus.). 88p. 1981. 19.95 (ISBN 0-7153-7960-7). David & Charles.
Overton, Robert. Palm Court. 1979. 17.95 (ISBN 0-241-10110-7, Pub. by Hamish Hamilton England). David & Charles.
Parker, A. K. & Pye, D. The Fenland. LC 76-29114. (British Topographical Ser.). (Illus.). 1977. 14.95 (ISBN 0-7153-7296-3). David & Charles.
Parkes, Joan. Travel in England in the Seventeenth Century. Repr. of 1925 ed. lib. bdg. 18.50x (ISBN 0-8371-4308-X, PATE). Greenwood.
Patterson, Allen. The Gardens of Britain, Two: Dorset, Hampshire and the Isle of Wight. 1978. 24.00 (ISBN 0-7134-0992-4, Pub. by Batsford England). David & Charles.
Peel, J. H. Along the Pennine Way. LC 79-52376. (Illus.). 1979. 19.95 (ISBN 0-7153-7833-3). David & Charles.
--Peel's England. LC 77-73586. 1977. 14.95 (ISBN 0-7153-7380-3). David & Charles.
--Portrait of Exmoor. LC 75-522868. (Portrait Bks.). (Illus.). 1970. 10.50x (ISBN 0-7091-1600-4). Intl Pubns Serv.
Pilcher, George W., ed. The Reverend Samuel Davies Abroad: The Diary of a Journey to England & Scotland, 1753-55. LC 67-12991. 1967. 12.50 (ISBN 0-252-74547-7). U of Ill Pr.
The Quest for Arthur's Britain. (Illus.). 1971. pap. 5.95x (ISBN 0-8464-0776-0). Beekman Pubs.
Rackham, Oliver. Trees & Woodland in the British Landscape. (Illus.). 176p. 1978. Repr. of 1976 ed. 15.75x (ISBN 0-460-04183-5, Pub. by J. M. Dent England). Biblio Dist.
Rees, Henry. British Isles: A Regional Geography. 2nd ed. (Illus.). 1972. text ed. 19.95x (ISBN 0-245-50745-0). Intl Ideas.
Renner, John, ed. Source Book on British Isles Geography. LC 75-315804. (Illus.). 256p. 1975. pap. 8.75x (ISBN 0-456-01760-7). Intl Pubns Serv.
Robinson, Cedric. Sand Pilot of Morecambe Bay. LC 79-56054. (Illus.). 168p. 1980. 14.95 (ISBN 0-7153-7915-1). David & Charles.
Robinson, G. W. Guernsey. LC 76-58788. 1977. 14.95 (ISBN 0-7153-7341-2). David & Charles.
Russell, Ronald. Lost Canals & Waterways of Britain. LC 81-80729. (Illus.). 352p. 1982. 24.50 (ISBN 0-7153-8072-9). David & Charles.
--Rivers. 1978. 7.50 (ISBN 0-7153-7473-7). David & Charles.
Rye, William B., ed. England As Seen by Foreigners in the Days of Elizabeth & James the First. LC 66-12288. 1967. Repr. of 1865 ed. 20.00 (ISBN 0-405-08903-1). Arno.
Sasek, Miroslav. This Is Historic Britain. LC 73-18345. 64p. (gr. 4-8). 1974. 8.95 (ISBN 0-02-778200-X). Macmillan.
Scowen, Kenneth. Unknown England. Niall, Ian. (Illus.). 128p. 1980. 24.00 (ISBN 0-7134-1843-5, Pub. by Batsford England). David & Charles.
Sharp, David. Ramblers' Ways. LC 79-56062. (Illus.). 192p. 1980. 19.95 (ISBN 0-7153-7972-0). David & Charles.
Shearwater Press, ed. The Isle of Man & the English Counties. 100p. 100.00x (ISBN 0-686-75610-X, Pub. by Shearwater England). State Mutual Bk.
Shepherd, E. W. The Story of Southend Pier...and It's Associations. 120p. 1979. 27.50x (ISBN 0-905858-11-5, Pub. by Egon England). State Mutual Bk.
Shillingford, A. E. England's Vanishing Windmills. 1981. 40.00x (ISBN 0-906223-15-6). State Mutual Bk.
Simond, Louis. An American in Regency England: The Journal of a Tour in 1810-1811. Hibbert, Christopher, ed. Repr. of 1815 ed. 3.95 (ISBN 0-686-05394-X). British Am Bks.
Southwart, Elizabeth. Bronte Moors & Villages from Thornton to Haworth. Repr. of 1923 ed. lib. bdg. 35.00 (ISBN 0-8495-5011-4). Arden Lib.
Spencer, Arthur. Gotland. (Islands Ser.). 1974. 12.95 (ISBN 0-7153-6373-5). David & Charles.
Storey, Edward. Portrait of the Fen Country. LC 77-876462. (Portrait Books Ser). 224p. 1975. 10.50x (ISBN 0-7091-5191-8). Intl Pubns Serv.
Synge, Patrick M. The Gardens of Britain, One: Devon & Cornwall. 1977. 24.00 (ISBN 0-7134-0927-4, Pub. by Batsford England). David & Charles.
Syson, Leslie. The Watermills of Britain. LC 80-66088. (Illus.). 192p. 1980. 24.00 (ISBN 0-7153-7824-4). David & Charles.
Thackrah, John R. The River Tweed. 136p. 1981. 30.00x (ISBN 0-900963-98-0, Pub. by Terence Dalton England). State Mutual Bk.
Thurston, Temple. Flower of Gloster Nineteen Eleven. (Illus.). 1972. 5.95 (ISBN 0-7153-4227-4). David & Charles.
Tibbs, Rodney. Fenland River. (Illus.). 1979. 8.95x (ISBN 0-900963-10-7, Pub. by Terence Dalton England). State Mutual Bk.
Tocqueville, Alexis De. Journeys to England & Ireland. Mayer, J. P., ed. Lawrence & Mayer, trs. 5.00 (ISBN 0-8446-0940-4). Peter Smith.
Toynbee, Margaret & Young, Peter. Cropredy Bridge, Sixteen Forty-Four. 1980. 21.00x (ISBN 0-900093-17-X, Pub. by Roundwood). State Mutual Bk.
Trent, C. Devon & Cornwall. (Motoring on Regional Byways Ser). 1969. 6.25x (ISBN 0-85429-094-X). Intl Pubns Serv.
Trent, Christopher. Midland England. (Motoring on Regional Byways Ser). (Illus.). 1967. 6.25x (ISBN 0-8002-1719-5). Intl Pubns Serv.
--Motoring Holidays in Britain. (Motoring on Regional Byways Ser). (Illus.). 1959. 6.25x (ISBN 0-8002-1727-6). Intl Pubns Serv.
U. K. Holiday & Tourism: 1980. 150p. 1981. 125.00x (ISBN 0-686-71960-3, Pub. by Euromonitor). State Mutual Bk.
Unsworth, Walt. Portrait of the River Derwent. LC 78-877927. (Portrait Books Ser). 208p. 1971. 10.50x (ISBN 0-7091-2337-X). Intl Pubns Serv.
Ure, John. The Trail of Tamerlane. 1981. 24.00x (ISBN 0-09-463350-9, Pub. by Constable Pubs). State Mutual Bk.
Wright, Tom. The Gardens of Britain, Four: Kent, Sussex & Surrey. 1978. 24.00 (ISBN 0-7134-1281-X, Pub. by Batsford England). David & Charles.
Yeadon, David. Hidden Corners of Britain. (Illus.). Date not set. 19.95 (ISBN 0-393-01460-6). Norton.
Young, Jimmy. Pubs That Welcome Children. LC 79-56580. (Illus.). 96p. 1980. 5.95 (ISBN 0-7153-7965-8). David & Charles.
Young, Peter. Edgehill, Sixteen Forty-Two. 344p. 1980. 24.00x (ISBN 0-900093-26-9, Pub. by Roundwood). State Mutual Bk.
--Marston Moor, Sixteen Forty-Four. 1980. 24.00x (ISBN 0-900093-07-2, Pub. by Roundwood). State Mutual Bk.
Young, Peter & Adair, John. From Hastings to Culloden. 1980. 36.00x (ISBN 0-906418-03-8, Pub. by Roundwood). State Mutual Bk.

GREAT BRITAIN–DESCRIPTION AND TRAVEL–GUIDEBOOKS

see also Restaurants, Lunchrooms, etc.–Great Britain

AA Around Britain's Seaside. rev. ed. 232p. 1980. pap. 9.95 (ISBN 0-86145-004-3, Pub. by B T A). Merrimack Bk Serv.
AA BTA Touring Map of Great Britain. rev. ed. pap. 2.95 (ISBN 0-86145-000-0, Pub. by B T A). Merrimack Bk Serv.
AA London Map. rev. ed. pap. 2.95 (ISBN 0-901088-99-4, Pub. by B T A). Merrimack Bk Serv.
AA Town Plans. rev. ed. 224p. 1980. pap. 9.95 (ISBN 0-86145-003-5, Pub. by B T A). Merrimack Bk Serv.
Anderson, Mary D. History by the Highway. 7.25 (ISBN 0-685-20592-4). Transatlantic.
Automobile Association. AA Camping & Caravanning in Britain. rev. ed. (Illus.). 256p. 1981. pap. 8.95 (ISBN 0-86145-041-8, Pub. by Auto Assn-British Tourist Authority England). Merrimack Bk Serv.
Automobile Association - British Tourist Authority. Britain: Stay at an Inn. 1979. pap. 2.50 (ISBN 0-85630-873-0, Pub. by B T a). Merrimack Bk Serv.
--Royal Britain. (Illus.). 1979. pap. 9.95 (ISBN 0-09-128200-4, Pub. by B T a). Merrimack Bk Serv.
--Touring Guide to Britain. (Illus.). 1979. pap. 13.95 (ISBN 0-85630-854-4, Pub. by B T a). Merrimack Bk Serv.
Automobile Association of England. Book of British Towns. (Illus.). 1979. 22.95 (ISBN 0-393-01232-8). Norton.
--Book of British Villages. (Automobile Association of England Series on Motorist Travelling in England). (Illus.). 1981. 27.95 (ISBN 0-393-01501-7). Norton.
--Hand-Picked Tours of Britain. (Illus.). 1979. 22.95 (ISBN 0-393-01228-X). Norton.
--New Book of the Road. rev. ed. (Illus.). 1979. 22.95 (ISBN 0-393-01229-8). Norton.
Automobile Association of England, ed. Treasures of Britain. 3rd ed. (Illus.). 1976. 24.95 (ISBN 0-393-08743-3). Norton.
Baedecker. The Baedecker Guide to Great Britain. (The Baedecker Travel Ser.). 424p. 1981. 19.95 (ISBN 0-13-055863-X); pap. 11.95 (ISBN 0-13-055855-9). P-H.
Bartholomew, John. Observer's Tourist Atlas of Great Britain & Ireland. (Observer Bks.). (Illus.). 1977. 2.95 (ISBN 0-684-15210-X, ScribT). Scribner.
Bellamy, Rex. The Peak District Companion: A Walker's Guide. LC 80-70294. (Illus.). 208p. 1981. 24.00 (ISBN 0-7153-8140-7). David & Charles.
Berry, Geoffrey. Across Northern Hills. 1981. 25.00x (ISBN 0-686-75520-0, Pub. by Westmorland Gazette). State Mutual Bk.
Britain by Britrail: 1980-1981. 5.95 (ISBN 0-89102-228-7). B Franklin.
British Tourist Authority. AA Motorists' Atlas of Great Britain. (Illus.). 1979. 12.95 (ISBN 0-09-211480-6, Pub. by BTA). Merrimack Bk Serv.
--AA Motorists' Map of Northern England. 1979. pap. 2.95 (ISBN 0-905522-31-1, Pub. by B T a). Merrimack Bk Serv.
--AA Motorists' Map of South East & East Midlands. 1979. pap. 2.95 (ISBN 0-905522-29-X, Pub. by B T a). Merrimack Bk Serv.
--AA Motorists' Map of Wales & West Midlands. 1979. pap. 2.95 (ISBN 0-09-211280-3, Pub. by B T a). Merrimack Bk Serv.
--AA Motorists's Map of West Country & South Wales. 1979. pap. 2.95 (ISBN 0-905522-28-1, Pub. by B T a). Merrimack Bk Serv.
--AA Touring Guide to England. (Illus.). 1979. 22.95 (ISBN 0-09-125890-1, Pub. by B T A). Merrimack Bk Serv.
--Bed & Breakfast Stops Nineteen Eighty-One. (Illus.). 96p. 1981. pap. 3.50 (ISBN 0-686-31831-5, Pub. by Auto Assn-British Tourist Authority England). Merrimack Bk Serv.
--Heart of England: Shakespeare Country. rev. ed. (Illus.). 122p. 1981. pap. 2.95 (ISBN 0-86143-041-7, Pub. by Auto Assn-British Tourist Authority England). Merrimack Bk Serv.
--North West England. rev. ed. (Illus.). 74p. 1981. pap. 2.95 (ISBN 0-86143-039-5, Pub. by Auto Assn-British Tourist Authority England). Merrimack Bk Serv.
--Northumbria. rev. ed. (Illus.). 82p. 1981. pap. 2.95 (ISBN 0-86143-038-7, Pub. by Auto Assn-British Tourist Authority England). Merrimack Bk Serv.
--Seeing Britain on a Budget. (Illus.). 1981. pap. 7.95 (ISBN 0-906318-07-6, Pub. by Auto Assn-British Tourist Authority England). Merrimack Bk Serv.
--South East England. rev. ed. (Illus.). 114p. 1981. pap. 2.95 (ISBN 0-86143-048-4, Pub. by Auto Assn-British Tourist Authority England). Merrimack Bk Serv.
--South of England. rev. ed. (Illus.). 114p. 1981. pap. 2.95 (ISBN 0-86143-047-6, Pub. by Auto Assn-British Tourist Authority). Merrimack Bk Serv.
--Thames & Chilterns. rev. ed. (Illus.). 66p. 1981. pap. 2.95 (ISBN 0-86143-043-3, Pub. by Auto Assn-British Tourist Authority England). Merrimack Bk Serv.
--West Country. rev. ed. (Illus.). 274p. 1981. pap. 2.95 (ISBN 0-86143-046-8, Pub. by Auto Assn-British Tourist Authority England). Merrimack Bk Serv.
--Yorkshire & Humberside. rev. ed. (Illus.). 106p. 1981. pap. 2.95 (ISBN 0-86143-040-9, Pub. by Auto Assn-British Tourist Authority England). Merrimack Bk Serv.
Brown, Karen. English, Welsh & Scottish Country Inns & Castle Hotels. LC 79-54714. (Country Inns Travel Guide Ser.). (Illus., Orig.). 1979. pap. 9.95 (ISBN 0-930328-02-7). Travel Pr.
Cheetham, J. H. & Piper, John. Whiltshire: A Shell Guide. (Illus.). 1968. 12.95 (ISBN 0-571-04633-9, Pub. by Faber & Faber). Merrimack Bk Serv.
Choco, John & Choco, Ronalyn. Traveling on Your Own in Great Britain. 164p. (Orig.). 1981. pap. 6.95 (ISBN 0-939596-00-8). County Rd.
Colorful Britain. rev. ed. 126p. 1980. 25.00 (ISBN 0-85306-838-0, Pub. by B T A). Merrimack Bk Serv.
Complete Atlas of Britain. rev. ed. 256p. 1980. pap. 24.95 (ISBN 0-86145-005-1, Pub. by B T A). Merrimack Bk Serv.
Courtenay, Ashley. Nineteen Eighty-Two Let's Halt Awhile in Great Britain Hotel Guide. (Orig.). 1982. pap. 14.95 (ISBN 0-8038-4339-9). Hastings.
Defoe, Daniel. A Tour Through the Whole Island of Great Britain. Date not set. 12.95x (ISBN 0-460-10820-4, Evman). Biblio Dist.
--Tour Through the Whole Island of Great Britain. 1978. pap. 3.95 (ISBN 0-14-043066-0). Penguin.
Eagle, Dorothy & Carnell, Hilary. The Oxford Literary Guide to the British Isles. LC 76-47430. (Illus.). 1977. 14.95 (ISBN 0-19-869123-8). Oxford U Pr.
Eagle, Dorothy & Carnell, Hilary, eds. The Oxford Illustrated Literary Guide to Great Britain & Ireland. (Illus.). 352p. 1981. 29.95 (ISBN 0-19-869125-4). Oxford U Pr.
Egon Ronay's Guide 1977: Hotels, Restaurants & Inns in Great Britain & Ireland. 1977. pap. 8.95 (ISBN 0-8277-4928-7). British Bk Ctr.
Evans, Craig. On Foot Through Europe: A Trail Guide to the British Isles. Whitney, Stephen, ed. (Illus.). 432p. 1980. lib. bdg. 12.95 (ISBN 0-933710-11-9); pap. 6.95 (ISBN 0-933710-10-0). Foot Trails.
Fisher, Lois. A Literary Gazetteer of England. (Illus.). 1980. 34.95 (ISBN 0-07-021098-5). McGraw.
Fodor's Budget Britain, 1981. 1980. pap. 4.95 (ISBN 0-679-00656-7). McKay.
Fodor's Great Britain, 1981. 1980. 12.95 (ISBN 0-679-00689-3); pap. 9.95 (ISBN 0-679-00690-7). McKay.
Goldstein, Frances. Children's Treasure Hunt Travel Guide to Britain. LC 78-71424. (Illus.). 1979. pap. 5.95 (ISBN 0-933334-00-1). Paper Tiger Pap.
Guide & Handbook (to Great Britain) 1980. LC 51-34691. (Royal Automobile Club Guides Ser.). (Illus.). 1980. 15.00x (ISBN 0-902628-90-9). Intl Pubns Serv.
Guide to Camping & Caravanning, 1978. (A.A. Guides Ser.). (Illus.). 1978. pap. 6.95x (ISBN 0-09-132011-9). Standing Orders.
Guide to Great Britain & Ireland. (Foreign Guides). 1981. pap. 7.95 (ISBN 0-528-84535-7). Rand.
Guide to Guesthouses, Farmhouses & Inns in Britain, 1980. (A. A. Guides Ser.). 256p. 1980. pap. 8.95x (ISBN 0-86145-008-6, Pub. by Auto Assn England). Standing Orders.
Guide to Guesthouses, Farmhouses & Inns, 1978. (A.A. Guides Ser.). (Illus.). 1978. pap. 6.95x (ISBN 0-09-131971-4). Standing Orders.
Guide to Hotels & Restaurants, 1978: Great Britain & Ireland. (A.A. Guides Ser.). (Illus.). 1978. pap. 8.95x (ISBN 0-09-132001-1). Standing Orders.
Guide to Stately Homes, Museums, Castles & Gardens (Britain), 1980. (A. A. Guides Ser.). 256p. (Orig.). 1980. pap. 8.95x (ISBN 0-86145-010-8, Pub. by Auto Assn England). Standing Orders.
Guide to Stately Homes, Museums, Castles & Gardens, 1978. (A.A. Guides Ser.). (Illus.). 1978. pap. 6.95x (ISBN 0-09-132171-9). Standing Orders.
Hadfield, Charles. Waterways Sights to See. LC 76-45513. (Illus.). 1977. 4.50 (ISBN 0-7153-7303-X). David & Charles.
Hammond, Reginald J. Lake District (Baddeley's) (A Ward Lock Red Guide). (Illus.). 313p. 1979. 12.95 (ISBN 0-7063-5072-3, Pub by Ward Lock England). Hippocrene Bks.

Hammond, Reginald J., ed. Complete Thames & Chilterns. (Ward Lock Red Guide Ser.). (Illus.). 1978. 10.95 (ISBN 0-686-66748-4). Hippocrene Bks.
--Complete Wales. (Ward Lock Red Guide Ser.). (Illus.). 1978. 12.95 (ISBN 0-7063-1712-2). Hippocrene Bks.
--Complete Yorkshire. (Ward Lock Red Guide Ser.). (Illus.). 1979. 10.95 (ISBN 0-7063-1530-8). Hippocrene Bks.
Hammond, Reginald J. & Lowther, Kenneth E., eds. Complete Wye Valley, Hereford & Worcester. (Ward Lock Red Guide Ser.). (Illus.). 1978. 10.95 (ISBN 0-686-66749-2). Hippocrene Bks.
Hardwick, Michael. Literary Atlas & Gazetteer of the British Isles. LC 73-7185. (Illus.). 208p. 1973. 38.00 (ISBN 0-8103-2004-5). Gale.
Harting, Emilie C. A Literary Tour Guide to England & Scotland. LC 75-22189. 192p. 1978. 6.95 (ISBN 0-688-02971-X); pap. 4.95 (ISBN 0-688-07971-7). Morrow.
Harvard Student Agencies. Let's Go, Britain & Ireland: The Budget Guide 1980 to 1981 Edition. (Illus.). 1980. pap. 5.50 (ISBN 0-525-93090-6). Dutton.
Hollingworth, Alan. Wales in Cameracolour. (Illus.). 1978. 18.95 (ISBN 0-7110-0802-7). Hippocrene Bks.
--West Country in Cameracolour. (Illus.). 1978. 17.95 (ISBN 0-7110-0803-5). Hippocrene Bks.
Hoskins, W. G. Leicestershire: A Shell Guide. 123p. 1970. 9.95 (ISBN 0-571-09467-8, Pub. by Faber & Faber). Merrimack Bk Serv.
Jennett, Sean. Suffolk & Essex: The Travellers Guides to the British Isles. LC 72-21513. (Illus.). 120p. (Orig.). 1970. pap. 5.00x (ISBN 0-232-35623-8). Intl Pubns Serv.
Jones, J. Sydney. Bike & Hike: Sixty Tours Around Great Britain & Ireland. (Illus., Orig.). 1978. pap. 3.95 (ISBN 0-8467-0439-0, Pub. by Two Continents). Hippocrene Bks.
Kent to Cornwall. pap. 2.95 (ISBN 0-8277-2412-8). British Bk Ctr.
The Lake District. pap. 4.50 (ISBN 0-8277-7248-3). British Bk Ctr.
Lake District 30 Miles Around. pap. 1.95 (ISBN 0-8277-2423-3). British Bk Ctr.
Michelin Guides & Maps. Michelin Red Guide to Great Britain & Ireland. (Red Guide Ser.). 1981. 12.95 (ISBN 2-06-006501-1). Michelin.
Mossman, Keith. Shell Book of Rural Britain. LC 77-85019. 1978. 8.50 (ISBN 0-7153-7394-3). David & Charles.
The Nagel Travel Guide to Great Britain & Ireland. (Nagel Travel Guide Ser.). (Illus.). 750p. 1974. 45.00 (ISBN 2-8263-0405-4). Hippocrene Bks.
Nicholson, Norman. The Lakes. (Hale Topographical Ser.). (Illus.). 1979. pap. 4.50 (ISBN 0-7091-6245-6). Hippocrene Bks.
Nicholson Publications. Nicholson's Guide to Great Britain. rev. ed. (Illus.). 1978. pap. 7.95 (ISBN 0-684-15928-7, SL816, ScribT). Scribner.
Nicolson, Adam. National Trust Book of Long Walks in England, Scotland, & Wales. (Illus.). 288p. 1981. 15.95 (ISBN 0-517-54509-8, Harmony). Crown.
Oakes, George W. Turn Left at the Pub. 1977. traveltex 4.95 (ISBN 0-679-50671-3). McKay.
Philips' Road Atlas of Great Britain. (Illus.). 141p. (YA) 1980. 12.50x (ISBN 0-540-05364-3). Intl Pubns Serv.
Ronay, Egon. Egon Ronay's Lucasa Guide 1981: To Hotels, Resturants, Inns in Great Britain & Ireland & Guide to 740 Furnished Apartments in London. rev. ed. LC 74-644899. (Illus.). 830p. 1981. pap. 12.95 (ISBN 0-03-058958-4). HR&W.
Royal Automobile Club. Guide & Handbook to Great Britain - 1980. LC 51-34691. (Royal Automobile Club Guides Ser.). (Illus.). 608p. 1980. 15.00x (ISBN 0-902628-90-9). Intl Pubns Serv.
Schofield, Bernard. Events in Britain. (Illus.). 256p. 1981. 19.95 (ISBN 0-7137-1230-9, Pub. by Blandford Pr England). Sterling.
Scott, Harry J. Yorkshire. (Hale Topographical Ser.). (Illus.). 1979. pap. 4.50 (ISBN 0-7091-6245-6). Hippocrene Bks.
Simpson, Norman T. Country Inns & Back Roads: Britain & Ireland. (Illus., Orig.). 1980. pap. 6.95 (ISBN 0-912944-58-7). Berkshire Traveller.
Simpson, W. Douglas. The Highlands of Scotland. (Hale Topographical Ser.). (Illus.). 1979. pap. 4.50 (ISBN 0-7091-5887-4). Hippocrene Bks.
Swanton, Michael. Exploring Early Britain. (Countryside Leisure Ser.). (Illus.). 1978. 9.95 (ISBN 0-7158-0472-3). Charles River Bks.
Swengle, Nicole. Britain. (Pocket Guides). 1981. pap. 3.95 (ISBN 0-528-84311-7). Rand.
Travel, I. Bitten by Britain: Enjoying England. LC 78-58515. (Illus.). 1978. pap. 3.25 (ISBN 0-915010-22-4). Sutter House.
Verstappen, Peter, ed. Rand McNally Guide to Great Britain & Ireland. LC 78-70556. (Illus.). 1981. pap. 7.95 (ISBN 0-528-84535-7). Rand.
Williams, Peter S. Recommended Wayside Inns of Britain: 1981. (Illus.). 168p. (Orig.). 1981. pap. cancelled (ISBN 0-933982-11-9, Herald Advisory Service). Bradt Ent.
Willis, Jenny, ed. British Tourist Authority Guide to the North of England. (Illus.). 158p. 1980. bds. 20.00x (ISBN 0-7099-0384-7, Pub. by Croom Helm Ltd England). Biblio Dist.
Winks, Robin. An American's Guide to Britain. LC 77-23341. 1977. pap. 6.95 (ISBN 0-684-15189-8, ScribT). Scribner.

GREAT BRITAIN–DESCRIPTION AND TRAVEL–HISTORY

Bord, Janet & Bord, Colin. A Guide to Ancient Sites in Britain. (Illus.). 183p. 1981. pap. 7.95 (ISBN 0-586-08309-X, Pub. by Granada England). Academy Chi Ltd.
Brown, Raymond L. Robert Burns's Tour of the Highlands & Stirlingshire 1787. (Illus.). 82p. 1973. 8.50x (ISBN 0-87471-439-7). Rowman.
Christian, Roy. Vanishing Britain. 1977. 8.95 (ISBN 0-7153-7346-3). David & Charles.
Clifford, James L. Dr. Campbell's Diary of a Visit to England in 1775. 1947. lib. bdg. 15.00 (ISBN 0-8414-3043-8). Folcroft.
Denney, Maryn. London & South-East England. 124p. 1980. 25.00x (ISBN 0-903485-71-0, Pub. by Moorland England). State Mutual Bk.
McKnight, Hugh. The Shell Book of Inland Waterways. (Illus.). 528p. 1981. 30.00 (ISBN 0-7153-8239-X). David & Charles.
Murray's Handbook for Devon & Cornwall. (Illus.). 293p. 1971. Repr. of 1859 ed. 4.50 (ISBN 0-7153-5293-8). David & Charles.
Robert Nicholson Publications. Nicholson's Guide to Historic Britain. 272p. (Orig.). 1981. pap. 7.95 (ISBN 0-684-17280-1, ScribT). Scribner.
Strugnell, Kenneth. Seagates to the Saxon Shore. (Illus.). 1979. 10.00 (ISBN 0-900963-20-4, Pub. by Terence Dalton England). State Mutual Bk.
Swanton, Michael. Exploring Early Britain. (Countryside Leisure Ser.). (Illus.). 1978. 9.95 (ISBN 0-7158-0472-3). Charles River Bks.

GREAT BRITAIN–DESCRIPTION AND TRAVEL–POETRY

Aubin, Robert A. Topographical Poetry in Eighteenth Century England. (MLA Rev. Fund Ser.). 1936. pap. 32.00 (ISBN 0-527-03800-8). Kraus Repr.
Daniell, William & Ayton, Richard. Voyage Round Great Britain, 2 vols. ltd. ed. (Illus.). 1248p. 1978. Repr. Set. slipcased 100.00x (ISBN 0-85967-472-X, Pub. by Scolar Pr England). Biblio Dist.
Drayton, Michael. Poly-Olbion: A Chronologic Description of Great Britain, 3 Vols. in One. (Spencer Soc.: Nos. 1-3). (Illus.). 1966. 78.50 (ISBN 0-8337-0921-6). B Franklin.
Knight, G. Wilson. This Sceptred Isle. 1940. lib. bdg. 12.50 (ISBN 0-8414-5490-6). Folcroft.

GREAT BRITAIN–DIPLOMATIC AND CONSULAR SERVICE

Bonham, Hilledge L. British Consuls in the Confederacy. LC 11-31660. (Columbia University Studies in the Social Sciences: No. 111). Repr. of 1911 ed. 12.50 (ISBN 0-404-51111-2). AMS Pr.
Inglis, Brian. Roger Casement. LC 73-15422. 1974. 8.95 (ISBN 0-15-178327-6). HarBraceJ.
Platt, D. C. Cinderella Service: British Consuls Since 1825. 1971. 17.50 (ISBN 0-208-01209-5, Archon). Shoe String.
Temperley, H. W. & Penson, L. M. Century of Diplomatic Blue Books 1814-1914. 600p. 1966. 32.50x (ISBN 0-7146-1519-6, F Cass Co). Biblio Dist.
Willson, Beckles. Friendly Relations. LC 71-90696. (Essay Index Reprint Ser). 1934. 22.00 (ISBN 0-8369-1266-7). Arno.

GREAT BRITAIN–DIRECTORIES

Anderson, I. G., ed. Councils, Committees & Boards: A Handbook of Advisory, Consultative, Executive & Similar Bodies in British Public Life. 4th ed. 500p. 1981. 115.00 (ISBN 0-686-71975-1, Pub. by CBD Research Ltd). Gale.
--Current British Directories. 9th ed. LC 53-26894. 1979. 105.00x (ISBN 0-900246-31-6). Intl Pubns Serv.
Henderson, G. P. & Henderson, S. P., eds. Directory of British Associations & Associations in Ireland. 6th ed. xiv, 486p. 1980. 125.00 (ISBN 0-686-74473-X). Gale.
--Directory of British Associations & Associations in Ireland. 6th ed. 488p. 1980. 120.00x (ISBN 0-900246-34-0). Intl Pubns Serv.
Kelly's Handbook 1977. 101st ed. LC 78-5253. 1977. 40.00x (ISBN 0-610-00493-X). Intl Pubns Serv.
The Times One Thousand, Nineteen Eighty to Nineteen Eighty One. 360p. 1980. 47.50x (ISBN 0-930466-31-4). Meckler Bks.

GREAT BRITAIN–ECONOMIC CONDITIONS

Aaronovitch, Sam. The Ruling Class: A Study of British Finance Capital. LC 78-23485. 1979. Repr. of 1961 ed. lib. bdg. 18.50x (ISBN 0-313-20764-X, AARC). Greenwood.
Addy, Sidney O. Church & Manor: A Study in English Economic History. LC 70-107902. (Illus.). Repr. of 1913 ed. 19.50x (ISBN 0-678-00632-6). Kelley.
Aldcroft, Derek H. & Richardson, Harry. British Economy Eighteen Seventy to Nineteen Thirty Nine. 1969. text ed. 8.75x (ISBN 0-333-10182-0). Humanities.
Aldcroft, Derek H. & Fearon, Peter, eds. British Economic Fluctuations: Seventeen-Ninety to Nineteen Thirty-Nine. LC 77-178900. 1972. text ed. 19.95 (ISBN 0-312-10045-0). St Martin.
Andrews, Charles M. British Committees, Commissions, & Councils of Trade & Plantations: 1622-1675. LC 78-63925. (Johns Hopkins University. Studies in the Social Sciences. Twenty-Sixth Ser. 1908: 1-3). Repr. of 1908 ed. 11.50 (ISBN 0-404-61175-3). AMS Pr.
--The Old English Manor: A Study in English Economic History. LC 78-64257. (Johns Hopkins University. Studies in the Social Sciences. Extra Volumes: 12). Repr. of 1892 ed. 25.50 (ISBN 0-404-61360-8). AMS Pr.
Appleby, Joyce O. Economic Thought & Ideology in Seventeenth-Century England. LC 77-85527. 304p. 1980. pap. 4.95 (ISBN 0-691-00779-9). Princeton U Pr.
--Economic Thought & Ideology in Seventeenth-Century England. LC 77-85527. 1978. text ed. 22.50 (ISBN 0-691-05265-4). Princeton U Pr.
Ashley, William J. An Introduction to English Economic History & Theory, 2 vols. in 1. Incl. Pt. 1. The Middle Ages. Repr. of 1888 ed; Pt. 2. The End of the Middle Ages. Repr. of 1893 ed. LC 65-26358. 27.50x (ISBN 0-678-00167-7). Kelley.
--Surveys: Historic & Economic. LC 66-21366. Repr. of 1900 ed. 22.50x (ISBN 0-678-00170-7). Kelley.
Ashton, Thomas S. An Economic History of England: The Eighteenth Century. 270p. 1972. pap. 12.95x (ISBN 0-416-57360-6). Methuen Inc.
--Industrial Revolution: 1760-1830. 1948. pap. 3.95x (ISBN 0-19-500252-0, 109). Oxford U Pr.
Atkinson, A. B., et al. Wealth & Personal Incomes. LC 77-30556. 1978. text ed. 37.00 (ISBN 0-08-022450-4). Pergamon.
Bacon, Robert & Eltis, Walter. Britain's Economic Problem: Too Few Producers. 2nd ed. LC 78-52386. 1978. 19.95x (ISBN 0-312-09941-X). St Martin.
Beales, H. L. Industrial Revolution, 1750-1850. 2nd ed. LC 67-17931. 1958. 10.00x (ISBN 0-678-00216-9). Kelley.
Beard, Charles A. Industrial Revolution. LC 69-13813. Repr. of 1927 ed. lib. bdg. 15.00 (ISBN 0-8371-2168-X, BEIR). Greenwood.
Beckerman, Wilfred, ed. Slow Growth in Britain: Causes & Consequences. (Illus.). 246p. 1979. text ed. 23.50x (ISBN 0-19-828420-9). Oxford U Pr.
Bellers, John. Essays About the Poor, Manufacturers, Trade Plantations, & Immorality, 3 vols. in 1. Bd. with A Discourse Touching Provision. Hale, Sir Matthew. Repr. of 1683 ed; A Discourse of the Poor. North, Roger. Repr. of 1753 ed. (History of English Economic Thought). Repr. of 1699 ed. 14.00 (ISBN 0-384-03860-3). Johnson Repr.
Berg, Maxine. The Machinery Question & the Making of Political Economy: 1815-1848. LC 79-51223. (Illus.). 1980. 39.50 (ISBN 0-521-22782-8). Cambridge U Pr.
Beveridge, Lord. Prices & Wages in England. (Illus.). 756p. 1965. Repr. of 1939 ed. 47.50x (ISBN 0-7146-1271-5, F Cass Co). Biblio Dist.
Birch, R. C. The Shaping of the Welfare State. (Seminar Studies in History Ser.). 126p. 1974. pap. text ed. 5.50x (ISBN 0-582-35200-2). Longman.
Bolton, J. L. The Medieval English Economy: Eleven Fifty to Fifteen Hundred. (Rowman & Littlefield University Library). (Illus.). 400p. 1980. 25.00x (ISBN 0-8476-6234-9); pap. 16.00x (ISBN 0-8476-6235-7). Rowman.
Bosanquet, Helen. The Strength of the People: A Study in Social Economics. 2nd ed. LC 79-56950. (The English Working Class Ser.). 1980. lib. bdg. 30.00 (ISBN 0-8240-0104-4). Garland Pub.
Botsford, J. B. English Society in the Eighteenth Century As Influenced from Oversea. 1965. lib. bdg. 20.00x (ISBN 0-374-90817-6). Octagon.
Bowley, A. L. & Burnett-Hurst, A. R. Livelihood & Poverty: A Study in the Economic Conditions of Working-Class Households in Northampton, Warrington, Stanley, & Reading. LC 79-59651. (The English Working Class Ser.). 1980. lib. bdg. 22.00 (ISBN 0-8240-0105-2). Garland Pub.
Branton, Noel. Economic Organization of Modern Britain. 1968. pap. 4.25x (ISBN 0-8426-1181-9). Verry.
Brentano, Lujo. Geschichte De Wirtschaftlichen Entwicklung Englands, 3 Vols. in 4. LC 68-56762. (Research & Source Works Ser.: No. 246). (Ger). 1969. Repr. of 1927 ed. Set. 101.00 (ISBN 0-8337-0367-6). B Franklin.
Budd, Alan. The Politics of Economic Planning. LC 78-66341. 1978. 20.95 (ISBN 0-03-046211-8). Praeger.
Cain, Peter J. Economic Foundations of British Overseas Expansion 1815-1914. (Studies in Economic & Social History). 1980. pap. text ed. 5.25x (ISBN 0-333-23284-4). Humanities.
Cairncross, Alec, ed. Britain's Economic Prospects Reconsidered. LC 71-37996. 1972. 19.00 (ISBN 0-87395-174-3). State U NY Pr.
Cannan, Edwin, ed. Paper Pound of 1797-1812. 2nd ed. 72p. 1970. Repr. of 1925 ed. 24.00x (ISBN 0-7146-1210-3, F Cass Co). Biblio Dist.
Carlson, Reynold E. British Block Grants & Central-Local Finance. LC 78-64203. (Johns Hopkins University. Studies in the Social Sciences. Sixty-Fifth Ser. 1947: 1). Repr. of 1947 ed. 21.00 (ISBN 0-404-61309-8). AMS Pr.
Chalmers, George. Estimate of the Comparative Strength of Great Britain. new ed. LC 67-29496. Repr. of 1794 ed. 19.50x (ISBN 0-678-00415-3). Kelley.
Chalmers, Thomas. An Enquiry into the Extent & Stability of National Resources. Repr. of 1808 ed. 17.50x (ISBN 0-678-01030-7). Kelley.
Chaloner, W. H. & Ratcliffe, Barrie M., eds. Trade & Transport: Essays in Economic History in Honour of T.S. Willan. 293p. 1977. 29.50x (ISBN 0-8476-6013-3). Rowman.
Chambers, Jonathan D. The Workshop of the World: British Economic History from 1820 to 1880. 2nd ed. 1968. pap. 5.95x (ISBN 0-19-888032-4). Oxford U Pr.
Chappell, D. J. An Economic History of England. 320p. 1980. pap. 12.95x (ISBN 0-7121-0587-5). Intl Ideas.
Chartres, J. A. Internal Trade in England 1500-1700. (Studies in Economic & Social History). 1977. pap. text ed. 4.00x (ISBN 0-333-18358-4). Humanities.
Cheyney, Edward P. Introduction to the Industrial & Social History of England. rev. ed. LC 79-92609. (BCL Ser.: No. I). (Illus.). Repr. of 1920 ed. 12.50 (ISBN 0-404-01524-7). AMS Pr.
--An Introduction to the Industrial & Social History of England. 1977. Repr. of 1912 ed. lib. bdg. 25.00 (ISBN 0-8414-1845-4). Folcroft.
Chisholm, M. & O'Sullivan, P. Freight Flows & Spatial Aspects of the British Economy. LC 72-83592. (Geographical Studies: No. 4). (Illus.). 140p. 1973. 27.50 (ISBN 0-521-08672-8). Cambridge U Pr.
Chrystal, K. A. Controversies in British Macroeconomics. 1981. pap. text ed. 15.00x (ISBN 0-86003-123-3). Verry.
Church, Roy A. Economic & Social Change in a Midland Town: Victorian Nottingham, 1815-1900. (Illus.). 409p. 1966. 27.50x (ISBN 0-7146-1290-1, F Cass Co). Biblio Dist.
Clapham, John H. A Concise Economic History of Britain, from the Earliest Times to 1750. LC 75-41059. (BCL Ser.: No. II). 1976. Repr. of 1949 ed. 25.00 (ISBN 0-404-14654-6). AMS Pr.
Clapp, B. W., ed. Documents in English Economic History, Vol. 2: England Since 1760. 544p. 1976. 40.00x (ISBN 0-8476-6085-0). Rowman.
Coats, B. E. & Tawstron, E. M. Regional Variations in Britain: Studies in Economic & Social Geography. 1972. 40.00 (ISBN 0-7134-2103-7, Pub. by Batsford England). David & Charles.
Coleman, D. C. Courtaulds: An Economic & Social History Vol. III: Crisis & Change 1940-65. (Illus.). 352p. 1980. 44.00x (ISBN 0-19-920111-0). Oxford U Pr.
--The Economy of England 1450-1750. (Opus 81). (Illus.). 1976. 11.50x (ISBN 0-19-215355-2); pap. 6.95x (ISBN 0-19-289070-0). Oxford U Pr.
--Industry in Tudor & Stuart England. (Studies in Economic & Social History Ser.). 80p. 1975. pap. text ed. 2.50x (ISBN 0-333-14351-5). Humanities.
Colquhoun, Patrick. A Treatise on the Wealth, Power & Resources of the British Empire. 2nd ed. 1815. 54.00 (ISBN 0-384-09710-3). Johnson Repr.
Court, W. H. Scarcity & Choice in History. LC 74-113460. 1970. lib. bdg. 15.00x (ISBN 0-678-08017-8). Kelley.
Court, William H. British Economic History, Eighteen Seventy - Nineteen Fourteen. (Orig.). 1966. 53.95 (ISBN 0-521-04731-5); pap. 19.50x (ISBN 0-521-09362-7). Cambridge U Pr.
--Concise Economic History of Britain. pap. 11.95x (ISBN 0-521-09217-5). Cambridge U Pr.

Cowherd, Raymond G. The Humanitarians & the Ten Hour Movement in England. (Kress Library of Business & Economics: No. 10). (Illus.). 1956. pap. 5.00x (ISBN 0-678-09905-7, Baker Lib). Kelley.

Crawford, Jonathan, ed. Directory of City Connections 1979-80. 1979. 85.00x (ISBN 0-903684-04-7). Nichols Pub.

Cunningham, William. The Growth of English Industry & Commerce, 3 vols. in 2. Incl. Vol. 1. Early & Middle Ages. 5th ed; Vol. 2. Modern Times: the Mercantile System. 4th ed; Vol. 3. Modern Times: Laissez Faire. 4th ed. LC 66-21667. Repr. of 1907 ed. Set. 50.00x (ISBN 0-678-00288-6). Kelley.

Davenport, Frances G. Economic Development of a Norfolk Manor, 1086-1565. (Illus.). 106p. 1967. Repr. 25.00x (ISBN 0-7146-1297-9, F Cass Co). Biblio Dist.

Davies, Brinley. Business Finance & the City of London. 2nd ed. (Studies in the British Economy). (Orig.). 1980. pap. text ed. 6.00x (ISBN 0-435-84579-9). Heinemann Ed.

--United Kingdom & the World Monetary System: Studies in the British Economy Ser. 1976. pap. text ed. 7.00x (ISBN 0-435-84350-8). Heinemann Ed.

Deane, Phyllis & Cole, W. A. British Economic Growth, Sixteen Eighty-Eight - Nineteen Fifty-Nine: Trends & Structure. 2nd ed. LC 67-21956. (Cambridge Department of Applied Economics Monographs). (Illus.). 1969. 47.50 (ISBN 0-521-04801-X); pap. 14.95x (ISBN 0-521-09569-7). Cambridge U Pr.

Deaton, Angus. Models & Projections of Demand in Post-War Britain. LC 74-19935. (Cambridge Studies in Applied Econometrics: Vol. 1). 261p. 1975. text ed. 29.95x (ISBN 0-412-13640-6, Pub. by Chapman & Hall England). Methuen Inc.

Decker, Mathew. An Essay on the Causes of the Decline of the Foreign Trade, Consequently of the Value of Lands of Britain, & on the Means to Restore Both. (History of English Economic Thought Ser). 1970. Repr. of 1744 ed. 15.50 (ISBN 0-384-11170-X). Johnson Repr.

Decker, Matthew. Essay on the Causes of the Decline of the Foreign Trade. 4th ed. LC 67-29502. Repr. of 1751 ed. 15.00x (ISBN 0-678-00864-7). Kelley.

D'Eichthal, Gustave. A French Sociologist Looks at Britain: Gustave d'Eichthal & British Society in 1828. Ratcliffe, Barrie M., ed. Chaloner, W. H., tr. LC 77-1899. 192p. 1977. 13.75x (ISBN 0-87471-963-1). Rowman.

Derry, T. K. & Blakeway, M. G. The Making of Britain, 2 vols. Incl. Vol. 1. Life & Work to the Close of the Middle Ages. pap. 6.95 (ISBN 0-7195-1816-4); Vol. 2. Life & Work from the Renaissance to the Industrial Revolution. pap. 6.95 (ISBN 0-7195-1834-2). (gr. 9-12). 10.00 (ISBN 0-7195-1833-4). Transatlantic.

Derry, T. K. & Jarman, T. L. Making of Modern Britain: Life & Work from George Third to Elizabeth Second. (Illus.). 1971. pap. 3.95 (ISBN 0-7195-0304-3). Transatlantic.

Devegh, Imre. The Pound Sterling. Wilkins, Mira, ed. LC 78-3908. (International Finance Ser.). 1978. Repr. of 1939 ed. lib. bdg. 10.00x (ISBN 0-405-11213-0). Arno.

A Discourse of the Common Weal of This Realm of England. LC 75-179393. (Research & Source Works Ser.). 284p. 1972. Repr. of 1893 ed. 20.50 (ISBN 0-8337-1533-X). B Franklin.

Dixon, R. J. & Thirlwall, A. P. Regional Growth & Unemployment in the United Kingdom. 1975. text ed. 35.00x (ISBN 0-8419-5010-5). Holmes & Meier.

Doty, C. Stewart, ed. The Industrial Revolution. LC 76-14929. (European Problem Studies Ser.). 142p. 1976. pap. text ed. 5.50 (ISBN 0-88275-433-5). Krieger.

Doubleday, Thomas. Financial, Monetary & Statistical History of England, from the Revolution of 1688 to the Present Time. LC 68-28626. 1968. Repr. of 1847 ed. lib. bdg. 21.00x (ISBN 0-8371-0388-6, DOFM). Greenwood.

Dugdale, J. S. Teach Yourself Economic & Social History. 2.50 (ISBN 0-486-21428-1). Dover.

Elliott, Sydney R. English Cooperatives. LC 73-156188. 1971. Repr. of 1937 ed. lib. bdg. 15.00x (ISBN 0-8371-6136-3, ELEN). Greenwood.

Engels, Frederick. The Condition of the Working Class in England. (Illus.). 336p. 1979. pap. 4.95 (ISBN 0-586-02880-3, Pub. by Granada England). Academy Chi Ltd.

Engels, Friedrich. The Condition of the Working Class in England. Henderson, W. O. & Chaloner, W. H., trs. (Illus.). 1958. 15.00x (ISBN 0-8047-0633-6); pap. 6.95x (ISBN 0-8047-0634-4). Stanford U Pr.

Evans, George H., Jr. British Corporation Finance, 1775-1850. LC 78-64292. (Johns Hopkins University. Studies in the Social Sciences. Extra Volumes.: 23). Repr. of 1936 ed. 20.00 (ISBN 0-404-61392-6). AMS Pr.

Fay, Charles R. Life & Labour in the Nineteenth Century. LC 73-90143. Repr. of 1920 ed. lib. bdg. 14.25x (ISBN 0-8371-2165-5, FALL). Greenwood.

--World of Adam Smith. 1960. 8.50x (ISBN 0-678-08053-4). Kelley.

Fetter, Frank W. The Economist in Parliament, Seventeen Eighty to Eighteen Sixty-Eight. LC 78-73944. 1980. 19.75 (ISBN 0-8223-0415-5). Duke.

Flinn, M. W. & Smout, T. C., eds. Essays in Social History. (Illus.). 304p. 1974. pap. 14.95x (ISBN 0-19-877017-0). Oxford U Pr.

Fraser, C. M. & Emsley, K. Tyneside. 1974. 3.50 (ISBN 0-7153-5764-6). David & Charles.

Gash, Norman, ed. Age of Peel. 1969. pap. 5.95x (ISBN 0-312-01260-8). St Martin.

Gee, Joshua. Trade & Navigation of Great Britain Considered: Shewing That Surest Way for a Nation to Increase in Riches, Is to Prevent the Importation of Such Foreign Commodities As May Be Rais'd at Home. LC 75-141123. (Research Library of Colonial Americana). 1971. Repr. of 1729 ed. 15.00 (ISBN 0-405-03335-4). Arno.

George, Mary D. England in Transition: Life & Work in the 18th Century. LC 75-41110. Repr. of 1931 ed. 19.50 (ISBN 0-404-14544-2). AMS Pr.

Giffen, Robert. Growth of Capital. LC 67-29505. Repr. of 1889 ed. 13.50x (ISBN 0-678-00664-4). Kelley.

Ginsburg, Norman. Class, Capital & Social Policy. (Critical Texts in Social Work & the Welfare State). 1979. text ed. 25.00 (ISBN 0-333-21581-8). Humanities.

Gordon, Barry. Economic Doctrine & Tory Liberalism Eighteen Twenty-Four to Eighteen Thirty. 1979. text ed. 26.50x (ISBN 0-06-492498-X). B&N.

Great Britain, Parliament, House of Commons, Select Committee on Artizans & Machinery. Six Reports from the Select Committee on Artizans & Machinery, 23 February - 21 May 1824. LC 68-110405. Date not set. Repr. of 1824 ed. lib. bdg. 45.00x (ISBN 0-678-05229-8). Kelley.

Gregg, Pauline. Black Death to Industrial Revolution: A Social & Economic History of England. LC 76-3815. (Illus.). 344p. 1976. Repr. of 1974 ed. text ed. 15.00x (ISBN 0-06-492540-4). B&N.

--Social & Economic History of Britain, 1760-1972. 7th ed. (Illus.). 1973. 22.50x (ISBN 0-245-51899-1). Intl Pubns Serv.

Grellier, J. J. History of the National Debt from the Revolution in 1688 to 1800. LC 73-121224. (Research & Source Works Ser: No. 764). 1971. Repr. of 1810 ed. lib. bdg. 26.00 (ISBN 0-8337-1452-X). B Franklin.

Harris, John R., ed. Liverpool & Merseyside: Essays in the Economic & Social History of the Port & Its Hinterland. 287p. 1969. 27.50x (ISBN 0-7146-1314-2, F Cass Co). Biblio Dist.

Harrod, Roy. The British Economy. LC 77-14391. (Economics Handbook Ser.). (Illus.). 1977. Repr. of 1963 ed. lib. bdg. 19.25x (ISBN 0-8371-9832-1, HABE). Greenwood.

Head, George. Home Tour Through the Manufacturing Districts of England in the Summer of 1835. LC 67-31559. Repr. of 1836 ed. 17.50x (ISBN 0-678-05057-0). Kelley.

Held, Adolf. Zwei Buecher Zur Socialen Geschichte Englands, 2 Vols. LC 75-146355. 1971. Repr. of 1881 ed. 46.50 (ISBN 0-8337-1646-8). B Franklin.

Hessen, B. The Social & Economic Roots of Newton's Principia. 12.50 (ISBN 0-86527-182-8). Fertig.

Higgins, Joan M. The Poverty Business: Britain & America. (Aspects of Social Policy Ser.). 162p. 1978. 22.00x (ISBN 0-631-16260-7, Pub. by Basil Blackwell). Biblio Dist.

Hilton, R. H. Peasants, Knights & Heretics. LC 76-1137. (Past & Present Publications Ser.). 320p. 1976. 34.50 (ISBN 0-521-21276-6). Cambridge U Pr.

Hobsbawm, Eric J. Pelican Economic History of Britain, Vol. 3: Industry & Empire. (Orig.). 1970. pap. 3.95 (ISBN 0-14-020898-4, Pelican). Penguin.

Holderness, B. A. Pre-Industrial England: Economy & Society from 1500 to 1750. 244p. 1976. 17.50x (ISBN 0-87471-910-0). Rowman.

Hoskins, W. G. The Age of Plunder: The England of Henry VIII, 1500-1547. LC 75-43647. (Social & Economic History of England Ser.). (Illus.). 1976. pap. text ed. 9.95x (ISBN 0-582-48544-4). Longman.

Hutchison, Keith. Decline & Fall of British Capitalism. 1966. Repr. of 1951 ed. 25.00 (ISBN 0-208-00013-5, Archon). Shoe String.

Hutton, Graham. Source Book on Restrictive Practices in Britain. (Institute of Economic Affairs Research Monographs: No. 7). (Orig.). 1969. pap. 3.75 (ISBN 0-255-69610-8). Transatlantic.

Jackson, Michael P. The Price of Coal (United Kingdom) 217p. 1975. text ed. 16.00x (ISBN 0-85664-121-9). Verry.

Johnson, Walford, et al. Short Economic & Social History of Twentieth Century England. LC 67-21370. 1967. 10.00x (ISBN 0-678-06002-9). Kelley.

Johnston, William. England As It Is: Political, Social & Industrial in the Middle of the Nineteenth Century, 2 vols. (The Development of Industrial Society Ser.). 721p. 1971. Repr. of 1857 ed. 60.00x (ISBN 0-7165-1774-4, Pub. by Irish Academic Pr). Biblio Dist.

Jones, W. J. The Foundations of English Bankruptcy: Statutes & Commissions in the Early Modern Period. LC 78-73169. (Transactions Ser.: Vol. 69, Pt. 3). 1979. 8.00 (ISBN 0-87169-693-2). Am Philos.

Joplin, Thomas. Outlines of a System of Political Economy. LC 68-30530. Repr. of 1823 ed. 22.50x (ISBN 0-678-00590-7). Kelley.

Jordan, Bill. Paupers: The Making of the New Claiming Class. 1973. 9.00x (ISBN 0-7100-7547-2); pap. 3.95 (ISBN 0-7100-7548-0). Routledge & Kegan.

Kent, H. S. War & Trade in the Northern Seas: Anglo-Scandinavian Economic Relations in the Mid-Eighteenth Century. LC 72-75304. (Studies in Economic History). (Illus.). 288p. 1973. 40.95 (ISBN 0-521-08579-9). Cambridge U Pr.

Kirby, M. W. The Decline of British Economic Power Since Eighteen Seventy. 216p. 1981. text ed. 19.95x (ISBN 0-04-942169-7). Allen Unwin.

Knights, Lionel C. Drama & Society in the Age of Jonson. 1968. pap. 2.25x (ISBN 0-393-00451-1, Norton Lib). Norton.

Knowles, Lillian C. Industrial & Commercial Revolutions in Great Britain During the Nineteenth Century. 4th ed. LC 67-27704. Repr. of 1961 ed. 17.50x (ISBN 0-678-06518-7). Kelley.

Lavington, F. English Capital Market. 1968. Repr. of 1921 ed. 30.00x (ISBN 0-7146-2265-6, F Cass Co). Biblio Dist.

Lee, Derek. Control of the Economy. 1974. pap. text ed. 4.00x (ISBN 0-435-84542-X). Heinemann Ed.

Lester, C. Edwards. The Glory & Shame of England, 2 vols. (The Development of Industrial Society Ser.). 905p. 1971. Repr. of 1866 ed. 36.00x (ISBN 0-7165-1789-2, Pub. by Irish Academic Pr). Biblio Dist.

Lester, Richard I. Confederate Finance & Purchasing in Great Britain. LC 74-13916. (Illus.). 1975. 17.50x (ISBN 0-8139-0513-3). U Pr of Va.

Levett, A. E. English Economic History. 1979. Repr. of 1929 ed. lib. bdg. 12.50 (ISBN 0-8495-3320-1). Arden Lib.

Levy, S. Leon. Nassau W. Senior, 1790-1864. rev. ed. LC 67-30861. 1970. 17.50x (ISBN 0-678-05676-5). Kelley.

Lieberman, Sima, ed. Europe & the Industrial Revolution. 457p. 1972. 14.80x (ISBN 0-87073-316-8); pap. text ed. 7.50 (ISBN 0-87073-317-6). Schenkman.

Little, Anthony J. Deceleration in the Eighteenth - Century British Economy. 111p. 1976. 15.00x (ISBN 0-87471-928-3). Rowman.

Livesey, Frank. Distributive Trades. (Studies in the British Economy). (Orig.). 1979. pap. text ed. 6.50x (ISBN 0-435-84553-5). Heinemann Ed.

Livingstone, James V. The British Economy in Theory & Practice. LC 74-13513. 240p. 1975. 18.95 (ISBN 0-312-10080-9). St Martin.

Lowe, Joseph. Present State of England in Regard to Agriculture, Trade & Finance. 2nd ed. LC 66-21682. Repr. of 1823 ed. 25.00x (ISBN 0-678-00320-3). Kelley.

McCloskey, Donald N., ed. Essays on a Mature Economy: Britain After 1840. LC 73-170254. (Quantitative Studies in History Ser.). 453p. 1972. 25.00x (ISBN 0-691-05198-4). Princeton U Pr.

MacDonagh, Oliver. Early Victorian Government, 1830-1870. LC 76-57957. 1977. text ed. 24.50x (ISBN 0-8419-0304-2). Holmes & Meier.

MacKay, Donald I. & Mackay, George A. The Political Economy of North Sea Oil. LC 75-25633. 208p. 1976. 26.50x (ISBN 0-89158-515-X). Westview.

Malthus, Thomas R. Pamphlets of Thomas Robert Malthus 1800-1817. LC 77-117389. Repr. lib. bdg. 17.50x (ISBN 0-678-00646-6). Kelley.

Matthews, R. C., et al. British Economic Growth: Studies of Economic Growth in Industrialized Countries. Date not set. price not set. Stanford U Pr.

Mayhew, N. J. Edwardian Monetary Affairs (1279-1344) 1977. 15.00x (ISBN 0-904531-64-3, Pub. by BAR). State Mutual Bk.

Medlicott, W. N. Contemporary England: 1914-1964. LC 67-26796. (Social & Economic History of England Ser.). 1976. pap. text ed. 12.95x (ISBN 0-582-48487-1). Longman.

Milward, A. S. Economic Effects of the World Wars on Britain. (Studies in Economic & Social History). (Illus.). 1970. pap. text ed. 4.00x (ISBN 0-333-10262-2). Humanities.

Mitchell, B. R. & Jones, H. G. Second Abstract of British Historical Statistics. LC 72-128502. (Department of Applied Economics Monographs: No. 18). (Illus.). 1971. 45.00 (ISBN 0-521-08001-0). Cambridge U Pr.

Moffit, L. W. England on Eve of Industrial Revolution. 312p. 1963. 25.00x (ISBN 0-7146-1345-2, F Cass Co). Biblio Dist.

Money, L. C. Chiozza. Riches & Poverty. LC 79-56955. (The English Working Class Ser.). 1980. lib. bdg. 30.00 (ISBN 0-8240-0109-5). Garland Pub.

Morishima, M., et al. The Working of Econometric Models. LC 79-184901. (Illus.). 300p. 1972. 44.50 (ISBN 0-521-08502-0). Cambridge U Pr.

Morris, Derek, ed. The Economic System in the United Kingdom. 2nd ed. 1977. 45.00x (ISBN 0-19-877141-X). Oxford U Pr.

Murphy, Michael J. Poverty in Cambridgeshire. (Cambridge Town, Gown & County Ser.: Vol. 23). (Illus.). 1978. pap. 4.50 (ISBN 0-900891-29-7). Oleander Pr.

Murray, Bruce K. The People's Budget Nineteen Hundred & Nine to Nineteen Hundred & Ten: Lloyd George & Liberal Politics. 360p. 1980. 49.95 (ISBN 0-19-822626-8). Oxford U Pr.

National Institute of Economic & Social Research. The United Kingdom Economy. 4th ed. (Studies in the British Economy). (1976. pap. text ed. 6.00x (ISBN 0-435-84581-0). Heinemann Ed.

Neale, Walter C. The British Economy: Toward a Decent Society. LC 79-16553. (Economics Ser.). 1980. pap. text ed. 9.95 (ISBN 0-88244-194-9); 12.95 (ISBN 0-686-65968-6). Grid Pub.

Nishimura, Shizuya. Decline of Inland Bills of Exchange in the London Money Market, 1855-1913. LC 70-134613. (Illus.). 1971. 41.00 (ISBN 0-521-08055-X). Cambridge U Pr.

O'Brien, D. P. & Presley, John R., eds. Pioneers of Modern Economics in Britain. LC 79-55496. (Illus.). 392p. 1981. text ed. 26.50x (ISBN 0-389-20181-2). B&N.

O'Brien, Patrick & Keyder, Caglar. Economic Growth in Britain & France 1780-1914: Two Paths to the Twentieth Century. 1978. text ed. 27.50x (ISBN 0-04-330288-2). Allen Unwin.

Offer, Avner. Property & Politics, Eighteen-Seventy to Nineteen-Fourteen: Landownership, Law, Ideology & Urban Development in England. LC 80-41010. (Illus.). 480p. Date not set. 55.00 (ISBN 0-521-22414-4). Cambridge U Pr.

Page, William, ed. Commerce & Industry, 2 Vols in One. LC 67-19709. Repr. of 1919 ed. 30.00x (ISBN 0-678-00404-8). Kelley.

Paish, F. W. How the Economy Works & Other Essays. 1970. text ed. 17.00x (ISBN 0-333-11067-6). Humanities.

Palmer, Stanley H. Economic Arithmetic: A Guide to the Statistical Sources of English Commerce, Industry & Finance, 1700-1850. LC 76-42890. (Reference Library of Social Science Ser.: Vol. 26). (Illus.). 1977. lib. bdg. 27.50 (ISBN 0-8240-9946-X). Garland Pub.

Parry, Edward A. The Law & the Poor. LC 79-56966. (The English Working Class Ser.). 1980. lib. bdg. 30.00 (ISBN 0-8240-0117-6). Garland Pub.

Parsons, Burke A. British Trade Cycles & American Bank Credit: Some Aspects of Economic Fluctuations in the United States, 1815-1840. Bruchey, Stuart, ed. LC 76-39839. (Nineteen Seventy-Seven Dissertations Ser.). (Illus.). 1977. lib. bdg. 25.00x (ISBN 0-405-09919-3). Arno.

Pemer Reeves, M. S. Round About a Pound a Week. LC 79-56968. (The English Working Class Ser.). 1980. lib. bdg. 25.00 (ISBN 0-8240-0119-2). Garland Pub.

Peston, M. H. The British Economy. 224p. 1980. 30.00x (ISBN 0-86003-014-8, Pub. by Allan Pubs England); pap. 19.95x (ISBN 0-86003-115-2). State Mutual Bk.

Pettman, William R. Resources of the United Kingdom. LC 68-56563. Repr. of 1830 ed. 17.50x (ISBN 0-678-00661-X). Kelley.

Pigou, Arthur Cecil. Aspects of British Economic History. 251p. 1971. Repr. 24.00x (ISBN 0-7146-2630-9, F Cass Co). Biblio Dist.

Porter, George R. Progress of the Nation. new ed. Hirst, F. W., ed. LC 77-85189. Repr. of 1912 ed. 25.00x (ISBN 0-678-00538-9). Kelley.

Posner, Michael, ed. Demand Management. (Economic Policy Papers Ser.). 1978. pap. text ed. 18.00x (ISBN 0-435-84601-9). Heinemann Ed.

Prest, A. R. & Coppock, D. J., eds. The UK Economy: Manual of Applied Economics. 6th ed. 1977. 19.95x (ISBN 0-8464-0942-9). Beekman Pubs.

Prest, Alan Richmond. Intergovernmental Financial Relations in the United Kingdom. (Centre for Research on Federal Financial Relations Research Monograph: No. 23). 1978. pap. 7.95 (ISBN 0-7081-0581-5, Pub by ANUP Australia). Bks Australia.
Redford, Arthur. The Economic History of England, 1760-1860. LC 73-15244. 244p. 1974. Repr. of 1960 ed. lib. bdg. 15.00x (ISBN 0-8371-7166-0, REEH). Greenwood.
Reed, Clyde G. Price Data & European Economic History: England 1300-1600. Bruchey, Stuart, ed. LC 80-2826. (Dissertations in European Economic History II). (Illus.). 1981. lib. bdg. 12.00x (ISBN 0-405-14010-X). Arno.
Reed, M. C., compiled by. Railways in the Victorian Economy. LC 69-10863. 1969. 13.50x (ISBN 0-678-05623-4). Kelley.
Rountree, B. Seebohm. Poverty: A Study of Town Life. 2nd ed. LC 79-56969. (The English Working Class Ser.). 1980. lib. bdg. 38.00 (ISBN 0-8240-0120-6). Garland Pub.
Rountree, B. Seebohm & Pigou, A. C. Lectures on Housing. LC 79-56971. (The English Working Class Ser.). 1980. lib. bdg. 12.00 (ISBN 0-8240-0122-2). Garland Pub.
Rowntree, B. Seebohm & Lasker, Bruno. Unemployment: A Social Study. LC 79-56970. (The English Workinh Class Ser.). 1980. lib. bdg. 28.00 (ISBN 0-8240-0121-4). Garland Pub.
Salzman, Louis T. English Industries of the Middle Ages. LC 74-8922. 1913. 30.00 (ISBN 0-8414-7770-1). Folcroft.
Sandford, Cedric. Taxation & Social Policy. 1981. text ed. 45.00x (ISBN 0-435-82789-8). Heinemann Ed.
Sant, Morgan & Moseley, Malcolm. Industrial Development of East Anglia. 207p. 1980. 15.70x (ISBN 0-86094-003-9, Pub. by GEO Abstracts England); pap. 10.60x (ISBN 0-686-27383-4, Pub. by GEO Abstracts England). State Mutual Bk.
Sayers, R. Vicissitudes of an Export Economy: Britain Since 1880. 1965. pap. 2.00x (ISBN 0-424-05080-3, Pub. by Sydney U Pr). Intl Schol Bk Serv.
Schilling, Bernard N. Human Dignity & the Great Victorians. LC 78-143883. 1972. Repr. of 1946 ed. 17.50 (ISBN 0-208-01113-7, Archon). Shoe String.
Sedgwick, Theodore. Public & Private Economy 3 Vols in 1. LC 68-27855. Repr. of 1936 ed. 27.50x (ISBN 0-678-01258-X). Kelley.
Smart, William. Economic Annals of the Nineteenth Century, 2 Vols. LC 63-23520. Repr. of 1910 ed. 50.00x set (ISBN 0-678-00027-1). Kelley.
Smith, Wilfred & Wise, M. J. A Historical Introduction to the Economic Geography of Great Britain. (Advanced Economic Geography Ser.). 1968. lib. bdg. 20.00x (ISBN 0-7135-1509-0). Westview.
Southampton Conf. on Short-Run Econometric Models of UK Economy. Econometric Study of the UK: Proceedings. Hilton, Kenneth & Heathfield, David, eds. LC 73-101418. 1970. lib. bdg. 25.00x (ISBN 0-678-07004-0). Kelley.
Sparkes, J. R. & Pass, C. L. Trade & Growth. (Studies in the British Economy). 1977. pap. text ed. 5.50x (ISBN 0-435-84555-1). Heinemann Ed.
Stamp, L. Dudley & Beaver, S. H. The British Isles. 6th ed. LC 70-17425. (Geographies for Advanced Studies). 1972. 35.00 (ISBN 0-312-10325-5). St Martin.
Supple, Barry, ed. Essays in British Business History. 1977. 37.50x (ISBN 0-19-877087-1); pap. 16.50x (ISBN 0-19-877088-X). Oxford U Pr.
Taylor, Arthur J., ed. The Standard of Living in Britain in the Industrial Revolution. (Debates in Economic History Ser.). 271p. 1975. text ed. 19.95x (ISBN 0-416-08250-5); pap. 8.95x (ISBN 0-416-08260-2). Methuen Inc.
Taylor, C. T. & Silberston, Z. A. The Economic Impact of the Patent System: A Study of the British Experiment. LC 73-77173. (Department of Applied Economics Monographs, No. 23). (Illus.). 400p. 1973. 54.00 (ISBN 0-521-20255-8). Cambridge U Pr.
Thompson, Allan. The Dynamics of the Industrial Revolution. LC 73-82224. 224p. 1973. text ed. 17.95 (ISBN 0-312-22330-7). St Martin.
Townsend, Peter. Poverty in the United Kingdom: A Survey of Household Resoures & Standards of Living. 1980. 46.50x (ISBN 0-520-03871-1); pap. 16.95x (ISBN 0-520-03976-9, CAMPUS NO. 242). U of Cal Pr.
Townsin, A. A. AEC-Blue Triangle. 252p. 1981. 40.00x (ISBN 0-903839-34-2, Pub. by Transport). State Mutual Bk.
Toynbee, Arnold J. Lectures on the Industrial Revolution in England. LC 68-59517. Repr. of 1884 ed. 15.00x (ISBN 0-678-05636-6). Kelley.
Treble, J. H. Urban Poverty in Britain, 1830-1914. 1979. 20.00x (ISBN 0-312-83463-2). St Martin.
Unwin, George. Studies in Economic History. Tawney, R. H., ed. LC 66-9002. Repr. of 1927 ed. 27.50x (ISBN 0-678-05198-4). Kelley.
Unwin, George, ed. Finance & Trade Under Edward III. Repr. of 1918 ed. 27.50x (ISBN 0-678-05199-2). Kelley.
--Finance & Trade Under Edward III. 2nd ed. 360p. 1962. 27.50x (ISBN 0-7146-1368-1, F Cass Co). Biblio Dist.
Vinogradoff, Paul. English Society in the Eleventh Century: Essays in English Medieval History. 1968. Repr. of 1908 ed. 43.00 (ISBN 0-403-00047-5). Scholarly.
Wade, John. History of the Middle & Working Classes. LC 66-18321. Repr. of 1833 ed. 25.00x (ISBN 0-678-00173-1). Kelley.
Wakefield, Edward G. England & America. LC 66-21699. Repr. of 1834 ed. 19.50x (ISBN 0-678-00236-3). Kelley.
Walker, J. British Economic & Social History. 3rd ed. 464p. (Orig.). 1981. pap. text ed. 18.95x (ISBN 0-7121-0288-4, Pub. by Macdonald & Evans England). Intl Ideas.
Wallace, Robert. Characteristics of the Present Political State of Great Britain. 2nd ed. LC 69-19551. Repr. of 1758 ed. 15.00x (ISBN 0-678-00496-X). Kelley.
Williams, John H. Postwar Monetary Plans & Other Essays. Wilkins, Mira, ed. LC 78-3957. (International Finance Ser.). 1978. Repr. of 1947 ed. lib. bdg. 28.00x (ISBN 0-405-11258-0). Arno.
Williams, Karel. From Pauperism to Poverty. 500p. 1981. 60.00 (ISBN 0-7100-0698-5). Routledge & Kegan.
Worswick, G. D., ed. The Medium Term: Models of the British Economy. Blackaby, F. 246p. 1974. 24.50x (ISBN 0-8448-0411-8). Crane-Russak Co.
Wright, John. Britain in the Age of Economic Management: An Economic History Since 1939. (Illus.). 1980. 16.95x (ISBN 0-19-219148-9); pap. 7.95x (ISBN 0-19-289135-9). Oxford U Pr.
Young, Arthur. Arthur Young on Industry & Economics. LC 72-38271. (The Evolution of Capitalism Ser.). 188p. 1972. Repr. of 1926 ed. 10.00 (ISBN 0-405-04142-X). Arno.
--Six Months Tour Through the North of England, 4 Vols. 2nd ed. LC 67-29461. Repr. of 1771 ed. 100.00x (ISBN 0-678-00332-7). Kelley.

GREAT BRITAIN–ECONOMIC CONDITIONS–BIBLIOGRAPHY

Hanson, Lawrence W. Contemporary Printed Sources for British & Irish Economic History, 1701-1750. 1964. 165.00 (ISBN 0-521-05196-7). Cambridge U Pr.
Williams, Judith B. Guide to the Printed Materials for English Social & Economic History, 1750-1850, 2 Vols. 1966. lib. bdg. 75.00x (ISBN 0-374-98608-8). Octagon.

GREAT BRITAIN–ECONOMIC CONDITIONS–1918-1945

Aldcroft, Derek H. The Inter-War Economy: Britain 1919-1939. LC 70-20963. 441p. 1971. 21.50x (ISBN 0-231-03517-9). Columbia U Pr.
Brown, William A., Jr. England & the New Gold Standard: 1919-1926. Wilkins, Mira, ed. LC 78-3901. (International Finance Ser.). (Illus.). 1978. Repr. of 1929 ed. lib. bdg. 21.00x (ISBN 0-405-11206-8). Arno.
Burridge, T. D. British Labour & Hitler's War. 1977. 15.00 (ISBN 0-233-96714-1). Transatlantic.
Clark, Colin. National Income Nineteen Twenty-Four to Nineteen Thirty-One. LC 67-33571. Repr. of 1932 ed. 24.00x (ISBN 0-678-05161-5). Kelley.
Fitzgerald, Patrick. Industrial Combination in England. Wilkins, Mira, ed. LC 76-29996. (European Business Ser.). 1977. Repr. of 1927 ed. lib. bdg. 15.00x (ISBN 0-405-09754-9). Arno.
Hurwitz, Samuel J. State Intervention in Great Britain: Study of Economic Control & Social Response, 1914-1919. 321p. 1968. Repr. of 1949 ed. 27.50x (ISBN 0-7146-1323-1, F Cass Co). Biblio Dist.
Law, Christopher M. British Regional Development Since World War I. LC 80-66425. 176p. 1980. 38.00 (ISBN 0-7153-7974-7). David & Charles.
McCloskey, Donald N., ed. Essays on a Mature Economy: Britain After 1840. LC 73-170254. (Quantitative Studies in History Ser.). 453p. 1972. 25.00x (ISBN 0-691-05198-4). Princeton U Pr.
Meakin, W. The New Industrial Revolution. Wilkins, Mira, ed. LC 76-29998. (European Business Ser.). 1977. Repr. of 1928 ed. lib. bdg. 17.00x (ISBN 0-405-09756-5). Arno.
Passfield, Sidney J., et al. Decay of Capitalist Civilization. Repr. of 1923 ed. lib. bdg. 15.75x (ISBN 0-8371-2037-3, PACI). Greenwood.
Pigou, Arthur C. Essays in Applied Economics. Repr. of 1930 ed. 21.00x (ISBN 0-678-05077-5). Kelley.
Pollard, Sidney, ed. The Gold Standard & Employment Policies Between the Wars. (Debates in Economic History Ser.). 1970. pap. text ed. 6.95x (ISBN 0-416-29950-4). Methuen Inc.
Stamp, Josiah. Wealth & Taxable Capacity. facsimile ed. LC 79-150200. (Select Bibliographies Reprint Ser.). Repr. of 1922 ed. 16.00 (ISBN 0-8369-5713-X). Arno.
Trotsky, Leon. Leon Trotsky on Britain. Drayton, Júlia, et al, trs. from Russ. & Fr. LC 72-92147. 336p. 1973. 25.00 (ISBN 0-913460-12-5, Dist. by Path Pr NY); pap. 5.45 (ISBN 0-913460-13-3). Monad Pr.
Youngson, A. J. Britain's Economic Growth, 1920-1966. LC 67-21371. 1967. 12.50x (ISBN 0-678-06004-5). Kelley.
--British Economy, 1920-1957. LC 60-5299. 1960. 14.00x (ISBN 0-674-08225-7). Harvard U Pr.

GREAT BRITAIN–ECONOMIC CONDITIONS–1945-

Aldcroft, Derek & Fearon, Peter. Economic Growth in Twentieth Century Britain. 1970. 8.75x (ISBN 0-333-10041-7); pap. text ed. 4.75x (ISBN 0-333-10595-8). Humanities.
Alt, James E. The Politics of Economic Decline. LC 78-67295. 1979. 24.95 (ISBN 0-521-22327-X). Cambridge U Pr.
Atkinson, A. B. & Harrison, A. J. Distribution of Personal Wealth in Britain. LC 77-2715. 1978. 41.50 (ISBN 0-521-21735-0). Cambridge U Pr.
Black, John. The Economics of Modern Britain: An Introduction to Macroeconomics. 2nd ed. 300p. 1980. cancelled (ISBN 0-85520-372-2, Pub. by Martin Robertson England); pap. 9.95x (ISBN 0-85520-371-4). Biblio Dist.
--The Economics of Modern Britain: An Introduction to Macroeconomics. 272p. 1979. 24.50x (ISBN 0-85520-274-2, Pub by Martin Robertson England); pap. 9.95x (ISBN 0-85520-273-4). Biblio Dist.
Brittan, Samuel. The Economic Consequences of Democracy. LC 78-20911. (Illus.). 1979. text ed. 24.50x (ISBN 0-8419-6901-9); pap. text ed. 9.75x (ISBN 0-8419-6902-7). Holmes & Meier.
Brunner, John. National Plan: A Preliminary Assessment. 2nd ed. (Institute of Economic Affairs, Eaton Papers Ser.: No. 4). (Illus.). 1968. pap. 2.50 (ISBN 0-255-69552-7). Transatlantic.
Cairncross, Alec, ed. Britain's Economic Prospects Reconsidered. LC 71-37996. 1972. 19.00 (ISBN 0-87395-174-3). State U NY Pr.
Cole, G. D. The Post-War Condition of Britain. LC 75-2625. 483p. 1975. Repr. of 1956 ed. lib. bdg. 22.50x (ISBN 0-8371-8043-0, COPC). Greenwood.
Cook, S. T. & Jackson, P. M., eds. Current Issues in Fiscal Policy. 238p. 1979. 36.00x (ISBN 0-85520-290-4, Pub. by Martin Robertson England). Biblio Dist.
Cornwall, J. Growth & Stability in a Mature Economy. 287p. 1972. 21.95 (ISBN 0-470-17508-7). Halsted Pr.
Cornwall, John. Growth & Stability in a Mature Economy. 1976. pap. 28.00x (ISBN 0-85520-100-2, Pub. by Martin Robertson England). Biblio Dist.
Dean, Andrew. Wages & Earnings. (Reviews of United Kingdom Statistical Sources Ser.: Vol. XIII). 1980. 45.00 (ISBN 0-08-024060-7). Pergamon.
Donaldson, Peter. Guide to the British Economy. 1965. lib. bdg. 11.50x (ISBN 0-88307-079-0). Gannon.
Eversley, David E., et al. Population Growth & Planning Policy: Housing & Employment Location in the West Midlands. (Illus.). 88p. 1965. 24.00x (ISBN 0-7146-1583-8, F Cass Co). Biblio Dist.
Facts on Europe, Economic & Labor Information for the U. S. Businessman. 1966. spiral bdg. 8.50 (ISBN 0-87330-020-3). Indus Rel.
Field, Frank, ed. The Wealth Report. (Inequality in Society Ser.). 1979. 20.00x (ISBN 0-7100-0164-9). Routledge & Kegan.
Forecasts of the United Kingdom Economy, 1975-1980. (Business Management & Investment Information Ser). 1975. pap. 45.00x (ISBN 0-903083-15-9). Intl Pubns Serv.
Gamble, Andrew. Britain in Decline: Economic Policy, Political Strategy, & the British State. LC 81-68354. 304p. 1982. 15.00 (ISBN 0-8070-4700-7). Beacon Pr.
Gower Economic Publications, ed. One Hundred Center Guide, 1976: Market Feasibility Studies of Major Business Areas in England. 1976. 40.00x (ISBN 0-8464-0686-1). Beekman Pubs.
Halsey, A. H. Change in British Society. (Illus.). 1978. 11.50x (ISBN 0-19-219132-2). Oxford U Pr.
Harbury, C. D. & Hitchens, D. M. Inheritance & Wealth Inequality in Britain. (Illus.). 1979. text ed. 27.50x (ISBN 0-04-330296-3). Allen Unwin.
Hicks, John. After the Boom: Thoughts on the 1966 Economic Crisis. (Institute of Economic Affairs, Occasional Papers Ser.: No. 11). pap. 2.50 (ISBN 0-255-69606-X). Transatlantic.
Jackson, Valerie J. Population in the Countryside: Growth & Stagnation in the Cotswolds. (Illus.). 176p. 1968. 24.00x (ISBN 0-7146-1584-6, F Cass Co). Biblio Dist.
Jordan, Bill. Automatic Poverty: The Ricardo Phenomenon. 208p. 1981. 22.50 (ISBN 0-7100-0824-4); pap. 12.95 (ISBN 0-7100-0825-2). Routledge & Kegan.
Lee, C. H. British Regional Employment Statistics: 1841-1971. LC 78-25698. 1980. 52.50 (ISBN 0-521-22666-X). Cambridge U Pr.
Lindley, Robert M., ed. Economic Change & Employment Policy. 160p. 1980. text ed. 42.25x (ISBN 0-8419-5071-7); pap. text ed. cancelled (ISBN 0-8419-5072-5). Holmes & Meier.
Livesey, Frank. Distributive Trades. (Studies in the British Economy). (Orig.). 1979. pap. text ed. 6.50x (ISBN 0-435-84553-5). Heinemann Ed.
Martin, J. P. & Smith, A. Trade & Payments Adjustment Under Flexible Exchange Rates. 220p. 1980. text ed. 48.50x (ISBN 0-8419-5067-9). Holmes & Meier.
Maunder, Peter, ed. British Economy in the Seventies. 1980. text ed. 40.50x (ISBN 0-435-84475-X). Heinemann Ed.
Mayes, David G. The Property Boom: The Effects of Building Society Behaviour on House Prices. 146p. 1979. 30.50x (ISBN 0-85520-296-3, Pub by Martin Robertson England). Biblio Dist.
Minns, Richard & Thornley, Jennifer. State Shareholding: The Role of Local & Regional Authorities. 1979. text ed. 35.00x (ISBN 0-333-23739-0). Verry.
Morgan, E. Victor, et al. City Lights: Essays on Financial Institutions & Markets in the City of London, No. 19. (Orig.). 1979. technical 5.95 (ISBN 0-255-36119-X). Transatlantic.
Nossiter, Bernard. Britain, a Future That Works. 1978. 9.95 (ISBN 0-395-27094-4). HM.
O'Dea, D. J. Cyclical Indicators for the Post War British Economy. LC 75-2738. (National Institute of Economic & Social Research, Occasional Papers Ser.: No. 28). (Illus.). 180p. 1975. 19.95x (ISBN 0-521-09963-3). Cambridge U Pr.
Pearce, I. F., et al, eds. A Model of Output, Employment, Wages & Prices in the UK. LC 75-46134. (Illus.). 1976. 29.95 (ISBN 0-521-21210-3). Cambridge U Pr.
Pollard, Sidney. Development of the British Economy: 1914-1967. 2nd ed. LC 71-82436. 1969. 17.95 (ISBN 0-312-19670-9). St Martin.
Ramanadham, V. V. Public Enterprise in Britain. 176p. 1950. 22.50x (ISBN 0-7146-1245-6, F Cass Co). Biblio Dist.
Schwartz, Eli. Trouble in Eden: A Comparison of the British & Swedish Economies. 160p. 1980. 19.95 (ISBN 0-03-057032-8). Praeger.
Sparkes, J. R. & Pass, C. L. Monopoly. 2nd ed. (Studies in the British Economy Ser.). (Orig.). 1980. pap. text ed. 10.00x (ISBN 0-435-84582-9). Heinemann Ed.
Stafford, G. B. Economic Growth in Post-War Britain. 200p. 1981. 19.95x (ISBN 0-85520-390-0, Pub. by Martin Robertson England); pap. 7.95x (ISBN 0-85520-396-X, Pub. by Martin Robertson England). Biblio Dist.
Stamp, L. Dudley & Beaver, S. H. The British Isles. 6th ed. LC 70-17425. (Geographies for Advanced Studies). 1972. 35.00 (ISBN 0-312-10325-5). St Martin.
Warren, Kenneth. North-East England. (Problem Regions in Europe Ser). (Illus.). 1973. pap. 7.95x (ISBN 0-19-913099-X). Oxford U Pr.
Whitaker, Ben, ed. Radical Future. 7.95 (ISBN 0-224-61204-2). Transatlantic.
Williamson, Rene & Greene, Lee, eds. Five Years of British Labour. 1950. pap. 2.00 (ISBN 0-910824-05-3). Kallman.
Youngson, A. J. Britain's Economic Growth, 1920-1966. LC 67-21371. 1967. 12.50x (ISBN 0-678-06004-5). Kelley.
--British Economy, 1920-1957. LC 60-5299. 1960. 14.00x (ISBN 0-674-08225-7). Harvard U Pr.

GREAT BRITAIN–ECONOMIC POLICY

Amery, Leopold S. The Forward View. facsimile ed. LC 75-179500. (Selected Bibliographies Reprint Ser). Repr. of 1935 ed. 22.00 (ISBN 0-8369-6629-5). Arno.
Ashford, Douglas E. Policy & Politics in Britain: The Limits of Consensus. (Policy & Politics in Industrial States Ser.). 400p. 1980. 19.50 (ISBN 0-87722-194-4); pap. text ed. 9.95 (ISBN 0-87722-195-2). Temple U Pr.
Baker, A. R. & Butlin, R. A., eds. Studies of Field Systems in the British Isles. LC 72-91359. (Illus.). 744p. 1973. 77.50 (ISBN 0-521-20121-7). Cambridge U Pr.

Barber, William J. British Economic Thought & India Sixteen Hundred to Eighteen Fifty-Eight: A Study in the History of Development Economics. 264p. 1975. 42.00x (ISBN 0-19-828265-6). Oxford U Pr.
Bartlett, C. J., ed. Britain Pre-Eminent: Studies in British World Influence in the Nineteenth Century. LC 75-93447. (Problems in Focus Ser). 1969. 18.95 (ISBN 0-312-09835-9). St Martin.
Beckerman, Wilfred, ed. Slow Growth in Britain: Causes & Consequences. (Illus.). 246p. 1979. text ed. 23.50x (ISBN 0-19-828420-9). Oxford U Pr.
Berkley, George. The Querist, Containing Several Queries Proposed to the Consideration of the Public. Repr. of 1737 ed. 12.50 (ISBN 0-384-04010-1). Johnson Repr.
Blackaby, F. T. British Economic Policy: Nineteen Sixty to Nineteen Seventy-Four. LC 77-28282. (NIESR Economic & Social Policy Studies: No. 31). (Illus.). 1979. 67.50 (ISBN 0-521-22042-4); pap. 19.95x (ISBN 0-521-29597-1). Cambridge U Pr.
Brassey, Thomas A. Problems of Empire. 2nd ed. LC 75-118478. 1971. Repr. of 1913 ed. 12.50 (ISBN 0-8046-1227-7). Kennikat.
Brisco, Norris A. Economic Policy of Robert Walpole. LC 7-36150. (Columbia University Studies in the Social Sciences: No. 72). Repr. of 1907 ed. 18.50 (ISBN 0-404-51072-8). AMS Pr.
British Association for the Advancement of Science, Section F, Economics. Public Sector Economics. Prest, A. R., ed. LC 68-6526. 1968. 12.50x (ISBN 0-678-06765-1). Kelley.
Brittan, Samuel. Government & the Market Economy. (Hobart Paperbacks). 1972. pap. 3.50 (ISBN 0-255-36018-5). Transatlantic.
--Steering the Economy: The British Experiment. LC 71-152814. 504p. 1971. 22.50 (ISBN 0-912050-05-5, Library Pr). Open Court.
Broadbridge, Seymour. Studies in Railway Expansion & the Capital Market in England: 1825-73. 216p. 1970. 30.00x (ISBN 0-7146-1287-1, F Cass Co). Biblio Dist.
Brown, E. H. Indicative Economic Planning in the the United Kingdom. 1969. 2.00x (ISBN 0-424-06020-5, Pub. by Sydney U Pr). Intl Schol Bk Serv.
Brunner, John. National Plan: A Preliminary Assessment. 2nd ed. (Institute of Economic Affairs, Eaton Papers Ser.: No. 4). (Illus.). 1968. pap. 2.50 (ISBN 0-255-69552-7). Transatlantic.
Chappell, D. J. An Economic History of England. 320p. 1980. pap. 12.95x (ISBN 0-7121-0587-5). Intl Ideas.
Chester, Daniel N., ed. Lessons of the British War Economy. LC 70-157956. 260p. 1972. Repr. of 1951 ed. lib. bdg. 16.25x (ISBN 0-8371-6175-4, CHWE). Greenwood.
Chisholm, M. & Manners, G., eds. Spatial Policy Problems of the British Economy. LC 70-160090. (Illus.). 1971. 38.50 (ISBN 0-521-08235-8). Cambridge U Pr.
Chrystal, K. A. Controversies in British Macroeconomics. 1979. 21.00x (ISBN 0-86003-022-9, Pub. by Allan Pubs England); pap. 10.50x (ISBN 0-86003-123-3). State Mutual Bk.
Cole, George D. The British Co-Operative Movement in a Socialist Society. LC 76-22523. 168p. 1976. Repr. of 1951 ed. lib. bdg. 15.00x (ISBN 0-8371-9002-9, COBCM). Greenwood.
--Economic Planning. LC 79-137935. (Economic Thought, History & Challenge Ser). 1971. Repr. of 1935 ed. 17.50 (ISBN 0-8046-1440-7). Kennikat.
--Fabian Socialism. LC 68-21432. Repr. of 1943 ed. 21.00x (ISBN 0-678-05020-1). Kelley.
Creedy. The Economics of Unemployment in Britain. 1981. text ed. 14.95 (ISBN 0-408-10703-0). Butterworth.
Cunningham, William. The Growth of English Industry & Commerce, 3 vols. in 2. Incl. Vol. 1. Early & Middle Ages. 5th ed; Vol. 2. Modern Times: the Mercantile System. 4th ed; Vol. 3. Modern Times: Laissez Faire. 4th ed. LC 66-21667. Repr. of 1907 ed. Set. 50.00x (ISBN 0-678-00288-6). Kelley.
Decker, Mathew. An Essay on the Causes of the Decline of the Foreign Trade, Consequently of the Value of Lands of Britain, & on the Means to Restore Both. (History of English Economic Thought Ser). 1970. Repr. of 1744 ed. 15.50 (ISBN 0-384-11170-X). Johnson Repr.
Decker, Matthew. Essay on the Causes of the Decline of the Foreign Trade. 4th ed. LC 67-29502. Repr. of 1751 ed. 15.00x (ISBN 0-678-00864-7). Kelley.
Farquhar, J. D. The National Economy. 184p. 1975. 18.00x (ISBN 0-86003-008-3, Pub. by Allan Pubs England); pap. 9.00x (ISBN 0-86003-109-8). State Mutual Bk.
Fay, Charles R. Imperial Economy & Its Place in the Formation of Economic Doctrine. LC 74-29638. 151p. 1975. Repr. of 1934 ed. lib. bdg. 15.00x (ISBN 0-8371-8007-4, FAIE). Greenwood.
Finberg, H. P. & Thirsk, J., eds. Agrarian History of England & Wales, Vol. 1, Pt. 2: A.D. 43-1042. LC 66-19763. (Illus.). 600p. 1972. 71.50 (ISBN 0-521-08423-7). Cambridge U Pr.
Floud, R. & McCloskey, D., eds. The Economic History of Britain Since Seventeen Hundred: Volume 2: 1860 to the 1970s. LC 79-41645. (Illus.). 504p. Date not set. price not set (ISBN 0-521-23167-1); pap. text ed. price not set (ISBN 0-521-29843-1). Cambridge U Pr.
Fogarty, Michael P. The Just Wage. LC 75-29076. 309p. 1975. Repr. of 1961 ed. lib. bdg. 16.25x (ISBN 0-8371-8404-5, FOJW). Greenwood.
Geale, R. G. International Commerce & Economic Theory. LC 68-30522. Repr. of 1925 ed. 13.50x (ISBN 0-678-01086-2). Kelley.
Gowland, David. Monetary Policy & Credit Control: The Uk Experience. 219p. 1978. 30.00x (ISBN 0-85664-327-0, Pub. by Croom Helm Ltd England). Biblio Dist.
Grant, Alexander T. Study of the Capital Market in Britain from 1919-1936. 2nd ed. 320p. 1967. 32.50x (ISBN 0-7146-1224-3, F Cass Co). Biblio Dist.
Hagen, Everett E. & White, Stephanie F. Great Britain: Quiet Revolution in Planning. (National Planning Ser.: No. 6). (Orig.). 1966. pap. 3.95x (ISBN 0-8156-2092-6). Syracuse U Pr.
Ham, Adrian. Treasury Rules: Recurrent Themes in British Economic Policy. 15.95 (ISBN 0-7043-2267-6, Pub. by Quartet England). Charles River Bks.
Hartley, Keith. Problems of Economic Policy. (Economics & Society Ser.). 1977. text ed. 18.95x (ISBN 0-04-339008-0). Allen Unwin.
Hirst, Francis W., ed. Free Trade & Other Fundamental Doctrines of the Manchester School. LC 68-27674. Repr. of 1903 ed. 19.50x (ISBN 0-678-00403-X). Kelley.
Howson, S. & Winch, D. The Economic Advisory Council 1930-1939. LC 75-38187. (Illus.). 1977. 68.50 (ISBN 0-521-21138-7). Cambridge U Pr.
Jevons, William S. Methods of Social Reform. LC 65-20925. Repr. of 1883 ed. 17.50x (ISBN 0-678-00108-1). Kelley.
Jha, Narmedeshwar. Age of Marshall: Aspects of British Economic Thought. 220p. 1973. 25.00x (ISBN 0-7146-2954-5, F Cass Co). Biblio Dist.
Johnson, Nevil & Cochrane, Allan. Economic Policy Making by Local Authorities in Britain & West Germany. (The New Local Government Ser.: No. 21). 212p. 1981. text ed. 37.50x (ISBN 0-04-352097-9). Allen Unwin.
Joplin, Thomas. Outlines of a System of Political Economy. LC 68-30530. Repr. of 1823 ed. 22.50x (ISBN 0-678-00590-7). Kelley.
Kahn, Alfred E. Great Britain in the World Economy. (Social & Economic History Ser). 1969. Repr. of 1946 ed. 19.50 (ISBN 0-384-28480-9). Johnson Repr.
Knowles, Lillian C. Industrial & Commercial Revolutions in Great Britain During the Nineteenth Century. 4th ed. LC 67-27704. Repr. of 1961 ed. 17.50x (ISBN 0-678-06518-7). Kelley.
Kramer, Stella. English Craft Gilds & the Government: An Examination of the Accepted Theory Regarding the Decay of the Craft Guilds. LC 68-5666. (Columbia University, Studies in the Social Sciences Ser.: No. 61). Repr. of 1905 ed. 16.50 (ISBN 0-404-51061-2). AMS Pr.
Lenin, V. I. British Labour & British Imperialism. 316p. 1969. 14.95x (ISBN 0-8464-0214-9). Beekman Pubs.
Longfield, Mountiford. Economic Writings of Mountiford Longfield. Black, R. D., ed. LC 73-144801. 1971. 35.00x (ISBN 0-678-00836-1). Kelley.
McCulloch, John R., ed. Select Collection of Scarce & Valuable Tracts & Other Publications on the National Debt & the Sinking Fund. LC 65-16989. Repr. of 1857 ed. 32.50x (ISBN 0-678-00148-0). Kelley.
--Select Collection of Scarce & Valuable Tracts & Other Publications on Paper Currency & Banking. LC 65-16986. Repr. of 1857 ed. 32.50x (ISBN 0-678-00149-9). Kelley.
--Select Collection of Scarce & Valuable Tracts on Money & Metallic Currency. LC 65-16987. Repr. of 1856 ed. 32.50x (ISBN 0-678-00147-2). Kelley.
Maclennan, Duncan & Parr, John B. Regional Policy: Past Experience & New Directions. 334p. 1979. o. p. 41.95x (ISBN 0-85520-217-3, Pub by Martin Robertson England); pap. 17.25x (ISBN 0-85520-216-5, Pub. by Martin Robertson England). Biblio Dist.
Major, Robin. Britain's Trade & Exchange Rate Policy. (Economic Policy Papers Ser.). 1979. text ed. 40.00x (ISBN 0-435-84467-9). Heinemann Ed.
Miller, Robert & Wood, John B. Exchange Control Forever? (Research Monographs: No. 33). (Orig.). 1979. 5.95 (ISBN 0-255-36117-3). Transatlantic.
Paish, F. W. How the Economy Works & Other Essays. 1970. text ed. 17.00x (ISBN 0-333-11067-6). Humanities.
Partington, Martin & Jowell, J. L., eds. Welfare Law & Policy: Studies in Teaching, Practice & Research. 1979. 37.50x (ISBN 0-89397-051-4). Nichols Pub.
Ponko, Vincent, Jr. Privy Council & the Spirit of Elizabethan Economic Management. LC 68-24356. (Transactions Ser.: Vol. 58, Pt. 4). 1968. pap. 1.00 (ISBN 0-87169-584-7). Am Philos.
Robertson, Dennis H. Utility & All That. LC 53-824. 1952. 12.50x (ISBN 0-678-06026-6). Kelley.
Rogow, A. A. & Shore, Peter. The Labour Government & British Industry, 1945-1951. LC 73-22508. 196p. 1974. Repr. of 1955 ed. lib. bdg. 15.00x (ISBN 0-8371-6374-9, ROLG). Greenwood.
Rooke, John. Inquiry into the Principles of National Wealth. LC 68-56573. Repr. of 1824 ed. 22.50x (ISBN 0-678-00566-4). Kelley.
Scrope & Poulett, G. J. Principles of Political Economy. LC 68-58008. Repr. of 1833 ed. 19.50x (ISBN 0-678-00563-X). Kelley.
Smart, William. Economic Annals of the Nineteenth Century, 2 Vols. LC 63-23520. Repr. of 1910 ed. 50.00x set (ISBN 0-678-00027-1). Kelley.
Spartacus. Growth Through Competition: An Alternative to the National Plan. (Institute of Economic Affairs, Hobart Papers Ser.: No. 35). (Orig.). 1969. pap. 2.50 (ISBN 0-255-69507-1). Transatlantic.
Stamp, A. H. A Social & Economic History of England from Seventeen Hundred to Nineteen Seventy. 334p. 1980. 22.50x (ISBN 0-7050-0070-2, Pub. by Skilton & Shaw England). State Mutual Bk.
Surrey, M. J. The Analysis & Forecasting of the British Economy. LC 75-171683. (National Institute of Economic & Social Research, Occasional Papers: No. 25). (Illus.). 100p. 1972. 15.50x (ISBN 0-521-09675-8). Cambridge U Pr.
Tariff Commission, London. Report of the Tariff Commission, 7 vols. in 6. 2512p. Repr. 215.50 (ISBN 0-384-59490-5). Johnson Repr.
Thirsk, Joan. Economic Policy & Projects: The Development of a Consumer Society in Early Modern England. 1978. 29.95x (ISBN 0-19-828274-5). Oxford U Pr.
Thomas, R. Resource Allocation & Cost Benefit Analysis. (Studies in the British Economy). Date not set. pap. text ed. write for info. (ISBN 0-435-84561-6). Heinemann Ed.
Tomlinson, Jim. Problems of British Economic Policy, 1870-1945. 1981. 21.00x (ISBN 0-416-30430-3). Methuen Inc.
Torrens, Robert. Budget. LC 68-58032. Repr. of 1844 ed. 19.50x (ISBN 0-678-00558-3). Kelley.
Tucker, Josiah. The Elements of Commerce & the Theory of Taxes. (History of English Economic Thought Ser). 1970. Repr. of 1755 ed. 38.50 (ISBN 0-384-61903-7). Johnson Repr.
Walker, J. British Economic & Social History. 448p. 1980. 12.00x (ISBN 0-7121-0266-3, Pub. by Macdonald & Evans). State Mutual Bk.
Walker, Peter. The Ascent of Britain. (Illus.). 1977. text ed. 18.95x (ISBN 0-8464-0154-1). Beekman Pubs.
Walters, Alan. Economists & the British Economy: Eight Wincott Memorial Lecture. (IEA Occasional Papers Ser.: No. 54). 1978. pap. 2.75 (ISBN 0-255-36106-8). Transatlantic.
Watson, Ian B. Foundation for Empire: English Private Trade in India, 1659 to 1760. (Illus.). 384p. 1980. text ed. 37.50 (ISBN 0-7069-1038-9, Pub. by Vikas India). Advent NY.
Wright, John. Britain in the Age of Economic Management: An Economic History Since 1939. (Illus.). 1980. 16.95x (ISBN 0-19-219148-9); pap. 7.95x (ISBN 0-19-289135-9). Oxford U Pr.
Wunderlich, Frieda. British Labor & the War. (Social Research Suppl.: No. 3). 1941. pap. 4.00 (ISBN 0-527-00863-X). Kraus Repr.

GREAT BRITAIN–ECONOMIC POLICY–1945-

Alt, James E. The Politics of Economic Decline. LC 78-67295. 1979. 24.95 (ISBN 0-521-22327-X). Cambridge U Pr.
Banting, Keith G. Poverty, Politics & Policy: Britain in the Nineteen Sixties. (Studies in Policy Making). 1979. text ed. 30.00x (ISBN 0-333-23324-7). Humanities.
British Association for the Advancement of Science. Conflicts in Policy Objects. Kaldor, Nicholas, ed. LC 70-166516. 189p. 1971. lib. bdg. 12.50x (ISBN 0-678-06276-5). Kelley.
Brittan, Samuel. Is There an Economic Consensus? An Attitude Survey. 1973. text ed. 7.00x (ISBN 0-333-14410-4). Humanities.
Brown, A. J. The Framework of Regional Economics in the United Kingdom. LC 72-83665. (Publications of the National Institute of Economic & Social Studies: No. 27). (Illus.). 384p. 1972. 42.50 (ISBN 0-521-08743-0). Cambridge U Pr.
Cairncross, Alec, ed. Britain's Economic Prospects Reconsidered. LC 71-37996. 1972. 19.00 (ISBN 0-87395-174-3). State U NY Pr.
Caves, Richard E., et al. Britain's Economic Prospects. 1968. 16.95 (ISBN 0-8157-1322-3). Brookings.
Coutts, K., et al. Industrial Pricing in the United Kingdom. LC 77-8976. (Applied Economics Monograph: No. 26). (Illus.). 1978. 31.50 (ISBN 0-521-21725-3). Cambridge U Pr.
Dorfman, Gerald A. Wage Politics in Britain, 1945-1967: Government Vs. the TUC. 160p. 1973. 7.95x (ISBN 0-8138-0300-4). Iowa St U Pr.
Fleming, John, et al. Catch Seventy-Six. (Occasional Paper: No. 47). 1977. pap. 5.95 (ISBN 0-255-36080-0). Transatlantic.
Friedman, Milton. From Galbraith to Economic Freedom. (Institute of Economic Affairs Occasional Papers: No. 49). 1977. pap. 4.25 (ISBN 0-255-36089-4). Transatlantic.
Galloway, David. The Public Prodigals. LC 77-373743. (Illus.). 1976. 15.00x (ISBN 0-85117-113-3). Intl Pubns Serv.
Hill, Arthur C. & Lubin, Isador. The British Attack on Unemployment. xiv, 325p. Repr. of 1934 ed. lib. bdg. 19.50x (ISBN 0-87991-087-9). Porcupine Pr.
Johnson, Peter S., ed. Structure of British Industry. 400p. 1980. 32.50x (ISBN 0-89397-086-7). Nichols Pub.
King, Anthony. Britain Says Yes: The 1975 Referendum on the Common Market. LC 77-83257. 1977. pap. 3.75 (ISBN 0-8447-3260-5). Am Enterprise.
Lindley, Robert M., ed. Economic Change & Employment Policy. 160p. 1980. text ed. 42.25x (ISBN 0-8419-5071-7); pap. text ed. cancelled (ISBN 0-8419-5072-5). Holmes & Meier.
Lowe, Joseph. Present State of England in Regard to Agriculture, Trade & Finance. 2nd ed. LC 66-21682. Repr. of 1823 ed. 25.00x (ISBN 0-678-00320-3). Kelley.
McEachern, D. A Class Against Itself. 245p. 1980. 29.50 (ISBN 0-521-22985-5); pap. cancelled (ISBN 0-521-28054-0). Cambridge U Pr.
McKie, David & Cook, Christopher. The Decade of Disillusion: Britain in the Sixties. LC 72-83416. 1972. 19.95 (ISBN 0-312-18900-1). St Martin.
Martin, J. P. & Smith, A. Trade & Payments Adjustment Under Flexible Exchange Rates. 220p. 1980. text ed. 48.50x (ISBN 0-8419-5067-9). Holmes & Meier.
Meade, James. The Structure & Reform of Direct Taxation. (Illus.). 1978. text ed. 50.00x (ISBN 0-04-336064-5); pap. text ed. 19.95x (ISBN 0-04-336065-3). Allen Unwin.
Mennell, William. British Economy. 1964. pap. 4.95x (ISBN 0-8464-0211-4). Beekman Pubs.
Morgan, D. J. Changes in British Aid Policy: 1951-1970, Vol. 4. 1980. text ed. cancelled (ISBN 0-391-01687-3). Humanities.
Nevin, E. T., ed. The Economics of Devolution: Proceedings of Section F of British Association for the Advancement of Science, Aston University 1977. 1978. pap. text ed. 10.00x (ISBN 0-7083-0698-5). Verry.
O'Brien, D. P., et al. Competition Policy, Profitability & Growth. 1979. text ed. 32.50x (ISBN 0-8419-5051-2). Holmes & Meier.
Stewart, Michael. The Jekyll & Hyde Years: Politics & Economic Policy Since 1964. 1977. 18.75x (ISBN 0-87471-940-2). Rowman.
--Politics & Economic Policy in the UK Since 1964: The Jekyll & Hyde Years. 1978. pap. 12.00 (ISBN 0-08-022469-5). Pergamon.
Strauss, E. European Reckoning: The Six & Britain's Future. LC 64-48224. 1962. 5.25x (ISBN 0-8002-0772-6). Intl Pubns Serv.
Whitaker, Ben, ed. Radical Future. 7.95 (ISBN 0-224-61204-2). Transatlantic.

GREAT BRITAIN–EMIGRATION AND IMMIGRATION

Allen, Sheila. New Minorities, Old Conflicts: Asian & West Indian Migrants in Britain. 1971. pap. text ed. 3.95x (ISBN 0-394-31477-8). Phila Bk Co.
Berthoff, Rowland T. British Immigrants in Industrial America, 1790-1950. LC 68-10901. (Illus.). 196p. 1968. Repr. of 1953 ed. 10.00 (ISBN 0-8462-1044-4). Russell.
Boston, Ray. British Chartists in America, 1839-1900. (Illus.). 110p. 1971. 10.00x (ISBN 0-87471-025-1). Rowman.

Bridenbaugh, Carl. Vexed & Troubled Englishman 1590-1642. LC 68-17604. 512p. 1976. pap. 6.95 (ISBN 0-19-502020-0, GB453, GB). Oxford U Pr.
--Vexed & Troubled Englishmen, 1590-1642. 1968. 19.95 (ISBN 0-19-500493-0). Oxford U Pr.
Carrothers, William A. Emigration from the British Isles. LC 66-5786. Repr. of 1929 ed. 25.00x (ISBN 0-678-05147-X). Kelley.
Cheetham, Juliet. Social Work with Immigrants. (Library of Social Work). 242p. 1972. 12.95x (ISBN 0-7100-7365-8); pap. 7.95 (ISBN 0-7100-7366-6). Routledge & Kegan.
Cunningham, William. Alien Immigrants to England. LC 72-94541. (Illus.). Repr. of 1897 ed. lib. bdg. 22.50x (ISBN 0-678-05098-8). Kelley.
Davison, Robert B. Black British: Immigrants to England. 1966. 8.00x (ISBN 0-19-218160-2). Oxford U Pr.
Dench, Geoff. Maltese in London. 1975. 25.00x (ISBN 0-7100-8067-0). Routledge & Kegan.
Ellis, June, ed. West African Families in Britain: A Meeting of Two Cultures. (Library of Social Work). 1978. 15.50 (ISBN 0-7100-8954-6). Routledge & Kegan.
Emigration, 28 vols. (British Parliamentary Papers Ser.). 1971. Set. 2196.00x (ISBN 0-7165-1494-X, Pub. by Irish Academic Pr Ireland). Biblio Dist.
French, Elizabeth. List of Emigrants to America from Liverpool, 1697-1707. LC 63-754. 1978. pap. 5.00 (ISBN 0-8063-0153-8). Genealog Pub.
Glass, D. V. & Taylor, P. A. Population & Emigration in Nineteenth Century Britain. (Commentaries on British Parlimentary Papers). 132p. 1976. 15.00x (ISBN 0-7165-2219-5, Pub. by Irish Academic Pr Ireland). Biblio Dist.
Guillet, Edwin C. The Great Migration: The Atlantic Crossing by Sailing-Ship Since 1770. LC 73-145482. (The American Immigration Library). xii, 316p. 1971. Repr. of 1937 ed. lib. bdg. 15.95x (ISBN 0-89198-013-X). Ozer.
Gunn, Hugh, ed. The British Empire, 12 vols. Incl. Vol. 1. Dominions & Dependencies of the British Empire. (Illus.). 20.00 (ISBN 0-404-54301-4); Vol. 2. The Story of the Empire. Lucas, C. 14.00 (ISBN 0-404-54302-2); Vol. 3. The Constitution, Administration & Laws of the Empire. Keith, A. B. 15.00 (ISBN 0-404-54303-0); Vol. 4. The Resources of the Empire & Their Development. Lewin, E. 15.00 (ISBN 0-404-54304-9); Vol. 5. Health Problems of the Empire, Past, Present & Future. Balfour, A. & Scott, H. H. 17.50 (ISBN 0-404-54305-7); Vol. 6. The Press & Communications of the Empire. Mills, J. S. 17.50 (ISBN 0-404-54306-5); Vol. 7. The Trade, Commerce... of the Empire. McLeod, C. C. 17.50 (ISBN 0-404-54307-3); Vol. 8. Makers of the Empire. Gunn, H. 17.50 (ISBN 0-404-54308-1); Vol. 9. The Native Races of the Empire. Lagden, G. 17.50 (ISBN 0-404-54309-X); Vol. 10. The Universities & Educational Systems of the British Empire. 17.50 (ISBN 0-404-54310-3); Vol. 11. The Literature of the Empire; the Art of the Empire. Salaman, E. & Longden, A. A. 17.50 (ISBN 0-404-54311-1); Vol. 12. Migration Within the Empire. Belcher, E. A. & Williamson, J. A. 17.50 (ISBN 0-404-54312-X). Repr. of 1924 ed. Set. 200.00 (ISBN 0-404-54300-6). AMS Pr.
Hargreaves-Mawdsley, R., ed. Bristol & America: A Record of the First Settlers in the Colonies of North America, 1654-1685. LC 64-19762. 1978. Repr. of 1929 ed. 12.50 (ISBN 0-8063-0170-8). Genealog Pub.
Jewson, Charles B. Transcript of Three Registers of Passengers from Great Yarmouth to Holland & New England, 1637-1639. LC 74-18558. (Norfolk Record Society Publications: Vol. 25). 1964. Repr. of 1954 ed. 10.00 (ISBN 0-8063-0192-9). Genealog Pub.
Johnson, Stanley C. History of Emigration from the United Kingdom to North America, 1763-1912. LC 66-5243. Repr. of 1913 ed. 25.00x (ISBN 0-678-05181-X). Kelley.
Johnston, H. J. British Emigration Policy, 1815-1830: Shovelling Out Paupers. 216p. 1972. 13.75x (ISBN 0-19-822353-6). Oxford U Pr.
Lobo, E. D. Children of Immigrants to Britain: Their Health & Social Problems. 1978. pap. text ed. 6.00x (ISBN 0-340-22840-7). Verry.
Malchow, Howard L. Population Pressures: Emigration & Government in Late Nineteenth-Century Britain. LC 79-64166. (Illus.). 1979. 18.00 (ISBN 0-930664-02-7). SPOSS.
Nicholson, Cregoe D. Some Early Emigrants to America. France, R. Sharpe, ed. Bd. with Early Emigrants to America from Liverpool. LC 65-25164. 110p. 1965. Repr. of 1955 ed. 10.00 (ISBN 0-8063-0260-7). Genealog Pub.
Parr, Joy. Labouring Children: British Immigrant Apprentices to Canada, Eighteen Sixty-Nine to Nineteen Twenty-Four. 240p. 1980. 25.95 (ISBN 0-7735-0517-2). McGill-Queens U Pr.
Rex, John & Tomlinson, Sally. Colonial Immigrants in a British City: A Class Analysis. (International Library of Sociology). 1979. 25.25x (ISBN 0-7100-0142-8). Routledge & Kegan.
Rose, E. J., et al. Colour & Citizenship: A Report on British Race Relations. 1969. pap. 14.50x (ISBN 0-19-218180-7). Oxford U Pr.
Shepperson, Wilbur S. Emigration & Disenchantment: Portraits of Englishmen Repatriated from the United States. 1965. 12.50x (ISBN 0-8061-0652-2). U of Okla Pr.
Sherwood, George. American Colonists in English Records: First & Second Series, 2 Vols. in 1. LC 63-528. 1978. 10.00 (ISBN 0-8063-0310-7). Genealog Pub.
Sookhdeo, Patrick. Asians in Britain. rev. ed. 1977. pap. 2.50 (ISBN 0-85364-207-9). Attic Pr.

GREAT BRITAIN–EXCHEQUER

Hall, Hubert. The Antiquites & Curiosities of the Exchequer. (Research & Source Works Ser.: No. 217). 1968. Repr. of 1893 ed. 21.50 (ISBN 0-8337-1537-2). B Franklin.
Madox, Thomas. History & Antiquities of the Exchequer of the Kings of England, 2 vols. Repr. of 1769 ed. Set. lib. bdg. 79.50x (ISBN 0-8371-1076-9, MAE). Greenwood.
--History & Antiquities of the Exchequer of the Kings of England, 2 Vols. 2nd ed. LC 68-57386. Repr. of 1769 ed. Set. 60.00x (ISBN 0-678-04500-3). Kelley.
--History & Antiquities of the Exchequer, 2 Vols. 2nd ed. LC 68-57386. 1969. Repr. of 1769 ed. Set. 60.00x (ISBN 0-8377-2426-0). Rothman.
Poole, Reginald Lane. Exchequer in the Twelfth Century. 196p. 1973. Repr. of 1912 ed. 27.50x (ISBN 0-7146-1510-2, F Cass Co). Biblio Dist.

GREAT BRITAIN–EXECUTIVE DEPARTMENTS

Clokie, Hugh M. & Robinson, J. William. Royal Commissions of Inquiry: The Significance of Investigation in British Politics. LC 70-86274. 1969. Repr. of 1937 ed. lib. bdg. 13.00x (ISBN 0-374-91710-8). Octagon.
Hewart, Gordon. The New Despotism. LC 75-25259. 307p. 1976. Repr. of 1945 ed. lib. bdg. 16.75x (ISBN 0-8371-8389-8, HEND). Greenwood.
MacKenzie, William J. & Grove, J. W. Central Administration in Britain. LC 74-33896. 487p. 1975. Repr. of 1957 ed. lib. bdg. 27.00x (ISBN 0-8371-7996-3, MACAB). Greenwood.
Sutherland, Gillian, ed. Studies in the Growth of Nineteenth-Century Government. 295p. 1972. 16.50x (ISBN 0-87471-080-4). Rowman.

GREAT BRITAIN–FOREIGN OFFICE

British Foreign Office : Russia Correspondence, 1906-1913 & 1919-1940: Indexes & Guides to the Microfilm Collection. LC 7-85235. 1977. 60.00 (ISBN 0-8420-2127-2). Scholarly Res Inc.
Great Britain. Foreign Office: Index to Foreign Office Correspondence, 1920-1949, 123 vols. lib. bdg. 6096.00 (ISBN 0-527-35675-1). Kraus Intl.
Great Britain - Her Majesty's Stationery Office, London. Catalogue of the Foreign Office Library, 1926-1968, 8 vols. 6423p. 1973. lib. bdg. 720.00 (ISBN 0-8161-0998-2). G K Hall.
Jones, Peter, et al. British Foreign Secretaries Since 1945. 1977. 9.50 (ISBN 0-7153-7381-1). David & Charles.
Jones, R. A. The Nineteenth Century Foreign Office of England. 240p. 1971. 17.50x (ISBN 0-8464-0674-8). Beekman Pubs.
Jones, Ray. Nineteenth Century Foreign Office: An Administrative History. (London School of Economics Research Monographs Ser: No. 9). 1971. bds. 14.00x (ISBN 0-297-00299-6). Humanities.
Steiner, Zara S. Foreign Office & Foreign Policy 1898-1914. LC 70-85739. (Illus.). 1970. 37.50 (ISBN 0-521-07654-4). Cambridge U Pr.

GREAT BRITAIN–FOREIGN RELATIONS

Austin, Dennis. Britain & South Africa. LC 81-4550. (Illus.). viii, 191p. 1981. Repr. of 1966 ed. lib. bdg. 22.50x (ISBN 0-313-22994-5, AUBS). Greenwood.
Bartlett, C. J., ed. Britain Pre-Eminent: Studies in British World Influence in the Nineteenth Century. LC 75-93447. (Problems in Focus Ser). 1969. 18.95 (ISBN 0-312-09835-9). St Martin.
Bell, H. C. Lord Palmerston, 2 Vols. (Illus.). 1966. Repr. of 1936 ed. Set. 37.50 (ISBN 0-208-00438-6, Archon). Shoe String.
Bellini, James & Pattie, Geoffrey. A New World Role for the Medium Power: The British Opportunity. 30.00x (ISBN 0-686-75613-4, Pub. by Royal United England). State Mutual Bk.
Beloff, Max. Future of British Foreign Policy. Crozier, Brian, ed. LC 73-86970. (World Realities Ser). 1969. 4.95 (ISBN 0-8008-3120-9). Taplinger.
Berard, Victor. British Imperialism & Commercial Supremacy. LC 70-80613. 298p. 1973. Repr. of 1906 ed. 24.00 (ISBN 0-86527-018-X). Fertig.
Brailsford, Henry N. The War of Steel & Gold: A Study of the Armed Peace. 3rd ed. (The Development of the Industrial Society Ser.). 340p. 1971. Repr. of 1915 ed. 25.00x (ISBN 0-7165-1767-1, Pub. by Irish Academic Pr). Biblio Dist.
Breslow, Marvin A. Mirror of England: English Puritan Views of Foreign Nations, 1618-1640. LC 70-89966. (Historical Studies: No. 84). 1970. 9.00x (ISBN 0-674-57638-1). Harvard U Pr.
Britain, Europe & the World, 4 bks. Incl. Bk 2. 1485-1713. Witcombe, Dennis. 1971. pap. text ed. 10.50x (ISBN 0-435-31101-8); Bk 3. 1714-1848. Symonds, Roger. 1975. pap. text ed. 10.50 (ISBN 0-435-31102-6); Bk 4. 1848-1918. Edwards, Tony & Bearman, Graham. 1971. pap. text ed. 11.95 (ISBN 0-435-31103-4); Bk 5. 1918-1977. Richardson, Paul. 1977. pap. text ed. 10.50x (ISBN 0-435-31105-0). Heinemann Ed.
British Imperialism: Three Documents. LC 70-141119. (Research Library of Colonial Americana). 1972. Repr. of 1720 ed. 17.00 (ISBN 0-405-03330-3). Arno.
Busch, Briton C. Britain & the Persian Gulf, 1894-1914. LC 67-24120. 1967. 24.50x (ISBN 0-520-00200-8). U of Cal Pr.
Canning, George. George Canning & His Friends, Containing Hitherto Unpublished Letters, Jeux D'espirit, Etc, 2 Vols. in 1. Bagot, J., ed. LC 9-14585. 1969. Repr. of 1909 ed. 34.00 (ISBN 0-527-14800-8). Kraus Repr.
Collins, D. Aspects of British Politics, 1904-1919. 1965. 25.00 (ISBN 0-08-010987-X); pap. 12.75 (ISBN 0-08-010986-1). Pergamon.
Crowson, P. S. Tudor Foreign Policy. LC 73-81733. 288p. 1973. 17.95 (ISBN 0-312-82285-5). St Martin.
Cyr, Arthur. British Foreign Policy & the Atlantic Area: The Techniques of Accommodation. LC 79-4331. 1979. text ed. 29.50x (ISBN 0-8419-0489-8). Holmes & Meier.
Datta, K. Anti-British Plots & Movements Before 1857. LC 72-915716. 1970. 8.00x (ISBN 0-8002-0955-9). Intl Pubns Serv.
Feiling, Keith. British Foreign Policy, Sixteen Sixty to Sixteen Seventy-Two. 385p. 1968. Repr. of 1930 ed. 28.50x (ISBN 0-7146-1473-4, F Cass Co). Biblio Dist.
Fowler, Wilton B. British-American Relations, 1917-1918: The Role of Sir William Wiseman. 1969. 22.50 (ISBN 0-691-04594-1). Princeton U Pr.
Frankel, Joseph. British Foreign Policy, Nineteen Forty-Five to Nineteen Seventy-Three. (Royal Institute of International Affairs Ser). 390p. 1975. text ed. 22.25x (ISBN 0-19-218306-0). Oxford U Pr.
Gooch, G. P. & Masterman, J. H. Century of British Foreign Policy. LC 70-118471. 1971. Repr. of 1917 ed. 11.00 (ISBN 0-8046-1220-X). Kennikat.
Gordon, Michael R. Conflict & Consensus in Labour's Foreign Policy, 1914-1965. 1969. 15.00x (ISBN 0-8047-0686-7). Stanford U Pr.
Great Britain Public Record Office. Syllabus in English of the Documents Relating to England & Other Kingdoms, 3 Vols. LC 78-168243. Repr. of 1885 ed. Set. 172.50 (ISBN 0-404-03130-7). AMS Pr.
Grenfell, Russell. Unconditional Hatred. 1953. 6.95 (ISBN 0-8159-7002-1). Devin.
Higgins, R. Administration of United Kingdom Foreign Policy Through the United Nations. LC 66-18648. 72p. 1967. 7.50 (ISBN 0-379-12101-8). Oceana.
Howard, Christopher. Britain & the Casus Belli 1822-1902: A Study of Britain's International Position from Canning to Salisbury. 204p. 1974. text ed. 21.00x (ISBN 0-485-11149-7, Athlone Pr). Humanities.
Howat, G. M. Stuart & Cromwellian Foreign Policy. LC 73-91111. 180p. 1974. 17.95 (ISBN 0-312-76895-8). St Martin.
Hume, Martin A. Great Lord Burghley: A Study in Elizabethan Statecraft. LC 68-25244. (English Biography Ser., No. 31). 1969. Repr. of 1898 ed. lib. bdg. 49.95 (ISBN 0-8383-0205-X). Haskell.
Israel, Milton, ed. Pax Britannica. LC 68-113032. (Selections from History Today Ser.: No. 9). (Illus.). 1968. 5.00 (ISBN 0-05-001653-9); pap. 3.95 (ISBN 0-685-09189-9). Dufour.
Jones, J. R. Britain & the World, Sixteen Forty-Nine to Eighteen Fifteen. (Fontana History of England Ser.: No. 6). 1980. text ed. 31.50x (ISBN 0-391-01776-4). Humanities.
Kennedy, Paul. The Realities Behind Diplomacy: Background Influences on British Foreign Policy 1865-1980. 416p. 1981. text ed. 27.50x (ISBN 0-04-902005-6). Allen Unwin.
Kent, H. S. War & Trade in the Northern Seas: Anglo-Scandinavian Economic Relations in the Mid-Eighteenth Century. LC 72-75304. (Studies in Economic History). (Illus.). 288p. 1973. 40.95 (ISBN 0-521-08579-9). Cambridge U Pr.
Knaplund, Paul. Gladstone & Britain's Imperial Policy. 256p. 1966. 25.00x (ISBN 0-7146-1489-0, F Cass Co). Biblio Dist.
--Gladstone's Foreign Policy. 1970. Repr. of 1935 ed. 24.00x (ISBN 0-7146-1490-4, F Cass Co). Biblio Dist.
Korr, Charles P. Cromwell & the New Model Foreign Policy. 1975. 23.50x (ISBN 0-520-02281-5). U of Cal Pr.
Kumar, Ravinder. India & the Persian Gulf Region, 1858-1907: A Study in British Imperial Policy. 1966. 10.75x (ISBN 0-210-27094-2). Asia.
Lammers, Donald N. Explaining Munich: The Search for Motive in British Policy. LC 65-26304. (Studies: No. 16). 1966. pap. 3.95 (ISBN 0-8179-3162-7). Hoover Inst Pr.
Langford, Paul. Eighteenth Century, Sixteen Eighty-Eight to Eighteen Fifteen. LC 76-8805. (Modern British Foreign Policy Ser.). 1976. 17.95x (ISBN 0-312-24010-4). St Martin.
Lee, Maurice, Jr., ed. Dudley Carleton to John Chamberlain 1603-1624: Jacobean Letters. LC 76-185391. 1972. 22.50 (ISBN 0-8135-0723-5). Rutgers U Pr.
Livingstone, J. M. Britain & the World Economy. 1966. lib. bdg. 11.50x (ISBN 0-88307-189-4). Gannon.
Low, Donald A. Lion Rampant: Essays in the Study of British Imperialism. 232p. 1973. 24.00x (ISBN 0-7146-2986-3, F Cass Co). Biblio Dist.
--Lion Rampant: Essays in the Study of British Imperialism. 232p. 1975. pap. 9.95x (ISBN 0-7146-4010-7, F Cass Co). Biblio Dist.
Lowe, C. J. & Dockrill, M. L. The Mirage of Power, British Foreign Policy. Incl. Vol. 1. 1902-1914. 13.95x (ISBN 0-7100-7092-6); Vol. 2. 1914-1922. 18.00x (ISBN 0-7100-7093-4); Vol. 3. The Documents. 24.00x (ISBN 0-7100-7094-2). (Foreign Policies of the Great Powers Ser). 1972. Set. 50.00 (ISBN 0-685-25614-6). Routledge & Kegan.
McIntyre, W. David. Imperial Frontier in the Tropics: Eighteen Sixty-Five to Eighteen Seventy-Five. 1969. 19.95 (ISBN 0-312-40985-0). St Martin.
Marlborough, John C. Letters & Dispatches of John Churchill, First Duke of Marlborough from 1702-1712, 5 Vols. Murray, George, ed. LC 68-54801. Repr. of 1845 ed. Set. lib. bdg. 150.00x (ISBN 0-8371-2663-0, MUJC). Greenwood.
Morel, E. D. Great Britain & the Congo: The Pillage of the Congo Basin. LC 68-9619. 1969. Repr. of 1909 ed. 22.50 (ISBN 0-86527-088-0). Fertig.
Morgan, D. J. The Origins of British Aid Policy Nineteen Twenty-Four to Nineteen Forty-Five. (Official History of Colonial Development Ser.). 1980. text ed. cancelled (ISBN 0-391-01684-9). Humanities.
--A Reassessment of British Aid Policy: 1951-1970, Vol. 3. (Official History of Colonial Development Ser.). 1980. text ed. cancelled (ISBN 0-391-01686-5). Humanities.
Morris, James. Outriders-a Liberal View of Britain. 1963. 4.00x (ISBN 0-8426-1393-5). Verry.
Murray, John J. George First, the Baltic & Whig Split of 1717: A Study in Diplomacy & Propaganda. LC 68-54009. 1969. 11.50x (ISBN 0-226-55380-9). U of Chicago Pr.
Neilson, Francis. England & the Balance of Power. 1979. lib. bdg. 39.95 (ISBN 0-685-96619-4). Revisionist Pr.
Raymond, Dora N. British Policy & Opinion During the Franco-Prussian War. LC 21-20208. (Columbia University. Studies in the Social Sciences: No. 227). 1921. 27.50 (ISBN 0-404-51227-5). AMS Pr.
Schoenfeld, Maxwell P. War Ministry of Winston Churchill. LC 72-153159. (Illus.). 1972. 9.95 (ISBN 0-8138-0260-1). Iowa St U Pr.
Scott, Thomas. Workes. LC 73-6158. (English Experience Ser.: No. 621). 1265p. 1973. Repr. of 1624 ed. 126.00 (ISBN 90-221-0621-7). Walter J Johnson.
Seeley, J. R. The Growth of British Policy: A Historical Essay, 2 vols. LC 72-145289. (Illus.). 838p. 1972. Repr. of 1903 ed. 45.00 (ISBN 0-403-01203-1). Scholarly.
Seton-Watson, R. W. Britain & the Dictators. 1968. Repr. of 1938 ed. 24.00 (ISBN 0-86527-015-5). Fertig.
Spring Rice, Cecil. The Letters & Friendships of Sir Cecil Spring Rice: A Record, 2 vols. facsimile ed. Gwynn, Stephen, ed. LC 79-37912. (Select Bibliographies Reprint Ser.). Repr. of 1929 ed. Set. 48.00 (ISBN 0-8369-6750-X). Arno.

Spring Rice, Cecil A. The Letters & Friendships of Sir Cecil Spring Rice, 2 vols. Gwynn, Stephen, ed. LC 73-110868. (Illus.). Repr. of 1929 ed. lib. bdg. 41.50x (ISBN 0-8371-4545-7, SPLE). Greenwood.

Steiner, Zara S. Foreign Office & Foreign Policy 1898-1914. LC 70-85739. (Illus.). 1970. 37.50 (ISBN 0-521-07654-4). Cambridge U Pr.

Strang, William. Britain in World Affairs: The Fluctuation in Power & Influence from Henry VIII to Elizabeth II. LC 75-32463. 426p. 1976. Repr. of 1961 ed. lib. bdg. 25.00x (ISBN 0-8371-8542-4, STBW). Greenwood.

Temperley, H. W. & Penson, Lillian M. Foundations of British Foreign Policy, 1792-1902. new ed. 573p. 1966. 32.50x (ISBN 0-7146-1520-X, F Cass Co). Biblio Dist.

Trotter, Ann. Britain & East Asia, 1933 to 1937. LC 74-76581. (International Studies). (Illus.). 292p. 1975. 31.50 (ISBN 0-521-20475-5). Cambridge U Pr.

Vogel, Robert, ed. A Breviate of British Diplomatic Blue Books, 1919-1939. 474p. 1963. 16.50x (ISBN 0-7735-0005-7). McGill-Queens U Pr.

Wallace, William. The Foreign Policy Process in Britain. 1975. text ed. 23.50x (ISBN 0-905031-00-8). Humanities.

--The Foreign Policy Process in Britain. 1976. pap. text ed. 9.95x (ISBN 0-04-327057-3). Allen Unwin.

Ward, A. W. & Gooch, G. P., eds. Cambridge History of British Foreign Policy, 1783-1918, 3 Vols. 1970. Repr. lib. bdg. 87.50x (ISBN 0-374-91248-3). Octagon.

Ward, John M. British Policy in the South Pacific: 1786-1893. LC 76-10622. 1976. Repr. of 1950 ed. lib. bdg. 22.75x (ISBN 0-8371-8821-0, WABP). Greenwood.

White, Carol. The New Dark Ages Conspiracy: Britain's Plot to Destroy Civilization. LC 80-23546. (Illus.). 400p. (Orig.). 1980. pap. 4.95 (ISBN 0-933488-05-X). New Benjamin.

Willer, Thomas F., compiled by. Southeast Asian References in the British Parliamentary Papers, 1801-1972-73: An Index. LC 77-620034. (Papers in International Studies: Southeast Asia: No. 48). 1977. pap. 8.50 (ISBN 0-89680-033-4). Ohio U Ctr Intl.

Williams, Basil. Stanhope: A Study in Eighteenth-Century War & Diplomacy. LC 78-26687. (Illus.). 1979. Repr. of 1932 ed. lib. bdg. 35.00x (ISBN 0-313-20918-9, WISW). Greenwood.

Winks, Robin W. British Imperialism: Gold, God, Glory. LC 63-14412. 1963. pap. text ed. 5.95 (ISBN 0-03-012260-0, HoltC). HR&W.

Wint, Guy. British in Asia. rev. ed. LC 71-139946. 1971. Repr. of 1954 ed. 13.00 (ISBN 0-8462-1547-0). Russell.

Winwood, Ralph. Memorials of Affairs of State in the Reigns of Queen Elizabeth & King James First, 3 Vols. Sawyer, Edmund, ed. LC 75-178310. Repr. of 1725 ed. lib. bdg. 195.00 (ISBN 0-404-07020-5). AMS Pr.

Wirthwein, Walter G. Britain & the Balkan Crisis 1875-1878. LC 35-8932. (Columbia University Studies in the Social Sciences: No. 407). Repr. of 1935 ed. 28.00 (ISBN 0-404-51407-3). AMS Pr.

Wiseman, H. V. The Cabinet in the Commonwealth: Post-War Developments in Africa, the West Indies & South East Asia. LC 74-10379. 1976. Repr. of 1958 ed. lib. bdg. 22.75x (ISBN 0-8371-7681-6, WICO). Greenwood.

Wolfers, Arnold. Britain & France Between Two Wars: Conflicting Strategies of Peace from Versailles to World War Two. 1966. pap. 5.95 (ISBN 0-393-00343-4, Norton Lib). Norton.

Wolfers, Arnold & Martin, Laurence W., eds. The Anglo-American Tradition in Foreign Affairs: Readings from Thomas More to Woodrow Wilson. 1956. text ed. 17.50x (ISBN 0-686-51345-2). Elliots Bks.

Younger, Kenneth G. Changing Perspectives in British Foreign Policy. LC 76-15296. (Chatham House Essays: No. 7). 1976. Repr. lib. bdg. 15.00x (ISBN 0-8371-8962-4, YOCP). Greenwood.

GREAT BRITAIN–FOREIGN RELATIONS–BIBLIOGRAPHY

Reynolds, Philip A. British Foreign Policy in the Inter-War Years. LC 73-22755. (Illus.). 182p. 1974. Repr. of 1954 ed. lib. bdg. 15.00x (ISBN 0-8371-7347-7, REBF). Greenwood.

Swanwick, Helena M. Builders of Peace: Ten Years of the Union of Democratic Control. LC 73-147460. (Library of War & Peace; Peace Leaders: Biographies & Memoirs). lib. bdg. 38.00 (ISBN 0-8240-0319-5). Garland Pub.

GREAT BRITAIN–FOREIGN RELATIONS–ADMINISTRATION

Bishop, Donald G. The Administration of British Foreign Relations. LC 74-3761. 410p. 1974. Repr. of 1961 ed. lib. bdg. 21.50x (ISBN 0-8371-7461-9, BIBF). Greenwood.

Watt, D. C. Personalities & Policies. LC 75-5005. 275p. 1975. Repr. of 1965 ed. lib. bdg. 15.50x (ISBN 0-8371-7692-1, WAPPO). Greenwood.

GREAT BRITAIN–FOREIGN RELATIONS–CATHOLIC CHURCH

Gasquet, Francis A. Monastic Life in the Middle Ages, 1792-1806. facs. ed. LC 76-137377. (Select Bibliographies Reprint Ser). 1922. 16.00 (ISBN 0-8369-5578-1). Arno.

Hachey, Thomas, ed. Anglo-Vatican Relations, Nineteen Fourteen to Nineteen Thirty-Nine: Confidential Annual Reports of the British Ministers to the Holy See. (Ser Seventy). 1972. lib. bdg. 18.00 (ISBN 0-8161-0991-5). G K Hall.

Wilkie, W. E. The Cardinal Protectors of England, Rome & the Tudors Before the Reformation. LC 73-82462. 224p. 1974. 35.50 (ISBN 0-521-20332-5). Cambridge U Pr.

GREAT BRITAIN–FOREIGN RELATIONS–TREATIES

Hertslet. Hertslet's Commercial Treaties: A Collection of Treaties & Conventions Between Great Britain & Foreign Powers, 1827-1925, 31 Vols. Repr. 90.00 ea. (ISBN 0-384-22701-5); 890.00, 10 vol. set (ISBN 0-685-02262-5). Johnson Repr.

Liverpool, Charles J. Collection of All the Treaties of Peace, Alliance & Commerce Between Great Britain & Other Powers, 3 Vols. LC 69-16554. Repr. of 1785 ed. 50.00x (ISBN 0-678-00486-2). Kelley.

GREAT BRITAIN–FOREIGN RELATIONS–19TH CENTURY

Cecil, Algernon. British Foreign Secretaries, Eighteen Seven to Nineteen Sixteen. LC 70-118463. 1971. Repr. of 1927 ed. 14.50 (ISBN 0-8046-1212-9). Kennikat.

Crawley, C. W. The Question of Greek Independence: A Study of British Policy in the Near East, 1821-1833. LC 74-144130. 272p. 1973. Repr. of 1930 ed. 23.50 (ISBN 0-86527-161-5). Fertig.

Eldridge, G. C. Victorian Imperialism. (Illus.). 1978. text ed. 18.75x (ISBN 0-391-00823-4); pap. text ed. 8.75x (ISBN 0-391-00824-2). Humanities.

Gallardo, Alexander. Britain & the First Carlist War. 1980. Repr. of 1978 ed. lib. bdg. 25.00 (ISBN 0-8414-4492-7). Folcroft.

Hayes, Paul. The Twentieth Century, 1880-1939. LC 77-93695. (Modern British Foreign Policy). 1978. 16.95x (ISBN 0-312-82409-2). St Martin.

Hayes, Paul M. The Nineteenth Century: Eighteen-Fourteen to Eighteen-Eighty. LC 75-10760. (Modern British Foreign Policy Ser.). 300p. 1975. 18.95 (ISBN 0-312-57470-3). St Martin.

Hood, Miriam. Gunboat Diplomacy. LC 76-24618. 1977. 8.95 (ISBN 0-498-01946-2). A S Barnes.

Johnston, W. Ross. Sovereignty & Protection: A Study of British Jurisdictional Imperialism in the Late Nineteenth Century. LC 72-96681. (Commonwealth Studies Center: No. 41). 360p. 1973. 16.75 (ISBN 0-8223-0282-9). Duke.

Knaplund, Paul. Gladstone's Foreign Policy. 1970. Repr. of 1935 ed. 16.50 (ISBN 0-208-00243-X, Archon). Shoe String.

Lane-Poole, Stanley. The Life of the Right Honourable Stratford Canning, Viscount Stratford de Redcliffe, 2 vols. LC 73-171653. Repr. of 1888 ed. 70.00 set (ISBN 0-404-07387-5). AMS Pr.

Middleton, Charles R. The Administration of British Foreign Policy, 1782-1846. LC 76-51017. 1977. 17.75 (ISBN 0-8223-0383-3). Duke.

Nish, Ian H. The Anglo-Japanese Alliance: The Diplomacy of Two Island Empires. LC 75-16853. 1977. Repr. of 1968 ed. lib. bdg. 28.75x (ISBN 0-8371-8264-6, NIAJ). Greenwood.

Porter, Bernard. The Lion's Share: A Short History of British Imperialism, 1850-1970. LC 75-16224. 400p. 1976. text ed. 22.00x (ISBN 0-582-48103-1); pap. text ed. 12.95x (ISBN 0-582-48104-X). Longman.

Seton-Watson, R. W. Disraeli, Gladstone & the Eastern Question. 1972. pap. 3.95x (ISBN 0-393-00594-1, Norton Lib). Norton.

Trollope, Anthony. Lord Palmerston. Hall, N. John, ed. LC 80-1901. (Selected Works of Anthony Trollope Ser.). 1981. Repr. of 1882 ed. lib. bdg. 25.00 (ISBN 0-405-14190-4). Arno.

Webster, Sir Charles. Foreign Policy of Castlereagh, 2 vols. Incl. Vol. 1. 1812-1815; Vol. 2. 1815-1822. 1963. Set. text ed. 19.25x (ISBN 0-391-00520-0). Humanities.

GREAT BRITAIN–FOREIGN RELATIONS–20TH CENTURY

Barnett, Correlli. The Collapse of British Power. (Illus.). 138p. 1972. 15.00 (ISBN 0-688-00001-0). Morrow.

Campbell-Johnson, Alan. Eden: The Making of a Statesman. LC 76-6056. (Illus.). 306p. 1976. Repr. of 1955 ed. lib. bdg. 19.00x (ISBN 0-8371-8813-X, CAED). Greenwood.

Carter, Gwendolen M. British Commonwealth & International Security. LC 71-114494. 1971. Repr. of 1947 ed. lib. bdg. 21.25x (ISBN 0-8371-4731-X, CABC). Greenwood.

Chamberlain, Neville. In Search of Peace. facsimile ed. LC 77-156627. (Essay Index Reprint Ser). Repr. of 1939 ed. 18.00 (ISBN 0-8369-2274-3). Arno.

Churchill, Winston. Step by Step, Nineteen Thirty-Six to Nineteen Thirty-Nine. facsimile ed. LC 72-156631. (Essay Index Reprint Ser). Repr. of 1939 ed. 19.00 (ISBN 0-8369-2310-3). Arno.

Churchill, Winston S. While England Slept: A Survey of World Affairs 1932-8. facsimile ed. LC 76-165621. (Select Bibliographies Reprint Ser). Repr. of 1938 ed. 23.00 (ISBN 0-8369-5928-0). Arno.

Colvin, Ian. Chamberlain Cabinet: How the Meetings in 10 Downing Street, 1937-9, Led to the Second World War. LC 73-155803. 1971. 8.95 (ISBN 0-8008-1433-9). Taplinger.

Cowling, M. The Impact of Hitler: British Politics & British Policy 1933-1940. LC 74-12968. (Studies in the History & Theory of Politics). 448p. 1975. 59.50 (ISBN 0-521-20582-4). Cambridge U Pr.

Cowling, Maurice. The Impact of Hitler: British Politics & British Policy, 1933-1940. 1977. pap. 7.95 (ISBN 0-226-11660-3, P747, Phoen). U of Chicago Pr.

Egerton, George W. Great Britain & the Creation of the League of Nations: Strategy, Politics, & International Organization, 1914-1919. LC 77-17897. (Supplementary Volume to The Papers of Woodrow Wilson). 1978. 19.00x (ISBN 0-8078-1320-6). U of NC Pr.

Fry, Michael G. Lloyd George & Foreign Policy Volume I: The Education of a Statesman, 1890-1916. 1977. lib. bdg. 18.50x (ISBN 0-7735-0274-2). McGill-Queens U Pr.

Halifax, Edward F. Speeches on Foreign Policy, 1934-1939. facsimile ed. Craster, H. H., ed. LC 72-156658. (Essay Index Reprint Ser). Repr. of 1940 ed. 20.00 (ISBN 0-8369-2401-0). Arno.

Hayes, Paul. The Twentieth Century, 1880-1939. LC 77-93695. (Modern British Foreign Policy). 1978. 16.95x (ISBN 0-312-82409-2). St Martin.

Higgins, Ronald. The Seventh Enemy. 1978. 12.50 (ISBN 0-07-028780-5, GB). McGraw.

Hinsley, F. H., ed. British Foreign Policy Under Sir Edward Grey. LC 76-19631. 1977. 93.00 (ISBN 0-521-21347-9). Cambridge U Pr.

Hogan, Michael J. Informal Entente: The Private Structure of Cooperation in Anglo-American Economic Diplomcy, 1918-1928. LC 76-45829. 1977. 12.50x (ISBN 0-8262-0217-9). U of Mo Pr.

Mackay, Ronald W. Towards a United States of Europe. LC 75-31435. 1976. Repr. of 1961 ed. lib. bdg. 15.00 (ISBN 0-8371-8509-2, MATU). Greenwood.

Maddox, William P. Foreign Relations in British Labour Politics: A Study of the Formation of Party Attitudes on Foreign Affairs, & the Application of Political Pressure Designed to Influence Government Policy, 1900-1924. (Perspectives in European History: No. 34). Repr. of 1934 ed. lib. bdg. 17.50x (ISBN 0-87991-635-4). Porcupine Pr.

Monger, George W. The End of Isolation: British Foreign Policy, 1900-1907. LC 75-36357. 343p. 1976. Repr. of 1963 ed. lib. bdg. 28.00x (ISBN 0-8371-8628-5, MOEI). Greenwood.

Porter, Bernard. The Lion's Share: A Short History of British Imperialism, 1850-1970. LC 75-16224. 400p. 1976. text ed. 22.00x (ISBN 0-582-48103-1); pap. text ed. 12.95x (ISBN 0-582-48104-X). Longman.

Rothstein, Andrew. British Foreign Policy & Its Critics, 1830-1950. 128p. 1969. 12.95x (ISBN 0-8464-0212-2). Beekman Pubs.

Royal Institute of International Affairs. British Foreign Policy: Some Relevant Documents, January, 1950 - April, 1955. LC 78-4467. 1978. Repr. of 1955 ed. lib. bdg. 15.50x (ISBN 0-313-20370-9, RIBF). Greenwood.

Shay, Robert P., Jr. British Rearmament in the Thirties: Politics & Profits. LC 76-45911. 1977. text ed. 23.50 (ISBN 0-691-05248-4). Princeton U Pr.

Spender, John. Great Britain: Empire & Commonwealth, 1886-1935. LC 79-110864. (Illus.). 906p. 1973. Repr. of 1936 ed. lib. bdg. 37.50x (ISBN 0-8371-4537-6, SPGB). Greenwood.

Stoler, Mark A. The Politics of the Second Front: American Military Planning & Diplomacy in Coalition Warfare, 1941-1943. LC 76-47171. (Contributions in Military History Ser.: No 12). 1977. lib. bdg. 18.95 (ISBN 0-8371-9438-5, SPF/). Greenwood.

Templewood, Samuel. Nine Troubled Years. LC 75-36363. (Illus.). 448p. 1976. Repr. of 1954 ed. lib. bdg. 25.00x (ISBN 0-8371-8633-1, TENT). Greenwood.

Trollope, Anthony. Lord Palmerston. Hall, N. John, ed. LC 80-1901. (Selected Works of Anthony Trollope Ser.). 1981. Repr. of 1882 ed. lib. bdg. 25.00 (ISBN 0-405-14190-4). Arno.

Watt, D. C. Personalities & Policies. LC 75-5005. 275p. 1975. Repr. of 1965 ed. lib. bdg. 15.50x (ISBN 0-8371-7692-1, WAPPO). Greenwood.

Wilson, Keith. The Policy of the Entente: The Determinants of British Foreign Policy, 1904-1914. 1981. text ed. 15.00 (ISBN 0-391-02198-2). Humanities.

Windrich, Elaine. British Labour's Foreign Policy. LC 73-147227. 1971. Repr. of 1952 ed. lib. bdg. 15.00x (ISBN 0-8371-5992-X, WIBL). Greenwood.

GREAT BRITAIN–FOREIGN RELATIONS–AFRICA

Aronson, Theo. Royal Ambassadors: British Royalties in Southern Africa, 1860-1947. (Illus.). 144p. 1975. 14.00x (ISBN 0-8476-2392-0). Rowman.

Barber, James. Imperial Frontier. LC 70-14208. (Illus.). 1968. 9.00x (ISBN 0-8002-1279-7). Intl Pubns Serv.

Carlson, Dennis G. African Fever: A Study of British Science, Technology, and Politics in West Africa, 1787-1864. Date not set. price not set. N Watson.

Channock, Martin. Britain, Rhodesia & South Africa, 1900-1945: The Unconsummated Union. (Illus.). 289p. 1977. 27.50x (ISBN 0-7146-6001-9, F Cass Co). Biblio Dist.

Fisher, Godfrey. Barbary Legend. LC 74-9166. (Illus.). 349p. 1974. Repr. of 1957 ed. lib. bdg. 21.00x (ISBN 0-8371-7617-4, FIBL). Greenwood.

Flourney, Francis R. British Policy Toward Morocco in the Age of Palmerston, 1830-1865. 1971. lib. bdg. 15.00x (ISBN 0-374-92759-6). Octagon.

Flournoy, Francis R. British Policy Towards Morocco in the Age of Palmerston, 1830-1865. LC 74-106835. Repr. of 1935 ed. 14.75x (ISBN 0-8371-3457-9, Pub. by Negro U Pr). Greenwood.

Froude, James A. Oceana; or, England & Her Colonies. LC 72-3974. (Black Heritage Library Collection Ser.). Repr. of 1886 ed. 18.75 (ISBN 0-8369-9096-X). Arno.

Hetherington, Penelope. British Paternalism & Africa 1920-1940. 196p. 1978. 22.50x (ISBN 0-7146-3051-9, F Cass Co). Biblio Dist.

Indakwa, John. Expansion of British Rule in the Interior of Central Africa. 316p. 1977. pap. text ed. 11.25 (ISBN 0-8191-0141-9). U Pr of Amer.

Okonjo, I. M. British Administration in Nigeria, 1900-1950: A Nigerian View. LC 73-84372. (The NOK Library of African Affairs). 450p. 1974. text ed. 18.50x (ISBN 0-88357-002-5). NOK Pubs.

Pyrah, G. B. Imperial Policy & South Africa, 1902-1910. LC 74-9170. (Illus.). 272p. 1975. Repr. of 1955 ed. lib. bdg. 15.50x (ISBN 0-8371-7619-0, PYIP). Greenwood.

Williams, A. Britain & France in the Middle East & North Africa. 1969. 6.95 (ISBN 0-312-09765-4). St Martin.

GREAT BRITAIN–FOREIGN RELATIONS–AMERICA

Great Britain. Parliament. Proceedings & Debates of the British Parliaments Respecting North America, 5 vols. Stock, Leo F., ed. LC 24-7105. 1976. Set. 200.00 (ISBN 0-527-35720-0). Kraus Repr.

Kneer, Warren G. Great Britain & the Caribbean: 1901-1913: a Study in Anglo-American Relations. 242p. 1975. 12.50x (ISBN 0-87013-187-7). Mich St U Pr.

GREAT BRITAIN–FOREIGN RELATIONS–ARGENTINE REPUBLIC

Cady, John F. Foreign Intervention in the Rio De La Plata 1838-50: A Study of French, British, & American Policy in Relation to the Dictator Juan Manuel Rosas. LC 71-100817. (BCL Ser. II). Repr. of 1929 ed. 24.00 (ISBN 0-404-01360-0). AMS Pr.

Ferns, Henry S. British & Argentina in the Nineteenth Century. Wilkins, Mira, ed. LC 76-29757. (European Business Ser.). 1977. Repr. of 1960 ed. lib. bdg. 30.00x (ISBN 0-405-09772-7). Arno.

GREAT BRITAIN–FOREIGN RELATIONS–AUSTRALIA

Goodwin, Craufurd D. The Image of Australia: British Perception of the Australian Economy from the Eighteenth to the Twentieth Century. LC 73-81711. (Commonwealth Center Publications Ser.). 275p. 1974. 14.75 (ISBN 0-8223-0310-8). Duke.

Madden, A. F. & Morris-Jones, W. H., eds. Australia & Britain: Studies in a Changing Relationship. 191p. 1981. 25.00x (ISBN 0-7146-3149-3, F Cass Co). Biblio Dist.

Mander-Jones, Phyllis, ed. Manuscripts in the British Isles Relating to Australia, New Zealand & the Pacific. LC 78-172122. 1972. text ed. 35.00x (ISBN 0-8248-0204-7). U Pr of Hawaii.

Morris, E. E. Australasian England. 59.95 (ISBN 0-87968-678-2). Gordon Pr.

Perkins, James O. Britain & Australia: Economic Relationships in the 1950's. 1962. 11.50x (ISBN 0-522-83701-8, Pub. by Melbourne U Pr). Intl Schol Bk Serv.

GREAT BRITAIN–FOREIGN RELATIONS–AUSTRIA

Pribram, Alfred F. Austria-Hungary & Great Britain, 1908-1914. LC 70-138174. 328p. 1972. Repr. of 1951 ed. lib. bdg. 15.00x (ISBN 0-8371-5631-9, PRAG). Greenwood.

GREAT BRITAIN–FOREIGN RELATIONS–BURMA

Banerjee, Anil C. Annexation of Burma. LC 77-87007. Repr. of 1944 ed. 25.00 (ISBN 0-404-16793-4). AMS Pr.

Hall, David G. Early English Intercourse with Burma, 1587-1743 & Tragedy of Negrais. 2nd ed. 342p. 1968. 30.00x (ISBN 0-7146-2010-6, F Cass Co). Biblio Dist.

Moscotti, Albert D. British Policy & the Nationalist Movement in Burma, 1917-1937. (Asian Studies at Hawaii Ser.: No. 11). 288p. (Orig.). 1973. pap. text ed. 7.50x (ISBN 0-8248-0279-9). U Pr of Hawaii.

Pollack, Oliver B. Empires in Collision: Anglo-Burmese Relations in the Mid-Nineteenth Century. LC 78-75239. (Contributions in Comparative Colonial Studies: No. 1). (Illus.). 1980. lib. bdg. 25.00 (ISBN 0-313-20824-7, PEC/). Greenwood.

GREAT BRITAIN–FOREIGN RELATIONS–CANADA

Brebner, John B. North Atlantic Triangle: The Interplay of Canada, the United States, & Great Britain. enl. ed. LC 77-110676. (Relations of Canada & the U. S. Ser). (Illus.). 385p. 1970. Repr. of 1966 ed. 25.00 (ISBN 0-8462-1195-5). Russell.

Raudzens, George. The British Ordinance Department & Canada's Canals, Eighteen Fifteen to Eighteen Fifty-Five. 204p. 1979. text ed. 14.95 (ISBN 0-88920-071-8, Pub. by Laurier U Pr Canada). Humanities.

Wigley, Philip G. Canada and the Transition to Commonwealth: British-Canadian Relations, 1917-1926. LC 76-11095. (Cambridge Commonwealth Ser.). 1977. 39.95 (ISBN 0-521-21157-3). Cambridge U Pr.

GREAT BRITAIN–FOREIGN RELATIONS–CHINA

Eames, James B. The English in China: Being an Account of the Intercourse & Relations Between England & China from the Year 1600. 1974. Repr. of 1909 ed. text ed. 17.00x (ISBN 0-7007-0043-9). Humanities.

Ellis, Henry. Journal of the Proceedings of the Late Embassy to China. (China Library Ser.). 1972. Repr. of 1817 ed. 30.00 (ISBN 0-8420-1382-2). Scholarly Res Inc.

Fox, Grace E. British Admirals & Chinese Pirates, 1832-1869. LC 73-873. (China Studies: from Confucius to Mao Ser.). (Illus.). xiv, 227p. 1973. Repr. of 1940 ed. 21.50 (ISBN 0-88355-068-7). Hyperion Conn.

Friedman, Irving S. British Relations with China, 1931-1939. 1972. lib. bdg. 14.50x (ISBN 0-374-92931-9). Octagon.

--British Relations with China, 1931-1939. LC 75-30056. (Institute of Pacific Relations). Repr. of 1940 ed. 21.50 (ISBN 0-404-59522-7). AMS Pr.

Greenberg, Michael. British Trade & the Opening of China, Eighteen Hundred to Eighteen Forty-Two. LC 78-20465. 1980. Repr. of 1951 ed. 19.50 (ISBN 0-88355-844-0). Hyperion Conn.

Kiernan, E. V. British Diplomacy in China, 1880-1885. LC 78-75999. 1969. Repr. of 1939 ed. lib. bdg. 17.50x (ISBN 0-374-94579-9). Octagon.

Owen, David E. British Opium Policy in China & India. 1968. Repr. of 1934 ed. 19.50 (ISBN 0-208-00676-1, Archon). Shoe String.

Pelcovits, Nathan A. Old China Hands & the Foreign Office. LC 78-76003. 1969. Repr. of 1948 ed. lib. bdg. 16.00x (ISBN 0-374-96365-7). Octagon.

Pritchard, Earl H. Anglo-Chinese Relations During the Seventeenth & Eighteenth Centuries. LC 74-96190. 1969. Repr. lib. bdg. 15.00x (ISBN 0-374-96612-5). Octagon.

--The Crucial Years of Early Anglo-Chinese Relations, 1750-1800. LC 78-96191. 1969. Repr. lib. bdg. 17.50x (ISBN 0-374-96631-1). Octagon.

Shai, Aron. The Origins of the War in the East: Britain, China & Japan, 1937-39. 267p. 1976. 32.00x (ISBN 0-85664-333-5, Pub. by Croom Helm Ltd England). Biblio Dist.

Stremski, Richard. The Shaping of British Policy During the Nationalist Revolution in China. LC 80-110682. Orig. Title: Soochow University Political Science Series. 179p. 1980. text ed. 20.00 (ISBN 0-931712-02-5). Alpine Guild.

Wang, Shen-Tsu. The Margary Affair & the Chefoo Agreement. LC 79-2844. (Illus.). 138p. 1981. Repr. of 1940 ed. 14.50 (ISBN 0-8305-0020-0). Hyperion Conn.

GREAT BRITAIN–FOREIGN RELATIONS–CONFEDERATE STATES OF AMERICA

Bonham, Hilledge L. British Consuls in the Confederacy. LC 11-31660. (Columbia University Studies in the Social Sciences: No. 111). Repr. of 1911 ed. 12.50 (ISBN 0-404-51111-2). AMS Pr.

GREAT BRITAIN–FOREIGN RELATIONS–EAST (FAR EAST)

Anderson, John. English Intercourse with Siam in the Seventeenth Century. 1976. Repr. of 1890 ed. 45.00 (ISBN 0-403-05983-6, Regency). Scholarly.

Bassett, D. K. British Trade & Policy in Indonesia & Malaysia in the Late Eighteenth Century. LC 72-195599. (Hull Monographs on South-East Asia Ser.: Vol. 3). 130p. 1971. 16.50x (ISBN 0-8002-1242-8). Intl Pubns Serv.

Clifford, Nicholas. Retreat from China: British Policy in the Far East, 1937-1941. (China in the 20th Century Ser.). 1976. Repr. of 1967 ed. lib. bdg. 22.50 (ISBN 0-306-70757-8). Da Capo.

Gull, Edward M. British Economic Interests in the Far East. LC 75-30058. (International Series of the Institute of Pacific Relations). Repr. of 1943 ed. 22.50 (ISBN 0-404-59528-6). AMS Pr.

Lee, Bradford A. Britain & the Sino-Japanese War, 1937-1939: A Study in the Dilemmas of British Decline. LC 77-190526. 320p. 1973. 15.00x (ISBN 0-8047-0799-5). Stanford U Pr.

Lowe, Peter. Britain in the Far East: A Survey from 1819 to the Present. (Illus.). 1981. text ed. 25.00x (ISBN 0-582-48730-7). Longman.

--Great Britain & the Origins of the Pacific War: A Study of British Policy in East Asia, 1937 to 1941. (Illus.). 330p. 1977. text ed. 45.00x (ISBN 0-19-822427-3). Oxford U Pr.

McCordock, Robert S. British Far Eastern Policy, 1894-1900. 1971. lib. bdg. 18.50x (ISBN 0-374-95437-2). Octagon.

GREAT BRITAIN–FOREIGN RELATIONS–EGYPT

Cottam, Richard W. Foreign Policy Motivation: A General Theory & a Case Study. LC 76-6659. 1977. 16.95 (ISBN 0-8229-3323-3). U of Pittsburgh Pr.

Fabunmi, L. A. The Sudan in Anglo-Egyptian Relations. LC 73-15242. (Illus.). 466p. 1974. Repr. of 1960 ed. lib. bdg. 20.75x (ISBN 0-8371-7165-2, FASU). Greenwood.

Royal Institute of International Affairs, Information Department. Great Britain & Egypt: 1914-1951. LC 78-2538. (Information Papers: No. 19). 1978. Repr. of 1952 ed. lib. bdg. 19.25x (ISBN 0-313-20350-4, RIGB). Greenwood.

GREAT BRITAIN–FOREIGN RELATIONS–ETHIOPIA

Dufton, Henry. Narrative of a Journey Through Abyssinia in 1862 & 1863. LC 76-106778. Repr. of 1867 ed. 17.75x (ISBN 0-8371-3534-6, Pub. by Negro U Pr). Greenwood.

Wylde, Augustus B. Eighty-Three to Eighty-Seven in the Saudan, with an Account of Sir William Hewett's Mission to King John of Abyssinia, 2 Vols. LC 72-82088. (Illus.). Repr. of 1888 ed. 28.00x (ISBN 0-8371-1525-6, Pub. by Negro U Pr). Greenwood.

GREAT BRITAIN–FOREIGN RELATIONS–EUROPE

Allen, H. C. Anglo-American Predicament: British Commonwealth & United States & European Unity. 1960. 17.95 (ISBN 0-312-03675-2). St Martin.

Butler, David & Marquand, David. European Elections & British Politics. 208p. 1981. text ed. 25.00x (ISBN 0-582-29528-9); pap. text ed. 11.95x (ISBN 0-582-29529-7). Longman.

Jowell, Roger, ed. Britain into Europe. 128p. 1976. 15.00x (ISBN 0-85664-264-9). Intl Pubns Serv.

MacDonald, Roger. Britain Versus Europe. Date not set. 14.00 (ISBN 0-392-15070-0, SpS). Sportshelf.

Pribram, A. F. England & the International Policy of the European Great Powers, 1871-1914. 156p. 1966. 24.00x (ISBN 0-7146-1511-0, F Cass Co). Biblio Dist.

Royal Institute of International Affairs. Britain in Western Europe: WEU & the Atlantic Alliance. LC 78-2451. 1978. Repr. of 1956 ed. lib. bdg. 15.25x (ISBN 0-313-20348-2, RIBW). Greenwood.

Thompson, Neville. Anti-Appeasers: Conservative Opposition to Appeasement in the 1930's. 1971. 28.50x (ISBN 0-19-821487-1). Oxford U Pr.

Wallace, William, ed. Britain in Europe. (Joint Studies in Public Policy Ser.). 1981. text ed. 34.50x (ISBN 0-435-83919-5). Heinemann Ed.

GREAT BRITAIN–FOREIGN RELATIONS–FRANCE

Cartwright, John. Commonwealth in Danger. 1968. Repr. of 1795 ed. 24.50 (ISBN 0-8337-0486-9). B Franklin.

Choiseul, Etienne F., ed. Memoire Historique Sur la Negociation De la France et De l'Angleterre. 1761. 12.50 (ISBN 0-384-08930-5). Johnson Repr.

Coville, Alfred, et al, eds. Studies in Anglo-French History During the Eighteenth, Nineteenth & Twentieth Centuries. facs. ed. LC 67-23197. (Essay Index Reprint Ser). 1935. 15.00 (ISBN 0-8369-0343-9). Arno.

De Salignac Fenelon, Bertrand. Correspondance diplomatique, 7 Vols. LC 73-168014. (Bannatyne Club, Edinburgh. Publications: No. 67). Repr. of 1840 ed. Set. 345.00 (ISBN 0-404-52780-9). AMS Pr.

Gates, Eleanor M. End of the Affair: The Collapse of the Anglo-French Alliance. LC 80-23585. 496p. 1981. 28.50x (ISBN 0-520-04292-1). U of Cal Pr.

Jordon, W. M. Great Britain, France & the German Problem,1918-1939: Study of Anglo-French Relations in the Making & Maintenance of the Versailles Settlement. 235p. 1971. Repr. of 1943 ed. 28.50x (ISBN 0-7146-2644-9, F Cass Co). Biblio Dist.

Knachel, Philip A. England & the Fronde: The Impact of the English Civil War & Revolution on France. (Monographs). 1978. 17.50x (ISBN 0-918016-33-9). Folger Bks.

Korr, Charles P. Cromwell & the New Model Foreign Policy. 1975. 23.50x (ISBN 0-520-02281-5). U of Cal Pr.

Laprade, William T. England & the French Revolution, 1789-1797. LC 77-109922. Repr. of 1909 ed. 12.50 (ISBN 0-404-03878-6). AMS Pr.

Lee, Maurice, Jr. James First & Henri Fourth: An Essay in English Foreign Policy, 1603-1610. LC 74-100377. (Illus.). 1970. 14.50 (ISBN 0-252-00084-6). U of Ill Pr.

Legg, L. Wickham. Matthew Prior: A Study of His Public Career & Correspondence. LC 72-5135. x, 348p. 1972. Repr. of 1921 ed. lib. bdg. 17.50x (ISBN 0-374-94890-9). Octagon.

Lord, Walter E. England & France in the Mediterranean 1660-1830. LC 73-110902. 1970. Repr. of 1901 ed. 14.00 (ISBN 0-8046-0894-6). Kennikat.

Rolo, P. J. Entente Cordiale: The Origins & Negotiations of the Anglo-French Agreements of April 8, 1904. LC 77-86588. 1970. 18.95 (ISBN 0-312-25690-6). St Martin.

Savelle, Maxwell H. Diplomatic History of the Canadian Boundary, 1749-1763. LC 68-27084. (Relations of Canada & the U. S. Ser). (Illus.). 1968. Repr. of 1940 ed. 8.00 (ISBN 0-8462-1213-7). Russell.

Spears, Edward. Fulfillment of a Mission: Syria & Lebanon, 1941-1944. 1978. 19.00 (ISBN 0-208-01695-3, Archon). Shoe String.

Swain, James E. The Struggle for the Control of the Mediterranean Prior to 1848: A Study in Anglo-French Relations. LC 72-85010. 152p. 1973. Repr. of 1933 ed. 12.00 (ISBN 0-8462-1677-9). Russell.

Teulet, Jean B. Papiers D'etat, 3 Vols. LC 70-176146. (Bannatyne Club, Edinburgh. Publications: No. 107). Repr. of 1860 ed. 210.00 (ISBN 0-404-52870-8). AMS Pr.

Thomas, R. T. Britain & Vichy: The Dilemma of Anglo-French Relations, 1940-42. (The Making of the Twentieth Century Ser.). 1979. 19.95 (ISBN 0-312-09822-7). St Martin.

GREAT BRITAIN–FOREIGN RELATIONS–GERMANY

Anderson, Pauline R. Background of Anti-English Feeling in Germany, 1890-1902. LC 78-86268. 1969. Repr. of 1939 ed. lib. bdg. 24.00x (ISBN 0-374-90209-7). Octagon.

Aydelotte, William O. Bismarck & British Colonial Policy: The Problem of South West Africa, 1883-1885. LC 71-111563. 1937. Repr. of 1937 ed. 10.25x (ISBN 0-8371-4584-8, Pub. by Negro U Pr). Greenwood.

Bruegel, J. W. Czechoslovakia Before Munich: The German Minority Problem & British Appeasement Policy. 41.95 (ISBN 0-521-08687-6). Cambridge U Pr.

Gardiner, Samuel R., ed. Letters & Other Documents Illustrating the Relations Between England & Germany at the Commencement of the Thirty Years' War, 2 Vols. LC 70-168100. (Camden Society, London. Publications, First Ser.: Nos. 90 & 98). Repr. of 1868 ed. Set. 42.00 (ISBN 0-404-50211-3); 21.00 ea. Vol. 1 (ISBN 0-404-50190-7). Vol. 2 (ISBN 0-404-50198-2). AMS Pr.

--Letters & Other Documents Illustrating the Relations Between England & Germany at the Commencement of the Thirty Years War, 2 Vols. Vol. 90. 23.00 ea. (ISBN 0-384-17640-2); Vol. 98. pap. (ISBN 0-384-17645-3). Johnson Repr.

Hale, O. J. Publicity & Diplomacy with Special Reference to England & Germany (1890-1914) 8.50 (ISBN 0-8446-1215-4). Peter Smith.

Henderson, Neville. Failure of a Mission: Berlin, 1937-1939. LC 75-41131. Repr. of 1940 ed. 15.50 (ISBN 0-404-14670-8). AMS Pr.

Kennedy, Paul. Rise of the Anglo-German Antagonism: 1860-1914. (Illus.). 616p. 1980. text ed. 60.00x (ISBN 0-04-940060-6). Allen Unwin.

Mander, John. Our German Cousins: Anglo-German Relations in the 19th & 20th Centuries. 273p. 1975. 12.50 (ISBN 0-7195-2894-1). Transatlantic.

Middlemas, Keith. The Strategy of Appeasement: The British Government & Germany, 1937-1939. LC 73-182509. 1972. 15.00 (ISBN 0-8129-0241-6). Times Bks.

Newman, Simon K. March Nineteen Thirty-Nine: A Study in the Continuity of British Foreign Policy. 1976. 45.00x (ISBN 0-19-822532-6). Oxford U Pr.

Peel, Peter H. British Public Opinion & the Wars of German Unification: 1864-1871. 537p. 1978. 19.95 (ISBN 0-940990-00-8). Intl Res Inst.

Sontag, Raymond J. Germany & England: Background of Conflict, 1848-1894. 1969. pap. 3.95x (ISBN 0-393-00180-6, Norton Lib). Norton.

--Germany & England: Background of Conflict, 1848-1894. LC 64-15034. 1964. Repr. of 1938 ed. 10.00 (ISBN 0-8462-0467-3). Russell.

Taylor, Telford. Munich: The Price of Peace. 1979. 17.50 (ISBN 0-385-02053-8). Doubleday.

Wood, Bryce. Peaceful Change & the Colonial Problem. LC 70-76639. (Columbia University. Teachers College. Contributions to Education: No. 464). Repr. of 1940 ed. 15.00 (ISBN 0-404-51464-2). AMS Pr.

GREAT BRITAIN–FOREIGN RELATIONS–HOLY ROMAN EMPIRE

Bradford, William, ed. Correspondence of the Emperor Charles Fifth. Repr. of 1850 ed. 27.50 (ISBN 0-404-00926-3). AMS Pr.

GREAT BRITAIN–FOREIGN RELATIONS–INDIA

Barrier, N. G. & Crane, Robert I., eds. British Imperial Policy in India and Sri Lanka, Eighteen Fifty-Eight to Nineteen Twelve: A Reassessment. 1981. 18.50x (ISBN 0-8364-0726-1). South Asia Bks.

Bhuyan, Suryya K. Anglo-Assamese Relations: Seventeen Seventy-One to Eighteen Twenty-Six. LC 77-87072. Repr. of 1949 ed. 46.00 (ISBN 0-404-16795-0). AMS Pr.

Chakravorty, Birendra C. British Relations with the Hill Tribes of Assam Since Eighteen Fifty-Eight. 1981. 12.50x (ISBN 0-8364-0705-9, Pub. by Mukhopadhyay). South Asia Bks.

Chamberlain, Muriel E. Britain & India: The Interraction of Two Peoples. (Library of Politics & Society Ser). 264p. 1974. 19.50 (ISBN 0-208-01423-3, Archon). Shoe String.

Hassnain, F. M. British Policy Towards Kashmir (Prior to 1974) 1974. 9.00x (ISBN 0-8426-0690-4). Verry.

Hoskins, Halford L. British Routes to India. new ed. (Illus.). 494p. 1966. 32.50x (ISBN 0-7146-2014-9, F Cass Co). Biblio Dist.

Hutchins, F. Illusion of Permanence: British Imperialism in India. 1967. 16.50 (ISBN 0-691-03023-5). Princeton U Pr.

Lipton, Michael. The Erosion of a Relationship: India & Britain Since 1960. (Illus.). 1976. 43.00x (ISBN 0-19-218310-9). Oxford U Pr.

Mims, Stewart L. Colbert's West India Policy. 1973. lib. bdg. 20.00x (ISBN 0-374-95764-9). Octagon.

Moore, R. J. Churchill, Cripps, & India, Nineteen Thirty-Nine to Nineteen Forty-Five. 1979. 33.00x (ISBN 0-19-822485-0). Oxford U Pr.

Panikkar, K. N. British Diplomacy in North India. 1968. 8.25x (ISBN 0-8426-1464-8). Verry.

Thompson, Edward J. The Other Side of the Medal. LC 78-144848. 142p. 1974. Repr. of 1926 ed. lib. bdg. 15.00x (ISBN 0-8371-5979-2, THOS). Greenwood.

Venkataramani, M. S. & Shrivastava, B. K. Roosevelt, Gandhi, Churchill. 300p. 1980. text ed. 18.50 (ISBN 0-391-01971-6). Humanities.

Watson, Ian B. Foundation for Empire: English Private Trade in India, 1659 to 1760. (Illus.). 384p. 1980. text ed. 37.50 (ISBN 0-7069-1038-9, Pub. by Vikas India). Advent NY.

GREAT BRITAIN–FOREIGN RELATIONS–IRELAND

Barzilay, David. British Army in Ulster. (Illus.). 1976. Repr. of 1973 ed. 29.95x set (ISBN 0-8464-0209-2). Beekman Pubs.

Cobden, Richard. England, Ireland, & America. LC 77-28350. 1980. text ed. 15.95x (ISBN 0-915980-44-4). Inst Study Human.

Dangerfield, George. The Damnable Question: A Study in Anglo-Irish Relations. pap. 5.95 (ISBN 0-316-17201-4, Atlantic-Little, Brown). Little.

--The Damnable Question: A Study of Anglo-Irish Relations. 1976. 14.95 (ISBN 0-316-17200-6, Pub. by Atlantic Monthly Pr). Little.

Hammond, J. L. Gladstone & the Irish Nation. 2nd ed. 785p. 1964. 32.50x (ISBN 0-7146-1479-3, F Cass Co). Biblio Dist.

Johnston, Edith M. Great Britain & Ireland Seventeen Sixty-Eighteen Hundred: A Study in Political Administration. LC 78-2887. (St. Andrews University Publications Ser.: No. 55). 1978. Repr. of 1963 ed. lib. bdg. 34.50x (ISBN 0-313-20341-5, JOGB). Greenwood.

Lebow, Richard N. White Britain & Black Ireland: The Influence of Stereotypes on Colonial Policy. LC 75-41333. 1976. text ed. 10.95x (ISBN 0-915980-01-0). Inst Study Human.

Murray, Alice E. History of the Commercial & Financial Relations Between England & Ireland from the Period of the Restoration. LC 75-122235. (Research & Source Works Ser: No. 482). 1970. Repr. of 1903 ed. lib. bdg. 29.00 (ISBN 0-8337-2491-6). B Franklin.

--A History of the Commercial & Financial Relations Between England & Ireland from the Period of the Restoration. facsimile ed. LC 70-133529. (Select Bibliographies Reprint Ser). Repr. of 1903 ed. 23.00 (ISBN 0-8369-5561-7). Arno.

GREAT BRITAIN–FOREIGN RELATIONS–ITALY

Giustiniani, Sebastiano. Four Years at the Court of Henry Eighth, 2 Vols. Brown, Rawdon, tr. from It. LC 75-133813. Repr. of 1854 ed. 37.50 (ISBN 0-404-02836-5). AMS Pr.

Glanville, James L. Italy's Relations with England, 1896-1905. LC 78-64153. (Johns Hopkins University. Studies in the Social Sciences. Fifty-Second Ser. 1934: 1). Repr. of 1934 ed. 18.50 (ISBN 0-404-61263-6). AMS Pr.

GREAT BRITAIN–FOREIGN RELATIONS–JAPAN

Chang, Chung-Fu. The Anglo-Japanese Alliance. LC 78-64282. (Johns Hopkins University. Studies in the Social Sciences. Extra Volumes-New Ser.: 12). Repr. of 1931 ed. 26.00 (ISBN 0-404-61382-9). AMS Pr.

Dennis, Alfred L. The Anglo-Japanese Alliance. 1923. pap. 6.00 (ISBN 0-384-11395-8). Johnson Repr.

Fox, Grace. Britain & Japan, 1858-1883. 1969. 22.00x (ISBN 0-19-821374-3). Oxford U Pr.

Ishii, Osamu. Cotton-Textile Diplomacy: Japan, Great Britain & the United States, 1930-1936. Bruchey, Stuart, ed. LC 80-2813. (Dissertations in European Economic History II). 1981. lib. bdg. 45.00x (ISBN 0-405-13996-9). Arno.

Kennedy, Malcolm D. The Estrangement of Great Britain & Japan, 1917-1935. LC 71-77517. (Illus.). 1969. 24.50x (ISBN 0-520-01431-6). U of Cal Pr.

Lowe, Peter. Great Britain & Japan Nineteen Eleven to Nineteen Fifteen: A Study of British Far Eastern Policy. (Illus.). 1969. lib. bdg. 25.00 (ISBN 0-312-34510-0). St Martin.

Nish, Ian H. Alliance in Decline: A Study in Anglo-Japanese Relations 1908-23. (University of London Historical Studies: No. 33). (Illus.). 472p. (Orig.). 1972. text ed. 47.00x (ISBN 0-485-13133-1, Athlone Pr). Humanities.

--The Anglo-Japanese Alliance: The Diplomacy of Two Island Empires. LC 75-16853. 1977. Repr. of 1968 ed. lib. bdg. 28.75x (ISBN 0-8371-8264-6, NIAJ). Greenwood.

Oliphant, Laurence. Elgin's Mission to China & Japan, 2 Vols. (Oxford in Asia Historical Reprints Ser). 1970. 22.25x (ISBN 0-19-641004-5). Oxford U Pr.

--Narrative of the Lord of Elgin's Mission to China & Japan, 2 Vols. LC 72-77056. Repr. of 1859 ed. 22.00x (ISBN 0-678-00498-6). Kelley.

Shai, Aron. The Origins of the War in the East: Britain, China & Japan, 1937-39. 267p. 1976. 32.00x (ISBN 0-85664-333-5, Pub. by Croom Helm Ltd England). Biblio Dist.

GREAT BRITAIN–FOREIGN RELATIONS–LATIN AMERICA

Burke, William. Additional Reasons for Our Immediately Emancipating Spanish America. LC 73-128426. Repr. of 1808 ed. 12.50 (ISBN 0-404-01240-X). AMS Pr.

Graham, R. Britain & the Onset of Modernization in Brazil, 1850-1914. LC 68-21393. (Latin American Studies: No. 4). (Illus.). 1972. 42.50 (ISBN 0-521-07078-3); pap. 10.95x (ISBN 0-521-09681-2). Cambridge U Pr.

Kaufmann, William W. British Policy & the Independence of Latin America, 1804-1828. 1967. Repr. of 1951 ed. 18.50 (ISBN 0-208-00351-7, Archon). Shoe String.

Rippy, J. Fred. Rivalry of the United States & Great Britain Over Latin America, 1808-1830. 1964. lib. bdg. 20.00x (ISBN 0-374-96821-7). Octagon.

Smith, Joseph. Illusions of Conflict: Anglo-American Diplomacy Toward Latin America, 1865-1896. LC 78-53602. (Pitt Latin American Ser.). 1979. 16.95 (ISBN 0-8229-3387-X). U of Pittsburgh Pr.

Webster, C. K. Britain & the Independence of Latin America, 1812-1830, 2 vols. LC 79-96194. 1969. Repr. Set. lib. bdg. 70.00x (ISBN 0-374-98303-8). Octagon.

GREAT BRITAIN–FOREIGN RELATIONS–MEXICO

Tischendorf, Alfred P. Great Britain & Mexico in the Era of Porfiro Dias. LC 61-6224. 1961. 12.75 (ISBN 0-8223-0180-6). Duke.

GREAT BRITAIN–FOREIGN RELATIONS–NEAR EAST

Busch, Briton C. Mudros to Lausanne: Britain's Frontier in West Asia, 1918-1923, Vol. 3. LC 76-21641. 1976. 34.00 (ISBN 0-87395-265-0). State U NY Pr.

Crawley, C. W. The Question of Greek Independence: A Study of British Policy in the Near East, 1821-1833. LC 74-144130. 272p. 1973. Repr. of 1930 ed. 23.50 (ISBN 0-86527-161-5). Fertig.

Cumming, Henry H. Franco-British Rivalry in the Post-War Near East: The Decline of French Influence. LC 79-2854. (Illus.). 229p. 1981. Repr. of 1938 ed. 19.75 (ISBN 0-8305-0029-4). Hyperion Conn.

Darwin, John. Britain, Egypt & the Middle East. LC 80-14718. 1980. write for info. (ISBN 0-312-09736-0). St Martin.

Fitzsimons, Matthew A. Empire by Treaty: Britain & the Middle East in the Twentieth Century. (International Studies Ser). 1964. 9.95x (ISBN 0-268-00088-3). U of Notre Dame Pr.

Gooch, John. The Prospect of War: British Defence Policy Eighteen Forty-Seven to Nineteen Forty-Two. 150p. 1981. 25.00x (ISBN 0-7146-3128-0, F Cass Co). Biblio Dist.

Hyamson, Albert M. Palestine under the Mandate, 1920-1948. LC 72-593. 210p. 1976. Repr. of 1950 ed. lib. bdg. 19.00x (ISBN 0-8371-5996-2, HYPU). Greenwood.

Hyamson, Albert M., ed. & intro. by. The British Consulate in Jerusalem in Relation to the Jews of Palestine, 1838-1914, 2 vols. LC 70-180348. Repr. of 1941 ed. Set. 49.50 (ISBN 0-404-56278-7). AMS Pr.

Joseph, Bernard. British Rule in Palestine. (Return to Zion Ser.). vii, 279p. 1980. Repr. of 1949 ed. lib. bdg. 20.00x (ISBN 0-87991-136-0). Porcupine Pr.

Kedourie, E. In the Anglo-Arab Labyrinth. LC 75-3975. (Studies in the History & Theory of Politics). (Illus.). 370p. 1976. 44.95 (ISBN 0-521-20826-2). Cambridge U Pr.

Kimche, Jon & Kimche, David. Both Sides of the Hill: Britain & the Palestine War. (Return to Zion Ser.). (Illus.). 287p. Repr. of 1960 ed. lib. bdg. 20.00x (ISBN 0-87991-145-X). Porcupine Pr.

Lee, Dwight E. Great Britain & the Cyprus Convention Policy of 1878. LC 35-2422. (Historical Studies: No. 38). (Illus.). 1934. 10.00x (ISBN 0-674-36100-8). Harvard U Pr.

Puryear, Vernon J. International Economics & Diplomacy in the Near East: A Study of British Commercial Policy in the Levant, 1834-1853. (Illus.). 1969. Repr. of 1935 ed. 18.50 (ISBN 0-208-00699-0, Archon). Shoe String.

Rubin, Barry. The Great Powers in the Middle East Nineteen Forty-One to Nineteen Forty-Seven: The Road to the Cold War. 254p. 1980. 26.00x (ISBN 0-7146-3141-8, F Cass Co). Biblio Dist.

Seton-Williams, M. V. Britain & the Arab States: A Survey of Anglo-Arab Relations, 1920-1948. LC 79-2881. (Illus.). 330p. 1981. Repr. of 1948 ed. 26.50 (ISBN 0-8305-0049-9). Hyperion Conn.

Williams, A. Britain & France in the Middle East & North Africa. 1969. 6.95 (ISBN 0-312-09765-4). St Martin.

Zeine, Zeine N. The Struggle for Arab Independence. 2nd ed. LC 77-5149. 280p. 1977. lib. bdg. 25.00x (ISBN 0-88206-002-3). Caravan Bks.

GREAT BRITAIN–FOREIGN RELATIONS–NETHERLANDS

An Answere to the Hollanders Declaration, Concerning the Occurrents of the East India. LC 72-168. (English Experience Ser.: No. 327). 1971. Repr. of 1622 ed. 7.00 (ISBN 90-221-0327-7). Walter J Johnson.

Dorsten, J. A. Ten Studies in Anglo-Dutch Relations. (Publications of Sir Thomas Browne Institute Ser: No. 5). 1974. lib. bdg. 34.00 (ISBN 90-6021-217-7, Pub. by Leiden Univ. Holland). Kluwer Boston.

Dudley, Robert. Correspondence of Robert Dudley. 1844. 46.00 (ISBN 0-384-32130-5). Johnson Repr.

Duke, A. C. & Tamse, C. A., eds. Britain & the Netherlands: War and Society. (Britain & the Netherland Ser: Vol. VI.). 1978. lib. bdg. 26.00 (ISBN 90-247-2012-5, Pub. by Martinus Nijhoff Netherlands). Kluwer Boston.

Edler, Friedrich. Dutch Republic & the American Revolution. LC 78-149686. Repr. of 1911 ed. 23.00 (ISBN 0-404-02246-4). AMS Pr.

The Hollanders Declaration of the Affaires of the East Indies. LC 72-187. (English Experience Ser.: No. 326). 12p. Repr. of 1622 ed. 7.00 (ISBN 90-221-0326-9). Walter J Johnson.

Scott, Thomas. Relation of Some Special Points Concerning the State of Holland...Shewing Why for the Security of the United Provinces Warre Is Better Than Peace. LC 73-6160. (English Experience Ser.: No. 623). 20p. 1973. Repr. of 1621 ed. 5.00 (ISBN 90-221-0623-3). Walter J Johnson.

Wilson, Charles. Queen Elizabeth & the Revolt of the Netherlands. LC 76-119009. 1970. 22.75x (ISBN 0-520-01744-7). U of Cal Pr.

GREAT BRITAIN–FOREIGN RELATIONS–PORTUGAL

Francis, A. D. Methuens & Portugal. 1966. 53.50 (ISBN 0-521-05028-6). Cambridge U Pr.

Prestage, Edgar, ed. Chapters in Anglo-Portuguese Relations. LC 73-109826. (Illus.). 1971. Repr. of 1935 ed. lib. bdg. 15.00x (ISBN 0-8371-4317-9, PRCA). Greenwood.

Shillington, Violet M. & Chapman, A. B. Commercial Relations of England & Portugal. LC 78-131458. (Research & Source Works Ser: No. 549). 1970. Repr. of 1907 ed. lib. bdg. 23.50 (ISBN 0-8337-3252-8). B Franklin.

GREAT BRITAIN–FOREIGN RELATIONS–RHODESIA, SOUTHERN

Windrich, Elaine. Britain & the Politics of Rhodesian Independence. LC 78-4070. 1978. text ed. 32.50x (ISBN 0-8419-0366-2, Africana). Holmes & Meier.

Young, Kenneth. Rhodesia & Independence. 1967. 7.25 (ISBN 0-685-11979-3). Heineman.

GREAT BRITAIN–FOREIGN RELATIONS–RUSSIA

British Foreign Office. British Foreign Office: Russia Correspondence, 1914 - 1918: Indexes & Guides to the Microfilm Collection. LC 76-44647. 1976. 20.00 (ISBN 0-8420-2107-8). Scholarly Res Inc.

Buchanan, George, 1854-1924. My Mission to Russia & Other Diplomatic Memories. LC 78-115510. (Russia Observed, Series 1). 1970. Repr. of 1923 ed. 22.00 (ISBN 0-405-03008-8). Arno.

Churchill, Rogers P. The Anglo-Russian Convention of 1907. LC 72-73. (Select Bibliographies Reprint Ser). 1972. Repr. of 1939 ed. 16.75 (ISBN 0-8369-9956-8). Arno.

--The Anglo-Russian Convention of 1907. 1939. 12.50x (ISBN 0-686-17413-5). R S Barnes.

Churchill, Rogers Platt. The Anglo-Russian Convention of 1907. 365p. 1975. Repr. of 1939 ed. lib. bdg. 17.50x (ISBN 0-374-91600-4). Octagon.

Cross, A. G., ed. Britain & Russia: Contacts & Comparisons, 1700-1800. (Illus.). 1979. 16.50 (ISBN 0-89250-109-X). Orient Res Partners.

Fletcher, Giles. Russia at the Close of the Sixteenth Century. Bond, Augustus, ed. (Hakluyt Soc., First Ser Publ.: Vol. 20). 32.00 (ISBN 0-8337-0334-X). B Franklin.

Gleason, John H. The Genesis of Russophobia in Great Britain. LC 70-159189. ix, 314p. 1971. Repr. of 1950 ed. lib. bdg. 16.50x (ISBN 0-374-93156-9). Octagon.

Gorodetsky. The Precarious Truce. LC 76-2279. (Soviet & East European Studies). 1977. 36.00 (ISBN 0-521-21226-X). Cambridge U Pr.

Middleton, K. W. Britain & Russia. LC 76-118489. 1971. Repr. of 1947 ed. 13.00 (ISBN 0-8046-1238-2). Kennikat.

Puryear, Vernon. England, Russia & the Straits Question, 1844-1856. 1965. Repr. of 1931 ed. 22.50 (ISBN 0-208-00104-2, Archon). Shoe String.

Smith, Arthur L., Jr. Churchill's German Army: Wartime Strategy & Cold War Politics, 1943-1947. LC 77-12683. (Sage Library of Social Research: Vol. 54). 159p. 1977. 20.00 (ISBN 0-8039-0928-4); pap. 9.95 (ISBN 0-8039-0929-2). Sage.

Solzhenitsyn, Alexander. Warning to the West. 146p. 1976. 7.95 (ISBN 0-374-26758-8); pap. 4.95 (ISBN 0-374-51334-1). FS&G.

Tolstoy, George, ed. First Forty Years of Intercourse Between England & Russia, 1553-1593. 1875. 32.00 (ISBN 0-8337-3545-4). B Franklin.

GREAT BRITAIN–FOREIGN RELATIONS–SPAIN

Childs, Wendy R. Anglo-Castilian Trade in the Later Middle Ages. (Illus.). 264p. 1978. 23.50x (ISBN 0-8476-6071-0). Rowman.

Coe, Samuel G. The Mission of William Carmichael to Spain. LC 78-64127. (Johns Hopkins University. Studies in the Social Sciences. Forty-Sixth Ser. 1928: 1). Repr. of 1928 ed. 15.50 (ISBN 0-404-61240-7). AMS Pr.

Francisco De Jesus. El Hecho De los Tratados Del Matrimonio Pretendido Pro el Principe De Gales Con la Serenissima Infa De Espana, Maria. Gardiner, Samuel R., tr. Repr. of 1869 ed. 23.00 (ISBN 0-384-16690-3). Johnson Repr.

--Narrative of the Spanish Marriage Treaty. Gardiner, Samuel R., tr. LC 72-168133. (Camden Society, London, Publications, First Ser.: No. 101). Repr. of 1869 ed. 21.00 (ISBN 0-404-50201-6). AMS Pr.

Gallardo, Alexander. Britain & the First Carlist War. 1980. Repr. of 1978 ed. lib. bdg. 25.00 (ISBN 0-8414-4492-7). Folcroft.

Loomie, Albert J. Spanish Elizabethans: The English Exiles at the Court of Philip Second. LC 63-14407. 1963. 25.00 (ISBN 0-8232-0560-6). Fordham.

--Toleration & Diplomacy: The Religious Issue in Anglo-Spanish Relations. LC 63-21166. (Transactions Ser.: Vol. 53, Pt. 6). (Illus.). 1963. pap. 1.00 (ISBN 0-87169-536-7). Am Philos.

Maltby, William S. Black Legend in England: The Development of Anti-Spanish Sentiment, 1558-1660. LC 78-161356. 1971. 9.75 (ISBN 0-8223-0250-0). Duke.

--Black Legend in England: The Development of Anti-Spanish Sentiment, 1558-1660. LC 78-161356. 1971. 9.75 (ISBN 0-8223-0250-0). Duke.

Powell, Philip W. Tree of Hate: Propaganda & Prejudices Affecting United States' Relations with the Hispanic World. LC 79-158442. (Illus.). 1971. text ed. 11.50x (ISBN 0-465-08750-7). Basic.

Scott, Thomas. Sir Walter Rawleighs Ghost or Englands Forewarner. LC 74-80222. (English Experience Ser.: No. 693). 42p. 1974. Repr. of 1626 ed. 5.00 (ISBN 90-221-0693-4). Walter J Johnson.

Silke, John J. Kinsale: The Spanish Intervention in Ireland at the End of the Elizabethan Wars. LC 77-96148. (Illus.). 1970. 25.00 (ISBN 0-8232-0865-6). Fordham.

Teulet, Jean B. Papiers D'etat, 3 Vols. LC 70-176146. (Bannatyne Club, Edinburgh. Publications: No. 107). Repr. of 1860 ed. 210.00 (ISBN 0-404-52870-8). AMS Pr.

GREAT BRITAIN–FOREIGN RELATIONS–TIBET

Addy, P. N. Anglo-Tibetan Relations Eighteen Ninety-Nine to Nineteen Forty-Seven. (Illus.). 1979. pap. text ed. 10.25x (ISBN 0-391-01125-1). Humanities.

GREAT BRITAIN–FOREIGN RELATIONS–TURKEY

Ashley, Percy. Modern Tariff History: Germany, United States, France. LC 68-9645. 1970. Repr. of 1926 ed. 24.00 (ISBN 0-86527-131-3). Fertig.

Bailey, Frank E. British Policy & the Turkish Reform Movement: A Study in Anglo-Turkish Relations, 1826-1853. LC 74-80519. 1970. Repr. of 1942 ed. 24.50 (ISBN 0-86527-019-8). Fertig.

Bent, James T., ed. Early Voyages & Travels in the Levant: The Diary of Thomas Dallam, 1599-1600 & Extracts from the Diaries of Dr. John Covel 1670-1679. 1670-79. 29.50 (ISBN 0-8337-0233-5). B Franklin.

Byrne, Leo G. Great Ambassador. LC 64-22404. 1965. 6.25 (ISBN 0-8142-0032-X). Ohio St U Pr.

Heller, Joseph. British Policy Towards the Ottoman Empire Nineteen Hundred Eight - Nineteen Fourteen. 1981. 26.00x (ISBN 0-7146-3127-2, F Cass Co). Biblio Dist.

Kedourie, Elie. England & the Middle East: The Destruction of the Ottoman Empire, 1914-1921. 1978. Repr. of 1956 ed. 20.00x (ISBN 0-87471-869-4). Rowman.

Millman, Richard. Britain & the Eastern Question 1875-1878. (Illus.). 1979. 79.00x (ISBN 0-19-822379-X). Oxford U Pr.

Skilliter, Susan. William Harborne & the Trade with Turkey: Secret Agent, 1578-1581. (Illus.). 1978. 49.00x (ISBN 0-19-725971-5). Oxford U Pr.

Weber, Frank G. The Evasive Neutral: Germany, Britain, & the Quest for a Turkish Alliance in the Second World War. LC 78-19641. 1979. text ed. 19.50x (ISBN 0-8262-0262-4). U of Mo Pr.

GREAT BRITAIN–FOREIGN RELATIONS–UNITED STATES

Adams, Charles F. Lee at Appomattox, & Other Papers. 2nd facs. ed. LC 77-134047. (Essay Index Reprint Ser). 1902. 23.00 (ISBN 0-8369-1901-7). Arno.

Adams, Ephraim D. British Interests & Activities in Texas, 1838-1846. 1963. 8.00 (ISBN 0-8446-1004-6). Peter Smith.

--Great Britain & the American Civil War, 2 Vols in 1. LC 58-5369. (Illus.). 1957. Repr. of 1924 ed. 16.50 (ISBN 0-8462-0102-X). Russell.

--Great Britain & the American Civil War, 2 vols. Set. 16.00 (ISBN 0-8446-1005-4). Peter Smith.

Allen, H. C. Anglo-American Predicament: British Commonwealth & United States & European Unity. 1960. 17.95 (ISBN 0-312-03675-2). St Martin.

Bemis, Samuel F. Jay's Treaty: A Study in Commerce & Diplomacy. LC 75-11844. (Illus.). 1975. Repr. of 1962 ed. lib. bdg. 29.50 (ISBN 0-8371-8133-X, BEJT). Greenwood.

Benns, F. Lee. American Struggle for the British West India Carrying-Trade 1815-1830. LC 68-55479. Repr. of 1923 ed. lib. bdg. 12.50x (ISBN 0-678-00793-4). Kelley.

Bernard, Mountague. Historical Account of the Neutrality of Great Britain During the American Civil War. LC 70-146237. 1971. Repr. of 1870 ed. lib. bdg. 32.00 (ISBN 0-8337-0246-7). B Franklin.

Bourne, Kenneth. Britain & the Balance of Power in North America, 1815-1908. LC 67-26632. 1967. 29.50x (ISBN 0-520-00153-2). U of Cal Pr.

Boyd, Julian P. Number Seven: Alexander Hamilton's Secret Attempts to Control American Foreign Policy. 1964. 13.50 (ISBN 0-691-04529-1). Princeton U Pr.

Brebner, John B. North Atlantic Triangle: The Interplay of Canada, the United States, & Great Britain. enl. ed. LC 77-110676. (Relations of Canada & the U. S. Ser). (Illus.). 385p. 1970. Repr. of 1966 ed. 25.00 (ISBN 0-8462-1195-5). Russell.

Brinton, Clarence C. United States & Britain. LC 75-97340. Repr. of 1948 ed. lib. bdg. 15.00x (ISBN 0-8371-2964-8, BRUS). Greenwood.

Brooks Bright Foundation. Aspects of Anglo-American Relations. 1928. 19.50x (ISBN 0-685-69830-0). Elliots Bks.

Burt, Alfred L. United States, Great Britain & British North America. LC 61-13768. (Relations of Canada & the U. S. Ser). (Illus.). 1961. Repr. of 1940 ed. 15.00 (ISBN 0-8462-0143-7). Russell.

Campbell, A. E. Great Britain & the United States, 1895-1903. LC 73-19122. 216p. 1974. Repr. of 1960 ed. lib. bdg. 15.00 (ISBN 0-8371-7302-7, CAGB). Greenwood.

Combs, Jerald A. The Jay Treaty: Political Battleground of the Founding Fathers. LC 70-84044. 1970. 21.50x (ISBN 0-520-01573-8). U of Cal Pr.

Cross, Jack L. London Mission: The First Critical Years. x, 180p. 1969. 6.00 (ISBN 0-87013-128-1). Mich St U Pr.

Davis, Forrest. The Atlantic System: The Story of Ango-American Control of the Seas. LC 73-3012. 363p. 1973. Repr. of 1941 ed. lib. bdg. 17.00x (ISBN 0-8371-6833-3, DAAS). Greenwood.

Dawes, Charles G. Journal As Ambassador to Great Britain. LC 72-109728. Repr. of 1939 ed. lib. bdg. 28.00x (ISBN 0-8371-4218-0, DAJO). Greenwood.

Dunning, William A. British Empire & the United States. LC 14-18567. 1969. Repr. of 1914 ed. 20.00 (ISBN 0-527-25800-8). Kraus Repr.

Ferris, Norman B. The Trent Affair: A Diplomatic Crisis. LC 76-28304. 1977. 16.50x (ISBN 0-87049-169-5). U of Tenn Pr.

Fox, Frank. Mastery of the Pacific. LC 75-111757. (American Imperialism: Viewpoints of United States Foreign Policy, 1898-1941). 1970. Repr. of 1928 ed. 15.00 (ISBN 0-405-02020-1). Arno.

Gelber, Lionel M. Rise of Anglo-American Friendship: A Study in World Politics, 1898-1906. 1966. Repr. of 1938 ed. 17.50 (ISBN 0-208-00506-4, Archon). Shoe String.

Hathaway, Robert M. Ambiguous Partnership: Britain & America, 1944-1947. LC 81-6153. (Contemporary American History Ser.). 448p. 1981. 22.50x (ISBN 0-231-04452-6). Columbia U Pr.

Hendrick, Burton J. Life & Letters of Walter H. Page, 3 Vols. LC 79-145079. (Illus.). 1971. Repr. of 1925 ed. Set. 89.00 (ISBN 0-403-00769-0). Scholarly.

Jenkins, Brian. Britain & the War for the Union, Vol. 2. 480p. 1980. 26.50 (ISBN 0-7735-0354-4). McGill-Queens U Pr.

--Fenians & Anglo-American Relations During Reconstruction. LC 79-81595. 1969. 22.50x (ISBN 0-8014-0500-9). Cornell U Pr.

Katz, Stanley N. Newcastle's New York: Anglo-American Politics, 1732-1753. LC 68-14261. (Illus.). 1968. 15.00x (ISBN 0-674-62051-8, Belknap Pr). Harvard U Pr.

Kernek, Sterling J. Distractions of Peace During War: The Lloyd George Government's Reactions to Woodrow Wilson, December 1916 - November 1918. LC 75-2608. (Transactions Ser.: Vol. 65, Pt. 2). 1975. pap. 6.00 (ISBN 0-87169-652-5). Am Philos.

Leuchtenburg, W. E., et al. Britain & the United States. LC 80-670039. (Orig.). 1980. pap. text ed. 7.95x (ISBN 0-435-32527-2). Heinemann Ed.

Mayo, B. Instructions to the British Ministers to the United States, 1791-1812. LC 70-75280. (Law, Politics & History Ser). 1971. lib. bdg. 42.50 (ISBN 0-306-71303-9). Da Capo.

Merk, Frederick. Oregon Question: Essays in Anglo-American Diplomacy & Politics. LC 67-14345. 1967. 20.00x (ISBN 0-674-64200-7, Belknap Pr). Harvard U Pr.

Neale, R. G. Great Britain & United States Expansion: 1898-1900. xxii, 230p. 1966. 6.00 (ISBN 0-87013-094-3). Mich St U Pr.

Neustadt, Richard E. Alliance Politics. LC 77-120855. 167p. 1970. 15.00x (ISBN 0-231-03066-5); pap. 6.00x (ISBN 0-231-08307-6). Columbia U Pr.

Nicholas, H. G. The United States & Britain. LC 74-16681. (The United States in the World: Foreign Perspectives). 1978. pap. 3.25 (ISBN 0-226-58003-2, P758, Phoen). U of Chicago Pr.

Nicholas, Herbert. Britain & the U. S. A. (Britain in the World Today Ser). 192p. 1963. 13.00x (ISBN 0-8018-0491-4). Johns Hopkins.

--Dispatches from Washington, 1941-45: Weekly Reports from the British Embassy. 784p. 1981. 40.00 (ISBN 0-226-58004-0). U of Chicago Pr.

Nicholas, Herbert G. The United States & Britain. Iriye, Akira, ed. LC 74-16681. (The United States in the World, Foreign Perspectives Ser.). viii, 196p. 1975. 10.00x (ISBN 0-226-58002-4). U of Chicago Pr.

O'Grady, Joseph P. Irish-Americans & Anglo-American Relations, 1880-1888. LC 76-6360. (Irish Americans Ser). 1976. 20.00 (ISBN 0-405-09353-5). Arno.

Perkins, Bradford. Castlereagh & Adams: England & the United States, 1812-1823. 1964. 25.00x (ISBN 0-520-00997-5). U of Cal Pr.

--The First Rapprochement: England & the United States, 1795-1805. 1967. Repr. 24.00x (ISBN 0-520-00998-3). U of Cal Pr.

--Prologue to War: England & the United States, 1805-1812. 1961. pap. 7.95x (ISBN 0-520-00996-7). U of Cal Pr.

Rippy, J. Fred. Rivalry of the United States & Great Britain Over Latin America, 1808-1830. 1964. lib. bdg. 20.00x (ISBN 0-374-96821-7). Octagon.

Ritcheson, Charles R. Aftermath of Revolution: British Policy Toward the United States, 1783-1795. 1971. pap. 3.25 (ISBN 0-393-00553-4, Norton Lib). Norton.

--Aftermath of Revolution: British Policy Toward the United States, 1783-1795. LC 77-76328. 1969. 12.50 (ISBN 0-87074-100-4). SMU Press.

Sargent, Fitzwilliam. England, the United States & the Southern Confederacy. Repr. of 1864 ed. 10.50x (ISBN 0-8371-2768-8, Pub. by Negro U Pr). Greenwood.

Smith, Goldwin A. Treaty of Washington, 1871: A Study in Imperial History. LC 70-139940. 1971. Repr. of 1941 ed. 10.00 (ISBN 0-8462-1567-5). Russell.

Spector, Margaret. The American Department of the British Government, 1768-1782. 1972. lib. bdg. 14.00x (ISBN 0-374-97535-3). Octagon.

Tappan, Lewis. Sidelight on Anglo-American Relations 1839-1858. Klingberg, Frank J. & Abel, Annie H., eds. LC 73-117503. Repr. of 1927 ed. 19.50x (ISBN 0-678-00650-4). Kelley.

Thorne, Christopher. Allies of a Kind: The United States, Britain, & the War Against Japan, 1941-1945. LC 79-14921. (Illus.). 1979. pap. 9.95 (ISBN 0-19-520173-6, GB 585, GB). Oxford U Pr.

Updyke, Frank A. The Diplomacy of the War of 1812. 8.50 (ISBN 0-8446-1455-6). Peter Smith.

Villiers, Brougham & Chesson, W. H. Anglo-American Relations, Eighteen Sixty-One to Sixty-Five. LC 70-159714. 1971. Repr. of 1919 ed. 12.50 (ISBN 0-8046-1673-6). Kennikat.

--Anglo-American Relations, Eighteen Sixty-One to Sixty-Five. LC 70-159714. 1971. Repr. of 1919 ed. 12.50 (ISBN 0-8046-1673-6). Kennikat.

Williams, Mary W. Anglo-American Isthmian Diplomacy, 1815-1915. LC 65-13935. 1965. Repr. of 1916 ed. 10.00 (ISBN 0-8462-0539-4). Russell.

--Anglo-American Isthmian Diplomacy, 1815-1915. (Illus., Authorized ed.). 1965. 8.00 (ISBN 0-8446-1479-3). Peter Smith.

Willson, Beckles. America's Ambassadors to England: 1785-1928. LC 70-93388. (Essay Index Reprint Ser). 1928. 32.00 (ISBN 0-8369-1436-8). Arno.

--Friendly Relations. LC 71-90696. (Essay Index Reprint Ser). 1934. 22.00 (ISBN 0-8369-1266-7). Arno.

Winant, John G. Letter from Grosvenor Square. Repr. of 1947 ed. lib. bdg. 15.00x (ISBN 0-8371-2563-4, WIGS). Greenwood.

Zimmerman, James F. Impressment of American Seamen. LC 65-27121. Repr. of 1925 ed. 10.50 (ISBN 0-8046-0516-5). Kennikat.

GREAT BRITAIN–GENEALOGY

Bankes, J. & Kerridge, E. The Early Records of the Banks Family at Winstanley. 114p. 1973. 33.00x (ISBN 0-7190-1158-2, Pub. by Manchester U Pr England). State Mutual Bk.

Birmingham & Midland Society for Genealogy & Heraldry, ed. The Registers of St. George Hockley, Marks. 1981. 13.50x (ISBN 0-905105-32-X, Pub. by Birmingham-Midland Soc England). State Mutual Bk.

--The Registers of Wednesfield, Staffs. 1981. 12.00x (ISBN 0-905105-38-9, Pub. by Birmingham-Midland Soc England). State Mutual Bk.

Burke, Bernard. A Genealogical History of the Dormant, Abeyant, Forfeited, & Extinct Peerages of the British Empire. LC 77-88158. (Illus.). 1978. Repr. of 1883 ed. 20.00 (ISBN 0-8063-0789-7). Genealog Pub.

Burke, John. Burke's Genealogical & Heraldic History of the Extinct & Dormant Baronetcies of England, Ireland, & Scotland. 2nd ed. LC 76-44268. 1977. 20.00 (ISBN 0-8063-0739-0). Genealog Pub.

--A Genealogical & Heraldic History of the Commoners of Great Britain & Ireland. LC 76-44267. 1977. 85.00 (ISBN 0-8063-0742-0). Genealog Pub.

Burke, John B. The General Armory of England, Scotland, Ireland, & Wales. LC 66-28797. (Illus.). 1976. 50.00 (ISBN 0-8063-0064-7). Genealog Pub.

Camp, Anthony J. Everyone Has Roots: An Introduction to English Genealogy. LC 78-62818. 1978. 9.50 (ISBN 0-8063-0828-1). Genealog Pub.

Charles, Nicholas. Visitation of the County of Huntingdon, Under the Authority of William Camden. Ellis, Henry, ed. LC 17-1223. (Camden Society, London. Publications, First Ser.: No. 43). Repr. of 1849 ed. 14.00 (ISBN 0-404-50143-5). AMS Pr.

Coventry, Eng. The Coventry Leet Book: Parts I & II. (EETS, OS Ser.: Nos. 134-35). Repr. of 1907 ed. Set. 31.00 (ISBN 0-527-00132-5). Kraus Repr.

--The Coventry Leet Book: Parts III & IV. (EETS, OS Ser.: No. 138). Repr. of 1909 ed. Set. 22.00 (ISBN 0-527-00133-3). Kraus Repr.

Crispin, M. Jackson & Macary, Leonce. Falaise Roll: Recording Prominent Companions of William Duke of Normandy at the Conquest of England. LC 76-86814. (Illus.). 1969. Repr. of 1938 ed. 15.00 (ISBN 0-8063-0080-9). Genealog Pub.

Dewhurst, Jack. Royal Confinements. 198p. 1981. 12.95 (ISBN 0-312-69466-0). St Martin.

Discovering (British) Surnames. 72p. 1980. pap. 2.95 (ISBN 0-85263-007-7, Pub. by B T A). Merrimack Bk Serv.

Durden, Robert F. The Dukes of Durham, Eighteen Sixty-Five-Nineteen Twenty Nine. LC 74-83785. (Illus.). xiv, 295p. 1975. 14.75 (ISBN 0-8223-0330-2). Duke.

Fitz-Thedmar, Arnold. De Antiquis Legibus Liber. Repr. of 1846 ed. 46.00 (ISBN 0-384-15820-X). Johnson Repr.

Glenn, Thomas A. Merion in the Welsh Tract. Historical & Genealogical Collections Concerning the Welsh Barony in the Province of Pennsylvania Settled by the Cymric Quakers in 1682. LC 74-91971. (Illus.). 1970. Repr. of 1896 ed. lib. bdg. 18.50 (ISBN 0-8063-0429-4). Genealog Pub.

Godstow Nunnery. The English Register of Godstow Nunnery, Pt. 1. Clark, A., ed. (EETS, OS Ser.: No. 129). Repr. of 1905 ed. 21.00 (ISBN 0-527-00124-4). Kraus Repr.

--The English Register of Godstow Nunnery, Pts. 2 & 3. Clark, A., ed. (EETS, OS Ser.: No. 130). Repr. of 1911 ed. Set. 26.00 (ISBN 0-527-00125-2). Kraus Repr.

Havran, Martin J. Caroline Courtier: The Life of Lord Cottington. LC 73-4510. (Illus.). 234p. 1973. 19.50x (ISBN 0-87249-284-2). U of SC Pr.

Jones, George A. Crown & Sword: The Milesian-Celtic Heritage of Ireland & Britain. LC 76-44145. 1977. pap. 3.95 (ISBN 0-917610-00-8). Rookfield.

Loyd, Lewis C. The Origins of Some Anglo-Norman Families. Clay, Charles T. & Douglas, David C., eds. LC 74-18109. 140p. 1980. Repr. of 1951 ed. 12.50 (ISBN 0-8063-0649-1). Genealog Pub.

Markwell, F. C. Tracing Your Ancestors in Warwickshire. 1981. 25.00x (ISBN 0-905105-45-1, Pub. by Birmingham-Midland Soc England). State Mutual Bk.

The Norman People & Their Existing Descendants in the British Dominions & in the United States of America. LC 74-18414. 484p. 1975. Repr. of 1874 ed. 17.50 (ISBN 0-8063-0636-X). Genealog Pub.

Oseney Abbey. The English Register of Oseney Abbey: Parts 1 & 2. (EETS, OS Ser.: No. 133). 1907-1913. Repr. of 1907 ed. 16.00 (ISBN 0-527-00130-9). Kraus Repr.

Ridge, Bradley B. The Bateman Connection. LC 79-63722. 291p. 1978. 30.00 (ISBN 0-686-30986-3). Ralling Hall.

Roth, Cecil. The Sassoon Dynasty. Wilkins, Mira, ed. LC 76-29982. (European Business Ser.). (Illus.). 1977. Repr. of 1941 ed. lib. bdg. 17.00x (ISBN 0-405-09747-6). Arno.

Round, Horace. Peerage & Pedigree: Studies in Peerage Law & Family History, 2 vols. (Genealogy Ser.: No. 1). 362p. 1971. Repr. of 1910 ed. Set. 65.00x (ISBN 0-7130-0020-1, Pub. by Woburn Pr England). Biblio Dist.

Round, John H. Family Origins & Other Studies. Page, William, ed. LC 79-124474. 1970. Repr. of 1930 ed. 15.00 (ISBN 0-8063-0424-3). Genealog Pub.

--Peerage & Pedigree: Studies in Peerage Law & Family History, 2 Vols. LC 76-124476. 1970. Repr. of 1910 ed. 30.00 (ISBN 0-8063-0425-1). Genealog Pub.

Smith, Frank. Genealogical Gazetteer of England. LC 68-23458. 1977. 20.00 (ISBN 0-8063-0316-6). Genealog Pub.

Thomson, T. R. A Catalogue of British Family Histories. 3rd rev. ed. LC 75-45516. 1976. 19.50 (ISBN 0-8048-1175-X). C E Tuttle.

Thorn, Caroline & Thorn, Frank, eds. Somerset: (from a Draft Translation Prepared by Frank Thorn) (Domesday Book Ser.). (Illus.). 405p. 1980. 32.50x (ISBN 0-8476-3261-X). Rowman.

Thorn, Frank, ed. Rutland. (Domesday Book Ser.). (Illus.). 52p. (From a draft translation prepared by Celia Parker). 1980. 15.00x (ISBN 0-8476-3260-1). Rowman.

Versailles, Elizabeth S. Hathaways Twelve Hundred to Nineteen-Eighty. 621p. (YA) 1980. lib. bdg. write for info. Versailles.

Wagner, Anthony R. English Genealogy. 2nd ed. (Illus.). 1972. 45.00x (ISBN 0-19-822334-X). Oxford U Pr.

Weis, Frederick L. & Adams, Arthur. The Magna Charta Sureties, Twelve Hundred Fifteen: The Barons Named in the Magna Charta, 1215, and Some of Their Descendants Who Settled in America, 1607 to 1650. LC 79-89349. vix, 125p. 1979. 12.50 (ISBN 0-8063-0866-4). Genealog Pub.

Whitehead, R. A. Garretts of Leiston. 1972. 5.00x (ISBN 0-85242-166-4). Intl Pubns Serv.

Wilkinson, Peter M. Genealogists Guide to the West Sussex Record Office. 109p. 1981. 4.00x (ISBN 0-686-75436-0, Pub. by County Archivist England). State Mutual Bk.

Yorke, James. The Union of Honour. LC 72-240. (English Experience Ser.: No. 148). 76p. 1969. Repr. of 1640 ed. 58.00 (ISBN 90-221-0148-7). Walter J Johnson.

GREAT BRITAIN–GENEALOGY–BIBLIOGRAPHY

Filby, P. William. American & British Genealogy & Heraldry: A Selected List of Books. 2nd ed. LC 75-29383. 1976. 25.00 (ISBN 0-8389-0203-0). ALA.

Gatfield, George. Guide to Printed Books & Manuscripts Relating to English & Foreign Heraldry & Genealogy. 1966. Repr. of 1892 ed. 30.00 (ISBN 0-8103-3121-7). Gale.

Marshall, George W. Genealogist's Guide. 4th ed. LC 66-23581. 1980. Repr. of 1903 ed. 30.00 (ISBN 0-686-66439-6). Genealog Pub.

Sims, Richard. Index to the Pedigrees & Arms Contained in the Herald's Visitations & Other Genealogical Manuscripts in the British Museum. LC 73-113835. 1970. Repr. of 1849 ed. 15.00 (ISBN 0-8063-0400-6). Genealog Pub.

GREAT BRITAIN–GENTRY

Brathwait, Richard. The English Gentleman: Containing Sundry Excellent Rules - How to Demeane or Accomodate Himselfe in the Manage of Publike or Private Affairs. LC 74-28836. (English Experience Ser.: No. 717). 1975. Repr. of 1630 ed. 35.00 (ISBN 90-221-0717-5). Walter J Johnson.

Kelso, Ruth. The Doctrine of the English Gentleman in the Sixteenth Century. 1964. 7.50 (ISBN 0-8446-1260-X). Peter Smith.

Mingay, G. E. The Gentry: The Rise & Fall of a Ruling Class. LC 76-13576. (Themes in British Social History). (Illus.). 1976. pap. text ed. 10.95x (ISBN 0-582-48403-0). Longman.

Slagle, Kenneth C. English Country Squire As Depicted in English Prose Fiction from 1740. LC 75-120667. 1970. Repr. lib. bdg. 12.00x (ISBN 0-374-97477-2). Octagon.

GREAT BRITAIN–GOVERNMENT PUBLICATIONS

Barrier, N. Gerald. Punjab History in Printed British Documents: A Bibliographic Guide to Parliamentary Papers & Select, Nonserial Publications, 1843-1947. LC 69-13332. 1969. 7.00x (ISBN 0-8262-0077-X). U of Mo Pr.

Chadwyck-Healey, Charles, intro. by. Catalogue of British Official Publications Not Published by HMSO 1980. 256p. 1981. lib. bdg. 190.00 (ISBN 0-85964-101-5). Chadwyck-Healey.

Cumulative Index to the Annual Catalogues of Her Majesty's Stationery Office Publications 1922-1972, 2 vols. LC 76-26730. 1976. 195.00 set (ISBN 0-685-74399-3); Vol. 1. (ISBN 0-8408-0140-8); Vol. 2. (ISBN 0-8408-0141-6). Carrollton Pr.

Ford, P. & Ford, G. Select List of British Parliamentary Papers 1833-1899. 188p. 1969. Repr. of 1953 ed. 20.00x (ISBN 0-7165-0574-6, Pub. by Irish Academic Pr Ireland). Biblio Dist.

Ford, P. & Ford, G. A. Breviate of Parliamentary Papers 1900-1916. 520p. 1970. Repr. of 1957 ed. 36.00x (ISBN 0-7165-0575-4, Pub. by Irish Academic Pr Ireland). Biblio Dist.

--Breviate of Parliamentary Papers 1917-1939. 624p. 1970. Repr. of 1951 ed. 36.00x (ISBN 0-7165-0576-2, Pub. by Irish Academic Pr Ireland). Biblio Dist.

Ford, P., et al. Select List of British Parliamentary Papers 1955-1964. 128p. 1970. 17.00x (ISBN 0-7165-0884-2, Pub. by Irish Academic Pr Ireland). Biblio Dist.

Ford, Percy & Ford, F. A Guide to Parliamentary Papers. 3rd rev. & enl. ed. 87p. 1972. 13.75x (ISBN 0-87471-100-2). Rowman.

Great Britain: Public Record Office. Lists & Indexes. (Supplementary Ser.: Nos. I-XVI, in 80 Vols. - 1980). Set. lib. bdg. 4156.00 (ISBN 0-527-02914-9). Kraus Intl.

Her Britannic Majesty's Stationery Office. The Sales Catalogues of British Government Publications, 1837-1921, 4 vols. LC 75-6964. 2000p. 1977. lib. bdg. 85.00 ea. Oceana.

Johansson, Eve. Current British Government Publishing. 1981. 10.00x (ISBN 0-902248-06-5, Pub. by AALSED England). State Mutual Bk.

Richard, Stephen. British Government Publications: An Index to Chairmen & Authors, Vol. 1. 320p. 1981. lib. bdg. 75.00x (ISBN 0-85365-743-2, Pub. by Lib Assn England). Oryx Pr.

--British Government Publications: An Index to Chairmen & Authors, Vol. 2. 174p. 1980. lib. bdg. 47.00x (ISBN 0-85365-427-1, Pub. by Lib Assn England). Oryx Pr.

--British Government Publications: An Index to Chairmen & Authors, Vol. 3. 250p. 1981. lib. bdg. 47.00x (ISBN 0-85365-753-X, Pub. by Lib Assn England). Oryx Pr.

Rodgers, Frank. A Guide to British Government Publications. 1980. 35.00 (ISBN 0-8242-0617-7). Wilson.

GREAT BRITAIN–HIGH COMMISSION FOR WESTERN PACIFIC ISLANDS

Scarr, Deryck. Fragments of Empire: A History of the Western Pacific High Commission, 1877-1914. LC 67-28350. (Illus.). 1968. text ed. 16.00x (ISBN 0-87022-730-0). U Pr of Hawaii.

GREAT BRITAIN–HISTORIC HOUSES, ETC.

Angus, W. The Seats of the Nobility & Gentry in Great Britain & Wales. Repr. of 1887 ed. 50.00 (ISBN 0-685-76580-6). Norwood Edns.

Calder, Jenni. The Victorian & Edwardian Home from Old Photographs. 1979. 19.95 (ISBN 0-7134-0793-X). David & Charles.

Castles & Palaces Map of Britain. pap. 2.95 (ISBN 0-8277-5156-7). British Bk Ctr.

Collinson, Hugh. Country Monuments & Their Families & Houses. LC 74-81065. 1975. 6.50 (ISBN 0-7153-6742-0). David & Charles.

Colourmaster. Historic Buildings. (Travel in England Ser.). (Illus.). 64p. 1975. 7.95 (ISBN 0-85933-129-6). Transatlantic.

Cormack, Patrick. Westminster: Place & Parliament. (Illus.). 192p. 1981. 25.00 (ISBN 0-7232-2681-4). Warne.

Cornforth, John. Pyne's Royal Residences. (Folio Miniature Ser.). 48p. 1976. 4.95 (ISBN 0-7181-1476-0, Pub. by Michael Joseph). Merrimack Bk Serv.

Davenport, Nicholas. The Honour of St Valery: The Story of an English Manor House. (Illus.). 168p. (Orig.). 1979. pap. 7.95 (ISBN 0-85967-463-0, Pub. by Scolar Pr England). Biblio Dist.

Delderfield, Eric R. West Country Historic Houses & Their Families, Vol. 2: Dorset, Wiltshire & N. Somerset. 13.50 (ISBN 0-7153-4910-4). David & Charles.

Foss, Arthur. Country House Treasures of Britain. (Illus.). 352p. 1980. 25.00 (ISBN 0-399-12549-3). Putnam.

Girouard, Mark. Historic Houses of Britain. LC 78-73973. (Illus.). 1979. 19.95 (ISBN 0-688-03467-5). Morrow.

Historic Houses, Castles & Gardens in Great Britain & Ireland. 1981 ed. LC 57-35834. (Illus.). 168p. (Orig.). 1981. pap. 4.50x (ISBN 0-900486-29-5). Intl Pubns Serv.

Historic Houses, Castles & Gardens in Great Britain & Ireland 1980. LC 57-35834. (Illus.). 167p. (Orig.). 1980. pap. 4.50x (ISBN 0-900486-26-0). Intl Pubns Serv.

Historic Houses, Castles & Gardens in Great Britain & Ireland, 1976. 1976. pap. 3.00x (ISBN 0-8277-0351-1). British Bk Ctr.

Hubbard, Elbert. Little Journeys to the Homes of Famous Women: Jane Austen, Elizabeth Browning, Madame de Stael, Mary Lamb, Mary Shelly, Etc. (Women Ser.). 1897. 20.00 (ISBN 0-685-43723-X). Norwood Edns.

Laws, Peter. A Guide to the National Trust in Devon & Cornwall. LC 77-91765. (Illus.). 1978. 14.95 (ISBN 0-7153-7581-4). David & Charles.

Lobel, M. D., ed. Historic Towns: Maps & Plans of Towns & Cities in the British Isles, with Historic Commentaries, from Earliest Times to Circa 1800. LC 72-131565. 182p. 1971. Vol. 1. 50.00x, oBE (ISBN 0-8018-1243-7); Vol. 2. 57.50, bBE (ISBN 0-8018-1753-6). Johns Hopkins.

Nicolson, Nigel. The National Trust Book of Great Houses of Britain. LC 78-53019. (Illus.). 1978. 30.00 (ISBN 0-87923-244-7). Godine.

Sandon, Eric. Suffolk Houses. (Illus.). 344p. 1977. 49.50 (ISBN 0-902028-68-5). Antique Collect.

GREAT BRITAIN–HISTORICAL GEOGRAPHY

Cook, Christopher & Stevenson, John. Longman Atlas of Modern British History: A Visual Guide to British Society & Politics, 1700-1970. (Illus.). 1978. text ed. 17.95x (ISBN 0-582-36485-X); pap. text ed. 10.95x (ISBN 0-582-36486-8). Longman.

Darby, H. C., ed. Domesday England. LC 76-11485. (The Domesday Geography of England Ser.). (Illus.). 1977. 77.50 (ISBN 0-521-21307-X). Cambridge U Pr.

--A New Historical Geography of England After 1600. LC 76-26029. 1978. 59.50 (ISBN 0-521-22123-4); pap. 19.50 (ISBN 0-521-29145-3). Cambridge U Pr.

--A New Historical Geography of England Before 1600. LC 76-26141. 1978. 49.50 (ISBN 0-521-22122-6); pap. 17.50 (ISBN 0-521-29144-5). Cambridge U Pr.

Dodgshon, R. A. & Butlin, R. A., eds. An Historical Geography of England & Wales. 1978. 44.00 (ISBN 0-12-219250-8); pap. 18.50 (ISBN 0-12-219252-4). Acad Pr.

Gardiner, Samuel R. A School Atlas of English History. 1905. Repr. 20.00 (ISBN 0-685-43036-7). Norwood Edns.

Gelling, Margaret. Signposts to the Past: Place-Names & the History of England. (Illus.). 256p. 1978. 15.75x (ISBN 0-460-04264-5, J M Dent England). Biblio Dist.

Madge, Sidney J. Domesday of Crown Lands. LC 67-31560. (Illus.). Repr. of 1938 ed. 26.00x (ISBN 0-678-05071-6). Kelley.

Rosing, Kenneth E. & Wood, Peter A. Character of a Conurbation: A Computer Atlas of Birmingham & the Black Country. (Illus.). 1971. 17.50x (ISBN 0-340-11879-2). Intl Pubns Serv.

GREAT BRITAIN–HISTORIOGRAPHY

Carter, James M. The Norman Conquest in English Historiography. 1980. pap. 12.00x (ISBN 0-89126-085-4). MA-AH Pub.

Elton, G. R. England: Twelve Hundred to Sixteen Forty. LC 69-63003. (Sources of History Ser). 255p. 1969. 22.50x (ISBN 0-8014-0490-8); pap. 4.95 (ISBN 0-8014-9123-1, CP123). Cornell U Pr.

Fredericq, Paul. The Study of History in England & Scotland. LC 78-63776. (Johns Hopkins University. Studies in the Social Sciences. Fifth Ser. 1887: 10). Repr. of 1887 ed. 11.50 (ISBN 0-404-61042-0). AMS Pr.

Galbraith, Vivian H. Historical Research in Medieval England. 1977. lib. bdg. 59.95 (ISBN 0-8490-1961-3). Gordon Pr.

Gransden, Antonia. Historical Writing in England: C. 550 to C. 1307. LC 73-3732. 634p. 1974. 55.00x (ISBN 0-8014-0770-2). Cornell U Pr.

--Historical Writing in England II: c. 1307 to the Early 16th Century, Vol. 2. LC 74-23267. 576p. 1980. 75.00x (ISBN 0-8014-1264-1). Cornell U Pr.

Hanning, Robert W. Vision of History in Early Britain: From Gildas to Geoffrey of Monmouth. LC 66-17856. 271p. 1966. 20.00x (ISBN 0-231-02826-1). Columbia U Pr.

Karlman, Roland. Evidencing Historical Classifications: In British & American Historiography 1930-1970. 1976. pap. text ed. 9.50x (ISBN 91-554-0414-6). Humanities.

King, W. British Isles. (Advanced Level Geography Ser.). 1976. 11.25x (ISBN 0-7121-0246-9). Intl Pubns Serv.

Peardon, Thomas P. Transition in English Historical Writing, 1760-1830. LC 34-967. (Columbia University. Studies in the Social Sciences: No. 390). 24.50 (ISBN 0-404-51390-5). AMS Pr.

Watson, Cahrles A. The Writing of History in Britain: A Bibliography of Post-1945 Writings About British Historians & Bibliographers. 1981. lib. bdg. 25.00 (ISBN 0-8240-9330-5). Garland Pub.

Winks, Robin W., ed. Historiography of the British Empire-Commonwealth. LC 66-15555. 1966. 22.75 (ISBN 0-8223-0193-8). Duke.

GREAT BRITAIN–HISTORY

Here are entered works on the history of Great Britain as a whole. For works on specific periods see the period subdivisions.

see also Great Britain–History–Juvenile Literature

A'Beckett, Gilbert A. Comic History of England, 2 Vols. LC 72-158218. (Illus.). Repr. of 1898 ed. Set. 62.50 (ISBN 0-404-00300-1). AMS Pr.

Addison, William. Understanding English Surnames. 1978. 19.95 (ISBN 0-7134-0295-4). David & Charles.

Almack, Edward. Eikon Basilike, or the King's Book. 1979. Repr. of 1907 ed. lib. bdg. 30.00 (ISBN 0-8495-0140-7). Arden Lib.

Andrews, C. M. The Old English Manor. 59.95 (ISBN 0-8490-0758-5). Gordon Pr.

Andrews, K. R., et al, eds. Westward Enterprise: English Activites in Ireland, the Atlantic & America 1480-1650. LC 79-13801. 1979. 19.95x (ISBN 0-8143-1647-6). Wayne St U Pr.

Anthony, Katherine. The Lambs: A Study of Pre-Victorian England. 1978. Repr. of 1948 ed. lib. bdg. 20.00 (ISBN 0-8495-0299-3). Arden Lib.

Ault, Norman. Life in Ancient Britain. LC 70-39667. (Select Bibliographies Reprint Ser). 1972. Repr. of 1920 ed. 16.50 (ISBN 0-8369-9927-4). Arno.

Bailey, Patrick. Orkney. (Island Ser.). (Illus.). 245p. 1974. 16.95 (ISBN 0-7153-5000-5). David & Charles.

Baring-Gould, S. An Old English Home & Its Dependencies. 59.95 (ISBN 0-8490-0756-9). Gordon Pr.

Beard, Charles A. Introduction to the English Historians. LC 68-56748. (Research & Source Works Ser: No. 231). 1968. Repr. of 1906 ed. 18.50 (ISBN 0-8337-0199-1). B Franklin.

Beaver, Patrick. Crystal Palace, 1851-36: A Portrait of Victorian Enterprise. (Illus.). 1970. 20.00x (ISBN 0-238-78961-6). Intl Pubns Serv.

Beckinsale, Robert & Beckinsale, Monica. The English Heartland. (Illus.). 446p. 1980. 39.50x (ISBN 0-7156-1389-8, Pub. by Duckworth England). Biblio Dist.

Bell, K. & Morgan, G. The Great Historians: An Anthology of British History Arranged in Chronological Order. 1924. 20.00 (ISBN 0-8482-7379-6). Norwood Edns.

Bellers, John. Essays About the Poor, Manufacturers, Trade Plantations, & Immorality, 3 vols. in 1. Bd. with A Discourse Touching Provision. Hale, Sir Matthew. Repr. of 1683 ed; A Discourse of the Poor. North, Roger. Repr. of 1753 ed. (History of English Economic Thought). Repr. of 1699 ed. 14.00 (ISBN 0-384-03860-3). Johnson Repr.

Benson, Forrest. The Saga of Seven Bays. 1979. 7.95 (ISBN 0-533-04032-9). Vantage.

Bohun, Edmund. The History of the Desertion, or an Account of All the Publick Affairs in England from the Beginning of September 1688 to the Twelfth of February Following. Straka, Gerald M., ed. LC 72-83158. (English Studies Ser). 1972. Repr. of 1689 ed. lib. bdg. 17.00 (ISBN 0-8420-1416-0). Scholarly Res Inc.

Bolingbroke. Lord Bolingbroke: Historical Writings. Kramnick, Isaac & Clive, John, eds. LC 72-75608. (Classics of British Historical Literature Ser). liv, 344p. 1974. pap. 3.45 (ISBN 0-226-06346-1, P491, Phoen). U of Chicago Pr.

Bollan, William. Continued Corruption, Standing Armies, & Popular Discontents Considered. LC 75-31083. Repr. of 1768 ed. 21.00 (ISBN 0-404-13502-1). AMS Pr.

Bond, John J. Handy-Book of Rules & Tables for Verifying Dates with the Christian Era. LC 66-29473. 1966. Repr. of 1889 ed. 10.00 (ISBN 0-8462-0797-4). Russell.

Boon, George C. Silchester: The Roman Town of Calleva. 1974. 12.50 (ISBN 0-7153-6339-5). David & Charles.

Booth, William. In Darkest England & the Way Out. LC 76-108240. (Criminology, Law Enforcement, & Social Problems Ser.: No. 142). Date not set. 10.00 (ISBN 0-87585-142-8). Patterson Smith.

Bord, Janet & Bord, Colin. Mysterious Britain. (Illus.). 1978. pap. text ed. 5.95x (ISBN 0-8464-0663-2). Beekman Pubs.

Brack, Alan. The Wirral. LC 79-56465. (Illus.). 176p. 1980. 30.00 (ISBN 0-7134-1378-6, Pub. by Batsford England). David & Charles.

Brackenridge, Hugh H. An Eulogium of the Brave Men Who Have Fallen in the Contest with Great Britain. 1976. Repr. 22.00 (ISBN 0-685-71956-1, Regency). Scholarly.

Bradbeer, Grace. The Land Changed Its Face: The Evacuation of Devon's South Hams 1943-44. (Illus.). 152p. 1973. 4.95 (ISBN 0-7153-5781-6). David & Charles.

Brailsford, Henry N. The War of Steel & Gold: A Study of the Armed Peace. 3rd ed. (The Development of the Industrial Society Ser.). 340p. 1971. Repr. of 1915 ed. 25.00x (ISBN 0-7165-1767-1, Pub. by Irish Academic Pr). Biblio Dist.

Brentano, Lujo. Geschichte De Wirtschaftlichen Entwicklung Englands, 3 Vols. in 4. LC 68-56762. (Research & Source Works Ser.: No. 246). (Ger). 1969. Repr. of 1927 ed. Set. 101.00 (ISBN 0-8337-0367-6). B Franklin.

Brownell, David & Knill, Harry, eds. Kings & Queens of England. 1978. pap. 2.50 (ISBN 0-88388-053-9). Bellerophon Bks.

Bryant, Arthur. Makers of England. 3.50 (ISBN 0-452-25001-3, Z5001, Plume). NAL.

Bulwer, Edward L. England & the English. Meacham, Standish, ed. LC 71-114959. (Classics of British Historical Literature Ser). 1972. pap. 3.45 (ISBN 0-226-08015-3, P384, Phoen). U of Chicago Pr.

--England & the English. Meacham, Standish, ed. LC 71-114959. (Classics of British Historical Literature Ser). 1970. 13.00x (ISBN 0-226-08014-5). U of Chicago Pr.

Burnet, Gilbert. A Collection of Eighteen Papers Relating to the Affairs of the Church & State. Straka, Gerald M., ed. LC 72-83159. (English Studies Ser.). 1972. Repr. of 1689 ed. lib. bdg. 20.00 (ISBN 0-8420-1417-9). Scholarly Res Inc.

Camden Society. Camden Society Publications: New Series, Vols. 1-62. Repr. of 1871 ed. Set. 1300.00 (ISBN 0-384-07232-1). Johnson Repr.

--Camden Society Publications: Series 1, Vols. 1-105. Repr. of 1838 ed. Set. 2420.00 (ISBN 0-384-07230-5). Johnson Repr.

Camden, William. Britannia, 4 vols. (Illus.). Repr. of 1806 ed. Set. 539.00 (ISBN 3-4870-5492-2). Adler.

--Remains Concerning Britain. 446p. 1974. Repr. of 1870 ed. 19.50x (ISBN 0-87471-543-1). Rowman.

Cameron, Kenneth. English Place-Names. 1977. 22.50 (ISBN 0-7134-0841-3). David & Charles.

Canning, Albert & Stratford, George. Literary Influence in British History. LC 76-10959. 1976. Repr. of 1904 ed. lib. bdg. 25.00 (ISBN 0-8414-3495-6). Folcroft.

Canning, Albert S. Literary Influence in British History. 202p. 1980. Repr. of 1904 ed. lib. bdg. 30.00 (ISBN 0-8495-0627-1). Arden Lib.

Catchpole, Brian. A Map History of the British People Since 1700. 1975. pap. text ed. 8.95x (ISBN 0-435-31160-3). Heinemann Ed.

Chancellor, Valerie E., ed. Master & Artisan in Victorian England. LC 69-17619. 1969. 15.00x (ISBN 0-678-07501-8). Kelley.

Chapman, Maybelle K. Great Britian & the Bagdad Railway. LC 48-8011. (Studies in History: No. 31). 1948. pap. 5.00 (ISBN 0-87391-001-X). Smith Coll.

Charlesworth, M. P. The Heritage of Early Britain. (Illus.). 1979. lib. bdg. 30.00 (ISBN 0-8495-0946-7). Arden Lib.

Cheney, C. R., ed. Handbook of Dates for Students of British History. (Royal Historical Society Ser.). 164p. 1970. Repr. of 1945 ed. 7.75x (ISBN 0-8476-1343-7). Rowman.

Cheyney, Edward P. Industrial & Social History of England. 1971. Repr. of 1901 ed. 10.50 (ISBN 0-87928-020-4). Corner Hse.

--Industrial & Social History of England. 1909. 25.00 (ISBN 0-685-43751-5). Norwood Edns.

--A Short History of England. 1904. 40.00 (ISBN 0-685-43753-1). Norwood Edns.

Church, Alfred J. Early Britain. 1978. Repr. of 1889 ed. lib. bdg. 35.00 (ISBN 0-89760-100-9, Telegraph). Dynamic Learn Corp.

Church, Alfred S. Early Britain. LC 73-16020. 1889. lib. bdg. 20.00 (ISBN 0-8414-3498-0). Folcroft.

Churchill, Winston S. Great Contemporaries. LC 73-77128. 1974. Repr. of 1938 ed. 7.95x (ISBN 0-226-10630-6). U of Chicago Pr.

--A History of the English-Speaking Peoples, 4 vols. Incl. Vol. 1. The Birth of Britain, 55 B.C. to 1485 (ISBN 0-396-03841-7); Vol. 2. The New World, 1485-1688 (ISBN 0-396-03905-7); Vol. 3. The Age of Revolution, 1688-1815 (ISBN 0-396-04008-X); Vol. 4. The Great Democracies, 1815-1901 (ISBN 0-396-04049-7). LC 56-6868. 10.00 ea.; boxed 40.00 (ISBN 0-396-04134-5). Dodd.

--History of the English-Speaking Peoples. 1976. pap. 14.95 (ISBN 0-553-18841-0). Bantam.

Clark, Grahame. Prehistoric England. 1979. Repr. of 1940 ed. lib. bdg. 30.00 (ISBN 0-8495-0948-3). Arden Lib.

Cobbett, William. Parliamentary History of England from the Norman Conquest in 1066 to the Year 1803, 36 Vols. 1966. Repr. of 1820 ed. Set. 1925.00 (ISBN 0-384-09496-1); 54.00 ea. Johnson Repr.

Cobbett, William, et al, eds. Parliamentary History of England from the Norman Conquest in 1066 to the Year 1803, 36 Vols. LC 54-54297. Repr. of 1820 ed. Set. 1750.00 (ISBN 0-404-01650-2); 49.00 ea. AMS Pr.

Cobbold, Richard. The History of Margaret Catchpole, a Suffolk Girl, 3 vols. in 2. LC 79-8253. (Illus.). Repr. of 1845 ed. Set. 84.50 (ISBN 0-404-61823-5). Vol. 1 (ISBN 0-404-61824-3). Vol. 2 (ISBN 0-404-61825-1). AMS Pr.

Cockburn, Henry. Memorials of His Time. Miller, Karl, ed. LC 74-5737. (Classics of British Historical Literature Ser). xxviii, 446p. 1974. text ed. 19.50x (ISBN 0-226-11164-4). U of Chicago Pr.

Cockerell, H. A. & Green, Edwin. The British Insurance Business 1547-1970: An Introduction & Guide to Historical Records in the United Kingdom. 142p. 1976. text ed. 16.50x (ISBN 0-8419-5315-5). Holmes & Meier.

Cox, George W. The Early Empire. Repr. 20.00 (ISBN 0-685-43695-0). Norwood Edns.

Cox, M. A History of Sir John Deane's Grammar School Northwich. 318p. 1976. 35.00x (ISBN 0-7190-1282-1, Pub. by Manchester U Pr England). State Mutual Bk.

Dawes, Frank. Not in Front of the Servants: A True Portrait of English Upstairs-Downstairs Life. LC 73-16961. 1974. 8.95 (ISBN 0-8008-5605-8). Taplinger.

De Guinard, Frances. From Brass Hat to Bowler Hat. 1979. 19.95 (ISBN 0-241-10165-4, Pub. by Hamish Hamilton England). David & Charles.

Donnachie, Ian L. & MacLeod, Innes. Old Galloway. (Old...Ser.). 1974. 6.00 (ISBN 0-7153-6459-6). David & Charles.

Doran, John. London in the Jacobite Times. Repr. 35.00 (ISBN 0-685-43701-9). Norwood Edns.

Dudley, Robert. A Briefe Report of the Militaire Services Done in the Low Countries by the Erle of Leicester. LC 72-192. (English Experience Ser.: No. 201). 36p. 1969. Repr. of 1587 ed. 7.00 (ISBN 90-221-0201-7). Walter J Johnson.

Dunning, R. W., ed. Somerset, Vol. IV. (Victoria History of the Counties of England Ser.). (Illus.). 1979. 99.00x (ISBN 0-19-722747-3). Oxford U Pr.

East, John. Gascony & the Pyrenees: England's First Empire. (Illus.). 1970. 7.50x (ISBN 0-85307-087-3). Intl Pubns Serv.

Ereira, Alan. The People's England. (Illus.). 288p. 1981. 24.95 (ISBN 0-7100-0596-2). Routledge & Kegan.

Faucher, Leon L. Manchester in 1844. Repr. of 1844 ed. 22.50x (ISBN 0-678-05211-5). Kelley.

Fishwick & Ditchfield, P. H., eds. Memorials of Old Lancashire, 2 vols. 1979. Repr. of 1909 ed. Set. lib. bdg. 125.00 (ISBN 0-8495-1628-5). Arden Lib.

Foxcroft, H. C. The Life & Letters of Sir George Savile First Marquis of Helifax, 2 vols. Straka, Gerald M., ed. LC 72-83170. (English Studies Ser.). 1972. Repr. of 1898 ed. Set. lib. bdg. 55.00 (ISBN 0-8420-1427-6). Scholarly Res Inc.

Frank, Joseph. Levellers: John Lilburne, Richard Overton, William Walwyn. LC 68-27058. 1969. Repr. of 1955 ed. 12.00 (ISBN 0-8462-1278-1). Russell.

Freeman-Grenville, G. S. Atlas of British History. (Illus.). 92p. 1979. 16.50x (ISBN 0-8476-6197-0); pap. 8.95x (ISBN 0-8476-6198-9). Rowman.

Gallardo, Alexander. Britain & the First Carlist War. 1980. Repr. of 1978 ed. lib. bdg. 25.00 (ISBN 0-8414-4492-7). Folcroft.

Garnier, Russell M. Annals of the British Peasantry. (Folklore Ser.). Repr. 25.00 (ISBN 0-685-43673-X). Norwood Edns.

Gilbert, Alan D. The Making of Post-Christian Britain. LC 80-40074. 173p. 1980. text ed. 23.00x (ISBN 0-582-48563-0). Longman.

Gipson, Lawrence H. The British Empire Before the American Revolution, 15 vols. Incl. Vol. 1. The British Isles & the American Colonies: Great Britain & Ireland, 1748-1754. rev. ed. 1958 (ISBN 0-394-41784-4); Vol. 2. The British Isles & the American Colonies: The Southern Plantations, 1748-1754. rev. ed. 1960 (ISBN 0-394-41782-8); Vol. 3. The British Isles & the American Colonies: The Northern Plantations, 1748-1754. rev. ed. 1960 (ISBN 0-394-41783-6); Vol. 4. Zones of International Friction: North America, South of the Great Lakes Region, 1748-1754 (ISBN 0-394-45340-9); Vol. 4. Zones of International Friction: The Great Lakes Frontier, Canada, the West Indies, India, 1748-1754014vol. 5 (ISBN 0-394-45341-7); Vol. 6. The Great War for the Empire: The Years of Defeat, 1754-1757 (ISBN 0-394-42718-1); Vol. 7. The Great War for the Empire: The Victorious Years, 1758-1760 (ISBN 0-394-45057-4); Vol. 8. The Great War for the Empire: The Culmination, 1760-1763 (ISBN 0-394-42719-X); Vol. 9. The Triumphant Empire: The Triumphant Empire. 1956 (ISBN 0-394-44963-0); Vol. 10. The Triumphant Empire: Thunder-Clouds Gather in the West, 1763-1766. 1961 (ISBN 0-394-41785-2); Vol. 11. The Triumphant Empire: The Rumbling of the Coming Storm, 1766-1770. 1965 (ISBN 0-394-41791-7); Vol. 12. The Triumphant Empire: Britain Sails into the Storm, 1770-1776. 1965 (ISBN 0-394-41795-X); Vol. 13. The Triumphant Empire: The Empire Beyond the Storm, 1770-1776. 1967 (ISBN 0-394-41797-6); Vol. 14. A Bibliographical Guide to the History of the British Empire, 1748-1776. 1968 (ISBN 0-394-41686-4); Vol. 15. A Guide to Manuscripts Relating to the History of the British Empire, 1748-1776. 1970 (ISBN 0-394-41786-0). Vols. 2-7, 9, 11-15. 15.00 ea. Knopf.

Goldsmid, Edmund. Some Political Satires of the Seventeenth Century, 2 vols. in 1. Straka, Gerald M., ed. LC 72-83162. (English Studies Ser.). 1972. Repr. of 1885 ed. lib. bdg. 16.00 (ISBN 0-8420-1421-7). Scholarly Res Inc.

Gooch, G. P. Under Six Reigns. 1971. Repr. of 1958 ed. 19.50 (ISBN 0-208-01263-X, Archon). Shoe String.

Gordon, L. L. British Battles & Medals. 1979. 42.00 (ISBN 0-685-51512-5, Pub by Spink & Son England). S J Durst.

Gough, Richard. The History of Myddle. 1979. Repr. text ed. 19.50x (ISBN 0-686-58501-1). Humanities.

Graham, Gerald S. A Concise History of the British Empire. (Illus.). 1978. pap. 10.95 (ISBN 0-500-27111-9). Thames Hudson.

Gray, Charles, et al. Harbrace History of England, 4 pts. Incl. Pt. 1. Ancient & Medieval England: Beginnings to 1509. Lander, J. R. pap. text ed. 10.95 (ISBN 0-15-535107-9); Pt. 2. Renaissance & Reformation England: 1509-1715. Gray, Charles. pap. text ed. 10.95 (ISBN 0-15-535108-7); The Birth & Growth of Industrial England: 1714-1867. Harrison, John F. pap. text ed. 10.95 (ISBN 0-15-535109-5); England Since 1867: Continuity & Change. Stansky, Peter. pap. text ed. 10.95 (ISBN 0-15-535110-9). 1973 (HC). HarBraceJ.

Gray, Howard L. English Field Systems. 1980. Repr. of 1915 ed. lib. bdg. 20.00x (ISBN 0-678-08069-0). Kelley.

Great Britain, Factories Inquiry Commission. First Report of the Central Board of His Majesty's Commissioners Appointed to Collect Information in the Manufacturing Districts: As to the Employment of Children in Factories. LC 71-367641. Date not set. Repr. of 1833 ed. lib. bdg. 75.00x (ISBN 0-678-05226-3). Kelley.

Green, John R. A Short History of the English People, 2 Vols. 1960. Vol. 1. 14.95x (ISBN 0-460-00727-0, Evman); Vol. 2. 14.95x (ISBN 0-460-00728-9). Biblio Dist.

Greenall, R. L. A History of Northamptonshire. (The Darwen County History Ser.). (Illus.). 128p. 1979. 20.75x (ISBN 0-8476-3167-2). Rowman.

Greenaway, George. English Historical Documents: 1042-1189, Vol. II. Douglas, David C., ed. (Illus.). 1088p. 1981. 98.00x (ISBN 0-19-520235-X). Oxford U Pr.

Greenberg, William. Flags of the Forgotten: Nationalism on the Celtic Fringe. 3.95 (ISBN 0-686-05398-2). British Am Bks.

Grose, Clyde L. Select Bibliography of British History, 1660-1760. 1967. lib. bdg. 25.00x (ISBN 0-374-93306-5). Octagon.

Gutch, John. Collectanea Curiosa, 2 vols. Straka, Gerald M., ed. LC 72-83163. (English Studies Ser.). 1972. Repr. of 1781 ed. Set. lib. bdg. 65.00 (ISBN 0-8420-1422-5). Scholarly Res Inc.

Hadfield, Charles. British Canals: An Illustrated History. 4th ed. LC 70-88654. 1969. lib. bdg. 16.95x (ISBN 0-678-05535-1). Kelley.

Hall, W. P., et al. History of England & the Empire Commonwealth. 5th ed. 1971. text ed. 28.95 (ISBN 0-471-00225-9). Wiley.

--History of England & the Empire Commonwealth. 5th ed. 1971. text ed. 28.95 (ISBN 0-471-00225-9). Wiley.

Halliday, F. E. A Concise History of England: From Stonehenge to the Atomic Age. (Illus.). 240p. 1980. pap. 10.95 (ISBN 0-500-27182-8). Thames Hudson.

Hamil, Fred C. The Valley of the Lower Thames, 1640-1850. LC 73-86461. (Illus.). 1973. pap. 8.50 (ISBN 0-8020-6220-2). U of Toronto Pr.

Hammond, John L. Age of the Chartists, to Eighteen Thirty-Two to Eighteen Fifty-Four. LC 66-22625. Repr. of 1919 ed. 17.50x (ISBN 0-678-00263-0). Kelley.

Hanham, Henry J. Scottish Nationalism. 1969. 12.50x (ISBN 0-674-79580-6). Harvard U Pr.

Hanson, Donald W. From Kingdom to Commonwealth: The Development of Civic Consciousness in English Political Thought. LC 77-105371. (Political Studies). xvi, 469p. 1970. 25.00x (ISBN 0-674-32475-7). Harvard U Pr.

Hardy, A. V. The British Isles. (Geography of the British Isles Ser.). 1974. text ed. 8.95x (ISBN 0-521-21656-7). Cambridge U Pr.

Hardyng, John. Chronicle of John Hardyng. LC 75-178538. Repr. of 1812 ed. 75.00 (ISBN 0-404-56621-9). AMS Pr.

Harris, B. E., ed. Victoria History of the Counties of England: Cheshire, Vol. 2. (Illus.). 282p. 1979. text ed. 115.00x (ISBN 0-19-722749-X). Oxford U Pr.

Harrison, Frederic. Chatham. 1979. Repr. of 1905 ed. lib. bdg. 20.00 (ISBN 0-8495-2261-7). Arden Lib.

Harvey, Nancy L. The Rose & the Thorn. (Illus.). 288p. 1975. 13.95 (ISBN 0-02-548550-4). Macmillan.

Haydn, Hiram C. Counter-Renaissance. LC 50-3937. 1967. pap. 3.95 (ISBN 0-15-622680-4, H056, Hbgr). HarBraceJ.

Hayward, Sir John. Answer to the First Part of a Certain Conference, Concerning Succession, Published...Under the Name of R. Dolman. LC 74-28861. (English Experience Ser.: No. 741). 1975. Repr. of 1603 ed. 13.00 (ISBN 90-221-0741-8). Walter J Johnson.

Herrtage, Sidney J., ed. The Sege off Melayne, Etc. (EETS, ES Ser.: No. 35). Repr. of 1880 ed. 12.00 (ISBN 0-527-00244-5). Kraus Repr.

Heylyn, Peter. Help to English History. Wright, Paul, ed. LC 70-130988. Repr. of 1773 ed. 40.00 (ISBN 0-404-03259-1). AMS Pr.

Heywood, Thomas. Troia Bretanica, or Great Britaines Troy. LC 74-80187. (English Experience Ser.: No. 667). 466p. 1974. Repr. of 1609 ed. 69.00 (ISBN 90-221-0667-5). Walter J Johnson.

Hoffman, Ross J. The Marquis: A Study of Lord Rockingham, 1730-1782. LC 72-93944. (Illus.). xiv, 397p. 1973. 25.00 (ISBN 0-8232-0970-9). Fordham.

Holmes, C. The Eastern Association in the English Civil War. LC 73-91616. (Illus.). 320p. 1974. 35.50 (ISBN 0-521-20400-3). Cambridge U Pr.

Howard, Philip. Royal Palaces. LC 70-118211. (Illus.). 1970. 10.00 (ISBN 0-87645-031-1). Gambit.

Hughan, Samuel. Hereditary Peers & Hereditary Paupers. LC 71-118477. 1971. Repr. of 1885 ed. 12.00 (ISBN 0-8046-1226-9). Kennikat.

Hume, David. History of England: From the Invasion of Julius Caesar to the Revolution of 1688. Kilcup, Rodney W., ed. LC 74-16685. (Classics of British Historical Literature Ser). lvi, 392p. 1975. text ed. 17.50x (ISBN 0-226-36065-2). U of Chicago Pr.

Hume, David & Tobias, George. History of England from the Invasion of Julius Caesar to the Revolution in 1688, Continued to the Death of George the Second by Tobias George Smollett, 13 Vols. LC 76-153594. Repr. of 1825 ed. Set. 260.00 (ISBN 0-404-08100-2); 20.00 ea. AMS Pr.

Hunt, William & Poole, Reginald L., eds. Political History of England, 12 Vols. Repr. of 1913 ed. Set. 270.00 (ISBN 0-404-50770-0); 22.50 ea. AMS Pr.

Hussey, W. D. Discovery, Expansion & Empire. text ed. 4.95x (ISBN 0-521-05352-8). Cambridge U Pr.

Hyams, Edward. The Changing Face of Britain. 1977. pap. 5.95x (ISBN 0-8464-0237-8). Beekman Pubs.

Jackson, K. H. Language & History in Early Britain. 1953. 42.50 (ISBN 0-85224-116-X, Pub. by Edinburgh U Pr Scotland). Columbia U Pr.

Johnson, Paul. British Cathedrals. LC 80-81171. (Illus.). 280p. 1980. 24.95 (ISBN 0-688-03672-4). Morrow.

Karsten, Peter. Patriot-Heroes in England & America: Political Symbolism & Changing Values Over Three Centuries. LC 78-53286. (Illus.). 268p. 1978. 25.00 (ISBN 0-299-07500-1). U of Wis Pr.

Kightly, Charles. Strongholds of the Realm: Defenses in Britain from Prehistory to the Twentieth Century. (Illus.). 1979. 19.95 (ISBN 0-500-25063-4). Thames Hudson.

King, Cecil. With Malice Toward None: A War Diary by Cecil King. Armstrong, William, ed. LC 70-175619. 343p. 1971. 28.50 (ISBN 0-8386-1067-6). Fairleigh Dickinson.

Kipling, Gordon. The Triumph of Honor. (Publications of the Sir Thomas Browne Institute: No. 6). 1977. lib. bdg. 24.00 (ISBN 90-6021-415-3, Pub. by Leiden Univ Holland). Kluwer Boston.

Kliger, Samuel. The Goths in England: A Study in Seventeenth & Eighteenth Century Thought. LC 78-159203. viii, 304p. 1971. Repr. of 1952 ed. lib. bdg. 16.50x (ISBN 0-374-94592-6). Octagon.

Knight, Charles. History of England, 8 vols. Set. 240.00 (ISBN 0-686-01771-4). Somerset Pub.

Lacey, C. Hightown Grammar: The School As a Social System. 230p. 1970. 15.00x (ISBN 0-7190-0485-3, Pub. by Manchester U Pr England). State Mutual Bk.

Laing, Jennifer. Britain's Mysterious Past. 1979. 7.50 (ISBN 0-7153-7587-3). David & Charles.

Lander, J. R. Government & Community: England, 1450-1509. LC 80-15. (The New History of England Ser.). 416p. 1981. pap. 7.95 (ISBN 0-674-35794-9). Harvard U Pr.

LeHuray, C. P. Bailiwick of Guernsey. rev. ed. LC 74-522873. (The Queen's Channel Islands Ser.). (Illus.). 182p. 1969. 8.75x (ISBN 0-340-00959-4). Intl Pubns Serv.

Lester, C. Edwards. The Glory & Shame of England, 2 vols. (The Development of Industrial Society Ser.). 905p. 1971. Repr. of 1866 ed. 36.00x (ISBN 0-7165-1789-2, Pub. by Irish Academic Pr). Biblio Dist.

Lysons, Daniel & Lysons, Samuel. Magna Britannia Bedfordshire. (Classical County Histories Ser.). 189p. 1978. Repr. of 1806 ed. 45.00x (ISBN 0-8476-6117-2). Rowman.

--Magna Britannia Berkshire. (Classical Country Histories Ser.). 342p. 1978. Repr. of 1806 ed. 57.50x (ISBN 0-8476-6118-0). Rowman.

Macaley, Thomas B. History of England, Vol. 2. Date not set. 14.95x (ISBN 0-460-00035-7, Evman). Biblio Dist.

Macaulay, Thomas. The History of England. Trevor-Roper, Hugh, ed. (English Library Ser.). 1979. pap. 3.95 (ISBN 0-14-043133-0). Penguin.

Macauley, Thomas B. History of England, Vol. 4. Date not set. 14.95x (ISBN 0-460-00037-3, Evman). Biblio Dist.

--History of England: From the Accession of James II. Date not set. 14.95x (ISBN 0-460-00035-7, Evman). Biblio Dist.

McCann, Timothy J., compiled by. Restricted Grandeur: Impressions of Chichester 1586-1948. 1981. 3.00x (ISBN 0-686-75439-5, Pub. by County Archivist England). State Mutual Bk.

McCord, Norman. North East England: The Region's Development 1760-1914. 1979. 50.00 (ISBN 0-7134-1261-5, Pub. by Batsford England). David & Charles.

McElwee, William. The Story of England. 3rd ed. (Story Ser.). (Illus.). 288p. 1969. 6.95 (ISBN 0-571-04662-2, Pub. by Faber & Faber). Merrimack Bk Serv.

MacKay, Hugh. Memoirs of the War Carried on in Scotland & Ireland. LC 70-172707. (Maitland Club, Glasgow. Publications: No. 22). Repr. of 1833 ed. 37.50 (ISBN 0-404-52755-8). AMS Pr.

Manning, Brian, ed. Politics, Religion & the English Civil War. LC 73-87138. 288p. 1974. text ed. 19.95 (ISBN 0-312-62755-6). St Martin.

Marshall, Peter & Williams, Glyn, eds. The British Atlantic Empire Before the American Revolution. 130p. 1980. 25.00x (ISBN 0-7146-3158-2, F Cass Co). Biblio Dist.

Martin, Margaret. Colleagues or Competitors. 103p. 1969. pap. text ed. 5.00x (ISBN 0-7135-1538-4, Pub. by Bedford England). Renouf.

Mather, F. C., ed. Chartism & Society. LC 80-15587. 488p. 1980. text ed. 45.00x (ISBN 0-8419-0625-4). Holmes & Meier.

Maurois, Andre. Histoire d'Angleterre. 26.25 (ISBN 0-685-36938-2). French & Eur.

Messenger, J. C. Inis Beag: Isle of Ireland. LC 70-87858. (Case Studies in Cultural Anthropology). 1969. pap. text ed. 4.95 (ISBN 0-03-081250-X, HoltC). HR&W.

Moore, Frances. Leycesters. LC 71-162914. (Bentley's Standard Novels: No. 123). Repr. of 1854 ed. 17.50 (ISBN 0-404-54523-8). AMS Pr.

Moore, John S., ed. The Goods & Chattels of Our Forefathers: Frampton, Cotterell & District Probate Inventories, 1539 to 1804. 364p. 1976. 26.50x (ISBN 0-8476-1378-X). Rowman.

Morley, John. Nineteenth Century Essays. Stansky, Peter, ed. LC 73-116380. (Classics of British Historical Literature Ser). 1972. pap. 3.45 (ISBN 0-226-53848-6, P387, Phoen). U of Chicago Pr.

Morton, A. L. People's History of England. (Illus.). 1980. pap. 2.95 (ISBN 0-7178-0150-0). Intl Pub Co.
Myers, A. R. England in the Late Middle Ages. lib. bdg. 9.50x (ISBN 0-88307-211-4). Gannon.
Neale, R. S. Class in English History: 1680-1850. (Illus.). 256p. 1981. 28.50x (ISBN 0-389-20177-4). B&N.
Nicholson, Norman. Greater Lakeland. (Illus.). 1969. 10.50x (ISBN 0-7091-0951-2). Intl Pubns Serv.
Nobbs, Douglas. England & Scotland, 1560-1707. LC 80-25749. xxi, 173p. 1981. Repr. of 1952 ed. lib. bdg. 19.75x (ISBN 0-313-22773-X, NOES). Greenwood.
Norgate, K. England Under the Angevin Kings, 2 Vols. LC 68-25255. (British History Ser., No. 30). 1969. Repr. of 1887 ed. lib. bdg. 79.95 (ISBN 0-8383-0184-3). Haskell.
Old England. (Illus.). 1978. Repr. of 1845 ed. 29.95 (ISBN 0-8317-6595-X, Mayflower Bks). Smith Pubs.
Oman, Charles. History of England. (Illus.). 760p. 1981. pap. text ed. write for info. (ISBN 0-86649-063-9). Twentieth Century.
--History of England. LC 71-39469. (Select Bibliographies Reprint Series). 1972. Repr. of 1902 ed. 30.75 (ISBN 0-8369-9920-7). Arno.
Ovennell, Marjorie & Ovennell, C. H. A History of Everyday Things in England, 5 vols. Incl. Volume I, 1066-1499. 1969 (ISBN 0-7134-1650-5); Volume II, 1500-1799. 1976 (ISBN 0-7134-1651-3); Volume III, 1733-1851. 1977 (ISBN 0-7134-1652-1); Volume IV, 1851-1914. 1976 (ISBN 0-7134-1653-X); Volume V, 1914-1968. Ellan, S. E. 1977 (ISBN 0-7134-1654-8). 17.95 ea. (Pub. by Batsford England). David & Charles.
Parry, Keith. Trans-Pennine Heritage: People & Transport. LC 80-68691. (Illus.). 1981. 24.00 (ISBN 0-7153-8019-2). David & Charles.
Patmore, K. A. Seven Edwards of England. LC 71-118493. 1971. Repr. of 1911 ed. 15.00 (ISBN 0-8046-1241-2). Kennikat.
Percy, F. H. A History of Whitgift School. 1976. 16.95 (ISBN 0-7134-3158-X, Pub. by Batsford England). David & Charles.
Perkin, Harold. The Structured Crowd: Essays in English Social History. 250p. 1981. 28.50x (ISBN 0-389-20116-2). B&N.
Phillips, John R. The Reformation of Images: Destruction of Art in England, 1530-1665. 1974. 25.00x (ISBN 0-520-02424-9). U of Cal Pr.
Pinches, J. J. & Pinches, R. V. Royal Heraldry of England. (Illus.). 1974. 35.00 (ISBN 0-8048-1228-4). C E Tuttle.
Plumb, J. The First Four Georges. 1956. pap. 2.25 (ISBN 0-531-06007-1, Fontana Pap). Watts.
Plumb, J. H., et al. The English Heritage. LC 77-92987. (Illus., Orig.). 1978. pap. text ed. 11.95x (ISBN 0-88273-350-8). Forum Pr MO.
Pomfret, John E. Struggle for Land in Ireland 1800-1923. LC 68-27079. (Illus.). 1969. Repr. of 1930 ed. 11.00 (ISBN 0-8462-1292-7). Russell.
Pound, John. Poverty & Vagrancy in Tudor England. 1971. pap. text ed. 4.50x (ISBN 0-582-31405-4). Longman.
Powell, W. R., ed. Essex, Vol. 7. (Victoria History of the Counties of England Ser.). (Illus.). 1979. 99.00 (ISBN 0-19-722720-1). Oxford U Pr.
Powicke, Maurice & Fryde, E. B., eds. Handbook of British Chronology. 2nd ed. (Royal Historical Society Ser.). 565p. 1961. 18.50x (ISBN 0-8476-1342-9). Rowman.
Presseisen, Ernst L. Amiens & Munich. (Comparisons in Appeasement). 1978. 31.50 (ISBN 90-247-2067-2, Pub. by Martinus Nijhoff Netherlands). Kluwer Boston.
The Quest for Arthur's Britain. (Illus.). 1971. pap. 5.95x (ISBN 0-8464-0776-0). Beekman Pubs.
Quinault, R. & Stevenson, J., eds. Popular Protest & Public Order: Six Studies in British History, 1790-1920. LC 74-26213. 256p. 1975. 19.95 (ISBN 0-312-63105-7). St Martin.
Ramsay, James H. The Foundations of England: Or, Twelve Centuries of British History, 2 vols. LC 80-2215. Repr. of 1898 ed. Set. 125.00 (ISBN 0-404-18780-3). Vol. 1 (ISBN 0-404-18781-1). Vol. 2 (ISBN 0-404-18782-X). AMS Pr.
Randle, John. Understanding Britain: A History of the British People & Their Culture. (Illus.). 232p. 1981. 19.95x (ISBN 0-631-12471-3, Pub. by Basil Blackwell England); pap. 8.95x (ISBN 0-631-12883-2). Biblio Dist.
Raymond, John. England on the Anvil. 1958. 20.00 (ISBN 0-8274-2248-2). R West.
Richmond, I. A. Roman Britain. 1978. pap. 2.95 (ISBN 0-14-020315-X, Pelican). Penguin.
Ridley, Jasper. The History of England. (Illus.). 400p. 1981. 18.95 (ISBN 0-7100-0794-9). Routledge & Kegan.
Ringler, William A. Stephen Gosson. 1971. lib. bdg. 13.00x (ISBN 0-374-96814-4). Octagon.
Roberts, Anthony, ed. Glastonbury: Ancient Avalon, New Jerusalem. 1979. pap. 7.50 (ISBN 0-00-913265-1, Pub. by Hutchinson). Merrimack Bk Serv.
Roberts, David & Roberts, Clayton. History of England, 2 vols. (Illus.). 1980. Vol. I To 1714. pap. text ed. 15.95 (ISBN 0-13-390005-3); Vol. II 1688 To Present. pap. text ed. 14.95 (ISBN 0-13-390013-4). P-H.
Robin, Jean. Elmdon, Continuity & Change in a Northwest Essex Village. LC 79-12964. (Illus.). 1980. 41.50 (ISBN 0-521-22820-4). Cambridge U Pr.
Rowlands, Richard. A Restitution of Decayed Intelligence: In Antiquities, Concerning the...English Nation. by the Studie & Travaile of R. Verstagen. Dedicated Unto the Kings Most Excellent Majestie. LC 79-84134. (English Experience Ser.: No. 952). 380p. 1979. Repr. of 1605 ed. lib. bdg. 35.00 (ISBN 90-221-0952-6). Walter J Johnson.
Royle, Edward. Radicals, Secularists & Republicans: Popular Freethought in Britain, 1866 to 1915. 380p. 1980. 29.50x (ISBN 0-8476-6294-2). Rowman.
Rubinstein, W. D. Men of Property: The Very Wealthy in Britain Since the Industrial Revolution. 256p. 1981. 22.00 (ISBN 0-8135-0927-0). Rutgers U Pr.
Sayles, George O. The King's Parliament of England. (Historical Controversies). 164p. 1974. 7.95 (ISBN 0-393-05508-6); pap. text ed. 4.95x (ISBN 0-393-09322-0). Norton.
Schiller, F. C. Cassandra or the Future of the British Empire. 92p. 1980. Repr. lib. bdg. 12.50 (ISBN 0-89984-400-6). Century Bookbindery.
Schultz, Harold J. History of England. 3rd ed. LC 79-153052. 1979. pap. 5.95 (ISBN 0-06-460188-9, CO 188, COS). Har-Row.
Scott, A. F. Every One a Witness Series. Incl. The Norman Age. (Illus.). 336p. 1976. 16.00x (ISBN 0-8476-6000-1); The Plantagenet Age. (Illus.). 328p. 1976. 13.50x (ISBN 0-8476-6001-X); The Stuart Age. (Illus.). 328p. 1974. 12.00x (ISBN 0-8476-6003-6); The Tudor Age. (Illus.). 291p. 1975. 13.50x (ISBN 0-8476-6002-8). (Illus.). Rowman.
Scott, Sir Walter. Woodstock. 1969. 9.95x (ISBN 0-460-00072-1, Evman). Biblio Dist.
Seabrook, Jeremy. What Went Wrong: Why Hasn't Having More Made People Happier. LC 78-20424. 1979. 10.00 (ISBN 0-394-50598-0); pap. 3.95 (ISBN 0-394-73773-3). Pantheon.
Seeley, J. R. The Growth of British Policy: A Historical Essay, 2 vols. LC 72-145289. (Illus.). 838p. 1972. Repr. of 1903 ed. 45.00 (ISBN 0-403-01203-1). Scholarly.
The Shaping of England. 1969. 4.50 (ISBN 0-395-06579-8). HM.
Sheppard, F. H., ed. Grosvenor Estate in Mayfair: The Buildings, Pt. 2. (Survey of London Ser.: Vol. 40). 429p. 1980. text ed. 143.00x (ISBN 0-485-48240-1, Athlone Pr). Humanities.
Six Old English Chronicles. 1885. 30.00 (ISBN 0-8274-3437-5). R West.
Smith, Lacey B., ed. A History of England, 4 vols. 3rd ed. Incl. Vol. 1. The Making of England, 55 B.C.-1399. Hollister, C. W. pap. text ed. 8.95x (ISBN 0-685-56522-X); Vol. 2. This Realm of England, 1399-1688. Smith, Lacey B. pap. text ed. 8.95x (ISBN 0-669-97949-X); Vol. 3. The Age of Aristocracy, 1688-1830. Willcox, William B. pap. text ed. 8.95x (ISBN 0-669-97956-2); Vol. 4. Britain Yesterday & Today, 1830 to the Present. Arnstein, Walter L. (Illus.). pap. text ed. 9.95x (ISBN 0-669-97964-3). 1975. Heath.
Smith, Lacey B. & Smith, Jean R., eds. The Past Speaks: Sources & Problems in English History to 1688. 368p. 1981. pap. text ed. 8.95 (ISBN 0-669-02920-3). Heath.
Stamp, A. H. A Social & Economic History of England from Seventeen Hundred to Nineteen Seventy. 334p. 1980. 22.50x (ISBN 0-7050-0070-2, Pub. by Skilton & Shaw England). State Mutual Bk.
Stenton, Frank. Anglo-Saxon England. 3rd ed. (Oxford History of England Ser.). 1971. 33.00x (ISBN 0-19-821716-1). Oxford U Pr.
Stephens, W. B. Sources for English Local History. (The Sources of History Ser.). 336p. Date not set. price not set (ISBN 0-521-23763-7); pap. price not set (ISBN 0-521-28213-6). Cambridge U Pr.
Stone, Lawrence. Family & Fortune: Studies in Aristocratic Finance in the Sixteenth & Seventeenth Centuries. (Illus.). 1973. 29.95x (ISBN 0-19-822401-X). Oxford U Pr.
--The Family, Sex & Marriage: England 1500-1800. LC 77-50. (Illus.). 1977. 30.00 (ISBN 0-06-014142-5, HarpT). Har-Row.
Sturt, Mary. Education of the People: A History of Primary Education in England & Wales in the 19th Century. 1966. text ed. 11.00x (ISBN 0-7100-2161-5). Humanities.
Sutcliffe, Sheila. Martello Towers. LC 72-9566. (Illus.). 181p. 1973. 12.50 (ISBN 0-8386-1313-6). Fairleigh Dickinson.
Sweet, Alfred H. History of England. 1931. Repr. 20.00 (ISBN 0-685-43460-5). Norwood Edns.
Taine, H. A. Notes on England. 1957. Repr. 30.00 (ISBN 0-8274-3875-3). R West.
Tatlock, John & Perry, S. Legendary History of Britain. LC 74-18288. 1975. Repr. of 1950 ed. 17.50 (ISBN 0-87752-168-9). Gordian.
Thorn, Caroline & Thorn, Frank, eds. Somerset: (from a Draft Translation Prepared by Frank Thorn) (Domesday Book Ser.). (Illus.). 405p. 1980. 32.50x (ISBN 0-8476-3261-X). Rowman.
Thorn, Frank, ed. Rutland. (Domesday Book Ser.). (Illus.). 52p. (From a draft translation prepared by Celia Parker). 1980. 15.00x (ISBN 0-8476-3260-1). Rowman.
Thornton-Cook, Elsie. Kings in the Making: The Princes of Wales. facs. ed. LC 68-22951. (Essay Index Reprint Ser). 1931. 19.50 (ISBN 0-8369-0937-2). Arno.
Tierney, Brian, et al, eds. English Liberalism: The New Democratic Way? 3rd ed. (Historical Pamphlets). 1977. pap. text ed. 1.95x (ISBN 0-394-32060-3). Random.
Tout, T. F. Political History of England from the Accession of Henry 3rd to the Death of Edward 3rd: 1216-1377. 1905. 24.00 (ISBN 0-527-00848-6). Kraus Repr.
Traill, Henry D. & Mann, James S., eds. Social England, 6 Vols. 1902-1904. Repr. Set. lib. bdg. 200.00x (ISBN 0-8371-1964-2, TRSO). Greenwood.
Trevelyan, G. M. Illustrated English Social History. LC 77-14065. (Illus.). 1978. text ed. 35.00x (ISBN 0-582-48488-X). Longman.
--Illustrated History of England. (Illus.). 824p. 1974. text ed. 31.00x (ISBN 0-582-48471-5). Longman.
--A Shortened History of England. 1976. pap. 5.95 (ISBN 0-14-020443-1, Pelican). Penguin.
Trevelyan, Sir George O. Marginal Notes by Lord Macaulay. 64p. 1980. Repr. of 1907 ed. lib. bdg. 15.00 (ISBN 0-89987-803-2). Darby Bks.
Turner, M. English Parliamentary Enclosure: Its Historical Geography & Economic History. (Studies in Historical Geography Ser.). (Illus.). 247p. 1980. 22.50 (ISBN 0-208-01786-0). Shoe String.
Vann, Richard T. Social Development of English Quakerism 1655-1755. LC 79-78524. 1969. 14.00x (ISBN 0-674-81290-5). Harvard U Pr.
Vexler, Robert I. England: A Chronology & Fact Book. LC 73-17607. (World Chronology Ser.). 160p. 1974. lib. bdg. 8.50x (ISBN 0-379-16306-3). Oceana.
Walker, J. British Economic & Social History. 448p. 1980. 12.00x (ISBN 0-7121-0266-3, Pub. by Macdonald & Evans). State Mutual Bk.
Watts, S. J. & Watts, S. I. From Border to Middle Shire: Northumberland 1586-1625. (Illus.). 256p. 1975. text ed. 21.00x (ISBN 0-7185-1127-1, Leicester). Humanities.
Webb, A. N. An Edition of the Cartulary of Burscough Prior. 330p. 1970. 33.00x (ISBN 0-7190-1152-3, Pub. by Manchester U Pr England). State Mutual Bk.
Wexler, Victor. David Hume & "The History of England". LC 78-68423. (Memoirs Ser.: Vol. 131). 1979. 8.00 (ISBN 0-87169-131-0). Am Philos.
White, Reginald J. Short History of England. (Illus.). 1967. 38.50 (ISBN 0-521-06784-7); pap. 10.50x (ISBN 0-521-09439-9). Cambridge U Pr.
Whitelock, Dorothy. The Pelican History of England: Beginnings of English Society, Vol. 2. 1952. pap. 2.95 (ISBN 0-14-020245-5, Pelican). Penguin.
Wiener, Joel H., ed. Great Britain: Foreign Policy & the Span of Empire, a Documentary History 1689-1971, 4 vols. LC 78-179375. 3600p. 1972. Set. 99.50 (ISBN 0-07-079730-7, P&RB); 30.00 ea. McGraw.
Williams, E. N. The Penguin Dictionary of English & European History 1485-1789. (Reference Ser.). 480p. 1980. pap. 6.95 (ISBN 0-14-051084-2). Penguin.
Williamson, James A. Great Britain & the Commonwealth. 3rd ed. 1965. text ed. 5.50x (ISBN 0-7136-0844-7). Humanities.
Willson, D. H. A History of England. 2nd ed. LC 74-182142. 1972. text ed. 20.95 (ISBN 0-03-085315-X, HoltC). HR&W.
Wilson, Derek. The Tower: The Tumultuous History of the Tower of London from 1078. (Illus.). 1979. 14.95 (ISBN 0-684-16261-X, ScribT). Scribner.
Wittke, Carl. History of English Parliamentary Privilege. LC 74-87623. (Law, Politics, & History Ser). 1969. Repr. of 1921 ed. lib. bdg. 25.00 (ISBN 0-306-71810-3). Da Capo.
Woodward, E. L. A History of England. 3rd ed. 1966. pap. 9.95x (ISBN 0-416-67910-2). Methuen Inc.
Wyatt, A. J. The Tutorial History of English History. 1978. Repr. of 1900 ed. lib. bdg. 20.00 (ISBN 0-8482-6983-7). Norwood Edns.
Young, G. V. From the Vikings to the Reformation: A Chronicle of the Faroe Islands up to 1538. (Illus.). 1979. text ed. 13.75x (ISBN 0-904980-20-0). Humanities.
Zimmern, Alfred E. The Third British Empire. 3rd ed. LC 79-4333. 1979. Repr. of 1934 ed. lib. bdg. 18.75x (ISBN 0-313-20990-1, ZITB). Greenwood.

GREAT BRITAIN–HISTORY–ADDRESSES, ESSAYS, LECTURES

Beresford, John. Storm & Peace. facs. ed. LC 67-28744. (Essay Index Reprint Ser). 1936. 15.00 (ISBN 0-8369-0201-7). Arno.
Burrow, John W. A Liberal Descent: Victorian Historians & the English Past. LC 81-3912. 336p. Date not set. price not set (ISBN 0-521-24079-4). Cambridge U Pr.
Clark, Dorothy K., et al. Essays on Modern English History in Honor of Wilbur Cortez Abbott. LC 74-118467. (Essay & General Literature Index Reprint Ser). 1971. Repr. of 1941 ed. 16.00 (ISBN 0-8046-1403-2). Kennikat.
Cronne, H. A., et al, eds. Essays in British & Irish History in Honour of James Eadie Todd. 1977. Repr. of 1949 ed. lib. bdg. 25.00 (ISBN 0-8495-0711-1). Arden Lib.
--Essays in British & Irish History in Honour of James Eadie Todd. Quinn, D. B. 1977. Repr. of 1949 ed. lib. bdg. 30.00 (ISBN 0-8482-3478-2). Norwood Edns.
Davies, Godfrey. Essays on the Later Stuarts. LC 74-20075. (Illus.). 133p. 1975. Repr. of 1958 ed. lib. bdg. 15.00x (ISBN 0-8371-7842-8, DAEL). Greenwood.
Essays in History Presented to Reginald Lane Poole. facs. ed. LC 67-30186. (Essay Index Reprint Ser). 1927. 20.00 (ISBN 0-8369-0424-9). Arno.
Lower, Mark A. Contributions to Literature: Historical, Antiquarian, & Metrical. LC 72-4578. (Essay Index Reprint Ser.). Repr. of 1854 ed. 18.00 (ISBN 0-8369-2959-4). Arno.
Macaulay, Thomas B. Selected Writings. Clive, John & Pinney, Thomas, eds. LC 78-171350. (Classics of British Historical Literature Ser). 544p. 1972. 15.00x (ISBN 0-226-49996-0). U of Chicago Pr.
Maitland, Frederic W. Selected Historical Essays. Cam, H. M., ed. 1957. 41.50 (ISBN 0-521-05659-4). Cambridge U Pr.
Malpass, E. Deanne, pref. by. Personalities & Policies: Essays on English & European History. LC 76-43381. (Illus.). 1977. lib. bdg. 6.00 (ISBN 0-912646-39-X). Tex Christian.
Namier, Lewis B. Crossroads of Power. LC 77-119604. (Essay Index Reprint Ser). 1962. 15.00 (ISBN 0-8369-1690-5). Arno.
Newman, Bertram. English Historians: Selected Passages. 1979. Repr. of 1957 ed. lib. bdg. 30.00 (ISBN 0-8495-4013-5). Arden Lib.
Rhodes, James F. Historical Essays. LC 66-25938. Repr. of 1909 ed. 12.75 (ISBN 0-8046-0378-2). Kennikat.
Rogers, Elizabeth F., ed. Letters of Sir John Hackett. LC 70-105570. (Archives of British History & Culture Ser). 419p. 1971. 15.00 (ISBN 0-937058-05-X). West Va U Pr.
Rowse, A. L. The English Spirit: Essays in History & Literature--George Herbert, Swift, Walpole, Wordsworth, Carlyle, Macaulay. 1977. Repr. of 1944 ed. lib. bdg. 30.00 (ISBN 0-8495-4508-0). Arden Lib.
Russell, George W. E. Prime Ministers & Some Others. 1919. Repr. 20.00 (ISBN 0-8274-3203-8). R West.
Steinberg, S. H., ed. Dictionary of British History. 2nd ed. LC 79-140431. 1971. 17.95 (ISBN 0-312-20020-X). St Martin.
Trevelyan, George M. Autobiography & Other Essays. facs. ed. LC 75-142707. (Essay Index Reprint Ser). 1949. 16.00 (ISBN 0-8369-2205-0). Arno.
Wainwright, Frederick T. Scandinavian England: Collected Papers. Finberg, H. P., ed. 387p. 1975. 27.50x (ISBN 0-87471-783-3). Rowman.

GREAT BRITAIN–HISTORY–BIBLIOGRAPHY

Bonser, Wilfrid. Romano-British Bibliography: 55B.C.-449A.D, Vol. 1 & 2. 1977. Set. 225.00x (ISBN 0-686-31733-5, Pub. by Basil Blackwell). Vol. 1 (ISBN 0-631-08370-7). Vol. 2 (ISBN 0-631-08380-4). Biblio Dist.
British History: Classification Schedule, Author & Title Listing, Chronological Listing, 2 vols. (Widener Library Shelflists Ser.: No. 53-54). 1328p. 1975. 85.00x set (ISBN 0-674-08240-0). Harvard U Pr.
Brown, Lucy M. & Christie, Ian R. Bibliography of British History Seventeen Eighty-Nine to Eighteen Fifty-One. 1977. 109.00x (ISBN 0-19-822390-0). Oxford U Pr.
Crawford, James L. Bibliography of Royal Proclamations of the Tudor & Stuart Sovereigns & of Others Published Under Authority, Fourteen Eighty-Five to Seventeen Fourteen, 3 vols. in 2. LC 68-1518. 661p. 1910-13. Repr. 153.00 (ISBN 0-8337-0724-8). B Franklin.

Day, Alan. History: A Reference Handbook. 1977. 19.50 (ISBN 0-208-01536-1, Linnet). Shoe String.
Elton, G., ed. Annual Bibliography of British & Irish History: Publications of 1977. 1978. text ed. 26.75x (ISBN 0-391-00881-1). Humanities.
--Annual Bibliography of British & Irish History: Publications of 1979, Vol. 5. 1981. text ed. 30.00x (ISBN 0-391-01774-8). Humanities.
--Annual Bibliography of British & Irish History, 1978. 1979. text ed. 26.75x (ISBN 0-391-01054-9). Humanities.
--Annual Bibliography of British & Irish History 1976. 1977. text ed. 28.50x (ISBN 0-391-00753-X). Humanities.
Elton, G. R. Modern Historians on British History, 1584-1945: A Critical Bibliography, 1945-1969. LC 77-137677. 248p. 1971. 19.50x (ISBN 0-8014-0611-0). Cornell U Pr.
Elton, Geoffrey R., ed. Annual Bibliography of British & Irish History, 1975. 1976. text ed. 31.25x (ISBN 0-391-00619-3). Humanities.
Graves, Edgar B., ed. Bibliography of British History to Fourteen Eighty-Five, 2 vols. 2nd ed. 1080p. 1974. Set. 129.00x (ISBN 0-19-822391-9). Oxford U Pr.
Hall, Hubert, ed. A Select Bibliography for the Study, Sources & Literature of English Medieval Economic History. 1960. Repr. of 1914 ed. 23.50 (ISBN 0-8337-1548-8). B Franklin.
Hanham, H. J., ed. Bibliography of British History Eighteen Fifty-One to Nineteen Fourteen. 1976. 174.00x (ISBN 0-19-822389-7). Oxford U Pr.
Hardy, Thomas D. Descriptive Catalogue of Materials Relating to the History of Great Britain & Ireland, to the End of the Reign of Henry 7th, 3 Vols. in 4. 1862-71. Set. 187.00 (ISBN 0-8337-1576-3). B Franklin.
Harrison, J. F. & Thompson, Dorothy. Bibliography of the Chartist Movement, Eighteen Thirty Seven to Nineteen Seventy-Seven. 1978. text ed. 25.00x (ISBN 0-391-00742-4). Humanities.
Shaw, William A. Bibliography of the Historical Works of Dr. Creighton, Dr. Stubbs, Dr. S. R. Gardiner, & the Late Lord Acton. 1969. 17.50 (ISBN 0-8337-3242-0). B Franklin.

GREAT BRITAIN–HISTORY–JUVENILE LITERATURE

see also Great Britain–History, Naval–Juvenile Literature

Clarke, Amanda. Growing up in Ancient Britain. (Growing up Ser.). (Illus.). 72p. (gr. 6 up). 1981. 14.95 (ISBN 0-7134-3557-7, Pub. by Batsford England). David & Charles.
--Growing up in Elizabethan Times. LC 79-56439. (Growing up Ser.). (Illus.). 72p. (gr. 7 up). 1980. text ed. 14.95 (ISBN 0-7134-3364-7, Pub. by Batsford England). David & Charles.
--Growing up in Puritan Times. LC 79-56452. (Growing up Ser.). (Illus.). 72p. (gr. 7 up). 1980. text ed. 14.95 (ISBN 0-7134-3366-3, Pub. by Batsford England). David & Charles.
Delderfield, Eric. Kings & Queens of England. LC 72-79138. 1972. 5.95 (ISBN 0-8128-1493-2); pap. 3.95 (ISBN 0-8128-1494-0). Stein & Day.
Dickens, Charles. Child's History of England. (gr. 4-6). 1970. 9.95x (ISBN 0-460-00291-0, Evman). Biblio Dist.
Hodges, Walter C. The Battlement Garden. LC 79-15849. (Illus.). (gr. 6 up). 1980. 10.95 (ISBN 0-395-29184-4, Clarion). HM.
Johnson, David. Clipper Ships & Cutty Sark. (Jackdaw Ser: No. 97). (gr. 7 up). 1971. 6.95 (ISBN 0-670-22518-5). Viking Pr.
Jones, Madeline. Growing up in Regency England. LC 79-56451. (Growing up Ser.). (Illus.). 72p. (gr. 7 up). 1980. text ed. 14.95 (ISBN 0-7134-3368-X, Pub. by Batsford England). David & Charles.
Lane, Peter. Georgian England. (Visual Sources Ser.). (Illus.). 96p. (gr. 7-9). 1981. 16.95 (ISBN 0-7134-3358-2, Pub. by Batsford England). David & Charles.
--Norman England. (Visual Sources Ser.). (Illus.). 96p. (gr. 7 up). 1980. text ed. 14.95 (ISBN 0-7134-3356-6, Pub. by Batsford England). David & Charles.
Little Arthur's History of England. (gr. 4-6). 1972. pap. 6.95 (ISBN 0-7195-3242-6). Transatlantic.
Reynolds, P. Iron Age Farming. (Cambridge Introduction to the History of Mankind Ser.). 48p. 1976. pap. 3.95 (ISBN 0-521-21084-4). Cambridge U Pr.
Richardson, Joanna. The Prince Regent. (Jackdaw Ser: No. 139). (gr. 7 up). 1976. 6.95 (ISBN 0-670-57656-5). Viking Pr.
Roll, Winifred. Mary I: The History of an Unhappy Tudor Queen. (Illus.). 1979. 9.95g (ISBN 0-13-559096-5). P-H.
Sasek, Miroslav. This Is Historic Britain. LC 73-18345. 64p. (gr. 4-8). 1974. 8.95 (ISBN 0-02-778200-X). Macmillan.
Snodin, David. A Mighty Ferment: Britain in the Age of Revolution, 1750-1850. LC 77-16482. (Illus.). 128p. (gr. 6 up). 1978. 8.95 (ISBN 0-395-28925-4, Clarion). HM.
Strickland, Agnes. Tales from English History: For Children. 1978. Repr. lib. bdg. 25.00 (ISBN 0-8492-8048-6). R West.
Tames, Richard. Gladstone. (Jackdaw Ser: No. 119). (gr. 7 up). 1976. 6.95 (ISBN 0-670-34178-9). Viking Pr.
Wilkins, Frances. Growing up During the Norman Conquest. LC 79-56440. (Growing up Ser.). (gr. 7-9). 1980. text ed. 14.95 (ISBN 0-7134-3360-4, Pub. by Batsford England). David & Charles.

GREAT BRITAIN–HISTORY–OUTLINES, SYLLABI, ETC.

Marwick, Arthur, et al, eds. The Illustrated Dictionary of British History. (Illus.). 320p. 1981. 19.95 (ISBN 0-500-25072-3). Thames Hudson.
Trenholme, Norman M. An Outline of English History. 1910. Repr. 10.00 (ISBN 0-685-43458-3). Norwood Edns.

GREAT BRITAIN–HISTORY–PHILOSOPHY

Christianson, Paul K. Reformers & Babylon: Apocalyptic Visions in England from the Reformation to the Outbreak of the Civil War. LC 77-16706. 1978. 25.00x (ISBN 0-8020-5365-3). U of Toronto Pr.
Colbourn, H. Trevor. Lamp of Experience: Whig History & the Intellectual Origins of the American Revolution. LC 65-23138. (Institute of Early American History & Culture Ser.). 1965. 17.00x (ISBN 0-8078-0958-6). U of NC Pr.
Cole, C. Robert & Moody, Michael E., eds. The Dissenting Tradition: Essays for Leland H. Carlson. LC 74-27706. xxiii, 272p. 1975. 17.00x (ISBN 0-8214-0176-9). Ohio U Pr.
Eroyle. Radicals, Secularists & Republicans: Popular Freethought in Britain, 1866-1915. 350p. 1981. 65.00x (ISBN 0-686-73068-2, Pub. by Manchester U Pr England). State Mutual Bk.

GREAT BRITAIN–HISTORY–PICTORIAL WORKS

Bishop, Coleman. Pictures from English History by the Great Historical Artists. 1977. lib. bdg. 59.95 (ISBN 0-8490-2441-2). Gordon Pr.
Escott, T. H. Platform, Press, Politics & Plays: Being Pen & Ink Sketches of Contemporary Celeberties. (Victorian Age Ser). 45.00 (ISBN 0-685-43402-8). Norwood Edns.
Household, G. A. & Smith, L. M., eds. To Catch a Sunbeam. (Illus.). 144p. 1980. 15.95 (ISBN 0-7181-1861-8, Pub. by Michael Joseph). Merrimack Bk Serv.
Pierce, A. J. & Pierce, D. K. Victorian & Edwardian Children from Old Photographs. LC 79-56442. (Illus.). 120p. 1980. 17.95 (ISBN 0-7134-2327-7, Pub. by Batsford England). David & Charles.
Strong, Roy. Recreating the Past: British History & the Victorian Painters. (Illus.). 1978. 19.95 (ISBN 0-500-23281-4). Thames Hudson.

GREAT BRITAIN–HISTORY–POETRY

Bates, Katharine L. & Coman, Katharine, eds. English History As Told by English Poets. facsimile ed. LC 71-103082. (Granger Index Reprint Ser.). 1902. 21.00 (ISBN 0-8369-6097-1). Arno.
Corson, Livingston. Finding List of Political Poems Referring to English Affairs of the 13th & 14th Centuries. LC 72-121222. (Bibliography & Reference Ser.: No. 331). 1970. Repr. of 1910 ed. lib. bdg. 18.50 (ISBN 0-8337-0684-5). B Franklin.
Ellis, Frank H., ed. Poems on Affairs of State: Augustan Satirical Verse, 1660-1714, Vol. 6, 1697-1704. (Illus.). 1970. 55.00x (ISBN 0-300-01194-6). Yale U Pr.
Firth, C. H. English History in English Poetry from the French Revolution to the Death of Queen Victoria. 59.95 (ISBN 0-8490-0111-0). Gordon Pr.
Gardner, Mary R. English History in Rhyme. 59.95 (ISBN 0-8490-0112-9). Gordon Pr.
Lord, George D., ed. Poems on Affairs of State: Augustan Satirical Verse 1660-1714, Vol. 1, 1669-1678. (Illus.). 1963. 40.00x (ISBN 0-300-00726-4). Yale U Pr.
Mengel, Elias F., ed. Poems on Affairs of State: Augustan Satirical Verse 1660-1714, Vol. 2, 1678-1681. (Illus.). 1965. 40.00x (ISBN 0-300-00766-3). Yale U Pr.
Rivet, A. L. & Smith, Colin. The Place-Names of Roman Britain. LC 79-21616. (Illus.). 584p. 1979. 100.00 (ISBN 0-691-03953-4). Princeton U Pr.
Warner, William. Albion's England. 1971. Repr. of 1612 ed. 64.00 (ISBN 3-4870-3325-9). Adler.
Windsor, M. E. & Turral, J., eds. Lyra Historica: Poems of British History, A. D. Sixty-One to Nineteen-Ten. LC 76-160913. (Granger Index Reprint Ser.). Repr. of 1911 ed. 16.00 (ISBN 0-8369-6278-8). Arno.
--Lyra Historica: Poems of British History, Ad 61-1910, 3 vols. in one. LC 79-50854. (Granger Poetry Library). 1979. Repr. of 1911 ed. 17.50x (ISBN 0-89609-174-0). Granger Bk.

GREAT BRITAIN–HISTORY–SOURCES

see also subdivision sources for various period subdivisions which follow, e.g., Great Britain–History–Medieval Period, 1066-1485–Sources; Great Britain–History–Sources

Agard, A. The Reportorie of Records at Westminster. LC 72-225. (English Experience Ser.: No. 291). 1971. Repr. of 1631 ed. 22.00 (ISBN 90-221-0291-2). Walter J Johnson.
Andrews, Ian. Boudicca's Revolt. (Introduction to the History of Mankind Ser.). 1972. 3.95 (ISBN 0-521-08031-2). Cambridge U Pr.
Bagley, J. J. Historical Interpretation. Incl. Vol. 1. Sources of English Medieval History, 1066-1540. 285p (ISBN 0-312-38045-3); Vol. 2. Sources of English History, 1540 to Present Day. 296p (ISBN 0-312-38080-1). LC 72-85263. (Illus.). 1973. 10.00x ea. St Martin.
Bickley, Francis L. An English Letter Book. LC 74-10521. 1925. 20.00 (ISBN 0-8414-3119-1). Folcroft.
Blakeley, Brian L. & Collins, Jacquelin. Documents in English History: Early Times to the Present. LC 74-18264. 448p. 1975. pap. text ed. 13.95 (ISBN 0-471-07946-4). Wiley.
Carpenter, Nathanael. Geography Delineated Forth in Two Books. LC 76-57369. (English Experience Ser.: No. 787). 1977. Repr. of 1625 ed. lib. bdg. 58.00 (ISBN 90-221-0787-6). Walter J Johnson.
Caxton, William. Begin Two A. LC 72-5980. (English Experience Ser.: No. 508). 1973. Repr. of 1480 ed. 61.00 (ISBN 90-221-0508-3). Walter J Johnson.
Cheyney, Edward P. Reading in English History Drawn from the Original Sources. 1908. 25.00 (ISBN 0-685-43752-3). Norwood Edns.
Colby, Charles W., ed. Selections from the Sources of English History: Being a Supplement to Text-Books of English History B.C. 55-A.D. 1832. 1978. Repr. of 1905 ed. lib. bdg. 35.00 (ISBN 0-89760-102-5, Telegraph). Dynamic Learn Corp.
A Discourse Concerning the Drayning of Fennes & Surrounded Ground. LC 76-57367. (English Experience Ser.: No. 784). 1977. Repr. of 1629 ed. lib. bdg. 3.50 (ISBN 90-221-0784-1). Walter J Johnson.
Ellis, Henry, ed. Original Letters Illustrative of English History, 11 Vols. Repr. of 1846 ed. Set. 192.50 (ISBN 0-404-02310-X); 17.50 ea. AMS Pr.
--Original Letters of Eminent Literary Men of the 16th, 17th & 18th Centuries. LC 71-166022. (Camden Society, London. Publications, First Ser.: No. 23). Repr. of 1843 ed. 35.00 (ISBN 0-404-50123-0). AMS Pr.
Great Britain Public Record Office. Syllabus in English of the Documents Relating to England & Other Kingdoms, 3 Vols. LC 78-168243. Repr. of 1885 ed. Set. 172.50 (ISBN 0-404-03130-7). AMS Pr.
Grey Friars Of London. Chronicle of the Grey Friars of London. 1852. 15.50 (ISBN 0-384-33445-8). Johnson Repr.
Guide to British Historical Manuscripts in the Huntington Library. (Huntington Library Manuscript Guide). 450p. 1981. price not set (ISBN 0-87328-117-9). Huntington Lib.
Hall, Hubert. Studies in English Official Historical Documents. LC 73-106063. (Bibliography & Reference Ser: No. 267). 1970. Repr. of 1908 ed. lib. bdg. 25.50 (ISBN 0-8337-1549-6). B Franklin.
Hall, Hubert, compiled by. Formula Book of English Historical Documents, 2 vols. (Bibliography & Reference Ser.: No. 266). 1970. Repr. of 1909 ed. 36.00 (ISBN 0-8337-1544-5). B Franklin.
Hutson, Arthur E. British Personal Names in the Historia Regun Britanniae. LC 75-19158. 1974. Repr. of 1940 ed. lib. bdg. 25.00 (ISBN 0-8414-4891-4). Folcroft.
Jackson, Michael, ed. Exploring England. (Illus.). 1979. pap. 6.95 (ISBN 0-8317-5773-6, Mayflower Bks). Smith Pubs.
Jensen, Merrill, ed. English Historical Documents: American Colonial Documents to 1776, Vol. 9. 69.00x (ISBN 0-19-519506-X). Oxford U Pr.
Lequesne, A. L. After Kilvert. (Illus.). 1978. 16.95x (ISBN 0-19-211748-3). Oxford U Pr.
Marlborough, Sarah J. Memoirs. King, William, ed. Repr. of 1930 ed. 24.00 (ISBN 0-527-61760-1). Kraus Repr.
Merewether, H. A. & Stephens, J. A. The History of the Boroughs & Municipal Corporations of the United Kingdom: From the Earliest to the Present Time, 3 vols. 1972. Repr. of 1835 ed. Set. text ed. 150.00x (ISBN 0-85527-402-6). Humanities.
Metrical Chronicle of England. (EETS, OS Ser.: No. 196). Repr. of 1935 ed. 14.00 (ISBN 0-527-00196-1). Kraus Repr.
Middleton, C. The Famous Historie of Chinon of England. (EETS, OS Ser.: No. 165). Repr. of 1925 ed. 10.00 (ISBN 0-527-00162-7). Kraus Repr.
Morris, John, ed. Nennius: British History & the Welsh Annals. (History from the Sources Ser.). 100p. 1980. 13.00x (ISBN 0-8476-6264-0). Rowman.
Nichols, John G., ed. Chronicle of the Grey Friars of London. (Camden Society, London. Publications, First Ser.: No. 53). Repr. of 1852 ed. 14.00 (ISBN 0-404-50153-2). AMS Pr.
Palmerston, Henry T. The Palmerston Papers, Gladstone & Palmerston. facsimile ed. Guedalla, Philip, ed. LC 73-157351. (Select Bibliographies Reprint Ser). Repr. of 1928 ed. 23.00 (ISBN 0-8369-5812-8). Arno.
Rothwell, Harry, ed. English Historical Documents: 1189-1327, Vol. 3. (Illus.). 1068p. 1975. 63.00x (ISBN 0-19-519744-5). Oxford U Pr.
Sachse, William L. English History in the Making: Readings from the Sources from 1689, 2 vols. LC 67-10154. 1970. Vol. 1. pap. text ed. 14.50x (ISBN 0-471-00494-4). Wiley.
Sawyer, P. H. Charters of Burton Abbey. (Anglo-Saxon Charters Ser.). (Illus.). 1979. 39.50x (ISBN 0-19-725940-5). Oxford U Pr.
Trevelyan. Trevelyan Papers, 1856-72, 3 Vols. Collier, J. Payne, et al, eds. (Camden Society, London, Publications, First Ser.: Nos. 67, 84, & 105). Set. 84.00 (ISBN 0-404-50206-7); 28.00 ea. No. 67 (ISBN 0-404-50167-2). No. 84 (ISBN 0-404-50184-2). No. 105 (ISBN 0-404-50205-9). AMS Pr.
Trevelyan Papers, 3 Vols. (Vol. 67, 0-384-61497-3; vol. 84, 0-384-61514-7; vol. 105, 0-384-61525-2). 1857-1872. 31.00 ea. Johnson Repr.
Vexler, Robert I. England: A Chronology & Fact Book. LC 73-17607. (World Chronology Ser.). 160p. 1974. lib. bdg. 8.50x (ISBN 0-379-16306-3). Oceana.
White, Albert Beebe & Notestein, Wallace. Source Problems in English History. Repr. 20.00 (ISBN 0-685-43253-X). Norwood Edns.
Willson, David H., ed. Parliamentary Diary of Robert Bowyer, 1606-1607. LC 72-120677. 1970. Repr. lib. bdg. 22.50x (ISBN 0-374-98636-3). Octagon.

GREAT BRITAIN–HISTORY–TO 449

Here are entered works on the early history of great britain to the end of the roman occupation as a whole, as well as books on parts of the period, such as the roman occupation.

Birley, Anthony. Life in Roman Britain. 1976. pap. 13.50 (ISBN 0-7134-3161-X, Pub. by Batsford England). David & Charles.
--The People of Roman Britain. LC 79-3604. 240p. 1980. 25.75x (ISBN 0-520-04119-4). U of Cal Pr.
Birley, Anthony R. The Fasti of Roman Britain. 410p. 1981. 79.00x (ISBN 0-19-814821-6). Oxford U Pr.
Burnham, Barry C. & Johnson, Helen B. Invasion & Response: The Case of Roman Britain. 1979. 50.00x (ISBN 0-86054-070-7, Pub. by BAR). State Mutual Bk.
Caesar. Invasion of Britain. 1969. 3.50x (ISBN 0-312-43470-7). St Martin.
Casey, P. J. The End of Roman Britain. 1979. 30.00x (ISBN 0-86054-069-3, Pub. by BAR). State Mutual Bk.
Chambers, Raymond W. England Before the Norman Conquest. LC 75-109718. Repr. of 1926 ed. lib. bdg. 15.25x (ISBN 0-8371-4208-3, CHNC). Greenwood.
Church, Alfred J. The Story of Early Britain. 375p. 1980. Repr. lib. bdg. 30.00 (ISBN 0-8495-0788-X). Arden Lib.
Clapham, John. The Historie of Great Britannie - from the Romans First Entrance, Untill the Raigne of Egbert, the West-Saxon Prince. LC 74-28837. (English Experience Ser.: No. 719). 1975. Repr. of 1606 ed. 22.00 (ISBN 90-221-0719-1). Walter J Johnson.
Collingwood, Robin G. & Myres, J. N. Roman Britain & the English Settlements. 2nd ed. (Oxford History of England Ser.). (Illus.). 1937. 34.50 (ISBN 0-19-821703-X). Oxford U Pr.
Divine, David. Hadrian's Wall: A Study of the North-West Frontier of Rome. LC 69-13122. (Illus.). 1969. 9.95 (ISBN 0-87645-017-6). Gambit.
Ellis, Peter B. Caesar's Invasion of Britain. LC 79-90167. 144p. 1979. 17.50x (ISBN 0-8147-2157-5). NYU Pr.
Fox, Aileen. Roman Britain. (Illus.). (gr. 7 up). 1968. 7.50 (ISBN 0-8023-1143-1). Dufour.
Frere, Sheppard. Britannia: A History of Roman Britain. rev. ed. (Illus.). 1978. 32.00x (ISBN 0-7100-8916-3). Routledge & Kegan.
Geoffrey of Monmouth. History of the Kings of Britain. Dunn, Charles W., ed. Evans, Sebastian, tr. 1958. pap. 3.95 (ISBN 0-525-47014-X). Dutton.
--Galfredi Monumentensis Historia Britonum. Giles, John A., ed. 1966. 24.00 (ISBN 0-8337-1344-2). B Franklin.

Hibbert, Christopher & Thomas, Charles. Search for King Arthur. LC 77-91594. (Horizon Caravel Bks). (Illus.). 153p. (gr. 6 up). 1969. 9.95 (ISBN 0-06-022313-8, Dist. by Har-Row); PLB 12.89 (ISBN 0-06-022314-6, Dist. by Har-Row). Am Heritage.

Hodgkin, Thomas. History of England from the Earliest Times to the Norman Conquest. LC 69-13933. Repr. of 1906 ed. lib. bdg. 23.00x (ISBN 0-8371-1023-8, HOHE). Greenwood.

Jones, David. Your Book of Roman Britain. (Your Book Ser.). (Illus.). 56p. 1978. 7.95 (ISBN 0-571-09903-3, Pub. by Faber & Faber). Merrimack Bk Serv.

Morris, John. The Age of Arthur. LC 72-11121. (Illus.). 656p. 1973. 17.50 (ISBN 0-684-13313-X, ScribT). Scribner.

Morrison, Alex. Early Man in Britain & Ireland. 1980. write for info. (ISBN 0-312-22463-X). St Martin.

Munby, Julian & Henjg, Martin. Roman Life & Art in Britain. 1977. 54.00x (ISBN 0-904531-91-0, Pub. by BAR). State Mutual Bk.

Parry, John J., ed. Brut Y Brenhinedd, Cotton Cleopatra Version. 1937. 12.00 (ISBN 0-910956-10-3). Medieval Acad.

Quennell, C. H. Everyday Life in Roman & Anglo-Saxon Times. 1969. 19.95 (ISBN 0-7134-1675-0, Pub. by Batsford England). David & Charles.

Rayson, Steven. The Crows of War. LC 74-19355. Orig. Title: Mai-Dun. 272p. (gr. 7 up). 1975. PLB 7.50 (ISBN 0-689-30455-2). Atheneum.

Rodwell, Warwick, ed. Temples, Churches & Religion: Recent Research in Roman Britain, with a Gazetteer of Roman-Celtic Temples in Continental Europe. 585p. 1980. 100.00x (ISBN 0-86054-085-5, Pub. by BAR). State Mutual Bk.

Salway, Peter. Roman Britain. (Oxford History of England Ser.). (Illus.). 784p. 1981. 49.95 (ISBN 0-19-821717-X). Oxford U Pr.

Sorrell, Alan. Roman Towns in Britain. 1976. 17.95 (ISBN 0-7134-3237-3). David & Charles.

Thomas, Charles. Christianity in Roman Britain to A. D. 500. (Illus.). 416p. 1981. 35.00x (ISBN 0-520-04392-8). U of Cal Pr.

Thwaite, Anthony. Beyond the Inhabited World: Roman Britain. LC 76-17526. (Illus.). (gr. 6 up). 1977. 8.95 (ISBN 0-395-28926-2, Clarion). HM.

Todd, Malcolm. Roman Britain. (Fontana History of the Ancient World Ser.). 288p. 1981. text ed. 23.75x (ISBN 0-391-02301-2, Pub. by Harvester England). Humanities.

Wacher, John. Roman Britain. (Illus.). 288p. 1978. 15.00x (ISBN 0-460-04307-2, J M Dent England). Biblio Dist.

Webster, Graham. Boudica: The British Revolt Against Rome A.D. 60. 1978. 33.00 (ISBN 0-7134-1064-7, Pub. by Batsford England). David & Charles.

Whatmore, Arthur W. Insulae Britannicae. LC 72-118508. 1971. Repr. of 1913 ed. 15.00 (ISBN 0-8046-1256-0). Kennikat.

GREAT BRITAIN–HISTORY–TO 1485

Here are entered works on the History of Great Britain to 1485 as a whole.

Adams, George B. History of England from the Norman Conquest to the Death of John. LC 77-5634. (The Political History of England: No. 2). Repr. of 1905 ed. 22.50 (ISBN 0-404-50772-7). AMS Pr.

Alcock, L. Arthur's Britain: History & Archaeology AD 367-634. 1972. 19.95 (ISBN 0-312-05530-7). St Martin.

Ashe, Geoffrey. The Quest for Arthur's Britain. (Illus.). 238p. 1980. pap. 6.95 (ISBN 0-586-08044-9, Granada Publishing Limited). Academy Chi Ltd.

Bingham, Caroline. The Crowned Lions: The Early Plantagenet Kings. (Illus.). 192p. 1978. 16.00x (ISBN 0-8476-6095-8). Rowman.

Blair, Peter H. Roman Britain & Early England 55 B. C. to A. D. 871. (Library History of England). (Illus.). 1966. pap. 5.95 (ISBN 0-393-00361-2, Norton Lib). Norton.

Bohn's Antiquarian Library, 28 titles in 38 vols. Repr. of 1892 ed. Set. 934.50 (ISBN 0-404-50000-5). AMS Pr.

Bradley, Richard. The Prehistoric Settlement of Britain. (The Archaeology of Britain Ser.). (Illus.). 1978. 24.00 (ISBN 0-7100-8993-7). Routledge & Kegan.

Briggs, Martin S. Goths & Vandals: A Study of the Destruction, Neglect & Preservation of Historical Buildings in England. 251p. Repr. of 1952 ed. 36.00 (ISBN 0-403-04087-6). Somerset Pub.

Brodeur, Arthur G. Arthur Dux Bellorum. LC 73-16320. 1939. lib. bdg. 7.50 (ISBN 0-8414-9864-4). Folcroft.

Carr, B. History of England from the Close of the Saxon Heptarchy to the Declaration of Independence. 10.00x (ISBN 0-87556-047-4). Saifer.

Deanesly, Margaret. Augustine of Canterbury. 1964. 8.50x (ISBN 0-8047-0771-5). Stanford U Pr.

De Hoveden, Roger. Annals of Roger De Hoveden, 2 Vols. Riley, H. T., tr. LC 68-57865. (Bohn's Antiquarian Library Ser). Repr. of 1853 ed. Set. 55.00 (ISBN 0-404-50060-9); Vol. 1. (ISBN 0-404-50061-7). Vol. 2 (ISBN 0-404-50062-5). AMS Pr.

De Wavrin, Jehan. Anchiennes Cronicques D'Engleterre, 3 Vols. 1858-1863. 83.00 (ISBN 0-384-66112-2); pap. 69.50 (ISBN 0-384-66113-0). Johnson Repr.

Freeman, Edward A. History of the Norman Conquest of England: Its Causes & Its Results, 5 Vols. Repr. of 1879 ed. Set. 265.00 (ISBN 0-404-07980-6). Vol. 1 (ISBN 0-404-07981-4). Vol. 2 (ISBN 0-404-07982-2). Vol. 3 (ISBN 0-404-07983-0). Vol. 4 (ISBN 0-404-07984-9). Vol. 5 (ISBN 0-404-07985-7). AMS Pr.

Gildas. De Excidio Brittaniae. Giles, J. A., tr. from Lat. pap. 3.95 (ISBN 0-686-25501-1). British Am Bks.

Great Britain, Laws, Statutes: England, Laws & Statutes. Incl. Laws of the Earliest English Kings, Aethelberth First to Aethelstan. Attenborough, F. L., ed. & tr. LC 76-178530. Repr. of 1922 ed. 14.00 (ISBN 0-404-56545-X); Laws of the Kings of England from Edmund to Henry First. Robertson, A. J., ed. & tr. LC 70-180687. Repr. of 1925 ed. 34.50 (ISBN 0-404-56547-6); Legal Code of Aelfred the Great. Turk, M. H., ed. & intro. by. LC 74-180688. Repr. of 1893 ed. 14.75 (ISBN 0-404-56546-8). AMS Pr.

Haines, R. M. The Church & Politics in Fourteenth Century England. LC 76-54062. (Studies in Medieval Life & Thought: No. 10). 1978. 42.50 (ISBN 0-521-21544-7). Cambridge U Pr.

Hanning, Robert W. Vision of History in Early Britain: From Gildas to Geoffrey of Monmouth. LC 66-17856. 271p. 1966. 20.00x (ISBN 0-231-02826-1). Columbia U Pr.

Harrison, George B. England to Shakespeare's Day. 1981. Repr. lib. bdg. 25.00 (ISBN 0-403-00620-1). Scholarly.

Henry Of Huntingdon. Chronicle of Henry of Huntingdon. Forester, T., ed. (Bohn's Antiquarian Library Ser). Repr. of 1853 ed. 27.50 (ISBN 0-404-50017-X). AMS Pr.

Henry Of Silgrave. Chronicon Henrici De Silegrave: A Chronicle of English History from the Earliest Period to 1274. Hook, C., ed. LC 71-107617. (Caxton Soc. Publications: No. 4). Repr. of 1849 ed. 24.00 (ISBN 0-8337-1730-8). B Franklin.

Hodgkin, Thomas. History of England from the Earliest Times to the Norman Conquest, 1066. Repr. of 1906 ed. 24.00 (ISBN 0-527-00846-X). Kraus Repr.

--The History of England from the Earliest Times to the Norman Conquest (to 1066) LC 79-5626. (Political History of England: No. 1). Repr. of 1906 ed. 22.50 (ISBN 0-404-50771-9). AMS Pr.

Holinshed, Raphael. Holinshed's Chronicles of England, Scotland & Ireland, 6 Vols. Ellis, Henry, ed. LC 75-44326. Repr. of 1808 ed. Set. 625.00 (ISBN 0-404-03330-X). Vol. 1 (ISBN 0-404-03331-8). Vol. 2 (ISBN 0-404-03332-6). Vol. 3 (ISBN 0-404-03333-4). Vol. 4 (ISBN 0-404-03334-2). Vol. 5 (ISBN 0-404-03335-0). Vol. 6 (ISBN 0-404-03336-9). AMS Pr.

Holmes, George. The Good Parliament. 210p. 1975. 37.50x (ISBN 0-19-822446-X). Oxford U Pr.

Lane, Peter. Roman Britain. (Visual Sources Ser.). (Illus.). 96p. (gr. 7 up). 1980. text ed. 14.95 (ISBN 0-7134-3354-X, Pub. by Batsford England). David & Charles.

Mackenzie, Agnes M. The Foundations of Scotland: From the Earliest Times to 1286. LC 75-41505. 1979. Repr. of 1938 ed. lib. bdg. 24.75x (ISBN 0-8371-8703-6, MAFN). Greenwood.

Matthew Of Westminster. Flowers of History, Especially Such As Relate to the Affairs of Britain, 2 Vols. Yonge, C. D., tr. LC 68-57870. (Bohn's Antiquarian Library). Repr. of 1853 ed. Set. 55.00 (ISBN 0-404-50030-7). AMS Pr.

Nennius. History of the Britons. Giles, J. A., tr. pap. 2.50 (ISBN 0-686-25503-8). British Am Bks.

Ordericus Vitalis. Ecclesiastical History of England & Normandy, 4 Vols. Forrester, T., tr. LC 68-57872. (Bohn's Antiquarian Library Ser). Repr. of 1856 ed. Set. 115.00 (ISBN 0-404-50040-4). AMS Pr.

Ordericus, Vitalis. Historiae Ecclesiasticae Libri Tredecim, 5 Vols. Le Prevost, A., ed. Repr. of 1838 ed. Set. 177.00 (ISBN 0-384-43511-4); Set. pap. 154.00 (ISBN 0-384-43512-2). Johnson Repr.

Partner, Nancy F. Serious Entertainments: The Writing of History in Twelfth-Century England. LC 77-4402. 1977. lib. bdg. 18.00x (ISBN 0-226-64763-3). U of Chicago Pr.

Pearson, Charles H. Early & Middle Ages of England. LC 75-118494. 1971. Repr. of 1861 ed. 18.00 (ISBN 0-8046-1242-0). Kennikat.

Saklatvala, Beram. Origins of the English People. LC 70-85491. (Illus.). 1970. 7.50 (ISBN 0-8008-6115-9). Taplinger.

Sawyer, P. H. From Roman Britain to Norman England. LC 78-17640. 1979. 19.95x (ISBN 0-312-30783-7). St Martin.

Sayles, G. O. The Medieval Foundations of England. 1961. pap. 4.95 (ISBN 0-498-04038-0, Prpta). A S Barnes.

Scullard, H. H. Roman Britain: Outpost of the Empire. (Illus.). 1979. 14.95 (ISBN 0-500-45019-6). Thames Hudson.

Searle, Eleanor, ed. The Chronicle of Battle Abbey. (Oxford Medieval Texts Ser.). 1980. 55.00x (ISBN 0-19-822238-6). Oxford U Pr.

Sharp, Buchanan. In Contempt of All Authority: Rural Artisans & Riot in the West of England. LC 78-54801. 1980. 21.50x (ISBN 0-520-03681-6). U of Cal Pr.

Simmons, Ian & Tooley, Michael, eds. The Environment in British Prehistory. LC 80-69818. (Illus.). 358p. 1981. 34.50x (ISBN 0-8014-1397-4). Cornell U Pr.

Smith, D. M. Episcopal Acta I: Lincoln Diocese, Ten Sixty-Seven to Eleven Eighty-Five, Pt. 1. (British Academy: English Episcopal Acta Ser.). 1980. 125.00x (ISBN 0-19-725986-3). Oxford U Pr.

Smith, H. Maymard. Pre-Reformation England. 1979. Repr. of 1938 ed. lib. bdg. 50.00 (ISBN 0-8495-4934-5). Arden Lib.

Vergilius, Polydorus. Polidore Vergil's English History. Repr. of 1846 ed. 31.00 (ISBN 0-384-64368-X). Johnson Repr.

--Polydore Vergil's English History, from an Early Translation. Ellis, Henry, ed. (Camden Society, London. Publications, First Ser.: No. 36). Repr. of 1846 ed. 28.00 (ISBN 0-404-50136-2). AMS Pr.

Webber, Ronald. The Peasants Revolt: The Uprising in Kent, Essex, East Anglia & London in 1381 During the Reign of King Richard II. 136p. 1981. 20.00x (ISBN 0-900963-44-1, Pub. by Terence Dalton England). State Mutual Bk.

Webster, Graham. Boudica: The British Revolt Against Rome A.D. 60. (Illus.). 152p. 1978. 12.50x (ISBN 0-8476-6043-5). Rowman.

--The Roman Invasion of Britain. (Illus.). 224p. 1980. 14.00x (ISBN 0-389-20107-3). B&N.

GREAT BRITAIN–HISTORY–TO 1485–SOURCES

Gildas. Gildas: The Ruin of Britain & Other Works. Winterbottom, Michael, ed. 162p. 1978. 16.00x (ISBN 0-8476-6079-6). Rowman.

GREAT BRITAIN–HISTORY–ANGLO-SAXON PERIOD, 449-1066

Here are entered works on the Anglo-Saxon period whether as a whole or portions of the period. For works on specific rulers of this period see the name of the ruler.

Allen, Grant. Early Britain: Anglo-Saxon Britain. (Illus.). 237p. 1980. Repr. of 1901 ed. lib. bdg. 25.00 (ISBN 0-89987-002-3). Darby Bks.

Ashdown, Margaret. English & Norse Documents Relating to the Reign of Ethelred the Unready. LC 78-173505. 1972. Repr. of 1930 ed. 17.50 (ISBN 0-8462-1506-3). Russell.

Ballard, Adolphus, ed. British Borough Charters,1042-1216. LC 80-2236. Repr. of 1913 ed. 49.50 (ISBN 0-404-18750-1). AMS Pr.

Blair, Peter H. World of Bede. LC 73-135524. 1971. 12.95 (ISBN 0-312-89215-2, W59000). St Martin.

Brandon, Peter, ed. The South Saxons. (Illus.). 262p. 1978. 29.50x (ISBN 0-8476-6154-7). Rowman.

Brodeur, Arthur G. Arthur Dux Bellorum. LC 73-16320. 1939. lib. bdg. 7.50 (ISBN 0-8414-9864-4). Folcroft.

Brooke, Christopher. From Alfred to Henry Third, 871-1272. (Illus.). 1966. pap. 4.95 (ISBN 0-393-00362-0, Norton Lib). Norton.

Brown, David. Anglo-Saxon England. (Illus.). 110p. 1978. 16.50x (ISBN 0-8476-6045-1). Rowman.

Brown, R. Allen, ed. Proceedings of the Battle Conference on Anglo-Norman Studies II: 1979. (Illus.). 210p. 1980. 49.50x (ISBN 0-8476-3455-8). Rowman.

Chambers, Raymond W. England Before the Norman Conquest. LC 75-109718. Repr. of 1926 ed. lib. bdg. 15.25x (ISBN 0-8371-4208-3, CHNC). Greenwood.

Chaney, William A. The Cult of Kingship in Anglo-Saxon England: The Transition from Paganism to Christianity. LC 72-79041. 1970. 21.50x (ISBN 0-520-01401-4). U of Cal Pr.

Clapham, John. The Historie of Great Britannie - from the Romans First Entrance, Untill the Raigne of Egbert, the West-Saxon Prince. LC 74-28837. (English Experience Ser.: No. 719). 1975. Repr. of 1606 ed. 22.00 (ISBN 90-221-0719-1). Walter J Johnson.

Clemoes, Peter A., ed. Anglo-Saxon England, 8 vols. Incl. Vol. 1. 320p. 1972. 47.50 (ISBN 0-521-08557-8); Vol. 2. 300p. 1973. 47.50 (ISBN 0-521-20218-3); Vol. 3. 320p. 1974. 47.50 (ISBN 0-521-20574-3); Vol. 4. 270p. 1975. 47.50 (ISBN 0-521-20868-8); Vol. 5. 1976. 47.50 (ISBN 0-521-21270-7); Vol. 6. 1977. 47.50 (ISBN 0-521-21701-6); Vol. 7. 1979. 47.50 (ISBN 0-521-22164-1); Vol. 8. 1980. 57.50 (ISBN 0-521-22788-7). LC 78-19043. (Illus.). Cambridge U Pr.

Collingwood, Robin G. & Myres, J. N. Roman Britain & the English Settlements. 2nd ed. (Oxford History of England Ser.). (Illus.). 1937. 34.50 (ISBN 0-19-821703-X). Oxford U Pr.

Eagles, Bruce N. The Anglo-Saxon Settlement of Humberside. 1979. 80.00x (ISBN 0-86054-057-X, Pub. by BAR). State Mutual Bk.

Finberg, H. P. The Formation of England 500-1042. 1974. 14.95x (ISBN 0-19-520117-5). Oxford U Pr.

Fisher, D. J. The Anglo-Saxon Age. LC 74-159804. (A History of England Ser.). 350p. 1973. text ed. 22.00x (ISBN 0-582-48277-1); pap. text ed. 11.95x (ISBN 0-582-48084-1). Longman.

Florence Of Worcester. Chronicle. Forester, Thomas, tr. LC 68-55550. (Bohn's Antiquarian Library Ser). 1968. Repr. of 1854 ed. 27.50 (ISBN 0-404-50008-0). AMS Pr.

Flower, Robin & Smith, Hugh, eds. The Parker Chronicle Laws: A Facsimile. (Early English Text Society Ser.). 116p. 1973. 39.95x (ISBN 0-19-722208-0). Oxford U Pr.

Gaimar, Geoffroy. L' Estoire des Engleis. Bell, Alexander, ed. 37.00 (ISBN 0-384-17555-4); pap. 31.00 (ISBN 0-384-17556-2). Johnson Repr.

Giles, J. A., ed. Six Old English Chronicles. LC 68-57866. (Bohn's Antiquarian Library Ser). Repr. of 1848 ed. 27.50 (ISBN 0-404-50010-2). AMS Pr.

Giles, John A., ed. Memorials of King Alfred, Being Essays on the History & Antiquities of England During the 9th Century, the Age of King Alfred. (Research & Source Works Ser: No. 287). 1969. Repr. of 1863 ed. 26.00 (ISBN 0-8337-1346-9). B Franklin.

Grohskopf, Bernice. The Treasure of Sutton Hoo Ship- Burial for an Anglo-Saxon King. LC 74-86555. (Illus.). 1973. pap. text ed. 2.95x (ISBN 0-689-70362-7, 199). Atheneum.

Hamilton, John & Sorrell, Alan. Saxon England. (Illus.). (gr. 6-9). 1968. 7.50 (ISBN 0-8023-1149-0). Dufour.

Hibbert, Christopher & Thomas, Charles. Search for King Arthur. LC 77-91594. (Horizon Caravel Bks). (Illus.). 153p. (gr. 6 up). 1969. 9.95 (ISBN 0-06-022313-8, Dist. by Har-Row); PLB 12.89 (ISBN 0-06-022314-6, Dist. by Har-Row). Am Heritage.

Hill, David. An Atlas of Anglo-Saxon England. 208p. 1981. 35.00x (ISBN 0-8020-2387-8); pap. 14.95x (ISBN 0-8020-6446-9). U of Toronto Pr.

Hodgkin, Thomas. History of England from the Earliest Times to the Norman Conquest. LC 69-13933. Repr. of 1906 ed. lib. bdg. 23.00x (ISBN 0-8371-1023-8, HOHE). Greenwood.

Holmes, Thomas R. Ancient Britain & the Invasions of Julius Caesar. facsimile ed. LC 71-175701. (Select Bibliographies Reprint Ser). Repr. of 1907 ed. 43.00 (ISBN 0-8369-6616-3). Arno.

Hugh The Chantor, pseud. The History of the Church of York, 1066-1127. Johnson, Charles, tr. from Lat. & intro. by. LC 80-2227. Repr. of 1961 ed. 34.50 (ISBN 0-404-18764-1). AMS Pr.

Johnson, David. Alfred the Great. (Jackdaw Ser: No. 89). 1969. 6.95 (ISBN 0-670-11252-6, Grossman). Viking Pr.

Jones, David. Your Book of Anglo Saxon England. (Your Book Ser.). (Illus.). 80p. 1978. 6.95 (ISBN 0-571-10778-8, Pub. by Faber & Faber). Merrimack Bk Serv.

Kapelle, William E. The Norman Conquest of the North: The Region & Its Transformation, 1000-1135. LC 79-10200. 1980. 19.00x (ISBN 0-8078-1371-0). U of NC Pr.

Kemble, John. Saxons in England, 2 Vols. rev. ed. Birch, Walter D., ed. LC 72-151600. Repr. of 1876 ed. 49.75 (ISBN 0-404-03647-3). AMS Pr.

Kirby, D. P. The Making of Early England. LC 68-11534. (Fabric of British History Ser). 1968. 10.00x (ISBN 0-8052-3151-X). Schocken.

Laing, Lloyd & Laing, Jennifer. Anglo-Saxon England. (Illus.). 1979. 15.95 (ISBN 0-684-16172-9, ScribT). Scribner.

Lappenberg, J. M. History of England Under the Anglo-Saxon Kings, 2 Vols. Thorpe, Benjamin, tr. from Ger. LC 70-118482. 1971. Repr. of 1845 ed. Set. 35.00x (ISBN 0-8046-1231-5). Kennikat.

Lappenberg, Johann M. A History of England Under the Anglo-Saxon Kings, 2 vols. Thorpe, Benjamin, rev. by. & tr. LC 80-2209. Repr. of 1845 ed. 97.50 (ISBN 0-404-18740-4). AMS Pr.

Loyn, H. R. Anglo-Saxon England & the Norman Conquest. (Social & Economic History of England). (Illus.). 1962. pap. text ed. 11.95x (ISBN 0-582-48232-1). Longman.

Miller, Thomas. History of the Anglo-Saxons: From the Earliest Period to the Norman Conquest. LC 77-23496. 1977. Repr. of 1852 ed. lib. bdg. 40.00 (ISBN 0-89341-159-0). Longwood Pr.

Morris, John. The Age of Arthur. LC 72-11121. (Illus.). 656p. 1973. 17.50 (ISBN 0-684-13313-X, ScribT). Scribner.

Page, R. I. Life in Anglo-Saxon England. 1972. 19.95 (ISBN 0-7134-1461-8, Pub. by Batsford England). David & Charles.

Parsons, F. G. Earlier Inhabitants of London. LC 78-118492. 1971. Repr. of 1927 ed. 13.00 (ISBN 0-8046-1240-4). Kennikat.

Rosenthal, Joel T. Angles, Angels & Conquerors, 400-1154, Vol. 1. (Borzoi History of England Ser.). (Illus.). 1973. 10.00 (ISBN 0-394-47949-1). Knopf.

Smith, A. H., ed. The Parker Chronicle. 1968. pap. 7.95x (ISBN 0-423-77160-4). Methuen Inc.

Stenton, F. M. Anglo-Saxon England. 1977. lib. bdg. 79.95 (ISBN 0-8490-1430-1). Gordon Pr.

Sydenham, G. England Before the Norman Conquest. LC 71-185966. (British History Ser., No. 30). vi, 196p. 1972. Repr. of 1861 ed. lib. bdg. 31.95 (ISBN 0-8383-1388-4). Haskell.

Turner, Sharon. The History of the Anglo-Saxons from the Earliest Period to the Norman Conquest, 3 vols. 7th ed. LC 80-2207. Repr. of 1852 ed. 160.00 (ISBN 0-404-18790-0). AMS Pr.

Whitlock, Ralph. Warrior Kings of Saxon England. 1977. text ed. 10.75x (ISBN 0-391-00719-X). Humanities.

GREAT BRITAIN–HISTORY–ANGLO-SAXON PERIOD, 449-1066–FICTION

Here are entered books of historical fiction of the Anglo-Saxon period. For biographical fiction, drama, etc. see subhead–Fiction, Drama, etc., under the name of the ruler, e.g. Alfred the Great–Fiction.

Trease, Geoffrey. Escape to King Alfred. LC 58-9224. (gr. 6 up). 1958. 6.95 (ISBN 0-8149-0428-9). Vanguard.

GREAT BRITAIN–HISTORY–ANGLO-SAXON PERIOD, 499-1066–SOURCES

Bede. History of the English Church & People. Sherley-Price, tr. (Classics Ser.). (Orig.). 1955. pap. 3.50 (ISBN 0-14-044042-9). Penguin.

Bede The Venerable. Ecclesiastical History of the English Nation. Stevens, John, tr. 1973. 9.95x (ISBN 0-460-00479-4, Evman). Biblio Dist.

Birch, Walter D., ed. Cartularium Saxonicum: A Collection of Charters Relating to Anglo-Saxon History, 3 vols. Repr. of 1893 ed. Set. with index. 192.50 (ISBN 0-384-04405-0); sep. index 14.00 (ISBN 0-685-13365-6). Johnson Repr.

Gaimar, Geoffrey. Anglo-Norman Metrical Chronicle of Geoffrey Gaimar. Wright, Thomas, ed. 1966. Repr. of 1850 ed. 24.00 (ISBN 0-8337-1263-2). B Franklin.

Plummer, Charles, ed. Anglo-Saxon Chronicle, 2 vols. 1899. Set. 75.00x (ISBN 0-19-811104-5). Oxford U Pr.

Whitelock, Dorothy, ed. English Historical Documents, C. Five Hundred to Ten Forty-Two. 2nd ed. (English Historical Documents Ser.). (Illus.). 984p. 1979. text ed. 89.00x (ISBN 0-19-520101-9). Oxford U Pr.

GREAT BRITAIN–HISTORY–MEDIEVAL PERIOD, 1066-1485

Here are entered works on the Medieval period as a whole as well as those on parts of the period. see also Barons' War, 1263-1267; Tyler's Insurrection, 1381

Adams, G. B. History of England from the Norman Conquest to the Death of John, 1066-1216. (Political History of England Monograph). Repr. of 1905 ed. 24.00 (ISBN 0-527-00847-8). Kraus Repr.

Adams, George B. History of England from the Norman Conquest to the Death of John, 1066-1216. LC 69-13801. 1969. Repr. of 1905 ed. lib. bdg. 23.00x (ISBN 0-8371-0922-1, ADHE). Greenwood.

Altschul, Michael. A Baronial Family in Medieval England: The Clares, 1217-1314. LC 78-64244. (Johns Hopkins University. Studies in the Social Sciences. Eighty-Third Ser. 1965: 2). Repr. of 1965 ed. 27.00 (ISBN 0-404-61349-7). AMS Pr.

Ballard, Adolphus, ed. British Borough Charters,1042-1216. LC 80-2236. Repr. of 1913 ed. 49.50 (ISBN 0-404-18750-1). AMS Pr.

Barber, Richard. Henry Plantagenet: A Biography. (Illus.). 278p. 1972. Repr. of 1964 ed. 15.00x (ISBN 0-87471-062-6). Rowman.

Bateson, Mary. Mediaeval England, 1066-1350. facsimile ed. LC 70-152973. (Select Bibliographies Reprint Ser). Repr. of 1903 ed. 29.00 (ISBN 0-8369-5725-3). Arno.

Bigelow, Melville M. History of Procedure in England from the Norman Conquest: The Norman Period (1066-1204) LC 80-2235. Repr. of 1880 ed. 44.50 (ISBN 0-404-18752-8). AMS Pr.

The Boke of Noblesse: Addressed to King Edward the Fourth on His Invasion of France in 1475. LC 73-80201. 95p. 1972. Repr. of 1860 ed. lib. bdg. 25.50 (ISBN 0-8337-2524-6). B Franklin.

Bolton, J. L. The Medieval English Economy: Eleven Fifty to Fifteen Hundred. (Rowman & Littlefield University Library). (Illus.). 400p. 1980. 25.00x (ISBN 0-8476-6234-9); pap. 16.00x (ISBN 0-8476-6235-7). Rowman.

Braddy, Haldeen. Chaucer's Parlement of Foules. LC 78-84176. 1969. Repr. of 1932 ed. lib. bdg. 12.00x (ISBN 0-374-90931-8). Octagon.

Brooke, Christopher. From Alfred to Henry Third, 871-1272. (Illus.). 1966. pap. 4.95 (ISBN 0-393-00362-0, Norton Lib). Norton.

Brooks, Janice Y. Kings & Queens: The Plantagenets of England. LC 75-17843. 160p. (gr. 6 up). 1975. 7.95 (ISBN 0-525-66438-6). Elsevier-Nelson.

Brown, R. Allen, ed. Battle Conference on Anglo-Norman Studies, 1st, 1978: Proceedings. (Illus.). 247p. 1979. 36.50x (ISBN 0-8476-6184-9). Rowman.

Bruce, John, ed. Historie of the Arrivall of Edward Fourth in England & the Finall Recoverye of His Kingdomes from Henry Sixth, A. D. 1471. LC 77-164757. (Camden Society, London. Publications. First Ser.: No. 1). Repr. of 1838 ed. 7.00 (ISBN 0-404-50101-X). AMS Pr.

--Historie of the Arrivall of Edward Fourth in England & the Finall Recouerye of His Kingdomes from Henry Sixth. 1838. 8.00 (ISBN 0-384-06035-8). Johnson Repr.

Cam, Helen M. Liberties & Communities in Medieval England: Collected Studies in Local Administration & Topography. (Illus.). 1963. lib. bdg. 12.50x (ISBN 0-678-08065-8). Kelley.

Charles, the Duke of Orleans. England & France in the Fifteenth Century. Pyne, Henry, tr. LC 78-63491. Repr. of 1870 ed. 27.50 (ISBN 0-404-17139-7). AMS Pr.

Chew, Helena M. The English Ecclesiastical Tenants-in-Chief & Knight Service, Especially in the Thirteenth & Fourteenth Centuries. LC 80-2310. Repr. of 1932 ed. 32.50 (ISBN 0-404-18558-4). AMS Pr.

Chrimes, S. B., et al, eds. Fifteenth-Century England. 190p. 1972. 22.00x (ISBN 0-7190-0511-6, Pub. by Manchester U Pr England). State Mutual Bk.

Chronicon Petroburgense. 1849. 19.50 (ISBN 0-384-08985-2). Johnson Repr.

Corfe, Tom. The Murder of Archbishop Thomas. LC 76-22419. (Cambridge Topic Bks). (Illus.). (gr. 5-10). 1977. PLB 5.95g (ISBN 0-8225-1202-5). Lerner Pubns.

Costain, Thomas B. The Conquering Family. LC 62-20488. 6.95 (ISBN 0-385-04088-1). Doubleday.

--The Last Plantagenets. LC 62-52105. 6.95 (ISBN 0-385-00142-8). Doubleday.

--Three Edwards. LC 62-52103. 1958. 8.95 (ISBN 0-385-05239-1). Doubleday.

Davies, James C. Baronial Opposition to Edward II: Its Character & Policy. 644p. 1967. 37.50x (ISBN 0-7146-1466-1, F Cass Co). Biblio Dist.

Davies, John S., ed. English Chronicle, of the Reigns of Richard Second, Henry Fourth, Henry Fifth, Henry Sixth, Written Before the Year 1471. LC 73-166036. (Camden Society, London. Publications. First Ser.: No. 64). Repr. of 1856 ed. 21.00 (ISBN 0-404-50164-8). AMS Pr.

Davis, H. W. C., ed. Medieval England. new ed. Orig. Title: Bernard's Companion to English History. 1977. Repr. of 1924 ed. lib. bdg. 45.00 (ISBN 0-8495-1006-6). Arden Lib.

Davis, R. H. C. King Stephen. LC 77-4291. (Illus.). 1977. pap. text ed. 9.95x (ISBN 0-582-48727-7). Longman.

De Angeli, Marguerite. The Door in the Wall: Story of Medieval London. LC 64-7025. (gr. 3-6). 7.95a (ISBN 0-385-07283-X); PLB (ISBN 0-385-05743-1); pap. 1.95 (ISBN 0-385-07909-5). Doubleday.

De Hoveden, Roger. Annals of Roger De Hoveden, 2 Vols. Riley, H. T., tr. LC 68-57865. (Bohn's Antiquarian Library Ser). Repr. of 1853 ed. Set. 55.00 (ISBN 0-404-50060-9); Vol. 1. (ISBN 0-404-50061-7). Vol. 2 (ISBN 0-404-50062-5). AMS Pr.

Denton, J. H. English Royal Free Chapels, Eleven Hundred to Thirteen Hundred. 216p. 1970. 31.00x (ISBN 0-7190-0401-2, Pub. by Manchester U Pr England). State Mutual Bk.

--Robert Winchelsey & the Crown, 1294-1313. (Cambridge Studies in Medieval Life & Thought: No. 14). 1980. 42.50 (ISBN 0-521-22963-4). Cambridge U Pr.

De Rishanger, William. Chronicle of William De Rishanger, of the Barons' Wars. Halliwell, James O., ed. (Camden Society, London. Publications, First Ser.: No. 15). Repr. of 1840 ed. 17.50 (ISBN 0-404-50115-X). AMS Pr.

Douglas-Irving, Helen. Extracts Relating to Medieval Markets & Fairs in England. 1978. Repr. of 1912 ed. lib. bdg. 15.00 (ISBN 0-8274-4184-3). R West.

Dunham, William H., Jr. Lord Hastings' Indentured Retainers, 1461-1483: The Lawfulness of Livery & Retaining Under the Yorkists & Tudors. (Connecticut Academy of Arts & Sciences Transactions: Vol. 39). 1970. Repr. of 1955 ed. 15.00 (ISBN 0-208-00989-2, Archon). Shoe String.

Dupont, Etienne. La Participation De la Bretagne a la Conquete De l'Angleterre Par les Normands. LC 80-2229. Repr. of 1911 ed. 17.50 (ISBN 0-404-18758-7). AMS Pr.

Dyer, Christopher. Lords & Peasants in a Changing Society: The Estates of the Bishopric of Worcester, 680-1540. LC 79-51225. (Past & Present Publications Ser.). (Illus.). 466p. 1980. 49.50 (ISBN 0-521-22618-X). Cambridge U Pr.

English Chronicle of the Reigns of Richard Second, Henry Fourth, Henry Fifth & Henry Sixth. 1856. 23.00 (ISBN 0-384-08975-5). Johnson Repr.

Fitz-Thedmar, Arnold. De Antiquis Legibus Liber. Repr. of 1846 ed. 46.00 (ISBN 0-384-15820-X). Johnson Repr.

Florence Of Worcester. Chronicle. Forester, Thomas, tr. LC 68-55550. (Bohn's Antiquarian Library Ser). 1968. Repr. of 1854 ed. 27.50 (ISBN 0-404-50008-0). AMS Pr.

Fortescue, Sir John. The Governance of England: Otherwise Called the Difference Between an Absolute & a Limited Monarchy. LC 78-62329. 1979. Repr. of 1885 ed. 29.50 (ISBN 0-88355-723-1). Hyperion Conn.

Freeman, Edward A. The History of the Norman Conquest of England. abr. ed. Burrow, J. W., ed. LC 73-87466. (Classics of British Historical Literature Ser). xxxv, 259p. 1974. Repr. 16.50x (ISBN 0-226-26171-9). U of Chicago Pr.

--Reign of William Rufus & the Accession of Henry the First, 2 Vols. Repr. of 1882 ed. Set. 67.50 (ISBN 0-404-00620-5); 35.00 ea. Vol. 1 (ISBN 0-404-00621-3). Vol. 2 (ISBN 0-404-00622-1). AMS Pr.

Froissart, Jean. Chronicle of Froissart, 6 Vols. Bourchier, John, tr. LC 70-168064. (Tudor Translations. First Ser.: Nos. 27-32). Repr. of 1903 ed. Set. 147.00 (ISBN 0-404-51930-X); 24.50 ea. Vol. 1 (ISBN 0-404-51931-8). Vol. 2 (ISBN 0-404-51932-6). Vol. 3 (ISBN 0-404-51933-4). Vol. 4 (ISBN 0-404-51934-2). Vol. 5 (ISBN 0-404-51935-0). Vol. 6 (ISBN 0-404-51936-9). AMS Pr.

--Here Begynneth the First Volum of Sir J. Froyssart. Bourchier, J., tr. LC 72-26004. (English Experience Ser.: No. 257). 644p. 1970. Repr. of 1523 ed. 104.00 (ISBN 90-221-0257-2). Walter J Johnson.

Giles, John A., ed. Chronicon Angliae Petriburgense. 1966. Repr. of 1845 ed. 24.00 (ISBN 0-8337-1342-6). B Franklin.

--Revolte Du Conte De Warwick Contre le Roi Edward 4e. (Fr). 1849. 24.00 (ISBN 0-8337-1347-7). B Franklin.

Given, James Buchanan. Society & Homicide in Thirteenth-Century England. LC 76-23372. 1977. 12.50x (ISBN 0-8047-0939-4). Stanford U Pr.

Goodman, Anthony. A History of England from Edward II to James I. LC 76-51405. (Illus.). 1977. text ed. 21.00x (ISBN 0-582-48281-X); pap. text ed. 12.95x (ISBN 0-582-48282-8). Longman.

Gray, Thomas. Scalacronica: A Chronicle of England & Scotland from A.D. 1066 to A. D. 1362. Stevenson, Joseph, ed. LC 70-168186. (Maitland Club. Glasgow. Publications: No. 40). Repr. of 1836 ed. 47.50 (ISBN 0-404-53015-X). AMS Pr.

Griffiths, Ralph, ed. Patronage, the Crown & the Provinces in Later Medieval England. 224p. 1980. text ed. 20.75x (ISBN 0-391-02096-X). Humanities.

Hall, Edward. Hall's Chronicle. Ellis, Henry, ed. LC 2-20847. Repr. of 1809 ed. 65.00 (ISBN 0-404-03029-7). AMS Pr.

Hall, Hubert. Court Life Under the Plantagenets: Reign of Henry the Second. facsimile ed. LC 70-109627. (Select Bibliographies Reprint Ser). 1899. 20.00 (ISBN 0-8369-5236-7). Arno.

Hallam. Rural England: Ten Sixty-Six to Twelve Seventy-Two. Date not set. text ed. 23.50 (ISBN 0-391-01775-6). Humanities.

Hanawalt, Barbara A. Crime & Conflict in English Communities, Thirteen Hundred to Thirteen Forty-Eight. LC 79-1211. 1979. text ed. 20.00x (ISBN 0-674-17580-8). Harvard U Pr.

Harvey, John. The Black Prince & His Age. (Illus.). 184p. 1976. 16.00x (ISBN 0-87471-818-X). Rowman.

Haskins, Charles H. Normans in European History. 1966. pap. 4.95x (ISBN 0-393-00342-6, Norton Lib). Norton.

Haskins, George L. The Statute of York & the Interest of the Commons. LC 77-4920. 1977. Repr. of 1935 ed. lib. bdg. 15.00 (ISBN 0-8371-9610-8, HASY); microfiche avail. (ISBN 0-8371-9612-4). Greenwood.

Hatcher, John. Plague, Population & the English Economy, 1348-1530. (Studies in Economic & Social History). 1977. pap. 4.75x (ISBN 0-333-21293-2). Humanities.

Hayward, Sir John. The First Part of the Life & Raigne of King Henrie the IIII. LC 74-28862. (English Experience Ser.: No. 742). 1975. Repr. of 1599 ed. 11.50 (ISBN 90-221-0742-6). Walter J Johnson.

Hilton, R. H. The English Peasantry in the Later Middle Ages: The Ford Lectures for 1973 & Related Studies. 264p. 1975. pap. 13.95x (ISBN 0-19-822631-4). Oxford U Pr.

Histoire Des Ducs De Normandie et Des Rois D'Angleterre. 1840. 35.50 (ISBN 0-384-23431-3); pap. 31.00 (ISBN 0-384-23430-5). Johnson Repr.

Historical Association, London. Social Life in Early England: Historical Association Essays. Barraclough, Geoffrey, ed. LÇ 79-16998. (Illus.). xi, 264p. 1980. Repr. of 1960 ed. lib. bdg. 34.50x (ISBN 0-313-21298-8, HASL). Greenwood.

Holinshed, Raphael. Holinshed's Chronicles: Richard II, 1398-1400, Henry IV & Henry V. Wallace, R. S. & Hansen, Alma, eds. LC 78-124. 1978. Repr. of 1923 ed. lib. bdg. 22.25x (ISBN 0-313-20259-1, HOHC). Greenwood.

Holmes, George. Later Middle Ages, 1272-1485. (History of England Ser). (Illus.). 1966. pap. 4.95 (ISBN 0-393-00363-9, Norton Lib). Norton.

Holmes, George A. The Estates of the Higher Nobility in Fourteenth-Century England. LC 80-2024. Repr. of 1957 ed. 25.00 (ISBN 0-404-18570-3). AMS Pr.

Holt, Emily S. Ye Olden Time: English Customs in the Middle Ages. LC 72-164343. 1971. Repr. of 1884 ed. 19.00 (ISBN 0-8103-3798-3). Gale.

Holt, James C. The Northerners: A Study in the Reign of King John. LC 80-27864. xiv, 272p. 1981. Repr. of 1961 ed. lib. bdg. 29.75x (ISBN 0-313-22764-0, HOTN). Greenwood.

Homans, George C. English Villagers of the Thirteenth Century. 496p. 1975. pap. 7.95 (ISBN 0-393-00765-0, Norton Lib). Norton.

Howarth, David. Ten Sixty-Six: The Year of the Conquest. 208p. 1981. pap. 4.95 (ISBN 0-14-005850-8). Penguin.

--Ten Sixty Six: The Year of the Conquest. 1978. 10.95 (ISBN 0-670-69601-3). Viking Pr.

Hudson, Anne, ed. Selections from English Wycliffite Writings. LC 77-1506. 234p. 1981. pap. 17.95 (ISBN 0-521-28258-6). Cambridge U Pr.

Hughes, Dorothy. Illustrations of Chaucer's England. 1978. Repr. of 1919 ed. lib. bdg. 30.00 (ISBN 0-8495-2313-3). Arden Lib.

Hunt, Richard W., et al, eds. Studies in Medieval History Presented to Frederick Maurice Powicke. LC 79-14227. 1979. Repr. of 1948 ed. lib. bdg. 35.00x (ISBN 0-313-21484-0, SMFM). Greenwood.

Jacob, Ernest F. Fifteenth Century, Thirteen Ninety-Nine to Fourteen Eighty-Five. (Oxford History of England Ser.). 1961. 33.00x (ISBN 0-19-821714-5). Oxford U Pr.

Jenkins, Elizabeth. The Princes in the Tower. LC 78-14459. (Illus.). 1978. 10.95 (ISBN 0-698-10842-6). Coward.

Jenks, Edward. Edward Plantagenet: The English Justinian or the Making of Common Law. (Select Bibliographies Reprint Ser). 1901. 15.00 (ISBN 0-8369-5070-4). Arno.

Jessopp, Augustus. The Coming of the Friars & Other Historic Essays. facsimile ed. (Select Bibliographies Reprint Ser). Repr. of 1892 ed. 19.00 (ISBN 0-8369-6696-1). Arno.

--Studies by a Recluse in Cloister, Town, & Country. 3rd ed. 1969. Repr. of 1883 ed. lib. bdg. 20.50 (ISBN 0-8337-1841-X). B Franklin.

Jusserand, J. J. English Wayfaring Life in the Middle Ages. (Illus.). 1974. Repr. of 1888 ed. 12.50 (ISBN 0-87928-048-4). Corner Hse.

Jusserand, Jean A. English Wayfaring Life in the Middle Ages. Smith, Lucy T., tr. LC 77-6979. 1977. Repr. of 1889 ed. lib. bdg. 30.00 (ISBN 0-89341-170-1). Longwood Pr.

Kapelle, William E. The Norman Conquest of the North: The Region & Its Transformation, 1000-1135. LC 79-10200. 1980. 19.00x (ISBN 0-8078-1371-0). U of NC Pr.

Keen, M. H. England in the Later Middle Ages. 455p. 1972. text ed. 27.00x (ISBN 0-416-75990-4); pap. 15.95 (ISBN 0-416-83570-8). Methuen Inc.

Kelley, Amy. Eleanor of Aquitaine & the Four Kings. LC 50-6545. (Illus.). 1950. 20.00x (ISBN 0-674-24250-5); pap. 7.95 (ISBN 0-674-24254-8). Harvard U Pr.

Kelly, Henry A. Divine Providence in the England of Shakespeare's Histories. LC 75-111485. 1970. 16.50x (ISBN 0-674-21292-4). Harvard U Pr.

King, Edmund. England, Eleven Seventy Five-Fourteen Twenty Five. (Illus.). 1979. 20.00 (ISBN 0-684-16140-0, ScribT). Scribner.

Kingsford, Charles L. Prejudice & Promise in Fifteenth Century England. 215p. 1962. 23.50x (ISBN 0-7146-1488-2, F Cass Co). Biblio Dist.

Knowles, David. Thomas Becket. LC 77-143785. 1971. 8.50x (ISBN 0-8047-0766-9). Stanford U Pr.

Kriehn, George. The English Rising in Fourteen Fifty. (Perspectives in European History Ser.: No. 37). vii, 131p. Repr. of 1882 ed. lib. bdg. 15.00x (ISBN 0-87991-081-X). Porcupine Pr.

Labarge, Margaret W. A Baronial Household of the Thirteenth Century. (Illus.). 235p. 1980. 22.50x (ISBN 0-389-20068-9); pap. 9.95x (ISBN 0-389-20034-4). B&N.

Lander, J. R. Government & Community: England, 1450-1509. (New History of England Ser.). 416p. 1980. 22.50x (ISBN 0-674-35793-0). Harvard U Pr.

Leach, H. G. Angevin Britain & Scandinavia. Repr. of 1921 ed. 22.00 (ISBN 0-527-03227-1). Kraus Repr.

Lennard, Reginald V. Rural England, Ten Eighty-Six to Eleven Thirty-Five: A Study of Social & Agrarian Conditions. LC 80-2222. Repr. of 1959 ed. 49.50 (ISBN 0-404-18767-6). AMS Pr.

Lodge, Eleanor C. Gascony Under English Rule. LC 74-118483. 1971. Repr. of 1926 ed. 13.50 (ISBN 0-8046-1232-3). Kennikat.

Longman, William. History of the Life & Times of Edward Third, 2 Vols. (Illus.). 1969. Repr. of 1869 ed. 40.50 (ISBN 0-8337-2141-0). B Franklin.

Mackinnon, James. The History of Edward the Third: 1327-1377. 625p. 1974. Repr. of 1900 ed. 23.50x (ISBN 0-87471-465-6). Rowman.

McKisack, May. Fourteenth Century, 1307-1399. (Oxford History of England Ser.). 1959. 34.00x (ISBN 0-19-821712-9). Oxford U Pr.

Mayhew, N. J. Edwardian Monetary Affairs (1279-1344) 1977. 15.00x (ISBN 0-904531-64-3, Pub. by BAR). State Mutual Bk.

Meisel, Janet. Barons of the Welsh Frontier: The Corbet, Pantulf, & Fitz Warin Families, 1066-1272. LC 80-10273. xx, 231p. 1980. 19.95x (ISBN 0-8032-3064-8). U of Nebr Pr.

Miller, Edward & Hatcher, John. Medieval England: Rural Society & Economic Change 1086-1348. LC 77-21445. (A Social & Economic History of England Ser.). 1979. text ed. 26.00x (ISBN 0-582-48218-6); pap. text ed. 13.95x (ISBN 0-582-48547-9). Longman.

Morris, W. A. The Medieval English to Thirteen Hundred. 310p. 1927. 40.00x (ISBN 0-7190-0342-3, Pub. by Manchester U Pr England). State Mutual Bk.

Morris, W. A. & Dunham, W. H., eds. English Government at Work, 1327-1336, Vol. 3 Local Administration & Justice. 1968. Repr. of 1950 ed. 12.00 (ISBN 0-910956-30-8). Medieval Acad.

Morris, W. A. & Strayer, J. R., eds. English Government at Work, 1327-1336, Vol. 2 Fiscal Administration. 1968. Repr. of 1947 ed. 12.00 (ISBN 0-910956-22-7). Medieval Acad.

Nash, Thomas. Description & First Procreation & Increase of the Towne of Great Yarmouth. Incl. Of the Praise of the Red Herring. 1975. text ed. 8.50 (ISBN 0-8277-3928-1); pap. text ed. 4.95 (ISBN 0-8277-2390-3). British Bk Ctr.

Norgate, Kate. England Under the Angevin Kings, 2 Vols. 1969. Repr. of 1887 ed. lib. bdg. 33.50 (ISBN 0-8337-2576-9). B Franklin.

Oman, C. W. History of England from the Accession of Richard Second to the Death of Richard Third: Thirteen Seventy-Seven to Fourteen Eighty-Five. Repr. of 1906 ed. 24.00 (ISBN 0-527-00849-4). Kraus Repr.

Oman, Charles W. History of England from the Accession of Richard Second to the Death of Richard Third. LC 71-5632. (Political History of England: No. 4). Repr. of 1906 ed. 22.50 (ISBN 0-404-50774-3). AMS Pr.

--History of England from the Accession of Richard Second to the Death of Richard Third 1377-1485. LC 69-14021. 1969. Repr. of 1906 ed. lib. bdg. 20.00x (ISBN 0-8371-0937-X, OMHE). Greenwood.

Oxford Essays in Medieval History, Presented to Herbert Edward Salter. facs. ed. LC 68-22115. (Essay Index Reprint Ser). 1934. 15.00 (ISBN 0-8369-0760-4). Arno.

Painter, Sidney. William Marshal: Knight-Errant, Baron, & Regent of England. LC 33-8958. 316p. 1933. 20.00x (ISBN 0-8018-0516-3); pap. 3.95x (ISBN 0-8018-0517-1). Johns Hopkins.

Paris, Matthew. English History, from the Year Twelve Hundred & Thirty-Five to Twelve Hundred & Seventy-Three, 3 Vols. Giles, J. A., tr. LC 68-55554. (Bohn's Antiquarian Library Ser). Repr. of 1852 ed. Set. 85.00 (ISBN 0-404-50050-1). AMS Pr.

Partner, Nancy F. Serious Entertainments: The Writing of History in Twelfth-Century England. LC 77-4402. 1977. lib. bdg. 18.00x (ISBN 0-226-64763-3). U of Chicago Pr.

Platt, Colin. The English Mediaeval Town. (Illus.). 272p. 1979. pap. 6.95 (ISBN 0-586-08272-7, Pub. by Granada England). Academy Chi Ltd.

--Medieval Southampton: The Port & Trading Community A. D. 1000-1600. (Illus.). 300p. 1973. 27.50x (ISBN 0-7100-7653-3). Routledge & Kegan.

--The Monastic Grange in Medieval England: A Reassessment. LC 73-80106. (Illus.). 272p. 1969. 22.50 (ISBN 0-8232-0845-1). Fordham.

Polybius. The Histories of Polybius, Discoursing of the Warres Betwixt the Romanes & Carthaginenses. Watson, Christopher, tr. LC 75-25683. (English Experience Ser.: No. 132). 1969. Repr. of 1568 ed. 30.00 (ISBN 90-221-0132-0). Walter J Johnson.

Poole, Austin L. From Domesday Book to Magna Carta, 1087-1216. 2nd ed. (Oxford History of England Ser). 1955. 33.00x (ISBN 0-19-821707-2). Oxford U Pr.

Powicke, Frederick M. Thirteenth Century, 1216-1307. 2nd ed. (Illus.). 1962. 33.00x (ISBN 0-19-821708-0). Oxford U Pr.

Powicke, Maurice. Medieval England, 1066-1485. (Oxford Paperbacks Ser). 1931. pap. 2.50x (ISBN 0-19-285027-X). Oxford U Pr.

Powicke, Michael. Military Obligation in Medieval England. LC 75-10217. 263p. 1975. Repr. of 1962 ed. lib. bdg. 15.00x (ISBN 0-8371-8171-2, POMO). Greenwood.

Prestwich, Michael. The Three Edwards: War & State in England, 1272-1377. LC 80-5095. 1980. 25.00 (ISBN 0-312-80251-X). St Martin.

Prestwich, Michael, ed. Documents Illustrating the Crisis of 1297-98 in England. (Royal Historical Society: Camden Society Fourth Ser.: Vol. 24). 216p. 1980. 20.00x (ISBN 0-8476-3307-1). Rowman.

Price, Mary R. Portrait of Britain in the Middle Ages, 1066-1485. (Oxford Introduction to British History Ser). (Illus.). 1951. pap. 12.50 (ISBN 0-19-832919-9). Oxford U Pr.

Ramsay, James H. The Angevin Empire: Or the Three Reigns of Henry II, Richard I, & John, 1154-1216. LC 76-29840. (Illus.). Repr. of 1903 ed. 46.50 (ISBN 0-404-15426-3). AMS Pr.

Rawcliffe, Carole. The Staffords, Earls of Stafford & Dukes of Buckingham 1394-1521. LC 77-71425. (Studies in Medieval Life & Thought: No. 11). (Illus.). 1978. 39.95 (ISBN 0-521-21663-X). Cambridge U Pr.

Razi, Zvi. Life, Marriage & Death in a Medieval Parish. LC 79-8491. (Past & Present Publications). (Illus.). 1980. 27.50 (ISBN 0-521-23252-X). Cambridge U Pr.

Reeves, A. Compton. Newport Lordship, Thirteen Seventeen to Fifteen Thirty-Six. LC 79-23817. (Illus.). 280p. (Orig.). 1979. pap. 20.75 (ISBN 0-8357-0487-4, SS-00119). Univ Microfilms.

Rishanger, William. The Chronicle of William of Rishanger. Repr. of 1840 ed. 19.50 (ISBN 0-384-50960-6). Johnson Repr.

Robbe-Grillet, Alain. La Maison de Rendez-vous. Howard, Richard, tr. from Fr. 1966. pap. 1.95 (ISBN 0-394-17120-9, B143, BC). Grove.

Roberts, Emma. Memoirs of the Rival Houses of York & Lancaster, 2 vols. 1981. Repr. of 1827 ed. lib. bdg. 200.00 (ISBN 0-89984-433-2). Century Bookbindery.

Robinson, David M. The Geography of Augustinian Settlement in Medieval England & Wales. 547p. 1980. 88.00x (ISBN 0-86054-093-6, Pub. by BAR). State Mutual Bk.

Roger Of Wendover. Flowers of History, 2 Vols. Giles, J. A., tr. LC 68-55556. (Bohn's Antiquarian Library Ser). Repr. of 1849 ed. Set. 55.00 (ISBN 0-404-50070-6). AMS Pr.

Rosenthal, Joel T. Angles, Angels & Conquerors, 400-1154, Vol. 1. (Borzoi History of England Ser.). (Illus.). 1973. 10.00 (ISBN 0-394-47949-1). Knopf.

Roskell, J. S. The Commons & Their Speakers in English Parliaments 1376-1523. 400p. 1965. 30.00x (ISBN 0-7190-0078-5, Pub. by Manchester U Pr England). State Mutual Bk.

Ross, Charles. Patronage, Pedigree & Power in Later Medieval England. (Illus.). 224p. 1980. text ed. 17.50x (ISBN 0-391-02099-4). Humanities.

Ross, Charles, ed. Patronage, Pedigree & Power in Later Medieval England. (Illus.). 225p. 1979. 18.50x (ISBN 0-8476-6205-5). Rowman.

Round, John H. Feudal England: Historical Studies on the Eleventh & Twelfth Centuries. LC 78-21143. 1979. Repr. of 1964 ed. lib. bdg. 28.75x (ISBN 0-313-21239-2, ROEN). Greenwood.

--Geoffrey De Mandeville: A Study of the Anarchy. (Illus.). 461p. 1972. Repr. of 1892 ed. 32.50 (ISBN 0-8337-3071-1). B Franklin.

Russell, Josiah C. British Medieval Population. (Perspectives in European History Ser.: No. 41). (Illus.). xvi, 389p. Repr. of 1949 ed. lib. bdg. 25.00x (ISBN 0-87991-052-6). Porcupine Pr.

Salusbury-Jones, G. T. Street Life in Medieval England. 2nd ed. 213p. 1975. Repr. of 1948 ed. 15.00x (ISBN 0-87471-615-2). Rowman.

--Street Life in Medieval England. 1979. Repr. of 1938 ed. lib. bdg. 25.00 (ISBN 0-8495-4945-0). Arden Lib.

Salzman, Louis F. Henry Second. LC 66-27144. (Illus.). 1967. Repr. of 1914 ed. 9.00 (ISBN 0-8462-1028-2). Russell.

Sanders, Ivor J. Feudal Military Service in England: A Study of the Constitutional & Military Powers of the Barones in Medieval England. LC 80-23778. (Oxford Historical Ser., British Ser.). xv, 173p. 1980. Repr. of 1956 ed. lib. bdg. 19.25x (ISBN 0-313-22725-X, SAFM). Greenwood.

Sayles, G. O. & Richardson, H. G. The Governance of Medieval England. 1963. 29.00 (ISBN 0-85224-102-X, Pub. by Edinburgh U Pr Scotland). Columbia U Pr.

Scofield, Cora L. Life & Reign of Edward the Fourth, 2 Vols. 1967. Set. lib. bdg. 55.00x (ISBN 0-374-97183-8). Octagon.

Scott, A. F. The Plantagenet Age. LC 75-4880. (Everyone a Witness Ser.). (Illus.). 328p. 1976. 9.95 (ISBN 0-690-01002-8). T Y Crowell.

Shelley, Percy V. English & French in England, Ten Sixty Six to Eleven Hundred. LC 72-194379. 1921. lib. bdg. 17.50 (ISBN 0-8414-8092-3). Folcroft.

Stenton, Doris M. English Society in the Early Middle Ages, 1066-1307. lib. bdg. 10.50x (ISBN 0-88307-258-0). Gannon.

Stevenson, Joseph, ed. Chronicon De Lanercost. LC 72-1036. (Maitland Club, Glasgow. Publications: No. 46). Repr. of 1839 ed. 55.00 (ISBN 0-404-53026-5). AMS Pr.

Stubbs, William. Historical Introduction to the Rolls Series. LC 77-158211. Repr. of 1902 ed. 11.50 (ISBN 0-404-06302-0). AMS Pr.

Tait, J. The Medieval English Borough: Studies on Its Origin & Constitutional History. 392p. 1936. 45.00x (ISBN 0-7190-0339-3, Pub. by Manchester U Pr England). State Mutual Bk.

Tanner, Norman P., ed. Heresy Trials in the Diocese of Norwich: 1428-31. (Royal Historical Society: Camden Society Fourth Ser.: Vol. 20). 233p. 1977. 20.00x (ISBN 0-8476-3305-5). Rowman.

Tout, T. F. Chapters in the Administrative History of Medieval England: The Wardrobe, the Chamber & the Small Seals, Vol. 1. 350p. 1920. 50.00x (ISBN 0-7190-0324-5, Pub. by Manchester U Pr England). State Mutual Bk.

--Chapters in the Administrative History of Medieval England: The Wardrobe, the Chamber & the Small Seals, Vol. 2. 382p. 1920. 50.00x (ISBN 0-7190-0325-3, Pub. by Manchester U Pr England). State Mutual Bk.

--Chapters in the Administrative History of Medieval England: The Wardrobe the Chamber & the Small Seals, Vol. 3. 514p. 1928. 50.00x (ISBN 0-7190-0326-1, Pub. by Manchester U Pr England). State Mutual Bk.

--Chapters in the Administrative History of Medieval England: The Wardrobe, the Chamber & the Small Seals, Vol. 5. 440p. 1930. 50.00x (ISBN 0-7190-0328-8, Pub. by Manchester U Pr England). State Mutual Bk.

--Chapters in the Administrative History of Medieval England: The Wardrobe, the Chamber & the Small Seals, Vol. 6. 458p. 1933. 50.00x (ISBN 0-7190-0329-6, Pub. by Manchester U Pr England). State Mutual Bk.

Tout, Thomas F. History of England from the Accession of Henry the Third to the Death of Edward the Third, 1216-1377. LC 71-5640. (Political History of England: No. 3). Repr. of 1905 ed. 22.50 (ISBN 0-404-50773-5). AMS Pr.

--History of England from the Accession of Henry Third to the Death of Edward Third, 1216-1377. LC 69-14120. 1969. Repr. of 1905 ed. lib. bdg. 20.00x (ISBN 0-8371-0941-8, TOHE). Greenwood.

--History of England from the Accession of Henry Third to the Death of Edward Third, 1216-1377. LC 68-25273. (British History Ser., No. 30). 1968. Repr. of 1905 ed. lib. bdg. 59.95 (ISBN 0-8383-0276-9). Haskell.

--The Place of the Reign of Edward Second in English History. 2nd rev. ed. Johnstone, Hilda, ed. LC 76-40284. (Ford Lectures at Oxford in 1913). 1976. Repr. of 1936 ed. lib. bdg. 26.25x (ISBN 0-8371-9046-0, TOES). Greenwood.

The Troublesome Reign of King John. LC 75-133750. (Tudor Facsimile Texts. Old English Plays: No. 59). Repr. of 1911 ed. 31.50 (ISBN 0-404-53359-0). AMS Pr.

Vergilius, Polydorus. Three Books of Polydore Vergil's English History, Comprising the Reigns of Henry Sixth, Edward Fourth, & Richard Third. Ellis, Henry, ed. (Camden Society, London. Publications, First Ser.: No. 29). Repr. of 1844 ed. 21.00 (ISBN 0-404-50129-X). AMS Pr.

--Three Books of Polydore Vergil's English History: Comprising the Reigns of Henry VI, Edward IV, & Richard III. Repr. of 1844 ed. 23.00 (ISBN 0-384-64245-4). Johnson Repr.

Vinogradoff, Paul. English Society in the Eleventh Century: Essays in English Medieval History. 1968. Repr. of 1908 ed. 43.00 (ISBN 0-403-00047-5). Scholarly.

Vitalis, Orderic. The Ecclesiastical History of Orderic Vitalis, Vol. 5, Bks. 9 & 10. Chibnall, Majorie, ed. & tr. from Fr. (Oxford Medieval Texts Ser). 434p. 1975. 65.00x (ISBN 0-19-822232-7). Oxford U Pr.

Wace. Master Wace: His Chronicle of the Norman Conquest from the Roman De Rou. LC 78-178501. (Illus.). Repr. of 1837 ed. 25.00 (ISBN 0-404-56682-0). AMS Pr.

Warkworth, John. Chronicle of the First Thirteen Years of the Reign of King Edward Fourth. Halliwell, J. O., ed. (Camden Society, London. Publications, First Series: No. 10). Repr. of 1839 ed. 14.00 (ISBN 0-404-50110-9). AMS Pr.

--A Chronicle of the First Thirteen Years of the Reign of King Edward the Fourth. 15.50 (ISBN 0-384-65830-X). Johnson Repr.

Wilkinson, B. The High Middle Ages in England, 1154-1377. LC 77-8490. (Conference on British Studies Bibliographical Handbooks). 1978. 15.50x (ISBN 0-521-21732-6). Cambridge U Pr.

Willard, J. F. & Morris, W. A., eds. English Government at Work, 1327-1336, Vol. 1 Central & Prerogative Administration. 1965. Repr. of 1940 ed. 18.00 (ISBN 0-910956-14-6). Medieval Acad.

William Of Malmesbury. Chronicle of the Kings of England. Giles, J. A., ed. Sharpe, J., tr. LC 68-55558. (Bohn's Antiquarian Library Ser). Repr. of 1847 ed. 27.50 (ISBN 0-404-50025-0). AMS Pr.

Wise, Terence. Ten Sixty Six, Year of Destiny. 1980. text ed. 19.50x (ISBN 0-85045-320-8). Humanities.

Woods, William. England in the Age of Chaucer. LC 76-13461. (Illus.). 1976. 10.00 (ISBN 0-685-70106-9). Stein & Day.

Wylie, James H. History of England Under Henry the Fourth, 4 Vols. LC 78-78505. 1968. Repr. of 1898 ed. Set. 130.00 (ISBN 0-404-07060-4); 32.50 ea. Vol. 1 (ISBN 0-404-07061-2). Vol. 2 (ISBN 0-404-07062-0). Vol. 3 (ISBN 0-404-07063-9). Vol. 4 (ISBN 0-404-07064-7). AMS Pr.

Young, Charles R. The Royal Forests of Medieval England. LC 78-65109. (The Middle Ages Ser.). (Illus.). 1979. 15.00x (ISBN 0-8122-7760-0). U of Pa Pr.

GREAT BRITAIN–HISTORY–MEDIEVAL PERIOD, 1066-1485–BIBLIOGRAPHY

Altschul, M. Anglo-Norman England, Ten Sixty-Six to Eleven Fifty-Four. LC 78-80816. (Bibliographical Handbooks of the Conference on British Studies). 1969. 17.50 (ISBN 0-521-07582-3). Cambridge U Pr.

Guth de Lloyd, J. Late-Medieval England, 1377-1485. LC 75-23845. (Conference on British Studies Bibliographical Handbooks Ser.). 164p. 1976. 17.95 (ISBN 0-521-20877-7). Cambridge U Pr.

GREAT BRITAIN–HISTORY–MEDIEVAL PERIOD, 1066-1485–FICTION

Here is entered historical Fiction on either the whole or portions of the period. Biographical fiction, drama, etc. will be found under the name of kings, e.g. Richard 2nd, King of England–Fiction.

Dolch, Edward W. & Dolch, M. P. Ivanhoe. (Pleasure Reading Ser). (gr. 3-12). 1961. PLB 6.57 (ISBN 0-8116-2612-1). Garrard.

Pyle, Howard. Men of Iron. (Classics Ser). (gr. 6 up). pap. 1.50 (ISBN 0-8049-0093-0, CL-93). Airmont.

--Men of Iron. LC 30-16249. (Illus.). (gr. 5 up). 1891. (HarpJ); PLB 9.89 (ISBN 0-06-024801-7). Har-Row.

Scott, Walter. Ivanhoe. (Great Il. Classics). (Illus.). (gr. 7-9). 1979. 8.95 (ISBN 0-396-07749-8). Dodd.

--Ivanhoe. (Classics Ser). (gr. 9 up). 1964. pap. 1.25 (ISBN 0-8049-0034-5, CL-34). Airmont.

--Ivanhoe. (Literature Ser). (gr. 7-12). 1970. pap. text ed. 3.83 (ISBN 0-87720-729-1). AMSCO Sch.

--Ivanhoe. (RL 7). pap. 2.95 (ISBN 0-451-51496-3, CE1496, Sig Classics). NAL.

Scott, Sir Walter. Ivanhoe. 1955. 12.95x (ISBN 0-460-00016-0, Evman); pap. 3.95x (ISBN 0-460-01016-6, Evman). Biblio Dist.

Stevenson, Robert L. Black Arrow. (Classics Ser). (gr. 6 up). 1964. pap. 1.25 (ISBN 0-8049-0020-5, CL-20). Airmont.

Wheeler, Thomas G. All Men Tall. LC 70-77313. (gr. 8 up). 1969. 9.95 (ISBN 0-87599-157-2). S G Phillips.

GREAT BRITAIN–HISTORY–MEDIEVAL PERIOD, 1066-1485–POETRY

Wright, Thomas, tr. Political Songs of England, from the Reign of John to That of Edward Second. (Camden Society, London. Publications, First Ser.: No. 6). Repr. of 1839 ed. 35.00 (ISBN 0-404-50106-0). AMS Pr.

GREAT BRITAIN–HISTORY–MEDIEVAL PERIOD, 1066-1485–SOURCES

Baker, Geoffrey. Chronicon Galfridi le Baker De Swynebroke Temporibus Edwardi Secund et Edwardi Tertii. Giles, John A., ed. 1966. Repr. of 1847 ed. 24.00 (ISBN 0-8337-1343-4). B Franklin.

Bullough, D. A. & Storey, R. L., eds. The Study of Medieval Records: Essays in Honour of Kathleen Major. (Illus.). 380p. 1971. 29.95x (ISBN 0-19-822347-1). Oxford U Pr.

Edward Fifth, King of England. Grants Etc. from the Crown During the Reign of Edward the Fifth. LC 70-164758. Repr. of 1854 ed. 14.00 (ISBN 0-404-50160-5). AMS Pr.

Gairdner, James, ed. Letters & Papers Illustrative to the Reigns of Richard III & Henry VII, 2 vols. LC 75-41107. Repr. of 1863 ed. Set. 72.50 (ISBN 0-404-14910-3). AMS Pr.

Giles, John A. Scriptores Rerum Gestarum Willelmi Conquestoris. 1966. 24.00 (ISBN 0-8337-1348-5). B Franklin.

Glasscock, Robin E., ed. The Lay Subsidy of 1334. (British Academy Records of Social & Economic History). 546p. 1975. 39.95x (ISBN 0-19-725933-2). Oxford U Pr.

Hughes, Dorothy. Illustrations of Chaucer's England. LC 72-5333. 1972. Repr. of 1919 ed. lib. bdg. 25.00 (ISBN 0-8414-0037-7). Folcroft.

James, Francis G. Pageant of Medieval England. LC 74-23679. 256p. (Orig.). 1974. pap. 5.95x (ISBN 0-88289-055-7). Pelican.

Lodge, E. C. & Thornton, G. A. English Constitutional Documents, 1307-1485. 1972. lib. bdg. 20.00x (ISBN 0-374-95076-8). Octagon.

Map, Walter. Gualteri Mapes De Nugis Curialium Distinctiones Quinque. Wright, Thomas, ed. (Camden Society. London. Publications, First Series: No. 50). Repr. of 1850 ed. 21.00 (ISBN 0-404-50150-8). AMS Pr.

Monro, Cecil, ed. Letters of Queen Margaret of Anjou & Bishop Beckington & Others. LC 17-1255. (Camden Society, London. Publications, First Series: No. 86). Repr. of 1863 ed. 14.00 (ISBN 0-404-50186-9). AMS Pr.

--Letters of Queen Margaret of Anjou & Bishop Beckington & Others. 1863. 15.50 (ISBN 0-384-39745-X). Johnson Repr.

Morris, John, ed. Bedfordshire. (The Domesday Book Ser.: Vol. 20). (Illus.). 170p. 1977. 18.00x (ISBN 0-8476-1426-3). Rowman.

--Buckinghamshire. (Domesday Bk.). 1977. 21.00x (ISBN 0-8476-1726-2). Rowman.

--Cheshire with Lancashire, Cumbria & North Wales. (Domesday Bk.). 170p. 1977. 21.00x (ISBN 0-8476-1725-4). Rowman.

Myers, A. R., ed. English Historical Documents, Vol. 4, 1327-1485. 1969. 69.00x (ISBN 0-19-519503-5). Oxford U Pr.

Ramsay, James H. History of the Revenues of the Kings of England 1066-1399, 2 Vols in 1. Repr. of 1925 ed. lib. bdg. 30.00x (ISBN 0-678-01237-7). Kelley.

Trevelyan, George M. England in the Age of Wycliffe. 3rd ed. LC 78-178560. Repr. of 1900 ed. 28.50 (ISBN 0-404-56677-4). AMS Pr.

GREAT BRITAIN–HISTORY–WARS OF THE ROSES, 1455-1485

Cole, Hubert. The Wars of the Roses. 1979. 11.95x (ISBN 0-8464-0099-5). Beekman Pubs.

Goodman, Anthony. The Wars of the Roses: Military Activity & English Society, 1452-1497. (Illus.). 300p. 1981. write for info. (ISBN 0-7100-0728-0). Routledge & Kegan.

Roberts, Emma. Memoirs of the Rival Houses of York & Lancaster, 2 vols. 1981. Repr. of 1827 ed. lib. bdg. 200.00 (ISBN 0-89984-433-2). Century Bookbindery.

Ross, Charles. The Wars of the Roses: A Concise History. (Illus.). 1977. 12.50 (ISBN 0-500-25049-9). Thames Hudson.

GREAT BRITAIN–HISTORY–MODERN PERIOD, 1485-

Bacon, Francis. History of the Reign of King Henry the Seventh. Levy, Fritz J., ed. LC 70-177471. (European Historiography Ser). 1972. pap. 6.95 (ISBN 0-672-61420-0). Bobbs.

Bowle, John. Charles I: A Biography. 1976. 12.50 (ISBN 0-316-10404-3). Little.

Capp, Bernard. English Almanacs: Fifteen Hundred to Eighteen Hundred: Astrology & the Popular Press. LC 78-74212. (Illus.). 1979. 42.50x (ISBN 0-8014-1229-3). Cornell U Pr.

Churchill, George B. Richard the Third up to Shakespeare. Repr. of 1900 ed. 44.50 (ISBN 0-384-09040-0); pap. 41.50 (ISBN 0-685-02232-3). Johnson Repr.

Cole, Gene D. Persons & Periods. LC 73-75412. Repr. of 1938 ed. 9.75x (ISBN 0-678-00495-1). Kelley.

Ferguson, Arthur B. CLIO Unbound: Perception of the Social & Cultural Past in Renaissance England. LC 78-67198. (Monographs in Medieval & Renaissance Studies: No. 2). 1979. 24.75 (ISBN 0-8223-0417-1). Duke.

Firth, Katherine R. The Apocalyptic Tradition in Reformation Britain 1530-1645. (Historical Monographs). (Illus.). 1979. 37.50x (ISBN 0-19-821868-0). Oxford U Pr.

Gooch, George P. Annals of Politics & Culture, 1492-1899. LC 79-170959. (History, Economics & Social Science Ser: No. 291). 1971. Repr. of 1905 ed. lib. bdg. 22.50 (ISBN 0-8337-1380-9). B Franklin.

Grants from the Crown During the Reign of Edward the Fifth: Great Britain Sovereigns. 1854. 15.50 (ISBN 0-384-19820-1). Johnson Repr.

Hatcher, John. Plague, Population & the English Economy, 1348-1530. (Studies in Economic & Social History). 1977. pap. 4.75x (ISBN 0-333-21293-2). Humanities.

Hunt, E. H. British Labour History, Eighteen Fifteen to Nineteen Fourteen. 428p. 1981. text ed. 48.25x (ISBN 0-391-02209-1, Pub. by Weidenfeld England). Humanities.

James, M. E. Family, Lineage & Civil Society: A Study of Society, Politics & Mentality in the Durham Region, 1500-1640. 240p. 1973. 33.00x (ISBN 0-19-822408-7). Oxford U Pr.

Kaye, Percy L. The Colonial Executive Prior to the Restoration. (Johns Hopkins University Studies in Historical & Political Science, Ser. 18: Nos. 5, 6). 84p. Repr. of 1900 ed. pap. 8.00 (ISBN 0-384-28800-6). Johnson Repr.

Kingsford, Charles L. Prejudice & Promise in Fifteenth Century England. 215p. 1962. 23.50x (ISBN 0-7146-1488-2, F Cass Co). Biblio Dist.

Lander, J. R. Government & Community: England, 1450-1509. (New History of England Ser.). 416p. 1980. 22.50x (ISBN 0-674-35793-0). Harvard U Pr.

Loades, D. M. Politics & the Nation, Fourteen Fifty-Sixteen Sixty: Obedience, Resistance & Public Order. Elton, Y. R., ed. (Fontana Library of English History). 484p. 1974. text ed. 22.25 (ISBN 0-901759-34-1). Humanities.

Misra, G. S. Survey of Modern British History, Vol. 1. 6.50x (ISBN 0-685-06522-7). Asia.

Williamson, James A. The Ocean in English History: Being the Ford Lectures. LC 78-12510. 1979. Repr. of 1941 ed. lib. bdg. 18.50x (ISBN 0-313-21157-4, WIOE). Greenwood.

Wilson, Derek. England in the Age of Thomas More. (Illus.). 1980. text ed. 15.50x (ISBN 0-246-10943-2). Humanities.

GREAT BRITAIN–HISTORY–MODERN PERIOD, 1485--SOURCES

Park, Thomas, ed. Harleian Miscellany, 10 Vols. LC 2-21219. Repr. of 1808 ed. Set. 495.00 (ISBN 0-404-03140-4); 49.50 ea. AMS Pr.

Somers. Somers Tracts: A Collection of Scarce & Valuable Tracts, 13 Vols. Scott, Walter, ed. Repr. of 1815 ed. Set. 812.50 (ISBN 0-404-06160-5); 62.50 ea. AMS Pr.

GREAT BRITAIN–HISTORY–TUDORS–1485-1603

Here are entered works on the period between 1485 and 1603 as a whole, as well as those on any part except the reign of Elizabeth, for which see Great Britain–History–Elizabeth–1558-1603.

Appleby, Andrew B. Famine in Tudor & Stuart England. LC 77-76151. 1978. 14.50x (ISBN 0-8047-0956-4). Stanford U Pr.

Ault, Susan & Worman, B. Tudors & Stuarts. (Illus.). 9.50x (ISBN 0-392-05218-0, SpS). Sportshelf.

Bachrach, A. G. Sir Constantine Huygens & Britain: 1597-1619, Vol. 1. (Publications of the Sir Thomas Browne Institute Ser: No. 1). 1962. pap. 26.00 (ISBN 90-6021-059-X, Pub. by Leiden Univ Holland). Kluwer Boston.

Beckingsale, B. W. Thomas Cromwell: Tudor Minister. (Illus.). 181p. 1978. 18.50x (ISBN 0-8476-6053-2). Rowman.

Bindoff, S. T. The Pelican History of England: Tudor England, Vol. 5. 1950. pap. 3.50 (ISBN 0-14-020212-9, Pelican). Penguin.

--Tudor England. lib. bdg. 10.50x (ISBN 0-88307-022-7). Gannon.

Brewer, John S. Reign of Henry Eighth from His Accession to the Death of Wolsey, 2 Vols. Gairdner, James, ed. LC 2-21517. Repr. of 1884 ed. Set. 45.00 (ISBN 0-404-01072-5). AMS Pr.

Brown, Daniel P. The Protectorate & The Northumberland Conspiracy: Political Intrigue in the Reign of Edward VI. LC 80-65156. (European History: Ser. I-1001). (Illus.). 74p. (Orig.). 1981. pap. 3.15 (ISBN 0-930860-02-0). Golden West Hist.

Capp, Bernard. English Almanacs: Fifteen Hundred to Eighteen Hundred: Astrology & the Popular Press. LC 78-74212. (Illus.). 1979. 42.50x (ISBN 0-8014-1229-3). Cornell U Pr.

Carr, Virginia M. The Drama As Propaganda: A Study of The Troublesome Reign of King John. (Salzburg Studies in English Literature, Elizabethan & Renaissance Studies: No. 28). 185p. 1974. pap. text ed. 25.00x (ISBN 0-391-01341-6). Humanities.

Chartres, J. A. Internal Trade in England 1500-1700. (Studies in Economic & Social History). 1977. pap. text ed. 4.00x (ISBN 0-333-18358-4). Humanities.

Clark, Peter, et al, eds. English Commonwealth Fifteen Forty-Seven to Sixteen Forty: Essays in Politics & Society. LC 78-32060. (Illus.). 1979. text ed. 30.00x (ISBN 0-06-491171-3). B&N.

Conway, Agnes. Henry Seventh's Relations with Scotland & Ireland, 1485-1498. 1972. lib. bdg. 15.00x (ISBN 0-374-91915-1). Octagon.

Copley, Gordon J., ed. Camden's Britannia, 2 vols. (Illus.). 1977. vol. 1 17.50 (ISBN 0-09-122000-9, Pub. by Hutchinson); vol. 2 17.50 (ISBN 0-09-125240-7). Merrimack Bk Serv.

Cornwall, Julian C. Revolt of the Peasantry, 1549. (Illus.). 1977. 22.00 (ISBN 0-7100-8676-8). Routledge & Kegan.

Davies, D. W. Dutch Influences on English Culture, 1558-1625. LC 64-18226. (Folger Guides to the Age of Shakespeare). 1964. pap. 3.95 (ISBN 0-918016-13-4). Folger Bks.

Dietz, Frederick C. English Government Finance, Fourteen Eighty-Five to Fifteen Fifty-Eight. Repr. of 1920 ed. 11.50 (ISBN 0-384-11750-3). Johnson Repr.

A Discourse of the Common Weal of This Realm of England. LC 75-179393. (Research & Source Works Ser.). 284p. 1972. Repr. of 1893 ed. 20.50 (ISBN 0-8337-1533-X). B Franklin.

Dodds, Madeleine H. & Dodds, Ruth. Pilgrimage of Grace, 1536-1537 & the Exeter Conspiracy, 1538, 2 vols. 1971. Repr. of 1915 ed. 62.50x set (ISBN 0-7146-1470-X, F Cass Co). Biblio Dist.

Edward Sixth. Literary Remains of King Edward Sixth, 2 Vols. Nichols, John G., ed. 1964. Repr. of 1857 ed. 52.00 (ISBN 0-8337-2528-9). B Franklin.

Einstein, Lewis. Tudor Ideals. LC 62-13833. 1962. Repr. of 1921 ed. 8.50 (ISBN 0-8462-0177-1). Russell.

Elton, G. R. England Under the Tudors. 2nd ed. (Illus.). 1974. text ed. 29.95 (ISBN 0-416-78720-7); pap. text ed. 15.95 (ISBN 0-416-70690-8). Methuen Inc.

--Reform & Reformation: England, 1509-1558. LC 77-6464. (Harvard Paperback Ser.: No. 146, The New History of England). 1979. 18.50x (ISBN 0-674-75245-7); pap. 7.95x (ISBN 0-674-75248-1). Harvard U Pr.

Erickson, Carolly. Great Harry. LC 79-21868. 1980. 14.95 (ISBN 0-671-40017-7). Summit Bks.

Fines, John. Tudor People. 1977. 16.95 (ISBN 0-7134-0283-0, Pub. by Batsford England). David & Charles.

Fisher, H. A. History of England from the Accession of Henry Seventh to the Death of Henry Eighth, 1485-1547. LC 79-592. Repr. of 1906 ed. 24.00 (ISBN 0-527-00850-8). Kraus Repr.

Fisher, Herbert A. History of England: From the Accession of Henry Seventh to the Death of Henry Eighth. LC 75-5625. (Political History of England: No. 5). 22.50 (ISBN 0-404-50775-1). AMS Pr.

--History of England from the Accession of Henry Seventh to the Death of Henry Eighth, 1485-1547. LC 69-18977. Repr. of 1906 ed. lib. bdg. 20.00x (ISBN 0-8371-1063-7, FIHE). Greenwood.

Fletcher, Anthony. Tudor Rebellions. 2nd rev. ed. (Seminar Studies in History). (Illus.). 176p. 1973. pap. text ed. 5.50x (ISBN 0-582-35205-3). Longman.

Fowler, Elaine W. English Sea Power in the Early Tudor Period, 1485-1558. LC 65-22933. (Folger Guides to the Age of Shakespeare). 1966. pap. 3.95 (ISBN 0-918016-15-0). Folger Bks.

Friedmann, Paul. Anne Boleyn: A Chapter of English History, 1527-1536, 2 Vols. Repr. of 1884 ed. Set. 52.50 (ISBN 0-404-09050-8). Vol. 1. Vol. 2 (ISBN 0-404-09051-6). AMS Pr.

Froude, James A. History of England from the Fall of Wolsey to the Defeat of the Spanish Armada, 12 Vols. LC 71-91303. Repr. of 1870 ed. Set. 420.00 (ISBN 0-404-02650-8); 35.00 ea. AMS Pr.

Gairdner, James. Henry the Seventh. LC 70-112639. Repr. of 1889 ed. 11.50 (ISBN 0-404-02667-2). AMS Pr.

--Henry the Seventh. 1889. 19.00 (ISBN 0-403-00020-3). Scholarly.

--History of the Life & Reign of Richard the Third, to Which Is Added the Story of Perkin Warbeck. Repr. of 1898 ed. lib. bdg. 17.25x (ISBN 0-8371-1061-0, GART). Greenwood.

Garvin, Katherine. The Great Tudors. LC 74-8259. 1935. lib. bdg. 40.00 (ISBN 0-8414-4503-6). Folcroft.

Goodman, Anthony. A History of England from Edward II to James I. LC 76-51405. (Illus.). 1977. text ed. 21.00x (ISBN 0-582-48281-X); pap. text ed. 12.95x (ISBN 0-582-48282-8). Longman.

Goodman, Christopher. How Superior Powers Oght to Be Obeyed of Their Subjects. LC 70-38197. (English Experience Ser.: No. 460). 240p. 1972. Repr. of 1548 ed. 22.00 (ISBN 90-221-0460-5). Walter J Johnson.

Graves, Michael A. The House of Lords in the Parliaments of Edward VI & Mary I: An Institutional Study. LC 80-42225. 312p. Date not set. price not set (ISBN 0-521-23678-9). Cambridge U Pr.

Gurney-Salter, Emma. Tudor England Through Venetian Eyes. 1977. lib. bdg. 59.95 (ISBN 0-8490-2778-0). Gordon Pr.

Haigh, C. Reformation & Resistance in Tudor Lancashire. LC 73-88308. (Illus.). 416p. 1974. 42.95 (ISBN 0-521-20367-8). Cambridge U Pr.

Hall, Edward. Hall's Chronicle. Ellis, Henry, ed. LC 2-20847. Repr. of 1809 ed. 65.00 (ISBN 0-404-03029-7). AMS Pr.

Harbison, E. Harris. Rival Ambassadors at the Court of Queen Mary. LC 73-107805. (Select Bibliographies Reprint Ser). 1940. 26.00 (ISBN 0-8369-5182-4). Arno.

Harrison, George B. England to Shakespeare's Day. 1981. Repr. lib. bdg. 25.00 (ISBN 0-403-00620-1). Scholarly.

Heinze, R. M. The Proclamations of Tudor Kings. LC 27-22983. 320p. 1976. 49.50 (ISBN 0-521-20938-2). Cambridge U Pr.

Helm, P. J. England Under the Yorkists & Tudors 1471 - 1603. (Illus.). 1968. text ed. 12.50x (ISBN 0-7135-0541-9); pap. text ed. 9.75x (ISBN 0-7135-0542-7). Humanities.

Hoeniger, F. D. & Hoeniger, J. F. Development of Natural History in Tudor England. LC 69-19336. (Folger Guides to the Age of Shakespeare). 1969. pap. 3.95 (ISBN 0-918016-14-2). Folger Bks.

Holinshed, Raphael. Holinshed's Chronicles of England, Scotland & Ireland, 6 Vols. Ellis, Henry, ed. LC 75-44326. Repr. of 1808 ed. Set. 625.00 (ISBN 0-404-03330-X). Vol. 1 (ISBN 0-404-03331-8). Vol. 2 (ISBN 0-404-03332-6). Vol. 3 (ISBN 0-404-03333-4). Vol. 4 (ISBN 0-404-03334-2). Vol. 5 (ISBN 0-404-03335-0). Vol. 6 (ISBN 0-404-03336-9). AMS Pr.

--Holinshed's Chronicles: Richard II, 1398-1400, Henry IV & Henry V. Wallace, R. S. & Hansen, Alma, eds. LC 78-124. 1978. Repr. of 1923 ed. lib. bdg. 22.25x (ISBN 0-313-20259-1, HOHC). Greenwood.

Hudson, Winthrop S. The Cambridge Connection & the Elizabethan Settlement of Fifteen Fifty-Nine. LC 79-56513. x, 158p. 1980. 14.75 (ISBN 0-8223-0440-6). Duke.

Hume, Martin A. Sir Walter Raleigh: The British Dominion of the West. 1977. Repr. of 1906 ed. lib. bdg. 40.00 (ISBN 0-8492-1143-3). R West.

Hurstfield, Joel, ed. The Tudors. LC 73-82823. 224p. 1973. 17.95 (ISBN 0-312-82320-7). St Martin.

Innes, Arthur D. Leading Figures in English History: Tudor & Stewart Period. facs. ed. LC 67-23233. (Essay Index Reprint Ser). 1931. 18.00 (ISBN 0-8369-0559-8). Arno.

--Ten Tudor Statesmen. LC 79-118479. 1971. Repr. of 1934 ed. 12.50 (ISBN 0-8046-1228-5). Kennikat.

Ives, E. W., et al, eds. Wealth & Power in Tudor England: Essays Presented to S. T. Bindoff. (Illus.). 1978. text ed. 47.00x (ISBN 0-485-11176-4, Athlone Pr). Humanities.

Jack Straw. LC 74-133687. (Tudor Facsimile Texts. Old English Plays: No. 64). Repr. of 1911 ed. 31.50 (ISBN 0-404-53364-7). AMS Pr.

Jack, Sybil M. Trade & Industry in Tudor & Stuart England. (Historical Problems - Studies & Documents). 1977. text ed. 29.95x (ISBN 0-04-942155-7); pap. text ed. 12.50x (ISBN 0-04-942156-5). Allen Unwin.

Jordan, W. K. Edward Sixth, the Young King: The Protectorship of the Duke of Somerset. (Illus.). 1968. 25.00x (ISBN 0-674-23965-2, Belknap Pr). Harvard U Pr.

Kennedy, W. P. Studies in Tudor History. LC 73-118480. 1971. Repr. of 1916 ed. 14.50 (ISBN 0-8046-1229-3). Kennikat.

Knox, D. B. Doctrine of Faith in the Reign of Henry Eighth. 1961. 12.50 (ISBN 0-227-67444-8). Attic Pr.

Lander, J. R. Conflict & Stability in Fifteenth Century England. 3rd ed. 1977. pap. 5.75x (ISBN 0-09-095741-5, Hutchinson U Lib). Humanities.

Lane, Peter. Tudor England. (Visual Source Ser.). 96p. 1980. 14.95 (ISBN 0-7134-0035-8, Pub. by Batsford England). David & Charles.

Lockyer, Roger. Tudor & Stuart Britain: Fourteen Seventy-One to Seventeen-Fourteen. (Illus.). 1964. 9.95 (ISBN 0-312-82250-2). St Martin.

London University, Board of Studies in History. Tudor Studies Presented to Albert Frederick Pollard. facs. ed. Seton-Watson, R. W., ed. LC 69-17582. (Essay Index Reprint Ser.). 1924. 16.00 (ISBN 0-8369-0083-9). Arno.

Mackie, John D. Earlier Tudors, 1485-1558. (Oxford History of England Ser.). (Illus.). 1952. 34.00x (ISBN 0-19-821706-4). Oxford U Pr.

Massie, Joseph. Bibliography of the Collection of Books & Tracts on Commerce, Currency & Poor Law Fifteen Fifty-Seven to Seventeen Sixty-Three Formed by Joseph Massie. Shaw, William A., ed. Repr. of 1937 ed. lib. bdg. 15.00x (ISBN 0-87991-825-X). Porcupine Pr.

Melanchthon, Philipp. The Epistle of P. Melancton Made Unto Kynge Henry the Eyght, for the Revokynge of the Six Artycles. Wesel, J. C., tr. from Lat. LC 72-216. (English Experience Ser.: No. 336). 32p. Repr. of 1547 ed. 7.00 (ISBN 90-221-0336-6). Walter J Johnson.

Millar, Gilbert J. Tudor Mercenaries & Auxiliaries, 1485-1547. LC 79-22164. 1980. 13.95x (ISBN 0-8139-0818-3). U Pr of Va.

Morris, Christopher. The Oxford Book of Tudor Anthems. 1978. pap. 10.00 (ISBN 0-19-353325-1). Oxford U Pr.

Munday, Anthony. The English Roman Life. Ayres, Phillip J., ed. (Studies in Tudor & Stewart Literature Ser.). (Illus.). 142p. 1980. 22.00 (ISBN 0-19-812635-2). Oxford U Pr.

Nichols, John G., ed. Chronicle of Queen Jane & of Two Years of Queen Mary & Especially of the Rebellion of Sir Thomas Wyat. (Camden Society, London. Publications, First Ser.: No. 48). Repr. of 1850 ed. 17.50 (ISBN 0-404-50148-6). AMS Pr.

Outhwaite, R. B. Inflation in Tudor & Early Stuart England. (Studies in Economic & Social History). 1970. pap. text ed. 1.25x (ISBN 0-333-10144-8). Humanities.

Palliser, D. M. Tudor York. (Historical Monographs). (Illus.). 346p. 1979. text ed. 32.50x (ISBN 0-19-821878-8). Oxford U Pr.

Palmer, R. Liddesdale. English Social History in the Making: The Tudor Revolution. 1934. Repr. 15.00 (ISBN 0-685-43457-5). Norwood Edns.

Plowden, Alison. The House of Tudor. LC 76-6936. 1976. 16.95 (ISBN 0-685-70111-5). Stein & Day.

Pollard, A. F. History of England from the Accession of Edward Sixth to the Death of Elizabeth: Fifteen Forty-Seven to Sixteen Hundred-Three. Repr. of 1910 ed. 24.00 (ISBN 0-527-00851-6). Kraus Repr.

Pollard, Albert F. England Under Protector Somerset. LC 66-15433. 1966. Repr. of 1900 ed. 9.00 (ISBN 0-8462-0726-5). Russell.

--History of England from the Accession of Edward Sixth to the Death of Elizabeth, 1547-1603. LC 69-14037. 1969. Repr. of 1910 ed. lib. bdg. 20.00x (ISBN 0-8371-1026-2, POHE). Greenwood.

--The History of England from the Accession of Edward Sixth to the Death of Elizabeth 1 (1547-1603) LC 75-5633. (The Political History of England Ser., No. 6). Repr. of 1910 ed. 22.50 (ISBN 0-404-50776-X). AMS Pr.

--Tudor Studies, Presented by the Board of Studies in History in the University of London to Albert Frederick Pollard. Seton-Watson, R. W., ed. LC 79-77681. 1970. Repr. of 1924 ed. 11.50 (ISBN 0-8462-1354-0). Russell.

Pollard, Alfred W. Tudor Tracts, Fifteen Thirty Two to Fifteen Eighty Eight. LC 64-16749. (Arber's an English Garner Ser.: Vol. 10). Repr. of 1890 ed. 13.50x (ISBN 0-8154-0180-9). Cooper Sq.

Powell, Ken & Cook, Chris. English Historical Facts, 1485-1603. 228p. 1977. 21.50x (ISBN 0-87471-865-1). Rowman.

Poynet, John, compiled by. A Shorte Treatise of Politike Power. LC 72-38220. (English Experience Ser.: No. 484). 184p. 1972. Repr. of 1556 ed. 11.50 (ISBN 90-221-0484-2). Walter J Johnson.

Price, Mary R. & Mather, C. E. Portrait of Britain Under Tudors & Stuarts, 1485-1688. (Oxford Introduction to British History Ser). (Illus.). 1954. pap. 12.50x (ISBN 0-19-832917-2). Oxford U Pr.

Rawcliffe, Carole. The Staffords, Earls of Stafford & Dukes of Buckingham 1394-1521. LC 77-71425. (Studies in Medieval Life & Thought: No. 11). (Illus.). 1978. 39.95 (ISBN 0-521-21663-X). Cambridge U Pr.

Razi, Zvi. Life, Marriage & Death in a Medieval Parish. LC 79-8491. (Past & Present Publications). (Illus.). 1980. 27.50 (ISBN 0-521-23252-X). Cambridge U Pr.

Read, Conyers. Tudors: Personalities & Practical Politics in Sixteenth Century England. facs. ed. LC 68-24854. (Essay Index Reprint Ser). 1936. 16.00 (ISBN 0-8369-0812-0). Arno.

--Tudors: Personalities & Practical Politics in Sixteenth-Century England. (Illus.). 1969. pap. 6.95 (ISBN 0-393-00129-6, Norton Lib). Norton.

Richardson, Walter C. Report of the Royal Commission of 1552. LC 72-86893. 1974. 22.00 (ISBN 0-937058-08-4). West Va U Pr.

Roots, Ivan, ed. Conflicts in Tudor & Stuart England. LC 68-97374. (Selections from History Today Ser.: No. 5). (Illus.). 1969. pap. 5.00 (ISBN 0-05-001536-2). Dufour.

Ross, Josephine. The Tudors: England's Golden Age. LC 79-84036. (Illus.). 1979. 15.95 (ISBN 0-399-12417-9). Putnam.

Roulstone, Michael. The Royal House of Tudor. (Illus.). 192p. 1975. 19.50 (ISBN 0-85944-005-2). Transatlantic.

Russell, Conrad. Crisis of Parliaments: English History 1509-1660. (Short Oxford History of the Modern World Ser.). 1971. pap. 6.95x (ISBN 0-19-501442-1). Oxford U Pr.

Schmidt, Albert J. Yeoman in Tudor & Stuart England. (Folger Guides to the Age of Shakespeare). 1961. 3.95 (ISBN 0-918016-20-7). Folger Bks.

Shirley, Evelyn P. The Sherley Brothers, an Historical Memoir of the Lives of Sir Thomas Sherley, Sir Anthony Sherley & Sir Robert Sherley, Knights, by One of the Same House. LC 77-80190. (Roxburghe Club Publications Ser: No. 66). viii, 110p. 1972. Repr. of 1848 ed. lib. bdg. 26.50 (ISBN 0-8337-3251-X). B Franklin.

Smith, Lucy T., ed. The Itinerary of John Leland in or About the Years 1535-1543, 5 vols. 1978. Repr. of 1906 ed. lib. bdg. 250.00 set (ISBN 0-8274-0003-9). R West.

Starkey, Thomas. England in the Reign of King Henry the Eighth. Cowper, J. M., ed. (EETS, ES Ser.: No. 12). Repr. of 1878 ed. 22.00 (ISBN 0-527-00228-3). Kraus Repr.

Synge, M. B., et al. The Tudors & Stuarts. Repr. of 1934 ed. 17.50 (ISBN 0-686-19864-6). Ridgeway Bks.

Taylor, William C., ed. Romantic Biography of the Age of Elizabeth: Or, Sketches of Life from the Bye-Ways of History, 2vols. LC 72-14121. (Essay Index Reprint Ser.). Repr. of 1842 ed. 46.50 (ISBN 0-518-10027-8). Arno.

Thompson, Craig R. Schools in Tudor England. LC 59-1347. (Folger Guides to the Age of Shakespeare). 1959. 3.95 (ISBN 0-918016-28-2). Folger Bks.

Tittler, Robert & Loach, Jennifer, eds. The Mid-Tudor Polity, c. Fifteen Forty to Fifteen Sixty. 227p. 1980. 20.00x (ISBN 0-8476-6257-8). Rowman.

Unwin, Rayner. The Defeat of John Hawkins: A Biography of His Third Slaving Voyage. 1960. 10.95 (ISBN 0-04-910027-0). Allen Unwin.

Van Cleave Alexander, Michael. The First of the Tudors: A Study of Henry VII & His Reign. 280p. 1980. 22.50x (ISBN 0-8476-6259-4). Rowman.

Verkamp, Bernard J. The Indifferent Mean: Adiaphorism in the English Reformation to 1554. Walton, Robert C. & Bebb, Philip N., eds. LC 77-13672. (Studies in the Reformation: Vol. I). 1978. text ed. 13.00x (ISBN 0-8143-1583-6). Wayne St U Pr.

Waldman, Milton. Some English Dictators. LC 77-112820. 1970. Repr. of 1940 ed. 12.50 (ISBN 0-8046-1087-8). Kennikat.

Washington, Booker T. Character Building. LC 75-38848. (Studies in Black History & Culture, No. 54). 291p. 1972. Repr. of 1902 ed. lib. bdg. 53.95 (ISBN 0-8383-1394-9). Haskell.

Wernham, R. B. Before the Armada: The Emergence of the English Nation, 1485-1588. 1972. pap. 6.95x (ISBN 0-393-00616-6, Norton Lib). Norton.

--The Making of Elizabethan Foreign Policy, 1558-1603. (Illus.). 120p. 1981. 15.50x (ISBN 0-520-03966-1); pap. 4.95x (ISBN 0-520-03974-2, CAMPUS 244). U of Cal Pr.

Whiting, J. R. A Handful of History. (Illus.). 201p. 1978. 18.50x (ISBN 0-8476-6036-2). Rowman.

Williams, Charles H. Making of the Tudor Despotism. rev ed. LC 66-27183. 1967. Repr. of 1935 ed. 7.50 (ISBN 0-8462-1000-2). Russell.

Williams, Penry. The Tudor Regime. 500p. 1981. 19.95 (ISBN 0-19-822678-0). Oxford U Pr.

--The Tudor Regime. 1979. 45.00x (ISBN 0-19-822491-5). Oxford U Pr.

Wilson, Derek. England in the Age of Thomas More. 1979. 17.95x (ISBN 0-8464-0106-1). Beekman Pubs.

Wriothesley, Charles W. A Chronicle of England During the Reigns of the Tudors, 2 Vols. Repr. of 1877 ed. 44.50 (ISBN 0-384-69570-1). Johnson Repr.

Youngs, F. A. The Proclamations of the Tudor Queens. LC 75-30442. 304p. 1976. 46.50 (ISBN 0-521-21044-5). Cambridge U Pr.

GREAT BRITAIN–HISTORY–TUDORS, 1485-1603–BIBLIOGRAPHY

Booty, John E., ed. The Godly Kingdom of Tudor England: Great Books of the English Reformation. LC 81-80626. (Illus.). 288p. 1981. 14.95 (ISBN 0-8192-1287-3). Morehouse.

Levine, Mortimer, ed. Bibliographical Handbook on Tudor England, Fourteen Eighty-Five to Sixteen Hundred Three. (Bibliographical Handbooks of the Conference on British Studies). 1968. 17.50 (ISBN 0-521-05543-1). Cambridge U Pr.

Millward, J. S., ed. Sixteen Century, Fourteen Eighty-Five to Sixteen Three. (Portraits & Documents Ser.). (Illus.). 1968. pap. text ed. 2.50x (ISBN 0-09-057725-6). Humanities.

Read, Conyers, ed. Bibliography of British History: Tudor Period, Fourteen Eighty-Five to Sixteen Hundred Three. 2nd ed. 624p. 1978. Repr. of 1959 ed. 35.00x (ISBN 0-8476-6074-5). Rowman.

Tucker, Lena L. Bibliography of Fifteenth Century Literature, with Special Reference to the History of English Culture. 1974. lib. bdg. 49.95 (ISBN 0-87968-738-X). Gordon Pr.

GREAT BRITAIN–HISTORY–TUDORS, 1485-1603–FICTION

Major, Charles. When Knighthood Was in Flower. LC 70-126656. Repr. of 1898 ed. 24.00 (ISBN 0-404-04169-8). AMS Pr.

GREAT BRITAIN–HISTORY–TUDORS, 1485-1603–SOURCES

Adair, E. R. Sources for the History of the Council in the Sixteenth & Seventeenth Centuries. LC 70-118458. 1971. Repr. of 1924 ed. 8.95 (ISBN 0-8046-1206-4). Kennikat.

Bucer, Martin. A Treatise How by the Worde of God, Christian Mens Almose Oght to Be Distributed. LC 76-57360. (English Experience Ser.). 1977. Repr. of 1557 ed. lib. bdg. 3.50 (ISBN 90-221-0779-5). Walter J Johnson.

Chronicle of Queen Jane, & of Two Years of Queen Mary, & Especially of the Rebellion of Sir Thomas Wyatt. 1850. 19.50 (ISBN 0-384-08965-8). Johnson Repr.

Dickens, Arthur G. & Carr, Dorothy. Reformation in England to the Accession of Elizabeth 1. (Documents of Modern History Ser). (Orig.). 1968. pap. 4.95 (ISBN 0-312-66815-5). St Martin.

Esdaile, Arundell. Age of Elizabeth Fifteen Forty-Seven to Sixteen Three. LC 72-190600. 1931. lib. bdg. 8.50 (ISBN 0-8414-1112-3). Folcroft.

Gairdner, James, ed. Letters & Papers Illustrative to the Reigns of Richard III & Henry VII, 2 vols. LC 75-41107. Repr. of 1863 ed. Set. 72.50 (ISBN 0-404-14910-3). AMS Pr.

Gardiner, Stephen. Letters of Stephen Gardiner. Muller, James A., ed. Repr. of 1933 ed. lib. bdg. 23.25x (ISBN 0-8371-4223-7, GALE). Greenwood.

--Obedience in Church & State: Three Political Tracts. Janelle, Pierre, ed. LC 68-19272. 1968. Repr. of 1930 ed. lib. bdg. 14.00x (ISBN 0-8371-0081-X, GABW). Greenwood.

Giustiniani, Sebastiano. Four Years at the Court of Henry Eighth, 2 Vols. Brown, Rawdon, tr. from It. LC 75-133813. Repr. of 1854 ed. 37.50 (ISBN 0-404-02836-5). AMS Pr.

Hardyng, John. The Chronicle of J. Hardyng from the Firste Begynnyng of Englande. LC 76-57387. (English Experience Ser.: No. 805). 1977. Repr. of 1543 ed. lib. bdg. 72.00 (ISBN 90-221-0805-8). Walter J Johnson.

Hughes, Paul L. & Larkin, James F., eds. Tudor Royal Proclamations, Vols. 2 - 3, The Later Tudors, 1553-1603. LC 63-13965. 1969. Set. 75.00x (ISBN 0-300-00103-7). Yale U Pr.

Machin, Henry. Diary of Henry Machyn. Nichols, John G., ed. (Camden Society, London. Publications. First Ser.: No. 42). Repr. of 1848 ed. 42.00 (ISBN 0-404-50142-7). AMS Pr.

Pollard, Albert F., ed. Reign of Henry Seventh from Contemporary Sources, 3 Vols. LC 73-181970. Repr. of 1914 ed. Set. 75.00 (ISBN 0-404-05140-5); 25.00 ea. Vol. 1 (ISBN 0-404-05141-3). Vol. 2 (ISBN 0-404-05142-1). Vol. 3 (ISBN 0-404-05143-X). AMS Pr.

Rutland, John H. Rutland Papers. Repr. of 1842 ed. 15.50 (ISBN 0-384-52640-3). Johnson Repr.

--Rutland Papers Original Documents Illustrative of the Courts & Times of Henry Seven & Henry Eight. Jerden, William, ed. LC 17-1204. (Camden Society, London. Publications. First Ser.: No. 21). Repr. of 1842 ed. 14.00 (ISBN 0-404-50121-4). AMS Pr.

Williams, C. H., ed. English Historical Documents, 1485-1558, Vol. 5. 1967. 69.00x (ISBN 0-19-519504-3). Oxford U Pr.

GREAT BRITAIN–HISTORY–16TH CENTURY

see Great Britain–History–Tudors–1485-1603

GREAT BRITAIN–HISTORY–ELIZABETH, 1558-1603

Aske, James. Elizabetha Triumphans: Conteyning the Damned Practizes Used Ever Sithence Her Highnesse First Comming to the Crowne. LC 73-6111. (English Experience Ser.: No. 78). 36p. 1969. Repr. of 1588 ed. 9.50 (ISBN 9-0221-0078-2). Walter J Johnson.

Barlow, William. The Summe & Substance of the Conference at Hampton Court, January 14, 1603. LC 74-28829. (English Experience Ser.: No. 711). 1975. Repr. of 1604 ed. 9.50 (ISBN 90-221-0711-6). Walter J Johnson.

Birch, Thomas. Memoirs of the Reign of Queen Elizabeth, 2 Vols. LC 79-131513. Repr. of 1754 ed. Set. lib. bdg. 65.00 (ISBN 0-404-00909-3). Vol. 1 (ISBN 0-404-00910-7). Vol. 2 (ISBN 0-404-00911-5). AMS Pr.

Black, J. B. Reign of Elizabeth, Fifteen Fifty-Eight to Sixteen Three. 2nd ed. (Oxford History of England Ser.). 1959. 39.00x (ISBN 0-19-821701-3). Oxford U Pr.

Bland, D. S. Three Revels from the Inns of Court. 1981. 45.00x (ISBN 0-86127-402-4, Pub. by Avebury Pub England). State Mutual Bk.

Boris, Edna Z. Shakespeare's English Kings, the People & the Law: A Study in the Relationship Between the Tudor Constitution & the English History Plays. LC 76-19838. 261p. 1978. 16.50 (ISBN 0-8386-1990-8). Fairleigh Dickinson.

A Breefe Declaration of That Which Is Happened As Well Within As Without Oastend. LC 70-171781. (English Experience Ser.: No. 406). 8p. Repr. of 1602 ed. 11.50 (ISBN 90-221-0406-0). Walter J Johnson.

Buchanan, George 1506-1582. Deiure Regni Apud Scotos Dialogus. LC 73-6075. (English Experience Ser.: No. 80). 106p. 1969. Repr. of 1579 ed. 14.00 (ISBN 90-221-0080-4). Walter J Johnson.

Camden, William. Britannia, 4 vols. 2nd ed. LC 73-113571. (Illus.). Repr. of 1806 ed. Set. 145.00 (ISBN 0-404-01370-8). Vol. 1 (ISBN 0-404-01371-6). Vol. 2 (ISBN 0-404-01372-4). Vol. 3 (ISBN 0-404-01373-2). Vol. 4 (ISBN 0-404-01374-0). AMS Pr.

--History of the Most Renowned & Victorious Princess Elizabeth Late Queen of England: Selected Chapters. MacCaffrey, Wallace T., ed. LC 74-115682. (Classics of British Historical Literature Ser). 1972. pap. 3.45 (ISBN 0-226-09219-4, P399, Phoen). U of Chicago Pr.

--History of the Most Renowned & Victorious Princess Elizabeth, Late Queen of England. MacCaffrey, Wallace T., ed. LC 74-115682. (Classics of British Historical Literature Ser). 1970. text ed. 12.50x (ISBN 0-226-09218-6). U of Chicago Pr.

Cheyney, Edward P. A History of England from the Defeat of the Armada to the Death of Elizabeth, 2 vols. Set. 18.00 (ISBN 0-8446-1112-3). Peter Smith.

Churchyard, Thomas. A Lamentable & Pitifull Description of the Wofull Warres in Flaunders. LC 76-57372. (English Experience Ser.: No. 790). 1977. Repr. of 1578 ed. lib. bdg. 8.00 (ISBN 90-221-0790-6). Walter J Johnson.

Clark, Peter, et al, eds. English Commonwealth Fifteen Forty-Seven to Sixteen Forty: Essays in Politics & Society. LC 78-32060. (Illus.). 1979. text ed. 30.00x (ISBN 0-06-491171-3). B&N.

Collins, Arthur. Letters & Memorials of State, in the Reigns of Queen Mary, Queen Elizabeth, King James, King Charles the First, Part of the Reign of King Charles the Second, & Oliver's Usurpation, 2 Vols. LC 72-997. Repr. of 1746 ed. lib. bdg. 185.00 (ISBN 0-404-01631-6). AMS Pr.

Copley, Thomas. Letters of Sir Thomas Copley to Queen Elizabeth & Her Ministers. Christie, Richard C., ed. LC 74-80263. (Research & Source Works Ser.: No. 631). 1971. Repr. lib. bdg. 32.00 (ISBN 0-8337-0655-1). B Franklin.

Creighton, Mandell. The Age of Elizabeth. 1898. 10.00 (ISBN 0-8482-7255-2). Norwood Edns.

Davis, D. W. Elizabethans Errant. LC 67-16462. 1967. 9.50 (ISBN 0-8014-0098-8). Brown Bk.

De Bacan, Alvaro. Relation of the Expongnable Attempt & Conquest of the Ylande of Tercera. LC 76-57352. (English Experience Ser.: No. 772). 1977. Repr. of 1584 ed. lib. bdg. 6.00 (ISBN 90-221-0772-8). Walter J Johnson.

Devereux, Robert & Wingfield, Anthony. True Copie of a Discourse Written by a Gentleman, Employed in the Late Voyage of Spaine & Portingale. LC 78-38172. (English Experience Ser.: No. 449). 1972. Repr. of 1589 ed. 9.50 (ISBN 90-221-0449-4). Walter J Johnson.

Devlin, Christopher. Hamlet's Divinity & Other Essays. facs. ed. (Essay Index Reprint Ser). 1963. 13.00 (ISBN 0-8369-1915-7). Arno.

Durant, David N. Bess of Hardwick. LC 77-24459. 1978. 10.95 (ISBN 0-689-10835-4). Atheneum.

Elizabeth, Queen. The True Copie of a Letter from the Queens Maiesty to the Lord Mayor of London. LC 70-25636. (English Experience Ser.: No. 167). 8p. 1969. Repr. of 1586 ed. 7.00 (ISBN 90-221-0167-3). Walter J Johnson.

Esdaile, Arundell J. The Age of Elizabeth. LC 74-22280. 1974. Repr. of 1931 ed. lib. bdg. 8.50 (ISBN 0-8414-3935-4). Folcroft.

Fletcher, Anthony. Elizabethan Village. (Then & There Ser.). (Illus.). 1972. pap. text ed. 2.65x (ISBN 0-582-20409-7). Longman.
Ford, John. Fames Memoriall, or the Earle of Devonshire Deceased. LC 70-25888. (English Experience Ser.: No. 188). 56p. 1969. Repr. of 1606 ed. 8.00 (ISBN 90-221-0188-6). Walter J Johnson.
Fraser, Antonia. Mary Queen of Scots. 1978. 17.95 (ISBN 0-440-05261-0). Delacorte.
Gainsford, Thomas. The True Exemplary & Remarkable History of the Earle of Tirone. LC 68-54644. (English Experience Ser.: No. 25). 1968. Repr. of 1619 ed. 8.00 (ISBN 90-221-0025-1). Walter J Johnson.
Greaves, Richard L. Society & Religion in Elizabethan England. 832p. 1981. 39.50x (ISBN 0-8166-1030-4). U of Minn Pr.
Greenlaw, Edwin. Studies in Spenser's Historical Allegory. 1967. lib. bdg. 14.00x (ISBN 0-374-93249-2). Octagon.
Hall, Hubert. Society in the Elizabethan Age. 1976. lib. bdg. 59.95 (ISBN 0-8490-2620-2). Gordon Pr.
Haller, William. Elizabeth One & the Puritans. LC 64-7541. 1965. pap. 3.95 (ISBN 0-918016-24-X). Folger Bks.
Harington, John. Nugae Antiquae, 2 Vols. Park, Thomas, ed. LC 2-21609. Repr. of 1804 ed. 50.00 (ISBN 0-404-03125-0). AMS Pr.
Harrison, G. B. The Elizabethan Journals, 2 vols. Incl. Vol. 1. 1591-1597; Vol. 2. 1598-1603. 12.00 (ISBN 0-8446-2211-7). Peter Smith.
Harrison, G. B., ed. An Elizabethan Journal. 1974. 25.50x (ISBN 0-7100-7881-1). Routledge & Kegan.
Harrison, George B. Elizabethan England. LC 72-194440. 1930. lib. bdg. 6.50 (ISBN 0-8414-5010-2). Folcroft.
Hayward, John. Annals of the First Four Years of the Reign of Queen Elizabeth. Bruce, John, ed. (Camden Society, London. Publications, First Series: No. 7). Repr. of 1840 ed. 14.00 (ISBN 0-404-50107-9). AMS Pr.
--Annals of the First Four Years of the Reign of Queen Elizabeth. 1840. 15.50 (ISBN 0-384-21870-9). Johnson Repr.
Hicks, Leo. Elizabethan Problem: Some Aspects of the Careers of Two Exile-Adventurers. LC 64-24786. 1965. 22.50 (ISBN 0-8232-0625-4). Fordham.
Hudson, Winthrop S. The Cambridge Connection & the Elizabethan Settlement of Fifteen Fifty-Nine. LC 79-56513. x, 158p. 1980. 14.75 (ISBN 0-8223-0440-6). Duke.
Hume, Martin A. Great Lord Burghley. LC 75-137244. Repr. of 1898 ed. 18.00 (ISBN 0-404-03386-5). AMS Pr.
--Great Lord Burghley: A Study in Elizabethan Statecraft. LC 68-25244. (English Biography Ser., No. 31). 1969. Repr. of 1898 ed. lib. bdg. 49.95 (ISBN 0-8383-0205-X). Haskell.
Jones, Eldred D. Elizabethan Image of Africa. LC 76-160290. (Folger Guides to the Age of Shakespeare). 1971. pap. 3.95 (ISBN 0-918016-27-4). Folger Bks.
Kempe, William. A Dutiful Inuective Against the Moste Haynous Treasons of Ballard & Babington. LC 74-38112. (English Experience Ser.: No. 395). 8p. 1971. Repr. of 1587 ed. 11.50 (ISBN 90-221-0395-1). Walter J Johnson.
Kinney, Arthur F., ed. Elizabethan Backgrounds: Historical Documents of the Age of Elizabeth I. (Illus.). xi, 412p. (Orig.). 1975. 32.50 (ISBN 0-208-01424-1, Archon). Shoe String.
Klein, Arthur J. Intolerance in the Reign of Elizabeth, Queen of England. LC 67-27614. 1968. Repr. of 1917 ed. 12.50 (ISBN 0-8046-0249-2). Kennikat.
Laing, Malcolm. Preliminary Dissertation on the Participation of Mary Queen of Scots, in the Murder of Darnley, 2 vols. Repr. 150.00 (ISBN 0-8274-3201-1). R West.
LaMar, Virginia A. English Dress in the Age of Shakespeare. LC 59-1285. (Folger Guides to the Age of Shakespeare). 1958. pap. 3.95 (ISBN 0-918016-31-2). Folger Bks.
Lewkenor, Lewis. A Discourse of the Usage of the English Fugitives by the Spaniard. LC 73-6149. (English Experience Ser.: No. 612). 80p. 1973. Repr. of 1595 ed. 8.00 (ISBN 90-221-0612-8). Walter J Johnson.
Lievsay, John L. Elizabethan Image of Italy. LC 64-9036. (Folger Guides to the Age of Shakespeare). 1964. pap. 3.95 (ISBN 0-918016-26-6). Folger Bks.
MacCaffrey, Wallace T. Queen Elizabeth & the Making of Policy, 1572-1588. LC 80-8564. 536p. 1981. 37.50x (ISBN 0-691-05324-3); pap. 15.00x (ISBN 0-691-10112-4). Princeton U Pr.
MacDonald, Michael. Mystical Bedlam: Madness, Anxiety, & Healing in Seventeenth Century England. LC 80-25787. (Cambridge Monographs on the History of Medicine). (Illus.). 300p. Date not set. price not set (ISBN 0-521-23170-1). Cambridge U Pr.
Milward, Peter. Religious Controversies of the Elizabethan Age: A Survey of Printed Sources. LC 77-80038. 1977. 21.00x (ISBN 0-8032-0923-1). U of Nebr Pr.
Percival, Rachel A. The Court of Elizabeth the First. (Illus.). 110p. 1976. 13.75x (ISBN 0-8476-6238-1). Rowman.
Plowden, Alison. Danger to Elizabeth. LC 72-83095. (Illus.). 240p. 1973. 25.00x (ISBN 0-8128-1620-X). Stein & Day.
Pollen, John H. English Catholics in the Reign of Queen Elizabeth: A Study of Their Politics, Civil Life & Government. 1971. Repr. of 1920 ed. lib. bdg. 24.50 (ISBN 0-8337-2798-2). B Franklin.
Pritchard, Arnold. Catholic Loyalism in Elizabethan England. LC 78-10208. 1979. 20.00x (ISBN 0-8078-1345-1). U of NC Pr.
Read, Conyers. The Government of England Under Elizabeth. LC 79-65980. (Folger Guides to the Age of Shakespeare). 1979. pap. 3.95 (ISBN 0-918016-07-X). Folger Bks.
Reynolds, George F. Elizabethan Studies & Other Studies: In Honor of George F. Reynolds. 1977. Repr. of 1945 ed. lib. bdg. 35.00 (ISBN 0-8495-4514-5). Arden Lib.
Ross, Williamson H. Sir Walter Raleigh. LC 78-17033. 1978. Repr. of 1951 ed. lib. bdg. 19.75x (ISBN 0-313-20577-9, ROSI). Greenwood.
Rowse, A. L. Elizabethan Renaissance: The Cultural Achievement. (Illus.). 1972. 12.50 (ISBN 0-684-12965-5, ScribT). Scribner.
--England of Elizabeth. LC 78-53293. 562p. 1978. 25.00 (ISBN 0-299-07720-9); pap. 8.95 (ISBN 0-299-07724-1). U of Wis Pr.
Rowse, Alfred L. The Elizabethans & America. LC 78-5090. (Illus.). 1978. Repr. of 1959 ed. lib. bdg. 23.50x (ISBN 0-8371-9350-8, ROELA). Greenwood.
Russell, John. Shakespeare's Country. (Illus.). 152p. 1980. Repr. lib. bdg. 25.00 (ISBN 0-89987-708-7). Darby Bks.
Sharpe, Kevin. Sir Robert Cotton, Fifteen Eighty-Six to Sixteen Thirty-One: History & Politics in Early Modern England. (OHM Ser.). (Illus.). 284p. 1979. 36.00x (ISBN 0-19-821877-X). Oxford U Pr.
Siegel, Paul. Shakespearean Tragedy & the Elizabethan Compromise. LC 78-39208. (Select Bibliographies Reprint Ser.). Repr. of 1957 ed. 17.00 (ISBN 0-8369-6810-7). Arno.
Skilliter, Susan. William Harborne & the Trade with Turkey: Secret Agent, 1578-1581. (Illus.). 1978. 49.00x (ISBN 0-19-725971-5). Oxford U Pr.
Smith, A. Hassell. County & Court: Government & Politics in Norfolk 1558-1603. 392p. 1974. 54.00x (ISBN 0-19-822407-9). Oxford U Pr.
Smith, Alan G. Servant of the Cecils: The Life of Sir Michael Hickes, 1543-1612. (Illus.). 221p. 1977. 17.50x (ISBN 0-87471-933-X). Rowman.
--William Cecil. LC 73-155113. (English Biography Ser., No. 31). 1971. Repr. of 1934 ed. lib. bdg. 37.95 (ISBN 0-8383-1286-1). Haskell.
Strong, Roy & Oman, Julia T. Elizabeth R. LC 71-179699. 1972. 25.00x (ISBN 0-8128-1432-0). Stein & Day.
Vale, Marcia. The Gentleman's Recreations: Accomplishments & Pastimes of the English Gentleman 1580-1630. (Elizabethan & Jacobean Culture Ser). (Illus.). 182p. 1977. 16.50x (ISBN 0-8476-6009-5). Rowman.
Wark, K. R. Elizabethan Recusancy in Cheshire. 208p. 1971. 33.00x (ISBN 0-7190-1154-X, Pub. by Manchester U Pr England). State Mutual Bk.
--Elizabethan Recusancy in Cheshire. (Illus.). 200p. 1971. 14.75x (ISBN 0-87471-389-7). Rowman.
Whetstone, George. The Censure of a Loyal Subject; Upon Certaine Noted Speach & Behaviours of Those Fourteene Notable Traitors, at the Place of Their Executions, the Xx & Xxi, of September Last Past. LC 73-6168. (English Experience Ser.: No. 631). 52p. 1973. Repr. of 1587 ed. 5.00 (ISBN 90-221-0631-4). Walter J Johnson.
Winstanley, Lilian. Hamlet & the Scottish Succession. facsimile ed. LC 78-109661. (Select Bibliographies Reprint Ser). 1921. 16.00 (ISBN 0-8369-5270-7). Arno.
Winstantley, Lilian. Hamlet & the Scottish Succession. LC 72-194431. 1921. lib. bdg. 10.00 (ISBN 0-8414-9778-8). Folcroft.
Winwood, Ralph. Memorials of Affairs of State in the Reigns of Queen Elizabeth & King James First, 3 Vols. Sawyer, Edmund, ed. LC 75-178310. Repr. of 1725 ed. lib. bdg. 195.00 (ISBN 0-404-07020-5). AMS Pr.
Wright, Louis B. Middle Class Culture in Elizabethan England. 733p. 1980. Repr. of 1935 ed. lib. bdg. 45.00x (ISBN 0-374-98780-7). Octagon.
Youngs, F. A. The Proclamations of the Tudor Queens. LC 75-30442. 304p. 1976. 46.50 (ISBN 0-521-21044-5). Cambridge U Pr.
Zins, Henryk. England & the Baltic in the Elizabethan Era. Stevens, H. S., tr. from Pol. 347p. 1972. 21.50x (ISBN 0-87471-117-7). Rowman.

GREAT BRITAIN–HISTORY–ELIZABETH, 1558-1603–FICTION

Kingsley, Charles. Westward Ho. (Classics Ser). (gr. 8 up). 1968. pap. 1.25 (ISBN 0-8049-0184-8, CL-184). Airmont.
Scott, Walter. Kenilworth. new ed. (Classics Series). (gr. 10 up). 1968. pap. 0.75 (ISBN 0-8049-0193-7, CL-193). Airmont.
Scott, Sir Walter. Kenilworth. 1955. 10.95x (ISBN 0-460-00135-3, Evman). Biblio Dist.
Trease, Geoffrey. Cue for Treason. (Illus.). (gr. 7 up). 1941. 6.95 (ISBN 0-8149-0434-3). Vanguard.
Trewin, John C. Portrait of the Shakespeare Country. LC 75-503070. (Portrait Bks.). (Illus.). 1970. 10.50x (ISBN 0-7091-1342-0). Intl Pubns Serv.

GREAT BRITAIN–HISTORY–ELIZABETH, 1558-1603–JUVENILE FICTION

Eagar, Frances. Time Tangle. LC 77-1612. (gr. 6 up). 1977. 7.95 (ISBN 0-525-66536-6). Elsevier-Nelson.
Horizon Magazine Editors. Shakespeare's England. LC 64-12231. (Horizon Caravel Bks.). 154p. (YA) (gr. 7 up). 1964. PLB 12.89 (ISBN 0-06-022591-2, HarpJ). Har-Row.
Lane, Peter. Elizabethan England. (Visual Sources Ser.). (Illus.). 96p. (gr. 7-12). 1981. 16.95 (ISBN 0-7134-3566-6, Pub. by Batsford England). David & Charles.

GREAT BRITAIN–HISTORY–ELIZABETH, 1558-1603–SOURCES

Camden, William. History of Elizabeth I: The History of the Renowned & Victorious Princess Elizabeth. 4th ed. LC 70-113570. Repr. of 1688 ed. 90.00 (ISBN 0-404-01366-X). AMS Pr.
Cecil, William. A Declaration of the Fauourable Dealing of Her Maiesties Commissioners Appointed for the Examination of Certaine Traitours. LC 73-25637. (English Experience Ser.: No. 113). 1969. Repr. of 1583 ed. 7.00 (ISBN 90-221-0113-4). Walter J Johnson.
Chamberlain, John. The Letters of John Chamberlain, 2 vols. McClure, Norman E., ed. LC 78-23784. 1979. Repr. of 1939 ed. Set. lib. bdg. 72.50x (ISBN 0-313-20710-0, CHLE). Greenwood.
--Letters Written by John Chamberlain During the Reign of Queen Elizabeth. Williams, Sarah, ed. (Camden Society, London. Publications. First Ser.: No. 79). Repr. of 1861 ed. 26.00 (ISBN 0-404-50179-6). AMS Pr.
--Letters Written by John Chamberlain During the Reign of Queen Elizabeth. 1861. 23.00 (ISBN 0-384-08425-7). Johnson Repr.
Copley, Thomas. Letters of Sir Thomas Copley to Queen Elizabeth & Her Ministers. Christie, Richard C., ed. LC 74-80263. (Research & Source Works Ser.: No. 631). 1971. Repr. lib. bdg. 32.00 (ISBN 0-8337-0655-1). B Franklin.
D'Ewes, Simonds, compiled by. A Compleat Journal of the Votes, Speeches & Debates Both of the House of Lords & House of Commons Throughout the Whole Reign of Queen Elizabeth, of Glorious Memory. LC 74-75952. 1974. Repr. of 1693 ed. 35.00 (ISBN 0-8420-1739-9). Scholarly Res Inc.
Egerton, Francis. Egerton Papers. Collier, J. Payne, ed. LC 74-164767. (Camden Society, London. Publications, First Ser.: No. 12). Repr. of 1840 ed. 38.50 (ISBN 0-404-50112-5). AMS Pr.
Elizabeth First Queen Of England. Letters of Queen Elizabeth & James Sixth of Scotland. Bruce, John, ed. LC 75-166015. (Camden Society, London. Publications, First Ser.: No. 46). Repr. of 1849 ed. 17.50 (ISBN 0-404-50146-X). AMS Pr.
Elizabeth - Queen Of England. Letters of Queen Elizabeth & King James Sixth of Scotland. 1849. 19.50 (ISBN 0-384-14135-8). Johnson Repr.
Ellesmere, Francis E. Egerton Papers. 1840. 42.50 (ISBN 0-384-14165-X). Johnson Repr.
Guicciardini, Ludovico. The Description of the Low Countreys Gathered into an Epitome. LC 76-57386. (English Experience Ser.: No. 804). 1977. Repr. of 1593 ed. lib. bdg. 18.50 (ISBN 90-221-0804-X). Walter J Johnson.
Hurstfield, Joel & Smith, Alan G., eds. Elizabethan People: State & Society. LC 72-85196. (Documents of Modern History Ser.). 1972. 5.95 (ISBN 0-312-24290-5). St Martin.
James First - King Of England. Correspondence of King James Sixth of Scotland with Sir Robert Cecil & Others in England, During the Reign of Queen Elizabeth. Bruce, John, ed. (Camden Society, London, Publications, First Ser.: No. 78). Repr. of 1861 ed. 14.00 (ISBN 0-404-50178-8). AMS Pr.
James First, King of Great Britain. Correspondence of King James Sixth of Scotland with Sir Robert Cecil & Others in England. 1861. 15.50 (ISBN 0-384-26740-8). Johnson Repr.
Kaula, David. Shakespeare & the Archpriest Controversy: A Study of Some New Sources. LC 74-78510. (Studies in English Literature: No. 85). 132p. 1975. pap. text ed. 26.25x (ISBN 90-2793-466-5). Mouton.
Machin, Henry. Diary of Henry Machyn. Nichols, John G., ed. (Camden Society, London. Publications. First Ser.: No. 42). Repr. of 1848 ed. 42.00 (ISBN 0-404-50142-7). AMS Pr.
Manningham, John. Diary of John Manningham. Bruce, John, ed. (Camden Society. London. Publications, First Series: No. 99). Repr. of 1868 ed. 17.50 (ISBN 0-404-50199-0). AMS Pr.
--Diary of John Manningham of the Middle Temple, & of Bradbourne, Kent, Barrister-at-Law, 1602-1603. Repr. of 1868 ed. 19.50 (ISBN 0-384-35175-1). Johnson Repr.
--The Diary of John Manningham of the Middle Temple, 1602-1603. Sorlien, Robert P., ed. LC 74-22553. 481p. 1976. text ed. 27.50x (ISBN 0-87451-113-5). U Pr of New Eng.
Strype, John. Historical Collections of the Life & Acts of John Aylmer, Bishop of London, in the Reign of Queen Elizabeth. LC 74-979. 244p. 1974. Repr. of 1821 ed. lib. bdg. 22.50 (ISBN 0-8337-4427-5). B Franklin.

GREAT BRITAIN–HISTORY–17TH CENTURY

see Great Britain–History–Stuarts, 1603-1714

GREAT BRITAIN–HISTORY–STUARTS, 1603-1714

Here are entered works on England in the Stuart period as a whole or in part, except for the subdivisions listed immediately below.

Aiken, William A. & Henning, Basil D., eds. Conflict in Stuart England: Essays in Honour of Wallace Notestein. 1970. Repr. of 1960 ed. 19.50 (ISBN 0-208-01029-7, Archon). Shoe String.
Andrews, Charles M. British Committees, Commissions, & Councils of Trade & Plantations: 1622-1675. LC 78-63925. (Johns Hopkins University. Studies in the Social Sciences. Twenty-Sixth Ser. 1908: 1-3). Repr. of 1908 ed. 11.50 (ISBN 0-404-61175-3). AMS Pr.
Appleby, Joyce O. Economic Thought & Ideology in Seventeenth-Century England. LC 77-85527. 304p. 1980. pap. 4.95 (ISBN 0-691-00779-9). Princeton U Pr.
Ashley, Maurice. England in the Seventeenth Century. new ed. 275p. 1980. 20.00x (ISBN 0-686-70947-0); pap. 9.95 (ISBN 0-686-70948-9). B&N.
--The House of Stuart: Its Rise & Fall. (Illus.). 237p. 1980. 22.50x (ISBN 0-460-04458-3, Pub. by J. M. Dent England). Biblio Dist.
--Life in Stuart England. 1967. 19.95 (ISBN 0-7134-1457-X, Pub. by Batsford England). David & Charles.
Ault, Susan & Worman, B. Tudors & Stuarts. (Illus.). 9.50x (ISBN 0-392-05218-0, SpS). Sportshelf.
Bachrach, A. G. Sir Constantine Huygens & Britain: 1597-1619, Vol. 1. (Publications of the Sir Thomas Browne Institute Ser: No. 1). 1962. pap. 26.00 (ISBN 90-6021-059-X, Pub. by Leiden Univ Holland). Kluwer Boston.
Barnes, Thomas G. List & Index to the Proceedings in Star Chamber for the Reign of James I (1603-1625) in the Public Record Office, London: Class STAC8, 3 vols. LC 75-542. 1975. 120.00 set (ISBN 0-910058-68-7). Am Bar Foun.
Blackwood, B. G. The Lancashire Gentry & the Great Rebellion 1640-60. (Illus.). 1978. text ed. 33.75x (ISBN 0-7190-1334-8). Humanities.
Borough, John. Notes of the Treaty Carried on at Ripon Between King Charles First & the Covenanters of Scotland, A. D. 1640. Bruce, John, ed. (Camden Society, London. Publications, First Ser.: No. 100). Repr. of 1869 ed. 14.00 (ISBN 0-404-50200-8). AMS Pr.
--Notes of the Treaty Carried on at Ripon Between King Charles First & the Covenanters of Scotland, A. D. 1640. 1869. 15.50 (ISBN 0-384-05145-6). Johnson Repr.
Braun, Montgomery W. The Life & Loves of Queen Anne & the History of Great Britain. (An Intimate Life of Man Library Book). (Illus.). 1979. 27.85 (ISBN 0-89266-172-0). Am Classical Coll Pr.
Bridenbaugh, Carl. Vexed & Troubled Englishman 1590-1642. LC 68-17604. 512p. 1976. pap. 6.95 (ISBN 0-19-502020-0, GB453, GB). Oxford U Pr.
--Vexed & Troubled Englishmen, 1590-1642. 1968. 19.95 (ISBN 0-19-500493-0). Oxford U Pr.
Brinkley, Roberta F. Arthurian Legend in the Seventeenth Century. LC 67-18755. 1970. Repr. lib. bdg. 14.50x (ISBN 0-374-90988-1). Octagon.
Cassavetti, Eillen. The Lion & the Lilies: The Stuarts & France. 1977. text ed. 20.75x (ISBN 0-354-04136-3). Humanities.

Chapman, Hester. Four Fine Gentlemen. LC 77-20589. (Illus.). 1978. 17.95x (ISBN 0-8032-1401-4). U of Nebr Pr.

Chartres, J. A. Internal Trade in England 1500-1700. (Studies in Economic & Social History). 1977. pap. text ed. 4.00x (ISBN 0-333-18358-4). Humanities.

Clark, George N. Later Stuarts, 1660-1714. 2nd ed. (Oxford History of England Ser.). 1955. 39.50x (ISBN 0-19-821702-1). Oxford U Pr.

Clark, Peter, et al, eds. English Commonwealth Fifteen Forty-Seven to Sixteen Forty: Essays in Politics & Society. LC 78-32060. (Illus.). 1979. text ed. 30.00x (ISBN 0-06-491171-3). B&N.

Clay, Christopher. Public Finance & Private Wealth: The Career of Sir Stephen Fox, 1627-1716. 1978. 54.00x (ISBN 0-19-822467-2). Oxford U Pr.

Cole, Rufus. Human History: The Seventeenth Century & the Stuart Family, 2 Vols. LC 59-8900. 1959. 10.00 set (ISBN 0-87027-042-7); Vol. 1. (ISBN 0-87027-047-8); Vol. 2. (ISBN 0-87027-048-6). Wheelwright.

Collins, Arthur. Letters & Memorials of State, in the Reigns of Queen Mary, Queen Elizabeth, King James, King Charles the First, Part of the Reign of King Charles the Second, & Oliver's Usurpation, 2 Vols. LC 72-997. Repr. of 1746 ed. lib. bdg. 185.00 (ISBN 0-404-01631-6). AMS Pr.

Cook, Chris & Wroughton, John. English Historical Facts: 1603-1688. 231p. 1980. 32.50x (ISBN 0-8476-6295-0). Rowman.

Cope, Esther S. & Coates, Willson H. Short Parliament of Sixteen-Forty: Proceedings. 340p. 1977. 18.50x (ISBN 0-8476-1473-5). Rowman.

Coward, Barry. The Stuart Age. LC 79-42887. (A History of England Ser.). (Illus.). 512p. 1980. text ed. 32.00x (ISBN 0-582-48279-8); pap. text ed. 18.95x (ISBN 0-582-48833-8). Longman.

Daly, James. Cosmic Harmony & Political Thinking in Early Stuart England. (Transactions Ser.: Vol. 69, Pt. 7). 1979. 6.00 (ISBN 0-87169-697-5). Am Philos.

Davies, D. W. Dutch Influences on English Culture, 1558-1625. LC 64-18226. (Folger Guides to the Age of Shakespeare). 1964. pap. 3.95 (ISBN 0-918016-13-4). Folger Bks.

Davies, Godfrey. Early Stuarts, 1603-1660. 2nd ed. (Illus.). 1959. 29.95 (ISBN 0-19-821704-8). Oxford U Pr.

--Essays on the Later Stuarts. LC 74-20075. (Illus.). 133p. 1975. Repr. of 1958 ed. lib. bdg. 15.00x (ISBN 0-8371-7842-8, DAEL). Greenwood.

D'Ewes, Simonds. Journal of Sir Simonds D'Ewes from the First Recess of the Long Parliament to the Withdrawal of King Charles from London. Coates, Willson H., ed. LC 71-122400. 1970. Repr. of 1942 ed. 27.50 (ISBN 0-208-00948-5, Archon). Shoe String.

Farmer, David L. Britain & the Stuarts 1603-1714. (The Bell Modern History Ser.). 1965. text ed. 7.25x (ISBN 0-7135-0445-5). Humanities.

Fedorowicz, J. K. England's Baltic Trade in the Early Seventeenth Century. LC 78-67629. (Cambridge Studies in the Economic History). (Illus.). 1980. 42.50 (ISBN 0-521-22425-X). Cambridge U Pr.

--England's Baltic Trade in the Early Seventeenth Century. LC 78-67629. (Cambridge Studies in the Economic History). (Illus.). 1980. 42.50 (ISBN 0-521-22425-X). Cambridge U Pr.

Feiling, Keith. British Foreign Policy, Sixteen Sixty to Sixteen Seventy-Two. 385p. 1968. Repr. of 1930 ed. 28.50x (ISBN 0-7146-1473-4, F Cass Co). Biblio Dist.

Firth, C. H. Stuart Tracts. LC 64-16747. (Arber's an English Garner Ser.). 1964. Repr. of 1890 ed. 13.50x (ISBN 0-8154-0071-3). Cooper Sq.

Firth, C. H., intro. by. Stuart Tracts, Sixteen Three to Sixteen Ninety-Three. Straka, Gerald M., ed. LC 72-83161. (English Studies Ser.). 1972. Repr. of 1903 ed. lib. bdg. 34.00 (ISBN 0-8420-1419-5). Scholarly Res Inc.

Fletcher, Anthony. A County Community in Peace & War: Sussex 1600-1660. (Illus.). 470p. 1976. text ed. 36.00x (ISBN 0-582-50024-9). Longman.

Franklin, J. H. John Locke & the Theory of Sovereignty. LC 77-80833. (Studies in the History & Theory of Politics). 1978. 19.95 (ISBN 0-521-21758-X). Cambridge U Pr.

Gardiner, Samuel R. The First Two Stuarts & the Puritan Revolution, 1603-1660. 1978. Repr. of 1911 ed. lib. bdg. 20.00 (ISBN 0-8492-4925-2). R West.

--The First Two Stuarts & the Puritan Revolution: 1603-1660. 1977. Repr. of 1891 ed. lib. bdg. 25.00 (ISBN 0-8495-1911-X). Arden Lib.

--History of England, 1603-1656, 18 vols. in 3 sections. Incl. From the Accession of James First to the Outbreak of Civil War. 1603-1642, 10 vols. 265.00 (ISBN 0-404-02740-7); History of the Great Civil War. 1642-1649, 4 vols. 105.00 (ISBN 0-404-02780-6); History of the Commonwealth & Protectorate. 1649-1656, 4 vols. 105.00 (ISBN 0-404-02760-1). LC 79-168096. Repr. of 1903 ed. Set. 475.00 (ISBN 0-404-02720-2). AMS Pr.

Gillespie, James E. The Influence of Oversea Expansion on England to 1700. 1972. lib. bdg. 17.50x (ISBN 0-374-93079-1). Octagon.

Glanvill, John & Martin, Henry. The Copies of Two Speeches in Parliament. The One by John Glanvill, Esquire. The Other by Sir Henry Martin, Knight. LC 74-28858. (English Experience Ser.: No. 739). 1975. Repr. of 1628 ed. 3.50 (ISBN 90-221-0739-6). Walter J Johnson.

Glassey, Lionel K. Politics & the Appointment of Justices of the Peace: 1675-1720. (Historical Monographs). 1979. 29.00x (ISBN 0-19-821875-3). Oxford U Pr.

Gough, Richard. History of Myddle, 17th Century England. 35.00 (ISBN 0-87556-105-5). Saifer.

Greene, Jack P. Great Britain & the American Colonies, Sixteen Six to Seventeen Sixty-Three. 1979. pap. text ed. write for info. (ISBN 0-391-01240-1). Humanities.

Gruenfelder, John K. Influence in Early Stuart Elections, 1604-1640. 294p. 1981. 22.50 (ISBN 0-8142-0316-7). Ohio St U Pr.

Guy, Henry. Moneys Received & Paid for Secret Services of Charles II & James II. 15.50 (ISBN 0-384-20490-2). Johnson Repr.

Hale, E. The Fall of the Stuarts & Western Europe from 1678 to 1697. 1892. Repr. 10.00 (ISBN 0-685-43047-2). Norwood Edns.

Haley, K. H., ed. The Stuarts. LC 73-82822. 224p. 1973. 17.95 (ISBN 0-312-76930-X). St Martin.

Haller, William. Tracts on Liberty in the Puritan Revolution, 1638-1647, 3 Vols. 1965. lib. bdg. 65.00x (ISBN 0-374-93401-0). Octagon.

Hartman, Cyril H. Cavalier Spirit & Its Influence on the Life & Work of Richard Lovelace. LC 74-11254. 1925. lib. bdg. 17.50 (ISBN 0-8414-4830-2). Folcroft.

Hartmann, Cyril H. The Cavalier Spirit. LC 72-3666. (English Literature Ser., No. 33). 1972. Repr. of 1925 ed. lib. bdg. 33.95 (ISBN 0-8383-1560-7). Haskell.

Hervey, Mary F. Life, Correspondence & Collections of Thomas Howard, Earl of Arundel. LC 21-10187. 1921. 24.00 (ISBN 0-527-39800-4). Kraus Repr.

Hexter, Jack H. Reign of King Pym. (Historical Studies: No. 48). 1941. 10.00x (ISBN 0-674-75401-8). Harvard U Pr.

Hill, Christopher. Century of Revolution, 1603-1714. 1966. pap. 5.95 (ISBN 0-393-00365-5, Norton Lib). Norton.

--Change & Continuity in Seventeenth-Century England. LC 74-12878. 1975. 17.50x (ISBN 0-674-10765-9). Harvard U Pr.

His Majesties Declaration Concerning His Proceedings with His Subjects of Scotland. LC 70-25707. (English Experience Ser.: No. 310). 1971. Repr. of 1640 ed. 9.50 (ISBN 90-221-0310-2). Walter J Johnson.

His Majesties Proclamation in Scotland with an Explanation of the Oath & Covenant. LC 74-80216. (English Experience Ser.: No. 692). 1974. Repr. of 1639 ed. 3.50 (ISBN 90-221-0692-6). Walter J Johnson.

Hoeniger, F. D. & Hoeniger, J. F. Growth of Natural History in Stuart England: From Gerard to the Royal Society. LC 69-17335. (Folger Guides to the Age of Shakespeare). 1969. pap. 3.95 (ISBN 0-8139-0264-9). Folger Bks.

Hook, Judith. The Baroque Age of England. (Illus.). 207p. 1976. 30.00 (ISBN 0-500-23229-6). Transatlantic.

Hughes, Ann, ed. Seventeenth-Century England: A Changing Culture, Vol. 1: Primary Sources. 1981. 28.50x (ISBN 0-389-20168-5). B&N.

Hume, Martin A. Sir Walter Raleigh: The British Dominion of the West. 1977. Repr. of 1906 ed. lib. bdg. 40.00 (ISBN 0-8492-1143-3). R West.

Innes, Arthur D. Leading Figures in English History: Tudor & Stewart Period. facs. ed. LC 67-23233. (Essay Index Reprint Ser). 1931. 18.00 (ISBN 0-8369-0559-8). Arno.

Jack, Sybil M. Trade & Industry in Tudor & Stuart England. (Historical Problems - Studies & Documents). 1977. text ed. 29.95x (ISBN 0-04-942155-7); pap. text ed. 12.50x (ISBN 0-04-942156-5). Allen Unwin.

Johnson, Robert C., et al, eds. Commons Debates 1628, 3 vols. Incl. Vol. I. Introduction & Reference Materials. 15.00x (ISBN 0-300-02033-3); Vol. II. 17 March-19 April 1628. 40.00x (ISBN 0-300-01946-7); Vol. III. 21 April-27 May 1628. 45.00x (ISBN 0-300-02048-1); Vol. IV. May 28 - June 26, 1628. (Illus.). 1978. 45.00x (ISBN 0-300-02050-3). LC 75-43321. 1977. Set. 80.00x (ISBN 0-300-02161-5). Yale U Pr.

Jones, James R. Britain & Europe in the Seventeenth Century. (Foundations of Modern History Ser). 1966. pap. 3.95x (ISBN 0-393-09465-0, NortonC). Norton.

Jones, Madeline. Stuart People. 1978. 16.95 (ISBN 0-7134-0617-8, Pub. by Batsford England). David & Charles.

Kenyon, J. P. Stuart England. 1978. pap. 3.50 (ISBN 0-14-022076-3, Pelican). Penguin.

Kenyon, J. R. Stuart England. LC 78-52750. 1978. 12.95x (ISBN 0-312-76909-1). St Martin.

Kepler, J. S. The Exchange of Christendom: The International Entrepot at Dover, 1622-1651. 200p. 1976. text ed. 19.50x (ISBN 0-7185-1144-1, Leicester). Humanities.

Lane, Peter. The Stuart Age. 96p. 1980. 14.95 (ISBN 0-7134-0037-4, Pub. by Batsford England). David & Charles.

Larkin, James F. & Hughes, Paul L., eds. Stuart Royal Proclamations: Royal Proclamations of King James I 1603-1625, Vol. 1. 716p. 1974. 19.00x (ISBN 0-19-822372-2). Oxford U Pr.

Larking, Lambert B., ed. Proceedings Principally in the County of Kent, in Connection with the Parliaments Called in 1640, & Especially with the Committee of Religion Appointed in That Year. (Camden Society, London. Publications, First Series: No. 80a). Repr. of 1862 ed. 28.00 (ISBN 0-404-50180-X). Ams Pr.

--Proceedings, Principally in the County of Kent, in Connection with the Parliaments Called in 1640. Repr. of 1862 ed. 31.00 (ISBN 0-384-31380-9). Johnson Repr.

Laurance Urdang Associates, ed. Lives of the Stuart Age: 1603-1714. LC 75-39126. (Illus.). 500p. 1976. text ed. 25.00x (ISBN 0-06-494330-5). B&N.

Lockyer, Roger. Tudor & Stuart Britain: Fourteen Seventy-One to Seventeen-Fourteen. (Illus.). 1964. 9.95 (ISBN 0-312-82250-2). St Martin.

Lodge, Richard. History of England from the Restoration to the Death of William Third 1660-1702. LC 69-13975. 1969. Repr. of 1910 ed. lib. bdg. 20.00x (ISBN 0-8371-0935-3, LOHE). Greenwood.

--History of England from the Restoration to the Death of William Third: Sixteen-Sixty to Seventeen Hundred-Two. Repr. of 1910 ed. 24.00 (ISBN 0-527-00853-2). Kraus Repr.

Luttrell, Narcissus. A Brief Historical Relation of State Affairs from September, 1678 to April, 1714, 6 vols. Straka, Gerald M., ed. LC 72-83165. (English Studies Ser.). 1972. Repr. of 1857 ed. Set. lib. bdg. 220.00 (ISBN 0-8420-1423-3). Scholarly Res Inc.

Lyon, Thomas. The Theory of Religious Liberty in England, 1603-1639. 1972. lib. bdg. 15.00x (ISBN 0-374-95212-4). Octagon.

Macfarlane, Alan. The Justice & the Mare's Ale: Law & Disorder in Seventeenth-Century England. (Illus.). 225p. 1981. 19.95 (ISBN 0-521-23949-4). Cambridge U Pr.

McGee, J. Sears. The Godly Man in Stuart England: Anglicans, Puritans & the Two Tables, 1620-1670. LC 74-43325. (Historical Publications, Miscellany Ser.: No. 110). 1976. 20.00x (ISBN 0-300-01637-9). Yale U Pr.

Mathew, David. The Age of Charles I. LC 77-24690. 1977. Repr. of 1951 ed. lib. bdg. 30.00 (ISBN 0-8414-6214-3). Folcroft.

--Jacobean Age. LC 72-118488. 1971. Repr. of 1938 ed. 16.50 (ISBN 0-8046-1237-4). Kennikat.

Montague, F. C. History of England from the Accession of James First to the Restoration: Sixteen Hundred-Three to Sixteen Sixty. Repr. of 1907 ed. 24.00 (ISBN 0-527-00852-4). Kraus Repr.

Montague, Francis C. History of England from the Accession of James First to the Restoration, 1603-1660. LC 78-5631. (Political History of England: No. 7). Repr. of 1907 ed. 22.50 (ISBN 0-404-50777-8). AMS Pr.

--History of England from the Accession of James First to the Restoration, 1603-1660. LC 69-14000. 1969. Repr. of 1907 ed. lib. bdg. 20.00x (ISBN 0-8371-0936-1, MOHE). Greenwood.

Morrill, J. S. Seventeenth Century Britain, Sixteen Hundred & Three to Seventeen Fourteen. (Critical Bibliographies Ser.). 188p. 1980. 17.50 (ISBN 0-208-01785-2, Archon). Shoe String.

Morris, Christopher. The Oxford Book of Tudor Anthems. 1978. pap. 10.00 (ISBN 0-19-353325-1). Oxford U Pr.

Munday, Anthony. The English Roman Life. Ayres, Phillip J., ed. (Studies in Tudor & Stewart Literature Ser.). (Illus.). 142p. 1980. 22.00 (ISBN 0-19-812635-2). Oxford U Pr.

Muriell, Christopher. An Answer Unto the Catholiques Supplication, Presented Unto the Kings Maiestie, for a Tolleration of Popish Religion in England...Annexed the Supplication of the Papists. LC 74-28874. (English Experience Ser.: No. 753). 1975. Repr. of 1603 ed. 3.50 (ISBN 90-221-0753-1). Walter J Johnson.

Newdigate-Newdegate, Lady Cavalier & Puritian in the Days of the Stuarts. 1902. 25.00 (ISBN 0-8274-2013-7). R West.

Notestein, Wallace. English People on the Eve of Colonization: English People on the Eve of Colonization: Sixteen Hundred & Three to Sixteen Thirty. (New American Nation Ser.). (Illus.). pap. 6.50x (ISBN 0-06-133006-X, TB3006, Torch). Har-Row.

Outhwaite, R. B. Inflation in Tudor & Early Stuart England. (Studies in Economic & Social History). 1970. pap. text ed. 1.25x (ISBN 0-333-10144-8). Humanities.

Owens, W. R., ed. Seventeenth-Century England: A Changing Culture, Vol. 2: Modern Studies. 352p. 1981. 28.50x (ISBN 0-389-20169-3). B&N.

Pennington, Donald & Thomas, Keith, eds. Puritans & Revolutionaries: Essays in Seventeenth-Century History Presented to Christopher Hill. 1978. 45.00x (ISBN 0-19-822439-7). Oxford U Pr.

Pepys, Samuel. Diary of Samuel Pepys, 10 Vols. Wheatley, Henry B., ed. Bright, Mynors, tr. LC 68-57227. Repr. of 1899 ed. Set. lib. bdg. 295.00 (ISBN 0-404-05030-1); 29.50 ea. AMS Pr.

--The Illustrated Pepys: Extracts from the Diary. Latham, Robert, ed. (Illus.). 1978. 15.95 (ISBN 0-520-03633-6). U of Cal Pr.

Powley, Edward B., ed. The Naval Side of King William's War. (Illus.). 400p. 1972. 20.00 (ISBN 0-208-01084-X, Archon). Shoe String.

Price, Mary R. & Mather, C. E. Portrait of Britain Under Tudors & Stuarts, 1485-1688. (Oxford Introduction to British History Ser). (Illus.). 1954. pap. 12.50x (ISBN 0-19-832917-2). Oxford U Pr.

Pruett, John H. The Parish Clergy Under the Later Stuarts: The Leicestershire Experience. LC 78-8174. 1978. 12.50 (ISBN 0-252-00662-3). U of Ill Pr.

Riley, P. W. The Union of England & Scotland: A Study in Anglo-Scottish Politics of the Eighteenth Century. 351p. 1978. 25.00x (ISBN 0-8476-6155-5). Rowman.

Roots, Ivan, ed. Conflicts in Tudor & Stuart England. LC 68-97374. (Selections from History Today Ser.: No. 5). (Illus.). 1969. pap. 5.00 (ISBN 0-05-001536-2). Dufour.

Ross, Williamson H. Sir Walter Raleigh. LC 78-17033. 1978. Repr. of 1951 ed. lib. bdg. 19.75x (ISBN 0-313-20577-9, ROSI). Greenwood.

Russell, Conrad. Crisis of Parliaments: English History 1509-1660. (Short Oxford History of the Modern World Ser.). 1971. pap. 6.95x (ISBN 0-19-501442-1). Oxford U Pr.

Schilling, Bernard N. Conservative England & the Case Against Voltaire. 1972. lib. bdg. 20.00x (ISBN 0-374-97099-8). Octagon.

Schmidt, Albert J. Yeoman in Tudor & Stuart England. (Folger Guides to the Age of Shakespeare). 1961. 3.95 (ISBN 0-918016-20-7). Folger Bks.

Scott, Eva. Six Stuart Sovereigns, 1512-1701. LC 73-118499. 1971. Repr. of 1935 ed. 16.50 (ISBN 0-8046-1247-1). Kennikat.

Scott, Thomas. Workes. LC 73-6158. (English Experience Ser.: No. 621). 1265p. 1973. Repr. of 1624 ed. 126.00 (ISBN 90-221-0621-7). Walter J Johnson.

Sellen, P. R. Daniel Heinisius & Stuart England. (Publications of Sir Thomas Browne Institute Ser: No. 3). 1968. lib. bdg. 26.00 (ISBN 90-6021-061-1, Pub. by Leiden Univ Holland). Kluwer Boston.

Sells, A. Lytton. Italian Influence on Englishmen in the 17th Century, the Paradise of Travellers. 14.50 (ISBN 0-686-10848-5). British Am Bks.

Sharpe, Kevin. Sir Robert Cotton, Fifteen Eighty-Six to Sixteen Thirty-One: History & Politics in Early Modern England. (OHM Ser.). (Illus.). 284p. 1979. 36.00x (ISBN 0-19-821877-X). Oxford U Pr.

Smith, Alan G., ed. The Reign of James VI & I. LC 73-79379. (Problems in Focus Ser.). 275p. 1973. 18.95 (ISBN 0-312-67025-7). St Martin.

Snow, Vernon F. Essex the Rebel: The Life of Robert Devereux, the Third Earl of Essex, 1591-1646. LC 71-81542. (Illus.). 1970. 24.50x (ISBN 0-8032-0719-0). U of Nebr Pr.

Solve, Norma Dobie. Stuart Politics in Chapman's Tragedy of Chabot. 1928. 20.00 (ISBN 0-8274-3530-4). R West.

Spenser, Benjamin. Vox Civitatis, or Londons Complaint Against Her Children in the Countrey. LC 79-84137. (English Experience Ser.: No. 954). 52p. (Eng.). 1979. Repr. of 1625 ed. lib. bdg. 8.00 (ISBN 90-221-0954-2). Walter J Johnson.

Straka, Gerald M., ed. State Tracts: Being a Further Collection of Several Choice Treatises Relating to the Government from the Year 1660 to 1689. LC 72-83171. (English Studies Ser.). 1972. Repr. of 1692 ed. lib. bdg. 44.00 (ISBN 0-8420-1428-4). Scholarly Res Inc.

Sylvester, Joshua. Lachrimae Lachrimarum. LC 72-234. (English Experience Ser.: No. 185). 32p. 1969. Repr. of 1612 ed. 7.00 (ISBN 90-221-0185-1). Walter J Johnson.

Synge, M. B., et al. The Tudors & Stuarts. Repr. of 1934 ed. 17.50 (ISBN 0-686-19864-6). Ridgeway Bks.

Tangye, Richard. Two Protectors: Oliver & Richard Cromwell. LC 78-118504. 1971. Repr. of 1899 ed. 13.50 (ISBN 0-8046-1252-8). Kennikat.

Thornton, Percy M. Brunswick Accession. LC 75-118506. 1971. Repr. of 1887 ed. 12.50 (ISBN 0-8046-1254-4). Kennikat.

Three Pamphlets on the Jacobean Antifeminist Controversy. LC 78-5847. 1978. Repr. of 1620 ed. 20.00 (ISBN 0-8201-1307-7). Schol Facsimiles.

Trevelyan, G. M. England Under the Stuarts. 21st ed. 1966. pap. text ed. 15.95x (ISBN 0-416-69240-0). Methuen Inc.

Trevelyan, George M. & Straka, Gerald M., eds. Select Documents for Queen Anne's Reign Down to the Union with Scotland, 1702-07. LC 72-83173. (English Studies Ser.). 1972. Repr. of 1929 ed. lib. bdg. 16.00 (ISBN 0-8420-1429-2). Scholarly Res Inc.

Vale, Marcia. The Gentleman's Recreations: Accomplishments & Pastimes of the English Gentleman 1580-1630. (Elizabethan & Jacobean Culture Ser). (Illus.). 182p. 1977. 16.50x (ISBN 0-8476-6009-5). Rowman.

Von Ranke, Leopold. History of England, Principally in the Seventeenth Century, 6 Vols. Kitchen, G. W., et al, trs. LC 78-182703. Repr. of 1875 ed. Set. 175.00 (ISBN 0-404-05240-1); 30.00 ea. Vol. 1 (ISBN 0-404-05241-X). Vol. 2 (ISBN 0-404-05242-8). Vol. 3 (ISBN 0-404-05243-6). Vol. 4 (ISBN 0-404-05244-4). Vol. 5 (ISBN 0-404-05245-2). Vol. 6 (ISBN 0-404-05246-0). AMS Pr.

Waldman, Milton. Some English Dictators. LC 77-112820. 1970. Repr. of 1940 ed. 12.50 (ISBN 0-8046-1087-8). Kennikat.

Wedgwood, Cicely V. Poetry & Politics Under the Stuarts. 1960. 32.00 (ISBN 0-521-06762-6). Cambridge U Pr.

--Strafford Fifteen Ninty-Three to Sixteen Forty-One. Repr. of 1935 ed. lib. bdg. 16.00x (ISBN 0-8371-4566-X, WEST). Greenwood.

Weston, Corinne & Greenberg, Janelle R. Subjects & Sovereigns: The Grand Controversy Over Legal Sovereignty in Stuart England. LC 80-40588. 400p. 1981. 39.50 (ISBN 0-521-23272-4). Cambridge U Pr.

Williamson, Arthur. Scottish National Consciousness in the Age of James VI: The Apocalypse, the Union & the Shaping of Scotland's Public Culture. 1979. text ed. 31.25x (ISBN 0-85976-036-7). Humanities.

Williamson, Jerry W. The Myth of the Conqueror: Prince Henry Stuart, a Study of 17th Century Personation. LC 77-78318. (AMS Studies in the Renaissance: No. 2). 1978. 21.00 (ISBN 0-404-16004-2). AMS Pr.

Wilson, Charles. England's Apprenticeship, 1603-1763. (Social & Economic History of England). (Illus.). 1965. pap. text ed. 12.95x (ISBN 0-582-48234-8). Longman.

--Profit & Power. (A Study of England & the Dutch Wars). 1978. pap. 18.50 (ISBN 90-247-2083-4, Pub. by Martinus Nijhoff Netherlands). Kluwer Boston.

Wingfield-Stratford, Esme. King Charles the Martyr, 1643-1649. LC 74-28760. (Illus.). 385p. 1975. Repr. of 1950 ed. lib. bdg. 26.00x (ISBN 0-8371-7922-X, WIKCM). Greenwood.

Winwood, Ralph. Memorials of Affairs of State in the Reigns of Queen Elizabeth & King James First, 3 Vols. Sawyer, Edmund, ed. LC 75-178310. Repr. of 1725 ed. lib. bdg. 195.00 (ISBN 0-404-07020-5). AMS Pr.

Wrong, E. M. History of England: 1688-1815. 1927. Repr. 10.00 (ISBN 0-685-43459-1). Norwood Edns.

GREAT BRITAIN–HISTORY–STUARTS, 1603-1714–BIBLIOGRAPHY

James, Brian, ed. A Catalogue of the Tract Collection of Saint David's University College, Lampeter. LC 76-353069. 336p. 1975. 56.50x (ISBN 0-7201-0538-2, Pub. by Mansell England). Merrimack Bk Serv.

Keeler, Mary F. Bibliography of British History: Stuart Period, Sixteen Hundred to Seventeen-Fourteen. 2nd ed. (Bibliography of British History Ser). 1970. 49.00x (ISBN 0-19-821371-9). Oxford U Pr.

GREAT BRITAIN–HISTORY–STUARTS, 1603-1714–FICTION

Scott, Sir Walter. Fortunes of Nigel. Link, Frederick M., ed. LC 65-18715. 1965. pap. 3.25x (ISBN 0-8032-5176-9, BB 321, Bison). U of Nebr Pr.

Wallace, M. Imelda, Sr. Outlaws of Ravenhurst. new ed. (Illus.). (gr. 6-10). 1950. 6.95 (ISBN 0-910334-25-0); pap. 2.95 (ISBN 0-910334-26-9). Cath Authors.

GREAT BRITAIN–HISTORY–STUARTS, 1603-1714–SOURCES

Articles of Peace: In a Treatie. LC 71-171753. (English Experience Ser.: No. 378). 1971. Repr. of 1605 ed. 7.00 (ISBN 90-221-0378-1). Walter J Johnson.

Chamberlain, John. The Letters of John Chamberlain, 2 vols. McClure, Norman E., ed. LC 78-23784. 1979. Repr. of 1939 ed. Set. lib. bdg. 72.50x (ISBN 0-313-20710-0, CHLE). Greenwood.

Christie, William D., ed. Letters Addressed from London to Sir Joseph Williamson While Plenipotentiary at the Congress of Cologne in the Years 1673 & 1674, 2 Vols. Repr. of 1874 ed. 44.50 (ISBN 0-384-08959-3). Johnson Repr.

Clay, Thomas. Briefe, Easie & Necessary Tables for the Valuation of Leases. LC 76-57373. (English Experience Ser.: No. 791). 1977. Repr. of 1622 ed. lib. bdg. 8.00 (ISBN 90-221-0791-4). Walter J Johnson.

Duncan, William J., ed. Miscellaneous Papers, Principally Illustrative of Events in the Reigns of Queen Mary & King James Sixth. LC 79-164807. (Maitland Club. Glasgow. Publications: No. 26). Repr. of 1834 ed. 17.50 (ISBN 0-404-52981-X). AMS Pr.

Edwards, Thomas. Gangraena. 824p. 1977. 60.00x (ISBN 0-904617-08-4, Pub. by Exeter Univ England). State Mutual Bk.

Egerton, Francis. Egerton Papers. Collier, J. Payne, ed. LC 74-164767. (Camden Society, London. Publications, First Ser.: No. 12). Repr. of 1840 ed. 38.50 (ISBN 0-404-50112-5). AMS Pr.

Ellesmere, Francis E. Egerton Papers. 1840. 42.50 (ISBN 0-384-14165-X). Johnson Repr.

Fortescue, George M. The Fortescue Papers. Gardiner, S. R., ed. Repr. of 1871 ed. 22.50 (ISBN 0-384-16440-4). Johnson Repr.

Gardiner, Samuel R., ed. Great Britain House of Lords: Notes of the Debates in the House of Lords, 1621. LC 75-168190. (Camden Society, London. Publications, First Ser.: No. 103). Repr. of 1870 ed. 14.00 (ISBN 0-404-50203-2). AMS Pr.

Great Britain House Of Commons. Debates in the House of Commons in 1625. Gardiner, Samuel R., ed. 1873. 22.50 (ISBN 0-384-19810-4). Johnson Repr.

Great Britain House Of Lords - 1621. Notes of the Debates in the House of Lords. 1870. 15.50 (ISBN 0-384-19790-6). Johnson Repr.

Great Britain House of Lords - 1624. Notes of the Debates in the House of Lords. Gardiner, Samuel R., ed. 1879. 22.50 (ISBN 0-384-19800-7). Johnson Repr.

Guy, Henry. Moneys Received & Paid for Secret Services of Charles Second & James Second from 30th March, 1679 to 25th December, 1688. Akerman, John Y., ed. LC 77-158238. (Camden Socity, London. Publications. First Ser.: No. 52). Repr. of 1851 ed. 14.00 (ISBN 0-404-50152-4). AMS Pr.

Haller, William & Davies, Godfrey, eds. The Leveller Tracts 1647-1653: 1647-1653. 1964. 8.50 (ISBN 0-8446-1218-9). Peter Smith.

Hamilton, James. Hamilton Papers. Gardiner, Samuel R., ed. 1880. 22.50 (ISBN 0-384-21160-7). Johnson Repr.

An Information to All Good Christians Within the Kingdome of England from the Noblemen & Commons of the Kingdome of Scotland. LC 76-57413. (English Experience Ser.: No. 828). 1977. Repr. of 1639 ed. lib. bdg. 3.50 (ISBN 90-221-0828-7). Walter J Johnson.

The Intentions of the Army of the Kingdome of Scotland. LC 76-57414. (English Experience Ser.: No. 829). 1977. Repr. of 1640 ed. lib. bdg. 3.50 (ISBN 90-221-0829-5). Walter J Johnson.

Kenyon, John P. Stuart Constitution, Sixteen Hundred Three to Sixteen Eighty Eight: Documents & Commentary. (Orig.). 1966. 62.00 (ISBN 0-521-05884-8); pap. 17.95x (ISBN 0-521-09370-8). Cambridge U Pr.

Knafla, L. A. Law & Politics in Jacobean England. LC 76-4757. (Cambridge Studies in English Legal History). (Illus.). 1977. 59.00 (ISBN 0-521-21191-3). Cambridge U Pr.

Lamont, William & Oldfield, Sybil, eds. Politics, Religion & Literature in the Seventeenth Century. (Rowman & Littlefield University Library). 248p. 1975. 13.75x (ISBN 0-87471-575-X); pap. 7.00x (ISBN 0-87471-576-8). Rowman.

Lowe, Roger. The Diary of Roger Lowe of Ashton-in-Makerfield, Lancashire Sixteen Sixty-Three to Sixteen Seventy-Four. Sachse, W. L., ed. 1938. 27.50 (ISBN 0-686-51372-X). Elliots Bks.

Manningham, John. Diary of John Manningham. Bruce, John, ed. (Camden Society. London. Publications, First Series: No. 99). Repr. of 1868 ed. 17.50 (ISBN 0-404-50199-0). AMS Pr.

--Diary of John Manningham of the Middle Temple, & of Bradbourne, Kent, Barrister-at-Law, 1602-1603. Repr. of 1868 ed. 19.50 (ISBN 0-384-35175-1). Johnson Repr.

--The Diary of John Manningham of the Middle Temple, 1602-1603. Sorlien, Robert P., ed. LC 74-22553. 481p. 1976. text ed. 27.50x (ISBN 0-87451-113-5). U Pr of New Eng.

Parker, Henry. The Case of Shipmony Briefly Discoursed, According to the Grounds of Law, Policy & Conscience. LC 76-57404. (English Experience Ser.: No. 820). 1977. Repr. of 1640 ed. lib. bdg. 7.00 (ISBN 90-221-0820-1). Walter J Johnson.

Read, Alexander. A Treatise of the First Part of Chirurgerie. LC 76-57411. (English Experience Ser.: No. 826). 1977. Repr. of 1638 ed. lib. bdg. 24.00 (ISBN 90-221-0826-0). Walter J Johnson.

Rous, John. Diary. Repr. of 1856 ed. 15.50 (ISBN 0-384-52180-0). Johnson Repr.

--Diary of John Rous, Incumbent of Santon Downham, Suffolk, from 1625 to 1642. Green, Mary A., ed. (Camden Society, London. Publications, First Ser.: No. 66). 1856. 14.00 (ISBN 0-404-50166-4). AMS Pr.

Totnes, George C. Letters from George Lord Carew to Sir Thomas Roe. Maclean, John, ed. (Camden Society, London. Publications. First Ser.: No. 76). Repr. of 1860 ed. 14.00 (ISBN 0-404-50176-1). AMS Pr.

--Letters from George Lord Carew to Sir Thomas Roe. Repr. of 1860 ed. 15.50 (ISBN 0-384-61030-7). Johnson Repr.

Villiers, Barbara. The Intimate Memoirs of Barbara, the Duchess of Cleveland. (The Memoirs Collection of Significant Historical Personalities Ser.). (Illus.). 1979. deluxe ed. 27.50 (ISBN 0-930582-24-1). Gloucester Art.

Whitelocke, James. Liber Famelicus. 15.50 (ISBN 0-384-68130-1). Johnson Repr.

--Liber Famelicus of Sir James Whitelocke. Bruce, John, ed. (Camden Society, London. Publications, First Ser.: No. 70). Repr. of 1858 ed. 14.00 (ISBN 0-404-50170-2). AMS Pr.

Yonge, Walter. Diary. 15.50 (ISBN 0-384-70375-5). Johnson Repr.

--Diary of Walter Yonge. Roberts, George, ed. (Camden Society, London. Publications. First Ser.: No. 41). Repr. of 1848 ed. 14.00 (ISBN 0-404-50141-9). AMS Pr.

GREAT BRITAIN–HISTORY–PURITAN REVOLUTION, 1642-1660

see also Edgehill, Battle of, 1642

Ashley, Maurice. The English Civil War: A Concise History. 1979. 12.50 (ISBN 0-500-82002-3). Thames Hudson.

--Financial & Commercial Policy Under Cromwellian Protectorate. 2nd ed. 190p. 1962. 25.00x (ISBN 0-7146-1265-0, F Cass Co). Biblio Dist.

--General Monck. (Illus.). 316p. 1977. 20.00x (ISBN 0-87471-934-8). Rowman.

Ashton, Robert. The English Civil War. 1979. 24.95 (ISBN 0-393-01207-7). Norton.

Barbary, James. Puritan & Cavalier: The English Civil War. LC 76-44979. (Illus.). 192p. (gr. 6 up). 1977. 7.95 (ISBN 0-525-66480-7). Elsevier-Nelson.

Barker, Arthur E. Milton & the Puritan Dilemma, 1641-1660. LC 58-3195. 1942. 22.50x (ISBN 0-8020-5025-5); pap. 7.50 (ISBN 0-8020-6306-3). U of Toronto Pr.

Boyce, Benjamin. Polemic Character, 1640-1661. 1969. lib. bdg. 14.00x (ISBN 0-374-90893-1). Octagon.

Broxap, E. The Great Civil War in Lancashire: 1642-51. (Illus.). xv, 226p. Repr. of 1910 ed. lib. bdg. 13.50x (ISBN 0-678-06792-9). Kelley.

Childs, John. The Army, James II & the Glorious Revolution. 25.00 (ISBN 0-312-04949-8). St Martin.

Clarenden, Edward & Hyde, Earlay. Selections from "The History of the Rebellion" & "The Life by Himself". Huehns, G., intro. by. 1979. 12.95x (ISBN 0-19-215852-X). Oxford U Pr.

Clarke, William. Clarke Papers, 4 Vols. Firth, C. H., ed. Set. 89.50 (ISBN 0-384-09232-2); 22.50 ea. Johnson Repr.

Coltman, Irene. Private Men & Public Causes: Philosophy & Politics in the English Civil War. 1962. text ed. 8.50x (ISBN 0-8401-0450-2). Allenson-Breckinridge.

Davies, Godfrey. Early Stuarts, 1603-1660. 2nd ed. (Illus.). 1959. 29.95 (ISBN 0-19-821704-8). Oxford U Pr.

Foster, Stephen. Notes from the Caroline Underground: Alexander Leighton, the Puritan Triumvirate, & the Laudian Reaction to Nonconformity. (Conference on British Studies: Vol. VI). 1978. 14.50 (ISBN 0-208-01758-5, Archon). Shoe String.

Gardiner, Samuel R. Cromwell's Place in History. LC 76-94270. (Select Bibliographies Reprint Ser). 1897. 15.00 (ISBN 0-8369-5044-5). Arno.

--The First Two Stuarts & the Puritan Revolution: 1603-1660. 1977. Repr. of 1891 ed. lib. bdg. 25.00 (ISBN 0-8495-1911-X). Arden Lib.

Haller, W. Liberty & Reformation in the Puritan Revolution. 8.00 (ISBN 0-8446-2190-0). Peter Smith.

Harrison, Frederic. Oliver Cromwell. LC 78-39196. (Select Bibliographies Reprint Ser.). Repr. of 1888 ed. 16.00 (ISBN 0-8369-6798-4). Arno.

Hause, Earl M. Tumble-Down Dick: The Fall of the House of Cromwell. LC 72-81386. 1972. 13.50 (ISBN 0-682-47514-9, University). Exposition.

Hill, Christopher. English Revolution, Sixteen Forty. 62p. 1966. pap. 4.95x (ISBN 0-8464-0379-X). Beekman Pubs.

--God's Englishman: Oliver Cromwell & the English Revolution. 324p. 1972. pap. 6.95x (ISBN 0-06-131666-0, TB1666, Torch). Har-Row.

--Good Old Cause: English Revolution of 1640-1660. 2nd, rev. ed. Dell, Edmund, ed. 488p. 1969. 27.50x (ISBN 0-7146-1483-1, F Cass Co). Biblio Dist.

--The World Turned Upside Down. 1976. pap. 3.95 (ISBN 0-14-021820-3, Pelican). Penguin.

Hill, John E. & Dell, Edmund, eds. Good Old Cause. LC 71-96377. Repr. of 1949 ed. 24.00x (ISBN 0-678-05105-4). Kelley.

Hobbes, Thomas. Behemoth: The History of the Causes of the Civil Wars in England & of the Counsels & Artifice by Which They Were Carried on. Molesworth, William, ed. 1962. Repr. of 1840 ed. 22.50 (ISBN 0-8337-1712-X). B Franklin.

Hodges, C. Walter. The Puritan Revolution: Story of Britain. (Illus.). 32p. (gr. 4-7). 1972. PLB 4.99 (ISBN 0-698-30426-8). Coward.

Howell, Roger, Jr. The Origins of the English Revolution. LC 73-81060. (The Forum Ser). 1975. pap. text ed. 1.60x (ISBN 0-88273-128-9). Forum Pr MO.

Hutchinson, Lucy. Memoirs of the Life of Colonel Hutchinson. 1965. pap. 3.25x (ISBN 0-460-01317-3, Evman). Biblio Dist.

Hutton, Ronald. The Royalist War Effort 1642-1646. (Illus.). 240p. 1981. pap. 28.00x (ISBN 0-582-50301-9). Longman.

Jacob, J. R. Robert Boyle & the English Revolution: A Study in Social & Intellectual Change. LC 77-2997. (Studies in the History of Science). (Illus.). 1978. lib. bdg. 18.95 (ISBN 0-89102-072-1). B Franklin.

Jones, J. R. Country & Court: England, Sixteen Fifty-Eight to Seventeen Fourteen. LC 78-5362. (New History of England). 1978. 18.50x (ISBN 0-674-17525-5); pap. 6.95x (ISBN 0-674-17535-2). Harvard U Pr.

Ketton-Cremer, R. W. Norfolk in the Civil War: A Portrait of a Society in Conflict. (Illus.). 1970. 22.50 (ISBN 0-208-00977-9, Archon). Shoe String.

Kishlansky, Mark A. The Rise of the New Model Army. LC 79-4285. 1979. 21.50 (ISBN 0-521-22751-8). Cambridge U Pr.

Knachel, Philip A. England & the Fronde: The Impact of the English Civil War & Revolution on France. (Monographs). 1978. 17.50x (ISBN 0-918016-33-9). Folger Bks.

Ludlow, Edmund. A Voyce from the Watch Tower: Part Five, 1660-1662. Worden, A. B., ed. (Royal Historical Society: Camden Society Fourth Ser.: Vol. 21). 370p. 1980. Repr. of 1978 ed. 20.00x (ISBN 0-8476-3308-X). Rowman.

Masson, David, ed. The Quarrel Between the Earl of Manchester & Oliver Cromwell: An Episode of the English Civil War. Repr. of 1875 ed. 22.50 (ISBN 0-384-35850-0). Johnson Repr.

Morrill, J. S. Cheshire Sixteen Thirty to Sixteen Sixty: County Government & Society During the English Revolution. (Oxford Historical Monographs Ser). 367p. 1974. 37.50x (ISBN 0-19-821855-9). Oxford U Pr.

Morton, A. L. World of Ranters-Religious Radicalism in the English Revolution. 1979. pap. 6.75x (ISBN 0-85315-497-X). Humanities.

--The World of the Ranters: Religious Radicalism in the English Revolution. 232p. 1970. 14.95x (ISBN 0-8464-0980-1). Beekman Pubs.

Nicholas, Edward. The Nicholas Papers, 3 Vols. 1886-1891. 22.50 ea. (ISBN 0-384-41400-1). Johnson Repr.

Parry, R. H., ed. The English Civil War & After, 1642-1658. LC 74-111423. 1970. pap. 4.95x (ISBN 0-520-01783-8, CAMPUS 30). U of Cal Pr.

Petegorsky, David W. Left-Wing Democracy in the English Civil War. LC 72-2021. (British History Ser., No. 30). 1972. Repr. of 1940 ed. lib. bdg. 33.95 (ISBN 0-8383-1472-4). Haskell.

Petrie, Sir Charles, ed. King Charles, Prince Rupert & the Civil War. 1975. 14.50 (ISBN 0-7100-7969-9). Routledge & Kegan.

Pocock, J. G., ed. Three British Revolutions: 1641, 1688, 1776. LC 79-27572. (Folger Institute Essays, Published for the Folger Shakespeare Library). 456p. 1980. 32.50 (ISBN 0-691-05293-X); pap. 12.50 (ISBN 0-691-10087-X). Princeton U Pr.

Prall, S. E. Puritan Revolution: A Documentary History. 8.75 (ISBN 0-8446-2756-9). Peter Smith.

Roe. Military Memoir of Colonel John Birch. Webb, ed. Repr. of 1873 ed. 22.50 (ISBN 0-384-51615-7). Johnson Repr.

Roots, Ivan A. Commonwealth & Protectorate: The English Civil War & Its Aftermath. LC 76-8164. 1976. Repr. of 1966 ed. lib. bdg. 19.00x (ISBN 0-8371-8854-7, ROCP). Greenwood.

Schenk, Wilhelm. The Concern for Social Justice in the Puritan Revolution. LC 74-29794. (Illus.). 180p. 1975. Repr. of 1948 ed. lib. bdg. 15.00x (ISBN 0-8371-8003-1, SCSJ). Greenwood.

Smith, Geoffrey R. & Toynbee, Margaret. Leaders of the Civil Wars, Sixteen Forty-Two to Sixteen Forty-Eight. 1980. 30.00x (ISBN 0-900093-56-0, Pub. by Roundwood). State Mutual Bk.

Solt, Leo F. Saints in Arms. LC 74-153355. (Stanford University. Stanford Studies in History, Economics & Political Science: No. 18). Repr. of 1959 ed. 16.00 (ISBN 0-404-50976-2). AMS Pr.

Stone, Lawrence. The Causes of the English Revolution. 1972. pap. 3.95x (ISBN 0-06-131678-4, TB1678, Torch). Har-Row.

Timmis, John H., III. Thine Is the Kingdom: The Trial for Treason of Thomas Wentworth, Earl of Strafford, First Minister of King Charles I, & the Last Hope of the English Crown. LC 73-22723. 1975. 18.25x (ISBN 0-8173-5403-4). U of Ala Pr.

Underdown, David. Royalist Conspiracy in England, 1649-1660. LC 74-122409. (Illus.). 1971. Repr. of 1960 ed. 22.50 (ISBN 0-208-00960-4, Archon). Shoe String.

Wenham, Peter. The Great & Close Siege of York, Sixteen Forty-Four. 1980. 24.00x (ISBN 0-900093-10-2, Pub. by Roundwood). State Mutual Bk.

Wolfe, Don M. Milton in the Puritan Revolution. 1963. text ed. 15.00x (ISBN 0-391-00477-8). Humanities.

Young, Peter. Naseby, Sixteen Forty-Five: The Campaign & Battle. 1980. 36.00x (ISBN 0-906418-02-X, Pub. by Roundwood). State Mutual Bk.

Young, Peter & Emberton, Wilfrid. Sieges of the Great Civil War. (Illus.). 159p. 1978. 19.50x (ISBN 0-8476-6096-6). Rowman.

GREAT BRITAIN–HISTORY–PURITAN REVOLUTION, 1642-1660–FICTION

Cowley, Abraham. Civil War. Pritchard, A. D., ed. LC 75-185731. 232p. 1973. 17.50x (ISBN 0-8020-5263-0). U of Toronto Pr.

Defoe, Daniel. Memoirs of a Cavalier. LC 74-13443. (Illus.). Repr. of 1895 ed. 27.50 (ISBN 0-404-07915-6). AMS Pr.

GREAT BRITAIN–HISTORY–PURITAN REVOLUTION, 1642-1660–SOURCES

Akerman, John Y., ed. Letters from Roundhead Officers. LC 73-158237. (Bannatyne Club, Edinburgh. Publications: No. 101). Repr. of 1856 ed. 37.50 (ISBN 0-404-52849-X). AMS Pr.

Atkyns, Richard & Gwyn, John. The Civil War. Young, Peter & Tucker, Norman, eds. (Military Memoirs Ser). 1967. 13.50 (ISBN 0-208-00632-X, Archon). Shoe String.

Charles First. Charles First 101, King of Great Britain: Letters of King Charles First to Queen Henrietta Maria. 1856. 15.50 (ISBN 0-384-08515-6). Johnson Repr.

Charles First, King of Great Britain. Charles First in 1646: Letters of King Charles First to Queen Henrietta Maria. Bruce, John, ed. LC 17-1236. (Camden Society, London. Publications. First Ser.: No. 63). Repr. of 1856 ed. 14.00 (ISBN 0-404-50163-X). AMS Pr.

Collins, Arthur. Letters & Memorials of State, in the Reigns of Queen Mary, Queen Elizabeth, King James, King Charles the First, Part of the Reign of King Charles the Second, & Oliver's Usurpation, 2 Vols. LC 72-997. Repr. of 1746 ed. lib. bdg. 185.00 (ISBN 0-404-01631-6). AMS Pr.

Langdon-Davies, John. Cromwell's Commonwealth & Protectorate. (Jackdaw Ser: No. 27). (Illus.). 1970. 6.95 (ISBN 0-670-24848-7, Grossman). Viking Pr.

Ludlow, Edmund. The Memoirs of Edmund Ludlow, Lieutenant-General of the Horse in the Army of the Commonwealth of England, 1625-1672, 2 vols. Firth, C. H., ed. LC 75-31098. (Illus.). Repr. of 1894 ed. 95.00 set (ISBN 0-404-13520-X). AMS Pr.

Ormerod, George, ed. Tracts Relating to Military Proceedings in Lancashire During the Great Civil War. 1844. 29.00 (ISBN 0-384-43700-1). Johnson Repr.

Sachse, William L. Restoration England, 1660-1689. (Conference on British Studies, Bibliographical Handbks). 1971. 17.50 (ISBN 0-521-08171-8). Cambridge U Pr.

Symonds, Richard. Diary of the Marches of the Royal Army During the Great Civil War. Long, Charles E., ed. (Camden Society, London. Publications, First Ser.: No. 74). Repr. of 1859 ed. 28.00 (ISBN 0-404-50174-5). AMS Pr.

--Diary of the Marches of the Royal Army During the Great Civil War. Repr. of 1859 ed. 31.00 (ISBN 0-384-59320-8). Johnson Repr.

GREAT BRITAIN–HISTORY–CIVIL WAR, 1642-1649

see Great Britain–History–Puritan Revolution, 1642-1660

GREAT BRITAIN–HISTORY–RESTORATION, 1660-1688

see also Dutch War, 1672-1678

Airy, Osmund. The English Restoration & Louis XIV. 1977. Repr. of 1900 ed. lib. bdg. 17.50 (ISBN 0-8492-0137-3). R West.

Ashley, Maurice. General Monck. (Illus.). 316p. 1977. 20.00x (ISBN 0-87471-934-8). Rowman.

Bebb, Evelyn D. Nonconformity & Social & Economic Life 1660-1800. LC 80-21180. Repr. of 1935 ed. lib. bdg. 15.00x (ISBN 0-87991-867-5). Porcupine Pr.

Burghclere, Winifred. George Villiers, Second Duke of Buckingham. LC 74-118511. 1971. Repr. of 1903 ed. 17.50 (ISBN 0-8046-1259-5). Kennikat.

Burnet, Gilbert. History of His Own Time. Date not set. 12.95x (ISBN 0-460-00085-3, Evman). Biblio Dist.

Christie, William D., ed. Letters Addressed from London to Sir Joseph Williamson While Plenipotentiary at the Congress of Cologne in the Years 1673 & 1674, 2 Vols. Repr. of 1874 ed. 44.50 (ISBN 0-384-08959-3). Johnson Repr.

Earle, Peter. Monmouth's Rebels: The Road to Sedgamoor 1685. LC 77-84928. (Illus.). 1977. 15.95x (ISBN 0-312-54512-6). St Martin.

Folsom, James K. & Slotkin, Richard, eds. So Dreadful a Judgement: Puritan Responses to King Philip's War, 1676-77. LC 77-14847. 25.00x (ISBN 0-8195-5027-2, Pub. by Wesleyan U Pr); pap. 10.00x (ISBN 0-8195-6058-8). Columbia U Pr.

Foxcroft, Helen C. Life & Letters of Sir George Savile, 2 Vols. LC 4-35272. 1969. Repr. of 1898 ed. Set. 50.00 (ISBN 0-384-16573-7). Johnson Repr.

Hunt, Leigh. Sir Ralph Esher. LC 78-162913. (Bentley's Standard Novels: No. 118). Repr. of 1849 ed. 20.00 (ISBN 0-404-54518-1). AMS Pr.

Jamison, Ted, Jr. George Monck & the Restoration: Victor Without Bloodshed. LC 74-28945. (History & Culture Monograph Ser., No. 11). 1975. pap. 4.50 (ISBN 0-912646-04-7). Tex Christian.

Jones, J. R. Country & Court: England, Sixteen Fifty-Eight to Seventeen Fourteen. LC 78-5362. (New History of England). 1978. 18.50x (ISBN 0-674-17525-5); pap. 6.95x (ISBN 0-674-17535-2). Harvard U Pr.

Jones, J. R., ed. Restored Monarchy, Sixteen Sixty to Sixteen Eighty-Eight. 232p. 1979. 15.75x (ISBN 0-8476-6139-3). Rowman.

Landon, Michael. Triumph of the Lawyers: Their Role in English Politics, 1678-1689. LC 69-15418. 303p. 1970. 19.95x (ISBN 0-8173-5401-8). U of Ala Pr.

Lodge, Richard. History of England from the Restoration to the Death of William Third. LC 70-5629. (Political History of England: No. 8). Repr. of 1910 ed. 22.50 (ISBN 0-404-50778-6). AMS Pr.

Ludlow, Edmund. A Voyce from the Watch Tower: Part Five, 1660-1662. Worden, A. B., ed. (Royal Historical Society: Camden Society Fourth Ser.: Vol. 21). 370p. 1980. Repr. of 1978 ed. 20.00x (ISBN 0-8476-3308-X). Rowman.

Macauley, Thomas B. History of England from the Accession of James Second, 6 Vols. Firth, C. H., ed. LC 14-14308. Repr. of 1915 ed. Set. 210.00 (ISBN 0-404-04110-8); 35.00 ea. Vol. 1 (ISBN 0-404-04111-6). Vol. 2 (ISBN 0-404-04112-4). Vol. 3 (ISBN 0-404-04113-2). Vol. 4 (ISBN 0-404-04114-0). Vol. 5 (ISBN 0-404-04115-9). Vol. 6 (ISBN 0-404-04116-7). AMS Pr.

McKeon, Michael. Politics & Poetry in Restoration England: The Case of Dryden's Annus Mirabilis. 322p. 1975. text ed. 16.50x (ISBN 0-674-68755-8). Harvard U Pr.

Mensing, Raymond C. Toleration & Parliament, 1660-1719. LC 79-63260. 1979. pap. text ed. 9.00 (ISBN 0-8191-0723-9). U Pr of Amer.

Ogg, David. England in the Reign of Charles II, 2 vols. LC 78-11572. 1979. Repr. of 1955 ed. Set. lib. bdg. 57.50x (ISBN 0-313-21038-1, OGER). Greenwood.

Swedenberg, H. T., Jr., ed. England in the Restoration & Early Eighteenth Century: Essays on Culture & Society. LC 72-149943. 272p. 1972. 25.00x (ISBN 0-520-01973-3). U of Cal Pr.

Thirsk, Joan. The Restoration. (Problems & Perspectives in History). 1975. pap. text ed. 4.95x (ISBN 0-582-35160-X). Longman.

Tschudi-Madsen, Stephan. Restoration & Anti-Restoration. 2nd ed. 180p. 1981. 19.00x (ISBN 82-00-05671-6). Universitet.

Wilburn, James R. The Hazard of the Die: Tolbert Fanning & the Restoration Movement. LC 74-77235. 1980. 9.95 (ISBN 0-932612-04-0). Pepperdine U Pr.

Wright, James. The History & Antiquities of the County of Rutland. (Classical County Histories Ser.). (Illus.). 229p. 1973. Repr. of 1790 ed. 27.50x (ISBN 0-87471-391-9). Rowman.

GREAT BRITAIN–HISTORY–RESTORATION, 1660-1688–SOURCES

Langdon-Davies, John. Restoration of Charles Second. (Jackdaw Ser: No. 29). (Illus.). 1968. 6.95 (ISBN 0-670-59538-1, Grossman). Viking Pr.

GREAT BRITAIN–HISTORY–REVOLUTION OF 1688

Foxcroft, Helen C. Life & Letters of Sir George Savile, 2 Vols. LC 4-35272. 1969. Repr. of 1898 ed. Set. 50.00 (ISBN 0-384-16573-7). Johnson Repr.

Hosford, David H. Nottingham, Nobles, & the North: Aspects of the Revolution of 1688. (Studies in British History & Culture: Vol. 4). (Illus.). xvi, 182p. 1976. 12.50 (ISBN 0-208-01565-5, Archon). Shoe String.

Pinkham, Lucile. William Third & the Respectable Revolution: The Part Played by William of Orange in the Revolution of 1688. 1969. Repr. of 1954 ed. 17.50 (ISBN 0-208-00724-5, Archon). Shoe String.

Pocock, J. G., ed. Three British Revolutions: 1641, 1688, 1776. LC 79-27572. (Folger Institute Essays, Published for the Folger Shakespeare Library). 456p. 1980. 32.50 (ISBN 0-691-05293-X); pap. 12.50 (ISBN 0-691-10087-X). Princeton U Pr.

Prall, Stuart E. The Bloodless Revolution: England, 1688. (Illus.). 6.00 (ISBN 0-8446-4454-4). Peter Smith.

Richardson, R. C. The Debate on the English Revolution. LC 77-73803. 1977. 15.95 (ISBN 0-312-18890-0). St Martin.

Straka, Gerald M., ed. Revolution of Sixteen Eighty-Eight & the Birth of the English Political Nation: Whig Triumph or Palace Revolution. 2nd ed. (Problems in European Civilization Ser.). 1973. pap. text ed. 4.94 (ISBN 0-669-82032-6). Heath.

Trevelyan, George M. English Revolution, Sixteen Eighty-Eight to Sixteen Eighty-Nine. (YA) (gr. 9 up). 1965. pap. 4.95 (ISBN 0-19-500263-6, GB). Oxford U Pr.

GREAT BRITAIN–HISTORY–1689-1714

Aitken, George A. Later Stuart Tracts. LC 64-16748. (Arber's an English Garner Ser.). 1964. Repr. of 1890 ed. 11.50x (ISBN 0-8154-0003-9). Cooper Sq.

Arnstein, Walter, ed. The Past Speaks: Sources & Problems in British History Since 1688. 448p. 1981. pap. text ed. 8.95 (ISBN 0-669-02919-X). Heath.

Aubrey, Philip. The Defeat of James Stuart's Armada, 1692. (Illus.). 192p. 1979. 15.00x (ISBN 0-8476-6156-3). Rowman.

Bennett, G. V. The Tory Crisis in Church & State 1688-1730: The Career of Francis Atterbury, Bishop of Rochester. (Illus.). 260p. 1975. 42.00x (ISBN 0-19-822444-3). Oxford U Pr.

Dern, John P. London Churchbooks & the German Emigration of 1709. (Illus.). 55p. (Ger. & Eng.). 1972. pap. 3.00 (ISBN 0-913186-01-5). Monocacy.

Ede, Mary. Arts & Society in England Under William & Mary. (Illus.). 218p. 1979. 23.50x (ISBN 0-8476-6261-6). Rowman.

Folsom, James K. & Slotkin, Richard, eds. So Dreadful a Judgement: Puritan Responses to King Philip's War, 1676-77. LC 77-14847. 25.00x (ISBN 0-8195-5027-2, Pub. by Wesleyan U Pr); pap. 10.00x (ISBN 0-8195-6058-8). Columbia U Pr.

Garrett, Jane. The Triumphs of Providence. (Illus.). 250p. 1981. 19.50 (ISBN 0-521-23346-1). Cambridge U Pr.

Holmes, Geoffrey, ed. Britain After the Glorious Revolution. (Problems in Focus Ser). 1969. text ed. 16.95 (ISBN 0-312-09730-1). St Martin.

Hyde, Mary. The Thrales of Streatham Park. (Illus.). 1977. 16.50x (ISBN 0-674-88746-8). Harvard U Pr.

Jacob, Margaret C. The Newtonians & the English Revolution, 1689-1720. LC 75-36995. 1976. 22.50x (ISBN 0-8014-0981-0). Cornell U Pr.

Jarrett. Britain: Sixteen Eighty-Eight to Eighteen Fifteen. 1976. pap. 9.95 (ISBN 0-312-09695-X). St Martin.

Jones, J. R. Country & Court: England, Sixteen Fifty-Eight to Seventeen Fourteen. LC 78-5362. (New History of England). 1978. 18.50x (ISBN 0-674-17525-5); pap. 6.95x (ISBN 0-674-17535-2). Harvard U Pr.

Landon, Michael. Triumph of the Lawyers: Their Role in English Politics, 1678-1689. LC 69-15418. 303p. 1970. 19.95x (ISBN 0-8173-5401-8). U of Ala Pr.

Leadam, I. S. History of England from the Accession of Anne to the Death of George Second: Seventeen Hundred-Two to Seventeen Sixty. (Political History of England). Repr. of 1909 ed. 24.00 (ISBN 0-685-13711-2). Kraus Repr.

Leadam, Isaac S. History of England from the Accession of Anne to the Death of George Second, 1702-1760. LC 69-13970. 1969. Repr. of 1909 ed. lib. bdg. 20.00x (ISBN 0-8371-0934-5, LEGV). Greenwood.

Legg, L. Wickham. Matthew Prior: A Study of His Public Career & Correspondence. LC 72-5135. x, 348p. 1972. Repr. of 1921 ed. lib. bdg. 17.50x (ISBN 0-374-94890-9). Octagon.

Lodge, Richard. History of England from the Restoration to the Death of William Third. LC 70-5629. (Political History of England: No. 8). Repr. of 1910 ed. 22.50 (ISBN 0-404-50778-6). AMS Pr.

Macauley, Thomas B. History of England from the Accession of James Second, 6 Vols. Firth, C. H., ed. LC 14-14308. Repr. of 1915 ed. Set. 210.00 (ISBN 0-404-04110-8); 35.00 ea. Vol. 1 (ISBN 0-404-04111-6). Vol. 2 (ISBN 0-404-04112-4). Vol. 3 (ISBN 0-404-04113-2). Vol. 4 (ISBN 0-404-04114-0). Vol. 5 (ISBN 0-404-04115-9). Vol. 6 (ISBN 0-404-04116-7). AMS Pr.

Mensing, Raymond C. Toleration & Parliament, 1660-1719. LC 79-63260. 1979. pap. text ed. 9.00 (ISBN 0-8191-0723-9). U Pr of Amer.

Swedenberg, H. T., Jr., ed. England in the Restoration & Early Eighteenth Century: Essays on Culture & Society. LC 72-149943. 272p. 1972. 25.00x (ISBN 0-520-01973-3). U of Cal Pr.

Turberville, Arthur S. The House of Lords in the Reign of William Third. LC 77-110877. vi, 264p. Repr. of 1913 ed. lib. bdg. 15.00x (ISBN 0-8371-4558-9, TULW). Greenwood.

Wolfgang, Michael. England Under George I: The Beginnings of the Hanoverian Dynasty. LC 81-6495. (Studies in Modern History). viii, 406p. 1981. Repr. of 1936 ed. lib. bdg. 29.75x (ISBN 0-313-23040-4, MIEG). Greenwood.

GREAT BRITAIN–HISTORY–1689-1714–SOURCES

Ewald, William B., Jr. Rogues, Royalty & Reporters: The Age of Queen Anne Through Its Newspapers. LC 78-17410. 1978. Repr. of 1956 ed. lib. bdg. 22.75x (ISBN 0-313-20506-X, EWRR). Greenwood.

Holmes, G. S. & Speck, W. A. Divided Society: Parties & Politics in England, 1694-1716. (Documents of Modern History Ser). (Orig.). 1968. pap. 4.95 (ISBN 0-312-21420-0, DMH2). St Martin.

Pepys, Samuel. Diary of Samuel Pepys. Morshead, O. F., ed. (Illus.). 1960. 8.50 (ISBN 0-8446-2727-5). Peter Smith.

GREAT BRITAIN–HISTORY–18TH CENTURY

Baugh, Daniel A., ed. Aristocratic Government & Society in Eighteenth-Century England: The Foundations of Stability. (Modern Scholarship on European History Ser). 288p. 1975. text ed. 6.95 (ISBN 0-531-05577-9). Watts.

Bebb, Evelyn D. Nonconformity & Social & Economic Life 1660-1800. LC 80-21180. Repr. of 1935 ed. lib. bdg. 15.00x (ISBN 0-87991-867-5). Porcupine Pr.

Bennett, G. V. The Tory Crisis in Church & State 1688-1730: The Career of Francis Atterbury, Bishop of Rochester. (Illus.). 260p. 1975. 42.00x (ISBN 0-19-822444-3). Oxford U Pr.

Bolingbroke, Henry S. Works of Lord Bolingbroke, 4 Vols. LC 67-16351. Repr. of 1844 ed. 90.00x (ISBN 0-678-05028-7). Kelley.

Bolingbroke, Lord. Works, 4 vols. 1967. Repr. of 1844 ed. Set. 165.00x (ISBN 0-7146-1011-9, F Cass Co). Biblio Dist.

Bowden, S. Industrial Society in England Towards the End of the Eighteenth Century. rev. & 2nd ed. 343p. 1965. 26.00x (ISBN 0-7146-1276-6, F Cass Co). Biblio Dist.

Briggs, Asa. Age of Improvement, 1783 to 1867. (A History of England Ser.). (Illus.). 1959. text ed. 20.00x (ISBN 0-582-48204-6); pap. text ed. 13.95x (ISBN 0-582-49100-2). Longman.

Brown, Philip A. The French Revolution in English History. 1918. 10.00 (ISBN 0-8482-7376-1). Norwood Edns.

--French Revolution in English History. 234p. 1965. Repr. 25.00x (ISBN 0-7146-1458-0, F Cass Co). Biblio Dist.

Buchan, John. Some Eighteenth Century Byways. LC 72-13299. 1972. Repr. of 1908 ed. lib. bdg. 20.00 (ISBN 0-8414-1178-6). Folcroft.

Campbell, R. H. & Wilson, R. G. Entrepreneurship in Britain, Seventeen Fifty to Nineteen Thirty-Nine. (Documents in Economic History). 1975. text ed. 13.00x (ISBN 0-7136-1524-9). Humanities.

Defoe, Daniel. A General History of the Pyrates. Schonhorn, Manuel, ed. LC 72-5341. (Illus.). xlviii, 732p. 1972. 27.50x (ISBN 0-87249-270-2). U of SC Pr.

De Remusat, Charles. L' Angleterre au XVIIIE siecle, 2 vols. in one. Mayer, J. P., ed. LC 78-67378. (L' Angleterre au XVIIIe siecle). (Fr.). 1979. Repr. of 1865 ed. lib. bdg. 62.00x (ISBN 0-405-11728-0). Arno.

Feldmann, Rodney M., et al. Field Guide: Southern Great Lakes. LC 77-75770. (Geology Field Guide Ser). (Illus.). 1977. pap. text ed. 7.95 (ISBN 0-8403-1730-1). Kendall-Hunt.

Flinn, M. W. British Population Growth 1700-1850. (Studies in Economic & Social History). (Orig.). 1970. pap. text ed. 3.50x (ISBN 0-333-10990-2). Humanities.

Glassey, Lionel K. Politics & the Appointment of Justices of the Peace: 1675-1720. (Historical Monographs). 1979. 29.00x (ISBN 0-19-821875-3). Oxford U Pr.

Glover, Michael. A Very Slippery Fellow: The Life of Sir Robert Wilson 1777-1849. (Illus.). 1978. 15.95x (ISBN 0-19-211745-9). Oxford U Pr.

Greene, Jack P. Great Britain & the American Colonies, Sixteen Six to Seventeen Sixty-Three. 1979. pap. text ed. write for info. (ISBN 0-391-01240-1). Humanities.

Hayter, Tony. The Army & the Crowd in Mid-Georgian England. 239p. 1979. 22.50x (ISBN 0-8476-6034-6). Rowman.

Henriques, Ursula R. Before the Welfare State: Social Administration in Early Industrial Britain. (Themes in British Social History Ser.). 1979. text ed. 23.00x (ISBN 0-582-48594-0); pap. text ed. 11.50x (ISBN 0-582-48595-9). Longman.

Hervey, John. Some Materials Towards Memoirs of the Reign of King George Second, 3 Vols. Sedgwick, Romney, ed. LC 79-119102. Repr. of 1931 ed. Set. 80.00 (ISBN 0-404-03300-8). AMS Pr.

Hilles, F. W., ed. The Age of Johnson: Essays Presented to Chauncey Brewster Tinker. LC 75-41004. Repr. of 1949 ed. 27.50 (ISBN 0-404-14770-4). AMS Pr.

Hook, Judith. The Baroque Age of England. (Illus.). 207p. 1976. 30.00 (ISBN 0-500-23229-6). Transatlantic.

Hunt, W. History of England from the Accession of George Third to the Close of Pitt's First Administration: Seventeen-Sixty to Eighteen Hundred-One. Repr. of 1905 ed. 28.00 (ISBN 0-527-00855-9). Kraus Repr.

Hunt, William. History of England from the Accession of George Third to the Close of Pitt's First Administration. (Political History of England: No. 10). Repr. of 1905 ed. 22.50 (ISBN 0-404-50780-8). AMS Pr.

Jarett, D. England in the Age of Hogarth. (Illus.). 256p. 1980. text ed. 13.75x (ISBN 0-246-64064-2). Humanities.

Jarrett, Derek. England in the Age of Hogarth. (Illus.). 223p. 1976. pap. 5.95 (ISBN 0-586-08251-4, Pub. by Granada England). Academy Chi Ltd.

--England in the Age of Hogarth. 1979. 17.95x (ISBN 0-8464-0101-0). Beekman Pubs.

Jones, Thomas M. Ward of the Generations: The Revolt of 1173-4. LC 80-18411. (Sponsor Ser.). 242p. (Orig.). 1980. pap. 18.50 (ISBN 0-8357-0528-5, SS-00141). Univ Microfilms.

Kelly, John A. England & the Englishman in German Literature of the Eighteenth Century. LC 21-7048. (Columbia University. Germanic Studies, Old Ser.: No. 24). Repr. of 1921 ed. 17.50 (ISBN 0-404-50424-8). AMS Pr.

Lambert, Sheila, ed. The House of Commons Sessional Papers of the Eighteenth Century, 147 vols. LC 74-33160. 1975. 14,000.00 (ISBN 0-8420-1892-1); 2 vols. folio list sold separately 95.00 (ISBN 0-8420-1911-1) (ISBN 0-8420-1912-X). Scholarly Res Inc.

Lawson, Murray B. Fur: A Study in English Mercantilism Seventeen Hundred to Seventeen Seventy-Five. (Illus.). Repr. of 1943 ed. lib. bdg. 13.50x (ISBN 0-87991-813-6). Porcupine Pr.

Leadam, I. S. History of England from the Accession of Anne to the Death of George Second: Seventeen Hundred-Two to Seventeen Sixty. (Political History of England). Repr. of 1909 ed. 24.00 (ISBN 0-685-13711-2). Kraus Repr.

Leadam, Isaac S. History of England from the Accession of Anne to the Death of George Second, 1702-1760. LC 69-13970. 1969. Repr. of 1909 ed. lib. bdg. 20.00x (ISBN 0-8371-0934-5, LEGV). Greenwood.

Leadam, Issac S. History of England from the Accession of Anne to the Death of George the Second. LC 76-5628. (Political History of England: No. 9). Repr. of 1909 ed. 22.50 (ISBN 0-404-50779-4). AMS Pr.

Lecky, William E. History of England in the Eighteenth Century, 7 Vols. rev. ed. LC 68-57226. Repr. of 1893 ed. Set. 210.00 (ISBN 0-404-03930-8); 30.00 ea. AMS Pr.

Lockmeyer, Seymour. Why Great Britain Failed: An Analysis in Political Stupidity. (Illus.). 1978. 49.75 (ISBN 0-89266-100-3). Am Classical Coll Pr.

Lough, John. The Encyclopedie in Eighteenth-Century England: And Other Studies. 1970. 16.50x (ISBN 0-85362-078-4, Oriel). Routledge & Kegan.

MacDonagh, Oliver. The Inspector-General: Sir Jeremiah Fitzpatrick & the Politics of Social Reform 1783-1802. 336p. 1981. 49.00x (ISBN 0-85664-421-8, Pub. by Croom Helm Ltd England). Biblio Dist.

MacDonald, John. Memoirs of an Eighteenth-Century Footman. 1928. Repr. 20.00 (ISBN 0-685-43104-5). Norwood Edns.

Marx, Karl & Hutchinson, Lester, eds. Secret Diplomatic History of the Eighteenth Century & the Story of the Life of Lord Palmerston. 1967. 14.00x (ISBN 0-686-73982-5). Beekman Pubs.

Mathias, Peter. The Transformation of England: Essays in the Economic & Social History of England in the Eighteenth Century. 302p. 1980. 18.50x (ISBN 0-231-05046-1). Columbia U Pr.

Michael, Wolfgang. England Under George First, 2 Vols. LC 79-123757. Repr. of 1939 ed. Set. 74.50 (ISBN 0-404-04314-3). Vol. 1 (ISBN 0-404-04315-1). Vol. 2 (ISBN 0-404-04316-X). AMS Pr.

Mills, Dennis R. Lord & Peasant in Nineteenth Century Britain. (Illus.). 232p. 1980. 31.50x (ISBN 0-8476-6806-1). Rowman.

Mowat, Robert B. England in the Eighteenth Century. LC 72-6111. 1972. Repr. of 1932 ed. lib. bdg. 25.00 (ISBN 0-8414-0120-9). Folcroft.

Owen, John B. Eighteenth Century, Seventeen Fourteen to Eighteen Fifteen. (Norton Library History of England Ser.). (Illus.). 384p. 1976. pap. 4.25 (ISBN 0-393-00366-3, Norton Lib). Norton.

--Eighteenth Century, Seventeen Fourteen to Eighteen Fifteen: 1714-1815. (History of England Ser: No. 6). (Illus.). 365p. 1975. 13.75x (ISBN 0-87471-622-5). Rowman.

Pares, Richard. The Historian's Business & Other Stories. LC 74-9228. (Illus.). 240p. 1974. Repr. of 1961 ed. lib. bdg. 14.00x (ISBN 0-8371-7622-0, PAHB). Greenwood.

Plumb, J. H. England in the Eighteenth Century. lib. bdg. 9.50x (ISBN 0-88307-233-5). Gannon.

Plumb, John H. Men & Centuries. LC 78-26300. 1979. Repr. of 1963 ed. lib. bdg. 20.50x (ISBN 0-313-20868-9, PLMC). Greenwood.

Pocock, J. G., ed. Three British Revolutions: 1641, 1688, 1776. LC 79-27572. (Folger Institute Essays, Published for the Folger Shakespeare Library). 456p. 1980. 32.50 (ISBN 0-691-05293-X); pap. 12.50 (ISBN 0-691-10087-X). Princeton U Pr.

Riely, John C. The Age of Horace Walpole in Caricature: An Exhibition of Satirical Prints & Drawings from the Collection of W. S. Lewis. LC 73-88450. 48p. 1981. pap. text ed. 5.00x (ISBN 0-300-03509-8). Yale U Pr.

Roberts, Michael. British Diplomacy & Swedish Politics, 1758-1773. LC 80-11499. 1980. 29.50x (ISBN 0-8166-0910-1). U of Minn Pr.

Scott, A. F. The Early Hanoverian Age 1714-1760: Commentaries of an Era. (Illus.). 175p. 1980. 20.00x (ISBN 0-7099-0145-3, Pub. by Croom Helm Ltd England). Biblio Dist.

Selley, W. T. England in the Eighteenth Century. 1978. Repr. of 1934 ed. lib. bdg. 30.00 (ISBN 0-8482-6373-1). Norwood Edns.

--England in the Eighteenth Century. 1934. Repr. 25.00 (ISBN 0-8274-2246-6). R West.

Stanhope, Philip H. History of England from the Peace of Utrecht to the Peace of Versaillles, 1713-1783, 7 vols. LC 79-176010. Repr. of 1858 ed. Set. 210.00 (ISBN 0-404-06240-7). AMS Pr.

Stephen, Leslie. English Literature & Society in the Eighteenth Century. Repr. of 1904 ed. lib. bdg. 15.00x (ISBN 0-87991-514-5). Porcupine Pr.

Stevenson, John. Popular Disturbances in England: 1700-1870. (Themes in British Social History Ser.). (Illus.). 1979. text ed. 24.00x (ISBN 0-582-48325-5); pap. text ed. 14.95x (ISBN 0-582-48326-3). Longman.

Toohey, Robert E. Liberty & Empire: British Radical Solutions to the American Problem, 1774-1776. LC 77-84068. 224p. 1978. 16.00 (ISBN 0-8131-1375-X). U Pr of Ky.

Turner, E. The Privy Council of England in the Seventeenth & Eighteenth Centuries, 1603-1784, 2 vols. 1972. lib. bdg. 55.00x (ISBN 0-374-98032-2). Octagon.

Walpole, Horace. Last Journals of Horace Walpole During the Reign of George Third, 2 Vols. Steuart, A. Frances, ed. LC 71-177879. Repr. of 1910 ed. Set. 75.00 (ISBN 0-404-06815-4). AMS Pr.

--Memoirs of the Reign of King George Second, 3 Vols. LC 70-121022. Repr. of 1846 ed. Set. 82.50 (ISBN 0-404-06830-8); 27.50 ea. Vol. 1 (ISBN 0-404-06831-6). Vol. 2 (ISBN 0-404-06832-4). Vol. 3 (ISBN 0-404-06833-2). AMS Pr.

Watson, J. Steven. Reign of George Third, Seventeen Sixty to Eighteen Fifteen. (Oxford History of England Ser). 1960. 35.00x (ISBN 0-19-821713-7). Oxford U Pr.

Webb, Robert K. Modern England: From the Eighteenth Century to the Present. 2nd ed. (Illus.). 685p. 1980. pap. text ed. 14.95 scp (ISBN 0-06-046974-9, HarpC). Har-Row.

Whiting, J. R. A Handful of History. (Illus.). 201p. 1978. 18.50x (ISBN 0-8476-6036-2). Rowman.

Winstanley, D. A. Lord Chatham & the Whig Opposition. 460p. 1966. Repr. 32.50x (ISBN 0-7146-1527-7, F Cass Co). Biblio Dist.

GREAT BRITAIN–HISTORY–18TH CENTURY–BIBLIOGRAPHY

Grose, Clyde L. Select Bibliography of British History, 1660-1760. 1967. lib. bdg. 25.00x (ISBN 0-374-93306-5). Octagon.

GREAT BRITAIN–HISTORY–18TH CENTURY–FICTION

Burton, Hester. To Ravensrigg. LC 76-54292. 1977. 8.95 (ISBN 0-690-01354-X, TYC-J). Har-Row.

Parker, R. A. Coke of Norfolk: A Financial & Agricultural Study, 1707-1842. (Illus.). 232p. 1975. 45.00x (ISBN 0-19-822403-6). Oxford U Pr.

GREAT BRITAIN–HISTORY–18TH CENTURY–SOURCES

George Third. Later Correspondence of George Third, 5 vols. Aspinall, A., ed. Incl. Vol. 1. 1783-1793 (ISBN 0-521-04066-3); Vol. 2. 1793-1797 (ISBN 0-521-04067-1); Vol. 3. 1798-1801 (ISBN 0-521-04068-X); Vol. 4. 1802-1807 (ISBN 0-521-06918-1); Vol. 5. 1807-1810, with Index to Vols. 1-5 (ISBN 0-521-07451-7). LC 61-52516. 700p. 120.00 ea. Cambridge U Pr.

MacDonald, John. Memoirs of an Eighteenth Century Footman. 256p. 1979. Repr. of 1927 ed. lib. bdg. 25.00 (ISBN 0-89984-326-3). Century Bookbindery.

Marlborough, Sarah J. Private Correspondence of Sarah, Duchess of Marlborough, Illustrative of the Court & Times of Queen Anne. Churchill, Sarah J., ed. 1838. Repr. 42.00 (ISBN 0-527-61770-9). Kraus Repr.

Quennell, Peter, ed. Memoirs of William Hickey. (Illus.). 470p. 1975. 25.00 (ISBN 0-7100-8129-4). Routledge & Kegan.

Williams, E. N. Eighteenth-Century Constitution: Documents & Commentary. (English Constitutional History Ser). 47.95 (ISBN 0-521-06810-X); pap. 14.95x (ISBN 0-521-09123-3). Cambridge U Pr.

GREAT BRITAIN–HISTORY–1714-1837

Here are entered works on the period between 1714 and 1837 as a whole or in part.

Arnstein, Walter, ed. The Past Speaks: Sources & Problems in British History Since 1688. 448p. 1981. pap. text ed. 8.95 (ISBN 0-669-02919-X). Heath.

Ashton, John. When William Fourth Was King. LC 67-23943. (Social History Reference Ser). 1968. Repr. of 1896 ed. 19.00 (ISBN 0-8103-3255-8). Gale.

Balderston, Marion & Syrett, David, eds. The Lost War: Letters from British Officers During the American Revolution. LC 75-18570. 237p. 1975. 11.95 (ISBN 0-8180-0813-X). Horizon.

Bhuyan, Suryya K. Anglo-Assamese Relations: Seventeen Seventy-One to Eighteen Twenty-Six. LC 77-87072. Repr. of 1949 ed. 46.00 (ISBN 0-404-16795-0). AMS Pr.

Brady, Alexander. William Huskisson & Liberal Reform. 2nd ed. 177p. 1967. 25.00x (ISBN 0-7146-1456-4, F Cass Co). Biblio Dist.

Brodrick, G. C. History of England from Addington's Administration to the Close of William Fourth's Reign, 1801-1837. Repr. of 1906 ed. 28.00 (ISBN 0-527-00856-7). Kraus Repr.

Calhoun, Craig. The Question of Class Struggle: The Social Foundation of Popular Radicalism During the Industrial Revolution. LC 81-2018. 1981. lib. bdg. 25.00x (ISBN 0-226-09090-6). U of Chicago Pr.

Chaplin, Arnold. Medicine in England During the Reign of George III. LC 75-23695. Repr. of 1919 ed. 15.50 (ISBN 0-404-13244-8). AMS Pr.

Clarke, John. The Price of Progress: Cobbett's England Seventeen Eighty to Eighteen Thirty-Five. 224p. 1980. text ed. 18.25x (ISBN 0-246-10604-2). Humanities.

Cobban, Alfred. Ambassadors & Secret Agents: The Diplomacy of the First Earl of Malmesbury at the Hague. LC 78-59012. (Illus.). 1979. Repr. of 1954 ed. 21.00 (ISBN 0-88355-687-1). Hyperion Conn.

Cook, Chris, et al. British Historical Facts Seventeen Sixty to Eighteen Thirty. ix, 197p. 1980. 32.50 (ISBN 0-208-01868-9, Archon). Shoe String.

Cowie, Leonard W. Hanoverian England, 1714-1837. (Bell Modern History Ser.). 1967. text ed. 18.00x (ISBN 0-7135-0234-7); pap. text ed. 14.50x (ISBN 0-7135-0235-5). Humanities.

Cunliffe, Marcus. Chattel Slavery & Wage Slavery: The Anglo-American Context, 1830-1860. LC 78-27195. (Mercer University Lamar Memorial Lectures: No. 22). (Illus.). 148p. 1979. 9.95 (ISBN 0-8203-0471-9). U of Ga Pr.

Darvall, Frank O. Popular Disturbances & Public Order in Regency England. LC 68-58973. Repr. of 1934 ed. lib. bdg. 17.50x (ISBN 0-678-00458-7). Kelley.

Dwyer, Fred. Georgian People. 1978. 16.95 (ISBN 0-7134-0045-5, Pub. by Batsford England). David & Charles.

Emsley, Clive. British Society & the French Wars, Seventeen Ninety Three - Eighteen Fifteen. (Illus.). 216p. 1979. 19.50x (ISBN 0-8476-6115-6). Rowman.

Floud, R. & McCloskey, D., eds. The Economic History of Britain Since Seventeen Hundred: Volume 2: 1860 to the 1970s. LC 79-41645. (Illus.). 504p. Date not set. price not set (ISBN 0-521-23167-1); pap. text ed. price not set (ISBN 0-521-29843-1). Cambridge U Pr.

Foord, Archibald S. His Majesty's Opposition, Seventeen Fourteen to Eighteen Thirty. LC 79-14245. 1979. Repr. of 1964 ed. lib. bdg. 35.00x (ISBN 0-313-21974-5, FOHM). Greenwood.

Fritz, Paul S. The English Ministers & Jacobitism Between the Rebellions of 1715 & 1745. LC 75-33706. (Illus.). 1975. 20.00x (ISBN 0-8020-5308-4). U of Toronto Pr.

Frost, Alan. Convicts & Empire: A Naval Question, 1776-1811. (Illus.). 280p. 1980. 45.00 (ISBN 0-19-554255-X). Oxford U Pr.

Galpin, W. F. The Grain Supply of England During the Napoleonic Period. 1973. lib. bdg. 15.50x (ISBN 0-374-92985-8). Octagon.

Gipson, Lawrence H. The British Empire Before the American Revolution, 15 vols. Incl. Vol. 1. The British Isles & the American Colonies: Great Britain & Ireland, 1748-1754. rev. ed. 1958 (ISBN 0-394-41784-4); Vol. 2. The British Isles & the American Colonies: The Southern Plantations, 1748-1754. rev. ed. 1960 (ISBN 0-394-41782-8); Vol. 3. The British Isles & the American Colonies: The Northern Plantations, 1748-1754. rev. ed. 1960 (ISBN 0-394-41783-6); Vol. 4. Zones of International Friction: North America, South of the Great Lakes Region, 1748-1754 (ISBN 0-394-45340-9); Vol. 4. Zones of International Friction: The Great Lakes Frontier, Canada, the West Indies, India, 1748-1754014vol. 5 (ISBN 0-394-45341-7); Vol. 6. The Great War for the Empire: The Years of Defeat, 1754-1757 (ISBN 0-394-42718-1); Vol. 7. The Great War for the Empire: The Victorious Years, 1758-1760 (ISBN 0-394-45057-4); Vol. 8. The Great War for the Empire: The Culmination, 1760-1763 (ISBN 0-394-42719-X); Vol. 9. The Triumphant Empire: The Triumphant Empire. 1956 (ISBN 0-394-44963-0); Vol. 10. The Triumphant Empire: Thunder-Clouds Gather in the West, 1763-1766. 1961 (ISBN 0-394-41785-2); Vol. 11. The Triumphant Empire: The Rumbling of the Coming Storm, 1766-1770. 1965 (ISBN 0-394-41791-7); Vol. 12. The Triumphant Empire: Britain Sails into the Storm, 1770-1776. 1965 (ISBN 0-394-41795-X); Vol. 13. The Triumphant Empire: The Empire Beyond the Storm, 1770-1776. 1967 (ISBN 0-394-41797-6); Vol. 14. A Bibliographical Guide to the History of the British Empire, 1748-1776. 1968 (ISBN 0-394-41686-4); Vol. 15. A Guide to Manuscripts Relating to the History of the British Empire, 1748-1776. 1970 (ISBN 0-394-41786-0). Vols. 2-7, 9, 11-15. 15.00 ea. Knopf.

Gordon, Barry. Economic Doctrine & Tory Liberalism Eighteen Twenty-Four to Eighteen Thirty. 1979. text ed. 26.50x (ISBN 0-06-492498-X). B&N.

Great Britain Historical Manuscripts Commission. Report of the Manuscripts of Mrs. Stopford-Sackville of Drayton House, Northamptonshire, 2 vols. Billias, George, ed. LC 72-8813. (American Revolutionary Ser.). Repr. of 1910 ed. Set. lib. bdg. 40.00x (ISBN 0-8398-0803-8). Irvington.

Henderson, W. O., ed. Industrial Britain Under the Regency. (Illus.). 188p. 1968. 23.50x (ISBN 0-7146-1318-5, F Cass Co). Biblio Dist.

Hunt, W. History of England from the Accession of George Third to the Close of Pitt's First Administration: Seventeen-Sixty to Eighteen Hundred-One. Repr. of 1905 ed. 28.00 (ISBN 0-527-00855-9). Kraus Repr.

Hunt, William. History of England from the Accession of George Third to the Close of Pitt's First Administration, 1760-1801. LC 69-13944. Repr. of 1905 ed. lib. bdg. 20.00x (ISBN 0-8371-1574-4, HUHE). Greenwood.

Ingram, Edward. The Beginning of the Great Game in Asia 1828-1834. (Illus.). 1979. 49.50x (ISBN 0-19-822470-2). Oxford U Pr.

--Commitment to Empire: Prophecies of the Great Game in Asia, 1797-1800. 400p. 1981. 66.50 (ISBN 0-19-822662-4). Oxford U Pr.

Jarrett. Britain: Sixteen Eighty-Eight to Eighteen Fifteen. 1976. pap. 9.95 (ISBN 0-312-09695-X). St Martin.

Johnson. Education & Society in England, 1780-1870. (Studies in Economic & Social History). 1980. pap. text ed. 11.50x (ISBN 0-391-01131-6). Humanities.

Kings, Lords & Wicked Libellers: Satire & Protest 1760-1837. (Illus.). 263p. 1974. 22.00 (ISBN 0-7195-2912-3). Transatlantic.

Lane, Peter. Success in British History Seventeen Sixty to Nineteen Fourteen. (Success Ser). (Illus.). 1978. pap. 9.95 (ISBN 0-7195-3483-6). Transatlantic.

Laprade, William T. England & the French Revolution, 1789-1797. LC 77-109922. Repr. of 1909 ed. 12.50 (ISBN 0-404-03878-6). AMS Pr.

Mensing, Raymond C. Toleration & Parliament, 1660-1719. LC 79-63260. 1979. pap. text ed. 9.00 (ISBN 0-8191-0723-9). U Pr of Amer.

Michael, Wolfgang. England Under George First, 2 Vols. LC 79-123757. Repr. of 1939 ed. Set. 74.50 (ISBN 0-404-04314-3). Vol. 1 (ISBN 0-404-04315-1). Vol. 2 (ISBN 0-404-04316-X). AMS Pr.

Namier, Lewis. England in the Age of the American Revolution. 2nd ed. 1974. 25.00 (ISBN 0-312-25270-6); pap. 10.95 (ISBN 0-312-25235-8). St Martin.

Pargellis, Stanley & Medley, D. J. Bibliography of British History: The Eighteenth Century, Seventeen Fourteen to Seventeen Eighty-Nine. 642p. 1977. Repr. of 1951 ed. 30.00x (ISBN 0-87471-953-4). Rowman.

Petrie, Charles. Four Georges. LC 72-118496. 1971. Repr. of 1935 ed. 13.50 (ISBN 0-8046-1244-7). Kennikat.

Society of Gentlemen. The History of the British Empire, from the Year 1765, to the End of 1783, 2 vols. Billias, George, ed. LC 72-10158. (American Revolutionary Ser.). 1979. Repr. of 1798 ed. Set. lib. bdg. 45.00x (ISBN 0-8398-1888-2). Irvington.

Speck, W. A. Stability & Strife: England 1714-1760. (New History of England Ser.). 1977. 15.00x (ISBN 0-674-83347-3). Harvard U Pr.

Stevens, John. England Last Revolution: Pentrich Eighteen Hundred and Seventeen. 167p. 1980. 27.00x (ISBN 0-903485-43-5, Pub. by Moorland England). State Mutual Bk.

Thomas, P. D. British Politics & the Stamp Act Crisis: The First Phase of the American Revolution 1763-1767. 395p. 1975. 45.00x (ISBN 0-19-822431-1). Oxford U Pr.

Trevelyan, George O. Early History of Charles James Fox. LC 79-158852. Repr. of 1880 ed. 31.00 (ISBN 0-404-06524-4). AMS Pr.

Vignoles, Keith H. Dick Burgess of Bosham. (Illus.). 1978. pap. text ed. 10.00x (ISBN 0-9504448-2-0, Pub by Ian Harrap Ltd.). State Mutual Bk.

--A Prisoner of Portchester. (Illus.). 1978. pap. text ed. 10.00x (ISBN 0-9504448-4-7, Pub. by Ian Harrap Ltd). State Mutual Bk.

Walpole, Horace. Memoirs of the Reign of King George the Third, 4 Vols. facs. ed. LC 70-126262. (Select Bibliographies Reprint Ser). 1894. Set. 90.00 (ISBN 0-8369-5489-0). Arno.

--Memoirs of the Reign of King George Third, 4 Vols. Barker, G. Russell, ed. LC 78-144698. (Illus.). Repr. of 1894 ed. Set. 78.50 (ISBN 0-404-06840-5). Vol. 1 (ISBN 0-404-06841-3). Vol. 2 (ISBN 0-404-06842-1). Vol. 3 (ISBN 0-404-06843-X). Vol. 4 (ISBN 0-404-06844-8). AMS Pr.

Ward, Adolphus W. Great Britain & Hanover: Some Aspects of the Personal Union. LC 68-25282. (British History Ser., No. 30). 1969. Repr. lib. bdg. 48.95 (ISBN 0-8383-0252-1). Haskell.

White, Reginald J. Waterloo to Peterloo. LC 72-90571. (Illus.). x, 202p. 1973. Repr. of 1957 ed. 18.00 (ISBN 0-8462-1718-X). Russell.

Williams, Basil. Whig Supremacy, 1714-1760. 2nd ed. Stuart, C. H., ed. (Oxford History of England Ser.). 1962. 35.00x (ISBN 0-19-821710-2). Oxford U Pr.

Williams, Gwyn A. Artisans & Sans-Culottes. LC 69-14476. (Foundations of Modern History Ser). 1969. pap. text ed. 3.95x (ISBN 0-393-09832-X, NortonC). Norton.

Wraxall, Nathaniel W. Historical & Posthumous Memoirs of Sir Nathanial Wraxall, 1772-1784, 5 Vols. Wheatley, Henry B., ed. LC 70-128981. Repr. of 1884 ed. Set. 95.00 (ISBN 0-404-06920-7); 19.00 ea. Vol. 1 (ISBN 0-404-06921-5). Vol. 2 (ISBN 0-404-06922-3). Vol. 3 (ISBN 0-404-06923-1). Vol. 4 (ISBN 0-404-06924-X). Vol. 5 (ISBN 0-404-06925-8). AMS Pr.

Wright, Thomas. Caricature History of the Georges. LC 68-56479. (Illus.). 1968. Repr. of 1868 ed. 35.00 (ISBN 0-405-09106-0). Arno.

Wrong, E. M. History of England: 1688-1815. 1927. Repr. 10.00 (ISBN 0-685-43459-1). Norwood Edns.

GREAT BRITAIN–HISTORY–1714-1837–SOURCES

Aspinall, Arthur & Smith, E. Anthony, eds. English Historical Documents: 1783-1832, Vol. 11. 1959. 69.00x (ISBN 0-19-519508-6). Oxford U Pr.

Care, Henry. English Liberties. LC 75-31087. Repr. of 1774 ed. 28.50 (ISBN 0-404-13505-6). AMS Pr.

Horn, D. B. & Ransome, Mary, eds. English Historical Documents Vol. 10: 1714-1783. 1957. 69.00x (ISBN 0-19-519507-8). Oxford U Pr.

Lambert, Sheila, ed. The House of Commons Sessional Papers of the Eighteenth Century, Part 2: George III, 126 vols. plus list vol. II. 1975. Set. 12,000.00 (ISBN 0-8420-2016-0). Scholarly Res Inc.

Naylor, John F., ed. British Aristocracy & the Peerage Bill of 1719. (Problems in European History Ser). (Orig.). 1968. pap. 4.95x (ISBN 0-19-501004-3). Oxford U Pr.

GREAT BRITAIN–HISTORY–19TH CENTURY

Here are entered works on the nineteenth century as a whole or any part except the reign of Victoria, for which see Great Britain–History–Victoria, 1837-1901.

Alison, A. England in 1815 & 1845. 98p. 1971. Repr. of 1845 ed. 15.00x (ISBN 0-7165-1699-3, Pub. by Irish Academic Pr Ireland). Biblio Dist.

Ashton, John. The Dawn of the Nineteenth Century in England: A Social Sketch of the Times. (Victorian Age Ser). 1936. Repr. 20.00 (ISBN 0-8482-7266-8). Norwood Edns.

--Social England Under the Regency. 1899. 40.00 (ISBN 0-685-43780-9). Norwood Edns.

Aston, John. Social England Under the Regency, Vol. I. (Illus.). 1976. 25.00x (ISBN 0-7158-1110-X). Charles River Bks.

Bagwell, P. S. Industrial Relations in Nineteenth Century Britain. 106p. 1974. 15.00x (ISBN 0-7165-2215-2, Pub. by Irish Academic Pr Ireland). Biblio Dist.

Baily, F. E. The Perfect Age. 187p. 1981. Repr. of 1946 ed. lib. bdg. 30.00 (ISBN 0-89987-064-3). Darby Bks.

Beales, Derek. From Castlereagh to Gladstone, Eighteen Fifteen to Eighteen Eighty Five. (History of England Ser.). (Illus.). 1969. pap. 5.95 (ISBN 0-393-00367-1, Norton Lib). Norton.

Bewes, Richard, ed. John Wesley's England: A Nineteenth Century Pictorial History Based on an 18th Century Journal. (Illus.). 128p. (Orig.). 1981. pap. 9.95 (ISBN 0-8164-2319-9). Seabury.

Brasher, N. H. Arguments in History: Britain in the 19th Century. LC 68-10753. (Illus.). 1969. 15.95 (ISBN 0-312-04900-5). St Martin.

Briggs, Asa. Age of Improvement, 1783 to 1867. (A History of England Ser.). (Illus.). 1959. text ed. 20.00x (ISBN 0-582-48204-6); pap. text ed. 13.95x (ISBN 0-582-49100-2). Longman.

Brock, Michael. The Great Reform Act. Hurstfield, Joel, ed. (Illus.). 411p. 1974. text ed. 18.25x (ISBN 0-09-115910-5, Hutchinson U Lib); pap. text ed. 11.75x (ISBN 0-09-115911-3, Hutchinson U Lib). Humanities.

Brock, William R. Lord Liverpool & Liberal Toryism: 1820-27. 2nd ed. (Illus.). 300p. 1967. 26.00x (ISBN 0-7146-1457-2, F Cass Co). Biblio Dist.

Brodrick, George C. History of England from Addington's Administration to the Close of William Fourth's Reign 1801-1837. rev. ed. Fotheringham, J. K., ed. LC 69-13841. Repr. of 1906 ed. lib. bdg. 20.00x (ISBN 0-8371-0924-8, BRHE). Greenwood.

Brodrick, George C. & Fotheringham, John K. History of England from Addington's Administration to the Close of William Fourth's Reign. LC 71-5624. (Political History of England). Repr. of 1906 ed. 22.50 (ISBN 0-404-50781-6). AMS Pr.

Cain, Peter J. Economic Foundations of British Overseas Expansion 1815-1914. (Studies in Economic & Social History). 1980. pap. text ed. 5.25x (ISBN 0-333-23284-4). Humanities.

Campbell, R. H. & Wilson, R. G. Entrepreneurship in Britain, Seventeen Fifty to Nineteen Thirty-Nine. (Documents in Economic History). 1975. text ed. 13.00x (ISBN 0-7136-1524-9). Humanities.

Chadwick, E. Report on the Sanitary Condition of the Labouring Population of Great Britain, 1842. Flinn, M., ed. 1965. 25.00x (ISBN 0-85224-145-3, Pub. by Edinburgh U Pr Scotland). Columbia U Pr.

Checkland, S. G. The Rise of Industrial Society: 1815-1855. (Social & Economic History of England). 1964. text ed. 12.95x (ISBN 0-582-48239-9). Longman.

Church, R. A. The Great Victorian Boom. (Studies in Economic & Social History Ser.). 1975. pap. text ed. 5.25x (ISBN 0-333-14350-7). Humanities.

Church, R. W. Oxford Movement Twelve Years, 1833-1845. Best, Geoffrey, ed. LC 77-115873. (Classics of British Historical Literature Ser). 1972. pap. 3.25 (ISBN 0-226-10619-5, P426, Phoen). U of Chicago Pr.

Cook, Chris & Keith, Brendan. British Historical Facts: 1830-1900. LC 74-76689. 400p. 1975. text ed. 29.95 (ISBN 0-312-10290-9). St Martin.

Datta, K. K. Anti-British Plots & Movements Before 1857. 1970. 5.50x (ISBN 0-8426-0169-4). Verry.

Davis, Henry W. Age of Grey & Peel. LC 64-15028. 1964. Repr. of 1929 ed. 10.00 (ISBN 0-8462-0461-4). Russell.

Dicey, Albert V. Lectures on the Relation Between Law & Public Opinion in England During the Nineteenth Century. LC 81-2391. (Social Science Classics Ser.). 506p. 1981. text ed. 19.95 cancelled (ISBN 0-87855-429-7); pap. text ed. 19.95 (ISBN 0-87855-869-1). Transaction Bk.

Digby. Children: School & Society in 19th Century England. 1980. text ed. 24.00x (ISBN 0-333-24678-0). Humanities.

Durey, Michael. The Return of the Plague: British Society & the Cholera 1831-32. 1979. text ed. 39.00x (ISBN 0-391-01038-7). Humanities.

Eldridge, G. C. Victorian Imperialism. (Illus.). 1978. text ed. 18.75x (ISBN 0-391-00823-4); pap. text ed. 8.75x (ISBN 0-391-00824-2). Humanities.

Escott, T. H. Platform, Press, Politics & Plays: Being Pen & Ink Sketches of Contemporary Celeberties. (Victorian Age Ser). 45.00 (ISBN 0-685-43402-8). Norwood Edns.

Fetter, F. W. & Gregory, D. Monetary & Financial Policy in Nineteenth Century Britain. (Government & Society in 19th Century Britain Ser.). 106p. 1973. 15.00x (ISBN 0-7165-2217-9, Pub. by Irish Academic Pr Ireland); pap. 6.00x o. p. (ISBN 0-7165-2218-7). Biblio Dist.

Focal Aspects of the Industrial Revolution: 1825-42, Five Pamphlets. (The Development of Industrial Society Ser.). 198p. 1971. Repr. of 1842 ed. 25.00x (ISBN 0-7165-1562-8, Pub. by Irish Academic Pr England). Biblio Dist.

Fremantle, Alan F. England in the Nineteenth Century, 2 vols. LC 30-6644. 1976. Repr. of 1929 ed. 48.00 (ISBN 0-527-31530-3). Kraus Repr.

Gallardo, Alexander. Britain & the First Carlist War. LC 78-26910. 1978. lib. bdg. 25.00 (ISBN 0-8482-4175-4). Norwood Edns.

Gladstone, William E. Gleanings of Past Years, 1843-1878, 8 Vols. LC 72-148788. Repr. of 1897 ed. Set. 180.00 (ISBN 0-404-08850-3). AMS Pr.

Gooch, G. P. History of Our Time: 1885-1911. 1977. Repr. lib. bdg. 12.50 (ISBN 0-8495-1905-5). Arden Lib.

Great Britain, Parliament, House of Commons, Select Committee on Artizans & Machinery. Six Reports from the Select Committee on Artizans & Machinery, 23 February - 21 May 1824. LC 68-110405. Date not set. Repr. of 1824 ed. lib. bdg. 45.00x (ISBN 0-678-05229-8). Kelley.

Halevy, Elie. History of the English People in 1815. 10.00 (ISBN 0-8446-0671-5). Peter Smith.

--History of the English People: 1815-1830. 10.00 (ISBN 0-8446-0672-3). Peter Smith.

--History of the English People: 1830-1841. 10.00 (ISBN 0-8446-0673-1). Peter Smith.

--History of the English People: 1841-1895. 10.00 (ISBN 0-8446-0674-X). Peter Smith.

--History of the English People: 1895-1905. 10.00 (ISBN 0-8446-0675-8). Peter Smith.

Hanham, H. J. Elections & Party Management: Politics in the Time of Disraeli & Gladstone. 2nd ed. 1978. 27.50 (ISBN 0-208-01550-7, Archon). Shoe String.

Hardy, Dennis. Alternative Communities in Nineteenth Century England. (Illus.). 1979. text ed. 30.00x (ISBN 0-582-50213-6). Longman.

Harrison, Royden, ed. The English Defence of the Commune, 1871. 1971. lib. bdg. 15.00x (ISBN 0-678-08070-4). Kelley.

Harvey, A. D. Britain in the Early Nineteenth Century. LC 77-15016. 1978. 25.00x (ISBN 0-312-09747-6). St Martin.

Hayter, Tony. The Army & the Crowd in Mid-Georgian England. 239p. 1979. 22.50x (ISBN 0-8476-6034-6). Rowman.

Henriques, Ursula R. Before the Welfare State: Social Administration in Early Industrial Britain. (Themes in British Social History Ser.). 1979. text ed. 23.00x (ISBN 0-582-48594-0); pap. text ed. 11.50x (ISBN 0-582-48595-9). Longman.

Hilton, Boyd. Corn, Cash, Commerce: The Economic Policies of the Tory Government, 1815-1830. (Oxford Historical Monographs). 1978. 29.00x (ISBN 0-19-821864-8). Oxford U Pr.

Hunt, William. History of England from the Accession of George Third to the Close of Pitt's First Administration. (Political History of England: No. 10). Repr. of 1905 ed. 22.50 (ISBN 0-404-50780-8). AMS Pr.

Hussey, W. D. British History, Eighteen Fifteen to Nineteen Thirty-Nine. LC 79-149429. (Illus.). 1972. 11.50 (ISBN 0-521-07985-3). Cambridge U Pr.

Jackson, J. Hampden. England Since the Industrial Revolution, 1815-1848. LC 75-7239. (Illus.). 298p. 1975. Repr. of 1949 ed. lib. bdg. 16.00x (ISBN 0-8371-8102-X, JAES). Greenwood.

James, Robert R. The British Revolution 1880-1939. 1977. 17.95 (ISBN 0-394-40761-X). Knopf.

Jenkins, Mick. The General Strike of Eighteen Forty-Two. (Illus.). 300p. 1980. text ed. 24.75x (ISBN 0-85315-488-0). Humanities.

Johnson. Education & Society in England, 1780-1870. (Studies in Economic & Social History). 1980. pap. text ed. 11.50x (ISBN 0-391-01131-6). Humanities.

Johnston, James P. A Hundred Years Eating: Food, Drink, & the Daily Diet in Britain Since the Late Nineteenth Century. (Illus.). 1977. 9.95 (ISBN 0-7735-0306-4). McGill-Queens U Pr.

Johnston, W. Ross. Sovereignty & Protection: A Study of British Jurisdictional Imperialism in the Late Nineteenth Century. LC 72-96681. (Commonwealth Studies Center: No. 41). 360p. 1973. 16.75 (ISBN 0-8223-0282-9). Duke.

Kent, Christopher. Brains & Numbers: Elitism, Comtism, & Democracy in Mid-Victorian England. LC 77-21722. 1978. 20.00x (ISBN 0-8020-5360-2). U of Toronto Pr.

Knights, B. The Idea of the Clerisy, in the Nineteenth Century. LC 77-80840. 1978. 42.00 (ISBN 0-521-21798-9). Cambridge U Pr.

Krein, David F. Last Palmerston Government: Foreign Policy, Domestic Politics, & the Genesis of "Splendid Isolation". replica ed. 1978. pap. 8.50x (ISBN 0-8138-1945-8). Iowa St U Pr.

Lacey, Robert. Peninsular War. (Jackdaw Ser: No. 72). 1971. 6.95 (ISBN 0-670-54625-9, Grossman). Viking Pr.

Lane, Peter. Success in British History Seventeen Sixty to Nineteen Fourteen. (Success Ser). (Illus.). 1978. pap. 9.95 (ISBN 0-7195-3483-6). Transatlantic.

Lean, E. Tangye. Napoleonists: A Study in Political Disaffection, 1760-1960. 1970. 17.00x (ISBN 0-19-215184-3). Oxford U Pr.

Lockmeyer, Seymour. Why Great Britain Failed: An Analysis in Political Stupidity. (Illus.). 1978. 49.75 (ISBN 0-89266-100-3). Am Classical Coll Pr.

McCarthy, Justin. The Epoch of Reform: 1830-1850. Repr. 10.00 (ISBN 0-685-43100-2). Norwood Edns.

MacDonald, D. F. Age of Transition: Britain in the Nineteenth Twentieth Centuries. 1967. 16.95 (ISBN 0-312-01330-2). St Martin.

MacKenzie, Robert. The Nineteenth Century: A History. Repr. of 1889 ed. 15.00 (ISBN 0-685-43417-6). Norwood Edns.

McLaren, Angus. Birth Control in Nineteenth Century England: A Social & Intellectual History. LC 77-16654. 1978. text ed. 26.00x (ISBN 0-8419-0349-2). Holmes & Meier.

Madden, L. How to Find Out About the Victorian Period. LC 74-116777. 1970. text ed. 22.00 (ISBN 0-08-015834-X); pap. text ed. 10.75 (ISBN 0-08-015833-1). Pergamon.

Marlow, Joyce. The Tolpuddle Martyrs. 1972. 12.50 (ISBN 0-233-95820-7). Transatlantic.

Martineau, Harriet. A History of the Thirty Years' Peace 1816-1846, 4 vols. (The Development of Industrial Society Ser.). 2007p. 1971. Repr. of 1878 ed. 160.00x (ISBN 0-7165-1753-1, Pub. by Irish Academic Pr). Biblio Dist.

Mills, Dennis R. Lord & Peasant in Nineteenth Century Britain. (Illus.). 232p. 1980. 31.50x (ISBN 0-8476-6806-1). Rowman.

Millward, Michael & Coe, Brian. Victorian Townscape: The Work of Samuel Smith. LC 76-16439. (Illus.). 120p. 1977. 25.00 (ISBN 0-87951-050-1). Overlook Pr.

Money, John. Experience & Identity: Birmingham & the West Midlands 1760-1800. 1977. lib. bdg. 18.00x (ISBN 0-7735-0290-4). McGill-Queens U Pr.
Nicholls, David. Nineteenth-Century Britian. 1978. 17.50 (ISBN 0-208-01730-5, Archon). Shoe String.
O'Farrell, P. J. England & Ireland Since 1800. 189p. 1975. pap. text ed. 3.95x (ISBN 0-19-289045-X). Oxford U Pr.
Oman, C. W. England in the Nineteenth Century. (Victorian Age Ser). 1905. Repr. 15.00 (ISBN 0-685-43422-2). Norwood Edns.
Parker, R. A. Coke of Norfolk: A Financial & Agricultural Study, 1707-1842. (Illus.). 232p. 1975. 45.00x (ISBN 0-19-822403-6). Oxford U Pr.
Peel, F. Rising of the Luddites, Chartists and Plug-Drawers. 4th ed. (Illus.). 348p. 1968. 27.50x (ISBN 0-7146-1350-9, F Cass Co). Biblio Dist.
Philips, David. Crime & Authority in Victorian England: The Black Country 1835-1860. 321p. 1977. 20.00x (ISBN 0-87471-866-X). Rowman.
Pickthall, Marmaduke, ed. The Glorious Koran. bilingual ed. 1696p. 1976. text ed. 50.00x (ISBN 0-04-297036-9). Allen Unwin.
Platt, D. C. Latin America & British Trade: 1806-1914. (Merchant Adventurers). (Illus.). 1972. text ed. 11.25x (ISBN 0-7136-1309-2). Humanities.
Powell, Geoffrey. The Kandyan Wars: The British Army in Ceylon, 1803-1818. (Nineteenth Century Military Campaigns Ser.). 320p. 1973. 18.50 (ISBN 0-85052-106-8). Shoe String.
Prentice, Archibald. History of the Anti-Corn Law League, 2 vols. 2nd ed. 1968. Repr. of 1853 ed. 65.00x (ISBN 0-7146-1352-5, F Cass Co). Biblio Dist.
Pyne, W. H. Picturesque Views of Rural Occupations in Early Nineteenth Century England, from Ackerman's Edition of Microcosm. 10.00 (ISBN 0-8446-5653-4). Peter Smith.
Ranger, C. Gray's Inn Journal. 1978. 50.00 (ISBN 0-379-20369-3). Oceana.
Roach, John. Social Reform in England 1780-1880. LC 78-6384. 1978. 22.50x (ISBN 0-312-73481-6). St Martin.
Schuyler, R. L. & Weston, C. C. British Constitutional History Since 1832. 5.00 (ISBN 0-8446-2891-3). Peter Smith.
Seeley, John R. The Expansion of England. Gross, John, ed. LC 73-152225. (Classics of British Historical Literature Ser). 1973. pap. 3.25 (ISBN 0-226-74429-9, P429, Phoen). U of Chicago Pr.
Shannon, Richard. Crisis of Imperialism Eighteen Sixty-Five to Nineteen Fifteen. 1974. 16.95x (ISBN 0-19-520119-1). Oxford U Pr.
Short, Kenneth. The Dynamite War: Irish-American Bombers in Victorian Britain. (Illus.). 1979. text ed. 23.25x (ISBN 0-391-00964-8). Humanities.
Somervell, D. C. English Thought in the Nineteenth Century. 1978. Repr. of 1938 ed. lib. bdg. 25.00 (ISBN 0-8492-2594-9). R West.
Stevens, J. England's Last Revolution: Pentrich 1817. 1977. 18.00 (ISBN 0-903485-43-5). State Mutual Bk.
Stevenson, John. Popular Disturbances in England: 1700-1870. (Themes in British Social History Ser.). (Illus.). 1979. text ed. 24.00x (ISBN 0-582-48325-5); pap. text ed. 14.95x (ISBN 0-582-48326-3). Longman.
Sturt, George. A Small Boy in the Sixties. 1977. Repr. of 1952 ed. text ed. 13.00x (ISBN 0-85527-244-9). Humanities.
Taylor, A. J. Essays in English History. (Pelican Ser.). 1976. pap. 2.95 (ISBN 0-14-021862-9, Pelican). Penguin.
Thomson, David. England in the Nineteenth Century, 1815-1914. lib. bdg. 10.50x (ISBN 0-88307-467-2). Gannon.
--England in the Nineteenth Century, 1815-1914. lib. bdg. 10.50x (ISBN 0-88307-467-2). Gannon.
Thomson, Dorothy. British People Seventeen Sixty to Nineteen Two. 1969. pap. text ed. 10.50 (ISBN 0-435-31890-X). Heinemann Ed.
Tobias, J. J. Prince of Fences: The Life & Crimes of Ikey Solomons. (Illus.). 178p. 1974. 18.00x (ISBN 0-85303-174-6, Pub. by Vallentine Mitchell England). Biblio Dist.
Turner, Frank M. Greek Heritage in Victorian Britain. LC 80-24013. (Illus.). 512p. 1981. 30.00x (ISBN 0-300-02480-0). Yale U Pr.
Turner, James. Reckoning with the Beast: Animals, Pain & Humanity in the Victorian Mind. LC 80-11559. 224p. 1980. text ed. 14.00x (ISBN 0-8018-2399-4). Johns Hopkins.
Unger, C. R., ed. Thomas Saga Erkipyskups. LC 80-1942. Repr. of 1869 ed. 72.00 (ISBN 0-404-18723-4). AMS Pr.
Uzoigwe, G. N. Britain & the Conquest of Africa: The Age of Salisbury. LC 73-80577. (Illus.). 1974. text ed. 14.00x (ISBN 0-472-08920-X). U of Mich Pr.
Von Raumer, Frederick. England in Eighteen Thirty Five, 3 vols. 908p. 1971. Repr. of 1836 ed. 84.00x (ISBN 0-686-28334-1, Pub. by Irish Academic Pr). Biblio Dist.
Webb, Robert K. Modern England: From the Eighteenth Century to the Present. 2nd ed. (Illus.). 685p. 1980. pap. text ed. 14.95 scp (ISBN 0-06-046974-9, HarpC). Har-Row.
White, Arnold. Efficiency & Empire. Searle, G. R., ed. LC 70-131993. (Society & Victorians: No. 15). 315p. 1973. Repr. of 1901 ed. text ed. 17.25x (ISBN 0-901759-42-2). Humanities.
Wiener, Martin. English Culture & the Decline of the Industrial Spirit, 1850-1980. (Illus.). 256p. 1981. 15.95 (ISBN 0-521-23418-2). Cambridge U Pr.
Woodward, Llewellyn. Age of Reform, Eighteen Fifteen to Eighteen Seventy. 2nd ed. 1962. 33.00x (ISBN 0-19-821711-0). Oxford U Pr.

GREAT BRITAIN–HISTORY–19TH CENTURY–SOURCES

Asquith, Herbert H. Occasional Addresses, Eighteen Ninety-Three - Nineteen Sixteen. facsimile ed. LC 76-99715. (Essay Index Reprint Ser). Repr. of 1918 ed. 16.00 (ISBN 0-8369-1368-X). Arno.
Brown, Bryan. The England of Henry Taunt, Victorian Photographer: His Thames, His Oxford, His Home Counties, & Travels, His Portraits, Times & Ephemera. (Illus.). 1974. 15.95 (ISBN 0-7100-7542-1). Routledge & Kegan.
Disraeli, Benjamin. The Works of Benjamin Disraeli, Earl of Beaconsfield, 20 vols. Incl. Vols. 1-2. Vivian Grey: A Romance of Youth. LC 76-12451; Vols. 3-4. The Young Duke, etc. LC 76-12450; Vols. 5-6. Contarini Fleming: A Psychological Romance, etc. LC 76-12449; Vol. 7. Alroy: Or, the Prince of the Captivity. LC 76-12448; Vols. 8-9. Henrietta Temple: A Love Story, etc. LC 76-12447; Vols. 10-11. Venetia, etc. LC 76-12445; Vols. 12-13. Coningsby: Or, the New Generation & Selected Speeches. LC 76-12444; Vols. 17-18. Lothair & Letters to His Sister. LC 76-12443; Vols. 19-20. Endymion, Miscellania. LC 76-12442; Vols. 14-16. Sybil; Tancred. LC 76-148746. (Illus.). Repr. of 1904 ed. Set. 550.00 (ISBN 0-404-08800-7); 27.50 ea. AMS Pr.
Handcock, W. D., ed. English Historical Documents: 1874-1914, Vol. XII, Part 2. (English Historical Documents Ser.). (Illus.). 1978. 55.00x (ISBN 0-19-519994-4). Oxford U Pr.
Jackman, Sydney W., ed. English Reform Tradition Seventeen Ninety to Nineteen Ten. 5.50 (ISBN 0-8446-2295-8). Peter Smith.
Levine, George L., ed. Emergence of Victorian Consciousness. LC 66-24458. 1967. pap. text ed. 6.95 (ISBN 0-02-918890-3). Free Pr.
National Reformer & Manx Weekly Review of Home & Foreign Affairs, Nos. 1-35. 1846-47. Repr. of 1846 ed. lib. bdg. 27.50x (ISBN 0-8371-9211-0, NB00). Greenwood.
Walpole, Horace. Horace Walpole's Correspondence with Mary & Agnes & Mary Berry Ii. Lewis, W. S. & Wallace, A. Dayle, eds. (Horace Walpole's Correspondence Ser.: Vol. 12). (Illus.). 1944. 40.00x (ISBN 0-300-00697-7). Yale U Pr.
Young, George M. & Handcock, W. D., eds. English Historical Documents: 1833-1874, Vol. 12, Pt. 1. 1956. 69.00x (ISBN 0-19-519509-4). Oxford U Pr.

GREAT BRITAIN–HISTORY–VICTORIA, 1837-1901

Altick, Richard D. Victorian People & Ideas. (Illus.). 338p. 1974. pap. 6.95x (ISBN 0-393-09376-X). Norton.
Ardizzone, Edward, illus. Ardizzone's Kilvert: Selections from the Diary of the Rev. Francis Kilvert 1870-79. abr. ed. (Illus.). 176p. (gr. 5-7). 1980. 7.95 (ISBN 0-224-01276-2, Pub. by Chatto Bodley Jonathan). Merrimack Bk Serv.
Arnstein, Walter, ed. The Past Speaks: Sources & Problems in British History Since 1688. 448p. 1981. pap. text ed. 8.95 (ISBN 0-669-02919-X). Heath.
Ashton, John. Gossip in the First Decade of Victoria's Reign. (Victorian Age Ser). Repr. of 1903 ed. 20.00 (ISBN 0-8482-7273-0). Norwood Edns.
Auchincloss, Louis. Persons of Consequence: Queen Victoria & Her Circle. LC 78-26626. (Illus.). 1979. 17.95 (ISBN 0-394-50427-5). Random.
Aydelotte, W. O. Bismarck & British Colonial Policy: The Problem of South West Africa, 1883-1885. LC 76-120225. 1970. Repr. lib. bdg. 14.00x (ISBN 0-374-90325-5). Octagon.
Banks, J. A. Victorian Values: Secularism & the Smaller Family. 288p. 1981. price not set (ISBN 0-7100-0807-4). Routledge & Kegan.
Baumann, Arthur. The Last Victorians. (Victorian Age Ser). 1927. Repr. 20.00 (ISBN 0-8482-7392-3). Norwood Edns.
Beaver, Patrick. Crystal Palace, 1851-36: A Portrait of Victorian Enterprise. (Illus.). 1970. 20.00x (ISBN 0-238-78961-6). Intl Pubns Serv.
--The Spice of Life: Pleasures of the Victorian Age. (Illus.). 1979. 24.00 (ISBN 0-241-89366-6, Pub. by Hamish Hamilton England). David & Charles.
Blair, R. & Hunter, David. In Victorian Days & Other Papers. 1979. Repr. of 1939 ed. lib. bdg. 25.00 (ISBN 0-8482-3415-4). Norwood Edns.
Bolt, Christine. Victorian Attitudes to Race. LC 79-151362. 1971. 17.50x (ISBN 0-8020-1751-7). U of Toronto Pr.
Bradley, Ian. The Optimists: Themes & Personalities in Victorian Liberalism. LC 80-670269. 301p. 1980. 37.00 (ISBN 0-571-11495-4, Pub. by Faber & Faber). Merrimack Bk Serv.
Brett, R. L., ed. Barclay Fox's Journal. (Illus.). 426p. 1979. 23.50x (ISBN 0-8476-6187-3). Rowman.
Briggs, Asa. Victorian People: A Reassessment of Persons & Themes, 1851-67. rev. ed. LC 55-7479. (Illus.). 1973. 15.00x (ISBN 0-226-07487-0). U of Chicago Pr.
--Victorian People: A Reassessment of Persons & Themes, 1851-67. new rev. ed. LC 55-5118. (Chicago Collectors Editions Ser.). (Illus.). x, 314p. 1975. pap. 4.95 (ISBN 0-226-07488-9, P365, Phoen). U of Chicago Pr.
Bromwich, D. & Dunning, R. Victorian & Edwardian Somerset. 1977. 19.95 (ISBN 0-7134-0405-1, Pub. by Batsford England). David & Charles.
Burgess, John W. The Middle Period. 1897. 30.00 (ISBN 0-8482-7399-0). Norwood Edns.
--Reconstruction & the Constitution 1866-1876. 1902. 15.00 (ISBN 0-685-43771-X). Norwood Edns.
Burn, William L. Age of Equipoise. 1965. pap. 3.95x (ISBN 0-393-00319-1, Norton Lib). Norton.
Butt, J. & Clarke, I. F., eds. The Victorians & Social Protest: A Symposium. 239p. 1973. 19.50 (ISBN 0-208-01329-6, Archon). Shoe String.
Conacher, J. B. The Peelites & the Party System, 1846-52. (Library of Politics & Society Ser.). 236p. 1972. 17.50 (ISBN 0-208-01268-0, Archon). Shoe String.
Coustillas, Pierre, ed. London & the Life of Literature in Late Victorian England: The Diary of George Gissing, Novelist. LC 77-72970. 617p. 1978. 40.00 (ISBN 0-8387-2145-1). Bucknell U Pr.
Crossick, Geoffrey. An Artisan Elite in Victorian Society: Kentish London 1840-1880. 306p. 1978. 24.50x (ISBN 0-8476-6098-2). Rowman.
Cunliffe, Marcus. Chattel Slavery & Wage Slavery: The Anglo-American Context, 1830-1860. LC 78-27195. (Mercer University Lamar Memorial Lectures: No. 22). (Illus.). 148p. 1979. 9.95 (ISBN 0-8203-0471-9). U of Ga Pr.
Dod, Charles. Electoral Facts from 1832-1853, Impartially Stated. A Complete Political Gazetteer. Hanham, H. J., ed. 388p. 1972. Repr. of 1853 ed. 25.00x (ISBN 0-8476-6051-6). Rowman.
Dunbar, Janet. The Early Victorian Woman: Some Aspects of Her Life, 1837-1857. LC 78-59019. (Illus.). 1979. Repr. of 1953 ed. 21.00 (ISBN 0-88355-693-6). Hyperion Conn.
Dyos, H. J. & Wolff, Michael, eds. The Victorian City-Images & Realities, Vol. 2: Shapes on the Ground & a Change of Accent. (Illus.). 1978. pap. 18.00 (ISBN 0-7100-8812-4). Routledge & Kegan.
Ensor, Robert C. England, 1870-1914. (Oxford History of England Ser.). 1936. 32.50x (ISBN 0-19-821705-6). Oxford U Pr.
Erickson, Arvel B. The Public Career of Sir James Graham. LC 74-382. 433p. 1974. Repr. of 1952 ed. lib. bdg. 20.00x (ISBN 0-8371-7383-3, ERJG). Greenwood.
Fay, Anna M. Victorian Days in England: Letters of an American Girl, 1851-1852. 1979. Repr. of 1923 ed. lib. bdg. 30.00 (ISBN 0-8482-3954-7). Norwood Edns.
Fletcher, Ronald. Biography of a Victorian Village. 1979. 19.95 (ISBN 0-7134-0787-5, Pub. by Batsford England). David & Charles.
Ford, Colin & Strong, Roy, eds. An Early Victorian Album. 1977. 35.00 (ISBN 0-394-49733-3). Knopf.
Goff, Martin. Victorian & Edwardian Surrey. 1972. 19.95 (ISBN 0-7134-0123-0, Pub. by Batsford England). David & Charles.
Gooch, John. The Prospect of War: British Defence Policy Eighteen Forty-Seven to Nineteen Forty-Two. 150p. 1981. 25.00x (ISBN 0-7146-3128-0, F Cass Co). Biblio Dist.
Grugel, Lee E. George Jacob Holyoake: A Study in the Evolution of a Victorian Radical. LC 76-8241. 225p. 1975. lib. bdg. 15.00x (ISBN 0-87991-619-2). Porcupine Pr.
--Society & Religion During the Age of Industrialization: Christianity in Victorian England. LC 78-65844. (Illus.). 1979. pap. text ed. 7.50 (ISBN 0-8191-0671-2). U Pr of Amer.
Harris, B. E., ed. A History of the County of Chester, Vol. 3. (Victoria History of the Counties of England Ser.). (Illus.). 260p. 1980. 169.00 (ISBN 0-19-722754-6). Oxford U Pr.
Harrison, Fraser. The Dark Angel: Aspects of Victorian Sexuality. LC 76-58096. (Illus.). 1978. 12.50x (ISBN 0-87663-229-0). Universe.
Hollis, Patricia, ed. Pressure from Without in Early Victorian England. LC 74-76016. 356p. 1974. 21.50 (ISBN 0-312-64155-9). St Martin.
Huggett, Frank E. Carriages at Eight. 1980. 15.95 (ISBN 0-684-16421-3). Scribner.
Hughes, M. Vivian. A Victorian Family, 3 vols. 608p. 1979. pap. text ed. 13.95 boxed set (ISBN 0-19-281280-7). Oxford U Pr.
Hurstfield, Joel. Queen's Wards: Wardship & Marriage Under Elizabeth I. (Illus.). 492p. 1973. 27.50x (ISBN 0-7146-2953-7, F Cass Co). Biblio Dist.
Hynes, William G. The Economics of Empire: Britain, Africa & the New Imperialism, 1870-1895. (Illus.). 1979. text ed. 22.00x (ISBN 0-582-64234-5); pap. text ed. 9.95x (ISBN 0-582-64235-3). Longman.
Inge, William R. The Victorian Age. 54p. Date not set. Repr. of 1922 ed. lib. bdg. 10.00 (ISBN 0-89987-411-8). Darby Bks.
--The Victorian Age. 1978. lib. bdg. 7.50 (ISBN 0-8495-2605-1). Arden Lib.
Ingle, Harold N. Nesselrode & the Russian Rapprochement with Britain, 1836-1843. LC 74-79764. 1976. 22.75x (ISBN 0-520-02795-7). U of Cal Pr.
Joyce, Patrick. Work, Society, & Politics: The Culture of the Factory in Later Victorian England. 1980. 25.00 (ISBN 0-8135-0899-1). Rutgers U Pr.
Kellett, Ernest E. Religion & Life in the Early Victorian Age. LC 76-6509. 1976. Repr. of 1938 ed. lib. bdg. 20.00 (ISBN 0-8414-5522-8). Folcroft.
Kemnitz, Thomas M. Structures of Working-Class Conciousness: The Chartist Experience. 1979. lib. bdg. 25.00 (ISBN 0-89824-001-8); pap. 10.00 (ISBN 0-89824-002-6). Trillium Pr.
Kingsford, P. W. Victorian Railwaymen: Emergence & Growth of Railway Labour, 1830-1870. (Illus.). 198p. 1970. 25.00x (ISBN 0-7146-1331-2, F Cass Co). Biblio Dist.
Knickerbocker, Frances W. Free Minds: John Morley & His Friends. Repr. of 1943 ed. lib. bdg. 15.00x (ISBN 0-8371-2803-X, KNFM). Greenwood.
Lasdun, Susan. Victorians at Home. 160p. 1981. 20.00 (ISBN 0-670-74600-2, Studio). Viking Pr.
Le May, G. H. The Victorian Constitution. 1979. 25.00x (ISBN 0-686-57422-2). St Martin.
Longford, Elizabeth, ed. Louisa, Lady in Waiting: The Personal Diaries & Albums of Louisa, Lady in Waiting to Queen Victoria & Queen Alexandra. LC 78-24247. (Illus.). 1979. 14.95 (ISBN 0-8317-5650-0, Mayflower Bks). Smith Pubs.
Low, S. & Sanders, L. C. History of England During the Reign of Victoria: Eighteen Thirty-Seven to Nineteen Hundred-One. Repr. of 1907 ed. 24.00 (ISBN 0-527-00857-5). Kraus Repr.
Low, Sidney & Sanders, Lloyd C. History of England During the Reign of Victoria, 1837-1907. LC 68-25247. (British History Ser., No. 30). (Illus.). 1969. Repr. of 1907 ed. lib. bdg. 57.95 (ISBN 0-8383-0267-X). Haskell.
Low, Sidney J. & Sanders, Lloyd C. History of England During the Reign of Victoria, 1837-1901. LC 74-5630. (Political History of England: No. 12). Repr. of 1907 ed. 22.50 (ISBN 0-404-50782-4). AMS Pr.
--History of England During the Reign of Victoria, 1837-1901. LC 69-13977. 1969. Repr. of 1907 ed. lib. bdg. 20.00x (ISBN 0-8371-1575-2, LOEV). Greenwood.
McCloskey, Donald N. Enterprise & Trade in Victorian Britain: Essays in Historical Economics. (Illus.). 240p. 1981. text ed. 37.50x (ISBN 0-04-942170-0); pap. text ed. 14.50x (ISBN 0-04-942171-9). Allen Unwin.
McKinlay, Brian. First Royal Tour, 1867-1868. (Illus.). 1970. 9.00x (ISBN 0-8426-1364-1). Verry.
Major, J. Kenneth & Watts, Martin. Victorian & Edwardian Windmills & Watermills. 1977. 17.95 (ISBN 0-7134-0621-6, Pub. by Batsford England). David & Charles.
Margetson, Stella. Victorian People. 1977. 16.95 (ISBN 0-7134-1010-8, Pub. by Batsford England). David & Charles.
Marshall, John & Davies-Spiell, Michael. Victorian & Edwardian Lake District. 1976. pap. 8.95 (ISBN 0-7134-3417-1, Pub. by Batsford England). David & Charles.
Martineau, Harriet. A History of the Thirty Years' Peace 1816-1846, 4 vols. (The Development of Industrial Society Ser.). 2007p. 1971. Repr. of 1878 ed. 160.00x (ISBN 0-7165-1753-1, Pub. by Irish Academic Pr). Biblio Dist.
Mastermar, C. F. The Heart of the Empire: Discussions of Problems of Modern City Life in England with an Essay on Imperialism. Gilbert, B., ed. (Society & the Victorians). 1973. Repr. text ed. 12.50x (ISBN 0-901759-82-1). Humanities.

Millman, Richard. Britain & the Eastern Question 1875-1878. (Illus.). 1979. 79.00x (ISBN 0-19-822379-X). Oxford U Pr.

Mingay, G. E., ed. The Victorian Countryside, 2 vols. (Illus.). 370p. 1981. Vol. 1. 85.00 (ISBN 0-7100-0734-5); Vol. 2. 45.00 (ISBN 0-7100-0735-3); Set. 85.00 (ISBN 0-7100-0736-1). Routledge & Kegan.

Mitchell, Donald G. English Lands, Letters & Kings: 1889-1897, 2 vols. Repr. lib. bdg. 40.00 (ISBN 0-8414-6626-2). Folcroft.

Mowat, Robert B. The Victorian Age. 1939. Repr. lib. bdg. 15.00 (ISBN 0-8414-6683-1). Folcroft.

Neff, Wanda F. Victorian Working Women. new ed. 288p. 1966. 25.00x (ISBN 0-7146-1347-9, F Cass Co). Biblio Dist.

Neilson, Francis. The English State in the Victorian Era. 1979. lib. bdg. 39.95 (ISBN 0-685-96620-8). Revisionist Pr.

Ormond, Richard. Early Victorian Portraits, 2 vol. (Illus.). 900p. 1980. Set. 160.00 (ISBN 0-312-22480-X). St Martin.

Parr, Joy. Labouring Children: British Immigrant Apprentices to Canada, Eighteen Sixty-Nine to Nineteen Twenty-Four. 240p. 1980. 25.95 (ISBN 0-7735-0517-2). McGill-Queens U Pr.

Paston, George. Little Memoirs of the Nineteenth Century. (Victorian Age Ser). 1902. Repr. 35.00 (ISBN 0-685-43420-6). Norwood Edns.

Pattison, Mark. Memoirs. 35.00x (ISBN 0-87556-231-0). Saifer.

Pearsall, Ronald. Victorian Sheet Music Covers. LC 72-6422. (Illus.). 116p. 1972. 16.00 (ISBN 0-8103-2001-0). Gale.

Pelling, Henry. Modern Britain, Eighteen Eighty Five to Nineteen Fifty Five. (Illus.). 1966. pap. 4.95 (ISBN 0-393-00368-X, Norton Lib). Norton.

Philips, Janet & Phillips, Peter. Victorians at Home & Away. (Illus.). 220p. 1978. 16.00x (ISBN 0-85664-688-1, Pub. by Croom Helm Ltd England). Biblio Dist.

Pirie, Valerie. A Frenchman Among the Victorians. (Victorian Age Ser). Repr. of 1936 ed. 15.00 (ISBN 0-685-43418-4). Norwood Edns.

Quennell, Peter. The Day Before Yesterday: A Photographic Album of Daily Life in Victorian & Edwardian England. (Illus.). 1979. 14.95 (ISBN 0-684-16066-8, ScribT). Scribner.

Ray, John & Ray, Mary. Victorian Age. 1969. pap. text ed. 9.95x (ISBN 0-435-31752-0). Heinemann Ed.

Rayska, Ursula. Victorian & Edwardian Shropshire. 1977. 19.95 (ISBN 0-7134-0445-0, Pub. by Batsford England). David & Charles.

Razzell, Peter. Victorian Working Class: Selections from the "Morning Chronicle". Wainwright, R. W, ed. (Illus.). 380p. 1973. 27.50x (ISBN 0-7146-2957-X, F. Cass Co). Biblio Dist.

Read, Donald. England, Eighteen Sixty-Eight to Nineteen Fourteen: The Age of Urban Democracy. (History of England Ser.). 1980. text ed. 32.00x (ISBN 0-582-48278-X); pap. text ed. 18.00x (ISBN 0-582-48835-4). Longman.

Reardon, Bernard M. Religious Thought in the Victorian Age: A Survey from Coleridge to Gore. (Illus.). 512p. 1980. pap. text ed. 15.95x (ISBN 0-582-49126-6). Longman.

Richter, Donald C. Riotous Victorians. LC 80-25055. (Illus.). xii, 185p. 1981. text ed. 14.95x (ISBN 0-8214-0571-3); pap. 5.95x (ISBN 0-8214-0618-3). Ohio U Pr.

Roberts, David. Paternalism in Early Victorian England. 1979. 24.00 (ISBN 0-8135-0868-1). Rutgers U Pr.

Routh, H. V. England Under Victoria. (Victorian Age Ser). 1930. Repr. 20.00 (ISBN 0-685-43423-0). Norwood Edns.

Russell, George W. E. Portraits of the Seventies. LC 73-117834. (Essay Index Reprint Ser). 1916. 20.00 (ISBN 0-8369-1717-0). Arno.

Schneewind, J. B. Sidgwick's Ethics & Victorian Moral Philosophy. 1977. 45.00x (ISBN 0-19-824552-1). Oxford U Pr.

Seaman, L. C. Life in Victorian London. 1973. 19.95 (ISBN 0-7134-1465-0, Pub. by Batsford England). David & Charles.

--Victorian England: Aspects of English & Imperial History 1837-1901. 500p. 1973. pap. 11.95x (ISBN 0-416-77550-0). Methuen Inc.

Skelley, Alan. The Victorian Army at Home: The Recruitment & Terms & Conditions of the British Regular, 1859-1899. (Illus.). 1977. lib. bdg. 20.00x (ISBN 0-7735-0304-8). McGill-Queens U Pr.

Snelling, Veram. Victorian Byeways. (Victorian Age Ser). 1949. Repr. 12.50 (ISBN 0-685-43103-7). Norwood Edns.

Somervell, D. C. The Victorian Age. 1937. Repr. 5.50 (ISBN 0-685-43426-5). Norwood Edns.

--The Victorian Age. LC 75-12768. Repr. of 1937 ed. lib. bdg. 8.50 (ISBN 0-8414-7846-5). Folcroft.

Thompson, Francis. Victorian & Edwardian Highlands. 1976. pap. 10.60 (ISBN 0-7134-3220-9, Pub. by Batsford England). David & Charles.

Tingsten, Herbert. Victoria & the Victorians. (Illus.). 1972. 15.00 (ISBN 0-440-09423-2, Sey Lawr). Delacorte.

Victoria, Queen. Queen & Mister Gladstone. Guedella, Philip, ed. LC 34-6053. 1969. Repr. of 1934 ed. 30.00 (ISBN 0-527-93152-7). Kraus Repr.

The Victorian Age. 1979. Repr. of 1921 ed. lib. bdg. 15.00 (ISBN 0-8495-0211-X). Arden Lib.

Wigley, J. The Rise & Fall of the Victorian Sunday. 208p. 1981. 49.00x (ISBN 0-686-73070-4, Pub. by Manchester U Pr England). State Mutual Bk.

Wingfield-Stratford, Esme. Those Earnest Victorians. 8.00 (ISBN 0-8446-0966-8). Peter Smith.

Woodham-Smith, Cecil. Queen Victoria. 1972. 17.95 (ISBN 0-394-48245-X). Knopf.

Wright, A. P., ed. Victoria History of the Counties of England: Cambridge & the Isle of Ely, Vol. 6. (Illus.). 330p. 1978. text ed. 85.00x (ISBN 0-19-722746-5). Oxford U Pr.

Wyndham, Horace. Victorian Sensations. (Victorian Age Ser). 1933. Repr. 30.00 (ISBN 0-685-43117-7). Norwood Edns.

Yarnall, Ellis. Wordsworth & the Coleridges. LC 77-21005. 1977. Repr. of 1909 ed. lib. bdg. 35.00 (ISBN 0-8414-9950-0). Folcroft.

Young, G. M. Portrait of an Age: Victorian England. 1977. 39.95x (ISBN 0-19-212961-9). Oxford U Pr.

Young, George M. Victorian England: Portrait of an Age. 2nd ed. 1964. pap. 7.95 (ISBN 0-19-500259-8, GB). Oxford U Pr.

GREAT BRITAIN–HISTORY–CRIMEAN WAR, 1853-1856

see Crimean War, 1853-1856

GREAT BRITAIN–HISTORY–20TH CENTURY

Adams, W. S. Edwardian Heritage; a Study in British History, 1901-1906. LC 49-4287. Repr. of 1949 ed. 12.00 (ISBN 0-527-00480-4). Kraus Repr.

Arnstein, Walter, ed. The Past Speaks: Sources & Problems in British History Since 1688. 448p. 1981. pap. text ed. 8.95 (ISBN 0-669-02919-X). Heath.

Bartlett, C. J. A History of Postwar Britain, 1945-74. LC 77-3000. 1977. pap. text ed. 12.95x (ISBN 0-582-48320-4). Longman.

Beaver, Patrick. Crystal Palace, 1851-36: A Portrait of Victorian Enterprise. (Illus.). 1970. 20.00x (ISBN 0-238-78961-6). Intl Pubns Serv.

Birch, A. H., et al. Britain: Progress & Decline, Vol. 17. 154p. 1980. lib. bdg. 17.50 (ISBN 0-930598-18-0). Tulane Stud Pol.

Boyle, Andrew. The Fourth Man. 1980. 12.95 (ISBN 0-8037-2321-0, J Wade). Dial.

Branson, Noreen. Britain in the Nineteen Twenties. Hobsbawm, E. J., ed. LC 75-27162. (History of British Society Ser). x, 264p. 1976. 20.00x (ISBN 0-8166-0770-2). U of Minn Pr.

Brendon, Piers. Eminent Edwardians. 1980. 10.95 (ISBN 0-395-29195-X). HM.

Burnet, Alastair & Landels, Willie. The Time of Our Lives. (Illus.). 208p. 1981. 28.00 (ISBN 0-241-10666-4, Pub. by Hamish Hamilton England). David & Charles.

Caffrey. The Nineteen-Hundreds Lady. (Illus.). 1976. 29.95 (ISBN 0-86033-014-1). Gordon-Cremonesi.

Cain, Peter J. Economic Foundations of British Overseas Expansion 1815-1914. (Studies in Economic & Social History). 1980. pap. text ed. 5.25x (ISBN 0-333-23284-4). Humanities.

Calder, K. J. Britain & the Origins of the New Europe, 1914-1918. LC 75-12161. (International Studies Ser.). 282p. 1976. 29.95 (ISBN 0-521-20897-1). Cambridge U Pr.

Calvocoressi, Peter. The British Experience, 1940-1975. LC 77-90401. 1978. 8.95 (ISBN 0-394-50067-9). Pantheon.

Campbell, R. H. & Wilson, R. G. Entrepreneurship in Britain, Seventeen Fifty to Nineteen Thirty-Nine. (Documents in Economic History). 1975. text ed. 13.00x (ISBN 0-7136-1524-9). Humanities.

Carr, Gordon. The Angry Brigade: The Cause & the Case - a History of Britain's First Urban Guerilla Group. (Illus.). 207p. 1975. text ed. 15.00x (ISBN 0-575-01992-1). Verry.

Childs, David. Britain Since Nineteen Forty-Five: A Political History. LC 79-8507. 1979. 22.50x (ISBN 0-312-09880-4). St Martin.

Clutterbuck, Richard. Britain in Agony. 320p. 1978. 18.95 (ISBN 0-571-11188-2, Pub. by Faber & Faber). Merrimack Bk Serv.

Cooke & Sted. Post-War Britain. 1980. text ed. write for info. (ISBN 0-391-00951-6). Humanities.

Cornwallis-West, George. Edwardian Heydays: A Little About a Lot of Things. (Illus.). 338p. 1975. Repr. of 1930 ed. 17.95x (ISBN 0-8464-0356-0). Beekman Pubs.

Coulton, Barbara. Louis MacNeice in the BBC. (Illus.). 224p. 1980. 31.00 (ISBN 0-571-11537-3, Pub. by Faber & Faber). Merrimack Bk Serv.

Creaton, Heather J., ed. Writings on British History, Nineteen Sixty-Two to Nineteen Sixty-Four. 350p. 1981. 50.00x (ISBN 0-7129-0992-3, Pub. by Dawson). State Mutual Bk.

Crow, Duncan. The Edwardian Woman. LC 77-83847. (Illus.). 1978. 10.95 (ISBN 0-312-23912-2). St Martin.

Donnelly, Peter, ed. Mrs. Milburn's Diaries: An English-Woman's Day-to-Day Reflections, 1935-45. LC 80-11442. (Illus.). 320p. 1980. 12.95 (ISBN 0-8052-3748-8). Schocken.

Douglas, Roy. Land, People & Politics. LC 75-32929. 250p. 1976. text ed. 17.95 (ISBN 0-312-46480-0). St Martin.

Ensor, Robert C. England, 1870-1914. (Oxford History of England Ser.). 1936. 32.50x (ISBN 0-19-821705-6). Oxford U Pr.

Evans, George E. Where Beards Wag All. (Illus.). 312p. 1977. pap. 6.95 (ISBN 0-686-19310-5, Pub. by Faber & Faber). Merrimack Bk Serv.

Ferguson, John. The Arts in Britain in World War One. (Illus.). 131p. 1980. 26.50x (ISBN 0-8476-6262-4). Rowman.

Florey, R. A. The General Strike of 1926. 1981. 28.95 (ISBN 0-7145-3698-9). Riverrun NY.

Forget Not: The Autobiography of Margaret, Duchess of Argyll. 248p. 1976. 8.95 (ISBN 0-491-01825-8). Transatlantic.

Fyson, Nance L. Growing up in Edwardian Britain. LC 79-56456. (Growing up Ser.). (Illus.). 72p. (gr. 7-9). 1980. text ed. 14.95 (ISBN 0-7134-3372-8, Pub. by Batsford England). David & Charles.

George, M. Dorothy. England in Johnson's Day. LC 72-7079. (Select Bibliographies Reprint Ser.). 1972. Repr. of 1928 ed. 18.00 (ISBN 0-8369-6933-2). Arno.

Gilbert, Bentley B. Britain Since Nineteen Eighteen. 2nd ed. 1980. 19.95 (ISBN 0-312-09876-6). St Martin.

Goldring, Douglas. The Nineteen Twenties. LC 75-28131. 1975. Repr. of 1945 ed. lib. bdg. 20.00 (ISBN 0-8414-4548-6). Folcroft.

Gooch, G. P. History of Our Time: 1885-1911. 1977. Repr. lib. bdg. 12.50 (ISBN 0-8495-1905-5). Arden Lib.

Gooch, John. The Prospect of War: British Defence Policy Eighteen Forty-Seven to Nineteen Forty-Two. 150p. 1981. 25.00x (ISBN 0-7146-3128-0, F Cass Co). Biblio Dist.

Great Britain, Cabinet Office: Principal War Telegrams & Memoranda 1940-1943, 7 vols. (Cabinet History Ser.). 1976. Per Vol. lib. bdg. 378.00 (ISBN 0-527-35650-6); lib. bdg. 54.00 ea. Kraus Intl.

Great Britain. Foreign Office: Index to Foreign Office Correspondence, 1920-1949, 123 vols. lib. bdg. 6096.00 (ISBN 0-527-35675-1). Kraus Intl.

Green, Martin. Children of the Sun: A Narrative of Decadence in England After 1918. LC 80-50549. (Illus.). 496p. 1980. pap. 6.95 (ISBN 0-87223-628-5, Dist. by Har-Row). Wideview Bks.

Haigh, R. H. & Turner, P. W. British Policies & Society, Nineteen Eighteen to Nineteen Thirty-Eight: The Effect on Appeasement. 1980. pap. 20.00x (ISBN 0-89126-093-5). MA-AH Pub.

Halevy, Elie. History of the English People: 1895-1905. 10.00 (ISBN 0-8446-0675-8). Peter Smith.

--History of the English People: 1905-1914, 2 pts. 10.00 ea. (ISBN 0-8446-0676-6). Peter Smith.

Havighurst, A. F. Modern England: 1901-1970. LC 75-23844. (Conference on British Studies Bibliographical Handbooks Ser.). 118p. 1976. 15.50 (ISBN 0-521-20941-2). Cambridge U Pr.

Havighurst, Alfred F. Britain in Transition: The Twentieth-Century. LC 78-16052. 1979. 25.00x (ISBN 0-226-31968-7); pap. text ed. 9.95 (ISBN 0-226-31969-5, P815, Phoen). U of Chicago Pr.

Hearnshaw, Fossey J., ed. Edwardian England, A.D. 1901-1910: A Series of Lectures Delivered at King's College, University of London. facs. ed. LC 68-22097. (Essay Index Reprint Ser). 1933. 16.00 (ISBN 0-8369-0529-6). Arno.

Henderson, Neville. Failure of a Mission: Berlin, 1937-1939. LC 75-41131. Repr. of 1940 ed. 15.50 (ISBN 0-404-14670-8). AMS Pr.

Higham, Robin. Britain's Imperial Air Routes, 1918 to 1939: The Story of Britain's Overseas Airlines. (Illus.). 405p. 1960. 19.50 (ISBN 0-208-00171-9). Shoe String.

Holland. Britain & the Commonwealth Alliance 1918-1939. 1979. text ed. 52.00x (ISBN 0-333-27295-1). Humanities.

Huggett, Frank E. Carriages at Eight. 1980. 15.95 (ISBN 0-684-16421-3). Scribner.

Hussey, W. D. British History, Eighteen Fifteen to Nineteen Thirty-Nine. LC 79-149429. (Illus.). 1972. 11.50 (ISBN 0-521-07985-3). Cambridge U Pr.

Inge, W. R. The Post Victorians. 648p. 1980. Repr. of 1933 ed. lib. bdg. 40.00 (ISBN 0-89987-401-0). Darby Bks.

Jackson, J. Hampden. England Since the Industrial Revolution, 1815-1848. LC 75-7239. (Illus.). 298p. 1975. Repr. of 1949 ed. lib. bdg. 16.00x (ISBN 0-8371-8102-X, JAES). Greenwood.

James, Robert R. The British Revolution 1880-1939. 1977. 17.95 (ISBN 0-394-40761-X). Knopf.

Johnston, James P. A Hundred Years Eating: Food, Drink, & the Daily Diet in Britain Since the Late Nineteenth Century. (Illus.). 1977. 9.95 (ISBN 0-7735-0306-4). McGill-Queens U Pr.

Joyce, William. Twilight Over England. 1978. pap. 4.50x (ISBN 0-911038-37-X). Noontide.

Kaufman, M. The Housing of the Working Classes & of the Poor. 146p. 1975. Repr. of 1907 ed. 9.50x (ISBN 0-87471-706-X). Rowman.

Kedourie, Elie. England & the Middle East: The Destruction of the Ottoman Empire, 1914-1921. 1978. Repr. of 1956 ed. 20.00x (ISBN 0-87471-869-4). Rowman.

Knaplund, Paul. Britain: Commonwealth & Empire, 1901-1955. LC 74-3744. (Illus.). 541p. 1974. Repr. of 1956 ed. lib. bdg. 32.50x (ISBN 0-8371-7467-8, KNBR). Greenwood.

Koss, Stephen. The Pro-Boers: The Anatomy of an Anti-War Movement. (Studies in Imperialism). 1973. text ed. 15.00x (ISBN 0-226-45134-8). U. of Chicago Pr.

Kramnick, Isaac, ed. Is Britain Dying? Perspectives on the Current Crisis. LC 79-12895. (Illus.). 1979. 17.50x (ISBN 0-8014-1234-X). Cornell U Pr.

Law, Christopher M. British Regional Development Since World War I. LC 80-66425. 176p. 1980. 38.00 (ISBN 0-7153-7974-7). David & Charles.

Lean, E. Tangye. Napoleonists: A Study in Political Disaffection, 1760-1960. 1970. 17.00x (ISBN 0-19-215184-3). Oxford U Pr.

Lebzelter, Gisela C. Political Anti-Semitism in England 1918-1939. LC 78-16795. 1979. text ed. 32.00x (ISBN 0-8419-0426-X). Holmes & Meier.

Lloyd, T. O. Empire to Welfare State: English History Nineteen Six to Nineteen Seventy-Six. 2nd ed. (Short Oxford History of the Modern World Ser.). (Illus.). 1979. 45.00x (ISBN 0-19-913132-5); pap. 19.95x (ISBN 0-19-913243-7). Oxford U Pr.

Lockmeyer, Seymour. Why Great Britain Failed: An Analysis in Political Stupidity. (Illus.). 1978. 49.75 (ISBN 0-89266-100-3). Am Classical Coll Pr.

Longford, Elizabeth, ed. Louisa, Lady in Waiting: The Personal Diaries & Albums of Louisa, Lady in Waiting to Queen Victoria & Queen Alexandra. LC 78-24247. (Illus.). 1979. 14.95 (ISBN 0-8317-5650-0, Mayflower Bks). Smith Pubs.

Louis, William R. Imperialism at Bay: The United States & the Decolonization of the British Empire, 1941-1945. 1978. 22.50x (ISBN 0-19-821125-2). Oxford U Pr.

Lowe, Peter. Great Britain & the Origins of the Pacific War: A Study of British Policy in East Asia, 1937 to 1941. (Illus.). 330p. 1977. text ed. 45.00x (ISBN 0-19-822427-3). Oxford U Pr.

MacDonald, D. F. Age of Transition: Britain in the Nineteenth Twentieth Centuries. 1967. 16.95 (ISBN 0-312-01330-2). St Martin.

McElwee, William L. Britain's Locust Years: Nineteen Eighteen to Nineteen Forty. LC 78-25900. 1979. Repr. of 1962 ed. lib. bdg. 22.00x (ISBN 0-313-21162-0, MCBL). Greenwood.

Mansergh, Nicholas. Survey of British Commonwealth Affairs: Problems of Wartime Cooperation & Post-War Change 1939-1952. 470p. 1968. Repr. of 1958 ed. 32.50x (ISBN 0-7146-1496-3, F Cass Co). Biblio Dist.

Marshall, John & Davies-Spiell, Michael. Victorian & Edwardian Lake District. 1976. pap. 8.95 (ISBN 0-7134-3417-1, Pub. by Batsford England). David & Charles.

Mauger, Peter. British People Nineteen Two to Nineteen Seventy-Five. 1976. pap. text ed. 13.95x (ISBN 0-435-31570-6). Heinemann Ed.

Monroe, Elizabeth. Britain's Moment in the Middle East: 1914-1971, New & Revised Edition. LC 80-8869. 250p. 1981. text ed. 20.00x (ISBN 0-8018-2616-0). Johns Hopkins.

Moore, R. J. Churchill, Cripps, & India, Nineteen Thirty-Nine to Nineteen Forty-Five. 1979. 33.00x (ISBN 0-19-822485-0). Oxford U Pr.

Morgan, Kenneth. Consensus & Disunity: The Lloyd George Coalition Government, 1918 to 1922. 448p. 1979. text ed. 54.00x (ISBN 0-19-822497-4). Oxford U Pr.

Morris, A. J. Edwardian Radicalism 1900-1914. 288p. 1974. 22.00 (ISBN 0-7100-7866-8). Routledge & Kegan.

Mowat, C. L. Great Britain Since 1914. Elton, G. R., ed. LC 79-146277. (Sources of History Ser). 1971. 22.50x (ISBN 0-8014-0632-3); pap. 6.95 (ISBN 0-8014-9118-5, CP118). Cornell U Pr.

Mowat, Charles L. Britain Between the Wars: Nineteen Eighteen-Forty. LC 55-5139. 1955. 13.50x (ISBN 0-226-54370-6). U of Chicago Pr.

Neilson, Francis. The British War Party in the Interwar Period: Nineteen Nineteen to Nineteen Thirty-Nine. 1979. lib. bdg. 39.95 (ISBN 0-685-96612-7). Revisionist Pr.

--Churchill & Yalta. (Revisionist Historiography Ser.). 1979. lib. bdg. 59.95 (ISBN 0-685-96613-5). Revisionist Pr.

Noble, Trevor. Modern Britain: Structure & Change. 1975. 38.00 (ISBN 0-7134-2987-9, Pub. by Batsford England); pap. 19.95 (ISBN 0-7134-2988-7). David & Charles.

O'Day, Alan, ed. The Edwardian Age: Conflict & Stability, 1900-1914. 199p. 1979. 18.50 (ISBN 0-208-01823-9, Archon). Shoe String.

O'Farrell, P. J. England & Ireland Since 1800. 189p. 1975. pap. text ed. 3.95x (ISBN 0-19-289045-X). Oxford U Pr.

Ovendale, Ritchie. Appeasement & the English Speaking World: Britain, the United States, the Dominions & the Policy of Appeasement; 1937-1939. 353p. 1975. text ed. 37.50x (ISBN 0-7083-0589-X). Verry.

Parr, Joy. Labouring Children: British Immigrant Apprentices to Canada, Eighteen Sixty-Nine to Nineteen Twenty-Four. 240p. 1980. 25.95 (ISBN 0-7735-0517-2). McGill-Queens U Pr.

Pelling, Henry. Modern Britain, Eighteen Eighty Five to Nineteen Fifty Five. (Illus.). 1966. pap. 4.95 (ISBN 0-393-00368-X, Norton Lib). Norton.

Phillips, Gregory D. The Diehards: Aristocratic Society & Politics in Edwardian England. LC 78-16949. (Historical Studies: No. 96). 1979. 18.50x (ISBN 0-674-20555-3). Harvard U Pr.

Pitt, Barrie. Churchill & His Generals. 224p. 1981. pap. 2.50 (ISBN 0-553-14610-6). Bantam.

Quennell, Peter. The Day Before Yesterday: A Photographic Album of Daily Life in Victorian & Edwardian England. (Illus.). 1979. 14.95 (ISBN 0-684-16066-8, ScribT). Scribner.

Ray, John. Britain Between the Wars. (History Broadsheets Ser.). 1975. pap. text ed. 6.95x (ISBN 0-435-31758-X). Heinemann Ed.

Read, Donald. England, Eighteen Sixty-Eight to Nineteen Fourteen: The Age of Urban Democracy. (History of England Ser.). 1980. text ed. 32.00x (ISBN 0-582-48278-X); pap. text ed. 18.00x (ISBN 0-582-48835-4). Longman.

Roberts, R. The Classic Slum: Salford Life in the First Quarter of the Century. 218p. 1978. 21.00x (ISBN 0-7190-0453-5, Pub. by Manchester U Pr England). State Mutual Bk.

Rothwell, V. H. British War Aims & Peace Diplomacy Nineteen-Fourteen to Nineteen-Eighteen. 1971. 33.00x (ISBN 0-19-822349-8). Oxford U Pr.

Schuyler, R. L. & Weston, C. C. British Constitutional History Since 1832. 5.00 (ISBN 0-8446-2891-3). Peter Smith.

Shannon, Richard. Crisis of Imperialism Eighteen Sixty-Five to Nineteen Fifteen. 1974. 16.95x (ISBN 0-19-520119-1). Oxford U Pr.

Sheail, John. Rural Conservation in Inter-War Britain. (ORSG Ser.). (Illus.). 278p. 1981. 49.50x (ISBN 0-19-823236-5). Oxford U Pr.

Sissons, Michael & French, Philip, eds. Age of Austerity. LC 75-45350. 349p. 1976. Repr. of 1963 ed. lib. bdg. 21.75x (ISBN 0-8371-8732-X, SIAA). Greenwood.

Snowman, Daniel. Britain & America: An Interpretation of Their Cultures, 1945-1975. LC 76-48858. (Orig.). 1977. pap. text ed. 6.50x (ISBN 0-06-131922-8, TB1922, Torch). Har-Row.

Spender, John. Great Britain: Empire & Commonwealth, 1886-1935. LC 79-110864. (Illus.). 906p. 1973. Repr. of 1936 ed. lib. bdg. 37.50x (ISBN 0-8371-4537-6, SPGB). Greenwood.

Steiner, Zara. Britain & the Origins of the First World War. LC 76-55861. (Making of the Twentieth Century Ser). 160p. 1978. 16.95x (ISBN 0-312-09818-9); pap. 6.95 (ISBN 0-312-09819-7). St Martin.

Tapp, Edwin. Policies of Survival. (Studies in Twentieth Century History). 1979. pap. text ed. 4.50x (ISBN 0-686-65413-7, 00549). Heinemann Ed.

Taylor, A. J. Essays in English History. (Pelican Ser.). 1976. pap. 2.95 (ISBN 0-14-021862-9, Pelican). Penguin.

Taylor, Alan J. English History, Nineteen Nineteen to Nineteen Forty-Five. (Oxford History of England Ser). 1965. 39.00x (ISBN 0-19-821715-3). Oxford U Pr.

--English History, Nineteen Nineteen to Nineteen Forty-Five. LC 65-27513. 1970. pap. 7.95 (ISBN 0-19-500304-7, GB311, GB). Oxford U Pr.

Taylor, Philip M. The Projection of Britain: British Overseas Publicity & Propaganda 1919-1939. LC 80-42291. 384p. Date not set. price not set (ISBN 0-521-23843-9). Cambridge U Pr.

Thompson, Edward R. Portraits of the New Century. LC 74-117853. (Essay Index Reprint Ser). 1928. 17.00 (ISBN 0-8369-1685-9). Arno.

Thompson, Francis. Victorian & Edwardian Highlands. 1976. pap. 10.50 (ISBN 0-7134-3220-9, Pub. by Batsford England). David & Charles.

Thompson, Neville. Anti-Appeasers: Conservative Opposition to Appeasement in the 1930's. 1971. 28.50x (ISBN 0-19-821487-1). Oxford U Pr.

Thompson, Paul. The Edwardians: The Remaking of British Society. (Illus.). 351p. 1977. pap. 6.50 (ISBN 0-586-08261-1, Pub. by Granada England). Academy Chi Ltd.

Thompson, Paul & Harkell, Gina. The Edwardians in Photographs. LC 79-928. (Illus.). 1979. text ed. 22.50x (ISBN 0-8419-0529-0). Holmes & Meier.

Thompson, Thea. Edwardian Childhoods. (Illus.). 256p. 1981. 27.50 (ISBN 0-7100-0676-4). Routledge & Kegan.

Thomson, David. England in the Twentieth Century. (Orig.). 1965. pap. 3.50 (ISBN 0-14-020691-4, Pelican). Penguin.

--England in the Twentieth Century, 1914-63. lib. bdg. 10.50x (ISBN 0-88307-269-6). Gannon.

Veerathappa, K. British Conservative Party & Indian Independence, 1930-1947. LC 76-900931. 1976. 15.00x (ISBN 0-88386-772-9). South Asia Bks.

White, Stephen. Britain & the Bolshevik Revolution: A Study of the Politics of Diplomacy, 1920-24. LC 79-12128. 1980. text ed. 35.50x (ISBN 0-8419-0513-4). Holmes & Meier.

Wiener, Martin. English Culture & the Decline of the Industrial Spirit, 1850-1980. (Illus.). 256p. 1981. 15.95 (ISBN 0-521-23418-2). Cambridge U Pr.

Wilson, Keith. The Policy of the Entente: The Determinants of British Foreign Policy, 1904-1914. 1981. text ed. 15.00 (ISBN 0-391-02198-2). Humanities.

Winkler. Twentieth-Century Britain. (Modern Scholarship on European History). 1976. 12.50 (ISBN 0-531-05381-4); pap. 6.95 (ISBN 0-531-05587-6). Watts.

Wood, Sydney. The British Welfare State 1900-1950. LC 81-3840. (Cambridge Introduction to the History of Mankind Ser.). (Illus.). 48p. Date not set. pap. price not set (ISBN 0-521-22843-3). Cambridge U Pr.

Woodhouse, C. M. Post-War Britain. 1967. 6.25 (ISBN 0-8023-1122-9). Dufour.

GREAT BRITAIN–HISTORY–20TH CENTURY–SOURCES

Asquith, Herbert H. Occasional Addresses, Eighteen Ninety-Three - Nineteen Sixteen. facsimile ed. LC 76-99715. (Essay Index Reprint Ser). Repr. of 1918 ed. 16.00 (ISBN 0-8369-1368-X). Arno.

Bettey, J. H., ed. English Historical Documents, 1906-1939. 1967. text ed. 5.00x (ISBN 0-7100-2883-0). Humanities.

Cook, Chris. Sources in British Political History, 1900-1951, Vols. 3 & 4. Incl. Vol. 3. A Guide to the Private Papers of Members of Parliament, A-K. LC 77-71207 (ISBN 0-312-74656-3); Vol. 4. A Guide to the Private Papers of Members of Parliament, L-Z. LC 77-71188 (ISBN 0-312-74657-1). 1977. 18.95x ea. St Martin.

Cook, Chris & Weeks, Jeffery. Sources in British Political History 1900-1951: A Guide to the Private Papers of Selected Writers, Intellectuals & Publicists, Vol. 5. LC 75-4012. 1978. 19.95 (ISBN 0-312-74658-X). St Martin.

Mayer, Sydney L. & Koenig, William, eds. The Two World Wars: A Guide to Manuscript Collections in the United Kingdom. LC 74-9187. 1976. 32.50 (ISBN 0-686-77113-3). Bowker.

GREAT BRITAIN–HISTORY, COMIC SATIRICAL, ETC.

Bingham, Madeline. Earls & Girls. (Illus.). 150p. 1980. 27.00 (ISBN 0-241-10270-7, Pub. by Hamish Hamilton England). David & Charles.

Sellar, Walter C. & Yeatman, Robert J. Ten Sixty-Six & All That. 1958. pap. 3.50 (ISBN 0-525-47025-5). Dutton.

GREAT BRITAIN–HISTORY, LOCAL

Borer, Mary C. Two Villages: Story of Chelsea & Kensington. (Illus.). 288p. 1974. 12.50 (ISBN 0-491-01061-3). Transatlantic.

Bulfield, Anthony. The Icknield Way. (Illus.). 1979. 16.50x (ISBN 0-900963-43-3, Pub. by Terence Dalton England). State Mutual Bk.

Coleman, B. I., ed. The Idea of the City in Nineteenth-Century Britain. (Birth of Modern Britain Ser). 256p. 1973. 16.00 (ISBN 0-7100-7591-X); pap. 7.95 (ISBN 0-7100-7592-8). Routledge & Kegan.

Farnie, D. A. The Manchester Ship Canal. 128p. 1981. 35.00x (ISBN 0-686-73063-1, Pub. by Manchester U Pr England). State Mutual Bk.

Finn, F. C. History of Chelsea. 12.50x (ISBN 0-392-07888-0, SpS). Sportshelf.

Gross, Charles. Bibliography of British Municipal History, Including Gilds & Parliamentary Representation. 1897. 32.50 (ISBN 0-8337-1465-1). B Franklin.

Norden, John. Speculum Britanniae: The First Parte, a Description of Middlesex. LC 70-171777. (English Experience Ser.: No. 402). 58p. 1971. Repr. of 1593 ed. 8.00 (ISBN 90-221-0402-8). Walter J Johnson.

Tate, W. E. Parish Chest. 3rd ed. LC 67-28686. (Illus.). 1969. 41.00 (ISBN 0-521-06603-4). Cambridge U Pr.

Trinder, Barrie, ed. The Most Extraordinary District in the World: Ironbridge & Coalbrookdale. (Illus.). 125p. 1977. 21.00x (ISBN 0-8476-1492-1). Rowman.

Upcott, William. Bibliographical Account of the Principal Works Relating to English Topography, 3 vols. LC 68-57921. (Illus.). 1968. Repr. of 1818 ed. 102.00 set (ISBN 0-8337-3598-5). B Franklin.

Watson, Godfrey. Goodwife Hot & Others: Northumberland's Past As Shown in Its Place Names. 1970. 10.50 (ISBN 0-85362-090-3, Oriel). Routledge & Kegan.

GREAT BRITAIN–HISTORY, MILITARY

see also Great Britain–Army

Abbey, Staton. Book of B.M.C. Eleven Hundred. pap. 4.50x (ISBN 0-392-02285-0, SpS). Sportshelf.

--Book of B.M.C. Minis. pap. 4.50x (ISBN 0-392-02299-0, SpS). Sportshelf.

Anglesey, Marquess of. A History of the British Cavalry 1816-1919, Vol. 1: 1816-1850. (Illus.). 325p. 1973. 25.00 (ISBN 0-208-01404-7, Archon). Shoe String.

Bancroft, Nathaniel W. From Recruit to Staff Sergeant. 1979. 15.00x (ISBN 0-86025-839-4, Pub. by Ian Henry Pubns England). State Mutual Bk.

Beeler, John. Warfare in England, 1066-1189. 1966. 29.50x (ISBN 0-8014-0030-9). Cornell U Pr.

Bond, Brian. British Military Policy Between the Two World Wars. 480p. 1980. 48.00x (ISBN 0-19-822464-8). Oxford U Pr.

Brett-James, Antony. Life in Wellington's Army. 1972. text ed. 13.50x (ISBN 0-04-940042-8). Allen Unwin.

Brookes, Kenneth. Battle Thunder: The Story of Britain's Artillery. (Illus.). 256p. 1973. 14.95x (ISBN 0-8464-0185-1). Beekman Pubs.

Chappell, Mike. British Infantry Equipments Eighteen-Eight to Nineteen-Eight. (Men at Arms Ser.). (Illus.). 1981. pap. 7.95 (ISBN 0-686-71700-7, Pub. by Osprey England). Hippocrene Bks.

--British Infantry Equipments Nineteen-Eight to Nighteen-Eighty. (Men at Arms Ser.). (Illus.). 1981. pap. 7.95 (ISBN 0-686-71701-5, Pub. by Osprey England). Hippocrene Bks.

Clammer, David. The Victorian Army in Photographs. LC 75-7908. (Illus.). 96p. 1975. 12.50 (ISBN 0-88254-352-0). Hippocrene Bks.

Cook, Samuel F. Drummond Island: The Story of the British Occupation 1815-1828. LC 73-90803. (Illus.). 124p. (YA) 1974. pap. 4.50 (ISBN 0-912382-14-7). Black Letter.

Donovan, Robert K., ed. Current Research in British Studies. 8th ed. 1980. pap. 14.00x (ISBN 0-89126-084-6). MA-AH Pub.

Dunnigan, Brian L. The British Army at Mackinac, Eighteen Tweleve - Eighteen Fifteen. Armour, David A., ed. (Reports in Mackinac History & Archaelogy Ser.: No. 7). (Illus.). 56p. (Orig.). 1981. pap. 5.00 (ISBN 0-911872-40-X). Mackinac Island.

--King's Men at Mackinac: The British Garrisons, 1780-1796. Armour, David A., ed. LC 74-172729. (Reports in Mackinac History & Archaeology Ser: No. 3). (Illus.). 38p. (Orig.). 1973. pap. 3.00 (ISBN 0-911872-19-1). Mackinac Island.

Fabb, John. Victorian & Edwardian Army from Old Photographs. 1975. 24.00 (ISBN 0-7134-2973-9). David & Charles.

Fortescue, John W. History of British Army from the Expedition to Egypt 1807, to the Battle of Coruna, January, 1809, Vol. 6. Repr. of 1910 ed. 27.50 (ISBN 0-404-02557-9). AMS Pr.

--History of British Army from the Fall of the Bastille to the Peace of Amiens, Pts. 1 & 2, Vol. 4. Repr. of 1915 ed. 47.50 (ISBN 0-404-02554-4). AMS Pr.

--History of British Army from the Fall of the Bastille to the Peace of Amiens: Supplementary Volume, Pt. 3, Vol. 4. Repr. of 1915 ed. 22.50 (ISBN 0-404-02555-2). AMS Pr.

--History of British Army from the Renewal of the War to the Evacuation of Rio De la Plata, Vol. 5. Repr. of 1910 ed. 27.50 (ISBN 0-404-02556-0). AMS Pr.

--History of British Army to the Close of the Seven Year's War, Vols. 1-2. Repr. of 1910 ed. 27.50 ea. Vol. 1 (ISBN 0-404-02551-X). Vol. 2 (ISBN 0-404-02552-8). AMS Pr.

--History of British Army to the Second Peace of Paris, Vol. 3. Repr. of 1911 ed. 27.50 (ISBN 0-404-02553-6). AMS Pr.

--History of British Army 1809-1810, Pt. 1., Vol. 7. Repr. of 1912 ed. 27.50 (ISBN 0-404-02558-7). AMS Pr.

--History of British Army 1809-1810: Supplementary Volume, Pt. 2, Vol. 7. (Illus.). Repr. of 1912 ed. 22.50 (ISBN 0-404-02559-5). AMS Pr.

--History of British Army 1811-1812, Pt. 1, Vol. 8. Repr. of 1917 ed. 27.50 (ISBN 0-404-02560-9). AMS Pr.

--History of British Army 1811-1812: Supplementary Volume, Pt. 2, Vol. 8. (Illus.). Repr. of 1917 ed. 22.50 (ISBN 0-404-02561-7). AMS Pr.

--History of British Army 1813-1815, Vols. 9-10. Repr. of 1920 ed. 27.50 ea. Vol. 9 (ISBN 0-404-02562-5). Vol. 10 (ISBN 0-404-02563-3). AMS Pr.

--History of British Army 1813-1815, Supplementary Volume, Pt. 2, Vol. 10. (Illus.). Repr. of 1920 ed. 22.50 (ISBN 0-404-02564-1). AMS Pr.

--History of British Army 1815-1838, Vol. 11. Repr. of 1923 ed. 27.50 (ISBN 0-404-02565-X). AMS Pr.

--History of British Army 1839-1852, Pt. 1, Vol. 12. Repr. of 1927 ed. 27.50 (ISBN 0-404-02566-8). AMS Pr.

--History of British Army 1839-1852: Supplementary Volume, Pt. 2, Vol. 12. (Illus.). Repr. of 1927 ed. 22.50 (ISBN 0-404-02567-6). AMS Pr.

--History of British Army 1852-1870, Pt. 1,vol. 13. Repr. of 1930 ed. 27.50 (ISBN 0-404-02568-4). AMS Pr.

--History of British Army 1852-1870: Supplementary Volume, Pt. 2, Vol. 13. (Illus.). Repr. of 1930 ed. 22.50 (ISBN 0-404-02569-2). AMS Pr.

--A History of the British Army, Vols. 1-13 & 6 Supplementary Vols. LC 70-116765. Repr. of 1930 ed. Set. 510.00 (ISBN 0-404-02550-1). AMS Pr.

Fremont, Jessie B. The Story of the Guard: A Chronicle of the War. 1863. Repr. 20.00 (ISBN 0-685-43083-9). Norwood Edns.

Frey, Sylvia R. The British Soldier in America: A Social History of Military Life in the Revolutionary Period. 223p. 1981. text ed. 25.00x (ISBN 0-292-78040-0). U of Tex Pr.

Gooch, John. The Plans of War: The General Staff & British Military Strategy c. 1900-1916. LC 74-511. 348p. 1974. 24.95 (ISBN 0-470-31321-8). Halsted Pr.

Goodman, Anthony. The Wars of the Roses: Military Activity & English Society, 1452-1497. (Illus.). 300p. 1981. write for info. (ISBN 0-7100-0728-0). Routledge & Kegan.

Halpern, P. G., ed. Keyes Papers, Vol. 2. (Illus.). 464p. 1980. text ed. 34.00x (ISBN 0-04-942165-4). Allen Unwin.

Hamilton, Angus. Somaliland. LC 75-94479. (Illus.). Repr. of 1911 ed. 24.00x (ISBN 0-8371-3292-4). Greenwood.

Hannah, W. H. Bobs, Kipling's General: The Life of Field-Marshall Earl Roberts of Kandahar, VC. (Illus.). 260p. (Orig.). 1972. 18.50 (ISBN 0-208-01139-0, Archon). Shoe String.

Harries-Jenkins, Gwyn. The Army in Victorian Society. 1977. 17.50x (ISBN 0-8020-2263-4). U of Toronto Pr.

Hastings, Max. Bomber Command: The Myths & Reality of the Strategic Bombing Offensive 1939-45. (Illus.). 1979. 12.95 (ISBN 0-8037-0154-3, J Wade). Dial.

Higham, Robin D. The Military Intellectuals in Britain, 1918 to 1939. LC 81-4917. xi, 267p. 1981. Repr. of 1966 ed. lib. bdg. 27.50x (ISBN 0-313-23008-0, HIMI). Greenwood.

Ingram, Edward. Commitment to Empire: Prophecies of the Great Game in Asia, 1797-1800. 400p. 1981. 66.50 (ISBN 0-19-822662-4). Oxford U Pr.

Kemp, Anthony. Castles in Color. LC 77-20984. (Arco Color Ser.). (Illus.). 1978. 8.95 (ISBN 0-668-04469-1); pap. 6.95 (ISBN 0-668-04480-2). Arco.

Kinross, John. The Battlefields of Britain. LC 79-84233. (Illus.). 1979. 14.95 (ISBN 0-88254-483-7). Hippocrene Bks.

Kishlansky, Mark A. The Rise of the New Model Army. LC 79-4285. 1979. 21.50 (ISBN 0-521-22751-8). Cambridge U Pr.

Morris, Thomas. Napoleonic Wars. Selby, John, ed. (Military Memoirs Ser.). 1968. 15.00 (ISBN 0-208-00631-1, Archon). Shoe String.

Newhall, Richard A. Muster & Review: A Problem of English Military Administration, Fourteen Twenty to Fourteen Forty. 1940. 27.50x (ISBN 0-686-51420-3). Elliots Bks.

Nicoll, Peter H. Britain's Blunder: How Britain Lost the Second World War. 134p. Date not set. pap. 4.00 (ISBN 0-911038-62-0). Inst Hist Rev.

Paget, Julian. The Story of the Guards. LC 77-89606. (Illus.). 1978. Repr. 28.50 (ISBN 0-89141-035-X). Presidio Pr.

Pfannes, Charles & Salamone, Victor. The Great Commanders of World War II: Vol. II, the British. (YA) 1981. pap. 2.75 (ISBN 0-89083-786-4). Zebra.

Powell, Geoffrey. The Kandyan Wars: The British Army in Ceylon, 1803-1818. (Nineteenth Century Military Campaigns Ser.). 320p. 1973. 18.50 (ISBN 0-85052-106-8). Shoe String.

Powicke, Michael. Military Obligation in Medieval England. LC 75-10217. 263p. 1975. Repr. of 1962 ed. lib. bdg. 15.00x (ISBN 0-8371-8171-2, POMO). Greenwood.

Prestwich, Michael. War, Politics & Finance Under Edward I. 317p. 1972. 17.50x (ISBN 0-87471-116-9). Rowman.

Proceedings of a Board of General Officers of the British Army at New York, 1781: Collections 1916. LC 16-17940. 5.00x (ISBN 0-685-73922-8, New York Historical Society). U Pr of Va.

Rogers, H. C. The British Army of the Eighteenth Century. LC 76-16779. (Illus.). 1977. 14.95 (ISBN 0-88254-418-7). Hippocrene Bks.

Seymour, William. Battles in Britain Ten Sixty-Six to Seventeen Forty-Six, 2 vols. in one. (Illus.). 1979. 19.95 (ISBN 0-88254-493-4). Hippocrene Bks.

--Battles in Britian & Their Political Background, 1642-1746, Vol. 2. LC 75-34555. (Illus.). 1976. 14.95 (ISBN 0-88254-379-2). Hippocrene Bks.

Sheppard, Eric W. A Short History of the British Army. LC 74-23642. (Illus.). 505p. 1975. Repr. of 1950 ed. lib. bdg. 35.50x (ISBN 0-8371-7567-4, SHBA). Greenwood.

Sherwig, John M. Guineas & Gunpowder: British Foreign Aid in the Wars with France, 1793-1815. LC 69-12736. (Illus.). 1969. 20.00x (ISBN 0-674-36775-8). Harvard U Pr.

Spiers, Edward M. The Arym & Society, 1815-1914. (Themes in British Social History Ser.). 336p. 1980. text ed. 25.00x (ISBN 0-582-48565-7). Longman.

Stafford, David. Britain & European Resistance, Nineteen Forty to Nineteen Forty-Five: A Survey of the Special Operations Executive, with Documents. LC 79-19224. 1980. 25.00 (ISBN 0-8020-2361-4). U of Toronto Pr.

Tanner, John, ed. The Lancaster Manual. LC 77-72264. (RAF Museum Ser.: Vol. 5). 1977. 19.95 (ISBN 0-88254-433-0). Hippocrene Bks.

Vere, Francis. True Newes from One of Sir F. Veres Companie. LC 78-38227. (English Experience Ser.: No. 491). 24p. 1972. Repr. of 1591 ed. 5.00 (ISBN 90-221-0491-5). Walter J Johnson.

Ward, Marjorie. The Blessed Trade. 1972. 15.00x (ISBN 0-7181-0951-1). Transatlantic.

Wolseley, G. J. Story of a Soldier's Life, 2 Vols. in 1. Repr. of 1903 ed. 35.00 (ISBN 0-527-97800-0). Kraus Repr.

Wood, Derek. Attack Warning Red. (Illus.). 355p. 1979. 17.95 (ISBN 0-356-08411-6, Pub. by Macdonald & Jane's England). Hippocrene Bks.

GREAT BRITAIN–HISTORY, NAVAL

see also Armada, 1588; Great Britain–Navy

Archibald, E. H. Wooden Fighting Ship in the Royal Navy AD 897-1860. LC 75-124422. (Illus.). 1968. 19.95 (ISBN 0-668-02369-4). Arco.

Aubrey, Philip. The Defeat of James Stuart's Armada, 1692. (Illus.). 192p. 1979. 15.00x (ISBN 0-8476-6156-3). Rowman.

Ballard, G. A. The Black Battlefleet. 264p. 1980. 66.00x (ISBN 0-245-53030-4, Pub. by Nautical England). State Mutual Bk.

Colledge, James J. Ships of the Royal Navy: An Historical Index, 2 vols. Incl. Vol. 1. Major Ships. 25.00x (ISBN 0-678-05300-6); Vol. 2. Navy-Built Trawlers, Drifters, Tugs & Requisitioned Ships. 17.50x (ISBN 0-678-05301-4). LC 69-10859. 1969-70. Set. 37.50x (ISBN 0-678-05514-9). Kelley.

Corbett, Julian S. Successors of Drake. (Research & Source Works Ser.: No. 176). 1968. Repr. of 1900 ed. 25.50 (ISBN 0-8337-0662-4). B Franklin.

Corbett, Julian S., ed. Papers Relating to the Navy During the Spanish War 1585-1587. LC 72-132676. (Research & Source Works: No. 562). 1970. Repr. of 1898 ed. lib. bdg. 22.50 (ISBN 0-8337-0661-6). B Franklin.

Course, A. G. Seventeenth Century Mariner. 6.95 (ISBN 0-685-20627-0). Transatlantic.

Dittmar, F. J. British Warships, Nineteen Fourteen to Nineteen Eighteen. (Illus.). 336p. 1972. 17.50x (ISBN 0-7110-0380-7). Intl Pubns Serv.

Ereira, Alan. Mutiny at Invergordon. 160p. 1981. price not set (ISBN 0-7100-0930-5). Routledge & Kegan.

Graham, Gerald S. Empire of the North Atlantic: The Maritime Struggle for North America. 2nd ed. LC 50-14296. 1958. 25.00x (ISBN 0-8020-7051-5). U of Toronto Pr.

Hagthorpe, John. Englands Exchequer, or, a Discourse of the Sea. LC 74-80181. (English Experience Ser.: No. 662). 50p. 1974. Repr. of 1625 ed. 6.00 (ISBN 90-221-0662-4). Walter J Johnson.

Halpern, P. G. The Keyes Papers, Vol. 1. (Illus.). 1979. text ed. 27.50x (ISBN 0-04-942164-6). Allen Unwin.

Halpern, P. G., ed. Keyes Papers, Vol. 2. (Illus.). 464p. 1980. text ed. 34.00x (ISBN 0-04-942165-4). Allen Unwin.

Higham, Robin, ed. A Guide to the Sources of British Military History. LC 74-104108. 1971. 45.00x (ISBN 0-520-01674-2). U of Cal Pr.

Lea, J., tr. An Answer to the Untruthes Published in Spaine, in Glorie of Their Supposed Victorie Against Our Enlish Navie. LC 72-25756. (English Experience Ser.: No. 189). 56p. 1969. Repr. of 1589 ed. 9.50 (ISBN 90-221-0189-4). Walter J Johnson.

Leutze, James R. Bargaining for Supremacy: Anglo-American Naval Collaboration, 1937-1941. LC 77-669. 1977. 22.50 (ISBN 0-8078-1305-2). U of NC Pr.

LeVeen, E. Phillip. British Slave Trade Suppression Policies 1821-1865: Impact & Implications. Bruchey, Stuart, ed. LC 77-77179. (Dissertations in European Economic History Ser.). (Illus.). 1977. lib. bdg. 18.00x (ISBN 0-405-10792-7). Arno.

Lloyd, Christopher. Nation & the Navy. LC 74-383. (Illus.). 314p. 1974. Repr. of 1961 ed. lib. bdg. 16.75x (ISBN 0-8371-7379-5, LLNN). Greenwood.

McKee, Alexander. King Henry Eighth's Mary Rose. LC 73-93035. (Illus.). 338p. 1974. 25.00x (ISBN 0-8128-1656-0). Stein & Day.

Mahan, Alfred T. Major Operations of the Navies in the War of American Independence. LC 69-10128. (Illus.). 1968. Repr. of 1913 ed. lib. bdg. 19.50x (ISBN 0-8371-1002-5, MAWI). Greenwood.

Marder, Arthur. The Anatomy of British Sea Power, 1880-1905. LC 73-2954. xix, 580p. 1974. Repr. lib. bdg. 42.00x (ISBN 0-374-95284-1). Octagon.

Marder, Arthur J. From the Dardanelles to Oran: Studies of the Royal Navy in War & Peace 1915-1940. (Illus.). 320p. 1974. 21.00x (ISBN 0-19-215802-3). Oxford U Pr.

--From the Dreadnought to Scapa Flow: The Royal Navy in the Fisher Era, 1904-1919, 5 vols. Incl. Vol. 1. The Road to War, 1904-1914. 1961. 28.50x (ISBN 0-19-215122-3); Vol. 3. Jutland & After. 2nd ed. 1978. 23.50x (ISBN 0-19-215841-4); Vol. 4. 1917: Year of Crisis. 1969. 24.00x (ISBN 0-19-215170-3); Vol. 5. Victory & Aftermath. 1970. 27.95x (ISBN 0-19-215187-8). Oxford U Pr.

Mattingly, Garrett. Armada. pap. 7.95 (ISBN 0-395-08366-4, 17, SenEd). HM.

Memoirs Relating to the Lord Torrington. 1889. 22.50 (ISBN 0-384-38100-6). Johnson Repr.

Parkes, Oscar. British Battleships, Eighteen Sixty to Nineteen Fifty: A History of Design, Construction and Armament. rev. ed. (Illus.). 1970. 50.00 (ISBN 0-208-01253-2, Archon). Shoe String.

Pepys, Samuel. Pepys' Memoires of the Royal Navy. LC 68-25260. (English Biography Ser., No. 31). 1969. Repr. of 1906 ed. lib. bdg. 28.95 (ISBN 0-8383-0228-9). Haskell.

Powley, Edward B., ed. The Naval Side of King William's War. (Illus.). 400p. 1972. 20.00 (ISBN 0-208-01084-X, Archon). Shoe String.

Richmond, Herbert W. Statesmen & Sea Power. LC 74-9222. (Illus.). 369p. 1974. Repr. of 1947 ed. lib. bdg. 17.75x (ISBN 0-8371-7632-8, RIST). Greenwood.

Robinson, Charles N. British Tar in Fact & Fiction. LC 68-26601. (Illus.). 1968. Repr. of 1909 ed. 24.00 (ISBN 0-8103-3514-X). Gale.

Rohwer, J. & Hummelchen, G. Chronology of the War at Sea, 1939-1945, 2 vols. Incl. Vol. 1. 1939-1942; Vol. 2. 1943-1945 (ISBN 0-668-03401-7). LC 73-78526. (Illus.). 256p. 1974. 12.50 ea. Arco.

Rose, J. Holland. Indecisiveness of Modern War. LC 68-15834. 1968. Repr. of 1927 ed. 11.00 (ISBN 0-8046-0392-8). Kennikat.

Russell, William C. Horatio Nelson & the Naval Supremacy of England. LC 73-14467. (Heroes of the Nation Ser.). Repr. of 1890 ed. 30.00 (ISBN 0-404-58285-0). AMS Pr.

Schurman, Donald M. Education of a Navy: The Development of British Naval Strategic Thought, 1867-1914. LC 65-24982. 1965. 7.00x (ISBN 0-226-74133-8). U of Chicago Pr.

Trotter, Wilfrid P. The Royal Navy in Old Photographs. LC 75-2890. 1975. 12.50 (ISBN 0-87021-959-6). Naval Inst Pr.

A True Relation of the Lives & Deaths of the Two English Pyrats, Purser & Clinton. LC 77-171784. (English Experience Ser.: No. 408). 1971. Repr. of 1639 ed. 7.00 (ISBN 90-221-0408-7). Walter J Johnson.

Tunstall, Brian. The Realities of Naval History. facsimile ed. LC 76-37914. (Select Bibliographies Reprint Ser.). Repr. of 1936 ed. 16.00 (ISBN 0-8369-6751-8). Arno.

Warner, Oliver & Nimitz, Chester W. Nelson & the Age of Fighting Sail. LC 63-10165. (Horizon Caravel Bks). (Illus.). 153p. (gr. 6 up). 1963. 9.95 (ISBN 0-8281-0397-6, J02414, Dist. by Har-Row); PLB 12.89 (ISBN 0-06-026380-6, Dist. by Har-Row). Am Heritage.

Williamson, James A. Sir Francis Drake. LC 74-30930. (Illus.). 160p. 1975. Repr. of 1951 ed. lib. bdg. 15.00x (ISBN 0-8371-7886-X, WIFD). Greenwood.

--Sir John Hawkins, the Time & the Man. Repr. of 1927 ed. lib. bdg. 22.00x (ISBN 0-8371-4569-4, WIJH). Greenwood.

GREAT BRITAIN–HISTORY, NAVAL–JUVENILE LITERATURE

Graham, G. S. Tides of Empire: Discursions on the Expansion of Britain Overseas. 1972. 7.00 (ISBN 0-7735-0137-1). McGill-Queens U Pr.

GREAT BRITAIN–HOME DEPARTMENT

National Academy of Sciences. Biographical Memoirs, Vol. 46, 47. 1975. Vol. 46. 10.00 (ISBN 0-309-02240-1); Vol. 47. 10.00 (ISBN 0-309-02245-2). Natl Acad Pr.

Nelson, R. R. The Home Office, Seventeen Eighty-Two-Eighteen One. LC 73-86481. (Historic Publication Ser). 1969. 9.00 (ISBN 0-8223-0210-1). Duke.

GREAT BRITAIN–IMPRINTS

see also England–Imprints

British Books in Print 1980. 1980. 130.00 (ISBN 0-85021-119-0). Bowker.

British Publishers' Catalogs Annual: 1979. 1979. 275.00x (ISBN 0-930466-22-5). Meckler Bks.

Frewer, Louis B. Bibliography of Historical Writings Published in Great Britain & the Empire: Nineteen Forty to Nineteen Forty-Five. LC 74-12628. 346p. 1974. Repr. of 1947 ed. lib. bdg. 19.75x (ISBN 0-8371-7735-9, FRHW). Greenwood.

Hardie, A. English Coloured Books. (Illus.). 32.00 (ISBN 0-87556-261-2). Saifer.

Jaggard, William. Catalogue of Such English Books As Lately Have Been, or Now Are, in Printing for Publication. LC 78-26323. (English Experience Ser.: No. 196). 1969. Repr. of 1618 ed. 7.00 (ISBN 90-221-0196-7). Walter J Johnson.

Maclean, D. Typographia Scoto-Gadelica. 384p. 1972. Repr. of 1915 ed. 31.00x (ISBN 0-7165-2058-3, Pub. by Irish Academic Pr Ireland). Biblio Dist.

Publications of the English Record Societies & the Index Library on Microfiche. (Orig.). 1979. pap. 6.00x (ISBN 0-914146-93-9). Somerset Hse.

Sawyer, Charles J. & Darton, F. Harvey. English Books, Fourteen-Hundred-Seventy-Five to Nineteen-Hundred, 2 vols. 1978. Repr. of 1927 ed. Set. 200.00 (ISBN 0-8492-8067-2). R West.

Stationery Office (Great Britain) Annual Catalogues of British Official & Parliamentary Publications 1910 to 1919. 2042p. 1975. Repr. lib. bdg. 65.00x (ISBN 0-914146-20-3). Somerset Hse.

--Annual Catalogues of British Official & Parliamentary Publications 1894 to 1909. 3076p. 1975. Repr. lib. bdg. 90.00x (ISBN 0-914146-19-X). Somerset Hse.

GREAT BRITAIN–INDIA OFFICE

Singh, S. N. Secretary of State for India & His Council. 1962. 5.50x (ISBN 0-8426-1539-3). Verry.

GREAT BRITAIN–INDUSTRY

Allen, G. C. The British Disease. 2nd ed. (Hobart Paperback Ser.: No. 67). (Orig.). 1979. technical 5.95 (ISBN 0-255-36082-7). Transatlantic.

Bairoch, Paul. Revolution Industrielle et Sous-Developpement. 4th ed. (Le Savoir Historique: No. 9). 1974. pap. 19.50x (ISBN 90-2797-295-8). Mouton.

Britain's Top One Thousand Foreign Owned Companies 1975-1976. 1976. 50.00x (ISBN 0-86010-018-9). Intl Pubns Serv.

Brittan, Samuel. The Economic Consequences of Democracy. LC 78-20911. (Illus.). 1979. text ed. 24.50x (ISBN 0-8419-6901-9); pap. text ed. 9.75x (ISBN 0-8419-6902-7). Holmes & Meier.

Chaloner, William H. People & Industries. (Illus.). 151p. 1963. 24.00x (ISBN 0-7146-1284-7, F Cass Co). Biblio Dist.

Cheyney, Edward P. Introduction to the Industrial & Social History of England. rev. ed. LC 79-92609. (BCL Ser.: No. I). (Illus.). Repr. of 1920 ed. 12.50 (ISBN 0-404-01524-7). AMS Pr.

Cunningham, William. Growth of the English Industry & Commerce. 5th ed. 1968. Repr. 95.00x (ISBN 0-7146-1296-0, F Cass Co). Biblio Dist.

Daunton, M. J. Coal Metropolis: Cardiff 1870-1914. 1977. text ed. 31.25x (ISBN 0-7185-1139-5, Leicester). Humanities.

Davis, Ralph. The Industrial Revolution & British Overseas Trade. (Illus.). 1978. text ed. 20.50x (ISBN 0-391-00925-7, Leicester); pap. text ed. 9.75x (ISBN 0-391-00927-3). Humanities.

Dunn, M. & Tranter, P. The Structure of British Industry. (Studies in the British Economy). 1979. pap. text ed. write for info. (ISBN 0-435-84544-6). Heinemann Ed.

Evans, E. W. & Creigh, S. W., eds. Industrial Conflict in Britain. 292p. 1977. 27.50x (ISBN 0-7146-3023-3, F Cass Co). Biblio Dist.

Florence, P. Sargant. The Logic of British & American Industry: A Realistic Analysis of Economic Structure & Government. 3rd ed. 1972. 22.75x (ISBN 0-7100-7155-8). Routledge & Kegan.

Fuel & Power, 5 pts. Incl. Pt. 1. Coal Trade, 5 vols. Set. 405.00x (ISBN 0-686-01141-4); Pt. 2. Gas, 6 vols. Set. 423.00x (ISBN 0-686-01142-2); Pt. 3. Mining Accidents, 12 vols. Set. 954.00x (ISBN 0-686-01143-0); Pt. 4. Mining Districts, 2 vols. Set. 153.00x (ISBN 0-686-01144-9); Pt. 5. Mining Royalties, 3 vols. Set. 216.00x (ISBN 0-686-01145-7). (British Parliamentary Papers Ser.). 1971 (Pub. by Irish Academic Pr Ireland). Biblio Dist.

Grant, Wyn & Marsh, David. The Confederation of British Industry. 1977. text ed. 16.50x (ISBN 0-8419-6205-7). Holmes & Meier.

Hart, P. E., et al. Mergers & Concentration in British Industry. (National Institute of Economic & Social Research, Occasional Papers: No. 26). (Illus.). 176p. 1973. 20.95 (ISBN 0-521-20238-8). Cambridge U Pr.

Henderson, William O. J. C. Fischer & His Diary of Industrial England, 1815-1841. LC 66-55759. (Illus.). 1966. 19.50x (ISBN 0-678-05059-7). Kelley.

Henderson, William O., ed. Industrial Britain Under the Regency. LC 67-30258. (Illus.). 1968. 19.50x (ISBN 0-678-05058-9). Kelley.

Her Majesty's Stationery Office. The Catalogue of the Translator's Library in the Department of Trade & Industry, London, 3 vols. LC 74-31406. 1600p. 1976. Set. lib. bdg. 90.00 ea. Oceana.

House, John W. Industrial Britain: The Northeast. LC 77-91239. 1969. 17.50x (ISBN 0-678-05569-6). Kelley.

Humphrys, Graham. Industrial Britain: South Wales. (Industrial Britain Ser.). (Illus.). 248p. 1972. 16.50 (ISBN 0-7153-5478-7). David & Charles.

Industrial Relations, 44 vols. (British Parliamentary Papers Ser.). 1971. Set. 3789.00x (ISBN 0-7165-1451-6, Pub. by Irish Academic Pr Ireland). Biblio Dist.

Jenkin, Michael. British Industry & the North Sea: State Intervention in a Developing Industrial Sector. 251p. 1981. text ed. 38.50x (ISBN 0-8419-5055-5). Holmes & Meier.

Jones, Philip N. & Lewis, Peter. Industrial Britain: The Humberside Region. (Industrial Britain Ser.). (Illus.). 235p. 1971. 16.50 (ISBN 0-7153-4897-3). David & Charles.

Jordan, Bill. Automatic Poverty: The Ricardo Phenomenon. 208p. 1981. 22.50 (ISBN 0-7100-0824-4); pap. 12.95 (ISBN 0-7100-0825-2). Routledge & Kegan.

Jordon Dataquest. Britain's Quoted Industrial Companies Nineteen Seventy-Nine. pap. text ed. 30.00 (ISBN 0-85938-091-2). State Mutual Bk.

Keeble, David. Industrial Location & Planning in the United Kingdom. (Illus.). 1976. pap. 16.95x (ISBN 0-416-80060-2). Methuen Inc.

Kemps London Directory, 1979. 1979. pap. 36.50 (ISBN 0-905255-56-9, KEMP 002, Kemps). Unipub.

Lee, Derek. Regional Planning & Location of Industry. 3rd ed. (Studies in the British Economy). 1980. pap. text ed. 7.50 (ISBN 0-435-84577-2). Heinemann Ed.

Little, A. D. New Technology-Based Firms in the United Kingdom & the Federal Republic of Germany. LC 78-301104. (Illus.). 1977. pap. 50.00x (ISBN 0-905492-04-8). Intl Pubns Serv.

MacDonald, J. R. The Zollverein & British Industry. Repr. of 1903 ed. 10.00 (ISBN 0-527-59380-X). Kraus Repr.

Macrosty, Henry W. Trust Movement in British Industry. LC 68-16355. 1968. Repr. of 1907 ed. 12.00x (ISBN 0-87586-007-9). Agathon.

Morris, J. A., ed. Growth of Industrial Britain: A Work Book & Study Guide in Social & Economic History. (Illus.). 1971. text ed. 16.95x (ISBN 0-245-50324-2). Intl Ideas.

Nef, John U. Industry & Government in France & England, 1540-1640. LC 68-25045. 1968. Repr. of 1940 ed. 8.00 (ISBN 0-8462-1172-6). Russell.

Pavitt, Keith. Technical Innovation & British Economic Performance. 353p. 1981. text ed. 50.00x (ISBN 0-333-26225-5, Pub. by Macmillan, England). Humanities.

Pryke, Richard. The Nationalised Industries: Policies & Performance Since 1968. 298p. 1981. 32.50x (ISBN 0-85520-241-6, Pub. by Martin Robertson England); pap. 12.95x (ISBN 0-85520-242-4). Biblio Dist.

Sanderson, Michael. The Universities & British Industry. (Illus.). 434p. 1972. 38.00x (ISBN 0-7100-7378-X). Routledge & Kegan.
Sell's British Exporters 1980. LC 75-640255. (Illus.). 230p. (Orig.). 1980. pap. 32.50x (ISBN 0-85499-547-1). Intl Pubns Serv.
Sharma, Arvind. Management Development in Public Enterprise. 1977. 18.00x (ISBN 0-686-22665-8). Intl Bk Dist.
Taylor, William C. Notes on Tour in the Manufacturing Districts of Lancashire. 3rd ed. 331p. 1968. 27.50x (ISBN 0-7146-1408-4, F Cass Co). Biblio Dist.
Thomas, W. A. The Finance of British Industry, 1918-1976. 1978. 49.95x (ISBN 0-416-67420-8). Methuen Inc.
Thomis, Malcolm I. Responses to Industrialisation: The British Experience, 1780-1850. (Orig.). 1976. 17.50 (ISBN 0-208-01588-4, Archon). Shoe String.
The Times One Thousand, Nineteen Eighty to Nineteen Eighty One. 360p. 1980. 47.50x (ISBN 0-930466-31-4). Meckler Bks.
Trade & Industry, 6 pts. Incl. Pt. 1. Navigation Laws, 2 vols. Set. 171.00x (ISBN 0-686-01135-X); Pt. 2. Trade Depression, 3 vols. Set. 216.00x (ISBN 0-686-01136-8); Pt. 3. Insurance (Friendly Soc, 10 vols. Set. 783.00x (ISBN 0-686-01137-6); Pt. 4. Explosives, 2 vols. Set. 153.00x (ISBN 0-686-01138-4); Pt. 5. Silver & Gold Wares, 2 vols. Set. 117.00x (ISBN 0-686-01139-2); Pt. 6. Tobacco, 2 vols. Set. 171.00x (ISBN 0-686-01140-6). (British Parliamentary Papers Ser.). 1971 (Pub. by Irish Academic Pr Ireland). Biblio Dist.
Transport & Communications, 3 pts. Incl. Pt. 1. General, 22 vols. Set. 1845.00x (ISBN 0-686-01146-5); Pt. 2. Shipping (Safety, 9 vols. Set. 792.00x (ISBN 0-686-01147-3); Pt. 3. Posts & Telegraphs, 8 vols. Set. 684.00x (ISBN 0-686-01148-1). (British Parliamentary Papers Ser.). 1971 (Pub. by Irish Academic Pr Ireland). Biblio Dist.
Wood, Peter A. Industrial Britain: West Midlands. 1976. 9.50 (ISBN 0-7153-7032-4). David & Charles.
Young, Arthur. Arthur Young on Industry & Economics. LC 72-38271. (The Evolution of Capitalism Ser.). 188p. 1972. Repr. of 1926 ed. 10.00 (ISBN 0-405-04142-X). Arno.

GREAT BRITAIN–INDUSTRY–HISTORY

Alderton, David & Booker, John. The Batsford Guide to the Industrial Archaeology of East Anglia. LC 79-56490. (Illus.). 150p. 1980. 39.00 (ISBN 0-7134-2233-5, Pub. by Batsford England). David & Charles.
Ashton, Thomas S. Eighteenth-Century Industrialist, Peter Stubs of Warrington. LC 40-5169. 1939. 12.50x (ISBN 0-678-06750-3). Kelley.
Babbage, Charles. Exposition of Eighteen Fifty One: Or Views of the Industry, the Science & Government of England. 2nd ed. 290p. 1968. Repr. of 1851 ed. 25.00x (ISBN 0-7146-1620-6, F Cass Co). Biblio Dist.
Baker, E. C. Sir William Preece F. R. S. Victorian Engineer Extraordinary. (Illus.). 377p. 1976. 19.75x (ISBN 0-8476-1369-0). Rowman.
Beales, H. L. Industrial Revolution, 1750-1850. 2nd ed. LC 67-17931. 1958. 10.00x (ISBN 0-678-00216-9). Kelley.
Beveridge, W. H. Unemployment: A Problem of Industry. LC 79-59646. (The English Workinh Class Ser.). 1980. lib. bdg. 35.00 (ISBN 0-8240-0101-X). Garland Pub.
British Association For The Advancement Of Science - Committee On Local Industries. Resources, Products & Industrial History of Birmingham & the Midland Hardware Districts. Timmins, Samuel, ed. LC 68-103772. (Illus.). Repr. of 1866 ed. lib. bdg. 32.50x (ISBN 0-678-05205-0). Kelley.
Broadway, Frank. State Intervention in British Industry 1964-68. LC 79-115974. 191p. 1970. 12.00 (ISBN 0-8386-7690-1). Fairleigh Dickinson.
Buchanan, Angus & Cossons, Neil. Industrial History in Pictures: Bristol. (Illus.). 112p. 1971. 5.50 (ISBN 0-7153-4745-4). David & Charles.
Buchanon, C. A. & Buchanon, R. A. The Batsford Guide to the Industrial Archaeology of Central Southern England. (Illus.). 192p. 1980. 45.00 (ISBN 0-7134-1364-6, Pub. by Batsford England). David & Charles.
Butt, John & Donnachie, Ian. Industrial Archaeology in the British Isles. LC 79-11955. (Illus.). 1979. text ed. 23.50x (ISBN 0-06-490837-2). B&N.
Buxton, Neil K. & Aldcroft, Derek H., eds. British Industry Between the Wars: Instability & Industrial Development 1919-1939. 308p. 1979. 40.00x (ISBN 0-85967-383-9, Pub. by Scolar Pr England). Biblio Dist.
Byatt, I. C. The British Electrical Industry Eighteen Seventy-Five to Nineteen Fourteen. 1979. 37.50x (ISBN 0-19-828270-2). Oxford U Pr.
Checkland, S. G. The Rise of Industrial Society: 1815-1855. (Social & Economic History of England). 1964. text ed. 12.95x (ISBN 0-582-48239-9). Longman.
Cheyney, Edward P. Industrial & Social History of England. 1971. Repr. of 1901 ed. 10.50 (ISBN 0-87928-020-4). Corner Hse.
--An Introduction to the Industrial & Social History of England. 1977. Repr. of 1912 ed. lib. bdg. 25.00 (ISBN 0-8414-1845-4). Folcroft.
Court, William H. British Economic History, Eighteen Seventy - Nineteen Fourteen. (Orig.). 1966. 53.95 (ISBN 0-521-04731-5); pap. 19.50x (ISBN 0-521-09362-7). Cambridge U Pr.
--Concise Economic History of Britain. pap. 11.95x (ISBN 0-521-09217-5). Cambridge U Pr.
Cunningham, William. The Growth of English Industry & Commerce, 3 vols. in 2. Incl. Vol. 1. Early & Middle Ages. 5th ed; Vol. 2. Modern Times: the Mercantile System. 4th ed; Vol. 3. Modern Times: Laissez Faire. 4th ed. LC 66-21667. Repr. of 1907 ed. Set. 50.00x (ISBN 0-678-00288-6). Kelley.
Dodd, George. Days at the Factories: Or, The Manufacturing Industry of Great Britain Described. (Illus.). 1978. Repr. of 1843 ed. 18.00x (ISBN 0-7158-1076-6). Charles River Bks.
Doty, C. Stewart, ed. The Industrial Revolution. LC 76-14929. (European Problem Studies Ser.). 142p. 1976. pap. text ed. 5.50 (ISBN 0-88275-433-5). Krieger.
Dummelow, John. The Wax Chandlers of London: A Short History of the Worshipful Company of Wax Chandlers of London. (Illus.). 204p. 1973. 47.50x (ISBN 0-8476-1381-X). Rowman.
Evans, Joan. The Endless Web: John Dickinson & Co. Ltd., Eighteen Hundred & Four to Nineteen Fifty-Four. LC 78-2673. (Illus.). xvi, 273p. 1978. Repr. of 1955 ed. lib. bdg. 26.75x (ISBN 0-313-20361-X, EVEW). Greenwood.
Falconer, Keith. Guide to England's Industrial Heritage. LC 80-8027. (Illus.). 270p. 1980. text ed. 29.50x (ISBN 0-8419-0646-7). Holmes & Meier.
Fell, A. Early Iron Industry of Furness & District. (Illus.). 462p. 1968. Repr. of 1908 ed. 30.00x (ISBN 0-7146-1393-2, F Cass Co). Biblio Dist.
Fitzgerald, Patrick. Industrial Combination in England. Wilkins, Mira, ed. LC 76-29996. (European Business Ser.). 1977. Repr. of 1927 ed. lib. bdg. 15.00x (ISBN 0-405-09754-9). Arno.
Floud, R. The British Machine-Tool Industry, 1850-1914. LC 75-46205. (Illus.). 180p. 1976. 29.95 (ISBN 0-521-21203-0). Cambridge U Pr.
George, Mary D. England in Transition: Life & Work in the 18th Century. LC 75-41110. Repr. of 1931 ed. 19.50 (ISBN 0-404-14544-2). AMS Pr.
Hamilton, Henry. English Brass & Copper Industries to 1880. 2nd rev. ed. (Illus.). 388p. 1967. 29.50x (ISBN 0-686-11102-8, F Cass Co). Biblio Dist.
Hart, Cyril. The Industrial History of Dean: With an Introduction to Its Industrial Archaeology. (Illus.). 466p. 1971. 22.50 (ISBN 0-7153-5288-1). David & Charles.
Hartwell, Ronald M., ed. Causes of the Industrial Revolution in England. 1967. pap. 9.95x (ISBN 0-416-48000-4). Methuen Inc.
Head, George. Home Tour Through the Manufacturing Districts of England in the Summer of 1835. 2nd, rev. ed. 1968. Repr. of 1836 ed. 23.50x (ISBN 0-7146-1397-5, F Cass Co). Biblio Dist.
Henderson, W. O. J. C. Fisher & His Diary of Industrial England: 1814-1851. (Illus.). 184p. 1966. 23.50x (ISBN 0-7146-1316-9, F Cass Co). Biblio Dist.
Hoffmann, Walther G. British Industry, Seventeen Hundred to Nineteen Fifty. Henderson, W. O. & Chaloner, W. H., trs. LC 77-1699. Repr. of 1955 ed. 17.50x (ISBN 0-678-06257-9). Kelley.
Howarth, Edward G. & Wilson, Mona. West Ham: A Study in Social & Industrial Problems. LC 79-56958. (The English Working Class Ser.). 1980. lib. bdg. 35.00 (ISBN 0-8240-0111-7). Garland Pub.
Hudson, Kenneth. Industrial Archaeology of Southern England. LC 68-23822. (Illus.). 1968. 14.95x (ISBN 0-678-05606-4). Kelley.
Industrial Revolution, 5 pts. Incl. Pt. 1. Children's Employment, 15 vols. Set. 1143.00x (ISBN 0-686-01154-6); Pt. 2. Design, 4 vols. Set. 342.00x (ISBN 0-686-01155-4); Pt. 3. Factories, 31 vols. Set. 2548.00x (ISBN 0-686-01156-2); Pt. 4. Textiles, 10 vols. Set. 783.00x (ISBN 0-686-01157-0); Pt. 5. Trade, 5 vols. Set. 351.00x (ISBN 0-686-01158-9). (British Parliamentary Papers Ser.). 1971 (Pub. by Irish Academic Pr Ireland). Biblio Dist.
Jack, Sybil M. Trade & Industry in Tudor & Stuart England. (Historical Problems - Studies & Documents). 1977. text ed. 29.95x (ISBN 0-04-942155-7); pap. text ed. 12.50x (ISBN 0-04-942156-5). Allen Unwin.
Jenkins, Rhys. Links in the History of Engineering & Technology from Tudor Times. facs. ed. LC 72-121481. (Essay Index Reprint Ser). 1936. 18.00 (ISBN 0-8369-2167-4). Arno.
Jones, George T. Increasing Returns: A Study of the Relation Between the Size & Efficiency of Industries with Special Reference to the History of Selected British & American Industries, 1850-1910. Clark, Colin G., ed. xi, 300p. Repr. of 1933 ed. lib. bdg. 19.50x (ISBN 0-87991-083-6). Porcupine Pr.
Joyce, Patrick. Work, Society & Politics: The Factory North of England in the Second Half of the Nineteenth Century. 1980. text ed. write for info. (ISBN 0-391-02215-6). Humanities.
Lord, John. Capital & Steam-Power, Seventeen Fifty to Eighteen Hundred. Repr. of 1923 ed. 19.50x (ISBN 0-678-05216-6). Kelley.
--Capital & Steam Power: Seventeen Fifty to Eighteen Hundred. 2nd ed. 253p. 1966. 23.50x (ISBN 0-7146-1339-8, F Cass Co). Biblio Dist.
Marshall, J. D. & Davies-Shiel, M. The Lake District at Work: Past & Present. (Industrial History in Pictures Ser.). (Illus.). 1971. 5.95 (ISBN 0-7153-5104-4). David & Charles.
Middlemas, Keith. Politics in Industrial Society: The Experience of the British System Since 1911. 512p. 1979. 37.50x (ISBN 0-8476-6872-X). Rowman.
Motherwell & Orbiston: The First Owenite Attempts at Cooperative Communities, 1822-1825. LC 72-2534. (British Labour Struggles Before 1850 Ser). 1972. 11.00 (ISBN 0-405-04427-5). Arno.
Musson, A. E. The Growth of British Industry. LC 78-178. 1978. text ed. 39.00x (ISBN 0-8419-0367-0). Holmes & Meier.
Nef, John U. Industry & Government in France & England, 1540-1640. 1957. pap. 3.95 (ISBN 0-8014-9053-7, CP53). Cornell U Pr.
Newell, Abraham. Hillside View of Industrial History. LC 73-119540. (Illus.). Repr. of 1925 ed. 15.00x (ISBN 0-678-00695-4). Kelley.
Nockolds, Harold. Lucas, Vol. 2. 1978. 17.50 (ISBN 0-7153-7316-1). David & Charles.
--Lucas: The First Hundred Years, Vol. 1. 1976. 17.50 (ISBN 0-7153-7306-4). David & Charles.
Page, William, ed. Commerce & Industry, 2 Vols in One. LC 67-19709. Repr. of 1919 ed. 30.00x (ISBN 0-678-00404-8). Kelley.
Pawson, Eric. The Early Industrial Revolution: Britain in the 18th Century. LC 78-17314. (Illus.). 1979. text ed. 18.50x (ISBN 0-06-495464-1). B&N.
Pike, Royston E., ed. Human Documents of the Industrial Revolution in Britain. 1966. pap. text ed. 12.50x (ISBN 0-04-942060-7). Allen Unwin.
Prais, S. J. The Evolution of Giant Firms in Britain: A Study in the Growth of Concentration in Manufacturing Industry in Britain, 1909-1970. LC 76-18410. (National Institute of Economic & Social Research Economic & Social Studies: No. 30). (Illus.). 321p. 1981. pap. 15.95 (ISBN 0-521-28273-X). Cambridge U Pr.
Raistrick, Arthur. Quakers in Science & Industry. LC 68-18641. (Illus.). Repr. of 1950 ed. 17.50x (ISBN 0-678-05622-6). Kelley.
--Two Centuries of Industrial Welfare: The London (Quaker) Lead Company, Sixteen Ninety-Two to Nineteen Hundred & Five. 168p. 1980. 19.75x (ISBN 0-903485-13-3, Pub. by & Moorland England). State Mutual Bks.
Roberts, Kenneth D. Some Nineteenth Century English Woodworking Tools. (Illus.). 496p. 1980. text ed. 40.00x (ISBN 0-913602-40-X). K Roberts.
Rowntree, B. Seebohm & Lasker, Bruno. Unemployment: A Social Study. LC 79-56970. (The English Workinh Class Ser.). 1980. lib. bdg. 28.00 (ISBN 0-8240-0121-4). Garland Pub.
Salzman, Louis T. English Industries of the Middle Ages. LC 74-8922. 1913. 30.00 (ISBN 0-8414-7770-1). Folcroft.
Seth-Smith, Michael. The Long Haul: A Social History of the British Commercial Vehicle Industry. (Illus.). 1975. text ed. 15.00x (ISBN 0-09-124440-4). Humanities.
Stanley Rule & Level, Eighteen Ninety-Two Price List Revised to Eighteen Ninety-Seven, Abbrigment. 1980. pap. 3.00 (ISBN 0-913602-36-1). K Roberts.
Supple, Barry, ed. Essays in British Business History. 1977. 37.50x (ISBN 0-19-877087-1); pap. 16.50x (ISBN 0-19-877088-X). Oxford U Pr.
Svedenstierna, Eric T. Svedenstierna's Tour in Great Britain 1802-3: The Travel Diary of an Industrial Spy. Dellow, E. L., tr. from Swed. 192p. 4.95 (ISBN 0-7153-5747-6). David & Charles.
Thompson, Allan. The Dynamics of the Industrial Revolution. LC 73-82224. 224p. 1973. text ed. 17.95 (ISBN 0-312-22330-7). St Martin.
Tierney, Brian, et al. Industrial Revolution in England. 1968. pap. text ed. 1.95 (ISBN 0-394-30874-3, RanC). Random.
Trinder, Barrie. The Industrial Revolution in Shropshire. (Illus.). 455p. 1973. 35.00x (ISBN 0-8476-1375-5). Rowman.
Underhill Edge Tool Co., Eighteen Fifty-Nine Price List Axes & Mechanics' Tools. 1980. pap. 3.00 (ISBN 0-913602-37-X). K Roberts.
Unwin, George. Studies in Economic History. Tawney, R. H., ed. LC 66-9002. Repr. of 1927 ed. 27.50x (ISBN 0-678-05198-4). Kelley.
Von Tunzelman, G. N. Steam Power & British Industrialization to 1860. (Illus.). 1978. 45.00x (ISBN 0-19-828273-7). Oxford U Pr.
Wadsworth, Alfred P. & Mann, Julia. Cotton Trade & Industrial Lancashire 1600-1780. LC 68-6121. (Illus.). Repr. of 1931 ed. 19.50x (ISBN 0-678-06768-6). Kelley.
Weatherill, Lorna. Pottery Trade & North Staffordshire 1660-1760. LC 79-141317. 1970. lib. bdg. 13.50x (ISBN 0-678-06783-X). Kelley.
William Chapple: Eighteen Seventy-Six Revised Price List Planes. 1980. pap. 2.50 (ISBN 0-913602-35-3). K Roberts.
Williams, Alfred. Life in a Railway Factory. LC 79-56941. 1980. lib. bdg. 28.00 (ISBN 0-8240-0126-5). Garland Pub.
Williams, Eric E. Capitalism & Slavery. LC 61-13088. 1961. Repr. of 1944 ed. 19.00 (ISBN 0-8462-0301-4). Russell.
Young, Stephen & Lowe, A. V. Intervention in the Mixed Economy: The Evolution of British Industrial Policy 1964-1972. 1974. 22.50x (ISBN 0-8448-0563-7). Crane-Russak Co.

GREAT BRITAIN–INTELLECTUAL LIFE

Allen, P. The Cambridge Apostles. LC 77-82482. (Illus.). 1979. 38.50 (ISBN 0-521-21803-9). Cambridge U Pr.
Allison, Thomas. Pioneers of English Learning. 1978. lib. bdg. 20.00 (ISBN 0-8495-0104-0). Arden Lib.
Asquith, H. H. Some Aspects of the Victorian Age. LC 74-13333. 1918. lib. bdg. 5.00 (ISBN 0-8414-2997-9). Folcroft.
Bax, E. Belfort. Reminiscences & Reflexions of a Mid & Late Victorian. LC 67-27466. 1918. 15.00x (ISBN 0-678-00313-0). Kelley.
Bonwick, Colin. English Radicals & the American Revolution. LC 76-12641. 1977. 21.50x (ISBN 0-8078-1277-3). U of NC Pr.
Boyd, Elizabeth F. Bloomsbury Heritage: Their Mothers & Their Aunts. LC 76-422. (Illus.). 1976. 10.50 (ISBN 0-8008-0821-5). Taplinger.
Brewer, Derek. Chaucer & His World. LC 77-10790. (Illus.). 1978. 20.00 (ISBN 0-396-07519-3). Dodd.
Bronson, Bertrand H. Printing As an Index of Taste in Eighteenth-Century England. rev. ed. (Illus.). 1963. pap. 4.00 (ISBN 0-87104-146-4). NY Pub Lib.
Buckley, Jerome H. Victorian Temper: A Study in Literary Culture. new ed. (Illus.). 282p. 1966. 25.00x (ISBN 0-7146-2052-1, F Cass Co). Biblio Dist.
Cox, C. B. & Dyson, A. E., eds. The Twentieth-Century Mind: History, Ideas, & Literature in Britain, Vol. I: Nineteen Hundred to Nineteen Eighteen. 540p. 1972. pap. text ed. 6.95x (ISBN 0-19-281118-5). Oxford U Pr.
--The Twentieth-Century Mind: History, Ideas, & Literature in Britain, Vol II: Nineteen Eighteen to Nineteen Forty-Five. 526p. 1972. pap. text ed. 16.75x (ISBN 0-19-212192-8). Oxford U Pr.
--The Twentieth Century Mind: History, Ideas, & Literature in Britain, Vol. III: Nineteen Forty-Five to Nineteen Sixty-Five. 522p. 1972. pap. text ed. 16.75x (ISBN 0-19-212193-6). Oxford U Pr.
Craig, Hardin. The Enchanted Glass: The Elizabethan Mind in Literature. LC 75-11492. 293p. 1975. Repr. of 1952 ed. lib. bdg. 16.75x (ISBN 0-8371-8200-X, CREG). Greenwood.
Cruse, Amy. After the Victorians. LC 76-158495. 1971. Repr. of 1938 ed. 24.00 (ISBN 0-403-01315-1). Scholarly.
--Englishman & His Books in the Early Nineteenth Century. LC 68-20218. (Illus.). 1968. Repr. of 1930 ed. 14.00 (ISBN 0-405-08412-9, Blom Pubns). Arno.
Daly, James. Cosmic Harmony & Political Thinking in Early Stuart England. (Transactions Ser.: Vol. 69, Pt. 7). 1979. 6.00 (ISBN 0-87169-697-5). Am Philos.
Davis, Garold N. German Thought & Culture in England, 1700-1770. (Studies in Comparative Literature Ser.: No. 47). 1969. 10.50x (ISBN 0-8078-7047-1). U of NC Pr.

Demiashkevich, Michael. The National Mind: English, French, German. 1979. Repr. of 1938 ed. lib. bdg. 45.00 (ISBN 0-8495-1104-6). Arden Lib.
Disraeli, Isaac. Amenities of Literature, Consisting of Sketches & Characters of English Literature, 2 Vols. Disraeli, B., ed. LC 68-57599. (Illus.). 1969. Repr. of 1871 ed. Set. lib. bdg. 37.00x (ISBN 0-8371-1970-7, DIAL). Greenwood.
Dobson, Austin. Eighteenth Century Vignettes, First, Second & Third Series, 3 Vols. LC 67-29812. (Illus.). 1968. Repr. of 1896 ed. Set. 50.00 (ISBN 0-686-66381-0, Pub. by Blom); Ser. 1. 16.50 (ISBN 0-686-66382-9); Ser. 2. 16.50 (ISBN 0-405-08448-X); Ser. 3. 17.00 (ISBN 0-405-08449-8). Arno.
--Miscellanies: Second Series. facs. ed. LC 67-28749. (Essay Index Reprint Ser). 1901. 16.00 (ISBN 0-8369-0380-3). Arno.
Ellis, Henry, ed. Original Letters of Eminent Literary Men of the 16th, 17th & 18th Centuries. LC 71-166022. (Camden Society, London. Publications, First Ser.: No. 23). Repr. of 1843 ed. 35.00 (ISBN 0-404-50123-0). AMS Pr.
Frantz, Ray W. English Traveller & the Movement of Ideas, 1660-1732. 1967. lib. bdg. 14.00x (ISBN 0-374-92870-3). Octagon.
Gadd, David. The Loving Friends-a Portrait of Bloomsbury. LC 74-26596. 1976. pap. 3.45 (ISBN 0-15-654300-1, Harv). HarBraceJ.
Garfield, Leon. The House of Hanover England in the Eighteenth Century. LC 75-42422. (Illus.). 128p. (gr. 6 up). 1976. 8.95 (ISBN 0-395-28904-1, Clarion). HM.
Green, Martin. Children of the Sun: A Narrative of "Decadence" in England After 1918. LC 74-25905. (Illus.). 454p. 1976. 18.00 (ISBN 0-465-01040-7). Basic.
Green, Michael & Wilding, Michael. Cultural Policy in Great Britain. (Studies & Documents on Cultural Policies). (Orig.). 1971. pap. 5.00 (ISBN 92-3-100852-8, U122, UNESCO). Unipub.
Harrison, G. B. The Elizabethan Journals, 2 vols. Incl. Vol. 1. 1591-1597; Vol. 2. 1598-1603. 12.00 (ISBN 0-8446-2211-7). Peter Smith.
Hazlitt, William. Spirit of the Age: Or, Contemporary Portraits. (World's Classics Ser.). 1904. 11.95 (ISBN 0-19-250057-0). Oxford U Pr.
Hewison, Robert. In Anger: British Culture in the Cold War, 1945-60. (Illus.). 212p. 1981. 19.95 (ISBN 0-19-520238-4). Oxford U Pr.
Hill, Christopher. Some Intellectual Consequences of the English Revolution. LC 79-5408. (Curti Lecture Ser.). 1980. 13.50 (ISBN 0-299-08140-0); pap. 4.95 (ISBN 0-299-08144-3). U of Wis Pr.
Himmelfarb, Gertrude. Victorian Minds. 8.25 (ISBN 0-8446-5117-6). Peter Smith.
Hunt, Violet. I Have This to Say. LC 78-64035. (Des Imagistes: Literature of the Imagist Movement). Repr. of 1926 ed. 26.00 (ISBN 0-404-17116-8). AMS Pr.
Johnson, Lesley. The Cultural Critics. (International Library of Sociology). 1979. 24.00x (ISBN 0-7100-7678-9). Routledge & Kegan.
Kelso, Ruth. The Doctrine of the English Gentleman in the Sixteenth Century. 1964. 7.50 (ISBN 0-8446-1260-X). Peter Smith.
Kingsmill, Hugh. The English Genius. 1973. lib. bdg. 25.00 (ISBN 0-8414-5587-2). Folcroft.
Knickerbocker, William S. Creative Oxford, Its Influence in Victorian Literature. LC 72-6165. 1925. lib. bdg. 20.00 (ISBN 0-8414-0124-1). Folcroft.
Knights, B. The Idea of the Clerisy, in the Nineteenth Century. LC 77-80840. 1978. 42.00 (ISBN 0-521-21798-9). Cambridge U Pr.
Knoepflmacher, U. C. & Tennyson, G. B., eds. Nature & the Victorian Imagination. LC 76-7761. 1978. 27.50 (ISBN 0-520-03229-2). U of Cal Pr.
Lester, John A. Journey Through Despair, 1880-1914: Transformations in British Literary Culture. LC 68-15767. 1968. 16.50 (ISBN 0-691-06144-0). Princeton U Pr.
Levine, Joseph M. Dr. Woodward's Shield: History, Science, & Satire in Augustan England. 1977. 32.75x (ISBN 0-520-03132-6). U of Cal Pr.
McLean. Humanism & the Rise of Science in Tudor England. 258p. 1972. text ed. 20.00 (ISBN 0-88202-001-3, Sci Hist). N Watson.
Mowat, Robert B. Americans in England. LC 79-99642. (Essay Index Reprint Ser). 1935. 23.00 (ISBN 0-8369-1423-6). Arno.
Patrides, C. A. & Waddington, Raymond B., eds. The Age of Milton: Backgrounds to Seventeenth-Century Literature. 400p. 1981. 60.00x (ISBN 0-686-73056-9, Pub. by Manchester U Pr England). State Mutual Bk.
Paulson, Ronald. Popular & Polite Art in the Age of Hogarth & Fielding. LC 79-63358. (Ward-Phillips Lectures in English Language & Literature Ser.: No. 10). 1979. text ed. 20.00x (ISBN 0-268-01534-1, 85-15348). U of Notre Dame Pr.
Regan, D. E. Local Government & Education. 2nd ed. (New Local Government Ser.). 1979. pap. text ed. 11.95x (ISBN 0-04-352065-0). Allen Unwin.
Robinson, Henry C. Henry Crabb Robinson on Books & Their Writers, 3 Vols. Morley, Edith J., ed. LC 75-182705. Repr. of 1938 ed. Set. 73.50 (ISBN 0-404-05410-2); 24.50 ea. Vol. 1 (ISBN 0-404-05411-0). Vol. 2 (ISBN 0-404-05412-9). Vol. 3 (ISBN 0-404-05413-7). AMS Pr.
Ross, Robert H. Georgian Revolt: Rise & Fall of a Poetic Ideal, 1910-1922. LC 65-12391. (Illus.). 320p. 1965. 9.95x (ISBN 0-8093-0164-4). S Ill U Pr.
Rudman, Harry. Italian Nationalism & English Letters. LC 72-182707. Repr. of 1940 ed. 17.50 (ISBN 0-404-05450-1). AMS Pr.
Smalley, Beryl. The Becket Conflict & the Schools: A Study of Intellectuals in Politics in the Twelfth Century. LC 72-14254. 257p. 1973. 21.50x (ISBN 0-87471-172-X). Rowman.
Somervell, D. C. English Thought in the Nineteenth Century. 1978. Repr. of 1938 ed. lib. bdg. 25.00 (ISBN 0-8492-2594-9). R West.
Somervell, David C. English Thought in the Nineteenth Century. LC 77-21468. 1977. Repr. of 1962 ed. lib. bdg. 18.50x (ISBN 0-8371-9793-7, SOET). Greenwood.
Sommerville, C. John. Popular Religion in Restoration England. LC 77-7618. (University of Florida Social Science Monographs: No. 59). 1977. pap. 4.50 (ISBN 0-8130-0564-7). U Presses Fla.
Staves, Susan. Players' Scepters: Fictions of Authority in the Restoration. LC 78-24346. (Illus.). 1979. 21.50x (ISBN 0-8032-4102-X). U of Nebr Pr.
Stephen, Leslie. Selected Writings in British Intellectual History. Annan, Noel, ed. LC 78-13218. (Classics of British Historical Literature). 1979. lib. bdg. 17.00x (ISBN 0-226-77255-1). U of Chicago Pr.
Thompson, Edward R. Portraits of the New Century. LC 74-117853. (Essay Index Reprint Ser). 1928. 17.00 (ISBN 0-8369-1685-9). Arno.
--Portraits of the Nineties. LC 78-117854. (Essay Index Reprint Ser). 1921. 19.50 (ISBN 0-8369-1686-7). Arno.
Tinker, Chauncey B. Salon & English Letters. LC 67-21716. 1967. Repr. of 1915 ed. 10.00 (ISBN 0-87752-113-1). Gordian.
Voltaire. Letters Concerning the English Nation. LC 74-728. 224p. 1974. Repr. of 1926 ed. lib. bdg. 19.00 (ISBN 0-8337-4467-4). B Franklin.
--Lettres Philosophiques. Pomeau, Rene, ed. 192p. 1964. 3.95 (ISBN 0-686-55754-9). French & Eur.
--Lettres Philosophiques. 18.95 (ISBN 0-686-55755-7). French & Eur.
Voltaire, Francois M. Philosophical Letters. Dilworth, Ernest N., tr. LC 60-53370. 1961. pap. 4.50 (ISBN 0-672-60326-8, LLA124). Bobbs.
Walker, Hugh. The Age of Tennyson. facsimile ed. LC 76-160999. (Select Bibliographies Reprint Ser.). Repr. of 1897 ed. 18.00 (ISBN 0-8369-5867-5). Arno.
Webster, Charles, ed. The Intellectual Revolution of the Seventeenth Century. (Past & Present Ser.). 452p. 1975. 25.00 (ISBN 0-7100-7844-7). Routledge & Kegan.
Willey, Basil. Nineteenth-Century Studies; Coleridge to Matthew Arnold. LC 80-40634. 288p. 1981. pap. 9.95 (ISBN 0-521-28066-4). Cambridge U Pr.
Williams, Raymond. The Long Revolution. LC 75-16613. 369p. 1975. Repr. of 1961 ed. lib. bdg. 22.75x (ISBN 0-8371-8244-1, WILR). Greenwood.
Wren, David. They Enriched Humanity (Shelley, William Morris) (Victorian Age Ser). 1948. Repr. 10.00 (ISBN 0-685-43116-9). Norwood Edns.

GREAT BRITAIN–JUVENILE LITERATURE

see also England–Juvenile Literature; Great Britain–History–Juvenile Literature

Coleman, Francis. Great Britain. LC 75-44870. (Macdonald Countries). (Illus.). (gr. 6 up). 1976. PLB 7.95 (ISBN 0-382-06102-0, Pub. by Macdonald Ed). Silver.
Fincham, Paul. East Anglia. (Discovering Britain Ser.). (Illus.). 149p. (gr. 5 up). 1976. 7.95 (ISBN 0-571-10344-8, Pub. by Faber & Faber). Merrimack Bk Serv.
Fletcher, David. Henry VIII. LC 77-188. (History Makers Ser.). (Illus.). (YA) 1977. 6.95 (ISBN 0-312-36802-X). St Martin.
Gilleo, Alma. Prince Charles, Growing up in Buckingham Palace. LC 78-18938. (Illus.). (gr. k-4). 1978. PLB 5.95 (ISBN 0-89565-029-0). Childs World.
Hinds, Lorna. Looking at Great Britain. LC 73-5947. (gr. 4-6). 1973. 8.95 (ISBN 0-397-31335-7, JBL-J). Har-Row.
Kendall, Alan. Elizabeth One. LC 77-304. (History Makers Ser.). (Illus.). 1977. 6.95 (ISBN 0-312-24247-6). St Martin.
Malmstrom, Vincent & Malmstrom, Ruth. British Isles. rev. ed. LC 77-83908. (World Cultures Ser). (Illus.). 164p. (gr. 6 up). 1978. text ed. 9.95 ea. 1-4 copies (ISBN 0-88296-173-X); text ed. 7.96 ea. 5 or more copies; tchrs'. guide 8.94 (ISBN 0-88296-369-4). Fideler.
Shaye, W. North Atlantic Neighbors: Britain, Canada, U.S.A. (The Life & Livelihood Geographies Ser.: Bk. 1). (Illus.). 8.95 (ISBN 0-7195-0829-0). Transatlantic.
Walsh, Jill P. The Island Sunrise: Prehistoric Culture in the British Isles. LC 75-4666. (Illus.). 128p. (gr. 6 up). 1976. 8.95 (ISBN 0-395-28928-9, Clarion). HM.
Warner, Marina. The Crack in the Teacup: Britain in the Twentieth Century. LC 78-27423. (Illus.). 160p. (gr. 6 up). 1979. 10.95 (ISBN 0-395-28972-6, Clarion). HM.
Wilkins, Frances. Growing up in Roman Britain. (Growing up Ser.). (Illus.). 72p. (gr. 7 up). 1980. text ed. 14.95 (ISBN 0-7134-0773-5, Pub. by Batsford England). David & Charles.

GREAT BRITAIN–KINGS AND RULERS

Auchincloss, Louis. Persons of Consequence: Queen Victoria & Her Circle. LC 78-26626. (Illus.). 1979. 17.95 (ISBN 0-394-50427-5). Random.
Barlow, Frank, ed. The Life of King Edward Who Rests at Westminster: Attributed to a Monk of St. Bertin. Barlow, Frank, tr. LC 80-2170. Repr. of 1962 ed. 34.50 (ISBN 0-404-18751-X). AMS Pr.
Baumer, Franklin L. Early Tudor Theory of Kingship. LC 66-13162. 1966. Repr. of 1940 ed. 8.50 (ISBN 0-8462-0715-X). Russell.
Brinkley, Roberta F. Arthurian Legend in the Seventeenth Century. LC 67-18755. 1970. Repr. lib. bdg. 14.50x (ISBN 0-374-90988-1). Octagon.
British Tourist Authority. Discovering Kings & Queens. (Illus.). 88p. 1981. pap. 2.95 (ISBN 0-85263-439-0, Pub. by Auto Assn-British Tourist Authority England). Merrimack Bk Serv.
Brooke-Little, John. The British Monarchy in Color. (Color Ser.). (Illus.). 1976. 9.95 (ISBN 0-7137-0774-7, Pub by Blandford Pr England). Sterling.
Brooks, Janice Y. Kings & Queens: The Plantagenets of England. LC 75-17843. 160p. (gr. 6 up). 1975. 7.95 (ISBN 0-525-66438-6). Elsevier-Nelson.
Brown, Michele. Queen Elizabeth II: The Silver Jubilee Book. LC 76-29855. 1977. 10.00 (ISBN 0-312-65975-X). St Martin.
Chaney, William A. The Cult of Kingship in Anglo-Saxon England: The Transition from Paganism to Christianity. LC 72-79041. 1970. 21.50x (ISBN 0-520-01401-4). U of Cal Pr.
Crompton, Richard. The Mansion of Magnanimitie: Wherein Is Shewed the Acts of Sundrie English Kings. LC 74-28841. (No. 722). 1975. Repr. of 1599 ed. 9.50 (ISBN 90-221-0722-1). Walter J Johnson.
Delderfield, Eric. Kings & Queens of England. LC 72-79138. 1972. 5.95 (ISBN 0-8128-1493-2); pap. 3.95 (ISBN 0-8128-1494-0). Stein & Day.
--Kings & Queens of England. LC 72-79138. 1972. 5.95 (ISBN 0-8128-1493-2); pap. 3.95 (ISBN 0-8128-1494-0). Stein & Day.
Erickson, Carolly. Great Harry. LC 79-21868. 1980. 14.95 (ISBN 0-671-40017-7). Summit Bks.
Fletcher, David. Henry VIII. LC 77-188. (History Makers Ser.). (Illus.). (YA) 1977. 6.95 (ISBN 0-312-36802-X). St Martin.
Fryde, Natalie. The Tyranny & Fall of Edward II: 1321-1326. LC 78-56179. 1979. 32.95 (ISBN 0-521-22201-X). Cambridge U Pr.
Gairdner, James, ed. Historical Collections of a Citizen of London in the Fifteenth Century. Repr. of 1876 ed. 22.50 (ISBN 0-384-17560-0). Johnson Repr.
Geoffrey of Monmouth. The History of the Kings of Britain. Thorpe, Lewis, tr. (Classic Ser). 1977. pap. 2.50 (ISBN 0-14-044170-0). Penguin.
--The History of the Kings of Britain. Thorpe, Lewis, tr. (Classic Ser). 1977. pap. 2.50 (ISBN 0-14-044170-0). Penguin.
Golding, Claude. The Throne of Britain. 1979. Repr. lib. bdg. 30.00 (ISBN 0-8495-2040-1). Arden Lib.
Harington, John. Tract on the Succession to the Crown, A.D. 1602. Markham, Clements R., ed. 1969. Repr. of 1880 ed. lib. bdg. 29.50 (ISBN 0-8337-1577-1). B Franklin.
Hasler, Charles. The Royal Arms: Its Graphic & Decorative Development. 1980. 75.00x (ISBN 0-904041-20-4, Pub. by Jupiter England). State Mutual Bk.
Henry the Lion: The Lothian Historical Essay for 1912. LC 80-2008. Repr. of 1912 ed. 18.50 (ISBN 0-404-18586-X). AMS Pr.
Higham, Florence M. Charles First: A Study. LC 78-21342. 1979. Repr. of 1932 ed. lib. bdg. 22.50x (ISBN 0-8371-6188-6, HICH). Greenwood.
Hudson, Mildred E. & Clark, Mary. Crown of a Thousand Years. 1978. 10.00 (ISBN 0-517-53452-5). Crown.
Kantorowicz, Ernest H. King's Two Bodies: A Study of Medieval Political Theology. 1957. 40.00 (ISBN 0-691-07120-9). Princeton U Pr.
Kendall, Alan. Elizabeth One. LC 77-304. (History Makers Ser.). (Illus.). 1977. 6.95 (ISBN 0-312-24247-6). St Martin.
Lacey, Robert. Majesty: Elizabeth II & the House of Windsor. LC 76-27424. 1977. 12.95 (ISBN 0-15-155684-9). HarBraceJ.
Levine, Mortimer. The Early Elizabethan Succession Question, 1558-1568. 1966. 15.00x (ISBN 0-8047-0299-3). Stanford U Pr.
MacDonagh, Michael. English King. LC 78-118484. 1971. Repr. of 1929 ed. 13.75 (ISBN 0-8046-1233-1). Kennikat.
Moncrieff, M. C. Kings & Queens of England. LC 74-18969. (Illus.). 160p. 1975. 5.95 (ISBN 0-88254-313-X). Hippocrene Bks.
Monmouth, Geoffrey Of. History of Kings of Britain. Date not set. 8.95x (ISBN 0-460-00577-4, Evman). Biblio Dist.
Montague-Smith, Patrick, ed. Debrett's Peerage & Baronetage Nineteen Eighty: Comprises Information Concerning the Royal Family, the Peerage, Privy Counsellors, Scottish Lords of Session, Baronets, & Chiefs of Names & Clans in Scotland. (Illus.). 1979. 135.00 (ISBN 0-8103-0949-1, Debretts Peerage Ltd). Gale.
Murray, Margaret A. The Divine King of England: A Study in Anthropology. LC 79-8115. Repr. of 1954 ed. 29.50 (ISBN 0-404-18428-6). AMS Pr.
Nichols, John. Collection of All the Wills, Now Known To Be Extant, Of The Kings & Queens Of England. LC 4-25875. Repr. of 1780 ed. 22.00 (ISBN 0-404-04759-9). AMS Pr.
Norgate, Kate. John Lackland. 75.00 (ISBN 0-8490-0455-1). Gordon Pr.
Parsons, Robert. Conference About the Next Succession to the Crown of England. LC 70-38217. (English Experience Ser.: No. 481). 1972. Repr. of 1594 ed. 32.50 (ISBN 90-221-0481-8). Walter J Johnson.
Plumb, J. H. The First Four Georges. (Illus.). 1975. 17.50 (ISBN 0-316-71126-8); pap. 3.95 (ISBN 0-316-71127-6). Little.
Plumb, J. H. & Wheldon, Huw. Royal Heritage: The Treasures of the Kings & Queens of England. LC 77-3832. (Illus.). 1977. 25.00 (ISBN 0-15-179011-6). HarBraceJ.
Roll, Winifred. Mary I: The History of an Unhappy Tudor Queen. (Illus.). 1979. 9.95g (ISBN 0-13-559096-5). P-H.
Taute, Anne & Brook-Little, John, eds. The Kings & Queens of Great Britain: A Genealogical Chart Showing Their Descent & Relationship. (Illus.). 1973. pap. 3.95 (ISBN 0-517-50344-1). Crown.
Thornton-Cook, Elsie. Royal Marys, Princess Mary & Her Predecessors. facs. ed. LC 67-23275. (Essay Index Reprint Ser). 1930. 17.00 (ISBN 0-8369-0940-2). Arno.
Trease, Geoffrey. Seven Kings of England. LC 55-7892. (gr. 6 up). 1955. 7.95 (ISBN 0-8149-0431-9). Vanguard.
Tree, Sir Herbert B. Henry VIII & His Court. 6th ed. LC 77-4446. 1977. lib. bdg. 17.50 (ISBN 0-8414-8545-3). Folcroft.
Wentworth, Peter. A Pithie Exhortation to Her Majestie for Establishing Her Successor, 2 pts. LC 72-6040. (English Experience Ser.: No. 519). 232p. 1973. Repr. of 1598 ed. 20.00 (ISBN 90-221-0519-9). Walter J Johnson.
Ziegler, Philip. Crown & People. LC 78-5397. (Illus.). 1978. 10.00 (ISBN 0-394-42124-8). Knopf.

GREAT BRITAIN–MAPS

A & B Roads & Motorways Atlas of Great Britain. 8th ed. 1973. pap. 4.95 (ISBN 0-8277-2403-9). British Bk Ctr.
Baker, A. R. & Butlin, R. A., eds. Studies of Field Systems in the British Isles. LC 72-91359. (Illus.). 744p. 1973. 77.50 (ISBN 0-521-20121-7). Cambridge U Pr.
Black, Jeannette D., ed. Blathwayt Atlas, Vol. 1, The Maps. LC 78-654217. (Illus.). 1970. Set. text ed. 500.00x unbound boxed (ISBN 0-87057-125-7, Pub. by Brown U Pr). U Pr of New Eng.
Complete Atlas of Britain. rev. ed. 256p. 1980. pap. 24.95 (ISBN 0-86145-005-1, Pub. by B T A). Merrimack Bk Serv.
Freeman-Grenville, G. S. Atlas of British History. (Illus.). 92p. 1979. 16.50x (ISBN 0-8476-6197-0); pap. 8.95x (ISBN 0-8476-6198-9). Rowman.
Fullard, Harold, ed. Esso Road Atlas Great Britain & Ireland. 6th ed. LC 73-160942. (Illus.). 235p. 1979. 13.50x (ISBN 0-540-05326-0). Intl Pubns Serv.

Goode, Clement T. & Shannon, Edgar F. An Atlas of English Literature. 1979. Repr. of 1925 ed. lib. bdg. 20.00 (ISBN 0-8495-2022-3). Arden Lib.
Handy Road Atlas of Great Britain & Northern Ireland. pap. 2.95 (ISBN 0-8277-2404-7). British Bk Ctr.
Harley. Ordnance Survey Maps. 5.50 ea. David & Charles.
Harley, J. B. Maps for the Local Historian- a Guide to the British Sources. 86p. 1972. pap. text ed. 6.25x (ISBN 0-7199-0834-5, Pub. by Bedford England). Renouf.
Johnston & Bacon. Great Britain, Road Atlas. (Illus.). 372p. 1978. pap. 11.95 (ISBN 0-7179-4239-2). Bradt Ent.
The Passenger Train Map of Britain. pap. 2.50 (ISBN 0-8277-5151-6). British Bk Ctr.
Pictorial Map Series: 1976. 2.50 ea. (ISBN 0-8277-0185-3). British Bk Ctr.
Pocket Road Atlas of Great Britain & Ireland 1973. pap. 1.95 (ISBN 0-8277-2402-0). British Bk Ctr.
Pritchard, C. West Midlands. (Geography of the British Isles Ser). (Illus.). 116p. 1975. 6.95x (ISBN 0-521-20029-6). Cambridge U Pr.
S. England & Wales Backed by N. England & Wales. pap. 2.50 (ISBN 0-8277-2406-3). British Bk Ctr.
Shirley, Rodney W. Early Printed Maps of the British Isles: A Bibliography: 1477-1650. (Holland Press Cartographica Ser.: Vol. 5). xxv, 188p. 70.00x (ISBN 0-934626-01-4). W G Arader.
Three Miles to One Inch Road Atlas of Great Britain: 1973. 7th ed. text ed. 8.50x (ISBN 0-8277-2400-4). British Bk Ctr.
White, T. P. Ordnance Survey of the United Kingdom. 1975. pap. text ed. 15.00x (ISBN 90-6041-118-8). Humanities.

GREAT BRITAIN–METROPOLITAN POLICE OFFICE–CRIMINAL INVESTIGATION DEPARTMENT

Browne, Douglas G. The Rise of Scotland Yard, a History of the Metropolitan Police. LC 73-6257. (Illus.). 392p. 1973. Repr. of 1956 ed. lib. bdg. 21.75x (ISBN 0-8371-6898-8, BRSY). Greenwood.
Leyland, Eric. Scotland Yard Detective. Date not set. 7.95 (ISBN 0-392-08491-0, SpS). Sportshelf.
Thomson, Basil. My Experiences at Scotland Yard. 1979. Repr. of 1922 ed. lib. bdg. 25.00 (ISBN 0-686-26798-2, Telegraph). Dynamic Learn Corp.
Tullett, Tom. Strictly Murder. 1980. 11.95 (ISBN 0-312-76632-7). St Martin.
Vickers, Roy. Department of Dead Ends: Fourteen Detective Stories. 1978. pap. 3.50 (ISBN 0-486-23669-2). Dover.
Wensley, Frederick P. Forty Years of Scotland Yard: The Record of a Lifetime's Service in the Criminal Investigation Department. LC 68-8075. (Illus.). 1968. Repr. of 1931 ed. lib. bdg. 15.00x (ISBN 0-8371-0264-2, WESY). Greenwood.

GREAT BRITAIN–MILITARY POLICY

Bartlett, C. J., ed. The Long Retreat. LC 79-177925. 1972. 18.95 (ISBN 0-312-49665-6). St Martin.
Baylis, John, ed. British Defence Policy in a Changing World. 295p. 1977. 29.00x (ISBN 0-85664-374-2, Pub. by Croom Helm Ltd England). Biblio Dist.
Bond, Brian. British Military Policy Between the Two World Wars. 480p. 1980. 48.00x (ISBN 0-19-822464-8). Oxford U Pr.
Dennis, Peter. Decision by Default: Peacetime Conscription & British Defence, 1919 - 1939. LC 72-190372. 320p. 1972. 14.75 (ISBN 0-8223-0272-1). Duke.
Di Roma, Edward & Rosenthal, Joseph A., eds. Numerical Finding List of British Command Papers Published 1833-1962. LC 70-137702. 1971. Repr. of 1967 ed. 12.00 (ISBN 0-87104-505-2). NY Pub Lib.
Gowing, Margaret. Independence & Deterrence-Britain & Atomic Energy 19445-52, Vol. 1: Policy Making. LC 74-81481. 500p. 1975. 32.50 (ISBN 0-312-41230-4). St Martin.
Johnson, Franklyn. Defence by Ministry. LC 79-28587. 234p. 1980. text ed. 42.50x (ISBN 0-8419-0598-3). Holmes & Meier.
Joshua, Wynfred & Hahn, Walter F. Nuclear Politics: America, France, & Britain. LC 73-83411. (The Washington Papers: No. 9). 80p. 1973. 4.00 (ISBN 0-8039-0282-4). Sage.
Kightly, Charles. Strongholds of the Realm: Defenses in Britain from Prehistory to the Twentieth Century. (Illus.). 1979. 19.95 (ISBN 0-500-25063-4). Thames Hudson.
Liddell Hart, Basil H. The Defence of Britain. LC 79-23041. 1980. Repr. of 1939 ed. lib. bdg. 29.75x (ISBN 0-313-22175-8, LHDB). Greenwood.
Military & Naval, 6 vols. (British Parliamentary Papers Ser.). 1971. Set. 459.00x (ISBN 0-7165-1496-6, Pub. by Irish Academic Pr Ireland). Biblio Dist.
Norman, A. & Pottinger, D. English Weapons & Warfare. 1979. 12.95 (ISBN 0-13-282871-5). P-H.
Peden, G. C. British Rearmament & the Treasury: 1932-39. 227p. 1979. 17.50x (ISBN 0-7073-0229-3, Pub. by Scottish Academic Pr Scotland). Columbia U Pr.
Pierre, Andrew J. Nuclear Politics: The British Experience with an Independent Strategic Force, 1939-1970. 388p. 1972. 20.00x (ISBN 0-19-212955-4). Oxford U Pr.
Rosecrance, Richard N. Defense of the Realm: British Strategy in the Nuclear Epoch. LC 67-26368. 1968. 20.00x (ISBN 0-231-03065-7). Columbia U Pr.
Schwoerer, Lois G. No Standing Armies! The Antiarmy Ideology in Seventeenth-Century England. LC 73-19337. 224p. 1974. 15.00x (ISBN 0-8018-1563-0). Johns Hopkins.
Snyder, William P. Politics of British Defense Policy, 1945-1962. LC 64-25606. 1965. 6.25 (ISBN 0-8142-0114-8). Ohio St U Pr.

GREAT BRITAIN–MILITIA

Castles, Town Defenses & Artillery Fortifications in Britain: Bibliography 1945 to 1974. 76p. 1978. pap. text ed. 10.50x (ISBN 0-900312-61-0, Pub. by Coun Brit Archaeology). Humanities.
Cust, Edward. Lives of the Warriors of the Civil Wars of France & England: Warriors of the Seventeenth Century, 2 vols. facsimile ed. LC 76-38737. (Essay Index Reprint Ser). Repr. of 1867 ed. 40.00 (ISBN 0-8369-2642-0). Arno.
Fitchett, W. H., ed. Wellington's Men: Some Soldier Autobiographies. 1977. Repr. of 1900 ed. 27.00 (ISBN 0-7158-1151-7). Charles River Bks.
Lewin, Ronald. The Chief: Field Marshal Lord Wavell, Commander-in-Chief & Viceroy 1939-47. 1980. 10.95 (ISBN 0-374-12112-5). FS&G.
Rowlandson, Thomas. Loyal Volunteers of London & Environs Infantry & Cavalry in Their Respective Uniforms. 1981. 300.00x (ISBN 0-238-78977-2). State Mutual Bk.
Skelley, Alan. The Victorian Army at Home: The Recruitment & Terms & Conditions of the British Regular, 1859-1899. (Illus.). 1977. lib. bdg. 20.00x (ISBN 0-7735-0304-8). McGill-Queens U Pr.
Wallis, Joseph T. Regiments of All Nations: A History of Britain Ltd. Lead Soldiers 1946-66. LC 81-90044. (Illus.). 260p. (Orig.). 1981. pap. 20.00 (ISBN 0-9605950-0-7). J Wallis.

GREAT BRITAIN–MORAL CONDITIONS

Bahlman, Dudley W. Moral Revolution of Sixteen Eighty Eight. 1968. Repr. of 1957 ed. 15.00 (ISBN 0-208-00494-7, Archon). Shoe String.
Chesney, Kellow. Anti-Society: An Account of the Victorian Underworld. LC 70-113999. (Illus.). 1970. 12.95 (ISBN 0-87645-022-2). Gambit.
Crick, Bernard. Crime, Rape & Gin. 96p. 1975. 7.95 (ISBN 0-87975-035-9). Prometheus Bks.
Haller, John S. & Haller, Robin M. The Physician & Sexuality in Victorian America. LC 73-2456. (Illus.). 280p. 1974. 19.95 (ISBN 0-252-00207-5). U of Ill Pr.
Markun, Leo. Mrs. Gruncy: A History of Four Centuries of Morals. LC 69-10130. 1969. Repr. of 1930 ed. lib. bdg. 32.00x (ISBN 0-8371-0560-9, MAMG). Greenwood.
--Mrs. Grundy: A History of Four Centuries of Morals Intended to Illuminate Present Problems in Great Britain & the United States. 1930. 31.00 (ISBN 0-403-00130-7). Scholarly.
Wohl, A. Victorian Family. LC 77-9234. 1978. 17.95x (ISBN 0-312-84276-7). St Martin.

GREAT BRITAIN–NATIONAL HEALTH SERVICE

Atkinson, Paul, et al, eds. Prospects for the National Health. 1981. 25.00x (ISBN 0-85664-741-1, Pub. by Croom Helm Ltd England). Biblio Dist.
Barnard, Keith & Lee, Kenneth, eds. Conflicts in the National Health Service. LC 76-57740. 1977. 18.00 (ISBN 0-88202-114-1, Prodist). N Watson.
Brown, R. G. Re-Organizing the National Health Service: A Case Study in Administrative Change. (Aspects of Social Policy Ser.). 232p. 1979. 24.50x (ISBN 0-631-18130-X, Pub. by Basil Blackwell). Biblio Dist.
CIBA Foundation. Health Care in a Changing Setting: The U. K. Experience. (CIBA Foundation Symposium: No. 43). 1976. 19.75 (ISBN 90-219-4048-5, Excerpta Medica). Elsevier.
Culyer, A. J. Need & the National Health Service: Economics & Social Choice. 163p. 1976. 13.50x (ISBN 0-87471-896-1). Rowman.
The Education & Training of Senior Managers in the National Health Service. 1977. text ed. 21.00x (ISBN 0-8464-0355-2). Beekman Pubs.
Haywood, Stuart & Alaszewski, Andy. Crisis in the Health Service: The Politics of Management. 154p. 1980. 30.00x (ISBN 0-7099-0013-9, Pub. by Croom Helm Ltd England). Biblio Dist.
Hyde, Gordon. The Soviet Health Service: Historical & Comparative Study. 356p. 1974. 20.00x (ISBN 0-8464-0872-4); pap. 12.95x (ISBN 0-686-77084-6). Beekman Pubs.
Levitt, Ruth. The Reorganised National Health Service. 2nd ed. 1981. pap. 9.00x (ISBN 0-85664-683-0, Pub. by Croom Helm Ltd England). Biblio Dist.
MacKenzie, W. J. Power & Responsibility in Health Care: The National Health Service As a Political Institution. (Nuffield Provincial Hospitals Trust Ser.). (Illus.). 1979. pap. 12.50x (ISBN 0-19-721222-0). Oxford U Pr.
Navarro, Vicente. Class Struggle, the State & Medicine: An Historical & Contemporary Analysis of the Medical Sector in Great Britain. 1978. lib. bdg. 16.95 (ISBN 0-88202-122-2). N Watson.
Paine, Leslie, ed. The Health Service Administrator: Innovator or Catalyst? (Selected Papers from a Kings Fund International Seminar). 1978. text ed. 18.00x (ISBN 0-8464-0473-7). Beekman Pubs.
Pritchard, Peter. Manual of Primary Health Care: Its Nature & Organization. (Illus.). 1979. pap. text ed. 10.95x (ISBN 0-19-264228-6). Oxford U Pr.
Walters, Vivienne. Class Inequality & Health Care: The Origins & Impact of the National Health Service. 175p. 1980. 26.00x (ISBN 0-85664-685-7, Pub. by Croom Helm Ltd England). Biblio Dist.
Watkin, Brian. The National Health Service: The First Phase 1948-1974 & After. 1978. text ed. 25.00x (ISBN 0-04-362025-6); pap. text ed. 8.95x (ISBN 0-04-362026-4). Allen Unwin.
Widgery, David. Health in Danger: The Crisis in the National Health Service. 1979. 17.50 (ISBN 0-208-01759-3, Archon). Shoe String.

GREAT BRITAIN–NAVY

see also Great Britain–History, Naval

Dingman, Roger. Power in the Pacific: The Origins of Naval Arms Limitation, 1914-1922. LC 75-36402. 1976. lib. bdg. 20.00x (ISBN 0-226-15331-2). U of Chicago Pr.
Edwards, Kenneth. The Navy of Today: The Status of the Royal Navy. 1977. lib. bdg. 59.95 (ISBN 0-8490-2334-3). Gordon Pr.
Fabb, John & McGowan, A. C. Victorian & Edwardian Navy. 1976. 17.95 (ISBN 0-7134-3122-9). David & Charles.
Halpern, P. G. The Keyes Papers, Vol. 1. (Illus.). 1979. text ed. 27.50x (ISBN 0-04-942164-6). Allen Unwin.
Manning, T. D. The British Destroyer. 1981. 40.00x (ISBN 0-906223-13-X). State Mutual Bk.
Marder, Arthur J. From the Dreadnought to Scapa Flow: The Royal Navy in the Fisher Era, 1904-1919, 5 vols. Incl. Vol. 1. The Road to War, 1904-1914. 1961. 28.50x (ISBN 0-19-215122-3); Vol. 3. Jutland & After. 2nd ed. 1978. 23.50x (ISBN 0-19-215841-4); Vol. 4. 1917: Year of Crisis. 1969. 24.00x (ISBN 0-19-215170-3); Vol. 5. Victory & Aftermath. 1970. 27.95x (ISBN 0-19-215187-8). Oxford U Pr.
Moore, John E. Warships of the Royal Navy. LC 79-84202. 1979. 12.95 (ISBN 0-87021-978-2). Naval Inst Pr.
Pears, Randolph. British Battleships Eighteen Ninety-Two to Nineteen Fifty-Seven. 1981. 40.00x (ISBN 0-906223-14-8). State Mutual Bk.

GREAT BRITAIN–NAVY–HISTORY

Allen, Joseph. Battles of the British Navy, 2 vols. 1977. Set. lib. bdg. 250.00 (ISBN 0-8490-1480-8). Gordon Pr.
Ballard, G. A. The Black Battlefleet: Early Ironclads of the Royal Navy. LC 79-49435. (Illus.). 245p. 1980. 38.95 (ISBN 0-87021-924-3). Naval Inst Pr.
Baugh, Daniel A. British Naval Administration in the Age of Walpole. (Illus.). 1965. 32.50 (ISBN 0-691-05107-0). Princeton U Pr.
Behrman, Cynthia F. Victorian Myths of the Sea. LC 76-51694. 188p. 1977. 12.95 (ISBN 0-8214-0351-6). Ohio U Pr.
Brownlee, Walter. The Navy That Beat Napoleon. (Cambridge Topic Bks.). (Illus.). 52p. (gr. 6 up). 1981. PLB 5.95 (ISBN 0-8225-1226-2). Lerner Pubns.
--The Navy That Beat Napoleon. LC 78-18091. (Cambridge Introduction to the History of Mankind Ser.). 1981. 3.95 (ISBN 0-521-22145-5). Cambridge U Pr.
Cable, Sir James. The Royal Navy & the Siege of Bilbao. LC 78-73238. (Illus.). 1980. 21.50 (ISBN 0-521-22516-7). Cambridge U Pr.
Clowes, William L., ed. Royal Navy: A History from the Earliest Times, 7 vols. Repr. of 1903 ed. Set. 290.00 (ISBN 0-404-01640-5); 41.50 ea. AMS Pr.
Cobden, R. Three Panics: An Historical Episode. 3rd. ed. Repr. of 1862 ed. 12.00 (ISBN 0-527-18230-3). Kraus Repr.
Cooper, Richard & Uden, Grant. British Ships & Seamen. (Illus.). 591p. 1981. lib. bdg. 40.00x (ISBN 0-312-20028-5). St Martin.
Davies, E. L. & Grove, E. J. Dartmouth: The Royal Naval College, Seventy-Five Years in Pictures. (Illus.). 96p. 1980. 14.95 (ISBN 0-85997-462-6). McCartan & Root.
Dee, John. General & Rare Memorials Pertayning to Perfecte Arte of Navigation. LC 68-54635. (English Experience Ser.: No. 62). 82p. 1968. Repr. of 1577 ed. 28.00 (ISBN 90-221-0062-6). Walter J Johnson.
Fabb, John & McGowan, A. C. Victorian & Edwardian Navy. 1976. 17.95 (ISBN 0-7134-3122-9). David & Charles.
Fowler, Elaine W. English Sea Power in the Early Tudor Period, 1485-1558. LC 65-22933. (Folger Guides to the Age of Shakespeare). 1966. pap. 3.95 (ISBN 0-918016-15-0). Folger Bks.
Fox, Frank. Great Ships: The Battlefleet of King Charles the Second. 208p. 1980. 69.75x (ISBN 0-85177-166-1, Pub. by Conway Maritime England). State Mutual Bk.
Graham, Gerald S. The China Station: War & Diplomacy 1830-1860. (Illus.). 1978. 64.00x (ISBN 0-19-822472-9). Oxford U Pr.
Grenfell, Russell. Horatio Nelson: A Short Biography. LC 78-6150. (Illus.). 1978. Repr. of 1968 ed. lib. bdg. 24.25x (ISBN 0-313-20481-0, GRHN). Greenwood.
Halpern, P. G. The Keyes Papers, Vol. 1. (Illus.). 1979. text ed. 27.50x (ISBN 0-04-942164-6). Allen Unwin.
Higham, Robin O. The British Rigid Airship, 1908-1931: A Study in Weapons Policy. LC 75-26603. (Illus.). 426p. 1975. Repr. of 1961 ed. lib. bdg. 27.25x (ISBN 0-8371-8247-6, HIBR). Greenwood.
Horsfield, John. The Art of Leadership in War: The Royal Navy from the Age of Nelson to the End of World War II. LC 79-54059. (Contributions in Military History: No. 21). (Illus.). xiv, 240p. 1980. lib. bdg. 25.00 (ISBN 0-313-20919-7, HLE/). Greenwood.
Knight, R. J., ed. Guide to the Manuscripts in the National Maritime Museum: The Personal Collections, Vol. 1. 1977. lib. bdg. 31.50 (ISBN 0-7201-0714-8, Pub. by Mansell England). Merrimack Bk Serv.
Longridge, C. Nepean. The Anatomy of Nelson's Ships. LC 80-84981. (Illus.). 283p. 1980. 24.95 (ISBN 0-87021-077-7). Naval Inst Pr.
MacKie, Charles P. With the Admiral of the Ocean Sea. 1891. Repr. 20.00 (ISBN 0-685-43097-9). Norwood Edns.
Mahan, Alfred T. Types of Naval Officers, Drawn from the History of the British Navy. facs. ed. LC 77-84323. (Essay Index Reprint Ser). 1901. 20.75 (ISBN 0-8369-1093-1). Arno.
Marder, Arthur. The Anatomy of British Sea Power, 1880-1905. LC 73-2954. xix, 580p. 1974. Repr. lib. bdg. 42.00x (ISBN 0-374-95284-1). Octagon.
Marder, Arthur J. From the Dardanelles to Oran: Studies of the Royal Navy in War & Peace 1915-1940. (Illus.). 320p. 1974. 21.00x (ISBN 0-19-215802-3). Oxford U Pr.
Masefield, John. Sea Life in Nelson's Time. facs. ed. LC 75-75513. (Select Bibliographies Reprint Ser). 1905. 20.00 (ISBN 0-8369-5011-9). Arno.
Military & Naval, 6 vols. (British Parliamentary Papers Ser.). 1971. Set. 459.00x (ISBN 0-7165-1496-6, Pub. by Irish Academic Pr Ireland). Biblio Dist.
Oppenheim, M. The Maritime History of Devon. 175p. 1968. 30.00x (ISBN 0-900771-00-3, Pub. by Exeter Univ England). State Mutual Bk.
Padfield, Peter. Rule Britannia: The Victorian & Edwardian Navy. (Illus.). 192p. 1981. 18.95 (ISBN 0-7100-0774-4). Routledge & Kegan.
Pool, Bernard. Navy Board Contracts, 1660-1832: Contract Administration Under the Navy Board. 1966. 15.00 (ISBN 0-208-00239-1, Archon). Shoe String.
Ralfe, James. The Naval Biography of Great Britain: Consisting of Historical Memoirs of Those Officers of the British Navy Who Distinguished Themselves During the Reign of His Majesty George III, 4 vols. LC 72-20833. (American Revolutionary Ser.). Repr. of 1828 ed. Set. lib. bdg. 140.00x (ISBN 0-8398-1773-8). Irvington.
Ranft, Bryan, ed. Technical Change & British Naval Policy, 1860-1939. 1977. text ed. 24.50x (ISBN 0-8419-6207-3). Holmes & Meier.
Rasor, Eugene L. Reform in the Royal Navy: A Social History of the Lower Deck, 1850-80. 1976. 17.50 (ISBN 0-208-01595-7, Archon). Shoe String.
Raven, Alan & Roberts, John. British Battleships of World War Two. LC 76-22915. (Illus.). 1976. 35.95 (ISBN 0-87021-817-4). Naval Inst Pr.
Rodgers, William L. Naval Warfare Under Oars Fourth to Sixteenth Centuries. LC 75-121794. (Illus.). 1967. Repr. of 1940 ed. 13.95 (ISBN 0-87021-487-X). Naval Inst Pr.

Scarlett, Bernard. Shipminder: The Story of Her Majesty's Coastguard. 1972. 9.75 (ISBN 0-7207-0480-4). Transatlantic.

Schurman, Donald M. Education of a Navy: The Development of British Naval Strategic Thought, 1867-1914. LC 65-24982. 1965. 7.00x (ISBN 0-226-74133-8). U of Chicago Pr.

Stapleton, N. B. Steam Picket Boats & Other Small Steam Craft of the Royal Navy. 120p. 1981. 30.00x (ISBN 0-900963-63-8, Pub. by Terence Dalton England). State Mutual Bk.

Stout, Neil R. The Royal Navy in America 1760-1775: A Study of Enforcement of British Colonial Policy in the Era of the American Revolution. LC 73-7771. 350p. 1973. 12.50 (ISBN 0-87021-553-1). Naval Inst Pr.

Tanner, Joseph R. Samuel Pepys & the Royal Navy. LC 79-163207. (English Literature Ser., No. 33). 1971. Repr. of 1920 ed. lib. bdg. 44.95 (ISBN 0-8383-1314-0). Haskell.

Warner, Oliver. The British Navy: A Concise History. (Illus.). 1977. 14.50 (ISBN 0-500-01139-7). Thames Hudson.

Whipple, A. B. Fighting Sail. new ed. Time-Life Books, ed. (Seafarers Ser.). (Illus.). 1978. 14.95 (ISBN 0-8094-2654-4). Time-Life.

White, Colin. The End of the Sailing Navy. LC 80-83938. (Illus.). 205p. 1981. 19.95 (ISBN 0-87021-931-6). Naval Inst Pr.

Winton, John. Find, Fix & Strike! The Fleet Air Arm at War 1939-45. (Illus.). 192p. 1981. 28.50 (ISBN 0-7134-3488-0, Pub. by Batsford England). David & Charles.

--Hurrah for the Life of a Sailor. (Illus.). 288p. 1980. 16.95 (ISBN 0-7181-1580-5, Pub. by Michael Joseph). Merrimack Bk Serv.

GREAT BRITAIN–NOBILITY

see also Great Britain–Baronetage

Brauer, George C. The Education of a Gentleman. 1959. pap. 1.95x (ISBN 0-8084-0115-7, P10). Coll & U Pr.

Coffin, Robert P. The Dukes of Buckingham. Repr. of 1931 ed. 30.00 (ISBN 0-686-19879-4). Ridgeway Bks.

The Decree & Establishment of the Kingsmaiestie, Upon a Controversie of Precedence, Betweene the Yonger Sonnes of Viscounts & Barons, & the Baronets. LC 74-28850. (English Experience Ser.: No. 731). 1975. Repr. of 1612 ed. 3.50 (ISBN 90-221-0731-0). Walter J Johnson.

Ferne, John. The Blazon of Gentrie. LC 72-5986. (English Experience Ser.: No. 513). (Illus.). 488p. 1973. Repr. of 1586 ed. 70.00 (ISBN 90-221-0513-X). Walter J Johnson.

Frankland, Noble. Prince Henry: Duke of Gloucester. (Illus.). 343p. 1980. 25.00x (ISBN 0-297-77705-X, Pub. by Weidenfeld & Nicolson England). Biblio Dist.

Herbert Of Cherbury, Edward. The Life of Edward, Lord Herbert of Cherbury. (Oxford English Memoirs and Travels Ser.). 1976. 17.50x (ISBN 0-19-255411-5). Oxford U Pr.

Jones, Paul V. Household of a Tudor Nobleman. (Illinois Studies in the Social Sciences: Vol. 6, No. 4). 1918. 18.50 (ISBN 0-384-27810-8). Johnson Repr.

Kinney, Arthur F. Titled Elizabethans: A Directory of Elizabethan State & Church Officers & Knights, with Peers of England, Scotland, & Ireland, 1558-1603. 89p. 1973. 12.50 (ISBN 0-208-01334-2, Archon). Shoe String.

Lewis, Wilmarth S. Rescuing Horace Walpole. LC 78-7590. (Illus.). 1978. 25.00x (ISBN 0-300-02278-6). Yale U Pr.

McFarlane, K. B. The Nobility of Later Medieval England: The Ford Lectures for 1953 & Related Studies. 1973. 29.95x (ISBN 0-19-822362-5). Oxford U Pr.

Rawcliffe, Carole. The Staffords, Earls of Stafford & Dukes of Buckingham 1394-1521. LC 77-71425. (Studies in Medieval Life & Thought: No. 11). (Illus.). 1978. 39.95 (ISBN 0-521-21663-X). Cambridge U Pr.

Sanford, John L. & Townsend, M. Great Governing Families of England, 2 vols. facsimile ed. LC 77-37862. (Essay Index Reprint Ser). Repr. of 1865 ed. 42.00 (ISBN 0-8369-2623-4). Arno.

Shaw, William A. Knights of England: A Complete Record from the Earliest Time to the Present Day of the Knights of All the Orders of Chivalry in England, Scotland & Ireland, & of Knights Bachelor, 2 Vols. LC 74-129966. 1971. Repr. of 1906 ed. Set. 42.50 (ISBN 0-8063-0443-X). Genealog Pub.

Stone, Lawrence. Crisis of the Aristocracy, Fifteen Fifty-Eight to Sixteen Forty-One. abr. ed. (Illus.). 1967. pap. 6.95 (ISBN 0-19-500274-1, GB). Oxford U Pr.

--Crisis of the Aristocracy, 1558-1641. 1965. 49.00x (ISBN 0-19-821314-X). Oxford U Pr.

Turner, E. S. Amazing Grace: The Great Day of Dukes. (Illus.). 316p. 1975. 17.50x (ISBN 0-7181-1362-4). Intl Pubns Serv.

Walpole, Horace. A Catalogue of Royal & Noble Authors, 5 vols. LC 76-149672. Repr. of 1806 ed. Set. 157.50 (ISBN 0-404-06820-0). AMS Pr.

GREAT BRITAIN–OFFICE OF THE REVELS

Chambers, Edmund K. Notes on the History of the Revels Office Under the Tudors. LC 68-56727. (Research & Source Works Ser.: No. 207). 1968. Repr. of 1906 ed. 14.50 (ISBN 0-8337-0523-7). B Franklin.

GREAT BRITAIN–OFFICIALS AND EMPLOYEES

Barnett, Richard C. Place, Profit, & Power: A Study of the Servants of William Cecil, Elizabethan Statesman. LC 77-97023. (James Sprunt Studies in History & Political Science: No. 51). 1969. pap. text ed. 7.50x (ISBN 0-8078-5051-9). U of NC Pr.

Heussler, Robert. British Rule in Malaya: The Malayan Civil Service & Its Predecessors, Eighteen Sixty-Seven to Nineteen Forty-Two. LC 80-658. (Contributions in Comparative Colonial Studies: No. 6). (Illus.). xx, 356p. 1981. lib. bdg. 37.50 (ISBN 0-313-22243-6, HBM/). Greenwood.

Steer, Francis W. A History of the Worshipful Company of Scriveners of London, Vol. 1. (Illus.). 92p. 1973. 35.00x (ISBN 0-8476-1379-8). Rowman.

GREAT BRITAIN–ORDNANCE SURVEY

Arden-Close, Charles F. Early Years of the Ordnance Survey. LC 69-12830. (Illus.). Repr. of 1926 ed. 12.50x (ISBN 0-678-05509-2). Kelley.

GREAT BRITAIN–PARLIAMENT

Acherley, Roger. Free Parliaments. Berkowitz, David S. & Thorne, Samuel E., eds. LC 77-89218. (Classics of English Legal History in the Modern Era Ser.: Vol. 65). 334p. 1979. lib. bdg. 40.00 (ISBN 0-8240-3164-4). Garland Pub.

Barker, A. & Rush, M. The Member of Parliament & His Information. (Political & Economic Planning Ser.). 1970. text ed. 27.50x (ISBN 0-04-329012-4). Allen Unwin.

Bentham, Jeremy. Plan of Parliamentary Reform, in the Form of a Catechism, with Reasons for Each Article. LC 75-41027. (BCL Ser. II). Repr. of 1818 ed. 16.50 (ISBN 0-404-14777-1). AMS Pr.

Black, Eugene C. The Association: British Extraparliamentary Political Organization, 1769-1793. LC 63-17195. (Historical Monographs Ser: No. 54). (Illus.). 1963. 17.50x (ISBN 0-674-05000-2). Harvard U Pr.

Bond, Maurice. The Houses of Parliament & the Palace of Westminster. 1974. pap. 1.95 (ISBN 0-8277-3314-3). British Bk Ctr.

Bromhead, P. A. Private Members' Bills in the British Parliament. LC 75-27677. 216p. 1976. Repr. of 1956 ed. lib. bdg. 14.00x (ISBN 0-8371-8462-2, BRPM). Greenwood.

Brunton, Douglas & Pennington, D. H. Members of the Long Parliament. 1968. Repr. of 1954 ed. 18.50 (ISBN 0-208-00686-9, Archon). Shoe String.

Burton, Ivor & Drewry, Gavin. Legislation & Public Policy: Public Bills in the Nineteen Seventy, Seventy-Four Parliament. 300p. 1981. text ed. 50.00x (ISBN 0-8419-5065-2). Holmes & Meier.

Checklist of British Parliamentary Papers in the Irish University Press: One Thousand Volume Series 1801-1899. 230p. 1972. 45.00x (ISBN 0-7165-0059-0, Pub. by Irish Academic Pr Ireland). Biblio Dist.

Cherry, George L. Convention Parliament, Sixteen Eighty-Nine: A Biographical Study of Its Members. LC 65-24394. 218p. 1966. text ed. 24.00x (ISBN 0-8290-0163-8). Irvington.

Chiao Wan-Hsuan. Devolution in Great Britain. LC 76-78010. (Columbia University Studies in the Social Sciences: No. 272). Repr. of 1926 ed. 22.50 (ISBN 0-404-51272-0). AMS Pr.

Clarke, Maude V. Medieval Representation & Consent: A Study of Early Parliaments in England & Ireland, with Special Reference to the Modus Tenendi Parliamentum. LC 64-15027. 1964. Repr. of 1936 ed. 10.00 (ISBN 0-8462-0460-6). Russell.

Cobbett, William. History of the Last Hundred Days of English Freedom. LC 73-114501. 1971. Repr. of 1921 ed. lib. bdg. 15.00x (ISBN 0-8371-4780-8, COLH). Greenwood.

Cope, Esther S. & Coates, Willson H. Short Parliament of Sixteen-Forty: Proceedings. 340p. 1977. 18.50x (ISBN 0-8476-1473-5). Rowman.

Cowling, Maurice. Eighteen Sixty-Seven Disraeli, Gladstone & Revolution. (Cambridge Studies in the History & Theory of Politics). 1967. 49.95 (ISBN 0-521-04740-4). Cambridge U Pr.

Craig, F. W., ed. Boundaries of Parliament Constituencies 1885-1972. LC 72-83549. (Illus.). 224p. 1973. 25.00x (ISBN 0-900178-09-4). Intl Pubns Serv.

Davidson, John M. Eminent English Liberals in & Out of Parliament. facsimile ed. LC 70-37521. (Essay Index Reprint Ser). Repr. of 1880 ed. 18.00 (ISBN 0-8369-2542-4). Arno.

Davies, R. G. & Denton, J. H., eds. The English Parliament in the Middle Ages. LC 81-3423. (Middle Ages Ser.). 212p. 1981. 22.50x (ISBN 0-8122-7802-X). U of Pa Pr.

D'Ewes, Simonds. Journal of Sir Simonds D'Ewes from the First Recess of the Long Parliament to the Withdrawal of King Charles from London. Coates, Willson H., ed. LC 71-122400. 1970. Repr. of 1942 ed. 27.50 (ISBN 0-208-00948-5, Archon). Shoe String.

Dod's Parliamentary Companion, 1977. 145th ed. 1977. 22.50x (ISBN 0-905702-00-X). Standing Orders.

Elsynge, H. Manner of Holding Parliaments in England. (Parliamentary & Congressional Ser). 608p. 1971. Repr. of 1768 ed. text ed. 48.00x (ISBN 0-7165-2013-3). Rothman.

Extracts from the Evidence Taken Before Committees of the Two Houses of Parliament Relative to the Slave Trade. LC 70-89032. (Illus.). Repr. of 1851 ed. 8.50x (ISBN 0-8371-1947-2, Pub. by Negro U Pr). Greenwood.

Foster, Elizabeth R. The Painful Labour of Mr. Elsyng. LC 72-89400. (Transactions Ser.: Vol. 62, Pt. 8). 1972. pap. 1.00 (ISBN 0-87169-628-2). Am Philos.

Fryde, E. B., ed. Historical Studies of the English Parliament, 2 vols. Incl. Vol. 1. Origins to 1399. 33.95 (ISBN 0-521-07613-7); pap. 11.50x (ISBN 0-521-09610-3); Vol. 2. 1399-1603. 33.95 (ISBN 0-521-07733-8); pap. 10.50x (ISBN 0-521-09611-1). 1970. Cambridge U Pr.

Great Britain House Of Commons. Parliamentary Debates in 1610. 1862. 19.50 (ISBN 0-384-19780-9). Johnson Repr.

Hanson, Albert & Wiseman, H. V. Parliament at Work. LC 74-29640. 358p. 1975. Repr. of 1962 ed. lib. bdg. 19.75x (ISBN 0-8371-8004-X, HAPA). Greenwood.

Hanson, Albert H. Planning & the Politicians. LC 75-95618. 1969. lib. bdg. 15.00x (ISBN 0-678-06524-1). Kelley.

Hartley, T. E., ed. Proceedings in the Parliaments of Elizabeth I. 572p. 1981. 87.00 (ISBN 0-89453-225-1). M Glazier.

Haskins, George L. Growth of English Representative Government. 7.50 (ISBN 0-8446-2216-8). Peter Smith.

--The Statute of York & the Interest of the Commons. LC 77-4920. 1977. Repr. of 1935 ed. lib. bdg. 15.00 (ISBN 0-8371-9610-8, HASY); microfiche avail. (ISBN 0-8371-9612-4). Greenwood.

His Majesties Declaration of the Causes Which Moved Him to Dissolve the Last Parliament. LC 79-38175. (English Experience Ser.: No. 450). 1972. Repr. of 1628 ed. 7.00 (ISBN 90-221-0450-8). Walter J Johnson.

Hobbes, Thomas. Behemoth or the Long Parliament. 2nd rev. ed. Tonnies, Ferdinand, ed. 204p. 1969. 29.50x (ISBN 0-7146-2539-6, F Cass Co). Biblio Dist.

Hollis, Christopher. Can Parliament Survive. LC 78-118476. 1971. Repr. of 1949 ed. 11.25 (ISBN 0-8046-1225-0). Kennikat.

Holmes, George. The Good Parliament. 210p. 1975. 37.50x (ISBN 0-19-822446-X). Oxford U Pr.

Hornyold-Strickland, H. Biographical Sketches of the Members of Parliament of Lancashire, 1290-1550. 1935. 13.00 (ISBN 0-384-24340-1). Johnson Repr.

Horwitz, Henry. Parliament, Policy & Politics in the Reign of William III. LC 76-27126. 385p. 27.50 (ISBN 0-87413-124-3). U Delaware Pr.

Jacob, Giles, et al. Laws of Liberty & Property. Berkowitz, David. S. & Thorne, Samuel E., eds. LC 77-89197. (Classics of English Legal History in the Modern Era Ser.: Vol. 56). 325p. 1979. lib. bdg. 40.00 (ISBN 0-8240-3156-3). Garland Pub.

Jennings, Ivor. Parliament. 1969. 53.95 (ISBN 0-521-07056-2); pap. 11.95x (ISBN 0-521-09532-8). Cambridge U Pr.

Jones, Andrew. Politics of Reform, Eighteen Eighty-Four. (Cambridge Studies in the History & Theory of Politics). 308p. 1972. 32.50 (ISBN 0-521-08376-1). Cambridge U Pr.

Larking, Lambert B., ed. Proceedings Principally in the County of Kent, in Connection with the Parliaments Called in 1640, & Especially with the Committee of Religion Appointed in That Year. (Camden Society, London. Publications, First Series: No. 80a). Repr. of 1862 ed. 28.00 (ISBN 0-404-50180-X). Ams Pr.

--Proceedings, Principally in the County of Kent, in Connection with the Parliaments Called in 1640. Repr. of 1862 ed. 31.00 (ISBN 0-384-31380-9). Johnson Repr.

Lehmberg, S. E. The Later Parliaments of Henry VIII, 1536-1547. LC 76-7804. 1977. 49.95 (ISBN 0-521-21256-1). Cambridge U Pr.

--Reformation Parliament Fifteen Twenty-Nine - Fifteen Thirty-Six. LC 70-85723. (Illus., Orig.). 1970. 35.50 (ISBN 0-521-07655-2). Cambridge U Pr.

Lloyd, Selwyn. Mr. Speaker, Sir. 1977. 12.50 (ISBN 0-224-01318-1). Transatlantic.

MacDonald, J. R. Parliament & Revolution. LC 20-26685. Repr. of 1920 ed. 12.00 (ISBN 0-527-59300-1). Kraus Repr.

Mackintosh, A. From Gladstone to Lloyd George: Parliament in Peace & War. Repr. of 1921 ed. 18.00 (ISBN 0-527-59800-3). Kraus Repr.

Mackintosh, John, ed. People & Parliament. LC 78-60433. 1978. 22.95 (ISBN 0-03-046231-2). Praeger.

Maclure, J. Stuart. Educational Documents: England & Wales 1816 to the Present. 4th ed. 1973. pap. 16.95 (ISBN 0-416-78290-6). Methuen Inc.

Malcolm, Ian Z. Vacant Thrones: A Volume of Political Portraits. facs. ed. LC 67-28760. (Essay Index Reprint Ser). 1931. 15.50 (ISBN 0-8369-0672-1). Arno.

Mantoux, Paul. Notes Sur les Comptes Rendus Des Seances Du Parlement Anglais Au Dix-Huitieme Siecle. LC 77-160017. (Research & Source Works Ser.: No. 744). 1971. Repr. of 1906 ed. lib. bdg. 19.50 (ISBN 0-8337-2209-3). B Franklin.

Markesinis, B. S. The Theory & Practice of Dissolution of Parliament. LC 70-189592. (Studies in International & Comparative Law). (Illus.). 300p. 1972. 37.50 (ISBN 0-521-08524-1). Cambridge U Pr.

May, E. Treatise Upon the Law, Privileges, Proceedings & Usage of Parliament. (Parliamentary & Congressional Ser). vixvi, 467p. 1971. Repr. of 1844 ed. 24.00x (ISBN 0-7165-2014-1). Rothman.

Menhennet, David & Palmer, John. Parliament in Perspective. 1967. 6.25 (ISBN 0-8023-1125-3). Dufour.

Mitchell, Williams M. The Rise of the Revolutionary Party in the English House of Commons, 1603-1629. LC 75-31471. 209p. 1976. Repr. of 1957 ed. lib. bdg. 14.00x (ISBN 0-8371-8535-1, MIRR). Greenwood.

Morgan, Janet, ed. The Backbench Diaries of Richard Crossman. 1072p. 1981. text ed. 35.00 (ISBN 0-8419-0686-6). Holmes & Meier.

Pettus, Sir John. The Constitution of Parliaments in England. Berkowitz, David S. & Thorne, Samuel E., eds. LC 77-89214. (Classics of English Legal History in the Modern Era Ser.: Vol. 63). 446p. 1979. lib. bdg. 40.00 (ISBN 0-8240-3162-8). Garland Pub.

Poor Law, 30 vols. (British Parliamentary Papers Ser.). 1973. Set. 2421.00x (ISBN 0-7165-1457-5, Pub. by Irish Academic Pr Ireland). Biblio Dist.

Pope-Hennessy, James. The Houses of Parliament. (Folio Miniature Ser.). 48p. 1975. 4.95 (ISBN 0-7181-1302-0, Pub. by Michael Joseph). Merrimack Bk Serv.

Port, Michael, ed. The Houses of Parliament. LC 76-3374. (Studies in British Art Ser.). 1976. 60.00x (ISBN 0-300-02022-8). Yale U Pr.

The Priviledges & Practice of Parliaments in England. LC 74-80218. (English Experience Ser.: No. 654). 1974. Repr. of 1628 ed. 5.00 (ISBN 90-221-0654-3). Walter J Johnson.

Prynne, Wiliam, et al. William Prynne. Berkowitz, David S. & Thorne, Samuel E., eds. (English Legal History Ser.: Vol. 124). 589p. 1979. lib. bdg. 55.00 (ISBN 0-8240-3161-X). Garland Pub.

Pulton, Ferdinand. De Pace Regis et Regni. Berkowitz, David S. & Thorne, Samuel E., eds. LC 77-86638. (Classics of English Legal History in the Modern Era Ser.: Vol.29). 574p. 1979. lib. bdg. 40.00 (ISBN 0-8240-3078-8). Garland Pub.

Raison, Timothy. Power & Parliament. 122p. 1979. 20.00x (ISBN 0-631-11301-0, Pub. by Basil Blackwell England); pap. 8.50x (ISBN 0-631-12892-1). Biblio Dist.

Ralegh, Walter. The Prerogative of Parliaments in England: Proved in a Dialogue. LC 74-80207. (English Experience Ser.: No. 686). 68p. 1974. Repr. of 1628 ed. 7.00 (ISBN 90-221-0686-1). Walter J Johnson.

Raleigh, Sir Walter, et al. The Prerogative of Parliaments in England, Proved in a Dialogue, 4 vols. in 1. Berkowitz, David S. & Thorne, Samuel E., eds. LC 77-89209. (Classics of English Legal History in the Modern Era Ser.: Vol. 123). 1979. lib. bdg. 55.00 (ISBN 0-8240-3160-1). Garland Pub.

Rogaly, Joe. Parliament for the People: British Electoral Reform. 181p. 1976. pap. 7.50x (ISBN 0-85117-099-4). Intl Pubns Serv.

Ruigh, Robert E. Parliament of 1624: Politics & Foreign Policy. LC 72-135548. (Historical Studies: No. 87). (Illus.). 1971. 20.00x (ISBN 0-674-65225-8). Harvard U Pr.

Rush, Michael. Parliamentary Government in Britain. 260p. 1981. pap. text ed. 30.00x (ISBN 0-8419-0680-7). Holmes & Meier.

Russell, Conrad. Parliaments & English Politics 1621-1629. LC 78-40498. 1979. 48.00x (ISBN 0-19-822482-6). Oxford U Pr.

Schuyler, Robert L. Parliament & the British Empire: Some Constitutional Controversies Concerning Imperial Legislative Jurisdiction. LC 75-31133. Repr. of 1929 ed. 22.50 (ISBN 0-404-13609-5). AMS Pr.

Selden, John. A Briefe Discourse Concerning the Power of the Peeres & Commons of Parliament. LC 74-25562. (English Experience Ser.: No. 344). 10p. 1971. Repr. of 1640 ed. 7.00 (ISBN 90-221-0344-7). Walter J Johnson.

Seymour, Charles. Electoral Reform in England & Wales: The Development & Operation of the Parliamentary Franchise, 1832-1885. (Illus.). 1970. Repr. of 1915 ed. 22.50 (ISBN 0-208-01042-4, Archon). Shoe String.

Sharpe, Kevin, ed. Faction & Parliament: Essays in Early Stuart History. LC 77-30635. 1978. 37.50x (ISBN 0-19-822468-0). Oxford U Pr.

Sheridan, Thomas. Some Revelations on Irish History. Bannister, Saxe, ed. LC 73-102592. (Irish Culture & History Ser). Repr. of 1870 ed. 14.50 (ISBN 0-8046-0769-9). Kennikat.

Smith, J. Berwick, intro. by. Dod's Parliamentary (Pocket) Companion. 161st ed. LC 6-7438. (Illus.). 653p. 1980. 57.50x (ISBN 0-905702-04-2). Intl Pubns Serv.

Snow, Vernon F. Parliament in Elizabethan England: John Hooker's "Order & Usage". LC 77-23301. (Illus.). 1977. 20.00x (ISBN 0-300-02093-7). Yale U Pr.

Stenton, Michael. Who's Who of British Members of Parliament: 1832-1885, Vol. 1. 380p. 1976. text ed. 50.00x (ISBN 0-391-00613-4). Humanities.

--Who's Who of British Members of Parliament: 1919-1945, Vol. 3. 1979. text ed. 86.50x (ISBN 0-391-00768-8). Humanities.

Stenton, Michael & Lees, Stephen. Who's Who of British Members of Parliament: Vol. 2, 1886-1918. 1978. 60.00x (ISBN 0-391-00745-9). Humanities.

Strenton, Michael & Lees, Stephen, eds. Who's Who of British Members of Parliament: Volume IV, 1945-1979. 413p. 1981. text ed. 84.00x (ISBN 0-391-01087-5, Pub. by Harvester England). Humanities.

Toland, John, et al. Anglia Libera. Berkowitz, David S. & Thorne, Samuel E., eds. LC 77-89231. (Classics of English Legal History in the Modern Era Ser.: Vol. 71). 400p. 1979. lib. bdg. 40.00 (ISBN 0-8240-3171-7). Garland Pub.

Wade, John, ed. Extraordinary Black Book. rev. ed. LC 79-104006. Repr. of 1832 ed. 27.50x (ISBN 0-678-00601-6). Kelley.

Walker, Ernestein. Struggle for the Reform of Parliament 1853-1867. 1977. 8.95 (ISBN 0-533-02690-3). Vantage.

Wang Chi-Kao. Dissolution of the British Parliament 1832-1931. LC 79-127433. (Columbia University Studies in the Social Sciences: No. 396). Repr. of 1934 ed. 12.50 (ISBN 0-404-51396-4). AMS Pr.

Wright, Arnold & Smith, Philip. Parliament: Past & Present: A Popular & Picturesque Account of a Thousand Years in the Palace of Westminster, the Home of the Mother of Parliament. 1978. Repr. lib. bdg. 150.00 (ISBN 0-89760-906-9, Telegraph). Dynamic Learn Corp.

GREAT BRITAIN–PARLIAMENT–BIBLIOGRAPHY

Bibliography of Parliamentary Papers: General Alphabetical Indexes 1696-1899, 8 vols. Incl. Vol. 1. Hansard's Catalogue & Breviate of Parliamentary Papers: 1696-1834. 89.00x (ISBN 0-686-27258-7); Vol. 2. Report of Selected Committees, 1801-1852. 103.00x (ISBN 0-686-27259-5); Vol. 3. Accounts & Papers, Reports of Commissioners, Etc., 1801-1852. 141.00x (ISBN 0-686-27260-9); Vol. 4. Bills, Reports, Estimates, Accounts & Papers, 1852-1869. 111.00x (ISBN 0-686-27261-7); Vol. 5. Bills, 1801-1852. 107.00x (ISBN 0-686-27262-5); Vol. 6. Bills, Reports, Estimates & Accounts & Papers, 1870-1879. 93.00x (ISBN 0-686-27263-3); Vol. 7. Bills, Reports, Estimates & Accounts & Papers, 1880-1889. 93.00x (ISBN 0-686-27264-1); Vol. 8. Bills, Reports, Estimates, Accounts & Papers, 1890-1899. 103.00x (ISBN 0-686-27265-X). Pub. by Irish Academic Pr). Biblio Dist.

Catalogue of British Parliamentary Papers 1801 - 1900. 310p. 1977. 45.00x (ISBN 0-686-19005-X, Pub. by Irish Academic Pr Ireland). Biblio Dist.

Ford, P. & Ford, G. Select List of British Parliamentary Papers 1833-1899. 188p. 1969. Repr. of 1953 ed. 20.00x (ISBN 0-7165-0574-6, Pub. by Irish Academic Pr Ireland). Biblio Dist.

Ford, P. & Ford, G. A. Breviate of Parliamentary Papers 1900-1916. 520p. 1970. Repr. of 1957 ed. 36.00x (ISBN 0-7165-0575-4, Pub. by Irish Academic Pr Ireland). Biblio Dist.

--Breviate of Parliamentary Papers 1917-1939. 624p. 1970. Repr. of 1951 ed. 36.00x (ISBN 0-7165-0576-2, Pub. by Irish Academic Pr Ireland). Biblio Dist.

Ford, P., et al. Select List of British Parliamentary Papers 1955-1964. 128p. 1970. 17.00x (ISBN 0-7165-0884-2, Pub. by Irish Academic Pr Ireland). Biblio Dist.

P. S. King & Son, Ltd., London. Catalogue of Parliamentary Papers: 1801-1900 with a Few of Earlier Date. Jones, Hilda V., compiled by. Bd. with Supplement I, 1901-1910. 81p; Supplement II, 1911-1920. 58p. LC 72-8810. vii, 317p. 1973. Repr. lib. bdg. 38.00 (ISBN 0-8337-1866-5). B Franklin.

Rodgers, Frank. Serial Publications in the British Parliamentary Papers, 1900-1968: A Bibliography. 166p. 1970. 7.50 (ISBN 0-8389-0086-0). ALA.

Stationery Office (Great Britain) Annual Catalogues of British Official & Parliamentary Publications 1910 to 1919. 2042p. 1975. Repr. lib. bdg. 65.00x (ISBN 0-914146-20-3). Somerset Hse.

--Annual Catalogues of British Official & Parliamentary Publications 1894 to 1909. 3076p. 1975. Repr. lib. bdg. 90.00x (ISBN 0-914146-19-X). Somerset Hse.

GREAT BRITAIN–PARLIAMENT–COMMITTEES

Herbert, A. P. Anything but Action. (Institute of Economic Affairs, Hobart Papers Ser.: No. 5). (Orig.). pap. 2.50 (ISBN 0-685-20561-4). Transatlantic.

GREAT BRITAIN–PARLIAMENT–ELECTIONS

Butler, David & Kavanagh, Dennis. The British General Election of October 1974. LC 75-21706. 350p. 1975. 25.00 (ISBN 0-312-10255-0). St Martin.

Butler, David E. & King, A. British General Election of 1966. 1966. 25.00 (ISBN 0-312-10150-3). St Martin.

Cook, Chris & Ramsden, John. By-Elections in British Politics. LC 73-87075. 224p. 1974. text ed. 22.50 (ISBN 0-312-11095-2). St Martin.

Craig, F. W. Minor Parties at British Parliamentary Elections, 1885-1974. 174p. 1975. 20.00x (ISBN 0-333-17152-7). Intl Pubns Serv.

Craig, F. W., ed. Britain Votes One: A Handbook of Parliamentary Election Results 1974-1977. (Illus.). 273p. (Orig.). 1977. pap. 17.50x (ISBN 0-900178-17-5). Intl Pubns Serv.

--British Parliamentary Election Results, 1832-1885. LC 77-371679. 692p. 1977. 52.50x (ISBN 0-333-17153-5). Intl Pubns Serv.

Craig, Fred W. British Parliamentary Election Results 1950-70. (Illus.). 780p. 1971. 55.00x (ISBN 0-900178-02-7). Intl Pubns Serv.

--British Parliamentary Election Results 1885-1918. (Illus.). 1974. 30.00x (ISBN 0-333-16903-4). Intl Pubns Serv.

Craig, Fred W., ed. British Parliamentary Election Results 1918-49. (British Political Reference Publications Ser). 1969. 45.00x (ISBN 0-900178-01-9). Intl Pubns Serv.

Grego, Joseph. A History of Parliamentary Elections & Electioneering: From the Stuarts to Queen Victoria. LC 73-141755. (Illus.). 403p. 1974. Repr. of 1892 ed. 43.00 (ISBN 0-8103-4030-5). Gale.

Morris, Homer L. Parliamentary Franchise Reform in England from 1885 to 1918. LC 73-78004. (Columbia University. Studies in the Social Sciences: No. 218). Repr. of 1921 ed. 18.50 (ISBN 0-404-51218-6). AMS Pr.

Pelling, Henry. Social Geography of British Elections: 1885-1910. (Maps). 1967. 22.50 (ISBN 0-312-73290-2). St Martin.

Ranney, Austin. Pathways to Parliament: Candidate Selection in Britain. 314p. 1965. 25.00 (ISBN 0-299-03560-3). U of Wis Pr.

Stobaugh, Beverly P. Women in Parliament Nineteen Eighteen-Nineteen Seventy. 1978. 9.00 (ISBN 0-682-49056-3, University). Exposition.

Vincent, J. R. & Stenton, M., eds. F. H. McCalmont's Parliamentary Poll Book: British Parliamentary Election Results, 1832-1918. 8th ed. 882p. 1971. Repr. of 1879 ed. 35.00x (ISBN 0-8476-6050-8). Rowman.

GREAT BRITAIN–PARLIAMENT–HOUSE OF COMMONS

Baker, Arthur. The House Is Sitting. LC 74-68. (Illus.). 264p. 1974. Repr. of 1958 ed. lib. bdg. 14.25x (ISBN 0-8371-7364-7, BAHS). Greenwood.

Berrington, Hugh B. Backbench Opinion in the House of Commons, 1945-1955. 1974. text ed. 32.00 (ISBN 0-08-016748-9). Pergamon.

Chester, D. N. & Bowring, Nona. Questions in Parliament. LC 74-9164. 335p. 1974. Repr. of 1962 ed. lib. bdg. 19.75x (ISBN 0-8371-7614-X, CHQP). Greenwood.

Dasent, Arthur I. Speakers of the House of Commons from the Earliest Times to the Present Day. (Illus.). 1965. 29.50 (ISBN 0-8337-0773-6). B Franklin.

Easterby, James H. & Green, Ruth S., eds. Journal of the Commons House of Assembly: Series One, 9 vols. Incl. November 10, 1736-June 7, 1739. xii, 764p. 1951 (ISBN 0-87249-900-6); September 12, 1739-March 26, 1741. xi, 613p. 1952 (ISBN 0-87249-901-4); May 18, 1741-July 10, 1742. xi, 620p. 1953 (ISBN 0-87249-902-2); September 14, 1742-January 27, 1744. xiv, 607p. 1954 (ISBN 0-87249-903-0); February 20, 1744-May 25, 1745. xi, 626p. 1955 (ISBN 0-87249-904-9); September 10, 1745-June 17, 1746. xiv, 291p. 1956 (ISBN 0-87249-905-7); September 10, 1746-June 13, 1747. Green, Ruth S., pref. by. xiv, 444p. 1958 (ISBN 0-87249-906-5); January 19, 1748-June 29, 1748. Rogers, George C., Jr., pref. by. xiv, 457p. 1961 (ISBN 0-87249-907-3); March 28, 1749-March 19, 1750. Lee, Charles E. & Rogers, George C., Jr.pref. by. xviii, 549p. 1962 (ISBN 0-87249-908-1). LC 51-62239. (Colonial Records of South Carolina Ser.). 27.50x ea. U of SC Pr.

Flegmann, Vilma. Called to Account: The Public Accounts Committee of the House of Commons. 328p. 1980. text ed. 31.50x (ISBN 0-566-00371-6, Pub. by Gower Pub Co England). Renouf.

Gregory, Roy & Hutchesson, Peter. The Parliamentary Ombudsman. (Royal Institute of Public Administration). 1975. text ed. 50.00x (ISBN 0-04-328009-9). Allen Unwin.

Hatsell, J. Precedents of the Proceedings in the House of Commons, with Observations, 5 vols. (Parliamentary & Congressional Ser). 1971. Repr. of 1818 ed. Set. text ed. 160.00x (ISBN 0-7165-2000-1). Rothman.

Johnson, Nevil. Parliament & Administration: The Estimates Committee, 1964-65. LC 67-3034. 1966. 12.50x (ISBN 0-678-06022-3). Kelley.

Judd, Gerrit Parmele. Members of Parliament, 1734-1832. LC 73-179572. vii, 389p. 1972. Repr. of 1955 ed. 21.50 (ISBN 0-208-01230-3, Archon). Shoe String.

King, Anthony. British Members of Parliament: A Self Portrait. 128p. 1975. 12.50 (ISBN 0-333-17170-5). Transatlantic.

Lacey, Douglas R. Dissent & Parliamentary Politics in England 1661-1689: A Study in the Perpetuation & Tempering of Parliamentarianism. 1969. 35.00 (ISBN 0-8135-0594-1). Rutgers U Pr.

Lambert, Sheila, ed. The House of Commons Sessional Papers of the Eighteenth Century, 147 vols. LC 74-33160. 1975. 14,000.00 (ISBN 0-8420-1892-1); 2 vols. folio list sold separately 95.00 (ISBN 0-8420-1911-1) (ISBN 0-8420-1912-X). Scholarly Res Inc.

--The House of Commons Sessional Papers of the Eighteenth Century, Pt. 1: George I & II, 19 vols. plus list vol. I. 1975. Set. 2000.00 (ISBN 0-8420-2014-4). Scholarly Res Inc.

--The House of Commons Sessional Papers of the Eighteenth Century, Part 2: George III, 126 vols. plus list vol. II. 1975. Set. 12,000.00 (ISBN 0-8420-2016-0). Scholarly Res Inc.

Laski, H. J. Reflections on the Constitution, the House of Commons, the Cabinet & the Civil Service. 220p. 1951. 30.00x (ISBN 0-7190-0223-0, Pub. by Manchester U Pr England). State Mutual Bk.

Leonard, Dick & Valentine, Herman, eds. The Backbencher & Parliament. LC 78-185906. 1972. 18.95 (ISBN 0-312-06475-6). St Martin.

Marsden, Philip. The Officers of the Commons 1363-1965. 5.95 (ISBN 0-686-05402-4). British Am Bks.

Maurice, Frederick D. Workman & the Franchise. LC 68-18601. Repr. of 1866 ed. 15.00x (ISBN 0-678-00592-3). Kelley.

Mellors, Colin. The British MP: A Socio-Economic Study of the House of Commons. (Illus.). 1978. 18.95 (ISBN 0-566-00138-1, 00708-0, Pub. by Saxon Hse England). Lexington Bks.

Muller, William D. The Kept Men? The First Century of Trade Union Representation in the British House of Commons, 1874-1975. (Illus.). 1977. text ed. 39.75x (ISBN 0-85527-184-1). Humanities.

Newman, Aubrey, ed. The Parliamentary Lists of the Early Eighteenth Century: Their Compilation & Use. 96p. 1973. text ed. 6.75x (ISBN 0-7185-1112-3, Leicester). Humanities.

Nicolson, Nigel. People & Parliament. LC 74-7612. 191p. 1974. Repr. of 1958 ed. lib. bdg. 15.00 (ISBN 0-8371-7588-7, NIPE). Greenwood.

Norton, Philip. Dissension in the House of Commons: Nineteen Seventy-Four to Nineteen Seventy-Nine. (Illus.). 560p. 1980. text ed. 97.50x (ISBN 0-19-827430-0). Oxford U Pr.

Notestein, Wallace, et al. Commons Debates, Sixteen Twenty-One, 7 vols. 1935. 450.00x (ISBN 0-685-69847-5). Elliots Bks.

Peel, R. The Speeches... Delivered in the House of Commons, 4 vols. Repr. of 1853 ed. Set. 145.00 (ISBN 0-527-70312-5). Kraus Repr.

Pitt, W. The Speeches in the House of Commons, 3 vols. Repr. of 1817 ed. Set. 62.00 (ISBN 0-527-71506-9). Kraus Repr.

Porritt, Edward. Unreformed House of Commons, 2 Vols. LC 63-21104. Repr. of 1903 ed. 45.00x (ISBN 0-678-00012-3). Kelley.

Redlich, Joseph. Procedure of the House of Commons, 3 Vols. Steinthal, A. Ernest, tr. LC 77-77895. Repr. of 1908 ed. Set. 62.50 (ISBN 0-404-05280-0). AMS Pr.

Reid, Gordon. Politics of Financial Control: The Role of the House of Commons. (Orig.). 1966. text ed. 5.00x (ISBN 0-09-079260-2, Hutchinson U Lib); pap. text ed. 2.50x (ISBN 0-09-079261-0, Hutchinson U Lib). Humanities.

Robinson, Ann. Parliament & Public Spending. 1978. text ed. 34.50x (ISBN 0-435-83750-8). Heinemann Ed.

Sedgwick, Romney, ed. House of Commons 1715-1754, Vols. 1 & 2. (Illus.). 1970. text ed. 39.95x (ISBN 0-19-519539-6). Oxford U Pr.

Strateman, Catherine. Liverpool Tractate. LC 38-6233. (Columbia University. Studies in the Social Sciences: No. 430). 1937. 12.50 (ISBN 0-404-51430-8). AMS Pr.

Taylor, Eric. The House of Commons at Work. 9th ed. 1979. text ed. 18.25x (ISBN 0-333-23319-0). Humanities.

Temple, Richard. Letters & Character Sketches from the House of Commons. Temple, Richard, ed. 1978. Repr. of 1912 ed. lib. bdg. 45.00 (ISBN 0-8492-2734-8). R West.

The Times Guide to the House of Commons. (Illus.). 350p. 1980. 45.00x (ISBN 0-930466-29-2). Meckler Bks.

The Times Guide to the House of Commons: May 1979. (Illus.). 1979. 45.00x (ISBN 0-7230-0225-8). Intl Pubns Serv.

Walkland, S. A., ed. The House of Commons in the Twentieth Century. 1979. 59.00x (ISBN 0-19-827193-X). Oxford U Pr.

White, William. Inner Life of the House of Commons, 2 Vols. facs. ed. LC 79-11949. (Select Bibliographies Reprint Ser). 1897. 30.50 (ISBN 0-8369-5392-4). Arno.

Willson, David H. Privy Councillors in the House of Commons, 1604-1629. LC 76-120678. 1970. Repr. lib. bdg. 17.50x (ISBN 0-374-98639-8). Octagon.

Willson, David H., ed. Parliamentary Diary of Robert Bowyer, 1606-1607. LC 72-120677. 1970. Repr. lib. bdg. 22.50x (ISBN 0-374-98636-3). Octagon.

Witmer, Helen E. Property Qualifications of Members of Parliament. LC 68-58644. (Columbia University. Studies in Social Sciences: No. 498). Repr. of 1943 ed. 20.00 (ISBN 0-404-51498-7). AMS Pr.

GREAT BRITAIN–PARLIAMENT–HOUSE OF LORDS

Bromhead, P. A. The House of Lords & Contemporary Politics: 1911-1957. LC 75-27676. 283p. 1976. Repr. of 1958 ed. lib. bdg. 16.75x (ISBN 0-8371-8458-4, BRHL). Greenwood.

House of Lords Sessional Papers, 1648-1790: Index, 4 vols. 400.00 (ISBN 0-379-20015-5). Oceana.

Marriott, John A. Second Chambers. LC 78-102250. (Select Bibliographies Reprint Ser). 1910. 24.00 (ISBN 0-8369-5135-2). Arno.

Morgan, Janet P. The House of Lords & the Labour Government, 1964-1970. (Illus.). 270p. 1975. text ed. 45.00x (ISBN 0-19-827191-3). Oxford U Pr.

Pike, Luke O. Constitutional History of the House of Lords. 1894. 24.50 (ISBN 0-8337-2770-2). B Franklin.

Stevens, Robert. Law & Politics: The House of Lords As a Judicial Body, 1800-1976. LC 78-8500. (Studies in Legal History). 1978. 33.00x (ISBN 0-8078-1321-4). U of NC Pr.

Torrington, William, ed. House of Lords Sessional Papers, 1641-1805, 60 vols. LC 70-141328. 1977. 75.00 ea. (ISBN 0-379-20014-7). Oceana.

Traill, H. D. Lord Strafford. 206p. 1981. Repr. of 1893 ed. lib. bdg. 20.00 (ISBN 0-8495-5167-6). Arden Lib.

Turberville, A. S. The House of Lords in the Age of Reform, 1784-1837. LC 74-11885. 1974. Repr. of 1958 ed. lib. bdg. 25.00x (ISBN 0-8371-7699-9, TUAR). Greenwood.

Turberville, Arthur S. The House of Lords in the Reign of William Third. LC 77-110877. vi, 264p. Repr. of 1913 ed. lib. bdg. 15.00x (ISBN 0-8371-4558-9, TULW). Greenwood.

GREAT BRITAIN–PEERAGE

see also Great Britain–Baronetage

Collins, Arthur. Collin's Peerage of England, 9 Vols. LC 70-115003. Repr. of 1812 ed. Set. 360.00 (ISBN 0-404-01740-1); 40.00 ea. AMS Pr.

Debrett's Correct Form. 1971. 30.00x (ISBN 0-8277-0409-7). British Bk Ctr.

Debrett's Correct Form. 1971. 30.00x (ISBN 0-8277-0409-7). British Bk Ctr.

Heylyn, Peter. Help to English History. Wright, Paul, ed. LC 70-130988. Repr. of 1773 ed. 40.00 (ISBN 0-404-03259-1). AMS Pr.

Montague-Smith, P., ed. Debrett's Correct Form. 375p. 1971. 15.00 (ISBN 0-905649-00-1). Intl Pubns Serv.

--Debrett's Correct Form. 375p. 1971. 15.00 (ISBN 0-905649-00-1). Intl Pubns Serv.

Montague-Smith, Patrick. Debrett's Peerage & Baronetage. new ed. (Illus.). 1978. 95.00 (ISBN 0-670-26234-X, Debrett's Peerage, Ltd.). Viking Pr.

Montaigne-Smith, Patrick, ed. Debrett's Peerage & Baronetage. LC 42-17925. 2336p. 1980. 112.50x (ISBN 0-905649-20-6). Intl Pubns Serv.

Naylor, John F., ed. British Aristocracy & the Peerage Bill of 1719. (Problems in European History Ser). (Orig.). 1968. pap. 4.95x (ISBN 0-19-501004-3). Oxford U Pr.

Pine, Leslie G. New Extinct Peerage, 1884-1971. LC 72-6707. (Illus.). 1973. 27.00 (ISBN 0-8063-0521-5). Genealog Pub.

Round, Horace. Peerage & Pedigree: Studies in Peerage Law & Family History, 2 vols. (Genealogy Ser.: No. 1). 362p. 1971. Repr. of 1910 ed. Set. 65.00x (ISBN 0-7130-0020-1, Pub. by Woburn Pr England). Biblio Dist.

--Studies in Peerage & Family History. (Genealogy Ser.: No. 2). 496p. 1971. Repr. of 1907 ed. 35.00x (ISBN 0-686-23098-1, Pub. by Woburn Pr England). Biblio Dist.

Round, John H. Peerage & Pedigree: Studies in Peerage Law & Family History, 2 Vols. LC 76-124476. 1970. Repr. of 1910 ed. 30.00 (ISBN 0-8063-0425-1). Genealog Pub.

--Studies in Peerage & Family History. LC 72-124475. 1970. Repr. of 1901 ed. 18.50 (ISBN 0-8063-0426-X). Genealog Pub.

Solly, Edward, ed. Index of Hereditary English, Scottish, & Irish Titles of Honour. LC 68-55167. (Index Society Ser: Vol. 5). 1968. Repr. of 1880 ed. 12.50 (ISBN 0-8063-0319-0). Genealog Pub.

GREAT BRITAIN–POLITICS AND GOVERNMENT

see also Great Britain–Parliament

Adams, Barbara, et al. Gypsies & Government Policy in England. 1975. text ed. 40.00x (ISBN 0-435-85080-6). Heinemann Ed.

Adelman, Paul. The Rise of the Labour Party, 1880-1945. 1972. pap. text ed. 5.50x (ISBN 0-582-31427-5). Longman.

Alderman, Geoffrey. British Elections. 1978. 30.00 (ISBN 0-7134-0195-8, Pub. by Batsford England); pap. 11.50 (ISBN 0-7134-0196-6). David & Charles.

Anderson, I. G., ed. Councils, Committees & Boards: A Handbook of Advisory, Consultative, Executive & Similar Bodies in British Public Life. 4th ed. 409p. 1980. 100.00x (ISBN 0-900246-32-4). Intl Pubns Serv.

Arthur, Terry. Ninety-Five Per-Cent Is Crap: A Plain Man's Guide to British Politics. (Illus.). 1976. 8.95 (ISBN 0-905004-01-9). Libertarian Bks.

Ashford, Douglas E. British Dogmatism & French Pragmatism: Central-Local Policy Making in the Welfare State. (New Local Government Ser.: No. 22). (Illus.). 432p. 1981. text ed. 60.00x (ISBN 0-04-352096-0). Allen Unwin.

--Policy & Politics in Britain: The Limits of Consensus. (Policy & Politics in Industrial States Ser.). 400p. 1980. 19.50 (ISBN 0-87722-194-4); pap. text ed. 9.95 (ISBN 0-87722-195-2). Temple U Pr.

Atkyns, Robert. The Power, Jurisdiction, & Privilege of Parliament. Straka, Gerald, ed. LC 72-83155. (English Studies Ser.). 1972. Repr. of 1689 ed. lib. bdg. 20.00 (ISBN 0-8420-1414-4). Scholarly Res Inc.

Atwood, William. The Fundamental Constitution of the English Government. Straka, Gerald, ed. LC 72-83157. (English Studies Ser). 1972. Repr. of 1690 ed. lib. bdg. 27.00 (ISBN 0-8420-1415-2). Scholarly Res Inc.

Babbage, Charles. Exposition of Eighteen Fifty One: Or Views of the Industry, the Science & Government of England. 2nd ed. 290p. 1968. Repr. of 1851 ed. 25.00x (ISBN 0-7146-1620-6, F Cass Co). Biblio Dist.

Backstrom, Philip N. Christian Socialism & Co-Operation in Victorian England: Edward Vansittart Neale & the Co-Operative Movement. 238p. 1974. 19.50x (ISBN 0-87471-582-2). Rowman.

Bagehot, Walter. The English Constitution. (Orig.). (YA) (gr. 9-12). 1966. pap. 5.95 (ISBN 0-8014-9023-5, CP23). Cornell U Pr.

--The English Constitution. LC 77-86594. (Classics of English Legal History in the Modern Era Ser.: Vol. 84). 1978. Repr. of 1867 ed. lib. bdg. 55.00 (ISBN 0-8240-3071-0). Garland Pub.

Bailey, Sydney D., ed. Political Parties & the Party System in Britain: A Symposium. LC 78-14099. 1979. Repr. of 1952 ed. 19.00 (ISBN 0-88355-773-8). Hyperion Conn.

Baldwin, Frances E. Sumptuary Legislation & Personal Regulation in England. LC 78-64119. (Johns Hopkins University. Studies in the Social Sciences. Forty-Fourth Ser. 1926: 1). Repr. of 1926 ed. 24.50 (ISBN 0-404-61233-4). AMS Pr.

Bauman, Zygmunt. Between Class & Elite: The Evolution of the British Labour Movement - a Sociological Study. Patterson, Sheila, tr. (Illus.). 334p. 1972. text ed. 16.00x (ISBN 0-7190-0502-7). Humanities.

Beer, Samuel H. British Political System. (Patterns of Government Ser.). 1974. pap. text ed. 8.95 (ISBN 0-394-31817-X). Random.

Bernstein, Eduard. Cromwell & Communism: Socialism & Democracy in the Great English Revolution. new ed. 287p. 1963. 25.00x (ISBN 0-7146-1454-8, F Cass Co). Biblio Dist.

Birch, A. H. Representative & Responsible Government; an Essay on the British Constitution. 1964. pap. 6.00 (ISBN 0-8020-6095-1). U of Toronto Pr.

Birch, Anthony H. British System of Government. 4th ed. (Minerva Series of Students Handbooks). (Illus.). 320p. 1980. text ed. 19.95x (ISBN 0-04-320142-3); pap. text ed. 7.95x (ISBN 0-04-320143-1). Allen Unwin.

--Political Integration & Disintegration in the British Isles. 1977. text ed. 17.95x (ISBN 0-04-320123-7); pap. text ed. 8.95x (ISBN 0-04-320124-5). Allen Unwin.

Birkenhead, Frederick E. Points of View, 2 Vols. facsimile ed. LC 77-111815. (Essay Index Reprint Ser.). 1923. 33.00 (ISBN 0-8369-1594-1). Arno.

Blackstone, Sir William. Tracts Chiefly Relating to the Antiquities & Laws of England. 3rd ed. Repr. of 1771 ed. lib. bdg. 30.00x (ISBN 0-87991-750-4). Porcupine Pr.

Bolton, Sarah K. Famous English Statesmen: Of Queen Victoria's Reign. LC 78-39705. (Essay Index Reprint Ser.). Repr. of 1891 ed. 25.00 (ISBN 0-8369-2749-4). Arno.

Bracton on the Laws & Customs of England, Vols. 1 & 2. 1968. Set. 65.00 (ISBN 0-674-08035-1). Harvard U Pr.

Brennan, T. Politics & Government in Britain. LC 78-171673. 9.95x (ISBN 0-521-08366-4). Cambridge U Pr.

Bryan, James W. The Devopment of the English Law of Conspiracy. LC 78-63932. (Johns Hopkins University. Studies in the Social Sciences. Twenty-Seventh Ser. 1909: 3-5). Repr. of 1909 ed. 14.50 (ISBN 0-404-61181-8). AMS Pr.

Bryson, W. H. The Equity Side of the Exchequer. LC 73-93394. (Cambridge Studies in English Legal History). 280p. 1975. 36.00 (ISBN 0-521-20406-2). Cambridge U Pr.

Bunyan, Tony. The Political Police in Britain. LC 75-45815. (Illus.). 304p. 1976. 17.95 (ISBN 0-312-62405-0). St Martin.

Butler, David E. & Sloman, Anne, eds. British Political Facts: Nineteen-Hundred to Nineteen Seventy-Four. 4th rev. ed. LC 74-24816. 352p. 1975. pap. 29.95 (ISBN 0-312-10465-0). St Martin.

Butler, James R. M. Passing of the Great Reform Bill. 2nd ed. 454p. 1964. 27.50x (ISBN 0-7146-1459-9, F Cass Co). Biblio Dist.

Care, Henry. English Liberties, or The Free-Born Subject's Inheritance. 6th ed. LC 75-31087. Repr. of 1774 ed. 28.50 (ISBN 0-404-13505-6). AMS Pr.

Chapman, Richard A., ed. The Role of Commissions in Policy Making (Britain) 1973. 12.50 (ISBN 0-04-350042-0). Verry.

Charry, George L. Early English Liberalism. 10.95 (ISBN 0-685-60122-6, Pub by Twayne). Cyrco Pr.

Chen Chih-Mai. Parliamentary Opinion of Delegated Legislation. LC 70-76628. (Columbia University Studies in the Social Sciences: No. 394). Repr. of 1933 ed. 15.00 (ISBN 0-404-51394-8). AMS Pr.

Chesterton, Gilbert K. Utopia of Usurers, & Other Essays. facs. ed. LC 67-26724. (Essay Index Reprint Ser). 1917. 15.00 (ISBN 0-8369-0299-8). Arno.

Cheyney, Edward P. European Background of American History. LC 65-29079. (American Classics Ser.). 15.00 (ISBN 0-8044-1155-7). Ungar.

Chiao Wan-Hsuan. Devolution in Great Britain. LC 76-78010. (Columbia University Studies in the Social Sciences: No. 272). Repr. of 1926 ed. 22.50 (ISBN 0-404-51272-0). AMS Pr.

Clifford, Frederick. A History of Private Bill Legislation, 2 vols. 1968. 75.00x (ISBN 0-7156-1563-7, F Cass Co). Biblio Dist.

Conquest, Robert. Present Danger: Towards a Foreign Policy. LC 79-2086. (Publication Ser.: 216). 170p. 1979. 15.95 (ISBN 0-8179-7161-0). Hoover Inst Pr.

Critchley, T. A. The Conquest of Violence: Order & Liberty in Britain. LC 70-128775. (Illus.). 1970. 8.50x (ISBN 0-8052-3376-8). Schocken.

Crook, David P. American Democracy in English Politics. 256p. 1965. text ed. 7.25x (ISBN 0-19-821338-7). Oxford U Pr.

Cross, J. A. British Public Administration. 1970. 6.00x (ISBN 0-7231-0628-2). Intl Pubns Serv.

Cyr, Arthur I. Liberal Party Politics in Britain. LC 76-702. 350p. 1977. text ed. 12.95 (ISBN 0-87855-145-X). Transaction Bks.

Daly, James. Sir Robert Filmer & English Political Thought. LC 78-25913. 1979. 25.00x (ISBN 0-8020-5433-1). U of Toronto Pr.

Dasent, Arthur I. Speakers of the House of Commons from the Earliest Times to the Present Day. (Illus.). 1965. 29.50 (ISBN 0-8337-0773-6). B Franklin.

David, Edward, ed. Inside Asquith's Cabinet: From the Diaries of Charles Hobhouse. LC 77-84941. (Illus.). 1978. 18.95x (ISBN 0-312-41868-X). St Martin.

Dearlove, John. The Reorganization of British Local Government. LC 78-18092. 1979. 39.95 (ISBN 0-521-22341-5); pap. 10.95 (ISBN 0-521-29456-8). Cambridge U Pr.

De Montmorency, J. E. The Legal System of England. 1928. 10.00 (ISBN 0-685-43880-5). Norwood Edns.

Denholm-Young, Noel. Seignorial Administration in England. 196p. 1963. 22.50x (ISBN 0-7146-1468-8, F Cass Co). Biblio Dist.

Derry, T. K. The United Kingdom: A Survey of British Institutions Today. LC 63-12058. 1963. 10.00x (ISBN 0-8147-0119-1); pap. 3.95 (ISBN 0-8147-0120-5). NYU Pr.

Dodd, A. H. The Growth of Responsible Government: From James I to Victoria. 1965. Repr. of 1956 ed. 12.95x (ISBN 0-7100-1288-8). Routledge & Kegan.

Dorfman, Gerald A. Government Versus Trade Unionism in British Politics Since 1968. LC 78-70886. (Publication 224 Ser.). 187p. 1979. 13.95 (ISBN 0-8179-7241-2). Hoover Inst Pr.

Epstein, Joel J. Francis Bacon: A Political Biography. LC 76-25617. xv, 187p. 1977. 13.50x (ISBN 0-8214-0232-3). Ohio U Pr.

Evans, Douglas. Britain in the EEC. LC 73-179437. 208p. 1973. 12.00x (ISBN 0-575-01682-5). Intl Pubns Serv.

Fielding, Nigel. The National Front. (International Library of Sociology). 228p. 1980. 38.50 (ISBN 0-7100-0559-8). Routledge & Kegan.

Finer, Samuel E. A Primer of Public Administration. LC 77-679. (Man & Society Ser.). 1977. Repr. of 1961 ed. lib. bdg. 15.00x (ISBN 0-8371-9492-X, FIPR). Greenwood.

Fraser, Derek. Urban Politics in Victorian England: The Structure of Politics in Victorian Cities. 320p. 1976. text ed. 30.00x (ISBN 0-7185-1145-X, Leicester). Humanities.

Gamble, Andrew. Britain in Decline: Economic Policy, Political Strategy, & the British State. LC 81-68354. 304p. 1982. 15.00 (ISBN 0-8070-4700-7). Beacon Pr.

--The Conservative Nation. 320p. 1974. 22.50x (ISBN 0-7100-8008-5). Routledge & Kegan.

Gash, Norman, et al. The Conservatives. Butler, Lord, ed. 1977. text ed. 28.00x (ISBN 0-04-942157-3). Allen Unwin.

Gifford, William, ed. Anti-Jacobin; or, Weekly Examiner. Nos. 1-36. 2 Vols. in 1. LC 68-57996. 1797-1798. lib. bdg. 57.50 (ISBN 0-685-05687-2). AMS Pr.

Ginsberg, Morris, ed. Law & Opinion in England in the Twentieth Century. LC 74-7537. 407p. 1974. Repr. of 1959 ed. lib. bdg. 35.00x (ISBN 0-8371-7576-3, GILO). Greenwood.

Goodnow, Frank J., ed. Comparative Administrative Law: An Analysis of the Administrative Systems of the U. S., England, France & Germany. 1970. Repr. of 1893 ed. Set. text ed. 44.50 (ISBN 0-8337-1384-1). B Franklin.

Government, 4 pts. Incl. Pt. 1. Civil Service, 12 vols. Set. 882.00x (ISBN 0-686-01119-8); Pt. 2. Diplomatic Service, 4 vols. Set. 306.00x (ISBN 0-686-01120-1); Pt. 3. Elections, 5 vols. Set. 432.00x (ISBN 0-686-01121-X); Pt. 4. Municipal Corporations, 9 vols. Set. 756.00x (ISBN 0-686-01122-8). (British Parliamentary Papers Ser.). 1971 (Pub. by Irish Academic Pr Ireland). Biblio Dist.

Grant, Wyn & Marsh, David. The Confederation of British Industry. 1977. text ed. 16.50x (ISBN 0-8419-6205-7). Holmes & Meier.

Greaves, H. R. The British Constitution. 1965. Repr. of 1938 ed. text ed. 4.50x (ISBN 0-04-342002-8). Humanities.

Green, David G. Power & Party in an English City. (New Local Government Ser.: No. 20). 256p. 1981. text ed. 37.50x (ISBN 0-04-352094-4). Allen Unwin.

Gross, Charles. Bibliography of British Municipal History, Including Gilds & Parliamentary Representation. 1897. 32.50 (ISBN 0-8337-1465-1). B Franklin.

Hale, Matthew. History of the Common Law of England. Gray, Charles M., ed. LC 70-155856. (Classics of British Historical Literature Ser.). 1971. pap. 2.45 (ISBN 0-226-31305-0, P428, Phoen). U of Chicago Pr.

Hall, Walter P. British Radicalism, 1791-1797. 1973. lib. bdg. 15.00x (ISBN 0-374-93383-9). Octagon.

Hamburger, Joseph. James Mill & the Art of Revolution. LC 77-8124. (Yale Studies in Political Science: No. 8). 1977. Repr. of 1963 ed. lib. bdg. 19.75x (ISBN 0-8371-9675-2, HAJM). Greenwood.

Harney, G. Julian, ed. The Democratic Review of British & Foreign Politics, History & Literature, 2 vols. 1968. Repr. of 1850 ed. lib. bdg. 27.50x (ISBN 0-678-08058-5). Kelley.

Harrington, James. The Political Writings of James Harrington: Representative Selections. Blitzer, Charles, ed. LC 80-21163. (The Library of Liberal Arts: No. 38). xlii, 165p. 1980. Repr. of 1955 ed. lib. bdg. 22.50x (ISBN 0-313-22670-9, HAWR). Greenwood.

Health, 5 pts. Incl. Pt. 1. General, 17 vols. Set. 1494.00x (ISBN 0-686-01159-7); Pt. 2. Food & Drugs, 5 vols. Set. 423.00x (ISBN 0-686-01160-0); Pt. 3. Infectious Diseases, 13 vols. Set. 1242.00x (ISBN 0-686-01161-9); Pt. 4. Medical Profession, 5 vols. Set. 342.00x (ISBN 0-686-01162-7); Pt. 5. Mental, 8 vols. Set. 558.00x (ISBN 0-686-01163-5). (British Parliamentary Papers Ser.). 1971 (Pub. by Irish Academic Pr Ireland). Biblio Dist.

Hearder, H. & Loyn, H. R., eds. British Government & Administration: Studies Presented to S. B. Chrimes. 250p. 1974. text ed. 25.00x (ISBN 0-7083-0538-5). Verry.

Hearnshaw, F. J. Conservatism in England. LC 67-24582. 1968. Repr. 23.50 (ISBN 0-86527-031-7). Fertig.

--Conservatism in England: An Analytical, Historical, & Political Survey. 1979. Repr. of 1933 ed. lib. bdg. 30.00 (ISBN 0-8482-4483-4). Norwood Edns.

Hechter, Michael. Internal Colonialism: The Celtic Fringe in British National Development. LC 73-84392. 1975. 25.00x (ISBN 0-520-02559-8); pap. 7.50x (ISBN 0-520-03512-7). U of Cal Pr.

Hill, Michael. The State, Administration & the Individual. 256p. 1976. 15.00x (ISBN 0-87471-909-7). Rowman.

Holmes, Colin. Anti-Semitism & British Society Eighteen Seventy-Six to Nineteen Thirty-Nine. LC 78-21023. 1979. text ed. 45.00x (ISBN 0-8419-0459-6). Holmes & Meier.

Hood, Christopher & Dunsire, Andrew. Bureaumetrics: The Quantitative Comparison of British Central Government Agencies. LC 80-54224. (Illus.). xiv, 312p. 1981. text ed. 27.50x (ISBN 0-8173-0058-9). U of Ala Pr.

Horwitz, Henry. Parliament, Policy & Politics in the Reign of William III. LC 76-27126. 385p. 27.50 (ISBN 0-87413-124-3). U Delaware Pr.

Howarth, Patrick. Questions in the House. LC 74-9627. 220p. 1974. Repr. of 1956 ed. lib. bdg. 15.00x (ISBN 0-8371-7600-X, HOHQ). Greenwood.

Hunt, W. & Poole, R., eds. Political History of England, 12vols. Repr. of 1905 ed. Set. 288.00 (ISBN 0-527-00845-1). Kraus Repr.

Jackson, Thomas A. Trials of British Freedom: Being Some Studies in the History of the Fight for Democratic Freedom in Britain. LC 68-56759. (Research & Source Works Ser.: No. 244). 1968. Repr. of 1940 ed. 17.00 (ISBN 0-8337-1816-9). B Franklin.

Jacobs, Dan N., et al. Comparative Politics: Introduction to the Politics of Britain, the United Kingdom, France, Germany, & the Soviet Union. 320p. 1982. pap. text ed. 9.95x (ISBN 0-934540-05-5). Chatham Hse Pubs.

Jeffares, A. Norman. Politics, Society & Nationhood, Vol. 1. (Collected Edition of the Writings of G. W. Russell Ser.: VI-1). 1980. text ed. write for info. (ISBN 0-391-01185-5). Humanities.

--Politics, Society & Nationhood, Vol. 2. (Collected Edition of the Writings of G. W. Russell Ser.: VI-2). 1980. text ed. write for info. (ISBN 0-391-01183-9). Humanities.

Jennings, Ivor. British Constitution. 5th ed. (English Institution Ser). (Illus.). 1961. pap. 9.95x (ISBN 0-521-09136-5, 136). Cambridge U Pr.

--Cabinet Government. 3rd ed. 1969. 54.50 (ISBN 0-521-05430-3); pap. 17.50x (ISBN 0-521-09570-0, 570). Cambridge U Pr.

--Parliament. 1969. 53.95 (ISBN 0-521-07056-2); pap. 11.95x (ISBN 0-521-09532-8). Cambridge U Pr.

Jephson, Henry. Platform Its Rise & Progress, 2 Vols. LC 68-133957. Repr. of 1892 ed. 45.00x (ISBN 0-678-05180-1). Kelley.

Jones, Bill & Kavanagh, Dennis, eds. British Politics Today. LC 78-21048. 1979. text ed. 14.75x (ISBN 0-8419-0473-1). Holmes & Meier.

Keir, David L. Constitutional History of Modern Britain Since 1485. 1967. pap. 6.95x (ISBN 0-393-00405-8). Norton.

Knappen, Marshall M. Constitutional & Legal History of England. 607p. 1964. Repr. of 1942 ed. 17.50 (ISBN 0-208-01439-X, Archon). Shoe String.

Kynaston, David. The Secretary of State. (Illus.). 1979. 18.50 (ISBN 0-900963-80-8, Pub. by Terence Dalton England). State Mutual Bk.

Larned, Josephus N., et al. English Leadership. LC 70-93353. (Essay Index Reprint Ser). 1918. 22.00 (ISBN 0-8369-1416-3). Arno.

Laski, H. J. Reflections on the Constitution, the House of Commons, the Cabinet & the Civil Service. 220p. 1951. 30.00x (ISBN 0-7190-0223-0, Pub. by Manchester U Pr England). State Mutual Bk.

Levine, Mortimer. The Early Elizabethan Succession Question, 1558-1568. 1966. 15.00x (ISBN 0-8047-0299-3). Stanford U Pr.

Lewis, Gordon. Slavery, Imperialism, & Freedom: Studies in English Radical Thought. LC 78-2826. 1979. pap. 6.50 (ISBN 0-85345-501-5, PB5015). Monthly Rev.

Lieber, Robert J. British Politics & European Unity: Parties, Elites & Pressure Groups. LC 70-104104. 1970. 24.00x (ISBN 0-520-01675-0). U of Cal Pr.

Lindsay, Kennedy. The British Intelligence Services in Action. (Illus.). 288p. (Orig.). 1980. pap. 12.50 (ISBN 0-86202-112-X, Pub. by Dunrod England). Facsimile Bk.

MacDonagh, Michael. English King. LC 78-118484. 1971. Repr. of 1929 ed. 13.75 (ISBN 0-8046-1233-1). Kennikat.

MacDonald, J. R. Parliament & Revolution. LC 20-26685. Repr. of 1920 ed. 12.00 (ISBN 0-527-59300-1). Kraus Repr.

McKechnie, William S. New Democracy & the Constitution. LC 71-118485. 1971. Repr. of 1912 ed. 12.50 (ISBN 0-8046-1234-X). Kennikat.

Mackintosh, John, ed. People & Parliament. LC 78-60433. 1978. 22.95 (ISBN 0-03-046231-2). Praeger.

Mackintosh, John P. Government & Politics of Britain. 4th rev. ed. 1977. pap. text ed. 8.50x (ISBN 0-09-118481-9, Hutchinson U Lib). Humanities.

Madgwick, P. J. Introduction to British Politics. (Illus.). 488p. 1976. pap. 8.50x (ISBN 0-09-127501-6). Intl Pubns Serv.

Marlin, John T. Government Auditing in Britain: An American Perspective. 34p. 1980. write for info. (ISBN 0-916450-40-6). Coun on Municipal.

Marriott, John A. English Political Institutions: An Introductory Study. 4th ed. LC 74-9169. 348p. 1975. Repr. of 1938 ed. lib. bdg. 22.50x (ISBN 0-8371-7621-2, MAEP). Greenwood.

Marx, Karl & Engels, Friedrich. Articles on Britain. 463p. 1975. 3.00 (ISBN 0-8285-0012-6, Pub. by Progress Pubs Russia). Imported Pubns.

Mathews, Anthony S. The Darker Reaches of Government: Access to Information About Public Administration in the United States, Britain & South Africa. LC 78-64475. (Perspectives on Southern Africa Ser.: No. 27). 1979. 30.00x (ISBN 0-520-03803-7). U of Cal Pr.

Miller, William L. The End of British Politics? (Illus.). 302p. 1981. 49.95x (ISBN 0-19-827422-X). Oxford U Pr.

Monetary Policy, 6 pts. Incl. Pt. 1. General, 12 vols. Set. 846.00x (ISBN 0-686-01126-0); Pt. 2. Commercial Distress, 4 vols. Set. 288.00x (ISBN 0-686-01127-9); Pt. 3. Currency, 8 vols. Set. 612.00x (ISBN 0-686-01128-7); Pt. 4. Decimal Coinage, 2 vols. Set. 153.00x (ISBN 0-686-01129-5); Pt. 5. Joint Stock Banks, 1 vol. Set. 121.00x (ISBN 0-686-01130-9); Pt. 6. Savings Banks, 4 vols. Set. 306.00x (ISBN 0-686-01131-7). (British Parliamentary Papers Ser.). 1971 (Pub. by Irish Academic Pr Ireland). Biblio Dist.

Moody, T. W. The Ulster Question, 1603-1973. (Illus.). 1974. pap. 4.95 (ISBN 0-85342-399-7). Irish Bk Ctr.

Morgan, Kenneth O. Wales in British Politics, 1868-1922. 3rd ed. 363p. 1980. text ed. 30.00 (ISBN 0-7083-0743-4). Verry.

Mosley, R. K. Westminster Workshop: A Student's Guide to the British Government. 4th ed. LC 78-41284. (Illus.). 1979. 28.00 (ISBN 0-08-020636-0); pap. 9.75 trade (ISBN 0-08-020635-2); pap. text ed. 7.00 (ISBN 0-08-024316-9). Pergamon.

National Finance, 3 pts. Incl. Pt. 1. General, 8 vols. 648.00x (ISBN 0-686-01123-6). Set; Pt. 2. Income Tax, 2 vols. Set. 171.00x (ISBN 0-686-01124-4); Pt. 3. Newspapers, 2 vols. Set. 135.00x (ISBN 0-686-01125-2). (British Parliamentary Papers Ser.). 1971 (Pub. by Irish Academic Pr Ireland). Biblio Dist.

Neilson, Francis. Birth of the Third Party in British Politics. 1979. lib. bdg. 39.95 (ISBN 0-685-96610-0). Revisionist Pr.

Nimocks, Walter. Milner's Young Men: The Kindergarten in Edwardian Imperial Affairs. LC 68-8588. 1968. 12.50 (ISBN 0-8223-0122-9). Duke.

Nugent, N. & King, R., eds. The British Right: Conservative & Right-Wing Politics in Britian. (Illus.). 1977. 23.95 (ISBN 0-566-00156-X, 00989-X, Pub by Saxon Hse England). Lexington Bks.

Ormond, Richard & Rogers, Malcolm. Dictionary of British Portraiture: Vol. 1, the Middle Ages to the Early Georgian; Historical Figures Born Before 1700. Davies, Adriana, ed. 168p. 1979. text ed. 45.00x (ISBN 0-19-520180-9). Oxford U Pr.

Osborne, Christine. The Gulf States & Oman. (Illus.). 208p. 16.00x (ISBN 0-85664-515-X, Pub. by Croom Helm Ltd. England). Biblio Dist.

Page, William, ed. Commerce & Industry, 2 Vols in One. LC 67-19709. Repr. of 1919 ed. 30.00x (ISBN 0-678-00404-8). Kelley.

Palmerston, H. J. Opinions & Policy. Repr. of 1852 ed. 24.00 (ISBN 0-527-69360-X). Kraus Repr.

Pelling, Henry. Popular Politics & Society in Late Victorian Britain. LC 68-29377. 1968. 17.95 (ISBN 0-312-63070-0). St Martin.

Petyt, George. Lex Parliamentaria; or, a Treatise of Law & Custom of the Parliaments of England. Berkowitz, David & Thorne, Samuel, eds. LC 77-89215. (Classics of English Legal History in the Modern Era Ser.: Vol. 126). 342p. 1979. Repr. of 1690 ed. lib. bdg. 40.00 (ISBN 0-8240-3163-6). Garland Pub.

Pike, E. Royston. Political Parties & Policies: A Popular Explanation of the Principles of the Chief Political Parties & a Guide to Understanding of Current Politics. LC 75-27656. 1976. Repr. of 1948 ed. lib. bdg. 15.00x (ISBN 0-8371-8449-5, PIPP). Greenwood.

Pole, J. R. Political Representation in England & the Origins of the American Republic. 1966. 21.50 (ISBN 0-312-62440-9). St Martin.

Polsby, Nelson W. & Smith, Geoffrey. British Government & Its Discontents. LC 79-56372. 208p. 1981. 12.95 (ISBN 0-465-00765-1). Basic.

Potter, Allen. Organized Groups in British National Politics. LC 74-11988. 395p. 1975. Repr. of 1961 ed. lib. bdg. 19.75x (ISBN 0-8371-7705-7, POOG). Greenwood.

Powell, Enoch & Ritchie, Richard. A Nation or No Nation? Six Years in British Politics. 1978. 24.00 (ISBN 0-7134-1542-8, Pub. by Batsford England). David & Charles.

Prynne, William, et al. William Prynne. Berkowitz, David S. & Thorne, Samuel E., eds. (English Legal History Ser.: Vol. 124). 589p. 1979. lib. bdg. 55.00 (ISBN 0-8240-3161-X). Garland Pub.

Pulzer, Peter G. Political Representation & Elections in Britain. 3rd ed. (Studies in Political Science). 1975. pap. text ed. 8.95x (ISBN 0-04-329023-X). Allen Unwin.

Punnett, R. M. British Government & Politics. 4th ed. 1981. text ed. 34.95x (ISBN 0-435-83739-7); pap. text ed. 15.95x (ISBN 0-435-83738-9). Heinemann Ed.

Randall, F. British Government & Politics. (Illus.). 288p. (Orig.). 1979. pap. text ed. 12.95x (ISBN 0-7121-0247-7, Pub. by Macdonald & Evans England). Intl Ideas.

Redlich, Josef & Hirst, Francis W. History of Local Government in England, Bk. 1. LC 71-110121. Repr. of 1903 ed. lib. bdg. 15.00x (ISBN 0-678-07005-9). Kelley.

Rees, Philip. Fascism in Britain: An Annotated Bibliography. 1978. text ed. 27.50x (ISBN 0-391-00908-7). Humanities.

Rempel, Richard A. Unionists Divided: Arthur Balfour, Joseph Chamberlain & the Unionist Free Traders. (Library of Politics & Society Ser.). 1972. 17.50 (ISBN 0-208-01308-3, Archon). Shoe String.

Rhodes, Gerald. Inspectorates in British Government. (Royal Institute of Public Administration Ser.). (Illus.). 276p. 1981. text ed. 35.00x (ISBN 0-04-351056-6). Allen Unwin.

Rose, Richard. Politics in England. 3rd ed. 392p. 1980. pap. text ed. 7.95 (ISBN 0-316-75641-5). Little.

--Politics in England. 401p. 1974. 17.00 (ISBN 0-571-10297-2, Pub. by Faber & Faber); pap. 10.95 (ISBN 0-571-10534-3). Merrimack Bk Serv.

--The Problem of Party Government. LC 74-30329. (Illus.). 1975. 17.95 (ISBN 0-02-926780-3). Free Pr.

Rush, Michael. Parliamentary Government in Britain. 260p. 1981. pap. text ed. 30.00x (ISBN 0-8419-0680-7). Holmes & Meier.

Russell, J. R. Essay on the History of the English Government & Constitution from the Reign of Henry Seventh to the Present Time. Repr. of 1865 ed. 18.00 (ISBN 0-527-78100-2). Kraus Repr.

Smellie, Kingsley B. A Hundred Years of English Government. 2nd ed. LC 75-41256. Repr. of 1950 ed. 24.50 (ISBN 0-404-14606-6). AMS Pr.

Smith, Brian & Stanyer, Jeffery. Administering Britain. 288p. 1976. 24.00x (ISBN 0-85520-139-8, Pub. by Martin Robertson England). Biblio Dist.

Smith, Brian C. Policy-Making in British Government: An Analysis of Power & Rationality. 210p. 1976. 13.50x (ISBN 0-87471-859-7). Rowman.

Smith, Dan. The Defence of the Realm in the Nineteen Eighty's. 276p. 1980. 38.00x (ISBN 0-85664-873-6, Pub. by Croom Helm Ltd England). Biblio Dist.

Smith, Lee & Jones, David. Deprivation, Participation & Community Action. (Community Work Ser.: No. 6). 240p. (Orig.). 1981. pap. 15.00 (ISBN 0-7100-0827-9). Routledge & Kegan.

Smith, Thomas. De Republica Anglorum, the Maner of Government of England. LC 73-25629. (English Experience Ser.: No. 219). 120p. 1970. Repr. of 1583 ed. 16.00 (ISBN 90-221-0219-X). Walter J Johnson.

Smith, Tony. The Pattern of Imperialism: The United States, Great Britain & the Late-Industrializing World Since 1815. LC 80-39676. (Illus.). 240p. Date not set. price not set (ISBN 0-521-23619-3); pap. price not set (ISBN 0-521-28076-1). Cambridge U Pr.

State Research. Review of Security & the State 1978. 1979. 27.50x (ISBN 0-685-94075-6). Nichols Pub.

Stewart, Michael. The British Approach to Politics. 1966. pap. text ed. 14.95x (ISBN 0-04-320038-9). Allen Unwin.

Tate, Joan. Your Town: A Child's Guide to the Functions & Organization of Local Government in England. 2.95 (ISBN 0-7153-5659-3). David & Charles.

Tawney, Richard H. The Attack: And Other Papers. facsimile ed. LC 70-152216. (Essay Index Reprint Ser). Repr. of 1953 ed. 16.00 (ISBN 0-8369-2376-6). Arno.

Thomson, Mark A. Secretaries of State, 1681-1782. LC 68-11126. Repr. of 1932 ed. 22.50x (ISBN 0-678-05089-9). Kelley.

Tierney, Brian, et al, eds. English Liberalism: The New Democratic Way? 3rd ed. (Historical Pamphlets). 1977. pap. text ed. 1.95x (ISBN 0-394-32060-3). Random.

Tite, C. G. Impeachment & Parlimentary Judicature in Early Stuart England. (University of London Historical Studies: No. 37). 256p. 1974. text ed. 37.25x (ISBN 0-485-13137-4, Athlone Pr). Humanities.

Transport & Communications, 3 pts. Incl. Pt. 1. General, 22 vols. Set. 1845.00x (ISBN 0-686-01146-5); Pt. 2. Shipping (Safety, 9 vols. Set. 792.00x (ISBN 0-686-01147-3); Pt. 3. Posts & Telegraphs, 8 vols. Set. 684.00x (ISBN 0-686-01148-1). (British Parliamentary Papers Ser.). 1971 (Pub. by Irish Academic Pr Ireland). Biblio Dist.

Trenchard, John & Gordon, Thomas. Cato's Letters, 4 Vols. in 2. LC 74-121105. (Civil Liberties in American History Ser). 1971. Repr. of 1775 ed. Set. lib. bdg. 75.00 (ISBN 0-306-71965-7). Da Capo.

Tsuzuki, C. Edward Carpenter: Eighteen Forty-Four to Nineteen Twenty Nine. LC 80-40152. 240p. 1980. 34.50 (ISBN 0-521-23371-2). Cambridge U Pr.

Twysden, Roger. Certaine Considerations Upon the Government of England. Kemble, John M., ed. (Camden Society, London. Publications, First Ser.: No. 45). Repr. of 1849 ed. 21.00 (ISBN 0-404-50145-1). AMS Pr.

Twysden, Roger B. Certain Considerations Upon the Government of England. Repr. of 1849 ed. 23.00 (ISBN 0-384-62155-4). Johnson Repr.

Tynwald: Symbol of an Ancient Kingdom. pap. 1.95 (ISBN 0-686-10860-4). British Am Bks.

Tyrrell, James. Bibliotheca Politica: or, an Inquiry into the Ancient Constitution of the English Government. Straka, Gerald M., ed. LC 72-83174. (English Studies Ser.). 1972. Repr. of 1694 ed. lib. bdg. 55.00 (ISBN 0-8420-1430-6). Scholarly Res Inc.

Underhill, Nicholas. The Lord Chancellor. (Illus.). 1979. 18.50 (ISBN 0-900963-81-6, Pub. by Terence Dalton England). State Mutual Bk.

Urry, J. & Wakeford, J. Power in Britain: Sociological Readings. 1973. text ed. 26.00x (ISBN 0-435-82900-9); pap. text ed. 16.50x (ISBN 0-435-82901-7). Heinemann Ed.

Verney, Douglas V. British Government & Politics: Life Without a Declaration of Independence. 3rd ed. (Comparative Government Ser.). 216p. 1976. pap. text ed. 9.95 scp (ISBN 0-06-046827-0, HarpC). Har-Row.

Wade, John. The Extraordinary Black Book. 2nd ed. (The Development of Industrial Society Ser.). 576p. 1971. Repr. of 1831 ed. 35.00x (ISBN 0-7165-1588-1, Pub. by Irish Academic Pr). Biblio Dist.

--History of the Middle & Working Classes. LC 66-18321. Repr. of 1833 ed. 25.00x (ISBN 0-678-00173-1). Kelley.

Walker, Peter. The Ascent of Britain. (Illus.). 1977. text ed. 18.95x (ISBN 0-8464-0154-1). Beekman Pubs.

Wang Chi-Kao. Dissolution of the British Parliament 1832-1931. LC 79-127433. (Columbia University Studies in the Social Sciences: No. 396). Repr. of 1934 ed. 12.50 (ISBN 0-404-51396-4). AMS Pr.

Webb, Sidney & Webb, Beatrice. A Constitution for the Socialist Commonwealth of Great Britain. LC 75-28805. 416p. 1975. Repr. of 1920 ed. 26.95 (ISBN 0-521-20851-3). Cambridge U Pr.

--History of English Local Government, 11 vols. Incl. Vol. 1. 28.50x (ISBN 0-7146-1372-X); Vols. 2 & 3. 57.50x set (ISBN 0-7146-1373-8); Vol. 4. 28.50x (ISBN 0-7146-1374-6); Vol. 5. 29.50x (ISBN 0-7146-1375-4); Vol. 6. 28.50x (ISBN 0-7146-1376-2); Vol. 7; Vols. 8 & 9; Vol. 10. 27.50x (ISBN 0-7146-1379-7); Vol. 11. 27.50x (ISBN 0-7146-1380-0). 1963 (F Cass Co). Biblio Dist.

Wheare, Kenneth C. Government by Committee: An Essay on the British Constitution. LC 78-31211. 1979. Repr. of 1955 ed. lib. bdg. 22.50x (ISBN 0-313-20955-3, WHGC). Greenwood.

Willis, John. The Parliamentary Powers of English Government Departments. Repr. of 1933 ed. 15.50 (ISBN 0-384-68640-0). Johnson Repr.

Wolff, Richard D. The Economics of Colonialism: Britain & Kenya, 1870-1930. (Economic History Ser.). 1974. 17.50x (ISBN 0-300-01639-5). Yale U Pr.

GREAT BRITAIN–POLITICS AND GOVERNMENT–SOURCES

Great Britain Public Record Office. Syllabus in English of the Documents Relating to England & Other Kingdoms, 3 Vols. LC 78-168243. Repr. of 1885 ed. Set. 172.50 (ISBN 0-404-03130-7). AMS Pr.

Greene, Douglas, ed. Diaries of the Popish Plot. LC 77-938. 1977. 40.00 (ISBN 0-8201-1288-7). Schol Facsimiles.

Marsh, Henry. British Documents of Liberty: From Earliest Times to Universal Suffrage. LC 76-174227. 224p. 1972. 14.50 (ISBN 0-8386-1066-8). Fairleigh Dickinson.

Minogue, M. Documents on Contemporary British Government: British Government & Constitutional Change, Vol. 1. LC 76-26374. 1977. 39.95 (ISBN 0-521-21437-8); pap. 12.95x (ISBN 0-521-29148-8). Cambridge U Pr.

Treharne, R. F. & Sanders, I. J., eds. Documents of the Baronial Movement of Reform & Rebellion, 1258-1267. (Oxford Medieval Texts Ser). 1973. 52.50x (ISBN 0-19-822222-X). Oxford U Pr.

GREAT BRITAIN–POLITICS AND GOVERNMENT–499-1066

Chadwick, Hector M. Studies on Anglo-Saxon Institutions. LC 63-15152. 1963. Repr. of 1905 ed. 16.00 (ISBN 0-8462-0361-8). Russell.

GREAT BRITAIN–POLITICS AND GOVERNMENT–1066-1485

Chrimes, S. B. An Introduction to the Administrative History of Mediaeval England. 3rd ed. (Studies in Mediaeval History: Vol. 7). 285p. 1966. 36.00x (ISBN 0-631-09170-X, Pub. by Basil Blackwell); pap. 8.95 (ISBN 0-631-12141-2, Pub. by Basil Blackwell). Biblio Dist.

Chrimes, Stanley B. English Constitutional Ideas in the Fifteenth Century. LC 75-41057. (BCL Ser.: No. II). Repr. of 1936 ed. 28.50 (ISBN 0-404-14653-8). AMS Pr.

Clarke, Maude V. Fourteenth Century Studies. facs. ed. Sutherland, L. G. & McKisack, M., eds. LC 67-30181. (Essay Index Reprint Ser). 1937. 18.50 (ISBN 0-8369-0310-2). Arno.

Edwards, Goronwy. The Second Century of the English Parliament. 1978. 22.50x (ISBN 0-19-822479-6). Oxford U Pr.

Hewitt, J. The Organization of War Under Edward III, 1338-62. 216p. 1966. 22.00x (ISBN 0-7190-0066-1, Pub. by Manchester U Pr England). State Mutual Bk.

Kealey, Edward J. Roger of Salisbury, Viceroy of England. LC 78-92681. (Illus.). 350p. 1972. 25.00x (ISBN 0-520-01985-7). U of Cal Pr.

Morris, W. A. & Dunham, W. H., eds. English Government at Work, 1327-1336, Vol. 3 Local Administration & Justice. 1968. Repr. of 1950 ed. 12.00 (ISBN 0-910956-30-8). Medieval Acad.

Morris, W. A. & Strayer, J. R., eds. English Government at Work, 1327-1336, Vol. 2 Fiscal Administration. 1968. Repr. of 1947 ed. 12.00 (ISBN 0-910956-22-7). Medieval Acad.

Ogilvie, Charles. The King's Government & the Common Law, Fourteen Seventy-One to Sixteen Forty-One. LC 78-6586. 1978. Repr. of 1958 ed. lib. bdg. 20.75x (ISBN 0-313-20492-6, OGKG). Greenwood.

Prestwich, Michael. War, Politics & Finance Under Edward I. 317p. 1972. 17.50x (ISBN 0-87471-116-9). Rowman.

White, Albert B. Self-Government at the King's Command. LC 74-5927. 130p. 1974. Repr. of 1933 ed. lib. bdg. 15.00 (ISBN 0-8371-7526-7, WHKC). Greenwood.

Willard, J. F. & Morris, W. A., eds. English Government at Work, 1327-1336, Vol. 1 Central & Prerogative Administration. 1965. Repr. of 1940 ed. 18.00 (ISBN 0-910956-14-6). Medieval Acad.

Young, Charles R. English Borough & Royal Administration, 1130-1307. LC 61-16910. 1961. 12.50 (ISBN 0-8223-0202-0). Duke.

GREAT BRITAIN–POLITICS AND GOVERNMENT–1485-1603

Abbott, L. W. Law Reporting in England Fourteen Eighty Five-Fifteen Eighty Five. (University of London Legal Ser.: No. 10). (Illus.). 328p. 1973. text ed. 65.00x (ISBN 0-485-13410-1, Athlone Pr). Humanities.

Barnett, Richard C. Place, Profit, & Power: A Study of the Servants of William Cecil, Elizabethan Statesman. LC 77-97023. (James Sprunt Studies in History & Political Science: No. 51). 1969. pap. text ed. 7.50x (ISBN 0-8078-5051-9). U of NC Pr.

Baumer, Franklin L. Early Tudor Theory of Kingship. LC 66-13162. 1966. Repr. of 1940 ed. 8.50 (ISBN 0-8462-0715-X). Russell.

Beer, Barrett L. Northumberland: The Political Career of John Dudley, Earl of Warwick & Duke of Northumberland. LC 73-77386. 180p. 1974. 12.00x (ISBN 0-87338-140-8). Kent St U Pr.

Chrimes, S. B. Henry VII. LC 72-78947. (English Monarch Ser.). (Illus.). 400p. 1973. 31.50x (ISBN 0-520-02266-1) (ISBN 0-520-04414-2). U of Cal Pr.

Crowder, C. M., ed. English Society & Government in the Fifteenth Century. LC 68-79460. (Selections from History Today Ser.,No. 2). (Illus.). 1967. 5.00 (ISBN 0-05-000809-9); pap. 3.95 (ISBN 0-685-09164-3). Dufour.

Elizabeth First Queen Of England. Public Speaking of Queen Elizabeth: Selections from the Official Addresses. Rice, George P., Jr., ed. Repr. of 1951 ed. 11.50 (ISBN 0-404-05288-6). AMS Pr.

Elton, G. R. Studies in Tudor & Stuart Politics & Government: Papers & Reviews, 1946-1972, 2 vols. LC 73-79305. 700p. 1974. 60.00 set (ISBN 0-521-20388-0); Vol. 1. 41.95 (ISBN 0-521-20282-5); Vol. 2. 29.95 (ISBN 0-521-20288-4). Cambridge U Pr.

Elton, Geoffrey R. Policy & Police: The Enforcement of the Reformation in the Age of Cromwell. LC 79-172831. 400p. 1972. 41.95 (ISBN 0-521-08383-4). Cambridge U Pr.

--Tudor Revolution in Government. 1959. 54.00 (ISBN 0-521-04892-3); pap. 15.95x (ISBN 0-521-09235-3, 235). Cambridge U Pr.

Esler, Anthony. Aspiring Mind of the Elizabethan Younger Generation. LC 66-26025. 1966. 12.75 (ISBN 0-8223-0054-0). Duke.

Gammon, Samuel R. Statesman & Schemer: William, First Lord Paget, Tudor Minister. (Illus.). 293p. 1973. 19.50 (ISBN 0-208-01405-5, Archon). Shoe String.

Gilkes, R. K. The Tudor Parliament. 192p. (Orig.). 1969. 5.00x (ISBN 0-87471-329-3). Rowman.

Greaves, Richard L. Elizabeth First, Queen of England. (Problems in European Civilization Ser). 1974. pap. text ed. 4.95x (ISBN 0-669-86371-8). Heath.

Greenleaf, W. H. Order, Empiricism & Politics: Two Traditions of English Political Thought, 1500-1700. LC 80-10499. (University of Hull Publications). vi, 299p. 1980. Repr. of 1964 ed. lib. bdg. 25.00x (ISBN 0-313-22324-6, GROE). Greenwood.

Ham, Randall E. The County & the Kingdom: Sir Herbert Croft & the Elizabethan State. 316p. 1977. pap. text ed. 11.75 (ISBN 0-8191-0260-1). U Pr of Amer.

Hicks, Michael. False Fleeting Perjur'd Clarence. (Illus.). 272p. 1980. text ed. 22.00x (ISBN 0-904387-44-5). Humanities.

Hirst, D. The Representative of the People? LC 75-9283. 320p. 1975. 35.50 (ISBN 0-521-20810-6). Cambridge U Pr.

Hurstfield, Joel. Freedom, Corruption, & Government in Elizabethan England. LC 73-76380. 368p. 1973. pap. text ed. 16.50x (ISBN 0-674-31925-7). Harvard U Pr.

--The Illusion of Power in Tudor Politics. (Creighton Lectures in History 1978 Ser.). (Orig.). 1979. pap. text ed. 4.75x (ISBN 0-485-14123-X, Athlone Pr). Humanities.

Kelly, J. Thomas. Thorns on the Tudor Rose: Monks, Rogues, Vagabonds, & Sturdy Beggars. LC 76-58547. 1977. 3.00x (ISBN 0-87805-029-9). U Pr of Miss.

Lander, J. R. Conflict & Stability in Fifteenth Century England. 3rd ed. 1977. pap. 5.75x (ISBN 0-09-095741-5, Hutchinson U Lib). Humanities.

Lehmberg, S. E. The Later Parliaments of Henry VIII, 1536-1547. LC 76-7804. 1977. 49.95 (ISBN 0-521-21256-1). Cambridge U Pr.

--Reformation Parliament Fifteen Twenty-Nine - Fifteen Thirty-Six. LC 70-85723. (Illus., Orig.). 1970. 35.50 (ISBN 0-521-07655-2). Cambridge U Pr.

Loades, D. M. Politics & the Nation, Fourteen Fifty-Sixteen Sixty: Obedience, Resistance & Public Order. Elton, Y. R., ed. (Fontana Library of English History). 484p. 1974. text ed. 22.25 (ISBN 0-901759-34-1). Humanities.

--The Reign of Mary Tudor: Politics, Government & Religions in England Fifteen Fifty-Three to Fifteen Fifty-Eight. LC 79-16479. 1979. 25.00x (ISBN 0-312-67029-X). St Martin.

Mosse, George L. Struggle for Sovereignty in England. 1968. lib. bdg. 14.50x (ISBN 0-374-95947-1). Octagon.

Ogilvie, Charles. The King's Government & the Common Law, Fourteen Seventy-One to Sixteen Forty-One. LC 78-6586. 1978. Repr. of 1958 ed. lib. bdg. 20.75x (ISBN 0-313-20492-6, OGKG). Greenwood.

Pickthorn, Kenneth. Early Tudor Government, 2 Vols. 1967. lib. bdg. 45.00x (ISBN 0-374-96441-6). Octagon.

Pollard, Albert F. Wolsey. LC 74-33897. (Illus.). 1978. Repr. of 1953 ed. lib. bdg. 32.25x (ISBN 0-8371-7997-1, POWO). Greenwood.

Ponko, Vincent, Jr. Privy Council & the Spirit of Elizabethan Economic Management. LC 68-24356. (Transactions Ser.: Vol. 58, Pt. 4). 1968. pap. 1.00 (ISBN 0-87169-584-7). Am Philos.

Poynet, John, compiled by. A Shorte Treatise of Politike Power. LC 72-38220. (English Experience Ser.: No. 484). 184p. 1972. Repr. of 1556 ed. 11.50 (ISBN 90-221-0484-2). Walter J Johnson.

Proclamations II, Chronological Series, 2 vols. Incl. No. 368. Proclamadion for the Marchauntes Adventurers. LC 74-171743. Repr. of 1559 ed (ISBN 90-221-0368-4); No. 369. By the Queene, Forbidding Unlicensed Plays. LC 78-171744. Repr. of 1559 ed (ISBN 90-221-0369-2); No. 370. A Proclamation Agaynst Breaking Monumentes of Antiquitie. LC 71-171745. Repr. of 1560 ed (ISBN 90-221-0370-6); No. 371. By the Queene, Forbidding Export of Armour to Russia. LC 75-171746. Repr. of 1561 ed (ISBN 90-221-0371-4); No. 372. This Is the Ordinance for the Quenes Swannes. LC 79-171747. Repr. of 1564 ed (ISBN 90-221-0371-4); No. 373. By the Queene, Against Ill-Treatment of "Informers". LC 72-171748. Repr. of 1566 ed (ISBN 90-221-0372-2); No. 374. By the Queene, Against the Earl of Northumberland. LC 76-171749. Repr. of 1569 ed (ISBN 90-221-0373-0); No. 375. By the Queene, a Proclamation Concerning Hattes & Cappes. LC 70-171750 (ISBN 90-221-0374-9); No. 376. By the Queene, for Discovering Authors of Libels. LC 74-171751. Repr. of 1576 ed (ISBN 90-221-0375-7); By the Queene, for Sowing Lands with Flax. LC 78-171752. (No. 377). Repr. of 1597 ed (ISBN 90-221-0376-5); No. 243. The King's Maiesties Declaration Concerning Lawfull Sports. LC 77-26398. Repr. of 1618 ed (ISBN 90-221-0377-3). (English Experience Ser.: Nos. 243, 368-377). 1970-71. Set. 21.00 (ISBN 90-221-0368-4). Walter J Johnson.

Saunders, Laurence. A Trewe Mirrour of Glase Wherin We Maye Beholde the Wofull State of Thys Our Realme of Englande. LC 74-28884. (English Experience Ser.: No. 761). 1975. Repr. of 1556 ed. 3.50 (ISBN 90-221-0761-2). Walter J Johnson.

Sharpe, Kevin. Sir Robert Cotton, Fifteen Eighty-Six to Sixteen Thirty-One: History & Politics in Early Modern England. (OHM Ser.). (Illus.). 284p. 1979. 36.00x (ISBN 0-19-821877-X). Oxford U Pr.

Stone, Lawrence. The Causes of the English Revolution. 1972. pap. 3.95x (ISBN 0-06-131678-4, TB1678, Torch). Har-Row.

Tawney, Richard H. Business & Politics Under James I: Lionel Cranfield As Merchant & Minister. LC 73-94147. (Illus.). xii, 325p. 1976. Repr. of 1958 ed. 20.00 (ISBN 0-8462-1790-2). Russell.

Youngs, F. A. The Proclamations of the Tudor Queens. LC 75-30442. 304p. 1976. 46.50 (ISBN 0-521-21044-5). Cambridge U Pr.

GREAT BRITAIN–POLITICS AND GOVERNMENT–1603-1714

Alexander, Michael V. Charles I's Lord Treasurer: Sir Richard Weston, Earl of Portland (1577-1635) LC 74-34370. 1975. text ed. 18.00x (ISBN 0-8078-1248-X). U of NC Pr.

Ashley, Maurice. Magna Carta in the Seventeenth Century. LC 65-23456. (Illus., Orig.). 1965. pap. 1.95x (ISBN 0-8139-0014-X). U Pr of Va.

Aylmer, G. E. The State's Servants: The Civil Service of the English Republic 1649-1660. (Illus.). 498p. 1973. 35.00x (ISBN 0-7100-7637-1). Routledge & Kegan.

Blackwood, B. G. The Lancashire Gentry & the Great Rebellion 1640-60. (Illus.). 1978. text ed. 33.75x (ISBN 0-7190-1334-8). Humanities.

Brailsford, H. N. The Levellers & the English Revolution. Hill, Christopher, ed. 1961. 22.50x (ISBN 0-8047-0095-8). Stanford U Pr.

Brown, Louise F. Political Activities of the Baptists & the Fifth Monarchy Men in England During the Interregnum. 1964. Repr. of 1911 ed. 20.50 (ISBN 0-8337-0399-4). B Franklin.

Brunton, Douglas & Pennington, D. H. Members of the Long Parliament. 1968. Repr. of 1954 ed. 18.50 (ISBN 0-208-00686-9, Archon). Shoe String.

Cannon, J. Parliamentary Reform: 1640-1832. LC 72-83588. (Illus.). 288p. 1973. pap. 11.50 (ISBN 0-521-09736-3). Cambridge U Pr.

Cope, Esther S. & Coates, Willson H. Short Parliament of Sixteen-Forty: Proceedings. 340p. 1977. 18.50x (ISBN 0-8476-1473-5). Rowman.

Cotton, Sir Robert B. The Danger Wherein the Kingdome Now Standeth, & the Remedie. LC 74-28839. (No. 721). 1975. Repr. of 1628 ed. 3.50 (ISBN 90-221-0721-3). Walter J Johnson.

Crowther-Hunt, Norman. Two Early Political Associations: The Quakers & the Dissenting Deputies in the Age of Sir Robert Walpole. LC 78-23805. 1979. Repr. of 1961 ed. lib. bdg. 18.75x (ISBN 0-313-21036-5, HUTW). Greenwood.

Defoe, Daniel. Best of Defoe's Review. facs. ed. Payne, William L., ed. LC 73-128233. (Essay Index Reprint Ser). 1951. 19.50 (ISBN 0-8369-1873-8). Arno.

D'Ewes, Simonds. Journal of Sir Simonds D'Ewes from the First Recess of the Long Parliament to the Withdrawal of King Charles from London. Coates, Willson H., ed. LC 71-122400. 1970. Repr. of 1942 ed. 27.50 (ISBN 0-208-00948-5, Archon). Shoe String.

Downie, J. A. Robert Harley & the Press. LC 78-67810. 1979. 33.50 (ISBN 0-521-22187-0). Cambridge U Pr.

Eccleshall, Robert. Order & Reason in Politics: Theories of Absolute & Limited Monarchy in Early Modern England. 1978. text ed. 24.95x (ISBN 0-19-713431-9). Oxford U Pr.

Elton, G. R. Studies in Tudor & Stuart Politics & Government: Papers & Reviews, 1946-1972, 2 vols. LC 73-79305. 700p. 1974. 60.00 set (ISBN 0-521-20388-0); Vol. 1. 41.95 (ISBN 0-521-20282-5); Vol. 2. 29.95 (ISBN 0-521-20288-4). Cambridge U Pr.

Foster, Elizabeth R., ed. Proceedings in Parliament 1610, 2 vols. Incl. Vol. 1. The House of Lords. (Illus.). lxix, 366p; Vol. 2. The House of Commons. (Illus.). xxi, 422p. (Historical Publications, Manuscripts & Edited Texts Ser.: No. 22 & 23). 1966. Set. 50.00x (ISBN 0-300-00462-1). Yale U Pr.

Gadave, Renne. Un Theoricien Anglais Du Droit Public Au Xvlle Siecle. Mayer, J. P., ed. LC 78-67351. (European Political Thought Ser.). (Fr.). 1979. Repr. of 1907 ed. lib. bdg. 16.00x (ISBN 0-405-11698-5). Arno.

Gardiner, Samuel R. The First Two Stuarts & the Puritan Revolution - 1603-1660. 5.25 (ISBN 0-8446-0103-9). Peter Smith.

Gardiner, Samuel R., ed. Great Britain House of Lords: Notes of the Debates in the House of Lords, 1621. LC 75-168190. (Camden Society, London. Publications, First Ser.: No. 103). Repr. of 1870 ed. 14.00 (ISBN 0-404-50203-2). AMS Pr.

Geikie, Roderick, et al. Dutch Barrier, 1705-1719. LC 69-10096. 1969. Repr. of 1930 ed. lib. bdg. 18.75x (ISBN 0-8371-0082-8, GEDB). Greenwood.

Glassey, Lionel K. Politics & the Appointment of Justices of the Peace: 1675-1720. (Historical Monographs). 1979. 29.00x (ISBN 0-19-821875-3). Oxford U Pr.

Great Britain House Of Commons. Debates in the House of Commons in 1625. Gardiner, Samuel R., ed. 1873. 22.50 (ISBN 0-384-19810-4). Johnson Repr.

Great Britain House Of Lords - 1621. Notes of the Debates in the House of Lords. 1870. 15.50 (ISBN 0-384-19790-6). Johnson Repr.

Great Britain House of Lords - 1624. Notes of the Debates in the House of Lords. Gardiner, Samuel R., ed. 1879. 22.50 (ISBN 0-384-19800-7). Johnson Repr.

Greenleaf, W. H. Order, Empiricism & Politics: Two Traditions of English Political Thought, 1500-1700. LC 80-10499. (University of Hull Publications). vi, 299p. 1980. Repr. of 1964 ed. lib. bdg. 25.00x (ISBN 0-313-22324-6, GROE). Greenwood.

Gruenfelder, John K. Influence in Early Stuart Elections, 1604-1640. 294p. 1981. 22.50 (ISBN 0-8142-0316-7). Ohio St U Pr.

Haller, William. Liberty & Reformation in the Puritan Revolution. LC 54-6482. 410p. 1955. pap. 7.50x (ISBN 0-231-08547-8, 47). Columbia U Pr.

Haller, William & Davies, Godfrey, eds. The Leveller Tracts 1647-1653: 1647-1653. 1964. 8.50 (ISBN 0-8446-1218-9). Peter Smith.

Ham, Randall E. The County & the Kingdom: Sir Herbert Croft & the Elizabethan State. 316p. 1977. pap. text ed. 11.75 (ISBN 0-8191-0260-1). U Pr of Amer.

Hexter, Jack H. Reign of King Pym. (Historical Studies: No. 48). 1941. 10.00x (ISBN 0-674-75401-8). Harvard U Pr.

Higham, Florence M. Charles First: A Study. LC 78-21342. 1979. Repr. of 1932 ed. lib. bdg. 22.50x (ISBN 0-8371-6188-6, HICH). Greenwood.

Hirst, D. The Representative of the People? LC 75-9283. 320p. 1975. 35.50 (ISBN 0-521-20810-6). Cambridge U Pr.

His Majesties Declaration of the Causes Which Moved Him to Dissolve the Last Parliament. LC 79-38175. (English Experience Ser.: No. 450). 1972. Repr. of 1628 ed. 7.00 (ISBN 90-221-0450-8). Walter J Johnson.

Holmes, Geoffrey S. British Politics in the Reign of Queen Anne. 1967. 25.00 (ISBN 0-312-10500-2). St Martin.

Howell, Roger, Jr. Cromwell. (Library of World Biography). 1977. 8.95 (ISBN 0-316-37581-0). Little.

Jones, Rufus M. Mysticism & Democracy in the English Commonwealth. 1965. lib. bdg. 12.50x (ISBN 0-374-94313-3). Octagon.

Jordan, Wilbur K. Men of Substance. 1967. lib. bdg. 15.00x (ISBN 0-374-94389-3). Octagon.

Judson, Margaret A. From Tradition to Political Reality: A Study of the Ideas Set Forth in Support of the Commonwealth Government in England, 1649-1653. (Studies in British History & Culture: Vol. Vii). 121p. 1980. 13.50 (ISBN 0-208-01836-0). Shoe String.

Kaplan, Lawrence. Politics & Religion during the English Revolution: The Scots & the Long Parliament 1643-1645. LC 76-13255. 1976. 16.50x (ISBN 0-8147-4563-6). NYU Pr.

Kenyon, J. P. Robert Spencer, Earl of Sunderland, 1641-1702. LC 75-8480. (Illus.). 396p. 1975. Repr. of 1958 ed. lib. bdg. 21.50x (ISBN 0-8371-8150-X, KERS). Greenwood.

Kirby, Ethyn W. William Prynne: A Study in Puritanism. LC 73-173528. (Illus.). 1972. Repr. of 1931 ed. 12.00 (ISBN 0-8462-1622-1). Russell.

Kitchin, George. Sir Roger L'Estrange: A Contribution to the History of the Press in the 17th Century. LC 74-120325. (English Book Trade). Repr. of 1913 ed. 17.50x (ISBN 0-678-00703-9). Kelley.

Lacey, Douglas R. Dissent & Parliamentary Politics in England 1661-1689: A Study in the Perpetuation & Tempering of Parliamentarianism. 1969. 35.00 (ISBN 0-8135-0594-1). Rutgers U Pr.

Loades, D. M. Politics & the Nation, Fourteen Fifty-Sixteen Sixty: Obedience, Resistance & Public Order. Elton, Y. R., ed. (Fontana Library of English History). 484p. 1974. text ed. 22.25 (ISBN 0-901759-34-1). Humanities.

Marriott, John A. Crisis of English Liberty, a History of the Stuart Monarchy & the Puritan Revolution. Repr. of 1930 ed. lib. bdg. 18.75x (ISBN 0-8371-4272-5, MAEL). Greenwood.

Mitchell, Williams M. The Rise of the Revolutionary Party in the English House of Commons, 1603-1629. LC 75-31471. 209p. 1976. Repr. of 1957 ed. lib. bdg. 14.00x (ISBN 0-8371-8535-1, MIRR). Greenwood.

Morgan, Wm. T. English Political Parties & Leaders in the Reign of Queen Anne, 1702-1710. (Yale Historical Studies, Miscellany: No. VII). 1920. 47:50x (ISBN 0-685-69845-9). Elliots Bks.

Morton, A. L., ed. Freedom in Arms: A Selection of Leveller Writings. LC 74-30435. 1976. pap. 2.25 (ISBN 0-7178-0425-9). Intl Pub Co.

Mosse, George L. Struggle for Sovereignty in England. 1968. lib. bdg. 14.50x (ISBN 0-374-95947-1). Octagon.

Nenner, Howard. By Colour of Law: Legal Culture & Constitutional Politics in England, 1660-1689. LC 76-25631. 1977. lib. bdg. 16.00x (ISBN 0-226-57275-7). U of Chicago Pr.

Notestein, Wallace. House of Commons, Sixteen Four to Sixteen Ten. LC 72-118733. 1971. 45.00x (ISBN 0-300-01356-6). Yale U Pr.

Ogilvie, Charles. The King's Government & the Common Law, Fourteen Seventy-One to Sixteen Forty-One. LC 78-6586. 1978. Repr. of 1958 ed. lib. bdg. 20.75x (ISBN 0-313-20492-6, OGKG). Greenwood.

Pease, T. C. The Leveller Movement. 8.00 (ISBN 0-8446-1345-2). Peter Smith.

Petyt, George. Lex Parliamentaria: or, a Treatise of the Law & Custom of the Parliaments of England. Straka, Gerald M., ed. Incl. The Defense of the Parliament of England in the Case of James II, 2 vols. in 1. Georgeson, B. Repr. of 1692 ed. LC 72-83167. (English Studies Ser.). 1974. 26.00 (ISBN 0-8420-1420-9). Scholarly Res Inc.

Ruigh, Robert E. Parliament of 1624: Politics & Foreign Policy. LC 72-135548. (Historical Studies: No. 87). (Illus.). 1971. 20.00x (ISBN 0-674-65225-8). Harvard U Pr.

Russell, Conrad. Parliaments & English Politics 1621-1629. LC 78-40498. 1979. 48.00x (ISBN 0-19-822482-6). Oxford U Pr.

Schwoerer, Lois. The Declaration of Rights, Sixteen Eighty-Nine. 384p. 1981. 26.50 (ISBN 0-8018-2430-3). Johns Hopkins.

Schwoerer, Lois G. The English Declaration of Rights, 1689. LC 81-2942. (Illus.). 384p. 1981. text ed. 26.50x (ISBN 0-8018-2430-3). Johns Hopkins.

Sensabaugh, George. That Grand Whig Milton. LC 67-29815. Repr. of 1952 ed. 14.00 (ISBN 0-405-08948-1, Blom Pubns). Arno.

Sharpe, Kevin. Sir Robert Cotton, Fifteen Eighty-Six to Sixteen Thirty-One: History & Politics in Early Modern England. (OHM Ser.). (Illus.). 284p. 1979. 36.00x (ISBN 0-19-821877-X). Oxford U Pr.

Sharpe, Kevin, ed. Faction & Parliament: Essays in Early Stuart History. LC 77-30635. 1978. 37.50x (ISBN 0-19-822468-0). Oxford U Pr.

Sheridan, Thomas. Some Revelations on Irish History. Bannister, Saxe, ed. LC 73-102592. (Irish Culture & History Ser). Repr. of 1870 ed. 14.50 (ISBN 0-8046-0769-9). Kennikat.

Snyder, Henry L., ed. Marlborough-Godolphin Correspondence, 3 vols. 1975. Set. 169.00x (ISBN 0-19-822381-1). Oxford U Pr.

Sutton, Harry T. For King or Commons: Story of Cavaliers & Roundheads. 1978. pap. 3.50 (ISBN 0-7134-1727-7, Pub. by Batsford England). David & Charles.

Thomson, Mark A. Secretaries of State, 1681-1782. 206p. 1968. 28.00x (ISBN 0-7146-1521-8, F Cass Co). Biblio Dist.

Turner, Edward R. Cabinet Council of England in the Seventeenth & Eighteenth Centuries, 1622-1784, 2 pts, Vol. 2. Megaro, Gaudence, ed. LC 79-81481. (Repr. of 1930, 1932 eds.). 1970. Set. 30.00 (ISBN 0-8462-1390-7). Russell.

Verney, Ralph. Verney Papers. Bruce, John, ed. (Camden Society, London. Publcations, First Ser.: No. 31). Repr. of 1845 ed. 21.00 (ISBN 0-404-50131-1). AMS Pr.

--Verney Papers: Notes of Proceedings in the Long Parliament. Repr. of 1845 ed. 23.00 (ISBN 0-384-64365-5). Johnson Repr.

Wadsworth, James. The English Spanish Pilgrime. LC 71-25682. (English Experience Ser.: No. 275). 96p. 1970. Repr. of 1629 ed. 11.50 (ISBN 90-221-0275-0). Walter J Johnson.

Walcott, Robert, Jr. English Politics in the Early Eighteenth Century. LC 79-180622. (Illus.). vi, 291p. 1972. Repr. of 1956 ed. 14.00 (ISBN 0-8462-1649-3). Russell.

Ward, Nathaniel. Simple Cobler of Aggawam in America. Zall, Paul M., ed. LC 69-19107. 1969. 7.50x (ISBN 0-8032-0188-5). U of Nebr Pr.

White, Stephen D. Sir Edward Coke & "The Grievances of the Commonwealth," 1621-1628. LC 78-16418. (Studies in Legal History). 22.50x (ISBN 0-8078-1335-4). U of NC Pr.

Willson, David H. Privy Councillors in the House of Commons, 1604-1629. LC 76-120678. 1970. Repr. lib. bdg. 17.50x (ISBN 0-374-98639-8). Octagon.

Willson, David H., ed. Parliamentary Diary of Robert Bowyer, 1606-1607. LC 72-120677. 1970. Repr. lib. bdg. 22.50x (ISBN 0-374-98636-3). Octagon.

Winstanley, Gerrard. Works of Gerrard Winstanley. Sabine, George H., ed. LC 64-66399. 1965. Repr. of 1941 ed. 20.00 (ISBN 0-8462-0572-6). Russell.

Wither, George. Respublica Anglicana: The Historie of the Parliament. 1966. 24.50 (ISBN 0-8337-3852-6). B Franklin.

Worden, B. The Rump Parliament, 1648-1653. LC 73-77264. 500p. 1974. 41.95 (ISBN 0-521-20205-1); pap. 14.95 (ISBN 0-521-29213-1). Cambridge U Pr.

Zagorin, Perez. Court & the Country: The Beginning of the English Revolution. LC 72-104129. 1971. pap. text ed. 3.25x (ISBN 0-689-70275-2, 181). Atheneum.

Zaller, Robert. The Parliament of 1621: A Study in Constitutional Conflict. LC 77-104106. 1971. 24.50x (ISBN 0-520-01677-7). U of Cal Pr.

GREAT BRITAIN–POLITICS AND GOVERNMENT–18TH CENTURY

The American Controversy: A Bibliographical Study of the British Pamphlets About the American Disputes, 1764 to 1783, 2 vols. 1980. 60.00 (ISBN 0-686-31071-3). Biblio Soc Am.

Barnes, Donald G. George Third & William Pitt, 1783-1806. 1965. lib. bdg. 25.00x (ISBN 0-374-90399-9). Octagon.

Barnes, Michael J., ed. Politics & Personality Seventeen Sixty-Eighteen Twenty-Seven. LC 68-97214. (Selections from History Today Ser.: No. 6). (Illus.). 1967. 5.00 (ISBN 0-05-001533-8); pap. 3.95 (ISBN 0-685-09195-3). Dufour.

Black, Eugene C. The Association: British Extraparliamentary Political Organization, 1769-1793. LC 63-17195. (Historical Monographs Ser: No. 54). (Illus.). 1963. 17.50x (ISBN 0-674-05000-2). Harvard U Pr.

Bolingbroke, Viscount. The Idea of a Patriot King. Jackman, Sydney W., ed. LC 64-66066. 1965. pap. text ed. 1.25x (ISBN 0-672-60433-7). Irvington.

Brewer, J. Party Ideology & Popular Politics at the Accession of George Third. (Illus.). 400p. 1916. 39.00 (ISBN 0-521-21049-6). Cambridge U Pr.

Brooke, John. The Chatham Administration 1766-1768. LC 76-6170. 1976. Repr. of 1956 ed. lib. bdg. 24.00x (ISBN 0-8371-8869-5, BRCAD). Greenwood.

Brown, P. Chathamites. (Illus.). 1967. 22.50 (ISBN 0-312-13160-7). St Martin.

Burke, Edmond. Reflections on the Revolution in France. Bd. with The Rights of Man. Paine, Thomas (Anchor). Doubleday. pap. 3.95 (ISBN 0-385-08190-1, Anch). Doubleday.

Burke, Edmund. A Letter to the Sheriffs of Bristol: A Speech at Bristol on Parliamentary Conduct; a Letter to a Noble Lord. Murison, W., ed. LC 76-29423. Repr. of 1920 ed. 34.00 (ISBN 0-404-15344-5). AMS Pr.

--Selected Works. Bate, Walter J., ed. LC 75-9946. 536p. 1975. Repr. of 1960 ed. lib. bdg. 25.50x (ISBN 0-8371-8122-4, BUSEW). Greenwood.

--Selected Writings & Speeches. Stanlis, J. P., ed. 8.50 (ISBN 0-8446-1094-1). Peter Smith.

Cannon, J. Fox-North Coalition. LC 70-85715. 1970. 35.50 (ISBN 0-521-07606-4). Cambridge U Pr.

Cartwright, John. Commonwealth in Danger. 1968. Repr. of 1795 ed. 24.50 (ISBN 0-8337-0486-9). B Franklin.

Christie, Ian R. Myth & Reality in Late Eighteenth-Century British Politics & Other Papers. LC 73-104105. 1970. 25.75x (ISBN 0-520-01673-4). U of Cal Pr.

Courtney, C. P. Montesquieu & Burke. LC 74-2586. 204p. 1975. Repr. of 1963 ed. lib. bdg. 15.00x (ISBN 0-8371-7406-6, COMB). Greenwood.

Cowherd, Raymond G. Political Economists & the English Poor Laws: A Historical Study of the Influence of Classical Economics on the Formation of Social Welfare Policy. LC 76-8301. xvii, 300p. 1977. 18.00x (ISBN 0-8214-0233-1). Ohio U Pr.

Crowther-Hunt, Norman. Two Early Political Associations: The Quakers & the Dissenting Deputies in the Age of Sir Robert Walpole. LC 78-23805. 1979. Repr. of 1961 ed. lib. bdg. 18.75x (ISBN 0-313-21036-5, HUTW). Greenwood.

Davidson, William L. Political Thought in England. 256p. 1980. Repr. text ed. 20.00 (ISBN 0-89760-129-7, Telegraph). Dynamic Learn Corp.

Davis, Richard W. Political Change & Continuity: A Buckinghamshire Study. (Library of Politics & Society Ser.). 256p. 1972. 17.50 (ISBN 0-208-01307-5, Archon). Shoe String.

Dawson, P. M. The Unacknowledged Legislator: Shelley & Politics. 320p. 1980. 48.00x (ISBN 0-19-812095-8). Oxford U Pr.

Defoe, Daniel. Defoe's Review, 9 Vols. Bd. in 22 Pts. facsimile ed. 1704-1713. Repr. of 1938 ed. Set. 605.00 (ISBN 0-404-02020-8). AMS Pr.

Dickinson, H. T. Liberty & Property: Political Ideology in Eighteenth-Century Britain. LC 77-13477. 1978. text ed. 41.00x (ISBN 0-8419-0351-4). Holmes & Meier.

Downie, J. A. Robert Harley & the Press. LC 78-67810. 1979. 33.50 (ISBN 0-521-22187-0). Cambridge U Pr.

Everett, C. W., ed. The Letters of Junius. 1978. Repr. of 1927 ed. lib. bdg. 50.00 (ISBN 0-89760-201-3, Telegraph). Dynamic Learn Corp.

Gardiner, Samuel R., ed. Great Britain House of Commons: Parliamantary Debates in 1610. LC 70-168189. (Camden Society, London. Publications, First Ser.: No. 81). Repr. of 1862 ed. 17.50 (ISBN 0-404-50181-8). AMS Pr.

Ginter, Donald E., ed. Whig Organization in the General Election of 1790: Selections from the Blair Adam Papers. 1967. 23.75x (ISBN 0-520-00477-9). U of Cal Pr.

Glassey, Lionel K. Politics & the Appointment of Justices of the Peace: 1675-1720. (Historical Monographs). 1979. 29.00x (ISBN 0-19-821875-3). Oxford U Pr.

Goodwin, Albert. The Friends of Liberty: The English Democratic Movement in the Age of the French Revolution. LC 78-15673. (Illus.). 1979. text ed. 25.00x (ISBN 0-674-32339-4). Harvard U Pr.

Gunn, J. A. Factions No More: Attitudes to Party in Government Opposition in Eighteenth Century England. 276p. 1972. 30.00x (ISBN 0-7146-2595-7, F Cass Co). Biblio Dist.

Hill, ed. Edmund Burke on Government, Politics & Society. 1976. pap. 5.95 (ISBN 0-531-06069-1, Fontana Pap). Watts.

Lamont, Hammond, ed. Speech of Conciliation with America. 1977. Repr. of 1897 ed. lib. bdg. 15.00 (ISBN 0-8482-3370-0). Norwood Edns.

Laprade, William T. Public Opinion & Politics in Eighteenth Century England to the Fall of Walpole. LC 70-114538. 1971. Repr. of 1936 ed. lib. bdg. 19.00x (ISBN 0-8371-4806-5, LAPO). Greenwood.

--Public Opinion & Politics in Eighteenth Century England to the Fall of Walpole. 1973. lib. bdg. 25.00x (ISBN 0-374-94784-8). Octagon.

Leeds, Francis O. The Political Memoranda of Francis Fifth Duke of Leeds. Browning, O., ed. Repr. of 1884 ed. 22.50 (ISBN 0-384-32055-4). Johnson Repr.

McCrea, Brian. Henry Fielding & the Politics of Mid-Eighteenth-Century England. LC 80-14711. (South Atlantic Modern Language Association Award Study, 1979). 272p. 1981. 20.00x (ISBN 0-8203-0531-6). U of Ga Pr.

Magnus, Philip, ed. Edmund Burke: Selected Prose. 1977. Repr. of 1948 ed. lib. bdg. 10.00 (ISBN 0-8482-3368-9). Norwood Edns.

Mansfield, Harvey C., Jr. Statesmanship & Party Government. LC 65-17298. 1965. 12.00x (ISBN 0-226-50367-4). U of Chicago Pr.

Montagu, Mary W. Nonsense of Common Sense, 1737-1738. Halsband, Robert, ed. LC 71-129373. (Northwestern University. Humanities Series: No. 17). Repr. of 1947 ed. 14.50 (ISBN 0-404-50717-4). AMS Pr.

Murray, John J. George First, the Baltic & Whig Split of 1717: A Study in Diplomacy & Propaganda. LC 68-54009. 1969. 11.50x (ISBN 0-226-55380-9). U of Chicago Pr.

Namier, Lewis. Structure of Politics at the Accession of George 3rd. 2nd ed. 1957. 9.95 (ISBN 0-312-76720-X). St Martin.

Newcastle, Phelman-Holles T. A Narrative of the Changes in the Ministry, 1765-1767. Bateson, M., ed. 1965. Repr. of 1898 ed. 22.50 (ISBN 0-384-41195-9). Johnson Repr.

Nobbe, George. North Briton: A Study in Political Propaganda. LC 39-24192. Repr. of 1939 ed. 17.50 (ISBN 0-404-04779-3). AMS Pr.

Oliver, Frederick S. Endless Adventure. LC 78-123762. Repr. of 1935 ed. 47.50 (ISBN 0-404-04840-4). AMS Pr.

Ormond, Richard & Rogers, Malcolm. Dictionary of British Portraiture: Vol. 2, the Later Georgians to the Early Victorians; Historical Figures Born Between 1700 & 1800. Kilmurray, Elaine, ed. 240p. 1979. text ed. 49.50 (ISBN 0-19-520181-7). Oxford U Pr.

Paine, Thomas. Rights of Man. 1935. 9.95x (ISBN 0-460-00718-1, Evman). Biblio Dist.

--Rights of Man. 1976. pap. 3.95 (ISBN 0-8065-0548-6). Citadel Pr.

Quinton, Anthony. The Politics of Imperfection. LC 79-670245. 92p. 1979. 13.50 (ISBN 0-571-11285-4, Pub. by Faber & Faber). Merrimack Bk Serv.

Ralph, James. Case of Authors by Profession or Trade, 1758, Champion 1739. LC 66-10008. 1966. 26.00x (ISBN 0-8201-1037-X). Schol Facsimiles.

Reilly, Robin. William Pitt the Younger. LC 78-13050. (Illus.). 1979. 19.95 (ISBN 0-399-12130-7). Putnam.

Sack, James J. The Grenvillites, 1801-29: Party Politics & Factionalism in the Age of Pitt & Liverpool. LC 78-23288. 1979. 15.00 (ISBN 0-252-00713-1). U of Ill Pr.

Sedgwick, Romney, ed. House of Commons 1715-1754, Vols. 1 & 2. (Illus.). 1970. text ed. 39.95x (ISBN 0-19-519539-6). Oxford U Pr.

Smith, Robert A. Eighteenth Century English Politics. 224p. 1972. pap. text ed. 6.50 (ISBN 0-03-079280-0, Pub. by HR&W). Krieger.

Stevens, David H. Party Politics & English Journalism, 1702-1742. LC 66-27155. 1967. Repr. of 1916 ed. 8.50 (ISBN 0-8462-0954-3). Russell.

Thomson, Mark A. Secretaries of State, 1681-1782. 206p. 1968. 28.00x (ISBN 0-7146-1521-8, F Cass Co). Biblio Dist.

Toohey, Robert E. Liberty & Empire: British Radical Solutions to the American Problem, 1774-1776. LC 77-84068. 224p. 1978. 16.00 (ISBN 0-8131-1375-X). U Pr of Ky.

Turberville, Arthur S. House of Lords in the Eighteenth Century. Repr. of 1927 ed. lib. bdg. 22.50x (ISBN 0-8371-4557-0, TUHL). Greenwood.

Turner, Edward R. Cabinet Council of England in the Seventeenth & Eighteenth Centuries, 1622-1784, 2 pts, Vol. 2. Megaro, Gaudence, ed. LC 79-81481. (Repr. of 1930, 1932 eds.). 1970. Set. 30.00 (ISBN 0-8462-1390-7). Russell.

Voltaire. Letters on England. Tancock, Leonard, tr. from Fr. (Classics Ser.). 1980. pap. 3.95 (ISBN 0-14-044386-X). Penguin.

Williams, Basil. Life of William Pitt, Earl of Chatham, 2 Vols. 1966. lib. bdg. 47.50x (ISBN 0-374-98626-6). Octagon.

--Whig Supremacy, 1714-1760. 2nd ed. Stuart, C. H., ed. (Oxford History of England Ser.). 1962. 35.00x (ISBN 0-19-821710-2). Oxford U Pr.

Williams, E. N. Eighteenth-Century Constitution: Documents & Commentary. (English Constitutional History Ser). 47.95 (ISBN 0-521-06810-X); pap. 14.95x (ISBN 0-521-09123-3). Cambridge U Pr.

Wright, Thomas. England Under the House of Hanover, 2 Vols. LC 78-118512. 1971. Repr. of 1848 ed. Set. 35.00x (ISBN 0-8046-1260-9). Kennikat.

GREAT BRITAIN–POLITICS AND GOVERNMENT–19TH CENTURY

Anderson, Olive. Liberal State at War: English Politics & Economics During the Crimean War. 1967. 17.95 (ISBN 0-312-48265-5). St Martin.

Aspinall, Arthur. Lord Brougham & the Whig Party. LC 78-179576. (Illus.). 322p. 1972. Repr. of 1927 ed. 19.50 (ISBN 0-208-01240-0, Archon). Shoe String.

Bagehot, Walter. Collected Works of Walter Bagehot, Vols. 3 & 4. St. John Stevas, Norman, ed. LC 66-1165. 1968. Set. 50.00x (ISBN 0-674-14002-8). Harvard U Pr.

Bailey, Victor, ed. Policing & Punishment in Nineteenth Century Britain. (Crime, Law, & Deviance). 365p. 1981. 23.00 (ISBN 0-8135-0932-7). Rutgers U Pr.

Barker, Ernest. Political Thought in England, Eighteen Forty-Eight to Nineteen Fourteen. 2nd ed. LC 80-19766. (Home University Library of Modern Knowledge: 104). 256p. 1980. Repr. of 1928 ed. lib. bdg. 22.50x (ISBN 0-313-22216-9, BAPL). Greenwood.

Barnes, Michael J., ed. Politics & Personality Seventeen Sixty-Eighteen Twenty-Seven. LC 68-97214. (Selections from History Today Ser.: No. 6). (Illus.). 1967. 5.00 (ISBN 0-05-001533-8); pap. 3.95 (ISBN 0-685-09195-3). Dufour.

Bell, H. C. Lord Palmerston, 2 Vols. (Illus.). 1966. Repr. of 1936 ed. Set. 37.50 (ISBN 0-208-00438-6, Archon). Shoe String.

Besant, Annie. Selection of the Social & Political Pamphlets of Annie Besant 1874-1890. LC 78-114024. 1970. 22.50x (ISBN 0-678-00638-5). Kelley.

Bogdanor, Vernon. The People & the Party System: The Referendum & Electoral Reform in British Politics. LC 81-3895. 280p. Date not set. price not set (ISBN 0-521-24207-X); pap. price not set (ISBN 0-521-28525-9). Cambridge U Pr.

Brock, William R. Lord Liverpool & Liberal Toryism 1820-1827. 1967. Repr. of 1941 ed. 19.50 (ISBN 0-208-00428-9, Archon). Shoe String.

Brodrick, George C. History of England from Addington's Administration to the Close of William Fourth's Reign 1801-1837. rev. ed. Fotheringham, J. K., ed. LC 69-13841. Repr. of 1906 ed. lib. bdg. 20.00x (ISBN 0-8371-0924-8, BRHE). Greenwood.

Brynn, Edward. Crown & Castle: British Rule in Ireland 1800-1830. (Illus.). 1978. text ed. 32.00x (ISBN 0-7705-1496-0). Humanities.

Burke, Edmund. Selected Works. Bate, Walter J., ed. LC 75-9946. 536p. 1975. Repr. of 1960 ed. lib. bdg. 25.50x (ISBN 0-8371-8122-4, BUSEW). Greenwood.

Butler, David, ed. Coalitions in British Politics. LC 77-17791. 1978. 17.95x (ISBN 0-312-14503-9). St Martin.

Buxton, Sydney C. Finance & Politics: An Historical Study, 1783-1885 2 Vols. LC 66-21367. Repr. of 1888 ed. Set. 35.00x (ISBN 0-678-00164-2). Kelley.

Calhoun, Craig. The Question of Class Struggle: The Social Foundation of Popular Radicalism During the Industrial Revolution. LC 81-2018. 1981. lib. bdg. 25.00x (ISBN 0-226-09090-6). U of Chicago Pr.

Canning, George. George Canning & His Friends, Containing Hitherto Unpublished Letters, Jeux D'espirit, Etc, 2 Vols. in 1. Bagot, J., ed. LC 9-14585. 1969. Repr. of 1909 ed. 34.00 (ISBN 0-527-14800-8). Kraus Repr.

Cartwright, John. Commonwealth in Danger. 1968. Repr. of 1795 ed. 24.50 (ISBN 0-8337-0486-9). B Franklin.

Catalogue of British Parliamentary Papers 1801 - 1900. 310p. 1977. 45.00x (ISBN 0-686-19005-X, Pub. by Irish Academic Pr Ireland). Biblio Dist.

Cecil, David. Melbourne. (Power & Personality Ser.). (Illus.). 1979. pap. 6.95 (ISBN 0-517-53782-6, Dist. by Crown). Crown.

Cecil, Gwendolen. Life of Robert, Marquis of Salisbury: By His Daughter, 4 Vols. in 2. Repr. of 1932 ed. Set. 54.00 (ISBN 0-527-15550-0). Kraus Repr.

Chester, Norman. The English Administrative System, Seventeen Eighty to Eighteen Seventy. 416p. 1981. 59.00x (ISBN 0-19-822643-8). Oxford U Pr.

Christie, Ian R. Myth & Reality in Late Eighteenth-Century British Politics & Other Papers. LC 73-104105. 1970. 25.75x (ISBN 0-520-01673-4). U of Cal Pr.

Clark, G. Kitson. Expanding Society: Britain 1830-1900. 1967. 23.95 (ISBN 0-521-05897-X). Cambridge U Pr.
Cobbett, William. History of the Last Hundred Days of English Freedom. LC 73-114501. 1971. Repr. of 1921 ed. lib. bdg. 15.00x (ISBN 0-8371-4780-8, COLH). Greenwood.
Conacher, J. B. Aberdeen Coalition, 1852-1855: A Study in Mid-Nineteenth-Century Party Politics. LC 68-10148. (Illus.). 1968. 64.00 (ISBN 0-521-04711-0). Cambridge U Pr.
Cookson, J. E. Lord Liverpool's Administration: The Crucial Years, 1815-1822. xii, 422p. (Orig.). 1975. 25.00 (ISBN 0-208-01495-0, Archon). Shoe String.
Cowherd, Raymond G. Political Economists & the English Poor Laws: A Historical Study of the Influence of Classical Economics on the Formation of Social Welfare Policy. LC 76-8301. xvii, 300p. 1977. 18.00x (ISBN 0-8214-0233-1). Ohio U Pr.
Cowling, Maurice. Eighteen Sixty-Seven Disraeli, Gladstone & Revolution. (Cambridge Studies in the History & Theory of Politics). 1967. 49.95 (ISBN 0-521-04740-4). Cambridge U Pr.
Cromwell, V., et al. Aspects of Government in Nineteenth Century Britain. (Government & Society in 19th Century Britain Ser.). 144p. 1978. 20.00x (ISBN 0-7165-2212-8, Pub. by Irish Academic Pr Ireland). Biblio Dist.
Crosby, Travis L. English Farmers & the Politics of Protection. 228p. 1977. text ed. 20.75x (ISBN 0-85527-116-7). Humanities.
Davidson, William L. Political Thought in England. 256p. 1980. Repr. text ed. 20.00 (ISBN 0-89760-129-7, Telegraph). Dynamic Learn Corp.
Dawson, P. M. The Unacknowledged Legislator: Shelley & Politics. 320p. 1980. 48.00x (ISBN 0-19-812095-8). Oxford U Pr.
Derry, John W. Radical Tradition: Tom Paine to Lloyd George. 1967. 19.95 (ISBN 0-312-66185-1). St Martin.
Disraeli, Benjamin. Whigs & Whiggism. LC 70-118466. 1971. Repr. of 1913 ed. 17.50 (ISBN 0-8046-1215-3). Kennikat.
--The Works of Benjamin Disraeli, Earl of Beaconsfield, 20 vols. Incl. Vols. 1-2. Vivian Grey: A Romance of Youth. LC 76-12451; Vols. 3-4. The Young Duke, etc. LC 76-12450; Vols. 5-6. Contarini Fleming: A Psychological Romance, etc. LC 76-12449; Vol. 7. Alroy: Or, the Prince of the Captivity. LC 76-12448; Vols. 8-9. Henrietta Temple: A Love Story, etc. LC 76-12447; Vols. 10-11. Venetia, etc. LC 76-12445; Vols. 12-13. Coningsby: Or, the New Generation & Selected Speeches. LC 76-12444; Vols. 17-18. Lothair & Letters to His Sister. LC 76-12443; Vols. 19-20. Endymion, Miscellania. LC 76-12442; Vols. 14-16. Sybil; Tancred. LC 76-148746. (Illus.). Repr. of 1904 ed. Set. 550.00 (ISBN 0-404-08800-7); 27.50 ea. AMS Pr.
Drescher, Seymour I. Tocqueville & England. LC 63-20764. (Historical Monographs Ser: No. 55). 1964. 14.00x (ISBN 0-674-89430-8). Harvard U Pr.
Dugdale, Blanche E. Arthur James Balfour, First Earl of Balfour. LC 70-97328. Repr. of 1936 ed. lib. bdg. 32.50x (ISBN 0-8371-2893-5, DUI&). Greenwood.
Elletson, D. H. Chamberlains. 1966. text ed. 6.00x (ISBN 0-7195-0352-3). Humanities.
Eyck, Erich. Gladstone. Miall, Bernard, tr. LC 68-56055. Repr. of 1938 ed. 25.00x (ISBN 0-678-05045-7). Kelley.
Flick, Carlos T. The Birmingham Political Union & the Movements for Reform in Britain, 1830-1839. (Illus.). 1978. 17.50 (ISBN 0-208-01752-6, Archon). Shoe String.
Gash, Norman. Politics in the Age of Peel. 1971. pap. 2.95x (ISBN 0-393-00564-X, Norton Lib). Norton.
--Politics in the Age of Peel: A Study in the Technique of Parliamentary Representation, 1830-1850. 2nd ed. 518p. 1977. text ed. 23.50x (ISBN 0-391-00676-2). Humanities.
--Reaction & Reconstruction in English Politics, 1832 to 1852. LC 81-1813. 227p. 1981. Repr. of 1965 ed. lib. bdg. 27.50x (ISBN 0-313-22927-9, GARR). Greenwood.
Gash, Norman, ed. Age of Peel. 1969. pap. 5.95x (ISBN 0-312-01260-8). St Martin.
Gillespie, Frances E. Labor & Politics in England: 1850-1867. 1967. lib. bdg. 15.00x (ISBN 0-374-93078-3). Octagon.
Goodwin, Albert. The Friends of Liberty: The English Democratic Movement in the Age of the French Revolution. LC 78-15673. (Illus.). 1979. text ed. 25.00x (ISBN 0-674-32339-4). Harvard U Pr.
Graham, Walter. Tory Criticism in the Quarterly Review, 1809 - 1853. LC 77-110570. 1970. Repr. of 1921 ed. 11.50 (ISBN 0-404-02889-6). AMS Pr.
Grey, Charles E. Colonial Policy of Lord John Russell's Administration, 2 vols. in 1. LC 79-118121. Repr. of 1853 ed. lib. bdg. 30.00x (ISBN 0-678-00660-1). Kelley.
Hamer, D. A. The Politics of Electoral Pressure: A Study in the History of Victorian Reform Agitation. 1977. text ed. 27.50x (ISBN 0-391-00682-7). Humanities.
Hanham, H. J., ed. Nineteenth Century Constitution, Eighteen Fifteen to Nineteen Fourteen. LC 69-11148. 1969. 44.50 (ISBN 0-521-07351-0); pap. 15.95x (ISBN 0-521-09560-3, 560). Cambridge U Pr.
Hardie, Frank. Political Influence of Queen Victoria 1861-1901. 1963. text ed. 10.00x (ISBN 0-7146-1481-5). Humanities.
Hearnshaw, Fossey J., ed. Political Principles of Some Notable Prime Ministers of the Nineteenth Century. LC 74-107710. (Essay Index Reprint Ser). 1926. 19.50 (ISBN 0-8369-1512-7). Arno.
Henderson, Alfred J. London & the National Government 1721-1742: A Study of City Politics & the Walpole Administration. LC 75-29086. (Perspectives in European History: No. 7). (Illus.). x, 242p. Repr. of 1945 ed. lib. bdg. 15.00x (ISBN 0-87991-609-5). Porcupine Pr.
Hudson, Derek. Thomas Barnes of the Times. Child, Harold, ed. LC 70-138623. (Illus.). 196p. 1972. Repr. of 1943 ed. lib. bdg. 15.00x (ISBN 0-8371-5735-8, HUTB). Greenwood.
Hyde, H. Montgomery. Carson: The Life of Sir Edward Carson. LC 73-8425. 515p. 1975. Repr. of 1953 ed. lib. bdg. 16.00x (ISBN 0-374-94078-9). Octagon.
Johnson, Nancy E., ed. The Diary of Gathorne Hardy, Later Lord Cranbook, 1866-1892: Political Selections. 650p. 1981. 125.00x (ISBN 0-19-822622-5). Oxford U Pr.
Lascelles, Edward C. Life of Charles James Fox. LC 78-96183. 1970. Repr. of 1936 ed. lib. bdg. 16.00x (ISBN 0-374-94788-0). Octagon.
Lipman, Vivian D. Local Government Areas, 1834-1945. LC 75-40918. 506p. 1976. Repr. of 1949 ed. lib. bdg. 25.00x (ISBN 0-8371-8695-1, LILG). Greenwood.
Llewellyn, Alexander. Decade of Reform: English Politics and Opinion in the 1830's. LC 71-182187. 1972. text ed. 17.95 (ISBN 0-312-18970-2). St Martin.
Lubenow, William C. Politics of Government Growth: Early Victorian Attitudes Towards State Intervention, 1833-1848. (Library of Politics & Society Ser.). 1971. 16.50 (ISBN 0-208-01227-3, Archon). Shoe String.
McBriar, A. M. Fabian Socialism & English Politics, Eighteen Eighty-Four - Nineteen Eighteen. 1962. pap. 14.95x (ISBN 0-521-09351-1). Cambridge U Pr.
MacCoby, Simon, ed. The English Radical Tradition: Seventeen Sixty-Three to Nineteen Fourteen. LC 78-681. 1978. Repr. of 1957 ed. lib. bdg. 20.50x (ISBN 0-313-20284-2, MAER). Greenwood.
MacDonagh, Oliver. Early Victorian Government, 1830-1870. LC 76-57957. 1977. text ed. 24.50x (ISBN 0-8419-0304-2). Holmes & Meier.
Martin, David E. & Rubinstein, David. Ideology & the Labour Movement: Essays Presented to John Saville. 276p. 1979. 21.50x (ISBN 0-8476-6123-7). Rowman.
Molesworth, William N. History of the Reform Bill of 1832. LC 68-30533. Repr. of 1865 ed. 17.50x (ISBN 0-678-00893-0). Kelley.
Monypenny, William F. & Buckle, George E. Life of Benjamin Disraeli, Earl of Beaconsfield, 4 Vols. rev. ed. LC 68-25044. (Illus.). 1968. Repr. of 1929 ed. Set. 85.00 (ISBN 0-8462-1171-8). Russell.
Nish, I & Steeds, D. China, Japan, & Nineteenth Century Britain. (Government & Society in Nineteenth Century Britain Ser.). 1977. 20.00x (ISBN 0-7165-2225-X, Pub. by Irish Academic Pr Ireland). Biblio Dist.
Park, Joseph H. British Prime Ministers of the Nineteenth Century. LC 76-111855. (Essay Index Reprint Ser). 1950. 23.00 (ISBN 0-8369-1892-4). Arno.
Politics for the People, Nos. 1-17. LC 69-13752. Repr. of 1848 ed. 20.00x (ISBN 0-678-00663-6). Kelley.
Quinton, Anthony. The Politics of Imperfection. LC 79-670245. 92p. 1979. 13.50 (ISBN 0-571-11285-4, Pub. by Faber & Faber). Merrimack Bk Serv.
Reilly, Robin. William Pitt the Younger. LC 78-13050. (Illus.). 1979. 19.95 (ISBN 0-399-12130-7). Putnam.
Russell, George W. E. Politics & Personalities, with Other Essays. facs. ed. (Essay Index Reprint Ser). 1917. 18.00 (ISBN 0-8369-0844-9). Arno.
Sanders, Lloyd. Holland House Circle. LC 70-82004. (Illus.). Repr. of 1908 ed. 20.00 (ISBN 0-405-08915-5). Arno.
Schapiro, J. Salwyn. Liberalism & the Challenge of Fascism. 1964. lib. bdg. 20.00x (ISBN 0-374-97087-4). Octagon.
Sontag, Raymond J. Germany & England: Background of Conflict, 1848-1894. 1969. pap. 3.95x (ISBN 0-393-00180-6, Norton Lib). Norton.
--Germany & England: Background of Conflict, 1848-1894. LC 64-15034. 1964. Repr. of 1938 ed. 10.00 (ISBN 0-8462-0467-3). Russell.
Spender, John A. Life of the Right Honorable Sir Henry Campbell-Bannerman, 2 Vols. in 1. LC 24-765. 1969. Repr. of 1923 ed. 30.00 (ISBN 0-527-85300-3). Kraus Repr.
Sutherland, Gillian, ed. Studies in the Growth of Nineteenth-Century Government. 295p. 1972. 16.50x (ISBN 0-87471-080-4). Rowman.
Taylor, George R. English Political Portraits of the Nineteenth Century. facs. ed. LC 67-23271. (Essay Index Reprint Ser). 1929. 18.00 (ISBN 0-8369-0927-5). Arno.
Thomis, Malcolm I. & Holt, Peter. Threats of Revolution in Britain, 1789-1848. 1977. 15.00 (ISBN 0-208-01657-0, Archon). Shoe String.
Trevelyan, George M. Life of John Bright. LC 72-110873. (Illus.). 1971. Repr. of 1913 ed. lib. bdg. 20.00x (ISBN 0-8371-4552-X, TRJB). Greenwood.
--Life of John Bright. 1913. 17.00 (ISBN 0-8274-2932-0). R West.
--Lord Grey of the Reform Bill, Being the Life of Charles, Second Earl Grey. Repr. of 1920 ed. lib. bdg. 17.75x (ISBN 0-8371-4553-8, TRLG). Greenwood.
Vincent, David, ed. Testaments of Radicalism: Memoirs of Working Class Politicians 1790-1885. LC 77-377253. 1977. 17.50 (ISBN 0-905118-01-4). Intl Pubns Serv.
Wade, John, ed. Extraordinary Black Book. rev. ed. LC 79-104006. Repr. of 1832 ed. 27.50x (ISBN 0-678-00601-6). Kelley.
White, Reginald J. Political Tracts of Wordsworth, Coleridge & Shelly. LC 74-31033. 1953. lib. bdg. 30.00 (ISBN 0-8414-9591-2). Folcroft.
Williams, W. E. The Rise of Gladstone to the Leadership of the Liberal Party, 1859-1868. LC 73-17482. 189p. 1973. Repr. of 1934 ed. lib. bdg. 13.50x (ISBN 0-374-98614-2). Octagon.
Woodward, Llewellyn. Age of Reform, Eighteen Fifteen to Eighteen Seventy. 2nd ed. 1962. 33.00x (ISBN 0-19-821711-0). Oxford U Pr.

GREAT BRITAIN–POLITICS AND GOVERNMENT–1837-1901

Chamberlain, Joseph. A Political Memoir, 1880-92. Howard, C. H., ed. LC 75-7235. (Illus.). 340p. 1975. Repr. of 1953 ed. lib. bdg. 20.75x (ISBN 0-8371-8101-1, CHPOM). Greenwood.
Chapman, J. K. Political Correspondence of the Gladstone Era: The Letters of Lady Sophia Palmer & Sir Arthur Gordon, 1884-1889. LC 79-143267. (Transactions Ser.: Vol. 61, Pt. 2). 1971. pap. 1.00 (ISBN 0-87169-612-6). Am Philos.
Churchill, R. H. Speeches Eighteen Eighty to Eighteen Eighty-Eight, 2 vols. Repr. of 1889 ed. Set. 36.00 (ISBN 0-527-17110-7). Kraus Repr.
Crosby, Travis L. Sir Robert Peel's Administration, 1841-46. (Elections & Administrations Ser.). 1976. 17.50 (ISBN 0-208-01517-5, Archon). Shoe String.
Fair, John D. British Interparty Conferences: A Study of the Procedure of Conciliation in British Politics, Eighteen Sixty-Seven to Nineteen Twenty-One. 366p. 1980. 59.00x (ISBN 0-19-822601-2). Oxford U Pr.
George, W. R. The Making of Lloyd George. (Illus.). 1976. 17.50 (ISBN 0-208-01627-9, Archon). Shoe String.
Hamilton, Edward W. Diary of Sir Edward Walter Hamilton, Eighteen-Eighty to Eighteen-Eighty Five, 2. Bahlman, Dudley W., ed. 1972. 54.00x (ISBN 0-19-822324-2). Oxford U Pr.
Hardie, Frank. Political Influence of Queen Victoria, 1861-1901. 2nd ed. 258p. 1963. 24.00x (ISBN 0-7146-1481-5, F Cass Co). Biblio Dist.
Harney, G. Julian, ed. The Democratic Review: 1849-1850. 1968. text ed. 30.25x (ISBN 0-85036-098-6). Humanities.
Hurst. Joseph Chamberlain & Liberal Reunion. 1972. 2.50 (ISBN 0-7153-5027-7). David & Charles.
Jalland, Patricia. The Liberals & Ireland: The Ulster Question in British Politics to 1914. LC 79-26719. 250p. 1980. 25.00x (ISBN 0-312-48347-3). St Martin.
Jenkins, Brian. Britain & the War for the Union, Vol. 2. 480p. 1980. 26.50 (ISBN 0-7735-0354-4). McGill-Queens U Pr.
Jones, Wilbur D. & Erickson, Arvel B. Peelites, 1846-1857. LC 79-157717. 1972. 10.00 (ISBN 0-8142-0162-8). Ohio St U Pr.
Koss, Stephen. Asquith. LC 76-20200. (British Political Biography Ser.). 1976. text ed. 15.95 (ISBN 0-312-05740-7). St Martin.
Le May, G. H. The Victorian Constitution. 1979. 25.00x (ISBN 0-686-57422-2). St Martin.
McDowell, Robert B. British Conservatism, 1832-1914. LC 74-11987. 191p. 1974. Repr. of 1959 ed. lib. bdg. 15.00 (ISBN 0-8371-7708-1, MCBC). Greenwood.
Matthew, H. C. The Liberal Imperialists: The Ideas & Politics of a Post-Gladstonian Elite. (Oxford Historical Monographs). 1973. 36.00x (ISBN 0-19-821842-7). Oxford U Pr.
Morley, John. The Life of William Ewart Gladstone, 3 vols. LC 70-145193. 1966p. 1972. Repr. of 1903 ed. Set. 359.00 (ISBN 0-403-01117-5). Scholarly.
Morley, John M. Life of William Ewart Gladstone, 3 Vols. LC 68-57630. (Illus.). 1969. Repr. of 1903 ed. Set. lib. bdg. 64.50x (ISBN 0-8371-0576-5, MOWG). Greenwood.
Park, Joseph H. English Reform Bill of Eighteen Sixty-Seven. LC 76-78002. (Columbia University. Studies in the Social Sciences: No.210). Repr. of 1920 ed. 22.50 (ISBN 0-404-51210-0). AMS Pr.
Pelling, Henry. Popular Politics & Society in Late Victorian Britain. 1979. text ed. 26.00x (ISBN 0-391-01205-3); pap. text ed. 12.50x (ISBN 0-391-01206-1). Humanities.
Pike, E. Royston, ed. Golden Times: Human Documents of the Victorian Age. LC 67-28725. (Illus.). 386p. 1972. pap. 3.95 (ISBN 0-8052-0335-4). Schocken.
Porter, Bernard. The Refugee Question in Mid-Victorian Politics. LC 78-73947. (Illus.). 1980. 41.50 (ISBN 0-521-22638-4). Cambridge U Pr.
Raymond, E. T. Man of Promise: Lord Rosebery. LC 72-1276. (Select Bibliographies Reprints Ser.). 1972. Repr. of 1923 ed. 16.00 (ISBN 0-8369-6834-4). Arno.
Rossi, John P. The Transformation of the British Liberal Party: A Study of the Tactics of the Liberal Opposition, 1874-1880. LC 77-91611. (Transactions Ser.: Vol. 68, Pt. 8). 1978. pap. 8.00 (ISBN 0-87169-688-6). Am Philos.
Searle, G. R. The Quest for National Efficiency: A Study in British Politics & Political Thought, 1899-1914. LC 75-126758. 1971. 25.00x (ISBN 0-520-01794-3). U of Cal Pr.
Seton-Watson, R. W. Disraeli, Gladstone & the Eastern Question. 1972. pap. 3.95x (ISBN 0-393-00594-1, Norton Lib). Norton.
Smith, P., ed. Lord Salisbury on Politics, 1860-1883. LC 74-174256. (Cambridge Studies in the History & Theory of Politics). 1972. 39.95 (ISBN 0-521-08386-9). Cambridge U Pr.
Trollope, Anthony. Lord Palmerston. Hall, N. John, ed. LC 80-1901. (Selected Works of Anthony Trollope Ser.). 1981. Repr. of 1882 ed. lib. bdg. 25.00 (ISBN 0-405-14190-4). Arno.
White, William. Inner Life of the House of Commons, 2 Vols. facs. ed. LC 79-11949. (Select Bibliographies Reprint Ser). 1897. 30.50 (ISBN 0-8369-5392-4). Arno.

GREAT BRITAIN–POLITICS AND GOVERNMENT–20TH CENTURY

Aster, Sidney. Anthony Eden. LC 76-22932. 1977. 8.95 (ISBN 0-312-04235-3). St Martin.
Baker, Arthur. The House Is Sitting. LC 74-68. (Illus.). 264p. 1974. Repr. of 1958 ed. lib. bdg. 14.25x (ISBN 0-8371-7364-7, BAHS). Greenwood.
Barker, Ernest. Political Thought in England, Eighteen Forty-Eight to Nineteen Fourteen. 2nd ed. LC 80-19766. (Home University Library of Modern Knowledge: 104). 256p. 1980. Repr. of 1928 ed. lib. bdg. 22.50x (ISBN 0-313-22216-9, BAPL). Greenwood.
Barnett, Correlli. The Collapse of British Power. (Illus.). 138p. 1972. 15.00 (ISBN 0-688-00001-0). Morrow.
Baumann, Arthur A. Last Victorians. facsimile ed. LC 70-104991. (Essay Index Reprint Ser). 1927. 19.50 (ISBN 0-8369-1445-7). Arno.
Beaverbrook, W. M. Men & Power, Nineteen Seventeen-Nineteen Eighteen. (Illus.). 1968. Repr. of 1956 ed. 22.50 (ISBN 0-208-00717-2, Archon). Shoe String.
--Politicians & the War, 1914-1916. (Illus.). 1968. Repr. of 1932 ed. 22.50 (ISBN 0-208-00718-0, Archon). Shoe String.
Begbie, Harold. Mirrors of Downing Street. facs. ed. LC 79-121448. (Essay Index Reprint Ser). 1923. 16.00 (ISBN 0-8369-1695-6). Arno.
--Mirrors of Downing Street. LC 70-9179. (Essay & General Literature Index Reprint Ser). 1970. Repr. of 1921 ed. 12.00 (ISBN 0-8046-0917-9). Kennikat.
--Windows of Westminster. facsimile ed. LC 77-104993. (Essay Index Reprint Ser). 1924. 17.00 (ISBN 0-8369-1447-3). Arno.
Bell, David S., ed. Labour into the Eighties. 168p. 1980. bds. 25.00x (ISBN 0-7099-0443-6, Pub. by Croom Helm Ltd England). Biblio Dist.
Beloff, Max & Peele, Gillian. The Government of the United Kingdom: Political Authority in a Changing Society. (Comparitive Modern Goverment Ser.). (Orig.). 1980. 17.95x (ISBN 0-393-01344-8); pap. text ed. 6.95x (ISBN 0-393-95135-9). Norton.
Bentley, M. The Liberal Mind 1914-1929. LC 76-11072. (Cambridge Studies in the History & Theory of Politics). 1977. 36.00 (ISBN 0-521-21243-X). Cambridge U Pr.

Berkeley, Humphry. The Myth That Will Not Die: The Formation of the National Government 1931. 143p. 1978. 25.00x (ISBN 0-85664-773-X, Pub. by Croom Helm Ltd England). Biblio Dist.

Bogdanor, Vernon. The People & the Party System: The Referendum & Electoral Reform in British Politics. LC 81-3895. 280p. Date not set. price not set (ISBN 0-521-24207-X); pap. price not set (ISBN 0-521-28525-9). Cambridge U Pr.

Brand, Jack. Local Government Reform in England, 1888-1974. 176p. 1974. 17.50 (ISBN 0-208-01480-2, Archon). Shoe String.

Brome, Vincent. Aneurin Bevan: A Biography. (Illus.). 1953. 5.95 (ISBN 0-686-00952-5). Wellington.

Buck, Philip W. Amateurs & Professionals in British Politics, 1918 to 1959. LC 63-13073. (Illus.). 1963. 7.50x (ISBN 0-226-07961-9). U of Chicago Pr.

Bunselmeyer, Robert E. The Cost of the War 1914-1919: British Economic War Aims and the Origins of Reparation. 249p. 1975. 17.50 (ISBN 0-208-01551-5, Archon). Shoe String.

Burton, Ivor & Drewry, Gavin. Legislation & Public Policy: Public Bills in the Nineteen Seventy, Seventy-Four Parliament. 300p. 1981. text ed. 50.00x (ISBN 0-8419-5065-2). Holmes & Meier.

Butler, David & Stokes, Donald. Political Change in Britain: The Evolution of Electoral Choice. 2nd ed. LC 75-29935. 300p. 1976. 25.00 (ISBN 0-312-62160-4); pap. 6.95 (ISBN 0-312-62195-7). St Martin.

Butler, David & Stokes, Donald E. Political Change in Britain, 1963-1970, 2 vols. 1972. codebooks 32.00 set (ISBN 0-89138-055-8). Vol. 1 (ISBN 0-89138-056-6). Vol. 2 (ISBN 0-89138-057-4). ICPSR.

Butler, David, ed. Coalitions in British Politics. LC 77-17791. 1978. 17.95x (ISBN 0-312-14503-9). St Martin.

Butler, David E. & King, A. British General Election of 1970. 350p. 1971. 25.00 (ISBN 0-312-10185-6). St Martin.

Butler, R. A. The Art of the Possible: The Memoirs of Lord Butler. LC 72-83705. (Illus.). 274p. 1972. 10.00 (ISBN 0-87645-067-2). Gambit.

Campbell-Johnson, Alan. Eden: The Making of a Statesman. LC 76-6056. (Illus.). 306p. 1976. Repr. of 1955 ed. lib. bdg. 19.00x (ISBN 0-8371-8813-X, CAED). Greenwood.

Ceadel, Martin. Pacifism in Britain Nineteen Fourteen to Nineteen Forty Five: The Defining of a Faith. 352p. 1980. 37.50x (ISBN 0-19-821882-6). Oxford U Pr.

Churchill, Winston J. Running in Place. LC 72-92832. 212p. 1973. 5.95 (ISBN 0-8076-0662-6). Braziller.

Citrine, W. M. Men & Work: An Autobiography. LC 75-36094. (Illus.). 1976. Repr. of 1964 ed. lib. bdg. 24.00x (ISBN 0-8371-8613-7, CIMW). Greenwood.

Clark, David. Colne Valley: Radicalism to Socialism. (Illus.). 240p. 1981. text ed. 27.00x (ISBN 0-582-50293-4). Longman.

Cline, Catherine A. Recruits to Labour: The British Labour Party, 1914-1931. LC 63-13888. 1963. 12.95x (ISBN 0-8156-2046-2). Syracuse U Pr.

Cole, George D. History of the Labour Party from 1914. LC 73-90407. Repr. of 1948 ed. 19.50x (ISBN 0-678-06505-5). Kelley.

Cook, Chris. Age of Alignment: Electorial Politics in Britain, 1922-1929. 1975. 27.50x (ISBN 0-8020-2204-9). U of Toronto Pr.

--Sources in British Political History, 1900-1951, Vols. 3 & 4. Incl. Vol. 3. A Guide to the Private Papers of Members of Parliament, A-K. LC 77-71207 (ISBN 0-312-74656-3); Vol. 4. A Guide to the Private Papers of Members of Parliament, L-Z. LC 77-71188 (ISBN 0-312-74657-1). 1977. 18.95x ea. St Martin.

--Sources in British Political History, 1900-1951: A Guide to the Papers of Selected Public Servants. LC 75-15220. 320p. 1975. Vol. 1. 18.95 (ISBN 0-312-74620-2); Vol. 2. 18.95 (ISBN 0-312-74655-5). St Martin.

Cook, Chris & Weeks, Jeffery. Sources in British Political History 1900-1951: A Guide to the Private Papers of Selected Writers, Intellectuals & Publicists, Vol. 5. LC 75-4012. 1978. 19.95 (ISBN 0-312-74658-X). St Martin.

Cook, Christopher. A Short History of the Liberal Party, 1900-1975. 192p. 1976. 19.95x (ISBN 0-312-72065-3). St Martin.

Corrin, Jay P. G. K. Chesterton & Hilaire Belloc: The Battle Against Modernity. LC 81-4756. 270p. 1981. text ed. 21.00x (ISBN 0-8214-0604-3). Ohio U Pr.

Cowling, M. The Impact of Hitler: British Politics & British Policy 1933-1940. LC 74-12968. (Studies in the History & Theory of Politics). 448p. 1975. 59.50 (ISBN 0-521-20582-4). Cambridge U Pr.

Cowling, Maurice. Impact of Labour, Nineteen Twenty-Twenty-Four: The Beginning of Modern British Politics. LC 73-127236. (Studies in History & Theory of Politics). 1971. 49.95 (ISBN 0-521-07969-1). Cambridge U Pr.

Cross, Colin. The Liberals in Power: 1905-1914. LC 75-40998. 1976. Repr. of 1963 ed. lib. bdg. 18.25x (ISBN 0-8371-8706-0, CRLP). Greenwood.

Daalder, Hans. Cabinet Reform in Britain, 1914-1963. 1963. 17.50x (ISBN 0-8047-0139-3). Stanford U Pr.

Dangerfield, George. Strange Death of Liberal England. 7.50 (ISBN 0-8446-1890-X). Peter Smith.

--Strange Death of Liberal England, 1910-1914. (Illus.). 1961. pap. 3.95 (ISBN 0-399-50227-0, 50, Perigee). Putnam.

Derry, John W. Radical Tradition: Tom Paine to Lloyd George. 1967. 19.95 (ISBN 0-312-66185-1). St Martin.

Douglas-Home, Alec. The Way the Wind Blows. LC 76-47153. (Illus.). 1977. 10.95 (ISBN 0-8129-0665-9). Times Bks.

Drucker, H. M., ed. Multi-Party Britain. LC 79-52940. (Praeger Special Studies). 256p. 1979. 25.95 (ISBN 0-03-053446-1). Praeger.

Dugdale, Blanche E. Arthur James Balfour, First Earl of Balfour. LC 70-97328. Repr. of 1936 ed. lib. bdg. 32.50x (ISBN 0-8371-2893-5, DUI&). Greenwood.

Elletson, D. H. Chamberlains. 1966. text ed. 6.00x (ISBN 0-7195-0352-3). Humanities.

Essays in Liberalism: Being the Lectures & Papers Which Were Delivered at the Liberal Summer School at Oxford. facs. ed. LC 68-16929. (Essay Index Reprint Ser). 1922. 15.00 (ISBN 0-8369-0426-5). Arno.

Fair, John D. British Interparty Conferences: A Study of the Procedure of Conciliation in British Politics, Eighteen Sixty-Seven to Nineteen Twenty-One. 366p. 1980. 59.00x (ISBN 0-19-822601-2). Oxford U Pr.

Fawcett, Millicent. What I Remember. LC 74-33939. (Pioneers of the Woman's Movement Ser.). (Illus.). 272p. 1975. Repr. of 1925 ed. 19.50 (ISBN 0-88355-261-2). Hyperion-Conn.

Fest, Wilfried. Peace or Partition: The Habsburg Monarchy & British Policy, 1914-1918. LC 77-92396. 1978. 16.95x (ISBN 0-312-59935-8). St Martin.

Garner, Joe. The Commonwealth Office. 1978. text ed. 60.00x (ISBN 0-435-32355-5). Heinemann Ed.

Gorodetsky. The Precarious Truce. LC 76-2279. (Soviet & East European Studies). 1977. 36.00 (ISBN 0-521-21226-X). Cambridge U Pr.

Grant, Wyn. Independent Local Politics in England. (Illus.). 1977. 19.95 (ISBN 0-566-00183-7, 01608-X, Pub. by Saxon Hse England). Lexington Bks.

Haigh, R. H. & Turner, P. W. British Policies & Society, Nineteen Eighteen to Nineteen Thirty-Eight: The Effect on Appeasement. 1980. pap. 20.00x (ISBN 0-89126-093-5). MA-AH Pub.

Halpern, P. G., ed. Keyes Papers, Vol. 2. (Illus.). 464p. 1980. text ed. 34.00x (ISBN 0-04-942165-4). Allen Unwin.

Harrison, J. F. & Thompson, Dorothy. Bibliography of the Chartist Movement, Eighteen Thirty Seven to Nineteen Seventy-Seven. 1978. text ed. 25.00x (ISBN 0-391-00742-4). Humanities.

Hayes, Carlton. British Social Politics. facsimile ed. LC 72-37885. (Select Bibliographies Reprint Ser). Repr. of 1913 ed. 29.00 (ISBN 0-8369-6722-4). Arno.

Hearnshaw, Fossey J., ed. Edwardian England, A.D. 1901-1910: A Series of Lectures Delivered at King's College, University of London. facs. ed. LC 68-22097. (Essay Index Reprint Ser). 1933. 16.00 (ISBN 0-8369-0529-6). Arno.

Howell, David. British Social Democracy: A Study in Development & Decay. LC 76-11701. 1976. 18.95 (ISBN 0-312-10535-5). St Martin.

Hudson Institute. The U. K. in 1980: The Hudson Report. LC 74-25234. 127p. 1974. 19.95 (ISBN 0-470-41855-9). Halsted Pr.

Hugo, Grant. Britain in Tomorrow's World: Principles of Foreign Policy. LC 78-84062. 1969. 20.00x (ISBN 0-231-03330-3). Columbia U Pr.

Hyde, H. Montgomery. Carson: The Life of Sir Edward Carson. LC 73-8425. 515p. 1975. Repr. of 1953 ed. lib. bdg. 16.00x (ISBN 0-374-94078-9). Octagon.

Jalland, Patricia. The Liberals & Ireland: The Ulster Question in British Politics to 1914. LC 79-26719. 250p. 1980. 25.00x (ISBN 0-312-48337-3). St Martin.

Jupp, James. British Radical Left Nineteen Thirty One - Nineteen Forty One. 423p. 1981. 27.50x (ISBN 0-7146-3123-X, F Cass Co). Biblio Dist.

Kennedy, Thomas C. The Hound of Conscience: A History of the No-Conscription Fellowship, 1914-1919. LC 80-39677. 304p. 1981. text ed. 22.00x (ISBN 0-938626-01-9). U of Mo Pr.

King, Cecil. With Malice Toward None: A War Diary by Cecil King. Armstrong, William, ed. LC 70-175619. 343p. 1971. 28.50 (ISBN 0-8386-1067-6). Fairleigh Dickinson.

Koss, Stephen. Asquith. LC 76-20200. (British Political Biography Ser.). 1976. text ed. 15.95 (ISBN 0-312-05740-7). St Martin.

--Nonconformity in Modern British Politics. 272p. 1975. 18.50 (ISBN 0-208-01553-1, Archon). Shoe String.

Lee, J. M. The Churchill Coalition, Nineteen Forty to Nineteen Forty-Five. 192p. 1980. 20.00 (ISBN 0-208-01880-8, Archon). Shoe String.

Le May, G. H. The Victorian Constitution. 1979. 25.00x (ISBN 0-686-57422-2). St Martin.

Lewis, Wyndham. Left Wings Over Europe. LC 72-82186. 1972. Repr. of 1936 ed. lib. bdg. 75.00 (ISBN 0-87968-004-0). Gordon Pr.

Lipman, Vivian D. Local Government Areas, 1834-1945. LC 75-40918. 506p. 1976. Repr. of 1949 ed. lib. bdg. 25.00x (ISBN 0-8371-8695-1, LILG). Greenwood.

Lowe, Peter. Great Britain & the Origins of the Pacific War: A Study of British Policy in East Asia, 1937 to 1941. (Illus.). 330p. 1977. text ed. 45.00x (ISBN 0-19-822427-3). Oxford U Pr.

Lugard, Frederick J. Political Memoranda: Revision of Instruction to Political Officers on Subjects Chiefly Political & Administrative, 1913-1918. 3rd rev. ed. 480p. 1970. 35.00x (ISBN 0-7146-1693-1, F Cass Co). Biblio Dist.

Lyman, Richard W. The First Labour Government, 1924. LC 73-92569. (Illus.). xi, 302p. 1975. Repr. of 1957 ed. 20.00 (ISBN 0-8462-1784-8). Russell.

McBriar, A. M. Fabian Socialism & English Politics, Eighteen Eighty-Four - Nineteen Eighteen. 1962. pap. 14.95x (ISBN 0-521-09351-1). Cambridge U Pr.

McDowell, Robert B. British Conservatism, 1832-1914. LC 74-11987. 191p. 1974. Repr. of 1959 ed. lib. bdg. 15.00 (ISBN 0-8371-7708-1, MCBC). Greenwood.

Mackintosh, John J., ed. British Prime Ministers in the Twentieth Century, Vol. 1. LC 77-76542. 1977. 19.95x (ISBN 0-312-10517-7). St Martin.

MacLean, John. In the Rapids of Revolution. Milton, Nan, ed. 256p. 1980. 14.00x (ISBN 0-686-65575-3, Pub. by Allison & Busby England); pap. 7.95 (ISBN 0-85031-175-6, Pub. by Allison & Busby England). Schocken.

Martin, David E. & Rubinstein, David. Ideology & the Labour Movement: Essays Presented to John Saville. 276p. 1979. 21.50x (ISBN 0-8476-6123-7). Rowman.

Masterman, Lucy B. C. F. G. Masterman: A Biography. LC 68-88329. (Illus.). Repr. of 1939 ed. 18.00x (ISBN 0-678-05187-9). Kelley.

Middlemas, Keith. Politics in Industrial Society: The Experience of the British System Since 1911. 512p. 1979. 37.50x (ISBN 0-8476-6872-X). Rowman.

Middlemas, Robert K. Clydesiders. LC 66-2916. (Illus.). 1965. 15.00x (ISBN 0-678-08040-2). Kelley.

Morgan, Kenneth. Consensus & Disunity: The Lloyd George Coalition Government, 1918 to 1922. 448p. 1979. text ed. 54.00x (ISBN 0-19-822497-4). Oxford U Pr.

Morgan, Kenneth & Morgan, Jane. Portrait of a Progressive: The Political Career of Christopher, Viscount Addison. (Illus.). 352p. 1980. 42.00x (ISBN 0-19-822494-X). Oxford U Pr.

Morgan, Kenneth O. The Age of Lloyd George: The Liberal Party & British Politics, 1880-1929. (Historical Problems: Studies & Documents). 1971. pap. text ed. 9.95x (ISBN 0-04-942093-3). Allen Unwin.

Peden, G. C. British Rearmament & the Treasury: 1932-39. 227p. 1979. 17.50x (ISBN 0-7073-0229-3, Pub. by Scottish Academic Pr Scotland). Columbia U Pr.

Peele, Gillian & Cook, Chris, eds. The Politics of Reappraisal: Nineteen-Eighteen to Nineteen Thirty-Nine. LC 75-13591. 250p. 1975. 25.00 (ISBN 0-312-62720-3). St Martin.

Pimlott, B. Labour & the Left in the 1930's. LC 76-27906. 1977. 19.95 (ISBN 0-521-21448-3). Cambridge U Pr.

Pugh, Martin. Electoral Reform in War & Peace, 1906-1918. 1978. 20.00 (ISBN 0-7100-8792-6). Routledge & Kegan.

Quinton, Anthony. The Politics of Imperfection. LC 79-670245. 92p. 1979. 13.50 (ISBN 0-571-11285-4, Pub. by Faber & Faber). Merrimack Bk Serv.

Raison, Timothy. Power & Parliament. 122p. 1979. 20.00x (ISBN 0-631-11301-0, Pub. by Basil Blackwell England); pap. 8.50x (ISBN 0-631-12892-1). Biblio Dist.

Read, Conyers. Mr. Secretary Walsingham & the Policy of Queen Elizabeth, 3 vols. LC 75-41223. Repr. of 1925 ed. Set. 84.50 (ISBN 0-404-13490-4). AMS Pr.

Rock, William R. British Appeasement in the 1930's. (Foundations of Modern History Ser.). 1978. 7.95 (ISBN 0-393-05668-6); pap. 3.95x (ISBN 0-393-09060-4). Norton.

Rowse, Alfred L. Appeasement: A Study in Political Decline, 1933-34. 1963. pap. 2.95x (ISBN 0-393-00139-3, Norton Lib). Norton.

Scally, Robert J. The Origins of the Lloyd George Coalition: The Politics of Social Imperialism, 1900-1918. LC 74-25608. (Illus.). 408p. 1975. 30.00x (ISBN 0-691-07570-0). Princeton U Pr.

Searle, G. R. The Quest for National Efficiency: A Study in British Politics & Political Thought, 1899-1914. LC 75-126758. 1971. 25.00x (ISBN 0-520-01794-3). U of Cal Pr.

Seton-Watson, R. W. Britain & the Dictators: A Survey of Post-War British Policy. 1979. Repr. of 1938 ed. lib. bdg. 40.00 (ISBN 0-8495-4933-7). Arden Lib.

Shay, Robert P., Jr. British Rearmament in the Thirties: Politics & Profits. LC 76-45911. 1977. text ed. 23.50 (ISBN 0-691-05248-4). Princeton U Pr.

Simon, John A. Comments & Criticisms. LC 74-118503. 1971. Repr. of 1930 ed. 13.00 (ISBN 0-8046-1251-X). Kennikat.

Smith, Brian C. & Stanyer, Jeffrey. Administering Britain. (Studies in Public Administrative Institutions Ser.). 288p. 1980. pap. 9.95x (ISBN 0-85520-374-9, Pub. by Martin Robertson England). Biblio Dist.

Spender, John A. Life of the Right Honorable Sir Henry Campbell-Bannerman, 2 Vols. in 1. LC 24-765. 1969. Repr. of 1923 ed. 30.00 (ISBN 0-527-85300-3). Kraus Repr.

--Short History of Our Times. LC 72-110865. (Illus.). 1971. Repr. of 1934 ed. lib. bdg. 14.25x (ISBN 0-8371-4538-4, SPSH). Greenwood.

Stannage, Tom. Baldwin Thwarts the Opposition: The British General Election of 1935. 320p. 1980. 50.00x (ISBN 0-7099-0341-3, Pub. by Croom Helm Ltd England). Biblio Dist.

Stanyer, Jeffrey. Understanding Local Government. (Studies in Public Administration Ser.). 320p. 1980. pap. 9.95x (ISBN 0-85520-373-0, Pub. by Martin Robertson England). Biblio Dist.

Sykes, Alan. Tariff Reform in British Politics, Nineteen Hundred Three to Nineteen Thirteen. 366p. 1979. text ed. 54.00x (ISBN 0-19-822483-4). Oxford U Pr.

Tapp, Edwin. Policies of Survival. (Studies in Twentieth Century History). 1979. pap. text ed. 4.50x (ISBN 0-686-65413-7, 00549). Heinemann Ed.

Taylor, G. R. Modern English Statesman. 1921. Repr. 12.50 (ISBN 0-685-43152-5). Norwood Edns.

Templewood, Samuel. Nine Troubled Years. LC 75-36363. (Illus.). 448p. 1976. Repr. of 1954 ed. lib. bdg. 25.00x (ISBN 0-8371-8633-1, TENT). Greenwood.

Townshend, Charles. The British Campaign in Ireland, Nineteen Nineteen to Nineteen Twenty-One. (Oxford Historical Monographs). (Illus.). 256p. 1978. pap. 12.95x (ISBN 0-19-821874-5). Oxford U Pr.

Trotsky, Leon. Leon Trotsky on Britain. Drayton, Julia, et al, trs. from Russ. & Fr. LC 72-92147. 336p. 1973. 25.00 (ISBN 0-913460-12-5, Dist. by Path Pr NY); pap. 5.45 (ISBN 0-913460-13-3). Monad Pr.

Walkland, S. A., ed. The House of Commons in the Twentieth Century. 1979. 59.00x (ISBN 0-19-827193-X). Oxford U Pr.

Warner, Marina. The Crack in the Teacup: Britain in the Twentieth Century. LC 78-27423. (Illus.). 160p. (gr. 6 up). 1979. 10.95 (ISBN 0-395-28972-6, Clarion). HM.

Watkins, K. W. Britain Divided. LC 75-36364. 270p. 1976. Repr. of 1963 ed. lib. bdg. 15.75x (ISBN 0-8371-8627-7, WABD). Greenwood.

Wilson, Trevor, ed. Political Diaries of C. P. Scott, 1911-1928. LC 75-110993. 512p. 1970. 25.00x (ISBN 0-8014-0569-6). Cornell U Pr.

Winter, J. M. Socialism & the Challenge of War: Ideas & Politics in Britain, 1912-1918. 1974. 24.00x (ISBN 0-7100-7839-0). Routledge & Kegan.

Wootton, Graham. Politics of Influence: British Ex-Servicemen, Cabinet Decisions & Cultural Change, 1917-1957. LC 63-5612. (Illus.). 1963. 16.50x (ISBN 0-674-68900-3). Harvard U Pr.

--Pressure Politics in Contemporary Britain. LC 77-26372. 1978. 21.95x (ISBN 0-669-02167-9). Lexington Bks.

GREAT BRITAIN–POLITICS AND GOVERNMENT–1945-

Bailey, Sydney D. British Parliamentary Democracy. 3rd ed. LC 77-18752. (Illus.). 1978. Repr. of 1971 ed. lib. bdg. 19.75x (ISBN 0-313-20195-1, BABR). Greenwood.

Barker, Rodney. Political Ideas in Modern Britain. 1978. 19.75x (ISBN 0-416-76250-6); pap. 8.95x (ISBN 0-416-76260-3). Methuen Inc.
Beer, Samuel H. Modern British Politics. 3rd ed. 1980. pap. 6.95 (ISBN 0-393-00952-1). Norton.
Behrens, Robert. The Conservative Party from Heath to Thatcher: Policy & Politics 1974 to 1979. 152p. 15.95x (ISBN 0-566-00268-X, 03778-8, Pub. by Gower Pub Co England). Lexington Bks.
Beloff, Max. Future of British Foreign Policy. Crozier, Brian, ed. LC 73-86970. (World Realities Ser). 1969. 4.95 (ISBN 0-8008-3120-9). Taplinger.
Berkeley, Humphry. The Odyssey of Enoch: A Political Memoir. (Illus.). 1978. 17.95 (ISBN 0-241-89623-1, Pub. by Hamish Hamilton England). David & Charles.
Bessell. Cover-Up: The Jeremy Thrope Affair. Brodie, Ian, ed. LC 80-52089. (Illus., Orig.). 1981. write for info. (ISBN 0-937812-01-3). Simons Bks.
Birch, A. H., et al. Britain: Progress & Decline, Vol. 17. 154p. 1980. lib. bdg. 17.50 (ISBN 0-930598-18-0). Tulane Stud Pol.
Brown, R. G. & Steel, D. R. The Administrative Process in Britain. 2nd ed. 1979. 24.00 (ISBN 0-416-85890-2). Methuen Inc.
Bruce-Gardyne, Jock & Lawson, Nigel. The Power Game: An Examination of Decision-Making in Government. (Illus.). 192p. 1976. 19.50 (ISBN 0-208-01598-1, Archon). Shoe String.
Butler, David & Kavanagh, Dennis. British General Elections of Nineteen Seventy-Nine. 416p. 1980. text ed. 50.00x (ISBN 0-8419-5081-4). Holmes & Meier.
Butler, David & Kitzinger, Uwe. The Nineteen Seventy-Five Referendum. LC 76-16701. 1976. 18.95x (ISBN 0-312-57435-5). St Martin.
Butler, David E. British General Election of 1955. 236p. 1969. Repr. of 1955 ed. 27.50x (ISBN 0-7146-1549-8, F Cass Co). Biblio Dist.
--British General Election of 1959. Rose, Richard, ed. (Illus.). 293p. 1970. Repr. of 1970 ed. 27.50x (ISBN 0-7156-1549-1, F Cass Co). Biblio Dist.
Cartwright, Timothy J. Royal Commissions & Departmental Committees in Britain. 320p. 1976. text ed. 25.50x (ISBN 0-340-17602-4). Verry.
Castle, Barbara. Castle Diaries Nineteen Seventy-Four to Seventy-Six. 788p. 1981. text ed. 42.50 (ISBN 0-8419-0689-0). Holmes & Meier.
Clarke, Charles F. Britain Today: A Review of Current Political & Social Trends. LC 70-100148. Repr. of 1951 ed. lib. bdg. 15.00x (ISBN 0-8371-3396-3, CLBT). Greenwood.
Clutterbuck, Richard. Britain in Agony. 320p. 1978. 18.95 (ISBN 0-571-11188-2, Pub. by Faber & Faber). Merrimack Bk Serv.
Cook, Chris & Ramsden, John, eds. Trends in British Politics Since 1945. LC 77-17789. 1978. 17.95x (ISBN 0-312-81754-1). St Martin.
Eden, Anthony. Days for Decision. LC 50-13062. 1969. Repr. of 1950 ed. 12.00 (ISBN 0-527-26300-1). Kraus Repr.
Fry, G. K. The Administrative Revolution in Whitehall. 256p. 1981. 29.50x (ISBN 0-7099-1010-X, Pub. by Croorn Helm Ltd England). Biblio Dist.
Fry, Geoffrey K. The Growth of Government: The Development of Ideas About the Role of the State & the Machinery & Functions of Government in Britain Since 1780. 295p. 1979. 25.00x (ISBN 0-7146-3116-7, F Cass Co). Biblio Dist.
Gilison, Jerome M. British & Soviet Politics: A Study of Legitimacy & Convergence. LC 72-4017. (Illus.). 208p. 1972. 13.50x (ISBN 0-8018-0710-7). Johns Hopkins.
Grimond, Joseph. The Liberal Challenge. LC 75-2696. 317p. 1975. Repr. of 1963 ed. lib. bdg. 16.50x (ISBN 0-8371-8025-2, GRLC). Greenwood.
Gwyn, William B. Democracy & the Cost of Politics in Britain. LC 79-28340. (Illus.). vii, 256p. 1980. Repr. of 1962 ed. lib. bdg. 22.50x (ISBN 0-313-22257-6, GWDC). Greenwood.
Hanson, Albert H. Planning & the Politicians. LC 75-95618. 1969. lib. bdg. 15.00x (ISBN 0-678-06524-1). Kelley.
Haseler, Stephen. The Death of British Democracy. 262p. 1976. 13.95 (ISBN 0-87975-087-1). Prometheus Bks.
Hatfield, Michael. The House That Left Built: Inside Labour Policy Making, 1970-1975. 1978. text ed. 25.00x (ISBN 0-575-02471-2). Verry.
Heren, Louis. Alas, Alas for England: What Went Wrong with Britain. 192p. 1981. 22.50 (ISBN 0-241-10538-2, Pub. by Hamish Hamilton England). David & Charles.
Hollis, Christopher. Can Parliament Survive. LC 78-118476. 1971. Repr. of 1949 ed. 11.25 (ISBN 0-8046-1225-0). Kennikat.
Irwin, John. Modern Britain: An Introduction. 1976. 15.00 (ISBN 0-208-01618-X, Archon). Shoe String.
Johnson, Nevil. In Search of the Constitution: Reflections on State & Society in Britain. LC 76-43316. 1977. text ed. 23.00 (ISBN 0-08-021379-0). Pergamon.
Johnson, Paul. The Recovery of Freedom. (Mainstream Ser.). 232p. 1981. pap. 7.95x (ISBN 0-631-12829-8, Pub. by Basil Blackwell England). Biblio Dist.
Jones, Grace. The Political Structure: Social Structure of Modern Britain. (Aspects of Modern Sociology Ser). (Orig.). 1969. pap. text ed. 2.00x (ISBN 0-582-48778-1). Humanities.
Jones, Kathleen, ed. The Year Book of Social Policy in Britain 1976. 1978. 33.00x (ISBN 0-7100-8765-9). Routledge & Kegan.
Katznelson, Ira. Black Men, White Cities: Race, Politics, & Migration in the United States, 1900-30, & Britain, 1948-68. LC 76-8376. 1976. pap. 3.95 (ISBN 0-226-42671-8, P679, Phoen). U of Chicago Pr.
Kavanagh, Dennis & Rose, Richard, eds. New Trends in British Politics: Issues for Study & Research. LC 76-56705. 254p. 1977. 18.50 (ISBN 0-8039-9869-4); pap. 9.95 (ISBN 0-8039-9864-3). Sage.
McCallum, R. B. & Readman, Alison. British General Election of 1945. 311p. 1964. 25.00x (ISBN 0-686-11190-7, F Cass Co). Biblio Dist.
McEachern, D. A Class Against Itself. 245p. 1980. 29.50 (ISBN 0-521-22985-5); pap. cancelled (ISBN 0-521-28054-0). Cambridge U Pr.
McKie, David & Cook, Christopher. The Decade of Disillusion: Britain in the Sixties. LC 72-83416. 1972. 19.95 (ISBN 0-312-18900-1). St Martin.
Mellors, Colin. The British MP: A Socio-Economic Study of the House of Commons. (Illus.). 1978. 18.95 (ISBN 0-566-00138-1, 00708-0, Pub. by Saxon Hse England). Lexington Bks.
Nairn, Tom. The Break-up of Britain: Crisis & Neo-Nationalism. 1977. 14.50 (ISBN 0-902308-57-2, Pub. by NLB). Schocken.
Nevin, E. T., ed. The Economics of Devolution: Proceedings of Section F of British Association for the Advancement of Science, Aston University 1977. 1978. pap. text ed. 10.00x (ISBN 0-7083-0698-5). Verry.
Nicholas, H. G. British General Election of 1950. (Illus.). 353p. 1968. Repr. of 1951 ed. 26.00x (ISBN 0-7146-1568-4, F Cass Co). Biblio Dist.
Noreng, Oystein. Economics & Politics of North Sea Oil. LC 80-81590. 1980. 27.50x (ISBN 0-918714-02-8). Intl Res Ctr Energy.
Norton, Philip. Dissension in the House of Commons: Nineteen Seventy-Four to Nineteen Seventy-Nine. (Illus.). 560p. 1980. text ed. 97.50x (ISBN 0-19-827430-0). Oxford U Pr.
Osmond, John. Creative Conflict: The Politics of Welsh Devolution. 1978. 14.95x (ISBN 0-7100-8741-1). Routledge & Kegan.
Owen, David. Face the Future. 552p. 1981. 29.95 (ISBN 0-224-01956-2, Pub. by Chatto-Bodley-Jonathan). Merrimack Bk Serv.
Oxford Liberal Group & McCallum, R. B. Radical Alternative: Studies in Liberalism. Watson, George, ed. LC 75-3869. 190p. 1975. Repr. of 1962 ed. lib. bdg. 15.00 (ISBN 0-8371-8085-6, OXRA). Greenwood.
Pateman, Trevor. Television & the February 1974 General Election. (BFI Television Monographs: No. 3). (Orig.). 1977. pap. 4.50 (ISBN 0-85170-043-8). NY Zoetrope.
Podmore, David. Solicitors & the Wider Community. 1980. text ed. 43.95x (ISBN 0-435-82696-4). Heinemann Ed.
Popham, G. T. Government in Britain. 1969. 22.00 (ISBN 0-08-013418-1); pap. 10.75 (ISBN 0-08-013417-3). Pergamon.
Pratt, Walter F. Privacy in Britain. LC 76-50289. 266p. 1979. 17.50 (ISBN 0-8387-2030-7). Bucknell U Pr.
Punnett, R. M. Front Bench Opposition. LC 73-85300. 508p. 1973. 21.50 (ISBN 0-312-30905-8). St Martin.
Rasmussen, Jorgen S. Retrenchment & Revival: A Study of the Contemporary British Liberal Party. LC 64-17263. 1964. 2.00 (ISBN 0-8165-0079-7). U of Ariz Pr.
Richardson, J. J. Policy-Making Process. (Library of Political Studies). 1969. text ed. 5.25x (ISBN 0-7100-6523-X). Humanities.
Robinson, Ann. Parliament & Public Spending. 1978. text ed. 34.50x (ISBN 0-435-83750-8). Heinemann Ed.
Rose, Paul. Backbencher's Dillemma. 224p. 1981. 40.00x (ISBN 0-584-10379-4, Pub. by Muller Ltd). State Mutual Bk.
Rose, Richard & McAllister, Ian. United Kingdom Facts. 240p. 1981. text ed. 70.00x (ISBN 0-8419-5578-6). Holmes & Meier.
Rose, Richard, ed. Studies in British Politics. 3rd. ed. LC 76-11279. 1977. text ed. 22.50x (ISBN 0-312-77070-7). St Martin.
Sampson, Anthony. The New Anatomy of Britain. LC 78-186150. 800p. 1973. pap. 10.95 (ISBN 0-8128-1583-1). Stein & Day.
Shanks, Michael. Planning & Politics: The British Experience 1960-76. (Political & Economic Planning Ser.). 1977. text ed. 17.95x (ISBN 0-04-330283-1); pap. text ed. 7.50x (ISBN 0-04-330284-X). Allen Unwin.
Shaw, Malcolm. Anglo-American Democracy. (Political Studies Library). 1967. text ed. 6.75x (ISBN 0-7100-6527-2); pap. text ed. 1.75x (ISBN 0-7100-5132-8). Humanities.
Shipley, Peter. Revolutionaries in Modern Britain. 256p. 1976. 16.95 (ISBN 0-370-11311-X). Transatlantic.
--Revolutionaries in Modern Britain. 1979. 12.95 (ISBN 0-370-11311-X, Pub. by Chatto Bodley Jonathan). Merrimack Bk Serv.
Stankiewicz, W. J., ed. Crisis in British Government. (Illus.). 1967. pap. text ed. 3.45x (ISBN 0-02-977880-8). Macmillan.
State Research. Review of Security & the State Nineteen Seventy-Nine. 2nd ed. 154p. 1980. 27.50x (ISBN 0-905290-04-6). Nichols Pub.
Stewart, John D. British Pressure Groups: Their Role in Relation to the House of Commons. LC 79-9838. 1979. Repr. of 1958 ed. lib. bdg. 25.00x (ISBN 0-313-21277-5, STBP). Greenwood.
Sutton, John. Understanding Politics in Modern Britain. 1977. pap. text ed. 11.00x (ISBN 0-245-52880-6). Intl Ideas.
Thornhill, William, ed. The Modernization of British Government. 322p. 1975. 23.50x (ISBN 0-87471-759-0). Rowman.
The Times Guide to the House of Commons. (Illus.). 350p. 1980. 45.00x (ISBN 0-930466-29-2). Meckler Bks.
Whitaker, Ben, ed. Radical Future. 7.95 (ISBN 0-224-61204-2). Transatlantic.
Wiseman, H. Victor, ed. Local Government in England 1958-69. 1970. 13.75x (ISBN 0-7100-6822-0). Routledge & Kegan.

GREAT BRITAIN–POPULATION

Banks, J. A. & Banks, Olive. Feminism & Family Planning in Victorian England. LC 63-18387. (Studies in the Life of Women). 154p. 1972. pap. 4.75 (ISBN 0-8052-0350-8). Schocken.
Carrothers, W. A. Emigration from the British Isles. 328p. 1965. Repr. 25.00x (ISBN 0-7146-1282-0, F Cass Co). Biblio Dist.
Chaloner, William H. People & Industries. (Illus.). 151p. 1963. 24.00x (ISBN 0-7146-1284-7, F Cass Co). Biblio Dist.
Chambers, Jonathan D. Population, Economy, & Society in Pre-Industrial England. (Oxford Paperbacks University Ser). 200p. 1972. pap. 3.95x (ISBN 0-19-888085-5). Oxford U Pr.
Cooper, William D., ed. List of Foreign Protestants, & Aliens, Resident in England, 1618-1688. 1862. 15.50 (ISBN 0-384-09795-2). Johnson Repr.
--Lists of Foreign Protestants & Aliens Resident in England 1618-1688. Repr. of 1862 ed. 14.00 (ISBN 0-404-50182-6). AMS Pr.
Cunningham, William. Alien Immigrants to England. 2nd ed. (Illus.). 286p. 1969. Repr. of 1897 ed. 25.00x (ISBN 0-7146-1295-2, F Cass Co). Biblio Dist.
Flinn, M. W. British Population Growth 1700-1850. (Studies in Economic & Social History). (Orig.). 1970. pap. text ed. 3.50x (ISBN 0-333-10990-2). Humanities.
Glass, D. V. & Taylor, P. A. Population & Emigration in Nineteenth Century Britain. (Commentaries on British Parlimentary Papers). 132p. 1976. 15.00x (ISBN 0-7165-2219-5, Pub. by Irish Academic Pr Ireland). Biblio Dist.
Gleason, Arthur. Inside the British. 1978. Repr. of 1917 ed. lib. bdg. 25.00 (ISBN 0-8495-1936-5). Arden Lib.
Great Britain, Census Office. Abstract of the Answers & Returns: The Census Report for 1801, 2 vols. LC 79-366591. Date not set. Repr. of 1802 ed. Set. lib. bdg. 90.00x (ISBN 0-678-05225-5). Vol. 1, Enumeration. Vol. 2, Parish Registers. Kelley.
Hiro, Dilip. Black British, White British. LC 72-92026. 384p. 1973. pap. 3.95 (ISBN 0-85345-304-7, PB3047). Monthly Rev.
Hobcraft, John & Rees, Philip, eds. Regional Demographic Development. (Illus.). 287p. 1977. 36.00x (ISBN 0-7099-0245-X, Pub. by Croom Helm Ltd England). Biblio Dist.
Howlett, John. Examination of Doctor Price's Essay on the Population of England & Wales. LC 67-29507. Repr. of 1781 ed. 13.50x (ISBN 0-678-00352-1). Kelley.
Jackson, Valerie J. Population in the Countryside: Growth & Stagnation in the Cotswolds. (Illus.). 176p. 1968. 24.00x (ISBN 0-7146-1584-6, F Cass Co). Biblio Dist.
Kelsall, R. K. Aspects of Modern Sociology, the Social Structure of Modern Britain Ser. rev. ed. (Aspects of Modern Sociology, the Social Structure of Modern Britain Ser). 1967. text ed. 4.25x (ISBN 0-582-48771-4); pap. text ed. 3.00x (ISBN 0-582-48709-9). Humanities.
Mitchison, Rosiland. British Population Change Since 1860. (Studies in Economic & Social History). 1977. pap. text ed. 4.75x (ISBN 0-333-13585-7). Humanities.
Newman, Arnold, photos by. The Great British. (Illus.). 118p. 1980. 10.00 (ISBN 0-297-77611-8, 56680-3, Pub. by Natl Portrait Gallery England). U of Chicago Pr.
Ohlin, Per G. The Positive & the Preventive Check: A Study of the Rate of Growth of Pre-Industrial Populations. Bruchey, Stuart, ed. LC 80-2819. (Dissertations in European Economic History II). (Illus.). 1981. lib. bdg. 45.00x (ISBN 0-405-14003-7). Arno.
Population, 25 vols. (British Parliamentary Papers Ser.). 1971. Set. 2142.00x (ISBN 0-7165-1497-4, Pub. by Irish Academic Pr Ireland). Biblio Dist.
Reed, Clyde G. Price Data & European Economic History: England 1300-1600. Bruchey, Stuart, ed. LC 80-2826. (Dissertations in European Economic History II). (Illus.). 1981. lib. bdg. 12.00x (ISBN 0-405-14010-X). Arno.
Tranter, Neil L. Population Since the Industrial Revolution: The Case of England & Wales. 1973. text ed. 10.50x (ISBN 0-85664-012-3). Humanities.
Williams, Michael. British Population. 2nd ed. (Studies in the British Economy Ser.). 1975. pap. text ed. 6.50x (ISBN 0-435-33960-5). Heinemann Ed.
Wrigley, E. A. & Schofield, R. S. The Population History of England 1541-1871: A Reconstruction. (Studies in Social & Demographic History). (Illus.). 704p. Date not set. text ed. 60.00x (ISBN 0-674-69007-9). Harvard U Pr.

GREAT BRITAIN–POST OFFICE

Robinson, Howard. British Post Office: A History. Repr. of 1948 ed. lib. bdg. 28.25x (ISBN 0-8371-3142-1, ROPO). Greenwood.

GREAT BRITAIN–PRINCES AND PRINCESSES

Fulford, Roger. Wicked Uncles: The Father of Queen Victoria - His Brothers. facs. ed. LC 68-8461. (Essay Index Reprint Ser). 1968. Repr. of 1933 ed. 17.00 (ISBN 0-8369-0466-4). Arno.
Gilleo, Alma. Prince Charles, Growing up in Buckingham Palace. LC 78-18938. (Illus.). (gr. k-4). 1978. PLB 5.95 (ISBN 0-89565-029-0). Childs World.
Pine, L. G. Princes of Wales. LC 72-104216. 1970. 5.00 (ISBN 0-8048-0896-1). C E Tuttle.
Thornton-Cook, Elsie. Kings in the Making: The Princes of Wales. facs. ed. LC 68-22951. (Essay Index Reprint Ser). 1931. 19.50 (ISBN 0-8369-0937-2). Arno.
--Royal Elizabeths: The Romance of Five Princesses, 1464-1840. facs. ed. LC 67-23274. (Essay Index Reprint Ser). 1967. Repr. of 1929 ed. 13.00 (ISBN 0-8369-0938-0). Arno.
--Royal Marys, Princess Mary & Her Predecessors. facs. ed. LC 67-23275. (Essay Index Reprint Ser). 1930. 17.00 (ISBN 0-8369-0940-2). Arno.

GREAT BRITAIN–PRIVY COUNCIL

Baldwin, James F. The King's Council in England During the Middle Ages. 1965. 10.00 (ISBN 0-8446-1045-3). Peter Smith.
Dicey, Albert V. The Privy Council. LC 79-1625. 1981. Repr. of 1887 ed. 16.00 (ISBN 0-88355-930-7). Hyperion Conn.
Howell, P. A. The Judicial Committee of the Privy Council: 1833-1876. LC 78-54326. (Cambridge Studies in English Legal History). (Illus.). 1979. 35.50 (ISBN 0-521-22146-3). Cambridge U Pr.
Ponko, Vincent, Jr. Privy Council & the Spirit of Elizabethan Economic Management. LC 68-24356. (Transactions Ser.: Vol. 58, Pt. 4). 1968. pap. 1.00 (ISBN 0-87169-584-7). Am Philos.
Pulman, Michael B. The Elizabethan Privy Council in the Fifteen Seventies. LC 73-115497. 1971. 26.75x (ISBN 0-520-01716-1). U of Cal Pr.
Smith, Joseph H. Appeals to the Privy Council from the American Plantations. 1965. lib. bdg. 30.00x (ISBN 0-374-97486-1). Octagon.
Washburne, George A. Imperial Control of the Administration of Justice in the Thirteen American Colonies 1684-1776. LC 70-109920. (Columbia Univesity. Studies in the Social Sciences: No. 238). Repr. of 1923 ed. 17.50 (ISBN 0-404-51238-0). AMS Pr.
Willson, David H. Privy Councillors in the House of Commons, 1604-1629. LC 76-120678. 1970. Repr. lib. bdg. 17.50x (ISBN 0-374-98639-8). Octagon.

GREAT BRITAIN–PROCLAMATIONS

Brigham, Clarence S., ed. British Royal Proclamations Relating to America, 1603-1783. Repr. of 1911 ed. pap. 23.00 (ISBN 0-384-19815-5). Johnson Repr.
Crawford, James L. Handlist of Proclamations Issued by Royal & Other Constitutional Authorities 1714-1910. 1966. Repr. of 1910 ed. 89.00 (ISBN 0-8337-0721-3). B Franklin.

Great Britain Sovereigns. British Royal Proclamations Relating to America, 1603-1783. 1964. Repr. of 1911 ed. 29.00 (ISBN 0-8337-0373-0). B Franklin.
Hughes, Paul L. & Larkin, James F., eds. Tudor Royal Proclamations, Vols. 2 - 3, The Later Tudors, 1553-1603. LC 63-13965. 1969. Set. 75.00x (ISBN 0-300-00103-7). Yale U Pr.
Youngs, F. A. The Proclamations of the Tudor Queens. LC 75-30442. 304p. 1976. 46.50 (ISBN 0-521-21044-5). Cambridge U Pr.

GREAT BRITAIN–PUBLIC RECORDS OFFICE

The British Public Record Office: History, Description, Record Groups, Finding Aids, & Materials for American History, with Special Reference to Virginia. LC 60-9753. (Publications Ser: No. 12). 1960. pap. 5.00 (ISBN 0-88490-048-7). VA State Lib.
Pong, David. A Critical Guide to the Kwangtung Provincial Archives Deposited at the Public Record Office, London. (East Asian Monographs: No. 63). 400p. 1976. pap. text ed. 9.00x (ISBN 0-674-17722-3). Harvard U Pr.

GREAT BRITAIN–QUEENS

Bates, Albert C. The Work of Hartford's First Printer. 1925. pap. 0.50 (ISBN 0-940748-47-9). Conn Hist Soc.
Benson, E. F. Queen Victoria's Daughters. (Victorian Age Ser). 1938. Repr. 25.00 (ISBN 0-685-43392-7). Norwood Edns.
Erlanger, Phillipe. Margaret of Anjou: Queen of England. Hyams, Edward, tr. LC 79-161438. (Illus.). 251p. 1970. 9.95x (ISBN 0-87024-214-8). U. of Miami Pr.
Froude, J. A. The Divorce of Catherine of Aragon. 1891. Repr. 15.00 (ISBN 0-685-43082-0). Norwood Edns.
Geoffrey of Monmouth. The History of the Kings of Britain. Thorpe, Lewis, tr. (Classic Ser). 1977. pap. 2.50 (ISBN 0-14-044170-0). Penguin.
Letters & Journals: Judge William Edmond, Judge Holbrook Curtis, Judge William Edmond Curtis, & Dr. Holbrook Curtis. 1926. plus three separate pamplhets 5.00 set (ISBN 0-940748-29-0). Conn Hist Soc.
McCann, Timothy J., ed. Goodwood: Royal Letters Mary Queen of Scots to Queen Elizabeth II. 1981. 5.00x (ISBN 0-686-75437-9, Pub. by County Archivist England). State Mutual Bk.
Meade, Marion. Eleanor of Aquitaine: A Biography. (Illus.). 1980. pap. 6.95 (ISBN 0-8015-2232-3, Hawthorn). Dutton.
Ponsonby, Frederick. Side Lights on Queen Victoria. (Victorian Age Ser). 1930. Repr. 12.50 (ISBN 0-685-43424-9). Norwood Edns.
Roberts, Kenneth D. The Contributions of Joseph Ives to Connecticut Clock Technology: Eighteen Ten to Eighteen Sixty-Two. 1970. 16.50x (ISBN 0-686-26753-2). Conn Hist Soc.
Softly, Barbara. The Queens of England. LC 76-14851. (Illus.). 1977. pap. 1.95 (ISBN 0-685-70103-4). Stein & Day.
Tappan, Eva. In the Days of Queen Victoria. (Victorian Age Ser). 1903. Repr. 12.50 (ISBN 0-685-43425-7). Norwood Edns.
Thornton-Cook, Elsie. Her Majesty: The Romance of the Queens of England, 1066-1910. facsimile ed. LC 78-105043. (Essay Index Reprint Ser). Repr. of 1926 ed. 23.00 (ISBN 0-8369-1688-3). Arno.
Weaver, Glenn. Jonathan Trumbull, Connecticut's Merchant Magistrate: Seventeen Ten to Seventeen Eighty-Five. 1956. 6.50x (ISBN 0-940748-27-4). Conn Hist Soc.

GREAT BRITAIN–RACE RELATIONS

Allen, Sheila. New Minorities, Old Conflicts: Asian & West Indian Migrants in Britain. 1971. pap. text ed. 3.95x (ISBN 0-394-31477-8). Phila Bk Co.
Banton, Michael P. White & Coloured: The Behavior of the British People Towards Coloured Immigrants. LC 76-43335. 1976. Repr. of 1960 ed. lib. bdg. 16.25x (ISBN 0-8371-9290-0, BAWAC). Greenwood.
Barker, Anthony J. The African Link: British Attitudes to the Negro in the Era of the Atlantic Slave Trade, 1550-1807. 263p. 1978. 26.00x (ISBN 0-7146-3081-0, F Cass Co). Biblio Dist.
Claiborne, Louis. Race & Law in Britain & the U. S. (Minority Rights Reports Ser.: No. 22). 1974. pap. 2.50 (ISBN 0-89192-108-7). Interbk Inc.
Freeman, Gary P. Immigrant Labor & Racial Conflict in Industrial Societies: The French & British Experience, 1945-1975. LC 78-70292. 1979. 25.00x (ISBN 0-691-07603-0). Princeton U Pr.
Hiro, Dilip. Black British, White British. LC 72-92026. 384p. 1973. pap. 3.95 (ISBN 0-85345-304-7, PB3047). Monthly Rev.
Katznelson, Ira. Black Men, White Cities: Race, Politics & Migration in the United States, 1900-1930 & in Britain, 1948-1968. 228p. 1973. 9.95 (ISBN 0-19-218193-9). Oxford U Pr.
--Black Men, White Cities: Race, Politics, & Migration in the United States, 1900-30, & Britain, 1948-68. LC 76-8376. 1976. pap. 3.95 (ISBN 0-226-42671-8, P679, Phoen). U of Chicago Pr.
Kirp, David L. Doing Good by Doing Little: Race & Schooling in Britain. LC 78-62824. 1979. 14.50x (ISBN 0-520-03740-5). U of Cal Pr.
Lester, Anthony & Bindman, Geoffrey. Race & Law in Great Britain. LC 73-189159. 1972. 22.50x (ISBN 0-674-74570-1). Harvard U Pr.
Miles, Robert & Phizacklea, Annie, eds. Racism & Political Action in Britain. 1978. 23.50x (ISBN 0-7100-0035-9); pap. 10.00 (ISBN 0-7100-0036-7). Routledge & Kegan.
Moore, Robert. Racism & Black Resistance in Britain. 128p. 1980. pap. 2.95 (ISBN 0-902818-76-7). Pluto Pr.
Richmond, Anthony H. Colour Prejudice in Britain: A Study of West Indian Workers in Liverpool, 1941-1951. LC 76-111496. (Illus.). 184p. 1954. Repr. 12.25x (ISBN 0-8371-4638-0, Pub. by Negro U Pr). Greenwood.
Rose, E. J., et al. Colour & Citizenship: A Report on British Race Relations. 1969. pap. 14.50x (ISBN 0-19-218180-7). Oxford U Pr.
Russell, A. G. Colour, Race & Empire. LC 72-89270. 280p. 1973. Repr. of 1944 ed. 13.50 (ISBN 0-8046-1756-2). Kennikat.
Sandford, Jeremy. Smiling David. LC 75-309907. (Illus.). 128p. 1979. 9.95 (ISBN 0-7145-1048-3, Pub. by M Boyars); pap. 5.95 (ISBN 0-7145-1049-1, Pub. by M Boyars). Merrimack Bk Serv.
Schaefer, Richard T. The Extent & Content of Racial Prejudice in Great Britain. LC 75-18121. 1976. softbound 12.00 (ISBN 0-88247-406-5). R & E Res Assoc.
Scobie, Edward. Black Britannia: A History of Blacks in Britain. LC 72-82184. (Illus.). 304p. 1972. 7.95 (ISBN 0-87485-056-8). Johnson Chi.

GREAT BRITAIN–REGISTERS

Haydn, Joseph T. Book of Dignities, Containing Lists of the Official Personages of the British Empire from the Earliest Period to the Present Time...the Orders and Knighthood of the United Kingdom and India, Etc.....Continued to the Present Time...by Horace Ockerby. 3rd ed. LC 70-140398. 1970. Repr. of 1894 ed. 35.00 (ISBN 0-8063-0431-6). Genealog Pub.

GREAT BRITAIN–RELATIONS (GENERAL) WITH FOREIGN COUNTRIES

Armytage, W. H. American Influence on English Education. (Students Library of Education). (Orig.). 1967. text ed. 5.50x (ISBN 0-7100-4201-9); pap. text ed. 3.25x (ISBN 0-7100-4206-X). Humanities.
Bastide, Charles. Anglo-French Entente in the 17th Century. LC 78-146136. (Research & Source Works Ser.: No. 825). 1971. Repr. of 1914 ed. lib. bdg. 21.00 (ISBN 0-8337-0185-1). B Franklin.
Chew, Samuel C. Crescent & the Rose: Islam & England During the Renaissance. 1965. lib. bdg. 27.50x (ISBN 0-374-91501-6). Octagon.
Davis, Garold N. German Thought & Culture in England, 1700-1770. (Studies in Comparative Literature Ser.: No. 47). 1969. 10.50x (ISBN 0-8078-7047-1). U. of NC Pr.
Davis, Ralph. English Overseas Trade Fifteen Hundred to Seventeen Hundred. (Studies in Economic & Social History). 1973. pap. 1.50x (ISBN 0-333-14419-8). Humanities.
De Vere, Aubrey. English Misrule & Irish Misdeeds. LC 77-102597. (Irish Culture & History Ser). 1970. Repr. of 1848 ed. 12.75 (ISBN 0-8046-0775-3). Kennikat.
Ferns, Henry S. British & Argentina in the Nineteenth Century. Wilkins, Mira, ed. LC 76-29757. (European Business Ser.). 1977. Repr. of 1960 ed. lib. bdg. 30.00x (ISBN 0-405-09772-7). Arno.
Gibbs, Philip H., ed. Bridging the Atlantic. facs. ed. LC 78-128245. (Essay Index Reprint Ser). 1943. 14.75 (ISBN 0-8369-1928-9). Arno.
Gordon, George S. Anglo-American Literary Relations: The Watson Chair Foundation Lectures of the Sulgrave Manor Board. LC 76-167346. (Essay Index Reprint Ser.). (Delivered in University College, London, March 1931). Repr. of 1942 ed. 11.00 (ISBN 0-8369-2649-8). Arno.
Heindel, Richard H. American Impact on Great Britain, 1898-1914. 1968. lib. bdg. 18.00x (ISBN 0-374-93800-8). Octagon.
Illick, Joseph E., ed. America & England, 1558-1776. LC 70-11183. 1970. pap. text ed. 5.95x (ISBN 0-89197-006-1). Irvington.
Jarrett, Derek. The Begetters of Revolution. 320p. 1973. 17.50x (ISBN 0-87471-136-3). Rowman.
Lyon, Peter, ed. Britain & Canada. 191p. 1976. 26.00x (ISBN 0-7146-3052-7, F Cass Co). Biblio Dist.
Manchester, Alan K. British Preeminence in Brazil. 1964. lib. bdg. 20.00x (ISBN 0-374-95263-9). Octagon.
Milton, John. Brief History of Moscovia. LC 72-195009. 1929. lib. bdg. 15.00 (ISBN 0-8414-6619-X). Folcroft.
Seaton, Ethel. Literary Relations of England & Scandinavia in the Seventeenth Century. LC 72-83605. 1973. Repr. of 1935 ed. lib. bdg. 17.00 (ISBN 0-405-08943-0). Arno.
Simmons, Ernest J. English Literature & Culture in Russia, 1553-1840. 1964. lib. bdg. 17.50x (ISBN 0-374-97448-9). Octagon.
Spencer, Terence. Fair Greece, Sad Relic: Literary Philhellenism from Shakespeare to Byron. LC 76-158507. (Illus.). 1971. Repr. of 1954 ed. 13.00 (ISBN 0-403-01307-0). Scholarly.
Tarling, Nicholas. Sulu & Sabah: A Study of the British Policy Towards the Philippines & North Borneo from the Late Eighteenth Century. (Illus.). 1978. 39.00x (ISBN 0-19-580337-X). Oxford U Pr.
Taylor, Philip M. The Projection of Britain: British Overseas Publicity & Propaganda 1919-1939. LC 80-42291. 384p. Date not set. price not set (ISBN 0-521-23843-9). Cambridge U Pr.
Thistlethwaite, Frank. Anglo-American Connection in the Early Nineteenth Century. LC 70-151558. 1971. Repr. of 1959 ed. 13.00 (ISBN 0-8462-1540-3). Russell.
Tout, Thomas F. France & England: Their Relations in the Middle Ages & Now. LC 74-5775. (U of Manchester Historical Ser.). 168p. 1975. Repr. of 1922 ed. lib. bdg. 15.00x (ISBN 0-8371-7514-3, TOFE). Greenwood.
Weber, Carl J. Hardy in America: A Study of Thomas Hardy & His American Readers. LC 66-15436. (Illus., Corrected ed.). 1966. Repr. of 1946 ed. 10.00 (ISBN 0-8462-0757-5). Russell.
Wheeler, Mark C. Britain & the War for Yugoslavia, Nineteen Forty to Nineteen Forty-Three. (East European Monographs: No. 64). 1980. 18.50x (ISBN 0-914710-57-5). East Eur Quarterly.

GREAT BRITAIN–RELATIONS (GENERAL) WITH THE CATHOLIC CHURCH

Lunt, William E. Financial Relations of the Papacy with England, 2 vols. Incl. Vol. 1. To 1327. 1967. Repr. of 1939 ed. 20.00 (ISBN 0-910956-13-8); Vol. 2. 1327-1534. 1962. 25.00 (ISBN 0-910956-48-0). Medieval Acad.

GREAT BRITAIN–RELIGION

Allison, Thomas. English Religious Life in the Eighth Century. LC 75-106708. Repr. of 1929 ed. lib. bdg. 15.00 (ISBN 0-8371-3438-2, ALRL). Greenwood.
--English Religious Life in the Eighth Century As Illustrated by Contemporary Letters. LC 70-136409. Repr. of 1929 ed. 9.00 (ISBN 0-404-00348-6). AMS Pr.
Bankes, J. & Kerridge, E. The Early Records of the Banks Family at Winstanley. 114p. 1973. 33.00x (ISBN 0-7190-1158-2, Pub. by Manchester U Pr England). State Mutual Bk.
Bell, G. K. The English Church. 10.00 (ISBN 0-8414-1634-6). Folcroft.
Buckley, George T. Atheism in the English Renaissance. LC 65-13936. 1965. Repr. of 1932 ed. 8.00 (ISBN 0-8462-0534-3). Russell.
Calderwood, David. A Solution of Doctor Resolutus, His Resolutions for Kneeling. LC 79-84093. (English Experience Ser.: No. 913). 60p. 1979. Repr. of 1619 ed. lib. bdg. 8.00 (ISBN 90-221-0913-5). Walter J Johnson.
Cashmore, Ernest. Rastaman: The Rastafarian Movement in England. (Illus.). 272p. 1980. pap. text ed. 8.95x (ISBN 0-04-301116-0). Allen Unwin.
--Rastaman: The Rastagarian Movement in England. (Illus.). 1979. text ed. 22.50x (ISBN 0-04-301108-X). Allen Unwin.
Cockshut, A. O. Religious Controversies of the Nineteenth Century: Selected Documents. LC 66-18225. 1966. 16.50x (ISBN 0-8032-0019-6). U of Nebr Pr.
Cowling, M. Religion & Public Doctrine in Modern England. (Cambridge Studies in the History & Theory of Politics). 498p. 1981. 49.50 (ISBN 0-521-23289-9). Cambridge U Pr.
Crosby, Thomas. History of the English Baptists: 1740 Ed, 4 vols. Set. 45.00 (ISBN 0-686-12405-7). Church History.
D'Aubigne, Merle. The Reformation in England, 2 vols. 1977. Vol. 1. 16.95 (ISBN 0-85151-059-0); Vol. 2. 16.95 (ISBN 0-85151-094-9); Set. 30.95 (ISBN 0-686-77101-X). Banner of Truth.
Davies, Horton. Worship & Theology in England: Vol. 2, From Andrews to Baxter & Fox, 1603-1690. LC 61-7402. (Illus.). 592p. 1975. 35.00x (ISBN 0-691-07121-7). Princeton U Pr.
Davies, Morton. The Ecumenical Century: 1900-1965. (Worship & Theology in England Ser.: Vol. 5). 1965. 24.00x (ISBN 0-691-07145-4). Princeton U Pr.
Firth, Katherine R. The Apocalyptic Tradition in Reformation Britain 1530-1645. (Historical Monographs). (Illus.). 1979. 37.50x (ISBN 0-19-821868-0). Oxford U Pr.
Gilbert, Alan D. Religion & Society in Industrial England. (Themes in British Social History Ser.). (Illus.). 260p. 1976. pap. text ed. 12.95x (ISBN 0-582-48323-9). Longman.
Greaves, Richard L. Society & Religion in Elizabethan England. 832p. 1981. 39.50x (ISBN 0-8166-1030-4). U of Minn Pr.
Hart, A. Tindal. Curate's Lot: The Story of the Unbeneficed English Clergy. 1970. text ed. 9.25x (ISBN 0-212-98380-6). Humanities.
Hick, John. God Has Many Names. 108p. 1981. text ed. 20.00x (ISBN 0-333-27747-3, Pub. by Macmillan, England); pap. text ed. 7.50 (ISBN 0-333-27758-9). Humanities.
Kelly, Faye L. Prayer in Sixteenth Century England. LC 66-64090. (U of Fla. Humanities Monographs: No. 22). 1966. pap. 2.50 (ISBN 0-8130-0127-7). U Presses Fla.
Knight, Helen C., compiled by. Lady Huntington & Her Friends. (Summit Bks). 1978. pap. 3.45 (ISBN 0-8010-5399-4). Baker Bk.
Knowles, David. The Religious Orders in England: The Tudor Age, Vol. 3. LC 78-73953. 1979. 59.50 (ISBN 0-521-05482-6); pap. 19.50 (ISBN 0-521-29568-8). Cambridge U Pr.
Manning, Bernard L. The People's Faith in the Time of Wyclif. 196p. 1975. Repr. of 1919 ed. 14.50x (ISBN 0-87471-616-0). Rowman.
Mensing, Raymond C. Toleration & Parliament, 1660-1719. LC 79-63260. 1979. pap. text ed. 9.00 (ISBN 0-8191-0723-9). U Pr of Amer.
Needham, G. I., ed. Lives of Three English Saints. rev. ed. 119p. 1979. pap. text ed. 5.00x (ISBN 0-85989-076-7, Pub. by U Exeter England). Humanities.
Owen, Gale R. Rites & Religions of the Anglo-Saxons. (Illus.). 216p. 1981. 18.50x (ISBN 0-389-20128-6). B&N.
Perman, David. Change & the Churches: An Anatomy of Religion in Britain. 1978. 18.00 (ISBN 0-370-10329-7). Transatlantic.
Pritchard, Arnold. Catholic Loyalism in Elizabethan England. LC 78-10208. 1979. 20.00x (ISBN 0-8078-1345-1). U of NC Pr.
Pruett, John H. The Parish Clergy Under the Later Stuarts: The Leicestershire Experience. LC 78-8174. 1978. 12.50 (ISBN 0-252-00662-3). U of Ill Pr.
Ransom, Stewart, et al. Clergy, Ministers & Priests. (International Library of Sociology Ser.). 1977. 20.00 (ISBN 0-7100-8713-6). Routledge & Kegan.
Religion, 3 vols. (British Parliamentary Papers Ser.). 1971. Set. 189.00x (ISBN 0-7165-1498-2, Pub. by Irish Academic Pr Ireland). Biblio Dist.
Selby-Lowndes, Joan. Your Book of the English Church. 3.25 (ISBN 0-685-91532-8). Transatlantic.
Smith, H. Maynard. Pre-Reformation England. LC 63-15182. 1963. Repr. of 1938 ed. 10.00 (ISBN 0-8462-0321-9). Russell.
Stoughton, John. History of Religion in England, 8 vols. 1977. lib. bdg. 800.00 (ISBN 0-8490-1984-2). Gordon Pr.
Sykes, Norman. The English Religious Tradition: Sketches of Its Influence on Church, State & Society. LC 78-59045. 1979. Repr. of 1953 ed. 13.50 (ISBN 0-88355-717-7). Hyperion Conn.
Thomas, Keith. Religion & the Decline of Magic. LC 74-141707. 1971. pap. text ed. 13.95x (ISBN 0-684-14542-1, ScribC). Scribner.
Voltaire. Letters Concerning the English Nation. LC 74-728. 224p. 1974. Repr. of 1926 ed. lib. bdg. 19.00 (ISBN 0-8337-4467-4). B Franklin.
--Lettres Philosophiques. Pomeau, Rene, ed. 192p. 1964. 3.95 (ISBN 0-686-55754-9). French & Eur.
--Lettres Philosophiques. 18.95 (ISBN 0-686-55755-7). French & Eur.
Voltaire, Francois M. Philosophical Letters. Dilworth, Ernest N., tr. LC 60-53370. 1961. pap. 4.50 (ISBN 0-672-60326-8, LLA124). Bobbs.

GREAT BRITAIN–RESTRICTIVE PRACTICES COURT

Brock, C. Control of Restrictive Practices from 1956. 1969. 6.95 (ISBN 0-07-094038-X, P&RB). McGraw.

GREAT BRITAIN–ROYAL AIR FORCE

Baker, E. C. Fighter Aces of the R. A. F., 1939-45. (Illus.). 1965. pap. 4.95 (ISBN 0-913076-00-7). Beachcomber Bks.
Barker, Ralph & Time-Life Book Editors. The RAF at War. (The Epic of Flight Ser.). (Illus.). 176p. 1981. 13.95 (ISBN 0-8094-3291-9). Time-Life.
Bowyer, Chaz. Airmen of World War One: Men of the British & Empire Air Forces in Old Photographs. LC 75-12847. (Illus.). 128p. 1976. 14.95 (ISBN 0-88254-356-3). Hippocrene Bks.
--Beaufighter at War. (Illus.). 1978. 14.95 (ISBN 0-684-15700-4, ScribT). Scribner.
Bowyer, Michael J. The Stirling Bomber. (Illus.). 240p. 1980. 29.00 (ISBN 0-571-11101-7, Pub. by Faber & Faber). Merrimack Bk Serv.
--Two Group R.A.F. LC 74-180641. (Illus.). 532p. 1979. 21.95 (ISBN 0-571-09491-0, Pub. by Faber & Faber); pap. 9.95 (ISBN 0-571-11460-1). Merrimack Bk Serv.

Foxley-Norris, Sir Christopher. A Lighter Shade of Blue. (Illus.). 1979. 14.95 (ISBN 0-7110-0858-2). Hippocrene Bks.
Fredette, Raymond H. The Sky on Fire: The First Battle of Britain. LC 75-33909. 290p. 1976. pap. 5.25 (ISBN 0-15-682750-6, HB329, Harv). HarBraceJ.
Gibson, Guy. Enemy Coast Ahead. LC 78-169417. (Literature & History of Aviation Ser). 1972. Repr. of 1946 ed. 15.00 (ISBN 0-405-03762-7). Arno.
Glubb, John B. War in the Desert: An R. A. F. Frontier Campaign. LC 80-1929. Repr. of 1961 ed. 38.00 (ISBN 0-404-18964-4). AMS Pr.
Goulding, James. Royal Air Force Bomber Command. (Illus.). 144p. 1976. 18.50x (ISBN 0-7110-0627-X). Intl Pubns Serv.
Haugland, Vern. The Eagle Squadrons: Yanks in the RAF 1940-1942. Slepyan, Norbert M., ed. (Illus.). 12.95 (ISBN 0-87165-028-2). Ziff-Davis Pub.
--The Eagles'war. (Illus.). 1982. 14.95 (ISBN 0-07-118766-9). Ziff-Davis Pub.
Hering, P. G. Customs & Traditions of the Royal Air Force. 1961. 7.95 (ISBN 0-685-56066-X). Beachcomber Bks.
King, H. F. Armament of British Aircraft Nineteen Hundred & Nine to Nineteen Thirty-Nine. (Putnam Aeronautical Ser.). (Illus.). 470p. 1980. 17.95 (ISBN 0-370-00057-9, Pub. by Chatto Bodley Jonathan). Merrimack Bk Serv.
Kinsey, Gordon. Martlesham Heath. (Illus.). 1979. 18.50 (ISBN 0-900963-48-4, Pub. by Terence Dalton England). State Mutual Bk.
Lawrence, T. E. Mint. 1963. pap. 4.95 (ISBN 0-393-00196-2, Norton Lib). Norton.
Macmillan, Norman. Into the Blue. LC 79-169430. (Literature & History of Aviation Ser). 1971. Repr. of 1969 ed. 15.00 (ISBN 0-405-03773-2). Arno.
Musgrove, Gordon. The Pathfinder Force: The History of 8 Group. (Illus.). 1977. 14.95 (ISBN 0-354-01017-4). Hippocrene Bks.
Powers, Barry D. Strategy Without Slide Rule: British Air Strategy 1914-39. 1976. text ed. 25.00x (ISBN 0-8419-5506-9). Holmes & Meier.
Richards, Denis. Portal of Hungerford: The Life of Marshal of the Royal Air Force Viscount Portal of Hungerford KG, GCB, OM, DSO, MC. (Illus.). 1978. text ed. 24.50x (ISBN 0-8419-6103-4). Holmes & Meier.
Saunders, Hillary S. Per Ardua: The Rise of British Air Power 1911-1939. LC 79-169436. (Literature & History of Aviation Ser). 1971. Repr. of 1945 ed. 18.00 (ISBN 0-405-03781-3). Arno.
Shores, Christopher F. Second Tactical Air Force: November 1943 to the End of World War II. (Illus.). 298p. 1970. 14.95x (ISBN 0-8464-0828-7). Beekman Pubs.
Tanner, John. Fighting in the Air. LC 78-60957. (RAF Museum Ser.: Vol. 7). (Illus.). 1979. 19.95 (ISBN 0-88254-472-1). Hippocrene Bks.
Tanner, John, ed. The Lancaster Manual. LC 77-72264. (RAF Museum Ser: Vol. 5). 1977. 19.95 (ISBN 0-88254-433-0). Hippocrene Bks.
Taylor, John W. Pictorial History of the R.A.F, 3 vols. Incl. Vol. 1. 1918-1939. 202p. 1969. 5.95 (ISBN 0-668-01857-7); Vol. 2. 1939-1945. Moyes, Philip J. 240p. 1968. o. p. 5.95 (ISBN 0-668-02137-3); Vol. 3. 1945-1969. Moyes, Philip J. 208p. 1970. LC 69-12569. (Illus.). Arco.
Taylor, John W., intro. by. Aircraft of the RAF Nineteen Eighteen to Nineteen Seventy-Eight. (Illus.). 1979. 14.95 (ISBN 0-354-01183-9). Hippocrene Bks.
Thetford, Owen. Aircraft of the Royal Air Force Since 1918. 7th ed. (Putnam Aeronautical Ser.). (Illus.). 656p. 1980. 26.95 (ISBN 0-370-30186-2, Pub. by Chatto Bodley Jonathan). Merrimack Bk Serv.
Voss, Vivian. Flying Minnows. LC 76-13831. (Illus.). 1977. 12.50 (ISBN 0-88254-410-1). Hippocrene Bks.
Wight, Basil. Arms & the Law. 1978. 6.95 (ISBN 0-533-03018-8). Vantage.

GREAT BRITAIN–ROYAL COMMISSION ON POOR LAWS AND THE RELIEF OF DEBTORS

Passfield & Webb, Sidney J., eds. Minority Report of the Poor Law Commission, 2 vols in 1. LC 73-18323. Repr. of 1909 ed. 35.00x (ISBN 0-678-01297-0). Kelley.

GREAT BRITAIN–ROYAL HOUSEHOLD

Cathcart, Helen. Prince Charles: The Making of a Prince. LC 77-73686. (Illus.). 1977. 8.50 (ISBN 0-8008-6555-3). Taplinger.
Clear, Celia. Royal Children Eighteen Forty to Nineteen Eighty: From Queen Victoria to Queen Elizabeth II. LC 81-5289. (Illus.). 166p. 1981. 12.95 (ISBN 0-8128-2826-7). Stein & Day.
Dewhurst, Jack. Royal Confinements. 198p. 1981. 12.95 (ISBN 0-312-69466-0). St Martin.
Edgar, Donald. Britain's Royal Family in the Twentieth Century. (Illus.). 1979. 14.95 (ISBN 0-517-53941-1). Crown.
Ford, Colin, ed. Happy & Glorious: Six Reigns of Royal Photography. LC 77-2297. (Illus.). 1977. 11.95 (ISBN 0-02-539590-4). Macmillan.
Hibbert, Christopher. The Court of St. James's: The Monarch at Work from Victoria to Elizabeth II. LC 79-28404. 1980. 12.95 (ISBN 0-688-03627-9). Morrow.
Larson, Laurence M. King's Household in England Before the Norman Conquest. LC 75-99885. Repr. of 1904 ed. 8.50 (ISBN 0-404-00617-5). AMS Pr.
--King's Household in England Before the Norman Conquest. Repr. of 1904 ed. lib. bdg. 15.00x (ISBN 0-8371-1805-0, LAKH). Greenwood.
--King's Household in England Before the Norman Conquest. 1904. 5.00 (ISBN 0-403-00042-4). Scholarly.
Packard, Jerrold M. The Queen & Her Court: A Guide to the British Monarchy Today. 256p. 1981. 14.95 (ISBN 0-684-16796-4, ScribT). Scribner.
Pinches, J. J. & Pinches, R. V. Royal Heraldry of England. (Illus.). 1974. 35.00 (ISBN 0-8048-1228-4). C E Tuttle.
Plowden, Alison. Marriage with My Kingdom: The Courtships of Queen Elizabeth I. LC 77-8768. (Illus.). 1978. 25.00x (ISBN 0-8128-2338-9). Stein & Day.
Round, Horace. King's Serjeants & Officers of State: With Their Coronation Service. (Genealogy Ser.: No. 3). 416p. 1971. Repr. of 1911 ed. 35.00x (ISBN 0-7130-0026-0, Pub. by Woburn Pr England). Biblio Dist.
Royal Family Souvenir. 1978. pap. 1.95 (ISBN 0-8277-5611-9). British Bk Ctr.
St. George, Noel. Royal Quotes. LC 81-67811. 96p. 1981. 8.00 (ISBN 0-7153-8257-8). David & Charles.
Seymour, William. Sovereign Legacy. LC 79-6041. (Illus.). 1980. 15.95 (ISBN 0-385-15930-7). Doubleday.
Vickers, Hugo. Debrett's Book of the Royal Wedding. LC 80-54659. (Illus.). 176p. 1981. 19.95 (ISBN 0-670-60997-8, Studio). Viking Pr.
--Gladys: Duchess of Marlborough. LC 79-3430. (Illus.). 336p. 1980. 12.95 (ISBN 0-03-044751-8). HR&W.
Warwick, Christopher. Two Centuries of Royal Weddings. LC 79-49276. (Illus.). 145p. 1980. 14.95 (ISBN 0-396-07838-9). Dodd.

GREAT BRITAIN–RURAL CONDITIONS

Archer, Fred. The Countryman Cottage Life Book. LC 74-82896. (Countryman Books). (Illus.). 192p. 1975. 4.95 (ISBN 0-7153-6580-0). David & Charles.
Barley, M. W. The English Farmhouse & Cottage. (Illus.). 1961. 22.50 (ISBN 0-7100-1050-8). Routledge & Kegan.
Bonham-Carter, Victor. Land & Environment: The Survival of the English Countryside. LC 72-3522. (Illus.). 240p. 1973. 15.00 (ISBN 0-8386-1195-8). Fairleigh Dickinson.
Bracey, H. E. People & the Countryside. 1970. 24.00x (ISBN 0-7100-6686-4). Routledge & Kegan.
Dunbabin, J. P. Rural Discontent in 19th Century Britain. LC 73-94070. 1975. text ed. 27.50x (ISBN 0-8419-0146-5). Holmes & Meier.
Evans, George E. Where Beards Wag All. (Illus.). 312p. 1977. pap. 6.95 (ISBN 0-686-19310-5, Pub. by Faber & Faber). Merrimack Bk Serv.
Fox, H. S. A. & Butlin, R. A., eds. Change in the Countryside: Essays on Rural England, 1500-1900. (The Special Publication of the Institute of British Geographers Ser.: No. 10). 1980. 20.00 (ISBN 0-12-264280-5). Acad Pr.
Havinden, Michael A. Estate Villages. LC 66-71443. (Illus.). 1966. 12.50x (ISBN 0-678-08032-1). Kelley.
Hobsbawm, Eric & Rude, George. Captain Swing: A Social History of the Great English Agricultural Uprising of 1830. (Illus.). 384p. 1975. pap. 5.95 (ISBN 0-393-00793-6, Norton Lib). Norton.
Howitt, William. The Rural Life of England. 615p. Repr. of 1844 ed. 31.00x (ISBN 0-686-28330-9, Pub. by Irish Academic Pr). Biblio Dist.
Johnston, William. England As It Is: Political, Social & Industrial in the Middle of the Nineteenth Century, 2 vols. (The Development of Industrial Society Ser.). 721p. 1971. Repr. of 1857 ed. 60.00x (ISBN 0-7165-1774-4, Pub. by Irish Academic Pr). Biblio Dist.
Jordan, Wilbur K. Charities of Rural England, Fourteen Eighty to Sixteen Sixty: The Aspirations & Achievements of the Rural Society. LC 78-1390. 1978. Repr. of 1961 ed. lib. bdg. 31.50x (ISBN 0-313-20304-0, JOCR). Greenwood.
Lester, C. Edwards. The Glory & Shame of England, 2 vols. (The Development of Industrial Society Ser.). 905p. 1971. Repr. of 1866 ed. 36.00x (ISBN 0-7165-1789-2, Pub. by Irish Academic Pr). Biblio Dist.
Mingay, G. E., ed. The Victorian Countryside, 2 vols. (Illus.). 370p. 1981. Vol. 1. 85.00 (ISBN 0-7100-0734-5); Vol. 2. 45.00 (ISBN 0-7100-0735-3); Set. 85.00 (ISBN 0-7100-0736-1). Routledge & Kegan.
Moseley, Malcolm J. Accessibility: The Rural Challenge. (Illus.). 1979. 24.00 (ISBN 0-416-71220-7). Methuen Inc.
Spufford, Margaret. Contrasting Communities: English Villagers in the Sixteenth & Seventeenth Centuries. LC 73-83105. (Illus.). 1974. 43.95 (ISBN 0-521-20323-6). Cambridge U Pr.
Sturt, George. Small Boy in the Sixties. 2nd ed. (Illus.). 14.50x (ISBN 0-85527-244-9). Intl Pubns Serv.
--A Small Boy in the Sixties. 1977. Repr. of 1952 ed. text ed. 13.00x (ISBN 0-85527-244-9). Humanities.

GREAT BRITAIN–SIGNET OFFICE

Crossick, Geoffrey, ed. The Lower-Middle Class in Britain, 1870-1914. LC 76-25410. 1977. 17.95x (ISBN 0-312-49980-9). St Martin.

GREAT BRITAIN–SOCIAL CONDITIONS

Allen, Eleanor. Victorian Children. (Junior Reference Ser.). (Illus.). 64p. (gr. 7 up). 7.95 (ISBN 0-7136-1324-6). Dufour.
Arnold, Matthew. Culture & Anarchy. 1932. 36.50 (ISBN 0-521-04061-2); pap. 7.95 (ISBN 0-521-09103-9, 103). Cambridge U Pr.
--Culture & Anarchy: An Essay in Political & Social Criticism. Gregor, Ian, ed. LC 79-95714. (Library of Literature Ser). 1971. pap. 6.95 (ISBN 0-672-60994-0, LL17). Bobbs.
Ashton, Thomas S. Economic & Social Investigations in Manchester, 1833-1933. LC 77-3570. Repr. of 1934 ed. 15.00x (ISBN 0-678-08067-4). Kelley.
Atkinson, A. B., et al. Wealth & Personal Incomes. LC 77-30556. 1978. text ed. 37.00 (ISBN 0-08-022450-4). Pergamon.
Beddis, R. A. The Land & People of Britain. 3rd ed. LC 68-104459. (New Secondary Geographies Ser: Pt. 1). 160p. 1969. 3.75x (ISBN 0-340-07412-4). Intl Pubns Serv.
Benn, Ernest. Happier Days, Recollections & Reflections. 222p. 1981. Repr. of 1949 ed. lib. bdg. 20.00 (ISBN 0-89987-068-6). Darby Bks.
Bernstein, Basil. Class, Codes & Control, Vol. 3: Towards a Theory of Educational Transmissions. (Primary Socialization, Language & Education Ser.). 1977. pap. 6.95 (ISBN 0-7100-8666-0). Routledge & Kegan.
Besant, Walter. East London. LC 79-56945. (The English Working Class Ser.). 1980. lib. bdg. 32.00 (ISBN 0-8240-0100-1). Garland Pub.
Black, Clementina. Married Women's Work: Being the Report of an Inquiry Undertaken by the Women's Industrial Council. LC 79-56947. (The Englishworking Class Ser.). 1980. lib. bdg. 25.00 (ISBN 0-8240-0102-8). Garland Pub.
Bosanquet, Bernard, ed. Aspects of the Social Problem by Various Writers. LC 9-5797. 1968. Repr. of 1895 ed. 19.00 (ISBN 0-527-10000-5). Kraus Repr.
Bosanquet, Helen. The Strength of the People: A Study in Social Economics. 2nd ed. LC 79-56950. (The English Working Class Ser.). 1980. lib. bdg. 30.00 (ISBN 0-8240-0104-4). Garland Pub.
Bouchier, David. Idealism & Revolution: New Ideologies of Liberation in Britain & the United States. LC 78-17007. 1979. 19.95 (ISBN 0-312-40439-5). St Martin.
Bowley, A. L. & Burnett-Hurst, A. R. Livelihood & Poverty: A Study in the Economic Conditions of Working-Class Households in Northampton, Warrington, Stanley, & Reading. LC 79-59651. (The English Working Class Ser.). 1980. lib. bdg. 22.00 (ISBN 0-8240-0105-2). Garland Pub.
Bracey, Howard E. Neighbours: Subdivision Life in England & the United States. LC 64-15877. 1964. 15.00 (ISBN 0-8071-0329-2). La State U Pr.
Branson, Noreen. Britain in the Nineteen Twenties. Hobsbawm, E. J., ed. LC 75-27162. (History of British Society Ser). x, 264p. 1976. 20.00x (ISBN 0-8166-0770-2). U of Minn Pr.
Brauer, George C. The Education of a Gentleman. 1959. pap. 1.95x (ISBN 0-8084-0115-7, P10). Coll & U Pr.
Bray, John F. Labour's Wrongs & Labour's Remedy. LC 66-21656. Repr. of 1839 ed. 12.50x (ISBN 0-678-00283-5). Kelley.
Bray, Reginald A. Boy Labour & Apprenticeship. LC 79-56952. (The English Working Class Ser.). 1980. lib. bdg. 22.00 (ISBN 0-8240-0106-0). Garland Pub.
Brown, Muriel & Baldwin, Sally, eds. The Year Book of Social Policy in Britain 1979. 272p. (Orig.). 1980. pap. 45.00 (ISBN 0-7100-0690-X). Routledge & Kegan.
--The Year Book of Social Policy in Britain, 1977. 1978. 36.50 (ISBN 0-7100-0066-9). Routledge & Kegan.
Burnett, John. Plenty & Want: A Social History of Diet in England from 1815 to the Present Day. 387p. 1979. Repr. of 1966 ed. 15.95 (ISBN 0-85967-461-4, Pub. by Scolar Pr England); pap. 7.95 (ISBN 0-85967-462-2). Biblio Dist.
Butler, C. V. Domestic Service. LC 79-56953. (The English Working Class Ser.). 1980. lib. bdg. 15.00 (ISBN 0-8240-0107-9). Garland Pub.
Butt, J. & Clarke, I. F., eds. The Victorians & Social Protest: A Symposium. 239p. 1973. 19.50 (ISBN 0-208-01329-6, Archon). Shoe String.
Bythell, Duncan. The Sweated Trade: Outwork in Nineteenth Century Britain. LC 78-451. 1979. 21.50 (ISBN 0-312-77999-2). St Martin.
Cadbury, Edward, et al. Women's Work & Wages. LC 79-56954. (The English Working Class). 1980. lib. bdg. 30.00 (ISBN 0-8240-0108-7). Garland Pub.
Caffrey. The Nineteen-Hundreds Lady. (Illus.). 1976. 29.95 (ISBN 0-86033-014-1). Gordon-Cremonesi.
Carlyle, Thomas. Past & Present. 1960. 7.95x (ISBN 0-460-00608-8, Evman). Biblio Dist.
--Past & Present. Altick, Richard D., ed. LC 77-70381. (Gotham Library). 294p. 1977. 12.00x (ISBN 0-8147-0561-8); pap. 8.00x (ISBN 0-8147-0562-6). NYU Pr.
Carlyle, Thomas & Mims, Edwin. Past & Present. 363p. 1981. Repr. of 1918 ed. lib. bdg. 20.00 (ISBN 0-8495-8770-0). Arden Lib.
Carlyle, Thomas, ed. Latter- Day Pamphlets. LC 72-37771. (Essay Index Reprint Ser.). Repr. of 1853 ed. 19.00 (ISBN 0-8369-2584-X). Arno.
Cashmore, Ernest. Rastaman: The Rastagarian Movement in England. (Illus.). 1979. text ed. 22.50x (ISBN 0-04-301108-X). Allen Unwin.
Caspari, Fritz. Humanism & Social Order in Tudor England. LC 68-29071. 1968. pap. text ed. 5.25x (ISBN 0-8077-1146-2). Tchrs Coll.
Chambers, Jonathan D. Population, Economy, & Society in Pre-Industrial England. (Oxford Paperbacks University Ser). 200p. 1972. pap. 3.95x (ISBN 0-19-888085-5). Oxford U Pr.
Charques, R. D. Contemporary Literature & Social Revolution. LC 68-2035. (Studies in Comparative Literature, No. 35). 1969. Repr. lib. bdg. 49.95 (ISBN 0-8383-0654-3). Haskell.
Chesterton, Gilbert K. Utopia of Usurers, & Other Essays. facs. ed. LC 67-26724. (Essay Index Reprint Ser). 1917. 15.00 (ISBN 0-8369-0299-8). Arno.
Cheyney, Edward P. Introduction to the Industrial & Social History of England. rev. ed. LC 79-92609. (BCL Ser.: No. I). (Illus.). Repr. of 1920 ed. 12.50 (ISBN 0-404-01524-7). AMS Pr.
--An Introduction to the Industrial & Social History of England. 1977. Repr. of 1912 ed. lib. bdg. 25.00 (ISBN 0-8414-1845-4). Folcroft.
--Social Changes in England in the Sixteenth Century As Reflected in Contemporary Literature. LC 76-168055. (Illus.). Repr. of 1895 ed. 12.50 (ISBN 0-404-01523-9). AMS Pr.
Church, Roy A. Economic & Social Change in a Midland Town: Victorian Nottingham, 1815-1900. (Illus.). 409p. 1966. 27.50x (ISBN 0-7146-1290-1, F Cass Co). Biblio Dist.
Clarke, P. F. Lancashire & the New Liberalism. (Illus.). 1971. 45.00 (ISBN 0-521-08075-4). Cambridge U Pr.
Clarkson, Leslie A. Death, Disease & Famine in Pre-Industrial England. LC 75-24755. 200p. 1975. 21.50 (ISBN 0-312-18550-2). St Martin.
Coats, B. E. & Tawstron, E. M. Regional Variations in Britain: Studies in Economic & Social Geography. 1972. 40.00 (ISBN 0-7134-2103-7, Pub. by Batsford England). David & Charles.
Cole, G. D. The Post-War Condition of Britain. LC 75-2625. 483p. 1975. Repr. of 1956 ed. lib. bdg. 22.50x (ISBN 0-8371-8043-0, COPC). Greenwood.
Cole, George. Studies in Class Structure. LC 76-2503. 195p. 1976. Repr. of 1955 ed. lib. bdg. 14.50x (ISBN 0-8371-8779-6, COSS). Greenwood.
Cole, George D. Labour in the Commonwealth: Book for the Younger Generation. facsimile ed. LC 75-157330. (Select Bibliographies Reprint Ser). Repr. of 1918 ed. 16.00 (ISBN 0-8369-5790-3). Arno.
--Persons & Periods: Studies. facs. ed. LC 67-26726. (Essay Index Reprint Ser). 1938. 16.00 (ISBN 0-8369-0323-4). Arno.
Coman, Peter W. Catholics & the Welfare State. LC 76-49523. (Illus.). 1977. text ed. 12.50x (ISBN 0-582-48543-6). Longman.

Constabulary Force Commissioners, Great Briain. First Report of the Constabulary Force Commissioners Appointed to Inquire As to the Best Means of Establishing an Efficient Constabulary Force in the Countries of England & Wales. LC 76-172561. (Criminology, Law Enforcement, & Social Problems Ser.: No. 165). (Intro. added). Date not set. 15.00 (ISBN 0-87585-165-7). Patterson Smith.

Cowie, L. W. A Dictionary of British Social History. (Illus.). 326p. 1973. 21.50x (ISBN 0-8476-6083-4). Rowman.

Daiches, David. Literature & Society. LC 74-95422. (Studies in Comparative Literature, No. 35). 1970. Repr. of 1938 ed. lib. bdg. 33.95 (ISBN 0-8383-0970-4). Haskell.

Daryl, Philippe. Public Life in England. Frith, Henry, tr. 1978. Repr. lib. bdg. 25.00 (ISBN 0-8495-1038-4). Arden Lib.

Davidoff, Lenore. The Best Circles. (Illus.). 127p. 1973. 16.75x (ISBN 0-87471-428-1). Rowman.

Defoe, Daniel. Best of Defoe's Review. facs. ed. Payne, William L., ed. LC 73-128233. (Essay Index Reprint Ser). 1951. 19.50 (ISBN 0-8369-1873-8). Arno.

D'Eichthal, Gustave. A French Sociologist Looks at Britain: Gustave d'Eichthal & British Society in 1828. Ratcliffe, Barrie M., ed. Chaloner, W. H., tr. LC 77-1899. 192p. 1977. 13.75x (ISBN 0-87471-963-1). Rowman.

Derry, T. K. & Blakeway, M. G. The Making of Britain, 2 vols. Incl. Vol. 1. Life & Work to the Close of the Middle Ages. pap. 6.95 (ISBN 0-7195-1816-4); Vol. 2. Life & Work from the Renaissance to the Industrial Revolution. pap. 6.95 (ISBN 0-7195-1834-2). (gr. 9-12). 10.00 (ISBN 0-7195-1833-4). Transatlantic.

Derry, T. K. & Jarman, T. L. Making of Modern Britain: Life & Work from George Third to Elizabeth Second. (Illus.). 1971. pap. 3.95 (ISBN 0-7195-0304-3). Transatlantic.

Dickinson, G. Lowes. Modern Symposium. LC 62-22258. (Milestones of Thought Ser.). 9.00 (ISBN 0-8044-5306-3); pap. 2.95 (ISBN 0-8044-6115-5). Ungar.

--A Modern Symposium. (Unwin Bks.). 1962. pap. 2.95 (ISBN 0-04-824003-6). Allen Unwin.

Digby, Anne & Searby, Peter. Children, School & Society in Nineteenth Century England. (Illus.). 282p. 1980. text ed. 24.00x (ISBN 0-333-24678-0). Humanities.

Dobbs, Archibald E. Education & Social Movements 1700-1850. LC 68-55702. Repr. of 1919 ed. 15.00x (ISBN 0-678-00501-X). Kelley.

Donnison, D. V. Social Policy & Administration Revisited. (National Institute Social Services Library). 1975. pap. text ed. 13.95x (ISBN 0-04-360038-7). Allen Unwin.

Dugdale, J. S. Teach Yourself Economic & Social History. 2.50 (ISBN 0-486-21428-1). Dover.

Dyos, H. J. & Wolff, Michael, eds. Victorian City: Images & Realities, 2 vols. (Illus.). 1001p. 1973. Set. 110.00 (ISBN 0-7100-7384-4); Vol. 1. 60.00 (ISBN 0-7100-7374-7); Vol. 2. 60.00 (ISBN 0-7100-7383-6). Routledge & Kegan.

Einstein, Lewis. Tudor Ideals. LC 62-13833. 1962. Repr. of 1921 ed. 8.50 (ISBN 0-8462-0177-1). Russell.

Emsley, Clive. British Society & the French Wars, Seventeen Ninety Three - Eighteen Fifteen. (Illus.). 216p. 1979. 19.50x (ISBN 0-8476-6115-6). Rowman.

Evans, Eric J., ed. Social Policy 1830-1914: Individualism, Collectivism & the Origins of the Welfare State. (Birth of Modern Britain Ser). 1978. 23.00x (ISBN 0-7100-8613-X); pap. 10.00 (ISBN 0-7100-8626-1). Routledge & Kegan.

Eyden, Joan L. Social Policy in Action. (Library of Social Policy & Administration). 1969. text ed. 5.50x (ISBN 0-7100-6402-0). Humanities.

Famine: Ireland, 8 vols. (British Parliamentary Papers Ser.). 1971. Set. 702.00x (ISBN 0-7165-1495-8, Pub. by Irish Academic Pr Ireland). Biblio Dist.

Finlayson, Geoffrey. Decade of Reform: England in the Eighteen Thirties. LC 79-102943. 1970. pap. 3.95x (ISBN 0-393-09915-6). Norton.

Fleming, Patricia H. Villagers & Strangers: An English Proletarian Village Over Four Centuries. 256p. 1979. 15.50x (ISBN 0-87073-818-6); pap. 7.95x (ISBN 0-87073-819-4). Schenkman.

Flinn, M. W. & Smout, T. C., eds. Essays in Social History. (Illus.). 304p. 1974. pap. 14.95x (ISBN 0-19-877017-0). Oxford U Pr.

Gash, Norman, ed. Age of Peel. 1969. pap. 5.95x (ISBN 0-312-01260-8). St Martin.

Gaston, Jerry. The Reward System in British & American Science. LC 77-17404. (Science, Culture & Society Ser.). 1978. 26.95x (ISBN 0-471-29293-1, Pub. by Wiley-Interscience). Wiley.

General Booth. In Darkest England & the Way Out. 15.00 (ISBN 0-8482-7387-7). Norwood Edns.

George, Mary D. England in Transition: Life & Work in the 18th Century. LC 75-41110. Repr. of 1931 ed. 19.50 (ISBN 0-404-14544-2). AMS Pr.

George, Victor. Social Security & Society. (Illus.). 164p. 1973. 20.00x (ISBN 0-7100-7642-8); pap. 6.50 (ISBN 0-7100-7643-6). Routledge & Kegan.

Gibbins, H. De B. English Social Reformers. 1978. Repr. of 1892 ed. lib. bdg. 20.00 (ISBN 0-8492-1045-3). R West.

Gilbert, Bentley B. British Social Policy, 1914-1939. LC 78-119702. 1970. 22.50x (ISBN 0-8014-0578-5). Cornell U Pr.

Girouard, Mark. Life in the English Country House: A Social & Architectural History. LC 78-9088. (Illus.). 1978. 29.95x (ISBN 0-300-02273-5). Yale U Pr.

Glass, David V., ed. Social Mobility in Britain. (International Library of Sociology & Social Reconstruction Ser.). 1963. text ed. 21.25x (ISBN 0-7100-3327-3). Humanities.

Graves, Robert & Hodge, Alan. Long Weekend: A Social History of Great Britain, 1918 to 1939. 1963. pap. 7.95 (ISBN 0-393-00217-9, Norton Lib). Norton.

Gregg, Pauline. Black Death to Industrial Revolution: A Social & Economic History of England. LC 76-3815. (Illus.). 344p. 1976. Repr. of 1974 ed. text ed. 15.00x (ISBN 0-06-492540-4). B&N.

--Social & Economic History of Britain, 1760-1972. 7th ed. (Illus.). 1973. 22.50x (ISBN 0-245-51899-1). Intl Pubns Serv.

Hall, Stuart, et al. Policing the Crisis: Mugging, the State, & Law & Order. Roberts, Brian, ed. LC 77-26859. 1978. text ed. 38.50x (ISBN 0-8419-0361-1); pap. text ed. 14.50x (ISBN 0-8419-5041-5). Holmes & Meier.

Halsey, A. H. Change in British Society. (Illus.). 1978. 11.50x (ISBN 0-19-219132-2). Oxford U Pr.

Hammond, J. L. & Hammond, Barbara. Age of the Chartists from Eighteen Thirty-Two to Eighteen Fifty-Four: A Study of Discontent. 1962. Repr. of 1930 ed. 22.50 (ISBN 0-208-00060-7, Archon). Shoe String.

Harris, John R., ed. Liverpool & Merseyside: Essays in the Economic & Social History of the Port & Its Hinterland. 287p. 1969. 27.50x (ISBN 0-7146-1314-2, F Cass Co). Biblio Dist.

Hay, J. R. The Development of the British Welfare State, 1880-1975. LC 77-28671. 1978. 18.95x (ISBN 0-312-19749-7). St Martin.

--The Origins of Liberal Welfare Reform, 1906-1914. (Studies in Economic & Social History Ser.). 78p. 1975. pap. text ed. 3.25x (ISBN 0-333-13588-1). Humanities.

Hayes, Carlton. British Social Politics. facsimile ed. LC 72-37885. (Select Bibliographies Reprint Ser). Repr. of 1913 ed. 29.00 (ISBN 0-8369-6722-4). Arno.

Hearnshaw, Fossey J., ed. Edwardian England, A.D. 1901-1910: A Series of Lectures Delivered at King's College, University of London. facs. ed. LC 68-22097. (Essay Index Reprint Ser). 1933. 16.00 (ISBN 0-8369-0529-6). Arno.

Held, Adolf. Zwei Buecher Zur Socialen Geschichte Englands, 2 Vols. LC 75-146355. 1971. Repr. of 1881 ed. 46.50 (ISBN 0-8337-1646-8). B Franklin.

Henderson, Philip. Literature & a Changing Civilization. LC 77-23493. 1935. lib. bdg. 15.00 (ISBN 0-8414-4904-X). Folcroft.

Hessen, B. The Social & Economic Roots of Newton's Principia. 12.50 (ISBN 0-86527-182-8). Fertig.

Hill, ed. Edmund Burke on Government, Politics & Society. 1976. pap. 5.95 (ISBN 0-531-06069-1, Fontana Pap). Watts.

Hill, John E. & Dell, Edmund, eds. Good Old Cause. LC 71-96377. Repr. of 1949 ed. 24.00x (ISBN 0-678-05105-4). Kelley.

Hill, Michael. The State, Administration & the Individual. 256p. 1976. 15.00x (ISBN 0-87471-909-7). Rowman.

Hilton, R. H. Peasants, Knights & Heretics. LC 76-1137. (Past & Present Publications Ser.). 320p. 1976. 34.50 (ISBN 0-521-21276-6). Cambridge U Pr.

Holderness, B. A. Pre-Industrial England: Economy & Society from 1500 to 1750. 244p. 1976. 17.50x (ISBN 0-87471-910-0). Rowman.

Hollis, Patricia, ed. Class & Conflict in Nineteenth-Century England, 1815-1850. (Birth of Modern Britain Ser). 402p. 1973. 20.00x (ISBN 0-7100-7419-0); pap. 10.00 (ISBN 0-7100-7420-4). Routledge & Kegan.

Hoskins, W. G. The Age of Plunder: The England of Henry VIII, 1500-1547. LC 75-43647. (Social & Economic History of England Ser.). (Illus.). 1976. pap. text ed. 9.95x (ISBN 0-582-48544-4). Longman.

Howarth, Edward G. & Wilson, Mona. West Ham: A Study in Social & Industrial Problems. LC 79-56958. (The English Working Class Ser.). 1980. lib. bdg. 35.00 (ISBN 0-8240-0111-7). Garland Pub.

Hutchins, B. L. Women in Modern Industry. LC 79-56959. (The English Working Class Ser.). 1980. lib. bdg. 28.00 (ISBN 0-8240-0112-5). Garland Pub.

Irwin, John. Modern Britain: An Introduction. 1976. 15.00 (ISBN 0-208-01618-X, Archon). Shoe String.

Jackson, Brian. Starting School. 156p. 1979. 19.00x (ISBN 0-85664-993-7, Pub. by Croom Helm Ltd England). Biblio Dist.

Jevons, William S. Methods of Social Reform. LC 65-20925. Repr. of 1883 ed. 17.50x (ISBN 0-678-00108-1). Kelley.

Johns, E. A. The Social Structure of Modern Britain. 3rd ed. 1979. text ed. 30.00 (ISBN 0-08-023343-0); pap. 12.00 (ISBN 0-08-023342-2). Pergamon.

Johnson. Education & Society in England, 1780-1870. (Studies in Economic & Social History). 1980. pap. text ed. 11.50x (ISBN 0-391-01131-6). Humanities.

Johnson, Walford, et al. Short Economic & Social History of Twentieth Century England. LC 67-21370. 1967. 10.00x (ISBN 0-678-06002-9). Kelley.

Jones, Catherine. Immigration & Social Policy in Britain. 275p. 1980. pap. 9.95 (ISBN 0-422-74680-0, 6363, Pub. by Tavistock England). Methuen Inc.

Jones, Kathleen, ed. The Year Book of Social Policy in Britain, 1971. annual 232p. 1972. 33.00x (ISBN 0-7100-7348-8). Routledge & Kegan.

--The Year Book of Social Policy in Britain 1976. 1978. 33.00x (ISBN 0-7100-8765-9). Routledge & Kegan.

--The Yearbook of Social Policy in Britain, 1973. 1974. 33.00x (ISBN 0-7100-7891-9). Routledge & Kegan.

--The Yearbook of Social Policy in Britain, 1974. 1975. 33.00x (ISBN 0-7100-8156-1). Routledge & Kegan.

Jones, Kathleen & Baldwin, Sally, eds. The Year Book of Social Policy in Britain, 1975. 1976. 33.00x (ISBN 0-7100-8380-7). Routledge & Kegan.

Jordon, Wilbur K. Philanthropy in England, Fourteen Eighty to Sixteen Sixty: A Study of the Changing Pattern of English Social Aspirations. LC 78-5651. (Illus.). 1978. Repr. of 1959 ed. lib. bdg. 30.00x (ISBN 0-313-20467-5, JOPH). Greenwood.

Judge, Ken & Matthews, James. Charging for Social Care. (National Institute Social Services Library: No. 39). (Illus.). 168p. (Orig.). 1980. text ed. 27.50x (ISBN 0-04-361040-4); pap. text ed. 12.95x (ISBN 0-04-361041-2). Allen Unwin.

Kay, Joseph. The Social Condition & Education of the People in England & Europe, 2 vols. (The Development of Industrial Society Ser.). 1156p. 1971. Repr. of 1850 ed. 50.00x (ISBN 0-7165-1565-2, Pub. by Irish Academic Pr). Biblio Dist.

Keating, Peter, ed. Into Unknown England, 1866-1913: Selections from the Social Explorers. 320p. 1976. 17.50x (ISBN 0-87471-820-1). Rowman.

Kelsall, R. K. Aspects of Modern Sociology, the Social Structure of Modern Britain Ser. rev. ed. (Aspects of Modern Sociology, the Social Structure of Modern Britain Ser). 1967. text ed. 4.25x (ISBN 0-582-48771-4); pap. text ed. 3.00x (ISBN 0-582-48709-9). Humanities.

King, Roger & Nugent, Neill, eds. Respectable Rebels: Middle Class Campaigns in Britain in the 1970's. 200p. 1980. text ed. 30.00x (ISBN 0-8419-6219-7); pap. text ed. 17.50x (ISBN 0-8419-6220-0). Holmes & Meier.

Knights, Lionel C. Drama & Society in the Age of Jonson. 1968. pap. 2.25x (ISBN 0-393-00451-1, Norton Lib). Norton.

Kussmaul, Ann. Servants in Husbandry in Early Modern England. (Interdisciplinary Perspectives on Modern History Ser.). (Illus.). 240p. Date not set. price not set (ISBN 0-521-23566-9). Cambridge U Pr.

Laslett, Peter. The World We Have Lost: England Before the Industrial Age. 2nd ed. LC 66-18543. 1971. pap. text ed. 9.95x (ISBN 0-684-13725-9, ScribC). Scribner.

Llewellyn, Alexander. Decade of Reform: English Politics and Opinion in the 1830's. LC 71-182187. 1972. text ed. 17.95 (ISBN 0-312-18970-2). St Martin.

Loane, M. From Their Point of View. LC 79-56961. (The English Working Class Ser.). 1980. lib. bdg. 27.00 (ISBN 0-8240-0113-3). Garland Pub.

London, Jack. The People of the Abyss. LC 77-73613. 134p. 1977. pap. 4.95 (ISBN 0-88208-079-2). Lawrence Hill.

Lynd, Helen M. England in the Eighteen-Eighties. LC 68-20035. Repr. of 1945 ed. 19.50x (ISBN 0-678-05069-4). Kelley.

McCullin, Don. Homecoming. LC 79-4721. 1979. 30.00 (ISBN 0-312-38865-9). St Martin.

MacDonagh, Oliver. Early Victorian Government, 1830-1870. LC 76-57957. 1977. text ed. 24.50x (ISBN 0-8419-0304-2). Holmes & Meier.

Macdonald, J. Ransay, ed. Women in the Printing Trades: A Sociological Study. LC 79-56961. (The English Working Class Ser.). 1980. lib. bdg. 18.00 (ISBN 0-8240-0114-1). Garland Pub.

Macfarlane, A. The Origins of English Individualism. LC 78-73956. 1979. 26.95 (ISBN 0-521-22587-6); pap. 7.50x (ISBN 0-521-29570-X). Cambridge U Pr.

McMillan, James. The Roots of Corruption. 210p. 1972. 7.50x (ISBN 0-85468-182-5). Intl Pubns Serv.

Macnicol, John. Movement for Family Allowances Nineteen -Eighteen to Forty-Five. (Studies in Social Policy & Welfare Ser.). 1981. text ed. 50.00x (ISBN 0-435-82555-0). Heinemann Ed.

Marsh, D. C. The Welfare State: Concept & Development. 2nd ed. (Aspects of Modern Sociology: Social Structure of Modern Britain Ser.). 144p. 1980. pap. text ed. 8.95x (ISBN 0-582-29531-9). Longman.

Marshall, Dorothy. English Poor in the Eighteenth Century 1662-1782. LC 77-80107. Repr. of 1926 ed. 15.00x (ISBN 0-678-06503-9). Kelley.

Marshall, T. H. Class, Citizenship, & Social Development. 1977. pap. text ed. 9.00x (ISBN 0-226-50702-5). U of Chicago Pr.

Marwick, Arthur. Deluge: British Society & the First World War. (Illus.). 1970. pap. 7.95 (ISBN 0-393-00523-2, Norton Lib). Norton.

Masterman, C. F. From the Abyss. of Its Inhabitants by One of Them. LC 79-56963. (The English Working Class Ser.). 1980. lib. bdg. 12.00 (ISBN 0-8240-0115-X). Garland Pub.

Medlicott, W. N. Contemporary England: 1914-1964. LC 67-26796. (Social & Economic History of England Ser.). 1976. pap. text ed. 12.95x (ISBN 0-582-48487-1). Longman.

Men Without Work: A Report Made to the Pilgrim Trust. Repr. of 1938 ed. lib. bdg. 20.25x (ISBN 0-8371-0169-7, MWW). Greenwood.

Money, L. C. Chiozza. Riches & Poverty. LC 79-56955. (The English Working Class Ser.). 1980. lib. bdg. 30.00 (ISBN 0-8240-0109-5). Garland Pub.

Moroney, R. M. The Family & the State: Considerations for Social Policy. LC 75-45230. (Illus.). 1976. pap. text ed. 9.50x (ISBN 0-582-48493-6). Longman.

Morris, James. Outriders-a Liberal View of Britain. 1963. 4.00x (ISBN 0-8426-1393-5). Verry.

The Movement: Anti-Persecution Gazette & Register of Progress. Bd. with The Circular of the Anti-Persecution Union. (No. 1 (May 1, 1845) - no. 4 (August 1, 1845)). LC 79-120546. (No. 1 (1843) - No. 68 (1845)). Repr. 35.00x (ISBN 0-678-00679-2). Kelley.

Mudie-Smith, Richard, ed. Handbook of the Daily News Sweated Industries Exhibition. LC 79-56964. (The English Working Class Ser.). 1980. lib. bdg. 16.00 (ISBN 0-8240-0116-8). Garland Pub.

Musgrave, P. W. Society & Education in England Since Eighteen Hundred. 1968. pap. text ed. 5.95x (ISBN 0-416-10790-7). Methuen Inc.

Musgrave, Peter. The Economic Structure. (Aspects of Modern Sociology Ser). 1969. text ed. 4.00x (ISBN 0-582-48804-4); pap. text ed. 2.50x (ISBN 0-582-48805-2). Humanities.

Neale, R. S. Class & Ideology in the Nineteenth Century. 1972. 17.50x (ISBN 0-7100-7331-3). Routledge & Kegan.

Newby, Howard. Social Change in Rural England. LC 79-21703. 272p. 1979. 21.50 (ISBN 0-299-08040-4). U of Wis Pr.

Oddy, Derek T. & Miller, Derek S., eds. The Making of the Modern British Diet. 235p. 1976. 17.50x (ISBN 0-87471-803-1). Rowman.

Pahl, R. E. Patterns of Urban Life. (Aspects of Modern Sociology Ser). 1970. pap. text ed. 5.25x (ISBN 0-582-48803-6). Humanities.

Parry, Edward A. The Law & the Poor. LC 79-56966. (The English Working Class Ser.). 1980. lib. bdg. 30.00 (ISBN 0-8240-0117-6). Garland Pub.

Paterson, Alexander. Across the Bridges or Life by the South London River-Side, LC 79-56967. (The English Working Class Ser.). 1980. lib. bdg. 25.00 (ISBN 0-8240-0118-4). Garland Pub.

Pelling, Henry. Popular Politics & Society in Late Victorian Britain. LC 68-29377. 1968. 17.95 (ISBN 0-312-63070-0). St Martin.

Perkin, Harold. Origins of Modern English Society: 1780-1880. LC 76-384509. 1969. pap. 12.50 (ISBN 0-8020-6141-9). U of Toronto Pr.

--The Structured Crowd: Essays in English Social History. 250p. 1981. 28.50x (ISBN 0-389-20116-2). B&N.

Pike, E. Royston. Human Documents of the Lloyd George Era. (Illus.). 378p. 1972. 9.95 (ISBN 0-312-39900-6). St Martin.
Porter, Bernard. The Refugee Question in Mid-Victorian Politics. LC 78-73947. (Illus.). 1980. 41.50 (ISBN 0-521-22638-4). Cambridge U Pr.
Porter, George R. Progress of the Nation. new ed. Hirst, F. W., ed. LC 77-85189. Repr. of 1912 ed. 25.00x (ISBN 0-678-00538-9). Kelley.
Pound, John. Poverty & Vagrancy in Tudor England. 1971. pap. text ed. 4.50x (ISBN 0-582-31405-4). Longman.
Powicke, Maurice. Medieval England, 1066-1485. (Oxford Paperbacks Ser). 1931. pap. 2.50x (ISBN 0-19-285027-X). Oxford U Pr.
Radford, Elizabeth, ed. The New Villagers: Urban Pressure on Rural Areas in Worchester. (Illus.). 76p. 1970. 22.50x (ISBN 0-7146-1585-4, F Cass Co). Biblio Dist.
Randle, John. Understanding Britain: A History of the British People & Their Culture. (Illus.). 232p. 1981. 19.95x (ISBN 0-631-12471-3, Pub. by Basil Blackwell England); pap. 8.95x (ISBN 0-631-12883-2). Biblio Dist.
Redford, Arthur. The Economic History of England, 1760-1860. LC 73-15244. 244p. 1974. Repr. of 1960 ed. lib. bdg. 15.00x (ISBN 0-8371-7166-0, REEH). Greenwood.
Roberts, David. Victorian Origins of the British Welfare State. 1969. Repr. of 1960 ed. 20.50 (ISBN 0-208-00692-3, Archon). Shoe String.
Roberts, Kenneth. Leisure. (Aspects of Modern Sociology, the Social Structure of Modern Britain Ser). 1970. pap. text ed. 9.75x (ISBN 0-582-48807-9). Humanities.
Roe, Frederick W. Social Philosophy of Carlyle & Ruskin. LC 74-93060. 1969. Repr. of 1921 ed. 14.75 (ISBN 0-8046-0682-X). Kennikat.
Rose, Richard & McAllister, Ian. United Kingdom Facts. 240p. 1981. text ed. 70.00x (ISBN 0-8419-5578-6). Holmes & Meier.
Rose, Richard, ed. Studies in British Politics. 3rd. ed. LC 76-11279. 1977. text ed. 22.50x (ISBN 0-312-77070-7). St Martin.
Rowntree, B. Seebohm & Lasker, Bruno. Unemployment: A Social Study. LC 79-56970. (The English Workinh Class Ser.). 1980. lib. bdg. 28.00 (ISBN 0-8240-0121-4). Garland Pub.
Rowse, A. L. The Elizabethan Renaissance: The Life of the Society. (Illus.). 320p. 1972. lib. rep. ed. 20.00x (ISBN 0-684-15656-3, ScribT). Scribner.
Rubinstein, David, ed. People for the People: (Radical Ideas & Personalities in British Social History Ser.). 216p. 1974. text ed. 8.75x (ISBN 0-391-00331-3); pap. text ed. 3.25x (ISBN 0-903729-03-2). Humanities.
Runciman, W. G. Relative Deprivation & Social Justice. (Reports of the Institute of Community Studies). 1980. Repr. pap. 35.00 (ISBN 0-7100-3923-9). Routledge & Kegan.
Ruskin, John. Fors Clavigera, Letters to the Workmen & Labourers of Great Britain, 8 Vols. in 4. LC 68-55326. (Illus.). 1968. Repr. of 1886 ed. Set. lib. bdg. 63.50x (ISBN 0-8371-0210-3, RUFO). Greenwood.
Russell, C. E. Social Problems of the North. LC 79-56944. (The English Working Class Ser.). 1980. lib. bdg. 20.00 (ISBN 0-8240-0123-0). Garland Pub.
Ryder, Judith & Silver, Harold. Modern English Society. 2nd ed. LC 77-8049. 1977. pap. text ed. 22.50x (ISBN 0-416-55490-3); pap. 10.95x (ISBN 0-416-55500-4). Methuen Inc.
Sandford, Cedric. Taxation & Social Policy. 1981. text ed. 45.00x (ISBN 0-435-82789-8). Heinemann Ed.
Sandford, Jeremy. Smiling David. LC 75-309907. (Illus.). 128p. 1979. 9.95 (ISBN 0-7145-1048-3, Pub. by M Boyars); pap. 5.95 (ISBN 0-7145-1049-1, Pub. by M Boyars). Merrimack Bk Serv.
Schenk, Wilhelm. The Concern for Social Justice in the Puritan Revolution. LC 74-29794. (Illus.). 180p. 1975. Repr. of 1948 ed. lib. bdg. 15.00x (ISBN 0-8371-8003-1, SCSJ). Greenwood.
Schilling, Bernard N. Human Dignity & the Great Victorians. LC 78-143883. 1972. Repr. of 1946 ed. 17.50 (ISBN 0-208-01113-7, Archon). Shoe String.
Schlatter, Richard B. Social Ideas of Religious Leaders, 1660-1688. LC 77-120663. 1970. Repr. lib. bdg. 14.50x (ISBN 0-374-97102-1). Octagon.
Scudder, Vida D. Social Ideals in English Letters. (Belles Lettres in English Ser). Repr. of 1898 ed. 27.00 (ISBN 0-384-54520-3). Johnson Repr.
Shaw, J. Martin. Rural Deprivation & Planning. 207p. 1980. 14.75x (ISBN 0-86094-020-9, Pub. by GEO Abstracts England); pap. 12.01x (ISBN 0-86094-019-5, Pub. by GEO Abstracts England). State Mutual Bk.
Simmie, J. M. Citizens in Conflict. 1974. pap. 7.95 (ISBN 0-09-119651-5, Pub. by Hutchinson). Merrimack Bk Serv.
Simon, John. English Sanitary Institutions, Reviewed in Their Course of Development & in Some of Their Political & Social Relations. (Social & Economic History, House Ser). 1970. Repr. of 1890 ed. 27.00 (ISBN 0-384-55400-8). Johnson Repr.
Simpson, M. A. & Lloyd, T. H., eds. Middle Class Housing in Britain. (Illus.). 1977. 17.50 (ISBN 0-208-01606-6, Archon). Shoe String.
Smelser, Neil J. Social Change in the Industrial Revolution. LC 59-10743. (Illus.). 1959. 12.00x (ISBN 0-226-76311-0). U of Chicago Pr.
Social Problems, 3 pts. Incl. Pt. 1. Drunkenness, 4 vols. Set. 306.00x (ISBN 0-686-01174-0); Pt. 2. Gambling, 2 vols. Set. 117.00x (ISBN 0-686-01175-9); Pt. 3. Sunday Observance, 3 vols. Set. 207.00x (ISBN 0-686-01176-7). (British Parliamentary Papers Ser.). 1971 (Pub. by Irish Academic Pr Ireland). Biblio Dist.
Solly, Henry. Working Men's Social Clubs & Educational Institutes. LC 79-56943. (The English Working Class Ser.). 1980. lib. bdg. 22.00 (ISBN 0-8240-0124-9). Garland Pub.
Spiers, Edward M. The Arym & Society, 1815-1914. (Themes in British Social History Ser.). 336p. 1980. text ed. 25.00x (ISBN 0-582-48565-7). Longman.
Sturgess, Roy. The Rural Revolution in an English Village. (Cambridge Introduction to the History of Mankind). (Illus.). 48p. Date not set. pap. price not set (ISBN 0-521-22800-X). Cambridge U Pr.
Tawney, Richard H. Religion & the Rise of Capitalism. 8.00 (ISBN 0-8446-1446-7). Peter Smith.
--Social History & Literature. LC 77-8952. 1977. lib. bdg. 8.50 (ISBN 0-8414-8635-2). Folcroft.
Taylor, Richard & Pritchard, Colin. The Protest Makers: The British Nuclear Disarmament Movement 1958-1965, Twenty Years on. (Illus.). 180p. 1980. 24.00 (ISBN 0-08-025211-7). Pergamon.
Teale, William H. Lives of English Laymen: Lord Falkland,Izaak Walton,Robert Nelson. LC 72-3363. (Essay Index Reprint Ser.). Repr. of 1842 ed. 19.50 (ISBN 0-8369-2930-6). Arno.
Thane, Pat, ed. The Origins of British Social Policy. 209p. 1978. 17.75x (ISBN 0-8476-6052-4). Rowman.
Tholfsen, Trygve. Working Class Radicalism in Mid-Victorian England. LC 76-43323. 1977. 22.50x (ISBN 0-231-04234-5). Columbia U Pr.
Thomas, D. S. Social Aspects of the Business Cycle. LC 67-25760. (Demographic Monographs Ser). 1968. 37.50x (ISBN 0-677-01570-4). Gordon.
Thomis, Malcolm I. Responses to Industrialisation: The British Experience, 1780-1850. (Orig.). 1976. 17.50 (ISBN 0-208-01588-4, Archon). Shoe String.
Thomis, Malcolm I. & Holt, Peter. Threats of Revolution in Britain, 1789-1848. 1977. 15.00 (ISBN 0-208-01657-0, Archon). Shoe String.
Thompson, Paul. The Edwardians: The Remaking of British Society. LC 75-10897. (Illus.). 396p. 1975. 15.00x (ISBN 0-253-31941-2). Ind U Pr.
Townsend, Peter. Poverty in the United Kingdom: A Survey of Household Resoures & Standards of Living. 1980. 46.50x (ISBN 0-520-03871-1); pap. 16.95x (ISBN 0-520-03976-9, CAMPUS NO. 242). U of Cal Pr.
Treble, J. H. Urban Poverty in Britain, Eighteen Thirty to Nineteen Sixty. 1979. 45.00 (ISBN 0-7134-1906-7, Pub. by Batsford England). David & Charles.
Trevelyan, G. M. Illustrated English Social History. LC 77-14065. (Illus.). 1978. text ed. 35.00x (ISBN 0-582-48488-X). Longman.
Urban Areas, 4 pts. Incl. Pt. 1. Housing, 3 vols. Set. 234.00x (ISBN 0-686-01164-3); Pt. 2. Planning, 10 vols. Set. 819.00x (ISBN 0-686-01165-1); Pt. 3. Sanitation, 7 vols. Set. 630.00x (ISBN 0-686-01166-X); Pt. 4. Water Supply, 9 vols. Set. 810.00x (ISBN 0-686-01167-8). (British Parliamentary Papers Ser.). 1971 (Pub. by Irish Academic Pr Ireland). Biblio Dist.
Urwick, E. J., ed. Study of Boy Life in Our Cities. LC 79-56942. (The English Working Class Ser.). 1980. lib. bdg. 28.00 (ISBN 0-8240-0125-7). Garland Pub.
Vicinus, Martha, ed. A Widening Sphere: Changing Roles of Victorian Women. LC 76-26433. 352p. 1977. 15.95x (ISBN 0-253-36540-6). Ind U Pr.
Vinogradoff, Paul. English Society in the Eleventh Century: Essays in English Medieval History. 1968. Repr. of 1908 ed. 43.00 (ISBN 0-403-00047-5). Scholarly.
Walker, J. British Economic & Social History. 448p. 1980. 12.00x (ISBN 0-7121-0266-3, Pub. by Macdonald & Evans). State Mutual Bk.
--British Economic & Social History. 3rd ed. 464p. (Orig.). 1981. pap. text ed. 18.95x (ISBN 0-7121-0288-4, Pub. by Macdonald & Evans England). Intl Ideas.
Walvin, James. Leisure & Society: 1830-1950. (Themes in British Social History). 1979. text ed. 18.00x (ISBN 0-582-48681-5); pap. text ed. 9.50x (ISBN 0-582-48682-3). Longman.
Ward, J. T. Popular Movements. LC 73-110257. (Problems in Focus Ser). 1970. 17.95 (ISBN 0-312-63035-2). St Martin.
Warner, Wellman J. Wesleyan Movement in the Industrial Revolution. LC 66-24768. 1967. Repr. of 1930 ed. 8.00 (ISBN 0-8462-0960-8). Russell.
White, Helen C. Social Criticism in Popular Religious Literature of the Sixteenth Century. 1965. lib. bdg. 16.50x (ISBN 0-374-98455-7). Octagon.
White, Reginald J. Waterloo to Peterloo. LC 72-90571. (Illus.). x, 202p. 1973. Repr. of 1957 ed. 18.00 (ISBN 0-8462-1718-X). Russell.
Williams, Basil. Whig Supremacy, 1714-1760. 2nd ed. Stuart, C. H., ed. (Oxford History of England Ser.). 1962. 35.00x (ISBN 0-19-821710-2). Oxford U Pr.
Williams, Judith B. Guide to the Printed Materials for English Social & Economic History, 1750-1850, 2 Vols. 1966. lib. bdg. 75.00x (ISBN 0-374-98608-8). Octagon.
Woods, Robert A. English Social Movements. LC 72-1150. (Essay Index Reprint Ser.). Repr. of 1891 ed. 21.00 (ISBN 0-8369-2880-6). Arno.
Woodward, John & Richards, David. Health Care & Popular Medicine in 19th Century England: Essays in Social History. LC 76-26910. 1977. text ed. 24.50x (ISBN 0-8419-0286-0). Holmes & Meier.
Woodward, Llewellyn. Age of Reform, Eighteen Fifteen to Eighteen Seventy. 2nd ed. 1962. 33.00x (ISBN 0-19-821711-0). Oxford U Pr.
Wootton, Barbara. Social Science & Social Pathology. Seal, Vera G. & Chambers, Rosalind, eds. LC 78-3616. 1978. Repr. of 1959 ed. lib. bdg. 28.75x (ISBN 0-313-20339-3, WOSO). Greenwood.
Zweig, F. Labour, Life & Poverty. 1975. Repr. of 1949 ed. 18.00x (ISBN 0-8464-0542-3). Beekman Pubs.

GREAT BRITAIN–SOCIAL LIFE AND CUSTOMS

see also England–Social Life and Customs

Abrams, P., et al, eds. Practice & Progress: British Sociology 1950-1980. 240p. 1981. text ed. 28.50 (ISBN 0-04-301131-4); pap. text ed. 12.50 (ISBN 0-04-301132-2). Allen Unwin.
Altholz, Josef L. Victorian England, Eighteen Thirty-Seven - Nineteen One. LC 71-108097. (Conference on British Studies Bibliographical Handbooks). 1970. 17.50 (ISBN 0-521-07880-6). Cambridge U Pr.
Ardizzone, Edward, illus. Ardizzone's Kilvert: Selections from the Diary of the Rev. Francis Kilvert 1870-79. abr. ed. (Illus.). 176p. (gr. 5-7). 1980. 7.95 (ISBN 0-224-01276-2, Pub. by Chatto Bodley Jonathan). Merrimack Bk Serv.
Ashton, John. Dawn of the Nineteenth Century in England. LC 67-23941. (Social History Reference Ser). 1968. Repr. of 1886 ed. 22.00 (ISBN 0-8103-3247-7). Gale.
--Eighteenth Century Waifs. LC 68-58971. 1968. Repr. of 1887 ed. 22.00 (ISBN 0-8103-3517-4). Gale.
--Eighteenth Century Waifs. facsimile ed. LC 71-38741. (Essay Index Reprint Ser). Repr. of 1887 ed. 21.00 (ISBN 0-8369-2634-X). Arno.
--Gossip in the First Decade of Victoria's Reign. LC 67-23942. 1968. Repr. of 1903 ed. 19.00 (ISBN 0-8103-3249-3). Gale.
--Old Times. LC 67-23944. (Illus.). 1969. Repr. of 1885 ed. 19.00 (ISBN 0-8103-3252-3). Gale.
--Social Life in the Reign of Queen Anne: Taken from Original Sources. LC 67-23939. (Illus.). 474p. 1968. Repr. of 1883 ed. 22.00 (ISBN 0-8103-3254-X). Gale.
Atkinson, Frank. Northeast England: People at Work 1860 to 1950. 1980. 25.00x (ISBN 0-86190-005-7, Pub. by Moorland England). State Mutual Bk.
Ausubel, Herman. In Hard Times: Reformers Among the Late Victorians. LC 72-9826. 403p. 1973. Repr. of 1960 ed. lib. bdg. 19.50x (ISBN 0-8371-6600-4, AUHT). Greenwood.
Bailey, Peter. Leisure & Class in Victorian England: Rational Recreation & the Contest for Control, 1830-1885. LC 78-40390. (Studies in Social History). 1978. 15.00x (ISBN 0-8020-2258-8). U of Toronto Pr.
Ball, Mia. The Worshipful Company of Brewers: A Short History. (Illus.). 1977. 14.95 (ISBN 0-09-127850-3, Pub. by Hutchinson). Merrimack Bk Serv.
Bebb, Evelyn D. Nonconformity & Social & Economic Life 1660-1800. LC 80-21180. Repr. of 1935 ed. lib. bdg. 15.00x (ISBN 0-87991-867-5). Porcupine Pr.
Bennett, Henry S. Pastons & Their England. 2nd ed. LC 68-23175. (Cambridge Studies in Medieval Life & Thought). 1968. 32.95 (ISBN 0-521-07173-9); pap. 8.95x (ISBN 0-521-09513-1). Cambridge U Pr.
Benson, E. F. As We Were: A Victorian Peep Show. (Victorian Age). 1930. Repr. 20.00 (ISBN 0-8482-0139-6). Norwood Edns.
Bland, D. S. Three Revels from the Inns of Court. 1981. 45.00x (ISBN 0-86127-402-4, Pub. by Avebury Pub England). State Mutual Bk.
Botsford, J. B. English Society in the Eighteenth Century As Influenced from Oversea. 1965. lib. bdg. 20.00x (ISBN 0-374-90817-6). Octagon.
Bott, Alan. Our Fathers (Eighteen Seventy to Nineteen Hundred) 249p. 1980. Repr. lib. bdg. 35.00 (ISBN 0-89987-061-9). Darby Bks.
Brand, John. Observations on the Popular Antiquities of Great Britain, 3 Vols. 3rd ed. Ellis, Henry, ed. LC 71-136368. (Bohn's Antiquarian Library Ser). Repr. of 1849 ed. Set. 37.50 (ISBN 0-404-50005-6); 12.50 ea. Vol. 1 (ISBN 0-404-50011-0). Vol. 2 (ISBN 0-404-50012-9). Vol. 3 (ISBN 0-404-50013-7). AMS Pr.
--Observations on the Popular Antiquities of Great Britain: Chiefly Illustrating the Origin of Our Vulgar & Provincial Customs, Ceremonies & Superstitions. LC 67-23896. 1969. Repr. of 1849 ed. 49.00 (ISBN 0-8103-3256-6). Gale.
Brett, R. L., ed. Barclay Fox's Journal. (Illus.). 426p. 1979. 23.50x (ISBN 0-8476-6187-3). Rowman.
Brown, John. An Estimate of the Manners & Principles of the Times. LC 75-31085. Repr. of 1758 ed. 21.50 (ISBN 0-404-13504-8). AMS Pr.
Butterworth, E. & Weir, D., eds. The Sociology of Modern Britain. 1970. pap. 2.25 (ISBN 0-531-06021-7, Fontana Pap). Watts.
Caffrey. The Nineteen-Hundreds Lady. (Illus.). 1976. 29.95 (ISBN 0-86033-014-1). Gordon-Cremonesi.
Caffrey, Kate. Nineteen Thirty Seven-Thirty Nine Last Look Round. LC 77-30508. (Illus.). 1978. 24.95 (ISBN 0-86033-066-4). Gordon-Cremonesi.
Campbell, Mildred. English Yeoman Under Elizabeth & the Early Stuarts. LC 68-4919. Repr. of 1942 ed. 17.50x (ISBN 0-678-08003-8). Kelley.
Chamberlain, John. The Letters of John Chamberlain, 2 vols. McClure, Norman E., ed. LC 78-23784. 1979. Repr. of 1939 ed. Set. lib. bdg. 72.50x (ISBN 0-313-20710-0, CHLE). Greenwood.
Clarke, Charles F. Britain Today: A Review of Current Political & Social Trends. LC 70-100148. Repr. of 1951 ed. lib. bdg. 15.00x (ISBN 0-8371-3396-3, CLBT). Greenwood.
Clout, Hugh D. & Dennis, Richard J. Social Geography of Great Britain: An Introduction. (Pergamon Oxford Geographies). 1980. 33.75 (ISBN 0-08-021802-4); pap. 14.50 (ISBN 0-08-021801-6). Pergamon.
Coate, Mary. Social Life in Stuart England. LC 77-109721. (Illus.). 1971. Repr. of 1924 ed. lib. bdg. 15.00x (ISBN 0-8371-4211-3, COSL). Greenwood.
Cooper, James F. Gleanings in Europe: Italy. (The Writings of James Fenimore Cooper Ser.). (Illus.). 377p. 1981. pap. text ed. 8.95x (ISBN 0-87395-460-2, COGI-P). State U NY Pr.
Cutts, Edward L. Parish Priests & Their People in the Middle Ages in England. LC 74-107457. Repr. of 1898 ed. 32.50 (ISBN 0-404-01898-X). Ams Pr.
Danielsson, Bror, ed. Middle English Falconry Treatises, Pt. 2. (Mediaeval English Hunt Ser.: Vol. 3). 1980. text ed. cancelled (ISBN 0-685-96753-0); pap. text ed. write for info. (ISBN 0-391-01177-4). Humanities.
Darwin, Bernard A. Dickens Advertiser: A Collection of the Advertisements in the Original Parts of Novels by Charles Dickens. LC 72-152553. (Studies in Dickens, No. 52). 1971. Repr. of 1930 ed. lib. bdg. 33.95 (ISBN 0-8383-1234-9). Haskell.
Daryl, Philippe. Public Life in England. Firth, Henry, tr. (Victorian Age Ser). 20.00 (ISBN 0-685-43396-X). Norwood Edns.
Ditchfield, P. H. Old English Customs Extant at the Present Time. LC 68-21765. 1968. Repr. of 1896 ed. 22.00 (ISBN 0-8103-3427-5). Gale.
Dyhouse, Carol. Girls Growing up in Late Victorian & Edwardian England. (Studies in Social History). 224p. 1981. price not set (ISBN 0-7100-0821-X). Routledge & Kegan.
Escott, Thomas H. Social Transformations of the Victorian Age. LC 73-12848. 1897. lib. bdg. 35.00 (ISBN 0-8414-3908-7). Folcroft.
Evans, Eric J. & Richards, Jeffrey. A Social History of Britain in Postcards, 1870 to 1930. LC 79-41449. 151p. (Orig.). 1980. 23.00x (ISBN 0-582-50292-6). Longman.
Ewald, William B., Jr. Rogues, Royalty & Reporters: The Age of Queen Anne Through Its Newspapers. LC 78-17410. 1978. Repr. of 1956 ed. lib. bdg. 22.75x (ISBN 0-313-20506-X, EWRR). Greenwood.

Foley, Winifred. As the Twig Is Bent: Sketches of a Bittersweet Life. LC 77-92766. 1978. 9.95 (ISBN 0-8008-0421-X). Taplinger.
Fox, Lilla M. Costumes & Customs of the British Isles. 1974. 6.95 (ISBN 0-8238-0154-3). Plays.
Furnivall, F. J., ed. Early English Meals & Manners. (EETS, OS Ser.: No. 32). Repr. of 1868 ed. 26.00 (ISBN 0-527-00032-9). Kraus Repr.
Gairdner, James, ed. Paston Letters, 1422-1509, 6 Vols. LC 77-168090. Repr. of 1904 ed. Set. 147.00 (ISBN 0-404-02690-7). AMS Pr.
Gash, Norman. Aristocracy & People: Britain, Eighteen Fifteen to Eighteen Sixty Five. (New History of England Ser.). 375p. 1980. 20.00x (ISBN 0-674-04490-8); pap. 9.95x (ISBN 0-674-04491-6). Harvard U Pr.
Gilbert, Bentley B. British Social Policy, 1914-1939. LC 78-119702. 1970. 22.50x (ISBN 0-8014-0578-5). Cornell U Pr.
Girouard, Mark. Life in the English Country House. 1980. pap. 12.95 (ISBN 0-14-005406-5). Penguin.
Haldane, Elizabeth S. From One Century to Another: The Reminiscences of Elizabeth S. Haldane. 1979. Repr. of 1937 ed. lib. bdg. 25.00 (ISBN 0-8492-5333-0). R West.
Hall, Ellen & Hall, Emily. Halls of Ravenswood. Mills, A. R., ed. (Illus.). 1968. 6.95 (ISBN 0-685-20591-6). Transatlantic.
Halsey, Albert H. & Heath, Anthony F. Origins & Destinations: Family, Class & Education in Modern Britain. (Illus.). 250p. 1980. text ed. 29.50x (ISBN 0-19-827224-3); pap. 12.95x (ISBN 0-19-827249-9). Oxford U Pr.
Harington, John. Nugae Antiquae, 2 Vols. Park, Thomas, ed. LC 2-21609. Repr. of 1804 ed. 50.00 (ISBN 0-404-03125-0). AMS Pr.
Harries-Jenkins, Gwyn. The Army in Victorian Society. 1977. 17.50x (ISBN 0-8020-2263-4). U of Toronto Pr.
Harrison, G. B. The Elizabethan Journals, 2 vols. Incl. Vol. 1. 1591-1597; Vol. 2. 1598-1603. 12.00 (ISBN 0-8446-2211-7). Peter Smith.
Hazlitt, William C. Faiths & Folklore of the British Isles, 2 Vols. LC 64-18758. 1905. Set. 40.00 (ISBN 0-405-08604-0, Blom Pubns); 20.00 ea. Vol. 1 (ISBN 0-405-08605-9). Vol. 2 (ISBN 0-405-08606-7). Arno.
Hole, Christina. British Folk Customs. (Illus.). 1977. 14.95x (ISBN 0-09-127340-4, Pub. by Hutchinson Pub. Group Ltd). Standing Orders.
Holloway, David. Derby Day. (Folio Miniature Ser.). 48p. 1975. 4.95 (ISBN 0-7181-1303-9, Pub. by Michael Joseph). Merrimack Bk Serv.
Hone, William. Every-Day Book, 2 Vols. LC 67-12945. 1967. Repr. of 1827 ed. Set. 84.00 (ISBN 0-8103-3005-9). Gale.
--Table Book, 2 Vols. LC 67-12946. Repr. of 1827 ed. Set. 37.00 (ISBN 0-8103-3006-7). Gale.
--The Year Book of Daily Recreation & Information. LC 67-12947. 1967. Repr. of 1832 ed. 37.00 (ISBN 0-8103-3007-5). Gale.
Huggett, Frank E. Carriages at Eight. 1980. 15.95 (ISBN 0-684-16421-3). Scribner.
Jekyll, Gertrude. Old English Household Life: Some Account of Cottage Objects & Country Folk. 2nd ed. (Illus.). 218p. 1975. 11.50x (ISBN 0-87471-791-4). Rowman.
Jekyll, Gertrude & Jones, Sydney R. Old English Household Life. 1978. Repr. of 1939 ed. lib. bdg. 27.50 (ISBN 0-89760-402-4, Telegraph). Dynamic Learn Corp.
Jenkins, Hugh. The Culture Gap: An Experience of Government & the Arts. 288p. 1981. 15.00 (ISBN 0-7145-2643-6, Pub. by M Boyars); pap. 9.95 (ISBN 0-7145-2742-4). Merrimack Bk Serv.
Jenkyns, Richard. The Victorians & Ancient Greece. (Illus.). 400p. 1980. 30.00x (ISBN 0-674-93686-8). Harvard U Pr.
Johnson, Wendell S. Living in Sin: The Victorian Sexual Revolution. LC 78-26845. 1979. 15.95x (ISBN 0-88229-445-8); pap. 7.95 (ISBN 0-88229-649-3). Nelson-Hall.
Johnston, James P. A Hundred Years Eating: Food, Drink, & the Daily Diet in Britain Since the Late Nineteenth Century. (Illus.). 1977. 9.95 (ISBN 0-7735-0306-4). McGill-Queens U Pr.
Judges, Arthur V., ed. Elizabethan Underworld. 1965. lib. bdg. 27.50x (ISBN 0-374-94446-6). Octagon.
Kendall, Paul M. Yorkist Age: Daily Life During the Wars of the Roses. (Illus.). 1970. pap. 6.95 (ISBN 0-393-00558-5, Norton Lib). Norton.
Kimber, Richard & Richardson, J. J., eds. Pressure Groups in Britain: A Reader. (Rowman & Littlefield University Library). 304p. 1974. 15.00x (ISBN 0-87471-524-5). Rowman.
Labarge, Margaret W. A Baronial Household of the Thirteenth Century. (Illus.). 235p. 1980. 22.50x (ISBN 0-389-20068-9); pap. 9.95x (ISBN 0-389-20034-4). B&N.
Lambert, Anthony J. Victorian & Edwardian Country House Life. LC 80-26606. (Illus.). 120p. 1981. 21.75x (ISBN 0-8419-0684-X). Holmes & Meier.
Langbridge, R. H. Edwardian Shopping. LC 75-24631. 1976. 25.00 (ISBN 0-7153-7068-5). David & Charles.
Lasdun, Susan. Victorians at Home. 160p. 1981. 20.00 (ISBN 0-670-74600-2, Studio). Viking Pr.
Lewis, Lesley. The Private Life of a Country House: Nineteen Twelve to Nineteen Thirty-Nine. LC 79-56437. (Illus.). 1980. 16.95 (ISBN 0-7153-7826-0). David & Charles.
Low, Donald A. That Sunny Dome: A Portrait of Regency Britain. (Illus.). 208p. 1977. 13.50x (ISBN 0-87471-978-X). Rowman.
Lowerson, John & Myerscough, John. Time to Spare in Victorian England. 1977. text ed. 13.00x (ISBN 0-391-00744-0). Humanities.
McKendrick, Neil, ed. Historical Perspectives: Studies in English Thought & Society in Honour of J. H. Plumb. 329p. 1974. 16.50x (ISBN 0-900362-77-4). Intl Pubns Serv.
Mallock, William H. The New Republic: Or, Culture, Faith & Philosophy in an English Country House. LC 75-30033. Repr. of 1878 ed. 34.50 (ISBN 0-404-14036-X). AMS Pr.
Mander, Raymond & Mitchenson, Joe. Victorian & Edwardian Entertainment. 1978. 22.50 (ISBN 0-7134-1257-7, Pub. by Batsford England). David & Charles.
Maplet, John. A Greene Forest, or a Naturall Historie. LC 79-84122. (English Experience Ser.: No.941). 244p. 1979. Repr. of 1567 ed. lib. bdg. 18.00 (ISBN 90-221-0941-0). Walter J Johnson.
Margetson, Stella. Victorian People. 1977. 16.95 (ISBN 0-7134-1010-8, Pub. by Batsford England). David & Charles.
Marshall, Sybil, ed. Fenland Chronicle. LC 66-21652. 1981. pap. 10.95 (ISBN 0-521-28043-5). Cambridge U Pr.
Mead, W. The English Medieval Feast. 59.95 (ISBN 0-8490-0114-5). Gordon Pr.
Meller, Walter C. Old Times. LC 68-26592. (Illus.). 1968. Repr. of 1925 ed. 19.00 (ISBN 0-8103-3453-4). Gale.
Miall, Antony & Miall, Peter. The Victorian Nursery Book. (Illus.). 1981. 14.95 (ISBN 0-394-51597-8). Pantheon.
Mogey, John M. Family & Neighbourhood: Two Studies in Oxford. LC 73-13033. (Illus.). 181p. 1974. Repr. of 1956 ed. lib. bdg. 15.00 (ISBN 0-8371-7105-9, MOFN). Greenwood.
Molloy, J. Fitzgerald. Court Life Below Stairs: or London Under the Last Georges. 427p. 1980. Repr. of 1897 ed. lib. bdg. 50.00 (ISBN 0-89984-337-9). Century Bookbindery.
--Court Life Below Stairs or London Under the Last Georges. 1760-1830. 1897. Repr. 25.00 (ISBN 0-685-43342-0). Norwood Edns.
Morgan, Robert B., ed. Readings in English Social History from Contemporary Literature, 5 Vols. in 1. LC 22-705. 1921-1922. 30.00 (ISBN 0-527-65060-9). Kraus Repr.
Morton, A. L. People's History of England. (Illus.). 1980. pap. 2.95 (ISBN 0-7178-0150-0). Intl Pub Co.
Murray, E. C. Side-Lights on English Society: Sketches from Life, Social & Satirical. rev ed. LC 75-83371. (Illus.). xii, 436p. 1969. Repr. of 1885 ed. 24.00 (ISBN 0-8103-3285-X). Gale.
--Sidelights on English Society: Sketches from Life, Social & Satirical. 1979. Repr. of 1885 ed. lib. bdg. 45.00 (ISBN 0-8492-6803-6). R West.
Murray, Grace A. Personalities of the Eighteenth Century. LC 72-7299. Repr. of 1927 ed. lib. bdg. 22.50 (ISBN 0-8414-0316-3). Folcroft.
Nadal, E. S. Impressions of London Social Life with Other Papers. (Victorian Age Ser). 1875. Repr. 30.00 (ISBN 0-685-43413-3). Norwood Edns.
Newman, Arnold, photos by. The Great British. (Illus.). 118p. 1980. 10.00 (ISBN 0-297-77611-8, 56680-3, Pub. by Natl Portrait Gallery England). U of Chicago Pr.
Obelkevich, James. Religion & Rural Society: South Lindsey, 1825-1875. (Illus.). 1976. 49.00x (ISBN 0-19-822426-5). Oxford U Pr.
Ogilvie, R. M. Latin & Greek: A History of the Influence of the Classics on English Life from 1600 to 1918. 1969. Repr. of 1964 ed. 15.00 (ISBN 0-208-00218-9, Archon). Shoe String.
Ogilvy, Mabell F. In Whig Society. LC 75-29167. 1975. Repr. of 1921 ed. lib. bdg. 30.00 (ISBN 0-8414-6145-7). Folcroft.
Old English Customs. (Illus.). 1972. Repr. 11.95 (ISBN 0-7153-5741-7). David & Charles.
Paget, Julian. The Pageantry of Britain. (Illus.). 224p. 1980. 25.95 (ISBN 0-686-28008-3, Pub. by Michael Joseph). Merrimack Bk Serv.
Paradis, James G. T. H. Huxley: Man's Place in Nature. LC 78-5492. 1978. 16.50x (ISBN 0-8032-0917-7). U of Nebr Pr.
Pelling, Henry. Popular Politics & Society in Late Victorian Britain. 1979. text ed. 26.00x (ISBN 0-391-01205-3); pap. text ed. 12.50x (ISBN 0-391-01206-1). Humanities.
Pepys, Samuel. Diary of Samuel Pepys. Morshead, O. F., ed. (Illus.). 1960. 8.50 (ISBN 0-8446-2727-5). Peter Smith.
--Diary of Samuel Pepys, 10 Vols. Wheatley, Henry B., ed. Bright, Mynors, tr. LC 68-57227. Repr. of 1899 ed. Set. lib. bdg. 295.00 (ISBN 0-404-05030-1); 29.50 ea. AMS Pr.
Petrie, Charles A. The Victorians. LC 79-12910. (Illus.). 1980. Repr. of 1960 ed. lib. bdg. 23.25x (ISBN 0-313-22003-4, PEVI). Greenwood.
Philips, Janet & Phillips, Peter. Victorians at Home & Away. (Illus.). 220p. 1978. 16.00x (ISBN 0-85664-688-1, Pub. by Croom Helm Ltd England). Biblio Dist.
Pike, Mary A. Town & Country Fare & Fable: A Collection of Regional Recipes & Customs. LC 78-60989. (Illus.). 1978. 11.95 (ISBN 0-7153-7720-5). David & Charles.
Plumb, John H., ed. Studies in Social History. facs. ed. LC 71-80395. (Essay Index Reprint Ser). 1955. 22.00 (ISBN 0-8369-1063-X). Arno.
Plumpton, Edward. Plumpton Correspondence. Stapleton, Thomas, ed. (Camden Society, London. Publications, First Series: No. 4). Repr. of 1839 ed. 35.00 (ISBN 0-404-50104-4). AMS Pr.
Plumpton, Sir Edward. Plumpton Correspondence. Repr. of 1839 ed. 38.50 (ISBN 0-384-46900-0). Johnson Repr.
Press Association. Album of a Nation: The Many Faces of Britain. LC 79-10692. (Illus.). 1979. 19.95 (ISBN 0-448-22839-4). Paddington.
Price, Mary R. Portrait of Britain in the Middle Ages, 1066-1485. (Oxford Introduction to British History Ser). (Illus.). 1951. pap. 12.50 (ISBN 0-19-832919-9). Oxford U Pr.
Price, Mary R. & Mather, C. E. Portrait of Britain Under Tudors & Stuarts, 1485-1688. (Oxford Introduction to British History Ser). (Illus.). 1954. pap. 12.50x (ISBN 0-19-832917-2). Oxford U Pr.
Quaife, G. R. Wanton Wenches & Wayward Wives: Peasants & Illicit Sex in Early Seventeenth Century England. 1979. 19.50 (ISBN 0-8135-0890-8). Rutgers U Pr.
Ratcliff, Rosemary. Dear Worried Brown Eyes. 1969. 10.00 (ISBN 0-08-007041-8). Pergamon.
Raven, Charles. Underworld Nights: Tales of London Underworld. Date not set. 7.95 (ISBN 0-392-16400-0, SpS). Sportshelf.
Rickert, Edith, et al, eds. Chaucer's World. LC 48-6059. 1948. 25.00x (ISBN 0-231-01568-2); pap. 12.50x (ISBN 0-231-08530-3). Columbia U Pr.
Robin, Jean. Elmdon, Continuity & Change in a Northwest Essex Village. LC 79-12964. (Illus.). 1980. 41.50 (ISBN 0-521-22820-4). Cambridge U Pr.
Rye, William B., ed. England As Seen by Foreigners in the Days of Elizabeth & James the First. LC 66-12288. 1967. Repr. of 1865 ed. 20.00 (ISBN 0-405-08903-1). Arno.
Salzman, Louis F. England in Tudor Times: An Account of Its Social Life & Industries. LC 72-81466. (Illus.). 1969. Repr. of 1926 ed. 12.50 (ISBN 0-8462-1373-7). Russell.
Sansom, W. M. & Chapman, Harold. Victorian Life in Photographs. (Illus.). 1977. 15.95 (ISBN 0-500-25042-1). Thames Hudson.
Seebohm, Frederic. The English Village Community. 1905. Repr. 20.00 (ISBN 0-685-43298-X). Norwood Edns.
Sitwell, Edith. Bath. LC 78-24153. 1980. Repr. of 1932 ed. lib. bdg. 21.75x (ISBN 0-313-20815-8, SIBT). Greenwood.
Snowman, Daniel. Britain & America: An Interpretation of Their Culture 1945-1975. LC 76-56927. 1977. usa 19.50x (ISBN 0-8147-7778-3). NYU Pr.
--Britain & America: An Interpretation of Their Cultures, 1945-1975. LC 76-48858. (Orig.). 1977. pap. text ed. 6.50x (ISBN 0-06-131922-8, TB1922, Torch). Har-Row.
Soffer, Reba N. Ethics & Society in England: The Revolution in the Social Sciences, 1870-1914. 1978. 28.50x (ISBN 0-520-03521-6). U of Cal Pr.
Southworth, James G. Vauxhall Gardens: A Chapter in the Social History of England. 1971. lib. bdg. 14.00x (ISBN 0-374-97516-7). Octagon.
Stamp, A. H. A Social & Economic History of England from Seventeen Hundred to Nineteen Seventy. 334p. 1980. 22.50x (ISBN 0-7050-0070-2, Pub. by Skilton & Shaw England). State Mutual Bk.
Stevenson, Bruce, compiled By. Reader's Guide to Great Britain. 558p. 1980. 35.00 (ISBN 0-85353-284-2, Pub. by Natl Bk League England). Bowker.
Stirling, A. M. Victorian Sidelights. 288p. 1980. Repr. lib. bdg. 25.00 (ISBN 0-89987-763-X). Darby Bks.
Sutherland, Douglas. The English Gentleman's Wife. (Illus.). 1979. 7.50 (ISBN 0-670-29680-5, Debrett's Peerage, Ltd.). Viking Pr.
Taylor, John H. The Half-Way Generation: A Study of Asian Youth in Newcastle-Upon-Tyne. 1976. pap. text ed. 18.75x (ISBN 0-85633-081-7, NFER). Humanities.
Tenison, Marika H. Book of Afternoon Tea. LC 79-56046. (Illus.). 96p. 1980. 11.95 (ISBN 0-7153-7929-1). David & Charles.
Thale, Mary. The Autobiography of Francis Place 1771-1854. LC 78-174265. (Illus.). 344p. 1972. 42.00 (ISBN 0-521-08399-0). Cambridge U Pr.
Thiselton-Dyer, T. F. Old English Social Life As Told by the Parish Registers. LC 2-8627. Repr. of 1898 ed. 17.00 (ISBN 0-527-89600-4). Kraus Repr.
Thiselton-Dyer, Thomas F. British Popular Customs, Present & Past. LC 79-136378. (Bohn's Antiquarian Lib). Repr. of 1875 ed. 12.50 (ISBN 0-404-50006-4). AMS Pr.
--British Popular Customs, Present & Past. LC 67-23908. (Social History Reference Ser.). (Illus.). 1968. Repr. of 1876 ed. 22.00 (ISBN 0-8103-3261-2). Gale.
Thornbury, George W. Shakspere's England: Or, Sketches of Our Social History in the Reign of Elizabeth, 2 Vols. LC 72-177453. Repr. of 1856 ed. Set. 42.50 (ISBN 0-404-06425-6). AMS Pr.
Traill, Henry D. & Mann, James S. Social England: A Record of the Progress of People in Religion, 6 Vols. LC 78-108550. 1902-1904. Set. 200.00 (ISBN 0-403-00269-9); 34.50 ea. Scholarly.
Trevelyan. Trevelyan Papers, 1856-72, 3 Vols. Collier, J. Payne, et al, eds. (Camden Society, London, Publications, First Ser.: Nos. 67, 84, & 105). Set. 84.00 (ISBN 0-404-50206-7); 28.00 ea. No. 67 (ISBN 0-404-50167-2). No. 84 (ISBN 0-404-50184-2). No. 105 (ISBN 0-404-50205-9). AMS Pr.
Trevelyan Papers, 3 Vols. (Vol. 67, 0-384-61497-3; vol. 84, 0-384-61514-7; vol. 105, 0-384-61525-2). 1857-1872. 31.00 ea. Johnson Repr.
Turner, Frank M. Greek Heritage in Victorian Britain. LC 80-24013. (Illus.). 512p. 1981. 30.00x (ISBN 0-300-02480-0). Yale U Pr.
Vassilyeva, Larissa. Lara in London. Franklin, Olga, tr. 1978. text ed. 15.00 (ISBN 0-08-023718-5); pap. text ed. 7.65 (ISBN 0-08-023717-7). Pergamon.
Waddell, L. A. British Edda. 331p. Date not set. Repr. of 1930 ed. 12.00 (ISBN 0-913022-41-1). Angriff Pr.
Westergaard, John, et al, eds. Modern British Society: A Bibliography. LC 76-51508. 1978. 17.95x (ISBN 0-312-53775-1). St Martin.
Whitelocke, James. Liber Famelicus. 15.50 (ISBN 0-384-68130-1). Johnson Repr.
--Liber Famelicus of Sir James Whitelocke. Bruce, John, ed. (Camden Society, London. Publications, First Ser.: No. 70). Repr. of 1858 ed. 14.00 (ISBN 0-404-50170-2). AMS Pr.
Whyman, John & Bruchey, Stuart, eds. Aspects of Holidaymaking & Resort Development with in the Isle of Thanet, with Particular Reference to Margate, Circa 1736 to Circa 1840. LC 80-2834. (Dissertations in European Economic History II). (Illus.). 1981. lib. bdg. 75.00x two vols. (ISBN 0-405-14018-5). Arno.
Wilmeth, Don B., ed. American & English Popular Entertainment: A Guide to Information Sources. LC 79-22869. (Performing Arts Information Guide Ser.: Vol. 7). 1980. 36.00 (ISBN 0-8103-1454-1). Gale.
Wilson, Violet A. Society Women of Shakespeare's Time. LC 73-113370. 1970. Repr. of 1924 ed. 12.50 (ISBN 0-8046-1040-1). Kennikat.
Wingfield-Stratford, Esme C. Before the Lamps Went Out. LC 78-12081. 1979. Repr. of 1945 ed. lib. bdg. 19.50x (ISBN 0-313-21067-5, WSBL). Greenwood.
Wohl, A. Victorian Family. LC 77-9234. 1978. 17.95x (ISBN 0-312-84276-7). St Martin.
Wood, Manfri F. In the Life of a Romany Gypsy. Brune, J. A., ed. (Illus.). 1979. pap. 6.95 (ISBN 0-7100-0197-5). Routledge & Kegan.
Wright, Thomas. Caricature History of the Georges. LC 68-56479. (Illus.). 1968. Repr. of 1868 ed. 35.00 (ISBN 0-405-09106-0). Arno.
--England Under the House of Hanover, 2 Vols. LC 78-118512. 1971. Repr. of 1848 ed. Set. 35.00x (ISBN 0-8046-1260-9). Kennikat.

GREAT BRITAIN–SPECIAL OPERATIONS EXECUTIVE

Masterman, J. C. The Double Cross System. cancelled (ISBN 0-686-28851-3). Academy Chi Ltd.

GREAT BRITAIN–STATISTICS

Buxton, N. K. & MacKay, D. I. British Employment Statistics: A Guide to Sources & Methods. 197p. 1977. 46.50x (ISBN 0-631-17240-8, Pub. by Basil Blackwell). Biblio Dist.
Cartwright, Timothy J. Royal Commissions & Departmental Committees in Britain. 320p. 1976. text ed. 25.50x (ISBN 0-340-17602-4). Verry.
Hey, John D. Britain in Context. 1979. 22.50 (ISBN 0-312-09741-7). St Martin.
Mitchell, B. R. & Jones, H. G. Second Abstract of British Historical Statistics. LC 72-128502. (Department of Applied Economics Monographs: No. 18). (Illus.). 1971. 45.00 (ISBN 0-521-08001-0). Cambridge U Pr.

Mitchell, Brian R. & Deane, P. Abstract of British Historical Statistics. (Department of Applied Economics Monographs: No. 17). 1962. 68.50 (ISBN 0-521-05738-8). Cambridge U Pr.
Newsholme, Arthur. The Elements of Vital Statistics. 3rd rev. ed. LC 75-38139. (Demography Ser.). (Illus.). 1976. Repr. of 1899 ed. 21.00 (ISBN 0-405-07992-3). Arno.
Ohlin, Per G. The Positive & the Preventive Check: A Study of the Rate of Growth of Pre-Industrial Populations. Bruchey, Stuart, ed. LC 80-2819. (Dissertations in European Economic History II). (Illus.). 1981. lib. bdg. 45.00x (ISBN 0-405-14003-7). Arno.
Page, William, ed. Commerce & Industry, 2 Vols in One. LC 67-19709. Repr. of 1919 ed. 30.00x (ISBN 0-678-00404-8). Kelley.
Thomas, D. S. Social Aspects of the Business Cycle. LC 67-25760. (Demographic Monographs Ser). 1968. 37.50x (ISBN 0-677-01570-4). Gordon.

GREAT BRITAIN–STATISTICS–BIBLIOGRAPHY

Harvey, Joan M. Sources of Statistics. 2nd ed. (Guides to Subject Literature Ser.). 1971. 13.50 (ISBN 0-208-01075-0, Linnet). Shoe String.
Palmer, Stanley H. Economic Arithmetic: A Guide to the Statistical Sources of English Commerce, Industry & Finance, 1700-1850. LC 76-42890. (Reference Library of Social Science Ser.: Vol. 26). (Illus.). 1977. lib. bdg. 27.50 (ISBN 0-8240-9946-X). Garland Pub.

GREAT BRITAIN–TREASURY

Chapman, R. A. Decision Making: A Case Study of the Decision to Raise the Bank Rate in September 1957. (Library of Political Studies). 1969. text ed. 5.75x (ISBN 0-7100-6302-4). Humanities.
Clark, Dora M. Rise of the British Treasury: Colonial Administration in the 18th Century. 1969. Repr. of 1960 ed. 18.00 (ISBN 0-208-00788-1, Archon). Shoe String.
Roseveare, Henry. The Treasury: The Evolution of a British Institution. 1970. 17.50x (ISBN 0-231-03405-9). Columbia U Pr.

GREAT BRITAIN–VICE-ADMIRALTY COURTS

Ubbelohde, Carl. Vice-Admiralty Courts & the American Revolution. (Institute of Early American History & Culture Ser.). 1960. 16.50x (ISBN 0-8078-0787-7). U of NC Pr.

GREAT BRITAIN–WAR OFFICE

Fay, Sir Sam. The War Office at War. 1976. Repr. 15.00x (ISBN 0-85409-883-6). Charles River Bks.

GREAT CENTRAL RAILWAY

Tuplin, W. A. Great Central Steam. 1967. 6.95 (ISBN 0-04-385039-1). Allen Unwin.

GREAT CRESTED GREBE

Huxley, Julian. Courtship Habits of the Great Crested Grebe. LC 68-55824. (Cape Editions Ser). 1968. 3.50 (ISBN 0-670-24426-0, Grossman). Viking Pr.

GREAT DANE DOGS

see Dogs–Breeds–Great Dane

GREAT LAKES

Callahan, J. M. Neutrality of the American Lakes & Anglo-American Relations. 1973. Repr. of 1898 ed. pap. 17.00 (ISBN 0-384-07195-3). Johnson Repr.
Cantor, George. The Great Lakes Guidebook: Lake Huron & Eastern Lake Michigan. LC 77-13606. (Illus.). 1979. pap. 5.95 (ISBN 0-472-19651-0). U of Mich Pr.
The Faces of the Great Lakes. LC 77-7666. 1977. write for info. (ISBN 0-87156-196-4, Pub. by Sierra). Black Ice.
Great Lakes Stack Charts 1979. 1980. 6.00 (ISBN 0-686-62312-6). Freshwater.
Hatcher, Harlan H. Lake Erie. (Illus.). Repr. of 1945 ed. lib. bdg. 18.50x (ISBN 0-8371-5790-0, HALA). Greenwood.
Komaiko, Jean, et al. Around Lake Michigan. 1980. pap. text ed. 7.95 (ISBN 0-395-29127-5). HM.
Kuchenberg, Thomas C. Reflections in a Tarnished Mirror: The Use & Abuse of the Great Lakes. LC 78-70548. (Illus.). 1978. pap. 9.50 (ISBN 0-933072-01-5). Golden Glow.
Kuttruff, Karl. Ships of the Great Lakes: A Pictorial History. LC 76-10383. 1976. 25.00 (ISBN 0-8143-1564-X). Wayne St U Pr.
Landon, Fred. Lake Huron. LC 71-180612. (Illus.). 398p. 1972. Repr. of 1944 ed. 21.00 (ISBN 0-8462-1660-4). Russell.
Mason, Ronald J. Great Lakes Archaeology. LC 80-2340. (New World Archaeological Record Ser.). 1981. 34.50 (ISBN 0-12-477850-X). Acad Pr.
Myers, Linda & Outdoor World Editors. The Great Lakes: North America's Inland Sea. LC 73-84641. (Illus.). 192p. 1974. 19.95 (ISBN 0-87294-052-7). Country Beautiful.
Ossoli, Margaret F. Summer on the Lakes. LC 68-24991. (Concordance Ser., No. 37). 1969. Repr. of 1844 ed. lib. bdg. 24.95 (ISBN 0-8383-0225-4). Haskell.
Our Inland Seas. 1979. 9.50 (ISBN 0-686-57986-0). Freshwater.
Piper, Don C. International Law of the Great Lakes: A Study of Canadian United States Co-Operation. LC 66-29860. (Commonwealth Studies Center: No. 30). 1967. 9.75 (ISBN 0-8223-0136-9). Duke.
Rousmaniere, John, ed. The Enduring Great Lakes: A Natural History Book. 1979. 14.95 (ISBN 0-393-01194-1). Norton.
Schoolcraft, Henry R. Narrative Journals of Travels Through the Northwestern Regions of the U.S. Extending from Detroit Through the Great Chain of American Lakes to the Sources of the Mississippi River. LC 73-125763. (American Environmental Studies). 1970. Repr. of 1821 ed. 18.00 (ISBN 0-405-02689-7). Arno.
Snook, Patricia K. Fishing the Great Lakes. 1979. pap. 6.95 o. p. (ISBN 0-8092-7319-5). Contemp Bks.

GREAT LAKES–HISTORY

Armour, David A. & Widder, Keith R. At the Crossroads: Michilimackinac During the American Revolution. (Illus.). 1978. 12.50 (ISBN 0-911872-24-8). Mackinac Island.
Ault, Phil. These Are the Great Lakes. LC 72-1533. (Illus.). 228p. (gr. 5 up). 1972. 5.95 (ISBN 0-396-06607-0). Dodd.
Barry, James P. Wrecks & Rescues of the Great Lakes: A Photographic History. LC 81-6199. (Illus.). 128p. 1981. 15.00 (ISBN 0-8310-7149-4). Howell-North.
Bowen, Dana T. Lore of the Lakes. 1940. 9.50 (ISBN 0-685-11634-4). Freshwater.
--Memories of the Lakes. 1946. 9.50 (ISBN 0-685-11635-2). Freshwater.
Boyer, Dwight. Great Stories of the Great Lakes. LC 66-21751. (Illus.). 1966. 8.95 (ISBN 0-396-05374-2). Dodd.
--Ships & Men of the Great Lakes. LC 77-5901. (Illus.). 1977. 8.95 (ISBN 0-396-07446-4). Dodd.
--Strange Adventures of the Great Lakes. LC 74-7771. (Illus.). 256p. 1974. 8.95 (ISBN 0-396-06996-7). Dodd.
Great Lakes Ship Wrecks: And Other Lake Stories. 5.00 (ISBN 0-686-26075-9). Voyager Pr.
Greenwood, John O. Namesakes 30-55. 1978. 19.75 (ISBN 0-685-87666-7). Freshwater.
Harwood, W. S., et al. Early Stories of the Great Lakes. LC 75-39086. Orig. Title: Stories of the Great Lakes. (Illus.). 186p. 1976. pap. 6.00 (ISBN 0-912382-18-X). Black Letter.
Havighurst, Walter. The Great Lakes Reader. (Illus.). 1978. pap. 6.95 (ISBN 0-02-080540-3, Collier). Macmillan.
--Long Ships Passing. 1961. 12.95 (ISBN 0-02-549100-8); pap. 1.65 (ISBN 0-02-033100-2). Macmillan.
Janzen, Donald E. The Naomikong Site & the Dimensions of Laurel in the Lake Superior Region. (Anthropological Papers: No. 36). (Illus.). 1968. pap. 3.00x (ISBN 0-932206-34-4). U Mich Mus Anthro.
Mansfield, J. B. History of the Great Lakes, Vols. 1-2. (Illus.). 2000p. 1972. Repr. 125.00 set (ISBN 0-686-01098-1). Freshwater.

GREAT LAKES REGION

Ault, Phil. These Are the Great Lakes. LC 72-1533. (Illus.). 228p. (gr. 5 up). 1972. 5.95 (ISBN 0-396-06607-0). Dodd.
Dewdney, Selwyn & Kidd, Kenneth E. Indian Rock Paintings of the Great Lakes. rev. ed. LC 67-98487. (Illus.). 1967. 15.00 (ISBN 0-8020-3172-2). U of Toronto Pr.
Eichenlaub, Val. Weather & Climate of the Great Lakes Region. LC 78-51526. (Illus.). 1979. text ed. 14.95x (ISBN 0-268-01929-0); pap. text ed. 5.95x (ISBN 0-268-01930-4). U of Notre Dame Pr.
Great Lakes Megalopolis: From Civilization to Ecumenization. (Illus.). 1977. pap. 7.40 (ISBN 0-660-00376-7, SSC). Unipub.
King, B. A. & Ela, Jonathan. The Faces of the Great Lakes. LC 77-7666. (Illus.). 1977. 24.50 (ISBN 0-87156-196-4). Sierra.
McKenney, Thomas L. Sketches of a Tour to the Lakes. (Illus.). Repr. 12.50 (ISBN 0-87018-042-8). Ross.
Peirce, Neal R. & Keefe, John. The Great Lakes State of America. (Illus.). 1980. 16.95 (ISBN 0-393-05619-8). Norton.
Taylor, Donna, ed. The Great Lakes Region in Children's Books: A Selected Annotated Bibliography. LC 80-13746. 1980. 16.95 (ISBN 0-931600-01-4). Green Oak Pr.

GREAT LAKES REGION–DESCRIPTION AND TRAVEL–GUIDEBOOKS

Cantor, George. The Great Lakes Guidebook: Lakes Ontario & Erie. LC 77-13606. 1978. pap. 5.95 (ISBN 0-472-19650-2). U of Mich Pr.
Gardner, Roberta H. Country Inns of America: The Great Lakes. LC 81-1618. (Illus.). 96p. 1981. pap. 8.95 (ISBN 0-03-059159-7, Owl Bk). HR&W.
Greenwood's Guide to Great Lakes Shipping, 1980. 1980. 35.00 (ISBN 0-686-57984-4). Freshwater.
Michigan United Conservation Clubs. Great Lakes Nature Guide. rev. ed. 1978. pap. 1.75 (ISBN 0-933112-05-X). Mich United Conserv.
Morris, Robert. Country Inns of the Great Lakes: A Guide to Inns, Lodges, & Historic Hostelries of the Upper Midwest. 180p. (Orig.). 1981. pap. 4.95 (ISBN 0-89286-165-7). One Hund One Prods.
Paul, Bil. Bicycling California's Spine: Touring the Length of the Sierra Nevada. LC 80-70010. (Bikeroots Ser.). (Illus.). 64p. (Orig.). 1981. pap. 3.95 (ISBN 0-9600650-3-2). Alchemist-Light.

GREAT NORTHERN RAILWAY

Great Northern Railway. Date not set. 49.50 (ISBN 0-686-75185-X). Chatham Pub CA.
Lines West. 9.95 (ISBN 0-685-83346-1). Chatham Pub CA.

GREAT PLAINS

Creigh, Dorothy W. Adams County, 2 vols. Incl. A Story of the Great Plains. 1972. 25.00 (ISBN 0-934858-00-4); The/People. 1971. 25.00 (ISBN 0-934858-01-2). (Illus.). Set. 45.00 (ISBN 0-934858-02-0). Adams County.
Inman, Henry. Buffalo Jones Adventures on the Plains. (Illus.). 6.00 (ISBN 0-8446-0721-5). Peter Smith.
Kraenzel, Carl F. Great Plains in Transition. (Illus.). 1970. Repr. of 1955 ed. 19.95x (ISBN 0-8061-0331-0). U of Okla Pr.
Lawson, Merlin P. & Baker, Maurice E., eds. The Great Plains: Perspectives & Prospects. LC 80-70962. (Illus.). x, 284p. pap. 9.95x (ISBN 0-938932-00-4). U of Nebr Pr.
Meacham, Mary, ed. Readings for Young People: The Great Plains. 7.50 (ISBN 0-686-74731-3). ALA.
Pierce, Neal R. The Great Plains States of America. 1973. 15.95 (ISBN 0-393-05349-0). Norton.
Tobin, Gregory M. The Making of a History: Walter Prescott Webb & "The Great Plains". 204p. 1976. 12.50x (ISBN 0-292-75029-3). U of Tex Pr.
Webb, Walter P. The Great Plains. LC 81-1821. (Illus.). xvi, 525p. 1981. pap. 9.95 (ISBN 0-8032-9702-5, BB 766, Bison). U of Nebr Pr.
Wilson, James C. & Wilson, Alice O. Grass Land. (Illus.). 32p. (Orig.). 1967. 10.00 (ISBN 0-939750-02-3); pap. 5.00 (ISBN 0-939750-03-1). Entheos.

GREAT PLAINS–ANTIQUITIES

Wedel, Waldo R. Prehistoric Man on the Great Plains. (Illus.). 1961. 16.95 (ISBN 0-8061-0501-1). U of Okla Pr.

GREAT PLAINS–DESCRIPTION AND TRAVEL

Custer, George A. My Life on the Plains. Quaife, Milo M., ed. LC 67-2618. (Illus.). 1966. pap. 6.95 (ISBN 0-8032-5042-8, BB 328, Bison). U of Nebr Pr.
Keller, George. A Trip Across the Plains. (California Heritage Ser.). 1955. lib. bdg. 12.00 (ISBN 0-685-86966-0). Sullivan Bks Intl.
Vestal, Stanley. Short Grass Country. Repr. of 1941 ed. lib. bdg. 15.00 (ISBN 0-8371-2978-8, VESG). Greenwood.
Wilson, Jim & Wilson, Alice. Grass Land. (Illus.). 1967. 5.95 (ISBN 0-686-00959-2); pap. 2.95 (ISBN 0-686-00960-6). Wide Skies.

GREAT PLAINS–DESCRIPTION AND TRAVEL–GUIDEBOOKS

Clark, Tom. A Short Guide to the High Plains. Miller, Jeffrey, ed. 48p. 1981. 15.00 (ISBN 0-932274-18-8); pap. 3.50 signed ltd. ed. (ISBN 0-932274-17-X). Cadmus Eds.

GREAT PLAINS–ECONOMIC CONDITIONS

Krutilla, John V., et al. Economic & Fiscal Impacts of Coal Development: Northern Great Plains. LC 77-89300. (Resources for the Future Ser.). (Illus.). 1978. text ed. 18.50x (ISBN 0-8018-2054-5). Johns Hopkins.

GREAT PLAINS–HISTORY

Blouet, Brian W. & Luebke, Frederick C., eds. The Great Plains: Environment & Culture. LC 79-1152. (Illus.). xxviii, 246p. 1979. 15.95x (ISBN 0-8032-1155-4). U of Nebr Pr.
Brill, Charles J. Conquest of the Southern Plains. LC 39-17554. 1975. Repr. of 1938 ed. 22.00 (ISBN 0-527-11068-X). Kraus Repr.
Emmons, David M. Garden in the Grasslands: Boomer Literature of the Central Great Plains. LC 70-125100. (Illus.). xiv, 220p. 1971. 15.50x (ISBN 0-8032-0753-0). U of Nebr Pr.
Fischer, John. From the High Plains: An Account of the Hard Men, High-Spirited Women -- & a Few Rascals -- Who Settled the Last Frontier of the Old West. LC 78-437. (Illus.). 1978. 10.00 (ISBN 0-06-011269-7, HarpT). Har-Row.
Luebke, Frederick C., ed. Ethnicity on the Great Plains. LC 79-17743. (Illus.). xxxiv, 237p. 1980. 15.95x (ISBN 0-8032-2855-4). U of Nebr Pr.
Sandoz, Mari. Love Song to the Plains. LC 61-6441. (Illus.). 1966. pap. 3.50 (ISBN 0-8032-5172-6, BB 349, Bison). U of Nebr Pr.
Sharrock, Floyd W. Prehistoric Occupation Patterns in Southwest Wyoming & Cultural Relationships with the Great Basin & Plains Culture Areas. (Utah Anthropological Papers: No. 77). Repr. of 1966 ed. 24.00 (ISBN 0-404-60677-6). AMS Pr.
Smith, G. Hubert. The Explorations of the La Verendryes in the Northern Plains, 1738-43. Wood, W. Raymond, ed. LC 79-26518. (Illus.). xx, 160p. 1980. 13.95x (ISBN 0-8032-4712-5). U of Nebr Pr.
Tobin, Gregory M. The Making of a History: Walter Prescott Webb & "The Great Plains". 204p. 1976. 12.50x (ISBN 0-292-75029-3). U of Tex Pr.
Vestal, Stanley. Short Grass Country. Repr. of 1941 ed. lib. bdg. 15.00 (ISBN 0-8371-2978-8, VESG). Greenwood.
Vyn, Kathleen. The Prairie Community. LC 78-6732. (Illus.). 64p. (gr. 3-5). 1978. PLB 6.97 (ISBN 0-671-32924-3). Messner.
Worster, Donald. Dust Bowl: The Southern Plains in the 1930's. (Illus.). 1979. 16.95 (ISBN 0-19-502550-4). Oxford U Pr.

GREAT PLAINS–JUVENILE LITERATURE

Vyn, Kathleen. The Prairie Community. LC 78-6732. (Illus.). 64p. (gr. 3-5). 1978. PLB 6.97 (ISBN 0-671-32924-3). Messner.

GREAT PYRENEES (DOGS)

see Dogs–Breeds–Great Pyrenees

GREAT SALT LAKE

Czermy, Peter G. Great, Great Salt Lake. LC 76-4080. (Illus.). 123p. 1976. pap. 4.95 (ISBN 0-8425-1073-7). Brigham.

GREAT SCHISM

see Schism; Schism–Eastern and Western Church; Schism, the Great Western, 1378-1417

GREAT SMOKY MOUNTAINS

Albright, Rod & Albright, Priscilla. Walks in the Great Smokies. LC 79-4898. (Illus.). 192p. 1979. pap. 6.95 (ISBN 0-914788-14-0). East Woods.
Cantu, Rita. Great Smoky Mountains: The Story Behind the Scenery. DenDooven, Gweneth R., ed. LC 78-78123. (Illus.). 1979. 7.95 (ISBN 0-916122-60-3); pap. 3.00 (ISBN 0-916122-59-X). KC Pubns.
Doane, Jim. Great Smoky Mountains Picture Book. Castaldo, George, ed. (Color Pictorial of Great Smoky Mountains Ser.: No. 1). (Illus.). 72p. (Orig.). 1981. 10.95 (ISBN 0-936672-13-7); pap. 7.50 (ISBN 0-936672-14-5). Aerial Photo.
Frome, Michael. Strangers in High Places: The Story of the Great Smoky Mountains. rev. ed. LC 79-19748. 1980. lib. bdg. 14.50x (ISBN 0-87049-281-0); pap. 7.50 (ISBN 0-87049-287-X). U of Tenn Pr.
Hall, Joseph S. Smoky Mountain Folks & Their Lore. (Illus.). 1964. pap. 1.75 (ISBN 0-9600168-0-5). Hollywood.
Murlless, Dick & Stallings, Constance. Hikers' Guide to the Smokies. LC 72-83981. (Totebook Ser.). (Illus.). 374p. 1973. pap. 8.95 (ISBN 0-87156-068-2); Hiker's Map of the Smokies 1.95 (ISBN 0-87156-095-X). Sierra.
Porter, Eliot. Appalachian Wilderness: The Great Smokey Mountains. 1973. 12.95 (ISBN 0-525-05686-6). Dutton.
Smokies. (Animal Friends Ser.). pap. 1.50 (ISBN 0-915266-12-1). Awani Pr.
Thornborough, Laura. Great Smoky Mountains. rev. ed. (Illus.). 1962. 7.50 (ISBN 0-87049-034-6). U of Tenn Pr.

GREAT SMOKY MOUNTAINS NATIONAL PARK

Campbell, Carlos C. Birth of a National Park in the Great Smoky Mountains. rev. ed. LC 60-12223. (Illus.). 1978. 8.50 (ISBN 0-87049-029-X). U of Tenn Pr.
Thornborough, Laura. Great Smoky Mountains. rev. ed. (Illus.). 1962. 7.50 (ISBN 0-87049-034-6). U of Tenn Pr.

GREAT SMOKY MOUNTAINS NATIONAL PARK–JUVENILE LITERATURE

Radlauer, Ruth. Great Smoky Mountains National Park. LC 76-9839. (Parks for People Ser.). (Illus.). (gr. 3 up). 1976. 3.95 (ISBN 0-516-17489-4, Elk Grove Bks); PLB 10.00 (ISBN 0-516-07489-X). Childrens.

GREAT WALL OF CHINA

see Wall of China

GREAT WESTERN RAILWAY (GREAT BRITAIN)

Booker, Frank. The Great Western Railway: A New History. 1977. 14.95 (ISBN 0-7153-7455-9). David & Charles.
Bourne, John C. History & Description of the Great Western Railway. LC 78-83361. (Illus.). Repr. of 1846 ed. lib. bdg. 37.50x (ISBN 0-678-05507-6). Kelley.
GWR Engines, Names, Numbers, Types & Classes: A Reprint of the Engine Books of 1911, 1928 & 1946 with Some Pages from That of 1938. (Illus.). 250p. 1971. 11.95 (ISBN 0-7153-5367-5). David & Charles.
Halcroft, H. An Outline of Great Western Locomotive Practice Eighteen Thirty-Seven to Nineteen Forty-Seven. Date not set. 13.95 (ISBN 0-392-08863-0, SpS). Sportshelf.

Hollingsworth, Brian. Great Western Adventure. LC 81-65959. (Illus.). 176p. 1981. 17.95 (ISBN 0-7153-8108-3). David & Charles.
Johnston & Casserly. Locomotives at the Grouping, Great Western Railway. 14.95x (ISBN 0-392-08054-0, SpS). Sportshelf.
Lucking, J. H. The Great Western at Weymouth: A Railway & Shipping History. (Illus.). 253p. 1971. 5.95 (ISBN 0-7153-5135-4). David & Charles.
Macdermat & Clinker. History of the Great Western Railway 1863-1921. 19.25x (ISBN 0-392-07891-0, SpS). Sportshelf.
Nock, O. S. History of the Great Western Railway Nineteen Twenty-Three to Nineteen Fourty-Eight. Date not set. 19.25x (ISBN 0-392-07907-0, SpS). Sportshelf.
Riley, R. C. Great Western Album. 14.50x (ISBN 0-392-07860-0, SpS). Sportshelf.
Thomas, David S. & Rocksborough Smith, Simon. Summer Saturdays in the West. (Illus.). 1973. 14.95 (ISBN 0-7153-5912-6). David & Charles.
Thomas, David St. John. The Great Way West: The History & Romance of the Great Western Railway's Route from Paddington to Penzanze. LC 75-10530. (Illus.). 1975. 14.95 (ISBN 0-7153-7063-4). David & Charles.
Wilson, Roger Burdett. Go Great Western: A History of GWR Publicity. (Illus.). 192p. 1970. 4.50 (ISBN 0-7153-4896-5). David & Charles.

GREAT WESTERN SCHISM
see Schism, the Great Western, 1378-1417

GREATER VEHICLE
see Mahayana Buddhism

GREATNESS
see Genius

GREBES
see also Great Crested Grebe
Pijlman, F. The Grebe. (Animal Environment Ser.). (Illus.). 30p. 1980. 4.95 (ISBN 0-8120-5377-X). Barron.

GRECIAN FIRE
see Greek Fire

GRECO-ROMAN ART
see Art, Greco-Roman

GRECO-ROMAN CIVILIZATION
see Civilization, Greco-Roman

GRECO-ROMAN PAINTING
see Painting, Greco-Roman

GRECO-ROMAN SCHISM
see Schism–Eastern and Western Church

GRECO-TURKISH WAR, 1897
Augustinos, Gerasimos. Consciousness & History: Nationalist Critics of Greek Society, 1897-1914. (East European Monographs: No. 32). 1977. 13.50x (ISBN 0-914710-25-7). East Eur Quarterly.
Stallman, R. W. & Hagemann, E. R., eds. The War Dispatches of Stephen Crane. LC 77-2994. (Illus.). 1977. Repr. of 1964 ed. lib. bdg. 21.25x (ISBN 0-8371-9549-7, CRWD). Greenwood.

GREECE
Here are entered only works on Ancient Greece. For books on Modern Greece, see Greece, Modern.
see also names of cities, towns and geographic areas in Greece
Billigmeier, Jon C.. Kadmos & the Possibility of a Semitic Presence in Halladic Greece. (Publications of the Henri Frankfort Foundation Ser.: No. 6). 1980. pap. text ed. write for info. (ISBN 90-6032-110-3). Humanities.
Horton, George. The Isles of Greece: Home of Nymphs & Vampires. 1977. lib. bdg. 59.95 (ISBN 0-8490-2082-4). Gordon Pr.
Jarde, Auguste. Formation of the Greek People. Dobie, M. R., tr. from Fr. LC 75-139998. (Illus.). 1971. Repr. of 1926 ed. lib. bdg. 17.50x (ISBN 0-8154-0369-0). Cooper Sq.
Knox, Bernard. Oedipus at Thebes: Sophocles Tragic Hero & His Time. 1971. pap. 1.95 (ISBN 0-393-00563-1, Norton Lib). Norton.
Marchant, E. C., ed. Thucydides, Book II. (Classical Ser.). 1891. 6.95 (ISBN 0-312-80395-8). St Martin.
Nawrath, Alfred. The Aegean World. LC 77-87872. (Illus.). 1977. 30.00 (ISBN 0-88331-097-X). J J Binns.
Nichols, R. & McLeish, K., eds. Through Greek Eyes. LC 74-80353. (Illus.). 144p. (gr. 7-12). 1975. 17.95 (ISBN 0-521-20632-4); pap. 6.50 (ISBN 0-521-08560-8). Cambridge U Pr.
Pillement, Georges. Unknown Greece, 3 vols. Incl. Vol. 1. Athens & the Peloponnesus. 200p (ISBN 0-85307-119-5); Vol. 2. Epirus, Thessaly, Corfu, & the Ionian Islands. 187p (ISBN 0-85307-122-5); Vol. 3. The Islands of the Aegean Sea. LC 73-161163. (Illus.). 1973. 12.50x ea. Intl Pubns Serv.
Proposals for Nature Conservation in Northern Greece. (Illus.). 1971. pap. 7.50x (ISBN 2-88032-052-6, IUCN42, IUCN). Unipub.
Vernant, Jean-Pierre. Myth & Society in Ancient Greece. 1980. text ed. 42.50x (ISBN 0-391-00915-X). Humanities.
Welsman, Ernest. Your Guide to Greece. LC 66-1651. (Your Guide Ser.). 1965. 5.25x (ISBN 0-8002-0779-3). Intl Pubns Serv.
Zimmern, Alfred. Greek Commonwealth: Politics & Economics in Fifth-Century Athens. 5th ed. 1931. pap. 5.95x (ISBN 0-19-500230-X). Oxford U Pr.

GREECE–ANTIQUITIES
Andronicos, Manolis. Vergina, the Prehistoric Necropolis & the Hellenistic Palace. (Studies in Mediterranean Archaeology Ser.: No. 13). (Illus.). 1964. pap. text ed. 4.25x (ISBN 91-85058-12-2). Humanities.
The Arrival of the Greeks: The Evidence of the Settlements, Pt. 3. (Publications of the Henri Frankfort Foundation: No. 5). 1978. pap. text ed. 16.50x (ISBN 90-6032-109-X). Humanities.
Beck, H. G., et al, eds. Kyklos: Griechisches und Byzantinisches: Rudolf Keydell Zum 90. Geburstag. 1978. 54.50x (ISBN 3-11-007211-4). De Gruyter.
Betancourt, Philip P. The Aeolic Style in Architecture: A Survey of Its Development in Palestine, the Halikarnassos Peninsula, & Greece, 1000-500 B.C. LC 76-45890. (Illus.). 1977. text ed. 35.00 (ISBN 0-691-03922-4). Princeton U Pr.
Biers, William R. The Archaeology of Greece: An Introduction. LC 79-22070. (Cornell Paperbacks Ser.). (Illus.). 344p. 1981. 29.95 (ISBN 0-8014-1023-1); pap. 14.95 (ISBN 0-8014-9229-7). Cornell U Pr.
Blumner, Hugo. Technologie und Terminologie der Gewerbe und Kunste bei Griechen und Romern, 4 vols. Finley, Moses, ed. LC 79-4963. (Ancient Economic History Ser.). (Illus., Ger.). 1980. Repr. of 1875 ed. Set. lib. bdg. 128.00x (ISBN 0-405-12350-7); 32.00x ea. Vol. 1 (ISBN 0-405-12351-5). Vol. 2 (ISBN 0-405-12352-3). Vol. 3 (ISBN 0-405-12484-8). Vol. 4 (ISBN 0-405-12485-6). Arno.
Boardman, John. The Greeks Overseas: Their Early Colonies & Trade. (Illus.). 1980. 22.50 (ISBN 0-500-25069-3). Thames Hudson.
Bol, Peter C. Grossplastik Aus Bronze in Olympia. (Olympische Forschungen: Vol. 14). 1978. 80.50x (ISBN 3-11-006701-3). De Gruyter.
Branigan, Keith, et al. Hellas: The Civilization of Ancient Greece. LC 80-18306. (Illus.). 224p. 1980. 39.95 (ISBN 0-07-007229-9). McGraw.
Cambitoglou, Alexander, et al, eds. Zagora 1: Excavation of a Geometric Settlement on the Island of Andros, Greece. LC 75-157251. (Australian Academy of the Humanities Monograph: No. 2). (Illus.). 96p. 1972. pap. 8.00x (ISBN 0-424-06200-3, Pub. by Sydney U Pr). Intl Schol Bk Serv.
Cameron, Fiona. Greek Bronze Hand-Mirrors in South Italy, with Special Reference to Calabria. 1979. 15.00x (ISBN 0-86054-056-1, Pub. by BAR). State Mutual Bk.
Carpenter, Rhys. Humanistic Value of Archaeology. LC 72-138582. 1971. Repr. of 1933 ed. lib. bdg. 15.00 (ISBN 0-8371-5781-1, CAHV). Greenwood.
Casson, S., ed. Essays in Aegean Archaeology: Presented to Sir Arthur Evans in Honour of His 75th Birthday. 1978. Repr. of 1927 ed. lib. bdg. 45.00 (ISBN 0-8495-0762-6). Arden Lib.
Coldstream, J. N. & Huxley, G. L., eds. Kythera: Excavation & Studies Conducted by the University of Pennsylvania Museum & the British School of Athens. LC 72-87476. (Illus.). 1973. 48.00 (ISBN 0-8155-5017-0, NP). Noyes.
Coleman, John E. Kephala: A Late Neolithic Settlement & Cemetery. LC 76-13187. (Keos Ser: Vol. 1). 1977. pap. 35.00x (ISBN 0-87661-701-1). Am Sch Athens.
Craik, Elizabeth M. The Dorian Aegean. (States & Cities of Ancient Greece Ser.). 1979. 22.50 (ISBN 0-7100-0378-1). Routledge & Kegan.
Davison, Michael. The Glory of Greece & World of Alexander. LC 79-92450. (Illus.). 172p. 1980. pap. 14.95 (ISBN 0-89659-104-2). Abbeville Pr.
De Ste. Croix, G. E. M. The Class Struggle in the Ancient Greek World: From the Archaic Age to the Arab Conquests. 672p. 1981. 49.50x (ISBN 0-8014-1442-3). Cornell U Pr.
Doumas, C., ed. Thera & the Aegean World Two. 427p. 1981. text ed. 85.00x (ISBN 0-686-72932-3, Pub. by Aris & Phillips England). Humanities.
Doumas, Christos. Early Bronze Age Burial Habits in the Cyclades. (Studies in Mediterranean Archaeology Ser.: No. XLVIII). (Illus.). 1977. pap. text ed. 60.00x (ISBN 91-85058-68-8). Humanities.
Gernet, Louis. The Anthropology of Ancient Greece. Hamilton, John D. B. & Nagy, Blaise, trs. from Fr. LC 81-47598. 336p. 1981. text ed. 27.50x (ISBN 0-8018-2112-6). Johns Hopkins.
Grace, Virginia R. Amphoras & the Ancient Wine Trade. (Excavations of the Athenian Agora Picture Bks.: No. 6). (Illus.). 1979. pap. 1.50x (ISBN 0-87661-619-8). Am Sch Athens.
Greece & Italy in the Classical World. 336p. 1979. 36.00x (ISBN 0-9506584-0-5). State Mutual Bk.
Grinnell, Isabel H. Greek Temples. LC 79-168420. (Metropolitan Museum of Art Publications in Reprint). (Illus.). 138p. 1972. Repr. of 1943 ed. 23.00 (ISBN 0-405-02258-1). Arno.
Grunauer-Von Hoerschelmann, Susanne. Die Muenzpraegung der Lakedaimonier. (Antike Muenzen und Geschnittene Steine: Vol. 7). (Illus.). 1978. 112.00x (ISBN 3-11-007222-X). De Gruyter.
Hall, H. R. Civilization of Greece in the Bronze Age. LC 78-124270. (Illus.). 1970. Repr. of 1928 ed. lib. bdg. 21.50x (ISBN 0-8154-0340-2). Cooper Sq.
Hansen, Hazel D. Early Civilization in Thessaly. LC 70-158855. Repr. of 1933 ed. 19.00 (ISBN 0-404-03106-4). AMS Pr.
Heilmeyer, Wolf-Dieter. Fruehe Olympische Bronzefiguren, Die Tiervotive. (Olympische Forschungen). 1979. 112.00x (ISBN 3-11-007208-4). De Gruyter.
--Fruehe Olympische Tonfiguren. (Olympische Forschungen, Vol. 7). 146p. 1972. 49.00x (ISBN 3-11-003962-1). De Gruyter.
Herbert, Kevin. Greek & Latin Inscriptions in the Brooklyn Museum. LC 72-139772. (Wilbour Monographs: No. 4). (Illus.). 1972. 8.00 (ISBN 0-913696-13-7). Bklyn Mus.
Hirsch, Ethel. Painted Decoration on the Floors of Bronze Age Structures on Crete & the Greek Mainland. (Studies in Mediterranean Archaeology Ser.: No. LIII). (Illus.). 1977. pap. text ed. 28.00x (ISBN 91-85058-76-9). Humanities.
Hodge, A. Trevor. Woodwork of Greek Roofs. (Cambridge Classical Studies). 1960. 17.95 (ISBN 0-521-05280-7). Cambridge U Pr.
Hoffmann, Herbert. Collecting Greek Antiquities. (Illus.). 1970. 15.00 (ISBN 0-685-92062-3, R01676). Crown.
Hoffmann, Herbert & Davidson, Patricia F. Greek Gold: Jewelry from the Age of Alexander. LC 65-26949. (Illus.). 1965. pap. 4.95 (ISBN 0-913696-02-1). Bklyn Mus.
Jeffery, L. H. Archaic Greece. LC 75-10758. (Illus.). 300p. 1976. 22.50 (ISBN 0-312-04760-6). St Martin.
Jenkyns, Richard. The Victorians & Ancient Greece. LC 79-25487. (Harvard Paperbacks Ser.). 400p. 1981. pap. 8.95 (ISBN 0-674-93687-6). Harvard U Pr.
Karouzou, Semni. The National Museum. (Illustrated Travel Guides Ser.). (Illus.). 1979. pap. 9.95 (ISBN 0-89241-100-7). Caratzas Bros.
Leekley, Dorothy & Noyes, Robert. Archaeological Excavations in the Greek Islands. LC 75-34931. 1976. 15.00 (ISBN 0-8155-5043-X, NP). Noyes.
--Archaeological Excavations in Southern Greece. LC 76-17378. 1977. 15.00 (ISBN 0-8155-5048-0, NP). Noyes.
Lehman, Karl. Samothrace, a Guide to the Excavation & the Museum. 4th ed. LC 55-8563. pap. 4.50 (ISBN 0-685-73230-4). J J Augustin.
Lehmann, Karl & Lehmann, P. W., eds. Samothrace Excavations: Conducted by the Institute of Fine Arts of New York University, 4 vols. Incl. Vol. 1. Ancient Literary Sources. Lewis, Naphtali, ed. & tr. 1958. 20.00x (ISBN 0-691-09820-4); Vol. 2, Pt. 1. Inscriptions on Stone. Fraser, P. M. 1960. 30.00 (ISBN 0-691-09821-2); Vol. 2, Pt. 2. Inscriptions on Ceramics & Minor Objects. Lehmann, Karl. 1960. 30.00 (ISBN 0-691-09822-0); Vol. 3. The Hieron. Lehmann, P. 1969. 3 vols. boxed set 75.00 (ISBN 0-691-09823-9); Vol. 4, Pt. 1. Hall of Votive Gifts. Lehmann, Karl. 1962. 30.00 (ISBN 0-691-09824-7); Vol. 4, Pt. 2. Altar Court. Lehmann, Karl & Spittle, Denys. 1964. 35.00 (ISBN 0-691-09825-5). (Bollingen Ser.: Vol. 60). Princeton U Pr.
Lewis, Naphtali. The Fifth Century B. C. LC 75-148096. (Greek Historical Documents Ser.). 124p. 1970. pap. text ed. 3.50 (ISBN 0-88866-504-0). Samuel Stevens.
McDonald, William A. & Rapp, George R., Jr., eds. The Minnesota Messenia Expedition: Reconstructing a Bronze Age Regional Environment. LC 75-187168. (Illus.). 304p. 1972. 22.50x (ISBN 0-8166-0636-6). U of Minn Pr.
MacKendrick, Paul. The Greek Stones Speak: The Story of Archaeology in Greek Lands. 2nd ed. (Illus.). 1981. 24.95 (ISBN 0-393-01463-0). Norton.
--The Greek Stones Speak: The Story of Archaeology in Greek Lands. 1979. pap. 5.95 (ISBN 0-393-00932-7). Norton.
McLeish, K. Greek Art & Architecture. (Aspects of Greek Life). (Illus.). 1975. pap. text ed. 2.95x (ISBN 0-582-20673-1). Longman.
Miller, Walter. Daedalus & Thespis: Volume II: Sculpture, Pts. 1 & 2. Repr. of 1931 ed. 10.00x (ISBN 0-8262-0590-9). U of Mo Pr.
Minns, Ellis H. Scythians & Greeks: A Survey of Ancient History & Archaeology on the North Coast of the Euxine from the Danube to the Caucasus. 1976. lib. bdg. 59.95 (ISBN 0-8490-2578-8). Gordon Pr.
Nicolaou, Kyriakos. The Historical Topography of Kition. (Studies in Mediterranean Archaeology Ser.: No. XLIII). (Illus.). 1976. pap. 42.00x (ISBN 91-85058-64-5). Humanities.
Nohlen, Klaus & Radt, Wolfgang. Kapikaya: Ein Felsheiligtum Bei Pergamon. (Altertumer Von Pergamon: Vol 12). (Illus.). 1978. 91.50x (ISBN 3-11-006710-2). De Gruyter.
Osborn, Henry F. Man Rises to Parnassus. 1927. 25.00 (ISBN 0-685-73488-9). Norwood Edns.
Papadopoulos, Athanasios. Excavations at Aigion Nineteen Seventy. (Studies in Mediterranean Archaeology Ser.: No. XLVI). (Illus.). 1976. pap. text ed. 56.00x (ISBN 91-85058-68-8). Humanities.
Papadopoulos, S. A., ed. Neolithic Greece. (Illus.). 356p. 1973. 75.00 (ISBN 0-89241-075-2). Caratzas Bros.
Papahatzis, Nicos. Ancient Corinth: The Museums of Corinth, Isthmia & Sicyon. (Illustrated Travel Guides Ser.). (Illus.). 1979. pap. 9.95 (ISBN 0-89241-103-1). Caratzas Bros.
Paris, Pierre. Lexique Des Antiquites Grecques. (Fr.). 1909. pap. 23.50 (ISBN 0-686-57066-9, M-6438). French & Eur.
Pausanias. Description of Greece, 6 Vols. 2nd ed. Frazer, J. G., tr. LC 65-13634. (Illus.). 1897. Set. 100.00x (ISBN 0-8196-0144-6). Biblo.
--Description of Greece, 5 Vols. (Loeb Classical Library: No. 93, 188, 272, 297-298). 1918-35. 11.00x ea. Vol. 1 (ISBN 0-674-99104-4). Vol. 2 (ISBN 0-674-99207-5). Vol. 3 (ISBN 0-674-99300-4). Vol. 4 (ISBN 0-674-99328-4). Vol. 5 (ISBN 0-674-99329-2). Harvard U Pr.
Pomerance, Leon. The Final Collapse of Santorini (Thera) 1400 B. C. or 1200? (Studies in Mediterranean Archaeology Ser.: No. XXVI). (Illus.). 1970. pap. text ed. 7.00x (ISBN 9-1850-5839-4). Humanities.
Potter, John. Archaeologica Graeca: Or, the Antiquities of Greece, 2 vols. Feldman, Burton & Richardson, Robert, eds. LC 78-60893. (Myth & Romanticism Ser.: Vol. 19). (Illus.). 1980. Set. lib. bdg. 120.00 (ISBN 0-8240-3568-2); lib. bdg. 66.00 ea. Garland Pub.
Price, Derek D. Gears from the Greeks: The Antikythera Mechanism - a Calendar Computer from c. 80 BC. new ed. LC 74-29043. (Illus.). 96p. 1975. Repr. text ed. 20.00 (ISBN 0-88202-019-6, Sci Hist). N Watson.
Ragghianti, Licia C. The Magnificent Heritage of Ancient Greece. La Farge, Henry A., ed. LC 78-8788. (Illus.). 1979. 19.95 (ISBN 0-88225-281-X). Newsweek.
Rapp, George R., Jr. & Aschenbrenner, S. E., eds. Excavations at Nichoria in Southwest Greece: Site, Environs, & Techniques, Vol. 1. LC 78-3198. (Illus.). 1978. 29.75x (ISBN 0-8166-0824-5). U of Minn Pr.
Rider, Bertha C. The Greek House: Its History & Development from the Neolithic Period to the Hellenistic Age. LC 77-94614. 1979. Repr. of 1916 ed. lib. bdg. 30.00 (ISBN 0-89341-248-1). Longwood Pr.
Rothenberg, Jacob. Descensus As Terram: The Acquisition & Reception of the Elgin Marbles. LC 76-23716. (Outstanding Dissertations in the Fine Arts Ser.). 1977. lib. bdg. 70.00x (ISBN 0-8240-2726-4). Garland Pub.
Rouse, William H. Greek Votive Offerings: An Essay in the History of Greek Religion. facsimile ed. LC 75-10654. (Ancient Religion & Mythology Ser.). (Illus.). 1976. Repr. of 1902 ed. 27.00x (ISBN 0-405-07262-7). Arno.
Runciman, Steven. Mistra. (Illus.). 1980. 17.50 (ISBN 0-500-25071-5). Thames Hudson.
Sakellarakis, J. A. Herakleion Museum. (Illustrated Travel Guides Ser.). (Illus.). 1979. pap. 9.95 (ISBN 0-89241-101-5). Caratzas Bros.
Schuchardt, C. Schliemann's Excavations: An Archaeological & Historical Study. LC 74-173145. (Illus.). Repr. of 1891 ed. 25.00 (ISBN 0-405-08938-4). Arno.
Schuchhardt, Carl. Schliemanns Excavations. Sellers, Eugenie, tr. LC 74-77893. (Illus.). 419p. 1975. 15.00 (ISBN 0-89005-034-1). Ares.
Smith, Robert H. Pella of the Decapolis, Vol. 1. LC 72-619700. (Illus.). 248p. 1973. 50.00 (ISBN 0-9604658-0-4). Coll Wooster.
Smith, William. Dictionary of Greek & Roman Antiquities, 2 vols. LC 77-6173. 1977. Repr. of 1890 ed. lib. bdg. 65.00 (ISBN 0-89341-166-3). Longwood Pr.
Snodgrass, Anthony. Archaic Greece: The Age of Experiment. (Orig.). 1981. pap. 5.95 (ISBN 0-520-04373-1, CAL 505). U of Cal Pr.
Stroud, Ronald. The Axones & Kyrbeis of Drakon & Solon. LC 77-20329. (Publications in Classical Studies: Vol. 19). 1979. 9.50x (ISBN 0-520-09590-1). U of Cal Pr.

Sturzebecker, Russell. An Anecdotal Photo-Atlas of Athletic-Cultural Archeological Sites in the Greco-Roman World, Vol. I. (Illus.). Date not set. price not set (ISBN 0-9600466-2-3). Sturzebecker.

Tataki, A. B. Lindos: The Acropolis & the Medieval Castle. (Illustrated Travel Guides Ser.). (Illus.). 1979. pap. 8.95 (ISBN 0-89241-105-8). Caratzas Bros.

--Sounion: The Temple of Poseidon. (Illustrated Travel Guides Ser.). (Illus.). 1979. pap. 8.95 (ISBN 0-89241-104-X). Caratzas Bros.

Vickers, M. Greek Vases. 103p. 1978. 15.00x (ISBN 0-686-75551-0, Pub. by Ashmolean Mus Oxford). State Mutual Bk.

Wace, Alan J. Prehistoric Thessaly. LC 75-41286. Repr. of 1912 ed. 42.50 (ISBN 0-404-14734-8). AMS Pr.

Webb, Virginia. Archaic Greek Faience: Miniature Scent Bottles & Related Objects from East Greece 650-500 B.C. (Illus.). 1978. 51.00x (ISBN 0-85668-081-8, Pub. by Aris & Phillips). Intl Schol Bk Serv.

Woodford, Susan. The Parthenon. (Cambridge Introduction to the History of Mankind Ser.). Date not set. pap. 3.95 (ISBN 0-521-22629-5). Cambridge U Pr.

GREECE–ARMY

Cassin-Scott, Jack. The Greek & Persian Armies. (Men-at-Arms Ser.). (Illus.). 48p. 1978. pap. 7.95 (ISBN 0-85045-271-6). Hippocrene Bks.

GREECE–BIBLIOGRAPHY

Clogg, Mary Jo & Clogg, Richard. Greece. (World Bibliographical Ser.: No. 17). 224p. 1981. 34.50 (ISBN 0-903450-30-5). ABC Clio.

Kenyon, Frederic G. Books & Readers in Ancient Greece & Rome. 136p. 1980. 12.50 (ISBN 0-89005-340-5). Ares.

Radice, Betty. Who's Who in the Ancient World. (Reference Ser.). (Orig.). 1973. pap. 4.95 (ISBN 0-14-051055-9). Penguin.

GREECE–BIOGRAPHY

see also Classical Biography

Cox, George W. Lives of Greek Statesmen. 1975. Repr. of 1885 ed. 15.00 (ISBN 0-8274-4046-4). R West.

--Lives of Greek Statesmen: Ephialtes to Hermokrates. LC 77-94560. 1979. Repr. of 1886 ed. lib. bdg. 30.00 (ISBN 0-89341-260-0). Longwood Pr.

Hopkinson, Leslie W. Greek Leaders. facs. ed. LC 75-76904. (Essay Index Reprint Ser). 1918. 16.00 (ISBN 0-8369-0017-0). Arno.

Lavell, Cecil F. A Biography of the Greek People. 1934. 20.00 (ISBN 0-686-20085-3). Quality Lib.

Nepos, Cornelius. Vitae. Winstedt, E. O., ed. (Oxford Classical Texts Ser). 1904. 14.95x (ISBN 0-19-814617-5). Oxford U Pr.

Plutarch. Parallel Lives, 11 vols. Incl. Vol. 1 (ISBN 0-674-99052-8); Vol. 2 (ISBN 0-674-99053-6); Vol. 3 (ISBN 0-674-99072-2); Vol. 4; Vol. 5; Vol. 6 (ISBN 0-674-99109-5); Vol. 7 (ISBN 0-674-99110-9); Vol. 8 (ISBN 0-674-99111-7); Vol. 9 (ISBN 0-674-99112-5); Vol. 10 (ISBN 0-674-99113-3); Vol. 11 (ISBN 0-674-99114-1). (Loeb Classical Library: No. 46-47, 65, 80, 87, 98-103). 11.00x ea. Harvard U Pr.

--Rise & Fall of Athens: Nine Greek Lives. Scott-Kilvert, Ian, tr. (Classics Ser.). 320p. 1975. pap. 4.95 (ISBN 0-14-044102-6). Penguin.

Plutarque. Les Vies des Homme Illustres, 2 vols. D'Amyot, tr. 37.50 ea. French & Eur.

Smith, William, ed. Dictionary of Greek & Roman Geography, 2 Vols. LC 4-14843. Repr. of 1873 ed. Set. 125.00 (ISBN 0-404-06134-6). AMS Pr.

Toynbee, Arnold J. Twelve Men of Action in Graeco-Roman History. facs. ed. LC 69-17592. (Essay Index Reprint Ser). 1952. 12.00 (ISBN 0-8369-0095-2). Arno.

Whibley, Leonard. Companion to Greek Studies. 4th rev. ed. (Illus.). 1963. Repr. of 1931 ed. 21.75 (ISBN 0-02-854700-4). Hafner.

GREECE–CIVILIZATION

see Civilization, Greek

GREECE–COLONIES

McLeish, Kenneth. Greek Exploration & Seafaring. (Aspects of Greek Life). 1972. pap. text ed. 2.95x (ISBN 0-582-34402-6). Longman.

Menetrier & Muterse. Antibes. 1975. pap. 4.00 (ISBN 0-89005-080-5). Ares.

GREECE–DESCRIPTION, GEOGRAPHY

Blue Guide - Greece. 1981. 46.95 (ISBN 0-528-84729-5); pap. 24.95 (ISBN 0-528-87428-4). Rand.

Burn, A. R. & Burn, Mary. The Living Past of Greece. (Illus.). 282p. 1980. 17.50 (ISBN 0-316-11710-2). Little.

Cramer, J. A. A Geographical & Historical Description of Ancient Greece, 3 vols. LC 77-6974. 1977. Repr. of 1828 ed. lib. bdg. 95.00 (ISBN 0-89341-211-2). Longwood Pr.

Dubin, Marc. Backpacker's Greece. (Backpacker's Guide Ser.). (Illus.). 128p. 1982. pap. 9.95 (ISBN 0-933982-19-4). Bradt Ent.

Durrell, Lawrence. Reflections on a Marine Venus. 1978. pap. 2.50 (ISBN 0-14-004686-0). Penguin.

Herodotus. Opys Skytii. (Ukrai.). 1968. pap. 8.00 (ISBN 0-918884-18-7). Slavia Lib.

Lazarides, P. Hossios Loukas. (Illus.). pap. 4.00 (ISBN 0-89005-135-6). Ares.

Myres, John Linton. Geographical History in Greek Lands. LC 74-9220. (Illus.). 381p. 1974. Repr. of 1953 ed. lib. bdg. 25.00x (ISBN 0-8371-7629-8, MYGL). Greenwood.

Pausanias. Description of Greece, 6 Vols. 2nd ed. Frazer, J. G., tr. LC 65-13634. (Illus.). 1897. Set. 100.00x (ISBN 0-8196-0144-6). Biblo.

--Description of Greece, 5 Vols. (Loeb Classical Library: No. 93, 188, 272, 297-298). 1918-35. 11.00x ea. Vol. 1 (ISBN 0-674-99104-4). Vol. 2 (ISBN 0-674-99207-5). Vol. 3 (ISBN 0-674-99300-4). Vol. 4 (ISBN 0-674-99328-4). Vol. 5 (ISBN 0-674-99329-2). Harvard U Pr.

--Guide to Greece. Levi, Peter, tr. (Penguin Classics Ser.). (Illus.). 1979. pap. 4.95 ea.; Vol. 1 Central Greece. (ISBN 0-14-044225-1); Vol. 2 Southern Greece. (ISBN 0-14-044226-X). Penguin.

Rapp, George R., Jr. & Aschenbrenner, S. E., eds. Excavations at Nichoria in Southwest Greece: Site, Environs, & Techniques, Vol. 1. LC 78-3198. (Illus.). 1978. 29.75x (ISBN 0-8166-0824-5). U of Minn Pr.

Smith, William, ed. Dictionary of Greek & Roman Biography & Mythology, 3 Vols. LC 11-24983. Repr. of 1890 ed. Set. 210.00 (ISBN 0-404-06130-3). AMS Pr.

Stuart, Jesse. Dandelion on the Acropolis. LC 78-1322. (Illus.). 1978. 10.00 (ISBN 0-89097-011-4); ltd. ed. 37.50 (ISBN 0-89097-012-2). Archer Edns.

Tozer, Henry F. Geography of Ancient Greece. LC 74-77868. 424p. 1975. 15.00 (ISBN 0-89005-024-4). Ares.

Whibley, Leonard. Companion to Greek Studies. 4th rev. ed. (Illus.). 1963. Repr. of 1931 ed. 21.75 (ISBN 0-02-854700-4). Hafner.

GREECE–ECONOMIC CONDITIONS

Andreades, A. M. & Finley, Moses, eds. A History of Greek Public Finance, Vol. I. rev. & enl. ed. Brown, Carroll N., tr. LC 79-4959. (Ancient Economic History Ser.). 1980. Repr. of 1933 ed. lib. bdg. 32.00x (ISBN 0-405-12347-7). Arno.

Austin, M. M. & Vidal-Naquet, P. Economic & Social History of Ancient Greece: An Introduction. 1978. 31.50x (ISBN 0-520-02658-6); pap. 8.95 (ISBN 0-520-04267-0). U of Cal Pr.

Calhoun, George M. Business Life of Ancient Athens. LC 68-18490. 175p. 1968. Repr. of 1926 ed. 8.50x (ISBN 0-8154-0043-8). Cooper Sq.

Du Mesnil-Marigny, Jules. Histoire De l'Economie Politique Des Anciens Peuples De l'Inde, De l'Egypte, De la Judee et De la Grece, 3 Vols. 3rd ed. 1967. Repr. of 1878 ed. 69.50 (ISBN 0-8337-4800-9). B Franklin.

Francotte, Henri. Les Finances des Cites Grecques. Finley, Moses, ed. LC 79-4971. (Ancient Economic History Ser.). (Fr.). 1980. Repr. of 1909 ed. lib. bdg. 23.00x (ISBN 0-405-12357-4). Arno.

--L' Industrie dans la Grece Ancienne, 2 vols. Finley, Moses, ed. LC 79-4972. (Ancient Economic History Ser.). (Fr.). 1980. Repr. of 1901 ed. Set. lib. bdg. 52.00x (ISBN 0-405-12358-2); lib. bdg. 26.00x ea. Vol. 1 (ISBN 0-405-12433-3). Vol. 2 (ISBN 0-405-12434-1). Arno.

Grace, Virginia R. Amphoras & the Ancient Wine Trade. (Excavations of the Athenian Agora Picture Bks.: No. 6). (Illus.). 1979. pap. 1.50x (ISBN 0-87661-619-8). Am Sch Athens.

Guiraud, Paul. Etudes Economiques Sur l'Antiquite. LC 77-126394. (Research & Source Ser.: No. 501). (Fr). 1970. Repr. of 1905 ed. 22.50 (ISBN 0-8337-1488-0). B Franklin.

Hasbroeck, J. Trade & Politics in Ancient Greece. Fraser, L. M., et al, trs. 1978. 15.00 (ISBN 0-89005-240-9). Ares.

Hasebroek, Johannes. Trade & Politics in Ancient Greece. LC 65-15245. 1933. 10.00x (ISBN 0-8196-0150-0). Biblo.

Heichelheim, Fritz M. Wirtschaftliche Schwankungen der zeit von Alexander bis Augustus. Finley, Moses, ed. LC 79-4981. (Ancient Economic History Ser.). (Illus., Ger.). 1980. Repr. of 1930 ed. lib. bdg. 14.00x (ISBN 0-405-12367-1). Arno.

Herfst, Pieter. Le Travail de la Femme dans la Grece Ancienne. Finley, Moses, ed. LC 79-4982. (Ancient Economic History Ser.). (Fr.). 1980. Repr. of 1922 ed. lib. bdg. 10.00x (ISBN 0-405-12368-X). Arno.

Hopper, R. J. Trade & Industry in Classical Greece. (Illus.). 1979. 19.95 (ISBN 0-500-40038-5). Thames Hudson.

Kofas, Jon V. Financial Relations of Greece & the Great Powers, 1832-1862. (East European Monograph: No. 91). 200p. 1981. text ed. 15.00x (ISBN 0-914710-85-0). East Eur Quarterly.

Korver, Jan. De Terminologie van het Crediet-Wezen in het Grieksch. Finley, Moses, ed. LC 79-4987. (Ancient Economic History Ser.). (Dutch.). 1980. Repr. of 1934 ed. lib. bdg. 14.00x (ISBN 0-405-12372-8). Arno.

Laistner, Max L. Greek Economics. LC 79-171641. (Library of Greek Thought: No. 3). Repr. of 1923 ed. 20.50 (ISBN 0-404-07802-8). AMS Pr.

Marder, Brenda L. Stewarts of the Land: The American Farm School & Modern Greece. (East European Monographs: No. 59). 1979. 14.50x (ISBN 0-914710-52-4). East Eur Quarterly.

Pringeheim, Fritz. Der Kauf Mit Frimdem Geld. Vlastos, Gregory, ed. (Morals & Law in Ancient Greece Ser.). 1979. Repr. of 1916 ed. lib. bdg. 12.00x (ISBN 0-405-11568-7). Arno.

Prodromichs, K. P. Forecasting Aggregate Consumer Expenditure in Greece: A Long-Run Analysis. LC 74-173139. (Center of Planning & Economic Research (Athens) Lecture Ser.). (Illus.). 62p. 1974. pap. 5.00x (ISBN 0-8002-1428-5). Intl Pubns Serv.

Riezler, Kurt. Uber Finanzen und Monopole Im Alten Griechenland: Zur Theorie und Geschichte der antiken Stadtwirtschaft. Finley, Moses, ed. LC 79-5002. (Ancient Economic History Ser.). (Ger.). 1980. Repr. of 1907 ed. lib. bdg. 10.00x (ISBN 0-405-12391-4). Arno.

Roebuck, Carl. Economy & Society in the Early Greek World: Collected Essays. Thomas, Carol G., ed. 1978. 25.00 (ISBN 0-89005-261-1). Ares.

Starr, Chester G. The Economic & Social Growth of Early Greece: 800--500 B.C. (Illus.). 1977. 15.95 (ISBN 0-19-502223-8). Oxford U Pr.

Toutain, Jules. The Economic Life of the Ancient World. Vlastos, Gregory, ed. Dobie, M. R., tr. LC 78-14600. (Morals & Law in Ancient Greece Ser.). (Illus.). 1979. Repr. of 1930 ed. lib. bdg. 25.00x (ISBN 0-405-11578-4). Arno.

Trever, Albert A. A History of Greek Economic Thought. LC 78-15142. Repr. of 1916 ed. lib. bdg. 15.00x (ISBN 0-87991-861-6). Porcupine Pr.

Van Lith, Jan A., ed. Change & the New International Economic Order. (Tilburg Studies in Economics: Vol. 20). 1980. lib. bdg. 14.95 (ISBN 0-89838-028-6, Pub. by Martinus Nijhoff Netherlands). Kluwer Boston.

Zimmern, Alfred. Greek Commonwealth: Politics & Economics in Fifth-Century Athens. 5th ed. 1931. pap. 5.95x (ISBN 0-19-500230-X). Oxford U Pr.

GREECE–FOREIGN RELATIONS

Dunbabin, Thomas J. The Greeks & Their Eastern Neighbours: Studies in the Relations Between Greece & the Countries of the Near East in the Eighth & Seventh Centuries B. C. Boardman, John, ed. LC 78-24477. (Illus.). 1979. Repr. of 1957 ed. lib. bdg. 15.75x (ISBN 0-313-20791-7, DUGR). Greenwood.

Kofas, Jon V. International & Domestic Politics in Greece During the Crimean War. (East European Monographs: No. 61). 1980. 12.00x (ISBN 0-914710-54-0). East Eur Quarterly.

Mallet, M. Dominique. Les Rapports des Grecs avec l'Egypte. 218p. 1980. 30.00 (ISBN 0-89005-299-9). Ares.

Sedlar, Jean W. India & the Greek World: A Study in the Transmission of Culture. (Illus.). 381p. 1980. 30.00x (ISBN 0-8476-6173-3). Rowman.

Vryonis, Speros, Jr., ed. Studies on Byzantium, Seljuks & Ottomans. (Byzantina Kai Metabyzantina Ser.). 350p. 1981. 25.00 (ISBN 0-89003-072-3); pap. 17.50 (ISBN 0-89003-071-5). Undena Pubns.

GREECE–HISTORIOGRAPHY

Mahaffy, John P. Problems of Greek History. Repr. of 1892 ed. 35.00 (ISBN 0-8274-3925-3). R West.

Miller, Molly. Sicilian Colony Dates: Studies in Chronography One. LC 69-14646. (Illus.). 1970. 21.50 (ISBN 0-87395-049-6); microfiche 21.50 (ISBN 0-87395-149-2). State U NY Pr.

Pearson, Lionel. Early Ionian Historians. LC 75-136874. 240p. 1975. Repr. of 1939 ed. lib. bdg. 16.50x (ISBN 0-8371-5314-X, PEIH). Greenwood.

--The Local Historians of Attica. LC 71-152621. 167p. 1972. Repr. of 1942 ed. lib. bdg. 15.00x (ISBN 0-8371-6020-0, PEHA). Greenwood.

GREECE–HISTORY

Adam, James. Religious Teachers of Greece. LC 72-2565. (Select Bibliographies Reprint Ser). 1972. Repr. of 1908 ed. 26.00 (ISBN 0-8369-6843-3). Arno.

Adock, Francis & Mosley, D. J. Diplomacy in Ancient Greece. LC 74-30066. 275p. 1975. text ed. 22.50x (ISBN 0-312-21105-8). St Martin.

Agard, Walter R. The Greek Mind. LC 78-25755. (Anvil Ser.). 190p. 1979. pap. text ed. 4.95 (ISBN 0-88275-811-X). Krieger.

Amos, H. D. & Lang, A. G. These Were the Greeks. (Illus.). 224p. 1980. 12.95 (ISBN 0-7175-0789-0). Dufour.

Andrewes, A. The Greek Tyrants. 1956. pap. 7.00x (ISBN 0-09-029564-1, Hutchinson U Lib). Humanities.

Andrewes, Antony. The Greeks. 1978. pap. 4.95 (ISBN 0-393-00877-0, N877, Norton Lib). Norton.

Asimov, Isaac. Greeks: A Great Adventure. (Illus.). (gr. 7 up). 1965. 12.95 (ISBN 0-395-06574-7). HM.

Austin, Norman. The Greek Historians: Introduction & Selected Readings. 6.50 (ISBN 0-8446-0466-6). Peter Smith.

Averoff-Tossizza, Evangelos. By Fire & Axe: The Communist Party & the Civil War in Greece, 1944-49. Rigos, Sarah A., tr. LC 77-91603. (Modern Greek History Ser.: No. 1). (Illus.). 438p. 1978. 15.00 (ISBN 0-89241-078-7). Caratzas Bros.

Badian, E. Studies in Greek & Roman History. 290p. 1964. 30.50x (ISBN 0-631-08140-2, Pub. by Basil Blackwell). Biblio Dist.

Baggally, John W. Klephtic Ballads in Relation to Greek History, 1715-1821. LC 73-92568. xiv, 109p. Date not set. Repr. of 1936 ed. 7.00 (ISBN 0-8462-1773-2). Russell.

Bees, N. A. Chronicon Monembasiae. 50p. 1979. 12.50 (ISBN 0-89005-279-4). Ares.

Bengtson, Hermann. The History of Greece. new ed. Bloedow, Edmund, tr. from Ger. Date not set. 17.95 (ISBN 0-88866-576-8). Samuel Stevens.

Bieber, Margarete. Griechische Kleidung. (Illus.). vi, 100p. 1977. Repr. of 1928 ed. 196.00x (ISBN 3-11-004835-3). De Gruyter.

Birtliff, John L. Natural Environment & Human Settlement in Prehistoric Greece. 1977. 75.00x (ISBN 0-904531-79-1, Pub. by BAR). State Mutual Bk.

Blaquiere, Edward, ed. Narrative of a Second Visit to Greece, Including Facts Connected with the Last Days of Lord Byron. LC 76-27677. 1976. Repr. of 1825 ed. lib. bdg. 50.00 (ISBN 0-8414-3336-4). Folcroft.

Boardman, John. The Greeks Overseas: Their Early Colonies & Trade. (Illus.). 1980. 22.50 (ISBN 0-500-25069-3). Thames Hudson.

Botsford, George W. A History of the Orient & Greece. 1902. 35.00 (ISBN 0-8274-3933-4). R West.

Brady, Donald, ed. Philosophy - in the Flesh: A Reader. 149p. 1975. pap. text ed. 6.95x (ISBN 0-8422-0492-X). Irvington.

Brice, William C., ed. Europa: Studien zur Geschichte und Epigraphik der fruehen Aegaeis Festschrift fuer Ernst Grumach. (Illus., Ger.). 1967. 75.00x (ISBN 3-11-005182-6). De Gruyter.

Brunt, P. A., ed. Thucydides: The Peloponnesian Wars (Revised & Abridged) Jowett, Benjamin, tr. (Illus.). 370p. 1963. text ed. 20.00x (ISBN 0-8290-0212-X). Irvington.

Burn, Andrew R. Pelican History of Greece. Orig. Title: Traveller's History of Greece. 1966. pap. 3.95 (ISBN 0-14-020792-9, Pelican). Penguin.

--Persia & the Greeks: The Defence of the West, 546-478 B. C. (Illus.). 1962. 25.00 (ISBN 0-312-60165-4). St Martin.

Bury, J. B. & Meiggs, Russell. A History of Greece. 4th rev. ed. LC 74-75836. (Illus.). 612p. 1975. 14.95 (ISBN 0-312-37940-4). St Martin.

Butcher, S. H. Harvard Lectures on Greek Subjects. 1978. Repr. of 1904 ed. lib. bdg. 30.00 (ISBN 0-8495-0386-8). Arden Lib.

Caldwell, Wallace E. Hellenic Conceptions of Peace. LC 19-18236. (Columbia University Studies in the Social Sciences: No. 195). Repr. of 1919 ed. 12.50 (ISBN 0-404-51195-3). AMS Pr.

Cambridge School Classics Project Foundation Course. Troy & the Early Greeks. Forrest, M., ed. (Illus.). 1973. text ed. 12.50x (ISBN 0-521-08467-9). Cambridge U Pr.

Cartledge, Paul. Sparta & Lakonia: A Regional History Thirteen Hundred to Three Sixty-Two B.C. (States & Cities of Ancient Greece Ser.). 1979. 25.00x (ISBN 0-7100-0377-3). Routledge & Kegan.

Cary, Max. A History of the Greek World: 323-146 B.C. 2nd rev. ed. (History of the Greek & Roman World Ser). (Illus.). 446p. 1972. pap. 14.95x (ISBN 0-416-70200-7). Methuen Inc.

Chambers, Mortimer. Ancient Greece. LC 73-75443. (AHA Pamphlets: No. 311). 60p. (Orig.). 1973. pap. text ed. 1.50 (ISBN 0-87229-012-3). Am Hist Assn.

Chapekar, Nalinee M. Ancient India & Greece. 1977. 10.00x (ISBN 0-686-22657-7). Intl Bk Dist.

Cheetham, Nicholas. The Feudal Age of Greece. 288p. cancelled. Yale U Pr.

Christopoulos, George A. Prehistory & Protohistory to 1100 B.C. Bastias, John C., ed. Sherrard, Philip, tr. LC 75-18610. (History of the Hellenic World Ser.: Vol. 1). (Illus.). 420p. 1975. 32.50 (ISBN 0-271-01199-8). Pa St U Pr.

Christopoulos, George A. & Bastias, John C., eds. The Archaic Period, 1100-479 BC. Sherrard, Philip, tr. LC 75-27171. (History of the Hellenic World Ser.: Vol. 2). (Illus.). 620p. 1975. 38.50 (ISBN 0-271-01214-5). Pa St U Pr.

Cohen, Edward E. Ancient Athenian Maritime Courts. LC 65-17135. 192p. 1973. 16.00 (ISBN 0-691-09227-3). Princeton U Pr.

Coldstream, J. N. Geometric Greece. LC 77-78085. (Illus.). 1977. 27.50x (ISBN 0-312-32365-4). St Martin.

Coleman, Kenneth, ed. Athens 1861 - 1865: As Seen Through Letters in the University of Georgia Libraries. LC 70-104399. 132p. 1969. pap. 5.95x (ISBN 0-8203-0253-8). U of Ga Pr.

Connor, W. R., ed. Greek History, 27 bks. 1973. Set. 649.00 (ISBN 0-405-04775-4). Arno.

Cornford, Francis M. Thucydides Mythistoricus. LC 69-13866. Repr. of 1907 ed. lib. bdg. 14.75x (ISBN 0-8371-1055-6, COTH). Greenwood.

Cox, George W. A General History of Greece. LC 77-94563. 1979. Repr. of 1892 ed. lib. bdg. 75.00 (ISBN 0-89341-258-9). Longwood Pr.

Craik, Elizabeth M. The Dorian Aegean. (States & Cities of Ancient Greece Ser.). 1979. 22.50 (ISBN 0-7100-0378-1). Routledge & Kegan.

Cramer, J. A. A Geographical & Historical Description of Ancient Greece, 3 vols. LC 77-6974. 1977. Repr. of 1828 ed. lib. bdg. 95.00 (ISBN 0-89341-211-2). Longwood Pr.

Dakin, Douglas. The Greek Struggle for Independence, 1821-1833. LC 72-89798. 1973. 25.00x (ISBN 0-520-02342-0). U of Cal Pr.

Detienne, Marcel & Vernant, Jean-Pierre. Cunning Intelligence in Greek Culture & Society. Lloyd, J., tr. from Greek. (European Philosophy & the Human Sciences Ser.). 1978. text ed. 33.75x (ISBN 0-391-00740-8). Humanities.

Devambez, Pierre. Diccionario de la Civilizacion Griega. 482p. (Espn.). 1972. 37.50 (ISBN 84-233-0645-3, S-50367). French & Eur.

Dover, Kenneth. The Greeks. (Illus.). 160p. 1981. 17.95 (ISBN 0-292-72723-2); pap. 8.95 (ISBN 0-292-72724-0). U of Tex Pr.

Duruy, Victor. Histoire Des Grecs, 3 Vols. (Orig.). Repr. of 1889 ed. Set. 242.00 (ISBN 0-384-13400-9). Johnson Repr.

Ehrenberg, Victor. From Solon to Socrates: Greek History & Civilization During the 6th & 5th Centuries B.C. 2nd ed. (Illus.). 500p. 1973. pap. 13.95x (ISBN 0-416-77760-0). Methuen Inc.

Ellis, J. R. Philip Second & Macedonian Imperialism. (Aspects of Greek & Roman Life Ser.). (Illus.). 1977. 19.95 (ISBN 0-500-40028-8). Thames Hudson.

Emlyn-Jones, C. J. The Ionians & Hellenism: A Study of the Cultural Achievement of the Early Greek Inhabitants of Asia Minor. (States & Cities of Ancient Greece Ser.). (Illus.). 256p. 1980. 30.00 (ISBN 0-7100-0470-2). Routledge & Kegan.

Ferguson, William S. Greek Imperialism. LC 63-18045. 1941. 10.50x (ISBN 0-8196-0127-6). Biblo.

Finlay, George. History of Greece, 7 Vols. 1970. Repr. of 1877 ed. Set. 245.00 (ISBN 0-404-02390-8); 35.00 ea. AMS Pr.

Finley, M. I. Ancient Greeks. 1977. pap. 2.95 (ISBN 0-14-020812-7, Pelican). Penguin.

--The World of Odysseus. rev. ed. 1979. pap. 2.95 (ISBN 0-14-020570-5, Pelican). Penguin.

Finley, M. I., ed. Problemes De la Terre En Grece Ancienne: Recueil De Travaux. (Civilisations et Societes: No. 33). (Illus.). 1973. pap. 29.50x (ISBN 0-686-21224-X). Mouton.

Forrest, William G. Emergence of Greek Democracy. (Illus., Orig.). 1966. pap. 3.95 (ISBN 0-07-021585-5, SP). McGraw.

Fritz, Kurt Von. Schriften zur griechischen und Roemischen Verfassungsgeschichte und Verfassungstheorie. 1976. 91.75x (ISBN 3-11-006567-3). De Gruyter.

Frost, Frank J. Greek Society. 2nd ed. 1980. pap. text ed. 8.95 (ISBN 0-669-02452-X). Heath.

Fyffe, C. A. History of Greece. 1884. 15.00 (ISBN 0-8274-3950-4). R West.

Garden, Glenn. Life B.C. (Orig.). 1980. 9.50x (ISBN 0-435-31200-6). Heinemann Ed.

Glotz, G. The Greek City & Its Institutions. Mallinson, N., tr. (History of Civilization Ser.). (Illus.). 1929. 35.00x (ISBN 0-7100-1451-1). Routledge & Kegan.

Gomme, Arnold W. Essays in Greek History & Literature. facs. ed. LC 67-23222. (Essay Index Reprint Ser). 1937. 19.00 (ISBN 0-8369-0481-8). Arno.

Graindor, Paul. Athens sous Hadrien. LC 72-7892. (Greek History Ser.). (Illus., Fr.). Repr. of 1934 ed. 20.00 (ISBN 0-405-04788-6). Arno.

Grant, Arthur J. Greece in the Age of Pericles. LC 72-91204. (Illus.). xvi, 331p. 1972. Repr. of 1893 ed. lib. bdg. 15.00x (ISBN 0-8154-0444-1). Cooper Sq.

Green, Peter. Ancient Greece: An Illustrated History. 1979. pap. 7.95 (ISBN 0-500-27161-5). Thames Hudson.

Green, R. L. Ancient Greece. (Young Historian Ser.). 1981. 10.75x (ISBN 0-392-08300-0, SpS). Sportshelf.

Greenhalgh, P. A. Early Greek Warfare. LC 72-87437. 228p. 1973. 32.50 (ISBN 0-521-20056-3). Cambridge U Pr.

Greenidge, Abel. A Handbook of Greek Constitutional History. 59.95 (ISBN 0-8490-0277-X). Gordon Pr.

Grote, George. History of Greece, 10 Vols. new ed. LC 75-137236. Repr. of 1888 ed. Set. 325.00 (ISBN 0-404-02950-7); 32.50 ea. AMS Pr.

Grundy, George B. Great Persian War. LC 71-84875. (Illus.). Repr. of 1901 ed. 37.50 (ISBN 0-404-02945-0). AMS Pr.

Hamilton, Charles D. Sparta's Bitter Victories: Politics & Diplomacy in the Corinthian War. LC 78-58045. 1978. 22.50x (ISBN 0-8014-1158-0). Cornell U Pr.

Hamilton, Edith. The Greek Way. 1973. pap. 2.75 (ISBN 0-380-00816-5, 53140, Discus). Avon.

Hammond, N. G. Studies in Greek History: A Companion Volume to A History of Greece to 322 B. C. (Illus.). 590p. 1973. 49.50x (ISBN 0-19-814801-1). Oxford U Pr.

Harrison, James A. The Story of Greece. 1827. 35.00 (ISBN 0-8274-3954-7). R West.

Harrison, Jane. Prolegomena to the Study of Greek Religion. 682p. 1981. text ed. 26.00x (ISBN 85036-262-8, Pub. by Merlin, England); pap. 13.25x (ISBN 0-686-69802-9). Humanities.

Hatzfeld, Jean & Aymard, Andre. History of Ancient Greece. Goddard, E. H., ed. Harrison, A. C., tr. (Illus.). 1968. pap. 5.95 (ISBN 0-393-00247-0, Norton Lib). Norton.

Hatzfield, Jean. History of Ancient Greece. 5.50 (ISBN 0-8446-0685-5). Peter Smith.

Hawkes, Charles & Hawkes, Sonia, eds. Greeks, Celts, & Romans: Studies in Venture & Resistance. LC 73-1223. (Archaeology into History Ser.). (Illus.). 162p. 1973. 13.50x (ISBN 0-87471-176-2). Rowman.

Henderson, Bernard W. The Great War Between Athens & Sparta. LC 72-7894. (Greek History Ser.). Repr. of 1927 ed. 28.00 (ISBN 0-405-04790-8). Arno.

Herodotus. Famous Hystory of Herodotus. LC 25-8760. (Tudor Translations, Second Series: No. 6). Repr. of 1924 ed. 24.50 (ISBN 0-404-51856-7). AMS Pr.

--Herodotus. LC 75-39478. (Select Bibliographies Reprint Series). 1972. Repr. of 1847 ed. 25.00 (ISBN 0-8369-9913-4). Arno.

--Historiae, 2 Vols. 3rd ed. Hude, Karl, ed. (Oxford Classical Texts Ser). 1927. Vol. 1. 18.95x (ISBN 0-19-814526-8); Vol. 2. 18.95x (ISBN 0-19-814527-6). Oxford U Pr.

--Histories. De Selincourt, Aubrey, tr. (Classics Ser.). (Orig.). 1954. pap. 5.95 (ISBN 0-14-044034-8). Penguin.

--History of the Persian Wars, 4 Vols. (Loeb Classical Library: No. 117-120). 11.00x ea. Vol. 1 (ISBN 0-674-99130-3). Vol. 2 (ISBN 0-674-99131-1). Vol. 3 (ISBN 0-674-99133-8). Vol. 4 (ISBN 0-674-99134-6). Harvard U Pr.

--Persian Wars. Rawlinson, George, tr. (YA) 1964. pap. 3.95 (ISBN 0-394-30954-5, T54, Mod LibC). Modern Lib.

--Tales from Herodotus. Goff, Marie & Farnell, G. S., eds. (Gr II). 1963. 5.95 (ISBN 0-312-78400-7). St Martin.

Hirzel, Rudolf. Der Eid: Ein Beitrag zu seiner Geschichte. Vlastos, Gregory, ed. LC 78-19361. (Morals & Law in Ancient Greece Ser.). (Ger. & Gr.). 1979. Repr. of 1902 ed. lib. bdg. 15.00x (ISBN 0-405-11553-9). Arno.

--Die Person: Begriff & Name Derselben Im Altertum. facsimile ed. Bd. with Griechische Kultur-Entstehungslehren. Uxkull-Gyllenband. LC 75-13275. (History of Ideas in Ancient Greece Ser.). (Ger.). 1976. Repr. 8.00x (ISBN 0-405-07315-1). Arno.

Hollinghurst, Hugh. Greeks & Romans. 1974. pap. text ed. 4.00x (ISBN 0-435-36406-5). Heinemann Ed.

Hooper, Finley. Greek Realities: Life & Thought in Ancient Greece. (Illus.). (YA) 1978. 15.00x (ISBN 0-8143-1596-8); pap. 7.50x (ISBN 0-8143-1597-6). Wayne St U Pr.

Immerwahr, Sara A. The Neolithic & Bronze Ages. (Athenian Agora Ser: Vol. 13). (Illus.). 1971. 25.00x (ISBN 0-87661-213-3). Am Sch Athens.

Jacoby, Felix. Apollodors Chronik: Eine Sammlung der Fragmente. LC 72-7896. (Greek History Ser.). (Ger.). Repr. of 1902 ed. 21.00 (ISBN 0-405-04795-9). Arno.

Jones, A. H. The Greek City from Alexander to Justinian. 404p. (Orig.). 1979. pap. text ed. 22.00x (ISBN 0-19-814842-9). Oxford U Pr.

Jones, C. P. The Roman World of Dio Chrysostom. LC 78-5869. (Loeb Classical Monograph). 1978. 15.00x (ISBN 0-674-77915-0). Harvard U Pr.

Jones, William H. Malaria & Greek History. LC 75-23729. Repr. of 1909 ed. 17.50 (ISBN 0-404-13287-1). AMS Pr.

Joy, James R. Grecian History: An Outline Sketch. 1892. 17.50 (ISBN 0-8274-3957-1). R West.

--Grecian History: An Outline Sketch. Repr. of 1892 ed. 17.50 (ISBN 0-686-20091-8). Quality Lib.

Kagan, Donald. Outbreak of the Peloponnesian War. LC 69-18212. 438p. 1969. 22.50x (ISBN 0-8014-0501-7). Cornell U Pr.

Kelly, Thomas. A History of Argos to 500 B.C. LC 76-11500. (Illus.). 1977. 15.75x (ISBN 0-8166-0790-7). U of Minn Pr.

Kerenyi, C. The Heroes of the Greeks. (Illus.). 1978. pap. 8.95 (ISBN 0-500-27049-X). Thames Hudson.

Killingray, Margaret. Ancient Greece. Yapp, Malcolm & O'Connor, Edmund, eds. (World History Ser.). Orig. Title: The Mediterranean. (Illus.). 32p. (gr. 10). 1980. Repr. of 1977 ed. lib. bdg. 5.95 (ISBN 0-89908-026-X); pap. text ed. 1.95 (ISBN 0-89908-001-4). Greenhaven.

Kinkaid, C. A. Successors of Alexander. 192p. 1980. 15.00 (ISBN 0-89005-352-9). Ares.

Kirchner, Johannes & Von Gaertringen, Friedrich, eds. Inscriptiones Atticae: Inscriptiones Graecae, Editio Minor, 5 vols. 2952p. 1974. 25.00 ea. Vol. 1 (ISBN 0-89005-014-7). Vol. 2 (ISBN 0-89005-015-5). Vol. 3 (ISBN 0-89005-016-3). Vol. 4 (ISBN 0-89005-017-1). Vol. 5 (ISBN 0-89005-018-X). Set. 125.00 (ISBN 0-89005-013-9). Ares.

Kitto, Humphrey O. Greeks. (Orig.). (YA) (gr. 9 up). 1950. pap. 2.95 (ISBN 0-14-020220-X, Pelican). Penguin.

Kofas, Jon V. Financial Relations of Greece & the Great Powers, 1832-1862. (East European Monograph: No. 91). 200p. 1981. text ed. 15.00x (ISBN 0-914710-85-0). East Eur Quarterly.

Koliopoulos, John S. Greece & the British Connection, 1935-1941. 1978. 45.00x (ISBN 0-19-822523-7). Oxford U Pr.

Koumoulides, John T., ed. Hellenic Perspectives: Essays in the History of Greece. LC 80-5475. 398p. 1980. lib. bdg. 20.75 (ISBN 0-8191-1107-4); pap. text ed. 12.75 (ISBN 0-8191-1108-2). U Pr of Amer.

Laistner, M. L. Greek History. 1932. 25.00 (ISBN 0-686-20092-6). Quality Lib.

Lambros, S. P. Ecthesis Chronica & Chronicon Athenarum. 1979. 12.50 (ISBN 0-89005-284-0). Ares.

Lancaster, Osbert. Classical Landscape with Figures. (Illus.). 224p. 1976. pap. 9.50 (ISBN 0-7195-3234-5). Transatlantic.

Legon, Ronald P. Megara: The Political History of a Greek City-State to 336 B. C. LC 80-69828. (Illus.). 344p. 1981. 25.00x (ISBN 0-8014-1370-2). Cornell U Pr.

Levi, Peter. Atlas of Greek World. 239p. 1981. 29.95 (ISBN 0-87196-448-1). Facts on File.

Lord, Louis E. Thucydides & the World War. LC 66-24725. 1967. Repr. of 1946 ed. 8.50 (ISBN 0-8462-0820-2). Russell.

Mahaffy, John P. Problems of Greek History. Repr. of 1892 ed. 35.00 (ISBN 0-8274-3925-3). R West.

--The Silver Age of the Greek World. 1978. Repr. of 1911 ed. lib. bdg. 65.00 (ISBN 0-8495-3718-5). Arden Lib.

Martin, Victor. La Vie Internationale Dans la Grece Des Cites. Vlastos, Gregory, ed. LC 78-19368. (Morals & Law in Ancient Greece Ser.). 1979. Repr. of 1940 ed. lib. bdg. 38.00x (ISBN 0-405-11559-8). Arno.

Mayer, Guenter. Index Philoneus. LC 73-81702. 312p. 1974. text ed. 98.50x (ISBN 3-11-004536-2). De Gruyter.

Meinardus, Otto F. St. John of Patmos & the Seven Churches of the Apocalypse. LC 78-51245. (In the Footsteps of the Saints Ser.). (Illus.). 1979. lib. bdg. 12.50 (ISBN 0-89241-070-1); pap. 5.95 (ISBN 0-89241-043-4). Caratzas Bros.

--St. Paul in Greece. LC 78-51244. (In the Footsteps of the Saints Ser.). 1979. lib. bdg. 12.50 (ISBN 0-89241-072-8); pap. 5.95 (ISBN 0-89241-045-0). Caratzas Bros.

Milchhoefer, A. Ancient Athens, Piraeus & Phaleron: Schriftquellen Zur Topographie Von Athen. 1977. 15.00 (ISBN 0-89005-215-8). Ares.

Miller, Molly. Sicilian Colony Dates: Studies in Chronography One. LC 69-14646. (Illus.). 1970. 21.50 (ISBN 0-87395-049-6); microfiche 21.50 (ISBN 0-87395-149-2). State U NY Pr.

Miller, W. A History of the Greek People, 1821-1921. (Illus.). 1976. 15.00 (ISBN 0-916710-28-9). Obol Intl.

Mosshammer, Alden A. The Chronicle of Eusebius & Greek Chronographic Tradition. LC 76-1029. 366p. 1979. 24.50 (ISBN 0-8387-1939-2). Bucknell U Pr.

Murray, Oswyn. Early Greece. (Fontana History of the Ancient World Ser.). 1980. text ed. 32.50x (ISBN 0-391-00767-X). Humanities.

Neumann, Carl. Griechische Geschichtsschreiber und Geschichtsquellen im Zwoelften Jahrhundert: Studien Anna Comnena, Theod. Prodromus, Joh. Cinnamus. (Research & Source Works Ser). 105p. (Ger.). 1972. Repr. of 1888 ed. lib. bdg. 21.00 (ISBN 0-8337-2516-5). B Franklin.

Ollier, Francois. Le Mirage Spartiate Part 1: Etude sur l'Idealisation de Sparte dans l'Antiquite Greque de ' Origine Jusqu'aux Cyniques, 2 vols. in 1. Bd. with La Mirage Spartiate Part 2: Etude sur l'Idealisation de Sparte dans ''Antiquite Greque du Debut de l'Ecole Cynique Jusqu'a la Fin de la Cite. LC 72-7903. (Greek History Ser.). (Fr.). Repr. of 1943 ed. 36.00 (ISBN 0-405-04799-1). Arno.

Oost, Stewart I. Roman Policy in Epirus & Acarnania in the Age of the Roman Conquest of Greece. LC 75-7333. (Roman History Ser.). 1975. Repr. 8.00x (ISBN 0-405-07050-0). Arno.

Osborn, E. B. The Heritage of Greece & the Legacy of Rome. 1979. Repr. lib. bdg. 20.00 (ISBN 0-8492-2046-7). R West.

Palmer, Leonard R. Mycenaeans & Minoans: Aegean Prehistory in the Light of the Linear B Tablets. 2nd ed. LC 79-22315. (Illus.). 368p. 1980. Repr. of 1965 ed. lib. bdg. 30.25x (ISBN 0-313-22160-X, PAMY). Greenwood.

Papadopoulos, Stelios, ed. The Greek Merchant Marine: 1453-1850. (Illus.). 510p. 1972. 100.00 (ISBN 0-89241-074-4). Caratzas Bros.

Polybe. Histoire. 1672p. 42.95 (ISBN 0-686-56553-3). French & Eur.

Polybius. Histories, 6 Vols. (Loeb Classical Library: No. 128, 137-138, 159-161). 11.00x ea. Vol. 1 (ISBN 0-674-99142-7). Vol. 2 (ISBN 0-674-99152-4). Vol. 3 (ISBN 0-674-99153-2). Vol. 4 (ISBN 0-674-99175-3). Vol. 5 (ISBN 0-674-99176-1). Vol. 6 (ISBN 0-674-99178-8). Harvard U Pr.

Pomerance, Leon. The Final Collapse of Santorini (Thera) 1400 B. C. or 1200? (Studies in Mediterranean Archaeology Ser.: No. XXVI). (Illus.). 1970. pap. text ed. 7.00x (ISBN 9-1850-5839-4). Humanities.

Pouncey, Peter. The Necessities of War: A Study of Thucydides' Pessimism. LC 80-16887. 232p. 1980. 19.50x (ISBN 0-231-04994-3). Columbia U Pr.

Preisigke, Friedrich. Sammelbuch griechischer Urkunden aus Aegypten, 3 vols. 1530p. 1974. Repr. of 1927 ed. 244.00x (ISBN 3-11-004756-). De Gruyter.

Reinhold, Meyer. Classics, Greek & Roman. LC 72-140633. (Orig.). (gr. 10 up). 1971. 6.95 (ISBN 0-8120-5020-7); pap. 2.95 (ISBN 0-8120-0044-7). Barron.

Roberts, W. Rhys. The Ancient Boeotians. 296p. 1974. 10.00 (ISBN 0-89005-031-7). Ares.

Robinson, Cyril E. Hellas: A Short History of Ancient Greece. 1955. pap. 4.95x (ISBN 0-8070-5791-6, BP8). Beacon Pr.

--A History of Greece. 9th ed. (Illus.). 1957. pap. 10.95 (ISBN 0-423-71290-X). Methuen Inc.

Rodgers, William L. Greek & Roman Naval Warfare. LC 79-121795. (Illus.). 1964. Repr. of 1937 ed. 13.95 (ISBN 0-87021-226-5). Naval Inst Pr.

Roebuck, Carl. Economy & Society in the Early Greek World: Collected Essays. Thomas, Carol G., ed. 1978. 25.00 (ISBN 0-89005-261-1). Ares.

Rostovtzeff, Mikhail I. Greece. Bickerman, Elias J., ed. Duff, J. D., tr. (Illus.). 1963. pap. 5.95x (ISBN 0-19-500368-3). Oxford U Pr.

Ryffel, Heinrich. Wandel der Staatsverfassungen. LC 72-7904. (Greek History Ser.). (Ger.). Repr. of 1949 ed. 17.00 (ISBN 0-405-04800-9). Arno.

Sarikakis, T. C. The Hoplite General in Athens. 1976. 15.00 (ISBN 0-89005-102-X). Ares.

Sealey, Raphael. A History of the Greek States, 700-388 BC. 1977. 29.50x (ISBN 0-520-03125-3); pap. 10.95x (ISBN 0-520-03177-6, CAMPUS 165). U of Cal Pr.

Smith, Morton. Ancient Greeks. (Development of Western Civilization Ser). 144p. (Orig.). (YA) (gr. 9-12). pap. 3.45x (ISBN 0-8014-9852-X). Cornell U Pr.

Snodgrass, A. M. The Dark Age of Greece. 1972. 26.50x (ISBN 0-85224-089-9, Pub. by Edinburgh U Pr Scotland). Columbia U Pr.

Snodgrass, Anthony. Archaic Greece: The Age of Experiment. (Illus.). 236p. 1980. 27.50x (ISBN 0-460-04338-2, Pub. by J M Dent England). Biblio Dist.

Starr, Chester G. Ancient Greeks. (Illus.). (gr. 9-12). 1971. pap. 8.95x (ISBN 0-19-501248-8). Oxford U Pr.

--The Economic & Social Growth of Early Greece, 800-500 B. C. (Illus.). 1977. pap. text ed. 4.95x (ISBN 0-19-502224-6). Oxford U Pr.

Ste. Croix, G. E. de. The Origins of the Peloponnesian War. 1972. 25.00x (ISBN 0-8014-0719-2). Cornell U Pr.
Stubbings, F. H. Prehistoric Greece. 1979. 12.95x (ISBN 0-8464-0104-5). Beekman Pubs.
Tarn, William W. Antigonos Gonatas. 1913. 13.50x (ISBN 0-19-814275-7). Oxford U Pr.
Tcherikover, Victor. Hellenistic Civilization & the Jews. Applebaum, S., tr. LC 59-8518. (Temple Bk). 1970. pap. 5.95 (ISBN 0-689-70248-5, T22). Atheneum.
Theodoracopulos, Taki. The Greek Upheaval: Kings, Demagogues & Bayonets. LC 77-91601. (Modern Greek History Ser.: No. 2). (Illus.). 262p. 1978. 12.50 (ISBN 0-89241-080-9). Caratzas Bros.
Thomson, George. Pre-Historic Aegean. 4th ed. 1978. pap. 18.00x (ISBN 0-8464-0746-9). Beekman Pubs.
Thucydides. Complete Writings. Crawley, Richard, tr. Bd. with Peloponnesian Wars. 1951. pap. 3.50x (ISBN 0-394-30951-0, T51, Mod LibC). Modern Lib.
--Historiae, 2 vols. Jones, H. W., ed. (Oxford Classical Texts Ser). 1942. Vol. 1 Bks.1-4. 18.95x (ISBN 0-19-814550-0); Vol. 2 Bks. 5-8. 18.95x (ISBN 0-19-814551-9). Oxford U Pr.
--Histories. Marchant, E. C., ed. (Classical Ser). Bk. 2. 5.95x (ISBN 0-312-80395-8). St Martin.
--History of the Peloponnesian War. Livingstone, Richard, ed. (Illus.). 1960. pap. 5.95x (ISBN 0-19-500218-0). Oxford U Pr.
--History of the Peloponnesian Wars, 4 Vols. (Loeb Classical Library: No. 108-110, 169). 11.00x ea. Vol. 1 (ISBN 0-674-99120-6). Vol. 2 (ISBN 0-674-99121-4). Vol. 3 (ISBN 0-674-99122-2). Vol. 4 (ISBN 0-674-99187-7). Harvard U Pr.
--The Peloponnesian War. rev. ed. Warner, Rex, tr. (Classic Ser.). (Orig.). 1954. pap. 4.95 (ISBN 0-14-044039-9). Penguin.
--Scholia in Thucydidem: Ad Optimos Codices Collata, Edidit Carolus Hude. LC 72-7895. (Greek History Ser.). (Gr.). Repr. of 1927 ed. 24.00 (ISBN 0-405-04801-7). Arno.
--Thucydides, Bks. 6 & 7. Dover, K. J., ed. 1965. Bk.6. 14.95x (ISBN 0-19-831832-4). Bk. 7 (ISBN 0-19-831829-4). pap. 12.95x (ISBN 0-19-872098-X). Oxford U Pr.
Tod, M. Sidelights of Greek History. 96p. 1974. 7.50 (ISBN 0-89005-039-2). Ares.
Topping, Peter. Studies on Latin Greece A. D. 1205-1715. 400p. 1980. 60.00x (ISBN 0-86078-012-0, Pub. by Variorum England). State Mutual Bk.
Toynbee, Arnold. The Greeks & Their Heritages. 352p. 1982. 25.00 (ISBN 0-19-215256-4). Oxford U Pr.
Tscherikower, V. Hellenistischen Stadtegrundungen Von Alexander Dem Grossen Bis Auf Die Romerzeit. LC 72-7907. (Greek History Ser.). (Ger.). Repr. of 1927 ed. 16.00 (ISBN 0-405-04803-3). Arno.
Tsigakou, Fani-Maria. The Rediscovery of Greece: Travellers & Painters of the Romantic Era. (Illus.). 208p. 1981. 45.00 (ISBN 0-89241-354-9). Caratzas Bros.
Vacalopoulos, Apostolos E. Origins of the Greek Nation: The Byzantine Period 1204-1461. Moles, Ian N., tr. (Byzantine Ser.). (Illus.). 1970. 27.50 (ISBN 0-8135-0659-X). Rutgers U Pr.
Vermeule, Emily. Greece in the Bronze Age. LC 64-23427. 406p. 1972. pap. 12.00 (ISBN 0-226-85354-3, P490, Phoen). U of Chicago Pr.
Walbank, F. W. A Historical Commentary on Polybius: Vol. 1, Commentary Books I-IV, Vol. 1. (Illus.). 804p. 1957. text ed. 59.00x (ISBN 0-19-814152-1). Oxford U Pr.
Wallbank, F. W. The Hellenistic World. (Fontana History of the Ancient World Ser.). 256p. 1981. text ed. 23.75x (ISBN 0-391-02302-0, Pub. by Harvester England). Humanities.
Wells, Joseph. Studies in Herodotus. facs. ed. LC 77-137388. (Select Bibliographies Reprint Ser). 1923. 15.00 (ISBN 0-8369-5589-7). Arno.
West, Allen B. The History of the Chalcidic League. LC 72-7908. (Greek History Ser.). Repr. of 1918 ed. 11.00 (ISBN 0-405-04804-1). Arno.
Westlake, H. D. Essays on the Greek Historians & Greek History. 338p. 1969. 42.00x (ISBN 0-7190-0366-0, Pub. by Manchester U Pr England). State Mutual Bk.
--Timolean & His Relations with Tyrants. 72p. 1952. 21.00x (ISBN 0-7190-1217-1, Pub. by Manchester U Pr England). State Mutual Bk.
Wheeler, Benjamin I. Alexander the Great: the Merging of East & West in Universal History. facsimile ed. LC 77-148907. (Select Bibliographies Reprint Ser). Repr. of 1900 ed. 36.00 (ISBN 0-8369-5670-2). Arno.
Whittle, Tyler. The World of Classical Greece. LC 77-150962. (History in Pictures Ser). (Illus.). 64p. 1972. PLB 6.49 (ISBN 0-381-99654-9, A91620, JD-J). Har-Row.
Woodhouse, C. M. The Greek War of Independence: Its Historical Setting. LC 73-92575. (Illus.). x, 167p. 1975. Repr. of 1952 ed. 14.00 (ISBN 0-8462-1782-1). Russell.
Xenophon. Hellenica, & Anabasis, 3 Vols. (Loeb Classical Library: No. 88-90). 11.00x ea. Vol. 1 (ISBN 0-674-99098-6). Vol. 2 (ISBN 0-674-99099-4). Vol. 3 (ISBN 0-674-99100-1). Harvard U Pr.
--A History of My Times. Warner, Rex, tr. (Penguin Classics Ser.). (Illus.). 1979. pap. 6.95 (ISBN 0-14-044175-1). Penguin.
--Opera Omnia, 4 vols. Marchant, E. C., ed. Incl. Vol. 1. Historia Graeca, Bks. 1-7. 2nd ed. 1909. 18.95x (ISBN 0-19-814552-7); Vol. 2. Commentarii, Oeconomicus, Convivium, Apologia Socratis. 2nd ed. 1921. 18.95x (ISBN 0-19-814553-5); Vol. 3. Expedito Cyri. 1904. 17.50x (ISBN 0-19-814554-3); Vol. 4. Institutio Cyri. 1919 (ISBN 0-19-814555-1); Vol. 5. Opuscula. 1920 (ISBN 0-19-814556-X). (Oxford Classical Texts Ser). Oxford U Pr.
Zakythinos, D. A. The Making of Modern Greece: From Byzantium to Independence. Johnstone, K. R., tr. 235p. 1976. 21.50x (ISBN 0-631-15360-8, Pub. by Basil Blackwell England). Biblio Dist.

GREECE–HISTORY–FICTION

Ehrenberg, Victor. The Greek State. 2nd ed. 1974. pap. 8.50x (ISBN 0-416-70110-8). Methuen Inc.

GREECE–HISTORY, MILITARY

Adcock, Frank E. The Greek & Macedonian Art of War. LC 57-10495. (Sather Classical Lectures: No. 30). 1957. 14.75x (ISBN 0-520-02807-4); pap. 2.25 (ISBN 0-520-00005-6, CAL54). U of Cal Pr.
Casson, Lionel. The Greek Conquerors. (Treasures of the World Ser.). (Illus.). 176p. 1981. 21.95 (ISBN 0-86706-001-8). Time-Life.
Delehaye, Hippolyte. Les Legendes Grecques Des Saints Militaires. LC 75-7314. (Roman History Ser.). (Fr.). 1975. Repr. 16.00x (ISBN 0-405-07196-5). Arno.
Griffith, G. T. The Mercenaries of the Hellenistic World. pap. 6.00 (ISBN 0-89005-085-6). Ares.
Griffith, Guy T. The Mercenaries of the Hellenistic World. LC 75-41123. Repr. of 1935 ed. 19.50 (ISBN 0-404-14667-8). AMS Pr.
Kagan, Donald. The Archidamian War. LC 74-4901. (Illus.). 392p. 1974. 25.00x (ISBN 0-8014-0889-X). Cornell U Pr.
Pritchett, W. Kendrick. The Greek State at War, Pt. 1. LC 71-633960. 1975. 22.50x (ISBN 0-520-02758-2). U of Cal Pr.
--The Greek State at War, Pt. 2. LC 74-77991. 1975. 24.50x (ISBN 0-520-02565-2). U of Cal Pr.
--The Greek State at War, Pt. 3. 1980. 27.50 (ISBN 0-520-03781-2). U of Cal Pr.
Schlatter, Richard. Hobbes's Thycydides. new ed. 1975. 30.00 (ISBN 0-8135-0782-0); pap. 8.95 (ISBN 0-8135-0783-9). Rutgers U Pr.
Tarn, W. W. Hellenistic Military & Naval Developments. 1975. pap. 6.00 (ISBN 0-89005-086-4). Ares.
Vernant, Jean-Pierre, ed. Problemes De la Guerre En Grece Ancienne. (Civilisations et Societes: No. 11). 1968. pap. 30.00x (ISBN 90-2796-080-1). Mouton.
Wright, Henry B. The Campaign of Plataea: Campaign of Plataea: September, Four Hundred & Seventy-Nine B.C. 1904. pap. 27.50x (ISBN 0-685-89737-0). Elliots Bks.

GREECE–HISTORY–SOURCES

Cary, Max. Documentary Sources of Greek History. LC 78-90478. Repr. of 1927 ed. lib. bdg. 15.00x (ISBN 0-8371-2215-5, CADS). Greenwood.
Dinsmoor, William B. Athenian Archon List in the Light of Recent Discoveries. LC 74-114512. (Illus.). 274p. 1974. Repr. of 1939 ed. lib. bdg. 18.75x (ISBN 0-8371-4735-2, DIAA). Greenwood.
Finley, M. I., ed. Portable Greek Historians. (Viking Portable Library: No. 65). 1959. 10.00 (ISBN 0-670-35244-6). Viking Pr.
Jacoby, David. La Feodalite En Grece Medievale: Les "Assises De Romanie", Sources, Application et Diffusion. (Documents et Recheroches Sur L'economie Des Pays Byzantins, Islamiques et Slaves et Leurs Relations Commerciales Au Moyen Age: No. 10). (Illus.). 1971. pap. 38.50x (ISBN 90-2796-876-4). Mouton.
Jacoby, Felix. Apollodors Chronik: Eine Sammlung der Fragmente. LC 72-7896. (Greek History Ser.). (Ger.). Repr. of 1902 ed. 21.00 (ISBN 0-405-04795-9). Arno.
Porter, Eliot. The Greek World. Levi, Peter, ed. (Illus.). 1980. 45.00 (ISBN 0-525-11812-8). Dutton.
Sherk, Robert K. Roman Documents from the Greek East: Senatus Consulta & Epistulae to the Age of Augustus. LC 68-19442. (Illus.). 396p. (Eng.,., Gr). 1969. 25.00x (ISBN 0-8018-0589-9). Johns Hopkins.
Verbrugghe, G. P. & Wickersham, J. The Fourth Century B. C. (Greek Historical Documents Ser.). 1973. pap. 3.50x (ISBN 0-88866-528-8). Samuel Stevens.
Wilson, J. Pylos Four Twenty-Five B.C. A Historical & Topographical Study of Thucydides' Account of the Campaign. (Illus.). 1979. 18.75x (ISBN 0-85668-145-8, Pub. by Aris & Phillips). Intl Schol Bk Serv.

GREECE–INTELLECTUAL LIFE

Agard, Walter R. The Greek Mind. LC 78-25755. (Anvil Ser.). 190p. 1979. pap. text ed. 4.95 (ISBN 0-88275-811-X). Krieger.
Butcher, Samuel H. Harvard Lectures on Greek Subjects. LC 78-101036. 1969. Repr. of 1904 ed. 12.50 (ISBN 0-8046-0703-6). Kennikat.
Capes, William W. University Life in Ancient Athens. 134p. 1980. Repr. of 1922 ed. lib. bdg. 17.50 (ISBN 0-8492-3864-1). R West.
Kimpel, Ben F. Philosophies of Life of Ancient Greeks & Israelites. LC 80-81697. 1981. 17.50 (ISBN 0-8022-2371-0). Philos Lib.
Nestle, Wilhelm. Vom Mythos Zum Logos: Die Selbstentfaltung Des Griechischen Denkens Von Homer Bis Auf Die Sophistik und Sokrates. Bolle, Kees W., ed. LC 77-79147. (Mythology Ser.). (Ger.). 1978. Repr. of 1942 ed. lib. bdg. 34.00x (ISBN 0-405-10556-8). Arno.
Pohlenz, M. Freedom in Greek Life & Thought: The History of an Ideal. Lofmark, C., tr. from Ger. 202p. 1966. lib. bdg. 26.00 (ISBN 90-277-0009-5, Pub. by Reidel Holland). Kluwer Boston.
Solmsen, Friedrich. Intellectual Experiments of the Greek Enlightenment. LC 74-25629. 296p. 1975. 22.00x (ISBN 0-691-07201-9). Princeton U Pr.
Vlastos, Gregory, ed. History of Ideas in Ancient Greece, 49 vols. 1976. Repr. Set. 1210.00 (ISBN 0-405-07285-6). Arno.
Walcot, P. Envy & the Greeks. 120p. 1978. text ed. 22.00x (ISBN 0-85668-146-6, Pub. by Aris & Phillips England). Humanities.

GREECE–JUVENILE LITERATURE

Antoniou, Jim. Greece. LC 75-44871. (Macdonald Countries). (Illus.). (gr. 6 up). 1976. PLB 7.95 (ISBN 0-382-06104-7, Pub. by Macdonald Ed.). Silver.
Coolidge, Oliver. Golden Days of Greece. LC 68-21599. (Illus.). (gr. 5 up). 1968. 10.95 (ISBN 0-690-33473-7, TYC-J). Har-Row.
Fagg, Christopher. Ancient Greece. LC 78-68532. (Modern Knowledge Library). (Illus.). (gr. 5 up). 1979. PLB 7.60 s&l (ISBN 0-531-09124-4, Warwick Press). Watts.
Gianakoulis, Theodore. The Land & People of Greece. rev. ed. LC 75-37745. (Portraits of the Nations Ser.). (Illus.). (gr. 6 up). 1972. 8.79 (ISBN 0-397-31523-6, JBL-J). Har-Row.
Robinson, Charles A., Jr. First Book of Ancient Greece. (First Bks). (Illus.). (gr. 4-6). 1960. PLB 6.90 (ISBN 0-531-00463-5). Watts.
Rutland, Jonathan. See Inside an Ancient Greek Town. LC 79-63368. (See Inside Bks.). (Illus.). (gr. 5 up). 1979. PLB 7.60 s&l (ISBN 0-531-09159-7, Warwick Press). Watts.
Stewart, Philippa. Growing up in Ancient Greece. LC 79-56475. (Growing up Ser.). (Illus.). 72p. (gr. 7 up). 1980. text ed. 14.95 (ISBN 0-7134-3376-0, Pub. by Batsford England). David & Charles.
Van Duyn, Janet. The Greeks. (Library of the Early Civilizations Ser.). (Illus.). 192p. (gr. 10 up). 1972. PLB 8.50 (ISBN 0-07-067038-2, 67038, GB). McGraw.

GREECE–NAVY

Lesky, Albin. Thalatta: Der Weg der Griechen Zum Meer. LC 72-7899. (Greek History Ser.). (Ger.). Repr. of 1947 ed. 21.00 (ISBN 0-405-04798-3). Arno.
McLeish, Kenneth. Greek Exploration & Seafaring. (Aspects of Greek Life). 1972. pap. text ed. 2.95x (ISBN 0-582-34402-6). Longman.
Morrison, John S. & Williams, R. T. Greek Oared Ships, Nine Hundred - Three Hundred Twenty-Two B.C. LC 67-19504. (Illus.). 1968. 72.00 (ISBN 0-521-05770-1). Cambridge U Pr.
Tarn, W. W. Hellenistic Military & Naval Developments. 1975. pap. 6.00 (ISBN 0-89005-086-4). Ares.

GREECE–POLITICS AND GOVERNMENT

Calhoun, George M. The Growth of Criminal Law in Ancient Greece. LC 73-10874. 179p. 1974. Repr. of 1927 ed. lib. bdg. 15.00x (ISBN 0-8371-7043-5, CACL). Greenwood.
Claster, Jill N., ed. Athenian Democracy: Triumph or Travesty? LC 78-7828. (European Problem Studies). 128p. 1978. pap. text ed. 5.50 (ISBN 0-88275-581-1). Krieger.
Crawley, C. W. The Question of Greek Independence: A Study of British Policy in the Near East, 1821-1833. LC 74-144130. 272p. 1973. Repr. of 1930 ed. 23.50 (ISBN 0-86527-161-5). Fertig.
Croiset, Maurice. Aristophanes & the Political Parties at Athens. Loeb, James, tr. LC 72-7886. (Greek History Ser). Repr. of 1909 ed. 15.00 (ISBN 0-405-04780-0). Arno.
Davies, J. K. Democracy & Classical Greece. (Fontana History of the Ancient World Ser.). 1978. text ed. 22.25x (ISBN 0-391-00766-1). Humanities.
De Coulanges, Fustel. Ancient City. 10.00 (ISBN 0-8446-1960-4). Peter Smith.
De Coulanges, Numa D. The Ancient City: A Classic Study of the Religious & Civil Institutions of Ancient Greece & Rome. LC 79-3703. 1980. pap. 5.95 (ISBN 0-8018-2304-8). Johns Hopkins.
Dyroff, Adolf. Die Ethik der Alten Stoa. Vlastos, Gregory, ed. LC 78-19350. (Morals & Law in Ancient Greece Ser.). (Ger. & Gr.). 1979. Repr. of 1897 ed. lib. bdg. 26.00x (ISBN 0-405-11540-7). Arno.
Ehrenberg, Victor. The Greek State. 2nd ed. 1974. pap. 8.50x (ISBN 0-416-70110-8). Methuen Inc.
--Greek State. (Orig.). 1964. pap. 5.95 (ISBN 0-393-00250-0, Norton Lib). Norton.
Erdman, Walter. Die Ehe Im Alten Griechenland. Vlastos, Gregory, ed. LC 78-19349. (Morals & Law in Ancient Greece Ser.). (Ger. & Gr.). 1979. Repr. of 1934 ed. lib. bdg. 26.00x (ISBN 0-405-11541-5). Arno.
Ferguson, William S. Greek Imperialism. LC 63-18045. 1941. 10.50x (ISBN 0-8196-0127-6). Biblo.
Fliess, Peter J. Thucydides & the Politics of Bipolarity. LC 66-17215. (Illus.). 1966. 15.00 (ISBN 0-8071-0448-5). La State U Pr.
Florance, A. Geographical Lexicon of Greek Coin Inscriptions. 1978. pap. 10.00 (ISBN 0-89005-232-8). Ares.
Francotte, Henri. Le Polis Greccue. pap. 15.50 (ISBN 0-384-16710-1). Johnson Repr.
Freeman, Kathleen. Greek City-States. (Illus.). 1963. pap. 4.95 (ISBN 0-393-00193-8, Norton Lib). Norton.
Glotz, Gustave. L'Ordalie Dans la Grece Primitive. Vlastos, Gregory, ed. LC 78-19352. (Morals & Law in Ancient Greece Ser.). 1979. Repr. of 1904 ed. lib. bdg. 10.00x (ISBN 0-405-11545-8). Arno.
Grene, David. Greek Political Theory: The Image of Man in Thucydides & Plato. 90p. 1965. pap. 1.95 (ISBN 0-226-30787-5, P201, Phoen). U of Chicago Pr.
Grosmann, Gustav. Politische Schlagworter Aus der Zeit Des Peloponnesischen Krieges. LC 72-7893. (Greek History Ser.). (Ger.). Repr. of 1950 ed. 13.00 (ISBN 0-405-04789-4). Arno.
Hamilton, Charles D. Sparta's Bitter Victories: Politics & Diplomacy in the Corinthian War. LC 78-58045. 1978. 22.50x (ISBN 0-8014-1158-0). Cornell U Pr.
Hasbroeck, J. Trade & Politics in Ancient Greece. Fraser, L. M., et al, trs. 1978. 15.00 (ISBN 0-89005-240-9). Ares.
Hausecullier, Bernard. La Vie Municipale En Antique. Vlastos, Gregory, ed. LC 78-19358. (Morals & Law in Ancient Greece Ser.). 1979. Repr. of 1883 ed. lib. bdg. 16.00x (ISBN 0-405-11550-4). Arno.
Hitzig, Hermann F. Das Griechische Pfandrecht. Vlastos, Gregory, ed. LC 78-14611. (Morals & Law in Ancient Greece Ser.). (Ger. & Gr.). 1979. Repr. of 1895 ed. lib. bdg. 10.00x (ISBN 0-405-11587-3). Arno.
Homelrijk, Jacob. Penia En Ploutos. Vlastos, Gregory, ed. LC 78-19360. (Morals & Law in Ancient Greece Ser.). 1979. Repr. of 1925 ed. lib. bdg. 12.00x (ISBN 0-405-11552-0). Arno.
Jones, A. H. The Greek City from Alexander to Justinian. 404p. (Orig.). 1979. pap. text ed. 22.00x (ISBN 0-19-814842-9). Oxford U Pr.
Jost, Karl. Das Beispiel und Vorbild der Vorfahren. Vlastos, Gregory, ed. LC 78-19366. (Morals & Law in Ancient Greece Ser.). (Ger. & Greek.). 1979. Repr. of 1935 ed. lib. bdg. 18.00x (ISBN 0-685-96158-3). Arno.
Kostler, Rudolf & Vos, Harm. Homerisches Reght & Themis, 2 vols. in one. Vlastos, Gregory, ed. LC 78-14606. (Morals & Law in Ancient Greece Ser.). (Ger. & Gr.). 1979. Repr. of 1956 ed. lib. bdg. 12.00x (ISBN 0-405-11582-2). Arno.
Larsen, J. A. Representative Government in Greek & Roman History. (Sather Classical Lectures Ser.: No. 28). 1976. 20.00x (ISBN 0-520-03240-3). U of Cal Pr.
Levi, Mario A. Political Power in the Ancient World. LC 75-18400. 194p. 1975. Repr. of 1965 ed. lib. bdg. 15.00x (ISBN 0-8371-8327-8, LEPOP). Greenwood.
Lotze, Detlef & Hample, Franz. Metary Eleutheron Kai Doulon & Die Lakesdaemonischen Perickon, 2 vols. in one. Vlastos, Gregory, ed. LC 78-14616. (Morals & Law in Ancient Greece Ser.). 1979. Repr. of 1937 ed. lib. bdg. 12.00x (ISBN 0-405-11591-1). Arno.
Markesinis, B. S. The Theory & Practice of Dissolution of Parliament. LC 70-189592. (Studies in International & Comparative Law). (Illus.). 300p. 1972. 37.50 (ISBN 0-521-08524-1). Cambridge U Pr.
Meier, Moritz H. & Schomann, Georg F. Der Attische Process. Vlastos, Gregory, ed. LC 78-19370. (Morals & Law in Ancient Greece Ser.). (Ger. & Greek.). 1979. Repr. of 1824 ed. lib. bdg. 48.00x (ISBN 0-405-11561-X). Arno.

Menzel, Adolf. Hellenika. Vlastos, Gregory, ed. LC 78-19372. (Morals & Law in Ancient Greece Ser.). (Ger. & Gr.). 1979. Repr. of 1938 ed. lib. bdg. 12.00x (ISBN 0-405-11562-8). Arno.
Minar, Edwin L., Jr. Early Pythagorean Politics in Practice & Theory. Vlastos, Gregory, ed. LC 78-19373. (Morals & Law in Ancient Greece Ser.). (Eng. & Gr.). 1979. Repr. of 1942 ed. lib. bdg. 10.00x (ISBN 0-405-11563-6). Arno.
Myres, John L. Political Ideas of the Greeks. LC 71-137278. Repr. of 1927 ed. 11.00 (ISBN 0-404-04549-9). AMS Pr.
--Political Ideas of the Greeks. LC 27-14202. Repr. of 1927 ed. lib. bdg. 10.50x (ISBN 0-678-08042-9). Kelley.
Oliver, James H. Demokratia, the Gods, & the Free World. Vlastos, Gregory, ed. LC 78-19378. (Morals & Law in Ancient Greece Ser.). (Illus., Eng. Gr. & Lat.). 1979. Repr. of 1960 ed. lib. bdg. 14.00x (ISBN 0-405-11564-4). Arno.
Rodewald, Cosmo. Democracy: Ideas and Realities. (The Ancient World Ser.). 138p. 1976. text ed. 8.00 (ISBN 0-88866-569-5); pap. text ed. 3.95 (ISBN 0-88866-570-9). Samuel Stevens.
Sagan, Eli. The Lust to Annihilate: A Psychoanalytic Study of Violence in Ancient Greek Culture. 1979. 12.00 (ISBN 0-914434-11-X). Psychohistory Pr.
Staveley, E. S. Greek & Roman Voting & Elections. Scullard, H. H., ed. LC 75-37004. (Aspects of Greek & Roman Life Ser.). (Illus.). 271p. 1972. 22.50x (ISBN 0-8014-0693-5). Cornell U Pr.
Theodoracopulos, Taki. The Greek Upheaval: Kings, Demagogues & Bayonets. LC 77-91601. (Modern Greek History Ser.: No. 2). (Illus.). 262p. 1978. 12.50 (ISBN 0-89241-080-9). Caratzas Bros.
Walbank, Michael B. Athenian Proxenies of the Fifth Century B.C. (Illus.). 1978. 15.00 (ISBN 0-89522-011-3). Samuel Stevens.
Whibley, L. Greek Oligarchies. 1975. 10.00 (ISBN 0-89005-166-6); pap. 6.00 (ISBN 0-89005-091-0). Ares.
Whibley, Leonard. Greek Oligarchies, Their Character & Organization. LC 68-25283. (World History Ser., No. 48). 1969. Repr. of 1896 ed. lib. bdg. 32.95 (ISBN 0-8383-0258-0). Haskell.
Willoughby, Westel W. Political Theories of the Ancient World. facsimile ed. LC 79-95083. (Select Bibliographies Reprint Ser). 1903. 25.00 (ISBN 0-8369-5082-8). Arno.
Wood, N. & Wood, E. M. Class Ideology & Ancient Political Theory: Socrates, Plato & Aristotle in Social Context. 1978. 17.95x (ISBN 0-19-520100-0). Oxford U Pr.
Zimmern, Alfred. Greek Commonwealth: Politics & Economics in Fifth-Century Athens. 5th ed. 1931. pap. 5.95x (ISBN 0-19-500230-X). Oxford U Pr.

GREECE–RELATIONS (GENERAL) WITH ASIA

Gladstone, W. E. Archaic Greece & the East. LC 77-94879. 1978. Repr. of 1892 ed. lib. bdg. 10.00 (ISBN 0-89341-177-9). Longwood Pr.

GREECE–RELATIONS (GENERAL) WITH GREAT BRITAIN

Spencer, Terence. Fair Greece, Sad Relic: Literary Philhellenism from Shakespeare to Byron. LC 76-158507. (Illus.). 1971. Repr. of 1954 ed. 13.00 (ISBN 0-403-01307-0). Scholarly.

GREECE–RELIGION

Abbott, Evelyn, ed. Hellenica: A Collection of Essays on Greek Poetry, Philosophy, History & Religion. LC 76-86577. (Classics Ser). 1971. Repr. of 1880 ed. 16.00 (ISBN 0-8046-1196-3). Kennikat.
Adam, James. The Religious Teachers of Greece. LC 65-22806. (Library of Religious & Philosophical Thought). Repr. of 1908 ed. lib. bdg. 17.50x (ISBN 0-678-09950-2, Reference Bk Pubs). Kelley.
Adeney, Walter F. The Greek & Eastern Churches. LC 65-22087. (Library of Religious & Philosophical Thought). Repr. of 1908 ed. lib. bdg. 22.50x (ISBN 0-678-09951-0, Reference Bk Pubs). Kelley.
Alexiou, Margaret. The Ritual Lament in Greek Tradition. LC 72-97879. (Illus.). 216p. 1974. 34.00 (ISBN 0-521-20226-4). Cambridge U Pr.
Angus, S. The Religious Quests of the Graeco-Roman World. 1929. 30.00 (ISBN 0-686-20108-6). Quality Lib.
Bevan, Edwyn R., ed. Later Greek Religion. LC 76-179282. (Library of Greek Thought: No. 9). Repr. of 1927 ed. 12.50 (ISBN 0-404-07807-9). AMS Pr.
Campbell, Lewis. Religion in Greek Literature: A Sketch in Outline. facsimile ed. LC 79-148874. (Select Bibliographies Reprint Ser). Repr. of 1898 ed. 22.00 (ISBN 0-8369-5645-1). Arno.
Cornford, Francis M., ed. Greek Religious Thought from Homer to the Age of Alexander. LC 79-98637. (Library of Greek Thought: No. 2). Repr. of 1923 ed. 21.50 (ISBN 0-404-01734-7). AMS Pr.
Cumont, Franz. Astrology & Religion Among the Greeks & Romans. 6.75 (ISBN 0-8446-1927-2). Peter Smith.
--Astrology & Religion Among the Greeks & Romans. 1912. pap. 2.75 (ISBN 0-486-20581-9). Dover.
Dietrich, B. C. Death, Fate & the Gods: Development of a Religious Idea in Greek Popular Belief & in Homer. (University of London Classical Studies: No. 3). 390p. 1967. Repr. text ed. 41.00x (ISBN 0-686-74103-X, Pub. by Aris England). Humanities.
--The Origins of Greek Religion. 314p. 1973. 79.50x (ISBN 3-11-003982-6). De Gruyter.
Earp, Frank R. Way of the Greeks. LC 75-136393. Repr. of 1929 ed. 21.50 (ISBN 0-404-02234-0). AMS Pr.
Farnell, L. R. The Higher Aspects of Greek Religion. 1977. 10.00 (ISBN 0-89005-206-9). Ares.
--Outline History of Greek Religion. 160p. 1974. 7.50 (ISBN 0-89005-025-2). Ares.
Farnell, Lewis R. Greece & Babylon: A Comparative Sketch of Mesopatamian, Anatolian & Hellenic Religions. 1977. lib. bdg. 59.95 (ISBN 0-8490-1906-0). Gordon Pr.
--The Higher Aspects of Greek Religion. LC 77-27158. (Hibbert Lectures: 1911). Repr. of 1912 ed. 16.00 (ISBN 0-404-60413-7). AMS Pr.
Ferguson, John. Greek & Roman Religion: A Source Book. LC 79-23009. (Classical Studies Ser.). 208p. 1980. 12.00 (ISBN 0-8155-5055-3, NP). Noyes.
Festugiere, Andre M. Epicurus & His Gods. Chilton, C. W., tr. LC 68-27057. 1969. Repr. of 1955 ed. 7.50 (ISBN 0-8462-1277-3). Russell.
Foucart, Paul F. Des Associations Religieuses Chez les Grecs: Thiases, Eranes, Orgeons. facsimile ed. LC 75-10637. (Ancient Religion & Mythology Ser.). (Fr.). 1976. Repr. of 1873 ed. 15.00x (ISBN 0-405-07014-4). Arno.
Foundation Course Folder III: Greek Religion. 1974. 11.50x (ISBN 0-521-08724-4). Cambridge U Pr.
Furley, William D. Studies in the Use of Fire in the Ancient Greek Religion. rev. ed. Connor, W. R., ed. LC 80-2650. (Monographs in Clasical Studies). (Illus.). 1981. lib. bdg. 29.00 (ISBN 0-405-14037-1). Arno.
Graf, Fritz. Eleusis und die orphische Dichtung Athens in vorhellenistischer Zeit. (Religionsgeschichtliche Versuche und Vorarbeiten, Vol. 33). xii, 224p. 1974. 42.50x (ISBN 3-11-004498-6). De Gruyter.
Grant, Frederick C., ed. Hellenistic Religions: The Age of Syncretism. 1953. pap. 8.95 (ISBN 0-672-60342-X, LLA134). Bobbs.
Gruppe, Otto. Griechische Mythologie und Religionsgeschichte, 2 vols. facsimile ed. LC 75-10638. (Ancient Religion & Mythology Ser.). (Ger.). 1976. Repr. of 1906 ed. 108.00x set (ISBN 0-405-07015-2). Arno.
Guthrie, William K. Greeks & Their Gods. (Orig.). 1968. pap. 5.95 (ISBN 0-8070-5793-2, BP2). Beacon Pr.
Harrison, Jane. Prolegomena to the Study of Greek Religion. 682p. 1981. text ed. 26.00x (ISBN 0-85036-262-8, Pub. by Merlin, England); pap. 13.25x (ISBN 0-686-69802-9). Humanities.
Harrison, Jane E. Prolegomena to the Study of Greek Religion. facsimile ed. LC 75-10639. (Ancient Religion & Mythology Ser.). (Illus.). 1976. Repr. of 1922 ed. 43.00x (ISBN 0-405-07018-7). Arno.
--The Religion of Ancient Greece. 1979. Repr. of 1905 ed. lib. bdg. 15.00 (ISBN 0-8495-2325-7). Arden Lib.
Hengel, Martin. Judaism & Hellenism: Studies in Their Encounter in Palestine During the Early Hellenistic Period. Bowden, John, tr. from Ger. 672p. 1981. Set. 19.95 (ISBN 0-8006-1495-X, 1-1495). Fortress.
Hyde, Walter W. Greek Religion & Its Survivals. LC 63-10268. (Our Debt to Greece & Rome Ser). 1963. Repr. of 1930 ed. 7.50x (ISBN 0-8154-0117-5). Cooper Sq.
Kephala, Euphrosyne. The Church of the Greek People. LC 77-87528. Repr. of 1930 ed. 14.50 (ISBN 0-404-16594-X). AMS Pr.
Kerenyi, Carl. Archetypal Images in Greek Religion, 5 vols. Manheim, R., tr. Incl. Vol. 1. Prometheus: Archetypal Image of Human Existence. 1963; Vol. 2. Dionysos: Archetypal Image of Industructible Life. 1976. 36.00x (ISBN 0-691-09863-8); Vol. 3. Asklepios: Archetypal Image of the Physician's Existence. 1959. 27.50 (ISBN 0-691-09703-8); Eleusis: Archetypal Image of Mother & Daughter. 1967; Vol. 5. Zeus & Hera-Archetypal Image of Father, Husband & Wife. 1975. 22.00 (ISBN 0-691-09864-6). (Bollingen Ser.: Vol. 65). Princeton U Pr.
Kerenyi, Karoly. The Religion of the Greeks & Romans. LC 72-9823. (Illus.). 303p. 1973. Repr. of 1962 ed. lib. bdg. 24.75x (ISBN 0-8371-6605-5, KERG). Greenwood.
Lloyd-Jones, Hugh. The Justice of Zeus. (Sather Classical Lectures: No. 41). 1971. 20.00x (ISBN 0-520-01739-0); pap. 3.45x (ISBN 0-520-02359-5). U of Cal Pr.
Mommsen, A. Athenae Christianae. 1977. 12.50 (ISBN 0-89005-216-6). Ares.
Murray, Gilbert. Five Stages of Greek Religion. LC 76-27675. 1976. Repr. of 1925 ed. lib. bdg. 20.00x (ISBN 0-8371-9080-0, MUFS). Greenwood.
--Five Stages of Greek Religion: Studies Based on a Course of Lectures Delivered in April 1912 at Columbia University. LC 75-41202. Repr. of 1925 ed. 12.50 (ISBN 0-404-14577-9). AMS Pr.
Nilsson, Martin P. Greek Folk Religion. (Illus.). 8.50 (ISBN 0-8446-0218-3). Peter Smith.
--Greek Folk Religion. 1972. pap. 4.95x (ISBN 0-8122-1034-4, Pa. Paperbacks). U of Pa Pr.
--A History of Greek Religion. Fielden, F. J., tr. from Swedish. LC 80-13430. 316p. 1980. Repr. of 1949 ed. lib. bdg. 27.50x (ISBN 0-313-22466-8, NIHG). Greenwood.
--History of Greek Religion. 2nd ed. (Orig.). 1964. pap. 4.45 (ISBN 0-393-00287-X, Norton Lib). Norton.
Otto, Walter F. The Homeric Gods. 1978. Repr. of 1954 ed. lib. bdg. 18.50x (ISBN 0-374-96151-4). Octagon.
--The Homeric Gods: The Spiritual Significance of Greek Religion. Hadas, Moses, tr. 1979. pap. 7.95 (ISBN 0-500-27144-5). Thames Hudson.
--The Homeric Gods: The Spiritual Significance of Greek Religion. Bolle, Kees W., ed. LC 77-79149. (Mythology Ser.). 1978. Repr. of 1954 ed. lib. bdg. 18.00x (ISBN 0-405-10558-4). Arno.
Parke, H. W. Festivals of the Athenians. LC 76-12819. (Aspects of Greek & Roman Life). (Illus.). 1977. 22.50x (ISBN 0-8014-1054-1). Cornell U Pr.
Reitzenstein, Richard. The Hellenistic Mystery-Religions. Steely, John E., tr. from Ger. LC 77-12980. (Pittsburgh Theological Monographs: No. 15). Orig. Title: Die Hellenistischen Mysterienreligionen Nach Ihren Arundgedanken und Wirkungen. 1978. pap. text ed. 13.95 (ISBN 0-915138-20-4). Pickwick.
Rexine, John E. Religion in Plato & Cicero. LC 68-28581. 72p. Repr. of 1959 ed. lib. bdg. 15.00x (ISBN 0-8371-0198-0, RERP). Greenwood.
Rice, David G. & Stambaugh, John E. Sources for the Study of Greek Religion. LC 79-18389. (Society of Biblical Literature. Sources for Biblical Study Ser.: No. 14). 1979. o.s.i 12.00 (ISBN 0-89130-346-4, 060314); pap. 7.50 (ISBN 0-89130-347-2). Scholars Pr Ca.
Rohde, Erwin. Psyche: The Cult of Souls & Belief in Immortality Among the Greeks. facsimile ed. LC 75-37911. (Select Bibliographies Reprint Ser). Repr. of 1920 ed. 32.00 (ISBN 0-8369-6749-6). Arno.
Rose, Herbert J. Religion in Greece & Rome. pap. 5.95x (ISBN 0-06-130055-1, TB55, Torch). Har-Row.
Rouse, William H. Greek Votive Offerings: An Essay in the History of Greek Religion. facsimile ed. LC 75-10654. (Ancient Religion & Mythology Ser.). (Illus.). 1976. Repr. of 1902 ed. 27.00x (ISBN 0-405-07262-7). Arno.
Smith, John S. Temples, Priests & Worship. (Greek & Roman Topics Ser.). 1975. pap. text ed. 3.95x (ISBN 0-04-930003-2). Allen Unwin.
Stengel, Paul. Die Griechischen Kultusaltertumer. facsimile ed. LC 75-10656. (Ancient Religion & Mythology Ser.). (Ger.). 1976. Repr. of 1920 ed. 16.00x (ISBN 0-405-07264-3). Arno.
Weil, Simone. Intimations of Christianity Among the Ancient Greeks. 1976. 12.50 (ISBN 0-7100-8524-9). Routledge & Kegan.
Zielinski, T. The Religion of Ancient Greece. 10.00 (ISBN 0-89005-168-2); pap. 6.00 (ISBN 0-89005-090-2). Ares.
Zielinski, Thaddeus. Religion of Ancient Greece. facsimile ed. Noyes, George R., tr. LC 76-107838. (Select Bibliographies Reprint Ser). 1926. 17.00 (ISBN 0-8369-5222-7). Arno.

GREECE–SOCIAL CONDITIONS

Beaubier, Jeff. High Life Expectancy on the Island of Paros, Greece. LC 75-22948. (Illus.). 160p. 1976. 10.00 (ISBN 0-8022-2172-6). Philos Lib.
Diller, Aubrey. Race Mixture Among the Greeks Before Alexander. LC 70-95094. Repr. of 1937 ed. lib. bdg. 14.00x (ISBN 0-8371-3086-7, DIRM). Greenwood.
Dyroff, Adolf. Die Ethik der Alten Stoa. Vlastos, Gregory, ed. LC 78-19350. (Morals & Law in Ancient Greece Ser.). (Ger. & Gr.). 1979. Repr. of 1897 ed. lib. bdg. 26.00x (ISBN 0-405-11540-7). Arno.
Erdman, Walter. Die Ehe Im Alten Griechenland. Vlastos, Gregory, ed. LC 78-19349. (Morals & Law in Ancient Greece Ser.). (Ger. & Gr.). 1979. Repr. of 1934 ed. lib. bdg. 26.00x (ISBN 0-405-11541-5). Arno.
Ferguson, John. Moral Values in the Ancient World. Vlastos, Gregory, ed. LC 78-19348. (Morals & Law in Ancient Greece Ser.). 1979. Repr. of 1958 ed. lib. bdg. 16.00x (ISBN 0-405-11542-3). Arno.
Garnet, Louis. Droit et Societe dans la Grece Ancienne. Vlastos, Gregory, ed. LC 78-19346. (Morals & Law in Ancient Greece Ser.). (Fr. & Gr.). 1979. Repr. of 1955 ed. lib. bdg. 16.00x (ISBN 0-405-11543-1). Arno.
Glotz, Gustave. L'Ordalie Dans la Grece Primitive. Vlastos, Gregory, ed. LC 78-19352. (Morals & Law in Ancient Greece Ser.). 1979. Repr. of 1904 ed. lib. bdg. 10.00x (ISBN 0-405-11545-8). Arno.
Heitland, William E. Agricola: A Study of Agriculture & Rustic Life in the Greco-Roman World from the Point of View of Labour. Repr. of 1921 ed. lib. bdg. 37.00 (ISBN 0-8371-4088-9, HEAG). Greenwood.
Hitzig, Hermann F. Das Griechische Pfandrecht. Vlastos, Gregory, ed. LC 78-14611. (Morals & Law in Ancient Greece Ser.). (Ger. & Gr.). 1979. Repr. of 1895 ed. lib. bdg. 10.00x (ISBN 0-405-11587-3). Arno.
Homelrijk, Jacob. Penia En Ploutos. Vlastos, Gregory, ed. LC 78-19360. (Morals & Law in Ancient Greece Ser.). 1979. Repr. of 1925 ed. lib. bdg. 12.00x (ISBN 0-405-11552-0). Arno.
Jost, Karl. Das Beispiel und Vorbild der Vorfahren. Vlastos, Gregory, ed. LC 78-19366. (Morals & Law in Ancient Greece Ser.). (Ger. & Greek.). 1979. Repr. of 1935 ed. lib. bdg. 18.00x (ISBN 0-685-96158-3). Arno.
Kostler, Rudolf & Vos, Harm. Homerisches Reght & Themis, 2 vols. in one. Vlastos, Gregory, ed. LC 78-14606. (Morals & Law in Ancient Greece Ser.). (Ger. & Gr.). 1979. Repr. of 1956 ed. lib. bdg. 12.00x (ISBN 0-405-11582-2). Arno.
Lotze, Detlef & Hample, Franz. Metary Eleutheron Kai Doulon & Die Lakedaemonischen Perickon, 2 vols. in one. Vlastos, Gregory, ed. LC 78-14616. (Morals & Law in Ancient Greece Ser.). 1979. Repr. of 1937 ed. lib. bdg. 12.00x (ISBN 0-405-11591-1). Arno.
Meier, Moritz H. & Schomann, Georg F. Der Attische Process. Vlastos, Gregory, ed. LC 78-19370. (Morals & Law in Ancient Greece Ser.). (Ger. & Greek.). 1979. Repr. of 1824 ed. lib. bdg. 48.00x (ISBN 0-405-11561-X). Arno.
Menzel, Adolf. Hellenika. Vlastos, Gregory, ed. LC 78-19372. (Morals & Law in Ancient Greece Ser.). (Ger. & Gr.). 1979. Repr. of 1938 ed. lib. bdg. 12.00x (ISBN 0-405-11562-8). Arno.
Nestle, Wilhelm. Vom Mythos Zum Logos: Die Selbstentfaltung Des Griechischen Denkens Von Homer Bis Auf Die Sophistik und Sokrates. Bolle, Kees W., ed. LC 77-79147. (Mythology Ser.). (Ger.). 1978. Repr. of 1942 ed. lib. bdg. 34.00x (ISBN 0-405-10556-8). Arno.
Roebuck, Carl. Economy & Society in the Early Greek World: Collected Essays. Thomas, Carol G., ed. 1978. 25.00 (ISBN 0-89005-261-1). Ares.
Sagan, Eli. The Lust to Annihilate: A Psychoanalytic Study of Violence in Ancient Greek Culture. 1979. 12.00 (ISBN 0-914434-11-X). Psychohistory Pr.
Schaps, David M. The Economic Rights of Women in Ancient Greece. 175p. 1979. 16.00x (ISBN 0-85224-343-X, Pub. by Edinburgh U Pr Scotland). Columbia U Pr.
Starr, Chester G. The Economic & Social Growth of Early Greece: 800--500 B.C. (Illus.). 1977. 15.95 (ISBN 0-19-502223-8). Oxford U Pr.
Thomson, George. Studies in Ancient Greek Society: The Prehistoric Aegean. 1966. pap. 2.95 (ISBN 0-8065-0047-6). Citadel Pr.
Vlastos, Gregory, ed. Morals & Law in Ancient Greece Series, 57 bks. 1979. Set. lib. bdg. 1165.00x (ISBN 0-405-11529-6). Arno.

GREECE–SOCIAL LIFE AND CUSTOMS

Andrewes, Antony. The Greeks. 1978. pap. 4.95 (ISBN 0-393-00877-0, N877, Norton Lib). Norton.
Arnheim, M. T. Aristocracy in Greek Society. (Aspects of Greek & Roman Life Ser.). (Illus.). 1977. 19.95 (ISBN 0-500-40031-8). Thames Hudson.
Austin, M. M. & Vidal-Naquet, P. Economic & Social History of Ancient Greece: An Introduction. 1978. 31.50x (ISBN 0-520-02658-6); pap. 8.95 (ISBN 0-520-04267-0). U of Cal Pr.
Blumner, Hugo. Home Life of the Ancient Greeks. Zimmern, A., tr. LC 66-30007. (Illus.). 548p. Repr. of 1893 ed. 17.50x (ISBN 0-8154-0025-X). Cooper Sq.

Burford, Alison. Craftsman in Greek & Roman Society. Scullard, H. H., ed. LC 71-37630. (Aspects in Greek & Roman Life Ser.). (Illus.). 256p. 1972. 22.50x (ISBN 0-8014-0717-6). Cornell U Pr.

Burns, C. Greek Ideals: A Study in Social Life. 59.95 (ISBN 0-8490-0264-8). Gordon Pr.

Burns, C. Delisle. Greek Ideals: A Study of Social Life. 1917. 14.50 (ISBN 0-686-20093-4). Quality Lib.

De Coulanges, Numa D. The Ancient City: A Classic Study of the Religious & Civil Institutions of Ancient Greece & Rome. LC 79-3703. 1980. pap. 5.95 (ISBN 0-8018-2304-8). Johns Hopkins.

Dover, K. J. Greek Homosexuality. 1978. 22.50x (ISBN 0-674-36261-6). Harvard U Pr.

Dugas, Ludovic. Le Amitie Antique D'apres les Moeurs Populaires & les Theories Des Philosophes. facsimile ed. LC 75-13263. (History of Ideas in Ancient Greeceser.). (Fr.). 1976. Repr. of 1894 ed. 26.00x (ISBN 0-405-07305-4). Arno.

Ehrenberg, Victor L. Society & Civilization in Greece & Rome. LC 64-19580. (Martin Classical Lectures Ser: No. 18). (Illus.). 1964. 6.95x (ISBN 0-674-81510-6). Harvard U Pr.

Firebaugh, W. C. The Inns of Greece & Rome. LC 76-175878. (Illus.). Repr. of 1928 ed. 18.00 (ISBN 0-405-08515-X, Blom Pubns). Arno.

Fisher, N. R. Social Values in Classical Athens. new ed. 1977. 8.00 (ISBN 0-88866-573-3); pap. 3.95 (ISBN 0-88866-574-1). Samuel Stevens.

Gulick, Charles B. The Life of the Ancient Greeks. LC 72-94074. (Illus.). 373p. 1973. Repr. of 1902 ed. lib. bdg. 16.50x (ISBN 0-8154-0456-5). Cooper Sq.

--Modern Traits in Old Greek Life. LC 63-10291. (Our Debt to Greece & Rome). 159p. Repr. of 1930 ed. 7.50x (ISBN 0-8154-0097-7). Cooper Sq.

Hausecullier, Bernard. La Vie Municipale En Antique. Vlastos, Gregory, ed. LC 78-19358. (Morals & Law in Ancient Greece Ser.). 1979. Repr. of 1883 ed. lib. bdg. 16.00x (ISBN 0-405-11550-4). Arno.

Klee, Theophil. Zur Geschichte der Gymnischen Agone an Griechischen Festen. 136p. 1980. 12.50 (ISBN 0-89005-336-7). Ares.

Lang, Mabel. The Athenian Citizen. (Excavations of the Athenian Agora Picture Bks.: No. 4). (Illus.). 1960. pap. 1.50x (ISBN 0-87661-604-X). Am Sch Athens.

Licht, Hans, pseud. Sexual Life in Ancient Greece. Dawson, Lawrence H., ed. Freese, J. H., tr. from Ger. LC 72-9622. (Illus.). Repr. of 1932 ed. 32.50 (ISBN 0-404-57417-3). AMS Pr.

McLeish, Kenneth. Food & Drink. (Greek & Roman Topics Ser.). (Illus.). 1978. pap. text ed. 3.95x (ISBN 0-04-930007-5). Allen Unwin.

Mahaffy, J. P. Greek Life & Thought from the Age of Alexander to the Roman Conquest. facsimile ed. LC 75-13278. (History of Ideas in Ancient Greece Ser.). 1976. Repr. of 1887 ed. 35.00x (ISBN 0-405-07318-6). Arno.

--Social Life in Greece from Homer to Menander. 457p. 1980. Repr. of 1883 ed. lib. bdg. 45.00 (ISBN 0-8495-3850-5). Arden Lib.

Miller, S. Arete: Ancient Writers, Papyri, & Inscriptions on the History & Ideals of Greek Athletics & Games. 1979. pap. 7.50 (ISBN 0-89005-273-5). Ares.

Mireaux, Emile. Daily Life in the Time of Homer. Sells, Iris, tr. 1959. 9.95 (ISBN 0-02-585090-3). Macmillan.

Nichols, R. & Nichols, S. Greek Everyday Life. (Aspects of Greek Life Ser.). (Illus.). 1978. pap. text ed. 2.95x (ISBN 0-582-20672-3). Longman.

Pollard, John. Birds in Greek Life & Myth. (Aspects of Greek & Roman Life Ser.). (Illus.). 1977. 19.95 (ISBN 0-500-40032-6). Thames Hudson.

Pope, Maurice. The Ancient Greeks: How They Lived & Worked. LC 75-41966. 192p. 1976. 11.95 (ISBN 0-8023-1264-0). Dufour.

Ramage, Edwin S. Urbanitas: Ancient Sophistication & Refinement. LC 72-9257. (Classical Studies Ser.: No. 3). 250p. 1973. 12.95x (ISBN 0-8061-1063-5). U of Okla Pr.

Richardson, Bessie E. Old Age Among the Ancient Greeks. LC 74-93775. (Illus.). Repr. of 1933 ed. 21.50 (ISBN 0-404-05289-4). AMS Pr.

--Old Age Among the Ancient Greeks: The Greek Portrayal of Old Age in Literature, Art & Inscriptions. Repr. of 1933 ed. lib. bdg. 23.50x (ISBN 0-8371-0637-0, RIOA). Greenwood.

Robinson, Cyril E. Everyday Life in Ancient Greece. LC 77-27627. 1978. Repr. of 1933 ed. lib. bdg. 20.75x (ISBN 0-8371-9078-9, ROEL). Greenwood.

--Everyday Life in Ancient Greece. LC 75-41232. Repr. of 1933 ed. 16.00 (ISBN 0-404-14592-2). AMS Pr.

Sambursky, S. Physical World of the Greeks. Dagut, Merton, tr. 1956. pap. 8.95 (ISBN 0-7100-4637-5). Routledge & Kegan.

Seymour, Thomas D. Life in the Homeric Age. LC 63-12451. (Illus.). 1907. 15.00x (ISBN 0-8196-0125-X). Biblo.

Symonds, John A. Problem in Greek Ethics. LC 71-163126. (Studies in Philosophy, No. 40). 1971. lib. bdg. 31.95 (ISBN 0-8383-1253-5). Haskell.

--Studies in Sexual Inversion. LC 72-9683. Repr. of 1928 ed. 14.50 (ISBN 0-404-57503-X). AMS Pr.

Tucker, T. G. Life in Ancient Athens. 1906. 40.00 (ISBN 0-8274-3983-0). R West.

Ure, P. N. The Greek Renaissance. 1921. 20.00 (ISBN 0-686-20094-2). Quality Lib.

Walcot, Peter. Envy & the Greeks: A Study of Human Behavior. 1978. 16.50x (ISBN 0-85668-146-6, Pub. by Aris & Phillips). Intl Schol Bk Serv.

Wright, Frederick A., ed. Greek Social Life. LC 70-179283. (Library of Greek Thought: No. 4). Repr. of 1925 ed. 11.50 (ISBN 0-404-07803-6). AMS Pr.

GREECE, MEDIEVAL

Cheetham, Nicholas. Mediaeval Greece. LC 80-13559. 352p. 1981. 27.50x (ISBN 0-300-02421-5). Yale U Pr.

Finlay, George. History of Greece, 7 Vols. 1970. Repr. of 1877 ed. Set. 245.00 (ISBN 0-404-02390-8); 35.00 ea. AMS Pr.

Hopf, Carl. Geschichte Griechenlands Vom Beginn Des Mittelalters Bis Auf Unsere Neure Zeit, 395-1821, 2 Vols. 1960. Repr. of 1868 ed. 55.50 (ISBN 0-8337-1734-0). B Franklin.

Littman, Robert J. The Greek Experiment: Imperialism & Social Conflict, 800-400 B.C. (Library of European Civilization Ser.). (Illus.). 180p. 1974. 8.75 (ISBN 0-500-32030-6). Transatlantic.

GREECE, MODERN

Dimen, Muriel & Friedl, Ernestine, eds. Regional Variation in Modern Greece & Cyprus: Toward a Perspective on the Ethnography of Greece. (Annals of the New York Academy of Sciences: Vol. 268). 465p. 1976. 30.00x (ISBN 0-89072-022-3). NY Acad Sci.

Gavin, Frank S. Some Aspects of Contemporary Greek Orthodox Thought. LC 73-133818. Repr. of 1923 ed. 29.00 (ISBN 0-404-02687-7). AMS Pr.

Iatrides, John O., ed. Greece in the Nineteen Forties: A Bibliographic Companion. LC 80-54473. 176p. 1981. text ed. 15.00x (ISBN 0-87451-199-2). U Pr of New Eng.

--Greece in the Nineteen Forties: A Nation in Crisis. LC 80-54472. 450p. 1981. 35.00x (ISBN 0-87451-198-4). U Pr of New Eng.

Jebb, R. C. Modern Greece: Two Lectures. 1979. Repr. of 1880 ed. lib. bdg. 30.00 (ISBN 0-8492-1363-0). R West.

Kellogg, William O. Greece & the Aegean. 1975. pap. text ed. 4.95x (ISBN 0-88334-066-6). Ind Sch Pr.

National Statistical Service. Statistical Yearbook of Greece, 1977. LC 61-45001. 1978. pap. 14.00x (ISBN 0-8002-0355-0). Intl Pubns Serv.

Szabo, George. The Robert Lehman Collection. LC 74-34207. (Illus.). 312p. 1975. pap. 7.50 (ISBN 0-87099-127-2). Metro Mus Art.

GREECE, MODERN-ANTIQUITIES

Leekley, Dorothy & Efstratiou, Nicholas. Archaeological Excavations in Central & Northern Greece. LC 80-11348. 184p. 1980. 15.00 (ISBN 0-8155-5056-1, NP). Noyes.

Prag, A. G., ed. Archaeological Reports 1979-80: Hellenic Sudies, No. 26. 89p. 1981. pap. text ed. 7.50x (ISBN 0-686-72931-5, Pub. by Aris & Phillips England). Humanities.

GREECE, MODERN-DESCRIPTION AND TRAVEL

Baird, Henry M. Modern Greece: Narrative of a Residence & Travels in That Country. LC 77-87533. (Illus.). Repr. of 1856 ed. 30.00 (ISBN 0-404-16593-1). AMS Pr.

Barret, Andre. Greece Observed. Hardman, Stephen, tr. (Illus.). 1974. 24.95 (ISBN 0-19-519779-8). Oxford U Pr.

De Stroumillo, Elisabeth. Greece. (Illus.). 1974. pap. 5.95 (ISBN 0-8038-2665-6). Hastings.

Dorizas, H. Workbook for Greek Children Reader. 1976. 2.20 (ISBN 0-685-79097-5). Divry.

Durrell, Lawrence. The Greek Islands. Date not set. 25.00 (ISBN 0-686-75009-8, Studio). Viking Pr.

Greek Island Hopping. LC 79-87874. (Illus.). 1979. pap. 14.95 (ISBN 0-88254-488-8). Hippocrene Bks.

Harvard Student Agencies. Let's Go, Greece, Israel & Europe: The Budget Guide 1981 to 1982 Edition. (Illus.). 352p. 1981. pap. 5.95 (ISBN 0-525-93146-5). Dutton.

Huxley, Anthony & Taylor, William. Flowers of Greece & the Aegean. (Illus.). 1977. 24.00 (ISBN 0-7011-2190-4). Transatlantic.

Keller, W. P. Dolphin off the Bow. 1979. 9.95 (ISBN 0-533-04150-3). Vantage.

Levi, Peter. The Hill of Kronos. (Illus.). 224p. 1981. 12.50 (ISBN 0-525-12495-0). Dutton.

Lucas, F. L. & Prudence. From Olympus to the Styx. 342p. 1981. Repr. of 1949 ed. lib. bdg. 30.00 (ISBN 0-89760-507-1). Telegraph Bks.

Lyle, Garry & Caldwell, John C. Let's Visit Greece. LC 77-143411. 96p. (gr. 3-7). 1972. PLB 7.89 (ISBN 0-381-99760-X, A42977, JD-J). Har-Row.

MacEwen, Gwendolyn. Mermaids & Ikons: A Greek Summer. 110p. (Orig.). 1978. pap. 6.95 (ISBN 0-88784-062-0, Pub. by Hse Anansi Pr Canada). U of Toronto Pr.

Mead, Robin. Greece. 1976. 22.50 (ISBN 0-7134-3080-X). David & Charles.

--The Greek Islands. LC 79-56491. (Illus.). 160p. 1980. 22.50 (ISBN 0-7134-0625-9, Pub. by Batsford England). David & Charles.

Miller, Henry. Colossus of Maroussi. LC 58-9511. pap. 2.95 (ISBN 0-8112-0109-0, NDP75). New Directions.

Moreau, Daniel, ed. La Grece. new ed. (Collection monde et voyages). 159p. (Fr.). 1973. 21.00x (ISBN 2-03-053105-7, 3897). Larousse.

Pentreath, Guy. The Hellenic Traveller. (Illus.). 338p. (Orig.). 1971. pap. 4.95 (ISBN 0-571-09718-9, Pub. by Faber & Faber). Merrimack Bk Serv.

Rose, Richard. The Problem of Party Government. LC 74-30329. (Illus.). 1975. 17.95 (ISBN 0-02-926780-3). Free Pr.

Senior, Nassau W. A Journal Kept in Turkey & Greece in the Autumn of 1857 & the Beginnings of 1858. Wilkins, Mira, ed. LC 76-29988. (European Business Ser.). (Illus.). 1977. Repr. of 1859 ed. lib. bdg. 22.00x (ISBN 0-405-09720-4). Arno.

Warburton, Minnie. Mykonos. LC 79-67. 1979. 9.95 (ISBN 0-698-10922-8). Coward.

Will, Frederic. From a Year in Greece. (Illus.). 195p. 1967. 11.50x (ISBN 0-292-73664-9). U of Tex Pr.

GREECE, MODERN-DESCRIPTION AND TRAVEL-GUIDEBOOKS

The Blue Jeans Guide to Greece. (Illus.). 176p. 1981. pap. 3.95 (ISBN 0-7064-1465-9, Pub. by Octopus). Smith Pubs.

De Stroumillo, Elizabeth. Travellers' Guide to Greece. Date not set. pap. 4.95 (ISBN 0-8038-2665-6). Hastings.

Dicks, Brian. Greece: The Traveller's Guide to History & Mythology. LC 79-91497. (Illus.). 1980. 17.95 (ISBN 0-7153-7797-3). David & Charles.

Durrell, Lawrence. The Greek Islands. 1980. pap. 12.95 (ISBN 0-14-005661-0). Penguin.

Evans, Craig. On Foot Through Europe: A Trail Guide to Italy, Greece & E. Europe. Whitney, Stephen, ed. (Illus.). 374p. 1980. lib. bdg. 10.95 (ISBN 0-933710-19-4); pap. 5.95 (ISBN 0-933710-18-6). Foot Trails.

Facaros, Dana. Greek Island Hopping. rev. ed. (Travel Ser.). 1981. pap. 14.95 (ISBN 0-88254-608-2). Hippocrene Bks.

Fodor's Greece, 1981. 1980. 12.95 (ISBN 0-679-00691-5); pap. 9.95 (ISBN 0-679-00692-3). McKay.

Greece & Yugoslavia on Fifteen & Twenty Dollars a Day: 1980-81 Edition. 1981. pap. 4.95 (ISBN 0-671-25176-7). Frommer-Pasmantier.

Harrison, John & Harrison, Shirley. Greece. LC 80-50995. (Rand McNally Pocket Guide Ser.). (Illus.). 1980. pap. 3.95 (ISBN 0-528-84307-9). Rand.

Iakovidis, S. E. Mycenae-Epidaurus: Argos-Tiryns-Nauplion. (Illustrated Travel Guides Ser.). (Illus.). 1979. pap. 9.95 (ISBN 0-89241-102-3). Caratzas Bros.

The Nagel Travel Guide to Greece. (Nagel Travel Guide Ser.). (Illus.). 980p. 1973. 45.00 (ISBN 0-685-31361-1). Hippocrene Bks.

Nagel's Encyclopedia Guide: Greece. (Illus.). 970p. 1978. 45.00 (ISBN 2-8263-0113-6). Masson Pub.

Ronay, Egon. Eating Out in Greece. LC 78-670077. (Illus.). 1977. pap. 8.50x (ISBN 0-8002-1930-9). Intl Pubns Serv.

Travelaid Staff. Travelaid Guide to Greece. (Travelaid Guides Ser.). (Illus., Orig.). 1978. pap. 5.95 (ISBN 0-8467-0435-8, Pub. by Two Continents). Hippocrene Bks.

GREECE, MODERN-ECONOMIC CONDITIONS

McNeill, William H. The Metamorphosis of Greece Since World War II. LC 77-26105. (Illus.). 1978. 12.95 (ISBN 0-226-56156-9). U of Chicago Pr.

Marder, Brenda L. Stewarts of the Land: The American Farm School & Modern Greece. (East European Monographs: No. 59). 1979. 14.50x (ISBN 0-914710-52-4). East Eur Quarterly.

Mouzelis, Nicos P. Modern Greece: Facets of Underdevelopment. LC 78-312273. 1980. text ed. 32.00x (ISBN 0-8419-0357-3); pap. text ed. 12.50x (ISBN 0-8419-0523-1). Holmes & Meier.

Skountzos, Th. A., et al. Input-Output Tables of the Greek Economy, 1958-1977. dual language ed. (Center of Planning & Economic Research (Athens) Monographs). 442p. (Orig., Eng. & Gr.). 1980. pap. 20.00x (ISBN 0-8002-2771-9). Intl Pubns Serv.

Zolotas, Xenophon. Monetary Equilibrium & Economic Development. 1965. 16.50x (ISBN 0-691-04148-2). Princeton U Pr.

GREECE, MODERN-FOREIGN RELATIONS

Bull, Hedley, et al. Greece & the European Community. 172p. 1979. text ed. 27.25x (ISBN 0-566-00232-9, Pub. by Gower Pub Co England). Renouf.

Lamanskii, Valdimar. Secrets D'Etat De Venise, 2 vols. LC 68-56771. (Research Source Works Ser.: No. 256). (Fr). 1968. Repr. of 1884 ed. 83.00 (ISBN 0-8337-1990-4). B Franklin.

Nicholas, Prince of Greece. Political Memoirs, 1914-17. LC 72-1274. (Select Bibliographies Reprint Ser.). 1972. Repr. of 1927 ed. 31.00 (ISBN 0-8369-6833-6). Arno.

GREECE, MODERN-HISTORY

see also Greco-Turkish War, 1897

Augustinos, Gerasimos. Consciousness & History: Nationalist Critics of Greek Society, 1897-1914. (East European Monographs: No. 32). 1977. 13.50x (ISBN 0-914710-25-7). East Eur Quarterly.

Baerentzen, Lars. Dmitri Kessel: Greece Nineteen Forty-Four: A Photographic Chronicle of Liberation & Civil War. (Illus.). 256p. 1980. 35.00 (ISBN 0-89241-133-3). Caratzas Bros.

Brandes, Georg M. Hellas: Travels in Greece. facs. ed. Hartmann, J. W., tr. LC 72-90613. (Essay Index Reprint Ser). 1926. 15.00 (ISBN 0-8369-1203-9). Arno.

Clogg, R. A Short History of Modern Greece. LC 78-72083. (Illus.). 1979. 29.95 (ISBN 0-521-22479-9); pap. 9.95 (ISBN 0-521-29517-3). Cambridge U Pr.

Clogg, Richard, ed. The Struggle for Greek Independence: Essays to Mark the 150th Anniversary of the Greek War of Independence. 224p. 1973. 18.50 (ISBN 0-208-01303-2, Archon). Shoe String.

Couvaras, Costa G. Photo Album of the Greek Resistance. new ed. LC 78-65147. (Illus.). 1978. pap. 5.95 (ISBN 0-918034-02-7). Wire Pr.

Crawley, C. W. The Question of Greek Independence: A Study of British Policy in the Near East, 1821-1833. LC 74-144130. 272p. 1973. Repr. of 1930 ed. 23.50 (ISBN 0-86527-161-5). Fertig.

Dakin, Douglas. The Unification of Greece: Seventeen-Seventy to Nineteen Twenty-Three. LC 76-187329. 1972. 17.95 (ISBN 0-312-83300-8). St. Martin.

Finlay, George. History of Greece, 7 Vols. 1970. Repr. of 1877 ed. Set. 245.00 (ISBN 0-404-02390-8); 35.00 ea. AMS Pr.

--History of the Greek Revolution & the Reign of King Otho, 2 vols. in 1. Dakin, Douglas, ed. (Illus.). 1971. Repr. of 1877 ed. text ed. 33.75x (ISBN 0-900834-12-9). Humanities.

Forster, Edward S. A Short History of Modern Greece, 1821-1956. Dakin, Douglas, ed. 1977. Repr. of 1958 ed. lib. bdg. 21.00x (ISBN 0-8371-9803-8, FOMG). Greenwood.

Gamba, Pietro. A Narrative of Lord Byron's Last Journey to Greece. LC 75-30618. 1975. Repr. of 1825 ed. lib. bdg. 45.00 (ISBN 0-8414-4441-2). Folcroft.

Hopf, Carl. Geschichte Griechenlands Vom Beginn Des Mittelalters Bis Auf Unsere Neure Zeit, 395-1821, 2 Vols. 1960. Repr. of 1868 ed. 55.50 (ISBN 0-8337-1734-0). B Franklin.

Iatrides, John E., ed. Ambassador MacVeagh Reports: Greece, Nineteen Thirty-Three to Nineteen Forty-Seven. LC 79-19079. 1980. 35.00x (ISBN 0-691-05292-1). Princeton U Pr.

Jacchinis, Chris. Greece. (Young Historian Ser.). Date not set. 10.75x (ISBN 0-392-15988-0, SpS). Sportshelf.

Kaltchas, Nicholas. Introduction to the Constitutional History of Modern Greece. LC 78-110573. Repr. of 1940 ed. 18.75 (ISBN 0-404-03627-9). AMS Pr.

Koumoulides, John T. Cyprus & the War of Greek Independence, 1821-29. LC 74-188678. (National Centre of Social Research Monographs). 141p. 1971. 10.00x (ISBN 0-8002-0734-3). Intl Pubns Serv.

Leon, George B. The Greek Socialist Movement and the First World War. (East European Monographs: No. 18). 200p. 1976. 12.00x (ISBN 0-914710-11-7). East Eur Quarterly.

Nicholas, Prince of Greece. Political Memoirs, 1914-17. LC 72-1274. (Select Bibliographies Reprint Ser.). 1972. Repr. of 1927 ed. 31.00 (ISBN 0-8369-6833-6). Arno.

Parry, William. The Last Days of Lord Byron. LC 75-29295. 1975. Repr. of 1825 ed. lib. bdg. 45.00 (ISBN 0-8414-6747-1). Folcroft.

Trelawney, Edward J. Records of Shelley, Byron & the Author, 2 vols. in 1. LC 68-20230. 1968. Repr. of 1878 ed. 25.00 (ISBN 0-405-09031-5). Arno.

Tsatsos, Jeanne. Sword's Fierce Edge: A Journal of the Occupation of Greece, 1941-1944. Demos, Jean, tr. LC 76-89473. (Illus.). 1969. 5.00 (ISBN 0-8265-1139-2). Vanderbilt U Pr.
Twentieth Century Fund. Report on the Greeks: Findings of a Twentieth Century Fund Team Which Surveyed Conditions in Greece in 1947. Repr. of 1948 ed. pap. 8.00 (ISBN 0-527-02839-8). Kraus Repr.
Vacalopoulos, Apostolos. The Greek Nation, 1453-1669: The Cultural & Economic Background of Modern Greek Society. 472p. 1976. 32.50 (ISBN 0-8135-0810-X). Rutgers U Pr.
Van Lith, Jan A., ed. Change & the New International Economic Order. (Tilburg Studies in Economics: Vol. 20). 1980. lib. bdg. 14.95 (ISBN 0-89838-028-6, Pub. by Martinus Nijhoff Netherlands). Kluwer Boston.
Vatikiotis, P. J. Greece: A Political Essay. LC 75-4208. (The Washington Papers, No. 22). 87p. 1975. 4.00 (ISBN 0-8039-0510-6). Sage.
Vryonis, S., Jr., ed. The "Past" in Medieval & Modern Greek Culture. LC 78-18624. (Byzantine Kai Metabyzantina Ser.: Vol. 1). (Illus.). 256p. 1978. 24.00 (ISBN 0-89003-026-X); pap. 19.00 (ISBN 0-89003-027-8). Undena Pubns.
Wagstaff, J. M. The Development of Rural Settlements: A Study of the Helos Plain in Southern Greece. 1981. 60.00x (ISBN 0-86127-302-8, Pub. by Avebury Pub England). State Mutual Bk.
Woodhouse, C. M. Modern Greece: A Short History. 336p. 1977. pap. 7.95 (ISBN 0-571-04936-2, Pub. by Faber & Faber). Merrimack Bk Serv.
--Struggle for Greece 1941-1949. (Illus.). 1979. 29.95x (ISBN 0-8464-0042-1). Beekman Pubs.

GREECE, MODERN–INDUSTRIES

Alexander, Alec P. Greek Industrialists. (Research Monograph Ser: No. 12). (Illus., Orig.). 1964. 7.50x (ISBN 0-8002-1473-0). Intl Pubns Serv.
ICAP Hellas (Athens), ed. ICAP Financial Directory of Greek Companies, 1980, 4 vols. 15th ed. (Illus.). 2960p. 1980. Set. pap. 180.00 (ISBN 0-8002-2762-X). Intl Pubns Serv.

GREECE, MODERN–JUVENILE LITERATURE

Johnson, Dorothy M. Greece: Wonderland of the Past & Present. LC 64-11673. (Illus.). (gr. 3-7). 1964. PLB 5.95 (ISBN 0-396-06709-3). Dodd.
Sasek, Miroslav. This Is Greece. (Illus.). (gr. 4-6). 1966. 8.95 (ISBN 0-02-778260-3). Macmillan.
Sterling Publishing Company Editors. Greece in Pictures. rev. ed. LC 62-12596. (Visual Geography Ser). (Illus., Orig.). (gr. 6 up). PLB 4.99 (ISBN 0-8069-1023-2); pap. 2.95 (ISBN 0-8069-1022-4). Sterling.
Zolotow, Charlotte & Getsug, Donald. Week in Yoni's World: Greece. LC 69-19574. (Face to Face Bks.). (Illus.). (gr. k-3). 1969. 4.50g (ISBN 0-02-735850-X, CCPr); text ed. 1.36 (ISBN 0-02-736010-5, CCPr). Macmillan.

GREECE, MODERN–POLITICS AND GOVERNMENT

Carey, Jane P. & Carey, Andrew G. The Web of Modern Politics. LC 68-28394. (Illus.). 240p. 1968. 18.00x (ISBN 0-231-03170-X). Columbia U Pr.
Couloumbis, T. A., et al. Foreign Interference in Greek Politics: An Historical Perspective. LC 76-45495. (Modern Greek Research Ser.). 1976. 10.00 (ISBN 0-918618-03-7); pap. 6.00 (ISBN 0-918618-02-9). Pella Pub.
Eudes, Dominique. The Kapetanios: Partisans & Civil War in Greece, 1943-1949. Howe, John, tr. from Fr. LC 72-92032. 1974. 11.95 (ISBN 0-85345-275-X, PB-3489); pap. 4.95 (ISBN 0-85345-348-9). Monthly Rev.
Freeman, Edward A. History of Federal Government in Greece & Italy. 2nd ed. Bury, J. B., ed. LC 72-39670. (Select Bibliographies Reprint Ser). 1972. Repr. of 1893 ed. 28.25 (ISBN 0-8369-9936-3). Arno.
Kuniholm, Bruce R. The Origins of the Cold War in the Near East: Great Power Conflict and Diplomacy in Iran, Turkey, and Greece. LC 79-83999. (Illus.). 1979. 27.50x (ISBN 0-691-04665-4); pap. 10.50 (ISBN 0-691-10083-7). Princeton U Pr.
Legg, Keith R. Politics in Modern Greece. LC 69-18495. 1969. 17.50x (ISBN 0-8047-0705-7). Stanford U Pr.
McNeill, William H. The Metamorphosis of Greece Since World War II. LC 77-26105. (Illus.). 1978. 12.95 (ISBN 0-226-56156-9). U of Chicago Pr.
Nicholas, Prince of Greece. Political Memoirs, 1914-17. LC 72-1274. (Select Bibliographies Reprint Ser.). 1972. Repr. of 1927 ed. 31.00 (ISBN 0-8369-6833-6). Arno.
Papacosma, S. Victor. The Military in Greek Politics: The 1909 Coup D'etat. LC 77-22391. 1977. 14.00x (ISBN 0-87338-208-0). Kent St U Pr.
Petropulos, John A. Politics & Statecraft in the Kingdom of Greece, 1833-1843. LC 66-21837. 1968. 27.50x (ISBN 0-691-05144-5). Princeton U Pr.
Poulantzas, Nicos. The Crisis of the Dictatorships: Portugal, Spain, Greece. 1976. 10.50 (ISBN 0-902308-77-7, Pub. by NLB). Schocken.
Smith, Michael L. Ionian Vision: Greece in Asia Minor, 1919-1922. LC 73-80083. 350p. 1973. 22.50 (ISBN 0-312-43540-1). St Martin.

GREECE, MODERN–RELATIONS (GENERAL) WITH FOREIGN COUNTRIES

Coufoudakis, Van, ed. Essays on the Cyprus Conflict. LC 76-10112. (Modern Greek Research Ser.). 1976. 8.00 (ISBN 0-918618-01-0); pap. 4.00 (ISBN 0-918618-00-2). Pella Pub.
Couloumbis, T. A., et al. Foreign Interference in Greek Politics: An Historical Perspective. LC 76-45495. (Modern Greek Research Ser.). 1976. 10.00 (ISBN 0-918618-03-7); pap. 6.00 (ISBN 0-918618-02-9). Pella Pub.
Couloumbis, Theodore A. Greek Political Reaction to American & NATO Influences. 1966. 20.00x (ISBN 0-300-00385-4). Yale U Pr.

GREECE, MODERN–SOCIAL CONDITIONS

Charioteer: An Annual Review of Modern Greek Culture, Nos. 3-22. Incl. No. 3 (ISBN 0-933824-02-5). No. 4 (ISBN 0-933824-03-3). No. 5 (ISBN 0-933824-04-1). No. 6 (ISBN 0-933824-05-X). Nos. 7 & 8 (ISBN 0-933824-06-8). No. 9 (ISBN 0-933824-07-6). No. 10 (ISBN 0-933824-08-4). Nos. 11 & 12 (ISBN 0-933824-09-2). No. 13 (ISBN 0-933824-10-6); No. 14 (ISBN 0-933824-11-4). No. 15 (ISBN 0-933824-12-2). Nos. 16 & 17 (ISBN 0-933824-13-0). No. 18 (ISBN 0-933824-14-9). No. 19 (ISBN 0-933824-15-7). No. 20 (ISBN 0-933824-16-5). No. 21 (ISBN 0-933824-17-3). Vols. 22 & 23 (ISBN 0-933824-18-1). Set. 60.00 (ISBN 0-686-62741-5); single issues 5.00 ea.; double issues 7.00 ea. Parnassos Ny.
DuBoulay, Juliet. Portrait of a Greek Mountain Village. (Oxford Monographs on Social Anthropology). (Illus.). 308p. text ed. 13.50 (ISBN 0-19-823198-9). Oxford U Pr.
Goodyear, William H. Greek Refinements. (Illus.). 1912. 100.00x (ISBN 0-685-69823-8). Elliots Bks.
McNeill, William H. The Metamorphosis of Greece Since World War II. LC 77-26105. (Illus.). 1978. 12.95 (ISBN 0-226-56156-9). U of Chicago Pr.
Mouzelis, Nicos P. Modern Greece: Facets of Underdevelopment. LC 78-312273. 1980. text ed. 32.00x (ISBN 0-8419-0357-3); pap. text ed. 12.50x (ISBN 0-8419-0523-1). Holmes & Meier.
Vlachos, Evan. Modern Greek Society: Continuity & Change. LC 77-87729. Repr. of 1969 ed. 29.50 (ISBN 0-404-16581-8). AMS Pr.

GREECE, MODERN–SOCIAL LIFE AND CUSTOMS

Campbell, J. K. Honour, Family & Patronage: A Study of Institutions & Moral Values in a Greek Mountain Community. (Illus.). 406p. 1973. 29.95x (ISBN 0-19-823122-9); pap. text ed. 6.95x (ISBN 0-19-519756-9). Oxford U Pr.
Charioteer: An Annual Review of Modern Greek Culture, Nos. 3-22. Incl. No. 3 (ISBN 0-933824-02-5). No. 4 (ISBN 0-933824-03-3). No. 5 (ISBN 0-933824-04-1). No. 6 (ISBN 0-933824-05-X). Nos. 7 & 8 (ISBN 0-933824-06-8). No. 9 (ISBN 0-933824-07-6). No. 10 (ISBN 0-933824-08-4). Nos. 11 & 12 (ISBN 0-933824-09-2). No. 13 (ISBN 0-933824-10-6); No. 14 (ISBN 0-933824-11-4). No. 15 (ISBN 0-933824-12-2). Nos. 16 & 17 (ISBN 0-933824-13-0). No. 18 (ISBN 0-933824-14-9). No. 19 (ISBN 0-933824-15-7). No. 20 (ISBN 0-933824-16-5). No. 21 (ISBN 0-933824-17-3). Vols. 22 & 23 (ISBN 0-933824-18-1). Set. 60.00 (ISBN 0-686-62741-5); single issues 5.00 ea.; double issues 7.00 ea. Parnassos Ny.
DuBoulay, Juliet. Portrait of a Greek Mountain Village. (Oxford Monographs on Social Anthropology). (Illus.). 308p. text ed. 13.50 (ISBN 0-19-823198-9). Oxford U Pr.

GREED

see Avarice

GREEK AMERICANS

Burgess, Thomas. Greeks in America. 1970. Repr. of 1913 ed. 11.00 (ISBN 0-685-40308-4). R & E Res Assoc.
--Greeks in America: An Account of Their Coming, Progress, Customs, Living & Aspirations. LC 72-129392. (American Immigration Collection, Ser. 2). (Illus.). 1970. Repr. of 1913 ed. 14.00 (ISBN 0-405-00547-4). Arno.
Buxbaum, Edwin C. The Greek American Group of Tarpon Springs, Florida: A Study of Ethnic Identification & Acculturation. Cordasco, Francesco, ed. LC 80-843. (American Ethnic Groups Ser.). 1981. lib. bdg. 45.00x (ISBN 0-405-13407-X). Arno.
Costantakos, Chrysie M. The American-Greek Subculture: Process of Continuity. Cordasco, Francesco, ed. LC 80-848. (American Ethnic Groups Ser.). 1981. lib. bdg. 65.00x (ISBN 0-405-13411-8). Arno.
Fenton, Heike & Hecker, Melvin. The Greeks in America: A Chronology & Fact Book. LC 77-93976. (Ethnic Chronology Ser.). 1978. lib. bdg. 8.50 (ISBN 0-379-00531-X). Oceana.
Georgas, Demitra. Greek Settlement of the San Francisco Bay Area: Thesis. LC 76-155643. 1974. soft bdg. 7.00 (ISBN 0-88247-259-3). R & E Res Assoc.
Jones, Jayne C. Greeks in America. rev. ed. LC 68-31504. (In America Bks.). (Illus.). (gr. 5-11). 1977. PLB 6.95g (ISBN 0-8225-0215-1). Lerner Pubns.
Karanikas, Alexander. Hellenes & Hellions: Modern Greek Characters in American Literature. LC 80-27482. 575p. 1981. 24.95 (ISBN 0-252-00792-1). U of Ill Pr.
Kourvetaris, George A. First & Second Generation Greeks in Chicago: An Inquiry into Their Stratification & Mobility Patterns. LC 71-171457. (National Centre of Social Research Monographs). 111p. 1971. 10.00x (ISBN 0-8002-0816-1). Intl Pubns Serv.
Moskos, Charles C., Jr. Greek Americans: Struggle & Success. 1980. text ed. 11.95 (ISBN 0-13-365106-1); pap. text ed. 8.95 (ISBN 0-13-365098-7). P-H.
Saloutos, Theodore. Greeks in America. LC 67-13192. 1967. pap. 2.95 (ISBN 0-8077-2089-5). Tchrs Coll.
Scourby, Alice. Third Generation Greek Americans: A Study of Religious Attitudes. Cordasco, Francesco, ed. LC 80-893. (American Ethnic Groups Ser.). lib. bdg. 14.00x (ISBN 0-405-13454-1). Arno.
Steffanides, G. F. America the Land of My Dreams. 1975. pap. 2.75 (ISBN 0-9600114-3-9). Steffanides.
Stephanides, Marios. The Greeks in Detroit: Authoritarianism - a Critical Analysis of Greek Culture, Personality, Attitudes & Behavior. LC 75-18134. 1975. soft bdg. 9.00 (ISBN 0-685-64834-6). R & E Res Assoc.
Vlachos, Evangelos C. Assimilation of Greeks in the United States. (National Centre of Social Researches Pubns - Greece). 1968. 9.50x (ISBN 0-8002-0667-3). Intl Pubns Serv.

GREEK ANTIQUITIES

see Classical Antiquities

GREEK ARCHITECTURE

see Architecture, Greek

GREEK ART

see Art, Greek

GREEK AUTHORS

see Authors, Greek

GREEK BALLADS AND SONGS

see also Folk-Songs, Greek (Modern)

GREEK CALENDAR

see Calendar, Greek

GREEK CHRONOLOGY

see Chronology, Greek

GREEK CHURCH

see Orthodox Eastern Church, Greek

GREEK CIVILIZATION

see Civilization, Greek; Hellenism

GREEK COSTUME

see Costume–Greece

GREEK CULTUS

see Cultus, Greek

GREEK DRAMA (COLLECTIONS)

Hadas, Moses, ed. Greek Drama. Incl. Agamemnon. Aeschylus; Antigone. Sophocles; Eumenides. Aeschylus; Frogs. Aristophanes; Hippolytus. Euripides; Medea. Euripides; Oedipus, the King. Sophocles; Philoctetes. Sophocles; Trojan Women. Euripides. (Orig.). (gr. 10-12). 1968. pap. 2.95 (ISBN 0-553-14284-4). Bantam.
McLeish, K., tr. Aristophanes: Clouds, Women in Power, Knights. LC 78-51680. (Translations from Greek & Roman Authors). 1980. 28.50 (ISBN 0-521-22009-2); pap. 7.95 (ISBN 0-521-29707-9). Cambridge U Pr.
Seneca, Lucius A. The Tragedies of L. Annaeus Seneca, the Philospher. LC 70-158326. 1976. Repr. of 1702 ed. 37.50 (ISBN 0-404-54136-4). AMS Pr.
Smyth, Herbert W. Aeschylean Tragedy. 59.95 (ISBN 0-87968-582-4). Gordon Pr.

GREEK DRAMA–HISTORY AND CRITICISM

Aristophanes. Aristophanes Plutos, with Commentary. Connor, W. R., ed. LC 78-18582. (Greek Texts & Commentaries Ser.). (Illus., Ger.). 1979. Repr. of 1940 ed. lib. bdg. 24.00x (ISBN 0-405-11425-7). Arno.
Baldry, H. C. The Greek Tragic Theatre. (Illus.). 160p. 1973. pap. 3.95x (ISBN 0-393-00585-2). Norton.
Barnett, Lionel. Greek Drama. LC 73-9662. 1900. lib. bdg. 8.50 (ISBN 0-8414-3143-4). Folcroft.
Barnett, Lionel D. The Greek Drama. 1979. Repr. of 1900 ed. lib. bdg. 15.00 (ISBN 0-8495-0450-3). Arden Lib.
Beede, Grace, ed. Greek Drama. 1967. pap. 4.95 (ISBN 0-88249-000-1). Dakota Pr.
Bieber, Margaret. History of the Greek & Roman Theater. rev. ed. (Illus.). 360p. 1980. 45.00 (ISBN 0-691-03521-0); pap. 15.00 (ISBN 0-691-00212-6). Princeton U Pr.
Bond, Godfrey W., ed. Euripides: Heracles: With Introduction & Commentary. 448p. 1981. 39.00x (ISBN 0-19-814012-6). Oxford U Pr.
Butler, James H. Theatre & Drama of Greece and Rome. LC 74-164495. 1972. pap. text ed. 10.50 scp (ISBN 0-8102-0439-8, HarpC). Har-Row.
Cameron, Howard D. Studies on the Seven Against Thebes of Aeschylus. LC 70-108138. (Studies in Classical Literature: No. 8). (Orig.). 1971. pap. text ed. 20.00x (ISBN 90-2791-614-4). Mouton.
Casaubon, Isaac. De Satyrica Graecorum Poesi & Romanorum Satira. LC 72-13784. 392p. (Lat.). 1973. Repr. of 1605 ed. lib. bdg. 39.00x (ISBN 0-8201-1115-5). Schol Facsimiles.
Collins, Charles W. Greek Love Stories of the Theatre. 1911. 25.00 (ISBN 0-685-84539-7). Norwood Edns.
Dale, A. M. Collected Papers. Webster, T. B. & Turner, E. G., eds. LC 69-10574. 1969. 48.00 (ISBN 0-521-04763-3). Cambridge U Pr.
Devereux, George. Dreams in Greek Tragedy: An Ethno-Psycho-Analytic Study. LC 74-27288. 400p. 1976. 28.50x (ISBN 0-520-02921-6). U of Cal Pr.
Donaldson, John W. The Theatre of the Greeks. LC 72-2095. (Studies in Drama, No. 39). 1972. Repr. of 1890 ed. lib. bdg. 46.95 (ISBN 0-8383-1495-3). Haskell.
Driver, Tom F. The Sense of History in Greek & Shakespearean Drama. LC 59-15146. 1960. pap. 6.00x (ISBN 0-231-08576-1). Columbia U Pr.
Egermann, Franz. Vom Attischen Menschenbild & Arete und Tragisches Bewusstheit Bei Sophokles und Herodot, 2 vols. in ne. Vlastos, Gregory, ed. LC 78-14613. (Morals & Law in Ancient Greece Ser.). (Ger. & Greek.). 1979. Repr. of 1957 ed. lib. bdg. 18.00x (ISBN 0-405-11588-1). Arno.
Flickinger, Roy C. Greek Theater & Its Drama. 4th ed. LC 36-11686. 1960. pap. 17.50x (ISBN 0-226-25369-4). U of Chicago Pr.
Flint, William W. Use of Myth to Create Suspense. (Studies in Comparative Literature, No. 35). 1970. pap. 12.95 (ISBN 0-8383-0030-8). Haskell.
Frye, Prosser H. Romance & Tragedy: A Study of the Classic & Romantic Elements in the Great Tragedies of European Literature. LC 61-10518. (Landmark Edns.). xiv, 372p. 1980. 21.00x (ISBN 0-8032-1955-5). U of Nebr Pr.
Goodell, Thomas D. Athenian Tragedy. LC 75-86018. 1969. Repr. of 1920 ed. 12.50 (ISBN 0-8046-0612-9). Kennikat.
Gould, John. Greek Tragedy. 1982. pap. 3.95 (ISBN 0-14-022100-X, Pelican). Penguin.
Gould, T. & Herington, J., eds. Yale Classical Studies: Greek Tragedy. LC 76-8156. (Yale Classical Studies). 1977. 36.00 (ISBN 0-521-21112-3). Cambridge U Pr.
Greek Poetry & Life: Essays Presented to Gilbert Murray on His Seventieth Birthday, January 2, 1936. facs. ed. LC 67-30192. (Essay Index Reprint Ser). 1936. 18.50 (ISBN 0-8369-0496-6). Arno.
Haigh, A. E. Attic Theatre. 3rd enl. ed. LC 73-94544. Repr. of 1907 ed. 16.00 (ISBN 0-527-37300-1). Kraus Repr.
--The Tragic Drama of the Greeks. 8.75 (ISBN 0-8446-0670-7). Peter Smith.
Haigh, Arthur E. Attic Theatre: A Description of the Stage & Theatre of the Athenians. LC 68-24965. (Studies in Drama, No. 39). (Illus.). 1969. Repr. of 1907 ed. lib. bdg. 53.95 (ISBN 0-8383-0951-8). Haskell.
Harry, Joseph E. Greek Tragic Poets. LC 68-789. (Studies in Poetry, No. 38). 1969. Repr. of 1914 ed. lib. bdg. 49.95 (ISBN 0-8383-0567-9). Haskell.
Harsh, Philip W. A Handbook of Classical Drama. 1944. 18.50x (ISBN 0-8047-0380-9); pap. 5.95 (ISBN 0-8047-0381-7, SP20). Stanford U Pr.
Henderson, J., ed. Aristophanes: Essays in Interpretation. LC 80-40042. (Yale Classical Studies: No. 26). 248p. 1981. 35.00 (ISBN 0-521-23120-5). Cambridge U Pr.
Henderson, Jeffrey. The Maculate Muse: Obscene Language in Attic Comedy. LC 74-82746. 272p. 1975. text ed. 20.00x (ISBN 0-300-01786-3). Yale U Pr.
Jones, John. On Aristotle & Greek Tragedy. LC 80-50895. 288p. 1980. 16.50x (ISBN 0-8047-1092-9); pap. 6.95 (ISBN 0-8047-1093-7, SP11). Stanford U Pr.
Kalechofsky, Roberta. Orestes in Progress. LC 76-12977. 1976. pap. 4.44x (ISBN 0-916288-02-1). Micah Pubns.
Kirk, G. S. The Bacchae of Euripides. LC 78-31827. 1979. 21.95 (ISBN 0-521-22675-9); pap. 5.50x (ISBN 0-521-29613-7). Cambridge U Pr.

Kitto, H. D. Form & Meaning in Drama: A Study of Six Greek Plays & of Hamlet. 2nd ed. 1979. pap. text ed. 10.95x (ISBN 0-416-67520-4). Methuen Inc.

Kitto, Humphrey D. Greek Tragedy: A Literary Study. 3rd rev. ed. 1966. pap. 12.95x (ISBN 0-416-68900-0). Methuen Inc.

Lattimore, Richmond. The Poetry of Greek Tragedy. 160p. 1958. 11.00x (ISBN 0-8018-0364-0). Johns Hopkins.

--Story Patterns in Greek Tragedy. 1964. pap. 1.95 (ISBN 0-472-06146-1, 146, AA). U of Mich Pr.

Legrand, Philippe E. New Greek Comedy. Loeb, James, tr. Repr. of 1917 ed. lib. bdg. 22.00x (ISBN 0-8371-3122-7, LEGC). Greenwood.

Lesky, Albin. Greek Tragedy. 3rd ed. LC 78-18440. 1979. pap. 7.95x (ISBN 0-06-494192-2). B&N.

Little, Alan M. Myth & Society in Attic Drama. 1967. lib. bdg. 8.50x (ISBN 0-374-95054-7). Octagon.

Loehrer, Robert. Mienenspiel und Maske in der Griechischen Tragodie. Repr. of 1927 ed. 12.50 (ISBN 0-384-33370-2). Johnson Repr.

McLeish, Kenneth. The Greek Theatre. (Aspects of Greek Life Ser.). (Illus.). 1972. pap. text ed. 2.95x (ISBN 0-582-34400-X). Longman.

Mastronarde, Donald. Contact & Discontinuity: Some Conventions of Speech & Action on the Greek Tragic Stage. (University of California Publications in Classical Studies: Vol. 21). 1979. pap. 16.00x (ISBN 0-520-09601-0). U of Cal Pr.

Mette, Hans J. Urkunden Dramatischer Auffuehrungen in Griechenland. (Texte und Kommentare: Vol. 8). 1977. 79.50x (ISBN 3-11-006782-X). De Gruyter.

Miller, Walter. Daedalus & Thespis: Volume II: Sculpture, Pts. 1 & 2. Repr. of 1931 ed. 10.00x (ISBN 0-8262-0590-9). U of Mo Pr.

Mueller, Martin. Children of Oedipus & Other Essays on the Imitation of Greek Tragedy Fifteen Fifty to Eighteen Hundred. 1980. 25.00x (ISBN 0-8020-5478-1); pap. 12.50 (ISBN 0-8020-6381-0). U of Toronto Pr.

Nietzsche, Friedrich. The Birth of Tragedy. Kaufmann, Walter, tr. Bd. with The Case of Wagner. (Orig.). 1967. pap. 2.95 (ISBN 0-394-70369-3, Vin). Random.

Prentice, William K. Those Ancient Dramas Called Tragedies. LC 78-75467. (Illus.). 1969. Repr. of 1942 ed. 9.50 (ISBN 0-8462-1339-7). Russell.

Reardon, A. A Study of Humor in Greek Tragedy. 59.95 (ISBN 0-8490-1153-1). Gordon Pr.

Reinhold, Meyer. Barron's Simplified Approach to Ten Greek Tragedies. LC 65-16321. (Orig.). 1965. pap. 1.50 (ISBN 0-8120-0188-5). Barron.

Ridgeway, William. Dramas & Dramatic Dances of Non-European Races. LC 63-23187. (Illus.). Repr. of 1910 ed. 25.00 (ISBN 0-405-08889-2, Blom Pubns). Arno.

--Origin of Tragedy. LC 65-19621. (Illus.). 1910. 15.00 (ISBN 0-405-08891-4, Blom Pubns). Arno.

Robinson, Cyril E. The Genius of the Greek Drama. 1921. 10.00 (ISBN 0-685-84589-3). Norwood Edns.

Romilly, Jacqueline de. Time in Greek Tragedy. LC 68-16380. 1968. 17.50x (ISBN 0-8014-0361-8). Cornell U Pr.

Rosenmeyer, Thomas G. Masks of Tragedy, Essays on Six Greek Dramas. LC 78-150417. 1971. Repr. of 1963 ed. text ed. 10.00 (ISBN 0-87752-140-9). Gordian.

Sandbach, F. H. The Comic Theatre of Greece & Rome. Finley, M. I., ed. (Ancient Culture & Society Ser.). 1977. 9.95x (ISBN 0-393-04483-1). Norton.

Sarma, M. V. The Eagle & the Phoenix. 108p. 1980. pap. text ed. 3.00x (ISBN 0-391-01914-7). Humanities.

Sheppard, J. T. Greek Tragedy. LC 73-4010. Repr. of 1920 ed. lib. bdg. 15.00 (ISBN 0-8414-7514-8). Folcroft.

Snell, Bruno. Scenes from Greek Drama. (Sather Classical Lectures: No. 34). 1964. 24.00x (ISBN 0-520-01191-0). U of Cal Pr.

Tapin, Oliver. The Stagecraft of Aeschylus: The Dramatic Use of Exists and Entrances in Greek Tragedy. 1978. 69.00x (ISBN 0-19-814006-1). Oxford U Pr.

Taplin, Oliver. Greek Tragedy in Action. 1979. 24.75x (ISBN 0-520-03704-9); pap. 4.95 (ISBN 0-520-03949-1). U of Cal Pr.

Thomson, George. Aeschylus & Athens. LC 67-30819. (Studies in Drama, No. 39). (Illus.). 1969. Repr. of 1940 ed. lib. bdg. 39.95 (ISBN 0-8383-0723-X). Haskell.

--Aeschylus & Athens: A Study of Athenian Drama & Democracy. 4th ed. 374p. 1974. 15.95x (ISBN 0-8464-0119-3); pap. 11.95x (ISBN 0-8464-0120-7). Beekman Pubs.

Walton, J. Michael. Greek Theatre Practice. LC 79-8580. (Contributions in Drama & Theatre Studies: No. 3). (Illus.). viii, 237p. 1980. lib. bdg. 23.95 (ISBN 0-313-22043-3, WGT/). Greenwood.

Watt, Laughlan M. Attic & Elizabethan Tragedy. LC 67-27661. 1968. Repr. of 1908 ed. 14.00 (ISBN 0-8046-0490-8). Kennikat.

Webster, T. Birth of Modern Comedy of Manners, No. 1. (Australian Humanities Research Council Occasional Paper Ser.: No. 1). 1959. pap. 2.00x (ISBN 0-424-05690-9, Pub. by Sydney U Pr). Intl Schol Bk Serv.

Webster, T. B. The Birth of Modern Comedy of Manners. LC 74-32030. 1959. lib. bdg. 8.50 (ISBN 0-8414-9369-3). Folcroft.

Webster, Thomas B. Studies in Later Greek Comedy. LC 81-5016. (Illus.). xiv, 282p. 1981. Repr. of 1970 ed. lib. bdg. 27.50x (ISBN 0-313-23050-1, WESL). Greenwood.

GREEK DRAMA–PRESENTATION, ANCIENT

see Theater–Greece

GREEK DRAMA–STORIES, PLOTS, ETC.

Reinhold, Meyer. Classical Drama, Greek & Roman. (Orig., Summaries, Critiques). (gr. 11 up). 1959. 6.00 (ISBN 0-8120-5018-5); pap. 2.95 (ISBN 0-8120-0042-0). Barron.

GREEK DRAMA–TRANSLATIONS INTO ENGLISH

Campbell, Lewis. A Guide to Greek Tragedy for English Readers. 1980. lib. bdg. 75.00 (ISBN 0-8490-3200-8). Gordon Pr.

Fitts, Dudley & MacNeice, Louis, trs. Four Greek Plays. Incl. Agamemnon. Aeschylus; Oedipus Rex. Sophocles; Alcestis. Euripides; The Birds. Aristophanes. LC 60-1871. 310p. 1960. pap. 3.95 (ISBN 0-15-632777-5, HB33, Harv). HarBraceJ.

Grene, David & Lattimore, Richmond, eds. Greek Tragedies. Incl. Vol. 1. Agamemnon, Prometheus Bound, Oedipus the King, Antigone. 1960. pap. 4.50 (ISBN 0-226-30774-3, P41); Vol. 2. The Libation Bearers, Electra (Sophocles), Iphigenia in Tauris, Electra (Euripides), the Trojan Women. 1960. pap. text ed. 3.95 (ISBN 0-226-30775-1, P42); Vol. 3. The Eumenides, Philoctetes, Oedipus at Colonus, the Bacchae, Alcestis. 1960. pap. text ed. 3.95 (ISBN 0-226-30777-8, P43). LC 60-950. 1960 (Phoen). U of Chicago Pr.

Hamilton, Edith, tr. Three Greek Plays: The Trojan Women of Euripedes & Prometheus Bound & Aggamemnon of Aeschylus. 1958. pap. 4.95 (ISBN 0-393-00203-9, Norton Lib). Norton.

Lind, Levi R., ed. Ten Greek Plays in Contemporary Translations. Incl. Prometheus Bound. Aeschylus; Agamemnon. Aeschylus; Antigone. Sophocles; Oedipus Rex. Sophocles; Philoctetes. Sophocles; Alcestis. Euripides; Suppliants. Euripides; Andromache. Euripides; Bacchae. Euripides; Lysistrata. Aristophanes. LC 57-59175. (YA) (gr. 9up). 1957. pap. 3.95 (ISBN 0-395-05117-7, C19, RivEd, 3-47653). HM.

Lowell, Robert, tr. Orestia of Aeschylus. 129p. 1978. 8.95 (ISBN 0-374-22723-3); pap. 6.95 (ISBN 0-374-51549-2). FS&G.

Oates, Whitney J. & O'Neill, Eugene, Jr., eds. Seven Famous Greek Plays. Incl. Prometheus Bound. Aeschylus; Agamemnon. Aeschylus; Oedipus the King. Sophocles; Medea. Euripides; Frogs. Aristophanes; Antigone. Sophocles; Alcestis. Euripides. 1955. pap. 3.45 (ISBN 0-394-70125-9, Vin). Random.

Robinson, Charles A., Jr., ed. Anthology of Greek Drama, Vol. 1. Incl. Agamemnon. Aeschylus; Oedipus Rex. Sophocles; Antigone. Sophocles; Medea. Euripides; Hippolytus. Euripides; Lysistrata. Aristophanes. LC 49-48280. (Rinehart Editions). 1949. pap. text ed. 7.50 (ISBN 0-03-009415-1, HoltC). HR&W.

Sophocles. Three Tragedies: Antigone, Oedipus the King, & Electra. Kitto, H. D., tr. from Gr. 1962. pap. text ed. 3.95x (ISBN 0-19-500374-8). Oxford U Pr.

GREEK EDUCATION

see Education, Greek

GREEK ESTHETICS

see Esthetics, Greek

GREEK ETHICS

see Ethics, Greek

GREEK FICTION–HISTORY AND CRITICISM

Glover, Terrot R. Life & Letters in the Fourth Century. LC 68-10923. 1968. Repr. of 1901 ed. 11.00 (ISBN 0-8462-1065-7). Russell.

Haight, Elizabeth H. Essays on Ancient Fiction. facs. ed. LC 67-22097. (Essay Index Reprint Ser). 1936. 12.25 (ISBN 0-8369-0506-7). Arno.

Perry, Ben E. The Ancient Romances: A Literary-Historical Account of Their Origins. (Sather Classical Lectures: No. 37). 1967. 24.50x (ISBN 0-520-01003-5). U of Cal Pr.

Todd, Frederick A. Some Ancient Novels. facs. ed. LC 68-29250. (Essay Index Reprint Ser). 1968. Repr. of 1940 ed. 13.00 (ISBN 0-8369-0947-X). Arno.

GREEK FIRE

Spears, W. H., Jr. Greek Fire: The Fabulous Secret Weapon That Saved Europe. LC 69-19967. 1969. 4.95 (ISBN 0-9600106-3-7). Spears.

GREEK FOLK-LORE

see Folk-Lore, Greek; Folk-Lore, Greek (Modern)

GREEK FOLK-SONGS

see Folk-Songs, Greek (Modern)

GREEK HISTORIANS

Austin, Norman. The Greek Historians: Introduction & Selected Readings. 6.50 (ISBN 0-8446-0466-6). Peter Smith.

Austin, Norman, ed. Greek Historians. (Orig.). 1969. pap. text ed. 8.95x (ISBN 0-442-00369-2). Van Nos Reinhold.

Cochrane, Charles N. Thucydides & the Science of History. LC 65-17885. 1965. Repr. of 1929 ed. 7.50 (ISBN 0-8462-0591-2). Russell.

Fritz, Kurt Von. Griechische Geschichtsschreibung: Von Den Anfaengen Bis Thukydides, Vol. 1. (Ger). 1967. 91.50 (ISBN 3-11-005167-2). De Gruyter.

Kagan, D., ed. Studies in the Greek Historians. LC 74-12982. (Yale Classical Studies: No. 24). 256p. 1975. 36.00 (ISBN 0-521-20587-5). Cambridge U Pr.

Muller, K. The Fragments of the Lost Historians of Alexander the Great. 162p. 1979. 35.00 (ISBN 0-89005-273-5). Ares.

Stadter, Philip A. Arrian of Nicomedia. LC 79-938. 1980. 18.50x (ISBN 0-8078-1364-8). U of NC Pr.

Usher, Stephen. Historians of Greece & Rome. LC 72-97192. 1970. 6.50 (ISBN 0-8008-3845-9). Taplinger.

GREEK HYMNS

see Hymns, Greek

GREEK INSCRIPTIONS

see Inscriptions, Greek

GREEK LANGUAGE

see also Classical Philology; Greek Philology; Hellenism; Inscriptions, Greek

Assimil. Assimil Language Courses: For French Speaking People Who Want to Learn Greek - Le Grec Sans Peine. 11.95 (ISBN 0-686-56076-0); accompanying records & tapes 75.00 (ISBN 0-686-56077-9). French & Eur.

Bardis, Panos D. The Future of the Greek Language in the United States. LC 75-36574. 1976. softbound 8.00 (ISBN 0-88247-396-4). R & E Res Assoc.

Beekes, R. S. Development of the Proto-Indo-European Laryngeals in Greek. (Janua Linguarum, Ser. Practica: No. 42). 1969. pap. text ed. 68.25x (ISBN 90-2790-693-9). Mouton.

Bien, Peter, et al. Workbook for Demotic Greek. 104p. 1973. pap. text ed. 3.00x (ISBN 0-87451-090-2). U Pr of New Eng.

Ellis, C. Douglas & Schachter, Albert. Ancient Greek: A Structural Programme. (Illus.). 1528p. 1973. wkbk. 18.00x (ISBN 0-7735-0196-7). McGill-Queens U Pr.

Foulkes, Irene. Griego del Nuevo Testamento: Texto Programado, Tomo III. 220p. (Span.). 1973. pap. text ed. 7.00 (ISBN 0-89922-054-1). Edit Caribe.

--Griego del Nuevo Testamento: Texto Programado, Tomo II. 203p. (Span.). 1973. pap. 7.00 (ISBN 0-89922-053-3). Edit Caribe.

--Griego del Nuevo Testamento: Texto Programado, Tomo I. 194p. (Span.). 1973. pap. 7.00 (ISBN 0-89922-052-5). Edit Caribe.

Gonda, Jan. Character of the Indo-European Moods, with Special Regard to Greek & Sanskrit. LC 56-5976. 220p. 1956. 48.50x (ISBN 3-447-00344-8). Intl Pubns Serv.

Humez, Alexander & Humez, Nicholas. Alpha to Omega: The Life & Times of the Greek Alphabet. 1981. 13.95 (ISBN 0-87923-377-X). Godine.

Joint Association of Classical Teachers. Greek Vocabulary. 1980. pap. 5.95 (ISBN 0-521-23277-5). Cambridge U Pr.

Levin, Saul. Indo-European & Semitic Languages: An Exploration of Structural Similarities Related to Accent, Chiefly in Greek, Sanskrit, & Hebrew. LC 67-28937. (Illus.). 1971. 47.00 (ISBN 0-87395-055-0); microfiche 47.00 (ISBN 0-87395-155-7). State U NY Pr.

Nagy, Gregory. Greek Dialects & the Transformation of an Indo-European Process. LC 69-12730. (Loeb Classical Monographs Ser). 1970. text ed. 10.00x (ISBN 0-674-36226-8). Harvard U Pr.

Palmer, L. R. The Greek Language. (Great Language Ser.). 1980. text ed. 57.50x (ISBN 0-391-01203-7). Humanities.

Rice, Allan L. Gothic Prepositional Compounds in Their Relation to the Greek Originals. 1932. pap. 8.00 (ISBN 0-527-00757-9). Kraus Repr.

Standerwick, H. F. Etymological Studies in the Greek Dialect Inscriptions. 1932. pap. 6.00 (ISBN 0-527-00756-0). Kraus Repr.

Stanford, W. B. The Sound of Greek: Studies in the Greek Theory & Practice of Euphony. (Sather Classical Lectures: No. 38). (YA) (gr. 9 up). 1967. 25.75x (ISBN 0-520-01204-6). U of Cal Pr.

Stanford, William B. Ambiguity in Greek Literature. xii, 185p. Repr. of 1939 ed. 19.50 (ISBN 0-384-57472-6). Johnson Repr.

--Greek Metaphor. xi, 156p. Repr. of 1936 ed. 18.50 (ISBN 0-384-57474-2). Johnson Repr.

Thumb, Albert. Handbuch der Neugriechischen Volkssprache. Grammatik, Texte, Glossar. 2nd ed. xxxii, 359p. 1974. Repr. of 1910 ed. 53.50x (ISBN 3-11-003340-2). De Gruyter.

Warburton, Irene P. On the Verb in Modern Greek. LC 68-65316. (Language Science Monographs: Vol. 4). (Illus., Orig.). 1970. pap. text ed. 10.00x (ISBN 0-87750-151-3). Res Ctr Lang Semiotic.

Wilding, L. A. Greek for Beginners. (gr. 7-12). text ed. 8.95 (ISBN 0-571-10402-9). Transatlantic.

GREEK LANGUAGE–ACCENTS AND ACCENTIVATION

Chandler, H. W. A Practical Introduction to Greek Accentuation. rev. 2nd ed. (College Classical Ser.). xxxiii, 292p. 1981. Repr. of 1881 ed. lib. bdg. 25.00x (ISBN 0-89241-112-0). Caratzas Bros.

Laum, Bernhard. Das Alexandrinische Akzentuationssystem Unter Zugrundelegung der Theoretischen Lehren der Grammatik. Repr. of 1928 ed. pap. 34.00 (ISBN 0-384-31620-4). Johnson Repr.

GREEK LANGUAGE–COMPOSITION AND EXERCISES

Chase, Alston H. & Phillips, Henry, Jr. New Introduction to Greek. 3rd ed. rev. & enl ed. LC 61-13748. (Illus.). 1961. 10.00x (ISBN 0-674-61600-6). Harvard U Pr.

Goodrick, Edward W. Do It Yourself Hebrew & Greek: Everybody's Guide to the Language Tools. 256p. (Orig.). 1980. pap. 9.95 (ISBN 0-310-41741-4). Zondervan.

Hayes, Walter M. Introductory Greek Program, 5 bks. 1966. pap. text ed. 15.00 with panels, post-tests, key, text aids (ISBN 0-8294-0130-X); 26 tapes 130.00 (ISBN 0-685-56942-X). Loyola.

Luschnig, C. A. E. Introduction to Ancient Greek. LC 76-17427. 1976. pap. text ed. 13.95x (ISBN 0-684-14710-6, ScribC). Scribner.

North, M. A. & Hillard, A. E. Greek Prose Composition. 2nd ed. 272p. 1978. 20.00x (ISBN 0-7156-1283-2, Pub. by Duckworth England); pap. 10.95x (ISBN 0-7156-1284-0, Pub. by Duckworth England). Biblio Dist.

Sidgwick, A. Introduction to Greek Prose Composition. (College Classical Ser). 1977. text ed. 12.50 (ISBN 0-89241-028-0). Caratzas Bros.

GREEK LANGUAGE–CONVERSATION AND PHRASE BOOKS

Constantinon, P. How to Say It in Modern Greek. 7.50 (ISBN 0-87559-171-X). Shalom.

Cortina Company. Conversational Modern Greek in Twenty Lessons. 288p. 1980. pap. 4.95 (ISBN 0-06-463604-6, EH 604, EH). Har-Row.

Holoway Staff. Greek. (Harper Phrase Books for the Traveler Ser.). (Orig.). 1977. pap. 1.00 (ISBN 0-8467-0311-4, Holloway). Hippocrene Bks.

Stangos, Nikos & Norman, Jillian. Greek Phrase Book. 5.00 (ISBN 0-8446-5248-2). Peter Smith.

Stern, A. Z. & Reif, Joseph A., eds. Useful Expressions in Greek. (Useful Expressions Ser.). 64p. (Orig.). 1980. pap. 2.00 (ISBN 0-86628-008-1). Ridgefield Pub.

GREEK LANGUAGE–DIALECTS

Buck, Carl D. Greek Dialects. 3rd ed. LC 55-5115. (Midway Reprint Ser). 1973. 17.00x (ISBN 0-226-07934-1). U of Chicago Pr.

Dawkins, Richard M. Modern Greek in Asia Minor. LC 78-67703. (The Folktale). Repr. of 1916 ed. 49.50 (ISBN 0-404-16077-8). AMS Pr.

Newton, B. The Generative Interpretation of Dialect: A Study of Modern Greek Phonology. LC 72-187080. (Studies in Linguistics: No. 8). (Illus.). 240p. 1973. 35.00 (ISBN 0-521-08497-0); pap. 11.95x (ISBN 0-521-29062-7). Cambridge U Pr.

Standerwick, H. F. Etymological Studies in the Greek Dialect Inscriptions. 1932. pap. 6.00 (ISBN 0-527-00756-0). Kraus Repr.

GREEK LANGUAGE–DICTIONARIES

Alexis de Sommevoire & Tomaso Da Parigi. Tesoro Della Linqua Greca-Volgare Ed Italiana, cioe Ricchissimo dizzionario greco-volgare et italiano, 2 vols. (Gr. & Ital.). 1981. Repr. of 1709 ed. lib. bdg. 175.00x (ISBN 0-686-72425-9). Pt. 1, Italian-Greek, Viii, 513 Pages. Pt. 2, Greek-Italian, Xxviii, 461 Pages. Caratzas Bros.

Bailly, Anatole. Dictionnaire Abrege Grec-Francais. 1012p. (Gr.-Fr.). 1969. pap. 22.95 (ISBN 0-686-56906-7, M-6019). French & Eur.
--Dictionnaire Grec-Francais. 2230p. (Gr.-Fr.). 1967. pap. 47.50 (ISBN 0-686-56907-5, M-6020). French & Eur.
Bauer, Walter. Griechisch-Deutsches Woerterbuch zu den Schriften des Neuen Testaments und der uebrigen urchristlichen Literatur. 5th rev. ed. (Ger). 1963. Repr. 61.00x (ISBN 3-11-002073-4). De Gruyter.
Buck, Carl D. & Petersen, Walter. A Reverse Index of Greek Nouns & Adjectives. (Midway Reprint Ser.). xviii, 766p. 1975. pap. text ed. 28.00x (ISBN 0-226-07936-8). U of Chicago Pr.
Chrysovitsiotis, I. Greek-English, English Greek Technical Dictionary. 2nd rev ed. 45.00 (ISBN 0-685-79112-2). Heinman.
Frisk, Hjalmar. Griechisches Etymologisches Woerterbuch, Vol. 1. (Gr. & Ger.). 1960. 95.00 (ISBN 3-533-00652-2, M-7434, Pub. by Carl Winter). French & Eur.
--Griechisches Etymologisches Woerterbuch, Vol. 2. (Gr. & Ger.). 1960. 132.00 (ISBN 3-533-00653-0, M-7435, Pub. by Carl Winter). French & Eur.
--Griechisches Etymologisches Woerterbuch, Vol. 3. (Gr. & Ger.). 1972. 45.00 (ISBN 3-533-02203-X, M-7436, Pub. by Carl Winter). French & Eur.
Georgin, Ch. Dictionnaire Grec-Francais. (Gr.-Fr.). pap. 14.95 (ISBN 0-686-57194-0, M-6268). French & Eur.
Hebrew-Aramaic & Greek Dictionary: The New American Standard Exhaustive Concordance of the Bible. 34.95 (ISBN 0-87981-197-8, 4690-98). Holman.
Hoffman, Horace Addison. Everyday Greek: Greek Words in English, Including Scientific Terms. (Midway Reprint). 1976. pap. 7.50x (ISBN 0-226-34787-7). U of Chicago Pr.
Lampe, G. W., ed. Patristic Greek Lexicon Nineteen Sixty-One to Sixty-Eight. 185.00x (ISBN 0-19-864213-X). Oxford U Pr.
Langenscheidt's Lilliput Greek-English Dictionary. 1972. 1.50 (ISBN 0-685-87395-1). Hippocrene Bks.
Liddell, H. G. & Scott, Robert, eds. Abridged Greek-English Lexicon. 1957. 24.95x (ISBN 0-19-910207-4). Oxford U Pr.
--Intermediate Greek-English Lexicon. 1959. text ed. 29.00x (ISBN 0-19-910206-6). Oxford U Pr.
Liddell, Henry G. & Scott, Robert. Greek-English Lexicon: A Supplement. Barber, E. A., et al, eds. 1968. 29.00x (ISBN 0-19-864210-5). Oxford U Pr.
Liddell, Henry G. & Scott, Robert, eds. Greek-English Lexicon. 9th ed. 1940. 79.00 (ISBN 0-19-864214-8). Oxford U Pr.
Moulton, Harold K., ed. The Analytical Greek Lexicon Revised. rev. ed. 1978. 14.95 (ISBN 0-310-20280-9). Zondervan.
Pabon, Jose M. Vox--Diccionario Manual Griego-Espanol. 11th ed. 724p. (Grie. -Espn.). 1979. leatherette 17.25 (ISBN 84-7153-192-5, S-12136). French & Eur.
Patsis, C. Greek-English, English Greek Dictionary, 2 vols. Set. 50.00 (ISBN 0-685-79111-4). Heinman.
Pessoneaux, Emile. Dictionnaire Grec-Francais. 896p. (Fr.-Gr.). 1953. 35.95 (ISBN 0-686-57071-5, M-6443). French & Eur.
Robinson, Maurice A., compiled by. Indexes to All Editions of Brown-Driver-Briggs Hebrew Lexicon & Thayer's Greek Lexicon. 1981. pap. 5.95 (ISBN 0-8010-7712-5). Baker Bk.
Stehle, Matthias. Greek Word Building. LC 76-14405. (Society of Biblical Literature). 1976. pap. 6.00 (ISBN 0-89130-108-9, 060310). Scholars Pr Ca.
Wharton, E. R. Etymological Lexicon of Classical Greek. LC 74-7787. 192p. 1975. Repr. 10.00 (ISBN 0-89005-033-3). Ares.

GREEK LANGUAGE-GLOSSARIES, VOCABULARIES, ETC.

Cheadle, John R. Basic Greek Vocabulary. 1939. text ed. 4.50 (ISBN 0-312-06790-9). St Martin.
Dornseiff, F. & Hansen, Bernard. Reverse Lexicon of Greek Proper Names. 1978. Repr. 25.00 (ISBN 0-89005-251-4). Ares.
McCulloch, James A. Medical Greek & Latin Workbook. 174p. 1977. pap. 8.50 (ISBN 0-398-01249-0). C C Thomas.
Stangos, Nikos & Norman, Jill. Greek Phrase Book. 256p. 1975. pap. 2.95 (ISBN 0-14-003559-1). Penguin.
Taylor, B. C. The Greeks Had a Word for It. 1973. pap. text ed. 2.00x (ISBN 0-8077-8018-9). Tchrs Coll.

GREEK LANGUAGE-GRAMMAR

Abbott, Evelyn & Mansfield, E. D. Primer of Greek Grammar. 246p. 1977. 20.00x (ISBN 0-7156-1257-3, Pub. by Duckworth England); pap. 10.95x (ISBN 0-7156-1258-1, Pub. by Duckworth England). Biblio Dist.
Allen, James T. First Year of Greek. rev. ed. 1931. text ed. 15.95x (ISBN 0-685-15120-4). Macmillan.
Belmont, David E. Approaching Greek. LC 76-47861. 1976. 19.75 (ISBN 0-8357-0190-5, SS-00019). Univ Microfilms.
Eklund, Bo-Lennart. Modern Greek: Verbal Aspect & Compound Nouns. (Acta Regiae Societatis Scientiarm et Litterarum Gothoburgensis, Humaniora: No. 11). 1976. pap. text ed. 5.75x (ISBN 91-85252-08-5). Humanities.
Fobes, Francis H. Philosophical Greek: An Introduction. LC 57-8580. 1957. pap. 15.00x (ISBN 0-226-25620-0). U of Chicago Pr.
Friedman, Victor A. The Grammatical Categories of the Macedonian Indicative. 1977. pap. 9.95 (ISBN 0-89357-042-7). Slavica.
Goodwin, W. W. & Gulick, Charles B. Greek Grammar. (College Classical Ser.). 460p. (gr. 11-12). 22.50 (ISBN 0-89241-118-X); pap. text ed. 12.50x (ISBN 0-89241-332-8). Caratzas Bros.
Goodwin, William W. Greek Grammar. 2nd ed. 1879. 14.95 (ISBN 0-312-34825-8). St Martin.
Joint Association of Classical Teachers. Reading Greek: Grammar, Vocabulary & Exercises. LC 77-91090. 1978. 10.95x (ISBN 0-521-21977-9). Cambridge U Pr.
--Reading Greek: Grammar, Vocabulary & Exercises. LC 77-91090. 1978. 10.95x (ISBN 0-521-21977-9). Cambridge U Pr.
Jones, Frank P. Ab Urbe Condita Construction in Greek, a Study of the Classification of the Participle. 1939. pap. 6.00 (ISBN 0-527-00774-9). Kraus Repr.
Marinone, N. & Guala, F. Complete Handbook of Greek Verbs. 353p. (YA) 1972. 9.95 (ISBN 0-685-20228-3). Schoenhof.
Mayor, Henry B. Primer of Attic Greek. 2nd ed. 1951. 4.50 (ISBN 0-312-64435-3). St Martin.
Paine, Stephen W. Beginning Greek: A Functional Approach. (YA) (gr. 9 up). 1961. 10.95x (ISBN 0-19-501013-2). Oxford U Pr.
Pharr, Clyde. Homeric Greek: A Book for Beginners. (Illus.). (YA) (gr. 9 up). 1980. Repr. of 1959 ed. 8.95x (ISBN 0-8061-1275-1). U of Okla Pr.
Smyth, Herbert W. Greek Grammar. rev. ed. Messing, Gordon M., ed. LC 57-2203. (gr. 10 up). 18.50x (ISBN 0-674-36250-0). Harvard U Pr.
Veitch, William. Greek Verbs, Irregular & Defective. 1967. Repr. of 1887 ed. 85.00 (ISBN 3-4870-1736-9). Adler.
Wilding, L. A. Greek for Beginners. (gr. 7-12). text ed. 8.95 (ISBN 0-571-10402-9). Transatlantic.

GREEK LANGUAGE-GRAMMAR, COMPARATIVE-LATIN

Buck, Carl D. Comparative Grammar of Greek & Latin. LC 33-11254. 1933. 22.00x (ISBN 0-226-07931-7). U of Chicago Pr.

GREEK LANGUAGE-GRAMMAR, HISTORICAL

Jannaris, Antonius N. Historical Greek Grammar. 1968. Repr. of 1897 ed. 94.00 (ISBN 3-4870-1636-2). Adler.

GREEK LANGUAGE-HISTORY

Costas, Procope S. An Outline History of the Greek Language. 1978. 15.00 (ISBN 0-89005-259-X). Ares.
Furnee, Edzard J. Die Wichtigsten Konsonantischen Erscheinungen Des Vorgriechischen Mit Einem Appendix Uber Den Vokalismus. (Janua Linguarum Ser: No. 150). 1972. pap. 80.00x (ISBN 90-2791-997-6). Mouton.
Gazes, Anthimos, ed. Lexikon tes Hellenikes Glosses Tritomon: Lexicon of the Greek Language in Three Volumes, 3 vols. 2627p. (Greek.). 1980. Repr. of 1835 ed. lib. bdg. 450.00x (ISBN 0-89241-136-8). Caratzas Bros.
Peabody, Berkley. The Winged Word. LC 72-91200. 1975. 44.00 (ISBN 0-87395-059-3); microfiche 44.00 (ISBN 0-87395-159-X). State U NY Pr.
Shipp, G. Essays in Mycenaean & Homeric Greek. 1961. pap. 3.00x (ISBN 0-424-05530-9, Pub. by Sydney U Pr). Intl Schol Bk Serv.
Teodorsson, Sven-Tage. The Phonology of Ptolemaic Koine. (Studia Graeca et Latina Gothoburgensia: No. 37). 1977. text ed. 40.50x (ISBN 91-7346-035-4). Humanities.
Valckenaer, L. C. Observationes Academicae. (Linguistics, 13th-18th Centuries Ser.). 97p. (Fr.). 1974. Repr. of 1805 ed. lib. bdg. 34.50x (ISBN 0-8287-0846-0, 5053). Clearwater Pub.
Van Lennep, J. D. Etymologicum Linguae Graecae, 2 vols. (Linguistics, 13th-18th Centuries Ser.). (Fr.). 1974. Repr. of 1790 ed. Set. lib. bdg. 337.50x (ISBN 0-8287-0849-5). Clearwater Pub.
--Praelectiones Academicae de Analogia Linguae Graecae, Sive Rationum Analogicarum Linguae Graecae Expositio. (Linguistics, 13th-18th Centuries Ser.). 520p. (Latin.). 1974. Repr. of 1805 ed. lib. bdg. 128.50x (ISBN 0-8287-0850-9, 5057). Clearwater Pub.

GREEK LANGUAGE-METRICS AND RHYTHMICS

Allen, W. Sidney. Accent & Rhythm: Prosodic Features of Latin & Greek. LC 72-91361. (Studies in Linguistics). 432p. 1973. 57.50 (ISBN 0-521-20098-9). Cambridge U Pr.
Georgiades, Thrasybulos. Greek Music, Verse & Dance. LC 73-4336. 156p. 1973. Repr. of 1955 ed. lib. bdg. 17.50 (ISBN 0-306-70561-3). Da Capo.
Lattimore, Richmond. The Poetry of Greek Tragedy. 160p. 1958. 11.00x (ISBN 0-8018-0364-0). Johns Hopkins.
Nagy, Gregory. Comparative Studies in Greek & Indic Meter. LC 73-90339. (Studies in Comparative Literature: Monograph No. 1). 360p. 1974. 16.50x (ISBN 0-674-15275-1). Harvard U Pr.
Rosenmeyer, Thomas W., et al. Meters of Greek & Latin Poetry. LC 62-21264. (Orig.). 1973. pap. text ed. 4.95x (ISBN 0-672-60328-4). Irvington.

GREEK LANGUAGE-PRONUNCIATION

Allen, W. Sidney. Vox Graeca. 2nd ed. (Illus.). 1968. 15.95x (ISBN 0-521-20626-X). Cambridge U Pr.
Drerup, Engelbert. Die Schulaussprache Des Griechischen Von der Renaissance Bis Zur Gegenwart, 2 Vols. 1930-32. Vol. 6. pap. 31.00 (ISBN 0-384-12825-4); Vol. 7. pap. 34.00 (ISBN 0-384-12830-0). Johnson Repr.
Sturtevant, E. H. The Pronunciation of Greek & Latin. pap. 6.00 (ISBN 0-89005-087-2). Ares.
Sturtevant, Edgar H. The Pronunciation of Greek & Latin. 2d ed. LC 77-1194. (William Dwight Whitney Linguistic Ser.). 1977. Repr. of 1940 ed. lib. bdg. 14.25x (ISBN 0-8371-9516-0, STPRO). Greenwood.
Teodorsson, Sven-Tage. The Phonology of Attic in the Hellenistic Period. (Studia Graeca et Latina Goteborg: No. 40). (Illus.). 1978. pap. text ed. 22.50x (ISBN 91-7346-060-5). Humanities.

GREEK LANGUAGE-READERS

Balme, M. G. & Warman, M. S. Aestimanda: Practical Criticism of Latin & Greek Poetry & Prose. 1965. pap. 6.95 (ISBN 0-19-831766-2). Oxford U Pr.
Chase, Alston H. & Phillips, Henry, Jr., eds. New Greek Reader. LC 54-12234. (Illus.). (gr. 10 up). 1954. pap. text ed. 12.00x (ISBN 0-674-61550-6). Harvard U Pr.
Fobes, Francis H. Philosophical Greek: An Introduction. LC 57-8580. 1957. pap. 15.00x (ISBN 0-226-25620-0). U of Chicago Pr.
Freeman, C. E. & Lowe, W. D., eds. Greek Reader for Schools. 1917. pap. 5.95x (ISBN 0-19-831831-6). Oxford U Pr.
Herodotus. Herodotus, Book 6: Erato. Shuckburgh, E. S., ed. text ed. 9.95x (ISBN 0-521-05248-3). Cambridge U Pr.
Kennedy, Eberhard C. Four Greek Authors. (Modern School Classics Ser.). 1969. text ed. 5.95 (ISBN 0-312-30135-9). St Martin.
Nairn, J. A. & Nairn, G. A. Greek Through Reading. 400p. 1975. text ed. 8.95 (ISBN 0-312-35000-7). St Martin.
Nash-Williams, Alvah H. Spirit of Greece. 1967. 7.95 (ISBN 0-312-75250-4). St Martin.
Paine, Stephen W. Beginning Greek: A Functional Approach. (YA) (gr. 9 up). 1961. 10.95x (ISBN 0-19-501013-2). Oxford U Pr.

GREEK LANGUAGE-SEMANTICS

Henderson, Jeffrey. The Maculate Muse: Obscene Language in Attic Comedy. LC 74-82746. 272p. 1975. text ed. 20.00x (ISBN 0-300-01786-3). Yale U Pr.
Lightfoot, David. Natural Logic & the Greek Moods. (Janua Linguarum, Series Practica: No. 230). 149p. 1975. pap. text ed. 33.25x (ISBN 90-2793-061-9). Mouton.
Lupas, Liana. Phonologie du Grec Attique. (Janua Linguarum, Ser. Practica: No. 164). 186p. (Orig., Fr.). 1972. pap. text ed. 40.00x (ISBN 90-2792-325-6). Mouton.
Stehle, Matthias. Greek Word Building. LC 76-14405. (Society of Biblical Literature). 1976. pap. 6.00 (ISBN 0-89130-108-9, 060310). Scholars Pr Ca.

GREEK LANGUAGE-STUDY AND TEACHING

Association of Assistant Masters in Secondary Schools: Teaching of Classics. rev. ed. 1962. 13.95 (ISBN 0-521-05363-3). Cambridge U Pr.
Bennett, Charles E. & Bristol, George P. The Teaching of Latin & Greek in the Secondary School. 1901. Repr. 35.00 (ISBN 0-685-43062-6). Norwood Edns.
Drerup, Engelbert. Die Schulaussprache Des Griechischen Von der Renaissance Bis Zur Gegenwart, 2 Vols. 1930-32. Vol. 6. pap. 31.00 (ISBN 0-384-12825-4); Vol. 7. pap. 34.00 (ISBN 0-384-12830-0). Johnson Repr.
Foreign Service Institute. Greek Basic Course, Vol. 1. 328p. (Gr.). 1980. 12 cassettes plus text 115.00x (ISBN 0-88432-034-0, R301, Audio-Forum). J Norton Pubs.
--Greek Basic Course, Vol. 2. 200p. (Gr.). 12 cassettes plus text 98.00x (ISBN 0-88432-035-9, R318, Audio-Forum). J Norton Pubs.
--Greek Basic Course, Vol. 3. 201p. (Gr.). 1980. 6 cassettes plus text 50.00 (ISBN 0-88432-036-7, R338, Audio-Forum). J Norton Pubs.
Forrest, M. Foundation Course Folders One to Five: Teacher's Handbook. (Cambridge School Classics Project). (Illus.). 160p. 1973. pap. 5.95x (ISBN 0-521-08548-9). Cambridge U Pr.
Modern Greek Readers: From Kindergarten to Sixth Year. 2.70 ea. Divry.
Stouriotis, S. D. Practical Modern Greek for English Speaking People. 1971. pap. 10.00 (ISBN 0-685-47304-X). Heinman.
Thumb, Albert. Die Griechische Sprache im Zeitalter des Hellenismus. viii, 273p. (Ger.). 1974. Repr. of 1901 ed. 55.00x (ISBN 3-1100-3433-6). De Gruyter.
Werner, John R. Greek: A Programed Primer, 3 vols. Set. 27.00x (ISBN 0-87552-532-6); 9.00x ea. Presby & Reformed.

GREEK LANGUAGE-SYNTAX

Bevier, L. Brief Greek Syntex. (College Classical Ser.). (gr. 11-12). 17.50x (ISBN 0-89241-344-1); pap. 12.50x (ISBN 0-89241-119-8). Caratzas Bros.
Denniston, John D. Greek Particles. 2nd ed. 1954. 59.00x (ISBN 0-19-814307-9). Oxford U Pr.
Kahn, C. H. The Verb Be in Ancient Greek. LC 74-183367. (Foundations of Language Supplementary Ser: No. 16). 486p. 1973. lib. bdg. 63.00 (ISBN 90-277-0222-5, Pub. by Reidel Holland); pap. text ed. 29.00 (ISBN 90-277-0313-2). Kluwer Boston.

GREEK LANGUAGE-TERMS AND PHRASES

Aristotle. Poetics. Bd. with On the Sublime. Longinus; On Style. Demetrius. (Loeb Classical Library: No. 199). 11.00x (ISBN 0-674-99219-9). Harvard U Pr.
Grosmann, Gustav. Politische Schlagworter Aus der Zeit Des Peloponnesischen Krieges. LC 72-7893. (Greek History Ser.). (Ger.). Repr. of 1950 ed. 13.00 (ISBN 0-405-04789-4). Arno.
Peters, F. E. Greek Philosophical Terms: A Historical Lexicon. LC 67-25043. 234p. 1967. o.p. 9.50x (ISBN 0-8147-0343-7); pap. 5.95 (ISBN 0-8147-6552-1). NYU Pr.

GREEK LANGUAGE (KOINE)

see Greek Language, Hellenistic (300 B.C.-600 A.D.)

GREEK LANGUAGE, BIBLICAL

Comprises the language of the Septuagint and the New Testament.

see also Greek Language, Hellenistic (300 B.C.-600 A.D.)

Alford, Henry A. Alford's Greek Testament, 4 vols. 1980. Repr. 75.00 (ISBN 0-8010-0158-7). Baker Bk.
Bienecker, Fritz. A Linguistic Key to the Greek New Testament, 2 vols. Vol. 1. 14.95 (ISBN 0-310-32020-8); Vol. 2. 17.95 (ISBN 0-686-77152-4); Set. 31.90 (ISBN 0-310-32048-8). Zondervan.
Boyer, James L. A Manual of Greek Forms. pap. 3.50 (ISBN 0-88469-007-5). BMH Bks.
Chapman, Benjamin. Card-Guide to New Testament Greek. 1.75 (ISBN 0-8010-2388-2). Baker Bk.
--New Testament Greek Notebook. 1976. looseleaf 9.95 (ISBN 0-8010-2389-0). Baker Bk.
Dicharry, Warren F. Greek Without Grief: An Outline Guide to New Testament Greek. rev. ed. 1981. 5.95 (ISBN 0-686-31337-2). St Thomas Seminary.
Eadie Greek Text Commentary, Vol. 5. pap. 7.95 (ISBN 0-8010-3347-0). Baker Bk.
Eadie, John. Eadie Greek Text Commentaries, 5 vols. Set. pap. 37.95 (ISBN 0-8010-3341-1). Baker Bk.
--Eadie Greek Text Commentary, Vol. 1. pap. 9.95 (ISBN 0-8010-3343-8). Baker Bk.
--Eadie Greek Text Commentary, Vol. 2. pap. 9.95 (ISBN 0-8010-3344-6). Baker Bk.
--Eadie Greek Text Commentary, Vol. 3. pap. 7.95 (ISBN 0-8010-3345-4). Baker Bk.
--Eadie Greek Text Commentary, Vol. 4. pap. 7.75 (ISBN 0-8010-3346-2). Baker Bk.
Goodrick, Edward W. Do It Yourself Hebrew & Greek. 2nd ed. LC 79-25463. 1980. pap. text ed. 9.95 (ISBN 0-930014-35-9); with cassette 12.95 (ISBN 0-930014-42-1). Multnomah.
Institut fuer Neutestamentliche Textforschung, Muenster-Westf. & Aland, Kurt, eds. Vollstaendige Konkordanz zum griechischon Neuen Testament, 2 vols, Fasc. 1. viii, 96p. 1975. 73.50x (ISBN 3-11-002258-3). De Gruyter.
Knoch, A. E., compiled by. Greek Elements. rev. ed. 176p. 1971. 5.00 (ISBN 0-910424-42-X). Concordant.
McGaughy, Lane C. A Descriptive Analysis of Einai. LC 72-88437. (Society of Biblical Literature, Dissertation Ser.). 1972. pap. 9.00 (ISBN 0-89130-162-3, 060106). Scholars Pr Ca.
Mare, W. Harold. Mastering New Testament Greek. 1979. 9.95 (ISBN 0-8010-6064-8). Baker Bk.

Martin, Raymond. An Introduction to New Testament Greek. 1980. text ed. 7.50x (ISBN 0-915948-07-9). Western NC Pr.

Peterson, David E. Greek New Testament Slidaverb Conjugation Chart. laminated plastic 3.95 (ISBN 0-310-31080-6). Zondervan.

Robertson, A. T. Minister & His Greek New Testament. (A. T. Robertson Library). 1977. pap. 3.95 (ISBN 0-8010-7647-1). Baker Bk.

Septuagint: Greek & English. 24.95 (ISBN 0-310-20420-8, Pub. by Bagster). Zondervan.

Story, Cullen I K. Greek to Me: An Easy Way to Learn New Testament Greek Through Memory Visualization. LC 79-1769. (Illus.). 1979. pap. text ed. 8.95x (ISBN 0-06-067705-8, RD 307, HarpR). Har-Row.

Walther, James A. New Testament Greek Workbook: An Inductive Study of the Complete Text of the Gospel of John. LC 80-23762. (Illus.). 1981. pap. 12.00x (ISBN 0-226-87239-4). U of Chicago Pr.

Zerwick, Max. A Grammatical Analysis of Greek New Testament. (Scripta Pontificii Instituti Biblici: Vol. 1). 1974. pap. 15.00 (ISBN 0-8294-0316-7). Loyola.

Zodhiates, Spiros, ed. Learn or Review New Testament Greek: The Answer Book. 1977. pap. 1.95 (ISBN 0-89957-519-6). AMG Pubs.

GREEK LANGUAGE, BIBLICAL–DICTIONARIES

Abbott-Smith, G. A Manual Greek Lexicon of the New Testament. 3rd ed. 528p. 1977. text ed. 20.95 (ISBN 0-567-01001-5). Attic Pr.

Berry, George R. Berry's Greek-English New Testament Lexicon with Synonyms: Numerically Coded to Strong's Exhaustive Concordance. 208p. (Orig.). 1980. pap. 5.95 (ISBN 0-8010-0791-7). Baker Bk.

--A Dictionary of New Testament Greek Synonyms. 1979. 5.95 (ISBN 0-310-21160-3). Zondervan.

Brown, Colin. The New International Dictionary of New Testament Theology, 3 vols. Set. 96.00 (ISBN 0-310-21928-0). Zondervan.

Cremer, Hermann. Biblico-Theological Lexicon of New Testament Greek. 4th ed. 960p. 1977. Repr. of 1895 ed. text ed. 36.00x (ISBN 0-567-01004-X). Attic Pr.

Gingrich, F. W. Shorter Lexicon of the Greek N. T. 12.00 (ISBN 0-310-25030-7). Zondervan.

Gingrich, F. Wilbur, ed. Shorter Lexicon of the Greek New Testament. LC 65-24434. 1965. 10.00x (ISBN 0-226-29520-6). U of Chicago Pr.

Gingrich, F. Wilbur, tr. from Ger. A Greek-English Lexicon of the New & Other Early Christian Literature. Arndt, William F., et al, eds. Danker, F. W., tr. from Ger. LC 78-14293. (2nd rev. & augmented edition). 1979. lib. bdg. 35.00x (ISBN 0-226-03932-3). U of Chicago Pr.

Holly, David. A Complete Categorized Greek-English New Testament Vocabulary. 1980. pap. 6.95 (ISBN 0-8010-4224-0). Baker Bk.

Kittel, Gerhard & Friedrich, Gerhard, eds. Theological Dictionary of the New Testament, 10 vols. Incl. Vol. 1. 1964. 25.00 (ISBN 0-8028-2243-6); Vol. 2. 1965. 27.50 (ISBN 0-8028-2244-4); Vol. 3. 1966. 27.50 (ISBN 0-8028-2245-2); Vol. 4. 1967. 27.50 (ISBN 0-8028-2246-0); Vol. 5. 1968. 27.50 (ISBN 0-8028-2247-9); Vol. 6. 1969. 27.50 (ISBN 0-8028-2248-7); Vol. 7. 1970. 27.50 (ISBN 0-8028-2249-5); Vol. 8. 1972. 25.00 (ISBN 0-8028-2250-9); Vol. 9. 1973. 25.00 (ISBN 0-8028-2322-X); Vol. 10. 1976. 25.00 (ISBN 0-8028-2323-8). 255.00 set (ISBN 0-8028-2324-6). Eerdmans.

Morrison, Clinton D. & Barnes, David H. New Testament Word Lists. 1964. pap. 2.95 (ISBN 0-8028-1141-8). Eerdmans.

Pitkin, ed. Index to the Theological Dictionary to the New Testament. (Theological Dictionary to the N. T. Ser.). 1976. text ed. 25.00 (ISBN 0-8028-2323-8). Eerdmans.

Smith, Jacob B., ed. Greek-English Concordance. 1955. 24.95 (ISBN 0-8361-1368-3). Herald Pr.

Souter, Alexander, ed. Pocket Lexicon to the Greek New Testament. 1916. 14.95x (ISBN 0-19-864203-2). Oxford U Pr.

Stegenga, J. Greek-English Analytical Concordance of the Greek-English New Testament. 1963. 14.95 (ISBN 0-910710-01-5). Hellenes.

Thayer, Joseph H. Greek-English Lexicon of the New Testament. 1956. 18.95 (ISBN 0-310-36850-2). Zondervan.

--Thayer's Greek-English Lexicon of the New Testament. LC 78-67264. 1978. pap. 10.95 (ISBN 0-8054-1376-6). Broadman.

Young, Robert. Young's Analytical Concordance to the Bible. 1955. 19.95 (ISBN 0-8028-8084-3); deluxe ed. 22.95 (ISBN 0-8028-8085-1). Eerdmans.

Zerwick, Maximilian. Biblical Greek. (Scripta Pontificci Instituti Biblica: Vol. 114). 1963. 8.00 (ISBN 0-8294-0317-5). Loyola.

GREEK LANGUAGE, BIBLICAL–GLOSSARIES, VOCABULARIES, ETC.

Hickie, W. J. Greek-English Lexicon of the New Testament. (Direction Bks.). 1977. pap. 2.95 (ISBN 0-8010-4164-3). Baker Bk.

Holly, David. A Complete Categorized Greek-English New Testament Vocabulary. 1978. 12.50 (ISBN 0-85150-119-2). Attic Pr.

Metzger, Bruce M. Lexical Aids for Students of New Testament Greek. 3rd ed. 1969. pap. 4.95x (ISBN 0-8401-1618-7). Allenson-Breckinridge.

Moulton, J. H. & Milligan, G. The Vocabulary of the Greek Testament: Illustrated from the Papyri & Other Non-Literary Sources, 2 vols. 1977. lib. bdg. 250.00 (ISBN 0-8490-2800-0). Gordon Pr.

Moulton, James H. & Milligan, George. Vocabulary of the Greek New Testament. 1949. 24.95 (ISBN 0-8028-2178-2). Eerdmans.

Vine, W. E. Expository Dictionary of New Testament Words. 12.95 (ISBN 0-8007-0089-9); thumb index ed. 14.95 (ISBN 0-8007-0090-2). Revell.

GREEK LANGUAGE, BIBLICAL–GRAMMAR

Argyle, Aubrey W. An Introductory Grammar of New Testament Greek. 156p. 1966. text ed. 14.50x (ISBN 0-8014-0018-X). Cornell U Pr.

Bienecker, Fritz. A Linguistic Key to the Greek New Testament, 2 vols. Vol. 1. 14.95 (ISBN 0-310-32020-8); Vol. 2. 17.95 (ISBN 0-686-77152-4); Set. 31.90 (ISBN 0-310-32048-8). Zondervan.

Chamberlain, William D. Exegetical Grammar of the Greek New Testament. 1979. pap. 7.95 (ISBN 0-8010-2438-2). Baker Bk.

Colwell, Ernest C. & Tune, E. W. Beginner's Reader-Grammar for New Testament Greek. 1965. 8.95x (ISBN 0-06-061530-3, HarpR). Har-Row.

Dana, H. E. & Mantey, R. Manual Grammar of the Greek New Testament: With Index. 1957. text ed. 15.95 (ISBN 0-02-327070-5, 32707). Macmillan.

Davis, Guillermo H. Gramatica Elemental Del Griego Del Nuevo Testamento. McKibben, Jorge F., tr. 1980. Repr. of 1978 ed. 4.05 (ISBN 0-311-42008-7). Casa Bautista.

Davis, William H. Beginner's Grammar of the Greek New Testament. 1923. 8.95x (ISBN 0-06-061710-1, HarpR). Har-Row.

Drumwright, Huber L. An Introduction to New Testament Greek. LC 78-59982. 1980. 9.95 (ISBN 0-8054-1368-5). Broadman.

Funk, Robert W., ed. Greek Grammar of the New Testament & Other Early Christian Literature. LC 61-8077. 1961. 20.00x (ISBN 0-226-27110-2). U of Chicago Pr.

Funk, Robert W., tr. Greek Grammar of the New Testament & Other Early Christian Literature. 22.00 (ISBN 0-310-24780-2). Zondervan.

Gignac, Francis T. An Introductory New Testament Greek Course. 4.20 (ISBN 0-8294-0223-3). Loyola.

Goetchius, E. V. Language of the New Testament. 1966. text ed. 11.95x (ISBN 0-684-41263-2, ScribC); wkbk. 9.95x (ISBN 0-684-41264-0). Scribner.

Greenlee, J. Harold. Concise Exegetical Grammar of New Testament Greek. (Orig.). 1963. pap. 1.95 (ISBN 0-8028-1092-6). Eerdmans.

Kubo, Sakae. A Beginner's New Testament Greek Grammar. LC 79-64247. 1979. pap. text ed. 9.50 (ISBN 0-8191-0761-1). U Pr of Amer.

LaSor, William S. Handbook of New Testament Greek: An Inductive Approach Based on the Greek Text of Acts, 2 vols. 1973. pap. text ed. 10.95x (ISBN 0-8028-2341-6). Eerdmans.

Machen, J. Gresham. New Testament Greek for Beginners. 1923. text ed. 17.95 (ISBN 0-02-373480-9). Macmillan.

Marshall, Alfred. New Testament Greek Primer. 176p. (Orig.). 1981. pap. 5.95 (ISBN 0-310-20401-1). Zondervan.

Moulton, J. H., et al. A Grammar of New Testament Greek: Accidence & Word Formation, Vol. 2. 572p. 1979. text ed. 21.50x (ISBN 0-567-01012-0). Attic Pr.

--A Grammar of New Testament Greek: Syntax, Vol. 3. 438p. 1978. Repr. of 1963 ed. text ed. 21.50x (ISBN 0-567-01013-9). Attic Pr.

--A Grammar of New Testament Greek: The Prolegomena, Vol. I. 3rd ed. 320p. 1978. 18.50x (ISBN 0-567-01011-2). Attic Pr.

Mueller, Walter. Grammatical Aids for Students of New Testament Greek. 1972. pap. 2.45 (ISBN 0-8028-1447-6). Eerdmans.

Nunn, Henry P. Short Syntax of New Testament Greek. 5th ed. 1931. text ed. 7.50x (ISBN 0-521-09941-2). Cambridge U Pr.

Rife, John M. A Beginning Greek Book. 5th rev. ed. LC 74-80276. 1964. 7.00 (ISBN 0-911246-01-0). Reiff Pr.

Robertson, Archibald T. Grammar of the Greek New Testament in the Light of Historical Research. 1947. 33.95 (ISBN 0-8054-1308-1). Broadman.

Summers, Ray. Essentials of New Testament Greek. 1950. text ed. 8.95 (ISBN 0-8054-1309-X). Broadman.

Vaughan, Curtis & Gideon, Virtus E. A Greek Grammar of the New Testament. LC 78-74504. 1979. 9.95 (ISBN 0-8054-1378-2). Broadman.

Wenham, John W. Elements of New Testament Greek. 1966. text ed. 7.50x (ISBN 0-521-09842-4); key 2.95x (ISBN 0-521-06769-3). Cambridge U Pr.

GREEK LANGUAGE, BIBLICAL–READERS

Colwell, Ernest C. & Tune, E. W. Beginner's Reader-Grammar for New Testament Greek. 1965. 8.95x (ISBN 0-06-061530-3, HarpR). Har-Row.

Kohlenberger, John R., ed. The NIV Triglot Old Testament. 1334p. 1981. 49.95 (ISBN 0-310-43820-9). Zondervan.

GREEK LANGUAGE, BIBLICAL–SEMANTICS

Butler, Roy F. The Meaning of Agapao & Phileo in the Greek New Testament. 1977. 6.50x (ISBN 0-87291-089-X). Coronado Pr.

Morris, Leon. Apostolic Preaching of the Cross. 1956. pap. 5.95 (ISBN 0-8028-1512-X). Eerdmans.

GREEK LANGUAGE, BIBLICAL–SYNTAX

Brooks, James A. & Winbery, Carlton L. Syntax of New Testament Greek. LC 78-51150. 1978. pap. text ed. 7.50x (ISBN 0-8191-0473-6). U Pr of Amer.

Burton, E. Syntax of Moods & Tenses of New Testament Greek. 3rd ed. 240p. 1976. Repr. of 1898 ed. text ed. 11.50x (ISBN 0-567-01002-3). Attic Pr.

Han, E. S. Parsing Guide to the Greek New Testament. LC 77-158175. 1971. 14.95 (ISBN 0-8361-1653-4). Herald Pr.

Moule, Charles F. Idiom Book of New Testament Greek. 2nd ed. 1959. 36.00 (ISBN 0-521-05774-4); pap. text ed. 9.95x (ISBN 0-521-09237-X). Cambridge U Pr.

GREEK LANGUAGE, BYZANTINE

see also Greek Language, Medieval and Late

GREEK LANGUAGE, HELLENISTIC (300 B.C.-600 A.D.)

Branigan, Keith, et al. Hellas: The Civilization of Ancient Greece. LC 80-18306. (Illus.). 224p. 1980. 39.95 (ISBN 0-07-007229-9). McGraw.

Funk, Robert W. A Beginning-Intermediate Grammar of Hellenistic Greek, 3 vols. 2nd, rev. ed. Incl. Vol. 1. Morphology; Vol. 2. Syntax; Vol. 3. Appendices. LC 72-88769. (Society of Biblical Literature. Sources for Biblical Studies). (Orig.). 1977. Set. pap. text ed. 18.00 (ISBN 0-89130-148-8). Scholars Pr Ca.

Lampe, G. W., ed. Patristic Greek Lexicon, Fascicle 5. 1968. 22.00x (ISBN 0-19-864212-1). Oxford U Pr.

McGaughy, Lane C. Workbook for a Beginning-Intermediate Grammar of Hellenistic Greek. LC 76-44351. (Society of Biblical Literature. Sources for Biblical Study). 1976. pap. text ed. 6.00 (ISBN 0-89130-093-7, 060306). Scholars Pr Ca.

Ruck, Carl A. Ancient Greek: A New Approach. 2nd ed. 1979. pap. text ed. 15.95x (ISBN 0-262-68031-9). MIT Pr.

GREEK LANGUAGE, MEDIEVAL AND LATE

Browning, Robert. Medieval & Modern Greek. (Illus.). 1969. pap. text ed. 6.00x (ISBN 0-09-099601-1, Hutchinson U Lib). Humanities.

Wagner, Wilhelm. Medieval Greek Texts: A Collection of the Earliest Compositions in Vulgar Greek, Prior to the Year 1500 (with Prolegomena & Critical Notes) 1970. 10.00 (ISBN 0-89005-211-5). Ares.

GREEK LANGUAGE, MODERN

Bien, Peter. Kazantzakis & Linguistic Revolution in Greek Literature. LC 79-154991. (Princeton Essays in Literature Ser.). 1972. 17.50 (ISBN 0-691-06206-4). Princeton U Pr.

Browning, Robert. Medieval & Modern Greek. (Illus.). 1969. pap. text ed. 6.00x (ISBN 0-09-099601-1, Hutchinson U Lib). Humanities.

Dawkins, Richard M. Modern Greek in Asia Minor. LC 78-67703. (The Folktale). Repr. of 1916 ed. 49.50 (ISBN 0-404-16077-8). AMS Pr.

Divry, George C. Divry's New Self Taught English Method for Greeks. 1956. 5.00 (ISBN 0-685-09032-9). Divry.

Eleftheriades, Olga. Modern Greek Reference Grammar. (Orig.). 1981. pap. text ed. 10.00x (ISBN 0-87840-173-3). Georgetown U Pr.

Harris, Katerina. Colloquial Greek. (Trubners Colloquial Manuals). 336p. 1975. 14.00 (ISBN 0-7100-8069-7); pap. 8.95 (ISBN 0-7100-8070-0). Routledge & Kegan.

Learn Greek for English Speakers. pap. 8.50 (ISBN 0-87557-031-3, 031-3). Saphrograph.

Newton, Brian. Cypriot Greek: The Phonology & Inflections. LC 72-88202. (Janua Linguarum, Ser. Practica: No. 121). (Illus.). 185p. (Orig.). 1973. pap. text ed. 47.50x (ISBN 90-2793-392-8). Mouton.

Obolensky, S., et al. FSI Greek Basic Course, Units 1-25. 1974. pap. text ed. 6.90x (ISBN 0-686-10726-8); 17 cassettes 102.00x (ISBN 0-686-10727-6). Intl Learn Syst.

--FSI Greek Basic Course, Units 26-50. 1975. pap. text ed. 6.95x (ISBN 0-686-10728-4); 19 cassettes 114.00x (ISBN 0-686-10729-2). Intl Learn Syst.

Revelis, B. G. Greek-English Letterwriting. 5.00 (ISBN 0-685-09036-1). Divry.

Seaman, P. David. Modern Greek & American English in Contact. LC 74-170005. (Janua Linguarum, Ser. Practica: No. 132). 312p. (Orig.). 1972. pap. text ed. 72.50x (ISBN 90-2792-148-2). Mouton.

Shipp, G. P. Modern Greek Evidence for the Ancient Greek Vocabulary. LC 80-670068. 1980. 35.00x (ISBN 0-424-00076-8, Pub. by Sydney U Pr). Intl Schol Bk Serv.

Swanson, Donald C. Modern Greek Studies in the West: A Critical Bibliography. LC 59-14103. 93p. 1960. 5.00 (ISBN 0-87104-122-7). NY Pub Lib.

GREEK LANGUAGE, MODERN–CONVERSATION AND PHRASE BOOKS

Divry, D. C. Divry's Greek-English Dialogues. 1947. pocket ed. 5.00 (ISBN 0-685-09028-0). Divry.

Divry, George C. Divry's English-To-Greek Phrase & Conversation Pronouncing Manual. 1966. flexible bdg. 5.00 (ISBN 0-685-09027-2). Divry.

Goodrick, Ed. Do It Yourself in Hebrew & Greek with Cassette. 9.95 (ISBN 0-8423-0672-2). Tyndale.

Greece--a Hugo Phrase Book. (Hugo's Language Courses Ser.: No. 562). 1971. pap. 1.50 (ISBN 0-8226-0562-7). Littlefield.

Modern Greek in Twenty Lessons. rev. ed. (Cortina Method Language Ser). (Illus.). 6.95 (ISBN 0-385-00488-5). Doubleday.

Pappageotes, George. Say It in Modern Greek. 1956. pap. 1.75 (ISBN 0-486-20813-3). Dover.

--Say It in Modern Greek. LC 57-804. 1956. lib. bdg. 8.50x (ISBN 0-88307-559-8). Gannon.

Settar, G. Worldwide Medical Interpreter: Greek, Vol. 12. 1977. pap. 12.00 (ISBN 0-87489-112-4). Med Economics.

Smith, F. K. & Melluish, T. W. Teach Yourself Greek. (Teach Yourself Ser.). pap. 3.95 (ISBN 0-679-10178-0). McKay.

Tsirpanlis, Constantine. Modern Greek Idiom & Phrase Book. LC 75-11952. 1978. pap. 8.95 (ISBN 0-8120-0476-0). Barron.

TYS Greek Phrase Book. 1980. pap. 2.95 (ISBN 0-679-10700-2). McKay.

GREEK LANGUAGE, MODERN–DICTIONARIES

Divry, George C., ed. Divry's New Modern Greek-English & English-Greek Handy Dictionary. rev. ed. 1978. pocket ed. 4.20 (ISBN 0-685-09029-9); with thumb indexes 5.50 (ISBN 0-685-09030-2); lea. 8.50 (ISBN 0-685-09031-0). Divry.

Divry's Modern English-Greek & Greek-English Desk Dictionary. 1976. 8.80 (ISBN 0-685-81638-9); thumble indexed 10.50 (ISBN 0-685-81639-7). Divry.

English-Greek Pocket Dictionary. pap. 7.00 (ISBN 0-685-77571-2, 030-5). Saphrograph.

Greek-English Dictionary "Modern". 12.50 (ISBN 0-87557-029-1, 028-3Y). Saphrograph.

Greek-English, English-Greek Pocket Dictionary. 9.00 (ISBN 0-685-58555-7). Heinman.

Greek-English Pocket Dictionary. pap. 7.00 (ISBN 0-685-77570-4, 030-5X). Saphrograph.

Institute for Language Study. Vest Pocket Modern Greek. LC 60-53247. (Illus.). 184p. (Modern Greek.). 1961. pap. 2.45 (ISBN 0-06-464904-0, BN4900, BN). Har-Row.

Mirambel, Andre. Petit Dictionnaire Francais-Grec Moderne et Grec Moderne-Francais. 486p. (Fr.-Mod. Gr.). 1969. 29.95 (ISBN 0-686-57051-0, M-6413). French & Eur.

Pring, Julian T., ed. Oxford Dictionary of Modern Greek. Greek-English. 1965. 13.50x (ISBN 0-19-864207-5). Oxford U Pr.

Rogers, Thomas. Greek Word Roots: A Practical List with Greek & English Derivatives. 32p. 1981. pap. 1.95 (ISBN 0-8010-7707-9). Baker Bk.

Settar, G. Worldwide Medical Interpreter: Greek, Vol. 12. 1977. pap. 12.00 (ISBN 0-87489-112-4). Med Economics.

GREEK LANGUAGE, MODERN–GRAMMAR

Bien, Peter, et al. Demotic Greek. 3rd ed. Alexiou, Christos, ed. LC 72-86870. (Illus.). 312p. 1972. pap. text ed. 7.50x (ISBN 0-87451-071-6). U Pr of New Eng.

Cherel, Albert O. Grec Sans Peine. 9.95 (ISBN 0-685-11224-1). French & Eur.

Divry, George C. Greek Made Easy. 3rd ed. 1953. 5.00 (ISBN 0-685-09037-X). Divry.

Eklund, Bo-Lennart. Modern Greek: Verbal Aspect & Compound Nouns. (Acta Regiae Societatis Scientiarm et Litterarum Gothoburgensis, Humaniora: No. 11). 1976. pap. text ed. 5.75x (ISBN 91-85252-08-5). Humanities.

Hansen, Hardy & Quinn, Gerald M. Greek: An Intensive Course, Preliminary Edition. LC 80-65601. 928p. (Orig.). 1980. pap. text ed. 17.50x (ISBN 0-8232-1064-2). Fordham.

Modern Greek in Twenty Lessons. rev. ed. (Cortina Method Language Ser). (Illus.). 6.95 (ISBN 0-385-00488-5). Doubleday.
Sofronious, S. A. Teach Yourself Modern Greek. (Teach Yourself Ser.). pap. 4.95 (ISBN 0-679-10189-6). McKay.
Thomson, George. Manual of Modern Greek. 10.50 (ISBN 0-8044-0661-8). Ungar.
Tsirpanlis, Constantine. Two Hundred & One Modern Greek Verbs. LC 80-13900. 1980. pap. 8.95 (ISBN 0-8120-0475-2). Barron.

GREEK LANGUAGE, MODERN–READERS

Bien, Peter, et al. The Flying Telephone Booth: Demotic Greek II. LC 81-51609. 500p. (Orig.). 1981. pap. text ed. 9.95 (ISBN 0-87451-208-5); wkbk. 5.00 (ISBN 0-87451-209-3). U Pr of New Eng.

GREEK LANGUAGE, MYCENAEAN

Chadwick, John. Decipherment of Linear B. (Illus.). 1970. 29.95 (ISBN 0-521-04599-1); pap. 7.50x (ISBN 0-521-09596-4, 596). Cambridge U Pr.

GREEK LAW

see Law, Greek

GREEK LETTER SOCIETIES

see also names of individual societies

Leemon, Thomas A. The Rites of Passage in a Student Culture. LC 72-81190. 1972. pap. text ed. 7.50x (ISBN 0-8077-1673-1). Tchrs Coll.
Sheldon, Henry D. Student Life & Customs. LC 70-89233. (American Education: Its Men, Institutions & Ideas, Ser. 1). 1969. Repr. of 1901 ed. 28.00 (ISBN 0-405-01470-8). Arno.

GREEK LETTERS

Aelian, Claudius. On the Characteristics of Animals, 3 Vols. (Loeb Classical Library: No. 446, 448, 449). 1958. 11.00x ea. Vol. 1 (ISBN 0-674-99491-4). Vol. 2 (ISBN 0-674-99493-0). Vol. 3 (ISBN 0-674-99494-9). Harvard U Pr.
Austin, Reginald P. The Stoichedon Style in Greek Inscriptions. LC 72-7884. (Greek History Ser). Repr. of 1938 ed. 14.00 (ISBN 0-405-04778-9). Arno.
Bailey, Shackelton D., ed. Cicero: Epistulae Ad Quintum Fratrem et M. Brutum. (Cambridge Classical Texts & Commentaries Ser.: No. 22). 300p. 1981. 49.50 (ISBN 0-521-23053-5). Cambridge U Pr.
Dionysius Of Halicarnassus. These Literary Letters. 232p. 1901. Repr. 19.00 (ISBN 0-403-04307-7). Somerset Pub.
White, John L. The Form & Function of the Body of the Greek Letter in the Non-Literary Papyri & in Paul the Apostle. LC 75-33088. (Society of Biblical Literature. Dissertation Ser.). (Illus.). 1975. pap. 7.50 (ISBN 0-89130-048-1, 060102). Scholars Pr Ca.
--The Form & Structure of the Official Petition: A Study in Greek Epistolography. LC 72-87889. (Society of Biblical Literature. Dissertations Ser.: No. 5). (Illus.). 1972. pap. 9.00 (ISBN 0-89130-161-5, 060105). Scholars Pr Ca.

GREEK LITERATURE (COLLECTIONS)

Here are entered collections in the Greek Language. For English translations see subdivision Translations into English.

Chase, Alston H. & Phillips, Henry, Jr., eds. New Greek Reader. LC 54-12234. (Illus.). (gr. 10 up). 1954. pap. text ed. 12.00x (ISBN 0-674-61550-6). Harvard U Pr.
Cook, Albert. Enactment: Greek Tragedy. LC 78-153076. 175p. 1971. 13.95x (ISBN 0-8040-0539-7). Swallow.
De Vogel, C. J. Greek Philosophy, 3 Vols. 1960-1964. Vol. 1. text ed. 24.00x (ISBN 90-04-02356-9); Vol. 2. text ed. 24.00x (ISBN 90-04-02357-7); Vol. 3. text ed. 42.25x (ISBN 90-040374-3-8). Humanities.
Grene, David & Lattimore, Richmond, eds. The Complete Greek Tragedies. Incl. Vol 1. Aeschylus. LC 60-950. 360p. 10.95 (ISBN 0-226-30768-9); Vol. 2. Sophocles. 468p. 12.50 (ISBN 0-226-30769-7); Vol. 3. Euripides. 672p. 15.00 (ISBN 0-226-30770-0); Vol. 4. Euripides. 624p. 15.00 (ISBN 0-226-30771-9). LC 60-950. 1942-1960. U of Chicago Pr.
Joint Association of Classical Teachers' Greek Course. A World of Heroes: Selections from Homer, Herodotus & Sophocles. LC 79-10740. (Illus.). 1979. pap. 9.95x (ISBN 0-521-22462-4). Cambridge U Pr.
Lysias. Orationes. Hude, Karl, ed. (Oxford Classical Texts). 290p. (Greek.). 1978. Repr. of 1912 ed. text ed. 17.50x (ISBN 0-19-814538-1). Oxford U Pr.
Miller, Walter. Daedalus & Thespis: Volume II: Sculpture, Pts. 1 & 2. Repr. of 1931 ed. 10.00x (ISBN 0-8262-0590-9). U of Mo Pr.
Wagner, Wilhelm, ed. Medieval Greek Texts: Being a Collection of the Earliest Composition in Vulgar Greek, Prior to the Year 1500. 190p. 1970. Repr. of 1870 ed. text ed. 28.50x (ISBN 90-6032-432-3). Humanities.
Warmington, E. H., ed. Greek Anthology, 5vols. Incl. Vol. 1. Book 1, Christian Epigrams. Book 2 Christoclorus of Thebes in Egypt. Book 3, Cyzicene Epigrams. Book 4, Proems of the Different Anthologies. Book 5, Amatory Epigrams. Book 6, Dedicatory Epigrams (ISBN 0-674-99074-9); Vol. 2. Book 7, Sepulchral Epigrams. Book 8, Epigrams of St. Gregory the Theologian (ISBN 0-674-99075-7); Vol. 3. Book 9, Declamatory Epigrams (ISBN 0-674-99093-5); Vol. 4. Book 10, Hortatory & Admonitory Epigrams. Book 11, Convivial & Satirical Epigrams. Book 12, Strato's Musa Puerilis (ISBN 0-674-99094-3); Vol. 5. Book 13, Epigrams in Various Metres. Book 14, Arithmetical Problems, Riddles, Oracles. Book 15, Miscellanea. Book 16, Epigrams of Planudean Anthology Not in the Palatine Manuscript (ISBN 0-674-99095-1). (Loeb Classical Library: No. 67-68, 84-86). (Gr. & Eng.). 11.00x ea. Harvard U Pr.
Wedeck, Harry E. Classics of Greek Literature. LC 63-11490. 1963. 6.00 (ISBN 0-8022-1826-1). Philos Lib.

GREEK LITERATURE–BIBLIOGRAPHY

Donlan, Walter, intro. by. The Classical World Bibliography of Greek Drama & Poetry. LC 76-52510. (Library of Humanities Reference Bks.: No. 93). lib. bdg. 34.00 (ISBN 0-8240-9880-3). Garland Pub.
Wilson, Nigel. Mediaeval Greek Bookhands: Examples Selected from Greek Manuscripts in Oxford Libraries, 2 vols. 1973. Set. 9.00 (ISBN 0-910956-55-3). Medieval Acad.

GREEK LITERATURE–CRITICISM, TEXTUAL

Cameron, Alan. Porphyrius the Charioteer. (Illus.). 297p. 1973. 56.00x (ISBN 0-19-814805-4). Oxford U Pr.
Hohendahl-Zoetelief, I. M. Manners in Homeric Epic. 191p. 1981. pap. text ed. 27.50x (ISBN 90-04-06223-8, Pub. by Brill Holland). Humanities.
Nickau, Klaus. Untersuchungen Zur Textkritischen Methode Des Zenodotos Von Ephesos. (Untersuchungen Zur Antiken Literatur und Geschichte: Vol. 16). 1977. 61.00x (ISBN 3-11-001827-6). De Gruyter.
Renehan, Robert. Greek Textual Criticism: A Reader. LC 72-82297. (Loeb Classical Monographs Ser). 1969. text ed. 8.95x (ISBN 0-674-36310-8). Harvard U Pr.

GREEK LITERATURE–DICTIONARIES

Avery, C. The New Century Handbook of Greek Literature. 1972. pap. 7.95 (ISBN 0-13-611988-3, Spec). P-H.
DuCange, Charles Du Fresne. Glossarium Ad Scriptores Mediae et Infimae Graecitatis. LC 60-21441. 1280p. 1958. Repr. of 1688 ed. 105.00x (ISBN 0-8002-1276-2). Intl Pubns Serv.
Mantinband, James, ed. Concise Dictionary of Greek Literature. LC 62-9769. 1962. 7.50 (ISBN 0-8022-1050-3). Philos Lib.
Mantinband, James H. Concise Dictionary of Greek Literature. Repr. of 1962 ed. lib. bdg. 15.50x (ISBN 0-8371-2289-9, MAGL). Greenwood.
--Dictionary of Greek Literature. (Quality Paperback: No. 145). 1966. pap. 3.95 (ISBN 0-8226-0145-1). Littlefield.

GREEK LITERATURE–HISTORY AND CRITICISM

Aeschines. Aeschines Against Ctesiphon: On the Crown. Connor, W. R. & Richardson, Rufus B., eds. LC 78-18596. (Greek Texts & Commentaries Ser.). (Illus., Gr. & Eng.). 1979. Repr. of 1889 ed. lib. bdg. 19.00x (ISBN 0-405-11437-0). Arno.
--Discours sur L'Ambasade. Connor, W. R., ed. LC 78-18585. (Greek Texts & Commentaries Ser.). (Gr. & Fr.). 1979. Repr. of 1902 ed. lib. bdg. 15.00x (ISBN 0-405-11427-3). Arno.
Apollonius, Rhodius. The Argonautica of Apollonius Rhodius, Bk. III. Connor, W. R., ed. LC 78-18578. (Greek Texts & Commendtaries Ser.). (Greek & Eng.). 1979. Repr. of 1928 ed. lib. bdg. 15.00x (ISBN 0-405-11421-4). Arno.
Baldry, H. C. Ancient Greek Literature in Its Living Context. LC 67-25806. (Illus.). 1967. pap. 3.25 (ISBN 0-07-003555-5, SP). McGraw.
Brandes, Georg M. Hellas: Travels in Greece. facs. ed. Hartmann, J. W., tr. LC 72-90613. (Essay Index Reprint Ser). 1926. 15.00 (ISBN 0-8369-1203-9). Arno.
Burns, C. D. Greek Ideals. LC 73-20390. (Studies in Classical Literature, No. 60). 1974. lib. bdg. 38.95 (ISBN 0-8383-1767-7). Haskell.
Butcher, ed. Odyssey. 1969. 5.50x (ISBN 0-312-58205-6). St Martin.
Butcher, S. H. Harvard Lectures on Greek Subjects. 1978. Repr. of 1904 ed. lib. bdg. 30.00 (ISBN 0-8495-0386-8). Arden Lib.
Butcher, Samuel H. Some Aspects of the Greek Genius. LC 79-101552. 1969. Repr. of 1891 ed. 15.00 (ISBN 0-8046-0721-4). Kennikat.
Campbell, Lewis. Religion in Greek Literature: A Sketch in Outline. facsimile ed. LC 79-148874. (Select Bibliographies Reprint Ser). Repr. of 1898 ed. 22.00 (ISBN 0-8369-5645-1). Arno.
Carpenter, Rhys. Folk Tale, Fiction & Saga in the Homeric Epics. LC 55-7555. (Sather Classical Lectures Ser.: No. 20). 1974. 19.50x (ISBN 0-520-02808-2). U of Cal Pr.
Clinton, Henry F. Fasti Hellenici: The Civil & Literary Chronology of Greece Through the Death of Augustus, 3 Vols. 1965. Repr. of 1834 ed. Set. 137.00 (ISBN 0-8337-0599-7). B Franklin.
--Fasti Romani: The Civil & Literary Chronology of Rome & Constantinople from the Death of Augustus to the Death of Justin the 2nd, 2 Vols. 1965. Repr. of 1850 ed. Set. 105.50 (ISBN 0-8337-0602-0). B Franklin.
Coleiro, E. Introduction to Vergil's Bucolics. 1979. pap. text ed. 46.00x (ISBN 90-6032-117-0). Humanities.
Columbia University - Department Of Classical Philology. Greek Literature. facs. ed. LC 69-18922. (Essay Index Reprint Ser.). 1912. 17.00 (ISBN 0-8369-0038-3). Arno.
Connor, W. R., ed. Chion of Heraclea. LC 78-18571. (Greek Texts & Commentaries Ser.). 1979. Repr. of 1951 ed. lib. bdg. 12.00x (ISBN 0-405-11415-X). Arno.
--Greek Texts & Commentaries Series, 40 bks. (Illus.). 1979. lib. bdg. 838.00x set (ISBN 0-405-11412-5). Arno.
Croiset, Alfred & Croiset, Maurice. Abridged History of Greek Literature. Heffelbower, G. F., tr. LC 78-131510. Repr. of 1904 ed. 32.50 (ISBN 0-404-01857-2). AMS Pr.
Demetrius. Demetrius on Style. Connor, W. R., ed. LC 78-18597. (Greek Texts & Commentaries Ser.). (Gr. & Eng.). 1979. Repr. of 1902 ed. lib. bdg. 22.00x (ISBN 0-405-11438-9). Arno.
Demosthenes. The First Philippic & the Olynthiacs of Demosthenes. Connor, W. R., ed. LC 78-18599. (Greek Texts & Commentaries Ser.). (Illus., Gr. & Eng.). 1979. Repr. of 1897 ed. lib. bdg. 22.00x (ISBN 0-405-11440-0). Arno.
--On the Peace: Second Philippic on Chersonesus & Third Philippic. Connor, W. R., ed. LC 78-18602. (Greek Text Commentaries Ser.). 1979. Repr. of 1900 ed. lib. bdg. 22.00x (ISBN 0-405-11443-5). Arno.
--Select Private Orations of Demosthenes, 2 vols. in 1, Pts. I & II. Connor, W. R., ed. LC 78-18601. (Greek Texts & Commentaries Ser.). (Illus.). 1979. Repr. of 1898 ed. lib. bdg. 42.00 (ISBN 0-405-11442-7). Arno.
Denniston, J. D. Greek Literary Criticism. 224p. 1981. Repr. of 1924 ed. lib. bdg. 35.00 (ISBN 0-89984-157-0). Century Bookbindery.
Denniston, John D. Greek Prose Style. LC 78-31880. 1979. Repr. of 1952 ed. lib. bdg. 15.00x (ISBN 0-313-20960-X, DEGP). Greenwood.
Dover, Kenneth. Ancient Greek Literature. 196p. 1980. 16.95x (ISBN 0-19-219137-3); pap. 6.95x (ISBN 0-19-289124-3). Oxford U Pr.
Drerup, Engelbert. Kulturprobleme Des Klassischen Griechentums. 1933. pap. 9.50 (ISBN 0-384-12820-3). Johnson Repr.
Eckstein, Jerome. The Death of Socrates: Living, Dying & Immortality--the Theater of Ideas in Plato's Phaedo. LC 81-924. 288p. 1981. 18.00 (ISBN 0-914366-19-X). Columbia Pub.
Fairclough, Henry R. Love of Nature Among the Greeks & Romans. LC 63-10298. (Our Debt to Greece & Rome Ser). (Illus.). Repr. of 1930 ed. 7.50x (ISBN 0-8154-0063-2). Cooper Sq.
Frankel, Hermann. Early Greek Poetry and Philosophy. Hadas, Moses & Willis, James, trs. LC 74-10724. (Helen & Kurt Wolff Bk.). 508p. 1975. 25.00 (ISBN 0-15-127190-9). HarBraceJ.
Geffcken, John. Die Oracula Sibyllina. Connor, W. R., ed. LC 78-18576. (Greek Texts Commentaries Ser.). (Illus.). 1979. Repr. of 1902 ed. lib. bdg. 20.00x (ISBN 0-405-11419-2). Arno.
Gomme, Arnold W. Essays in Greek History & Literature. facs. ed. LC 67-23222. (Essay Index Reprint Ser). 1937. 19.00 (ISBN 0-8369-0481-8). Arno.
Greek Literature. 316p. 1980. Repr. of 1912 ed. lib. bdg. 40.00 (ISBN 0-8492-3432-8). R West.
Grey, Henry. The Classics for the Million: Being an Epitome in English of the Works of the Principal Greek & Latin Authors. 1898. 30.00 (ISBN 0-89984-221-6). Century Bookbindery.
Gutas, Dimitri. Greek Wisdom Literature in Arabic Translation: A Study of the Graeco-Arabic Gnomologia. (American Oriental Ser.: Vol. 60). 1975. pap. 9.00x (ISBN 0-940490-60-9). Am Orient Soc.
Hadas, Moses. History of Greek Literature. LC 50-7015. 1950. 17.50x (ISBN 0-231-01767-7). Columbia U Pr.
Harvard University Library. Ancient Greek Literature. (Widener Library Shelflist Ser.: No. 58). 1977. 55.00x (ISBN 0-674-03310-8). Harvard U Pr.
Heller, John L., ed. Serta Turyniana: Studies in Greek Literature & Palaeography in Honor of Alexander Turyn. LC 73-81567. (Illus.). 670p. 1974. 37.50 (ISBN 0-252-00405-1). U of Ill Pr.
Isocrates. Ad Demonicum et Panegyricus. Connor, W. R. & Sandys, J. E., eds. LC 78-18604. (Greek Texts & Commentaries Ser.). (Illus., Gr. & Eng.). 1979. Repr. of 1872 ed. lib. bdg. 15.00x (ISBN 0-405-11444-3). Arno.
--Cyprian Orations. Connor, R. W. & Forster, Edward S., eds. LC 78-18574. (Greek Texts & Commentaries Ser). 1979. lib. bdg. 15.00x (ISBN 0-405-11418-4). Arno.
Jaeger, Werner. Paideia: The Ideals of Greek Culture, 3 vols. Highet, Gilbert, tr. from Ger. Incl. Vol. 1. Archaic Greece; The Mind of Athens. 2nd ed. 1945 (ISBN 0-19-500399-3); Vol. 2. In Search of the Divine Center. 1943 (ISBN 0-19-500592-9); Vol. 3. The Conflict of Cultural Ideals in the Age of Plato. 1944 (ISBN 0-19-500593-7). 20.00 ea. Oxford U Pr.
--Paideia: The Ideals of Greek Culture, Vol. 1. Archaic Greece & Mind Of Athens. Highet, Gilbert, tr. (YA) (gr. 9 up). 1965. pap. 7.95 (ISBN 0-19-500425-6, 144, GB). Oxford U Pr.
Kessels, A. H. Studies on the Dream in Greek Literature. 280p. 1980. pap. text ed. 34.25x (ISBN 90-6194-491-0). Humanities.
Kirkwood, G. M., ed. Poetry & Poetics from Ancient Greece to the Renaissance: Studies in Honor of James Hutton. LC 74-10410. (Studies in Classical Philology). (Illus.). 256p. 1975. 24.50x (ISBN 0-8014-0847-4). Cornell U Pr.
Kitto, H. D. Poiesis: Structure & Thought. (Sather Classical Lectures: No. 36). 1966. 25.00x (ISBN 0-520-00651-8). U of Cal Pr.
Lawrence, Eugene. A Primer of Greek Literature. 1877. 15.00 (ISBN 0-8274-3960-1). R West.
Lesky, Albin. History of Greek Literature. LC 65-25033. 1966. 19.95 (ISBN 0-690-38372-X). T Y Crowell.
--A History of Greek Literature. LC 65-25033. (Apollo Eds.). 1976. pap. 9.95 (ISBN 0-8152-0394-2, A-394). T Y Crowell.
Longus. The Story of Daphnis & Chloe. Connor, W. R., ed. LC 78-18586. (Greek Texts & Commentaries Ser.). (Illus.). 1979. Repr. of 1908 ed. lib. bdg. 15.00x (ISBN 0-405-11428-1). Arno.
Lumb, T. W. Authors of Greece. LC 75-101046. 1969. Repr. of 1924 ed. 11.75 (ISBN 0-8046-0711-7). Kennikat.
Lysias. Lysia Epitaphios, Pts. I & II. Connor, W. R., ed. LC 78-18608. (Greek Texts & Commentaries Ser.). 1979. Repr. of 1887 ed. lib. bdg. 10.00x (ISBN 0-405-11448-6). Arno.
MacGregor, Marshall. Leaves of Hellas: Essays on Some Aspects of Greek Literature. LC 68-8222. 1969. Repr. of 1926 ed. 12.00 (ISBN 0-8046-0285-9). Kennikat.
--Studies & Diversions in Greek Literature. LC 79-101047. 1969. Repr. of 1937 ed. 14.00 (ISBN 0-8046-0712-5). Kennikat.
Mahaffy, J. A. A History of Classical Greek Literature, 4 vols. 400.00 (ISBN 0-8490-0320-2). Gordon Pr.
Marcovich, Miroslav, ed. Illinois Classical Studies, Vol. IV. 1979. 20.00 (ISBN 0-252-00694-1). U of Ill Pr.
Meritt, Benjamin D. & Traill, John S. Inscriptions: The Athenian Councillors. LC 54-5697. (The Athenian Agora Ser.: Vol. 15). 1975. 45.00x (ISBN 0-87661-215-X). Am Sch Athens.
Muller, Karl O. & Donaldson, John W. History of the Literature of Ancient Greece, 3 Vols. LC 70-113282. (Classics Ser). 1971. Repr. of 1858 ed. Set. 52.00x (ISBN 0-8046-1201-3). Kennikat.
Oxford Lectures on Classical Subjects, 1909-1920, 10 vols. in 1. facs. ed. LC 68-8486. (Essay Index Reprint Ser). 1968. Repr. of 1924 ed. 15.00 (ISBN 0-8369-0761-2). Arno.
Philo. Philonis Alexandrini in Flaccum. Connor, W. R., ed. LC 78-18570. (Greek Texts & Commentaries Ser.). 1979. Repr. of 1939 ed. lib. bdg. 15.00x (ISBN 0-405-11414-1). Arno.
Plutarch. Life of Aratus. Connor, W. R., ed. LC 78-18593. (Greek Texts & Commentaries Ser.). (Illus.). 1979. Repr. of 1937 ed. lib. bdg. 15.00x (ISBN 0-405-11434-6). Arno.
--Life of Dion. Connor, W. R., ed. LC 78-18594. (Greek Texts & Commentaries Ser.). (Illus.). 1979. Repr. of 1952 ed. lib. bdg. 12.00x (ISBN 0-405-11435-4). Arno.
Ramage, Craufurd T. Beautiful Thoughts from Greek Authors. 1979. Repr. of 1864 ed. lib. bdg. 40.00 (ISBN 0-8495-4567-6). Arden Lib.
Reinhold, Meyer. Classics, Greek & Roman. LC 72-140633. (Orig.). (gr. 10 up). 1971. 6.95 (ISBN 0-8120-5020-7); pap. 2.95 (ISBN 0-8120-0044-7). Barron.
Reynolds, L. D. & Wilson, N. G. Scribes & Scholars: A Guide to the Transmission of Greek & Latin Literature. 2nd ed. (Illus.). 266p. 1974. pap. text ed. 11.50x (ISBN 0-19-814372-9). Oxford U Pr.

Richardson, Bessie E. Old Age Among the Ancient Greeks. LC 74-93775. (Illus.). Repr. of 1933 ed. 21.50 (ISBN 0-404-05289-4). AMS Pr.

--Old Age Among the Ancient Greeks: The Greek Portrayal of Old Age in Literature, Art & Inscriptions. Repr. of 1933 ed. lib. bdg. 23.50x (ISBN 0-8371-0637-0, RIOA). Greenwood.

Roberts, William R. Greek Rhetoric & Literary Criticism. LC 63-10296. (Our Debt to Greece & Rome Ser). Repr. of 1930 ed. 7.50x (ISBN 0-8154-0194-9). Cooper Sq.

Robinson, David M. A Study of the Greek Love Names. LC 78-22238. (The Gay Experience). Repr. of 1937 ed. 22.50 (ISBN 0-404-61529-5). AMS Pr.

Robinson, Thomas M. Contrasting Arguments. new ed. Connor, W. R., ed. LC 78-18598. (Greek Texts & Commentaries Ser.). (Illus., Gr. & Eng.). 1979. lib. bdg. 22.00x (ISBN 0-405-11439-7). Arno.

Russell, D. A. & Wilson, N. G., eds. Menander Rhetor. 438p. 1981. 98.00 (ISBN 0-19-814013-4). Oxford U Pr.

Sinclair, T. A. A History of Classical Greek Literature. LC 72-8691. (Studies in European Literature, No. 56). 1973. Repr. of 1934 ed. lib. bdg. 46.95 (ISBN 0-8383-1674-3). Haskell.

Stuart, Duane R. Epochs of Greek & Roman Biography. LC 67-19532. 1928. 12.00x (ISBN 0-8196-0193-4). Biblo.

Taylor, Thomas. Eleusinian & Bacchic Mysteries. Wilder, Alexander, ed. LC 78-59603. (Secret Doctrine Reference Ser.). 1978. Repr. of 1875 ed. 9.95 (ISBN 0-913510-29-7). Wizards.

Theognis. The Elegies of Theognis. Connor, W. R., ed. LC 78-18584. (Greek Texts & Commentaries Ser.). (Gr. & Eng.). 1979. Repr. of 1910 ed. lib. bdg. 20.00x (ISBN 0-405-11426-5). Arno.

Theophrastus. The Characters of Theophrastus. Connor, W. R., ed. LC 78-18600. (Greek Texts & Commentaries Ser.). (Greek & Eng.). 1979. Repr. of 1909 ed. lib. bdg. 16.00x (ISBN 0-405-11441-9). Arno.

Thomson, James A. The Greek Tradition: Essays in the Reconstruction of Ancient Thought. facsimile ed. LC 71-157356. (Select Bibliographies Reprint Ser.). Repr. of 1915 ed. 16.00 (ISBN 0-8369-5817-9). Arno.

Trypanis, C. A. The Homeric Epics. Phelps, W. W., tr. 1977. 18.00x (ISBN 0-85668-085-0, Pub. by Aris & Phillips); pap. 10.00x (ISBN 0-85668-086-9, Pub. by Aris & Phillips). Intl Schol Bk Serv.

Versenyi, Laszlo. Man's Measure: A Study of the Greek Image of Man from Homer to Sophocles. LC 73-17420. 1974. 19.00 (ISBN 0-87395-254-5); microfiche 19.00 (ISBN 0-87395-255-3). State U Ny Pr.

Vickers, Brian. Towards Greek Tragedy. (Illus.). 416p. 1980. pap. text ed. 18.00x (ISBN 0-582-49062-6). Longman.

Vollgraff, Carl W. L'Oraison Funedbre De Gorgias. Vlastosd, Gregory, ed. LC 78-14601. (Morals & Law in Ancient Greece Ser.). 1979. Repr. of 1952 ed. lib. bdg. 12.00x (ISBN 0-405-11580-6). Arno.

Wacholder, Ben Z. Eupolemus: A Study of Graeco-Judean Literature. 1974. 20.00x (ISBN 0-87820-401-6). Ktav.

Warr, George C. The Greek Epic. 1975. Repr. of 1895 ed. 20.00 (ISBN 0-8274-4096-0). R West.

Webster, Thomas B. Art & Literature in Fourth Century Athens. Repr. of 1956 ed. lib. bdg. 15.00x (ISBN 0-8371-0743-1, WEAL). Greenwood.

Wheeler, J. R. Greek Literature. 1912. 25.00 (ISBN 0-8274-3987-3). R West.

Whibley, Leonard. Companion to Greek Studies. 4th rev. ed. (Illus.). 1963. Repr. of 1931 ed. 21.75 (ISBN 0-02-854700-4). Hafner.

Wilson, Elkin C. The Lamentation of Troy for the Death of Hector. 1973. lib. bdg. 12.50 (ISBN 0-8414-9745-1). Folcroft.

Wilson, N. G. Saint Basil on the Value of Greek Literature. (Illus.). 75p. 1975. 17.95x (ISBN 0-7156-0872-X, Pub. by Duckworth England). Biblio Dist.

Wilson, N. G., ed. Saint Basil on the Value of Greek Literature. 1975. 21.00x (ISBN 0-685-88342-6); pap. 11.95x (ISBN 0-7156-0872-X). Intl Ideas.

Wright, John H. Masterpieces of Greek Literature. 1902. 35.00 (ISBN 0-8274-3992-X). R West.

Wright, Wilmer C. A Short History of Greek Literature: From Homer to Julian. 1975. Repr. of 1907 ed. 35.00 (ISBN 0-8274-4098-7). R West.

Xenophon. Hellendica. Connor, W. R., ed. LC 78-18613. (Greek Texts & Commentaries Ser.). 1979. Repr. of 1906 ed. lib. bdg. 30.00x (ISBN 0-405-11452-4). Arno.

--La Republique Des Lacedemoniens. Connor, W. R., ed. LC 78-18589. (Greek Texts Commentaries Ser.). (Illus.). 1979. Repr. of 1934 ed. lib. bdg. 12.00x (ISBN 0-405-11431-1). Arno.

GREEK LITERATURE–TRANSLATIONS INTO ENGLISH

Anderson, David, tr. from Greek. On the Divine Images: St. John of Damascus. LC 80-13409. 106p. 1980. pap. 3.95 (ISBN 0-913836-62-1). St Vladimirs.

Barbour, Amy L., ed. Selections from Herodotus. (Illus.). 1977. pap. 7.95x (ISBN 0-8061-1427-4). U of Okla Pr.

Barker, Ernest, ed. Library of Greek Thought, 9 Vols. Repr. of 1934 ed. Set. 147.00 (ISBN 0-404-07800-1). AMS Pr.

Brueggemann, Ludwig W. View of English Editions, Translations & Illustrations of the Ancient Greek & Latin Authors, 2 Vols. Repr. of 1797 ed. Set. 61.50 (ISBN 0-8337-0403-6). B Franklin.

Cornford, Francis M., ed. Greek Religious Thought from Homer to the Age of Alexander. LC 79-98637. (Library of Greek Thought: No. 2). Repr. of 1923 ed. 21.50 (ISBN 0-404-01734-7). AMS Pr.

Dickinson, G. Lowes & Meredith, H. O., eds. Temple Greek & Latin Classics, 5 Vols. Repr. of 1907 ed. Set. 120.00 (ISBN 0-404-07900-8). AMS Pr.

Gaselee, S., tr. from Greek. Achilles Tatius. LC 76-48065. 1977. Repr. of 1917 ed. lib. bdg. 27.25x (ISBN 0-8371-9315-X, ACTA). Greenwood.

Holton, Milne, ed. The Big Horse & Other Stories of Modern Macedonia. LC 73-93892. 224p. 1974. 12.50x (ISBN 0-8262-0162-8). U of Mo Pr.

Homer. The Odyssey. Shewring, Walter, tr. (The World's Classics Ser.). 384p. 1981. pap. 3.95x (ISBN 0-19-281542-3). Oxford U Pr.

--Odyssey, 2 vols. 2nd ed. Incl. Vol. 1, Bks. 1-12. 432p. 1959. 12.95 (ISBN 0-312-58135-1); Vol. 2, Bks. 13-24. 454p. 1958. 12.95 (ISBN 0-312-58170-X). (Classic Ser). St Martin.

Howe, George & Harrer, Gustave A. Greek Literature in Translation. 1979. Repr. of 1924 ed. lib. bdg. 40.00 (ISBN 0-8495-2255-2). Arden Lib.

Joint Association of Classical Teachers-Greek Course. The Intellectual Revolution: Selections from Euripides, Thucydides & Plato. LC 79-16754. (Illus.). 160p. 1980. pap. 9.95x (ISBN 0-521-22461-6). Cambridge U Pr.

Livingstone, Richard W., ed. The Mission of Greece: Some Views of Life in the Roman World. LC 75-17473. (Illus.). 1976. Repr. of 1928 ed. lib. bdg. 19.00x (ISBN 0-8371-8312-X, LIMGR). Greenwood.

Lucian. True History & Lucius or the Ass. Turner, Paul, tr. from Gr. LC 58-8065. (Midland Bks.: No. 176). (Illus.). 120p. 1974. 5.95x (ISBN 0-253-36090-0); pap. 1.95x (ISBN 0-253-20176-4). Ind U Pr.

MacKendrick, Paul L & Howe, Herbert M, eds. Classics in Translation, 2 vols. Incl. Vol. 1. Greek Literature. 444p (ISBN 0-299-80895-5); Vol. 2. Latin Literature. 452p (ISBN 0-299-80896-3). 1952. text ed. 7.95 ea. U of Wis Pr.

Plato. Plato Apology & Crito. Dyer, Louis, ed. (College Classical Ser.). 246p. 1976. Repr. of 1908 ed. lib. bdg. 11.00 (ISBN 0-89241-000-0). Caratzas Bros.

Underdowne, Thomas. An Aethiopian History of Helidorus. 1974. lib. bdg. 20.00 (ISBN 0-685-45190-9). Folcroft.

Von Hildebrand, Alice, ed. Greek Culture. LC 66-15756. (Cultures of Mankind Ser). (Illus.). 1966. 6.95 (ISBN 0-8076-0366-X). Braziller.

Wallace, Malcolm W. The Birthe of Hercules: A Free Translation or Adaptation of the Amphitruo of Plautus. LC 73-13606. 1974. Repr. of 1903 ed. lib. bdg. 30.00 (ISBN 0-8414-9410-X). Folcroft.

Wedeck, Harry E., ed. Classics of Greek Literature. (Quality Paperback: No. 157). 1964. pap. 3.95 (ISBN 0-8226-0157-5). Littlefield.

Wright, John H., ed. Masterpieces of Greek Literature. facs. ed. LC 72-132136. (Play Anthology Reprint Ser). 1902. 18.25 (ISBN 0-8369-8213-4). Arno.

GREEK LITERATURE–TRANSLATIONS INTO ENGLISH–BIBLIOGRAPHY

Foster, Finley M. English Translations from the Greek. LC 70-168127. Repr. of 1918 ed. 15.00 (ISBN 0-404-02541-2). AMS Pr.

Howe, George. Greek Literature in Translation. Harrer, Gustave A., ed. 1978. Repr. of 1924 ed. lib. bdg. 35.00 (ISBN 0-8495-2334-6). Arden Lib.

GREEK LITERATURE, HELLENISTIC (COLLECTIONS)

Spencer, Terence. Fair Greece, Sad Relic: Literary Philhellenism from Shakespeare to Byron. LC 76-158507. (Illus.). 1971. Repr. of 1954 ed. 13.00 (ISBN 0-403-01307-0). Scholarly.

Stebbing, William. Some Greek Masterpieces in Dramatic & Burolic Poetry. 1919. 25.00 (ISBN 0-8274-3979-2). R West.

Wikgren, Allen P., et al. Hellenistic Greek Texts. LC 47-4029. 1947. 15.00x (ISBN 0-226-89688-9). U of Chicago Pr.

GREEK LITERATURE, HELLENISTIC–HISTORY AND CRITICISM

Dover, Kenneth. Ancient Greek Literature. 196p. 1980. 16.95x (ISBN 0-19-219137-3); pap. 6.95x (ISBN 0-19-289124-3). Oxford U Pr.

Murray, Gilbert. History of Ancient Greek Literature. Repr. lib. bdg. 30.00 (ISBN 0-8414-6689-0). Folcroft.

Page, Denys, ed. Epigrammata Graeca: From the Beginning to the Garland of Phillip. (Oxford Classical Texts Ser). 350p. 1975. 24.95x (ISBN 0-19-814581-0). Oxford U Pr.

GREEK LITERATURE, MODERN–HISTORY AND CRITICISM

Bien, Peter. Kazantzakis & Linguistic Revolution in Greek Literature. LC 79-154991. (Princeton Essays in Literature Ser.). 1972. 17.50 (ISBN 0-691-06206-4). Princeton U Pr.

Dimaras, C. T. History of Modern Greek Literature. Gianos, Mary P., tr. LC 73-112610. 1973. 36.00 (ISBN 0-87395-071-2); pap. 11.00 (ISBN 0-87395-230-8); microfiche o.p. 36.00 (ISBN 0-87395-171-9). State U NY Pr.

Doulis, Thomas. Disaster & Fiction: The Impact of the Asia Minor Disaster of 1922 on Modern Greek Fiction. LC 75-22654. 1977. 21.50x (ISBN 0-520-03112-1). U of Cal Pr.

Gianos, Mary P., ed. Introduction to Modern Greek Literature. LC 67-30722. 1969. text ed. 29.50x (ISBN 0-8057-3125-3); pap. text ed. 16.50x (ISBN 0-89197-801-1). Irvington.

Henderson, G. P. Revival of Greek Thought, 1620-1830. LC 75-112608. 1970. 14.00 (ISBN 0-87395-069-0); microfiche 14.00 (ISBN 0-87395-169-7). State U NY Pr.

Keeley, Edmund & Bien, Peter, eds. Modern Greek Writers. LC 78-166379. (Princeton Essays in Literature Ser.). 266p. 1972. 19.00 (ISBN 0-691-06215-3). Princeton U Pr.

Politis, Linos. A History of Modern Greek Literature. 341p. 1973. 37.50x (ISBN 0-19-815721-5). Oxford U Pr.

Powell, J. U. & Barber, E. A., eds. New Chapters in the History of Greek Literature. 1921. 15.00x (ISBN 0-8196-0286-8). Biblo.

--New Chapters in the History of Greek Literature. (Second Ser). 1929. 15.00x (ISBN 0-8196-0287-6). Biblo.

Sherrard, Philip. The Wound of Greece: Studies in Neo-Hellenism. LC 78-27758. 1979. 11.95x (ISBN 0-312-89300-0). St Martin.

GREEK LITERATURE, MODERN–TRANSLATIONS INTO ENGLISH

Decavalles, Adonis, et al, eds. Voice of Cyprus. 1966. 8.50 (ISBN 0-8079-0132-6). October.

GREEK MATHEMATICS

see Mathematics, Greek

GREEK MEDICINE

see Medicine, Greek and Roman

GREEK MUSIC

see Music, Greek and Roman

GREEK MYTHOLOGY

see Mythology, Greek

GREEK ORACLES

see Oracles

GREEK ORATIONS

Connor, W. Robert, ed. Greek Orations: Lysias, Isocrates, Demosthenes, Aeschines, Hyperides. (Orig.). 1966. pap. 5.95 (ISBN 0-472-06116-X, 116, AA). U of Mich Pr.

Jebb, Richard C., ed. Attic Orators: Selections from Antiphon, Andocides, Lysias, Isocrates & Isaeus. 2nd ed. (Gr). 1888. 9.95 (ISBN 0-312-06020-3). St Martin.

Maidment, K. J. & Burtt, J. O., trs. Minor Attic Orators, Vol. 1. Incl. Antiphon & Andocides. (Loeb Classical Library: No. 308). 11.00x (ISBN 0-674-99340-3). Harvard U Pr.

--Minor Attic Orators, Vol. 2. Incl. Lycurgus; Dinarchus; Demades; Hyperides. (Loeb Classical Library: No. 395). 11.00x (ISBN 0-674-99434-5). Harvard U Pr.

GREEK ORATIONS–HISTORY AND CRITICISM

Connor, Robert W., ed. Greek Orations: Lysias, Isocrates, Demosthenes, Aeschines, Hyperides. LC 66-17355. 1966. 5.95 (ISBN 0-472-24250-4). U of Mich Pr.

Dionysius Of Halicarnassus. Critical Essays, Vol. 1. Usher, Stephen, tr. from Gr. (Loeb Classical Library: No. 465). 640p. (Eng.). 1974. text ed. 11.00x (ISBN 0-674-99512-0). Harvard U Pr.

Dobson, J. F. The Greek Orators. 336p. 1974. 10.00 (ISBN 0-89005-050-3). Ares.

Dobson, John F. Greek Orators. facs. ed. LC 67-23205. (Essay Index Reprint Ser). 1919. 19.00 (ISBN 0-8369-0381-1). Arno.

Jebb, Richard C. Attic Orators from Antiphon to Isaeos, 2 Vols. LC 62-8230. 1962. Repr. of 1875 ed. Set. 20.00 (ISBN 0-8462-0208-5). Russell.

Miller, Walter. Daedalus & Thespis: Volume II: Sculpture, Pts. 1 & 2. Repr. of 1931 ed. 10.00x (ISBN 0-8262-0590-9). U of Mo Pr.

GREEK PAINTING

see Painting, Greek

GREEK PAPYRI

see Manuscripts (Papyri)

GREEK PHILOLOGY

see also Classical Philology; Greek Language; Greek Literature (Collections); Inscriptions, Greek

Egger, E. L' Hellenisme En France, 2 Vols. 1964. Repr. of 1869 ed. 50.50 (ISBN 0-8337-1022-2). B Franklin.

Geanakoplos, Deno J. Byzantium & the Renaissance: Greek Scholars in Venice: Studies in the Dissemination of Greek Learning from Byzantium to Western Europe. (Illus.). xiii, 348p. 1973. Repr. of 1962 ed. 17.50 (ISBN 0-208-01311-3, Archon). Shoe String.

Greek Poetry & Life: Essays Presented to Gilbert Murray on His Seventieth Birthday, January 2, 1936. facs. ed. LC 67-30192. (Essay Index Reprint Ser). 1936. 18.50 (ISBN 0-8369-0496-6). Arno.

Laum, Bernhard. Das Alexandrinische Akzentuationssystem Unter Zugrundelegung der Theoretischen Lehren der Grammatik. Repr. of 1928 ed. pap. 34.00 (ISBN 0-384-31620-4). Johnson Repr.

Lloyd-Jones, Hugh, ed. The Greeks. (New Reprints in Essay & General Literature Index Ser.). 1975. Repr. of 1962 ed. 20.75 (ISBN 0-518-10204-1, 10204). Arno.

Oikonomides, Al. N. Greek Abbreviations in Inscriptions, Papyri, Manuscripts & Early Printed Books. 214p. 1975. 15.00 (ISBN 0-89005-049-X). Ares.

Thomson, J. A. The Greek Tradition. 1971. Repr. of 1915 ed. 10.00 (ISBN 0-911858-23-7). Appel.

Whibley, Leonard. Companion to Greek Studies. 4th rev. ed. (Illus.). 1963. Repr. of 1931 ed. 21.75 (ISBN 0-02-854700-4). Hafner.

GREEK PHILOSOPHY

see Philosophy, Ancient

GREEK POETRY (COLLECTIONS)

Here are entered collections in the Greek Language. For English translations see subdivision Translations into English.

Campbell, D. A., ed. Greek Lyric Poetry. (Gr). 1967. 10.95 (ISBN 0-312-34860-6). St Martin.

Daitz, Stephen G. A Recital of Ancient Greek Poetry. (Sound Seminars Ser.). 1978. 4 audio cassettes incl. 48.00x (ISBN 0-88432-029-4). J Norton Pubs.

Edmonds, J. M., tr. Lyra Graeca, 3 Vols. (Loeb Classical Library: No. 142-144). 11.00x ea. Vol. 1 (ISBN 0-674-99157-5). Vol. 2 (ISBN 0-674-99158-3). Vol. 3 (ISBN 0-674-99159-1). Harvard U Pr.

Gow, Andrew S. & Page, D. L. Greek Anthology: Garland of Philip & Other Contemporary Epigrams, 2 Vols. LC 68-10149. (Eng. & Gr.). 1968. 130.00 set (ISBN 0-521-05874-0). Cambridge U Pr.

Gow, Andrew S., ed. Bucolici Graeci. (Oxford Classical Texts). 1952. 14.95x (ISBN 0-19-814517-9). Oxford U Pr.

Greek Bucolic Poets: Theocritus, Bion & Moschus. (Loeb Classical Library: No. 28). 11.00x (ISBN 0-674-99031-5). Harvard U Pr.

Greek Elegy, Iambus, & Anacreontea, 2 Vols. (Loeb Classical Library: No. 258-259). 11.00x ea. Vol. 1 (ISBN 0-674-99284-9). Vol. 2 (ISBN 0-674-99285-7). Harvard U Pr.

Holton, Milne & Reid, Graham W., eds. Reading the Ashes: An Anthology of the Poetry of Modern Macedonia. LC 76-41758. 1977. 10.95 (ISBN 0-8229-3337-3); pap. 4.95 (ISBN 0-8229-5282-3). U of Pittsburgh Pr.

Page, Denys, ed. Supplementum Lyricum: Poetarum Lyricorum Graecorum Fragmenta Qua Recens Innotuerunt. 160p. (Greek.). 1974. 32.50x (ISBN 0-19-814002-9). Oxford U Pr.

Page, Denys L., ed. Lyrica Graece Selecta. (Oxford Classical Texts). 1968. 17.50x (ISBN 0-19-814567-5). Oxford U Pr.

--Poetae Melici Graeci. 1962. 44.50x (ISBN 0-19-814333-8). Oxford U Pr.

Radhakrishnan, S. Eastern Religions & Western Thought. 2nd ed. 396p. 1975. pap. text ed. 6.95x (ISBN 0-19-560604-3). Oxford U Pr.

Smyth, Herbert W., ed. Greek Melic Poets. LC 63-10769. 1899. 12.50 (ISBN 0-8196-0120-9). Biblo.

GREEK POETRY–HISTORY AND CRITICISM

Alcman. The Partheneion. Connor, W. R., ed. LC 78-81590. (Greek Texts Commentaries Ser.). 1979. Repr. of 1951 ed. lib. bdg. 15.00x (ISBN 0-405-11432-X). Arno.

Arnold, Edwin. Poets of Greece. LC 70-39680. (Essay Index Reprint Ser.). Repr. of 1869 ed. 16.00 (ISBN 0-8369-2738-9). Arno.

Barnstone, Willis, tr. from Gr. Greek Lyric Poetry. LC 67-25140. (Illus.). 320p. 1972. 11.00x (ISBN 0-8052-3447-0); pap. 5.95 (ISBN 0-8052-0339-7). Schocken.

Bergren, Ann L. The Etymology & Usage of Peirar in Early Greek Poetry. (American Philological Association, American Classical Studies). 1975. pap. 6.00 (ISBN 0-89130-242-5, 400402). Scholars Pr Ca.
Bowie, Angus M. The Poetic Dialect of Sappho & Alcaeus. rev ed. Connor, W. R., ed. LC 80-2641. (Monographs in Classical Studies). 1981. lib. bdg. 22.00 (ISBN 0-405-14029-0). Arno.
Cairns, F. Genetic Composition in Greek & Roman Poetry. 1973. 18.50x (ISBN 0-85224-224-7, Pub. by Edinburgh U Pr Scotland). Columbia U Pr.
De Almeida, Hermione. Byron & Joyce Through Homer: Don Juan & Ulysses. 256p. 1981. 20.00x (ISBN 0-231-05092-5). Columbia U Pr.
Elliger, Winfried. Die Darstellung der Landschaft in der griechischen Dichtung: Untersuchungen Zur Antiken Literatur und Geschicht, Vol.15. LC 73-93160. (Ger.). 1975. 103.00x (ISBN 3-11-004794-2). De Gruyter.
Greek Poetry & Life. 399p. 1981. Repr. of 1936 ed. lib. bdg. 45.00 (ISBN 0-89987-310-3). Darby Bks.
Greek Poetry & Life: Essays Presented to Gilbert Murray on His Seventieth Birthday, January 2, 1936. facs. ed. LC 67-30192. (Essay Index Reprint Ser). 1936. 18.50 (ISBN 0-8369-0496-6). Arno.
Halporn, James, et al. The Meters of Greek & Latin Poetry. rev. ed. LC 79-6718. 138p. 1980. pap. 4.95x (ISBN 0-8061-1558-0). U of Okla Pr.
Hirzel, Rudolf & Marg, Walter. Agraphcs Nomos & der Charakter in der Sprache der Fruhgriechischen Dichtung, 2 vols. in one. Vlastos, Gregory, ed. LC 78-14615. (Morals & Law in Ancient Greece Ser.). (Ger. & Greek.). 1979. Repr. of 1938 ed. lib. bdg. 16.00x (ISBN 0-405-11590-3). Arno.
Irwin, Eleanor. Colour Terms in Greek Poetry. LC 72-78018. 1973. 15.00 (ISBN 0-88866-519-9). Samuel Stevens.
Jebb, R. C. Growth & Influence of Classical Greek Poetry. LC 71-101045. 1969. Repr. of 1893 ed. 13.00 (ISBN 0-8046-0710-9). Kennikat.
Jebb, Richard C. Growth & Influence of Classical Greek Poetry. LC 79-93247. 1970. Repr. of 1893 ed. 8.50 (ISBN 0-87752-054-2). Gordian.
Kindstrand, Jan F. The Bion of Borysthenes. (Sudia Graeca Upsaliensia: No. 11). 1976. pap. text ed. 24.00x (ISBN 91-554-0486-3). Humanities.
Kirkwood, G. M. Early Greek Monody: The History of a Poetic Type, Vol. 37. LC 73-8411. (Studies in Classical Philology). 317p. 1974. 24.50x (ISBN 0-8014-0795-8). Cornell U Pr.
Levi, Peter, ed. Agenda: Greek Poetry Special Issue, Vol. 7 No. 1. 1977. lib. bdg. 8.50 (ISBN 0-8495-0008-7). Arden Lib.
Lorenzatos, Zissimos. The Lost Center & Other Essays in Greek Poetry. Cicellis, Kay, tr. from Gr. LC 79-3221. (Princeton Essays in Literature Ser.). 224p. 1980. 15.00x (ISBN 0-691-06246-3). Princeton U Pr.
Mackail, J. W. Lectures on Greek Poetry. LC 66-23520. 1910. 10.50x (ISBN 0-8196-0180-2). Biblo.
--Lectures on Greek Poetry. 59.95 (ISBN 0-8490-0495-0). Gordon Pr.
Montagu, Elizabeth. Essay on the Writings & Genius of Shakespeare Compared with the Greek & French Dramatic Poets: 1785-1839. 292p. 1970. Repr. of 1839 ed. 25.00x (ISBN 0-7146-2515-9, F Cass Co). Biblio Dist.
Nagy, Gregory. The Best of the Achaeans: Concepts of the Hero As Reflected in the Archaic Forms of Greek Poetry. LC 79-9907. 1980. text ed. 15.00x (ISBN 0-8018-2200-9). Johns Hopkins.
--The Best of the Achaens: Concepts of the Hero in Archaic Greek Poetry. LC 79-9907. 414p. 1981. pap. 7.95 (ISBN 0-8018-2388-9). Johns Hopkins.
Nicander. The Poems & Poetical Fragments. Connor, W. R., ed. LC 78-18579. (Greek Texts & Commentaries Ser.). (Illus.). 1979. Repr. of 1887 ed. lib. bdg. 18.00x (ISBN 0-405-11422-2). Arno.
Parry, Hugh. The Lyric Poems of Greek Tragedy. 1978. 15.95 (ISBN 0-89522-014-8). Samuel Stevens.
Richardson, N. J. The Homeric Hymn to Demeter. 380p. 1979. Repr. of 1974 ed. text ed. 29.50x (ISBN 0-19-814199-8). Oxford U Pr.
Sen, Ramendra K. A Brief Introduction to a Comparative Study of Greek & Indian Poetics & Aesthetics. LC 76-14407. 1976. Repr. of 1954 ed. lib. bdg. 7.50 (ISBN 0-8414-7837-6). Folcroft.
Sikes, Edward E. The Greek View of Poetry. LC 78-20494. 1980. Repr. of 1931 ed. 21.00 (ISBN 0-88355-870-X). Hyperion Conn.
Silk, M. S. Interaction in Poetic Imagery. LC 73-90813. 304p. 1974. 42.00 (ISBN 0-521-20417-8). Cambridge U Pr.
Snell, Bruno. Poetry & Society: The Role of Poetry in Ancient Greece. LC 73-165808. (Select Bibliographies Reprint Ser.). Repr. of 1961 ed. 12.00 (ISBN 0-8369-5965-5). Arno.
Soutar, George. Nature in Greek Poetry, Studies Partly Comparative. Repr. of 1939 ed. 23.00 (ISBN 0-384-56750-9). Johnson Repr.
Thomson, George. Pre-Historic Aegean. 4th ed. 1978. pap. 18.00x (ISBN 0-8464-0746-9). Beekman Pubs.
Trypanis, Constantine A. Greek Poetry from Homer to Seferis. LC 81-1160. 896p. 1981. lib. bdg. 50.00x (ISBN 0-226-81316-9). U of Chicago Pr.
West, M. L., ed. Iambi et Elegi Graeci Ante Alexandrum Cantati: Archilochus, Hipponax, Theognidea, Vol. 1. 276p. 1972. 34.50x (ISBN 0-19-814184-X). Oxford U Pr.
West, Martin. Studies in Greek Elegy & Iambus. LC 73-93168. (Untersuchungen zur antiken Literatur & Geschichte, Vol. 14). ix, 198p. 1974. 57.10x (ISBN 3-11-004585-0). De Gruyter.
White, Heather. Essays in Hellenistic Poetry. (London Studies in Classical Philology: Vol. 5). 81p. 1981. pap. text ed. 17.25x (ISBN 90-70265-52-4, Pub. by Gieben Holland). Humanities.
--Studies in Theocritus & Other Hellenistic Poets. (London Studies in Classical Philology: Vol. 3). 1980. text ed. 17.25x (ISBN 90-70265-81-8). Humanities.
Willcock, Malcolm M. A Companion to the "Iliad". LC 75-20894. 1976. pap. 6.95 (ISBN 0-226-89855-5, P677, Phoen). U of Chicago Pr.

GREEK POETRY–TRANSLATIONS INTO ENGLISH

Aldington, Richard, ed. The Poet's Translation Series, 2 vols. Incl. Series One. LC 78-64005 (ISBN 0-404-17101-X); Second Series. LC 78-64016 (ISBN 0-404-17102-8). (Des Imagistes: Literature of the Imagist Movement). Repr. of 1920 ed. Set. 49.00 (ISBN 0-404-17100-1); 25.00 ea. AMS Pr.
Anthologia Graeca Selections. Poems from the Greek Anthology, in English Paraphrase. Fitts, Dudley, tr. LC 78-13574. 1978. Repr. of 1956 ed. lib. bdg. 18.50 (ISBN 0-313-21017-9, AGPG). Greenwood.
Elytis, Odysseus. The Axion Esti. Keeley, Edmund & Savidis, George, trs. from Gr. LC 79-49274. (Pitt Poetry Ser.). 1979. pap. 4.95 (ISBN 0-8229-5318-8). U of Pittsburgh Pr.
Gow, A. S., tr. The Greek Bucolic Poets. LC 72-179529. 156p. 1972. Repr. of 1953 ed. 15.00 (ISBN 0-208-01250-8, Archon). Shoe String.
Greek Bucolic Poets: Theocritus, Bion & Moschus. (Loeb Classical Library: No. 28). 11.00x (ISBN 0-674-99031-5). Harvard U Pr.
Greek Elegy, Iambus, & Anacreontea, 2 Vols. (Loeb Classical Library: No. 258-259). 11.00x ea. Vol. 1 (ISBN 0-674-99284-9). Vol. 2 (ISBN 0-674-99285-7). Harvard U Pr.
Hine, Daryl. The Homeric Hymns. LC 72-82685. 1972. 7.95 (ISBN 0-689-10515-0). Atheneum.
Jay, Peter, ed. & intro. by. The Greek Anthology & Other Ancient Greek Epigrams. 1973. 14.95 (ISBN 0-19-519745-3). Oxford U Pr.
Keeley, Edmund & Sherrard, Phillip, eds. Voices of Modern Greece: Cavafy, Sikelianos, Seferis, Elytis & Gatsos. rev. & expanded ed. LC 81-47282. (Lockert Library of Poetry in Translation). 210p. 1981. 18.50x (ISBN 0-691-06473-3); pap. 5.95x (ISBN 0-691-01382-9). Princeton U Pr.
Lattimore, Richmond, tr. Greek Lyrics. rev. ed. LC 60-51619. (Orig.). 1960. pap. 2.50 (ISBN 0-226-46944-1, P48, Phoen). U of Chicago Pr.
Rexroth, Kenneth, tr. Poems from the Greek Anthology. (Illus.). 1962. pap. 2.50 (ISBN 0-472-06063-5, 63, AA). U of Mich Pr.
Sappho. Memoir. 4th ed. Wharton, H. T., tr. 217p. 1974. Repr. of 1898 ed. text ed. 21.75x (ISBN 90-6090-002-2). Humanities.
Spanias, Nikos, tr. from Gr. Resistance, Exile & Love: An Anthology of Greek Post-War Poetry. LC 77-81189. 1977. 10.00 (ISBN 0-918618-05-3); pap. 6.00 (ISBN 0-918618-04-5). Pella Pub.

GREEK POETRY, MODERN–HISTORY AND CRITICISM

Sherrard, Philip. Marble Threshing Floor. facs. ed. LC 73-117893. (Select Bibliographies Reprint Ser). 1956. 20.00 (ISBN 0-8369-5346-0). Arno.

GREEK POETRY, MODERN–TRANSLATIONS INTO ENGLISH

Cavafy, C. P. C. P. Cavafy: Collected Poems. Savidis, George, ed. Keeley, Edmund & Sherrard, Philip, trs. from Gr. LC 74-2977. (Lockert Library of Poetry in Translation). 508p. (Eng. & Gr.). 1975. 27.50 (ISBN 0-691-06279-X); pap. 5.95 (ISBN 0-691-01320-9). Princeton U Pr.
Dalven, Rae, ed. & tr. Modern Greek Poetry. 2nd enl. ed. LC 78-151544. 1971. Repr. of 1949 ed. 27.50 (ISBN 0-8462-1595-0). Russell.
Friar, Kimon, ed. Modern Greek Poetry: Translation, Introduction, an Essay on Translation, & Notes by Kimon Friar. LC 70-171604. 1973. 20.00 (ISBN 0-671-21025-4). S&S.
Palamas, Kostes. The Twelve Words of the Gypsy. new ed. Stephanides, Theodore & Katsimbalis, George, trs. from Gr. LC 75-12894. 336p. 1975. text ed. 15.00x (ISBN 0-87870-025-0); pap. text ed. 6.95x (ISBN 0-87870-029-3). Memphis St Univ.

GREEK POTTERY

see Pottery, Greek

GREEK RHETORIC

see Rhetoric, Ancient

GREEK REVIVAL (ARCHITECTURE)

see also Architecture, Greek; Neoclassicism (Architecture)

GREEK SATIRE

see Satire, Greek

GREEK SCULPTURE

see Sculpture, Greek

GREEK TALES

see Tales, Greek

GREEK VASES

see Vases–Greece

GREEKS

Applebaum, Shimon. Jews & Greeks in Ancient Cyrene. (Illus.). 367p. 1980. text ed. 64.00x (ISBN 90-04-05970-9). Humanities.
Crosher, Judith & Strongman, Harry. The Greeks. LC 77-86190. (Peoples of the Past Ser.). (Illus.). 1977. lib. bdg. 7.95 (ISBN 0-686-51157-3). Silver.
Dunbabin, T. J. The Western Greeks. 504p. 1979. 30.00 (ISBN 0-89005-300-6). Ares.
O'Connell, Brian. Greek & Celtic. 1978. 8.95 (ISBN 0-533-02474-9). Vantage.

GREEKS IN FOREIGN COUNTRIES

Antoniou, Mary. Welfare Activities Among the Greek People in Los Angeles: Thesis. LC 74-7650. 1974. Repr. of 1939 ed. soft bdg. 8.00 (ISBN 0-88247-283-6). R & E Res Assoc.
Bottomley, Gillian. After the Odyssey. (Studies in Society & Culture). 1980. 24.95x (ISBN 0-7022-1399-3). U of Queensland Pr.
Burgess, Thomas. Greeks in America. 1970. Repr. of 1913 ed. 11.00 (ISBN 0-685-40308-4). R & E Res Assoc.
--Greeks in America: An Account of Their Coming, Progress, Customs, Living & Aspirations. LC 72-129392. (American Immigration Collection, Ser. 2). (Illus.). 1970. Repr. of 1913 ed. 14.00 (ISBN 0-405-00547-4). Arno.
Cutsumbis, Michael N. A Bibliographic Guide to Materials on Greeks in the United States, 1890-1968. LC 74-130283. 100p. 1970. pap. text ed. 8.95x (ISBN 0-913256-02-1, Dist. by Ozer). Ctr Migration.
Dimitras, Elie. Sociological Survey on Greek Emigrants: Upon the Return to Greece. (National Centre of Social Research Monographs). (Illus.). 131p. 1971. 7.50x (ISBN 0-8002-1988-0). Intl Pubns Serv.
Dunbabin, T. J. The Western Greeks. 504p. 1979. 30.00 (ISBN 0-89005-300-6). Ares.
Gavaki, Efrosini. The Integration of Greeks in Canada. LC 76-55962. 1977. soft bdg. 8.00 (ISBN 0-88247-436-7). R & E Res Assoc.
Geanakoplos, Deno J. Byzantium & the Renaissance: Greek Scholars in Venice: Studies in the Dissemination of Greek Learning from Byzantium to Western Europe. (Illus.). xiii, 348p. 1973. Repr. of 1962 ed. 17.50 (ISBN 0-208-01311-3, Archon). Shoe String.
Panagopoulos, Epaminodes P. New Smyrna: An Eighteenth Century Greek Odyssey. 2nd ed. LC 77-16303. (Illus.). 1978. 10.00 (ISBN 0-916586-13-8); pap. 4.95 (ISBN 0-916586-14-6). Holy Cross Orthodox.
Randall-MacIver, David. Greek Cities in Italy & Sicily. Repr. of 1931 ed. lib. bdg. 14.25x (ISBN 0-8371-4318-7, RAGC). Greenwood.
Saloutos, Theodore. Greeks in the United States. LC 64-13428. (Illus.). 1964. 18.50x (ISBN 0-674-36325-6). Harvard U Pr.
Stathopoulos, Peter. The Greek Community of Montreal. LC 70-174583. (National Centre of Social Research Monographs). 68p. 1971. 7.50x (ISBN 0-8002-1472-2). Intl Pubns Serv.
Steffanides, G. F. America the Land of My Dreams. 1974. 6.95 (ISBN 0-9600114-2-0). Steffanides.
Teske, Robert T. Votive Offerings Among Greek-Philadelphians: A Ritual Perspective. Dorson, Richard M., ed. LC 80-735. (Folklore of the World Ser.). 1980. lib. bdg. 29.00x (ISBN 0-405-13325-1). Arno.
Toynbee, Arnold J. The Western Question in Greece & Turkey: A Study in the Contrast of Civilizations. 2nd ed. LC 68-9598. (Illus., Maps). 1970. Repr. of 1922 ed. 25.00 (ISBN 0-86527-209-3). Fertig.

GREELEY, HORACE 1811-1872

Fahrney, Ralph R. Horace Greeley & the Tribune in the Civil War. LC 77-135663. (American Scene Ser). 1970. Repr. of 1936 ed. lib. bdg. 25.00 (ISBN 0-306-71120-6). Da Capo.
Horner, Harlan H. Lincoln & Greeley. LC 74-135247. viii, 432p. Repr. of 1953 ed. lib. bdg. 20.00x (ISBN 0-8371-5166-X, HOLG). Greenwood.
Ingersoll, Lurton D. Life of Horace Greeley: Founder of the N. Y. Tribune. (American Newspapermen 1790-1933 Ser.). (Illus.). 688p. 1974. Repr. 26.50x (ISBN 0-8464-0018-9). Beekman Pubs.
Isely, Jeter A. Horace Greeley & the Republican Party, 1853-1861. 1965. lib. bdg. 25.00x (ISBN 0-374-94123-8). Octagon.
Linn, W. A. Horace Greeley. LC 80-26831. (American Men & Women of Letters Ser.). 275p. 1981. pap. 5.95 (ISBN 0-87754-165-5). Chelsea Hse.
Linn, William A. Horace Greeley. (Amer. Newspapermen Ser.: 1790-1933). 267p. 1975. 17.50x (ISBN 0-8464-0015-4). Beekman Pubs.
Lunde, Erik S. Horace Greeley. (United States Author Ser.: No. 413). 1981. lib. bdg. 9.95 (ISBN 0-8057-7343-6). Twayne.
Parton, James. Life of Horace Greeley. LC 70-125711. (The American Journalists). 442p. 1972. Repr. of 1855 ed. 24.00 (ISBN 0-405-01692-1). Arno.
Seitz, Don C. Horace Greeley, Founder of the New York Tribune. LC 74-112297. (Illus.). Repr. of 1926 ed. 28.00 (ISBN 0-404-00210-2). AMS Pr.
Sotheran, Charles. Horace Greeley & Other Pioneers of American Socialism. LC 75-333. (The Radical Tradition in America Ser). 367p. 1975. Repr. of 1915 ed. 23.50 (ISBN 0-88355-236-1). Hyperion Conn.
Southeran, Charles. Horace Greeley & Other Pioneers of American Socialism. LC 70-122999. (American Biography Ser., No. 32). 1970. Repr. lib. bdg. 53.95 (ISBN 0-8383-1132-6). Haskell.
Zabriskie, Frances. Horace Greeley, the Editor. (Amer. Newspapermen Ser.: 1790-1933). 398p. 1977. Repr. of 1890 ed. 19.50x (ISBN 0-8464-0000-6). Beekman Pubs.
Zabriskie, Francis N. Horace Greeley. 1977. Repr. of 1890 ed. lib. bdg. 20.00 (ISBN 0-686-19808-5). Havertown Bks.
--Horace Greeley: The Editor. 398p. 1980. Repr. of 1890 ed. lib. bdg. 25.00 (ISBN 0-89984-548-7). Century Bookbindery.

GREEN, FLETCHER MELVIN, 1895-

Link, Arthur S. & Patrick, Rembert W., eds. Writing Southern History: Essays in Historiography in Honor of Fletcher M. Green. LC 65-23761. 1967. pap. text ed. 8.95x (ISBN 0-8071-0123-0). La State U Pr.

GREEN, GEORGE, 1743-1808

Wordsworth, Dorothy. George & Sarah Green. De Selincourt, ed. LC 72-196429. 1936. lib. bdg. 20.00 (ISBN 0-8414-9797-4). Folcroft.

GREEN, HENRY, 1905-

Bassoff, Bruce. Toward Loving: The Poetics of the Novel & the Practice of Henry Green. LC 75-22071. 180p. 1975. lib. bdg. 14.95x (ISBN 0-87249-324-5). U of SC Pr.
Ryf, Robert S. Henry Green. LC 67-27360. (Columbia Essays on Modern Writers Ser.: No. 29). 1968. pap. 2.00 (ISBN 0-231-02897-0). Columbia U Pr.
Weatherhead, A. Kingsley. A Reading of Henry Green. LC 61-8767. 180p. 1961. 11.00 (ISBN 0-295-73902-9). U of Wash Pr.

GREEN, JULIAN, 1900-

Burne, Glenn S. Julian Green. (World Authors Ser.: France: No. 195). lib. bdg. 10.95 (ISBN 0-8057-2404-4). Twayne.
Dunaway, John M. The Metamorphoses of the Self: The Mystic, the Sensualist, & the Artist in the Works of Julien Green. LC 78-88007. (Studies in Romance Languages: No. 19). 128p. 1978. 11.50x (ISBN 0-8131-1364-4). U Pr of Ky.
Kostis, Nicholas. The Exorcism of Sex & Death in Julien Green's Novels. (De Proprietatibus Litterarum Ser. Practica: No. 71). 1973. pap. text ed. 18.75x (ISBN 90-2792-602-6). Mouton.
Stokes, Samuel E. Julian Green & the Thorn of Puritanism. LC 72-5655. 155p. 1972. Repr. of 1955 ed. lib. bdg. 15.00x (ISBN 0-8371-6444-3, STJG). Greenwood.

GREEN, PAUL ELIOT, 1894-

Clark, Barrett H. Paul Green. LC 74-1164. (Studies in Drama, No. 39). 1974. lib. bdg. 22.95 (ISBN 0-8383-2016-3). Haskell.
Kenny, Vincent. Paul Green. LC 79-125254. (United States Authors Ser.). 1971. lib. bdg. 8.95x (ISBN 0-89197-880-1); pap. text ed. 4.95x (ISBN 0-8290-0007-0). Irvington.

GREEN, SARAH, 1763-1808

Wordsworth, Dorothy. George & Sarah Green. De Selincourt, ed. LC 72-196429. 1936. lib. bdg. 20.00 (ISBN 0-8414-9797-4). Folcroft.

GREEN, THEODORE FRANCIS, 1867-1966

Levine, Erwin L. Theodore Francis Green: The Rhode Island Years, 1906-1936. LC 63-18096. (Illus.). x, 222p. 1963. 10.00 (ISBN 0-87057-077-3, Pub. by Brown U Pr). U Pr of New Eng.

--Theodore Francis Green: The Rhode Island Years, 1906-1936. LC 63-18096. (Illus.). 232p. 1963. text ed. 10.00x (ISBN 0-87057-077-3, Pub. by Brown U Pr). U Pr of New Eng.
--Theodore Francis Green: The Washington Years, 1937-1960. LC 73-127366. (Illus.). xii, 179p. 1971. 10.00 (ISBN 0-87057-126-5, Pub. by Brown U Pr). U Pr of New Eng.
--Theodore Francis Green: The Washington Years, 1937-1960. LC 73-127366. (Illus.). 191p. 1971. text ed. 10.00x (ISBN 0-87057-126-5, Pub. by Brown U Pr). U Pr of New Eng.

GREEN, THOMAS HILL 1836-1882
Greengarten, I. M. Thomas Hill Green & the Development of Liberal-Democratic Thought. 194p. 1981. 20.00x (ISBN 0-8020-5503-6). U of Toronto Pr.
Leland, Abby P. The Educational Theory & Practice of T. H. Green. LC 78-176984. (Columbia University. Teachers College. Contributions to Education: No. 46). Repr. of 1911 ed. 17.50 (ISBN 0-404-55046-0). AMS Pr.
MacCunn, John. Six Radical Thinkers: Bentham, J. S. Mill, Cobden, Carlyle, Mazzini, T. H. Green. LC 64-20669. 1964. Repr. of 1910 ed. 7.50 (ISBN 0-8462-0502-5). Russell.
--Six Radical Thinkers: Bentham, J.S. Mill, Codden, Carlyle, Massine, T.H. Green. Mayer, J. P., ed. LC 78-67370. (European Political Thought Ser.). 1979. Repr. of 1907 ed. lib. bdg. 16.00x (ISBN 0-405-11720-5). Arno.
Ritchie, David G. Principles of State Interference. facsimile ed. LC 70-94282. (Select Bibliogrpahies Reprint Ser). 1902. 17.00 (ISBN 0-8369-5060-7). Arno.
Sidgwick, Henry. Lectures on the Ethics of T. H. Green, Herbert Spencer, & J. Martineau. LC 3-865. 1968. Repr. of 1902 ed. 22.00 (ISBN 0-527-82812-2). Kraus Repr.

GREEN BAY, WISCONSIN, FOOTBALL CLUB (NATIONAL LEAGUE)
Bengtson, Phil & Hunt, Todd. Packer Dynasty. LC 75-78716. 1969. 6.95 (ISBN 0-385-07164-7). Doubleday.
Kramer, Jerry. Instant Replay: The Green Bay Diary of Jerry Kramer. Schaap, Dick, ed. (RL 7). 1969. pap. 2.50 (ISBN 0-451-07377-0, E9657, Sig). NAL.
May, Julian. The Green Bay Packers. (The NFL Today Ser.). (gr. 4-8). 1980. lib. bdg. 6.45 (ISBN 0-87191-727-0); pap. 2.95 (ISBN 0-89812-230-9). Creative Ed.
--Green Bay Packers. LC 74-905. (Superbowl Champions Ser). 48p. 1974. 6.45 (ISBN 0-87191-330-5); pap. 2.95 (ISBN 0-89812-086-1). Creative Ed.
--Green Bay Packers. LC 74-905. (Superbowl Champions Ser). 48p. 1974. 6.45 (ISBN 0-87191-330-5); pap. 2.95 (ISBN 0-89812-086-1). Creative Ed.

GREEN BELTS
see Greenbelts

GREEN BERETS
see United States–Army

GREEN RIVER AND VALLEY
Crocker, Helen B. The Green River of Kentucky. LC 76-4433. (Kentucky Bicentennial Bookshelf Ser.). (Illus.). 120p. 1976. 6.95 (ISBN 0-8131-0226-X). U Pr of Ky.
Evans, Laura & Belknap, Buzz. Desolation River Guide: Green River Wilderness. LC 74-80877. (Illus.). 56p. 1974. waterproof 8.95 (ISBN 0-916370-06-2); pap. 5.95 (ISBN 0-916370-05-4). Westwater.
Goldwater, Barry M. Delightful Journey: Down the Green & Colorado Rivers. LC 77-94876. 1970. 15.00 (ISBN 0-910152-01-2). AZ Hist Foun.
Staveley, Gaylord. Broken Waters Sing: Rediscovering Two Great Rivers of the West. 1971. 6.95 (ISBN 0-316-81095-9). Little.

GREEN SEA TURTLE
see Green Turtle

GREEN TURTLE
Cromie, William J. Steven & the Green Turtle. LC 77-85040. (Science I Can Read Books). (Illus.). (gr. k-3). 1970. PLB 7.89 (ISBN 0-06-021374-4, HarpJ). Har-Row.
Waters, John F. Green Turtle Mysteries. LC 70-158701. (A Let's-Read-&-Find-Out Science Bk). (Illus.). (gr. k-3). 1972. (TYC-J); PLB 8.79 (ISBN 0-690-35995-0). Har-Row.

GREENAWAY, KATE, 1846-1901
Engen, Rodney. Kate Greenaway: A Biography. LC 81-40407. (Illus.). 240p. 1981. 22.50 (ISBN 0-8052-3775-5). Schocken.
Kate Greenaway. LC 77-78654. (Illus.). 1977. pap. 8.50 (ISBN 0-8478-0130-6). Rizzoli Intl.
Kiger, Robert, et al, eds. Kate Greenaway: Catalogue of an Exhibition of Original Artworks & Related Materials Selected from the Frances Hooper Collection at the Hunt Institute. (Illus.). 112p. 1980. 22.00x (ISBN 0-913196-33-9). Hunt Inst Botanical.
Spielmann, M. H. & Layard, G. S. Kate Greenaway. LC 68-58917. (Illus.). 1968. Repr. of 1905 ed. 22.00 (ISBN 0-405-08990-2). Arno.
--Kate Greenaway. 1977. lib. bdg. 150.95 (ISBN 0-8490-2113-8). Gordon Pr.
Thomson, Susan R., ed. Kate Greenaway: A Catalogue of the Kate Greenaway Collection, Rare Book Room, Detroit Public Library. LC 77-5222. (Illus.). 1977. 30.00x (ISBN 0-8143-1581-X). Wayne St U Pr.

GREENBACKS
Barrett, Don C. The Greenbacks & the Resumption of Specie Payments. 1965. 8.00 (ISBN 0-8446-1057-7). Peter Smith.
Berkey, William A. Money Question. LC 78-75562. Repr. of 1876 ed. lib. bdg. 15.00x (ISBN 0-8371-1078-5, BEMQ). Greenwood.
Hessler, Gene. U. S. Essay, Proof & Specimen Notes. LC 79-7481. 1979. 19.50 (ISBN 0-931960-04-5). BNR Pr.
Mitchell, Wesley C. Gold, Prices & Wages Under the Greenback Standard. pap. 27.00 (ISBN 0-384-39220-2). Johnson Repr.
--Gold, Prices, & Wages Under the Greenback Standard. LC 66-21688. Repr. of 1908 ed. 25.00x (ISBN 0-678-00200-2). Kelley.
--History of the Greenbacks with Special Reference to the Economic Consequences of Their Issue: 1862-1865. LC 3-22564. 1960. Repr. of 1903 ed. 15.00x (ISBN 0-226-53212-7). U of Chicago Pr.
Newcomb, Simon. Critical Examination of Our Financial Policy During the Southern Rebellion. Repr. of 1865 ed. lib. bdg. 15.00 (ISBN 0-8371-0589-7, NEFP). Greenwood.
Sharkey, Robert. Money, Class, & Party: An Economic Study of Civil War & Reconstruction. LC 59-15423. (Studies in Historical & Political Science: No. 2, 77th Series). 346p. 1959. pap. 5.95x (ISBN 0-8018-0586-4). Johns Hopkins.
Spaulding, Elbridge G. Resource of War: The Credit of the Government Made Immediately Available-History of the Legal Tender Paper Money Issued During the Great Rebellion Being a Loan Without Interest & a National Currency. LC 69-19681. (Money Markets Ser). 1971. Repr. of 1869 ed. lib. bdg. 14.75x (ISBN 0-8371-0662-1, SPRW). Greenwood.
Unger, I. Greenback Era: A Social & Political History of American Finance, 1865-1879. 1964. 26.50x (ISBN 0-691-04517-8). Princeton U Pr.

GREENBELTS
see also Garden Cities
Little, C. Challenge of the Land. 1969. 12.25 (ISBN 0-08-006913-4). Pergamon.
Osborn, Frederic J. Green-Belt Cities. 2nd ed. LC 77-85678. 1971. pap. 2.45 (ISBN 0-8052-0301-X). Schocken.
Platt, Rutherford H. Open Land in Urban Illinois: Roles of the Citizen Advocate. LC 78-146641. 132p. 1971. pap. 5.00 (ISBN 0-87580-506-X). N Ill U Pr.

GREENBERG, CLEMENT
Kuspit, Donald B. Clement Greenberg, Art Critic. LC 79-3967. 1979. 15.00 (ISBN 0-299-07900-7). U of Wis Pr.

GREENE, GRAHAM, 1904-
Allott, Kenneth & Farris, Miriam. Art of Graham Greene. LC 63-15146. (Illus.). 1963. Repr. of 1951 ed. 15.00 (ISBN 0-8462-0371-5). Russell.
Atkins, John. Graham Greene. 240p. 1980. Repr. lib. bdg. 30.00 (ISBN 0-8492-3447-6). R West.
--Graham Greene. 2nd rev. ed. 1970. text ed. 10.00x (ISBN 0-7145-0262-6). Humanities.
--Graham Greene. 1979. Repr. of 1957 ed. lib. bdg. 35.00 (ISBN 0-8495-0139-3). Arden Lib.
Boardman, Gwenn R. Graham Greene: The Aesthetics of Exploration. LC 78-126425. 1971. 7.25 (ISBN 0-8130-0312-1). U Presses Fla.
Cassis, A. F. Graham Greene: An Annotated Bibliography of Criticism. LC 81-770. (Scarecrow Author Bibliographies Ser.: No. 55). 423p. 1981. 22.50 (ISBN 0-8108-1418-8). Scarecrow.
Evans, Robert O., ed. Graham Greene: Some Critical Considerations. LC 63-22005. 304p. 1967. pap. 6.00x (ISBN 0-8131-0114-X). U Pr of Ky.
Greene, Graham. Ways of Escape. 1981. 13.95 (ISBN 0-671-41219-1). S&S.
Kulshrestha, J. P. Graham Greene the Novelist. 1977. text ed. 9.00x (ISBN 0-333-90174-6). Humanities.
Kunkel, Francis L. The Labyrinthine Ways of Graham Greene: A Critical Study. 2nd. & enl. ed. Repr. of 1960 ed. 12.00 (ISBN 0-911858-25-3). Appel.
Mesnet, Marie B. Graham Greene & the Heart of the Matter: An Essay. LC 72-6404. 115p. 1972. Repr. of 1954 ed. lib. bdg. 15.00 (ISBN 0-8371-6490-7, MEGG). Greenwood.
--Graham Greene & the Heart of the Matter. LC 77-28959. 1954. 10.00 (ISBN 0-8482-1843-4). Norwood Edns.
Miller, Robert H. Graham Greene: A Descriptive Catalogue. LC 77-92925. 88p. 1979. 12.50x (ISBN 0-8131-1383-0). U Pr of Ky.
Phillips, Gene D. Graham Greene: The Films of His Fiction. LC 73-85252. 1974. pap. 7.95 (ISBN 0-8077-2376-2). Tchrs Coll.
Roy, Gregor. Monarch Notes on Graham Greene's Major Novels. (Orig.). pap. 1.95 (ISBN 0-671-00838-2). Monarch Pr.
Stratford, Philip. Faith & Fiction: Creative Process in Greene & Mauriac. 1964. pap. 2.95x (ISBN 0-268-00379-3). U of Notre Dame Pr.
Vann, J. Don. Graham Greene: A Checklist of Criticism. LC 70-113763. (Serif Ser.: No. 14). 1970. 5.50x (ISBN 0-87338-101-7). Kent St U Pr.
Wolfe, Peter. Graham Greene the Entertainer. LC 72-188700. (Crosscurrents-Modern Critiques Ser.). 191p. 1972. 11.95 (ISBN 0-8093-0580-1). S Ill U Pr.

GREENE, NATHANAEL, 1742-1786
Abbazia, Patrick. Nathanael Greene, Commander of the American Continental Army in the South. Rahmas, Steve, ed. (Outstanding Personalities Ser.: No. 87). 1976. lib. bdg. 2.95 incl. catalog cards (ISBN 0-686-15818-0); pap. 1.50 vinyl laminated covers (ISBN 0-686-15819-9). SamHar Pr.
Greene, Francis V. General Greene. LC 72-120878. (American Bicentennial Ser). 1970. Repr. of 1893 ed. 16.75 (ISBN 0-8046-1271-4). Kennikat.
Greene, George W. The Life of Nathanael Greene: Major-General in the Army of the Revolution. LC 72-5507. (Select Bibliographies Reprint Ser.). 1972. Repr. of 1867 ed. 75.00 (ISBN 0-8369-6910-3). Arno.
Greene, Nathanael. The Papers of Nathanael Greene, Seventeen Sixty-Six to Seventeen Eighty-Six, Vol. 2: 1 January 1777 to 16 October 1778. Showman, Richard K., et al, eds. 650p. 1980. 22.00 (ISBN 0-8078-1384-2). U of NC Pr.
Johnson, William. Sketches of the Life & Correspondences of Nathanael Green, 2 vols. LC 78-119063. 516p. 1974. Repr. of 1822 ed. lib. bdg. 65.00 (ISBN 0-306-71953-3). Da Capo.
Peckham, Howard H. Nathanael Greene: Independent Boy. (Childhood of Famous Americans Ser). (Illus.). (gr. 3-7). 1956. 3.95 (ISBN 0-672-50139-2). Bobbs.
Showman, Richard K., ed. The Papers of General Nathanael Greene, Dec. 1766-Dec. 1776, Vol. 1. 1976. 18.00 (ISBN 0-685-67666-8). RI Hist Soc.
Showman, Richard K., et al, eds. The Papers of General Nathanael Greene, Vol. 1: December, 1766 to December 1776. LC 76-20441. 1976. 18.00x (ISBN 0-8078-1285-4). U of NC Pr.
--The Papers of General Nathanael Greene: January 1st. 1777-October 16th. 1778, Vol. 2. LC 76-20441. 1980. 22.00x (ISBN 0-8078-1384-2). U of NC Pr.
Treacy, Mildred F. Prelude to Yorktown: The Southern Campaign of Nathanael Greene, 1780-1781. 1963. 17.50x (ISBN 0-8078-0887-3). U of NC Pr.

GREENE, ROBERT, 1558-1592
Bratchell, D. F. Robert Greene's Planetomachia & the Text of the Third Tragedy: A Bibliographical Explanation & a New Edition of the Text. 1979. 40.00x (ISBN 0-86127-201-3, Pub. by Avebury Pub England). State Mutual Bk.
Chapman, W. William Shakespeare & Robert Greene: The Evidence. LC 73-18209. (Studies in Shakespeare, No. 24). 1974. lib. bdg. 49.95 (ISBN 0-8383-1731-6). Haskell.
Harvey, Gabriel. Foure Letters & Certaine Sonnets. 1973. Repr. of 1922 ed. 10.50 (ISBN 0-8274-1364-5). R West.
--Foure Letters & Certeine Sonnets, Especially Touching Robert Greene & Other Parties by Him Abused, 1592. facs. ed. LC 70-119960. (Select Bibliographies Reprint Ser). 1922. 11.00 (ISBN 0-8369-5403-3). Arno.
Hayashi, Tetsumaro. Robert Greene Criticism: A Comprehensive Bibliography. LC 79-142235. (Author Bibliographies Ser.: No. 6). 1971. 10.00 (ISBN 0-8108-0340-2). Scarecrow.
Jordan, John C. Robert Greene. 1965. lib. bdg. 14.50x (ISBN 0-374-94408-3). Octagon.
Robertson, John M. Did Shakespeare Write Titus Andronicus. LC 77-39875. Repr. of 1905 ed. 10.00 (ISBN 0-404-05361-0). AMS Pr.
Simpson, Richard, ed. School of Shakespeare, 2 vols. LC 78-176026. Repr. of 1878 ed. Set. 47.50 (ISBN 0-404-06058-7). AMS Pr.
Stein, Charles H. Robert Greene's the Scottish History of James IV: A Critical, Old Spelling Edition. (Salzburg Studies in English Literature: Elizabethan & Renaissance Studies: No. 59). 1977. pap. text ed. 22.75x (ISBN 0-391-01531-1). Humanities.

GREENE COUNTY, NEW YORK
Beecher, Raymond. Out to Greenville & Beyond, Historical Sketches of Greene County. (Illus.). 1977. pap. 5.50 (ISBN 0-685-88519-4). Hope Farm.
Burgner, Goldene F. Greene County Marriages, 1783 to 1868. 310p. Date not set. 25.00 (ISBN 0-89308-202-3). Southern Hist.
History of Greene County: New York with Biographical Sketches of Its Prominent Men. Repr. of 1884 ed. 12.50 (ISBN 0-685-61127-2). Hope Farm.

GREENE COUNTY, NEW YORK–DESCRIPTION AND TRAVEL
Atkinson, Oriana. Not Only Ours, a Story of Greene County, N. Y. 1974. pap. 3.75 (ISBN 0-685-48725-3). Hope Farm.
Chadwick, George H. Rocks of Greene County. 1973. pap. 2.00 (ISBN 0-685-40640-7). Hope Farm.
De Lisser, R. Lionel. Picturesque Catskills, Greene County. (Illus.). 1894. pap. 5.50 (ISBN 0-685-12167-4). Hope Farm.

GREENHEAD
see Striped Bass

GREENHOUSES
see also Artificial Light Gardening; Forcing (Plants)
Abraham, George & Abraham, Katy. Organic Gardening Under Glass. LC 75-19310. 1975. 10.95 (ISBN 0-87857-104-3). Rodale Pr Inc.
Beckett, Kenneth A. Amateur Greenhouse Gardening. 1980. 14.95 (ISBN 0-8464-0991-7). Beekman Pubs.
Blake, Claire. Greenhouse Gardening for Fun. (Illus.). 1967. pap. 3.95 (ISBN 0-688-06737-9). Morrow.
Boodley, James W. The Commercial Greenhouse. LC 78-74806. (Agriculture Ser.). 576p. 1981. 16.40 (ISBN 0-8273-1719-0); instr's. guide 1.45 (ISBN 0-8273-1718-2). Delmar.
--The Commerical Greenhouse Handbook. 544p. 1981. 24.95 (ISBN 0-442-23146-6). Van Nos Reinhold.
Brann, Donald R. How to Build Greenhouses - Walk-in, Window, Sun House, Garden Tool House. LC 80-67650. 210p. 1980. pap. 5.95 (ISBN 0-87733-811-6). Easi-Bild.
--How to Build Greenhouses-Sun Houses. rev ed. LC 72-91056. (Illus.). 1976. lib. bdg. 5.95 (ISBN 0-87733-011-5); pap. 3.50 (ISBN 0-87733-611-3). Easi-Bild.
Byers, Anthony. Growing Under Glass. 144p. 1974. 7.95 (ISBN 0-7207-0549-5, Pub. by Michael Joseph). Merrimack Bk Serv.
Clegg, Peter & Watkins, Derry. The Complete Greenhouse Book: From Cold Frames to Solar Structures. 1978. o. p. 14.95 (ISBN 0-88266-142-6); pap. 10.95 (ISBN 0-88266-141-8). Garden Way Pub.
Downs, R. G. & Hellmers, H. Environment & the Experimental Control of Plant Growth. (Experimental Botany Ser.). 1975. 24.50 (ISBN 0-12-221450-1). Acad Pr.
Eaton, Jerome A. Gardening Under Glass: An Illustrated Guide to Living with a Greenhouse. LC 75-189678. 224p. 1973. 8.95 (ISBN 0-02-534700-4). Macmillan.
Ellwood, Charles. How to Build & Operate Your Greenhouse. LC 77-89600. (Illus.). 1977. pap. 5.95 (ISBN 0-912656-55-7). H P Bks.
Fenten. Greenhousing for Purple Thumbs. LC 76-26055. (Illus.). 192p. (Orig.). 1976. 4.95 (ISBN 0-89286-105-3); pap. 4.95 (ISBN 0-89286-104-5). One Hund One Prods.
Fontanetta, John & Heller, Al. Building & Using a Solar-Heated Geodesic Greenhouse. (Illus.). pap. 9.95 (ISBN 0-88266-161-2). Garden Way Pub.
Fuel Saving in Greenhouses. 1981. 15.00x (ISBN 0-686-75416-6, Pub. by Grower Bks). State Mutual Bk.
Gardiner, G. F. Greenhouse Gardening. 1968. 17.00 (ISBN 0-8206-0052-0). Chem Pub.
The Greenhouse Book. LC 74-22566. (Illus.). 1976. pap. 4.95 (ISBN 0-8473-1347-6). Sterling.
Greenhouse Handbook for the Amateur. 1.95 (ISBN 0-686-21137-5). Bklyn Botanic.
Hanan, J. J., et al. Greenhouse Management. LC 77-21211. (Advanced Series in Agricultural Sciences: Vol 5). 1978. 49.40 (ISBN 0-387-08478-9). Springer-Verlag.
Kramer, Jack. Your Homemade Greenhouse. 1980. pap. 5.95 (ISBN 0-346-12442-5). Cornerstone.
--Your Homemade Greenhouse: And How to Build It. LC 74-31926. (Illus.). 98p. 1975. 7.95 (ISBN 0-8027-0495-6). Walker & Co.
Langhans, Robert W. Greenhouse Management: A Guide to Structures, Environmental Control, Materials Handling, Crop Programming & Business Analysis. (Illus.). 239p. 1980. 14.50 (ISBN 0-9604006-0-5). Halcyon Ithaca.
Laurie, Alex, et al. Commercial Flower Forcing. 7th ed. 1968. text ed. 19.00 (ISBN 0-07-036632-2, C). McGraw.
--Commercial Flower Forcing. 8th ed. (Illus.). 1979. text ed. 20.00 (ISBN 0-07-036633-0, C). McGraw.
McCullagh, James, ed. The Solar Greenhouse Book. LC 77-17028. 1978. 14.95 (ISBN 0-87857-198-1); pap. 9.95 (ISBN 0-87857-222-8). Rodale Pr Inc.
McDonald, Elvin. The Greenhouse Gardener. rev ed. (Orig.). 1976. pap. 1.75 (ISBN 0-451-09037-3, E9037, Sig). NAL.

Mastalerz, John W. The Greenhouse Environment: The Effect of Environmental Factors on Flower Crops. LC 77-6793. 1977. 28.95 (ISBN 0-471-57606-9). Wiley.
Menage, Ronald. Woolman's Greenhouse Gardening: A Comprehensive Guide to Cultivation Under Glass. (Illus.). 253p. 1975. 12.50 (ISBN 0-241-89032-2). Transatlantic.
Menage, Ronald H. The Unheated Greenhouse: How to Maximize Its Potential. LC 80-52346. (Illus.). 128p. 1980. pap. 5.95 (ISBN 0-8069-8954-8). Sterling.
Minar, William M. Greenhouse Gardening in the South. LC 76-1685. (Illus.). 96p. 1976. pap. 3.95 (ISBN 0-88415-327-4). Pacesetter Pr.
Neal, Charles D. Build Your Own Greenhouse: How to Construct, Equip, & Maintain It. (Illus.). 180p. 1975. 10.95 (ISBN 0-8019-5968-3). Chilton.
--Build Your Own Greenhouse: How to Construct, Equip & Maintain It. (Illus.). 1978. pap. 6.95 (ISBN 0-8019-6683-3). Chilton.
Nearing, Helen & Nearing, Scott. Building & Using Our Sun-Heated Greenhouse: Grow Vegetables All Year-Round. (Illus.). 1977. 11.95 (ISBN 0-88266-112-4); pap. 7.95 (ISBN 0-88266-111-6). Garden Way Pub.
Nearing, Scott & Nearing, Helen. Our Sun-Heated Greenhouse. (Illus.). 7.00 (ISBN 0-685-51041-7). Soc Sci Inst.
Nearing, Scott & Nearing, Helen K. Building & Using Our Sun-Heated Greenhouse. (Illus.). 1979. pap. 7.00 (ISBN 0-686-57438-9). Soc Sci Inst.
Nelson, Kennard S. Flower & Plant Production in the Greenhouse. 3rd ed. LC 77-79741. (Illus.). (gr. 9-12). 1978. 15.35 (ISBN 0-8134-1965-4). Interstate.
--Greenhouse Management for Flower & Plant Production. 4th ed. 1980. 15.35 (ISBN 0-8134-2070-9, 2070); text ed. 11.50x (ISBN 0-8134-2070-9). Interstate.
Nelson, P. Greenhouse Operation & Management. 1978. 19.95 (ISBN 0-87909-319-6); instrs'. manual avail. Reston.
Nelson, Paul. Greenhouse Operation & Management. 2nd ed. 520p. 1981. text ed. 19.95 (ISBN 0-8359-2576-5); instr's. manual free (ISBN 0-8359-2577-3). Reston.
Nicholls, Richard. The Handmade Greenhouse: From Windowsill to Backyard. LC 74-31541. (Illus.). 128p. (Orig.). 1975. lib. bdg. 12.90 (ISBN 0-914294-11-3); pap. 5.95 (ISBN 0-914294-12-1). Running Pr.
Northen, Henry T. & Northen, Rebecca T. Greenhouse Gardening. 2nd ed. (Illus.). 350p. 1973. 18.95 (ISBN 0-8260-6785-9, 72583, Pub. by Wiley-Interscience). Wiley.
Ortho Books Editorial Staff, ed. How to Build & Use Greenhouses. LC 78-57889. (Illus.). 1979. pap. 4.95 (ISBN 0-917102-74-6). Ortho.
Pierce, John H. Greenhouse Grow How. (Illus.). 1978. 19.95 (ISBN 0-918730-01-5, ScribT). Scribner.
--Greenhouse Grow-How. Hollis, Angela & Johnson, Emily, eds. (Illus.). 1977. 19.95 (ISBN 0-918730-01-5). Plants Alive.
Scheller, William. Successful Home Greenhouses. LC 76-51747. (Illus.). 134p. 1977. 13.95 (ISBN 0-912336-40-4); pap. 6.95 (ISBN 0-912336-41-2). Structures Pub.
Sherrill Britz, Billie. The Greenhouse at Lyndhurst: Construction & Development of the Gould Greenhouse, 1881. LC 76-50813. (Illus., Orig.). 1977. pap. 5.00 (ISBN 0-89133-046-1). Preservation Pr.
Shewell-Cooper, W. E. Basic Book of Greenhouse Growing. (Illus.). 1978. 15.00 (ISBN 0-214-20499-5). Transatlantic.
Simmons, Ted C. Greenhouse. 1977. pap. 1.50 (ISBN 0-912664-35-5). VPC Pr.
Steffek, Edwin, ed. The Complete Book of Houseplants & Indoor Gardening. (Illus.). 1976. 16.95 (ISBN 0-517-52614-X). Crown.
Sunset Editors. Greenhouse Gardening. LC 75-26490. (Illus.). 96p. 1976. pap. 2.95 (ISBN 0-376-03262-6, Sunset Bks). Sunset-Lane.
Time-Life Books, ed. Greenhouse Gardening. (The Encyclopedia of Gardening). (Illus.). 1977. 12.95 (ISBN 0-8094-2562-9). Time-Life.
Walls, Ian. Making the Most of Your Greenhouse. LC 77-90053. (Illus.). 1978. pap. 2.95 (ISBN 0-8120-0869-3). Barron.
Walls, Ian G. The Complete Book of Greenhouse Gardening. LC 75-8219. pap. 8.95 (ISBN 0-8129-6304-0). Times Bks.
--The Complete Book of Greenhouse Gardening. LC 75-8291. (Illus.). 448p. 1975. 14.95 (ISBN 0-8129-0577-6). Times Bks.
Yanda, Bill & Fisher, Rick. The Food & Heat Producing Solar Greenhouse. rev. ed. LC 79-91276. (Illus.). 208p. (Orig.). 1980. pap. 8.00 (ISBN 0-912528-20-6). John Muir.
Yanda, W. F. & Yanda, Susan. An Attached Solar Greenhouse. (Sp. & Eng.). 1976. pap. 2.00 (ISBN 0-89016-028-7). Lightning Tree.

GREENLAND

Banks, Michael. Greenland. (Illus.). 208p. 1975. 15.00x (ISBN 0-87471-722-1). Rowman.
Berg, Karin & Berg, Hans. Greenland Through the Year. LC 72-90689. (Illus.). 24p. (gr. k-4). 1973. 4.75 (ISBN 0-87592-023-3). Scroll Pr.
Berry, Francis. I Tell of Greenland: An Edited Translation of the Sautharkrokur Manuscripts. 1977. 17.50 (ISBN 0-7100-8591-5). Routledge & Kegan.
Birket-Smith, Kaj. Ethnography of the Egedesminde District, with Aspects of the General Culture of West Greenland. LC 74-5827. (Illus.). Repr. of 1924 ed. 73.00 (ISBN 0-404-11630-2). AMS Pr.
De Laguna, Frederica. Voyage to Greenland: A Personal Initiation into Anthropology. (Illus.). 1977. 9.95 (ISBN 0-393-06413-1). Norton.
Fristrup, Borge. The Greenland Ice Cap. LC 67-31985. (Illus.). 312p. 1967. 25.00 (ISBN 0-295-95209-1). U of Wash Pr.
Greenland Criminal Code. (American Series of Foreign Penal Codes: Vol. 16). x, 47p. 1970. 10.00x (ISBN 0-8377-0036-1). Rothman.
Kent, Rockwell. Greenland Journal. deluxe ed. 50.00 (ISBN 0-686-77011-0). Astor-Honor.
Markham, Clements R., ed. The Voyages of William Baffin, 1612-1622. LC 74-20893. (Illus.). 192p. 1881. Repr. 28.50 (ISBN 0-8337-2240-9). B Franklin.
Rink, Henrik. Danish Greenland: Its People & Products. (Illus.). 480p. 1975. Repr. of 1877 ed. 25.00x (ISBN 0-7735-0217-3). McGill-Queens U Pr.
Svarlien, Oscar. Eastern Greenland Case in Historical Perspective. LC 64-63740. (U of Fla. Social Sciences Monographs: No. 21). 1964. pap. 3.00 (ISBN 0-8130-0221-4). U Presses Fla.

GREENLAND–BIBLIOGRAPHY

Hermannsson, Halldor. Northmen in America, Nine Eighty Two-Fifteen Hundred. LC 9-18976. (Islandica Ser.: Vol. 2). 1909. pap. 8.00 (ISBN 0-527-00332-8). Kraus Repr.

GREENLAND–DESCRIPTION AND TRAVEL

Egede, H. P. A Description of Greenland. Repr. of 1818 ed. 25.00 (ISBN 0-527-26550-0). Kraus Repr.
Graah, Wilhelm A. Narrative of an Expedition to the East Coast of Greenland. LC 74-5842. Repr. of 1837 ed. 14.50 (ISBN 0-404-11647-7). AMS Pr.
Hermannsson, Halldor. Two Cartographers: Gudbrandur Thorlaksson & Thordur Thorlaksson. LC 27-13445. (Islandica Ser.: Vol. 17). 1926. pap. 14.00 (ISBN 0-527-00347-6). Kraus Repr.
Hobbs, William H. Exploring About the North Pole of the Winds. LC 68-55196. (Illus.). Repr. of 1930 ed. lib. bdg. 18.75x (ISBN 0-8371-0478-5, HONP). Greenwood.
Kent, Rockwell. N by E. LC 77-13530. (Illus.). 1978. Repr. of 1930 ed. 15.00x (ISBN 0-8195-5018-3, Pub. by Wesleyan U Pr). Columbia U Pr.
Nagel Travel Guide to Denmark-Greenland. (Nagel Travel Guide Ser). 1975. 43.00 (ISBN 2-8263-0640-5). Hippocrene Bks.
Nagel's Encyclopedia Guide: Denmark-Greenland. (Illus.). 544p. 1975. 43.00 (ISBN 2-8263-0640-5). Masson Pub.
Pellham, Edward. God's Power & Providence: Shewed in the Miraculous Preservation of Eight Englishmen, Left by Mischance in Green-Land. with a Description of That Countey. LC 68-54656. (English Experience Ser.: No. 45). 36p. 1968. Repr. of 1631 ed. 9.50 (ISBN 90-221-0045-6). Walter J Johnson.
Rasmussen, Knud. The People of the Polar North. LC 75-167126. 1975. Repr. of 1908 ed. 22.00 (ISBN 0-685-52348-9). Gale.
Rasmussen, Knud J. Greenland by the Polar Sea. LC 74-5867. (Illus.). Repr. of 1921 ed. 67.50 (ISBN 0-404-11674-4). AMS Pr.
Tillman, H. W. Ice with Everything. (Illus.). 144p. 8.95 (ISBN 0-686-74148-X). Superior Pub.
White, Adam, ed. Collection of Documents on Spitzbergen & Greenland. LC 71-134706. (Hakluyt Soc. Ser.: No. 18). 1970. lib. bdg. 32.00 (ISBN 0-8337-3766-X). B Franklin.

GREENLAND–HISTORY

Gad, Finn. History of Greenland: Earliest Times to 1700, Vol. 1. (Illus.). 356p. 1971. 22.95x (ISBN 0-7735-0119-3). McGill-Queens U Pr.
--The History of Greenland: 1700-1782, Vol. 2. (Illus.). 350p. 1973. 27.95x (ISBN 0-7735-0156-8). McGill-Queens U Pr.
Lethbridge, Thomas C. Herdsmen & Hermits. 1950. text ed. 4.25x (ISBN 0-391-01986-4). Humanities.
Norlund, P. Viking Settlers in Greenland & Their Descendants During Five Hundred Years. LC 37-14674. Repr. of 1936 ed. 13.00 (ISBN 0-527-67600-4). Kraus Repr.

GREENLAND–SOCIAL LIFE AND CUSTOMS

Kent, Rockwell. Greenland Journal. (Illus.). 1962. 12.50 (ISBN 0-8392-1042-6). Astor-Honor.
Rasmussen, Knud J. Knud Rasmussen's Posthumous Notes on the Life & Doings of the East Greenlanders in Olden Times. Osterman, H., ed. LC 74-19915. (Illus.). Repr. of 1938 ed. 37.50 (ISBN 0-404-12297-3). AMS Pr.
Rink, Hinrich J. Danish Greenland: Its People & Its Products. LC 74-5870. (Illus.). Repr. of 1877 ed. 32.50 (ISBN 0-404-11677-9). AMS Pr.

GREENLANDIC LANGUAGE

see Eskimo Language

GREENOUGH, HENRY, 1807-1883

Greenough, Horatio. Letters of Horatio Greenough to His Brother Henry Greenough. Greenough, Frances B., ed. LC 78-168199. Repr. of 1887 ed. 19.00 (ISBN 0-404-02897-7). AMS Pr.
Metzger, Charles R. Emerson & Greenough: Transcendental Pioneers of an American Esthetic. LC 74-139140. 1971. Repr. of 1954 ed. lib. bdg. 15.00 (ISBN 0-8371-5756-0, MEEG). Greenwood.

GREENOUGH, HORATIO, 1805-1852

Metzger, Charles R. Emerson & Greenough: Transcendental Pioneers of an American Esthetic. LC 74-139140. 1971. Repr. of 1954 ed. lib. bdg. 15.00 (ISBN 0-8371-5756-0, MEEG). Greenwood.
Tuckerman, Henry, ed. Memorial of Horatio Greenough. LC 68-57194. 1968. Repr. of 1853 ed. 15.00 (ISBN 0-405-09033-1, Pub. by Blom). Arno.
Wright, Nathalia, ed. Letters of Horatio Greenough, American Sculptor. LC 77-176417. (Illus.). 486p. 1972. 37.50x (ISBN 0-299-06070-5). U of Wis Pr.

GREEN'S FUNCTIONS

Doniach, S. & Sondheimer, E. G. Green's Functions for Solid State Physicists. LC 73-13723. (Frontiers in Physics Ser.: No. 44). (Illus.). 304p. 1974. pap. text ed. 16.50 (ISBN 0-8053-2397-X, Adv Bk Prog). Benjamin-Cummings.
Keilson, Julian. Green's Function Methods in Probability Theory. (Griffin's Statistical Monographs & Courses Ser: Vol. 17). (Illus.). 1965. pap. 14.25 (ISBN 0-02-847580-1). Hafner.
Rickayzen, G. Green's Functions & Condensed Matter. 1981. 55.00 (ISBN 0-12-587950-4). Acad Pr.
Stakgold, Ivar. Green's Functions & Boundary Value Problems. LC 78-27259. (Pure & Applied Mathematics: Texts, Monographs & Tracts). 638p. 1979. 39.50 (ISBN 0-471-81967-0, Pub. by Wiley-Interscience). Wiley.

GREEN'S THEOREM

see Potential, Theory Of

GREENSLET, FERRIS, 1875-

Greenslet, Ferris. Under the Bridge. 1943. 3.00 (ISBN 0-395-07755-9). HM.

GREENWATER (COPPER CAMP)

Weight, Harold O. Greenwater - Death Valley's Greatest Copper Camp. LC 78-83290. 1969. pap. 1.00 (ISBN 0-912714-02-6). Calico Pr.

GREENWICH VILLAGE, NEW YORK (CITY)

Barnes, Djuna. Greenwich Village As It Is. Wilson, Robert A., ed. (Illus.). 1978. 20.00 (ISBN 0-916228-08-8). Phoenix Bk Shop.
Chapin, Anna A. Greenwich Village. Repr. of 1917 ed. 20.00 (ISBN 0-685-64773-0). Norwood Edns.
Humphrey, Robert E. Children of Fantasy: The First Rebels of Greenwich Village. LC 77-28242. 1978. 21.95 (ISBN 0-471-42100-6, Pub. by Wiley-Interscience). Wiley.
Manville, Bill. Saloon Society. 192p. 1980. pap. 2.25 (ISBN 0-515-05490-9). Jove Pubns.
Ware, Caroline F. Greenwich Village, 1920-1930: A Comment on American Civilization in the Post-War Years. LC 76-51282. 1977. Repr. lib. bdg. 30.00x (ISBN 0-374-98230-9). Octagon.

GREENWOOD, CALEB, 1763-1853

Crosby, Alexander. Old Greenwood: Pathfinder of the West. LC 67-26263. (Illus.). (gr. 5-10). 1968. 3.95 (ISBN 0-934612-00-5). Talisman.

GREENWOOD, GRANVILLE GEORGE, SIR, 1850-1928

Beeching, Henry C. William Shakespeare, Player, Playmaker & Poet. LC 77-168571. (Illus.). Repr. of 1909 ed. 8.50 (ISBN 0-404-00724-4). AMS Pr.

GREETING CARDS

Chase, Ernest D. Romance of Greeting Cards: An Historical Account of the Origin, Evolution, & Development. LC 76-159914. (Tower Bks). (Illus.). 1971. Repr. of 1926 ed. 30.00 (ISBN 0-8103-3903-X). Gale.
Freeman, L. Collecting Prang Mark Greeting Cards. 1974. pap. 2.50 (ISBN 0-87282-042-4). Century Hse.
Freymann, Sara J. Season's Greetings. 1974. 2.50 (ISBN 0-517-51649-7). Crown.
Goeller, Carl. Writing & Selling Greeting Cards. 1980. 10.95 (ISBN 0-87116-124-9). Writer.
Hardt, Lorraine. How to Make Money Writing Greeting Cards. LC 68-18134. (Illus.). 180p. 1968. 8.95 (ISBN 0-8119-0096-7). Fell.
Holtje, Bert & Holtje, Adrienne. Cardcraft: Twenty-Two Techniques for Making Your Own Greeting Card & Notepaper. (Creative Crafts Ser.). 1978. 13.95 (ISBN 0-8019-6655-8); pap. 7.95 (ISBN 0-8019-6656-6). Chilton.
Kovash, Sr. Emily. How to Have Fun Making Cards. LC 74-10532. (Creative Craft Bks.). (Illus.). 32p. (gr. 2-6). 1974. PLB 5.95 (ISBN 0-87191-360-7). Creative Ed.
Purdy, Susan. Holiday Cards for You to Make. LC 67-10375. (Illus.). (gr. 4-9). 1967. 9.89 (ISBN 0-397-31574-0, JBL-J). Har-Row.
Sandman, Larry, ed. A Guide to Greeting Card Writing. LC 80-19737. 256p. 1980. 10.95 (ISBN 0-89879-022-0). Writers Digest.
Shinn, Bev & Shinn, Duane. How to Create Your Own Stationery, Christmas Cards Arrangements, Invitations, Greeting Cards, Posters, Note Paper, Etc. 1979. pap. 3.95 (ISBN 0-912732-36-9). Duane Shinn.

GREGARINIDA

Kamm, Minnie E. Studies on Gregarines. 1916. 18.50 (ISBN 0-384-28550-3). Johnson Repr.
--Studies on Gregarines 2: Synopsis of the Polycystid Gregarines of the World, Excluding Those from the Myriapoda, Orthoptera and Coleoptera. (Illinois Biological Monographs: Vol. 7, No. 1). 1922. 6.00 (ISBN 0-384-28560-0). Johnson Repr.

GREGG, JOHN ROBERT, 1867-1948

Symonds, Francis A. John Robert Gregg: The Man & His Work. 1963. 10.00 (ISBN 0-07-062655-3, G). McGraw.

GREGG, WILLIAM, 1800-1867

Mitchell, Broadus. William Gregg, Factory Master of the Old South. 1966. lib. bdg. 16.50x (ISBN 0-374-95795-9). Octagon.

GREGOIRE, HENRI, ABBE, 1750-1831

Necheles, Ruth F. Abbe Gregoire, 1787-1831: The Odyssey of an Egalitarian. LC 75-105987. 1971. lib. bdg. 15.95 (ISBN 0-8371-3312-2, NAG/&). Greenwood.

GREGORIAN CHANT

see Chants (Plain, Gregorian, etc.)

GREGORIUS 1ST, THE GREAT, SAINT, POPE, 540-604

Dudden, Frederick H. Gregory the Great: His Place in History & Thought, 2 Vols. LC 66-24687. (Illus.). 1967. Repr. of 1905 ed. Set. 25.00 (ISBN 0-8462-0921-7). Russell.
King Alfred's West-Saxon Version of Gregory's Pastoral Care, 2 pts. (EETS, OS Ser.: No. 50). Repr. of 1872 ed. Pt. I. 17.00 (ISBN 0-527-00041-8); Pt. II. 13.00 (ISBN 0-527-00042-6). Kraus Repr.
Richards, Jeffrey. Consul of God. 1980. 25.00x (ISBN 0-7100-0346-3). Routledge & Kegan.

GREGORIUS 7TH, SAINT, POPE, 1015-1085

Gregory Seventh, Pope The Correspondence of Pope Gregory VII. Emerton, E., tr. (Columbia University Records of Civilization Ser.). 1969. pap. 5.95x (ISBN 0-393-09859-1). Norton.
Macdonald, Allan J. Hildebrand: A Life of Gregory the Seventh. (Great Medieval Churchmen Ser). 254p. 1977. Repr. of 1932 ed. lib. bdg. 15.00x (ISBN 0-915172-26-7). Richwood Pub.

GREGORIUS DE ARNIMINO, d. 1358

Gregorii Ariminensis, O. E. S. A. Super Primum et Secundum Sententiarum. (Text Ser). 1955. Repr. of 1522 ed. 20.00 (ISBN 0-686-11553-8). Franciscan Inst.

GREGORY, SAINT, BP. OF NYSSA, 322-398

Burghardt, W. J., et al, eds. St. Gregory the Great: Pastoral Care. (ACW Ser.: No. 11). 282p. 1950. 11.95 (ISBN 0-8091-0251-X). Paulist Pr.
Cherniss, Harold F. Platonism of Gregory of Nyssa. 1971. Repr. of 1930 ed. lib. bdg. 18.50 (ISBN 0-8337-0556-3). B Franklin.
Malherbe, Abraham, tr. Gregory of Nyssa: The Life of Moses. LC 78-56352. (Classics of Western Spirituality). 224p. 1978. 11.95 (ISBN 0-8091-0239-0); pap. 7.95 (ISBN 0-8091-2112-3). Paulist Pr.

GREGORY, ISABELLA AUGUSTA (PERSSE) LADY, 1852-1932

Adams, Hazard. Lady Gregory. (Irish Writers Ser.). 106p. 1973. 4.50 (ISBN 0-8387-1085-9); pap. 1.95 (ISBN 0-8387-1207-X). Bucknell U Pr.
Coxhead, Elizabeth. Lady Gregory: A Literary Portrait. rev. ed. 1976. Repr. of 1961 ed. text ed. 4.75x (ISBN 0-900675-74-8). Humanities.
Gregory, Anne. Me & Nu: Childhood at Coole. 1970. text ed. 5.00x (ISBN 0-900675-48-9). Humanities.
Gregory, Isabella A. The Journals of Lady Gregory, Vol. 1: Book 1-29, 1916-1925. (Coole Edition of the Works of Lady Gregory). 1978. 39.95x (ISBN 0-19-519886-7). Oxford U Pr.
Kopper, Edward J., Jr. Lady Isabella Persse Gregory. (English Authors Ser: No. 194). 1976. lib. bdg. 12.95 (ISBN 0-8057-6658-8). Twayne.
Mikhail, E. H., ed. Lady Gregory: Interviews & Recollections. LC 77-1322. 113p. 1977. 13.50x (ISBN 0-87471-961-5). Rowman.

Von Klenze, Hilda. Lady Gregorys Leben und Werke. 1940. pap. 7.00 (ISBN 0-384-29775-7). Johnson Repr.

GREGORY, JOHN MILTON, 1822-1898

Kersey, Harry A., Jr. John Milton Gregory & the University of Illinois. LC 67-21854. 1968. 16.50 (ISBN 0-252-72563-8). U of Ill Pr.

GREGORY OF NAZIANZENUS, PATRIARCH OF CONSTANTINOPLE

Galavaris, George. Illustrations of the Liturgical Homilies of Gregory Nazianzenus. (Illuminated Manuscripts of the Middle Ages Ser.: Vol. 6). (Illus.). 1969. 50.00x (ISBN 0-691-03860-0). Princeton U Pr.

GRELLET, STEPHEN, 1773-1855

Dalglish, Doris N. People Called Quakers. facsimile ed. LC 78-90628. (Essay Index Reprint Ser). 1938. 15.00 (ISBN 0-8369-1254-3). Arno.

GRENADA, WEST INDIES

Constitucion De Grenada, 1973. (Span.). 1977. pap. 1.00 (ISBN 0-8270-5575-7). OAS.

Hay, John. Narrative of the Insurrection in the Island of Grenada, Which Took Place in 1795. LC 72-110010. Repr. of 1823 ed. 10.25x (ISBN 0-8371-4164-8, Pub. by Negro U Pr). Greenwood.

GRENFELL, GEORGE, 1849-1906

Johnston, Harry H. George Grenfell & the Congo, 2 Vols. Repr. of 1908 ed. Set. 60.00 (ISBN 0-527-46500-3). Kraus Repr.

--George Grenfell & the Congo, 2 vols. (Illus.). Repr. of 1908 ed. 88.00x (ISBN 0-8371-2482-4, Pub. by Negro U Pr). Greenwood.

GRENFELL, WILFRED THOMASON, SIR, 1865-1940

Kerr, James L. Wilfred Grenfell. His Life & Work. LC 73-21177. 1977. lib. bdg. 19.50x (ISBN 0-8371-6068-5, KEWG). Greenwood.

Martin, R. G. Knight of the Snows (Willfred Grenfell) 1966. pap. 1.50 (ISBN 0-87508-609-8). Chr Lit.

Ready, Dolores. Wilfred's Hospital Ship: Wilfred Grenfell. LC 77-86603. (Stories About Christian Heroes). (Illus.). (gr. 1-5). 1977. pap. 1.95 (ISBN 0-03-041651-5). Winston Pr.

Starr, Stephen Z. Colonel Grenfell's Wars: The Life of a Soldier of Fortune. LC 71-142339. 1971. 22.50x (ISBN 0-8071-0921-5). La State U Pr.

GRENVILLE, RICHARD, SIR, 1541-1591

Ralegh, Walter. A Report of the Truth of the Fight About the Iles of Acores. LC 72-26280. (English Experience Ser.: No. 183). 32p. 1969. Repr. of 1591 ed. 7.00 (ISBN 90-221-0183-5). Walter J Johnson.

GRENVILLE, RICHARD, SIR, 1600-1658

Miller, Amos C. Sir Richard Grenville of the Civil War. (Illus.). 215p. 1979. 16.50x (ISBN 0-8476-6160-1). Rowman.

Thomson, James E. The Grenville Problem. LC 57-3022. vii, 119p. 1956. 10.00x (ISBN 0-8020-7022-1). U of Toronto Pr.

GRESHAM, THOMAS, SIR, 1519-1579

Bindoff, S. T. The Fame of Sir Thomas Gresham. (Neale Lecture in English History Ser.: No. 4). 1973. pap. 2.00x (ISBN 0-224-00928-1). Humanities.

Burgon, John W. Life & Times of Sir Thomas Gresham, 2 Vols. (Illus.). 1965. Repr. of 1839 ed. Set. 53.00 (ISBN 0-8337-0422-2). B Franklin.

Ward, John. Lives of the Professors of Gresham College. (Illus.). Repr. of 1740 ed. 31.00 (ISBN 0-384-65740-0). Johnson Repr.

GRESHAM, WALTER QUINTIN, 1832-1895

Gresham, Matilda. Life of Walter Quintin Gresham 1832-1895, 2 Vols. facs. ed. LC 70-137378. (Select Bibliographies Reprint Ser). 1919. Set. 48.00 (ISBN 0-8369-5579-X). Arno.

GRESHAM COLLEGE

Ward, John. Lives of the Professors of Gresham College. (Illus.). Repr. of 1740 ed. 31.00 (ISBN 0-384-65740-0). Johnson Repr.

GREVILLE, FULKE, 1554-1628

Rees, Joan. Fulke Greville, Lord Brooke, 1554-1628: A Critical Biography. LC 79-132064. (Illus.). 1971. 22.75x (ISBN 0-520-01824-9). U of Cal Pr.

GREW, JOSEPH CLARK, 1880-1965

Heinrichs, Waldo H., Jr. American Ambassador: Joseph C. Grew & the Development of the United States Diplomatic Tradition. Freidel, Frank, ed. LC 78-66536. (The History of the United States Ser.: Vol. 7). 474p. 1979. lib. bdg. 35.00 (ISBN 0-8240-9705-X). Garland Pub.

GREY, CHARLES, 2ND EARL, 1764-1845

Trevelyan, George M. Lord Grey of the Reform Bill, Being the Life of Charles, Second Earl Grey. Repr. of 1920 ed. lib. bdg. 17.75x (ISBN 0-8371-4553-8, TRLG). Greenwood.

GREY, EDWARD GREY, 1ST VISCOUNT, 1862-1933

Hinsley, F. H., ed. British Foreign Policy Under Sir Edward Grey. LC 76-19631. 1977. 93.00 (ISBN 0-521-21347-9). Cambridge U Pr.

GREY, JANE, LADY

see Dudley, Jane, Lady, Known As Lady Jane Grey, 1537-1554

GREY, ZANE, 1875-1939

Gruber, Frank. Zane Grey. 1978. pap. 1.95 (ISBN 0-505-51281-5). Tower Bks.

--Zane Grey: A Biography. Repr. lib. bdg. 15.95x (ISBN 0-89190-756-4). Am Repr-Rivercity Pr.

--Zane Grey: A Biography. 298p. Repr. of 1969 ed. lib. bdg. 15.95x (ISBN 0-89190-756-4). Am Repr-Rivercity Pr.

Jackson, Carlton. Zane Grey. (U. S. Authors Ser.: No. 218). 1973. lib. bdg. 10.95 (ISBN 0-8057-0338-1). Twayne.

Scott, Kenneth W. Zane Grey, Born to the West. (Reference Bks.). 1979. lib. bdg. 21.50 (ISBN 0-8161-7875-5). G K Hall.

GREY DE WILTON, ARTHUR GREY, 14TH BARON, 1536-1593

Jones, Harry S. Spenser's Defense of Lord Grey. 1919. pap. 5.50 (ISBN 0-384-27770-5). Johnson Repr.

GREY DE WILTON, WILLIAM GREY, 13TH BARON, d. 1562

Grey De Wilton, Arthur G. Commentary of the Services & Charge of William Lord Grey of Wilton. De Malpas Grey Egerton, Philip, ed. LC 71-161716. (Camden Society, London. Publications. First Ser.: No. 40). Repr. of 1847 ed. 14.00 (ISBN 0-404-50140-0). AMS Pr.

GREY FRIARS

see Franciscans

GREYHOUNDS

see Dogs–Breeds–Greyhounds

GRIDDLE CAKES

see Pancakes, Waffles, etc.

GRIDWORK (STRUCTURAL ENGINEERING)

see Grillages (Structural Engineering)

GRIEF

see also Church Work with the Bereaved; Consolation

Allen, R. Earl. For Those Who Grieve. LC 77-75558. 1978. pap. 2.95 (ISBN 0-8054-2411-3). Broadman.

Anderson. It's O. K. to Cry. Date not set. lib. bdg. 7.35 (ISBN 0-516-06431-2). Childrens.

BerNstein, Joanne. Loss & How to Cope with It. LC 76-50027. (gr. 6 up). 8.95 (ISBN 0-395-28891-6, Clarion). HM.

Brown, Velma D. After Weeping, a Song. LC 79-53321. 1980. 6.50 (ISBN 0-8054-5425-X). Broadman.

Cain, Albert C., ed. Survivors of Suicide. (Illus.). 324p. 1972. pap. 26.75 photocopy edition, spiral (ISBN 0-398-02252-6). C C Thomas.

Chenard, Marcelle. Working Through Grief. (Thantology Service Ser.). 70p. 1982. 6.95 (ISBN 0-930194-05-5). Highly Specialized.

Claypool, John R. Tracks of a Fellow Struggler. LC 73-91553. 1976. pap. 1.25 (ISBN 0-87680-863-1, 91008, Key Word Bks). Word Bks.

Coniaris, A. M. Christ's Comfort for Those Who Sorrow. 1978. pap. 2.95 (ISBN 0-937032-00-X). Light&Life Pub Co MN.

Danto, Bruce & Kutscher, Austin H., eds. Suicide & Bereavement. (Thanatology Ser.). 1976. text ed. 13.50x (ISBN 0-8422-7298-4). Irvington.

D'Arcy, Paula. Song for Sarah: A Young Mother's Journey Through Grief, & Beyond. LC 79-14684. 1979. 6.95 (ISBN 0-87788-778-0); pap. 2.50 (ISBN 0-87788-780-2). Shaw Pubs.

Day, Gwynn M. The Joy Beyond. 1979. 3.95 (ISBN 0-8010-2893-0). Baker Bk.

Doyle, Polly. Grief Counseling & Sudden Death: A Manual & Guide. (Illus.). 352p. 1980. 26.50 (ISBN 0-398-04060-5). C C Thomas.

The Dynamics of Grief. LC 74-112333. 1970. 8.95 (ISBN 0-687-11313-X). Abingdon.

Freese, Arthur. GRIEF: Living Through It & Growing with It. 1978. pap. 3.50 (ISBN 0-06-464024-8, BN 4024, BN). Har-Row.

Freese, Arthur S. Help for Your Grief: Turning Emotional Loss into Growth. LC 76-44538. 1977. 9.95 (ISBN 0-8052-3640-6). Schocken.

Fulton, Robert. Death, Grief & Bereavement: A Bibliography, 1845-1975. Kastenbaum, Robert, ed. LC 76-19572. (Death and Dying Ser.). 1976. PLB 20.00 (ISBN 0-405-09570-8). Arno.

Fulton, Robert J. & Bendiksen, Robert. Death & Identity. rev. ed. 1978. text ed. 17.95 (ISBN 0-913486-78-7). Charles.

Furman, Erna. A Child's Parent Dies: Studies in Childhood Bereavement. LC 73-86894. 1974. 25.00x (ISBN 0-300-01719-7); pap. 7.95x (ISBN 0-300-02645-5). Yale U Pr.

Geaney, Dennis. Living with Sorrow. 1977. pap. 5.95 (ISBN 0-88347-074-8). Thomas More.

Guthmann, Robert F., Jr. & Womack, Sharon K. Death, Dying & Grief: A Bibliography. LC 77-82084. 1978. pap. text ed. 5.50 (ISBN 0-918626-01-3, Pied Publications). Word Serv.

Harper, Ralph. The Path of Darkness. 1968. 8.00 (ISBN 0-8295-0131-2). UPB.

Hegarty, Carol. The Conquering Spirit. (Illus.). 1977. pap. 2.50 (ISBN 0-89638-003-3). CompCare.

Helmlinger, Trudy. After You've Said Goodbye: How to Recover After Ending a Relationship. 1977. 8.95 (ISBN 0-8467-0214-2, Pub. by Two Continents). Hippocrene Bks.

Howard, Donald. Christians Grieve Too. 1980. pap. 1.45 (ISBN 0-85151-315-8). Banner of Truth.

Jackson, Edgar N. The Many Faces of Grief. LC 77-4363. 1977. 7.95 (ISBN 0-687-23203-1). Abingdon.

--Understanding Grief. LC 57-9786. 1957. 7.95 (ISBN 0-687-42854-8). Abingdon.

--You & Your Grief. 1961. 3.95 (ISBN 0-8015-9036-1, Hawthorn). Dutton.

Klopfenstein, Janette. My Walk Through Grief. LC 76-3937. 120p. 1976. pap. 1.75 (ISBN 0-8361-1799-9). Herald Pr.

Kutscher, A. & Kutscher, Lillian G., eds. Religion & Bereavement: Counsel for the Physician, Advice for the Bereaved. LC 74-187977. 350p. 1972. 12.50 (ISBN 0-88238-515-1). H S Pub Corp.

Lindemann, Erich & Lindemann, Elizabeth. Beyond Grief: Studies in Crisis Intervention. LC 79-50155. 1979. 22.50x (ISBN 0-87668-363-4). Aronson.

Linzer, N., ed. Understanding Bereavement & Grief. 20.00x (ISBN 0-87068-497-3). Ktav.

MacDuff, John R. The Bow in the Cloud: And the First Bereavement. (Summit Bks.). 148p. 1980. pap. 2.45 (ISBN 0-8010-6108-3). Baker Bk.

Marshall, George. Facing Death & Grief. LC 80-84402. (Library of Liberal Religion Ser.). 250p. 1981. 16.95 (ISBN 0-87975-140-1); pap. 8.95 (ISBN 0-87975-169-X). Prometheus Bks.

Miller, Jolonda. You Can Become Whole Again: A Guide to Healing for Christians in Grief. LC 80-84652. 1981. pap. 5.00 (ISBN 0-8042-1156-6). John Knox.

Moriarty, David M. The Loss of Loved Ones. 288p. 1981. 18.50 (ISBN 0-87527-198-7). Green.

Murphey, Cecil. Comforting Those Who Grieve. LC 78-71052. 64p. 1979. pap. 3.25 (ISBN 0-8042-1099-3). John Knox.

Nimeth, Albert J. In Your Time of Sorrow. 1976. pap. 0.25 (ISBN 0-685-77503-8). Franciscan Herald.

Novak, Michael, ed. Democracy & Mediating Structures: A Theological Inquiry. 1980. 13.25 (ISBN 0-8447-2175-1); pap. 7.25 (ISBN 0-8447-2176-X). Am Enterprise.

Oates, Wayne E. Your Particular Grief. LC 81-3328. 1981. pap. 6.95 (ISBN 0-664-24376-2). Westminster.

Parkes, Colin M. Bereavement: Studies of Grief in Adult Life. LC 72-82121. 1973. text ed. 17.50 (ISBN 0-8236-0485-3). Intl Univs Pr.

Pike, Diane K. Life Is Victorious. 1977. pap. 1.95 (ISBN 0-671-81241-6). PB.

Pollard, Albert J. The Salad Bar Syndrome. 1981. 6.95 (ISBN 0-533-04573-8). Vantage.

Ramsay, Ronald W. & Noorbergen, Rene. Living with Loss: A Dramatic New Breakthrough in Grief Therapy. LC 81-756. 196p. 1981. 8.95 (ISBN 0-688-00485-7). Morrow.

Robinson, Haddon W. Grief. 24p. 1976. Repr. pap. 1.50 (ISBN 0-310-32261-8). Zondervan.

Rodriguez, Roger. Senhor, Faze-Me Chorar! Date not set. 1.50 (ISBN 0-686-76439-0). Life Pubs Intl.

Schoenberg, Bernard, et al, eds. Loss & Grief: Psychological Management in Medical Practice. LC 75-118356. 398p. 1973. 22.50x (ISBN 0-231-03329-X); pap. 10.00x (ISBN 0-231-08331-9). Columbia U Pr.

Silverman, Phyllis. Helping Bereaved Women. (Sage Human Services Guides Ser.: Vol. 25). 96p. 1981. 6.00 (ISBN 0-8039-1735-X). Sage.

Simos, Bertha G. A Time to Grieve: Loss As a Universal Human Experience. LC 75-27964. 1979. 14.95 (ISBN 0-87304-141-0); pap. 9.95 (ISBN 0-87304-153-4). Family Serv.

Simpson, M. A., ed. Dying, Death, & Grief: A Critically Annotated Bibliography & Source Book of Thanatology & Terminal Care. LC 78-27273. 300p. 1979. 21.95 (ISBN 0-306-40147-9, Plenum Pr). Plenum Pub.

Smidt, Christine. An Acquaintance with Grief. LC 77-9253. 1977. 6.00 (ISBN 0-8309-0183-3). Herald Hse.

Smith, Kathleen. The Stages of Sorrow. 96p. 1978. 22.00 (ISBN 0-7156-1309-X, Pub. by Duckworth England); pap. 7.00 (ISBN 0-7156-1310-3, Pub. by Duckworth England). Biblio Dist.

Speck, P. Loss & Grief in Medicine. 1978. pap. text ed. 9.95 (ISBN 0-02-859250-6). Macmillan.

Spiegel, Yorick. The Grief Process: Analysis & Counseling. Duke, Elsbeth, tr. LC 77-1547. 1977. 5.95 (ISBN 0-687-15880-X). Abingdon.

Sumrall, Lester. You Can Conquer Grief Before It Conquers You. 144p. 1981. pap. 3.95 (ISBN 0-8407-5776-X). Nelson.

Swindoll, Chuck. For Those Who Hurt. 2.95 (ISBN 0-8423-0893-8). Tyndale.

Tallmer, Margot, et al, eds. Children, Dying, & Grief. (Thanatology Service Ser.). 200p. 1982. pap. 9.95 (ISBN 0-930194-26-8). Highly Specialized.

Tanner, Ira J. Healing the Pain of Everyday Loss. 184p. 1980. pap. 4.95 (ISBN 0-03-057849-3). Winston Pr.

Tatelbaum, Judy. The Courage to Grieve: Creative Living, Recovery, & Growth Through Grief. LC 80-7868. 192p. 1980. 10.00 (ISBN 0-690-01930-0). Har-Row.

Taylor, June. But for Our Grief: A Look at How Comfort Comes. 1977. pap. 3.95 (ISBN 0-87981-078-5). Holman.

Teicher, Elizabeth. A Grief Endured. 1980. pap. 3.95 (ISBN 0-89293-064-0). Beta Bk.

Temes, Roberta. Living with an Empty Chair: A Guide Through Grief. (Illus.). 80p. 1980. 10.95 (ISBN 0-8290-0183-2); pap. 5.95 (ISBN 0-8290-0184-0). Irvington.

Tuck, William P. Facing Grief & Death. LC 75-2977. 1975. 4.95 (ISBN 0-8054-2409-1). Broadman.

Werner-Beland, Jean A. Grief Response for the Critically Ill. (Illus.). 1980. text ed. 14.95 (ISBN 0-8359-2591-9); pap. text ed. 9.95 (ISBN 0-8359-2590-0). Reston.

Williams, Mary L. Sorrow Speaks. 1968. pap. 1.25 (ISBN 0-8272-3405-8). Bethany Pr.

Williams, Steve. The Death of a Child. 1977. 3.95 (ISBN 0-686-23229-1). Firm Foun Pub.

Zanca, Kenneth J. Mourning: The Healing Journey 1980. (Orig.). 1.75 (ISBN 0-914544-30-6). Living Flame Pr.

GRIEG, EDVARD HAGERUP, 1843-1907

Abraham, Gerald E., ed. Grieg: A Symposium. LC 71-138196. 144p. 1972. Repr. of 1950 ed. lib. bdg. 15.00 (ISBN 0-8371-5549-5, ABGR). Greenwood.

Acker, Helen. Four Sons of Norway. facsimile ed. LC 72-117318. (Biography Index Reprint Ser). 1948. 20.00 (ISBN 0-8369-8010-7). Arno.

Finck, H. Greig & His Music. Repr. lib. bdg. 25.00 (ISBN 0-403-08976-X). Scholarly.

Gilman, Lawrence. Nature in Music, & Other Studies in the Tone Poetry of Today. facs. ed. LC 67-22096. (Essay Index Reprint Ser). 1914. 13.00 (ISBN 0-8369-0475-3). Arno.

Horton, John. Grieg. (Master Musicians: No. M169). (Illus.). 1975. pap. 7.95 (ISBN 0-8226-0711-5). Littlefield.

Johansen, David M. Edward Grieg. LC 73-181193. 400p. 1938. Repr. 29.00 (ISBN 0-403-01599-5). Scholarly.

GRIERSON, FRANCIS, 1848-1927

Simonson, Harold P. Francis Grierson. (Twayne's United States Authors Ser). 1966. pap. 3.45 (ISBN 0-8084-0133-5, T97, Twayne). Coll & U Pr.

GRIERSON'S CAVALRY RAID, 1863

Underwood, Larry D. The Butternut Guerillas: A Story of Grierson's Raid. 1981. write for info. Cook-McDowell.

GRIESE, BOB

Burchard, S. H. Sports Star: Bob Griese. LC 75-11779. (Sports Star Ser). (Illus.). 64p. (gr. 1-5). 1975. 5.25 (ISBN 0-15-277997-3, HJ). HarBraceJ.

--Sports Star: Bob Griese. LC 75-11779. (Sports Star Ser.). (Illus.). (gr. 1-5). 1975. pap. 2.95 (ISBN 0-15-278026-2, VoyB). HarBraceJ.

GRIEVANCE PROCEDURES

American Arbitration Association. Lawyers' Arbitration Letters, 1970 to 1979. LC 80-39817. 1981. 15.95 (ISBN 0-02-900570-1). Free Pr.

Baer, Walter E. Grievance Handling. LC 72-114202. 1970. 12.50 (ISBN 0-8144-5213-2). Am Mgmt.

Blockhaus, Arthur P. Grievance Arbitration Case Studies. LC 74-8433. 416p. 1974. 19.95 (ISBN 0-8436-0722-X). CBI Pub.

BNA Editorial Staff. Grievance Guide. 5th ed. 322p. 1978. pap. 7.00 (ISBN 0-87179-283-4). BNA.

Didactic Systems Staff. Grievance Handling: Industrial. 1970. pap. 24.90 (ISBN 0-89401-027-1); pap. 21.50 two or more (ISBN 0-685-78105-4); pap. 24.90 french ed. (ISBN 0-89401-028-X); pap. 21.50 ea. two or more french eds. Didactic Syst.

--Grievance Handling: Non-Industrial. 1971. pap. 24.90 (ISBN 0-89401-029-8); pap. 21.50 two or more (ISBN 0-685-78107-0); pap. 24.90 french ed. (ISBN 0-89401-030-1); pap. 21.50 ea. two or more french eds. Didactic Syst.

Geary, Dick. European Labour Protest. 1981. price not set (ISBN 0-312-26974-9). St Martin.

Goldmann, Robert B., ed. Roundtable Justice: Case Studies in Conflict Resolution. (Westview Special Studies in Peace, Conflict, & Conflict Resolution). 231p. 1980. lib. bdg. 25.75x (ISBN 0-89158-962-7); pap. text ed. 9.00x (ISBN 0-86531-139-0). Westview.

How to Handle Grievances. 1974. 7.50 (ISBN 0-8144-6950-7). Am Mgmt.

Kaplan, Abbott. Making Grievance Procedures Work. 1964. 2.00 (ISBN 0-89215-074-2). U Cal LA Indus Rel.

Lazar, Joseph. Due Process in Disciplinary Hearings: Decisions of the National Railroad Adjustment Board. (Monograph Ser.: No. 25). 300p. 1980. 10.50 (ISBN 0-89215-108-0). U Cal LA Indus Rel.
Robinson, James W. & Dernoncourt, Wayne L. The Grievance Procedure & Arbitration: Text & Cases. LC 77-18573. 1978. pap. text ed. 11.00 (ISBN 0-8191-0411-6). U Pr of Amer.
Stern, James L. & Dennis, Barbara D., eds. Decisional Thinking of Arbitrators & Judges: National Academy of Arbitrators, 33rd Annual Meeting. 320p. 1981. text ed. 20.00 (ISBN 0-87179-346-6). BNA.
Trotta, Maurice S. Handling Grievances: A Guide for Management & Labor. LC 76-42311. 184p. 1976. 10.00 (ISBN 0-87179-237-0). BNA.

GRIFFES, CHARLES TOMLINSON, 1884-1920

Anderson, Donna K. The Works of Charles T. Griffes: A Descriptive Catalog. LC 75-23552. (Bibliographies in American Music Ser.: No. 3). 1977. 12.00 (ISBN 0-911772-87-1). Info Coord.

GRIFFIN, ROBERT

Griffin, Robert. In the Kingdom of the Lonely God. LC 72-94181. 1973. pap. 3.50 (ISBN 0-8091-1747-9). Paulist Pr.

GRIFFIN, WALTER BURLEIGH, 1876-1937

Birrell, James. Walter Burley Griffen. (Illus.). 1964. 25.00x (ISBN 0-7022-0389-0). U of Queensland Pr.
Johnson, Donald. Canberra & Walter Burley Griffin: A Bibliography of Eighteen Seventy-Six to Nineteen Seventy-Six & a Guide to Published Sources. (Illus.). 128p. (Orig.). 1980. pap. 7.50x (ISBN 0-19-554203-7). Oxford U Pr.
Love, Richard H. Walter Griffin: American Impressionist (1861-1935) (Illus.). 25p. 1975. pap. 5.00 (ISBN 0-940114-01-1). Love Galleries.
Van Zanten, David T., ed. Walter Burley Griffin: Selected Designs. LC 70-126770. (Illus.). 1970. 35.00 (ISBN 0-685-42429-4). Prairie Sch.

GRIFFITH, DAVID WARK, 1875-1948

Brown, Karl. Adventures with D. W. Griffith. Brownlow, Kevin, ed. LC 75-31755. 1976. pap. 4.95 (ISBN 0-306-80032-2). Da Capo.
Henderson, Robert M. D. W. Griffith: The Years at Biograph. (Illus.). 1970. pap. 2.95 (ISBN 0-374-50958-1). FS&G.
Niver, Kemp R. D. W. Griffith: His Biograph Films in Perspective. LC 74-81838. (Illus.). 1974. 15.00 (ISBN 0-913986-06-2). Locare.
--D. W. Griffith's "the Battle at Elderbush Gulch". LC 72-85599. (Illus.). 1972. 7.50 (ISBN 0-913986-04-6). Locare.
O'Dell, Paul. Griffith & the Rise of Hollywood. LC 71-119640. (International Film Guide Ser). 1970. pap. 4.95 (ISBN 0-498-07718-7). A S Barnes.
Phillips, Jill & Phillips, Leona. D. W. Griffith & His Films. 490p. 1975. lib. bdg. 75.00 (ISBN 0-87968-334-1). Gordon Pr.
Stern, Seymour. Index to the Films of D.W. Griffith. (Film Ser.). 1979. lib. bdg. 75.00 (ISBN 0-8490-2947-3). Gordon Pr.
Williams, Martin. Griffith: First Artist of the Movies. (Illus.). 1980. 12.95 (ISBN 0-19-502685-3). Oxford U Pr.

GRIFFITH, REGINALD HARVEY, 1873-1957

Osborne, Mary T., ed. The Great Torch Race: Essays in Honor of Reginald Harvey Griffith. LC 61-10425. (Illus.). 1961. 4.95 (ISBN 0-87959-063-7). U of Tex Hum Res.

GRIGNARD REAGENTS

Felkin, H. & Swierczewski, G. Activation of Grignard Reagents by Transition Metal Compounds. 1976. pap. text ed. 12.75 (ISBN 0-08-020465-1). Pergamon.

GRILLAGES (STRUCTURAL ENGINEERING)

Bares, Richard & Massonnet, Charles. Analysis of Beam Grids & Orthotropic Plates by the Guyon-Massonnet-Bares Method. Vanek, Jiri, tr. LC 68-20521. (Illus.). 1968. 16.00 (ISBN 0-8044-4089-1). Ungar.
Borrego, John. Space Grid Structures: Skeletal Frameworks & Stressed Skin Systems. (Report Ser.: No. 11). 1968. pap. 7.95 (ISBN 0-262-52009-5). MIT Pr.
Otto, Frei, et al. Grid Shells. (Information of the Institute for Lightweight Structures, University of Stuttgart Ser.: No. 10). (Illus., Orig., Eng. & Ger.). 1974. pap. 27.50x (ISBN 0-8150-0664-0). Wittenborn.

GRILLPARZER, FRANZ, 1791-1872

Alker, E. Franz Grillparzer: Ein Kampf Um Leben und Kunst. (Beitraege Zur Deutschen Literaturwissenschaft: No. 36). pap. 15.50 (ISBN 0-384-00750-3). Johnson Repr.
Buecher, W. Grillparzers Verhaeltnis Zur Politik Seiner Zeit. 1913. pap. 7.00 (ISBN 0-384-06220-2). Johnson Repr.
Burkhard, Arthur. Franz Grillparzer in England & America. (Illus.). 3.00x (ISBN 0-685-57216-1). M S Rosenberg.
--Grillparzer Im Ausland. (Illus., Ger.). 5.00x (ISBN 0-685-57215-3). M S Rosenberg.
Coenen, Frederic E. Franz Grillparzer's Portraiture of Men. LC 72-1013. (North Carolina. University. Studies in the Germanic Languages & Literatures: No. 4). Repr. of 1951 ed. 18.50 (ISBN 0-404-50904-5). AMS Pr.
De Walsh, Faust C. Grillparzer As a Poet of Nature. LC 73-164827. (Columbia University. Germanic Studies, Old Ser.: No. 12). Repr. of 1910 ed. 11.50 (ISBN 0-404-50412-4). AMS Pr.
Thompson, Bruce. Franz Grillparzer. (World Authors Ser.: No. 637). 14.95 (ISBN 0-8057-6481-X). Twayne.
Wells, G. A. The Plays of Grillparzer. 1969. 16.50 (ISBN 0-08-012950-1); pap. 7.75 (ISBN 0-08-012949-8). Pergamon.
Yates, Douglas. Franz Grillparzer, a Critical Biography. 188p. 1980. Repr. of 1946 ed. lib. bdg. 22.50 (ISBN 0-8482-3111-2). Norwood Edns.
--Franz Grillparzer: A Critical Biography. LC 74-9599. 1946. 20.00 (ISBN 0-8414-9764-8). Folcroft.

GRIMALDI, JOSEPH, 1779-1837

Disher, Maurice W. Clowns & Pantomimes. LC 68-21211. (Illus.). 1968. Repr. of 1925 ed. 19.50 (ISBN 0-405-08446-3, Blom Pubns). Arno.
Findlater, R. Joe Grimaldi: His Life & Theatre. LC 78-7465. 1979. 42.00 (ISBN 0-521-22221-4); pap. 12.95x (ISBN 0-521-29407-X). Cambridge U Pr.
Mayer, David, 3rd. Harlequin in His Element: The English Pantomime, 1806-1836. LC 79-88809. (Illus.). 1969. 20.00x (ISBN 0-674-37275-1). Harvard U Pr.
Neville, Giles. Incidents in the Life of Joseph Grimaldi. (Illus.). 64p. 1981. 10.95 (ISBN 0-224-01869-8, Pub. by Chatto-Bodley-Jonathan). Merrimack Bk Serv.

GRIMKE, SARAH MOORE, 1792-1873, AND ANGELINA EMILY, 1805-1809

Birney, C. M. Grimke Sisters-Sarah & Angelina Grimke, the First American Women Advocates of Abolition & Women's Rights. LC 68-24971. (American Biography Ser., No. 32). 1969. Repr. of 1885 ed. lib. bdg. 29.95 (ISBN 0-8383-0912-7). Haskell.
Birney, Catherine H. Grimke Sisters: Sarah & Angelina Grimke, the First American Women Advocates of Abolition & Women's Rights. LC 69-13828. Repr. of 1885 ed. lib. bdg. 15.00x (ISBN 0-8371-1303-2, BIGS). Greenwood.
--Grimke Sisters, Sarah & Angelina Grimke: The First America Women Advocates of Abolition & Women's Rights. LC 70-108461. 1970. Repr. of 1855 ed. 9.00 (ISBN 0-403-00230-3). Scholarly.
Lerner, Gerda. The Grimke Sisters from South Carolina: Pioneers for Women's Rights & Abolition. LC 67-25218. (Studies in the Life of Women). 1971. pap. 5.95 (ISBN 0-8052-0321-4). Schocken.

GRIMM BROTHERS

Grimm Library, 18 Vols. Repr. of 1909 ed. Set. 287.50 (ISBN 0-404-53550-X); Volumes. individual avail. AMS Pr.
Hamann, Hermann. Literarischen Vorlagen der Kinder-und-Hausmaerchen und Ihre Bearbeitung Durch Die Brueder Grimm. (Ger). Repr. of 1906 ed. 14.00 (ISBN 0-384-21130-5); pap. 12.00 (ISBN 0-685-02258-7). Johnson Repr.
Sexton, Anne. Transformations. 1972. 7.95 (ISBN 0-395-12721-1); ltd. ed. 25.00 (ISBN 0-395-13155-3); pap. 3.95 (ISBN 0-395-12722-X). HM.

GRIMMELSHAUSEN, HANS JACOB CHRISTOFFEL VON, 1625-1676

Koschlig, Manfred. Grimmelshausen und Seine Verleger. Repr. of 1939 ed. 29.00 (ISBN 0-384-30231-9); pap. 26.00 (ISBN 0-384-30230-0). Johnson Repr.
Von Bloedau, Carl A. Grimmelshausens Simplicissimus und Seine Vorganger. 1908. 14.00 (ISBN 0-384-04736-X); pap. 11.00 (ISBN 0-384-04735-1). Johnson Repr.

GRIMOND, JOSEPH

Jo Grimond: Memoirs. (Illus.). 316p. 1980. text ed. 27.50x (ISBN 0-8419-6106-9). Holmes & Meier.

GRIMSHAW, WILLIAM, 1708-1763

Harrison, G. E. Haworth Parsonage: Study of Wesley & the Brontes. 1937. lib. bdg. 7.50 (ISBN 0-8414-5008-0). Folcroft.

GRIMWADE, RUSSELL, SIR, 1897-1955

Poynter, J. R. Russell Grimwade. 1967. 18.50x (ISBN 0-522-83827-8, Pub. by Melbourne U Pr). Intl Schol Bk Serv.

GRINDAL, EDMUND, 1519-1583

Collinson, Patrick. Archbishop Grindal, 1519-1589: The Struggle for a Reformed Church in England. LC 78-65474. 1979. 35.00x (ISBN 0-520-03831-2). U of Cal Pr.
Strype, John. The History of the Life & Acts of Edmund Grindal. LC 78-183700. 640p. 1974. Repr. of 1821 ed. lib. bdg. 32.00 (ISBN 0-8337-3445-8). B Franklin.

GRINDING AND POLISHING

see also Metals–Finishing; Sharpening of Tools

Allen, J., et al, eds. Grinding, Vol. 1. (Engineering Craftsmen: No. H5). 1968. spiral bdg. 21.00x (ISBN 0-85083-013-3). Intl Ideas.
Barlow, D. W., et al, eds. Grinding, Vol. 2. (Engineering Craftsmen: No. H.31). 1972. spiral bdg. 28.50x (ISBN 0-85083-380-9). Intl Ideas.
Bellows, Guy. Low Stress Grinding. (Machining Process Ser.: MDC 78-103). (Illus.). 112p. 1978. pap. 10.00 (ISBN 0-936974-06-0). Metcut Res Assocs.
Coes, L. Abrasives. LC 78-153451. (Applied Minerology: Vol. 1). (Illus.). 1971. 26.30 (ISBN 0-387-80968-6). Springer-Verlag.
Farago, Francis T. Abrasive Methods Engineering, Vol. 1. LC 76-14970. (Illus.). 366p. 1976. 45.00 (ISBN 0-8311-1112-7). Indus Pr.
Fletcher, Edward. Rock & Gem Polishing. (Illus.). 1973. 4.95 (ISBN 0-7137-0617-1, Pub by Blandford Pr England). Sterling.
Krar, S. F. & Oswald, J. W. Grinding Technology. LC 72-7935. 1974. pap. text ed. 11.60 (ISBN 0-8273-0208-8); instructor's guide 1.60 (ISBN 0-8273-0209-6). Delmar.
Pinkstone, William G. The Abrasive Ages. LC 74-23797. (Illus.). 132p. 1975. 10.00 (ISBN 0-915010-01-1). Sutter House.
Springborn, R. K., ed. Cutting & Grinding Fluids: Selection & Application. LC 67-17077. (Manufacturing Data Ser). 1967. pap. 8.75 (ISBN 0-87263-001-3). SME.
Turner, Sue. Wheels & Grindstones. 1980. pap. 4.95 (ISBN 0-87397-180-9). Strode.
Twist Drills & Grinding Wheels. (Machine Tool Ser.: Vol. 6). 1974. pap. text ed. 3.95x (ISBN 0-88462-247-9). Ed Methods.

GRINNEL EXPEDITION, 2ND, 1853-1855

Corner, George W. Dr. Kane of the Arctic Seas. LC 72-88531. 330p. 1972. 17.50x (ISBN 0-87722-022-0). Temple U Pr.

GRIPER (SHIP)

Lyon, George F. A Brief Narrative of an Unsuccessful Attempt to Reach Repulse Bay, Through Sir Thomas Rowe's Welcome, in His Majesty's Ship Griper, in the Year 1824. LC 74-5852. Repr. of 1825 ed. 14.50 (ISBN 0-404-11659-0). AMS Pr.
Parry, William E. Journal of a Voyage for the Discovery of a Northwest Passage from the Atlantic to the Pacific, Performed in the Years 1819-20. LC 68-55209. 1968. Repr. of 1821 ed. lib. bdg. 28.50x (ISBN 0-8371-0608-7, PANP). Greenwood.

GRIPPE

see Influenza

GRISELDA

Griffith, Dudley. Origin of the Griselda Story. LC 73-9823. 1931. lib. bdg. 12.50 (ISBN 0-8414-2042-4). Folcroft.
Griselda. Story of Griselda in Iceland. Hermannsson, Halldor, ed. (Islandica: Vol. 7). Repr. of 1914 ed. pap. 6.00 (ISBN 0-527-00337-9). Kraus Repr.
Severs, J. Burke. Literary Relationships of Chaucer's Clerkes Tale. (Yale Studies in English Ser.: No. 96). 1972. Repr. of 1942 ed. 18.50 (ISBN 0-208-01138-2, Archon). Shoe String.

GRISONS (CANTON)

Arielli, A. D. Grisons. (Panorama Bks). (Illus.). 62p. (Fr.). 4.95 (ISBN 0-685-23347-2). French & Eur.

GRIST-MILLS

see Flour Mills

GRISTLE

see Cartilage

GRIZZLY BEAR

Craighead, Frank C., Jr. Track of the Grizzly. LC 78-8563. (Illus.). 1979. 10.95 (ISBN 0-87156-223-5). Sierra.
Hanna, Warren L. The Grizzlies of Glacier. LC 77-23004. (Illus.). 154p. 1978. pap. 5.95 (ISBN 0-87842-072-X). Mountain Pr.
Haynes, Bessie D. & Haynes, Edgar. The Grizzly Bear: Portraits from Life. (Illus.). 1979. pap. 8.95 (ISBN 0-8061-1481-9). U of Okla Pr.
Hubbard, W. P. & Harris, Peggy. Notorious Grizzly Bears. LC 60-14583. (Illus.). 205p. 1960. pap. 5.95 (ISBN 0-8040-0617-2, SB). Swallow.
McClung, Robert M. Samson, Last of the California Grizzlies. (Illus.). 96p. (gr. 3-7). 1973. PLB 6.48 (ISBN 0-688-31935-1). Morrow.
May, Julian. Glacier Grizzly. LC 78-174892. (gr. 3-6). 1973. PLB 7.95 (ISBN 0-87191-092-6). Creative Ed.
Mills, Enos A. The Grizzly. 1976. pap. 2.25 (ISBN 0-89174-006-6). Comstock Edns.
Schneider, Bill. Where the Grizzly Walks. LC 76-58451. (Illus.). 208p. 1977. 8.95 (ISBN 0-87842-067-3). Mountain Pr.
Seton, Ernest T. Monarch: The Big Bear of Tallac. Jones, William R., ed. (Illus.). 1978. pap. 6.95 (ISBN 0-89646-040-1). Outbooks.
Storer, Tracy I. & Tevis, Lloyd P., Jr. California Grizzly. LC 78-17671. (Illus.). 1978. 19.50x (ISBN 0-8032-4101-1); pap. 4.95 (ISBN 0-8032-9101-9, BB 688, Bison). U of Nebr Pr.
Wright, William H. The Grizzly Bear: The Narrative of a Hunter-Naturalist. LC 77-1772. (Illus.). 1977. 17.50x (ISBN 0-8032-0927-4); pap. 4.95 (ISBN 0-8032-5865-8, BB 646, Bison). U of Nebr Pr.
Young, Ralph W. Grizzlies Don't Come Easy. (Illus.). 176p. 1981. 13.95 (ISBN 0-87691-349-4). Winchester Pr.

GRIZZLY BEAR–LEGENDS AND STORIES

Russell, Andy. Grizzly Country. (Illus.). (YA) 1967. 10.95 (ISBN 0-394-42736-X). Knopf.
Seton, Ernest T. The Biography of a Grizzly. 1977. Repr. of 1910 ed. lib. bdg. 20.00 (ISBN 0-8414-8123-7). Folcroft.

GROCERIES–PACKAGING

see Food–Packaging

GROCERY TRADE

see also Supermarkets

Book Div. Research Staff. SN Distribution Study of Grocery Store Sales - 1981. 250p. 1981. pap. 30.00 (ISBN 0-87005-370-1). Fairchild.
Book Division Research. SN Distribution Study Grocery Store Sales - 1980. 1980. pap. text ed. 27.50 (ISBN 0-87005-313-2). Fairchild.
Bussel, Norman, ed. Progressive Grocer's Market Scope. 7th ed. 1981. 129.00 (ISBN 0-911790-01-2). Prog Grocer.
Cohen, Harold. The Crime That No One Talks About. Daykin, Len, ed. LC 74-26240. (Illus.). 1974. 11.95 (ISBN 0-911790-50-0). Prog Grocer.
Dyer, Lee. Idea Sketchbook. (Illus.). 1974. looseleaf bdg 12.95 (ISBN 0-911790-63-2). Prog Grocer.
Five Seasons Merchandising Kit. (Illus.). 1974. 9.95 (ISBN 0-911790-53-5). Prog Grocer.
Haas, Harold M. Social & Economic Aspects of the Chain Store Movement. Bruchey, Stuart & Carosso, Vincent P., eds. LC 78-18962. (Small Business Enterprise in America Ser.). 1979. lib. bdg. 20.00x (ISBN 0-405-11466-4). Arno.
Hightower, Jim. Eat Your Heart Out: How Food Profiteers Victimize the Consumer. 1976. pap. 1.95 (ISBN 0-394-72094-6, Vin). Random.
Jenkins, Herbert T. Food, Fairs & Farmers' Markets in Atlanta. LC 77-1228. (Illus.). 1977. pap. 4.00 (ISBN 0-89937-000-4). Ctr Res Soc Chg.
Lynch, R. L. & Lunch, Richard L., eds. Food Marketing. (Career Competencies in Marketing Ser.). (Illus.). 1979. pap. text ed. 5.36 (ISBN 0-07-051483-6, G); teacher's manual & key 3.00 (ISBN 0-07-051484-4). McGraw.
Marion, Bruce W., et al. The Food Retailing Industry: Market Structure, Profits, & Prices. LC 78-19751. 1979. 22.95 (ISBN 0-03-046106-5). Praeger.
Mittendorf, H. J. Planning of Urban Wholesale Markets for Perishable Food with Particular Reference to Developing Countries. (Illus.). 174p. 1976. pap. 27.25 (ISBN 92-5-100021-2, F1064, FAO). Unipub.
Progressive Grocer Magazine Staff. Grocery Retailing in the Eighties. (Illus.). 1980. 14.95 (ISBN 0-911790-75-6). Prog Grocer.
Tarzian, Lucy, ed. Progressive Grocer's Marketing Guidebook. LC 68-126162. 1981. 159.00 (ISBN 0-911790-20-9). Prog Grocer.
--Progressive Grocer's Marketing Guidebook. LC 68-126162. 1982. 175.00 (ISBN 0-911790-21-7). Prog Grocer.

GROESBECK, ALEXANDER JOSEPH, 1873-1953

Woodford, Frank B. Alex J. Groesbeck: Portrait of a Public Man. LC 62-7209. 383p. 1962. 8.95x (ISBN 0-8143-1212-8). Wayne St U Pr.

GROLIER, JEAN, VICOMTE D'AGUISY, 1479-1565

Andrews, W. L. Jean Grolier. 59.95 (ISBN 0-8490-0437-3). Gordon Pr.
Austin, Gabriel. The Library of Jean Grolier. LC 78-85855. (Illus.). viii, 137p. 1971. 35.00x (ISBN 0-8139-0458-7, Grolier Club). U Pr of Va.
--Library of Jean Grolier: A Preliminary Catalogue. LC 78-85855. (Illus.). 1971. 35.00x (ISBN 0-8139-0458-7, Dist. by U Pr of Va). Grolier Club.
Leroux De Lincy, Antoine J. Researches Concerning Jean Grolier, His Life & His Library, with a Partial Catalogue of His Books. Portalis, Roger, ed. Shipman, Carolyn, tr. LC 70-80254. (Essays in Literature & Criticism Ser.: No. 137). (Illus.). 1971. Repr. of 1907 ed. lib. bdg. 43.00 (ISBN 0-8337-2078-3). B Franklin.

--Researches Concerning Jean Grolier, His Life & His Library, with a Partial Catalogue of His Books. Portalis, Roger, ed. Shipman, Carolyn, tr. LC 70-80254. (Essays in Literature & Criticism Ser.: No. 137). (Illus.). 1971. Repr. of 1907 ed. lib. bdg. 43.00 (ISBN 0-8337-2078-3). B Franklin.

GROLIER CLUB, NEW YORK

Barrett, C. Waller & Davidson, Alexander, Jr. Exhibition Celebrating the Seventy-Fifth Anniversary of the Grolier Club. 44p. 1959. pap. 4.00x (ISBN 0-8139-0449-8, Dist. by U Prof Va). Grolier Club.

--An Exhibition Celebrating the 75th Anniversary of the Grolier Club. 1959. pap. 4.00x (ISBN 0-8139-0449-8). U Pr of Va.

Winterich, John T. Grolier Club, Eighteen Eighty-Four to Nineteen Sixty-Seven: An Informal History. (Illus.). 1967. boxed 10.00x (ISBN 0-8139-0454-4, Dist. by U Pr of Va). Grolier Club.

--The Grolier Club, 1884-1967: An Informal History. (Illus.). 49p. 1967. 10.00x (ISBN 0-8139-0454-4, Grolier Club). U Pr of Va.

GROOMBRIDGE, WILLIAM, 1748-1811

Pleasants, Jacob H. Four Late Eighteenth Century Anglo-American Landscape Painters. LC 78-128288. (Essay Index Reprint Ser). 1943. 16.00 (ISBN 0-8369-1894-0). Arno.

GROOMING, PERSONAL

see Beauty, Personal

GROOMING FOR WOMEN

see Beauty, Personal

GROOMING OF DOGS

see Dog Grooming

GROPIUS, WALTER, 1883-1969

Gay, Peter. Art & Act: On Causes in History - Manet, Gropius, Mondrian. LC 75-12291. (Icon Editions). (Illus.). 320p. 1976. 20.00 (ISBN 0-06-433248-9, HarpT). Har-Row.

Gropius, et al. Four Great Makers of Modern Architecture: Gropius, le Corbusier, Mies Van der Rohe, Wright. LC 78-130312. (Architecture & Decorative Art Ser.: Vol. 37). 1970. Repr. of 1963 ed. lib. bdg. 29.50 (ISBN 0-306-70065-4). Da Capo.

O'Neal, William B., ed. American Association of Architectural Bibliographers' Papers, Vol. 9. Incl. A Supplement to the Bibliography of Walter Gropius. Gropius, Ise, ed; A Bibliography of Works About Sir Christopher Wren. Stringer, Gail G., ed; Benjamin Henry Latrobe. Norton, Paul F., ed; Frank Lloyd Wright in Print 1959-1970. Muggenberg, James, compiled by.. LC 65-14273. 1972. 10.00x (ISBN 0-8139-0391-2). U Pr of Va.

GROS VENTRE INDIANS

see Indians of North America-The West

GROS VENTRE MOUNTAINS

Nelson, Vincent E. The Structural Geology of the Cache Creek Area, Gros Ventre Mountains, Wyoming. LC 43-15519. (Augustana College Library Ser.: No. 18). 1942. pap. 3.00 (ISBN 0-910182-13-2). Augustana Coll.

Swenson, Frank A. Geology of the Northwest Flank of the Gros Ventre Mountains, Wyoming. LC 50-5669. (Augustana College Library Ser.: No. 21). 1949. pap. 3.50 (ISBN 0-910182-16-7). Augustana Coll.

GROSS, CHAIM, 1904-

Getlein, Frank. Chaim Gross. LC 73-13807. (Contemporary Art Ser.). (Illus.). 225p. 1975. 65.00 (ISBN 0-8109-0160-9). Abrams.

GROSS NATIONAL PRODUCT

see also Income; National Income

Adair, Bryan. The Estimation of a State's Gross Product: A Procedure Applied to Texas. 69p. 1975. pap. 4.00 (ISBN 0-87755-220-7). U of Tex Busn Res.

Bowers, J. The Anatomy of Regional Activity Rates. Bd. with Regional Social Accounts for the U.K. Woodward, V. H. (Economic & Social Research Ser: No. 1). 1971. 13.95 (ISBN 0-521-07719-2). Cambridge U Pr.

Conference on Research in Income & Wealth, 88th Congress, 2nd Session. Measuring the Nation's Wealth: Proceedings. LC 75-19737. (National Bureau of Economic Research Ser.). (Illus.). 1975. Repr. 48.00x (ISBN 0-405-07614-2). Arno.

Kendrick, John W. The National Wealth of the United States: By Major Sectors & Industry. LC 76-41080. (Report Ser: No. 698). (Illus., Orig.). 1976. pap. 30.00 (ISBN 0-8237-0132-8). Conference Bd.

Kravis, Irving B., et al. A System of International Comparisons of Gross Product & Purchasing Power. LC 73-19352. (World Bank Ser). (Illus.). 308p. 1975. 25.00x (ISBN 0-8018-1606-8); pap. 7.50x (ISBN 0-8018-1669-6). Johns Hopkins.

Kuznets, Simon. National Product in Wartime. LC 75-19721. (National Bureau of Economic Research Ser.). (Illus.). 1975. Repr. 12.00x (ISBN 0-405-07600-2). Arno.

--National Product Since 1869. LC 75-19722. (National Bureau of Economic Research Ser.). (Illus.). 1975. Repr. 17.00x (ISBN 0-405-07601-0). Arno.

Pesek, Boris P. Gross National Product of Czechoslovakia in Monetary & Real Terms, 1946-58. LC 65-14429. 1965. 5.50x (ISBN 0-226-66187-3). U of Chicago Pr.

Polenske, Karen R. State Estimates of the Gross National Product 1947, 1958, 1963. LC 79-145900. (Multiregional Input Output Study: Vol. 1). 320p. 1972. 29.95 (ISBN 0-669-62539-6). Lexington Bks.

Rimmer, Douglas. Macromancy: The Ideology of Development Economics. (Institute of Economic Affairs, Hobart Papers Ser.: No. 55). 64p. 1973. pap. 2.50 (ISBN 0-255-36042-8). Transatlantic.

Scheppach, Raymond C., Jr. State Projection of the Gross National Product, 1970, 1980. LC 72-8038. (Multiregional Input-Output Study: Vol. 3). (Illus.). 320p. 1972. 28.95 (ISBN 0-669-84996-0). Lexington Bks.

Schultze, Charles L. National Income Analysis. 3rd ed. LC 72-140763. (Foundations of Modern Economics). (Illus.). 1971. pap. 9.95 ref. ed. (ISBN 0-13-609420-1). P-H.

GROSSES VOLLSTANDIGES UNIVERSAL LEXICON

Shorr, Philip. Science & Superstition in the Eighteenth Century: A Study of the Treatment of Science in Two Encyclopedias of 1725-1750. LC 33-3916. (Columbia University. Studies in the Social Sciences: No. 364). Repr. of 1932 ed. 10.00 (ISBN 0-404-51364-6). AMS Pr.

GROSSETESTE, ROBERT, BP. OF LINCOLN, 1175-1253

Callus, D. A., ed. Robert Grosseteste: Scholar & Bishop. 1955. 22.50x (ISBN 0-19-821387-5). Oxford U Pr.

Stevenson, F. S. Robert Grosseteste, Bishop of Lincoln: A Contribution to the Religious, Political & Intellectual History of the Thirteenth Century. (Medieval Studies Ser.). Repr. of 1899 ed. lib. bdg. 28.50x (ISBN 0-697-00018-4). Irvington.

GROSSULIARIA

Hutchinson, G. E. Some Continental European Aberrations of Abraxas Grossulariata Linn, Lepidoptera: With a Note on the Theoretical Significance of the Variation Observed in the Species. (Connecticut Academy of Arts & Sciences - Transaction: Vol. 43). (Illus.). 1969. pap. 7.50 (ISBN 0-208-00832-2). Shoe String.

GROSVENOR FAMILY

Sheppard, F. H., ed. Grosvenor Estate in Mayfair: The Buildings, Pt. 2. (Survey of London Ser.: Vol. 40). 429p. 1980. text ed. 143.00x (ISBN 0-485-48240-1, Athlone Pr). Humanities.

GROSVENTRE LANGUAGE

see Hidatsa Language

GROSZ, GEORGE, 1893-1959

Grosz, George. Ecce Homo. LC 76-26191. (Illus.). 96p. 1976. pap. 4.00 (ISBN 0-486-23410-X). Dover.

Scheede, Uwe M., et al. George Grosz: His Life & Work. Flatauer, Susanne, tr. LC 78-64969. (Illus.). 184p. 1980. 12.50x (ISBN 0-87663-333-5); pap. 8.95 (ISBN 0-87663-990-2). Universe.

Whitford, Frank. Grosz. (Oresko-Jupiter Art Bks). (Illus.). 96p. 1981. 17.95 (ISBN 0-933516-88-6, Pub. by Oresko-Jupiter England). Hippocrene Bks.

GROTESQUE

Bridaham, Lester B. Gargoyles, Chimeres, & the Grotesque in French Gothic Sculpture. enl. & 2nd ed. LC 68-27724. (Architecture & Decorative Art Ser.: Vol. 22). (Illus.). 1969. Repr. of 1930 ed. lib. bdg. 55.00 (ISBN 0-306-71152-4). Da Capo.

Campbell, Lily. The Grotesque in the Poetry of Robert Browning. 1978. Repr. of 1907 ed. lib. bdg. 12.50 (ISBN 0-8495-0770-7). Arden Lib.

Farnham, Willard. Shakespearean Grotesque: Its Genesis & Transformations. (Illus.). 1971. 12.95x (ISBN 0-19-811699-3). Oxford U Pr.

Kayser, Wolfgang. The Grotesque in Art & Literature. Weisstein, Ulrich, tr. from Ger. LC 81-3882. 256p. 1981. 22.50x (ISBN 0-231-05337-1, Pub. by Morningside); pap. 8.00x (ISBN 0-231-05336-3, Pub. by Morningside). Columbia U Pr.

Muller, Gilbert H. Nightmares & Visions: Flannery O'Connor & the Catholic Grotesque. LC 75-184777. 134p. 1972. 9.95x (ISBN 0-8203-0284-8). U of Ga Pr.

Northey, Margot. The Haunted Wilderness: The Gothic & Grotesque in Canadian Fiction. LC 76-23329. 1976. 17.50x (ISBN 0-8020-5357-2); pap. 6.50 (ISBN 0-8020-6296-2). U of Toronto Pr.

Rhodes, Neil. Elizabeth Grotesque. 208p. 1980. 35.00 (ISBN 0-7100-0599-7). Routledge & Kegan.

Rollins, Yvonne B. Baudelaire et le Grotesque. LC 78-54094. (Fr.). 1978. pap. text ed. 9.75 (ISBN 0-8191-0498-1). U Pr of Amer.

Thomson, Philip. The Grotesque. (Critical Idiom Ser.). 1979. pap. text ed. 5.50x (ISBN 0-416-08180-0). Methuen Inc.

Wildridge, Thomas T. Grotesque in Church Art. LC 68-30633. 1969. Repr. of 1899 ed. 19.00 (ISBN 0-8103-3077-6). Gale.

Wright, Thomas. A History of Caricature & Grotesque in Literature & Art. LC 78-58186. 1978. Repr. of 1875 ed. lib. bdg. 40.00 (ISBN 0-89341-353-4). Longwood Pr.

GROTHENDIECK, ALEXANDRE

Hartshorne, R. Residues & Duality. (Lecture Notes in Mathematics: Vol. 20). 1966. pap. 21.90 (ISBN 0-387-03603-2). Springer-Verlag.

GROTIUS, HUGO, 1583-1645

Dumbauld, Edward. Life & Legal Writings of Hugo Grotius. LC 68-31373. 1969. 7.95x (ISBN 0-8061-0848-7). U of Okla Pr.

Edwards, Charles S. Hugo Grotius, the Miracle of Holland: A Study of Political & Legal Thought. LC 81-4592. 288p. 1981. text ed. 19.95x (ISBN 0-88229-624-8). Nelson-Hall.

Sotirovich, William V. Grotius Universe: Divine Law & a Quest for Harmony. 1978. 5.95 (ISBN 0-533-02274-6). Vantage.

GROTTOES

see Caves

GROUND, PATTERNED

see Patterned Ground

GROUND COVER PLANTS

Crockett, James U. Lawns & Ground Covers. (Encyclopedia of Gardening Ser). (Illus.). 1971. 12.95 (ISBN 0-8094-1093-1); lib. bdg. avail. (ISBN 0-685-00194-6). Time-Life.

Crockett, James V. Lawns & Ground Covers. LC 78-140420. (Time-Life Encyclopedia of Gardening). (Illus.). (gr. 6 up). 1971. lib. bdg. 11.97 (ISBN 0-8094-1094-X, Pub. by Time-Life). Silver.

Duble, Richard & Kell, J. Carroll. Southern Lawns & Groundcovers. LC 77-73533. (Illus.). 96p. 1977. pap. 3.95 (ISBN 0-88415-426-2). Pacesetter Pr.

Foley, Daniel J. Ground Covers for Easier Gardening. (Illus.). 224p. 1972. pap. 4.00 (ISBN 0-486-20124-4). Dover.

Ortho Books Editorial Staff, ed. All About Ground Covers. LC 77-89688. (Illus.). 1978. pap. 4.95 Midwest-Northeast ed. (ISBN 0-917102-55-X); pap. 4.95 South ed. (ISBN 0-917102-56-8); pap. 4.95 West ed. (ISBN 0-917102-57-6). Ortho.

Sunset Editors. Lawns & Ground Covers. LC 78-70267. (Illus.). 96p. 1979. pap. 3.95 (ISBN 0-376-03506-4, Sunset Bks.). Sunset-Lane.

Symonds, George W. The Shrub Identification Book. LC 63-7388. 1963. 17.95 (ISBN 0-688-00040-1, Barrows & Co); pap. 7.95 (ISBN 0-688-05040-9). Morrow.

Thompson, H. C. & Bonnie, Fred. Growing Lawns & Ground Covers. LC 75-12125. (Family Guidebooks Ser.). (Illus.). 96p. 1975. pap. 1.95 (ISBN 0-8487-0383-9). Oxmoor Hse.

Wyman, Donald & Koller, Gary, eds. Ground Covers & Vines. 1978. 1.95 (ISBN 0-686-00615-1). Bklyn Botanic.

GROUND-EFFECT MACHINES

see also Helicopters; Vertically Rising Aircraft

Croome, Angela. Hovercraft. (Illus.). (gr. 5 up). 1962. 4.50 (ISBN 0-8392-3008-7). Astor-Honor.

Instrumentation for Ground Vibration & Earthquakes. 176p. 1980. pap. 65.00x (ISBN 0-7277-0052-9, Pub. by Telford England). State Mutual Bk.

McLeavy, Roy & Wood, John W. Hovercraft & Hydrofoils. LC 76-27703. (Arco Color Books). (Illus.). 1977. 7.95 (ISBN 0-668-04105-6, 4105); pap. 5.95 (ISBN 0-668-04254-0, 4254). Arco.

Symposium on Air Cushion Handling. Proceedings. 1974. pap. 34.00 (ISBN 0-900983-34-5, Dist. by Air Science Co.). BHRA Fluid.

GROUND HOGS

see Marmots

GROUND NUTS

see Peanuts

GROUND PROXIMITY MACHINES

see Ground-Effect Machines

GROUND-RENT

see Rent

GROUND SQUIRRELS

McClung, Robert M. Stripe: The Story of a Chipmunk. (Illus.). (gr. 1-5). 1951. pap. 3.80 (ISBN 0-688-35005-4). Morrow.

GROUND SUPPORT SYSTEMS (ASTRONAUTICS)

Geddes, James D. Ground Movements & Structures. 972p. 1981. 75.00 (ISBN 0-470-27208-2). Halsted Pr.

Jane's Motor Veh. & Grnd. Supp. Equip. Date not set. 125.00x (ISBN 0-531-03954-4). Key Bk Serv.

GROUND TEMPERATURE

see Earth Temperature

GROUND WATER

see Water, Underground

GROUNDS MAINTENANCE

Castellano, Carmine C. & Seitz, Clifford P. You Fix It: Lawn Mowers. (Illus.). 192p. 1974. pap. 6.95 (ISBN 0-668-02705-3). Arco.

Conover, Herbert S. Grounds Maintenance Handbook. 3rd ed. (Illus.). 512p. 1976. 29.50 (ISBN 0-07-012412-4, P&RB). McGraw.

Rorison, I. & Hunt, R. Amenity Grassland: An Ecological Perspective. 261p. 1980. 59.50 (ISBN 0-471-27666-9, Pub. by Wiley-Interscience). Wiley.

Rudman, Jack. Chief Groundskeeper. (Career Examination Ser.: C-1574). (Cloth bdg. avail. on request). pap. 10.00 (ISBN 0-8373-1574-3). Natl Learning.

--Principal Groundskeeper. (Career Examination Ser.: C-1573). (Cloth bdg. avail. on request). pap. 10.00 (ISBN 0-8373-1573-5). Natl Learning.

--Senior Groundskeeper. (Career Examination Ser.: C-1572). (Cloth bdg. avail. on request). pap. 8.00 (ISBN 0-8373-1572-7). Natl Learning.

GROUP COUNSELING

see also Group Psychotherapy; Self-Help Groups

Allen, Bud & Bosta, Diana. How to Be a Successful Trainer: Without Being Tarred & Feathered. 62p. 1981. vinyl 8.95x (ISBN 0-9605226-8-9). Rae John.

Berg, Robert & Landreth, Garry. Group Counseling: Concepts & Procedures. 1979. pap. text ed. 8.95x (ISBN 0-915202-20-4). Accel Devel.

Cohen, Arthur M. & Smith, R. Douglas. The Critical Incident in Growth Groups: A Manual for Group Leaders. LC 75-18139. 262p. 1976. 12.50 (ISBN 0-88390-107-2). Univ Assocs.

Corey, Gerald. Manual for Theory & Practice of Group Counseling. 150p. 1980. pap. text ed. 5.95 (ISBN 0-8185-0432-3). Brooks-Cole.

--Theory & Practice of Group Counseling. LC 80-18985. 500p. 1980. text ed. 15.95 (ISBN 0-8185-0400-5). Brooks-Cole.

Dinkmeyer, Don C. & Muro, James J. Group Counseling: Theory & Practice. 2nd ed. LC 77-83357. 1979. text ed. 15.95 (ISBN 0-87581-206-6). Peacock Pubs.

Fenton, Norman. Group Counseling. LC 73-9254. 109p. 1974. Repr. of 1961 ed. lib. bdg. 15.00x (ISBN 0-8371-6997-6, FEGC). Greenwood.

Fullmer, Daniel W. Counseling: Group Theory & System. 2nd ed. LC 78-9058. 1978. 27.00 (ISBN 0-910328-12-9); pap. 16.50 (ISBN 0-686-52428-4). Carroll Pr.

Gazda, George M. Group Counseling: A Developmental Approach. 2nd ed. 1978. pap. text ed. 20.95 (ISBN 0-205-05958-9). Allyn.

--Theories & Methods of Group Counseling in the Schools. 2nd ed. (Illus.). 384p. 1976. 20.00 (ISBN 0-398-03547-4). C C Thomas.

Gazda, George M., ed. Basic Approaches to Group Psychotherapy & Group Counseling. 2nd ed. (Illus.). 560p. 1979. 21.50 (ISBN 0-398-03212-2). C C Thomas.

Gordon, Myron & Liberman, Norman. Theme-Centered Interaction: An Original Focus on Counseling & Education. new ed. LC 72-76599. (Illus.). 250p. 1973. text ed. 10.00x (ISBN 0-87971-004-7). Natl Educ Pr.

Hall, Dale M. Dynamics of Group Action. LC 64-22544. (Illus.). 1964. 10.00 (ISBN 0-8134-0457-6). Interstate.

Hardy, Richard E. & Cull, John G., eds. Techniques & Approaches in Marital & Family Counseling. (American Lectures in Social & Rehabilitation Psychology Ser.). 240p. 1974. text ed. 18.75 (ISBN 0-398-03093-6). C C Thomas.

Jackins, Harvey. Multiplied Awareness. 1969. pap. 0.50 (ISBN 0-911214-18-6). Rational Isl.

Jones, John E. & Pfeiffer, J. William, eds. Annual Handbook for Group Facilitators, 1977. LC 73-92841. (Series in Human Relations Training). 288p. 1977. pap. 20.00 (ISBN 0-88390-091-2); looseleaf ntbk. 44.50 (ISBN 0-88390-090-4). Univ Assocs.

Kemp, C. Gratton. Perspectives on the Group Process: A Foundation for Counseling with Groups. 2nd ed. LC 64-346. 1970. text ed. 18.50 (ISBN 0-395-04723-4, 3-29410). HM.

Kidd, Worth R. Edgar Cayce & Group Dynamics. rev. ed. 1971. pap. 2.00 (ISBN 0-87604-046-6). ARE Pr.

Lee, James L. & Pulvino, Charles J. Group Counseling: Theory, Research & Practice. (APGA Reprint Ser: No. 4). 1973. pap. 9.50 (ISBN 0-686-05523-3, 029). Am Personnel.

Lewis, Judith A. & Lewis, Michael D. Community Counseling: A Human Services Approach. LC 76-15274. (Wiley Series in Counseling & Human Development). 1977. text ed. 21.95 (ISBN 0-471-53203-7). Wiley.

Lifton, Walter. Groups: Facilitating Individual Growth & Societal Change. LC 72-566. 1972. 21.50 (ISBN 0-471-53491-9). Wiley.

Maclennan, Beryce W. & Felsenfeld, Naomi. Group Counseling & Psychotherapy with Adolescents. LC 68-18998. 1968. 15.00x (ISBN 0-231-03093-2); pap. 5.00x (ISBN 0-231-08640-7). Columbia U Pr.

Merritt, Ray E., Jr. & Walley, Donald D. The Group Leader's Handbook: Resources, Techniques, & Survival Skills. LC 77-81297. (Illus.). 1977. pap. text ed. 10.95 (ISBN 0-87822-139-5). Res Press.

Ohlsen, M. M. Counseling Children in Groups: A Forum. LC 73-6531. 1973. pap. text ed. 9.95 (ISBN 0-03-085943-3, HoltC). HR&W.

--Group Counseling. 2nd ed. LC 76-51307. 1977. text ed. 18.95 (ISBN 0-03-089848-X, HoltC). HR&W.

Ohlsen, Merle M. Marriage Counseling in Groups. LC 79-66180. (Illus., Orig.). 1979. pap. text ed. 8.95 (ISBN 0-87822-201-4). Res Press.

Pfeiffer, J. William & Jones, John E., eds. The Annual Handbook for Group Facilitators, 1980. LC 73-92841. (Series in Human Relations Training). 296p. 1980. pap. 20.00 (ISBN 0-88390-097-1); looseleaf notebook 44.50 (ISBN 0-88390-096-3). Univ Assocs.

Samuels, Mimi & Samuels, Don. The Complete Handbook of Peer Counseling. (Educational Bks.). 192p. (Orig.). 1975. pap. text ed. 5.95 (ISBN 0-88473-025-5). Fiesta Pub.

Seligman, Milton. Group Counseling & Group Psychotherapy with the Handicapped. 415p. 1981. pap. text ed. 25.95 (ISBN 0-8391-1691-8). Univ Park.

--Group Psychotherapy & Group Counseling with the Handicapped. 415p. 1981. pap. text ed. 25.95 (ISBN 0-8391-1691-8). Univ Park.

Thompson, S. & Kahn, J. H. The Group Process As a Helping Technique. LC 79-124667. 1970. 15.00 (ISBN 0-08-016220-7); pap. 7.00 (ISBN 0-08-016219-3). Pergamon.

Trotzer, James P. The Counselor & the Group: Integrating Theory, Training & Practice. LC 77-7306. (Illus.). 1977. text ed. 13.95 (ISBN 0-8185-0233-9). Brooks-Cole.

GROUP DISCUSSION

see Discussion; Forums (Discussion and Debate)

GROUP DYNAMICS

see Social Groups

GROUP GUIDANCE IN EDUCATION

Belka, Bro. Marion S. Being & Becoming, An Action Approach to Group Guidance: Commitment. 1970. pap. text ed. 2.96 (ISBN 0-685-07622-9, 81061); leader's manual 3.76 (ISBN 0-02-810620-2). Glencoe.

Belka, Bro. Marion S., ed. Being & Becoming, An Action Approach to Group Guidance: Identity. 1967. pap. text ed. 2.96 (ISBN 0-02-810600-8); leader's manual 3.76 (ISBN 0-685-07644-X). Glencoe.

--Being & Becoming, An Action Approach to Group Guidance: Involvement. 1968. pap. text ed. 2.96 (ISBN 0-02-810550-8); leader's manual 3.76 (ISBN 0-02-810560-5). Glencoe.

Bruck, Charlott M. Discovery Through Guidance-Group Guidance for Elementary Schools: Build. 1969. pap. text ed. 2.48 (ISBN 0-02-811770-0); teachers manual 3.52 (ISBN 0-02-811780-8). Glencoe.

--Discovery Through Guidance-Group Guidance for Elementary Schools: Quest. 1968. pap. text ed. 2.48 (ISBN 0-02-811740-9); teacher's manual 3.52 (ISBN 0-02-811760-3). Glencoe.

--Discovery Through Guidance-Group Guidance for Elementary Schools: Search. 1969. pap. text ed. 2.48 (ISBN 0-02-811720-4); teachers manual 3.52 (ISBN 0-02-811730-1). Glencoe.

Bruck, Charlotte M. Discovery Through Guidance, Group Guidance for Elementary Schools: Focus. 1968. pap. text ed. 2.48 (ISBN 0-02-812000-0); teachers' manual 3.52 (ISBN 0-02-812020-5). Glencoe.

Dye, H. Allan. Fundamental Group Procedures for School Counselors. (Guidance Monograph). 1968. pap. 2.40 (ISBN 0-395-09922-6). HM.

Fedder, Ruth. Guidance in the Homeroom. LC 67-24642. 1967. pap. text ed. 5.00x (ISBN 0-8077-1308-2). Tchrs Coll.

Fox, C. Lynn. Communicating with Friends: A Program for the Classroom Teacher. (Illus.). 130p. (Orig.). 1980. pap. 12.95x (ISBN 0-935266-04-6). B L Winch.

Hansen, James & Cramer, Stanley, eds. Group Guidance & Counseling in the Schools: Selected Readings. 1971. pap. text ed. 14.95 (ISBN 0-13-365304-8). P-H.

Kawin, Ethel. Manual for Group Leaders & Participants: Parenthood in a Free Nation, Vol. 4. 1970. pap. 1.75 (ISBN 0-931682-08-8). Purdue Univ Bks.

GROUP HEALTH

see Medical Care, Prepaid

GROUP INDENTITY, ETHNIC

see Ethnicity

GROUP INSURANCE

see Insurance, Group

GROUP MEDICAL PRACTICE

see also Clinics; Health Maintenance Organizations

Bryant, John H., et al. Community Hospitals & Primary Care. LC 76-14833. 1975. text ed. 20.00 (ISBN 0-88410-121-5). Ballinger Pub.

Center for Research in Ambulatory Health Care Administration, et al. Medical Group Practice Management. LC 77-3330. 1977. prof. ref. 29.00 (ISBN 0-88410-511-3). Ballinger Pub.

Douglas, Tom. Groupwork Practice. LC 76-1316. 1976. 17.50 (ISBN 0-8236-2265-7). Intl Univs Pr.

Field, John W. Group Practice Development: A Practical Handbook. LC 76-56948. 252p. 1976. 32.00 (ISBN 0-912862-26-2). Aspen Systems.

Goldsmith, Seth B. Ambulatory Care: Theory & Practice. LC 77-10315. 135p. 1977. 21.50 (ISBN 0-912862-46-7). Aspen Systems.

Group Medical Practice in the U. S. 1975. 15.00 (ISBN 0-89970-047-0, OP-047). AMA.

Group Practice Guidelines to Joining or Forming a Medical Group. pap. 1.50 (ISBN 0-89970-048-9, OP-456). AMA.

Jerge, Charles R., et al, eds. Group Practice & the Future of Dental Care. LC 74-708. (Illus.). 420p. 1974. text ed. 18.50 (ISBN 0-8121-0462-5). Lea & Febiger.

Medical Group Management Association. Organization and Development of a Medical Group Practice. LC 76-26953. 1976. 50.00 (ISBN 0-88410-143-6). Ballinger Pub.

Medical Group Practice Terminology with Accompanying Definitions. LC 81-65571. 75p. (Orig.). 1981. pap. 15.00 three ring binder (ISBN 0-933948-09-3). Med Group Mgmt.

Sampson, Edward E. & Sampson, Marya. Group Process for the Health Professions. 2nd ed. LC 80-26487. 320p. 1981. pap. 13.95 (ISBN 0-471-08279-1, Pub. by Wiley Med). Wiley.

Shouldice, Robert G. & Shouldice, Katherine H. Medical Group Practice & Health Maintenance Organizations. LC 78-53824. (Illus.). 1978. text ed. 27.50 (ISBN 0-87815-020-X). Info Resources.

Survey of Medical Groups in the U.S. - 1969. 128p. 1971. pap. 2.50 (ISBN 0-89970-080-2, OP-261). AMA.

Wasserman, Fred W. & Miller, Michael C. Building a Group Practice. 188p. 1973. text ed. 11.75 (ISBN 0-398-02774-9); pap. text ed. 8.50 (ISBN 0-398-02793-5). C C Thomas.

GROUP MEDICAL PRACTICE, PREPAID

see Health Maintenance Organizations

GROUP MEDICAL SERVICE

see Medical Care, Prepaid

GROUP PRAYER

see Prayer Groups

GROUP PSYCHOANALYSIS

see also Group Psychotherapy

Bion, W. R. Experiences in Groups. LC 61-7884. 1981. text ed. 12.95x (ISBN 0-465-02174-3). Basic.

Foulkes, Siegmund H. Therapeutic Group Analysis. 1965. text ed. 20.00 (ISBN 0-8236-6480-5). Intl Univs Pr.

Grotjahn, Martin. Psychoanalysis & the Family Neurosis. 1960. 5.95x (ISBN 0-393-01037-6, NortonC). Norton.

Hamilton, David L., ed. Cognitive Processes in Stereotyping & Intergroup Behavior. LC 80-29408. 384p. 1981. text ed. 24.95 (ISBN 0-89859-081-7). L Erlbaum Assocs.

Kissen, M. From Group Dynamics to Group Psychoanalysis: The Therapeutic Application of Group Dynamics Understanding. LC 76-14844. (The Ser. in Classical & Community Psychology). 1976. 21.95 (ISBN 0-470-15132-3). Halsted Pr.

Scheidlinger, Saul, ed. Psychoanalytic Group Dynamics: Basic Reading. LC 79-20604. 315p. 1980. text ed. 25.00 (ISBN 0-8236-4445-6, 004445). Intl Univs Pr.

Slavson, S. R. Textbook in Analytic Group Psychotherapy. LC 64-15375. 1964. text ed. 27.50 (ISBN 0-8236-6460-0). Intl Univs Pr.

Stierlin, Helm. Psychoanalysis Family Therapy. LC 76-45568. 1977. 25.00x (ISBN 0-87668-257-3, 25734). Aronson.

GROUP PSYCHOTHERAPY

see also Family Psychotherapy; Group Psychoanalysis; Prayer Groups; Psychodrama

Agazarian, Yvonne & Peters, Richard. The Visible & Invisible Group: Two Perspectives on Group Psychotherapy & Group Process. (Illus.). 304p. 1981. 27.50 (ISBN 0-7100-0692-6). Routledge & Kegan.

Anders, Robert L., et al. Group Therapy: A Source of New Meaning for Nurses. 350p. 1982. price not set (ISBN 0-8036-0142-5). Davis Co.

Berkovitz, Irving H. Adolescents Grow in Groups: Clinical Experiences in Adolescent Group Psychotherapy. LC 72-190076. 364p. 1972. pap. 8.95 (ISBN 0-87630-055-7). Brunner-Mazel.

Beukenkamp, Cornelius, Jr. Fortunate Strangers. LC 80-19260. 269p. 1980. Repr. of 1971 ed. lib. bdg. 9.95x (ISBN 0-89370-600-0). Borgo Pr.

Brandes, Norman S. Group Therapy for the Adolescent. LC 72-96530. (Illus.). 1973. 20.00x (ISBN 0-87668-060-0). Aronson.

The Classics of Group Psychotherapy, 27 vols. 594.00 (ISBN 0-685-25825-4); pap. 486.00 (ISBN 0-685-25826-2). Beacon Hse.

Cohen. Group Psychotherapy. (Post Graduate Psychiatry Ser.). Date not set. price not set (ISBN 0-407-00130-1). Butterworth.

Corey, Gerald & Corey, Marianne S. Groups: Process & Practice. LC 77-8324. (Illus.). 1977. pap. text ed. 10.95 (ISBN 0-8185-0235-5). Brooks-Cole.

Cox, Murray. Structuring the Therapeutic Process: Compromise with Chaos - a Therapist's Response to the Individual & the Group. LC 77-4181. 1978. text ed. 37.00 (ISBN 0-08-020403-1); pap. text ed. 12.50 (ISBN 0-08-020402-3). Pergamon.

Cumming, John & Cumming, Elaine. Ego & Milieu: Theory & Practice of Environmental Therapy. LC 62-18829. 1962. pap. 9.95x (ISBN 0-202-26044-5). Aldine Pub.

De Schill, Stefan, ed. The Challenge for Group Psychotherapy: Present & Future. 1st ed. LC 73-19952. 1974. text ed. 22.50 (ISBN 0-8236-0710-0). Intl Univs Pr.

Driver, Helen I., et al. Counseling & Learning Through Small-Group Discussion. library ed. (Illus.). 1970. lib. bdg. 8.95 (ISBN 0-910982-02-3). Monona.

Drum, David J. & Knott, J. Eugene. Structured Groups for Facilitating Development: Acquiring Life Skills, Resolving Life Themes, & Making Life Transitions. LC 77-1947. (New Vistas in Counseling Ser.: Vol. 1). 1977. 19.95 (ISBN 0-87705-308-1). Human Sci Pr.

Durkin, Helen. The Group in Depth. LC 64-7550. 1966. text ed. 20.00 (ISBN 0-8236-2240-1). Intl Univs Pr.

Durkin, Helen E. Group Psychotherapy for Mothers. (American Lecture Psychology). 144p. 1969. ed. spiral bdg. 14.50photocopy (ISBN 0-398-00488-9). C C Thomas.

Durkin, James E., ed. Living Groups: Group Psychotherapy & General Systems Theory. 400p. 1981. 32.50 (ISBN 0-87630-253-3). Brunner-Mazel.

Dyer, William G. Modern Theory & Method in Group Training. 256p. 1981. Repr. of 1972 ed. text ed. write for info. (ISBN 0-89874-280-3). Krieger.

Encounter Groups & Psychiatry. (Task Force Report: No. 1). 27p. 1970. pap. 5.00 (ISBN 0-685-24863-1, P246-0). Am Psychiatric.

Ernst, Franklin H., Jr. Get-on-with, Getting Well & Get Winners. 3rd ed. 1974. softbound 1.00x (ISBN 0-916944-00-X). Addresso'set.

--Leaving Your Mark. 2nd ed. 1973. softbound 2.00x (ISBN 0-916944-05-0). Addresso'set.

--Outline of the Activity of Listening. 3rd ed. 1973. softbound 1.95x (ISBN 0-916944-09-3). Addresso'set.

--Who's Listening - Handbook of the Listening Activity. LC 73-84380. 1973. 9.95x (ISBN 0-916944-15-8). Addresso'set.

Feder, Bud & Ronall, Ruth E., eds. Beyond the Hot Seat: Gestalt Approaches to Group. LC 79-20648. 1980. 17.50 (ISBN 0-87630-205-3). Brunner-Mazel.

Feldman, Ronald A. & Wodarski, John S. Contemporary Approaches to Group Treatment: Traditional, Behavior-Modification, & Group-Centered. LC 74-27913. (Social & Behavioral Science Ser.). (Illus.). 256p. 1975. 16.95x (ISBN 0-87589-249-3). Jossey-Bass.

Friedman, William H. How to Do Groups. LC 79-51933. 1979. 20.00x (ISBN 0-87668-335-9). Aronson.

Gardiner, Cyril F. A First Course in Group Therapy. (Universitext Ser.). 177p. 1981. pap. 14.80 (ISBN 0-387-90545-6). Springer-Verlag.

Gazda, George M. Innovations to Group Psychotherapy. 2nd ed. (Illus.). 344p. 1981. 16.75 (ISBN 0-398-04152-0). C C Thomas.

--Innovations to Group Psychotherapy. (Illus.). 326p. 1971. 15.50 (ISBN 0-398-00659-8). C C Thomas.

Gazda, George M., ed. Basic Approaches to Group Psychotherapy & Group Counseling. 2nd ed. (Illus.). 560p. 1979. 21.50 (ISBN 0-398-03212-2). C C Thomas.

Gibbard, Graham S., et al, eds. Analysis of Groups: Contributions to Theory, Research & Practice. LC 73-10941. (Social & Behavioral Science Ser.). 384p. 1973. 18.95x (ISBN 0-87589-205-1). Jossey-Bass.

Ginott, Haim G. Group Psychotherapy with Children: The Theory & Practice of Play-Therapy. (Psychology & Human Development in Education). 1961. text ed. 15.95 (ISBN 0-07-023268-7, C). McGraw.

Goldberg, Carl & Goldberg, Merle C. The Human Circle: An Existential Approach to the New Group Therapies. LC 73-75523. 1973. 18.95x (ISBN 0-911012-67-2). Nelson-Hall.

Grotjahn, Martin. The Art & Technique of Analytic Group Therapy. LC 76-22916. 1977. 25.00x (ISBN 0-87668-252-2). Aronson.

Haas, Kurt. Growth Encounter: A Guide for Groups. LC 75-2180. 1975. 16.95x (ISBN 0-88229-225-0). Nelson-Hall.

Hardy, Richard E. & Cull, John G., eds. Group Counseling & Therapy Techniques in Special Settings. (American Lectures in Social & Rehabilitation Psychology Ser.). 180p. 1974. text ed. 14.50 (ISBN 0-398-03001-4). C C Thomas.

Harris, Gloria G., ed. The Group Treatment of Human Problems: A Social Learning Approach. LC 77-22371. 288p. 1977. 37.25 (ISBN 0-8089-1023-X). Grune.

Harris, Jay & Joseph, Cliff. Murals of the Mind. LC 72-8793. (Illus.). 1973. text ed. 20.00 (ISBN 0-8236-3490-6). Intl Univs Pr.

Heckel, Robert V. & Salzburg, H. C. Group Psychotherapy: A Behavioral Approach. (Behavioral Science Ser.: No. 2). (Illus.). 224p. 1976. 14.95x (ISBN 0-87249-340-7). U of SC Pr.

Hogan, Richard. Group Psychotherapy: A Peer-Focused Approach. 304p. 1980. text ed. 21.95 (ISBN 0-03-051076-7, HoltC). HR&W.

Jacobs, Alfred & Spradlin, Wilford, eds. The Group As Agent of Change. LC 73-12805. 492p. 1974. text ed. 29.95 (ISBN 0-87705-128-3); pap. text ed. 14.95 (ISBN 0-87705-129-1). Human Sci Pr.

Johnson, James A. Group Therapy: A Practical Approach. 1963. 22.00 (ISBN 0-07-032632-0, HP). McGraw.

Jurjevich, Ratibor-Ray M. No Water in My Cup. LC 68-9415. 1968. 5.00 (ISBN 0-87212-010-4). Libra.

Kellerman, Henry. Group Psychotherapy & Personality: Intersecting Structures. 368p. 1979. 22.50 (ISBN 0-8089-1182-1). Grune.

Klapman, J. W. Group Psychotherapy. 2nd rev. ed. LC 58-11400. 312p. 1959. 29.25 (ISBN 0-8089-0233-4). Grune.

Kroth, Jerome A. Counseling Psychology & Guidance: An Overview in Outline. 272p. 1973. 12.75 (ISBN 0-398-02726-9). C C Thomas.

Levine, Baroch. Group Psychotherapy: Practice & Development. 1979. 18.95 (ISBN 0-13-365296-3). P-H.

Lewin, Karl K. Brief Encounters (Brief Psychotherapy) LC 78-96987. 288p. 1970. 15.00x (ISBN 0-87527-048-4). Green.

Lifton, Walter. Groups: Facilitating Individual Growth & Societal Change. LC 72-566. 1972. 21.50 (ISBN 0-471-53491-9). Wiley.

Lubin, Bernard & Lubin, Alice W. Group Psychotherapy: A Bibliography of the Literature from 1956 Through 1964. viii, 186p. 1966. 5.00 (ISBN 0-87013-102-8). Mich St U Pr.

Maclennan, Beryce W. & Felsenfeld, Naomi. Group Counseling & Psychotherapy with Adolescents. LC 68-18998. 1968. 15.00x (ISBN 0-231-03093-2); pap. 5.00x (ISBN 0-231-08640-7). Columbia U Pr.

Malamud, Daniel I. & Machover, Solomon. Toward Self-Understanding: Group Techniques in Self-Confrontation. (American Lecture Psychology Ser.). 288p. 1975. 15.50 (ISBN 0-398-01204-0). C C Thomas.

Mintz, Elizabeth E. Marathon Groups: Reality & Symbol. LC 73-157796. (Century Psychology Ser.). 1971. 24.00x (ISBN 0-89197-293-5); pap. text ed. 6.95x (ISBN 0-89197-294-3). Irvington.

Moreno, J. L. Group Psychotherapy: A Symposium. 13.00 (ISBN 0-685-06812-9); pap. 11.00 (ISBN 0-685-06813-7). Beacon Hse.

--International Handbook of Group Psychotherapy. LC 65-10661. 1966. 17.50 (ISBN 0-8022-1143-7). Philos Lib.

Mullan, Hugh & Rosenbaum, Max. Group Psychotherapy. 2nd ed. LC 78-3208. 1978. 17.95 (ISBN 0-02-922080-7). Free Pr.

Naar, Ray. A Primer of Group Psychotherapy. 1981. 18.95 (ISBN 0-89885-027-4). Human Sci Pr.

Pinney, Edward L., Jr. A First Group Therapy Book. 224p. 1970. text ed. 11.50 (ISBN 0-398-01490-6). C C Thomas.

Polsky, Howard W. Cottage Six: Social System of Delinquent Boys in Residential Treatment. LC 76-50144. (Illus.). 192p. 1977. pap. text ed. 4.95 (ISBN 0-88275-475-0). Krieger.

Polsky, Howard W., et al. Dynamics of Residential Treatment: A Social System Analysis. 1968. 15.00x (ISBN 0-8078-1069-X). U of NC Pr.

Powdermaker, Florence B. & Frank, Jerome D. Group Psychotherapy, Studies in Methodology of Research & Therapy. LC 72-6188. (Illus.). 615p. 1973. Repr. of 1953 ed. lib. bdg. 36.50x (ISBN 0-8371-6450-8, POGP). Greenwood.

Rabin, H. M. & Rosenbaum, Max, eds. How to Begin a Psychotherapy Group: Six Approaches. new ed. 144p. 1976. 21.00 (ISBN 0-677-15800-9). Gordon.

Remocker, A. Jane & Storch, Elizabeth T. Action Speaks Louder: Handbook of Non-Verbal Group Techniques. 2nd ed. (Illus.). 1979. pap. text ed. 15.75 (ISBN 0-443-01919-3). Churchill.

Roback, Howard B., et al, eds. Group Psychotherapy Research: Commentaries & Selected Readings. LC 77-29216. 256p. 1979. lib. bdg. 14.50 (ISBN 0-88275-655-9). Krieger.

Rogers, Carl. Carl Rogers on Encounter Groups. 172p. 1973. pap. 2.95 (ISBN 0-06-080376-2, P376, PL). Har-Row.

Rose, Sheldon D. A Casebook in Group Therapy: A Behavioral-Cognitive Approach. (Social Work Practice Ser.). (Illus.). 1979. text ed. 15.95 (ISBN 0-13-117408-8). P-H.

--Group Therapy: A Behavioral Approach. (Illus.). 1977. 18.95 (ISBN 0-13-365239-4). P-H.

Rosenbaum, Max & Berger, Milton M., eds. Group Psychotherapy & Group Function. 2nd ed. LC 73-91084. 1975. 17.95x (ISBN 0-465-02721-0). Basic.

Sager, Clifford J. & Kaplan, Helen S. Progress in Group & Family Therapy. LC 72-153376. 960p. 1972. 35.00 (ISBN 0-87630-048-4); pap. 15.95 (ISBN 0-87630-073-5). Brunner-Mazel.

Saretsky, Theodore. Active Techniques & Group Psychotherapy. LC 77-88834. 1978. 25.00x (ISBN 0-87668-272-7). Aronson.

Scheidlinger, Saul. Focus on Group Psychotherapy. 1981. write for info. (ISBN 0-8236-1990-7). Intl Univs Pr.

Seligman, Milton. Group Counseling & Group Psychotherapy with Rehabilitation Clients. (Illus.). 352p. 1977. 22.00 (ISBN 0-398-03585-7); pap. 17.00 (ISBN 0-398-03588-1). C C Thomas.

--Group Counseling & Group Psychotherapy with the Handicapped. 415p. 1981. pap. text ed. 25.95 (ISBN 0-8391-1691-8). Univ Park.

--Group Psychotherapy & Group Counseling with the Handicapped. 415p. 1981. pap. text ed. 25.95 (ISBN 0-8391-1691-8). Univ Park.

Shaffer, John B. & Galinsky, M. David. Models of Group Therapy & Sensitivity Training. (Personal, Clinical & Social Psychology Ser). 228p. 1974. 18.95 (ISBN 0-13-586081-4). P-H.

Shapiro, Jerrold L. Methods of Group Psychotherapy & Encounter: A Tradition of Innovation. LC 77-83390. 1978. text ed. 14.95 (ISBN 0-87581-229-5). Peacock Pubs.

Slavson, S. R. Introduction to Group Therapy. 1970. text ed. 17.50 (ISBN 0-8236-2780-2); pap. text ed. 5.95 (ISBN 0-8236-8095-9, 022780). Intl Univs Pr.

Slavson, S. R. & Schiffer, Mortimer. Dynamics of Group Psychotherapy. LC 78-68010. 1979. 40.00x (ISBN 0-87668-372-3). Aronson.

Slavson, S. R., ed. Fields of Group Psychotherapy. LC 64-15375. 1956. text ed. 20.00 (ISBN 0-8236-1940-0); pap. text ed. 5.95x (ISBN 0-8236-8053-3, 021940). Intl Univs Pr.

--Practice of Group Therapy. 1965. text ed. 15.00 (ISBN 0-8236-4200-3). Intl Univs Pr.

Smith, Robert L. & Alexander, Ann M. Counseling Couples in Groups: A Manual for Improving Troubled Relationships. (Illus.). 128p. 1974. 12.75 (ISBN 0-398-03191-6). C C Thomas.

Speers, Rex W. & Lansing, Cornelius. Group Therapy in Childhood Psychosis. (Illus.). 1965. 12.50x (ISBN 0-8078-0945-4). U of NC Pr.

Stephenson, Richard & Scarpitti, Frank. Group Interaction As Therapy. LC 72-810. (Contributions in Sociology Ser.: No. 13). 228p. 1974. lib. bdg. 14.75 (ISBN 0-8371-6399-4, SCG/). Greenwood.

Swamy, et al. Physical Applications of Group the0ry. Date not set. price not set. Gordon.

Thompson, S. & Kahn, J. H. The Group Process As a Helping Technique. LC 79-124667. 1970. 15.00 (ISBN 0-08-016220-7); pap. 7.00 (ISBN 0-08-016219-3). Pergamon.

Upper, Dennis & Ross, Steven M., eds. Behavioral Group Therapy, 1980: An Annual Review. LC 80-642109. (Illus., Orig.). 1980. text ed. 24.95 (ISBN 0-87822-210-3). Res Press.

--Behavioral Group Therapy, 1981: An Annual Review. LC 80-642109. (Illus.). 340p. 1981. text ed. 24.95 (ISBN 0-87822-256-1, 2561). Res Press.

Verny, Thomas R. Inside Groups: A Practical Guide to Encounter Groups & Group Therapy. LC 73-10392. (McGraw-Hill Paperbacks). 272p. 1975. pap. 3.95 (ISBN 0-07-067407-8, SP). McGraw.

Whitaker, D. S. & Lieberman, M. A. Psychotherapy Through the Group Process. 1964. 19.95x (ISBN 0-202-26056-9). Aldine Pub.

Wolberg, Lewis R. & Aronson, Marvin L. Group Therapy 1978. LC 72-10881. (Group Therapy Ser.). 1978. pap. 19.75 (ISBN 0-913258-55-5). Thieme-Stratton.

Wolberg, Lewis R. & Aronson, Marvin L., eds. Group & Family Therapy: 1980. LC 72-10881. 432p. 1980. 25.00 (ISBN 0-87630-238-X). Brunner-Mazel.

--Group & Family Therapy 1981. LC 72-10881. 350p. 1981. price not set (ISBN 0-87630-275-4). Brunner-Mazel.

--Group Therapy: 1979 An Overview. LC 72-10881. (Illus.). 1979. pap. text ed. 19.75 (ISBN 0-913258-63-6). Thieme-Stratton.

Wolf, Alexander, et al. Beyond the Couch: Dialogues in Teaching & Learning Psychoanalysis in Groups. LC 70-11256. 1970. 25.00x (ISBN 0-87668-029-5). Aronson.

Yalom, Irvin D. The Theory & Practice of Group Psychotherapy. 2nd ed. LC 75-7637. 1975. 14.50x (ISBN 0-465-08446-X). Basic.

Zuk, Gerald H. & Boszormenyi-Nagy, Ivan, eds. Family Therapy & Disturbed Families. LC 66-28684. (Orig.). 1967. pap. 6.95x (ISBN 0-8314-0012-9). Sci & Behavior.

GROUP PSYCHOTHERAPY–STUDY AND TEACHING

Bradford, Leland P., et al, eds. T-Group Theory & Laboratory Method: Innovation in Re-Education. LC 64-11499. 1964. 28.00 (ISBN 0-471-09510-9). Wiley.

Milman, Donald S. & Goldman, George D., eds. Group Process Today: Evaluation & Perspective. 336p. 1974. 19.75 (ISBN 0-685-50187-6). C C Thomas.

Mosak, Harold H. & Pollack, Howard. Group Psychotherapy, a Syllabus. 30p. (Orig.). 1975. pap. text ed. 2.00 (ISBN 0-918560-04-7). Adler.

GROUP RELATIONS LEARNING

Schutz, William C. Here Comes Everybody: Bodymind & Encounter Culture. 1981. Repr. of 1971 ed. text ed. 18.00x (ISBN 0-8290-0044-5). Irvington.

--Joy: Expanding Human Awareness. 1967. pap. 1.95 (ISBN 0-394-17255-8, B323, BC). Grove.

Van Kreveld, D. Structure & Outcomes of Study Groups: A Method of Determining Several Properties of Group Structure & Some Relationships Observed with Group Outcome. (Orig.). 1970. pap. text ed. 4.75x (ISBN 90-232-0700-9). Humanities.

Zook, Wilbur. From Self to Group Action: A Group Planning Process. 1978. pap. 3.95 (ISBN 0-933222-00-9). Zook.

GROUP RELATIONS TRAINING

Allen, Bud & Bosta, Diana. Library of Lesson Plans: Team Building & Listening Workshop. 75p. 1981. vinyl 49.95x (ISBN 0-939438-16-X). Rae John.

Back, Kurt W. Beyond Words: The Story of Sensitivity Training & the Encounter Movement. LC 73-182935. 260p. 1972. 9.95 (ISBN 0-87154-077-0). Russell Sage.

Bailes, Frederick. How to Get Along with Troublesome People. 1972. pap. 0.75 (ISBN 0-87516-128-6). De Vorss.

Ballard, Jim. Stop a Moment: A Group Leader's Handbook of Energizing Experiences. LC 77-81459. (Mandala Ser. in Education). (Illus.). 73p. 1977. pap. 4.95 (ISBN 0-916250-24-5). Irvington.

Berger, M. L. & Berger, P. J., eds. Group Training Techniques: Cases, Applications & Research. LC 72-9008. 191p. 1973. 24.95 (ISBN 0-470-06960-0). Halsted Pr.

Bertcher, Harvey J. Group Participation: Techniques for Leaders & Members. LC 79-175. (Sage Human Services Guides: Vol. 10). 1979. pap. 8.00 (ISBN 0-8039-1204-8). Sage.

Blumberg, Arthur. Sensitivity Training: Processes, Problems & Applications. LC 74-157409. (Notes & Essays Ser No. 68). 1971. pap. 2.50 (ISBN 0-87060-040-0). Syracuse U Cont Ed.

Carter, Stephen J. & McKinney, Charles. Keeping a Good Thing Going. 1979. pap. 2.95 (ISBN 0-570-03787-5, 12-2745). Concordia.

Casella, Cono. Training Exercises to Improve Interpersonal Relations in Health Care Organizations. LC 77-72280. 404p. 1977. 21.00x (ISBN 0-916592-17-0). Panel Pubs.

Cathcart, Robert S. & Samovar, Larry A. Small Group Communication: A Reader. 3rd ed. 556p. 1979. pap. text ed. write for info. (ISBN 0-697-04156-5). Wm C Brown.

Clinebell, Howard. Growth Groups: Marriage & Family Enrichment, Creative Singlehood, Human Liberation, Youth Work, Social Change. LC 77-80169. 1977. pap. 4.95 (ISBN 0-687-15975-X). Abingdon.

Cohen, Arthur M. & Smith, R. Douglas. The Critical Incident in Growth Groups: Theory & Technique. LC 75-22510. 292p. 1976. pap. 14.95 (ISBN 0-88390-102-1). Univ Assocs.

Cooper, Cary L. Theories of Group Processes. LC 74-28089. (Individuals, Groups & Organizations Ser.). 275p. 1975. 40.75 (ISBN 0-471-17117-4, Pub. by Wiley-Interscience); pap. text ed. 20.00 (ISBN 0-471-99452-9). Wiley.

Cooper, Cary L. & Alderfer, Clayton. Advances in Experiential Social Processes. LC 77-22060. (Advances in Experimental Social Processes Ser.: Vol. 1). 1978. 36.25 (ISBN 0-471-99546-0, Pub. by Wiley-Interscience). Wiley.

Coulson, William R. A Sense of Community: That Education Might Be Personal. LC 73-76604. 1973. pap. text ed. 5.95x (ISBN 0-675-08929-8). Merrill.

Doob, Leonard W. Resolving Conflict in Africa: The Fermeda Workshop. 1970. pap. 3.95x (ISBN 0-300-01376-0). Yale U Pr.

Durkin, Henry P. Forty Four Hours to Change Your Life. LC 74-80349. 96p. (Orig.). 1974. pap. 1.75 (ISBN 0-8091-1849-1). Paulist Pr.

Dyer, William G. Modern Theory & Methods in Group Training. (Natl. Learning Resources Ser.). 1972. 14.95x (ISBN 0-442-22218-1). Van Nos Reinhold.

Egan, Gerard. Encounter: Group Processes for Interpersonal Growth. LC 71-113403. (Orig.). 1970. pap. text ed. 11.95 (ISBN 0-8185-0301-7). Brooks-Cole.

--Face to Face: The Small Group Experience & Interpersonal Growth. LC 72-90673. (Orig.). 1973. pap. text ed. 8.95 (ISBN 0-8185-0075-1). Brooks-Cole.

Elliot, James. The Theory & Practice of Encounter Group Leadership. pap. 14.50 (ISBN 0-685-85015-3). Explorations Inst.

Farrell, Warren. The Liberated Man. 384p. 1975. pap. 2.95 (ISBN 0-553-02275-X, G13599-6). Bantam.

Fearn, Leif, et al. Human Development Program Supplementary Idea Guide. rev. ed. 1975. 7.95 (ISBN 0-86584-008-3). Human Dev Train.

Gallagher, Chuck. Marriage Encounter: As I Have Loved You. LC 75-12224. 168p. 1975. 6.95 (ISBN 0-385-00991-7). Doubleday.

Goldberg, Carl. Encounter: Group Sensitivity Training Experience. LC 70-133292. 1971. 25.00x (ISBN 0-87668-035-X). Aronson.

Gosling, R., et al. The Use of Small Groups in Training. 144p. 1967. pap. 15.75 (ISBN 0-8089-0630-5). Grune.

Heisel, D. The Kairos Dimension. 304p. 1974. 19.25 (ISBN 0-677-04910-2); pap. 8.95 (ISBN 0-685-42134-1). Gordon.

Hoeper, Claus-Juergen, et al. Awareness Games: Personal Growth Through Group Interaction. Davies, Hilary, tr. 160p. 1976. pap. 4.95 (ISBN 0-312-06300-8). St Martin.

Holt, Herbert. Free to Be Good or Bad: An Anti Self-Improvement Book. LC 75-38523. 206p. 1976. 6.95 (ISBN 0-87131-203-4). M Evans.

Howard, Jane. Please Touch. 1971. pap. 3.95 (ISBN 0-440-56798-X, Delta). Dell.

Jones, John E. & Pfeiffer, J. William, eds. Annual Handbook for Group Facilitators,1975. LC 73-92841. (Series in Human Relations Training). 290p. 1975. pap. 20.00 (ISBN 0-88390-079-3); looseleaf 44.50 (ISBN 0-88390-078-5). Univ Assocs.

Katz, Richard. Preludes to Growth: An Experiential Approach. LC 72-94013. 1973. pap. text ed. 7.95 (ISBN 0-02-917190-3). Free Pr.

Klein, Alan F. Effective Groupwork: An Introduction to Principle & Method. LC 77-189011. 1972. 12.95 (ISBN 0-8096-1845-1, Assn Pr). New Century.

Lakin, Martin. Interpersonal Encounter Theory & Practice in Sensitivity Training. (Psychology Ser.). (Illus.). 320p. 1971. text ed. 17.50 (ISBN 0-07-036065-0, C). McGraw.

Lawrence, W. Gordon. Exploring Individual & Organizational Boundaries: A Tavistock Open Systems Approach. LC 78-8603. (Individuals, Groups & Organizations Ser.). 256p. 1979. 34.95 (ISBN 0-471-99679-3, Pub. by Wiley-Interscience). Wiley.

Lieberman, M. A., et al. Encounter Groups: First Facts. LC 72-89174. 1973. 15.95x (ISBN 0-465-01968-4). Basic.

Liff, Zavel A. The Leader in the Group. LC 75-10862. 370p. 1975. 25.00x (ISBN 0-87668-213-1). Aronson.

Lifton, Walter. Groups: Facilitating Individual Growth & Societal Change. LC 72-566. 1972. 21.50 (ISBN 0-471-53491-9). Wiley.

Lucero, Maryetta. Why Don't You Love Yourself: Some Information on Dealing with Yourself & Others. LC 75-46072. 1976. pap. 3.50 (ISBN 0-89016-021-X). Lightning Tree.

Luft, Joseph. Of Human Interaction. LC 76-84008. (Illus.). 179p. 1969. pap. 6.95 (ISBN 0-87484-198-4). Mayfield Pub.

McConnell, Taylor. Group Leadership for Self-Realization. 1974. text ed. 16.95x (ISBN 0-442-80028-2). Van Nos Reinhold.

Maslowski, Raymond M. & Morgan, Lewis B. Interpersonal Growth & Self Actualization in Groups. LC 72-13775. (Illus.). 1973. 29.50x (ISBN 0-8422-5082-4); pap. text ed. 8.95x (ISBN 0-8422-0289-7). Irvington.

Mason, Russell E. Informational Guides for Groups, Communication, Living & Change, Set-GL. 1975. pap. 25.00x (ISBN 0-89533-019-9); tape-2, t-16, t-17, Notes, Clinical Applications, rev. ed., 1979, H.E.S.T-a, SET incl. F I Comm.

Morris, Kenneth T. & Cinnamon, Kenneth M. Controversial Issues in Human Relations Training Groups. 168p. 1975. 13.75 (ISBN 0-398-03456-7); pap. 8.50 (ISBN 0-398-03458-3). C C Thomas.

Moustakas, Clark. Individuality & Encounter: A Brief Journey into Loneliness & Sensitivity Groups. LC 68-25353. 1968. pap. 3.45 (ISBN 0-87299-002-8). Howard Doyle.

Napier, Rodney W. & Gershenfeld, Matti K. Groups: Theory & Experience. LC 72-7925. 325p. 1973. text ed. 17.95 (ISBN 0-395-12658-4, 3-40200); instructors' manual pap. 4.50 (ISBN 0-395-14048-X, 3-40201). HM.

O'Banion, Terry & O'Connell, April. Shared Journey: An Introduction to Encounter. 1970. pap. text ed. 11.95 (ISBN 0-13-807834-3). P-H.

Oden, Thomas C. The Intensive Group Experience: The New Pietism. 1972. pap. 3.45 (ISBN 0-664-24951-5). Westminster.

O'Neill, Michael E. & Martensen, Kai R. Criminal Justice Group Training: A Facilitator's Handbook. LC 75-11040. 290p. 1975. pap. 15.00 (ISBN 0-88390-100-5). Univ Assocs.

Pfeiffer, J. William & Jones, John E., eds. Annual Handbook for Group Facilitators, 1974. LC 73-92841. (Series in Human Relations Training). 290p. 1974. pap. 20.00 (ISBN 0-88390-082-3); looseleaf ntbk. 44.50 (ISBN 0-88390-074-2). Univ Assocs.

--Annual Handbook for Group Facilitators, 1976. LC 73-92841. (Series in Human Relations Training). 292p. 1976. pap. 20.00 (ISBN 0-88390-088-2); looseleaf notebk. 44.50 (ISBN 0-88390-087-4). Univ Assocs.

--Annual Handbook for Group Facilitators, 1978. LC 73-92841. (Series in Human Relations Training). 296p. 1978. pap. 20.00 (ISBN 0-88390-099-8); looseleaf notebook 44.50 (ISBN 0-88390-098-X). Univ Assocs.

--A Handbook of Structured Experiences for Human Relations Training, 8 vols. LC 73-92840. (Series in Human Relations Training). 1973-81. pap. 9.50 ea.; Vol. 1. Rev. Ed. (ISBN 0-88390-041-6); Vol. 2. Rev. Ed. (ISBN 0-88390-042-4); Vol. 3. Rev. Ed. (ISBN 0-88390-043-2); Vol. 4. (ISBN 0-88390-044-0). Vol. 5 (ISBN 0-88390-045-9). Vol. 6 (ISBN 0-88390-046-7). Vol. 7 (ISBN 0-88390-047-5). Vol.8 (ISBN 0-88390-048-3). Univ Assocs.

Pfeiffer, J. William, et al. Instrumentation in Human Relations Training, 2nd Ed. A Guide to 92 Instruments with Wide Application to the Behavioral Sciences. LC 76-6621. 324p. 1976. pap. 17.50 (ISBN 0-88390-116-1). Univ Assocs.

Rosenbaum, Max & Snadowsky, Alvin. The Intensive Group Experience. LC 76-8147. 1976. 13.95 (ISBN 0-02-926950-4). Free Pr.

Schoenberg, B. Mark. A Strange Breed of Cat: An Encounter in Human Sexuality. LC 74-5281. 336p. 1975. 12.95 (ISBN 0-88280-015-9). ETC Pubns.

Schutz, William C. Elements of Encounter. 1973. text ed. 8.95x (ISBN 0-8290-0043-7); pap. text ed. 3.50x (ISBN 0-8290-0107-7). Irvington.

Shaffer, John B. & Galinsky, M. David. Models of Group Therapy & Sensitivity Training. (Personal, Clinical & Social Psychology Ser). 228p. 1974. 18.95 (ISBN 0-13-586081-4). P-H.

Sheehan, Valerie H., ed. Unmasking: Ten Women in Metamorphosis. LC 72-96163. 286p. 1973. 12.95 (ISBN 0-8040-0626-1). Swallow.

Smith, Gerald W. & Phillips, Alice I. Couple Therapy. 160p. 1973. pap. 1.95 (ISBN 0-02-078000-1, Collier). Macmillan.

Smith, Henry C. Sensitivity Training: The Scientific Understanding of Individuals. 1973. text ed. 15.95 (ISBN 0-07-058481-8, C). McGraw.

Solomon, Lawrence N. & Berzon, Betty, eds. New Perspectives on Encounter Groups. LC 73-186583. (Social & Behavioral Science Ser). 1972. 17.95x (ISBN 0-87589-128-4). Jossey-Bass.

Taylor, Margaret. Creative Movement: Steps Towards Understanding. 1979. 2.00 (ISBN 0-686-22743-3). Sharing Co.

Weschler, Irving R. & Reisel, Jerome. Inside a Sensitivity Training Group. (Monograph Ser.: No. 4). 1959. 5.00 (ISBN 0-89215-006-8). U Cal LA Indus Rel.

Wexley, Kenneth N. & Yukl, Gary A., eds. Organizational Behavior & Industrial Psychology: Readings with Commentary. (Illus.). 650p. 1975. pap. text ed. 10.95x (ISBN 0-19-501930-X). Oxford U Pr.

GROUP REPRESENTATION (MATHEMATICS)

see Representations of Groups

GROUP TEACHING

see Group Work in Education

GROUP THEATER

Kubicki, Jan. The Theatre Student: Techniques of Group Theatre. LC 73-86317. (Theatre Student Ser). (Illus.). 190p. (gr. 7-12). 1975. PLB 12.50 (ISBN 0-8239-0292-7). Rosen Pr.

GROUP WORK, CHURCH

see Church Group Work

GROUP WORK, SOCIAL

see Social Group Work

GROUP WORK IN EDUCATION

Arends, Richard I. & Arends, Jane H. Systems Change Strategies in Educational Settings. Walz, Garry R. & Benjamin, Libby, eds. LC 77-22315. (New Vista in Counseling Ser.: Vol. III). 120p. 1977. 14.95 (ISBN 0-87705-310-3). Human Sci Pr.

Cooper, Cary L. Learning from Others in Groups: Experimental Learning Approaches. LC 78-26987. (Illus.). 1979. lib. bdg. 23.95x (ISBN 0-313-20922-7, COL/). Greenwood.

Hanson, Philip G. Learning Through Groups: A Trainer's Basic Guide. LC 81-50701. 216p. 1981. pap. 17.95 (ISBN 0-88390-165-X). Univ Assocs.

Hawley, Robert C. & Hawley, Isabel L. Developing Human Potential: More Activities for Person & Social Growth, Vol. 2. LC 76-51467. 1977. pap. 6.95 (ISBN 0-913636-09-6). Educ Res MA.

Klopf, Donald. Interacting in Groups-Theory & Practice. 225p. (Orig.). 1980. pap. text ed. 9.95 (ISBN 0-89582-060-9). Morton Pub.

Kounin, Jacob S. Discipline & Group Management in Classrooms. LC 76-57243. 192p. 1977. Repr. of 1970 ed. lib. bdg. 9.50 (ISBN 0-88275-504-8). Krieger.

Malnati, Richard J. & Trembley, Edward L. Group Procedures for Counselors in Educational & Community Settings. 1974. 24.50x (ISBN 0-8422-5161-8); pap. text ed. 8.95x (ISBN 0-8422-0385-0). Irvington.

Miel, Alice. Cooperative Procedures in Learning. LC 77-168965. 512p. 1972. Repr. of 1952 ed. lib. bdg. 21.25x (ISBN 0-8371-6238-6, MIPL). Greenwood.

Robinson, Russell D. Group Dynamics for Student Activities. 1977. pap. 3.00 (ISBN 0-88210-082-3). Natl Assn Principals.

Schmuck, Richard A. & Schmuck, Patricia A. Group Processes in the Classroom. 3rd ed. 234p. 1979. pap. text ed. write for info. (ISBN 0-697-06091-8). Wm C Brown.

Stanford, Gene. Developing Effective Classroom Groups: A Practical Guide for Teachers. 256p. 1977. 10.95 (ISBN 0-89104-230-X); pap. 6.95 (ISBN 0-89104-188-5). A & W Pubs.

Turney, C., et al. Sydney Micro Skills, Series 4 Handbook: Guiding Small Group Discussion, Small Group Teaching & Individualized Instruction. (Illus.). 1976. pap. 5.00x (ISBN 0-424-00026-1, Pub. by Sydney U Pr). Intl Schol Bk Serv.

GROUPING BY ABILITY

see Ability Grouping in Education

GROUPS, AGE

see Age Groups

GROUPS, CONTINUOUS

see also Differential Forms; Differential Invariants; Ergodic Theory; Fiber Bundles (Mathematics); Topological Groups; Transformations, Infinitesimal

Campbell, John R. Introductory Treatise on Lie's Theory. LC 65-28441. 14.95 (ISBN 0-8284-0183-7). Chelsea Pub.

Dieudonne, Jean & Hua, L. K. On the Automorphisms of the Classical Groups. LC 52-42839. (Memoirs: No. 2). 1980. pap. 11.20 (ISBN 0-8218-1202-5, MEMO-2). Am Math.

Ferraro, John R. & Ziomek, Joseph S. Introductory Group Theory & Its Applications to Molecular Structure. 2nd ed. LC 68-28096. 292p. 1975. 25.00 (ISBN 0-306-30768-5, Plenum Pr). Plenum Pub.

Loewner, Charles, et al. Charles Loewner: Theory of Continuous Groups. (Mathematicians of Our Time Ser). 1971. 17.50x (ISBN 0-262-06041-8). MIT Pr.

Palais, Richard S. Global Formulation of the Lie Theory of Transformation Groups. LC 52-42839. (Memoirs: No. 22). 1971. pap. 8.40 (ISBN 0-8218-1222-X, MEMO-22). Am Math.

Sehgal, S. Topics in Group Rings, Vol. 50. (Pure & Applied Mathematics Ser.). 1978. 27.50 (ISBN 0-8247-6755-1). Dekker.

Tondeur, Philippe. Introduction to Lie Groups & Transformation Groups. 2nd ed. LC 78-99012. (Lecture Notes in Mathematics: Vol. 7). 1969. pap. 10.70 (ISBN 0-387-04599-6). Springer-Verlag.

Von Neumann, John. Continuous Geometry. (Mathematical Ser.: Vol. 25). 1960. 22.00x (ISBN 0-691-07928-5). Princeton U Pr.

Weyl, Hermann. Classical Groups, Their Invariants & Representations. rev ed. (Mathematical Ser.: Vol. 1). 1946. 22.00x (ISBN 0-691-07923-4). Princeton U Pr.

GROUPS, ETHNIC

see Ethnic Groups

GROUPS, LIE

see Lie Groups

GROUPS, REPRESENTATION THEORY OF

see Representations of Groups

GROUPS, SELF-HELP

see Self-Help Groups

GROUPS, SMALL

see Small Groups

GROUPS, SOCIAL

see Social Groups

GROUPS, THEORY OF

see also Abelian Groups; Algebra, Boolean; Categories (Mathematics); Crystallography, Mathematical; Finite Groups; Fourier Transformations; Functions, Modular; Galois Theory; Games of Strategy (Mathematics); Lattice Theory; Matrix Groups; Representations of Groups; Semigroups; Transformation Groups; Transformations (Mathematics)

Adian, S. I. The Burnside Problem & Identities in Groups. Lennox, J. & Wiegold, J., trs. from Russian. (Ergebnisse der Mathematik und Ihrer Grenzgebiete: Vol. 95). 1979. 41.00 (ISBN 0-387-08728-1). Springer-Verlag.

American Mathematical Society Special Session, San Francisco, Jan, 1974. A Crash Course on Kleinian Groups: Proceedings. Bers, L. & Kra, I., eds. (Lecture Notes in Mathematics Ser.: Vol. 400). vii, 130p. 1974. pap. 9.90 (ISBN 0-387-06840-6). Springer-Verlag.

Andrianov, A. N., et al. Thirteen Papers on Group Theory, Algebraic Geometry & Algebraic Topology. LC 51-5559. (Translations Ser.: No. 2, Vol. 66). 1968. 30.00 (ISBN 0-8218-1766-3, TRANS 2-66). Am Math.

Arbib, Michael A. Algebraic Theory of Machines, Languages & Semigroups. LC 68-18654. 1968. 55.00 (ISBN 0-12-059050-6). Acad Pr.

Arkowitz, M. & Curjel, C. R. Groups of Homotopy Classes: Rank Formulaas & Homotopy - Commutativity. 2nd ed. (Lecture Notes in Mathematics: Vol. 4). (Orig.). 1967. pap. 10.70 (ISBN 0-387-03900-7). Springer-Verlag.

Aschbacher, Michael. The Finite Simple Groups & Their Classifications. LC 79-20927. (Yale Mathematical Monograph: No. 7). (Orig.). 1980. pap. text ed. 8.00 (ISBN 0-300-02449-5). Yale U Pr.

Babakhanian, A. Cohomological Methods in Group Theory. (Pure & Applied Mathematics Ser.: Vol. 11). 254p. 1972. 28.50 (ISBN 0-8247-1031-2). Dekker.

Bacry, Henri. Lecons sur la Theorie des Groupes & les Symetries des Particules Elementaires. (Cours & Documents de Mathematiques & de Physique Ser.). (Orig.). 1967. 74.25x (ISBN 0-677-50190-0). Gordon.

--Lectures on Group Theory & Particle Theory. LC 72-78879. (Documents on Modern Physics Ser.). (Illus.). 1977. 104.00 (ISBN 0-677-30190-1). Gordon.

Bargmann, V., ed. Group Representations in Mathematics & Physics: Battelle Seattle 1969 Rencontres. LC 75-146233. (Lecture Notes in Physics: Vol. 6). 1971. pap. 18.30 (ISBN 0-387-05310-7). Springer-Verlag.

Baumslag, C. B. & Chandler, B. Group Theory. LC 68-6033. (Schaum's Outline Ser). (Illus.). 1968. pap. 6.95 (ISBN 0-07-004124-5, SP). McGraw.

Baumslag, Gilbert. Notes on Nilpotent Groups. LC 78-145636. (CBMS Regional Conference Series in Mathematics: No. 2). 1971. 8.40 (ISBN 0-8218-1651-9, CBMS-2). Am Math.

Baumslag, Gilbert, ed. Reviews on Infinite Groups. LC 73-21521. 1974. 92.00 (ISBN 0-686-66983-5, REVINFIN). Am Math.

Beaumont, Ross A. & Pierce, Richard S. Torsion Free Groups of Rank Two. LC 52-42839. (Memoirs: No. 38). 1968. pap. 7.20 (ISBN 0-8218-1238-6, MEMO-38). Am Math.

Beiglboeck, W., et al, eds. Group Theoretical Methods in Physics, Vol. 94. (Lecture Notes in Physics Ser.). 1979. pap. 24.20 (ISBN 0-387-09238-2). Springer-Verlag.

Berman, S. D., et al. Nine Papers on Logic & Group Theory. LC 51-5559. (Translations Ser.: No. 2, Vol. 64). 1967. 28.80 (ISBN 0-8218-1764-7, TRANS 2-64). Am Math.

Bhagavantam, S. & Venkatarayudu, T. Theory of Groups & Its Application to Physical Problems. 1969. 26.50 (ISBN 0-12-095460-5). Acad Pr.

Biggs, N. L. & White, A. T. Permutation Groups & Combinatorial Structures. LC 78-21485. (London Mathematical Society Lecture Note: No. 33). (Illus.). 1979. pap. 17.95x (ISBN 0-521-22287-7). Cambridge U Pr.

Birkhoff, Garrett. Hydrodynamics: A Study in Logic, Fact, & Similitude. LC 77-18143. (Illus.). 1978. Repr. of 1960 ed. lib. bdg. 19.75x (ISBN 0-313-20118-8, BIHY). Greenwood.

Bishop, David M. Group Theory & Chemistry. (Illus.). 310p. 1973. 59.00x (ISBN 0-19-855140-1). Oxford U Pr.

Boruvka, O. Foundations of the Theory of Groupoids & Groups. 216p. 1975. 34.00 (ISBN 3-7643-0780-3). Birkhauser.

Boruvka, Otakar. Foundations of the Theory of Groupoids & Groups. LC 75-8625. 215p. 1976. Repr. of 1960 ed. 41.95 (ISBN 0-470-08965-2). Halsted Pr.

Bruck, R. H. Survey of Binary Systems. 3rd ed. LC 79-143906. (Ergebnisse der Mathematik und Ihrer Grenzebiete: Vol. 20). 1971. 18.50 (ISBN 0-387-03497-8). Springer-Verlag.

Bryce, R. A., et al. Group Theory. (Lectures Notes in Mathematics: Vol. 573). 1977. pap. 10.10 (ISBN 0-387-08131-3). Springer-Verlag.

Burns, Gerald. Introduction to Group Theory with Applications. (Material Science & Technology Ser.). 1977. 21.50 (ISBN 0-12-145750-8). Acad Pr.

Butzer, P. L. & Berens, H. Semi-Groups of Operators & Approximation. LC 68-11980. (Grundlehren der Mathematischen Wissenschaften: Vol. 145). 1967. 33.90 (ISBN 0-387-03832-9). Springer-Verlag.

Carmeli, Moshe. Group Theory & General Relativity. (Pure & Applied Physics Ser.). (Illus.). 1977. text ed. 40.50x (ISBN 0-07-009986-3, C). McGraw.

Cernikov, S. N., et al. Fourteen Papers on Groups & Semigroups. LC 51-5559. (Translations Ser.: No. 2, Vol. 36). 1964. 26.80 (ISBN 0-8218-1736-1, TRANS 2-36). Am Math.

Clifford, A. H. & Preston, G. B. Algebraic Theory of Semigroups, 2 Vols. LC 61-15686. (Mathematical Surveys Ser.: Vol. 7). 1977. Repr. of 1961 ed. Vol. 1. with corrections 23.60 (ISBN 0-8218-0271-2, SURV-7-1); Vol. 2. with corrections 30.00 (ISBN 0-8218-0272-0, SURV-7.2). Am Math.

Conference in Orders, Group Rings & Related Topics. Proceedings. Hsia, J. S., et al, eds. (Lecture Notes in Mathematics: Vol. 353). 224p. 1974. pap. 12.20 (ISBN 0-387-06518-0). Springer-Verlag.

Conference on Group Theory, University of Wisconsin-Parkside, 1972. Proceedings. Gatterdam, R. W. & Weston, K. W., eds. LC 73-76679. (Lecture Notes in Mathematics: Vol. 319). v, 188p. 1973. pap. 9.90 (ISBN 0-387-06205-X). Springer-Verlag.

Conference, 5th, Oberwolfach, Germany, Jan. 29 - Feb. 4, 1978. Probability Measures on Groups: Proceedings. Heyer, H., ed. (Lecture Notes in Mathematics: Vol. 706). 1979. pap. 18.70 (ISBN 0-387-09124-6). Springer-Verlag.

Cotton, F. Albert. Chemical Applications of Group Theory. 2nd ed. LC 76-129657. 1971. 32.50 (ISBN 0-471-17570-6, Pub. by Wiley-Interscience). Wiley.

Coxeter, H. S. Twisted Honeycombs. LC 75-145638. (CBMS Regional Conference Series in Mathematics: Vol. 4). iv, 47p. 1970. 7.40 (ISBN 0-8218-1653-5, CBMS-4). Am Math.

Coxeter, H. S. & Moser, W. O. Generators & Relations for Discrete Groups. 4th ed. (Engebnisse der Mathematik und ihrer Grenzgebiete: Vol. 14). (Illus.). 1980. 37.40 (ISBN 0-387-09212-9). Springer-Verlag.

Cracknell, A. P. Applied Group Theory. 1968. 46.00 (ISBN 0-08-013328-2); pap. 12.75 (ISBN 0-08-012286-8). Pergamon.

Demazure, M. Lectures on P-Divisible Groups. LC 72-94595. (Lecture Notes in Mathematics: Vol. 302). 98p. 1973. pap. 7.70 (ISBN 0-387-06092-8). Springer-Verlag.

DeWitt, Bryce S. Dynamical Theory of Groups & Fields. (Documents on Modern Physics Ser). 1965. 54.50x (ISBN 0-677-00985-2). Gordon.

Dieudonne, Jean & Hua, L. K. On the Automorphisms of the Classical Groups. LC 52-42839. (Memoirs: No. 2). 1980. pap. 11.20 (ISBN 0-8218-1202-5, MEMO-2). Am Math.

Dixon, John D. Problems in Group Theory. LC 72-76597. 1973. pap. 3.50 (ISBN 0-486-61574-X). Dover.

Dunkl, Charles F. & Ramirez, Donald E. Topics in Harmonic Analysis. LC 73-153387. 1971. 28.00x (ISBN 0-89197-454-7); pap. text ed. 15.95x (ISBN 0-89197-969-7). Irvington.

Dynkin, E. B., et al. Five Papers on Algebra & Group Theory. LC 51-5559. (Translations Ser.: No. 2, Vol. 6). 1957. 47.20 (ISBN 0-8218-1706-X, TRANS 2-6). Am Math.

Dyson, Freeman J., ed. Symmetry Groups in Nuclear & Particle Physics: A Lecture Note & Reprint Volume. (Mathematical Physics Monographs: No. 4). 1966. 17.50 (ISBN 0-8053-2370-8, Adv Bk Prog). Benjamin-Cummings.

Edwards, R. E., ed. Integration & Harmonic Analysis on Compact Groups. LC 77-190412. (London Mathematical Society Lecture Notes Ser.: No. 8). 228p. 1972. 20.50 (ISBN 0-521-09717-7). Cambridge U Pr.

Evanston Conference, Oct. 11-15, 1975. Brauer Groups: Proceedings. Zelinsky, D., ed. (Lecture Notes in Mathematics: Vol. 549). 1976. soft cover 9.90 (ISBN 0-387-07989-0). Springer-Verlag.

Fackler, John P., Jr., ed. Symmetry in Chemical Theory: The Application of Group Theoretical Techniques to the Solution of Chemical Problems. LC 73-12620. (Benchmark Papers in Inorganic Chemistry Ser.). 528p. 1974. text ed. 51.00 (ISBN 0-12-786453-9). Acad Pr.

Falicov, L. M. Group Theory & Its Physical Applications. Luehrmann, A., ed. LC 66-13867. (Chicago Lectures in Physics Ser). (Orig.). 1966. 7.00x (ISBN 0-226-23540-8). U of Chicago Pr.

Fossum, R. M. The Divisor Class Group of a Krull Domain. LC 72-918901. (Ergebnisse der Mathematik und Ihrer Grenzgebiete: Vol. 74). (Illus.). 148p. 1973. 26.20 (ISBN 0-387-06044-8). Springer-Verlag.

Fulkerson, D. R., ed. Studies in Graph Theory: Part II. LC 75-24987. (MAA Studies: No. 11). 1976. 12.50 (ISBN 0-88385-112-1). Math Assn.

Gel'fand, I. M., et al. Eight Papers on Group Theory. LC 51-5559. (Translations, Ser.: No. 2, Vol. 2). 1956. 24.40 (ISBN 0-8218-1702-7, TRANS 2-2). Am Math.

Gerardin, P. Construction de Series Discretes p-Adiques. LC 75-16187. (Lecture Notes in Mathematics: Vol. 462). 180p. 1975. pap. 10.70 (ISBN 0-387-07172-5). Springer-Verlag.

Goodman, R. W. Nilpotent Lie Groups: Structure & Applications to Analysis. (Lecture Notes on Mathematics Ser.: Vol. 562). 1976. soft cover 13.10 (ISBN 0-387-08055-4). Springer-Verlag.

Green, J. A. Sets & Groups. (Library of Mathematics). 1971. pap. 5.00 (ISBN 0-7100-4356-2). Routledge & Kegan.

Grothendieck, A. & Murre, J. P. Tame Fundamental Group of a Formal Neighbourhood of a Divisor with Normal Crossing on a Scheme. (Lecture Notes in Mathematics: Vol. 208). 1971. pap. 8.20 (ISBN 0-387-05499-5). Springer-Verlag.

Gruenberg, Karl W. Cohomological Topics in Group Theory. LC 70-127042. (Lecture Notes in Mathematics: Vol. 143). 1970. pap. 14.70 (ISBN 0-387-04932-0). Springer-Verlag.

Guillemin, V. W. & Sternberg, Shlomo. Deformation Theory of Pseudogroup Structures. LC 52-42839. (Memoirs: No. 64). 1966. pap. 7.20 (ISBN 0-8218-1264-5, MEMO-64). Am Math.

Hall, Marshall, Jr. The Theory of Groups. 2nd ed. LC 75-42306. xiii, 434p. text ed. 11.95 (ISBN 0-8284-0288-4). Chelsea Pub.

Hamermesh, Morton. Group Theory & Its Application to Physical Problems. (Illus.). 1962. 22.95 (ISBN 0-201-02780-1). A-W.

Harish-Chandra. Harmonic Analysis on Reductive P-adic Groups. LC 79-138810. (Lecture Notes in Mathematics: Vol. 162). 1970. pap. 8.20 (ISBN 0-387-05189-9). Springer-Verlag.

Heine, V. Group Theory in Quantum Mechanics. 1963. 30.00 (ISBN 0-08-009242-X). Pergamon.

Hermann, Robert. Fourier Analysis on Groups & Partial Wave Analysis. (Math Lecture Notes Ser.: No. 32). 1969. 19.50 (ISBN 0-8053-3940-X, Adv Bk Prog); pap. 9.50 (ISBN 0-8053-3941-8, Adv Bk Prog). Benjamin-Cummings.

--Lie Groups for Physicists. (Mathematical Physics Monographs: No. 5). 1966. pap. 11.50 (ISBN 0-8053-3951-5, Adv Bk Prog). Benjamin-Cummings.

Hewitt, E. & Ross, K. A. Abstract Harmonic Analysis: Vol. 1, Structure of Topological Groups, Integration Theory, Group Representations. (Grundlehren der Mathematischen Wissenschaften: Vol. 115). 1963. 54.30 (ISBN 0-387-02983-4). Springer-Verlag.

--Abstract Harmonic Analysis: Vol. 2, Structure & Analysis for Compact Groups, Analysis on Locally Compact Abelian Groups. LC 63-12898. (Grundlehren der Mathematischen Wissenschaften: Vol. 152). 1970. 76.00 (ISBN 0-387-04832-4). Springer-Verlag.

Hill, Victor E. Groups, Representations, and Characters. LC 75-43362. 1976. text ed. 14.25 (ISBN 0-02-846790-6). Hafner.

Hilton, P., et al. Localization of Nilpotent Groups & Spaces. (Mathematics Studies Ser: Vol. 15). 156p. 1975. pap. 24.50 (ISBN 0-444-10776-2, North-Holland). Elsevier.

Hilton, P. J., ed. Localization in Group Theory & Homotopy Theory & Related Topics. (Lecture Notes in Mathematics: Vol. 418). 185p. 1975. pap. 10.90 (ISBN 0-387-06963-1). Springer-Verlag.

Hochschild, G. H. Basic Theory of Algebraic Groups & Lie Algebras. (Graduate Texts in Mathematics Ser.: Vol. 75). 350p. 1981. 32.00 (ISBN 0-387-90541-3). Springer-Verlag.

Humphreys, J. E. Ordinary & Modular Representations of Chevalley Groups. (Lecture Notes in Mathematics: Vol. 528). 1976. soft cover 9.90 (ISBN 0-387-07796-0). Springer-Verlag.

Husseini, S. Y. Lectures on the Topology of Classical Groups & Related Topics. (Notes on Mathematics & Its Applications Ser). 1969. 22.50x (ISBN 0-677-02160-7). Gordon.

International Conference on the Theory of Groups, 1969. Proceedings. Neumann, B. H. & Kovacs, L. G., eds. 414p. 1969. 54.00 (ISBN 0-677-10780-3). Gordon.

International Conference on the Theory of Groups, 2nd. Proceedings. Newman, M. F., ed. (Lecture Notes in Mathematics Ser.: Vol. 372). vii, 740p. 1974. pap. 26.20 (ISBN 0-387-06845-7). Springer-Verlag.

International Conference On Theory Of Groups - Australian National University - 1965. Theory of Groups. Kovacs, L. G. & Neumann, B. H., eds. 1967. 54.00x (ISBN 0-677-10780-3). Gordon.

Istanbul Summer School Of Theoretical Physics - 1962. Group Theoretical Concepts & Methods in Elementary Particle Physics. Gursey, F., ed. (Quantum Physics & Its Applications Ser.). 1964. 83.75x (ISBN 0-677-10140-6). Gordon.

Janner, A., et al, eds. Group Theoretical Methods in Physics. (Lecture Notes in Physics: Vol. 50). 1976. 27.30 (ISBN 3-540-07789-8). Springer-Verlag.

Janssen, T. Crystallographic Groups. LC 72-96140. 300p. 1973. 34.25 (ISBN 0-444-10436-4, North-Holland-). Elsevier.

Joshi, A. W. Elements of Group Therapy for Physicists. 2nd ed. LC 76-51385. 1977. 14.95 (ISBN 0-470-99062-7). Halsted Pr.

Kambayashi, T., et al. Unipotent Algebraic Groups. (Lecture Notes in Mathematics: Vol. 414). vi, 165p. 1975. pap. 10.50 (ISBN 0-387-06960-7). Springer-Verlag.

Kargapolov, M. I. & Merzljakov, Ju. I. Fundamentals of the Theory of Groups, Vol. Sixty-Two. Burns, R., tr. from Rus. (Graduate Texts in Mathematics Ser.). 1979. 18.40 (ISBN 0-387-90396-8). Springer-Verlag.

Kervaire, M. & Ojanguren, M., eds. Groupe De Brauer: Proceedings. (Lecture Notes in Mathematics Ser.: Vol. 844). 274p. 1981. pap. 16.80 (ISBN 0-387-10562-X). Springer-Verlag.

Kokorin, A. I. & Kopytov, V. M. Fully Ordered Groups. Louvish, D., tr. from Rus. LC 73-22108. 147p. 1974. 36.95 (ISBN 0-470-49887-0). Halsted Pr.

Kolchin, E. R. Differential Algebra & Algebraic Groups. (Pure & Applied Mathematics Ser.: Vol. 55). 1973. 55.50 (ISBN 0-12-417650-X). Acad Pr.

Koster, George F. Space Groups & Their Representations. (Solid State Reprint Ser.). 1964. 12.00 (ISBN 0-12-608468-8). Acad Pr.

Kowalewski, Gerhard. Kontinuierliche Gruppen. LC 51-3003. (Ger). 14.95 (ISBN 0-8284-0070-9). Chelsea Pub.

Kra, Irwin. Automorphic Forms & Kleinian Groups. LC 72-187423. (Math Lecture Notes Ser.: No. 51). xiv, 464p. 1972. text ed. 23.50 (ISBN 0-8053-2342-2, Adv Bk Prog); pap. text ed. 13.50 (ISBN 0-8053-2343-0, Adv Bk Prog). Benjamin-Cummings.

Kramer, P. & Rieckers, A., eds. Group Theoretical Methods in Physics: Sixth International Colloquium, Tuebingen 1977. (Lecture Notes in Physics: Vol. 79). 1978. pap. 27.20 (ISBN 0-387-08848-2). Springer-Verlag.

Kurosh, Alexander G. Group Theory, Vol. 1. LC 60-8965. 1979. text ed. 12.50 (ISBN 0-8284-0107-1). Chelsea Pub.

--Group Theory, Vol. 2. 2nd ed. LC 60-8965. 1979. text ed. 12.50 (ISBN 0-8284-0109-8). Chelsea Pub.

--Group Theory, Vol. 3. 2nd ed. Hirsch, K. A., tr. LC 60-8965. write for info. (ISBN 0-685-07978-3). Chelsea Pub.

Kurth, Rudolf. Dimensional Analysis & Group Theory in Astrophysics. 249p. 1972. text ed. 55.00 (ISBN 0-08-016616-4). Pergamon.

Lax, Melvin. Symmetry Principles in Solid State & Molecular Physics. LC 74-1215. 499p. 1974. (Pub. by Wiley-Interscience); pap. 23.95x (ISBN 0-471-51904-9). Wiley.

Lazard, M. P. Communative Formal Groups. (Lecture Notes in Mathematics Ser.: Vol. 443). ii, 236p. 1975. pap. 12.60 (ISBN 0-387-07145-8). Springer-Verlag.

Ledermann, W. Introduction to Group Characters. LC 76-46858. (Illus.). 1977. 47.00 (ISBN 0-521-21486-6); pap. 12.95 (ISBN 0-521-29170-4). Cambridge U Pr.

--Introduction to Group Theory. (Illus.). 176p. 1973. pap. 7.50x (ISBN 0-06-494125-6). B&N.

Lee, Chung-Nim & Wasserman, Arthur G. On the Groups JO(G) (Memoirs: No. 159). 1975. pap. 8.40 (ISBN 0-8218-1859-7, MEMO-159). Am Math.

Leech, J. H-Coextensions of Monoids & the Structure of a Band of Groups. 1975. 8.80 (ISBN 0-8218-1857-0, MEMO-157). Am Math.

Ljapin, E. S. Semigroups. rev. ed. LC 63-15659. (Translations of Mathematical Monographs: Vol. 3). 1974. 40.00 (ISBN 0-8218-1553-9, MMONO-3). Am Math.

Loebl, Ernest M., ed. Group Theory & Its Applications, 3 vols. LC 67-23166. Vol. 1 1968. 63.00 (ISBN 0-12-455150-5); Vol. 2 1971. 55.00 (ISBN 0-12-455152-1); 76.00 (ISBN 0-12-455153-X). Vol. 3, 1975. Acad Pr.

Lusztig, George. The Discrete Series Representations of the General Linear Groups Over a Finite Field. (Annals of Mathematics Studies: No. 81). 150p. 1974. 10.00 (ISBN 0-691-08154-9). Princeton U Pr.

Lyapin, E. S., et al. Exercises in Group Theory. LC 78-141243. 240p. 1972. 29.50 (ISBN 0-306-30505-4, Plenum Pr). Plenum Pub.

Lyndon, R. & Schapp, P. E. Combinatorial Group Theory. (Ergebnisse der Mathematik und Ihrer Grenzgebiete: Vol. 89). 1976. 42.20 (ISBN 0-387-07642-5). Springer-Verlag.

MacDonald, Ian D. Theory of Groups. 1968. pap. 16.95x (ISBN 0-19-853138-9). Oxford U Pr.

Mackenzie. A Theory of Group Structures, 2 vols. 1976. Set. 59.00 (ISBN 0-677-05330-4). Gordon.

Magnus, Wilhelm. Noneuclidian Tesselations & Their Groups. 1974. 30.00 (ISBN 0-12-465450-9). Acad Pr.

Magnus, Wilhelm, et al. Combinational Group Theory: Presentations of Groups in Terms of Generators & Relations. 1976. pap. text ed. 6.00 (ISBN 0-486-63281-4). Dover.

Mann, Henry B. Addition Theorems: The Addition Theorems of Group Theory & Number Theory. LC 76-16766. 124p. 1976. Repr. of 1965 ed. text ed. 12.50 (ISBN 0-88275-418-1). Krieger.

Meijer, P. H., ed. Group Theory & Solid State Physics. (International Science Review Ser.). 1964. 43.00x (ISBN 0-677-00530-X). Gordon.

Mennicke, J. L., ed. Burnside Groups. (Lecture Notes in Mathematics: Vol. 806). 274p. 1980. pap. 16.80 (ISBN 0-387-10006-7). Springer-Verlag.

Miller, Charles F., 3rd. On Group-Theoretic Decision Problems & Their Classification. (Annals of Mathematics Studies: No. 68). 1971. 11.50 (ISBN 0-691-08091-7). Princeton U Pr.

Moshinsky, M. Group Theory & the Many-Body Problem. 1968. 28.50 (ISBN 0-677-01740-5, DMP). Gordon.

Mura, R. & Rhemtulla, A., eds. Orderable Groups. (Lecture Notes in Pure & Applied Mathematics: Vol. 27). 1977. 23.75 (ISBN 0-8247-6579-6). Dekker.

Napier, Rodney & Gershenfeld, Matti. Groups: Theory & Experience. 2nd ed. LC 80-82844. (Illus.). 448p. 1981. text ed. 17.95 (ISBN 0-395-29703-6); instr's manual 1.00 (ISBN 0-395-29704-4). HM.

Netto, Eugen. Theory of Substitutions. 2nd ed. LC 64-10289. 1964. 9.50 (ISBN 0-8284-0165-9). Chelsea Pub.

Neumann, H. Varieties of Groups. (Ergebnisse der Mathematik und Ihrer Grenzgebiete: Vol. 37). 1967. 28.10 (ISBN 0-387-03779-9). Springer-Verlag.

Neuwirth, L. P., ed. Knots, Groups, & 3-Manifolds: Papers Dedicated to the Memory of R. H. Fox. LC 75-5619. (Annals of Mathematics Studies: No. 84). 345p. 1975. 24.00 (ISBN 0-691-08170-0); pap. 9.50 (ISBN 0-691-08167-0). Princeton U Pr.

Newman, Morris. Integral Matrices. (Pure & Applied Mathematics Ser.: Vol. 45). 1972. 38.00 (ISBN 0-12-517850-6). Acad Pr.

Pyatekskii-Shapiro, I. I. Automorphic Functions & the Geometry of Classical Domains. (Mathematics & Its Applications Ser.). 1969. 44.00x (ISBN 0-677-20310-1). Gordon.

Reiner, I. & Roggenkamp, K. W. Integral Representations. (Lecture Notes in Mathematics: Vol. 744). 1979. pap. 15.00 (ISBN 0-387-09546-2). Springer-Verlag.

Reiner, Irving. Class Groups & Picard Groups of Group Rings & Orders. LC 76-10337. (CBMS Regional Conference Ser. in Mathematics: Vol. 26). 1976. 10.60 (ISBN 0-8218-1676-4, CBMS-26). Am Math.

Reviews on Group Theory. 144.00 (ISBN 0-685-91810-6, REVGRP). Am Math.

Robinson, D. J. Finiteness Conditions & Generalized Soluble Groups, Pt. 1. (Ergebnisse der Mathematik und Ihrer Grenzgebiete: Vol. 62). (Illus.). 240p. 1972. 22.70 (ISBN 0-387-05620-3). Springer-Verlag.

Rose, John S. A Course on Group Theory. LC 76-22984. (Illus.). 1978. 57.50 (ISBN 0-521-21409-2); pap. 18.50x (ISBN 0-521-29142-9). Cambridge U Pr.

Rotman, Joseph J. The Theory of Groups: An Introduction. 2nd ed. 352p. 1973. text ed. 26.95x (ISBN 0-205-03655-4, 5636558). Allyn.

Ruehl, Werner. Lorentz Group & Harmonic Analysis. (Mathematical Physics Monographs: No. 13). 1970. 16.00 (ISBN 0-8053-8362-X, Adv Bk Prog). Benjamin-Cummings.

Rutherford, Daniel E. Substitutional Analysis. 1968. Repr. of 1948 ed. 10.75 (ISBN 0-02-851220-0). Hafner.

Satake, I. Classification Theory of Semi-Simple Algebraic Groups. (Lecture Notes in Pure & Applied Mathematics Ser.: Vol. 3). 1971. 16.25 (ISBN 0-8247-1607-8). Dekker.

Sattinger, D. H. Group Theoretic Methods in Bifurcation Theory. (Lecture Notes in Mathematics: Vol. 762). 241p. 1980. pap. 14.70 (ISBN 0-387-09715-5). Springer-Verlag.

Schenkman, Eugene. Group Theory. LC 75-23321. 304p. 1975. Repr. of 1965 ed. 18.50 (ISBN 0-88275-070-4). Krieger.

Schonland, David. Molecular Symmetry. (Illus.). 1965. 14.95 (ISBN 0-442-07423-9). Van Nos Reinhold.

Singmaster, David. Notes on Rubik's Magic Cube. LC 80-27751. (Illus.). 73p. 1981. text ed. 9.95x (ISBN 0-89490-057-9). Enslow Pubs.

Smith, J., et al, eds. Ordered Groups. (Lecture Notes in Pure & Applied Mathematics: Vol. 62). 192p. 1980. 25.50 (ISBN 0-8247-6943-0). Dekker.

Springer, T. A. Jordan Algebras & Algebraic Groups. LC 72-96718. (Ergebnisse der Mathematik und Ihrer Grenzgebiete: Vol. 75). vii, 169p. 1973. 28.40 (ISBN 0-387-06104-5). Springer-Verlag.

--Linear Algebraic Groups. (Progress in Mathematics Ser.). 312p. 1981. 18.00 (ISBN 3-7643-3029-5). Birkhauser.

Stammbach, U. Homology in Group Theory. LC 73-19547. (Lecture Notes in Mathematics: Vol. 359). 183p. 1974. pap. 10.30 (ISBN 0-387-06569-5). Springer-Verlag.

Steinberg, Robert. Endomorphisms of Linear Algebraic Groups. LC 52-42839. (Memoirs: No. 80). 1968. pap. 7.20 (ISBN 0-8218-1280-7, MEMO-80). Am Math.

Steklov Institute of Mathematics, Academy of Sciences, U S S R, No. 85 & Adjan, S. I. Defining Relations & Algorithmic Problems for Groups & Semigroups: Proceedings. 1967. 31.20 (ISBN 0-8218-1885-6, STEKLO-85). Am Math.

Stillwell, J. Classical Topology & Combinatorial Group Theory. (Graduate Texts in Mathematics Ser.: Vol. 72). (Illus.). 301p. 1980. 32.00 (ISBN 0-387-90516-2). Springer-Verlag.

Streitwolf, H. W. Group Theory in Solid-State Physics. (Illus.). 248p. 1971. 17.95x (ISBN 0-8464-0458-3). Beekman Pubs.

Suprenenko, F. A. Soluble & Nilpotent Linear Groups. LC 63-20676. (Translations of Mathematical Monographs: Vol. 9). 1970. Repr. of 1963 ed. 20.00 (ISBN 0-8218-1559-8, MMONO-9). Am Math.

Suprunenko, D. A. Matrix Groups. LC 75-45115. (Translations of Mathematical Monographs: Vol. 45). 1976. 48.40 (ISBN 0-8218-1595-4, MMONO-45). Am Math.

Swamy, N. V. & Samuel, Mark A. Group Theory Made Easy for Scientists & Engineers. LC 78-11733. 174p. 1979. 23.00 (ISBN 0-471-05128-4, Pub. by Wiley-Interscience). Wiley.

Symposia in Pure Mathematics-Boulder, 1965. Algebraic Groups & Discontinous Subgroups: Proceedings, Vol. 9. Borel, A. & Mostow, G. D., eds. LC 66-18581. 1966. 29.60 (ISBN 0-8218-1409-5, PSPUM-9). Am Math.

Symposia in Pure Mathematics-New York-1959. Finite Groups: Proceedings, Vol. 1. Albert, A. A. & Kaplansky, I., eds. LC 50-1183. 1959. 19.60 (ISBN 0-8218-1401-X, PSPUM-1). Am Math.

Symposium in Pure Mathematics - Monterey Calif - 1959. Lattice Theory: Proceedings, Vol. 2. Dilworth, R. P., ed. LC 50-1183. 1961. 21.20 (ISBN 0-8218-1402-8, PSPUM-2). Am Math.

Tinkham, Michael. Group Theory & Quantum Mechanics. (International Series in Pure & Applied Physics). 1964. text ed. 24.95 (ISBN 0-07-064895-6, C). McGraw.

Van Der Waerden, B. L. Group Theory & Quantum Mechanics. (Grundlehren der Mathematischen Wissenschaften Ser.: Vol. 214). (Illus.). 211p. 1981. 39.00 (ISBN 0-387-06740-X). Springer-Verlag.

Wallace, D. A. Groups. (Problem Solvers). (Illus.). 1974. pap. text ed. 6.50x (ISBN 0-04-519013-5). Allen Unwin.

Warfield, R. B., Jr. Nilpotent Groups. (Lecture Notes in Mathematics Ser.: Vol. 513). 1976. pap. 9.90 (ISBN 0-387-07683-2). Springer-Verlag.

Waterhouse, W. Introduction to Affine Group Schemes. LC 79-12231. (Graduate Texts in Mathematics: Vol. 66). 1979. 20.80 (ISBN 0-387-90421-2). Springer-Verlag.

Weiss, E. Cohomology of Groups. (Pure & Applied Mathematics Ser.: Vol. 34). 1969. 46.50 (ISBN 0-12-742750-3). Acad Pr.

Weyl, Hermann. Classical Groups, Their Invariants & Representations. rev ed. (Mathematical Ser.: Vol. 1). 1946. 22.00x (ISBN 0-691-07923-4). Princeton U Pr.

--Theory of Groups & Quantum Mechanics. 1950. pap. text ed. 5.50 (ISBN 0-486-60269-9). Dover.

White, A. T. Graphs, Groups & Surfaces. LC 73-86088. (Mathematical Studies Ser.: No. 8). 156p. 1974. pap. 22.00 (ISBN 0-444-10570-0, North-Holland). Elsevier.

Wooster, W. A. Tensors & Group Theory for the Physical Properties of Crystals. (Illus.). 349p. 1973. 28.50x (ISBN 0-19-851137-X). Oxford U Pr.

Yanagihara, H. Theory of Hopf Algebras Attached to Group Schemes. (Lecture Notes in Mathematics: Vol. 614). 1977. pap. text ed. 18.30 (ISBN 0-387-08444-4). Springer-Verlag.

Zassenhaus, Hans J. Theory of Groups. 2nd ed. LC 56-13058. 12.95 (ISBN 0-8284-0053-9). Chelsea Pub.

Zieschang, H., et al. Surfaces & Planar Discontinuous Groups: Revised & Expanded Translation. (Lecture Notes in Mathematics Ser.: Vol. 835). 334p. 1981. pap. 19.50 (ISBN 0-387-10024-5). Springer-Verlag.

GROUPS, TOPOLOGICAL

see Topological Groups

GROUPS OF POINTS

see also Convex Domains

GROUPS OF TRANSFORMATIONS

see Transformation Groups

GROUSE

Johnsgard, Paul A. Grouse & Quails of North America. LC 77-181596. (Illus.). xx, 533p. 1973. 35.00 (ISBN 0-8032-0810-3). U of Nebr Pr.

Robinson, William L. Fool Hen: The Spruce Grouse on the Yellow Dog Plains. LC 79-3962. (Illus.). 1980. 18.50 (ISBN 0-299-07960-0). U of Wis Pr.

Rue, Leonard L., 3rd. The World of the Ruffled Grouse. Terres, John, ed. LC 72-748. (Living World Bks). (Illus.). 291p. 1972. 8.95 (ISBN 0-397-00817-1). Har-Row.

Sisley, Nick. Grouse & Woodcock: An Upland Hunter's Book. (Illus.). 192p. 1980. 11.95 (ISBN 0-8117-0717-2). Stackpole.

Spiller, Burton. Drummer in the Woods. (Illus.). 240p. 1980. Repr. of 1962 ed. text ed. 13.95 (ISBN 0-8117-0528-5). Stackpole.

GROUTING

Bowen, R. Grouting in Engineering Practice. 2nd ed. (Illus.). ix, 275p. 1981. 45.50x (ISBN 0-85334-943-6). Intl Ideas.

Bowen, Robert. Grouting in Engineering Practice. 2nd ed. LC 81-1015. 240p. 1981. 47.95 (ISBN 0-470-27147-7). Halsted Pr.

--Grouting in Engineering Practice. LC 75-20111. 186p. 1975. 47.95 (ISBN 0-470-09221-1). Halsted Pr.

GROVE FARM CO., INC.

Krauss, Bob & Alexander, W. P. Grove Farm Plantation: The Biography of a Hawaiian Sugar Plantation. LC 65-18124. (Illus.). 1965. 10.00 (ISBN 0-87015-140-1). Pacific Bks.

GROWTH

see also Developmental Biology; Developmental Genetics; Growth (Plants); Heterosis; Regeneration (Biology)

also subdivision Growth under subjects, e.g. Bone–Growth; cities and towns - growth

Babcock, Dorothy E. Introduction to Growth, Development & Family Life. 3rd ed. 192p. 1972. pap. text ed. 6.00 (ISBN 0-8036-0541-2). Davis Co.

Baer, Melvyn J. Growth & Maturation: An Introduction to Physical Development. new ed. LC 72-81296. (Illus.). 224p. 1973. pap. text ed. 5.95 (ISBN 0-87299-016-8). Howard Doyle.

Barnett, S. A., ed. Ethology & Development. (Clinics in Developmental Medicine Ser.: Vol. 47). 128p. 1973. 17.00 (ISBN 0-685-59042-9). Har-Row.

Bayer, Leona M. & Bayley, Nancy. Growth Diagnosis: Selected Methods for Interpreting & Predicting Physical Development from One Year to Maturity. 2nd ed. LC 75-19240. 256p. 1976. pap. text ed. 20.00x (ISBN 0-226-03958-7). U of Chicago Pr.

Becker, Robert O. Mechanisms of Growth Control. (Illus.). 528p. 1981. 39.75 (ISBN 0-398-04469-4). C C Thomas.

Bergsma, Daniel, ed. Growth Problems & Clinical Advances. LC 76-21714. (Alan R. Liss, Inc. Ser.: Vol. 12, No. 6). 1976. 30.00 (ISBN 0-686-18083-6). March of Dimes.

Berrill, Norman J. Growth, Development, & Pattern. LC 61-8356. (Illus.). 1961. 26.95x (ISBN 0-7167-0607-5). W H Freeman.

Birren, James E. & Stein, Leon, eds. Relations of Development & Aging. LC 79-8659. (Growing Old Ser.). (Illus.). 1980. Repr. of 1964 ed. lib. bdg. 24.00x (ISBN 0-405-12775-8). Arno.

Boyd, Edith. The Growth of the Surface Area of the Human Body. LC 75-14249. (Univ. of Minnesota, the Institute of Child Welfare Monograph: No. 10). (Illus.). 145p. 1975. Repr. of 1935 ed. lib. bdg. 14.00x (ISBN 0-8371-8069-4, CWBS). Greenwood.

--Origins of the Study of Human Growth. Bhim Sen Savara & Schilke, John F., eds. (Illus.). 700p. 1981. 65.00 (ISBN 0-686-30702-X). U of Oreg Health Sci.

Carter, Nicholas, ed. Development, Growth, & Aging. 176p. 1980. 25.00x (ISBN 0-85664-861-2, Pub. by Croom Helm England). State Mutual Bk.

Coleman & Davidson, Bill. Gary Coleman: Medical Miracle. (Illus.). 1981. 9.95 (ISBN 0-698-11093-5). Coward.

Conference On The Biology Of Normal And A-Typical Pigment Cell Growth - 3rd - New York - 1951. Pigment Cell Growth: Proceedings. Gordon, Myron, ed. 1953. 48.50 (ISBN 0-12-290956-9). Acad Pr.

Crow, Lester D. & Crow, Alice. Human Development & Learning. 2nd ed. LC 74-26685. 590p. 1975. Repr. of 1965 ed. 21.50 (ISBN 0-88275-252-9). Krieger.

Deevey, E. S., ed. Growth by Intussusception: Ecological Essays in Honor of G. Evelyn Hutchinson. (Conn. Academy of Arts & Sciences Transactions, Vol. 44). (Illus.). 500p. 1973. pap. 25.00 (ISBN 0-208-01293-1). Shoe String.
Di Leo, Joseph. Physical Factors in Growth & Development: A Manual for Educators, Nurses, & Social Workers. LC 75-106235. 1970. pap. 3.50 (ISBN 0-8077-1244-2). Tchrs Coll.
Eiben. Growth & Development Physique. 1977. 34.50 (ISBN 0-9960000-9-7, Pub. by Kaido Hungary). Heyden.
Elkind, David. The Hurried Child: Growing up Too Fast Too Soon. 224p. 1981. 10.95 (ISBN 0-201-03966-4); pap. 5.95 (ISBN 0-201-03967-2). A-W.
Encounter. (Being & Becoming Ser.: Bk. 1). 2.22 (ISBN 0-685-61776-9, 81057); group leader's manual 2.82 (ISBN 0-02-810580-X). Benziger Pub Co.
Falkner, F. & Tanner, J. M., eds. Human Growth, Vol. 1: Principles & Prenatal Growth. LC 78-1440. (Illus.). 654p. 1978. 35.00 (ISBN 0-306-34461-0, Plenum Pr). Plenum Pub.
--Human Growth, Vol. 2: Postnatal Growth. LC 78-1440. (Illus.). 652p. 1978. 35.00 (ISBN 0-306-34462-9, Plenum Pr). Plenum Pub.
Focus. (Discovery Through Guidance Ser.). (gr. 8). 1.86 (ISBN 0-02-812000-0); tchr's manual 2.64 (ISBN 0-02-812020-5). Benziger Pub Co.
Gedda, L. Auxology: Human Growth in Health & Disorder. Parisi, P., ed. (Serono Symposia Ser.). 1978. 50.50 (ISBN 0-12-279050-2). Acad Pr.
Goldspink, G., ed. Differentiation & Growth of Cells in Vertebrate Tissues. LC 74-4173. 323p. 1974. text ed. 37.95x (ISBN 0-412-11390-2, Pub. by Chapman & Hall). Methuen Inc.
Goss, Richard J. Adaptive Growth. 1965. 44.50 (ISBN 0-12-292750-8). Acad Pr.
--The Physiology of Growth. 1978. 42.50 (ISBN 0-12-293055-X). Acad Pr.
Grow. (gr. 1). 1973. 1.98 (ISBN 0-02-649590-2); tchr's annotated ed. 6.00 (ISBN 0-02-649610-0); activity bk. 1.74 (ISBN 0-685-61677-0, 64061); activity bk. tchr's ed. 2.16 (ISBN 0-685-61678-9, 64073); parents' handbk. 0.75 (ISBN 0-685-61679-7, 64960); testing program 0.69 (ISBN 0-02-640820-1); testing program tchr's manual 0.33 (ISBN 0-02-641070-2). Benziger Pub Co.
Growth & Development: An Anthology. 1975. pap. 6.00 (ISBN 0-912452-12-9). Am Phys Therapy Assn.
Heidenreich, Alfred. Growing Point. (Illus.). 17.95 (ISBN 0-903540-17-7, Pub. by Floris Books). St George Bk Serv.
Heinmets, Ferdinand. Analysis of Normal & Abnormal Cell Growth: Model-System Formulations & Analog Computer Studies. LC 66-11882. 288p. 1966. 34.50 (ISBN 0-306-30225-X, Plenum Pr). Plenum Pub.
Hofstein, Sadie & Bauer, W. W. Human Story: Facts on Birth, Growth & Reproduction. LC 69-16819. (Illus.). (gr. 7-12). 1969. 7.25 (ISBN 0-688-41361-7); PLB 6.96 (ISBN 0-688-51361-1). Lothrop.
Johnston, F. E., et al, eds. Human Physical Growth & Maturation: Methodologies & Factors. (NATO Advanced Study Institute Series, Series A: Life Sciences: Vol. 30). 375p. 1980. 42.50 (ISBN 0-306-40420-6, Plenum Pr). Plenum Pub.
Kastenbaum, Robert. Humans Developing: A Lifespan Perspective. 1979. text ed. 19.95x (ISBN 0-205-06513-9); instr's man. avail. (ISBN 0-205-06536-8); student guide avail. (ISBN 0-205-06535-X). Allyn.
LoBue, Joseph & Gordon, Albert S., eds. Humoral Control of Growth & Differentiation, 2 vols. Incl. Vol. 1. Vertebrate Regulatory Factors. 1973. 60.00 (ISBN 0-12-453801-0); Vol. 2. Nonvertebrate Neuroendocrinology & Ageing. 1974. 51.00 (ISBN 0-12-453802-9). Set. 90.50 (ISBN 0-686-77005-6). Acad Pr.
Locke, Michael & Locke, Michael, eds. Cellular Membranes in Development. 1964. 51.50 (ISBN 0-12-454168-2). Acad Pr.
--Control Mechanisms in Developmental Processes. 1968. 43.00 (ISBN 0-12-612950-9). Acad Pr.
McCormick, Maurice D. An Invitation to Grow. 135p. 1977. pap. text ed. 6.75 (ISBN 0-8191-0034-X). U Pr of Amer.
Meredith, Howard V. Human Body Growth in the First Ten Years of Life. LC 78-63120. (Illus., Orig.). 1978. pap. text ed. 4.90 (ISBN 0-9603120-0-5). H V Meredith.
Otto, Herbert A. & Mann, John. Ways of Growth. 1979. pap. 2.25 (ISBN 0-671-82691-3). PB.
Parpart, Arthur K., ed. Chemistry & Physiology of Growth. LC 79-159099. 1971. Repr. of 1949 ed. 13.50 (ISBN 0-8046-1642-6). Kennikat.
Prahl-Andersen, B. & Kowalski, Charles J., eds. A Mixed-Longitudinal, Interdisciplinary Study of Growth & Developement. LC 78-3346. 1979. 45.50 (ISBN 0-12-563350-5). Acad Pr.
Rarick, G. Lawrence, ed. Physical Activity: Human Growth & Development. 1973. 42.50 (ISBN 0-12-581550-6). Acad Pr.
Ritzen, Martin, et al, eds. Biology of Normal Human Growth. 350p. 1981. 38.50 (ISBN 0-686-77676-3). Raven.
Robbins, William J., et al. Growth. 1928. 29.50x (ISBN 0-685-89755-9). Elliots Bks.
Rudman, Jack. Human Growth & Development. (College Level Examination Ser.: CLEP-17). 14.95 (ISBN 0-8373-5367-X); pap. 9.95 (ISBN 0-8373-5317-3). Natl Learning.
Rudnick, Dorothea, ed. Rhythmic & Synthetic Processes in Growth. (Growth Symposia, Vol. 15). 1957. 22.50x (ISBN 0-691-08025-9). Princeton U Pr.
Runner, Meredith N. & Runner, Meredith N., eds. Changing Syntheses in Development. 1971. 43.00 (ISBN 0-12-612971-1); pap. 28.50 (ISBN 0-12-612972-X). Acad Pr.
Shizume, Kazuo. Growth & Growth Factors. 296p. text ed. 39.95 (ISBN 0-8391-4128-9). Univ Park.
Sidorova, Vera F. The Postnatal Growth & Restoration of Internal Organs in Vertebrates. Carlson, Bruce M., ed. & intro. by. LC 77-88071. (Illus.). 210p. 1978. 20.00 (ISBN 0-88416-212-5). Wright-PSG.
Sinclair, David. Human Growth After Birth. 3rd ed. 1978. pap. text ed. 14.95x (ISBN 0-19-263329-5). Oxford U Pr.
Smith, David W. Growth & Its Disorders: Basics & Standards, Approach & Classifications, Growth Deficiency Disorders, Growth Excess Disorders, Obesity. LC 76-20114. (Major Problems in Clinical Pediatrics Ser: Vol. 15). (Illus.). 1977. text ed. 17.95 (ISBN 0-7216-8378-9). Saunders.
Smith, David W. & Bierman, Edwin L., eds. The Biologic Ages of Man: From Conception Through Old Age. LC 73-81837. (Illus.). 211p. 1973. text ed. 8.00 (ISBN 0-7216-8423-8). Saunders.
Swenson, Allan. Big Fun to Grow Book. 1980. pap. 3.50 (ISBN 0-679-20510-1). McKay.
Temerlin, Maurice K. Lucy: Growing up Human-A Chimpanzee Daughter in a Psychotherapist's Family. LC 75-12455. (Illus.). 1975. 8.95 (ISBN 0-8314-0045-5). Sci & Behavior.
Thompson, D'Arcy W. On Growth & Form, 2 Vols. 1952. Set. 125.00 (ISBN 0-521-06622-0). Cambridge U Pr.
--On Growth & Form. abr. ed. Bonner, John T., ed. 49.50 (ISBN 0-521-06623-9); pap. 13.95x (ISBN 0-521-09390-2). Cambridge U Pr.
WHO Scientific Group. Geneva, 1971. Human Development & Public Health: Report. (Technical Report Ser.: No. 485). (Also avail. in French, Russian & Spanish). 1972. pap. 1.60 (ISBN 92-4-120485-0). World Health.
Wigglesworth, Vincent B. Control of Growth & Form: A Study of the Epidermal Cell in an Insect. (Illus.). 1959. 22.50x (ISBN 0-8014-0450-9). Cornell U Pr.

GROWTH–JUVENILE LITERATURE

Lytle, Jim, ed. Color Me Growing up, No. 3. (Illus.). (gr. 1-6). 1977. pap. 2.80 (ISBN 0-935040-06-4). Tri-Science Pubs.
Mason, Sheila. The Toddler. (Illus.). 1977. 3.95x (ISBN 0-521-21391-6). Cambridge U Pr.
Swenson, Allan A. Allan Swenson's Big Fun to Grow Book. (Illus.). (gr. 3-7). 1980. 3.50 (ISBN 0-679-20510-1). McKay.
Zim, Herbert S. How Things Grow. (Illus.). (gr. 3-7). 1960. PLB 6.00 (ISBN 0-688-31409-0). Morrow.

GROWTH (PLANTS)

see also Growth Promoting Substances; Heterosis; Plant Hormones; Tree Rings

Advanced Study Institute,Izmir,1971 & Kaldewey, Harald. Hormonal Regulation in Plant Growth & Development: Proceedings. LC 72-86049. 1972. 75.00x (ISBN 3-527-25436-6). Intl Pubns Serv.
Agerter, Sharlene & Glock, Waldo S. An Annotated Bibliography of Tree Growth & Growth Rings, 1950-62. LC 64-17274. 1965. 2.00 (ISBN 0-8165-0002-9). U of Ariz Pr.
Ayres, P. G. Effects of Disease on the Physiology of the Growing Plant: Seminar 11. LC 80-42175. (Society for Experimental Biology). (Illus.). 200p. Date not set. price not set (ISBN 0-521-23306-2); pap. price not set (ISBN 0-521-29898-9). Cambridge U Pr.
Bickford, Elwood D. & Dunn, Stuart. Lighting for Plant Growth. LC 70-157464. (Illus.). 264p. 1972. 18.00x (ISBN 0-87338-116-5). Kent St U Pr.
Browse, P. D. Hardy Wood Plants from Seeds. 1979. 17.95x (ISBN 0-901361-21-6, Pub. by Grower Books England). Intl Schol Bk Serv.
Donahue, Roy L., et al. Soils: An Introduction to Soils & Plant Growth. 4th ed. (Illus.). 1977. 22.95 (ISBN 0-13-821918-4). P-H.
Downs, R. G. & Hellmers, H. Environment & the Experimental Control of Plant Growth. (Experimental Botany Ser.). 1975. 24.50 (ISBN 0-12-221450-1). Acad Pr.
Downs, Robert J. Controlled Environments for Plant Research. LC 74-20878. (Illus.). 175p. 1975. 17.50x (ISBN 0-231-03561-6). Columbia U Pr.
Duffield, Mary R. & Jones, Warren D. Plants for Dry Climates: How to Select, Grow & Enjoy. LC 80-82535. (Illus.). 176p. 1981. pap. 7.95 (ISBN 0-89586-042-2). H P Bks.
Evans, G. Clifford. The Quantitative Analysis of Plant Growth. LC 77-183156. (Studies in Ecology: Vol. 1). 1973. 23.75x (ISBN 0-520-09432-8). U of Cal Pr.
Galston, Arthur W. & Davies, Peter J. Control Mechanisms in Plant Development. (Foundations of Developmental Biology Ser). 1970. pap. 12.95x ref. ed. (ISBN 0-13-171801-0). P-H.
Hillman, J. R., ed. Isolation of Plant Growth Substances. LC 77-83997. (Society for Experimental Biology Seminar Ser.: No. 4). (Illus.). 1978. 39.50 (ISBN 0-521-21866-7); pap. 13.95x (ISBN 0-521-29297-2). Cambridge U Pr.
Hunt. Plant Growth Analysis. (Studies in Biology: No. 96). 1978. 5.95 (ISBN 0-7131-2696-5). Univ Park.
Huxley, Julian. Problems of Relative Growth. 2nd ed. (Illus.). 6.00 (ISBN 0-8446-4561-3). Peter Smith.
Kaldewey, Harald & Vardar, Yusuf. Hormonal Regulation in Plant Growth & Development. LC 72-86049. (Illus.). 1972. 55.90 (ISBN 3-527-25436-6). Verlag Chemie.
Kirby, Celia. Hormone Weedkillers. 60p. (Orig.). 1981. pap. 10.00x (ISBN 0-901436-62-3, Pub. by British Crop Protection England). Intl Schol Bk Serv.
Knapp, Ruediger. Gegenseitige Beeinflussung und Temperatur-Wirkung bei tropischen und subtropischen Pflanzen: Bericht ueber neue experimentelle Untersuchungen an Nutzpflanzen und Arten der spontanen Vegetation. (Illus.). 1967. pap. 6.00 (ISBN 3-7682-0576-2). Lubrecht & Cramer.
Kolisko, L. Moon & Growth of Plants. (Illus.). 1979. pap. 7.95x (ISBN 0-906492-13-0, Pub. by Kolisko Archives). St George Bk Serv.
Kozlowski, Theodore T., ed. Tree Growth. (Illus.). 442p. 1962. 22.50 (ISBN 0-8260-5090-5, Pub. by Wiley-Interscience). Wiley.
--Water Deficits & Plant Growth, 5 vols. LC 68-14658. Vol. 1 1968. 55.00 (ISBN 0-12-424150-6); Vol. 2 1968. 46.50 (ISBN 0-12-424152-2); Vol. 3 1972. 46.50 (ISBN 0-12-424153-0); Vol. 4 1976. 55.50 (ISBN 0-12-424154-9); Vol. 5, 1978. 45.50 (ISBN 0-12-424155-7); Set. 202.50 (ISBN 0-686-76859-0). Acad Pr.
Krishnamoorthy, H. N. Gibberellins & Plant Growth. LC 74-10469. 1976. 28.95 (ISBN 0-470-50797-7). Halsted Pr.
Leopold, A., et al. Plant Growth & Development. rev. ed. 1975. 24.95 (ISBN 0-07-037200-4, C). McGraw.
Mandava, N. Bhushan, ed. Plant Growth Substances. LC 79-18933. (ACS Symposium Ser.: No. 111). 1979. 29.00 (ISBN 0-8412-0518-3). Am Chemical.
Mitchell, Roger L. Crop Growth & Culture. 1st ed. LC 72-88006. (Illus.). 1970. 14.95x (ISBN 0-8138-0377-2). Iowa St U Pr.
Rapp, Joel & Rapp, Lynn. Mother Earth's Hassle-Free Indoor Plant Book. LC 73-76660. 128p. 1973. 6.95 (ISBN 0-87477-026-2); pap. 3.95 (ISBN 0-87477-007-6). J P Tarcher.
Skoog, F., ed. Plant Growth Substances, Nineteen Seventy-Nine: Proceedings. (Proceedings in Life Sciences Ser.). (Illus.). 527p. 1981. 57.90 (ISBN 0-387-10182-9). Springer-Verlag.
Steward, F. C. & Krikorian, A. D. Plants, Chemicals & Growth. 1971. text ed. 25.00 (ISBN 0-12-668662-9); pap. 8.95 (ISBN 0-12-668660-2). Acad Pr.
Stutte, Charles A., ed. Plant Growth Regulators. LC 77-7934. (Advances in Chemistry Ser.: No. 159). 1977. 17.25 (ISBN 0-8412-0344-X). Am Chemical.
Thimann, Kenneth V. Hormone Action in the Whole Life of Plants. LC 76-26641. (Illus.). 1977. 40.00x (ISBN 0-87023-224-X). U of Mass Pr.
Torrey, John G. Development in Flowering Plants. (Orig.). 1967. pap. text ed. 6.95x (ISBN 0-02-420960-0). Macmillan.
Wareing, P. F. & Phillips, I. D. The Control of Growth & Differentiation in Plants. 2nd ed. LC 78-30561. 1979. text ed. 45.00 (ISBN 0-08-021526-2); pap. text ed. 18.50 (ISBN 0-686-68007-3). Pergamon.
--Growth & Diffentiation in Plants. 3rd ed. Orig. Title: The Control of Growth & Differentiation in Plants. (Illus.). 176p. 1981. 38.00 (ISBN 0-08-026351-8); pap. 19.00 (ISBN 0-08-026350-X). Pergamon.
Williams, R. F. The Shoot Apex & Leaf Growth. (Illus.). 280p. 1975. 35.50 (ISBN 0-521-20453-4). Cambridge U Pr.
Wolf, Ray, ed. Rodale Plans Solar Growing Frame. (Illus.). 80p. 1980. pap. 14.95 (ISBN 0-87857-305-4). Rodale Pr Inc.

GROWTH (PLANTS)–JUVENILE LITERATURE

Rahn, Joan E. More About What Plants Do. LC 74-19280. (Illus.). 80p. (gr. 3-5). 1975. PLB 6.95 (ISBN 0-689-30454-4). Atheneum.
--Watch It Grow, Watch It Change. LC 78-6287. (Illus.). (gr. 4-7). 1978. 7.95 (ISBN 0-689-30665-2). Atheneum.

GROWTH CABINETS AND ROOMS

Controlled Climates & Plant Research. (Technical Note: No. 148). 1976. pap. 12.00 (ISBN 0-685-68368-0, WMO 436, WMO). Unipub.
Downs, R. G. & Hellmers, H. Environment & the Experimental Control of Plant Growth. (Experimental Botany Ser.). 1975. 24.50 (ISBN 0-12-221450-1). Acad Pr.
Downs, Robert J. Controlled Environments for Plant Research. LC 74-20878. (Illus.). 175p. 1975. 17.50x (ISBN 0-231-03561-6). Columbia U Pr.

GROWTH HORMONE

see Somatotropin

GROWTH PROMOTING SUBSTANCES

see also Plant Hormones

Bickford, Elwood D. & Dunn, Stuart. Lighting for Plant Growth. LC 70-157464. (Illus.). 264p. 1972. 18.00x (ISBN 0-87338-116-5). Kent St U Pr.
International Conference on Plant Growth Substances, 7th, Canberra, 1970. Plant Growth Substances, 1970: Proceedings. Carr, D. J., ed. LC 72-80291. (Illus.). 849p. 1972. pap. 29.30 (ISBN 0-387-05850-8). Springer-Verlag.
Leffert, H. L., ed. Growth Regulation by Ion Fluxes. LC 80-13986. (Annals of the New York Academy of Sciences: Vol. 339). 335p. 60.00x (ISBN 0-89766-049-8). NY Acad Sci.

GRUB-STREET JOURNAL

Hillhouse, James T. Grub-Street Journal. LC 67-12466. Repr. of 1928 ed. 15.00 (ISBN 0-405-08621-0, Pub. by Blom). Arno.

GRUBER, FRANZ XAVIER, 1787-1863

Rosel, Paul. Silent Night, Holy Night. (Illus.). 1969. 3.25 (ISBN 0-8066-0928-1, 11-9388). Augsburg.

GRUBER, FRANZ XAVIER, 1787-1863–JUVENILE LITERATURE

Moore, John Travers. Story of Silent Night. LC 65-19252. (gr. 2-3). 1965. 5.50 (ISBN 0-570-03430-2, 56-1056). Concordia.

GRUMMAN F6F HELLCAT

see Hellcat (Fighter Planes)

GRUNDTVIG, NICOLAI FREDERIK SEVERIN 1783-1872

Knudsen, Johannes, ed. N. F. S. Grundtvig: Selected Writings. LC 76-7873. 192p. 1976. pap. 5.95 (ISBN 0-8006-1238-8, 1-1238). Fortress.

GRUNER, JOHN WALTER, 1890-

Doe, Bruce R. & Smith, D. K., eds. Studies in Mineralogy & Precambrian Geology: A Volume in Honor of John W. Gruner. LC 70-190173. (Memoir: No. 135). (Illus.). viii, 304p. 1972. 22.25x (ISBN 0-8137-1135-5). Geol Soc.

GRUNEWALD, MATHIAS, 16TH CENTURY

Burkhard, Arthur. Matthias Grunewald: Personality & Accomplishment. LC 75-10712. 1976. Repr. of 1936 ed. lib. bdg. 40.00 (ISBN 0-87817-186-X). Hacker.
Nochlin, Linda. Mathis at Colmar: A Visual Confrontation. LC 63-2298. (Illus., Orig.). 1963. 5.25 (ISBN 0-87376-002-6). Red Dust.

GRYPHIUS, ANDREAS, 1616-1664

Kimmich, Flora. Sonnets of Catharina von Greiffenberg: Methods of Composition. (Studies in the Germanic Languages & Literatures: No. 83). 1975. 11.50x (ISBN 0-8078-8083-3). U of NC Pr.
Schindler, Marvin S. Sonnets of Andreas Gryphius: The Use of the Poetic Word in the 17th Century. LC 79-630254. 1971. 9.50 (ISBN 0-8130-0301-6). U Presses Fla.

GRYPHONS

see Animals, Mythical

GUADALAJARA, SPAIN–CHARTERS, GRANTS, PRIVILEGES

Keniston, Hayward, ed. Fuero De Guadalajara Twelve Nineteen. (Elliott Monographs: Vol. 16). 1924. pap. 5.00 (ISBN 0-527-02619-0). Kraus Repr.

GUADALUPE, NUESTRA SENORA DE

Dooley, L. M. That Motherly Mother of Guadalupe. 2.25 (ISBN 0-8198-0634-X); pap. 1.25 (ISBN 0-8198-0635-8). Dghtrs St Paul.
Lafaye, Jacques. Quetzalcoatl & Guadalupe: The Formation of Mexican National Consciousness, 1531-1813. Keen, Benjamin, tr. from Fr. LC 75-20889. 1976. lib. bdg. 22.00x (ISBN 0-226-46794-5). U of Chicago Pr.

GUADELOUPE

A Handbook on Guadalupe: For All Americans-a Pledge of Hope. pap. 4.25 (ISBN 0-686-30916-2, 101-16). Prow Bks-Franciscan.

GUAIANOLIDES
Sorm, Frantisek. Guaianolides & Germacranolides. LC 67-1773. (Chemistry of Natural Products Ser.). 153p. 1965. 13.75x (ISBN 0-8002-1479-X). Intl Pubns Serv.
Sorm, Frantisek & Dolejs, Ladislaw. Guaianolides & Germacranolides. LC 66-16515. 1966. 20.00x (ISBN 0-8162-8261-7). Holden-Day.
GUAICURUAN LANGUAGES
see Guaycuruan Languages
GUAM
Beardsley, Charles. Guam: Past & Present. LC 63-22540. (gr. 9 up). 1964. bds. 12.95 (ISBN 0-8048-0223-8). C E Tuttle.
Carano, Paul & Sanchez, Pedro C. A Complete History of Guam. LC 64-21619. (Illus.). 1964. 19.50 (ISBN 0-8048-0114-2). C E Tuttle.
Ishikawa, Wes. The Elder Guamanian. Valle, Ramon, ed. LC 77-83489. (Elder Minority Ser.). 1978. pap. 3.50x (ISBN 0-916304-39-6). Campanile.
Thompson, Laura. Guam & Its People. rev. 3rd ed. Repr. of 1947 ed. lib. bdg. 24.25x (ISBN 0-8371-1170-6, THGP). Greenwood.
GUARA LANGUAGES
see also Agau Language
GUARANTEED ANNUAL INCOME
see also Wages-Annual Wage
Bowler, M. Kenneth. The Nixon Guaranteed Income Proposal: Substance & Process in Policy Change. LC 74-3093. (Illus.). 224p. 1974. text ed. 17.50 (ISBN 0-88410-011-1). Ballinger Pub.
Lurie, Irene, ed. Integrating Income Maintenance Programs. (Institute for Research on Poverty Monographs). 1975. 23.50 (ISBN 0-12-460450-1). Acad Pr.
Moynihan, Daniel P. Politics of a Guaranteed Income: The Nixon Administration & the Family Assistance Plan. 1973. pap. 2.95 (ISBN 0-394-71931-X, Vin). Random.
Theobald, Robert, ed. Committed Spending: A Route to Economic Security. LC 77-16172. (Illus.). 1978. Repr. of 1968 ed. lib. bdg. 17.25x (ISBN 0-313-20018-1, THCS). Greenwood.
--Middle Class Support: A Route to Socioeconomic Security. LC 72-91921. 199p. 1972. pap. 5.95x (ISBN 0-8040-0612-1). Swallow.
Wallace, Frank. Poker a Guaranteed Income for Life by Using the Advanced Concepts. 9th ed. LC 76-3223. 1976. 17.50 (ISBN 0-911752-22-6). I & O Pub.
GUARANTEED ANNUAL WAGE
see Wages-Annual Wage
GUARANTY
see Suretyship and Guaranty
GUARD DOGS
see Watchdogs
GUARDI, FRANCESCO, 1712-1793
Guardi. (Watercolor Ser.). (Illus.). (gr. 12). 1979. 29.95 (ISBN 0-8120-5146-7). Barron.
THE GUARDIAN, LONDON, 1713
Drake, Nathan. Essays: Biographical, Critical & Historical, Illustrative of the Tatler, Spectator, & Guardian, 3 vols. (Belles Letters in English Ser). 1969. Repr. of 1805 ed. Set. 77.00 (ISBN 0-384-12700-2). Johnson Repr.
GUARDIAN AND WARD
see also Adoption; Custody of Children; Executors and Administrators; Parent and Child (Law)
Decedent's Estate & Fiduciary Relations, District of Columbia Code Annotated. pap. 3.95 (ISBN 0-685-14178-0). Lerner Law.
Faber, Stuart J. Handbook of Guardianships & Conservatorships. 2nd ed. 1979. 21.50 (ISBN 0-89074-063-1). Lega Bks.
Field, G. W. The Legal Relations of Infants, Parent & Child, & Guardian & Ward: And a Particular Consideration of Guardianship in the State of New York. xx, 376p. 1981. Repr. of 1888 ed. lib. bdg. 28.50x (ISBN 0-8377-0537-1). Rothman.
MacKay, Richard V. The Law of Guardianships. 3rd ed. Sloan, Irving J., ed. LC 79-28375. 125p. 1980. lib. bdg. 5.95 (ISBN 0-379-11128-4). Oceana.
GUARINI LANGUAGE
Gregores, Emma & Suarez, Jorge A. Description of Colloquial Guarani: Containing a Phonology & Grammar of Spoken Guarani & a Guarani-English Vocabulary of 1130 Entries. (Janua Linguarum, Ser. Practica: No. 27). 1967. pap. text ed. 52.50x (ISBN 90-2790-644-0). Mouton.
GUATEMALA
Adams, Richard N. Crucifixion by Power: Essays on Guatemalan National Social Structure, 1944-1966. 567p. 1970. 22.50x (ISBN 0-292-70035-0). U of Tex Pr.
--Cultural Surveys of Panama, Nicaragua, Guatemala, El Salvador, Honduras. LC 76-41776. 1976. Repr. of 1957 ed. 35.00 (ISBN 0-87917-056-5). Blaine Ethridge.
Anderson, Marilyn. Guatemalan Textiles Today. (Illus.). 1978. 24.50 (ISBN 0-8230-2158-0). Watson-Guptill.
Atwater, Mary M. Guatemala Visited. LC 47-24720. (Shuttle Craft Guild Monograph: No. 15). (Illus.). 46p. 1965. pap. 6.50 (ISBN 0-916658-15-5). HTH Pubs.
Bjerregaard, Lena. Techniques of Guatemalan Weaving. (Illus.). 1977. 13.95 (ISBN 0-442-20785-9). Van Nos Reinhold.
Brigham, W. Guatemala. 1976. lib. bdg. 59.95 (ISBN 0-8490-1909-5). Gordon Pr.
Brigham, William T. Guatemala: The Land of the Quetzal. 1976. lib. bdg. 59.95 (ISBN 0-8490-1916-8). Gordon Pr.
Coe, William R. Piedras Negras Archaeology: Artifacts, Caches & Burials. (Museum Monographs). (Illus.). 245p. 1959. soft bound 10.00 (ISBN 0-934718-11-3). Univ Mus of U PA.
Ferggusson, E. Guatemala. 1977. lib. bdg. 59.95 (ISBN 0-8490-1910-9). Gordon Pr.
Franklin, Woodman B. Guatemala. (World Bibliographical Ser.: No. 9). 1981. write for info. (ISBN 0-903450-24-0). Abc-Clio.
Hoppenot, J. Guatemala. 1976. lib. bdg. 59.95 (ISBN 0-8490-1911-7). Gordon Pr.
Jones, Chester L. Guatemala Past & Present. 1976. lib. bdg. 59.95 (ISBN 0-8490-1914-1). Gordon Pr.
Mayers, Marvin, ed. Languages of Guatemala. (Janua Linguarum, Ser. Practica: No. 23). (Orig.). 1966. pap. text ed. 55.00x (ISBN 90-2790-642-4). Mouton.
Olivera, Otto. La Literatura en publicaciones periodicas de Guatemala: Siglo XIX, Vol. 5. 273p. 1974. pap. 7.00 (ISBN 0-912788-04-6). Tulane Romance Lang.
Whetten, Nathan L. Guatemala, the Land & the People. LC 74-6787. (Caribbean Ser.: No. 4). (Illus.). 399p. 1974. Repr. of 1961 ed. lib. bdg. 23.50x (ISBN 0-8371-7561-5, WHGU). Greenwood.
Wolf, Eric. Sons of the Shaking Earth. LC 59-12290. (Illus.). 1959. 15.00x (ISBN 0-226-90499-7, Phoen); pap. 4.95x (ISBN 0-226-90500-4, P90, Phoen). U of Chicago Pr.
Woods, Clyde M. & Graves, Theodore D. The Process of Medical Change in a Highland Guatemalan Town. LC 72-97396. (Latin American Studies Ser.: Vol. 21). 61p. 1973. pap. text ed. 5.00 (ISBN 0-87903-021-6). UCLA Lat Am Ctr.
GUATEMALA-ANTIQUITIES
Brigham, William T. Guatemala, Land of the Quetzal. Popenoe, William, ed. LC 65-14894. (Latin American Gateway Ser). 1965. Repr. of 1887 ed. 12.50 (ISBN 0-8130-0028-9). U Presses Fla.
Carr, Robert F. & Hazard, James E. Tikal Reports No. 11: Map of the Ruins of Tikal,El Peten, Guatemala. (Musuem Monograph). (Illus.). iv, 24p. 1961. 10.00 (ISBN 0-934718-13-X). Univ Mus of U PA.
Dillon, Brian. Salinas De los Nueve Cerros Guatemala: Preliminary Archaeological Investigations. (Ballena Press Studies in Mesoamerican Art, Archaeology & Ethnohistory: No. 2). 1978. pap. 5.95 (ISBN 0-87919-070-1). Ballena Pr.
Excavations at Seibal: Department of Peten, Guatemala. Incl. Vol. 14, No. 1. Artifacts. Willey, Gordon R; Vol. 14, No. 2. A Reconnaissance of Cancuen. Tourtellot, Gair, 3rd, et al.; Vol. 14, No. 3. A Brief Reconnaissance of Itzan. Tourtellot, Gair, et al.. LC 76-53126. (Memoirs of the Peabody Museum: Vol. 14). 1978. Set. 35.00 (ISBN 0-87365-686-5). Peabody Harvard.
Feldman, Lawrence H. Riverine Maya: The Torquegua & Other Chols of the Lower Motagua Valley. LC 75-621315. (Museum Brief: No. 15). (Illus.). 25p. 1975. pap. 1.20x (ISBN 0-913134-14-7). Mus Anthro Mo.
Feldman, Lawrence H. & Walters, Gary H., eds. Excavations in Southeastern Guatemala: 1976-1978. (Miscellaneous Publications in Anthropology Ser.: No. 9, Reports 1 & 2). (Illus.). 1980. pap. 5.00x (ISBN 0-913134-80-5). Mus Anthro Mo.
Feldman, Lawrence H., et al. Jade Workers in the Motagua Valley: The Late Classic Terzuola Site. LC 75-325233. (Museum Brief: No. 17). (Illus.). 1975. pap. 0.85x (ISBN 0-913134-16-3). Mus Anthro Mo.
Gann, Thomas W. Mystery Cities: Exploration & Adventure in Labaantun. LC 76-44721. 1977. Repr. of 1925 ed. 28.50 (ISBN 0-404-15925-7). AMS Pr.
Kidder, A. V., et al. Excavations at Kaminaljuyu, Guatemala. LC 77-14658. (Monograph Ser. on Kaminaljuyu). (Illus.). 1978. Repr. text ed. 23.50x (ISBN 0-271-00535-1). Pa St U Pr.
Kidder, Alfred V. The Artifacts of Uaxactun, Guatemala. LC 77-11502. (Carnegie Institution of Washington. Publication: No. 576). Repr. of 1947 ed. 17.50 (ISBN 0-404-16265-7). AMS Pr.
Kidder, Alfred V., et al. Excavations at Kaminaljuyu, Guatemala. LC 77-11505. Repr. of 1946 ed. 44.00 (ISBN 0-404-16266-5). AMS Pr.
Lothrop, Samuel K. Atitlan: An Archaeological Study of Ancient Remains on the Borders of Lake Atitlan, Guatemala. LC 77-11509. (Carnegie Institution of Washington. Publication: No. 444). Repr. of 1933 ed. 22.00 (ISBN 0-404-16268-1). AMS Pr.
Maler, T. Explorations in the Department of Peten, Guatemala, & Adjacent Region, 2 vols. Repr. of 1910 ed. Vol. 1. pap. 30.00 (ISBN 0-527-01163-0); Vol. 2. pap. 21.00 (ISBN 0-527-01164-9). Kraus Repr.
--Explorations of the Upper Usumatsintla & Adjacent Region. Repr. of 1908 ed. pap. 14.00 (ISBN 0-527-01162-2). Kraus Repr.
--Researches in the Central Portion of the Usumatsintla Valley. Repr. of 1901 ed. pap. 30.00 (ISBN 0-527-01156-8). Kraus Repr.
--Researches in the Usumatsintla Valley, Pt. 2. Repr. of 1903 ed. pap. 48.00 (ISBN 0-527-01157-6). Kraus Repr.
Merwin, R. E. & Vaillant, G. C. Ruins of Holmul, Guatemala. Repr. of 1932 ed. pap. 35.00 (ISBN 0-527-01160-6). Kraus Repr.
Michels, Joseph W. The Kaminaljuyu Chiefdom. LC 79-15181. (Monograph Ser. on Kaminaljuyu). (Illus.). 1979. text ed. 22.50x (ISBN 0-271-00224-7). Pa St U Pr.
Recinos, Adrian & Goetz, Delia, trs. Popol Vuh: The Sacred Book of the Ancient Quiche Maya: Spanish Version of the Original Maya. (Civilization of the American Indian Ser.: No. 29). (Eng). 1978. Repr. of 1950 ed. 10.95 (ISBN 0-8061-0205-5). U of Okla Pr.
Sanders, William T. & Michels, Joseph W., eds. Teotihuacan & Kaminaljuyu: A Study in Culture Contact. LC 77-21061. (Monograph Ser. on Kaminaljuyu). (Illus.). 1978. text ed. 23.50x (ISBN 0-271-00529-7). Pa St U Pr.
Smith, Augustus L. Uaxactun, Guatemala: Excavations of 1931-1937. LC 77-11523. (Carnegie Institution of Washington. Publication: No. 588). Repr. of 1950 ed. 30.50 (ISBN 0-404-16288-6). AMS Pr.
Smith, Ledyard. Excavations at Seibal: Major Architecture & Caches & Analysis of Fine Paste Ceramics, Vol. 15, No. 1 & 2. Subloff, Jeremy A., ed. (Peabody Museum Memoirs Ser.: Vol. 15, No. 1 & 2). 1981. pap. write for info. (ISBN 0-87365-687-3). Peabody Harvard.
Tozzer, A. M. Preliminary Study of the Prehistoric Ruins of Nakum, Guatemala. Repr. of 1913 ed. pap. 18.00 (ISBN 0-527-01167-3). Kraus Repr.
Uaxactun, Guatemala. Group E - 1926-1931 & Ricketson, Oliver G., Jr. The Excavations & the Artifacts, 2 pts. LC 77-11516. (Carnegie Institution of Washington. Publication: No. 477). Repr. of 1937 ed. 43.00 (ISBN 0-404-16276-2). AMS Pr.
GUATEMALA-DESCRIPTION AND TRAVEL
Brigham, William T. Guatemala, Land of the Quetzal. Popenoe, William, ed. LC 65-14894. (Latin American Gateway Ser). 1965. Repr. of 1887 ed. 12.50 (ISBN 0-8130-0028-9). U Presses Fla.
Burbank, A. Guatemala Profile. 1976. lib. bdg. 59.95 (ISBN 0-8490-1915-X). Gordon Pr.
Carlson, Loraine. TraveLeer Guide to Yucatan & Guatemala. LC 79-53283. (Illus.). 365p. (Orig.). 1980. pap. 6.95 (ISBN 0-932554-01-6). Upland Pr.
Frommer & Pasmantier. Mexico & Guatemala on Ten Dollars a Day. 1977. pap. 4.95 (ISBN 0-671-10893-X). S&S.
Glassman, Paul. Guatemala Guide. (Orig.). 1983. pap. 15.00x (ISBN 0-930016-02-5). Passport Pr.
--Guatemala Guide. LC 77-74034. (Illus.). 1978. 10.00 (ISBN 0-930016-00-9). Passport Pr.
--Lake Atitlan & Chichicastenango: The Complete Guide. LC 76-364141. 1976. 3.50 (ISBN 0-930016-01-7). Passport Pr.
Greenberg, Harriet & Greenberg, Arnold. Guatemala Alive. 1976. pap. 2.50 (ISBN 0-686-23068-X). Alive Pubns.
Lister, Robert H. In Search of Maya Glyphs. (Illus.). 1970. 8.95 (ISBN 0-89013-044-2); pap. 4.95 (ISBN 0-89013-045-0). Museum NM Pr.
Lloyd, Joan. Guatemala, Land of the Mayas. LC 74-2557. (Illus.). 175p. 1974. Repr. of 1963 ed. lib. bdg. 14.00x (ISBN 0-8371-7415-5, LLGU). Greenwood.
Maudslay, Anne C. & Maudslay, Alfred P. A Glimpse at Guatemala, & Some Notes on the Ancient Monuments of Central America. LC 79-15012. (Illus.). 1979. Repr. of 1899 ed. 47.50 (ISBN 0-87917-070-0). Blaine Ethridge.
Morton, Friedrich. In the Land of the Quetzal Feather. (Illus.). 1960. 5.00 (ISBN 0-8159-5807-2). Devin.
Pettersen, Carmen L. The Maya of Guatemala: Their Life & Dress. LC 76-42102. (Illus.). 276p. 1977. 45.00 (ISBN 0-295-95537-6). U of Wash Pr.
Tedlock, Barbara. Time & the Highland Maya. LC 80-54569. 304p. 1981. 27.50 (ISBN 0-8263-0577-6). U of NM Pr.
Weekley, Richard J. Mayan Night. LC 81-65782. (Illus.). 224p. (Orig.). 1981. pap. 6.50 (ISBN 0-915392-08-9, Domina Bks). Double M Pr.
GUATEMALA-ECONOMIC CONDITIONS
Adler, John H. Public Finance & Economic Development in Guatemala. LC 77-138097. (Illus.). xix, 282p. Repr. of 1952 ed. lib. bdg. 15.00 (ISBN 0-8371-5672-6, ADPF). Greenwood.
Melville, T. & Melville, M. Guatemala: The Politics of Land Ownership. LC 70-143523. 1971. 12.95 (ISBN 0-02-920840-8). Free Pr.
Roberts, Bryan R. Organizing Strangers: Poor Families in Guatemala City. LC 72-3513. (Texas Pan American Ser.). 378p. 1973. 17.50x (ISBN 0-292-76000-0). U of Tex Pr.
Tax, Sol. Penny Capitalism: A Guatemalan Indian Economy. LC 78-159254. x, 230p. 1971. Repr. of 1953 ed. lib. bdg. 16.00x (ISBN 0-374-97785-2). Octagon.
Wagley, Charles. Economics of a Guatemalan Village. LC 41-19381. 1941. pap. 6.00 (ISBN 0-527-00557-6). Kraus Repr.
Wilson-Grau, Richard. Latin America's Underdevelopment in the Case of Rural Development in Guatemala: A Macro-Analysis. 1974. 69.95 (ISBN 0-8490-0489-6). Gordon Pr.
GUATEMALA-HISTORY
Annis, Verle L. The Architecture of Antigua Guatemala, 1543-1773. (Illus.). 35.00x (ISBN 0-686-11833-2). R Reed.
De Alvarado, Pedro. An Account of the Conquest of Guatemala in 1524. Mackie, Sedley J., ed. 1924. 12.00 (ISBN 0-527-19723-8). Kraus Repr.
--An Account of the Conquest of Guatemala in 1524. Mackie, Sedley J., ed. LC 77-88568. 1977. Repr. of 1924 ed. lib. bdg. 15.00 (ISBN 0-89341-275-9). Longwood Pr.
Fox, John W. Quiche Conquest. LC 77-89437. 1978. 15.00x (ISBN 0-8263-0461-3). U of NM Pr.
Grieb, Kenneth J. Guatemalan Caudillo: The Regime of Jorge Ubica, Guatemala, 1931-1944. LC 78-14339. 384p. 1979. 20.00x (ISBN 0-8214-0379-6). Ohio U Pr.
Holleran, Mary P. Church & State in Guatemala. LC 73-19956. 359p. 1974. Repr. of 1949 ed. lib. bdg. 17.00x (ISBN 0-374-93929-2). Octagon.
Juarros, Domingo. Statistical & Commercial History of the Kingdom of Guatemala. LC 76-128432. Repr. of 1823 ed. 35.00 (ISBN 0-404-03622-8). AMS Pr.
Kennedy, Paul. Middle Beat: A Correspondent's View of Mexico, Guatemala, & El Salvador. LC 71-144045. (Illus.). 1971. text ed. 12.00 (ISBN 0-8077-1603-0). Tchrs Coll.
Maler, T. Explorations in the Department of Peten, Guatemala. Bd. with Prehistoric Ruins of Tikal, Guatemala. Tozzer, A. M. 1911. pap. 48.00 (ISBN 0-527-01166-5). Kraus Repr.
Sperlich, Norbert & Sperlich, Elizabeth K. Guatemalan Backstrap Weaving. LC 79-56663. (Illus.). 275p. 1980. 25.00 (ISBN 0-8061-1571-8). U of Okla Pr.
GUATEMALA-JUVENILE LITERATURE
Buff, Mary & Buff, Conrad. Magic Maize. (Illus.). (gr. 4-6). 1953. Dolphin bdg. 3.57 (ISBN 0-395-06666-2). HM.
Jenness, Aylette & Kroeber, Lisa. A Life of Their Own: An Indian Family in Latin America. LC 75-15964. (Illus.). (gr. 5 up). 1975. 8.95 (ISBN 0-690-00572-5, TYC-J). Har-Row.
U. S. Committee For UNICEF. Hi Neighbor Book No. 5: Burma, Guatemala, Spain, Sudan, UAR. (Illus.). (gr. 4-6). 1961. 4.95 (ISBN 0-8038-2983-3); pap. 2.00 (ISBN 0-8038-2982-5). Hastings.
GUATEMALA-SOCIAL CONDITIONS
Asturias, Miguel. Guatemalan Sociology. Ahern, Maureen, tr. LC 77-8270. 1977. pap. 7.95x (ISBN 0-87918-037-4). ASU Lat Am St.
Colby, Benjamin N. & Van Den Berghe, Pierre L. Ixil Country: A Plural Society in Highland Guatemala. LC 68-16740. 1969. 21.50x (ISBN 0-520-01515-0). U of Cal Pr.
Forrest, Colburn D. Guatemala's Rural Health Paraprofessionals. (Special Series on Paraprofessionals). 53p. (Orig.). 1981. pap. 3.50 (ISBN 0-86731-048-0). RDC Ctr Intl Stud.
Tumin, Melvin M. Caste in a Peasant Society. LC 75-29328. (Illus.). 300p. 1975. Repr. of 1952 ed. lib. bdg. 18.75x (ISBN 0-8371-8390-1, TUPS). Greenwood.
Wilson-Grau, Richard. Latin America's Underdevelopment in the Case of Rural Development in Guatemala: A Macro-Analysis. 1974. 69.95 (ISBN 0-8490-0489-6). Gordon Pr.
Winter, N. Guatemala & Her People of Today. 1976. lib. bdg. 59.95 (ISBN 0-8490-1913-3). Gordon Pr.
GUAYCURUAN LANGUAGES
Najlis, Elena. Lengua Abipona, 2 vols. 1966. Set. 49.95 (ISBN 0-686-56663-7, S-33069). French & Eur.
GUERILLAS
see Guerrillas

GUERRE, MME. BERTRANDE (DE ROIS) 1539-1560–FICTION
Lewis, Janet. Wife of Martin Guerre. LC 70-135357. 109p. 1967. pap. 4.95 (ISBN 0-8040-0321-1). Swallow.
GUERRE, MARTIN, 1539-1560- FICTION
Lewis, Janet. Wife of Martin Guerre. LC 70-135357. 109p. 1967. pap. 4.95 (ISBN 0-8040-0321-1). Swallow.
GUERRERO, MEXICO (COAHUILA)–HISTORY
Weddle, Robert S. San Juan Bautista: Gateway to Spanish Texas. (Illus.). 485p. 1968. 17.95 (ISBN 0-292-73306-2). U of Tex Pr.
GUERRILLA WARFARE
Australian Military Forces. Ambush & Counter Ambush. (Illus.). 80p. 1977. pap. 4.00 (ISBN 0-87364-098-5). Paladin Ent.
Bayo, Alberto. One Hundred Fifty Questions for a Guerrilla. Brown, Robert K., ed. Hartenstein, Hugo & Harber, Dennis, trs. from Span. LC 63-2215. (Illus.). 86p. 1963. pap. 5.00 (ISBN 0-87364-022-5). Paladin Ent.
Burchett, Wilfred. Grasshoppers & Elephants. 1977. pap. 4.95 (ISBN 0-916354-65-2); pap. 5.95 (ISBN 0-916354-66-0). Urizen Bks.
Callwell, C. E. Small Wars: Their Principles & Practices. (Illus.). 1977. Repr. of 1906 ed. 35.00x (ISBN 0-7158-1200-9). Charles River Bks.
Camejo, Pedro M. La Guerrilla: For Que "Fracaso" Como Estrategia. 48p. (Span.). 1974. pap. 0.85 (ISBN 0-87348-337-5). Path Pr NY.
Colby, C. B. Special Forces: The U.S. Army's Experts in Unconventional Warfare. (Illus.). (gr. 4-7). 1964. PLB 5.29 (ISBN 0-698-30326-1). Coward.
Cross, James E. Conflict in the Shadows. LC 75-17468. 180p. 1975. Repr. of 1963 ed. lib. bdg. 15.00x (ISBN 0-8371-8305-7, CRCS). Greenwood.
Davidson. The People's Cause. (Longman Studies in African History). (Illus.). 224p. (Orig.). 1981. text ed. 24.00x (ISBN 0-582-64680-4); pap. text ed. 11.95x (ISBN 0-582-64681-2). Longman.
Debray, Regis. Revolution in the Revolution? Ortiz, Bobbye, tr. from Fr. 1967. pap. 1.50 (ISBN 0-394-17121-7, B144, BC). Grove.
Dept. of the Army, Washington D. C. Counterguerilla Operations: FM 1-16. (Illus.). 163p. 1967. pap. 8.00 (ISBN 0-87364-038-1). Paladin Ent.
Dept. of the Navy, U. S. Marine Corps. Sniping: U. S. Marine Corps Manual FMFM-1-3B. (Illus.). 270p. 1969. pap. 6.95 (ISBN 0-87364-042-X). Paladin Ent.
Gann, Lewis. Guerrillas in History. LC 76-132819. (Studies Ser.: No. 28). 1971. pap. 5.95 (ISBN 0-8179-3281-X). Hoover Inst Pr.
Giap, Vo Nguyen. Military Art of People's War: Selected Writings. Stetler, Russell, ed. LC 75-105317. (Illus.). 1970. pap. 5.95 (ISBN 0-85345-193-1, PB-1931). Monthly Rev.
Guevara, E. Che. Guerrilla Warfare. 1968. pap. 1.65 (ISBN 0-394-70430-4, Vin). Random.
Halperin, Ernst. Terrorism in Latin America. LC 76-4103. (The Washington Papers: No. 33). 90p. 1976. 4.00x (ISBN 0-8039-0648-X). Sage.
Hesketh-Prichard, H. Sniping in France. (Illus.). 268p. 1976. pap. 6.00 (ISBN 0-87364-046-2). Paladin Ent.
James, Daniel, ed. Complete Bolivian Diaries of Che Guevara & Other Captured Documents. LC 68-55642. 1969. pap. 2.95 (ISBN 0-8128-1229-8). Stein & Day.
Klonis, N. I. Guerrilla Warfare. 12.50 (ISBN 0-8315-0134-0). Speller.
Levy, Bert Y. Guerrilla Warfare. Brown, Robert K., ed. LC 64-6189. (Illus.). 119p. 1965. pap. 5.00 (ISBN 0-87364-020-9). Paladin Ent.
Mao Tse-Tung. Selected Military Writings, 1928-1949. 1967-1968. 6.95 (ISBN 0-8351-0321-8); red plastic 3.95 (ISBN 0-8351-0323-4); pap. 4.95 (ISBN 0-8351-0322-6). China Bks.
Pomeroy, William J., ed. Guerrilla Warfare & Marxism: A Collection of Writings from Karl Marx to the Present. LC 65-55606. 1969. 5.95 (ISBN 0-7178-0082-2); pap. 2.95 (ISBN 0-7178-0248-5). Intl Pub Co.
Rhodesian Government. Rhodesian Leader's Guide. (Illus.). 55p. 1980. pap. 6.00 (ISBN 0-87364-194-9). Paladin Ent.
Sable, Martin H. The Guerrilla Movement in Latin America Since 1950: A Bibliography. LC 77-89822. (Center Bibliographic Ser.: No. 3). 1977. pap. 4.00 (ISBN 0-930450-00-0). Univ of Wis Latin Am.
Sarkesian. Revolutionary Guerrilla Warfare. 1975. 12.95 (ISBN 0-07-054745-9, I). McGraw.
Sarkesian, Sam C., ed. Revolutionary Guerrilla Warfare. LC 74-12995. 1975. 16.95 (ISBN 0-913750-05-0). Precedent Pub.
Senich, Peter R. Limited War Sniping. LC 77-86752. (Illus.). 150p. 1978. 17.95 (ISBN 0-87364-125-6). Paladin Ent.
Smith, Bradley F. Heinrich Himmler: A Nazi in the Making, 1900-1926. LC 79-137403. (Publications Ser.: No. 93). (Illus.). 1971. 10.95 (ISBN 0-8179-1931-7). Hoover Inst Pr.
Taber, Robert. War of the Flea: A Study of Guerrilla Warfare. (Theory & Practise Ser). 1970. pap. 1.95 (ISBN 0-8065-0225-8). Citadel Pr.
Thorhoffen, Alex, ed. The Citizen's Guide to Guerrilla Warfare. 4th ed. LC 79-66802. (Illus.). 245p. 1979. pap. 33.00 (ISBN 0-939856-05-0, Magick Circle). Tech Group.
U.S. Army. Boobytraps: FM 5-13. (Illus.). 133p. 1977. pap. 5.00 (ISBN 0-87364-092-6). Paladin Ent.
Whipp, Derek. Street & Guerrillar Fighting. (Interservice Combat in Cities Ser.). (Illus.). Date not set. pap. 6.95x (ISBN 0-86695-013-3). Interserv Pub.
GUERRILLAS
see also United States–History–Civil War, 1861-1865–Guerrillas; World War, 1939-1945–Underground Movements
Bell, J. Bowyer. On Revolt: Strategies of National Liberation. 368p. 1976. 15.00x (ISBN 0-674-63655-4). Harvard U Pr.
Clutterbuck, Richard. Guerrillas & Terrorists. LC 80-83219. 125p. 1980. 12.00x (ISBN 0-8214-0590-X); pap. 5.95x (ISBN 0-8214-0592-6). Ohio U Pr.
Drum, Karl. Airpower & Russian Partisan Warfare. LC 68-22553. (German Air Force in World War 2 Ser.). (Illus.). 1968. Repr. of 1962 ed. 11.00 (ISBN 0-405-00041-3). Arno.
El-Rayyes, Riad. Guerrillas for Palestine. LC 76-15869. 1976. 17.95 (ISBN 0-312-35280-8). St Martin.
Feit, Edward. Urban Revolt in South Africa, 1960-1964: A Case Study. 1971. 15.95x (ISBN 0-8101-0344-3). Northwestern U Pr.
Idriess, Ion L. Sniping. 120p. 1978. pap. 4.00 (ISBN 0-87364-104-3). Paladin Ent.
James, Daniel, ed. Complete Bolivian Diaries of Che Guevara & Other Captured Documents. LC 68-55642. 1969. pap. 2.95 (ISBN 0-8128-1229-8). Stein & Day.
Laffin, John. Fedayeen. LC 73-10577. 1973. 6.95 (ISBN 0-02-917770-7). Free Pr.
Laqueur, Walter. Guerrilla: A Historical & Critical Study. LC 76-22552. 1976. 17.50 (ISBN 0-316-51469-1). Little.
McCorkle, John. Three Years with Quantrell. Barton, D. S., ed. LC 67-6851. (American Biography Ser., No. 32). 1970. lib. bdg. 45.95 (ISBN 0-8383-1107-5). Haskell.
Mallin, Jay, ed. Terror & Urban Guerillas: A Study of Tactics & Documents. LC 79-163842. 1971. 8.95x (ISBN 0-87024-223-7). U of Miami Pr.
Miksche, Ferdinand O. Secret Forces: The Technique of Underground Movements. LC 73-110273. (Illus.). 181p. Repr. of 1950 ed. lib. bdg. 18.00 (ISBN 0-8371-4499-X, MISF). Greenwood.
Paz, Nestor. My Life for My Friends: The Guerilla Journal of Nestor Paz, Christian. Garcia, Ed & Eagleson, John, trs. from Sp. LC 74-21107. 128p. 1975. 4.95x (ISBN 0-88344-320-1); pap. 2.95x (ISBN 0-88344-319-8). Orbis Bks.
Porzecanski, Arturo C. Uruguay's Tupamaros: The Urban Guerilla. LC 73-13340. (Special Studies in International Politics & Government). 1973. 21.00x (ISBN 0-275-28802-1). Irvington.
Special Operations Research Office, U. S. Army. Secrets of Underground Organization & Operations. LC 74-25006. 1974. 12.95 (ISBN 0-685-16394-6); pap. 8.95 (ISBN 0-685-16395-4). Phoenix Assocs.
Tanham, George K. Trial in Thailand. LC 74-75314. 189p. 1974. 19.50x (ISBN 0-8448-0318-9). Crane-Russak Co.
Venter, Al, Jr. Report on Portugal's War in Guinea-Bissau. (Illus.). 1973. 3.00 (ISBN 0-686-23287-9). Munger Africana Lib.
GUESTS
see Entertaining; Etiquette
GUEVARA, ERNESTO, 1928-1967
Fat Capitalist's Song on the Death of Che Guevara. (Illus., Orig.). 1971. pap. 0.50 (ISBN 0-87810-003-2). Times Change.
Guevara, Che. Che Speaks: Selected Speeches & Writings. 1980. pap. 3.45 (ISBN 0-87348-602-1). Path Pr NY.
Harris, Richard L. Death of a Revolutionary: The Last Days of Che Guevara. LC 79-77405. (Illus.). 1970. 6.95 (ISBN 0-393-07445-5). Norton.
Hodges, Donald C. Legacy of Che Guevara: a Documentary Study. 1977. 14.95 (ISBN 0-500-25056-1). Thames Hudson.
James, Daniel. Che Guevara. LC 68-19566. (Illus.). 1970. pap. 5.95 (ISBN 0-8128-1348-0). Stein & Day.
James, Daniel, ed. Complete Bolivian Diaries of Che Guevara & Other Captured Documents. LC 68-55642. 1969. pap. 2.95 (ISBN 0-8128-1229-8). Stein & Day.
Lowy, Michael. The Marxism of Che Guevara: Philosophy, Economics, & Revolutionary Warfare. Pearce, Brian, tr. from Fr. LC 72-92030. 128p. 1973. pap. 3.95 (ISBN 0-85345-307-1, PB-3071). Monthly Rev.
Mallin, Jay. Ernesto 'Che' Guevara: Modern Revolutionary, Guerilla Theorist. Rahmas, D. Steve, ed. (Outstanding Personalities Ser.: No. 53). 32p. (Orig.). (gr. 7-12). 1973. lib. bdg. 2.95 incl. catalog cards (ISBN 0-87157-556-6); pap. 1.50 vinyl laminated covers (ISBN 0-87157-056-4). SamHar Pr.
GUGGENHEIM FAMILY
Davis, John H. Guggenheims: An American Epic. LC 77-20069. (Illus.). 1979. pap. 6.95 (ISBN 0-688-08273-4, Quill). Morrow.
--The Guggenheims: An American Epic. 1978. 14.95 (ISBN 0-688-03273-7). Morrow.
Guggenheim, Peggy. Out of This Century: Confessions of an Art Addict. LC 78-68475. (Illus.). 456p. 1979. 17.50 (ISBN 0-87663-337-8). Universe.
O'Connor, Harvey. The Guggenheims: The Making of an American Dynasty. Bruchey, Stuart & Bruchey, Eleanor, eds. LC 76-5026. (American Business Abroad Ser.). (Illus.). 1976. Repr. of 1937 ed. 30.00x (ISBN 0-405-09292-X). Arno.
Vidal, Gore, et al. Great American Families. (Illus.). 1977. 15.95 (ISBN 0-393-08752-2). Norton.
GUGGENHEIM MUSEUM, NEW YORK CITY
Barnett, Vivian E. The Guggenheim Museum: Justin K. Thannhauser Collection. new ed. LC 78-66357. (Illus.). 1978. 24.50 (ISBN 0-89207-016-1); pap. 15.50 (ISBN 0-685-91431-3). S R Guggenheim.
--Handbook: The Guggenheim Museum Collection, 1900-1980. LC 79-66597. (Illus.). 1980. 14.85 (ISBN 0-89207-021-8). S R Guggenheim.
Rudenstine, Angelica Z. The Guggenheim Museum: Paintings 1880-1945. LC 75-37356. 750p. 1976. 85.00 (ISBN 0-8390-0188-6). Allanheld & Schram.
GUI DE CAMBRAI, 13TH CENTURY
Armstrong, Edward C. Authorship of the Vengement Alixandre & of the Venjance Alixandre. 1926. pap. 5.00 (ISBN 0-527-02622-0). Kraus Repr.
--French Metrical Versions of Barlaam & Josaphat. (Elliott Monographs: Vol. 10). 1922. pap. 7.00 (ISBN 0-527-02614-X). Kraus Repr.
Edwards, Bateman. Classification of the Manuscripts of Gui De Cambrai's Vengement Alixandre. (Elliott Monographs: Vol. 20). 1926. pap. 5.00 (ISBN 0-527-02623-9). Kraus Repr.
GUIANA
see also Guyana
Comitas, Lambros. Caribbeana, 1900-1965: A Topical Bibliography. LC 68-14239. (Illus.). 930p. 1968. 18.50 (ISBN 0-295-73970-3). U of Wash Pr.
Fletcher, Alan M. The Land & People of the Guianas. rev. ed. LC 78-37743. (Portraits of the Nations Ser.). (Illus.). (gr. 6 up). 1972. 8.95 (ISBN 0-397-31541-4). Lippincott.
Harcourt, Robert. A Relation of a Voyage to Guiana. LC 73-6135. (English Experience Ser.: No. 600). 71p. 1973. Repr. of 1613 ed. 10.50 (ISBN 90-221-0600-4). Walter J Johnson.
Keymis, Lawrence. A Relation of the Second Voyage to Guiana. LC 76-6258. (No. 65). 48p. 1968. Repr. of 1596 ed. 11.50 (ISBN 90-221-0065-0). Walter J Johnson.
Palgrave, William G. Dutch Guiana. LC 75-107520. Repr. of 1876 ed. 12.75x (ISBN 0-8371-3767-5, Pub. by Negro U Pr). Greenwood.
A Publication of Guiana's Plantation. LC 72-7836. (English Experience Ser.: No. 525). 24p. 1972. Repr. of 1632 ed. 6.00 (ISBN 90-221-0726-4). Walter J Johnson.
Ralegh, Walter. The Discoverie of the Large, Rich & Bewtiful Empire of Guiana, Performed in the Yeare 1595, by Sir W. Ralegh. LC 68-27482. (English Experience Ser.: No. 3). 112p. 1968. Repr. of 1596 ed. 11.50 (ISBN 90-221-0003-0). Walter J Johnson.
Raleigh, Walter. Discovery of the Large, Rich and Beautiful Empire of Guiana. Schomburgk, Richard H, ed. LC 74-134704. (Hakluyt Society Ser., No. 3). 1970. lib. bdg. 25.50 (ISBN 0-8337-2886-5). B Franklin.
Rodway, James. In the Guiana Forest: Studies of Nature in Relations to the Struggle for Life. LC 69-18997. (Illus.). Repr. of 1894 ed. 15.50x (ISBN 0-8371-1027-0). Greenwood.
Roth, Walter. An Introductory Study of the Arts, Crafts & Customs of the Guiana Indians. LC 24-29840. (Illus.). Repr. of 1924 ed. 54.00 (ISBN 0-384-52140-1). Johnson Repr.
GUICCIARDINI, FRANCESCO, 1482-1540
Bondanella, Peter E. Francesco Guicciardini. LC 75-41388. (World Authors Ser.,: Italy: No.389). 1976. lib. bdg. 10.95 (ISBN 0-8057-6231-0). Twayne.
Gilbert, Felix. Machiavelli & Guicciardini: Politics & History in Sixteenth Century Florence. LC 63-23405. 1965. 22.50x (ISBN 0-691-05133-X); pap. 8.95 (ISBN 0-691-00771-3). Princeton U Pr.
GUIDANCE, STUDENT
see Personnel Service in Education; Vocational Guidance
GUIDANCE, VOCATIONAL
see Vocational Guidance
GUIDANCE IN EDUCATION
see Personnel Service in Education
GUIDANCE SYSTEMS (FLIGHT)
Here are entered works on systems for supervising the navigation of aircraft and space vehicles from one location to another.
Gysbers, N. & Moore, E. Improving Guidance Programs. 1981. 14.95 (ISBN 0-13-452656-2). P-H.
GUIDE-BOOKS
see Voyages and Travels–Guidebooks
GUIDE DOGS
Curtis, Patricia. Cindy, a Hearing Ear Dog. LC 80-24487. (Illus.). (gr. 3-5). 1981. 9.95 (ISBN 0-525-27950-4). Dutton.
Ford, Lee E. Animal Welfare Encyclopedia: Guide Dog Training & Schools in U. S. A. & Abroad. 1975. Set. pap. 30.00 (ISBN 0-686-13726-4); Vol. 16. pap. (ISBN 0-686-13727-2, 4672119801); Vol. 16A. pap. (ISBN 0-686-13728-0, 4672119802); Vol. 16B. pap. (ISBN 0-686-13729-9, 4672119803). Ford Assocs.
Holmes, Burnham. The First Seeing Eye Dogs. LC 78-14804. (Famous Firsts Ser.). (Illus.). 1978. lib. bdg. 7.35 (ISBN 0-686-51104-2). Silver.
McPhee, Richard. Tom & Bear: The Training of a Guide Dog Team. LC 81-43031. (Illus.). 160p. (gr. 5 up). 1981. 9.95 (ISBN 0-690-04136-5, TYC-J); PLB 9.89 (ISBN 0-690-04137-3). Har-Row.
Pfaffenberger, C., et al. Guide Dogs for the Blind: Their Selection, Development & Training. (Developments in Animal & Veterinary Sciences Ser.: Vol. 1). 1976. 31.25 (ISBN 0-444-41520-3). Elsevier.
Pfaffenberger, Clarence J. New Knowledge of Dog Behavior. LC 63-13674. (Illus.). 1963. 10.95 (ISBN 0-87605-704-0). Howell Bk.
Putnam, Peter. Triumph of the Seeing Eye. LC 62-21294. (Breakthrough Books). (Illus.). (gr. 5 up). 1963. PLB 7.89 (ISBN 0-06-024776-2, HarpJ). Har-Row.
Putnam, Peter B. Love in the Lead: The Fifty-Year Miracle of the Seeing Eye Dog. 1979. 10.95 (ISBN 0-87690-309-X). Dutton.
Scheffer, Victor B. The Seeing Eye. LC 70-140773. (Illus.). (gr. 5-9). 1971. 5.95 (ISBN 0-684-92311-4, ScribJ). Scribner.
GUIDE-POSTS
see Signs and Signboards
GUIDEBOOKS
see Travel
GUIDED MISSILES
see also Antimissile Missiles; Ballistic Missiles; Rockets (Aeronautics)
also names of specific missiles
Gatland, Kenneth. Missiles and Rockets. LC 75-15641. (Illus.). 256p. 1975. 9.95 (ISBN 0-02-542860-8, 54286). Macmillan.
Greenwood, Ted. Making the Mirv: A Study of Defense Decision-Making. LC 75-11635. 256p. 1975. text ed. 17.50 (ISBN 0-88410-033-2). Ballinger Pub.
Huisken, Ron. The Cruise Missile & Arms Control. LC 80-68052. (Canberra Papers on Strategy & Defence: No. 13). 84p. (Orig.). 1980. pap. text ed. 12.95 (ISBN 0-908160-54-2, 0370). Bks Australia.
Huisken, Ronald. The Origin of the Strategic Cruise Missile. 220p. 1981. 23.95 (ISBN 0-03-059378-6). Praeger.
Jane's Pocket Books. Jane's Pocket Book of Missiles. Pretty, Ron, ed. LC 74-10314. (Jane's Pocket Books Ser.). (Illus.). 288p. 1976. pap. 5.95 (ISBN 0-02-080410-5, Collier). Macmillan.
Owen-Smith, M. S. High Velocity Missile Wounds. (Illus.). 192p. 1981. 38.50x (ISBN 0-7131-4371-1). Intl Ideas.
Pfaltzgraff, Robert L., Jr. & Davis, Jacquelyn K. The Cruise Missile: Bargaining Chip or Defense Bargain? LC 76-51854. (Special Reports Ser.). 1977. 3.00 (ISBN 0-89549-001-3). Inst Foreign Policy Anal.
Scoville, Herbert, Jr. The MX: Design for Disaster. (Illus.). 224p. 1981. 15.00 (ISBN 0-262-19199-7); pap. 6.95 (ISBN 0-262-69077-2). MIT Pr.
Slow to Take Offense: Bombers, Cruise Missles & Prudent Deterrence. 136p. 1980. pap. 15.00 (ISBN 0-89206-015-8, CSIS017, CSIS). Unipub.
Taylor, Michael J. Missiles of the World. 3rd, rev. ed. 1980. 14.95 (ISBN 0-684-16593-7, ScribT). Scribner.

Tucker, D. E. & Garland-Collins, T. K. Guided Weapons. (Brassey's Battlefield Weapons Systems & Technology: Vol. 8). 160p. 1982. 40.00 (ISBN 0-08-028336-5); pap. 16.00 (ISBN 0-08-028337-3). Pergamon.

GUIDED MISSILES–GUIDANCE SYSTEMS

Blakelock, John H. Automatic Control of Aircraft & Missiles. LC 65-16402. 1965. 45.00 (ISBN 0-471-07930-8, Pub. by Wiley-Interscience). Wiley.

Northrop Institute of Technology. Electricity & Electronics for Aerospace Vehicles. 2nd ed. 1972. text ed. 16.95 (ISBN 0-07-047485-0, G). McGraw.

Roberson, R. E. & Farrior, J. S., eds. Guidance & Control. (Progress in Astronautics & Aeronautics: Vol. 8). 1962. 21.00 (ISBN 0-12-535108-9). Acad Pr.

GUIDED MISSILES–JUVENILE LITERATURE

Colby, C. B. Countdown: Rockets & Missiles for National Defense. rev. ed. LC 70-125328. (Illus.). (gr. 4-7). 1970. PLB 5.29 (ISBN 0-698-30056-4). Coward.

GUILD SOCIALISM

see Gild Socialism

GUILDFORD, RICHARD, SIR, 1455-1506

Ellis, Henry, ed. Pylgrymage of Sir Richard Guylforde to the Holy Land, A. D. 1506. LC 75-166023. (Camden Society, London. Publications, First Ser.: No. 51). Repr. of 1851 ed. 14.00 (ISBN 0-404-50151-6). AMS Pr.

GUILDS

see Gilds

GUILLAUME (CHANSON DE GESTE)

Robertson, Howard S. La Chanson de Willaume: A Critical Study. (Studies in the Romance Languages & Literatures: No. 65). 1967. pap. 5.00x (ISBN 0-8078-9065-0). U of NC Pr.

GUILLAUME D'AUVERGNE, BP. OF PARIS, d. 1249

Valois, Noel. Guillaume d'Auvergne: Eveque De Paris (1228-1249), Sa vie & Ses ouvrages (Medieval Studies Ser.) (Medieval Studies Ser.). (Fr.). Repr. of 1880 ed. lib. bdg. 27.50x (ISBN 0-697-00019-2). Irvington.

GUILLAUME DE CHAMPEAUX, BP., 1070?-1121

Michaud, E. Guillaume de Champeaux et les Ecoles de Paris. 2nd ed. (Medieval Studies Reprint Ser.). (Fr.). Repr. of 1867 ed. lib. bdg. 28.00x (ISBN 0-697-00011-7). Irvington.

GUILLAUME DE DEGUILLEVILLE, 14TH CENTURY

Wharey, James B. Study of the Sources of Bunyan's Allegories(with Special Reference to Deguileville's Pilgrimage of Man. LC 68-59038. 1968. Repr. of 1904 ed. 7.50 (ISBN 0-87752-120-4). Gordian.

GUILLAUME DE MACHAULT, 1284-1370

Calin, William. A Poet at the Fountain: Essays on the Narrative Verse of Guillaume de Machaut. LC 72-91663. (Studies in Romance Languages: No. 9). 264p. 1974. 13.00x (ISBN 0-8131-1297-4). U Pr of Ky.

Levarie, Siegmund. Guillaume De Machaut. LC 70-98309. (Music Ser). 1969. Repr. of 1954 ed. lib. bdg. 15.00 (ISBN 0-306-71831-6). Da Capo.

Reaney, Gilbert. Guillaume De Machaut. (Oxford Studies of Composers Ser). 72p. (Fr.). 1971. pap. 8.95x (ISBN 0-19-315218-5). Oxford U Pr.

Wimsatt, James I. The Marguerite Poetry of Guillaume de Machaut. (Studies in the Romance Languages & Literatures: No. 87). 1969. pap. 5.00x (ISBN 0-8078-9087-1). U of NC Pr.

GUILLAUME DE PALERNE

De Palerne, Guillaume. William of Palerne. LC 75-37599. 1975. lib. bdg. 40.00 (ISBN 0-8414-7549-0). Folcroft.

GUILLAUME D'ORANGE (CHANSON DE GESTE)

Suchier, Hermann, ed. Narbonnais, 2 Vols. 1965. Repr. of 1898 ed. Set. 61.50 (ISBN 0-384-40887-7); Set. pap. 54.00 (ISBN 0-685-92802-0). Johnson Repr.

GUILLEN, JORGE, 1893-

Guillen, Jorge. Guillen on Guillen: The Poetry & the Poet. Gibbons, Reginald & Geist, Anthony L., trs. LC 78-70299. 1979. 16.50x (ISBN 0-691-06392-3); pap. 5.95 (ISBN 0-691-01356-X). Princeton U Pr.

MacCurdy, C. Grant. Jorge Guillen. (World Author Ser.: No. 641). 1981. lib. bdg. 15.95 (ISBN 0-8057-6485-2). Twayne.

Yudin, Florence. The Vibrant Silence in Jorge Guilleu's Aire Nuestro. (Studies in the Romance Languages & Literatures: No. 141). 1974. pap. 6.00x (ISBN 0-8078-9141-X). U of NC Pr.

GUILT

see also Atonement; Shame; Sin

Agudo, Philomena, et al. Guilt: Issues of Emotional Living in an Age of Stress for Clergy & Religious. LC 80-10747. 144p. 1980. pap. 5.00 (ISBN 0-89571-008-0). Affirmation.

Becker, Arthur H. Guilt: Curse or Blessing. LC 77-72455. 1977. 7.95 (ISBN 0-8066-1599-0, 10-2913); pap. 3.95 (ISBN 0-8066-1588-5, 10-2912). Augsburg.

Caldwell, Louis O. You Can Stop Feeling Guilty. (Christian Counseling Aids Ser.). 1978. pap. 0.75 (ISBN 0-8010-2414-5). Baker Bk.

Cavanagh, Michael E. What to Do When You're Feeling Guilty. (Illus.). 1978. pap. 1.95 (ISBN 0-89570-149-9). Claretian Pubns.

Drakeford, John W. Integrity Therapy. LC 67-19396. 1974. pap. 4.95 (ISBN 0-8054-6702-5). Broadman.

Dyer, Wayne W. Your Erroneous Zones. LC 75-35621. (Funk & W Bk.). 256p. 1976. 10.95 (ISBN 0-308-10228-2). T Y Crowell.

Houselander, Caryll. Guilt. LC 76-131251. (Illus.). 1971. Repr. of 1952 ed. text ed. 10.00 (ISBN 0-87752-053-4). Gordian.

Hughes, Don. Free from Guilt & Condemnation. (Orig.). 1977. pap. 0.60 (ISBN 0-89274-048-5, HH-048). Harrison Hse.

Kurtz, E. Shame & Guilt: An Historical Perspective for Professionals. 1981. 3.50 (ISBN 0-89486-132-8). Hazelden.

Lewis, Helen B. Shame & Guilt in Neurosis. LC 75-128622. 1971. text ed. 22.50 (ISBN 0-8236-6075-3); pap. 6.95x (ISBN 0-8236-8307-9, 026075). Intl Univs Pr.

McKeating, Henry. Living with Guilt. LC 71-133000. 1971. pap. 1.95 (ISBN 0-8170-0515-3). Judson.

Mitscherlich, Alexander & Mitscherlich, Margarete. The Inability to Mourn: Principles of Collective Behavior. Placzek, Beverly R., tr. from Ger. LC 78-26060. 1978. pap. 27.50 (ISBN 0-8357-0343-6, ST-00020, Pub. by Grove). Univ Microfilms.

Moore, Marvin. How to Handle Guilt. (Better Living Ser.). 1977. pap. 0.95 (ISBN 0-8127-0158-5). Review & Herald.

Morano, Donald V. Existential Guilt: A Phenomenological Study. 175p. 1973. pap. text ed. 7.00x (ISBN 0-391-00674-6). Humanities.

Morris, Herbert. On Guilt & Innocence: Essays in Legal Philosophy & Moral Psychology. LC 72-89789. 1976. pap. 3.95 (ISBN 0-520-03944-0). U of Cal Pr.

Narramore, Bruce & Counts, Bill. Freedom from Guilt. LC 73-92358. 159p. 1974. pap. 4.95 (ISBN 0-88449-003-3, A424408). Vision Hse.

--Freedom from Guilt. LC 74-19862. Orig. Title: Guilt & Freedom. (Orig.). 1976. pap. 4.95 (ISBN 0-89081-001-X, 001X). Harvest Hse.

Piers, Gerhart & Singer, Milton B. Shame & Guilt. 112p. 1972. pap. 1.95x (ISBN 0-393-00649-2, Norton Lib). Norton.

Ross, Alf. On Guilt, Responsibility & Punishment. LC 73-94446. 1975. 21.50x (ISBN 0-520-02717-5). U of Cal Pr.

Shuler, J. L. Give Your Guilt Away. LC 72-79605. 1972. pap. 0.95 (ISBN 0-8163-0134-4, 07150-6). Pacific Pr Pub Assn.

Stein, Edward V. Guilt: Theory & Therapy. 1968. 6.00 (ISBN 0-664-20819-3). Westminster.

Tournier, Paul. Guilt & Grace. LC 62-7305. 1962. 8.95 (ISBN 0-06-068330-9, HarpR). Har-Row.

Trudeau, Garry. Guilty, Guilty, Guilty. LC 73-15162. (Illus.). 1974. pap. 1.95 (ISBN 0-03-012511-1). HR&W.

Warner, Paul L. Feeling Good About Feeling Bad. LC 78-59431. 1979. 4.95 (ISBN 0-8499-0104-9, 0104-9). Word Bks.

GUILT (LAW)

see also Criminal Intent; Negligence

Dyer, Wayne W. Your Erroneous Zones. 1981. pap. 2.75 (ISBN 0-380-01669-9, 51706). Avon.

GUINEA–POLITICS AND GOVERNMENT

Adamolekun, Ladipo. Sekou Toure's Guinea: An Eperiment in National Building. LC 76-17220. (Studies in African History: No. 12). 200p. 1976. 17.50x (ISBN 0-416-77840-2); pap. 10.95x (ISBN 0-416-77850-X). Methuen Inc.

Cabral, Amilcar. Revolution in Guinea: Selected Texts. Handyside, Richard, ed. & tr. LC 73-124084. 144p. 1970. pap. 3.95 (ISBN 0-85345-222-9, PB-2229). Monthly Rev.

Riviere, Claude. Guinea: The Mobilization of a People. Adloff, Virginia & Adloff, Richard, trs. LC 76-50262. (Africa in the Modern World Ser). (Illus.). 1977. 22.50x (ISBN 0-8014-0904-7). Cornell U Pr.

GUINEA (REGION)

Bergeron, Pierre. Les Voyages Fameux du Sieur Vincent le Blanc marseillais. (Bibliotheque Africaine Ser.). 625p. (Fr.). 1974. Repr. of 1649 ed. lib. bdg. 151.00x (ISBN 0-8287-0081-8, 72-2134). Clearwater Pub.

Bosman, Willem. Voyage de Guinee Contenant une Description Nouvelle et Tres Exacte de Cette Cote. (Bibliotheque Africaine Ser.). 565p. (Fr.). 1974. Repr. of 1705 ed. lib. bdg. 138.00x (ISBN 0-8287-0122-9, 72-2117). Clearwater Pub.

Bosman, William. New & Accurate Description of the Coast of Guinea: 1705. 4th & rev. ed. (Illus.). 577p. 1967. 40.00x (ISBN 0-7146-1793-8, F Cass Co). Biblio Dist.

De Zurara, Gomes E. Chronicle of the Discovery & Conquest of Guinea, 2 Vols. (Hakluy Society Ser.: Nos. 95 & 100). (Illus.). 1963. Repr. Set. 57.50 (ISBN 0-8337-0209-2). B Franklin.

Isert, Paul E. Voyages en Guinee et dans les Isles Caraibes, en Amerique. (Bibliotheque Africaine Ser.). 400p. (Fr.). 1974. Repr. of 1793 ed. lib. bdg. 101.50 (ISBN 0-8287-0458-9, 72-2116). Clearwater Pub.

Loyer, Godefroy. Relation du Voyage du Royaume d'Issigny, Cote d'Or, Pays de Guinee, en Afrique. (Bibliotheque Africaine Ser.). 318p. (Fr.). 1974. Repr. of 1714 ed. lib. bdg. 84.00x (ISBN 0-8287-0556-9, 72-2121). Clearwater Pub.

Montauban. Relation du Voyage du Sieur de Montauban en l'Annee 1695. (Bibliotheque Africaine Ser.). 44p. (Fr.). 1974. Repr. of 1698 ed. lib. bdg. 24.00x (ISBN 0-8287-0633-6, 72-2136). Clearwater Pub.

Mouser, Bruce L., ed. Guinea Journals: Journeys into Guinea-Conakry During the Sierra Leone Phase, 1800-1821. LC 79-62896. 1979. pap. text ed. 10.25 (ISBN 0-8191-0713-1). U Pr of Amer.

O'Toole, Thomas E. Historical Dictionary of Guinea: Republic of Guinea-Conakry. LC 77-28145. (African Historical Dictionaries Ser.: No. 16). 1978. 10.00 (ISBN 0-8108-1112-X). Scarecrow.

Smith, William. New Voyage to Guinea. 282p. 1967. Repr. of 1744 ed. 24.00x (ISBN 0-7146-1018-6, F Cass Co). Biblio Dist.

Snelgrave, William. New Account of Some Parts of Guinea & the Slave Trade. 1971. Repr. of 1734 ed. 24.00x (ISBN 0-7146-1898-5, F Cass Co). Biblio Dist.

U. S. Committee For UNICEF. Hi Neighbor Book No. 4: Guinea, India, Iran, Mexico, Portugal. (Illus.). (gr. 4-6). 4.95 (ISBN 0-8038-2981-7); pap. 2.00 (ISBN 0-8038-2980-9). Hastings.

GUINEA, FRENCH–SOCIAL LIFE AND CUSTOMS

Laye, Camara. The Dark Child. Kirkup, James, et al, trs. from Fr. 188p. 1954. 5.95 (ISBN 0-374-13472-3); pap. 3.95 (ISBN 0-374-50768-6, N365). FS&G.

GUINEA-BISSAU

Cabral, Amilcar. Return to the Source: Selected Speeches of Amilcar Cabral. Africa Information Service, ed. LC 74-7788. (Illus.). 128p. 1974. pap. 2.95 (ISBN 0-85345-347-0; PB3470). Monthly Rev.

Goulet, Denis. Looking at Guinea-Bissau: A New Nation's Development Strategy. LC 78-55460. (Occasional Papers: No. 9). 72p. 1978. 2.50 (ISBN 0-686-28695-2). Overseas Dev Council.

McCarthy, Joseph M. Guinea-Bissau & Cape Verde: A Comprehensive Bibliography. LC 76-24770. (Reference Library of Social Science Ser.: Vol. 27). 1977. lib. bdg. 21.00 (ISBN 0-8240-9908-7). Garland Pub.

Sarrazin, Chantal & Gjerstad, Ole. Sowing the First Harvest: Reconstruction in Guinea-Bissau. LC 78-50380. 2.95 (ISBN 0-919914-29-2). LSM Pr.

GUINEA-BISSAU–HISTORY

Benezet, A. Some Historical Account of Guinea. 131p. 1968. Repr. of 1788 ed. 24.00x (ISBN 0-7146-1888-8, F Cass Co). Biblio Dist.

Cabral, Amilcar. Unity & Struggle: Speeches & Writings. LC 79-2327. 1980. 16.50 (ISBN 0-85345-510-4, CL5104). Monthly Rev.

Chaliand, Gerard. Armed Struggle in Africa: With the Guerrillas in Portuguese Guinea. LC 72-81789. 1969. pap. 2.95 (ISBN 0-85345-179-6, PB1796). Monthly Rev.

Davidson, Basil. No Fist Is Big Enough to Hide the Sky: The Liberation of Guinea Bissau & Cape Verde. 208p. 1981. 25.00 (ISBN 0-905762-86-X, Pub. by Zed Pr England). Lawrence Hill.

Lobban, Richard. Historical Dictionary of the Republics of Guinea-Bissau & Cape Verde. LC 79-18227. (African Historical Dictionaries Ser.: No. 22). 209p. 1979. 11.00 (ISBN 0-8108-1240-1). Scarecrow.

Rodney, Walter. A History of the Upper Guinea Coast, 1545-1800. 1980. pap. 7.95 (ISBN 0-85345-546-5). Monthly Rev.

Urdang, Stephanie. Fighting Two Colonialisms: Women in Guinea-Bissau. LC 79-2329. (Illus.). 1979. 16.50 (ISBN 0-85345-511-2, CL5112); pap. 6.50 (ISBN 0-85345-524-4, PB5244). Monthly Rev.

Venter, Al, Jr. Report on Portugal's War in Guinea-Bissau. (Illus.). 1973. 3.00 (ISBN 0-686-23287-9). Munger Africana Lib.

GUINEA-PIGS

Axelrod, Jennifer. Breeding Guinea Pigs. 1980. 2.95 (ISBN 0-87666-929-1, KW-073). TFH Pubns.

Cooper, Gale & Schiller, Alan L. Anatomy of the Guinea Pig. LC 74-81866. (Commonwealth Fund Ser.). (Illus.). 432p. 1975. text ed. 40.00x (ISBN 0-674-03159-8). Harvard U Pr.

Elward, Margaret & Whiteway, Catherine E. Encyclopedia of Guinea Pigs. (Illus.). 224p. 1980. 9.95 (ISBN 0-87666-916-X, H-975). TFH Pubns.

Guinea Pigs. 1976. pap. text ed. 0.87 (ISBN 0-08-016237-1). British Bk Ctr.

Hammer, Gunnar. A Quantitative Cytochemical Study of Shock Wave Effects on Spiral Ganglion Cells. 1956. pap. 9.00 (ISBN 0-384-21250-6). Johnson Repr.

Keeling, C. H. Guinea Pigs. LC 79-126566. (The Pet Library). (Illus.). 67p. 1972. bds. 1.95 (ISBN 0-668-02380-5). Arco.

Mosesson, G. & Scher, S. Guinea Pigs & Other Laboratory Animals. 1972. text ed. 4.95 (ISBN 0-87666-200-9, PS689). TFH Pubns.

Ragland, Kay. Guinea Pigs. (Illus.). 1979. 2.95 (ISBN 0-87666-925-9, KW-016). TFH Pubns.

Roberts, Mervin F. Guinea Pigs for Beginners. (Illus.). 1972. pap. 2.00 (ISBN 0-87666-198-3, M-541). TFH Pubns.

Saiga Editors. Cavies (Guinea Pigs) 1981. 10.00x (ISBN 0-86230-010-X, Pub. by Saiga Pub). State Mutual Bk.

Wagner, Joseph E. & Manning, Patrick J., eds. The Biology of the Guinea Pig. 1976. 55.00 (ISBN 0-12-730050-3). Acad Pr.

Wersall, Jan. Studies in the Structure & Innervation of the Sensory Epithelium of the Cristae Ampullares in the Guinea Pig. Repr. of 1956 ed. pap. 9.00 (ISBN 0-384-66900-X). Johnson Repr.

GUINEY, LOUISE IMOGEN, 1861-1920

Fairbanks, Henry G. Louise Imogen Guiney. (U. S. Authors Ser.: No. 224). 1973. lib. bdg. 10.95 (ISBN 0-8057-0342-X). Twayne.

--Louise Imogen Guiney: Laureate of the Lost. LC 73-176128. 1972. 12.95x (ISBN 0-87343-039-5). Magi Bks.

GUITAR

Brosnac, Donald. The Electric Guitar: Its History & Constuction. (Illus.). 204p. 1975. pap. 6.95 (ISBN 0-915572-00-1). Panjandrum.

--An Introduction to Scientific Guitar Design. Clarke, Nicholas, ed. LC 79-50925. (Illus.). 1979. pap. text ed. 8.95 (ISBN 0-933224-01-X). Bold Strummer Ltd.

--The Steel String Guitar: Its History & Construction. 2nd rev ed. (Illus.). 112p. 1976. pap. 6.95 (ISBN 0-915572-26-5). Panjandrum.

Duncan, Charles. The Art of Classical Guitar Playing. (The Art of Ser.). (Illus.). 132p. (Orig.). 1980. pap. text ed. write for info. (ISBN 0-87487-079-8). Summy.

Evans, Tom & Evans, Mary A. Guitars: From the Renaissance to Rock. LC 77-4461. (Illus.). 1977. 19.95 (ISBN 0-448-22240-X). Paddington.

--Guitars: Music, History, Construction & Players from the Renaissance to Rock. (Illus.). 479p. 1978. 24.95 (ISBN 0-87196-321-3). Facts on File.

Fradd, Dale. Guitar. (Teach Yourself Ser.). 1975. pap. 5.95 (ISBN 0-679-10365-1). McKay.

Grunfeld, Frederic V. The Art & Times of the Guitar: An Illustrated History of Guitars & Guitarists. (Illus.). 340p. 1974. pap. 5.95 (ISBN 0-02-060670-2, Collier). Macmillan.

Guitar Player Magazine, ed. Putting a Band Together. 2.95 (ISBN 0-8256-9509-0). Guitar Player.

Guitar Player Magazine & Kriss, Eric, eds. Fix Your Axe: Easy Guitar Repairs You Can Do at Home. LC 75-27790. (Illus.). 72p. (Orig.). 1976. pap. 5.95 (ISBN 0-8256-9503-1). Guitar Player.

The Guitars Friend: Mail Order Guide to Musical Instruments & Supplies. LC 76-8072. (Orig.). 1977. pap. 4.95 (ISBN 0-8256-3072-X, Quick Fox). Music Sales.

Kamimoto, Hideo. Complete Guitar Repair. LC 74-76821. (Illus.). 192p. (Orig.). 1975. pap. 7.95 (ISBN 0-8256-0156-8, Oak). Music Sales.

Mongan, Norman. The History of the Guitar in Jazz. (Illus.). 240p. pap. 14.95 (ISBN 0-8256-0255-6). Music Sales.

Mottola, Tony. Play the Guitar in Thirty Minutes. (Orig.). 1964. pap. 3.95 (ISBN 0-346-12331-3). Cornerstone.

Noad, Frederick. The Classical Guitar. 1976. pap. 6.95 (ISBN 0-394-73138-7). Knopf.

--The Classical Guitar. (Illus., Orig.). 1976. pap. 7.95 (ISBN 0-8256-9952-5, Noad). Music Sales.

Overholtzer, Arthur E. Classic Guitar Making. LC 74-1079. (Illus.). 360p. (Orig.). 1974. 22.95 (ISBN 0-930534-01-8); pap. 14.95 (ISBN 0-930534-00-X). Brock Pub.

Pollack, Richard & Sloane, Irving. Guitar Repair: A Manual of Repair for Guitars & Fretted Instruments. 1973. 14.95 (ISBN 0-525-12002-5). Dutton.

Roth, Arlen. Slide Guitar. pap. 6.95 with recording (ISBN 0-8256-0162-2, Oak). Music Sales.

Sloane, Irving. Classic Guitar Construction. 1966. 10.95 (ISBN 0-525-08200-X). Dutton.

Straw Dog & Saslow, Richard. The Art of Ragtime Guitar. LC 73-94403. (Guitar Heritage Ser.). 96p. 1974. pap. 8.95 (ISBN 0-912910-04-6). Green Note Music.
Teeter, Don E. The Acoustic Guitar: Adjustment, Care, Maintenance, & Repair, Vol. II. LC 79-5962. (Illus.). 202p. 1980. 20.00 (ISBN 0-8061-1607-2). U of Okla Pr.
--The Acoustic Guitar: Adjustment, Care, Maintenance, & Repair, Vol. I. LC 74-5962. (Illus.). 250p. 1975. 22.50 (ISBN 0-8061-1219-0). U of Okla Pr.
Traum, Happy. Bluegrass Guitar. LC 74-77312. (Illus.). 1974. pap. 6.95 with recording (ISBN 0-8256-0153-3, 000153, Oak). Music Sales.
Turnbull, Harvey. The Guitar: From the Sixteenth Century to the Present. LC 72-9038. 1974. 12.50 (ISBN 0-684-13215-X, ScribT). Scribner.
Tyler, James. The Early Guitar: A History & Handbook. (Early Music Ser.). (Illus.). 176p. (Orig.). 1980. pap. text ed. 22.95x (ISBN 0-19-323182-4). Oxford U Pr.
Wade, Graham. Traditions of the Classical Guitar. (Illus.). 270p. 1981. 25.00 (ISBN 0-7145-3794-2). Riverrun NY.
--Your Book of the Guitar. (Your Book Ser.). (Illus.). 64p. (gr. 3-8). 1980. 8.95 (ISBN 0-571-11553-5, Pub. by Faber & Faber). Merrimack Bk Serv.
Young, David R. The Steel String Guitar: Construction & Repair. 208p. 1975. 14.95 (ISBN 0-8019-5959-4). Chilton.

GUITAR-INSTRUCTION AND STUDY

Abe & Malka. One Hundred Guitar Accompaniment Patterns. LC 73-92398. (Orig.). 1974. pap. 7.95 (ISBN 0-8256-2812-1, Amsco Music). Music Sales.
Adler, Joseph. Guitar for a Singing Planet. 1976. pap. text ed. 9.95 (ISBN 0-8403-1428-0). Kendall-Hunt.
Almeida, Laurindo. Guitar Tutor. 8.95 (ISBN 0-685-52340-3). Criterion Mus.
Alzofon, David. Mastering Guitar. LC 80-24682. 1981. write for info. (ISBN 0-671-25421-9, Fireside). S&S.
Baxter, Bob. Baxter's Complete Beginning Folk Guitar Manual. (Illus.). 168p. pap. 8.95 (ISBN 0-8256-2601-3, Amsco Music). Music Sales.
--Baxter's Private Guitar Lessons, 2 bks. LC 76-17437. 1976. pap. 2.95 ea. (Acorn); Bk. 1. pap. (ISBN 0-8256-2371-5); Bk. 2. pap. (ISBN 0-8256-2372-3). Music Sales.
Bickford, Vahadah O. Method for Classic Guitar. pap. 8.00 (ISBN 0-686-09073-X). Peer-Southern.
Bobri, Valdimir. The Segovia Technique. (Illus.). 1977. pap. 5.95 (ISBN 0-02-079240-9, Collier). Macmillan.
Buckingham, Jack. The Accompaniment Guitar: A Beginner's Guide to Song Accompaniment for Individual or Classroom Use. (Illus.). 80p. (gr. 6-12). 1979. pap. 5.95 (ISBN 0-686-64082-9, 05065). Fischer Inc NY.
Camp, Christopher. How to Play Ragtime Guitar. LC 75-16976. (Illus., Orig.). 1976. pap. 2.95 (ISBN 0-8256-2351-0, Acorn). Music Sales.
Carcassi, M. Classical Guitar Method. rev. ed. 128p. 1962. pap. 4.95 (ISBN 0-686-64092-6, 0762). Fischer Inc NY.
Christiansen, Michael. Strumming, Finger-Picking, Playing the Melody: A Beginning Guitar Method for Group, Individual, or Self-Instruction. 112p. 1980. pap. text ed. 9.95 (ISBN 0-8403-2247-X). Kendall-Hunt.
Daniels, Richard. The Heavy Guitar Bible. (Illus.). 104p. (YA) 1979. pap. 10.00 (ISBN 0-89524-066-1, 9105). Cherry Lane.
Darling, Erik & Riker, Tom. Chords for Guitar. LC 79-9702. (Illus.). 1980. pap. 5.95 (ISBN 0-02-870410-X). Schirmer Bks.
DeJay, Ralph. Guitar-Plus. (Illus.). 1979. pap. 4.00 (ISBN 0-682-49408-9). Exposition.
De Mause, Alan. Guitar Power. LC 75-16979. (Illus., Orig.). 1976. pap. 5.95 (ISBN 0-8256-2816-4, Amsco Music). Music Sales.
Elements of Guitar: Workbook One. (Self Teaching Education Ser.). 1975. spiral bdg 1.95 (ISBN 0-685-52517-1). Macgregor.
Erbsen, Wayne. The Complete & Painless Guide to the Guitar for Young Beginner. (Illus.). 64p. (gr. 4-12). 1979. pap. 5.95 (ISBN 0-686-64085-3, PCB 111). Fischer Inc NY.
Evans, Roger. How to Play Guitar. 1980. 8.95 (ISBN 0-312-39608-2); pap. 4.95 (ISBN 0-312-39609-0). St Martin.
Fahey, John. The Best of John Fahey. Lescroat, John, ed. LC 77-82830. (Illus.). 176p. 1978. pap. 7.95 (ISBN 0-8256-9515-5). Guitar Player.
Friedman, Jay. Bass Guitar Chords, Arpeggios & Studies. 4.95 (ISBN 0-686-15876-8). D Zdenek Pubns.
--Bass Guitar Complete. 7.95 (ISBN 0-686-15877-6). D Zdenek Pubns.
--Bass Guitar Scales & Melodic Patterns. 4.95 (ISBN 0-686-15875-X). D Zdenek Pubns.
Gidcomb, Johnny & Barron, Emily. How to Play the Guitar. LC 72-128458. (Illus.). 1970. pap. 4.95 (ISBN 0-87695-102-7). Aurora Pubs.
--How to Play the Guitar. LC 72-128458. (Illus.). 1970. pap. 4.95 (ISBN 0-87695-102-7). Aurora Pubs.
Goran, Ulf., et al. Play a Tune on Recorder & Guitar. Pehrsson, Clas, ed. (Illus.). 32p. (Incl. a 33.3 record). 1975. pap. 6.00 (ISBN 0-19-322206-X). Oxford U Pr.
Green Note Music Publications Staff. Country Rock Guitar. Straw Dog, ed. (Contemporary Guitar Styles Ser.). (Illus.). 1978. pap. 8.95 (ISBN 0-912910-07-0). Green Note Music.
--Electric Blues Guitar. (Contemporary Guitar Styles Ser). (Illus.). 96p. (Orig., Prog. Bk.). 1977. pap. 8.95 (ISBN 0-912910-05-4). Green Note Music.
Greene, Ted. Chord Chemistry. 5.95 (ISBN 0-686-15871-7). D Zdenek Pubns.
--Modern Chord Progressions, Vol. 1. 5.95 (ISBN 0-686-15873-3). D Zdenek Pubns.
Gregory, Jim & Vinson, Harvey. Bass Guitar. new ed. (Illus., Orig.). 1973. pap. 4.95 (ISBN 0-8256-4061-X, Consolidated). Music Sales.
Gross, David. Teach Yourself Rock Bass. 64p. pap. 3.95 (ISBN 0-8256-2202-6). Music Sales.
Grossman, Stefan. Contemporary Fingerpicking Guitar Workshop. 1981. 5.95 (ISBN 0-89898-055-0). Almo Pubns.
Guide for the Guitarist. LC 75-14546. 1974. pap. 1.95 (ISBN 0-915866-06-4). Am Cath Pr.
Heinz, Cecilia & Straw Dog. Improvising Blues Guitar: A Programmed Manual of Instruction. LC 70-143775. (Contemporary Guitar Styles Ser.). (Illus.). 84p. (Prog. Bk.). 1970. pap. 6.95 (ISBN 0-912910-01-1). Green Note Music.
How to Arrange for Solo Guitar. (Illus.). pap. 2.50 (ISBN 0-686-09071-3). Peer-Southern.
How to Play the Guitar. 1981. 1.95 (ISBN 0-88284-152-1). Alfred Pub.
Irving, Darrel. A Fingerboard Foundation for the Classical Guitar. (Illus.). 96p. 1981. pap. text ed. 7.95 (ISBN 0-9605912-0-6). Calliope Music.
Ives, Burl. Guitar for Beginners. 1976. 9.95 (ISBN 0-89328-003-8); pap. 5.95 (ISBN 0-89328-002-X). Lorenz Pr.
Jacobs, Ruth T. The Guitar Experience: Learning the E-Z Numbers Way to Play Guitar Even If You Do Not Read Music. (Illus.). 304p. 1980. 21.95 (ISBN 0-13-371625-2, Spec); pap. 9.95 (ISBN 0-13-371617-1). P-H.
Jahnel, Franz. Manual of Guitar Technology. (Illus.). 240p. 1981. Repr. of 1963 ed. 80.00x (ISBN 0-686-74791-7). Bold Strummer Ltd.
Kessel, Barney. The Guitar. LC 66-29862. 1967. 19.95 (ISBN 0-685-52341-1). Criterion Mus.
Knuth, Alice & Berg, Richard C. Learning Music with the Guitar. 1976. pap. text ed. 10.95x (ISBN 0-534-00308-7). Wadsworth Pub.
Laine, Denny. Denny Laine: How to Play the Guitar. (Illus.). 110p. 1980. 10.95 (ISBN 0-517-54207-2, Harmony); pap. 6.95 (ISBN 0-517-54208-0, Harmony). Crown.
Lawrence, Victor J. Easy Steps to Playing Guitar, Vol. I. 1946. 1.75 (ISBN 0-913650-27-7). Volkwein Bros.
--Easy Steps to Playing Guitar, Vol. II. 1954. 1.75 (ISBN 0-913650-28-5). Volkwein Bros.
--Easy Steps to Playing Guitar, Vol. III. 1954. 2.50 (ISBN 0-913650-29-3). Volkwein Bros.
--Elementary Guitar Method. 1943. 3.00 (ISBN 0-913650-30-7). Volkwein Bros.
--Teaching Spanish Guitar: In Advanced Modern Style. 1942. 3.50 (ISBN 0-913650-31-5). Volkwein Bros.
Lehrer, Oscar J. Complete Method for Voice & Guitar: Instruction Manual in Accompaniment Playing & Singing. 1941. 1.00 (ISBN 0-913650-26-9). Volkwein Bros.
Michaels, Mark. Teach Yourself Rhythm Guitar. 64p. pap. 3.95 (ISBN 0-8256-2201-8). Music Sales.
Murants, Ivare. Play the Plectrum Guitar. (Illus.). 4.50x (ISBN 0-392-04179-0, LTB). Sportshelf.
Niles, John J. Ballad Book of John Jacob Niles. 1971. Repr. of 1960 ed. 6.00 (ISBN 0-486-22716-2). Dover.
Noad, Frederick. Solo Guitar Playing. (Illus., Orig.). 1968. pap. 3.95 (ISBN 0-02-870720-6, Collier). Macmillan.
Noad, Frederick M. The Guitar Songbook. LC 69-16492. 1969. pap. 6.95 (ISBN 0-02-871730-9). Schirmer Bks.
--Playing the Guitar. 3rd ed. LC 80-5494. (Illus.). 1981. pap. 9.95 (ISBN 0-02-871990-5). Schirmer Bks.
--Playing the Guitar. 2nd ed. (Quick & Easy Ser.). (Illus.). 160p. 1972. pap. 2.95 (ISBN 0-02-871710-4, Collier). Macmillan.
--Solo Guitar Playing, Book 1. 2nd ed. LC 76-12833. 1976. pap. 9.95 (ISBN 0-02-871680-9). Schirmer Bks.
--Solo Guitar Playing, Book II. LC 77-2529. (Illus.). 1978. pap. 7.95 (ISBN 0-02-871690-6). Schirmer Bks.
Novick, Adam. Harmonics for Electric Bass. (Illus.). 76p. (Orig.). 1981. pap. 7.95 (ISBN 0-8256-9943-6, 640000). Free-Bass.
Pearse, John. Frets & Fingers: A Guitar Player's Manual. LC 77-20937. (Illus.). 1978. 9.95 (ISBN 0-448-22837-8). Paddington.
--The Guitarist's Picture Chord Encyclopedia. (Illus.). 310p. 1978. pap. 9.95 (ISBN 0-8256-2199-2, Amsco Music). Music Sales.
Reed, Harry D. Classroom Guitar: A Teacher's Guide to Self-Taught Instruction. 4.00 (ISBN 0-88247-178-3). R & E Res Assoc.
Ring, Ken. Hey! Let's Play the Folk Guitar. 1972. 5.50x (ISBN 0-8002-1490-0). Intl Pubns Serv.
Roth, Arlen. How to Play Blues Guitar. LC 75-32888. (Illus., Orig.). 1976. pap. 2.95 (ISBN 0-8256-2350-2, Acorn). Music Sales.
Saslow, Richard & Straw Dog. Slide Guitar: A Record Book Guide to Electric Lead & Traditional Slide & Bottleneck Styles. LC 72-76529. (Contemporary Guitar Styles Ser.). (Illus.). 82p. (Orig., Prog. Bk.). 1972. pap. 8.95 (ISBN 0-912910-02-X). Green Note Music.
Segovia, Andres & Mendoza, George. Andres Segovia, My Book of the Guitar: Guidance for the Young Beginner. LC 79-10277. (Illus.). 1979. 9.95 (ISBN 0-529-05539-2). Philomel.
Shinn, Duane. How to Play "Chord" Guitar in Ten Days. 32p. 1975. pap. 6.95 (ISBN 0-912732-12-1). Duane Shinn.
Silverman, Jerry. Beginning the Folk Guitar. (Illus.). 96p. 1964. pap. 7.95 (ISBN 0-8256-0015-4, 000015, Oak). Music Sales.
--Folk Guitar - Folk Song. LC 77-71706. (Illus.). 1977. 35.00x (ISBN 0-8128-2264-1); pap. 5.95 (ISBN 0-8128-2255-2). Stein & Day.
--Folksinger's Guitar Guide. (Illus.). 1962. pap. 4.95 (ISBN 0-8256-0013-8, 000013, Oak). Music Sales.
--How to Play the Guitar. LC 68-14557. 1968. pap. 5.95 (ISBN 0-385-09862-6, Dolp). Doubleday.
Sloane, Irving. Steel-String Guitar Construction. (Illus.). 1975. 14.95 (ISBN 0-87690-172-0). Dutton.
Smith, Gary R. & Stuart, Martin. Studies in Modern Guitar. LC 77-75479. 1977. pap. 9.95 (ISBN 0-8497-5500-X, WE4, Pub by Kjos West). Kjos.
Sor, F. Method for the Spanish Guitar. LC 77-158960. (Music Ser). 1971. Repr. lib. bdg. 17.50 (ISBN 0-306-70188-X). Da Capo.
Sor, Ferdinand. Method for the Spanish Guitar. Merrick, A., tr. (Illus.). 1980. pap. text ed. 5.95 (ISBN 0-306-80121-3). Da Capo.
Straw Dog. The Art of Ragtime Guitar. LC 73-94403. (Green Note Musical Publications Ser.). (Illus.). 1975. Repr. of 1974 ed. 10.95 (ISBN 0-02-871300-1); pap. 6.95 (ISBN 0-02-870990-X). Schirmer Bks.
--Improvising Blues Guitar. LC 70-143775. (Green Note Musical Publications Ser.). (Illus.). 1975. 10.95 (ISBN 0-02-871290-0); pap. 6.95 (ISBN 0-02-870980-2). Schirmer Bks.
--Improvising Rock Guitar. LC 72-92915. (Green Note Music Publications Ser.). (Illus.). 1975. Repr. of 1973 ed. 12.95 (ISBN 0-02-871280-3); pap. 5.95 (ISBN 0-02-870970-5). Schirmer Bks.
--Slide Guitar. LC 72-76529. (Green Note Musical Publications Ser.). (Illus.). 1975. 10.95 (ISBN 0-02-871310-9); pap. 6.95 (ISBN 0-02-871000-2). Schirmer Bks.
Straw Dog, et al. Improvising Rock Guitar: The Most Comprehensive Guide to Lead-Style Rock Guitar Ever Devised. LC 72-92915. (Contemporary Guitar Styles Ser.). (Illus.). 112p. (Orig., Prog. Bk.). 1973. pap. 8.95 (ISBN 0-912910-03-8). Green Note Music.
Swanson. Music Fund Through Folksong. 1977. 12.95x (ISBN 0-534-00505-5). Wadsworth Pub.
Swears, Linda. Discovering the Guitar: Teach Yourself to Play. (Illus.). 96p. 1981. PLB 7.20 (ISBN 0-688-00718-X); pap. 6.95 (ISBN 0-688-00717-1). Morrow.
Tarshis, Steve. Teach Yourself Lead Guitar. 64p. pap. 3.95 (ISBN 0-8256-2200-X). Music Sales.
Taussig, Harry. Teach Yourself Guitar. (Illus.). 150p. pap. 6.95 (ISBN 0-8256-0010-3, Pub. by Oak). Music Sales.
Taussig, Harry A. Advanced Guitar. 128p. 1981. pap. 5.95 (ISBN 0-8256-0163-0). Music Sales.
Teachers Guide for the Classroom Guitar. 1974. spiral bdg. 4.95 (ISBN 0-685-40268-1). Macgregor.
Timmerman, Maurine & Griffith, Celeste. Guitar in the Classroom. 2nd ed. 144p. 1976. pap. text ed. write for info. plastic comb (ISBN 0-697-03470-4). Wm C Brown.
Traum, Happy. Children's Guitar Guide. (Illus., Orig.). (gr. 4-6). 1969. pap. 3.95 (ISBN 0-8256-2141-0, Amsco Music). Music Sales.
--Finger-Picking Styles for Guitar. (Illus.). 1967. pap. 4.95 (ISBN 0-8256-0005-7, 000005, Oak). Music Sales.
--Folk Guitar As a Profession. Milano, Dominic, ed. LC 76-57470. (Illus.). 70p. 1977. pap. 5.95 (ISBN 0-8256-9507-4). Guitar Player.
--The Guitarist's Chord Manual. (Illus.). pap. 2.95 (ISBN 0-8256-2134-8, Amsco). Music Sales.
--The Joy of Guitar. (Orig.). 1967. pap. 4.95 (ISBN 0-8256-8000-X, Yorktown). Music Sales.
Vinson, Harvey. Lead Guitar. (Orig.). 1972. pap. 5.95 (ISBN 0-8256-4058-X, Consolidated). Music Sales.
--Rhythm Guitar. (Orig.). 1969. pap. 5.95 (ISBN 0-8256-4082-2, Consolidated). Music Sales.
--Rock Chord Guide. LC 70-85514. (Illus., Orig.). 1970. pap. 6.95 (ISBN 0-8256-2147-X, Amsco Music). Music Sales.
Wheeler, Tom. The Guitar Book: A Handbook for Electric & Acoustic Guitarists. rev. ed. LC 77-11791. 1978. 21.95 (ISBN 0-06-014579-X, HarpT). Har-Row.
White, Verdine & Satterfield, Louis. Playing the Bass Guitar. Schwartz, Norman, ed. (Illus.). 100p. (Orig.). 1978. pap. 6.95 (ISBN 0-89705-011-8). Almo Pubns.

GUITAR MUSIC

Atkins, Chet & Knowles, John. Chet Atkins Note-for-Note. LC 75-14957. 72p. (Orig.). 1978. pap. 5.95 (ISBN 0-8256-9510-4). Guitar Player.
Bobri, V. & Miller, Carl. Two Guitars. 1972. pap. 3.95 (ISBN 0-02-060140-9, Collier). Macmillan.
Bobri, Vladimir & Miller, Carl. A Musical Voyage with Two Guitars. LC 73-10568. (Illus.). 176p. 1974. pap. 5.95 (ISBN 0-02-060150-6, Collier). Macmillan.
The Flamenco Guitar. (Illus.). 200p. 15.00 (ISBN 0-686-09074-8); companion instruction lp 6.98 (ISBN 0-686-09075-6). Peer-Southern.
Folk Music Accompaniment for Guitar. pap. 2.95 (ISBN 0-686-09070-5). Peer-Southern.
Goran, Ulf. Play Guitar. Britten, Paul, tr. (Illus.). 48p. 1974. pap. 5.75 (ISBN 0-19-322210-8). Oxford U Pr.
--Play Together for Voices & Guitar. Britten, Paul, tr. 16p. 1974. pap. 3.25 (ISBN 0-19-322212-4). Oxford U Pr.
Green Note Music Publications Staff. Country Rock Guitar, Vol. 2. (Guitar Transcription Ser.). 1980. pap. 7.25 (ISBN 0-912910-10-0). Green Note Music.
--Improvising Blues Guitar, Vol. 2. (Guitar Transcription Ser.). 1980. pap. 7.25 (ISBN 0-912910-11-9). Green Note Music.
--Improvising Rock Guitar, Vol. 2. (Guitar Transcription Ser.). 1980. pap. 7.25 (ISBN 0-912910-08-9). Green Note Music.
--Improvising Rock Guitar, Vol. 3. (Guitar Transcription Ser.). 1980. pap. 7.25 (ISBN 0-912910-09-7). Green Note Music.
Guitar Chord Dictionary. 1981. 3.50 (ISBN 0-88284-153-X). Alfred Pub.
Guitar Chord Encyclopedia. 256p. 1980. pap. 2.49 (ISBN 0-8256-3206-4, Quick Fox). Music Sales.
Guitar Player Magazine, ed. Jazz Guitarists. (Illus.). 120p. 5.95 (ISBN 0-8256-9508-2). Guitar Player.
La Guitarra Flamenco: Spanish Text Edition of 'the Flamenco Guitar' 15.00 (ISBN 0-686-09076-4). Peer-Southern.
Insta Chord for Guitar. pap. 2.95 (ISBN 0-686-09072-1). Peer-Southern.
Knuth, Alice & Berg, Richard C. Learning Music with the Guitar. 1976. pap. text ed. 10.95x (ISBN 0-534-00308-7). Wadsworth Pub.
McKeown, Beverly. Guitar Songbook with Instructions. 1975. pap. text ed. 9.95 (ISBN 0-395-18648-X). HM.
Noad, Frederick. The Classical Guitar. (Illus., Orig.). 1976. pap. 7.95 (ISBN 0-8256-9952-5, Noad). Music Sales.
Noad, Frederick M. The Guitar Songbook. LC 69-16492. 1969. pap. 6.95 (ISBN 0-02-871730-9). Schirmer Bks.
Nunes, Warren, ed. Jazz Guitar Chord Bible. 190p. (Orig.). 1979. pap. 9.95 (ISBN 0-89705-049-5). Almo Pubns.
Okun, Milton & Fox, Dan, eds. Pocket Guitar. (Pocket Guitar Ser.). (Orig.). (YA) 1980. pap. 3.95 (ISBN 0-89524-113-7, 8801). Cherry Lane.
Pennington, Neid D. & Buelow, George. The Spanish Baroque Guitar, Including a Transcription of Santiago de Murcia's Passacalles y Orbas (1732) (Studies in Musicology: No. 46). 1981. price not set (ISBN 0-8357-1188-9, Pub. by UMI Res Pr). Univ Microfilms.
Pinnell, Richard T. Francesco Corbetta & the Baroque Guitar: With a Transcription of His Works, 2 vols. Buelow, George, ed. (Studies in Musicology: No. 25). 714p. 1980. Set. 49.95 (ISBN 0-8357-1140-4, Pub. by UMI Res Pr); Vol. 1. (ISBN 0-8357-1141-2); Vol. 2. (ISBN 0-8357-1142-0). Univ Microfilms.
Preas, Jerry L. Having Fun with Guitar & Electronic Music. 52p. (Orig.). 1981. pap. 3.95 (ISBN 0-686-73273-1). Texan-Am Pub.
Tyler, James. The Early Guitar: A History & Handbook. (Early Music Ser.). (Illus.). 176p. (Orig.). 1980. pap. text ed. 22.95x (ISBN 0-19-323182-4). Oxford U Pr.

Washington, Joe, ed. The Beatles for Classical Guitar. LC 74-32651. (Illus.). 88p. 1975. pap. 6.95 (ISBN 0-8256-2661-7, Amsco Music). Music Sales.

GUITAR MUSIC–DISCOGRAPHY

Pickow, Peter. The Original Guitar Case Chord Book. 48p. pap. 1.95 (ISBN 0-8256-2367-7). Music Sales.

Rezits, Joseph. Guitar Music in Print. LC 80-84548. 500p. (Orig.). 1981. pap. 65.00 (ISBN 0-8497-7802-6, PM9, Pub. by Palma). Kjos.

GUITARISTS

Crockett, Jim, ed. The Guitar Player Book. rev. ed. LC 79-2350. (Illus.). 416p. 1979. pap. 9.95 (ISBN 0-394-17169-1, E739, Ever). Grove.

Guitar Player Magazine, ed. Rock Guitarists, Vol. I. LC 74-25845. (Illus.). 176p. (Orig.). 1975. pap. 6.95 (ISBN 0-8256-9505-8). Guitar Player.

Segovia, Andres. Segovia: An Autobiography of the Years 1893-1920. (Illus.). 1976. 14.95 (ISBN 0-02-609080-5, 60908). Macmillan.

Tobler, John. Guitar Heroes. LC 78-439. (Illus.). 1978. 8.95 (ISBN 0-312-35320-0). St Martin.

GUITEAU, CHARLES JULIUS, 1841-1882

Rosenberg, Charles E. Trial of the Assassin Guitean: Psychiatry & Law in the Gilded Age. LC 68-16713. 1976. pap. 4.95 (ISBN 0-226-72717-3, P682, Phoen). U of Chicago Pr.

--Trial of the Assassin Guiteau: Psychiatry & the Law in the Gilded Age. LC 68-16712. (Illus.). 1968. 8.00x (ISBN 0-226-72716-5). U of Chicago Pr.

GUITRY, SACHA, 1885-

Knapp, Bettina L. Sacha Guitry. (Theatrical Arts Ser.). 1981. lib. bdg. 14.95 (ISBN 0-8057-9278-3). Twayne.

GUIZOT, FRANCOIS PIERRE GUILLAUME, 1787-1874

Brush, Elizabeth P. Guizot in the Early Years of the Orleanist Monarchy. LC 74-2319. (University of Illinois Studies in the Social Sciences). 236p. 1975. Repr. of 1929 ed. 21.00 (ISBN 0-86527-090-2). Fertig.

Bullen, Roger. Palmerston, Guizot & the Collapse of the Entente Cordiale. (University of London Historical Studies: No. 36). 380p. 1974. text ed. 36.50x (ISBN 0-485-13136-6, Athlone Pr). Humanities.

Johnson, Douglas W. Guizot: Aspects of French History, 1787-1874. LC 75-35335. (Illus.). 469p. 1976. Repr. of 1963 ed. lib. bdg. 25.00x (ISBN 0-8371-8566-1, JOGUZ). Greenwood.

GUJARAT

Chaube, Jharkhande. History of Gujarat Kingdom: 1458-1537. LC 75-901629. 1975. 14.00 (ISBN 0-88386-573-4). South Asia Bks.

Neubauer, Jutta J. The Stepwells of Gujarat: In Art - Historical Perspective. 118p. 1981. text ed. 65.00x (ISBN 0-391-02284-9). Humanities.

Pearson, M. N. Merchants & Rulers in Gujarat: The Response to the Portuguese in the Sixteenth Century. 1976. 22.75x (ISBN 0-520-02809-0). U of Cal Pr.

GUJARAT, INDIA (STATE)

Majmudar, M. R. Gujarat: Its Art Heritage. (Illus.). 1968. 11.00x (ISBN 0-8002-1485-4). Intl Pubns Serv.

Pocock, David. Mind, Body & Wealth: A Study of Belief & Practice in an Indian Village. 187p. 1973. 16.50x (ISBN 0-87471-415-X). Rowman.

Shah, Ghanshyam. Protest Movements in Two Indian States: A Study of Gujarat & Bihar Movements. 1977. 11.00x (ISBN 0-8364-0449-1). South Asia Bks.

GUJARATI LANGUAGE

Lambert, H. M. Gujarati Language Course. LC 68-23180. 1970. 44.00 (ISBN 0-521-07157-7). Cambridge U Pr.

Tisdall, William S. Simplified Grammar of the Gujarati Language. LC 61-13642. 13.50 (ISBN 0-8044-0711-8). Ungar.

GUJRI LANGUAGE

see Urdu Language

GULAB SINGH, MAHARAJAH OF KASHMIR, 1792-1857

Singh, Bawa S. The Jammu Fox: A Biography of Maharaja Gulab Singh of Kashmir, 1792-1857. LC 73-23023. (Illus.). 291p. 1974. 15.00x (ISBN 0-8093-0652-2). S Ill U Pr.

GULF STATES

Delanglez, Jean. El Rio Del Espiritu Santo: An Essay on the Cartography of the Gulf Coast & the Adjacent Territory During the 16th & 17th Centuries. LC 48-2640. (Monograph Ser.: No. 21). (Illus.). 1945. 6.50x (ISBN 0-930060-03-2). US Cath Hist.

Gulf Coast History & Humanities Conference. The Americanization of the Gulf Coast: Proceedings. Ellsworth, Lucius F., ed. 1972. pap. 6.95 (ISBN 0-686-05551-9). Historic Pensacola.

Gulf Coast History & Humanities Conference 1975. The Cultural Legacy of the Gulf Coast 1870-1940: Proceedings. Ellsworth, Linda V., ed. (Illus.). 1977. 10.95 (ISBN 0-686-16729-5); pap. 6.95 (ISBN 0-686-16730-9). Historic Pensacola.

McWilliams, Richebourg G., ed. & tr. Iberville's Gulf Journals. (Illus.). 208p. 1981. 16.50 (ISBN 0-8173-0049-X). U of Ala Pr.

GULF STREAM

Brindze, Ruth. Gulf Stream. (Illus.). (gr. 4-7). 1945. 6.95 (ISBN 0-8149-0279-0). Vanguard.

Kohl, J. G. Geschichte des Golfstroms und Seiner Erforschung. (Illus., Ger.). 1868. text ed. 13.25x (ISBN 90-6041-031-9). Humanities.

Stommmel, Henry. The Gulf Stream: A Physical & Dynamical Description. (California Library Reprint Ser). 1977. Repr. of 1964 ed. 24.00x (ISBN 0-520-03307-8). U of Cal Pr.

Worthington, L. V. On the North Atlantic Circulation. LC 76-17244. (Oceanographic Studies: No. 6). (Illus.). 112p. 1977. 16.50x (ISBN 0-8018-1742-0). Johns Hopkins.

GULICK, LUTHER HALSEY, 1865-1918

Dorgan, Ethel J. Luther Halsey Gulick: 1865-1918. LC 75-176726. (Columbia University. Teachers College. Contributions to Education: No. 635). Repr. of 1934 ed. 17.50 (ISBN 0-404-55635-3). AMS Pr.

GULLS

see also California Gull; Herring-Gull

Bent, Arthur C. Life Histories of North American Gulls & Terns. (Illus.). 9.50 (ISBN 0-8446-1637-0). Peter Smith.

--Life Histories of North American Gulls & Terns. (Illus.). 1921. pap. 5.50 (ISBN 0-486-21029-4). Dover.

Howell, Thomas R., et al. Breeding Biology of the Gray Gull, Larus Modestus. (Publications in Zoology: Vol. 104). 1975. pap. 8.50x (ISBN 0-520-09516-2). U of Cal Pr.

Paca, Lillian G. Sea Gulls & Such: Shore Birds of the Pacific Coast. LC 61-17177. (Illus., Orig.). 1961. pap. 1.95 (ISBN 0-87015-103-7). Pacific Bks.

Schreiber, Elizabeth Ann & Schreiber, Ralph W. Wonders of Sea Gulls. LC 75-11437. (Wonders Ser.). (Illus.). 80p. (gr. 3-7). 1975. PLB 5.95 (ISBN 0-396-07200-3). Dodd.

Scott, Jack D. & Sweet, Ozzie. The Gulls of Smuttynose Island. LC 77-7870. (Illus.). (gr. 6-8). 1977. 8.95 (ISBN 0-399-20618-3). Putnam.

Wright, Dare. Look at a Gull. (Illus.). (gr. k-3). 1967. PLB 4.99 (ISBN 0-394-91628-X, BYR). Random.

GUM ELASTIC

see Rubber

GUMBRIN

see Bentonite

GUMS–DISEASES

see also Oral Manifestations of General Diseases

Cross. Gingivitis. 1977. 10.95 (ISBN 0-8151-2018-4). Year Bk Med.

GUMS AND RESINS

see also Gums and Resins, Synthetic; Ion Exchange Resins; Naval Stores; also names of specific gums and resins

Future for Water-Based Resins. 1978. 725.00 (ISBN 0-89336-120-8, C-012). BCC.

Glicksman, M. Gum Technology in the Food Industry. (Food Science & Technology Ser). 1969. 68.00 (ISBN 0-12-286350-X). Acad Pr.

Knop, A. & Scheib, W. Chemistry & Application of Phenolic Resins. LC 78-10967. (Polymers: Properties & Applications Vol. 3). (Illus.). 1979. 56.60 (ISBN 0-387-09051-7). Springer-Verlag.

Mantell, Charles L. Water-Soluble Gums. (Illus.). 1965. Repr. of 1947 ed. 19.75 (ISBN 0-02-848800-8). Hafner.

May, Clayton A., ed. Resins for Aerospace. LC 80-15342. (ACS Symposium Ser.: No. 132). 1980. 48.00 (ISBN 0-8412-0567-1). Am Chemical.

Whistler, R. L. & BeMiller, J. N., eds. Industrial Gums: Polysaccharides & Their Derivatives. 2nd ed. 1973. 75.50 (ISBN 0-12-746252-X). Acad Pr.

GUMS AND RESINS, SYNTHETIC

see also Acrylic Resins; Epoxy Resins; Thermoplastics

Davidson, Robert L. & Sittig, Marshall. Water-Soluble Resins. 2nd ed. (Illus.). 1968. 15.95x (ISBN 0-442-15606-5). Van Nos Reinhold.

Lawrence, John R. Polyester Resins. 261p. 1960. 12.50 (ISBN 0-442-15056-3, Pub. by Van Nos Reinhold). Krieger.

Virgines, George E. Famous Guns & Gunners. LC 77-92857. (Illus.). 1980. 12.95 (ISBN 0-89769-035-4); pap. 6.95 (ISBN 0-89769-010-9). Pine Mntn.

GUN CONTROL

see Firearms–Laws and Regulations

GUN DOGS

see Hunting Dogs

GUNDOLF, FRIEDRICH, 1880-1931

Evans, Arthur R., Jr., ed. On Four Modern Humanists: Hofmannsthal, Gundolf, Curtius, Kantorowicz. LC 76-90945. (Princeton Essays Literature). 1970. 16.00 (ISBN 0-691-06174-2). Princeton U Pr.

GUNN OSCILLATORS

see Oscillators, Microwave

GUNNERY

see also Ammunition; Antitank Guns; Artillery; Ballistics; Explosives; Firearms; Gunpowder; Naval Gunnery; Ordnance; Rifle Practice

The Compleat Gunner. 1974. Repr. of 1672 ed. text ed. 12.50x (ISBN 0-8277-1539-0). British Bk Ctr.

GUNNING

see Hunting; Shooting

GUNPOWDER

see also Ammunition

Fadala, Sam. The Complete Black Powder Handbook. (Illus.). 288p. 1979. pap. 8.95 (ISBN 0-695-81311-0). DBI.

Grancsay, Stephen V. American Engraved Powder Horns. LC 76-20385. (Illus.). 1976. 25.00 (ISBN 0-686-15790-7). Ray Riling.

Macchiavelli, Niccolo. The Arte of Warre, (Certain Waies of the Orderyng of Souldiours) Whitehorne, P., tr. LC 79-26097. (English Experience Ser.: No. 135). 1969. Repr. of 1562 ed. 42.00 (ISBN 90-221-0135-5). Walter J Johnson.

Warner, Ken, ed. Handloader's Digest Bullet & Powder Update. (Illus.). 128p. 1980. pap. 4.95 (ISBN 0-910676-17-8). DBI.

GUNPOWDER PLOT, 1605

Gardiner, Samuel. What Gunpowder Plot Was. LC 68-25234. (British History Ser., No. 30). (Illus.). 1969. Repr. of 1897 ed. lib. bdg. 33.95 (ISBN 0-8383-0941-0). Haskell.

Gardiner, Samuel R. What Gunpowder Plot Was. LC 73-131718. 1971. 9.00 (ISBN 0-403-00605-8). Scholarly.

--What Gunpowder Plot Was. LC 76-89457. (BCL Ser.: I). Repr. of 1897 ed. 11.50 (ISBN 0-404-02677-X). AMS Pr.

--What Gunpowder Plot Was. Repr. of 1897 ed. lib. bdg. 15.00x (ISBN 0-8371-1806-9, GAGP). Greenwood.

Herring, Francis. Mischeefs Mysterie: Or, Treasons Masterpeece. Vicars, J., tr. from Lat. LC 79-171763. (No. 317). 122p. 1971. Repr. of 1617 ed. 14.00 (ISBN 90-221-0317-X). Walter J Johnson.

Parkinson, C. Northcote. Gunpowder, Treason & Plot. LC 76-28660. 1977. 8.95 (ISBN 0-312-35350-2). St Martin.

Taylor, Jeremy. A Sermon Preached Upon the Anniversary of the Gunpowder Treason. LC 78-25673. (English Experience Ser.: No. 354). 64p. 1971. Repr. of 1638 ed. 11.50 (ISBN 90-221-0354-4). Walter J Johnson.

GUNS

see Firearms; Ordnance; Revolvers; Rifles; Shot-Guns

GUNSHOT WOUNDS

Fatteh, Adbullah. Medicolegal Investigation of Gunshot Wounds. LC 76-6957. (Illus.). 1976. 23.75 (ISBN 0-397-50356-3, JBL-Med-Nursing). Har-Row.

Swan, Kenneth G. & Swan, Roy C. Gunshot Wounds: Pathophysiology & Management. LC 79-16118. (Illus.). 1980. 27.50 (ISBN 0-88416-196-X). Wright-PSG.

Wilber, Charles G. Medicolegal Investigation of the President John F. Kennedy Murder. (Illus.). 336p. 1978. 19.50 (ISBN 0-398-03679-9). C C Thomas.

GUNSMITHING

Angier, R. H. Firearms Blueing & Browning. 160p. 1936. 9.95 (ISBN 0-686-76905-8). Stackpole.

Bailey, De Witt & Nie, Douglas A. English Gunmakers: The Birmingham & Provincial Gun Trade in the 18th & 19th Century. LC 77-29162. (Illus.). 1978. 18.95 (ISBN 0-668-04566-3, 4566). Arco.

Carmichael, Jim. Do-It-Yourself Gunsmithing. LC 77-12450. (Outdoor Life Book). (Illus.). 1978. 16.95 (ISBN 0-06-010638-7, HarpT). Har-Row.

Demeritt, Dwight B., Jr. Maine Made Guns & Their Makers. LC 73-91769. (Maine Heritage Ser.: No. 2). (Illus.). 1973. 22.00 (ISBN 0-913764-04-3). Maine St Mus.

Dunlap, Roy F. Gunsmithing. LC 63-21755. (Illus.). 848p. 1963. 19.95 (ISBN 0-8117-0770-9). Stackpole.

Gill, Harold B., Jr. Gunsmith in Colonial Virginia. (Williamsburg Research Studies Ser). (Illus.). 200p. 1974. 7.50x (ISBN 0-8139-0334-3); pap. 4.50x 0.p. (ISBN 0-8139-0526-5). U Pr of Va.

Gill, Harold, Jr. The Gunsmith in Colonial Virgina. LC 73-78366. (Williamsburg Research Studies Ser). 1974. pap. 4.50 (ISBN 0-87935-008-3). Williamsburg.

Hartzler, Daniel D. Arms Makers of Maryland. LC 74-24434. (Longrifle Ser.). (Illus.). 312p. 1977. 35.00 (ISBN 0-87387-054-9). Shumway.

Howe, Walter J. Professional Gunsmithing. (Illus.). 518p. 1946. 24.95 (ISBN 0-8117-1375-X). Stackpole.

Hutslar, Donald A. Gunsmiths of Ohio: 18th & 19th Centuries, Vol. I. LC 72-87114. (Illus.). 448p. casebound 35.00 (ISBN 0-87387-026-3). Shumway.

Mitchell, Jack. Gun Digest Book of Pistolsmithing. LC 80-66470. (Illus.). 288p. (Orig.). 1980. pap. 8.95 (ISBN 0-910676-18-6). DBI.

Newell, A. Donald. Gunstock Finishing & Care. (Illus.). 512p. 1949. 22.95 (ISBN 0-8117-0780-6). Stackpole.

Norton(R.W.) Art Gallery. Artistry in Arms: The Art of Gunsmithing & Gun Engraving. LC 75-164699. (Illus.). 1971. pap. 2.50x (ISBN 0-9600182-4-7). Norton Art.

Shelton, Lawrence P. California Gunsmiths. (Illus.). 302p. 1977. casebound 29.65 (ISBN 0-87387-081-6). Shumway.

Steindler, Robert A. Home Gunsmithing Digest. 2nd ed. (Illus.). 288p. 1978. pap. 8.95 (ISBN 0-695-81212-2). DBI.

Stelle & Harrison. The Gunsmith's Manual: A Complete Handbook for the American Gunsmith. (Illus.). Repr. of 1883 ed. 12.95 (ISBN 0-88227-002-8). Gun Room.

Traister, John. Clyde Baker's Modern Gunsmithing. (Illus.). 608p. 1981. 24.95 (ISBN 0-8117-0983-3). Stackpole.

Traister, John E. Basic Gunsmithing. (Illus.). 1979. pap. 8.95 (ISBN 0-8306-1140-1, 1140). TAB Bks.

--First Book of Gunsmithing. (Illus.). 192p. 1981. 14.95 (ISBN 0-8117-0633-8). Stackpole.

--Gun Digest of Gunsmithing Tools...& Their Uses. 1980. pap. 7.95 (ISBN 0-910676-08-9). DBI.

Walker, Ralph. Hobby Gunsmithing. (Illus.). 320p. 1972. pap. 8.95 (ISBN 0-695-80361-1). DBI.

Walker, Ralph T. Black Powder Gunsmithing. (Illus.). 288p. 1978. pap. 8.95 (ISBN 0-695-80943-1). DBI.

GUNTER'S LINE

see Slide-Rule

GUNTHER, JOHN, 1929-1947

Gunther, John. Death Be Not Proud. 1953. 3.95 (ISBN 0-394-60286-2, M286). Modern Lib.

--Death Be Not Proud: A Memoir. 1965. pap. 1.95 (ISBN 0-06-080111-5, P111, PL). Har-Row.

GUPPIES

Axelrod, Herbert R. & Whitern, Wilfred H. Guppies. (Orig.). pap. 2.00 (ISBN 0-87666-082-0, M505). TFH Pubns.

Emmens, C. W. Guppy Handbook. (Illus.). pap. 3.95 (ISBN 0-87666-084-7, PS668). TFH Pubns.

Emmens, C. W. & Axelrod, Herbert. Fancy Guppies for the Advanced Hobbyist. 1968. pap. 3.95 (ISBN 0-87666-086-3, M526). TFH Pubns.

Simon, Seymour. What Do You Want to Know About Guppies? LC 77-5930. (Illus.). 80p. (gr. 2-5). 1977. 7.95 (ISBN 0-590-07412-1, Four Winds). Schol Bk Serv.

Stein, Sara B. How to Raise Goldfish & Guppies: A Child's Book of Pet Care. LC 76-8139. (Illus.). (ps-5). 1976. PLB 5.99 (ISBN 0-394-93225-0, BYR); pap. 3.95 (ISBN 0-394-83225-6). Random.

Wasserman, Lou. Raise & Show Guppies. (Illus.). 1977. pap. 4.95 (ISBN 0-87666-453-2, PS-738). TFH Pubns.

White, William, Jr. The Guppy: Its Life Cycle. LC 73-83441. (Colorful Nature Ser.). 64p. (gr. 5 up). 1974. 9.95 (ISBN 0-8069-3476-X); PLB 9.29 (ISBN 0-8069-3477-8). Sterling.

Whitern, Wilfred L. & Gordon, Myron. Guppies. (Illus.). 96p. 1980. 2.95 (ISBN 0-87666-523-7, KW058). TFH Pubns.

Whitney, Leon F. All About Guppies. (Orig.). pap. 5.95 (ISBN 0-87666-083-9, PS603). TFH Pubns.

GURAGE LANGUAGE

Leslau, Wolf. Ethiopic Documents: Gurage. Repr. of 1950 ed. pap. 15.50 (ISBN 0-384-32330-8). Johnson Repr.

GURDJIEFF, GEORGE IVANOVITCH, 1872-1949

Anderson, Margaret. The Unknowable Gurdjieff. (Illus.). 212p. (Orig.). 1973. pap. 3.95 (ISBN 0-87728-219-6). Weiser.

Bennett, J. G. Gurdjieff: Making a New World. 1976. pap. 5.95 (ISBN 0-06-090474-7, CN474, CN). Har-Row.

De Hartmann, Thomas. Our Life with Mister Gurdjieff. LC 64-22661. (Illus.). 1964. 8.00x (ISBN 0-8154-0058-6). Cooper Sq.

Hulme, Kathryn. Undiscovered Country: In Search of Gurdjieff. 1972. pap. 4.95 (ISBN 0-316-38138-1, Pub. by Atlantic Monthly Pr). Little.

Moore, James. Gurdjieff & Mansfield. (Illus.). 304p. 1980. 25.00 (ISBN 0-7100-0488-5). Routledge & Kegan.

Nicoll, M. Psychological Commentaries on Teaching of Gurdjieff & Ouspensky, 5 vols. Vols. 1-3. 15.00 ea.; Vols. 4 & 5. 17.50 ea. Weiser.

Nott, C. S. Teachings of Gurdjieff: The Journal of a Pupil. (Illus.). 1970. pap. 5.95 (ISBN 0-87728-396-6). Weiser.

Ouspensky, P. D. Fourth Way. 1971. pap. 3.95 (ISBN 0-394-71672-8, Vin). Random.

--In Search of the Miraculous: Fragments of an Unknown Teaching. 1965. pap. 4.50 (ISBN 0-15-644508-5, HB86, Harv). HarBraceJ.
Peters, Fritz. Boyhood with Gurdjieff. 192p. 1980. pap. 4.95 (ISBN 0-88496-146-X). Capra Pr.
Popoff, Irmis B. Gurdjieff: His Work on Myself... with Others... for the Work. rev ed. LC 73-79122. 198p. 1973. pap. 5.95 (ISBN 0-87728-417-2). Weiser.
Speeth, Kathleen R. The Gurdjieff Work. LC 76-384044. 1976. pap. 5.95 (ISBN 0-915904-19-5). And-or Pr.
--The Gurdjieff Work. 1978. pap. 2.95 (ISBN 0-671-83238-7). PB.
Speeth, Kathleen R. & Friedlander, Ira. Gurdjieff Seeker of the Truth. LC 78-24696. (Illus.). 1979. pap. 5.95 (ISBN 0-06-090693-6, CN-693, CN). Har-Row.
Staveley, A. L. Memories of Gurdjieff. 1978. 6.95 (ISBN 0-89756-025-6). Two Rivers.
--Themes. xvi, 100p. 1981. 20.00 (ISBN 0-89756-005-1). Two Rivers.
Vaysse, Jean. Toward Awakening: An Approach to the Teaching of Gurdjieff. LC 79-1779. 1979. pap. 3.95 (ISBN 0-06-068860-2, RD 304, HarpR). Har-Row.
Waldberg, Michael. Gurdjieff: An Approach to His Ideas. Cox, Steve, tr. 160p. (Orig.). 1981. pap. 9.50 (ISBN 0-7100-0811-2). Routledge & Kegan.
Walker, Kenneth. Gurdjieff: A Study of His Teaching. (Unwin Paperback Ser.). 221p. (Orig.). 1980. pap. text ed. 5.95 (ISBN 0-04-294106-7). Allen Unwin.
--The Making of Man. 1963. 12.95 (ISBN 0-7100-2248-4). Routledge & Kegan.
Webb, James. The Harmonious Circle. LC 77-16261. (Illus.). 1980. 19.95 (ISBN 0-399-11465-3). Putnam.
Zuber, Rene. Who Are You Monsieur Gurdjieff? Koralek, Jenny, tr. 80p. 1980. pap. 7.50 (ISBN 0-7100-0674-8). Routledge & Kegan.

GURJARI LANGUAGE
see Urdu Language

GURKHAS
Nicholson, J. B. The Gurkha Rifles. LC 74-76623. (Men-at-Arms Ser). (Illus.). 40p. (Orig.). 1974. pap. 7.95 (ISBN 0-88254-235-4). Hippocrene Bks.
Northey, W. Brook & Morris, C. J. The Gurkhas: Their Manners, Customs & Country. 282p. 1975. text ed. 22.00x (ISBN 0-8426-0772-2). Verry.
Northey, William B. The Land of the Gurkhas. LC 78-179229. (Illus.). Repr. of 1937 ed. 27.50 (ISBN 0-404-54856-3). AMS Pr.

GURNEY, EDMUND, 1847-1888
Gauld, Alan. The Founders of Psychical Research. LC 68-13562. 1968. 10.00x (ISBN 0-8052-3076-9). Schocken.
Hall, Trevor H. The Strange Case of Edmund Gurney. 2nd ed. (Illus.). 219p. 1980. 26.50x (ISBN 0-7156-1154-2, Pub. by Duckworth England). Biblio Dist.

GURNEY, JOSEPH, 1788-1847
Channing, William E. Emancipation. LC 75-82181. (Anti-Slavery Crusade in America Ser). 1969. Repr. of 1840 ed. 9.00 (ISBN 0-405-00619-5). Arno.
--Slavery & Emancipation. LC 68-55928. Repr. of 1841 ed. 13.00x (ISBN 0-8371-0347-9). Greenwood.

GUROWSKI, ADAM, HRABIA, 1805-1866
Fischer, LeRoy H. Lincoln's Gadfly, Adam Gurowski. (Illus.). 1964. 16.95x (ISBN 0-8061-0621-2). U of Okla Pr.

GURUITCH, GEORGES, 1894-
Bosserman, Phillip. Dialectical Sociology: Analysis of French Sociologist, Georges Gurvitch. LC 67-31430. (Extending Horizons Ser). 1968. 7.95 (ISBN 0-87558-040-8). Porter Sargent.

GURURUMBA (NEW GUINEA TRIBE)
Newman, Philip L. Knowing the Gururumba. LC 65-13211. (Case Studies in Cultural Anthropology). (Orig.). 1965. pap. text ed. 5.95 (ISBN 0-03-050510-0, HoltC). HR&W.

GUSII (BANTU TRIBE)
LeVine, Robert A. & LeVine, B. B. Nyansongo: A Gusii Community in Kenya. LC 76-52994. 240p. 1977. pap. 6.50 (ISBN 0-88275-514-5). Krieger.
LeVine, Sarah & LeVine, Robert A. Mothers & Wives: Gusii Women of East Africa. LC 78-21573. 1979. 21.00x (ISBN 0-226-47548-4). U of Chicago Pr.

GUSTAF 3RD, KING OF SWEDEN, 1746-1792
Bain, Robert N. Gustavus III & His Contemporaries, Vols. 1 & 2. 1970. Repr. of 1894 ed. 28.50x (ISBN 0-685-80726-6). Humanities.

GUSTAV 2ND ADOLF, KING OF SWEDEN, 1594-1632
Bowen, Marjorie. Sundry Great Gentlemen: Some Essays in Historical Biography. facs. ed. LC 68-29192. (Essay Index Reprint Ser). 1968. Repr. of 1928 ed. 18.00 (ISBN 0-8369-0230-0). Arno.
Liddell Hart, Basil. Great Captains Unveiled. facs. ed. LC 67-23240. (Essay Index Reprint Ser). 1928. 19.50 (ISBN 0-8369-0618-7). Arno.

GUSTAV 2ND ADOLF, KING OF SWEDEN, 1594-1632-DRAMA
Strindberg, August. Gustav Adolf. Johnson, Walter, tr. from Swedish. LC 57-5153. (American-Scandinavian Foundation Scandinavian Studies). (Illus.). 245p. 1957. 11.50 (ISBN 0-295-73800-6). U of Wash Pr.

GUSTAV 3RD, KING OF SWEDEN, 1746-1792-DRAMA
Strindberg, August. Queen Christina, Charles XII, Gustav III. Johnson, Walter, tr. LC 55-7573. (American-Scandinavian Foundation Scandinavian Studies). (Illus.). 293p. 1968. 11.50 (ISBN 0-295-73899-5); pap. 2.95 (ISBN 0-295-78570-5, WP45). U of Wash Pr.

GUSTON, PHILIP, 1912-
Feld, Ross. Philip Couston. LC 79-27425. (Illus.). 152p. 1980. 25.00 (ISBN 0-8076-0962-5); pap. 11.95 (ISBN 0-8076-0962-5). Braziller.
Hess, Thomas B. & Feldman, Morton. Six Painters: Mondrian, DeKooning, Guston, Kline, Pollock, Rothko. LC 67-30452. (Illus.). 1968. pap. 3.00 (ISBN 0-914412-22-1). Inst for the Arts.

GUTENBERG, JOHANN, 1397-1468
Goff, Frederick R. The Permanence of Johann Gutenberg. LC 78-89558. (Bibliographical Monograph: No. 3). 1974. Repr. of 1970 ed. 5.95 (ISBN 0-87959-048-3). U of Tex Hum Res.
Johann Gutenburg, the Inventor of Printing. 1981. 9.00x (ISBN 0-7141-0376-4, Pub. by Brit Lib England); pap. 6.00x (ISBN 0-7141-0288-1). State Mutual Bk.
Lamartine, A. de. Gutenberg Inventaire de l'Imprimerie. 1960. 6000.00 (ISBN 0-686-54274-6). French & Eur.
McMurtrie, D. C. & McMurtrie, D. C., eds. The Gutenberg Documents. (Eng.-ger.). 1949. limited to 900 copies 17.50x (ISBN 0-686-17400-3). R S Barnes.
McMurtrie, Douglas C. Wings for Words: The Story of Johann Gutenberg & His Invention of Printing. LC 78-167061. (Tower Bks). (Illus.). 175p. 1972. Repr. of 1940 ed. 24.00 (ISBN 0-8103-3936-6). Gale.

GUTHRIE, ALFRED BERTRAM, JR., 1901-
Ford, Thomas W. A. B. Guthrie, Jr. (U. S. Authors Ser.: No. 396). 1981. 10.95 (ISBN 0-8057-7327-4). Twayne.

GUTHRIE, WOODY, 1912-1967
Klein, Joe. Woody Guthrie: A Life. LC 80-7634. (Illus.). 512p. 1980. 15.95 (ISBN 0-394-50152-7). Knopf.
Robbin, Ed. Woody Guthrie & Me: An Intimate Reminiscence. (Illus.). 1980. pap. 6.95 (ISBN 0-89581-015-8). Lancaster-Miller.

GUTZKOW, KARL, 1811-1878
Muller, P. Beitraege Zur Wurdigung Von Karl Gutzkow Als Lustspieldichter. pap. 7.00 (ISBN 0-384-40420-0). Johnson Repr.
Schinnerer, Otto P. Woman in the Life & Works of Gutzkow. LC 24-19780. (Columbia University. Germanic Studies, Old Ser.: No. 28). Repr. of 1924 ed. 14.50 (ISBN 0-404-50428-0). AMS Pr.
Weiglin, Paul. Gutzkows Und Laubes Literaturdramen. (Ger). Repr. of 1910 ed. 14.00 (ISBN 0-384-66500-4); pap. 11.00 (ISBN 0-685-02148-3). Johnson Repr.

GUY, FRANCIS, 1760-1820
Colwill, Stiles T. Francis Guy: Seventeen-Sixty to Eighteen-Twenty. LC 81-81085. (Illus.). 140p. (Orig.). 1981. pap. 15.00 (ISBN 0-938420-20-8). Md Hist.
Pleasants, Jacob H. Four Late Eighteenth Century Anglo-American Landscape Painters. LC 78-128288. (Essay Index Reprint Ser). 1943. 16.00 (ISBN 0-8369-1894-0). Arno.

GUYANA
Carew, Jan. Black Midas. 2nd ed. 184p. 1981. 10.00x (ISBN 0-89410-124-2); pap. 5.00x (ISBN 0-89410-125-0). Three Continents.
Cultural Policy in Guyana. (Studies & Documents on Cultural Policy). 1978. pap. 5.00 (ISBN 92-3-101511-7, U792, UNESCO). Unipub.
Glasgow, Roy A. Guyana: Race & Politics Among Africans & East Indians. (Studies in Social Life: No. 14). 1970. 20.00x (ISBN 90-247-5005-9). Intl Pubns Serv.
Hope, Kempe R. Development Policy in Guyana: Planning, Finance, & Administration. LC 79-5229. (Westview Replica Editions). lib. bdg. 27.75x (ISBN 0-89158-583-4). Westview.
Irving, Brian, et al. Guyana: A Composite Monograph. LC 72-91600. (Illus.). 87p. (Orig.). 1972. 10.00 (ISBN 0-913480-04-5); pap. 5.00 (ISBN 0-913480-05-3). Inter Am U Pr.
James, Henry. Richard Olney & His Public Service. LC 70-87445. (American Scene Ser). (Illus.). 1971. Repr. of 1923 ed. lib. bdg. 32.50 (ISBN 0-306-71516-3). Da Capo.
Kirke, Henry. Twenty-Five Years in British Guiana. LC 77-106841. (Illus.). Repr. of 1898 ed. 20.75x (ISBN 0-8371-3463-3). Greenwood.
Manley, Robert. Guyana Emergent: The Post-Independence Struggle for Nondependent Development. (Reference Bks.). 1979. lib. bdg. 14.50 (ISBN 0-8161-9001-1). G K Hall.
Rodney, Walter. A History of the Guyanese Working People, 1881-1905. 26.50x (ISBN 0-8018-2428-1); pap. 6.95 (ISBN 0-8018-2447-8). Johns Hopkins.
Sanders, Ron. Broadcasting in Guyana. (Case Studies on Broadcasting Systems). (Orig.). 1978. pap. 14.00 (ISBN 0-7100-0025-1). Routledge & Kegan.
Simms, Peter. Trouble in Guyana. (Illus.). 1966. 7.50x (ISBN 0-8002-2114-1). Intl Pubns Serv.
Sterling Editors. Guyana - in Pictures. LC 74-31702. (Visual Geography Ser.). (Illus.). 64p. (gr. 5 up). 1975. pap. 2.95 (ISBN 0-8069-1160-3). Sterling.
Sukdeo, Iris D. The Emergence of a Multiracial Society: The Sociology of Multiracism with Reference to Guyana. 224p. 1981. 9.50 (ISBN 0-682-49686-3). Exposition.
Trade Directory of Guyana: 1975. 1976. text ed. 50.00x (ISBN 0-8277-4297-5). British Bk Ctr.
Waterton, Charles. Wanderings in South America, the Northwest of the United States, & the Antilles in the Years Eighteen Twelve, Eighteen Sixteen, Eighteen Twenty, & Eighteen Twenty-Four. 341p. 1968. Repr. of 1828 ed. 25.00 (ISBN 0-8398-2157-3). Parnassus Imprints.

GUYNEMER, GEORGES MARIE, 1894-1917
Bordeaux, Henry. Georges Guynemer, Knight of the Air. LC 73-169405. (Literature & History of Aviation Ser). 1972. Repr. of 1918 ed. 13.00 (ISBN 0-405-03751-1). Arno.

GUYON JEANNE MARIE (BOUVIER DE LA MOTTE) 1648-1717
Madame Guyon. Madame Guyon. new ed. 382p. 1974. pap. 6.95 (ISBN 0-8024-5135-7). Moody.
Upham, T. C. Life of Madam Guyon. 1961. Repr. of 1905 ed. 10.00 (ISBN 0-227-67521-5). Attic Pr.

GUZMAN BLANCO, ANTONIO, 1828-1899
Brancaforte, Benito. Guzman de Alfarache: Conversion O Degradacion. 350p. 1980. 11.00 (ISBN 0-686-27986-7). Hispanic Seminary.
Wise, George S. Caudillo, a Portrait of Antonio Guzman Blanco. Repr. of 1951 ed. lib. bdg. 15.00x (ISBN 0-8371-3349-1, WICA). Greenwood.

GWEMBE VALLEY
Reynolds, B. The Material Culture of the Peoples of the Gwembe Valley. (Kariba Studies: Vol. III). 276p. 1968. 36.00x (ISBN 0-7190-1241-4, Pub. by Manchester U Pr England). State Mutual Bk.

GWYN, NELL, 1650-1687
Bax, Clifford. Pretty Witty Nell: An Account of Nell Gwyn & Her Environment. LC 76-83871. (Illus.). Repr. of 1932 ed. 17.00 (ISBN 0-405-08243-6, Blom Pubns). Arno.
Dasent, Arthur I. Nell Gwyn Sixteen Fifty-Sixteen Eighty-Seven. LC 70-82824. 1924. 15.00 (ISBN 0-405-08432-3, Blom Pubns). Arno.

GYMNASTICS
see also Acrobats and Acrobatism; Callisthenics; Exercise; Gymnastics for Women; Physical Education and Training; Schools-Exercises and Recreations
Allen, Joyce E. Sense & Sensitivity in Gymnastics. 1969. pap. text ed. 6.00x (ISBN 0-435-80020-5). Heinemann Ed.
--Sense & Sensitivity in Gymnastics: A Teacher's Guide to Educational Gymnastics. LC 72-407844. (Illus.). 1969. 4.50x (ISBN 0-435-80020-5). Intl Pubns Serv.
Alt, Doug & Glossbrenner, Alfred. Introduction to Men's Gymnastics. LC 79-84327. (Illus., Orig.). 1979. pap. 6.95 (ISBN 0-8015-4081-X, Hawthorn). Dutton.
American Alliance for Health, Physical Education & Recreation. Gymnastics Guide 1978-80. 1978. plastic bdg. 4.50 (ISBN 0-685-52988-6, 243-26192). AAHPERD.
--Gymnastics Selected Articles, 1971. pap. 0.60 (ISBN 0-685-42004-3, 243-25164). AAHPERD.
Arnold, Eddie & Stocks, Broan. Men's Gymanastics. (EP Sport Ser.). (Illus.). 1979. 12.95 (ISBN 0-8069-9128-3, Pub. by EP Publishing England); pap. 6.95 (ISBN 0-8069-9130-5). Sterling.
Aykrord, Peter. Skills & Tactics of Gymnastics. LC 78-18628. (Skills & Tactics Ser.). (Illus.). 152p. 1980. 9.95 (ISBN 0-668-04838-7). Arco.
Bare, Frank L. The Complete Gymnastics Book. 192p. 1980. pap. 6.95 (ISBN 0-695-81427-3). New Century.
Boone, William. Illustrated Handbook of Gymnastics, Tumbling & Trampolining. 1976. 11.95 (ISBN 0-13-451203-0). P-H.
Boone, William T. Better Gymnastics: How to Spot the Performer. LC 78-368. (Illus.). 225p. 1979. pap. 10.00 (ISBN 0-89037-127-X). Anderson World.
Bott, Jenny. Modern Rhythmic Gymnastics. (Illus.). 1981. 12.95 (ISBN 0-8069-9064-3, Pub. by EP Publishing England). Sterling.
Brown, James R. & Wardell, David B. Teaching & Coaching Gymnastics for Men & Women. 1980. text ed. 19.95 (ISBN 0-471-10798-0). Wiley.
Buckland, D. G. In the Primary School. 1969. pap. text ed. 4.50x (ISBN 0-435-80601-7). Heinemann Ed.
Burchard, S. H. Sports Star: Nadia Comaneci. LC 77-3967. (Sports Star Ser.). (Illus.). (gr. 1-5). 1977. pap. 2.50 (ISBN 0-15-278037-8, VoyB). HarBraceJ.
Carr, Gerald A. Safety in Gymnastics: A Manual of Spotting & Safety Techniques. (Illus.). 250p. (Orig.). 1981. pap. 9.95x (ISBN 0-87663-642-3, Pub. by Hancock Hse). Universe.
Connock, Marion. Nadia of Romania. (Illus.). 132p. 1977. 13.50 (ISBN 0-7156-1241-7, Pub. by Duckworth England); pap. 8.95 (ISBN 0-7156-1249-2, Pub. by Duckworth England). Biblio Dist.
Cureton, T. K., et al. Endurance of Young Men, Analysis of Endurance Exercises & Methods of Evaluating Motor Fitness. 1945. pap. 16.00 (ISBN 0-527-01534-2). Kraus Repr.
Diagram Group. Enjoying Gymnastics. LC 76-3810. (Enjoying Sports Ser.). (Illus., Orig.). (YA) 1976. pap. 3.95 (ISBN 0-448-23311-8). Paddington.
Engel. Gymnastics: The New Era. Date not set. 10.15 (ISBN 0-448-13614-7). G&D.
Faria, Irvin & Peek, Ronald W. Gymnastics: Floor Exercise. LC 79-109498. (Sports Techniques Ser). 1972. 3.95 (ISBN 0-87670-008-3); pap. 1.95 (ISBN 0-87670-056-3). Athletic Inst.
--Gymnastics: Horizontal Bar. LC 79-109498. (Sports Techniques Ser). 1972. 3.95 (ISBN 0-87670-009-1); pap. 1.95 (ISBN 0-87670-055-5). Athletic Inst.
--Gymnastics: Parallel Bars. LC 79-109498. (Sports Techniques Ser). 1972. 3.95 (ISBN 0-87670-010-5); pap. 1.95 (ISBN 0-87670-057-1). Athletic Inst.
--Gymnastics: Rings. LC 79-109498. (Sports Techniques Ser). 1972. 3.95 (ISBN 0-87670-011-3); pap. 1.95 (ISBN 0-87670-053-9). Athletic Inst.
--Gymnastics: Side Horse, Long Horse-Vaulting. LC 79-109498. (Sports Techniques Ser). 1972. 3.95 (ISBN 0-87670-012-1); pap. 1.95 (ISBN 0-87670-054-7). Athletic Inst.
Fontaine, Robert. Humorous Skits for Young People. rev. ed. LC 65-22677. (gr. 6-12). 1976. 10.00 (ISBN 0-8238-0210-8). Plays.
Frederick, A. Bruce. Gymnastics for Men. (Physical Education Activities Ser.). 80p. 1969. pap. text ed. write for info. (ISBN 0-697-07014-X); tchr's man. 0.50 (ISBN 0-686-66581-3). Wm C Brown.
Friedlaender, Elizabeth. Vaulting. LC 72-118228. 1979. pap. 5.95 (ISBN 0-8289-0343-3). Greene.
Friendly Gathering of Gymnasts. 1980. pap. 7.95 (ISBN 0-8351-0702-7). China Bks.
Fukushima, Sho & Russell, Wrio. Men's Gymnastics. (Illus.). 224p. 1980. 25.00 (ISBN 0-571-11478-4, Pub. by Faber & Faber). Merrimack Bk Serv.
Golubev, V. Soviet Gymnastics Stars. 220p. 1979. 22.00 (ISBN 0-8285-1650-2, Pub. by Progress Pubs Russia). Imported Pubns.
Grumeza, Ion. Nadia: The Success Secrets of the Amazing Romanian Gymnast. 1977. pap. 3.95 (ISBN 0-8015-5296-6, Pub. by Giniger). Dutton.
Guraedy, Ila. Illustrated Gymnastics Dictionary for Young People. LC 79-93357. (Illustrated Dictionary Ser.). (Illus.). 120p. (gr. 4 up). 1980. PLB 7.29 (ISBN 0-8178-0002-6). Harvey.
--Illustrated Gymnastics Dictionary for Young People. (Illus., Orig.). pap. 2.50 (ISBN 0-13-450932-3). P-H.
Guts Muths, Johann C. Gymnastics for Youth. (Physical Education Reprint Ser.). Repr. of 1800 ed. lib. bdg. 28.00x (ISBN 0-697-00103-2). Irvington.
Gymnastics. 1976. pap. 2.50 (ISBN 0-8277-4849-3). British Bk Ctr.
Holbrook, Jennifer K. Movement Activity in Gymnastics. 1974. 9.95 (ISBN 0-8238-0158-6). Plays.
Hughes, Eric L. Gymnastics for Men: A Competitive Approach for Teacher & Coach. (Illus.). 1966. 16.95 (ISBN 0-471-07122-6). Wiley.
Inner London Council. Educational Gymnastics. 1973. 2.95 (ISBN 0-8238-0164-0). Plays.
Jaques-Dalcroze, Emile. Eurhythmics, Art & Education. LC 78-180927. Repr. of 1930 ed. 18.00 (ISBN 0-405-08665-2, Blom Pubns). Arno.
--Rhythm, Music & Education. LC 77-187829. (Illus.). Repr. of 1921 ed. 18.00 (ISBN 0-405-08666-0, Blom Pubns). Arno.
K. S. Giniger Company. Complete Gymnastics. 12.95 (ISBN 0-686-31260-0); pap. 6.95 (ISBN 0-686-31261-9). New Century.

Learmouth, John. The Young Gymnast. LC 76-62781. (Illus.). 1977. 6.95 (ISBN 0-312-89723-5). St Martin.

Learmouth, John & Whitaker, Keith. Movement in Practice. LC 76-41142. (Illus.). 1977. pap. 7.95 (ISBN 0-8238-0209-4). Plays.

Loken, Newton C. Gymnastics. LC 66-16202. (Athletic Institute Ser). (Illus.). (gr. 9-12). 1969. 6.95 (ISBN 0-8069-4314-9); PLB 7.49 (ISBN 0-8069-4315-7). Sterling.

Loken, Newton C. & Willoughby, Robert J. The Complete Book of Gymnastics. 3rd ed. (Illus.). 256p. 1977. text ed. 17.50 (ISBN 0-13-157172-9). P-H.

Maddux, Gordon T. Men's Gymnastics. (Phys. Ed. Ser.). 1970. pap. text ed. 4.25 (ISBN 0-87620-570-8). Goodyear.

Mercurialis-Hieronymus. De Arte Gymnastica, Libri Sex. Tanis, Norman E., ed. (Northridge Facsimile Ser.: Pt. X). 1978. pap. 5.00 (ISBN 0-937048-09-7). CSUN.

Moran, Lyn. The Young Gymnasts. (Illus.). 1979. pap. 1.95 (ISBN 0-448-17019-1, Tempo). Ace Bks.

Morison, Ruth. A Movement Approach to Educational Gymnastics. 1974. 8.95 (ISBN 0-8238-0153-5). Plays.

O'Quinn, Garland. Developmental Gymnastics: Horizontal Bar, Tumbling Table, & Beam. (Illus.). 118p. 1979. 19.00x (ISBN 0-292-71520-X). U of Tex Pr.

Prestige, Pauline. Better Gymnastics. (Illus.). 1979. 10.00 (ISBN 0-8238-0233-7). Plays.

Price, Hartley D., et al. Gymnastics & Tumbling. LC 72-91942. (Illus.). 414p. 1972. pap. 6.95 (ISBN 0-668-02720-7). Arco.

Rodwell, Peter. Gymnastics. 1978. pap. 2.95 (ISBN 0-346-12360-7). Cornerstone.

--Gymnastics: Progressive Practices and Modern Coaching. (Illus.). 184p. 1976. 8.95 (ISBN 0-87523-116-0). Emerson.

Ryser, Otto E. & Brown, James R. A Manual for Tumbling & Apparatus Stunts. 7th ed. 256p. 1980. write for info. plastic comb. (ISBN 0-697-07170-7). Wm C Brown.

Salmela, J. H. Competitive Behaviors of Olympic Gymnasts. (Illus.). 164p. 1980. 19.75 (ISBN 0-398-04019-2); pap. 14.50 (ISBN 0-398-04021-4). C C Thomas.

Sands, Bill. Beginning Gymnastics. (Illus.). 1981. 14.95 (ISBN 0-8092-5948-6); pap. 6.95 (ISBN 0-8092-5947-8). Contemp Bks.

Schmid, Andrea B. Modern Rhythmic Gymnastics. LC 75-21074. 379p. 1976. pap. text ed. 11.95 (ISBN 0-87484-280-8). Mayfield Pub.

Smither, Graham B. Gymnastics. (Illus.). 128p. 1981. pap. 7.95 (ISBN 0-906071-36-4). Proteus Pub NY.

Spackman, Robert R., Jr. Conditioning for Gymnastics: Pre-Season, Regular Season & Off-Season. (Illus.). 120p. 1970. 12.75 (ISBN 0-398-01820-0). C C Thomas.

Sprague, Ken. The Gold's Gym Book of Strength Training. LC 78-65364. 1979. 13.50 (ISBN 0-87477-154-4); pap. 8.95 (ISBN 0-87477-153-6). J P Tarcher.

Stedwell, Paki. Vaulting: Gymnastics on Horseback. LC 79-11556. (Illus.). 128p. (gr. 7 up). 1980. PLB 7.79 (ISBN 0-671-34023-9). Messner.

Straus, Hal, ed. The Gymnastics Guide. LC 78-55790. (Illus.). 390p. 1978. pap. 7.95 (ISBN 0-89037-139-3). Anderson World.

Stuart, Nik. Gymnastics for Men. (Illus.). 1979. 14.95 (ISBN 0-09-131280-9, Pub. by Hutchinson); pap. 7.95 (ISBN 0-09-131281-7). Merrimack Bk Serv.

Szypula, June & Szypula, George. Contemporary Gymnastics. 1979. pap. 4.95 (ISBN 0-8092-7701-8). Contemp Bks.

Tatlow, Peter, et al. The World of Gymnastics. LC 78-5389. (Illus.). 1978. 13.95 (ISBN 0-689-10899-0). Atheneum.

Taylor, Bryce, et al. Olympic Gymnastics for Men & Women. (P-H Physical Education Ser). 1972. ref. ed. 16.95 (ISBN 0-13-633925-5). P-H.

Thomas, Kurt & Hannon. Kurt Thomas on Gymnastics. 1980. pap. 8.95 (ISBN 0-671-25508-8, 25508). S&S.

Trevor, M. D. The Development of Gymnastic Skills. (Development Skills Ser.). 64p. 1981. pap. 5.95x (ISBN 0-631-12577-9, Pub. by Basil Blackwell England). Biblio Dist.

Warren, Meg. The New Book of Gymnastics. 8th rev. ed. (Illus.). 120p. 1980. 13.50x (ISBN 0-213-16772-7, Pub. by Weidenfeld & Nicolson England). Biblio Dist.

--The New Book of Gymnastics. rev. ed. (Illus.). 120p. (Orig.). 1980. pap. 8.50x (ISBN 0-213-16773-5). Intl Pubns Serv.

Wettstone, Eugene, ed. Gymnastics Safety Manual: The Official Manual of the United States Gymnastics Safety Association. 2nd ed. LC 79-65860. (Illus.). 1979. text ed. 11.95x (ISBN 0-271-00242-5); pap. text ed. 7.95x (ISBN 0-271-00244-1). Pa St U Pr.

Wiley, Jack. Men's Gymnastics. LC 78-65024. (Illus.). 192p. (Orig.). 1980. pap. 6.95 (ISBN 0-89037-165-2). Anderson World.

Williams, Jean. Themes for Educational Gymnastics. 10.00 (ISBN 0-8238-0202-7). Plays.

GYMNASTICS–JUVENILE LITERATURE

Braun, Thomas. Nadia Comaneci. (Sports Superstars Ser.). (Illus.). (gr. 3-9). 1977. PLB 5.95 (ISBN 0-87191-592-8); pap. 2.95 (ISBN 0-89812-195-7). Creative Ed.

Dolan, Edward F., Jr. The Complete Beginner's Guide to Gymnastics. LC 78-60286. (Illus.). 1980. 8.95a (ISBN 0-385-13434-7); PLB (ISBN 0-385-13435-5). Doubleday.

Gagnier, Ed & Bender, Jack. Inside Gymnastics. new ed. LC 73-20676. (Illus.). 112p. (gr. 5-8). 1974. 7.95 (ISBN 0-8092-8876-1); pap. 5.95 (ISBN 0-8092-8875-3). Contemp Bks.

Haney, Lynn. Perfect Balance: The Story of an Elite Gymnast. LC 78-11634. (Illus.). (gr. 5-12). 1979. 8.95 (ISBN 0-399-20661-2). Putnam.

Hansen, Rosanna. Gymnastics. LC 79-55009. (Illus.). (gr. 3-7). 1980. pap. 5.95 (ISBN 0-448-16581-3). G&D.

Hayhurst, Brian. Gymnastics. LC 80-50303. (Illus.). 48p. (gr. 3-7). 1980. 6.95 (ISBN 0-528-82373-6). Rand.

Jacobs, Linda. Cathy Rigby: On the Beam. LC 74-31424. (Women Who Win Ser.: No. 2). 1974. lib. bdg. 5.95 (ISBN 0-88436-168-3); pap. 3.50 (ISBN 0-88436-169-1). EMC.

Litsky, Frank. Winners in Gymnastics. (gr. 6 up). 1979. pap. 1.25 (ISBN 0-380-43299-4, 43299, Camelot). Avon.

--Winners in Gymnastics. (Picture Life Books Ser.). (Illus.). (gr. 2 up). 1978. PLB 6.45 s&l (ISBN 0-531-02887-9). Watts.

Olney, Ross R. Gymnastics. 1980. pap. 1.75 (ISBN 0-380-49213-X, 49213, Camelot). Avon.

--Gymnastics. (First Bks.). (Illus.). 96p. (gr. 4-6). 1976. PLB 6.90 (ISBN 0-531-00849-5). Watts.

Prestidge, Pauline & Prestidge, Jim. Your Book of Gymnastics. 3rd ed. 60p. (gr. 4 up). 1979. 6.50 (ISBN 0-571-04970-2, Pub. by Faber & Faber). Merrimack Bk Serv.

Radlauer, Ed & Radlauer, Ruth. Some Basics About Women's Gymnastics. LC 79-21826. (Gemini Bks.). (Illus.). 32p. (gr. 3 up). 1980. PLB 8.65 (ISBN 0-516-07687-6, Elk Grove Bks.); pap. 2.95 (ISBN 0-516-47687-4). Childrens.

Resnick, Michael. Gymnastics & You: The Whole Story of the Sport. LC 77-8345. (Illus.). (gr. 5-9). 1977. pap. 3.95 (ISBN 0-528-87052-1). Rand.

Sullivan, George. Better Gymnastics for Girls. LC 77-6484. (Better Sports Ser.). (Illus.). (gr. 4 up). 1977. PLB 5.95 (ISBN 0-396-07453-7). Dodd.

--The Picture Story of Nadia Comaneci. LC 77-21345. (Illus.). 64p. (gr. 3-6). 1977. PLB 6.97 (ISBN 0-671-32925-1). Messner.

Taylor, Paula. Gymnastics' Happy Superstar: Olga Korbut. (The Allstars Ser.). (Illus.). (gr. 2-6). 1977. PLB 5.95 (ISBN 0-87191-581-2); pap. 2.95 (ISBN 0-89812-197-3). Creative Ed.

Traetta, John & Traetta, MaryJean. Gymnastics Basics. LC 79-15092. (Sports Basics Ser.). (Illus.). (gr. 3-7). 1979. PLB 6.95 (ISBN 0-13-371757-7). P-H.

Washington, Rosemary G. Gymnastics Is for Me. LC 79-4496. (Sports for Me Bks.). (Illus.). (gr. 2-5). 1979. PLB 5.95 (ISBN 0-8225-1078-2). Lerner Pubns.

GYMNASTICS–STUDY AND TEACHING

Cooper & Trnka. Teaching Gymnastic Skills to Men & Women. (Illus.). 224p. 1982. price not set spiral bdg. Burgess.

Kaneko, Akitomo. Olympic Gymnastics. LC 76-1171. (Illus.). 256p. 1980. pap. 7.95 (ISBN 0-8069-8926-2). Sterling.

Mauldon, E. & Layson, J. Teaching Gymnastics. 288p. 1980. 12.00x (ISBN 0-7121-2024-6, Pub. by Macdonald & Evans). State Mutual Bk.

Murdock, Tony. Gymnastics for Girls. (Illus.). (gr. 3-12). 1980. bds. 8.95 (ISBN 0-8238-0239-6). Plays.

O'Quinn, Garland. Developmental Gymnastics: Building Physical Skills for Children. LC 77-91498. (Illus.). 243p. 1979. 35.00x (ISBN 0-292-71521-8). U of Tex Pr.

Salmela, John. The Advanced Study of Gymnastics. (Illus.). 288p. 1976. 27.50 (ISBN 0-398-03438-9). C C Thomas.

Williams, Jean. Themes for Educational Gymnastics. 2nd ed. 192p. 1980. 12.00x (ISBN 0-86019-038-2, Pub. by Kimpton). State Mutual Bk.

GYMNASTICS, MEDICAL

see Exercise Therapy

GYMNASTICS FOR WOMEN

Babbitt, Diane H. & Haas, Werner. Gymnastic Apparatus Exercises for Girls. (Illus.). 130p. 1964. 11.95 (ISBN 0-8260-0590-X). Wiley.

Bowers, Carolyn O., et al. Judging & Coaching Women's Gymnastics. 2nd ed. 365p. 1981. text ed. 18.95 (ISBN 0-87484-391-X). Mayfield Pub.

Brown, James R. & Wardell, David B. Teaching & Coaching Gymnastics for Men & Women. 1980. text ed. 19.95 (ISBN 0-471-10798-0). Wiley.

Carter, Ernestine R. Gymnastics for Girls & Women. (Illus.). 1968. text ed. 11.95 (ISBN 0-13-371781-X). P-H.

Comaneci, Nadia. Nadia: The Autobiography of Nadia Comaneci. (Illus.). 160p. 1981. 14.95 (ISBN 0-906071-78-X). Proteus Pub NY.

Cooper, Phyllis. Feminine Gymnastics. 3rd rev. ed. 1980. pap. 12.95x spiral bdg. (ISBN 0-8087-2962-4). Burgess.

Coulton, Jill. Women's Gymnastics. (EP Sport Ser.). (Illus.). 116p. 1979. 12.95 (ISBN 0-8069-9168-2, Pub. by EP Publishing England); pap. 6.95 (ISBN 0-8069-9170-4, Pub. by EP Publishing England). Sterling.

--Women's Gymnastics. (Sports Ser.). (Illus.). 1977. 7.95 (ISBN 0-7158-0592-4). Charles River Bks.

Davis, H. Beginning Gymnastics for College Women. (Illus.). pap. 4.50 wrappers (ISBN 0-8363-0011-4). Jenkins.

Drury, Blanche J. & Schmid, Andrea B. Introduction to Women's Gymnastics. LC 72-88952. (Illus.). 112p. 1973. pap. text ed. 4.95 (ISBN 0-87484-242-5). Mayfield Pub.

--Introduction to Women's Gymnastics. 1976. pap. 4.95 (ISBN 0-8015-4084-4, Hawthorn). Dutton.

Frederick, A. Bruce. Gymnastics for Women. (Physical Education Activities Ser.). 94p. 1966. pap. text ed. write for info. (ISBN 0-697-07015-8); teacher's man. 0.50 (ISBN 0-686-66582-1). Wm C Brown.

Gault, Jim & Grant, Jack. The World of Women's Gymnastics. LC 76-11354. (Illus.). 1976. pap. 4.95 (ISBN 0-89087-166-3). Celestial Arts.

George, Gerald S. Biomechanics of Women's Gymnastics. 1980. text ed. 16.50 (ISBN 0-13-077461-8). P-H.

Ito, Robert & Dolney, Pam C. Mastering Women's Gymnastics. LC 77-23696. 1978. 9.95 (ISBN 0-8092-7744-1); pap. 6.95 (ISBN 0-8092-7743-3). Contemp Bks.

Johnson, Barry L. & Boudreaux, Patricia D. Basic Gymnastics for Girls & Women. LC 74-129091. (Illus.). 1971. pap. text ed. 9.95x spiral bdg. (ISBN 0-89197-041-X). Irvington.

Krementz, Jill. A Very Young Gymnast. LC 78-5502. (YA) 1978. 10.95 (ISBN 0-394-50080-6). Knopf.

Maddux, Gordon & Shay, Arthur. Forty Common Errors in Women's Gymnastics & How to Correct Them. 1979. o. p. 9.95 (ISBN 0-8092-7384-5); pap. 5.95 (ISBN 0-8092-7383-7). Contemp Bks.

Murray, Mimi. Women's Gymnastics: Coach, Participant, Spectator. 1979. text ed. 19.95x (ISBN 0-205-06162-1, 6261620). Allyn.

Ryan, Frank. Gymnastics for Girls. LC 75-25773. (Illus.). 352p. 1976. 16.95 (ISBN 0-670-35822-3). Viking Pr.

--Gymnastics for Girls. (Handbooks Ser). 1977. pap. 9.95 (ISBN 0-14-046271-6). Penguin.

Schmid, Andrea B. & Drury, Blanche J. Gymnastics for Women. 4th ed. LC 76-56510. 396p. 1977. pap. text ed. 12.95 spiral bdg. (ISBN 0-87484-364-2). Mayfield Pub.

Schmidt, Darlene. Scientific Approach to Women's Gymnastics. (Brighton Ser. in Health & Physical Education). 1980. text ed. 12.95x (ISBN 0-89832-011-9). Brighton Pub Co.

Schreiber, Mary L. Women's Gymnastics. LC 69-17995. (Physical Education Activites Ser). 1969. pap. text ed. 5.95 (ISBN 0-87620-971-1). Goodyear.

Shelly, Kathleen. Women's Gymnastics: Balance Beam. LC 79-109498. (Sports Techniques Ser). 1973. 3.95 (ISBN 0-87670-020-2); pap. 1.95 (ISBN 0-87670-079-2). Athletic Inst.

--Women's Gymnastics: Floor Exercise - Vaulting. LC 79-109498. (Sports Techniques Ser). 1973. 3.95 (ISBN 0-87670-046-6); pap. 1.95 (ISBN 0-87670-080-6). Athletic Inst.

--Women's Gymnastics: Uneven Parallel Bars. LC 79-109498. (Sports Techniques Ser). 1972. 3.95 (ISBN 0-87670-047-4); pap. 1.95 (ISBN 0-87670-078-4). Athletic Inst.

Sullivan, George. Better Gymnastics for Girls. LC 77-6484. (Better Sports Ser.). (Illus.). (gr. 4 up). 1977. PLB 5.95 (ISBN 0-396-07453-7). Dodd.

Temple, Cliff & Tatlow, Peter. Gymnastics for Girls. (Pelham Pictorial Sports Instruction Ser.). (Illus.). 1978. 12.50 (ISBN 0-7207-1013-8). Transatlantic.

Tonry, Don. Sports Illustrated Women's Gymnastics: The Floor Exercise Event. (Sports Illustrated Books). (Illus.). 1980. 8.95 (ISBN 0-690-01908-4); pap. 5.95 (ISBN 0-690-01907-6). T Y Crowell.

--Sports Illustrated Women's Gymnastics: The Vaulting, Balance Beam, & Uneven Parallel Bars Events. (Sports Illustrated Books). (Illus.). 192p. 1980. 8.95 (ISBN 0-690-01909-2); pap. 5.95 (ISBN 0-690-01906-8). T Y Crowell.

Wachtel, Erna & Loken, Newton C. Girls' Gymnastics. rev ed. LC 63-19163. (gr. 6 up). 1967. 6.95 (ISBN 0-8069-4310-6); PLB 7.49 (ISBN 0-8069-4311-4). Sterling.

Warren, Meg. The Book of Gymnastics. (Illus.). 106p. (YA) 1972. 7.50x (ISBN 0-213-00384-8). Intl Pubns Serv.

Wiley, Jack. Women's Gymnastics. LC 79-64732. (Illus.). 176p. (Orig.). 1980. pap. 7.95 (ISBN 0-89037-223-3). Anderson World.

GYMNOSPERMS

see also Coniferae

Chamberlain, Charles J. Gymnosperms: Structure & Evolution. (Illus.). 1935. 28.00 (ISBN 0-384-08415-X). Johnson Repr.

Kern, Frank D. A Revised Taxonomic Account of Gymnosporangium. new ed. LC 79-165358. (Illus.). 136p. 1973. 12.25x (ISBN 0-271-01105-X). Pa St U Pr.

Rendle, Alfred B. Classification of Flowering Plants, 2 bks. Incl. Bk. 1. Gymnosperms & Monocotyledons. 72.50 (ISBN 0-521-06056-7); Bk. 2. Dicotyledons. 85.00 (ISBN 0-521-06057-5). Cambridge U Pr.

Singh, Hardev. Embryology of Gymnosperms. LC 78-326641. (Encyclopedia of Plant Anatomy Ser.). (Illus.). 302p. 1978. 90.00x (ISBN 3-443-14011-4). Intl Pubns Serv.

--Embryology of Gymnosperms. (Encyclopedia of Plant Anatomy: Vol. X, No. 2). (Illus.). 302p. 1978. lib. bdg. 84.20x (ISBN 3-443-14011-4). Lubrecht & Cramer.

Sporne, K. R. Morphology of Gymnosperms: The Structure & Evolution of Primitive Seed Plants. 1967. text ed. 12.50x (ISBN 0-09-077151-6, Hutchinson U Lib); pap. text ed. 9.25x (ISBN 0-09-077152-4, Hutchinson U Lib). Humanities.

GYNECOCRACY

see Matriarchy

GYNECOLOGIC ENDOCRINOLOGY

see Endocrine Gynecology

GYNECOLOGIC NURSING

Dean, Patricia G. Self-Assessment of Current Knowledge in Gynecologic Nursing & Women's Health Care. LC 79-92917. 1980. pap. 9.50 (ISBN 0-87488-268-0). Med Exam.

Fream, W. C. Notes on Gynaecological Nursing. (Churchill Livingstone Nursing Notes). (Illus.). 1979. pap. text ed. 6.50 (ISBN 0-443-01480-9). Churchill.

Lytle, Nancy A. Nursing of Women in the Age of Liberation. 1977. pap. text ed. 6.95x (ISBN 0-697-05516-7). Wm C Brown.

McNall, Lee. Contemporary Obstetric & Gynecologic Nursing, Vol. 3. LC 79-27333. (Current Practice Ser.). 1980. pap. 13.95 (ISBN 0-8016-3325-7). Mosby.

McNall, Leota K., ed. Current Practice in Obstetric & Gynecologic Nursing, Vol. 2. Galeener, Janet. LC 75-29240. (Current Practice Ser.). (Illus.). 1978. 11.95 (ISBN 0-8016-3326-5); pap. 8.95 (ISBN 0-8016-3327-3). Mosby.

GYNECOLOGY

see also Endocrine Gynecology; Gynecologic Nursing; Pathology, Gynecological; Pediatric Gynecology; Women–Diseases

Ahrens, Uwe, et al. Birth. LC 77-2603. (Illus.). 176p. 1981. pap. 9.95 (ISBN 0-06-090867-X, CN 867, CN). Har-Row.

Baba, S., et al, eds. The Biology of the Fluids of the Female Genital Tract. 456p. 1979. 80.50 (ISBN 0-444-90069-1, Excerpta Medica). Elsevier.

Bacchus, Habeeb. Essentials of Gynecologic & Obstetric Endocrinology. (Illus.). 232p. 1975. 14.50 (ISBN 0-8391-0814-1). Univ Park.

Barber, Hugh R. Manual of Gynecologic Oncology. 356p. 1980. pap. text ed. 19.50 (ISBN 0-397-50474-8, JBL-Med-Nursing). Har-Row.

Barber, Hugh R., et al. Quick Reference to OB-Gyn Procedures. 2nd ed. 1979. pap. text ed. 19.50 (ISBN 0-397-50423-3, JBL-Med-Nursing). Har-Row.

Barnes, Allan C., ed. The Social Responsibility of Gynecology & Obstetrics. 225p. 1965. 15.50x (ISBN 0-8018-0055-2). Johns Hopkins.

Beller, F. K., et al. Gynecology: A Textbook for Students. LC 73-77004. (Illus.). 385p. 1974. pap. 15.90 (ISBN 0-387-90087-X). Springer-Verlag.

Benson, Ralph C. Handbook of Obstetrics & Gynecology. 7th ed. LC 80-81205. (Illus.). 808p. 1980. lexotone cover 10.00 (ISBN 0-87041-144-6). Lange.

Benson, Ralph C., ed. Current Obstetric & Gynecologic Diagnosis & Treatment. 3rd ed. LC 80-82160. (Illus.). 1001p. 1980. lexotone cover 21.00 (ISBN 0-87041-212-4). Lange.

Bericht ueber die Jahresversammlung, 19-21 Juni 1975 in Nyon, Schweizerische Gesellschaft. Gynaekologie. Erb, H., ed. (Gynaekologische Rundschau: Vol. 15, Suppl. 1). (Illus.). 128p. 1976. 28.75 (ISBN 3-8055-2313-0). S Karger.

Boon, Mathilde E. Gynaecological Cytology. 78p. 1980. pap. 29.95 (ISBN 0-8391-4105-X). Univ Park.

Bradley, Robert A. Husband Coached Childbirth. 3rd ed. LC 80-8683. (Illus.). 256p. 1981. 9.95 (ISBN 0-06-014850-0, HarpT). Har-Row.

Breen, James L. & Jaffurs, William. Atlas of Gynecologic-Obstetric Pathology. (Complete print edition available). 1973. Two Parts. 90.00 (ISBN 0-8036-1136-6). Davis Co.

Brown, D. Obstetrics, Contraception, & Gynecology. 1977. 29.50 (ISBN 0-8391-1171-1). Univ Park.

Brush, M. G. & Taylor, R. W. Gynaecological Malignancy: Clinical & Experimental Studies. (Illus.). 1975. text ed. 28.50 (ISBN 0-02-857340-4). Macmillan.

Burnett, C. W. A Summary of Gynaecology. new ed. 150p. 1974. pap. text ed. 3.95 (ISBN 0-571-04846-3, Pub. by Faber & Faber). Merrimack Bk Serv.

Cantor, Edward B. Female Urinary Stress Incontinence. (Illus.). 360p. 1979. text ed. 30.25 (ISBN 0-398-03819-8). C C Thomas.

Caplan & Sweeney. Advances in Obstetrics & Gynecology. 1978. lib. bdg. 53.00 (ISBN 0-683-01435-8). Williams & Wilkins.

Carmichael, D. Erskine. The Pap Smear: Life of George N. Papanicolaou. (Illus.). 140p. 1973. 10.25 (ISBN 0-398-02716-1). C C Thomas.

Castelazo-Ayala, L., et al, eds. Gynecology & Obstetrics: Proceedings of the VII World Congress of Gynecology & Obstertics, Mexico City, October, 1976. (International Congress Ser: No. 412). 1978. 103.50 (ISBN 0-444-15251-2, Excerpta Medica). Elsevier.

Chabon, Irwin. Awake & Aware: Participating in Childbirth Through Psychoprophylaxis. 1966. 6.95 (ISBN 0-440-00351-2). Delacorte.

Chamberlain, Geoffrey. Contemporary Obstetrics & Gynaecology, Vol. 1. 440p. 90.00x (ISBN 0-7198-2546-6, Pub. by Northwood Bks). State Mutual Bk.

Chamberlain, Geoffrey & Dewhurst, C. J. Practice of Obstetrics & Gynecology. (Illus.). 271p. 1977. 21.00x (ISBN 0-8464-1120-2). Beekman Pubs.

Chamberlain, Geoffrey & Dewhurst, G. J. A Practice of Obstetrics & Gynocology. 1976. 19.00 (ISBN 0-685-85058-7). State Mutual Bk.

Chamberlin, Geoffrey. Contemporary Obstetrics & Gynaecology. (Illus.). 1977. 46.50x (ISBN 0-7198-2546-6). Intl Ideas.

Channing, C. P., et al, eds. Ovarian Follicular & Corpus Luteum Function. LC 79-48. (Advances in Experimental Medicine & Biology Ser.: Vol. 112). 824p. 1979. 59.50 (ISBN 0-306-40149-5, Plenum Pr). Plenum Pub.

Charles, David. Infections in Obstetrics & Gynecology. LC 79-67789. (Major Problems in Obstetrics & Gynecology Ser.: Vol. 12). (Illus.). 440p. 1980. text ed. 32.50 (ISBN 0-7216-2492-8). Saunders.

--Self-Assessment of Current Knowledge in Obstetrics & Gynecology. 3rd ed. LC 79-91970. 1980. pap. 16.50 (ISBN 0-87488-260-5). Med Exam.

Chef, R., ed. Real Time Ultrasound in Perinatal Medicine. (Contributions to Gynecology & Obstetrics: Vol. 6). (Illus.). 1979. pap. 47.50 (ISBN 3-8055-2976-7). S Karger.

Cianfrani, Theodore. A Short History of Obstetrics & Gynecology. (Illus.). 466p. 1960. ed. spiral bdg. 44.00photocopy (ISBN 0-398-00308-4). C C Thomas.

Clayton, et al. Gynecology. 12th ed. 600p. 1971. 24.00 (ISBN 0-685-72296-1, Pub. by Williams & Wilkins). Krieger.

Clayton, Stanley & Newton, John R. A Pocket Gynaecology. 9th ed. (Illus.). 1979. pap. text ed. 8.75 (ISBN 0-443-02007-8). Churchill.

Clayton, Stanley G., et al, eds. Gynaecology by Ten Teachers. 13th ed. (Illus.). 400p. 1981. pap. text ed. 18.95x (ISBN 0-7131-4394-0). Intl Ideas.

Cohen, Arnold W. Emergencies in Obstetrics & Gynecology. (Clinics in Emergency Medicine Ser.). (Illus.). 224p. Date not set. lib. bdg. price not set (ISBN 0-443-08130-1). Churchill.

Cumulative Index to Obstetrics & Gynecology, Vols. 1-40 (1953-1972) new ed. LC 74-10594. iv, 427p. 1975. 40.00 (ISBN 0-88471-033-5). Numarc Bk Corp.

Daly, Mary. Gyn-Ecology: The Metaethics of Radical Feminism. LC 78-53790. 1979. pap. 7.95 (ISBN 0-8070-1511-3, BP601). Beacon Pr.

Danforth, David N., ed. Obstetrics & Gynecology. 3rd ed. (Illus.). 1977. text ed. 52.50x (ISBN 0-06-140684-8, Harper Medical). Har-Row.

Davidson, Christine V. & Abramowitz, Stephen I. Women As Patients. LC 80-80350. (Special Issue of Psychology of Women Quarterly: Vol. 4, No. 3). 1980. pap. 9.95 (ISBN 0-89885-015-0). Human Sci Pr.

De Alvarez, Russell R., ed. Textbook of Gynecology. LC 76-10816. (Illus.). 546p. 1977. text ed. 42.50 (ISBN 0-8121-0515-X). Lea & Febiger.

Dean, Patricia G. Self-Assessment of Current Knowledge in Gynecologic Nursing & Women's Health Care. LC 79-92917. 1980. pap. 9.50 (ISBN 0-87488-268-0). Med Exam.

DeCherney, Alan. Patient Management Problems: Obstetrics & Gynecology. LC 79-24563. 128p. (Orig.). 1980. pap. text ed. 9.00 (ISBN 0-668-04364-4). Arco.

De Cherney, Alan, ed. Obstetrics & Gynecology: PreTest Self-Assessment & Review. LC 77-78446. (Clinical Sciences: PreTest Self-Assessment & Review Ser.). (Illus.). 1978. pap. 9.95 (ISBN 0-07-051602-2). McGraw-Pretest.

Delgado, Gregorio & Smith, Julian P. Management of Complications in Gynecologic Oncology. 344p. 1982. 35.00 (ISBN 0-471-05993-5, Pub. by Wiley Med). Wiley.

Dennerstein, Lorraine, et al. Gynaecology, Sex & Psyche. LC 79-670113. 1978. pap. 17.00x (ISBN 0-522-84148-1, Pub. by Melbourne U Pr). Intl Schol Bk Serv.

Dilts, P. V., Jr., et al. Core Studies in Obstetrics & Gynecology. 3rd ed. (Illus.). 272p. 1981. softcover 17.95 (ISBN 0-686-77755-7, 2572-4). Williams & Wilkins.

DiSaia, Philip J. & Creasman, William T. Clinical Gynecologic Oncology. LC 80-18687. (Illus.). 478p. 1980. text ed. 30.50 (ISBN 0-8016-1314-0). Mosby.

DiSaia, Philip J., et al. Synopsis of Gynecologic Oncology. LC 74-34307. (Clinical Monographs in Obstetrics & Gynecology Ser). 344p. 1975. 37.50 (ISBN 0-471-21590-2, Pub. by Wiley-Med). Wiley.

Dixon, G., ed. Undergraduate Obstetrics & Gynecology. (Illus.). 280p. 1980. pap. text ed. 17.50 (ISBN 0-7236-0564-5). Wright-PSG.

Dreher, E., ed. Schweizerische Gesellschaft fuer Gynaekologie, Bericht ueber die Jahresversammlung, Montreux, Juni 1979. (Journal: Gynaekologische Rundschau: Vol. 19, Suppl. 2). 1980. pap. 19.75 (ISBN 3-8055-0456-X). S Karger.

--Schweizerische Gesellschaft fuer Gynaekologie Bericht ueber die Jahresversammlung, St. Gallen. J 1980. (Journal: Gynaekologische Rundschau: Vol. 20, No. 1). (Illus.). iv, 144p. 1981. pap. 19.75 (ISBN 3-8055-2126-X). S Karger.

Elazo-Ayala, Cast & MacGregor, C., eds. Eighth World Congress of Gynecology & Obstetrics: Abstracts. (International Congress Ser.: No. 396). 1976. pap. 33.75 (ISBN 0-444-15235-0, Excerpta Medica). Elsevier.

Elder, M. G. & Hendricks, C. H. Obstetrics & Gynecology: Preterm Labor, Vol. 1. (Butterworths International Medical Reviews Ser.). 1981. text ed. 29.95 (ISBN 0-407-02300-3). Butterworth.

Emans, S. J. & Goldstein, Donald P. Pediatric & Adolescent Gynecology. 1977. text ed. 17.95 (ISBN 0-316-23400-1). Little.

Ephron, Nora. Crazy Salad: Some Things About Women. 1975. 9.95 (ISBN 0-394-49735-X). Knopf.

Farrer, Helen. Gynecological Care. (Illus.). 174p. 1981. pap. 14.95 (ISBN 0-8261-3600-1). Springer Pub.

Frangenheim, H. Laparoscopy & Culdoscopy in Gynecology: Textbook & Atlas. Finzer, K. H., tr. from Ger. (Illus.). 114p. 1972. 19.95 (ISBN 0-407-90100-0). Butterworth.

Garrey, Matthew M., et al. Gynaecology Illustrated. 2nd ed. (Illus.). 1978. pap. text ed. 21.75 (ISBN 0-443-01842-1). Churchill.

Glass, Robert. Office Gynecology. 2nd ed. (Illus.). 352p. 1981. lib. bdg. 26.50 (ISBN 0-683-03548-7). Williams & Wilkins.

Glass, Robert H. Office Gynecology. 250p. 1976. 25.50 (ISBN 0-683-03549-5). Williams & Wilkins.

Goldfarb, W. Office Gynecology: An Audiovisual Book. 1971. including three cassettes 37.95 (ISBN 0-685-54393-5). Krieger.

Goldhirsch, A., ed. Mammakarzinom: Neue Aspekte fuer die Praxis, 1981. (Journal: Gynaekologische Rundschau: Vol. 21, No. 1). (Illus.). xii, 68p. 1981. pap. 21.00 (ISBN 3-8055-2188-X). S Karger.

Goldsmith, Jay P. & Karotkin, Edward H. Assisted Ventilation of the Neonate. LC 80-53489. (Illus.). 390p. Date not set. text ed. price not set (ISBN 0-7216-4154-7). Saunders.

Goodlin, Robert C. Care of the Fetus. LC 78-62542. (Illus.). 580p. 1979. 43.50x (ISBN 0-89352-021-7). Masson Pub.

Green, Thomas H., Jr. Gynecology: Essentials of Clinical Practice. 3rd ed. 1977. pap. 13.95 (ISBN 0-316-32632-1). Little.

Greenhill, J. P. Office Gynecology. 9th ed. (Illus.). 1971. 25.50 (ISBN 0-8151-3951-9). Year Bk Med.

Hassani, N. Ultrasound in Gynecology & Obstetrics. 1977. 26.30 (ISBN 0-387-90260-0). Springer-Verlag.

Hawkins, D. F. Gynecological Therapeutics. 2nd ed. 1981. text ed. 45.00x (ISBN 0-02-858040-0). Macmillan.

Hector, Winifred & Bourne, Gordon. Modern Gynaecology with Obstetrics for Nurses. 6th ed. (Illus.). 282p. 1980. pap. 18.50x (ISBN 0-433-14210-3). Intl Ideas.

Heller. Emergencies in Gynecology & Obstetrics. 1981. 13.95 (ISBN 0-8151-4225-0). Year Bk Med.

Hibbard, Lester T. Infections in Obstetrics & Gynecology. LC 80-18670. (Discussions in Patient Management Ser.). 1980. pap. 8.00 (ISBN 0-87488-896-4). Med Exam.

History of ACOG 1950-1976. 5.00 (ISBN 0-686-24124-X). Am Coll Obstetric.

Howkins, John & Hudson, Christopher N. Shaw's Textbook of Operative Gynaecology. 4th ed. (Illus.). 1977. 89.50 (ISBN 0-443-01394-2). Churchill.

Howkins, John & Stallworthy, John. Bonney's Gynaecological Survey. 8th ed. (Illus.). 1974. text ed. 37.50 (ISBN 0-02-858070-2). Macmillan.

Huff, R. W. & Pauerstein, C. J. Human Reproduction: Physiology & Pathophysiology. 497p. 1979. pap. 18.00 (ISBN 0-471-03562-9). Wiley.

Huffman, John W., et al. The Gynecology of Childhood & Adolescence. 2nd ed. (Illus.). 600p. Date not set. text ed. price not set (ISBN 0-7216-4816-9). Saunders.

Hurt, W. Glenn. Textbook Study Guide of Gynecology. 2nd ed. (Medical Examination Review Book: Vol. 4A). 1976. pap. 8.50 (ISBN 0-87488-152-8). Med Exam.

Insler, Vaclav & Homburg, Roy. Practical Obstetrics & Gynecology: Manual of Selected Procedures & Treatments. (Illus.). 1979. bookblock 49.25 (ISBN 3-8055-2945-7). S Karger.

International Congress of Psychosomatic Obsterics & Gynecology, 5th. Emotion & Reproduction: Proceedings, Vol. 20B, Pt. B. Carenza, L. & Zinchella, L., eds. LC 78-54528. 1980. 86.50 (ISBN 0-12-159402-5). Acad Pr.

International Congress of Psychosomatic Medicine in Obstetrics & Gynecology, 3rd, London, 1971. Psychosomatic Medicine in Obstetrics & Gynecology: Proceedings. Morris, Norman, ed. (Illus.). 1972. 90.00 (ISBN 3-8055-1314-3). S Karger.

International Congress on Obstetrics & Gynecology, 12th, Moscow, 1973. Recent Progress in Obstetrics & Gyna Ecology: Proceedings. Persianinov, L. S., et al, eds. (International Congress Ser.: No. 329). 575p. 1975. 111.75 (ISBN 0-444-15081-1, Excerpta Medica). Elsevier.

Jaluvka, V. Surgical Geriatric Gynecology. (Contributions to Gynecology & Obstetrics: Vol. 7). (Illus.). 1980. soft cover 49.25 (ISBN 3-8055-3070-6). S Karger.

Jameson, Edwin M. Gynecology & Obstetrics. LC 75-24905. (Clio Medica: No. 17). (Illus.). Repr. of 1936 ed. 15.00 (ISBN 0-404-58917-0). AMS Pr.

Janisch, Herbert, et al. Selected Urologic Operations in Gynecology. 1979. 61.25x (ISBN 3-11007-418-4). De Gruyter.

Jeffcoate, N. Principles of Gynecology. 4th ed. 1975. 67.50 (ISBN 0-407-00000-3). Butterworth.

Jones, Howard, Jr. & Jones, Georgeanna S. Novak's Textbook of Gynecology. 3rd, student ed. (Illus.). 450p. 1981. soft cover 16.50 (ISBN 0-686-77750-6, 4467-2). Williams & Wilkins.

Jones, Howard W. & Jones, Georgeanna S. Novak's Textbook of Gynecology. 10th ed. (Illus.). 634p. 1981. pap. 48.00 (ISBN 0-683-04468-0). Williams & Wilkins.

Karim, S. Obstetric & Gunecological Uses of Prostaglandins. (Illus.). 1976. 34.50 (ISBN 0-8391-0950-4). Univ Park.

Kaufman, Sherwin A. From a Gynecologist's Notebook: Questions Women Ask. LC 74-79423. 276p. 1974. 25.00x (ISBN 0-8128-1706-0). Stein & Day.

Keller, Paul J. Hormornal Disorders in Gynecology. (Illus.). 113p. 1981. pap. 16.60 (ISBN 0-387-10341-4). Springer-Verlag.

Kern, G. Gynecology. 2nd ed. (Illus.). 1976. pap. 14.50 (ISBN 0-8151-5015-6). Year Bk Med.

Kistner, Robert W. Gynecology: Principles & Practice. 3rd ed. (Illus.). 1979. 59.50 (ISBN 0-8151-5081-4). Year Bk Med.

Kobayashi, Mitsunao. Illustrated Manual of Ultrasonography in Obstetrics & Gynecology. 2nd ed. LC 79-92555. (Illus.). 1980. 37.50 (ISBN 0-89640-040-9). Igaku-Shoin.

Kreutner, A. Karen & Reycroft-Hollingsworth, Dorothy. Adolescent Obstetrics & Gynecology. (Illus.). 1978. 44.95 (ISBN 0-8151-5200-0). Year Bk Med.

Kroger, William S. Psychosomatic Obstetrics, Gynecology & Endocrinology: Including Diseases of Metabolism. (American Lecture Gynecology & Obstetrics). (Illus.). 848p. 1962. photocopy ed. spiral 79.50 (ISBN 0-398-01052-8). C C Thomas.

Lackritz, Richard M. Current Literature Reveiw in Obstetrics & Gynecology. 175p. 1981. 18.50 (ISBN 0-8385-1409-X). ACC.

Lanson, Lucienne. From Woman to Woman: A Gynecologist Answers Questions About You & Your Body. rev. ed. LC 80-11226. (Illus.). 352p. 1981. 15.00 (ISBN 0-394-51293-6); pap. 8.95 (ISBN 0-394-73996-5). Knopf.

--From Woman to Woman: A Gynecologist Answers Questions About You & Your Body. 1975. 10.00 (ISBN 0-394-49099-1); pap. 5.95 (ISBN 0-394-73341-X). Knopf.

Lees, David H. & Singer, Albert. A Color Atlas of Gynecological Surgery: Vol. 4, Surgery of Vulva & Lower Genital Tract. (Illus.). 1980. 72.50 (ISBN 0-8151-5354-6). Year Bk Med.

Lifshitz, Samuel & Buchsbaum, Herbert. Gynecologic Oncology Case Studies. 1978. spiral bdg. 14.75 (ISBN 0-87488-005-X). Med Exam.

Llewellyn-Jones, Derek. Everywoman: A Gynaecological Guide for Life. (Illus.). 368p. 1978. 13.50 (ISBN 0-571-04961-3, Pub. by Faber & Faber); pap. 4.95 (ISBN 0-571-04960-5). Merrimack Bk Serv.

--Fundamental of Obstetrics & Gynaecology, Vol. I: Obstetrics. rev. 2nd ed. (Illus.). 472p. 1977. 32.00 (ISBN 0-571-04913-3, Pub. by Faber & Faber); pap. 25.00 (ISBN 0-571-04914-1). Merrimack Bk Serv.

--Fundamentals of Obstetrics & Gynaecology, Vol. 2: Gynaecology. (Illus.). 296p. 1978. 29.00 (ISBN 0-571-04929-X, Pub. by Faber & Faber); pap. 18.00 (ISBN 0-571-04958-3). Merrimack Bk Serv.

Loch, E. G. Ultrasonic Tomography in Obstetrics & Gynaecology. (Advances in Obstetrics & Gynaecology: Vol. 51). (Illus.). 1973. 24.00 (ISBN 3-8055-1585-5). S Karger.

Loose Leaf Reference Services. Gynecology & Obstetrics, 6 vols. Sciarra, John J., ed. Set. loose leaf bdg. 300.00 (ISBN 0-06-148008-8, Harper Medical); yearly revision pages 50.00 (ISBN 0-685-88067-2). Har-Row.

Ludwig, Alfred O., et al. Psychosomatic Aspects of Gynecological Disorders: Seven Psychoanalytic Case Studies. LC 69-18039. (Commonwealth Fund Publications Ser). 1969. text ed. 7.95x (ISBN 0-674-72215-9). Harvard U Pr.

McClure-Browne, J. C. Postgraduate Obstetrics & Gynaecology. 4th ed. (Illus.). 1973. 39.50 (ISBN 0-407-36121-9). Butterworth.

Macdonald, Ronald R., ed. Scientific Basis of Obstetrics & Gynecology. 2nd ed. (Illus.). 1978. text ed. 49.00 (ISBN 0-443-01580-5). Churchill.

McGowan, Larry, ed. Gynecologic Oncology. (Illus.). 435p. 1978. 42.00 (ISBN 0-8385-3529-1). ACC.

Malik, M. Basu. Textbook of Gynaecology. 786p. 1981. 30.00x (ISBN 0-686-72971-4, Pub. by Oxford & IBH India). State Mutual Bk.

Marcus, C. C. & Marcus, S. L. Advances in Obstetrics & Gynecology. 717p. 1966. 23.50 (ISBN 0-683-05551-8, Pub. by Williams & Wilkins). Krieger.

Martin, Purvis L. Ambulatory Gynecologic Surgery. LC 78-55286. (Illus.). 394p. 1979. 34.00 (ISBN 0-88416-209-5). Wright-PSG.

Menon, M. K., et al. Post Graduate Obstetrics & Gynaecology. 450p. 1979. cloth with jacket 50.00x (ISBN 0-86131-207-4, Pub. by Orient Longman India). State Mutual Bk.

Meudt, R. O. & Hinselmann, M. Ultrasonoscopic Differential Diagnosis in Obstetrics & Gynecology. (Illus.). x, 138p. 1975. 51.00 (ISBN 0-387-06991-7). Springer-Verlag.

Midgley, A. Rees & Sadler, William A., eds. Ovarian Follicular Development & Function. LC 77-17750. 310p. 1978. 30.00 (ISBN 0-89004-186-5). Raven.

Monif, Gilles R., ed. Infectious Diseases in Obstetrics & Gynecology. (Illus.). 1974. text ed. 37.00x (ISBN 0-06-141795-5, Harper Medical). Har-Row.

Morselli, P. L., et al, eds. Basic & Therapeutic Aspects of Perinatal Pharmacology. LC 74-21981. (Monograph of the Mario Negri Institute of Pharmacological Research). 456p. 1975. 37.50 (ISBN 0-89004-016-8). Raven.

Naftolin, Frederick & Stubblefield, Phillip G., eds. Dilation of the Uterine Cervix: Connective Tissue Biology & Clinical Management. 406p. 1979. text ed. 38.50 (ISBN 0-89004-300-0). Raven.

Neuwirth, Robert S. Hysteroscopy. LC 75-296. (Major Problems in Obstetrics & Gynecology Ser., Vol. 8). (Illus.). 116p. 1975. 14.50 (ISBN 0-7216-6762-7). Saunders.

Niswander, Kenneth R. Obstetrics & Gynecology. 4th ed. (Medical Examination Review Book: Vol. 4). 1971. spiral bdg. 8.50 (ISBN 0-87488-104-8). Med Exam.

Page, Ernest W., et al. Human Reproduction: Essentials of Obstetrics, Gynecology, & Reproductive Medicine. 1981. text ed. write for info. (ISBN 0-7216-7053-9). Saunders.

Paletta, Jeanne L., et al. Gynecologic Nursing. (Nursng Outline Ser.). pap. 9.50 (ISBN 0-87488-388-1). Med Exam.

Parsons, Langdon & Sommers, Sheldon C. Gynecology, 2 vols. 2nd ed. LC 75-8184. (Illus.). 1660p. 1978. text ed. 80.00 set (ISBN 0-7216-7084-9); text ed. 70.00 single vol. (ISBN 0-7216-7081-4); Vol. 1. text ed. 45.00 (ISBN 0-7216-7082-2); Vol. 2. text ed. 35.00 (ISBN 0-7216-7083-0). Saunders.

Pauerstein, C. J., ed. Seminar on Tubal Physiology & Biochemistry. (Gynecologic Investigation: Vol. 6, Nos. 3-4). iv, 160p. 1975. Repr. 33.75 (ISBN 3-8055-2252-5). S Karger.

Philipp, Elliott E., et al, eds. Scientific Foundations of Obstetrics & Gynecology. 2nd ed. (Illus.). 1977. 79.50 (ISBN 0-8151-6669-9). Year Bk Med.

Phillips, Jordan M., et al. Laparoscopy. (Illus.). 500p. 1977. 66.00 (ISBN 0-683-06876-8). Williams & Wilkins.

Pitkin, Roy M., ed. Yearbook of Obstetrics & Gynecology, 1981. 1981. 29.95 (ISBN 0-8151-6690-7). Year Bk Med.

Pitkin, Roy M. & Zlatnik, Frank J., eds. Year Book of Obstetrics & Gynecology 1980. (Illus.). 1980. 29.95 (ISBN 0-8151-6689-3). Year Bk Med.

--Year Book of Obstetrics & Gynecology 1979. (Illus.). 1979. 27.50 (ISBN 0-8151-6688-5). Year Bk Med.

Precis: An Update in Obstetrics & Gynecology. 35.00 (ISBN 0-686-24130-4). Am Coll Obstetric.

Probst, Raymond E., ed. Obstetrics & Gynecology Specialty Board Review. 5th ed. 1977. spiral bdg. 16.50 (ISBN 0-87488-304-0). Med Exam.

Quilligan, Edward J. Current Therapy in Obstetrics & Gynecology. LC 79-65461. (Illus.). 224p. 1980. text ed. 22.50 (ISBN 0-7216-7414-3). Saunders.

Reid, Duncan E. & Christian, C. Donald, eds. Controversy in Obstetrics & Gynecology Two. 2nd ed. LC 73-93432. (Illus.). 365p. 1974. text ed. 38.00 (ISBN 0-7216-7528-X). Saunders.

Reinold, E., ed. Jahrestagung der Oesterreichischen Gesellschaft Fuer Gyaekologie und Geburtshilfe. (Gynaekologische Rundschau: Vol. 20, Suppl. 2, 1981). (Illus.). xviii, 294p. 1981. pap. 39.75 (ISBN 3-8055-2191-X). S Karger.

Robinson, Aletha. The Lao Handbook of Maternal & Child Health. 1980. pap. 1.95 (ISBN 0-9602790-1-6). The Garden.

Roland, Beryl, ed. Medieval Women's Guide to Health: The First English Gynecological Handbook. Rowland, Beryl, tr. (Middle English Texts & Contexts Ser.: No. 4). (Illus.). Date not set. lib. bdg. 18.95x (ISBN 0-89102-122-1). B Franklin.

Romney, S., et al. Gynecology & Obstetrics: The Health Care of Women. 1975. 37.00 (ISBN 0-07-053581-7, HP). McGraw.

Romney, Seymour, et al, eds. Gynecology & Obstetrics: The Health Care of Women. 2nd ed. (Illus.). 1980. text ed. 48.50 (ISBN 0-07-053582-5, HP). McGraw.

Ryan, George M., Jr., ed. Ambulatory Care in Obstetrics & Gynecology. 544p. 1980. 43.50 (ISBN 0-8089-1253-4). Grune.

Rydberg, Erik. The Mechanism of Labour. (American Lecture Gynecology & Obstetrics). (Illus.). 192p. 1954. photocopy ed. spiral 19.50 (ISBN 0-398-01636-4). C C Thomas.

Sanders, Roger C. & James, A. E., Jr., eds. Principles & Practice of Ultrasonography in Obstetrics & Gynecology. 2nd ed. (Illus.). 466p. 1980. 52.50 (ISBN 0-8385-7955-8). ACC.

Scarpelli, Emile M. & Cosmi, Ermelando V., eds. Reviews in Perinatal Medicine, Vol. 2. LC 77-74616. 405p. 1978. 34.50 (ISBN 0-89004-195-4). Raven.

Schams, H. & Bretscher, J. Ultrasonographic Diagnosis in Obstetrics & Gynecology. (Illus.). 230p. 1975. text ed. 42.60 (ISBN 0-387-07254-3). Springer-Verlag.

Schreiner, W. E., ed. Schweizerische Gesellschaft fuer Senologie, Kongress in Zuerich, November 1979. (Journal: Gynaekolgishe Rundschau: Vol. 21, Supplement 1). (Illus.). vi, 202p. 1981. pap. 36.00 (ISBN 3-8055-2837-X). S Karger.

--Schweizerische Gesellschaft Fuer Senologie, Kongress in Zuerich, November Nineteen Seventy-Nine. (Journal: Gynaekologische Rundschau: Vol.21, Supplement 1). (Illus.). vi, 198p. 1981. pap. 36.00 (ISBN 3-8055-2837-X). S Karger.

Schweizerische Gesellschaft fuer Gynaekologie, Bericht ueber die Jahresversammlung, Lugano, Juni 30 - Juli 2, 1977. Praeventivmassnahmen in der Gynaekologie und ihre oekonomischen Aspekte. Dreher, E., ed. (Gynaekologische Rundschau: Vol. 17, Suppl. 1). (Illus., Fr. & Ger.). 1977. 21.00 (ISBN 3-8055-2867-1). S Karger.

Schweizerische Gesellschaft fuer Gynaekologie, Bericht ueber die Jahresversammlung Davos 1976. (Gynaekologische Rundschau: Vol. 16, Suppl. 1). (Illus.). 1977. 20.00 (ISBN 3-8055-2669-5). S Karger.

Scientific Abstracts, 24th Annual Meeting, Tucson, Ariz. March 1977. Society for Gynecologic Investigation: Proceedings. (Gynecologic Investigation: Vol. 8, No. 1-2). 1977. 36.00 (ISBN 3-8055-2673-3). S Karger.

Scott, Joseph W. Woman Know Thyself. LC 76-14588. (Illus.). 1976. 12.50 (ISBN 0-913590-44-4). C B Slack.

Semm, K. Atlas of Gynecologic Laparoscopy & Hysteroscopy. Borow, Lawrence S., ed. Rice, Allan L., tr. LC 76-20941. (Illus.). 352p. 1977. text ed. 57.50 (ISBN 0-7216-8063-1). Saunders.

Sloane, Ethel. Biology of Women. LC 79-15256. 1980. 18.95 (ISBN 0-471-02165-2, Pub. by Wiley-Medical). Wiley.

Speroff, Leon, et al. Clinical Gynecologic Endocrinology & Infertility. 2nd ed. (Illus.). 444p. 1978. 35.00 (ISBN 0-683-07894-1). Williams & Wilkins.

Stage, Sarah. Female Complaints: Lydia Pinkham & the Business of Women's Medicine. (Illus.). 1979. 14.95 (ISBN 0-393-01178-X). Norton.

Stallworthy, John & Bourne, Gordon, eds. Recent Advances in Obstetrics & Gynaecology, No. 13. 1980. text ed. 42.50 (ISBN 0-443-01887-1). Churchill.

Standards for Obstetric-Gynecologic Services. 1974. 10.00 (ISBN 0-686-24132-0). Am Coll Obstetric.

Stewart, F. H., et al. My Body, My Health: The Concerned Woman's Guide to Gynecology. LC 78-31499. 567p. 1979. 17.95 (ISBN 0-471-04517-9); (Pub. by Wiley Medical). Wiley.

Stewart, Felicia & Hatcher, Robert. My Body, My Health. 592p. 1981. pap. 9.95 (ISBN 0-553-01299-1). Bantam.

Stoll, Peter. Gynecological Vital Cytology. Function. Microbiology. Neoplasia. Atlas of Phase-Contrast Microscopy. LC 74-99013. (Illus.). 1969. 35.30 (ISBN 0-387-04725-5). Springer-Verlag.

Sturgis, Somers H. Gynecologic Patient: A Psycho-Endocrine Study. LC 61-18639. (Illus.). 256p. 1962. 38.25 (ISBN 0-8089-0491-4). Grune.

Swartz, William H., ed. Obstetrics & Gynecology: PreTest Self-Assessment & Review. 2nd ed. (Illus.). 225p. 1981. pap. 9.95 (ISBN 0-07-050975-1, HP). McGraw.

Sweeney, William J., 3rd & Stern, Barbara L. Woman's Doctor. 352p. 1974. pap. 1.75 (ISBN 0-445-08271-2). Popular Lib.

Taber, Ben-Zion. Manual of Gynecologic & Obstetric Emergencies. new ed. LC 77-84692. (Illus.). 1979. pap. text ed. 26.00 (ISBN 0-7216-8721-0). Saunders.

Taylor, R. W. & Brush, M. G. Obstetrics & Gynaecology: Concise Medical Textbook. (Illus.). 1979. pap. text ed. 13.95 (ISBN 0-02-859450-9). Macmillan.

Taymor, Melvin L. Infertility. LC 77-18735. 224p. 1978. 29.50 (ISBN 0-8089-1075-2). Grune.

Thoms, Herbert. Classic Contributions to Obstertrics & Gynecology. (Historia Medicinae Ser.). (Illus.). Repr. of 1935 ed. lib. bdg. 17.50 (ISBN 0-87991-715-6). Porcupine Pr.

--Classical Contributions to Obstetrics & Gynecology. (Illus.). 265p. 1935. photocopy ed. spiral 26.50 (ISBN 0-398-04421-X). C C Thomas.

Tindall, V. R. Color Atlas of Clinical Gynecology. 1981. 41.50 (ISBN 0-8151-8204-X). Year Bk Med.

--Self Assessment in Obstetrics & Gynecology, Part 1: Basic Sciences. 1978. pap. 12.95 (ISBN 0-8151-8806-4). Year Bk Med.

Tovell, Harold & Dank, Leonard. Operaciones Ginecologicas. (Span.). 1981. pap. text ed. price not set (ISBN 0-06-319301-9, Pub. by HarLA Mexico). Har-Row.

Van Nagell, John R., Jr. & Barber, Hugh R., eds. Modern Concepts of Gynecological Oncology. (Illus.). 600p. 1981. text ed. 54.50 (ISBN 0-88416-268-0). Wright-PSG.

Vokaer, Roger & De Maubeuge, M. Sexual Endocrinology. LC 77-86694. (Illus.). 280p. 1978. 37.50x (ISBN 0-89352-017-9). Masson Pub.

Vontver, Louis A. Obstetrics & Gynecology Review. 2nd ed. LC 78-6768. (Arco Medical Review Ser.). (Illus.). 1978. pap. text ed. 9.00 (ISBN 0-668-03450-5). Arco.

Vontver, Louis A. & Gamette, Kent R. Differential Diagnosis in Gynecology. LC 77-17629. 1978. pap. text ed. 12.00x (ISBN 0-668-04129-3, 4129). Arco.

Wachstein, Alison E. Pregnant Moments. LC 79-88347. 1979. pap. 10.95 (ISBN 0-87100-153-5, 2153). Morgan.

Walker, J., et al. Combined Textbook of Obstetrics & Gynecology. 9th ed. LC 76-8406. (Illus.). 1976. 98.00 (ISBN 0-443-01072-2). Churchill.

Weller, Robert H. & Heuser, Robert L. Wanted & Unwanted Childbearing in the United States: National Natality Surveys 1968-1969 & 1972. Stevenson, Taloria, ed. (Ser. 21: No. 32). 1978. pap. text ed. 1.75 (ISBN 0-8406-0140-9). Natl Ctr Health Stats.

Williams, Preston P. Specialty Board Review: Obstetrics & Gynecology. 2nd ed. LC 78-8734. (Arco Medical Review Ser.). (Illus.). 1979. pap. 14.00 (ISBN 0-668-03477-7). Arco.

Willocks, James. Essential Obstetrics & Gynaecology: A Guide for Postgraduates. (Illus.). 1978. pap. text ed. 14.50 (ISBN 0-443-01390-X). Churchill.

Willson, J. Robert. Obstetrics & Gynecology. 5th ed. LC 74-28270. 698p. 1975. text ed. 25.50 (ISBN 0-8016-5592-7). Mosby.

Willson, J. Robert & Carrington, Elsie R. Obstetrics & Gynecology. 6th ed. LC 78-31642. (Illus.). 1979. text ed. 34.50 (ISBN 0-8016-5595-1). Mosby.

Wolman, B. B., ed. Psychological Aspects of Gynecology & Obstetrics. 1978. 22.50 (ISBN 0-87489-009-8). Med Economics.

Wren, Barry G. Handbook of Obstetrics & Gynaecology. (Illus.). 454p. 1979. pap. text ed. 14.95 (ISBN 0-02-859810-5). Macmillan.

Wynn, ed. Obstetrics & Gynecology Annual: 1977, Vol. 6. (Illus.). 1977. 28.75 (ISBN 0-8385-7181-6). ACC.

Wynn, Ralph M. Obstetrics & Gynecology: The Clinical Core. 2nd ed. LC 78-12821. 296p. 1979. text ed. 15.00 (ISBN 0-8121-0658-X). Lea & Febiger.

Wynn, Ralph M., ed. Obstetrics & Gynecology Annual 1978, Vol. 7. (Illus.). 476p. 1978. 32.50 (ISBN 0-8385-7182-4). ACC.

--Obstetrics & Gynecology Annual 1979, Vol. 8. (Illus.). 481p. 1979. 32.50 (ISBN 0-8385-7183-2). ACC.

--Obstetrics & Gynecology Annual 1980. (Obstetrics & Gynecology Ser.). (Illus.). 390p. 1980. 32.50x (ISBN 0-8385-7186-7). ACC.

--Obstetrics & Gynecology Annual, 1981. (Obstetrics & Gynecology Annual Series). (Illus.). 448p. 1981. 32.50 (ISBN 0-8385-7188-3). ACC.

Youngs, David D. & Ehrhardt, Anke A. Psychosomatic Obstetrics & Gynecology. (Illus.). 306p. 1980. 19.50 (ISBN 0-8385-8041-6). ACC.

GYNECOLOGY-DICTIONARIES

Cumulative Index to Clinical Obstetrics & Genecology, Vols. 1-17 (1958-1974) new ed. LC 75-45525. 1976. lib. bdg. 25.00 (ISBN 0-88471-035-1). Numarc Bk Corp.

GYNECOLOGY-OUTLINES, SYLLABI, ETC.

Beacham, Daniel W. & Beacham, Woodard D. Synopsis of Gynecology. 9th ed. LC 77-3544. (Illus.). 1977. pap. 19.95 (ISBN 0-8016-0525-3). Mosby.

NAACOG Conference Manual. 1978. 5.00 (ISBN 0-686-24127-4). Am Coll Obstetric.

NAACOG Officers Manual. 1976. 5.00 (ISBN 0-686-24128-2). Am Coll Obstetric.

GYNECOLOGY, OPERATIVE

Bush, Raymond S. Malignancies of the Ovary, Uterus & Cervix. (Management of Malignant Diseases Ser.: Vol. 2). (Illus.). 200p. 1980. 29.50 (ISBN 0-8151-1384-6). Year Bk Med.

Greenhill, J. P. Surgical Gynecology. 4th ed. (Illus.). 1969. 27.50 (ISBN 0-8151-3954-3). Year Bk Med.

Howkins, John & Stallworthy, John. Bonney's Gynaecological Survey. 8th ed. (Illus.). 1974. text ed. 37.50 (ISBN 0-02-858070-2). Macmillan.

Lees, David & Singer, Albert. Color Atlas of Gynecological Surgery: Abdominal Operations for Bening Conditions Vol. 2. 1978. 62.50 (ISBN 0-8151-5352-X). Year Bk Med.

--Color Atlas of Gynecological Surgery: Abdominal Operations for Benign Conditions, Vol. 2. 1978. 62.50 (ISBN 0-8151-5352-X). Year Bk Med.

Lees, David H. & Singer, Albert. Cirugia De la Vulva y Del Tracto Genital, Vol. 4. Date not set. price not set (ISBN 0-8151-5361-9). Year Bk Med.

--A Color Atlas of Gynecological Surgery Vol. 1: Vaginal Operations. (Illus.). 1978. 55.00 (ISBN 0-8151-5351-1). Year Bk Med.

--Color Atlas of Gynecological Surgery: Vol. 3, Operations for Malignant Diseases. (Illus.). 1979. 79.95 (ISBN 0-8151-5353-8). Year Bk Med.

Masterson, B. J. Manual of Gynecologic Surgery. (Comprehensive Manuals of Surgical Specialities). (Illus.). 1979. 83.80 (ISBN 0-387-90372-0). Springer-Verlag.

Mattingly, Richardf. Te Linde's Operative Gynegology. 5th ed. LC 77-12490. (Illus.). 1977. 79.50 (ISBN 0-397-50375-X, JBL-Med-Nursing). Har-Row.

Parsons, Langdon & Ulfelder, Howard. Atlas of Pelvic Operations. 2nd ed. LC 68-18283. (Illus.). 1968. 37.50 (ISBN 0-7216-7096-2). Saunders.

Phillips, Jordan M., et al. Laparoscopy. (Illus.). 500p. 1977. 66.00 (ISBN 0-683-06876-8). Williams & Wilkins.

Ridley, John H. Gynecologic Surgery: Errors, Safeguards & Salvage. 2nd. ed. (Illus.). 397p. 1981. lib. bdg. 39.00 (ISBN 0-683-07277-3). Williams & Wilkins.

Roberts, D. W. Gynecology & Obstetrics. (Operative Surgery Ser.). 1977. 49.95 (ISBN 0-407-00615-X). Butterworth.

Schaefer, George & Graber, Edward A., eds. Complications in Obstetric & Gynecologic Surgery. (Illus.). 492p. 1981. text ed. 40.00 (ISBN 0-06-142330-0, Harper Medical). Har-Row.

Schweizerische Gesellschaft fuer Gynackologie, Bericht ueber die Jahresversammlung, Lugano, Juni 30 - Juli 2, 1977. Aesthetisch-Plastische Operationen in der Gynaekologie. Dreher, E., ed. (Gynaekologische Rundschau: Vol. 18, No. 1). (Illus., Fr., Ger. & Etal.). 1978. 21.00 (ISBN 3-8055-2908-2). S Karger.

Tovell, Harold M. & Dank, Leonard D. Gynecologic Operations: As Performed by Members of the Staff of Woman's Hospital, St. Luke's Hospital Center, New York, New York. (Illus.). 1978. text ed. 37.50x (ISBN 0-06-142553-2, Harper Medical). Har-Row.

Uyttenbroeck, Frans. Gynecologic Surgery: Treatment of Complications & Prevention of Injuries. LC 80-80968. 288p. 1980. 29.50x (ISBN 0-89352-088-8). Masson Pub.

GYPSIES

see Gipsies

GYPSY LANGUAGE

see Gipsies–Language

GYPSY TALES

see Tales, Gypsy

GYRO COMPASS

see also Automatic Pilot (Airplanes)

GYRO PILOT

see Automatic Pilot (Airplanes)

GYRODYNAMICS

see Rotational Motion

GYROPILOT

see Automatic Pilot (Airplanes)

GYROSCOPE

see also Gyroscopic Instruments; Stability of Airplanes; Stability of Ships

CISM (International Center for Mechanical Sciences), Dept. for General Mechanics, 1970. Critical Speeds of Gyroscopes. Schweitzer, G., ed. (CISM Pubns. Ser.: No. 55). (Illus.). 95p. 1972. pap. 13.50 (ISBN 0-387-81150-8). Springer-Verlag.

CISM (International Center for Mechanical Sciences), Dept. for General Mechanics, Vienna, 1970. Gas-Lubricated Bearings of Gyroscopes. Heinrich, G., ed. (CISM Pubns. Ser.: No. 43). (Illus.). 57p. 1972. pap. 10.00 (ISBN 0-387-81147-8). Springer-Verlag.

CISM (International Center for Mechanical Scineces) Gyrodynamics. Magnus, K., ed. (CISM Intl. Centre for Mechanical Science, Courses & Lectures Ser.: No. 53). (Illus.). x, 280p. 1974. pap. 15.40 (ISBN 0-387-81229-6). Springer-Verlag.

Crabtree, Harold. Spinning Tops & Gyroscopic Motion. LC 66-23755. (Illus.). 1977. text ed. 9.95 (ISBN 0-8284-0204-3). Chelsea Pub.

Euromech 38 Colloquium, Louvain-la-Neuve, Belgium, 3-5 September, 1973. Gyrodynamics: Proceedings. Willems, P. Y., ed. (Illus.). 300p. 1974. 28.40 (ISBN 0-387-06776-0). Springer-Verlag.

Greenhill, George. Gyroscopic Theory. LC 66-30616. 17.50 (ISBN 0-8284-0205-1). Chelsea Pub.

Klein, Felix. Ueber Die Theorie Des Kreisels. 1965. 46.00 (ISBN 0-384-29720-X). Johnson Repr.

Leimanis, E. General Problem of the Motion of Coupled Rigid Bodies About a Fixed Point. (Springer Tracts in Natural Philosophy: Vol. 7). (Illus.). 1965. 29.70 (ISBN 0-387-03408-0). Springer-Verlag.

Ziegler, Hans, ed. Gyrodynamics. (Illus., Eng. & Fr.). 1963. 46.70 (ISBN 0-387-03017-4). Springer-Verlag.

GYROSCOPIC INSTRUMENTS

see also Astronautical Instruments;

also names of specific instruments and uses, e.g. Automatic Pilot (Airplanes); Gyro Compass; Inertial Navigation

CISM (International Center for Mechanical Sciences), Dept. for General Mechanics, 1970. Special Problems in Gyrodynamics. Muller, P. C., ed. (CISM Pubns. Ser.: No. 63). (Illus.). 96p. 1973. pap. 14.20 (ISBN 0-387-81085-4). Springer-Verlag.

Siff, Elliott J. & Emmerich, Claude L. Engineering Approach to Gyroscopic Instruments. 1961. 7.50 (ISBN 0-8315-0028-X). Speller.

Ziegler, Hans, ed. Gyrodynamics. (Illus., Eng. & Fr.). 1963. 46.70 (ISBN 0-387-03017-4). Springer-Verlag.

H

H-T-P TEST
see House-Tree-Person Technique

HAAK, THEODORE, 1605-1690

Barnett, Pamela R. Theodore Haak, F. R. S. 1605-1690, the First German Translator of Paradise Lost. 1962. text ed. 19.00x (ISBN 0-686-22468-X). Mouton.

HAAR INTERVAL
see Integrals, Haar

HABANS
see Anabaptists

HABE (AFRICAN PEOPLE)
see Dogons (African People)

HABEAS CORPUS

Duker, William F. A Constitutional History of Habeas Corpus. LC 79-6834. (Contributions in Legal Studies: No. 13). 349p. 1980. lib. bdg. 29.95 (ISBN 0-313-22264-9, DHC/). Greenwood.

Hurd, Rollin Carlos. A Treatise on the Right of Personal Liberty & on Writ of Habeas Corpus. LC 77-37767. (American Constitutional & Legal History Ser). 670p. 1972. Repr. of 1876 ed. lib. bdg. 59.50 (ISBN 0-306-70431-5). Da Capo.

Klaus, Samuel, ed. Milligan Case. LC 78-118031. (Civil Liberties in American History Ser). 1970. Repr. of 1929 ed. lib. bdg. 42.50 (ISBN 0-306-71945-2). Da Capo.

Sharpe, Robert J. The Law of Habeas Corpus. 1976. 42.00x (ISBN 0-19-825332-X). Oxford U Pr.

Sokol, Ronald P. Federal Habeas Corpus. 2nd ed. 1969. 35.00 (ISBN 0-87215-052-6). Michie-Bobbs.

HABER, FRITZ, 1868-1934

Goran, Morris. Story of Fritz Haber. (Illus.). 1967. 10.95x (ISBN 0-8061-0756-1). U of Okla Pr.

HABERSHAM FAMILY

Habersham, Josephine. Ebb Tide: As Seen Through the Diary of Josephine Clay Habersham, 1863. King, Spencer B., Jr., ed. LC 58-59847. (Illus.). 129p. 1958. 9.00 (ISBN 0-8203-0054-3). U of Ga Pr.

HABIMAH

Levy, Emanuel. The Habima--Israel's National Theater 1917-1977. LC 79-12486. 384p. 1979. 25.00x (ISBN 0-231-04582-4). Columbia U Pr.

HABIT
see also Inhibition; Instinct

Azrin, Nathan & Nunn, Gregory. Habit Control in a Day. 1978. pap. 1.95 (ISBN 0-671-81540-7). PB.

Dunlap, Knight. Habits: Their Making & Unmaking. LC 77-184102. 336p. 1949. pap. 3.95 (ISBN 0-87140-072-3). Liveright.

Glover, John A. & Gary, Albert L. Behavior Modification: An Empirical Approach to Self-Control. LC 79-88. 208p. 1979. 15.95x (ISBN 0-88229-298-6). Nelson-Hall.

Hartness, James. The Human Factor in Works Management. LC 73-10284. (Management History Ser.: No. 46). 168p. Repr. of 1912 ed. 12.50 (ISBN 0-87960-047-0). Hive Pub.

Hyde, Margaret O. Addictions. 1978. 7.95 (ISBN 0-07-031645-7, GB). McGraw.

Kane, Cornelius T. Habit: A Theological & Psychological Analysis. LC 78-64370. 1978. pap. text ed. 6.50 (ISBN 0-8191-0630-5). U Pr of Amer.

Kestenbaum, Victor. The Phenomenological Sense of John Dewey: Habit & Meaning. 1977. text ed. 8.50x (ISBN 0-391-00668-1). Humanities.

Klubertanz, George P. Habits & Virtues: A Philosophical Analysis. LC 65-23606. 1965. 29.50x (ISBN 0-89197-196-3). Irvington.

Maine De Biran, Pierre. Influence of Habit on the Faculty of Thinking. Boehm, Margaret D., tr. Repr. of 1929 ed. lib. bdg. 15.00 (ISBN 0-8371-3124-3, MBTH). Greenwood.

Peeke, Harmon V. & Herz, Michael J., eds. Habituation, 2 vols. Incl. Vol. 1. Behavioral Studies. 1973. 46.50 (ISBN 0-12-549801-2); Vol. 2. Electrophysiological Substrates. 1973. 40.50 (ISBN 0-12-549802-0). Set. 70.00 (ISBN 0-685-40604-0). Acad Pr.

Peele, Stanton. How Much Is Too Much? Healthy Habits of Destructive Addictions. (Illus.). 160p. 1980. 10.95 (ISBN 0-13-424192-4, Spec); pap. 4.95 (ISBN 0-13-424184-3). P-H.

Smith, Frederick H. Nail-Biting: The Beatable Habit. LC 80-11687. (Illus., Orig.). 1980. pap. 7.95 (ISBN 0-8425-1806-1). Brigham.

Stiller, Richard. Habits. 158p. 1980. pap. 3.95 (ISBN 0-346-12437-9). Cornerstone.

--Habits: How We Get Them, Why We Keep Them, How We Kick Them. LC 76-47004. (Illus.). (gr. 8 up). 1977. 7.95 (ISBN 0-525-66511-0). Elsevier-Nelson.

HABITS OF ANIMALS
see Animals, Habits and Behavior Of

HABITUAL CRIMINALS
see Recidivists

HABSBURG, HOUSE OF

Carsten, F. L., et al, eds. The Hapsburg Monarchy, 2 vols. (Studies in Russian & East European History Ser.). 1981. text ed. 25.00x ea. Vol. 1, Austria & Bohemia 1835-1918 (ISBN 0-06-490991-3). Vol. 2, Hungary 1835-1918. B&N.

Chmel, Joseph, ed. Urkunde, Briefe und Actenstuecke Zur Geschichte der Habsburgischen Fuersten K. Ladislaus Posth: Erzherzog Albrecht Vi, & Herzog Siegmund Von Oesterreich. (Ger). Repr. of 1850 ed. pap. 52.00 (ISBN 0-384-08898-8). Johnson Repr.

Cone, Polly, ed. The Imperial Style: Fashions of the Hapsburg Era. (Illus.). 168p. 1980. 25.00 (ISBN 0-87099-232-5). Metro Mus Art.

Evans, R. J. The Making of the Habsburg Monarchy: Fifteen Fifty to Seventeen Hundred. 1979. 59.00x (ISBN 0-19-822560-1). Oxford U Pr.

Fest, Wilfried. Peace or Partition: The Habsburg Monarchy & British Policy, 1914-1918. LC 77-92396. 1978. 16.95x (ISBN 0-312-59935-8). St Martin.

Ingrao, Charles W. In Quest & Crisis: Emperor Joseph I & the Habsburg Monarchy. LC 77-88358. (Illus.). 1979. 12.95 (ISBN 0-911198-53-9). Purdue.

Jaszi, Oscar. Dissolution of the Habsburg Monarchy. LC 29-22812. 1961. pap. 3.45 (ISBN 0-226-39568-5, P70, Phoen). U of Chicago Pr.

Jelavich, Barbara. The Habsburg Empire in European Affairs, 1814-1918. viii, 190p. 1974. Repr. of 1969 ed. 16.50 (ISBN 0-208-01485-3, Archon). Shoe String.

Kann, Robert A. A History of the Habsburg Empire, 1526-1918. LC 72-97733. 1974. 36.50x (ISBN 0-520-02408-7); pap. 10.95x (ISBN 0-520-04206-9, CAMPUS 265). U of Cal Pr.

Koenigsberger, H. G. Habsburgs & Europe, 1516-1660. LC 73-145868. (Illus.). 320p. 1971. 20.00x (ISBN 0-8014-0624-2). Cornell U Pr.

Lockyer, Roger. Habsburg & Bourbon Europe, 1470-1720. LC 75-328564. (Illus.). 1974. pap. text ed. 10.95x (ISBN 0-582-35029-8). Longman.

Mamatey, Victor S. Rise of the Habsburg Empire: 1526-1815. LC 77-15525. (Berkshire Studies). 192p. 1978. pap. text ed. 5.50 (ISBN 0-88275-639-7). Krieger.

Metropolitan Museum of Art. The Imperial Style: Fashions of the Hapsburg Era. (Illus.). 1980. 40.00 (ISBN 0-8478-5322-5). Rizzoli Intl.

Spielman, John P. Leopold the First of Austria. 1977. 17.50 (ISBN 0-8135-0836-3). Rutgers U Pr.

Sulzberger, C. L. Fall of Eagles. (Illus.). 1977. 17.95 (ISBN 0-517-52817-7). Crown.

Taylor, A. J. The Habsburg Monarchy, 1809-1918: A History of the Austrian Empire & Austria-Hungary. 1976. pap. 5.50x (ISBN 0-226-79145-9, P683, Phoen). U of Chicago Pr.

Trevor-Roper, Hugh. Princes & Artists: Patronage & Ideology at Four Habsburg Courts, 1517-1633. LC 75-34681. (Illus.). 176p. 1977. 20.00 (ISBN 0-06-014362-2, HarpT). Har-Row.

Wandruszka, Adam. The House of Habsburg: Six Hundred Years of a European Dynasty. Epstein, Cathleen & Epstein, Hans, trs. LC 75-5004. 212p. 1975. Repr. of 1964 ed. lib. bdg. 14.00x (ISBN 0-8371-7928-9, WAHH). Greenwood.

Wangermann, Ernst. From Joseph Second to the Jacobin Trials: Government Policy & Public Opinion in the Habsburg Dominions in the Period of the French Revolution. 2nd ed. LC 78-26290. (Oxford Historical Monographs). 1979. Repr. of 1969 ed. lib. bdg. 19.50x (ISBN 0-313-20852-2, WAFJ). Greenwood.

Wedgewood, Cicily V. Thirty Years War. 1962. text ed. 18.75x (ISBN 0-224-00690-8). Humanities.

HACK WRITERS

Pinkus, Philip. Grub Street Stripped Bare: The Scandalous & Pornographic Works of the Original Grub Street Writers. (Illus.). 1968. 19.50 (ISBN 0-208-00756-3, Archon). Shoe String.

HACKS (CARRIAGES)
see Carriages and Carts

HADES
see Future Life; Hell

HADITH
Here are entered works on the oral traditions concerning the deeds and sayings of Muhammad, the prophet, solely.

Ali, Maulana M. A Manual of Hadith: Arabic Text & English Translation. 2nd, 1944 ed. 1978. text ed. 13.00x (ISBN 0-391-00548-0). Humanities.

Azami, M. M. Studies in Early Hadith Literature. LC 77-90341. 1978. 8.25 (ISBN 0-89259-012-2). Am Trust Pubns.

Azami, Mustafa. Studies in Hadith Methodology & Literature. Beg, Anwer, ed. LC 77-90335. 1978. 7.00 (ISBN 0-89259-011-4). Am Trust Pubns.

Azizullah. Glimpses of Hadith, 3. pap. 3.75 (ISBN 0-686-18380-0). Kazi Pubns.

Doi, A. R. Hadith: An Introduction. 1980. pap. 4.95 (ISBN 0-686-64661-4). Kazi Pubns.

Guillaume, Alfred. The Traditions of Islam. LC 79-52552. (Islam Ser.). 1980. Repr. of 1924 ed. lib. bdg. 16.00x (ISBN 0-8369-9260-1). Arno.

Historical Association of Kenya. Hadith: Proceedings, 7 vols. Ogot, Bethwell A., ed. (Illus.). Vol. 1. 1968. 6.25x (ISBN 0-8002-0574-X); Vol. 2. 1970. 12.50x (ISBN 0-8002-0501-4); Vol. 3. 1971. 7.50x (ISBN 0-8002-0572-3); Vol. 4. 1972. 12.50x (ISBN 0-8002-0600-2); Vol. 5. 1973. 12.50x (ISBN 0-8002-0601-0); Vol. 6. 1974. 12.50x (ISBN 0-8002-0602-9); Vol. 7. 1975. 13.50x (ISBN 0-8002-0603-7). Intl Pubns Serv.

Qazi, M. A. Bilal in Hadith. pap. 1.00 (ISBN 0-686-18324-X). Kazi Pubns.

Rauf, A. Hadilh for Children. pap. 3.95 (ISBN 0-686-63901-4). Kazi Pubns.

HADLEY, MASSACHUSETTS

Judd, Sylvester. The History of Hadley, Mass. LC 75-29635. 784p. 1976. Repr. of 1905 ed. 35.00 (ISBN 0-912274-57-3). NH Pub Co.

HADRAMI INSCRIPTIONS
see Inscriptions, Hadrami

HADRIAN, EMPEROR OF ROME, 76-138

Benario, Herbert W. A Commentary on the Vita Hadriana in the Historia Augusta. LC 80-11953. (American Classical Studies: No. 7). 1980. 13.50x (ISBN 0-89130-391-X, 400407); pap. 9.00x (ISBN 0-686-29276-6). Scholars Pr CA.

Perowne, Stewart. Hadrian. LC 75-43946. (Illus.). 192p. 1976. Repr. of 1960 ed. lib. bdg. 15.75x (ISBN 0-8371-8723-0, PEHAD). Greenwood.

Rolfe, F. Hadrian the Seventh. 1982. pap. 3.95 (ISBN 0-14-002031-4). Penguin.

Trease, Geofrey. Message to Hadrian. (gr. 7 up). 1955. 6.95 (ISBN 0-8149-0429-7). Vanguard.

HADRIAN, EMPEROR OF ROME, 76-138–FICTION

Trease, Geofrey. Message to Hadrian. (gr. 7 up). 1955. 6.95 (ISBN 0-8149-0429-7). Vanguard.

Yourcenar, Marguerite. Memoirs of Hadrian. (Illus.). 347p. 1963. 17.50 (ISBN 0-374-20728-3); pap. 9.95 (ISBN 0-374-50348-6). FS&G.

HADRIAN'S WALL

Bergstrom, Theo. Hadrian's Wall. (Illus.). 1978. pap. 3.95 (ISBN 0-8467-0502-8, Pub. by Two Continents). Hippocrene Bks.

Divine, David. Hadrian's Wall: A Study of the North-West Frontier of Rome. LC 69-13122. (Illus.). 1969. 9.95 (ISBN 0-87645-017-6). Gambit.

Forde-Johnston, James. Hadrian's Wall. (Illus.). 240p. 1980. 15.95 (ISBN 0-7181-1652-6, Pub. by Michael Joseph). Merrimack Bk Serv.

Phillips, E. J. Corpus Signorium Imperii Romani: Hadrian's Wall, East of North Tyne, Vol. I, Fsc. I. (British Academy Ser.). (Illus.). 1977. 69.00x (ISBN 0-19-725954-5). Oxford U Pr.

HADRONS

Cabibbo, N. & Sertorio, L., eds. Hadronic Matter at Extreme Energy Density. (Ettore Majoana International Science Ser., Physical Sciences: Vol. 2). 365p. 1980. 42.50 (ISBN 0-306-40303-X, Plenum Pr). Plenum Pub.

Cumming, J. & Osborn, H., eds. Hadronic Interactions of Electronics & Photons. 1971. 103.50 (ISBN 0-12-198750-7). Acad Pr.

Donnachie, A. & Shaw, G., eds. Electromagnetic Interactions of Hadrons. (Nuclear Physics Monographs). (Illus.). 1978. Vol. 1, 458 Pp. 49.50 (ISBN 0-306-31052-X, Plenum Pr); Vol. 2, 400 Pp. 57.50 (ISBN 0-306-31106-2). Plenum Pub.

Feynman, Richard P. Photon-Hadron Interactions. (Frontiers in Physics Ser.: No. 37). 1972. 19.50 (ISBN 0-8053-2510-7, Adv Bk Prog). Benjamin-Cummings.

Fries & Wess, eds. New Phenomena in Lepton-Hadron Physics. (NATO Advanced Study Institutes, Ser. B, Physics: Vol. 49). 1979. 49.50 (ISBN 0-306-40301-3, Plenum Pr). Plenum Pub.

Hofmann, W. Jets of Hadrons. (Springer Tracts in Modern Physics Ser.: Vol. 90). (Illus.). 210p. 1981. 32.50 (ISBN 0-387-10625-1). Springer-Verlag.

Horn, David & Zachariasen, Fredrik. Hadron Physics at Very High Energies. LC 73-9616. (Frontiers in Physics Ser: No. 40). xvi, 378p. 1973. text ed. 17.50 (ISBN 0-8053-4402-0, Adv Bk Prog); pap. text ed. 9.50 (ISBN 0-8053-4403-9, Adv Bk Prog). Benjamin-Cummings.

Humpert, B., ed. Dynamical Concepts on Scaling Violation & the New Resonances in e Positive e Negative Annihilation. (Lecture Notes in Physics Ser: Vol. 45). 1975. pap. 13.80 (ISBN 0-387-07539-9). Springer-Verlag.

Levy, et al, eds. Hadron Structure & Lepton-Hadron Interactions. (NATO Advanced Study Institutes Ser.: Series B, Physics, Vol. 39). 1979. 65.00 (ISBN 0-306-40072-3, Plenum Pr). Plenum Pub.

Morpurgo, G., ed. Quarks & Hadronic Structure. LC 76-47490. (International Physics Workshop Ser.: Vol. 1). 318p. 1977. 35.00 (ISBN 0-306-38141-9, Plenum Pr). Plenum Pub.

Perl, Martin L. High Energy Hadron Physics. LC 74-6348. 584p. 1974. 41.00 (ISBN 0-471-68049-4, Pub. by Wiley-Interscience). Wiley.

Preparata, G. & Aubert, J. J., eds. Probing Hadrons with Leptons. (Ettore Majorana International Science Ser., Physical Sciences: Vol. 5). 502p. 1980. 59.50 (ISBN 0-306-40438-9, Plenum Pr). Plenum Pub.

Thomas, A. W., ed. Modern Three-Hadron Physics. (Topics in Current Physics: Vol. 2). 1976. 38.70 (ISBN 3-540-07950-5). Springer-Verlag.

Zichichi, A., ed. Laws of Hadronic Matter: Proceedings. Ettore Majorana Course on Subnuclear Physics, Eleventh, Held at Erice, Italy, July 1973. 1975. 111.00 (ISBN 0-12-780588-5). Acad Pr.

--Lepton & Hadron Structure. 1975. 111.00 (ISBN 0-12-780589-3). Acad Pr.

HADWIG, DUCHESS OF SWABIA, d. 994–FICTION

Scheffel, Josef V. Ekkehard. abridged ed. Delffs, Sofie, tr. LC 64-20049. 1965. 9.00 (ISBN 0-8044-2767-4); pap. 4.75 (ISBN 0-8044-6802-8). Ungar.

HAECKEL, ERNST HEINRICH PHILIPP AUGUST, 1834-1919

Slosson, Edwin E. Major Prophets of To-Day. facs. ed. LC 68-8493. (Essay Index Reprint Ser). 1914. 18.00 (ISBN 0-8369-0882-1). Arno.

HAEMOSTASIS
see Hemostasis

HAENDEL, GEORG FRIEDRICH, 1685-1759

Abraham, Gerald E., ed. Handel: A Symposium. LC 80-11679. (Illus.). vi, 328p. 1980. Repr. of 1954 ed. lib. bdg. 27.25x (ISBN 0-313-22358-0, ABHA). Greenwood.

Bradbury, William & Guild, Courtenay. History of the Handel & Haydn Society, Vol. 2. (Music Reprint Ser.). 1979. Repr. of 1893 ed. lib. bdg. 32.50 (ISBN 0-306-79506-X). Da Capo.

Clarke, Eliza. Handel. LC 70-158201. (Studies in Music, No. 42). 1971. Repr. of 1885 ed. lib. bdg. 48.95 (ISBN 0-8383-1250-0). Haskell.

Coxe, William. Anecdotes of Frederick Handel & John Christopher Smith. (Music Reprint Ser.). 1979. Repr. of 1799 ed. 22.50 (ISBN 0-306-79512-4). Da Capo.

Cudworth, Charles. Handel: A Biography, with a Survey of Books, Editions & Recordings. (Concertgoer's Companion Ser). 1972. 11.50 (ISBN 0-208-01068-8, Linnet). Shoe String.

Dean, Winton. Handel & the Opera Seria. LC 79-78567. (Ernest Bloch Lectures). 1969. 31.75x (ISBN 0-520-01438-3). U of Cal Pr.

--Handel's Dramatic Oratorios & Masques. 1959. 65.00x (ISBN 0-19-315203-7). Oxford U Pr.

Deutsch, Otto. Handel: A Documentary Biography. LC 74-3118. (Music Ser.). 942p. 1974. Repr. of 1954 ed. lib. bdg. 55.00 (ISBN 0-306-70624-5). Da Capo.

Eisenschmitt, Joachim. Die Szenische Darstellung der Opern G. F. Haendels Auf der Londoner Buhne Seiner Zeit, 2 vols. in 1. LC 80-2275. Repr. of 1940 ed. 29.50 (ISBN 0-404-18843-5). AMS Pr.

Flower, Newman. Handel, His Personality & His Times. 383p. 1972. pap. 4.95 (ISBN 0-586-03778-0, Pub. by Granada England). Academy Chi Ltd.

Hadden, James C. Life of Handel: The Kelkel Edition. LC 74-24096. Repr. of 1904 ed. 15.00 (ISBN 0-404-12941-2). AMS Pr.

Hall, James S. G. F. Handel. LC 61-1995. (Great Masters Ser). 50p. 1961. pap. 3.00 (ISBN 0-913932-22-1). Boosey & Hawkes.

Handel. Handel's "Messiah". The Conducting Score. 460p. 1979. Repr. of 1974 ed. 75.00x (ISBN 0-85967-158-5, Pub. by Scolar Pr England). Biblio Dist.

Handel's Messiah: Complete Score, Music & Words. 1973. pap. 2.95 (ISBN 0-85150-265-2). Attic Pr.

Lang, Paul H. George Frideric Handel. 1966. 22.95 (ISBN 0-393-02131-9, Norton Lib); pap. 8.95 (ISBN 0-393-00815-0). Norton.

Mainwaring, John. Memoirs of the Life of George Frederick Handel. (Music Ser.). 1980. Repr. of 1760 ed. 22.50 (ISBN 0-306-76042-8). Da Capo.
--Memoirs of the Life of the Late George Frederic Handel. (Facsimilies of Early Biographies Ser.: Vol. 2). 1975. Repr. of 1760 ed. 17.50 (ISBN 90-6027-016-9, Pub. by Frits Knuf Netherlands). Pendragon NY.
Myers, Robert H. Handel, Dryden, & Milton. 1978. Repr. of 1956 ed. lib. bdg. 20.00 (ISBN 0-8492-6708-0). R West.
Myers, Robert M. Handel, Dryden & Milton. 1956. lib. bdg. 20.00 (ISBN 0-8414-6129-5). Folcroft.
--Handel's Messiah: A Touchstone of Taste. LC 72-159747. 338p. 1971. Repr. of 1948 ed. lib. bdg. 21.00x (ISBN 0-374-96035-6). Octagon.
Rackwitz, Werner & Steffens, Helmut. George Frederic Handel: A Biography in Pictures. LC 74-181232. 191p. 1962. Repr. 18.00 (ISBN 0-403-01653-3). Scholarly.
Robinson, Percy. Handel & His Orbit. (Music Reprint Ser.). 1979. Repr. of 1908 ed. lib. bdg. 27.50 (ISBN 0-306-79522-1). Da Capo.
Rolland, Romain. Haendel. (Illus.). 320p. 1975. 14.95 (ISBN 0-686-55253-9). French & Eur.
--Handel. LC 75-151597. (Illus.). Repr. of 1916 ed. 18.50 (ISBN 0-404-05388-2). AMS Pr.
--Handel. Hull, A. Eaglefield, tr. (Music: Practice & Theory, House Ser). (Illus.). Repr. of 1916 ed. 14.00 (ISBN 0-384-51860-5). Johnson Repr.
Sadie, Stanley. Handel Concertos. LC 72-6085. (BBC Music Guide Ser.: No. 29). (Illus.). 64p. (Orig.). 1973. pap. 1.95 (ISBN 0-295-95227-X). U of Wash Pr.
Schoelcher, Victor. The Life of Handel. (Music Reprint Ser.). 1979. Repr. of 1857 ed. lib. bdg. 35.00 (ISBN 0-306-79572-8). Da Capo.
Smith, William C. Concerning Handel: His Life & Works. LC 78-59044. (Encore Music Editions). (Illus.). 1979. Repr. of 1948 ed. 25.00 (ISBN 0-88355-716-9). Hyperion Conn.
Streatfeild, Richard A. Handel. LC 77-28261. (The New Library of Music). 1978. Repr. of 1909 ed. lib. bdg. 31.50x (ISBN 0-313-20248-6, STHA). Greenwood.
Streatfield, Richard A. Handel. 2nd ed. LC 64-18991. (Music Ser). 1964. 25.00 (ISBN 0-306-70901-5). Da Capo.
Taylor, Sedley. The Indebtedness of Handel to Works by Other Composers. (Music Reprint Ser.). 1979. Repr. of 1906 ed. lib. bdg. 22.50 (ISBN 0-306-79513-2). Da Capo.
--The Indebtedness of Handel to Works by Other Composers, a Presentation of Evidence. Repr. of 1906 ed. 19.50 (ISBN 0-384-59609-6). Johnson Repr.
Tobin, John. Handel's Messiah. LC 69-13491. (Illus.). 1969. 35.00 (ISBN 0-312-35840-7). St Martin.
Weinstock, Herbert. Handel. 2nd rev. ed. LC 78-11991. 1979. Repr. of 1959 ed. lib. bdg. 25.50x (ISBN 0-313-21109-4, WEHD). Greenwood.
Young, Percy M. Handel. rev. ed. (The Master Musicians Ser.: No. M-165). (Illus.). 1978. pap. 7.95 (ISBN 0-8226-0712-3). Littlefield.
--Handel. rev. ed. (Master Musicians Ser). (Illus.). 256p. 1975. 9.95x (ISBN 0-460-03161-9, Pub. by J. M. Dent England). Biblio Dist.
--Messiah, a Study in Interpretation. 1961. 6.95 (ISBN 0-234-77215-8). Dufour.

HAENDEL, GEORG FRIEDRICH, 1685-1759–BIBLIOGRAPHY

Sasse, Konrad. Handel Bibliographie. 2nd ed. 512p. 1965. 37.50x (ISBN 0-8002-0882-X). Intl Pubns Serv.

HAENDEL, GEORG FRIEDRICH, 1685-1759–JUVENILE LITERATURE

Berk, Phyllis L. Duke's Command. (Illus.). (gr. 2-5). PLB 6.19 (ISBN 0-685-13772-4). Lantern.
Young, Percy M. Handel. (gr. 7 up). 1967. 3.50 (ISBN 0-87250-213-9); PLB 3.27 (ISBN 0-87250-413-1). D White.

HAFEN, ANN (WOODBURY), 1893-1970

Hafen, LeRoy R. Joyous Journey. (Illus.). 1973. 11.50 (ISBN 0-87062-102-5). A H Clark.

HAFEN, LE ROY REUBEN, 1893-

Hafen, LeRoy R. Joyous Journey. (Illus.). 1973. 11.50 (ISBN 0-87062-102-5). A H Clark.

HAFNIUM

Manual on Zirconium & Hafnium. (Special Technical Publications Ser.). 108p. 1977. 9.50x (ISBN 0-686-76083-2, 639, 04-639000-35). ASTM.
Mukherji, A. K. Analytical Chemistry of Zirconium & Hafnium. LC 71-109236. 1970. 49.00 (ISBN 0-08-006886-3). Pergamon.
Thomas, D. E. & Hayes, E. T., eds. The Metallurgy of Hafnium. 384p. 1960. pap. 47.80 (ISBN 0-686-75853-6); microfilm 23.90 (ISBN 0-686-75854-4). DOE.

HAGANAH

Syrkin, Marie. Blessed Is the Match: The Story of Jewish Resistance. LC 76-22216. 366p. 1977. pap. 4.95 (ISBN 0-8276-0086-0, 396). Jewish Pubn.

HAGGARD, HENRY RIDER, SIR, 1856-1925

Haggard, Lilias R. The Cloak That I Left: A Biography of the Author, Henry Rider Haggard, K. B. E. 1976. 12.00x (ISBN 0-8476-1419-0). Rowman.
Higgins, D. S., ed. The Private Diaries of Sir H. Rider Haggard, Nineteen Fourteen to Nineteen Twenty-Five. LC 80-5496. 326p. 1980. 19.95 (ISBN 0-8128-2738-4). Stein & Day.

HAGIOGRAPHY

Here are entered works on the lives of the saints, and how to write them. The lives themselves are entered under the heading Saints.

Delehaye, Hippolyte. Legends of the Saints. Attwater, Donald, tr. LC 61-18761. 1962. 20.00 (ISBN 0-8232-0440-5). Fordham.
Petin, L. M. Dictionnaire Hagiographique, 2 vols. Migne, J. P., ed. (Encyclopedie Theologique Ser.: Vols. 40-41). 1580p. (Fr.). Date not set. Repr. of 1850 ed. lib. bdg. 240.00x (ISBN 0-89241-246-1). Caratzas Bros.

HAGUE, FRANK, 1876-1956

Connors, Richard J. A Cycle of Power: The Career of Jersey City Mayor Frank Hague. LC 71-168603. 1971. 10.00 (ISBN 0-8108-0435-2). Scarecrow.

HAGUE–DESCRIPTION–VIEWS

Slechte, C. H. The Hague in Pen & Pencil: Den Haag in Pen en Penseel. (Illus.). 1977. 25.00 (ISBN 90-247-2029-X). Heinman.

HAGUE–INTERNATIONAL COURT OF JUSTICE

Academie De Droit International Recueil Des Cours, Collected Courses of the Hague Academy of International Law, 1980, Vol. I, Tome 166. 448p. 1981. 37.50x (ISBN 90-286-2731-6). Sijthoff & Noordhoff.
Bernhardt, R., et al, eds. Digest of the Decisions of the International Court of Justice, 1959-1975. (Fontes Iuris Gentium, A-I-6). 1978. 200.60 (ISBN 0-387-08550-5). Springer-Verlag.
Clarke. Aspects of the Hague Rules. 1976. pap. 45.00 (ISBN 90-247-1806-6, Pub. by Martinus Nijhoff Netherlands). Kluwer Boston.
Fleming, D. F. The United States & the World Court, 1920-1966. 2nd ed. LC 66-24690. 1968. Repr. of 1945 ed. 10.00 (ISBN 0-8462-1046-0). Russell.
Foster, John W. Arbitration & the Hague Court. vi, 148p. 1980. Repr. of 1904 ed. lib. bdg. 18.50x (ISBN 0-8377-0535-5). Rothman.
Gross, Leo. The Future of the International Court of Justice, 2 vols. LC 76-2646. 1976. Set. text ed. 76.00 (ISBN 0-379-00298-1); Vol 1. text ed. 38.00 (ISBN 0-379-00298-1); Vol 2. text ed. 38.00 (ISBN 0-379-00299-X). Oceana.
Hudson, Manley O. The Permanent Court of International Justice, 1920-1942: A Treatise. LC 72-4277. (World Affairs Ser.: National & International Viewpoints). 832p. 1972. Repr. of 1943 ed. 37.00 (ISBN 0-405-04571-9). Arno.
--Permanent Court of International Justice, 1920-1942: A Treatise. LC 74-147605. (Library of War & Peace; Kellogg Pact & the Outlawry of War). lib. bdg. 38.00 (ISBN 0-8240-0366-7). Garland Pub.
Jessup, Philip C. United States & the World Court. LC 30-269. 1971. Repr. of 1929 ed. 10.00 (ISBN 0-384-27190-1). Johnson Repr.
Lissitzyn, Oliver J. The International Court of Justice. LC 72-159207. 118p. 1971. Repr. of 1951 ed. lib. bdg. 13.00x (ISBN 0-374-95043-1). Octagon.
--The International Court of Justice. LC 72-159207. 118p. 1971. Repr. of 1951 ed. lib. bdg. 13.00x (ISBN 0-374-95043-1). Octagon.
--The International Court of Justice: Its Role in the Maintenance of International Peace & Security. LC 78-2885. (Carnegie Endowment for International Peace, United Nations Studies: No. 6). 1978. Repr. of 1951 ed. lib. bdg. 15.25x (ISBN 0-313-20333-4, LICJ). Greenwood.
Pomerance, Michla. The Advisory Function of the International Court in the League & U N Eras. LC 72-4024. 456p. 1973. 28.50x (ISBN 0-8018-1291-7). Johns Hopkins.
Rosenne, S. Documents in International Court Justice. 2nd ed. 1979. 50.00 (ISBN 0-379-20460-6). Oceana.
Sumanpouw, Mathilde. Les Nouvelles Conventions De la Haye: Leur Application Par les Juges Nationaux, Vol. II. 260p. (Fr.). 1981. 45.00x (ISBN 90-286-0870-2). Sijthoff & Noordhoff.
Syatauw, J. Decisions of the International Court of Justice, a Digest. 1963. 12.00 (ISBN 0-379-00187-X). Oceana.
United Nations Charter & Statute of the International Court of Justice. 87p. 0.75 (ISBN 0-686-30397-0, Co-Pub. by Addams Peace). WILPF.

HAGUE–INTERNATIONAL COURT OF JUSTICE–BIBLIOGRAPHY

Recueil Des Cours De L'academie De Droit International De la Haye-Collected Courses of the Hague Academy of International Law: General Index to Volumes 126 to 151. 1980. 40.00 (ISBN 90-286-0630-0). Sijthoff & Noordhoff.

HAGUE PEACE CONFERENCE, 1899

Choate, Joseph H. Two Hague Conferences. (Reprints in Government & Political Science Ser). 1970. Repr. of 1913 ed. 11.50 (ISBN 0-384-08915-1). Johnson Repr.
--Two Hague Conferences. LC 13-4133. 1969. Repr. of 1913 ed. 9.00 (ISBN 0-527-16850-5). Kraus Repr.
Davis, Calvin D. The United States & the First Hague Peace Conference. (Beveridge Award Books Ser.). 248p. 1962. 22.50x (ISBN 0-8014-0099-6). Cornell U Pr.
Hull, W. I. Two Hague Conferences & Their Contributions to International Law. LC 8-28855. Repr. of 1908 ed. 24.00 (ISBN 0-527-43200-8). Kraus Repr.
Hull, William I. Two Hague Conferences & Their Contributions to International Law. LC 73-147582. (Library of War & Peace; Int'l. Organization, Arbitration & Law). lib. bdg. 38.00 (ISBN 0-8240-0346-2). Garland Pub.
--The Two Hague Conferences & Their Contributions to International Law. 1978. Repr. of 1908 ed. lib. bdg. 30.00 (ISBN 0-8495-2253-6). Arden Lib.
Scott, James B. Hague Conference of Eighteen Ninety-Nine & Nineteen Seven, 2 vols. LC 79-147589. (Library of War & Peace; Int'l. Organization, Arbitration & Law). Set. lib. bdg. 76.00 (ISBN 0-8240-0350-0); lib. bdg. 38.00 ea. Garland Pub.

HAGUE PEACE CONFERENCE, 2ND, 1907

Choate, Joseph H. Two Hague Conferences. (Reprints in Government & Political Science Ser). 1970. Repr. of 1913 ed. 11.50 (ISBN 0-384-08915-1). Johnson Repr.
--Two Hague Conferences. LC 13-4133. 1969. Repr. of 1913 ed. 9.00 (ISBN 0-527-16850-5). Kraus Repr.
Davis, Calvin D. United States & the Second Hague Peace Conference: American Diplomacy & International Organization, 1899-1914. LC 75-17353. 1976. 18.75 (ISBN 0-8223-0346-9). Duke.
Hull, W. I. Two Hague Conferences & Their Contributions to International Law. LC 8-28855. Repr. of 1908 ed. 24.00 (ISBN 0-527-43200-8). Kraus Repr.
Hull, William I. Two Hague Conferences & Their Contributions to International Law. LC 73-147582. (Library of War & Peace; Int'l. Organization, Arbitration & Law). lib. bdg. 38.00 (ISBN 0-8240-0346-2). Garland Pub.
--The Two Hague Conferences & Their Contributions to International Law. 1978. Repr. of 1908 ed. lib. bdg. 30.00 (ISBN 0-8495-2253-6). Arden Lib.
Jacobson, Jon. Locarno Diplomacy: Germany & the West. LC 74-154998. 1972. 28.00 (ISBN 0-691-05190-9). Princeton U Pr.
Scott, James B. Hague Conference of Eighteen Ninety-Nine & Nineteen Seven, 2 vols. LC 79-147589. (Library of War & Peace; Int'l. Organization, Arbitration & Law). Set. lib. bdg. 76.00 (ISBN 0-8240-0350-0); lib. bdg. 38.00 ea. Garland Pub.

HAHN, EMILY, 1905-

Hahn, Emily. China to Me: A Partial Autobiography. LC 74-23432. (China in the 20th Century Ser). 429p. 1975. Repr. of 1944 ed. lib. bdg. 35.00 (ISBN 0-306-70695-4). Da Capo.

HAI, JUI, 1514-1587–DRAMA

Han, Wu. Hai Jui Dismissed from Office. Huang, C. C., tr. from Chinese. (Asian Studies at Hawaii Ser.: No. 7). 120p. 1972. pap. text ed. 5.00x (ISBN 0-8248-0215-2). U Pr of Hawaii.
Wu, Han. Dismissal of Hai Jui. LC 68-24313. 1968. pap. 2.75 (ISBN 0-685-06836-6, 911970-02). Bede.

HAIDA INDIANS

see Indians of North America–Northwest, Pacific

HAIDA LANGUAGE

Swanton, John R. Haida Texts & Myths: Skidegate Dialect. LC 5-41613. (Landmarks in Anthropology Ser). Repr. of 1905 ed. pap. 28.00 (ISBN 0-384-59020-9). Johnson Repr.
--Haida Texts & Myths; Skidgate Dialect. Repr. of 1905 ed. 43.00 (ISBN 0-403-03401-9). Scholarly.

HAIG, DOUGLAS, 1ST EARL, 1861-1928

Boraston, J. H., ed. Sir Douglas Haig's Despatches. (Illus.). 371p. 1979. Repr. of 1919 ed. 25.00x (ISBN 0-460-04371-4, Pub by J. M. Dent England). Biblio Dist.

HAIKU

see also Senryu

Akmakjian, Hiag. Snow Falling from a Bamboo Leaf: The Art of Haiku. (A Noel Young Bks.). 1979. pap. 4.95 (ISBN 0-88496-095-1). Capra Pr.
Andrews, J. David. Oh, My Comet, Shine! Found Haiku and Senryu, Based on "Thought Forms" by Mirtala Bentov. 60p. (Orig.). 1979. pap. 5.00 (ISBN 0-686-29308-8). Planetary Pr.
Atwood, Ann. Haiku: The Mood of the Earth. LC 70-162737. (Illus.). (gr. 3 up). 1971. reinforced bdg. 9.95 (ISBN 0-684-12494-7, ScribJ); pap. 4.95 (ISBN 0-684-16214-8, ScribJ). Scribner.
--Haiku Vision: In Poetry & Photography. LC 76-42287. (Illus.). (gr. 3 up). 1977. reinforced bdg. 7.95 (ISBN 0-684-14858-7, ScribJ). Scribner.
Behn, Harry, tr. Cricket Songs: Japanese Haiku. LC 64-11489. (Illus.). (gr. 4 up). 1964. 4.95 (ISBN 0-15-220890-9, HJ). HarBraceJ.
--More Cricket Songs: Japanese Haiku. LC 77-137755. (Illus., Photos). (gr. 4 up). 1971. 4.50 (ISBN 0-15-255440-8, HJ). HarBraceJ.
Blyth, R. H. Haiku, 4 vols. 1981. pap. 8.95 ea. Vol. 1 (ISBN 0-89346-158-X). Vol. 2 (ISBN 0-89346-159-8). Vol. 3, Date Not Set (ISBN 0-89346-160-1). Vol. 4, 39.80 (ISBN 0-89346-161-X). Heian Intl.
Brower, Gary L. Haiku in Western Languages: An Annotated Bibliography (with Some Reference to Senryu) LC 70-187878. 1972. 10.00 (ISBN 0-8108-0472-7). Scarecrow.
Buchanan, Daniel, tr. One Hundred Famous Haiku. LC 72-95667. 1977. pap. 5.95 (ISBN 0-87040-222-6). Japan Pubns.
Cherry Blossoms: Haiku Three. 1960. 2.95 (ISBN 0-442-82157-3). Peter Pauper.
Henderson, Harold G. The Bamboo Broom: An Introduction to Japanese Haiku. LC 77-22366. lib. bdg. 15.00 (ISBN 0-8414-4884-1). Folcroft.
--Introduction to Haiku. LC 58-11314. (Illus.). 1958. pap. 2.50 (ISBN 0-385-09376-4, A150, Anch). Doubleday.
Isaacson, Harold J., tr. Peonies Kana: Haiku by the Upasaka Shiki. (The Bhaisajaguru Ser.). pap. 1.85 (ISBN 0-87830-547-5). Theatre Arts.
Japanese Haiku. (Haiku Ser: No. 1). 1956. 2.95 (ISBN 0-442-82280-4). Peter Pauper.
Kimbro, Harriet. Tamotzu in Haiku. LC 77-10844. (Illus.). 1977. pap. 4.95 (ISBN 0-913270-78-4). Sunstone Pr.
Klinge, Gunther. Day into Night: A Haiku Journey. Atwood, Ann, tr. LC 79-92729. (Illus.). 184p. 1980. 12.50 (ISBN 0-8048-1340-X). C E Tuttle.
Lahr, Georgiana L. Songs of Many Colors. 1980. 5.95 (ISBN 0-533-04406-5). Vantage.
Los Altos Writers Roundtable. Borrowed Water: A Book of American Haiku. LC 66-26103. (Illus.). (gr. 9 up). 1966. 3.95 (ISBN 0-8048-0070-7). C E Tuttle.
Lytle, Ruby. What Is the Moon? Japanese Haiku Sequence. LC 65-12861. (Illus., Orig.). (gr. 7 up). 1965. pap. 1.10 (ISBN 0-8048-0626-8). C E Tuttle.
Miyamori, Asataro, ed. Anthology of Haiku, Ancient & Modern. Repr. of 1932 ed. lib. bdg. 57.50x (ISBN 0-8371-3987-2, MIHA). Greenwood.
Mizumura, Kazue. Flower Moon Snow: A Book of Haiku. LC 76-41180. (Illus.). (gr. k-4). 1977. 7.95 (ISBN 0-690-01291-8, TYC-J); PLB 7.89 (ISBN 0-690-01290-X). Har-Row.
Morrow, Annette S. Haiku of Hawaii. LC 74-104203. (Illus.). 1970. 2.75 (ISBN 0-8048-0229-7). C E Tuttle.
Oldenburg, Carl. Frog Croaks: Haiku Tongue in Cheek. (Illus.). 65p. 1975. 3.95 (ISBN 0-517-52341-8). Crown.
Seegal, David. Victories & Foibles: Some Western Haiku. LC 77-86327. 1977. 6.50 (ISBN 0-8048-1222-5). C E Tuttle.
Shiki, et al. Thistle Brilliant Morning. Higginson, William J., tr. from Japanese. (Xtras Ser.: No. 1). 24p. (Orig.). 1975. pap. 1.50 (ISBN 0-89120-000-2). From Here.
Stewart, Harold. Chime of Windbells: A Year of Japanese Haiku in English Verse. LC 69-12084. (Illus.). 1969. 17.50 (ISBN 0-8048-0092-8). C E Tuttle.
--Net of Fireflies: Japanese Haiku & Haiku Painting. LC 60-15603. (Illus.). 1960. 17.50 (ISBN 0-8048-0421-4). C E Tuttle.
Stock, Dennis, photos by. A Haiku Journey. LC 74-24903. (Illus.). 111p. 1975. 22.50 (ISBN 0-87011-239-2). Kodansha.
Ueda, Makato, compiled by. Modern Japanese Haiku: An Anthology. LC 74-75035. 1976. pap. 8.50 (ISBN 0-8020-6245-8). U of Toronto Pr.

HAIKU–HISTORY AND CRITICISM

Akmakjian, Hiag. Snow Falling from a Bamboo Leaf: The Art of Haiku. (A Noel Young Bks.). 1979. pap. 4.95 (ISBN 0-88496-095-1). Capra Pr.
Blyth, R. H. History of Haiku, Vol. 1. (Illus.). 1963. 19.95 (ISBN 0-89346-066-4, Pub. by Hokuseido Pr). Heian Intl.
--History of Haiku, Vols. 1 & 2. (Illus.). 1964. Set. 39.90 (ISBN 0-89346-068-0, Pub. by Hokuseido Pr). Heian Intl.
--History of Haiku, Vol. 2. (Illus.). 1964. 19.95 (ISBN 0-89346-067-2, Pub. by Hokuseido Pr). Heian Intl.

Gillon. In the Manner of Haiku. 3.50 (ISBN 0-913994-02-2). Hippocrene Bks.
Hillier, Jack. The Art of Hokusai in Book-Illustration. LC 79-9687. 1980. 110.00 (ISBN 0-520-04137-2). U of Cal Pr.
Yasuda, Ken. Japanese Haiku: Its Essential Nature, History & Possibilities in English, with Examples. LC 57-8795. pap. 5.95 (ISBN 0-8048-1096-6). C E Tuttle.

HAIL

Aviation Hail Problem (Includes Other Notes on Forecasting for Jet Aircraft) (Technical Note Ser.: Nos. 37-40). pap. 17.00 (ISBN 0-685-57276-5, WMO109, WMO). Unipub.
Flora, Snowden D. Hailstorms of the United States. (Illus.). 1956. 9.95x (ISBN 0-8061-0359-0). U of Okla Pr.
Gokhale, Narayan R. Hailstorms & Hailstone Growth. LC 75-19480. 550p. 1976. 34.00 (ISBN 0-87395-312-6); microfiche 34.00 (ISBN 0-87395-313-4). State U NY Pr.

HAILE SELASSIE 1ST EMPEROR OF ETHIOPIA, 1891-1975

Haile Sellasie I. The Autobiography of Emperor Haile Sellasis I: My Life & Ethiopia's Progress 1892-1937. Ullendorff, Edward, ed. & tr. (Illus.). 1976. 24.50x (ISBN 0-19-713589-7). Oxford U Pr.
Nicholas, Tracy. Rastafari: A Way of Life. LC 77-76285. (Illus.). 1979. pap. 7.95 (ISBN 0-385-11575-X, Anch). Doubleday.
Sandford, Christine. The Lion of Judah Hath Prevailed: Being the Biography of His Imperial Majesty Haile Selassie I. LC 73-135611. (Illus.). 192p. 1972. Repr. of 1955 ed. lib. bdg. 20.25x (ISBN 0-8371-5198-8, SLJ&). Greenwood.
Schwab, Peter. Haile Selassie I: Ethiopia's Lion of Judah. LC 79-9897. (Illus.). 1979. 15.95x (ISBN 0-88229-342-7). Nelson-Hall.

HAINAN

American Presbyterian Mission. The Isle of Palms: Sketches of Hainan. LC 78-74354. (The Modern Chinese Economy Ser.: Vol. 21). 141p. 1980. lib. bdg. 16.50 (ISBN 0-8240-4269-7). Garland Pub.
Schafer, Edward H. Shore of Pearls: Hainan Island in Early Times. LC 78-94990. (Illus.). 1970. 22.75x (ISBN 0-520-01592-4). U of Cal Pr.
Stubel, Hans. Le Stamme der Insel Hainan, 2 vols. (Asian Folklore & Social Life Monographs: Vol. 83-84). (Ger.). 1935. 15.00 (ISBN 0-89986-293-4). E Langstaff.
Stubel, Hans & Mitsuo, Shimizu. Le Stamme der Insel Hainan, 2 vols. (Asian Folklore & Social Life Monographs: Vols. 85-86). (Ger.). 1935. 15.00 (ISBN 0-89986-294-2). E Langstaff.

HAIR

see also Hypertrichosis; Wigs and Wigmakers

Abta, Nitza. The Complete Guide to Hair Replacement. 1975. 29.95x (ISBN 0-685-81806-3). New You Pub.
Alexander, Dale. Healthy Hair & Common Sense. LC 69-12841. 1969. 9.95 (ISBN 0-911638-02-4). Witkower.
Bragg, Paul C. & Bragg, Patricia. Your Health & Your Hair. 13th ed. LC 68-24217. pap. 2.95 (ISBN 0-87790-009-4). Health Sci.
Ceres. Herbs for Healthy Hair. LC 80-50747. (Everybody's Home Herbal Ser.). (Illus.). 62p. (Orig.). 1980. pap. 1.95 (ISBN 0-394-73947-7). Shambhala Pubns.
Colletti, Anthony B. Trichology: The Keystone Guide to Hair Analysis As Related to the Practice of Cosmetology & Barbering. (Illus.). 1981. text ed. 11.36 (ISBN 0-912126-57-4). Keystone Pubns.
Cordwell, Miriam & Rudoy, Marion. The Complete Book of Men's Hair Styles & Hair Care. LC 75-147328. (Illus.). 128p. 1974. 4.95 (ISBN 0-517-51533-4). Crown.
Dale, Alexander. Healthy Hair & Common Sense. 8.95 (ISBN 0-686-29855-1). Cancer Bk Hse.
Feinberg, Herbert S. All About Hair. LC 77-92355. 1978. 10.00 (ISBN 0-930988-01-9). Wallingford NJ.
Ferriman, David. Human Hair Growth in Health & Disease. (American Lectures in Living Chemistry Ser.). (Illus.). 76p. 1971. 11.75 (ISBN 0-398-00560-5). C C Thomas.
Galvin, Daniel. The World of Hair Color: The Art & Techniques of Modern, Natural & Synthetic Hair Coloring. 1977. pap. 7.95 (ISBN 0-442-21451-0). Van Nos Reinhold.
Goldin, Augusta. Straight Hair, Curly Hair. LC 66-12669. (A Let's-Read-&-Find-Out Science Bk). (Illus.). (gr. k-3). 1966. PLB 8.79 (ISBN 0-690-77921-6, TYC-J); filmstrip with record 11.95 (ISBN 0-690-77924-0); filmstrip with cassette 14.95 (ISBN 0-690-77926-7). Har-Row.
Guy'D, Louis & Warsaw, Jacqueline. Everything You Need to Know to Have Great Looking Hair. LC 80-51999. (Illus.). 144p. 1981. 15.95 (ISBN 0-670-30040-3). Viking Pr.
How to Keep Your Hair on. 1980. 15.00x (ISBN 0-85032-191-3, Pub. by Daniel Co England). State Mutual Bk.
Lavan, Fay. The Natural Way to Healthy Hair. LC 74-77435. 128p. 1975. pap. 1.50 (ISBN 0-668-03497-1). Arco.
Law, Donald. How to Keep Your Hair On. 70p. 1968. pap. 4.00x (ISBN 0-8464-1025-7). Beekman Pubs.
Lerner, Marguerite R. Fur, Feathers, Hair. LC 62-16851. (Medical Books for Children). (Illus.). (gr. 3-9). 1962. PLB 3.95 (ISBN 0-8225-0014-0). Lerner Pubns.
Margo. Growing New Hair! How to Keep What You Have & Fill in Where It's Thin, by Margo for Men Only. LC 81-66699. (Illus.). 112p. 1981. pap. 5.95 (ISBN 0-914398-32-6). Autumn Pr.
Norris, Clarice. Classroom Experiments in Hair Structure & Chemistry. (Illus.). 1976. 25.50 (ISBN 0-87350-068-7). Milady.
Norwood, O'Tar T. Hair Transplant Surgery. (Illus.). 148p. 1973. 14.75 (ISBN 0-398-02892-3). C C Thomas.
Null, Gary. Handbook of Skin & Hair. 1976. pap. 1.75 (ISBN 0-515-03619-6). Jove Pubns.
Powitt, A. H. Hair Structure & Chemistry Simplified. new ed. (Illus.). 300p. 1977. text ed. 15.95 (ISBN 0-87350-080-6). Milady.
--Lectures in Hair Structure & Chemistry for Cosmetology Teachers. (Illus.). 1971. 16.95 (ISBN 0-87350-013-X). Milady.
Reynolds, Reginald. Beards. LC 75-34138. 302p. 1976. pap. 3.95 (ISBN 0-15-610845-3, HB334, Harv). HarBraceJ.
Robbins, Clarence R. The Chemical & Physical Behavior of Human Hair. 1979. text ed. 22.50 (ISBN 0-442-26818-1). Van Nos Reinhold.
Savage, John. The Biodynamics of Hair Growth. 1980. 17.50x (ISBN 0-686-64691-6, Pub. by Daniel Co England). State Mutual Bk.
--The Biodynamics of Hair Growth. 88p. 1977. pap. 6.50x (ISBN 0-8464-0996-8). Beekman Pubs.
Schoen, Linda A., ed. The AMA Book of Skin & Hair Care. (Illus.). 1976. (JBL-Med-Nursing); pap. 4.95 (ISBN 0-397-01158-X). Har-Row.
Thomson, James C. & Thomson, Leslie C. Healthy Hair. LC 69-19822. 1969. pap. 1.50 (ISBN 0-668-01902-6). Arco.
Unger, Walter P. & Katz, Sidney. The Intelligent Man's Guide to Hair Transplants & Other Methods of Hair Replacement. 1979. 9.95 (ISBN 0-8092-7436-1). Contemp Bks.
Valkovic, Vlado. Trace Elements in the Human Hair. (Vol. 14). (LC 76-052705). 1977. lib. bdg. 27.50 (ISBN 0-8240-9861-7, Garland STPM Pr). Garland Pub.
Yahm, J. J. Lesson Plans for Hair Structure & Chemistry. 1973. 37.50 (ISBN 0-87350-052-0); wkbk. 11.50 (ISBN 0-87350-053-9). Milady.

HAIR–DISEASES

see also Baldness

Toda, et al, eds. Biology & Disease of the Hair. (Illus.). 1976. 97.50 (ISBN 0-8391-0958-X). Univ Park.
Unger. Hair Transplantation. 1978. 47.50 (ISBN 0-8247-6789-6). Dekker.

HAIR–JUVENILE LITERATURE

Tether, Graham. The Hair Book. LC 77-93772. (Bright & Early Ser.: No. 24). (Illus.). (ps-1). 1979. 3.95 (ISBN 0-394-83665-0); PLB 4.99 (ISBN 0-394-93665-5). Random.

HAIR, REMOVAL OF

Hinkel, Arthur R. & Lind, Richard W. Electrolysis, Thermolysis & the Blend: The Principles & Practice of Permanent Hair Removal. LC 68-19191. (Illus.). 1968. 21.50x (ISBN 0-9600284-1-2). Arroway.
Shapiro, Julius. Electrolysis: Beauty & Confidence Through Permanent Hair Removal. LC 80-24691. (Illus.). 207p. 1981. 10.95 (ISBN 0-396-07903-2). Dodd.

HAIRDRESSING

see also Costume

Bent, Bob & Bozzi. How to Cut Your Own or Anybody Else's Hair. LC 75-2295. 1975. 6.95 (ISBN 0-671-22012-8). S&S.
Colletti, Anthony B. A Complete Question & Answer Guide to Hairdressing & Cosmetology. 1978. text ed. 16.00 (ISBN 0-912126-48-5, 1258-01); pap. text ed. 14.21 (ISBN 0-912126-49-3, 1258-00). Keystone Pubns.
--Cosmetology Instructor's Guide, No. 1. (Keystone Publications' Audio-Visual Program Ser.). 88p. 1976. 7.10 (ISBN 0-912126-16-7). Keystone Pubns.
--Cosmetology Instructor's Guide, No. 2. (Keystone Publications' Audio-Visual Program Ser.). 80p. 1976. 7.10311 (ISBN 0-912126-17-5). Keystone Pubns.
--Cosmetology Instructor's Guide, No. 3. (Keystone's Publications' Audio-Visual Program Ser.). 136p. 1976. 7.10 (ISBN 0-912126-18-3). Keystone Pubns.
--Cosmetology Instructor's Guide, No. 4. (Keystone Publications' Audio-Visual Program Ser.). 112p. 1976. 7.10 (ISBN 0-912126-19-1). Keystone Pubns.
--Twenty-Four Practice Hairstyles. rev. ed. 1981. pap. text ed. 5.00 (ISBN 0-912126-47-7, 1265-00). Keystone Pubns.
Cordwell, Miriam & Rudoy, Marion. The Complete Book of Men's Hair Styles & Hair Care. LC 75-147328. (Illus.). 128p. 1974. 4.95 (ISBN 0-517-51533-4). Crown.
--Hair Design & Fashion: Principles & Relationships. 6th & rev. ed. (Illus.). 1977. 14.95 (ISBN 0-517-53121-6). Crown.
Cumine, Earl. Shringar: The Golden Book of Indian Hair Styles. (Illus.). 1975. pap. 2.50 English, Urdu, & Tamil (ISBN 0-88253-454-8). Ind-US Inc.
Fine, Linda S. The Complete Book of Hair Care, Hairstyling, & Hairstylists. LC 79-22594. (Illus.). 192p. 1980. pap. 6.95 (ISBN 0-668-04870-0, 4870-0). Arco.
Fletcher, Helen J. Your Hair Can Be Beautiful. pap. 1.00 (ISBN 0-686-00718-2). Key Bks.
Goei, Jacques S. How to Be Your Own Hairdresser for Fun & Profit. (Illus.). 1981. 7.50 (ISBN 0-682-49128-4). Exposition.
Hurley, Marie. Beauty for Sale. 1978. 6.95 (ISBN 0-533-03475-2). Vantage.
Lee, C. M. & Inglis, J. K. Science for Hairdressing Students. 2nd ed. 1972. text ed. 16.50 (ISBN 0-08-016665-2); pap. text ed. 7.75 (ISBN 0-08-016666-0). Pergamon.
Leighton, Harold. Haircutting for Everyone. LC 78-72508. (Illus.). 1979. 9.95 (ISBN 0-89104-132-X); pap. 4.95 (ISBN 0-89104-097-8). A & W Pubs.
Masters, T. W. Hairdressing in Theory & Practice. 280p. 1980. 25.00x (ISBN 0-291-39618-6, Pub. by Tech Pr). State Mutual Bk.
--Hairdressing in Theory & Practice. 5th ed. (Illus.). 280p. 1981. pap. text ed. 12.95x (ISBN 0-291-39624-0). Intl Ideas.
--Hairdressing in Theory & Practice. 5th, rev. ed. (Illus.). 1979. pap. 15.00 (ISBN 0-291-39624-0). Heinman.
Michael, George & Lindsay, Ray. George Michael's Secrets for Beautiful Hair. LC 79-7693. (Illus.). 256p. 1981. 19.95 (ISBN 0-385-15465-8). Doubleday.
Milady Barber Textbook Committee. Standard Textbook of Professional Barber Styling. 1977. text ed. 16.50 (ISBN 0-87350-116-0). Milady.
Milady Editors. Exam Reviews in Hair Structure & Chemistry. 1977. 6.30 (ISBN 0-87350-014-8). Milady.
--Tecnicas Modernas Del Peinado. (Span.). 1977. 14.95 (ISBN 0-87350-076-8). Milady.
Moro, Michael D. Air Jet Hairstyling. 7.50 (ISBN 0-8497-6325-8, 1577-00). Keystone Pubns.
Papagno, et al. Desairology: Hairdressing for Decedents. LC 80-82330. (The Family, the Funeral & the Hairdresser). (Illus.). 104p. (Orig.). 1980. 17.95x (ISBN 0-9604610-0-0); lib. bdg. 13.95 (ISBN 0-686-27695-7); pap. 13.95x (ISBN 0-9604610-1-9). JJ Pub Fl.
Papagno, Noella C. The Hairdresser at the Funeral Home: Desairology Handbook Questions & Answers. LC 80-82330. 30p. (Orig.). 1981. spiral bound 5.95 (ISBN 0-686-73674-5). JJ Pub FL.
Parr, A. F. Techniques of Hairdressing. (Illus.). 1979. pap. 11.25x (ISBN 0-434-91520-3). Intl Pubns Serv.
Schroder, David. Engagement in the Mirror: Hairdressers & Their Work. LC 77-90358. 1978. soft cover 10.00 (ISBN 0-88247-501-0). R & E Res Assoc.
Suga, Yusuke & Penney, Alexandra. Beautiful Hair by Suga. (Illus.). 1980. 12.95 (ISBN 0-394-50750-9). Random.
Textbook Committee of Barbering. Advanced Textbook of Barbering & Men's Hairstyling. 1969. 12.95 (ISBN 0-87350-101-2); pap. avail (ISBN 0-87350-102-0). Milady.
Thaine, Marina & Griffin, Robert. Working in Hair-Dressing. 1980. 16.95 (ISBN 0-7134-3323-X). David & Charles.
Yahm, J. J. Lesson Plans for Hair Structure & Chemistry. 1973. 37.50 (ISBN 0-87350-052-0); wkbk. 11.50 (ISBN 0-87350-053-9). Milady.

HAIRDRESSING–HISTORY

Andrews, William. At the Sign of the Barber's Pole. LC 74-77164. 1969. Repr. of 1904 ed. 19.00 (ISBN 0-8103-3846-7). Gale.
Corson, Richard. Fashions in Hair: The First Five Thousand Years. 3rd rev. ed. (Illus.). 1971. text ed. 75.00x (ISBN 0-391-00167-1). Humanities.

HAITI

Bellegarde, Dantes. Haiti & Her Problems. 1976. lib. bdg. 59.95 (ISBN 0-8490-1925-7). Gordon Pr.
Bissainthe, Max. Dictionnaire De Bibliographie Haitienne: Premier Supplement. LC 51-12164. 1973. 10.00 (ISBN 0-8108-0667-3). Scarecrow.
Bordes, Ary & Couture, Andrea. For the People, for a Change: Bringing Health to the Families of Haiti. LC 77-88372. (Illus.). 1978. 11.95 (ISBN 0-8070-2166-0). Beacon Pr.
Courlander, Harold & Bastien, Remy. Religion & Politics in Haiti. LC 66-26633. (Illus.). 1970. 3.95 (ISBN 0-911976-00-0). ICR.
Franklin, James. Present State of Hayti - Saint Domingo - with Remarks on Its Agriculture, Commerce, Laws, Religion, Finance & Population. LC 79-109325. Repr. of 1828 ed. 19.00x (ISBN 0-8371-3591-5). Greenwood.
--Present State of Hayti: (Saint Domingo) 412p. 1972. Repr. of 1828 ed. 32.50x (ISBN 0-7146-2707-0, F Cass Co). Biblio Dist.
Haiti, Mission d'Assistance Technique Integree 1972. (Fr.). 50.00 (ISBN 0-8270-3940-9). OAS.
Logan, Rayford W. Haiti & the Dominican Republic. (Royal Institute of International Affairs Ser.). 1968. 13.95x (ISBN 0-19-214966-0). Oxford U Pr.
Lundahl, Mats. Peasants & Poverty. LC 78-11918. 1979. 37.50x (ISBN 0-312-59994-3). St Martin.
Redpath, James. Guide to Hayti. LC 75-107484. Repr. of 1861 ed. 10.75x (ISBN 0-8371-3786-1, Pub. by Negro U Pr). Greenwood.
Roman, Selden. Haiti: The Story of the Black Republic. rev. ed. LC 54-97025. (Illus.). 1974. pap. 5.00 (ISBN 0-8159-5701-7). Devin.
Steedman, Mabel. Haiti: Unknown to the World. 1976. lib. bdg. 59.95 (ISBN 0-8490-1928-1). Gordon Pr.

HAITI–ANTIQUITIES

Rainey, Froelich G. Excavations in the Ft. Liberte Region, Haiti. LC 76-44780. Repr. of 1941 ed. 21.00 (ISBN 0-404-15965-6). AMS Pr.
Rouse, Irving. Prehistory in Haiti: A Study in Method. LC 64-21834. (Yale University Publications in Anthropology Reprints Ser: No. 21). 202p. 1964. pap. 7.50x (ISBN 0-87536-504-3). HRAFP.

HAITI–DESCRIPTION AND TRAVEL

Caimite. Don't Get Hit by a Coconut. 1979. 10.00 (ISBN 0-682-49246-9). Exposition.
Courlander, Harold. The Drum & the Hoe: Life & Lore of the Haitian People. (California Library Reprint Ser.: No. 31). (Illus.). 436p. 1981. Repr. of 1973 ed. 25.00x (ISBN 0-520-02364-1). U of Cal Pr.
Kuser, John D. Haiti: Its Dawn of Progress After Years in a Night of Revolution. LC 77-106876. Repr. of 1921 ed. 10.50x (ISBN 0-8371-3294-0, Pub. by Negro U Pr). Greenwood.
Mackenzie, Charles. Notes on Haiti: Made During a Residence in That Republic, 2 vols. (Illus.). 1972. Repr. of 1830 ed. 68.50x set (ISBN 0-7146-2710-0, F Cass Co). Biblio Dist.
Prichard, Hesketh. Where Black Rules White. facsimile ed. LC 70-161272. (Black Heritage Library Collection). Repr. of 1900 ed. 18.75 (ISBN 0-8369-8831-0). Arno.
--Where Black Rules White: A Journey Across & About Hayti. (Illus.). 298p. 1971. Repr. of 1900 ed. 24.00x (ISBN 0-7165-1819-8, Pub. by Irish Academic Pr Ireland). Biblio Dist.
Taft, Edna. Puritan in Voodoo-Land. LC 73-174115. (Tower Bks). (Illus.). 1971. Repr. of 1938 ed. 24.00 (ISBN 0-8103-3919-6). Gale.

HAITI–FOREIGN RELATIONS

Healy, David. Gunboat Diplomacy in the Wilson Era: The U.S. Navy in Haiti, 1915-1916. LC 75-32074. 1976. 21.50x (ISBN 0-299-06980-X). U of Wis Pr.
Logan, Rayford W. Diplomatic Relations of the United States with Haiti, 1776-1891. LC 41-6260. 1969. Repr. of 1941 ed. 27.00 (ISBN 0-527-58000-7). Kraus Repr.

HAITI–HISTORY

Balch, Emily G. Occupied Haiti. LC 75-14988. Repr. of 1927 ed. 10.00x (ISBN 0-8371-2785-8, Pub. by Negro U Pr). Greenwood.
Balch, Emily G., ed. Occupied Haiti: Being the Report of a Committee of Six Disinterested Americans Representing Organizations Exclusively American. LC 79-147491. (Library of War & Peace; the Political Economy of War). lib. bdg. 38.00 (ISBN 0-8240-0284-9). Garland Pub.
Beard, John R. Life of Toussaint L'ouverture, the Negro Patriot of Hayti. LC 75-109316. (Illus.). Repr. of 1853 ed. 14.50x (ISBN 0-8371-3572-9, Pub. by Negro U Pr). Greenwood.
Bird, M. B. The Black Man. facsimile ed. LC 70-164380. (Black Heritage Library Collection). Repr. of 1869 ed. 24.00 (ISBN 0-8369-8839-6). Arno.
Christophe, Henri. Henry Christophe & Thomas Clarkson, a Correspondence. Griggs, Earl L. & Praton, Clifford H., eds. LC 68-23281. (Illus.). 1968. Repr. of 1952 ed. lib. bdg. 14.75x (ISBN 0-8371-0091-7). Greenwood.
Edwards, Bryan. History, Civil & Commercial, of the British West Indies, 5 Vols. LC 79-164760. Repr. of 1819 ed. Set. 135.00 (ISBN 0-404-02270-7). AMS Pr.
Fouchard, Jean. The Haitian Maroons: Liberty or Death. Watts, A. Faulkner, tr. from Fr. 500p. 1981. write for info. (ISBN 0-914110-11-X). Blyden Pr.
Harvey, William W. Sketches of Hayti: From the Expulsion of the French to the Death of Christophe. LC 77-111578. Repr. of 1827 ed. 20.75x (ISBN 0-8371-4604-6). Greenwood.

--Sketches of Hayti from the Expulsion of the French to the Death of Christophe. 416p. 1972. Repr. of 1827 ed. 32.50x (ISBN 0-7146-2708-9, F Cass Co). Biblio Dist.

Healy, David. Gunboat Diplomacy in the Wilson Era: The U.S. Navy in Haiti, 1915-1916. LC 75-32074. 1976. 21.50x (ISBN 0-299-06980-X). U of Wis Pr.

Heinl, Robert D., Jr. & Heinl, Nancy G. Written in Blood: The Story of the Haitian People 1492-1971. 1978. 21.95 (ISBN 0-395-26305-0). HM.

James, Cyril L. Black Jacobins: Toussaint L'Ouverture & the San Domingo Revolution. 1963. pap. 4.95 (ISBN 0-394-70242-5, 242, Vin). Random.

Jerome, Yves J. Toussaint L'ouverture. 1978. 5.95 (ISBN 0-533-03200-8). Vantage.

Korngold, Ralph. Citizen Toussaint. LC 78-21026. 1979. Repr. of 1965 ed. lib. bdg. 22.50x (ISBN 0-313-20794-1, KOCT). Greenwood.

Kuser, J. Dryden. Haiti: Its Dawn of Progress After Years in a Night of Revolution. 1976. lib. bdg. 59.95 (ISBN 0-8490-1927-3). Gordon Pr.

Leger, Jacques N. Haiti, Her History & Her Detractors. LC 78-107482. Repr. of 1907 ed. 20.75x (ISBN 0-8371-3784-5, Pub. by Negro U Pr). Greenwood.

Legger, J. N. Haiti: Her History & Her Detractors. 1976. lib. bdg. 59.95 (ISBN 0-8490-1926-5). Gordon Pr.

L'Ouverture, Toussaint. Toussaint L'Ouverture: A Biography & Autobiography. facs. ed. LC 77-152924. (Black Heritage Library Collection Ser). 1863. 21.00 (ISBN 0-8369-8768-3). Arno.

Millspaugh, Arthur C. Haiti Under American Control Nineteen Fifteen to Nineteen-Thirty. LC 74-106878. Repr. of 1931 ed. 13.75x (ISBN 0-8371-3296-7, Pub. by Negro U Pr). Greenwood.

Nicholls, David. From Dessalines to Duvalier: Race, Colour & National Independence in Haiti. LC 78-56817. (Cambridge Latin American Studies: No. 34). 1979. 39.95 (ISBN 0-521-22177-3). Cambridge U Pr.

Ott, Thomas O. The Haitian Revolution, 1789-1804. LC 72-85085. (Illus.). 1973. 12.50x (ISBN 0-87049-143-1). U of Tenn Pr.

Perusse, Roland I. Historical Dictionary of Haiti. LC 76-30264. (Latin American Historical Dictionaries Ser: No. 15). (Illus.). 1977. 10.00 (ISBN 0-8108-1006-9). Scarecrow.

Rouse, Irving. Prehistory in Haiti: A Study in Method. LC 64-21834. (Yale University Publications in Anthropology Reprints Ser: No. 21). 202p. 1964. pap. 7.50x (ISBN 0-87536-504-3). HRAFP.

St. John. Sir Spenser Hayti, or the Black Republic, 1889. (Illus.). 389p. 1972. Repr. of 1889 ed. 29.50x (ISBN 0-7146-2705-4, F Cass Co). Biblio Dist.

Saunders, Prince, ed. Haytian Papers. a Collection of the Very Interesting Proclamations, & Other Official Documents. LC 77-89058. Repr. of 1816 ed. 12.75x (ISBN 0-8371-2023-3, Pub. by Negro U Pr). Greenwood.

Schmidt, Hans R., Jr. The United States Occupation of Haiti, 1915-1934. 1971. 22.00 (ISBN 0-8135-0690-5). Rutgers U Pr.

Stephen, James. Crisis of the Sugar Colonies: Or, an Enquiry into the Objects & Probable Effects of the French Expedition to the West Indies. LC 70-88418. Repr. of 1802 ed. 12.25x (ISBN 0-8371-1832-8, Pub. by Negro U Pr). Greenwood.

Steward, Theophilus G. Haitian Revolution, 1791 to 1804; or Side Lights on the French Revolution. LC 73-83865. (Illus.). 1971. Repr. of 1914 ed. 14.00 (ISBN 0-8462-1417-2). Russell.

Syme, Ronald. Toussaint, the Black Liberator. LC 72-152072. (Illus.). (gr. 5-9). 1971. 6.50 (ISBN 0-688-21806-7). Morrow.

Telemaque, Eleanor W. Haiti Through Its Holidays. LC 79-52858. (Illus.). 64p. (gr. 4-6). 1980. 7.50 (ISBN 0-914110-12-8). Blyden Pr.

Vastey, Pompee. Essay on the Causes of the Revolution & Civil Wars of Hayti. LC 70-97442. Repr. of 1823 ed. 15.75x (ISBN 0-8371-2709-2, Pub. by Negro U Pr). Greenwood.

HAITI–HISTORY–FICTION

Galvan, Manuel D. Manuel De Jesus Galvan's Enriquillo: The Cross & the Sword. LC 75-153323. Repr. of 1954 ed. 28.00 (ISBN 0-404-02675-3). AMS Pr.

Gilliam, E. W. Seventy Ninety-One: A Tale of San Domingo. facsimile ed. LC 70-37591. (Black Heritage Library Collection). Repr. of 1890 ed. 17.25 (ISBN 0-8369-8967-8). Arno.

HAITI–POLITICS AND GOVERNMENT

Calixte, Demosthenes P. Haiti: The Calvary of a Soldier. LC 75-98715. Repr. of 1939 ed. 10.00x (ISBN 0-8371-2760-2, Pub. by Negro U Pr). Greenwood.

Constitution of Haiti, 1964. 34p. 1974. pap. 1.00 (ISBN 0-8270-5620-6). OAS.

Levilain, Guy V. Cultural Identity, Negritude & Decolonization: A Study of the Haitian Situation in the Light of the Socialist Humanism of Jacques Romain & Rene Depestre. (Occasional Papers: No. 29). 1978. 1.50 (ISBN 0-89977-015-0). Am Inst Marxist.

Nicholls, David. From Dessalines to Duvalier: Race, Colour & National Independence in Haiti. LC 78-56817. (Cambridge Latin American Studies: No. 34). 1979. 39.95 (ISBN 0-521-22177-3). Cambridge U Pr.

Pratt, Frances H. La Belle Zoa; or, the Insurrection of Haiti. LC 72-1820. (Black Heritage Library Collection Ser.). Repr. of 1853 ed. 12.25 (ISBN 0-8369-9049-8). Arno.

Prichard, Hesketh. Where Black Rules White. facsimile ed. LC 70-161272. (Black Heritage Library Collection). Repr. of 1900 ed. 18.75 (ISBN 0-8369-8831-0). Arno.

--Where Black Rules White: A Journey Across & About Hayti. (Illus.). 298p. 1971. Repr. of 1900 ed. 24.00x (ISBN 0-7165-1819-8, Pub. by Irish Academic Pr Ireland). Biblio Dist.

Roman, Selden. Haiti: The Story of the Black Republic. rev. ed. LC 54-97025. (Illus.). 1974. pap. 5.00 (ISBN 0-8159-5701-7). Devin.

HAITI–SOCIAL LIFE AND CUSTOMS

Courlander, Harold. The Drum & the Hoe: Life & Lore of the Haitian People. (California Library Reprint Ser.: No. 31). (Illus.). 436p. 1981. Repr. of 1973 ed. 25.00x (ISBN 0-520-02364-1). U of Cal Pr.

--Haiti Singing. LC 72-95270. (Illus.). 274p. 1973. Repr. of 1939 ed. lib. bdg. 15.00x (ISBN 0-8154-0461-1). Cooper Sq.

Herskovits, Melville J. Life in a Haitian Valley. 1964. lib. bdg. 18.00x (ISBN 0-374-93857-1). Octagon.

Leyburn, James G. The Haitian People. rev. ed. Mintz, Sidney W., intro. by. LC 80-476. (Caribbean Ser.: No. 9). (Illus.). xlviii, 342p. 1980. Repr. lib. bdg. 28.25x (ISBN 0-313-22155-3, LEHA). Greenwood.

Romain, J. B. Quelques Moeurs et Coutumes des Paysans Haitiens. LC 75-1057. Repr. of 1958 ed. lib. bdg. 45.00 (ISBN 0-8414-7370-6). Folcroft.

Secret History. facsimile ed. LC 73-161273. (Black Heritage Library Collection). Repr. of 1808 ed. 16.00 (ISBN 0-8369-8832-9). Arno.

Taft, Edna. Puritan in Voodoo-Land. LC 73-174115. (Tower Bks). (Illus.). 1971. Repr. of 1938 ed. 24.00 (ISBN 0-8103-3919-6). Gale.

HAITIAN BALLADS AND SONGS

see also Folk-Songs, Haitian

HAITIAN FOLK-LORE

see Folk-Lore, Haitian

HAITIAN FOLK SONGS

see Folk-Songs, Haitian

HAITIAN MAGIC

see Magic, Haitian

HAITIAN POETRY

Cobb, Martha. Harlem, Haiti, & Havana: A Comparative Critical Study of Langston Hughes, Jacques Roumain, & Nicolas Guillen. LC 78-19962. (Illus.). 1979. 15.00 (ISBN 0-914478-90-7); pap. 8.00 (ISBN 0-914478-91-5). Three Continents.

Underwood, Edna W., ed. The Poets of Haiti. 1977. lib. bdg. 34.95 (ISBN 0-8490-2449-8). Gordon Pr.

HAITIAN TALES

see Tales, Haitian

HAJAR AL HUMAYD

Van Beek, Gus W. Hajar Bin Humeid: Investigations at a Pre-Islamic Site in South Arabia. LC 68-16275. (American Foundation for the Study of Man Ser: Vol. V). (Illus.). 421p. 1969. 40.00x (ISBN 0-8018-1000-0). Johns Hopkins.

HAKLUYT, RICHARD, 1552-1616

David, Richard. Hakluyt's Voyages. 672p. 1981. 27.50 (ISBN 0-395-31556-5). HM.

Hakluyt, Richard. Hakluyts Voyages II. Date not set. 8.95x (ISBN 0-460-00265-1, Evman). Biblio Dist.

--Hakluyts Voyages III. Date not set. 8.95x (ISBN 0-460-00388-7, Evman). Biblio Dist.

--Hakluyts Voyages 1. Date not set. 8.95x (ISBN 0-460-00264-3, Evman). Biblio Dist.

Parks, George B. Richard Hakluyt & the English Voyages. 2nd ed. LC 61-13628. 1961. 13.50 (ISBN 0-8044-1719-9). Ungar.

HAKLUYT, RICHARD, d. 1591

Parks, George B. Richard Hakluyt & the English Voyages. 2nd ed. LC 61-13628. 1961. 13.50 (ISBN 0-8044-1719-9). Ungar.

HALACHA

see Jewish Law; Talmud; Tradition (Judaism)

HALAS, GEORGE, 1895-

Halas, George & Morgan, Gwen. Halas by Halas. (Illus.). 1979. 12.95 (ISBN 0-07-025549-0). McGraw.

HALBERG, ARVO

see Hall, Gus (Pseud.), 1910-

HALDANE, RICHARD BURDON HALDANE, 1ST VISCOUNT, 1856-1928

Ashby, Eric & Anderson, Mary. Portrait of Haldane at Work on Education. xvi, 202p. 1974. 17.50 (ISBN 0-208-01463-2, Archon). Shoe String.

Koss, Stephen E. Lord Haldane: Scapegoat for Liberalism. LC 69-19460. (Illus.). 263p. 1969. 17.50x (ISBN 0-231-03201-3). Columbia U Pr.

Maurice, Frederick B. Haldane, Eighteen Hundred Fifty-Six to Nineteen Fifteen: The Life of Viscount Haldane of Cloan, K.T., O.M, 2 Vols. Repr. of 1939 ed. Set. lib. bdg. 35.50x (ISBN 0-8371-4524-4, MAHA). Greenwood.

Spiers, E. M. Haldane: An Army Reformer. 232p. 1980. 21.00x (ISBN 0-85224-370-7, Pub. by Edinburgh U Pr Scotland). Columbia U Pr.

Teagarden, Ernest M. Haldane at the War Office. 1974. lib. bdg. 69.95 (ISBN 0-87968-400-3). Gordon Pr.

HALE, EDWARD EVERETT, 1822-1909

Adams, John R. Edward Everett Hale. (U.S. Authors Ser.: No. 284). 1977. lib. bdg. 9.95 (ISBN 0-8057-7186-7). Twayne.

Hartnett, Connor. Monarch Notes on Hales's Man Without a Country. (Orig.). pap. 1.50 (ISBN 0-671-00669-X). Monarch Pr.

HALE, GEORGE ELLERY, 1868-1938

Wright, Helen, et al, eds. Legacy of George Ellery Hale. 1972. 32.50x (ISBN 0-262-23049-6). Mit Pr.

HALE, LILLIAN WESTCOTT, 1881-1963

Hale, Nancy. The Life in the Studio. 1980. pap. 2.75 (ISBN 0-380-75721-4, 75721, Discus). Avon.

HALE, NATHAN, 1755-1776–JUVENILE LITERATURE

Brown, Marion M. Young Nathan. (Illus.). (gr. 5-9). 1949. 4.75 (ISBN 0-664-32050-3). Westminster.

Mann, Martha. Nathan Hale, Patriot. LC 44-8683. (Illus.). (gr. 6-9). 1944. 5.00 (ISBN 0-396-02565-X). Dodd.

Poole, Susan. Nathan Hale. LC 78-64421. (Illus.). (gr. 1-4). 1979. 3.50 (ISBN 0-89799-128-1); pap. 1.50 (ISBN 0-89799-035-8). Dandelion Pr.

HALE, PHILIP LESLIE, 1865-1931

Hale, Nancy. The Life in the Studio. 1980. pap. 2.75 (ISBN 0-380-75721-4, 75721, Discus). Avon.

HALE, SARAH JOSEPHA (BUELL), 1788-1879

Finley, Ruth E. The Lady of Godey's: Sara Josephia Hale. LC 74-3949. (Women in America Ser). (Illus.). 378p. 1974. Repr. of 1931 ed. 25.00x (ISBN 0-405-06095-5). Arno.

HALES, STEPHEN, 1677-1761

Allan, D. G. & Schofield, R. E. Stephen Hales: Scientist & Philanthropist. (Illus.). 220p. 1980. 50.00x (ISBN 0-85967-482-7, Pub. by Scolar Pr England). Biblio Dist.

Darwin, Francis. Rustic Sounds & Other Studies in Literature & Natural History. facs. ed. LC 69-17572. (Essay Index Reprint Ser). 1917. 15.00 (ISBN 0-8369-0069-3). Arno.

HALEY, BERNARD FRANCIS

Abramovitz, Moses, et al. The Allocation of Economic Resources. LC 59-7420. 1959. pap. 4.85x (ISBN 0-8047-0569-0). Stanford U Pr.

HALF-TIMBERED HOUSES

see also Framing (Building)

HALF TONE PROCESS

see Photoengraving

HALF-TRACK VEHICLES, MILITARY

Ellis, Chris & Chamberlain, Peter. American Half-Tracks of World War 2. LC 78-314050. (Illus., Orig.). 1978. pap. 8.50x (ISBN 0-85242-581-3). Intl Pubns Serv.

Feist, Uwe & Spielberger, Walter. Halbkettenfahrzeuge: German Halftrack Vehicles. LC 68-22558. (Armor Ser: Vol. 7). (Illus., Orig.). 1968. pap. 3.00 (ISBN 0-8168-2024-4). Aero.

Milsom, John. German Half-Tracked Vehicles of World War Two. LC 75-12783. (Illus.). 96p. 1975. 12.50 (ISBN 0-88254-354-7). Hippocrene Bks.

HALF-TRACKS (MILITARY SCIENCE)

see Half-Track Vehicles, Military

HALF-WAY COVENANT

see Covenants (Church Polity)

HALFWAY HOUSES

Apte, Robert Z. Halfway Houses. 125p. 1968. pap. text ed. 5.00x (ISBN 0-7135-1522-8, Pub. by Bedford England). Renouf.

Bradley, V. Deinstitutionalization of Developmentally Disabled Persons. 1978. 12.50 (ISBN 0-8391-1254-8). Univ Park.

Budson, Richard D. The Psychiatric Halfway House: A Handbook of Theory & Practice. LC 77-74548. (Contemporary Community Health Ser.). 1978. 10.95 (ISBN 0-8229-3350-0). U of Pittsburgh Pr.

Goulet, Bertrand H., Jr. & Rochefort, David A. Barriers to the Establishment & Operation of Halfway Houses. (State Institutional Care Ser.). (Illus.). 55p. (Orig.). 1978. pap. 4.95 (ISBN 0-89995-056-6, M 405-6). Social Matrix.

Hughes, Patrick H. Behind the Wall of Respect: Experiments in Heroin Addiction Control in Chicago Neighborhoods. LC 76-25640. 1977. 10.95 (ISBN 0-226-35930-1). U of Chicago Pr.

Moseley, Sr. Riccarda & James, Howard. Knock On Our Door: A Home for Troubled Girls. LC 79-65849. 1979. 11.95 (ISBN 0-89526-683-0). Regnery-Gateway.

Mulligan, Elizabeth. Hoodlum's Priest. 174p. 1979. 9.95 (ISBN 0-86629-000-1). Sunrise MO.

Rothwell, Naomi D. & Doniger, Joan M. The Psychiatric Halfway House: A Case Study. (Illus.). 284p. 1966. photocopy ed. spiral 27.50 (ISBN 0-398-01615-1). C C Thomas.

Sales, Grover. John Maher of Delancey Street: A Guide for Peaceful Revolution in America. (Illus.). 176p. 1976. 7.95 (ISBN 0-393-07499-4). Norton.

HALIBURTON, THOMAS CHANDLER, 1796-1865

Chittick, Victor L. Thomas Chandler Haliburton, "Sam Slick". LC 24-29336. Repr. of 1924 ed. 20.00 (ISBN 0-404-01525-5). AMS Pr.

Haliburton, Thomas C. Sam Slick. Baker, Ray P., ed. 420p. 1981. Repr. of 1923 ed. lib. bdg. 45.00 (ISBN 0-8495-2373-7). Arden Lib.

HALIDES

Clever, H. L. & Gerrard, W. Hydrogen Halides in Non-Aqueous Solvents: Gas Solubilities. (Solubility Data Ser.). Date not set. 100.01 (ISBN 0-08-023925-0). Pergamon.

Huang, C. C., et al. Molecular Studies on Halogenated Deoxynucleosides. 256p. 1972. text ed. 34.50x (ISBN 0-8422-7013-2). Irvington.

Patai, S., ed. Chemistry of Acyl Halides. LC 70-37114. (Chemistry of Functional Groups Ser.). 576p. 1972. 87.50 (ISBN 0-471-66936-9, Pub. by Wiley-Interscience). Wiley.

Wilcox. Lead Tin Telluride, Silver Halides & Czochralski Growth. (Preparation & Properties of Solid State Materials Ser.: Vol. 6). 1981. write for info. (ISBN 0-8247-1354-0). Dekker.

HALIFAX, GEORGE SAVILE, 1ST MARQUIS OF, 1633-1695

Foxcroft, Helen C. Life & Letters of Sir George Savile, 2 Vols. LC 4-35272. 1969. Repr. of 1898 ed. Set. 50.00 (ISBN 0-384-16573-7). Johnson Repr.

HALIFAX, NOVA SCOTIA

Rompkey, Ronald, ed. Expeditions of Honour: The Journal of John Salusbury in Halifax, Nova Scotia, 1749-1753. LC 79-13797. (Illus.). 180p. 1981. 16.00 (ISBN 0-87413-169-3). U Delaware Pr.

HALIFAX, NOVA SCOTIA–EXPLOSION, 1917

Prince, Samuel H. Catastrophe & Social Change, Based Upon a Sociological Study of the Halifax Disaster. LC 68-56683. (Columbia University. Studies in the Social Sciences: No. 212). Repr. of 1920 ed. 15.00 (ISBN 0-404-51212-7). AMS Pr.

HALITE

see Salt

HALKETT, ANNE (MURRAY) LADY, 1622-1699

Halkett, Anne. Autobiography. Nichols, J. G., ed. 1875. 22.50 (ISBN 0-384-20970-X). Johnson Repr.

HALL, ELLEN AUGUSTA, b. 1822

Hall, Ellen & Hall, Emily. Halls of Ravenswood. Mills, A. R., ed. (Illus.). 1968. 6.95 (ISBN 0-685-20591-6). Transatlantic.

HALL, EMILY MARY, b. 1819

Hall, Ellen & Hall, Emily. Halls of Ravenswood. Mills, A. R., ed. (Illus.). 1968. 6.95 (ISBN 0-685-20591-6). Transatlantic.

HALL, GRANVILLE STANLEY, 1844-1924

Pruette, Lorine. G. Stanley Hall. facs. ed. LC 73-126247. (Select Bibliographies Reprint Ser). 1926. 16.00 (ISBN 0-8369-5474-2). Arno.

Rosenzweig, Saul. Freud & the Kingmaker: The Visit to America - The Letters of Sigmund Freud & G. S. Hall, 1908 to 1923 & Freud's Five Lectures at Clark University. LC 78-65156. 1981. 13.50 (ISBN 0-930172-03-5). Rana Hse.

--The Rosenzweig Picture-Frustration (P-F) Study--Basic Manual. LC 77-95428. 1978. 8.00 (ISBN 0-930172-02-7). Rana Hse.

Ross, Dorothy. G. Stanley Hall: The Psychologist As Prophet. LC 75-165180. 482p. 1972. 17.50x (ISBN 0-226-72821-8). U of Chicago Pr.

HALL, GUS (PSEUD.), 1910-

North, Joseph, et al. Gus Hall - the Man & the Message. 1970. pap. 0.50 (ISBN 0-87898-060-1). New Outlook.

HALL, JAMES, 1793-1868

Burtschi, Mary. James Hall of Lincoln's Frontier World. LC 77-87957. (Illus.). 1978. 9.95 (ISBN 0-9601648-2-0). Little Brick Hse.

Flanagan, John T. James Hall: Literary Pioneer of the Ohio Valley. LC 77-102491. (Illus.). 1971. Repr. of 1941 ed. 11.50 (ISBN 0-8462-1511-X). Russell.

Randall, Randolph C. James Hall: Spokesman of the New West. LC 63-18578. (Illus.). 1964. 7.50 (ISBN 0-8142-0103-2). Ohio St U Pr.

HALL, JAMES NORMAN, 1887-1951

Monarch Notes on Nordhoff & Hall's Mutiny on the Bounty. (Orig.). pap. 1.50 (ISBN 0-671-00857-9). Monarch Pr.

Roulston, Robert. James Norman Hall. (Twayne United States Authors Ser.). 1978. lib. bdg. 9.95 (ISBN 0-8057-7255-3). G K Hall.

--James Norman Hall. (United States Authors Ser.: No. 323). 1978. 12.50 (ISBN 0-8057-7255-3). Twayne.

HALL, JOHN, 1575-1635

Huntington, R. T. Hall's Breechloaders: John H. Hall's Invention & Development of a Breechloading Rifle with Precision-Made Interchangeable Parts, & Its Introduction into the United States Service. LC 71-91843. (Illus.). 369p. 1972. pap. 20.00 softbound (ISBN 0-87387-049-2). Shumway.

Mitchell, C. M. The Shakespeare Circle. LC 76-30693. (Studies in Shakespeare, No. 24). 1977. lib. bdg. 46.95 (ISBN 0-8383-2166-6). Haskell.

Morlan, George. America's Heritage from John Stuart Hall. 1973. lib. bdg. 14.00x (ISBN 0-374-95877-7). Octagon.

HALL EFFECT

Campell, Leslie L. Galvanomagnetic & Thermogmagnetic Effects: The Hall & Allied Phenomena. (Illus.). 1923. 19.50 (ISBN 0-384-07280-1). Johnson Repr.

Chien, C. L. & Westgate, C. R., eds. The Hall Effect & Its Applications. 560p. 1980. 59.50 (ISBN 0-306-40556-3, Plenum Pr). Plenum Pub.

Hurd, Colin M. The Hall Effect in Metals & Alloys. LC 76-157936. (International Cryogenics Monographs). 400p. 1972. 39.50 (ISBN 0-306-30530-5, Plenum Pr). Plenum Pub.

HALL FAMILY

Hall, Septimius & William, Tasker H. Genealogy of Thomas Hall, His Children & Grandchildren. (Illus.). 1967. pap. 3.50 (ISBN 0-87012-064-6). McClain.

HALL-MARKS

see also Clocks and Watches; Jewelry; Pewter; Plate

Barber, E. A. & Lockwood, L. V. The Ceramic, Furniture & Silver Collectors' Glossary. (Architecture & Decorative Art Ser.). 1976. pap. 6.95 (ISBN 0-306-80049-7). Da Capo.

Belden, Louise C. Marks of American Silversmiths in the Ineson-Bissell Collection. LC 78-31816. 1980. 50.00x (ISBN 0-8139-0798-5). U Pr of Va.

Bohan, Peter & Hammerslough, Philip. Early Connecticut Silver, 1700-1840. LC 76-82543. (Illus.). 1970. 45.00x (ISBN 0-8195-4008-0, Pub. by Wesleyan U Pr). Columbia U Pr.

Chaffers, William. Chaffer's Handbook to Hallmarks on Gold & Silver Plate. Bunt, Cyril, ed. 9.50 (ISBN 0-685-07214-2). Borden.

Cripps, W. Old French Silver Marks. LC 73-78444. (Illus.). 1972. Repr. of 1880 ed. 8.00 (ISBN 0-912728-01-9). Newbury Bks.

Currier, E. M. E. A. Silvermarks, Sixteen Ninety to Eighteen Forty. LC 78-96937. 15.00 (ISBN 0-87282-021-1). Century Hse.

Currier, Ernest M. Marks of Early American Silversmiths. limited ed. LC 74-111387. (Illus.). 192p. 1970. deluxe ed. 35.00x (ISBN 0-9600266-1-4). R A Green.

French, Hollis. Silver Collector's Glossary & a List of Early American Silversmiths & Their Marks. LC 67-27454. (Architecture & Decorative Art Ser). 1967. lib. bdg. 17.50 (ISBN 0-306-70969-4). Da Capo.

Kovel, Ralph M. & Kovel, Terry H. Directory of American Silver, Pewter & Silver Plate. (Illus.). 1961. 9.95 (ISBN 0-517-50636-X). Crown.

MacDonald-Taylor, Margaret. Dictionary of Marks. (Illus.). 1962. pap. 4.95 (ISBN 0-8015-2089-4, Hawthorn). Dutton.

Norton(R.W.) Art Gallery. American Silver & Pressed Glass. LC 67-24712. (Illus.). 1967. pap. 3.50x (ISBN 0-9600182-0-4). Norton Art.

Wilkinson, W. R. T. History of Hallmarks. 11.95x (ISBN 0-8464-0482-6). Beekman Pubs.

Wyler, Seymour B. Book of Old Silver: English, American, Foreign. (Illus.). 1937. 11.95 (ISBN 0-517-00089-X). Crown.

HALLAM, ARTHUR HENRY, 1811-1833

Gladstone, William E. Arthur Henry Hallam. LC 73-15672. 1898. lib. bdg. 6.50 (ISBN 0-8414-4454-4). Folcroft.

Kolb, Jack, ed. The Letters of Arthur Henry Hallam. LC 79-13490. (Illus.). 835p. 1981. 45.00x (ISBN 0-8142-0300-0). Ohio St U Pr.

HALLECK, CHARLES A. 1900-

Kennedy, Michael, ed. The Autobiography of Charles Halle. (Illus.). 216p. 1981. Repr. of 1972 ed. lib. bdg. 22.50 (ISBN 0-306-76094-0). Da Capo.

HALLEIN, AUSTRIA

Powell, G. Bingham, Jr. Social Fragmentation & Political Hostility: An Austrian Case Study. LC 74-83119. 1970. 12.50x (ISBN 0-8047-0715-4). Stanford U Pr.

HALLEY, EDMOND, 1656-1742

Halley, Edmond. Correspondence & Papers of Edmond Halley. LC 74-26268. (History, Philosophy & Sociology of Science Ser). 1975. Repr. 22.00x (ISBN 0-405-06596-5). Arno.

HALLEY'S COMET

Anderson, Norman D. & Brown, Walter R. Halley's Comet. (Illus.). 80p. (gr. 4 up). 1981. PLB 7.95 (ISBN 0-396-07974-1). Dodd.

HALLIBURTON, RICHARD, 1900-1939

Halliburton, Richard. Complete Book of Marvels. 1981. Repr. lib. bdg. 30.00 (ISBN 0-89987-371-5). Darby Bks.

HALLOCK, GERARD, 1800-1866

Hallock, William H. Life of Gerald Hallock, Thirty-Three Years Editor of the New York Journal of Commerce. LC 78-125696. (American Journalists Ser). 1970. Repr. of 1869 ed. 20.00 (ISBN 0-405-01675-1). Arno.

HALLOWEEN

Barth, Edna. Witches, Pumpkins, & Grinning Ghosts: The Story of the Halloween Symbols. (Illus.). 96p. (gr. 3-6). 1981. pap. 3.95 (ISBN 0-89919-040-5, Clarion). HM.

--Witches, Pumpkins & Grinning Ghosts: The Story of the Halloween Symbols. LC 72-75705. (Illus.). 96p. (gr. 3-6). 1972. 8.95 (ISBN 0-395-28847-9, Clarion). HM.

Borten, Helen. Halloween. LC 65-16184. (Holiday Ser.). (Illus.). (gr. 1-3). 1965. PLB 7.89 (ISBN 0-690-36314-1, TYC-J). Har-Row.

Dobrin, Arnold. Make a Witch, Make a Goblin: A Book of Halloween Crafts. LC 77-177. (Illus.). 128p. (gr. 2-5). 1977. 7.95 (ISBN 0-590-07450-4, Four Winds). Schol Bk Serv.

Gibbons, Gail. Things to Make & Do for Halloween. LC 75-19396. (Things to Make & Do Ser.). (Illus.). 48p. (gr. k-2). 1976. PLB 8.40 (ISBN 0-531-01103-8). Watts.

Harper, Wilhelmina, ed. Ghosts & Goblins. rev. ed. (Illus.). (gr. 2 up). 1965. 7.95 (ISBN 0-525-30516-5). Dutton.

Hathaway, Nancy. Halloween Crafts & Cookbook. LC 78-73829. (Craft & Cookbook Ser.). (Illus.). (gr. 2-5). 1979. PLB 5.79 (ISBN 0-8178-6130-0). Harvey.

Hopkins, Lee B., ed. Hey-How for Halloween. LC 74-5601. 32p. (gr. 1-5). 1974. 4.95 (ISBN 0-15-233900-0, HJ). HarBraceJ.

Katz, Ruth. Pumpkin Personalities. (Illus.). (gr. k-4). 1979. 5.95 (ISBN 0-8027-6364-2); PLB 5.85 (ISBN 0-8027-6365-0). Walker & Co.

Kessler, Leonard. Riddles That Rhyme for Halloween Time. LC 77-13140. (Imagination Ser.). (Illus.). (gr. 1-5). 1978. PLB 6.18 (ISBN 0-8116-4409-X). Garrard.

McGovern, Ann. Squeals & Squiggles & Ghostly Giggles. LC 72-87083. (Illus.). 80p. (gr. 2-5). 1973. 6.95 (ISBN 0-590-17306-5, Four Winds). Schol Bk Serv.

Owens, Judy. Hallowe'en Fun. (Illus.). (gr. k-3). 1973. pap. 1.50 (ISBN 0-590-08700-2, Schol Pap). Schol Bk Serv.

Patterson, Lillie. Halloween. LC 63-13626. (Holiday Books Ser). (Illus.). (gr. 2-5). 1963. PLB 6.87 (ISBN 0-8116-6552-6). Garrard.

Prelutsky, Jack. It's Halloween. (Illus.). 48p. 1980. Repr. pap. 1.50 (ISBN 0-590-03275-5, Schol Pap). Schol Bk Serv.

--It's Halloween. LC 77-2141. (Greenwillow Read-Alone Bks.). (Illus.). (gr. 1-4). 1977. 5.95 (ISBN 0-688-80102-1); PLB 5.71 (ISBN 0-688-84102-3). Greenwillow.

Racioppo, Larry. Halloween. LC 80-19119. (Illus.). 32p. (gr. 1 up). 1980. 8.95 (ISBN 0-684-16708-5). Scribner.

Sandak, Cass R. Halloween. (gr. 2-4). 1980. PLB 8.60 (ISBN 0-531-04149-2). Watts.

Sechrist, Elizabeth H. Heigh-Ho for Halloween. (Illus.). (gr. 7-11). 1948. PLB 6.71 (ISBN 0-8255-8139-7). Macrae.

Supraner, Robyn. Happy Halloween: Things to Make & Do. LC 80-23889. (Illus.). 48p. (gr. 1-5). 1981. lib. bdg. 6.92 (ISBN 0-89375-420-X); pap. 1.95 (ISBN 0-89375-421-8). Troll Assocs.

Werner, Ken. Halloween. LC 81-80643. (Illus.). 64p. (Orig.). 1981. pap. 12.95x (ISBN 0-9605882-0-5). Octavia Pr.

HALLS OF RESIDENCE

see Dormitories

HALLUCINATIONS AND ILLUSIONS

see also Apparitions; Conjuring; Ghosts; Magic; Optical Illusions; Perception, Disorders of; Personality, Disorders of

Brierre De Boismont, Alexandre-Jacques-Francois. Hallucinations. LC 75-16689. (Classics in Psychiatry Ser.). 1976. Repr. of 1853 ed. 31.00x (ISBN 0-405-07419-0). Arno.

Campbell, Coyne H. Induced Delusions. 187p. 1981. Repr. of 1957 ed. 10.95x (ISBN 0-686-76737-3). Regent House.

Goodman, F. D., et al. Trance, Healing, & Hallucination: Three Field Studies in Religious Experience. 414p. 1981. Repr. of 1974 ed. text ed. write for info. (ISBN 0-89874-246-3). Krieger.

Johnson, Fred H. The Anatomy of Hallucinations. LC 77-22711. 1978. 19.95x (ISBN 0-88229-155-6). Nelson-Hall.

Keup, Wolfram, ed. Origin & Mechanisms of Hallucinations. LC 71-139579. 479p. 1970. 35.00 (ISBN 0-306-30515-1, Plenum Pr). Plenum Pub.

Kleps, Art. Millbrook: The True Story of the Early Years of the Psychedelic Revolution. LC 76-54660. (Illus.). 1977. 10.00 (ISBN 0-916534-05-7); pap. 4.95 (ISBN 0-916534-06-5). Bench Pr.

MacDermot, Violet. The Cult of the Seer in the Ancient Middle East: A Contribution to Current Research on Hallucinations Drawn from Coptic & Other Texts. LC 79-152047. (Wellcome Institute of the History of Medicine). 1971. 65.00x (ISBN 0-520-02030-8). U of Cal Pr.

Meerloo, A. M. Delusion & Mass Delusion. (Nervous & Mental Disease Monographs). Repr. of 1949 ed. 11.50 (ISBN 0-384-37950-8). Johnson Repr.

Reed, Graham. The Psychology of Anomalous Experience: A Cognitive Approach. 1972. text ed. 8.25x (ISBN 0-09-113240-1, Hutchinson U Lib). Humanities.

Siegel, R. K. & West, L. J., eds. Hallucinations: Behavior, Experience, & Theory. LC 75-12670. 322p. 1975. 50.00 (ISBN 0-471-79096-6, Pub. by Wiley Medical). Wiley.

Supraner, Robyn. Stop & Look! Illusions. LC 80-23799. (Illus.). 48p. (gr. 1-5). 1981. PLB 6.92 (ISBN 0-89375-434-X); pap. 1.95 (ISBN 0-89375-435-8). Troll Assocs.

HALLUCINOGENIC DRUGS

see also Lysergic Acid Diethylamide

Brown, F. Christine. Hallucinogenic Drugs. (Amer. Lec. Living Chemistry Ser.). (Illus.). 164p. 1972. 19.75 (ISBN 0-398-02249-6). C C Thomas.

Castaneda, Carlos. Journey to Ixtlan. (gr. 10-12). 1976. pap. 2.50 (ISBN 0-671-80424-3, 82768). PB.

Cavanna, Roberto & Servadio, Emilio. ESP Experiments with LSD Twenty-Five & Psilocybin. LC 64-24271. (Parapsychological Monograph No. 5). 1964. pap. 3.00 (ISBN 0-912328-08-8). Parapsych Foun.

Drug Abuse Council. Altered States of Consciousness. LC 75-4022. 1975. 5.00 (ISBN 0-686-15286-7). Drug Abuse.

Durr, Robert A. Poetic Vision & the Psychedelic Experience. LC 78-112038. 1970. 14.95x (ISBN 0-8156-0067-4). Syracuse U Pr.

Feldman, Harvey W., et al, eds. Angel Dust: An Ethnographic Study of Phencyclidine Users. LC 79-8319. 240p. 1979. 14.95 (ISBN 0-669-03379-0). Lexington Bks.

Furst, Peter T. Hallucinogens & Culture. LC 75-25442. (Cross-Cultural Themes Ser.). (Illus.). 208p. 1976. pap. text ed. 5.95 (ISBN 0-88316-517-1). Chandler & Sharp.

Gamage, J. R. & Zerkin, E. L., eds. Hallucinogenic Drug Research: Impact on Science & Society. LC 72-133456. 1970. pap. 5.00x (ISBN 0-932204-01-5). Stash.

Go Ask Alice. 1972. pap. 1.95 (ISBN 0-380-00523-9, 51730). Avon.

Grinspoon, Lester & Bakalar, James B. Psychedelic Drugs Reconsidered. 1981. pap. 7.95 (ISBN 0-465-06451-5). Basic.

--Psychedelic Drugs Reconsidered. LC 79-7336. 1979. 15.95 (ISBN 0-465-06450-7). Basic.

Haining, Peter, ed. The Hashish Club: An Anthology of Drug Literature. Incl. Vol. 1. Founding of the Modern Tradition: from Coleridge to Crowley. Aldiss, Brian W., pref. by. text ed. 11.75x (ISBN 0-7206-0303-X); Vol. 2. Psychedelic Era: from Huxley to Lennon. text ed. 8.50x (ISBN 0-7206-0014-6). 1975. Humanities.

Hoffer, Abram & Osmond, H. Hallucinogens. 1967. 64.00 (ISBN 0-12-351850-4). Acad Pr.

Hollister, Leo E. Chemical Psychoses: LSD & Related Drugs. (Amer. Lec. Living Chemistry Ser). (Illus.). 200p. 1972. 11.75 (ISBN 0-398-00860-4). C C Thomas.

Huxley, Aldous. Moksha: Writings on Psychedelics & the Visionary Experience, 1953-1963. Palmer, Cynthia, ed. LC 77-71224. 320p. 1977. 12.95 (ISBN 0-88373-042-1). Stonehill Pub Co.

Karczmar, A. G. & Koella, W. P. Neurophysiological & Behavioral Aspects of Psychotropic Drugs. (Illus.). 224p. 1969. photocopy ed. spiral 19.75 (ISBN 0-398-00972-4). C C Thomas.

Marshall, William & Taylor, Gilbert W. Psychedelic Ecstasy. pap. 2.00 (ISBN 0-87980-126-3). Wilshire.

Metzner, Ralph, ed. Ecstatic Adventure. LC 68-15269. (Psychedelic Paintings). 1968. 10.95 (ISBN 0-02-584450-4). Macmillan.

Norland, Richard H. Psilocybin Bibliography: Companion to What's in a Mushroom, Pt. 3. 1977. pap. text ed. 5.95x (ISBN 0-918578-06-X). Pear Tree.

--What's in a Mushroom, 3 pts. Incl. Pt. 1. Nutritional & Medical Mushrooms. 13.95 (ISBN 0-918578-12-4); pap. 9.95 (ISBN 0-918578-01-9); Pt. 2. Four Hundred Twenty-Six Toxic Mushrooms. 11.95 (ISBN 0-918578-14-0); pap. 7.95 (ISBN 0-918578-03-5); Pt. 3. Psycho-Active Mushrooms. 9.95 (ISBN 0-918578-16-7); pap. 5.95 (ISBN 0-918578-05-1). (Illus.). 1977. 29.95 (ISBN 0-918578-11-6). Pear Tree.

Oeric, O. N. & Oss, O. T. Psilocybin: Magic Mushroom Grower's Guide. LC 76-381457. (Illus.). 1976. pap. 5.95 (ISBN 0-915904-13-6). And-or Pr.

Ott, Jonathan & Bigwood, Jeremy, eds. Teonanacatl: Hallucinogenic Mushrooms of North America. LC 78-14794. 1978. 14.50x (ISBN 0-914842-32-3); pap. 8.95 (ISBN 0-914842-29-3). Madrona Pubs.

Perrero, Laurie & Perrero, Louis. Hallucinogenic Mushrooms. Romashko, Sandra, ed. (Illus.). Date not set. pap. 3.25 (ISBN 0-89317-021-6). Windward Pub.

Schultes, Richard E. & Hofmann, Albert. The Botany & Chemistry of Hallucinogens. 2nd ed. (Amer. Lec Living Chemistry). (Illus.). 464p. 1980. text ed. 29.75 (ISBN 0-398-03863-5). C C Thomas.

--Plants of the Gods: Origins of Hallucinogenic Use. LC 79-13382. (Illus.). 1980. 34.95 (ISBN 0-07-056089-7). McGraw.

Smith, Michael V. Psychedelic Chemistry. pap. 14.95 (ISBN 0-686-30636-8). Loompanics.

Stafford, Peter. Psychedelics Encyclopedia. LC 77-89430. (Illus.). 1977. pap. 10.95 (ISBN 0-915904-21-7). And-or Pr.

Stillman, R. C. & Willette, R. E., eds. The Psychopharmacology of Hallucinogens. LC 78-14019. 1979. 40.00 (ISBN 0-08-021938-1). Pergamon.

Watts, Alan W. Joyous Cosmology. (Illus.). 1965. pap. 1.95 (ISBN 0-394-70299-9, Vin). Random.

Watts, W. David, Jr. The Psychedelic Experience. LC 78-127997. 256p. 1971. 16.95 (ISBN 0-8039-0081-3). Sage.

Weil, Gunther M., et al, eds. Psychedelic Reader. 1971. pap. 3.95 (ISBN 0-8065-0255-X). Citadel Pr.

WHO Scientific Group. Geneva, 1970. Use of Cannabis: Report. (Technical Report Ser.: No. 478). (Also avail. in French & Spanish). 1971. pap. 2.00 (ISBN 92-4-120478-8). World Health.

Young, Lawrence A., et al. Recreational Drugs. 1979. pap. 2.75 (ISBN 0-425-04682-6). Berkley Pub.

HALLUCINOGENIC DRUGS AND RELIGIOUS EXPERIENCE

Castaneda, Carlos. Journey to Ixtlan. 1981. pap. 2.95 (ISBN 0-671-43673-2). PB.

--Separate Reality. 1981. pap. 2.95 (ISBN 0-671-43672-4). PB.

--Separate Reality. LC 79-139617. 1971. pap. 4.95 (ISBN 0-671-21074-2, Touchstone Bks). S&S.

--Separate Reality. LC 79-139617. 1971. 11.95 (ISBN 0-671-20897-7). S&S.

--A Separate Reality. (gr. 10-12). 1976. pap. 2.50 (ISBN 0-671-83132-1). PB.

--Tales of Power. 1981. pap. 2.95 (ISBN 0-671-43674-0). PB.

--Tales of Power. (gr. 10 up). 1976. pap. 2.50 (ISBN 0-671-83121-6). PB.

--Teachings of Don Juan. 1981. pap. 2.95 (ISBN 0-671-42216-2). PB.

--The Teachings of Don Juan. 1976. pap. 2.50 (ISBN 0-671-82767-7). PB.

--The Teachings of Don Juan: A Yaqui Way of Knowledge. LC 68-17303. 1968. 12.95x (ISBN 0-520-00217-2); pap. 3.95 (ISBN 0-520-02258-0, CAL253). U of Cal Pr.

Gowan, J. C. The Development of the Psychedelic Indiviual. 300p. 1974. pap. 4.00 (ISBN 0-686-27924-7). Snyder Inst Res.

Hall, Manly P. Drugs of Vision. pap. 0.25 (ISBN 0-89314-313-8). Philos Res.

Harner, Michael J., ed. Hallucinogens & Shamanism. (Illus.). 224p. 1973. 15.95 (ISBN 0-19-501650-5). Oxford U Pr.

--Hallucinogens & Shamanism. (Illus.). 216p. 1973. pap. 4.95 (ISBN 0-19-501649-1, 386, GB). Oxford U Pr.

Kleps, Arthur J. Boo Hoo Bible: The Neo-American Church Catechism & Handbook. rev. ed. LC 73-29356. Orig. Title: Neo-American Church Catechism. (Illus.). 218p. 1971. pap. 2.95 (ISBN 0-9600388-1-7). Neo-Am Church.

Leary, Timothy. Psychedelic Prayers. 2.95 (ISBN 0-8216-0002-8). Univ Bks.

Leary, Timothy & Metzner, Ralph. The Psychedelic Experience: A Manual Based on the Tibetan Book of the Dead. 1976. pap. 3.95 (ISBN 0-8065-0552-4). Citadel Pr.

Regardie, Israel. Roll Away the Stone. 250p. 1974. pap. 3.95 (ISBN 0-87542-692-1). Llewellyn Pubns.
Wasson, R. Gordon. The Wonderous Mushroom: Mycolatry in Mesoamerica. LC 79-26895. (Illus.). 178p. 1980. 14.95 (ISBN 0-07-068441-3); deluxe ed. 435.00 (ISBN 0-07-068442-1); pap. 10.95 (ISBN 0-07-068443-X). McGraw.

HALOGENATION

Gann, Richard G., ed. Halogenated Fire Suppressants. LC 75-25638. (ACS Symposium Ser.: No. 16). 1975. 27.75 (ISBN 0-8412-0297-4). Am Chemical.

HALOGENS

see also Chlorine; Fluorine; Iodine

Gutmann, Viktor, ed. International Review of Halogen Chemistry, 3 Vols. LC 66-30147. (Illus.). Vol. 1, 1967. 64.50 (ISBN 0-12-310901-9); Vol. 2, 1967. 66.00 (ISBN 0-12-310902-7); Vol. 3, 1968. 64.50 (ISBN 0-12-310903-5). Acad Pr.
Guttman, V. Main Group Elements: Groups 6-7. (MTP International Review of Science: Inorganic Chemistry Ser. 2: Vol. 3). (Illus.). 400p. 1975. 37.50 (ISBN 0-8391-0202-X). Univ Park.
Guttman, Viktor. Main Group Elements - Group 7 & Noble Gases. (Mtp International Review of Science-Inorganic Chemistry Ser. 1: Vol. 3). (Illus.). 24.50, index vol. 12.50 (ISBN 0-8391-1006-5). Univ Park.
Khan, M. A. & Stanton, R. H., eds. Toxicology of Halogenated Hydrocarbons: Health & Ecological Effects. (Illus.). 350p. 1981. 60.00 (ISBN 0-08-027530-3). Pergamon.
Nicholson, William J. & Moore, John A., eds. Health Effects of Halogenated Aromatic Hydrocarbons. LC 79-12253. (Annals of the New York Academy of Sciences: Vol. 320). 730p. 1979. 115.00x (ISBN 0-89766-008-0). NY Acad Sci.

HALOPHYTES

Poljakoff-Mayber, A. & Gale, J., eds. Plants in Saline Environments. LC 75-1272. (Ecological Studies: Vol. 15). (Illus.). 215p. 1975. 40.70 (ISBN 0-387-07193-8). Springer-Verlag.
Reimold, Robert J. & Queen, William H. Ecology of Halophytes. 1974. 43.00 (ISBN 0-12-586450-7). Acad Pr.
Waisel, Yoav. Biology of Halophytes. (Physiological Ecology Ser). 1972. 51.00 (ISBN 0-12-730850-4). Acad Pr.

HALS, FRANS, 1580-1666

Beard, H. P. Frans Hals. Stuyck, George, tr. (Illus.). 168p. 1981. 40.00 (ISBN 0-8109-1055-1). Abrams.
Van Der Groot, Georg, ed. Frans Hals, His Life, His Paintings: A Critique of His Art. 1979. deluxe ed. 27.50 (ISBN 0-930582-27-6). Gloucester Art.

HALSEY, WILLIAM FREDERICK, 1882-1959

Halsey, William & Bryan, J. Admiral Halsey's Story. (Politics & Strategy of World War II Ser.). 1976. Repr. of 1917 ed. lib. bdg. 27.50 (ISBN 0-306-70770-5). Da Capo.
Halsey, William F., 3rd & Bryan, Joseph. Admiral Halsey's Story. Repr. of 1947 ed. 15.00 (ISBN 0-89201-093-2). Zenger Pub.
Keating, Lawrence A. Fleet Admiral: The Story of William F. Halsey. (Illus.). (gr. 7 up). 1965. 3.95 (ISBN 0-664-32343-X). Westminster.

HALSTED, WILLIAM STEWART, 1852-1922

Crowe, Samuel J. Halsted of John Hopkins: The Man & His Men. (Illus.). 268p. 1957. ed. spiral bdg. 27.50photocopy (ISBN 0-398-00371-8). C C Thomas.

HAM

Peterson, Thomas V. Ham & Japheth: The Mythic World of Whites in the Antebellum South. LC 78-15716. (ATLA Monograph: No. 12). 1978. lib. bdg. 11.00 (ISBN 0-8108-1162-6). Scarecrow.
Recommended International Standards for Cooked Ham & for Cooked Cured Pork Shoulder. 1979. pap. 4.50 (ISBN 92-5-100637-7, F1570, FAO). Unipub.

HAMANN, JOHANN GEORG, 1730-1788

Dunning, Stephen N. The Tongues of Men. LC 79-10729. (American Academy of Religion, Dissertation Ser.: No. 27). 1979. 12.00 (ISBN 0-89130-283-2, 010127); pap. 7.50 (ISBN 0-89130-302-2). Scholars Pr Ca.
O'Flaherty, James C. Unity & Language: A Study in the Philosophy of Johann Georg Hamann. LC 52-4007. (North Carolina. University. Studies in the Germanic Languages & Literatures: No. 6). Repr. of 1952 ed. 18.50 (ISBN 0-404-50906-1). AMS Pr.

HAMBLIN, JACOB

Corbett, Pearson H. Jacob Hamblin, Peacemaker. 7.95 (ISBN 0-87747-128-2). Deseret Bk.
Little, James A. Jacob Hamblin. facsimile ed. LC 72-164615. (Select Bibliographies Reprint Ser). Repr. of 1881 ed. 15.00 (ISBN 0-8369-5899-3). Arno.

HAMBURG-AMERICAN LINES

Cecil, Lamar. Albert Ballin: Business & Politics in Imperial Germany, 1888-1918. 1967. 26.50 (ISBN 0-691-05101-1). Princeton U Pr.

HAMBURG, GERMANY

Comfort, Richard A. Revolutionary Hamburg: Labor Politics in the Early Weimar Republic. 1966. 15.00x (ISBN 0-8047-0284-5). Stanford U Pr.
Fox, Ogden & Orsi, Roberto. Hamburg After Dark-Rome After Dark. 1977. pap. 1.50 (ISBN 0-532-15239-5). Woodhill.
Reissner, Larissa. Hamburg at the Barricades. Chappell, Richard, tr. from Rus. (Illus.). 228p. 1980. text ed. 12.00 (ISBN 0-904383-36-9). Pluto Pr.
Rodnick, David. A Portrait of Two German Cities: Lubeck & Hamburg. LC 79-54321. 1980. 20.00x (ISBN 0-912570-06-7). Caprock Pr.
Spoehr, Florence M. White Falcon: The House of Godeffroy & Its Commercial & Scientific Role in the Pacific. LC 63-18693. (Illus.). 1963. 7.95 (ISBN 0-87015-119-3). Pacific Bks.

HAMBURG, GERMANY-THEATERS

Robertson, John G., ed. Lessing's Dramatic Theory. LC 63-14713. (Illus.). 1939. 25.00 (ISBN 0-405-08894-9). Arno.

HAMBURGER

see Cookery (Beef)

HAMDEN, CONNECTICUT-HISTORY, JUVENILE

Hartley, Rachel. The Story of Hamden: Land of the Sleeping Giant. rev. ed. 1966. 10.00 (ISBN 0-208-01648-1). Shoe String.

HAMELN, GLUCKEL OF, 1646-1724

Gluckel. The Memoirs of Gluckel of Hameln. Lowenthal, Marvin, tr. from Ger. LC 77-75290. 1977. pap. 6.95 (ISBN 0-8052-0572-1). Schocken.

HAMER, FANNIE LOU

Jordan, June. Fannie Lou Hammer. LC 70-184982. (Crocodile Paperbacks Ser.). (Illus.). 48p. (gr. 1-4). 1975. pap. 1.45 (ISBN 0-690-00634-9, TYC-J). Har-Row.

HAMID IBN MUHAMMAD, CALLED TIPPO TIB, d. 1905

Brode, Heinrich. Tippoo Tib, the Story of His Career in Central Africa. Havelock, H., tr. LC 78-99351. 1969. Repr. of 1907 ed. lib. bdg. 12.00 (ISBN 0-8411-0022-5). Metro Bks.

HAMILTON, ALEXANDER, 1757-1804

Alexander, Holmes. To Covet Honor. LC 77-75276. 1977. 10.00 (ISBN 0-88279-232-6). Western Islands.
Baldwin, Joseph G. Party Leaders: Sketches of Thomas Jefferson, Alexander Hamilton, Andrew Jackson, Henry Clay John Randolph of Roanoke; Including Notices of Many Other Distinguished American Statesmen. LC 72-39654. (Essay Index Reprint Ser.). Repr. of 1885 ed. 21.00 (ISBN 0-8369-2741-9). Arno.
Boyd, Julian P. Number Seven: Alexander Hamilton's Secret Attempts to Control American Foreign Policy. 1964. 13.50 (ISBN 0-691-04529-1). Princeton U Pr.
Bryce, James B. Predictions of Hamilton & De Tocqueville. LC 78-63775. (Johns Hopkins University. Studies in the Social Sciences. Fifth Ser. 1887: 9). Repr. of 1887 ed. 11.50 (ISBN 0-404-61041-2). AMS Pr.
Coleman, William. A Collection of the Facts & Documents Relative to the Death of Major General Alexander Hamilton. LC 72-95422. (Illus.). 238p. 1973. Repr. of 1804 ed. 2.95 (ISBN 0-88319-012-5). Shoal Creek Pub.
Crouse, Anna & Crouse, Russell. Alexander Hamilton & Aaron Burr. (Landmark Ser.: No. 85). 1963. PLB 5.99 (ISBN 0-394-90385-4, BYR). Random.
Culbertson, William S. Alexander Hamilton: An Essay. 1916. 22.50x (ISBN 0-686-50039-3). Elliots Bks.
Emery, Noemie. Alexander Hamilton. (Illus.). 1979. 12.95 (ISBN 0-399-12367-9). Putnam.
Flexner, James T. The Young Hamilton: A Biography. LC 77-13877. 1978. 15.00 (ISBN 0-316-28594-3). Little.
Ford, Paul L. Bibliotheca Hamiltoniana. Repr. of 1886 ed. 12.50 (ISBN 0-8363-0013-0). Jenkins.
Goebel, Julius, Jr. & Smith, Joseph H., eds. The Law Practice of Alexander Hamilton, Vol. 1. LC 64-13900. 1964. 50.00x (ISBN 0-231-08944-9). Columbia U Pr.
--The Law Practice of Alexander Hamilton, Vol. 2. 1969. 50.00x (ISBN 0-231-08945-7). Columbia U Pr.
--The Law Practice of Alexander Hamilton, Vol. 3. 1980. 50.00x (ISBN 0-231-08946-5). Columbia U Pr.
--The Law Practice of Alexander Hamilton, Vol. 4. 1980. 50.00x (ISBN 0-231-08930-9). Columbia U Pr.
--The Law Practice of Alexander Hamilton, Vol. 5. 1981. 50.00x (ISBN 0-231-08929-5). Columbia U Pr.
Griggs, Edward H. American Statesmen: An Interpretation of Our History & Heritage. LC 76-121474. (Essay Index Reprint Ser). 1927. 19.50 (ISBN 0-8369-1810-X). Arno.
Hacker, Louis. Alexander Hamilton in the American Tradition. LC 74-25994. 273p. 1975. Repr. of 1957 ed. lib. bdg. 15.50x (ISBN 0-8371-7878-9, HAAL). Greenwood.
Hall, Margaret E., ed. Alexander Hamilton Reader. LC 57-6014. (Orig.). 1957. 7.50 (ISBN 0-379-11309-0); pap. 2.50 (ISBN 0-379-11309-0). Oceana.
Hamilton, Alexander. Collection of the Facts & Documents, Relative to the Death of Major-General Alexander Hamilton. Coleman, William, ed. LC 72-95068. (Select Bibliographies Reprint Ser). 1904. 25.00 (ISBN 0-8369-5025-9). Arno.
--The Papers of Alexander Hamilton, Vol. 23. Syrett, Harold C., ed. 624p. 1976. 22.50x (ISBN 0-231-08922-8). Columbia U Pr.
--The Papers of Alexander Hamilton, Vol. 24. Syrett, Harold C., ed. 664p. 1976. 20.00x (ISBN 0-231-08923-6). Columbia U Pr.
--The Papers of Alexander Hamilton, Vol. 19 August 1795-December 1795. Syrett, Harold C., et al, eds. 640p. 1973. text ed. 20.00x (ISBN 0-231-08918-X). Columbia U Pr.
--The Papers of Alexander Hamilton, Vol. 18 January 1795-july 1795. Syrett, Harold C., et al, eds. 608p. 1973. text ed. 20.00x (ISBN 0-231-08917-1). Columbia U Pr.
--The Papers of Alexander Hamilton, Vol. 20 Jan 1796-1797. Syrett, Harold C., et al, eds. 1974. 20.00x (ISBN 0-231-08919-8). Columbia U Pr.
--Papers of Alexander Hamilton: Index, Vol. 27. LC 61-15593. 1981. 20.00x (ISBN 0-231-08926-0). Columbia U Pr.
--The Papers of Alexander Hamilton: July 1798-March 1799, Vol. 22. Syrett, Harold C., et al, eds. 640p. 1975. 22.50x (ISBN 0-231-08921-X). Columbia U Pr.
--Papers of Alexander Hamilton: May 1802-July 1804, Vol. 26. 1978. 20.00x (ISBN 0-231-08925-2). Columbia U Pr.
Hamilton, Allan McLane. The Intimate Life of Alexander Hamilton. 1979. Repr. of 1910 ed. lib. bdg. 85.00 (ISBN 0-8492-5263-6). R West.
Hendrickson, Robert. The Rise & Fall of Alexander Hamilton. 800p. 1981. 24.95 (ISBN 0-442-26113-6). Van Nos Reinhold.
Kent, James. Memoirs & Letters of James Kent. Kent, William, ed. LC 78-99481. (American Public Figures Ser). 1970. Repr. of 1898 ed. lib. bdg. 32.50 (ISBN 0-306-71847-2). Da Capo.
Lodge, Henry C. Alexander Hamilton. LC 80-22082. (American Statesmen Ser.). 310p. 1981. pap. 4.95 (ISBN 0-87754-179-5). Chelsea Hse.
--Alexander Hamilton. Morse, John T., Jr., ed. LC 72-128971. (American Statesmen: No. 7). Repr. of 1898 ed. 16.00 (ISBN 0-404-50857-X). AMS Pr.
--Alexander Hamilton. Repr. of 1917 ed. lib. bdg. 16.25x (ISBN 0-8371-1928-6, LOAH). Greenwood.
--Alexander Hamilton. Repr. of 1890 ed. 20.00 (ISBN 0-686-19876-X). Ridgeway Bks.
Lycan, Gilbert L. Alexander Hamilton & American Foreign Policy: A Design for Greatness. LC 69-16730. (Illus.). 1970. 24.95x (ISBN 0-8061-0880-0). U of Okla Pr.
McDonald, Forrest. Alexander Hamilton: A Biography. LC 78-26554. 1979. 19.50 (ISBN 0-393-01218-2). Norton.
Miller, John C. Alexander Hamilton: Portrait in Paradox. LC 78-27607. 1979. Repr. of 1959 ed. lib. bdg. 38.75x (ISBN 0-313-20908-1, MIAH). Greenwood.
Mitchell, Broadus. Alexander Hamilton, 2 vols. 1981. Repr. of 1957 ed. lib. bdg. 75.00x (ISBN 0-374-95792-4). Octagon.
--Alexander Hamilton: A Concise Biography. LC 75-16899. (Illus.). 384p. 1976. 17.95x (ISBN 0-19-501979-2). Oxford U Pr.
Morse, John T. The Life of Alexander Hamilton, 2 vols. LC 75-31123. Repr. of 1876 ed. 64.50 (ISBN 0-404-13750-4). AMS Pr.
Otenasek, Mildred B. Alexander Hamilton's Financial Policies. Bruchey, Stuart, ed. LC 76-39837. (Nineteen Seventy-Seven Dissertations Ser.). 1977. lib. bdg. 15.00x (ISBN 0-405-09917-7). Arno.
Pancake, John S. Jefferson & Hamilton. Colegrove, Kenneth, ed. LC 74-750. (Shapers of History Ser). (gr. 10 up). 1974. pap. text ed. 4.95 (ISBN 0-8120-0463-9). Barron.
Parks, Robert J. European Origins of the Economic Ideas of Alexander Hamilton. Bruchey, Stuart, ed. LC 76-39838. (Nineteen Seventy-Seven Dissertations Ser.). 1977. lib. bdg. 15.00x (ISBN 0-405-09918-5). Arno.
Prescott, F. C. Hamilton & Jefferson. 422p. 1980. Repr. lib. bdg. 40.00 (ISBN 0-8495-4381-9). Arden Lib.
Rocher, Rosane. Alexander Hamilton (1762-1824) A Chapter in the Early History of Sanskrit Philology. (American Oriental Ser.: Vol. 51). 1968. pap. 5.00 (ISBN 0-940490-51-X). Am Orient Soc.
Schachner, Nathan. Alexander Hamilton. 1961. pap. 4.95 (ISBN 0-498-04027-5). A S Barnes.
Schouler, James. Alexander Hamilton. 1978. Repr. of 1901 ed. 17.50 (ISBN 0-8492-8052-4). R West.
Stourzh, Gerald. Alexander Hamilton & the Idea of Republican Government. LC 69-18496. 1970. 12.50x (ISBN 0-8047-0724-3). Stanford U Pr.
Swanson, Donald F. Origins of Hamilton's Fiscal Policies. LC 63-63264. (U of Fla. Social Sciences Monographs Ser.: No. 17). 1963. pap. 3.00 (ISBN 0-8130-0222-2). U Presses Fla.

HAMILTON, ALEXANDER, 1757-1804–BIBLIOGRAPHY

Ford, Paul L. Bibliotheca Hamiltoniana. LC 74-168120. Repr. of 1886 ed. 11.50 (ISBN 0-404-02513-7). AMS Pr.
--List of Treasury Reports & Circulars Issued by Alexander Hamilton, 1789-1795. LC 72-131451. (Bibliography & Reference Ser.: No. 390). 1971. Repr. of 1886 ed. lib. bdg. 13.50 (ISBN 0-8337-1200-4). B Franklin.

HAMILTON, ALEXANDER, 1757-1804–JUVENILE LITERATURE

Kurland, Gerald. Alexander Hamilton: Architect of American Nationalism. Rahmas, D. Steve, ed. LC 73-190245. (Outstanding Personalities Ser). 32p. (Orig.). (gr. 7-9). 1972. PLB 2.95 incl. catalog cards (ISBN 0-87157-527-2); pap. 1.50 vinyl laminated covers (ISBN 0-87157-027-0). SamHar Pr.

HAMILTON, ANDREW JACKSON

Konkle, Burton A. The Life of Andrew Hamilton, 1676-1741. LC 72-27. (Select Bibliographies Reprint Ser). 1972. Repr. of 1941 ed. 15.00 (ISBN 0-8369-9962-2). Arno.

HAMILTON, EMMA, LADY, 1761-1815

Jeaffreson, John C. Lady Hamilton & Lord Nelson. Repr. of 1897 ed. lib. bdg. 35.00 (ISBN 0-8495-2724-4). Arden Lib.
Lofts, Norah. Emma Hamilton. LC 77-26868. (Illus.). 1978. 14.95 (ISBN 0-698-10912-0). Coward.

HAMILTON, HENRY, d. 1796–JUVENILE LITERATURE

Havighurst, Walter. Proud Prisoner. LC 64-19641. (Younger Readers Ser.). (Illus.). (gr. 4-7). 1964. 3.95 (ISBN 0-910412-61-8). Williamsburg.

HAMILTON, WILLIAM, SIR, 1788-1856

Graves, Robert P. Life of Sir William Rowan Hamilton, 3 vols. LC 74-26266. (History, Philosophy & Sociology of Science Ser). 1975. Repr. 120.00x (ISBN 0-405-06594-9). Arno.

HAMILTON, WILLIAM ROWAN, SIR, 1805-1865

Graves, Robert P. Life of Sir William Rowan Hamilton, 3 vols. 2nd ed. Date not set. price not set (ISBN 0-8284-9003-1). Chelsea Pub.
Hankins, Thomas L. Sir William Rowan Hamilton: A Biography. LC 80-10627. 512p. 1980. text ed. 32.50 (ISBN 0-8018-2203-3). Johns Hopkins.
Mill, John S. An Examination of Sir William Hamilton's Philosophy. Robson, John M., ed. LC 63-25976. (Collected Works of John Stuart Mill Ser.). 1979. 35.00x (ISBN 0-8020-2329-0). U of Toronto Pr.

HAMILTON COUNTY, OHIO–ANTIQUITIES

Willoughby, C. C. Turner Group of Earthworks, Hamilton County, Ohio. 1922. pap. 8.00 (ISBN 0-527-01214-9). Kraus Repr.

HAMITES

see also Berbers; Masai; Somalis

HAMITIC LANGUAGES

see also Agau Language; Berber Languages; Hausa Language; Nubian Language

Historical Section of the Linguistics Association (Great Britain) at the School of Oriental & African Studies, U of London, March 1970. Hamito-Semitica: Proceedings. Bynon, James & Bynon, Theodora, eds. (Janua Linguarum, Series Practica: No. 200). (Illus.). 1975. pap. 105.50x (ISBN 90-2793-092-9). Mouton.

HAMITO-SEMITIC LANGUGES

see also Semitic Languages

HAMLET

Scofield, Martin. The Ghosts of Hamlet. LC 79-21297. 180p. 1981. 39.50 (ISBN 0-521-22735-6). Cambridge U Pr.
Tolman, Albert. A View of the Views About Hamlet. LC 73-9665. Repr. of 1898 ed. lib. bdg. 6.50 (ISBN 0-8414-2685-6). Folcroft.
Werder, Karl. The Heart of Hamlet's Mystery. LC 74-32199. 1972. Repr. of 1907 ed. lib. bdg. 17.50 (ISBN 0-8414-9365-0). Folcroft.

HAMLIN, HANNIBAL, 1809-1891

Hamlin, Charles E. Life & Times of Hannibal Hamlin, 2 Vols. LC 70-137914. (American History & Culture in the Nineteenth Century Ser). 1971. Repr. of 1899 ed. Set. 35.00x (ISBN 0-8046-1482-2). Kennikat.
Hunt, H. Draper. Hannibal Hamlin of Maine: Lincoln's First Vice-President. LC 70-88709. (Illus.). 1969. 14.95x (ISBN 0-8156-2142-6). Syracuse U Pr.

HAMMARSKJOLD, DAG HJALMAR AGNE CARL, 1905-1961

Cordier, Andrew W., ed. Paths to World Order. LC 67-19877. 161p. (Orig.). 1967. pap. 4.00x (ISBN 0-231-08578-8). Columbia U Pr.

Cordier, Andrew W. & Foote, Wilder, eds. Public Papers of the Secretaries-General of the United Nations: Dag Hammarskjold, 1953-1956, Vol. 2. LC 68-8873. 115p. 1972. 30.00x (ISBN 0-231-03633-7). Columbia U Pr.

--Public Papers of the Secretaries General of the United Nations: Dag Hammarskjold, 1956-1957, Vol. 3. 729p. 1973. 30.00x (ISBN 0-231-03735-X). Columbia U Pr.

--The Quest for Peace: The Dag Hammarskjold Memorial Lectures. LC 65-10357. 390p. 1964. 20.00x (ISBN 0-231-02770-2); pap. 5.00x (ISBN 0-231-08575-3). Columbia U Pr.

Dayal, Rajeshwar. Mission for Hammarskold: The Congo Crisis. LC 75-3484. (Illus.). 244p. 1976. 26.00 (ISBN 0-691-05660-9). Princeton U Pr.

Hammarskjold, Dag. Markings. (YA) 1964. 11.95 (ISBN 0-394-43532-X). Knopf.

--Markings. 9th ed. 186p. 1966. (Pub. by Faber & Faber); pap. 4.95 (ISBN 0-571-06591-0). Merrimack Bk Serv.

Lash, Joseph P. Dag Hamarskjold, Custodian of the Brushfire Peace. LC 73-22637. 304p. 1974. Repr. of 1961 ed. lib. bdg. 15.25x (ISBN 0-8371-6995-X, LADJ). Greenwood.

Lichello, Robert. Dag Hammarskjold: A Giant in Diplomacy. Rahmas, D. Steve, ed. LC 73-185657. (Outstanding Personalities Ser.: No. 1). 32p. (Orig.). (gr. 7-12). 1972. lib. bdg. 2.95 incl. catalog cards (ISBN 0-87157-501-9); pap. 1.50 vinyl laminated covers (ISBN 0-87157-001-7). SamHar Pr.

Montgomery, Elizabeth R. Dag Hammarskjold: Peacemaker for the UN. LC 73-570. (Century Biographies Ser.). (Illus.). (gr. 4-8). 1973. PLB 4.28 (ISBN 0-8116-4757-9). Garrard.

Zacher, Mark W. Dag Hammarskjold's United Nations. LC 71-101593. (International Organization Ser.: No. 7). 1969. 20.00x (ISBN 0-231-03275-7). Columbia U Pr.

HAMMERED STRINGED INSTRUMENTS

see Stringed Instruments

HAMMERSMITH, ENGLAND–LYRIC THEATRE

Playfair, Nigel R. Story of the Lyric Theatre, Hammersmith. LC 77-84524. (Illus.). 1925. 15.00 (ISBN 0-405-08858-2). Arno.

HAMMERSTEIN, OSCAR, 1895-1960

Green, Stanley. The Rodgers & Hammerstein Story. (Illus.). 187p. 1980. pap. 6.95 (ISBN 0-306-80124-8). Da Capo.

Green, Stanley, ed. Rodgers & Hammerstein Fact Book. (Illus.). 804p. (Orig.). 1980. pap. 17.95 (ISBN 0-686-61676-6). L Farnol Group.

--Rodgers & Hammerstein Fact Book. (Illus.). 804p. (Orig.). 1980. pap. 17.95 (ISBN 0-9604002-0-6). Drama Bk.

Hammerstein, Oscar. Songs of Oscar Hammerstein II. LC 74-21637. (Illus.). 1975. 14.95 (ISBN 0-02-871020-7); pap. 8.95 (ISBN 0-02-871010-X). Schirmer Bks.

Nolan, Frederick. The Sound of Their Music: The Story of Rodgers & Hammerstein. LC 77-90488. (Illus.). 1978. 12.95 (ISBN 0-8027-0594-4). Walker & Co.

Taylor, Deems. Some Enchanted Evenings: The Story of Rodgers & Hammerstein. LC 73-138132. (Illus.). 244p. 1972. Repr. of 1953 ed. lib. bdg. 16.75x (ISBN 0-8371-5414-6, TAEE). Greenwood.

HAMMETT, DASHIELL, 1894-1961

Herron, Don. Dashiell Hammett Tour. (Illus.). 20p. 1979. pap. 2.00 (ISBN 0-939790-01-7). Dawn Heron.

Layman, Richard. Dashiell Hammett: A Descriptive Bibliography. LC 78-53600. (Pittsburgh Ser. in Bibliography). (Illus.). 1979. 17.50x (ISBN 0-8229-3394-2). U of Pittsburgh Pr.

--The Shadow Man: A Documentary Life of Dashiell Hammett. LC 80-8752. 300p. 1981. 14.95 (ISBN 0-15-181459-7). HarBraceJ.

Mundell, E. H., ed. List of the Original Appearances of Dashiell Hammett's Magazine Work. LC 75-97620. (Serif Ser.: No. 13). 1970. 6.00x (ISBN 0-87338-033-9). Kent St U Pr.

Wolfe, Peter. Beams Falling: Art of Dashiell Hammett. LC 79-84639. 1979. 13.95 (ISBN 0-87972-139-1); pap. 6.95 (ISBN 0-87972-140-5). Bowling Green Univ.

HAMMOCKS

Andrews, Denison. Hammock: How to Make Your Own & Lie in It. rev. ed. LC 77-18433. (Illus.). 1978. pap. 2.95 (ISBN 0-89480-028-0). Workman Pub.

HAMMOND, JOHN, 1910-

Hammond, John & Townsend, Irving. John Hammond on Record. Date not set. Repr. price not set (ISBN 0-685-65348-X, Wallaby). PB.

--John Hammond on Record: An Autobiography. 1981. pap. 5.95 (ISBN 0-14-005705-6). Penguin.

HAMMOND, JOHN HAYS, 1855-1936

Hammond, John H. The Autobiography of John Hays Hammond, 2 vols. in 1, Vol. 17. LC 74-351. (Gold Ser.). (Illus.). 813p. 1974. Repr. of 1935 ed. 44.00x (ISBN 0-405-05913-2). Arno.

HAMMON, JUPITER, 1720-1800

Hammon, Jupitor. America's First Negro Poet. Ransom, Stanley A., Jr., ed. LC 74-8265. (Empire State Historical Publications Ser: No. 82). 1969. 12.50 (ISBN 0-87198-082-7). Friedman.

Wegelin, Oscar. Jupiter Hammon, American Negro Poet. pap. 1.50 (ISBN 0-685-16788-7, N218P). Mnemosyne.

--Jupiter Hammon: American Negro Poet. 59.95 (ISBN 0-8490-0467-5). Gordon Pr.

HAMPSHIRE, ENGLAND–DESCRIPTION AND TRAVEL

Dutton, Ralph. Hampshire. (Batsford Britain Ser.). 1970. 8.95 (ISBN 0-8038-3011-4). Hastings.

Hudson, William H. Hampshire Days. Repr. of 1923 ed. 21.50 (ISBN 0-404-03401-2). AMS Pr.

Jowitt, R. L. History, People & Places in Hampshire. LC 76-352170. (Illus.). 1975. 12.50x (ISBN 0-902875-93-0). Intl Pubns Serv.

Moutray Read, D. H. Highways & Byways in Hampshire. Repr. of 1932 ed. 20.00 (ISBN 0-89987-011-2). Darby Bks.

Patterson, A. Temple. Hampshire & the Isle of Wight. 1976. 17.95 (ISBN 0-7134-3221-7, Pub. by Batsford England). David & Charles.

HAMPSHIRE, ENGLAND–HISTORY

Carpenter-Turner, Barbara. A History of Hampshire. (The Darwen County History Ser.). (Illus.). 128p. 1978. Repr. of 1963 ed. 18.00x (ISBN 0-8476-2312-2). Rowman.

Norwood, John. Victorian & Edwardian Hampshire. 1973. 19.95 (ISBN 0-7134-0130-3, Pub. by Batsford England). David & Charles.

HAMPSHIRE COUNTY, WEST VIRGINIA

Brannon, Selden. Historic Hampshire: A Symposium of Hampshire County & Its People, Past & Present. 1976. Repr. of 1978 ed. 25.00 (ISBN 0-87012-236-3). McClain.

Sage, Clara McC. & Jones, Laura S. Early Records, Hampshire County, Virginia. LC 75-90051. 1976. Repr. of 1939 ed. 15.00 (ISBN 0-8063-0305-0). Genealog Pub.

HAMPSTEAD NURSERIES

Freud, Anna & Burlingham, Dorothy T. Infants Without Families: Reports on the Hampstead Nurseries. LC 72-8788. (Writings of Anna Freud: Vol. 3). 1973. text ed. 25.00 (ISBN 0-8236-6872-X). Intl Univs Pr.

--Infants Without Families: The Case Against Residential Nurseries. 128p. 1947. text ed. 12.50 (ISBN 0-8236-2640-7). Intl Univs Pr.

--War & Children. Lehrman, Philip R., ed. LC 73-7699. 191p. 1973. Repr. of 1943 ed. lib. bdg. 15.00x (ISBN 0-8371-6942-9, FRWC). Greenwood.

HAMPTON, WADE, 1818-1902

Jarrell, Hampton M. Wade Hampton & the Negro: The Road Not Taken. LC 50-5796. 1969. Repr. of 1949 ed. 14.95x (ISBN 0-87249-017-3). U of SC Pr.

Williams, Alfred B. Hampton & His Red Shirts. facs. ed. LC 72-124266. (Select Bibliographies Reprint Ser). 1935. 21.00 (ISBN 0-8369-5454-8). Arno.

HAMPTON, VIRGINIA NORMAL AND AGRICULTURAL INSTITUTE

Talbot, Edith A. Samuel Chapman Armstrong, a Biographical Study. LC 73-79811. (Illus.). Repr. of 1904 ed. 16.25x (ISBN 0-8371-1512-4). Greenwood.

HAMPTON COURT CONFERENCE, 1604

Barlow, William. Summe & Substance of the Conference. LC 65-10395. 1965. Repr. of 1604 ed. 20.00x (ISBN 0-8201-1004-3). Schol Facsimiles.

HAMPTON INSTITUTE, HAMPTON, VIRGINIA

Armstrong, Mrs. M. & Ludlow, Helen W. Hampton & Its Students. facs. ed. Fenner, Thomas P., ed. LC 75-149862. (Black Heritage Library Collection Ser). 1874. 14.00 (ISBN 0-8369-8744-6). Arno.

Armstrong, Mary F. & Ludlow, Helen W. Hampton & Its Students. LC 71-132385. 256p. Repr. of 1874 ed. 11.00 (ISBN 0-404-07234-8). AMS Pr.

--Hampton & Its Students by Two of Its Teachers, with Fifty Cabin & Plantation Songs. LC 77-99332. 1969. Repr. of 1874 ed. lib. bdg. 11.50 (ISBN 0-8411-0003-9). Metro Bks.

Schall, Keith L., ed. Stony the Road: Essays from the Hampton Institute Archives. LC 76-56224. (Hampton Institute Archives). (Illus.). 1977. 12.50x (ISBN 0-8139-0720-9). U Pr of Va.

HAMPTON ROADS, BATTLE OF–FICTION, JUVENILE

Werstein, Irving. Civil War Sailor. LC 62-114361. (gr. 6-9). 5.95 (ISBN 0-385-01263-2). Doubleday.

HAMSTERS

Folk, G. Edgar, Jr. Hamster Guide. rev. ed. (Illus.). 1958. pap. 3.95 (ISBN 0-87666-203-3, AP7200). TFH Pubns.

Keyser, A. The Development of the Diencephalon of the Chinese Hamster: An Investigation of the Validity of the Criteria of Subdivision of the Brain. (Acta Anatomica: Vol. 83, Suppl.). (Illus.). 1972. pap. 21.74 (ISBN 3-8055-1593-6). S Karger.

Murschetz, Luis. A Hamster's Journey. Allard, Harry, tr. from German. LC 76-9788. (Illus.). (ps-3). 1976. PLB 5.95 (ISBN 0-13-372383-6). P-H.

Parslow, Percy. Hamsters. (Illus.). 1979. 2.95 (ISBN 0-685-96898-7, KW-015). TFH Pubns.

Roberts, Mervin F. How to Raise Hamsters. pap. 2.00 (ISBN 0-87666-205-X, M508). TFH Pubns.

--Teddy Bear Hamsters. (Illus.). 96p. (Orig.). 1974. pap. 2.50 (ISBN 0-87666-206-8, PS710). TFH Pubns.

Robinson, David. Exhibition & Pet Hamsters & Gerbils. 1981. 30.00x (ISBN 0-904558-39-8, Pub. by Saiga Pub). State Mutual Bk.

Saiga Editors. Hamster Keeping. 1981. 10.00x (ISBN 0-86230-001-0, Pub. by Saiga Pub). State Mutual Bk.

Silverstein, Alvin & Silverstein, Virginia. Hamsters: All About Them. LC 74-8863. (Illus.). 160p. (gr. 3-6). 1974. PLB 6.96 (ISBN 0-688-50056-0). Lothrop.

Streilein, Jacob W., et al, eds. Hamster Immune Responses in Infectious & Oncologic Diseases. (Advances in Experimental Medicine & Biology Ser.: Vol. 134). 474p. 1981. 55.00 (ISBN 0-306-40642-X, Plenum Pr). Plenum Pub.

Symposium on the Syrian Hamster in Toxicology & Carcinogenesis Research, Boston, November 30-December 2, 1977. The Syrian Hamster in Toxicology & Carcinogenesis: Proceedings. Homburger, F., ed. (Progress in Experimental Tumor Research: Vol. 24). (Illus.). 1979. 97.75 (ISBN 3-8055-2890-6). S Karger.

Zim, Herbert S. Golden Hamsters. (Illus.). (gr. 3-7). 1951. 6.48 (ISBN 0-688-31353-1). Morrow.

HAMSUN, KNUT, b. 1859

Larsen, H. A. Knut Hamsun. 59.95 (ISBN 0-87968-385-6). Gordon Pr.

HAMTRAMCK, MICHIGAN

Wood, Arthur E. Hamtramck: A Sociological Study of a Polish-American Community. (Orig.). 1955. pap. 2.45 (ISBN 0-8084-0148-3, B1). Coll & U Pr.

Wood, Arthur Evans. Hamtramck: A Sociological Study of a Polish-American Community. 253p. 1975. Repr. of 1955 ed. lib. bdg. 14.50x (ISBN 0-374-98714-9). Octagon.

HAN-SHAN, 1546-1623

Luk, Charles, pseud. Practical Buddhism. LC 72-91124. 177p. 1973. 5.95 (ISBN 0-8356-0212-5). Theos Pub Hse.

HANCOCK, JOHN, 1737-1793

Baxter, William T. House of Hancock: Business in Boston, 1724-1775. LC 65-24090. (Illus.). 1965. Repr. of 1945 ed. 9.00 (ISBN 0-8462-0611-0). Russell.

Fowler, William M. The Baron of Beacon Hill: A Biography of John Hancock. 1979. 15.00 (ISBN 0-395-27619-5). HM.

Sears, Lorenzo. John Hancock, the Picturesque Patriot. LC 72-8733. (American Revolutionary Ser.). Repr. of 1912 ed. lib. bdg. 25.00x (ISBN 0-8398-1880-7). Irvington.

Umbreit, Kenneth B. Founding Fathers: Men Who Shaped Our Tradition. LC 68-26228. Repr. of 1941 ed. 13.00 (ISBN 0-8046-0469-X). Kennikat.

HANCOCK, JOHN, 1737-1793–JUVENILE LITERATURE

Fritz, Jean. Will You Sign Here, John Hancock? LC 75-33243. (Illus.). 48p. (gr. 2-6). 1976. 6.95 (ISBN 0-698-20308-9). Coward.

HANCOCK, THOMAS, 1703-1764

Baxter, William T. House of Hancock: Business in Boston, 1724-1775. LC 65-24090. (Illus.). 1965. Repr. of 1945 ed. 9.00 (ISBN 0-8462-0611-0). Russell.

HAND, LEARNED, 1872-1961

Griffith, Kathryn P. Judge Learned Hand & the Role of the Federal Juciciary. LC 72-9254. 363p. 1973. 13.50x (ISBN 0-8061-1071-6); pap. 6.95x (ISBN 0-8061-1369-3). U of Okla Pr.

Schick, Marvin. Learned Hand's Court. LC 78-17390. 1978. Repr. of 1970 ed. lib. bdg. 29.25x (ISBN 0-313-20508-6, SCLH). Greenwood.

HAND

see also Gesture; Left- and Right-Handedness; Palmistry

Alexander, Harold L. V. Classifying Palmprints: A Complete System of Coding, Filing & Searching Palmprints. (Illus.). 136p. 1973. 15.25 (ISBN 0-398-02652-1). C C Thomas.

Ariyan. The Hand Book. 1978. pap. 12.95 (ISBN 0-683-00251-1). Williams & Wilkins.

Association of Bone & Joint Surgeons. Wrist & Hand: Clinical Orthopaedics & Related Research Ser. No. 83. Urist, Marshall R. & De Palma, Anthony F., eds. (Illus.). 1971. 15.00 (ISBN 0-685-24744-9, JBL-Med-Nursing). Har-Row.

Bell, Charles. The Hand: Its Mechanism & Vital Endowments. LC 78-72789. (Brainedness, Handedness, & Mental Ability Ser.). Repr. of 1885 ed. 27.50 (ISBN 0-404-60853-1). AMS Pr.

Blauth, W. & Schneider-Sickert, F. R. Congenital Deformities of the Hand: An Atlas of Their Surgical Treatment. (Illus.). 394p. 1980. 230.00 (ISBN 0-387-10084-9). Springer-Verlag.

Bulwer, John. Chirologia, 2 vols. in 1. LC 75-147955. (Language, Man & Society Ser.). Repr. of 1644 ed. 27.00 (ISBN 0-404-08205-X). AMS Pr.

Byrne, John J. The Hand: Its Anatomy & Diseases. (Illus.). 408p. 1959. ed. spiral bdg. 36.50photocopy (ISBN 0-398-00269-X). C C Thomas.

Carter, Mildred. Hand Reflexology: Key to Perfect Health. 1975. 9.95 (ISBN 0-13-383612-6, Reward); pap. 3.95 (ISBN 0-13-383604-5). P-H.

Costello, Maurice J. & Gibbs, Richard C. Palms & Soles in Medicine. (American Lecture Dermatology Ser.). (Illus.). 720p. 1967. pap. 60.25 photocopy ed. spiral (ISBN 0-398-00351-3). C C Thomas.

Flatt, Adrian E. The Care of Coqenital Hand Anomalies. LC 77-5932. (Illus.). 1977. text ed. 40.50 (ISBN 0-8016-1586-0). Mosby.

Flory, Charles D. Osseous Development in the Hand As an Index of Skeletal Development. 1936. pap. 10.00 (ISBN 0-527-01488-5). Kraus Repr.

Greulich, William W. & Pyle, S. Idell. Radiographic Atlas of Skeletal Development of the Hand & Wrist. 2nd ed. (Illus.). 1959. 27.50x (ISBN 0-8047-0398-1). Stanford U Pr.

Henninger, Joseph. Drawing of the Hand & Its Anatomy. 7.50 (ISBN 0-685-38494-2). Borden.

Humphry, George M. The Human Foot & the Human Hand. LC 78-72803. Repr. of 1861 ed. 21.50 (ISBN 0-404-60866-3). AMS Pr.

Jacobs, P. Atlas of Hand Radiographs. (Illus.). 1973. 29.50 (ISBN 0-8391-0728-5). Univ Park.

Jaegers, Beverly C. You & Your Hand. 4.00 (ISBN 0-89861-012-5). Esoteric Pubns.

Johnson, Moulton K. The Hand Book. (Illus.). 130p. 1973. 12.50 (ISBN 0-398-02595-9). C C Thomas.

Johnson, Moulton K. & Cohen, Myles J. The Hand Atlas. (Illus.). 108p. 1975. 28.00 (ISBN 0-398-03203-3). C C Thomas.

Kricun, Morrison E. & Edeiken, Jack. Hand & Wrist in Systemic Disease. 324p. 1973. 23.50 (ISBN 0-683-04783-3). Krieger.

Landsmeer, Johan M. Atlas of Anatomy of the Hand. (Illus.). 448p. 1976. text ed. 79.00 (ISBN 0-443-01154-0). Churchill.

Lister, Graham. The Hand: Diagnosis and Indications. (Illus.). 288p. 1977. 42.00 (ISBN 0-443-01482-5). Churchill.

Lucas, George L. Examination of the Hand. (Illus.). 248p. 1972. text ed. 19.75 (ISBN 0-398-02347-6). C C Thomas.

Napier, John. Hands. (Illus.). 1980. 13.95 (ISBN 0-394-50783-5). Pantheon.

--The Human Hand. Head, J. J., ed. LC 76-29377. (Carolina Biology Readers Ser.). (Illus.). (gr. 11 up). 1976. pap. 1.65 (ISBN 0-89278-261-7, 45-9661). Carolina Biological.

Rose, Linda. Hands. 1980. 14.95 (ISBN 0-671-24944-4). S&S.

Schamber, Dean. Diagnostic Tests of the Hand. Date not set. price not set (ISBN 0-89874-319-2). Krieger.

Stack, H. Graham. The Palmar Fascia. LC 73-180327. 1974. text ed. 37.50 (ISBN 0-443-01000-5). Churchill.

Steinbach, Howard L., et al. Roentgen Appearance of the Hand in Diffuse Disease. (Illus.). 674p. 1975. 65.00 (ISBN 0-8151-8191-4). Year Bk Med.

Temtamy, Samia & McKusick, Victor, eds. Genetics of Hand Malformations. (Alan R. Liss Inc. Ser.: Vol. 14, No. 3). 1978. 90.00 (ISBN 0-686-26119-4). March of Dimes.

Temtamy, Samia A. & McKusick, Victor A. The Genetics of Hand Malformation. LC 77-27829. (Birth Defects Original Article Ser.: Vol. 14, No. 3). 620p. 1978. 104.00 (ISBN 0-8451-1017-9). A R Liss.

HAND–JUVENILE LITERATURE

Aliki. My Hands. LC 62-12810. (A Let's-Read-&-Find-Out Science Bk). (Illus.). (gr. k-3). 1962. PLB 8.79 (ISBN 0-690-56834-7, TYC-J). Har-Row.

Blumenthal, Lassor A. The Hand Book: All Kinds of Jokes, Tricks & Games to Do with Your Hands. LC 73-21219. 96p. (gr. 1-5). 1976. PLB 5.95 (ISBN 0-385-04308-2). Doubleday.

Goode, Ruth. Hands up! The Story of Hands. (Illus.). 64p. (gr. 2-5). 1981. 7.95 (ISBN 0-02-736550-6). Macmillan.

Perkins, Al. Hand, Hand, Fingers, Thumb. LC 76-77841. (Bright & Early Bk.). (Illus.). (ps-1). 1969. 3.95 (ISBN 0-394-81076-7, BYR); PLB 4.99 (ISBN 0-394-91076-1). Random.

Rasch, Gerald. Hands Are Handy. 20p. (Orig.). 1981. pap. 3.50 (ISBN 0-86629-011-7). Sunrise MO.

Watson, Elizabeth E. All About Hands. LC 81-50676. (A Happy Day Bk.). (Illus.). 24p. (Orig.). (ps-1). 1981. pap. 0.98 (ISBN 0-87239-460-3, 3593). Standard Pub.

HAND–SURGERY

Association of Bone & Joint Surgeons. Hand, Pt. 2. Urist, Marshall, ed. (Clinical Orthopaedics Ser.). (Illus.). 1959. 15.00 (ISBN 0-686-76889-2, JBL-Med-Nursing). Har-Row.

Blauth, W. & Schneider-Sickert, F. R. Congenital Deformities of the Hand: An Atlas of Their Surgical Treatment. (Illus.). 394p. 1980. 230.00 (ISBN 0-387-10084-9). Springer-Verlag.

Chase, Robert A. Atlas of Hand Surgery. LC 72-97907. (Illus.). 438p. 1973. text ed. 50.00 (ISBN 0-7216-2495-2). Saunders.

Cowen. Hand Surgery. 1981. 65.00 (ISBN 0-8151-1871-6). Year Bk Med.

Cowen, George W., ed. Hand Surgery. 1980. write for info. (ISBN 0-8151-1871-6). Symposia Special.

Dellon, A. Lee. Evaluation of Sensibility & Reeducation of Sensation in the Hand. (Illus.). 388p. 1981. 35.00 (ISBN 0-686-77746-8, 2427-2). Williams & Wilkins.

Flatt, Adrian E. The Care of the Rheumatoid Hand. 3rd ed. LC 74-2478. 1974. 32.50 (ISBN 0-8016-1584-4). Mosby.

Flynn, J. Edward. Hand Surgery. (Illus.). 850p. 1981. lib. bdg. 80.00 (ISBN 0-683-03268-2). Williams & Wilkins.

--Hand Surgery. 2nd ed. 850p. 1975. 53.00 (ISBN 0-683-03267-4). Williams & Wilkins.

Kilgore, Eugene S., Jr. & Graham, William P., III, eds. The Hand: Surgical & Non-surgical Management. LC 76-40478. (Illus.). 502p. 1977. text ed. 48.50 (ISBN 0-8121-0534-6). Lea & Febiger.

Lister, Graham. The Hand: Diagnosis and Indications. (Illus.). 288p. 1977. 42.00 (ISBN 0-443-01482-5). Churchill.

Littler, J. William, et al, eds. Symposium on Reconstructive Hand Surgery (Plastic Surgery Symposia, Vol. 9. LC 74-12410. 1974. 49.50 (ISBN 0-8016-3022-3). Mosby.

Meals, Roy & Lesavoy, Malcolm A. Hand Surgery Review. 184p. 1980. soft cover 16.95 (ISBN 0-683-05899-1). Williams & Wilkins.

Mittelbach, H. R. The Injured Hand: A Handbook for General & Clinical Practice. (Illus.). 1979. 20.80 (ISBN 0-387-90365-8). Springer-Verlag.

Nicolle, F. V. & Dickson, R. A. Surgery of the Rheumatoid Hand: A Practical Manual. (Illus.). 166p. 1980. 73.95 (ISBN 0-8151-6390-8). Year Bk Med.

Pulvertaft, R. G. Hand. 3rd ed. (Operative Surgery Ser.). 1977. 94.95 (ISBN 0-407-00618-4). Butterworth.

Rank, B. K., et al. Surgery of Repair As Applied to Hand Injuries. 4th ed. LC 73-595469. (Illus.). 408p. 1973. 27.50 (ISBN 0-443-00934-1). Churchill.

Usoltseva, E. V. & Mashkara, K. I. Surgery of Diseases & Injuries of the Hand, 2 vols. LC 78-26990. (Illus.). 1979. Set. 39.50 (ISBN 0-8016-5198-0). Mosby.

Verdan, Claude G., ed. Tendon Surgery of the Hand. (G.E.M. Monographs: Vol. 4). (Illus.). 1979. text ed. 55.00 (ISBN 0-443-01881-2). Churchill.

Wynn-Parry, C. E. Rehabilitation of the Hand. 3rd ed. 1973. Repr. of 1977 ed. 49.95 (ISBN 0-407-38501-0). Butterworth.

HAND–WOUNDS AND INJURIES

Beasley. Hand Injuries. (Illus.). 320p. 1981. text ed. write for info. (ISBN 0-7216-1607-0). Saunders.

Cailliet, Rene. Hand Pain & Impairment. 2nd ed. LC 75-6660. (Illus.). 180p. 1975. pap. text ed. 7.95 (ISBN 0-8036-1617-1). Davis Co.

Carter, Sylvester J. Infections of the Hand: A Modern Approach to Treatment. (Illus.). 325p. 1982. price not set (ISBN 0-8121-0821-3). Lea & Febiger.

Conolly, W. Bruce. Color Atlas of Hand Conditions. (Illus.). 366p. 1980. 87.50 (ISBN 0-8151-1836-8). Year Bk Med.

Conolly, W. Bruce & Kilgore, Eugene S. Hand Injuries & Infections: An Illustrated Guide. (Illus.). 1979. 37.95 (ISBN 0-8151-1833-3). Year Bk Med.

Flatt, Adrian E. The Care of Minor Hand Injuries. 4th ed. LC 79-12082. (Illus.). 1979. text ed. 38.50 (ISBN 0-8016-1581-X). Mosby.

Hunter, James M., et al. Rehabilitation of the Hand. LC 78-59659. 1978. text ed. 74.50 (ISBN 0-8016-2317-0). Mosby.

Kilgore, Eugene S., Jr. & Graham, William P., III, eds. The Hand: Surgical & Non-surgical Management. LC 76-40478. (Illus.). 502p. 1977. text ed. 48.50 (ISBN 0-8121-0534-6). Lea & Febiger.

Lister, Graham. The Hand: Diagnosis and Indications. (Illus.). 288p. 1977. 42.00 (ISBN 0-443-01482-5). Churchill.

Mittelbach, H. R. The Injured Hand: A Handbook for General & Clinical Practice. (Illus.). 1979. 20.80 (ISBN 0-387-90365-8). Springer-Verlag.

Newmeyer, William L. Primary Care of Hand Injuries. LC 78-31444. (Illus.). 297p. 1979. text ed. 22.50 (ISBN 0-8121-0669-5). Lea & Febiger.

Rank, B. K., et al. Surgery of Repair As Applied to Hand Injuries. 4th ed. LC 73-595469. (Illus.). 408p. 1973. 27.50 (ISBN 0-443-00934-1). Churchill.

Reid, D. A. & Gosset, J. Mutilating Injuries of the Hand. (G. E. M. Monographs: Vol. 3). (Illus.). 1979. text ed. 52.00 (ISBN 0-443-01684-4). Churchill.

Sandzen, S. C., Jr. Atlas of Acute Hand Injuries. LC 79-21848. (Illus.). 456p. 1980. 95.00 (ISBN 0-88416-030-0, Dist. by McGraw). Wright-PSG.

--Atlas of Wrist & Hand Fractures. LC 75-12036. (Illus.). 442p. 1979. 54.50 (ISBN 0-88416-032-7). Wright-PSG.

Segmuller, Gottfried. Surgical Stabilization of the Skeleton of the Hand. (Illus.). 170p. 1977. pap. 22.50 (ISBN 0-683-07751-1). Krieger.

Semple, Campbell. Primary Management of Hand Injuries. (Illus.). 1979. 21.00 (ISBN 0-8151-7592-2). Year Bk Med.

Tubiana, Raoul. The Hand. (Illus.). 800p. Date not set. Vol. 1. price not set (ISBN 0-7216-8907-8); Vol. 2. pap. price not set (ISBN 0-7216-8908-6). Saunders.

Weckesser, Elden. Treatment of Hand Injuries. (Illus.). 274p. 1974. 27.50 (ISBN 0-8151-9163-4). Year Bk Med.

Weeks, Paul M. Acute Bone & Joint Injuries of the Hand & Wrist: A Clinical Guide to Management. LC 80-24813. (Illus.). 299p. 1981. text ed. 37.50 (ISBN 0-8016-5373-8). Mosby.

Weeks, Paul M. & Wray, R. Christie. Management of Acute Hand Injuries: A Biological Approach. 2nd ed. LC 78-5718. 1978. text ed. 49.50 (ISBN 0-8016-5371-1). Mosby.

Wolfort, Francis G., ed. Acute Hand Injuries: A Multispecialty Approach. LC 79-90896. 1980. text ed. 27.50 (ISBN 0-316-95112-9). Little.

Wynn-Parry, C. B. Rehabilitation of the Hand. 4th rev. ed. LC 80-41761. (Illus.). 1981. text ed. 69.00 (ISBN 0-407-38502-9). Butterworth.

HAND-BAGS

see Handbags

HAND IN ART

Borden, Emanuel, ed. Hand in Art. (Master Draughtsman Ser). (Illus.). 1963. treasure trove bdg. 6.47x (ISBN 0-685-07327-0); pap. 2.95 (ISBN 0-685-07328-9). Borden.

Bridgman, George B. Book of One-Hundred Hands. (Illus.). 1972. pap. 3.50 (ISBN 0-486-22709-X). Dover.

Hogarth, Burne. Drawing Dynamic Hands. (Illus.). 1977. 14.95 (ISBN 0-8230-1367-7). Watson-Guptill.

Loomis, Andrew. Drawing the Head & Hands. (Illus.). 1956. 13.95 (ISBN 0-670-28385-1). Viking Pr.

HAND PLANES

see Planes (Hand Tools)

HAND PRESS

see Handpress

HAND SHADOWS

see Shadow-Pictures

HAND TEST

Bricklin, Barry, et al. Hand Test: A New Projective Test with Special Reference to the Prediction of Overt Aggressive Behavior. (American Lecture in Psychology Ser.). 112p. 1978. 12.75 (ISBN 0-398-00223-1). C C Thomas.

HAND-TO-HAND FIGHTING

see also Self-Defense

Baltazzi, Evan S. A Stick for Self-Protection: Stick-Foot Fighting for Men & Women. LC 79-84945. (Illus.). 10.00 (ISBN 0-918948-02-9). Evanel.

Birkenhead. Fifty Famous Fights in Fact & Fiction. 1932. Repr. 20.00 (ISBN 0-8274-2344-6). R West.

Campbell, Sid. Falcon Claw: The Motion Picture. Morales, Mahi, ed. 115p. 1980. pap. 7.50 (ISBN 0-937610-01-1). Dimond Pubs.

Campbell, Sid, et al. Two Thousand & One Martial Arts Questions, Kung Fu, Karate, Tae Kwon Do, Kenpo Students Should Know. LC 80-67769. (Illus.). 150p. 1980. pap. text ed. 8.95 (ISBN 0-686-28062-8). Dimond Pubs.

Cassidy, William L. The Basic Manual of Knife Fighting. 48p. 1978. pap. 4.00 (ISBN 0-87364-129-9). Paladin Ent.

Cheong Cheng Leong & Draeger, Donn F. Phoenix-Eye Fist: A Shaolin Fighting Art of South China. LC 77-23373. (Illus.). 1977. pap. 7.95 (ISBN 0-8348-0127-2). Weatherhill.

Cooper, Jeff. Principles of Personal Defense. Brown, Robert K. & Lund, Peder C., eds. 30p. 1972. pap. 4.00 (ISBN 0-87364-001-2). Paladin Ent.

Corcoran, John & Farkas, Emil. The Complete Martial Arts Catalogue. 1977. 10.95 (ISBN 0-685-76281-5); pap. 7.95 (ISBN 0-671-22668-1). S&S.

Diagram Group. Enjoying Combat Sports. LC 77-5024. (Enjoying Sports Ser.). (Illus.). 1977. pap. 3.95 (ISBN 0-448-22189-6). Paddington.

Draeger, Don. Budo: Classical. 1975. 10.00 (ISBN 0-685-83518-9). Wehman.

--Bujutso & Budo: Modern. 1974. 15.00 (ISBN 0-685-83520-0). Wehman.

--Bujutso: Classical. 1973. 10.00 (ISBN 0-685-83519-7). Wehman.

Draeger, Donn F. Modern Bujutsu & Budo. LC 74-76779. (Martial Arts of Japan Ser: Vol. 3). (Illus.). 192p. 1974. 17.95 (ISBN 0-8348-0099-3). Weatherhill.

Draeger, Donn F. & Smith, Robert. Asian Fighting Arts. (Illus.). 1969. 16.50 (ISBN 0-685-21878-3, Pub. by Kodansha). Wehman.

Draeger, Donn F. & Smith, Robert W. Comprehensive Asian Fighting Arts. LC 80-82527. (Illus.). 207p. 1981. pap. 11.95 (ISBN 0-87011-436-0). Kodansha.

Echanis, Michael D. Knife Self-Defence for Combat. LC 77-89614. (Ser. 127). 1977. pap. 5.95 (ISBN 0-89750-022-9). Ohara Pubns.

Fairbairn, W. E. Get Tough. (Illus.). 121p. 1974. Repr. 12.95 (ISBN 0-87364-002-0). Paladin Ent.

Fitzbarnard, L. Fighting Sports. 1981. 60.00x (ISBN 0-904558-09-6, Pub. by Saiga Pub). State Mutual Bk.

Gilbey, J. F. Fighting Arts of World. 6.50 (ISBN 0-685-21946-1). Wehman.

Gilbey, John F. Secret Fighting Arts of the World. LC 63-7910. (Illus.). 1963. bds. 9.75 (ISBN 0-8048-0515-6). C E Tuttle.

Hayes, Stephen K. The Ninja & Their Secret Fighting Art. LC 81-50105. (Illus.). 160p. 1981. 16.50 (ISBN 0-8048-1374-4). C E Tuttle.

Khim, P'Ng C. & Draeger, Donn F. Shaolin: An Introduction to Lohan Fighting Techniques. LC 78-62671. (Illus.). 1979. 19.50 (ISBN 0-8048-1213-6). C E Tuttle.

Kiong & Draeger. Shantung Black Tiger. 1976. 6.95 (ISBN 0-685-83535-9). Wehman.

Laiken, Deidre S. Mind - Body - Spirit: The Martial Arts & Oriental Medicine. LC 77-29101. (Illus.). 192p. (gr. 7 up). 1978. PLB 7.79 (ISBN 0-671-32894-8). Messner.

Lee, Jae M. & Wayt, David H. Hapkido: The Korean Art of Self Defense. LC 75-6079. (Illus.). 1977. pap. 3.95 (ISBN 0-668-03806-3). Arco.

Marchini, Ronald L. The Ultimate Martial Art: Renbukai, Vol. 1. 128p. (Orig.). 1981. pap. 6.95 (ISBN 0-940522-00-4). ROMARC Inc.

Mashiro, N. Black Medicine I: The Dark Art of Death. LC 78-2210. (Illus.). 88p. 1978. pap. 8.00 (ISBN 0-87364-101-9). Paladin Ent.

Maslak, Paul. Strategy in Unarmed Combat. 1977. 10.00 (ISBN 0-685-83177-9). Wehman.

Ribner, Susan & Chin, Richard. The Martial Arts. LC 77-58713. (Illus.). 1978. (HarpJ); PLB 7.49 (ISBN 0-06-025000-3). Har-Row.

Schultz, D. O. & Slepecky, M. Police Unarmed Defense Tactics. 102p. 1973. pap. 7.50 (ISBN 0-398-02666-1). C C Thomas.

Steele, David E. Secrets of Modern Knife Fighting. LC 75-37196. (Illus.). 1975. 15.95 (ISBN 0-685-16327-X); pap. 9.95 (ISBN 0-685-16328-8). Phoenix Assocs.

Steiner, Bradley J. Manuals on Mayhem: An Annotated Bibliography of Books on Combat Martial Arts & Self-Defense. 1979. pap. 6.00 (ISBN 0-686-26031-7). Loompanics.

Tjoa Khek Kiorg, et al. Shantung Black Tiger: A Fighting Art of North China. LC 76-18800. (Illus.). 1976. pap. 7.95 (ISBN 0-8348-0122-1). Weatherhill.

Walston, Gerald. The Legal Implications of Self-Defense: A Reference Text for the Martial Arts. 1979. 6.95 (ISBN 0-533-03539-2). Vantage.

Winderbaum, Larry, et al. The Martial Arts Encyclopedia. Brown, Roger G., ed. LC 76-43250. 1978. 19.50 (ISBN 0-87953-600-4). Inscape Corp.

Yamada, Yoshimitsu. Aikido Complete. (Illus.). 128p. 1974. pap. 4.95 (ISBN 0-8065-0417-X). Citadel Pr.

Zarrilli, Phillip B., ed. Martial Arts in Actor Training. (Illus.). 1981. 13.95x (ISBN 0-89676-052-9); pap. 10.00x (ISBN 0-89676-053-7). Drama Bk.

HAND WEAVING

Albaum, Charlet. Ojo De Dios: Eye of God. (Illus.). 96p. (Orig.). 1972. pap. 2.50 (ISBN 0-448-01149-2). G&D.

Anderson, Beryl. Creative Spinning, Weaving, & Plant-Dyeing. LC 72-4194. 1973. pap. 3.25 (ISBN 0-668-02703-7). Arco.

Atwater, M. Shuttle-Craft Book of American Hand Weaving. 16.95 (ISBN 0-87245-026-0). Textile Bk.

Atwater, Mary M. Byways in Handweaving. 1968. 12.95 (ISBN 0-02-504320-X). Macmillan.

--Design & the Handweaver. LC 61-4138. (Shuttle Craft Guild Monograph: No. 3). (Illus.). 26p. 1961. pap. 5.50 (ISBN 0-916658-03-1). HTH Pubs.

--Handwoven Rugs. LC 76-24018. (Shuttle Craft Guild Monograph: No. 29). (Illus.). 28p. 1948. pap. 6.50 (ISBN 0-916658-29-5). HTH Pubs.

--Shuttle-Craft Book of American Hand-Weaving. rev. ed. (Illus.). 1951. 16.95 (ISBN 0-02-504380-3). Macmillan.

Belfer, Nancy. Weaving: Design & Expression. LC 74-27624. (Illus.). 168p. 1975. 13.95 (ISBN 0-87192-068-9). Davis Mass.

Beveridge, June H. Warp, Weft & Sett: A Reference Manual for Handweavers. 176p. 1980. 22.95 (ISBN 0-442-26129-2). Van Nos Reinhold.

Blumenau, Lili. Creative Design in Wall Hangings. (Arts & Crafts Ser). (Illus.). 1966. 9.95 (ISBN 0-517-02559-0). Crown.

Bronson, J. & Bronson, R. Early American Weaving & Dyeing: The Domestic Manufacturer's Assistant, & Family Directory in the Arts of Weaving & Dyeing. (Illus.). 224p. 1977. pap. 3.50 (ISBN 0-486-23440-1). Dover.

Burnham, Harold B. & Burnham, Dorothy K. Keep Me Warm One Night: Early Handweaving in Eastern Canada. LC 72-83388. (Illus.). 1972. 37.50 (ISBN 0-8020-1896-3). U of Toronto Pr.

Collingwood, Peter. Peter Collingwood: His Weaves & Weaving. Tidball, Harriet, ed. LC 63-2332. (Shuttle Craft Guild Monograph: No. 8). (Illus.). 46p. 1963. pap. 7.50 (ISBN 0-916658-08-2). HTH Pubs.

--Techniques of Rug Weaving. LC 68-24486. (Illus.). 1969. 35.00 (ISBN 0-8230-5200-1). Watson-Guptill.

Complete Guide to Handspinning. (Illus.). 1979. pap. 2.50 (ISBN 0-910458-09-X). Select Bks.

Creager, Clara. Weaving: A Creative Approach for Beginners. LC 73-16503. 192p. 1974. pap. 6.95 (ISBN 0-385-02901-2). Doubleday.

Crockett, Candace. Card Weaving. (Illus.). 144p. 1973. 14.50 (ISBN 0-8230-0562-3). Watson-Guptill.

Davenport, Elsie G. Your Handweaving. (Illus.). 1981. pap. 5.50 (ISBN 0-910458-03-0). Select Bks.

Davison, Marguerite P. A Handweavers Pattern Book. rev ed. (Illus.). 1951. 15.00 (ISBN 0-9603172-0-1). M P Davison.

--A Handweavers Source Book. (Illus.). 1953. pap. text ed. 8.95 (ISBN 0-9603172-1-X). M P Davison.

Dendel, Esther W. The Basic Book of Fingerweaving. (Illus.). 1974. 8.95 (ISBN 0-671-21697-X). S&S.

--Basic Book of Twining. 1978. 13.95 (ISBN 0-442-22076-6); pap. 7.95 (ISBN 0-442-22078-2). Van Nos Reinhold.

Douglas, Harriet C. Handweaver's Instruction Manual. LC 76-24020. (Illus.). 41p. 1949. pap. 8.00 (ISBN 0-916658-30-9). HTH Pubs.

Educational Research Council of America. Hand Weaver. Ferris, Theodore N. & Marchak, John P., eds. (Real People at Work Ser: A). (Illus.). 1974. pap. text ed. 2.25 (ISBN 0-89247-000-3). Changing Times.

Ely, Evelyn & Hughes, Phyllis. Ojos De Dios. (Illus.). 1972. pap. 1.95 (ISBN 0-89013-056-6). Museum NM Pr.

Fannin, Allen. Handloom Weaving Technology. 1979. 26.50 (ISBN 0-442-22370-6). Van Nos Reinhold.

Frey, Berta. Designing & Drafting for Handweavers. (Illus.). 240p. 1975. pap. 5.95 (ISBN 0-02-011400-1, Collier). Macmillan.

--Designing & Drafting for Handweavers. 240p. 1975. 10.95 (ISBN 0-02-541460-7). Macmillan.

Gilby, Myriam. Free Weaving. LC 75-34530. (Encore Edition). 1976. 6.95 (ISBN 0-684-15945-7, ScribT). Scribner.

Gilmurray, Susan. Weaving Tricks. 128p. 1981. 12.95 (ISBN 0-442-26132-2). Van Nos Reinhold.

Groff, Russell E. Card Weaving or Tablet Weaving. (Illus.). 3.50 (ISBN 0-686-09825-0). Robin & Russ.

Hall, Joanne. Mexican Tapestry Weaving. LC 77-351132. (Illus.). 1976. wrap-around spiral bdg., leatherette 12.95 (ISBN 0-9602098-0-8). J Arvidson.

Harvey, Virginia I. & Tidball, Harriet. Weft Twining. LC 76-24017. (Shuttle Craft Guild Monograph: No. 28). (Illus.). 39p. 1969. pap. 6.50 (ISBN 0-916658-28-7). HTH Pubs.

Harvey, Virginia I., et al. Multiple Tabby Weaves, Based on Dr. William G. Bateman's Manuscript. LC 81-80587. (Shuttle Craft Guild Monograph: No. 35). (Illus.). 90p. 1981. pap. 9.95 (ISBN 0-916658-37-6). HTH Pubs.

Holland, Nina. Inkle Loom Weaving. (Illus.). 144p. 1973. 13.95 (ISBN 0-8230-2551-9). Watson-Guptill.

--The Weaving Primer. LC 77-147443. (Creative Craft Ser.). (Illus.). 1978. 13.95 (ISBN 0-8019-6624-8); pap. 7.95 (ISBN 0-8019-6625-6). Chilton.

Hooper, Luther. Hand Loom Weaving. LC 78-21372. (Illus.). 1979. pap. 9.95 (ISBN 0-8008-3805-X, Pentalic). Taplinger.

Howar, V. Weaving, Spinning & Dyeing: A Beginner's Manual. 1976. 10.95 (ISBN 0-13-947812-4, Spec); pap. 4.95 (ISBN 0-13-947804-3). P-H.

Hull, Raymond. The Off Loom Weaving Book. LC 72-11139. (Encore Edition). (Illus.). 192p. 1973. 4.95 (ISBN 0-684-15950-3, ScribT). Scribner.

Kelly, Karin. Weaving. LC 72-13336. (Early Crafts Bks.). (Illus.). 36p. (gr. 1-4). 1973. PLB 3.95 (ISBN 0-8225-0861-3). Lerner Pubns.

King, William A. Warp & Weft from Tibet. Repr. 4.95 (ISBN 0-686-09827-7). Robin & Russ.

Krevitsky, Nik & Ericson, Lois. Shaped Weaving: Making Garments & Accessories with Simple Needle-&-Finger Weaving Techniques. (Illus.). 120p. 1974. pap. 4.95 (ISBN 0-442-22321-8). Van Nos Reinhold.

Kroncke, Grete. Simple Weaving: Designs, Material, Technique. (Illus.). 95p. 1973. 6.95 (ISBN 0-442-29972-9). Van Nos Reinhold.

Laughlin, Mary E. More Than Four: A Book for Multiple Harness Weavers. 2nd rev. ed. LC 76-370952. (Illus.). 179p. 1979. 11.95 (ISBN 0-933604-01-7). Laughlin Enter.

Mason, Otis T. A Primitive Frame for Weaving Narrow Fabric. (Illus.). Repr. of 1901 ed. pap. 7.95 (ISBN 0-8466-4075-9, SJ175). Shorey.

Mattera, Joanne. Navajo Techniques for Today's Weaver. (Illus.). 160p. 1975. 15.95 (ISBN 0-8230-3153-5). Watson-Guptill.

Mead, S. M. The Art of Taaniko Weaving. (Illus.). 96p. 1968. 7.50 (ISBN 0-589-00005-5, Pub. by Reed Books Australia). C E Tuttle.

Murray, Rosemary. Practical Modern Weaving. (Illus.). 96p. 1975. 10.95 (ISBN 0-442-30077-8); pap. 6.95 (ISBN 0-442-30078-6). Van Nos Reinhold.

Parker, Xenia L. Creative Handweaving. (Illus.). 224p. (YA) 1976. 14.95 (ISBN 0-8037-1405-X); pap. 6.95 (ISBN 0-8037-4491-9). Dial.

Paulin, Lynn. Weaving for Beginners. (Future Crafts Today Ser.). (Illus.). 1977. pap. 2.50 (ISBN 0-918170-26-5, HP-502). Gick.

Pocock, Sylvia D. A Basic Approach to Designing & Drafting Original Overshot Patterns. 1976. pap. 3.95 (ISBN 0-913078-23-9). Sheriar Pr.

Powell, Marian. One Thousand-Plus Patterns in Four, Six & Eight Harness Shadow Weaves. 1976. Repr. 9.95 (ISBN 0-686-15734-6). Robin & Russ.

Rainey. Weaving Without a Loom. 1977. 7.95 (ISBN 0-13-947796-9, Spec). P-H.

Redman, Jane. Frame-Loom Weaving. (Illus.). 144p. 1976. 14.50 (ISBN 0-442-26860-2). Van Nos Reinhold.

Regensteiner, Else. Art of Weaving. (Illus.). 1970. 15.95 (ISBN 0-442-11442-7); pap. 8.95 (ISBN 0-442-26872-6). Van Nos Reinhold.

Romberg, Jenean. Let's Discover Weaving. (Arts & Crafts Discovery Units Ser.). (Illus.). 1974. pap. 5.95x (ISBN 0-87628-532-9). Ctr Appl Res.

Russell, Elfleda. Off-Loom Weaving: A Basic Manual. (The Crafts Ser). (Illus.). 1975. 7.95 (ISBN 0-316-76295-4); pap. 5.95 (ISBN 0-316-76296-2). Little.

Seagroatt, Margaret. Basic Textile Book. 1975. 10.95 (ISBN 0-442-25064-9); pap. 6.95 (ISBN 0-442-25066-5). Van Nos Reinhold.

Sectional Warping Made Easy. (Illus.). Repr. 3.50 (ISBN 0-686-09826-9). Robin & Russ.

Specht, Sally & Rawlings, Sandra. Creating with Card Weaving. (Arts & Crafts Ser.). 96p. 1973. 4.95 (ISBN 0-517-50348-4); pap. 2.95 (ISBN 0-517-50379-4). Crown.

Stephens, Cleo. Willow Spokes & Wickerwork. LC 74-297. (Illus.). 192p. 1975. 11.95 (ISBN 0-8117-1900-6). Stackpole.

Swanson, Karen. Rigid Heddle Weaving. (Illus.). 232p. 1975. 18.95 (ISBN 0-8230-4555-2). Watson-Guptill.

Taber, Barbara & Anderson, Marilyn. Backstrap Weaving. (Illus.). 160p. 1975. 14.95 (ISBN 0-8230-0422-8). Watson-Guptill.

Tacker, Harold & Tacker, Sylvia B. Band Weaving. 1974. 11.95 (ISBN 0-442-28404-7). Van Nos Reinhold.

Thomas, Diane. The Creative Ojo Book. LC 76-7023. 1976. pap. 2.95 (ISBN 0-918126-00-2). Hunter Ariz.

Tidball, Harriet. Brocade. LC 68-5499. (Shuttle Craft Guild Monographs: No. 22). (Illus.). 50p. 1967. pap. 8.00 (ISBN 0-916658-22-8). HTH Pubs.

--Contemporary Costume: Strictly Handwoven. LC 76-24014. (Shuttle Craft Guild Monograph: No. 24). (Illus.). 44p. 1968. pap. 8.00 (ISBN 0-916658-24-4). HTH Pubs.

--The Handloom Weaves. LC 57-49779. (Illus.). 38p. pap. 6.50 (ISBN 0-916658-00-7). HTH Pubs.

--Merry Christmas, Handweavers. LC 76-24002. (Shuttle Craft Guild Monograph: No. 10). (Illus.). 29p. 1963. pap. 5.50 (ISBN 0-916658-10-4). HTH Pubs.

Tod, Osma G. The Joy of Hand Weaving. LC 76-42959. (Illus.). 352p. 1977. pap. 5.00 (ISBN 0-486-23458-4). Dover.

--The Joy of Handweaving. LC 76-42959. 1977. lib. bdg. 12.50x (ISBN 0-88307-603-9). Gannon.

Todd, Mattie P. Hand Loom Weaving. (Illus.). 170p. pap. 16.00 (ISBN 0-8466-6022-9, SJU22). Shorey.

Weigle, Palmy. Double Weave. (Illus.). 1978. 13.95 (ISBN 0-8230-1355-3). Watson-Guptill.

West, Virginia. Finishing Touches for the Handweaver. 102p. 1967. pap. 6.95 (ISBN 0-8231-5016-X). Branford.

White, A. V. Weaving Is Fun. LC 74-27568. (Illus.). 96p. 1975. pap. 1.75 (ISBN 0-486-22724-3). Dover.

Williams, Elsa S. Bargello. (Illus.). 1967. 8.95 (ISBN 0-442-11248-3); pap. 5.95 (ISBN 0-442-29481-6). Van Nos Reinhold.

Wilson, Jean. The Pile Weaves: Twenty Six Techniques & How to Do Them. rev. ed. (Illus., Orig.). 1979. pap. 9.95 (ISBN 0-684-16085-4, SL843, ScribT). Scribner.

Wood, Irene. The Fanciest Twills of Them All: One Hundred Fifty Patterns in Sixteen Harness Weaves. 1976. pap. 8.95 (ISBN 0-686-16296-X). Robin & Russ.

Worst, Edward F. Weaving with Foot-Power Looms. LC 74-75270. (Illus.). 275p. 1974. pap. 5.00 (ISBN 0-486-23064-3). Dover.

Zielinski, Stanislaw. Encyclopedia of Handweaving. LC 75-45519. (Funk & W Bk.). (Illus.). 200p. 1976. pap. 4.95 (ISBN 0-308-10072-7). T Y Crowell.

Znamierowski, Nell. Weaving, Step by Step. (Step by Step Craft Ser.). 1967. (Golden Pr); pap. 2.95 (ISBN 0-307-42002-7). Western Pub.

HANDBAGS

Aiken, Joyce & Laury, Jean Ray. The Total Tote Bag Book: Designer Totes to Craft & Carry. LC 76-11058. (Illus.). 128p. 1977. 12.50 (ISBN 0-8008-7793-4); pap. 5.95 (ISBN 0-8008-7794-2). Taplinger.

Ericson, Lois & Ericson, Diane. The Bag Book. 1976. pap. 6.95 (ISBN 0-442-22327-7). Van Nos Reinhold.

Frager, Dorothy. Cloth Hats, Bags 'n Baggage. LC 77-6116. (Creative Crafts Ser.). (Illus.). 1978. 12.50 (ISBN 0-8019-6367-2, 6367); pap. 6.95 (ISBN 0-8019-6368-0, 6368). Chilton.

Handbag Buyers Guide Directory. Date not set. 6.00 (ISBN 0-686-31376-3). Diesel Pubns.

Houck, Carter & Miller, Myron. The Big Bag Book: How to Make All Kinds of Carry-Alls. (Encore Edition). (Illus.). 1977. pap. 2.95 (ISBN 0-684-16903-7). Scribner.

Loomis, Mary W. Custom Make Your Own Shoes & Handbags. (Illus.). 1978 (1978 ed. (ISBN 0-517-53138-0). pap. 4.95 (ISBN 0-517-53139-9). Crown.

Mackall, Lucy. Lucy's Bag Book. 1978. 12.95 (ISBN 0-395-26302-6); pap. 6.95 (ISBN 0-395-26473-1). HM.

Montagna, Pier. How to Make Handbags. pap. 2.00 (ISBN 0-686-00686-0). Key Bks.

Proper, Churchill. Leathercraft: Bags, Cases, Purses. LC 72-185670. (Handicraft Ser.: No. 2). (Illus.). 32p. (Orig.). (gr. 7-12). 1971. lib. bdg. 2.45 incl. catalog cards (ISBN 0-87157-902-2); pap. 1.25 vinyl laminated covers (ISBN 0-87157-402-0). SamHar Pr.

HANDBALL

see also Racquetball

Haber, Paul. Inside Handball. LC 72-126157. (Illus.). 1970. 7.95 (ISBN 0-8092-8868-0); pap. 5.95 (ISBN 0-8092-8867-2). Contemp Bks.

Johnson, Dewayne J. & Oliver, Robert A. Handball. (Illus.). 64p. (Orig.). 1981. pap. text ed. 2.95x (ISBN 0-89641-043-9). American Pr.

Lowy, Lance. The Handball Handbook: Strategies & Techniques. (Illus.). 107p. 1979. pap. text ed. 3.95x (ISBN 0-89641-031-5). American Pr.

McFarland, Wayne J. & Smith, Philip. Sports Illustrated Handball. LC 75-28486. (Sports Illustrated Ser). (Illus.). 1976. 5.95 (ISBN 0-397-01095-8); pap. 2.95 (ISBN 0-397-01106-7). Har-Row.

Nelson, Richard & Berger, H. Handball. (Prentice-Hall Sports Ser). 1971. pap. 4.95 ref. ed. (ISBN 0-13-372433-6). P-H.

Reznik, John, ed. Championship Handball by the Experts. LC 76-27946. (West Point Sports Fitness Ser.: Vol. 11). (Illus.). 1976. pap. text ed. 4.95 (ISBN 0-918438-04-7). Leisure Pr.

Team Handball-Racketball-Orienteering Guide 1976-78. 1976. 2.75x (ISBN 0-685-67027-9, 243-25850). AAHPERD.

Tyson, Pete. Handball. LC 73-141160. (Physical Education Ser). (Illus.). 1971. pap. text ed. 5.95 (ISBN 0-87620-375-6). Goodyear.

--Handball. LC 79-109498. (Sports Techniques Ser). 1972. 3.95 (ISBN 0-87670-013-X); pap. 1.95 (ISBN 0-87670-052-0). Athletic Inst.

Yessis, Michael. Handball. 3rd ed. (Physical Education Activities & Dance Ser). 1977. pap. text ed. write for info. (ISBN 0-697-07076-X). Wm C Brown.

Zafferano, George J. Handball Basics. LC 76-19798. 1977. 9.95 (ISBN 0-8069-4104-9); PLB 9.29 (ISBN 0-8069-4105-7). Sterling.

HANDBOOKS, VADE-MECUMS, ETC.

see also Recipes;

also subdivision Handbooks, Manuals, etc. under subjects

Adams, Florence. I Took a Hammer in My Hand. (Illus.). 1977. pap. 4.95 (ISBN 0-688-05165-0). Morrow.

Bacharach, Bert. How to Do Almost Everything. 1979. 9.95 (ISBN 0-671-24384-5). S&S.

Beaudouin, John T. & Mattlin, Everett. The Phrase-Dropper's Handbook. 1977. pap. 1.50 (ISBN 0-440-36790-5, LE). Dell.

Davids, Jules, ed. The Inquiry Handbooks. LC 74-21632. (41 vols. in 20). 1975. Repr. of 1918 ed. 795.00 (ISBN 0-8420-1798-4). Scholarly Res Inc.

Enquire Within: A Facsimile of the First Ed. 1978. 8.95 (ISBN 0-374-14853-8). FS&G.

Hohman, Edward J. & Leary, Norma E. The Greeting Card Handbook. (Barnes & Noble Everyday Handbook). (Illus.). 160p. (Orig.). 1981. pap. 4.95 (ISBN 0-06-463532-5, EH532, BN). Har-Row.

Lancaster. Prospect Park Handbook. LC 72-88263. 1972. 3.50 (ISBN 0-913252-06-9). LIU Univ.

Linton, Calvin D. & Litchfield, Edward H., eds. Complete Reference Handbook. (Illus.). 1964. 12.50 (ISBN 0-87396-011-4). Stravon.

McKenzie, E. C. Salted Peanuts: Eighteen Hundred Little Known Facts. (Direction Bks). 1976. pap. 3.95 large print ed. (ISBN 0-8010-6013-3); pap. 1.25 (ISBN 0-8010-5914-3). Baker Bk.

Pierson, K. K. Principles of Prosection: A Guide for the Anatomic Pathologist. 236p. 1974. 22.95 (ISBN 0-471-05811-4, Pub. by Wiley Med). Wiley.

Reit, Seymour. The Easy How-to Book. 48p. (gr. k-4). 1973. PLB 9.15 (ISBN 0-307-63573-2, Golden Pr). Western Pub.

Rushton, William. Superpig: The Gentleman's Guide to Everyday Survival. (Illus.). 1976. 15.95x (ISBN 0-8464-0899-6). Beekman Pubs.

Southwick, Albert P. Quizzism & Its Key. LC 68-22051. 1970. Repr. of 1884 ed. 19.00 (ISBN 0-8103-3094-6). Gale.

Timbs, John. Things Not Generally Known. Wells, David A., ed. LC 68-30584. 1968. Repr. of 1857 ed. 28.00 (ISBN 0-8103-3101-2). Gale.

Wallechinsky, David & Wallace, Irving. The People's Almanac. LC 75-2856. 1536p. 1975. 15.95 (ISBN 0-385-04186-1); pap. 10.95 (ISBN 0-385-04060-1). Doubleday.

The World Book Student Handbook, 2 vols. rev. ed. LC 77-95232. 1979. Repr. of 1978 ed. 27.00 (ISBN 0-685-88170-9). Vol. 1 (ISBN 0-7166-2053-7). Vol. 2 (ISBN 0-7166-2054-5). World Bk-Childcraft.

HANDEL, GEORG FRIEDRICH, 1685-1759

see Haendel, Georg Friedrich, 1685-1759

HANDICAPPED

see also Church Work with the Handicapped; Disability Evaluation; Mentally Handicapped; Physical Education for Handicapped Persons; Physically Handicapped; Sick; Socially Handicapped

Anderson, Hoyt. The Disabled Homemaker. (Illus.). 356p. 1981. 19.50 (ISBN 0-398-04077-X); pap. 12.75 (ISBN 0-398-04078-8). C C Thomas.

Arts and the Handicapped: An Issue of Access. LC 75-27022. (Illus.). 80p. 1975. pap. 4.00 (ISBN 0-89192-041-2). Interbk Inc.

Ayrault, Evelyn W. Sex, Love & the Physically Handicapped. 172p. 1981. 11.95 (ISBN 0-8264-0051-5). Continuum.

Baron, Henrietta. Everybody Can Cook: Techniques for the Handicapped, Vol. 1: Breakfast. LC 74-84845. (Illus.). 1977. pap. 10.50x tchr's manual (ISBN 0-87562-041-8); pap. 5.00x student manual (ISBN 0-87562-042-6). Spec Child.

Becker, Gaylene. Growing Old in Silence. LC 79-63548. 160p. 1980. 10.00 (ISBN 0-520-03900-9). U of Cal Pr.

Becker, Howard S., ed. Other Side: Perspectives on Deviance. LC 64-16953. 1967. pap. 5.95 (ISBN 0-02-902210-X). Free Pr.

Belgum, David. What Can I Do About the Part of Me I Don't Like? LC 73-88609. 96p. (Orig.). 1974. pap. 3.50 (ISBN 0-8066-1412-9, 10-7025). Augsburg.

Bergsma, Daniel, ed. Developmental Disabilities: Psychologic & Social Implications. LC 76-44446. (Alan R. Liss, Inc. Ser.: Vol. 12, No. 4). 1976. 18.00 (ISBN 0-686-18080-1). March of Dimes.

Berkler, Margo. Current Behavioral Trends for the Developmentally Disabled. 1978. 12.95 (ISBN 0-8391-1215-7). Univ Park.

Berkowitz, Monroe, et al. Public Policy Toward Disability. LC 76-25081. (Illus.). 1976. 23.95 (ISBN 0-275-23290-5). Praeger.

Bilovsky, David & Matson, Jane. Community Colleges & the Developmentally Disabled. 1977. 5.00 (ISBN 0-87117-052-3). Am Assn Comm Jr Coll.

Boswell, David M., ed. The Handicapped Person in the Community. Wingrove, Janet M. 1974. pap. 17.95x (ISBN 0-422-74760-2, Pub. by Travistock England). Methuen Inc.

Bowe, Frank. Handicapping America: Barriers to Disabled People. LC 77-11816. 1978. 14.95 (ISBN 0-06-010422-8, HarpT). Har-Row.

--Rehabilitating America: Toward Independence for Disabled & Elderly People. LC 79-1654. 1980. 11.95 (ISBN 0-06-010436-8, HarpT). Har-Row.

Boy Scouts of America. Handicapped Awareness. (Illus.). 48p. (gr. 6-12). 1981. pap. 0.70x (ISBN 0-8395-3370-5, 3370). BSA.

Burgdorf, Robert L., Jr., ed. The Legal Rights of Handicapped Persons: Cases, Materials, & Text. LC 79-26311. 1180p. 1980. text ed. 24.50 (ISBN 0-933716-01-X). P H Brookes.

Campling, Jo, ed. Image of Ourselves: Women with Disabilities Talking. 160p. 1981. pap. 9.75 (ISBN 0-7100-0822-8). Routledge & Kegan.

Carling, Finn & Haecker, Theodor. And Yet We Are Human & Kierkegaard: The Cripple, 2 vols. in 1. Bruyn, C. V., tr. from Norwegian. Phillips, William R. & Rosenberg, Janet, eds. LC 79-6897. (Physically Handicapped in Society Ser.). (Illus.). 1980. Repr. of 1962 ed. lib. bdg. 20.00x (ISBN 0-405-13108-9). Arno.

Cary, Jane R. How to Create Interiors for the Disabled: A Guidebook for Family & Friends. LC 77-88781. 1978. 15.00 (ISBN 0-394-41376-8); pap. 5.95 (ISBN 0-394-73595-1). Pantheon.

Charity Organisation Society. The Epileptic & Crippled Child & Adult. Phillips, William R. & Rosenberg, Janet, eds. LC 79-6899. (Physically Handicapped in Society Ser.). 1980. Repr. of 1893 ed. lib. bdg. 15.00x (ISBN 0-405-13109-7). Arno.

Chartered Society of Physiotherapy. Handling the Handicapped. 1977. Repr. 7.00 (ISBN 0-85941-012-9). State Mutual Bk.

Clelland, Richard W. Civil Rights for the Handicapped. 1978. pap. 4.95 (ISBN 0-686-12213-5, 021-00327). Am Assn Sch Admin.

Cohen, Herbert J. & Kligler, David. Urban Community Care for the Developmentally Disabled. (Illus.). 360p. 1980. text ed. 25.50 (ISBN 0-398-03945-3). C C Thomas.

Cohen, Uriel, et al. Mainstreaming the Handicapped: A Design Guide. (Publications in Architecture & Urban Planning Ser.: R79-5). (Illus.). iv, 64p. 1979. 5.00 (ISBN 0-686-27456-3). U of Wis Ctr Arch-Urban.

Copeland, Keith, ed. Aids for the Severely Handicapped. (Illus.). 150p. 1975. 27.00 (ISBN 0-8089-0866-9). Grune.

Cox-Gedmark, Jan. Coping with Physical Disability. LC 79-28275. (Christian Care Books). 1980. pap. 5.95 (ISBN 0-664-24297-9). Westminster.

Darnbrough, Ann & Kinrade, Derek. Directory for the Disabled: A Handbook of Information & Opportunities for Disabled & Handicapped People. 2nd ed. 208p. 1980. 27.00x (ISBN 0-85941-106-0, Pub. by Woodhead-Faulkner England); pap. 12.00x (ISBN 0-85941-108-7). State Mutual Bk.

Eakin, Billy J. How to Grow Rich Helping the Elderly & Handicapped. 1978. pap. 9.95 (ISBN 0-89668-007-X). Bridgeport Pub.

Eareckson, Joni & Estes, Steve. A Step Further. 2nd ed. (Illus.). 192p. 1980. pap. 4.95 (ISBN 0-310-23971-0). Zondervan.

Eareckson, Joni & Musser, Joe. Joni. (Illus.). 1977. pap. 3.95 (ISBN 0-89066-002-6). World Wide Pubs.

Edgar, Betsy J. We Live with the Wheel Chair. (Illus.). 1970. 5.00 (ISBN 0-87012-081-6). B J Edgar.

Eisenberg, Myron G., et al. Disabled People As Second Class Citizens. (Springer Ser. on Rehabilitation: Vol. 2). 1981. text ed. price not set (ISBN 0-8261-3220-0); pap. text ed. price not set (ISBN 0-8261-3221-9). Springer Pub.

Fielding, P. P. PIP College "HELPS" - Handicapped & Exceptional Learners Programs & Services: (College - Handicapped & Exceptional Learners Programs & Services, Vol. 1. 1976. pap. 10.00 (ISBN 0-686-18916-7). PIP.

Fischer, Henry L., et al. Sex Education for the Developmentally Disabled: A Guide for Parents, Teachers & Professionals. 1976. 7.50 (ISBN 0-8391-0750-1). Univ Park.

Gallender, Carolyn N. & Gallender, Demos. Dietary Problems & Diets for the Handicapped. 224p. 1979. 16.25 (ISBN 0-398-03838-4). C C Thomas.

Gallender, Demos. Eating Handicaps: Illustrated Techniques for Feeding Disorders. (Illus.). 312p. 1979. 21.75 (ISBN 0-398-03771-X). C C Thomas.

Garee, Betty, ed. Accent on Living Buyer's Guide: Your Number One Source of Information on Products for the Disabled. 1977. pap. 10.00 (ISBN 0-915708-05-1). Cheever Pub.

Gelfand, Ravina & Patterson, Letha. They Wouldn't Quit. LC 62-16852. (Medical Bks for Children). (gr. 3-9). 1962. PLB 3.95 (ISBN 0-8225-0013-2). Lerner Pubns.

Gilbreth, Frank B. Motion Study for the Handicapped. LC 72-9511. (Management History Ser.: No. 20). 169p. 1973. Repr. of 1920 ed. 17.50 (ISBN 0-87960-025-X). Hive Pub.

Giralestone, Gathrone R. The Care & Cure of Cripple Children. Phillips, William R. & Rosenberg, Janet, eds. LC 79-6900. (Physically Handicapped in Society Ser.). (Illus.). 1980. Repr. of 1924 ed. lib. bdg. 10.00x (ISBN 0-405-13111-9). Arno.

Goffman, Irving. Stigma: Notes on the Management of Spoiled Identity. (Orig.). 1963. pap. 3.45 (ISBN 0-13-846626-2, Spec). P-H.

Goldenson, Robert M., et al. Disability & Rehabilitation Handbook. (Illus.). 1978. text ed. 27.50 (ISBN 0-07-023658-5, P&RB). McGraw.

Goldsworthy, Maureen. Clothes for Disabled People. (Illus.). 120p. 1981. 22.50 (ISBN 0-7134-3928-9, Pub. by Batsford England); 14.50 (ISBN 0-7134-3929-7). David & Charles.

Goodzeit, Jack M. The Multihandicapped: Serving the Severely Disabled. 300p. 1981. text ed. 24.50x (ISBN 0-8290-0268-5); pap. text ed. 12.95x (ISBN 0-8290-0269-3). Irvington.

Gordon, Neil & McKinlay, Ian, eds. Helping Clumsy Children. (Illus.). 200p. 1980. pap. text ed. 16.00x (ISBN 0-443-01868-5). Churchill.

Gordon, Sol. Sexual Rights for People Who Happen to Be Handicapped. 1979. 1.00 (ISBN 0-937540-04-8, HPP-10). Human Policy Pr.

Grainger, Stuart E. Making Aids for Disabled Living. (Illus.). 88p. 1981. 16.95 (ISBN 0-7134-3934-3, Pub. by Batsford England). David & Charles.

Greer, John G., et al. Strategies for Helping Severely & Multiply Handicapped Citizens. 450p. 1981. pap. text ed. 24.95 (ISBN 0-8391-1692-6). Univ Park.

Guess, Doug, et al. Functional Speech & Language Training for the Severely Handicapped, Pt. 2. 1976. 8.95 (ISBN 0-89079-025-6); scoring form set 2.00 (ISBN 0-89079-026-4). H & H Ent.

Haj, Fareed. Disability in Antiquity. LC 70-92087. 1970. 6.50 (ISBN 0-8022-2316-8). Philos Lib.

Hale, Gloria, ed. The Source Book for the Disabled. LC 80-50722. (Illus.). 228p. Date not set. 15.95 (ISBN 0-03-057988-0); pap. 10.95 (ISBN 0-03-057654-7). HR&W.

--The Source Book for the Disabled. LC 78-31463. (Illus.). 1979. 15.95 (ISBN 0-448-22426-7); pap. 9.95 (ISBN 0-448-22429-1). Paddington.

Hamerlynck, L. A. Behavioral Systems for the Developmentally Disabled: Institutional, Clinic & Community Environments, Vol. 2. LC 78-21643. 1979. 17.50 (ISBN 0-87630-187-1). Brunner-Mazel.

Handicapping Conditions & Services Directory. 405p. 1981. Repr. of 1976 ed. 28.00 (ISBN 0-8103-0995-5). Gale.

Hart, V. Beginning with the Handicapped. (Illus.). 140p. 1978. pap. 8.75 (ISBN 0-398-03179-7). C C Thomas.

Haskins, James & Stifle, J. M. The Quiet Revolution: The Struggle for the Rights of Disabled Americans. LC 77-27664. (Illus.). (gr. 7 up). 1979. 7.95 (ISBN 0-690-03981-6, TYC-J); PLB 8.89 (ISBN 0-690-03982-4). Har-Row.

Haskins, James S. Who Are the Handicapped? LC 76-2777. (gr. 4-7). 1978. 6.95a (ISBN 0-385-09609-7); PLB (ISBN 0-385-09610-0). Doubleday.

Hoffman, Adeline M. Clothing for the Handicapped, the Aged & Other People with Special Needs. (Illus.). 212p. 1979. text ed. 14.75 (ISBN 0-398-03860-0). C C Thomas.

Hoopes, G. Gertrude. Out of the Running. (Illus.). 158p. 1939. photocopy ed. spiral 14.95 (ISBN 0-398-04286-1). C C Thomas.

Kamien, Janet. What If I Couldn't...? A Book About Special Needs. LC 78-26659. (Illus.). (gr. 4 up). 1979. reinforced bdg 9.95 (ISBN 0-684-15970-8, ScribJ). Scribner.

Kenedi, R. M. Disability. 524p. text ed. 89.50 (ISBN 0-8391-1464-8). Univ Park.

Kleinfield, Sonny. The Hidden Minority: America's Handicapped. LC 79-14812. 1979. 9.95 (ISBN 0-316-49842-4, Pub. by Atlantic-Little Brown). Little.

LaMore, Gregory S. Handicapped...How Does It Feel. (Illus.). 70p. (gr. 2-3). 1981. pap. text ed. 10.95 (ISBN 0-935266-06-2). B L Winch.

Lancaster-Gaye, Derek, ed. Personal Relationships, the Handicapped & the Community: Some European Thoughts & Solutions. (Illus.). 156p. 1972. 12.00 (ISBN 0-7100-7478-6). Routledge & Kegan.

Landis, Carney & Bolles, M. Marjorie. Personality & Sexuality in the Physically Handicapped Woman. Phillips, William R. & Rosebberg, Janet, eds. LC 79-6912. (Physically Handicapped in Society Ser.). 1980. Repr. of 1942 ed. lib. bdg. 15.00x (ISBN 0-405-13121-6). Arno.

LaRocca, Joseph & Turen, Jerry. The Application of Technological Developments to Physically Disabled People. (An Institute Paper). 113p. 1978. pap. 3.50 (ISBN 0-87766-225-8, 23200). Urban Inst.

Lees, Dennis & Shaw, Stella. Impairment, Disability & Handicap. 1974. text ed. 24.50x (ISBN 0-435-82530-5). Heinemann Ed.

Leonard, Joe H., Jr. Living with the Handicapped. (Christian Living Ser). 16p. 1976. pap. 0.30 (ISBN 0-8170-0726-1). Judson.

Lippman, Leopold. Attitudes Toward the Handicapped: A Comparison Between Europe & the United States. (American Lecture in Special Education Ser.). 136p. 1972. text ed. 10.50 (ISBN 0-398-02341-7). C C Thomas.

Lockhart, Terence. Housing Adaptations for Disabled People. 144p. (Orig.). 1981. pap. 21.95 (ISBN 0-89397-115-4). Nichols Pub.

Lombana, Judy H. Guidance for Handicapped Students. (Illus.). 450p. 1981. 34.75 (ISBN 0-398-04498-8). C C Thomas.

Ludlow, Norman H., Jr. Clip Book Number Fourteen: Disabled People at Work & Play. (Illus.). 64p. (Orig.). 1981. pap. 15.95x (ISBN 0-916706-24-9). N H Ludlow.

Luft, Harold S. Poverty & Health: Economic Causes & Consequences of Health Problems. 160p. 1978. professional reference 15.50 (ISBN 0-88410-515-6). Ballinger Pub.

McGrath, Martin G. Give Us the Knife: Carving a Lifestyle. 1978. pap. 4.95 (ISBN 0-932534-00-7). Ashlar Pr.

Mack, Nancy. Tracy. LC 76-12557. (Moods & Emotions Ser.). (Illus.). 32p. (gr. k-4). 1976. PLB 10.25 (ISBN 0-8172-0013-4). Raintree Pubs.

McMurrie, Douglas C. The Disabled Soldier. Phillips, William R. & Rosenberg, Janet, eds. LC 79-6921. (Physically Handicapped in Society Ser.). (Illus.). 1980. Repr. of 1919 ed. lib. bdg. 20.00x (ISBN 0-405-13140-2). Arno.

Magrab, Phyllis R. & Elder, Jerry O., eds. Planning for Services to Handicapped Persons: Community, Education, Health. LC 79-21474. 1979. text ed. 14.50 (ISBN 0-933716-04-4). P H Brookes.

Mallinson, Vernon. None Can Be Called Deformed. Phillips, William R. & Rosenberg, Janet, eds. LC 79-6917. (Physically Handicapped in Society Ser.). 1980. Repr. of 1956 ed. lib. bdg. 19.00x (ISBN 0-405-13124-0). Arno.

Marais, Elizabeth & Marais, Michael. Lives Worth Living: The Right of All the Handicapped. (Illus.). 1977. pap. 8.95 (ISBN 0-285-64831-4, Pub. by Souvenir Pr). Intl Schol Bk Serv.

Martmer, Edgare. The Child with a Handicap: A Team Approach to His Care & Guidance. (Illus.). 434p. 1959. ed. spiral bdg. 39.50photocopy (ISBN 0-398-04354-X). C C Thomas.

May, Elizabeth E., et al. Independent Living for the Handicapped & the Elderly. 1974. text ed. 17.95 (ISBN 0-395-18108-9). HM.

Mickhaus, Louisa. The Physically Handicapped & the Community: Some Challenging Breakthroughs. (Illus.). 132p. 1970. photocopy ed. spiral 12.75 (ISBN 0-398-01304-7). C C Thomas.

Milunsky, Aubrey, ed. Coping with Crisis & Handicap. 352p. 1981. 19.50 (ISBN 0-306-40660-8, Plenum Pr). Plenum Pub.

Morris, Robert. Allocating Health Resources for the Aged & Disabled: Technology Versus Politics. 160p. 1981. 16.95x (ISBN 0-669-04329-X). Lexington Bks.

Myers, Caroline C. & Barbe, Walter B., eds. Challenge of a Handicap. (Highlights Handbooks Ser.). (Illus.). (gr. 2-6). 1977. pap. 1.95 (ISBN 0-87534-168-3). Highlights.

Myers, J. S. Orientation to Chronic Disease & Disablity. 1965. text ed. 15.95 (ISBN 0-02-385850-8). Macmillan.

Nelson, Roberta. Creating Community Acceptance for Handicapped People. (Illus.). 240p. 1978. 17.50 (ISBN 0-398-03788-4). C C Thomas.

Nelson-Walker, Roberta. Planning, Creating & Financing Housing for Handicapped People. (Illus.). 240p. 1981. 24.50 (ISBN 0-398-04485-6). C C Thomas.

Northrup, James P. Old Age, Handicapped & Vietnam-Era Antidiscrimination Legislation. rev. ed. 1980. pap. 15.00 (ISBN 0-89546-020-3). Indus Res Unit-Wharton.

Novak, Angela R. & Heal, Laird W., eds. Integration of Developmentally Disabled Individuals into the Community. LC 80-21082. (Illus.). 262p. 1980. pap. text ed. 12.95 (ISBN 0-933716-10-9). P H Brookes.

Oppe, T. E. & Woodford, F. Peter, eds. Early Management of Handicapping Disorders. (Reviews of Research & Practice: 19). 1976. 18.00 (ISBN 90-219-5003-0, Excerpta Medica). Elsevier.

Orlansky, Michael D. & Heward, William L. Voices: Interviews with Handicapped People. (Special Education Ser.). (Illus.). 352p. (Orig.). 1981. pap. text ed. 8.95 (ISBN 0-675-08024-X). Merrill.

Orr, H. Winnett. On the Contributions of Hugh Owen Thomas of Liverpool, Sir Robert Jones of Liverpool & London, John Ridlon, M. D. of New York & Chicago to Modern Orthopedic Surgery. Phillips, William R. & Rosenberg, Janet, eds. LC 79-6920. (Physically Handicapped in Society Ser.). 1980. Repr. of 1949 ed. lib. bdg. 21.00x (ISBN 0-405-13129-1). Arno.

Paul, James M., et al, eds. Deinstitutionalization: Program & Policy Development. (Special Education & Rehabilitation Monograph: No. 12). 1977. 13.95x (ISBN 0-8156-0132-8). Syracuse U Pr.

Pearman, William A. & Starr, Philip. The Physically Handicapped: An Annotated Bibliography. 1981. lib. bdg. 30.00 (ISBN 0-8240-9484-0). Garland Pub.

People with Disabilities: Toward Acquiring Information Which Reflects More Sentively Their Problems & Needs. write for info. (ISBN 0-939986-23-X). World Rehab Fund.

Perske, Robert. New Life in the Neighborhood: How Persons with Retardation & Other Disabilities Can Help Make a Good Community Better. LC 80-15517. (Illus.). 80p. (Orig.). 1980. pap. 4.95 (ISBN 0-687-27800-7). Abingdon.

Petrie, Joyce A. Mainstreaming in the Media Center. 1981. lib. bdg. write for info. (ISBN 0-89774-006-8). Oryx Pr.

Phillips, William R. & Rosenberg, Janet, eds. Changing Patterns of Law: The Courts & the Handicapped. an original anthology ed. LC 79-6009. (Physically Handicapped in Society Ser.). 1980. lib. bdg. 35.00x (ISBN 0-405-13101-1). Arno.

--Cleveland Symposium on Behavioral Research in Rehabilitation. rev. ed. LC 79-6898. (Physically Handicapped in Society Ser.). 1980. Repr. of 1959 ed. lib. bdg. 20.00x (ISBN 0-405-13110-0). Arno.

--Physically Handicapped in Society Series, 39 bks. 1980. Set. lib. bdg. 838.00x (ISBN 0-405-13100-3). Arno.

--Social Scientists & the Physically Handicapped: An Original Anthology. LC 79-6011. (Physically Handicapped in Society Ser.). 1980. lib. bdg. 28.00x (ISBN 0-405-13103-8). Arno.

Pilling, Doria. The Handicapped Child, Research Review, Vol. 3: Mental Handicaps. (Studies in Child Development). 635p. (Orig.). 1973. pap. text ed. 19.50x (ISBN 0-582-36510-4). Humanities.

Pitner, Rudolf & Eisenson, Jon. The Psychology of the Physically Handicapped. Phillips, William R. & Rosenberg, Janet, eds. LC 79-6922. (Physically Handicapped in Society Ser.). 1980. Repr. of 1941 ed. lib. bdg. 30.00x (ISBN 0-405-13130-5). Arno.

Powell, T. Hennessy & Hecimovic, Anton. Respite Care for the Handicapped: Helping Individuals & Their Families. (Illus.). 104p. 1981. 12.75 (ISBN 0-398-04536-4). C C Thomas.

Readings in Human Growth & Development of the Exceptional Individual. (Special Education Ser.). 1978. pap. 10.95 (ISBN 0-89568-080-7). Spec Learn Corp.

Reddoch, Mildred L. So White, the Lilies. 1981. 5.95 (ISBN 0-8062-1629-8). Carlton.

Rehabilitation & Handicapped Literature, Nineteen Seventy Nine Update: A Guide to the Microform Collection. 61p. 1981. write for info. Microfilming Corp.

Rehabilitation & Handicapped Literature, 1950-1978: A Bibliographic Guide to the Microfiche Collection. 409p. 1981. 50.00 (ISBN 0-667-00614-1). Microfilming Corp.

Robinault, Isabel P. Sex, Society, & the Disabled: A Developmental Inquiry into Roles, Reactions, & Responsibilities. (Illus.). 1978. text ed. 18.00x (ISBN 0-06-142274-6, Harper Medical). Har-Row.

Roessler, R. Psychosocial Adjustment to Disability. 1978. 12.95 (ISBN 0-8391-1244-0). Univ Park.

Rosen, M., et al, eds. Habilitation of the Handicapped. 1977. 18.50 (ISBN 0-8391-1137-1). Univ Park.

Roth, William. The Handicapped Speak. LC 80-20297. 223p. 1981. lib. bdg. 15.95x (ISBN 0-89950-022-6). McFarland & Co.

Sainsbury, Sally. Measuring Disability. 125p. 1973. pap. text ed. 6.25x (ISBN 0-7135-1899-5, Pub. by Bedford England). Renouf.

--Registered As Disabled. 205p. 1970. pap. text ed. 6.25x (ISBN 0-7135-1619-4, Pub. by Bedford England). Renouf.

Sargent, Jean V. An Easier Way: A Handbook for the Elderly & Handicapped. (Illus.). 216p. 1981. pap. 9.95 (ISBN 0-8138-0870-7). Iowa St U Pr.

Saunders, Franklin F. Attitudes Toward Handicapped Persons: A Study of the Differential Effects of Fine Variables. LC 74-29579. 1975. soft bdg. 8.00 (ISBN 0-88247-323-9). R & E Res Assoc.

Savitz, Harriet M. Wheelchair Champions: A History of Wheelchair Sports. LC 77-11561. (Illus.). (gr. 4 up). 1978. 7.95 (ISBN 0-381-90057-6, JD-J); PLB 7.79 (ISBN 0-381-99555-0). Har-Row.

Sha'ked, Ami. Human Sexuality in Physical & Mental Illnesses & Disabilities: An Annotated Bibliography. LC 78-17813. 320p. 1979. 22.50x (ISBN 0-253-10100-X). Ind U Pr.

Shakespeare, Rosemary. The Psychology Handicap. (Essential Psychology Ser.). 1975. pap. 4.50x (ISBN 0-416-81720-3). Methuen Inc.

Shaw, Ann M. & Stevens, C. J., eds. Drama, Theatre & the Handicapped. 121p. 1979. 7.00x (ISBN 0-686-29488-2). Am Theatre Assoc.

Sherrill, Claudine. Creative Arts for the Severely Handicapped. 2nd ed. (Illus.). 304p. 1979. text ed. 15.50 (ISBN 0-398-03908-9). C C Thomas.

Siantz, M. The Nurse & the Developmentally Disabled Adolescent. 1977. pap. 9.95 (ISBN 0-8391-1131-2). Univ Park.

Smith, Ernest. Workshops for the Handicapped in the United States: An Historical & Developmental Perspective. 480p. 1971. pap. 20.25 spiral (ISBN 0-686-77575-9). C C Thomas.

Stein, Sarah B. About Handicaps. LC 73-15270. (Open Family Ser). (Illus.). 48p. (gr. 1 up). 1974. 7.95 (ISBN 0-8027-6174-7). Walker & Co.

Stewart, Jim, et al. Community Competencies for the Handicapped: School Graduation Requirements: A Basis for Curriculum & IEP Development. 208p. 1978. spiral bdg. 14.50 (ISBN 0-398-03765-5). C C Thomas.

Stubbins, J. Social & Psychological Aspects of Disability. 1977. 24.95 (ISBN 0-8391-1119-3). Univ Park.

Topliss, Eda. Provision for the Disabled. 2nd ed. (Aspects of Social Policy Ser.). 179p. 1975. 22.50x (ISBN 0-631-10821-1, Pub. by Basil Blackwell); pap. 8.95x (ISBN 0-631-11691-5). Biblio Dist.

Topliss, Eda & Gould, Bryan. Charter for the Disabled: The Chronically Sick & Disabled Persons Act 1970. (Aspects of Social Policy Ser.). 160p. 1981. 19.95x (ISBN 0-631-12833-6, Pub. by Basil Blackwell England); pap. 7.95 (ISBN 0-631-12748-8). Biblio Dist.

--A Charter for the Disabled: The Chronically Sick & Disabled Persons Act Nineteen Seventy. (Aspects of Social Policy Ser.). 160p. 1981. pap. 7.95x (ISBN 0-631-12748-8, Pub. by Basil Blackwell). Biblio Dist.

Wambold, Clark, et al. Instructional Programs & Activities for the Severely Handicapped. (Illus.). 238p. 1981. spiral bdg. 27.50 (ISBN 0-398-04162-8). C C Thomas.

Watson, Frederick. Civilization & the Cripple. Phillips, William R. & Rosenberg, Janet, eds. LC 79-6927. (Physically Handicapped in Society Ser.). (Illus.). 1980. Repr. of 1930 ed. lib. bdg. 12.00x (ISBN 0-405-13134-8). Arno.

Weiss, Louise. Access to the World: A Travel Guide for the Handicapped. LC 77-10792. 1977. 7.95 (ISBN 0-89456-003-4). Chatham Sq.

Wright, Henry C. Survey of Cripples in New York City: Under the Auspices of a Special Committee on Survey of Cripples. Phillips, William R. & Rosenberg, Janet, eds. LC 79-6014. (Physically Handicapped in Society Ser.). 1980. Repr. of 1920 ed. lib. bdg. 10.00x (ISBN 0-405-13137-2). Arno.

Wright, Kieth C. Library & Information Services for Handicapped Individuals. LC 78-26472. 1979. lib. bdg. 17.50x (ISBN 0-87287-129-0). Libs Unl.

Wurtz, Hans. Das Seelenleben des Kruppels: Kruppelseelen Kundliche Erziehung und das Gesetz Betr. Phillips, William R. & Rosenberg, Janet, eds. LC 79-6007. (Physically Handicapped in Society Ser.). (Ger.). 1980. Repr. of 1921 ed. lib. bdg. 10.00x (ISBN 0-405-13138-0). Arno.

HANDICAPPED–BIOGRAPHY

Brown, Helene. Yesterday's Child. LC 76-171. 216p. 1976. 7.95 (ISBN 0-87131-194-1). M Evans.

Cleland, Max. Strong at the Broken Places. 180p. 1980. 6.95 (ISBN 0-912376-55-4). Chosen Bks Pub.

Giddings, Robert. You Should See Me in Pyjamas. 192p. 1981. 25.00 (ISBN 0-241-10534-X, Pub. by Hamish Hamilton England). David & Charles.

Hathaway, Katharine B. The Little Locksmith. Phillips, William R. & Rosenberg, Janet, eds. LC 79-6904. (Physically Handicapped in Society Ser.). 1980. Repr. of 1943 ed. lib. bdg. 20.00x (ISBN 0-405-13113-5). Arno.

Hearst, James. My Shadow Below Me. 224p. 1981. 13.50 (ISBN 0-8138-1136-8). Iowa St U Pr.

Helms, Tom. Against All Odds. 1979. pap. 2.50 (ISBN 0-446-81546-2). Warner Bks.

Hunt, Agnes. This Is My Life. Phillips, William R. & Rosenberg, Janet, eds. LC 79-6013. (Physically Handicapped in Society Ser.). 1980. Repr. of 1942 ed. lib. bdg. 19.00x (ISBN 0-405-13116-X). Arno.

Kenny, Elizabeth. And They Shall Walk. Phillips, William R. & Rosenberg, Janet, eds. LC 79-6907. (Physically Handicapped in Society Ser.). (Illus.). 1980. Repr. of 1943 ed. lib. bdg. 24.00x (ISBN 0-405-13117-8). Arno.

Kimmel, Neita. Reaching for the Stars. 1978. 5.95 (ISBN 0-533-03438-8). Vantage.

Lotz, Philip H., ed. Unused Alibis, Creative Personalities, Vol. 7. facs. ed. LC 79-126322. (Biography Index Reprint Ser.). 1951. 12.00 (ISBN 0-8369-8028-X). Arno.

Meyers, Jeff. One of a Kind: The Legend of Carl Joseph. 200p. 1980. pap. 6.95 (ISBN 0-86629-028-1); 11.95 (ISBN 0-86629-025-7). Sunrise MO.

Russell, Harold & Ferullo, Dan. The Best Years of My Life. (Illus.). 192p. 1981. 11.95 (ISBN 0-8397-1026-7). Eriksson.

Sandness, Grace L. Brimming Over. pap. 5.95 (ISBN 0-686-31395-X). NACAC.

Watson, Frederick. The Life of Sir Robert Jones. Phillips, William R. & Rosenberg, Janet, eds. LC 79-6928. (Physically Handicapped in Society Ser.). (Illus.). 1980. Repr. of 1934 ed. lib. bdg. 25.00x (ISBN 0-405-13135-6). Arno.

HANDICAPPED–EDUCATION

Anderson, Robert M. & Greer, John G., eds. Educating the Severely & Profoundly Retarded. (Illus.). 1976. 16.95 (ISBN 0-8391-0945-8). Univ Park.

Calhoun, Mary L. & Hawisher, Margaret. Teaching & Learning Strategies for Physically Handicapped Students. 384p. 1979. pap. text ed. 18.50 (ISBN 0-8391-1394-3). Univ Park.

Cave, Cyril & Maddison, Pamela. A Survey of Recent Research in Special Education. (General Ser.). 229p. 1979. text ed. 27.50x (ISBN 0-85633-148-1, NFER). Humanities.

Eaton, Peggy & Eiring, Leslie. Joy of Learning. 10.50 (ISBN 0-86575-027-0). Dormac.

Fielding, P. PIP College "HELPS". Handicapped & Exceptional Learners Programs & Services. (College Handicapped & Exceptional Programs & Services Ser.: Vol. 3). 1978. pap. 10.00 (ISBN 0-686-27591-8). PIP.

Fischer, Henry L., et al. Sex Education for the Developmentally Disabled: A Guide for Parents, Teachers & Professionals. 1976. 7.50 (ISBN 0-8391-0750-1). Univ Park.

Frederick Muller, Ltd., ed. The Source Book for the Disabled. 40.00x (ISBN 0-7092-0324-1, Pub. by Muller Ltd); soft cover 27.00x (ISBN 0-686-75471-9). State Mutual Bk.

Fredericks, H. D. & Baldwin, Victor. The Teaching Research Curriculum for Moderately & Severely Handicapped. (Illus.). 340p. 1978. pap. 23.75 photocopy ed. spiral (ISBN 0-398-03330-7). C C Thomas.

Fredericks, H. D., et al. The Teaching Research Curriculum for Moderately & Severely Handicapped: Self-Help & Cognitive. (Illus.). 280p. 1980. pap. 17.75 (ISBN 0-398-04034-6); developmental chart 3.50 (ISBN 0-686-65146-4). C C Thomas.

Gillet, Pamela. Of Work & Worth: Career Ed. for Exceptional Children & Youth. LC 80-84931. 340p. 1981. text ed. 19.95 (ISBN 0-913420-90-5). Olympus Pub Co.

Hofman, Helenmarie & Ricker, Kenneth S., eds. Sourcebook, Science Education & the Physically Handicapped. (Orig.). 1979. pap. 6.00 (ISBN 0-87355-014-5). Natl Sci Tchrs.

Hoyer, Louis & Hay, Charles K. Services to the Orthopedically Handicapped. Phillips, William R. & Rosenberg, Janet, eds. LC 79-6906. (Physically Handicapped in Society Ser.). (Illus.). 1980. Repr. of 1942 ed. lib. bdg. 12.00x (ISBN 0-405-13115-1). Arno.

Jacobson, David W., ed. Management of Accessibility for Handicapped Students in Higher Education. LC 81-82617. (Illus., Orig.). 1981. pap. write for info. (ISBN 0-915164-13-2). Natl Assn Coll.

Jones, Clarence J. & Rabold, Ted F. Public Law Ninety-Four To One Forty-Two: A Guide for the Education for All Handicapped Children Act. 1979. pap. 3.75x (ISBN 0-931992-32-X). Penns Valley.

Jones, Clarence J. & Yerger, William M. The Primer for the Training of ESEA Title One Parent Advisory Council. rev. ed. 1979. pap. 3.75 (ISBN 0-931992-33-8). Penns Valley.

Kissinger, Ellen M. A Sequential Curriculum for the Severely & Profoundly Mentally Retarded-Multi-Handicapped. 276p. 1981. pap. 22.75 spiral (ISBN 0-398-04145-8). C C Thomas.

Lazarus, Mitchell. Educating the Handicapped: Where We've Been, Where We're Going. 1980. pap. 11.95 (ISBN 0-87545-019-9). Natl Sch PR.

Lufburrow, Bill. The Most Honest People. LC 80-69253. (Illus., Orig.). 1980. pap. 4.95 (ISBN 0-918464-23-4). D Armstrong.

McGeough, Charles & Jungjohan, Barbara. College Facilities & Services for the Handicapped. 1000p. 1982. write for info. (ISBN 0-89774-004-1). Oryx Pr.

McLoughlin, James & Lewis, Rena. Assessing Special Students. (Special Education Ser.). (Illus.). 640p. 1981. text ed. 19.95 (ISBN 0-675-08151-3). Merrill.

Marsh, George E. Methods for Teaching the Mildly Handicapped Adolescent. LC 80-13396. (Illus.). 1980. pap. text ed. 14.95 (ISBN 0-8016-3115-7). Mosby.

Moss, John R., et al. A College Level Program for Learning Disabled Students. 1980. pap. 15.95 (ISBN 0-686-23977-6). PIP.

National Information Center for Educational Media. Special Education Index to Learner Materials. LC 79-84454. 462p. 1979. pap. 60.00 (ISBN 0-89320-024-7). Univ SC Natl Info.

National Information Center for Special Education Materials (NICSEM) Special Education Index to Assessment Materials. LC 79-84457. (Orig.). 1980. pap. 21.00 (ISBN 0-89320-026-3). Univ. SC Natl Info.

--Special Education Index to Inservice Training Materials. LC 79-84458. (Orig.). 1980. pap. 12.00 (ISBN 0-89320-027-1). Univ. SC Natl Info.

National Information Center for Special Education Materials (NISCEM) Special Education Index to Parent Materials. LC 79-84456. (Orig.). 1979. pap. 21.00 (ISBN 0-89320-025-5). Univ SC Natl Info.

Panckhurst, John & McAllister, Arthur G. An Approach to the Further Education of the Physically Handicapped. (Illus.). 139p. 1980. pap. text ed. 13.75x (ISBN 0-85633-195-3, NFER). Humanities.

Pasanella, Anne L. & Volkmor, Cara B. Teaching Handicapped Students in the Mainstream: Coming Back...or Never Leaving. 2nd ed. (Special Education Ser.). (Illus.). 384p. 1981. pap. text ed. 11.95 (ISBN 0-675-08026-6). Merrill.

Phillips, William R. & Rosenberg, Janet, eds. Education & Occupations of Cripples: Juveniles & Adults. LC 79-6924. (Physically Handicapped in Society Ser.). 1980. Repr. of 1918 ed. lib. bdg. 15.00x (ISBN 0-405-13131-3). Arno.

Readings in Career & Vocational Education for the Handicapped. (Special Education Ser.). 1978. pap. 10.95 (ISBN 0-89568-083-1). Spec Learn Corp.

Sailor, Wayne, et al, eds. Methods of Instruction for Severely Handicapped Students. LC 80-16668. (Illus.). 352p. (Orig.). 1980. pap. text ed. 16.95 (ISBN 0-933716-06-0). P H Brookes.

Siegel, Ernest & Gold, Ruth. Educating the Learning Disabled. 1982. text ed. 17.95 (ISBN 0-686-75026-8). Macmillan.

Stolurow, Lawrence M. & Hildebrand, Myrene R. Resource Utilization & Dissemination of Information by REGI Projects. (RTF Report Ser.: No. 5). 24p. (Orig.). 1981. pap. text ed. 2.50 (ISBN 0-939984-03-2). U IA Ctr Ed Experiment.

Sullivan, Oscar M. & Snortum, Kenneth O. Disabled Persons: Their Education & Rehabilitation. Phillips, William R. & Rosenberg, Janet, eds. LC 79-6925. (Physically Handicapped in Society Ser.). 1980. Repr. of 1926 ed. lib. bdg. 48.00x (ISBN 0-405-13132-1). Arno.

Turnbull, Ann P. & Schulz, Jane B. Mainstreaming Handicapped Students: A Guide for the Classroom Teacher. 1979. text ed. 19.95 (ISBN 0-205-06107-9) (ISBN 0-205-06107-9). Allyn.

Van Etten, Glen & Arkell, Claudia. The Severely & Profoundly Handicapped: Programs, Methods & Materials. LC 79-28841. 1980. pap. text ed. 19.95 (ISBN 0-8016-5215-4). Mosby.

Ward, Michael J., et al. Everybody Counts! A Workshop Manual to Increase Awareness of Handicapped People. LC 79-63014. 73p. 1979. pap. 12.50 (ISBN 0-86586-027-0). Coun Exc Child.

Weatherley, Richard A. Reforming Special Education: Policy Implementation from State Level to Street Level. 1979. text ed. 17.50x (ISBN 0-262-23094-1). MIT Pr.

Wilcox, Barbara & Bellamy, G. Thomas. Design of High School Programs for Severely Handicapped Students. 210p. (Orig.). 1981. pap. text ed. 15.95 (ISBN 0-933716-18-4). P H Brookes.

HANDICAPPED–EMPLOYMENT

Adaptation of Jobs for the Disabled. 6th ed. (Illus.). 1978. 7.15 (ISBN 92-2-100032-X). Intl Labour Office.

Anderson, Roy N. The Disabled Man & His Vocational Adjustment: A Study of the Types of Jobs Held by 4,404 Orthopedic Cases in Relation to the Specific Disability. Phillips, William R. & Rosenberg, Janet, eds. LC 79-6893. (Physically Handicapped in Society Ser.). 1980. Repr. of 1932 ed. lib. bdg. 12.00x (ISBN 0-405-13104-6). Arno.

Cheever, Raymond C., ed. Home Operated Business Opportunities for the Disabled. (Illus.). 1977. pap. 4.50 (ISBN 0-915708-04-3). Cheever Pub.

Complying with Equal Employment Regulations for Handicapped Persons. 1979. pap. 3.00 (ISBN 0-917386-84-1). Exec Ent.

Darnbrough, Ann & Kinrade, Derek. Directory for the Disabled: A Handbook of Information & Opportunities for Disabled & Handicapped People. 2nd ed. 208p. 1980. 27.00x (ISBN 0-85941-106-0, Pub. by Woodhead-Faulkner England); pap. 12.00x (ISBN 0-85941-108-7). State Mutual Bk.

Gearheart, Bill R. Special Education for the Eighties. LC 79-20647. (Illus.). 1980. text ed. 17.95 (ISBN 0-8016-1759-6). Mosby.

Ginglend, David R. & Carlson, Bernice W. Ready to Work? Development of Occupational Skills, Attitudes, & Behaviors with Mentally Retarded Persons. LC 76-58841. 1977. 6.95 (ISBN 0-687-35559-1). Abingdon.

Grossman, Vigdor. Employing Handicapped Persons: Meeting EEO Obligations. 154p. 1980. pap. 15.00 (ISBN 0-87179-319-9). BNA.

Institute for Information Studies, et al. Financial Resources for Disabled Individuals. Vash, Carolyn & Crane, Marjorie Boyer, eds. LC 80-84166. 70p. 1980. pap. write for info. (ISBN 0-935294-06-6). Inst Info Stud.

Kunc, Norman. Ready, Willing & Disabled. 192p. 1981. 7.95 (ISBN 0-920510-56-6, Pub. by Personal Lib). Everest Hse.

Levitan, Sar A. & Taggart, Robert. Jobs for the Disabled. LC 76-49910. (Policy Studies in Employment & Welfare: No. 28). (Illus.). 144p. 1977. 9.00x (ISBN 0-8018-1925-3); pap. 3.50x (ISBN 0-8018-1926-1). Johns Hopkins.

Lufburrow, Bill. The Most Honest People. LC 80-69253. (Illus., Orig.). 1980. pap. 4.95 (ISBN 0-918464-23-4). D Armstrong.

Marais, Elizabeth & Marais, Michael. Lives Worth Living: The Right of All the Handicapped. (Illus.). 1977. pap. 8.95 (ISBN 0-285-64831-4, Pub. by Souvenir Pr). Intl Schol Bk Serv.

Mawson, Thomas. The Imperial Obligation: Industrial Villages for the Partialy Disabled Soldiers & Sailors. Phillips, William R. & Rosenberg, Janet, eds. LC 79-6918. (Physically Handicapped in Society Ser.). 1980. Repr. of 1917 ed. lib. bdg. 12.00x (ISBN 0-405-13125-9). Arno.

Northrup, James P. Old Age, Handicapped & Vietnam-Era Anti-Discrimination Legislation (Supplement) LC 78-70927. (Labor Relations & Public Policy Ser.: No. 14). 1978. pap. 3.00 (ISBN 0-89546-008-4). Indus Res Unit-Wharton.

Rabby, Rami. Locating, Recruiting, & Hiring the Disabled. LC 80-39779. 1981. pap. 3.95 (ISBN 0-87576-095-3). Pilot Bks.

Taylor, Vernon R. Employment of the Disadvantaged in the Public Service. 1971. 3.00 (ISBN 0-87373-283-9). Intl Personnel Mgmt.

Vocational Assessment & Work Preparation Centers for the Disabled. 3rd ed. 1974. 4.55 (ISBN 92-2-100993-9). Intl Labour Office.

Vocational Rehabilitation & the Employment of the Disabled. 182p. pap. 9.50 (ISBN 92-2-002571-X, ILO177, ILO). Unipub.

Wehman, Paul. Competitive Employment: New Horizons for Severely Disabled Individuals. LC 80-24926. (Illus.). 278p. (Orig.). 1981. pap. text ed. 13.95 (ISBN 0-933716-12-5). P H Brookes.

Zimmer, A. B. Employing the Handicapped: A Practical Compliance Manual. 530p. 1981. 12.95 (ISBN 0-8144-5525-5). Am Mgmt.

HANDICAPPED–RECREATION

Adams, Ronald C., et al. Games, Sports & Excercises for the Physically Handicapped. 3rd. ed. LC 81-7288. (Illus.). 400p. 1982. pap. text ed. price not set (ISBN 0-8121-0785-3). Lea & Febiger.

American National Red Cross. Adapted Aquatics: Swimming for Persons with Physical or Mental Impairments. LC 76-43131. 320p. 1977. pap. 3.95 (ISBN 0-385-12611-5). Doubleday.

Anderson, Enid. A Handbook of Crafts for the Disabled & Their Teachers. (Illus.). 168p. 1981. 22.00 (ISBN 0-7134-2181-9, Pub. by Batsford England). David & Charles.

Arnheim, Daniel D., et al. Principles & Methods of Adapted Physical Education & Recreation. 3rd ed. LC 76-46427. (Illus.). 1977. text ed. 19.95 (ISBN 0-8016-0320-X). Mosby.

Clark, Cynthia & Chadwick, Donnacompiled by. Clinically Adapted Instruments for the Multiply Handicapped: A Sourcebook. rev. ed. 1980. Repr. of 1979 ed. 12.95 (ISBN 0-918812-13-5). Magnamusic.

Geddes, Dolores. Physical Activities for Individuals with Handicapping Conditions. 2nd ed. LC 77-26228. (Illus.). 1978. pap. text ed. 10.50 (ISBN 0-8016-1793-6). Mosby.

Hamill, Charlotte & Oliver, Robert C. Therapeutic Activities for the Handicapped Elderly. LC 80-19661. 295p. 1980. text ed. 24.00 (ISBN 0-89443-326-1). Aspen Systems.

Hunt, Valerie V. Recreation for the Handicapped. 1955. text ed. 16.50 (ISBN 0-13-767640-9). P-H.

Jones, Ron. The Acorn People. 1978. Repr. of 1976 ed. 4.95 (ISBN 0-687-00707-0). Abingdon.

Kay, Jane G. Crafts for the Very Disabled & Handicapped: For All Ages. (Illus.). 224p. 1977. spiral bdg. 19.75 (ISBN 0-398-03661-6). C C Thomas.

Kelly, Thomas J., et al, eds. School & Community Resources for the Behaviorally Handicapped. 333p. 1974. text ed. 29.50x (ISBN 0-8422-5163-4); pap. text ed. 9.75x (ISBN 0-8422-0392-3). Irvington.

Lane, Jim & Schaaf, Dick. Wheelchair Bowling: A Complete Guide to Bowling for the Handicapped. LC 78-24103. (Illus.). 96p. (Orig.). 1980. pap. 7.95 (ISBN 0-9605306-0-6). Wheelchair Bowlers.

Merrill, Toni. Activities for the Aged & Infirm: A Handbook for the Untrained Worker. (Illus.). 392p. 1979. 16.50 (ISBN 0-398-01294-6). C C Thomas.

--Party Packets: For Hospitals & Homes Shortcuts for a Single Activity Worker. (Illus.). 196p. 1970. pap. 17.50 photocopy ed. (ISBN 0-398-01295-4). C C Thomas.

Overs, Robert P., et al. Avocational Activities for the Handicapped: A Handbook for Avocational Counseling. (American Lectures in Social & Rehabilitation Psychology Ser.). 208p. 1974. 13.75 (ISBN 0-398-02975-X). C C Thomas.

Shivers, Jay S. & Fait, Hollis F. Therapeutic & Adapted Recreational Services. LC 75-16377. (Illus.). 366p. 1975. text ed. 14.50 (ISBN 0-8121-0464-1). Lea & Febiger.

Wehman, Paul & Schleien, Stuart. Leisure Programs for Handicapped Persons: Adaptations, Techniques & Curriculum. 288p. 1981. pap. text ed. 21.95 (ISBN 0-8391-1643-8). Univ Park.

HANDICAPPED–REHABILITATION

see Rehabilitation; Vocational Rehabilitation

HANDICAPPED CHILDREN

see also Aphasia; Brain-Damaged Children; Mentally Handicapped Children; Physically Handicapped Children; Socially Handicapped Children

Andersen, Linda. Classroom Activities for Helping Perceptually Handicapped Children. 1974. pap. 5.95x (ISBN 0-87628-201-X). Ctr Appl Res.

Axford, Wendy A. & McMurtrie, Douglas C. Handicapped Children in Britain: Their Problems & Education & Index Catalogue of a Library of Rehabilitation of the Disabled, 2 vols. in 1. Phillips, William R. & Rosenberg, Janet, eds. LC 79-6894. (Physically Handicapped in Society Ser.). 1980. Repr. of 1959 ed. lib. bdg. 15.00x (ISBN 0-405-13105-4). Arno.

Barsch, Ray H. Parent of the Handicapped Child: The Study of Child-rearing Practices. (American Lecture in Special Education Ser.). (Illus.). 452p. 1976. pap. 14.75 (ISBN 0-398-03559-8). C C Thomas.

Baumgartner, Diane. Melissa. (Orig.). 1980. pap. 4.95 (ISBN 0-89191-233-9). Cook.

Benson, Hazel B. Behavior Modification & the Child: An Annotated Bibliography. LC 79-7358. (Contemporary Problems of Childhood: No. 3). 1979. lib. bdg. 27.50 (ISBN 0-313-21489-1, BBM/). Greenwood.

Biklen, Douglas. Let Our Children Go. 1974. 3.50 (ISBN 0-937540-02-1, HPP-1). Human Policy Pr.

Birch, Herbert G. & Gussow, Joan D. Disadvantaged Children: Health, Nutrition & School Failure. LC 78-102443. (Illus.). 320p. 1970. 25.75 (ISBN 0-8089-0643-7). Grune.

Bleck, Eugene E. & Nagel, Donald, eds. Physically Handicapped Children: A Medical Atlas for Teachers. 2nd ed. 1981. price not set (ISBN 0-8089-1391-3, 790623). Grune.

Bondo, Ulla. Ida: Life with My Handicapped Child. (Illus.). 128p. 1981. 23.00 (ISBN 0-571-11589-6, Pub. by Faber & Faber); pap. 8.95 (ISBN 0-571-11590-X). Merrimack Bk Serv.

Bowley, Agatha H. Children at Risk. LC 74-29080. (Illus.). 88p. 1975. pap. text ed. 3.25 (ISBN 0-443-01271-7). Churchill.

Bowley, Agatha H. & Gardner, Leslie. The Handicapped Child. 4th ed. (Illus.). 1980. pap. text ed. 18.25 (ISBN 0-443-02084-1). Churchill.

Braun, Samuel J. & Lasher, Miriam G. Are You Ready to Mainstream: Helping Preschoolers with Learning & Behavior Problems. 1978. pap. text ed. 7.95 (ISBN 0-675-08443-1). Merrill.

Bremner, Robert H., ed. Care of Handicapped Children, Vol. 7. LC 74-1671. (Children & Youth Ser.). 1974. 13.00x (ISBN 0-405-05951-5). Arno.

Brown, Diana L. Developmental Handicaps in Babies & Young Children: A Guide for Parents. 100p. 1972. 11.75 (ISBN 0-398-02534-7). C C Thomas.

Brown, Helene. Yesterday's Child. LC 76-171. 216p. 1976. 7.95 (ISBN 0-87131-194-1). M Evans.

Coyner, Athleen B. & Zelle, Raeone. Nursing of Developmentally Disabled Infants & Children. (Illus.). 200p. Date not set. pap. price not set (ISBN 0-8036-1995-2). Davis Co.

Crow, Gary A. Children at Risk: A Handbook of the Signs & Symptoms of Early Childhood Difficulties. LC 77-87859. 1978. 12.95x (ISBN 0-8052-3675-9). Schocken.

--Children at Risk: Handbook of the Signs & Symptoms of Early Childhood Disabilities. LC 77-87859. 288p. 1980. pap. 6.95 (ISBN 0-8052-0655-8). Schocken.

Cunningham, Cliff & Sloper, Patricia. Helping Your Exceptional Baby: A Practical & Honest Approach to Raising a Mentally Handicapped Baby. (Illus.). 1981. 6.95 (ISBN 0-394-73867-5). Pantheon.

Darling, Rosalyn B. Families Against Society: A Study of Reactions to Children with Birth Defects. LC 79-14148. (Sage Library of Social Research: No. 88). (Illus.). 256p. 1979. 20.00x (ISBN 0-8039-1285-4); pap. 9.95x (ISBN 0-8039-1286-2). Sage.

Doman, Glenn. What to Do About Your Brain Injured Child. LC 72-92202. 312p. 1974. 9.95 (ISBN 0-385-02139-9). Doubleday.

Downey, John A. & Low, Niels L., eds. The Child with Disabling Illness. 1981. text ed. 49.00 (ISBN 0-89004-664-6). Raven.

Elder, Jerry O. & Magrab, Phyllis R., eds. Coordinating Services to Handicapped Children: A Handbook for Interagency Collaboration. LC 80-16033. (Illus.). 264p. (Orig.). 1980. pap. text ed. 13.95 (ISBN 0-933716-11-7). P H Brookes.

Evans, Joyce. Working with Parents of Handicapped Children. LC 76-41192. 1976. pap. text ed. 3.50 (ISBN 0-86586-094-7). Coun Exc Child.

Fallen, Nancy & McGovern, Jill. Young Children with Special Needs. (Special Education Ser.). 1978. text ed. 17.95 (ISBN 0-675-08382-6). study guide 3.95 (ISBN 0-675-08383-4). Merrill.

Featherstone, Helen. A Difference in the Family: Life with a Disabled Child. LC 79-56668. 262p. 1980. 13.95 (ISBN 0-465-01654-5). Basic.

Feingold, S. Norman & Miller, Norma R. Your Future: A Guide for the Handicapped Teenager. (Careers in Depth Ser.). 140p. 1981. lib. bdg. 7.97 (ISBN 0-8239-0424-5). Rosen Pr.

Foott, Sydney, et al. The Disabled Schoolchild and Kitchen Sense. (Illus.). 96p. 1976. pap. 10.00x (ISBN 0-433-10666-2). Intl Ideas.

Fredericks, H. D., et al. The Teaching Research Curriculum for Moderately & Severely Handicapped: Gross & Fine Motor. (Illus.). 264p. 1980. pap. 17.75 (ISBN 0-398-04035-4); developmental chart 3.50 (ISBN 0-686-77473-6). C C Thomas.

Gliedman, John & Roth, William. The Unexpected Minority: Handicapped Children in America. LC 79-1823. 1979. 17.95 (ISBN 0-15-192845-2). HarBraceJ.

Guralnick. Early Intervention & the Integration of Handicapped & Nonhandicapped Children. (Illus.). 1977. 18.95 (ISBN 0-8391-1165-7). Univ Park.

Hare, Betty A., et al. Teaching Young Handicapped Children: A Guide for Preschool & the Primary Grades. 288p. 1977. 12.75 (ISBN 0-8089-1065-5). Grune.

Haring, Norris G., ed. Behavior of Exceptional Children: An Introduction to Special Education. 2nd ed. 1978. text ed. 18.95x (ISBN 0-675-08398-2); instructor's manual 3.95 (ISBN 0-686-67970-9). Merrill.

Hawley, Gloria H. Laura's Psalm. 192p. 1981. pap. 5.95 (ISBN 0-86608-000-7, 14014P). Impact Tenn.

Hennon, M. L. Identifying Handicapped Children for Child Development Programs: A Recruitment & Selection Manual. 96p. 1974. 5.00 (ISBN 0-89269-001-1, 202). Humanics Ltd.

Hofmann, Ruth B. How to Build Special Furniture & Equipment for Handicapped Children. (Illus.). 100p. 1974. photocopy ed. spiral 10.50 (ISBN 0-398-00854-X). C C Thomas.

Hong, Edna. Bright Valley of Love. LC 75-22723. 160p. 1979. pap. 2.95 (ISBN 0-8066-1700-4, 10-0911). Augsburg.

Jobling, Megan. Helping the Handicapped Child, No. 1: In the Family. (Illus.). 40p. 1975. pap. text ed. 2.50x (ISBN 0-85633-058-2, NFER). Humanities.

Kershaw, John D. Handicapped Children. 3rd ed. 1973. 17.50x (ISBN 0-433-18381-0). Intl Ideas.

Kok, J. F. Structopathic Children. Incl. Pt. 1. Description of Disturbance Type & Strategies. (Modern Approaches to the Diagnosis & Instruction of Milti-Handicapped Children: Vol. 9). 126p (ISBN 90-237-4109-9); Pt. 2. Results of Experimental Research of Structuring Group Therapy. (Modern Approaches to the Diagnosis & Instruction of Multi-Handicapped: Vol. 10). 122p (ISBN 90-237-4110-2). 1972. text ed. 26.00 ea. (Pub. by Swets Pub Serv Holland). Swets North Am.

Lansdown, Richard. More Than Sympathy: The Everyday Needs of Sick & Handicapped Children & Their Families. 1980. 19.95x (ISBN 0-422-76630-5, Pub. by Tavistock); pap. 10.95x (ISBN 0-422-76640-2). Methuen Inc.

Lear, Roma. Play Helps: Toys & Activities for Handicapped Children. 1977. pap. 12.95x (ISBN 0-433-19085-X). Intl Ideas.

Loring, James & Burn, Graham, eds. Integration of Handicapped Children in Society. 172p. 1975. 16.00x (ISBN 0-7100-8269-X). Routledge & Kegan.

McDonald, Eugene T. Understand Those Feelings. LC 61-18740. 1962. 11.25x (ISBN 0-87076-807-7). Stanwix.

MacDonald, James & Horstmeier, Deanna. Environmental Language Intervention Program. (Special Education Ser.). 1978. 59.95 (ISBN 0-675-08379-6); instructor's manual 3.95 (ISBN 0-686-67977-6). Merrill.

McMichael, Joan K. Handicap: A Study of Physically Handicapped Children & Their Families. LC 77-189858. (Contemporary Community Health Ser.). 1972. 9.95x (ISBN 0-8229-1106-X). U of Pittsburgh Pr.

Manciaux, M., ed. Handicaps in Childhood. (Child Health in the Community Ser.: Vol. 1). (Illus.). viii, 180p. 1981. 30.00 (ISBN 3-8055-2935-X). S Karger.

Menolascino, Frank J. & Pearson, Paul H., eds. Beyond the Limits: Innovations in Services for the Severely & Profoundly Retarded. LC 74-84668. 1974. pap. 8.50x (ISBN 0-87562-053-1). Spec Child.

Mitchell, Joyce S. See Me More Clearly: Career & Life Planning for Teens with Physical Disabilities. LC 79-3768. (gr. 7 up). 1980. 8.95 (ISBN 0-15-272460-5, HJ). HarBraceJ.

Mopsik, Stanley I., ed. An Education Handbook for Parents of Handicapped Children. Agard, Judith A. LC 78-67848. 1980. 22.50 (ISBN 0-89011-511-7). Abt Assoc.

Orton, Samuel T. Reading Writing & Speech Problems in Children. 1973. 3.50x (ISBN 0-393-01107-0). Norton.

Parfit, Jessie. Helping the Handicapped Child: In Day & Residential Care, No. 3. (General Ser.). (Illus.). 48p. 1975. pap. text ed. 2.25x (ISBN 0-85633-060-4, NFER). Humanities.

Paterson, George. Helping Your Handicapped Child. LC 74-14185. 112p. (Orig.). 1975. pap. 3.50 (ISBN 0-8066-1467-6, 10-3005). Augsburg.

Phillips, William R. & Rosenberg, Janet, eds. The Origins of Modern Treatment & the Education of Physically Handicapped Children: An Original Anthology. LC 79-6010. (Physically Handicapped in Society Ser.). 1980. lib. bdg. 35.00x (ISBN 0-405-13102-X). Arno.

Prensky, Arthur L. & Palkes, Helen. Care of the Neurologically Handicapped Child. (Illus.). 350p. 1981. text ed. 18.95x (ISBN 0-19-502917-8). Oxford U Pr.

Price, Robert J. Physical Education & the Physically Handicapped Child. 192p. 1980. 21.00x (ISBN 0-86019-035-8, Pub. by Kimpton). State Mutual Bk.

Readings in Diagnosis & Placement. (Special Education Ser.). 1978. pap. text ed. 10.95 (ISBN 0-89568-009-2). Spec Learn Corp.

Rich, Mildred K. Handcrafts for the Homebound Handicapped. (Illus.). 116p. 1960. photocopy ed. spiral 11.75 (ISBN 0-398-01585-6). C C Thomas.

Riley, Mary T. Laton: The Parent Book. new ed. LC 77-79313. (Illus.). 1978. pap. 10.00 (ISBN 0-89334-012-X). Humanics Ltd.

Roberts, Nancy. Help for the Parents of a Handicapped Child. 1981. pap. 2.25 (ISBN 0-570-08254-4, 12YY2926). Concordia.

Routledge, Linda. Only Child's Play: Developing the Capicities of Handicapped Children. (Illus.). 1978. pap. 13.95x (ISBN 0-433-28350-5). Intl Ideas.

Schopler, E. Individualized Assessment & Treatment for Autistic & Developmentally Disabled Children. Incl. Vol. I. Psycho-Educational Profile. 1978. 29.50 (ISBN 0-8391-1279-3); Vol. II. Teaching Strategies for Parents & Professionals. 1979. 19.95 (ISBN 0-8391-1521-0). Univ Park.

Seligman, Milton. Strategies for Helping Parents of Exceptional Children: A Guide for Teachers. LC 78-24764. (Illus.). 1979. 14.95 (ISBN 0-02-928420-1). Free Pr.

Siegel, Dorothy S. Winners: Eight Special Young People. LC 77-27985. 192p. (gr. 7 up). 1978. PLB 7.79 (ISBN 0-671-32861-1). Messner.

Stewart, Jack C. Counseling Parents of Exceptional Children. (Special Education Ser.). 1978. pap. text ed. 8.95 (ISBN 0-675-08386-9). Merrill.

Taft, Jessie. Dynamics of Therapy in a Controlled Relationship. 7.50 (ISBN 0-8446-3045-4). Peter Smith.

Thain, Wilbur S., et al. Normal & Handicapped Children: A Growth & Development Primer for Parents & Professionals. LC 79-9402. (Illus.). 256p. 1980. text ed. 16.50 (ISBN 0-88416-227-3). Wright-PSG.

Thompson, Robert J., Jr. & O'Quinn, Aglaia N. Developmental Disabilities: Etiologies, Manifestations, Diagnoses & Treatment. (Illus.). 1979. text ed. 15.95x (ISBN 0-19-502421-4); pap. text ed. 9.95x (ISBN 0-19-502422-2). Oxford U Pr.

Turnbull, A. C. & Woodford, F. P. Prevention of Handicap Through Antenatal Care. (The Institute for Research into Mental & Multiple Handicap, Review of Research & Practice: 18). 1976. 21.50 (ISBN 0-444-15210-5, Excerpta Medica). Elsevier.

Turnbull, Ann & Turnbull, H. R. Parents Speak Out: Views from the Other Side of the Two-Way Mirror. 1978. pap. 7.50 (ISBN 0-675-08385-0). Merrill.

Turnbull, Ann P. & Turnbull, H. Rutherford, III. Parents Speak Out: Growing with a Handicapped Child. 210p. pap. 5.95 (ISBN 0-675-01043-8). Merrill.

Tymchuk, Alexander J. Parent & Family Therapy: An Integrative Approach to Family Interventions. new ed. LC 79-1085. 1979. text ed. 14.95 (ISBN 0-89335-080-X). Spectrum Pub.

Voysey, Margaret. A Constant Burden: The Reconstitution of Family Life. 320p. 1975. 20.00 (ISBN 0-7100-8183-9). Routledge & Kegan.

Wakefield, Tom. Some Mothers I Know: Living with Handicapped Children. 1978. 10.95 (ISBN 0-7100-8783-7). Routledge & Kegan.

Walberg, Franette. Dancing to Learn. (Illus.). (gr. 6-12). 1979. pap. text ed. 6.00x (ISBN 0-87879-218-X). Acad Therapy.

Webster, Elizabeth J. Counseling with Parents of Handicapped Children: Guidlines for Improving Communication. 176p. 1977. 17.50 (ISBN 0-8089-1036-1). Grune.

--Professional Approaches with Parents of Handicapped Children. 292p. 1976. 16.75 (ISBN 0-398-03521-0). C C Thomas.

Weihs, Thomas J. Children in Need of Special Care. LC 79-13412. 1979. text ed. 9.95x (ISBN 0-8052-3717-8). Schocken.

Wexler, Susan S. The Story of Sandy. rev. ed. 176p. (RL 10). pap. 1.50 (ISBN 0-451-08102-1, W8102, Sig). NAL.

White House Conference on Child Health & Protection. Organization for the Care of Handicapped Children, National, State, Local. LC 74-1715. (Children & Youth Ser.: Vol. 14). 390p. 1974. Repr. of 1932 ed. 23.00x (ISBN 0-405-05990-6). Arno.

Wolf, Bernard. Don't Feel Sorry for Paul. LC 74-9925. (Illus.). 96p. (gr. 3-6). 1974. 8.95 (ISBN 0-397-31588-0). Lippincott.

--No Sientan Lastima Por Paul. Ortiz, Victoria, ed. Lois, Ximena, tr. LC 78-20549. (Libros Lippincott En Espanol). (Illus.). (gr. 3-7). 1979. 6.95 (ISBN 0-397-31848-0). Lippincott.

Wolf, James M. & Anderson, Robert. The Multiply Handicapped Child. 488p. 1973. photocopy ed. spiral 48.75 (ISBN 0-398-02105-8). C C Thomas.

Younghusband, E., et al. Living with Handicap. 390p. 1970. 43.00x (ISBN 0-677-65140-6). Gordon.

Zang, Barbara, ed. How to Get Help for Kids: A Reference Guide to Services for Handicapped Children. 245p. 1980. pap. 29.95 (ISBN 0-915794-18-7). Gaylord Prof Pubns.

Ziegler, Carlos R. The Image of the Physically Handicapped in Children's Literature. Phillips, William R. & Rosenberg, Janet, eds. LC 79-6008. (Physically Handicapped in Society Ser.). 1980. lib. bdg. 15.00x (ISBN 0-405-13139-9). Arno.

HANDICAPPED CHILDREN–EDUCATION

see also Religious Education of Mentally Handicapped Children

Adler, Sol, et al. An Interdisciplinary Language Intervention Program for the Moderately to Profoundly Language-Retarded Child. 1980. 19.50 (ISBN 0-8089-1301-8). Grune.

Alvin, Juliette. Music for the Handicapped Child. 1976. pap. 9.95x (ISBN 0-19-314920-6). Oxford U Pr.

Anderson, D. R., et al. Instructional Programming for the Handicapped Student. (Illus.). 1024p. 1976. 49.75 (ISBN 0-398-03339-0); pap. 37.50 (ISBN 0-398-03340-4). C C Thomas.

Anderson, Elizabeth M. Disabled Schoolchild: A Study of Integration in Primary Schools. 377p. 1973. pap. 12.95x (ISBN 0-416-78190-X). Methuen Inc.

Anderson, R. Individualizing Educational Materials for Special Children in the Mainstream. 1978. 16.50 (ISBN 0-8391-1253-X). Univ Park.

Arena, John. How to Write an IEP. LC 78-12880. 1978. pap. 4.00 (ISBN 0-87879-208-2). Acad Therapy.

Bailey, Phillip. They Can Make Music. (Illus.). 160p. 1973. 9.95x (ISBN 0-19-311913-7). Oxford U Pr.

Banas, Norma & Wills, I. H. WISC-R Prescriptions. LC 78-12881. 1978. pap. 4.00x (ISBN 0-87879-206-6). Acad Therapy.

Bangs, Tina E. Language & Learning Disorders of the Pre-Academic Child. (Illus.). 1968. 18.95 (ISBN 0-13-522797-6). P-H.

Bannatyne, Alexander. Language, Reading & Learning Disabilities: Psychology, Neuropsychology, Diagnosis & Remediation. (Illus.). 800p. 1976. 21.50 (ISBN 0-398-02182-1). C C Thomas.

Barnard, Kathryn E. & Erickson, Marcene L. Teaching Children with Developmental Problems, a Family Care Approach. 2nd ed. LC 75-31520. (Illus.). 184p. 1976. pap. 10.50 (ISBN 0-8016-0486-9). Mosby.

Bender, Michael & Valletuhi, Peter J. Teaching the Moderately & Severely Handicapped: Curriculum, Objectives, Strategies & Activites, 3 vols. (Illus.). 1000p. 1976. Set. ed. 3 vol. set 39.50 (ISBN 0-686-77132-X); vol. 1 & 2 28.50 (ISBN 0-686-77133-8); Vol. 1. 14.95 (ISBN 0-8391-0869-9); Vol. 2. 19.95 (ISBN 0-8391-0868-0); Vol. 3. 16.95 (ISBN 0-8391-0963-6). Univ Park.

Berkler, Margo. Current Behavioral Trends for the Developmentally Disabled. 1978. 12.95 (ISBN 0-8391-1215-7). Univ Park.

Bigge, June L. & O'Donnell, Patrick A. Teaching the Physically & Multiply Disabled. (Special Education Ser.). 1977. text ed. 19.95 (ISBN 0-675-08527-6). Merrill.

Birch, Jack W. & Johnstone, B. Kenneth. Designing Schools & Schooling for the Handicapped. (Illus.). 244p. 1975. 22.50 (ISBN 0-398-03362-5). C C Thomas.

Blackwell, Peter M., et al. Sentences & Other Systems: A Language & Learning Curriculum for Hearing-Impaired Children. LC 78-51922. 1978. pap. text ed. 11.75 (ISBN 0-88200-118-3, C2557). Alexander Graham.

Blanco, Ralph F. Prescriptions for Children with Learning & Adjustment Problems. 2nd ed. 352p. 1981. 14.75 (ISBN 0-398-04511-9). C C Thomas.

Blumenfeld, Jane, et al. Help Them Grow: A Pictorial Handbook for Parents of Handicapped Children. LC 79-148858. (Illus., Orig.). 1971. pap. 2.75 (ISBN 0-687-16856-2). Abingdon.

Brolin, Donn E. & Kokaska, Charles J. Career Education for Handicapped Children & Youth. (Special Education Ser.). 1979. text ed. 19.50 (ISBN 0-675-08278-1). Merrill.

Brown, Sara L. & Moersch, Martha S., eds. Parents on the Team. LC 78-18517. (Illus.). 1978. lib. bdg. 8.95x (ISBN 0-472-09302-9); pap. 5.95 (ISBN 0-472-06302-2). U of Mich Pr.

Bruce, V. Awakening the Slower Mind. 1969. 22.00 (ISBN 0-08-006387-X); pap. 10.75 (ISBN 0-08-006386-1). Pergamon.

Buscaglia, Leo F. & Williams, Eddie H. Human Advocacy & Pl 94-142: The Educator's Roles. 1979. pap. 9.50 (ISBN 0-685-91502-6). C B Slack.

Butler, Dorothy. Cushla & Her Books. LC 79-25695. (Illus.). 128p. 1980. Repr. 13.50 (ISBN 0-87675-279-2). Horn Bk.

Caldwell, Bettye & Stedman, Donald, eds. Infant Education. 1977. 9.95 (ISBN 0-8027-9042-9); pap. 8.95 (ISBN 0-8027-7110-6). Walker & Co.

Campbell, Bob & Baldwin, Victor, eds. Severely Handicapped-Hearing Impaired Students: Strengthening Service Delivery. LC 81-10203. 260p. (Orig.). 1981. pap. text ed. 15.95 (ISBN 0-933716-24-9). P-H Brookes.

Campbell, Harold. Measuring the Abilities of Severely Handicapped Students. (Illus.). 90p. 1981. spiral bdg. 13.75 (ISBN 0-398-04526-7). C C Thomas.

Casto, Glendon, ed. CAMS Training Manual. LC 79-64723. (Curriculum & Monitoring System Ser.). 102p. 1979. tchrs. ed. 9.70 (ISBN 0-8027-9061-5). Walker Educ.

Charles, C. M. & Malian, Ida. The Special Student: Practical Help for the Classroom Teacher. LC 80-13053. (Illus.). 1980. pap. text ed. 10.45 (ISBN 0-8016-1132-6). Mosby.

Cohen, Sandra B. & Plaskon, Stephen P. Language Arts for the Mildly Handicapped. (Special Education Ser.). 544p. 1980. text ed. 17.95x (ISBN 0-675-08131-9). Merrill.

Connor, Frances P., et al. Program Guide for Infants & Toddlers with Neuromotor & Other Developmental Disabilities. LC 77-28188. 1978. pap. 14.50x (ISBN 0-8077-2546-3). Tchrs Coll.

Consilia, Sr. Mary. The Noncoping Child. new ed. LC 78-12889. 1978. 3-ring binder program 31.50x (ISBN 0-87879-200-7). Acad Therapy.

Constructive Education for Special Groups: Handicapped & Deviant Children. 1979. pap. 13.25 (ISBN 92-3-101588-5, U913, UNESCO). Unipub.

Corrigan, Dean C. & Howey, Kenneth R., eds. Special Education in Transition: Concepts to Guide the Education of Experienced Teachers with Implications for PL 94-142. LC 80-68281. 208p. 1980. pap. 12.95 (ISBN 0-86586-109-0). Coun Exc Child.

Cratty, Bryant J. Some Educational Implications of Movements. LC 78-123868. (Orig.). 1971. pap. 7.00x (ISBN 0-87562-022-1). Spec Child.

Curtis, Audrey & Hill, Sheelagh. My World. (General Ser.). 1978. pap. text ed. 9.00x (ISBN 0-85633-156-2, NFER). Humanities.

Davis, Sharon & Ward, Michael. Vocational Education of Handicapped Students: A Guide for Policy Development. LC 78-63156. 1978. pap. text ed. 6.00 (ISBN 0-86586-092-0). Coun Exc Child.

Day, Dabney, et al. Learning to Remember: Procedures for Teaching Recall. 1978. pap. text ed. 18.50 (ISBN 0-87879-194-9). Acad Therapy.

Designing Environments for Handicapped Children. LC 79-89670. 95p. (Orig.). 1979. pap. 8.00 (ISBN 0-88481-211-1). Ed Facilities.

Dexter, Beverly L. Special Education & the Classroom Teacher: Concepts, Perspectives & Strategies. (Illus.). 272p. 1977. 22.50 (ISBN 0-398-03607-1). C C Thomas.

Donlon, Edward T. & Burton, Louise F., eds. The Severely & Profoundly Handicapped: A Practical Approach to Teaching. LC 76-17293. 272p. 1976. 29.00 (ISBN 0-8089-0952-5). Grune.

Doyle, Phyllis B., et al. Helping the Severely Handicapped Child: A Guide for Parents & Teachers. LC 78-3300. (John Day Bk. in Special Education). (Illus.). 1979. 10.95 (ISBN 0-381-90063-0). T Y Crowell.

Economic Aspects of Special Education. (Special Education Ser.). 1979. pap. 9.25 (ISBN 92-3-101514-1, U869, UNESCO). Unipub.

Ellis, Norman E. & Cross, Lee, eds. Planning Programs for Early Education of the Handicapped. (First Chance Ser.). 1976. 9.95 (ISBN 0-8027-9039-9). Walker & Co.

Everard, Margaret P., ed. An Approach to Teaching Autistic Children. 156p. 1976. 16.50 (ISBN 0-08-020895-9); pap. 7.00 (ISBN 0-08-019923-2). Pergamon.

Featherstone, Helen. A Difference in the Family: Living with a Disabled Child. 288p. 1981. pap. 6.95 (ISBN 0-14-005941-5). Penguin.

Featherstone, William B. Curriculum of the Special Class: Its Underlying Principles. LC 74-176766. (Columbia University. Teachers College. Contributions to Education: No. 544). Repr. of 1932 ed. 17.50 (ISBN 0-404-55544-6, CE544). AMS Pr.

Federlin, Anne C. Play in Preschool Mainstreamed & Handicapped Settings. LC 80-65612. 135p. 1981. perfect bdg. 10.50 (ISBN 0-86548-035-4). Century Twenty One.

Fielding, P. P. PIP College "HELPS" - Handicapped & Exceptional Learners Programs & Services, Vol. 2. 1977. pap. 10.00 (ISBN 0-686-23403-0), PIP.

Finkle, Louis J. Math Lesson Plans for Teachers for Assisting Handicapped Children. 383p. 1977. pap. text ed. 10.50 (ISBN 0-8191-0026-9). U Pr of Amer.

Francis-Williams, Jesse. Children with Specific Learning Difficulties. 2nd ed. LC 74-4021. 240p. 1974. text ed. 23.00 (ISBN 0-08-017967-3); pap. text ed. 10.75 (ISBN 0-08-017968-1). Pergamon.

Fredericks, H. D., et al. The Teaching Research Curriculum for Moderately & Severely Handicapped: Gross & Fine Motor. (Illus.). 264p. 1980. pap. 17.75 (ISBN 0-398-04035-4); developmental chart 3.50 (ISBN 0-686-77473-6). C C Thomas.

Frostig, Marianne. Education for Dignity. 224p. 1976. 25.75 (ISBN 0-8089-0951-7). Grune.

Frostig, Marianne & Maslow, Phyllis. Learning Problems in the Classroom. LC 73-1578. 368p. 1973. 23.75 (ISBN 0-8089-0783-2). Grune.

Gallender, Demos. Teaching Eating & Toileting Skills to the Multi-Handicapped in the School Setting. (Illus.). 384p. 1980. text ed. 22.75 (ISBN 0-398-03879-1). C C Thomas.

Garwood, S. Gray. Educating Young Handicapped Children: A Developmental Approach. LC 79-13200. 572p. 1979. text ed. 24.75 (ISBN 0-89443-099-8). Aspen Systems.

Gearheart, Bill R. & Weishahn, Mel W. The Handicapped Student in the Regular Classroom. 2nd ed. LC 79-23706. 1980. text ed. 17.95 (ISBN 0-8016-1760-X). Mosby.

Goldberg, I. Ignacy. Selected Bibliography of Special Education. LC 67-19388. (Orig.). 1967. pap. 3.25x (ISBN 0-8077-1434-8). Tchrs Coll.

Griffiths, Anita. Teaching the Dyslexic Child. LC 78-12875. 1978. pap. 4.00x (ISBN 0-87879-205-8). Acad Therapy.

Gulliford, R. Helping the Handicapped Child, No. 2: At School. (Illus.). 40p. 1975. pap. text ed. 2.50x (ISBN 0-85633-059-0, NFER). Humanities.

Guralnick. Early Intervention & the Integration of Handicapped & Nonhandicapped Children. (Illus.). 1977. 18.95 (ISBN 0-8391-1165-7). Univ Park.

Hales, Ann. The Children of Skylard Ward. LC 77-80836. 1978. 12.95 (ISBN 0-521-21752-0). Cambridge U Pr.

Hamerlynck, L. A. Behavioral Systems for the Developmentally Disabled: School & Family Environment, Vol. 1. LC 78-21562. 1979. 17.50 (ISBN 0-87630-193-6). Brunner-Mazel.

Hammill, Donald & Wiederholt, J. Lee. The Resource Room: Rationale & Implementation. 87p. 1972. pap. 12.00 (ISBN 0-8089-0895-2). Grune.

Hare, Betty A., et al. Teaching Young Handicapped Children: A Guide for Preschool & the Primary Grades. 288p. 1977. 12.75 (ISBN 0-8089-1065-5). Grune.

Haring, Norris G. & Phillips, E. L. Teaching Special Children. (Special Education Ser). 1976. text ed. 15.95 (ISBN 0-07-026430-9, C). McGraw.

Harrison, Betty D. Dial-a-Skill: A Manual of Procedures for Team Members of Special Education & Related Services. LC 77-16371. (Illus.). 1978. pap. 9.95x (ISBN 0-8425-0907-0). Brigham.

Hart, Verna. Mainstreaming Children with Special Needs. (Illus.). 224p. (Orig.). 1980. pap. text ed. 8.95x (ISBN 0-582-28211-X). Longman.

Hasazi, Susan E. Under One Cover: Implementing the Least Restrictive Environment Concept. LC 80-68096. 208p. 1980. pap. 11.25 (ISBN 0-86586-106-4). Coun Exc Child.

Haskell, Simon H., et al. The Education of Motor & Neurologically Handicapped Children. 1977. 21.95 (ISBN 0-470-99276-X). Halsted Pr.

Hawisher, Margaret F. & Calhoun, Mary L. The Resource Room: An Educational Asset for Children with Special Needs. (Special Education Ser.). 1978. pap. text ed. 9.95x (ISBN 0-675-08354-0); instructor's manual 3.95 (ISBN 0-686-67987-3). Merrill.

Hayden, Torey L. Somebody Else's Kids. 384p. 1981. 11.95 (ISBN 0-399-12602-3). Putnam.

Heasley, Bernice E. & Grosklos, Jacqueline R. Programmed Lessons for Young Language-Disabled Children: A Handbook for Therapists, Educators & Parents. (Illus.). 172p. 1976. pap. text ed. 12.75 spiral (ISBN 0-398-03526-1). C C Thomas.

Heinich, Robert, ed. Educating All Handicapped Children. LC 78-12749. 384p. 1979. 18.95 (ISBN 0-87778-131-1). Educ Tech Pubns.

Heller, Jack. Typing for the Physically Handicapped: Methods & Keyboard Presentation Charts. (gr. 10-12). 1978. text ed. 100.00 (ISBN 0-07-028079-7, G). McGraw.

Hughes, Thomas & Hughes, Kendall S. Casebook for Special Education & Elementary Education. LC 76-57115. 1977. pap. 7.50x (ISBN 0-8134-1905-0, 1905). Interstate.

Hyde, Sarah & Engle. The Potomac Program. 439p. 1977. 34.95 (ISBN 0-86575-037-8). Dormac.

Jones, Reginald L., ed. Mainstreaming & the Minority Child. 1976. pap. text ed. 5.00x (ISBN 0-86586-051-3). Coun Exc Child.

Jordan, June B., ed. Exceptional Students in Secondary Schools: A Report from the Invisible College on Learning & Behavioral Problems of Handicapped Students in Secondary School Programs. LC 78-62325. 1978. pap. text ed. 8.75 (ISBN 0-86586-030-0). Coun Exc Child.

Kalish, Ruth A., ed. Therapy in Educational Environments for Handicapped Children. 500p. 1982. 17.95 (ISBN 0-8036-5207-0). Davis Co.

Koegel, Robert L., et al. Educating & Understanding Autistic Children. 350p. 1981. 25.00 (ISBN 0-933014-68-6). College-Hill.

Kokaska, Sharen M. Creative Movement for Special Education. LC 74-81747. 1974. pap. 4.50 (ISBN 0-8224-1662-X). Pitman Learning.

Kozloff, M. Educating Children with Learning & Behavior Problems. LC 74-11304. 459p. 1974. 32.95 (ISBN 0-471-50630-3, Pub. by Wiley-Interscience). Wiley.

Larsen, L. Competencies for Effective Teaching of the Severely & Profoundly Handicapped in Classroom Settings. Date not set. 16.50 (ISBN 0-8391-1260-2). Univ Park.

Light, Janice B. The Joy of Listening. LC 78-52752. 1978. pap. text ed. 7.50 (ISBN 0-88200-119-1, M7992). Alexander Graham.

Lillie, David L., ed. Teaching Parents to Teach: Education for the Handicapped. (First Chance Ser.). (Illus.). 1976. 12.95 (ISBN 0-8027-0550-2). Walker & Co.

Ling, Daniel & Ling, Agnes H. Aural Habilitation: The Foundations of Verbal Learning in Hearing-Impaired Children. LC 78-56077. 1978. pap. text ed. 12.50 (ISBN 0-88200-121-3, C2441). Alexander Graham.

--Basic Vocabulary & Language Thesaurus for Hearing-Impaired Children. LC 76-52826. 1977. 4.50 (ISBN 0-88200-078-0, C1437). Alexander Graham.

Long, Kate. Johnny's Such a Bright Boy, What a Shame He's Retarded. 1977. 10.00 (ISBN 0-395-25346-2); pap. 4.95 (ISBN 0-395-27164-9). HM.

Lovaas, O. Ivar. Teaching Developmentally Disabled Children: The Me Book. 264p. 1981. pap. text ed. 14.95 (ISBN 0-8391-1567-9). Univ Park.

Lowenbraun, Sheila, et al. Teaching the Mildly Handicapped in the Regular Classroom. 2nd ed. (Special Education Ser.). 192p. pap. text ed. 7.50 (ISBN 0-675-08132-7). Merrill.

McCormack, James E. & Chalmers, Amanda J. Early Cognitive Instruction for the Moderately & Severely Handicapped. LC 78-62903. (Illus.). 1978. loose-leaf & program guide 44.95 (ISBN 0-87822-188-3). Res Press.

McGivern, A. B., et al. Language Stories: Teaching Language to Developmentally Disabled Children. LC 76-27347. (John Day Bk.). 1978. 29.95x (ISBN 0-381-98108-8). T y Crowell.

Mackie, Romaine. Special Education in the United States: Statistics 1948-1966. LC 69-18776. 1969. pap. 4.25x (ISBN 0-8077-1721-5). Tchrs Coll.

McNeal, Brenda. Springboards for Writing. (gr. 8-12). 1979. pap. text ed. 7.00x (ISBN 0-87879-222-8). Acad Therapy.

Markel, Geraldine & Greenbaum, Judith L. Parents Are to Be Seen & Heard: Assertiveness in Educational Planning for Handicapped Children. LC 79-12924. 1979. pap. 6.95 (ISBN 0-915166-28-3). Impact Pubs Cal.

Marshall, Margaret. The Librarian & the Handicapped Child. LC 80-51349. (Grafton Books on Library & Information Science). 160p. 1981. lib. bdg. 26.75x (ISBN 0-86531-056-4, Pub. by Andre Deutsch). Westview.

Martin, Reed. Educating Handicapped Children: The Legal Mandate. LC 79-63389. 1979. pap. text ed. 8.95 (ISBN 0-87822-196-4). Res Press.

Meisels, S. Special Education & Development. 1979. 17.95 (ISBN 0-8391-1351-X). Univ Park.

Mithaug, Dennis E. How to Teach Prevocational Skills to Severely Handicapped Persons. 1981. 4.00 (ISBN 0-89079-056-6). H & H Ent.

Moore, Mary H. Parent Partnership Training Program, 8 bks. Incl. Bk. 1. Introductory Guide. LC 78-68013. 128p. pap. text ed. 12.90 (ISBN 0-8027-9053-4); Bk. 2. Parent's Manual. LC 78-68014. 192p. pap. text ed. 17.80 (ISBN 0-8027-9054-2); Bk. 3. Basic Communications Skills. LC 78-68015. 288p. pap. text ed. 39.10 (ISBN 0-8027-9055-0); Bk. 4. Developing Social Acceptability. LC 78-62918. 216p. pap. text ed. 29.70 (ISBN 0-8027-9056-9); Bk. 5. Developing Responsible Sexuality. LC 78-62919. 160p. pap. text ed. 19.50 (ISBN 0-8027-9057-7); Bk. 6. Light Housekeeping & In-Home Assistance. LC 78-61387. 272p. pap. text ed. 32.60 (ISBN 0-8027-9058-5); Bk. 7. Heavy Duty Cleaning & Yards & Ground Care. LC 78-62939. 240p. pap. text ed. 32.60 (ISBN 0-8027-9059-3); Bk. 8. Skills of Daily Living. LC 78-62940. 304p. pap. text ed. 29.80 (ISBN 0-8027-9060-7). (For use with K-12 handicapped). 1979. Walker Educ.

Murphy, Albert T. Special Children, Special Parents: Personal Issues with Handicapped Children. 192p. 1980. text ed. 10.95 (ISBN 0-13-826412-0, Spec); 4.95 (ISBN 0-13-826404-X). P-H.

Musselwite, Caroline R. & St. Louis, Karen W. Communication Programming for the Severely Handicapped: Vocal & Non-Vocal Strategies. (Illus.). 338p. 1981. 29.50 (ISBN 0-933014-64-3). College-Hill.

Myklebust, Helmer R., ed. Progress in Learning Disabilities, Vol. 1. LC 67-24545. 282p. 1967. 32.00 (ISBN 0-8089-0340-3). Grune.

Neff, Herbert & Pilch, Judith. Teaching Handicapped Children Easily: A Manual for the Average Classroom Teacher Without Specialized Training. (Illus.). 264p. 1976. 16.50 (ISBN 0-398-03439-7). C C Thomas.

Noland, Robert L., ed. Counseling Parents of the Ill & the Handicapped. (Illus.). 628p. 1979. pap. 12.95 (ISBN 0-398-01404-3). C C Thomas.

Nordoff, Paul & Robbins, Clive. Therapy in Music for Handicapped Children. 1971. text ed. 4.25x (ISBN 0-575-00755-9). Humanities.

Northcott, Winifred H., ed. Curriculum Guide: Hearing-Impaired Children, Birth to Three Years, & Their Parents. LC 76-56634. 1977. pap. text ed. 9.50 (ISBN 0-88200-077-2, D1998). Alexander Graham.

Ochoa, Anna S. & Shuster, Susan K. Social Studies in the Mainstreamed Classroom, K-6. LC 80-12323. 1980. pap. 11.95 (ISBN 0-89994-242-3). Soc Sci Ed.

O'Connor, Katherine H. Removing Roadblocks in Reading. new ed. LC 72-96305. (Illus.). 200p. 1976. text ed. 12.95 (ISBN 0-910812-10-1); pap. text ed. 8.75 (ISBN 0-910812-11-X). Johnny Reads.

Pasanella, Anne L. & Volkmor, Cara B. Coming Back...or Never Leaving: Instructional Programming for Handicapped Students in the Mainstream. 1977. pap. text ed. 13.95 (ISBN 0-675-08460-1); filmstrip & cassette 150.00 (ISBN 0-675-08459-8); 2-5 sets 85.00, 6 or more sets 65.00 (ISBN 0-685-75490-1); instructor's manual 3.95 (ISBN 0-686-67642-4). Merrill.

Paul, James L., et al. Mainstreaming: A Practical Guide. LC 78-26112. 1979. pap. 4.95 (ISBN 0-8052-0617-5). Schocken.

Peter, Laurence J. Prescriptive Teaching. (Illus.). 1965. text ed. 13.95 (ISBN 0-07-049575-0, C); instructor's manual 3.95 (ISBN 0-07-049576-9). McGraw.

Phillips, William R. & Rosenberg, Janet, eds. The Origins of Modern Treatment & the Education of Physically Handicapped Children: An Original Anthology. LC 79-6010. (Physically Handicapped in Society Ser.). 1980. lib. bdg. 35.00x (ISBN 0-405-13102-X). Arno.

Popovich, Dorothy. Effective Educational & Behavioral Programming for Severely & Profoundly Handicapped Students. LC 80-27706. (Illus.). 272p. (Orig.). 1981. pap. text ed. 14.95 (ISBN 0-933716-14-1). P H Brookes.

Preen, Brian S. Schooling for the Mentally Retarded: An Historical Perspective. LC 76-15867. 1977. 14.95x (ISBN 0-312-70175-6). St Martin.

Rarick, L., et al. The Motor Domain & Its Correlates in Educationally Handicapped Children. (Illus.). 208p. 1976. 18.95 (ISBN 0-13-604116-7). P-H.

Raynor, Sherry & Drouillard, Richard. Get a Wiggle on. Alonso, Lou, ed. (Illus.). 1978. pap. 2.25 (ISBN 0-685-29041-7, 245-26174). AAHPERD.

--Move It!!! Alonso, Lou, ed. 1978. pap. 2.25 (ISBN 0-685-29043-3, 245-26176). AAHPERD.

Readings in Pre-School Education for the Handicapped. (Special Education Ser.). 1978. pap. 10.95 (ISBN 0-89568-082-3). Spec Learn Corp.

Reger, Roger. Preschool Programming of Children with Disabilities. (Illus.). 136p. 1974. 13.75 (ISBN 0-398-01564-3). C C Thomas.

Roberts, Joseph & Hawk, Bonnie. Legal Rights Primer: In & Out of the Classroom. 96p. (Orig.). 1980. pap. 5.00 (ISBN 0-87879-241-4). Acad Therapy.

Romanczyk, Raymond G. & Lockshin, Stephanie. How to Create a Curriculum for Autistic & Other Handicapped Children. 1981. 4.00 (ISBN 0-89079-057-4). H & H Ent.

Ross, Mark. Hard of Hearing Children in Regular Schools. (Illus.). 272p. 1982. 18.95 (ISBN 0-13-383802-1). P-H.

Rudman, Jack. Homebound. (Teachers License Examination Ser.: T-27). (Cloth bdg. avail. on request). pap. 10.00 (ISBN 0-8373-8027-8). Natl Learning.

--Teaching Orthopedically Handicapped. (National Teachers Examination Ser.: NT-25). (Cloth bdg. avail. on request). pap. 9.95 (ISBN 0-8373-8435-4). Natl Learning.

Rush, Mary L. The Language of Directions: A Programmed Workbook. LC 77-87703. 1977. pap. text ed. 7.75 (ISBN 0-88200-113-2, C1321). Alexander Graham.

Sabatino, David A., ed. Describing Learner Characteristics of Handicapped Children & Youth. 640p. 1978. 29.50 (ISBN 0-8089-1127-9). Grune.

Satz, Paul & Ross, J. L., eds. The Disabled Learner, Early Detection & Intervention. (Modern Approaches to the Diagnosis & Instruction of Multi-Handicapped Children Ser.: Vol. 8). 298p. 1973. text ed. 34.25 (ISBN 90-237-4107-2, Pub. by Swets Pub Serv Holland). Swets North Am.

Schattner, Regina. Early Childhood Curriculum for Multiply Handicapped Children. (John Day Bk.). 1971. 8.95 (ISBN 0-381-97033-7, A20700). T Y Crowell.

Schleier, Louis M. Problems in the Training of Certain Special-Class Teachers. LC 70-177809. (Columbia University. Teachers College. Contributions to Education: No. 475). Repr. of 1931 ed. 17.50 (ISBN 0-404-55475-X). AMS Pr.

Schmid, Rex E., et al. Contemporary Issues in Special Education. (Special Education Ser.). (Illus.). 1976. text ed. 9.95 (ISBN 0-07-055330-0, C). McGraw.

Schopler, E. Individualized Assessment & Treatment for Autistic & Developmentally Disabled Children. Incl. Vol. I. Psycho-Educational Profile. 1978. 29.50 (ISBN 0-8391-1279-3); Vol. II. Teaching Strategies for Parents & Professionals. 1979. 19.95 (ISBN 0-8391-1521-0). Univ Park.

Segal, S. S. No Child Is Ineducable. 2nd ed. LC 73-21571. 412p. 1974. text ed. 18.75 (ISBN 0-08-017815-4). Pergamon.

Shanker, Uday. Exceptional Children: India. 1977. text ed. 13.50x (ISBN 0-8426-0949-0). Verry.

Shearer, Ann. Handicapped Children in Residential Care: A Study of Policy Failure. 114p. 1980. pap. text ed. 12.25 (ISBN 0-7199-1035-8, Pub. by Bedford England). Renouf.

Silver, Rawley. Developing Cognitive & Creative Skills Through Art. 1978. 17.50 (ISBN 0-8391-1248-3). Univ Park.

Simmons-Martin, Audrey A. Chats with Johnny's Parents. LC 75-15380. 1975. pap. text ed. 4.50 (ISBN 0-88200-069-1, 17640). Alexander Graham.

Snell, Martha E., ed. Systematic Instructional of the Moderately & Severely Handicapped. (Special Education Ser.). 1978. text ed. 19.95 (ISBN 0-675-08390-7). Merrill.

Steenburgen, Fran. Steenburgen Diagnostic-Prescriptive Math Program. 1978. complete program 12.00 (ISBN 0-87879-209-0). Acad Therapy.

Stephens, Thomas M. Directive Teaching of Children with Learning & Behavioral Handicaps. 2nd ed. 272p. 1976. pap. text ed. 9.95 (ISBN 0-675-08590-X). Merrill.

Strauss, Alfred A. & Lehtinen, L. E. Psychopathology & Education of the Brain-Injured Child. Incl. Vol. I. Fundamentals & Treatment. Strauss, Lehtinen. (Illus.). 206p. 1947. 24.00 (ISBN 0-8089-0487-6); Vol. II. Progress in Theory & Clinic. Strauss, Kephart. (Illus.). 277p. 1955. 24.00 (ISBN 0-8089-0488-4). Grune.

Sutton, Dorothy & Whitworth, John R. WISC-R Compilation. 1978. 3-ring binder program 22.50x (ISBN 0-87879-202-3). Acad Therapy.

Tarnopol, Lester. Learning Disabilities: Introduction to Educational & Medical Management. (Illus.). 412p. 1974. 18.75 (ISBN 0-398-01897-9); pap. 13.50 (ISBN 0-398-02894-X). C C Thomas.

Tawney, James, et al. Programmed Environments Curriculum for the Handicapped. (Special Education Ser.). 1979. text ed. 21.95 (ISBN 0-675-08265-X); instructor's manual 3.95 (ISBN 0-686-67290-9). Merrill.

Thomas, Carol H. & Thomas, James L., eds. Meeting the Needs of the Handicapped. 1980. lib. bdg. 18.50x (ISBN 0-912700-54-8). Oryx Pr.

Thomas, M. Angele. Hey, Don't Forget About Me! Education's Investment in the Severely, Profoundly, & Multiply Handicapped. LC 76-41565. 1976. pap. text ed. 7.50x (ISBN 0-86586-041-6). Coun Exc Child.

Thomas, M. Angele, ed. Very Special Children Series: Developing Skills in Severely & Profoundly Handicapped Children. 1977. pap. text ed. 5.00 (ISBN 0-86586-091-2). Coun Exc Child.

Thorum, Arden R., et al. Instructional Materials for the Handicapped: Birth Through Early Childhood. (Illus.). 208p. 1976. pap. 6.95 (ISBN 0-913420-69-7). Olympus Pub Co.

Tomat, Jean H. & Krutzky, Carmel D. Learning Through Music for Special Children & Their Teachers. LC 75-25031. 82p. (Orig.). 1975. pap. 5.00 (ISBN 0-914562-02-9). Merriam-Eddy.

Tuckey, L., et al. Handicapped School-Leavers: Their Further Education Training & Employment. 1973. pap. text ed. 4.50x (ISBN 0-85633-017-5, NFER). Humanities.

Van Witsen, Betty. Teaching Children with Severe Behavior Communication Disorders. LC 77-10483. 1977. pap. text ed. 10.50x (ISBN 0-8077-2465-3). Tchrs Coll.

Wallin, J. Wallace. The Education of Handicapped Children. (Educational Ser.). 1924. Repr. 17.50 (ISBN 0-685-43639-X). Norwood Edns.

Weatherley, Richard A. Reforming Special Education: Policy Implementation from State Level to Street Level. 1979. text ed. 17.50x (ISBN 0-262-23094-1). MIT Pr.

Webb, L. Children with Special Needs in the Infants School. 1967. pap. 1.25 (ISBN 0-531-06003-9, Fontana Pap). Watts.

Wehman, Paul H. Curriculum Design for Severely & Profoundly Handicapped. LC 78-23704. 1979. text ed. 19.95 (ISBN 0-87705-365-0). Human Sci Pr.

Weisgerber, Robert A., ed. Vocational Education: Teaching the Handicapped in Regular Classes. LC 78-68174. 1978. pap. text ed. 8.50 (ISBN 0-86586-093-9). Coun Exc Child.

Wiig, Elisabeth H. & Semel, Eleanor M. Language Assessment & Intervention for the Learning Disabled. (Special Education Ser.). 464p. 1980. text ed. 19.95 (ISBN 0-675-08180-7). Merrill.

HANDICAPPED CHILDREN-REHABILITATION

Batshaw, Mark L. & Perret, Yvonne M. Children with Handicaps: A Medical Primer. (Illus.). 364p. 1981. 18.95 (ISBN 0-933716-16-8). P H Brookes.

Bonner, Cleon R. A Black Principal's Struggle to Survive. 1982. 8.95 (ISBN 0-686-76760-8). Vantage.

Collins, Maurice & Collins, Doreen. Kith & Kids: Self-Help for Families of the Handicapped. (Illus.). 1977. pap. 6.95 (ISBN 0-285-64819-5, Pub. by Souvenir Pr). Intl Schol Bk Serv.

Cross, Lee & Goin, Kenneth, eds. Identifying Handicapped Children. LC 76-52246. (First Chance Ser.). 1977. pap. 7.95 (ISBN 0-8027-7111-4). Walker & Co.

Designing Environments for Handicapped Children. LC 79-89670. 95p. (Orig.). 1979. pap. 8.00 (ISBN 0-88481-211-1). Ed Facilities.

Doyle, Phyllis B., et al. Helping the Severely Handicapped Child: A Guide for Parents & Teachers. LC 78-3300. (John Day Bk. in Special Education). (Illus.). 1979. 10.95 (ISBN 0-381-90063-0). T Y Crowell.

Fredericks, H. D., et al. The Teaching Research Curriculum for Moderately & Severely Handicapped: Gross & Fine Motor. (Illus.). 264p. 1980. pap. 17.75 (ISBN 0-398-04035-4); developmental chart 3.50 (ISBN 0-686-77473-6). C C Thomas.

Hennen, M. L. Identifying Handicapped Children for Child Development Programs. Hooper, Katherine A., ed. (Illus.). 1977. pap. 5.95 (ISBN 0-89334-008-1). Humanics Ltd.

Karren, Keith J. & Hundley, Sherril A. God's Special Children: Helping the Handicapped Achieve. (Illus.). 1977. 8.50 (ISBN 0-88290-086-2). Horizon Utah.

King, Roy D., et al. Patterns of Residential Care: Sociological Studies in Institutions for Handicapped Children. (International Library of Sociology). 1978. Repr. of 1971 ed. 23.50 (ISBN 0-7100-7038-1). Routledge & Kegan.

Kline, Judy. Children Move to Learn: A Guide to Planning Gross Motor Activities. 1977. pap. text ed. 4.95 (ISBN 0-88450-771-8, 2036-B). Communication Skill.

Kok, J. F. W. Structopathic Children, 2 pts. Incl. Pt. 1. Description of Disturbance Type & Strategies. 1126p (ISBN 90-237-4109-9); Pt. 2. Results of Experimental Research of Structuring Group Therapy. 122p (ISBN 90-237-4110-2). (Modern Approaches to the Diagnosis & Instruction of Multi-Handicapped Children Ser.: Vols. 9 & 10). 1972. text ed. 26.00 ea. (Pub. by Swets Pub Serv Holland). Swets North Am.

Murray, Joseph N. Developing Assessment Programs for the Multi-Handicapped Child. (Illus.). 304p. 1980. 17.50 (ISBN 0-398-04052-4); pap. 11.75 (ISBN 0-398-04076-1). C C Thomas.

Pearson, Paul H. & Williams, Carol E., eds. Physical Therapy Services in the Developmental Disabilities. (Illus.). 448p. 1980. 25.50 (ISBN 0-398-02377-8). C C Thomas.

Robertson, Elizabeth. Rehabilitation of Arm Amputees & Limb Deficient Children. (Illus.). 1979. text ed. 25.00 (ISBN 0-02-858950-5). Macmillan.

Safford, Philip L. & Arbitman, Dena C. Developmental Intervention with Young Physically Handicapped Children. (Illus.). 336p. 1975. 28.75 (ISBN 0-398-03326-9). C C Thomas.

Thomas, Carol H. & Thomas, James L., eds. Meeting the Needs of the Handicapped. 1980. lib. bdg. 18.50x (ISBN 0-912700-54-8). Oryx Pr.

Viscardi, Henry, Jr. The Phoenix Child. LC 74-30858. 224p. 1975. 8.95 (ISBN 0-8397-6500-2). Eriksson.

Zang, Barbara, ed. How to Get Help for Kids: A Reference Guide to Services for Handicapped Children. 245p. 1981. 29.95x (ISBN 0-915794-18-7). Neal-Schuman.

HANDICAPPING

see Horse Race Betting

HANDICRAFT

see also Artisans; Arts and Crafts Movement; Basket Making; Beadwork; Bookbinding; Candlemaking; China Painting; Creative Activities and Seatwork; Decoration and Ornament; Design, Decorative; Embroidery; Enamel and Enameling; Folk Art; Furniture; Glass Painting and Staining; Home Workshops; Illumination of Books and Manuscripts; Industrial Arts; Jewelry; Lace and Lace Making; Lacquer and Lacquering; Leather Work; Manual Training; Metal-Work; Modeling; Models and Modelmaking; Mosaics; Mural Painting and Decoration; Needlework; Occupational Therapy; Occupations; Paper Work; Pottery; Pottery Craft; Rugs; Sand Craft; Shellcraft; Stencil Work; Tapestry; Wood-Carving

Abeles, Kim V. Crafts, Cookery & Country Living. (Illus.). 1976. pap. 8.95 (ISBN 0-442-20236-9). Van Nos Reinhold.

Addison, Julia. Arts & Crafts in the Middle Ages. 59.95 (ISBN 0-87968-665-0). Gordon Pr.

Aldrich, Dot & Aldrich, Genevieve. Creating with Cattails, Cones & Pods. LC 68-8521. (Illus.). 1971. 6.95 (ISBN 0-686-76844-2). Hearthside.

Alkema, Chester J. Alkema's Scrap Magic. LC 76-19769. (Illus.). (YA) 1976. 12.95 (ISBN 0-8069-5352-7); PLB 11.69 (ISBN 0-8069-5353-5). Sterling.

--Crafting with Nature's Materials. LC 72-81038. (Little Craft Book Ser.). (Illus.). 48p. (gr. 6 up). 1972. 5.95 (ISBN 0-8069-5214-8); PLB 6.69 (ISBN 0-8069-5215-6). Sterling.

Allen, Dorothy S. Plaster Art: Step by Step. Cole, Tom, ed. LC 80-70317. (Illus.). 172p. (Orig.). 1981 (ISBN 0-686-28861-0). pap. 12.95 (ISBN 0-686-28861-0). Dots Pubns.

Allen, Janet. Exciting Things to Do with Color. LC 76-39906. (gr. 3 up). 1977. 2.95 (ISBN 0-397-31742-5, JBL-J). Har-Row.

Allen, Judy. Exciting Things to Do with Nature Materials. LC 76-39960. (gr. 3 up). 1977. 2.95 (ISBN 0-397-31743-3, JBL-J). Har-Row.

Allison, Linda & Allison, Stella. Rags: Making a Little Something Out of Almost Nothing. 1979. 14.95 (ISBN 0-517-53498-3); pap. 7.95 (ISBN 0-517-53499-1). Crown.

American Craft Council. Clay: A Bibliography. rev. ed. 1979. 4.70 (ISBN 0-88321-011-8). Am Craft.

--Packing-Shipping Crafts. 1977. 2.70 (ISBN 0-88321-031-2). Am Craft.

--Photographing Crafts. 66p. 1974. 6.20 (ISBN 0-88321-006-1). Am Craft.

American Womans Club of Shanghai, ed. Arts & Crafts of Ancient China. 1976. lib. bdg. 59.95 (ISBN 0-87968-666-9). Gordon Pr.

Andersen, Gretchen. Creative Exploration in Crafts. (Illus.). 368p. 1976. 17.00 (ISBN 0-87909-169-X); pap. 9.95 (ISBN 0-87909-168-1). Reston.

Anderson, Enid. A Handbook of Crafts for the Disabled & Their Teachers. (Illus.). 168p. 1981. 22.00 (ISBN 0-7134-2181-9, Pub. by Batsford England). David & Charles.

Andrew, H. E. Laye. The Arco Encyclopedia of Crafts. LC 78-2841. 1978. 19.95 (ISBN 0-668-04630-9, 4630). Arco.

Angier, Bradford. We Like It Wild. (Illus.). 176p. 1973. pap. 2.95 (ISBN 0-02-097200-8, Collier). Macmillan.

--Wilderness Gear You Can Make Yourself. (Illus.). 176p. 1973. pap. 2.95 (ISBN 0-02-011150-9, Collier). Macmillan.

Appel, Ellen. The Fibercraft Sampler. LC 78-7144. 1978. 13.95 (ISBN 0-8019-6643-4); pap. 7.95 (ISBN 0-8019-6644-2). Chilton.

Arnold, Arnold. The Complete Book of Arts & Crafts: An Encyclopedic Sourcebook of Techniques, Tools, Ideas & Instruction. 1977. pap. 4.95 (ISBN 0-452-25147-8, Z5147, Plume). NAL.

--The Crowell Book of Arts & Crafts for Children. LC 75-2333. (Illus.). 356p. (YA) 1975. 10.00 (ISBN 0-690-00567-9). T Y Crowell.

Baer, Barbara. Very New Christmas-Make It Book. LC 68-8523. (Illus.). 1968. 4.95 (ISBN 0-8208-0328-6). Hearthside.

Bailey, Jocelyn. Country Wheelwright. 1978. 19.95 (ISBN 0-7134-1563-0, Pub. by Batsford England). David & Charles.

Baldwin, ed. Makin' Things for Kids. LC 78-73845. 1981. 12.95 (ISBN 0-916752-46-1). Dorison Hse.

Baldwin, Ed & Baldwin, Stevie. Makin' Things for Kids. LC 78-73845. (Illus.). 120p. 1980. 8.95 (ISBN 0-498-00533-X). A S Barnes.

Ball, W. W. Fun with String Figures. LC 76-173664. (gr. k-3). 1971. Repr. of 1920 ed. pap. 1.75 (ISBN 0-486-22809-6). Dover.

Barrie, H. Practical Homecraft Handbook: How to Do It Manual. 15.00 (ISBN 0-87559-108-6). Shalom.

Barss, Peter & Gordon, Joleen. Older Ways: Traditional Nova Scotian Craftsman. 1981. 16.95 (ISBN 0-442-29628-2). Van Nos Reinhold.

Barton, Peggy Ann. Step-by-Step Sugar Artistry. LC 74-75055. 1974. 6.00 (ISBN 0-682-47741-9, Banner). Exposition.

Baxter, William T. Jewelry, Gem Cutting & Metalcraft. 3rd ed. 1950. 10.00 (ISBN 0-07-004149-0, GB). McGraw.

BCC Staff. Hobbies & Crafts, GB-040. 1976. 350.00 (ISBN 0-89336-098-8). BCC.

Beaney, Jan. Buildings, in Picture, Collage & Design. (Illus.). 1980. cancelled (ISBN 0-8120-5168-8). Barron.

Beard, Lina & Beard, Adelia. American Girls Handy Book. LC 69-11086. (Illus.). (gr. 2-8). 1968. Repr. of 1888 ed. 10.00 (ISBN 0-8048-0008-1). C E Tuttle.

Becker, Joyce. Jewish Holiday Crafts. (Illus.). (gr. 1 up). 1977. 9.95 (ISBN 0-88482-757-7, Bonim Bks); pap. 6.95 (ISBN 0-88482-755-0, Bonim Bks). Hebrew Pub.

Becker, Lois. How to Make & Sell Your Arts & Crafts. LC 75-29939. (Illus.). 1975. 8.95 (ISBN 0-8119-0250-1); pap. 4.95 (ISBN 0-88391-056-X). Fell.

Benbow, Mary, et al. Dolls: Traditional & Topical & How to Make Them. LC 75-133316. (Illus.). 1970. 10.00 (ISBN 0-8238-0090-3). Plays.

Benson, Kenneth R. Creative Crafts for Children. 1958. text ed. 9.95 (ISBN 0-13-189340-8). P-H.

Benson, Kenneth R. & Frankson, Carl E. Creative Nature Crafts. (Illus.). 1968. pap. text ed. 9.95 (ISBN 0-13-190470-1). P-H.

Better Homes & Gardens Books Editors. Better Homes & Gardens Treasury of Christmas Crafts & Foods. (Illus.). 384p. 1980. 21.95 (ISBN 0-696-00025-3). Meredith Corp.

--Easy Bazaar Crafts. (Illus.). 96p. 1981. 5.95 (ISBN 0-696-00665-0). Meredith Corp.

Biddle, Maureen. Fifty Craft Projects with Bible Verses & Patterns. LC 80-53862. (Illus.). 64p. (Orig.). 1981. pap. 3.50 (ISBN 0-87239-428-X, 2148). Standard Pub.

Blackburn, Charles. The Pillow Book. LC 77-93302. (Illus.). 1979. 12.95 (ISBN 0-8149-0799-7); pap. 7.95 (ISBN 0-8149-0801-2). Vanguard.

Blandford, Percy W. Country Craft Tools. LC 73-22569. (Illus.). 240p. 1974. 22.00 (ISBN 0-8103-2011-8). Gale.

--Country Craft Tools. LC 75-27176. (Funk & W Bk.). (Illus.). 240p. 1976. pap. 5.95 (ISBN 0-308-10242-8). T Y Crowell.

Blood, Charles L. American Indian Games & Crafts. (Easy-Read Activity Bks.). (Illus.). 32p. (gr. 1-3). 1981. PLB 8.90 (ISBN 0-531-04304-5). Watts.

Bodger, Lorraine & Ephron, Delia. Crafts for All Seasons. LC 79-6410. (Illus.). 112p. 1980. pap. 5.95 (ISBN 0-87663-996-1). Universe.

Bodkin, Cora, et al. Crafts for Your Leisure Years. 1976. 14.95 (ISBN 0-395-24767-5); pap. 7.95 (ISBN 0-395-24837-X). HM.

Bowler, Vivien, ed. Forty-Four String & Nail Art Projects. (Illus.). 96p. 1975. 6.95 (ISBN 0-517-51887-2). Crown.

Bowles, Ella S. Homespun Handicrafts. LC 75-183343. Repr. of 1931 ed. 15.00 (ISBN 0-405-08298-3, Blom Pubns). Arno.

Bowman, Bruce. Toothpick Sculpture & Ice-Cream Stick Art. LC 76-19808. (Illus.). (gr. 5 up). 1976. 7.95 (ISBN 0-8069-5372-1); PLB 7.49 (ISBN 0-8069-5373-X). Sterling.

Brabec, Barbara. Creative Cash: How to Sell Your Crafts, Needlework, Designs & Know-How. 1981. 7.95 (ISBN 0-89586-129-1). H P Bks.

--Creative Cash: How to Sell Your Crafts, Needlework, Designs, & Know-How. LC 79-64792. (Illus.). 1979. pap. 9.95 (ISBN 0-88453-017-5). Barrington.

Brokering, Lois. Constructions. (A Nice Place to Live Ser.). 1978. pap. 1.95 (ISBN 0-570-07755-9, 12-2714). Concordia.

--Odds & Ends. (A Nice Place to Live Ser.). 1978. pap. 2.25 (ISBN 0-570-07754-0, 12-2713). Concordia.

Brooks, William. Fun for Boys. pap. 1.00 (ISBN 0-686-04907-1). Key Bks.

Brotherton, Germaine. Rush & Leafcraft. 1977. 7.95 (ISBN 0-395-25787-5). HM.

Brown, Opal. Fun with Handcraft. 1973. pap. 1.00 (ISBN 0-8341-0250-1, Beacon). Nazarene.

--Fun with Handcraft: Forty-Four Projects for Group or Personal Enjoyment. 64p. 1975. pap. 1.25 (ISBN 0-8010-0628-7). Baker Bk.

Bruce, Marjory. The Book of Craftsmen: The Story of Man's Handiwork Through the Ages. LC 70-185352. (Illus.). 283p. 1974. Repr. of 1937 ed. 22.00 (ISBN 0-8103-3960-9). Gale.

Brunner, Marguerite A. Pass It on: How to Make Your Own Family Keepsakes. LC 78-10294. (Illus.). 1979. 10.95 (ISBN 0-671-18377-X); pap. 5.95 (ISBN 0-671-18376-1). Sovereign Bks.
Burch, Monte. The Outdoorsman's Workshop. 1977. 12.95 (ISBN 0-87691-239-0). Winchester Pr.
Butterworth, Nancy & Broad, Laura. Kits for Kids. (Illus.). 256p. 1980. 15.95 (ISBN 0-312-45701-4); pap. 7.95 (ISBN 0-312-45702-2). St Martin.
The Camera & the Craftsman: A Travelling Exhibition of Photographs & Objects. LC 79-670112. 1979. pap. 5.95 (ISBN 0-903798-14-X, Pub. by Crafts Advis Comm). Intl Schol Bk Serv.
Chamberlain, Marcia & Crockett, Candace. Beyond Weaving. (Illus.). 192p. 1974. 18.95 (ISBN 0-8230-0486-4). Watson-Guptill.
Chatterton, Pauline. Coordinated Crafts for the Home. (Illus.). 1980. 19.95 (ISBN 0-399-90060-8). Marek.
Chinese Arts & Crafts. (Illus.). 1973. 35.00 (ISBN 0-8351-0031-6). China Bks.
Chinese Folk Toys & Ornaments. 1980. pap. 4.95 (ISBN 0-8351-0735-3). China Bks.
Clark, Robert J., ed. The Arts & Crafts Movement in America. LC 72-77734. (Publications of the Art Museum Ser.). (Illus.). 182p. 1972. 35.00 (ISBN 0-691-03883-X); pap. 12.95 (ISBN 0-691-03884-8). Princeton U Pr.
Colorcraft. 1977. text ed. 17.00x (ISBN 0-8277-5118-4). British Bk Ctr.
A Complete Guide to Fancy Paper Flowers. (Handicraft Ser.). (Illus.). 1979. pap. 5.50 (ISBN 0-87040-454-7). Japan Pubns.
Conaway, Judith. Great Indoor Games from Trash & Other Things. LC 77-7383. (Games & Activities Ser.). (Illus.). (gr. k-4). 1977. PLB 10.65 (ISBN 0-8172-0952-2). Raintree Pubs.
--Great Outdoor Games from Trash & Other Things. LC 77-7785. (Games & Activities Ser.). (Illus.). (gr. k-4). 1977. PLB 10.65 (ISBN 0-8172-0950-6). Raintree Pubs.
Constantine, Mildred & Larsen, Jack L. Beyond Craft: The Art Fabric. (Illus.). 304p. 1973. 35.00 (ISBN 0-442-21634-3). Van Nos Reinhold.
Contemporary Arts & Crafts. 1978. 1.50 (ISBN 0-911410-46-5). Applied Arts.
Corbett, Edith O. The Playtime Shoebox. LC 78-24438. (Illus.). 128p. (gr. 3-5). 1979. PLB 7.79 (ISBN 0-671-32927-8). Messner.
Cosas Que Hacer Para Navidad. (Editorial Mundo Hispano). (YA) 1980. 2.75 (ISBN 0-311-26607-X). Casa Bautista.
Country New England Antiques, Crafts & Factory Outlets. 1981. 4.95 (ISBN 0-89102-178-7). B Franklin.
Craft: A Handbook of Classroom Ideas to Motivate the Teaching of Intermediate Art. (Spice Ser.). 1977. 6.50 (ISBN 0-89273-124-9). Educ Serv.
Craftworkers Market. 672p. 1980. 13.00 (ISBN 0-686-62448-3). B Klein Pubns.
Crater, Don R. Cone Crafting. (Illus.). 52p. (Orig.). 1981. pap. 5.95 (ISBN 0-940654-00-8). Tribune Pub.
Crommelin, Jennyfer. Fabric Crafts. LC 79-20121. (Pegasus Books: No. 26). 1970. 10.50x (ISBN 0-234-77275-1). Intl Pubns Serv.
Csiba, E. Leathercraft. (Illus.). 8.50 (ISBN 963-13-4641-2). Newbury Bks Inc.
D'Amato, Alex & D'Amato, Janet. American Indian Craft Inspirations. LC 72-83734. (Illus.). 224p. (YA) 1972. 7.95 (ISBN 0-87131-031-7). M Evans.
--Italian Crafts: Inspirations from Folk Art. LC 76-30523. (Illus.). 160p. 1977. 7.95 (ISBN 0-87131-227-1). M Evans.
D'Amato, Janet & D'Amato, Alex. African Crafts for You to Make. LC 70-75690. (Illus.). 64p. (gr. 4 up). 1969. PLB 7.79 (ISBN 0-671-32130-7). Messner.
Dank, Michael. Scrap Craft: One Hundred & Five Projects. (Illus.). 1969. pap. 3.00 (ISBN 0-486-21999-2). Dover.
Dank, Michael C. Scrap Craft: 105 Projects. (Illus.). 5.50 (ISBN 0-8446-0572-7). Peter Smith.
Davis, Katrina. Toothpick Building Illustrated. (Illus.). 48p. (Orig.). 1980. pap. 3.95 (ISBN 0-937242-04-7). Scandia Pubs.
Decorations from Dried Flowers & Grasses. 1976. pap. 1.50 (ISBN 0-8277-5705-0). British Bk Ctr.
De Cristoforo, R. J. How to Build Your Own Furniture. (Illus.). 176p. pap. 3.50 (ISBN 0-06-463352-7, EH 352, EH). Har-Row.
De Menezes, Patricia. Crafts from the Countryside. LC 81-81454. (Illus.). 176p. 1981. 14.95 (ISBN 0-88332-256-0, 8190). Larousse.
Derendinger, Gertrud. It's Fun Making Things. (Handicraft Ser). (Illus.). 1965. 8.00x (ISBN 0-8002-1601-6). Intl Pubns Serv.
Deutch, Yvonne. Crafts Jamboree. (Illus.). 1977. 19.95 (ISBN 0-442-21351-4). Van Nos Reinhold.
Dhamija, Jasleen. Living Tradition of Iran's Crafts. (Illus.). 81p. 1979. 40.00x (ISBN 0-7069-0728-0, Pub. by Croom Helm Ltd England). Biblio Dist.
Diagram Group. Handtools of Arts & Crafts. (Illus.). 320p. 1981. 19.95 (ISBN 0-312-35860-1). St Martin.
Dick, Stewart. Arts & Crafts of Old Japan. LC 77-94574. 1979. Repr. of 1905 ed. lib. bdg. 20.00 (ISBN 0-89341-237-6). Longwood Pr.
Dickey, Roland. New Mexico Village Arts. LC 71-107101. (Illus.). 264p. 1970. pap. 5.95 (ISBN 0-8263-0168-1). U of NM Pr.
Dittrick, Mark. Hard Crochet. 1979. 12.95 (ISBN 0-8015-3279-5, Hawthorn); pap. 7.95 (ISBN 0-8015-3280-9, Hawthorn). Dutton.
Doan, Eleanor. Two Hundred Sixty-One Handcrafts & Fun for Little Ones. (Illus.). 1953. pap. 3.95 (ISBN 0-310-23721-1). Zondervan.
Donald, Elsie B., ed. The Book of Creative Crafts. (Octopus Book). (Illus.). 1978. 19.95 (ISBN 0-7064-0757-1). Smith Pubs.
Droge & Glander-Bandyk. Woman's Day Book of Calligraphy. 1980. 12.95 (ISBN 0-671-25018-3, 25018). S&S.
Dubane, Janet. Kid Crafts. Friend, Diane, ed. (Illus.). 64p. (Orig.). 1981. pap. 2.00 (ISBN 0-918178-23-1). Simplicity.
DuBane, Janet & Kuman, Alexandra, eds. Americana Crafts. (Illus.). 64p. (Orig.). 1980. pap. 2.00 (ISBN 0-918178-22-3). Simplicity.
--Pillow Ideas. (Illus.). 64p. (Orig.). 1980. pap. 1.75 (ISBN 0-918178-19-3). Simplicity.
Eaton, Allen H. Handicrafts of the Southern Highlands. (Illus.). 10.00 (ISBN 0-8446-4732-2). Peter Smith.
--Immigrant Gifts to American Life: Some Experiments in Appreciation of the Contributions of Our Foreign Born. LC 73-129395. (American Immigration Collection, Ser. 2). (Illus.). 1970. Repr. of 1932 ed. 12.00 (ISBN 0-405-00576-8). Arno.
Eckstein, Artis A. How to Make Treasures from Trash. (Illus.). 1972. 8.95 (ISBN 0-8208-0348-0). Hearthside.
Editorial Staff, ed. Beautiful Crafts Book. LC 76-21846. (Illus.). (YA) 1976. 16.95 (ISBN 0-8069-5366-7); PLB 14.99 (ISBN 0-8069-5367-5). Sterling.
Edlin, Herbert L. Woodland Crafts in Britain: An Account of the Traditional Uses of Trees & Timbers in the British Countryside. new ed. (Illus.). 182p. 1973. 14.95 (ISBN 0-7153-5852-9). David & Charles.
Edwards, Lauton. Industrial Arts Plastics. rev. ed. (gr. 10-12). 1974. 13.12 (ISBN 0-87002-146-X). Bennett IL.
Edwards, Ron. Australian Traditional Bush Crafts. LC 76-48813. (Illus.). 1977. 10.95x (ISBN 0-8052-3654-6); pap. 6.95 (ISBN 0-8052-0560-8). Schocken.
Erdahl, Berlyn. Cyclopedic Treasury of Arts & Crafts Activities Using Scrap Materials. 1977. 13.95 (ISBN 0-13-196600-6, Parker). P-H.
Eshmeyer, R. E. Ask Any Vegetable: Low-Cost Family Crafts Fun. 1981. pap. 4.95 (ISBN 0-13-049742-8). P-H.
Estrin, Michael. Treasury of Hobbies & Crafts. pap. 2.00 (ISBN 0-686-00715-8). Key Bks.
Ethe, Jane. Easy-to-Make Felt Bean Bag Toys. (Illus., Orig.). 1981. pap. 2.50 (ISBN 0-486-23884-9). Dover.
Ethe, Jane & Kirshon, Josephine. Easy & Attractive Gifts You Can Sew: Step-by-Step Instructions for 20 Presents. (Illus.). 1978. pap. 3.50 (ISBN 0-486-23638-2). Dover.
Everist, Burton. The Christian Family Craftbook. LC 78-62064. 1978. pap. 4.95 (ISBN 0-8192-1239-3). Morehouse.
Farlie, Barbara & Abell, Vivian. Flower Craft. LC 78-55664. (Illus.). 1978. 14.95 (ISBN 0-685-53358-1). Bobbs.
Favorite Do-It-Yourself Projects. LC 75-42915. (Family Circle Books). 144p. 1976. 3.98x (ISBN 0-405-06682-1). Arno.
Fell, Dereck. House Plants & Crafts: For Fun & Profit. (Fun & Profit Ser.). (Illus.). 1978. 9.95 (ISBN 0-916302-16-4); pap. 5.50 (ISBN 0-916302-04-0). Bookworm Pub.
Fettner, Ann T. Potpourri. LC 77-5931. (Illus.). 1977. pap. 3.50 (ISBN 0-911104-97-6). Workman Pub.
Fiarotta, Phyllis. Phyllis Fiarotta's Nostalgia Crafts Book. LC 75-8812. (Illus.). 224p. 1974. 10.95 (ISBN 0-911104-43-7); pap. 5.95 (ISBN 0-911104-44-5). Workman Pub.
--Snips & Snails & Walnut Whales. LC 75-9574. (Parents & Children Together). (Illus.). 288p. (ps up). 1975. 9.95 (ISBN 0-911104-75-5); pap. 5.95 (ISBN 0-911104-49-6). Workman Pub.
Fiberarts Magazine, ed. The Fiberarts Design Book: The Best of Contemporary Weaving, Needlework, Wearables, Quilting, Surface Design, Papermaking, Basketry & Felting. LC 80-67315. (Illus.). 176p. (Orig.). 1980. 24.95 (ISBN 0-937274-00-3); pap. 15.95 (ISBN 0-937274-01-1). Lark Comm.
Finlay, Ian. Scottish Crafts. (Illus.). 1977. Repr. of 1948 ed. 29.00x (ISBN 0-7158-1171-1). Charles River Bks.
Fischer, E. & Shah, H. Rural-Craftsmen & Their Work. 20.00 (ISBN 0-88253-403-3). Ind-US Inc.
Fleming, Gerry. Scrap Craft for Youth Groups. (John Day Bk.). (Illus.). 1969. 9.95x (ISBN 0-381-97015-9, A68200). T Y Crowell.
Fobel, Jim & Boleach, Jim. The Big Book of Fabulous, Fun'filled Celebrations & Holiday Crafts. LC 78-4698. (Illus.). 1978. 14.95 (ISBN 0-03-040446-0). HR&W.
Foreman, Gloria. Four Hundred-Twenty Handicrafts Illustrated in Simple Steps. 30th ed. (Illus.). 1964. pap. 3.50 (ISBN 0-915198-02-9). G Foreman.
Foy, Elizabeth & Schurer, John. Construction of Assemblages. new ed. Rahmas, D. Steve, ed. (Handicraft Ser.: No. 7). (Illus.). 32p. (Orig.). (gr. 7-12). 1973. lib. bdg. 2.45 incl. catalog cards (ISBN 0-87157-907-3); pap. 1.25 vinyl laminated covers (ISBN 0-87157-407-1). SamHar Pr.
Frankson, Carl & Benson, Kenneth R. Crafts Activities: Featuring Sixty-Five Holiday Ideas. 1970. 13.95 (ISBN 0-13-188755-6, Parker). P-H.
Frederick, Filis. Design & Sell Toys, Games & Crafts. LC 76-55417. 1977. 12.50 (ISBN 0-8019-6223-4). Chilton.
Freeman, C. & Holdsworth, D. Arts & Crafts of Papua & New Guinea. (Illus.). 7.95 (ISBN 0-912728-02-7). Newbury Bks.
Frost, Marie. Crafts for Preschoolers. (Peter Panda Ser.). 1977. pap. 1.25 (ISBN 0-87239-144-2, 42036). Standard Pub.
Fun with Seeds. pap. 1.50 (ISBN 0-8277-5722-0). British Bk Ctr.
Gaines, Patricia E. Soft: An Irresistible Collection of Pillows, Toys, Bags, Objects to Sit on, Ornaments for the Body, & Various Malleable Oddities... & How to Make Them. 1977. o.p. 14.95 (ISBN 0-688-03215-X); pap. 7.95 (ISBN 0-688-08215-7). Morrow.
Garrison, William E. Selling Your Handcrafts. LC 74-16304. (Creative Crafts Series). 1974. 10.95 (ISBN 0-8019-6042-8); pap. 6.95 (ISBN 0-8019-6043-6). Chilton.
Gault, Elizabeth & Sykes, Susan. Crafts for the Disabled: A New Kind of Craft Book for People with Special Needs. LC 78-20625. (Illus.). 1979. 14.95 (ISBN 0-690-01806-1); pap. 7.95 (ISBN 0-690-01825-8, TYC-T). T Y Crowell.
Gelman, Rita G. & Buxbaum, Susan K. Boats That Float. (Easy-Read Activity Bks.). (Illus.). 32p. (gr. 1-3). 1981. PLB 8.90 (ISBN 0-531-04305-3). Watts.
Genfan, Herb & Taetzsch, Lyn. How to Start Your Own Craft Business. (Illus.). 208p. 1974. 10.95 (ISBN 0-8230-2470-9). Watson-Guptill.
Gick, James E. Ferns from Mother Nature. (Future Crafts Today Ser.). (Illus.). 1977. pap. 2.50 (ISBN 0-918170-25-7, HP-501). Gick.
Gisby, Jane. Making Posh Paws & His Prehistoric Friends. (Illus.). 96p. 1979. 9.50 (ISBN 0-263-06379-8). Transatlantic.
Gjersvik, Maryanne. Green Fun. LC 74-75042. 1975. pap. 2.50 (ISBN 0-85699-104-X). Chatham Pr.
Gleason, Norma. Cryptograms & Spygrams. 128p. (Orig.). 1981. pap. 3.50 (ISBN 0-486-24036-3). Dover.
The Golden Book of Colonial Crafts. (Illus.). 160p. 1975. (Golden Pr); pap. 5.95 (ISBN 0-307-43251-3). Western Pub.
Gottesman, Rita S. Arts & Crafts in New York, Seventeen Twenty-Six to Seventeen Seventy-Six. LC 70-127254. (Architecture & Decorative Art Ser.: Vol. 35). 1970. Repr. of 1938 ed. lib. bdg. 39.50 (ISBN 0-306-71129-X). Da Capo.
Gould, Elaine & Gould, Loren. Arts & Crafts for Physically & Mentally Disabled: The How, What & Why of It. (Illus.). 368p. 1978. 38.00 (ISBN 0-398-03783-3). C C Thomas.
Grater, Michael. Creative Paper Toys & Crafts. Orig. Title: Paper Play. (Illus.). 224p. 1981. pap. price not set (ISBN 0-486-24184-X). Dover.
Griswold, Lester & Griswold, Kathleen. The New Handicraft: Process & Projects. 10th ed. (Illus.). 480p. 1972. 9.95 (ISBN 0-442-22863-5); pap. 5.95 (ISBN 0-442-22862-7). Van Nos Reinhold.
Grogg, Evelyn. Kindergarten Pattern Book. Eberle, Sarah, rev. by. (Illus.). 48p. (Orig.). 1981. pap. 3.95 (ISBN 0-87239-431-X, 2159). Standard Pub.
Guttman, Dena. Teacher's Arts & Crafts Almanac. (Illus.). 1978. 13.95 (ISBN 0-13-887984-2, Parker). P-H.
Hall, Carolyn V. Soft Sculpture. LC 80-67546. (Illus.). 112p. 1981. 14.95 (ISBN 0-87192-129-4). Davis Mass.
Hand Printed Fabrics. 1977. pap. 1.50 (ISBN 0-8277-5732-8). British Bk Ctr.
Handcrafts: A Golden Hands Pattern Book. (Illus.). 1973. 4.95 (ISBN 0-394-48796-6). Random.
Handicraft Series, 10 vols. (Orig.). (gr. 7-12). Set. lib. bdg. 21.95 incl. catalog cards (ISBN 0-686-07234-0); Set. pap. 11.50 vinyl laminated covers (ISBN 0-686-07235-9). SamHar Pr.
Harp. Nature Crafts. (Carstens Hobby Bks.: C-24). 52p. 1972. pap. 2.00 (ISBN 0-911868-24-0). Carstens Pubns.
Harp, Sybil C., ed. Creative Crafts Sampler. (Carstens Hobby Bks.: C-20). (Orig.). 1971. pap. 2.00 (ISBN 0-911868-20-8). Carstens Pubns.
Hawkes, Patricia & Darnell, Jane. Pods & Odd Bodikins. LC 79-50697. (Illus.). 1979. pap. 4.95 (ISBN 0-87106-029-9). Globe Pequot.
Hayes, Phyllis. Food Fun. (Easy-Read Activity Bks.). (Illus.). 32p. (gr. 1-3). 1981. lib. bdg. 8.90 (ISBN 0-531-04308-8). Watts.
Hershoff, Evelyn G. It's Fun to Make Things from Scrap Materials. Orig. Title: Scrap Fun for Everyone. (Illus.). (gr. 4 up). 1944. pap. 3.50 (ISBN 0-486-21251-3). Dover.
Higgingbotham, Bill. Living Country Characters: Step-by-Step Instructions for Eighteen Projects. (Illus., Orig.). 1981. pap. 2.50 (ISBN 0-486-24135-1). Dover.
Hill, Jack. The Complete Practical Book of Country Crafts. LC 79-51091. (Illus.). 1979. 22.50 (ISBN 0-7153-7706-X). David & Charles.
Himel, Susan & Lambert, Elaine. Handmade in Ontario: A Guide to Crafts & Craftsmen. LC 75-43064. 1976. pap. 5.95 (ISBN 0-442-29931-1). Van Nos Reinhold.
Hodgson, Harriet W. I Made It Myself. (Illus., Orig.). 1979. pap. 4.95 (ISBN 0-446-97083-2). Warner Bks.
Holz, Loretta. Make It & Sell It. LC 78-1271. 1978. 7.95 (ISBN 0-684-15563-X, ScribT). Scribner.
Horwitz, Elinor L. Mountain People, Mountain Crafts. LC 73-19665. (Illus.). 144p. 1974. 8.95 (ISBN 0-397-31498-1, JBL-J); pap. 3.95 (ISBN 0-397-31499-X). Har-Row.
Howard, Constance. Textile Crafts. (Illus.). 1978. encore edition 5.95 (ISBN 0-684-16358-6, ScribT). Scribner.
Howlett, Carolyn. Art in Craftmaking: Basic Methods & Materials. 1974. 19.95 (ISBN 0-442-23559-3). Van Nos Reinhold.
Hughes, George B. Living Crafts. facsimile ed. LC 70-156660. (Essay Index Reprints). Repr. of 1954 ed. 25.00 (ISBN 0-8369-2509-2). Arno.
Hulbert, Anne. Victorian Crafts. (Illus.). 1978. 10.95 (ISBN 0-8038-7762-5). Hastings.
Hull, Clinton, ed. Complete Plans, Specifications, Instructions & Bill of Materials for Building. Incl. Ten Foot Chassis Mount. 4.95 (ISBN 0-87593-060-3); Folding Tent Camper for Pickup Truck; Folding Tent Roll-a-Way Camper for Pickup Truck. 4.95 (ISBN 0-87593-072-7); Folding Hard Top Tent Trailer. 4.95 (ISBN 0-87593-034-4); Pickup Camper Cover. 4.95 (ISBN 0-87593-061-1); Cab Over Shell with Removable Furniture. 4.95 (ISBN 0-87593-053-0); Folding Tent Trailer. 4.95 (ISBN 0-87593-055-7); Ten Foot Trailer. 4.95 (ISBN 0-87593-073-5); Twelve Foot Trailer. 4.95 (ISBN 0-87593-074-3); Fifteen Foot Travel Trailer. 4.95 (ISBN 0-87593-056-5); Eighteen Foot Travel Trailer. 4.95 (ISBN 0-87593-057-3); Twenty One-Twenty Four Foot Trailer. 4.95 (ISBN 0-87593-050-6); Eight Foot Slide-in Camper. 4.95 (ISBN 0-87593-058-1); Ten Foot Slide-in Camper. 4.95 (ISBN 0-87593-059-X). (Build-It-Yourself Plans Ser.). Trail-R.
Hunt, B. The Complete How-to Book of Indian craft. Orig. Title: Ben Hunt's Big Indian Craft Book. 1973. pap. 4.95 (ISBN 0-02-011690-X, Collier). Macmillan.
Hutchings, Margaret. Nature's Toyshop. (Illus.). 128p. 1976. 9.75 (ISBN 0-263-05595-7). Transatlantic.
--Teddy Bears & How to Make Them. LC 76-70049. (Illus.). 1978. pap. 5.95 (ISBN 0-486-23487-8). Dover.
Hyde, Christopher S. & Matthews, Richard A. The Complete Book of Rock Tumbling. LC 77-70331. (Creative Crafts Ser.). (Illus.). 1977. 13.95 (ISBN 0-8019-6236-6); pap. 7.95 (ISBN 0-8019-6237-4). Chilton.
Ickis, Marguerite & Esh, Reba S. Book of Arts & Crafts. (Illus.). 1965. pap. 3.00 (ISBN 0-486-21472-9). Dover.
Jaeger, Ellsworth. Nature Crafts. (Illus.). (gr. 9 up). 1950. 8.95 (ISBN 0-02-558770-6). Macmillan.
James, Mary & Shinn, Bev. Clothes Hanger Projects: One Hundred One Fun & Useful Items You Can Make from Wire Clothes Hangers. 1979. pap. 4.95 (ISBN 0-912732-35-0). Duane Shinn.
Janitch, Valerie. Crafts on the Counter. 160p. 1981. 35.00x (ISBN 0-584-10374-3, Pub. by Muller Ltd). State Mutual Bk.

Jeffery, Vera. The Flower Workshop. LC 79-89824. 160p. 1980. 16.95 (ISBN 0-87851-203-9). Hearst Bks.

Jeffs, Angela, ed. Creative Crafts. (Illus.). 1977. 35.00 (ISBN 0-8069-5378-0); lib. bdg. 32.99 (ISBN 0-8069-5379-9). Sterling.

Jenkins, J. Geraint. Exploring Country Crafts. (Countryside Leisure Ser.). (Illus.). 1978. 9.95 (ISBN 0-7158-0469-3). Charles River Bks.

--Traditional Country Craftsmen. (Illus.). 1968. Repr. of 1965 ed. 20.00 (ISBN 0-7100-1610-7). Routledge & Kegan.

--Traditional Country Craftsmen. 2nd ed. (Illus.). 1978. 15.00 (ISBN 0-7100-8726-8). Routledge & Kegan.

Johns-Brian, Ann. Make Your Choice: 80 Things to Make for Yourself & the Home. (Illus.). 127p. 1975. 7.50 (ISBN 0-263-05515-9). Transatlantic.

Johnson, Jerry M. Down Home Ways: Old-Fangled Skills for Making Hundreds of Simple, Useful Things. LC 78-58164. 1978. 12.50 (ISBN 0-8129-0788-4); pap. 6.95 (ISBN 0-8129-6305-9). Times Bks.

Johnson, Mary E. Pillows. LC 77-75687. (Illus.). 1978. 14.95 (ISBN 0-8487-0477-0). Oxmoor Hse.

Johnson, Mary E. & Pearson, Katherine. Naturecrafts: Seasonal Projects from Natural Materials. LC 79-83705. (Illus.). 1980. 17.95 (ISBN 0-8487-0494-0). Oxmoor Hse.

Johnson, Ruth. What to Do till the Garbageman Arrives: A Miser's Craft Manual. (Illus.). 1977. 7.95 (ISBN 0-7715-9951-X). Vanguard.

Johnston, Randolph W. The Book of Country Crafts. (Illus.). 3.95 (ISBN 0-498-06127-2, Encore). A S Barnes.

--The Book of Country Crafts: Large Type Editions Ser. LC 64-19168. (Illus.). 211p. 1975. 9.95 (ISBN 0-498-01601-3). A S Barnes.

Joly, Henri L. & Tomita, Kumasaku. Japanese Art & Handicraft. limited ed. LC 76-24135. (Illus.). 1977. Repr. of 1916 ed. 70.00 (ISBN 0-8048-1205-5). C E Tuttle.

Jones, John L. Crafts from the Countryside. LC 75-10516. (Illus.). 144p. 1975. 5.95 (ISBN 0-7153-7049-9). David & Charles.

Jones, Mary E. Welsh Crafts. 1978. 19.95 (ISBN 0-7134-1087-6, Pub. by Batsford England). David & Charles.

Kafka, Francis J. Batik, Tie Dyeing, Stenciling, Silk Screen, Block Printing. 9.00 (ISBN 0-8446-5707-7). Peter Smith.

Kahn, Deborah, ed. The Handspun Project Book. LC 78-64613. (Illus.). 1980. pap. 4.00 (ISBN 0-910458-13-8). Select Bks.

Kay, Jane G. Crafts for the Very Disabled & Handicapped: For All Ages. (Illus.). 224p. 1977. spiral bdg. 19.75 (ISBN 0-398-03661-6). C C Thomas.

Ketchum, William C., Jr. The Collector's Book of American Crafts. Date not set. 9.95 (ISBN 0-671-24823-5). S&S.

Kicklighter, Clois E. & Baird, Ronald J. Crafts, Illustrated Designs & Techniques. LC 79-23955. (Illus.). 384p. 1980. text ed. 14.64 (ISBN 0-87006-298-0). Goodheart.

King, Bucky & Martin, Jude. Ecclesiastical Crafts. 1978. 16.95 (ISBN 0-442-22966-6). Van Nos Reinhold.

Kirsch, Dietrich & Kirsch-Korn, Jutta. Make Your Own Rugs. 1970. 11.95 (ISBN 0-7134-2461-3, Pub. by Batsford England). David & Charles.

Klamkin, Marian. Hands to Work: Shaker Folk Art & Industries. LC 72-3922. (Illus.). 250p. 1973. 8.95 (ISBN 0-396-06647-X). Dodd.

Kreischer, Lois. String Art: Symmography. (Arts & Crafts Ser). (Illus.). 62p. 1971. 4.95 (ISBN 0-517-50274-7, N04901); pap. 3.95 (ISBN 0-517-54310-9). Crown.

Kudo, Kazuyoshi. Japanese Bamboo Baskets. LC 78-71255. (Form & Function Ser.: Vol. 4). (Illus.). 80p. 1981. pap. 8.95 (ISBN 0-87011-394-1). Kodansha.

Lang, N. Getting Started in Egg Decorating. 1971. pap. 2.95 (ISBN 0-685-01118-6, 80387). Glencoe.

Lapin, L., ed. Craftworker's Market, 1981. 1981. 12.95 (ISBN 0-89879-030-1). Writers Digest.

Lappin, Alvin R. Plastics - Projects & Techniques. (gr. 9 up). 1965. text ed. 13.28 (ISBN 0-87345-159-7). McKnight.

Laskin, Joyce. Arts & Crafts Activities Desk Book. (Illus.). 1972. 10.95 (ISBN 0-13-048769-4, Parker). P-H.

Laury, Jean R. & Aiken, Joyce. The Pantyhose Craft Book: Making Things from Run Pantyhose & Nylons. LC 76-53871. (Illus.). 1977. 12.95 (ISBN 0-8008-6235-X); pap. 5.95 (ISBN 0-8008-6234-1). Taplinger.

Lawrence, Martin, compiled by. The Compleat Craftsman: Yesterday's Handicrafts for Today's Family. LC 77-70473. (Illus.). 1977. pap. 14.95x (ISBN 0-87663-300-9). Universe.

Leed, Gretel & Goodman, L. M., eds. New York Crafts: A Historical Survey Seventeen Hundred to Eighteen Seventy Five. new ed. (Illus.). 54p. 1972. pap. 3.00 (ISBN 0-87282-083-1). Century Hse.

Leisure Crafts Series. 1976. pap. 1.50 ea. (ISBN 0-8277-0472-0). British Bk Ctr.

Lewis, Ralph. Making & Managing an Art & Craft Shop. LC 80-68685. (Making & Managing Ser.). (Illus.). 128p. 1981. 19.95 (ISBN 0-7153-8065-6). David & Charles.

Lidstone, John & Bunch, Clarence. Working Big. (Illus.). 96p. 1975. pap. 7.95 (ISBN 0-442-24795-8). Van Nos Reinhold.

Lindbeck, et al. Basic Crafts. (gr. 7-12). 1979. text ed. 12.40 (ISBN 0-87002-275-X); student guide 3.00 (ISBN 0-87002-296-2). Bennett IL.

Linderman, Earl W. & Linderman, Marlene M. Crafts in the Classroom. (Illus.). 1977. 17.95 (ISBN 0-02-370780-1). Macmillan.

Linse, Barbara B. Arts & Crafts for All Seasons. LC 68-57698. (Illus., Orig.). 1969. pap. 5.50 (ISBN 0-8224-0490-7). Pitman Learning.

Linsley, Leslie. Custom Made. LC 78-69623. (Illus.). 1979. 14.95 (ISBN 0-06-012633-7, HarpT). Har-Row.

Lippman, Deborah & Colin, Paul. Craft Sources: The Ultimate Catalog for Craftspeople. LC 75-12543. (Illus.). 240p. 1975. 12.50 (ISBN 0-87131-183-6); pap. 5.95 (ISBN 0-87131-184-4). M Evans.

Lobley, Priscilla. Flower Making. LC 69-11682. (Illus.). 1969. 7.50 (ISBN 0-8008-2800-3). Taplinger.

Lucie-Smith, Edward. The Story of Craft: The Craftsman's Role in Society. LC 81-65992. (Cornell-Phaidon Bks.). (Illus.). 228p. 1981. 29.95 (ISBN 0-8014-1428-8, Pub. by Phaidon England). Cornell U Pr.

Ludlow, Norman H., Jr., compiled by. The Y-Indian Guides What to Do Book. (Illus.). 1959. pap. 1.50x (ISBN 0-916706-00-1). N H Ludlow.

McCay, Jeanette B. Create with Cones. (Nature Crafts for Leisure Years). (Illus.). 32p. (Orig.). 1972. pap. 1.95 (ISBN 0-8200-0506-1). Great Outdoors.

MacIntosh, Harold C. The Chain Saw Craft Book. (Illus.). 1980. pap. 6.95 (ISBN 0-87108-516-X). Pruett.

MacKay, James A. Rural Crafts in Scotland. (Illus.). 1977. 8.75 (ISBN 0-7091-5460-7). Transatlantic.

McNair, Paul C. The Sportsman's Crafts Book. 1978. 12.95 (ISBN 0-87691-263-3). Winchester Pr.

Maile, Ann. Tie-&-Dye As a Present Day Craft. LC 76-107018. 1970. 6.95 (ISBN 0-8008-7700-4). Taplinger.

Making Cushions. 1977. pap. 1.50 (ISBN 0-8277-5736-0). British Bk Ctr.

Manners, John. Country Crafts Today. LC 74-4355. (Illus.). 208p. 1974. 26.00 (ISBN 0-8103-2013-4). Gale.

--Crafts of the Highlands & Islands. LC 77-91724. 1978. 11.95 (ISBN 0-7153-7485-0). David & Charles.

Margie, Victor. Crafts Philosophy. 1980. pap. 10.00x (ISBN 0-903798-50-6, Pub. by Crafts Council England). Intl Schol Bk Serv.

Marsters, Ted & Marsters, Bridget. The Big Ideas for Little People Book. (Illus., Orig.). 1981. pap. 4.95 (ISBN 0-939562-00-6). Parker Pr.

Martens, Rachel. Modern Patchwork. LC 75-150285. 1971. pap. 3.50 (ISBN 0-385-03024-X). Doubleday.

Mason, Bernard S. The Book of Indian Crafts & Costumes. (Illus.). 1946. 16.95 (ISBN 0-8260-5720-9). Wiley.

--Woodcraft & Camping. (Illus.). 580p. 1974. pap. 4.00 (ISBN 0-486-21951-8). Dover.

Master's Theses: Crafts - a National Directory. LC 76-17433. 153p. 1976. spiral bdg. 8.20 (ISBN 0-88321-019-3). Am Craft.

Mattil, Edward L. Meaning in Crafts. 3rd ed. LC 73-123087. 1971. ref. ed. 17.50 (ISBN 0-13-567156-6). P-H.

Meras, Phyllis. Vacation Crafts. 1978. 11.95 (ISBN 0-395-26309-3); pap. 6.95 (ISBN 0-395-26498-7). HM.

Metcalf, Harlan G. The Pioneer Book of Nature Crafts. Orig. Title: Whittlin, Whistlin & Thingama Jigs. 1977. pap. 4.95 (ISBN 0-8065-0568-0). Citadel Pr.

Mitchell, Peggy. Country Crafts. Pringle, P., ed. LC 70-468023. (Pegasus Bks.: No. 19). (Illus.). 1968. 10.50x (ISBN 0-234-77157-7). Intl Pubns Serv.

Morris, William, et al. Arts & Crafts Essays. LC 76-17783. (Arts & Crafts Movement Ser.: Vol. 34). 1977. Repr. of 1893 ed. lib. bdg. 44.00x (ISBN 0-8240-2483-4). Garland Pub.

--Arts & Crafts Essays. LC 76-17783. (Arts & Crafts Movement Ser.: Vol. 34). 1977. Repr. of 1893 ed. lib. bdg. 44.00x (ISBN 0-8240-2483-4). Garland Pub.

Moseley, Spencer, et al. Crafts Design: An Illustrated Guide. 1967. 25.95x (ISBN 0-534-00243-9). Wadsworth Pub.

Naturecraft. 112p. 1981. 25.00x (ISBN 0-686-72938-2, Pub. by Search & Burns & Oates England). State Mutual Bk.

Naylor, Gillian. Arts & Crafts Movement: A Study of Its Sources, Ideals & Influence on Design Theory. 1971. pap. 10.95 (ISBN 0-262-64018-X). MIT Pr.

Needleman, Carla. The Work of Craft. 160p. 1981. pap. 2.95 (ISBN 0-380-55871-8, Discus). Avon.

Newman, Thelma R. Contemporary African Arts & Crafts: An on-Site Working with Art Forms & Processes. LC 73-91515. (Arts & Crafts Ser.). (Illus.). 320p. 1974 (ISBN 0-517-51466-4). pap. 5.95 (ISBN 0-517-51467-2). Crown.

Nicklaus, Carol. Flying, Gliding, and Whirling: Making Things That Fly. (Easy-Read Activity Bks.). (Illus.). 32p. (gr. 1-3). 1981. lib. bdg. 8.90 (ISBN 0-531-04313-4). Watts.

North Carolina Museum of Art, ed. North Carolina Craftsmen Exhibition, 1971. LC 79-198388. (Illus.). 20p. pap. 0.50x (ISBN 0-88259-059-6). NCMA.

Norton, Margaret. Infant Crafts for School & Home. (Illus.). 1975. 8.50 (ISBN 0-7137-0671-6, Pub by Blandford Pr England). Sterling.

Nueckel, Susan, ed. A Selected Guide to Make-It, Fix-It, Do-It-Yourself Books. LC 72-82609. (Selected Guide Ser.). 300p. 1973. 14.50 (ISBN 0-8303-0125-9); pap. 6.50 (ISBN 0-8303-0123-2). Fleet.

Nylen, Anna-Maja. Swedish Handcraft. (Illus.). 1977. 39.95 (ISBN 0-442-26090-3). Van Nos Reinhold.

Olsheim, Linda, ed. Creative Handicrafts Course. (Illus.). 1976. pap. 5.95 (ISBN 0-517-52631-X). Crown.

Ondori Staff. Cross Stitch in Small Designs. LC 79-66300. (Illus.). 1980. pap. 5.95 (ISBN 0-87040-464-4). Japan Pubns.

Parish, Peggy. Sheet Magic: Games, Toys & Gifts from Old Sheets. (Illus.). (gr. 4-6). 1971. 6.95g (ISBN 0-02-769870-X). Macmillan.

Patten, Marjorie. Arts Workshop of Rural America. LC 37-15722. Repr. of 1937 ed. 16.00 (ISBN 0-404-04907-9). AMS Pr.

Paz, Octavio & World Crafts Council. In Praise of Hands: Contemporary Crafts of the World. LC 73-89960. (Illus.). 224p. 1974. 27.50 (ISBN 0-8212-0558-7, 418501). NYGS.

Petrie, W. M. Arts & Crafts of Ancient Egypt. (Illus.). 158p. 1974. pap. 8.00 (ISBN 0-915018-05-5). Attic Bks.

Pettit, Rosemary. Craft Business in England. 1975. pap. 19.75x (ISBN 0-8464-0297-1). Beekman Pubs.

Pfeiffer, Charles M. The Art of Making Wax Flowers & Fruit As an Interesting & Profitable Career. (Illus.). 117p. 1981. 39.85 (ISBN 0-930582-87-X). Gloucester Art.

Philippoff, Diane M. Fiber Arts: Crochet, Wrapping, Coiling, Weaving. LC 78-7143. 1978. 13.95 (ISBN 0-8019-6659-0); pap. 7.95 (ISBN 0-8019-6660-4). Chilton.

Pin & Thread. 1977. pap. 1.50 (ISBN 0-8277-5735-2). British Bk Ctr.

Pownall, Glen. Fun Crafts: Photograms; Wire Jewelry; Candle-Making, Etc. LC 72-10509. (Creative Leisure Ser.). (Illus.). 71p. 1973. 7.50x (ISBN 0-87749-326-X). Intl Pubns Serv.

Preslan, Kristina. Group Crafts for Teachers & Librarians on Limited Budgets. LC 80-13145. (Illus.). 105p. 1980. pap. 9.00x (ISBN 0-87287-218-1). Libs Unl.

Price, Belinda. Presents & Decorations on a Shoestring. (Illus.). 1972. 7.95 (ISBN 0-571-09762-6). Transatlantic.

Price, Lowi & Wronsky, Marilyn. Concoctions: Recipes for Creeping Crystals, Invisible Ink, Self-Stick Plastic, Grease Paint, Playdough, & Other Inedibles. (Illus.). (gr. 1-5). 1976. 7.95 (ISBN 0-525-28137-1). Dutton.

Prieto, Mariana. Fun Jewelry. Rahmas, D. Steve, ed. (Handicraft Ser.: No. 10). (Illus.). 32p. (Orig.). (gr. 7-12). 1973. lib. bdg. 2.45 incl. catalog cards (ISBN 0-87157-910-3); pap. 1.25 vinyl laminated covers (ISBN 0-87157-410-1). SamHar Pr.

Proper, Churchill. Indian Crafts. LC 70-185672. (Handicraft Ser.: No. 4). (Illus.). 32p. (Orig.). (gr. 7-12). 1971. lib. bdg. 2.45 incl. catalog cards (ISBN 0-87157-904-9); pap. 1.25 vinyl laminated covers (ISBN 0-87157-404-7). SamHar Pr.

Rabineau, Phyllis. Feather Arts: Beauty, Wealth, & Spirit from Five Continents. Williams, Patricia, ed. LC 78-774595. (Illus.). 88p. (Orig.). 1979. pap. 7.95 (ISBN 0-914868-08-X). Field Mus.

Reese, Loretta. Fifty Craft Ideas with Patterns. LC 80-53363. (Illus.). 64p. (Orig.). pap. 3.50 (ISBN 0-87239-427-1, 2144). Standard Pub.

--Fifty-Four Crafts with Easy Patterns. LC 78-62788. (Illus.). 1979. pap. 3.50 (ISBN 0-87239-175-2, 2134). Standard Pub.

Reeves, Robert. Make-It-Yourself Games Book. (Illus.). (gr. 9 up). 1964. 6.95 (ISBN 0-87523-152-7). Emerson.

Regensteiner, Else. Art of Weaving. (Illus.). 1970. 15.95 (ISBN 0-442-11442-7); pap. 8.95 (ISBN 0-442-26872-6). Van Nos Reinhold.

Reinhold. Reinhold Book of Art & Craft Techniques. 1976. 11.95 (ISBN 0-442-26875-0); pap. 7.95 (ISBN 0-442-26876-9). Van Nos Reinhold.

Rendell, Joan. Country Crafts. (Local Search Ser.). (Illus.). (gr. 6-11). 1977. 6.95 (ISBN 0-7100-8604-0). Routledge & Kegan.

Rich, Mildred K. Handcrafts for the Homebound Handicapped. (Illus.). 116p. 1960. photocopy ed. spiral 11.75 (ISBN 0-398-01585-6). C C Thomas.

Riviere, Marie-Claude. Pin Pictures with Wire & Thread. Egan, E. W., tr. from Fr. LC 75-14521. (Little Craft Book Ser.). (Illus.). 48p. 1975. 5.95 (ISBN 0-8069-5340-3); PLB 6.69 (ISBN 0-8069-5341-1). Sterling.

Robbins, Royal. Advanced Rockcraft. (Illus.). 1973. wrappers 3.95 (ISBN 0-910856-56-7). La Siesta.

Robertson, Seonaid M. Creative Crafts in Education. (Illus.). 1967. Repr. of 1952 ed. 20.00 (ISBN 0-7100-2045-7). Routledge & Kegan.

Rodway, Pamela. Gifts Galore: Gifts to Make for Everyone. LC 74-19758. (Leisuretime Ser.). (Illus.). 96p. 1975. bds. 5.95 (ISBN 0-668-03696-6). Arco.

Rogers, Rachelle. Creative Crafts Desk Handbook. 223p. 1981. 13.95 (ISBN 0-686-73451-3, Parker). P-H.

Rome, John, frwd. by. The Blandford Book of Traditional Handicrafts. (Illus.). 169p. 1981. cancelled (ISBN 0-8069-9734-6, Pub. by Blandford Pr England); lib. bdg. 17.99 (ISBN 0-8069-9735-4). Sterling.

Rothenberg, Polly. Decorating Glass. (Illus.). 1976. 6.95 (ISBN 0-517-52391-4). Crown.

Rowen, Dolores & Self, Margaret, eds. Easy to Make Crafts: Children 3-11 Years. (Orig.). 1976. pap. 2.75 (ISBN 0-8307-0416-7, 52-017-05). Regal.

Ruthberg, Helen. Contemporary Miniature Room Settings. 192p. 1980. 14.95 (ISBN 0-8019-6915-8); pap. 8.95 (ISBN 0-8019-6916-6). Chilton.

Saraf, D. N. Crafts of India. (Illus.). 380p. 1981. cancelled (ISBN 0-7069-0735-3, Pub. by Croom Helm Ltd England). Biblio Dist.

Sari. How I Turn Junk into Fun & Profit. 1974. pap. 3.00 (ISBN 0-87980-278-2). Wilshire.

Sasaki, June. Polynesian Crafts. (Illus.). 1978. pap. 4.50 (ISBN 0-912180-33-1). Petroglyph.

Sattler, Helen R. Recipes for Art & Craft Materials. LC 73-4950. (Illus.). 160p. (gr. k up). 1973. PLB 6.96 (ISBN 0-688-51557-6). Lothrop.

Saurman, Judith & Pierce, Judith. Ready-to-Use Marbelized Papers. 1979. pap. 3.50 (ISBN 0-486-23901-2). Dover.

Sayer, Chloe. Crafts of Mexico. LC 76-51863. 1977. 9.95 (ISBN 0-385-13118-6). Doubleday.

Schiffer, Margaret B. Arts & Crafts of Chester County, Pa. (Illus.). 356p. 1981. write for info. (ISBN 0-916838-35-8). Schiffer.

Schiffer, Susan B. Making It in Less Than an Hour. (Illus.). 1976. 8.95 (ISBN 0-916838-03-X). Schiffer.

Schneider, Mary Jane. Contemporary Indian Crafts. LC 75-326254. (Museum Brief: No. 11). (Illus.). 1972. pap. 2.50x (ISBN 0-913134-12-0). Mus Anthro Mo.

Schomas, Rhonda. My Book of Gospel Treasures. (Illus.). 63p. (Orig.). 1980. pap. 2.95 (ISBN 0-87747-839-2). Deseret Bk.

Schuman, Jo M. Art from Many Hands: Multicultural Art Projects for Home & School. (Illus.). 320p. 1981. 19.95 (ISBN 0-13-047217-4, Spec); pap. 10.95 (ISBN 0-13-047209-3). P-H.

Scott, Michael. The Crafts Business Encyclopedia: Marketing, Management, & Money. LC 78-24336. 1979. pap. 3.95 (ISBN 0-15-622725-8, Harv). HarBraceJ.

Scott, Valerie. Bright Ideas. (Illus.). 85p. 1977. 7.50 (ISBN 0-589-00982-6). C E Tuttle.

Seager, Elizabeth, ed. The Countryman Book of Village Trades & Crafts. LC 77-91719. (Countryman Bks.). (Illus.). 1978. 7.50 (ISBN 0-7153-7493-1). David & Charles.

The Selected Handicrafts from the Collections of the Palace Museum. (Illus.). 1974. 35.00 (ISBN 0-8351-0320-X). China Bks.

Sharon, Ruth. Arts & Crafts the Year Round, 2 Vols. (Illus.). 1965. Set. 29.00x (ISBN 0-8381-0213-1). United Syn Bk.

Sharpton, Robert. String Art: Step-by-Step. (Illus.). 224p. 1975. 12.50 (ISBN 0-8019-6131-9); pap. 6.95 (ISBN 0-8019-6132-7). Chilton.

Shepard, Mary & Shepard, Ray. Vegetable Soup Activities. 96p. 1975. text ed. 6.95 (ISBN 0-590-07443-1, Citation); pap. text ed. 2.25 (ISBN 0-590-09603-6). Schol Bk Serv.

Shivers, Jay S. & Calder, Clarence R. Recreational Crafts. (Health, Physical Education, Recreation Ser.). (Illus.). 448p. 1974. 16.50 (ISBN 0-07-056980-0, C). McGraw.

Shoemaker, Kathryn. Creative Christmas: Simple Crafts from Many Lands. 1978. pap. 7.95 (ISBN 0-03-045716-5). Winston Pr.

Sjovaag, Elsa. Rosemaling (Advanced Stage) 4th ed. Ofstad, Ingjerd, tr. from Norwegian. (Illus.). 72p. 1977. pap. 15.00x (ISBN 8-250-10132-4, N522). Vanous.
Slayton, Mariette P. Early American Decorating Techniques: Step-by-Step Directions for Mastering Traditional Crafts. (Illus.). 1979. pap. 8.95 (ISBN 0-02-006950-2, Collier). Macmillan.
Smaridge, Norah. Choosing Your Retirement Hobby. 160p. 1976. 5.95 (ISBN 0-396-07205-4). Dodd.
Smedley, Norman. East Anglian Crafts. 1977. 19.95 (ISBN 0-7134-0637-2, Pub. by Batsford England). David & Charles.
Smith, D. J. Discovering Country Crafts. (Discovering Ser.). (Illus.). 64p. (Orig.). 1977. pap. 2.00 (ISBN 0-913714-35-6). Legacy Bks.
Smith, David & Hann, Scott. Wire Art. LC 78-22149. 1979. 10.95 (ISBN 0-8019-6712-0); pap. 6.95 (ISBN 0-8019-6713-9). Chilton.
Smith, Sharon, ed. Handcraft Centers of New England. LC 80-85481. (Guidebook Ser.). (Illus.). 176p. (Orig.). 1981. pap. 7.95 (ISBN 0-911658-26-2). Yankee Bks.
Snyder, Steven. Can Do Art. (Illus.). 200p. 1981. pap. 29.95 (ISBN 0-9603530-1-1). Southwest Screen Print.
Sommer, Elyse. Career Opportunities in Crafts: The First Complete Guide for Success As a Crafts Professional. 1977. 10.95 (ISBN 0-517-52873-8); pap. 5.95 (ISBN 0-517-52874-6). Crown.
--Rock & Stone Craft. (Arts & Crafts Ser.). (Illus.). 96p. 1973. 5.95 (ISBN 0-517-50353-0). Crown.
Sommer, Elyse & Sommer, Mike. Wearable Crafts. 1976. o. p. 10.95 (ISBN 0-517-52395-7); pap. 5.95 (ISBN 0-517-52518-6). Crown.
Soper, Gill & Stuart, Monica. Come, Hear & See: Creative Activities for Use with Bible Stories. 96p. pap. 5.95 (ISBN 0-571-11099-1, Pub. by Faber & Faber). Merrimack Bk Serv.
Stalberg, Roberta & Nesi, Ruth. China's Crafts: The Story of How They're Made & What They Mean. 1980. pap. 10.95 (ISBN 0-8351-0740-X). China Bks.
Stapleton, Marjorie. Make Things Sailors Made. LC 74-33171. (Illus.). 64p. 1975. 6.95 (ISBN 0-8008-5053-X). Taplinger.
Stein, Sara B. A Family Dollhouse. (Illus.). 1979. 16.95 (ISBN 0-670-30614-2, Studio). Viking Pr.
Stephan, Barbara B. Decorations for Holidays & Celebrations. (Illus.). 1978. 16.95 (ISBN 0-517-51593-8); pap. 8.95 (ISBN 0-517-51594-6). Crown.
Sterling Editors. Christmas Crafts Book. LC 79-65064. (Illus.). 1979. 16.95 (ISBN 0-8069-5396-9); lib. bdg. 13.99 (ISBN 0-8069-5397-7). Sterling.
--Easy Crafts Book. LC 75-14517. (Illus.). 112p. (gr. 4 up). 1975. 9.95 (ISBN 0-8069-5328-4); PLB 9.29 (ISBN 0-8069-5329-2). Sterling.
Stevens, Austin N., ed. Mysterious New England. LC 74-172976. (Illus.). 1979. pap. 9.95 (ISBN 0-911658-86-6). Yankee Bks.
Stevenson, Violet. Flowercraft. (Illus.). 1978. 12.95 (ISBN 0-600-33606-9). A & W Pubs.
Stiles, David R. Fun Projects for Dad & the Kids. LC 63-9634. (Illus., Orig). 1963. pap. 3.95 (ISBN 0-668-01104-1). Arco.
Stockham, Peter. Little Book of Early American Crafts & Trades. (Illus.). 4.50 (ISBN 0-8446-5488-4). Peter Smith.
Stockham, Peter, ed. Little Book of Early American Crafts & Trades. LC 75-46194. (Illus.). 192p. 1976. pap. 2.50 (ISBN 0-486-23336-7). Dover.
Stoltz, Sandra G. Be Your Own Santa Claus. (Illus.). 1978. pap. 3.95 (ISBN 0-686-25032-X). Pathfinder Pubns.
Stoutenburgh, John L., ed. Dictionary of Arts & Crafts. 1956. 6.00 (ISBN 0-8022-1661-7). Philos Lib.
Stranks, Susan. Family Fun: Things to Make, Do & Play. LC 78-71829. (Illus.). 1979. 11.95 (ISBN 0-8120-5319-2). Barron.
Stringer, Leslea & Bowman, Lea. Crafts Handbook for Children's Church: Graded Activities for Ages 3-7. (Teaching Help Ser.). (Orig.). 1981. pap. 6.95 (ISBN 0-8010-8197-1). Baker Bk.
Stuart, Monica & Soper, Gill. The Bazaar Stall. 64p. 1979 (Pub. by Faber & Faber). pap. 5.95 (ISBN 0-571-11289-7). Merrimack Bk Serv.
Temko, Florence. Folk Crafts for World Friendship. new ed. LC 76-4215. (Illus.). (gr. 3 up). 1976. pap. 4.00 (ISBN 0-385-12349-3, 5038). US Comm Unicef.
Terp, Pop-Top & Patton, Kenneth. Pop-Topping. 12.50 (ISBN 0-8019-6226-9); pap. 6.95 (ISBN 0-8019-6227-7). Chilton.
The Thatcher's Craft. 1980. 55.00x (ISBN 0-686-75588-X, Pub. by CoSira Pubns). State Mutual Bk.
Things to Do in a Day. LC 76-2035. 1976. 8.95 (ISBN 0-02-578240-1). Macmillan.
Things to Make from Odds & Ends. pap. 1.50 (ISBN 0-8277-5712-3). British Bk Ctr.
Thomas, Diane. The Advanced Creative Ojo Book. LC 75-44655. 1976. pap. 2.95 (ISBN 0-918126-01-0). Hunter Ariz.
--The Anthology of Creative Ojo Books. LC 79-89670. (Illus.). 1980. pap. 15.95 (ISBN 0-918126-07-X). Hunter Ariz.
--The Handcrafter's Creative Ojo Book. LC 76-28911. 52p. 1976. pap. 2.95 (ISBN 0-918126-03-7). Hunter Ariz.
--The Regional Creative Ojo Book. LC 75-44654. 1976. pap. 2.95 (ISBN 0-918126-02-9). Hunter Ariz.
Thomson, Ruth. Exciting Things to Make with Paper. LC 76-39905. (gr. 3 up). 1977. 2.95 (ISBN 0-397-31741-7). Lippincott.
Titley, Paul. The Roman World. (Let's Make History Ser.). (Orig.). 1980. pap. 3.50 (ISBN 0-263-06336-4). Transatlantic.
To Survey American Crafts: A Planning Study. (National Endowment for the Arts Research Division Reports: No. 2). 1977. pap. 2.50x (ISBN 0-89062-112-8, Pub by Natl Endow Arts). Pub Ctr Cult Res.
Torbet, Laura. The Scribner Encyclopedia of Crafts, 3 vols. (Illus.). 1980. Set. 100.00 (ISBN 0-684-16409-4, ScribT). Scribner.
Trowell, Margaret. Tribal Crafts of Uganda, by M.T. & K.P. Wachsmann. LC 74-15098. (Illus.). Repr. of 1953 ed. 57.50 (ISBN 0-404-12147-0). AMS Pr.
Trupp, Phillip. Art of Craftsmanship. (Illus.). 1976. pap. 3.50 (ISBN 0-87491-043-9). Acropolis.
Tudor, Tasha & Allen, Linda. Tasha Tudor's Old-Fashioned Gifts, Presents & Favors for All Occasions. (Illus.). 1979. 10.95 (ISBN 0-679-20981-6); pap. 7.95 (ISBN 0-679-20984-0). McKay.
Tuthill, Marge. Arts & Crafts for Children: Fifty-Two Projects for Children to Create on Their Own. LC 78-51588. (Illus.). 120p. 1978. pap. 5.95 (ISBN 0-8091-2114-X). Paulist Pr.
Upadhyay, M. N. Economics of Handicraft Industry: India. 1972. 6.50x (ISBN 0-8426-0464-2). Verry.
Van Nostrand Reinhold. New Reinhold Paperback Craft Series. 1975. pap. 190.75 5 copies of 12 titles (ISBN 0-442-28905-7). Van Nos Reinhold.
Van De Smissen, Betty & Goering, Oswald H. A Leader's Guide to Nature-Oriented Activities. 3rd ed. (Illus.). 1977. pap. text ed. 7.95x (ISBN 0-8138-1125-2). Iowa St U Pr.
Van Hoesen, Walter H. Crafts & Craftsmen of New Jersey. LC 72-421. (Illus.). 251p. 1973. 14.50 (ISBN 0-8386-1080-3). Fairleigh Dickinson.
Van Zandt, Eleanor. The Complete Book of Babycrafts. LC 81-67322. (Illus.). 1982. 18.95 (ISBN 0-668-05342-9, 5342). Arco.
Vermeer, Jackie & Frew, Marian L. Making Decorative Planters: From Practically Anything. LC 77-92755. 1978. 9.95 (ISBN 0-8008-5065-3); pap. 4.95 (ISBN 0-8008-5066-1). Taplinger.
Vienna. Create & Celebrate: A Book of Simple Crafts. pap. 2.50 (ISBN 0-8192-1145-1). Morehouse.
Walker, Louisa. Graded Lessons in Macrame, Knotting & Netting. Orig. Title: Varied Occupations in String Work. (Illus.). 254p. 1896. pap. 3.50 (ISBN 0-486-22754-5). Dover.
Walkin, Carol. Using Letters in Art & Craft. 1975. 17.95 (ISBN 0-7134-2867-8, Pub. by Batsford England). David & Charles.
Waltner, Elma & Waltner, Willard. Heritage Hobbycraft. LC 77-19087. 1978. lib. bdg. 7.95 (ISBN 0-8313-0105-8); pap. 7.95 (ISBN 0-686-76952-X). Lantern.
Waltner, Willard & Waltner, Elma. Hobbycraft Around the World. (Illus.). (gr. 6 up). 1966. 6.70 (ISBN 0-8313-0097-3). Lantern.
--New Hobbycraft Book. (Illus.). (gr. 6 up). 1963. 6.70 (ISBN 0-8313-0095-7). Lantern.
--New Look at Old Crafts. LC 70-143700. (Illus.). 142p. (gr. 9 up). 1971. 6.70 (ISBN 0-8313-0098-1). Lantern.
--Year Round Hobbycraft. (Illus.). (gr. 4 up). 6.70 (ISBN 0-8313-0100-7). Lantern.
Wankelman, Willard F. & Wigg, Philip. A Handbook of Arts & Crafts for Elementary & Junior High School Teachers. 4th ed. 274p. 1978. write for info. plastic comb. (ISBN 0-697-03298-1). Wm C Brown.
Wargo, Stephanie. Soft Crafts for All Occasions: A Wrights Idea Book. (Illus.). 144p. 1981. 9.95 (ISBN 0-916752-51-8). Dorison Hse.
Weills, Christopher. The Goodfellow Catalog of Wonderful Things: Traditional & Contemporary Crafts. 1977. pap. 8.95 (ISBN 0-425-03402-X, Windhover). Berkley Pub.
Welch, Nancy & Hoover, Doris. Tassels. LC 78-55562. (Illus.). 1978. pap. 5.00 (ISBN 0-9601602-0-5). Apple Tree Ln.
Wells, Marjorie. Micronesian Handicraft Books of the Trust Territory of the Pacific Islands. 1981. 6.50 (ISBN 0-8062-1781-2). Carlton.
Whitlock, Richard. A Calendar of Country Customs. 1978. 19.95 (ISBN 0-7134-0571-6). David & Charles.
Wigginton, Eliot. Foxfire Books, Bks. 1-3. (Illus.). 1312p. 1975. Set. pap. 20.85 (ISBN 0-385-11253-X, Anch). Doubleday.
--Foxfire Six: Shoemaking, Gourd Banjos & Song-Bows, 100 Toys & Games, Wooden Locks, a Water-Powered Sawmill & Other Affairs of Just Plain Living. LC 79-6541. (Illus.). 512p. 1980. 14.95 (ISBN 0-385-15271-X, Anchor Pr); pap. 7.95 (ISBN 0-385-15272-8). Doubleday.
Wigginton, Eliot, ed. The Foxfire Book: Hog Dressing, Log Cabin Building, Mt. Crafts, Foods Planting by the Signs, Snake Lore, Hunting Tales, Faith Healing, Moonshining & Other Affairs of Plain Living. 320p. 1972. 12.95 (ISBN 0-385-07350-X, Anch); pap. 7.95 (ISBN 0-385-07353-4, Anch). Doubleday.
--Foxfire Five. LC 78-55859. 1979. 14.95 (ISBN 0-385-14307-9, Anchor Pr); pap. 7.95 (ISBN 0-385-14308-7). Doubleday.
--Foxfire Four. LC 76-50803. 1977. 12.95 (ISBN 0-385-12086-9, Anchor Pr); pap. 7.95 (ISBN 0-385-12087-7, Anch). Doubleday.
--Foxfire Three. LC 73-9183. 512p. 1975. 10.00 (ISBN 0-385-02265-4, Anchor Pr); pap. 7.95 (ISBN 0-385-02272-7, Anch). Doubleday.
--Foxfire Two. LC 70-163087. 12.95 (ISBN 0-385-02254-9, Anchor Pr); pap. 7.95 (ISBN 0-385-02267-0, Anch). Doubleday.
Willcox, Don. New Design in Craft Series, Vols. 1-5. Incl. Vol. 1. Ceramics. pap. 6.95 (ISBN 0-442-29471-9); Vol. 2. Stitchery. pap. 6.95 (ISBN 0-442-29473-5); Vol. 3. Weaving. pap. 6.95 (ISBN 0-442-29474-3); Vol. 5. Jewelry (ISBN 0-442-29472-7). 1970. pap. 6.95 ea. Van Nos Reinhold.
Winsor, Maryan T. Arts & Crafts for Special Education. LC 72-83323. 1972. pap. 4.50 (ISBN 0-8224-0500-8). Pitman Learning.
Wirtenberg, Pat Z. All-Around-The-House Art Book. (gr. 5 up). 1968. 6.95 (ISBN 0-395-07209-3). HM.
Wiseman, Ann. Bread Sculpture: The Edible Art. LC 75-26909. (Illus.). 96p. (Orig.). 1975. 3.95 (ISBN 0-912238-74-7); pap. 2.95 (ISBN 0-912238-72-0). One Hund One Prods.
--Making Things, Bk. 2. (Illus.). 176p. 1975. 9.95 (ISBN 0-316-94850-0); pap. 4.95 (ISBN 0-316-94851-9). Little.
Woman's Day Editors. The Woman's Day Book of Weekend Crafts: More Than 100 Quick-to-Finish Projects. LC 77-15496. 1978. 11.95 (ISBN 0-395-26284-4). HM.
Woods, Mary. Turn Your Craft Hobbies into Cash. 2nd ed. 110p. 1981. pap. 12.95 (ISBN 0-939640-01-5). MWS Pubns.
Wroth, William, ed. Hispanic Crafts of the Southwest. 8.00 (ISBN 0-686-15924-1). Taylor Museum.
Yanagi, Soetsu & Leach, Bernard. The Unknown Craftsman: A Japanese Insight into Beauty. LC 72-77798. (Illus.). 231p. 1980. pap. 11.95 (ISBN 0-87011-352-6). Kodansha.

HANDICRAFT–INDEXES

Alt, E. Winifred. Index to Handicrafts, Modelmaking & Workshop Projects, Suppl. 4. LC 36-27324. (The Useful Reference Ser. of Library Bks: Vol. 96). 1969. lib. bdg. 16.00x (ISBN 0-87305-096-7). Faxon.
American Craft Council. Pricing & Promotion: A Guide for Craftspeople. McGuire, Patrick & Moran, Lois, eds. 93p. 1979. 7.20 (ISBN 0-88321-024-X). Am Craft.
Chicorel, Marietta, ed. Chicorel Index to the Crafts: Ceramics, Leather, Wood, Vol. 13B. 1977. 85.00 (ISBN 0-934598-58-4). Am Lib Pub Co.
--Chicorel Index to the Crafts: Education, Recreation, & Therapy, Vol. 13C. 1975. 85.00x (ISBN 0-934598-60-6). Am Lib Pub Co.
--Chicorel Index to the Crafts: Glass, Enamel, Metal, Vol. 13A. 1975. 85.00 (ISBN 0-934598-59-2). Am Lib Pub Co.
--Chicorel Index to the Crafts: Needlework, Crochet to Tie Dye, Vol. 13. LC 74-195924. 500p. 1974. 85.00 (ISBN 0-934598-57-6). Am Lib Pub Co.
Gallivan, Marion F. Fun for Kids: An Index to Children's Craft Books. LC 81-5649. vii, 340p. 1981. 15.00 (ISBN 0-8108-1439-0). Scarecrow.
Glassman, Judith. National Guide to Craft Supplies. 1975. 14.95 (ISBN 0-442-22704-3); pap. 7.95 (ISBN 0-442-22702-7). Van Nos Reinhold.
Lovell, Eleanor C. & Hall, Ruth M. Index to Handicrafts, Modelmaking & Workshop Projects. (The Useful Reference Ser of Library Bks: Vol. 57). 1936. lib. bdg. 14.00x (ISBN 0-87305-057-6). Faxon.
--Index to Handicrafts, Modelmaking & Workshop Projects, Suppl. 1. (The Useful Reference Ser of Library Bks: Vol. 70). 1943. lib. bdg. 14.00x (ISBN 0-87305-070-3). Faxon.
--Index to Handicrafts, Modelmaking & Workshop Projects, Suppl. 2. (The Useful Reference Ser of Library Bks: Vol. 79). 1950. lib. bdg. 14.00x (ISBN 0-87305-079-7). Faxon.
Satterlee, Sarah & Auerbach, Debbie, eds. The Third Goodfellow Catalog of Wonderful Things: A Mail Order Treasury of America's Finest Crafts. (Illus.). 704p. 1981. 32.50 (ISBN 0-936016-00-0); pap. 19.95 (ISBN 0-936016-00-0). Goodfellow.
Shields, Joyce F. Make It: An Index to Projects & Materials. LC 74-17114. 1975. 18.50 (ISBN 0-8108-0772-6). Scarecrow.
Turner, Pearl. Index to Handicrafts, Modelmaking, & Workshop Projects, Fifth Supplement. LC 36-27324. (Useful Reference Ser. of Library Bks: Vol. 102). 1975. lib. bdg. 20.00x (ISBN 0-87305-102-5). Faxon.

HANDICRAFT–JUVENILE LITERATURE

Adams, Adrienne. The Great Valentine's Day Balloon Race. LC 80-19527. (Illus.). 32p. (gr. k-3). 1980. 9.95 (ISBN 0-684-16640-2). Scribner.
Allen, Judy. Exciting Things to Do with Nature Materials. LC 76-39960. (gr. 3 up). 1977. 2.95 (ISBN 0-397-31743-3, JBL-J). Har-Row.
Allison, Linda. The Reasons for Seasons: The Great Cosmic Megagalactic Trip Without Moving from Your Chair. (A Brown Paper School Book). (Illus.). 128p. (gr. 4 up). 1975. 8.95 (ISBN 0-316-03439-8); pap. 5.95 (ISBN 0-316-03440-1). Little.
Arnold, Susan. Eggshells to Objects. LC 79-4328. (Illus.). (gr. 6 up). 1979. 7.95 (ISBN 0-03-043981-7). HR&W.
Arnold, Wesley F. & Cardy, Wayne C. Fun with Next to Nothing: Handicraft Projects for Boys & Girls. LC 62-8039. (Illus.). (gr. 2-6). 1962. PLB 8.89 (ISBN 0-06-020146-0, HarpJ). Har-Row.
Arts & Crafts Discovery Units: Arts & Crafts Discovery Units. Incl. Crayon (ISBN 0-87628-523-X); Mobiles (ISBN 0-87628-524-8); Paper (ISBN 0-87628-525-6); Papier Mache (ISBN 0-87628-526-4); Printing (ISBN 0-87628-527-2); Puppets (ISBN 0-87628-528-0); Tempera (ISBN 0-87628-529-9); Tissue (ISBN 0-87628-530-2); Watercolor (ISBN 0-87628-531-0); Weaving (ISBN 0-87628-532-9). (ps-2). 1974. 5.95x ea. Ctr Appl Res.
Barkin, Carol & James, Elizabeth. Slapdash Decorating. LC 77-22241. (Illus.). (gr. 5 up). 1977. 7.25 (ISBN 0-688-41813-9); PLB 6.96 (ISBN 0-688-51813-3). Lothrop.
Barwell, Eve. Make Your Pet a Present. LC 76-30663. (Lothrop Craft Ser). (Illus.). (gr. 3 up). 1977. 7.75 (ISBN 0-688-41788-4); PLB 7.44 (ISBN 0-688-51788-9). Lothrop.
Beegle, Shirley, ed. Creative Craft Ideas for All Ages. (Illus., Orig.). (gr. k up). 1966. pap. 5.50 (ISBN 0-87239-321-6, 2795). Standard Pub.
Belen, Hermogenes F. Philippine Creative Handicrafts. (Illus.). (gr. k-4). 1977. 5.75 (ISBN 0-686-09536-7). Cellar.
Bennett, Marian. Preschool Pattern Book. (Illus., Orig.). (gr. k). 1973. pap. 3.95 (ISBN 0-87239-339-9, 2145). Standard Pub.
Boden, Arthur & Woodside, John. Boden's Beasts. (Illus.). (gr. 1-5). 1964. 4.50 (ISBN 0-8392-3045-1). Astor-Honor.
Bowman, Bruce. Toothpick Sculpture & Ice-Cream Stick Art. LC 76-19808. (Illus.). (gr. 5 up). 1976. 7.95 (ISBN 0-8069-5372-1); PLB 7.49 (ISBN 0-8069-5373-X). Sterling.
Boy Scouts Of America. Crafts for Cub Scouts. (Illus.). 80p. 1963. pap. 1.25x (ISBN 0-8395-3843-X, 3843). BSA.
Braga, Meg. Easter Make & Tell: Family Fun & Crafts for Easter Time. (Illus.). 32p. (gr. 1-6). 1980. wkbk. 1.95 (ISBN 0-87788-210-X). Shaw Pubs.
Byrnes, Patricia & Krenz, Nancy. Southwestern Arts & Crafts Projects. Smith, James C., Jr., ed. LC 77-18988. (Illus.). (gr. 1-8). 1979. pap. 12.95 (ISBN 0-913270-62-8). Sunstone Pr.
Caney, Steven. Steven Caney's Playbook. LC 75-9816. (Parents & Children Together Ser). (Illus.). 240p. (ps-7). 1975. 9.95 (ISBN 0-911104-37-2); pap. 5.95 (ISBN 0-911104-38-0). Workman Pub.
Carlbom, Hans. Horseshoe-Nail Crafting. LC 73-83450. (Little Craft Book Ser.). 48p. (gr. 7 up). 1973. 5.95 (ISBN 0-8069-5280-6); PLB 6.69 (ISBN 0-8069-5281-4). Sterling.
Carlson, Bernice W. Picture That! LC 76-25813. (Illus.). (gr. k-3). 1977. 7.95 (ISBN 0-687-31419-4). Abingdon.
Choate, Judith & Green, Jane. Scrapcraft: 50 Easy-to-Make Handicrafts Projects. LC 72-89814. 64p. (gr. 4-7). 1973. 4.95 (ISBN 0-385-09419-1). Doubleday.
Christian, Mary B. The Goosehill Gang Craft Book. (Goosehill Gang Ser.: No. 3). (Illus.). (gr. 1-4). 1978. pap. 0.95 (ISBN 0-570-07362-6, 39-1054). Concordia.
Cobb, Vicki. Arts & Crafts You Can Eat. LC 73-13864. (Illus.). 128p. (gr. 6 up). 1974. 8.95 (ISBN 0-397-31491-4, JBL-J); pap. 2.75 (ISBN 0-397-31492-2). Har-Row.
Cogniat, Maurice. Wild West Toys You Can Make. LC 76-609. (Easy Craft Ser.). (Illus.). (gr. 4 up). 1976. 5.95 (ISBN 0-8069-5414-0); PLB 5.89 (ISBN 0-8069-5415-9). Sterling.

Colby, C. B. Early American Crafts: Tools, Shops & Products. (Illus.). (gr. 4-7). 1967. PLB 5.29 (ISBN 0-698-30066-1). Coward.
Cole, Ann, et al. A Pumpkin in a Pear Tree - Creative Ideas for Twelve Months of Holiday Fun. (Illus.). 112p. (gr. 1 up). 1976. 8.95g (ISBN 0-316-15110-6); pap. 5.95 (ISBN 0-316-15111-4). Little.
Comins, Jeremy. Chinese & Japanese Crafts & Their Cultural Backgrounds. LC 77-28835. (Lothrop Craft Ser.). (Illus.). (gr. 5 up). 1978. 7.95 (ISBN 0-688-41844-9); PLB 7.63 (ISBN 0-688-51844-3). Lothrop.
--Latin American Crafts. LC 73-17704. (Illus.). 128p. (gr. 5 up). 1974. PLB 6.96 (ISBN 0-688-51582-7). Lothrop.
Conaway, Judith. City Crafts from Secret Cities. LC 77-88640. (Illus.). (gr. 3-7). 1978. lib. bdg. 8.97 (ISBN 0-695-40874-7). Follett.
Condit, Martha O. Something to Make, Something to Think About. LC 75-15464. (Illus.). 40p. (gr. k-3). 1976. 5.95g (ISBN 0-590-07442-3, Four Winds). Schol Bk Serv.
Cooper, Michael. Things to Make & Do for George Washington's Birthday. (Things to Make & Do Ser.). (Illus.). (gr. k-3). 1979. PLB 8.40 s&l (ISBN 0-531-02294-3). Watts.
Cutler, Katherine N. From Petals to Pinecones: A Nature Art & Craft Book. LC 70-81753. (Illus.). (gr. 4 up). 1969. PLB 7.92 (ISBN 0-688-51594-0). Lothrop.
Cutler, Katherine N. & Bogle, Kate. Crafts for Christmas. LC 74-8750. (Illus.). 128p. (gr. 3 up). 1974. PLB 7.44 (ISBN 0-688-51663-7). Lothrop.
Cutler, Katherine N. & Bogle, Kate C. Crafts for Christmas. (Illus.). 96p. (gr. 3 up). 1975. pap. 1.95 (ISBN 0-688-46663-X). Lothrop.
Cuyler, Margery. All Around Pumpkin Book. LC 79-4820. (Illus.). (gr. 3-7). 1980. 8.95 (ISBN 0-03-047101-X); pap. 3.95 (ISBN 0-03-568188-8). HR&W.
Dahl, Anna. Handiwork Patterns for the Whole Year. (Illus.). 48p. (Orig.). (gr. 3 up). 1951. pap. 3.95 (ISBN 0-87239-329-1, 2146). Standard Pub.
D'Amato, Jane & D'Amato, Alex. Algonquian & Iroquois Crafts for You to Make. LC 79-15487. (Illus.). 96p. (gr. 3 up). 1979. PLB 8.29 (ISBN 0-671-32979-0). Messner.
D'Amato, Janet & D'Amato, Alex. African Crafts for You to Make. LC 70-75690. (Illus.). 64p. (gr. 4 up). 1969. PLB 7.79 (ISBN 0-671-32130-7). Messner.
--Colonial Crafts for You to Make. LC 74-19005. (Illus.). 64p. (gr. 4-6). 1975. 8.29 (ISBN 0-671-32706-2). Messner.
--Handicrafts for Holidays. (Illus.). (gr. 1-4). 1967. PLB 7.21 (ISBN 0-87460-086-3). Lion Bks.
--Indian Crafts. (Illus.). (gr. 1-4). PLB 7.95 (ISBN 0-87460-088-X). Lion Bks.
Deacon, Eileen. Making Jewelry. LC 77-7942. (Beginning Crafts Ser.). (Illus.). (gr. k-3). 1977. PLB 9.30 (ISBN 0-8393-0116-2). Raintree Child.
Dean, Audrey V. Make a Prehistoric Monster. LC 77-76580. (Illus.). (gr. 2-7). 1977. 7.50 (ISBN 0-8008-5049-1). Taplinger.
De Paola. Things to Make & Do for Valentine's Day. (gr. k-3). 1978. pap. 1.50 (ISBN 0-590-11821-8, Schol Pap). Schol Bk Serv.
Doan, Eleanor. Creative Handcrafts for Juniors. LC 72-93601. 118p. (Orig.). (gr. 4-6). 1973. pap. text ed. 1.65 (ISBN 0-8307-0210-5, 5008700). Regal.
Doan, Robert L. Arts & Crafts Achievement Activities. (Early Childhood Achievement Units Ser.). 1979. pap. 5.95x (ISBN 0-87628-282-6). Ctr Appl Res.
Dobrin, Arnold. Make a Witch, Make a Goblin: A Book of Halloween Crafts. LC 77-177. (Illus.). 128p. (gr. 2-5). 1977. 7.95 (ISBN 0-590-07450-4, Four Winds). Schol Bk Serv.
Duda, Margaret B. Useful Gifts Children Can Make. LC 81-38404. (Illus.). 112p. (Orig.). 1981. pap. 8.95 (ISBN 0-916392-66-X). Oak Tree Pubns.
Eckstein, Joan & Gleit, Joyce. Fun with Making Things. (gr. 3-7). 1979. pap. 1.50 (ISBN 0-380-43315-X, 43315, Camelot). Avon.
Eisner, Vivien & Shisler, William. Crafting with Newspapers. LC 76-19771. (Little Craft Bk.). (gr. 5up). 1976. 5.95 (ISBN 0-8069-5368-3); PLB 6.69 (ISBN 0-8069-5369-1). Sterling.
Eisner, Vivienne & Weiss, Adelle. A Boat, a Bat & a Beanie: Things to Make from Newspaper. LC 77-493. (Illus.). (gr. 1-5). 1977. 7.75 (ISBN 0-688-41789-2); PLB 7.44 (ISBN 0-688-51789-7). Lothrop.
Elliott, Ann. Eyes to See God. (Illus.). 1977. pap. 5.95 (ISBN 0-8192-1225-3). Morehouse.
Fiarotta, Phyllis. Sticks & Stones & Ice Cream Cones. LC 74-160843. (Parents & Children Together Ser.). (Illus.). 316p. (ps up). 1973. 9.95 (ISBN 0-911104-29-1); pap. 5.95 (ISBN 0-911104-30-5). Workman Pub.
Fiarotta, Phyllis & Fiarotta, Noel. Be What You Want to Be. LC 76-52860. (Parents & Children Together Ser.). (Illus.). (gr. k-7). 1977. 10.95 (ISBN 0-911104-94-1); pap. 5.95 (ISBN 0-911104-95-X). Workman Pub.
--Pin It, Tack It, Hang It. LC 75-20211. (Parents & Children Together). (Illus.). 160p. (gr. 1 up). 1975. 9.95 (ISBN 0-911104-61-5); pap. 4.95 (ISBN 0-911104-63-1). Workman Pub.
--The You & Me Heritage Tree. LC 75-44133. (Parents & Children Together Ser.). (Illus.). 288p. (gr. 1-5). 1976. 10.95 (ISBN 0-911104-74-7); pap. 4.95 (ISBN 0-911104-73-9). Workman Pub.
Fiedler, Mildred. Prarie Crafts. (Illus.). 96p. 1981. PLB 8.95 (ISBN 0-87460-380-3). Lion Bks.
Filstrup, Chris & Filstrup, Janie. Beadazzled. LC 81-3426. (Illus.). 192p. (gr. 7 up). 1981. price not set (ISBN 0-7232-6204-7). Warne.
Fisher, Timothy. Hammocks, Hassocks & Hideaways. (Illus.). 1980. 7.95g (ISBN 0-201-02936-7, 2936); pap. 4.95 (ISBN 0-201-02938-3, 2938). A-W.
--Huts, Hovels & Houses. LC 76-57168. (Illus.). (gr. 6-12). 1977. PLB 6.95 (ISBN 0-201-02464-0, A-W Childrens). A-W.
Fletcher, Helen. Carton Crafts. (Illus.). 64p. (gr. 3-7). 1981. PLB 7.95 (ISBN 0-87460-268-8). Lion Bks.
Foreman, Gloria. Busy Hands. (Illus.). (gr. 3-8). 1959. pap. 1.00 (ISBN 0-915198-01-0). G Foreman.
Forte, Imogene, et al. Pumpkins, Pinwheels & Peppermint Packages: Teacher's Edition. LC 74-18906. (gr. 2-6). 1974. 12.95 (ISBN 0-913916-10-2, IP 10-2). Incentive Pubns.
Frost, Marie. Fifty-Two Nursery Patterns. (Illus.). 48p. (Orig.). (ps-k). 1979. pap. 3.95 (ISBN 0-87239-341-0, 42046). Standard Pub.
Gallivan, Marion F. Fun for Kids: An Index to Children's Craft Books. LC 81-5649. vii, 340p. 1981. 15.00 (ISBN 0-8108-1439-0). Scarecrow.
Gates, Frieda. Monsters & Ghouls: Costumes & Lore. LC 79-5385. (Illus.). 48p. (gr. 4-9). 1980. PLB 8.85 (ISBN 0-8027-6379-0). Walker & Co.
Gelman, Rita G. & Buxbaum, Susan K. Boats That Float. (Easy-Read Activity Bks.). (Illus.). 32p. (gr. 1-3). 1981. PLB 8.90 (ISBN 0-531-04305-3). Watts.
Gerson, Trina. Holiday Crafts. 80p. (ps-7). 1981. pap. text ed. write for info. (ISBN 0-9605878-1-0). Anirt Pr.
Gibbons, Gail. Things to Make & Do for Columbus Day. (Things to Make & Do Ser.). (Illus.). (gr. 1-3). 1977. PLB 8.40 s&l (ISBN 0-531-01274-3). Watts.
--Things to Make & Do for Your Birthday. (Things to Make & Do Ser.). (Illus.). (gr. 1-3). 1978. PLB 8.40 s&l (ISBN 0-531-01462-2). Watts.
Gilbert, Dorothy. Can I Make One: A Craft Book for the Pre-School Child. (Illus.). (ps). 1970. 11.95 (ISBN 0-571-09303-5). Transatlantic.
Gilbreath, Alice. Fun & Easy Things to Make. (Illus.). (gr. 5-8). 1974. pap. 1.50 (ISBN 0-590-04837-6, Schol Pap). Schol Bk Serv.
--More Fun & Easy Things to Make. (gr. k-3). 1977. pap. 1.50 (ISBN 0-590-10408-X, Schol Pap). Schol Bk Serv.
--Slab, Coil, & Pinch: A Beginners Pottery Book. (Illus.). (gr. 3-7). 1977. 6.75 (ISBN 0-688-22105-X); PLB 6.48 (ISBN 0-688-32105-4). Morrow.
--Spouts, Lids, Cans, Fun with Familiar Metal Objects. (Illus.). 48p. (gr. 3-7). 1973. PLB 6.00 (ISBN 0-688-30064-2). Morrow.
Ginsberg, Ruth. Crafts for the Jewish Child. (Illus.). (gr. 2-7). 1976. 5.00 (ISBN 0-914080-61-X). Shulsinger Sales.
Glovach, Linda. The Little Witch's Thanksgiving Book. LC 76-9847. (Illus.). 48p. (gr. 1-4). 1976. PLB 5.95 (ISBN 0-13-537993-8). P-H.
Greene, Peggy R. Things to Make. LC 77-91652. (Picturebacks Ser.). (Illus.). 32p. (ps-3). 1981. PLB 4.99 (ISBN 0-394-93834-8); pap. 1.25 (ISBN 0-394-83834-3). Random.
Guth, Phyllis. Crafts for Kids. LC 75-4287. 182p. (gr. 4-8). 1975. pap. 6.95 (ISBN 0-8306-4766-X, 766). TAB Bks.
Haddad, Helen R. Potato Printing. LC 80-2458. (Illus.). 64p. (gr. 3-6). 1981. 8.95 (ISBN 0-690-04088-1, TYC-J); PLB 8.89 (ISBN 0-690-04089-X). Har-Row.
Haley, Gail E. Costumes for Plays & Playing. (Illus.). (gr. 3 up). 1978. 7.95 (ISBN 0-416-30581-4). Methuen Inc.
Harding, Mary & Coughtrie, Margo, eds. Make It Yourself: The Complete Step by Step Library of Needlework & Crafts, 20 vols. rev. ed. LC 77-23734. (Illus.). 1977. Repr. of 1975 ed. Set. lib. bdg. 199.50 set (ISBN 0-8393-6012-6). Purnell Ref Bks.
Hart, Tony. Fun with Historial Projects. new ed. (Learning with Fun Ser). (Illus.). 64p. (gr. 5 up). 1976. 12.50x (ISBN 0-7182-0074-8, SpS). Sportshelf.
Hautzig, Esther. Let's Make More Presents: Easy & Inexpensive Gifts for Every Occasion. LC 72-92445. (How-to Bk.). (Illus.). 160p. (gr. 5 up). 1973. 8.95 (ISBN 0-02-743490-7). Macmillan.
--Let's Make Presents: One Hundred Gifts for Less Than One Dollar. LC 61-14532. (Illus.). (gr. 4 up). 1962. 8.95 (ISBN 0-690-48951-X, TYC-J). Har-Row.
--Life with Working Parents: Practical Hints for Everyday Situations. LC 76-15223. (Illus.). (gr. 5 up). 1976. 8.25 (ISBN 0-02-743500-8, 74350). Macmillan.
Helfman, Harry. Making Pictures Without Paint. LC 72-4234. (Illus.). 48p. (gr. 3-7). 1973. PLB 6.00 (ISBN 0-688-30068-5). Morrow.
Hetzer, Linda. Creative Crafts. LC 77-28864. (Illustrated Crafts for Beginners). (Illus.). (gr. 3-7). Date not set. PLB cancelled (ISBN 0-8172-1194-2). Raintree Pubs.
--Decorative Crafts. LC 77-28702. (Illustrated Crafts for Beginners). (Illus.). (gr. 3-7). 1978. PLB 11.15 (ISBN 0-8172-1178-0). Raintree Pubs.
--Designer Crafts. LC 77-28784. (Illustrated Crafts for Beginners). (Illus.). (gr. 3-7). PLB 11.15 (ISBN 0-8172-1188-8). Raintree Pubs.
--Hobby Crafts. LC 77-28949. (Illustrated Crafts for Beginners). (Illus.). (gr. 3-7). 1978. PLB 11.15 (ISBN 0-8172-1180-2). Raintree Pubs.
--Paper Crafts. LC 77-28796. (Illustrated Crafts for Beginners). (Illus.). (gr. 3-7). 1978. PLB 11.15 (ISBN 0-8172-1186-1). Raintree Pubs.
--Playtime Crafts. LC 77-28790. (Illustrated Crafts for Beginners Ser.). (Illus.). (gr. 3-7). 1978. PLB 11.15 (ISBN 0-8172-1182-9). Raintree Pubs.
--Traditional Crafts. LC 77-28740, (Illustrated Crafts for Beginners). (Illus.). (gr. 3-7). 1978. PLB 11.15 (ISBN 0-8172-1190-X). Raintree Pubs.
--Workshop Crafts. LC 77-28707. (Illustrated Crafts for Beginners). (Illus.). (gr. 3-7). 1978. PLB 11.15 (ISBN 0-8172-1184-5). Raintree Pubs.
--Yarn Crafts. LC 77-29052. (Illustrated Crafts for Beginners). (Illus.). (gr. 3-7). 1978. PLB 11.15 (ISBN 0-8172-1176-4). Raintree Pubs.
Highlights Editors. Creative Craft Activities. LC 67-28201. (Jumbo Handbooks Ser.). (gr. 1-6). 1967. text ed. 4.95 (ISBN 0-87534-554-9). Highlights.
--One Hundred Thirty-Two Gift Crafts Kids Can Make. (Handbooks Ser.). (Illus.). 48p. (Orig.). (gr. 1-6). 1981. pap. 2.95 (ISBN 0-87534-308-2). Highlights.
--One Hundred Twenty-Eight Crafts Kids Can Make. (Handbooks Ser.). (Illus.). 48p. (Orig.). (gr. 1-6). 1981. pap. 2.95 (ISBN 0-87534-309-0). Highlights.
--One Hundred Twenty-Seven Anytime Crafts Kids Can Make. (Handbooks Ser.). (Illus.). 48p. (Orig.). (gr. 1-6). 1981. pap. 2.95 (ISBN 0-87534-307-4). Highlights.
--One Hundred Twenty Twenty-Five Crafts Kids Can Make from Throw-Always. (Handbooks Ser.). (Illus.). 48p. (Orig.). (gr. 1-6). 1981. pap. 2.95 (ISBN 0-87534-306-6). Highlights.
--Party Ideas with Crafts Kids Can Make. (Handbooks Ser.). (Illus.). 48p. (Orig.). (gr. 1-6). 1981. pap. 2.95 (ISBN 0-87534-310-4). Highlights.
Holz, Loretta. The Christmas Spider: A Puppet Play from Poland & Other Traditional Games, Crafts & Activities. (gr. 3-7). 5.95 (ISBN 0-399-20754-6); lib. bdg. 5.99g (ISBN 0-399-61164-9). Philomel.
Holzenthaler, Jean. My Hands Can. (ps-k). 1978. 7.95 (ISBN 0-525-35490-5). Dutton.
Horn, George F. Crafts for Today's Schools. LC 79-181784. (Illus.). 144p. 1972. 11.95 (ISBN 0-87192-045-X). Davis Mass.
Horner, Deborah R. The Great Disguise Book: A Book of Disguises to Cut Out & Wear. (Illus.). 12p. (gr. 1-4). 1980. 6.95 (ISBN 0-684-16629-1). Scribner.
Hutchings, Margaret. Wool-Bag Book. (Make & Play Ser.). (Illus.). 48p. (gr. 5-6). 1976. pap. 1.50 (ISBN 0-263-05911-1). Transatlantic.
Janvier, Jeannine. Fantastic Fish You Can Make. LC 76-19819. (Illus.). (gr. 4 up). 1976. 5.95 (ISBN 0-8069-5406-X); PLB 5.89 (ISBN 0-8069-5407-8). Sterling.
Johnson, Ruth. What to Do till the Garbageman Arrives: A Miser's Craft Manual. (Illus.). 1977. 7.95 (ISBN 0-7715-9951-X). Vanguard.
Jordan, Nina R. Holiday Handicraft. LC 38-27801. (Illus.). 245p. (gr. 4-6). 6.95 (ISBN 0-15-234868-9, HJ). HarBraceJ.
Kerina, Jane. African Crafts. LC 69-18916. (Illus.). (gr. 2-6). 1970. PLB 7.21 (ISBN 0-87460-084-7). Lion Bks.
Kinney, Jean & Kinney, Cle. How to Make Nineteen Kinds of American Folk Art from Maska to TV Commercials. LC 73-91014. (Illus.). 128p. (gr. 5 up). 1974. 7.95 (ISBN 0-689-30400-5). Atheneum.
--Twenty-Three Varieties of Ethnic Art & How You Can Make Each One. LC 76-5409. (Illus.). (gr. 4-7). 1976. 8.95 (ISBN 0-689-30541-9). Atheneum.
Klimo, Joan F. What Can I Do Today? A Treasury of Crafts for Children. LC 73-15110. (Illus.). 64p. (gr. k-3). 1974. PLB 4.99 (ISBN 0-394-92309-X); pap. 2.95 (ISBN 0-394-82809-7). Pantheon.
Kuehnemann, Ursula. Presents for Dad. LC 67-11512. (Illus.). (gr. k-3). 1966. 2.95 (ISBN 0-8008-6525-1). Taplinger.
Lane, Jane & Lane, John. How to Make Play Places & Secret Hidy Holes. (Illus.). 1979. 6.95a (ISBN 0-385-13048-1); PLB (ISBN 0-385-13056-2). Doubleday.
Lasky, Kathryn. The Weaver's Gift. LC 80-12042. (Illus.). 64p. (gr. 4-7). 1981. 8.95g (ISBN 0-7232-6191-1). Warne.
Lawson. Terrific Gifts to Make & Give. (gr. 7-12). 1980. pap. 1.25 (ISBN 0-590-30885-8, Schol Pap). Schol Bk Serv.
Lazar, Wendy Phillips. Jewish Holiday Book. LC 76-42342. (gr. 6-12). 1977. 8.95a (ISBN 0-385-11426-5); PLB (ISBN 0-385-11427-3). Doubleday.
Lewis, Shari. Toy Store-in-a-Book. (Kids-Only Club Books). (Illus.). (gr. 3-6). 1979. pap. 1.95 (ISBN 0-03-049706-X). HR&W.
Lofgren, Ulf. Swedish Toys, Dolls, & Gifts You Can Make Yourself: Traditional Swedish Handicrafts. LC 78-8619. (Unicef Storycraft Bks.). (Illus.). (ps-3). 1978. 5.95 (ISBN 0-529-05448-5); PLB 5.91 (ISBN 0-529-05449-3). Philomel.
Lopshire, Robert. The Beginner Book of Things to Make. LC 64-22011. (Beginner Bk: No. 37). (Illus.). (gr. k-3). 1977. 3.95 (ISBN 0-394-83493-3); PLB 4.39 (ISBN 0-394-93493-8). Beginner.
McPhee Gribble Publishers. Presents: Making Them to Match People. (Practical Puffins Ser.). (Illus.). 1978. pap. 1.50 (ISBN 0-14-049163-5, Puffin). Penguin.
Manley, Seon. Adventures in Making: Romance of Crafts Around the World. LC 59-12397. (Illus.). (gr. 7 up). 1959. 7.95 (ISBN 0-8149-0361-4). Vanguard.
Marshall Cavendish Editorial Board. Modelling Is Easy - When You Know How. LC 74-76266. (gr. 2-9). 4.95 (ISBN 0-668-03483-1). Arco.
Mayer, Mercer. Little Monster's You-Can-Make-It Book. (Illus.). (gr. k-7). 1978. 3.95 (ISBN 0-307-15802-0, Golden Pr). Western Pub.
Meyer, Carolyn. People Who Make Things: How American Craftsmen Live & Work. LC 74-18189. (Illus.). 208p. (gr. 7 up). 1975. 6.50 (ISBN 0-689-50012-2, McElderry Bk). Atheneum.
Middler-Junior Pocketbook of Crafts. LC 74-28720. (Illus.). 96p. (gr. 3-6). 1975. pap. text ed. 1.95 (ISBN 0-87239-047-0, 2137). Standard Pub.
Miller, Jay & Miller, Frank. Making Gifts. LC 74-33532. (Early Craft Bks). (Illus.). 32p. (gr. 1-4). 1975. PLB 3.95 (ISBN 0-8225-0867-2). Lerner Pubns.
--Nature Crafts. LC 74-33535. (Early Craft Bks). (Illus.). 32p. (gr. 1-4). 1975. PLB 3.95 (ISBN 0-8225-0866-4). Lerner Pubns.
Miller, Joni & Thompson, Lowry. Rubber Stamp Album. LC 78-7118. (Illus.). 1978. 12.50 (ISBN 0-89480-046-9, IBM 2127); pap. 6.95 (ISBN 0-89480-045-0, IBM 2119). Workman Pub.
Mooser, Stephen. Monster Fun. LC 79-16000. (Illus.). 96p. (gr. 4-6). 1979. PLB 7.29 (ISBN 0-671-33016-0). Messner.
Myers, Caroline C., ed. More Creative Craft Activities. LC 73-8898. (Jumbo Handbooks Ser.). 96p. (gr. 1-6). 1973. text ed. 4.95 (ISBN 0-87534-556-5). Highlights.
Norvell, Flo A. The Great Big Book. LC 78-22500. (Illus.). (gr. 3 up). 1979. 8.95 (ISBN 0-690-03939-5, TYC-J); PLB 8.79 (ISBN 0-690-03940-9). Har-Row.
Parish, Peggy. Beginning Mobiles. LC 79-9950. (Ready-to-Read Handbook). (Illus.). (gr. 1-4). 1979. 6.95 (ISBN 0-02-770030-5). Macmillan.
--Let's Be Indians. LC 62-13314. (Illus.). (gr. 1-5). 1962. PLB 8.79 (ISBN 0-06-024651-0, HarpJ). Har-Row.
Petrich, Patricia & Dalton, Rosemary. The Kid's Arts & Crafts Book. Walsh, Jackie, ed. (Illus.). 192p. (Orig.). (gr. 1-6). 1975. pap. 4.95 (ISBN 0-911954-33-3). Nitty Gritty.
Pettit, Florence H. The Stamp-Pad Printing Book. LC 78-22504. (Illus.). (gr. 5-9). 1979. 7.95 (ISBN 0-690-03967-0, TYC-J); PLB 7.89 (ISBN 0-690-03968-9). Har-Row.
Pinto, Andrew & Berman, Norman. Art from Clutter. 128p. (gr. 7-12). 1976. PLB 9.66 (ISBN 0-8239-0341-9). Rosen Pr.
Pluckrose, Henry, compiled by. The Art & Craft Book. (Illus.). 190p. (gr. 4 up). 1975. 15.00 (ISBN 0-237-35141-2). Transatlantic.
--Art & Craft Today. (Illus.). 192p. (gr. 4 up). 1975. 15.00 (ISBN 0-237-35226-5). Transatlantic.

Pountney, Kate. Creative Crafts for Children. (Illus.). 64p. 1977. 7.95 (ISBN 0-571-10948-9, Pub. by Faber & Faber). Merrimack Bk Serv.
Primary Pocketbook of Crafts. LC 74-28721. (Illus.). 96p. (gr. 1-3). 1975. pap. text ed. 1.95 (ISBN 0-87239-046-2, 2136). Standard Pub.
Purdy, Susan. Holiday Cards for You to Make. LC 67-10375. (Illus.). (gr. 4-9). 1967. 9.89 (ISBN 0-397-31574-0, JBL-J). Har-Row.
Racioppo, Larry. Halloween. LC 80-19119. (Illus.). 32p. (gr. 1 up). 1980. 8.95 (ISBN 0-684-16708-5). Scribner.
Rasmussen, Richard M. & Rasmussen, Rhonda L. The Kid's Encyclopedia of Things to Make & Do. (Illus.). 320p. (gr. 4-10). 1981. pap. 14.95 (ISBN 0-916392-71-6). Oak Tree Pubns.
Riviere, Marie-Claude. Pin Pictures with Wire & Thread. Egan, E. W., tr. from Fr. LC 75-14521. (Little Craft Book Ser.). (Illus.). 48p. 1975. 5.95 (ISBN 0-8069-5340-3); PLB 6.69 (ISBN 0-8069-5341-1). Sterling.
Rockwell, Harlow. Look at This. LC 77-12716. (Ready-to-Read Ser.). (Illus.). (gr. 1-4). 1978. 7.95 (ISBN 0-02-777590-9, 77759). Macmillan.
Rowen, Dolores. Easy to Make Crafts: Preteens & Youth. 2.75 (ISBN 0-8307-0417-5, 5201802). Regal.
Saeger, Glen. String Designs. LC 74-31703. (Little Craft Book Ser.). (Illus.). 48p. (gr. 5 up). 1975. 5.95 (ISBN 0-8069-5320-9); PLB 6.69 (ISBN 0-8069-5321-7). Sterling.
St. Tamara. Asian Crafts. LC 71-86983. (Activity Book Ser., Vol. 6). (Illus.). (gr. 2-6). 1972. PLB 6.87 (ISBN 0-87460-148-7). Lion Bks.
Scarry, Richard. Richard Scarry's Best Make-It Book Ever. (Illus.). (gr. k-3). 1977. pap. 5.95 (ISBN 0-394-83492-5, BYR). Random.
Seidelman, James E. & Mintonye, Grace. Shopping Cart Art. LC 78-93279. (Creating Activity Bks). (Illus.). (gr. 3-6). 1970. 4.95g (ISBN 0-02-767230-1, CCPr). Macmillan.
--Shopping Cart Art. abr. ed. LC 78-93279. 48p. (gr. 3-6). 1973. pap. 0.95 (ISBN 0-02-045100-8, Collier). Macmillan.
Self, Margaret, ed. One Hundred Fifty-Eight Things to Make. LC 70-121625. (Orig.). (gr. 1-6). 1971. pap. 1.95 (ISBN 0-8307-0078-1, 50-026-05). Regal.
Seyling, Barbara & Glasgow, Winnette. Fun with Crafts. (Elephant Bks). (gr. 1-6). 1977. pap. 1.25 (ISBN 0-448-14450-6). G&D.
Shely, Patricia. Pre-School Pocketbook of Crafts. LC 74-28722. (Illus.). 96p. (ps-1). 1975. pap. 1.95 (ISBN 0-87239-045-4, 2135). Standard Pub.
Shoemaker, Kathryn. Creative Classroom. 1980. pap. 7.95 (ISBN 0-03-053441-0). Winston Pr.
Simons, Robin. Recyclopedia. (Illus.). (gr. 3-7). 1976. 9.95 (ISBN 0-395-24390-4). HM.
Soleillant, Claude. Activities & Projects: India in Color. LC 77-79499. (Activities & Projects Ser.). (Illus.). (gr. 2 up). 1977. 9.95 (ISBN 0-8069-4550-8); PLB 9.29 (ISBN 0-8069-4551-6). Sterling.
Sparkes, Roy. Exploring Materials with Young Children. 1975. pap. 13.50 (ISBN 0-7134-2926-7, Pub. by Batsford England). David & Charles.
Stapleton, Marjorie. Make Things Grandma Made. LC 74-21672. (Illus.). 64p. (gr. 6). 1975. 6.95 (ISBN 0-8008-5052-1). Taplinger.
Sterling Editors. Easy Crafts Book. LC 75-14517. (Illus.). 112p. (gr. 4 up). 1975. 9.95 (ISBN 0-8069-5328-4); PLB 9.29 (ISBN 0-8069-5329-2). Sterling.
Stine, Bob. The Dynamite Do-It-Yourself Pen Pal Kit. 48p. (gr. 3 up). 1980. pap. 3.95 (ISBN 0-590-11818-6, Schol Pap). Schol Bk Serv.
Sunset Editors. Children's Crafts. 2nd ed. LC 75-26496. (Illus.). 96p. 1976. pap. 3.95 (ISBN 0-376-04124-2, Sunset Bks.). Sunset-Lane.
Supraner, Robyn. Fun-to-Make Nature Crafts. LC 80-23999. (Illus.). 48p. (gr. 1-5). 1981. PLB 6.92 (ISBN 0-89375-440-4); pap. 1.95 (ISBN 0-89375-441-2). Troll Assocs.
--Rainy Day Surprises You Can Make. LC 80-19858. (Illus.). 48p. (gr. 1-5). 1981. PLB 6.92 (ISBN 0-89375-428-5); pap. 1.95 (ISBN 0-89375-429-3). Troll Assocs.
Symons, Arthur. Fix-It Book. 1974. pap. 2.00 (ISBN 0-87980-289-8). Wilshire.
Temko, Florence. Folk Crafts for World Friendship. LC 76-4215. (gr. 3-5). 1976. 9.95 (ISBN 0-385-11115-0). Doubleday.
Things to Make. (Ladybird Stories Ser.). (Illus., Arabic.). 2.50x (ISBN 0-86685-238-7). Intl Bk Ctr.
Things to Make & Do for Thanksgiving. (Things to Make & Do Ser.). (gr. 1-3). 1977. lib. bdg. 7.90 (ISBN 0-531-01324-3). Watts.
The Treasure Series. Incl. Ragbag Treasures; Tasty Treasures. (Illus.). (gr. 4 up). 1973. 3.95 ea. Transatlantic.
Vermeer, Jackie. The Little Kid's Americana Craft Book. LC 74-21698. (Illus.). 128p. (ps-2). 1975. 9.95 (ISBN 0-8008-4927-2). Taplinger.
Vonk, Idalee W. Elementary Activity Patterns: For Year 'Round Use. (Illus.). 48p. (Orig.). (gr. 3 up). 1973. pap. 3.95 (ISBN 0-87239-323-2, 2142). Standard Pub.
--Fifty-Two Elementary Patterns. (Illus.). 48p. (Orig.). (gr. 1-6). 1979. pap. 3.95 (ISBN 0-87239-340-2, 3366). Standard Pub.
--Patterns for Fifty-Two Visual Lessons. (Illus., Orig.). (gr. 3-6). 1951. pap. 3.95 (ISBN 0-87239-362-3, 2143). Standard Pub.
Walt Disney Productions. The Mickey Mouse Make-It Book. LC 74-5241. (Disney's Wonderful World of Reading Ser). (Illus.). 48p. (ps-3). 1974. 4.95 (ISBN 0-394-82555-1, BYR). Random.
Waltner, Willard & Waltner, Elma. Hobbycraft for Juniors. (Illus.). (gr. 2-10). 6.70 (ISBN 0-8313-0096-5). Lantern.
--Hobbycraft Toys & Games. (Illus.). (gr. 6 up). 6.70 (ISBN 0-8313-0094-9). Lantern.
Weiss, Harvey. Sticks, Spools & Feathers. LC 62-51701. (gr. 4-9). 1962. PLB 8.95 (ISBN 0-685-21700-0, A-W Childrens). A-W.
Weiss, Peter. Scrap Wood Craft. LC 77-24769. (Lothrop Craft Ser.). (Illus.). (gr. 4 up). 1977. 7.25 (ISBN 0-688-41791-4); PLB 6.96 (ISBN 0-688-51791-9). Lothrop.
Wilkins, Marne. Long Ago Lake: A Child's Book of Nature Lore & Crafts. (gr. 5 up). 1978. reinforced bdg. 8.95 (ISBN 0-684-15614-8, ScribJ); pap. 5.95 (ISBN 0-684-15613-X, SL788, ScribT). Scribner.
--The Long Ago Lake: A Child's Book of Nature Lore & Crafts. LC 77-18173. (Sierra Club-Scribner Juvenile Ser.). (Illus.). (gr. 5 up). 1978. 8.95 (ISBN 0-684-15614-8); pap. 5.95 (ISBN 0-684-15613-X). Sierra.
Williams, Barbara & Arnold, Susan. Pins, Picks, & Popsicle Sticks. LC 76-41164. (Illus.). (gr. 6 up). 1977. PLB 7.95 (ISBN 0-03-017786-3). HR&W.
Wilson, Jim. Uncle Jim's Book of Things to Make for Children & Adults. LC 76-45360. (Illus.). 128p. 1976. lib. bdg. 12.90 (ISBN 0-914294-61-X); pap. 3.95 (ISBN 0-914294-62-8). Running Pr.
Winter, Gary, ed. Junior Mechanics Handbook. LC 64-21153. (Illus.). (gr. 5-9). 1964. PLB 3.50 (ISBN 0-668-01208-0). Arco.
Wirtenberg, Patricia Z. The All-Around-the-House Art & Craft Book. (Illus.). (gr. 1 up). 1974. pap. 3.95 (ISBN 0-395-19974-3, Sandpiper). HM.
Wiseman, Ann. Making Things: The Hand Book of Creative Discovery. (Illus.). 192p. (gr. 4 up). 1973. 7.95 (ISBN 0-316-94847-0); pap. 4.95 (ISBN 0-316-94849-7). Little.
Wonson, Agnes. Year Round Creative Activity Pattern Book. (Illus., Orig.). (gr. 1 up). 1956. pap. 3.95 (ISBN 0-87239-337-2, 2149). Standard Pub.
World Book-Childcraft International Inc. Staff. Childcraft Annual-Mathemagic. LC 65-25105. (Childcraft--the How & Why Library). (Illus.). (gr. k-6). 1978. PLB write for price info (ISBN 0-7166-0678-X). World Bk-Childcraft.
Wrigley, Elsie. Soft Toys. LC 77-81969. (Fingertips Ser.: No. 2). (Illus.). (gr. 3 up). 1978. PLB 3.95 (ISBN 0-7232-2000-X). Warne.
--Wool Toys. LC 77-81970. (Fingertips Ser.: No. 1). (Illus.). (gr. 1 up). 1978. PLB 3.95 (ISBN 0-7232-1998-2). Warne.
Yonck, Barbara. Candle Crafts. (Illus.). (gr. 4-8). 1981. PLB 7.95 (ISBN 0-87460-376-5). Lion Bks.
Zechlin, Katharina. Games You Can Build Yourself. LC 74-82327. (Illus.). 64p. (gr. 6 up). 1975. 9.95 (ISBN 0-8069-5308-X); PLB 9.29 (ISBN 0-8069-5309-8). Sterling.
Zubrowski, Bernie. Messing Around with Drinking Straw Construction. (Illus.). 1981. write for info. (ISBN 0-316-98873-1, Pub. by Atlantic Pr); pap. write for info. (ISBN 0-316-98875-8). Little.

HANDKE, PETER
Hern, Nicholas. Peter Handke. LC 76-190349. (Modern Literature Ser.). 1972. 10.95 (ISBN 0-8044-2380-6). Ungar.
Schlueter, June. The Plays & Novels of Peter Handke. LC 81-50242. (Critical Essays in Modern Literature). 256p. 1981. 13.95 (ISBN 0-8229-3443-4); pap. 7.95 (ISBN 0-8229-5330-7). U of Pittsburgh Pr.

HANDKERCHIEFS
Braun-Ronsdorf, M. History of the Handkerchief. 33.50 (ISBN 0-87245-499-1). Textile Bk.

HANDLIN, OSCAR, 1915-
Bushman, Richard L., et al, eds. Uprooted Americans: Essays to Honor Oscar Handlin. LC 79-11095. 1979. 15.00 (ISBN 0-316-11810-9). Little.

HANDLING OF BULK SOLIDS
see Bulk Solids Handling

HANDLING OF FOOD
see Food Handling

HANDLING OF MATERIALS
see Materials Handling

HANDPRESS
see also Printing, Practical; Printing Press
Allen, Lewis. Printing with the Handpress. LC 75-42044. 78p. 1976. Repr. of 1969 ed. 11.50 (ISBN 0-88275-379-7). Krieger.
Harris, Elizabeth & Sisson, Clinton. The Common Press. LC 77-79005. (Illus.). 1978. 20.00x (ISBN 0-87923-211-0). Godine.
Mason, Billy. How to Build Your Own Rubber Stamp Press. 1978. 5.00 (ISBN 0-686-23414-6). Kelso.

HANDWRITING
see Autographs; Graphology; Paleography; Penmanship; Writing

HANDY, WILLIAM C., 1873-1958
Handy, W. C. Father of the Blues. 1970. pap. 1.95 (ISBN 0-02-060700-8, Collier). Macmillan.
Wayne, Bennett, ed. Three Jazz Greats. LC 72-6801. (Target Ser.). (Illus.). 168p. (gr. 5-12). 1973. PLB 7.29 (ISBN 0-8116-4901-6). Garrard.

HANFF, HELENE
Hanff, Helene. The Duchess of Bloomsbury Street. LC 73-1801. 144p. 1973. 6.95 (ISBN 0-397-00976-3). Har-Row.

HANG GLIDING
Adleson, Joe & Williams, Bill. Hang Flight: Flight Instruction Manual for Beginner & Intermediate Pilots. (Illus.). 66p. 1975. pap. 3.25 (ISBN 0-911720-71-5, Pub. by Eco-Nautics). Aviation.
Dedera, Don. Hang Gliding: The Flyingest Flying. LC 74-31616. (Illus.). 1975. pap. 9.95 (ISBN 0-87358-136-9). Northland.
Doyle, Lorraine M. Hang Gliding: Rapture of the Heights. (Illus.). 96p. 1975. pap. 1.95 (ISBN 0-911720-83-9, Pub. by Lion). Aviation.
Hadley, Dunstan. Hang Gliding. (Black's Picture Sports Ser.). (Illus.). 96p. 1979. 8.95 (ISBN 0-7136-1914-7). Transatlantic.
Markowski, Michael A. The Hang Glider's Bible. (Illus.). 1977. 12.95 (ISBN 0-8306-7886-7); pap. 8.95 (ISBN 0-8306-6886-1, 886). TAB Bks.
Mrazek, James. Hang Gliding. rev. ed. (Illus.). 160p. 1981. 17.95 (ISBN 0-312-35912-8). St Martin.
Mrazek, James E. Hang Gliding & Soaring: A Complete Introduction to the Newest Way to Fly. (Illus.). 160p. 1976. pap. 6.95 (ISBN 0-312-35910-1). St Martin.
Olney, Ross R. Hang Gliding. LC 76-16193. (Illus.). (gr. 6-8). 1976. 7.50 (ISBN 0-399-20537-3). Putnam.
Pagen, Dennis. Hang Gliding & Flying Skills. (Illus.). 124p. (Orig.). 1977. pap. 6.95 (ISBN 0-936310-01-4). Black Mntn.
--Hang Gliding for Advanced Pilots. LC 78-112581. (Illus.). 124p. (Orig.). 1978. pap. 6.95 (ISBN 0-936310-02-2). Black Mntn.
Paul, Eddie. Skysurfing: A Guide to Hang Gliding. 1975. pap. 3.95 (ISBN 0-8306-2234-9, 2234). Tab Bks.
Penzler, Otto. Hang Gliding: Riding the Wind. new ed. LC 75-21843. (Illus.). 32p. (gr. 5-10). 1976. PLB 6.89 (ISBN 0-89375-008-5); pap. 2.50 (ISBN 0-89375-024-7). Troll Assocs.
Poynter, Dan. Hang Gliding Manual with Log. 6th ed. LC 76-14105. (Illus.). 1980. pap. 1.50 (ISBN 0-915516-12-8). Para Pub.
--Hang Gliding: The Basic Handbook of Skysurfing. 10th ed. LC 75-46185. (Illus.). 1981. 11.95 (ISBN 0-915516-08-X); pap. 7.95 (ISBN 0-915516-07-1). Para Pub.
--Para-Gliding, the Basic Handbook of Tow Launched Parachuting. LC 81-9596. (Illus.). 104p. (Orig.). 1981. pap. 5.95 (ISBN 0-915516-30-6). Para Pub.
Radlauer, Edward. Some Basics About Hang Gliding. LC 79-11584. (Gemini Bks). (Illus.). (gr. 3 up). 1979. PLB 9.25 (ISBN 0-516-07685-X, Elk Grove Bks.); pap. 2.95 (ISBN 0-516-47685-8, Elk Grove Bks). Childrens.
Richards, Norman. The Complete Beginner's Guide to Soaring & Hang Gliding. LC 74-18827. 144p. (gr. 6 up). 1976. 5.95 (ISBN 0-385-08318-1). Doubleday.
Robison, Nancy. Hang Gliding. LC 77-15892. (Free Time Fun Ser.). (Illus.). (gr. 4-9). 1978. PLB 6.99 (ISBN 0-8178-5772-9). Harvey.
Schmitz, Dorothy C. Hang Gliding. Schroeder, Howard, ed. LC 78-6200. (Funseekers Ser.). (Illus.). (gr. 3-4). 1978. PLB 6.95 (ISBN 0-913940-94-1); pap. 3.25 (ISBN 0-89686-015-9). Crestwood Hse.
Severance, Don. Reach for the Sky-the Romance & Techniques of Hang Gliding. LC 78-52130. (Illus.). 1978. pap. 6.00 (ISBN 0-915190-13-3). Jalmar Pr.
Siposs, George. Hang Gliding Handbook: Fly Like a Bird. LC 75-1699. (Illus.). 210p. 1975. 8.95 (ISBN 0-8306-5776-2); pap. 5.95 (ISBN 0-8306-4776-7, 776). TAB Bks.
Welch, Ann & Breen, Gerry. Hang Glider Pilot. (Illus.). 128p. 1981. pap. 7.95 (ISBN 0-8117-2138-8). Stackpole.
Wolters, Richard. The World of Silent Flight. LC 78-15822. (Illus.). 1979. 15.95 (ISBN 0-07-071561-0, GB). McGraw.

HANGING
Bleakley, Horace. The Hangmen of England. (Illus.). 1977. Repr. of 1929 ed. 29.00x (ISBN 0-7158-1184-3). Charles River Bks.
Duff, Charles. A Handbook on Hanging. 192p. 1974. Repr. of 1961 ed. 10.00x (ISBN 0-87471-459-1). Rowman.
Teeters, Negley K. & Hedblom, Jack. Hang by the Neck: The Legal Use of Scaffold & Noose, Gibbet, Stake, & Firing Squad from Colonial Times to the Present. 504p. 1967. pap. 44.75 (ISBN 0-398-01906-1). C C Thomas.

HANGING PLANTS
Container & Hanging Gardens. 96p. 1977. pap. 3.98 ea.; midwest-northeast ed. (ISBN 0-917102-15-0); pap. west ed. (ISBN 0-917102-14-2); pap. south ed. (ISBN 0-917102-16-9). Ortho.
Helmer, M. Jane. Hanging Plants for Modern Living. (Modern Living Ser.). (Illus.). 80p. (Orig.). 1975. pap. 2.95 (ISBN 0-89484-001-0, 10102). Merchants Pub Co.

HANGOVER CURES
Outerbridge, David. Hangover Handbook. (Illus.). 96p. 1981. 8.95 (ISBN 0-517-54584-5, Harmony). Crown.

HANKEY, MAURICE PASCHAL ALERS, 1877-1963
Roskill, Stephen. Hankey: Man of Secrets 1919-1931, Vol. 2. LC 75-156341. (Illus.). 576p. 1972. 15.00 (ISBN 0-312-36015-0, H03270). St Martin.

HANKS, NANCY, 1784-1818
see Lincoln, Nancy (Hanks), 1784-1818

HANNA, MARCUS ALONZO, 1837-1904
Beer, Thomas. Hanna. LC 73-3036. 325p. 1973. Repr. of 1929 ed. lib. bdg. 17.50x (ISBN 0-374-90518-5). Octagon.
Stern, Clarence A. Resurgent Republicanism: The Handiwork of Hanna. 1968. pap. 1.25 (ISBN 0-9600116-3-3). Stern.
Thompson, Charles W. Presidents I've Known & Two Near Presidents. LC 71-93383. (Essay Index Reprint Ser). 1929. 22.00 (ISBN 0-8369-1728-6). Arno.

HANNA PERKINS SCHOOL
Furman, Robert A. & Katan, Anny, eds. Therapeutic Nursery School. LC 78-75187. 1969. text ed. 17.50 (ISBN 0-8236-6500-3). Intl Univs Pr.
McDonald, Marjorie. Not by the Color of Their Skin: The Impact of Racial Differences on the Child's Development. LC 73-134334. Orig. Title: Integration & Skin Color. 1971. text ed. 17.50 (ISBN 0-8236-3690-9); pap. text ed. 5.95 (ISBN 0-8236-8166-1, 023690). Intl Univs Pr.

HANNAY FAMILY
Hannay, Patrick. Poetical Works of Patrick Hannay. LC 68-21217. 1968. Repr. of 1875 ed. 15.00 (ISBN 0-405-08596-6, Blom Pubns). Arno.

HANNIBAL, 247-183 B.C.
Abbott, Jacob. History of Hannibal the Carthaginian. Repr. of 1854 ed. 15.00 (ISBN 0-686-20100-0). Quality Lib.
Bradford, E. Hannibal. 288p. 1981. 14.95 (ISBN 0-07-007081-4). McGraw.
Dodge, Theodore A. Hannibal, a History of the Art of War Among the Cartaginians & Romans Down to the Battle of Pydna, 168 B.C. with a Detailed Account of the Second Punic War. 1977. Repr. 75.00 (ISBN 0-403-08284-6). Scholarly.
Lazenby, J. F. Hannibal's War. 340p. 1978. text ed. 36.00x (ISBN 0-85668-080-X, Pub. by Aris & Phillips England). Humanities.
--Hannibal's War: A Military History of the Second Punic War. (Illus.). 1978. 29.00x (ISBN 0-85668-080-X, Pub. by Aris & Phillips). Intl Schol Bk Serv.
Livy. War with Hannibal. De Selincourt, Aubrey, tr. (Classics Ser.). (Orig.). 1965. pap. 5.95 (ISBN 0-14-044145-X). Penguin.
Morris, William O. Hannibal. LC 73-14457. (Heroes of the Nations Series). Repr. of 1897 ed. 30.00 (ISBN 0-404-58275-3). AMS Pr.
Nash-Williams, A. H., ed. Hannibal Triumphant: Selections from Nepos & Livy. (Modern School Classics Ser.). 1969. 4.50 (ISBN 0-312-36085-1). St Martin.

HANNIBAL, 247-183 B.C.-JUVENILE LITERATURE
Hannibal. (MacDonald Educational Ser.). (Illus., Arabic.). 3.50 (ISBN 0-686-53097-7). Intl Bk Ctr.

HANNINGTON, JAMES, BP., 1847-1885
Dawson, Edwin C. James Hannington First Bishop of Eastern Equatorial Africa. LC 69-19355. (Illus.). Repr. of 1887 ed. 21.75x (ISBN 0-8371-0985-X, Pub. by Negro U Pr). Greenwood.

HANO, ARIZONA
Dozier, Edward P. Hano: A Tewa Indian Community in Arizona. LC 65-26674. (Case Studies in Cultural Anthropology). (Orig.). 1966. pap. text ed. 4.95 (ISBN 0-03-055115-3, HoltC). HR&W.

HANOI

Berrigan, Daniel. Night Flight to Hanoi: Daniel Berrigan's War Diary with Eleven Poems. 1968. 4.95 (ISBN 0-685-15654-0). Macmillan.

McCarthy, Mary. Hanoi. LC 68-54313. 1968. pap. 1.45 (ISBN 0-15-138450-9). HarBraceJ.

HANOVER

Ford, Guy S. Hanover & Prussia, 1795-1803. LC 72-168054. (Columbia University. Studies in the Social Sciences: No. 48). 18.00 (ISBN 0-404-51048-5). AMS Pr.

Fulford, R. Hanover to Windsor. 1960. pap. 2.25 (ISBN 0-531-06010-1, Fontana Pap). Watts.

Hodgskin, Thomas. Travels in the North of Germany, 2 Vols. LC 68-55735. Repr. of 1820 ed. 45.00x (ISBN 0-678-00587-7). Kelley.

Ward, Adolphus W. Great Britain & Hanover: Some Aspects of the Personal Union. LC 68-25282. (British History Ser., No. 30). 1969. Repr. lib. bdg. 48.95 (ISBN 0-8383-0252-1). Haskell.

HANOVER, HOUSE OF

Fulford, Roger. Wicked Uncles: The Father of Queen Victoria - His Brothers. facs. ed. LC 68-8461. (Essay Index Reprint Ser). 1968. Repr. of 1933 ed. 17.00 (ISBN 0-8369-0466-4). Arno.

Garfield, Leon. The House of Hanover England in the Eighteenth Century. LC 75-42422. (Illus.). 128p. (gr. 6 up). 1976. 8.95 (ISBN 0-395-28904-1, Clarion). HM.

Sinclair-Stevenson, Christopher. Blood Royal: The Illustrious House of Hanover. LC 74-33662. (Illus.). 1980. 10.95 (ISBN 0-385-09663-1). Doubleday.

Thornton, Percy M. Brunswick Accession. LC 75-118506. 1971. Repr. of 1887 ed. 12.50 (ISBN 0-8046-1254-4). Kennikat.

Ward, Adolphus W. Great Britain & Hanover: Some Aspects of the Personal Union. LC 68-25282. (British History Ser., No. 30). 1969. Repr. lib. bdg. 48.95 (ISBN 0-8383-0252-1). Haskell.

HANOVER, NEW HAMPSHIRE

Lee, Lawrence. New Hanover County: a Brief History. rev. ed. (Illus.). 1977. pap. 2.00 (ISBN 0-86526-128-8). NC Archives.

HANSEATIC LEAGUE

Dollinger, Philippe. The German Hansa. Ault, D. S. & Steinberg, S. H., trs. from Ger. LC 77-120697. 1970. 20.00x (ISBN 0-8047-0742-1). Stanford U Pr.

Worms, Emile. Histoire Commerciale De la Ligue Hanseatique. LC 68-56738. (Research & Source Works Ser.: No. 218). (Fr). 1968. Repr. of 1864 ed. 32.50 (ISBN 0-8337-3884-4). B Franklin.

Zimmern, Helen. Hansa Towns. Repr. of 1889 ed. 20.00 (ISBN 0-527-99960-1). Kraus Repr.

HANSEN'S DISEASE

see Leprosy

HANSON, JOSEPH MELLOR, 1900-

Ziff, Paul J. J. M. Hanson. (Illus.). 1962. 14.50x (ISBN 0-8014-0469-X). Cornell U Pr.

HANUKKAH (FEAST OF LIGHTS)

Bloch, Charles E. The First Chanukah. LC 56-12405. (Illus.). 1957. pap. 1.50 (ISBN 0-8197-0450-4). Bloch.

Butler, Debra G. A Classroom Hanukah. (Illus.). 32p. (Orig.). (gr. k-4). 1980. pap. 3.00 (ISBN 0-938836-01-3). Pascal Pubs.

Chaikin, Miriam. Light Another Candle: The Story & Meaning of Hanukkah. LC 80-28137. (Illus.). 80p. (gr. 3-6). 1981. 9.95 (ISBN 0-395-31026-1, Clarion); pap. 3.95 (ISBN 0-89919-057-X). HM.

Goodman, Philip, ed. The Hanukkah Anthology. LC 75-44637. (Illus.). xxxiv, 466p. 1976. 10.95 (ISBN 0-8276-0080-1, 392). Jewish Pubn.

Greenberg, David & Bernards, Solomon S. The Living Heritage of Hanukkah. 47p. 1.50 (ISBN 0-686-74963-4). ADL.

Hirsh, Marilyn. The Hanukkah Story. LC 77-22183. (Illus.). (gr. k-4). 1977. 7.95 (ISBN 0-88482-756-9, Bonim Bks). Hebrew Pub.

Kaplan, Aryeh. The Laws of Chanukah. 124p. pap. 5.45 (ISBN 0-940118-28-9). Maznaim.

Lieberman, Donald. Heroes of Hanukkah. Date not set. 8.95x (ISBN 0-87068-866-9). Ktav.

Rockland, Mae S. The Hanukkah Book. LC 75-10609. (Illus.). 160p. 1975. 4.95 (ISBN 0-8052-3590-6). Schocken.

Rosenberg, David. A Blazing Fountain: A Book for Hanukkah. LC 78-54388. 1978. 9.95 (ISBN 0-8052-3690-2). Schocken.

Sanders, James. Fun-in-Learning About Chanukah. LC 76-189390. (Illus.). (gr. 2-6). 1972. 2.95 (ISBN 0-8246-0135-1). Jonathan David.

Saypol, Judyth R. & Wikler, Madeline. My Very Own Chanukah Book. LC 77-23682. (Illus.). (gr. k-5). 1977. pap. 2.50 (ISBN 0-930494-03-2). Kar-Ben.

Wengrov, Charles. Hanukkah Song & Story. (Illus.). 1960. pap. 4.00 (ISBN 0-914080-29-6). Shulsinger Sales.

HANUKKAH (FEAST OF LIGHTS)-JUVENILE LITERATURE

Adler, David A. Hanukkah Fun Book: Puzzles, Riddles, Magic & More. LC 76-47459. (Illus.). (gr. 3-7). 1976. pap. 1.95 (ISBN 0-88482-754-2, Bonim Bks). Hebrew Pub.

--Hanukkah Game Book: Games, Riddles, Puzzles & More. (Fun-to-Do Bk). (Illus.). (gr. 1-5). 1978. pap. 1.95 (ISBN 0-88482-764-X, Bonim Bks). Hebrew Pub.

Bearman, Jane. The Eight Nights: A Chanukah Counting Book. Syme, Daniel B., ed. LC 78-60781. (Illus.). 1979. pap. 4.50 (ISBN 0-8074-0025-4, 102562). UAHC.

Becker, Joyce. Hanukkah Crafts. (Illus.). (gr. 1 up). 1978. 9.95 (ISBN 0-88482-763-1, Bonim Bks); pap. 6.95 (ISBN 0-88482-765-8, Bonim Bks). Hebrew Pub.

Chaikin, Miriam. Light Another Candle: The Story & Meaning of Hanukkah. LC 80-28137. (Illus.). 80p. (gr. 3-6). 1981. 9.95 (ISBN 0-395-31026-1, Clarion); pap. 3.95 (ISBN 0-89919-057-X). HM.

Chiel, Kinneret. Complete Book of Hanukah. (Illus.). (gr. 6-8). pap. 4.95x (ISBN 0-87068-367-5). Ktav.

Drucker, Malka. Hanukkah: Eight Nights, Eight Lights. LC 80-15852. (A Jewish Holidays Book). (Illus.). 96p. (gr. 5 up). 1980. PLB 8.95 (ISBN 0-8234-0377-7). Holiday.

Greenfeld, Howard. Chanukah. LC 76-6527. 1976. 5.95 (ISBN 0-03-015566-5). HR&W.

Hirsh, Marilyn. The Hanukkah Story. LC 77-22183. (Illus.). (gr. k-4). 1977. 7.95 (ISBN 0-88482-756-9, Bonim Bks). Hebrew Pub.

Parish, Peggy. December Decorations. LC 75-14285. (Illus.). 64p. (gr. 1-4). 1975. 6.95 (ISBN 0-02-769920-X, 76992). Macmillan.

Scharfstein, Eythe & Scharfstein, Sol. Book of Chanukah. (Illus.). (gr. 2-4). 1959. 4.00x (ISBN 0-87068-357-8). Ktav.

Simon, Norma. Hanukah in My House. (Festival Series of Picture Story Books). (Illus.). (ps-k). 1960. plastic cover 3.95 (ISBN 0-8381-0705-2). United Syn Bk.

--Hanukkah. LC 66-10065. (Holiday Ser.). (Illus.). (gr. k-3). 1966. PLB 7.89 (ISBN 0-690-36953-0, TYC-J). Har-Row.

Stuhlman, Daniel D. My Own Hanukah Story. (Illus., Orig.). (ps-5). 1980. pap. 3.95 (ISBN 0-934402-07-8); decorations 1.00 (ISBN 0-934402-08-6); reg. ver. 3.55 (ISBN 0-934402-12-4). BYLS Pr.

Vered, Ben. Why Is Hanukkah. (Illus.). (ps-5). 1961. 4.00 (ISBN 0-914080-59-8). Shulsinger Sales.

Wengrov, Charles. The Story of Hanukkah. (Holiday Ser.). (Illus.). (gr. k-7). 1965. pap. 1.50 (ISBN 0-914080-52-0). Shulsinger Sales.

HANUMAN-MAHANATAKA

Aryan, K. C. Hanuman in Art & Mythology. 1976. 45.00x (ISBN 0-88386-817-2). South Asia Bks.

HAPPENING (ART)

Cardew, Cornelius, ed. Scratch Music. 128p. 1974. pap. 3.95 (ISBN 0-262-53025-2). MIT Pr.

Hansen, Al. A Primer of Happenings & Time Space Art. LC 65-26157. (Illus.). 1965. 14.00 (ISBN 0-89366-057-4). Ultramarine Pub.

Henri, Andrian. Total Art: Environments, Happenings, & Performances. (World of Art Ser.). (Illus.). 1974. pap. 9.95 (ISBN 0-19-519934-0). Oxford U Pr.

Vostell, Wolf. Miss Vietnam & Texts of Other Happenings. Weissner, Carl, tr. from Ger. (Nova Broadcast Ser.: No. 2). (Illus.). 39p. (Orig.). 1968. pap. 3.50 (ISBN 0-89366-027-2). Ultramarine Pub.

HAPPINESS

see also Joy and Sorrow; Mental Health; Pleasure

Alain, pseud. Alain on Happiness. Cottrell, Robert D. & Cottrell, Jane E., trs. from Fr. LC 76-186356. Orig. Title: Propos Sur le Bonheur. 272p. 1973. 10.50 (ISBN 0-8044-5033-1); pap. 4.95 (ISBN 0-8044-6004-3). Ungar.

Boethius. The Consolation of Philosophy. Green, Richard H., tr. LC 62-11788. 1962. pap. 3.95 (ISBN 0-672-60273-3, LLA86). Bobbs.

--Consolation of Philosophy. Buchanan, James J., ed. LC 57-8649. (Milestones of Thought Ser.). 7.00 (ISBN 0-8044-5149-4); pap. 2.95 (ISBN 0-8044-6057-4). Ungar.

Boethius, Anicius. Boecius De Consolacione Philosophie. Chaucer, Geoffrey, tr. LC 74-80164. (English Experience Ser.: No. 644). 1974. Repr. of 1478 ed. 28.00 (ISBN 90-221-0644-6). Walter J Johnson.

Bradburn, Norman M. Structure of Psychological Well-Being. LC 67-27388. (NORC Monographs in Social Research Ser.: No. 15). (Illus.). 1969. 12.95x (ISBN 0-202-25029-6). NORC.

Bradburn, Norman M. & Caplovitz, David. Reports on Happiness: A Pilot Study of Behavior Related to Mental Health. LC 64-15605. (NORC Monographs in Social Research Ser.: No. 3). 1965. 9.95x (ISBN 0-202-30020-X). NORC.

Brandt, Henry. Querio la Felicidad Ahora. (Span.). Date not set. 2.25 (ISBN 0-686-76338-6). Life Pubs Intl.

Collie, Erroll S. Quimby's Science of Happiness. 119p. (Orig.). 1980. pap. 5.50 (ISBN 0-87516-410-2). De Vorss.

Cooper, Irving S. Secret of Happiness. LC 75-26815. 75p. 1976. pap. 1.75 (ISBN 0-8356-0469-1, Quest). Theos Pub Hse.

Curtis, Donald. How to Be Happy & Successful. rev. ed. pap. 1.00 (ISBN 0-87707-051-2). CSA Pr.

Da Free, John. What to Remember to Be Happy. (Illus.). pap. 4.95 (ISBN 0-913922-36-6). Dawn Horse Pr.

Duffin, Henry C. Way of Happiness: A Reading of Wordsworth. LC 72-192021. 1947. lib. bdg. 12.50 (ISBN 0-685-10893-7). Folcroft.

Edwards, John F. How to Quit the Rat Race - Successfully! LC 80-82676. (Illus.). 159p. (Orig.). 1981. 9.95 (ISBN 0-937590-00-2); pap. 5.95 (ISBN 0-937590-01-0). New Era.

Elbin, Paul N. Making Happiness a Habit. 1981. pap. 2.75 (ISBN 0-687-23030-6). Aberigdow.

Gibson, Robert M. The Miracle of Smilepower. Neoh, Stephen B., ed. write for info. (ISBN 0-685-83840-4). Smilepower.

Gray, John. A Lecture on Human Happiness. LC 66-21675. (Reprints of Economic Classics). 83p. Repr. of 1826 ed. lib. bdg. 9.50x (ISBN 0-678-00293-2). Kelley.

Greenbie, Marjorie L. In Quest of Contentment. LC 72-121473. (Essay Index Reprint Ser). 1936. 17.00 (ISBN 0-8369-1752-9). Arno.

Greenwald, Harold. The Happy Person. LC 80-6154. 192p. 1981. 10.95 (ISBN 0-8128-2783-X). Stein & Day.

Gutridge, D. Foster, II. Your Secret Power: Creating Harmony with Others, Vol. 4. 96p. (Orig.). 1981. pap. 5.95 (ISBN 0-938014-04-8, 301D). Freedom Unltd.

Hadfield, John, compiled by. A Book of Delights: An Anthology of Words & Pictures. LC 77-78720. (Illus.). 1977. 10.00x (ISBN 0-87663-286-X). Universe.

Heywood, Ellis. Il Moro: Ellis Heywood's Dialogue in Memory of Thomas More. Deakins, Roger L., tr. LC 75-184107. 176p. 1972. 10.00x (ISBN 0-674-58735-9). Harvard U Pr.

Houston, John. The Pursuit of Happiness. 1981. pap. text ed. 7.95x (ISBN 0-673-15421-1). Scott F.

Hughes, Don. Happiness Is...! (Orig.). 1976. pap. 0.60 mini (ISBN 0-89274-033-7, HH-033). Harrison Hse.

Humphreys, Gertrude. Adventures in Good Living. (Illus.). 1972. 5.50 (ISBN 0-87012-133-2). McClain.

Hutschnecker, A. The Will to Happiness. 1964. 6.95 (ISBN 0-13-960211-9). P-H.

Hutschnecker, Arnold A. Will to Happiness. 1972. pap. 1.95 (ISBN 0-346-12024-1). Cornerstone.

Johnson, James L. How to Enjoy Life & Not Feel Guilty. LC 79-85748. 176p. 1980. pap. 4.95 (ISBN 0-89081-121-0). Harvest Hse.

Johnson, Spencer. Precious Present. LC 80-46478. (Illus.). 80p. 1981. 7.95 (ISBN 0-89087-286-4). Celestial Arts.

Jones, Howard M. Pursuit of Happiness. 1966. pap. 3.95 (ISBN 0-8014-9026-X, CP26). Cornell U Pr.

Keyes, Ken, Jr. Prescriptions for Happiness. LC 80-84855. (Illus.). 132p. 1981. pap. 2.00 (ISBN 0-915972-02-6); cancelled pocketbook edition (ISBN 0-915972-03-4). Living Love.

Krimm, Irwinn F. Health, Success & Happiness for You. LC 56-12200. 3.50 (ISBN 0-686-08991-X). Happy Health.

Kurtz, Paul. Exuberance: Your Guide to Happiness & Fulfillment. 1977. pap. 3.00 (ISBN 0-87980-353-3). Wilshire.

Ludwig, Emil. Of Life & Love. LC 72-128273. (Essay Index Reprint Ser). 1945. 16.00 (ISBN 0-8369-1984-X). Arno.

Magic of Joy. (Gifts of Gold Ser.). 1972. 3.50 (ISBN 0-442-82496-3). Peter Pauper.

Maltz, Maxwell. Five Minutes to Happiness. 1962. 4.95 (ISBN 0-8392-1033-7). Astor-Honor.

Marra, William A. Happiness & Christian Hope: A Phenomenological Analysis. 1979. 8.95 (ISBN 0-8199-0770-7). Franciscan Herald.

Maybaum, Ignaz. Happiness Outside the State. 128p. 1980. 25.00 (ISBN 0-85362-183-7). Routledge & Kegan.

Minirth, Frank B. & Meier, Paul. Happiness Is a Choice. 1977. pap. 4.95 (ISBN 0-8010-6025-7). Baker Bk.

Montapert, Alfred A. The Way to Happiness. 1977. 5.95 (ISBN 0-13-946228-7, Busn). P-H.

Muller, Robert. Most of All They Taught Me Happiness. LC 78-52110. 1978. 8.95 (ISBN 0-385-14310-9). Doubleday.

Nickels, William G. The Happiness Games: Have Fun Keeping Score As You Learn Happiness Skills. (Illus.). 1981. 9.95 (ISBN 0-87491-070-6). Acropolis.

On True Happiness. 1969. 2.95 (ISBN 0-442-82359-2). Peter Pauper.

Peale, Norman V. & Blanton, Smiley. The Art of Real Happiness. 1976. pap. 2.25 (ISBN 0-449-24062-2, Crest). Fawcett.

Pearson, Charles & Eyres, Alfred. A Happier Life. LC 72-79092. 270p. 1969. 10.95 (ISBN 0-87716-005-8, Pub. by Moore Pub Co). F Apple.

Robbins, Caroline. Pursuit of Happiness. (Bicentennial Lecture Ser.). 21p. 1974. pap. 1.00 (ISBN 0-8447-1305-8). Am Enterprise.

Sailer, Randolph C. Happiness Self-Estimates of Young Men. LC 74-177223. (Columbia University. Teachers College. Contributions to Education: No. 467). Repr. of 1931 ed. 17.50 (ISBN 0-404-55467-9). AMS Pr.

Schauffler, Robert H. Joyful Heart. facsimile ed. LC 77-156714. (Essay Index Reprint Ser). Repr. of 1914 ed. 16.00 (ISBN 0-8369-2296-4). Arno.

Shelly, Maynard & Buck, Johanna. How to Be Happy, Happier, Happiest. LC 77-22217. 1977. 7.95 (ISBN 0-89456-006-9). Chatham Sq.

Sherman, Harold. Your Key to Happiness. 1979. pap. 1.75 (ISBN 0-449-14300-7, GM). Fawcett.

Siddiqui, M. A. A. Quest for True Happiness. pap. 0.70 (ISBN 0-686-18467-X). Kazi Pubns.

Silver, Samuel M. How to Enjoy This Moment. LC 67-28141. 1967. 4.95 (ISBN 0-671-33230-9). Trident.

Tatarkiewicz. Analysis of Happiness. (Melbourne International Philosophy Ser: No. 3). 1976. lib. bdg. 47.50 (ISBN 90-247-1807-4, Pub. by Martinus Nijhoff Netherlands). Kluwer Boston.

Telfer, Elizabeth. Happiness. LC 79-16373. 1980. cancelled (ISBN 0-312-36171-8). St Martin.

Trinkaus, Charles. Adversity's Noblemen. rev. ed. 1965. lib. bdg. 11.50x (ISBN 0-374-97999-5). Octagon.

Vandeman, George E. Happiness Wall to Wall. LC 68-56328. (Stories That Win Ser.). 92p. 1968. pap. 0.95 (ISBN 0-8163-0054-2, 08105-9). Pacific Pr Pub Assn.

Zodhiates, Spiros. Formula for Happiness. 256p. (Orig.). 1980. pap. 6.25 (ISBN 0-89957-046-1). AMG Pubs.

HAPPINESS-QUOTATIONS, MAXIMS, ETC.

Hay, Gilbert. Happiness Is... 1967. pap. 1.00 (ISBN 0-671-10228-1, Fireside). S&S.

HAPSBURG, HOUSE OF

see Habsburg, House Of

HAPTICS

see Touch

HARALD 3RD, KING OF NORWAY, 1015-1066

see Harold 3rd, King of Norway, 1015-1066

HARA, SATOSHI, 1856-1921

Najita, Tetsuo. Hara Kei in the Politics of Compromise 1905-1915. LC 67-27090. (East Asian Ser: No. 31). (Illus.). 1967. 16.50x (ISBN 0-674-37250-6). Harvard U Pr.

HARA-KARI

see Bushido

HARBORS

see also Docks; Free Ports and Zones; Piers; Pilots and Pilotage; Shore Protection; Wharves

American Society of Civil Engineers, compiled by. Ports Seventy-Seven. 1024p. 1977. pap. text ed. 36.00 (ISBN 0-87262-084-0). Am Soc Civil Eng.

--Report on Small Craft Harbors. (Manual & Report on Engineering Practice Ser.: No. 50). 148p. 1969. pap. 10.00 (ISBN 0-87262-224-X). Am Soc Civil Eng.

--Source Book on Environmental & Safety Considerations for Planning & Design of LNG Marine Terminals. 48p. 1976. pap. text ed. 7.00 (ISBN 0-87262-158-8). Am Soc Civil Eng.

Begg, A. Charles. Port Preservation. 1973. 21.90x (ISBN 0-7233-0379-7). Intl Pubns Serv.

Bennathan, Esra & Walters, Alan A. Port Pricing & Investment Policy for Developing Countries. 1979. 19.95x (ISBN 0-19-520092-6); pap. 9.95x (ISBN 0-19-520093-4). Oxford U Pr.

Bruun, Per. Port Engineering. 3rd ed. 800p. 1981. 79.95x (ISBN 0-87201-739-7). Gulf Pub.

Clark, John, et al. Small Seaports: Revitalization Through Conserving Heritage Resources. LC 79-67736. (Illus.). 64p. (Orig.). 1979. pap. 6.50 (ISBN 0-89164-059-2). Conservation Foun.

Cornick, H. F. Dock & Harbour Engineering: The Design of Docks, Vol. 1. 338p. 80.00x (ISBN 0-85264-037-4, Pub. by Griffin England). State Mutual Bk.

De Frondeville, Betrand L., et al. Foreign Deep Water Ports: Lessons for America. 1973. pap. 10.00 (ISBN 0-87659-411-9). Gryphon Hse.

Dock & Harbour Engineering: The Design of Harbours, Vol. 2. 352p. 1969. 80.00x (ISBN 0-85264-041-2, Pub. by Griffin England). State Mutual Bk.

Facilities in Ports for the Reception of Oil Residues: Results of an Enquiry Made in 1972. 145p. 1973. 16.50 (ISBN 0-686-70797-4, IMCO). Unipub.

Greenhill, Basil. A Quayside Camera, 1845-1917. LC 74-20469. (Illus.). 112p. 1975. 14.95x (ISBN 0-8195-4088-9, Pub. by Wesleyan U Pr). Columbia U Pr.

Guidelines on the Provision of Adequate Reception Facilities in Ports: Oily Wastes, Pt. 1. 16p. 1976. 7.00 (ISBN 0-686-70794-X, IMCO). Unipub.

Guidelines on the Provision of Adequate Reception Facilities in Ports: Sewage, Pt. 3. 27p. 1978. 7.00 (ISBN 0-686-70795-8, IMCO). Unipub.

Guidelines on the Provision of Adequate Reception Facilities in Ports: Garbage, Pt. 4. 27p. 1978. 7.00 (ISBN 0-686-70796-6, IMCO). Unipub.

Hoyle, B. S. Seaports of East Africa. (East African Studies). (Illus.). 1967. 6.50x (ISBN 0-8002-1959-7). Intl Pubns Serv.

Hoyle, Brian & Pinder, David, eds. Spatial Analysis & Planning Strategies Cityport Industrialization, 15-18 Nov. 1978: Spatial Analysis & Planning Strategies Cityport Industrialization,15-18 Nov. 1978, Univ. Ofsouthampton. LC 80-40837. (Urban & Regional Planning Ser.). (Illus.). 350p. 1981. 60.00 (ISBN 0-08-025815-8). Pergamon.

Inland & Maritime Waterways & Ports: Proceedings of the XXV Congress of the Permanent International Association of Navigation Congresses, (PIANC) Edinburgh, Scotland, 11 vols. (Illus.). 2750p. 1981. 400.00 (ISBN 0-08-026750-5). Pergamon.

Inter-American Convention on Facilitation of International Waterborne Transportation: Convention of Mar Del Plata. (Treaty Ser.: No. 30). (Span. , Eng. , Fr. & Port.). 1963. pap. 1.00 (ISBN 0-8270-0425-7). OAS.

Karmon, Yehuda. Ports Around the World. (Illus.). 1979. 15.95 (ISBN 0-517-53378-2). Crown.

Nagorski, Bohdan. Port Problems in Developing Countries. (Illus.). 293p. 1972. 20.00x (ISBN 0-8002-1822-1). Intl Pubns Serv.

Oram, R. B. Cargo Handling in a Modern Port. 1964. 27.00 (ISBN 0-08-011306-0); pap. 14.00 (ISBN 0-08-011305-2). Pergamon.

Ports of the World 1980. (Benn Directories Ser.). 1979. 85.00x (ISBN 0-686-60660-4, Pub by Benn Pubns). Nichols Pub.

Riethmuller, John. Ports of the World, Nineteen Eighty. 33rd ed. LC 48-3083. (Illus.). 1076p. 1980. 100.00x (ISBN 0-510-49156-1). Intl Pubns Serv.

Winters, Tobey L. Deepwater Ports in the United States: An Economic & Environmental Impact Study. LC 76-12885. (Special Studies). 1977. text ed. 27.50 (ISBN 0-275-23250-6). Praeger.

HARBORS–JUVENILE LITERATURE

Safety Considerations in the Use of Ports & Approaches by Nuclear Merchant Ships. (Safety Ser.: No. 27). 1968. pap. 5.50 (ISBN 92-0-123168-7, ISP206, IAEA). Unipub.

Scotti, Paul. Seaports: Ships, Piers, & People. LC 80-21655. (Illus.). 64p. (gr. 4-6). 1980. PLB 7.29 (ISBN 0-671-34032-8). Messner.

HARBORS–AUSTRALIA

Bird, James. Seaport Gateways of Australia. 1968. 11.75x (ISBN 0-19-212940-6). Oxford U Pr.

HARBORS–CHINA

Fairbank, John K. Trade & Diplomacy on the China Coast: The Opening of the Treaty Ports, 1842-1854, 2 Vols. in 1. LC 65-100264. (Historical Studies: No. 62-63). 1954. Set. 18.00x (ISBN 0-674-89835-4). Harvard U Pr.

--Trade & Diplomacy on the China Coast: The Opening of the Treaty Ports 1842-1854. LC 69-10365. (Illus.). 1953. pap. 5.95 (ISBN 0-8047-0648-4, SP94). Stanford U Pr.

Liu Kwang-Ching, ed. Anglo-American Steamship Rivalry in China, 1862-1874. LC 62-9426. (East Asian Ser: No. 8). (Illus.). 1962. 12.50x (ISBN 0-674-03601-8). Harvard U Pr.

Tai, En-Sai. Treaty Ports in China: A Study in Diplomacy. (Studies in Chinese History & Civilization). 202p. 1977. 17.50 (ISBN 0-89093-083-X). U Pubns Amer.

HARBORS–EUROPE

Baxter, R. E. & Phillips, C. Ports, Inland Waterways & Civil Aviation. Maunder, W. F., ed. 1979. text ed. 55.00 (ISBN 0-08-022460-1). Pergamon.

Greenhill, Basil & Giffard, Ann. Victorian & Edwardian Ships & Harbours from Early Photographs. 1978. 19.95 (ISBN 0-7134-1079-5, Pub. by Batsford England). David & Charles.

Joicey, Richard. Harbour Sketches: With Pen & Brush. (Illus.). 1978. pap. text ed. 13.95x (ISBN 0-9504448-6-3, Pub. by Ian Harrap Ltd.). State Mutual Bk.

Konvitz, Josef W. Cities & the Sea: Port City Planning in Early Modern Europe. LC 77-12976. (Illus.). 1978. text ed. 17.00x (ISBN 0-8018-2038-3). Johns Hopkins.

Maka, Henryk. Szczecin-Stettin: Yesterday, Today & Tomorrow. Brice-Wojciechowska, Susan, tr. from Polish. LC 79-320867. (Illus.). 1979. 13.50x (ISBN 0-8002-2288-1). Intl Pubns Serv.

Wren, Wilfred. Ports of the Eastern Counties. (Illus.). 1979. 16.00 (ISBN 0-900963-70-0, Pub. by Terence Dalton England). State Mutual Bk.

HARBORS–UNITED STATES

Adams, John S., ed. Contemporary Metropolitan America: Twenty Geographical Vignettes: Nineteenth Century Ports, Pt. 2. (Comparative Metropolitan Analysis Project Ser.). (Illus.). 1976. 25.00 (ISBN 0-88410-464-8). Ballinger Pub.

--Contemporary Metropolitan America: Twenty Geographical Vignettes: Nineteenth Century Inland Centers & Ports, Pt. 3. (Comparative Metropolitan Analysis Project Ser.). (Illus.). 1976. 33.50 (ISBN 0-88410-465-6). Ballinger Pub.

California Coastal Commission. The California Coastal Access Guide. 250p. (Orig.). 1981. pap. 7.95 (ISBN 0-520-04576-9). U of Cal Pr.

Chase, Ed. Plymouth Beach: Protective Barrier of Plymouth Harbor. (Pilgrim Society Notes Ser.: No. 22). 1.00 (ISBN 0-686-30065-3). Pilgrim Hall.

Converse, James R., ed. Southern California Ports Maritime Directory & Guide. 1979. 11.60 (ISBN 0-937628-01-8). Civic Data.

De Frondeville, Betrand L., et al. Foreign Deep Water Ports: Lessons for America. 1973. pap. 10.00 (ISBN 0-87659-411-9). Gryphon Hse.

Gambee, Robert. Manhattan Seascape. (Illus.). 256p. 1975. 15.00 (ISBN 0-8038-5043-3). Hastings.

Jenks, Fred L. The Wharves of Plymouth. (Pilgrim Society Notes Ser.: No. 3). 1955. 1.00 (ISBN 0-686-30047-5). Pilgrim Hall.

Landon, Charles E. North Carolina State Ports Authority. LC 63-9009. (Illus.). 1963. 9.75 (ISBN 0-8223-0104-0). Duke.

Marcus, Henry S., et al. Federal Port Policy in the United States. LC 76-10853. 376p. 1976. 26.00x (ISBN 0-262-13125-0). MIT Pr.

Maritime Transportation Research Board, National Research Council. Port Development in the United States. LC 76-5180. xv, 244p. 1976. pap. 6.50 (ISBN 0-309-02448-X). Natl Acad Pr.

HARD OF HEARING CHILDREN

see Children, Deaf

HARD WOODS

see Hardwoods

HARDBOARD

see also Particle Board

Abbina, Bruno & Baldisseri, M., eds. Plywood, Fibreboard & Particle Board. (Terminolgy Bulletin: No. 30). 1977. pap. 17.75 (ISBN 0-686-67773-0, F1218, FAO). Unipub.

HARDENBERG, FRIEDRICH LEOPOLD, FREIHERR VON, 1772-1801

Birrell, Gordon. The Boundless Present: Space & Time in the Literary Fairy Tales of Novalis & Tieck. (Studies in the Germanic Languages & Literatures: No. 95). 1979. 13.75x (ISBN 0-8078-8095-7). U of NC Pr.

Dyck, Martin. Novalis & Mathematics. LC 76-164817. (North Carolina. University. Studies in the Germanic Languages & Literatures: No. 27). Repr. of 1960 ed. 18.50 (ISBN 0-404-50927-4). AMS Pr.

Havenstein, Eduard. Friedrich Von Haerdenbergs Asthetische Anschauungen. 1909. 21.50 (ISBN 0-384-21831-8); pap. 18.50 (ISBN 0-384-21830-X). Johnson Repr.

Hiebel, Friedrich. Novalis: German Poet, European Thinker, Christian Mystic. LC 54-62201. (North Carolina. University. Studies in the Germanic Languages & Literatures: No. 10). Repr. of 1953 ed. 18.50 (ISBN 0-404-50910-X). AMS Pr.

Neubauer, John. Bifocal Vision: Novalis' Philosophy of Nature & Disease. (Studies in the Germanic Languages & Literatures Ser.: No. 68). 1971. 14.00x (ISBN 0-8078-8068-X). U of NC Pr.

Neuberger, John. Novalis. (World Authors Ser.: Germany: No. 556). 1980. lib. bdg. 11.95 (ISBN 0-8057-6398-8). Twayne.

HARDIE, KEIR, 1856-1915

McLean, Iain. Keir Hardie. LC 75-18038. (British Political Biography Ser.). 192p. 1975. 17.95 (ISBN 0-312-45115-6). St Martin.

Reid, Fred. Keir Hardie: The Making of a Socialist. 211p. 1978. 19.00x (ISBN 0-85664-624-5, Pub. by Croom Helm Ltd England). Biblio Dist.

Stewart, William. J. Keir Hardie, a Biography. Repr. of 1921 ed. lib. bdg. 14.25x (ISBN 0-8371-3746-2, STKH). Greenwood.

HARDIN, JOHN WESLEY, 1853-1895

Parsons, Chuck. The Capture of John Wesley Hardin. LC 78-67552. (Illus.). 134p. 1978. 9.95 (ISBN 0-932702-00-7); collector's edition 70.00 (ISBN 0-932702-01-5). Creative Texas.

HARDING, WARREN GAMALIEL, PRES. U. S., 1865-1923

Adams, Samuel H. Incredible Era: The Life & Times of Warren Gamaliel Harding. LC 78-27383. 1979. Repr. of 1939 ed. lib. bdg. 25.00x (ISBN 0-374-90051-5). Octagon.

Bates, James L. The Origins of Teapot Dome: Progressive Parties & Petroleum. LC 78-5265. (Illus.). viii, 278p. 1978. Repr. of 1963 ed. lib. bdg. 25.75 (ISBN 0-313-20383-0, BAOT). Greenwood.

Daugherty, Harry M. The Inside Story of the Harding Tragedy. facsimile ed. (Select Bibliographies Reprint Ser). Repr. of 1932 ed. 23.00 (ISBN 0-8369-5833-0). Arno.

--Inside Story of the Harding Tragedy. LC 75-27054. 348p. 1975. pap. 2.00 (ISBN 0-88279-118-4). Western Islands.

Downes, Randolph C. Rise of Warren Gamaliel Harding, 1865-1920. LC 68-31421. (Illus.). 1970. 17.50 (ISBN 0-8142-0140-7). Ohio St U Pr.

Grieb, Kenneth J. The Latin American Policy of Warren G. Harding. LC 74-26229. (Series on the American Presidency: Vol. 1). (Illus.). 1978. text ed. 8.00 (ISBN 0-912646-46-2). Tex Christian.

Kurland, Gerald. Warren Harding: President Betrayed by Friends. Rahmas, D. Steve, ed. LC 72-185662. (Outstanding Personalities No. 6). 32p. (Orig.). (gr. 7-12). 1972. lib. bdg. 2.95 incl. catalog cards (ISBN 0-87157-506-X); pap. 1.50 vinyl laminated covers (ISBN 0-87157-006-8). SamHar Pr.

Mee, Charles L., Jr. The Ohio Gang: The World of Warren G. Harding. Katz, Herbert M., ed. (Illus.). 256p. 1981. 14.95 (ISBN 0-87131-340-5). M Evans.

Moran, P. Warren G. Harding, 1865-1923: Chronology, Documents, Bibliographical Aids. LC 78-95013. (Presidential Chronology Ser). 1970. 8.00 (ISBN 0-379-12064-X). Oceana.

Murray, Robert K. Harding Era: Warren G. Harding & His Administration. LC 74-91797. (Illus.). 1969. 19.50x (ISBN 0-8166-0541-6). U of Minn Pr.

--The Politics of Normalcy: Governmental Theory & Practice in the Harding-Coolidge Era. (Norton Essays in American History Ser.). 160p. 1973. pap. text ed. 3.95x (ISBN 0-393-09422-7). Norton.

Trani, Eugene P. & Wilson, David L. The Presidency of Warren G. Harding. LC 76-26110. (The American Presidency Ser.). (Illus.). 1977. 12.00x (ISBN 0-7006-0152-X). Regents Pr KS.

HARDINGE, CHARLES, BARON, 1858-1944

Busch, Briton C. Hardinge of Penshurst: A Study in the Old Diplomacy. (Conference on British Studies (Cbs): Vol. 1). (Illus.). 381p. 1980. 19.50 (ISBN 0-208-01830-1). Shoe String.

HARDNESS

Ivan' ko, A. A. Handbook of Hardness Data. 126p. 1971. 10.50x (ISBN 0-7065-1166-2, Pub. by IPST). Intl Schol Bk Serv.

HARDT FAMILY

Hardt, Anton. Johann Hardt, 1753-1825: His Family, the History. (Illus.). 1969. 10.50 (ISBN 0-911708-02-2). Greenwich Pr.

HARDWARE

see also Building Fittings; Cutlery; Knives; Locks and Keys; Nails and Spikes; Saws; Tools

Benn's Hardware Directory 1979. (Benn Directories Ser.). 1979. 40.00 (ISBN 0-510-48511-1, Pub by Benn Pubns). Nichols Pub.

Philbin, Tom. The Encyclopedia of Hardware. LC 78-52965. 1978. 12.00 (ISBN 0-8015-2335-4, Hawthorn); pap. 6.95 (ISBN 0-8015-2336-2, Hawthorn). Dutton.

Roberts, Kenneth D., ed. Stanley Rule & Level Co. 1879 Price List of Tools & Hardware. 1973. 4.50 (ISBN 0-913602-05-1). K Roberts.

Ryder, G. H., ed. Gates' Jigs, Fixtures, Tools & Gauges. 6th ed. (Illus.). 1973. 17.50x (ISBN 0-291-39432-9). Intl Ideas.

Schiffer, Herbert F. Early Pennsylvania Hardware. (Illus.). 64p. 1966. pap. 3.75 (ISBN 0-916838-42-0). Schiffer.

Stanley Rule & Level Co. 1870 Catalogue of Tools & Hardware. 1973. 5.00 (ISBN 0-913602-04-3). K Roberts.

Tinkham, Sandra S., ed. Catalog of Tools, Hardware, Firearms, & Vehicles. (Index of American Design Ser.: Pt. 4). (Orig.). 1979. pap. 30.00x (ISBN 0-914146-69-6); incl. color microfiche 260.00x (ISBN 0-914146-68-8). Somerset Hse.

HARDWOODS

see also names of hardwoods, e.g. Mahogany

Nutting, Wallace. Furniture Treasury, 3 Vols. (Illus.). Vols. 1 & 2 In 1. 29.95 (ISBN 0-02-590980-0); Vol. 3. 24.95 (ISBN 0-02-591040-X). Macmillan.

Tropical Hardwoods Conference: Proceedings. 1969. 10.00 (ISBN 0-686-20720-3). SUNY Environ.

HARDY, EMMA LAVINIA (GIFFORD) 1840-1912

Hardy, Godfrey H. The Collected Papers of G. H. Hardy: Theory of Series, Vol. 6. London Mathematical Society Committee, ed. 1974. 74.00 (ISBN 0-19-853340-3). Oxford U Pr.

Kay-Robinson, Denys. The First Mrs. Thomas Hardy. LC 79-14065. (Illus.). 1979. 18.50x (ISBN 0-312-29246-5). St Martin.

HARDY, OLIVER, 1892-1957

Barr, Charles. Laurel & Hardy. movie ed. LC 68-31074. (Illus.). 1968. pap. 2.95 (ISBN 0-520-00085-4, CAL170). U of Cal Pr.

Everson, Bill. Films of Laurel & Hardy. 1969. 12.00 (ISBN 0-685-08133-8); pap. 6.95 (ISBN 0-8065-0146-4). Citadel Pr.

McCabe, John. Mr. Laurel & Mr. Hardy. (RL 9). pap. 1.50 (ISBN 0-451-07313-4, W7313, Sig). NAL.

Scagnetti, Jack. The Laurel & Hardy Scrapbook. LC 76-6566. (Illus.). 160p. 1976. 12.95 (ISBN 0-8246-0207-2). Jonathan David.

HARDY, THOMAS, 1840-1928

Abercrombie, Lascelles. Thomas Hardy, a Critical Study. LC 64-8920. 1964. Repr. of 1912 ed. 11.00 (ISBN 0-8462-0117-8). Russell.

Ackerman, Robert. Monarch Notes on Hardy's Tess of the D'Urbervilles. (Orig.). pap. 1.95 (ISBN 0-671-00619-3). Monarch Pr.

Bailey, J. O. Poetry of Thomas Hardy: A Handbook & Commentary. LC 77-97015. 1970. 35.00x (ISBN 0-8078-1135-1). U of NC Pr.

--Thomas Hardy & the Cosmic Mind: A New Reading of "the Dynasts". LC 77-24118. 1977. Repr. of 1956 ed. lib. bdg. 18.00x (ISBN 0-8371-9743-0, BATH). Greenwood.

Bayley, J. An Essay on Hardy. LC 77-80826. 1978. 23.95 (ISBN 0-521-21814-4). Cambridge U Pr.

Bayley, John. An Essay on Hardy. LC 77-80826. 237p. (Orig.). Date not set. pap. 13.95 (ISBN 0-521-28462-7). Cambridge U Pr.

Beach, Joseph W. Technique of Thomas Hardy. LC 61-14870. 1962. Repr. of 1922 ed. 14.00 (ISBN 0-8462-0120-8). Russell.

Bebbington, W. G. The Original Manuscript of Thomas Hardy's "the Trumpet Major". LC 73-4599. 1973. lib. bdg. 6.50 (ISBN 0-8414-1753-9). Folcroft.

Berle, Lina W. George Eliot & Thomas Hardy: A Contrast. 174p. 1981. lib. bdg. 30.00 (ISBN 0-8495-0468-6). Arden Lib.

Bjork, Lennart A. The Literary Notes of Thomas Hardy, Vol. 1 In 2 Pts. (Gothenburg Studies in English: No. 29). 479p. 1975. Set. text ed. 27.50x (ISBN 91-7346-002-8). Humanities.

Blunden, Edmund. Thomas Hardy. 1942. pap. 2.25 (ISBN 0-312-80080-0, Papermac). St Martin.

Bowra, C. M. The Lyrical Poetry of Thomas Hardy. LC 75-22227. (Studies in Thomas Hardy, No. 14). 1975. lib. bdg. 22.95 (ISBN 0-8383-2098-8). Haskell.

Bowra, Cecil M. Lyrical Poetry of Thomas Hardy. LC 73-2719. 1946. lib. bdg. 6.00 (ISBN 0-8414-1787-3). Folcroft.

Braybrooke, E. Hardy & His Philosophy. LC 73-9581. (Studies in Thomas Hardy, No. 14). 1973. lib. bdg. 32.95 (ISBN 0-8383-1716-2). Haskell.

Brennecke, E. The Life of Thomas Hardy. LC 72-8648. (Studies in Thomas Hardy, No. 14). 1973. Repr. of 1925 ed. lib. bdg. 42.95 (ISBN 0-8383-1672-7). Haskell.

--Thomas Hardy's Universe: A Study of a Poet's Mind. LC 68-689. (Studies in Thomas Hardy, No. 14). 1969. Repr. of 1924 ed. lib. bdg. 49.95 (ISBN 0-8383-0651-9). Haskell.

Brennecke, Ernest. Thomas Hardy's Universe. LC 73-15715. 1974. Repr. of 1924 ed. lib. bdg. 5.75 (ISBN 0-8414-3318-6). Folcroft.

Brooks, Jean R. Thomas Hardy: The Poetic Structure. Hough, Graham, ed. LC 78-164670. (Novelists & Their World Ser). 1971. 24.50x (ISBN 0-8014-0679-X); pap. 7.95 (ISBN 0-8014-9125-8). Cornell U Pr.

Brown, Douglas. Thomas Hardy. LC 79-19057. (Illus.). 1980. Repr. of 1954 ed. lib. bdg. 18.25x (ISBN 0-313-22105-7, BRTH). Greenwood.

Butler, L. J. Thomas Hardy. LC 77-23532. (British Authors Ser.). 1978. 23.95 (ISBN 0-521-21743-1); pap. 7.95x (ISBN 0-521-29271-9). Cambridge U Pr.

Butler, Lance St. J., ed. Thomas Hardy: After Fifty Years. LC 77-3057. 153p. 1977. 17.50x (ISBN 0-87471-980-1). Rowman.

Canby, Henry S. Thomas Hardy: Notes on His Life & Work. LC 74-11144. 1925. lib. bdg. 7.50 (ISBN 0-8414-3515-4). Folcroft.

Canby, Henry S., et al. Thomas Hardy: Notes on His Life & Work. 1978. Repr. lib. bdg. 8.50 (ISBN 0-8495-0812-6). Arden Lib.

Carpenter, Richard. Thomas Hardy. LC 74-80240. (Griffin Authors Ser). 223p. 1974. pap. 4.95 (ISBN 0-312-80115-7). St Martin.

Carpenter, Richard C. Thomas Hardy. (English Authors Ser.: No. 13). 1964. lib. bdg. 9.95 (ISBN 0-8057-1244-5). Twayne.

Casagrande, Peter J. Unity in Hardy's Novels: "Repetitive Symmetries". 272p. 1981. 20.00x (ISBN 0-7006-0209-7). Regents Pr KS.

Cecil, David. Hardy the Novelist. 235p. Repr. of 1946 ed. 10.00 (ISBN 0-911858-10-5). Appel.

Chakravarty, Amiya. Dynasts & the Post-War Age in Poetry. 1938. lib. bdg. 13.50 (ISBN 0-8414-3634-7). Folcroft.

Chase, Mary E. Thomas Hardy, from Serial to Novel. LC 64-18595. 1964. Repr. of 1927 ed. 12.00 (ISBN 0-8462-0482-7). Russell.
Chew, S. C. Thomas Hardy: Poet & Novelist. 59.95 (ISBN 0-8490-1200-7). Gordon Pr.
Chew, Samuel C. Thomas Hardy, Poet & Novelist. LC 64-18597. (Illus.). 1964. Repr. of 1928 ed. 17.00 (ISBN 0-8462-0422-3). Russell.
Child, Harold. Thomas Hardy. LC 72-3631. (Studies in Thomas Hardy, No. 14). 1972. Repr. of 1916 ed. lib. bdg. 29.95 (ISBN 0-8383-1584-4). Haskell.
--Thomas Hardy. LC 78-8740. 1916. lib. bdg. 12.50 (ISBN 0-8414-3366-6). Folcroft.
Chilton, Eleanor Carroll & Agar, Herbert. The Garment of Praise. 1929. Repr. 30.00 (ISBN 0-8274-2391-8). R West.
Clemens, Cyril. My Chat with Thomas Hardy. LC 77-1147. 1944. lib. bdg. 6.50 (ISBN 0-8414-3592-8). Folcroft.
Clements, Patricia & Grindle, Juliet, eds. The Poetry of Thomas Hardy. (Critical Studies Ser.). 194p. 1980. 26.00x (ISBN 0-389-20057-3). B&N.
Cliff's Notes Editors. Mayor of Casterbridge Notes. (Orig.). pap. 1.95 (ISBN 0-8220-0816-5). Cliffs.
Collins, Vere H. Talks with Thomas Hardy at Max Gate. 2nd ed. 85p. 1978. 13.50x (ISBN 0-7156-1280-8, Pub. by Duckworth England). Biblio Dist.
--Talks with Thomas Hardy at Max Gate, 1920-1922. LC 74-28383. 1928. 15.00 (ISBN 0-8414-3615-0). Folcroft.
Davie, Donald. Thomas Hardy & British Poetry. LC 70-188291. 208p. 1972. 12.95 (ISBN 0-19-501572-X). Oxford U Pr.
De Ridder-Barzin, Louise. Le Pessimisme De Thomas Hardy. LC 76-16485. 1976. Repr. of 1932 ed. lib. bdg. 25.00 (ISBN 0-8414-3776-9). Folcroft.
D'Exideuil, Pierre. Human Pair in the Work of Thomas Hardy. LC 79-105779. 1970. Repr. of 1930 ed. 12.00 (ISBN 0-8046-1012-6). Kennikat.
Duffin, Henry C. Thomas Hardy: A Study of the Wessex Novels, the Poems, & the Dynasts. LC 77-17945. 1978. Repr. of 1937 ed. lib. bdg. 30.25x (ISBN 0-313-20109-9, DUTH). Greenwood.
Elliott, Albert P. Fatalism in the Works of Thomas Hardy. LC 74-10791. 1972. lib. bdg. 8.75 (ISBN 0-8414-3950-8). Folcroft.
--Fatalism in the Works of Thomas Hardy. LC 66-11360. 1966. Repr. of 1935 ed. 9.00 (ISBN 0-8462-0663-3). Russell.
Enstice, Andrew. Thomas Hardy: Landscapes of the Mind. (Illus.). 1979. 18.95x (ISBN 0-312-80153-X). St Martin.
Firor, Ruth A. Folkways in Thomas Hardy. pap. 2.45 (ISBN 0-498-04069-0, Prpta). A S Barnes.
--Folkways in Thomas Hardy. LC 68-25031. 1968. Repr. of 1931 ed. 11.00 (ISBN 0-8462-1143-2). Russell.
Force, Lorraine M. Tess of the D'Urbervilles Notes. (Orig.). pap. 1.95 (ISBN 0-8220-1273-1). Cliffs.
Fowler, J. H. Novels of Thomas Hardy. LC 77-873. 1928. lib. bdg. 6.00 (ISBN 0-8414-4184-7). Folcroft.
Gardner, W. H. Some Thoughts on the Mayor of Casterbridge. 52p. 1980. Repr. of 1930 ed. lib. bdg. 7.50 (ISBN 0-8492-4959-7). R West.
--Some Thoughts on the Mayor of Casterbridge. LC 74-16131. 1930. lib. bdg. 6.00 (ISBN 0-8414-4554-0). Folcroft.
Garrison, Chester A. The Vast Venture: Hardy's Epic-Drama The Dynasts. (Salzburg Studies in English Literature, Poetic Drama & Poetic Theory: No. 18). 250p. 1973. pap. text ed. 25.00x (ISBN 0-391-01381-5). Humanities.
Garwood, Helen. Thomas Hardy: An Illustration of the Philosophy of Schopenhauer. LC 74-10776. 1911. lib. bdg. 15.00 (ISBN 0-8414-4521-4). Folcroft.
Gittings, Robert. Thomas Hardy's Later Years. 1978. 12.50 (ISBN 0-316-31454-4, Atlantic-Little, Brown). Little.
--Young Thomas Hardy. 1975. 10.95 (ISBN 0-316-31453-6, Atlantic-Little, Brown). Little.
Grimsditch, Herbert. Character & Environment in the Novels of Thomas Hardy. LC 68-788. (Studies in Thomas Hardy, No. 14). 1969. Repr. of 1925 ed. lib. bdg. 29.95 (ISBN 0-8383-0662-4). Haskell.
Grimsditch, Herbert B. Character & Environment in the Novels of Thomas Hardy. LC 62-13835. 1962. Repr. of 1925 ed. 8.50 (ISBN 0-8462-0189-5). Russell.
Grundy, Joan. Hardy & the Sister Arts. LC 78-20834. 1979. text ed. 24.50x (ISBN 0-06-492576-5). B&N.
Hardy, Emma. Some Recollections - Together with 'Some Relevant Poems' by Thomas Hardy. Hardy, Evelyn & Gittings, Robert, eds. (Illus.). 82p. 1979. 14.95x (ISBN 0-19-211764-5). Oxford U Pr.
Hardy, Evelyn. Thomas Hardy, a Critical Biography. LC 73-12879. 1953. lib. bdg. 14.50 (ISBN 0-8414-4748-9). Folcroft.
--Thomas Hardy: A Critical Biography. LC 75-83860. (Illus.). 1970. Repr. of 1954 ed. 20.00 (ISBN 0-8462-1411-3). Russell.
Hardy, Florence E. Early Life of Thomas Hardy: 1840-1891. 1971. Repr. of 1928 ed. 14.00 (ISBN 0-403-00772-0). Scholarly.
--Life of Thomas Hardy: 1840-1928. (Illus.). 1970. Repr. of 1962 ed. 22.50 (ISBN 0-208-00986-8, Archon). Shoe String.
Hardy, Thomas. The Collected Letters of Thomas Hardy, 1840-1842, Vol. 1. Purdy, Richard L., ed. (Illus.). 1978. 49.00x (ISBN 0-19-812470-8). Oxford U Pr.
--Jude the Obscure. Southerington, F. R., ed. LC 76-140800. (Library of Literature Ser: No. 35). 1972. pap. 8.50 (ISBN 0-672-61022-1, LL35). Bobbs.
--Return of the Native with Reader's Guide. (AMSCO Literature Program). (gr. 10-12). 1970. pap. 4.17 (ISBN 0-87720-807-7); with model ans. s.p. 2.70 (ISBN 0-87720-907-3). AMSCO Sch.
--The Variorum Edition of the Complete Poems of Thomas Hardy. Gibson, James, ed. (Illus.). 1980. 50.00 (ISBN 0-02-548170-3). Macmillan.
Harper, Charles. The Hardy Country. 1973. Repr. of 1904 ed. 40.00 (ISBN 0-8274-0028-4). R West.
Harper, Charles G. The Hardy Country. LC 76-16031. 1976. Repr. of 1925 ed. lib. bdg. 35.00 (ISBN 0-8414-4810-8). Folcroft.
Hatch, Benton L. & Peirce, Walter. Three Notes on Thomas Hardy. 1978. Repr. of 1966 ed. 7.50 (ISBN 0-8492-5310-1). R West.
Hatch, Benton L., et al. Three Papers on Hardy. 1966. lib. bdg. 5.00 (ISBN 0-8414-5018-8). Folcroft.
Hawkins, Desmond. Hardy: Novelist and Poet. LC 75-41575. (Illus.). 247p. 1979. Repr. of 1976 ed. text ed. 18.50x (ISBN 0-06-492752-0). B&N.
--Thomas Hardy. LC 76-9790. 1950. lib. bdg. 12.50 (ISBN 0-8414-4745-4). Folcroft.
Hickson, Elizabeth. Versification of Thomas Hardy. LC 72-191601. 1931. lib. bdg. 12.50 (ISBN 0-8414-0891-2). Folcroft.
Holland, C. Thomas Hardy, O.M. LC 68-952. (Studies in Thomas Hardy, No. 14). 1969. Repr. of 1933 ed. lib. bdg. 29.95 (ISBN 0-8383-0570-9). Haskell.
Hornback, Bert G. Metaphor of Chance: Vision & Technique in the Works of Thomas Hardy. LC 77-122099. viii, 177p. 1971. 12.00x (ISBN 0-8214-0077-0). Ohio U Pr.
Howe, Irving. Thomas Hardy. (Masters of World Literature Ser.). 226p. 1973. pap. 2.95 (ISBN 0-02-052000-X, Collier). Macmillan.
Hugman, Bruce. Hardy: Tess of the D'urbervilles. (Studies in English Literature Ser.). 1974. pap. text ed. 3.95x (ISBN 0-7131-5506-X). Dynamic Learn Corp.
Hurst, Alan. Hardy: An Illustrated Dictionary. (Illus.). 216p. 1980. 15.95 (ISBN 0-312-36218-8). St Martin.
Hyman, Virginia R. Ethical Perspective in the Novels of Thomas Hardy. (National University Publications Literary Criticism Ser.). 1975. 12.50 (ISBN 0-8046-9128-2, Natl U). Kennikat.
Hynes, Samuel. Pattern of Hardy's Poetry. 1961. 13.50x (ISBN 0-8078-0815-6). U of NC Pr.
Jackson, Arlene M. Illustration & the Novels of Thomas Hardy. (Illus.). 168p. 1981. 25.00x (ISBN 0-8476-6275-6). Rowman.
Johnson, Lionel. Art of Thomas Hardy. LC 72-11548. (Studies in Thomas Hardy, No. 14). 1969. Repr. of 1923 ed. lib. bdg. 33.95 (ISBN 0-8383-0575-X). Haskell.
Kay-Robinson, Denys. Hardy's Wessex Re-appraised. LC 76-186155. (Illus.). 262p. 1972. 9.95 (ISBN 0-312-36260-9). St Martin.
Kimball, Arthur G. & Weatherford, Richard M. Barron's Simplified Approach to Hardy's Mayor of Casterbridge. LC 68-31482. (Orig.). 1968. pap. text ed. 1.50 (ISBN 0-8120-0351-9). Barron.
Kramer, Dale. Thomas Hardy: The Forms of Tragedy. LC 74-17084. 184p. 1975. text ed. 12.95x (ISBN 0-8143-1530-5). Wayne St U Pr.
Kramer, Dale, ed. Critical Approaches to the Fiction of Thomas Hardy. LC 79-53441. 1979. text ed. 28.50x (ISBN 0-06-493951-0). B&N.
Lea, H. Thomas Hardy's Wessex. 35.00 (ISBN 0-8490-1201-5). Gordon Pr.
Lea, Hermann. Handbook to the Wessex Country of Thomas Hardy's Novels. LC 74-3274. 1906. lib. bdg. 20.00 (ISBN 0-8414-5714-X). Folcroft.
--Thomas Hardy's Wessex. 1979. Repr. of 1913 ed. lib. bdg. 35.00 (ISBN 0-8495-3326-0). Arden Lib.
--Thomas Hardy's Wessex. LC 76-58449. 1977. Repr. of 1913 ed. lib. bdg. 72.50 (ISBN 0-8414-5736-0). Folcroft.
Leeming, Glenda. Who's Who in Thomas Hardy. LC 74-24527. (Who's Who in Literature Ser). 144p. 1975. 8.95 (ISBN 0-8008-8271-7). Taplinger.
Lerner, Laurence. Thomas Hardy's "The Mayor of Casterbridge: Tragedy or Social History? (Text & Context Ser.). 1975. text ed. 6.25x (ISBN 0-85621-042-0). Humanities.
Levi, Peter. John Clare & Thomas Hardy. (John Coffin Memorial Lecture Ser., 1975). 1976. pap. text ed. 2.50x (ISBN 0-485-16210-5, Athlone Pr). Humanities.
Lewis, C. Day. Lyrical Poetry of Thomas Hardy. LC 74-8077. 1953. lib. bdg. 5.00 (ISBN 0-8414-3743-2). Folcroft.
Lucas, E. V. Reading, Writing & Remembering: A Literary Record. Meredith, James, Dickens, Thackeray, Conrad, & Hardy. Repr. of 1932 ed. lib. bdg. 30.00 (ISBN 0-8495-3315-5). Arden Lib.
Macdonell, Annie. Thomas Hardy. LC 72-4841. 1895. lib. bdg. 14.95 (ISBN 0-8414-0000-8). Folcroft.
--Thomas Hardy. LC 77-148276. Repr. of 1895 ed. 19.45 (ISBN 0-404-08885-6). AMS Pr.
McDowall. Thomas Hardy. 59.95 (ISBN 0-8490-1197-3). Gordon Pr.
McDowall, Arthur S. Thomas Hardy: A Critical Study. LC 74-19300. 1974. Repr. of 1931 ed. lib. bdg. 20.00 (ISBN 0-8414-5913-4). Folcroft.
Mahon, Maureen. Thomas Hardy's Novels: A Study Guide. 1976. pap. text ed. 3.95x (ISBN 0-435-18552-7). Heinemann Ed.
Maxwell, Donald. The Landscape of Thomas Hardy. LC 74-7212. 1928. Repr. lib. bdg. 20.00 (ISBN 0-8414-6130-9). Folcroft.
Meisel, Perry. Thomas Hardy: The Return of the Repressed, a Study of the Major Fiction. LC 77-182211. 192p. 1972. 15.00x (ISBN 0-300-01440-6). Yale U Pr.
Mickelson, Anne Z. Thomas Hardy's Women & Men: The Defeat of Nature. LC 76-28366. 1976. 10.00 (ISBN 0-8108-0985-0). Scarecrow.
Miller, Joseph H. Thomas Hardy: Distance & Desire. LC 75-102670. 1970. 16.50x (ISBN 0-674-88505-8, Belknap Pr). Harvard U Pr.
Monarch Notes on Hardy's Mayor of Casterbridge. (Orig.). pap. 1.50 (ISBN 0-671-00617-7). Monarch Pr.
Monarch Notes on Hardy's Return of the Native. (Orig.). pap. 1.75 (ISBN 0-671-00618-5). Monarch Pr.
Morrell, Roy. Thomas Hardy: The Will & the Way. LC 78-27475. 1978. lib. bdg. 30.00 (ISBN 0-8414-6332-8). Folcroft.
Morris, Robert. Barron's Simplified Approach to Hardy's The Return of the Native. LC 66-19207. 1966. pap. text ed. 1.50 (ISBN 0-8120-0174-5). Barron.
Nelson, Elizabeth R. Monarch Notes on Hardy's Far from the Madding Crowd. (Orig.). pap. 1.95 (ISBN 0-671-00890-0). Monarch Pr.
Nevinson, Henry W. Thomas Hardy. LC 72-2084. (Studies in Thomas Hardy, No. 14). 1972. Repr. of 1941 ed. lib. bdg. 22.95 (ISBN 0-8383-1466-X). Haskell.
--Thomas Hardy. LC 74-23622. 1974. Repr. of 1941 ed. lib. bdg. 8.75 (ISBN 0-8414-6283-6). Folcroft.
Newton, A. Edward. Thomas Hardy, Novelist Or Poet. LC 76-41673. 1929. lib. bdg. 12.50 (ISBN 0-8414-6294-1). Folcroft.
Newton, Alfred E. Thomas Hardy: Novelist or Poet. LC 70-160428. (Studies in Thomas Hardy, No. 14). 1971. Repr. of 1929 ed. lib. bdg. 22.95 (ISBN 0-8383-1298-5). Haskell.
Orel, Harold. Thomas Hardy's Epic-Drama: A Study of the Dynasts. Repr. of 1963 ed. lib. bdg. 15.00 (ISBN 0-8371-0602-8, ORTD). Greenwood.
Orel, Harold, ed. Thomas Hardy's Personal Writings. 295p. 1981. text ed. 10.00x (ISBN 0-333-05493-8, Pub. by Macmillan, England). Humanities.
Page, Norman. Thomas Hardy. 212p. (Orig.). 1981. pap. write for info. (ISBN 0-7100-8615-6). Routledge & Kegan.
--Thomas Hardy. 1977. 18.00 (ISBN 0-7100-8614-8). Routledge & Kegan.
--Thomas Hardy: The Writer & His Background. LC 80-5188. 1980. 27.50 (ISBN 0-312-80132-7). St Martin.
Palmer, Cecil. The Thomas Hardy Calendar. 133p. 1980. Repr. lib. bdg. 20.00 (ISBN 0-8492-2172-2). R West.
Paterson, John. The Making of the Return of the Native. LC 77-18909. (University of California Publications English Ser.: No. 19). 1978. Repr. of 1963 ed. lib. bdg. 15.25x (ISBN 0-313-20064-5, PAMR). Greenwood.
Paulin, Thomas. Thomas Hardy: The Poetry of Perception. 225p. 1975. 18.50x (ISBN 0-87471-753-1). Rowman.
Pinion, F. B. Thomas Hardy: Art & Thought. 214p. 1977. 17.50x (ISBN 0-87471-975-5). Rowman.
Purdy, Richard L. Thomas Hardy: A Bibliographical Study. (Illus.). 1978. text ed. 29.95x (ISBN 0-19-818131-0). Oxford U Pr.
Purdy, Richard Little & Millgate, Michael, eds. The Collected Letters of Thomas Hardy: Vol. 2 1893-1901. (Illus.). 320p. 1980. 49.50x (ISBN 0-19-812619-0). Oxford U Pr.
Ranald, Ralph. Monarch Notes on Hardy's Jude, the Obscure. (Orig.). pap. 1.95 (ISBN 0-671-00713-0). Monarch Pr.
Richardson, James. Thomas Hardy: The Poetry of Necessity. LC 76-8100. 1977. lib. bdg. 12.00x (ISBN 0-226-71237-0). U of Chicago Pr.
Rutland, William R. Thomas Hardy: A Study of His Writings & Their Background. LC 62-13851. (Illus.). 1962. Repr. of 1938 ed. 23.00 (ISBN 0-8462-0268-9). Russell.
Salter, C. H. Good Little Thomas Hardy. 210p. 1981. 23.50x (ISBN 0-389-20126-X). B&N.
Saxelby, F. Outwin. A Thomas Hardy Dictionary: The Characters & Scenes of the Novels & Poems Alphabetically Arranged & Described. LC 79-17624. (Illus.). 1980. Repr. of 1911 ed. lib. bdg. 25.00x (ISBN 0-313-22078-6, SATD). Greenwood.
Sherman, G. W. The Pessimism of Thomas Hardy: A Social Study. LC 74-4982. 518p. 1976. 25.00 (ISBN 0-8386-1582-1). Fairleigh Dickinson.
Sime, J. G. Thomas Hardy of the Wessex Novels. LC 74-10581. Repr. of 1928 ed. lib. bdg. 10.00 (ISBN 0-8414-7504-0). Folcroft.
Stewart, J. I. Thomas Hardy: A Critical Biography. LC 78-159830. 1971. 6.95 (ISBN 0-396-06338-1). Dodd.
Strong, Archibald. The Poetry of Thomas Hardy in Four Studies. 1973. Repr. of 1932 ed. 10.00 (ISBN 0-8274-0420-4). R West.
Summer, Rosemary. Thomas Hardy, Psychologist Novelist. 19.95 (ISBN 0-312-80161-0). St Martin.
Symons, Arthur. Study of Thomas Hardy. LC 77-160427. (Studies in Thomas Hardy, No. 14). 1971. Repr. of 1927 ed. lib. bdg. 27.95 (ISBN 0-8383-1297-7). Haskell.
Taylor, Richard H. The Personal Notebooks of Thomas Hardy. 1979. 25.00x (ISBN 0-231-04696-0). Columbia U Pr.
Thompson, Frank, Jr. Jude the Obscure Notes. (Orig.). pap. 2.25 (ISBN 0-8220-0690-1). Cliffs.
--Return of the Native Notes. (Orig.). pap. 1.75 (ISBN 0-8220-1138-7). Cliffs.
Thurley, Geoffrey. The Psychology of Handy's Novels: The Nervous & the Statuesque. 252p. 1975. text ed. 17.50x (ISBN 0-7022-0872-8). Humanities.
Tomlinson, Henry J. Thomas Hardy. 1979. Repr. of 1929 ed. lib. bdg. 10.00 (ISBN 0-8492-8425-2). R West.
Tomlinson, Henry M. Thomas Hardy. LC 70-160129. (Studies in Thomas Hardy, No. 14). 1971. lib. bdg. 40.95 (ISBN 0-8383-1283-7). Haskell.
--Thomas Hardy. LC 73-11383. 74. Repr. of 1929 ed. lib. bdg. 9.50 (ISBN 0-8414-2691-0). Folcroft.
Van Doren, Mark. Thomas Hardy, Poet in Modern Writers at Work. Piercy, J. K., ed. 1973. Repr. of 1930 ed. 45.00 (ISBN 0-8274-0432-8). R West.
Vigar, Penelope. The Novels of Thomas Hardy: Illusion & Reality. 236p. 1974. text ed. 17.50x (ISBN 0-391-00932-X). Humanities.
Waldock, Arthur J. James, Joyce & Others. facs. ed. LC 67-23277. (Essay Index Reprint Ser). 1937. 13.00 (ISBN 0-8369-0963-1). Arno.
Weber, Carl. Thomas Hardy in Maine. 1942. Repr. 10.50 (ISBN 0-8274-3610-6). R West.
--Thomas Hardy in Maine. LC 75-22203. (Studies in Thomas Hardy, No. 14). 1975. lib. bdg. 40.95 (ISBN 0-8383-2077-5). Haskell.
--The Tragedy of Little Hintock: New Light on Thomas Hardy's Novel, 'The Woodlanders' in Booker Memorial Studies Edited by Hill Shine. 1950. Repr. 25.00 (ISBN 0-8274-3642-4). R West.
Weber, Carl J. Hardy & the Lady from Madison Square. LC 72-85323. 280p. 1973. Repr. of 1952 ed. 14.25 (ISBN 0-8046-1739-2). Kennikat.
--Hardy in America: A Study of Thomas Hardy & His American Readers. LC 66-15436. (Illus., Corrected ed.). 1966. Repr. of 1946 ed. 10.00 (ISBN 0-8462-0757-5). Russell.
Whitfield, A. Stanton. Thomas Hardy. 1921. lib. bdg. 20.00 (ISBN 0-8414-9715-X). Folcroft.
Williams, Merryn. A Preface to Hardy. LC 75-28382. (Preface Books). (Illus.). 192p. 1976. pap. text ed. 5.95x (ISBN 0-582-35114-6). Longman.
--Thomas Hardy & Rural England. LC 72-318. 1972. 17.50x (ISBN 0-231-03674-4). Columbia U Pr.
Williams, Randall. Wessex Novels of Thomas Hardy. LC 74-31361. 1924. lib. bdg. 20.00 (ISBN 0-8414-9374-X). Folcroft.
Windle, Bertram C. Wessex of Thomas Hardy. LC 78-610. 1906. lib. bdg. 25.00 (ISBN 0-8414-9586-6). Folcroft.
Winner, Anthony. Characters in the Twilight: Hardy, Zola, & Chekhov. 1981. 14.95x (ISBN 0-8139-0894-9). U Pr of Va.

Winslow, D. J. Thomas Hardy: His British & American Critics. 59.95 (ISBN 0-8490-1199-X). Gordon Pr.
Wright, Walter F. Shaping of "The Dynasts". A Study in Thomas Hardy. LC 67-19159. (Illus.). 1968. 19.95x (ISBN 0-8032-0200-8). U of Nebr Pr.
Zachrisson, R. E. Thomas Hardy, 2 vols. 200.00 (ISBN 0-8490-1198-1). Gordon Pr.
--Thomas Hardy As a Man, Writer & Philosopher. (Studies in Thomas Hardy, No. 14). 1970. pap. 8.95 (ISBN 0-8383-0104-5). Haskell.
--Thomas Hardy's Twilight View of Life. (Studies in Thomas Hardy, No. 14). 1970. pap. 8.95 (ISBN 0-8383-0105-3). Haskell.
Zietlow, Paul. Moments of Vision: The Poetry of Thomas Hardy. LC 73-85184. 304p. 1974. text ed. 16.50x (ISBN 0-674-58215-2). Harvard U Pr.

HARDY, THOMAS, 1840-1928–BIBLIOGRAPHY

Danielson, Henry. First Editions of the Writings of Thomas Hardy. LC 77-1239. 1916. lib. bdg. 7.50 (ISBN 0-8414-3818-8). Folcroft.
Gerber, Helmut E. & Davis, W. Eugene, eds. Thomas Hardy: An Annotated Bibliography of Writings About Him. LC 72-7514. (Annotated Secondary Bibliography Ser. on English Literature in Transition, 1880-1920). 841p. 1973. 25.00x (ISBN 0-87580-039-4). N Ill U Pr.
Holland, C. Hardy's Wessex Scene. LC 79-119090. (Studies in Thomas Hardy, No. 14). 1970. Repr. of 1948 ed. lib. bdg. 29.95 (ISBN 0-8383-1086-9). Haskell.
Johnson, Lionel. Art of Thomas Hardy. LC 72-11548. (Studies in Thomas Hardy, No. 14). 1969. Repr. of 1923 ed. lib. bdg. 33.95 (ISBN 0-8383-0575-X). Haskell.
Prasad, Birjadish. The Poetry of Thomas Hardy, 2 vols. (Salzburg Studies in English Literature, Romantic Reassessment Ser: 57). 1977. Set. pap. text ed. 50.25x (ISBN 0-391-01501-X). Humanities.
Webb, A. P. Bibliography of the Works of Thomas Hardy, Eighteen Sixty-Five to Nineteen Fifteen. LC 68-56597. (Bibliography & Reference Ser: No. 110). 1968. Repr. of 1916 ed. 20.50 (ISBN 0-8337-3702-3). B Franklin.
Webb, A. P., ed. Bibliography of Thomas Hardy Eighteen Sixty-Five to Nineteen Fifteen. LC 77-85613. 1979. Repr. of 1916 ed. lib. bdg. 15.00 (ISBN 0-89341-157-4). Longwood Pr.
Weber, Carl J., compiled by. First Hundred Years of Thomas Hardy, 1840-1940: A Centenary Bibliography of Hardiana. LC 64-66384. 1965. Repr. of 1942 ed. 12.00 (ISBN 0-8462-0538-6). Russell.
Weber, Carl J. & Weber, Clara C., eds. Thomas Hardy's Correspondence at Max Gate: A Descriptive Check List. 1968. 6.50 (ISBN 0-910394-07-5). Colby.
Yamamoto, Bunnosuke, ed. Bibliography of Thomas Hardy in Japan: With Reference Books in England & America, Outlines of His Principal Works. 1978. Repr. lib. bdg. 85.00 (ISBN 0-8492-3112-4). R West.

HARDY SPACES

see also Functional Analysis; Functions of Complex Variables

Neville, Charles W. Invariant Subspaces of Hardy Classes on Infinitely Connected Open Surfaces. (Memoirs: No. 160). 1975. pap. 10.00 (ISBN 0-8218-1860-0, MEMO-160). Am Math.
Petersen, K. E. Brownian Motion, Hardy Spaces & Bounded Mean Oscillation. LC 76-46860. (London Mathematical Society Lecture Notes: No. 28). (Illus.). 1977. limp bdg. 14.50x (ISBN 0-521-21512-9). Cambridge U Pr.

HARE, AUGUSTUS JOHN CUTHBERT, 1834-1903

Leslie, Shane. Men Were Different: Five Studies in Late Victorian Biography. facs. ed. LC 67-26754. (Essay Index Reprint Ser). 1937. 16.00 (ISBN 0-8369-0615-2). Arno.

HARE KRISHNA SECT

Yamamoto, J. Isamu. Hare Krishna, Hare Krishna. 32p. 1978. pap. 0.50 (ISBN 0-87784-164-0). Inter-Varsity.
Yanoff, Morris. Where Is Joey? Lost Among the Hare Krishnas. 230p. 1981. 15.95 (ISBN 0-8040-0414-5). Swallow.

HAREBELLS

Shetler, St. G. Variation & Evolution of the Neartic Harebells: Campanula Subsect. Heterophylla. (Phanerogamarum Monographiae: No. XI). (Illus.). 1980. lib. bdg. 75.00x (ISBN 3-7682-1241-6). Lubrecht & Cramer.

HARELIP

Bzoch, Kenneth. Communicative Disorders Related to Cleft Lip & Palate. 2nd ed. 1979. 18.95 (ISBN 0-316-11936-9). Little.
Grabb, William C., et al. Cleft Lip & Palate: Surgical, Dental, & Speech Aspects. 916p. 1971. 68.50 (ISBN 0-316-32266-0). Little.
International Symposium First - August 1979, Bern, Switzerland. Long Term Treatment in Cleft Lip & Palate: Proceedings. Kehrer, et al, eds. (Illus.). 340p. 1981. text ed. 30.00 (ISBN 3-456-80988-3, Pub. by Hans Huber Switzerland). J K Burgess.
Ross, R. B. & Johnston, M. C. Cleft Lip & Palate. LC 78-9746. 330p. 1978. Repr. of 1972 ed. lib. bdg. 34.50 (ISBN 0-88275-702-4). Krieger.

HAREM

Miller, Barnette. Beyond the Sublime Porte. LC 79-111774. Repr. of 1931 ed. 32.45 (ISBN 0-404-04329-1). AMS Pr.
Penzer, Norman M. The Harem. LC 77-180304. (Illus.). Repr. of 1937 ed. 37.50 (ISBN 0-404-56316-3). AMS Pr.

HARES

see also Rabbits

Hughes, Lynn, ed. Hares. (Illus.). 64p. 1981. 4.95 (ISBN 0-312-92284-1). Congdon & Lattes.
MacLulich, D. A. Fluctuations in the Numbers of the Varying Hare (Lepus Americanus) LC 38-22317. (Lepus Americanus). 1937. 12.50x (ISBN 0-8020-7039-6). U of Toronto Pr.
Silverstein, Alvin & Silverstein, Virginia. Rabbits: All About Them. LC 73-4952. (Illus.). 128p. (gr. 3-7). 1973. PLB 7.44 (ISBN 0-688-51564-9). Lothrop.

HARIJANS

see Untouchables

HARINGTON, JOHN, 1520-1582

Ariosto, Ludovico. Orlando Furioso. Harrington, John, tr. 1972. 79.00x (ISBN 0-19-812407-4). Oxford U Pr.
Hughey, Ruth. John Harington of Stepney, Tudor Gentleman: His Life & Works. LC 71-125863. (Illus.). 1971. 15.00 (ISBN 0-8142-0150-4). Ohio St U Pr.

HARIOT, THOMAS, 1560-1621

Shirley, John W. A Source Book for the Study of Thomas Harriot. Cohen, I. Bernard, ed. LC 80-2111. (Development of Science Ser.). (Illus.). 1981. lib. bdg. 50.00x (ISBN 0-405-13831-8). Arno.
--Thomas Harriott: Renaissance Scientist. (Illus.). 1974. 37.50x (ISBN 0-19-858140-8). Oxford U Pr.
Stevens, Henry. Thomas Hariot, the Mathematician, the Philosopher & the Scholar. LC 72-82433. 213p. 1972. Repr. of 1900 ed. 19.50 (ISBN 0-8337-3399-0). B Franklin.

HARLAN, JOHN MARSHALL, 1833-1911

Clark, Floyd B. The Constitutional Doctrines of Justice Harlan. LC 74-87560. (Law, Politics & History Ser). 1969. Repr. of 1915 ed. lib. bdg. 25.00 (ISBN 0-306-71391-8). Da Capo.
--The Constitutional Doctrines of Justice Harlan. LC 78-63945. (Johns Hopkins University. Studies in the Social Sciences. Thirty-Third Ser. 1915: 4). Repr. of 1915 ed. 14.50 (ISBN 0-404-61202-4). AMS Pr.
Latham, Frank. Great Dissenter: Supreme Court Justice John Marshall Harlan 1833-1911. (Illus.). (gr. 7 up). 1970. 4.95 (ISBN 0-8092-8509-6). Contemp Bks.

HARLAN, RICHARD, 1796-1843

Fauna Americana. LC 73-17819. (Natural Sciences in America Ser.). 424p. 1974. Repr. 21.00x (ISBN 0-405-05735-0). Arno.

HARLAN COUNTY, KENTUCKY

Gumpert, Robert. Harlan County, a Photo-Document. (Illus.). 1976. 5.00 (ISBN 0-685-79287-0, Pub. by Red Hill). SBD.

HARLEM, NEW YORK (CITY)

Brown, Claude. Manchild in the Promised Land. (RL 7). 1971. pap. 2.25 (ISBN 0-451-08206-0, E9282, Sig). NAL.
Chung, Hyung C. The Economics of Residential Rehabilitation: Social Life of Housing in Harlem. LC 73-5167. (Special Studies in Economic, Social, & Political Issues). 1973. 27.50x (ISBN 0-275-07180-4). Irvington.
Clark, Kenneth B. Dark Ghetto: Dilemmas of Social Power. pap. 3.50x (ISBN 0-06-131317-3, TB1317, Torch). Har-Row.
Clarke, John H., ed. Harlem: A Community in Transition. (Orig.). 1969. pap. 2.45 (ISBN 0-8065-0132-4, 180). Citadel Pr.
Ellis, Arthur L. A Mind on Harlem. LC 78-62232. 1978. soft cover 12.00 (ISBN 0-88247-537-1). R & E Res Assoc.
Goering, John M. The Best Eight Blocks in Harlem. 1977. pap. text ed. 9.50 (ISBN 0-8191-0261-X). U Pr of Amer.
Gurock, Jeffrey. When Harlem Was Jewish, Eighteen Seventy to Nineteen Thirty. 1979. 17.50x (ISBN 0-231-04666-9). Columbia U Pr.
Halliburton, Warren J. & Kaiser, Ernest. Harlem: A History of Broken Dreams. LC 72-79392. 128p. 1974. pap. 2.50 (ISBN 0-385-05840-3, Zenith). Doubleday.
Johnson, James W. Black Manhattan. LC 68-29003. (American Negro: His History & Literature, Ser. No. 1). 1968. Repr. of 1940 ed. 15.00 (ISBN 0-405-01822-3). Arno.
Lewis, David L. When Harlem Was in Vogue. LC 80-2704. (Illus.). 400p. 1981. 17.95 (ISBN 0-394-49572-1). Knopf.
Osofsky, Gilbert. Harlem: The Making of a Ghetto-Negro New York, 1890-1930. LC 66-10913. (Illus.). 1966. 20.00x (ISBN 0-8290-0019-4). Irvington.
--Harlem: The Making of a Ghetto, 1890-1930. pap. 5.95x (ISBN 0-06-131572-9, TB1572, Torch). Har-Row.
Ottley, Roi. New World A-Coming: Inside Black America. LC 68-29014. (American Negro: His History & Literature Ser., No. 1). 1968. Repr. of 1943 ed. 13.00 (ISBN 0-405-01833-9). Arno.
Perry, Margaret. The Harlem Renaissance: An Annotated Bibliography. 1981. lib. bdg. 25.00 (ISBN 0-8240-9320-8). Garland Pub.
Pinkney, Alphonso & Woock, Roger R. Poverty & Politics in Harlem. 1970. 6.00 (ISBN 0-8084-0249-8); pap. 2.95 (ISBN 0-8084-0250-1, B51). Coll & U Pr.
Riker, James. Harlem: Its Origins & Early Annals. LC 78-104551. Repr. of 1881 ed. lib. bdg. 38.50x (ISBN 0-8398-1759-2). Irvington.
Schoener, Allen. Harlem on My Mind. 1979. pap. 8.95 (ISBN 0-440-53888-2, Delta). Dell.

HARLEM, NEW YORK (CITY)–DESCRIPTION–POETRY

Russell, Mariann. Melvin B. Tolson's Harlem Gallery: A Literary Analysis. LC 80-50306. 160p. 1981. text ed. 15.00x (ISBN 0-8262-0309-4). U of Mo Pr.
Tolson, Melvin B. Harlem Gallery: Book I, the Curator. 1971. lib. bdg. 8.95 (ISBN 0-8057-5808-9). Twayne.

HARLEM, NEW YORK (CITY)–RIOT, 1935

Mayor la Guardia's Commission on the Harlem Riot. Complete Report of Mayor La Guardia's Commission on the Harlem Riot of March 19, 1935. LC 76-90204. (Mass Violence in America). Repr. of 1936 ed. 10.00 (ISBN 0-405-01328-0). Arno.

HARLEM, NEW YORK (CITY)–RIOT, 1943

Capeci, Dominic J., Jr. The Harlem Riot of 1943. LC 77-70328. 1977. 17.50x (ISBN 0-87722-094-8). Temple U Pr.

HARLEM HEIGHTS, BATTLE OF, 1776

Johnston, Henry P. Battle of Harlem Heights. LC 79-115990. Repr. of 1897 ed. 19.50 (ISBN 0-404-03594-9). AMS Pr.

HARLEQUIN

Beaumont, Cyril W. History of Harlequin. LC 65-27909. (Illus.). 1967. Repr. of 1926 ed. 18.00 (ISBN 0-405-08248-7, Blom Pubns). Arno.
Mayer, David, 3rd. Harlequin in His Element: The English Pantomime, 1806-1836. LC 79-88809. (Illus.). 1969. 20.00x (ISBN 0-674-37275-1). Harvard U Pr.

HARLEY, EDWARD, SIR, 1624-1700

Harley, Brilliana. Letters of the Lady Brilliana Harley, Wife of Sir Roberto Harley, of Brampton Bryan Knight of the Bath. 1854. 31.00 (ISBN 0-384-21380-4). Johnson Repr.

HARLEY, ROBERT, SIR, 1579-1656

Harley, Brilliana. Letters of the Lady Brilliana Harley, Wife of Sir Robert Harley, of Brampton Bryan, Knight of the Bath. Lewis, Thomas T., ed. LC 73-6768. (Camden Society, London. Publications, First Ser.: No. 58). Repr. of 1854 ed. 28.00 (ISBN 0-404-50158-3). AMS Pr.
--Letters of the Lady Brilliana Harley, Wife of Sir Roberto Harley, of Brampton Bryan Knight of the Bath. 1854. 31.00 (ISBN 0-384-21380-4). Johnson Repr.

HARLEY-DAVIDSON MOTORCYCLE

Arman, Mike & Heinrichs, Kurt. What Fits What on Harley Davidson 1936-1981. 4th ed. (Illus.). 1981. pap. 5.00 (ISBN 0-933078-04-8). M Arman.
Clew, Jeff. Harley Davidson Owners Workshop Manual: Sportster '75 on. new ed. (Owners Workshop Manuals Ser.: No. 250). 1979. 8.50 (ISBN 0-85696-250-3, Pub. by J H Haynes England). Haynes Pubns.
Clymer Publications. Harley-Davidson Service--Repair Handbook: Sportster Series, 1959-1980. Robinson, Jeff, ed. (Illus.). pap. 9.95 (ISBN 0-89287-126-1, M419). Clymer Pubns.
Harley Davidson Owners Workshop Manual: Super & Electraglide Thru '77. new ed. (Owners Workshop Manuals Ser.: No. 330). 1979. 8.50 (ISBN 0-85696-330-5, Pub. by J H Haynes England). Haynes Pubns.
Jorgensen, Eric, ed. Harley-Davidson Service, Repair Handbook: All 74 Cu. in. Models, 1959-1980. (Illus.). pap. 9.95 (ISBN 0-89287-190-3, M420). Clymer Pubns.

HARLOW, JEAN, 1911-1937

Conway, Michael & Ricci, Mark. Films of Jean Harlow. 1969. pap. 6.95 (ISBN 0-8065-0147-2). Citadel Pr.

HARMON, DANIEL WILLIAMS, 1778-1845

Harmon, Daniel W. A Journal of Voyages & Travels in the Interior of North America. LC 72-2829. (American Explorers Ser.). (Illus.). Repr. of 1922 ed. 27.00 (ISBN 0-404-54911-X). AMS Pr.

HARMONIC ANALYSIS

see also Bessel's Functions; Fourier Series; Fourier Transformations; Harmonic Functions; Lame's Functions; Spherical Harmonics; Time-Series Analysis

Ash, Marshall J., ed. Studies in Harmonic Analysis. LC 76-16431. (MAA Studies Ser.: No. 13). 1976. 16.00 (ISBN 0-88385-113-X). Math Assn.
Benedetto, J. Harmonic Analysis on Totally Disconnected Sets. LC 77-163741. (Lecture Notes in Mathematics: Vol. 202). 1971. pap. 11.20 (ISBN 0-387-05488-X). Springer-Verlag.
--Harmonic Analysis on Totally Disconnected Sets. LC 77-163741. (Lecture Notes in Mathematics: Vol. 202). 1971. pap. 11.20 (ISBN 0-387-05488-X). Springer-Verlag.
Benedetto, J. J., ed. Euclidean Harmonic Analysis: Proceedings. (Lecture Notes in Mathematics: Vol. 779). 177p. 1980. pap. 11.80 (ISBN 0-387-09748-1). Springer-Verlag.
Bochner, Salomon. Fouriersche Integrale. LC 49-22695. (Ger). 8.95 (ISBN 0-8284-0042-3). Chelsea Pub.
Bracewell, R. The Fourier Transform & Its Applications. 2nd ed. (Electrical Engineering Ser.). (Illus.). 1978. text ed. 24.50 (ISBN 0-07-007013-X, C); solutions manual 10.95 (ISBN 0-07-007014-8). McGraw.
Brezin, J. P. Harmonic Analysis on Compact Solvmanifolds. LC 77-22142. (Lecture Notes in Mathematics: Vol. 602). 1977. pap. text ed. 10.70 (ISBN 0-387-08354-5). Springer-Verlag.
Carmona, J. & Vergne, M., eds. Non-Commutative Analysis: Proceedings. (Lecture Notes in Mathematics: Vol. 728). 1979. pap. 13.10 (ISBN 0-387-09516-0). Springer-Verlag.
--Non-Commutative Harmonic Analysis. (Lecture Notes in Mathematics Ser.: Vol. 587). 1977. soft cover 14.10 (ISBN 0-387-08245-X). Springer-Verlag.
Carmona, J., et al, eds. Non-Commutative Harmonic Analysis. 231p. 1975. pap. 12.00 (ISBN 0-387-07183-0). Springer-Verlag.
Coifman, Ronald & Weiss, Guido. Transference Methods in Analysis. LC 77-24098. (Conference Board of the Mathematical Sciences Ser.: No. 31). 1977. 11.20 (ISBN 0-8218-1681-0, CBMS 31). Am Math.
Conference on Harmonic Analysis, College Park, Md., 1971. Proceedings. Gulick, D. & Lipsman, R. L., eds. LC 72-80302. (Lecture Notes in Mathematics: Vol. 266). 329p. 1972. pap. 9.40 (ISBN 0-387-05856-7). Springer-Verlag.
Dobrev, V. K., et al. Harmonic Analysis. (Lecture Notes in Physics: Vol. 63). 1977. pap. 14.10 (ISBN 0-387-08150-X). Springer-Verlag.
Dunkl, Charles F. & Ramirez, Donald E. Topics in Harmonic Analysis. LC 73-153387. 1971. 28.00x (ISBN 0-89197-454-7); pap. text ed. 15.95x (ISBN 0-89197-969-7). Irvington.
Graham, C. C. & McGehee, O. C. Essays in Commutative Harmonic Analysis. LC 79-13096. (Grundlehren der Mathematischen Wissenschaften: Vol. 238). (Illus.). 1979. 44.10 (ISBN 0-387-90426-3). Springer-Verlag.
Gross, Leonard. Harmonic Analysis on Hilbert Space. LC 52-42839. (Memoirs: No. 46). 1971. pap. 7.20 (ISBN 0-8218-1246-7, MEMO-46). Am Math.
Harish-Chandra. Harmonic Analysis on Reductive P-adic Groups. LC 79-138810. (Lecture Notes in Mathematics: Vol. 162). 1970. pap. 8.20 (ISBN 0-387-05189-9). Springer-Verlag.
Harrington, Roger F. Time-Harmonic Electromagnetic Fields. (Electronic & Electrical Engineering Ser.). 1961. text ed. 27.95 (ISBN 0-07-026745-6, C). McGraw.
Helgason, Sigurdur. Analysis on Lie Groups & Homogeneous Spaces. LC 72-10153. (CBMS Regional Conference Series in Mathematics: Vol. 14). 64p. 1977. pap. text ed. 8.80 (ISBN 0-8218-1664-0, CBMS-14). Am Math.
--Topics in Harmonic Analysis on Homgeneous Spaces. 160p. 1981. text ed. 12.00 (ISBN 3-7643-3051-1). Birkhauser.
Hewitt, E. & Ross, K. A. Abstract Harmonic Analysis: Vol. 1, Structure of Topological Groups, Integration Theory, Group Representations. (Grundlehren der Mathematischen Wissenschaften: Vol. 115). 1963. 54.30 (ISBN 0-387-02983-4). Springer-Verlag.
--Abstract Harmonic Analysis: Vol. 2, Structure & Analysis for Compact Groups, Analysis on Locally Compact Abelian Groups. LC 63-12898. (Grundlehren der Mathematischen Wissenschaften: Vol. 152). 1970. 76.00 (ISBN 0-387-04832-4). Springer-Verlag.
Hewitt, E. F. & Ross, K. A. Abstract Harmonic Analysis: Vol. 1, Structure of Topological Groups, Integration Theory, Group Representations. 2nd ed. (Grundlehren der Mathematischen Wissenchaften: Vol. 115). 1979. 53.10 (ISBN 0-387-09434-2). Springer-Verlag.

Heyer, H. Probability Measures on Locally Compact Groups. (Ergebnisse der Mathematik und ihrer Grenzgbiete: Vol. 94). 1977. 70.20 (ISBN 0-387-08332-4). Springer-Verlag.
Hua, L. K. Harmonic Analysis of Functions of Several Complex Variable in the Classical Domains. rev. ed. LC 63-16769. 1979. 24.00 (ISBN 0-8218-1556-3, MMONO-6). Am Math.
Katznelson, Yitzhak. An Introduction to Harmonic Analysis. 264p. 1976. pap. text ed. 4.00 (ISBN 0-486-63331-4). Dover.
Levinson, Norman. Gap & Density Theorems. LC 41-6147. (Colloquium, Pbns. Ser.: Vol. 26). 1963. Repr. of 1940 ed. 19.60 (ISBN 0-8218-1026-X, COLL-26). Am Math.
Lindahl, L. A. & Poulsen, F. Thin Sets in Harmonic Analysis. (Lecture Notes in Pure & Applied Mathematics Ser.: Vol. 2). 1971. 17.50 (ISBN 0-8247-1317-6). Dekker.
Marcus, Michael B. & Pisier, Gilles. Random Fourier Series with Application to Harmonic Analysis. LC 81-47145. (Annals of Mathematical Studies: No.101). 192p. 1981. 17.50x (ISBN 0-691-08289-8); pap. 7.00x (ISBN 0-691-08292-8). Princeton U Pr.
Meyer, Y. Algebraic Numbers & Harmonic Analysis. 1972. 34.25 (ISBN 0-444-10357-0, North-Holland). Elsevier.
Moshinsky, M. Harmonic Oscillator in Modern Physics: From Atoms to Quark. (Documents on Modern Physics Ser.). 1969. 24.75x (ISBN 0-677-02450-9). Gordon.
Paley, Raymond E. & Wiener, Norbert. Fourier Transforms in the Complex Domain. LC 35-3273. (Colloquium, Pbns. Ser.: Vol. 19). 1978. Repr. of 1934 ed. 27.60 (ISBN 0-8218-1019-7, COLL-19). Am Math.
Petridis, N., et al, eds. Harmonic Analysis, Iraklion Nineteen Seventy-Eight: Proceedings. (Lecture Notes in Mathematics: Vol. 781). 213p. 1980. pap. text ed. 14.00 (ISBN 0-387-09756-2). Springer-Verlag.
Riesz, Frigyes & Sz-Nagy, Bela. Functional Analysis. Boron, Leo. F, tr. LC 55-8437. xii, 468p. 25.00 (ISBN 0-8044-4821-3); appendix 2.50 (ISBN 0-8044-4822-1). Ungar.
Ruehl, Werner. Lorentz Group & Harmonic Analysis. (Mathematical Physics Monographs: No. 13). 1970. 16.00 (ISBN 0-8053-8362-X, Adv Bk Prog). Benjamin-Cummings.
Silberger, Allan J. Introduction to Harmonic Analysis on Reductive P-Adic Groups. LC 79-19020. (Mathematical Notes Ser.: 23). 376p. 1979. pap. 13.50x (ISBN 0-691-08246-4). Princeton U Pr.
Stein, E. M. Singular Integrals & Differentiability Properties of Functions. (Mathematical Ser.: No. 30). 1971. 20.00 (ISBN 0-691-08079-8). Princeton U Pr.
Stein, Elias M. Topics in Harmonic Analysis Related to the Littlewood-Paley Theory. LC 72-83688. (Annals of Mathematics Studies: No. 63). 1969. 15.00 (ISBN 0-691-08067-4). Princeton U Pr.
Stein, Elias M. & Weiss, Guido. Introduction to Fourier Analysis on Euclidean Spaces. LC 73-106394. (Mathematical Ser.: No. 32). 1971. 22.00x (ISBN 0-691-08078-X). Princeton U Pr.
Varadarajan, V. S. Harmonic Analysis on Real Reductive Groups. LC 77-2216. (Lecture Notes in Mathematics: Vol. 576). 1977. pap. 21.90 (ISBN 0-387-08135-6). Springer-Verlag.
Wallach, Nolan. Harmonic Analysis on Homogeneous Spaces. (Pure & Applied Mathematics Ser: Vol. 19). 384p. 1973. 39.75 (ISBN 0-8247-6010-7). Dekker.
Weiss, Guido & Wainger, Steve, eds. Harmonic Analysis in Euclidean Spaces, 2 pts. LC 79-12726. (Proceedings of Symposia in Pure Mathematics: Vol. 35). 1979. Set. 49.20 (ISBN 0-8218-1436-2); Pt. 1. 29.20 (ISBN 0-686-67540-1, PSPUM 35, 1); Pt. 2. pap. 26.80 (ISBN 0-8218-1438-9, PSPUM 35, 2). Am Math.
Whittaker, Edmund T. & Watson, George N. A Course of Modern Analysis. 4th ed. 1927. 74.50 (ISBN 0-521-06794-4); pap. text ed. 19.95x (ISBN 0-521-09189-6). Cambridge U Pr.
Williams, F. L. Tensor Products of Principal Series Representations, Reduction of Tensor Products of Principal Series Representations of Complex Semisimple Lie Groups. LC 73-19546. (Lecture Notes in Mathematics: Vol. 358). 132p. 1974. pap. 9.10 (ISBN 0-387-06567-9). Springer-Verlag.
Williams, W. E. Fourier Series & Boundary-Value Problems. (Problem Solvers). (Illus.). 1973. pap. text ed. 4.95x (ISBN 0-04-512023-4). Allen Unwin.

HARMONIC DICTATION
see Musical Dictation

HARMONIC FUNCTIONS
see also Bessel's Functions; Fourier Series; Functions, Spheroidal; Harmonic Analysis; Lame's Functions; Spherical Harmonics

Agrest, M. M. & Maksimov, M. S. Theory of Incomplete Cylindrical Functions & Their Applications. Fettis, H. E., et al, trs. from Rus. LC 78-139673. (Die Grundlehren der Mathematischen Wissenschaften: Vol. 160). (Illus.). 1971. 48.00 (ISBN 0-387-05111-2). Springer-Verlag.
Bland, D. R. Solutions of Laplace's Equation. (Library of Mathematics). 1967. Repr. of 1961 ed. 3.50 (ISBN 0-7100-4353-8). Routledge & Kegan.
Constantinescu, C. & Cornea, A. Potential Theory on Harmonic Spaces. LC 72-86117. (Die Grundlehren der Mathematischen Wissenschaften: Vol. 158). 1972. 58.70 (ISBN 0-387-05916-4). Springer-Verlag.
Farrell, Orin J. & Ross, Bertram. Solved Problems in Analysis: As Applied to Gamma, Beta, Legendre and Bessel Function. 7.50 (ISBN 0-8446-0091-1). Peter Smith.
Fuglede, B. Finely Harmonic Functions. LC 72-90194. (Lecture Notes in Mathematics: Vol. 289). 188p. 1972. pap. 7.00 (ISBN 0-387-06005-7). Springer-Verlag.
Glasner, M. S. Proximal Flows. (Lecture Notes in Mathematics: Vol. 517). 1976. pap. 9.90 (ISBN 0-387-07689-1). Springer-Verlag.
Hayman, W. K. & Kennedy, P. B. Subharmonic Functions, Vol. 1. (London Mathematical Society Ser.). 1977. 45.50 (ISBN 0-12-334801-3). Acad Pr.
Herve, M. Analytic & Plurisubharmonic Functions in Finite & Infinite Dimensional Spaces. (Lecture Notes in Mathematics: Vol. 198). 1971. pap. 8.20 (ISBN 0-387-05472-3). Springer-Verlag.
Kantorovich, L. V., et al. Tables for the Numerical Solution of Boundary Value Problems of the Theory of Harmonic Functions. Obolensky, Alexis N., tr. LC 63-12908. 1963. 25.00 (ISBN 0-8044-4497-8). Ungar.
Lelong, P. Fonctions Plurisousharmoniques et Formes Differentielles Positives. (Cours & Documents de Mathematiques & de Physique Ser.). 1968. 18.75x (ISBN 0-677-50220-6). Gordon.
--Plurisubharmonic Functions & Positive Differential Forms. (Notes on Mathematics & Its Applications Ser.). 1969. 18.75 (ISBN 0-677-30220-7). Gordon.
Maeda, F. Y. Dirichlet Integrals on Harmonic Spaces. (Lecture Notes in Mathematics: Vol. 803). 180p. 1980. pap. 11.80 (ISBN 0-387-09995-6). Springer-Verlag.
Rado, T. On the Problem of Plateau - Subharmonic Functions. LC 71-160175. (Illus.). 1971. pap. 20.90 (ISBN 0-387-05479-0). Springer-Verlag.
Ronkin, L. I. Introduction to the Theory of Entire Functions of Several Variables. LC 74-12068. (Translations of Mathematical Monographs: Vol. 44). 1974. 50.80 (ISBN 0-8218-1594-6, MMONO-44). Am Math.
Sario, L. & Oikawa, K. Capacity Functions. LC 69-20300. (Die Grundlehren der Mathematischen Wissenschaften: Vol. 149). (Illus.). 1969. 52.50 (ISBN 0-387-04503-1). Springer-Verlag.
Sario, L., et al. Classification Theory of Riemannian Manifolds. LC 77-22197. (Lecture Notes in Mathematics: Vol. 605). 1977. pap. text ed. 21.80 (ISBN 0-387-08358-8). Springer-Verlag.
Stein, E. M. Boundary Behavior of Holomorphic Functions of Several Complex Variables. LC 71-183062. (Mathematical Notes Ser.: No. 11). 84p. 1972. pap. 8.50x (ISBN 0-691-08109-3). Princeton U Pr.
Stein, Elias M. & Weiss, Guido. Introduction to Fourier Analysis on Euclidean Spaces. LC 73-106394. (Mathematical Ser.: No. 32). 1971. 22.00x (ISBN 0-691-08078-X). Princeton U Pr.
Steklov Institute of Mathematics, No. 120. Selected Problems of Weighted Approximation & Spectral Analysis: Proceedings. LC 76-46375. 1976. 58.40 (ISBN 0-8218-3020-1, STEKLO-120). Am Math.
Stockman, Harry E. Steinmetz & Laplace Solutions to Modern Network Problems. 1977. pap. 3.25 (ISBN 0-918332-07-9). Sercolab.
Tsuji, Masatugu. Potential Theory in Modern Function Theory. 2nd ed. LC 74-4297. 600p. 1975. text ed. 19.50 (ISBN 0-8284-0281-7). Chelsea Pub.
Walsh, Joseph L. Location of Critical Points of Analytic & Harmonic Functions. LC 50-12177. (Colloquium Pbns. Ser.: Vol. 34). 1950. 20.00 (ISBN 0-8218-1034-0, COLL-34). Am Math.

HARMONICA, MOUTH
see Mouth-Organ

HARMONISTS

Lockwood, George B. New Harmony Movement. LC 68-56245. (Illus.). Repr. of 1905 ed. 9.25x (ISBN 0-678-00667-9). Kelley.

HARMONY
see also Chromatic Alteration (Music); Melody; Musical Intervals and Scales; Thorough Bass; Tonality; Twelve-Tone System

Abbott, Lawrence. The Listener's Book on Harmony. LC 74-27325. Repr. of 1943 ed. 19.50 (ISBN 0-404-12850-5). AMS Pr.
Aldwell, Edward & Schachter, Carl. Harmony & Voice Leading, Vol. 2. 276p. 1979. text ed. 12.95 (ISBN 0-15-531517-X, HC); wkbk. 6.95 (ISBN 0-15-531518-8). HarBraceJ.
Brandt, William, et al. The Comprehensive Study of Music: Piano Reductions for Harmonic Music. 1979. pap. text ed. 11.50 scp (ISBN 0-06-161421-1, HarpC). Har-Row.
Breidger, J. Henry. How to Harmonize Melodies. 1976. lib. bdg. 19.00 (ISBN 0-403-03607-0). Scholarly.
Budge, H. Study of Chord Frequencies Based on the Music of the Eighteenth & Nineteenth Centuries. LC 75-176604. (Columbia University. Teachers College. Contributions to Education: No. 882). Repr. of 1943 ed. 17.50 (ISBN 0-404-55882-8). AMS Pr.
Burkhart, Charles. Anthology for Musical Analysis. 3rd ed. LC 78-15566. 1979. pap. text ed. 18.95 (ISBN 0-03-018866-0, HoltC). HR&W.
Burns, Samuel T. Harmonic Skills Used by Selected High School Choral Leaders. LC 79-176605. (Columbia University. Teachers College. Contributions to Education: No. 905). Repr. of 1945 ed. 17.50 (ISBN 0-404-55905-0). AMS Pr.
Chadwick, George. Harmony: A Course of Study, 2 vols. in 1. Incl. A Key to Chadwick's Harmony. vii, 103p. LC 74-36316. (Music Reprint Ser). xiv, 231p. 1975. Repr. of 1897 ed. lib. bdg. 32.50 (ISBN 0-306-70663-6). Da Capo.
Clough, John. Scales, Intervals, Keys & Triads: A Self-Instruction Program. (Orig., Prog. Bk.). 1964. pap. 6.95x (ISBN 0-393-09625-4, NortonC). Norton.
Copley, R. Evan. Harmony: Baroque to Contemporary, Pt. II. 198p. 1979. pap. text ed. 10.60x (ISBN 0-87563-175-4). Stipes.
De Coussemaker, Edmond. L'art harmonique aux XIIe et XIIIe Siecles. (Illus.). 550p. (Fr.). 1964. Repr. of 1865 ed. 55.00x (ISBN 0-8450-2501-5). Broude.
Ellsworth, A. Eugene. Aural Harmony. LC 72-138243. 1970. spiral bdg. 12.95 (ISBN 0-910842-00-0, GE9, Pub. by GWM); 34 tapes 134.50 set (ISBN 0-8497-6325-8, GE9T). Kjos.
Foote, Arthur W. & Spalding, Walter R. Foote & Spalding: Harmony. LC 78-176. 1978. Repr. of 1969 ed. lib. bdg. 25.75x (ISBN 0-313-20265-6, FOHA). Greenwood.
Forte, Allen. Tonal Harmony in Concept & Practice. 3rd ed. LC 78-12229. 1979. text ed. 18.95 (ISBN 0-03-020756-8, HoltC). HR&W.
Friedheim, P. First-Year Harmony Workbook. 1966. pap. text ed. 5.95 (ISBN 0-02-910710-5). Free Pr.
Goetschius, Percy. The Theory & Practice of Tone-Relations. LC 72-109968. 187p. 1973. Repr. of 1931 ed. lib. bdg. 15.00x (ISBN 0-8371-6182-7, GOTR). Greenwood.
Goldman, Richard F. Harmony in Western Music. 1965. 11.95x (ISBN 0-393-09746-3, NortonC). Norton.
Haydon, Glen. Evolution of the Six-Four Chord: A Chapter in the History of Dissonant Treatment. LC 75-125052. (Music Ser). 1971. Repr. of 1933 ed. lib. bdg. 19.50 (ISBN 0-306-70017-4). Da Capo.
Hindemith, Paul. A Concentrated Course in Traditional Harmony, Book 1. 1943. pap. 7.50 (ISBN 0-901938-42-4). Eur-Am Music.
--A Concentrated Course in Traditional Harmony: Book Two, Exercises for Advanced Students. 1953. pap. 6.00 (ISBN 0-901938-43-2). Eur-Am Music.
Hunt, Reginald. A First Harmony Book. LC 77-23413. 1977. lib. bdg. 17.00x (ISBN 0-8371-9703-1, HUFH). Greenwood.
--Second Harmony Book. (Illus.). 1965-66. 8.95 (ISBN 0-257-66450-5). Dufour.
Jacobs, Robert L. Understanding Harmony: An Unconventional Textbook. (Illus.). 1958. pap. 5.95x (ISBN 0-19-317504-5). Oxford U Pr.
Jeppesen, Knud. Style of Palestrina & the Dissonance. 1970. pap. 4.50 (ISBN 0-486-22386-8). Dover.
Katz, Adele T. Challenge to Musical Tradition. LC 79-180046. 408p. 1972. Repr. of 1945 ed. lib. bdg. 32.50 (ISBN 0-306-70428-5). Da Capo.
Keys, Ivor C. Texture of Music: From Purcell to Brahms. (Illus.). 1961. 6.95 (ISBN 0-234-77414-2). Dufour.
Kitson, Charles H. Contrapuntal Harmony for Beginners. LC 78-5507. viii, 93p. 1978. Repr. of 1931 ed. lib. bdg. 15.00x (ISBN 0-313-20441-1, KICH). Greenwood.
--Elementary Harmony, 3 Vols. (YA) (gr. 9 up). 1920. 17.50 (ISBN 0-686-76895-7). Vol. 1 (ISBN 0-19-317210-0). Vol. 2 (ISBN 0-19-317209-7). Vol. 3 (ISBN 0-19-317208-9). 3 vols. in 1 11.55 (ISBN 0-19-317207-0). Oxford U Pr.
Lenormand, Rene & Carner, Mosco. A Study of Twentieth-Century Harmony: Harmony in France to 1914 & Contemporary Harmony, 2 vols. in 1. LC 76-40058. (Music Reprint Ser). 1975. Repr. of 1940 ed. lib. bdg. 22.50 (ISBN 0-306-70717-9). Da Capo.
Logier, Johann B. A System of the Science of Music & Practical Composition: Incidentally Comprising What Is Usally Understood by the Term Through Bass. LC 76-20715. (Music Reprint Ser). 1976. Repr. of 1897 ed. lib. bdg. 32.50 (ISBN 0-306-70793-4). Da Capo.
McHose, Allen I. Contrapuntal Harmonic Technique of the Eighteenth Century. 1947. 20.95 (ISBN 0-13-171843-6). P-H.
McKay, George F. Creative Harmony. Date not set. price not set (ISBN 0-685-52883-9). Pacific Bks.
Madden, Edward J. Fundamental Harmony Workbook. pap. 2.50 (ISBN 0-8008-3101-2, Crescendo). Taplinger.
Markewich, Reese. Inside Outside: Substitute Harmony in Modern Jazz & Pop Music. LC 67-7697. 102p. 1967. pap. 4.95 (ISBN 0-9600160-0-7). Markewich.
Melcher, Robert A. & Warch, Willard F. Music for Advanced Study. (Orig.). 1964. pap. text ed. 14.95 (ISBN 0-13-607317-4). P-H.
Mickelsen, William C., ed. & tr. Hugo Riemann's Theory of Harmony. Bd. with History of Music Theory, Book III. LC 76-15366. 1977. 17.50x (ISBN 0-8032-0891-X). U of Nebr Pr.
Mitchell, William J. Elementary Harmony. 3rd ed. 1965. 17.95x (ISBN 0-13-257279-6). P-H.
Morris, Reginald O. Foundations of Practical Harmony & Counterpoint. 2nd ed. LC 79-10541. (Illus.). xii, 148p. 1980. Repr. of 1931 ed. lib. bdg. 15.75x (ISBN 0-313-21465-4, MOPH). Greenwood.
Morris, Reginald O. & Andrews, H. K. Oxford Harmony, 2 Vols. 1946-50. Vol. 1. pap. 12.00 (ISBN 0-19-317315-8); Vol. 2. pap. text ed. 12.00 (ISBN 0-19-317314-X). Oxford U Pr.
Murphy, Howard A. & Stringham, E. J. Creative Harmony & Musicianship: An Introduction to the Structure of Music. 1951. pap. 16.95 (ISBN 0-13-189704-7). P-H.
Murphy, Howard A., et al. Music for Study: A Sourcebook of Excerpts. 2nd ed. 192p. 1973. pap. text ed. 14.95 (ISBN 0-13-607515-0). P-H.
Norden, Hugo. Fundamental Harmony. LC 73-123576. 7.50 (ISBN 0-8008-3103-9, Crescendo). Taplinger.
Ottman, Robert W. Advanced Harmony: Theory & Practice. 2nd ed. LC 72-173655. (Illus.). 304p. 1972. text ed. 17.95 (ISBN 0-13-012955-0). P-H.
--Elementary Harmony: Theory & Practice. 2nd ed. LC 70-105451. 1970. text ed. 17.50 (ISBN 0-13-257451-9); wkbk 10.95 (ISBN 0-13-257469-1). P-H.
Persichetti, Vincent. Twentieth-Century Harmony. (Illus.). 1961. 12.95x (ISBN 0-393-09539-8, NortonC). Norton.
Piston, Walter. Harmony. 4th ed. De Voto, Mark, ed. 500p. 1978. text ed. 17.95 (ISBN 0-393-09034-5). Norton.
--Principles of Harmonic Analysis. 1933. pap. 7.50 (ISBN 0-911318-05-4). E C Schirmer.
Pound, Ezra. Antheil & the Treatise on Harmony. 2nd ed. LC 68-27463. (Music Ser). (gr. 9 up). 1968. Repr. of 1927 ed. lib. bdg. 17.50 (ISBN 0-306-70981-3). Da Capo.
Prout, Ebenezer. Harmony: Its Theory & Practice. LC 70-108524. 1971. Repr. of 1903 ed. 11.00 (ISBN 0-403-00326-1). Scholarly.
--Harmony, Its' Theory & Practice. rev. ed. LC 79-151598. Repr. of 1903 ed. 16.00 (ISBN 0-404-05144-8). AMS Pr.
Rameau, Jean-Phillipe. Treatise on Harmony. Gossett, Philip, tr. 17.50 (ISBN 0-486-22461-9). Dover.
Ratner, Leonard G. Harmony: Structure & Style. (Music Ser.). 1962. text ed. 14.95 (ISBN 0-07-051213-2, C). McGraw.
Ricigliano, Daniel A. Popular & Jazz Harmony. LC 66-26789. 1967. pap. 9.95 (ISBN 0-935058-03-6). Donato Music.
Salzer, Felix. Structural Hearing: Tonal Coherence in Music, 2 Vols. (Illus.). 1952. text ed. 7.50 ea.; Vol. 1. text ed. (ISBN 0-486-22275-6); Vol. 2. text ed. (ISBN 0-486-22276-4). Dover.
Schenker, Heinrich. Harmony. Jonas, Oswald, ed. Borgese, Elizabeth M., tr. LC 54-11213. 396p. 1980. pap. 8.95 (ISBN 0-226-73734-9, P894, Phoen). U of Chicago Pr.
Schoenberg, Arnold. Structural Functions of Harmony. rev. ed. Stein, Leonard, ed. (Illus.). 1969. pap. 5.95 (ISBN 0-393-00478-3, Norton Lib). Norton.
--Theory of Harmony. Carter, Roy E., tr. LC 77-73502. 1978. 57.50x (ISBN 0-520-03464-3). U of Cal Pr.

Scholes, Percy A. Beginner's Guide to Harmony. 2nd ed. 1924. pap. 3.95x (ISBN 0-19-317502-9). Oxford U Pr.
Serly, Tibor. Second Look at Harmony. 1965. 10.45 (ISBN 0-573-69022-7). French.
Sessions, Roger. Harmonic Practice. 1951. text ed. 20.95 (ISBN 0-15-531509-9, HC). HarBraceJ.
Shinn, Duane. How to Teach Yourself Harmony-Instantly. 40p. 1973. pap. 6.95 (ISBN 0-912732-10-5). Duane Shinn.
Shir-Cliff, J., et al. Chromatic Harmony. LC 64-23079. 1965. text ed. 10.95 (ISBN 0-02-928630-1); wkbk. 9.95 (ISBN 0-02-928640-9). Free Pr.
Shirlaw, Matthew. Theory of Harmony. LC 72-87348. (Music Reprint Ser). 1969. Repr. of 1917 ed. lib. bdg. 29.50 (ISBN 0-306-71658-5). Da Capo.
Siegmeister, Elie. Harmony & Melody, 2 vols. Incl. The Diatonic Style. 1965. Vol. 1 (ISBN 0-534-00245-5); Modulation, Chromatic & Modern Styles. 1966. Vol. 2 (ISBN 0-534-00247-1). 19.95x ea.; wkbks. 9.95x ea. Wadsworth Pub.
Thompson, David M. A History of Harmonic Theory in the United States. LC 80-82202. (Illus.). 211p. 1980. 14.50x (ISBN 0-87338-246-3). Kent St U Pr.
Tschaikowsky, P. Guide to the Practical Study of Harmony. 2nd ed. Juon, P., et al, trs. from Ger. LC 77-122510. 1970. 15.00 (ISBN 0-87786-001-7). Gold Penny.
Wedge, George A. Applied Harmony, 2 bks. 1930. Bk. 1. pap. 7.95 (ISBN 0-02-872760-6); Bk. 2. pap. 6.95 (ISBN 0-02-872770-3). Schirmer Bks.
Whitehall Company. Basic Harmony. LC 77-168634. pap. 2.95x (ISBN 0-87655-525-3). Whitehall Co.
Whitney, Maurice. Backgrounds in Harmony. 1961. pap. 6.95 (ISBN 0-02-872860-2). Schirmer Bks.
Yost, Gaylord. Studies in Pizzicato & Harmonics. 1951. 2.50 (ISBN 0-913650-21-8). Volkwein Bros.

HARMONY-PROGRAMMED INSTRUCTION

Green, Douglass. Harmony Through Counterpoint: A Programmed Introduction to the Theory of Tonal Music-Harmonic Counterpoint in Two & Three Parts. 1970. pap. text ed. 19.50x (ISBN 0-89197-209-9). Irvington.

HARMONY (COSMOLOGY)

see Harmony of the Spheres

HARMONY (ESTHETICS)

Bacon, Edmund N. Design of Cities. rev ed. (Illus.). 336p. 1976. pap. 18.95 (ISBN 0-14-004236-9). Penguin.
Bronstein, Leo. Five Variations on the Theme of Japanese Painting. LC 65-27614. (Illus.). 1969. 25.00 (ISBN 0-87027-105-9). Wheelwright.
Koenigsberger, Dorothy. Renaissance Man & Creative Thinking: A History of Concepts of Harmony 1400-1700. LC 78-956. 1979. text ed. 27.50x (ISBN 0-391-00851-X). Humanities.
Moore, Charles & Allen, Gerald. Dimensions: Space, Scale & Shape in Architecture. 2nd ed. LC 76-28406. (Illus.). 1976. 15.95 (ISBN 0-07-002336-0, Architectural Res Bks). McGraw.
Ricigliano, Daniel A. Melody & Harmony in Contemporary Songwriting. LC 78-51645. 1978. pap. text ed. 12.50 (ISBN 0-935058-01-X); wrbk. 8.50 (ISBN 0-935058-02-8). Donato Music.

HARMONY, KEYBOARD

Berkowitz, Sol. Improvisation Through Keyboard Harmony. (Illus.). 288p. 1975. pap. 14.50 (ISBN 0-13-453472-7). P-H.
Brings, Allen, et al. A New Approach to Keyboard Harmony. (Illus.). 1979. pap. text ed. 9.95x (ISBN 0-393-95001-8). Norton.
Chastek, Winifred K. Keyboard Skills: Sight Reading, Transposition, Harmonization, Improvisation. 1967. 12.95x (ISBN 0-534-00666-3). Wadsworth Pub.
Diller, Angela. Keyboard Harmony Course, 2 bks. 1937. pap. 2.95 ea. Bk. I (ISBN 0-02-870730-3). Bk. II (ISBN 0-02-870740-0). Schirmer Bks.
Frackenpohl, Arthur. Harmonization at the Piano. 4th ed. 275p. 1981. write for info. plastic comb binding (ISBN 0-697-03559-X). Wm C Brown.
Hunt, Reginald. Harmony at the Keyboard. 100p. 1970. 11.25 (ISBN 0-19-321382-6). Oxford U Pr.
Johnson, J. Barham. Keyboard Harmony for Beginners. 1947. 4.35 (ISBN 0-19-321410-5). Oxford U Pr.
Kern, Alice M. Harmonization-Transposition at the Keyboard. rev. ed. 1968. pap. 12.50 (ISBN 0-87487-059-3). Summy.
Kleinhammer, Edward. Art of Trombone Playing. (Illus.). 1963. pap. 11.75 (ISBN 0-87487-058-5). Summy.
Kochevitsky, George. Art of Piano Playing: A Scientific Approach. (Illus.). (gr. 9 up). 1967. pap. text ed. 8.95 (ISBN 0-87487-068-2). Summy.
Lefkoff, Gerald. Analyzed Examples of Four-Part Harmony: For the Study of Harmonic Dictation, Part Singing & Keyboard Reading. LC 79-92507. 140p. 1980. pap. text ed. 12.50 (ISBN 0-935964-00-2). Glyphic Pr.
Lehmer, Isabel. Keyboard Harmony. LC 66-24048. 1967. pap. 9.95 (ISBN 0-935058-00-1). Donato Music.
Lloyd, Ruth & Lloyd, Norman. Creative Keyboard Musicianship: Fundamentals of Music & Keyboard Harmony Through Improvisation. 1975. pap. text ed. 16.50 scp (ISBN 0-06-044063-5, HarpC). Har-Row.
McHose, Allen I. & White, Donald F. Keyboard & Dictation Manual. (Eastman School of Music Ser.). 1949. 29.50x (ISBN 0-89197-255-2); pap. text ed. 18.50x (ISBN 0-89197-819-4). Irvington.
Melcher, Robert A. & Warch, Willard F. Music for Keyboard Harmony. 1966. pap. text ed. 14.50 (ISBN 0-13-607432-4). P-H.
Morris, Reginald O. Figured Harmony at the Keyboard, 2 Vols. 1932. Pt. 1. 4.50x (ISBN 0-19-321471-7); Pt. 2. 4.50x (ISBN 0-19-321472-5). Oxford U Pr.
Pelz, William. Basic Keyboard Skills: An Introduction to Accompaniment Improvisation, Transposition & Modulation, with an Appendix on Sight Reading. LC 80-22820. vii, 173p. 1981. Repr. of 1963 ed. PLB 23.50x (ISBN 0-313-22882-5, PEBK). Greenwood.
Shumway, Stanley. Harmony & Ear Training at the Keyboard. 3rd ed. 285p. 1980. write for info. plastic comb. (ISBN 0-697-03601-4). Wm C Brown.
Wedge, George A. Keyboard Harmony. 1924. pap. 8.95 (ISBN 0-02-872790-8). Schirmer Bks.

HARMONY OF THE SPHERES

Hammill, Carrie E. Celestial Journey & the Harmony of the Spheres. LC 79-28416. 183p. 1980. pap. 13.50 (ISBN 0-686-77617-8). Carrollton Pr.
Kayser, Hans. Akroasis: The Theory of World Harmonics. Lilienfeld, Robert, tr. LC 71-92587. (gr. 8 up). 1970. 5.95 (ISBN 0-87368-067-7). Plowshare.
Murchie, Guy. Music of the Spheres: The Material Universe from Atom to Quasar, Simply Explained, 2 Vols. rev. ed. (Illus.). (YA) (gr. 7-12). Vol. 1. pap. 5.00 (ISBN 0-486-21809-0); Vol. 2. pap. 5.00 (ISBN 0-486-21810-4). Dover.
--Music of the Spheres: The Material Universe from Atom to Quasar, Simply Explained, 2 vols. (Illus.). 20.00 set (ISBN 0-8446-0815-7). Peter Smith.

HARMONY SOCIETY

Bole, John A. The Harmony Society: A Chapter in German American Culture History. LC 72-2981. Repr. of 1904 ed. 14.50 (ISBN 0-404-10744-3). AMS Pr.
--The Harmony Society: A Chapter in German American Culture History. 1976. lib. bdg. 59.95 (ISBN 0-8490-1933-8). Gordon Pr.
Duss, John S. The Harmonists: A Personal History. LC 79-187439. (The American Utopian Adventure Ser.). (Illus.). xviii, 425p. Repr. of 1943 ed. lib. bdg. 19.50x (ISBN 0-87991-013-5). Porcupine Pr.
Kring, Hilda A. The Harmonists: A Folk-Cultural Approach. (ATLA Monograph: No. 3). 1973. 10.00 (ISBN 0-8108-0603-7). Scarecrow.
Lockwood, George B. The New Harmony Communities. LC 72-134410. Repr. of 1902 ed. 22.50 (ISBN 0-404-08456-7). AMS Pr.
--New Harmony Movement. LC 76-134411. Repr. of 1905 ed. 9.50 (ISBN 0-404-08457-5). AMS Pr.
Maclure, William & Fretageot, Marie D. Education & Reform at New Harmony: Correspondence of Wm. Maclure & Marie Duclos Fretageot, 1820-1833. Bestor, Arthur E., Jr., ed. LC 72-77059. Repr. of 1948 ed. lib. bdg. 12.50x (ISBN 0-678-00722-5). Kelley.
Williams, Aaron. Harmony Society at Economy, Penn. Founded by George Rapp, A.D. 1805: With Thoughts on the Destiny of Man, by George Rapp, 1824. LC 68-58669. Repr. of 1866 ed. lib. bdg. 17.50x (ISBN 0-678-00681-4). Kelley.
--Harmony Society at Economy, Pennsylvania. LC 70-134412. Repr. of 1866 ed. 12.50 (ISBN 0-404-08478-8). AMS Pr.

HARNESS

see also Bridle

HARNESS MAKING AND TRADE

Bloodgood, Lida. Saddle of the Queens. (Illus.). 12.50x (ISBN 0-87556-028-8). Saifer.
FitzGerald, W. N. The Harness Makers Illustrated Manual. (Illus.). 1974. 17.95 (ISBN 0-918778-17-4). Printed Horse.
Fitz-Gerald, William. The Harness Maker's Illustrated Manual. 16.95 (ISBN 0-88427-014-9). Green Hill.
--The Harness Makers' Illustrated Manual. (Illus.). 1977. Repr. of 1875 ed. 16.95x (ISBN 0-88427-014-9, Dist. by Caroline House Pubs). North River.
Hasluck, Paul N. Saddlery & Harness Making. (Illus.). 12.25 (ISBN 0-85131-148-2, Dist. by Sporting Book Center). J A Allen.

HARNESS RACING

Ainsley, Tom. Ainsley's New Complete Guide to Harness Racing. rev. ed. 1981. Repr. of 1971 ed. 17.95 (ISBN 0-671-25257-7). S&S.
Bernstein, Aaron. Beating the Harness Races. LC 75-18956. (Illus.). 224p. 1976. pap. 5.95 (ISBN 0-668-03872-1). Arco.
Cammarano, Nick. Winning at the Harness Races. 1977. pap. 3.00 (ISBN 0-87980-326-6). Wilshire.
Chaplin, Steve. Bettor's Guide to Harness Racing. 1977. 15.00 (ISBN 0-686-65434-X). Landau.
Emerson, Elliot. Bet & Win at Harness Racing. 1966. pap. 0.75 (ISBN 0-911996-24-9). Gamblers.
Evans, Donald P. Hanover: The Greatest Name in Harness Racing. LC 75-20589. (Illus.). 224p. 1976. 12.00 (ISBN 0-498-01694-3). A S Barnes.
--Still Hooked on Harness Racing. LC 78-55445. 1978. 9.95 (ISBN 0-498-02243-9). A S Barnes.
Evans, Donald P. & Pikelny, Philip S. Rambling Willie: The Horse That God Loved. LC 80-26884. (Illus.). 240p. 1981. 8.95 (ISBN 0-498-02542-X). A S Barnes.
Gibson, Walter B. How to Bet the Harness Races. (Gambler's Book Shelf). 72p. 1975. pap. 2.95 (ISBN 0-911996-57-5). Gamblers.
Henry, Marguerite. One Man's Horse. LC 77-10080. (Illus.). (gr. 3-6). 1977. 4.95 (ISBN 0-528-82092-3); PLB 4.97 (ISBN 0-528-80057-4). Rand.
Hill, Marie. Adios: The Big Daddy of Harness Racing. LC 72-92308. (Illus.). 1971. 9.95 (ISBN 0-668-02742-8). Arco.
--Gentleman Joe: The Story of Harness Driver Joe O'Brien. LC 74-14204. (Illus.). 160p. 1975. 7.95 (ISBN 0-668-03624-9). Arco.
How to Win at the Trotters. 1977. 14.95 (ISBN 0-685-86781-1). J&M Pub.
Kellogg, Charles. Driving the Horse in Harness: Training & Technique for Pleasure & Performance. LC 77-92777. (Illus.). 1978. 12.95 (ISBN 0-8289-0332-8); pap. 7.95 (ISBN 0-8289-0333-6). Greene.
Lehrman, Steve. Your Career in Harness Racing. LC 75-38343. (YA) (gr. 9 up). 1976. 6.95 (ISBN 0-689-10714-5). Atheneum.
Meadow, Barry. Success at Harness Racing. 2.45 (ISBN 0-685-22120-2). Wehman.
--Success at the Harness Races. 1970. 4.95 (ISBN 0-685-08136-2); pap. 2.45 (ISBN 0-8065-0005-0). Citadel Pr.
--Success at the Harness Races. 1976. pap. 3.00 (ISBN 0-87980-320-7). Wilshire.
Pines, Philip A. The Complete Book of Harness Racing. 3rd ed. LC 77-722. (Illus.). 1978. pap. 9.95 (ISBN 0-668-04258-3, 4258). Arco.
Sullivan, George. Harness Racing. LC 64-24733. (Illus.). 1964. 6.95 (ISBN 0-8303-0004-X). Fleet.
--Harness Racing. 1975. pap. 1.95 (ISBN 0-346-12180-9). Cornerstone.
Watney, Sanders, rev. by. The Harness Horse. 1981. 25.00x (ISBN 0-904558-21-5, Pub. by Saiga Pub). State Mutual Bk.
Welsh, Peter C. Track & Road: The American Trotting Horse. LC 67-29351. (Illus.). 174p. 1967. 15.00 (ISBN 0-87474-097-5). Smithsonian.

HAROLD, KING OF ENGLAND, 1022-1066

Birch, Williiam D., ed. Vita Haroldi: The Romance of the Life of Harold, King of England. Birch, William D., tr. LC 80-2232. Repr. of 1885 ed. 32.50 (ISBN 0-404-18753-6). AMS Pr.
Lytton, Dward. Harold, the Last of the Saxon Kings. 1970. 9.95x (ISBN 0-460-00015-2, Evman). Biblio Dist.

HAROLD, KING OF ENGLAND, 1022-1066-FICTION

Muntz, Hope. Golden Warrior. 1949. 8.95 (ISBN 0-684-13585-X, ScribT). Scribner.

HAROLD 3RD, KING OF NORWAY, 1015-1066

Magnusson, Magnus & Palsson, Hermann, trs. King Harald's Saga: Harald Hardradi of Norway. (Penguin Classics Ser.). 1976. pap. 1.95 (ISBN 0-14-044183-2). Penguin.

HARP

Anderson, Otto. The Bowed Harp. Repr. lib. bdg. 19.00 (ISBN 0-403-03851-0). Scholarly.
Andersson, Otto. The Bowed Harp. Schlesinger, Kathleen, tr. from Ger. LC 77-8733. 1977. Repr. of 1930 ed. lib. bdg. 30.00 (ISBN 0-89341-080-2). Longwood Pr.
Cuthbert, Sheila L. The Irish Harp Book - a Tutor & Companion. 1977. pap. text ed. 27.00 large format limp bdg. (ISBN 0-85342-279-6). Irish Bk Ctr.
Flood, William Grattan. The Story of the Harp. LC 76-42036. 1977. Repr. of 1905 ed. lib. bdg. 25.00 (ISBN 0-89341-057-8). Longwood Pr.
Jaffrennou, Gildas. Folk Harps. (Illus.). 103p. 1973. 11.00x (ISBN 0-85242-313-6). Intl Pubns Serv.
Meltzer, David. Harps. 1974. 5.00 (ISBN 0-685-56671-4, Pub. by Oyez); pap. 2.00 (ISBN 0-685-56672-2). SBD.

HARP-HISTORY

Inglefield, Ruth K. Marcel Grandjany: Concert Harpist. 1977. pap. text ed. 7.50 (ISBN 0-8191-0348-9). U Pr of Amer.
Rensch, Roslyn. The Harp: Its History, Technique & Repertoire. (Illus.). 246p. 1971. Repr. of 1969 ed. 40.00x (ISBN 0-7156-0467-8, Pub. by Duckworth England). Biblio Dist.
Rimmer, Joan. The Irish Harp. 2nd ed. (Irish Life & Culture Ser.). (Illus.). 1977. pap. 3.50 (ISBN 0-85342-151-X). Irish Bk Ctr.
Thomas, John. History of the Harp. Repr. lib. bdg. 19.00 (ISBN 0-403-03853-7). Scholarly.

HARPER, ROBERT GOODLOE, 1765-1825

Cox, Joseph W. Champion of Southern Federalism: Robert Goodloe Harper of South Carolina. LC 78-189554. 1972. 15.00 (ISBN 0-8046-9025-1, Natl U). Kennikat.

HARPER, WILLIAM RAINEY, 1856-1906

Storr, Richard J. Harper's University: The Beginnings. LC 66-13890. (Illus.). 1966. 10.00 (ISBN 0-226-77616-6). U. of Chicago Pr.

HARPER, FIRM, PUBLISHERS, NEW YORK

Exman, Eugene. Brothers Harper. LC 65-14651. (Illus.). 1965. 7.95 (ISBN 0-06-011200-X, HarpT). Har-Row.

HARPER'S BAZAAR

Erte. Designs by Erte: Fashion Drawings & Illustrations from "Harper's Bazar". LC 76-24054. (Illus.). 1976. pap. 6.00 (ISBN 0-486-23397-9). Dover.

HARPER'S FERRY, WEST VIRGINIA

American Anti-Slavery Society. Anti-Slavery History of the John Brown Year: Being the Twenty-Seventh Report of the American Anti-Slavery Society. LC 70-82169. (Anti-Slavery Crusade in America Ser). 1969. Repr. of 1861 ed. 15.00 (ISBN 0-405-00604-7). Arno.
Brown, Stephen D. Harpers Ferry. 3rd ed. LC 75-15007. (Illus.). 40p. 1979. pap. 1.95 (ISBN 0-685-93080-7). The Little Brown House.
--Places to Visit Near Harpers Ferry. 2nd rev. ed. (Illus.). 1979. pap. 2.00 (ISBN 0-685-93630-9). The Little Brown House.
Conway, Martin. Harpers Ferry-Time Remembered. Mehrkam, Deborah, ed. LC 80-65777. (Illus.). 160p. 1982. 14.95 (ISBN 0-938634-00-3); pap. 9.95 (ISBN 0-938634-01-1). Carabelle.
Roberts, Bruce & McNally, William. Harpers Ferry in Pictures. (Orig.). pap. 2.50 (ISBN 0-87461-004-4). McNally.
Smith, Merritt R. Harpers Ferry Armory & the New Technology: The Challenge of Change. LC 76-28022. (Illus.). 1977. 24.50x (ISBN 0-8014-0984-5); pap. 8.95 (ISBN 0-8014-9181-9). Cornell U Pr.

HARPER'S FERRY, WEST VIRGINIA-JOHN BROWN RAID, 1859

American Anti-Slavery Society. Anti-Slavery History of the John Brown Year. LC 76-76852. Repr. of 1861 ed. 16.50x (ISBN 0-8371-1165-X, Pub. by Negro U Pr). Greenwood.
Boteler, Alexander R., et al. John Brown's Raid at Harpers Ferry, West Virginia, 1859. (Illus.). 1980. pap. 2.00 (ISBN 0-89646-055-X). Outbooks.
Brown, John. Life, Trial & Execution of Captain John Brown, Known As "Old Brown of Ossawatomie". LC 69-18827. (Law, Politics & History Ser). 1969. Repr. of 1859 ed. lib. bdg. 17.50 (ISBN 0-306-71250-4). Da Capo.
Hinton, Richard J. John Brown & His Men. LC 68-29001. (American Negro: His History & Literature, Ser., No. 1). (Illus.). 1968. Repr. of 1894 ed. 26.00 (ISBN 0-405-01820-7). Arno.
Life, Trial & Execution of Captain John Brown: With a Full Account of the Attempted Insurrection at Harper's Ferry. facs. ed. LC 70-89398. (Black Heritage Library Collection Ser). 1859. 8.75 (ISBN 0-8369-8621-0). Arno.
Rosenberg, Daniel. Mary Brown: From Harper's Ferry to California. (Occasional Papers: No. 17). 1976. pap. 1.50 (ISBN 0-89977-024-X). Am Inst Marxist.
Teetor, Paul R. A Matter of Hours: Treason at Harper's Ferry. LC 80-65576. (Illus.). 360p. 1981. 27.50 (ISBN 0-8386-3012-X). Fairleigh Dickinson.
Williams, James. South Vindicated. LC 79-99425. 1969. Repr. of 1862 ed. lib. bdg. 12.00 (ISBN 0-8411-0099-3). Metro Bks.

HARPOONS

Mason, Otis T. Aboriginal American Harpoons. (Illus.). Repr. of 1902 ed. pap. 12.50 (ISBN 0-8466-4058-9, SJ158). Shorey.

HARPSICHORD

see also Piano

Bremner, Robert. Harpsichord or Spinnet Miscellany. Darling, James S., ed. LC 75-165365. 1972. pap. 2.95 (ISBN 0-910412-94-4). Williamsburg.

Corrette, Michel. Le Maitre De Clavecin. (Monuments of Music and Music Literature in Facsimile, Ser II, Vol. 13). 1976. Repr. of 1753 ed. 35.00x (ISBN 0-8450-2213-X). Broude.
Dale, William. Tschudi: The Harpsichord Maker. LC 77-75208. 1977. Repr. of 1913 ed. lib. bdg. 12.50 (ISBN 0-89341-069-1). Longwood Pr.
Hubbard, Frank T. Three Centuries of Harpsichord Making. LC 65-12784. (Illus.). 1965. 20.00 (ISBN 0-674-88845-6). Harvard U Pr.
Kern, Evan J. The Harpsichord: Design & Construction. 144p. 1980. 16.95 (ISBN 0-442-23348-5). Van Nos Reinhold.
Klop, G. C. Harpsichord Tuning. Wilson, Glen, tr. from Dutch. (Illus.). 30p. 1974. pap. 3.75x (ISBN 0-915548-10-0). Sunbury Pr.
Naylor, E. W. An Elizabethan Virginal Book. (Keyboard Studies Ser.: Vol. 1). (Illus.). 1981. Repr. of 1905 ed. 32.50 (ISBN 90-6027-304-4, Pub. by Frits Knuf Netherlands). Pendragon NY.
Russell, Raymond. The Harpsichord & Clavichord. (Illus.). 1980. 30.00 (ISBN 0-684-16466-3, ScribT). Scribner.
Scheurwater, W. & Van Acht, R. Oude Klavecimbels, Hun Bouw En Restauratie: Old Harpsichords, Their Construction & Restauration. (Haags Gemeentemuseum, 'kijkboekjes' Ser.: Vol. 2). (Dutch & Eng.). 1976. wrappers 15.00 (ISBN 90-6027-337-0, Pub. by Frits Knuf Netherlands). Pendragon NY.
Schott, Howard. Playing the Harpsichord: With Revised Introduction. LC 78-11951. 1979. pap. 5.95 (ISBN 0-312-61636-8). St Martin.

HARPISICHORD AND VIOLA DA GAMBA MUSIC
see Viola Da Gamba and Harpsichord Music

HARPSICHORD MUSIC
Bach, Johann. Harpsichord Music. (Bach-Gesellschaft ed.). 8.75 (ISBN 0-8446-0467-4). Peter Smith.
Bach, Johann S. Two & Three Part Inventions (Fifteen Inventions & Fifteen Symphonies) Simon, Eric, ed. LC 68-11918. (Facsimile Series of Musical Manuscripts). (Orig.). 1969. pap. 4.00 (ISBN 0-486-21982-8). Dover.
Bedford, Frances & Conant, Robert. Twentieth-Century Harpsichord Music: A Classified Catalog. 1974. pap. 8.50 (ISBN 0-913574-08-2). Eur-Am Music.
Bremner, Robert. The Harpsichord or Spinnet Miscellany. Darling, James S., ed. LC 75-165365. 32p. 1972. 5.95x (ISBN 0-8139-0383-1, Colonial Williamsburg). U Pr of Va.
Byrd, William. My Ladye Nevells Booke of Virginal Music. Andrews, Hilda, ed. LC 68-55532. 1969. pap. 7.50 (ISBN 0-486-22246-2). Dover.
Chilcot, Thomas. Two Suites for Harpsichord. Beechey, Gwilym, ed. LC 72-626211. (Penn State Music Series, No. 22). pap. 4.00 (ISBN 0-271-09122-3). Pa St U Pr.
Glyn, Margaret H. Elizabethan Virginal Music & Its Composers. LC 77-75230. 1977. Repr. of 1934 ed. lib. bdg. 20.00 (ISBN 0-89341-086-1). Longwood Pr.
Gustafson, Bruce. French Harpsichord Music of the Seventeenth Century: A Thematic Catalog of the Sources with Commentary, 3 vols, No. 11. Buelow, George, ed. (Studies in Musicology). 1979. Set. 59.95 (ISBN 0-8357-1069-6, Pub. by UMI Res Pr). Vol. 1 (ISBN 0-8357-1066-1). Vol. 2 (ISBN 0-8357-1067-X). Univ Microfilms.
Hopkinson, Francis. Seven Songs for the Harpsichord or Forte Piano. (Illus.). 1954. pap. 10.00x (ISBN 0-8450-2597-X, Musical Americana). Broude.
Maitland, J. A. & Squire, W. B. Fitzwilliam Virginal Book, 2 Vols. Set. 18.00 (ISBN 0-8446-2514-0). Peter Smith.
Maitland, John A. & Squire, W. Barclay. Fitzwilliam Virginal Book. 2 Vols. 1963. Vol. 1. pap. 9.95 (ISBN 0-486-21068-5); Vol. 2. pap. 9.95 (ISBN 0-486-21069-3). Dover.
Naylor, E. W. An Elizabethan Virginal Book. LC 70-87638. (Music Ser). 1970. Repr. of 1905 ed. lib. bdg. 25.00 (ISBN 0-306-71792-1). Da Capo.
Poglietti, Alessandro. Harpsichord Music. Nettles, William E., ed. LC 65-26098. (Penn State Music Series, No. 9). 44p. 1965. pap. 3.75x (ISBN 0-271-73066-8). Pa St U Pr.
Purcell, Henry. Choice Collection of Lessons for the Harpsichord or Spinnet. (Monuments of Music Literature in Facsimile: Ser. I, Vol. 26). (Illus.). 1978. Repr. of 1696 ed. 25.00x (ISBN 0-8450-2026-9). Broude.
Roseingrave, Thomas. Compositions for Organ & Harpsichord. Stevens, Denis, ed. LC 63-21370. (Penn State Music Series, No. 2). 44p. 1964. pap. 3.75x (ISBN 0-271-73054-4). Pa St U Pr.

HARPSICHORD MUSIC–HISTORY AND CRITICISM
Apel, Willi. The History of Keyboard Music to 1700. Tischler, Hans, tr. LC 79-135015. 896p. 1972. 30.00x (ISBN 0-253-32795-4). Ind U Pr.
Bedford, Frances & Conant, Robert. Twentieth-Century Harpsichord Music: A Classified Catalog. 1974. pap. 8.50 (ISBN 0-913574-08-2). Eur-Am Music.
Borren, Charles V. Sources of Keyboard Music in England. Matthew, James E., tr. LC 78-106714. Repr. of 1914 ed. lib. bdg. 16.25x (ISBN 0-8371-3444-7, BOKM). Greenwood.
Gillespie, John. Five Centuries of Keyboard Music. (Illus.). xii, 463p. 1972. pap. 6.95 (ISBN 0-486-22855-X). Dover.
Kenyon, Max. Harpsichord Music: A Survey. LC 78-181197. 256p. 1949. Repr. 19.00 (ISBN 0-403-01605-3). Scholarly.

HARRIMAN, EDWARD HENRY, 1848-1909
Eckenrode, H. J. & Edmunds, Pocahontas W. E. H. Harriman: The Little Giant of Wall Street. Bruchey, Stuart, ed. LC 80-1304. (Railroads Ser.). 1981. Repr. of 1933 ed. lib. bdg. 22.00x (ISBN 0-405-13773-7). Arno.
Kennan, George. E. H. Harriman, 2 Vols. LC 77-99663. (Select Bibliographies Reprint Ser). 1922. Set. 55.00 (ISBN 0-8369-5092-5). Arno.
--E. H. Harriman: A Biography, 2 vols. Bruchey, Stuart, ed. LC 80-1322. (Railroads Ser.). 1981. Repr. of 1922 ed. lib. bdg. 75.00x (ISBN 0-405-13795-8). Arno.

HARRINGTON, JAMES, 1611-1677
Blitzer, Charles. Immortal Commonwealth: The Political Thought of James Harrington. 1970. Repr. of 1960 ed. 20.00 (ISBN 0-208-00811-X, Archon). Shoe String.
Downs, Michael. James Harrington. (English Authors Ser.: No. 188). 1977. lib. bdg. 12.50 (ISBN 0-8057-6693-6). Twayne.
Macpherson, Crawford B. Political Theory of Possessive Individualism: Hobbes to Locke. (Oxford Paperbacks Ser). 1962. pap. 5.95x (ISBN 0-19-881084-9). Oxford U Pr.
Russell-Smith, Hugh F. Harrington & His Oceana. LC 70-159228. xi, 223p. 1971. Repr. of 1914 ed. lib. bdg. 14.00x (ISBN 0-374-96996-5). Octagon.
Tawney, R. H. Harrington's Interpretation of His Age. 1974. lib. bdg. 69.95 (ISBN 0-8490-0283-4). Gordon Pr.

HARRIOT, THOMAS
see Hariot, Thomas, 1560-1621

HARRIS, ELEANOR VAN BUSKIRK
Harris, Eleanor B. The Ship That Never Returned. LC 73-84912. (Illus.). 256p. 1973. 8.95 (ISBN 0-8158-0310-9). Chris Mass.

HARRIS, FRANK, 1855-1931
Brome, Vincent. Frank Harris. LC 79-8057. Repr. of 1959 ed. 20.00 (ISBN 0-404-18368-9). AMS Pr.
Harris, Frank. My Life & Loves. Gallagher, John F., ed. & intro. by. 1963. pap. 4.95 (ISBN 0-394-17124-1, B152, BC). Grove.
Kingsmill, Hugh. Frank Harris. LC 74-7348. (English Literature Ser., No. 33). 1974. lib. bdg. 32.95 (ISBN 0-8383-1854-1). Haskell.
Sherrard, Robert H. Bernard Shaw, Frank Harris, & Oscar Wilde. LC 74-30469. (English Literature Ser., No. 33). 1974. lib. bdg. 41.95 (ISBN 0-8383-2019-8). Haskell.
Tobin, A. I. & Gertz, Elmer. Frank Harris: A Study in Black & White. LC 71-133279. (English Biography Ser., No. 31). 1970. Repr. of 1931 ed. lib. bdg. 56.95 (ISBN 0-8383-1178-4). Haskell.
Viereck, George S. Glimpses of the Great. 1978. Repr. of 1930 ed. lib. bdg. 25.00 (ISBN 0-89760-903-4, Telegraph). Dynamic Learn Corp.

HARRIS, GEORGE WASHINGTON, 1814-1869
Rickels, Milton. George Washington Harris. (U. S. Authors Ser.: No. 91). 10.95 (ISBN 0-8057-0344-6). Twayne.
--George Washington Harris. (Twayne's United States Authors Ser). 1965. pap. 3.45 (ISBN 0-8084-0144-0, T91, Twayne). Coll & U Pr.
--George Washington Harris. LC 65-24244. (United States Authors Ser.). 1965. lib. bdg. 7.95x (ISBN 0-89197-770-8); pap. text ed. 2.95x (ISBN 0-8290-0009-7). Irvington.

HARRIS, JOEL CHANDLER, 1848-1908
Bickley, R. Bruce, et al, eds. Joel Chandler Harris: A Reference Guide. 1978. lib. bdg. 30.00 (ISBN 0-8161-7873-9). G K Hall.
Bickley, R. Bruce, Jr. Critical Essays on Joel Chandler Harris. (Critical Essays on American Literature Ser.). 1981. 25.00 (ISBN 0-8161-8381-3). Twayne.
--Joel Chandler Harris. (United States Authors Ser.: No. 308). 1978. lib. bdg. 12.50 (ISBN 0-8057-7215-4). Twayne.
Cousins, Paul M. Joel Chandler Harris: A Biography. LC 68-13452. (Southern Literary Studies). (Illus.). 1968. 17.50 (ISBN 0-8071-0411-6). La State U Pr.
Harris, Julia C. Life & Letters of Joel Chandler Harris. LC 72-168247. (Illus.). Repr. of 1918 ed. 21.00 (ISBN 0-404-00059-2). AMS Pr.

HARRIS, THOMAS LAKE, 1823-1906
Cuthbert, Arthur A. The Life & World-Work of Thomas Lake Harris, Written from Direct Personal Knowledge. LC 72-2954. Repr. of 1909 ed. 21.50 (ISBN 0-404-10719-2). AMS Pr.
Ericson, Jack T., ed. Thomas Lake Harris & the Brotherhood of the New Life: Books, Pamphlets, Serials & Manuscripts, 1854-1942; a Guide to the Microfilm Edition. LC 75-2398. 48p. 1975. pap. 15.00 (ISBN 0-88455-061-3). Microfilming Corp.
Schneider, Herbert & Lawton, George. Prophet & a Pilgrim. LC 78-134433. (Illus.). Repr. of 1942 ed. 36.50 (ISBN 0-404-05610-5). AMS Pr.

HARRIS, THOMAS MEALEY, 1817-1906
Crittenden, H. Temple. Maine Scenic Route. 1966. 12.50 (ISBN 0-87012-060-3). McClain.
Matheny, H. E. Major General Thomas Maley Harris, Including Roster of 10th West Virginia Volunteer Infantry Regiment, 1861-1865. 1963. 12.50 (ISBN 0-87012-003-4). McClain.

HARRIS, TOWNSEND, 1804-1878
Gowen, Herbert H. Five Foreigners in Japan. facs. ed. LC 67-28735. (Essay Index Reprint Ser). 1936. 18.00 (ISBN 0-8369-0491-5). Arno.
Griffis, William E. Townsend Harris: First American Envoy in Japan. facsimile ed. LC 74-175698. (Select Bibliographies Reprint Ser). Repr. of 1895 ed. 19.00 (ISBN 0-8369-6613-9). Arno.

HARRIS, WILLIAM TORREY, 1835-1909
Leidecker, K. F. Yankee Teacher: The Life of William Torrey Harris. Repr. of 1946 ed. 24.00 (ISBN 0-527-56000-6). Kraus Repr.
McCluskey, Neil Gerard. Public Schools & Moral Education. LC 74-12848. 315p. 1975. Repr. of 1958 ed. lib. bdg. 17.50x (ISBN 0-8371-7762-6, MCPS). Greenwood.
Pochmann, Henry A. New England Transcendentalism & St. Louis Hegelianism. LC 68-55163. (Studies in Comparative Literature, No. 35). 1969. Repr. of 1948 ed. lib. bdg. 26.95 (ISBN 0-8383-0610-1). Haskell.

HARRIS, WILLIAM WADE
Haliburton, Gordon M. The Prophet Harris: A Study of an African Prophet & His Mass-Movement in the Ivory Coast & the Gold Coast, 1913-1915. (Illus.). 192p. 1973. pap. 3.50x (ISBN 0-19-501625-4). Oxford U Pr.

HARRIS TWEED ASSOCIATION
Thompson, Francis G. Harris Tweed. LC 69-10864. (Illus.). 1968. 11.95x (ISBN 0-678-05634-X). Kelley.

HARRISON, BENJAMIN, PRES. U. S., 1833-1901
Harrison, Benjamin. Speeches of Benjamin Harrison. Hedges, Charles, ed. LC 74-137915. (American History & Culture in the Nineteenth Century Ser). 1971. Repr. of 1892 ed. 22.50 (ISBN 0-8046-1494-6). Kennikat.
McIlwaine, H. R., ed. The Letters of Thomas Nelson & Benjamin Harrison. LC 27-2700. (Official Letters of the Governors of Virginia Ser: Vol. 3). 1929. 7.50 (ISBN 0-88490-020-7). VA State Lib.
Sievers, H. J., ed. Benjain Harrison, Eighteen Thirty-Three to Nineteen Hundred & One: Chronology, Documents, Bibliographical Aids. LC 74-83746. 1969. 8.00 (ISBN 0-379-12059-3). Oceana.

HARRISON, WILLIAM HENRY, PRES. U. S., 1773-1841
Goebel, Dorothy B. William Henry Harrison: A Political Biography. LC 73-20129. (Perspectives in American History Ser.: No. 11). (Illus.). xi, 456p. Repr. of 1926 ed. lib. bdg. 22.50x (ISBN 0-87991-326-6). Porcupine Pr.
Hall, James. Memoir of the Public Services of William Henry Harrison, of Ohio. facs. ed. LC 70-117879. (Select Bibliographies Reprint Ser). 1836. 20.00 (ISBN 0-8369-5332-0). Arno.
Harrison, William H. Messages & Letters of William Henry Harrison, 2 vols. facsimile ed. Esarey, Logan, ed. LC 75-99. (Mid-American Frontier Ser.). 1975. Repr. of 1922 ed. Set. 90.00x (ISBN 0-405-06865-4); 45.00x ea. Vol. 1 (ISBN 0-405-06866-2). Vol. 2 (ISBN 0-405-06867-0). Arno.
Peckham, Howard H. William Henry Harrison: Young Tippecanoe. (Childhood of Famous Americans Ser.). (Illus.). (gr. 3-7). 1951. 3.95 (ISBN 0-672-50189-9). Bobbs.
Todd, Charles S. & Drake, Benjamin. Sketches of the Civil & Military Services of William Henry Harrison. facsimile ed. LC 75-128. (Mid-American Frontier Ser.). 1975. Repr. of 1840 ed. 9.00x (ISBN 0-405-06893-X). Arno.

HARSDORFER, GEORGE PHILIPP, 1607-1658
Kayser, Wolfgang J. Klangmalerei Bei Harsdoerffer. 1932. 21.50 (ISBN 0-384-28831-6); pap. 18.50 (ISBN 0-384-28830-8). Johnson Repr.

HARSHA (OR HARSHAVARDHANA), RAJAH, d. 648
Mookerji, R. K. Harsha. 3rd ed. (Illus.). 1965. 1.95 (ISBN 0-89684-212-6). Orient Bk Dist.

HART, MOSS, 1904-1961
Hart, Moss. Act One. LC 75-28169. 1976. pap. 2.95 (ISBN 0-394-71633-7, Vin). Random.

HART FAMILY
Frame, Katherine H. The Harts of Randolph. 1977. 24.00 (ISBN 0-87012-266-5). McClain.

HARTE, BRET, 1836-1902
Boynton, Henry W. Bret Harte. LC 70-133513. (Select Bibliographies Reprint Ser.). 1972. Repr. of 1903 ed. 10.00 (ISBN 0-8369-5545-5). Arno.
--Bret Harte. LC 70-133513. (Select Bibliographies Reprint Ser.). 1972. Repr. of 1903 ed. 10.00 (ISBN 0-8369-5545-5). Arno.
Bret Harte: A Reference Guide. 1980. lib. bdg. 38.00 (ISBN 0-8161-8197-7). G K Hall.
Gaer, Joseph. Bret Harte: Bibliography & Biographical Data. 1967. Repr. of 1935 ed. 23.50 (ISBN 0-8337-1254-3). B Franklin.
Harte, Bret. The Letters of Bret Harte. LC 70-161761. Repr. of 1926 ed. 32.50 (ISBN 0-404-09024-9). AMS Pr.
Harte, Geoffrey B. The Letters of Bret Harte. 40.00 (ISBN 0-932062-78-4). Sharon Hill.
Kozlay, Charles. Lectures of Bret Harte. LC 77-28745. 1909. lib. bdg. 10.00 (ISBN 0-8414-5463-9). Folcroft.
Leaves from a Life: Thackeray, Dickens, Browning, Bret Harte, Du Maurier, Trollope. 1978. Repr. of 1908 ed. lib. bdg. 25.00 (ISBN 0-8492-1595-1). R West.
Merwin, Henry C. Life of Bret Harte, with Some Account of the California Pioneers. LC 67-23887. 1967. Repr. of 1911 ed. 24.00 (ISBN 0-8103-3042-3). Gale.
Morrow, Patrick. Bret Harte. LC 72-619588. (Western Writers Ser: No. 5). (Illus.). 51p. (Orig.). 1972. pap. 2.00 (ISBN 0-88430-004-8). Boise St Univ.
--Bret Harte, Literary Critic. LC 78-71393. 1979. 10.95 (ISBN 0-87972-133-2). Bowling Green Univ.
Pemberton, Thomas E. The Life of Bret Harte. facsimile ed. LC 74-133530. (Select Bibliographies Ser). Repr. of 1903 ed. 19.00 (ISBN 0-8369-5562-5). Arno.
Stewart, George R. Bret Harte, Argonaut & Exile. LC 76-6593. Repr. of 1931 ed. 30.00 (ISBN 0-404-15298-8). AMS Pr.
Stewart, George R., Jr. Bibliography of the Writings of Bret Harte. LC 76-26851. 1933. lib. bdg. 15.00 (ISBN 0-8414-7839-2). Folcroft.
The Works of Bret Harte, 18 vols. 1981. Repr. of 1899 ed. Set. lib. bdg. 300.00 (ISBN 0-8495-2356-7). Arden Lib.

HARTFORD (SLOOP)
Jameson, Edwin M. & Sternlicht, Sanford. The Black Devil of the Bayous: The Life & Times of the United States Steam Sloop Hartford, 1858 - 1957. 205p. 1970. 12.50 (ISBN 0-8398-0951-4). Parnassus Imprints.

HARTFORD, CONNECTICUT
Andrews, Charles M. The River Towns of Connecticut: A Study of Wethersfield, Hartford & Windsor. LC 78-63790. (Johns Hopkins University. Studies in the Social Sciences. Seventh Ser. 1889: 7-9). Repr. of 1889 ed. 11.50 (ISBN 0-404-61055-2). AMS Pr.
Andrews, Kenneth R. Nook Farm: Mark Twain's Hartford Circle. LC 50-9751. (Illus.). 302p. 1960. pap. 2.95 (ISBN 0-295-78576-4, WP49). U of Wash Pr.
Close, F. Perry. History of Hartford Streets. facsimile ed. 1969. pap. 2.50x (ISBN 0-940748-24-X). Conn Hist Soc.
Delana, Alice & Reik, Cynthia, eds. On Common Ground: A Selection of Hartford Writers. (Illus.). 1975. pap. 5.95 (ISBN 0-917482-03-4). Stowe-Day.
Grant, Marion H. In & About Hartford: Tours & Tales. (Illus.). 1977. 6.95x (ISBN 0-940748-26-6); pap. 1.00x (ISBN 0-686-26746-X). Conn Hist Soc.
Henning, Alyson & MacColl, Gwynne. A Guide to Hartford. LC 78-51227. (Illus.). 1978. pap. 4.95 (ISBN 0-87106-094-9). Globe Pequot.
Love, William D. The Colonial History of Hartford. LC 73-85465. (Illus.). 416p. 1974. casebound 15.00 (ISBN 0-87106-133-3). Globe Pequot.
--The Colonial History of Hartford: Bicentennial Edition. (Illus.). 1974. Repr. of 1914 ed. 15.00x (ISBN 0-686-26742-7). Conn Hist Soc.
Silverman, Morris. Hartford Jews: Sixteen Fifty-Nine to Nineteen Seventy. (Illus.). 448p. 1970. 17.50x (ISBN 0-940748-21-5). Conn Hist Soc.
Van Why, Joseph S. Nook Farm. French, Earl A., ed. LC 75-20778. (Illus.). 1975. pap. 3.00 (ISBN 0-917482-02-6). Stowe-Day.

HARTFORD, MICHIGAN
Arrow Pub Staff, ed. Arrow Street Guide of Greater Hartford. 1976. pap. 2.25 (ISBN 0-685-70907-8). Arrow Pub.

HARTFORD CONVENTION, 1814
Dwight, Theodore. History of the Hartford Convention. facs. ed. (Select Bibliographies Reprint Ser). 1833. 25.00 (ISBN 0-8369-5326-6). Arno.
--History of the Hartford Convention. LC 77-99474. (American Constitutional & Legal History Ser). 1970. Repr. of 1833 ed. 45.00 (ISBN 0-306-71855-3). Da Capo.
HARTFORD COURANT
Smith, James E. One Hundred Years of Hartford's Courant, from Colonial Times Through the Civil War. LC 74-121759. 1970. Repr. of 1949 ed. 19.50 (ISBN 0-208-00962-0, Archon). Shoe String.
HARTLEY, DAVID, 1705-1757
Hazlitt, William. Essay on the Principles of Human Action, 1805. LC 70-75943. (Hist. of Psych. Ser.). 1969. 28.00x (ISBN 0-8201-1053-1). Schol Facsimiles.
HARTLEY, LESLIE POLES, 1895-
Bloomfield, P. L. P. Hartley. pap. 2.95 (ISBN 0-685-31890-7, WTW217, WTW217). British Bk Ctr.
Schardt, Alois J., et al. Feininger-Hartley. LC 66-26122. (Museum of Modern Art Publications in Reprint Ser.). Repr. of 1944 ed. 14.00 (ISBN 0-405-01511-9). Arno.
HARTMAN FAMILY
Shank, Merna B. & Shank, Sanford L., eds. Hartman History. 1959. loose leaf bdg. 3.25x (ISBN 0-87813-127-2). Park View.
HARTMANN, NICOLAI, 1882-1951
Samuel, Otto. Foundation of Onthology. 1954. 3.75 (ISBN 0-8022-1477-0). Philos Lib.
HARTMANN VON AUE, 12TH CENTURY
Cutting, Starr W. Der Conjunctiv Bei Hartmann Von Aue. LC 76-173037. (Chicago. University. Germanic Studies: No. 1). Repr. of 1894 ed. 14.00 (ISBN 0-404-50271-7). AMS Pr.
Fischer, Rudolf. Zu Den Kunstformen Des Mittelalterlichen Epos. 1965. pap. 21.00 (ISBN 0-384-15765-3). Johnson Repr.
Hartmann Von Aue. Der Arme Heinrich nebst einer Auswahl aus der Klage, dem Gregorius und Den liedern: Mit einem Woerterverzeichnis. 2nd rev. ed. Mauer, Friedrich, ed. (Sammlung Goeschen, No. 18). (Ger). 1968. 3.25x (ISBN 3-11-002723-2). De Gruyter.
--Iwein: Eine Erzaehlung, 2 vols. 7th ed. Benecke, G. F., et al, eds. Incl. Vol. 1. Text. xii, 196p. 1968. 17.75x (ISBN 3-11-000329-5); Vol. 2. Handschriftenuebersicht: Anmerkungen und Lesarten. iv, 227p. 1968. 17.75 (ISBN 3-11-000330-9). (Ger.). De Gruyter.
--Die Klage: Das (zweite) Buechlein aus dem Ambraser Heldenbuch. Zutt, Herta, ed. xx, 177p. (Ger.). 1968. 15.25x (ISBN 3-11-000549-2). De Gruyter.
Hartmann von Ave. Iwein. 2nd ed. Benecke, G. F., et al, eds. Cramer, Thomas, tr. & notes by. vi, 232p. (Ger.). 1974. 20.00x (ISBN 3-11-004860-4). De Gruyter.
HARTSHORNE, CHARLES, 1897-
Ford, Lewis S., ed. Two Process Philosophers: Hartshorne's Encounter with Whitehead. LC 73-85592. (American Academy of Religion. Studies in Religion). 1973. pap. 7.50 (ISBN 0-88420-104-X, 010005). Scholars Pr Ca.
Goodwin, George L. The Ontological Argument of Charles Hartshorne. LC 78-2821. 1978. pap. 7.50 (ISBN 0-89130-228-X). Scholars Pr Ca.
Gragg, Alan. Hartshorne, Charles. new ed. Patterson, Bob E., ed. LC 70-188063. (Makers of Modern Theological Minds Ser.). 128p. 1973. 5.95 (ISBN 0-87680-270-6, 80270). Word Bks.
Gunton, Colin E. Becoming & Being: The Doctrine of God in Charles Hartshorne & Karl Barth. (Theological Monographs). 1978. text ed. 37.50x (ISBN 0-19-826713-4). Oxford U Pr.
Peters, Eugene H. Hartshorne & Neoclassical Metaphysics: An Interpretation. LC 77-116531. 1970. 10.75x (ISBN 0-8032-0766-2). U of Nebr Pr.
HARTUNG, HANS, 1904-
Geldzahler, Henry, intro. by. Hans Hartung: Paintings, 1971-1975. LC 75-31609. (Illus.). 1975. pap. 2.95 (ISBN 0-87099-145-0). Metro Mus Art.
HARUN AL-RASHID, CALIPH, 763-809
Buckler, Francis W. Harunu'l-Rashid & Charles the Great. LC 75-41041. (BCL Ser. II). Repr. of 1931 ed. 11.50 (ISBN 0-404-14761-5). AMS Pr.
Palmer, E. H. Haroun Al-Raschid: Caliph of Bagdad. 1976. lib. bdg. 59.95 (ISBN 0-8490-1934-6). Gordon Pr.
HARUNOBU, 1725-1770
Chiba, Reiko. Making of a Japanese Print. LC 59-14277. (Illus.). 1960. brocade 6.95 (ISBN 0-8048-0393-5). C E Tuttle.
HARVARD (TRAINING PLANES)
see T-Six (Training Planes)
HARVARD-RADCLIFFE VOLUNTEER PROGRAM FOR SERVICE TO MENTAL PATIENTS
Umbarger, Carter C., et al. College Students in a Mental Hospital. LC 62-14136. 192p. 1962. pap. 19.75 (ISBN 0-8089-0513-9). Grune.
HARVARD UNIVERSITY
Buck, Paul H., ed. Social Sciences at Harvard, 1860-1920: From Inculcation to the Open Mind. LC 65-22059. 1965. 17.50x (ISBN 0-674-81420-7). Harvard U Pr.
Bush, George G. Harvard: The First American University. 1978. Repr. of 1886 ed. lib. bdg. 30.00 (ISBN 0-8492-3703-3). R West.
Eliot, Charles W. Harvard Memories. LC 76-93336. (Essay Index Reprint Ser). 1923. 16.00 (ISBN 0-8369-1289-6). Arno.
Harris, Seymour E. Economics of Harvard. 1970. 20.50 (ISBN 0-07-026832-0, C). McGraw.
Harvard University Library. Philosophy & Psychology: Classification Schedule, Author & Title Listing, Chronological Listing, 2 vols. LC 72-83389. (Widener Library Shelflist Ser: No. 42-43). 1973. 95.00x (ISBN 0-674-66486-8). Harvard U Pr.
Harvard University Museum of Comparative Zoology. Catalogue of the Library of the Museum of Comparative Zoology, First Supplement. 1976. lib. bdg. 120.00 (ISBN 0-8161-0811-0). G K Hall.
Jones, Bessie Z. & Boyd, Lyle G. Harvard College Observatory: The First Four Directorships, 1838-1919. LC 73-143228. (Illus.). 1971. 25.00x (ISBN 0-674-37460-6, Belknap Pr). Harvard U Pr.
LeBoutillier, John. Harvard Hates America. LC 78-60229. 1978. 7.95 (ISBN 0-89526-689-X). Regnery-Gateway.
Lopez, Enrique H. The Harvard Mystique: The Power Syndrome That Effects Our Lives from Sesame Street to the White House. 1979. 10.00 (ISBN 0-02-575120-4). Macmillan.
Lowell, Abbott L. At War with Academic Traditions in America. LC 79-108395. (Illus.). xiv, 357p. Repr. of 1934 ed. lib. bdg. 15.75x (ISBN 0-8371-3818-3, LOAT). Greenwood.
Spalding, Walter R. Music at Harvard: A Historical Review of Men & Events. LC 76-58921. (Music Reprint Series). 1977. Repr. of 1935 ed. lib. bdg. 27.50 (ISBN 0-306-70871-X). Da Capo.
HARVARD UNIVERSITY-BIOGRAPHY
Change Magazine Editors. The Great Core Curriculum Debate: Education As a Mirror of Culture. LC 79-51332. 108p. (Orig.). 1980. pap. 7.95 (ISBN 0-915390-22-1). Change Mag.
Peabody, Andrew P. Harvard Reminiscences. LC 72-39149. (Essay Index Reprint Ser.). Repr. of 1888 ed. 16.00 (ISBN 0-8369-2708-7). Arno.
Shipton, Clifford K. New England Life in the Eighteenth Century: Representative Biographies from Sibley's Harvard Graduates. LC 63-9562. (Illus.). 1963. 30.00x (ISBN 0-674-61250-7, Belknap Pr). Harvard U Pr.
Sibley, John L. Biographical Sketches of Graduates of Harvard University in Cambridge, Massachusetts. (Vols. 1-3). Repr. of 1873 ed. Set. 127.00 (ISBN 0-384-55240-4). Johnson Repr.
HARVARD UNIVERSITY-DESCRIPTION
Change Magazine Editors. The Great Core Curriculum Debate: Education As a Mirror of Culture. LC 79-51332. 108p. (Orig.). 1980. pap. 7.95 (ISBN 0-915390-22-1). Change Mag.
HARVARD UNIVERSITY-GRADUATE SCHOOL OF BUSINESS ADMINISTRATION
Cohen, Peter. The Gospel According to the Harvard Business School. 336p. 1974. pap. 2.95 (ISBN 0-14-003912-0). Penguin.
Harvard University, Graduate School of Business Administration. Subject Catalog of the Baker Library: First Supplement. 1974. 115.00 (ISBN 0-8161-1180-4). G K Hall.
Roethlisberger, Fritz J. The Elusive Phenomena: An Autobiographical Account of My Work in the Field of Organizational Behavior at the Harvard Business School. Lombard, George F., ed. 1978. 18.50x (ISBN 0-87584-116-3). Harvard Busn.
HARVARD UNIVERSITY-GRADUATE SCHOOL OF EDUCATION
Change Magazine Editors. The Great Core Curriculum Debate: Education As a Mirror of Culture. LC 79-51332. 108p. (Orig.). 1980. pap. 7.95 (ISBN 0-915390-22-1). Change Mag.
Harvard Committee. Graduate Study of Education. LC 66-27587. 1966. 5.95x (ISBN 0-674-36000-1). Harvard U Pr.
HARVARD UNIVERSITY-HISTORY
Abbot, Francis E. Professor Royce's Libel. Bd. with A Public Remonstrance Addressed to the Board of Overseers of Harvard University. LC 75-3011. Repr. of 1892 ed. 11.50 (ISBN 0-404-59003-9). AMS Pr.
Adams, Henry. Historical Essays. Repr. of 1891 ed. 39.50 (ISBN 3-4870-4645-8). Adler.
Anderson, Robert C. Directions of a Town: A History of Harvard Massachusetts. 1976. soft bdg. 5.95 (ISBN 0-916782-01-8). Harvard Common Pr.
Bentinck-Smith, William, ed. Harvard Book: Selections from Three Centuries. LC 53-11123. 1953. 16.50x (ISBN 0-674-37300-6). Harvard U Pr.
Foster, Margery S. Out of Smalle Beginings: An Economic History of Harvard College in the Puritan Period, 1636-1712. LC 62-13266. (Illus.). 1962. 12.50x (ISBN 0-674-64800-5, Belknap Pr). Harvard U Pr.
McCord, David T. In Sight of Sever: Essays from Harvard. LC 63-19143. 1963. 16.00x (ISBN 0-674-44701-8). Harvard U Pr.
Morison, Samuel E. Founding of Harvard College. LC 35-4941. (Illus.). 1935. 20.00x (ISBN 0-674-31450-6). Harvard U Pr.
--Harvard College in the Seventeeth Century, 2 Vols. LC 36-6926. (Illus.). 1936. Set. 30.00x (ISBN 0-674-37450-9). Harvard U Pr.
--Three Centuries of Harvard, 1636-1936. facsim. ed. LC 36-14160. 1936. 20.00x (ISBN 0-674-88890-1, Belknap Pr). Harvard U Pr.
Powell, Arthur G. The Uncertain Profession: Harvard & the Search for Educational Authority. LC 79-260960. (Illus.). 1980. 18.50x (ISBN 0-674-92045-7). Harvard U Pr.
Quincy, Joseph. The History of Harvard University, 2 vols. Metzger, Walter P., ed. LC 76-55188. (The Academic Profession Ser.). (Illus.). 1977. Repr. of 1840 ed. Set. lib. bdg. 76.00x (ISBN 0-405-10015-9); lib. bdg. 38.00x ea. Vol. 1 (ISBN 0-405-10016-7). Vol. 2 (ISBN 0-405-10017-5). Arno.
Shipton, Clifford K. Biographical Sketches of Those Who Attended Harvard College in the Classes 1690-1771. (Sibley's Harvard Graduates Ser.: Vols. 4-17). (Illus.). 1933-1975. 35.00 ea. Mass Hist Soc.
Synnott, Marcia G. The Half-Opened Door: Discrimination & Admissions at Harvard, Yale, & Princeton, 1900-1970. LC 78-66714. (Contributions in American History: No. 80). (Illus.). 1979. lib. bdg. 23.95 (ISBN 0-313-20617-1, SHO/). Greenwood.
Wheatland, David & Carson, Barbara. Apparatus of Science at Harvard, 1765-1800. LC 68-8298. (Illus.). 1968. 20.00x (ISBN 0-674-04085-6). Harvard U Pr.
HARVARD UNIVERSITY-HOUGHTON LIBRARY
Amory, Hugh. Bute Broadsides in the Houghton Library Harvard University, Guide & Index to the Microfilm Collection. 1981. write for info. (ISBN 0-89235-025-3). Res Pubns Conn.
Magocsi, Paul R. & Mayo, Olga K. Carpatho-Ruthenica at Harvard: A Catalog of Holdings. 125p. (Orig.). 1977. pap. 6.00x (ISBN 0-917242-03-3, Pub. by Transworld). Carpatho-Rusyn Res Ctr.
HARVARD UNIVERSITY-LAW SCHOOL
Sutherland, Arthur E. Law at Harvard: A History of Ideas & Men, 1817-1967. LC 67-17320. (Illus.). 1967. 20.00x (ISBN 0-674-51500-5, Belknap Pr). Harvard U Pr.
Turow, Scott. One L: An Inside Account of Life in the First Year at Harvard Law School. 1978. pap. 2.95 (ISBN 0-14-004913-4). Penguin.
Warren, Charles. History of the Harvard Law School & of Early Legal Conditions in America. LC 72-112311. (American Constitutional & Legal History Ser). 1970. Repr. of 1908 ed. lib. bdg. 75.00 (ISBN 0-306-71913-4). Da Capo.
HARVARD UNIVERSITY-PEABODY MUSEUM OF ARCHAEOLOGY AND ETHNOLOGY
Peabody Museum of Archaeology & Ethnology. Author & Subject Catalogues of the Library of the Peabody Museum of Archaeology & Ethnology: Fourth Supplement, 7 vols. (Library Catalogs Bib Guides). 1979. lib. bdg. 980.00 set (ISBN 0-8161-0253-8). G K Hall.
HARVARD UNIVERSITY-SCHOOL OF PUBLIC HEALTH-CENTER FOR RESEARCH IN CHILD HEALTH AND DEVELOPMENT
Stuart, Harold C. Center, the Group Under Observation, Sources of Information & Studies in Progress. 1939. pap. 14.00 (ISBN 0-527-01508-3). Kraus Repr.
HARVEST FESTIVALS
see also Sukkoth; Thanksgiving Day
HARVESTERS
see Harvesting Machinery
HARVESTING MACHINERY
see also Mowing Machines
Casson, Herbert N. Cyrus Hall McCormick: His Life & Work. LC 74-152977. (Select Bibliographies Reprint Ser.). 1972. Repr. of 1909 ed. 22.00 (ISBN 0-8369-5729-6). Arno.
Hutchinson, William T. Cyrus Hall Maccormick, 2 Vols. 2nd ed. LC 68-8127. (American Scene Ser). 1969. Repr. of 1935 ed. lib. bdg. 69.50 (ISBN 0-306-71162-1). Da Capo.
McCormick, Cyrus. The Century of the Reaper: An Account of Cyrus Hall McCormick, the Inventor of the Reaper, of the McCormick Harvesting Machine Company, the Business He Created & of the International Harvester Company, His Heir & Chief Memorial. LC 31-9940. Repr. of 1931 ed. 23.00 (ISBN 0-384-34740-1). Johnson Repr.
HARVEY, GABRIEL, 1550?-1631
Harman, Edward G. Gabriel Harvey & Thomas Nashe. LC 74-2009. 1932. Repr. lib. bdg. 30.00 (ISBN 0-8414-4809-4). Folcroft.
Stern, Virginia F. Gabriel Harvey: A Study of His Life, Marginalia & Library. (Illus.). 306p. 1979. text ed. 44.00x (ISBN 0-19-812091-5). Oxford U Pr.
HARVEY, WILLIAM, 1578-1657
Cohen, I. Bernard, ed. Studies on William Harvey. LC 80-2101. (Development of Science Ser.). (Illus.). 1981. lib. bdg. 65.00x (ISBN 0-405-13866-0). Arno.
Curtis, John G. Harvey's Views on the Use of the Circulation of the Blood. (Historia Medicinae). (Illus.). Repr. of 1915 ed. lib. bdg. 15.00x (ISBN 0-87991-701-6). Porcupine Pr.
Frank, Robert G., Jr. Harvey & the Oxford Physiologists: Scientific Ideas & Social Interaction. LC 79-63553. (Illus.). 1981. 27.50x (ISBN 0-520-03906-8). U of Cal Pr.
Meyer, Arthur W. An Analysis of the De Generatione Animalium of William Harvey. (Historia Medicinae). Repr. of 1936 ed. lib. bdg. 15.00x (ISBN 0-87991-702-4). Porcupine Pr.
Pagel, W. New Light on William Harvey. (Illus.). 200p. 1975. 54.00 (ISBN 3-8055-2209-6). S Karger.
Webster, Charles, et al. William Harvey & His Age: The Professional & Social Context of the Discovery of Circulation. LC 78-20526. 1979. 12.50x (ISBN 0-8018-2213-0). Johns Hopkins.
HASAN, MIR, fl. 1796
Russell, Ralph & Islam, Khurshidul. Three Mughal Poets: Mir, Sauda, Mir Hasan. LC 68-15643. 1968. 15.00x (ISBN 0-674-88980-0). Harvard U Pr.
HASHISH
Baudelaire, Charles P. Les Paradis Artificiels: Opium et haschisch. LC 77-10248. Repr. of 1860 ed. 23.50 (ISBN 0-404-16304-1). AMS Pr.
Berke, Joseph & Hernton, Calvin C. The Cannabis Experience: An Interpretative Study of the Effects of Marijuana & Hashish. 288p. 1974. text ed. 17.00x (ISBN 0-7206-0073-1). Humanities.
Cherniak, Laurence. The Great Books of Hashish, Vol. I, Bk. I. LC 79-17557. (Illus.). 1979. pap. 14.95 (ISBN 0-915904-41-1). And-or Pr.
Drake, William D., Jr. International Cultivators Handbook. LC 74-80865. 100p. 1974. pap. 5.00 (ISBN 0-914728-02-4). Wingbow Pr.
Grob, Gerald N. The Medical Professions & Drug Addiction: Six Studies, 1882 to 1932, An Original Anthology. LC 80-1206. (Addiction in America Ser.). 1981. lib. bdg. 32.00x (ISBN 0-405-13560-2). Arno.
Kimmens, Andrew, ed. Tales of Hashish. (Illus.). 1977. 8.95 (ISBN 0-688-03194-3); pap. 4.95 (ISBN 0-688-08194-0). Morrow.
Mickel, Emanuel J., Jr. The Artificial Paradises: The Influence of Opium & Hashish on the Literature of French Romanticism & "les Fleurs du Mal". (Studies in the Romance Languages & Literatures: No. 84). 1969. pap. 10.50x (ISBN 0-8078-9084-7). U of NC Pr.
Moreau, J. J., et al. Hashish & Mental Illness. Peters, H. & Nahas, G., eds. Barnett, G. J., tr. from Fr. LC 76-107227. Orig. Title: Du Haschish et De l'Alienation Mentale. 267p. 1973. pap. 18.00 (ISBN 0-911216-14-6). Raven.
Stefanis, et al, eds. Hashish: Studies of Long-Term Use. LC 76-19848. 195p. 1977. 15.50 (ISBN 0-89004-138-5). Raven.
HASIDIC SONGS
see Songs, Hasidic
HASIDIC TALES
see Tales, Hassidic
HASIDISM
Aron, Milton. Ideas & Ideals of the Hassidim. 1980. pap. 5.95 (ISBN 0-8065-0722-5). Citadel Pr.
--Ideas & Ideals of the Hassidim. 1969. 7.95 (ISBN 0-8065-0319-X). Citadel Pr.
Ben-Amos, Dan & Mintz, Jerome R., eds. In Praise of the Baal Shem Tov (Shivhei ha-Besht) The Earliest Collection of Legends About the Founder of Hasidism. Ben-Amos, Dan & Mintz, Jerome R., trs. LC 76-98986. (Illus.). 384p. 1970. 15.00x (ISBN 0-253-14050-1); pap. 5.95x (ISBN 0-253-14051-X). Ind U Pr.
Buber, Martin. For the Sake of Heaven. Lewisohn, Ludwig, tr. LC 77-97311. Repr. of 1953 ed. lib. bdg. 15.00x (ISBN 0-8371-2592-8, BUSH). Greenwood.

--For the Sake of Heaven: A Chronicle. Lewisohn, Ludwig, tr. LC 58-8531. (Temple Books). 1969. pap. 3.45 (ISBN 0-689-70026-1, T2). Atheneum.

--Hasidism & Modern Man. LC 58-10225. 256p. 1972. pap. 5.95 (ISBN 0-8180-1326-5). Horizon.

--The Legend of the Baal-Shem. LC 76-86849. 1969. pap. 4.75 (ISBN 0-8052-0233-1). Schocken.

--Mamre, Essays in Religion. Hort, Greta, tr. LC 72-97271. Repr. of 1946 ed. lib. bdg. 15.00x (ISBN 0-8371-2591-X, BUMA). Greenwood.

--The Origin & Meaning of Hasidism. LC 60-8161. 256p. 1972. 7.50 (ISBN 0-8180-1315-X). Horizon.

--Tales of the Hasidim, 2 vols. Incl. The Early Masters. pap. 5.95 (ISBN 0-8052-0001-0); The Later Masters. pap. 4.95 (ISBN 0-8052-0002-9). LC 47-2952. 1961. Schocken.

--Ten Rungs: Hasidic Sayings. LC 62-13135. 1962. pap. 2.95 (ISBN 0-8052-0018-5). Schocken.

--Way of Man. 1966. pap. 1.50 (ISBN 0-8065-0024-7, 219). Citadel Pr.

Carlebach, Shlomo. Holy Beggar Teachings: Jewish Hasidic Stories, 1975-1977. Maimes, Steven L. & Rappaport, Elana, eds. 1979. pap. 5.95 (ISBN 0-917246-06-3). Maimes.

DeA'Morelli, Richard. Psychic Power: How to Increase Your ESP. 176p. (Orig.). 1976. pap. 1.50 (ISBN 0-89041-096-8, 3096). Major Bks.

Fleer, Gedaliah. Rabbi Nachman's Foundation. 1976. pap. 2.95 (ISBN 0-87203-063-6, Ohr Mibreslav). Hermon.

Green, Arthur. Tormented Master: A Life of Rabbi Nahman of Bratslav. LC 80-14668. 408p. 1981. pap. 11.95 (ISBN 0-8052-0663-9). Schocken.

--Tormented Master: A Life of Rabbi Nahman of Bratslav. LC 78-16674. (Judaic Studies: No. 9). (Illus.). 400p. 1979. 27.50x (ISBN 0-8173-6907-4). U of Ala Pr.

Heifetz, Harold, ed. Zen & Hasidism. LC 78-9073. 1978. 10.95 (ISBN 0-8356-0514-0, Quest); pap. 5.25 (ISBN 0-8356-0512-4, Quest). Theos Pub Hse.

Horodezky, Samuel A. Religiose Stromungen Judentum: Mit besondered Berucksichtigung des Chassidismus. Katz, Steven, ed. LC 79-7137. (Jewish Philosophy, Mysticism & History of Ideas Ser.). 1980. Repr. of 1920 ed. lib. bdg. 20.00x (ISBN 0-405-12263-2). Arno.

Jacobs, Louis. Hasidic Thought. LC 76-15825. 1976. pap. 3.95x (ISBN 0-87441-242-0). Behrman.

Kantor, Mattis. Chassidic Insights: A Guide for the Entangled. pap. 5.95x (ISBN 0-87068-679-8). Ktav.

Katz, Steven, ed. Studies by Samuel Horodezky: An Original Anthology. LC 79-51391. (Jewish Philosophy, Mysticism & History of Ideas Ser.). 1980. lib. bdg. 15.00x (ISBN 0-405-12233-0). Arno.

Langer, Jiri. Nine Gates to the Chassidic Mysteries. new ed. Rossel, Seymour, ed. Jolly, Stephen, tr. from Czech, Fr. LC 76-5859. (Jewish Legacy Ser.). 266p. 1976. pap. text ed. 3.95x (ISBN 0-87441-241-2). Behrman.

Minkin, Jacob S. Romance of Hassidism. pap. 2.50 (ISBN 0-87980-130-1). Wilshire.

Mintz, Jerome R. Legends of the Hasidim: An Introduction to Hasidic Culture & Oral Tradition in the New World. LC 68-16702. (Illus.). 1968. 15.00x (ISBN 0-226-53102-3). U of Chicago Pr.

--Legends of the Hasidim: An Introduction to Hasidic Culture & Oral Tradition in the New World. LC 68-16707. 504p. 1974. pap. 6.95 (ISBN 0-226-53103-1, P612, Phoen). U of Chicago Pr.

Newman, Louis I., ed. The Hasidic Anthology: Tales & Teachings of the Hasidim. LC 63-11041. 1963. pap. 6.95 (ISBN 0-8052-0046-0). Schocken.

Poll, Solomon. The Hasidic Community of Williamsburg: A Study in the Sociology of Religion. 2nd ed. LC 69-19419. 1969. pap. 4.95 (ISBN 0-8052-0209-9). Schocken.

Rabinowicz, Harry M. Hasidism & the State of Israel. LC 80-70271. (Littman Library of Jewish Civilization). (Illus.). 320p. 1981. 24.00 (ISBN 0-8386-3034-0). Fairleigh Dickinson.

--World of Hasidism. LC 79-113413. 1970. 8.95 (ISBN 0-87677-005-7). Hartmore.

Rabinowitsch, Wolf Z. Lithuanian Hasidism. LC 72-148840. (Illus.). 1971. 7.00x (ISBN 0-8052-3402-0). Schocken.

Rubin, Israel. Satmar: An Island in the City. LC 79-182505. 320p. 1972. 8.95 (ISBN 0-8129-0245-9). Times Bks.

Singer, Isaac B. Hasidim. LC 72-84288. (Illus.). 160p. 1973. 10.00 (ISBN 0-517-50047-7). Crown.

Wiesel, Elie. Four Hasidic Masters & Their Struggle Against Melancholy. LC 78-1419. (Ward-Phillips Lectures in English Language & Literature Ser: No. 9). (Illus.). 1978. 7.95 (ISBN 0-268-00944-9). U of Notre Dame Pr.

--Four Hasidic Masters & Their Struggle Against Melancholy. LC 78-1419. (Ward-Phillips Lectures in English Language & Literature: No. 9). (Illus.). 1979. pap. text ed. 3.95x (ISBN 0-268-00947-3). U of Notre Dame Pr.

HASMONAEANS

see Maccabees

HASSAM, CHILDE, 1859-1935

Hassam, Childe. Ninety-Four Prints by Childe Hassam. 12.50 (ISBN 0-8446-5771-9). Peter Smith.

--Ninety-One Prints by Childe Hassam. Czestochowski, Joseph S., ed. (Illus., Orig.). 1980. 6.00 (ISBN 0-486-23981-0). Dover.

Hoopes, Donelson F. Childe Hassam. (Illus.). 1979. 22.50 (ISBN 0-8230-0622-0). Watson-Guptill.

HASSE, JOHANN ADOLF, 1699-1783

Hansell, S. H. Works for Solo Voice of Johann Adolf Hasse, 1699-1783. (Detroit Studies in Music Bibliography Ser.: No. 12). 1968. pap. 2.00 (ISBN 0-911772-32-4). Info Coord.

Millner, Fredrick L. The Operas of Johann Adolf Hasse. Buelow, George, ed. LC 79-11832. (Studies in Musicology: No. 2). 1979. 34.95 (ISBN 0-8357-1006-8, Pub. by UMI Res Pr). Univ Microfilms.

HASTINGS, WARREN, 1732-1818

Busteed, H. E. Echoes from Old Calcutta. (Illus.). 454p. 1972. Repr. of 1908 ed. 31.00x (ISBN 0-7165-2115-6, Pub. by Irish Academic Pr Ireland). Biblio Dist.

Feiling, Keith G. Warren Hastings. (Illus.). 1966. Repr. of 1954 ed. 22.50 (ISBN 0-208-00287-1, Archon). Shoe String.

Lyall, Alfred. Warren Hastings. facsimile ed. LC 73-140364. (Select Bibliographies Reprint Ser). Repr. of 1889 ed. 16.00 (ISBN 0-8369-5607-9). Arno.

The Trial of Warren Hastings in House of Lords Sessional Papers: 1794-95, 9 vols, Vols. 1-9. LC 70-141328. 1974. 750.00 set (ISBN 0-685-88686-7). Oceana.

HASTINGS, WILLIAM HASTINGS, LORD, 1430?-1483

Dunham, William H., Jr. Lord Hastings' Indentured Retainers, 1461-1483: The Lawfulness of Livery & Retaining Under the Yorkists & Tudors. (Connecticut Academy of Arts & Sciences Transactions: Vol. 39). 1970. Repr. of 1955 ed. 15.00 (ISBN 0-208-00989-2, Archon). Shoe String.

HASTINGS, BATTLE OF, 1066

Howarth, David. Ten Sixty Six: The Year of the Conquest. 1978. 10.95 (ISBN 0-670-69601-3). Viking Pr.

Korner, Sten. The Battle of Hastings, England & Europe, 1035-1066. LC 80-2221. Repr. of 1964 ed. 38.00 (ISBN 0-404-18765-X). AMS Pr.

HASTON, DOUGAL

Haston, Dougal. In High Places. (Illus.). 176p. 1973. 9.95 (ISBN 0-02-548980-1). Macmillan.

HATBOXES

see also Bandboxes

Carlisle, Lilian B. Hat Boxes & Bandboxes at Shelburne Museum. (Museum Pamphlet Ser.: No. 4). (Illus., Orig.). 1960. pap. 4.50 (ISBN 0-939384-02-7). Shelburne.

HATE

see also Self-Hate (Psychology)

Bychowski, Gustav. Evil in Man: Anatomy of Hate & Violence. LC 68-13447. 104p. 1968. pap. 16.75 (ISBN 0-8089-0090-0). Grune.

Carrol, Donald, ed. Dear, Drop Dead! Hate Mail Through the Ages. 1979. pap. 4.95 (ISBN 0-02-040360-7, Collier). Macmillan.

Holbrook, David. The Masks of Hate: The Problem of False Solutions in the Culture of an Acquisitive Society. 276p. 1976. Repr. of 1972 ed. 26.00 (ISBN 0-08-015799-8). Pergamon.

HATFIELD-MCCOY FEUD

Jones, Virgil C. Hatfields & the McCoys. 1948. 9.95 (ISBN 0-8078-0524-6). U of NC Pr.

--The Hatfields and the McCoys. new ed. 246p. 1976. pap. 1.95 (ISBN 0-89176-014-8, 6014). Mockingbird Bks.

Rice, Otis K. The Hatfields & the McCoys. LC 78-57388. (Kentucky Bicentennial Bookshelf Ser.). (Illus.). 160p. 1978. 6.95 (ISBN 0-8131-0235-9). U Pr of Ky.

HATHA YOGA

see Yoga, Hatha

HATHORNE FAMILY (WILLIAM HATHORNE, 1601-1681)

Loggins, Vernon. Hawthornes: The Story of Seven Generations of an American Family. LC 69-10121. (Illus.). 1968. Repr. of 1951 ed. lib. bdg. 17.25x (ISBN 0-8371-0149-2, LOH). Greenwood.

HATS

see also Millinery

Alton, W. G. Hats Galore. (Make & Play Ser.). (Illus.). 48p. (gr. k-6). 1976. pap. 1.50 (ISBN 0-263-05936-7). Transatlantic.

Couldridge, Alan. The Hat Book. (Illus.). 128p. 1980. 19.95 (ISBN 0-7134-2385-4, Pub. by Batsford England). David & Charles.

Couldridge, Alan & Dowell, Celia. The Hat Book. 128p. 1981. 16.95 (ISBN 0-13-384222-3, Spec); pap. 8.95 (ISBN 0-13-384214-2). P-H.

Feldman, Annette. The Hat Book. 1978. 11.95 (ISBN 0-442-21559-2); pap. 7.95 (ISBN 0-442-21557-6). Van Nos Reinhold.

Frager, Dorothy. Cloth Hats, Bags 'n Baggage. LC 77-6116. (Creative Crafts Ser.). (Illus.). 1978. 12.50 (ISBN 0-8019-6367-2, 6367); pap. 6.95 (ISBN 0-8019-6368-0, 6368). Chilton.

Kenworthy, Leonard S. Hats, Caps, & Crowns. LC 77-23800. (Illus.). 64p. (gr. 3-5). 1977. PLB 6.64 (ISBN 0-671-32874-3). Messner.

McClellan, Mary Elizabeth. Felt-Silk-Straw Handmade Hats: Tools & Processes, Vol. III. (Illus.). 1978. pap. 3.50 (ISBN 0-685-46329-X). Bucks Co Hist.

Morgan, Peter. Making Hats. 1978. 11.95 (ISBN 0-7134-1078-7, Pub. by Batsford England). David & Charles.

Neamtu, Cella. Woman's Ritual Headwear (Romania) Popescu-Judetz, Eugenia, tr. from Fr. (Illus.). 110p. (Orig.). 1981. pap. 7.00 (ISBN 0-936922-03-6). Tamburitza.

Rankin, Robert H. Military Headdress: A Pictorial History of Military Headgear from 1660-1914. LC 75-43821. (Illus.). 1976. 14.95 (ISBN 0-88254-371-7). Hippocrene Bks.

Tomlinson, Jill. Lady Bee's Bonnets. 32p. 1971. pap. 2.95 (ISBN 0-571-11133-5, Pub. by Faber &Faber). Merrimack Bk Serv.

HATS-JUVENILE LITERATURE

Kenworthy, Leonard S. Hats, Caps, & Crowns. LC 77-23800. (Illus.). 64p. (gr. 3-5). 1977. PLB 6.64 (ISBN 0-671-32874-3). Messner.

Shortall, Leonard. The Hat Book. (Illus.). 24p. (gr. k-1). 1976. PLB 5.38 (ISBN 0-307-68976-X, Golden Pr). Western Pub.

HATTON FAMILY

Thompson, Edward M., ed. Correspondence of the Family of Hatton. Repr. of 1878 ed. 45.00 (ISBN 0-384-60252-5). Johnson Repr.

Trzebinski, Errol. Silence Will Speak: A Study of the Life of Denys Finch Hatton & His Relationship with Karen Blixen. LC 77-93000. (Illus.). 1978. 15.00 (ISBN 0-226-81286-3). U of Chicago Pr.

Vines, Alice G. Neither Fire nor Steel: Sir Christopher Hatton. LC 77-21424. 1978. 17.95x (ISBN 0-88229-372-9). Nelson-Hall.

HAUGE, HANS NIELSEN, 1771-1824

Aarflot, Andreas. Hans Nielsen Hauge: His Life & Message. LC 77-84101. 1979. pap. 8.95 (ISBN 0-8066-1627-X, 10-2965). Augsburg.

Shaw, Joseph M. Pulpit Under the Sky: A Life of Hans Nielson Hauge. LC 78-12391. 1979. Repr. of 1955 ed. lib. bdg. 18.50x (ISBN 0-313-21123-X, SHPU). Greenwood.

HAUGEN, EINER INGVALD, 1906- -BIBLIOGRAPHY

Firchow, Evelyn S., ed. Studies for Einar Haugen Presented by Friends & Colleagues. LC 72-889779. (Janua Linguarum, Ser. Major: No. 59). (Illus.). 573p. 1972. text ed. 92.50x (ISBN 90-2792-338-8). Mouton.

HAUNTED HOUSES

see Ghosts

HAUPT, HERMAN 1817-1905

Haupt, Herman. Reminiscences of General Herman Haupt. LC 80-1314. (Railroads Ser.). (Illus.). 1981. Repr. of 1901 ed. lib. bdg. 30.00x (ISBN 0-405-13786-9). Arno.

Lord, Francis A. Lincoln's Railroad Man: Herman Haupt. LC 69-20296. 325p. 1969. 16.50 (ISBN 0-8386-7343-0). Fairleigh Dickinson.

Ward, James A. That Man Haupt: A Biography of Herman Haupt. LC 73-82420. (Illus.). 288p. 1973. 20.00x (ISBN 0-8071-0225-3). La State U Pr.

HAUPTMANN, BRUNO RICHARD, 1899-1936

Haring, J. Vreeland. Hand of Hauptmann: The Handwriting Expert Tells the Story of the Lindbergh Case. (Illus.). 1937. 10.00 (ISBN 0-87585-702-7). Patterson Smith.

HAUPTMANN, GERHARD JOHANN ROBERT, 1862-1946

Heller, Otto. Studies in Modern German Literature. facs. ed. LC 67-26748. (Essay Index Reprint Ser). 1905. 16.00 (ISBN 0-8369-0531-8). Arno.

Holl, Karl. Gerhart Hauptmann. LC 72-7083. (Select Bibliographies Reprint Ser.). 1972. Repr. of 1913 ed. 13.00 (ISBN 0-8369-6941-3). Arno.

Klenze, Camillo Von. From Goethe to Hauptmann: Studies in a Changing Culture. LC 66-23519. 1926. 10.50x (ISBN 0-8196-0178-0). Biblo.

Viereck, George S. Glimpses of the Great. 1978. Repr. of 1930 ed. lib. bdg. 25.00 (ISBN 0-89760-903-4, Telegraph). Dynamic Learn Corp.

HAURIOU, MAURICE

Broderick, Albert, ed. French Institutionalists: Maurice Hauriou, Georges Renard, Joseph T. Delos. Welling, Mary, tr. from Fr. (Twentieth Century Legal Philosophy Ser: No. 8). 1970. 20.00x (ISBN 0-674-32125-1). Harvard U Pr.

HAUSA FOLK-LORE

see Folk-Lore, Hausa

HAUSA LANGUAGE

Cowan, J. Ronayne & Schuh, Russell G. Spoken Hausa. LC 75-15184. (Spoken Language Ser). 350p. (Programmed book). 1976. pap. text ed. 10.00x (ISBN 0-87950-401-3); book & cassettes for units 1-12 70.00x (ISBN 0-87950-403-X); cassettes for units 1-12, six dual track 65.00x (ISBN 0-87950-402-1); cassettes for units 13-25 (14 hours) 100.00x (ISBN 0-87950-404-8). Spoken Lang Serv.

Kraft, Charles H. & Kraft, Marguerite G. Introductory Hausa. LC 70-161997. 1974. 25.75x (ISBN 0-520-01988-1). U of Cal Pr.

Newman, Paul & Newman, Roxanna M., eds. Modern Hausa-English Dictionary. 168p. 1979. pap. text ed. 6.95x (ISBN 0-19-575303-8). Oxford U Pr.

Skinner, Neil. Hausa Readings: Selections from Edgar's Tatsuniyoyi. LC 68-9836. 302p. (Hausa). 1968. 7.50x (ISBN 0-299-05130-7). U of Wis Pr.

Zima, P. Problems of Categories & Word Classes in Hausa. (Oriental Institute Czechoslovakia Dissertationes Orientales, Vol. 33). 1972. 6.00x (ISBN 0-685-33017-6). Paragon.

HAUSA LANGUAGE-TEXTS

Hodge, C. T. Outline of Hausa Grammar. Repr. of 1947 ed. pap. 6.00 (ISBN 0-527-00787-0). Kraus Repr.

Kraft, Charles H. Hausa Reader: Cultural Materials with Helps for Use in Teaching Intermediate & Advanced Hausa. LC 70-161997. 1974. pap. 25.75x (ISBN 0-520-02067-7). U of Cal Pr.

Rattray, Robert S., ed. Hausa Folk-Lore, Customs, Proverbs, Etc, 2 Vols. LC 71-79274. (Illus.). 1913. 26.00x (ISBN 0-8371-1464-0, Pub. by Negro U Pr). Greenwood.

HAUSA TALES

see Tales, Hausa

HAUSAS

Backwell, H. Occupation of Hausaland: 1900-1904. 80p. 1969. Repr. of 1927 ed. 27.50x (ISBN 0-7146-1631-1, F Cass Co). Biblio Dist.

Cohen, Abner. Custom & Politics in Urban Africa: A Study of Hausa Migrants in Yoruba Towns. LC 68-55743. 1969. 20.00x (ISBN 0-520-01571-1); pap. 6.95x (ISBN 0-520-01836-2, CAMPUS43). U of Cal Pr.

Hill, Polly. Population, Prosperity, & Poverty. LC 77-23167. (Illus.). 1977. 27.50 (ISBN 0-521-21511-0). Cambridge U Pr.

--Rural Hausa: A Village & a Setting. LC 75-161287. 1972. 34.50 (ISBN 0-521-08242-0). Cambridge U Pr.

Jackson, James G., ed. El Hage Abd Salam Shabeeny Account of Timbuctoo & Housa Territories. 547p. 1967. 35.00x (ISBN 0-7146-1054-2, F Cass Co). Biblio Dist.

Robinson, Charles H. Nigeria, Our Latest Protectorate. LC 69-16569. Repr. of 1900 ed. 18.00x (ISBN 0-8371-1542-6, Pub. by Negro U Pr). Greenwood.

Smith, Mary F. Baba of Karo: A Woman of the Muslin Hausa. LC 81-40433. 304p. 1981. text ed. 25.00x (ISBN 0-300-02734-6); pap. 6.95x (ISBN 0-300-02741-9, Y-408). Yale U Pr.

Tremearne, A. J. Hausa Superstitions & Customs. (Illus.). 548p. 1970. Repr. of 1913 ed. 32.50x (ISBN 0-7146-1729-6, F Cass Co). Biblio Dist.

Whitaker, C. S., Jr. Politics of Tradition: Continuity & Change in Northern Nigeria, 1946-1966. LC 68-56323. (Center of International Studies Ser). 1969. 28.50x (ISBN 0-691-03079-0). Princeton U Pr.

Works, John A., Jr. Pilgrims in a Strange Land: Hausa Communities in Chad. LC 76-23138. 1976. 17.50x (ISBN 0-231-03976-X). Columbia U Pr.

HAUSER, KASPAR, 1812-1833

Cleveland, Catherine. The True Story of Kaspar Hauser. 1976. lib. bdg. 59.95 (ISBN 0-8490-2774-8). Gordon Pr.

Wassermann, Jacob. Caspar Hauser. 1956. 6.95 (ISBN 0-87140-818-X). Liveright.

HAUSHOFER, KARL, 1869-1946

Dorpalen, Andreas. World of General Haushofer: Geopolitics in Action. LC 66-21393. 1942. Repr. 12.50 (ISBN 0-8046-0112-7). Kennikat.

HAUSSMANN, GEORGES EUGENE, BARON, 1809-1891

Saalman, Howard. Haussmann: Paris Transformer. LC 76-143399. (Planning & Cities Ser). (Illus.). 1971. 7.95 (ISBN 0-8076-0583-2); pap. 3.95 (ISBN 0-8076-0582-4). Braziller.

HAUTERIVE, ALEXANDRE MAURICE BLANC DE LANAUTTE, COMTE D', 1754-1830

Von Gentz, Friedrich. On the State of Europe Before & After the French Revolution. Herries, John C., tr. LC 73-118630. Repr. of 1802 ed. 34.50 (ISBN 0-404-02711-3). AMS Pr.

HAVASUPAI INDIANS

see Indians of North America-Southwest, New

HAVELOCK THE DANE

Havelok The Dane. The Lay of Havelok the Dane. 2nd ed. Skeat, Walter W. & Sisam, K., eds. LC 75-41129. Repr. of 1915 ed. 11.50 (ISBN 0-404-14551-5). AMS Pr.

HAVERFORDWEST, WALES-HISTORY-SOURCES

Charles, B. G., ed. Calendar of the Records of the Borough of Haverfordwest, 1539-1600. (History & Law Ser.: No. 24). 1967. 12.00x (ISBN 0-7083-0002-2). Verry.

HAVILAND CHINA

Jacobson, Gertrude T. Haviland China: Vol. Two, a Pattern Identification Guide. (Illus.). 19.95 (ISBN 0-87069-291-7). Wallace-Homestead.

Schleiger, Arlene. Two Hundred Patterns of Haviland China, 5 vols, Vols. 1-5. 6.00 ea. Schleiger.

Young, Harriet. Grandmother's Haviland. rev. ed. (Illus.). 1970. 9.95 (ISBN 0-87069-031-0). Wallace-Homestead.

HAWAII

Bryan, Edwin H., Jr. Stars Over Hawaii. (Illus.). 1977. pap. 4.50 (ISBN 0-912180-30-7). Petroglyph.

Calisch, Rus. Paumalu: A Story of Modern Hawaii. LC 78-78037. (Orig.). 1979. pap. 3.95 (ISBN 0-9602354-1-8). Paumalu Pr.

Cameron, Robert. Above Hawaii. LC 77-88840. 1977. 19.95 (ISBN 0-918684-02-1). Cameron & Co.

Clemens, Samuel L. Letters from the Sandwich Islands. LC 72-2113. (American Literature Ser., No. 49). 1972. Repr. of 1938 ed. lib. bdg. 49.95 (ISBN 0-8383-1471-6). Haskell.

Coulter, J. W. Population & Utilization of Land & Sea in Hawaii. Repr. of 1853 ed. pap. 5.00 (ISBN 0-527-02194-6). Kraus Repr.

Department of Geography, University of Hawaii, compiled by. Atlas of Hawaii. LC 72-91236. (Illus.). 232p. 1973. 19.95 (ISBN 0-8248-0259-4). U Pr of Hawaii.

Elliott, Rex R. Hawaiian Bottles of Long Ago. 3rd ed. LC 78-134504. (Illus.). 1971. pap. 4.95 (ISBN 0-930492-13-7). Hawaiian Serv.

Galtsoff, P. S. Pearl & Hermes Reef, Hawaii, Hydrographical & Biographical Observations. Repr. of 1933 ed. pap. 6.00 (ISBN 0-527-02213-6). Kraus Repr.

Gavan Daws, O. A. & Bushnell, Andrew J. Illustrated Atlas of Hawaii. LC 70-152566. (Illus.). 1970. pap. 5.95 (ISBN 0-89610-034-0). Island Her.

Gerould, Katharine F. Hawaii: Scenes & Impressions. 1923. 15.00 (ISBN 0-8495-1967-5). Arden Lib.

Handy, E. Craighill, et al. Ancient Hawaiian Civilization. rev. ed. LC 65-23709. (gr. 9 up). 1965. 15.00 (ISBN 0-8048-0023-5). C E Tuttle.

Handy, E. S. & Pukui, Mary K. The Polynesian Family System in Kau, Hawaii. LC 75-171998. 1972. 15.00 (ISBN 0-8048-1031-1). C E Tuttle.

Hawaii. 23.00 (ISBN 0-89770-087-2). Curriculum Info Ctr.

Myhre, Ethelyn. Hawaiian Yesterdays. (Illus.). 1978. pap. 3.50 (ISBN 0-912180-25-0). Petroglyph.

Nickerson, Roy. Hawaii, the Volcano State. (Illus.). 1978. 1.95 (ISBN 0-930492-01-3). Hawaiian Serv.

Pollock, J. B. Fringing & Fossil Reefs of Oahu. Repr. of 1928 ed. pap. 7.00 (ISBN 0-527-02161-X). Kraus Repr.

Pratt, Julius. Expansionists of 1898: The Acquisition of Hawaii & the Spanish Islands. 8.00 (ISBN 0-8446-1364-9). Peter Smith.

Roes, Carol. Eight Islands. 1963. pap. 3.50 (ISBN 0-930932-12-9). M Loke.

--It Can Happen Only in Hawaii. 1965. pap. 3.50 (ISBN 0-930932-14-5). M Loke.

--Santa's Hawaiian Party. 1966. pap. 4.50 with record (ISBN 0-930932-19-6). M Loke.

Roes, Carol & Loke, M. Hulas from Hawaii. (Hula Book Ser.: Bk. 6). 1968. pap. 4.50 with record (ISBN 0-930932-11-0). M Loke.

Rubano, Judith. Culture & Behavior in Hawaii: An Annotated Bibliography. (Social Science & Linguistics Institute Publications). 147p. 1971. pap. 5.00x (ISBN 0-8248-0242-X). U Pr of Hawaii.

Sager, Gordon. Hawaii. LC 69-16369. (This Beautiful World Ser.: Vol. 8). (Illus.). 1969. pap. 4.95 (ISBN 0-87011-072-1). Kodansha.

Sterling Editors, ed. Hawaii - in Pictures. rev. ed. LC 61-10398. (Visual Geography Ser.). (Illus.). (gr. 5 up). 1977. pap. 2.95 (ISBN 0-8069-1006-2). Sterling.

Tabrah, Ruth. Hawaii. (States of the Nation Ser.). (Illus.). 1980. 12.95 (ISBN 0-393-05680-5). Norton.

Titcomb, Margaret. The Ancient Hawaiians: How They Clothed Themselves. Hazama, Dorothy, ed. (Hawaii's Cultural Heritage Ser.: Vol. 1). (Illus.). 64p. (gr. 4 up). 1974. pap. 2.50 (ISBN 0-911776-24-9). Hogarth.

Tuggle, H. David & Griffin, P. Bion, eds. Lapakahi, Hawaii: Archaeological Studies. (Social Science & Linguistics Institute Special Publications). (Illus.). 380p. 1973. pap. 6.00x (ISBN 0-8248-0246-2). U Pr of Hawaii.

Twain, Mark, pseud. Mark Twain in Hawaii. Jones, William R., ed. (Illus.). 96p. 1981. pap. 4.95 (ISBN 0-89646-070-3). Outbooks.

Wallace, Robert. Hawaii. LC 73-179462. (American Wilderness Ser). (Illus.). (gr. 6 up). 1973. lib. bdg. 11.97 (ISBN 0-8094-1177-6, Pub. by Time-Life). Silver.

Young, Lucien. Real Hawaii: Its History & Present Conditions Including the True Story of the Revolution. LC 77-111760. (American Imperialism: Viewpoints of United States Foreign Policy, 1898-1941). 1970. Repr. of 1899 ed. 17.00 (ISBN 0-405-02054-6). Arno.

HAWAII-ANTIQUITIES

Cordy, Ross. A Study of Prehistoric Social Change: The Development of Complex Societies in the Hawaiian Islands. (Studies in Archaeology). 1981. price not set (ISBN 0-12-188450-3). Acad Pr.

Malo, David. Hawaiian Antiquities. (Special Publication Ser: No. 2). 278p. 1971. Repr. 6.00 (ISBN 0-910240-15-9). Bishop Mus.

Snow, Charles E. Early Hawaiians: An Initial Study of Skeletal Remains from Mokapu, Oahu. LC 72-81317. (Illus.). 192p. 1974. 17.50x (ISBN 0-8131-1277-X). U Pr of Ky.

HAWAII-BIBLIOGRAPHY

Day, A. Grove. Books About Hawaii: Fifty Basic Authors. LC 77-7997. 1977. text ed. 8.95x (ISBN 0-8248-0561-5). U Pr of Hawaii.

Hunnewell, James F. Bibliography of the Hawaiian Islands. 1869. 9.00 (ISBN 0-527-43400-0). Kraus Repr.

HAWAII-BIOGRAPHY

De Varigny, Charles. Fourteen Years in the Sandwich Islands. Korn, Alfons L., tr. LC 80-26141. (Illus.). 320p. (Fr.). 1981. 24.95 (ISBN 0-8248-0709-X). U Pr of Hawaii.

Gast, Ross H. Contentious Consul: A Biography of John Coffin Jones First United States Counselor Agent at Hawai. 1976. 10.00 (ISBN 0-87093-175-X). Dawsons.

Sinclair, Marjorie. Nahi'ena 'ena: Sacred Daughter of Hawaii. LC 76-27896. 1976. 9.95 (ISBN 0-8248-0367-1). U Pr of Hawaii.

Sutherland, Audrey. Paddling My Own Canoe. LC 78-16374. (Illus.). 1978. 7.95 (ISBN 0-8248-0618-2, Kolowalu Bk). U Pr of Hawaii.

HAWAII-CIVIL DEFENSE

Ogawa, Dennis M. Kodomo No Tame Ni-for the Sake of the Children: The Japanese American Experience in Hawaii. LC 77-18368. 639p. 1980. pap. 8.95 (ISBN 0-8248-0730-8). U Pr of Hawaii.

HAWAII-DESCRIPTION AND TRAVEL

Abramson, Joan, ed. Photographers of Old Hawaii. 3rd ed. LC 76-1504. (Illus.). 228p. 1981. 12.50 (ISBN 0-89610-082-0). Island Her.

Arrigoni, Edward. A Nature Walk to Ka'ena Point. 1978. pap. 3.95 (ISBN 0-914916-30-0). Topgallant.

Ashdown, Inez M. Kahoolawe: Recollections of Kahoolawe. 1979. pap. 5.95 (ISBN 0-914916-48-3). Topgallant.

Barrot, Theodore-Adolphe. Unless Haste Is Made: A French Skeptic's Account of the Sandwich Islands in 1836. Pagliaro, Penny, ed. Dole, Daniel, tr. from Fr. LC 77-27597. Orig. Title: Visit of the French Frigate Sloop of War to the Sandwich Islands, 1836. (Illus.). 1978. 10.00 (ISBN 0-916630-05-6); pap. 4.95 (ISBN 0-916630-04-8). Pr Pacifica.

Barrow, Terence. Incredible Hawaii. LC 74-77226. (Illus.). 1974. pap. 3.25 (ISBN 0-8048-1137-7). C E Tuttle.

Berry, Dick & Berry, Pat. Hawaii by Condominium. Bryan, Greta, ed. LC 78-69737. (Travel Guides Ser.). (Illus.). 1978. pap. 6.95 (ISBN 0-932422-01-2). Discovery Pub.

Bird, Isabella L. Six Months in the Sandwich Islands. LC 73-77575. (Illus.). 1973. pap. 4.95 (ISBN 0-8048-1112-1). C E Tuttle.

Brown, Alexander C. Longboat to Hawaii. LC 74-22317. (Illus.). 254p. 1974. 12.50 (ISBN 0-87033-201-5). Cornell Maritime.

Buffet, Guy. Guy Buffet's Hawaii. LC 80-67292. 1981. 9.95 (ISBN 0-918684-11-0). Cameron & Co.

Chisholm, Craig. Hawaiian Hiking Trails. LC 75-13696. (Illus.). 1975. pap. 7.95 (ISBN 0-911518-35-5). Touchstone Pr Ore.

Clark, John R. The Beaches of O'ahu. LC 77-8244. (Illus., Orig.). 1977. pap. 4.95 (ISBN 0-8248-0510-0). U Pr of Hawaii.

Dampier, Robert. To the Sandwich Islands on H.M.S. Blonde. Joerger, Pauline K., ed. LC 73-147156. 1971. 12.00 (ISBN 0-87022-176-0). U Pr of Hawaii.

Davis, Lynn. Na Pa'i Ki'i: The Photographers in the Hawaiian Islands, 1900-1945. LC 80-70100. (Special Publication Ser.: No. 69). (Illus.). 48p. 1980. pap. 5.50 (ISBN 0-910240-29-9). Bishop Mus.

Edmonson, Charles H. Hawaii's Seashore Treasures. 144p. 1974. pap. 5.25 (ISBN 0-912180-21-8). Petroglyph.

Gleasner, Bill & Gleasner, Diana. Hawaiian Gardens: Photographed on Kauai. LC 77-73322. (Illus.). 1978. pap. 4.00 (ISBN 0-932596-01-0, Pub. by Oriental). Intl Schol Bk Serv.

--Kauai Traveler's Guide. (Illus.). 1978. pap. 4.00 (ISBN 0-932596-03-7, Pub. by Oriental). Intl Schol Bk Serv.

Golt, Rick & Lagundimao, Clemente, Jr. Hawai'i Hawai'i. LC 81-50935. (Illus.). 128p. 1981. 19.95 (ISBN 0-8248-0772-3). U Pr of Hawaii.

Grigg, Richard W. Hawaii's Precious Corals. LC 77-78113. (Illus.). 1977. pap. 4.95 (ISBN 0-89610-069-3). Island Her.

Hawaii on Twenty-Five Dollars a Day: 1981-82 Edition. 1981. pap. 5.95 (ISBN 0-671-41457-7). Frommer-Pasmantier.

Holt, John D., ed. An Account of the Sandwich Islands: The Hawaiian Journal of John B. Whitman, 1813-1815. (Illus.). 1979. 9.95 (ISBN 0-914916-49-1). Topgallant.

Howard, Alan. Ain't No Big Thing: Coping Strategies in a Hawaiian-American Community. LC 73-86029. 336p. 1974. text ed. 14.00x (ISBN 0-8248-0300-0, Eastwest Ctr). U Pr of Hawaii.

Kane, Robert S. Hawaii A to Z Guide. (Illus.). 1980. pap. 6.95 (ISBN 0-528-84339-7). Rand.

Krauss, Bob. Kauai. LC 77-82233. (Illus.). 1978. pap. 4.95 (ISBN 0-89610-083-9). Island Her.

Lewis, Paul M. Beautiful Hawaii. rev. ed. (Illus.). 72p. 1980. 14.95 (ISBN 0-89802-109-X); pap. 7.95 (ISBN 0-89802-108-1). Beautiful Am.

--Beautiful Hawaii: The Big Island. Shangle, Robert D., ed. (Illus.). 72p. 1981. 14.95 (ISBN 0-89802-281-9); pap. 7.95 (ISBN 0-89802-280-0). Beautiful Am.

Lind, Andrew W. Hawaii's People. rev. ed. LC 80-10764. 1980. pap. text ed. 5.00x (ISBN 0-8248-0704-9). U Pr of Hawaii.

McGaw, Martha M., Sr. Stevenson in Hawaii. LC 77-13757. (Illus.). 1978. Repr. of 1950 ed. lib. bdg. 18.25x (ISBN 0-8371-9864-X, MCSH). Greenwood.

Martin, Henry B. The Polynesian Journal of Henry Byam Martin. Dodd, Edward, ed. (Illus.). 200p. 1981. write for info. (ISBN 0-87577-060-6). Peabody Mus Salem.

Michener, James A. Hawaii. 1959. pap. 3.45 (ISBN 0-394-70306-5, Vin). Random.

Moon, Jan. Living with Nature in Hawaii. rev. ed. 136p. 1979. pap. 6.50 (ISBN 0-912180-06-4). Petroglyph.

Nordhoff, Charles. Northern California, Oregon & the Sandwich Islands. (Illus.). 226p. 1975. pap. 3.95 (ISBN 0-913668-25-7). Ten Speed Pr.

Parker, Samuel. Journal of Exploring Tour Etc. Repr. 10.00 (ISBN 0-87018-046-0). Ross.

Pratt, Helen G. Hawaiians: An Island People. LC 63-22620. (Illus.). (YA) (gr. 7-9). 1963. 8.95 (ISBN 0-8048-0242-4). C E Tuttle.

Radford, Georgia F. & Radford, Warren H. Sculpture in the Sun: Hawaii's Art for Open Spaces. LC 77-92972. 1978. pap. 7.95 (ISBN 0-8248-0526-7). U Pr of Hawaii.

Radlauer, Ruth. Hawaii Volcanoes National Park. LC 78-19718. (Parks for People Ser.). (Illus.). (gr. 3 up). 1979. PLB 10.00 (ISBN 0-516-07498-9, Elk Grove Bks). Childrens.

Rapson, Richard L. Fairly Lucky You Live Hawaii! LC 80-5530. 166p. 1980. lib. bdg. 13.50 (ISBN 0-8191-1167-8); pap. text ed. 6.50 (ISBN 0-8191-1168-6). U Pr of Amer.

Reynolds, Stephen. Voyage of the New Hazard to the Northwest Coast, Hawaii & China, 1810-1813. 1970. 14.95 (ISBN 0-87770-076-1). Ye Galleon.

Roes, Carol. The Streets of Waikiki. 1965. pap. 3.50 (ISBN 0-930932-13-7). M Loke.

Sannebeck, Norvelle. All-About Living in Hawaii. LC 77-23732. (Illus.). 1977. 9.95 (ISBN 0-87015-224-6). Pacific Bks.

Shangle, Robert D., ed. Hawaii. LC 78-102325. (Illus.). 72p. 1976. 14.95 (ISBN 0-915796-16-3); pap. 7.95 (ISBN 0-915796-15-5). Beautiful Am.

Skottsberg, C. Juan Fernandez & Hawaii: A Phytogeographical Discussion. (BMB Ser.: BMB 16). Repr. of 1925 ed. pap. 5.00 (ISBN 0-527-02119-9). Kraus Repr.

Smith, Robert. Hiking Hawaii. Winnett, Thomas, ed. LC 79-93247. (Wilderness Press Trail Guide Ser.). (Illus.). 112p. (Orig.). 1981. write for info. (ISBN 0-89997-000-1). Wilderness Pr.

Stearns, Harold T. Quaternary Shorelines in the Hawaiian Islands. LC 78-57837. (Bulletin Ser.: No. 237). (Illus.). 1978. 6.50 (ISBN 0-910240-25-6). Bishop Mus.

Stevenson, Robert L. Travels in Hawaii. Day, A. Grove, ed. & intro. by. LC 72-91621. (Illus.). 250p. 1973. 9.50 (ISBN 0-8248-0257-8). U Pr of Hawaii.

Stewart, C. S. Journal of a Residence in the Sandwich Islands, 1823-1825. LC 71-135064. (Sandwich Islands Publications). (Illus.). 1971. Repr. of 1830 ed. 7.50 (ISBN 0-87022-772-6). U Pr of Hawaii.

Stone, Scott C. Volcano!! (Illus.). 1978. pap. 4.95 (ISBN 0-89610-064-2). Island Her.

Street, John M. & Morgan, Joseph R. Oahu Environments. 1979. pap. 6.00 (ISBN 0-932596-06-1, Pub. by Oriental). Intl Schol Bk Serv.

Sunset Editors. Beautiful Hawaii. 2nd ed. LC 77-72508. (Illus.). 208p. 1977. pap. 8.95 (ISBN 0-376-05373-9, Sunset Bks). Sunset-Lane.

--Hawaii: Travel Guide. 5th ed. LC 74-20023. (Illus.). 160p. 1975. pap. 4.95 (ISBN 0-376-06307-6, Sunset Bks.). Sunset-Lane.

Twain, Mark. Mark Twain's Letters from Hawaii. Day, A. Grove, ed. LC 74-31359. (Pacific Classics Ser.: No. 5). 320p. 1975. pap. 4.95 (ISBN 0-8248-0288-8). U Pr of Hawaii.

--Roughing It. (Classics Ser). (gr. 8 up). pap. 1.25 (ISBN 0-8049-0134-1, CL-134). Airmont.

--Roughing It. LC 28-1234. (Illus.). Repr. of 1875 ed. 10.95 (ISBN 0-06-014420-3, HarpT). Har-Row.

--Roughing It. (RL 10). pap. 2.50 (ISBN 0-451-51454-8, CE1454, Sig Classics). NAL.

Wallace, Robert. Hawaii. (The American Wilderness Ser.). (Illus.). 1973. 12.95 (ISBN 0-8094-1176-8). Time-Life.

Webb, William & Webb, Mary. Exploring Hawaii, 2 bks. Incl. Bk. I. Ohau; Bk. II. Maui. (Illus.). Date not set. pap. 2.95 ea. World Wide.

Wenkam, Robert. Hawaii: Kauai, Oahu, Maui, Molokai, Lanai, & Hawaii. LC 72-4186. (Illus.). 160p. 1972. pap. 7.95 (ISBN 0-528-88160-4). Rand.

--Kauai: Hawaii's Garden Island. (Illus.). 1979. 25.00 (ISBN 0-528-81040-5). Rand.

White, Sheryl S. Beautiful Oahu. Shangle, Robert D., ed. (Illus.). 72p. 1981. 14.95 (ISBN 0-89802-279-7); pap. 7.95 (ISBN 0-89802-278-9). Beautiful Am.

Wilder, Kinau. Wilders of Waikiki. 1978. pap. 7.95 (ISBN 0-914916-28-9). Topgallant.

Wilkes, Charles. United States Exploring Expedition During the Years 1838-42 Under the Command of Charles Wilkes: Botanical Section, Vols. 15-17. Incl. Vol. 15. Phanoregamia. Gray, A. 240.00 (ISBN 3-7682-0714-5); Vol. 16. Cryptogamia, Filices, Lycopodiaceae & Hydropterides. Brackenridge, W. D. (Illus.). 90.00 (ISBN 3-7682-0715-3); Vol. 17. Cryptogamia Musci, Lichenes, Algae, Fungi Phanerogamia of Pacific North America. Sullivent, W. B., et al. (Illus.). 100.00 (ISBN 3-7682-0716-1). 1968. Repr. of 1854 ed. Set. 420.00 (ISBN 3-7682-0709-9). Lubrecht & Cramer.

HAWAII-DESCRIPTION AND TRAVEL-GUIDEBOOKS

Arthur Frommer's Guide to Hawaii, 1981-82. 224p. 1981. pap. 2.95 (ISBN 0-671-41430-5). Frommer-Pasmantier.

Bone, Robert W. Maverick Guide to Hawaii: 1980 Edition. LC 78-71963. 437p. 1980. pap. 8.95 (ISBN 0-88289-262-2). Pelican.

--Maverick Guide to Hawaii: 1981 Edition. LC 80-25076. (Illus.). 437p. (Orig.). 1981. pap. 8.95 (ISBN 0-88289-277-0). Pelican.

Clemens, Samuel L. Letters from the Sandwich Islands. LC 72-2113. (American Literature Ser., No. 49). 1972. Repr. of 1938 ed. lib. bdg. 49.95 (ISBN 0-8383-1471-6). Haskell.

Fodor's Hawaii in Japanese. (Fodor's Travel Guide Ser.). (Illus., Japanese.). 1979. 9.95 (ISBN 0-679-00436-X); pap. 6.95 (ISBN 0-679-00437-8). McKay.

Fodor's Hawaii, 1981. 1980. 12.95 (ISBN 0-679-00693-1); pap. 9.95 (ISBN 0-679-00694-X). McKay.

Gleasner, Bill & Gleasner, Diana. Big Island Traveler's Guide. (Illus.). 1978. pap. 3.50 (ISBN 0-932596-05-3, Pub. by Oriental). Intl Schol Bk Serv.

--Oahu Traveler's Guide. 1978. pap. 3.50 (ISBN 0-932596-04-5, Pub. by Oriental). Intl Schol Bk Serv.

Hawaii Bus & Travel Guide. 30p. 1981. pap. 1.50 (ISBN 0-9601256-9-8). Singletary.

Head, Timothy E. Going Native in Hawaii: A Poor Man's Guide to Paradise. LC 65-14212. (Illus., Orig.). pap. 3.25 (ISBN 0-8048-0209-2). C E Tuttle.

Immler, Robert. Bicycling in Hawaii. Winnett, Thomas, ed. LC 78-52745. (Illus., Orig.). 1978. pap. 4.95 (ISBN 0-911824-72-3). Wilderness.

Inglott, Irene. Tutu Grandma & Vic in Hawaii. (Illus., Orig.). 1970. pap. 1.50 (ISBN 0-686-00265-2). Aquarius.

Johnson, Rubellite K. & Mahelona, John. Na Inoa Hoku: A Catalogue of Hawaiian & Pacific Star Names. LC 75-23889. 1975. pap. 4.95 (ISBN 0-914916-09-2). Topgallant.

Kane, Robert S. The A to Z Travel Guides. 6.95 (ISBN 0-686-73303-7). Rand.

Krauss, Bob. Kauai. 2nd ed. LC 77-82233. (Illus.). 72p. 1981. pap. 4.95 (ISBN 0-89610-083-9). Island Her.

Mitchell, Charles & Shifflette, Colleen. Hawaii for You & the Family. (Illus., Orig.). 1979. pap. 6.95 (ISBN 0-87663-999-6, Pub. by Hancock Hse). Universe.

Paitson, Hupi & Paitson, Lloyd. Maui: Notes from a Private Guidebook. (Illus., Orig.). 1970. pap. 1.50 (ISBN 0-686-00264-4). Aquarius.
Piercy, LaRue W. Hawaii, This & That. (Illus.). 64p. 1981. pap. 2.50 (ISBN 0-912180-39-0). Petroglyph.
Randall, John E. The Underwater Guide to Hawaiian Reef Fishes. (Illus.). 1980. plastic bdg. 8.95 (ISBN 0-915180-02-2). Harrowood Bks.
Rathbun, Linda M. Bicycler's Guide to Hawaii. 1976. pap. 3.25 (ISBN 0-912180-28-5). Petroglyph.
Riegert, Ray. Hidden Hawaii: An Adventurer's Guide. LC 79-20871. (Illus.). 1979. pap. 9.95 (ISBN 0-915904-48-9). And-Or Pr.
Rizzuto, Shirley. Hawaiian Camping. Winnett, Thomas, ed. LC 79-67012. (Illus., Orig.). 1979. pap. 4.95 (ISBN 0-911824-92-8). Wilderness.
Saltonstall, Maxine. Dining in Hawaii. (Dining In Ser.). 200p. (Orig.). 1981. pap. 7.95 (ISBN 0-89716-066-5). Peanut Butter.
Singletary, Milly. Discover Hawaii Minute by Minute, Vol. 1 Oahu. (Illus.). 1978. pap. 1.95 (ISBN 0-685-31954-7). Singletary.
--Hawaii Bus & Travel Guide. (Illus., Orig.). 1981. pap. 1.50 (ISBN 0-9601256-9-8). Sunset Pubns.
--Restaurant Encyclopedia of Hawaii. Hindle, Susan, ed. (Illus.). 64p. 1980. pap. 4.95 (ISBN 0-9601256-7-1). Singletary.
Singletary, Milly & Hindle, Susan, eds. Restaurant Encyclopedia of Hawaii, Nineteen Eighty. (Illus.). 64p. (Orig.). 1980. pap. 4.95x (ISBN 0-9601256-7-1). Sunset Pubns.
Smith, Robert. Hiking Hawaii: The Big Island. 2nd ed. Winnett, Thomas, ed. LC 79-93248. (Wilderness Press Trail Guide Ser.). (Illus.). 112p. 1980. pap. 4.95 (ISBN 0-89997-000-1). Wilderness Pr.
--Hiking Hawaii: The Big Island. Winnett, Thomas, ed. LC 79-93248. (Wilderness Press Trail Guide Ser.). (Illus.). 112p. 1980. pap. 4.95 (ISBN 0-89997-000-1). Wilderness Pr.
Van Campen, Shirley. Hawaii: A Woman's Guide. 150p. 1979. pap. 5.95 (ISBN 0-916032-07-8). Chicago Review.

HAWAII–ECONOMIC CONDITIONS

Creighton, Thomas H. The Lands of Hawaii: Their Use & Misuse. LC 77-16124. 1978. text ed. 15.00x (ISBN 0-8248-0482-1). U Pr of Hawaii.
Lim, Adam P. Y. Job Searching in Hawaii, Practicalities & Realities. LC 77-83968. (Illus.). 1978. pap. 4.95 (ISBN 0-916630-06-4). Pr Pacifica.
Lind, Andrew W. Island Community: Ecological Succession in Hawaii. LC 68-28639. 1968. Repr. of 1938 ed. lib. bdg. 22.75x (ISBN 0-8371-0538-2, LIIC). Greenwood.
Porteus, Stanley D. Century of Social Thinking in Hawaii. LC 62-21039. 1962. 14.95x (ISBN 0-87015-113-4). Pacific Bks.
Whitney, Caspar. Hawaiian America: Something of Its History, Resources & Prospects. facsimile ed. McCurry, Dan C. & Rubenstein, Richard E., eds. LC 74-30665. (American Farmers & the Rise of Agribusiness Ser.). (Illus.). 1975. Repr. of 1899 ed. 32.00x (ISBN 0-405-06841-7). Arno.

HAWAII–HISTORY

Abramson, Joan, ed. Photographers of Old Hawaii. 3rd ed. LC 76-1504. (Illus.). 228p. 1981. 12.50 (ISBN 0-89610-082-0). Island Her.
Allen, Gwenfread E. Hawaii's War Years, 1941-1945. LC 70-136889. (Illus.). 1971. Repr. of 1950 ed. lib. bdg. 27.75 (ISBN 0-8371-5331-X, ALHW). Greenwood.
Armitage, George T. A Brief History of Hawaii. 1973. soft bdg. 1.95 (ISBN 0-930492-04-8). Hawaiian Serv.
Bailey, Paul. Those Kings & Queens of Old Hawaii: A Mele to Their Memory. LC 75-259. (Illus.). 381p. 1975. 16.00 (ISBN 0-87026-035-9). Westernlore.
Barnes, Harry E. Pearl Harbor After a Quarter of a Century. 1981. lib. bdg. 59.95 (ISBN 0-686-73185-9). Revisionist Pr.
Barrow, Terence. Captain Cook in Hawaii. LC 76-1506. (The Island Heritage Collection Ser.). (Illus.). 1978. 12.50 (ISBN 0-89610-063-4). Island Her.
Bingham, Hiram. A Residence of Twenty-One Years in the Sandwich Islands: A Civil, Religious, & Political History. rev. 3rd ed. LC 77-83041. 1981. 27.50 (ISBN 0-8048-1252-7). C E Tuttle.
Blackman, William F. The Making of Hawaii: A Study in Social Evolution. 2nd ed. LC 75-35175. Repr. of 1906 ed. 22.50 (ISBN 0-404-14204-4). AMS Pr.
Bradley, Harold W. The American Frontier in Hawaii: The Pioneers 1789-1843. 9.00 (ISBN 0-8446-0505-0). Peter Smith.
Burns, Eugene. Last King of Paradise. LC 72-10607. (Select Bibliographies Reprint Ser.). 1973. Repr. of 1952 ed. 19.00 (ISBN 0-8369-7102-7). Arno.
Calisch, Rus. Paumalu: A Story of Modern Hawaii. LC 78-78037. (Orig.). 1979. pap. 3.95 (ISBN 0-9602354-1-8). Paumalu Pr.
Campbell, Archibald. Voyage Around the World from 1806 to 1812. (Fasc, of 1822 Ed). 1967. Repr. 5.95 (ISBN 0-87022-100-0). U Pr of Hawaii.
Campbell, James K., et al, eds. Kaulana na Pua: A Hawaiian Album, 1890-1930. LC 77-156041. (Illus.). 1977. pap. 6.95 (ISBN 0-917850-01-7). Pueo Pr.
Chambers, Henry E. Constitutional History of Hawaii. LC 78-63846. (Johns Hopkins University. Studies in the Social Sciences. Fourteenth Ser. 1896: 1). Repr. of 1896 ed. 11.50 (ISBN 0-404-61103-6). AMS Pr.
Chaplin, George & Paige, Glenn D., eds. Hawaii Two Thousand: Continuing Experiment in Anticipatory Democracy. 500p. 1973. 12.95 (ISBN 0-8248-0252-7). U Pr of Hawaii.
Chickering, William H. Within the Sound of These Waves: The Story of the Kings of Hawaii Island, Containing a Full Account of the Death of Captain Cook, Together with the Hawaiian Adventures of George Vancouver & Sundry Other Mariners. LC 70-138584. (Illus.). 1971. Repr. of 1941 ed. lib. bdg. 21.75x (ISBN 0-8371-5783-8, CHSW). Greenwood.
Creighton, Thomas H. The Lands of Hawaii: Their Use & Misuse. LC 77-16124. 1978. text ed. 15.00x (ISBN 0-8248-0482-1). U Pr of Hawaii.
Dahlgren, Erik W. Were the Hawaiian Islands Visited by the Spaniards Before Their Discovery by Captain Cook in 1778? LC 75-35187. (Illus.). Repr. of 1916 ed. 43.50 (ISBN 0-404-14216-8). AMS Pr.
Daws, Gavan. Shoal of Time: A History of the Hawaiian Islands. LC 73-92053. 507p. 1974. pap. 6.95 (ISBN 0-8248-0324-8). U Pr of Hawaii.
DeFrancis, John. Things Japanese in Hawaii. (Illus.). 224p. 1973. pap. 8.50 (ISBN 0-8248-0233-0). U Pr of Hawaii.
Dorita, Mary. Filipino Immigration to Hawaii. LC 75-5373. 1975. Repr. of 1954 ed. soft bdg. 9.00 (ISBN 0-88247-354-9). R & E Res Assoc.
Ellis, William. The Journal of William Ellis. LC 78-54936. (Illus.). 1979. 18.50 (ISBN 0-8048-1298-5). C E Tuttle.
Estep, Gerald A. Social Placement of the Portuguese in Hawaii As Indicated by Factors in Assimilation: Thesis. LC 73-78062. 1974. Repr. of 1941 ed. soft bdg. 7.00 (ISBN 0-88247-271-2). R & E Res Assoc.
Farrell, Bryan. Hawaii: The Legend That Sells. 300p. 1981. 20.00x (ISBN 0-8248-0766-9). U Pr of Hawaii.
Gillis, J. A. Hawaiian Incident. facs. ed. LC 77-117878. (Select Bibliographies Reprint Ser). 1897. 12.00 (ISBN 0-8369-5331-2). Arno.
Gowen, Herbert H. The Napoleon of the Pacific, Kamehameha the Great. LC 75-35193. Repr. of 1919 ed. 26.00 (ISBN 0-404-14221-4). AMS Pr.
Hazama, Dorothy. The Ancient Hawaiians: Who Were They? How Did They Live? O'Connell, J. Patrick, ed. (Hawaii's Cultural Heritage Ser.: Vol. 2). (Illus.). 80p. (gr. 4 up). 1974. pap. 2.50 (ISBN 0-911776-23-0). Hogarth.
Holt, John D., ed. An Account of the Sandwich Islands: The Hawaiian Journal of John B. Whitman, 1813-1815. (Illus.). 1979. 9.95 (ISBN 0-914916-49-1). Topgallant.
Joesting, Edward. Hawaii: An Uncommon History. (Illus.). 353p. 1972. 10.95 (ISBN 0-393-05382-2). Norton.
Joseting, Edward. Hawaii: An Uncommon History. (Illus.). 1978. pap. 5.95 (ISBN 0-393-00907-6). Norton.
Judd, Bernice. Voyages to Hawaii Before 1860. LC 74-78864. 1974. text ed. 10.00x (ISBN 0-8248-0329-9). U Pr of Hawaii.
Judd, Gerrit P. Doctor Judd, Hawaii's Friend: A Biography of Gerrit Parmele Judd, 1803-1873. (Illus.). 1960. 12.00 (ISBN 0-87022-385-2). U Pr of Hawaii.
--Hawaii. LC 66-17588. (Orig.). 1966. pap. 2.95 (ISBN 0-8077-1596-4). Tchrs Coll.
--Hawaii: An Informal History. 5.50 (ISBN 0-8446-2345-8). Peter Smith.
Judd, Gerritt P. Hawaii: An Informal History. 1961. pap. 1.95 (ISBN 0-02-033980-1, Collier). Macmillan.
Judd, Lawrence M. Lawrence M. Judd & Hawaii: An Autobiography. Lytle, Hugh W., as told to. LC 71-147177. 1971. 8.00 (ISBN 0-8048-0910-0). C E Tuttle.
Judd, Walter F. Palaces & Forts of the Hawaiian Kingdom. LC 73-91595. (Illus.). 1975. 14.95 (ISBN 0-87015-216-5). Pacific Bks.
Kane, Herb K. Voyage: The Discovery of Hawaii. LC 76-1503. (Illus.). 1976. 9.95 (ISBN 0-89610-031-6). Island Her.
Keesing, Felix M. Hawaiian Homesteading on Molokai. LC 75-35196. Repr. of 1936 ed. 15.50 (ISBN 0-404-14224-9). AMS Pr.
Krauss, Bob & Alexander, W. P. Grove Farm Plantation: The Biography of a Hawaiian Sugar Plantation. LC 65-18124. (Illus.). 1965. 10.00 (ISBN 0-87015-140-1). Pacific Bks.
Kuykendall, R. & Day, A. Hawaii: A History. 1978. pap. 5.95 (ISBN 0-13-384305-X). P-H.
Kuykendall, Ralph S. The Hawaiian Kingdom, 3 vols. Incl. Vol. 1. 1778-1854, Foundation & Transformation. 462p. 1938. 14.00 (ISBN 0-87022-431-X); Vol. 2. 1854-1874, Twenty Critical Years. 320p. 1953. 12.00 (ISBN 0-87022-432-8); Vol. 3. 1874-1893, the Kalakaua Dynasty. 776p. 1967. 17.50 (ISBN 0-87022-433-6). (Illus.). U Pr of Hawaii.
Loomis, Albertine. The Best of Friends: The Story of Hawaii's Libraries & Their Friends, 1879-1979. Pagliaro, Penny, ed. (Illus.). 1979. pap. 3.95 (ISBN 0-916630-10-2). Pr Pacifica.
--For Whom Are the Stars? LC 76-16778. 256p. 1976. 9.95 (ISBN 0-8248-0416-3). U Pr of Hawaii.
Mack, Jim. Haleakala: The Story Behind the Scenery. DenDooven, Gweneth R., ed. LC 78-51407. (Illus.). 1979. 7.95 (ISBN 0-916122-54-9); pap. 3.50 (ISBN 0-916122-53-0). KC Pubns.
March, Alden. History & Conquest of the Philippines & Our Other Island Possessions. LC 4-111744. (American Imperialism: Viewpoints of United States Foreign Policy, 1898-1941). 1970. Repr. of 1899 ed. 19.00 (ISBN 0-405-02038-4). Arno.
Martin, Henry B. The Polynesian Journal of Henry Byam Martin. Dodd, Edward, ed. (Illus.). 200p. 1981. write for info. (ISBN 0-87577-060-6). Peabody Mus Salem.
Mellen, Kathleen D. Island Kingdom Passes. 1958. 8.95 (ISBN 0-8038-3357-1). Hastings.
Miyamoto, Kazuo. Hawaii: The End of the Rainbow. LC 63-20213. 1964. pap. 5.25 (ISBN 0-8048-0233-5). C E Tuttle.
Murray-Oliver, Anthony. Captain Cook's Hawaii. (Illus.). 215p. 1975. 29.00x (ISBN 0-8002-0456-5). Intl Pubns Serv.
Nickerson, Roy. Lahaina: Royal Capital of Hawaii. Wirtz, Richard, ed. LC 77-94277. (Illus.). 1978. pap. 4.95 (ISBN 0-930492-03-X). Hawaiian Serv.
Nordhof, Charles. Hawaii-Nei: 1873. Apple, Russell A., ed. (Illus.). 40p. 1977. Repr. of 1873 ed. pap. 2.95 (ISBN 0-89646-030-4). Outbooks.
Ogawa, Dennis M. Kodomo No Tame Ni-for the Sake of the Children: The Japanese American Experience in Hawaii. LC 77-18368. 639p. 1980. pap. 8.95 (ISBN 0-8248-0730-8). U Pr of Hawaii.
Osborne, Thomas J. Empire Can Wait: American Opposition to Hawaiian Annexation, 1893 - 1898. LC 81-8156. (Illus.). 200p. 1981. 18.00x (ISBN 0-87338-259-5). Kent St U Pr.
Pogue, John F. Moolelo of Ancient Hawaii. Kenn, Charles W., tr. from Hawaiian. 1978. pap. 3.95 (ISBN 0-914916-31-9). Topgallant.
Pratt, Julius W. Expansionists of 1898: The Acquisition of Hawaii & the Spanish Islands. 1972. pap. 3.45 (ISBN 0-8129-6015-7, QP15). Times Bks.
Pukui, Mary K., et al. Place Names of Hawaii. 2nd ed. LC 73-85582. 320p. 1974 (ISBN 0-8248-0208-X). pap. 5.95 (ISBN 0-8248-0524-0). U Pr of Hawaii.
--Nana I Ke Kumu, Vol. 2. LC 72-93779. 1980. 16.00 (ISBN 0-916630-15-3); write for info. lea. bdg. ltd. to 100 copies (ISBN 0-916630-16-1); pap. 8.00 (ISBN 0-916630-14-5). Hui-Hanai-Queen.
Queen Liliuokalani. Hawaii's Story by Hawaii's Queen. LC 63-23301. (Illus.). 1964. pap. 6.95 (ISBN 0-8048-1066-4). C E Tuttle.
Rose, Roger G. Hawaii: The Royal Isles. LC 80-65718. (Special Publications: No. 67). (Illus.). 225p. 1980. pap. 18.00 (ISBN 0-910240-27-2). Bishop Mus.
Schmitt, Robert C. Historical Statistics of Hawaii. LC 77-90997. 1978. text ed. 25.00x (ISBN 0-8248-0505-4). U Pr of Hawaii.
Stevens, Sylvester K. American Expansion in Hawaii, 1842-1898. LC 68-25049. 1968. Repr. of 1945 ed. 12.50 (ISBN 0-8462-1180-7). Russell.
Tate, Merze. Hawaii: Reciprocity or Annexation. LC 68-15011. (Illus.). xl, 300p. 1968. 8.50 (ISBN 0-87013-126-5). Mich St U Pr.
--The United States & the Hawaiian Kingdom: A Political History. LC 80-14045. (Illus.). ix, 374p. 1980. Repr. of 1965 ed. lib. bdg. 29.25x (ISBN 0-313-22441-2, TAUS). Greenwood.
Westervelt, William D. Hawaiian Historical Legends. LC 75-35216. Repr. of 1923 ed. 17.50 (ISBN 0-404-14239-7). AMS Pr.
Whitson, Skip, compiled by. Hawaii-Nei, the Kingdom of Hawaii: One Hundred Years Ago. (Sun Historical Ser). (Illus., Orig.). 1976. pap. 3.50 (ISBN 0-89540-035-9, SB035). Sun Pub.
Wong, Helen H. & Carey, Robert K. Hawaii's Royal History. O'Connell, J. Patrick, ed. (Illus.). 272p. (gr. 7). 1980. lib. bdg. 11.95 (ISBN 0-911776-39-7). Hogarth.
Wooden, Wayne S. What Price Paradise? Changing Social Patterns in Hawaii. LC 80-6240. 157p. 1981. lib. bdg. 17.00 (ISBN 0-8191-1520-7); pap. text ed. 8.25 (ISBN 0-8191-1521-5). U Pr of Amer.
Young, Lucien. Real Hawaii: Its History & Present Conditions Including the True Story of the Revolution. LC 77-111760. (American Imperialism: Viewpoints of United States Foreign Policy, 1898-1941). 1970. Repr. of 1899 ed. 17.00 (ISBN 0-405-02054-6). Arno.

HAWAII–HISTORY–BIBLIOGRAPHY

Swindler, W. F. Chronology & Documentary Handbook of the State of Hawaii. 1978. 8.50 (ISBN 0-379-16136-2). Oceana.
Vance, Mary. Historical Society Architectural Publications: Georgia, Hawaii, Idaho, Illinois & Indiana. (Architecture Ser.: Bibliography A-157). 54p. 1980. pap. 6.00 (ISBN 0-686-26906-3). Vance Biblios.

HAWAII–HISTORY–FICTION

Bushnell, O. A. Ka'a'awa: A Novel About Hawaii in the 1850's. LC 72-83490. 350p. 1972. 10.00 (ISBN 0-8248-0206-3). U Pr of Hawaii.
Michener, James A. Hawaii. 1959. 16.95 (ISBN 0-394-42797-1). Random.
--Hawaii. 1978. pap. 3.50 (ISBN 0-449-23761-3, Crest). Fawcett.

HAWAII–HISTORY–SOURCES

Johnson, Rubellite K., ed. Kukini 'aha 'ilono: Over a Century of Native Hawaiian Life & Thought from Hawaiian Newpapers, 1834-1948. (Illus.). 1976. pap. text ed. 20.00 (ISBN 0-914916-26-2). Topgallant.
Korn, Alfons L. Victorian Visitors. 1958. 12.95 (ISBN 0-87022-421-2). U Pr of Hawaii.
Korn, Alfons L., ed. News from Molokai: Letters Between Peter Kaeo & Queen Emma, 1873-1876. LC 76-16823. 448p. 1976. 14.95 (ISBN 0-8248-0399-X). U Pr of Hawaii.
Liliuokalani. The Kumulipo: A Hawaiian Creation Myth. Campbell, James K. & Vorhies, Aleen, eds. LC 78-60923. (Illus.). 1978. pap. 7.95 (ISBN 0-917850-02-5). Pueo Pr.
Remy, M. Jules. Contributions of a Venerable Native to the Ancient History of the Hawaiian Islands. Alexander, W. D. & Brigham, William T., trs. (Illus.). 1979. pap. 2.95 (ISBN 0-89646-056-8). Outbooks.

HAWAII–JUVENILE LITERATURE

Bailey, Bernadine. Picture Book of Hawaii. rev. ed. LC 62-10660. (Illus.). (gr. 3-5). 1978. 5.50g (ISBN 0-8075-9513-6). A Whitman.
Carpenter, Allan. Hawaii. new ed. LC 79-9991. (New Enchantment of America State Bks.). (Illus.). (gr. 4 up). 1979. PLB 10.60 (ISBN 0-516-04111-8). Childrens.
Chambers, H. E. Constitutional History of Hawaii. 1973. Repr. of 1896 ed. pap. 7.00 (ISBN 0-384-08450-8). Johnson Repr.
Fradin, Dennis. Hawaii: In Words & Pictures. LC 79-25605. (Young People's Stories of Our States Ser.). (Illus.). 48p. (gr. 2-5). 1980. PLB 9.25 (ISBN 0-516-03913-X). Childrens.
Lewis, Oscar. Hawaii, Gem of the Pacific. (Illus.). (gr. 7-9). 1954. PLB 4.39 (ISBN 0-394-90349-8). Random.
Radlauer, Ruth. Haleakala National Park. LC 79-10500. (Parks for People Ser.). (Illus.). (gr. 3 up). 1979. 3.95 (ISBN 0-516-17499-1, Elk Grove Bks.); PLB 10.00 (ISBN 0-516-07499-7). Childrens.
Rublowsky, John. Born in Fire: A Geological History of Hawaii. LC 79-2001. (Illus.). 96p. (gr. 5 up). 1981. 9.95 (ISBN 0-06-025088-7, HarpJ); PLB 9.89g (ISBN 0-06-025089-5). Har-Row.

HAWAII–POLITICS AND GOVERNMENT

Anthony, J. Garner. Hawaii Under Army Rule. 213p. 1975. pap. 3.95 (ISBN 0-8248-0377-9). U Pr of Hawaii.
Apple, Russ & Apple, Peg. Land, Lili'uokalani & Annexation. 1979. pap. 4.95 (ISBN 0-914916-40-8). Topgallant.
Gething, Judith. Sex Discrimination & the Law in Hawaii: A Guide to Your Legal Rights. LC 78-10636. 1979. pap. 3.95 (ISBN 0-8248-0620-4). U Pr of Hawaii.
Holt, John D. Monarchy in Hawaii. rev., 2nd ed. 1971. pap. 3.50 (ISBN 0-914916-00-9). Topgallant.
Hooper, Paul F. Elusive Destiny: The Internationalist Movement in Modern Hawaii. LC 79-24540. 1980. text ed. 15.00x (ISBN 0-8248-0631-X). U Pr of Hawaii.
Judd, Lawrence M. Lawrence M. Judd & Hawaii: An Autobiography. Lytle, Hugh W., as told to. LC 71-147177. 1971. 8.00 (ISBN 0-8048-0910-0). C E Tuttle.
Myers, Phyllis. Zoning Hawaii: An Analysis of the Passage & Implementation of Hawaii's Land Classification Law. LC 76-5914. (Illus.). 1976. 8.95 (ISBN 0-89164-033-9); pap. 4.95 (ISBN 0-89164-032-0). Conservation Foun.
Zalburg, Sanford. A Spark Is Struck! Jack Hall & the ILWU in Hawaii. LC 79-91284. (Illus.). 1980. pap. 5.95 (ISBN 0-8248-0672-7). U Pr of Hawaii.

HAWAII–POPULATION

Adams, Romanzo. Interracial Marriage in Hawaii: A Study of Mutually Conditioned Processes of Acculturation & Amalgamation. LC 69-14907. (Criminology, Law Enforcement, & Social Problems Ser.: No. 65). (Illus.). 1969. Repr. of 1937 ed. 12.50 (ISBN 0-87585-065-0). Patterson Smith.

Burrows, Edwin G. Hawaiian Americans: An Account of the Mingling of Japanese, Chinese, Polynesian, & American Cultures. 1970. Repr. of 1947 ed. 16.00 (ISBN 0-208-00949-3, Archon). Shoe String.

Coman, Katherine & Lind, Andrew W. The History of Contract Labor in the Hawaiian Islands & Hawaii's Japanese, 2 vols. in 1. Daniels, Roger, ed. LC 78-54813. (Asian Experience in North America Ser.). (Illus.). 1979. Repr. of 1946 ed. lib. bdg. 22.00x (ISBN 0-405-11269-6). Arno.

Conroy, Hilary. The Japanese Frontier in Hawaii, 1868-1898. Daniels, Roger, ed. LC 78-54840. (Asian Experience in North America). 1979. Repr. of 1953 ed. lib. bdg. 11.00x (ISBN 0-405-11306-4). Arno.

Embree, John F. Acculturation Among the Japanese of Kona, Hawaii. LC 43-1209. (American Anthropological Association Memoirs). pap. 12.00 (ISBN 0-527-00558-4). Kraus Repr.

Glick, Clarence E. Sojourners & Settlers: Chinese Migrants in Hawaii. LC 80-13799. 480p. 1980. text ed. 20.00x (ISBN 0-8248-0707-3). U Pr of Hawaii.

Hazama, Dorothy. Hawaii's People from Japan. O'Connell, Patrick, ed. (Hawaii Cultural Heritage Ser.: Vol. 10). (Illus.). (gr. 4 up). 1975. pap. 2.50 (ISBN 0-911776-35-4). Hogarth.

Lind, Andrew W. Island Community: Ecological Succession in Hawaii. LC 68-28639. 1968. Repr. of 1938 ed. lib. bdg. 22.75x (ISBN 0-8371-0538-2, LIIC). Greenwood.

McDermott, John F., Jr., et al, eds. People & Cultures of Hawaii: A Psychocultural Profile. LC 80-11959. 242p. 1980. pap. 7.50 (ISBN 0-8248-0706-5). U Pr of Hawaii.

Nordyke, Eleanor C. The Peopling of Hawaii. LC 77-8842. (Illus.). 1977. pap. 4.95 (ISBN 0-8248-0511-9, Eastwest Ctr). U Pr of Hawaii.

Samuels, Frederick. The Japanese & the Haoles of Honolulu: Durable Group Interaction. 1970. 6.00 (ISBN 0-8084-0175-0); pap. 2.95 (ISBN 0-8084-0176-9, B50). Coll & U Pr.

Schmitt, Robert C. Demographic Statistics of Hawaii, 1778-1965. LC 67-50840. (Illus.). 1968. pap. text ed. 6.00x (ISBN 0-87022-740-8). U Pr of Hawaii.

HAWAII–RELIGION

Kepelino. Kepelino's Traditions of Hawaii. Beckwith, Martha W., ed. Repr. of 1932 ed. pap. 17.00 (ISBN 0-527-02201-2). Kraus Repr.

Melville, Leinani. Children of the Rainbow: The Religions, Legends & Gods of Pre-Christian Hawaii. LC 69-17715. (Illus.). 1969. pap. 1.95 (ISBN 0-8356-0002-5, Quest). Theos Pub Hse.

Nau, Erika S. Self-Awareness Through Huna-Hawaii's Ancient Wisdom. Grunwald, Stefan, ed. LC 80-27842. (Orig.). 1981. pap. 5.95 (ISBN 0-89865-099-2, Unilaw). Donning Co.

Rodman, Julius S. The Kahuna Sorcerers of Hawaii, Past & Present: With a Glossary of Ancient Religious Terms & the Books of the Hawaiian Royal Dead. 1979. 15.00 (ISBN 0-682-49196-9, Banner). Exposition.

Spurrier, Joseph H. Great Are the Promises Unto the Isle of the Sea: The Church of Jesus Christ of Latter-day Saints in the Hawaiian Islands. (Orig.). 1978. pap. 3.95 (ISBN 0-89036-114-2). Hawkes Pub Inc.

Van Woerkom, Dorothy. The Lands of Fire & Ice. (gr. 2-5). 1979. 4.95 (ISBN 0-570-03472-8, 56-1338). Concordia.

HAWAII–SOCIAL CONDITIONS

Adams, Romanzo. Interracial Marriage in Hawaii: A Study of the Mutually Conditioned Processes of Acculturation & Amalgamation. LC 75-96473. (BCL Ser.: No. I). Repr. of 1937 ed. 12.00 (ISBN 0-404-00293-5). AMS Pr.

Clemens, Samuel L. Letters from the Sandwich Islands. LC 72-2113. (American Literature Ser., No. 49). 1972. Repr. of 1938 ed. lib. bdg. 49.95 (ISBN 0-8383-1471-6). Haskell.

Du Puy, William A. Hawaii & Its Race Problem. LC 75-35214. Repr. of 1932 ed. 19.50 (ISBN 0-404-14237-0). AMS Pr.

Fuchs, Lawrence H. Hawaii Pono: A Social History. LC 61-13347. (Illus.). 1961. 14.95 (ISBN 0-15-139539-X). HarBraceJ.

Gething, Judith. Sex Discrimination & the Law in Hawaii: A Guide to Your Legal Rights. LC 78-10636. 1979. pap. 3.95 (ISBN 0-8248-0620-4). U Pr of Hawaii.

Holt, John D. On Being Hawaiian. (Illus.). 1973. pap. 3.50 (ISBN 0-914916-23-8). Topgallant.

Lasker, Bruno. Filipino Immigration to the Continental United States & to Hawaii. LC 69-18783. (American Immigration Collection Ser., No. 1). (Illus.). 1969. Repr. of 1931 ed. 18.00 (ISBN 0-405-00531-8). Arno.

Lind, Andrew W. Hawaii's People. rev. ed. LC 80-10764. 1980. pap. text ed. 5.00x (ISBN 0-8248-0704-9). U Pr of Hawaii.

Lyon, Fred. Week in Windley's World: Hawaii. (Face to Face Bks.). (Illus.). (gr. k-3). 1970. 8.95 (ISBN 0-02-761500-6, CCPr). Macmillan.

Ogawa, Dennis M. Jan Ken Po: The World of Hawaii's Japanese Americans. new ed. LC 78-9513. (Illus.). 1978. pap. 3.95 (ISBN 0-8248-0398-1). U Pr of Hawaii.

Ogawa, Dennis M. & Grant, Glen. Kodomo No Tame Ni-for the Sake of the Children: The Japanese American Experience in Hawaii. LC 77-18368. 1978. 15.00 (ISBN 0-8248-0528-3). U Pr of Hawaii.

Porteus, Stanley D. Century of Social Thinking in Hawaii. LC 62-21039. 1962. 14.95x (ISBN 0-87015-113-4). Pacific Bks.

Pukui, Mary K., et al. Nana I Ke Kumu, Vol. 1. LC 72-93779. 1972. pap. 8.00 (ISBN 0-916630-13-7). Hui-Hanai-Queen.

Rapson, Richard L. Fairly Lucky You Live Hawaii! LC 80-5530. 166p. 1980. lib. bdg. 13.50 (ISBN 0-8191-1167-8); pap. text ed. 6.50 (ISBN 0-8191-1168-6). U Pr of Amer.

Research Committee on the Study of Honolulu Residents, compiled by. Honolulu Residents in Multi-Ethnic Perspective: Toward a Theory of the American National Character. 1980. pap. text ed. 7.50x (ISBN 0-8248-0717-0). U Pr of Hawaii.

Smith, William C. Americans in Process: A Study of Our Citizens of Oriental Ancestry. LC 76-129413. (American Immigration Collection, Ser. 2). 1970. Repr. of 1937 ed. 19.00 (ISBN 0-405-00567-9). Arno.

Vallangca, Roberto V. Pinoy: The First Wave. LC 76-47180. (Illus., Orig.). 1977. pap. 6.95 (ISBN 0-89407-000-2). Strawberry Hill.

Zalburg, Sanford. A Spark Is Struck! Jack Hall & the ILWU in Hawaii. LC 79-91284. (Illus.). 1980. pap. 5.95 (ISBN 0-8248-0672-7). U Pr of Hawaii.

HAWAIIAN BALLADS AND SONGS

see also Folk-Songs, Hawaiian; Songs, Hawaiian

Beckwith, Martha W., ed. The Kumulipo: A Hawaiian Creation Chant. LC 79-188978. 276p. 1981. pap. 5.95 (ISBN 0-8248-0771-5). U Pr of Hawaii.

Pukui, Mary K. & Korn, Alfons L., trs. The Echo of Our Song: Chants & Poems of the Hawaiians. LC 72-91620. 1979. pap. 4.95 (ISBN 0-8248-0668-9). U Pr of Hawaii.

HAWAIIAN FOLK-LORE

see Folk-Lore, Hawaiian

HAWAIIAN FOLK-SONGS

see Folk-Songs, Hawaiian

HAWAIIAN LANGUAGE

Alexander, W. C. Short Synopsis of the Most Essential Points in Hawaiian Grammar. LC 68-13866. pap. 2.95 (ISBN 0-8048-0528-8). C E Tuttle.

Andrews, Lorrin. Grammar of the Hawaiian Language. LC 75-35173. Repr. of 1854 ed. 13.50 (ISBN 0-404-14202-8). AMS Pr.

Counts, David R. Grammar of Kaliai-Kove. LC 72-627917. (Oceanic Linguistics Special Publication: No. 6). (Orig.). 1970. pap. text ed. 5.00x (ISBN 0-87022-156-6). U Pr of Hawaii.

Donnelly, Milly L. Me Spik English. 31p. soft bdg. 1.95 (ISBN 0-930492-08-0). Hawaiian Serv.

Elbert, Samuel H. Spoken Hawaiian. LC 77-98134. (Illus., Orig.). 1970. pap. 5.00 (ISBN 0-87022-216-3). U Pr of Hawaii.

Elbert, Samuel H. & Pukui, Mary K. Hawaiian Grammar. LC 78-21692. 1979. text ed. 12.00x (ISBN 0-8248-0494-5). U Pr of Hawaii.

Helbig, W. Ray. Let's Learn a Little Hawaiian. 1970. soft bdg. 1.95 (ISBN 0-930492-07-2). Hawaiian Serv.

Kahananui, Dorothy M. & Anthony, Alberta P. Let's Speak Hawaiian - E Kama'ilio Hawai'i Kakou. rev. ed. (Illus.). 1974. pap. text ed. 8.00x (ISBN 0-8248-0283-7). U Pr of Hawaii.

Soper, J. H., ed. Hawaiian Phrase Book. LC 68-13868. 1968. pap. 3.50 (ISBN 0-8048-0241-6). C E Tuttle.

University of Hawaii, Honolulu. Sinclair Library: Dictionary Catalog of the Hawaiian Collection, 4 vols. 1963. Set. lib. bdg. 340.00 (ISBN 0-8161-0650-9). G K Hall.

HAWAIIAN LANGUAGE–BIBLIOGRAPHY

Judd, Bernice, et al, eds. Hawaiian Language Imprints, 1822-1899: A Bibliography. LC 77-21295. 1978. text ed. 12.00x (ISBN 0-8248-0529-1). U Pr of Hawaii.

HAWAIIAN LANGUAGE–DICTIONARIES–ENGLISH

Andrews, Lorrin. A Dictionary of the Hawaiian Language. LC 72-89745. 1973. 17.50 (ISBN 0-8048-1087-7). C E Tuttle.

Hitchcock, Harvey R. English-Hawaiian Dictionary. LC 68-13870. (gr. 7 up). 1968. Repr. 7.25 (ISBN 0-8048-0168-1). C E Tuttle.

Judd, Henry P. The Hawaiian Language & Hawaiian-English Dictionary. LC 78-101212. 1966. soft bdg. 3.95 (ISBN 0-930492-06-4). Hawaiian Serv.

Pukui, Mary K. & Elbert, Samuel H. Hawaiian Dictionary. rev. ed. Orig. Title: Hawaiian-English Dictionary English-Hawaiian Dictionary. 1971. 17.50 (ISBN 0-87022-662-2). U Pr of Hawaii.

Pukui, Mary K., et al. The Pocket Hawaiian Dictionary: With a Concise Hawaiian Grammar. LC 74-78865. 280p. 1975. pap. 1.95 (ISBN 0-8248-0307-8). U Pr of Hawaii.

Rehg, Kenneth L. & Sohl, Damian G. Ponapean-English Dictionary. LC 79-19451. (Pali Language Texts: Micronesia). 1979. pap. text ed. 8.00x (ISBN 0-8248-0562-3). U Pr of Hawaii.

HAWAIIAN LEGENDS

see Legends, Hawaiian

HAWAIIAN MAGIC

see Magic, Hawaiian

HAWAIIAN MUSIC

see Music, Hawaiian

HAWAIIAN MYTHOLOGY

see Mythology, Hawaiian

HAWAIIAN POETRY

Lombard, Shirley C. Iliahi: Poems of Hawaii. (Illus.). 1975. pap. 3.95 (ISBN 0-914916-03-3). Topgallant.

Pukui, Mary K. & Korn, Alfons L., eds. The Echo of Our Song: Chants & Poems of the Hawaiians. Pukui, Mary K. & Korn, Alfons L., trs. from Hawaiian. LC 72-91620. 250p. 1973. 14.00 (ISBN 0-8248-0248-9); deluxe ed. 30.00 (ISBN 0-8248-0285-3). U Pr of Hawaii.

HAWAIIAN POETRY–TRANSLATIONS INTO ENGLISH

Pukui, Mary K. & Korn, Alfons L., eds. The Echo of Our Song: Chants & Poems of the Hawaiians. Pukui, Mary K. & Korn, Alfons L., trs. from Hawaiian. LC 72-91620. 250p. 1973. 14.00 (ISBN 0-8248-0248-9); deluxe ed. 30.00 (ISBN 0-8248-0285-3). U Pr of Hawaii.

Roes, Carol. Mahalo Nui Translations. 1980. pap. 3.00 (ISBN 0-930932-20-X). M. Loke.

Stewart, Frank & Unterecker, John, eds. Poetry Hawaii: A Contemporary Anthology. LC 79-63338. (Illus., Orig.). 1979. pap. 4.95 (ISBN 0-8248-0642-5). U Pr of Hawaii.

HAWAIIAN SONGS

see Songs, Hawaiian

HAWAIIAN TALES

see Tales, Hawaiian

HAWEIS, THOMAS, 1724-1820

Wood, Arthur S. Thomas Haweis. (Church Historical Society Ser.: No. 70). 1957. 11.50x (ISBN 0-8401-5070-9). Allenson-Breckinridge.

HAWKEN RIFLE

Baird, John D. Fifteen Years in Hawken Lode. 15.00 (ISBN 0-88227-011-7). Gun Room.

--Hawken Rifles: The Mountain Man's Choice. 15.00 (ISBN 0-88227-010-9). Gun Room.

HAWKER AIRCRAFT, LIMITED

Rice, Michael S. Pilot's Manual for Hawker Hurricane. (Illus.). 56p. 1974. pap. 2.95 (ISBN 0-87994-030-1, Pub. by AvPubns). Aviation.

HAWKERS AND HAWKING

see Peddlers and Peddling

HAWKES, JOHN, 1925-

Berry, Eliot. A Poetry of Force & Darkness: The Fiction of John Hawkes. LC 79-282. (The Milford Ser.: Popular Writers of Today: Vol. 22). 1979. lib. bdg. 8.95x (ISBN 0-89370-132-7); pap. 2.95 (ISBN 0-89370-232-3). Borgo Pr.

Busch, Frederick. Hawkes: A Guide to His Fictions. LC 72-7765. 210p. 1973. 10.00x (ISBN 0-8156-0089-5). Syracuse U Pr.

Graham, John. Merrill Studies in Second Skin. LC 71-160518. 1971. pap. text ed. 2.50x (ISBN 0-675-09496-8). Merrill.

Greiner, Donald J. Comic Terror: The Novels of John Hawkes. rev. ed. LC 78-16886. 1978. pap. 6.95x (ISBN 0-87870-044-7). Memphis St Univ.

--Comic Terror: The Novels of John Hawkes. LC 73-81555. 1973. 11.95x (ISBN 0-87870-017-X). Memphis St Univ.

Hryciw, Carol A. John Hawkes: An Annotated Bibliography. LC 77-700. (Author Bibliographies Ser.: No. 32). 1977. 10.00 (ISBN 0-8108-1024-7). Scarecrow.

Kuehl, John. John Hawkes & the Craft of Conflict. 1975. 14.00 (ISBN 0-8135-0802-9). Rutgers U Pr.

Santore, Anthony C. & Pocalyko, Michael N., eds. A John Hawkes Symposium: Design & Debris. LC 77-7031. (Insights: Working Papers in Contemporary Criticism Ser.). 1977. pap. 4.95 (ISBN 0-8112-0671-8, NDP446). New Directions.

Scotto, Robert M. Three Contemporary Novelists: An Annotated Bibliography of Works by & About John Hawkes, Joseph Heller & Thomas Pynchon. LC 75-42889. (Reference Library of the Humanities Ser.: Vol. 52). 1977. lib. bdg. 16.00 (ISBN 0-8240-9948-6). Garland Pub.

HAWKESWORTH, JOHN, 1715?-1773

Drake, Nathan. Essays: Biographical, Critical & Historical Illustrative of the Rambler, Adventurer & Idler, 2 Vols. (Belles Lettres in English Ser). 1969. Repr. of 1810 ed. Set. 66.50 (ISBN 0-384-12650-2). Johnson Repr.

HAWKING

see Falconry

HAWKINS, ANTHONY HOPE, SIR, 1863-1933

Mallet, Charles. Anthony Hope & His Books. LC 68-16280. (Illus.). 1968. Repr. of 1935 ed. 12.50 (ISBN 0-8046-0298-0). Kennikat.

HAWKINS, JOHN, SIR, 1532-1595

Markham, Clements R., ed. Hawkins' Voyages During the Reigns of Henry Eighth, Queen Elizabeth, & James First. LC 73-126271. (Hakluyt Society First Ser.: No. 57). (Illus.). 1970. 32.00 (ISBN 0-8337-2229-8). B Franklin.

Unwin, Rayner. The Defeat of John Hawkins: A Biography of His Third Slaving Voyage. 1960. 10.95 (ISBN 0-04-910027-0). Allen Unwin.

HAWKINS, JOHN, SIR, 1719-1789

Davis, Bertram H. Johnson Before Boswell. LC 72-12309. 222p. 1973. Repr. of 1960 ed. lib. bdg. 15.00x (ISBN 0-8371-6691-8, DAJA). Greenwood.

Miller, C. A. Sir John Hawkins: Samuel Johnson. LC 72-10377. 1951. lib. bdg. 6.00 (ISBN 0-8414-0450-X). Folcroft.

Scholes, Percy A. The Life & Activities of Sir John Hawkins: Musician, Magistrate & Friend of Johnson. LC 77-26652. (Music Reprint Ser., 1978). (Illus.). 1978. Repr. of 1953 ed. lib. bdg. 27.50 (ISBN 0-306-77571-9). Da Capo.

Williamson, James A. Sir John Hawkins, the Time & the Man. Repr. of 1927 ed. lib. bdg. 22.00x (ISBN 0-8371-4569-4, WIJH). Greenwood.

HAWKINS, WILLIAM, d. 1554

Markham, Clements R., ed. Hawkins' Voyages During the Reigns of Henry Eighth, Queen Elizabeth, & James First. LC 73-126271. (Hakluyt Society First Ser.: No. 57). (Illus.). 1970. 32.00 (ISBN 0-8337-2229-8). B Franklin.

HAWKS, HOWARD, 1896-1977

Belton, John. The Hollywood Professionals, Vol. 3: Hawks, Borzage, & Ulmer. LC 73-13190. (International Film Guide Ser). (Illus.). 192p. 1974. pap. 4.95 (ISBN 0-498-01448-7). A S Barnes.

McBride, Joseph. Hawks on Hawks. LC 81-362. (Illus.). 172p. 1981. 14.95 (ISBN 0-520-04344-8). U of Cal Pr.

HAWKS

Beebe, Frank L. & Webster, Harold M., eds. North American Falconry & Hunting Hawks. 4th ed. (Illus.). 330p. 1976. 30.00x (ISBN 0-685-66290-X). North Am Fal Hunt.

Craighead, John J. & Craighead, Frank C., Jr. Hawks, Owls & Wildlife. LC 74-81670. 1969. pap. 6.00 (ISBN 0-486-22123-7). Dover.

Fisher, Albert K. The Hawks & Owls of the United States in Their Relation to Agriculture. LC 73-17820. (Natural Sciences in America Ser.). (Illus.). 266p. 1974. Repr. 15.00x (ISBN 0-405-05736-9). Arno.

Heintzelman, Donald. Hawks & Owls of North America: A Complete Guide to North American Birds of Prey. LC 78-65623. 1979. 18.50x (ISBN 0-87663-335-1). Universe.

Heintzelman, Donald S. A Guide to Hawk Watching in North America. LC 78-21003. (Keystone Bks.). (Illus.). 1979. 12.95 (ISBN 0-271-00212-3); pap. 6.95 (ISBN 0-271-00217-4). Pa St U Pr.

Holly, H. H. Sparrow Hawk. Date not set. 0.75 (ISBN 0-686-30043-2). Pilgrim Hall.

Lavine, Sigmund A. Wonders of the Hawk World. LC 70-38564. (Wonders Ser.). (Illus.). 64p. (gr. 3-7). 1972. PLB 5.95 (ISBN 0-396-06509-0). Dodd.

Mavrogordato, Jack. A Hawk for the Bush: A Treatise on the Training of the Sparrow Hawk & Other Short-Wings Hawks. (Illus.). 224p. 1974. 12.50 (ISBN 0-517-51434-6). Potter.

Wallig, Gaird. A Red-Tailed Hawk Named Bucket. LC 76-57546. (Illus.). 224p. 1980. 9.95 (ISBN 0-89087-276-7). Celestial Arts.

--A Red-Tailed Hawk Named Bucket: City Life with a Hawk in the Family. LC 79-57546. 202p. 1980. 9.95 (ISBN 0-89087-276-7). Gusto Pr.

HAWLEY, JOSEPH, 1723-1788

Brown, E. Francis. Joseph Hawley: Colonial Radical. LC 31-29646. Repr. of 1931 ed. 15.00 (ISBN 0-404-01128-4). AMS Pr.

HAWSH AL HARIMAH

Williams, Judith R. Youth of Haouch el Harimi, a Lebanese Village. LC 68-23032. (Middle Eastern Monographs Ser: No. 20). 1968. pap. 4.50x (ISBN 0-674-96675-9). Harvard U Pr.

HAWTHORNE, JULIAN, 1846-1934

Bassan, Maurice. Hawthorne's Son: The Life & Literary Career of Julian Hawthorne. LC 70-83142. (Illus.). 1970. 10.00 (ISBN 0-8142-0003-6). Ohio St U Pr.

HAWTHORNE, MONT, b. 1865

McKeown, Martha F. Them Was the Days: An American Saga of the '70's. LC 50-7450. (Illus.). 1961. pap. 2.95 (ISBN 0-8032-5131-9, BB 117, Bison). U of Nebr Pr.

HAWTHORNE, NATHANIEL, 1804-1864

Arie, Staal. Hawthorne's Narrative Art. 1976. lib. bdg. 59.95 (ISBN 0-685-68943-3). Revisionist Pr.

Arvin, Newton. Hawthorne. LC 61-12123. (Illus.). 1961. Repr. of 1929 ed. 18.00 (ISBN 0-8462-0110-0). Russell.

Asselineau, Roger. Studies in the House of Seven Gables. LC 73-146037. 1971. pap. text ed. 2.50x (ISBN 0-675-09246-9). Merrill.

Babiiha, Thaddeo K. The James-Hawthorne Relation: Biographical Essays. (Scholarly Reference Publications). 1980. lib. bdg. 20.00 (ISBN 0-8161-8431-3). G K Hall.

Baym, Nina. The Shape of Hawthorne's Career. LC 75-36994. 1976. 19.50x (ISBN 0-8014-0996-9). Cornell U Pr.

Beers, Henry A. Four Americans. facs. ed. LC 68-54324. (Essay Index Reprint Ser). 1919. 11.50 (ISBN 0-8369-0182-7). Arno.

Bell, Millicent. Hawthorne's View of the Artist. LC 62-13566. 1962. 16.50 (ISBN 0-87395-008-9); microfiche 16.50 (ISBN 0-87395-108-5). State U NY Pr.

Bewley, Marius. Complex Fate: Hawthorne, Henry James, & Some American Writers. LC 67-28474. 1967. Repr. of 1954 ed. 9.00 (ISBN 0-87752-008-9). Gordian.

Bridge, Horatio. Personal Recollections of Nathaniel Hawthorne. LC 68-24931. (Studies in Hawthorne, No. 15). 1969. Repr. of 1893 ed. lib. bdg. 49.95 (ISBN 0-8383-0916-X). Haskell.

Brodhead, Richard H. Hawthorne, Melville & the Novel. LC 75-5071. (Phoenix Ser). 1977. pap. 4.50 (ISBN 0-226-07523-0, P730, Phoen). U of Chicago Pr.

Browne, Nina E. Bibliography of Nathaniel Hawthorne. 1967. Repr. of 1908 ed. 16.50 (ISBN 0-8337-0400-1). B Franklin.

--Bibliography of Nathaniel Hawthorne. 1905. 10.50 (ISBN 0-384-06005-6). Johnson Repr.

Byron, May. A Day with Nathaniel Hawthorne. LC 78-4080. Repr. 15.00 (ISBN 0-8414-0159-4). Folcroft.

Byron, May C. A Day with Nathaniel Hawthorne. 1979. Repr. of 1912 ed. lib. bdg. 10.00 (ISBN 0-8482-3441-3). Norwood Edns.

Cantwell, Robert. Nathaniel Hawthorne: The American Years. LC 77-159172. xiv, 499p. 1971. Repr. of 1948 ed. lib. bdg. 30.00x (ISBN 0-374-91277-7). Octagon.

Chandler, Elizabeth L. A Study of the Source of the Tales & Romances Written by Nathaniel Hawthorne. LC 75-9569. Repr. of 1926 ed. lib. bdg. 10.00 (ISBN 0-8414-3645-2). Folcroft.

--A Study of the Source of the Tales & Romances Written by Nathaniel Hawthorne. LC 75-9569. Repr. of 1926 ed. lib. bdg. 10.00 (ISBN 0-8414-3645-2). Folcroft.

--A Study of the Sources of the Tales & Romances Written by Nathaniel Hawthorne Before 1853. 1978. Repr. of 1926 ed. lib. bdg. 12.50 (ISBN 0-8495-0832-0). Arden Lib.

Clark, C. E. Frazer, Jr., ed. Hawthorne at Auction 1894-1971. LC 70-38939. (A Bruccoli Clark Book, Authors at Auction Ser.). 400p. 1972. 30.00 (ISBN 0-8103-0919-X). Gale.

--Nathaniel Hawthorne Journal. Incl. 1973. 22.00 (ISBN 0-685-83820-X); 1974. 23.00 (ISBN 0-685-83821-8); 1975. Bruccoli.

Clark, C. E., Jr., ed. Nathaniel Hawthorne Journal, Nineteen Seventy-Seven. (Illus.). 1980. 32.00 (ISBN 0-8103-0926-2, Bruccoli Clark Bk). Gale.

Clark, C. Frazer, Jr. Nathaniel Hawthorne: A Descriptive Bibliography. LC 76-50885. (Pittsburgh Ser. in Bibliography). 1978. 30.00x (ISBN 0-8229-3343-8). U of Pittsburgh Pr.

Clark, C. Frazer, Jr., frwd. by. Letters of Hawthorne to William D Ticknor. LC 72-76250. 1972. 18.00 (ISBN 0-910972-19-2). IHS-PDS.

--Love Letters of Nathaniel Hawthorne. LC 72-76251. 1972. 18.00 (ISBN 0-910972-18-4). IHS-PDS.

Clark, C. Frazer, Jr., ed. Nathaniel Hawthorne Journal Nineteen Seventy-Eight. (Bruccoli Clark Bk.). (Illus.). 400p. 1981. 32.00 (ISBN 0-8103-0929-7). Gale.

Clark, Thomas Arkle. Nathaniel Hawthorne: Selections from His Writings. 1900. Repr. 10.00 (ISBN 0-8274-3011-6). R West.

Clarke, Helen Archibald. Hawthorne's Country. LC 73-12227. 1910. lib. bdg. 35.00 (ISBN 0-8414-3390-9). Folcroft.

Conway, M. D. Life of Nathaniel Hawthorne. LC 68-24935. (Studies in Hawthorne, No. 15). 1969. Repr. of 1890 ed. lib. bdg. 36.95 (ISBN 0-8383-0931-3). Haskell.

Crowley, J. Donald, ed. Hawthorne: The Critical Heritage. 1971. 36.00 (ISBN 0-7100-6886-7). Routledge & Kegan.

Curl, Vega. Pasteboard Masks: Fact As Spiritual Symbol in the Novels of Hawthorne & Melville. LC 72-193943. 1931. lib. bdg. 10.00 (ISBN 0-8414-2432-2). Folcroft.

Dauber, Kenneth. Rediscovering Hawthorne. LC 76-45893. 1977. text ed. 17.50 (ISBN 0-691-06323-0). Princeton U Pr.

Davidson, Edward H. Hawthorne's Last Phase. (Yale Studies in English Ser.: No. 111). 172p. 1967. Repr. of 1949 ed. 17.50 (ISBN 0-208-00297-9, Archon). Shoe String.

Della Buono, Carmen J. Rare Early Essays on Nathaniel Hawthorne. 200p. 1979. lib. bdg. 22.50 (ISBN 0-8482-0635-5). Norwood Edns.

Dhaleine, L. N. Hawthorne, sa vie et son oeuvre. LC 77-164828. (BCL Ser. I). Repr. of 1905 ed. 24.50 (ISBN 0-404-02122-0). AMS Pr.

Doubleday, Neal F. A Study of Hawthorne's Early Tales. LC 76-185462. 1972. 15.75 (ISBN 0-8223-0267-5). Duke.

Dryden, Edgar A. Nathaniel Hawthorne: The Poetics of Enchantment. LC 76-28010. 1977. 17.50x (ISBN 0-8014-1028-2). Cornell U Pr.

Elder, Marjorie J. Nathaniel Hawthorne: Transcendental Symbolist. LC 69-18476. vi, 215p. 1969. 12.95x (ISBN 0-8214-0051-7). Ohio U Pr.

Faust, Bertha. Hawthorne's Contemporaneous Reputation. 1967. lib. bdg. 10.00x (ISBN 0-374-92717-0). Octagon.

Fick, Leonard J. Light Beyond: A Study of Hawthorne's Theology. LC 74-8995. 1955. lib. bdg. 20.00 (ISBN 0-8414-4195-2). Folcroft.

Fields, Annie. Nathaniel Hawthorne. LC 74-11032. 1899. lib. bdg. 7.50 (ISBN 0-8414-4224-X). Folcroft.

--Nathaniel Hawthorne. LC 74-7223. (American Literature Ser., No. 49). 1974. lib. bdg. 31.95 (ISBN 0-8383-1859-2). Haskell.

Fields, James T. Yesterdays with Authors. 1977. Repr. of 1882 ed. lib. bdg. 20.00 (ISBN 0-8414-4250-9). Folcroft.

Fogle, Richard H. Hawthorne's Fiction: The Light & the Dark. rev. ed. 1975. pap. 5.95x (ISBN 0-8061-1263-8). U of Okla Pr.

Folsom, James K. Man's Accidents & God's Purposes: Multiplicity in Hawthorne's Fiction. 1963. pap. 2.95 (ISBN 0-8084-0208-0, L16). Coll & U Pr.

Fossum, Robert H. Hawthorne's Inviolable Circle: The Problem of Time. 2nd ed. LC 74-172791. 229p. 1973. lib. bdg. 12.00 (ISBN 0-912112-10-7). Everett-Edwards.

Frazer Clark, C. E., Jr., ed. The Nathaniel Hawthorne Journal 1971. (Illus.). 1976. 22.00 (ISBN 0-685-77416-3). Bruccoli.

--The Nathaniel Hawthorne Journal 1972. (Illus.). 1977. 22.00 (ISBN 0-685-77417-1). Bruccoli.

Frazer Clark, C. E., Jr., compiled by. Hawthorne at Auction. (Illus.). 30.00 (ISBN 0-685-77411-2). Bruccoli.

Frazer Clark, C. E., Jr., frwd. by. Letters of Hawthorne to William D. Ticknor. 17.00 (ISBN 0-685-77419-8). Bruccoli.

--Love Letters of Nathaniel Hawthorne. 17.00 (ISBN 0-685-77418-X). Bruccoli.

Gaeddert, LouAnn. A New England Love Story: Nathaniel Hawthorne & Sophia Peabody. LC 80-16329. (Illus.). 160p. (gr. 7 up). 1980. 8.95 (ISBN 0-8037-6153-8). Dial.

Gale, Robert L. Plots & Characters - Hawthorne. 172p. 1972. pap. 2.95 (ISBN 0-262-57030-0). MIT Pr.

--Plots & Characters in the Fiction & Sketches of Nathaniel Hawthorne. (Plots & Characters Ser.). 1968. 17.50 (ISBN 0-208-00649-4, Archon). Shoe String.

Gerber, John C., ed. Twentieth Century Interpretations of The Scarlet Letter. LC 68-23438. (Twentieth Century Interpretations Series). (Orig.). 1968. 8.95 (ISBN 0-13-791582-9, Spec). P-H.

Gollin, Rita K. Nathaniel Hawthorne & the Truth of Dreams. LC 78-14952. 1979. 17.50x (ISBN 0-8071-0467-1). La State U Pr.

Goodspeed, Charles E. Nathaniel Hawthorne & the Museum of the East India Marine Society. 1946. pap. 0.50 (ISBN 0-87577-035-5). Peabody Mus Salem.

Gordon, John D. Nathaniel Hawthorne: The Years of Fulfillment 1804-1853. 1973. Repr. of 1954 ed. 10.00 (ISBN 0-8274-0381-X). R West.

Gorman, Herbert S. Hawthorne. LC 66-13474. 1927. 9.50x (ISBN 0-8196-0170-5). Biblo.

Hawthorne. The Scarlet Letter. Date not set. pap. price not set. Cliffs.

Hawthorne, Julian. Hawthorne & His Circle. 1903. lib. bdg. 30.00 (ISBN 0-8414-5024-2). Folcroft.

--Hawthorne & His Circle. (Illus.). 1968. Repr. of 1903 ed. 19.50 (ISBN 0-208-00673-7, Archon). Shoe String.

--Hawthorne Reading, an Essay. LC 72-194977. 1902. lib. bdg. 17.50 (ISBN 0-8414-5025-0). Folcroft.

--Nathaniel Hawthorne & His Wife, a Biography, 2 Vols. LC 17-21573. 1969. Repr. of 1885 ed. Set. 30.00 (ISBN 0-403-00084-X). Scholarly.

--Nathaniel Hawthorne & His Wife: A Biography, 2 vols. (Illus.). 1968. Repr. of 1884 ed. Set. 37.50 (ISBN 0-208-00672-9, Archon). Shoe String.

--Nathaniel Hawthorne and His Wife a Biography, 2 vols. 1973. Repr. of 1889 ed. 27.00 set (ISBN 0-8274-0038-1). R West.

Hawthorne, Nathaniel. The Blithdale Romance. Gross, Seymore & Murphy, Rosalie, eds. (Critical Edition Ser.). 1978. 12.95 (ISBN 0-393-04449-1); pap. 4.95x (ISBN 0-393-09150-3). Norton.

--First Editions of the Works of Nathaniel Hawthorne Together with Some Manuscripts, Letters & Portraits. Repr. of 1904 ed. lib. bdg. 15.00 (ISBN 0-8414-5026-9). Folcroft.

--The French & Italian Notebooks: The Centenary Edition of the Works of Nathaniel Hawthorne, Vol.14. Woodson, Thomas, ed. 1980. 36.00 (ISBN 0-8142-0256-X). Ohio St U Pr.

--Hawthorne's Lost Notebook, Eighteen Thirty-Five to Eighteen Forty-One. Waggoner, Hyatt H. & Mouffe, Barbara S., eds. LC 78-50772. 1978. 12.75x (ISBN 0-271-00549-1). Pa St U Pr.

--House of the Seven Gables. rev. ed. Dixson, Robert J., ed. (American Classics Ser.: Bk. 1). 113p. (gr. 9 up). 1973. pap. 2.95 (ISBN 0-88345-197-2, 18120); cassettes 40.00 (ISBN 0-685-38988-X); tapes 40.00 (ISBN 0-685-38989-8). Regents Pub.

--Nathaniel Hawthorne: Representative Selections. 1971. Repr. of 1934 ed. 49.00 (ISBN 0-403-01017-9). Scholarly.

--Scarlet Letter. Bradley, Sculley, et al, eds. (Critical Editions). (Annotated). (gr. 9-12). 1966. text ed. 5.50 (ISBN 0-393-05318-0); pap. text ed. 2.45x (ISBN 0-393-09562-2, 9562). Norton.

Hull, Raymona E. Nathaniel Hawthorne: The English Experience 1853-1864. LC 79-26616. (Illus.). 1980. 21.95 (ISBN 0-8229-3418-3). U of Pittsburgh Pr.

Ives, Charles. Essays Before a Sonata, the Majority, & Other Writings. Boatwright, Howard, ed. 1970. pap. 4.95 (ISBN 0-393-00528-3, Norton Lib). Norton.

Jacobson, Richard J. Hawthorne's Conception of the Creative Process. LC 66-14445. (LeBaron Russell Briggs Prize Honors Essays in English Ser). 1965. pap. 1.75x (ISBN 0-674-38275-7). Harvard U Pr.

James, Henry. Hawthorne. Morley, John, ed. LC 68-58383. (English Men of Letters). Repr. of 1887 ed. 12.50 (ISBN 0-404-51715-3). AMS Pr.

--Hawthorne. Repr. of 1879 ed. lib. bdg. 30.00 (ISBN 0-8414-5357-8). Folcroft.

--Hawthorne. pap. 4.95 (ISBN 0-686-10845-0). British Am Bks.

James, Henry, Jr. Hawthorne. 59.95 (ISBN 0-8490-1935-4). Gordon Pr.

Johnson, Claudia D. The Productive Tension of Hawthorne's Art. LC 80-15634. 176p. 1981. text ed. 14.00x (ISBN 0-8173-0050-3); pap. text ed. 5.95x (ISBN 0-8173-0051-1). U of Ala Pr.

Kesselring, Marion L. Hawthorne's Reading 1828-1850. LC 75-43961. 1949. lib. bdg. 10.50 (ISBN 0-8414-5520-1). Folcroft.

--Hawthorne's Readings. LC 75-22074. (Studies in Hawthorne, No. 15). 1975. lib. bdg. 29.95 (ISBN 0-8383-2076-7). Haskell.

Kesterson, David. Merrill Studies in The Marble Faun. LC 74-15279. 1971. pap. text ed. 2.50x (ISBN 0-675-09199-3). Merrill.

Lathrop, George P. Study of Hawthorne. LC 70-86168. Repr. of 1876 ed. 17.50 (ISBN 0-404-03884-0). AMS Pr.

--Study of Hawthorne. LC 78-107178. 1970. Repr. of 1876 ed. 15.00 (ISBN 0-403-00237-0). Scholarly.

Lathrop, R. Memories of Hawthorne. 59.95 (ISBN 0-8490-0606-6). Gordon Pr.

Lathrop, Rose H. Memories of Hawthorne. LC 79-96474. Repr. of 1897 ed. 10.00 (ISBN 0-404-03885-9). AMS Pr.

Levin, Harry. The House of the Seven Gables. (gr. 9-12). 1969. pap. text ed. 1.95x (ISBN 0-675-09470-4). Merrill.

--The Power of Blackness: Hawthorne, Poe, Melville. LC 80-83221. xxii, 263p. 1980. pap. 6.95x (ISBN 0-8214-0581-0). Ohio U Pr.

Lewin, Walter. Nathaniel Hawthorne. LC 77-9015. 1977. Repr. of 1906 ed. lib. bdg. 10.00 (ISBN 0-8414-5822-7). Folcroft.

Long, Robert E. The Great Succession: Henry James & the Legacy of Hawthorne. LC 79-922. (Critical Essays in Modern Literature Ser.). 1979. 12.95 (ISBN 0-8229-3398-5). U of Pittsburgh Pr.

Lundblad, J. Nathaniel Hawthorne & the Tradition of Gothic Romance. LC 65-15898. (Studies in Hawthorne, No. 15). 1969. Repr. of 1946 ed. lib. bdg. 49.95 (ISBN 0-8383-0589-X). Haskell.

Lundblad, Jane. Nathaniel Hawthorne & European Literary Tradition. LC 65-13950. 1965. Repr. of 1947 ed. 6.50 (ISBN 0-8462-0525-4). Russell.

McPherson, Hugo. Hawthorne as Myth Maker: A Study in Imagination. LC 76-430856. 1969. 17.50x (ISBN 0-8020-5200-2). U of Toronto Pr.

Mani, Lakshmi. The Apocalyptic Vision in Nineteenth Century Fiction: A Study of Cooper, Hawthorne, & Melville. LC 80-69060. 348p. 1981. lib. bdg. 20.75 (ISBN 0-8191-1602-5); pap. text ed. 11.75 (ISBN 0-8191-1603-3). U Pr of Amer.

Manley, Seon. Nathaniel Hawthorne: Captain of the Imagination. LC 69-10907. (Illus.). (gr. 8-10). 1969. 7.95 (ISBN 0-8149-0358-4). Vanguard.

Martin, Terence. Nathaniel Hawthorne. (Twayne's United States Authors Ser). 1964. pap. 3.45 (ISBN 0-8084-0226-9, T75, Twayne). Coll & U Pr.

--Nathaniel Hawthorne. (U. S. Authors Ser.: No. 75). 1964. lib. bdg. 11.95 (ISBN 0-8057-0348-9). Twayne.

Mather Jackson, Edward A. Nathaniel Hawthorne, a Modest Man. Repr. of 1940 ed. lib. bdg. 21.00x (ISBN 0-8371-2594-4, MANH). Greenwood.

Mellow, James R. Nathaniel Hawthorne in His Time. 672p. 1980. 19.95 (ISBN 0-395-27602-0). HM.

Monarch Notes on Hawthorne's House of the Seven Gables, Marble Faun. (Orig.). pap. 1.95 (ISBN 0-671-00670-3). Monarch Pr.

Monarch Notes on Hawthorne's Scarlet Letter. (Orig.). pap. 1.95 (ISBN 0-671-00620-7). Monarch Pr.

Nathaniel Hawthorne: New York University Index to Early American Periodical Literature, 1820-1870, Pt. 6. 1981. 12.50 (ISBN 0-87164-093-7). William-F.

Newman, Lea B. A Reader's Guide to the Short Stories of Nathaniel Hawthorne. 380p. 1979. lib. bdg. 32.50 (ISBN 0-8161-8398-8). G K Hall.

Nicoll, Bruce. House of the Seven Gables. (Orig.). pap. 1.75 (ISBN 0-8220-0595-6). Cliffs.

Page, H. A. Memoir of Nathaniel Hawthorne. LC 76-15613. 1872. lib. bdg. 25.00 (ISBN 0-8414-6795-1). Folcroft.

Pickard, Samuel T. Hawthorne's First Diary. LC 72-285. (Studies in Hawthorne, No. 15). 1972. Repr. of 1897 ed. lib. bdg. 29.95 (ISBN 0-8383-1408-2). Haskell.

--Hawthorne's First Diary. 1973. Repr. of 1897 ed. 8.75 (ISBN 0-8274-1363-7). R West.

Rohrberger, Mary. Hawthorne & the Modern Short Story: A Study in Genre. (Orig.). 1966. pap. text ed. 17.25x (ISBN 90-2790-315-8). Mouton.

Rosa, Alfred. Salem, Transcendentalism, & Hawthorne. LC 77-89784. 108p. 1980. 15.50 (ISBN 0-8386-2159-7). Fairleigh Dickinson.

Sanborn, Franklin B. Hawthorn & His Friends. LC 73-3465. 1908. lib. bdg. 10.00 (ISBN 0-8414-2624-4). Folcroft.

Stearns, F. Life & Genius of Nathaniel Hawthorne. LC 76-40459. 1906. lib. bdg. 25.00 (ISBN 0-8414-7710-8). Folcroft.

Stein, William B. Hawthorne's Faust, a Study of the Devil Archetype. 1968. Repr. of 1953 ed. 15.00 (ISBN 0-208-00648-6, Archon). Shoe String.

Stewart, Paul. Scarlet Letter Notes. (Orig.). pap. 2.25 (ISBN 0-8220-1165-4). Cliffs.

Stoehr, Taylor. Hawthorne's Mad Scientists: Pseudoscience & Social Science in Nineteenth-Century Life & Letters. 1978. 19.50 (ISBN 0-208-01710-0, Archon). Shoe String.

Taylor, J. Golden. Hawthorne's Ambivalence Toward Puritanism. LC 77-24154. 1977. lib. bdg. 15.00 (ISBN 0-8414-8586-0). Folcroft.

Ticknor, C. Hawthorne & His Publisher. 1973. Repr. of 1913 ed. 13.00 (ISBN 0-8274-0429-8). R West.

Ticknor, Caroline. Hawthorne & His Publisher. 339p. 1981. Repr. of 1913 ed. lib. bdg. 30.00 (ISBN 0-89984-456-1). Century Bookbindery.

--Hawthorne & His Publisher. LC 68-8240. 1969. Repr. of 1913 ed. 13.50 (ISBN 0-8046-0463-0). Kennikat.

Turner, Arlin. Hawthorne As Editor. LC 76-23265. 1941. lib. bdg. 20.00 (ISBN 0-8414-8590-9). Folcroft.

--Nathaniel Hawthorne: A Biography. (Illus.). 1980. 20.00 (ISBN 0-19-502547-4). Oxford U Pr.

Van Doren, Mark. Nathaniel Hawthorne. LC 72-7878. (American Men of Letters Ser.). (Illus.). 285p. 1973. Repr. of 1949 ed. lib. bdg. 17.75x (ISBN 0-8371-6552-0, VANH). Greenwood.

Von Abele, Rudolph. Death of the Artist: A Study of Hawthorne's Disintegration. LC 77-7534. 1955. lib. bdg. 20.00 (ISBN 0-8414-9180-1). Folcroft.

Waggoner, Hyatt H. Hawthorne: A Critical Study. rev. ed. LC 63-17215. 1963. 15.00x (ISBN 0-674-38250-1, Belknap Pr). Harvard U Pr.

--The Presence of Hawthorne. LC 79-14573. 1980. text ed. 12.95x (ISBN 0-8071-0576-7). La State U Pr.
Walker, Kenneth E. Barron's Simplified Approach to Hawthorne's House of Seven Gables. (Orig.). 1968. pap. text ed. 1.50 (ISBN 0-8120-0280-6). Barron.
Warren, A. Nathaniel Hawthorne. 368p. 1980. Repr. lib. bdg. 30.00 (ISBN 0-89984-502-9). Century Bookbindery.
White, Sidney H. Barron's Simplified Approach to Hawthorne's Scarlet Letter. LC 66-26624. 1967. pap. text ed. 1.50 (ISBN 0-8120-0254-7). Barron.
Wood, James P. Unpardonable Sin: A Life of Nathaniel Hawthorne. LC 71-117461. (Illus.). (gr. 7 up). 1970. PLB 5.99 (ISBN 0-394-90443-5). Pantheon.
Woodberry, George E. Nathaniel Hawthorne. LC 80-23480. (American Men & Women of Letters Ser.). 304p. 1981. pap. 4.95 (ISBN 0-87754-154-X). Chelsea Hse.
--Nathaniel Hawthorne. LC 67-23888. 1967. Repr. of 1902 ed. 22.00 (ISBN 0-8103-3043-1). Gale.

HAWTHORNE, SOPHIA AMELIA (PEABODY) 1811-1871

Clark, C. Frazer, Jr., frwd. by. Love Letters of Nathaniel Hawthorne. LC 72-76251. 1972. 18.00 (ISBN 0-910972-18-4). IHS-PDS.
Gaeddert, LouAnn. A New England Love Story: Nathaniel Hawthorne & Sophia Peabody. LC 80-16329. (Illus.). 160p. (gr. 7 up). 1980. 8.95 (ISBN 0-8037-6153-8). Dial.
Hawthorne, Julian. Nathaniel Hawthorne & His Wife, a Biography, 2 Vols. LC 17-21573. 1969. Repr. of 1885 ed. Set. 30.00 (ISBN 0-403-00084-X). Scholarly.
--Nathaniel Hawthorne & His Wife: A Biography, 2 vols. (Illus.). 1968. Repr. of 1884 ed. Set. 37.50 (ISBN 0-208-00672-9, Archon). Shoe String.

HAWTHORNE-CEDAR KNOLLS SCHOOL, HAWTHORNE, NEW YORK

Polsky, Howard W., et al. Dynamics of Residential Treatment: A Social System Analysis. 1968. 15.00x (ISBN 0-8078-1069-X). U of NC Pr.

HAWTHORNE FAMILY

see Hathorne Family (William Hathorne, 1601-1681)

HAY, JOHN MILTON, 1838-1905

Brown University Library. The Life & Works of John Hay, Eighteen Thirty-Eight to Nineteen Hundred & Five: A Commemorative Catalogue of the Exhibition Shown at the John Hay Library of Brown University in Honor of the Centennial of His Graduation at the Commencement of 1858. LC 61-3289. (Illus.). xii, 51p. 1961. 8.00x (ISBN 0-87057-063-3, Pub. by Brown U Pr). U Pr of New Eng.
Clymer, Kenton J. John Hay: The Gentleman As Diplomat. LC 74-78986. 1975. 15.00 (ISBN 0-472-23400-5). U of Mich Pr.
Gale, Robert L. John Hay. (United States Authors Ser.: No. 296). 1978. lib. bdg. 12.50 (ISBN 0-8057-7199-9). Twayne.
Kushner, Howard I. & Sherrill, Anne H. John Milton Hay. (World Leaders Ser.: No. 69). 1977. lib. bdg. 12.50 (ISBN 0-8057-7719-9). Twayne.
Monteiro, George. Henry James & John Hay: The Record of a Friendship. LC 65-24094. (Illus.). xiv, 205p. 1965. 10.00 (ISBN 0-87057-091-9, Pub. by Brown U Pr). U Pr of New Eng.
Monteiro, George & Murphy, Brenda, eds. John Hay-Howells Letters: The Correspondence of John Milton Hay & William Dean Howells. (American Literary Manuscripts Ser.). 1981. lib. bdg. 17.50 (ISBN 0-8057-9652-5). Twayne.
Montiero, George & Murphy, Brenda, eds. Correspondence of John Hay & William Dean Howells. (American Literature Manuscripts Ser.). 1980. 17.50 (ISBN 0-8057-9652-5). Twayne.
Sears, Lorenzo. John Hay: Author & Statesman. 1973. Repr. of 1914 ed. 20.00 (ISBN 0-8274-0917-6). R West.
Thayer, William R. John Hay, 2 Vols. Morse, John T., Jr., ed. LC 75-128945. (American Statesmen: Vols. 36-37). Repr. of 1916 ed. Set. 47.00 (ISBN 0-404-50895-2); 23.50 ea. Vol. 1 (ISBN 0-404-50886-3). Vol. 2 (ISBN 0-404-50887-1). AMS Pr.
--John Hay, 2 vols. 1973. Repr. of 1916 ed. 35.00 set (ISBN 0-8274-1361-0). R West.
--Life & Letters of John Hay, 2 Vols. 1915. Set. 42.00 (ISBN 0-527-89500-8). Kraus Repr.
--The Life & Letters of John Hay, 2 vols. 1977. Repr. of 1908 ed. lib. bdg. 35.00 (ISBN 0-8414-8452-X). Folcroft.
Thurman, Kelly. John Hay As a Man of Letters. 85p. 1974. 8.00 (ISBN 0-87881-017-X). Mojave Bks.

HAY-FEVER

Anderson, E. W. New Fundamental Discoveries in the Causation & Prevention of Hay Fever & Colds. 128p. 1980. 5.95 (ISBN 0-8059-2701-8). Dorrance.
Frompovich, Catherine J. Attacking Hay Fever & Winning. Koppenhaver, April M., ed. 32p. 1981. pap. 2.50 (ISBN 0-935322-15-9). C J Frompovich.
Knight, Allan. Asthma & Hay Fever. LC 80-22839. (Positive Health Guides Ser.). (Illus.). 112p. 1981. 11.95 (ISBN 0-668-04675-9); pap. 5.95 (ISBN 0-668-04681-3). Arco.
Swineford, Oscar, Jr. Asthma & Hay Fever. (Amer. Lec. Allergy & Immunology Ser.). (Illus.). 508p. 1971. 26.75 (ISBN 0-398-02390-5). C C Thomas.
--Asthma & Hay Fever & Other Allergic Diseases for Victims & Their Families. (Illus.). 186p. 1973. pap. 18.75 photocopy ed. (ISBN 0-398-02767-6). C C Thomas.

HAYA (AFRICAN TRIBE)

Cory, H. & Hartnoll, M. Customary Law of the Haya Tribe, Tanganyika Territory. 362p. 1971. Repr. of 1945 ed. 30.00x (ISBN 0-7146-2476-4, F Cass Co). Biblio Dist.
Cory, Hans. Customary Law of the Haya Tribe, Tanganyika Territory. LC 75-111572. (Illus.). 299p. Repr. of 1945 ed. 21.00x (ISBN 0-8371-4597-X, Pub. by Negro U Pr). Greenwood.

HAYA DE LA TORRE, VICTOR RAUL, 1895-

Alexander, Robert J., ed. Aprismo: The Ideas & Doctrines of Victor Raul Haya De la Torre. LC 78-181083. 370p. 1973. 13.50x (ISBN 0-87338-125-4). Kent St U Pr.

HAYDEN, BENJAMIN ROBERT, 1786-1846

Raynor, Henry & Landon, H. Robbins. Haydn. (Great Composers Ser.). (Illus.). 108p. 1972. 8.95 (ISBN 0-571-08361-7, Pub. by Faber & Faber). Merrimack Bk Serv.

HAYES, ROLAND, 1887-

Helm, MacKinley. Angel Mo' & Her Son, Roland Hayes. Repr. of 1942 ed. lib. bdg. 15.00 (ISBN 0-8371-2449-2, HEAM). Greenwood.

HAYDN, HIRAM COLLINS, 1907-1973

Haydn, Hiram. Words & Faces. LC 74-7184. 352p. 1974. 8.95 (ISBN 0-15-198460-3). HarBraceJ.

HAYDN, JOSEPH, 1732-1809

Barrett-Ayres, Reginald. Joseph Haydn & the String Quartet. LC 74-494. (Illus.). 1975. Repr. of 1974 ed. 19.95 (ISBN 0-02-870400-2). Schirmer Bks.
Bradbury, William & Guild, Courtenay. History of the Handel & Haydn Society, Vol. 2. (Music Reprint Ser.). 1979. Repr. of 1893 ed. lib. bdg. 32.50 (ISBN 0-306-79506-X). Da Capo.
Brenet, Michel. Haydn. LC 72-80497. Repr. of 1926 ed. 14.00 (ISBN 0-405-08304-1, Blom Pubns). Arno.
Burke, Cornelius G. The Collector's Haydn. LC 77-28259. (Keystone Books in English Ser.: No. KB 7). (Addendum by Arthur Cohn). 1978. Repr. of 1959 ed. lib. bdg. 19.75x (ISBN 0-313-20239-7, BUCH). Greenwood.
Butterworth, Neil. Haydn: His Life & Times. expanded ed. (Life & Times Ser.). (Illus.). 176p. 1980. Repr. of 1977 ed. 19.95 (ISBN 0-87666-645-4, Z-44). Paganiniana Pubns.
--Haydn: His Life & Times. (Illus.). 1978. 16.95 (ISBN 0-8467-0417-X, Pub. by Two Continents); pap. 9.95 (ISBN 0-8467-0418-8). Hippocrene Bks.
Geiringer, Karl, ed. & pref. by. Haydn: Symphony No. One Hundred & Three in E-Flat Major (Drum Roll) LC 73-20231. (Illus.). 116p. 1974. pap. 4.95x (ISBN 0-393-09349-2). Norton.
Gotwals, Vernon, ed. Haydn: Two Contemporary Portraits. Orig. Title: Joseph Haydn: Eighteenth-Century Gentleman & Genius. 1963. 17.50 (ISBN 0-299-02791-0); pap. 5.95x (ISBN 0-299-02794-5). U of Wis Pr.
Hadden, James C. Haydn. LC 74-24267. (The Master Musicians). (Illus.). Repr. of 1934 ed. 20.00 (ISBN 0-404-12940-4). AMS Pr.
Hodgson, Antony. The Music of Joseph Haydn. LC 75-21259. (A New Ser. of Music Bks). (Illus.). 208p. 1977. 15.00 (ISBN 0-8386-1684-4). Fairleigh Dickinson.
Hughes, Rosemary. Haydn. rev. ed. (The Master Musicians Ser.: No. M160). (Illus.). 1978. pap. 7.95 (ISBN 0-8226-0713-1). Littlefield.
--Haydn. rev. ed. (Master Musicians Ser). (Illus.). 274p. 1978. 11.00x (ISBN 0-460-03160-0, J M Dent England). Biblio Dist.
Jacob, Heinrich E. Joseph Haydn: His Art, Times & Glory. Winston, Richard & Winston, Clara, trs. LC 76-138591. (Illus.). 1971. Repr. of 1950 ed. lib. bdg. 20.00x (ISBN 0-8371-5792-7, JAJH). Greenwood.
Landon, H. C. Chronicle & Works, 5 vols. Incl. Vol. 1 Haydn: the Early Years, 1732-1765. 656p. 1981. 85.00x (ISBN 0-253-37001-9); Vol. 2. Haydn at Eszterhaza; 1766-1790. 820p. 1978. 60.00x (ISBN 0-253-37002-7); Vol. 3. Haydn in England, 1791-1795. 640p. 1976. 70.00x (ISBN 0-253-37003-5); Vol. 4. Haydn: the Years of "the Creation" 1796-1800. 640p. 1976. 55.00x (ISBN 0-253-37004-3); Vol. 5. Haydn: the Late Years, 1801-1809. 496p. 1977. 55.00x (ISBN 0-253-37005-1). Set. 260.00x (ISBN 0-686-70203-4). Ind U Pr.
Larsen, Jens P. Three Haydn Catalogues: Second Facsimile Edition with a Survey of Haydn's Oeuvre. (Thematic Catalogues Ser: No. 4). 1979. lib. bdg. 27.50 (ISBN 0-918728-10-X). Pendragon NY.
Larsen, Jens P., et al, eds. Haydn Studies. 1981. 35.00x (ISBN 0-393-01454-1). Norton.
Lasker, David. The Boy Who Loved Music. LC 79-14651. (Illus.). (gr. 2-5). 1979. PLB 8.95 (ISBN 0-670-18385-7). Viking Pr.
Lowens, Irving. Haydn in America. LC 79-92140. (Bibliographies in American Music Ser.: No. 5). 1980. 11.50 (ISBN 0-911772-99-5). Info Coord.
Nohl, Louis. Life of Haydn. 1889. Repr. 17.00 (ISBN 0-403-00343-1). Scholarly.
Nohl, Ludwig. Life of Haydn. 7th ed. Upton, George P., tr. LC 73-173796. Repr. of 1902 ed. 18.45 (ISBN 0-404-04786-6). AMS Pr.
--Life of Haydn. 7th ed. Upton, George P., tr. LC 73-173796. Repr. of 1902 ed. 18.45 (ISBN 0-404-04786-6). AMS Pr.
Pohl, C. F. Mozart & Haydn in London, 2 vols. in 1. LC 70-125059. (Music Ser). 1970. Repr. of 1867 ed. lib. bdg. 35.00 (ISBN 0-306-70024-7). Da Capo.
Raynor, Henry. Joseph Haydn. LC 61-44249. (Great Masters Ser). 50p. 1961. pap. 3.00 (ISBN 0-913932-21-3). Boosey & Hawkes.
Redfern, Brian. Haydn: A Biography, with a Survey of Books, Editions & Recordings. (Concertgoer's Companion Ser). 1970. 10.50 (ISBN 0-208-00886-1). Shoe String.
Rosen, Charles. The Classical Style: Haydn, Mozart, Beethoven. LC 72-8920. (Illus.). 464p. 1972. pap. 6.95 (ISBN 0-393-00653-0, Norton Lib). Norton.
Somfai, Laszlo. Joseph Haydn: His Life in Contemporary Pictures. LC 68-10725. (Illus.). 1969. 12.95 (ISBN 0-8008-4425-4). Taplinger.
Stendhal. Vie de Haydn, de Mozart et de Metastase. 48.00 (ISBN 0-686-55083-8). French & Eur.
Stendhal, et al. Haydn, Mozart et Metatase. (Illus.). 9.95 (ISBN 0-686-55061-7). French & Eur.
Young, Percy M. Haydn. LC 77-96897. Orig. Title: Haydn Masters of Music Ser. (gr. 7 up). 1970. 3.95 (ISBN 0-87250-214-7); PLB 3.76 (ISBN 0-87250-414-X). D White.

HAYDON, BENJAMIN ROBERT, 1786-1846

Barrett, Elizabeth B. & Haydon, Benjamin R. Invisible Friends: The Correspondence of Elizabeth Barrett Barrett & Benjamin Robert Haydon, 1842-1845. Pope, Willard B., ed. LC 72-80659. (Illus.). 220p. 1972. 10.00x (ISBN 0-674-46586-5). Harvard U Pr.
George, Eric. Life & Death of Benjamin Robert Haydon, Historical Painter, 1786-1846. 2nd ed. 1967. 16.95x (ISBN 0-19-817156-0). Oxford U Pr.
Haydon, Benjamin R. Diary: 1825-1846, Vols. 3-5. Willard, B., ed. (Illus.). 2012p. 1977. Set. 50.00x (ISBN 0-674-20351-8). Harvard U Pr.
Paston, George. B. R. Haydon & His Friends. 306p. 1981. Repr. of 1905 ed. lib. bdg. 35.00 (ISBN 0-8495-4401-7). Arden Lib.

HAYES, RUTHERFORD BIRCHARD, PRES. U. S., 1822-1893

Barnard, Harry. Rutherford B. Hayes & His America. LC 66-24667. (Illus.). 1967. Repr. of 1954 ed. 17.50 (ISBN 0-8462-0863-6). Russell.
Bishop, A., ed. Rutherford B. Hayes, 1822-1893: Chronology, Documents, Bibliographical Aids. LC 69-15394. (Presidential Chronology Ser.). 1969. 8.00 (ISBN 0-379-12062-3). Oceana.
Davison, Kenneth E. The Presidency of Rutherford B. Hayes. LC 79-176289. (Contributions in American Studies: No. 3). 1972. lib. bdg. 16.00 (ISBN 0-8371-6275-0, DPH/); pap. 4.95 (ISBN 0-8371-7564-X, DPH). Greenwood.
Hayes, R. B. Teach the Freeman: The Correspondence of Rutherford B. Hayes & the Slater Fund for Negro Education 1881-1887, 2 Vols. in 1. Repr. of 1959 ed. 26.00 (ISBN 0-527-38930-7). Kraus Repr.
Howells, William D. Sketch of the Life & Character of Rutherford B. Hayes. LC 72-78758. 1876. Repr. 16.00 (ISBN 0-403-04285-2). Somerset Pub.
--Sketch of the Life & Character of Rutherford B. Hayes. 25.00 (ISBN 0-8414-4786-1). Folcroft.
--Sketch of the Life & Character of Rutherford B. Haynes: Also a Biographical Sketch of William A. Wheeler, with Portraits of Both Candidates. 226p. 1980. Repr. of 1876 ed. lib. bdg. 30.00 (ISBN 0-8492-5269-5). R West.
The Spoils System in New York. LC 73-19191. (Politics & People Ser.). 187p. 1974. Repr. 12.00x (ISBN 0-405-05900-0). Arno.
Williams, Charles R. Life of Rutherford Birchard Hayes, 2 Vols. LC 79-87678. (American Scene Ser). 1970. Repr. of 1914 ed. lib. bdg. 85.00 (ISBN 0-306-71714-X). Da Capo.

HAYMARKET SQUARE RIOT, 1866

see Chicago–Haymarket Square Riot, 1886

HAYMERLE, HEINRICH VON, 1828-1881

Brown, Marvin L., Jr. Heinrich von Haymerle: Austro-Hungarian Career Diplomat 1828-81. LC 79-183904. (Illus.). xii, 238p. 1973. 14.95x (ISBN 0-87249-243-5). U of SC Pr.

HAYNE, PAUL HAMILTON, 1830-1886

DeBellis, Jack, ed. Sidney Lanier, Henry Timrod & Paul Hamilton Hayne: A Reference Guide. 1978. lib. bdg. 20.00 (ISBN 0-8161-7967-0). G K Hall.
Moore, Rayburn S. Paul Hamilton Hayne. (U. S. Authors Ser.: No. 202). lib. bdg. 10.95 (ISBN 0-8057-0352-7). Twayne.

HAYNES, FRANK JAY

Montana Historical Society Staff. F. Jay Haynes, Photographer. (Illus.). 192p. 1981. 29.95 (ISBN 0-917298-04-7). MT Hist Soc.

HAYNES, LEMUEL, 1753-1833

Cooley, Timothy M. Sketches of the Life & Character of the Rev. Lemuel Haynes. LC 70-88426. Repr. of 1837 ed. 15.25x (ISBN 0-8371-1888-3). Greenwood.

HAYWARD, SUSAN

Andersen, Christopher P. A Star, Is a Star, Is a Star: The Life & Loves of Susan Hayward. LC 80-908. (Illus.). 288p. 1980. 12.95 (ISBN 0-385-15598-0). Doubleday.
Linet, Beverly. Susan Hayward: Portrait of a Survivor. LC 80-66003. 1980. 12.95 (ISBN 0-689-11079-0). Atheneum.
--Susan Haywood: Portrait of a Survivor. 352p. 1981. pap. 2.95 (ISBN 0-425-05030-0). Berkley Pub.

HAYWOOD, WILLIAM DUDLEY, 1869-1928

Conlin, Joseph R. Big Bill Haywood & the Radical Union Movement. LC 79-80015. (Men & Movements Ser). (Illus.). 1969. 10.00x (ISBN 0-8156-2140-X). Syracuse U Pr.
Grover, David H. Debaters & Dynamiters: The Story of the Haywood Trial. LC 64-63331. (Studies in History Ser: No. 4). (Illus.). 1964. 10.00 (ISBN 0-87071-074-5); pap. 6.00 (ISBN 0-87071-318-3). Oreg St U Pr.
Haywood, William D. Autobiography of Big Bill Haywood. LC 74-2407. 1966. pap. 2.95 (ISBN 0-7178-0011-3). Intl Pub Co.

HAYWOOD FAMILY

James, Richard. Iter Lancastrense. 1845. 17.00 (ISBN 0-384-26780-7). Johnson Repr.

HAYWORTH, RITA

Kobal, John. Rita Hayworth: The Time, the Place, the Woman. (Illus.). 1978. 12.95 (ISBN 0-393-07526-5). Norton.
Moreno, Eduardo. The Films of Susan Hayward. (Illus.). 1979. 14.95 (ISBN 0-8065-0682-2). Citadel Pr.
Ringgold, Gene. The Films of Rita Hayworth. 1977. pap. 6.95 (ISBN 0-8065-0574-5). Citadel Pr.

HAZARDOUS SUBSTANCES

see also Inflammable Materials

American Water Works Association. Hazardous Materials Spills Seminar. (AWWA Handbooks - Proceedings). (Illus.). 72p. 1977. pap. text ed. 7.00 (ISBN 0-89867-054-3). Am Water Wks Assn.
Bierlein, Lawrence W. Red Book on Transportation of Hazardous Materials. LC 76-44394. 1977. 90.00 (ISBN 0-8436-1407-2). CBI Pub.
Block, J. Bradford. The Signs & Symptoms of Chemical Exposure. 164p. 1980. text ed. 12.75 lexotone (ISBN 0-398-03958-5). C C Thomas.
Bretherick, L. Handbook of Reactive Chemical Hazards. 2nd ed. 1979. text ed. 130.00 (ISBN 0-408-70927-8). Butterworth.
Canadian Law & the Control of Exposure to Hazards. (Science Council of Canada Background Study: No. 39). 1978. pap. 7.50 (ISBN 0-660-01484-X, SSC 110, SSC). Unipub.
Cheremisinoff, Nicholas P. & Cheremisinoff, Paul N. Industrial & Hazardous Wastes Impoundment. LC 78-71428. 1979. 37.50 (ISBN 0-250-40280-7). Ann Arbor Science.
Committee on Hazardous Substances in the Laboratory, National Research Council. Prudent Practices for Handling Hazardous Chemicals in Laboratories. 1981. pap. text ed. 12.00 (ISBN 0-309-03128-1). Natl Acad Pr.
Committee on the Transport of Dangerous Goods, U N. Transport of Dangerous Goods, Vol. 1. LC 81-82269. (Illus.). 472p. 1981. 35.00 (ISBN 0-940394-00-6). INTEREG.
Control of Hazardous Material Spills, Nineteen Seventy-Eight. (Illus.). 1978. 30.00 (ISBN 0-686-26028-7); softcover 25.00 (ISBN 0-686-26029-5). Info Transfer.
Cranberg, Lawrence & Moghissi, A. Alan, eds. Hazardous Waste Sites in the U. S. 175p. 1981. pap. 38.50 (ISBN 0-08-026274-0). Pergamon.
De Renzo, D. J., ed. Biodegradation Techniques for Industrial Organic Wastes. LC 80-12834. (Pollution Technology Review Ser. 65; Chemical Technology Review Ser. 158). (Illus.). 358p. 1980. 28.00 (ISBN 0-8155-0800-X). Noyes.

A Guide for Control & Cleanup of Hazardous Materials. 1975. 0.75 (ISBN 0-686-29464-5). AASHTO.

Handling of Tritium-Bearing Wastes. (Technical Reports Ser.: No. 203). 137p. 1981. pap. 21.75 (ISBN 92-0-125081-9, IDC 203, IAEA). Unipub.

Hazardous Chemicals Data. (Forty Ser). 298p. 1973. pap. 3.50 (ISBN 0-685-44170-9, 49). Natl Fire Prot.

Institute of Civil Engineers, UK. Transport of Hazardous Materials. 160p. 1980. 39.00x (ISBN 0-7277-0058-8, Pub. by Telford England). State Mutual Bk.

International Maritime Dangerous Goods (IMDG) Code (Amendments 17-79 & 18-79) 1050p. 1981. pap. 71.00 (ISBN 92-801-1109-4, IMCO 68, IMCO). Unipub.

J. J. Keller & Assoc. Hazardous Materials Shipments. LC 77-8927. 1977. pap. 10.00 (ISBN 0-934674-15-9). J J Keller.

J. J. Keller & Associates, Inc. Driver's Pocket Guide to Hazardous Materials. LC 77-90372. (Orig.). 1977. pap. 1.75 (ISBN 0-934674-26-4, 0RS2). J J Keller.

Mallow, Alex. Hazardous Waste Regulations: An Interpretive Guide. 640p. 1981. 40.00 (ISBN 0-442-21935-0). Van Nos Reinhold.

Management of Alpha-Contaminated Wastes. 714p. 1981. pap. 95.50 (ISBN 92-0-020081-8, ISP 562, IAEA). Unipub.

Marine Board. Responding to Casualties of Ships Bearing Hazardous Cargoes. 1979. pap. 8.25 (ISBN 0-309-02935-X). Natl Acad Pr.

Meidl, James. Explosive & Toxic Hazardous Materials. Gruber, Harvey, ed. (Glencoe Press Fire Science Ser). 1970. text ed. 18.95x (ISBN 0-02-476380-2, 47638). Macmillan.

--Hazardous Materials Handbook. (Fire Science Ser). 1972. pap. text ed. 12.95x (ISBN 0-02-476370-5, 47637). Macmillan.

Meyer, Eugene. Chemistry of Hazardous Materials. (Illus.). 1977. 18.95 (ISBN 0-13-129239-0). P-H.

Peirce, J. Jeffery, et al. Hazardous Waste Management. 200p. 1981. text ed. 29.95 (ISBN 0-250-40459-1). Ann Arbor Science.

--Hazardous Waste Management. 200p. 1981. text ed. 29.95 (ISBN 0-250-40459-1). Ann Arbor Science.

Pelnar, Premysl U. Health Effects of Asbestos & of Some Other Minerals & Fibres As Reflected in the World Literature: A Compendium of References, 1906-1979. 1981. 25.00 set (ISBN 0-930376-25-0). Pathotox Pubs.

Pojasek, Robert B. Options for Stabilization-Solidification, Vol. 2. LC 78-50312. (Toxic & Hazardous Waste Disposal Ser.). 1979. 39.95 (ISBN 0-250-40252-1). Ann Arbor Science.

--Processes for Stabilization-Solidification, Vol. 1. LC 78-50312. (Toxic & Hazardous Waste Disposal Ser.). 1979. 39.95 (ISBN 0-250-40251-3). Ann Arbor Science.

Quirk, Terence J., ed. Hazardous Materials Guide: Shipping, Materials Handling & Transportation. rev. ed. LC 76-40627. 1979. looseleaf 79.00 (ISBN 0-934674-10-8). J J Keller.

Regulatory Processes & Jurisdictional Issues in the Regulation of Hazzardous Products in Canada. (Science Council of Canada Background Study: No. 41). 1978. pap. 10.25 (ISBN 0-660-01490-4, SSC 108, SSC). Unipub.

Robinson, J. S., ed. Hazardous Chemical Spill Cleanup. LC 79-16362. (Pollution Technology Review Ser.: No. 59). (Illus.). 1980. 48.00 (ISBN 0-8155-0767-4). Noyes.

Royal Society of London. Long-Term Hazards from Environmental Chemicals. Doll, Richard & McClean, A. E., eds. 1979. 25.00x (ISBN 0-85403-110-3, Pub. by Royal Soc London). Scholium Intl.

Sax, N. Irving. Cancer Causing Chemicals. 400p. 1981. text ed. 39.95 (ISBN 0-442-21919-9). Van Nos Reinhold.

Schieler, Leroy & Pauze, Denis. Hazardous Materials. LC 75-19526. 1976. pap. 9.20 (ISBN 0-8273-0593-1); instructor's guide 1.60 (ISBN 0-8273-0594-X). Delmar.

Scottish Schools Science Equipment Research Centre, ed. Hazardous Chemicals: A Manual for Schools & Colleges. 1979. pap. 12.95x lab. manual (ISBN 0-05-003204-6). Longman.

Sittig, M. Toxic Metals-Pollution Control & Worker Protection. LC 76-24142. (Pollution Technology Review: No. 30). (Illus.). 1977. 39.00 (ISBN 0-8155-0636-8). Noyes.

Sittig, Marshall. Handbook of Toxic & Hazardous Chemicals. LC 81-4950. 729p. 1981. 64.00 (ISBN 0-8155-0841-7). Noyes.

--Landfill Disposal of Hazardous Wastes & Sludges. LC 79-20359. (Pollution Technology Review: No. 62). (Illus.). 1980. 48.00 (ISBN 0-8155-0773-9). Noyes.

Turner & McCreery. Chemistry of Fire & Hazardous Materials. 1980. text ed. 18.95 (ISBN 0-205-06912-6, 826912-2). Allyn.

Walters, Douglas B., ed. Safe Handling of Chemical Carcinogens, Mutagens Teratogens & Highly Toxic Substances. LC 79-88922. 1980. Vol. 1. 33.95 (ISBN 0-250-40303-X); Vol. 2. 33.95 (ISBN 0-250-40354-4). Ann Arbor Science.

Watson, Thomas, et al. R C R A-Hazardous Waste Handbook. 850p. 1980. 65.00 (ISBN 0-86587-086-1). Gov Insts.

Weiss, G., ed. Hazardous Chemicals Data Book. LC 80-21634. (Environmental Health Review: No. 4). 1188p. 1981. 64.00 (ISBN 0-8155-0831-X). Noyes.

Zajic, J. E. & Himmelman, W. A. Highly Hazardous Material Spills & Emergency Planning. (Hazardous & Toxic Substances Ser.: Vol. 1). 1978. 29.75 (ISBN 0-8247-6622-9). Dekker.

HAZEN, WILLIAM BABCOCK, 1830-1887

Kroeker, Marvin E. Great Plains Command: William B. Hazen in the Frontier West. LC 75-17709. (Illus.). 200p. 1976. 11.95 (ISBN 0-8061-1318-9). U of Okla Pr.

HAZING

see also Greek Letter Societies; Secret Societies

Leemon, Thomas A. The Rites of Passage in a Student Culture. LC 72-81190. 1972. pap. text ed. 7.50x (ISBN 0-8077-1673-1). Tchrs Coll.

HAZLITT, WILLIAM, 1778-1830

Albrecht, W. P. Hazlitt & the Creative Imagination. LC 65-26727. 1965. 4.00x (ISBN 0-7006-0001-9). Regents Pr KS.

Albrecht, William P. William Hazlitt & the Malthusian Controversy. LC 70-85980. 1969. Repr. of 1950 ed. 12.50 (ISBN 0-8046-0597-1). Kennikat.

Birrell, Augustine. William Hazlitt. LC 70-98817. Repr. of 1902 ed. lib. bdg. 15.00x (ISBN 0-8371-2848-X, BIWH). Greenwood.

--William Hazlitt. 1973. Repr. of 1902 ed. 11.00 (ISBN 0-8274-1359-9). R West.

Chandler, Zelphs E. Analysis of the Stylistic Technique of Addison, Johnson, Hazlitt & Pater. 1928. lib. bdg. 10.00 (ISBN 0-8414-3633-9). Folcroft.

Douady, Jules. Liste chronologique des oeuvres de William Hazlitt. LC 78-164776. Repr. of 1906 ed. 12.50 (ISBN 0-686-77062-5). AMS Pr.

Douday, Jules. Vie De William Hazlitt L'essayiste. 1973. Repr. of 1907 ed. 50.00 (ISBN 0-8274-0065-9). R West.

Houck, James A., ed. William Hazlitt: A Reference Guide. (Reference Publications Ser.). 1977. lib. bdg. 22.50 (ISBN 0-8161-7826-7). G K Hall.

Howe, Percival. The Life of William Hazlitt. LC 72-7505. (Illus.). 433p. 1973. Repr. of 1947 ed. lib. bdg. 19.75x (ISBN 0-8371-6512-1, HOWH). Greenwood.

Ireland, A. William Hazlitt. lib. bdg. 69.95 (ISBN 0-8490-1305-4). Gordon Pr.

Ireland, Alexander. List of the Writings of William Hazlitt, Leigh Hunt & Charles Lamb. LC 70-102856. (Bibliography & Reference Ser: No. 299). 1970. Repr. of 1868 ed. lib. bdg. 13.00 (ISBN 0-8337-1806-1). B Franklin.

--William Hazlitt, Essayist & Critic. 1973. Repr. of 1889 ed. 30.00 (ISBN 0-8274-1360-2). R West.

Keynes, Geoffrey L. Bibliography of William Hazlitt. 1931. lib. bdg. 20.00 (ISBN 0-8414-5572-4). Folcroft.

Kinnaird, John. William Hazlitt, Critic of Power. (Illus.). 429p. 1978. 25.00x (ISBN 0-231-04600-6). Columbia U Pr.

Law, Marie H. English Familiar Essay in the Early Nineteenth Century: The Elements Old & New Which Went into Its Making, As Exemplified in the Writings of Hunt, Hazlitt & Lamb. LC 65-17906. 1965. Repr. of 1934 ed. 7.50 (ISBN 0-8462-0580-7). Russell.

Mahoney, John L. The Logic of Passion: The Literary Criticism of William Hazlitt. 120p. 1981. cloth 17.50 (ISBN 0-8232-1073-1); pap. 8.00 (ISBN 0-8232-1074-X). Fordham.

--The Logic of Passion: The Literary Criticism of William Hazlitt. (Salzburg Studies in English Literature Romantic Reassessment Ser.: No. 75). 1978. pap. text ed. 25.00x (ISBN 0-391-01468-4). Humanities.

Murray, Grace A. Personalities of the Eighteenth Century: (Samuel Foote, Christopher Smart, William Hazlitt) 230p. 1980. Repr. of 1927 ed. lib. bdg. 25.00 (ISBN 0-8495-3772-X). Arden Lib.

Ready, Robert. Hazlitt at Table. LC 79-22811. 126p. 1981. 13.50 (ISBN 0-8386-2414-6). Fairleigh Dickinson.

Schneider, Elisabeth. Aesthetics of William Hazlitt. LC 71-86285. 1969. Repr. of 1952 ed. lib. bdg. 14.50x (ISBN 0-374-97125-0). Octagon.

Sikes, Herschel M., et al, eds. The Letters of William Hazlitt. LC 78-54079. 1978. cobee 25.50x (ISBN 0-8147-4986-0); pap. 12.50x (ISBN 0-8147-4987-9). NYU Pr.

Stoddard, Richard H. Personal Recollections of Lamb, Hazlitt, & Others. 1978. Repr. of 1875 ed. lib. bdg. 30.00 (ISBN 0-8492-2584-1). R West.

Wardle, Ralph M. Hazlitt. LC 75-130870. (Illus.). xiv, 530p. 1971. 23.50x (ISBN 0-8032-0790-5). U of Nebr Pr.

HEAD

see also Brain; Ear; Eye; Face; Hair; Jaws; Mouth; Nose; Skull

Batsakis, John G. Tumors of the Head & Neck: Clinical & Pathological Considerations. 2nd ed. (Illus.). 584p. 1979. 53.50 (ISBN 0-683-00476-X). Williams & Wilkins.

Brand, Richard W. & Isselhard, Donald E. Anatomy of Orofacial Structures. LC 77-14586. 1977. pap. text ed. 19.95 (ISBN 0-8016-0740-X). Mosby.

Bridgman, George B. Heads, Features, & Faces. LC 74-78681. (Illus.). 64p. 1974. pap. 2.00 (ISBN 0-486-22708-1). Dover.

Cohn, Sidney A. & Gottlieb, Marvin I. Head & Neck Anatomy Review. (Basic Science Review Bks.). 1976. spiral bdg. 8.50 (ISBN 0-87488-222-2). Med Exam.

Conley, John. Regional Flaps of the Head & Neck. LC 76-11603. (Illus.). 1976. text ed. 70.00 (ISBN 0-7216-2647-5). Saunders.

Fried, Lawerence A. Anatomy of the Head, Neck, Face, & Jaws. 2nd ed. LC 80-16800. (Illus.). 299p. 1980. text ed. 17.50 (ISBN 0-8121-0717-9). Lea & Febiger.

Gerrick, David J. Surface Anatomy: The Head. (Illus.). 1978. 20.00 (ISBN 0-916750-60-4). Dayton Labs.

Hiatt, James L. & Gartner, Leslie P. Textbook of Head & Neck Anatomy. 416p. 1982. 24.50 (ISBN 0-8385-8876-X). ACC.

Montgomery, Royce L. Head & Neck Anatomy: With Clinical Correlations. (Illus.). 352p. 1981. text ed. 25.00 (ISBN 0-07-042853-0). McGraw.

Paff, George H. Anatomy of the Head & Neck. LC 72-93117. (Illus.). 235p. 1973. text ed. 19.95 (ISBN 0-7216-7041-5). Saunders.

Palacios, Enrique, et al. Multiplanar Anatomy of the Head & Neck: For Computed Tomography. LC 80-11368. 206p. 1980. 160.00 (ISBN 0-471-05820-3, Pub. by WileyMed). Wiley.

Pernkoph, Eduard. Atlas of Topographical & Applied Human Anatomy: Head & Neck, Vol. 1. rev. 2nd ed. Ferner, Helmut, ed. Monsen, Harry, tr. from Ger. LC 79-25264. Orig. Title: Atlas der Topographischen und Angewamdten Anatomie Des Menschen. (Illus.). 308p. 1980. Repr. of 1963 ed. text ed. 98.00 (ISBN 0-7216-7198-5). Saunders.

Potter, Guy D. Sectional Anatomy & Tomography of the Head. LC 71-158948. (Illus.). 352p. 1971. 82.50 (ISBN 0-8089-0700-X). Grune.

Reed, Gretchen M. & Sheppard, Vincent F. Basic Structures of the Head & Neck: A Programmed Instruction in Clinical Anatomy for Dental Professionals. LC 75-298. (Illus.). 640p. 1976. pap. text ed. 24.50 (ISBN 0-7216-7516-6). Saunders.

Riviere, Holliston L. Anatomy & Embryology of the Head & Neck. 1981. text ed. 22.95 (ISBN 0-8359-0211-0). Reston.

Sicher, Harry & DuBrul, E. Lloyd. Oral Anatomy. 6th ed. LC 74-20890. 1975. text ed. 24.50 (ISBN 0-8016-4604-9). Mosby.

HEAD-ABNORMITIES AND DEFORMITIES

Goodman, Richard M. & Gorlin, Robert J. Atlas of the Face in Genetic Disorders. 2nd ed. LC 76-40327. (Illus.). 1977. 69.50 (ISBN 0-8016-1895-9). Mosby.

HEAD-DISEASES

see also Head-Radiography; Headache

Anderson, Robin & Hoopes, John, eds. Symposium on Malignancies of the Head & Neck, Vol. 11. LC 74-22108. 1975. 45.00 (ISBN 0-8016-0183-5). Mosby.

Barbosa, Jorge F. Surgical Treatment of Head & Neck Tumors. Von Becker Froon, Rosemarie, tr. from Portuguese. LC 74-3460. (Illus.). 416p. 1974. 67.75 (ISBN 0-8089-0811-1). Grune.

Chambers, R. G., et al. Cancer of the Head & Neck: Proceedings of the International Symposium, Switzerland, 1976. (International Congress Ser.: No. 365). 1975. 72.25 (ISBN 0-444-15190-7, Excerpta Medica). Elsevier.

Gelb, Harold. Clinical Management of Head, Neck & TMJ Pain & Dysfunction: A Multi-Disciplinary Approach to Diagnosis & Treatment. LC 76-50148. (Illus.). 1977. text ed. 49.50 (ISBN 0-7216-4072-9). Saunders.

Gorlin, R. V., et al. Syndromes of the Head & Neck. 2nd ed. (Illus.). 1976. text ed. 48.00 (ISBN 0-07-023790-5, HP). McGraw.

Pendergrass, Eugene P., et al. The Head & Neck in Roentgen Diagnosis, 2 vols. 2nd ed. (Illus.). 1880p. 1956. photocopy ed. spiral 188.00 (ISBN 0-398-01473-6). C C Thomas.

HEAD-RADIOGRAPHY

Djindjian, R. & Merland, J. J. Super-Selective Arteriography of the External Carotid Artery. LC 77-2949. (Illus.). 1977. 251.40 (ISBN 0-387-08118-6). Springer-Verlag.

Newton, Thomas H. & Potts, D. Gordon, eds. Radiology of the Skull & Brain: The Skull, Vol. 1. LC 78-173600. (Illus.). 1971. 136.00 (ISBN 0-8016-3646-9). Mosby.

Potter, Guy D. Sectional Anatomy & Tomography of the Head. LC 71-158948. (Illus.). 352p. 1971. 82.50 (ISBN 0-8089-0700-X). Grune.

HEAD-SURGERY

see also Brain-Surgery

Beder, Oscar E. Surgical & Maxillofacial Prosthesis. rev. ed. LC 49-50002. (Illus.). 94p. 1959. pap. 10.00 spiral bdg. (ISBN 0-295-74090-6). U of Wash Pr.

Bernstein, Leslie, ed. Third International Symposium in Plastic & Reconstructive Surgery of the Head & Neck: Aesthetic Surgery, Vol. 1. 1981. price not set (ISBN 0-8089-1372-7). Grune.

--Third International Symposium in Plastic & Reconstructive Surgery of the Head & Neck: Rehabilitative Surgery, Vol.2. 1981. price not set (ISBN 0-8089-1373-5). Grune.

Conley, John. Complications of Head & Neck Surgery. LC 79-416. (Illus.). 1979. text ed. 39.00 (ISBN 0-7216-2649-1). Saunders.

--Concepts in Head & Neck Surgery. (Illus.). 300p. 1970. 98.25 (ISBN 0-8089-0631-3). Grune.

Freund, H. R. Principles of Head & Neck Surgery. 2nd ed. (Illus.). 459p. 1979. 45.50 (ISBN 0-8385-7922-1). ACC.

Hollinshead, W. Henry. Anatomy for Surgeons Vol. 1: The Head & the Neck. 2nd ed. (Illus.). 1968. 37.00x (ISBN 0-06-141241-4, Harper Medical). Har-Row.

Lesavoy, Malcolm A. Reconstruction of the Head & Neck. (Illus.). 258p. 1981. 43.00 (ISBN 0-683-04949-6). Williams & Wilkins.

Naumann, H. H. Head & Neck Surgery, 2 vols. LC 79-3798. (Illus.). 1980. Vol. 1, 473 Pp. text ed. 97.50 (ISBN 0-7216-6663-9); Vol. 2, 475 Pp. 97.50 (ISBN 0-7216-6664-7). Saunders.

Pollack, R. S. Tumor Surgery of the Head & Neck. (Illus.). x, 206p. 1975. 43.75 (ISBN 3-8055-2092-1). S Karger.

Stell, P. M. & Maran, A. G. Head & Neck Surgery. 2nd ed. LC 78-66407. 1979. 35.00 (ISBN 0-397-58241-2). Lippincott.

Wilson, John S. Head & Neck: Volumes 1 & 2. (Operative Surgery Ser.). 1981. Set. text ed. price not set (ISBN 0-407-00624-9). Vol. 1 (ISBN 0-407-00622-2). Vol. 2 (ISBN 0-407-00623-0). Butterworth.

Wise, Robert A. & Baker, Harvey W. Surgery of the Head & Neck. 3rd ed. (Handbook of Operative Surgery Ser). (Illus.). 1968. 27.50 (ISBN 0-8151-9335-1). Year Bk Med.

Zacarian, Setrag A. Cryosurgical Advances in Dermatology & Tumors of the Head & Neck. (Illus.). 296p. 1977. 41.75 (ISBN 0-398-03597-0). C C Thomas.

HEAD-WOUNDS AND INJURIES

Bagchi, Asoke K. An Introduction to Head Injuries. (Illus.). 1981. text ed. 15.95x (ISBN 0-19-561151-9). Oxford U Pr.

Bakay, Louis & Glasauer, Franz E. Head Injury. 1980. text ed. 28.95 (ISBN 0-316-07774-7). Little.

Bolton, Brian. Rehabilitation Counseling Research. 293p. pap. text ed. 14.95 (ISBN 0-8391-1501-6). Univ Park.

Cartlidge, Niall & Shaw, David. Head Injury. (Major Problems in Neurosurgery Ser.: Vol. III). 1980. text ed. write for info. (ISBN 0-7216-2443-X). Saunders.

Frowein, R. A., ed. Head Injuries: Tumors of the Cerebellar Region. Proceedings of the 28th Annual Meeting of the German Society of Neurosurgery, Koeln, Sept. 18-21, 1977. LC 78-15592. (Advances in Neurosurgery: Vol. 5). (Illus.). 1979. pap. 54.70 (ISBN 0-387-08964-0). Springer-Verlag.

Gurdjian, E. S. Head Injury from Antiquity to the Present with Special Reference to Penetrating Head Wounds. (Beaumont Lecture Ser.). (Illus.). 148p. 1973. 16.75 (ISBN 0-398-02689-0). C C Thomas.

--Impact Head Injury: Mechanistic, Clinical & Preventative Correlations. (Illus.). 388p. 1975. 43.00 (ISBN 0-398-03301-3). C C Thomas.

Hooper, R. Patterns of Acute Head Injury. 175p. 1969. 13.50 (ISBN 0-683-04134-7, Pub. by Williams & Wilkins). Krieger.

Jamieson, K. G. A First Notebook of Head Injury. 2nd ed. (Illus.). 1971. 14.95 (ISBN 0-407-17350-1). Butterworth.

Jennett, Bryan. Epilepsy After Non-Missile Head Injuries. 2nd ed. 1975. 23.00 (ISBN 0-8151-4866-6). Year Bk Med.

Jennett, Bryan & Teasdale, Graham. Management of Head Injuries. LC 80-16785. (Contemporary Neurology Ser.: Vol. 20). (Illus.). 361p. 1981. text ed. 35.00 (ISBN 0-8036-5017-5). Davis Co.

Krayenbuehl, H., et al, eds. Craniocerebral Trauma. (Progress in Neurological Surgery: Vol. 10). (Illus.). 1981. 78.50 (ISBN 3-8055-0134-X). S Karger.
Lanksch, W., et al. Computed Tomography in Head Injuries. Dougherty, F. C., tr. from Ger. (Illus.). 1979. 45.10 (ISBN 0-387-09634-5). Springer-Verlag.
Luria, A. R. Man with a Shattered World: A History of a Brain Wound. LC 78-174809. 1972. 11.00x (ISBN 0-465-04371-2). Basic.
Walker, A. Earl & Erculei, Franco. Head Injured Men: Fifteen Years Later. (Illus.). 128p. 1969. photocopy ed. spiral 12.75 (ISBN 0-398-02006-X). C C Thomas.
Walker, A. Earl, et al. The Late Effects of Head Injury. (Illus.). 580p. 1969. pap. 57.75 (ISBN 0-398-02005-1). C C Thomas.
Zimmerman, Robert A. Pediatric Head Trauma. LC 78-50207. (Modern Concepts of Pediatrics). Date not set. write for info. (ISBN 0-87527-182-0). Green.
Zomeren, A. H. Reaction Time & Attention After Closed Head Injury. 176p. 1981. pap. text ed. 15.75 (ISBN 90-265-0369-5, Pub. by Swets Pub Serv Holland). Swets North Am.

HEAD-GEAR
see Costume; Hats; Millinery

HEAD-HUNTERS
Baumann, Peter & Patzelt, Erwin. Moquimbio: Memoirs of a Headhunter. LC 79-21939. (Illus.). 1980. 12.95 (ISBN 0-448-22076-8). Paddington.
Curtis, Edward S. In the Land of Head-Hunters. (Illus.). 1978. 7.95 (ISBN 0-913668-48-6); pap. 3.95 (ISBN 0-913668-47-8). Ten Speed Pr.
Rosaldo, Renato. Ilongot Headhunting, 1883-1974: A Study in Society & History. LC 79-64218. (Illus.). 1980. 18.50x (ISBN 0-8047-1046-5). Stanford U Pr.

HEAD IN ART
Bridgeman, George B. Heads, Features & Faces. LC 74-78681. 1974. lib. bdg. 9.50x (ISBN 0-88307-602-0). Gannon.
Bridgman, George B. Heads, Features, & Faces. LC 74-78681. (Illus.). 64p. 1974. pap. 2.00 (ISBN 0-486-22708-1). Dover.
Emerson, Ellen R. Masks, Heads, & Faces with Some Considerations Respecting the Rise & Development of Art. (Illus.). 1979. Repr. of 1891 ed. lib. bdg. 45.00 (ISBN 0-8495-1324-3). Arden Lib.
Gordon, Louise. How to Draw the Human Head. (Illus.). 1977. 9.95 (ISBN 0-670-38328-7, Studio). Viking Pr.
Hamm, Jack. Cartooning the Head & Figure. (Illus., Orig.). (gr. 9 up). 1967. pap. 4.95 (ISBN 0-448-01541-2). G&D.
Hogarth, Burne. Drawing the Human Head. (Illus.). 1965. 14.95 (ISBN 0-8230-1375-8). Watson-Guptill.
Loomis, Andrew. Drawing the Head & Hands. (Illus.). 1956. 13.95 (ISBN 0-670-28385-1). Viking Pr.
Sanden, John H. Painting the Head in Oil. (Illus.). 152p. 1976. 18.95 (ISBN 0-8230-3640-5). Watson-Guptill.
Zaidenberg, Arthur. How to Draw Heads & Faces. LC 66-10314. (How to Draw Ser). (Illus.). (gr. 5-10). 1966. PLB 8.79 (ISBN 0-200-71813-4, B37801, AbS-J). Har-Row.

HEAD NURSE
see Nursing Service Administration

HEADACHE
see also Migraine
Biermann, June & Toohey, Barbara. The Woman's Holistic Headache Relief Book. LC 78-62973. 1979. 7.95 (ISBN 0-312-90971-3). St Martin.
--Women's Holistic Headache Relief Book. LC 78-62973. 1979. 8.95 (ISBN 0-87477-086-6). J P Tarcher.
Critchley, Macdonald, et al, eds. International Headache Congress, 1980. 500p. 1981. 55.00 (ISBN 0-686-77787-5). Raven.
Diamond & Dalessio. The Practicing Physicians Approach to Headache. 2nd ed. 235p. 1978. lib. bdg. 23.50 (ISBN 0-683-02502-3). Williams & Wilkins.
Di Fiore, Frank R. You Can Conquer Your Headaches. (Illus.). 66p. (Orig.). 1980. pap. 10.00 (ISBN 0-932896-03-0). Westcliff Pubns.
Ehrmantraut, Harry C. Headaches: The Lasting Way to Drugless Relief. LC 80-66697. (Illus.). 152p. 1981. pap. 6.95 (ISBN 0-914398-41-5). Autumn Pr.
Freese, Arthur S. Headaches: The Kinds & the Cures. LC 74-10152. 192p. 1974. pap. 2.75 (ISBN 0-8052-0467-9). Schocken.
Friedman, A. P. & Granger, M. E., eds. Epidemiology & Non-Drug Treatment of Head Pain. (Research & Clinical Studies in Headache: Vol. 5). (Illus.). 1978. 37.25 (ISBN 3-8055-2803-5). S Karger.
Friedman, A. P., et al, eds. Headache Today - an Update by 21 Experts. (Research & Clinical Studies in Headache: Vol. 6). (Illus.). 1978. 39.00 (ISBN 3-8055-2924-4). S Karger.
Friedman, Arnold P. & Harms, Ernest. Headaches in Children. (Illus.). 160p. 1967. ed. spiral bdg. 16.50photocopy (ISBN 0-398-00619-9). C C Thomas.
Granger, Mary E., et al, eds. Pathophysiologic, Diagnostic & Therapeutic Aspects of Headache. (Research & Clinical Studies in Headache: Vol. 4). 135p. 1976. 37.25 (ISBN 3-8055-2282-7). S Karger.
Hanington, Edda. The Headache Book. LC 80-52621. (Illus.). 226p. 1981. 12.50 (ISBN 0-87762-292-2). Technomic.
Harpe, Shideler & Salazar, Jose L. Doctor Discuss Headaches. (Illus.). 1979. pap. 2.50 (ISBN 0-686-65548-6). Budlong.
International Migraine-Headache Symposium, Florence, 1970. Selected Papers of the International Migraine-Headache Symposium: Proceedings. Sicuteri, F., ed. (Research & Clinical Studies in Headache: Vol. 3). 1972. 84.00 (ISBN 3-8055-1295-3). S Karger.
Kudrow, Lee. Cluster Headache: Mechanisms & Management. (Illus.). 172p. 1981. 29.50 (ISBN 0-19-261169-0). Oxford U Pr.
Kurland, Howard D. Quick Headache Relief Without Drugs: How to Relieve Your Headache in Seconds: a Physician's Do-It-Yourself Technique. LC 76-28184. (A Bernard Geis Associates Book). (Illus.). 1977. 7.95 (ISBN 0-688-03147-1). Morrow.
Lance, James W. Headache: Understanding, Alleviation. LC 75-11809. (Illus.). 1975. pap. 8.95 (ISBN 0-684-14372-0, ScribT); pap. 0.95 (ISBN 0-684-16373-X, SL657, ScribT). Scribner.
Ostfeld, Adrian M. The Common Headache Syndromes: Biochemistry, Pathophysiology, Therapy. (American Lecture Living Chemistry). (Illus.). 100p. 1962. photocopy ed. spiral 10.50 (ISBN 0-398-01435-3). C C Thomas.
Pearce, John. Migraine: Clinical Features, Mechanisims & Management. (American Lecture Living Chemistry). (Illus.). 116p. 1969. photocopy ed. spiral 11.75 (ISBN 0-398-01457-4). C C Thomas.
Raskin, Neil H. & Appenzeller, Otto. Headache. LC 79-66042. (Monograph in Major Problems in Internal Medicine: No. 19). (Illus.). 244p. 1980. 19.50 (ISBN 0-7216-7467-4). Saunders.
Ryan, Robert E. & Ryan, Robert E., Jr., eds. Headache & Head Pain: Diagnosis & Treatment. LC 78-8973. 1978. text ed. 42.50 (ISBN 0-8016-4242-6). Mosby.
Saper, Joel & Magee, Kenneth. Freedom from Headaches. 1979. 8.95 (ISBN 0-671-24302-0). S&S.
Saper, Joel R. & Magge, Kenneth R. Freedom from Headaches. 1980. pap. 3.95 (ISBN 0-671-25404-9, Fireside). S&S.
Star, Cima. Understanding Headaches. (Illus.). 1977. pap. 2.95 (ISBN 0-671-18088-6). Monarch Pr.
Tourtellotte, Wallace W., et al. Post-Lumbar Puncture Headaches. (Illus.). 132p. 1964. photocopy ed. spiral 13.75 (ISBN 0-398-01937-1). C C Thomas.
Turin, Alan C. No More Headaches! 288p. 1981. 12.95 (ISBN 0-395-30516-0). HM.
Wolff, Harold G. Headache & Other Head Pain. 4th ed. Dalessio, Donald J., ed. (Illus.). 1980. text ed. 35.00x (ISBN 0-19-502624-1). Oxford U Pr.

HEADDRESS
see Hairdressing

HEADE, MARTIN J.
Stebbins, Theodore E., Jr. The Life & Works of Martin Johnson Heade. LC 74-83794. (Pubns. in the History of Art Ser.: No. 26). (Illus.). 328p. 1975. 40.00x (ISBN 0-300-01808-8). Yale U Pr.

HEADINGS, SUBJECT
see Subject Headings

HEADLIGHTS
see Automobiles-Lighting

HEADLINE WRITING
see Newspapers-Headlines

HEADS OF STATE
see also Statesmen
Bidwell, Robin, ed. Guide to Government Ministers: Arab World 1900-1972, Vol.2. 124p. 1973. 35.00x (ISBN 0-7146-3001-2, F Cass Co). Biblio Dist.
--Guide to Government Ministers: Major Powers & Western Europe 1900-1971, Vol.1. 298p. 1973. 35.00x (ISBN 0-7146-2977-4, F Cass Co). Biblio Dist.
--Guide to Government Ministers: The British Empire & Successor States 1900-1972, Vol. 3. 168p. 1974. 35.00x (ISBN 0-7146-3017-9, F Cass Co). Biblio Dist.
Binion, R. Hitler Among the Germans. 1976. 23.95 (ISBN 0-444-99033-X, Pub. by Elsevier). Greenwood.
Brezhnev, Leonid I. A Short Biography. LC 77-30493. 1978. text ed. 15.00 (ISBN 0-08-022266-8). Pergamon.
Ferrero, Guglielmo. The Life of Caesar. Zimmern, A. E., tr. LC 77-9520. 1977. Repr. of 1933 ed. lib. bdg. 33.75x (ISBN 0-8371-9090-8, FELC). Greenwood.
Langville, Alan R., compiled By. Modern World Rulers: A Chronology. LC 79-19294. 372p. 1979. 20.00 (ISBN 0-8108-1251-7). Scarecrow.
Schwartenberg, Roger-Gerard. Super Star Show of Government: Government Star System. LC 77-17696. 1980. 11.95 (ISBN 0-8120-5258-7). Barron.
Spencer, Donald S. Louis Kossuth & Young America: A Study of Sectionalism & Foreign Policy, 1848-1852. LC 77-2123. 1977. 12.50x (ISBN 0-8262-0223-3). U of Mo Pr.
Waite, Robert G. Psychopathic God: Adolf Hitler. LC 76-43484. (Illus.). 1977. 13.50 (ISBN 0-465-06743-3). Basic.
Worcester, Donald E. Bolivar. (Library of World Biography). 1977. 8.95 (ISBN 0-316-95390-3). Little.

HEALEY AUTOMOBILE
see Automobiles, Foreign-Types-Healey

HEALING (IN RELIGION, FOLK-LORE, ETC.)
see also Faith-Cure
Althouse, Lawrence W. Rediscovering the Gift of Healing. LC 77-9290. 1977. pap. 4.95 (ISBN 0-687-35860-4). Abingdon.
Answers to the Difficult Questions Concerning Healing. (Divine Healing & Health Ser.). 0.95 (ISBN 0-89985-025-1). Christ Nations.
Bennett, George. In His Healing Steps. LC 76-48507. 1977. pap. 2.95 (ISBN 0-8170-0748-2). Judson.
Bleich, David J. Judaism & Healing: Halakhic Perspectives. Date not set. 15.00x (ISBN 0-686-73601-X). Ktav.
Catholic Health Association. The Misnistry of Healing: Readings in the Catholic Health Care Ministry. 120p. 1981. pap. write for info. Cath Health.
Chaitow, Boris R. My Healing Secrets. 128p. 1980. 14.95 (ISBN 0-8464-1066-4). Beekman Pubs.
Challoner, H. K. The Path of Healing. LC 76-3660. 175p. 1976. pap. 3.25 (ISBN 0-8356-0480-2, Quest). Theos Pub Hse.
Coleman, William & Coleman, Patricia. The Sacraments of Healing. rev. ed. (Mine Is the Morning Ser.). 160p. (gr. 9-12). 1978. tchrs. manual & duplicator masters 16.95 (ISBN 0-89622-065-6). Twenty-Third.
Davidson, Ronald H. & Day, Richard. Symbol & Realization: A Contribution to the Study of Magic & Healing. (Research Monograph: No. 12). 1974. 8.75 (ISBN 0-686-23615-7, Ctr South & Southeast Asia Studies). Cellar.
Durodola, James I. Scientific Insights into Yoruba Traditional Medicine. (Traditional Healing Ser.). 1981. 27.50 (ISBN 0-932426-17-4). Conch Mag.
East, Reginald. Heal the Sick. LC 77-80678. (Orig.). 1977. pap. 1.95 (ISBN 0-87123-232-4, 200232). Bethany Hse.
Eddy, Mary B. Science & Health with Key to the Scriptures. (Polish.). 20.00 (ISBN 0-686-09421-2). First Church.
--Science & Health with Key to the Scriptures. Spanish Ed. pap. 5.00 (ISBN 0-686-09422-0); pap. 9.00 ger. ed (ISBN 0-686-09423-9). First Church.
Firas, Shihab. Healer, Ash-Shafuja, an Ismaili Treatise. Makarem, Sami N., ed. 1966. pap. 15.95x (ISBN 0-8156-6026-X, Am U Beirut). Syracuse U Pr.
Fishbein, Morris. Fads & Quackery in Healing. LC 75-23708. Repr. of 1932 ed. 31.00 (ISBN 0-404-13260-X). AMS Pr.
Flammonde, Paris. Mystic Healers. LC 73-91856. 1975. pap. 2.45 (ISBN 0-8128-1858-X). Stein & Day.
Gardner, Joy. Healing Yourself. 6th, rev. ed. (Illus.). 1977. pap. 2.00 (ISBN 0-9601688-1-8). Healing Yourself.
Hall, Manly P. Healing: Divine Art. 9.90 (ISBN 0-89314-390-1); pap. 4.95 (ISBN 0-686-68489-3). Philos Res.
Harner, Michael. The Way of the Shaman: A Guide to Power & Healing. LC 79-2995. 192p. 1980. 8.95 (ISBN 0-06-063710-2, HarpR). Har-Row.
Jilek, Wolfgang G. Indian Healing: Shamanic Ceremonialism in the Pacific Northwest Today. rev. ed. (Cultures in Review Ser.). Orig. Title: Salish Indian Mental Health & Culture Change. 184p. 1981. pap. text ed. 7.95 (ISBN 0-88839-120-X, Pub. by Hancock Hse). Universe.
Jones, Lloyd. Healing Forces. 1969. pap. 1.50 (ISBN 0-910140-25-1). Anthony.
King, Pat, ed. Healed. 92p. 1974. 2.25 (ISBN 0-930756-04-5, 4230-KI2). Women's Aglow.
Ki-Zerbo, J., ed. African Traditional Medicine & Pharmacopoeia. (Traditional Healing Ser.). 750p. 1981. 100.00 (ISBN 0-932426-22-0). Conch Mag.
Kuhlman, Kathryn. Never Too Late. LC 75-32235. 80p. 1975. pap. 1.95 (ISBN 0-87123-397-5, 200387). Bethany Hse.
Lawrence, Roy. Christian Healing Rediscovered. LC 80-7470. 128p. (Orig.). 1980. pap. 3.95 (ISBN 0-87784-621-9). Inter-Varsity.
Lindsay, Gordon. How You Can Be Healed. (Divine Healing & Health Ser.). 0.95 (ISBN 0-89985-026-X). Christ Nations.
Long, Joseph. Psyche Versus Soma: Traditional Healing Choices in Jamaica. (Traditional Healing Ser.). 300p. 1981. 17.50 (ISBN 0-932426-20-4); pap. 9.95 (ISBN 0-932426-21-2). Conch Mag.
Lovett, C. S. Jesus Wants You Well. 1973. pap. 5.45 (ISBN 0-938148-29-X). Personal Christianity.
Luckert, Karl W. Coyoteway: A Navajo Holyway Healing Ceremonial. LC 78-10358. 1979. pap. 13.95x (ISBN 0-8165-0655-8). U of Ariz Pr.
MacDougall, Mary K. Healing Now. 219p. 1970. 2.95 (ISBN 0-87159-054-9). Unity Bks.
McKechnie, R. E., II. Strong Medicine: A History of Healing on the Northwest Coast. 10.50 (ISBN 0-88894-074-2, Pub. by Douglas & McIntyre); pap. 6.50 (ISBN 0-88894-011-4, Pub. by Douglas & McIntyre). Intl Schol Bk Serv.
McNutt, Francis. The Power to Heal. 1979. pap. 2.25 (ISBN 0-553-12649-0). Bantam.
Martin, George. Healing: Reflections on the Gospel. 1977. pap. 1.75 (ISBN 0-89283-043-3). Servant.
Morningland Publications, Inc., ed. Healing: As It Is, 2 vols. (Illus.). 320p. (Orig.). 1981. Set. pap. 10.00 (ISBN 0-935146-59-8). Morningland.
Nowell, Henry F. Metaphysical Healing: Principles & Practice. 1979. 6.00 (ISBN 0-682-49239-6). Exposition.
Parkhurst, Genevieve. Positive Living Through Inner Healing. 1978. pap. 3.95 (ISBN 0-88270-283-1). Logos.
Peterson, John H. Healing Touch. LC 81-80629. (Illus.). 112p. (Orig.). 1981. pap. 4.95 (ISBN 0-8192-1291-1). Morehouse.
Ripley, John W. & Richmind, Robert W., eds. A Century of Healing Arts-Eighteen Fifty to Nineteen Fifty. (Illus.). 176p. 1980. pap. 5.95 (ISBN 0-686-70064-3). Shawnee County Hist.
Roebling, Karl. Is There Healing Power? LC 72-83072. (Pivot Family Reader Ser.). 112p. (Orig.). 1972. pap. 0.95 (ISBN 0-87983-029-8). Keats.
Rogers, E. P. Syrian Leper. (Summit Books). 1977. Repr. pap. 0.95 (ISBN 0-8010-7655-2). Baker Bk.
Rosenberg, Charles E., ed. Healing & History: Essays for George Rosen. 1979. lib. bdg. 27.00 (ISBN 0-88202-180-X). N Watson.
Sanford, Agnes. The Healing Gifts of the Spirit. (Trumpet Bks). 1976. pap. 1.75 (ISBN 0-87981-056-4). Holman.
--The Healing Power of the Bible. (Trumpet Bks). 1976. pap. 1.95 (ISBN 0-87981-059-9). Holman.
Sanford, John A. Healing & Wholeness. LC 77-83576. 180p. 1977. 9.95 (ISBN 0-8091-0225-0); pap. 6.95 (ISBN 0-8091-2044-5). Paulist Pr.
Shlemon, Barbara L., et al. To Heal As Jesus Healed. LC 78-54126. 112p. 1978. pap. 1.95 (ISBN 0-87793-152-6). Ave Maria.
Smith, Cushing. I Can Heal Myself & I Will. new ed. LC 62-14344. 315p. 1980. pap. 5.95 (ISBN 0-8119-0384-2). Fell.
Stanger, Frank B. God's Healing Community. LC 78-8017. 1978. 4.95 (ISBN 0-687-15332-8). Abingdon.
Stapleton, Ruth C. Experiencing Inner Healing. 1979. pap. 2.25 (ISBN 0-8499-4120-2, Key-Word Bks). Word Bks.
--The Gift of Inner Healing. LC 75-36180. 1976. 5.95 (ISBN 0-87680-809-7, Key Word Bks.); pap. 1.75 (ISBN 0-686-67399-9, 91030). Word Bks.
Sterner, Eugene. Healing & Wholeness. (Doctrinal Material of the Church of God: No. 2). 1978. pap. text ed. 3.50 (ISBN 0-87162-201-7, D4285). Warner Pr.
Suber, S. H. Faith Healing in the Twentieth Century. pap. 3.98 (ISBN 0-911734-09-0). Commonsense.
Tapscott, Betty. Inner Healing Through Healing of Memories. 1975. pap. 2.95 (ISBN 0-917726-29-4). Hunter Bks.
Tournier, Paul. The Violence Within. 2nd ed. LC 78-3139. 208p. 1982. pap. 6.95 (ISBN 0-06-068295-7, HarpR). Har-Row.
White, Anne S. Healing Devotions. LC 75-5218. 138p. 1975. pap. 3.25 (ISBN 0-8192-1192-3). Morehouse.
Wilson, Jim. Healing Through the Power of Christ. 1969. pap. 3.25 (ISBN 0-227-67478-2). Attic Pr.
Yogi Ramacharaka. Practical Water Cure. leatherette 2.50 (ISBN 0-911662-12-X). Yoga.
Zodhiates, Spiros. Healing, Confession, Prayer. (Illus.). 1974. pap. 2.25 (ISBN 0-89957-506-4). AMG Pubs.

HEALING, MENTAL
see Mental Healing

HEALING, PSYCHIC
see Mental Healing
HEALTH
Here are entered works on optimal physical, mental, and social well-being, as well as how to achieve and preserve it. Works on personal body care and cleanliness are entered under Hygiene. Works on muscular efficiency and physical endurance are entered under Physical fitness.
see also Climatology, Medical; Diet; Environmental Health; Executives–Health Programs; Exercise; Health Education; Hygiene; Longevity; Mental Health; Nutrition; Physical Fitness; Public Health; Relaxation; Rest; Sleep; Temperance;
also subdivision Care and Hygiene under parts of the body, or under age groups dependent on the assistance of others, e.g. Eye–Care and Hygiene; Infants–Care and Hygiene; and subdivision Health and Hygiene under classes of persons or ethnic groups, e.g. Students–Health and Hygiene; Afro-Americans–Health and Hygiene

A P L Project, University of Texas at Austin. The A P L Series: Coping in Today's Society. Incl. Community Resources. 1980. pap. 3.24 reading bk. (ISBN 0-15-502865-0); tchr's. manual 2.94 (ISBN 0-15-502889-8); wkbk. 1.94 (ISBN 0-15-502866-9); tchr's. kit incl. manual 25.00 (ISBN 0-15-502867-7); Consumer Economics I. 1980. pap. 3.24 reading bk. (ISBN 0-15-502868-5); tchr's. manual 2.94 (ISBN 0-15-502890-1); wkbk. 2.94 (ISBN 0-15-502869-3); tchr's. kit incl. manual 25.00 (ISBN 0-15-502870-7); Consumer Economics II. 1980. pap. 3.24 reading bk. (ISBN 0-15-502871-5); tchr's. manual 2.94 (ISBN 0-15-502891-X); wkbk. 2.94 (ISBN 0-15-502872-3); tchr's. kit incl. manual 25.00 (ISBN 0-15-502873-1); Consumer Economics III. 1980. pap. 3.24 reading bk. (ISBN 0-15-502874-X); tchr's. manual 2.94 (ISBN 0-15-502892-8); wkbk. 1.94 (ISBN 0-15-502875-8); tchr's. kit incl. manual 20.00 (ISBN 0-15-502876-6); Government & Law. 1980. pap. 3.24 reading bk. (ISBN 0-686-65010-7); tchr's. manual 2.94 (ISBN 0-15-502893-6); wkbk. 1.94 (ISBN 0-15-502878-2); tchr's. kit incl. manual 20.00 (ISBN 0-15-502879-0); Health I. 1979. pap. 3.24 reading bk. (ISBN 0-15-502880-4); tchr's. manual 2.94 (ISBN 0-15-502894-4); wkbk. 1.94 (ISBN 0-15-502881-2); tchr's. kit incl. manual 20.00 (ISBN 0-15-502882-0); Health II. 1979. pap. 3.24 reading bk. (ISBN 0-15-502883-9); tchr's. manual 2.94 (ISBN 0-15-502895-2); wkbk. 1.94 (ISBN 0-15-502884-7); tchr's. kit incl. manual 20.00 (ISBN 0-15-502885-5); Occupational Knowledge. 1980p. pap. 3.24 reading bk. (ISBN 0-15-502886-3); tchr's. manual 2.94 (ISBN 0-15-502897-9); wkbk. 2.94 (ISBN 0-686-65011-5); tchr's. kit incl. manual 25.00 (ISBN 0-15-502888-X). HC). HarBraceJ.

Abehsera, Michel. Healing Clay. 1979. 9.95 (ISBN 0-918282-10-1); pap. 3.95 (ISBN 0-918282-11-X). Bolder Bks.

Abriel, Vera. The Woman's Total Reshape Program: Have the Figure You Always Wanted. (Illus.). 256p. 1981. 12.95 (ISBN 0-525-93148-1). Dutton.

Abstracts of Research Papers, 1979. 1979. 3.50 (ISBN 0-685-96292-X, 248-26486). AAHPERD.

Airola, Paavo. How to Get Well. 12.95 (ISBN 0-686-29849-7). Cancer Bk Hse.

--How to Get Well. 1974. cloth 12.95 (ISBN 0-932090-03-6). Health Plus.

Airola, Paavo O. Health Secrets from Europe. LC 79-135618. 1971. pap. 1.65 (ISBN 0-668-02411-9). Arco.

Alexander, Dale. Good Health & Common Sense. 8.95 (ISBN 0-686-29856-X). Cancer Bk Hse.

Alexander, F. Matthias. The Resurrection of the Body. 256p. 1974. pap. 4.95 (ISBN 0-440-57374-2, Delta). Dell.

Allen, Anne S. Introduction to Health Professions. 3rd ed. LC 79-26136. (Illus.). 1980. pap. text ed. 11.50 (ISBN 0-8016-0113-4). Mosby.

Allen, David T. & Wells, John P. Passport to Good Health. LC 78-51737. 1978. 3.50 (ISBN 0-917634-02-0). Creative Infomatics.

Allen, Robert & Linde, Shirley. Lifegain: The Exciting New Program That Will Change Your Health - & Your Life. (Appleton Consumer Health Guides). 288p. 1981. 12.95 (ISBN 0-8385-5671-X). ACC.

Allinson, T. R. Hygienic Medicine: A Rational Way to Treat Disease. 1974. lib. bdg. 69.95 (ISBN 0-685-51382-3). Revisionist Pr.

Altman, Philip L. & Katz, Dorothy D., eds. Human Health & Disease. LC 76-53166. (Biological Handbks: Vol. 2). (Illus.). 1977. 55.00 (ISBN 0-913822-11-6). FASEB.

American Alliance for Health, Physical Education & Recreation. Abstracts of Research Papers, 1973. pap. 2.50 (ISBN 0-685-42022-1, 248-25436). AAHPERD.

--Completed Research in Health, Physical Education, & Recreation, Vol. 15. 1973. pap. 4.25x (ISBN 0-685-42024-8, 248-25462). AAHPERD.

--Completed Research in Health, Physical Education, & Recreation, Vol. 16. 1974. 8.95x (ISBN 0-685-42023-X, 248-25686). AAHPERD.

American Health Foundation. The Book of Health: A Complete Guide to Making Health Last a Lifetime. Wynder, Ernst L., ed. (Illus.). 736p. 1981. 19.95 (ISBN 0-531-09929-6). Watts.

American National Red Cross. Family Health & Home Nursing. (Illus.). 1979. pap. 3.95 (ISBN 0-385-15281-7). Doubleday.

Anderson, Ernest C. & Sullivan, Elizabeth M., eds. Impact of Energy Production on Human Health: An Evaluation of Means for Assessment, Proceedings. LC 76-22540. (ERDA Symposium Ser.). 152p. 1976. pap. 6.75 (ISBN 0-686-75826-9); microfiche 3.00 (ISBN 0-686-75827-7). DOE.

Antonetti, Vincent W. Fitness Management. LC 76-42583. (Illus., Orig.). 1976. pap. 4.95x (ISBN 0-918278-01-5). Fitness.

Archart-Treichel, Joan. Biotypes: The Critical Link Between Your Personality & Your Health. 1980. 12.95 (ISBN 0-686-65923-6). Times Bks.

Ardell, Donald B. Fourteen Days to a Wellness Lifestyle. (Illus.). 290p. (Orig.). (YA) 1981. pap. 6.95 (ISBN 0-931432-11-1). Whatever Pub.

--High Level Wellness. 1979. pap. 2.75 (ISBN 0-553-12165-0). Bantam.

Ardell, Donald B., ed. High-Level Wellness. LC 77-10993. 1977. pap. 8.95 (ISBN 0-87857-194-9). Rodale Pr Inc.

Arola, Paavo. Health Secrets from Europe. 1.65 (ISBN 0-686-29850-0). Cancer Bk Hse.

Asai, Kazuhiko. Miracle Cure: Organic Germanium. LC 79-91512. (Illus.). 256p. 1980. 12.95 (ISBN 0-87040-474-1). Japan Pubns.

Ashton, Leila M. My Feel Good Secrets. (My Church Teaches Ser.). (Illus.). 1978. pap. 1.25 (ISBN 0-8127-0178-X). Review & Herald.

Aumiller, Dr. Jochen. You Don't Have to Be Next. 1980. pap. 5.95 (ISBN 0-8065-0683-0). Lyle Stuart.

Bach, Marcus. The Power of Total Living. LC 77-13279. (Illus.). 1977. 7.95 (ISBN 0-396-07510-X). Dodd.

Bachman, David C. & Preston, Marilyn. Dear Dr. Jock. (Illus.). 1980. pap. 8.95 (ISBN 0-525-93066-3). Dutton.

Bailey, Covert. Fit or Fat. 1978. 6.95 (ISBN 0-395-27161-4); pap. 3.95 (ISBN 0-395-27162-2). HM.

Bane, Bernard M. Guidelines to Authenticity Stepping Stones to Health. LC 77-87980. 60p. 1977. soft bdg. 3.00 (ISBN 0-9600164-6-5). BMB Pub Co.

Barrett, Stephen, ed. The Health Robbers. 2nd ed. 396p. 1981. 12.95 (ISBN 0-89313-023-0). G F Stickley Co.

Bartlett, Albert B. Improve Your Health & Save Money at the Same Time. 1977. pap. 3.50 (ISBN 0-89036-077-4). Hawkes Pub Inc.

Barton, John & Barton, Margaret. How to Take Care of Yourselves Naturally. 4th ed. LC 77-80393. Orig. Title: Flow Lines to Health. (Illus.). 158p. 1980. pap. 8.00 (ISBN 0-937216-04-6). J&M Barton.

Basch, Paul F. International Health. 1978. text ed. 11.95x (ISBN 0-19-502328-5); pap. text ed. 10.95x (ISBN 0-19-502329-3). Oxford U Pr.

Basic Health Science Series: 1974 Edition. Bk. D. 4.76 (ISBN 0-397-43595-9, JBL-Med-Nursing); Bk. D. tchr's ed 4.76 (ISBN 0-397-43596-7); Bk. E. 5.08 (ISBN 0-397-43597-5); Bk. E. tchr's ed 5.08 (ISBN 0-397-43598-3); Bk. F. tchr's ed 5.08 (ISBN 0-397-43599-1). Bk. F. Har-Row.

Baumslag, Naomi, ed. Family Care. 392p. 1973. 13.50 (ISBN 0-683-00412-3, Pub. by W & W). Krieger.

Bauwens, Eleanor E., ed. The Anthropology of Health. LC 78-6776. 1978. pap. text ed. 11.95 (ISBN 0-8016-0516-4). Mosby.

Becker, Gail L. High Points for Healthful Living. 1981. write for info. (ISBN 0-87502-091-7). Benjamin Co.

Beebe, Brooke, et al. Nutrition & Good Health. LC 78-731300. (Illus.). 1978. pap. text ed. 135.00 (ISBN 0-89290-099-7, A576-SATC). Soc for Visual.

Beecher, Catharine. Letters to the People on Health & Happiness. LC 70-180554. (Medicine & Society in America Ser). (Illus.). 228p. 1972. Repr. of 1855 ed. 12.00 (ISBN 0-405-03934-4). Arno.

Beenstock, Michael. Health, Migration & Development. 192p. 1980. text ed. 27.75x (ISBN 0-566-00369-4, Pub. by Gower Pub Co England). Renouf.

Bergson, Anika, ed. Zone Therapy. Tuchak, Vladimir. (Illus.). 160p. 1980. pap. 1.95 (ISBN 0-523-40861-7). Pinnacle Bks.

Berk, William R., ed. Chinese Healing Arts: Internal Kung-Fu. LC 79-1566. (Illus.). 240p. 1979. pap. 8.95 (ISBN 0-915238-29-2). Peace Pr.

Berkeley Holistic Health Center. Holistic Health Handbook. LC 78-54344. (Illus.). 1978. pap. 9.95 (ISBN 0-915904-32-2). And-or Pr.

Berle, Beatrice B. Eighty Puerto Rican Families in New York City: Health & Disease Studied in Context. LC 74-14221. (The Puerto Rican Experience Ser). (Illus.). 356p. 1975. Repr. 20.00x (ISBN 0-405-06211-7). Arno.

Better Homes & Gardens, ed. After--Forty Health & Medical Guide. 1981. 24.95 (ISBN 0-696-00810-6). BH&G.

Better Homes & Gardens Books Editors. Better Homes & Gardens After-40 Health & Medical Guide. (Illus.). 480p. 1980. 24.95 (ISBN 0-696-00810-6). Meredith Corp.

Bieliauskas, Linas A. The Influence of Indiviual Differences in Health & Illness. (Behavioral Sciences for Health Care Professionals). 128p. (Orig.). Date not set. lib. bdg. 15.00x (ISBN 0-86531-004-1); pap. text ed. 6.75x (ISBN 0-86531-005-X). Westview.

Birch, C. C., et al. Health & Food. 224p. 1972. 21.95 (ISBN 0-470-07322-5). Halsted Pr.

Bittner, Vernon J. You Can Help with Your Healing: A Guide for Recovering Wholeness in Body, Mind, & Spirit. LC 78-66946. 1979. pap. 3.95 (ISBN 0-8066-1698-9, 10-7411). Augsburg.

Blanda, George & Herskowitz, Mickey. Over Forty: Feeling Great & Looking Good! 1980. pap. 2.95 (ISBN 0-671-25189-9, Fireside). S&S.

--Over Forty Feeling Great & Looking Good. 1978. 9.95 (ISBN 0-671-22472-7). S&S.

Blide, Richard R. - Seven Steps to Heart & Lung Fitness. Darden, Ellington, ed. LC 77-75763. (Physical Fitness & Sports Medicine Ser). (Illus.). 1977. pap. 3.95 (ISBN 0-89305-005-9). Anna Pub.

Blum, Henrik L. Planning for Health: Generics for the Eighties. 2nd ed. LC 80-23461. 1981. 29.95 (ISBN 0-89885-013-4). Human Sci Pr.

Boff, Vic. You Can Be Physically Perfect, Powerfully Strong. LC 74-82866. (Orig.). 1975. PLB 7.95 (ISBN 0-668-02700-2); pap. 1.95 (ISBN 0-668-03783-0). Arco.

Boston Women's Health Collective. Our Bodies, Ourselves. rev. ed. 1976. pap. 7.95 (ISBN 0-671-22146-9, Touchstone Bks). S&S.

Boyd, Nathaniel W., III. How to Stay Out of the Hospital. LC 76-39730. 190p. 1979. pap. 4.95 (ISBN 0-8119-0404-0). Fell.

Bragg, Paul C. & Bragg, Patricia. Building Health & Youthfulness. 11th ed. pap. 1.75 (ISBN 0-87790-017-5). Health Sci.

--Building Powerful Nerve Force. 9th ed. LC 79-76538. pap. 2.95 (ISBN 0-87790-003-5). Health Sci.

--Golden Keys to Internal Physical Fitness. 9th ed. LC 66-30394. pap. 2.95 (ISBN 0-87790-006-X). Health Sci.

--New Science of Health. 7th ed. pap. 1.75 (ISBN 0-87790-021-3). Health Sci.

--Philosophy of Super Health. 10th ed. pap. 1.75 (ISBN 0-87790-022-1). Health Sci.

Brenner, M. Harvey. Assessing the Contribution of the Social Sciences & Health. 1979. lib. bdg. 20.00 (ISBN 0-89158-291-6). Westview.

Brenner, Paul. Health Is a Question of Balance. 143p. 1980. pap. 4.95 (ISBN 0-87516-415-3). De Vorss.

Breyfogle, Newell D. The Common Sense Medical Guide & Outdoor Reference. McGraw, Robert P., ed. (Illus.). 416p. 1981. text ed. 11.95 (ISBN 0-07-007672-3, HP); pap. text ed. 6.95 (ISBN 0-07-007673-1). McGraw.

Bricklin, Mark & Claessens, Charon. Natural Healing Cookbook: Over Four Hundred Fifty Delicious Ways to Get Better & Stay Healthy. (Illus.). 416p. 1981. 19.95 (ISBN 0-87857-338-0). Rodale Pr Inc.

Bronwen, Meredith. Natural Health & Beauty. (Illus.). 304p. 1981. 19.95 (ISBN 0-03-057976-7). HR&W.

Brooke, Eileen M. Current & Future Use of Registers in Health Information Systems. (Offset Pub.: No. 8). (Also avail. in French). 1974. pap. 5.60 (ISBN 92-4-170008-4). World Health.

Brooks, Natalie & Brooks, Stewart M. Turner's Personal & Community Health. 15th ed. LC 78-31647. (Illus.). 1979. text ed. 15.95 (ISBN 0-8016-5536-6). Mosby.

Bucher, Charles & Olsen, Einar. Foundations of Health. 2nd ed. (Illus.). 448p. 1976. Ref. Ed. 16.95 (ISBN 0-13-329896-5). P-H.

Bucher, Charles A., et al. Foundations of Health. LC 67-10700. (Illus.). 1967. 18.95x (ISBN 0-89197-174-2). Irvington.

Buchman, Dian Dincin. Complete Herbal Guide to Natural Health & Beauty. LC 73-79653. 216p. 1973. pap. 3.50 (ISBN 0-385-08815-9). Doubleday.

Buck, Albert H. A Treatise on Hygiene & Public Health, 2 vols. Rosenkrantz, Barbara G., ed. LC 76-25654. (Public Health in America Ser.). 1977. Repr. of 1879 ed. Set. lib. bdg. 80.00x (ISBN 0-405-09810-3); lib. bdg. 40.00x ea. Vol. 1 (ISBN 0-405-09811-1). Vol. 2 (ISBN 0-405-09812-X). Arno.

Burd, James J. & Serfustini, Leonard T. Quest One: Active Living, a Guide to Fitness, Conditioning, & Health. 1978. pap. 9.95 (ISBN 0-8403-1536-8). Kendall Hunt.

Burns, Dolores, ed. The Greatest Health Discovery. (Illus., Orig.). 1972. pap. 2.25 (ISBN 0-914532-05-7). Natural Hygiene.

Burstein, John. Slim Goodbody: The Inside Story. (Illus.). (gr. k-6). 1977. 7.95 (ISBN 0-07-009240-0, GB); pap. 4.95 (ISBN 0-07-009241-9). McGraw.

Cantu, Robert C., ed. Health Maintenance Through Physical Conditioning. LC 80-15622. 180p. 1981. pap. 12.50 (ISBN 0-88416-312-1). Wright-PSG.

Caplan, Arthur L., et al. Concepts of Health & Disease: Interdisciplinary Perspectives. 608p. 1981. pap. text ed. write for info. (ISBN 0-201-00973-0). A-W.

Carroll, Charles & Miller, Dean. Health: The Science of Human Adaptation. 3rd ed. 672p. 1982. pap. text ed. price not set (ISBN 0-697-07393-9); instructor's manual avail. Wm C Brown.

Carroll, Charles R. & Miller, Dean F. Health: The Science of Human Adaptation. 2nd ed. 620p. 1979. pap. text ed. write for info. (ISBN 0-697-07382-3); instr. manual avail. (ISBN 0-685-91863-7). Wm C Brown.

Carroll, Walter J., ed. Hospital-Health Care Training Media Profiles, Vol. 8. 1981. 85.00 (ISBN 0-88367-208-1). Olympic Media.

Carson, Rachel. Silent Spring. 1.50 (ISBN 0-686-29884-5). Cancer Bk Hse.

Carter, Craig. Your Handbook for Healing. 1981. pap. 6.95 (ISBN 0-911336-86-9). Sci of Mind.

Chacko, G. K., ed. Health Handbook: An International Reference on Care & Cure. 1979. 146.50 (ISBN 0-444-85254-9, North Holland). Elsevier.

Chancellor, Phillip. Handbook on the Bach Flower Remedies. LC 79-93435. 254p. (Orig.). 1980. pap. 5.95 (ISBN 0-87983-196-0). Keats.

Chaney, Earlyne. The Book of Beginning Again. (Illus.). 240p. 1981. pap. 12.50 (ISBN 0-918936-09-8). Astara.

Chang, Stephen T. & Miller, Richard C. The Book of Internal Exercises. LC 78-18320. (Illus., Orig.). 1978. pap. 6.95 (ISBN 0-89407-017-7). Strawberry Hill.

Cheyne, George. An Essay of Health & Long Life. 1977. 40.00 (ISBN 0-85362-166-7, Oriel). Routledge & Kegan.

Chomicki, William P. Your Secret to Vibrant Good Health. 1981. 4.95 (ISBN 0-8062-1802-9). Carlton.

Christopher, John R. The Incurables. 1.50 (ISBN 0-89557-032-7). Bi World Indus.

Cilento. You Don't Have to Live with: Chronic Ill Health. 1978. 7.50x (ISBN 0-7233-5297-6). Intl Pubns Serv.

--You Don't Have to Live with: Vitamin & Mineral Deficiences. 1978. 7.50x (ISBN 0-7233-5299-2). Intl Pubns Serv.

Cizmar, Paula & Drolet, Judy. An Invitation to Health: Your Personal Responsibility: Instructor's Guide. 1980. 3.95 (ISBN 0-8053-2302-3). Benjamin Cummings.

Clark, Carolyn C. Enhancing Wellness. 1981. text ed. 26.95 (ISBN 0-8261-2950-1); pap. text ed. 16.95 (ISBN 0-8261-2951-X). Springer Pub.

Clark, Linda. Be Slim & Healthy. (Spanish ed.). 1980. pap. 5.95 (ISBN 0-87983-187-1). Keats.

--Get Well Naturally. 5.95 (ISBN 0-686-29889-6); pap. 1.95 (ISBN 0-686-29890-X). Cancer Bk Hse.

--Go-Caution-Stop Carbohydrate Computer. (Pivot Health Book Ser.). 48p. (YA) 1973. pap. 1.95 (ISBN 0-87983-056-5). Keats.

--How to Improve Your Health. LC 78-61329. 1979. 8.95 (ISBN 0-87983-181-2); pap. 4.95 (ISBN 0-87983-180-4). Keats.

--Light on Your Health Problems. LC 72-83522. (Pivot Original Health Book). 240p. 1972. pap. 1.50 (ISBN 0-87983-026-3). Keats.

Clark, Linda A. Secrets of Health & Beauty: How to Make Yourself Over. 1969. 5.95 (ISBN 0-8159-6807-8). Devin.

Colby, Benjamin. A Guide to Health. rev. & enl. ed. 6.95 (ISBN 0-89557-013-0). Bi World Indus.

Combs, B., et al. An Invitation to Health: Your Personal Responsibility. 1980. pap. 13.95 (ISBN 0-8053-2301-5); instrs manual 3.95 (ISBN 0-8053-2302-3). A-W.

Combs, Barbara, et al. An Invitation to Health: Your Personal Responsibility. 1979. 13.95 (ISBN 0-8053-2301-5). Benjamin-Cummings.

Communications Research Machines, Inc. Essentials of Life & Health. 2nd ed. (CRM Bks.). 1977. pap. text ed. 11.95x (ISBN 0-394-31191-4). Random.

--Life & Health. 3rd ed. 589p. 1980. text ed. 19.95 (ISBN 0-394-32207-X). Random.
Community Service Society of New York. Family in a Democratic Society. facsimile ed. LC 77-167330. (Essay Index Reprint Ser). Repr. of 1949 ed. 18.00 (ISBN 0-8369-2491-6). Arno.
Complete Book of Minerals for Health. rev. ed. 1981. 16.95 (ISBN 0-87857-360-7). Rodale Pr Inc.
Corcoran, Eileen L. Meeting Basic Competencies in Practical Science & Health: A Workstudy Book to Improve Daily Living Skills. (Illus.). 1979. 2.50x (ISBN 0-88323-146-8, 237); tchrs answer key free (ISBN 0-88323-154-9, 245). Richards Pub.
Corder, Brice W., et al. Health: Current Perspectives. 3rd ed. 403p. 1981. pap. text ed. write for info. (ISBN 0-697-07388-2); instructor's manual avail. (ISBN 0-697-07389-0). Wm C Brown.
Cornacchia, Harold J. & Staton, Wesley M. Health in the Elementary Schools. 5th ed. LC 78-21076. (Illus.). 1979. text ed. 16.95 (ISBN 0-8016-1062-1). Mosby.
Cousins, Norman. Anatomy of an Illness As Perceived by the Patient: Reflections on Healing & Regeneration. 1979. 9.95 (ISBN 0-393-01252-2). Norton.
Cox, Anthony & Groves, Philip. Design for Health. (Newnes-Butterworth Design Ser.). 1981. text ed. 48.95 (ISBN 0-408-00389-8, Newnes-Butterworth). Butterworth.
Cox, S., et al. Wellness R.S.V.P. 1981. 4.95 (ISBN 0-8053-2304-X). A-W.
Cox, Stafford G., et al. Wellness R. S. V. P. Your Personal Invitation. 1981. pap. 3.95 (ISBN 0-8053-2304-X, 800100). Benjamin Cummings.
Cullis, John G. & West, Peter A. The Economics of Health: An Introducton. LC 79-50451. 1979. 22.50x (ISBN 0-8147-1377-7). NYU Pr.
Cundiff, David E. & Brynteson, Paul. Health Fitness: Guide to a Life Style. (Illus.). 1979. pap. text ed. 9.95 (ISBN 0-8403-2016-7). Kendall-Hunt.
Curtis, John D. & Papenfuss, Richard L. Health Instruction: A Task Approach. 1980. pap. 10.95x (ISBN 0-8087-2914-4). Burgess.
Dalet, Roger. How to Safeguard Your Health & Beauty with the Simple Pressure of a Finger. LC 80-5497. (Illus.). 160p. 1981. 10.95 (ISBN 0-8128-2742-2). Stein & Day.
Dankenbring, William F. The Keys to Radiant Health. LC 74-19241. 281p. 1974. 7.50 (ISBN 0-685-61404-2). Triumph Pub.
--Your Keys to Radiant Health. LC 74-19241. (Illus.). 288p. 1975. pap. 1.95 (ISBN 0-87983-119-7). Keats.
Danowski, T. S. Sustained Weight Control: The Individual Approach. 2nd ed. 1973. pap. text ed. 3.75 (ISBN 0-8036-2331-3). Davis Co.
Davis, Flora. Living Alive. LC 79-7490. 456p. 1980. 12.95 (ISBN 0-385-14506-3). Doubleday.
Day, Harvey. Encyclopaedia of Natural Health & Healing. LC 78-24666. (Illus.). 1979. 7.95 (ISBN 0-912800-62-3). Woodbridge Pr.
Day, Stacey B., et al. Biopsychosocial Health. 225p. 1980. pap. 15.00 (ISBN 0-934314-02-0). Intl Found Biosocial Dev.
Dean, Herbert M. & Massarelli, John J. Look to Your Health: What You Should Know About the Body, Common Diseases & Healthful Living. 320p. 1980. 13.95 (ISBN 0-442-24742-7). Van Nos Reinhold.
De Castille, Vernon. Health & Physical Well Being: The Essential Knowledge of the Basic Rules on Being Healthy, Staying Healthy & Live a Long & Happy Life Which Everyone, but Absolutely Everyone Ought to Possess for the Benefit & Success of His Existence. (The Essential Knowledge Ser. Books). (Illus.). 1978. plastic spiral bdg. 27.35 (ISBN 0-89266-121-6). Am Classical Coll Pr.
Deichmann, William B. Safe Farming & Gardening. 1972. pap. 3.00 (ISBN 0-89970-077-2, OP-389). AMA.
Deimel, Diana. Vision Victory. 3.00 (ISBN 0-686-29907-8). Cancer Bk Hse.
De Langre, Jacques. Food Consciousness for Spiritual Development. LC 80-84993. (Illus., Orig.). 1980. pap. 6.00 (ISBN 0-916508-05-6). Happiness Pr.
Derbyshire, Caroline. The New Woman's Guide to Health & Medicine. (Appleton Consumer Health Guides). (Illus.). 316p. 1980. 12.95 (ISBN 0-8385-6759-2); pap. 5.95 (ISBN 0-8385-6758-4). ACC.
Devries, Herbert & Briley, Michael. Health Science. LC 78-27588. (Illus.). 1978. text ed. 13.95 (ISBN 0-87620-380-2); inst. manual avail. (ISBN 0-87620-381-0). Goodyear.
De Waters, Lillian. How to Have Health. pap. 0.95 (ISBN 0-686-05708-2). L De Waters.
Dextreit, ed. Our Earth Our Cure. Abehsera, Michel, tr. 1979. 14.95 (ISBN 0-918282-08-X); pap. 5.95 (ISBN 0-918282-09-8). Bolder Bks.
Diagram Group. The Healthy Body: A Maintenance Manual. 1981. pap. 6.95 (ISBN 0-452-25294-6, Z5294, Plume). NAL.
Diehl, H. S., et al. Health & Safety for You. 4th ed. text ed. 12.92 (ISBN 0-07-016860-1, W); tchr's. ed. 14.12 (ISBN 0-07-016861-X); tests 1.96 (ISBN 0-07-016862-8). McGraw.
Diehl, Harold S. & Dalrymple, Willard. Healthful Living: A Textbook of Personal & Community Health. 9th ed. (Illus.). 576p. 1973. text ed. 15.95 (ISBN 0-07-016835-0, C); instructor's manual 3.95 (ISBN 0-07-016836-9). McGraw.
Diehl, Harold S., et al. Health & Safety for You. 3rd ed. (gr. 9 up). 1969. text ed. 12.20 (ISBN 0-07-016856-3, W); teachers' ec. 11.36 (ISBN 0-07-016857-1). McGraw.
Diekelman, Nancy. Primary Health Care of the Well Adult. (Illus.). 1977. pap. text ed. 8.50 (ISBN 0-07-016879-2, HP). McGraw.
Dinaburg & Akel. Nutrition Survival Kit. (Orig.). pap. 1.75 (ISBN 0-515-04654-X). Jove Pubns.
Dincin, Dian. How to Look Good & Feel Great: Secrets of Clear Skin, Beautiful Hair, Good Health. (gr. 7-9). 1976. pap. 1.25 (ISBN 0-590-10245-1). Schol Bk Serv.
Dingwall, Robert, et al, eds. Health Care & Health Knowledge. LC 76-55745. 1977. lib. bdg. 22.50 (ISBN 0-88202-113-3). N Watson.
Dintiman, George B. & Greenberg, Jerrold S. Health Through Discovery. LC 79-20714. (Illus.). 1980. pap. text ed. 14.95 (ISBN 0-201-01256-1). A-W.
Donsbach, Kurt. Passport to Good Health. 5.95 (ISBN 0-686-29910-8). Cancer Bk Hse.
Dorfman, John, et al. Well-Being: An Introduction to Health. 1980. pap. text ed. 11.95x (ISBN 0-673-15088-7). Scott F.
Dougherty, Bro. Patricius & Leifer, Sr. Carmel. Review Text in Health. (30 Line Drawings, Index, 336p). (gr. 7-12). 1962. pap. text ed. 5.58 (ISBN 0-87720-161-7). AMSCO Sch.
Dunglison, Robley. Human Health. Rosenkrantz, Barbara G., ed. LC 76-25660. (Public Health in America Ser.). 1977. Repr. of 1844 ed. lib. bdg. 26.00x (ISBN 0-405-09815-4). Arno.
Dunn, H. L. High Level Wellness. LC 61-1785. 1977. pap. 8.95 (ISBN 0-686-74259-1). C B Slack.
DuPont, Herbert & DuPont, Margaret. Travel with Health. (Appleton Consumer Health Guides). 195p. 1981. 13.95 (ISBN 0-8385-9009-8); pap. 7.95 (ISBN 0-8385-9008-X). ACC.
Dupuy, R. J., ed. The Right to Health As a Human Right: Colloquim 1978 of the Hague Academy of International Law. 513p. 1980. 40.00x (ISBN 90-286-1028-6). Sijthoff & Noordhoff.
Duskis, Ronald A. Back to Health. Johnson, Michael & Drill, Helen, eds. LC 79-91243. (Illus.). 1979. pap. text ed. 5.95 (ISBN 0-935670-00-9). Herrick Hse.
Easter, Jade. The Healing Handbook. (Illus.). 128p. (Orig.). 1981. pap. 6.95 (ISBN 0-913300-15-2). Unity Pr.
Eckholm, Erik P. The Picture of Health: Environmental Sources of Disease. 1977. 9.95 (ISBN 0-393-06434-4); pap. 4.95 (ISBN 0-393-06440-9). Norton.
Editorial Department of ARE. An Edgar Cayce Health Anthology. 198p. (Orig.). 1979. pap. 3.95 (ISBN 0-87604-119-5). ARE Pr.
Education, Health & Housing. 1979. text ed. 28.25x (ISBN 0-566-00298-1, Pub. by Gower Pub Co England). Renouf.
Eliopoulos, Nicholas C. Thine Health. Phystiklakis, Nicholas G., ed. (Orig.). 1980. pap. text ed. 18.00x (ISBN 0-9605396-2-X). Eliopoulos.
Elrick, Harold, et al. Living Longer & Better: Guide to Optimal Health. LC 78-366. (Illus.). 303p. 1978. pap. 5.95 (ISBN 0-89037-125-3). Anderson World.
Elwood, Catharyn. Feel Like a Million. 1.95 (ISBN 0-686-29914-0). Cancer Bk Hse.
Enger, Eldon D., et al. Essentials of Allied Health Science. 250p. 1978. pap. text ed. write for info. (ISBN 0-697-04547-1). Wm C Brown.
Ensor, Phyllis G., et al. Personal Health: Confronting Your Health Behavior. 1977. pap. text ed. 15.95 (ISBN 0-205-05737-3, 6257372); instr's manual avail. (ISBN 0-205-05738-1, 6257380). Allyn.
Essentials of Life & Health. 3rd ed. 425p. 1981. pap. text ed. 12.95 (ISBN 0-394-32570-2). Random.
Ewington, E. J. & Moore, D. F. Human Biology & Hygiene: Biology, Bk. 2. (Secondary Science Ser). (Illus., Orig.). (gr. 8-11). 1980. pap. 6.95 (ISBN 0-7100-7079-9). Routledge & Kegan.
Faber, Marilyn M. & Reinhardt, Adina M. Promoting Health Through Risk Reduction. 1982. text ed. 24.95 (ISBN 0-686-75046-2). Macmillan.
Fader, Wendy. Qualifying Procedures for Health Visitors. (General Ser.). (Orig.). 1977. pap. text ed. 13.75x (ISBN 0-85633-111-2, NFER). Humanities.
Fancher, Carlton M. Personal Ecology. 2nd ed. 272p. 1981. pap. text ed. 13.95 (ISBN 0-8403-2352-2). Kendall-Hunt.
Fassbender, William. You & Your Health. 2nd ed. LC 79-12472. 1980. text ed. 13.95 (ISBN 0-471-04936-0); tchrs' manual (ISBN 0-471-06384-3). Wiley.
Fast, Julius. Psyching up. LC 76-46584. 1978. 8.95 (ISBN 0-8128-2154-8). Stein & Day.
Feachem, Richard, et al. Water, Health & Development-an Interdisciplinary Evaluation. 286p. 1981. 35.00x (ISBN 0-905402-06-5, Pub. by Tri-Med England). State Mutual Bk.
Feel Younger, Live Longer. LC 76-56979. (Illus.). 1977. pap. 7.95 (ISBN 0-528-88195-7). Rand.
Feinman, Max L. & Wilson, Josleen. Live Longer. 1978. pap. 2.50 (ISBN 0-515-05722-3). Jove Pubns.
Feldenkrais, Moshe. Awareness Through Movement: Health Exercises for Personal Growth. LC 74-184419. 192p. 1972. 10.95 (ISBN 0-06-062345-4, HarpR). Har-Row.
Feldstein, M. S., et al. Resource Allocation Model for Public Health Planning: A Case Study of Tuberculosis Control. (WHO Bulletin Supplement: Vol. 48). (Summary in French). 1973. pap. 6.40 (ISBN 92-4-068481-6). World Health.
Ferguson, Tom. Medical Self-Care: Access to Health Tools. LC 80-14678. 320p. 1980. 19.95 (ISBN 0-671-40033-9); pap. 8.95 (ISBN 0-671-44816-1). Summit Bks.
Ferrara, Peter L. & Kahn, Frederick E. Natural Cures for Common Ills. 256p. Date not set. pap. 9.95 (ISBN 0-8329-0111-3). New Century.
Fink, Arlene & Kosecoff, Jacqueline. An Evaluation Primer Workbook: Practical Exercises for Health Professionals. LC 77-88463. (Illus.). 89p. 1980. pap. 8.95 (ISBN 0-8039-1482-2). Sage.
Fisher, M. F. A Cordiall Water: A Garland of Odd & Old Receipts to Assuage the Ills of Man & Beast. LC 80-28409. 160p. 1981. 10.00 (ISBN 0-86547-035-9); pap. 5.00 (ISBN 0-86547-036-7). N Point Pr.
Fitch, Kenneth & Johnson, Perry. Human Life Science. LC 76-46987. 1977. text ed. 22.95 (ISBN 0-03-018876-8, HoltC). HR&W.
Flatto, Edwin. Look Younger, Think Clearer, Live Longer. 1978. pap. 3.95 (ISBN 0-935540-04-0). Plymouth Pr.
--The Restoration of Health: Nature's Way. 1970. 9.95 (ISBN 0-935540-03-2). Plymouth Pr.
Flaxman, Ruth. Health Hints. 160p. 1981. pap. 4.95 (ISBN 0-8256-3238-2, Quick Fox). Music Sales.
Flynn, Patricia A. Holistic Health: The Art & Science of Care. (Illus.). 259p. 1980. pap. text ed. 12.95 (ISBN 0-87619-626-1). R J Brady.
Forbes, Alec. Try Being Healthy. 184p. 1976. pap. 5.50x (ISBN 0-8464-1057-5). Beekman Pubs.
Foresman, Ethel. Health & Happiness Are Twins. 1961. 3.95 (ISBN 0-8315-0034-4). Speller.
Franklyn, Robert A. & Gould, Helen. The Art of Staying Young. 1967. pap. 1.00 (ISBN 0-671-10197-8, Fireside). S&S.
Fredericks, Carlton. Look Younger, Feel Healthier. 2.95 (ISBN 0-686-29925-6). Cancer Bk Hse.
French, Ruth. Dynamics of Health Care. 3rd ed. (Illus.). 1979. pap. text ed. 7.95 (ISBN 0-07-022143-X, HP). McGraw.
Furst, Jeffrey. The Over Twenty Nine Health Book. LC 79-12269. (Illus.). 1979. pap. 5.95 (ISBN 0-915442-79-5, Unilaw). Donning Co.
Gall, Morris. Health & Leisure. new ed. LC 73-83981. (Consumer Education Ser). (Illus., Orig.). (gr. 7-12). 1973. pap. text ed. 1.45 (ISBN 0-88301-120-4). Pendulum Pr.
Gandhi, M. K. The Health Guide. LC 78-2592. 1978. 7.95 (ISBN 0-89594-005-1); pap. 4.95 (ISBN 0-89594-002-7). Crossing Pr.
Garrison, Omar. Dicto Crats, Our Unelected Rulers. 1.25 (ISBN 0-686-29926-4). Cancer Bk Hse.
Gay, John, et al. Current Health Problems. LC 77-72798. 1979. pap. 9.95 (ISBN 0-7216-4057-5). HR&W.
Gentile, Augustine. Physician Visits-Volume & Interval Since Last Visit: United States-1975. Stevenson, Taloria, ed. (Ser. 10: No. 128). 1978. pap. text ed. 1.75 (ISBN 0-8406-0150-6). Natl Ctr Health Stats.
Germann, Donald R. Too Young to Die. LC 74-84337. 1974. 9.95 (ISBN 0-87863-081-3). Farnswth Pub.
Gibson, John. Health, Personal & Communal. 4th ed. (Illus.). 206p. 1976. 8.95 (ISBN 0-571-04908-7, Pub. by Faber & Faber); pap. 4.95 (ISBN 0-571-04909-5). Merrimack Bk Serv.
Gilbert, Mitchell. An Owner's Manual for the Human Being. 1980. pap. 4.95 (ISBN 0-686-69316-7). Weiser.
Gillie, Oliver & Mercer, Derrick. The Complete Book of Body Maintenance. (Illus.). 1980. 19.95 (ISBN 0-393-01267-0); pap. 9.95 (ISBN 0-393-00941-6). Norton.
Gimbel, Theo. Healing Through Colour. 108p. 1980. 23.95x (ISBN 0-8464-1017-6). Beekman Pubs.
Gish, Oscar. Doctor Migration & World Health. 151p. 1971. pap. text ed. 6.75x (ISBN 0-7135-1611-9, Pub. by Bedford England). Renouf.
Gmur, B. Making Health Decisions. 2nd ed. 1975. 15.96 (ISBN 0-13-547927-4). P-H.
Go to Health. 1973. pap. 3.95 (ISBN 0-440-53070-9, Delta). Dell.
Goldberg, Philip. Executive Health. (A BusinessWeek Bk.). 1979. pap. 4.95 (ISBN 0-07-023638-0). McGraw.
Goldwag, E. M., et al, eds. The Joy of Life. (Octopus Book). (Illus.). 1978. 19.95 (ISBN 0-7064-0755-5, Mayflower Bks); pap. 8.95 (ISBN 0-7064-0897-7). Smith Pubs.
Gomez, Joan. How Not to Die Young. LC 79-160343. 1972. 25.00x (ISBN 0-8128-1418-5). Stein & Day.
Good Health Club Handbook for Doctors & Nurses. 1981. 5.95 (ISBN 0-913290-34-3). Camaro Pub.
Good Housekeeping Editors. Family Health & Medical Guide. LC 78-51129. (Illus.). 960p. 1979. 22.95 (ISBN 0-87851-023-0). Hearst Bks.
Gore, Irene. Add Years to Your Life & Life to Your Years. LC 73-92183. 1975. pap. 1.95 (ISBN 0-8128-1849-0). Stein & Day.
Gray, Stephen E. & Matson, Hollis N. Health Now. (Illus.). 352p. 1976. pap. text ed. 9.95 (ISBN 0-02-346140-3, 34614). Macmillan.
Greenwald, Howard P. Social Problems in Cancer Control. LC 79-15385. 304p. 1979. reference 24.50 (ISBN 0-88410-708-6). Ballinger Pub.
Griffin, LaDean. Is Any Sick Among You? 7.95 (ISBN 0-686-29930-2). Cancer Bk Hse.
--Is Any Sick Among You. 8.95 (ISBN 0-89557-001-7). Bi World Indus.
Grinims, Mark & Fischman, Walter. M.R.T. Music Response Test. LC 78-15488. (Illus.). 1979. 9.95 (ISBN 0-399-90011-X). Marek.
Guggenheim, B., ed. Health & Sugar Substitutes. 1979. pap. 57.50 (ISBN 3-8055-2961-9). S Karger.
Guild, W., et al. Science of Health. 1969. 16.95 (ISBN 0-13-794818-2). P-H.
Gwatkin, Davidson R. & Wilcox, Janet R. Can Health & Nutrition Interventions Make a Difference? LC 80-80500. 76p. 1980. pap. 5.00 (ISBN 0-686-28117-9). Overseas Dev Council.
Haas, Elson. Staying Healthy with the Seasons. LC 80-69469. (Illus.). 192p. (Orig.). 1981. pap. 9.95 (ISBN 0-89087-306-2). Celestial Arts.
Hafen, Brent Q., et al. Health Perspectives. LC 78-18283. (Illus.). 1979. pap. 12.95x (ISBN 0-8425-1280-2). Brigham.
Halpern, Reuben & Halpern, Joshua. Live Your Health: The Art & Practice of Holistic Healing. (Healing Arts Ser.). 220p. 1980. 10.95 (ISBN 0-89496-028-8); pap. 5.95 (ISBN 0-89496-020-2). Ross Bks.
Hamill, Peter V., et al. Forced Vital Capacity of Children 6-11 Years, United States. (Series 11, No. 164). 1977. pap. text ed. 1.75 (ISBN 0-8406-0102-6). Natl Ctr Health Stats.
Harihar Das, Swami & Ito, Dee. The Healthy Body Handbook: A Basic Guide to Diet & Nutrition, Yoga for Health, & Natural Cures for a Healthy Body. LC 79-2802. (Illus.). 1980. pap. 5.95 (ISBN 0-06-090730-4, CN 730, CN). Har-Row.
Harmer, Ruth. American Medical Avarice "Live As You Go". 8.95 (ISBN 0-686-29736-9). Cancer Bk Hse.
Haro, Michael S., et al. Explorations in Personal Health. LC 76-10900. (Illus.). 1977. text ed. 15.75 (ISBN 0-395-24478-1); inst. manual 1.25 (ISBN 0-395-24479-X). HM.
Harris. Overdrive: A Human Maintenance Manual. 1978. 5.95 (ISBN 0-7153-7399-4). David & Charles.
Hasler, Doris & Hasler, Norman B. Personal, Home & Community Health. (Orig.). 1967. pap. text ed. 8.95 (ISBN 0-02-351650-X). Macmillan.
Hauser, Gayelord. Gayelord Hauser's New Treasury of Secrets. 432p. 1978. pap. 2.95 (ISBN 0-449-24026-6, Crest). Fawcett.
--Mirror, Mirror on the Wall: An Invitation to Beauty. (Illus.). 364p. 1961. 5.95 (ISBN 0-374-21009-8). FS&G.
Hauser, Gaylord. Gaylord Hauser's New Treasury of Secrets. rev. ed. LC 74-22102. 424p. 1974. 8.95 (ISBN 0-374-22150-2). FS&G.
Hayden, Naura. Energy: Always Wanted to Know. 1.95 (ISBN 0-686-29741-5). Cancer Bk Hse.
Health, 5 pts. Incl. Pt. 1. General, 17 vols. Set. 1494.00x (ISBN 0-686-01159-7); Pt. 2. Food & Drugs, 5 vols. Set. 423.00x (ISBN 0-686-01160-0); Pt. 3. Infectious Diseases, 13 vols. Set. 1242.00x (ISBN 0-686-01161-9); Pt. 4. Medical Profession, 5 vols. Set. 342.00x (ISBN 0-686-01162-7); Pt. 5. Mental, 8 vols. Set. 558.00x (ISBN 0-686-01163-5). (British Parliamentary Papers Ser.). 1971 (Pub. by Irish Academic Pr Ireland). Biblio Dist.
Health Aspects of Human Rights with Special Reference to Developments in Biology & Medicine. (Also avail. in French). 1976. pap. 4.00 (ISBN 92-4-156050-9). World Health.

Heath, Gordon R. Live Longer & Love It. LC 80-81595. (Illus.). 78p. (Orig.). 1980. pap. 5.95 (ISBN 0-937092-00-2). Methuselah Bks.
Hegne, Barbara. Everywoman's Every Day Exercise & Nutrition Book. LC 78-57649. (Illus.). 1979. pap. 10.95 (ISBN 0-87983-152-9). Keats.
Heller, Alfred L. Your Body, His Temple. 192p. 1981. pap. 4.95 (ISBN 0-8407-5769-7). Nelson.
Henkel, Barbara O., et al. Foundations of Health Science. 3rd ed. 1977. text ed. 19.95 (ISBN 0-205-05739-X). Allyn.
Henry, J. P. & Stephens, P. M. Stress, Health, & the Social Environment: A Sociobiologic Approach to Medicine. LC 77-10500. (Topics in Environmental Physiology & Medicine). (Illus.). 1977. 37.80 (ISBN 0-387-90293-7). Springer Verlag.
Hepner, J. O. Case Studies in Health Administration, 2 vols. Incl. Vol. 1. Health Planning for Emerging Multi-Hospital Systems. LC 77-17008. (Illus.). 1978. pap. text ed. 15.95 (ISBN 0-8016-2156-9); Vol. 2. Hospital Administrator-Physician Relationships. LC 80-16073. 1980. pap. text ed. 22.95 (ISBN 0-8016-2158-5). Mosby.
Ho, Betty Y. A Chinese & Western Guide to Better Health & Longer Life. LC 74-12332. (Orig.). 1974. pap. 2.00 (ISBN 0-87576-046-5). Pilot Bks.
--A Chinese & Western Guide to Better Health & Longer Life. LC 74-12332. pap. 2.00 (ISBN 0-87576-046-5). Juvenescent.
--How to Stay Healthy a Lifetime Without Medicines. LC 77-86248. 1979. pap. 10.00 (ISBN 0-9600148-3-7). Juvenescent.
--Scientific Guide to Peaceful Living. LC 77-142457. (Illus., Orig.). 1973. pap. 7.50 (ISBN 0-9600148-2-9). Juvenescent.
Hochbaum, Godfrey M. Health Behavior. 1970. pap. 5.95x (ISBN 0-534-00662-0). Wadsworth Pub.
Hoffman, Norman S. A New World of Health. (Illus.). 1976. pap. text ed. 10.95 (ISBN 0-07-029203-5, C); instructor's manual 3.95 (ISBN 0-07-029204-3). McGraw.
Holmes, Ernest. This Thing Called You. 1948. 4.95 (ISBN 0-396-02867-5). Dodd.
Homola, Samuel. Secrets of Naturally Youthful Health & Vitality. LC 70-152523. (Illus.). 1971. 10.95 (ISBN 0-13-797514-7, Parker). P-H.
Hood, Lamartine F. & Wardrip, E. K. Carbohydrates & Health. (Illus.). 1977. text ed. 23.50 (ISBN 0-87055-223-6). AVI.
Hoover, J. Gary & Maher, Charles A., eds. School Psychology & Program Evaluation. 1979. pap. 8.95 (ISBN 0-87705-387-1). Human Sci Pr.
Hosford, Bowen. Who's in Charge of This Body Anyhow? LC 81-40464. 250p. 1981. 10.95 (ISBN 0-8044-5502-3). Ungar.
Hrachovec, Josef P. Keeping Young & Living Longer. 256p. 1972. 6.95 (ISBN 0-8202-0150-2). Sherbourne.
Huber, Helen, et al. Homemaker-Home Health Aide. LC 78-66616. 1980. pap. 8.80 (ISBN 0-8273-1704-2); instr's. guide 1.50 (ISBN 0-8273-1705-0). Delmar.
Hughes, David T. & Marshall, P. T. Human Health, Biology & Hygiene. LC 79-128501. (Illus.). 1970. text ed. 8.50x (ISBN 0-521-07731-1). Cambridge U Pr.
Hunter, Beatrice T., et al. Your Natural Health Sampler. LC 73-80031. (Pivot Health Bk.). 128p. 1973. pap. 1.25 (ISBN 0-87983-058-1). Keats.
Hunter, Charles & Hunter, Frances. How to Heal the Sick. 208p. 1981. pap. 4.95 (ISBN 0-917726-40-5). Hunter Bks.
Hurdle, J. Frank. A Country Doctor's Common Sense Health Manual. 1976. 8.95 (ISBN 0-13-184358-3, Reward); pap. 3.45 (ISBN 0-13-184341-9). P-H.
Hyman, Herbert H. Health Planing: A System Approach. 2nd ed. 550p. 1981. text ed. price not set (ISBN 0-89443-379-2). Aspen Systems.
Hynovich, Debra & Barnard, Martha. Family Health Care, Vol. II. 1979. pap. text ed. 8.95 (ISBN 0-07-031676-7, HP). McGraw.
Idleman, H. K. & Stanton, E. N. Health, Education & Recreation. (Contemporary Consumer Ser.). 1974. text ed. 4.24 (ISBN 0-07-031698-8, G); tchr's manual & key 4.95 (ISBN 0-07-031699-6). McGraw.
Insel, Paul M. & Roth, Walton T. Core Concepts in Health. 2nd ed. LC 78-71611. 1979. pap. text ed. 14.95 (ISBN 0-87484-498-3). Mayfield Pub.
--Health in a Changing Society. LC 75-39358. (Illus.). 584p. 1976. text ed. 17.95 (ISBN 0-87484-361-8). Mayfield Pub.
Instructional Aides, Inc. Health--a Concern of Every American. (Instructional Aides Ser.). 1981. pap. 9.95 (ISBN 0-936474-10-6). Instruct Aides TX.
International Conference of National Committees on Vital & Health Statistics. Copenhagen, 1973, 2nd. New Approaches in Health Statistics: Report. (Technical Report Ser.: No. 559). (Also avail. in French & Spanish). 1974. pap. 2.00 (ISBN 92-4-120559-8). World Health.
Isaacs, Benno & Kobler, Jay. The Nickolaus Technique: What It Takes to Feel Good. LC 79-6559. (Illus.). 160p. 1980. pap. 5.95 (ISBN 0-89104-173-7). A & W Pubs.
Jansky, Robert C. Astrology, Nutrition & Health. Anderson, Margaret, ed. 1977. pap. 6.95 (ISBN 0-914918-08-7). Para Res.
Jazairi, N. T. Approaches to the Development of Health Indicators: Special Studies, No. 2. (Social Indicator Development Programme Ser.). 1976. 3.00x (ISBN 92-64-11493-9). OECD.
Jensen, Bernard. World Keys to Health & Long Life. 5.95 (ISBN 0-89557-020-3). Bi World Indus.
Jensen, Bernard D. Survive-This Day. 5.95 (ISBN 0-686-29763-6). Cancer Bk Hse.
--World Keys to Health. 6.95 (ISBN 0-686-29761-X). Cancer Bk Hse.
--You Can Master Disease. 4.95 (ISBN 0-686-29760-1). Cancer Bk Hse.
Jensen, William E. & Winters, Donna. Keep Healthy Keep Active. 1979. pap. 1.95 (ISBN 0-910286-73-6). Boxwood.
Jiyu-Kennett, Roshi & MacPhillamy, Daizui. The Book of Life. (Illus.). 1979. pap. 7.95 (ISBN 0-930066-04-9). Shasta Abbey.
Johns, Edward B., et al. Health for Effective Living. 6th ed. (Illus.). 512p. 1975. pap. text ed. 12.50 (ISBN 0-07-032572-3, C); 4.95 (ISBN 0-07-032574-X). McGraw.
Johnson. Your Guide to Better Health, Greater Energy. 1944. 1.50 (ISBN 0-910140-28-6). Anthony.
Johnson, Bruce L. Chinese Wand Exercise. LC 77-3534. (Illus.). 1979. pap. 4.50 (ISBN 0-688-08183-5, Quill). Morrow.
Johnson, G. Timothy & Goldfinger, Stephen E., eds. The Harvard Medical School Health Letter Book. LC 80-27215. (Illus.). 460p. 1981. 15.95 (ISBN 0-686-71097-5). Harvard U Pr.
Jones, Boisfeuillet, ed. Health of Americans. LC 70-120793. 1970. 5.95 (ISBN 0-13-385070-6); pap. 2.45 (ISBN 0-13-385062-5). Am Assembly.
Jones, David A. The Health Risks of Imprisonment. LC 76-5620. (Illus.). 1976. 21.50 (ISBN 0-669-00651-3). Lexington Bks.
Jones, Kenneth L., et al. Dimensions: A Changing Concept of Health. 4th ed. LC 78-26220. 1979. pap. text ed. 16.50 scp (ISBN 0-06-043438-4, HarpC). Har-Row.
--Health Science. 4th ed. 1978. text ed. 20.95 scp (ISBN 0-06-043432-5, HarpC); inst. manual free (ISBN 0-06-363434-1). Har-Row.
--Principles of Health Science. 2nd ed. (Illus.). 1980. pap. text ed. 16.95 scp (ISBN 0-06-043437-6, HarpC); instr's. resource manual free. Har-Row.
Jordan, Sara M. Health & Happiness. 1962. 5.95 (ISBN 0-8159-5702-5). Devin.
Josephson, Elmer A. God's Key to Health & Happiness. 1976. pap. 3.95 (ISBN 0-8007-5018-7, Spower Bks). Revell.
Joyce, Verner F. The Management of Your Body. (The International Council for Excellence in Management Library). (Illus.). 113p. 1980. plastic spiral bdg. 28.45 (ISBN 0-89266-250-6). Am Classical Coll Pr.
Kaibara, Ekiken. Yojokun: Japanese Secret of Good Health. 1974. 9.95 (ISBN 0-89346-101-6, Pub. by Tokuma Shoten); pap. 2.95 (ISBN 0-89346-047-8). Heian Intl.
Katch, Frank I., et al. Getting in Shape: An Optimum Approach to Fitness & Weight Control. 1979. 7.95 (ISBN 0-395-27782-5). HM.
Kathren, Ronald L. Health Physics: A Backward Glance. 1980. text ed. 28.00 (ISBN 0-08-021531-9). Pergamon.
Kiell, Paul J. & Frelinghuysen, Joseph. Keep Your Heart Running. 1976. 11.95 (ISBN 0-87691-182-3). Winchester Pr.
Kime, Zane R. Sunlight Could Save Your Life. LC 80-51038. 312p. 1980. 15.95 (ISBN 0-9604268-0-9); pap. 11.95 (ISBN 0-9604268-1-7). World Health.
Kiphuth, Robert. How to Be Fit: New Revised Edition with Exercises for Men & Women. (Illus.). 1963. 14.50x (ISBN 0-300-00628-4). Yale U Pr.
Kirban, Salem. Health Guide for Survival. (Illus.). 1976. 7.95 (ISBN 0-912582-24-3); pap. 3.95 (ISBN 0-685-67495-9). Kirban.
Kirschner, H. E. Nature's Seven Doctors. 2.45 (ISBN 0-686-29770-9). Cancer Bk Hse.
Klingbeil, Reinhold L. Hazards to Health. LC 78-17381. (Better Living Ser.). 1978. pap. 0.95 (ISBN 0-8127-0185-2). Review & Herald.
Kloss, Jethro. Back to Eden. 2.50 (ISBN 0-686-29774-1). Cancer Bk Hse.
--Back to Eden. 1981. pap. 2.95 (ISBN 0-87904-000-9). Lust.
Kogan, Benjamin. Health. 3rd ed. 511p. 1980. pap. text ed. 13.95 (ISBN 0-15-535588-0, HC); instructor's manual avail. (ISBN 0-15-535585-6). HarBraceJ.
Kogan, Gerald. Your Body Works. LC 81-10938. (Illus.). 184p. 1981. pap. 9.95 (ISBN 0-915904-57-8). And-or Pr.
Konecci, Eugene B., ed. Health Care Systems. (Science & Technology Ser.: Vol. 32). (Illus.). 262p. 1974. lib. bdg. 25.00 (ISBN 0-87703-067-7). Am Astronaut.
Kordel, Lelord. Stay Alive Longer. 2nd ed. 224p. 1977. pap. 1.50 (ISBN 0-532-15182-8). Woodhill.
Krimm, Irwinn F. Health, Success & Happiness for You. LC 56-12200. 3.50 (ISBN 0-686-08991-X). Happy Health.
Kugler, Hans J. Dr. Kugler's Seven Keys to a Longer Life. 1979. pap. 2.25 (ISBN 0-449-23811-3, Crest). Fawcett.
--Your First Hundred Years of Health: A Practical Guide to Preventive Medicine. LC 78-56945. 1979. cancelled (ISBN 0-8128-2524-1). Stein & Day.
Kulvinskas, Viktoras. Survival into the Twenty-First Century. Hurlbut, Hermine & Newman, Joan, eds. (Illus.). 1975. pap. 12.95 (ISBN 0-933278-04-7). OMango.
Kunin, Richard A. Mega-Nutrition: The New Prescription for Maximum Health, Energy & Longevity. 1981. pap. 6.95 (ISBN 0-452-25271-7, Plume). NAL.
Kuntzleman, Charles T. Maximum Personal Energy: Enjoy Life More, Keep Fit & Eat Well Through Your Choice of Energy Plans. Wallace, Dan, ed. (Illus.). 256p. 1981. 14.95 (ISBN 0-87857-364-X); pap. 11.95 (ISBN 0-87857-363-1). Rodale Pr Inc.
Kunz-Bircher, Ruth. The Bircher-Benner Health Guide. Shed, Rosemarie, tr. from Fr. LC 80-93644. Orig. Title: Le Guide De Sante Bircher. 160p. 1980. pap. 3.95 (ISBN 0-912800-87-9). Woodbridge Pr.
Kushi, Michio. Natural Healing Through Macrobiotics. LC 79-1959. (Illus.). 1979. pap. 10.95 (ISBN 0-87040-457-1). Japan Pubns.
Lambing, Mary Lou & King, Mary Frances. On the Health Scene. LC 75-44060. 1976. text ed. 6.95 (ISBN 0-8261-2090-3). Springer Pub.
Lande, Nathaniel. Self-Health: The Lifelong Fitness Book. LC 79-14671. (Illus.). 192p. 1980. 9.95 (ISBN 0-03-048316-6). HR&W.
LaPlace, John. Health. 3rd ed. (Illus.). 1980. text ed. 14.95 (ISBN 0-13-385393-4); cloth 17.95 (ISBN 0-13-385427-2). P-H.
Larson, Bruce. There's a Lot More to Health Than Not Being Sick. 1981. 6.95 (ISBN 0-686-72234-5). Word Bks.
Lauersen, Niels. Listen to Your Body. (Illus.). 256p. (Orig.). 1981. pap. 7.95 (ISBN 0-671-43648-1, Fireside). S&S.
Lawson-Wood, D. & Lawson-Wood, J. Glowing Health Through Diet & Posture. 62p. 1973. pap. 2.50x (ISBN 0-686-68110-X). Beekman Pubs.
Leblond, Wilfrid. Hygiene: Manuel De Medicine Preventive. (Fr). 1964. 12.00x (ISBN 2-7637-6511-4, Pub. by Laval). Intl Schol Bk Serv.
Lebowitz, Gordon. Exploring Health Careers Ser., Bk. 1: You & a Health Career. 128p. 1973. 3.00 (ISBN 0-87005-115-6); tchrs' guide 1.50 (ISBN 0-87005-125-3). Fairchild.
Lehrer, Steven. Explorers of the Body. LC 78-14685. 1979. 12.95 (ISBN 0-385-13497-5). Doubleday.
Leichtman, Robert R. & Japikse, Carl. The Way to Health. (Art of Living Ser.). 90p. Date not set. pap. 3.00 (ISBN 0-89804-037-X). Ariel Pr.
Leonard, George. The Silent Pulse. 208p. 1981. pap. 2.95 (ISBN 0-553-14368-9). Bantam.
Leonard, Jon N., et al. Live Longer Now. 236p. 1981. pap. 2.50 (ISBN 0-441-48516-2, Pub. by Charter Bks). Ace Bks.
Levin, Arthur & Rapoport, Mitchell, eds. Focus on Health: Issues & Events of 1978 from the New York Times Information Bank. LC 78-31464. (News in Print Ser.). 1979. lib. bdg. 24.95x (ISBN 0-405-12874-6). Arno.
Levin, Lowell S., et al. Self-Care: Lay Initiatives in Health. LC 76-29361. 1976. 15.00 (ISBN 0-686-57948-8); pap. 7.95 (ISBN 0-88202-111-7). N Watson.
Levine, Seymour & Ursin, Holger, eds. Coping & Health. (NATO Conference Ser.: Series III: Human Factors, Volume 12). 370p. 1980. 35.00 (ISBN 0-306-40422-2, Plenum Pr). Plenum Pub.
Lewin, Stephen, ed. Nation's Health. (Reference Shelf Ser: Vol. 43, No. 3). 1971. 6.25 (ISBN 0-8242-0448-4). Wilson.
Linde, Shirley. Wholehealth Catalogue. 6.95 (ISBN 0-686-29785-7). Cancer Bk Hse.
Linde, Shirley M. The Whole Health Catalogue. LC 77-77890. 1978. 12.95 (ISBN 0-89256-012-6); pap. 6.95 (ISBN 0-89256-035-5). Rawson Wade.
Lindegren, Carl C. The Theory & Practice of Natural Healing. LC 80-50132. 1981. 7.95 (ISBN 0-533-04595-9). Vantage.
Lindlahr, Victor H. The Natural Way to Health. LC 80-19863. 255p. 1980. Repr. of 1973 ed. lib. bdg. 9.95x (ISBN 0-89370-617-5). Borgo Pr.
--The Natural Way to Health. 255p. 1973. pap. 2.95 (ISBN 0-87877-017-8, H-17). Newcastle Pub.
Lindsay, Gordon. How You Can Have Divine Health. (Divine Healing & Health Ser.). 0.95 (ISBN 0-89985-027-8). Christ Nations.
Litchfield, Harry R. Live & Be Well. LC 72-76583. 300p. 1972. 6.00 (ISBN 0-87212-022-8). Libra.
Lobb, Nancy. Basic Health, Bk. 1. 1979. pap. 2.50x (ISBN 0-88323-155-7, 244). Richards Pub.
London, Mel. Easy Going: A Guide to Good Health & Good Spirits on Your Journey Away from Home. (Illus.). 320p. (Orig.). 1981. 12.95 (ISBN 0-87857-331-3); pap. 9.95 (ISBN 0-87857-345-3). Rodale Pr Inc.
Lumiere, Cornel. Feeling Younger Longer. Brand, Eileen, ed. LC 72-76846. 224p. 1973. 7.95 (ISBN 0-8184-0032-3). Lyle Stuart.
Lunin, Lois F., ed. Health Sciences & Services: A Guide to Information Sources. LC 77-80614. (Management Information Guide Ser.: No. 36). 1979. 36.00 (ISBN 0-8103-0836-3). Gale.
Lupus, Peter & Homola, Samuel. Peter Lupus' Guide to Radiant Health & Beauty: Mission Possible for Women. (Illus.). 1977. 9.95 (ISBN 0-13-661884-7, Parker). P-H.
Lust, John B. Lust for Living. 1978. pap. 2.95 (ISBN 0-87904-036-X). Lust.
Lynch, L. Riddick, ed. Cross-Cultural Approach to Health Behavior. LC 73-84199. 356p. 1970. 20.00 (ISBN 0-8386-7439-9); pap. 8.95 (ISBN 0-8386-1377-2). Fairleigh Dickinson.
Lynch, Richard. Secret of Health. 1.00 (ISBN 0-87159-143-X). Unity Bks.
Lyon, Lisa & Hall, Douglas K. Lisa Lyon's Body Magic. LC 80-70864. (Illus.). 183p. 1981. pap. 9.95 (ISBN 0-553-01296-7). Bantam.
McCaughan, Lindsay. Five Phase Fitness: A Handbook to Health. 1976. 4.40x (ISBN 0-7233-0419-X). Intl Pubns Serv.
McCoy, Kathy & Wibbelsman, Charles. The Teenage Body Book. (gr. 9-12). 1979. pap. 5.95 (ISBN 0-671-79012-9, Wallaby). PB.
McGee, Charles T. How to Survive Modern Technology. LC 80-82327. 256p. (Orig.). 1981. pap. 2.95 (ISBN 0-87983-230-4). Keats.
Machan, Lorraine. The Practitioner-Teacher Role: Practice What You Teach. LC 80-80814. (Nursing Dimensions Education Ser.). 185p. 1980. pap. text ed. 9.50 (ISBN 0-913654-65-5). Nursing Res.
Machinery & Allied Products Institute Seminar on Occupational Safety & Health, Washington, D.C., 1973. Occupational Safety & Health: A Transcript. LC 73-166354. 173p. 1973. 15.00 (ISBN 0-686-05728-7). M & A Products.
MacKichan, N. D. The GP & the Primary Health Care Team. (Illus.). 1976. text ed. 22.00x (ISBN 0-685-83074-8). State Mutual Bk.
McMillen, S. I. None of These Diseases. (Orig.). pap. 1.50 (ISBN 0-515-04604-3). Jove Pubns.
McMurtray, Frances. Allied Health Reading Vocabulary Workbook. 1978. pap. text ed. 3.95x (ISBN 0-89641-008-0). American Pr.
McVerry, V. Early Warning Health Guide. 1977. pap. 4.95 (ISBN 0-89019-058-5). O'Sullivan Woodside.
Malasanos, Lois. Health Assessment. 2nd ed. LC 80-27518. (Illus.). 723p. 1981. text ed. 24.95 (ISBN 0-8016-3073-8). Mosby.
Marten, Michael & Chesterman, John. Man to Man: New Answers to Old Questions About Your Health, Fitness & Sexuality. LC 78-8292. 1978. 8.95 (ISBN 0-448-22681-2). Paddington.
Martin, W. Coda. A Matter of Life. 1965. 4.95 (ISBN 0-8159-6202-9). Devin.
Martine, Yvonne. Health, Youth, & Beauty Through Color Breathing. 1977. pap. 1.50 (ISBN 0-425-03792-4, Medallion). Berkley Pub.
--Health, Youth, & Beauty Through Color Breathing. 1977. pap. 1.50 (ISBN 0-425-03792-4, Medallion). Berkley Pub.
Maxwell, Jessica. The Eye-Body Connection. (Illus., Orig.). 1980. pap. 6.95 (ISBN 0-446-87950-9). Warner Bks.
Mazzanti, Deborah S. Secrets of the Golden Door. rev. ed. 1979. pap. 2.95 (ISBN 0-553-12695-4). Bantam.
--Secrets of the Golden Door. LC 77-2722. 1977. 12.50 (ISBN 0-688-03237-0). Morrow.
Mellor, Constance. How to Be Healthy, Wealthy & Wise. 112p. 1976. pap. 6.00x (ISBN 0-8464-1023-0). Beekman Pubs.
Messenger, David L. & Souter, John C. Dr. Messenger's Guide to Better Health. 1981. 9.95 (ISBN 0-8007-1113-0). Revell.

Messing, Simon D., ed. Target of Health in Ethiopia: A Holistic Reader in Applied Anthropology. 285p. 1973. text ed. 29.50x (ISBN 0-8422-5074-3); pap. text ed. 12.50x (ISBN 0-8422-0261-7). Irvington.

Miller, B. F., et al. Investigating Your Health. new ed. LC 74-111257. (Illus.). 564p. 1974. text ed. 11.25 (ISBN 0-395-17078-8, 2-37394). HM.

Miller, Benjamin F., et al. Freedom from Heart Attacks. 1972. 7.95 (ISBN 0-671-21319-9); pap. 4.95 (ISBN 0-671-21759-3). S&S.

Miller, Don E. Bodymind. 1980. pap. 1.95 (ISBN 0-523-40858-7). Pinnacle Bks.

Miller, Fred. Passport to Better Health Through Eating. Date not set. pap. 3.95 (ISBN 0-89404-028-6). Aztex.

Miller, Jonas E. Prescription for Total Health & Longevity. 1979. 2.95 (ISBN 0-88270-353-6). Logos.

Monteiro, Lois A. Monitoring Health Status & Medical Care. LC 76-2483. 144p. 1976. text ed. 17.50 (ISBN 0-88410-106-1). Ballinger Pub.

Moore, Marcia & Douglas, Mark. Diet, Sex & Yoga. rev. ed. LC 66-28086. (Illus.). 1970. 10.00 (ISBN 0-912240-00-8). Arcane Pubns.

Morrison, Marsh. Doctor Morrison's Miracle Body Tune-up for Rejuvenated Health. 1977. 12.95 (ISBN 0-13-216341-1, Reward); pap. 2.95 (ISBN 0-13-216358-6). P-H.

Moynihan, Fergus & Moynihan, Liz. The Positive Way to Good Health. 1977. 8.95 (ISBN 0-236-40030-4, Pub. by Paul Elek). Merrimack Bk Serv.

Mulcahy, Risteard. Beat Heart Disease! LC 78-24490. (Positive Health Guide Ser.). (Illus.). 1979. 8.95 (ISBN 0-668-04678-3, 4678-3); pap. 4.95 (ISBN 0-668-04685-6, 4685-6). Arco.

Murata, Alice K. & Farquhar, Judith, eds. Issues in Pacific-Asian American Health & Mental Health. (Occasional Paper Ser.). (Orig.). 1981. pap. write for info. (ISBN 0-934584-10-9). Pacific-Asian.

Murdock, George P. Theories of Illness: A World Survey. LC 80-5257. (Illus.). 160p. 1980. 9.95 (ISBN 0-8229-3428-0). U of Pittsburgh Pr.

Murray, Al & Bettsworth, Mike. Towards Total Health: A Realistic Approach to Better Living. (Illus.). 144p. 1981. 16.95 (ISBN 0-7134-3413-9, Pub. by Batsford England). David & Charles.

Mushkin, Selma J. & Dunlop, David W., eds. Health: What Is It Worth? Measures of Health Benefits. (Pergamon Policy Studies). 1979. 19.25 (ISBN 0-08-023898-X). Pergamon.

Napoli, Maryann. Health Facts: A Critical Evaluation of the Major Problems, Treatments, & Alternatives Facing Medical Consumers. LC 81-2127. 352p. 1981. 15.00 (ISBN 0-87951-132-X). Overlook Pr.

National Negro Health News, Vol. 1-18. 1933-1950. Repr. 270.00x (ISBN 0-8371-9115-7, Pub. by Negro U Pr). Greenwood.

Nature's Big, Beautiful, Bountiful, Feel-Good Book. LC 76-24504. (Illus.). 1977. 11.95 (ISBN 0-87983-136-7); pap. 6.95 (ISBN 0-87983-133-2). Keats.

Neimark, Paul & Matlin, Samuel. Doctor Discusses Female Surgery. (Illus.). 1979. pap. 2.50 (ISBN 0-686-65550-8). Budlong.

Neimark, Paul G. & Schmidt, Jay. A Doctor Discusses How to Stay Young & Live Longer. (Illus.). 1977. pap. 2.50 (ISBN 0-685-46340-0). Budlong.

Nigh, Edward & Stark Research Associates. The Formula Book 3. new ed. (Formula Bks). (Illus.). 1978. 12.00 (ISBN 0-8362-2202-4); pap. 5.95 (ISBN 0-8362-2205-9). Andrews & McMeel.

NIH Factbook (National Institutes of Health) LC 75-32699. 1976. 44.50 (ISBN 0-8379-3401-X). Marquis.

Noder, Walter. Hablando De Actividad y Salud Despues De Cuarenta. (Medical Adviser Ser.). (Illus.). 1979. pap. 3.95 (ISBN 0-686-26833-4). Edit Pr Serv.

Norfolk, Donald. The Habits of Health: The Prudent Person's Guide to Well-Being. 224p. 1977. 9.95 (ISBN 0-312-35630-7). St Martin.

Nutrition Almanac. LC 75-4193. 1975. pap. 6.95 (ISBN 0-685-72753-X, Pub. by McGraw). Formur Intl.

Oehm, Rudolph. The Joy of Good Health. LC 80-65169. (Orig.). 1980. pap. 3.95 (ISBN 0-89081-222-5). Harvest Hse.

Oliver, Lincoln I. Association of Health Attitudes & Perceptions for Youths 12-17 Years of Age & Their Parents, United States, 1966-70. Stevenson, Taloria, ed. LC 76-7213. (Series 11: No. 161). 60p. 1976. pap. text ed. 1.25 (ISBN 0-8406-0071-2). Natl Ctr Health Stats.

Oppenheim, Mike. Common Sense Health: A Doctor's Frank Prescriptions for Getting the Best Care for Less. 1981. 5.95 (ISBN 0-686-72115-2). Wideview Bks.

Ott, John. Light & Health. 7.50 (ISBN 0-686-29819-5). Cancer Bk Hse.

Ott, John N. The Dynamics of Color & Light: How They Affect Human Health & Behavior. (Illus.). 256p. 1981. 10.00 (ISBN 0-8159-5314-3). Devin.

Otto, James H., et al. Modern Health. rev. ed. (gr. 9-12). 1971. text ed. 14.00 (ISBN 0-03-084991-8, HoltE); tchr's ed. 18.64 (ISBN 0-03-080187-7); exercises 3.24 (ISBN 0-685-03787-8). HR&W.

Page, Melvin E. & Abrams, H. Leon, Jr. Your Body Is Your Best Doctor. (Pivot Health Book). Orig. Title: Health Versus Disease. 256p. 1972. pap. 1.95 (ISBN 0-87983-021-2). Keats.

Parizkova, J. Nutrition, Physical Fitness & Health. 1978. 26.95 (ISBN 0-8391-1263-7). Univ Park.

Parkhill, Joe. Health, Beauty & Happiness. spiral 5.95 (ISBN 0-936744-00-6). Green Hill.

Pearse, I. The Quality of Life. 272p. 1979. 15.00x (ISBN 0-7073-0141-6, Pub. by Scottish Academic Pr Scotland). Columbia U Pr.

Pearson, Durk. Life Extension: Adding Years to Your Life & Life to Your Years, a Practical Approach. (Orig.). 1981. 12.95 (ISBN 0-446-51229-X). Warner Bks.

Perkoff, Gerald T. Changing Health Care: Perspectives from a New Medical Care Setting. 1980. 18.50 (ISBN 0-914904-38-8). Health Admin Pr.

Petulengro, Leon. Herbs, Health & Astrology. LC 76-58769. (Living with Herbs Ser.: Vol. 1). (Illus.). 100p. 1977. pap. 2.50 (ISBN 0-87983-148-0). Keats.

Phillips, David A. From Soil to Psyche: Total Health for the New Age. LC 77-79907. (Orig.). 1977. pap. 4.95 (ISBN 0-912800-43-7). Woodbridge Pr.

Phillips, David S. Basic Statistics for Health Science Students. LC 77-13865. (Psychology Ser.). (Illus.). 1978. text ed. 14.95x (ISBN 0-7167-0051-4); pap. text ed. 7.95x (ISBN 0-7167-0050-6). W H Freeman.

Phillips, Phoebe & Hatch, Pamela. The Complete Book of Good Health: The Illustrated Family Guide to Diet, Fitness & Beauty. LC 78-4768. 1978. 12.95 (ISBN 0-690-01781-2). T Y Crowell.

Pilcher, Joseph. Fast Health. (Orig.). 1977. pap. cancelled (ISBN 0-425-03406-2, Medallion). Berkley Pub.

Pilsner, Ray C. Your Health & Life Are in Your Hands. 1974. pap. 2.75 (ISBN 0-685-57204-8). Byzantine Pr.

A Pocketguide to Health & Health Problems in School Physical Activities. LC 81-66886. 1981. pap. 4.50 (ISBN 0-917160-13-4). Am Sch Health.

Pohaska, Steve. Little Known Secrets: Health - Long Life. 1.45 (ISBN 0-686-29942-6). Cancer Bk Hse.

Pollock, Michael L., et al. Health & Fitness Through Physical Activity. LC 78-495. (College of Sports Medicine Ser). 1978. text ed. 16.50 (ISBN 0-471-69285-9). Wiley.

Ponder, Catherine. Dynamic Laws of Healing. 1972. pap. 4.95 (ISBN 0-87516-156-1). De Vorss.

Ports Designated in Applications of the International Health Regulations 1969: Situation As at 1 January 1974. 1974. 1.60 (ISBN 92-4-058003-4). World Health.

Powell, Eric F. Health from the Kitchen. 64p. 1969. pap. 2.50x (ISBN 0-8464-1018-4). Beekman Pubs.

Preas, Jerry L. You & Your Health: Large, Medium or Small. (Illus.). 96p. (Orig.). 1981. pap. 3.95 (ISBN 0-935622-06-3). Texan-Am Pub.

Priest, M. A. Modern Textbook of Personal & Communal Health for Nurses. 5th ed. 1979. pap. text ed. 14.95x (ISBN 0-433-26204-4). Intl Ideas.

Program On Hospital-Finance-Accounting And Administration - 26th. Financial Implications for Hospitals in Comprehensive Health Care Planning: Proceedings. Pressler, Stanley A., ed. (Business Paper Ser: No. 17). (Illus.). 1968. pap. 3.95 (ISBN 0-685-12533-5). Ind U Busn Res.

Prosser, Elizabeth. A to Z of Health, Sickness & First Aid. 1978. pap. 2.75 (ISBN 0-86072-012-8). Transatlantic.

Public Interest Economics Foundation. Benefits of Health & Safety Regulation. Ferguson, Allen R. & Behn, Judith, eds. 1981. 26.50 (ISBN 0-88410-721-3). Ballinger Pub.

Raeburn, Janet K. & Raeburn, H. A. Anatomy, Physiology & Hygiene. 4th ed. 1975. pap. 7.95 (ISBN 0-7195-3213-2). Transatlantic.

Rathbone, R. S. & Rathbone, E. Health & the Nature of Man. 1971. 9.95 (ISBN 0-07-051205-1, C); pap. 9.95 (ISBN 0-07-051206-X); instructors' manual 2.95 (ISBN 0-07-051207-8). McGraw.

Rawls, Walter, Jr. & Davis, Albert R. The Rainbow in Your Hands. 5.95 (ISBN 0-686-29947-7). Cancer Bk Hse.

Read, Donald A. Looking in: Exploring One's Personal Health Values. (Health Education Ser.). (Illus.). 1977. pap. text ed. 8.95 (ISBN 0-13-540484-3). P-H.

Read, Donald A., et al. Health & Modern Man. Zulch, Joan C., ed. (Illus.). 640p. 1973. text ed. 16.95 (ISBN 0-02-398740-5). Macmillan.

Readings in Health 1976-1977. new ed. LC 75-26099. (Annual Edition Ser.). 224p. (Orig.). 1975. pap. text ed. 4.95 (ISBN 0-87967-132-7). Dushkin Pub.

Readings in Health 78-79. LC 75-26099. (Annual Editions Ser.). (Illus.). 1978. pap. text ed. 5.75 (ISBN 0-87967-236-6). Dushkin Pub.

Reams, Carey A. Choose! Life or Death: Reams Biological Theory of Ionization. 1978. pap. 3.95 (ISBN 0-89221-046-X). New Leaf.

Reeves, Philip N., et al. Introduction to Health Planning. 2nd ed. LC 79-53114. (Illus.). 1979. text ed. 24.95 (ISBN 0-87815-027-7). Info Resources.

Reid, George. Sound of the Trumpet. (Horizon Ser.). 224p. 1981. write for info. (ISBN 0-8127-0328-6); pap. write for info. (ISBN 0-8127-0321-9). Review & Herald.

Reilly, Harold J. & Brod, Ruth H. Edgar Cayce Handbook for Health Through Drugless Therapy. 1977. pap. 3.50 (ISBN 0-515-05825-4). Jove Pubns.

Reinke, Williams A., ed. The Functional Analysis of Health Needs & Services. 1976. 14.00 (ISBN 0-210-40582-1). Dept Intl Health.

Reldnas, William A. El Metodo Para Aumentar Su Estatura: Spanish Edition. Triana, Manual, tr. LC 78-75228. Orig. Title: The Height Increase Method. (Illus.). 1979. pap. 25.00 (ISBN 0-88473-026-3). Fiesta Pub.

Reuben, David. Save Your Life Diet. pap. 1.95 (ISBN 0-686-29951-5). Cancer Bk Hse.

Rhodes, Helen. Doctor, What Can I Do? (Horizon Ser.). 128p. 1981. pap. write for info. (ISBN 0-8127-0327-8). Review & Herald.

Rhodes, Russell L. Man at His Best - How to Be More Youthful, Virile, Healthy & Handsome. LC 73-22791. 384p. 1974. 8.95 (ISBN 0-385-05906-X). Doubleday.

Richardson, Joseph G. Long Life & How to Reach It. Rosenkrantz, Barbara G., ed. LC 76-40640. (Public Health in America Ser.). 1977. Repr. of 1886 ed. lib. bdg. 12.00x (ISBN 0-405-09828-6). Arno.

Robinson, David & Henry, Stuart. Self-Help & Health: Mutual Aid for Modern Problems. 1977. pap. 12.50x (ISBN 0-85520-317-X, Pub by Martin Robertson England). Biblio Dist.

Roe, Daphne A. Clinical Nutrition for the Health Scientist. 144p. 1980. 44.95 (ISBN 0-8493-5417-X). CRC Pr.

Roes, Mimi. The Do Nothing Way to Health & Beauty. (Illus.). 1979. pap. 3.95 (ISBN 0-89780-000-1). Teacher Update.

Roglieri, John L. Odds on Your Life: How to Make Informed Decisions About the Health Factors You Control. LC 79-67551. (Illus.). 288p. 10.95 (ISBN 0-87223-595-5, Dist. by Har-Row). Seaview Bks.

Rona, Luanne. Total Glow: Dr. Rona's Unbeatable Health Program. 2nd ed. Dwight, pref. by. LC 78-62657. (Illus.). 1979. 9.95 (ISBN 0-913864-37-4). Enterprise Del.

Roper, Nancy. Man's Anatomy, Physiology, Health & Environment. 5th ed. LC 76-25811. 1977. pap. text ed. 16.00 (ISBN 0-443-01497-3). Churchill.

Rose, Jeanne. Jeanne Rose's Herbal Guide to Inner Health. (Illus.). 1978. pap. 6.95 1980 (ISBN 0-448-14522-7). G&D.

Rosenkrantz, Barbara G., ed. Selections from the Health-Education Series: An Original Anthology. LC 76-40664. (Public Health in America Ser.). 1977. Repr. of 1977 ed. lib. bdg. 10.00x (ISBN 0-405-09873-1). Arno.

Rothenberg, Robert. Health in the Later Years. 1972. pap. 2.25 (ISBN 0-451-08073-4, E8073, Sig). NAL.

Rowan, Robert L. & Gillette, Paul G. The Gay Health Guide. (Modern Medicine Ser.). 1978. 9.95 (ISBN 0-316-31356-4). Little.

Rudman, Jack. Health One: Personal Health, Physical Aspects. (ACT Proficiency Examination Program: PEP-33). 14.95 (ISBN 0-8373-5583-4); pap. 9.95 (ISBN 0-8373-5533-8). Natl Learning.

--Health Restoration: Area I. (ACT Proficiency Examination Program Ser.: PEP-51). pap. 9.95 (ISBN 0-8373-5901-5). Natl Learning.

--Health Restoration: Area II. (ACT Proficiency Examination Program Ser.: PEP-52). (Cloth bdg. avail. on request). pap. 9.95 (ISBN 0-8373-5902-3). Natl Learning.

Rudy, Ellen & Gray, Ruth. Handbook of Health Assessment. (Illus.). 184p. 1981. pap. text ed. 10.95 (ISBN 0-87619-843-4). R J Brady.

Rueveni, Uri & Speck, Ross. Interventions: Healing Human Systems. 1982. in prep. (ISBN 0-89885-086-X). Human Sci Pr.

Rumsey, Tim. The Health Solution: A Complete & Practical Guide to Medical Self-Care. (Illus.). 256p. 1981. 12.95 (ISBN 0-8317-4450-2, Rutledge Pr). Smith Pubs.

Runyan, John W., Jr. Primary Care Guide. (Illus.). 1975. pap. 16.50x (ISBN 0-06-142304-1, Harper Medical). Har-Row.

Rutter, Michael, et al, eds. Education, Health & Behaviour. 496p. 1981. Repr. of 1970 ed. text ed. 19.50 (ISBN 0-89874-268-4). Krieger.

Ryan, Regina S. & Travis, John W. Wellness Workbook: A Guide to Attaining High Level Wellness. 15.95 (ISBN 0-89815-033-7); pap. 9.95 (ISBN 0-89815-032-9). Ten Speed Pr.

Salk, Lee. Dear Dr. Salk: Answers to Your Questions About Your Family. 1980. pap. 2.50 (ISBN 0-446-91486-X). Warner Bks.

Salloway, J. C. Introduction to Social Epidemiology. (Behavioral Science for Health Care Professionals Ser.). 128p. (Orig.). Date not set. lib. bdg. 15.00x (ISBN 0-86531-014-9); pap. text ed. 6.75x (ISBN 0-86531-015-7). Westview.

Saltzman, Barry, et al. Wholly Alive: The Handbook of Holistic Health. LC 78-67852. 1979. pap. 4.95 (ISBN 0-89087-237-6). Celestial Arts.

Samuels, Mike & Bennett, Hal Z. Be Well. LC 74-8134. 160p. 1975. pap. 3.95 (ISBN 0-394-70685-4). Random.

Sarkar, K. An Easy Guide to Sound Health. (Illus.). 1976. pap. 3.00 (ISBN 0-89071-264-6). Matagiri.

Sassoon, Beverly & Sassoon, Vidal. A Year of Beauty & Health. 1979. pap. 4.95 (ISBN 0-671-24379-9, Fireside). S&S.

Saussele, H. P. Health & Vigor After Fifty. 1981. 7.95x (ISBN 0-686-76736-5). Regent House.

Saxon, Edgar J. A Sense of Wonder. 64p. 1980. pap. 3.25x (ISBN 0-8464-1048-6). Beekman Pubs.

Scanlon, James. Self-Reported Health Characteristics, Behavior, & Attitudes of Youths: U. S., 1966-70. LC 75-12433. (Data from the Health Examination Survey Ser. 11: No. 147). 80p. 1974. pap. text ed. 1.25 (ISBN 0-8406-0026-7). Natl Ctr Health Stats.

Schaffner, M. H. & Schaffner, Dorthy. Mieux Vivre-Imibereho Myiza. Gutekunst, D. & Munyambuga, E., trs. (Illus., In French & the language of Rwanda). 1977. pap. 3.95 (ISBN 0-930192-03-6, Union De l'afrique Centrale). Gazelle Pubns.

Schifferes, Justus J. & Peterson, Louis J. Healthier Living Highlights. 2nd ed. LC 74-24339. (Illus.). 289p. 1975. text ed. 16.50x (ISBN 0-471-76071-4); thcrs. manual o.p. avail. (ISBN 0-471-76072-2). Wiley.

Schneider, L. L. & Stone, Robert B. Old Fashioned Health Remedies That Work Best. 1977. 12.95 (ISBN 0-13-633701-5, Parker). P-H.

Schroeder, Henry A. The Poisons Around Us. LC 73-15283. 1978. pap. 4.95 (ISBN 0-87983-188-X). Keats.

Schulberg, Herbert C. & Baker, Frank, eds. Program Evaluation in the Health Fields, Vol. II. LC 78-102679. 1979. text ed. 29.95x (ISBN 0-87705-339-1). Human Sci Pr.

Schuller, Robert H. Discover Health & Happiness. (Orig.). 1978. pap. 1.25 (ISBN 0-89081-143-1). Harvest Hse.

Schwarz, Jack. Human Energy Systems. (Illus.). 1980. pap. 6.95 (ISBN 0-525-47556-7). Dutton.

Scott, John B. & Hutton, E. L. Mathematics for the Health Sciences. 1978. pap. text ed. 13.95x (ISBN 0-89641-009-9). American Pr.

Scrutton, Robert. Nature's Way to Nutrition & Vibrant Health. 1977. pap. 3.00 (ISBN 0-87980-344-4). Wilshire.

Seebohm, Caroline & Pool, Mary J., eds. The House & Garden's Book of Total Health. LC 78-5048. (Illus.). 1978. 11.95 (ISBN 0-399-12154-4). Putnam.

Seeger, Francis M. Until My Last Breath. 1980. pap. text ed. 5.50x (ISBN 0-932194-06-0). Health Comm.

Segal, Maybelle. Reflexology. (Illus.). 1976. 5.95 (ISBN 0-87426-040-X). Whitmore.

Shadman, Alonzo J. Who Is Your Doctor & Why? LC 80-82320. 446p. 1980. pap. 3.95 (ISBN 0-87983-227-4). Keats.

Shaftesbury, Edmund. Goal of Creation. 9.95 (ISBN 0-685-21956-9). Wehman.

Shakman, Robert A. Poison-Proof Your Body. 192p. 1980. 12.95 (ISBN 0-87000-478-6). Arlington Hse.

Shealy, C. Norman. Ninety Days to Self-Health: Biogenics: How to Control All Types of Stress by Yourself Through a Complete Health Program of Autogenics, Diet, Vitamins & Exercise. (YA) 1977. 7.95 (ISBN 0-8037-6386-7). Dial.

Shealy, Norman C. Ninety Ways to Self-Health. 1978. Repr. of 1977 ed. pap. 2.50 (ISBN 0-553-14485-5). Bantam.

Shelton, Herbert M. Health for the Millions. (Orig.). 1968. pap. 1.95 (ISBN 0-914532-02-2). Natural Hygiene.

Shipley, Roger R. & Plonsky, Carolyn G. Consumer Health: Protecting Your Health & Money. (Illus.). 1980. text ed. 18.95 scp (ISBN 0-06-045231-5, HarpC). Har-Row.

Shonick, William. Elements of Planning for Area-Wide Personal Health Services. LC 76-6445. (Issues & Problems in Health Care Ser.). (Illus.). 288p. 1976. pap. text ed. 8.50 (ISBN 0-8016-4592-1). Mosby.
Shute, Wilfrid E. The Health Preserver. LC 77-14086. 1977. 8.95 (ISBN 0-87857-189-2). Rodale Pr Inc.
Shute, Wilfrid E. & Taub, Harald. Vitamin E for Ailing & Healthy Hearts. 1972. pap. 2.50 (ISBN 0-515-05724-X). Jove Pubns.
Silverman, Samuel. How Will You Feel Tomorrow? LC 73-82111. 1975. pap. 2.95 (ISBN 0-8128-1855-5). Stein & Day.
Simmons, Jeannette, ed. Making Health Education Work. 1976. 6.00x (ISBN 0-87553-080-X, 073). Am Pub Health.
Simonton, Carl, et al. Getting Well Again. 256p. (Orig.). 1980. pap. 2.95 (ISBN 0-553-20442-4). Bantam.
Sinacore, J. S. Health: A Quality of Life. 2nd ed. 1974. 18.95 (ISBN 0-02-410700-X). Macmillan.
Sinacore, John S. & Sinacore, A. S. Introductory Health: A Vital Issue. 1975. pap. 9.95 (ISBN 0-02-410690-9). Macmillan.
Singer, Philip & Titus, Elizabeth A. Selected W.H.O. Documents Relating to Traditional Healing. (Traditional Healing Ser.: Vol. 3). Date not set. text ed. 19.50x (ISBN 0-932426-02-6); pap. text ed. 10.00x (ISBN 0-932426-06-9). Trado-Medic.
Singer, Philip & Titus, Elizabeth M. Selected Readings in Traditional Healing. (Traditional Healing Ser.: Vol. 2). Date not set. text ed. 15.75x (ISBN 0-932426-01-8); pap. text ed. 10.00x (ISBN 0-932426-05-0). Trado-Medic.
Skeist, Robert J. To Your Good Health: A Practical Guide for Older Americans, Their Families & Friends. (Illus.). 200p. (Orig.). 1980. pap. 5.95 (ISBN 0-914090-83-6). Chicago Review.
Smith, Philip. Total Breathing. (McGraw-Hill Paperbacks Ser.). 1980. pap. 6.95 (ISBN 0-07-058989-5). McGraw.
Snyder, Paul. Health & Human Nature. 256p. 1980. pap. 10.95 (ISBN 0-8019-6798-8). Chilton.
Sonntag, Ida M. Don't Drink the Water. (Illus.). 128p. 1980. 7.50 (ISBN 0-8158-0393-1). Chris Mass.
Sorochan, Walter D. Personal Health Appraisal. LC 75-31788. 302p. Date not set. Repr. of 1976 ed. pap. 9.95 (ISBN 0-686-76754-3). Krieger.
--Promoting Your Health. LC 80-24347. 577p. 1981. pap. text ed. 14.95 (ISBN 0-471-04681-7). Wiley.
Speight, Phyllis. Before Calling the Doctor. 1976. pap. 3.00x (ISBN 0-8464-0994-1). Beekman Pubs.
Spino, Dyveke. New Age Training for Fitness & Health. LC 78-65254. (Illus.). 288p. 1980. pap. 7.95 (ISBN 0-394-17738-X, E766, Ever). Grove.
Spontaneous Images: Relationship Between Psyche & Soma. (Illus.). 123p. (Orig., Eng. Fr. & Ger.). 1980. pap. text ed. 16.00 (ISBN 0-89192-311-X). Interbk Inc.
Sprug, Joseph. Index to Nutrition & Health. (Useful Reference Ser. of Library Books: Vol. 119). 1981. 20.00 (ISBN 0-87305-125-4). Faxon.
Stark, Norman, et al. The Formula Book One, Two, & Three Slipcased Gift Pack. (Formula Ser.). (Illus.). 1979. pap. 17.85 (ISBN 0-8362-2208-3). Andrews & McMeel.
Staton, Wesley M., et al. Health for Better Living. 2nd ed. LC 69-14400. 464p. 1972. 13.95x (ISBN 0-675-09538-7). Merrill.
Stewart, Andrew. Live to Ninety & Stay Young. 184p. 1968. 5.25x (ISBN 0-8464-1029-X). Beekman Pubs.
Stewart, Jane E. Home Health Care. LC 78-31116. (Illus.). 1979. pap. text ed. 11.50 (ISBN 0-8016-4801-7). Mosby.
Stewart, Rosemarie. The Best Days of Your Life. 1977. pap. 1.95 (ISBN 0-515-03660-9). Jove Pubns.
Stoppard, Miriam. Healthcare: With an A to Z of Common Medical Complaints & How to Treat Them. (Illus.). 208p. 1980. 17.50x (ISBN 0-297-77724-6, Pub. by Weidenfeld & Nicolson England). Biblio Dist.
Stoppard, Miriam, ed. The Good Looks Book. LC 80-5367. (Illus.). 256p. 1980. 25.00 (ISBN 0-670-34547-4, Studio). Viking Pr.
Stransky, Judith & Stone, Robert B. The Alexander Technique: Joy in the Life of Your Body. LC 80-26380. (Illus.). 320p. 1981. 14.95 (ISBN 0-8253-0000-2). Beaufort Bks NY.
Strickland, Stephen P. Research & Health of Americans. LC 77-25779. (Illus.). 1978. 17.95x (ISBN 0-669-02165-2). Lexington Bks.
Swami Rama. A Practical Guide to Holistic Health. 2nd ed. LC 80-81598. 156p. 1980. 7.95 (ISBN 0-89389-066-9); pap. 5.95 (ISBN 0-89389-065-0). Himalayan Intl Inst.
Tansley, David V. Dimensions of Radionics. 224p. 1977. 18.95x (ISBN 0-8464-1005-2). Beekman Pubs.
--Radionics & the Subtle Anatomy of Man. 1980. 5.50 (ISBN 0-8464-1044-3). Beekman Pubs.
--Radionics Interface with the Ether Fields. 112p. 1979. pap. text ed. 10.95x (ISBN 0-8464-1045-1). Beekman Pubs.
Tatai, Kichinosuke. Biorhythm for Health Design. LC 76-29337. (Illus.). 152p. 1977. pap. 8.95 (ISBN 0-87040-393-1). Japan Pubns.
Taub, Harald. Keep Healthy: Polluted World. 5.00 (ISBN 0-686-29973-6). Cancer Bk Hse.
Taylor, Renee. Hunza Health Secrets. 5.00 (ISBN 0-686-29974-4). Cancer Bk Hse.
--Hunza Health Secrets for Long Life & Happiness. LC 63-19916. 1978. pap. 4.95 (ISBN 0-87983-189-8). Keats.
--The New Hunza Health Plan. 192p. (Orig.). 1979. pap. 1.95 (ISBN 0-441-57151-4, Pub. by Charter Bks). Ace Bks.
Ticknor, Caleb. The Philosophy of Living or, the Way to Enjoy Life & Its Comforts. LC 72-180595. (Medicine & Society in America Ser). 342p. 1972. Repr. of 1836 ed. 17.00 (ISBN 0-405-03977-8). Arno.
Tilden, J. H. Food: Its Influence As a Factor in Disease & Health. LC 76-2984. 1976. pap. 3.50 (ISBN 0-87983-125-1). Keats.
Tomlinson, H. The Divination of Disease. 1980. 9.50x (ISBN 0-8464-1006-0). Beekman Pubs.
Toms, Agnes. Eat, Drink & Be Healthy. 1968. pap. 1.50 (ISBN 0-515-04606-X). Jove Pubns.
Toohey, Jack V. & Dezelsky, Thomas L. Activities for Health Science. 1978. pap. text ed. 8.95 (ISBN 0-8403-1881-2). Kendall-Hunt.
Topics for the Health Care Manager. 133p. pap. 10.00 (ISBN 0-686-05274-9). Preston.
Topics in Health Care Financing. (A quarterly topical journal). annual subscription 43.50 (ISBN 0-912862-75-0). Aspen Systems.
Trop, Jack D. A Gift of Love & Health. 2nd ed. LC 78-70059. 1980. pap. 7.95 (ISBN 0-914532-24-3). Natural Hygiene.
--You Don't Have to Be Sick. LC 60-15988. 1961. pap. 1.95 (ISBN 0-914532-01-4). Natural Hygiene.
Turner, C. E. Personal & Community Health. 14th rev. ed. LC 79-129655. (Illus.). 1971. text ed. 11.95 (ISBN 0-8016-5126-3). Mosby.
Ubell, Earl. How to Save Your Life. LC 73-7520. 1973. 7.50 (ISBN 0-15-142179-X). HarBraceJ.
Ulene, Arthur & Fried, John. Feeling Fine. LC 76-29221. 1977. 7.95 (ISBN 0-312-90533-5). St Martin.
Ullrich, Helen D., ed. Health Maintenance Through Food & Nutrition: A Guide to Information Sources. (Health Affairs Information Guide Ser.: Vol. 7). 350p. 1981. 34.00 (ISBN 0-8103-1500-9). Gale.
Utt, Richard. New Frontiers in Good Health. (Uplook Ser.). 1979. pap. 0.75 (ISBN 0-8163-0325-8, 14400-6). Pacific Pr Pub Assn.
Verdesca, Arthur S. Live, Work, & Be Healthy: A Top Medical Director's Common-Sense Advice & Observations for the Working Person. 319p. 1980. 10.95 (ISBN 0-442-25779-1). Van Nos Reinhold.
Vernon, Ann. Help Yourself to a Heathier You. LC 80-5125. 186p. 1980. pap. text ed. 8.50 (ISBN 0-8191-1048-5). U Pr of Amer.
Vickery, Donald M. Lifeplan for Your Health. (Illus.). 1978. 10.95 (ISBN 0-201-08175-X); pap. 5.95 (ISBN 0-201-08176-8). A-W.
Vincent, L. M. Competing with the Sylph: Dancers & the Pursuit of the Ideal Body Form. 1979. 12.95 (ISBN 0-8362-2405-1). Andrews & McMeel.
Vincent, Larry. The Dancer's Book of Health. (Illus.). 1978. 8.95 (ISBN 0-8362-2401-9); pap. 5.95 (ISBN 0-8362-2402-7). Andrews & McMeel.
Vogt, Dorothee K. Health Attitudes & Behavior of Youths Twelve to Seventeen Years, Demographic & Socioeconomic Factors: U.S. Stevenson, Taloria, ed. LC 75-11667. (Data from the Health Examination Survey Ser 11: No. 153). 56p. 1975. pap. text ed. 1.25 (ISBN 0-8406-0042-9). Natl Ctr Health Stats.
Von Furstenberg, Ira. Young at Any Age. (Illus.). 208p. 1981. 12.95 (ISBN 0-02-622100-4). Macmillan.
Wade, Carlson. Healing & Revitalizing Your Vital Organs. 1978. 10.95 (ISBN 0-13-384354-8, Parker). P-H.
Wadsworth, Michael & Robinson, David, eds. Studies in Everyday Medical Life. (Medicine in Society Ser.). 232p. 1981. 23.50x (ISBN 0-85520-147-9, Pub. by Martin Robertson England). Biblio Dist.
Wagman, Richard J. New Complete Medical & Health Encyclopedia, 4 vols. LC 77-81669. 1977. Set. lib. bdg. 42.50 (ISBN 0-89434-007-7). Purnell Ref Bks.
Wagman, Richard J., M.D. The New Concise Family Health & Medical Guide. 400p. 1972. 12.95 (ISBN 0-385-08075-1). Doubleday.
Walker, Morton. Total Health. 9.95 (ISBN 0-686-29990-6). Cancer Bk Hse.
--Total Health. 276p. Date not set. pap. cancelled (ISBN 0-346-12444-1). Cornerstone.
Walker, N. W. Discover Your Fountain of Health. 60p. 1979. pap. 0.95 (ISBN 0-89019-070-4). O'Sullivan Woodside.
Walton, Lewis, et al. Now You Can Live Six Extra Years. (Illus.). 160p. 1981. pap. 3.95 (ISBN 0-912800-84-4). Woodbridge Pr.
Watson, John. The Massage & Bodywork Resource Guide. (Illus.). 360p. (Orig.). 1981. pap. 7.95 (ISBN 0-913300-13-6). Unity Pr.
Weber, Walter. Health Hazards from Pigeons, Starlings & English Sparrows. LC 79-55324. Date not set. 13.00 (ISBN 0-913702-10-2). Thomson Pub Ca.
Weed, Lawrence L. Your Health Care & How to Manage It. 2nd ed. LC 74-33815. 1978. 5.00 (ISBN 0-686-24752-3, Pub. by Essex Pub Co). PROMIS Lab.
Weiner, Albert. Doctor Weiner's Miracle Diet for Health & Longevity. 1978. 9.95 (ISBN 0-13-217109-0, Parker). P-H.
Wells, R. B. Good Health & How to Secure It. 1975. lib. bdg. 69.95 (ISBN 0-685-51372-6). Revisionist Pr.
Welt, I., ed. Drug Information for the Health Professions, Vol. 2. 1970. 54.50x (ISBN 0-677-14090-8). Gordon.
Whaley, Russell F. Basic Health Science Ser. Incl. Book A. D'Agostino, Muriel M. (Illus.). 116p. text ed. 4.00 (ISBN 0-397-43429-4); tchr's ed. 4.00 (ISBN 0-397-43430-8); duplicating masters 11.60 (ISBN 0-685-27016-5); Book B. D'Agostino, Muriel M. (Illus.). 138p. text ed. 4.24 (ISBN 0-397-43431-6); tchr's ed 4.24 (ISBN 0-397-43432-4); duplicating masters 11.60 (ISBN 0-685-27017-3); Book C. D'Agostino, Muriel M. (Illus.). 186p. text ed. 4.56 (ISBN 0-397-43433-2); tchr's. ed. 4.56 (ISBN 0-397-43434-0); duplicating masters 11.60 (ISBN 0-685-27018-1); Book D. Lampe, John M., et al. (Illus.). 248p. text ed. 4.76 (ISBN 0-397-43435-9); tchr's ed. 4.76 (ISBN 0-397-43436-7); duplicating masters 10.64 (ISBN 0-685-27019-X); Book E. Lampe, John M., et al. (Illus.). 258p. text ed. 5.08 (ISBN 0-397-43437-5); tchr's. ed. 5.08 (ISBN 0-397-43438-3); duplicating masters 10.64 (ISBN 0-685-27020-3); Book F. Lampe, John M., et al. (Illus.). 258p. text ed. 5.08 (ISBN 0-397-43439-1); tchr's ed. 5.08 (ISBN 0-397-43440-5); duplicating masters 10.64 (ISBN 0-685-27021-1). (gr. 1-6). 1971. Lippincott.
Whitbread, Jane. Stop Hurting! Start Living! 1981. 11.95 (ISBN 0-440-08377-X). Delacorte.
WHO Expert Committee. Geneva, 1973. Health Aspects of Environmental Pollution Control-Planning & Implementation of Nationnal Programmes: Report. (Technical Report Ser.: No. 554). (Also avail. in French & Spanish). 1974. pap. 2.40 (ISBN 92-4-120554-7). World Health.
WHO Meeting of Experts. Geneva, 1971. Reuse of Effluents - Methods of Wastewater Treatment & Health Safeguards: Report. (Technical Report Ser.: No. 517). (Also avail. in French & Spanish). 1973. pap. 2.00 (ISBN 92-4-120517-2). World Health.
WHO Study Group. Statistical Indices of Family Health: Report. (Technical Report Ser.: No. 587). (Also avail. in French & Spanish). 1976. pap. 3.20 (ISBN 92-4-120587-3). World Health.
WHO Study Group. Geneva, 1974. Early Detection of Health Impairment in Occupational Exposure to Health Hazards: Report. (Technical Report Ser.: No. 571). (Also avail. in French & Spanish). 1975. pap. 3.50 (ISBN 92-4-120571-7). World Health.
WHO Study Group, Geneva, 1974. Health Hazards from New Environmental Pollutants: Report. (Technical Report Ser.: No. 586). (Also avail. in french & spanish). 1976. pap. 3.20 (ISBN 92-4-120586-5). World Health.
Wigmoe, Ann. Be Your Own Doctor. 1.95 (ISBN 0-686-29998-1). Cancer Bk Hse.
Wilder, Charles S. Health Characteristics of Persons with Chronic Activity Limitation, U.S., 1974. Stevenson, Taloria, ed. (Series 10: No. 112). 1976. pap. 1.50 (ISBN 0-8406-0079-8). Natl Ctr Health Stats.
--Prevalence of Selected Chronic Circulatory Conditions, U. S., 1972. LC 74-8148. (Data from the Health Interview Survey Ser. 10: No. 94). 50p. 1974. pap. text ed. 0.50 (ISBN 0-8406-0021-6). Natl Ctr Health Stats.
Wilder, Mary H. & Moy, Claudia S. Persons Hospitalized by Number of Episodes & Days Hospitalized in a Year: United States, 1972. Stevenson, Taloria, ed. (Ser. 10, No. 116). 1977. pap. text ed. 1.50 (ISBN 0-8406-0104-2). Natl Ctr Health Stats.
Williamson, G. Scott & Pearse, Innes H. Science, Synthesis, & Sanity. 352p. 1980. pap. 13.00x (ISBN 0-7073-0259-5, Pub. by Scottish Academic Pr Scotland). Columbia U Pr.
Williamson, John D. & Danaher, Kate. Self-Care in Health. 1978. lib. bdg. 22.50 (ISBN 0-85664-484-6). N Watson.
Willie, Ralph G. Health Is Happiness. LC 79-62988. 4.50 (ISBN 0-686-24645-4). R G Willie DDS.
Wilson, Tom, ed. Home Remedies: A Guide for Residential Retrofit. LC 81-80269. (Illus.). 253p. 1981. pap. 10.00 (ISBN 0-9601884-0-1). MASEA.
Wood, Corinne S. Human Sickness & Health: A Bio-Cultural View. LC 78-71608. 376p. 1979. pap. text ed. 12.95 (ISBN 0-87484-418-5). Mayfield Pub.
Woodruff, Diana. Can You Live to Be One Hundred? 1979. pap. 2.25 (ISBN 0-451-08468-3, E8468, Sig). NAL.
World Health Assembly, 1974, 27th. Promoting Health in the Human Environment: Technical Discussions Review. Meyer, E. E. & Sainsbury, P., eds. 1975. pap. 4.80 (ISBN 92-4-156046-0). World Health.
World Health Statistics Annual: 1973-76, Vol. 1. 1976. pap. 54.40 (ISBN 92-4-067761-5). World Health.
Wren, George R. Modern Health Administration. LC 72-91995. 238p. 1974. 9.95x (ISBN 0-8203-0268-6). U of Ga Pr.
Wright, H. Beric. Executive Ease & Dis-Ease. LC 75-1072. 1975. 21.95 (ISBN 0-470-96450-2). Halsted Pr.
Wyatt, David E. The Good Health Book: A Guide to the Origins & Symptoms of Illnesses & What You Can Do to Get Well & Stay Well. LC 80-20456. (Illus.). 1981. 19.95 (ISBN 0-88229-411-3); pap. 9.95 (ISBN 0-88229-769-4). Nelson- Hall.
Yes Bookshop. Wellness: Health Book Directory. 4.95 (ISBN 0-686-30006-8). Cancer Bk Hse.
Young, Bob. How to Stay Healthy While Traveling: A Guide to Today's World Traveler. LC 80-5320. (Illus.). 119p. (Orig.). 1980. pap. 4.95 (ISBN 0-915520-31-1). Ross-Erikson.
Zamm, Alfred. Why Your House May Endanger Your Health. 1980. 10.95 (ISBN 0-671-24128-1). S&S.
Zarren, Harvey. Health, Infection & Diseases. (Clinical Monograph Ser.). (Illus.). 1975. pap. 7.95 (ISBN 0-87618-064-0). R J Brady.

HEALTH–AUTHORSHIP

see Medical Writing

HEALTH–BIBLIOGRAPHY

Ardell, Donald & James, John, eds. Author's Guide to Journals in the Health Field. LC 80-13403. (Author's Guide to Journals Ser.). 176p. 1980. 16.95 (ISBN 0-917724-09-7). Haworth Pr.
Ash, Joan, ed. Health: A Multimedia Source Guide. LC 76-28297. 1976. 16.50 (ISBN 0-8352-0905-9). Bowker.
Barkas, J. L., ed. Personal Concerns Directory: A Guide to Companies, Associations, Organizations, Programs, Research Centers, Publications & Audio Visual Materials in the Areas of Health, Family & Work, 3 issues. Set. pap. 64.00 (ISBN 0-8103-1187-9). Gale.
Culyer, A. J., et al, eds. An Annotated Bibliography of Health Economics. LC 77-79018. 1977. 29.95x (ISBN 0-312-03873-9). St Martin.
The Dictionary Catalog of the Applied Life Studies Library, University of Illinois at Urbana-Champaign, 4 vols. 1976. 300.00 (ISBN 0-8161-0047-0). G K Hall.
Free Stuff Editors, ed. Free Stuff for Better Health. (Illus.). 120p. (Orig.). 1982. pap. 2.95 (ISBN 0-915658-40-2). Meadowbrook Pr.
Rees, Alan M. & Young, Blanche A. Consumer Health Information Source Book. (Consumer Health Information Publications Program Ser.). 472p. 1981. 32.50 (ISBN 0-8352-1336-6). Bowker.
Roper, Fred & Boorkman, JoAnne. Introduction to Reference Sources in the Health Sciences. 256p. 1980. text ed. 18.00 (ISBN 0-912176-08-3). Med Lib Assn.
Singer & Titus. Resources for Third World Health Planners: A Selected Subject Bibliography. (Traditional Healing Ser.: No. 6). 1980. 17.50 (ISBN 0-932426-11-5, Trado-Medic Bks); pap. 9.95 (ISBN 0-932426-12-3, Trado-Medic Bks). Conch Mag.
Ullrich, Helen D., ed. Health Maintenance Through Food & Nutrition: A Guide to Information Sources. (Health Affairs Information Guide Ser.: Vol. 7). 350p. 1981. 34.00 (ISBN 0-8103-1500-9). Gale.
U. S. Department of Health, Education and Welfare Washington D. C. Author-Title Catalog of the Department Library, 29 Vols. 1965. Set. 2755.00 (ISBN 0-8161-0717-3). G K Hall.
Weise, Frieda O., ed. Health Statistics: A Guide to Information Sources. LC 80-12039. (Health Affairs Information Guide Ser.: Vol. 4). 1980. 36.00 (ISBN 0-8103-1412-6). Gale.

HEALTH–DICTIONARIES

Appleton Book Display Unit, 30 bks. 1980. prepack 178.50 (ISBN 0-8385-0199-0). ACC.
Gardner, A. Ward. Good Housekeeping Dictionary of Symptoms. 256p. 1982. pap. 2.95 (ISBN 0-441-29822-2). Ace Bks.

Gesundheits - Brockhaus. 2nd rev. ed. 848p. (Gr.). 38.50 (ISBN 3-7653-0026-8, M-7422, Pub. by Brockhaus). French & Eur.

Hughes, Harold K. A Dictionary of Abbreviations in Medicine & the Health Sciences. 1977. 25.95 (ISBN 0-669-00688-2). Lexington Bks.

Kruzas, Anthony T., ed. Medical & Health Information Directory: A Guide to Professional & Nonprofit Organizations, Government Agencies, Educational Institutons, Grant Award Sources, Health Care Insurers, Journals, Newsletters, Review Serials, Etc. 2nd ed. LC 77-82802. 1980. 110.00 (ISBN 0-8103-0267-5). Gale.

Lindeke, Wolfgang. Dictionary of Ventilation & Health. 186p. 1980. 25.00x (ISBN 0-569-08522-5, Pub. by Collet's). State Mutual Bk.

The New American Medical Dictionary & Health Manual. 1975. pap. 2.25 (ISBN 0-685-57129-7, Pub. by NAL). Formur Intl.

Tver, David F. & Russell, Percy. The Nutrition & Health Encyclopedia. LC 80-19933. (Illus.). 544p. 1981. text ed. 26.50 (ISBN 0-442-24859-8). Van Nos Reinhold.

HEALTH–EARLY WORKS TO 1800

Cummins, Patricia W. A Critical Edition of Le Regime Tresutile et Tresproufitable Pour Conserver et Garder la Sante du Corps Humain. LC 76-25778. (North Carolina Studies in Romance Languages & Literatures: 177). 1976. 24.50 (ISBN 0-8357-0182-4, IS-00013, Pub. by U of North Carolina at Chapel Hill). Univ Microfilms.

Faust, Bernhard C. Catechism of Health. Basse, J. H., tr. from Ger. LC 74-180574. (Medicine & Society in America Ser). 116p. 1972. Repr. of 1794 ed. 10.00 (ISBN 0-405-03951-4). Arno.

Gratarolus, Gulielmus. A Direction for the Health of Magistrates & Students. Newton, Thomas, tr. LC 72-38192. (English Experience Ser.: No. 462). 172p. 1972. Repr. of 1574 ed. 15.00 (ISBN 90-221-0462-1). Walter J Johnson.

In This Tretyse That Is Cleped Gouernayle of Helthe. LC 72-200. (English Experience Ser.: No. 192). 1969. Repr. of 1489 ed. 11.50 (ISBN 90-221-0192-4). Walter J Johnson.

Regimen Sanitatis Salernitanum, et al. School of Salernum. LC 79-95627. (Illus.). 1920. 13.50x (ISBN 0-678-03751-5). Kelley.

HEALTH–EXAMINATIONS, QUESTIONS, ETC.

Ferguson, L. Kraeer & Kerr, John H. Explain It to Me, Doctor. LC 69-14856. 1971. 16.50 (ISBN 0-397-55951-8, JBL-Med-Nursing). Har-Row.

Hamrick, Michael & Anspaugh, David. Health Decisions. 224p. (Orig.). 1980. pap. 9.95x wkbk. (ISBN 0-89459-108-8). Hunter NC.

Rudman, Jack. Health - Jr. H.S. (Teachers License Examination Ser.: T-24a). (Cloth bdg. avail on request). pap. 10.00 (ISBN 0-8373-8024-3). Natl Learning.

--Health - Sr. H.S. (Teachers License Examination Ser.: T-24b). (Cloth bdg. avail. on request). pap. 10.00 (ISBN 0-685-18755-1). Natl Learning.

--Health Aide. (Career Examination Ser.: C-1301). (Cloth bdg. avail. on request). pap. 8.00 (ISBN 0-8373-1301-5). Natl Learning.

--Health & Physical Education - Jr. H.S. (Teachers License Examination Ser.: T-24). (Cloth bdg. avail. on request). pap. 10.00 (ISBN 0-8373-8025-1). Natl Learning.

--Health & Physical Education - Sr. H.S. (Teachers License Examination Ser.: T-25). (Cloth bdg. avail. on request). pap. 10.00 (ISBN 0-685-18748-9). Natl Learning.

--Health Conservation. (Teachers License Examination Ser.: T-23). (Cloth bdg. avail. on request). pap. 10.00 (ISBN 0-8373-8023-5). Natl Learning.

--Health One. (College Proficiency Examination Ser.: CPEP-17). 14.95 (ISBN 0-8373-5467-6); pap. 9.95 (ISBN 0-8373-5417-X). Natl Learning.

--Health Support: Area I. (ACT Proficiency Examination Program: PEP-48). 14.95 (ISBN 0-8373-5598-2); pap. 9.95 (ISBN 0-8373-5548-6). Natl Learning.

--Health Support: Area I. (Regents External Degree Ser.: REDP-24). 14.95 (ISBN 0-8373-5674-1); pap. 9.95 (ISBN 0-8373-5624-5). Natl Learning.

--Health Support: Area II. (ACT Proficiency Examination Program: PEP-49). 14.95 (ISBN 0-8373-5599-0); pap. 9.95 (ISBN 0-8373-5549-4). Natl Learning.

--Health Support: Area II. (Regents External Degree Ser.: REDP-25). 14.95 (ISBN 0-8373-5675-X); pap. 9.95 (ISBN 0-8373-5625-3). Natl Learning.

--Health Three. (College Proficiency Examination Ser.: CPEP-19). 14.95 (ISBN 0-8373-5469-2); pap. 9.95 (ISBN 0-8373-5419-6). Natl Learning.

--Health Two. (College Proficiency Examination Ser.: CPEP-18). 14.95 (ISBN 0-8373-5468-4); pap. 9.95 (ISBN 0-8373-5418-8). Natl Learning.

--Swimming & Health Instructors - Sr. H.S. (Teachers License Examination Ser.: T-62). (Cloth bdg. avail. on request). pap. 10.00 (ISBN 0-8373-8062-6). Natl Learning.

Wilson, Michael. Health Is for People. 134p. 1980. 12.95x (ISBN 0-232-51326-0, Pub. by Darton-Longman-Todd England). State Mutual Bk.

Wunderlich, Ray C., Jr. Explanatory Notes to Accompany Wunder-Form No. 11: Health & Developmental Questionnaire. new ed. 1974. pap. 1.55 (ISBN 0-910812-16-0). Johnny Reads.

HEALTH–HISTORY

Bosson, Linda. Soap & Water. (Readers Ser.: Stage 3). 1977. pap. text ed. 2.95 (ISBN 0-88377-089-X). Newbury Hse.

Haley, Bruce. The Healthy Body & Victorian Culture. LC 78-6933. 1978. 18.50x (ISBN 0-674-38610-8). Harvard U Pr.

Risse, Guenter B., et al, eds. Medicine Without Doctors: Home Health Care in American History. 1977. pap. 8.95 (ISBN 0-88202-165-6). N Watson.

Thom, Burton P. Hygieia or Disease & Evolution. 1978. Repr. of 1926 ed. lib. bdg. 12.50 (ISBN 0-8495-5119-6). Arden Lib.

HEALTH–JUVENILE LITERATURE

Abrams, Joy, et al. Look Good - Feel Good Through Yoga. LC 78-4288. (Illus.). (gr. 6 up). 1978. 7.95 (ISBN 0-03-019436-9). HR&W.

Anderson, James L. & Cohen, Martin. The West Point Fitness & Diet Book. 1978. pap. 3.95 (ISBN 0-380-01894-2, 37342). Avon.

Bennett, Hal & Samuels, Michael. The Well-Body Book. (YA) 1973. pap. 8.95 (ISBN 0-394-70969-1). Random.

Burstein, John. Lucky You! LC 80-14641. (Illus.). 32p. (ps-3). 1980. 4.95 (ISBN 0-07-009243-5). McGraw.

--Slim Goodbody: What Can Go Wrong & How to Be Strong. (Illus.). (gr. k-6). 1978. 6.95 (ISBN 0-07-009242-7, GB). McGraw.

Diehl, Harold S., et al. Health & Safety for You. 5th ed. 1979. text ed. 12.92 (ISBN 0-07-016863-6); tchr's ed. 6.40 (ISBN 0-07-016864-4). McGraw.

Donahue, Parnell & Capellaro, Helen. Germs Make Me Sick: A Health Handbook for Kids. LC 74-15309. (Illus.). 96p. (gr. 4 up). 1975. PLB 5.99 (ISBN 0-394-92909-8); pap. 2.95 (ISBN 0-394-82909-3). Knopf.

Good Thing Inc. & Burstein, John. Slim Goodbody: Your Body, Health & Feelings. (gr. 1-3). 1978. pap. text ed. 190.00 (ISBN 0-89290-098-9, CM-43). Soc for Visual.

Jacobsen, Karen. Health. (The New True Bks.). (Illus.). (gr. k-4). 1981. PLB 9.25 (ISBN 0-516-01622-9). Childrens.

Kettelkamp, Larry. The Healing Arts. (gr. 4-6). 1978. 6.95 (ISBN 0-688-22161-0); PLB 6.67 (ISBN 0-688-32161-5). Morrow.

Lappin, Myra & Feinglass, Sanford. Need a Doctor? (On Your Own Ser.). (Illus.). 64p. (gr. 7-12). 1981. pap. text ed. 3.10 (ISBN 0-915510-58-8). Janus Bks.

Moncure, Jane B. Magic Monsters Learn About Health. LC 79-24240. (Magic Monster Ser.). (Illus.). (ps-3). 1980. PLB 5.95 (ISBN 0-89565-117-3). Childs World.

Neff, Fred. Fred Neff's Keeping Fit Handbook for Physical Conditioning & Better Health. LC 75-38478. (Fred Neff's Self-Defense Library). (Illus.). 56p. (gr. 5 up). 1977. PLB 5.95g (ISBN 0-8225-1157-6). Lerner Pubns.

Newman, Gerry, compiled by. Encyclopedia of Health & the Human Body. (Illus.). (gr. 7 up). 1977. PLB 16.90 s&l (ISBN 0-531-01331-6). Watts.

Odor, Ruth. What's a Body to Do? A Handbook About Health. LC 80-17584. (Living the Good Live Ser.). (Illus.). 112p. (Orig.). (gr. 1-6). 1980. pap. 5.95 (ISBN 0-89565-176-9). Childs World.

Parkinson, Virginia. Going to Bed. (Pointers for Little Persons Ser). (Illus.). (gr. k-3). 1961. PLB 5.99 (ISBN 0-8178-5022-8). Harvey.

Resnick, Charlotte A. & Resnick, Gloria R. To Your Good Health! (gr. 7-12). 1979. text ed. 14.50 (ISBN 0-87720-164-1); pap. text ed. 9.54 (ISBN 0-87720-163-3). AMSCO Sch.

Sneve, Virginia D. Three Lakota Grandmother Stories: Health Lessons for Young Readers. LC 76-24676. 1975. pap. 1.00 (ISBN 0-686-24338-2). Assn Am Indian.

Stiller, Richard. Your Body Is Trying to Tell You Something: How to Understand Its Signals & Respond to Its Needs. LC 79-87529. (gr. 7-9). 1979. 7.95 (ISBN 0-15-299894-2, HJ). HarBraceJ.

Wilson, Charles C. & Wilson, Elizabeth A. Health & Fun. (Health for Young America Ser). (gr. 3). 1968. text ed. 2.88 (ISBN 0-672-70822-1); tchrs' ed. 2.88 (ISBN 0-685-07150-2); tchrs' manual 1.20 (ISBN 0-685-07151-0). Bobbs.

--Health & Growth. (Health for Young America Ser). (gr. 4). text ed. 3.12 (ISBN 0-672-70826-4); tchrs' ed. 3.12 (ISBN 0-685-07152-9); tchrs' manual 1.20 (ISBN 0-685-07153-7). Bobbs.

--Health & Happiness. (Health for Young America Ser). (Illus.). (gr. 6). text ed. 3.52 (ISBN 0-672-70834-5); tchrs' ed. 3.52 (ISBN 0-685-07154-5); tchrs' manual 1.20 (ISBN 0-685-07155-3). Bobbs.

--Health & Living. (Health for Young America Ser). (gr. 5). text ed. 3.16 (ISBN 0-672-70830-2); tchrs' ed. 3.16 (ISBN 0-685-07156-1); tchrs' manual 1.20 (ISBN 0-685-07157-X). Bobbs.

--Health Day by Day. (Health for Young America Ser). (gr. 2). text ed. 2.76 (ISBN 0-672-70818-3); tchrs' ed. 2.76 (ISBN 0-685-07160-X); tchrs' manual 1.20 (ISBN 0-685-07161-8). Bobbs.

--Health, Fitness & Safety. (Health for Young America Ser). (gr. 8). text ed. 3.80 (ISBN 0-672-70842-6); tchrs' ed. 3.80 (ISBN 0-685-07162-6); tchrs' manual 1.20 (ISBN 0-685-07163-4). Bobbs.

--Men, Science & Health. (Health for Young America Ser). (gr. 7). text ed. 3.80 (ISBN 0-672-70838-8); tchrs' ed. 3.80 (ISBN 0-685-07172-3); 1.20 (ISBN 0-685-07173-1). Bobbs.

Winn, Marie. The Sick Book: Questions & Answers About Hiccups & Mumps, Sneezes & Bumps & Other Things That Go Wrong with Us. LC 75-34470. (Illus.). 160p. (gr. 2-6). 1976. 9.95 (ISBN 0-590-07259-5, Four Winds). Schol Bk Serv.

HEALTH–PROGRAMMED INSTRUCTION

Gallagher, Neil E. & Peregoy, Stephen M. Health in Our Lives: An Introductory Workbook. 112p. 1981. pap. text ed. 6.95 (ISBN 0-8403-2401-4). Kendall-Hunt.

HEALTH–READERS

see Readers–Health

HEALTH–STUDY AND TEACHING

see Health Education

HEALTH, COMMUNITY

see Public Health

HEALTH, INDUSTRIAL

see Industrial Health

HEALTH, MENTAL

see Mental Health

HEALTH, PUBLIC

see Public Health

HEALTH, PUBLIC–ADMINISTRATION

see Public Health Administration

HEALTH, RURAL

Alford, Terry W. Facility Planning, Design, & Construction of Rural Health Centers. LC 78-31993. (Rural Health Center Ser.). (Illus.). 1979. 18.50 (ISBN 0-88410-539-3); pap. 10.95 (ISBN 0-88410-545-8). Ballinger Pub.

Barton, S. N., ed. Rural Health & Health Communications. (Biosciences Communications: Vol. 4, No. 1). (Illus.). 1977. 15.75 (ISBN 3-8055-2838-8). S Karger.

Bernstein, James D. & Hege, Frederick P. Rural Health Centers in the United States. LC 79-903. (Rural Health Center Ser.: Vol. I). (Illus.). 1979. 15.00 (ISBN 0-88410-535-0); pap. 7.95 (ISBN 0-88410-541-5). Ballinger Pub.

Bioconversion of Organic Residues for Rural Communities. (Food & Nutrition Bulletin Supplement Ser.: No. 2). 176p. 1980. pap. 15.00 (ISBN 92-808-0043-4, TUNU 039, UNU). Unipub.

Brooks, Edward F. & Wade, Torlen L. Planning & Managing Rural Health Centers. LC 78-27667. (Rural Health Center Ser.). (Illus.). 1979. reference 17.50 (ISBN 0-88410-536-9); pap. 9.95 (ISBN 0-88410-542-3). Ballinger Pub.

Denham, John W. & Pickard, C. Glenn. Clinical Roles in Rural Health Centers. LC 78-27733. (Rural Health Center Ser.). (Illus.). 1979. 12.50 (ISBN 0-88410-537-7); pap. 9.95 (ISBN 0-88410-543-1). Ballinger Pub.

D'Onofrio, Carol & Wang, Virginia, eds. Cooperative Rural Health Education. 1976. pap. 9.00x (ISBN 0-913590-35-5). C B Slack.

Forrest, Colburn D. Guatemala's Rural Health Paraprofessionals. (Special Series on Paraprofessionals). 53p. (Orig.). 1981. pap. 3.50 (ISBN 0-86731-048-0). RDC Ctr Intl Stud.

Hall, Robert E. The Village Health Worker Approach to Rural Health Care: The Case of Senegal. (Special Series on Paraprofesionals). 64p. (Orig.). 1981. pap. 3.50 (ISBN 0-86731-050-2). RDC Ctr Intl Stud.

Health Care Delivery in Rural Areas. pap. 1.50 (ISBN 0-89970-052-7, OP-465). AMA.

Long, Ernest C., ed. Health Objectives for the Developing Society: Responsibility of Individual, Physician & Community. LC 65-19451. (Illus.). 1965. 9.75 (ISBN 0-8223-0109-1). Duke.

Low-Cost Rural Health Care & Health Manpower Training, Vol. 3. 1977. pap. 10.00 (ISBN 0-88936-138-X, IDRC 93, IDRC). Unipub.

Low-Cost Rural Health Care & Health Manpower Training, Vol. 4. 1979. pap. 10.00 (ISBN 0-88936-201-7, IDRC125, IDRC). Unipub.

McNerney, Walter J. & Riedel, Donald C., eds. Regionalization & Rural Health Care: An Experiment in Three Communitiies, No. 2. LC 78-7392. 1978. pap. 20.00 (ISBN 0-8357-0316-9, ST-00007, Pub. by U of Mich GSBA BHA). Univ Microfilms.

North Central Regional Center for Rural Development. Rural Health Services: Organization, Delivery, & Use. Whiting, Larry & Hassinger, E., eds. 384p. 1976. text ed. 7.50x (ISBN 0-8138-1465-0). Iowa St U Pr.

Reynolds, Richard C., et al, eds. The Health of Rural County: Perspectives & Problems. LC 75-35753. 1976. 7.50 (ISBN 0-8130-0525-6). U Presses Fla.

Roemer, Milton I. Rural Health Care. LC 76-6880. (Issues & Problems in Health Care). 128p. 1976. pap. 7.50 (ISBN 0-8016-4166-7). Mosby.

Royal Society of London Publications, et al. Technologies for Rural Health. LC 79-670285. (Illus.). 1978. text ed. 19.50x (ISBN 0-85403-094-8). Scholium Intl.

Smith, Harvey L. Society & Health in a Mountain Community. 25p. 1961. pap. text ed. 1.50 (ISBN 0-89143-053-9). U NC Inst Res Soc Sci.

Tyrrell, D. A., et al. More Technologies for Rural Health. (Proceedings of the Royal Society, Series B.: Vol. 209). 186p. 1980. text ed. 30.00x (ISBN 0-85403-148-0, Pub. by Royal Soc London). Scholium Intl.

United States Children's Bureau. Rural Children in Selected Counties of North Carolina. Bradley, Francis S. & Williamson, Margaretta A., eds. LC 76-78778. (Illus.). Repr. of 1918 ed. 10.75x (ISBN 0-8371-1399-7). Greenwood.

Warren, David G. A Legal Guide for Rural Health Programs. LC 78-27621. (Rural Health Center Ser.). (Illus.). 1979. reference 17.50 (ISBN 0-88410-538-5); pap. 8.95 (ISBN 0-88410-544-X). Ballinger Pub.

HEALTH ADMINISTRATION

see Public Health Administration

HEALTH AGENCIES, VOLUNTARY

see Voluntary Health Agencies

HEALTH BOARDS–UNITED STATES

Chapin, Charles V. A Report on State Public Health Work, Based on a Survey of State Boards of Health. Rosenkrantz, Barbara G., ed. LC 76-25657. (Public Health in America Ser.). (Illus.). 1977. Repr. of 1915 ed. lib. bdg. 15.00x (ISBN 0-405-09807-3). Arno.

Municipal Health Department Practice for the Year 1923: In America's 100 Largest Cities. LC 73-11911. (Metropolitan America Ser.). 810p. 1974. Repr. 38.00x (ISBN 0-405-05429-7). Arno.

HEALTH CARE

see Medical Care

HEALTH CARE ADMINISTRATION

see Public Health Administration

HEALTH CARE DELIVERY ORGANIZATIONS, COMPREHENSIVE

see Health Maintenance Organizations

HEALTH COMMUNICATION

see Communication in Medicine

HEALTH ECONOMICS

see Medical Economics

HEALTH EDUCATION

see also Cancer Education; School Health

Alexander, Dale. Good Health & Common Sense. 1st ed. LC 60-13133. 1960. 9.95 (ISBN 0-911638-03-2). Witkower.

American Alliance for Health, Physical Education & Recreation. Abstracts of Research Papers, 1972. pap. 2.00x (ISBN 0-685-42021-3, 248-25306). AAHPERD.

--Abstracts of Research Papers, 1975. 1975. pap. 2.75x (ISBN 0-685-52989-4, 248-25696). AAHPERD.

American Alliance for Health, Physical Education, & Recreation. Evaluation Instruments in Health Education. rev. ed. Solleder, M. K., ed. 1969. pap. 1.25x (ISBN 0-685-05086-6, 244-25024). AAHPERD.

American Alliance for Health, Physical Education & Recreation. Health Education 1975. 1975. pap. 9.25x (ISBN 0-685-57478-4, 244-25732). AAHPERD.

--Professional Preparation in Dance, Physical Education, Recreation Education, Safety Education, & School Health Education. 1974. pap. 6.50 (ISBN 0-685-42017-5, 240-25556). AAHPERD.

--Professional Preparation in Physical Education & Coaching. 1974. pap. 1.25x (ISBN 0-685-42018-3, 245-25574). AAHPERD.

--Professional Preparation in Safety Education & School Health Education. 1974. pap. 1.25x (ISBN 0-685-42019-1, 244-25572). AAHPERD.

American Alliance for Health, Physical Education, & Recreation. Programmed Instruction in Health & Physical Education. 1970. pap. 3.50x (ISBN 0-685-05099-8, 245-25028). AAHPERD.

American Hospital Association. Educational Programs in the Health Field. LC 79-24621. 48p. 1979. pap. 7.50 (ISBN 0-87258-283-3, 3502). Am Hospital.

Anderson, Digby C., ed. Health Education in Practice. 207p. 1979. 29.00x (ISBN 0-85664-962-7, Pub. by Croom Helm Ltd England). Biblio Dist.

Barrett, Morris. Health Education Guide: A Design for Teaching. 2nd ed. LC 73-20279. (Illus.). 338p. 1974. pap. 12.00 (ISBN 0-8121-0481-1). Lea & Febiger.

Bedworth, David A. & Bedworth, Albert E. Health Education: A Process for Human Effectiveness. 1978. text ed. 16.95 scp (ISBN 0-06-040575-9, HarpC); inst. manual free (ISBN 0-06-360557-0). Har-Row.

Braunstein, Bruce. The Daily Plan-It R. 180p. (Orig.). 1980. pap. 6.95 (ISBN 0-686-27615-9). Tetragrammaton.

Bryant, John H. Education & Training of Health Manpower for Prevention. LC 76-15084. 1976. pap. 5.00 (ISBN 0-88202-106-0). N Watson.

Chafetz, M. C. Health Education: An Annotated Bibliography of Lifestyle, Behavior & Health. 258p. 1981. 29.50 (ISBN 0-306-40754-X, Plenum Pr). Plenum Pub.

Chappelear, Claude S. Health Subject Matter in Natural Sciences. LC 78-176637. (Columbia University. Teachers College. Contributions to Education: No. 341). Repr. of 1929 ed. 17.50 (ISBN 0-404-55341-9). AMS Pr.

Clarke, H. Harrison. Application of Measurement to Health & Physical Education. 5th ed. (Illus.). 464p. 1976. 17.50x (ISBN 0-13-039024-0). P-H.

Commission on Education for Health Administration. Report of the Commission on Education for Health Administration, Vol. 1. LC 74-17538. 220p. 1975. 10.00 (ISBN 0-914904-04-3). Health Admin Pr.

--Selected Papers of the Commission on Education for Health Administration, Vol. 2. LC 74-17537. 350p. 1975. 12.50 (ISBN 0-914904-05-1). Health Admin Pr.

Cowley, J. Health Education in Schools. 1981. text ed. 26.50 (ISBN 0-06-318178-9, Pub. by Har-Row England Ltd); pap. text ed. 15.50 (ISBN 0-06-318179-7). Har-Row.

Curriculum Guide for Health Education: Nutrition. 112p. 1975. 12.50 (ISBN 0-686-29253-7). Natl Cath Educ.

Dalis, G. & Strasser, B. Teaching Strategies for Values Awareness & Decision-Making in Health Education. LC 77-82319. 1977. 7.95 (ISBN 0-913590-46-0). C B Slack.

Daum, Susan L., ed. Guide to Audiovisual Resources for the Health Care Field. 1981 ed. 200p. (Orig.). 1981. 18.00 (ISBN 0-939450-00-3). Med Info Pubns.

Davis, Elwood C. Methods & Techniques Used in Surveying Health & Physical Education in City Schools: An Analysis & Evaluation. LC 70-176711. (Columbia University. Teachers College. Contributions to Education: No. 515). Repr. of 1932 ed. 17.50 (ISBN 0-404-55515-2). AMS Pr.

De Land, E. C., ed. Information Technology in Health Science Education. (Computers in Biology & Medicine Ser.). 608p. 1978. 42.50 (ISBN 0-306-31113-5, Plenum Pr). Plenum Pub.

Development of Educational Programmes for the Health Professions. (Public Health Paper: No. 52). (Also avail. in French & Spanish). 1973. pap. 4.80 (ISBN 92-4-130052-3). World Health.

Dignan, Mark B. & Carr, Patricia A. Introduction to Program Planning: A Basic Text for Community Health Education. LC 81-865. (Illus.). 156p. 1981. text ed. 13.00 (ISBN 0-8121-0787-X). Lea & Febiger.

D'Onofrio, Carol & Wang, Virginia, eds. Cooperative Rural Health Education. 1976. pap. 9.00x (ISBN 0-913590-35-5). C B Slack.

Eisner, Victor & Callan, Laurence B. Dimensions of School Health. 192p. 1974. 14.75 (ISBN 0-398-02948-2). C C Thomas.

Engs, Ruth & Wantz, Molly. Teaching Health Education in the Elementary School. (Illus., LC 77-079371). 1978. text ed. 17.75 (ISBN 0-395-25483-3); inst. manual 0.75 (ISBN 0-395-25484-1). HM.

Engs, Ruth C., et al. Health Games Students Play: Creative Strategies for Health Education. 1976. perfect bdg. 7.50 (ISBN 0-8403-1238-5). Kendall-Hunt.

Ensor, Phyllis A. & Means, Richard K. Health Education Instructor's Resource & Method Handbook. 2nd rev. ed. 1979. pap. text ed. 20.95 (ISBN 0-205-06750-6). Allyn.

Feldman, Jacob J. Dissemination of Health Information: A Case Study in Adult Learning. LC 66-14570. (NORC Monographs in Social Research Ser.: No. 11). 1966. 9.95x (ISBN 0-202-27001-7). NORC.

Fodor, John T. & Dalis, Gus T. Health Instruction: Theory & Application. 3rd ed. LC 80-24484. (Illus.). 150p. 1981. text ed. 9.75 (ISBN 0-8121-0776-4). Lea & Febiger.

Ford, Beryl I. Health Education: A Source Book for Teaching. 1978. text ed. 21.00 (ISBN 0-08-021327-8); pap. text ed. 15.75 (ISBN 0-08-021326-X). Pergamon.

Ford, Charles W. Clinical Education for the Allied Health Professions. LC 78-3620. 1978. text ed. 15.95 (ISBN 0-8016-1623-9). Mosby.

Galli, Nicholas. Foundations & Principles of Health Education. LC 77-21586. 1978. text ed. 19.95 (ISBN 0-471-29065-3). Wiley.

Green, Lawrence W., et al. Health Education Planning: A Diagnostic Approach. LC 79-89920. 306p. 1980. text ed. 16.95 (ISBN 0-87484-471-1). Mayfield Pub.

Greenberg, Jerrold S. Student-Centered Health Instruction: A Humanistic Approach. LC 76-55642. (Illus.). 1978. pap. text ed. 7.95 (ISBN 0-201-02627-9). A-W.

Greene, Walter H., et al. Health in the Elementary School: Teaching for Relevance. (Illus.). 1978. 14.95 (ISBN 0-02-346590-5). Macmillan.

Groomer, Vera. Growing Stronger: Two - Two. (Come Unto Me Ser.: Year 2, Bk. 2). 32p. (ps). 1980. pap. 1.50 (ISBN 0-8127-0271-9). Review & Herald.

Growth: A Handbook of Classroom Ideas to Motivate the Teaching of Elementary Health. (Spice Ser.). 1975. 6.50 (ISBN 0-89273-119-2). Educ Serv.

Hakim, David. My ABC of Health Coloring Book. pap. 1.50 (ISBN 0-686-11513-9). Hakims Pubs.

Hamburg, Joseph, ed. Review of Allied Health Education, No. 1. LC 74-7876. (Illus.). 244p. 1974. 13.00x (ISBN 0-8131-1322-9). U Pr of Ky.

--Review of Allied Health Education, No. 2. LC 74-7876. 200p. 1977. 13.00 (ISBN 0-8131-1336-9). U Pr of Ky.

--Review of Allied Health Education, No. 3. LC 74-7876. 168p. 1979. 13.00x (ISBN 0-8131-1367-9). U Pr of Ky.

--Review of Allied Health Education, No. 4. LC 74-7876. 1981. 13.00x (ISBN 0-8131-1455-1). U Pr of Ky.

Health Education. 1961. pap. 8.00 (ISBN 0-89970-053-5, OP-201). AMA.

Health Education: A Programmes Review. (Offset Pub.: No. 7). (Also avail. in French). 1974. pap. 6.80 (ISBN 92-4-170007-6). World Health.

Health Education by Radio & Television: Proceedings of the Conference . . . Munich 1980 with an Annotated Bibliography. (Communication Research & Broadcasting Ser.). 240p. 1981. 24.00 (ISBN 3-598-20203-2, Pub. by K G Saur). Shoe String.

Health Education in the USSR. (Public Health Papers Ser: No. 19). 69p. (Eng, Fr, Rus, & Span.). 1963. pap. 2.00 (ISBN 92-4-130019-1). World Health.

Health Instruction II: Guidelines for Planning Health Education Programs K-12. LC 81-66887. 1981. 4.50 (ISBN 0-917160-14-2). Am Sch Health.

Health Instruction: Suggestions for Teachers. 1973. 3.00 (ISBN 0-917160-08-8). Am Sch Health.

Hellmuth, George A. & Hellmuth, Phillip J., eds. Prevention of Heart Attack: A Challenge to the Health Professions. LC 76-52609. (Illus.). 1977. 25.75 (ISBN 0-8357-0194-8, SS-00023). Univ Microfilms.

Hudson, Margaret W. & Weaver, Ann A. Plans for Living: Your Guide to Health & Safety. (gr. 4-9). 1973. text ed. 3.20 (ISBN 0-8224-5465-3); tchrs.' manual free (ISBN 0-8224-5466-1). Pitman Learning.

Hughes, William L. The Administration of Health & Physical Education for Men in Colleges & Universities. LC 77-176886. (Columbia University. Teachers College. Contributions to Education: No. 541). Repr. of 1932 ed. 17.50 (ISBN 0-404-55541-1). AMS Pr.

Insel, Paul M. & Roth, Walton T. Core Concepts in Health. 2nd ed. LC 78-71611. 1979. pap. text ed. 14.95 (ISBN 0-87484-498-3). Mayfield Pub.

Introducing Tobacco Education in the Elementary School, K-4. 1978. 1.50 (ISBN 0-917160-10-X). Am Sch Health.

Jones, Evelyn G., et al. Living in Safety & Health. rev. ed. 495p. 1966. text ed. 6.92 (ISBN 0-397-40134-5, JBL-Med-Nursing); annotated tchrs'. ed. 6.92 (ISBN 0-397-40135-3); mastery tests 0.48 (ISBN 0-397-40136-1); key to mastery tests incl. (ISBN 0-397-40137-X). Har-Row.

Jones, Hiram A. The Administration of Health & Physical Education in New York State. LC 74-176916. (Columbia University. Teachers College. Contributions to Education: No. 622). Repr. of 1934 ed. 17.50 (ISBN 0-404-55622-1). AMS Pr.

Kime, R., et al. Health Instruction: An Action Approach. 1977. text ed. 16.95 (ISBN 0-13-385252-0). P-H.

Knutson, Andie L. The Individual, Society, & Health Behavior. LC 80-20075. 533p. (Orig.). 1982. pap. 9.95 (ISBN 0-87855-685-0). Transaction Bks.

Laton, Anita D. The Psychology of Learning Applied to Health Education Through Biology: An Experimental Application of Psychology in the Junior High School. LC 73-176980. (Columbia University. Teachers College. Contributions to Education: No. 344). Repr. of 1929 ed. 17.50 (ISBN 0-404-55344-3). AMS Pr.

Lazes, Peter, ed. The Handbook of Health Education. LC 79-50. 456p. 1979. 29.95 (ISBN 0-89443-085-8). Aspen Systems.

Lerrigo, Marion O. Health Problem Sources. LC 76-176989. (Columbia University. Teachers College. Contributions to Education: No. 224). Repr. of 1926 ed. 17.50 (ISBN 0-404-55224-2). AMS Pr.

Litwack, Lawrence, et al. Health Counseling. (Illus.). 290p. 1980. 14.95 (ISBN 0-8385-3665-4). ACC.

Lorentzen, Karen M. A New Approach to the Secondary School Health Education Curriculum: Reading Proficiency. 1981. 11.95 (ISBN 0-533-04633-5). Vantage.

Mace, D. R. & Bannermann, R. H. Teaching of Human Sexuality in Schools for Health Professionals. (Public Health Paper: No. 57). 1974. pap. 2.00 (ISBN 92-4-130057-4). World Health.

McGrath, Ruth E. Developing Concepts of Health in Early Childhood. (Illus.). 1977. 2.95 (ISBN 0-914634-44-5, 7703). DOK Pubs.

Mayer, Jean. Health. Orig. Title: Health & the Patterns of Life. 550p. 1974. text ed. 12.95 (ISBN 0-442-25183-1). D Van Nostrand.

Meeks, Linda B., et al. Teaching Health Science in Middle & Secondary Schools. 400p. 1981. pap. text ed. write for info. (ISBN 0-697-07392-0). Wm C Brown.

Miller, G. E. & Fulop, T. Educational Strategies for the Health Professions. (Public Health Paper: No. 61). (Also avail. in French & Spanish). 1974. pap. 2.80 (ISBN 92-4-130061-2). World Health.

National Commission on Allied Health Education. The Future of Allied Health Education: New Alliances for the 1980s. LC 79-9666. (Higher Education Ser.). 1980. text ed. 15.95x (ISBN 0-87589-457-7). Jossey-Bass.

Odegaard, Charles E. Area Health Education Centers: The Pioneering Years, 1972-1978. LC 79-56245. (Carnegie Council on Policy Studies in Higher Education). 124p. 1980. pap. 5.00 (ISBN 0-295-95787-5). U of Wash Pr.

--Eleven Area Health Education Centers: The View from the Grass Roots. LC 80-50250. (Carnegie Council on Policy Studies in Higher Education). (Illus.). 808p. (Orig.). 1980. pap. 20.00 (ISBN 0-295-95748-4, Pub. by Carnegie Coun Policy). U of Wash Pr.

Open University. The Good Health Guide. 1980. text ed. 22.95 (ISBN 0-06-318150-9, IntlDept). Har-Row.

Paul, Benjamin D., ed. Health, Culture & Community. LC 55-10583. 1955. pap. 6.95 (ISBN 0-87154-653-1). Russell Sage.

Pennsylvania State University Nutrition Education Curriculum Study. Nutrition in a Changing World: Grade Four. LC 80-20736. (Illus.). 152p. (Orig.). (gr. 4). 1981. pap. text ed. 11.95x (ISBN 0-8425-1864-9). Brigham.

Pisharoti, K. A. Guide to the Inegration of Health Education in Environmental Health Programmes. (Offset Pub.: No. 20). (Also avail. in French). 1975. pap. 6.00 (ISBN 92-4-170020-3). World Health.

Rash, J. Keogh & Pigg, R. Morgan. Health Education Curriculum: A Guide for Curriculum Development in Health Education. LC 78-24493. 1979. text ed. 18.95 (ISBN 0-471-03765-6). Wiley.

Read, D., et al. Health Education: The Search for Values. 1977. 13.50 (ISBN 0-13-384511-7). P-H.

Read, D. A. New Directions in Health Education: Some Contemporary Issues for the Emerging Age. 1971. pap. text ed. 5.95x (ISBN 0-02-398760-X). Macmillan.

Read, Donald A. & Greene, Walter H. Creative Teaching in Health. 3rd ed. (Illus.). 1980. text ed. 18.95 (ISBN 0-02-398700-6). Macmillan.

Rose, Clare & Nyre, G. F., eds. Agents of Academic Change: The Pandora's Box. (Health Communications & Informatics Ser.: Vol. 6, No. 1, 1980). 1980. soft cover 11.50 (ISBN 3-8055-0554-X). S Karger.

Ross, Helen S. & Mico, Paul. Theory & Practice in Health Education. LC 80-82564. (Illus.). 338p. 1980. text ed. 16.95 (ISBN 0-87484-406-1). Mayfield Pub.

Rudman, Jack. Teaching Health Conservation. (National Teachers Examination Ser.: NT-23). (Cloth bdg. avail. on request). pap. 9.95 (ISBN 0-8373-8433-8). Natl Learning.

Ruef, Dorothy N. Health Education in Senior High Schools. LC 79-177219. (Columbia University. Teachers College. Contributions to Education: No. 636). Repr. of 1934 ed. 17.50 (ISBN 0-404-55636-1). AMS Pr.

Russell, Robert D. Health Education. LC 75-12809. 264p. 1975. pap. text ed. 8.00 (ISBN 0-8106-1354-9, Co-Pub. with AMA). NEA.

Schaller, Warren E. The School Health Program. 1981. 18.95 (ISBN 0-03-057702-0, HoltC). HR&W.

Scott, Gwendolyn D. & Carlo, Mona. Learning, Feeling, Doing: Designing Creative Learning Experiences for Elementary Health Education. (Illus.). 1978. ref. ed. 15.95 (ISBN 0-13-527689-6). P-H.

Scott, Gwendolyn D. & Carlo, Mona W. On Becoming a Health Educator. 2nd ed. 200p. 1979. pap. text ed. write for info. (ISBN 0-697-07374-2). Wm C Brown.

Seaton, Ronald S. & Seaton, Edith B. Here's How: Health Education by Extension. LC 76-40599. 1976. pap. 3.95 (ISBN 0-87808-150-X). William Carey Lib.

Sheps, Cecil B. Higher Education for Public Health: A Report of the Milbank Memorial Fund Commission. LC 76-6951. 1976. 15.00 (ISBN 0-88202-065-X); pap. 9.50 (ISBN 0-685-83790-4). N Watson.

Simmons, Jeannette, ed. Making Health Education Work. 1976. 6.00x (ISBN 0-87553-080-X, 073). Am Pub Health.

Sleet, David A. & Hileman, Laurie. Guide to Health Instruction: Simulations, Games & Related Activities. 80p. (Orig.). 1981. pap. 14.95 (ISBN 0-939552-06-X, 006). Human Behavior.

Snyder, Raymond A. Professional Preparation in Health, Physical Education, & Recreation. LC 78-100177. viii, 421p. Repr. of 1954 ed. lib. bdg. 21.75 (ISBN 0-8371-4026-9, SNPH). Greenwood.

Somers, Anne, ed. Promoting Health: Consumer Education & National Policy. LC 76-21444. 240p. 1976. 12.95 (ISBN 0-912862-25-4). Aspen Systems.

Somers, Anne R. Health Promotion & Consumer Health Education. LC 76-15082. 1976. pap. 7.99 (ISBN 0-88202-104-4). N Watson.

Sorochan, Walter D. & Bender, Stephen J. Teaching Elementary Health Science. 2nd ed. LC 78-62551. (Health Education Ser.). (Illus.). 1979. text ed. 16.95 (ISBN 0-201-07492-3). A-W.

--Teaching Secondary Health Science. LC 78-1760. 1978. text ed. 23.50 (ISBN 0-471-81387-7). Wiley.

Spencer, Mary E. Health Education for Teachers: A Critical Study of the Pre-Service Preparation of Classroom Teachers for the School Health Program. LC 73-177752. (Columbia University. Teachers College. Contributions to Education: No. 589). Repr. of 1933 ed. 17.50 (ISBN 0-404-55589-6). AMS Pr.

Strang, Ruth M. Subject Matter in Health Education: An Analysis & Evaluation of the Contents of Some Courses of Study & Textbooks Dealing with Health & Suggestions for Using Such an Analysis. LC 70-177814. (Columbia University. Teachers College. Contributions to Education: No. 222). Repr. of 1926 ed. 17.50 (ISBN 0-404-55222-6). AMS Pr.

Sutherland, Ian, ed. Health Education: Perspectives & Choices. (Illus.). 1980. text ed. 22.50x (ISBN 0-04-371069-7). Allen Unwin.

Topical Index to JOSH: Nineteen Sixty-Three to Nineteen Seventy-Four. 2.50 (ISBN 0-917160-03-7). Am Sch Health.

Topical Theses & Dissertations in Health Education, Vols. 2 & 3. 1978. 7.00 (ISBN 0-685-92018-6, 244-26368). AAHPERD.

Training Programs for Health Care Workers: Pediatric Nursing Aides - Caring for Children in the Hospital. 1973. student manual 6.95 (ISBN 0-87914-020-8, 9772); instructor's guide 6.95 (ISBN 0-87914-021-6, 9773). Hosp Res & Educ.

Turner, Clair E. Planning for Health Education in Schools. 1966. 6.50 (ISBN 92-3-100626-6, U452, UNESCO). Unipub.

U. S. Senate, Committee on Labor & Public Welfare. Bilingual Education, Health, & Manpower Programs. Cordasco, Francesco, ed. LC 77-90563. (Bilingual-Bicultural Education in the U. S. Ser.). 1978. Repr. of 1973 ed. lib. bdg. 14.00x (ISBN 0-405-11101-0). Arno.

Values for Health Series, (a Values Approach to Health Education, 6 bks. Incl. Bk. A. pap. 4.00 (ISBN 0-8224-7200-7); tchrs' guide 1.50 (ISBN 0-8224-7206-6); Bk. B. pap. 4.00 (ISBN 0-8224-7201-5); tchrs guide 1.50 (ISBN 0-8224-7207-4); Bk. C. pap. 4.40 (ISBN 0-8224-7202-3); tchrs' guide 1.50 (ISBN 0-8224-7208-2); Bk. D. pap. 4.80 (ISBN 0-8224-7203-1); tchrs' guide 1.50 (ISBN 0-8224-7209-0); Bk. E. pap. 4.80 (ISBN 0-8224-7204-X); tchrs' guide 1.50 (ISBN 0-8224-7210-4); Bk. F. pap. 4.80 (ISBN 0-8224-7205-8); tchrs guide 1.50 (ISBN 0-8224-7211-2). (gr. 4-9). 1976. Pitman Learning.

WHO Expert Committee. Geneva, 1967. Planning & Evaluation of Health Education Services: Report. (Technical Report Ser.: No. 409). (Also avail. in French, Russian & Spanish). 1969. pap. 2.40 (ISBN 92-4-120409-5). World Health.

WHO Scientific Group. Geneva,1968. Research in Health Education: Report. (Technical Report Ser.: No. 432). 1969. pap. 2.00 (ISBN 92-4-120432-X). World Health.

WHO Study Group, Geneva, 1970. Health Education in Health Aspects of Family Planning: Report. (Technical Report Ser.: No. 483). (Also avail. in French & spanish). 1971. pap. 2.40 (ISBN 92-4-120483-4). World Health.

WHO Study Group. Geneva, 1971. Education & Training for Family Planning in Health Services: Report. (Technical Report Ser.: No. 508). (Also avail. in French & Spanish). 1972. pap. 2.00 (ISBN 92-4-120508-3). World Health.

WHO Study Group. Geneva, 1973. Selection of Teaching-Learning Materials in Health Sciences Education: Report. (Technical Report Ser.: No. 538). (Also avail. in French & Spanish). 1974. pap. 1.60 (ISBN 92-4-120538-5). World Health.

Wigmore, Ann. New Naturama: Living Textbook. 400p. pap. text ed. 12.95 (ISBN 0-686-29394-0). Hippocrates.

Willgoose, Carl E. Health Teaching in Secondary Schools. 2nd ed. LC 76-8587. (Illus.). 1977. text ed. 15.95 (ISBN 0-7216-9370-9). HR&W.

HEALTH EDUCATION–BIBLIOGRAPHY

Completed Research in Health, Physical Education & Recreation 1977, Vol. 19. 1977. pap. 8.00x (ISBN 0-685-81577-3, 248-264094). AAHPERD.

Completed Research in Health, Physical Education & Recreation 1978, Vol. 20. 1978. pap. 7.00x (ISBN 0-685-31239-9, 248-26170). AAHPERD.

Health Education: Drugs & Alcohol -- an Annotated Bibliography. LC 75-5753. 1975. pap. 2.50 (ISBN 0-8106-1351-4). NEA.

Horkheimer, Foley A. & Alley, Louis E., eds. Educators Guide to Free Health, Physical Education & Recreation Materials. 13th rev. ed. LC 68-57948. 1980. pap. 16.50 (ISBN 0-87708-109-3). Ed Prog.

HEALTH FACILITIES

see also Halfway Houses; Health Resorts, Watering-Places, Etc.; Mental Retardation Facilities

American Hospital Association. Directory of Architects for Health Facilities, 1981 Edition. 4th, rev. ed. LC 80-641180. 56p. 1981. 19.50 (ISBN 0-87258-350-3, 1329). Am Hospital.

--A Portfolio of Architecture for Health. LC 77-23782. (Illus.). 168p. 1977. 22.00 (ISBN 0-87258-219-1, 2300). Am Hospital.

Beales, J. Gerald. Sick Health Centers & How to Make Them Better. 147p. 1978. 14.95x (ISBN 0-8464-1136-9). Beekman Pubs.

Berriman, W. Thomas, et al. Capital Projects for Health Care Facilities. LC 76-15771. 224p. 1976. 27.50 (ISBN 0-912862-24-6). Aspen Systems.

Boyer, John M., et al. Employee Relations & Collective Bargaining in Health Care Facilities. 2nd ed. LC 75-15677. (Illus.). 350p. 1975. text ed. 21.50 (ISBN 0-8016-0726-4). Mosby.

Broyles, Robert. Financial & Managerial Accounting in Health Care Facilities, Vol. 1. 600p. 1981. text ed. price not set (ISBN 0-89443-340-7). Aspen Systems.

Chase, Mildred L. Housekeeping Management for Health Care Facilities. rev. ed. LC 78-23436. 1978. pap. 11.00 (ISBN 0-87125-045-4). Cath Health.

Coleman, J. R. & Kaminsky, F. C. Ambulatory Care Systems, Vol. 5: Financial Design & Administration of Health Maintenance Organizations. LC 76-55865. 1977. 26.95 (ISBN 0-669-01328-5). Lexington Bks.

Egdahl, R. H. & Walsh, D. C., eds. Health Services & Health Hazards: The Employee's Need to Know. LC 78-18241. (Springer Ser. on Industry & Health Care: Vol. 4). (Illus.). 1978. pap. 13.90 (ISBN 0-387-90335-6). Springer-Verlag.

Ethical & Religious Directives for Catholic Health Facilities. 1975. pap. 0.40 (ISBN 0-87125-051-9). Cath Health.

Falcier, Robert. Facilitated Self-Care: An Apologia: Health at the Millenium. 1978. write for info. (ISBN 0-915852-04-7). Ctr Human Servs.

Field, John W. Group Practice Development: A Practical Handbook. LC 76-56948. 252p. 1976. 32.00 (ISBN 0-912862-26-2). Aspen Systems.

Furst, Richard W. Financial Management for Health Care Institutions. 350p. 1981. text ed. 19.95 (ISBN 0-205-07214-3, 1072145). Allyn.

Havighurst, Clark C., ed. Regulating Health Facilities Construction. 1974. 16.25 (ISBN 0-8447-2044-5); pap. 8.25 (ISBN 0-8447-2043-7). Am Enterprise.

Hyman, Herbert H. Health Regulation: Certificate of Need & 1122. LC 76-45524. 204p. 1977. 22.00 (ISBN 0-912862-34-3). Aspen Systems.

Hyman, Stanley. Supplies Management for Health Services. 250p. 1981. 30.00x (ISBN 0-85664-707-1, Pub. by Croom Helm Ltd England). Biblio Dist.

Lasdon, Gail S. Improving Ambulatory Health Care Delivery. LC 77-75659. (Ambulatory Care Systems Ser.). 1977. 19.95 (ISBN 0-669-01514-8). Lexington Bks.

McConnell, Charles, et al. Hospital Energy Management Manual. LC 80-19015. 184p. 1980. text ed. 34.95 (ISBN 0-89443-296-6). Aspen Systems.

Malkin, Jain. The Design of Medical & Dental Facilities. 288p. 1981. text ed. price not set (ISBN 0-442-24493-2). Van Nos Reinhold.

Margulies, N. & Adams, J. D. Organizational Development in Health Care Organizations. 1982. price not set (ISBN 0-201-04505-2). A-W.

Metzger, Norman. The Health Care Supervisor's Handbook. LC 78-12513. 156p. 1978. text ed. 21.50 (ISBN 0-89443-078-5). Aspen Systems.

Rothenberg, Eleanore. Regulation & Expansion of Health Facilities. LC 76-7381. (Special Studies). (Illus.). 130p. 1976. text ed. 22.95 (ISBN 0-275-23080-5). Praeger.

Sloane, Robert M. & Sloane, Beverly L. A Guide to Health Facilities: Personnel and Management. 2nd ed. LC 76-39863. (Illus.). 1977. pap. 13.95 (ISBN 0-8016-4653-7). Mosby.

Sutton, Jeannie F., et al. Inpatient Health Facilities As Reported from the MFI Survey, United States, Nineteen Seventy-Six. (Ser. 14: No. 23). 1979. pap. text ed. 1.75 (ISBN 0-8406-0170-0). Natl Ctr Health Stats.

Turban, Ephraim, et al. Cost Containment in Hospitals. LC 80-13272. 648p. 1980. text ed. 39.75 (ISBN 0-89443-279-6). Aspen Systems.

Wasserman, Paul, ed. Health Organizations of the United States & Canada: A Directory of Voluntary Associations, Professional Societies & Other Groups Concerned with Health & Related Fields. 5th ed. 500p. 1981. 65.00 (ISBN 0-8103-0466-X). Gale.

Wing, Kenneth R., ed. Health Facility Regulation: The North Carolina Law Review Symposium. LC 80-5446. 336p. 1980. text ed. 25.00 (ISBN 0-89946-043-7). Oelgeschlager.

Wren, George R. & Knobel, Roland J., Jr. Health Planning for a Rural Model Cities Program. (Research Monograph: No. 58). 1974. spiral bdg. 3.00x (ISBN 0-88406-087-X). Ga St U Busn Pub.

HEALTH FOOD

see Food, Natural

HEALTH INSURANCE

see Insurance, Health

HEALTH MAINTENANCE ORGANIZATIONS

Christman, Luther & Counte, Michael A. Hospital Organization & Health Care Delivery. (Behavioral Science for Health Care Professionals Ser.). 128p. 1981. lib. bdg. 15.00 (ISBN 0-86531-006-8); pap. 6.75 (ISBN 0-86531-007-6). Westview.

Donabedian, Avedis, et al. Medical Care Chartbook. 7th ed. (Illus.). 420p. 1980. text ed. 42.50 (ISBN 0-914904-61-2); pap. 22.50 (ISBN 0-914904-62-0). Health Admin Pr.

Falkson, Joseph L. HMOs & the Politics of Health System Reform. LC 79-21932. 224p. (Orig.). 1980. casebound 12.75 (ISBN 0-87258-288-4, 1183); pap. 9.75 (ISBN 0-87258-276-0, 1182). Am Hospital.

Goldsmith, Seth. Health Care Management: Perspectives for Today. LC 80-25645. 263p. 1981. text ed. 26.50 (ISBN 0-89443-336-9). Aspen Systems.

Grupenhoff, John T., ed. National Directory of Health - Medicine Organization, 1980-1981. 185p. Date not set. text ed. 29.75 (ISBN 0-89443-349-0). Aspen Systems.

Harrsi, Louis. American Attitudes Towards Health Maintenance Organizations. (Louis Harris Publications Ser.). 1981. lib. bdg. 30.00 (ISBN 0-8240-9374-7). Garland Pub.

HMO's: Health Maintenance Organizations, 2 vols. Incl. Vol. 1. Carey, Sarah C., et al. 161p; Vol. 2. Stoeckle, John D., et al. 174p (ISBN 0-8422-7243-7). 1976. text ed. 29.00x ea. Irvington.

Kress, John R. & Singer, James. HMO Handbook. LC 75-18637. 206p. 1975. text ed. 27.50 (ISBN 0-912862-14-9). Aspen Systems.

Luft, Harold S. Health Maintenance Organization: Dimensions of Performance. LC 80-22420. (Health, Medicine & Society Ser.). 468p. 1981. 33.50 (ISBN 0-471-01695-0, Pub. by Wiley-Interscience). Wiley.

Prussin, Jeffrey A. Employee Health Benefits: HMOs & Mandatory Dual Choice. LC 76-24131. 230p. 1976. 49.50 (ISBN 0-912862-27-0). Aspen Systems.

Rosser, James M. & Mossberg, Howard E. An Analysis of Health Care Delivery. LC 80-11611. 188p. 1981. Repr. of 1977 ed. lib. bdg. write for info. (ISBN 0-89874-158-0). Krieger.

Salus: Low Cost Rural Health Care & Health Manpower Training, Vol. 6. 157p. 1980. pap. 10.00 (ISBN 0-88936-249-1, IDRC153, IDRC). Unipub.

Scammells, B. The Administration of Health Welfare Services: A Study of the Provision of Care to Elderly People. 134p. 1971. 21.00x (ISBN 0-7190-0462-4, Pub. by Manchester U Pr England). State Mutual Bk.

Wasserman, Paul & Bossart, Jane, eds. Health Organizations of the U.S., Canada, & Internationally: A Directory of Voluntary Associations, Professional Societies & Other Groups Concerned with Health & Related Fields. 4th ed. LC 77-79000. 500p. 1977. 36.00 (ISBN 0-686-27874-7). Kruzas Assoc.

White, Stephen L. Managing Health & Human Service Programs: A Guide for Managers. LC 80-1057. (Illus.). 1981. 17.95 (ISBN 0-02-934550-2). Free Pr.

HEALTH OF CHILDREN

see Children–Care and Hygiene

HEALTH OF INFANTS

see Infants–Care and Hygiene

HEALTH OF WOMEN

see Women–Health and Hygiene

HEALTH OF WORKERS

see Industrial Health

HEALTH OFFICERS

Baker, S. Josephine. Fighting for Life. LC 78-156075. 296p. 1980. Repr. of 1939 ed. lib. bdg. 14.50 (ISBN 0-88275-611-7). Krieger.

Dingwall, Robert. The Social Organisation of Health Visitor Training. 249p. 1977. 30.00x (ISBN 0-85664-487-0, Pub. by Croom Helm Ltd England). Biblio Dist.

McConnell, Charles R. The Effective Health Care Supervisor. 375p. 1981. text ed. price not set (ISBN 0-89443-390-3). Aspen Systems.

MacNutt, J. Scott. A Manual for Health Officers. Rosenkrantz, Barbara G., ed. LC 76-40634. (Public Health in America Ser.). (Illus.). 1977. Repr. of 1915 ed. lib. bdg. 37.00x (ISBN 0-405-09825-1). Arno.

Salus: Low Cost Rural Health Care & Health Manpower Training, Vol. 6. 157p. 1980. pap. 10.00 (ISBN 0-88936-249-1, IDRC153, IDRC). Unipub.

Village Health Workers. (Illus.). 48p. 1977. pap. 4.00 (ISBN 0-88936-106-1, IDRC 74, IDRC). Unipub.

WHO Chronicle. Education & Training of Health Workers, Vol. 24, No. 10. (Also avail. in French, Russian & Spanish). 1970. pap. 1.20 (ISBN 0-686-16781-3). World Health.

Wilson, Margaret. Equivalency Evaluation in Development of Health Practitioners. LC 76-56984. 1976. pap. text ed. 7.00 (ISBN 0-685-79297-8). C B Slack.

HEALTH PROFESSIONS

see Medical Personnel

HEALTH RECORDS

see Medical Records

HEALTH RESORTS, WATERING-PLACES, ETC.

see also Seaside Resorts; Summer Resorts

Amory, Cleveland. The Last Resorts. LC 72-10976. (Illus.). 527p. 1973. Repr. of 1952 ed. lib. bdg. 28.00x (ISBN 0-8371-6644-6, AMLR). Greenwood.

Mazzanti, Deborah S. Secrets of the Golden Door. LC 77-2722. 1977. 12.50 (ISBN 0-688-03237-0). Morrow.

Van Cleef, A. The Hot Springs of Arkansas, 1878. Jones, William R., ed. (Illus.). 20p. 1977. Repr. of 1878 ed. pap. 2.00 (ISBN 0-89646-008-8). Outbooks.

Wechsberg, Joseph. The Lost World of the Great Spas. LC 79-1691. (Illus.). 1979. 24.95 (ISBN 0-06-014584-6, HarpT). Har-Row.

Yaller, Raye & Yaller, Robert. The Health Spas: World Guidebook to Health Spas, Mineral Baths, & Nature-Cure Centers. LC 74-21128. (Lifeline Bks). (Illus.). 160p. (Orig.). 1975. pap. 2.95 (ISBN 0-912800-10-0). Woodbridge Pr.

Yaller, Robert & Yaller, Raye. Health Spas: World Guidebook. 2.95 (ISBN 0-686-30005-X). Cancer Bk Hse.

HEALTH SCIENCES ADMINISTRATION

see Public Health Administration

HEALTH SERVICES

see Public Health

HEALTH SURVEYS

Abraham, Sidney, et al. Caloria & Selected Nutrient Values of Persons Age 1-74 Years, U. S., 1971-74. Stevenson, Taloria, ed. (Ser. 11: No. 209). 1978. pap. 1.50 (ISBN 0-8406-0147-6). Natl Ctr Health Stats.

--Preliminary Findings of the First Health & Nutrition Examination Survey, U.S., Nineteen Seventy-One to Nineteen Seventy-Two, Dietary Intake & Biochemical Findings. 70p. 1974. pap. 1.25 (ISBN 0-8406-0028-3). Natl Ctr Health Stats.

Andersen, Ronald, et al. Total Survey Error: Applications to Improve Health Surveys. LC 79-88104. (Social & Behavioral Science Ser.). 1979. text ed. 16.95x (ISBN 0-87589-409-7). Jossey-Bass.

Chapin, Charles V. A Report on State Public Health Work, Based on a Survey of State Boards of Health. Rosenkrantz, Barbara G., ed. LC 76-25657. (Public Health in America Ser.). (Illus.). 1977. Repr. of 1915 ed. lib. bdg. 15.00x (ISBN 0-405-09807-3). Arno.

Clark, Margaret. Health in the Mexican-American Culture: A Community Study. 2nd ed. 1970. 18.50x (ISBN 0-520-01666-1); pap. 3.85 (ISBN 0-520-01668-8, CAL192). U of Cal Pr.

Emerson, Haven & Luginbuhl, Martha. Local Health Units for the Nation. Rosenkrantz, Barbara G., ed. LC 76-25661. (Public Health in America Ser.). (Illus.). 1977. Repr. of 1945 ed. lib. bdg. 21.00x (ISBN 0-405-09816-2). Arno.

Falk, Isidore S., et al. The Incidence of Illness & the Receipt & Costs of Medical Care Among Representative Families: Experiences in Twelve Consecutive Months During 1928-1931. LC 75-17220. (Social Problems & Social Policy Ser.). (Illus.). 1976. Repr. of 1933 ed. 19.00x (ISBN 0-405-07491-3). Arno.

John Hopkins University, Department of International Health. The Functional Analysis of Health Needs & Services. (Illus.). 1976. lib. bdg. 14.00x (ISBN 0-210-40582-1). Asia.

Kessier, Irving I. & Levin, Morton L., eds. The Community as an Epidemiologic Laboratory: A Casebook of Community Studies. LC 79-109096. (Illus.). 325p. 1970. 22.50x (ISBN 0-8018-1119-8). Johns Hopkins.

Levy, Paul S. & Lemeshow, Stanley. Sampling for Health Professionals. LC 80-14733. 320p. 1980. pap. text ed. 24.95 solutions manual (ISBN 0-534-97986-6). Lifetime Learn.

Mass Health Examinations. (Public Health Paper: No. 45). (Also avail. in French & Spanish). 1971. pap. 2.80 (ISBN 92-4-130045-0). World Health.

Maunder, W. F., ed. Health Surveys & Related Studies. LC 78-40963. (Reviews of United Kingdom Statistical Sources Ser.: Vol. IX). 1979. 55.00 (ISBN 0-08-022459-8). Pergamon.

Paul, Benjamin D., ed. Health, Culture & Community. LC 55-10583. 1955. pap. 6.95 (ISBN 0-87154-653-1). Russell Sage.

Roberts, Jean & Maurer, Kurt. Blood Pressure Levels of Persons 6-74 Years, United States, 1971-1974. Stevenson, Taloria, ed. (Ser. II: No. 203). 1977. pap. 1.75 (ISBN 0-8406-0087-9). Natl Ctr Health Stats.

Schaible, Wesley L., et al. Small Area Estimation: An Empirical Comparison of Conventional & Synthetic Estimators for States. Shipp, Audrey, ed. (Ser. 2: No. 82). 1979. pap. text ed. 1.75 (ISBN 0-8406-0176-X). Natl Ctr Health Stats.

Schoenborn, Charlotte A., et al. Basic Data from Wave I of the National Survey of Personal Health Practices & Consequences: United States, 1979. (Series 15: No. 2). 40p. 1981. pap. text ed. 1.50 (ISBN 0-8406-0230-8). Natl Ctr Health Stats.

Sheldon, J. H. Social Medicine of Old Age: Report of an Inquiry in Wolverhampton. LC 79-8688. (Growing Old Ser.). 1980. Repr. of 1948 ed. lib. bdg. 19.00 (ISBN 0-405-12804-5). Arno.

Weinberg, Eve. Community Surveys with Local Talent: A Handbook. (Report Ser: No. 123). 1971. 5.00 (ISBN 0-932132-15-4). NORC.

Wilson, Florence & Neuhauser, Duncan. Health Services in the U. S. rev. ed. Date not set. 15.50 (ISBN 0-88410-713-2). Ballinger Pub.

Worth, Robert M. & Shah, Narayan K. Nepal Health Survey, 1965-1966. LC 72-76764. (Illus., Orig.). 1969. pap. text ed. 8.00x (ISBN 0-87022-870-6). U Pr of Hawaii.

HEALTH THOUGHTS

see Mental Healing

HEALTHS, DRINKING OF

see Drinking Customs; Toasts

HEALY, JAMES AUGUSTINE, BISHOP, 1830-1900

Foley, Albert S. Bishop Healy: Beloved Outcaste. LC 79-94130. (American Negro: His History & Literature, Ser. No. 3). 1970. Repr. of 1954 ed. 12.00 (ISBN 0-405-01925-4). Arno.

HEARD, GERALD, 1889-

Savage, D. S. Mysticism & Aldous Huxley. LC 77-23247. 1947. lib. bdg. 7.50 (ISBN 0-8414-7805-8). Folcroft.

HEARING

see also Audiometry; Deafness; Ear; Labyrinth (Ear)

Baker, Donald, et al. Fundamentals of Hearing & Speech Science. Hamlet, Sandra, ed. LC 72-92716. (Illus.). 160p. 1973. text ed. 5.95 (ISBN 0-88429-001-8). Collegiate Pub.

Baltaxe, Christiane A. Foundations of Distinctive Feature Theory. 1978. 19.50 (ISBN 0-8391-1212-2). Univ Park.

Barbara, Dominick A. Art of Listening. (Illus.). 208p. 1974. 9.25 (ISBN 0-398-00086-7). C C Thomas.

Barr, David F. & Miller, Richard K. Basic Industrial Hearing Conservation. 26.95 (ISBN 0-686-74625-2). Fairmont Pr.

Baru, A. V. The Brain & Hearing: Hearing Disturbances Associated with Local Brain Lesions. LC 72-82624. (Neuropsychology Ser). 116p. 1972. 22.50 (ISBN 0-306-10876-3, Consultants). Plenum Pub.

Bateman, Hugh E. A Clinical Approach to Speech Anatomy & Physiology. (Illus.). 440p. 1977. 33.75 (ISBN 0-398-03633-0); pap. 26.75 (ISBN 0-398-03634-9). C C Thomas.

Blache, Stephen E., ed. The Acquisition of Distinctive Features. 1978. pap. 17.95 (ISBN 0-8391-1208-4). Univ Park.

Bond, Guy L. The Auditory & Speech Characteristics of Poor Readers. LC 72-176578. (Columbia University. Teachers College. Contributions to Education: No. 657). Repr. of 1935 ed. 17.50 (ISBN 0-404-55657-4). AMS Pr.

British Society of Audiology, 1st Conference, Univ. of Dundee, July 1971. Disorders of the Auditory Function: Proceedings. Taylor, W., ed. 1973. 43.50 (ISBN 0-12-684750-9). Acad Pr.

Brown, R. Don & Daigneault, Ernest A. Pharmacology of Hearing: Experimental & Clinical Bases. 376p. 1980. 45.00 (ISBN 0-471-05074-1, Pub. by Wiley-Interscience). Wiley.

Carnell, C. Mitchell, Jr. Development, Management, & Evaluation of Community Speech & Hearing Centers. (Illus.). 148p. 1976. 16.25 (ISBN 0-398-03524-5). C C Thomas.

Ciocco, A. Hearing of School Children. 1941. pap. 5.00 (ISBN 0-527-01519-9). Kraus Repr.

Cohen, Leslie B. & Salapatek, Philip, eds. Infant Perception: From Sensation to Cognition, 2 vols. Incl. Vol. 1. Basic Visual Processes. 1975. 44.50 (ISBN 0-12-178601-3); Vol. 2. Perception of Space, Speech, & Sound. 1975. 36.00 (ISBN 0-12-178602-1). (Child Psychology Ser.). 1975. 64.50 set (ISBN 0-685-72441-7). Acad Pr.

Creutzfeldt, O., ed. Hearing Mechanisms & Speech. (Experimental Brain Research Supplementum Ser.: No. 2). (Illus.). 1980. pap. 27.20 (ISBN 0-387-09655-8). Springer-Verlag.

Dallos, Peter. The Auditory Periphery: Biophysics & Physiology. 1973. 57.00 (ISBN 0-12-200750-6). Acad Pr.

Davis, Hallowell & Silverman, Richard S. Hearing & Deafness. 4th ed. LC 77-22533. 1978. pap. 21.95 (ISBN 0-03-089980-X, HoltC). HR&W.

Denes, Peter B. & Pinson, Elliot N. The Speech Chain: The Physics & Biology of Spoken Language. LC 74-180069. 192p. 1973. pap. 2.50 (ISBN 0-385-04238-8, Anch). Doubleday.

Deutsch, L. Elements of Hearing Science. 1978. 12.95 (ISBN 0-8391-1255-6). Univ Park.

Deutsch, Lawrence J. Elementary Hearing Science. 191p. pap. text ed. 12.95 (ISBN 0-8391-1255-6). Univ Park.

Dittrich, F. L. Biophysics of the Ear. (American Lecture Biochemistry & Biophysics). (Illus.). 136p. 1963. ed. spiral bdg. 16.75photocopy (ISBN 0-398-00461-7). C C Thomas.

Durrant, John D. & Lovrinic, Jean H. Bases of Hearing Science. 1977. pap. 17.50 (ISBN 0-683-02696-8). Williams & Wilkins.

Duverney, Guichard J. A Treatise of the Organ of Hearing. LC 77-147969. Repr. of 1737 ed. 21.50 (ISBN 0-404-08221-1). AMS Pr.

Evans, E. F. & Wilson, J. P., eds. Psychophysics & Physiology of Hearing. 1978. 45.00 (ISBN 0-12-244050-1). Acad Pr.

Freese, Arthur S. You & Your Hearing: How to Protect It, Preserve It, & Restore It. 1980. 10.00 (ISBN 0-684-16240-7, ScribT). Scribner.

Fulton, R. Auditory Stimulus-Response Control. 1974. 16.50 (ISBN 0-8391-0685-8). Univ Park.

Gelfano. Hearing: An Introduction to Psychological & Physiological Acoustics. 392p. 1981. 29.75 (ISBN 0-8247-1189-0). Dekker.

Gerber, Sanford E. Introductory Hearing Science: Physical & Psychological Concepts. LC 73-89177. (Illus.). 305p. 1974. text ed. 17.00 (ISBN 0-7216-4104-0). Saunders.

Gersuni, G. V., ed. Sensory Processes at the Neuronal & Behavioral Levels. 1971. 53.50 (ISBN 0-12-281350-2). Acad Pr.

Gerwin, K. S. & Glorig, A. Detection of Hearing Loss & Ear Disease in Children. (Illus.). 208p. 1974. 16.75 (ISBN 0-398-03175-4). C C Thomas.

Gillet, Pamela. Auditory Processes. LC 74-80092. 1974. pap. 4.00x (ISBN 0-87879-094-2). Acad Therapy.

Goldstein, Karen J., ed. Annual Abstracts of Speech, Voice, Language & Hearing. 1979. text ed. 15.95 (ISBN 0-316-31948-1). Little.

Gulick, W. Lawrence. Hearing: Physiology & Psychophysics. (Illus.). 1971. 16.95x (ISBN 0-19-501299-2). Oxford U Pr.

Harris, J. Donald. Anatomy & Physiology of the Peripheral Hearing Mechanism. LC 73-12474. (Studies in Communicative Disorders Ser). 1974. pap. text ed. 4.50 (ISBN 0-672-61304-2). Bobbs.

--Psychoacoustics. pap. text ed. 1.95x (ISBN 0-8290-0327-4). Irvington.

Hawley, Mones E., ed. Speech Intelligibility & Speaker Recognition. (Benchmark Papers in Acoustics Ser.: Vol. 5). 1977. 50.00 (ISBN 0-12-786643-4). Acad Pr.

Henderson, Donald, et al, eds. Effects of Noise on Hearing. LC 75-14576. 580p. 1976. 43.50 (ISBN 0-89004-012-5). Raven.

Hirsch, Ira J. Measurement of Hearing. (Psychology Ser.). 1952. text ed. 24.00 (ISBN 0-07-029045-8, C). McGraw.

How We Hear. 1977. tchrs'. guide 8.00 (ISBN 0-87453-155-1). Denoyer.

Hull, Raymond H. & Traynor, Robert M. Hearing Impairment Among Aging Persons. LC 77-70100. (Cliffs Speech & Hearing Ser.). (Illus.). 1977. pap. text ed. 2.75 (ISBN 0-8220-1826-8). Cliffs.

International Congress of Logopedics & Phoniatrics, 17th, Copenhagen, August 1977. Main Lectures: Proceedings. Loebell, E., et al, eds. (Folia Phoniatrics: Vol. 29, No. 1). (Illus.). 1977. 20.00 (ISBN 3-8055-2780-2). S Karger.

International Symposium on Hearing, Fifth, Noordwijkerhout, the Netherlands, April 8-12, 1980. Psychophysical Physiological & Behavioral Studies in Hearing: Proceedings. Van den Brink, G. & Bilsen, F. A., eds. 480p. 1980. 42.50x (ISBN 90-286-0780-3). Sijthoff & Noordhoff.

Irwin, Ruth B. Speech & Hearing Therapy. rev. ed. LC 65-21220. (Illus.). 1969. 13.00x (ISBN 0-87076-820-4). Stanwix.

Keidel, W. D. & Neff, W. D. Auditory System: Physiology (CNS), Behavioral Studies, Psychoacoustics, Vol. 5. (Handbook of Sensory Physiology: Pt. 2). (Illus.). 580p. 1976. 126.50 (ISBN 0-387-07000-1). Springer-Verlag.

Kuroda, Ryo. Experimental Researches Upon the Sense of Hearing in Lower Vertebrates, Including Reptiles, Amphibians, & Fishes. LC 26-12355. 1926. pap. 5.00 (ISBN 0-527-24851-7). Kraus Repr.

Lass, Norman J., ed. Speech & Hearing Science: Selected Readings. 382p. 1974. text ed. 35.50x (ISBN 0-8422-5154-5); pap. text ed. 14.50x (ISBN 0-8422-0377-X). Irvington.

Leavitt, G. S. Oral-Aural Communications (OAC) A Teacher's Manual. (Illus.). 136p. 1974. 11.75 (ISBN 0-398-03061-8); pap. 8.25 (ISBN 0-398-03063-4). C C Thomas.

Martin, F. M. & Murray, Kathleen, eds. Children's Hearing. 1976. 15.00x (ISBN 0-7073-0123-8, Pub. by Scottish Academic Pr Scotland). Columbia U Pr.

Maurer, James F. & Rupp, Ralph R. Hearing & Aging: Tactics for Intervention. 304p. 1979. 21.00 (ISBN 0-8089-1171-6). Grune.

Miller, Alfred L., et al. Your Child's Hearing & Speech: A Guide for Parents. (Illus.). 104p. 1974. pap. 6.25 (ISBN 0-398-03013-8). C C Thomas.

Miller, Diane M. & Miller, Alfred L. Carryover Articulation Manual: A Language Approach to the (S) & (R) Phonemes. (Illus.). 80p. 1971. photocopy ed. spiral 7.75 (ISBN 0-398-01310-1). C C Thomas.

Minifie, Fred D., et al. Normal Aspects of Speech, Hearing, & Language. (Illus.). 528p. 1973. ref. ed. 20.95 (ISBN 0-13-623702-9). P-H.

Moller, Aage R. & Boston, Pamela, eds. Basic Mechanisms in Hearing. 1973. 56.00 (ISBN 0-12-504250-7). Acad Pr.

Moore. Introduction to the Psychology of Hearing. (Illus.). 1977. 14.50 (ISBN 0-8391-0996-2). Univ Park.

Neuschutz, Louise M. How to Help Your Hearing. 1940. 20.00 (ISBN 0-8492-9971-3). R West.

Nieder, Philip C. The Cochlea As an Opto-Acoustic Device: A Unified Theory for the Function of the End Organ of Hearing in Mammals. LC 74-29191. (Illus.). 1974. 2.00x (ISBN 0-915176-05-X). Woods Hole.

Ogden, R. M. Hearing. 59.95 (ISBN 0-8490-0287-7). Gordon Pr.

Ogden, Robert M. Hearing. LC 73-97562. Repr. of 1924 ed. 19.50 (ISBN 0-404-04812-9). AMS Pr.

--Hearing. LC 75-124248. (Select Bibliographies Reprint Ser). 1924. 26.00 (ISBN 0-8369-5137-9). Arno.

Paparella, ed. Biochemical Mechanisms in Hearing & Deafness. (Illus.). 416p. 1970. 27.50 (ISBN 0-398-01445-0). C C Thomas.

Popelka, Gerald, ed. Hearing Assessment with the Acoustic Reflex. (Illus.). 1981. 17.50 (ISBN 0-8089-1361-1). Grune.

Popper, A. N. & Fay, R. R., eds. Comparative Studies of Hearing in Invertebrates. (Proceedings in Life Sciences Ser.). (Illus.). 512p. 1980. 39.80 (ISBN 0-387-90460-3). Springer-Verlag.

Ptacek, Paul H., et al. Index to Speech, Language & Hearing Journal Titles, 1954-78. LC 79-20058. 305p. 1979. text ed. 25.00 (ISBN 0-933014-54-6). College-Hill.

Reagan, Cora L. Handbook of Auditory Perceptual Training. 168p. 1973. 11.75 (ISBN 0-398-02885-0). C C Thomas.

Reed, Vicki. Basic Anatomy & Physiology of Speech & Hearing: A Learning Guide. 2nd ed. 1981. text ed. write for info. (ISBN 0-8134-2195-0). Interstate.

Roberts, Jean & Ahuja, Elizabeth. Hearing Levels of U. S. Youths 12-17 Years. LC 74-11318. (Data from Health Examination Survey Ser. 11: No. 145). 65p. 1975. pap. 1.50 (ISBN 0-8406-0024-0). Natl Ctr Health Stats.

Rosenblum, Estelle. Fundamentals of Hearing for Health Professionals. 1979. 8.95 (ISBN 0-316-75730-6). Little.

Rossignol, Lois J. The Relationships Among Hearing Acuity, Speech Production, & Reading Performance in Grades 1a, 1b, & 2a. LC 73-177212. (Columbia University. Teachers College. Contributions to Education: No. 936). Repr. of 1948 ed. 17.50 (ISBN 0-404-55936-0). AMS Pr.

Rudman, Jack. Audiologist - Speech Pathologist. (Career Examination Ser.: C-59). (Cloth bdg. avail. on request). pap. 10.00 (ISBN 0-8373-0059-2). Natl Learning.

--Senior Speech & Hearing Therapist. (Career Examination Ser.: C-2273). (Cloth bdg. avail. on request). 1977. pap. 10.00 (ISBN 0-8373-2273-1). Natl Learning.

--Speech & Hearing Therapist. (Career Examination Ser.: C-754). (Cloth bdg. avail. on request). pap. 10.00 (ISBN 0-8373-0754-6). Natl Learning.

Sanders, Derek A. Auditory Perception of Speech: An Introduction to Principles & Problems. LC 76-27320. (Illus.). 1977. text ed. 16.95 (ISBN 0-13-052787-4). P-H.

Schow, Ronald L., et al, eds. Communication Disorders of the Aged. 1978. pap. 16.95 (ISBN 0-8391-1237-8). Univ Park.

Schubert, E. D. Hearing: Its Function & Dysfunction. (Disorders of Human Communications: Vol. 1). (Illus.). 200p. 1980. 29.50 (ISBN 0-387-81579-1). Springer-Verlag.

Schuijf, A. & Hawkins, A. D., eds. Sound Reception in Fish. LC 76-54648. (Developments in Aquaculture & Fisheries Science: Vol. 5). 1977. 40.00 (ISBN 0-444-41540-8). Elsevier.

Singh, Roderick P. Anatomy of Hearing & Speech. (Illus.). 176p. 1980. text ed. 13.95x (ISBN 0-19-502665-9); pap. text ed. 7.95x (ISBN 0-19-502666-7). Oxford U Pr.

Singh, S. Diagnostic Procedures in Hearing, Language & Speech. 1978. 29.50 (ISBN 0-8391-1217-3). Univ Park.

--Distinctive Features: Theory & Validation. (Illus.). 300p. 1976. 16.50 (ISBN 0-8391-0754-4). Univ Park.

Skinner, Paul H. & Shelton, Ralph L. Speech, Language & Hearing: Normal Processes & Disorders. LC 77-73956. (Speech Pathology & Audiology Ser.). 1978. text ed. 16.95 (ISBN 0-201-07461-3); instr's man. price not set (ISBN 0-201-07462-1). A-W.

Smith, Clarissa R. & Karp, Adrienne. A Workbook in Auditory Training for Adults: With a Special Section on the Institutionalized Geriatric Patient. 112p. 1978. 12.75 (ISBN 0-398-03760-4); pap. 7.75 (ISBN 0-398-03768-X). C C Thomas.

Strong, William J. & Plitnik, George R. Music, Speech, & High Fidelity: A Descriptive Acoustics Workbook. (Illus.). 1977. pap. 12.95x (ISBN 0-8425-0797-3). Brigham.

Syka, Josef & Aitkin, Lindsay, eds. Neuronal Mechanisms of Hearing. 430p. 1981. 45.00 (ISBN 0-306-40656-X). Plenum Pub.

Szende. Intervallic Hearing: Its Nature & Pedagogy. 1977. 13.00 (ISBN 0-9960013-3-6, Pub. by Kaido Hungary). Heyden.

Tobias, Jerry V., ed. Foundations of Modern Auditory Theory, 2 vols. LC 78-91432. 1970-72. Vol. 1. 57.00 (ISBN 0-12-691901-1); Vol. 2. 57.00 (ISBN 0-12-691902-X). Acad Pr.

Tobias, Jerry V. & Schubert, Earl D., eds. Hearing & Research Theory, Vol. I. (Serial Publication). 1980. 18.50 (ISBN 0-12-312101-9). Acad Pr.

Von Bekesy, Georg. Experiments in Hearing. LC 77-4715. 756p. 1980. Repr. of 1960 ed. lib. bdg. 32.50 (ISBN 0-88275-552-8). Krieger.

Voroba, Barry. Experimenting in the Hearing & Speech Sciences: 1978. LC 78-63106. (Illus.). 204p. 1978. 21.95 (ISBN 0-9601970-2-8); pap. 14.95 (ISBN 0-9601970-1-X); ring binder 29.95 (ISBN 0-9601970-0-1). Starkey Labs.

Warren, Richard M. Aspects of Auditory Perception: Non-Verbal Sounds & Speech. (Pergamon General Psychology Ser.). 225p. Date not set. write for info. (ISBN 0-08-025957-X). Pergamon.

Welles, Henry H. The Measurement of Certain Aspects of Personality Among Hard of Hearing Adults. LC 72-177654. (Columbia University. Teachers College. Contributions to Education: No. 138). Repr. of 1932 ed. 17.50 (ISBN 0-404-55545-4). AMS Pr.

Wever, Glen & Lawrence, M. Physiological Acoustics. 1954. 32.50x (ISBN 0-691-08018-6). Princeton U Pr.

Yost, William A. & Nielsen, Donald W. Fundamentals of Hearing: An Introduction. LC 76-54247. 1977. text ed. 19.95 (ISBN 0-03-016781-7, HoltC). HR&W.

Zemlin, W. R. Speech & Hearing Science: Anatomy & Physiology. 2nd ed. (Illus.). 704p. 1981. text ed. 23.95 (ISBN 0-13-827378-2). P-H.

Zemlin, Willard R. Speech & Hearing Science: Anatomy & Physiology. 1968. ref. ed. 24.95 (ISBN 0-13-827386-3). P-H.

HEARING–BIBLIOGRAPHY

Ptacek, Paul, et al, eds. Index to Speech, Language & Hearing: Journal Titles, 1954-78. 25.00 (ISBN 0-933014-54-6). College-Hill.

HEARING–JUVENILE LITERATURE

Allington, Richard L. & Cowles, Kathleen. Hearing. LC 79-28387. (Beginning to Learn About Ser.). (Illus.). 32p. (ps-2). 1980. PLB 10.65 (ISBN 0-8172-1291-4). Raintree Pubs.

Fryer, Judith. How We Hear: The Story of Hearing. LC 61-13575. (Medical Bks for Children). (Illus.). (gr. 3-9). 1961. PLB 3.95 (ISBN 0-8225-0012-4). Lerner Pubns.

Rosner, Jerome. Auditory Analysis Skillsbook. (gr. k-3). 1981. 17.50 (ISBN 0-8027-9127-1). Walker & Co.

Silverstein, Alvin & Silverstein, Virginia B. The Story of Your Ear. 64p. (gr. 5-9). Date not set. lib. bdg. 6.99 (ISBN 0-698-30704-6). Coward.

Ward, Brian. The Ear and Hearing. (The Human Body Ser.). (Illus.). 48p. (gr. 4 up). 1981. lib. bdg. 7.90 (ISBN 0-531-04289-8). Watts.

HEARING–TESTING

see Audiometry

HEARING AIDS

Craig, et al. Hearing Aids & You. 121p. (gr. 4 up). 3.95 (ISBN 0-86575-028-9). Dormac.

--Your Child's Hearing Aid. 46p. 1976. write for info (ISBN 0-86575-029-7). Dormac.

Donnelly, Kenneth, ed. Interpreting Hearing Aid Technology. (Illus.). 320p. 1974. text ed. 21.50 (ISBN 0-398-03087-1). C C Thomas.

Ewing, A. & Ewing, E. C. Hearing Aids, Lip Reading & Clear Speech. 128p. 1967. 18.00x (ISBN 0-7190-0315-6, Pub. by Manchester U Pr England). State Mutual Bk.

Gauger, Jaclyn S. Orientation to Hearing Aids. 1978. 9.45 (ISBN 0-88200-132-9, N6362). Alexander Graham.

Haug, Olaf & Haug, Scott. Help for the Hard of Hearing: A Speech, Reading & Auditory Training Manual for Home & Professionally Guided Training. 144p. 1977. 13.00 (ISBN 0-398-03674-8); pap. 8.75 (ISBN 0-398-03675-6). C C Thomas.

Heasley, Bernice E. Auditory Processing Disorders & Remediation. 2nd ed. (Illus.). 168p. 1980. pap. 16.50 spiral bdg. (ISBN 0-398-04047-8). C C Thomas.

Hodgson, W. R. & Skinner, Paul. Hearing Aid Assessment & Use in Audiologic Rehabilitation. 2nd ed. (Illus.). 343p. 1981. 32.00 (ISBN 0-683-04092-8). Williams & Wilkins.

Levitt & Pickett. Sensory Aids for the Hearing Impaired. LC 76-28875. 566p. 1980. 46.95 (ISBN 0-471-08436-0, Pub. by Wiley-Interscience); pap. 30.50 (ISBN 0-471-08437-9). Wiley.

Levitt, H., et al, eds. Sensory Aids for the Hearing Impaired. LC 76-28875. 1980. 46.95 (ISBN 0-87942-087-1). Inst Electrical.

Loavenbruck, Angela M. & Madell, Jane, eds. Hearing Aid Dispensing for Audiologists: A Guide for Clinical Service. (Illus.). 203p. 1980. 16.50 (ISBN 0-8089-1323-9). Grune.

Markides, Andreas. Binaural Hearing Aids. 1977. 41.00 (ISBN 0-12-472650-X). Acad Pr.

Miller, A. L. Hearing Loss, Hearing Aids & Your Child. (Illus.). 112p. 1980. lexotone 7.50 (ISBN 0-398-03979-8). C C Thomas.

Miller, Maurice. Hearing Aids. LC 72-190707. (Studies in Communicative Disorders Ser). 1972. pap. 2.50 (ISBN 0-672-61284-4). Bobbs.

Peterson, Dean R. Hearing Aids New Era. 9.95 (ISBN 0-89741-005-X). Roadrunner Tech.

Rosenthal, Richard. The Hearing-Loss Handbook. LC 75-9496. (Illus.). 225p. 1975. 8.95 (ISBN 0-312-36540-3). St Martin.

Rubin, Martha, ed. Hearing Aids: Current Developments & Concepts. (Illus.). 1976. 19.50 (ISBN 0-8391-0939-3). Univ Park.
Staab, Wayne J. The Hearing Aid Book. (Illus.). 1978. 12.95 (ISBN 0-8306-8987-7); pap. 8.95 (ISBN 0-8306-7987-1, 987). TAB Bks.
Studebaker, Gerald A. Acoustical Factors Affecting Hearing Aid Performance. 450p. text ed. 34.50 (ISBN 0-8391-1553-9). Univ Park.
Watson, Leland & Tolan, Thomas. Hearing Tests & Hearing Instruments. 1967. Repr. of 1949 ed. 24.00 (ISBN 0-02-854500-1). Hafner.
Yanick, Paul, Jr. & Freifield, Stephen, eds. The Application of Signal Processing Concepts to Hearing Aids. 256p. 1978. text ed. 19.50 (ISBN 0-8089-1106-6). Grune.

HEARING DISORDERS
see also Deafness

Barrager, Diane & Perkins, Rodney. The Hearing Book. Orig. Title: Come Again, Please... (Illus.). 128p. 1980. pap. 8.95 (ISBN 0-89106-016-2, 7274). Consulting Psychol.
Bradford, Larry J. & Hardy, William G., eds. Hearing & Hearing Impairment. 672p. 1979. 53.50 (ISBN 0-8089-1145-7). Grune.
Frisina, Robert, ed. Bicentennial Monograph on Hearing Impairment. LC 76-16454. 1976. softcover 4.95 (ISBN 0-88200-100-0, L9338). Alexander Graham.
Gentile, Augustine. Persons with Impaired Hearing, U. S., 1971. Knox, Kathleen, ed. LC 75-619226. (Data from the Health Interview Survey Ser 10: No. 101). 65p. 1975. pap. text ed. 1.75 (ISBN 0-8406-0048-8). Natl Ctr Health Stats.
Gerber, Sanford E. & Mencher, George T. Auditory Dysfunction. (Illus.). 256p. 1980. text ed. 20.00 (ISBN 0-933014-60-0). College-Hill.
Gerber, Sanford E. & Mencher, George T., eds. Early Diagnosis of Hearing Loss. 384p. 1978. 22.75 (ISBN 0-8089-1153-8). Grune.
Giolas, Thomas G. Hearing-Handicapped Adults. (Illus.). 240p. 1982. 18.95 (ISBN 0-13-384693-8). P-H.
Griffith, Jerry. Persons with Hearing Loss. (Illus.). 240p. 1969. photocopy ed. spiral 24.50 (ISBN 0-398-00737-3). C C Thomas.
Hamernik, Roger P., et al, eds. New Perspectives on Noise-Induced Hearing Loss. 525p. 1981. text ed. 58.00 (ISBN 0-89004-601-8). Raven.
Heasley, Bernice E. Auditory Processing Disorders & Remediation. 2nd ed. (Illus.). 168p. 1980. pap. 16.50 spiral bdg. (ISBN 0-398-04047-8). C C Thomas.
Helleberg, Marilyn M. Your Hearing Loss: How to Break the Sound Barrier. LC 78-8663. 1979. 15.95 (ISBN 0-88229-341-9). Nelson-Hall.
Henoch, Miriam A., ed. Aural Rehabilitation for the Elderly. 240p. 1979. 20.25 (ISBN 0-8089-1186-4). Grune.
Information Center for Hearing, Speech & Disorders of Human Communication of the Johns Hopkins Medical Institution, compiled by. Hearing, Speech & Communication Disorders. Incl. Cumulated Citations: 1973. 772p. 1974. 85.00 (ISBN 0-306-67311-8); Cumulated Citations: 1974. 789p. 1975. 75.00 (ISBN 0-306-67312-6). LC 74-9879. IFI Plenum.
Jeffers, Janet & Barley, Margaret. Look, Now Hear This: Combined Auditory Training & Speechreading Instruction. (Illus.). 230p. 1979. text ed. 17.75 (ISBN 0-398-03830-9). C C Thomas.
Keith, Robert W., ed. Central Auditory Dysfunction. LC 77-10777. 400p. 1977. 21.00 (ISBN 0-8089-1061-2). Grune.
Kelly, J. C. Clinician's Handbook for Auditory Training. LC 73-88227. 1973. pap. text ed. 6.25 (ISBN 0-88200-065-9, A1770). Alexander Graham.
Larson, Vernon D., et al, eds. Current Trends in Auditory & Hearing Prosthesis Research. 480p. 1979. 24.50 (ISBN 0-685-67602-1). Grune.
Lass, Norman J., et al. Speech, Language & Hearing: Normal Processes & Clinical Disorders. LC 77-77198. (Illus.). 1000p. Date not set. text ed. price not set (ISBN 0-7216-5634-X). Saunders.
Levin, Stefan & Knight, Connie H., eds. Genetic & Environmental Hearing Loss: Syndromic & Nonsyndromic. (Alan R. Liss Ser.: Vol. 16, No. 7). 1980. 16.00 (ISBN 0-8451-1040-3). March of Dimes.
Lysons, Kenneth. Your Hearing Loss & How to Cope with It. 1978. 5.50 (ISBN 0-7153-7472-9). David & Charles.
Madden, Richard. The School Status of the Hard of Hearing Child: An Analysis of the Intelligence, the Achievement & Certain Personality Traits of the Hard of Hearing School Child. LC 76-177044. (Columbia University. Teachers College. Contributions to Education: No. 499). Repr. of 1931 ed. 17.50 (ISBN 0-404-55499-7). AMS Pr.
Martin, Frederick N., ed. Medical Audiology: Disorders of Hearing. (Illus.). 512p. 1981. text ed. 32.00 (ISBN 0-13-572677-8). P-H.
Mencher, George T. & Gerber, Sanford, eds. Early Management of Hearing Loss. (Illus.). 468p. 1980. 19.50 (ISBN 0-8089-1346-8). Grune.
Noble, W. G. The Assessment of Hearing Loss & Handicap in Adults. 1978. 26.50 (ISBN 0-12-520050-1). Acad Pr.
Northern, Jerry L., ed. Hearing Disorders. 1976. pap. 13.95 (ISBN 0-316-61195-6). Little.
Nova Scotia Conference on Early Identification of Hearing Loss, Halifax, Nova Scotia, September 9-11, 1974. Proceedings. Mencher, Georges T., ed. 1976. 29.50 (ISBN 3-8055-2296-7). S Karger.
Oyer, Herbert J., ed. Communication for the Hearing Handicapped: An International Perspective. (Illus.). 1976. 24.50 (ISBN 0-8391-0826-5). Univ Park.
Paparella, Michael M., et al. Ear Clinics International Sensorineural Hearing Loss, Vertigo & Tinnitus. (Ear Clinics International). 232p. 1981. 25.00 (ISBN 0-686-77768-9, 6750-8). Williams & Wilkins.
Pollack, Michael C. Amplification for the Hearing Impaired. 2nd ed. 480p. 1980. 24.50 (ISBN 0-8089-1212-7). Grune.
Prescod, Stephen V. Audiological Handbook of Hearing Disorders. 1978. text ed. 19.50x (ISBN 0-442-26632-4). Van Nos Reinhold.
Readings in Speech & Hearing. (Special Education Ser.). 1978. pap. text ed. 10.95 (ISBN 0-89568-005-X). Spec Learn Corp.
Rosenthal, Richard. The Hearing-Loss Handbook. LC 75-9496. (Illus.). 225p. 1975. 8.95 (ISBN 0-312-36540-3). St Martin.
--The Hearing Loss Handbook. LC 77-87894. 1978. pap. 4.95 (ISBN 0-8052-0587-X). Schocken.
Sataloff, Joseph. Hearing Loss. 2nd ed. 1980. text ed. 34.00 (ISBN 0-397-50426-8, JBL-Med-Nursing). Har-Row.
Sataloff, Joseph & Michael, Paul. Hearing Conservation. (Illus.). 376p. 1973. 21.75 (ISBN 0-398-02822-2). C C Thomas.
Shambaugh, George & Shea, John J. Proceedings of the Shambaugh Fifth International Workshop on Middle Ear Microsurgery and Fluctant Hearing Loss. LC 77-79552. 1977. 35.00 (ISBN 0-87397-125-6). Strode.
Skinner, Paul H. & Shelton, Ralph L. Speech, Language & Hearing: Normal Processes & Disorders. LC 77-73956. (Speech Pathology & Audiology Ser.). 1978. text ed. 16.95 (ISBN 0-201-07461-3); instr's man. price not set (ISBN 0-201-07462-1). A-W.
Small, Arnold M. Elements of Hearing Science: A Programmed Text. LC 77-20110. (Communications Disorders Ser.). 1978. 12.95 (ISBN 0-471-01732-9). Wiley.
Yanick, Paul, Jr., ed. Rehabilitation Strategies for Sensorineural Hearing Loss: Proceedings of the Second Conference on Auditory Techniques. 256p. 1979. 15.00 (ISBN 0-8089-1215-1). Grune.
Yeates, Sybil. Development of Hearing. (Studies in Developmental Pediatrics Ser.: Vol. 2). 240p. 1981. text ed. 17.50 (ISBN 0-88416-378-4). Wright-PSG.
Yules, Richard B., et al. Speech-Hearing Pathology & Surgery. LC 79-51131. (Cliffs Speech & Hearing Ser.). (Illus., Orig.). 1980. pap. text ed. 4.95 (ISBN 0-8220-1828-4). Cliffs.

HEARING DISORDERS IN CHILDREN
see also Children, Deaf

Blackwell, Peter M., et al. Sentences & Other Systems: A Language & Learning Curriculum for Hearing-Impaired Children. LC 78-51922. 1978. pap. text ed. 11.75 (ISBN 0-88200-118-3, C2557). Alexander Graham.
Boothroyd, Arthur. Hearing Impairments in Young Children. (Illus.). 266p. 1982. 19.95 (ISBN 0-13-773408-5). P-H.
Freeman, Roger D., et al. Can't Your Child Hear? 368p. 1981. pap. text ed. 16.95 (ISBN 0-8391-1616-0). Univ Park.
Graham, Malcolm D. Cleft Palate: Middle Ear Disease & Hearing Loss. (Illus.). 168p. 1978. 18.25 (ISBN 0-398-03667-5). C C Thomas.
Harford, Earl R., et al, eds. Impedance Screening for Middle Ear Diseases in Children. LC 78-57629. 320p. 1978. 19.00 (ISBN 0-8089-1097-3). Grune.
Hasenstab, M. Suzanne & Horner, John S. Comprehensive Services for Hearing Impaired Infants & Preschool Children. 300p. 1981. text ed. price not set (ISBN 0-89443-384-9). Aspen Systems.
Jaffe, B. F. Hearing Loss in Children. (Illus.). 1977. 34.50 (ISBN 0-8391-0824-9). Univ Park.
Johnson, J. C. Educating Hearing-Impaired Children in Ordinary Schools. 130p. 1962. 21.00x (ISBN 0-7190-0361-X, Pub. by Manchester U Pr England). State Mutual Bk.
Keith, Robert W., ed. Central Auditory & Language Disorders in Children. (Illus.). 198p. 1981. text ed. 29.00 (ISBN 0-933014-61-9). College-Hill.
Light, Janice B. The Joy of Listening. LC 78-52752. 1978. pap. text ed. 7.50 (ISBN 0-88200-119-1, M7992). Alexander Graham.
Ling, Daniel & Ling, Agnes H. Aural Habilitation: The Foundations of Verbal Learning in Hearing-Impaired Children. LC 78-56077. 1978. pap. text ed. 12.50 (ISBN 0-88200-121-3, C2441). Alexander Graham.
--Basic Vocabulary & Language Thesaurus for Hearing-Impaired Children. LC 76-52826. 1977. 4.50 (ISBN 0-88200-078-0, C1437). Alexander Graham.
Miller, A. L. Hearing Loss, Hearing Aids & Your Child. (Illus.). 112p. 1980. lexotone 7.50 (ISBN 0-398-03979-8). C C Thomas.
Nix, Gary W., ed. The Rights of the Hearing-Impaired Child. LC 77-85240. 1977. 3.95 (ISBN 0-88200-112-4, P5543). Alexander Graham.
Northcott, Winifred H., ed. Curriculum Guide: Hearing-Impaired Children, Birth to Three Years, & Their Parents. LC 76-56634. 1977. pap. text ed. 9.50 (ISBN 0-88200-077-2, D1998). Alexander Graham.
Northern, Jerry L. Hearing in Children. 2nd ed. (Illus.). 350p. 1978. 23.00 (ISBN 0-683-06572-6). Williams & Wilkins.
Phillips, Phyllis P. Speech & Hearing Problems in the Classroom. LC 74-78838. (Speech & Hearing Ser.). (Illus.). 134p. (Orig.). 1975. pap. text ed. 3.95 (ISBN 0-8220-1807-1). Cliffs.
Rampp, Donald L. Classroom Activities for Auditory Perceptual Disorders. 1976. pap. text ed. 2.95x (ISBN 0-8134-1794-5, 1794). Interstate.
Ross, Mark. Hard of Hearing Children in Regular Schools. (Illus.). 272p. 1982. 18.95 (ISBN 0-13-383802-1). P-H.
Rush, Mary L. The Language of Directions: A Programmed Workbook. LC 77-87703. 1977. pap. text ed. 7.75 (ISBN 0-88200-113-2, C1321). Alexander Graham.
Whitehurst, Mary W. Auditory Training for Children. 1966. pap. text ed. 6.75 (ISBN 0-88200-125-6, M8107). Alexander Graham.

HEARING-IMPAIRED CHILDREN
see Children, Deaf

HEARINGS (CRIMINAL PROCEDURE)
see Preliminary Examinations (Criminal Procedure)

HEARN, LAFCADIO, 1850-1904

Ball, Charles E. Lafcadio Hearn: An Appreciation. LC 74-13639. 1926. lib. bdg. 5.00 (ISBN 0-8414-3251-1). Folcroft.
Bisland, Elizabeth. The Japanese Letters of Lafcadio Hearn. 1973. Repr. of 1911 ed. 35.00 (ISBN 0-8274-1217-7). R West.
Bisland, Elizabeth, ed. The Japanese Letters of Lafcadio Hearn. LC 72-82097. (Japan Library Ser.). (Illus.). 1973. Repr. of 1910 ed. lib. bdg. 26.00 (ISBN 0-8420-1391-1). Scholarly Res Inc.
Hearn, Lafcadio. Editorials of Lafacadio Hearn. Hutson, Charles W., ed. (American Newspapermen 1790-1933 Ser). xx, 356p. 1974. Repr. of 1926 ed. 17.50x (ISBN 0-8464-0020-0). Beekman Pubs.
--Manuscript Facsimiles of Various Lafcadio Hearn Writings in the Tenri Central Library Collection, Tokyo, Japan, 5 titles. Repr. of 1975 ed. 260.00 set (ISBN 0-685-73260-6). Ams Pr.
Hearn, Setsu K. Reminiscences of Lafcadio Hearn. 87p. 1979. Repr. of 1918 ed. lib. bdg. 30.00 (ISBN 0-8482-1225-8). Norwood Edns.
Kennard, Nina H. Lafcadio Hearn. LC 67-27613. 1968. Repr. of 1912 ed. 14.50 (ISBN 0-8046-0248-4). Kennikat.
--Lafcadio Hearn. 1977. Repr. of 1912 ed. lib. bdg. 35.00 (ISBN 0-8492-1409-2). R West.
McWilliams, Vera. Lafcadio Hearn. LC 79-129462. 1971. Repr. of 1949 ed. 16.50x (ISBN 0-8154-0350-X). Cooper Sq.
Noguchi, Y. Lafcadio Hearn in Japan. lib. bdg. 59.95 (ISBN 0-8490-0480-2). Gordon Pr.
Noguchi, Yone. Latcadio Hearn in Japan. LC 78-2870. 1973. lib. bdg. 25.00 (ISBN 0-8414-0284-1). Folcroft.
Perkins, Percival D. & Perkins, Ione. Lafcadio Hearn: A Bibliography of His Writings. 1934. 29.50 (ISBN 0-8337-2726-5). B Franklin.
Reminiscences of Lafcadio Hearn. LC 78-16202. 1978. Repr. of 1918 ed. lib. bdg. 20.00 (ISBN 0-8414-2226-5). Folcroft.
Rexroth, Kenneth, ed. The Buddhist Writings of Lafcadio Hearn. LC 77-2496. 312p. 1977. lib. bdg. 12.95 (ISBN 0-915520-05-2). Ross-Erikson.
Stevenson, Elizabeth. Lafcadio Hearn: A Biography. 1979. Repr. of 1961 ed. lib. bdg. 17.50x (ISBN 0-374-97625-2). Octagon.
Temple, J. Blue Ghost: Lafcadio Hearn's Work. LC 74-16485. (American Literature Ser., No. 49). 1974. lib. bdg. 49.95 (ISBN 0-8383-2027-9). Haskell.
Thomas, Edward. Lafcadio Hearn. LC 77-7488. 1977. Repr. of 1912 ed. lib. bdg. 10.00 (ISBN 0-8414-8630-1). Folcroft.
Tinker, Edward L. Lafcadio Hearn's American Days. LC 71-99064. (Library of Lives & Letters). (Illus.). 1970. Repr. of 1924 ed. 24.00 (ISBN 0-8103-3366-X). Gale.

HEARNE, SAMUEL

Laut, Agnes C. Pathfinders of the West. LC 74-90651. (Essay Index Reprint Ser). 1904. 25.00 (ISBN 0-8369-1220-9). Arno.

HEARST, PATRICIA, 1954-

Alexander, Shana. Anyone's Daughter. 1979. 14.95 (ISBN 0-670-12949-6). Viking Pr.
Avery, Paul & McLellan, Vin. The Voices of Guns. (Illus.). 388p. 1977. 14.95 (ISBN 0-399-11738-5). Putnam.
Chaney, Lindsay & Ciepli, Michael. The Hearsts: Family & Empire, the Later Years. 1981. 16.95 (ISBN 0-671-24765-4). S&S.
Maguire, John G. & Dunn, Mary L. Patty Hearst. 2nd ed. 1975. pap. 1.50 (ISBN 0-89596-233-0, Success). Merit Pubns.

HEARST, WILLIAM RANDOLPH, 1863-1951

Carlisle, Rodney P. Hearst & the New Deal - The Progressive As Reactionary. Freidel, Frank, ed. LC 78-62378. (Modern American History Ser.: Vol. 4). 1979. lib. bdg. 28.00 (ISBN 0-8240-3628-X). Garland Pub.
Carlson, Oliver & Bates, Ernest S. Hearst, Lord of San Simeon. LC 70-98830. Repr. of 1936 ed. lib. bdg. 15.00 (ISBN 0-8371-2847-1, CAHE). Greenwood.
--Hearst, Lord of San Simeon. (American Studies). 1969. Repr. of 1936 ed. 19.50 (ISBN 0-384-07575-4). Johnson Repr.
Chaney, Lindsay & Ciepli, Michael. The Hearsts: Family & Empire, the Later Years. 1981. 16.95 (ISBN 0-671-24765-4). S&S.
Littlefield, Roy E., III. William Randolph Hearst: His Role in American Progressivism. LC 80-5729. 405p. 1980. lib. bdg. 22.75 (ISBN 0-8191-1320-4); pap. text ed. 13.75 (ISBN 0-8191-1321-2). U Pr of Amer.
Lundberg, Ferdinand. Imperial Hearst. LC 73-125704. (American Journalists). 1970. Repr. of 1927 ed. 19.00 (ISBN 0-405-01685-9). Arno.
--Imperial Hearst, a Social Biography. Repr. of 1936 ed. lib. bdg. 15.25x (ISBN 0-8371-2963-X, LUIH). Greenwood.
Older, Mrs. Fremont. William Randolph Hearst, American. LC 72-7195. (Select Bibliographies Reprints Ser.). 1972. Repr. of 1936 ed. 35.00 (ISBN 0-8369-6951-0). Arno.
O'Loughlin, Edward T., ed. Hearst & His Enemies. LC 76-125710. (American Journalists). 1970. Repr. of 1919 ed. 9.00 (ISBN 0-405-01691-3). Arno.
Swanberg, W. A. Citizen Hearst. 600p. 1981. pap. 4.95 (ISBN 0-684-17147-3, ScribT). Scribner.
--Citizen Hearst. (Illus.). 1961. lib. rep. ed. 25.00x (ISBN 0-684-14503-0, ScribT). Scribner.

HEART
see also Blood-Circulation; Cardiography; Pericardium; Pulse

Aegerter, Ernest. Save Your Heart. 1981. write for info. (ISBN 0-442-23112-1). Van Nos Reinhold.
Alpert, Norman. Cardiac Hypertrophy. 642p. 1971. 59.50 (ISBN 0-12-053550-5). Acad Pr.
American Heart Association, Scientific Sessions, 52nd. Abstracts. (AHA Monograph: No. 65). 1979. pap. 8.00 (ISBN 0-686-58031-1). Am Heart.
Bajusz, E. & Rona, G., eds. Cardiomyopathies. (Recent Advances in Studies on Cardiac Structure & Metabolism: Vol. 2). (Illus.). 1973. 39.50 (ISBN 0-8391-0700-5). Univ Park.
Bishop, Vernon S. Cardiac Performance, Vol. 1. Granger, Harris J., ed. (Annual Research Reviews). 1979. 18.00 (ISBN 0-88831-060-9). Eden Med Res.
Blaine, Tom R. Nutrition & Your Heart. LC 79-87833. 1979. pap. 2.25 (ISBN 0-87983-178-2). Keats.
Borchard, Franz. The Adrenergic Nerves of the Normal & Hypertrophied Heart: Biochemical, Histochemical, Electron-Microscopic, & Morphometric Studies. Bergmann, Wolfgang & Doerr, Wilhelm, eds. Hirsch, H. J., tr. from Ger. LC 77-92112. (Normal & Pathologic Anatomy Ser.). (Illus.). 72p. 1978. pap. 24.50 (ISBN 0-88416-240-0). Wright-PSG.
Bourne, Geoffrey H., ed. Hearts & Heart-Like Organs: Comparative Anatomy & Development, Vol. I. LC 80-760. 1980. 51.00 (ISBN 0-12-119401-9). Acad Pr.
--Hearts & Heart-Like Organs, Vol. 2: Physiology. LC 80-18121. 1980. 57.00 (ISBN 0-12-119402-7). Acad Pr.
--Hearts & Heart-Like Organs: Vol. 3, Physiology. 1980. subscription 45.00 53.00 (ISBN 0-12-119403-5); Set: Vols. 1-3. 138.00 (ISBN 0-686-77476-0). Acad Pr.
Braunwald, Eugene, ed. Symposium on Myocardial Metabolism. (AHA Monograph: No. 44). 1974. 6.00 (ISBN 0-87493-042-1, 73-031A). Am Heart.

Cantwell, John D. Endurance for Your Heart. (Illus.). 250p. Date not set. text ed. price not set. Saunders.
Comparative Physiology of the Heart: Current Trends-Proceedings. LC 70-443604. (Illus.). 270p. 1969. 65.00x (ISBN 3-7643-0116-3). Intl Pubns Serv.
Cranefield, Paul. Conduction of the Cardiac Impulse. LC 74-19921. 418p. 1975. 27.50 (ISBN 0-87993-056-X). Futura Pub.
Cranefield, Paul F. & Hoffman, Brian F., eds. Paired Pulse Stimulation of the Heart. 1968. 10.00 (ISBN 0-87470-009-4). Rockefeller.
De La Cruz, Maria V., et al. Development of the Chick Heart. LC 71-169907. 87p. 1972. 20.00x (ISBN 0-8018-1320-4). Johns Hopkins.
De Mello, Walmor C., ed. Electrical Phenomena in the Heart. (Clinical Engineering Ser). 1972. 54.00 (ISBN 0-12-208950-2). Acad Pr.
Dhalla, N. Myocardial Biology. (Recent Advances in Studies on Cardiac Structure & Metabolism Ser.: Vol. 4). (Illus.). 1974. 39.50 (ISBN 0-8391-0698-X). Univ Park.
--Myocardial Metabolism. (Recent Advances in Studies on Cardiac Structure & Metabolism Ser.: Vol. 3). (Illus.). 1973. 39.50 (ISBN 0-8391-0699-8). Univ Park.
Dhalla, N. & Sano, Toyomi, eds. Heart Function & Metabolism. (Recent Advances in Studies of Cardiac Structure & Metabolism Ser: Vol. 11). 1977. 57.50 (ISBN 0-8391-0671-8). Univ Park.
Dorman, Peter J., ed. The Book of Hearts. LC 78-14898. (Illus.). 1978. lib. bdg. 12.90 (ISBN 0-89471-045-1); pap. 3.95 (ISBN 0-89471-044-3). Running Pr.
Edwards, Jesse E. & Goott, Bernard. Illustrated Coronary Fact Book. pap. 1.50 (ISBN 0-668-02935-8). Arco.
Edwards, Jesse E., ed. The Heart. LC 73-11319. 270p. 1964. 29.50 (ISBN 0-683-02958-4). Krieger.
Ferrer, M. Irene. Pre-Excitation. LC 76-480. 1976. 27.50 (ISBN 0-87993-062-4). Futura Pub.
Fisher, Arthur. The Healthy Heart. Time-Life Bks. Eds., ed. (Library of Health). (Illus.). 176p. 1981. 12.95 (ISBN 0-8094-3750-3). Time-Life.
Garfiel, Evelyn. Service of the Heart. pap. 4.00 (ISBN 0-87980-140-9). Wilshire.
Gey, H. F., et al. Structure & Chemistry of the Aging Heart. 238p. 1974. text ed. 24.00x (ISBN 0-8422-7168-6). Irvington.
Gotto, Antonio M., Jr., et al. The Living Heart Diet. 1981. text ed. price not set (ISBN 0-89004-672-7). Raven.
Guyton, Arthur C., et al. Circulatory Physiology I: Cardiac Output & Its Regulation. 2nd ed. LC 72-90721. (Illus.). 556p. 1973. 25.00 (ISBN 0-7216-4360-4). Saunders.
Harris, P., et al. Biochemistry & Pharmacology of Myocardial Hypertrophy, Hypoxia, & Infarction. (Recent Advances in Studies on Cardiac Structure & Metabolism: Vol. 7). (Illus.). 600p. 1976. 39.50 (ISBN 0-8391-0667-X). Univ Park.
Harvey, William. De Motu Cordis: Anatomical Studies on the Motion of the Heart & Blood. 5th ed. Leake, Chauncey D., tr. (Illus.). 186p. 1978. pap. 6.75 (ISBN 0-398-00793-4). C C Thomas.
Heyden, Siegfried. Keep Your Heart in Shape. 96p. (Orig.). 1981. pap. 1.95 (ISBN 0-8326-2249-4, 7446). Delair.
Hoffman, Brian F. & Cranefield, Paul F. Electrophysiology of the Heart. LC 76-18003. 1976. Repr. of 1960 ed. 17.50 (ISBN 0-87993-083-7). Futura Pub.
Hurst, J. W. Update Three: The Heart. (Illus.). 288p. 1980. text ed. 30.00 (ISBN 0-07-031492-6, HP). McGraw.
Hurst, J. W., et al. The Heart, 2 vol. ed. 5th ed. 2120p. 1981. 82.00 (ISBN 0-07-031482-9, HP). McGraw.
Hurst, J. Willis. Update IV: The Heart. (Updates Ser.). (Illus.). 224p. 1980. text ed. 30.00 (ISBN 0-07-031493-4, HP). McGraw.
Hurst, J. Willis & Hurst, John W., Jr. Hurst, the Heart Self-Assessment & Review with CME. (Illus.). 270p. (Orig.). 1980. 65.00 (ISBN 0-07-079066-3, HP). McGraw.
Hurst, J. Willis, ed. Update I: The Heart. 1979. text ed. 29.95 (ISBN 0-07-031490-X, HP). McGraw.
Hurst, J. Willis, et al. The Heart. 5th ed. (Illus.). 352p. 1981. One Vol. Ed. price not set (ISBN 0-07-031481-0, HP). McGraw.
Johnson, J. Alan & Anderson, Ralph R., eds. The Renin-Angiotensin System. (Advances in Experimental Medicine & Biology Ser.: Vol. 130). 315p. 1980. 37.50 (ISBN 0-306-40469-9, Plenum Pr). Plenum Pub.
Jokl, Ernst. Heart & Sport. (American Lecture in Sports Medicine). (Illus.). 120p. 1964. photocopy ed. spiral 12.50 (ISBN 0-398-00935-X). C C Thomas.
Katz, Arnold M. Physiology of the Heart. LC 75-14580. 464p. 1977. 31.00 (ISBN 0-89004-053-2); pap. 15.95 (ISBN 0-686-67627-0). Raven.
Kezdi, Paul. You & Your Heart. LC 76-53757. (Illus.). 1977. 9.95 (ISBN 0-689-10743-9); pap. 4.95 (ISBN 0-689-70575-1, 243). Atheneum.
Knoll. Symposium on Pharmacology of the Heart. 1979. 23.00 (ISBN 0-9960007-9-8, Pub. by Kaido Hungary). Heyden.
Kobayashi, T., et al, eds. Cardiac Adaptation. (Recent Advances in Studies on Cardiac Structure & Metabolism Ser.: Vol. 12). 1977. 57.50 (ISBN 0-8391-0672-6). Univ Park.
Kones, Richard. Glucose, Insulin, Potassium & the Heart. LC 74-21391. (Illus.). 464p. 1975. text ed. 48.00 (ISBN 0-87993-054-3). Futura Pub.
Laane, Henk-Maarten. The Arterial Pole of the Embryonic Heart. 160p. 1978. pap. text ed. 26.50 (ISBN 90-265-0297-4, Pub. by Swets Pub Serv Holland). Swets North Am.
Left Ventricular Performance. (Landmark Ser.). 1979. 22.50x (ISBN 0-8422-4122-1). Irvington.
Longmore, Donald. Heart. LC 74-104743. (Illus., Orig.). 1971. pap. 2.45 (ISBN 0-07-038678-1, SP). McGraw.
Luederitz, B., ed. Cardiac Pacing: Diagnostic & Therapeutic Tools. (Illus.). 1976. 23.80 (ISBN 0-387-07711-1). Springer-Verlag.
McAlpine, W. A. Heart & Coronary Arteries. LC 74-20634. (Illus.). 240p. 1975. 99.30 (ISBN 0-387-06985-2). Springer-Verlag.
Meerson, F. Z. Myocardium in Hyperfunction, Hypertrophy & Heart Failure. (AHA Monograph Ser.: Vol. 26). (Illus., Orig.). 1969. pap. text ed. 5.00 (ISBN 0-87493-009-X, 73-018A). Am Heart.
National Heart, Lung & Blood Institute. A Handbook of Heart Terms. (Illus.). 64p. 1981. text ed. 6.95 (ISBN 0-89490-052-8). Enslow Pubs.
Navarantham, V. The Human Heart & Circulation. 1975. 13.50 (ISBN 0-12-514750-3). Acad Pr.
Phibbs, Brendan. The Human Heart: A Guide to Heart Disease. 4th ed. LC 79-17665. 1979. pap. text ed. 14.95 (ISBN 0-8016-3917-4). Mosby.
Roskamm, H. & Hahn, C., eds. Ventricular Function at Rest & During Exercise. 1976. pap. 21.30 (ISBN 0-387-07707-3). Springer-Verlag.
Roy, P. E. & Harris, Peter, eds. The Cardiac Sarcoplasm. (Recent Advances in Studies on Cardiac Structure & Metabolism Ser.: Vol. 8). (Illus.). 600p. 1975. 39.50 (ISBN 0-8391-0668-8). Univ Park.
Sambhi, Mohinder P., ed. Renin-Substrate Reaction. (AHA Monograph: No. 56). 1977. pap. 4.00 (ISBN 0-87493-058-8, 73-042A). Am Heart.
Sano, T., et al, eds. Electrophysiology & Ultrastructure of the Heart. (Illus.). 267p. 1967. 59.50 (ISBN 0-8089-0613-5). Grune.
Symbas, Panagiotis N. Traumatic Injuries of the Heart & Great Vessels. (Illus.). 204p. 1972. text ed. 19.75 (ISBN 0-398-02425-1). C C Thomas.
Symposium on Pharmacology of the Heart. (Congress of the Hungarian Pharmacology Society Ser.). 1977. 25.00x (ISBN 963-05-0976-8). Intl Pubns Serv.
Szentivanyi, M. & Juhasz-Nagy, A., eds. Factors Influencing Adrenergic Mechanisms in the Heart: Proceedings of a Satellite Symposium of the 28th International Congress of Physiological Sciences, Visegrad, Hungary, 1980. LC 80-42203. (Advances in Physiological Sciences: Vol. 27). (Illus.). 265p. 1981. 35.00 (ISBN 0-08-027348-3). Pergamon.
Tavel, Morton E. Heart Sounds & Murmurs: An Audiovisual Presentation. 1975. 185.00 (ISBN 0-8151-8728-9). Year Bk Med.
Vaquez, H. & Bordet, E. The Heart & the Aorta. 1920. 49.50x (ISBN 0-685-69879-3). Elliots Bks.
Vassale, Mario, ed. Cardiac Physiology for the Clinician. 1976. 35.00 (ISBN 0-12-715050-1). Acad Pr.
Vassalle, Mario. The Human Heart. rev. ed. Head, J. J., ed. LC 76-62985. (Carolina Biology Readers Ser.). (Illus.). (gr. 11 up). 1979. pap. 1.65 (ISBN 0-89278-208-0, 45-9608). Carolina Biological.
Walmsley, R. & Watson, H. Clinical Anatomy of the Heart. (Illus.). 1978. 65.00 (ISBN 0-443-01524-4). Churchill.
Wellens, H. J. Electrical Stimulation of the Heart in the Study & Treatment of Tachycardias. (Illus.). 1971. 24.50 (ISBN 0-8391-0602-5). Univ Park.
Wellens, H. J., et al, eds. The Conduction System of the Heart: Structure, Function & Clinical Implications. (Illus.). 708p. 1976. text ed. 58.00 (ISBN 0-8121-0564-8). Lea & Febiger.
Wildenthal, Kern, et al, eds. Regulation of Cardiac Metabolism. LC 76-1516. (AHA Monograph: No. 49). 1976. pap. 4.00 (ISBN 0-87493-050-2, 73-035A). Am Heart.
Willems, Jos L., et al, eds. Cardiac Function & Aging. LC 74-11160. 159p. 1974. text ed. 21.00x (ISBN 0-8422-7245-3). Irvington.
Zabriskie, John. Clinical Immunology of the Heart. LC 80-17927. (Perspectives in Clinical Immunology Ser.). 238p. 1981. 35.00 (ISBN 0-471-02676-X, Pub. by Wiley Med). Wiley.
Zelenin, V. Strengthen Your Heart. 110p. 1979. pap. 3.00 (ISBN 0-8285-0835-6, Pub. by Mir Pubs Russia). Imported Pubns.

HEART-ABNORMITIES

Adams, Forrest H., et al, eds. Pathophysiology of Congenital Heart Disease. LC 69-16626. (UCLA Forum in Medical Sciences: No. 10). (Illus.). 1970. 65.00x (ISBN 0-520-01630-0). U of Cal Pr.
Amsterdam & James. Cardiac Ischemia & Arrhythmias. 1980. 43.00 (ISBN 0-8151-4848-8). Year Bk Med.
Anderson & Becker. Pathology of Congenital Heart Disease. 1982. text ed. write for info. (ISBN 0-407-00137-9). Butterworth.
Billig, Donal M. & Kreidberg, Marshall B. The Management of Neonates & Infants with Congenital Heart Disease. LC 72-11559. (A Modern Surgical Monograph). 192p. 1973. 33.75 (ISBN 0-8089-0792-1). Grune.
Dry, Thomas J., et al. Congenital Anomalies of the Heart & Great Vessels. (Clinicopathologic Study of 132 Cases). (Illus.). 83p. 1949. ed. spiral bdg. 24.50photocopy (ISBN 0-398-04247-0). C C Thomas.
DuShane, James W. & Weidman, William H., eds. Five Congenital Cardiac Defects: Profile & Natural History. (AHA Monograph Ser: Vol. 12). pap. 5.00 (ISBN 0-87493-000-6, 73-008A). Am Heart.
Edwards, Jesse, et al. An Atlas of Congenital Anomalies of the Heart & Great Vessels. 2nd ed. (Illus.). 216p. 1954. ed. spiral bdg. 24.75photocopy (ISBN 0-398-04251-9). C C Thomas.
Feldt, Robert H., ed. Atrioventricular Canal Defects. LC 76-8574. (Illus.). 1976. text ed. 22.00 (ISBN 0-7216-3615-2). Saunders.
Fink, Burton W. Congenital Heart Disease: A Deductive Approach to Its Diagnosis. (Illus.). 183p. 1975. pap. 15.75 (ISBN 0-8151-3222-0). Year Bk Med.
Friedman, William F., et al, eds. Neonatal Heart Disease. LC 73-4449. (Illus.). 386p. 1973. 49.00 (ISBN 0-8089-0802-2). Grune.
Gerrick, David J. Congenital Heart Defects. (Illus.). 1978. 20.00 (ISBN 0-916750-18-3). Dayton Labs.
--Murmurs in Man. (Illus.). 1978. 20.00 (ISBN 0-916750-39-6). Dayton Labs.
Goor, Daniel A. & Lillehei, C. Walton. Congenital Malformations of the Heart. (Illus.). 450p. 1975. 62.75 (ISBN 0-8089-0810-3). Grune.
Gyepes, Michael T. & Vincent, William R. Cardiac Catheterization & Angiocardiography in Severe Neonatal Heart Disease. (Illus.). 184p. 1974. text ed. 18.50 (ISBN 0-398-03088-X). C C Thomas.
International Workshop on Morphogenesis & Malformation, 4th, Grand Canyon, Ariz., 1977. Morphogenesis & Malformation of the Cardiovascular System: Proceedings. Rosenquist, Glenn C. & Bergsma, Daniel, eds. LC 78-14527. (Birth Defects Original Article Ser.: Vol. 14, No. 7). 452p. 1978. 53.00x (ISBN 0-8451-1023-3). A R Liss.
Kidd, B. Langford & Rowe, Richard D., eds. The Child with Congenital Heart Disease After Surgery. LC 76-4618. (Illus.). 1976. 29.50 (ISBN 0-87993-076-4). Futura Pub.
Kidd, B. S. & Keith, John D. The Natural History & Progress in Treatment of Congenital Heart Defects. (Illus.). 360p. 1971. 26.50 (ISBN 0-398-02174-0). C C Thomas.
Lev, Maurice. Autopsy Diagnosis of Congenitally Malformed Hearts. (Illus.). 195p. 1953. photocopy ed. spiral 19.50 (ISBN 0-398-04336-1). C C Thomas.
Lev, Maurice & Vass, Aloysius. Spitzer's Architecture of Normal & Malformed Hearts: A Phylogenetic Theory of Their Development. (Illus.). 176p. 1951. photocopy ed. spiral 17.50 (ISBN 0-398-01114-1). C C Thomas.
Lundstrom, Nils-Rune, ed. Echocardiography in Congenital Heart Disease. LC 78-70262. 1979. 30.00x (ISBN 0-397-58243-9, JBL-Med-Nursing). Har-Row.
McCollum, Audrey T. Coping with Prolonged Health Impairment in Your Child. 242p. 1975. 12.95 (ISBN 0-316-54185-0). Little.
Nadas, Alexander. Natural History Study of Congenital Heart Defects. LC 77-7732. (AHA Monograph: No. 53). 1977. pap. 3.00 (ISBN 0-87493-057-X, 73-039A). Am Heart.
Okamoto, Naomasa. Congenital Anomalies of the Heart. LC 79-89192. (Illus.). 1980. 51.00 (ISBN 0-89640-036-0). Igaku-Shoin.
Pexieder, T. Cell Death in the Morphogenesis & Teratogenesis of the Heart. (Advances in Anatomy, Embryology & Cell Biology Ser.: Vol. 51, Pt. 3). (Illus.). 100p. (Orig.). 1975. pap. 42.50 (ISBN 0-387-07270-5). Springer-Verlag.
Schad, N., et al. Differential Diagnosis of Congenital Heart Disease. Bar, Hans, ed. LC 64-12879. 450p. 1966. 96.00 (ISBN 0-8089-0403-5). Grune.
Snider, Arthur J. & Adatto, I. J. A Doctor Discusses Learning to Live with Heart Trouble. (Illus.). 1980. pap. 2.50 (ISBN 0-685-35677-9). Budlong.
Stanger, Paul, et al. Diagrammatic Portrayal of Variations in Cardiac Structure, Vol. 21. (AHA. Monograph,). (Illus.). 1968. pap. 4.00 (ISBN 0-87493-006-5, 73-014A). Am Heart.
Taussig, Helen B. Congenital Malformations of the Heart, 2 vols. 2nd ed. Incl. Vol. 1. General Considerations. 12.50x (ISBN 0-674-16150-5); Vol. 2. Specific Malformations. 32.50x (ISBN 0-674-16151-3). (Commonwealth Fund Publications Ser.). 1960. Harvard U Pr.
--Congenital Malformations of the Heart, 2 vols. 2nd ed. LC 60-5739. (Commonwealth Fund Publications Ser). 1960. Vol. 1. 10.00x (ISBN 0-674-16150-5); Vol. 2. 27.50x (ISBN 0-674-16151-3). Harvard U Pr.
Tilikian, Ara G. & Conover, Mary B. Understanding Heart Sounds & Murmurs. LC 77-27760. (Illus.). 1979. pap. text ed. 18.95 (ISBN 0-7216-8869-1). Saunders.
Vlodaver, Zeev, et al. Coronary Arterial Variations in the Normal Heart & in Congenital Heart Disease. 1975. 27.50 (ISBN 0-12-722450-5). Acad Pr.

HEART-CALCIFICATION

Shapiro, Jerome H., et al. Calcifications of the Heart. (Illus.). 208p. 1963. photocopy ed. spiral 19.75 (ISBN 0-398-01732-8). C C Thomas.

HEART-DISEASES

see also Blood-Circulation, Disorders Of; Cardiacs; Cardiology; Chest-Diseases; Cor Pulmonale; Endocarditis; Heart-Radiography; Heart Failure

Alpert, Joseph S. The Heart Attack Handbook: A Commonsense Guide to Treatment, Recovery, & Staying Well. 1978. 5.95 (ISBN 0-316-03501-7). Little.
Asmussen, N. W., et al, eds. Aldosterone Antagonists in Clinical Medicine. (International Congress Ser.: No. 460). 1979. 78.00 (ISBN 0-444-90062-4, Excerpta Medica). Elsevier.
Baldry, P. E. Battle Against Heart Disease. LC 75-108098. (Illus.). 1971. 29.95 (ISBN 0-521-07490-8). Cambridge U Pr.
Bayer, Leona M. & Honzik, Marjorie P. Children with Congenital Intracardiac Defects: A Pictorial Atlas of Individual Somatic & Neuropsychologic Development Before & After Open Heart Surgery. (Illus.). 276p. 1976. 45.50 (ISBN 0-398-03185-1). C C Thomas.
Bennett, David H. Cardiac Arrhythmias: Practical Notes on Interpretation & Treatment. (Illus.). 176p. 1981. pap. text ed. 25.00 (ISBN 0-7236-0590-4). Wright-PSG.
Bircks, W., et al, eds. Medical & Surgical Management of Tacharrhythmias. (Illus.). 190p. 1980. pap. 28.40 (ISBN 0-387-09929-8). Springer-Verlag.
Bloor, Colin M. & Liebow, Averill A. The Pulmonary & Bronchial Circulations in Congenital Heart Disease. (Topics in Cardiovascular Disease Ser.). (Illus.). 284p. 1980. 32.50 (ISBN 0-306-40383-8, Plenum Pr). Plenum Pub.
Bonchek, Lawrence I. & Brooks, Harold L. Medical & Surgical Management of Heart Disease: A Concise Guide for Non-Cardiologists. 1981. text ed. 22.50 (ISBN 0-316-10121-4). Little.
Braunwald, Eugene. Heart Disease: A Textbook of Cardiovasular Medicine, 2 vols. LC 79-3923. (Illus.). 1943p. 1980. Set. text ed. 75.00 set (ISBN 0-7216-1924-X); Vol. 1. text ed. (ISBN 0-7216-1928-2); Vol. 2. text ed. (ISBN 0-7216-1929-0); text ed. 65.00 single vol. (ISBN 0-7216-1923-1). Saunders.
Brest, Albert N., et al, eds. Innovations in the Diagnosis & Management of Acute Myocardial Infraction. LC 75-25778. (Cardiovascular Clinics Ser.: Vol. 7, No. 2). 336p. 1975. text ed. 32.00 (ISBN 0-8036-1190-0). Davis Co.
Buchner, et al. Cardiomyopathy Associated with Systemic Myopathy: Genetic Defect of Actomyosin Influencing Muscular Structure & Function. LC 78-12364. (Illus.). 108p. 1978. pap. text ed. 19.50 (ISBN 0-8067-0241-9). Urban & S.
Cardiovascular Conference, 3rd, Aspen, Colo., Jan. 1972. Myocardial Infraction: A New Look at an Old Subject. Vogel, J. H., ed. (Advances in Cardiology: Vol. 9). 1973. 58.75 (ISBN 3-8055-1373-9). S Karger.
Chazov, E. Myocardial Infarction. 380p. 1976. 8.50 (ISBN 0-8285-0763-5, Pub. by Mir Pubs Russia). Imported Pubns.
Cohen, Michael V. Correlative Atlas of Adult Cardiac Disorders: Noninvasive Diagnostic Techniques. LC 80-66333. (Illus.). 432p. 1980. 48.50 (ISBN 0-87993-149-3). Futura Pub.

Cohn, Jules & Shah, Prauin M., eds. Symposium on Cardiachypertrophy and Cardiomyopathy. (AHA Monograph: No. 43). 210p. 1974. 5.00 (ISBN 0-87493-039-1, 73-030A). Am Heart.
Cohn, Lawrence H. The Treatment of Acute Myocardial Ischemia: An Integrated Medical-Surgical Approach. LC 78-61505. (Illus.). 1979. monograph 23.00 (ISBN 0-87993-116-7). Futura Pub.
Cone, Judson P. Heart: An Owner's Manual. new ed. 69p. (Orig.). 1974. pap. 1.95 (ISBN 0-685-52022-6). Good Life.
Corday, Eliot, ed. Controversies in Cardiology. LC 76-54825. (Cardiovascular Clinics Ser: Vol, 8, No. 1). 1977. text ed. 35.00 (ISBN 0-8036-1980-4). Davis Co.
Crawford. Pathology of Ischaemic Heart Disease. (Postgraduate Pathology Ser.). 1978. 27.50 (ISBN 0-407-00091-7). Butterworth.
Dalen, James E. & Alpert, Joseph E. Valvular Heart Disease. 1981. text ed. 27.50 (ISBN 0-316-17170-0). Little.
Day, Charles E., ed. Atherosclerosis Drug Discovery. LC 76-5395. (Advances in Experimental Medicine & Biology: Vol. 67). 468p. 1976. 42.50 (ISBN 0-306-39067-1, Plenum Pr). Plenum Pub.
De Faire, Ulf & Theorell, Tores. Life Stress & Coronary Heart Disease. 250p. 1981. 18.50 (ISBN 0-87527-201-0). Green.
Detry, Jean-Marie R. Exercise Testing & Training in Coronary Heart Disease. 80p. 1973. pap. 17.50 (ISBN 0-686-65360-2, Pub. by Williams & Wilkens). Krieger.
East, T. Story of Heart Disease. (Illus.). 148p. 1958. 10.95x (ISBN 0-8464-0886-4). Beekman Pubs.
Eglash, Albert, ed. Psychogenesis of Coronary Heart Disease: A Syllabus for Medical Researchers. (Bibliographies in Psychosomatic Medicine Ser.: No. 1, Myocardial Infraction). (Illus.). 110p. (Orig.). 1980. 30.00 (ISBN 0-935320-20-2). Quest Pr.
Eldredge, W. Jay, et al, eds. Current Problems in Congenital Heart Disease. LC 78-15311. 1979. text ed. 25.00 (ISBN 0-89335-060-5). Spectrum Pub.
Eliot, Robert S., et al, eds. Cardiac Emergencies. LC 76-41062. (Contemporary Problems in Cardiology Ser: Vol. 3). 1977. 22.50 (ISBN 0-87993-075-6). Futura Pub.
Engle, Mary A., ed. Pediatric Cardiovascular Disease. LC 80-15616. (Cardiovascular Clinics Ser.: Vol. 11, No. 2). (Illus.). 475p. 1980. text ed. 48.00 (ISBN 0-8036-3204-5). Davis Co.
Farrer-Brown, Geoffrey. Color Atlas of Cardiac Pathology. (Illus.). 1977. 32.50 (ISBN 0-8151-3209-3). Year Bk Med.
Fowler, Noble O. Cardiac Diagnosis & Treatment. 3rd ed. 1980. text ed. 67.50 (ISBN 0-06-140818-2, Harper Medical). Har-Row.
Friedman, Meyer & Rosenman, Ray H. Type A Behavior & Your Heart. 1974. 12.95 (ISBN 0-394-48011-2). Knopf.
--Type A Behavior & Your Heart. 320p. 1981. pap. 6.95 (ISBN 0-449-90059-2, Crest). Fawcett.
Gage, Gloria. Fully Alive. LC 80-68884. 160p. (Orig.). 1981. pap. 3.95 (ISBN 0-89636-064-4). Accent Bks.
Garson, Arthur, Jr., et al. A Guide to Cardiac Dysrhythmias in Children. (Clinical Cardiology Monographs). 208p. 1980. 19.50 (ISBN 0-8089-1261-5). Grune.
Geist, Harold. The Emotional Aspects of Heart Disease. LC 76-16319. 1977. 6.95 (ISBN 0-87212-062-7). Libra.
Gertler, M. & White, P. D. Coronary Heart Disease: A Twenty-Five Year Study in Retrospect. 1976. 29.95 (ISBN 0-87489-093-4). Med Economics.
Goldberger, Ary L. Myocardial Infarction. 2nd ed. LC 78-31981. (Illus.). 1979. text ed. 29.50 (ISBN 0-8016-1860-6). Mosby.
Goldberger, Emanuel. A Textbook of Clinical Cardiology. LC 81-38350. (Illus.). 992p. 1981. text ed. 36,00 (ISBN 0-8016-1864-9). Mosby.
--Treatment of Cardiac Emergencies. 2nd ed. LC 77-5070. (Illus.). 1977. 25.95 (ISBN 0-8016-1854-1). Mosby.
Gordon, A. J., et al. Hemodynamics of Aortic & Mitral Valve Disease. 144p. 1961. 22.00 (ISBN 0-8089-0157-5). Grune.
Gould, Lawrence & Reddy, C. V., eds. Vasodilator Therapy for Cardiac Disorders. LC 79-65372. (Illus.). 1979. 29.50 (ISBN 0-87993-125-6). Futura Pub.
Grandis, Sue L. Instrumentation for Coronary Care. (Techniques of Measurement in Medicine: No. 5). (Illus.). 150p. Date not set. price not set (ISBN 0-521-23548-0); pap. price not set (ISBN 0-521-28024-9). Cambridge U Pr.
Gross, Peter F., ed. The Cardioprotective Action of Beta-Blockers: Facts & Theories. LC 77-13243. 1978. 24.50 (ISBN 0-8391-1178-9). Univ Park.
Haft, Jacob I. & Bailey, Charles P., eds. Acute Myocardial Infarction & Coronary Artery Disease. LC 78-53403. (Advances in the Management of Clinical Heart Disease Ser.: Vol. II). (Illus.). 1978. medical monograph 19.75 (ISBN 0-87993-110-8). Futura Pub.
--Advances in the Management of Clinical Heart Disease, Vol. 1. LC 76-4112. (Illus.). 456p. 1976. 34.95 (ISBN 0-87993-064-0). Futura Pub.
--Therapeutics, Hypertension & Aspects of Echocardiography. LC 78-52967. (Advances in the Management of Clinical Heart Disease Ser.: Vol. III). (Illus.). 1978. medical monograph 19.75 (ISBN 0-87993-111-6). Futura Pub.
Halhuber, Carola & Halhuber, Max J. Speaking of Heart Attacks. Heyden, Francoise, tr. from Ger. LC 78-72876. (Medical Adviser Ser.). (Illus.). 1979. pap. 3.95 (ISBN 0-8326-2232-X, 7450). Delair.
Halhuber, M. J. & Siegrist, J., eds. Myocardial Infarction & Psychosocial Risks. (Illus.). 152p. 1981. pap. 17.60 (ISBN 0-387-10386-4). Springer-Verlag.
Hamer, John, ed. Drugs for Heart Disease. 1979. 47.50 (ISBN 0-8151-4109-2). Year Bk Med.
Harris, Cecelia C. A Primer of Cardiac Arrhythmias: A Self Instructional Program. LC 78-27022. 1979. pap. text ed. 9.50 (ISBN 0-8016-2070-8). Mosby.
Huisman, P. H. & Schipperheypn, J. J. The Isolated Heart-Lung Preparation. (Illus.). 1978. pap. 16.00 (ISBN 90-247-2107-5, Pub. by Martinus Nijhoff Netherlands). Kluwer Boston.
James, William E. & Amsterdam, Ezra A., eds. Coronary Heart Disease: Exercise Testing & Cardiac Rehabilitation. (Illus.). 1977. 31.00 (ISBN 0-8151-4846-1, Pub. by Symposia Special). Year Bk Med.
Jatene, A. D. & Lichtlen, P. New Therapy of Ischemic Heart Disease. (International Congress Ser.: No. 388). 1976. 51.25 (ISBN 90-219-0318-0, Excerpta Medica). Elsevier.
Jeresaty, Robert M. Mitral Valve Prolapse. LC 78-66350. 263p. 1979. 27.00 (ISBN 0-89004-230-6). Raven.
Joint ISC-WHO Symposium, Geneva, 1971. Metabolism of the Hypoxic & Ischaemic Heart. Moret, P. R. & Feifar, Z., eds. (Cardiology: Pt. 1: Vol 56, Nos. 1-6; Pt. 2: Vol. 57, Nos. 1-2). (Illus.). 1972. pap. 58.75 (ISBN 3-8055-1447-6). S Karger.
Jokl, E. Exercise & Cardiac Death. 1971. 19.50 (ISBN 0-8391-0529-0). Univ Park.
Jordan, S. C. & Scott, Olive. Heart Disease in Pediatrics. 2nd ed. 1981. text ed. write for info. (ISBN 0-407-19941-1). Butterworth.
Karassi, Arthur H. Acute Myocardial Infarction. (Illus.). 559p. 1980. text ed. 49.50 (ISBN 0-07-033296-7, HP). McGraw.
Katz, Arnold M. Physiology of the Heart. LC 75-14580. 464p. 1977. 31.00 (ISBN 0-89004-053-2); pap. 15.95 (ISBN 0-686-67627-0). Raven.
Kellermann, J. J., ed. Exercise in Diagnosis & Treatment of Coronary Heart Disease. (Cardiology: Vol. 62, No. 3 (1977)). (Illus.). 1977. 18.00 (ISBN 3-8055-2805-1). S Karger.
Kezdi, Paul. You & Your Heart. LC 76-53757. (Illus.). 1977. 9.95 (ISBN 0-689-10743-9); pap. 4.95 (ISBN 0-689-70575-1, 243). Atheneum.
Krikler, Dennis M. & Goodwin, John F., eds. Cardiac Arrhythmias. LC 75-11582. (Illus.). 255p. 1975. text ed. 26.00 (ISBN 0-7216-5516-5). Saunders.
Lee, Won R. Essentials of Clinical Cardiology. (Illus.). 443p. (Orig.). 1980. pap. text ed. 24.95 (ISBN 0-89303-008-2). Charles.
Limburg, Peter. The Story of Your Heart. LC 78-24308. (Health Bk.). (Illus.). (gr. 3-7). 1979. PLB 6.59 (ISBN 0-698-30705-4). Coward.
Liss, Joseph. Victory Over Heart Attacks. 144p. 1977. 5.95 (ISBN 0-8059-2367-5). Dorrance.
Lochner, W., et al. Second International Nifedipine Adalat Symposium. (Illus.). 400p. 1976. pap. 27.20 (ISBN 0-387-07471-6). Springer-Verlag.
McBride, Helena & Moses, Dorothy. Acute Myocardial Infarction. (Illus.). 1979. pap. 6.95 (ISBN 0-8385-0049-8). ACC.
McIntyre, H. Mildred, ed. Heart Disease: New Dimensions of Nursing Care. LC 73-18483. 331p. 1974. soft cover 16.95 (ISBN 0-686-63968-5). Trainex Pr.
Mason, Dean T. Advances in Heart Disease, Vol. 2. (Clinical Cardiology Monographs). 1978. 47.75 (ISBN 0-8089-1067-1). Grune.
Mitral Valve Prolapse. (Landmark Ser.). 1979. 22.50x (ISBN 0-8422-4123-X). Irvington.
Mo, Sam. Why Heart Attack? 1981. 6.95 (ISBN 0-8062-1546-1). Carlton.
Moss, Arthur J., et al, eds. Heart Disease in Infants & Adolescents. 2nd ed. (Illus.). 788p. 1977. 71.00 (ISBN 0-683-06130-5). Williams & Wilkins.
Naito, H., ed. Nutrition & Heart Disease. (Monographs of the American College of Nutrition: Vol. 5). 1981. text ed. 25.00 (ISBN 0-89335-119-9). Spectrum Pub.
Oram, Samuel. Clinical Heart Disease. (Illus.). 1971. 68.50x (ISBN 0-685-83723-8). Intl Ideas.
Peacock, Thomas B. On Malformations of the Human Heart. LC 77-91537. 1977. Repr. of 1858 ed. lib. bdg. 20.00 (ISBN 0-89341-506-5). Longwood Pr.
Perloff, Joseph K. The Clinical Recognition of Congenital Heart Disease. 2nd ed. LC 77-84680. (Illus.). 1978. text ed. 48.00 (ISBN 0-7216-7191-8). Saunders.
Phibbs, Brendan. The Cardiac Arrhythmias. 3rd ed. LC 78-7265. 1978. pap. text ed. 17.50 (ISBN 0-8016-3911-5). Mosby.
--The Human Heart: A Guide to Heart Disease. 3rd ed. LC 75-9753. (Illus.). 280p. 1975. pap. text ed. 10.95 (ISBN 0-8016-3916-6). Mosby.
Pupillo, John. An Atlas of Cardiac Arrhythmias. (Illus.). Date not set. price not set (ISBN 0-9602206-1-5). Vismar.
Pyle, Gerald F. Heart Disease, Cancer & Stroke in Chicago: A Geographical Analysis with Facilities Plans for 1980. LC 77-167941. (Research Paper Ser.: No. 134). (Illus.). 292p. (Orig.). 1971. pap. 8.00 (ISBN 0-89065-041-1). U Chicago Dept Geog.
Rapaport, Elliot. Current Controversies in Cardiovascular Disease. LC 79-64600. (Illus.). 761p. 1980. text ed. 39.50 (ISBN 0-7216-7459-3). Saunders.
Reich, Nathaniel E. The Uncommon Heart Diseases. (Illus.). 528p. 1954. photocopy ed. spiral 52.75 (ISBN 0-398-04387-6). C C Thomas.
Resnekov, Leon & Julian, Desmond, eds. Friedberg's: Diseases of the Heart. 4th ed. (Illus.). Date not set. write for info. (ISBN 0-443-08003-8). Churchill.
Riedman, Sarah. Heart. (Golden Guide Ser). (Illus.). 160p. 1974. PLB 10.38 (ISBN 0-307-64354-9, Golden Pr). Western Pub.
Ritota, Michael C. Congestive Heart Failure & Cardiac Impedance. Mancini, L. Phillip, ed. LC 77-91511. (Illus.). 1977. pap. 14.75 (ISBN 0-916420-02-7); set of slides & 1 bk. 94.50 (ISBN 0-685-81125-5); cassettes, set of 4 1 hr. tapes 7.00 ea.; slides, bk. & tapes 115.00 (ISBN 0-686-67868-0). Meds Corp.
Roberts, Jean. Cardiovascular Conditions of Children 6-11 Years & Youth 12-17 Years United States, 1963-1965 & 1966-1970. Stevenson, Taloria, ed. (Ser. 11: No. 166). 1978. pap. text ed. 1.75 (ISBN 0-8406-0119-0). Natl Ctr Health Stats.
Roberts, William C. Congenital Heart Disease in Adults. LC 78-21460. (Cardiovascular Clinics Ser.: Vol. 10, No. 1). (Illus.). 574p. 1979. 60.00 (ISBN 0-8036-7419-8). Davis Co.
Roberts, William C., et al. Cardiology: 1981. (Illus.). 388p. 1981. text ed. 39.50 (ISBN 0-914316-22-2). Yorke Med.
Rosenthal, Amnon, et al, eds. Postoperative Congenital Heart Disease. 176p. 1975. 33.50 (ISBN 0-8089-0934-7). Grune.
Ross, J. & O'Rourke, R. A. Understanding the Heart & Its Disease. 1975. 9.95 (ISBN 0-07-053861-1, C); pap. 6.95 (ISBN 0-07-053862-X). McGraw.
Rowe, Richard D., et al. The Neonate with Congenital Heart Disease. 2nd ed. (Illus.). 450p. 1981. text ed. 42.50 (ISBN 0-7216-7775-4). Saunders.
Sanne, Harold. Readaptation After Myocardial Infection. write for inof. (ISBN 0-939986-01-9). World Rehab Fund.
Schmidt, F. L. Ergometrie bei Herzkranken. Elektrokardiogramm, Herzschlagfrequenz und Blutdruck bei Belastungsuntersuchungen. 1977. 58.75 (ISBN 3-8055-2409-9). S Karger.
Scott, Ralph C., ed. Fundamental Considerations in Cardiology & Diabetes. (Clinical Cardiology & Diabetes Ser.: Vol. I Part I). (Illus.). 384p. 1981. 36.00 (ISBN 0-87993-135-3). Futura Pub.
Selzer, Arthur. The Heart: Its Function in Health & Disease. rev. ed. (Perspectives in Medicine: No. 1). (YA) (gr. 9 up). 1968. 16.50x (ISBN 0-520-01162-7). U of Cal Pr.
Silber, Earl N. & Katz, Louis N. Heart Disease. (Illus.). 1975. text ed. 50.00 (ISBN 0-02-410450-7). Macmillan.
Speedby, Henry J. Twentieth Century & Your Heart. 4.50 (ISBN 0-685-06607-X). Assoc Bk.
Stocksmeier, U., ed. Psychological Approach to the Rehabilitation of Coronary Patients. LC 76-14831. 1976. pap. 17.60 (ISBN 0-387-07721-9). Springer-Verlag.
Strauer, B. E. Hypertensive Heart Disease. (Illus.). 106p. 1980. pap. 16.60 (ISBN 0-387-10041-5). Springer-Verlag.
Swischuk, Leonard. Plain Film Interpretation in Congenital Heart Disease. 2nd ed. (Illus.). 1979. pap. 29.95 (ISBN 0-683-08041-5). Williams & Wilkins.
Symbas, P. Trauma to the Heart & Great Vessels. 208p. 1978. 33.00 (ISBN 0-8089-1099-X). Grune.
Symposium on Cardiomyopathy. 36p. 1972. pap. 1.00 (ISBN 0-87493-031-6, 73-308A). Am Heart.
Symposium on Comparative Pathology of the Heart, Boston, Sept. 1973. Comparative Pathology of the Heart: Proceedings. Homburger, F. & Lucas, I., eds. (Advances in Cardiology: Vol. 13). 250p. 1974. 155.75 (ISBN 3-8055-1697-5). S Karger.
Symposium on Congenital Heart Disease with Cyanosis, Amsterdam, 1968. Proceedings. Klinkhammer, A. C., ed. (Radiologia Clinica et Biologica: Vol. 39, No. 2). 1970. pap. 19.25 (ISBN 3-8055-0802-6). S Karger.
Szekely, Paul & Snaith, Linton. Heart Disease & Pregnancy. (Illus.). 208p. 1974. text ed. 35.00x (ISBN 0-443-01135-4). Churchill.
Thomson, James C. Your Heart. 1980. 25.00x (ISBN 0-85207-126-4, Pub. by Daniel Co England). State Mutual Bk.
--Your Heart. Thomson, C. Leslie, ed. 80p. 1974. pap. 3.50x (ISBN 0-8464-1058-3). Beekman Pubs.
Tripp, Alice. Basic Mechanism of Congestive Heart Failure. 1978. pap. text ed. 5.95 (ISBN 0-07-065223-6, HP). McGraw.
Tucker, Bernard L. & Lindesmith, George G. Congenital Heart Disease. 368p. 1979. 26.00 (ISBN 0-8089-1199-6). Grune.
Tully, Marianne & Tully, Alice. Heart Disease. (gr. 4 up). 1980. PLB 6.90 (ISBN 0-531-04163-8). Watts.
Ulodaver, Z., et al. Coronary Heart Disease: Clinical Angiographic & Pathologic Profiles. LC 75-35842. 1976. 84.30 (ISBN 0-387-90165-5). Springer-Verlag.
Van Praagh, Richard & Takao, Atsuyoshi. Etiology & Morphogenesis of Congenital Heart Disease. LC 79-65371. (Illus.). 550p. 1980. 47.50 (ISBN 0-87993-126-4). Futura Pub.
Vineberg, Arthur. How to Live with Your Heart: The Family Guide to Heart Health. LC 74-25204. 219p. 1977. 8.95 (ISBN 0-8129-0549-0); pap. 3.50 (ISBN 0-8129-6282-6). Times Bks.
Waldo, Albert L. & Maclean, William A. Diagnosis & Treatment of Cardiac Arrythmias Following Open Heart Surgery: Emphasis on the Use of Atrial Ventricular Epicardial Wire Electrodes. LC 80-65680. (Illus.). 280p. 1980. monograph 29.50 (ISBN 0-87993-132-9). Futura Pub.
Wheatley, David, ed. Stress & the Heart. 2nd ed. 430p. 1981. 39.50 (ISBN 0-89004-520-8). Raven.
White, Paul D. Clues in the Diagnosis & Treatment of Heart Disease. 2nd ed. (American Lecture Circulation). (Illus.). 204p. 1956. photocopy ed. spiral 19.75 (ISBN 0-398-04428-7). C C Thomas.
WHO Scientific Group, Geneva, 1969. Pathological Diagnosis of Acute Ischaemic Heart Disease: Report. (Technical Report Ser.: No. 441). (Also avail. in French, Russian & Spanish). 1970. pap. 1.20 (ISBN 92-4-120441-9). World Health.
Zavodskaya, I. S., et al. Neurogenic Heart Lesions. LC 80-40436. (Illus.). 150p. 1980. 58.00 (ISBN 0-08-025482-9). Pergamon.
Zoneraich, Samuel. Diabetes & the Heart. (Illus.). 320p. 1978. 35.75 (ISBN 0-398-03644-6). C C Thomas.

HEART–DISEASES–DIAGNOSIS

see also Angiocardiography; Auscultation; Ballistocardiography; Cardiac Catheterization; Cardiography; Electrocardiography; Percussion; Pulse

Adolph, A. L. & Lorenz, Rita. Enzyme Diagnosis in Diseases of the Heart, Liver & Pancreas. (Illus.). 128p. 1981. pap. 13.25 (ISBN 3-8055-3079-X). S Karger.
Adolph, L. & Lorenz, Rita. Diagnostico enzimatico En las Enfermedades De corazon, higado y Pancreas. (Illus.). 126p. 1980. soft cover 13.25 (ISBN 3-8055-0506-X). S Karger.
Alexander, Gilbert H. The Heart & Its Action: Roentgenkymographic Studies. LC 78-96979. (Illus.). 272p. 1971. 25.00 (ISBN 0-87527-001-8). Green.
Alpert, Martin A. Cardiac Arrhythmias: A Bedside Guide to Diagnosis & Treatment. (Illus.). 256p. 1980. pap. 21.95 (ISBN 0-8151-0118-X). Year Bk Med.
Armstrong, Gail & Friis, Robert. Stress-Heart Disease Connection. 50p. (Orig.). 1981. pap. 14.95 (ISBN 0-939552-05-1, 007). Human Behavior.
Bloomfield, Dennis A. & Simon, Hansjorg. Cardio Active Drugs: A Pharmacological Basis for Practice. 1982. price not set (ISBN 0-8067-1851-X). Urban & S.
Diethrich, Edward B., ed. Noninvasive Cardiovascular Diagnosis. rev. ed. LC 80-11233. (Illus.). 630p. 1980. text ed. 59.50 (ISBN 0-88416-288-5). Wright-PSG.
Dressler, William. Clinical Aids in Cardiac Diagnosis. LC 74-82556. 256p. 1970. 44.50 (ISBN 0-8089-0120-6). Grune.

Elliott, Larry P. & Schiebler, Gerold L. The X-Ray Diagnosis of Congenital Heart Disease in Infants, Children & Adults: Pathologic, Hemodynamic, & Clinical Correlations As Related to Chest Film. 2nd ed. (Illus.). 424p. 1979. text ed. 36.50 (ISBN 0-398-03857-0). C C Thomas.

Gruberg, Edward & Raymond, Stephen. Beyond Cholesterol. 208p. 1981. 9.95 (ISBN 0-312-07779-3). St Martin.

Haft, Jacob I., ed. Differential Diagnosis of Chest Pain & Other Cardiac Symptoms. LC 80-68061. (Advances in the Management of Clinical Heart Disease Monograph: Vol. 4). (Illus.). 230p. 1980. 26.50 (ISBN 0-87993-150-7). Futura Pub.

Jacob, Alphons. Clinical Cardiac Roentgen Diagnosis. new ed. LC 70-96985. (Illus.). 384p. 1971. 19.50 (ISBN 0-87527-044-1). Green.

Josephson, Mark E. & Seides, Stuart F. Clinical Cardiac Electrophysiology: Techniques & Interpretations. LC 79-10744. (Illus.). 1979. text ed. 24.50 (ISBN 0-8121-0675-X). Lea & Febiger.

Kellermann, J. J., ed. Exercise in Diagnosis & Treatment of Coronary Heart Disease. (Cardiology: Vol. 62, No. 3 (1977)). (Illus.). 1977. 18.00 (ISBN 3-8055-2805-1). S Karger.

Kingsley, B., et al. Advances in Non-Invasive Diagnostic Cardiology. LC 76-367. 1976. 40.00x (ISBN 0-913590-29-0). C B Slack.

Lindsay, Alan E. & Budkin, Alberto. The Cardiac Arrhythmias: An Approach to Their Electrocardiographic Recognition. 2nd ed. (Illus.). 178p. 1975. pap. 19.95 (ISBN 0-8151-5428-3). Year Bk Med.

Luisada, Aldo A. The Sounds of the Diseased Heart. LC 74-176171. (Illus.). 416p. 1973. text ed. 25.50 (ISBN 0-87527-113-8). Green.

Luisada, Aldo A. & Sainani, Gurmukh S. A Primer of Cardiac Diagnosis: The Physical & Technical Study of the Cardiac Patient. LC 68-20943. (Illus.). 262p. 1968. 10.50 (ISBN 0-87527-049-2). Green.

McCutcheon, Ernest P., ed. Chronically Implanted Cardiovascular Instrumentation. (Clinical Engineering Ser). (Based upon a Symposium). 1973. 34.00 (ISBN 0-12-483150-8). Acad Pr.

Mason, Dean T., ed. Advances in Heart Disease, Vol. 3. (Clinical Cardiology Monograph). 811p. 1980. 49.50 (ISBN 0-8089-1284-4). Grune.

New York Heart Association. Nomenclature & Criteria for Diagnosis of Diseases of the Heart & Great Vessels. 8th ed. LC 78-71219. 349p. 1979. text ed. 14.95 (ISBN 0-316-60536-0); pap. text ed. 11.95 (ISBN 0-316-60537-9). Little.

Noninvasive Cardiac Diagnosis. (Landmark Ser.). 1979. 22.50x (ISBN 0-8422-4108-6). Irvington.

Parkey, Robert W., et al, eds. Clinical Nuclear Cardiology. LC 78-12673. (Illus.). 1979. 36.50 (ISBN 0-8385-1146-5). ACC.

Schad, N., et al. Differential Diagnosis of Congenital Heart Disease. Bar, Hans, ed. LC 64-12879. 450p. 1966. 96.00 (ISBN 0-8089-0403-5). Grune.

Scott, Ralph C., ed. Diagnostic Procedures. (Clinical Cardiology & Diabetes: Vol. I, Part II). (Illus.). 352p. 1981. 32.00 (ISBN 0-87993-142-6). Futura Pub.

Serafini, Aldo. Nuclear Cardiology: Principles & Methods. LC 76-39783. (Topics in Cardiovascular Disease Ser.). (Illus.). 249p. 1977. 27.50 (ISBN 0-306-30952-1, Plenum Pr). Plenum Pub.

Surawicz, Borys & Pellegrino, E. D., eds. Sudden Cardiac Death. LC 64-22052. (Illus.). 222p. 1964. 39.00 (ISBN 0-8089-0493-0). Grune.

Tardos,., et al, eds. Pharmacological Control of Heart & Circulation: Proceedings of the Third Congress of the Hungarian Pharmacological Society, Budapest, 1979. LC 80-41281. (Advances in Pharmacological Research & Practice Ser.: Vol. I). 445p. 1981. 84.00 (ISBN 0-08-026386-0). Pergamon.

Weissler, Arnold M., ed. Noninvasive Cardiology. (Clinical Cardiology Monograph). 384p. 1974. 46.75 (ISBN 0-8089-0815-4). Grune.

Willerson, James T., ed. Nuclear Cardiology. LC 78-31500. (Cardiovascular Clinics Ser.: Vol. 10, No. 2). (Illus.). 1979. text ed. 35.00 (ISBN 0-8036-9329-X). Davis Co.

Williams, Roberta G. & Tucker, Charles R. Echocardiographic Diagnosis of Congenital Heart Disease. 1977. text ed. 25.00 (ISBN 0-316-94351-7). Little.

Zoneraich, Samuel. Non-Invasive Methods in Cardiology. (Illus.). 596p. 1975. text ed. 59.75 (ISBN 0-398-03107-X). C C Thomas.

HEART-DISEASES-PERSONAL NARRATIVES

Geary, Kenneth E. Heart Attack (Mine... & Yours?) 1979. 4.00 (ISBN 0-682-49348-1). Exposition.

Johnson, James L. Coming Back: One Man's Journey to the Edge of Eternity & Spiritual Rediscovery. LC 79-672450. 1979. 6.95 (ISBN 0-89952-001-4). Springhouse.

Lair, Jess & Lair, Jacqueline. Hey, God, What Should I Do Now? 240p. 1978. pap. 2.50 (ISBN 0-449-23586-6, Crest). Fawcett.

McDowell, Mildred. With an Open Heart. 1978. pap. 2.45 (ISBN 0-8091-2075-5). Paulist Pr.

Singh, John R. A Coronary Experience. 2nd ed. LC 80-82823. (Illus.). 128p. (Orig.). 1980. text ed. 9.95 (ISBN 0-9604672-0-3); pap. text ed. 4.95 (ISBN 0-9604672-1-1). Mid Am Pr.

Weiss, Elizabeth & Rubenstein, Stephen. Recovering from the Heart Attack Experience: Emotional Feeling, Medical Facts. 160p. 1980. 12.95 (ISBN 0-02-625830-7). Macmillan.

HEART-DISEASES-PREVENTION

Bailey, Herbert. Gerovital (GH3) Will It Keep You Young Longer. 2.50 (ISBN 0-686-29863-2). Cancer Bk Hse.

--Vitamin E: Your Key to a Healthy Heart. 1.65 (ISBN 0-686-29862-4). Cancer Bk Hse.

--Vitamin E: Your Key to a Healthy Heart. LC 64-23349. (Orig.). 1968. pap. 1.65 (ISBN 0-668-01514-4). Arco.

Barnes, Broda. Solved: Riddle-Heart Attacks. 4.00 (ISBN 0-686-29860-8). Cancer Bk Hse.

Blaine, Tom R. Prevent That Heart Attack. 6.95 (ISBN 0-8065-0299-1). Citadel Pr.

Braunwald, Eugene, ed. Protection of the Ischemic Myocardium. LC 76-1517. (AHA Monograph: No. 48). 1976. 6.00 (ISBN 0-87493-049-9, 73-034A). Am Heart.

Cantwell, John D. Stay Young at Heart. LC 75-25958. (Illus.). 212p. 1975. 14.95 (ISBN 0-88229-247-1). Nelson-Hall.

Czerwinski, Barara S. A Manual of Patient Education for Cardiopulmonary Dysfunction. LC 79-21435. (Illus.). 1980. pap. text ed. 13.95 (ISBN 0-8016-1197-0). Mosby.

Detry, Jean-Marie R. Exercise Testing & Training in Coronary Heart Disease. 80p. 1973. pap. 17.50 (ISBN 0-686-65360-2, Pub. by Williams & Wilkens). Krieger.

Diethrich, Edward. The Heart Test: The Arizona Heart Institute Program for the Detection, Prevention & Treatment of Heart Disease. 224p. (Orig.). 1981. pap. 6.95 (ISBN 0-346-12551-0). Cornerstone.

Farber, Thomas. Hazards to the Human Heart. 1980. 10.95 (ISBN 0-525-15424-8). Dutton.

Hurst, J. Willis & Luciano, Dorothy S. The Healthy Heart Book: A Guide for Patients & Their Families. 1980. 12.95 (ISBN 0-525-12241-9, Painter-Hopkins). Dutton.

Kavanagh, Terence. The Healthy Heart Program. 328p. 1981. pap. 6.95 (ISBN 0-442-29768-8). Van Nos Reinhold.

--Heart Attack? - Counterattack! 1976. 9.95 (ISBN 0-442-29927-3). Van Nos Reinhold.

Kezdi, Paul. You & Your Heart. LC 76-53757. (Illus.). 1977. 9.95 (ISBN 0-689-10743-9); pap. 4.95 (ISBN 0-689-70575-1, 243). Atheneum.

Loughran, John X. Ninety Days to a Better Heart. LC 58-12625. (Orig.). 1968. pap. 1.45 (ISBN 0-668-01793-7). Arco.

Maness, William. Exercise Your Heart. 1969. pap. 1.95 (ISBN 0-02-059350-3, Collier). Macmillan.

Murray, Frank. Program Your Heart for Health. 368p. (Orig.). 1977. pap. 2.95 (ISBN 0-915962-20-9). Larchmont Bks.

Nora, James J. The Whole Heart Book. LC 80-387. 352p. 1980. 17.95 (ISBN 0-03-048251-8); pap. 9.95 (ISBN 0-03-048246-1). HR&W.

Passwater, Richard. Supernutrition for Healthy Hearts. 1978. pap. 2.95 (ISBN 0-515-05725-8). Jove Pubns.

Powell, Eric F. Building a Healthy Heart. 1980. 19.50 (ISBN 0-85032-177-8, Pub. by Daniel Co England). State Mutual Bk.

Raab, Wilheim. Prevention of Ischemic Heart Disease: Principles & Practice. (Illus.). 504p. 1966. photocopy ed. spiral 49.75 (ISBN 0-398-01532-5). C C Thomas.

Raab, Wilhelm. Preventive Myocardiology: Fundamentals & Targets. (American Lecture Living Chemistry). (Illus.). 248p. 1970. photocopy ed. spiral 24.75 (ISBN 0-398-01533-3). C C Thomas.

Shute, Evan V. & Shute Institute Staff. The Heart & Vitamin E. LC 77-86547. 1977. pap. 4.95 (ISBN 0-87983-165-0). Keats.

Shute, Wilfrid. Vitamin E: Ailing & Healthy Hearts. pap. 1.95 (ISBN 0-686-29960-4). Cancer Bk Hse.

Sonnenblick, E. & Lesch, M., eds. Exercise & Heart Disease. 256p. 1977. 29.50 (ISBN 0-8089-1016-7). Grune.

Super-Nutrition-Healthy Hearts. 2.50 (ISBN 0-686-29823-3). Cancer Bk Hse.

Towse, G., ed. Myocardial Protection & Exercise Tolerance: The Role of Lidoflazine, a New Anti-Anginal Agent. (Royal Society of Medicine International Congress & Symposium Ser.: No. 29). 112p. 1980. pap. 19.50 (ISBN 0-8089-1290-9). Grune.

Vineberg, Arthur. How to Live with Your Heart: The Family Guide to Heart Health. LC 74-25204. 219p. 1977. 8.95 (ISBN 0-8129-0549-0); pap. 3.50 (ISBN 0-8129-6282-6). Times Bks.

Walker, Morton. How Not to Have a Heart Attack. 7.95 (ISBN 0-686-29991-4). Cancer Bk Hse.

--How Not to Have a Heart Attack. 1980. pap. 7.95 (ISBN 0-531-09919-9). Watts.

Warmbrand, Max. Add Years to Your Heart. 1969. pap. 2.50 (ISBN 0-515-05720-7, N2046). Jove Pubns.

Weisfeldt, Myron L., ed. The Aging Heart: Its Function & Response to Stress. (Aging Ser.: Vol. 12). 335p. 1980. 32.00 (ISBN 0-89004-307-8, 382). Raven.

Westberg, Marita. Eat Well, Live Longer: A Manual for a Healthy Heart. 4.95 (ISBN 0-7043-3219-1, Pub. by Quartet England). Charles River Bks.

HEART-INFARCTION

Cologne Symposium, Third, June 16-19, 1976. Brain & Heart Infarct: Proceedings. Zulch, K. J., et al, eds. (Illus.). 1977. 39.40 (ISBN 0-387-08270-0). Springer-Verlag.

Eliot, Robert S., et al, eds. Cardiac Emergencies. LC 76-41062. (Contemporary Problems in Cardiology Ser: Vol. 3). 1977. 22.50 (ISBN 0-87993-075-6). Futura Pub.

Friedberg, Charles K., ed. Acute Myocardial Infarction & Coronary Care Units. 296p. 1969. 44.50 (ISBN 0-8089-0144-3). Grune.

--Myocardial Infarction. 1972. pap. 5.00 (ISBN 0-87493-027-8, 73-025A). Am Heart.

Friedman, Meyer & Rosenman, Ray H. Type A Behavior & Your Heart. 1974. 12.95 (ISBN 0-394-48011-2). Knopf.

--Type A Behavior & Your Heart. 320p. 1981. pap. 6.95 (ISBN 0-449-90059-2, Crest). Fawcett.

Garcia, Rebecca M. Rehabilitation After Myocardial Infarction. LC 78-10450. (CECN Ser.). (Illus.). 83p. 1979. 6.95 (ISBN 0-8385-8312-1). ACC.

Gentry, W. Doyle & Williams, Redford B. Psychological Aspects of Myocardial Infarction & Coronary Care. 2nd ed. LC 79-2554. (Illus.). 1979. pap. text ed. 12.95 (ISBN 0-8016-1796-0). Mosby.

Greenbaum, Dennis & Gianelli, Stanley, Jr. Acute Cardiovascular Failure. (Clinics in Critical Care Medicine Ser.). (Illus.). 224p. 1981. lib. bdg. 22.50 (ISBN 0-443-08111-5). Churchill.

Gunnar, Rolf M., et al, eds. Shock in Myocardial Infarction. (Illus.). 272p. 1974. 44.50 (ISBN 0-8089-0830-8). Grune.

Haft, Jacob I. & Berlin, Saretta. Consultation with a Cardiologist: Coronary Heart Disease & Heart Attacks: Prevention. LC 78-26660. 1979. 19.95 (ISBN 0-88229-320-6). Nelson-Hall.

Haft, Jacob I. & Bailey, Charles P., eds. Acute Myocardial Infarction & Coronary Artery Disease. LC 78-53403. (Advances in the Management of Clinical Heart Disease Ser.: Vol. II). (Illus.). 1978. medical monograph 19.75 (ISBN 0-87993-110-8). Futura Pub.

Harrison, Donald C., ed. Management of Acute Myocardial Infarction. 89p. 1972. pap. 9.95 (ISBN 0-685-90284-6, Pub. by W & W). Krieger.

WHO Scientific Group, Geneva, 1969. Pathological Diagnosis of Acute Ischaemic Heart Disease: Report. (Technical Report Ser.: No. 441). (Also avail. in French, Russian & Spanish). 1970. pap. 1.20 (ISBN 92-4-120441-9). World Health.

HEART-INNERVATION

Abraham, A. Microscopic Innervation of the Heart & Blood Vessels in Vertebrates Including Man. 1969. 64.00 (ISBN 0-08-012342-2). Pergamon.

Hainsworth, R., et al, eds. Cardiac Receptors. LC 77-12404. (Illus.). 1980. 83.50 (ISBN 0-521-21853-5). Cambridge U Pr.

Khabarova, A. Y. The Afferent Innervation of the Heart. LC 62-15548. 175p. 1963. 25.00 (ISBN 0-306-10656-6, Consultants). Plenum Pub.

Randall, W. C. Nervous Control of the Heart. 251p. 1965. 15.00 (ISBN 0-683-07108-4, Pub by Williams & Wilkens). Krieger.

Randall, Walter C. Neural Regulation of the Heart. (Illus.). 375p. 1976. 24.95x (ISBN 0-19-502080-4). Oxford U Pr.

HEART-JUVENILE LITERATURE

Elgin, Kathleen. The Heart. (Human Body Ser). (Illus.). (gr. 4-6). 1968. PLB 6.90 (ISBN 0-531-01174-7). Watts.

Showers, Paul. Hear Your Heart. LC 68-11067. (A Let's Read & Find Out Science Bk). (Illus.). (gr. k-3). 1968. (TYC-J); PLB 8.79 (ISBN 0-690-37379-1); filmstrip with record 11.95 (ISBN 0-690-37380-5); film with cassette 14.95 (ISBN 0-690-37382-1). Har-Row.

--Hear Your Heart. LC 68-11067. (Crocodile Paperbacks Ser.). (Illus.). 40p. (gr. k-3). 1975. pap. 2.95 (ISBN 0-690-00636-5, TYC-J). Har-Row.

Simon, Seymour. About Your Heart. LC 73-8019. (Illus.). 48p. (ps-4). 1974. PLB 6.95 (ISBN 0-07-057440-5, GB). McGraw.

Zim, Herbert S. Your Heart & How It Works. (Illus.). (gr. 3-7). 1959. PLB 6.48 (ISBN 0-688-31552-6). Morrow.

HEART-MUSCLE

Clark, Nancy Fairchild. Normal Conduction System & the Electrocardiogram: A Programmed Instruction Unit. LC 75-2393. (Illus.). 96p. 1975. pap. text ed. 3.95 (ISBN 0-8036-1840-9). Davis Co.

Fleckenstein, A. Basic Functions of Cations in Myocardial Activity. (Recent Advances in Studies on Cardiac Structure & Metabolism Ser.: Vol. 5). (Illus.). 1975. 39.50 (ISBN 0-8391-0665-3). Univ Park.

--Pathophysiology & Morphology of Myocardial Cell Alterations. (Recent Advances in Studies on Cardiac Structure & Metabolism Ser.: Vol. 6). (Illus.). 1974. 39.50 (ISBN 0-8391-0666-1). Univ Park.

Fowler, Noble O., ed. Myocardial Diseases. LC 73-1685. (Clinical Cardiology Monograph). (Illus.). 392p. 1973. 51.50 (ISBN 0-8089-0799-9). Grune.

Harris, P. & Opie, L., eds. Calcium & the Heart. 198p. 1971. 32.00 (ISBN 0-12-326950-4). Acad Pr.

Langer, Glenn A. & Brady, Allan J., eds. The Mammalian Myocardium. LC 73-9906. 310p. 1974. 25.00 (ISBN 0-471-51600-7, Pub. by Wiley). Krieger.

Lieberman, M. & Sano, T., eds. Developmental & Physiological Correlates of Cardiac Muscle: Perspectives in Cardiovascular Research, Vol. 1. LC 74-21979. 336p. 1976. 34.50 (ISBN 0-89004-027-3). Raven.

Morad, Martin & Smith, Susan, eds. Biophysical Aspects of Cardiac Muscle. 1978. 29.50 (ISBN 0-12-506150-1). Acad Pr.

Paavo Nurmi Symposium, 3rd, Helsinki, 1975. Physical Activity & Coronary Heart Disease: Proceedings. Manninen, V., ed. (Advances in Cardiology: Vol. 18). (Illus.). 240p. 1976. 72.00 (ISBN 3-8055-2356-4). S Karger.

Rakusan, Karel. Oxygen in the Heart Muscle. (Illus.). 108p. 1971. photocopy ed. spiral 12.00 (ISBN 0-398-01541-4). C C Thomas.

Tanz, Ralph D., et al, eds. Factors Influencing Myocardial Contractility. 1967. 78.50 (ISBN 0-12-683450-4). Acad Pr.

HEART-PALPITATION

see also Arrhythmia

Summerall, C. P., 3rd, et al. Monitoring Heart Rhythm. 208p. 1976. 16.50 (ISBN 0-471-83556-0). Wiley.

HEART-RADIOGRAPHY

Cooley, Robert N. & Schreiber, M. H. Radiology of the Heart & Great Vessels. 3rd ed. (Golden's Diagnostic Radiology Ser: Section 4). (Illus.). 676p. 1978. 73.00 (ISBN 0-683-02103-6). Williams & Wilkins.

Elliott, Larry P. & Schiebler, Gerold L. The X-Ray Diagnosis of Congenital Heart Disease in Infants, Children & Adults: Pathologic, Hemodynamic, & Clinical Correlations As Related to Chest Film. 2nd ed. (Illus.). 424p. 1979. text ed. 36.50 (ISBN 0-398-03857-0). C C Thomas.

Jefferson, K. & Rees, S. Clinical Cardiac Radiology. 1973. 39.95 (ISBN 0-407-13575-8). Butterworth.

HEART-SOUNDS

Baragan, Joseph, et al. Dynamic Auscultation & Phonocardiography. Tavel, Morton E. & Tavel, Morton E., eds. (Illus.). 314p. 1979. 31.95 (ISBN 0-87619-458-7). Charles.

Butterworth, J. Scott, et al. Cardiac Auscultation. 2nd enl. ed. LC 60-6018. (Illus.). 1960. 32.00 (ISBN 0-8089-0089-7). Grune.

Deuchar, Dennis C. Clinical Phonocardiography. (Illus.). 1965. 5.95x (ISBN 0-442-02085-6). Van Nos Reinhold.

Gerrick, David J. Sounds of the Heart. (Illus.). 1978. 20.00 (ISBN 0-916750-55-8). Dayton Labs.

Guenther, K. H. Comparative Extracardiac & Intracardiac Phonocardiography on Hemodynamic Basis. (Illus., Ger. & Eng.). 1969. plastics 46.25 (ISBN 0-685-37419-X). Adler.

Leatham, Aubrey. Auscultation of the Heart & Phonocardiography. 2nd ed. LC 75-7547. (Illus.). 176p. 1975. pap. text ed. 23.75x (ISBN 0-443-01155-9). Churchill.

Leon, Donald F., ed. Physiologic Principles of Heart Sounds & Murmurs. (AHA Monograph Ser.: Vol. 46). 1975. 4.00 (ISBN 0-87493-045-6, 73-032A). Am Heart.

Luisada, Aldo A. The Sounds of the Diseased Heart. LC 74-176171. (Illus.). 416p. 1973. text ed. 25.50 (ISBN 0-87527-113-8). Green.

--The Sounds of the Normal Heart. LC 78-176172. (Illus.). 264p. 1972. 22.50 (ISBN 0-87527-051-4). Green.

Luisada, Aldo A., et al. An Atlas of Non-Invasive Techniques: Sound & Pulse Tracings-Echograms. (Illus.). 568p. 1976. vinyl 45.75 (ISBN 0-398-03555-5). C C Thomas.

Ravin, A. Auscultation of the Heart. 3rd ed. (Illus.). 1977. 21.50 (ISBN 0-8151-7101-3). Year Bk Med.
Segal, Bernard L. & Likoff, William. Auscultation of the Heart. LC 65-14909. (Illus.). 208p. 1965. 39.50 (ISBN 0-8089-0419-1); record o.p. 20.50 (ISBN 0-8089-0420-5); tape at 3 3/4 44.75 (ISBN 0-8089-0421-3); tape at 7 1/2 34.50 (ISBN 0-8089-0422-1). Grune.
Tavel, Morton E. Clinical Phonocardiography & External Pulse Recording. 3rd ed. (Illus.). 1978. 29.95 (ISBN 0-8151-8725-4). Year Bk Med.
Wartak, Josef. Phonocardiology. (Illus.). 1972. 25.00x (ISBN 0-06-142613-X, Harper Medical). Har-Row.

HEART–SURGERY
see also Cardiac Catheterization
Adelman, Allen G. & Goldman, Bernard S., eds. Unstable Angina: Recognition & Management. LC 80-13211. 358p. 1981. 32.50 (ISBN 0-88416-271-0). Wright-PSG.
Aspinall, Mary Jo. Aortic Arch Surgery. (Surgical Aspects of Cardiovascular Disease: Nursing Intervention Series). (Illus.). 105p. 1980. pap. 6.95 (ISBN 0-8385-0171-0). ACC.
Behrendt, Douglas M. & Austen, W. Gerald. Patient Care in Cardiac Surgery. 3rd ed. (Little, Brown SPIRAL TM Manual Ser.). 1980. pap. 12.95 (ISBN 0-316-08756-4). Little.
Buckley, Mortimer J., ed. Cardiovasular Surgery, Nineteen Seventy-Seven. (AHA Monograph: No. 59). 1979. 5.00 (ISBN 0-685-49694-5, 73-045-A). Am Heart.
Buis, B. Aorto-Coronary Bypass Surgery. 1974. lib. bdg. 24.00 (ISBN 90-207-0474-5, Pub. by Martinus Nijhoff Netherlands). Kluwer Boston.
Burrows, Susan G. & Gassert, Carole A. Moving Right Along Open Heart Surgery. Hull, Nancy R., ed. (Illus.). 52p. (Orig.). (gr. 8-10). 1979. pap. text ed. 5.00 (ISBN 0-939838-03-6). Pritchett & Hull.
Campbell, Charles D., ed. The Surgical Treatment of Aortic Aneurysms. (Illus.). 185p. 1981. price not set monograph (ISBN 0-87993-162-0). Futura Pub.
Chow, Rita. Cardiosurgical Nursing Care. LC 74-79408. (Illus.). 1976. text ed. 15.50 (ISBN 0-8261-1233-1). Springer Pub.
Conference on Cardiovascular Disease, 2nd, Snowmass-at-Aspen, Colorado, 1971. Long-Term Prognosis Following Valve Replacement: Proceedings. Vogel, J. H., ed. (Advances in Cardiology: Vol. 7). 1972. 59.50 (ISBN 3-8055-1299-6). S Karger.
Davila, Julio C., ed. The Second Henry Ford Hospital International Symposium on Cardiac Surgery. (Illus.). 732p. 1977. 72.00 (ISBN 0-8385-8526-4). ACC.
Dyde, J. A. & Smith, R. E., eds. Surgery of the Heart. LC 76-14827. 209p. 1976. 27.50 (ISBN 0-306-30944-0, Plenum Pr). Plenum Pub.
Galletti, Pierre M. & Brecher, Gerhard A. Heart Lung Bypass. (Illus.). 400p. 1962. 56.25 (ISBN 0-8089-0146-X). Grune.
Harken, Dwight. Cardiac Surgery One. (Illus.). 1971. 15.00 (ISBN 0-8036-4567-8). Davis Co.
--Cardiac Surgery 2. (Illus.). 1971. 15.00 (ISBN 0-8036-4568-6). Davis Co.
Harlan, B. J., et al. Manual of Cardiac Surgery, Vol. I. (Comprehensive Manuals of Surgical Specialities Ser.). (Illus.). 204p. 1980. 140.00 (ISBN 0-387-90393-3). Springer-Verlag.
Hurst, J. Willis. Update Two: the Heart: Bypass Surgery for Obstructive Coronary Disease. (Illus.). 1979. text ed. 30.00 (ISBN 0-07-031491-8). McGraw.
Kennedy, John H., ed. Cardiovascular Surgery 1973. 265p. 1974. pap. 6.00 (ISBN 0-87493-041-3, 73-005L). Am Heart.
King, Ouida M. Care of the Cardiac Surgical Patient. LC 75-2460. (Illus.). 272p. 1975. text ed. 16.50 (ISBN 0-8016-3434-2). Mosby.
Lawton, George. Straight to the Heart. LC 56-11027. 1956. text ed. 15.00 (ISBN 0-8236-6160-1). Intl Univs Pr.
Longmore, D. Modern Cardiac Surgery. 1978. 29.50 (ISBN 0-8391-1285-8). Univ Park.
Longmore, D. B. Current Status of Cardiac Surgery. 1975. 29.50 (ISBN 0-8391-0820-6). Univ Park.
Longmore, Donald P. Towards Safer Cardiac Surgery. 1981. lib. bdg. 35.00 (ISBN 0-8161-2232-6, Hall Medical). G K Hall.
McGoon, Dwight C., ed. Cardiac Surgery. (Cardiovascular Clints Ser.: Vol. 12, No. 3). (Illus.). 250p. 1982. 40.00 (ISBN 0-8036-5982-2). Davis Co.
Minetree, Harry. Cooley: The Career of a Great Heart Surgeon. LC 72-79716. (Illus.). 310p. 1973. 13.95 (ISBN 0-06-126382-6). Har-Row.
Ochsner, John L. & Mills, Noel L. Coronary Artery Surgery. LC 77-17476. (Illus.). 275p. 1978. text ed. 25.00 (ISBN 0-8121-0620-2). Lea & Febiger.
Pothuizen, L. M., et al, eds. Coronary Artery Surgery. (International Congress Ser.: No. 343). 84p. 1975. pap. 15.75 (ISBN 0-444-15137-0, Excerpta Medica). Elsevier.
Powers, Maryann & Storlie, Frances. Cardiac Surgical Patient. (Illus.). 1969. text ed. 9.25x (ISBN 0-02-396300-X). Macmillan.
Rahimtoola, Shahbudin H. Coronary Bypass Surgery. LC 77-8284. (Cardiovascular Clinics Ser.: Vol. 8, No. 2). 1977. text ed. 35.00 (ISBN 0-8036-7270-5). Davis Co.
Richardson, Robert G. Surgeon's Heart: History of Cardiac Surgery. (Illus.). 1969. 21.00x (ISBN 0-433-27590-1). Intl Ideas.
Roskamm, H. & Schmuziger, M. Coronary Heart Surgery: A Rehabilitation Measure. (Illus.). 1979. pap. 45.10 (ISBN 0-387-09345-1). Springer-Verlag.
Ross, James O. The Heart Machine: A Personal Account of Open-Heart Surgery. LC 73-6183. 144p. 1973. 5.50 (ISBN 0-8008-3821-1). Taplinger.
Sade, Robert M. Infant & Child Care in Heart Surgery. (Illus.). 1977. pap. 14.95 (ISBN 0-8151-7504-3). Year Bk Med.
Stark, J. & De Leval, M., eds. Surgery for Congenital Heart Disease in Infants. 1981. write for info. (ISBN 0-8089-1161-9, 794309). Grune.
Tyers, G. Frank, ed. Self-Assessment of Current Knowledge in Cardiothoracic Surgery. 2nd. ed. LC 79-92911. 1980. pap. 18.00 (ISBN 0-87488-276-1). Med Exam.
Vineberg, Arthur. How to Live with Your Heart: The Family Guide to Heart Health. LC 74-25204. 219p. 1977. 8.95 (ISBN 0-8129-0549-0); pap. 3.50 (ISBN 0-8129-6282-6). Times Bks.

HEART–TRANSPLANTATION
Poole, Victoria. Thursday's Child. 1980. 10.95 (ISBN 0-316-71334-1). Little.
Symposium Mondiale - 2nd - 1969. Transplantation Cardiaque: Proceedings. (Fr). 1970. 21.60x (ISBN 2-7637-6485-1, Pub. by Laval). Intl Schol Bk Serv.

HEART, ARTIFICIAL
Here are entered intracorporeal pumping mechanisms that duplicate the function of the natural heart. Extracorporeal pumping mechanisms that duplicate the function of the natural heart are entered under Heart, Mechanical.
see also Heart, Mechanical; Pacemaker, Artificial (Heart)
Bolooki, Hooshang, ed. Clinical Application of Intra-Aortic Balloon Pump. LC 77-84351. (Illus.). 1977. 34.50 (ISBN 0-87993-104-3). Futura Pub.
Bregman, David. Mechanical Support of the Failing Heart & Lungs. (Illus.). 210p. 1977. 21.50 (ISBN 0-8385-6196-9). ACC.

HEART, MECHANICAL
Here are entered extracorporeal pumping mechanisms that duplicate the function of the natural heart. Intracorporeal pumping mechanisms that duplicate the function of the natural heart are entered under Heart, Artificial.
Bartosek, I., et al, eds. Isolated Liver Perfusion & Its Applications. LC 72-95635. (Mario Negri Institute for Pharmacological Research Monographs). (Illus.). 1973. 25.50 (ISBN 0-911216-43-X). Raven.
Castellanos, Agustin, ed. Cardiac Arrhythmias: Mechanisms & Management. LC 79-24345. (Cardiovascular Clinics Ser.: Vol. 11, No. 1). (Illus.). 296p. 1980. text ed. 40.00 (ISBN 0-8036-1684-8). Davis Co.
Rapaport, Felix T. & Merrill, John P., eds. Artificial Organs & Cardiopulmonary Support Systems. LC 77-183645. (Illus.). 200p. 1972. 42.50 (ISBN 0-8089-0748-4). Grune.
Symposium, Boston, 1970. Mechanical Devices for Cardiopulmonary Assistance: Proceedings. Bartlett, R. H., et al, eds. (Advances in Cardiology: Vol. 6). 1971. 40.75 (ISBN 3-8055-1163-9). S Karger.

HEART ATTACK
see Coronary Heart Disease; Heart–Diseases; Heart–Infarction

HEART-BEAT
see also Pacemaker, Artificial (Heart); Pulse
Boas, Ernest P. & Golschmidt, Ernst F. The Heart Rate. (Illus.). 160p. 1932. ed. spiral bdg. 14.75photocopy (ISBN 0-398-04215-2). C C Thomas.
Kitney, R. I. & Rompelman, O. The Study of Heart-Rate Variability. (Illus.). 220p. 1980. text ed. 65.00x (ISBN 0-19-857533-5). Oxford U Pr.
Kulbertus, M. Re-Entrant Arrythmias. 1977. 44.50 (ISBN 0-8391-1120-7). Univ Park.
Noble, Denis. The Initiation of the Heartbeat. 2nd ed. 1977. 19.95x (ISBN 0-19-857177-1); pap. text ed. 9.95x (ISBN 0-19-857178-X). Oxford U Pr.
Phillips, Raymond E. The Cardiac Rhythms: A Kit for Instructors. 2nd ed. 64p. 1981. 100.00 (ISBN 0-7216-9958-8). Saunders.

HEART CATHETERIZATION
see Cardiac Catheterization

HEART FAILURE
see also Cardiac Resuscitation
Bander, Joseph J., et al. Cardiac Arrest & CPR: Assessment, Planning & Intervention. LC 80-18748. 202p. 1980. text ed. 24.50 (ISBN 0-89443-328-8). Aspen Systems.
Brest, Albert, ed. Congestive Heart Failure. 157p. 1975. pap. 15.00 (ISBN 0-683-01054-9, Pub. by W & W). Krieger.
Chazov, Evgenii I., ed. Myocardial Infarction. LC 77-99143. (Illus.). 314p. 1979. 23.00 (ISBN 0-88416-119-6). Wright-PSG.
Fishman, Alfred P., ed. Heart Failure. (Illus.). 1978. text ed. 19.95 (ISBN 0-07-021118-3, HP). McGraw.
Friedberg, Charles K., ed. Congestive Heart Failure. LC 58-8981. (Illus.). 320p. 1970. 50.00 (ISBN 0-8089-0670-4). Grune.
Gelb, Donald. Heart Attack: You Can Survive. 1979. pap. 2.95 (ISBN 0-89260-128-0). Hwong Pub.
Hamilton, William P. & Lavin, Mary A. Decision Making in the Coronary Care Unit. 2nd ed. LC 75-30994. (Illus.). 184p. 1976. pap. text ed. 9.50 (ISBN 0-8016-2026-0). Mosby.
Jarcho, Saul. The Concept of Heart Failure: From Avicenna to Albertini. (Commonwealth Fund Ser.). 1980. text ed. 45.00x (ISBN 0-674-15635-8). Harvard U Pr.
Kones, Richard J. Cardiogenic Shock: Mechanisms & Management. LC 73-89311. 400p. 1974. 22.95 (ISBN 0-87993-032-2). Futura Pub.
Mason, Dean T. Cardiac Emergencies. (Illus.). 280p. 1978. 31.50 (ISBN 0-683-05904-1). Williams & Wilkins.
Mason, Dean T., ed. Congestive Heart Failure. LC 76-3321. (Illus.). 448p. 1976. 35.00 (ISBN 0-914316-05-2). Yorke Med.
Pinneo, Rose. Congestive Heart Failure. (Illus.). 1978. pap. 6.95 (ISBN 0-8385-1169-4). ACC.
Prinzmetal, Myron. Heart Attack. rev. ed. pap. 2.95 (ISBN 0-671-20863-2, Fireside). S&S.
Purcell, Julia A. & Johnston, Barbara. A Stronger Pump. Hull, Nancy R., ed. (Illus., Orig.). (gr. 8-10). 1980. pap. text ed. 4.50 (ISBN 0-939838-05-2). Pritchett & Hull.
Rawlings, M. D., et al, eds. Prazosin: Pharmacology, Hypertension & Congestive Heart Failure. LC 80-41965. (Royal Society of Medicine International Congress & Symposium Ser.: No. 41). 1981. 27.50 (ISBN 0-8089-1370-0). Grune.
Riecker, G., et al, eds. Myocardial Failure. Weber, A. & Goodwin, J. LC 77-5159. 1977. pap. 28.20 (ISBN 0-387-08225-5). Springer-Verlag.
Rose. Fundamentals of Mobile Coronary Care. 2nd ed. (Illus.). 174p. 1979. pap. 15.95 (ISBN 0-683-07362-1). Williams & Wilkins.
Roth, Oscar & Galton, Lawrence. Heart Attack: A Question & Answer Book. 1980. pap. 4.95 (ISBN 0-8092-7054-4). Contemp Bks.
Rubinson, Ann. Heart Attacks: Is Your Family a Risk Factor? 1981. 8.95 (ISBN 0-533-04217-8). Vantage.
Snider, Arthur J. & Adatto, I. J. A Doctor Discusses Learning to Live with Heart Trouble. (Illus.). 1980. pap. 2.50 (ISBN 0-685-35677-9). Budlong.
Symposium On Congestive Heart Failure. Proceedings. rev. ed. Blumgart, Herrman L., ed. (AHA Monograph Ser.: Vol. 1). 1966. pap. text ed. 5.00 (ISBN 0-87493-011-1, 73-001A). Am Heart.

HEART FUNCTION TESTS
see also Function Tests (Medicine)
Bleifeld, W., et al, eds. Evaluation of Cardiac Function by Echocardiography. (Illus.). 210p. 1980. 37.80 (ISBN 0-387-10045-8). Springer-Verlag.
Chung, Edward K. Exercise Electrocardiography: Practical Approach. 1979. 33.00 (ISBN 0-683-01569-9). Williams & Wilkins.
Curran, J. T. Fetal Heart Monitoring. 1975. 21.95 (ISBN 0-407-00014-3). Butterworth.
Mullins, L. J. Ion Transport in Heart. 144p. 1981. 16.50 (ISBN 0-89004-645-X). Raven.
Weissler, Arnold M., ed. Noninvasive Cardiology. (Clinical Cardiology Monograph). 384p. 1974. 46.75 (ISBN 0-8089-0815-4). Grune.

HEART-LUNG MACHINE
see Heart, Mechanical

HEART MUSCLE
see Heart–Muscle

HEART OF JESUS, DEVOTION TO
see Sacred Heart, Devotion To

HEART PATIENTS
see Cardiacs

HEART VALVE PROSTHESIS
Advances in Heart Valve Prostheses. 1981. write for info. (ISBN 0-89004-670-0). Raven.
Conference on Cardiovascular Disease, 2nd, Snowmass-at-Aspen, Colorado, 1971. Long-Term Prognosis Following Valve Replacement: Proceedings. Vogel, J. H., ed. (Advances in Cardiology: Vol. 7). 1972. 59.50 (ISBN 3-8055-1299-6). S Karger.
Ionescu, M. I. Tissue Heart Values. 112p. 1979. text ed. 64.95 (ISBN 0-407-00139-5). Butterworth.
Ionescu, M. I., et al, eds. Biological Tissue in Heart Valve Replacement. (Illus.). 956p. 1971. 94.95 (ISBN 0-407-11730-X). Butterworth.
Lefrak, Edward & Starr, Albert. Cardiac Valve Prostheses. LC 79-46. (Illus.). 419p. 1979. 27.00 (ISBN 0-8385-1049-3). ACC.

HEAT
see also Aerodynamic Heating; Animal Heat; Atmospheric Temperature; Calorimeters and Calorimetry; Cold; Combustion; Entropy; Fire; Gases–Liquefaction; Heat Engineering; High Temperatures; Metals at High Temperatures; Pyrometers and Pyrometry; Solidification; Steam; Temperature; Thermochemistry; Thermodynamics; Thermoelectricity; Thermography (Copying Process); Thermomagnetism; Thermometers and Thermometry; Waste Heat
Andronov, A. A., et al. Seven Papers on Equations Related to Mechanics & Heat. LC 51-5559. (Translations Ser.: No. 2, Vol. 75). 1968. 28.80 (ISBN 0-8218-1775-2, TRANS 2-75). Am Math.
Becker, R. Theory of Heat. 2nd. ed. Leibfried, G., tr. (Illus.). 1967. 40.70 (ISBN 0-387-03730-6). Springer-Verlag.
Beggerow, G. Heats of Mixing & Solution. (Landolt-Bornstein New Ser.: Group IV, Vol. 2). 1977. 377.60 (ISBN 0-387-07443-0). Springer-Verlag.
Bierman, Sheldon L., et al. Geothermal Energy in the Western United States: Innovation Versus Monopoly. LC 77-16078. 1978. 34.50 (ISBN 0-03-041470-9). Praeger.
Chapple, M. A Level Physics: Mechanics & Heat, Vol. 1. 2nd ed. (Illus.). 336p. (Orig.). 1979. pap. text ed. 10.95x (ISBN 0-7121-0154-3, Pub. by Macdonald & Evans England). Intl Ideas.
Cohen, I. Bernard, ed. Gravitation, Heat & X-Rays. LC 80-2104. (Development of Science Ser.). (Illus.). 1981. lib. bdg. 35.00x (ISBN 0-405-13869-5). Arno.
Cornwell, Keith. The Flow of Heat. 1977. 21.00x (ISBN 0-442-30177-4); pap. 11.50x (ISBN 0-442-30168-5). Van Nos Reinhold.
Hannequin, Arthur. Essai Critique sur L'hypothese Atomesdans La Sciene Contemporaine. Cohen, I. Bernard, ed. LC 80-2127. (Development of Science Ser.). (Illus.). 1981. lib. bdg. 40.00x (ISBN 0-405-13876-8). Arno.
In Situ Heating Experiments in Geological Formations, Ludvika, Sweden, September 1978. 1979. 16.50x (ISBN 92-64-01872-7). OECD.
Lavoisier, A. L. & Laplace, P. S. Memoirs on Heat. Guerlac, Henry, ed. 1981. write for info. (ISBN 0-88202-195-8). N Watson.
Long, T. S. Boiling Crisis & Critical Heat Flux. LC 72-600190. (AEC Critical Review Ser.). 89p. 1972. pap. 3.00 (ISBN 0-686-75887-0); microfiche 3.00 (ISBN 0-686-75888-9). DOE.
McKenzie, Arthur E. Physics. 4th ed. 1970. 17.95x (ISBN 0-521-07698-6). Cambridge U Pr.
Maleh, Issac. Mechanics, Heat, & Sound. (Merrill Physical Science Library). pap. text ed. 3.75x (ISBN 0-675-09638-3). Merrill.
Maxwell, James C. Theory of Heat. 3rd ed. LC 77-173064. Repr. of 1872 ed. 11.25 (ISBN 0-404-04277-5). AMS Pr.
--Theory of Heat. 3rd ed. Repr. of 1872 ed. lib. bdg. 15.00x (ISBN 0-8371-4097-8, MATH). Greenwood.
Millikan, Robert, et al. Mechanics, Molecular Physics, Heat, & Sound. (Illus.). 1965. pap. 4.95x (ISBN 0-262-63001-X). MIT Pr.
Mott-Smith, Morton. Concept of Heat & Its Workings. Orig. Title: Heat & Its Workings. 1933. pap. 2.75 (ISBN 0-486-20978-4). Dover.
--The Concept of Heat & Its Workings Simply Explained. 1962. lib. bdg. 9.50 (ISBN 0-88307-627-6). Gannon.
Olszewski. Utilization of Reject Heat. (Energy, Power & Environment Ser.: Vol. 10). 189p. 1980. 29.50 (ISBN 0-8247-1168-8). Dekker.
Pincherle, L. Worked Problems in Heat, Thermodynamics & Kinetic Theory. 1966. pap. 10.75 (ISBN 0-08-012015-6). Pergamon.
Portman, Donald J. & Ryznar, Edward. An Investigation of Heat Exchange. (International Indian Ocean Expedition Meteorological Monographs: No. 5). 1971. 12.00x (ISBN 0-8248-0097-4, Eastwest Ctr). U Pr of Hawaii.
Saha, M. N. & Srivastava, B. N. A Textbook of Heat for Junior Students. 368p. 1981. 10.00x (ISBN 0-86125-639-5, Pub. by Orient Longman India). State Mutual Bk.
Sears, Francis W. Mechanics, Heat, & Sound. 2nd ed. (Illus.). 1950. 17.95 (ISBN 0-201-06905-9). A-W.
--Mechanics, Wave Motion & Heat. 1958. 15.95 (ISBN 0-201-06910-5). A-W.
Truesdell, C. & Bharatha, S. The Concept & Logic of Classical Thermodynamics As a Theory of Heat Engines. Rigorously Constructed Upon Foundations Laid by S. Carnot & F. Reech. LC 76-48115. (Texts & Monographs in Physics). (Illus.). 1978. 31.60 (ISBN 0-387-07971-8). Springer-Verlag.

United Nations Economic Commission for Europe. Combined Production of Electric Power & Heat: Proceedings of a Seminar Organized by the Committee on Electric Power of the United Nations Economic Commission for Europe, Hamburg, FR Germany, 6-9 November 1978. LC 80-755. (Illus.). 150p. 32.00 (ISBN 0-08-025677-5). Pergamon.
Widder, D. V. The Heat Equation. (Pure & Applied Mathematics Ser.). 1975. 40.50 (ISBN 0-12-748540-6). Acad Pr.
Wilkinson, Bruce W. & Barnes, Richard W. Cogeneration of Electricity & Useful Heat. 272p. 1980. 74.95 (ISBN 0-8493-5615-6). CRC Pr.
Young, Hugh D. Fundamentals of Mechanics & Heat. 2nd ed. (Fundamentals of Physics Ser). (Illus.). 736p. 1973. text ed. 19.95 (ISBN 0-07-072638-8, C); instructo's manual 2.50 (ISBN 0-07-072639-6). McGraw.
--Fundamentals of Mechanics & Heat. 2nd ed. (Fundamentals of Physics Ser). (Illus.). 736p. 1973. text ed. 19.95 (ISBN 0-07-072638-8, C); instructo's manual 2.50 (ISBN 0-07-072639-6). McGraw.
Zemansky, Mark & Dittman, Richard. Heat & Thermodynamics. 6th ed. (Illus.). 560p. 1981. text ed. 22.95 (ISBN 0-07-072808-9, C). McGraw.
Zemansky, Mark W. Heat & Thermodynamics. 5th ed. LC 67-26891. (Illus.). 1968. text ed. 20.95 (ISBN 0-07-072807-0, C). McGraw.

HEAT-ABSORPTION

see Heat-Radiation and Absorption

HEAT-CONDUCTION

Arpaci, Vedat S. Conduction Heat Transfer. 1966. 23.95 (ISBN 0-201-00359-7). A-W.
Berman, R. Thermal Conductions in Solids. (Oxford Studies in Physics). (Illus.). 1976. 34.50 (ISBN 0-19-851429-8). Oxford U Pr.
Carslaw, Horatio S. & Jaeger, J. C. Conduction of Heat in Solids. 2nd ed. (Illus.). 1959. 39.50x (ISBN 0-19-853303-9). Oxford U Pr.
CISM (International Center for Mechanical Sciences) Structural Dynamics Heat Conduction. De Veubeke, B. F., et al, eds. (CISM Pubns. Ser.: No. 126). (Illus.). 256p. 1974. pap. 25.60 (ISBN 0-387-81201-6). Springer-Verlag.
Conductivity - Heat & Mass Transfer - Refrigerants. 1964. pap. 10.75 (ISBN 0-685-99130-X, IIR58, IIR). Unipub.
Ho, C. Y. & Taylor, R. D. Thermal Conductivity. LC 79-80957. 1169p. 1969. 95.00 (ISBN 0-306-30413-9, Plenum Pr). Plenum Pub.
Klemens, P. G. & Chu, T. K. Thermal Conductivity, No. 14. LC 76-10951. 566p. 1976. 55.00 (ISBN 0-306-33114-4, Plenum Pr). Plenum Pub.
Mirkovich, ed. Thermal Conductivity, Vol. 15. 1978. 45.00 (ISBN 0-306-40054-5, Plenum Pr). Plenum Pub.
Myers, G. E. Analytical Methods in Conduction Heat Transfer. 1971. text ed. 26.00 (ISBN 0-07-044215-0, C). McGraw.
Ozisik, M. Necati. Heat Conduction. LC 79-990. 1980. 32.95 (ISBN 0-471-05481-X, Pub. by Wiley-Interscience). Wiley.
--Radiative Transfer & Interactions with Conduction & Convection. LC 72-12824. 608p. 1973. 40.00 (ISBN 0-471-65722-0, Pub. by Wiley-Interscience). Wiley.
Pal, L. & Pal, L., eds. Organic Conductors & Semiconductors: Proceedings of the International Conference Siofok, Hungary,1976. (Lecture Notes in Physics: Vol. 65). 1977. pap. text ed. 28.80 (ISBN 0-387-08255-7). Springer-Verlag.
Peggs, ed. Thermal Expansion Six. 1978. 39.50 (ISBN 0-306-40056-1, Plenum Pr). Plenum Pub.
Tsederberg, N. V. Thermal Conductivity of Gases & Liquids. 1965. 19.50x (ISBN 0-262-20004-X). MIT Pr.
Tye, R. P., ed. Thermal Conductivity, 2 Vols. 1969. Vol. 1. 67.00 (ISBN 0-12-705401-4); Vol. 2. 56.00 (ISBN 0-12-705402-2). Acad Pr.

HEAT-CONVECTION

Heat & Mass Transfer During Cooling & Storage of Agricultural Products As Influenced by Natural Convection. 158p. 1980. pap. 32.50 (ISBN 90-220-0728-6, PDC 208, Pudoc). Unipub.
International Heat Transfer Conference, 6th, Toronto, Aug. 1978. Heat Transfer Nineteen Seventy-Eight: Proceedings, 8 vols. new ed. Banerjee, S. & Rogers, J. T., eds. 1978. Set. text ed. 324.90 (ISBN 0-89116-130-9). Hemisphere Pub.
Jaluria, Y. Natural Convection Heat & Mass Transfer. LC 79-41176. (HMT Ser.). (Illus.). 400p. 1980. 59.00 (ISBN 0-08-025432-2). Pergamon.
Kakac, Sadik & Spalding, D. Brian, eds. Turbulent Forced Convection in Channels & Bundles: Theory & Applications to Heat Exchangers & Nuclear Reactors, 2 vols. LC 79-12842. 1132p. 1979. Set. 92.50 (ISBN 0-89116-148-1). Hemisphere Pub.
Kays, William M. Convective Heat & Mass Transfer. (Mechanical Engineering Ser.). 1966. text ed. 25.50 (ISBN 0-07-033393-9, C). McGraw.
Launder, B. E., ed. Studies in Convection: Theory Measurement & Applications, Vol. 2. 1978. 35.00 (ISBN 0-12-438002-6). Acad Pr.
Ozisik, M. Necati. Radiative Transfer & Interactions with Conduction & Convection. LC 72-12824. 608p. 1973. 40.00 (ISBN 0-471-65722-0, Pub. by Wiley-Interscience). Wiley.
Shah, Ramesh & London, A. L. Laminar Flow Forced Convection in Ducts: Supplement 1 to Advances in Heat Transfer. (Supplement 1 to Advances in Heat Transfer). 1978. 60.00 (ISBN 0-12-020051-1). Acad Pr.
Spalding, D. Brian & Afgan, N., eds. Heat Transfer & Turbulent Buoyant Convection: Studies & Applications for Natural Environment, Buildings Engineering Systems, 2 vols. new ed. LC 77-1868. (Thermal and Fluids Engineering Ser.). (Illus.). 1977. text ed. 129.50 set (ISBN 0-89116-163-5, Co-Pub. by McGraw Intl). Hemisphere Pub.

HEAT-JUVENILE LITERATURE

Balestrino, Philip. Hot As an Ice Cube. LC 70-139092. (A Let's-Read-&-Find-Out Science Bk). (Illus.). (gr. k-3). 1971. PLB 7.89 (ISBN 0-690-40415-8, TYC-J). T Y Crowell.
Liss, Howard. Heat. (Science Is What & Why Ser). (Illus.). (gr. k-4). 1965. PLB 4.49 (ISBN 0-698-30186-2). Coward.
Wade, Harlan. El Calor. Contreras, Mamie M., tr. from Eng. LC 78-26916. (A Book About Ser.). Orig. Title: Heat. (Illus., Sp.). (gr. k-3). 1979. PLB 7.95 (ISBN 0-8172-1487-9). Raintree Pubs.
--La Chaleur. Potvin, Claude & Potvin, Rose-Ella, trs. from Eng. (A Book About Ser.). Orig. Title: Heat. (Illus., Fr.). (gr. k-3). 1979. PLB 7.95 (ISBN 0-8172-1462-3). Raintree Pubs.
--Heat. rev. ed. LC 78-20959. (A Book About Ser.). (Illus.). (gr. k-3). 1979. PLB 7.95 (ISBN 0-8172-1536-0). Raintree Pubs.
Willis, John V. BTU Heat Values & Conservation. LC 79-63232. (Illus.). (gr. k-12). 1980. pap. 8.50 (ISBN 0-913732-18-4). J V Willis.

HEAT-PHYSIOLOGICAL EFFECT

Aldrete, J. Antonio & Britt, Beverly A., eds. The Second International Symposium on Malignant Hyperthermia, 1978: International Symposium. 1978. 37.00 (ISBN 0-8089-1073-6). Grune.
Dintenfass, Leopold. Hyperviscosity in Hypertension. (Illus.). 192p. 1981. 52.50 (ISBN 0-08-024816-0). Pergamon.
Kerslake, D. M. The Stress of Hot Environments. LC 74-168896. (Physiological Society Monographs: No. 29). (Illus.). 300p. 1972. 59.50 (ISBN 0-521-08343-5). Cambridge U Pr.
Kirmiz, John P. Adaptation to Desert Environment: A Study of the Jerboa, Rat & Man. 168p. 1962. 24.50 (ISBN 0-306-30658-1, Plenum Pr). Plenum Pub.
Mazumdar, N. C. Indices of Heat Stress. 132p. 1980. 4.95x (ISBN 0-89955-318-4, Pub. by Interprint India). Intl Schol Bk Serv.
Schmidt-Nielsen, Knut. Desert Animals: Physiological Problems of Heat & Water. 9.00 (ISBN 0-8446-5811-1). Peter Smith.
WHO Scientific Group, Geneva, 1967. Health Factors Involved in Working Under Conditions of Heat Stress: Report. (Technical Report Ser.: No. 412). (Also avail. in French, Russian & Spanish). 1969. pap. 2.00 (ISBN 92-4-120412-5). World Health.

HEAT-RADIATION AND ABSORPTION

see also Radiative Transfer

Armstrong, B. H. & Nicholls, R. W. Emission, Absorption & Transfer of Radiation in Heated Atmospheres. 319p. 1972. text ed. 50.00 (ISBN 0-08-016774-8). Pergamon.
Giordano, Carmelo, ed. Sorbents & Their Clinical Applications. 1980. 55.00 (ISBN 0-12-285250-8). Acad Pr.
Gray, W. A. & Muller, R. Engineering Calculations in Radiative Heat Transfer. LC 73-17321. 176p. 1974. text ed. 29.00 (ISBN 0-08-017786-7); pap. text ed. 13.25 (ISBN 0-08-017787-5). Pergamon.
Penner, S. S. Quantitative Molecular Spectroscopy & Gas Emissivities. 1959. 21.50 (ISBN 0-201-05760-3). A-W.
Ritchie, Ralph W. & Ritchie, Fern J. Electric Kiln Handbook, Vol. 6. LC 81-90074. (Energy Conservation in the Crafts-a Craft Monograph). (Illus.). 60p. (Orig.). 1981. pap. 4.00 (ISBN 0-939656-05-1). Studios West.
Siegel, R. & Howell, J. R. Thermal Radiation Heat Transfer. 1971. text ed. 26.50 (ISBN 0-07-057318-2, C); solution manual 5.00 (ISBN 0-07-057319-0). McGraw.
Svet, Darii Y. Thermal Radiation: Metals, Semiconductors, Ceramics, Partly Transparent Bodies, & Films. LC 65-25260. 93p. 1965. 25.00 (ISBN 0-306-10737-6, Consultants). Plenum Pub.

HEAT-TRANSMISSION

see also Heat Exchangers

Afgan, N. H. & Beer, J. M., eds. Heat Transfer in Flames. LC 74-8747. (Advances in Thermal Engineering Ser.). 501p. 1974. 28.50 (ISBN 0-470-00931-4). Halsted Pr.
Application of Numerical Heat Transfer. 1979. 33.75 (ISBN 92-3-101399-8, UM 38, UNESCO). Unipub.
Backhurst, J. R., et al. Problems in Heat & Mass Transfer. (Illus.). 1974. pap. text ed. 14.95x (ISBN 0-7131-3327-9). Intl Ideas.
Bankoff, S. George, et al, eds. Heat Transfer in Nuclear Reactor Safety. (International Centre for Heat & Mass Transfer Ser.). (Illus.). 1981. text ed. 95.00 (ISBN 0-89116-223-2). Hemisphere Pub.
Bergles, A. E., et al. Two-Phase Flow & Heat Transfer in the Power & Process Industries. (Illus.). 695p. 1981. 55.00 (ISBN 0-07-004902-5, P&RB). McGraw.
Bergles, Arthur E. & Ishigai, Seiken, eds. Two-Phase Flow Dynamics & Reactur Safety: The Japan-U. S. Seminar 1979. LC 81-4295. (Illus.). 554p. 1981. text ed. 75.00 (ISBN 0-89116-198-8). Hemisphere Pub.
Bergles, Arthur E., et al, eds. Two-Phase Flow & Heat Transfer in the Power & Process Industries. LC 80-22025. (Illus.). 707p. 1980. text ed. 55.00 (ISBN 0-89116-197-X). Hemisphere Pub.
Blackshear, P. L. Heat Transfer in Fires: Thermo-Physics, Social Aspects, Economic Impact. LC 74-8824. (Advances in Thermal Engineering Ser.). 516p. 1974. 28.50 (ISBN 0-470-07780-8). Halsted Pr.
Botterill, J. S. Fluid-Bed Heat Transfer: Gas-Fluidized Bed Behavior & Its Influence on Bed Thermal Properties. 1975. 47.50 (ISBN 0-12-118750-0). Acad Pr.
Brown, Aubrey I. & Marco, S. M. Introduction to Heat Transfer. 3rd ed. 1958. text ed. 23.00 (ISBN 0-07-008458-0, C). McGraw.
Butterworth, D. & Hewitt, G. F. Two-Phase Flow & Heat Transfer. (Harwell Ser.). (Illus.). 1977. 49.50x (ISBN 0-19-851715-7); pap. 29.00x (ISBN 0-19-851718-1). Oxford U Pr.
Chapman, Alan J. Heat Transfer. 3rd ed. (Illus.). 653p. 1974. text ed. 24.95 (ISBN 0-02-321450-3). Macmillan.
Chemical Engineering Magazine. Process Heat Exchange. (Chemical Engineering Book Ser.). (Illus.). 624p. 1980. 34.50 (ISBN 0-07-010742-4, P&RB). McGraw.
Chenoweth, J. M., et al, eds. Advances in Enhanced Heat Transfer. 168p. 1979. 24.00 (ISBN 0-686-59659-5, I00122). ASME.
Collier, J. G. Convective Boiling & Condensation. 2nd ed. (Illus.). 460p. 1981. text ed. 59.50 (ISBN 0-07-011798-5). McGraw.
Croft, David R. & Lilley, David G. Heat Transfer Calculations Using Finite Difference Equations. (Illus.). 1977. 55.90x (ISBN 0-85334-720-4, Pub. by Applied Science). Burgess-Intl Ideas.
Dalrymple, Paul, et al. A Year of Snow Accumulation at Plateau Station; Thermal Properties & Heat Transfer Processes of Low-Temperature Snow; Radiative Heat Transfer; Process in Snow & Ice; Papers 1, 2, 3 & 4: Meteorological Studies at Plateau Station, Antarctica. Businger, Joost A., ed. (Antarctic Research Ser.: Vol. 25). 1977. pap. 10.40 (ISBN 0-87590-125-5). Am Geophysical.
DeVries, D. A. & Afgan, N. H., eds. Heat & Mass Transfer in the Biosphere: Pt. 1, Transfer Processes in the Plant Environment. LC 74-28072. (Advances in Thermal Engineering Ser.). 594p. 1975. 28.50 (ISBN 0-470-20985-2). Halsted Pr.
Durst, Franz, et al, eds. Two-Phase Momentum, Heat & Mass Transfer in Chemical, Process, & Energy Engineering Systems, 2 vols. LC 79-12405. (Thermal & Fluid Engineering, Proceedings of the International Centre for Heat & Mass Transfer). (Illus.). 1079p. 1979. text ed. 105.00 set (ISBN 0-89116-154-6, Co-Pub by McGraw International). Hemisphere Pub.
Dwyer, O. E. Boiling Liquid-Metal Heat Transfer. LC 75-11012. (Nuclear Science Technology Ser.). (Illus.). 1976. text ed. 37.95 (ISBN 0-89448-000-6). Am Nuclear Soc.
Eckert, E. R. Heat & Mass Transfer. 2nd ed. LC 81-359. 344p. 1981. Repr. lib. bdg. 29.50 (ISBN 0-89874-332-X). Krieger.
Eckert, Ernest R. & Drake, R. M. Analysis of Heat & Mass Transfer. LC 73-159305. (Mechanical Engineering Ser). (Illus.). 832p. 1971. text ed. 26.95 (ISBN 0-07-018925-0, C). McGraw.
Eckert, Ernest R. & Drake, R. M., Jr. Heat & Mass Transfer. 2nd ed. (Mechanical Engineering Ser.). 1959. text ed. 23.50 (ISBN 0-07-018924-2, C). McGraw.
Eckert, Ernest R. & Goldstein, Richard J., eds. Measurement in Heat Transfer. (McGraw-Hill - Hemisphere Ser. in Thermal & Fluids Engineering). (Illus.). 1976. text ed. 33.95 (ISBN 0-07-018926-9, C). McGraw.
Edwards, D. K., et al. Transfer Processes. (Illus.). 1976. Repr. of 1973 ed. text ed. 18.00 (ISBN 0-07-019040-2, C). McGraw.
--Transfer Processes. 2nd ed. LC 78-7883. (Series in Thermal and Fluids Engineering). (Illus.). 1979. text ed. 28.95 (ISBN 0-07-019041-0, C). McGraw.
Edwards, Don K. Radiation Heat Transfer Notes. LC 81-4539. (Illus.). 370p. (Orig.). 1981. pap. text ed. 19.95 (ISBN 0-89116-231-3). Hemisphere Pub.
Fenech, Henri, ed. Heat Transfer & Fluid Flow in Nuclear Systems. 300p. 1981. 49.51 (ISBN 0-08-027181-2). Pergamon.
Frank-Kamenetskii, D. A. Diffusion & Heat Transfer in Chemical Kinetics. LC 68-26770. 574p. 1969. 45.00 (ISBN 0-306-30349-3, Plenum Pr). Plenum Pub.
Frost, Walter, ed. Heat Transfer at Low Temperatures. LC 71-186257. (International Cryogenics Monographs). (Illus.). 362p. 1975. 39.50 (ISBN 0-306-30575-5, Plenum Pr). Plenum Pub.
Gebhart, B. Heat Transfer. 2nd ed. 1971. text ed. 26.00 (ISBN 0-07-023127-3, C); solutions manual 2.50 (ISBN 0-07-023132-X). McGraw.
Geiringer, Paul L. Handbook of Heat Transfer Media. LC 76-57170. (Illus.). 272p. 1977. Repr. of 1962 ed. lib. bdg. 18.50 (ISBN 0-88275-498-X). Krieger.
Ginoux, Jean J. Two Phase Flows & Heat Transfer with Application to Nuclear Reactor Design Problems. LC 77-2090. (McGraw-Hill - Hemisphere Thermal & Fluids Engineering Ser). (Illus.). 1978. text ed. 39.50x (ISBN 0-07-023305-5, C). McGraw.
Goldstein, R. J., et al. Heat Transfer in Energy Conservation. (Bk. No. H00106). 136p. 1977. 18.00 (ISBN 0-685-46848-8). ASME.
Gray, W. A., et al. Heat Transfer from Flames. (Topics in Fuel Science Ser.). 1977. pap. 9.95 (ISBN 0-236-40044-4, Pub. by Paul Elek). Merrimack Bk Serv.
Hartnett, J. P., et al. Studies in Heat Transfer: A Festschrift for E.R.G. Eckert. LC 79-15633. (Illus.). 1979. text ed. 42.50 (ISBN 0-07-026962-9). McGraw.
Heat & Mass Transfer During Cooling & Storage of Agricultural Products As Influenced by Natural Convection. 158p. 1980. pap. 32.50 (ISBN 90-220-0728-6, PDC 208, Pudoc). Unipub.
Heat & Mass Transfer in Porous Structures. 1976. pap. 14.50 (ISBN 0-685-99143-1, IIR49, IIR). Unipub.
Heat & Mass Transfer in Refrigeration Systems & in Air Conditioning. 1972. pap. 41.25 (ISBN 0-685-99145-8, IIR52, IIR). Unipub.
Heat Flow Below One Hundred Degrees Kelvin. 1965. pap. 17.75 (ISBN 0-685-99149-0, IIR48, IIR). Unipub.
Heat Transfer & Air Conditioning. 1969. pap. 30.25 (ISBN 0-685-99150-4, IIR55, IIR). Unipub.
Heat Transfer & Fluid Mechanics Institute. Proceedings. Incl. 1958 Sessions. viii, 264p. pap. 12.50x (ISBN 0-8047-0422-8); 1959 Sessions. x, 242p. pap. 12.50x (ISBN 0-8047-0423-6); 1960 Sessions. Mason, David M, et al, eds. x, 260p. 12.50x (ISBN 0-8047-0424-4); 1961 Sessions. Binder, Raymond C., et al, eds. xi, 236p. 12.50x (ISBN 0-8047-0425-2); 1962 Sessions. Ehlers, F. Edward, et al, eds. x, 294p. 12.50x (ISBN 0-8047-0426-0); 1963 Sessions. Roshko, Anatol, et al, eds. xii, 280p. 12.50x (ISBN 0-8047-0427-9); 1964 Sessions. Giedt, Warren H. & Levy, Salomon, eds. x, 275p. 12.50x (ISBN 0-8047-0428-7); 1965 Sessions. Charwat, Andrew F., et al, eds. xii, 372p. 16.50x (ISBN 0-8047-0429-5); 1966 Sessions. Saad, Michel A. & Miller, James A., eds. xii, 444p. 17.50x (ISBN 0-8047-0430-9); 1967 Sessions. Libby, Paul A., et al, eds. x, 468p. 17.50x (ISBN 0-8047-0431-7); 1968 Sessions. Emery, Ashley F. & Depew, Creighton A., eds. ix, 272p. 12.50x (ISBN 0-8047-0438-4); 1970 Sessions. Sarpkaya, Turgut, ed. xii, 370p. 15.00x (ISBN 0-8047-0744-8); 1974 Sessions. Davis, Lorin R. & Wilson, Robert E., eds. 17.50x (ISBN 0-8047-0865-7); 1976 Sessions. McKillop, Allan A., et al, eds. 29.50x (ISBN 0-8047-0917-3); 1978 Sessions. Crowe, Clayton T. & Grosshandler, William L., eds. 344p. text ed. 28.50x (ISBN 0-8047-1002-3); 1980 Sessions. Gerstein, Melvin & Choudhury, P. Roy, eds. text ed. 22.50x (ISBN 0-8047-1087-2). (Illus.). Stanford U Pr.
Heat Transfer in Refrigeration. 1966. pap. 17.75 (ISBN 0-685-99151-2, IIR56, IIR). Unipub.
Heat Transmission Measurements in Thermal Insulations. 1974. 30.75 (ISBN 0-686-52110-2, 04-544000-10). ASTM.
Hills, D. A. Heat Transfer & Vulcanisation of Rubber. (Illus.). 1971. text ed. 22.30x (ISBN 0-444-20075-4, Pub. by Applied Science). Burgess-Intl Ideas.
Hoffman, E. G. Heat Transfer Rate Analysis. 702p. 1980. 40.00 (ISBN 0-87814-139-1). Pennwell Pub.

Holland, F. A., et al. Heat Transfer Problems. 1971. 27.50 (ISBN 0-444-19626-9). Elsevier.
Holman, J. P. Heat Transfer. 5th ed. (Illus.). 672p. 1981. text ed. 28.95x (ISBN 0-07-029618-9, C); solutions manual 12.50 (ISBN 0-07-029619-7). McGraw.
Holman, Jack P. Heat Transfer. 4th ed. (Illus.). 1976. text ed. 24.50 (ISBN 0-07-029598-0, C); solutions manual 5.95 (ISBN 0-07-029600-6); audio cassettes 110.00 (ISBN 0-07-075380-6). McGraw.
Hsu, Y. & Graham, Robert W. Transport Processes in Boiling & Two-Phase Systems Including Near-Critical Fluids. LC 75-38662. (McGraw-Hill - Hemisphere Ser. in Thermal & Fluids Engineering). (Illus.). 1976. text ed. 31.50 (ISBN 0-07-030637-0, C). McGraw.
Ibele, Warren E., ed. Modern Developments in Heat Transfer. 1963. 63.50 (ISBN 0-12-369550-3). Acad Pr.
Incropera, Frank P. Fundamentals of Heat Transfer. DeWitt, David P., ed. LC 80-17209. 819p. 1981. text ed. 28.95 (ISBN 0-471-42711-X). Wiley.
International Heat Transfer Conference, 6th, Toronto, Aug. 1978. Heat Transfer Nineteen Seventy-Eight: Proceedings, 8 vols. new ed. Banerjee, S. & Rogers, J. T., eds. 1978. Set. text ed. 324.90 (ISBN 0-89116-130-9). Hemisphere Pub.
International Heat Transfer Conference, 5th, Tokyo. Heat Transfer Nineteen Seventy Four: Proceedings, 7 vols. Mizushina, T., ed. LC 75-12763. (Illus.). 2300p. 1975. pap. text ed. 180.00 (ISBN 0-89116-001-9). Hemisphere Pub.
International Institute of Refrigeration. Heat Transfer-Current Application of Air Conditioning. Van Iherbeek, A., ed. 1971. 90.00 (ISBN 0-08-016597-4). Pergamon.
Irvine, T. F. & Hartnett, J. P., eds. Advances in Heat Transfer, Vol. 15. 1981. price not set (ISBN 0-12-020015-5); price not set lib. ed. (ISBN 0-12-020082-1); price not set microfiche (ISBN 0-12-020083-X). Acad Pr.
Irvine, Thomas F., Jr. & Hartnett, James P., eds. Advances in Heat Transfer, 14 vols. Incl. Vol. 1. 1964. 58.00 (ISBN 0-12-020001-5); Vol. 2. 1965. 58.00 (ISBN 0-12-020002-3); Vol. 3. 1966. 58.00 (ISBN 0-12-020003-1); Vol. 4. 1967. 58.00 (ISBN 0-12-020004-X); Vol. 5. 1968. 63.00 (ISBN 0-12-020005-8); Vol. 6. 1970. 63.00 (ISBN 0-12-020006-6); Vol. 7. 1970. 58.50 (ISBN 0-12-020007-4); Vol. 8. 1972. 58.50 (ISBN 0-12-020008-2); Vol. 9. 1973. 58.50 (ISBN 0-12-020009-0); Vol. 10. 1974. 58.50 (ISBN 0-12-020010-4); Vol. 11. 1975. 67.50 (ISBN 0-12-020011-2); lib. bdg. 86.50 lib. ed. (ISBN 0-12-020074-0); microfiche 48.50 (ISBN 0-12-020075-9); Vol. 12. 1976. 56.00 (ISBN 0-12-020012-0); lib. bdg. 72.00 lib. ed. (ISBN 0-12-020076-7); microfiche 40.50 (ISBN 0-12-020077-5); Vol. 13. 1977. 56.00 (ISBN 0-12-020013-9); lib. ed. 72.00 (ISBN 0-12-020078-3); microfiche 40.50 (ISBN 0-12-020079-1); Vol. 14. 1979. 49.50 (ISBN 0-12-020014-7); lib. ed. 63.00 (ISBN 0-12-020080-5); microfiche 35.50 (ISBN 0-12-020081-3). Acad Pr.
Isachenko, V., et al. Heat Transfer. Semyonov, S., tr. from Russian. (Illus.). 552p. 1969. 17.00x (ISBN 0-8464-0475-3). Beekman Pubs.
Isachenko, V. P., et al. Heat Transfer. 493p. 1977. 13.00 (ISBN 0-8285-1761-4, Pub. by Mir Pubs Russia). Imported Pubns.
Jakob, Max & Hawkins, G. A. Elements of Heat Transfer. 3rd ed. LC 57-12230. 1957. text ed. 27.95x (ISBN 0-471-43725-5). Wiley.
Jones, James B. & Hawkins, George A. Engineering Thermodynamics: An Introductory Textbook. LC 60-10316. (Illus.). 724p. 1960. text ed. 30.95x (ISBN 0-471-44946-6). Wiley.
Jones, Owen C., Jr., ed. Nuclear Reactor Safety Heat Transfer. LC 81-2932. (Proceedings of the International Centre for Heat & Mass Transfer Ser.). (Illus.). 1981. text ed. 99.00 (ISBN 0-89116-224-0). Hemisphere Pub.
Karlekar, Bhalchandra V. & Desmond, Robert M. Engineering Heat Transfer. (Illus., Orig.). 1977. text ed. 25.95 (ISBN 0-8299-0054-3); solutions manual avail. (ISBN 0-8299-0497-2). West Pub.
Kay, J. M. & Nedderman, R. M. An Introduction to Fluid Mechanics & Heat Transfer. 3rd. rev. ed. LC 74-77383. 300p. 1975. 44.50 (ISBN 0-521-20533-6); pap. 17.50x (ISBN 0-521-09880-7). Cambridge U Pr.
Kays, William M. & Crawford, Michael. Convective Heat & Mass Transfer. 2nd ed. (Mechanical Engineering Ser.). (Illus.). 1980. text ed. 31.50 (ISBN 0-07-033457-9); solutions manual 8.95 (ISBN 0-07-033458-7). McGraw.
Kern, Donald Q. Process Heat Transfer. 1950. text ed. 29.50 (ISBN 0-07-034190-7, C). McGraw.
Knudsen, James G. & Katz, Donald L. Fluid Dynamics & Heat Transfer. LC 79-9748. 586p. 1979. Repr. lib. bdg. 29.50 (ISBN 0-88275-917-5). Krieger.
Konakov, P. K., ed. Progress in Heat Transfer. Incl. Pt. I. Laminar Boundary Layer Flow in Transparent & Grey Media; Pt. II. Equipment for the Preparation of Semiconductor Materials. LC 65-26629. 157p. 1966. 29.50 (ISBN 0-306-10753-8, Consultants). Plenum Pub.
Kothandaraman, C. P. & Subramanyan, S. Heat & Mass Transfer Data Book. 3rd ed. 149p. 1977. 13.95 (ISBN 0-470-99078-3). Halsted Pr.
Kreith, Frank. Principles of Heat Transfer. 3rd ed. LC 73-1784. (Chemical Engineering Ser.). 672p. 1973. text ed. 29.50 scp (ISBN 0-7002-2422-X, HarpC); scp solution manual 5.50 (ISBN 0-685-28246-5). Har-Row.
Kreith, Frank & Black, William Z. Basic Heat Transfer. 1980. text ed. 26.50 scp (ISBN 0-7002-2518-8, HarpC); solutions manual free (ISBN 0-06-363760-X). Har-Row.
Kutateladze, S. S., et al. Liquid-Metal Heat Transfer Media. LC 59-9228. 155p. 1959. 27.50 (ISBN 0-306-10548-9, Consultants). Plenum Pub.
Lewis, R. W. & Morgan, K. Numerical Methods in Heat Transfer. Zienkiewicz, O. C., ed. LC 80-49973. (Numerical Methods in Engineering Ser.). 536p. 1981. 78.75 (ISBN 0-471-27803-3, Pub. by Wiley-Interscience). Wiley.
Lienhard, John. A Heat Transfer Textbook. (Illus.). 480p. 1981. text ed. 24.95 (ISBN 0-13-385112-5). P-H.
Loh, W. H. Modern Developments in Gas Dynamics. LC 69-14561. 386p. 1969. 42.50 (ISBN 0-306-30377-9, Plenum Pr). Plenum Pub.
Luikov, A. V. Analytical Heat Diffusion Theory. 1969. 50.00 (ISBN 0-12-459756-4). Acad Pr.
Lunardini, Virgil J. Heat Transfer in Cold Climates. 704p. 1981. text ed. 39.50 (ISBN 0-442-26250-7). Van Nos Reinhold.
McAdams, William H. Heat Transmission. 3rd ed. (Chemical Engineering Ser.). (Illus.). 1954. text ed. 24.50 (ISBN 0-07-044799-3, C); answers 1.00 (ISBN 0-07-044800-0). McGraw.
Manrique, Jose. Transferencia De Calor. 1977. pap. text ed. 9.80 (ISBN 0-06-315511-7, IntlDept). Har-Row.
Marto, P. J. & Kroeger, P. G. Condensation Heat Transfer. 118p. 1979. 18.00 (ISBN 0-686-59660-9, I00123). ASME.
Marto, P. J. & Nunn, R. H. Power Condenser Heat Transfer Technology: Computer Modeling-Design-Fouling. 496p. 1981. 47.50 (ISBN 0-07-040662-6, P&RB). McGraw.
Modern Research Laboratories for Heat & Mass Transfer. (Engineering Laboratories: No. 5). (Illus.). 148p. 1975. pap. 12.25 (ISBN 92-3-101103-0, U389, UNESCO). Unipub.
Mohsenin, Nuri N. Thermal Properties of Food & Agriculture Materials. 420p. 1980. 53.00 (ISBN 0-677-05450-5). Gordon.
Mooney, David A. Introduction to Thermodynamics & Heat Transfer. 1955. text ed. 26.95 (ISBN 0-13-499681-X). P-H.
Multi-Phase Flow & Heat Transfer Symposium-Workshop, 2nd, Miami Beach, Apr. 16-18, 1979. Multiphase Transport: Fundamentals, Reactor Safety, Applications: Proceedings, 5 vols. Veziroglu, T. Nejat, ed. LC 80-11157. 3500p. 1980. Set. text ed. 350.00 (ISBN 0-89116-159-7). Hemisphere Pub.
Muncey, R. W. Heat Transfer Calculations for Buildings. (Illus.). 1979. 23.20x (ISBN 0-85334-852-9, Pub. by Applied Science). Burgess-Intl Ideas.
Myers, G. E. Analytical Methods in Conduction Heat Transfer. 1971. text ed. 26.00 (ISBN 0-07-044215-0, C). McGraw.
NATO Advanced Study Institute on Two-Phase Flows & Heat Transfer, Istanbul, Aug. 1976. Two-Phase Flows & Heat Transfer: Proceedings, 3 vols. new ed. Kakac, S., et al, eds. LC 77-8801. 1977. Set. text ed. 155.00 (ISBN 0-89116-167-8). Hemisphere Pub.
Nogotov, E. F. Applications of Numerical Methods to Heat Transfer. (Illus.). 1978. pap. text ed. 28.50 (ISBN 0-07-046852-4, C). McGraw.
Norris, Hosmer, et al. Heat Transfer & Fluid Flow Data Books, 2 vols. (Illus.). 921p. 1981. 350.00 (ISBN 0-931690-02-1). GE Tech Marketing.
Obert & Young. Elements of Thermodynamics & Heat Transfer. 2nd ed. (Illus.). 1962. text ed. 23.50 (ISBN 0-07-047592-X, C). McGraw.
Obert, Edward F. & Young, Robert L. Elements of Thermodynamics & Heat Transfer. 2nd ed. LC 79-23780. 558p. 1980. Repr. of 1962 ed. lib. bdg. 28.00 (ISBN 0-89874-005-3). Krieger.
Ozisik, M. Necati. Basic Heat Transfer. (Illus.). 1976. text ed. 23.95 (ISBN 0-07-047980-1, C); student manual 4.95 (ISBN 0-07-047981-X). McGraw.
Parker, J. D., et al. Introduction to Fluid Mechanics & Heat Transfer. (Engineering Ser). 1969. text ed. 25.95 (ISBN 0-201-05710-7). A-W.
Patankar, Suhas V. Numerical Heat Transfer & Fluid Flow. LC 79-28286. (Hemisphere Series on Computational Methods in Mechanics & Thermal Sciences). (Illus.). 208p. 1980. text ed. 22.50 (ISBN 0-07-048740-5). McGraw.
Patterson, G. A. Energy Analysis with a Pocket Calculator. 2ns ed. LC 77-88128. (Illus.). 1981. 9.95 (ISBN 0-917410-04-1). Basic Sci Pr.
Pratt, A. W. Heat Transmission in Building. LC 80-42021. 304p. 1981. 49.00 (ISBN 0-471-27971-4, Pub. by Wiley-Interscience). Wiley.
Rohsenow, Warren & Hartnett, J. P. Handbook of Heat Transfer. 1504p. 1973. 54.50 (ISBN 0-07-053576-0, P&RB). McGraw.
Rohsenow, Warren M. & Choi, H. Heat, Mass & Momentum Transfer. (Illus.). 1961. text ed. 27.95 (ISBN 0-13-385187-7). P-H.
Schneider, Paul J. Conduction Heat Transfer. 1955. 16.50 (ISBN 0-201-06750-1). A-W.
Seagrave, Richard C. Biomedical Applications of Heat & Mass Transfer. LC 71-146930. (Illus.). 1971. 8.95 (ISBN 0-8138-0195-8). Iowa St U Pr.
--Biomedical Applications of Heat & Mass Transfer. LC 71-146930. (Illus.). 1971. 8.95 (ISBN 0-8138-0195-8). Iowa St U Pr.
Siegel, R. & Howell, J. R. Thermal Radiation Heat Transfer. 1971. text ed. 26.50 (ISBN 0-07-057318-2, C); solution manual 5.00 (ISBN 0-07-057319-0). McGraw.
Siegel, Robert & Howell, John R. Thermal Radiation Heat Transfer. 2nd ed. LC 79-17242. (Thermal & Fluids Engineering Hemisphere Ser.). (Illus.). 928p. 1980. text ed. 32.00 (ISBN 0-07-057316-6, C); solutions manual 16.95 (ISBN 0-07-057317-4). McGraw.
Somerscales, Euan F. & Knudsen, James G., eds. Fouling of Heat Transfer Equipment: International Conference 1979. LC 80-28694. (Illus.). 743p. 1981. text ed. 75.00 (ISBN 0-89116-199-6). Hemisphere Pub.
Spalding, D. Brian & Afgan, N., eds. Heat Transfer & Turbulent Buoyant Convection: Studies & Applications for Natural Environment, Buildings Engineering Systems, 2 vols. new ed. LC 77-1868. (Thermal and Fluids Engineering Ser.). (Illus.). 1977. text ed. 129.50 set (ISBN 0-89116-163-5, Co-Pub. by McGraw Intl). Hemisphere Pub.
Spalding, D. Brian & Afgan, Naim H., eds. Heat & Mass Transfer in Metallurgical Systems. LC 80-27193. (International Center for Heat & Mass Transfer Ser.). (Illus.). 758p. 1981. text ed. 85.50 (ISBN 0-89116-169-4). Hemisphere Pub.
Spalding, Dudley B., ed. Progress in Heat & Mass Transfer, Vol. 19, No. 10 - Alan Ede Memorial Issue: Developments in Heat & Mass Transfer. 1977. pap. 32.00 (ISBN 0-08-021285-9). Pergamon.
Sparrow, E. M. & Cess, R. D. Radiation Heat Transfer: Augmented Edition. LC 77-24158. (McGraw-Hill Series in Thermal & Fluids Engineering). (Illus.). 1978. text ed. 25.95 (ISBN 0-07-059910-6, Hemisphere Pub. Corp.). McGraw.
Styrikovich, M. A., et al. Heat & Mass Transfer Source Book: Fifth All-Union Conference, Minsk, 1976. LC 77-22337. 1977. 42.95 (ISBN 0-470-99234-4). Halsted Pr.
Sukhatme, S. P. A Textbook on Heat Transfer. 238p. 1981. 20.00x (ISBN 0-86131-073-X, Pub. by Orient Longman India). State Mutual Bk.
Thermal Transmission Measurements of Insulation. (Special Technical Publications Ser.). 458p. 1979. 39.50x (ISBN 0-686-76095-6, 660, 04-660000-10). ASTM.
Thomas, Lindon. Fundamentals of Heat Transfer. (Illus.). 1980. text ed. 27.95 (ISBN 0-13-339903-6). P-H.
Tong, L. S. Boiling Heat Transfer & Two-Phase Flow. LC 74-26607. 256p. 1975. Repr. of 1965 ed. 18.50 (ISBN 0-88275-251-0). Krieger.
Tong, L. S. & Weisman, Joel. Thermal Analysis of Pressurized Water Reactors. LC 77-119001. (ANS Monographs). 320p. 1970. 24.00 (ISBN 0-89448-005-7). Am Nuclear Soc.
Turner, G. Alan. Heat & Concentration Waves: Analysis & Applications. 1972. 40.00 (ISBN 0-12-704050-1). Acad Pr.
Two-Phase Flow & Heat Transfer Workshop, Ft. Lauderdale, Oct. 1976. Two-Phase Transport & Reactor Safety: Proceedings, 4 vols. Veziroglu, T. N. & Kakac, S., eds. LC 77-14094. 1978. Set. text ed. 225.00 (ISBN 0-89116-168-6). Hemisphere Pub.
Welty, James R. Engineering Heat Transfer, SI Version. LC 78-5179. 1978. text ed. 34.95 (ISBN 0-471-02860-6). Wiley.
Welty, James R., et al. Fundamentals of Momentum, Heat & Mass Transfer. 2nd ed. LC 76-16813. 897p. 1976. text ed. 36.95 (ISBN 0-471-93354-6). Wiley.
Whitaker, S. Elementary Heat Transfer Analysis (in SI-Metric Units) LC 74-3246. 1977. text ed. 16.50 (ISBN 0-08-018959-8). Pergamon.
--Fundamental Principles of Heat Transfer. 1977. 38.50 (ISBN 0-08-017866-9). Pergamon.
Wong, H. Y. Handbook of Essential Formulae & Data on Heat Transfer for Engineers. LC 77-5681. (Illus.). 1977. pap. text ed. 14.50x (ISBN 0-582-46050-6). Longman.
Zabrodsky, S. S. Hydrodynamics & Heat Transfer in Fluidized Beds. 1966. 31.50x (ISBN 0-262-24007-6). MIT Pr.
Zaric, Z., ed. Heat & Mass Transfers in Flows with Separated Regions. LC 72-85858. 232p. 1975. pap. text ed. 29.00 (ISBN 0-08-017156-7). Pergamon.

HEAT (IN RELIGION, FOLK-LORE, ETC.)
see also Fire (In Religion, Folk-Lore, etc.)

HEAT, SPECIFIC
see Specific Heat

HEAT ABSORPTION
see Heat-Radiation and Absorption

HEAT BARRIER
see Aerodynamic Heating; High Temperatures

HEAT BUDGET (GEOPHYSICS)
see also Atmospheric Temperature; Ocean Temperature

HEAT ENGINEERING
see also Heat-Engines; Heating

Arpaci, Vedat S. Conduction Heat Transfer. 1966. 23.95 (ISBN 0-201-00359-7). A-W.
Burghardt, David M. Engineering Thermodynamics with Applications. (Illus.). 1978. text ed. 25.50 scp (ISBN 0-06-041041-8, HarpC); sol. manual free (ISBN 0-06-361040-X). Har-Row.
Chernov, A. & Bessrebrennikov, N. Fundamentals of Heat Engineering & Hydraulics. Troitsky, A., tr. from Rus. (Illus.). 407p. 1969. 17.00x (ISBN 0-8464-0437-0). Beekman Pubs.
Dean, Thomas S. Thermal Storage. LC 78-3211. (Solar Ser). (Illus.). 1977. pap. text ed. 2.25 (ISBN 0-89168-005-5). Franklin Inst Pr.
Duffie, J. A. & Beckman, W. A. Solar Energy Thermal Processes. LC 74-12390. 1974. 31.00 (ISBN 0-471-22371-9, Pub. by Wiley-Interscience). Wiley.
Gutfinger, Chaim, ed. Topics in Transport Phenomena: Bioprocesses, Mathematical Treatment, Mechanisms. LC 75-15867. 622p. 1975. 39.50 (ISBN 0-470-33712-5). Halsted Pr.
International Union of Pure & Applied Chemistry. High Temperature Technology-3: Proceedings of an International Symposium, Pacific Grove, Calif., 1967. 764p. 1976. 110.00 (ISBN 0-08-020760-X). Pergamon.
Preobrazhensky, V. Measurements & Instrumentation in Heat Engineering, 2 vols. 1980. Set. 18.00 (ISBN 0-8285-1804-1, Pub. by Mir Pubs Russia). Imported Pubns.
Rohsenow, Warren M. & Choi, H. Heat, Mass & Momentum Transfer. (Illus.). 1961. text ed. 27.95 (ISBN 0-13-385187-7). P-H.
Schaetzle. Thermal Energy Storage in Aquifiers. (Design & Applications). 275p. 1980. text ed. 24.50 (ISBN 0-08-025977-4). Pergamon.
Solberg, Harry L., et al. Thermal Engineering. LC 60-11730. 1960. text ed. 29.95x (ISBN 0-471-81147-5). Wiley.
Stoecker, W. F. Design of Thermal Systems. 1971. text ed. 24.95 (ISBN 0-07-061617-5). McGraw.
Turner, Robert H. High Temperature Thermal Energy Storage. LC 77-18603. (Solar Ser). (Illus.). 1978. 8.95 (ISBN 0-89168-007-1). Franklin Inst Pr.
Wahl, Edward C. Geothermal Energy Utilization. LC 77-546. 1977. 37.50 (ISBN 0-471-02304-3, Pub. by Wiley-Interscience). Wiley.

HEAT-ENGINES
see also Gas and Oil Engines; Heat Engineering; Heat Pumps; Steam-Engines; Thermodynamics

Bennett, J. V. Heat Engines: Questions & Answers. (Marine Engineering Ser.). 116p. 1975. pap. 9.50x (ISBN 0-540-07340-7). Sheridan.
Campbell, Ashley S. Thermodynamic Analysis of Combustion Engines. LC 78-16181. 1979. text ed. 29.95 (ISBN 0-471-03751-6). Wiley.
Cardwell, D. S. From Watt to Clausius: The Rise of Thermodynamics in the Early Industrial Age. LC 72-163129. (Illus.). 352p. 1971. 25.00x (ISBN 0-8014-0678-1). Cornell U Pr.
Jones, James B. & Hawkins, George A. Engineering Thermodynamics: An Introductory Textbook. LC 60-10316. (Illus.). 724p. 1960. text ed. 30.95x (ISBN 0-471-44946-6). Wiley.
Mott-Smith, Morton. Concept of Energy Simply Explained. Orig. Title: Story of Energy, Il. 1934. pap. 3.00 (ISBN 0-486-21071-5). Dover.
Sandfort, John F. Heat Engines: Thermodynamics in Theory & Practice. LC 78-25847. (Illus.). Repr. of 1962 ed. lib. bdg. 20.00x (ISBN 0-313-20784-4, SAEN). Greenwood.

HEAT EXCHANGERS

Afgan, N. H. & Schlunder, E. U. Heat Exchangers: Design & Theory. (Illus.). 928p. 1974. 53.50 (ISBN 0-07-000460-9, P&RB). McGraw.

Chisholm, D., ed. Developments in Heat Exchanger Technology - One. (Illus.). x, 288p. 1980. 65.00x (ISBN 0-85334-913-4). Burgess-Intl Ideas.

Coen, V. & Holtbecker, H. Post Accident Heat Removal. (European Applied Research Reports Special Topics Ser.). 402p. 1980. pap. text ed. 101.25 (ISBN 3-7186-0025-0). Harwood Academic.

Fraas, Arthur P. & Ozisik, M. N. Heat Exchanger Design. LC 65-21441. 1965. 48.50 (ISBN 0-471-27432-1, Pub. by Wiley-Interscience). Wiley.

Heat Exchange in Refrigerating Systems. 1970. pap. 19.25 (ISBN 0-685-99146-6, IIR53, IIR). Unipub.

Heat Exchanger Tubes. 1971. 17.00 (ISBN 0-85501-393-1). Heyden.

Kakac, S., et al. Heat Exchangers: Thermal-Hydraulic Fundamentals & Design. 1981. price not set (ISBN 0-07-033284-3). McGraw.

Kays, William M. & London, A. L. Compact Heat Exchangers. 2nd ed. (Mechanical Engineering Ser.). 1964. text ed. 35.50 (ISBN 0-07-033391-2, P&RB). McGraw.

Mahajan, Kanti. K. Design of Process Equipment: Selected Topics. (Illus.). 1979. 26.00 (ISBN 0-914458-06-X). Pressure.

Ranney, M. W. Heat Exchange Fluids & Techniques. LC 79-20336. (Energy Tech Review, No. 50, Chemical Review Ser.: No. 143). (Illus.). 1980. 42.00 (ISBN 0-8155-0778-X). Noyes.

HEAT INSULATING MATERIALS

see Insulation (Heat)

HEAT PIPES

Here are entered works on heat transfer cylinders that absorb heat at one end by vaporization of a liquid and release heat by condensation of the liquid at the other end. Works on pipes which are components of heating installations in structures are entered under Heating-Pipes.

Chi, S. W. Heat Pipe Theory & Practice: A Sourcebook. LC 76-9761. (McGraw-Hill-Hemisphere Ser. Thermal & Fluids Engineering). (Illus.). 1976. text ed. 24.50 (ISBN 0-07-010718-1, C). McGraw.

Dunn, P. D. & Reay, D. A. Heat Pipes. 2nd ed. 1977. text ed. 45.00 (ISBN 0-08-022127-0); pap. text ed. 17.00 (ISBN 0-08-022128-9). Pergamon.

HEAT POLLUTION OF RIVERS, LAKES, ETC.

see Thermal Pollution of Rivers, Lakes, etc.

HEAT PUMPS

Ambrose, E. R. Heat Pumps & Electric Heating: Residential, Commercial, Industrial Year-Round Air Conditioning. LC 65-27664. 205p. 1966. 26.00 (ISBN 0-471-02530-5, Pub. by Wiley-Interscience). Wiley.

BCC Staff. The Heat Pump, E-020r: Commercial Forecasts. rev. ed. (Illus.). 1979. 600.00 (ISBN 0-89336-104-6). BCC.

Camatini, E. & Kester, T., eds. Heat Pumps Their Contribution to Energy Conservation, No. 15. (NATO Advanced Study Applied Science Ser.). 428p. 1976. 42.50x (ISBN 90-286-0056-6). Sijthoff & Noordhoff.

Collie, M. J., ed. Heat Pump Technology for Saving Energy. LC 79-83902. (Energy Technology Review Ser.: No. 39). (Illus.). 1979. 39.00 (ISBN 0-8155-0744-5). Noyes.

Gordian Associates for the U. S. Department of Energy. Heat Pump Technology: A Survey of Technical Developments, Market Prospects & Research Needs. 464p. 1980. 44.95 (ISBN 0-89934-016-4, H-010PP); pap. 39.95 (ISBN 0-89934-017-2). Solar Energy Info.

Heap, R. D. Heat Pumps. 1979. 21.00x (ISBN 0-419-11330-4, Pub. by E & FN Spon). Methuen Inc.

The Heat Pump E-020R: Commercial Forecasts. 1979. 600.00 (ISBN 0-89336-191-7). BCC.

Lord, N. W., et al. Heat Pump Technology. LC 79-56112. (Electrotechnology Ser.: Vol. 4). (Illus.). 1980. 29.95 (ISBN 0-250-40341-2). Ann Arbor Science.

McGuigan, Dermot. Heat Pumps: An Efficient Heating & Cooling Alternative. (Illus.). 160p. 1981. pap. 6.95 (ISBN 0-88266-255-4). Garden Way Pub.

Von Cube, Hans L. & Staimle, Fritz. Heat Pump Technology. Goodall, E. G., tr. 1981. text ed. write for info. (ISBN 0-408-00497-5, Newnes-Butterworth). Butterworth.

HEAT RESISTANT ALLOYS

see also Nimonic Alloys; Steel, Heat Resistant

Frank, Robert G. & Zimmerman, William F. Materials for Rockets & Missiles. 1959. 7.95 (ISBN 0-02-339400-5, 33940). Macmillan.

Machlin, I., et al, eds. Refractory Metal Alloys: Metallurgy & Technology. LC 69-13684. 491p. 1968. 49.50 (ISBN 0-306-30375-2, Plenum Pr). Plenum Pub.

Plansee Seminar De Re Metallica - 5th - Reutte - 1964. Metals for the Space Age: Papers presented at the Fifth Plansee Seminar. Benesovsky, F., ed. (Illus.). 1965. 51.40 (ISBN 0-387-80729-2). Springer-Verlag.

Samsonov, G. V., et al. Chemical Properties & Analysis of Refractory Compounds. LC 70-37619. 127p. 1972. 27.50 (ISBN 0-306-10867-4, Consultants). Plenum Pub.

Savitskii, E. M. & Burkhanov, G. S. Physical Metallurgy of Refractory Metals & Alloys. LC 69-12519. 287p. 1970. 45.00 (ISBN 0-306-10841-0, Consultants). Plenum Pub.

Sims, Chester T. & Hagel, William C., eds. The Superalloys. LC 72-5904. (Science & Technology of Materials Ser.). 688p. 1972. 56.00 (ISBN 0-471-79207-1, Pub. by Wiley-Interscience). Wiley.

Tietz, T. E. & Wilson, J. W. Behavior & Properties of Refractory Metals. 1965. 20.00x (ISBN 0-8047-0162-8). Stanford U Pr.

Wilkinson, Walter D. Fabrication of Refractory Metals. LC 70-115054. 429p. 1970. 29.50 (ISBN 0-685-58269-8). Am Nuclear Soc.

--Properties of Refractory Metals. LC 72-75349. 355p. 1969. 27.50 (ISBN 0-685-58275-2). Am Nuclear Soc.

HEAT RESISTANT CONCRETE

Petzold, A. & Rohrs, M. Concrete for High Temperatures. 2nd ed. Phillips, A. R. & Turner, F. H., trs. from Ger. (Illus.). 1970. text ed. 37.30x (ISBN 0-85334-033-1, Pub. by Applied Science). Burgess-Intl Ideas.

HEAT RESISTANT MATERIALS

see also Ceramic Materials; Refractory Materials

Kennedy, A. J., ed. High Temperature Materials: The Controlling Physical Processes. 1968. 6.65 (ISBN 0-934454-48-5). Lubrecht & Cramer.

Preston, J. & Economy, J., eds. High-Temperature & Flame-Resistant Fibers. 232p. (Orig.). 1973. 21.50 (ISBN 0-686-74168-4). Krieger.

HEAT RESISTANT PLASTICS

Critser, James R., Jr. Flame Retardants for Plastics, Rubber Textiles & Paper (July 1972 - June 1973) (Ser. 2-7273). 112p. 1973. 100.00 (ISBN 0-914428-14-4). Lexington Data.

HEAT RESISTANT STEEL

see Steel, Heat Resistant

HEAT SENSITIVE COPYING PROCESSES

see Thermography (Copying Process)

HEAT STRESS (BIOLOGY)

see Heat-Physiological Effect

HEAT TRANSFER

see Heat-Transmission

HEAT TRANSFER IMAGES

see Thermography (Copying Process)

HEAT TREATMENT OF METALS

see Metals-Heat Treatment

HEAT TREATMENT OF STEEL

see Steel-Heat Treatment

HEATH, EDWARD, 1916-

Heath, Edward. Travels: People & Places in My Life. (Illus.). 1979. 12.95 (ISBN 0-8317-8810-0, Mayflower Bks). Smith Pubs.

Laing, Margaret. Edward Heath: Prime Minister. LC 72-95089. 258p. 1973. 10.00 (ISBN 0-89388-086-8). Okpaku Communications.

Roth, A. Heath & the Heathmen. 1972. 3.25 (ISBN 0-7100-7428-X). Routledge & Kegan.

HEATHENISM

see Paganism

HEATHER

Proudley, Brian & Proudley, Valerie. Heathers in Color. (Color Ser.). (Illus.). 1974. 9.95 (ISBN 0-7137-0635-X, Pub by Blandford Pr England). Sterling.

HEATHS

see Moors and Heaths

HEATING

see also Boilers; Electric Heating; Fans (Machinery); Fireplaces; Fuel; Furnaces; Heating From Central Stations; Hot-Water Heating; Insulation (Heat); Oil Burners; Solar Heating; Stoves; Ventilation; Waste Heat

Adams, Jeannette T. Complete Home Plumbing & Heating Handbook. LC 76-28519. 1977. 12.95 (ISBN 0-668-03939-6). Arco.

Argonne National Laboratory. Thermal Energy Storage: Design & Installation Manual. rev., 2nd ed. 372p. 1981. 44.50 (ISBN 0-89934-009-1, H.929); pap. 29.50 (ISBN 0-89934-010-5, H.029). Solar Energy Info.

Bartok, John W. Heating with Coal. (Illus.). 160p. 1980. pap. 6.95 (ISBN 0-88266-243-0). Garden Way Pub.

Berl, W. G. & Powell, W. R. Efficient Comfort Conditioning. 1979. lib. bdg. 24.25x (ISBN 0-89158-290-8). Westview.

Bierman, Sheldon L., et al. Geothermal Energy in the Western United States: Innovation Versus Monopoly. LC 77-16078. 1978. 34.50 (ISBN 0-03-041470-9). Praeger.

Bowyer, John. Central Heating. LC 76-40808. (Illus.). 1977. 13.50 (ISBN 0-7153-7037-5). David & Charles.

Bronthon & McLaughlin. Heating Service Design. 1981. text ed. 49.95 (ISBN 0-408-00380-4). Butterworth.

Browne, Dan. Alternative Home Heating. LC 79-3445. (Illus.). 208p. (Orig.). 1980. 12.95 (ISBN 0-03-041531-4); pap. 6.95 (ISBN 0-03-041536-5). HR&W.

Burberry, Peter & Aldersey-Williams, Arthur. Guide to Domestic Central Heating Installation & Controls. LC 78-16062. 1979. 17.50 (ISBN 0-85139-207-5, Pub. by Architectural Pr). Nichols Pub.

Cassiday, Bruce. The Complete Solar House. 1978. pap. 2.50 (ISBN 0-446-81780-5). Warner Bks.

Copson, David A. Microwave Heating. 2nd ed. (Illus.). 1975. lib. bdg. 49.00 (ISBN 0-87055-182-5). AVI.

Daniels, George. Home Guide to Plumbing, Heating, & Air Conditioning. 2nd ed. LC 67-10841. (Popular Science Skill Bk). (Illus.). 1976. pap. 3.95 (ISBN 0-06-010957-2, TD-271, HarpT). Har-Row.

Daniels, M. E. Fireplaces & Wood Stoves. LC 76-26948. (Illus.). 1977. 13.95 (ISBN 0-672-52175-X). Bobbs.

Day, Richard. The Home Owner Handbook of Plumbing & Heating. (The Home Owner Handbooks Ser.). (Illus.). 124p. 1974. 1.98 (ISBN 0-517-51441-9). Crown.

Doring, G. & Rudolphi. Tiefkuhl Lexikon. 239p. (Ger.). 10.95 (ISBN 3-87150-020-8, M-7666, Pub. by Deutscher Fachverlag). French & Eur.

Down, P. G. Heating & Cooling Load Calculations. 1969. 26.00 (ISBN 0-08-013001-1). Pergamon.

Dundas, James L. Heating Service. (Illus.). 1978. text ed. 14.95 (ISBN 0-8403-1866-9). Kendall-Hunt.

Edwards, Harry J., Jr. Automatic Controls for Heating & Air Conditioning: Pneumatic-Electric Control Systems. (Illus.). 1980. 16.95 (ISBN 0-07-019046-1). McGraw.

Egan, M. David. Concepts in Thermal Comfort. (Illus.). 224p. 1975. 15.95 (ISBN 0-13-166447-6). P-H.

Eisinger, Larry, ed. Handy Man's Plumbing & Heating Guide. (Illus.). 1952. lib. bdg. 3.95 (ISBN 0-668-00372-3). Arco.

Emerick, Robert H. Heating Handbook: A Manual of Standards, Codes & Methods. (Illus.). 1964. 29.50 (ISBN 0-07-019312-6, P&RB). McGraw.

Fanger, P. O. Thermal Comfort. 256p. 1973. text ed. 24.50 (ISBN 0-07-019915-9, C). McGraw.

Federal Construction Council - Building Research Advisory Board. Evaluation of Components for Underground Heat Distribution Systems. 1964. pap. 2.75 (ISBN 0-309-01196-5). Natl Acad Pr.

Gasman, A. B. Home Owner's Guide to Gas Heat. 1967. pap. 2.00 (ISBN 0-87164-004-X). William-F.

Gay, Larry. Central Heating with Wood & Coal. (Illus.). 128p. 1981. write for info. (ISBN 0-8289-0419-7); pap. 8.95 (ISBN 0-8289-0420-0). Greene.

--The Complete Book of Heating with Wood. LC 74-83144. 128p. 1974. pap. 4.95 (ISBN 0-88266-035-7). Garden Way Pub.

Haines, R. W. Control Systems for Heating, Ventilating & Air Conditioning. LC 78-56751. 1978. pap. text ed. 8.00 (ISBN 0-8273-1804-9). Delmar.

Haines, Roger W. Control Systems for Heating, Ventilating, & Air Conditioning. 2nd ed. 1977. text ed. 17.95x (ISBN 0-442-23031-1). Van Nos Reinhold.

Harrington, Geri, et al. Total Warmth: A Resource Book for the Cold, Dark Days Ahead. (Illus.). 192p. 1981. 15.95 (ISBN 0-02-548460-5); pap. 8.95 (ISBN 0-02-080070-3). Macmillan.

Havrella, Raymond. Heating, Ventilating & Air Conditioning Fundamentals. LC 80-17155. (Contemporary Construction Ser.). (Illus.). 288p. (gr. 10-12). 1981. text ed. 16.95x (ISBN 0-07-027281-6, G); wkbk. avail. (ISBN 0-07-027283-2). McGraw.

Hedden, Jay. Heating, Cooling & Ventilation: Solar & Conventional Solutions. Kummings, Gail S., ed. (Illus.). 144p. 1981. 17.95 (ISBN 0-932944-39-6); pap. 6.95 (ISBN 0-932944-40-X). Creative Homeowner.

Hornung, William J. Plumbing & Heating. (Illus.). 224p. 1982. 14.95 (ISBN 0-13-683920-7). P-H.

Industrial Heating Equipment Assn. The Directory of Industrial Heat Processing & Combustion Equipment: U. S. Manufacturers, 1981-1982. 3rd biennial ed. 224p. (Orig.). 1981. pap. 38.50 (ISBN 0-931634-05-9). Info Clearing House.

Jennings, Burgess H. Environmental Engineering: Analysis & Practice. 765p. 1970. text ed. 30.50 scp (ISBN 0-7002-2259-6, HarpC); scp solution manual 5.50 (ISBN 0-685-12705-2). Har-Row.

Jones, Peter. Homeowner's Guide to Plumbing, Heating & Air Conditioning. (Illus.). 1980. text ed. 13.95 (ISBN 0-8359-2845-4). Reston.

--How to Cut Heating & Cooling Costs. Machtiger, B., ed. LC 79-15207. (Home Environment "Help" Bks). (Illus.). 1981. pap. 4.95 (ISBN 0-88421-092-8). New Century.

Kern, Donald Q. Process Heat Transfer. 1950. text ed. 29.50 (ISBN 0-07-034190-7, C). McGraw.

Khashab, A. Heating, Ventilating & Air Conditioning Estimating Manual. (Illus.). 1977. 27.50 (ISBN 0-07-034535-X, P&RB). McGraw.

Kut, D. Heating & Hot Water Services in Buildings. 1968. 32.00 (ISBN 0-08-012218-3). Pergamon.

--Warm Air Heating. LC 71-122009. 1971. 42.00 (ISBN 0-08-015853-6); pap. 32.00 (ISBN 0-08-019006-5). Pergamon.

Lang, V. Paul. Heating & Cooling Safety. LC 76-24983. (gr. 9-12). 1977. pap. 3.80 (ISBN 0-8273-1011-0); instructor's guide 1.00 (ISBN 0-8273-1012-9). Delmar.

Langley, Billy C. Comfort Heating. 2nd ed. (Illus.). 1978. ref. 17.50 (ISBN 0-87909-091-X); instrs'. manual avail. Reston.

Lefax Pub. Co. Editors. Home Heating. (Lefax Data Bks.: No. 610). (Illus.). looseleaf bdg. 3.00 (ISBN 0-685-14143-8). Lefax.

McQuiston, Faye C. & Parker, Jerald D. Heating, Ventilating, & Air Conditioning: Analysis & Design. LC 77-8033. 1977. 29.95 (ISBN 0-471-01722-1). Wiley.

Morrison, James W. The Complete Energy-Saving Home Improvement Guide. 4th ed. LC 80-23996. (Illus.). 1981. pap. 2.50 (ISBN 0-668-05085-3, 5085-3). Arco.

Oliker, I., ed. Cogeneration District Heating Applications. 52p. 1978. 7.00 (ISBN 0-685-66792-8, H00128). ASME.

Olivieri, Joseph B. How to Design Heating-Cooling Comfort Systems. 3rd ed. LC 75-84355. (Illus.). 1973. 24.00 (ISBN 0-912524-09-X). Busn News.

Orchard, W. R. & Sherratt, A. F. Combined Heat & Power Whole City Heating Planning: Tomorrows Energy Economy. LC 80-41444. 234p. 1980. 65.95 (ISBN 0-470-27088-8). Halsted Pr.

Osgood, William. Wintering in Snow Country. LC 78-58680. (Illus.). 1977. 9.95 (ISBN 0-8289-0319-0); pap. 4.95 (ISBN 0-8289-0320-4). Greene.

Page, John S. Estimator's Man-Hour Manual on Heating, Air Conditioning, Ventilating & Plumbing. 2nd ed. (Estimators Man-Hour Library). 240p. 1978. 25.00x (ISBN 0-87201-364-2). Gulf Pub.

Parks, Alexis. People Heaters: A People's Guide to Keeping Warm in Winter. LC 80-21930. (Illus.). 128p. (Orig.). 1980. pap. 4.95 (ISBN 0-931790-16-6). Brick Hse Pub.

Price, Billy L. & Price, James T. The Master Handbook of ALL Home Heating Systems: Tune-Up, Repair, Installation & Maintenance. (Illus.). 1979. 12.95 (ISBN 0-8306-9757-8); pap. 7.95 (ISBN 0-8306-1176-2, 1176). TAB Bks.

Reay, David A. Heat Recovery Systems: A Directory of Equipment & Techniques. LC 79-10877. (Energy Ser.). 590p. 1979. text ed. 59.95x (ISBN 0-419-11400-9, Pub. by E & FN Spon England). Methuen Inc.

Rizzi, Ennio A. Design & Estimating for Heating, Ventilating, & Air Conditioning. 480p. 1980. text ed. 27.95 (ISBN 0-442-26952-8). Van Nos Reinhold.

Rudman, Jack. Automatic Heating. (Occupational Competency Examination Ser.: OCE-6). 14.95 (ISBN 0-8373-5756-X); pap. 9.95 (ISBN 0-8373-5706-3). Natl Learning.

--Senior Heating & Ventilating Engineer. (Career Examination Ser.: C-1918). (Cloth bdg. avail. on request). pap. 10.00 (ISBN 0-8373-1918-8). Natl Learning.

--Superintendent of Heating & Ventilation. (Career Examination Ser.: C-2380). (Cloth bdg. avail. on request). pap. 10.00 (ISBN 0-8373-2380-0). Natl Learning.

Russell, Allen. Getting Stated in Heating & Air Conditioning Service. 3rd ed. LC 77-13571. 1977. text ed. 22.00 (ISBN 0-912524-17-0). Busn News.

Schneider, Raymond K. HVAC Control Systems. LC 80-23588. 358p. 1981. text ed. 21.95 (ISBN 0-471-05180-2). Wiley.

Severns, William H. & Fellows, Julian R. Air Conditioning & Refrigeration. LC 58-7908. 1958. text ed. 30.95x (ISBN 0-471-77781-1). Wiley.

Shaw, E. W. Heating & Hot Water Services. 1979. 32.95 (ISBN 0-8464-0048-0); pap. 18.95 (ISBN 0-8464-0049-9). Beekman Pubs.

--Heating & Hot-Water Services: Selected Subjects with Worked Examples in SI Units. 4th ed. 241p. pap. text ed. 22.75x (ISBN 0-246-11229-8, Pub. by Granada England). Renouf.

Shelton, Jay W. Wood Heat Safety. (Illus.). 1979. pap. 9.95 (ISBN 0-88266-160-4). Garden Way Pub.

Sherman, Steve. Home Heating with Coal. (Illus.). 192p. 1980. pap. 8.95 (ISBN 0-8117-2081-0). Stackpole.

Stoecker, W. F. Using SI Units (Standard International Metric) in Heating, Air Conditioning, & Refrigeration. LC 74-26697. (Illus.). 1975. 7.50 (ISBN 0-912524-12-X). Busn News.

Tattersall, Robert. Home Heating & Fireplaces: A Do-It-Yourself Guide. (Illus.). 1977. pap. 3.95 (ISBN 0-09-128061-3, Pub. by Hutchinson). Merrimack Bk Serv.
Time-Life Books, ed. Heating & Cooling. LC 77-80200. (Home Repair & Improvement Ser.). (Illus.). (gr. 7 up). 1977. lib. bdg. 11.97 (ISBN 0-685-77684-0, Pub. by Time-Life). Silver.
--Heating & Cooling. (Home Repair & Improvement Ser.). 1977. 10.95 (ISBN 0-8094-2378-2). Time-Life.
Traister, John. Practical Drafting for the HVAC Trades. LC 75-5404. (Illus.). 1975. pap. 12.95 (ISBN 0-672-21082-7). Sams.
Traister, John E. Do-It-Yourselfer's Guide to Modern Energy-Efficient Heating & Cooling Systems. (Illus.). 1978. 9.95 (ISBN 0-8306-7903-0); pap. 5.95 (ISBN 0-8306-6903-5, 903). TAB Bks.
Urban District Heating Using Nuclear Heat. (Panel Proceedings Ser). (Illus.). 1977. pap. text ed. 22.75 (ISBN 92-0-051077-9, IAEA). Unipub.
Vivian, John. Wood Heat. new & improved ed. 1978. 12.95 (ISBN 0-87857-241-4); pap. 9.95 (ISBN 0-87857-242-2). Rodale Pr Inc.
Warm Air Heating & Air Conditioning System. (Eighty-Ninety Ser). 1973. pap. 2.00 (ISBN 0-685-58162-4, 90B). Natl Fire Prot.
Whillier, Austin. Solar Energy Collection & Its Utilization for House Heating. Bruchey, Stuart, ed. LC 78-22712. (Energy in the American Economy Ser.). (Illus.). 1979. lib. bdg. 14.00x (ISBN 0-405-12022-2). Arno.
Wright, Lawrence. Home Fires Burning: The History of Domestic Heating & Cooking. 1964. 15.00 (ISBN 0-7100-2332-4). Routledge & Kegan.
Zurick, Timothy. Air Conditioning, Heating & Refrigeration Dictionary. LC 77-10318. 1977. sewn lexotone 5.95 (ISBN 0-912524-16-2). Busn News.

HEATING-TABLES, CALCULATIONS, ETC.

Barton, John J. Estimating for Heating & Ventilating. 3rd ed. (Illus.). 29.50x (ISBN 0-408-00072-4). Transatlantic.
Stamper, Eugene & Koral, Richard L., eds. Handbook of Air Conditioning, Heating & Ventilating. 3rd ed. LC 78-71559. (Illus.). 1420p. 1979. 59.00 (ISBN 0-8311-1124-0). Indus Pr.

HEATING, AERODYNAMIC

see Aerodynamic Heating

HEATING FROM CENTRAL STATIONS

Diamant, R. M. & Kut, David. District Heating & Cooling for Energy Conservation. 350p. 1981. 54.95 (ISBN 0-470-27182-5). Halsted Pr.
Din Standards for Central-Heating & Ventilating Plants. 229.00 (ISBN 0-01-005732-3, 10057-3/23). Heyden.
Federal Construction Council - Building Research Advisory Board. Supplementary Field Investigation of Underground Heat Distribution Systems. 1966. pap. 3.25 (ISBN 0-309-01481-6). Natl Acad Pr.
MacKenzie. District Heating Thermal Generation & Distribution. 1979. text ed. 37.00 (ISBN 0-08-022711-2). Pergamon.

HEATING-PIPES

Here are entered works on pipes which are components of heating installations in structures. Works on heat transfer cylinders that absorb heat at one end by vaporization of a liquid and release heat by condensation of the liquid at the other end are entered under Heat Pipes.

Building Research Advisory Board. Criteria for Underground Heat Distribution Systems. LC 74-32581. 1975. pap. 4.75 (ISBN 0-309-02320-3). Natl Acad Pr.

HEAVEN

see also Angels; Beatific Vision; Future Life; Paradise

Arendzen, J. P. Purgatory & Heaven. (Canterbury Ser.). Orig. Title: What Becomes of the Dead? 1972. pap. 1.50 (ISBN 0-89555-045-8, 778). TAN Bks Pubs.
Becker, Ernest J. A Contribution to the Comparative Study of the Medieval Visions of Heaven & Hell. 1976. Repr. of 1899 ed. 25.00 (ISBN 0-403-06507-0, Regency). Scholarly.
Beiderwieden, George. Heaven. 1957. 1.05 (ISBN 0-570-03680-1, 74-1008). Concordia.
Les Bons Iront-Ils Au Ciel? Date not set. 14.50 (ISBN 0-686-76384-X). Life Pubs Intl.
Bounds, E. M. Heaven: A Place, a City, a Home. (Direction Bks). 152p. 1975. pap. 1.45 (ISBN 0-8010-0648-1). Baker Bk.
Bunyan, John. The Strait Gate. pap. 2.25 (ISBN 0-685-88394-9). Reiner.
Carothers, Merlin, tr. El Cielo Baja Al Infierno. (Spanish Bks.). (Span.). 1978. 1.75 (ISBN 0-8297-0766-2). Life Pubs Intl.
Clutton-Brock, A. What Is the Kingdom of Heaven. 1979. Repr. of 1919 ed. lib. bdg. 20.00 (ISBN 0-8492-3855-2). R West.
Cornwall, Judson. Heaven. 1978. pap. 3.50 (ISBN 0-89728-008-3, 704649). Bible Voice.
Daughters of St. Paul. Heaven. 1977. 3.50 (ISBN 0-8198-0419-3); pap. 2.50 (ISBN 0-8198-0420-7). Dghtrs St Paul.
Everett, Donald L. People & the Mind: The Mind & Me. 64p. 1980. 5.95 (ISBN 0-533-03421-3). Vantage.
Ford, W. Herschel. Simple Sermons on Heaven, Hell, & Judgment. pap. 3.95 (ISBN 0-310-24481-1). Zondervan.
Hurnard, Hannah. Temples of the Living God. LC 81-50723. 174p. (Orig.). 1981. pap. 4.95 (ISBN 0-9603634-9-1). Rahamah Pubns.
Keith, M. R. How I Found Out About Heaven. 1970. 3.50 (ISBN 0-910122-23-7). Amherst Pr.
--So You're Going to Heaven. 3.50 (ISBN 0-910122-22-9). Amherst Pr.
Kohler, Kaufmann. Heaven & Hell in Comparative Religion. 1923. 15.00 (ISBN 0-8414-5601-1). Folcroft.
Kreeft, Peter J. Heaven: The Heart's Deepest Longing. LC 80-7747. 160p. 1980. 8.95 (ISBN 0-06-064776-0, HarpR). Har-Row.
Lauterbach, William A. Heaven Bound. LC 74-34277. 128p. 1974. pap. 4.50 (ISBN 0-570-03028-5, 6-1156). Concordia.
Lightner, Robert P. Heaven for Those Who Can't Believe. LC 76-50303. 1977. pap. 1.95 (ISBN 0-87227-035-1). Reg Baptist.
Lindsay, Gordon. Within the Gates. (Sorcery & Spirit World Ser.). 1.25 (ISBN 0-89985-095-2). Christ Nations.
Mayer, Fred S. Why Two Worlds: Relation of Physical to Spiritual Realities. LC 78-134425. Repr. of 1934 ed. 21.00 (ISBN 0-404-08465-6). AMS Pr.
Mayle, Peter. Will I Go to Heaven? LC 76-1190. (Illus.). 1976. 7.95 (ISBN 0-498-01983-7); pap. 3.95 (ISBN 0-89474-015-6). Corwin.
Mullen, E. Theodore, Jr. The Assembly of the Gods: The Divine Council in Canaanite & Hebrew Literature. LC 80-10128. (Harvard Semitic Museum Monographs: No. 24). 10.50x (ISBN 0-89130-380-4, 04 00 24). Scholars Pr CA.
Nee, Watchman. The King & the Kingdom of Heaven. Kaung, Stephen, tr. from Chinese. 1978. 6.95 (ISBN 0-935008-23-3); pap. 4.50 (ISBN 0-935008-24-1). Christian Fellow Pubs.
Patch, Howard R. Other World, According to Descriptions in Medieval Literature. LC 77-96164. 1970. Repr. of 1950 ed. lib. bdg. 24.00x (ISBN 0-374-96289-8). Octagon.
Quadrupani, R. P. Light & Peace. LC 79-67860. 193p. 1980. pap. 3.00 (ISBN 0-89555-133-0). Tan Bks Pubs.
Sayers, Stanley E. The Nature of Things to Come. 1972. 3.95 (ISBN 0-686-21491-9). Firm Foun Pub.
Schillebeeck, Edward & Iersel, Van B., eds. Heaven. (Concilium Ser.: Vol. 123). 1979. pap. 4.95 (ISBN 0-8245-0284-1). Crossroad NY.
Smith, Wilbur M. The Biblical Doctrine of Heaven. 1980. text ed. 6.95 (ISBN 0-8024-0705-6). Moody.
Springer, Rebecca R. My Dream of Heaven. 1979. 6.95 (ISBN 0-8007-0989-6). Revell.
Swedenborg, Emanual. Heaven & Hell. 1976. pap. 1.95 (ISBN 0-89129-110-5). Jove Pubns.
Swedenborg, Emanuel. Heaven & Hell. LC 77-93044. trade ed. 8.25 (ISBN 0-87785-067-4); student ed 6.50 (ISBN 0-87785-066-6); pap. 1.95 (ISBN 0-87785-153-0). Swedenborg.
Thompson, Fred, Jr. What the Bible Says About Heaven & Hell. (What the Bible Says Ser.). 400p. 1982. 13.50 (ISBN 0-89900-081-9). College Pr Pub.
Travis, Arthur E. Where on Earth Is Heaven. LC 74-78967. 1974. 4.95 (ISBN 0-8054-1928-4). Broadman.
Van Note, Gene. The Glad Reunion Day. 1976. pap. 1.50 (ISBN 0-8341-0397-4). Beacon Hill.

HEAVISIDE LAYER

see Ionosphere

HEAVY ELECTRONS

see Mesons

HEAVY HYDROGEN

see Hydrogen-Isotopes

HEAVY IONS

Bethge, K., ed. Experimental Methods in Heavy Ion Physics. LC 78-12583. (Lecture Notes in Physics: Vol. 83). 1978. pap. 16.50 (ISBN 0-387-08931-4). Springer-Verlag.
Broglia, R. A. & Winther, Aage. Heavy Ion Reactions: Elastic & Inelastic Reactions, Vol. 1. 1980. write for info. (ISBN 0-8053-1302-8). A-W.
McVoy & Friedman, eds. Theoretical Methods in Medium-Energy Heavy Iron Physics. (NATO Advanced Study Institutes Ser.: Series B: Physics, Vol. 38). 1979. 65.00 (ISBN 0-306-40062-6, Plenum Pr). Plenum Pub.
Noerenberg, W. & Weidenmueller, H. -A. Introduction to the Theory of Heavy-Ion Collisions. 2nd enl ed. (Lecture Notes in Physics: Vol. 51). 345p. 1980. pap. 19.80 (ISBN 0-387-09753-8). Springer-Verlag.
Tamura, T., et al, eds. Continuum Spectra of Heavy-Ion Reactions. (Nuclear Science Research Conference Ser.: Vol. 2). 490p. 1980. 53.50 (ISBN 3-7186-0028-5). Harwood Academic.
Von Oertzen, W., ed. Deep Inelastic & Fusion Reactions with Heavy Ions. (Lecture Notes in Physics: Vol. 117). 410p. 1980. pap. 29.00 (ISBN 0-387-09965-4). Springer-Verlag.

HEAVY WATER REACTORS

Heavy Water Lattices. (Illus., Orig.). 1960. pap. 5.00 (ISBN 92-0-151060-8, ISP17, IAEA). Unipub.
Heavy Water Lattices: Second Panel Report. (Technical Reports Ser.: No. 20). (Illus., Orig.). 1963. pap. 31.50 (ISBN 92-0-051063-9, IDC20, IAEA). Unipub.
Heavy-Water Power Reactors. (Illus., Orig., Eng. & Fr.). 1968. pap. 58.50 (ISBN 92-0-050268-7, ISP163, IAEA). Unipub.
Kirshenbaum, Isidor. Utilization of Heavy Water. (National Nuclear Energy Ser.: Division III, Vol. 4B). 208p. 1951. pap. 25.00 (ISBN 0-686-75885-4); microfilm (35 mm) 12.50 (ISBN 0-686-75886-2). DOE.

HEBBEL, FRIEDRICH, 1813-1863

Danton, Annina P. Hebbel's Nibelungen. LC 71-163666. (Columbia University. Germanic Studies, Old Ser.: No. 8). Repr. of 1906 ed. 17.00 (ISBN 0-404-50408-6). AMS Pr.
Flygt, Sten G. Friedrich Hebbel. LC 68-20810. (World Authors Ser.). 1968. lib. bdg. 12.95x (ISBN 0-8057-2412-5). Irvington.
--Friedrich Hebbel's Conception of Movement in the Absolute & in History. LC 71-168051. (North Carolina. University. Studies in the Germanic Languages & Literatures: No. 7). Repr. of 1952 ed. 18.50 (ISBN 0-404-50907-X). AMS Pr.
Garland, Mary. Hebbel's Prose Tragedies. LC 72-88621. (Anglica Germanica Ser.: No. 2). 364p. 1973. 60.00 (ISBN 0-521-20090-3). Cambridge U Pr.
Gubelmann, Albert. Studies in the Lyric Poems of Friedrich Hebbel. 1973. Repr. of 1912 ed. 25.00 (ISBN 0-8274-1570-2). R West.
Gubelmann, Albert E. Studies in the Lyric Poems of Friedrich Hebbel. 1912. 22.50x (ISBN 0-685-89788-5). Elliots Bks.
Kuh, Emil. Biographie Friedrich Hebbel's, 2 Vols. Repr. of 1877 ed. Set. 64.50 (ISBN 0-404-03784-4). AMS Pr.
Schultze-Jahde, Karl. Motivanalyse Von Hebbels Agnes Bernauer. Repr. of 1925 ed. 14.00 (ISBN 0-384-54300-6); pap. 11.00 (ISBN 0-685-02060-6). Johnson Repr.

HEBER, REGMALD, 1783-1826

Laird, M. A., ed. Bishop Heber in Northern India: Selections from Heber's Journal. LC 70-123673. (European Understanding of India Ser). (Illus.). 1971. 32.50 (ISBN 0-521-07873-3). Cambridge U Pr.

HEBREW ART

see Art, Jewish

HEBREW CALENDAR

see Calendar, Jewish

HEBREW CHRONOLOGY

see Chronology, Jewish

HEBREW DRAMA

Abramson, Glenda. Modern Hebrew Drama. LC 79-16608. (Illus.). 1979. 25.00x (ISBN 0-312-53988-6). St Martin.

HEBREW IMPRINTS

Edelmann, Martin & Schmelzer, Menahem, eds. The Damascus Bible, Vol. 1, Pt. 1. Orig. Title: Early Hebrew Manuscripts in Facsimile. 1979. text ed. 5.28 (ISBN 0-8018-1337-9); pap. text ed. 4.95 (ISBN 0-8018-1349-2). Johns Hopkins.
Harvard University Library. Catalogue of Hebrew Books, 6 Vols. LC 68-22146. (Yiddish & Heb). 1968. Set. 225.00x (ISBN 0-674-10150-2). Harvard U Pr.

HEBREW LANGUAGE

see also Yiddish Language

American National Standards Institute, Standards Committee Z39 on Library Work, Documentation & Related Publishing Practices. American National Standard System for Romanization of Hebrew. 1975. 4.50 (ISBN 0-686-15232-8, Z39.25). ANSI.
Bar-Adon, Aaron. Modern Israeli Hebrew. wrappers 8.00 (ISBN 0-8363-0072-6). Jenkins.
--The Rise & Decline of a Dialect: A Study in the Revival of Modern Hebrew. LC 74-80121. (Janua Linguarum, Ser. Practica: No. 197). 116p. (Orig.). 1975. pap. text ed. 28.25x (ISBN 90-2793-206-9). Mouton.
Birnbaum, Philip. Fluent Hebrew. 491p. 1966. 6.00x (ISBN 0-88482-681-3). Hebrew Pub.
Butin, Romain. Ten Nequdoth of the Torah. rev. ed. (Library of Biblical Studies). 1969. 15.00x (ISBN 0-87068-043-9). Ktav.
Chomsky, Noam. Morphophonemics of Modern Hebrew. Hankamer, Jorge, ed. LC 78-66579. (Outstanding Dissertations in Linguistics Ser.). 1979. lib. bdg. 13.00 (ISBN 0-8240-9688-6). Garland Pub.
Coffin, Edna A. Lessons in Modern Hebrew, 2 vols. LC 76-49149. 1977. Vol. I. 12.50x (ISBN 0-472-08225-6); Vol. II. 12.50x (ISBN 0-472-08226-4). U of Mich Pr.
Cross, Frank M., Jr. & Freedman, David N. Early Hebrew Orthography: A Study of the Epigraphic Evidence. (American Oriental Ser.: Vol. 36). 1952. pap. 9.00x (ISBN 0-940490-36-6). Am Orient Soc.
Davis, John J. Hebrew Language Chart. pap. 1.75 (ISBN 0-8010-2865-5). Baker Bk.
D'Olivet, Fabre. The Hebraic Tongue Restored. Redfield, Louise N., tr. 1976. 27.50 (ISBN 0-87728-332-X). Weiser.
Efros, Israel I. Philosophical Terms in the Moreh Nebukim. LC 73-164764. (Columbia University. Oriental Studies: No. 22). Repr. of 1924 ed. 17.00 (ISBN 0-404-50512-0). AMS Pr.
Eitan, Israel. Contribution to Biblical Lexicography. (Columbia University. Contributions to Oriental History & Philology: No. 10). Repr. of 1924 ed. 12.50 (ISBN 0-404-50540-6). AMS Pr.
Encyclopedia Hebraica, 32 vols. Incl. Supplement. (Heb.). 1949. 1250.00 (ISBN 0-686-77001-3). Maxwell Sci Intl.
Feinstein, Marnin. Basic Hebrew: A Textbook of Contemporary Hebrew. LC 73-77286. 1973. 6.75x (ISBN 0-8197-0287-0). Bloch.
Fellman, Jack. The Revival of a Classical Tongue: Elizer Ben Yehuda & the Modern Hebrew Language. (Contributions to the Sociology of Language: No. 6). 1973. pap. text ed. 21.75x (ISBN 90-2792-495-3). Mouton.
Finley, Harvey E. & Isbell, Charles D. Biblical Hebrew. pap. 9.95 (ISBN 0-8010-3477-9). Baker Bk.
--Biblical Hebrew. 213p. 1975. pap. text ed. 9.95 (ISBN 0-8341-0350-8). Beacon Hill.
Fish, Sidney M. Reshith Binah: A Hebrew Primer. 1976. pap. 2.50x (ISBN 0-8197-0035-5). Bloch.
Foreign Service Institute. Hebrew Basic Course. 552p. (Hebrew.). 1980. 185.00x (ISBN 0-88432-040-5, H345); 24 audiocassettes incl. J Norton Pubs.
Gray, G. B. Forms of Hebrew Poetry. rev. ed. (Library of Biblical Studies). 1970. 16.95x (ISBN 0-87068-064-1). Ktav.
Greenspan, Jay Seth. Hebrew Calligraphy: A Step-by-Step Guide. LC 79-12718. (Illus.). 1980. 14.95 (ISBN 0-8052-3720-8); pap. 7.95 (ISBN 0-8052-0664-7). Schocken.
Haden, Peter. Elementary Knowledge: A Story of the Creation of the Hebrew Alaphabet. (Illus.). 68p. 1981. 22.50 (ISBN 0-87663-357-2). Universe.
Hayon, Yehiel. Relativization in Hebrew: A Transformational Approach. (Janua Linguarum Ser. Practica: No. 189). (Illus.). 238p. (Orig.). 1973. pap. text ed. 56.50x (ISBN 90-2792-391-4). Mouton.
Heuman, Fred S. The Uses of Hebraisms in Recent Bible Translations. 1977. 8.50 (ISBN 0-8022-2190-4). Philos Lib.
Jakubowski, Sarah & Lipscitz, Arieh. Be'al Peh U'bchtav: Parts A & B. (Illus.). 1977. Pt.A. pap. text ed. 4.95x (ISBN 0-930038-00-2); Pt.B. pap. text ed. 5.25x (ISBN 0-930038-01-0). Arbit.
James, J. Courtenay. Hebrew & English: Some Likenesses, Psychic & Linguistic. Repr. of 1920 ed. lib. bdg. 20.00 (ISBN 0-8495-2723-6). Arden Lib.
Kamhi, D. J. Modern Hebrew: An Introductory Course. (OUP for the School of Oriental & African Studies Ser.). 1981. 14.95x (ISBN 0-19-713594-3). Oxford U Pr.
Klatzkin. Thesaurus Philosophicus Linguae Hebraica, 4 pts. in 2 vols. 47.50 (ISBN 0-87306-118-7). Feldheim.
Kugel, James L. The Idea of Biblical Poetry: Parallelism & Its History. LC 80-25227. 320p. 1981. 27.50x (ISBN 0-300-02474-6). Yale U Pr.
Landmann, Michael. Reform of the Hebrew Alphabet. Parent, David J., tr. LC 76-14595. 321p. (Illinois Language & Culture Ser., Vol. One). 1976. 31.75 (ISBN 0-8357-0177-8, IS-00012, Pub by Applied Literature Press). Univ Microfilms.
LaSor, William S. Handbook of Biblical Hebrew, 3 vols. Set. 12.95x (ISBN 0-8028-2379-3). Eerdmans.
Leaf, Reuben. Hebrew Alphabets - 400 B. C. E. to Our Days: Specimens of Hebrew Lettering & Graphic Art. LC 73-77285. 1975. 17.50 (ISBN 0-8197-0278-1). Bloch.
Learn Hebrew for English Speakers. pap. 8.50 (ISBN 0-87557-032-1, 032-1). Saphrograph.
Levin, Saul. Indo-European & Semitic Languages: An Exploration of Structural Similarities Related to Accent, Chiefly in Greek, Sanskrit, & Hebrew. LC 67-28937. (Illus.). 1971. 47.00 (ISBN 0-87395-055-0); microfiche 47.00 (ISBN 0-87395-155-7). State U NY Pr.
Marks, Cara G. A Handbook of Hebrew Calligraphy: The ABC's of the Alef-Bet. (Illus.). 128p. 1981. 10.95 (ISBN 0-89961-010-2); pap. 5.95 (ISBN 0-89961-011-0). SBS Pub.

Miller, Edward F. Influence of Gesenius on Hebrew Lexicography. LC 28-3581. (Columbia University. Contributions to Oriental History & Philology: No. 11). Repr. of 1927 ed. 14.00 (ISBN 0-404-50541-4). AMS Pr.

Nahir, Moshe, ed. Hebrew Teachings & Applied Linguistics. LC 80-8142. (Illus.). 396p. (Orig.). 1981. lib. bdg. 21.75 (ISBN 0-8191-1708-0); pap. text ed. 12.75 (ISBN 0-8191-1709-9). U Pr of Amer.

Paper, H. H., ed. Jewish Languages: Theme & Variations. 10.00x (ISBN 0-915938-01-4, Pub. by Assoc for Jewish Studies). Ktav.

Polzin, Robert. Late Biblical Hebrew: Toward an Historical Typology of Biblical Hebrew Prose. LC 76-3559. (Harvard Semitic Monographs). (Illus.). 1976. 7.50 (ISBN 0-89130-101-1, 040012). Scholars Pr Ca.

Revell, E. J. Biblical Texts with Palestinian Pointing. LC 77-8893. (Society of Biblical Literature. Masoretic Studies). 1977. pap. 9.00 (ISBN 0-89130-141-0, 060504). Scholars Pr Ca.

Rosen, H. Contemporary Hebrew. (Trends in Linguistics). 1977. 40.00x (ISBN 90-279-3106-2). Mouton.

Rosen, Haiim B. A Textbook of Israeli Hebrew: With an Introduction to the Classical Language. 2nd ed. LC 62-9116. 1976. pap. text ed. 8.95 (ISBN 0-226-72603-7, P689, Phoen, P684). U of Chicago Pr.

Saulex, William H. The Romance of the Hebrew Language. 243p. Date not set. Repr. of 1913 ed. lib. bdg. 25.00 (ISBN 0-8482-6303-0). Norwood Edns.

Saulez, William H. The Romance of the Hebrew Language. 1979. Repr. of 1913 ed. lib. bdg. 25.00 (ISBN 0-8414-8013-3). Folcroft.

Saulson, Scott B. Institutionalized Language Planning: Documents & Analysis of the Revival of Hebrew. (Contributions to the Sociology of Language Ser.: No. 23). 1979. text ed. 36.50x (ISBN 90-279-7567-1). Mouton.

Sawyer, John F. A Modern Introduction to Biblical Hebrew. (Orig.). 1976. pap. 12.50 (ISBN 0-85362-159-4, Oriel). Routledge & Kegan.

Simon, Ethelyn, et al. A Simple Approach to Old Testament Hebrew. (Orig.). 1981. pap. text ed. 14.95 (ISBN 0-939144-03-4). EKS Pub Co.

Soloff, et al. Torataynu. (Sacred Hebrew Ser.). (Illus.). 168p. (gr. 2-8). 1981. pap. text ed. 4.95 (ISBN 0-86628-026-X). Ridgefield Pub.

Talmage, Frank, et al. Sifron la Student (Alef-Bet) Study Guide. 2nd ed. 1977. pap. 8.50x (ISBN 0-8020-2256-1). U of Toronto Pr.

Uveeler & Bronznick. Hayesod: Fundamentals of Hebrew. LC 72-86858. 12.95 (ISBN 0-87306-071-7). Feldheim.

Vaughan, P. H. Meaning of Bama in the Old Testament. LC 73-89004. (Society for Old Testament Study Monographs: No. 3). (Illus.). 96p. 1974. 23.95 (ISBN 0-521-20425-9). Cambridge U Pr.

Wickes, William. Two Treatises on the Accentuation of the Old Testament. rev. ed. 1970. 25.00x (ISBN 0-87068-004-8). Ktav.

Yates, Kyle M. & Owens, J. J. Nociones Esenciales Del Hebreo Biblico. Daglio, S. Daniel, tr. 1980. Repr. of 1978 ed. 5.65 (ISBN 0-311-42056-7). Casa Bautista.

HEBREW LANGUAGE–COMPOSITION AND EXERCISES

Harper, William R. Introductory Hebrew: Method & Manual. rev. ed. Smith, James M., ed. LC 59-7624. (Midway Reprint Ser). 1974. pap. 6.00x (ISBN 0-226-31683-1). U of Chicago Pr.

Sellers, Ovid R. & Voigt, E. E. Biblical Hebrew for Beginners. 12th corr ed. 1963. pap. 2.95x (ISBN 0-8401-2163-6). Allenson-Breckinridge.

Weingreen, Jacob. Classical Hebrew Composition. 1957. 13.95x (ISBN 0-19-815423-2). Oxford U Pr.

HEBREW LANGUAGE–CONVERSATION AND PHRASE BOOKS

see also Hebrew Language–Self-Instruction

Beare, Aleeza C. Say It in Hebrew. LC 53-2919. 1959. lib. bdg. 8.50x (ISBN 0-88307-558-X). Gannon.

Benjamin, Ben A. Let's Talk Hebrew. 1961. 4.00 (ISBN 0-914080-01-6). Shulsinger Sales.

Cerf, Aleeza. Say It in Modern Hebrew. (Orig.). pap. 2.00 (ISBN 0-486-20805-2). Dover.

Lambdin, Thomas O. An Introduction to Biblical Hebrew. 1971. text ed. 17.95x (ISBN 0-684-41322-1, ScribC). Scribner.

Mansoor, Menahem. Contemporary Hebrew. LC 75-1813. 1976. pap. text ed. 6.95x (ISBN 0-87441-251-X). Behrman.

Stern, A. Z. & Reif, Joseph A., eds. Useful Expressions in Hebrew. (Useful Expressions Ser.). 64p. (Orig.). 1980. pap. 2.00 (ISBN 0-86628-009-X); cassette 4.95 (ISBN 0-86628-014-6). Ridgefield Pub.

HEBREW LANGUAGE–DICTIONARIES

Ben-Yehuda, Eliezer, ed. Dictionary & Thesaurus of the Hebrew Language, 8 Vols. Set. 150.00 (ISBN 0-498-07038-7, Yoseloff); lea. bd. set o.p. 250.00 (ISBN 0-498-08915-0). A S Barnes.

Cohn, Marc M. Dictionnaire Francais-Hebreu. 760p. (Fr.-Heb.). 1966. 27.50 (ISBN 0-686-56955-5, M-6077). French & Eur.

--Nouveau Dictionnaire Hebreu-Francais. 792p. (Fr.-Heb.). 1974. 32.50 (ISBN 0-686-56956-3, M-6078). French & Eur.

Davidson, Benjamin. Analytical Hebrew & Chaldee Lexicon. 19.95 (ISBN 0-310-20290-6, Pub. by Bagster). Zondervan.

Debahy, M. Dictionary Hebrew Verbs. 1974. 15.00x (ISBN 0-86685-123-2). Intl Bk Ctr.

Einspahr, Bruce, compiled by. Index to the Brown, Driver & Briggs Hebrew Lexicon. 1976. 19.95 (ISBN 0-8024-4082-7). Moody.

Jastrow, Marcus. Hebrew-Aramaic-English Dictionary, a Dictionary of Talmud Babli & Talmud Yerushalmi Targum & Midrash, 2 Vols. 55.00 (ISBN 0-87559-019-5). Shalom.

Levenston, Edward A. & Sivan, Reuven. The New Bantam-Megiddo Hebrew Dictionary. 736p. 1975. pap. 2.95 (ISBN 0-553-02094-3, G14420-0). Bantam.

Nouveau Dictionnaire francais-hebreu. 1973. 26.00 (ISBN 0-685-55772-3). Larousse.

Nouveau dictionnaire hebreu-francais. 1973. 39.25 (ISBN 0-685-55771-5). Larousse.

Robinson, Maurice A., compiled by. Indexes to All Editions of Brown-Driver-Briggs Hebrew Lexicon & Thayer's Greek Lexicon. 1981. pap. 5.95 (ISBN 0-8010-7712-5). Baker Bk.

Skoss, Solomon, ed. Hebrew-Arabic Dictionary of the Bible Known As Kitab Jami-Al-Alfaz, 2 vols. (Yale Oriental Researches Ser.: No. XX, XXI). 1945. 50.00x ea.; 95.00x set (ISBN 0-686-57837-6). Elliots Bks.

Stutchkoff, Nahum. Hebrew Thesaurus. 1968. 24.00 (ISBN 0-914080-40-7). Shulsinger Sales.

HEBREW LANGUAGE–DICTIONARIES–ENGLISH

Alcalay, Reuben. Complete English-Hebrew, Hebrew-English Dictionary, 3 vols. 7180p. 1980. Repr. of 1965 ed. 62.00 set (ISBN 0-89961-017-X). Vol. 1 (ISBN 0-89961-003-X). Vol. 2 (ISBN 0-89961-007-2). Vol. 3 (ISBN 0-89961-008-0). SBS Pub.

--The Massada English-Hebrew Student Dictionary. 734p. 1980. Repr. 18.95 (ISBN 0-89961-006-4). SBS Pub.

Armstrong, Terry, et al, eds. A Reader's Hebrew-English Lexicon of the Old Testament: (Genesis-Deuteronomy, Vol. 1. 1978. 9.95 (ISBN 0-310-37020-5). Zondervan.

Ben-Yehuda's English-Hebrew Hebrew-English Dictionary. (gr. 8-12). 1976. pap. 2.95 (ISBN 0-671-83358-8). PB.

Dov Ben Abba. The Signet Hebrew-English - English-Hebrew Dictionary. (Orig.). 1978. pap. 2.95 (ISBN 0-451-09654-1, E9654, Sig). NAL.

Ettinger, David. Hebrew-English Pictorial Dictionary. 22.50 (ISBN 0-87559-018-7). Shalom.

Furst, Gesenius. Hebrew-English Dictionary: Hebrew & Chaldee Lexicon to the Old Testament. rev. ed. Mitchell, Edward C., ed. 27.50 (ISBN 0-87559-021-7); thumb indexed 32.50 (ISBN 0-87559-022-5). Shalom.

Gesenius, William. Hebrew & Chaldee Lexicon, Tregelles Translation. 1949. 11.95 (ISBN 0-8028-8029-0). Eerdmans.

--Hebrew & English Lexicon to the Old Testament. 2nd ed. Brown, Francis, et al, eds. Robinson, Edward, tr. 1959. 29.95x (ISBN 0-19-864301-2). Oxford U Pr.

Goldberg, Nathan. New Functional Hebrew-English, English-Hebrew Dictionary. (gr. 9-12). 1958. 5.00x (ISBN 0-87068-379-9). Ktav.

--New Illustrated Hebrew-English Dictionary for Young Readers. (Illus.). (gr. 4-7). 1958. pap. 6.95x (ISBN 0-87068-370-5). Ktav.

Hebrew-Aramaic & Greek Dictionary: The New American Standard Exhaustive Concordance of the Bible. 34.95 (ISBN 0-87981-197-8, 4690-98). Holman.

Hebrew-English Lexicon. 6.95 (ISBN 0-310-20360-0, Pub. by Bagster). Zondervan.

Hebrew-English Lexicon of the Bible. LC 74-26705. 296p. (Orig.). 1975. pap. 6.50 (ISBN 0-8052-0481-4). Schocken.

Hebrew Pocket Dictionary. 10.00 (ISBN 0-685-12022-8). Heinman.

Sivan, Reuven & Levenston, Edward A. The New Bantam-Megiddo Hebrew & English Dictionary. LC 77-75289. 1977. 18.95 (ISBN 0-8052-3666-X). Schocken.

Waldstein, A. Hebrew-English, English-Hebrew Dictionary. 15.00 (ISBN 0-87559-016-0); thumb indexed 18.50 (ISBN 0-87559-017-9). Shalom.

Weinberg, W. How Do You Spell Chanukah? A General-Purpose Romanization of Hebrew for Speakers of English. (Bibliographica Judaica Ser: No. 5). 7.50x (ISBN 0-87820-903-4, HUC Pr). Ktav.

Young, Robert. Young's Analytical Concordance to the Bible. 1955. 19.95 (ISBN 0-8028-8084-3); deluxe ed. 22.95 (ISBN 0-8028-8085-1). Eerdmans.

HEBREW LANGUAGE–DICTIONARIES–GERMAN

Herstig, David. Deutsch-Hebraeisches Woerterbuch. (Ger. -Heb.). 1971. 17.50 (ISBN 3-19-006285-4, M-7330, Pub. by Max Hueber). French & Eur.

--Hebraeisch - Deutsches Woerterbuch. (Heb. & Ger.). 1971. 17.50 (ISBN 3-19-006289-7, M-7441, Pub. by Max Hueber). French & Eur.

Lavy, Jaacom. Langenscheidt's Hebrew-German Dictionary. 638p. 1978. 32.00 (ISBN 0-685-64071-X). Hippocrene Bks.

HEBREW LANGUAGE–EXAMINATIONS, QUESTIONS, ETC.

Rudman, Jack. Hebrew - Jr. & Sr. H.S. (Teachers License Examination Ser.: T-26). (Cloth bdg. avail. on rquest). pap. 10.00 (ISBN 0-8373-8026-X). Natl Learning.

HEBREW LANGUAGE–GLOSSARIES, VOCABULARIES, ETC.

Kushner, Lawrence. The Book of Letters. LC 75-9323. (Illus.). 64p. 1975. 9.95 (ISBN 0-06-064900-3, HarpR). Har-Row.

Landes, George M. Student's Vocabulary of Biblical Hebrew: Listed According to Frequency & Cognate. (Orig.). 1961. pap. text ed. 4.50x (ISBN 0-684-41323-X, ScribC). Scribner.

Payne, J. Barton. Hebrew Vocabularies. pap. 2.95 (ISBN 0-8010-6949-1). Baker Bk.

Watts, John D. Lists of Words Occurring Frequently in the Hebrew Bible. (Heb, & Eng). 1960. pap. 1.95 (ISBN 0-8028-1214-7). Eerdmans.

HEBREW LANGUAGE–GRAMMAR

Berman, Ruth A. Modern Hebrew Structure. LC 79-119963. 1979. 20.00x (ISBN 965-20-0024-8, Pub by Turtledove Pub Ltd Israel); pap. 16.00x (ISBN 0-686-66009-9). Intl Schol Bk Serv.

Blau, Joshua. A Grammar of Biblical Hebrew. LC 76-375136. 1976. pap. 42.50x (ISBN 3-447-01554-3). Intl Pubns Serv.

Chomsky, William. Hebrew: The Eternal Language. LC 57-8140. 1975. 4.95 (ISBN 0-8276-0077-1, 384). Jewish Pubn.

Davidson, A. B. An Introductory Hebrew Grammar, with Progressive Exercises in Reading & Writing. 26th ed. Mauchline, John, ed. 336p. 1976. Repr. of 1966 ed. text ed. 15.50x (ISBN 0-567-01005-8). Attic Pr.

Gesunius, William. Gesenius' Hebrew Grammar. 2nd ed. Kautzsch, E. & Cowley, A. E., eds. 1910. 25.00x (ISBN 0-19-815406-2). Oxford U Pr.

Greenberg, Moshe. Introduction to Hebrew. 1964. text ed. 15.95 (ISBN 0-13-484469-6). P-H.

Halkin, A. S. Two Hundred & One Hebrew Verbs Fully Conjugated in All the Forms. LC 70-102878. (Orig.). 1970. text ed. 10.50 (ISBN 0-8120-6061-X); pap. text ed. 5.50 (ISBN 0-8120-0331-4). Barron.

Harper, William R. Elements of Hebrew by an Inductive Method. LC 59-7625. (Midway Reprint Ser). 204p. 1974. pap. 6.00x (ISBN 0-226-31681-5). U of Chicago Pr.

--Introductory Hebrew: Method & Manual. rev. ed. Smith, James M., ed. LC 59-7624. (Midway Reprint Ser). 1974. pap. 6.00x (ISBN 0-226-31683-1). U of Chicago Pr.

Harris, R. Laird. Introductory Hebrew Grammar. pap. 3.95 (ISBN 0-8028-1100-0). Eerdmans.

Hebrew Verb Tables. Date not set. pap. 4.95 (ISBN 0-686-76516-8). Feldheim.

Horowitz, Edward. How the Hebrew Language Grew. rev. ed. 1967. 6.95 (ISBN 0-87068-066-8). Ktav.

Marks, John H. & Rogers, Virgil M. Beginner's Handbook to Biblical Hebrew. LC 58-7434. 1958. 9.50 (ISBN 0-687-02616-4). Abingdon.

Mauchline, John. A Key to the Exercises in the Introductory Hebrew Grammar. 146p. Repr. of 1967 ed. 13.50x (ISBN 0-567-01006-6). Attic Pr.

Segal, M. H. A Grammar of Mishnaic Hebrew. 1979. pap. text ed. 12.95x (ISBN 0-19-815454-2). Oxford U Pr.

Sellers, Ovid R. & Voigt, E. E. Biblical Hebrew for Beginners. 12th corr ed. 1963. pap. 2.95x (ISBN 0-8401-2163-6). Allenson-Breckinridge.

Simon, Ethelyn, et al. The First Hebrew Primer for Adults. (Orig.). 1981. pap. text ed. 14.95 (ISBN 0-939144-01-8). EKS Pub Co.

Weingreen, Jacob. Practical Grammar for Classical Hebrew. 2nd ed. 1959. 11.95x (ISBN 0-19-815422-4). Oxford U Pr.

Yates, Kyle M. Essentials of Biblical Hebrew. rev. ed. Owens, J. J., ed. 1955. 8.00x (ISBN 0-06-069710-5, HarpR). Har-Row.

HEBREW LANGUAGE–GRAMMAR, COMPARATIVE

Languages of the Pentatevch in Its Relation to Egyptian. Date not set. 27.50 (ISBN 0-686-76534-6). Feldheim.

HEBREW LANGUAGE–PROGRAMMED INSTRUCTION

Bridger, David. Programmed Hebrew Series, 2 vols. Incl. Vol. 1. 1971. pap. text ed. 2.50x (ISBN 0-87441-079-7); Vol. 2. 1971. pap. text ed. 2.50x (ISBN 0-87441-080-0). (Reshit Tefillah V'lashon). 62p. (Prog. Bk.). (YA) Behrman.

Chavez, Moises. Hebreo Biblico Juego De Dos Tomos, 2 vols. (Span., Vol. I - 568 pgs., Vol. II - 240 pgs.). pap. write for info. (ISBN 0-311-42070-2, Edit Mundo). Casa Bautista.

HEBREW LANGUAGE–READERS

Adler, L. W. & Castberg, C. Reading Hebrew. 1972. pap. 3.50x (ISBN 0-87441-042-8). Behrman.

Harper, William R. Introductory Hebrew: Method & Manual. rev. ed. Smith, James M., ed. LC 59-7624. (Midway Reprint Ser). 1974. pap. 6.00x (ISBN 0-226-31683-1). U of Chicago Pr.

Harvard University Library. Catalogue of Hebrew Books: Supplement I, 3 vols. LC 68-22416. 1972. Set. 170.00x (ISBN 0-674-10173-1). Harvard U Pr.

Koch, Anna P. Let's Read Hebrew. rev. ed. 1974. pap. 2.95x (ISBN 0-8197-0029-0). Bloch.

Kohlenberger, John R., ed. The NIV Triglot Old Testament. 1334p. 1981. 49.95 (ISBN 0-310-43820-9). Zondervan.

Rabin, Chaim. Hebrew. 1977. Repr. of 1949 ed. lib. bdg. 12.50 (ISBN 0-8492-2311-3). R West.

HEBREW LANGUAGE–SELF-INSTRUCTION

see also Hebrew Language–Conversation and Phrase Books

Carlson, E. Leslie. Elementary Hebrew. 1978. pap. 5.95 (ISBN 0-8010-2419-6). Baker Bk.

Goodrick, Ed. Do It Yourself in Hebrew & Greek with Cassette. 9.95 (ISBN 0-8423-0672-2). Tyndale.

Goodrick, Edward W. Do It Yourself Hebrew & Greek. 2nd ed. LC 79-25463. 1980. pap. text ed. 9.95 (ISBN 0-930014-35-9); with cassette 12.95 (ISBN 0-930014-42-1). Multnomah.

--Do It Yourself Hebrew & Greek: Everybody's Guide to the Language Tools. 256p. (Orig.). 1980. pap. 9.95 (ISBN 0-310-41741-4). Zondervan.

Harrison, Roland K. Teach Yourself Biblical Hebrew. (Teach Yourself Ser.). pap. 4.50 (ISBN 0-679-10180-2). McKay.

Levy, Harold. Hebrew for All. 260p. 1976. Repr. of 1970 ed. 12.50x (ISBN 0-85303-191-6, Pub. by Vallentine Mitchell England). Biblio Dist.

Living Hebrew for Spanish-Speaking People. 1959. 14.95, with 4 lp records conversation manual & dictionary (ISBN 0-517-50823-0). Crown.

Mansoor, Menahem. Biblical Hebrew Step by Step: A Significant Breakthrough for Learning Biblical Hebrew. 1978. pap. 9.95 (ISBN 0-8010-6041-9). Baker Bk.

Reif, Joseph A. & Levinson, Hanna. FSI Hebrew Basic Course. 1976. pap. text ed. 12.50x (ISBN 0-686-10730-6); 35 cassettes 210.00x (ISBN 0-686-10731-4). Intl Learn Syst.

--Spoken Modern Hebrew. (Spoken Language Ser.). 590p. 1980. pap. 10.00x (ISBN 0-87950-683-0); text & cassettes 170.00 (ISBN 0-87950-685-7); cassettes, 31 dual track 165.00x (ISBN 0-87950-684-9). Spoken Lang Serv.

Simon, Ethelyn, et al. Teach Yourself to Read Hebrew. (Orig.). 1981. pap. text ed. 2.95 (ISBN 0-939144-02-6). EKS Pub Co.

Steinberg, Samuel. Living Hebrew. (YA) (gr. 6-12). 1958. 14.95, with 4 lp records conversation manual & dictionary (ISBN 0-517-00133-0). Crown.

HEBREW LANGUAGE–SYNONYMS

Girdlestone, Robert B. Synonyms of the Old Testament. 1948. pap. 3.95 (ISBN 0-8028-1548-0). Eerdmans.

HEBREW LANGUAGE–SYNTAX

Andersen, Francis I. The Sentence in Biblical Hebrew. (Janua Linguarum, Ser. Practica: No. 231). 209p. 1974. pap. text ed. 34.10x (ISBN 90-2792-673-5). Mouton.

Cole, Peter, ed. Studies in Modern Hebrew Syntax & Semantics: Transformational Generative Approach. new ed. (North Holland Linguistics Ser.: Vol. 32). 1976. 22.00 (ISBN 0-7204-0543-2, North-Holland). Elsevier.

Davidson, A. B. Hebrew Syntax. 3rd ed. 248p. 1976. pap. text ed. 13.50x (ISBN 0-567-21007-3). Attic Pr.

HEBREW LANGUAGE–TEXTBOOKS FOR CHILDREN

Haramati, Schlomo. Alfon Ivri, a Hebrew Primer. (Illus.). 1979. pap. text ed. 3.95x (ISBN 0-87441-321-4). Behrman.

Kishon, Ephraim & Baron, Leora. Hebrew with Kishon. 200p. 1975. text ed. 5.00x (ISBN 0-88482-901-4). Hebrew Pub.

Lapine, Jennifer & Lapine, Susan. My First Hebrew Alphabet Book. (Illus.). 1977. 4.00 (ISBN 0-685-76975-5); pap. 2.95 (ISBN 0-8197-0399-0). Bloch.

Shumsky, Abraham & Shumsky, Adaia. Ahavat Chesed - Love Mercy: Reader. (Mah Tov Hebrew Teaching Ser.: Bk. 2). (Illus.). (gr. 4 up). 1970. text ed. 5.00 (ISBN 0-8074-0175-7, 405304); tchrs'. guide 3.50 (ISBN 0-8074-0176-5, 205305); wkbk. 3.50 (ISBN 0-8074-0177-3, 405303). UAHC.
--Alef-Bet: A Hebrew Primer. (Illus.). (gr. k-6). 1979. pap. text ed. 5.00 (ISBN 0-8074-0026-2, 405309). UAHC.
--Asot Mishpat. (Mah Tov Hebrew Teaching Ser.: Bk. 1). (Illus.). (gr. 4-8). 1969. text ed. 5.00 (ISBN 0-8074-0178-1, 405301); tchrs'. guide 3.50 (ISBN 0-8074-0179-X, 205302); wkbk. 3.50 (ISBN 0-8074-0180-3, 405300). UAHC.
Wengrov, Charles. The Hebrew Alef-Bet. (Illus.). (ps-3). pap. 0.99 (ISBN 0-914080-66-0). Shulsinger Sales.

HEBREW LAW
see Jewish Law

HEBREW LITERATURE
see also Apocalyptic Literature; Cabala; Rabbinical Literature; Talmud
Abbott, Lyman. The Life & Literature of the Ancient Hebrews. 1976. Repr. of 1901 ed. 39.00 (ISBN 0-403-05671-3, Regency). Scholarly.
Bleiweiss, Robert M., ed. Torah at Brandeis Institute: The Layman Expounds. LC 76-7776. 1976. 8.95 (ISBN 0-916952-00-2). Brandeis-Bardin Inst.
Clay, Albert T. Hebrew Deluge Story. (Yale Oriental Researches Ser.: No. V, Pt. III). 1922. 19.50x (ISBN 0-685-69802-5). Elliots Bks.
Fishbane, Michael. Text & Texture: Close Readings of Selected Biblical Passages. LC 79-14083. 1979. text ed. 12.95x (ISBN 0-8052-3724-0). Schocken.
Gaster, Moses. Studies & Texts in Folklore, Magic, Medieval Romance, Hebrew Apocrypha & Samaritan Archaeology, 3 Vols. rev. ed. 1970. Set. 45.00x (ISBN 0-87068-056-0). Ktav.
Guber, Rivka. Village of the Brothers. LC 78-54568. (Illus.). 1979. 10.00 (ISBN 0-88400-059-1). Shengold.
Kaplan, Aryeh, tr. The Bahir. 1979. 15.00 (ISBN 0-87728-343-5). Weiser.
Kee, Howard C. The Origins of Christianity: Sources & Documents. LC 73-4830. 320p. 1973. 10.95 (ISBN 0-13-642553-4). P-H.
Lowy, Albert & Society of Hebrew Literature, eds. Miscellany of Hebrew Literature, 2 vols, Pt. 1. LC 72-97298. (Repr. of 1872-77 Ed.). lib. bdg. 24.50x (ISBN 0-8371-4623-2, LOMH). Greenwood.
Mansoor, Menahem. Modern Hebrew Literature Reader for Advanced Students, 2 vols. 1971. Vol. 1. 8.95x (ISBN 0-685-27920-0); Vol. 2. 8.95x (ISBN 0-685-27921-9). Ktav.
Pearl, Chaim & Brookes, Reuben. The Guide to Jewish Knowledge. rev. ed. LC 75-187866. 123p. 1973. 4.95 (ISBN 0-87677-046-4). Hartmore.

HEBREW LITERATURE–BIBLIOGRAPHY
Adler, Elkan N. About Hebrew Manuscripts. LC 78-136769. (Illus.). 1971. Repr. of 1905 ed. 12.50 (ISBN 0-87203-025-3). Hermon.
Berlin, Charles. Hebrew Printing & Bibliography. 1973. 50.00x (ISBN 0-87068-204-0). Ktav.
Fletcher, Harris F. Milton's Rabbinical Readings. LC 67-30701. 1967. Repr. of 1930 ed. 8.50 (ISBN 0-87752-034-8). Gordian.
--Milton's Rabbinical Readings. 1967. Repr. of 1930 ed. 19.50 (ISBN 0-208-00335-5, Archon). Shoe String.
Harvard University Library. Catalogue of Hebrew Books: Supplement I, 3 vols. LC 68-22416. 1972. Set. 170.00x (ISBN 0-674-10173-1). Harvard U Pr.
Steinschneider, Moritz. Die Geschichtsliteratur der Juden. Katz, Steven, ed. LC 79-7153. (Jewish Philosophy, Mysticism & History of Ideas Ser.). 1980. Repr. of 1905 ed. lib. bdg. 14.00x (ISBN 0-405-12290-X). Arno.
Zeitlin, William & Katz, Steven, eds. Bibliotheca Hebraica Post-Mendelssohniana. LC 79-7154. (Jewish Philosophy, Mysticism & History of Ideas Ser.). 1980. Repr. of 1895 ed. lib. bdg. 39.00x (ISBN 0-405-12291-8). Arno.

HEBREW LITERATURE–HISTORY AND CRITICISM
Abrahams, Israel. By-Paths in Hebraic Bookland. LC 77-174368. Repr. of 1920 ed. 15.00 (ISBN 0-405-08177-4, Pub by Blom Publications). Arno.
Bloch, Joshua, et al. Hebrew Printing & Bibliography. Berlin, Charles, ed. LC 72-12075. (Illus.). 1976. text ed. 35.00 (ISBN 0-87104-515-X, Co-Pub by Ktav). NY Pub Lib.
Bridger, David. Hebrew & Heritage, 4 vols. LC 75-1812. (Illus.). 1976. Vol. I. pap. 2.95x (ISBN 0-87441-254-4); Vol. II. pap. 2.95x (ISBN 0-87441-252-8); Vol. III. pap. 2.95x (ISBN 0-87441-259-5); Vol. IV. pap. 2.95x (ISBN 0-87441-274-9). Behrman.
Burke, David G., ed. The Poetry of Baruch: A Reconstruction & Analysis of the Original Hebrew Text of Baruch 3: 9-5: 9. LC 80-10271. (Society of Biblical Literature, Septuagint & Cognate Studies: No. 10). pap. write for info. (ISBN 0-89130-382-0). Scholars Pr CA.
Driver, S. R. Introduction to the Literature of the Old Testament. 8.50 (ISBN 0-8446-1998-1). Peter Smith.
Edelmann, Martin & Schmelzer, Menahem, eds. The Damascus Bible, Vol. 1, Pt. 1. Orig. Title: Early Hebrew Manuscripts in Facsimile. 1979. text ed. 5.28 (ISBN 0-8018-1337-9); pap. text ed. 4.95 (ISBN 0-8018-1349-2). Johns Hopkins.
Fischman, Naomi. Western & Eastern Cultures Reflected in Modern Hebrew Literature. 124p. 1976. text ed. 7.95 (ISBN 0-8197-0478-4, A716647). Bloch.
Fletcher, Harris F. Milton's Rabbinical Readings. LC 67-30701. 1967. Repr. of 1930 ed. 8.50 (ISBN 0-87752-034-8). Gordian.
--Milton's Rabbinical Readings. 1967. Repr. of 1930 ed. 19.50 (ISBN 0-208-00335-5, Archon). Shoe String.
Golb, Norman & Pritsak, Omeljan. Khazarian Hebrew Documents of the Tenth Century. 1981. 25.00 (ISBN 0-8014-1221-8). Cornell U Pr.
Kersten, John C. Understanding Hebrew Literature: A Guide to a Better Understanding of the Bible As a Source Book for the Humanities. 2.25 (ISBN 0-686-14328-0, 145/04). Catholic Bk Pub.
Kravitz, Nathaniel. Three Thousand Years of Hebrew Literature: From the Earliest Time Through the 20th Century. LC 73-150752. 586p. 1971. 20.00 (ISBN 0-8040-0505-2); limited ed. 50.00 (ISBN 0-8040-0728-4). Swallow.
Mullen, E. Theodore, Jr. The Assembly of the Gods: The Divine Council in Canaanite & Hebrew Literature. LC 80-10128. (Harvard Semitic Museum Monographs: No. 24). 10.50x (ISBN 0-89130-380-4, 04 00 24). Scholars Pr CA.
Pardee, Dennis. Handbook of Ancient Hebrew Letters. LC 79-22372. (Society of Biblical Literature, Sources for Biblical Study: 15). Date not set. pap. price not set (ISBN 0-89130-360-X). Scholars Pr CA.
Popper, William. Censorship of Hebrew Books. rev. ed. LC 68-19728. (Illus.). 1969. Repr. of 1899 ed. 12.50x (ISBN 0-87068-120-6). Ktav.
Rosner, Joseph. The Story of the Writings. Borowitz, Eugene B., ed. LC 78-116680. (Illus.). 159p. (gr. 6-7). 1975. pap. text ed. 4.95x (ISBN 0-87441-229-3). Behrman.
Shepard, Sanford. Shem Tov: His World & His Words. LC 76-62685. (Coleccion De Estudios Hispanicos). 1978. pap. 9.95 (ISBN 0-89729-189-1). Ediciones.
Silberschlag, Eisig. From Renaissance to Renaissance: Hebrew Literature 1492-1967, Vol. I. 1972. 25.00x (ISBN 0-87068-184-2). Ktav.
Slouschz, Nahum. The Renascence of Hebrew Literature. 1973. Repr. of 1909 ed. 35.00 (ISBN 0-8274-0897-8). R West.
Wacholder, Ben Z. Eupolemus: A Study of Graeco-Judean Literature. 1974. 20.00x (ISBN 0-87820-401-6). Ktav.
Yalon, Reuven. He & She; the Chocolate. (Illus.). 1972. pap. 0.60 (ISBN 0-912022-19-1). EMC.
--Hungry Dan; Lemech, the Soldier. (Illus.). 1972. pap. 0.60 (ISBN 0-912022-21-3). EMC.
--Package, a Package; Halot & Candles for the Sabbath. (Illus.). 1972. pap. 0.60 (ISBN 0-912022-18-3). EMC.
--Where from; Hello; So Long. (Illus.). 1972. pap. 0.60 (ISBN 0-912022-16-7). EMC.

HEBREW LITERATURE–TRANSLATIONS INTO ENGLISH
Leviant, Curt. Masterpieces of Hebrew Literature: A Treasury of Two Thousand Years of Jewish Creativity. 1969. pap. 9.95 (ISBN 0-87068-079-X). Ktav.
Neusner, Jacob. The Tosefta, Translated from the Hebrew: Pt. III Nashim. The Order of Women. 35.00x (ISBN 0-87068-684-4). Ktav.
Tronik, Ruth. Israeli Periodicals & Serials in English & Other European Languages: A Classified Bibliography. LC 73-14901. 1974. 10.00 (ISBN 0-8108-0682-7). Scarecrow.

HEBREW LITERATURE, MODERN–BIBLIOGRAPHY
Goell, Yohai. Bibliography of Modern Hebrew Literature in English Translation. 1969. 15.00x (ISBN 0-87068-062-5). Ktav.
--Bibliography of Modern Hebrew Literature in English Translation. 132p. 1968. casebound 14.95 (ISBN 0-87855-187-5). Transaction Bks.

HEBREW LITERATURE, MODERN–HISTORY AND CRITICISM
Epstein, George L. & Zeldner, Max. Modern Hebrew Literature. 257p. 1965. 4.95x (ISBN 0-88482-668-6). Hebrew Pub.
Halkin, Simon. Modern Hebrew Literature: From the Enlightenment to the Birth of the State of Israel: Trends & Values. LC 71-110610. 1970. pap. 3.75 (ISBN 0-8052-0252-8). Schocken.
Klausner, Joseph. A History of Modern Hebrew Literature, 1785-1930. Simon, Leon, ed. Danby, Herbert, tr. from Heb. LC 79-97289. 204p. 1972. Repr. of 1932 ed. lib. bdg. 15.00x (ISBN 0-8371-2612-6, KLHL). Greenwood.
Popper, William. Censorship of Hebrew Books. (Judaica Ser.: No. 6). (Illus.). Repr. of 1899 ed. 11.50 (ISBN 0-8337-2809-1). B Franklin.
Rabinovich, Isaiah. Major Trends in Modern Hebrew Fiction. Rosten, M., tr. LC 68-15035. 1968. 17.00x (ISBN 0-226-70132-8). U of Chicago Pr.
Stern, Nathan. The Jewish Historico-Critical School of the Nineteenth Century. LC 73-2228. (The Jewish People; History, Religion, Literature). Repr. of 1901 ed. 12.00 (ISBN 0-405-05289-8). Arno.
Waldstein, Abraham S. Evolution of Modern Hebrew Literature, 1850-1912. LC 16-7654. (Columbia University. Oriental Studies: No. 9). Repr. of 1916 ed. 15.25 (ISBN 0-404-50499-X). AMS Pr.

HEBREW PHILOLOGY
Ben Horin, Meir. Studies & Essays in Honor of Abraham A. Neuman. 1962. 35.00x (ISBN 0-685-13745-7, Pub. by Dropsie U Pr). Ktav.
Miller, Edward F. Influence of Gesenius on Hebrew Lexicography. LC 28-3581. (Columbia University. Contributions to Oriental History & Philology: No. 11). Repr. of 1927 ed. 14.00 (ISBN 0-404-50541-4). AMS Pr.

HEBREW POETRY
Brooke, Avery, ed. The Vineyard Bible: A Central Narrative & Index. 416p. 1980. 12.95 (ISBN 0-8164-0144-6). Seabury.
Carmi, T. The Penguin Book of Hebrew Verse. 1981. 25.00 (ISBN 0-670-36507-6). Viking Pr.
Meyer, F. B. Great Verses Through the Bible. 13.95 (ISBN 0-310-29130-5). Zondervan.
Schwartz, Benjamin & Athanassakis, Apostolos N., eds. The Judaeo-Greek Hymns of Jannina. Schwartz, Benjamin & Athanassakis, Apostolos N., trs. Date not set. price not set (ISBN 0-918618-06-1). Pella Pub.

HEBREW POETRY (COLLECTIONS)
Boerman, Vernon, ed. Poetry of the Bible. LC 77-86038. (Illus., Orig.). (gr. 10-12). pap. text ed. 3.50 (ISBN 0-932816-08-8). Lit Bible.
Carmi, T., ed. The Penguin Book of Hebrew Verse. 448p. (Orig., Hebrew & Eng.). 1981. pap. 9.95 (ISBN 0-14-042197-1). Penguin.
Davidson, Israel. Thesaurus of Medieval Hebrew Poetry, 4 Vols. rev. ed. (Library of Jewish Classics). 1970. Set. 150.00x (ISBN 0-87068-003-X). Ktav.
Lasker-Schuler, Else. Hebrew Ballads & Other Poems. Durchslang, A. & Litman-Demeestere, J., trs. LC 80-13282. (Jewish Poetry Ser.). 103p. 1981. 10.95 (ISBN 0-8276-0179-4); pap. 6.95 (ISBN 0-8276-0180-8, 459). Jewish Pubn.
Mintz, Ruth F. Modern Hebrew Poetry: A Bilingual Anthology. 1966. pap. 3.95 (ISBN 0-520-00868-5, CAL165). U of Cal Pr.
Weinberger, Leon J. Anthology of Hebrew Poetry in Greece, Anatolia & the Balkans. LC 75-34119. 270p. 1975. pap. 15.00 (ISBN 0-8173-8525-8). U of Ala Pr.

HEBREW POETRY–HISTORY AND CRITICISM
Freedman, D. N. Pottery, Poetry, & Prophecy: Studies in Hebrew Poetry. 1980. text ed. 15.00x (ISBN 0-931464-04-8). Eisenbrauns.
Geller, Stephen A. Parallelism in Early Biblical Poetry. LC 78-27255. (Harvard Semitic Monographs: No. 20). 1979. 12.00 (ISBN 0-89130-275-1, 040020). Scholars Pr Ca.
Gevirtz, Stanley. Patterns of Early Poetry of Israel. 2nd ed. 1973. pap. 7.50x (ISBN 0-226-62405-6, SAOC 32). U of Chicago Pr.
Gray, G. B. Forms of Hebrew Poetry. rev. ed. (Library of Biblical Studies). 1970. 16.95x (ISBN 0-87068-064-1). Ktav.
Helprin, Michael. The Historical Poetry of the Ancient Hebrews, 2 vols. 200.00 (ISBN 0-8490-0310-5). Gordon Pr.
Kugel, James L. The Idea of Biblical Poetry: Parallelism & Its History. LC 80-25227. 320p. 1981. 27.50x (ISBN 0-300-02474-6). Yale U Pr.
O'Connor, Michael. Hebrew Verse Structure. 1980. 15.00x (ISBN 0-931464-02-1). Eisenbrauns.
Robinson, Theodore H. The Poetry of the Old Testament. LC 75-41233. Repr. of 1947 ed. 15.00 (ISBN 0-404-14593-0). AMS Pr.
Smith, George A. The Early Poetry of Israel in Its Physical & Social Origins. LC 77-26078. 1977. Repr. of 1912 ed. lib. bdg. 15.00 (ISBN 0-8414-7872-4). Folcroft.
Taylor, Isaac. Spirit of Hebrew Poetry. LC 74-30247. (Studies in Poetry, No. 38). 1974. lib. bdg. 56.95 (ISBN 0-8383-1988-2). Haskell.
White, John B. A Study of the Language of Love in the Song of Songs & Ancient Egyptian Poetry. LC 77-13399. (Society of Biblical Literature. Dissertation Ser.: Vol. 38). 1978. pap. 7.50 (ISBN 0-89130-192-5, 060138). Scholars Pr Ca.
Yoder, Sanford C. Poetry of the Old Testament. 1948. pap. 7.95 (ISBN 0-8361-1709-3). Herald Pr.

HEBREW POETRY–TRANSLATIONS INTO ENGLISH
Frank, Bernhard, tr. from Heb. & intro. by. Modern Hebrew Poetry. LC 80-20037. (Iowa Translations Ser.). 240p. 1980. text ed. 15.00x (ISBN 0-87745-106-0); pap. 9.95 (ISBN 0-87745-107-9). U of Iowa Pr.
Mezey, Robert, ed. Poems from the Hebrew. LC 75-132299. (Poems of the World Ser.). (Illus.). 156p. (gr. 9-12). 1973. 8.95 (ISBN 0-690-63685-7, TYC-J). Har-Row.
Mintz, Ruth F. Modern Hebrew Poetry: A Bilingual Anthology. 1966. pap. 3.95 (ISBN 0-520-00868-5, CAL165). U of Cal Pr.

HEBREW PRIMERS
see Hebrew Language–Textbooks for Children

HEBREW THEATER
see Theater–Jews

HEBREW WIT AND HUMOR
see also Jewish Wit and Humor
Chotzner, J. Hebrew Humour & Other Essays. 1979. Repr. of 1905 ed. lib. bdg. 20.00 (ISBN 0-8414-9985-3). Folcroft.
--Hebrew Humour & Other Essays. 1977. Repr. of 1905 ed. lib. bdg. 25.00 (ISBN 0-8495-0703-0). Arden Lib.
Israel: Wit & Wisdom. 1969. 2.95 (ISBN 0-442-82273-1). Peter Pauper.

HEBREWS
see Jews

HEBRIDES
Cooper, D. Hebridean Connection. (Illus.). 1977. 14.95 (ISBN 0-7100-8484-6). Routledge & Kegan.
Darling, F. F. Naturalist on Rona: Essays of a Biologist in Isolation. LC 42-5414. Repr. of 1939 ed. 10.00 (ISBN 0-527-21400-0). Kraus Repr.
Knowlton, Derrick. Naturalist in the Hebrides. 1977. 8.95 (ISBN 0-7153-7446-X). David & Charles.
McKay, Margaret M. The Rev. Dr. John Walker's Report on the Hebrides of 1764 to 1771. 263p. 1980. text ed. 39.00x (ISBN 0-85976-043-X). Humanities.

HEBRIDES–DESCRIPTION AND TRAVEL
Banks, Noel. Six Inner Hebrides. 1977. 16.95 (ISBN 0-7153-7368-4). David & Charles.
Boswell, James. Boswell's Journal of a Tour to the Hebrides with Samuel Johnson. (Oxford Standard Authors Ser.). 1970. pap. 8.95x (ISBN 0-19-281072-3, OPB). Oxford U Pr.
--The Journal of a Tour to the Hebrides with Samuel Johnson. Powell, Lawrence F., ed. 1957. 9.95x (ISBN 0-460-00387-9, Evman). Biblio Dist.
Cooper, Derek. Road to the Isles: Travellers in the Hebrides, 1770-1914. 1979. 18.00 (ISBN 0-7100-0256-4). Routledge & Kegan.
Johnson, Samuel & Boswell, James. A Journey to the Western Islands of Scotland. Wendt, Allan, ed. Bd. with The Journal of a Tour to the Hebrides. LC 66-175. (YA) (gr. 9 up). 1965. pap. 3.95 (ISBN 0-395-05181-9, B86, RivEd, 3-47720). HM.
Simpson, W. Douglas. Portrait of Skye & the Outer Hebrides. LC 67-74411. (Portrait Bks.). 1967. 12.50x (ISBN 0-7091-0650-5). Intl Pubns Serv.
Thompson, Francis. The Uists & Barra. LC 74-81056. (Islands Ser). (Illus.). 192p. 1974. 16.95 (ISBN 0-7153-6676-9). David & Charles.
Weir, Tom. Scottish Islands. LC 76-8618. (Leisure & Travel Ser.). (Illus.). 128p. 1976. 7.50 (ISBN 0-7153-7214-9). David & Charles.

HEBRIDES–HISTORY
Sillar, F. C. & Meyler, Ruth. Skye. (Islands Ser). (Illus.). 248p. pap. 10.50 (ISBN 0-7153-5751-4). David & Charles.
Thompson, Francis. Highlands & Islands. LC 74-181926. (Illus.). 315p. 1974. 15.00x (ISBN 0-7091-4576-4). Intl Pubns Serv.
Walker, John. Report on the Hebrides Seventeen Sixty-Four. McKay, Margaret, ed. 1980. text ed. 39.00x (ISBN 0-85976-043-X). Humanities.

HEBRIDES–SOCIAL LIFE AND CUSTOMS
Brown, Jean. A Song to Sing & a Tale to Tell. 174p. 1980. 14.95 (ISBN 0-906191-43-2, Pub. by Thule Pr England). Intl Schol Bk Serv.

HECIA (SHIP)
Parry, William E. Journal of a Second Voyage for the Discovery of a Northwest Passage from the Atlantic to the Pacific. Repr. of 1824 ed. lib. bdg. 34.00x (ISBN 0-8371-1448-9, PASV). Greenwood.

--Journal of a Voyage for the Discovery of a Northwest Passage from the Atlantic to the Pacific, Performed in the Years 1819-20. LC 68-55209. 1968. Repr. of 1821 ed. lib. bdg. 28.50x (ISBN 0-8371-0608-7, PANP). Greenwood.

HECKER, ISAAC THOMAS, 1819-1888

Elliott, Walter. The Life of Father Hecker. LC 75-38446. (Religion in America, Ser. 2). 456p. 1972. Repr. of 1891 ed. 23.00 (ISBN 0-405-04065-2). Arno.

Farina, John. An American Experience of God: The Spirituality of Isaac Hecker. LC 81-80875. 240p. 1981. 11.95 (ISBN 0-8091-0321-4). Paulist Pr.

Holden, Vincent F. The Early Years of Isaac Thomas Hecker (1819-1844) LC 73-3583. (Catholic University of America. Studies in American Church History: No. 29). Repr. of 1939 ed. 22.00 (ISBN 0-404-57779-2). AMS Pr.

McSorley, Joseph. Isaac Hecker & His Friends. 1972. pap. 1.45 (ISBN 0-8091-1605-7). Paulist Pr.

HEDGEHOGS

Griffiths, G. D. Mattie: The Story of a Hedgehog. LC 76-47240. (gr. 3-6). 1977. 5.95 (ISBN 0-440-05490-7); PLB 5.47 (ISBN 0-440-05491-5). Delacorte.

Poduschka, Walter & Poduschka, Christl. Dearest Prickles: The Story of a Hedgehog Family. LC 72-2182. (Illus.). 128p. 1972. 6.50 (ISBN 0-8008-2124-6). Taplinger.

HEDGES

see also Fences; Shrubs

Howland, Joseph E. How to Select & Care for Shrubs & Hedges. Ortho Books Editorial Staff, ed. LC 80-66346. (Illus.). 96p. (Orig.). 1981. pap. 4.95 (ISBN 0-917102-88-6). Ortho.

Jennings, Terry. The World of a Hedge. (Illus.). 128p. 1978. 8.95 (ISBN 0-571-11179-3, Pub. by Faber & Faber). Merrimack Bk Serv.

Pollard, E., et al. Hedges. LC 75-5816. (New Naturalist Ser). (Illus.). 256p. 1974. text ed. 14.95x (ISBN 0-8008-3828-9). Taplinger.

HEDONISM

see also Altruism; Egoism; Happiness; Pleasure; Self-Interest; Utilitarianism

Edwards, Rem B. Pleasures & Pains: A Theory of Qualitative Hedonism. LC 79-4168. 1979. 15.00x (ISBN 0-8014-1241-2). Cornell U Pr.

Gosling, J. C. Pleasure & Desire: The Case for Hedonism Reviewed. 1969. 32.00x (ISBN 0-19-824339-1). Oxford U Pr.

Powys, Llewelyn. Rats in the Sacristy. facs. ed. LC 67-30226. (Essay Index Reprint Ser). 1937. 15.00 (ISBN 0-8369-0798-1). Arno.

Sedgwick, Henry D. Art of Happiness or the Teachings of Epicurus. LC 70-117841. (Essay Index Reprint Ser). 1933. 15.00 (ISBN 0-8369-1814-2). Arno.

HEERMANN, JOHANN, 1585-1647

Hitzeroth, C. Johann Heermann, 1585-1647. 1907. pap. 7.00 (ISBN 0-384-23490-9). Johnson Repr.

HEGEL, GEORG WILHELM FRIEDRICH, 1770-1831

Althusser, Louis. Politics & History: Montesquieu, Rousseau, Hegel, Marx. 1978. pap. 5.50 (ISBN 0-902308-96-3, Pub by NLB). Schocken.

Angehrn, Emil. Freiheit und System Bei Hegel. 1977. 73.00x (ISBN 3-11-006969-5). De Gruyter.

Avineri, Shlomo. Hegel's Theory of the Modern State. LC 70-186254. (Cambridge Studies in the History & Theory of Politics Ser.). 266p. 1973. 32.50 (ISBN 0-521-08513-6); pap. 8.95x (ISBN 0-521-09832-7). Cambridge U Pr.

Beach, Edward. Dance of the Dialectic: A Dramatic Dialogue Presenting Hegel's Philosophy of Religion. LC 78-63255. pap. text ed. 5.50 (ISBN 0-8191-0615-1). U Pr of Amer.

Bryant, William M. Hegel's Educational Idea. 1896. 8.00 (ISBN 0-403-00005-X). Scholarly.

--Hegel's Educational Ideas. LC 72-136415. Repr. of 1896 ed. 14.00 (ISBN 0-404-01144-6). AMS Pr.

Butler, Clark. G. W. F. Hegel. (World Authors Ser.: Germany: No. 461). 1977. lib. bdg. 12.50 (ISBN 0-8057-6298-1). Twayne.

Caird, Edward. Hegel. LC 71-181924. (BCL Ser. I). Repr. of 1883 ed. 16.50 (ISBN 0-404-01362-7). AMS Pr.

Chiodi, Pietro. Sartre & Marxism. Soper, Kate, tr. from It. (European Philosophy & the Human Sciences Ser.). 1976. text ed. 26.25x (ISBN 0-391-00590-1); pap. text ed. 10.50x (ISBN 0-391-00886-2). Humanities.

Colletti, Lucio. Marxism & Hegel. 1979. 20.00x (ISBN 0-86091-715-0, Pub. by NLB); pap. 7.95 (ISBN 0-686-67432-4). Schocken.

Cook, Daniel. Language in the Philosophy of Hegel. (Janua Linguarum, Ser. Minor: No. 135). 198p. (Orig.). 1973. pap. text ed. 28.75x (ISBN 90-2792-402-3). Mouton.

Cooper, Rebecca. The Logical Influence of Hegel on Marx. 1974. lib. bdg. 75.00 (ISBN 0-8490-0550-7). Gordon Pr.

Crites, Stephen. In the Twilight of Christendom: Hegel Vs. Kierkegaard on Faith & History. LC 77-188905. (American Academy of Religion. Studies in Religion). 1972. pap. text ed. 7.50 (ISBN 0-89130-154-2, 010002). Scholars Pr Ca.

Croce, Benedetto. Ce qui est vivant et Ce qui est morte De la philosophie De Hegel: Etude Critique Suivie d,un Essai De Bibliographie Hegelienne. Buriot, Henri, tr. from Ital. (Reprints in Philosophy Ser.). (Fr.). Repr. of 1910 ed. lib. bdg. 24.00x (ISBN 0-697-00051-6). Irvington.

Cullen, Bernard. Hegel's Social & Political Thought. LC 79-10730. 1979. 19.95x (ISBN 0-312-36674-4). St Martin.

Degrood, David. Dialectics & Revolution. (Philosophical Currents Ser.: No. 25). 1980. pap. text ed. 27.50x (ISBN 9-0603-2154-5). Humanities.

Drue, Hermann. Psychologie Aus Dem Begriff. 1976. 77.25 (ISBN 3-11-004603-2). De Gruyter.

Dunning, Stephen N. The Tongues of Men. LC 79-10729. (American Academy of Religion, Dissertation Ser.: No. 27). 1979. 12.00 (ISBN 0-89130-283-2, 010127); pap. 7.50 (ISBN 0-89130-302-2). Scholars Pr Ca.

Easton, Loyd D. Hegel's First American Followers: The Ohio Hegelians. LC 66-20062. ix, 353p. 1966. 17.00 (ISBN 0-8214-0026-6). Ohio U Pr.

Elder, Crawford. Appropriating Hegel. Brennan, Andrew & Lyons, William, eds. (Scots Philosophical Monographs: Vol. 3). 116p. 1980. 12.00 (ISBN 0-08-025729-1). Pergamon.

Findlay, J. N. Hegel: A Re-Examination. LC 76-12155. 366p. 1976. pap. 4.95 (ISBN 0-19-519879-4, 473, GB). Oxford U Pr.

Flaccus, Louis W. Artists & Thinkers. facs. ed. LC 67-23218. (Essay Index Reprint Ser). 1916. 15.00 (ISBN 0-8369-0444-3). Arno.

Gadamer, Hans-Georg. Hegel's Dialectic: Five Hermeneutical Studies. Smith, P. Christopher, tr. LC 75-18171. 130p. 1976. 12.50x (ISBN 0-300-01909-2). Yale U Pr.

Harris, H. S. Hegel's Development: Toward the Sunlight, 1770-1801. 606p. 1972. text ed. 48.00x (ISBN 0-19-824358-8). Oxford U Pr.

Harris, William T. Hegel's Doctrine of Reflection. LC 75-3160. Repr. of 1881 ed. 22.50 (ISBN 0-404-59165-5). AMS Pr.

Hartmann, Klaus. Sartre's Ontology: A Study of Being & Nothingness in the Light of Hegel's Logic. (Studies in Phenomenology & Existential Philosophy Ser). 1966. 15.95x (ISBN 0-8101-0115-7); pap. 6.95x (ISBN 0-8101-0610-8). Northwestern U Pr.

Hegel. The Essential Writings. Weiss, Frederick G., ed. 7.50 (ISBN 0-8446-5198-2). Peter Smith.

Hegel, G. W. The Difference Between the Fichtean & Schellingian Systems of Philosophy. Surber, Jere P., tr. from Ger. 1978. pap. text ed. 6.50x (ISBN 0-917930-12-6); lib. bdg. 21.00 (ISBN 0-917930-32-0). Ridgeview.

--The Essential Writings. Weiss, Frederick G., ed. 1974. pap. 7.50x (ISBN 0-06-131831-0, TB1831, Torch). Har-Row.

--Hegel: Phenomenology of Spirit. Miller, A. V. & Findlay, J. N., trs. 1977. 29.50x (ISBN 0-19-824530-0). Oxford U Pr.

--Hegel's System of Ethical Life & First Philosophy of Spirit. Harris, H. S. & Knox, T. M., eds. LC 79-11477. 1979. 26.50 (ISBN 0-87395-386-X). State U NY Pr.

Hegel, Georg W. The Ethics of Hegel. Sterret, James M., tr. 1976. lib. bdg. 59.95 (ISBN 0-8490-1791-2). Gordon Pr.

--Hegel's Doctrine of Reflection. Harris, William T., tr. 1976. lib. bdg. 59.95 (ISBN 0-8490-1936-2). Gordon Pr.

--Hegel's First Principle. Harris, William T., tr. 1976. lib. bdg. 59.95 (ISBN 0-8490-1937-0). Gordon Pr.

--Hegel's Philosophy of Mind. Wallace, William, tr. 1976. lib. bdg. 59.95 (ISBN 0-8490-1938-9). Gordon Pr.

--The Introduction to Hegel's Philosophy of Fine Art. Bosanquet, Bernard, tr. 1976. lib. bdg. 59.95 (ISBN 0-8490-2066-2). Gordon Pr.

--The Metaphysical Vision of the Roman World. (Essential Library of the Great Philosophers). (Illus.). 121p. 1980. deluxe ed. 49.85 (ISBN 0-89266-265-4). Am Classical Coll Pr.

Hegel Society of America Conference, 1976. Hegel's Social & Political Thought: The Philosophy of Objective Spirit Proceedings of the 1976th Hegel Society of America. Verene, Donald P., ed. LC 77-26183. 250p. 1980. text ed. 17.50x (ISBN 0-391-00543-X). Humanities.

Heiss, Robert. Hegel, Kierkegaard, Marx. 448p. 1975. pap. 3.95 (ISBN 0-440-53529-8, Delta). Dell.

Hook, Sidney. From Hegel to Marx: Studies in the Intellectual Development of Karl Marx. 1962. pap. 4.95 (ISBN 0-472-06066-X, 66, AA). U of Mich Pr.

Hyppolite, Jean. Genesis & Structure of Hegel's Phenomenology of Spirit. Cherniak, Samuel & Heckman, John, trs. from Fr. LC 73-94431. (Studies in Phenomenology & Existential Philosophy). 1974. text ed. 26.95x (ISBN 0-8101-0594-2); pap. 11.95x (ISBN 0-686-67046-9). Northwestern U Pr.

--Studies on Marx & Hegel. O'Neill, John, tr. LC 70-77231. 1969. 7.50x (ISBN 0-465-08284-X). Basic.

Idea y Figura (el Concepto Hegeliano Del Arte) LC 78-15075. 1979. pap. 6.25 (ISBN 0-8477-2819-6). U of PR Pr.

Kainz, Howard P. Hegel's Phenomenology Pt. 1: Analysis & Commentary. LC 73-22587. (Studies in the Humanities: No. 12). 224p. 1976. pap. 6.95 (ISBN 0-8173-6618-0). U of Ala Pr.

Kaminsky, Jack. Hegel on Art: An Interpretation of Hegel's Aesthetics. LC 61-14335. 1962. 14.00 (ISBN 0-87395-007-0); pap. 7.95 (ISBN 0-87395-065-8); microfiche 17.00 (ISBN 0-87395-107-7). State U NY Pr.

Kaufmann, Walter. Discovering the Mind, Vol. 1: Goethe, Kant, & Hegel. LC 79-18004. 1980. 14.95 (ISBN 0-07-033311-4). McGraw.

--Hegel: A Reinterpretation. LC 77-89765. 1978. text ed. 12.95x (ISBN 0-268-01070-6); pap. text ed. 6.95x (ISBN 0-268-01068-4). U of Notre Dame Pr.

Kaufmann, Walter, ed. Hegel's Political Philosophy. LC 79-105606. (Controversy Ser). 179p. 1970. text ed. 9.95x (ISBN 0-202-24077-0); pap. text ed. 3.95x (ISBN 0-202-24078-9). Lieber-Atherton.

Kelly, George A. Hegel's Retreat from Eleusis: Studies in Political Thought. LC 77-85542. 1978. text ed. 19.00 (ISBN 0-691-07589-1). Princeton U Pr.

--Idealism, Politics & History. LC 72-85721. (Studies in the History & Theory of Politics). 1969. 34.50 (ISBN 0-521-07510-6). Cambridge U Pr.

Knox, Israel. Aesthetic Theories of Kant, Hegel & Schopenhauer. 1978. Repr. of 1936 ed. text ed. 12.50x (ISBN 0-391-00929-X). Humanities.

Laffleur, Mark H. Anti-Hegelianism & the Theory of the Infinite. (Illus.). 131p. 1981. 41.45 (ISBN 0-89266-281-6). Am Classical Coll Pr.

Lamb, D. Language & Perception in Hegel & Wittgenstein. 1979. 45.00x (ISBN 0-86127-101-7, Pub. by Avebury Pub England). State Mutual Bk.

Lamb, David. Hegel: From Foundation to System. (Martinus Nijhoff Philosophy Library: No. 1). 252p. 1980. lib. bdg. 34.50 (ISBN 90-247-2359-0, Pub. by Martinus Nijhoff Netherlands). Kluwer Boston.

--Language & Perception in Hegel & Wittgenstein. LC 80-505. 135p. 1980. 18.95 (ISBN 0-312-46612-9). St Martin.

Lauer, Quentin. Essays in Hegelian Dialectic. LC 76-18465. 1977. 20.00 (ISBN 0-8232-1021-9); pap. 8.00 (ISBN 0-8232-1022-7). Fordham.

--A Reading of Hegel's Phenomenology of Spirit. rev ed. LC 75-41657. 1978. 25.00 (ISBN 0-8232-1000-6); pap. 10.00 (ISBN 0-8232-1001-4). Fordham.

Lichtheim, George. From Marx to Hegel. LC 70-167871. 1971. pap. 3.95 (ISBN 0-8164-9188-7); (Continuum). Continuum.

Loewenberg, J. Hegel's Phenomenology: Dialogues on the Life of Mind. LC 65-15621. xv, 377p. 1965. 19.95 (ISBN 0-87548-022-5). Open Court.

Loewenberg, J., ed. Hegel: Selections. 1971. pap. text ed. 7.95x (ISBN 0-684-14346-1, ScribC). Scribner.

Lucas, George R. Two Views of Freedom in Process & Thought. LC 79-12287. (American Academy of Religion, Dissertation Ser.: No. 28). 1979. 12.00 (ISBN 0-89130-285-9, 010128); pap. 7.50 (ISBN 0-89130-304-9). Scholars Pr Ca.

Lukacs, Georg. The Young Hegel: Studies on the Relations Between Dialectics & Economics. Livingstone, Rodney, tr. from Ger. LC 75-29628. 608p. 1975. pap. 9.95 (ISBN 0-262-54032-0). MIT Pr.

Luqueer, Frederick L. Hegel As Educator. LC 3-12359. Repr. of 1896 ed. 14.50 (ISBN 0-404-04068-3). AMS Pr.

McClellan, David. Young Hegelians & Karl Marx. 1918. Repr. of 1964 ed. text ed. 9.95x (ISBN 0-333-08788-7). Humanities.

MacIntyre, Alasdair, ed. Hegel: A Collection of Critical Essays. LC 76-42278. (Modern Studies in Philosophy). 1976. text ed. 14.95x (ISBN 0-268-01066-8); pap. text ed. 4.95x (ISBN 0-268-01067-6). U of Notre Dame Pr.

Mackenzie, H. Millicent. Hegel's Educational Theory & Practice. Repr. of 1909 ed. lib. bdg. 15.00 (ISBN 0-8371-4478-7, MAHE). Greenwood.

Mackenzie, Hettie M. Hegel's Educational Theory & Practice. LC 79-122985. (Studies in Philosophy, No. 40). 1971. Repr. of 1909 ed. lib. bdg. 33.95 (ISBN 0-8383-1118-0). Haskell.

McTaggart, John M. Commentary on Hegel's Logic. LC 64-10391. 1964. Repr. of 1910 ed. 18.00 (ISBN 0-8462-0425-8). Russell.

--Studies in the Hegelian Dialectic. 2nd ed. LC 64-10392. 1964. Repr. of 1922 ed. 20.00 (ISBN 0-8462-0420-7). Russell.

Macvannel, John A. Hegel's Doctrine of the Will. LC 3-12358. Repr. of 1896 ed. 12.45 (ISBN 0-404-04146-9). AMS Pr.

Maier, Josef. On Hegel's Critique of Kant. LC 39-31564. Repr. of 1939 ed. 16.45 (ISBN 0-404-04168-X). AMS Pr.

Marcuse, Herbert. Reason & Revolution: Hegel & the Rise of Social Theory. 1960. pap. 5.95 (ISBN 0-8070-1557-1, BP110). Beacon Pr.

--Reason & Revolution: Hegel & the Rise of Social Theory. 2nd ed. 1968. text ed. 13.50x (ISBN 0-391-00458-1). Humanities.

Marx, Karl. Critique of Hegel's "Philosophy of Right". O'Malley, J., ed. LC 74-112471. (Cambridge Studies in the History & Theory of Politics). 1970. 23.95 (ISBN 0-521-07836-9); pap. 8.50x (ISBN 0-521-29211-5). Cambridge U Pr.

Marx, Werner. Hegel's Phenomenology of Spirit. LC 74-4635. 144p. 1975. pap. 4.50x (ISBN 0-06-065463-5, RD88, HarpR). Har-Row.

Mehta, V. R. Hegel & the Modern State. 1968. 7.50 (ISBN 0-686-20237-6). Intl Bk Dist.

--Hegel & the Modern State: An Introduction to Hegel's Political Thought. 1968. 5.50x (ISBN 0-8426-0215-1). Verry.

--Hegel & the Modern State: An Introduction to Hegel's Political Thought. 1968. text ed. 7.00x (ISBN 0-391-00501-4). Humanities.

Morris, George S. Hegel's Philosophy of the State & of History: An Exposition. 2nd ed. LC 75-3287. Repr. of 1887 ed. 21.50 (ISBN 0-404-59275-9). AMS Pr.

Mure, G. R. Idealist Epilogue. 1978. text ed. 22.50x (ISBN 0-19-824583-1). Oxford U Pr.

Myers, Henry A. Spinoza-Hegel Paradox: A Study of the Choice Between Traditional Idealism & Systematic Pluralism. Repr. of 1944 ed. 15.00 (ISBN 0-8337-4914-5). B Franklin.

Norman, Richard. Hegel's Phenomenology. LC 76-12235. 1976. 15.95x (ISBN 0-312-36680-9). St Martin.

--Hegel's Phenomenology: A Philosophical Introduction. (Philosophy Now). 1980. text ed. 19.50 (ISBN 0-391-01720-9); pap. text ed. 4.50x (ISBN 0-391-01721-7). Humanities.

O'Brien, George D. Hegel on Reason & History: A Contemporary Interpretation. 1977. pap. 3.95 (ISBN 0-226-61647-9, P722, Phoen). U of Chicago Pr.

Orynski, Wanda, ed. Hengel Highlights. 1960. 4.75 (ISBN 0-8022-1245-X). Philos Lib.

Ottmann, Henning. Individuum und Gemeinschaft Bei Hegel: Hegel Im Spiegel der Interpretationen, Vol. 1. (Quellen und Studien Zur Philosophie). 1977. 73.50x (ISBN 3-11-007134-7). De Gruyter.

Peddle, Frank. Thought & Being: Hegel's Criticism of Kant's System of Cosmological Ideas. LC 79-9695. 204p. 1980. text ed. 17.75 (ISBN 0-8191-0987-8); pap. text ed. 9.50 (ISBN 0-8191-0988-6). U Pr of Amer.

Pelczynski, Z. A., ed. Hegel's Political Philosophy: Problems & Perspectives. LC 71-160096. 1971. pap. 8.95x (ISBN 0-521-09987-0). Cambridge U Pr.

Petry, Michael J., ed. & tr. Hegel's Philosophy of Subjective Spirit, 3 vols. new ed. 1976. Set. lib. bdg. 113.00 (ISBN 90-277-0718-9, Pub. by Reidel Holland). Kluwer Boston.

Plant, Raymond. Hegel. LC 72-93910. (Political Thinkers Ser). 216p. 1973. 7.95x (ISBN 0-253-32714-8). Ind U Pr.

Pochmann, Henry A. New England Transcendentalism & St. Louis Hegelianism. LC 68-55163. (Studies in Comparative Literature, No. 35). 1969. Repr. of 1948 ed. lib. bdg. 26.95 (ISBN 0-8383-0610-1). Haskell.

Prokopczyk, Czeslaw. Truth & Reality in Marx & Hegel: A Reassessment. LC 80-7976. 142p. 1980. lib. bdg. 13.50x (ISBN 0-87023-307-6). U of Mass Pr.

Rauch, Leo. Monarch Notes on Hegel's Philosophy. (Orig.). pap. 1.50 (ISBN 0-671-00528-6). Monarch Pr.

Reardon, Bernard M. Hegel's Philosophy of Religion. LC 76-51703. (Library of Philosophy & Religion Ser.). 1977. text ed. 23.50x (ISBN 0-06-495806-X). B&N.

Ripalda, Jose-Maria. The Divided Nation: The Roots of a Bourgeois Thinker, G. W. F. Hegel. (Dialectic & Society: No. 3). 1977. text ed. 31.25x (ISBN 90-232-1514-1). Humanities.

Robinson, Jonathan. Duty & Hypocracy in Hegel's Phenomenology of Mind. 1977. 17.50x (ISBN 0-8020-5380-7). U of Toronto Pr.

Rosen, Stanley. G. W. F. Hegel: An Introduction to the Science of Wisdom. LC 73-86916. 320p. 1974. 20.00x (ISBN 0-300-01688-3). Yale U Pr.

Sarlemijn, Andries. Hegelsche Dialektik. 206p. 1971. 36.25x (ISBN 3-11-001839-X). De Gruyter.
Schacht, Richard. Hegel & After: Studies in Continental Philosophy Between Kant & Sartre. LC 74-4526. 1975. pap. 6.25x (ISBN 0-8229-5254-8). U of Pittsburgh Pr.
Schmidt, Erik. Hegels System der Theologie. LC 73-81703. (Theologische Bibliothek Toepelmann 26). 210p. 1974. 33.75x (ISBN 3-11-004463-3). De Gruyter.
Seth, Andrew. The Development from Kant to Hegel, with Chapters on the Philosophy of Religion. Beck, Lewis W., ed. LC 75-32044. (The Philosophy of Immanuel Kant Ser.: Vol. 7). 1977. Repr. of 1882 ed. lib. bdg. 20.00 (ISBN 0-8240-2331-5). Garland Pub.
Seth Pringle Pattison, Andrew. The Development from Kant to Hegel. 1975. lib. bdg. 49.95 (ISBN 0-8490-0020-3). Gordon Pr.
--Hegelianism & Personality. 1971. Repr. of 1887 ed. lib. bdg. 21.00 (ISBN 0-8337-3236-6). B Franklin.
--Hegelianism & Personality. 1975. lib. bdg. 59.95 (ISBN 0-8490-0288-5). Gordon Pr.
Siebert, Rudolf J. Hegel's Concept of Marriage & Family: The Origin of Subjective Freedom. LC 78-78401. 1979. pap. text ed. 7.50 (ISBN 0-8191-0710-7). U Pr of Amer.
--Hegel's Philosophy of History: Theological, Humanistic & Scientific Elements. LC 78-66279. 1979. pap. text ed. 9.00 (ISBN 0-8191-0689-5). U Pr of Amer.
Soll, Ivan. Introduction to Hegel's Metaphysics. LC 75-85447. 1969. 7.50x (ISBN 0-226-76794-9); pap. 5.00x (ISBN 0-226-76795-7). U of Chicago Pr.
Stace, W. T. The Philosophy of Hegel: A Systematic Exposition. LC 55-1374. lib. bdg. 13.50x (ISBN 0-88307-256-4). Gannon.
Stace, Walter T. Philosophy of Hegel: A Systematic Exposition. 1923. pap. text ed. 6.00 (ISBN 0-486-20254-2). Dover.
Steinhauer, Kurt. Hegel Bibliography: Background Material on the International Reception of Hegel Within the Context of the History of Philosophy. 894p. 1981. 129.50 (ISBN 0-686-30080-7). K G Saur.
Steinhauer, Kurt, ed. Hegel: Bibliography. 896p. 1981. 129.50 (ISBN 3-598-03184-X). Bowker.
Steinkraus, W., et al, eds. Art & Logic in Hegel's Philosophy, the Georgetown Conference: The Hegel Society of America 1974. 1980. text ed. 17.50x (ISBN 0-391-00542-1). Humanities.
Stirling, J. H. The Secret of Hegel: Being the Hegelian System in Origin Principle Form & Matter. 2nd, rev. ed. (Reprints in Philosophy Ser.). Repr. of 1898 ed. lib. bdg. 30.00x (ISBN 0-697-00058-3). Irvington.
Taylor, C. Hegel. LC 74-25642. 700p. 1975. 57.50 (ISBN 0-521-20679-0); pap. 14.95 (ISBN 0-521-29199-2). Cambridge U Pr.
--Hegel & Modern Society. LC 78-54727. (Modern European Philosophy). 1979. 28.95 (ISBN 0-521-22083-1); pap. 6.95 (ISBN 0-521-29351-0). Cambridge U Pr.
Taylor, Mark C. Journeys to Selfhood: Hegel & Kierkegaard. 264p. 1981. 22.50x (ISBN 0-520-04167-4); pap. 7.95 (ISBN 0-520-04176-3, CAL 483). U of Cal Pr.
Theunissen, Michael. Sein und Schein: Die Kritische Funktion der Hegelschen Logik. (Suhrkamp Taschenbucher Wissenschaft: Vol. 314). 501p. (Orig.). 1980. pap. text ed. 11.70 (ISBN 3-518-07914-X, Pub. by Suhrkamp Verlag Germany). Suhrkamp.
Thulstrup, Niels. Kierkegaard's Relation to Hegel. Stengren, George L., tr. LC 79-3233. 1980. 27.50x (ISBN 0-691-07243-4); pap. 10.75 limited ed. (ISBN 0-691-10079-9). Princeton U Pr.
Toews, John E. Hegelianism: The Path Toward Dialectic Humanism, 1805 to 1841. LC 80-16370. 512p. 1981. 39.50 (ISBN 0-521-23048-9). Cambridge U Pr.
Wallace, William. The Logic of Hegel: Translated from the Encyclopedia of the Philosophical Sciences. with Prolegomena. 1979. Repr. of 1874 ed. lib. bdg. 100.00 (ISBN 0-8495-5718-6). Arden Lib.
--Prolegomena to the Study of Hegel's Philosophy, & Especially of His Logic. 2nd ed. LC 68-15169. 1968. Repr. of 1894 ed. 12.00 (ISBN 0-8462-1302-8). Russell.
Watson, Gerald H. Incongruities, Inconsistencies, Absurdities in Hegel's Conception of the Universe. (Illus.). 1980. 37.75 (ISBN 0-89266-220-4). Am Classical Coll Pr.
Westphal, Merold. History & Truth in Hegel's Phenomenology. 1979. text ed. 12.50x (ISBN 0-391-00557-X). Humanities.
Wilkins, Burleigh T. Hegel's Philosophy of History. LC 73-16831. 224p. 1974. 16.50x (ISBN 0-8014-0819-9). Cornell U Pr.
Yerkes, James. The Christology of Hegel. LC 78-6563. 1978. pap. 9.00 (ISBN 0-89130-233-6). Scholars Pr Ca.
Young, William. Hegel's Dialectical Method. pap. 4.95 (ISBN 0-934532-28-1). Presby & Reformed.

HEIDEGGER, MARTIN, 1889-1976

Bartels, Martin. Selbstbewusstsein und Unbewusstes: Studien Zu Freud und Heidegger. (Quellen und Studien Zur Philosophie Ser.: Vol. 10). 1976. 48.75x (ISBN 3-11-005778-6). De Gruyter.
Biemel, Walter. Martin Heidegger. Mehta, J. L., tr. 1976. 6.95 (ISBN 0-15-657301-6, HB327). HarBraceJ.
Bindeman, Steven L. Heidegger & Wittgenstein: The Poetics of Silence. LC 80-6066. 159p. 1980. lib. bdg. 15.75 (ISBN 0-8191-1350-6); pap. text ed. 7.50 (ISBN 0-8191-1351-4). U Pr of Amer.
Blitz, Mark. Heidegger's "Being & Time" & the Possibility of Political Philosophy. LC 81-3258. 288p. 1981. 19.50x (ISBN 0-8014-1320-6). Cornell U Pr.
Bove, Paul A. Destructive Poetics: Heidegger & Modern American Poetry. 1980. text ed. 17.50x (ISBN 0-231-04690-1). Columbia U Pr.
Caputo, John D. The Mystical Element in Heidegger's Thought. LC 77-92251. xvi, 292p. 1978. 20.00x (ISBN 0-8214-0372-9). Ohio U Pr.
Casares, Angel J. Sobre la Esencia del Hombre. LC 78-15645. 1979. pap. 6.00 (ISBN 0-8477-2818-8). U of PR Pr.
Cousineau, Robert H. Humanism & Ethics: An Introduction to the Letter on Humanism by Heidegger. 137p. 1972. text ed. 13.75x (ISBN 0-391-00407-7). Humanities.
Decleve. Heidegger und Kant. (Phaenomenologica Ser: No. 40). 1970. lib. bdg. 45.00 (ISBN 90-247-5016-4, Pub. by Martinus Nijhoff Netherlands). Kluwer Boston.
Elliston, Frederick, ed. Heidegger's Existential Analytic. 1978. text ed. 37.75x (ISBN 90-279-7514-0). Mouton.
Erickson, Stephen A. Language & Being: An Analytic Phenomenology. LC 74-99823. 1970. 15.00 (ISBN 0-300-01195-4). Yale U Pr.
Fay. Heidegger: The Critique of Logic. 1977. pap. 26.00 (ISBN 90-247-1931-3, Pub. by Martinus Nijhoff Netherlands). Kluwer Boston.
Fell, Joseph P. Heidegger & Sartre: An Essay or Being & Place. LC 78-27437. (Illus.). 560p. 1979. 25.00x (ISBN 0-231-04554-9). Columbia U Pr.
Frings, Manfred S. Heidegger & the Quest for Truth. LC 67-21643. 1968. pap. 2.95 (ISBN 0-8129-6061-0). Times Bks.
Goldmann, Lucien. Lukacs & Heidegger: Towards a New Philosophy. Boelhower, William Q., tr. 1979. pap. 7.95 (ISBN 0-7100-8794-2). Routledge & Kegan.
--Lukacs & Heidegger: Towards a New Philosophy. Boelhower, William Q., tr. 15.00x (ISBN 0-7100-8625-3). Routledge & Kegan.
Hines, Thomas J. The Later Poetry of Wallace Stevens: Phenomenological Parallels with Husserl & Heidegger. LC 74-6773. 298p. 1975. 18.50 (ISBN 0-8387-1613-X). Bucknell U Pr.
Hofstadter, Albert & Kuhns, Richard, eds. Philosophies of Art & Beauty: Selected Readings in Aesthetics from Plato to Heidegger. 1976. pap. 8.95 (ISBN 0-226-34812-1, P685, Phoen). U of Chicago Pr.
Kockelmans, J. A. Martin Heidegger: A First Introduction to His Philosophy. 1965. text ed. 5.50x (ISBN 0-8207-0066-5, J26198). Duquesne.
Macomber, W. B. Anatomy of Disillusion: Martin Heidegger's Notion of Truth. LC 67-27474. (Studies in Phenomenology & Existential Philosophy Ser). 1967. 13.95x (ISBN 0-8101-0153-X). Northwestern U Pr.
Macquarrie, John. Martin Heidegger. LC 68-11970. (Makers of Contemporary Theology Ser). 1968. pap. 3.45 (ISBN 0-8042-0659-7). John Knox.
Marx, Werner. Heidegger & the Tradition. LC 70-126901. (Studies in Phenomenology & Existential Philosophy). 1971. 15.95x (ISBN 0-8101-0331-1). Northwestern U Pr.
Mehta, J. L. Martin Heidegger: The Way & the Vision. rev ed. 512p. 1976. Repr. of 1967 ed. text ed. 17.50x (ISBN 0-8248-0254-3). U Pr of Hawaii.
Mongis, H. Heidegger et la Critique De la Notion De Valeur. (Phaenomenologica Ser: No. 74). 1976. lib. bdg. 47.50 (ISBN 90-247-1904-6, Pub. by Martinus Nijhoff Netherlands). Kluwer Boston.
Murray, Michael, ed. Heidegger & Modern Philosophy. LC 77-21684. 1978. 25.00x (ISBN 0-300-02100-3); pap. 8.95x (ISBN 0-300-02236-0). Yale U Pr.
--Heidegger & Modern Philosophy. LC 77-21684. 1978. 25.00x (ISBN 0-300-02100-3); pap. 8.95x (ISBN 0-300-02236-0). Yale U Pr.
Naess, Arne. Four Modern Philosophers: Carnap, Wittgenstein, Heidegger & Sartre. Hannay, Alastair, tr. LC 68-14011. 1968. 13.50x (ISBN 0-226-56731-1). U of Chicago Pr.
--Four Modern Philosophers: Carnap, Wittgenstein, Heidegger & Sartre. Hannay, Alastair, tr. LC 68-14011. 1969. pap. 3.25 (ISBN 0-226-56733-8, P337, Phoen). U of Chicago Pr.
Perotti, James L. Heidegger on the Divine: The Thinker, the Poet & God. LC 73-92904. x, 134p. 1974. 10.00x (ISBN 0-8214-0144-0). Ohio U Pr.
Richardson. Heidegger. 3rd ed. (Phaenomenologica Ser: No. 13). 1974. lib. bdg. 50.00 (ISBN 90-247-0246-1, Pub. by Martinus Nijhoff Netherlands). Kluwer Boston.
Robinson, James M. & Cobb, John B., Jr., eds. The Later Heidegger & Theology. LC 78-23619. 1979. Repr. of 1963 ed. lib. bdg. 17.75x (ISBN 0-313-20783-6, ROLH). Greenwood.
Rose, Gillian. Hegel Contra Sociology. 1981. text ed. 45.00x (ISBN 0-391-02289-X, Athlone); pap. text ed. 17.50x (ISBN 0-391-02288-1). Humanities.
Sallis, John, ed. Heidegger & the Path of Thinking. LC 79-107355. (Philosophical Ser). 1970. text ed. 8.50x (ISBN 0-8207-0128-9). Duquesne.
Schmitt, Richard. Martin Heidegger on Being Human: An Introduction to Sein und Zeit. 8.50 (ISBN 0-8446-2881-6). Peter Smith.
Seidel, George J. Martin Heidegger & the Pre-Socratics: An Introduction to His Thought. LC 64-17224. (Landmark Edition). 1978. 12.50x (ISBN 0-8032-0171-0). U of Nebr Pr.
Shahan, Robert W. & Mohanty, J. N. Thinking About Being: Aspects of Heidegger's Thought. LC 81-40297. 208p. 1981. 12.95 (ISBN 0-8061-1780-X). U of Okla Pr.
Sheehan, Thomas, ed. Heidegger, the Man & the Thinker. LC 77-82476. 1980. 21.95 (ISBN 0-913750-16-6). Precedent Pub.
Sherover, Charles M. Heidegger, Kant & Time. LC 74-135011. 344p. 1971. 15.00x (ISBN 0-253-32720-2). Ind U Pr.
Spanos, William V., ed. Martin Heidegger & the Question of Literature: Toward a Postmodern Literary Hermeneutics. LC 79-84261. (Studies in Phenomenology & Existential Philosophy). 352p. 1980. 15.00x (ISBN 0-253-17575-5). Ind U Pr.
Steiner, George. Martin Heidegger. (Penguin Modern Masters Ser.). 1980. pap. 3.95 (ISBN 0-14-005501-0). Penguin.
--Martin Heidegger. (Modern Masters Ser.). 1979. 10.95 (ISBN 0-670-45909-7). Viking Pr.
Sternberger, Adolf. Der Verstandene Tod: Eine Untersuchung Zu Martin Heideggers Existenzialontologie. Natanson, Maurice, ed. LC 78-66753. (Phenomenology Ser.: Vol. 14). 165p. 1979. lib. bdg. 17.00 (ISBN 0-8240-9556-1). Garland Pub.
Ussher, Arland. Journey Through Dread. LC 68-54234. 1955. 9.00x (ISBN 0-8196-0221-3). Biblo.
Vail, L. M. Heidegger & Ontological Difference. LC 70-165361. 224p. 1972. 16.95x (ISBN 0-271-01108-4). Pa St U Pr.
Warnock, Mary. Existentialist Ethics. (Orig.). 1967. pap. 4.50 (ISBN 0-312-27510-2, E73250). St Martin.
Waterhouse, Roger. A Heidegger Critique: A Critical Examination of the Existential Phenomenology of Martin Heidegger. (Philosophy Now Ser.: No. 15). 239p. 1981. text ed. 49.00x (ISBN 0-391-02225-3, Pub. by Harvester England). Humanities.
White, David A. Heidegger & the Language of Poetry. LC 78-5610. 1978. 15.75x (ISBN 0-8032-4703-6). U of Nebr Pr.
Williams, John R. Martin Heidegger's Philosophy of Religion. 190p. 1977. pap. text ed. 6.75 (ISBN 0-919812-03-1, Pub. by Laurier U Pr Canada). Humanities.
Wisser, Richard, ed. Martin Heidegger in Conversation. Murthy, B. S., tr. from Ger. 1977. text ed. 2.75x (ISBN 0-391-01090-5). Humanities.

HEIDELBERG

Heidelberg. (Panorama Bks.). (Illus., Fr.). 3.95 (ISBN 0-685-11230-6). French & Eur.

HEIDELBERG CATECHISM

Barth, Karl. Learning Jesus Christ Through the Heidelberg Catechism. 144p. (Orig.). 1981. pap. 4.95 (ISBN 0-8028-1893-5). Eerdmans.
Heidelberg Catechism with Scripture Texts. (Orig.). 1981. pap. 3.45 (ISBN 0-933140-21-5). Bd of Pubns CRC.
Hoeksema, Herman. Triple Knowledge: Heidelberg Catechism, 3 Vols. LC 71-129740. 1972. Set. 29.95 (ISBN 0-8254-2813-0). Kregel.
Theleman. Aid to Heidelberg Catechism. 5.95 (ISBN 0-686-23483-9). Rose Pub MI.
Thompson, Bard, et al. Essays on the Heidelberg Catechism. LC 63-21522. 1963. pap. 5.95 (ISBN 0-8298-0325-4). Pilgrim NY.

HEIFETZ, JASCHA, 1901-

Axelrod, Herbert R., ed. Heifetz. 2nd ed. (Illus.). 640p. 1981. 20.00 (ISBN 0-87666-578-4, Z-24). Paganiniana Pubns.

HEILBRONER, ROBERT

Leon, Joseph M. Worldly Philosophers Notes. (Orig.). pap. 1.95 (ISBN 0-8220-1385-1). Cliffs.

HEINE, HEINRICH, 1797-1856

Braun, Wilhelm A. Types of Weltschmerz in German Poetry. LC 5-33195. (Columbia University. Germanic Studies, Old Ser.: No. 6). Repr. of 1905 ed. 14.50 (ISBN 0-404-50406-X). AMS Pr.
Brod, Max. Heinrich Heine: The Artist in Revolt. Witriol, Joseph, tr. from Ger. LC 76-21292. (Illus.). 355p. 1976. Repr. of 1957 ed. lib. bdg. 21.50x (ISBN 0-8371-8992-6, BRHA). Greenwood.
Butler, E. M. Heinrich Heine. 291p. 1981. Repr. of 1956 ed. lib. bdg. 30.00 (ISBN 0-89984-070-1). Century Bookbindery.
Butler, Eliza M. Heinrich Heine, a Biography. LC 70-106684. Repr. of 1956 ed. lib. bdg. 14.25x (ISBN 0-8371-3607-5, BUHH). Greenwood.
Canaan, Gilbert. Heinrich Heine's Memoirs, 2 vols. Karpeles, Gustav, ed. Repr. of 1893 ed. 15.00 (ISBN 0-8274-3846-X). R West.
Dexter, Arthur. Heinrich Heine's Life Told in His Own Words. Karpeles, Gustav, ed. 1893. Repr. 15.00 (ISBN 0-8274-3845-1). R West.
Ellis, Havelock. New Spirit. LC 39-224. 1969. Repr. of 1935 ed. 12.00 (ISBN 0-527-26920-4). Kraus Repr.
Evans, Thomas W. The Memoirs of Henrich Heine. 1973. Repr. of 1884 ed. 30.00 (ISBN 0-8274-0414-X). R West.
Ewen, Frederic. Heinrich Heine Self-Portrait & Other Prose Writings. Ewen, Frederic, tr. 550p. 1974. pap. 5.95 (ISBN 0-8065-0452-8). Citadel Pr.
Fairley, Barker. Heinrich Heine: An Interpretation. LC 77-709. 1977. Repr. of 1954 ed. lib. bdg. 15.00x (ISBN 0-8371-9338-9, FAHH). Greenwood.
Fejto, Francois. Heine. LC 78-103187. 1970. Repr. of 1946 ed. 13.50 (ISBN 0-8046-0824-5). Kennikat.
--Heine, a Biography. 1979. Repr. of 1946 ed. lib. bdg. 30.00 (ISBN 0-8492-4633-4). R West.
Heine, Heinrich. Family Life of Heinrich Heine. Von Embden, Ludwig, ed. LC 76-133280. (Studies in German Literature, No. 13). 1970. Repr. of 1892 ed. lib. bdg. 54.95 (ISBN 0-8383-1179-2). Haskell.
--The Works of Heinrich Heine, 20 vols. Leland, Charles G., tr. LC 76-13343. Repr. of 1906 ed. 20.00 ea.; 400.00 set (ISBN 0-404-15250-3). AMS Pr.
Hessel, K. R. Heinrich Heines Verhaeltnis Zur Bildenden Kunst. 1931. pap. 15.50 (ISBN 0-384-22720-1). Johnson Repr.
Loewenthal, Erich. Studien Zu Heines Reisebildern. 14.00 (ISBN 0-384-33391-5); pap. 11.00 (ISBN 0-384-33390-7). Johnson Repr.
Monahan, Michael. Heinrich Heine. 1973. Repr. of 1924 ed. 20.00 (ISBN 0-8274-1018-2). R West.
Reeves, Nigel. Heirich Heine: Poetry & Politics. (Oxford Modern Languages & Literature Monographs). 215p. 1974. 29.95x (ISBN 0-19-815524-7). Oxford U Pr.
Sachs, H. B. Heine in America. 59.95 (ISBN 0-8490-0289-3). Gordon Pr.
Sammons, Jeffrey L. Heinriche Heine. LC 79-84015. (Illus.). 1979. 27.50x (ISBN 0-691-06321-4); PLB 9.75 (ISBN 0-691-10081-0). Princeton U Pr.
Sharp, Elizabeth. Heine in Art & Letters. 1973. 20.00 (ISBN 0-8274-0913-3). R West.
Sharp, William. Life of Heinrich Heine. 1973. Repr. of 1888 ed. 20.00 (ISBN 0-8274-0448-4). R West.
--Life of Heinrich Heine. 1977. Repr. of 1888 ed. lib. bdg. 15.00 (ISBN 0-8495-4810-1). Arden Lib.
Siebert, W. Heinrich Heines Beziehungen Zu E. T. A. Hoffmann. Repr. of 1908 ed. pap. 7.00 (ISBN 0-384-55290-0). Johnson Repr.
Stanberry, D. Elaine C. Love's Perplexing Obsession, Experienced by Two Geniuses: Heinrich Hein & Percy Bysshe Shelley. 1981. 8.95 (ISBN 0-533-04826-5). Vantage.
Untermeyer, Louis. Heinrich Heine, 2 vols. 1937. Repr. 65.00 set (ISBN 0-8274-2477-9). R West.
Vallentin, Antonina. Poet in Exile. LC 72-113327. 1970. Repr. of 1934 ed. 12.50 (ISBN 0-8046-1003-7). Kennikat.
Von Embden, Ludwig. The Family Life of Heinrich Heine. De Kay, Charles, tr. from Ger. 1979. Repr. of 1892 ed. lib. bdg. 30.00 (ISBN 0-8495-5515-9). Arden Lib.
Weidekampf, Ilse. Traum und Wirklichkeit in der Romantik und Bei Heine. Repr. of 1932 ed. 14.00 (ISBN 0-685-92806-3); pap. 11.00 (ISBN 0-384-66455-5). Johnson Repr.

HEINKEL (FIGHTER PLANES)

Aeronautical Staff of Aero Publishers, et al. Heinkel HE162. LC 65-26827. (Aero Ser: Vol. 4). 1965. pap. 3.00 (ISBN 0-8168-0512-1). Aero.

Feist, Uwe & Hirsch, R. S. Heinkel HE100, 112. LC 67-16730. (Aero Ser: Vol. 12). (Illus.). 1967. pap. 3.00 (ISBN 0-8168-0544-X). Aero.

HEINKEL ONE HUNDRED SEVENTY-SEVEN (BOMBERS)

Feist, Uwe & Hirsch, R. S. Heinkel HE177 Greif. LC 67-16732. (Aero Ser: Vol. 13). (Illus.). 1967. pap. 3.00 (ISBN 0-8168-0548-2). Aero.

HEINLEIN, ROBERT ANSON, 1907-

Franklin, H. Bruce. Robert A. Heinlein: America As Science Fiction. (Science Fiction Writers Ser.: No. Gb 610). (Illus.). 250p. 1980. 18.95 (ISBN 0-19-502746-9, GB); pap. 4.95 (ISBN 0-19-502747-7). Oxford U Pr.

Olander, Joseph D. & Greenberg, Martin H., eds. Robert A. Heinlein. LC 76-11054. (Writers of the 21st Century Ser.). (Orig.). 1978. 12.95 (ISBN 0-8008-6801-3); pap. 5.95 (ISBN 0-8008-6802-1). Taplinger.

Panshin, Alexei. Heinlein in Dimension. rev. ed. LC 68-2797. 1968. 9.00 (ISBN 0-911682-01-5); pap. 5.00 (ISBN 0-911682-12-0). Advent.

Searles, Baird. Stranger in a Strange Land & Other Works Notes. 59p. (Orig.). 1975. pap. text ed. 1.95 (ISBN 0-8220-1231-6). Cliffs.

Slusser, George E. The Classic Years of Robert A. Heinlein. LC 77-24626. (The Milford Ser.: Popular Writers of Today Ser.: Vol. 11). 1977. lib. bdg. 8.95x (ISBN 0-89370-116-5); pap. 2.95x (ISBN 0-89370-216-1). Borgo Pr.

--Robert A. Heinlein: Stranger in His Own Land. 2nd rev. ed. LC 77-5657. (The Milford Ser: Popular Writers of Today Vol. 1). 1977. lib. bdg. 8.95x (ISBN 0-89370-110-6); pap. 2.95 (ISBN 0-89370-210-2). Borgo Pr.

HEINRICH 4TH, 1050-1106

see Henry 4th, King of Germany, 1050-1106

HEINRICH 7TH, EMPEROR OF GERMANY, 1269-1313

Bowsky, William M. Henry Seventh in Italy: The Conflict of Empire & City-State, 1310-1313. LC 74-10014. (Illus.). 301p. 1974. Repr. of 1960 ed. lib. bdg. 20.50x (ISBN 0-8371-7656-5, BOHS). Greenwood.

HEINRICH VON DEM TURLIN, fl. 1220

Boll, Lawrence L. Relation of Diu Krone to La Mule Sanz Frain. LC 77-140018. (Catholic University Studies in German Ser.: No. 2). Repr. of 1929 ed. 14.50 (ISBN 0-404-50222-9). AMS Pr.

HEINRICH VON VELDEKE, 12TH CENTURY

Sinnema, John R. Hendrik van Veldeke. (World Authors Ser.: Netherlands: No. 223). lib. bdg. 10.95 (ISBN 0-8057-2936-4). Twayne.

HEINRICH, ANTHONY PHILIP, 1781-1861

Upton, William T. Anthony Philip Heinrich: A Nineteenth Century Composer in America. LC 39-2473. Repr. of 1939 ed. 18.50 (ISBN 0-404-06706-9). AMS Pr.

HEINSE, JOHANN JAKOB WILHELM, 1749-1803

Jessen, Karl D. Heinses Stellung Zur Bildenden Kunst und Ihrer Aesthetik. 1901. 21.50 (ISBN 0-384-27170-7); pap. 18.50 (ISBN 0-685-13451-2). Johnson Repr.

HEINSIUS, DANIEL, 1580-1655

Becker-Cantarino, Baerbel. Daniel Heinsius. (World Author Ser.: No. 477). 1978. lib. bdg. 12.50 (ISBN 0-8057-6318-X). Twayne.

Sellen, P. R. Daniel Heinisius & Stuart England. (Publications of Sir Thomas Browne Institute Ser: No. 3). 1968. lib. bdg. 26.00 (ISBN 90-6021-061-1, Pub. by Leiden Univ Holland). Kluwer Boston.

HEINZE, FREDERICK AUGUSTUS, 1869-1914

Fahey, John. Inland Empire: D. C. Corbin & Spokane. LC 65-10816. (Illus.). 286p. 1965. 10.00 (ISBN 0-295-73815-4). U of Wash Pr.

HEIRS

see Inheritance and Succession

HELDENSAGE

see also Byliny; Chansons de Geste; Legends, Germanic

De Vries, Jan. Heroic Song & Heroic Legend. Bolle, Kees W., ed. LC 77-79157. (Mythology Ser.). 1978. Repr. of 1963 ed. lib. bdg. 16.00x (ISBN 0-405-10566-5). Arno.

Dickins, Bruce, ed. Runic & Heroic Poems of the Old Teutonic Peoples. LC 16-16313. 1968. Repr. of 1915 ed. 10.00 (ISBN 0-527-22600-9). Kraus Repr.

Friese, Hans. Thidrekssaga und Dietrichsepos. 21.50 (ISBN 0-384-16981-3); pap. 18.50 (ISBN 0-384-16980-5). Johnson Repr.

Jiriczek, Otto L. Northern Hero Legends. LC 76-30761. 1977. Repr. of 1902 ed. lib. bdg. 15.00 (ISBN 0-8414-5280-6). Folcroft.

Thurneysen, Rudolf. Die Irische Helden-und Konigssage bis zum Siebzehnten Jahrhundert. LC 78-72650. (Celtic Language & Literature: Goidelic & Brythonic). Repr. of 1921 ed. 49.50 (ISBN 0-404-17599-6). AMS Pr.

HELEN OF TROY

Giraudoux, Jean. Guerre De Troie N'Aura Pas Lieu. 1963. pap. 7.95 (ISBN 0-685-11227-6). French & Eur.

--La Guerre de Troie n'aura pas lieu. (Classiques Larousse). (Illus., Fr.). pap. 1.95 (ISBN 0-685-13933-6, 113). Larousse.

Lindsay, Jack. Helen of Troy: Woman & Goddess. (Illus.). 448p. 1974. 18.50x (ISBN 0-87471-581-4). Rowman.

HELEN OF TROY-POETRY

H. D., pseud. Helen in Egypt. LC 74-8563. 320p. 1974. pap. 3.25 (ISBN 0-8112-0544-4, NDP380). New Directions.

HELENA, SAINT, ca. 246-326

Shine, I. Serendipity in St. Helena. 1970. 34.00 (ISBN 0-08-012794-0). Pergamon.

HELICOPTERS

see also Heliports

Aviation Mechanincs Journal. Nineteen Eighty Aircraft & Helicopter Digest. (Illus.). 204p. 1980. text ed. 13.25 (ISBN 0-89100-184-0, E*A-184-0). Aviation Maintenance.

Beall, James R. & Downing, Robert E. Helicopter Utilization in Municipal Law Enforcement: Administrative Considerations. (Illus.). 96p. 1973. text ed. 14.75 (ISBN 0-398-02780-3). C C Thomas.

Bramwell, A. R. Helicopter Dynamics. LC 76-4944. 1976. 65.95 (ISBN 0-470-15067-X). Halsted Pr.

Branch, Melville C. Urban Air Traffic & City Planning: Case Study of Los Angeles County. LC 73-1090. (Special Studies in U.S. Economic, Social & Political Issues). 1973. 39.50x (ISBN 0-275-28701-7). Irvington.

Brown, E. M. The Helicopter in Civil Operations. 208p. 1981. 17.95 (ISBN 0-442-24528-9). Van Nos Reinhold.

Brown, Joseph M. Helicopter Directory. LC 75-44234. (Illus.). 128p. 1976. 15.95 (ISBN 0-88254-382-2). Hippocrene Bks.

Davis, Ann N. & Richardson, Robert A. The Helicopter: Its Importance to Commerce & to the Public. 138p. 1978. 10.00 (ISBN 0-911721-70-3, Pub. by Helicopter Assn). Aviation.

Dzik, Stanley J. Helicopter Design & Data Manual. 2nd rev. ed. (Illus.). 120p. 1974. pap. 7.95 (ISBN 0-87994-010-7, Pub. by AvPubns). Aviation.

Fay, John. The Helicopter: History, Piloting & How It Flies. LC 76-54073. (Illus.). 1977. 16.95 (ISBN 0-7153-7249-1). David & Charles.

Gessow, Alfred & Myers, Garry C., Jr. Aerodynamics of the Helicopter. LC 67-26126. 1967. 20.00 (ISBN 0-8044-4275-4). Ungar.

Gunston, Bill. An Illustrated Guide to Military Helicopters. LC 81-67084. (Illus.). 160p. 1981. 8.95 (ISBN 0-668-05345-3, 5345). Arco.

Hallman, Ruth. Rescue Chopper. LC 80-15593. (A Hiway Bk.). 1980. 8.95 (ISBN 0-664-32667-6). Westminster.

Johnson, Wayne. Helicopter Theory. LC 79-83995. 1000p. 1980. 95.00x (ISBN 0-691-07971-4). Princeton U Pr.

Polmar, Norman & Kennedy, Floyd. Military Helicopters of the World: Military Rotary-Wing Aircraft Since 1917. LC 80-84060. 1981. 28.95 (ISBN 0-87021-383-0). Naval Inst Pr.

Saunders, George H. Dynamics of Helicopter Flight. LC 74-30261. (Illus.). 304p. 1975. 28.50 (ISBN 0-471-75509-5, Pub. by Wiley-Interscience). Wiley.

Schafer, Joseph. Helicopter Fundamentals. (Aviation Technician Training Course Ser.). (Illus.). 400p. 1980. pap. text ed. 8.95 (ISBN 0-89100-118-2). Aviation Maintenance.

Taylor, John W., ed. Jane's Pocket Book of Helicopters. (Illus.). 260p. 1981. pap. 8.95 (ISBN 0-686-69548-8, Collier). Macmillan.

Taylor, Michael J. & Taylor, John W. Helicopters of the World. LC 76-18634. (Illus.). 1979. 9.95 (ISBN 0-684-15865-5, ScribT). Scribner.

--Helicopters of the World. 2nd rev. ed. 1978. 12.50x (ISBN 0-7110-0685-7). Intl Pubns Serv.

HELICOPTERS-JUVENILE LITERATURE

Croome, Angela. Hovercraft. (Illus.). (gr. 5 up). 1962. 4.50 (ISBN 0-8392-3008-7). Astor-Honor.

Delear, Frank J. The New World of Helicopters. rev. ed. LC 67-10442. (New World Ser.). (Illus.). (gr. 4 up). 1978. 5.95 (ISBN 0-396-07563-0). Dodd.

Harris, Susan. Helicopters. (Easy-Read Fact Bks.). (Illus.). (gr. 2-4). 1979. s&l 6.90 (ISBN 0-531-02850-X). Watts.

Kaufmann, John. Fly It: Making & Flying Your Own Kites, Boomerangs, Helicopters, Hang Gliders & Hand-Launched Gliders. LC 78-60292. (Illus.). (gr. 4-5). 1980. 8.95a (ISBN 0-385-14292-7); PLB (ISBN 0-385-14293-5). Doubleday.

Knight, Clayton S. Big Book of Helicopters. (Illus.). (gr. 4-6). 1971. 1.95 (ISBN 0-448-02253-2). G&D.

Sikorsky, Igor. Story of the Winged-S. rev. ed. (Illus.). 1967. 6.95 (ISBN 0-396-01829-7). Dodd.

HELICOPTERS-PILOTING

Collier, Larry. How to Fly Helicopters. (Modern Aviation Ser.). (Illus.). 1979. 9.95 (ISBN 0-8306-9840-X); pap. 7.95 (ISBN 0-8306-2264-0, 2264). TAB Bks.

Educational Research Council of America. Helicopter Pilot. Kunze, Linda J. & Marchak, John P., eds. (Real People at Work Ser: K). (Illus.). 1976. pap. text ed. 2.25 (ISBN 0-89247-082-8). Changing Times.

Federal Aviation Administration. Basic Helicopter Handbook. 3rd ed. (Pilot Training Ser.). (Illus.). 111p. 1978. pap. 3.75 (ISBN 0-89100-162-X, E*A-A*C61-13B). Aviation Maintenance.

--Flight Test Guide: Private & Commericial Pilots (Helicopter) Ac 61-59A. 1977. pap. 2.25 (ISBN 0-686-74530-2, Pub. by Astro). Aviation.

Safford, Edward L. Flying Model Airplanes & Helicopters by Radio Control. (Illus.). 1977. pap. 5.95 (ISBN 0-8306-6825-X, 825). TAB Bks.

Saunders, George H. Dynamics of Helicopter Flight. LC 74-30261. (Illus.). 304p. 1975. 28.50 (ISBN 0-471-75509-5, Pub. by Wiley-Interscience). Wiley.

HELICOPTERS, USED

see Used Aircraft

HELIOCHROMY

see Color Photography

HELIOMETER

Lietze, Ernst. Modern Heliographic Processes: A Manual of Instruction. Lyons, Nathan, ed. LC 73-22265. (Visual Studies Reprint Ser.). 1974. 12.50 (ISBN 0-87992-001-7); pap. 7.95 (ISBN 0-87992-000-9). Light Impressions.

Precisions des Mesures Pyheliometriques. (Technical Note Ser.). pap. 22.00 (ISBN 0-685-57272-2, WMO). Unipub.

HELIOZOA

Cash, J. & Hopkinson, J. British Freshwater Rhizopoda & Heliozoa, 5 Vols. 1905-21. Set. 77.00 (ISBN 0-384-07835-4). Johnson Repr.

HELIPORTS

see also Aeronautics, Commercial; Airports; Helicopters

Roof-Top Heliport Construction & Protection. (Four Hundred Ser). 1973. pap. 2.00 (ISBN 0-685-58237-X, 418). Natl Fire Prot.

HELIUM

see also Liquid Helium; Solid Helium

Armitage, Jonathan G. & Farquhar, Ian E., eds. The Helium Liquid. (A NATO Advanced Study Institute). 1976. 83.50 (ISBN 0-12-062550-4). Acad Pr.

Clever, H. L. Helium & Neon: Gas Solubilities. (Solubility Data Ser.: Vol. 1). 1979. 100.00 (ISBN 0-08-022351-6). Pergamon.

Daunt, John G. & Lerner, E., eds. Monolayer & Submonolayer Helium Films. 160p. 1973. 25.00 (ISBN 0-306-30757-X, Plenum Pr). Plenum Pub.

Galasiewicz, Z. M. Helium Four. 1971. 25.00 (ISBN 0-08-015816-1). Pergamon.

Helium Study Committee. Helium: A Public Policy Program. 1978. pap. 10.50 (ISBN 0-309-02742-X). Natl Acad Pr.

Ziegler, James F., ed. Helium: Stopping Powers & Ranges in All Elemental Matter. LC 77-13219. 1977. text ed. 40.00 (ISBN 0-08-021606-4). Pergamon.

HELIUM-ISOTOPES

Keller, William E. Helium-Three & Helium-Four. LC 68-25382. (International Cryogenics Monographs). (Illus.). 431p. 1969. 42.50 (ISBN 0-306-30346-9, Plenum Pr). Plenum Pub.

HELL

see also Future Punishment

Becker, Ernest J. A Contribution to the Comparative Study of the Medieval Visions of Heaven & Hell. 1976. Repr. of 1899 ed. 25.00 (ISBN 0-403-06507-0, Regency). Scholarly.

Braun, Jon. Whatever Happened to Hell? LC 79-218. 1979. 7.95 (ISBN 0-8407-5158-3). Nelson.

Carothers, Merlin, tr. El Cielo Baja Al Infierno. (Spanish Bks.). (Span.). 1978. 1.75 (ISBN 0-8297-0766-2). Life Pubs Intl.

Cribb, C. C. The Devil's Empire. LC 77-70211. pap. 1.95 (ISBN 0-932046-02-9). Manhattan Ltd NC.

Ferguson, John. The Place of Suffering. 137p. 1972. 10.00 (ISBN 0-227-67803-6). Attic Pr.

Ford, W. Herschel. Simple Sermons on Heaven, Hell, & Judgment. pap. 3.95 (ISBN 0-310-24481-1). Zondervan.

Fox, Samuel J. Hell in Jewish Literature. LC 76-101511. 1969. pap. 6.95x (ISBN 0-87655-515-6). Whitehall Co.

Kater, John. The Letter of John to James. (Illus.). 64p. (Orig.). (gr. k-5). 1981. pap. 6.95 (ISBN 0-8164-2344-X). Seabury.

Kelley, P. J. So High the Price. LC 68-28104. (St. Paul Editions). 1968. 3.00 (ISBN 0-8198-0148-8). Dghtrs St Paul.

Kohler, Kaufmann. Heaven & Hell in Comparative Religion. 1923. 15.00 (ISBN 0-8414-5601-1). Folcroft.

Lehner, Ernst & Lehner, Johanna. Picture Book of Devils, Demons, & Witchcraft. LC 72-137002. 1972. pap. 5.50 (ISBN 0-486-22751-0). Dover.

Lindsay, Gordon. Hades-Abode of the Unrighteous Dead. (Sorcery & Spirit World Ser.). 0.95 (ISBN 0-89985-082-0). Christ Nations.

Macculloch, John A. The Harrowing of Hell: A Comparative Study of an Early Christian Doctrine. LC 79-8113. Repr. of 1930 ed. 33.50 (ISBN 0-404-18426-X). AMS Pr.

Mew, James. Traditional Aspects of Hell. LC 73-140321. 1971. Repr. of 1903 ed. 28.00 (ISBN 0-8103-3693-6). Gale.

Patch, Howard R. Other World, According to Descriptions in Medieval Literature. LC 77-96164. 1970. Repr. of 1950 ed. lib. bdg. 24.00x (ISBN 0-374-96289-8). Octagon.

Sayers, Stanley E. The Nature of Things to Come. 1972. 3.95 (ISBN 0-686-21491-9). Firm Foun Pub.

Swedenborg, Emanual. Heaven & Hell. 1976. pap. 1.95 (ISBN 0-89129-110-5). Jove Pubns.

Swedenborg, Emanuel. Heaven & Hell. LC 77-93044. trade ed. 8.25 (ISBN 0-87785-067-4); student ed 6.50 (ISBN 0-87785-066-6); pap. 1.95 (ISBN 0-87785-153-0). Swedenborg.

Thompson, Fred, Jr. What the Bible Says About Heaven & Hell. (What the Bible Says Ser.). 400p. 1982. 13.50 (ISBN 0-89900-081-9). College Pr Pub.

Walker, Daniel P. Decline of Hell: Seventeenth-Century Discussions of Eternal Torment. LC 64-19849. (Illus.). 1964. 12.00x (ISBN 0-226-87106-1). U of Chicago Pr.

Woodson, Leslie H. What the Bible Says About Hell. (Direction Bks). 128p. 1976. pap. text ed. 1.45 (ISBN 0-8010-9582-4). Baker Bk.

Worley, Win. Annihilating the Hosts of Hell: The Battle Royal, Vol. 1. 1981. 5.00 (ISBN 0-686-75479-4). HBC.

HELLCAT (FIGHTER PLANES)

Anderton, David A. Hellcat. (Crown's World War II Fighter Planes Ser.). 1981. 15.95 (ISBN 0-517-54259-5). Crown.

Rice, Michael S., ed. Pilot's Manual for the Grumman F6F Hellcat. (Illus.). 60p. 1975. pap. 4.95 (ISBN 0-87994-033-6, Pub. by AvPubns). Aviation.

Tillman, Barrett. Hellcat: F6F in World War Two. LC 78-58824. 1979. 17.95 (ISBN 0-87021-265-6). Naval Inst Pr.

HELLENICA OXYRHYNCHIA

Bruce, I. A. Historical Commentary on the Hellenica Cxyrhynchia. (Cambridge Classical Studies). 1967. 19.95 (ISBN 0-521-04352-2). Cambridge U Pr.

HELLENISM

see also Neoplatonism

Avi-Yonah, Michael. Hellenism & the East: Contacts & Interrelations from Alexander to the Roman Conquest. LC 78-410. 1978. pap. 20.00 (ISBN 0-8357-0301-0, SS00061). Univ Microfilms.

Banerjee, Gauranga N. Hellenism in Ancient India. rev. ed. 276p. 1981. text ed. 20.25x (ISBN 0-391-02417-5, Pub. by Munshiram Manoharlal India). Humanities.

Bevan, Edwyn R. Hellenism & Christianity. facs. ed. LC 67-26714. (Essay Index Reprint Ser). 1921. 16.00 (ISBN 0-8369-0207-6). Arno.

Bowersock, Glen W., et al, eds. Arktouros: Hellenic Studies Presented to Bernard M. W. Knox on the Occasion of His 65th Birthday. 471p. 1979. 88.00 (ISBN 3-11-007798-1). De Gruyter.

Dimaras, C. T. History of Modern Greek Literature. Gianos, Mary P., tr. LC 73-112610. 1973. 36.00 (ISBN 0-87395-071-2); pap. 11.00 (ISBN 0-87395-230-8); microfiche o.p. 36.00 (ISBN 0-87395-171-9). State U NY Pr.

Egger, E. L' Hellenisme En France, 2 Vols. 1964. Repr. of 1869 ed. 50.50 (ISBN 0-8337-1022-2). B Franklin.

Ferguson, W. Scott. Hellenistic Athens. 512p. 1974. 15.00 (ISBN 0-89005-021-X). Ares.

Glover, Terrot R. Greek Byways. LC 74-101043. 1969. Repr. of 1932 ed. 13.75 (ISBN 0-8046-0709-5). Kennikat.

Hadas, Moses. Hellenistic Culture. 1972. pap. 4.95x (ISBN 0-393-00593-3, Norton Lib.). Norton.

Humphreys, S. C. Anthropology & the Greeks. (International Library of Anthropology Ser.). 1978. 30.00x (ISBN 0-7100-8785-3). Routledge & Kegan.

Hutton, Maurice. Greek Point of View. LC 72-105840. (Classics Ser). 1971. Repr. of 1926 ed. 12.00 (ISBN 0-8046-1200-5). Kennikat.

Kleines Woerterbuch Des Hellenismus. 1st ed. (Ger. -Gr.). 1972. 30.95 (ISBN 0-686-56625-4, M-7515, Pub. by Harrassowitz). French & Eur.

Kraeling, Carl H. Anthropos & Son of Man. LC 27-23162. (Columbia University. Oriental Studies: No. 25). Repr. of 1927 ed. 18.50 (ISBN 0-404-50515-5). AMS Pr.

Langlois, Walter G., ed. The Persistent Voice: Essays on Hellenism in French Literature Since the 18th Century In Honor of Henri M. Peyre. LC 71-150982. 1971. 12.00x (ISBN 0-8147-4952-6). NYU Pr.
Livingstone, Richard W. Greek Ideals & Modern Life. LC 72-82814. 1969. Repr. of 1935 ed. 10.50x (ISBN 0-8196-0245-0). Biblo.
Mahaffy, J. P. Greek Life & Thought from the Age of Alexander to the Roman Conquest. facsimile ed. LC 75-13278. (History of Ideas in Ancient Greece Ser.). 1976. Repr. of 1887 ed. 35.00x (ISBN 0-405-07318-6). Arno.
Makrakis, Apostolos. Hellenism & the Unfinished Revolution. Orthodox Christian Educational Society, ed. Stephanou, Archimandrite E., tr. from Hellenic. 191p. (Orig.). 1968. pap. 3.00x (ISBN 0-938366-26-2). Orthodox Chr.
Peters, F. E. Harvest of Hellenism. LC 74-116509. 1971. pap. 8.95 (ISBN 0-671-20659-1, Touchstone Bks). S&S.
Peyre, Henri. Bibliographie critique de l'hellenisme en France de 1843 a 1870. LC 72-1698. (Yale Romanic Studies: No. 6). Repr. of 1932 ed. 14.00 (ISBN 0-404-53206-3). AMS Pr.
Scarborough, John. Facets of Hellenic Life. LC 75-29704. (Illus.). 320p. 1976. pap. text ed. 14.25 (ISBN 0-395-20368-6). HM.
Schofield, Malcolm, et al, eds. Doubt & Dogmatism: Studies in Hellenistic Epistemology. 354p. 1980. text ed. 37.50x (ISBN 0-19-824601-3). Oxford U Pr.
Stern, Bernard H. Rise of Romantic Hellenism in English Literature, 1732-1786. LC 72-86288. 1969. Repr. of 1940 ed. lib. bdg. 13.50x (ISBN 0-374-97619-8). Octagon.
Tarn, William W. Hellenistic Civilization. rev. ed. 1961. pap. 4.95 (ISBN 0-452-00457-8, F457, Mer). NAL.
Tcherikover, Victor. Hellenistic Civilization & the Jews. Applebaum, S., tr. LC 59-8518. (Temple Bk). 1970. pap. 5.95 (ISBN 0-689-70248-5, T22). Atheneum.
Toynbee, Arnold J. Hellenism: The History of a Civilization. LC 80-27772. xii, 272p. 1981. Repr. of 1959 ed. lib. bdg. 25.00x (ISBN 0-313-22742-X, TOHM). Greenwood.
Vacalopoulos, Apostolos E. Origins of the Greek Nation: The Byzantine Period 1204-1461. Moles, Ian N., tr. (Byzantine Ser.). (Illus.). 1970. 27.50 (ISBN 0-8135-0659-X). Rutgers U Pr.
Webb, Timothy. English Romantic Hellenism: 1700-1824. (Literature in Context Ser.). 150p. 1982. 25.00x (ISBN 0-389-20029-8). B&N.
Webster, Thomas B. Art of Greece: The Age of Hellenism. (Art of the World Library). (Illus.). 1966. 6.95 (ISBN 0-517-50841-9). Crown.

HELLENISTIC GREEK
see Greek Language, Hellenistic (300 B.C.-600 A.D.)

HELLER, JOSEPH, 1923-
Peek, C. A. Catch Twenty-Two Notes. 48p. pap. 1.75 (ISBN 0-8220-0296-5). Cliffs.

HELLMAN, LILLIAN, 1905-
Estrin, Mark. Lillian Hellman: Plays, Films, Memoirs. 1980. lib. bdg. 24.00 (ISBN 0-8161-7907-7). G K Hall.
Falk, Doris V. Lillian Hellman. LC 78-4299. (Modern Literature Ser.). 1978. 10.95 (ISBN 0-8044-2194-3); pap. 4.95 (ISBN 0-8044-6144-9). Ungar.
Hellman, Lillian. Pentimento: A Book of Portraits. 1973. 11.95 (ISBN 0-316-35520-8). Little.
--Scoundrel Time. 1977. lib. bdg. 8.95 (ISBN 0-8161-6446-0, Large Print Bks). G K Hall.
--An Unfinished Woman. 256p. 1974. pap. 2.75 (ISBN 0-553-14551-7, 12710-1). Bantam.
Lederer, Katherine. Lillian Hellman. (United States Authors Ser.: No. 338). 1979. 9.95 (ISBN 0-8057-7275-8). Twayne.
Triesch, Manfred, ed. The Lillian Hellman Collection at the University of Texas. LC 67-64819. (Tower Bibliographical Ser.: No. 3). (Illus.). 1966. 10.00 (ISBN 0-87959-044-0). U of Tex Hum Res.

HELLMAN, LILLIAN, 1905- --BIBLIOGRAPHY
Riordan, Mary M. Lillian Hellman; A Bibliography, 1926-1978. LC 80-16147. (Author Bibliographies Ser.: No. 50). 244p. 1980. 12.50 (ISBN 0-8108-1320-3). Scarecrow.

HELL'S ANGELS
Morgan, Raymond C. The Angels Do Not Forget. (Illus., Orig.). 1979. pap. text ed. 7.95 (ISBN 0-9602718-0-5). Law & Justice.
Thompson, Hunter S. Hell's Angels. 1975. pap. 2.75 (ISBN 0-345-29238-3). Ballantine.
Wethern, George & Colnett, Vincent. A Wayward Angel. LC 78-1989. 1978. 8.95 (ISBN 0-399-90006-3). Marek.

HELMETS
Hencken, Hugh. The Earliest European Helmets: Bronze Age or Early Iron Age. LC 78-152525. (ASPR Bulletin: No. 28). 1971. pap. text ed. 17.00 (ISBN 0-87365-530-3). Peabody Harvard.

HELMHOLTZ, HERMANN LUDWIG FERDINAND VON, 1821-1894
Koenigsberger, Leo. Herman Von Helmholtz. Welby, tr. 5.50 (ISBN 0-8446-2390-3). Peter Smith.

HELMINTHOLOGY
see also Veterinary Helminthology; Worms, Intestinal and Parasitic
Davis, A. Drug Treatment in Intestinal Helminthiasis. (Also avail. in French). 1973. 6.40 (ISBN 92-4-156036-3). World Health.
Jeffrey, Hugh C. & Leach, R. M. Atlas of Medical Helminthology & Protozoology. 2nd ed. LC 74-81190. (Illus.). 126p. 1975. 35.00 (ISBN 0-443-01222-9). Churchill.
Muller, Ralph. Worms & Disease: A Manual of Medical Helminthology. (Illus.). 1975. 49.95x (ISBN 0-433-17580-X). Intl Ideas.
Nuclear Techniques in Helminthology Research. (Illus.). 187p. 1975. pap. 19.50 (ISBN 92-0-111075-8, ISP390, IAEA). Unipub.
Production & Utilization of Radiation Vaccines Against Helminthic Diseases. (Technical Reports: No. 30). 1964. pap. 10.25 (ISBN 92-0-115164-0, IDC30, IAEA). Unipub.
Rysavy, B. & Ryzhikov, K. M., eds. Helminths of Fish Eating Birds of the Palaearctic Region: Volume 1, Nematoda. (Illus.). 1978. lib. bdg. 50.00 (ISBN 90-6193-551-2, Pub. by Junk Pubs Nethherlands). Kluwer Boston.
WHO Expert Committee on Helminthiasis, Rio De Janeiro, 1963. Soil Transmitted Helminths: A Report. (Technical Report Ser: No. 277). 70p. (Eng, Fr, Rus, & Span.). 1964. pap. 2.00 (ISBN 92-4-120277-7). World Health.

HELMINTHS
see Worms, Intestinal and Parasitic

HELOISE, 1101-1164
Gilson, Etienne. Heloise & Abelard. 1960. pap. 4.95 (ISBN 0-472-06038-4, 38, AA). U of Mich Pr.

HELOISE, 1101-1164–DRAMA
Forsyth, James. Heloise. (Orig.). 1959. pap. 1.00x (ISBN 0-87830-542-4). Theatre Arts.

HELOISE, 1101-1164–FICTION
Meade, M. Stealing Heaven: The Love Story of Heloise & Abelard. LC 79-1182. 1979. 10.95 (ISBN 0-688-03477-2). Morrow.

HELPER, HINTON ROWAN, 1829-1909
Bailey, Hugh C. Hinton Rowan Helper: Abolitionist-Racist. LC 65-16384. (Southern Historical Ser: Vol. 7). 1965. 18.50x (ISBN 0-8173-5212-0). U of Ala Pr.
Peissner, Elias. American Question in Its National Aspect. facs. ed. LC 71-152928. (Black Heritage Library Collection Ser). 1861. 13.50 (ISBN 0-8369-8772-1). Arno.
--American Question in Its National Aspect. LC 72-109350. Repr. of 1861 ed. 10.25x (ISBN 0-8371-3624-5, Pub. by Negro U Pr). Greenwood.
Wolfe, Samuel M. Helper's Impending Crisis Dissected. LC 77-92768. Repr. of 1860 ed. 12.25x (ISBN 0-8371-2174-4, Pub. by Negro U Pr). Greenwood.

HELPERN, MILTON, 1902-1977
Helpern, Milton & Knight, Bernard. Autopsy: The Memoirs of a Medical Detective. LC 77-76639. 1977. 10.00 (ISBN 0-312-06211-7). St Martin.
--Autopsy: The Memoirs of Milton Helpern-the World's Greatest Medical Detective. 1979. pap. 2.50 (ISBN 0-451-08607-4, E8607, Sig). NAL.

HELPLESSNESS (PSYCHOLOGY)
Garber, Judy & Seligman, Martin E., eds. Human Helplessness: Theory & Applications. LC 79-6773. 1980. 18.50 (ISBN 0-12-275050-0). Acad Pr.
Seligman, Martin E. Helplessness: On Depression, Development, & Death. LC 74-23125. (Psychology Ser.). (Illus.). 1975. text ed. 17.95x (ISBN 0-7167-0752-7); pap. text ed. 9.95x (ISBN 0-7167-0751-9). W H Freeman.

HELSINKI
Dominick, Mary F., ed. Human Rights & the Helsinki Accord. LC 81-80195. 422p. 1981. lib. bdg. 27.50 (ISBN 0-89941-095-2). W S Hein.
Helsinki. (Panorama Bks.). (Illus., Fr.). 3.95 (ISBN 0-685-11231-4). French & Eur.

HELVETIUS, CLAUDE ADRIEN, 1715-1771
Grossman, M. Philosophy of Helvetius with Special Emphasis on the Educational Implications of Sensationalism. LC 79-176822. (Columbia University. Teachers College. Contributions to Education: No. 210). Repr. of 1926 ed. 17.50 (ISBN 0-404-55210-2). AMS Pr.
Guillois, Antoine. Salon de Madame Helvetius: Cabanis et les Ideologues. LC 74-159698. (Research & Source Works Ser: No. 892). 250p. (Selected essays in History, Economics, & Social Science, No. 323). 1972. Repr. of 1894 ed. lib. bdg. 23.50 (ISBN 0-8337-4145-4). B Franklin.
Hazlitt, William. Essay on the Principles of Human Action, 1805. LC 70-75943. (Hist. of Psych. Ser.). 1969. 28.00x (ISBN 0-8201-1053-1). Schol Facsimiles.
Helvetius, Claude A. De l'Espirit: Or Essays on the Mind & Its Several Faculties. LC 70-80251. (Research & Source Works Ser.: No. 515). 1970. Repr. of 1810 ed. 32.50 (ISBN 0-8337-1649-2). B Franklin.
Plekhanov, G. V. Essays in the History of Materialism. 1968. 25.00 (ISBN 0-86527-061-9). Fertig.
Smith, D. W., et al, eds. Correspondance Generale D'Helvetius, Vol. I: 1737-1756. (Romance Ser.). 384p. 1981. 45.00x (ISBN 0-8020-5517-6). U of Toronto Pr.

HEMATOENCEPHALIC BARRIER
see Blood-Brain Barrier

HEMATOLOGY
see also Blood; Immunohematology; Pediatric Hematology
Andrew, Warren. Comparative Hematology. LC 64-25851. (Illus.). 1965. 72.75 (ISBN 0-8089-0012-9). Grune.
Baker, Brian H. Fundamental Skills in Hematology. 508p. 1980. pap. 28.50 spiral ed. (ISBN 0-398-04101-6). C C Thomas.
Ballas, Samir K. Self-Assessment of Current Knowledge in Hematology, Part One: Textbook Review. 2nd ed. 1977. 15.00 (ISBN 0-87488-248-6). Med Exam.
Baum, S. J. & Ledney, G. D., eds. Experimental Hematology Today. (Illus.). 1977. soft cover 36.00 (ISBN 0-387-90208-2). Springer-Verlag.
--Experimental Hematology Today 1978. LC 78-8054. (Illus.). 1978. 40.20 (ISBN 0-387-90323-2). Springer-Verlag.
--Experimental Hematology Today 1979. (Illus.). 1979. 61.70 (ISBN 0-387-90380-1). Springer-Verlag.
Baum, S. J., et al, eds. Experimental Hematology Today: 1980. (Illus.). xiv, 342p. 1981. 98.00 (ISBN 3-8055-1705-X). S Karger.
--Experimental Hematology Today 1981. (Illus.). xiv, 250p. 1981. 98.00 (ISBN 3-8055-2255-X). S Karger.
Beck, William S., ed. Hematology. 3rd ed. (Illus.). 448p. 1981. text ed. 27.50x (ISBN 0-262-02163-3); pap. text ed. 15.00x (ISBN 0-262-52067-2). MIT Pr.
Bessis, M. Living Blood Cells & Their Ultrastructure. Weed, R. I., tr. from Fr. LC 72-88924. (Illus.). 800p. 1973. 86.80 (ISBN 0-387-05981-4). Springer-Verlag.
Bessis, M. & Brecher, G., eds. Hemopoietic Dysplasias: Proceedings of a Symposium, Held on Oct.11-12, 1974 at the Institute of Cell Pathology, Hopital De Bicetre, Paris, France. (Illus.). 1977. pap. 28.20 (ISBN 0-387-07597-6). Springer-Verlag.
Blood Component Therapy: A Physician's Handbook. 56p. 1981. 3.00 (ISBN 0-914404-63-6). Am Assn Blood.
Bowring, C. S. Radionuclide Tracer Techniques in Hematology. 1981. text ed. write for info. (ISBN 0-407-00183-2). Butterworth.
Brown, Barbara A. Hematology: Principles & Procedures. 3rd ed. LC 80-16943. (Illus.). 358p. 1980. text ed. 22.00 (ISBN 0-8121-0707-1). Lea & Febiger.
Brown, Elmer, ed. Progress in Hematology, Vol. XII. 1981. price not set (ISBN 0-8089-1410-3). Grune.
Brown, Elmer B., ed. Progress in Hematology, Vol. XI. 335p. 1979. 34.50 (ISBN 0-8089-1223-2). Grune.
--Progress in Hematology, Vol. VIII. LC 56-58463. (Illus.). 384p. 1973. 54.00 (ISBN 0-8089-0821-9). Grune.
--Progress in Hematology, Vol. IX. (Illus.). 352p. 1975. 59.00 (ISBN 0-8089-0912-6). Grune.
Brown, Elmer B. & Moore, Carl V., eds. Progress in Hematology, Vols. 4-7. LC 56-58463. 1964-71. Vol.iV, 309pps. 54.25 (ISBN 0-8089-0332-2); Vol. V, 408pps. 62.00 (ISBN 0-8089-0079-X); Vol. VI,400pps. 62.00 (ISBN 0-8089-0080-3); Vol.vII, 448pps. 62.00 (ISBN 0-8089-0722-0). Grune.
Cavill, I., et al. Computers in Hematology. (Computers in Medicine Ser.). 1975. 7.95 (ISBN 0-407-00037-2). Butterworth.
Cawley, J. C. & Hayhoe, F. G. Ultrastructures of Haemic Cells. LC 73-80975. (Illus.). 285p. 1973. text ed. 21.00 (ISBN 0-7216-2470-7). Saunders.
Clarke, Cyril A. Rhesus Hemolytic Disease. 320p. 1975. 49.50 (ISBN 0-8391-0809-5). Univ Park.
Cline, Martin, ed. Leukocyte Function, Vol. 3. (Methods in Hematology). (Illus.). 224p. 1981. lib. bdg. write for info. (ISBN 0-686-28872-6). Churchill.
Clinical Hematology for Blood Bankers. 181p. 1979. 20.00 (ISBN 0-914404-47-4). Am Assn Blood.
Conference on Mononuclear Phagocytes, Third, Noorwijk aan Zee, The Netherlands, Sept. 17-24, 1978. Functional Aspects of Mononuclear Phagocytes: Proceedings, 2 vols. Ralph, ed. 1980. Set. lib. bdg. 189.50 (ISBN 90-247-2211-X, Pub. by Martinus Nijhoff Netherlands). Kluwer Boston.
Congress on Haematology Society, 13th International, Munich, 1970. Nucleic Acid Metabolism in Normal & Leukemic Cells: Proceedings. Polli, E., ed. 1971. pap. 12.00 (ISBN 3-8055-1230-9). S Karger.
Corsaut, Maurine J. Hematology Laboratory Manual. (Illus.). 136p. 1981. pap. 14.75 (ISBN 0-398-04524-0). C C Thomas.
Dacie, J. V. & Lewis, S. M. Practical Haematology. 5th ed. LC 75-24019. (Illus.). 576p. 1975. text ed. 24.00 (ISBN 0-443-01262-8). Churchill.
Delaney, J. W. & Garratty, G. Handbook of Hematological & Blood Transfusion Technique. 2nd ed. (Illus.). 1969. pap. text ed. 11.95x (ISBN 0-407-72852-X). Butterworth.
Dimitrov, Nikolay V. & Nodine, John H., eds. Drugs & Hematologic Reactions: The Twenty-Ninth Hahnemann Symposium. 416p. 1974. 65.25 (ISBN 0-8089-0812-X). Grune.
Dougherty, William M. Introduction to Hematology. 2nd ed. LC 75-33097. (Illus.). 400p. 1976. 19.95 (ISBN 0-8016-1444-9). Mosby.
Eastham, R. D. Clinical Haematology. 5th ed. (Illus.). 1977. pap. 12.95 (ISBN 0-8151-3009-0). Year Bk Med.
Fairbanks, Virgil F. Current Hematology, Vol. 1. 640p. 1981. 55.00 (ISBN 0-471-09504-4, Pub. by Wiley Med). Wiley.
Figueroa, William G. Hematology: UCLA Postgraduate Medicine for the Internist. (Illus.). 1981. write for info. (ISBN 0-89289-377-X). HM.
Forrai, J. Radiology of Haemophilic Arthropathies. 1976. 30.00x (ISBN 963-05-1012-X). Intl Pubns Serv.
Forrai, Jeno. Radiology of Haemophilic, 1979. lib. bdg. 26.00x (ISBN 9-0247-2130-X, Pub. by Martinus Nijhoff Netherlands). Kluwer Boston.
Garrick, Barbara L., ed. Hematology for Medical Technologists PreTest Self-Assessment & Review. LC 78-51704. (PreTest Self-Assessment & Review Ser.). (Illus.). 1979. pap. 10.95 (ISBN 0-07-051573-5). McGraw-Pretest.
Gross, R., ed. Strategies in Clinical Hematology. (Recent Results in Cancer Research Ser.: Vol. 69). (Illus.). 1979. 27.70 (ISBN 0-387-09578-0). Springer-Verlag.
Harper. The Peripheral Blood Film. 2nd ed. (Illus.). 1974. 18.95 (ISBN 0-407-76001-6). Butterworth.
Harris, John W. & Horrigan, Daniel L. Case Development Problems in Hematology: Ser. 1, the Red Cell. LC 63-6774. (Commonwealth Fund Publications Ser). (Illus.). 1963. pap. 3.25x (ISBN 0-674-09850-1). Harvard U Pr.
Hartmann, Peter M., ed. Guide to Hematologic Disorders. (Monographs in Family Medicine). 304p. 1980. 22.75 (ISBN 0-8089-1221-6). Grune.
Hawkey, Christine M. Comparative Mammalian Haematology: Cellular Components & Blood Coagulation in Captive Wild Animals. 1975. 60.00x (ISBN 0-433-13390-2). Intl Ideas.
Heckner, Fritz. Practical Microscopic Hematology: A Manual for the Clinical Laboratory & Clinical Practice. Lehmann, H. Peter & Yuan Kao, eds. Lehmann, H. L., tr. from Ger. LC 79-28562. (Illus.). 127p. 1980. pap. 19.50 (ISBN 0-8067-0811-5). Urban & S.
Hillman, Robert S. & Finch, Clement A. Red Cell Manual. 4th ed. (Illus.). 90p. 1974. pap. text ed. 2.50 (ISBN 0-8036-4633-X). Davis Co.
Hoffbrand, A. V., et al. Recent Advances in Haematology, No. 2. (Recent Advances in Haematology Ser.). (Illus.). 1977. text ed. 52.50 (ISBN 0-443-01621-6). Churchill.
Huser, H. J. Atlas of Comparative Primate Hematology. 1970. 62.00 (ISBN 0-12-362750-8). Acad Pr.
Hyun, Bong H., et al. Practical Hematology: A Lab Manual in Filmstrip. LC 75-8179. (Illus.). 384p. 1975. pap. text ed. 14.95 (ISBN 0-7216-9865-4); 65.00 (ISBN 0-7216-9864-6). Saunders.
International Society of Blood Transfusion Congress, 12th, Moscow, 1969. Proceedings, 2 pts. Stampfli, K., ed. Incl. Pt. 1. Immunhematology-Immunology, Transplantation Problems, Leukemia, Coagulation; Pt. 2. Organization & Technical Problems of Transfusion; Clinical Problems of Transfusion. (Bibliotheca Haematologica: Vol. 38). 1972. Set. 383.25 (ISBN 3-8055-1287-2); Pt. 1. 191.75 (ISBN 3-8055-1240-6); Pt. 2. 191.75 (ISBN 3-8055-1241-4). S Karger.
International Symposium on Hemodilution, 2nd, Rottach-Egern Tegernsee, Oct 1974. Intentional Hemodilution: Proceedings. Messmer, K. & Schmid-Schonbein, H., eds. (Bibliotheca Haematologica: Vol. 41). 200p. 1975. 57.50 (ISBN 3-8055-2167-7). S Karger.
Karr, Scott M. Blood Cells in Man. 1978. wkbk. 20.00 (ISBN 0-916750-12-4, CX-13). Dayton Labs.

Lamberg, Stanley L. & Rothstein, Robert. Hematology & Urinalysis: Functional Medical Lboratory Manual. (Illus.). 1978. write for info. (ISBN 0-87055-268-6). AVI.
Leavell, Byrd S. & Thorup, Oscar A. Fundamentals of Clinical Hematology. 4th ed. LC 75-19845. (Illus.). 750p. 1976. text ed. 29.00 (ISBN 0-7216-5678-1). Saunders.
Libansky, L., ed. Current Problems in Haematology. (International Congress Ser.: No. 336). 300p. 1975. 58.00 (ISBN 0-444-15138-9, Excerpta Medica). Elsevier.
Lichtman, Marshall A. Hematology for Practitioners. 1978. text ed. 27.50 (ISBN 0-316-52480-8). Little.
Lichtman, Marshall A., ed. Hematology & Oncology. (The Science & Practice of Clinical Medicine). 368p. 1980. 24.50 (ISBN 0-8089-1231-3). Grune.
Linman, J. W. Principles of Hematology. 1966. text ed. 14.95x (ISBN 0-02-370940-5). Macmillan.
Linman, James W. Hematology: Physiologic, Pathophysiologic, & Clinical Principles. (Illus.). 1975. text ed. 39.50 (ISBN 0-02-370920-0). Macmillan.
Livingstone, Frank B. Data on the Abnormal Hemoglobins & Glucose-Six-Phosphate Dehydrogenase Deficiency in Human Populations. (Technical Reports Ser.: No. 3). (Contribution 1 in Contributions in Human Biology). 1973. pap. 2.50x (ISBN 0-932206-12-3). U Mich Mus Anthro.
LoBue, J., et al, eds. The Year in Hematology: 1977. LC 77-8412. 595p. 1977. 29.50 (ISBN 0-306-32401-6, Plenum Pr). Plenum Pub.
LoBue, Joseph, et al, eds. Contemporary Hematology-Oncology, Vol. 1. (Illus.). 346p. 1980. 29.50 (ISBN 0-306-40246-7, Plenum Pr). Plenum Pub.
Mammen, et al, eds. Treatment of Bleeding Disorders with Blood Compounds. LC 80-80246. (Reviews of Hematology: Vol. I). 384p. 1980. 39.95 (ISBN 0-915340-01-1). PJD Pubns.
Manual on Radiation Haematology. (Technical Reports Ser.: No. 123). (Illus., Orig.). 1971. pap. 33.00 (ISBN 92-0-115071-7, IDC123, IAEA). Unipub.
Mathe, Georges, et al. Bone Marrow Transplantation & Leucocyte Transfusions. (American Lecture Living Chemistry). (Illus.). 224p. photocopy ed. spiral 19.75 (ISBN 0-398-01235-0). C C Thomas.
Mengel, Charles E. Hematology: Principles & Practice. (Illus.). 1977. 27.95 (ISBN 0-8151-5884-X). Year Bk Med.
Miale, John B. Laboratory Medicine: Hematology. 5th ed. LC 76-30575. (Illus.). 1977. text ed. 49.50 (ISBN 0-8016-3425-3). Mosby.
Milnor, William R. Hemodynamics. (Illus.). 518p. 1981. lib. bdg. 55.00 (ISBN 0-683-06050-3). Williams & Wilkins.
Mitruka, Brij M. & Rawnsley, Howard M. Clinical Biochemical & Hematological Reference Values in Normal Experimental Animals. LC 77-84608. (Illus.). 286p. 1977. 28.75x (ISBN 0-89352-006-3). Masson Pub.
Morrison, Frances S., et al, eds. Self-Assessment of Current Knowledge in Hematology, Part 2: Literature Review. 1975. spiral bdg. 13.00 (ISBN 0-87488-283-4). Med Exam.
Nathan, David G. & Oski, Frank A. Hematology of Infancy & Childhood. LC 73-89190. (Illus.). 720p. 1974. text ed. 42.50 (ISBN 0-7216-6660-4). Saunders.
Necheles, Thomas F. The Acute Leukemias. LC 78-12701. (Clinical Monographs in Hematology: Vol. 1). (Illus.). 1979. pap. 14.75 (ISBN 0-913258-57-1). Thieme-Stratton.
Neuwirt, J. & Ponka, P. Regulation of Haemoglobin Synthesis. 1977. lib. bdg. 26.00 (ISBN 90-247-1999-2, Pub. by Martinus Nijhoff Netherlands). Kluwer Boston.
Nour-Eldin, F. Revision Haematology: With Examination Exercises. (Illus.). 1973. 7.95 (ISBN 0-407-76700-2). Butterworth.
Nussbaum, Murray. Understanding Hematology. 1973. 12.00 (ISBN 0-87488-977-4). Med Exam.
Piomelli, Sergio & Yachnin, Stanley. Current Topics in Hematology, Vol. 1. LC 78-19681. 247p. 1978. 28.00x (ISBN 0-8451-0350-4). A R Liss.
Piomelli, Sergio & Yachnin, Stanley, eds. Current Topics in Hematology, Vol. 2. LC 78-19681. 290p. 1979. 28.00x (ISBN 0-8451-0351-2). A R Liss.
--Current Topics in Hematology, Vol. 3. LC 78-19681. 280p. 1980. 32.00x (ISBN 0-8451-0352-0). A R Liss.
Platt, William R. Color Atlas & Textbook of Hematology. 2nd ed. LC 78-21851. (Illus.). 1979. text ed. 62.50 (ISBN 0-397-50407-1, JBL-Med-Nursing). Har-Row.
Prasad, Ananda S.. Trace Elements & Iron in Human Metabolism. LC 78-13446. (Topics in Hematology Ser.). (Illus.). 408p. 1978. 29.50 (ISBN 0-306-31142-9, Plenum Pr). Plenum Pub.
Rapaport, Samuel I. Introduction to Hematology. (Illus.). 1971. pap. 17.50x (ISBN 0-06-142232-0, Harper Medical). Har-Row.
Reich, Paul R. Hematology: Physiopathologic Basis for Clinical Practice. 1978. text ed. 22.95 (ISBN 0-316-73860-3); pap. text ed. 17.95 (ISBN 0-316-73861-1). Little.
Remuzzi, Giuseppe, et al, eds. Hemostasis, Prostaglandins & Renal Disease. (Monographs of the Mario Negri Institute for Pharmacological Research). 475p. 1980. text ed. 52.50 (ISBN 0-89004-484-8). Raven.
Rifkind, R. A. Fundamentals of Hematology. 1980. 19.95 (ISBN 0-8151-7336-9). Year Bk Med.
Roath, S., ed. Topical Reviews in Haemotology, Vol. 1. (Topical Reviews Ser.). (Illus.). 240p. 1980. text ed. 29.50 (ISBN 0-7236-0540-8). Wright-PSG.
Rondanelli, E. G., et al. Pathology of Erythroblastic Mitosis in Occupational Benzenic Erythropathy & Erythremia. (Bibliotheca Haematologica: No. 35). (Illus.). 1970. pap. 45.50 (ISBN 3-8055-0139-0). S Karger.
Ross, D. W., et al, eds. Automation in Hematology: What to Measure & Why. (Illus.). 338p. 1981. pap. 46.00 (ISBN 0-387-10225-6). Springer-Verlag.
Rudman, Jack. Hematology. (College Level Examination Ser.: CLEP-33). 14.95 (ISBN 0-8373-5383-1); pap. 9.95 (ISBN 0-8373-5333-5). Natl Learning.
Samson, P. Glossary of Hematological & Seriological Terms. (Illus.). 128p. 1973. text ed. 7.95 (ISBN 0-407-72720-5). Butterworth.
Schmid-Schoenbein, H., et al, eds. Hemodilution & Flow Improvement. (Bibliotheca Haematologica Ser.: No. 47). (Illus.). viii, 296p. 1981. pap. 96.00 (ISBN 3-8055-2899-X). S Karger.
Schmidt, Robert M., ed. Hematology: Section I-Hematology. 544p. 1979-80. 67.95 (ISBN 0-8493-7091-4). CRC Pr.
Seiverd, Charles E. Hematology for Medical Technologists. 5th ed. (Illus.). 840p. 1982. price not set (ISBN 0-8121-0805-1). Lea & Febiger.
Seno, S. Topics on Hematology. (International Congress Ser: No. 415). 1978. 185.50 (ISBN 0-444-15250-4, Excerpta Medica). Elsevier.
Silber, R., et al. The Year in Hematology: 1978. (Illus.). 547p. 1978. 29.50 (ISBN 0-306-32402-4, Plenum Pr). Plenum Pub.
Silber, R., et al, eds. Contemporary Hematology-Oncology, Vol. 2. 536p. 1981. 49.50 (ISBN 0-306-40683-7, Plenum Pr). Plenum Pub.
Simmons, Arthur. Basic Hematology: An Introduction for Student Medical Technologists & Medical Assistants. (Illus.). 296p. 1973. text ed. 24.75 photocopy ed. spiral (ISBN 0-398-02536-3). C C Thomas.
--Technical Hematology. 3rd ed. (Illus.). 559p. 1980. text ed. 29.75 (ISBN 0-397-50350-4). Lippincott.
Spivak, Jerry L. Fundamentals of Clinical Hematology. (Illus.). 405p. 1980. 25.00 (ISBN 0-06-142465-X, Harper Medical). Har-Row.
Szirmai, E., ed. Nuclear Hematology. 1965. 64.00 (ISBN 0-12-681650-6). Acad Pr.
Ungaro, Peter C. Hematologic Diseases - New Directions in Therapy. 2nd ed. 1979. pap. 15.50 (ISBN 0-87488-682-1). Med Exam.
The Urokinase Pulmonary Embolism Trial by a National Cooperative Study. (AHA Monograph: No. 39). 1973. pap. 5.00 (ISBN 0-87493-033-2, 73-028A). Am Heart.
Verstraete, M. Haemostatic Drugs. 1977. lib. bdg. 29.00 (ISBN 90-247-2020-6, Pub. by Martinus Nijhoff Netherlands). Kluwer Boston.
Ward, F. A. Primer of Hematology. 1971. 6.95 (ISBN 0-407-62506-2). Butterworth.
Waterbury, Larry. Hematology for the House Officer. (House Officer Ser.). (Illus.). 152p. 1981. soft cover 9.95 (ISBN 0-683-08851-3). Williams & Wilkins.
Williams, William J., et al. Hematology. 2nd ed. (Illus.). 1977. text ed. 48.00 (ISBN 0-07-070376-0, HP). McGraw.
Wintrobe, Maxwell M. Blood, Pure & Eloquent. new ed. (Illus.). 1980. text ed. 30.00 (ISBN 0-07-071135-6, HP). McGraw.
Wintrobe, Maxwell M., et al. Clinical Hematology. 8th ed. (Illus.). 1900p. 1981. text ed. price not set (ISBN 0-8121-0718-7). Lea & Febiger.

HEMATOLOGY-ATLASES

Begemann, H. & Rastetter, J. W. Atlas of Clinical Haematology. 3rd ed. Hirsch, H. J., tr. from Ger. LC 79-12768. (Illus.). 1979. 172.10 (ISBN 0-387-09404-0). Springer-Verlag.
Block, Matthew H. Text-Atlas of Hematology. LC 75-38565. (Illus.). 651p. 1976. text ed. 76.50 (ISBN 0-8121-0014-X). Lea & Febiger.
Kapff, Carola T. & Jandl, James H. Blood: Atlas & Sourcebook of Hematology. 1981. text ed. price not set. Little.
McDonald, G. A., et al. Atlas of Haematology. 4th ed. LC 77-30131. (Illus.). 1978. 50.00 (ISBN 0-443-01376-4). Churchill.
Platt, William R. Color Atlas & Textbook of Hematology. 2nd ed. LC 78-21851. (Illus.). 1979. text ed. 62.50 (ISBN 0-397-50407-1, JBL-Med-Nursing). Har-Row.
Sanderson, J. H. & Phillips, Christine E. An Atlas of Laboratory Animal Haematology. (Illus.). 200p. 1981. text ed. 225.00x (ISBN 0-19-857520-3). Oxford U Pr.

HEMATOLOGY, FORENSIC

see Forensic Hematology

HEMATOLOGY, VETERINARY

see Veterinary Hematology

HEMATOPHILA

see Hemophilia

HEMATOPOIESIS

see also Blood; Blood Cells; Erythropoiesis; Hematopoietic System

Albert, Soloman N., et al. The Hematocrit in Clinical Practice. (American Lecture Anesthesiology). (Illus.). 80p. 1965. ed. spiral bdg. 9.75photocopy (ISBN 0-398-00025-5). C C Thomas.
CIBA Foundation. Haemopoietic Stem Cells. (Ciba Foundation Symposium Ser.: No.13). 356p. 1973. 26.00 (ISBN 0-444-15009-9, Excerpta Medica). Elsevier.
Cronkite, E. P. & Carstens, A. L. Diffusion Chamber Culture: Hemopoiesis, Cloning of Tumors, Cytogenetic & Carinogenic Assays. (Illus.). 270p. 1980. pap. 46.00 (ISBN 0-387-10064-4). Springer-Verlag.
Keleman, E., et al. Atlas of Human Hemopoietic Development. (Illus.). 1979. 207.90 (ISBN 0-387-08741-9). Springer-Verlag.

HEMATOPOIETIC SYSTEM

see also Marrow; Reticulo-Endothelial System; Spleen

Akazaki, K. Malignant Diseases of the Hematopoietic System. (Gann Monographs on Cancer Research: No. 15). (Illus.). 1976. 44.50 (ISBN 0-8391-0721-8). Univ Park.
Block, Matthew H. Text-Atlas of Hematology. LC 75-38565. (Illus.). 651p. 1976. text ed. 76.50 (ISBN 0-8121-0014-X). Lea & Febiger.
Dreyfus, J. C. & Dreyfus, B. Hematopoietic Agents. 1971. 55.00 (ISBN 0-08-016211-8). Pergamon.
Golde, David W., et al, eds. Hematopoietic Cell Differentiation. (ICN-UCLA Symposia on Molecular Biology, 1978 Ser.: Vol. 10). 1978. 32.50 (ISBN 0-12-287750-0). Acad Pr.
Lieberman, Philip H. & Good, Robert A., eds. Diseases of Hematopoietic System. LC 81-4946. (Anatomic Pathology Slide Seminar Ser.). (Illus.). 137p. 1981. pap. text ed. 18.00 (ISBN 0-89189-085-8). Am Soc Clinical.
Luriya, E. A., ed. Hematopoietic & Lymphoid Tissue in Cultures. LC 76-55703. (Studies in Soviet Science: Life Science). (Illus.). 181p. 1977. 42.50 (ISBN 0-306-10934-4, Consultants). Plenum Pub.
Lymphosarcoma & Other Neoplasms of Lymphatic & Hematopoietic System. (World Health Statistics Report: Vol. 18, No. 11). 1965. pap. 2.00 (ISBN 0-686-09175-2). World Health.
Maslow, William C., et al. Practical Diagnosis: Hematologic Disease. 1980. kroydenflex bdg. 22.00 (ISBN 0-471-09488-9, Pub. by Wiley Med). Wiley.

HEMATOPOIETIC SYSTEM-RADIATION EFFECTS

see Hematopoietic System, Effect of Radiation on the

HEMATOPOIETIC SYSTEM, EFFECT OF RADIATION ON THE

Manual on Radiation Haematology. (Technical Reports Ser.: No. 123). (Illus., Orig.). 1971. pap. 33.00 (ISBN 92-0-115071-7, IDC123, IAEA). Unipub.

HEME

Chance, Britton, et al, eds. Hemes & Hemoproteins. 1967. 55.00 (ISBN 0-12-167856-3). Acad Pr.
International Research Conference, Marburg an der Lahn, June 28 - July 1, 1973. Regulation of Porphyrin & Heme Biosynthesis: Proceedings. rev. ed. Doss, Manfred, ed. (Enzyme: Vol. 16, No. 1-6 & Vol. 17, No. 1-2). 384p. 1974. Repr. of 1973 ed. 85.25 (ISBN 3-8055-1652-5). S Karger.
Matteis, F. De & Aldridge, W. N., eds. Heme & Hemoproteins. LC 77-13134. (Handbook of Experimental Pharmacology: Vol. 44). (Illus.). 1977. 111.10 (ISBN 0-387-08460-6). Springer-Verlag.

HEMENWAY, AUGUSTUS, 1805-1876

Bandelier, Adolf F. Hemenway Southwestern Archaeological Expedition. LC 74-7922. Repr. of 1890 ed. 16.00 (ISBN 0-404-58057-2). AMS Pr.

HEMIC CELLS

see Blood Cells

HEMINGWAY, ERNEST, 1899-1961

Arnold, Lloyd. Hemingway: High on the Wild. (Illus.). 1977. 5.95 (ISBN 0-448-14290-2). G&D.
Asselineau, Roger, ed. The Literary Reputation of Hemingway in Europe. LC 65-22740. (Orig.). 1965. pap. 3.95x, uSA (ISBN 0-8147-0016-0). NYU Pr.
Astro, Richard & Benson, Jackson J., eds. Hemingway in Our Time. LC 73-18428. 1974. 10.95 (ISBN 0-87071-445-7). Oreg St U Pr.
Baker, Carlos. Ernest Hemingway: A Life Story. 1980. pap. 4.95 (ISBN 0-380-50039-6, 50039, Discus). Avon.
--Ernest Hemingway: A Life Story. LC 68-57079. 1969. lib. rep. ed. 27.50x (ISBN 0-684-14740-8, ScribT). Scribner.
--Hemingway: The Writer As Artist. rev. 4th ed. 440p. 1972. 27.50 (ISBN 0-691-06231-5); pap. 6.95 (ISBN 0-691-01305-5, 86). Princeton U Pr.
Baker, Carlos, ed. Ernest Hemingway: Selected Letters 1917-1961. 27.50 (ISBN 0-684-16765-4, ScribT); deluxe ed. 75.00 (ISBN 0-684-16961-4). Scribner.
Barger, James. Ernest Hemingway: American Literary Giant. new ed. Rahmas, D. Steve, ed. (Outstanding Personalities Ser.). 32p. 1975. lib. bdg. 2.95 incl. catalog cards (ISBN 0-686-11245-8); pap. 1.50 vinyl laminated covers (ISBN 0-686-11246-6). SamHar Pr.
Benson, Jackson J., ed. The Short Stories of Ernest Hemingway: Critical Essays. LC 74-75815. xv, 375p. 1975. 16.75 (ISBN 0-8223-0320-5); pap. 8.95 (ISBN 0-8223-0386-8). Duke.
Brasch, James D. & Sigman, Joseph. Hemingway's Library: A Composite Record. LC 80-8488. 1981. lib. bdg. 75.00 (ISBN 0-8240-9499-9). Garland Pub.
Brown, John, et al. Hemingway: A New Critical & Personal Assessment. Wiener, Amy D., tr. from Fr. LC 79-88630. (Illus.). Date not set. 12.95 (ISBN 0-85690-080-X). Peebles Pr.
Bruccoli, Mathew J. & Layman, Richard, eds. Fitzgerald-Hemingway Annual, 1978. 44.00 (ISBN 0-686-63977-4). Bruccoli.
--Fitzgerald-Hemingway Annual, 1979. 44.00 (ISBN 0-686-63978-2). Bruccoli.
Bruccoli, Matthew J., ed. Ernest Hemingway's Apprenticeship. 13.00 (ISBN 0-685-77404-X). Bruccoli.
--Fitzgerald-Hemingway Annual 1969. 18.00 (ISBN 0-685-77405-8). Bruccoli.
--Fitzgerald-Hemingway Annual 1976. 24.00 (ISBN 0-685-84829-9). Bruccoli.
Bruccoli, Matthew J. & Clark, C. E., eds. Fitzgerald-Hemingway Annual 1970. 18.00 (ISBN 0-685-77406-6). Bruccoli.
Bruccoli, Matthew J. & Clark, C. E. Frazer, Jr., eds. Fitzgerald-Hemingway Annual 1974. 23.00 (ISBN 0-685-84827-2). Bruccoli.
--Fitzgerald-Hemingway Annual 1975. 23.00 (ISBN 0-685-84828-0). Bruccoli.
Bruccoli, Matthew J. & Clark, C. E., Jr., eds. Fitzgerald-Hemingway Annual 1971. 22.00 (ISBN 0-685-77407-4). Bruccoli.
--Fitzgerald-Hemingway Annual 1972. 22.00 (ISBN 0-685-77408-2). Bruccoli.
--Fitzgerald-Hemingway Annual 1973. 20.00 (ISBN 0-685-77409-0). Bruccoli.
Bruccoli, Matthew J. & Layman, Richard, eds. Fitzgerald-Hemingway Annual, 3 vols. Incl. 1977 Annual. 1978 (ISBN 0-8103-0909-2); 1978 Annual. 1979 (ISBN 0-8103-0910-6); 1979 Annual. 1980 (ISBN 0-8103-0911-4). LC 75-83781. (Illus.). 44.00 ea. (Bruccoli Clark). Gale.
Burgess, Anthony. Ernest Hemingway & His World. LC 77-93899. (Illus.). 1978. 12.50 (ISBN 0-684-15661-X, ScribT). Scribner.
Callaghan, Morley. That Summer in Paris: Memories of Tangled Friendships with Hemingway, Fitzgerald & Some Others. (Illus.). 1979. pap. 3.95 (ISBN 0-14-005074-4). Penguin.
Capellan, Angel. El Viejo y el Mar, Hemingway. (Portico Ser.). 1976. pap. 1.50 (ISBN 0-671-08080-6). Monarch Pr.
Carey, Gary. Sun Also Rises Notes. (Orig.). pap. 1.95 (ISBN 0-8220-1237-5). Cliffs.
Carey, Gary K. The Old Man & the Sea Notes. 59p. (Orig.). 1973. pap. 2.25 (ISBN 0-8220-0935-8). Cliffs.
Cooperman, Stanley. Monarch Notes on Hemingway's Major Novels. (Orig.). pap. 1.95 (ISBN 0-671-00621-5). Monarch Pr.
Defalco, Joseph. The Hero in Hemingway's Short Stories. LC 78-16871. Repr. of 1963 ed. lib. bdg. 30.00 (ISBN 0-8414-1884-5). Folcroft.
--The Hero in Hemingway's Short Stories. 1977. Repr. of 1963 ed. lib. bdg. 27.50 (ISBN 0-8495-1000-7). Arden Lib.
Donaldson, Scott. By Force of Will: The Life & Art of Ernest Hemingway. 1978. pap. 3.95 (ISBN 0-14-004689-5). Penguin.
Duggan, Margaret M. & Layman, Richard, eds. Fitzgerald-Hemingway Annual 1977. 44.00 (ISBN 0-685-84830-2). Bruccoli.
F. Scott Fitzgerald & Ernest Hemingway in Paris. 5.00 (ISBN 0-89723-009-4). Bruccoli.
Fenton, Charles A. The Apprenticeship of Ernest Hemingway. 302p. 1975. Repr. of 1954 ed. lib. bdg. 17.50x (ISBN 0-374-92737-5). Octagon.

Fowler, Austin. Monarch Notes on Hemingway's the Snows of Kilimanjaro. (Orig.). pap. 1.50 (ISBN 0-671-00839-0). Monarch Pr.
Gellens, Jay, ed. Twentieth Century Interpretations of A Farewell to Arms. (Twentieth Century Interpretations Ser). 1970. 8.95 (ISBN 0-13-303180-2, Spec). P-H.
Grebstein, Sheldon. Studies in For Whom the Bell Tolls. LC 77-146318. 1971. pap. text ed. 2.50x (ISBN 0-675-09221-3). Merrill.
Grebstein, Sheldon N. Hemingway's Craft. LC 70-183304. (Crosscurrents-Modern Critiques Ser.). 1973. 9.95 (ISBN 0-8093-0611-5). S Ill U Pr.
Hanneman, Audre. Ernest Hemingway: A Comprehensive Bibliography. 1967. 35.00x (ISBN 0-691-06039-8); supplement 28.00x (ISBN 0-691-06284-6); Set. 55.00x (ISBN 0-686-57570-9). Princeton U Pr.
Hayashi, Tetsumaro, ed. Steinbeck & Hemingway: Dissertation Abstracts & Research Opportunities. LC 80-15540. 242p. 1980. 12.50 (ISBN 0-8108-1321-1). Scarecrow.
Heiney, Donald W. Barron's Simplified Approach to Hemingway: Novels & Other Works. rev. ed. LC 65-16319. (Orig.). (gr. 9-12). 1967. pap. text ed. 1.50 (ISBN 0-8120-0175-3). Barron.
Hemingway, Ernest. Ernest Hemingway's Apprenticeship. Bruccoli, Matthew J., ed. LC 74-155140. (Illus.). 122p. 1971. 14.00 (ISBN 0-910972-05-2). IHS-PDS.
Hemingway, Gregory H. Papa: A Personal Memoir. 1976. 7.95 (ISBN 0-395-24348-3). HM.
Hemingway, Mary W. How It Was. 1976. 12.50 (ISBN 0-394-40109-3). Knopf.
Isabelle, J. Hemingway's Religious Experience. 1970. 17.50 (ISBN 0-912378-02-6). Chips.
Killinger, John. Hemingway & the Dead Gods: A Study in Existentialism. LC 60-15379. 128p. 1960. 9.00x (ISBN 0-8131-1055-6). U Pr of Ky.
Klebbe, Lawrence. Monarch Notes on Hemingway's the Sun Also Rises. (Orig.). pap. 1.95 (ISBN 0-671-00674-6). Monarch Pr.
Klibbe, Lawrence. Monarch Notes on Hemingway's Farewell to Arms. (Orig.). pap. 1.95 (ISBN 0-671-00671-1). Monarch Pr.
--Monarch Notes on Hemingway's for Whom the Bell Tolls. (Orig.). pap. 1.95 (ISBN 0-671-00672-X). Monarch Pr.
Kvam, Wayne E. Hemingway in Germany. LC 79-181689. x, 214p. 1973. 12.95x (ISBN 0-8214-0126-2). Ohio U Pr.
Laurence, Frank M. Hemingway & the Movies. LC 79-1437. 336p. 1980. 20.00x (ISBN 0-87805-115-5). U Pr of Miss.
Lewis, Robert, Jr. Hemingway on Love. LC 72-6772. (Studies in Fiction, No. 34). 1972. Repr. of 1965 ed. lib. bdg. 24.95 (ISBN 0-8383-1650-6). Haskell.
McCaffery, John K. Ernest Hemingway: The Man & His Work. LC 69-17516. Repr. of 1950 ed. 12.50x (ISBN 0-8154-0277-5). Cooper Sq.
Monarch Notes on Hemingway's Old Man & the Sea. (Orig.). pap. 1.95 (ISBN 0-671-00673-8). Monarch Pr.
Nahal, Chaman. The Narrative Pattern in Ernest Hemingway's Fiction. 245p. 1971. 16.50 (ISBN 0-8386-7795-9). Fairleigh Dickinson.
--The Narrative Pattern in Ernest Hemingway's Fiction. 245p. 1971. 16.50 (ISBN 0-8386-7795-9). Fairleigh Dickinson.
Nelson, Raymond S. Hemingway: Expressionist Artist. (Illus.). 1979. text ed. 9.95 (ISBN 0-8138-1025-6); pap. text ed. 6.95 (ISBN 0-8138-1305-0). Iowa St U Pr.
Oldsey, Bernard. Ernest Hemingway: The Papers of a Writer. LC 80-9031. 1981. lib. bdg. 20.00 (ISBN 0-8240-9303-8). Garland Pub.
--Hemingway's Hidden Craft: The Writing of "A Farewell to Arms". LC 79-743. (Illus.). 1979. 9.50 (ISBN 0-271-00213-1). Pa St U Pr.
Pearsall, Robert B. The Life & Writings of Ernest Hemingway. LC 72-93573. 282p. (Orig.). 1973. pap. text ed. 20.00x (ISBN 0-391-02005-6). Humanities.
Peterson, Richard. Hemingway: Direct & Oblique. LC 68-23810. (Studies in American Literature: No. 14). 1969. text ed. 32.50x (ISBN 90-2797-527-2). Mouton.
Rajan, B. Focus Two (Symposium; the Realist Novel in the Thirties, Ernest Hemingway) LC 72-13481. Repr. of 1946 ed. lib. bdg. 15.00 (ISBN 0-8414-1278-2). Folcroft.
Reynolds, Michael S. Hemingway's First War: The Making of A Farewell to Arms. LC 75-30202. 1976. 22.00 (ISBN 0-691-06302-8). Princeton U Pr.
--Hemingway's Reading, Nineteen Ten to Nineteen Forty: Commentary & Inventory. LC 80-7549. 200p. 1980. 17.50 (ISBN 0-691-06447-4). Princeton U Pr.
Roberts, James L. Farewell to Arms Notes. (Orig.). pap. 1.95 (ISBN 0-8220-0461-5). Cliffs.
--For Whom the Bell Tolls Notes. (Orig.). pap. 2.25 (ISBN 0-8220-0497-6). Cliffs.
Rovit, Earl H. Ernest Hemingway. (Twayne's United States Authors Ser). 1963. pap. 3.45 (ISBN 0-8084-0123-8, T41, Twayne). Coll & U Pr.
--Ernest Hemingway. (U. S. Authors Ser.: No. 41). 1963. lib. bdg. 9.95 (ISBN 0-8057-0364-0). Twayne.
Ryan, Frank L. The Immediate Critical Reception of Ernest Hemingway. LC 79-6026. 77p. 1980. text ed. 12.75 (ISBN 0-8191-0970-3); pap. text ed. 6.50 (ISBN 0-8191-0971-1). U Pr of Amer.
Sarason, Bertram D. Hemingway & The Sun Set. LC 72-76990. (Illus.). 270p. 1972. 16.00 (ISBN 0-910972-06-0). IHS-PDS.
--Hemingway & THE SUN Set. 15.00 (ISBN 0-685-77410-4). Bruccoli.
Shaw, Samuel. Ernest Hemingway. LC 78-134827. (Modern Literature Ser.). 10.95 (ISBN 0-8044-2823-9). Ungar.
Stephens, Robert O., ed. Ernest Hemingway: The Critical Reception. (American Critical Tradition: No. 3). 600p. 1976. lib. bdg. 23.50 (ISBN 0-89102-052-7). B Franklin.
Stoltzfus, Ben. Gide & Hemingway: Rebels Against God. (National University Pubns. Literary Criticism Ser.). 1978. 9.95 (ISBN 0-8046-9214-9). Kennikat.
Unfried, Sarah P. Man's Place in the Natural Order: A Study of Ernest Hemingway's Major Works. 1976. lib. bdg. 69.95 (ISBN 0-87968-458-5). Gordon Pr.
Wagner, Linda W. Hemingway & Faulkner: Inventors-Masters. LC 75-23367. 1975. 13.50 (ISBN 0-8108-0862-5). Scarecrow.
Wagner, Linda W., ed. Ernest Hemingway: Five Decades of Criticism. 325p. 1974. 10.00 (ISBN 0-87013-182-6). Mich St U Pr.
Waldhorn, Arthur. Ernest Hemingway. 160p. (Orig.). 1973. pap. 1.95 (ISBN 0-07-067800-6, SP). McGraw.
--A Reader's Guide to Ernest Hemingway. 1977. Repr. of 1972 ed. lib. bdg. 15.00x (ISBN 0-374-98146-9). Octagon.
Watkins, Floyd C. Flesh & the Word: Eliot, Hemingway, Faulkner. LC 75-157740. 1971. 8.95 (ISBN 0-8265-1169-4). Vanderbilt U Pr.
Watts, Emily S. Ernest Hemingway & the Arts. LC 77-146456. (Illus.). 259p. 1971. 10.95 (ISBN 0-252-00169-9). U of Ill Pr.
Williams, Wirt. The Tragic Art of Ernest Hemingway. LC 81-4740. 264p. 1981. text ed. 17.95x (ISBN 0-8071-0884-7). La State U Pr.
Young, Philip. Ernest Hemingway. rev. ed. (Pamphlets on American Writers Ser: No. 1). 1965. pap. 1.25x (ISBN 0-8166-0191-7, MPAW1). U of Minn Pr.
--Ernest Hemingway: A Reconsideration. 2nd ed. LC 65-26101. 1966. 13.95 (ISBN 0-271-73060-9). Pa St U Pr.

HEMINGWAY, ERNEST, 1899-1961-BIBLIOGRAPHY

Cohn, Louis. A Bibliography of the Writings of Ernest Hemingway. LC 73-2635. (American Literature Ser., No. 49). 1973. Repr. of 1931 ed. lib. bdg. 49.95 (ISBN 0-8383-1694-8). Haskell.
Cohn, Louis H. A Bibliography of the Works of Ernest Hemingway. LC 73-13845. 1931. lib. bdg. 8.75 (ISBN 0-8414-3466-2). Folcroft.
Harmon, Robert B. The First Editions of Ernest Hemingway. LC 77-26500. (First Edition Pocket Guides Ser.). 1978. pap. 3.95 (ISBN 0-910720-11-8). Hermes.
John F. Kennedy Memorial Library. Ernest Hemingway: Catalog of the Manuscripts, Correspondence & Other Material in the John F. Kennedy Library. (Library Catalogs & Supplements Ser.). 1981. lib. bdg. 120.00 (ISBN 0-8161-0380-1). G K Hall.
Wagner, Linda W. Ernest Hemingway: A Reference Guide. (Reference Publications Ser.). 1977. lib. bdg. 22.00 (ISBN 0-8161-7976-X). G K Hall.
Waldhorn, Arthur. A Reader's Guide to Ernest Hemingway. 1977. Repr. of 1972 ed. lib. bdg. 15.00x (ISBN 0-374-98146-9). Octagon.
Young, Philip & Mann, Charles W., eds. Hemingway Manuscripts: An Inventory. LC 68-8189. 1969. 9.95 (ISBN 0-271-00080-5); ltd. ed. 16.00x (ISBN 0-271-00231-X). Pa St U Pr.

HEMIPLEGIA

see Paralysis

HEMIPTERA

see also Homoptera; Scale-Insects

Furth, David G. The Stink Bugs of Ohio (Hemiptera: Pentatomidae) 1974. 3.00 (ISBN 0-686-30331-8). Ohio Bio Survey.
Hungerford, H. B. The Corixidae of the Western Hemisphere (Hemiptera) LC 75-43673. (Illus.). 827p. 1977. Repr. of 1948 ed. 25.00 (ISBN 0-911836-07-1). Entomological Repr.
Menke, Arnold, ed. The Semi-Aquatic & Aquatic Hemiptera of California (Herteroptera: Hemiptera) (California Insect Survey Ser.: Vol. 21). 1979. pap. 21.50x (ISBN 0-520-09592-8). U of Cal Pr.
Slater, James A. & Baranowski, Richard M. How to Know the True Bugs: (Hemiptera: Heteroptera) (Pictured Key Nature Ser). 1978. text ed. 8.95x (ISBN 0-697-04893-4); wire coil 6.95x (ISBN 0-697-04894-2). Wm C Brown.
Usinger, R. L. Genus Nysius & Its Allies in the Hawaiian Islands. Repr. of 1942 ed. pap. 15.00 (ISBN 0-527-02281-0). Kraus Repr.
Van Duzee, E. P. Checklist of Hemiptera (Excepting the Aphididae, Aleurodidae & Coccidae) of America, North of Mexico. 1916. pap. 5.00 (ISBN 0-934454-23-X). Lubrecht & Cramer.
Weber, H. Biologie der Hemipteren. (Illus.). 1968. 50.00 (ISBN 90-6123-179-5). Lubrecht & Cramer.

HEMOCHROMATOSIS

see also Blood-Diseases; Liver-Diseases

HEMOCYANIN

Ghiretti, F., ed. Physiology & Biochemistry of Haemocyanins. LC 68-17675. (Illus.). 1968. 21.00 (ISBN 0-12-281550-5). Acad Pr.

HEMODIALYSIS

see also Artificial Kidney; Peritoneal Dialysis

Bailey, George L., ed. Hemodialysis: Principles & Practice. 1972. 50.00 (ISBN 0-12-072950-4). Acad Pr.
Bazzato, Giorgio & Onesti, Gaddo. Hemodialysis in the Home: Techniques & Clinical Results. (Illus.). 120p. 1975. 12.00 (ISBN 0-398-03156-8). C C Thomas.
Czaczkes, J. W. & De-Nour, A. Kaplan. Chronic Hemodialysis As a Way of Life. LC 78-3605. 1978. 17.50 (ISBN 0-87630-165-0). Brunner-Mazel.
Daily, Elaine K. & Schroeder, John S. Techniques in Bedside Hemodynamic Monitoring. 2nd ed. LC 80-16594. (Illus.). 198p. 1980. pap. text ed. 12.45 (ISBN 0-8016-4363-5). Mosby.
European Dialysis & Transplant Assoc. Dialysis, Transplantation & Nephrology: Proceedings, Vol. 12. Moorhead, J. F., ed. (Illus.). 1976. text ed. 49.00x (ISBN 0-8464-0327-7). Beekman Pubs.
Fox, Renee C. & Swazey, Judith P. The Courage to Fail: A Social View of Organ Transplants & Dialysis. 2nd ed. LC 78-56332. 1979. pap. 6.95 (ISBN 0-226-25944-7, P778, Phoen). U of Chicago Pr.
--The Courage to Fail: A Social View of Organ Transplants & Dialysis. 2nd rev. ed. LC 78-56332. (Illus.). 1979. lib. bdg. 17.00x (ISBN 0-226-25943-9). U of Chicago Pr.
Kagan, Lynn W. Renal Disease: A Manual of Patient Care. (Illus.). 1979. text ed. 17.95 (ISBN 0-07-033190-1, HP). McGraw.
Kenedi, R. M. Artificial Organs. (Illus.). 1977. 49.50 (ISBN 0-8391-0999-7). Univ Park.
Levy, Norman. Living or Dying: Adaptation to Hemodialysis. 164p. 1974. pap. 16.75 photocopy ed., spiral (ISBN 0-398-02987-3). C C Thomas.
Levy, Norman B., ed. Psychonephrology One: Psychological Factors in Hemodialysis & Transplantation. 280p. 1981. 25.00 (ISBN 0-306-40586-5, Plenum Pr). Plenum Pub.
Wright, Lucius F. Maintaince Hemodialysis. 1981. lib. bdg. 28.50 (ISBN 0-8161-2172-9, Hall Medical). G K Hall.

HEMOGLOBIN

see also Anoxemia; Bile Pigments

Antonini, E. & Brunori, M. Hemoglobin & Myoglobin in Their Reactions with Ligands. (Frontiers of Biology Ser. Vol. 21). 1971. 85.50 (ISBN 0-444-10096-2, North-Holland). Elsevier.
Brewer, George J. Hemoglobin & Red Cell Structure & Function. LC 72-86140. (Advances in Experimental Medicine & Biology Ser.: Vol. 28). 526p. 1972. 47.50 (ISBN 0-306-39028-0, Plenum Pr). Plenum Pub.
Bunn, H. Franklin, et al. Hemoglobinopathies. LC 76-14678. (Major Problems in Internal Medicine: Vol. 12). 1977. text ed. 16.00 (ISBN 0-7216-2179-1). Saunders.
--Human Hemoglobins. LC 76-14677. 1977. text ed. 20.00 (ISBN 0-7216-2178-3). Saunders.
Fairbanks, Virgil. Hemoglobinopathies & Thalassemias. LC 80-51938. 1980. 35.00 (ISBN 0-686-29379-7). Thieme Stratton.
Hanash, Samir M. & Brewer, George J., eds. Advances in Hemoglobin Analysis. LC 81-3686. (Progress in Clinical & Biological Research Ser.: Vol. 60). 222p. 1981. 22.00 (ISBN 0-8451-0060-2). A R Liss.
Huisman, Titus A. J. & Jonxis, J. H. P. The Hemoglobinopathies: Techniques of Identification. (Clinical & Biochemical Analysis: Vol. 6). 1977. 54.50 (ISBN 0-8247-6529-X). Dekker.
Ingram, Vernon M. Hemoglobins in Genetics & Evolution. LC 63-10416. (Biology Ser.). (Illus.). 1963. 15.00x (ISBN 0-231-02585-8). Columbia U Pr.
Lehmann, H. & Huntsman, R. G. Man's Haemoglobins. 2nd ed. LC 74-11653. (Illus.). 478p. 1974. 32.00 (ISBN 0-397-58148-3, JBL-Med-Nursing). Har-Row.
Lehmann, H. & Kynoch, P. A., eds. Human Haemoglobin Variants & Their Characteristics. 1976. 36.75 (ISBN 0-7204-0585-8, North-Holland). Elsevier.
McElroy, Samuel R. The Handbook on the Psychology of Hemoglobin-S: A Perspicacious View of Sickle Cell Disease. LC 80-8170. 133p. 1980. pap. text ed. 7.50 (ISBN 0-8191-1132-5). U Pr of Amer.
Maclean. Haemoglobin. (Studies in Biology: No. 93). 1978. 5.95 (ISBN 0-7131-2698-1). Univ Park.
Neuwirt, J. & Ponka, P. Regulation of Haemoglobin Synthesis. 1977. lib. bdg. 26.00 (ISBN 90-247-1999-2, Pub. by Martinus Nijhoff Netherlands). Kluwer Boston.
Schreeder & Huisman. The Chromatography of Hemoglobin. (Clinical & Biochemical Analysis Ser.: Vol. 9). 256p. 1980. 29.75 (ISBN 0-8247-6941-4). Dekker.
Stamatoyannopoulos, G. & Nienhuis, A., eds. Cellular & Molecular Regulation of Hemoglobin Switching. 856p. 1979. 79.50 (ISBN 0-686-63983-9). Grune.
Symposium On Hemoglobin - 1st Inter-American - Caracas - 1969. Genetical, Functional & Physical Studies of Hemoglobins: Proceedings. Arends, T., et al, eds. 1971. 48.00 (ISBN 3-8055-1255-4). S Karger.
Van Assendelft, O. W. Spectrophotometry of Haemoglobin Derivatives. 1970. 18.30x (ISBN 90-232-0560-X, Pub by Van Gorcum). Intl Schol Bk Serv.
Weissbluth, M. Hemoglobin: Cooperativity & Electronic Properties. LC 73-19106. (Molecular Biology, Biochemistry & Biophysics Ser.: Vol. 15). (Illus.). 175p. 1974. 39.30 (ISBN 0-387-06582-2). Springer-Verlag.

HEMOGLOBIN, ABNORMAL

see Hemoglobinopathy

HEMOGLOBINOPATHY

Bunn, H. Franklin, et al. Hemoglobinopathies. LC 76-14678. (Major Problems in Internal Medicine: Vol. 12). 1977. text ed. 16.00 (ISBN 0-7216-2179-1). Saunders.
Caughey, Winslow, ed. Clinical & Biochemical Aspects of Hemoglobin Abnormalities. 1978. 48.00 (ISBN 0-12-164350-6). Acad Pr.
Huisman, Titus A. J. & Jonxis, J. H. P. The Hemoglobinopathies: Techniques of Identification. (Clinical & Biochemical Analysis: Vol. 6). 1977. 54.50 (ISBN 0-8247-6529-X). Dekker.
Lehmann, H. & Huntsman, R. G. Man's Haemoglobins. 2nd ed. LC 74-11653. (Illus.). 478p. 1974. 32.00 (ISBN 0-397-58148-3, JBL-Med-Nursing). Har-Row.
Schmid, Rudi, et al, eds. Physiology & Disorders of Hemoglobin Degradation. LC 72-4766. (Illus.). 149p. 1972. 29.00 (ISBN 0-8089-0791-3). Grune.
Schwartz, Elias, et al, eds. Hemoglobinopathies in Children. LC 78-55277. (Progress in Pediatric Hematology & Oncology Ser.: Vol. 3). (Illus.). 400p. 1979. 27.50 (ISBN 0-88416-204-4). Wright-PSG.
Stamatoyannopoulos, George & Nienhuis, Arthur W., eds. Organization & Expression of Globin Genes. LC 81-3677. 368p. 1981. 52.00 (ISBN 0-8451-0211-7). A R Liss.
WHO Scientific Group. Geneva, 1971. Treatment of Haemoglobinopathies & Allied Disorders: Report. (Technical Report Ser.: No. 509). (Also avail. in French & Spanish). 1972. pap. 2.00 (ISBN 92-4-120509-1). World Health.

HEMOLYSIS AND HEMOLYSINS

Beutler, Ernest. Hemolytic Anemia in Disorders of Red Cell Metabolism. LC 78-2391. (Topics in Hematology). (Illus.). 280p. 1978. 23.50 (ISBN 0-306-31112-7, Plenum Pr). Plenum Pub.
Ponder, Eric. Hemolysis & Related Phenomena. reissued ed. LC 48-3833. (Illus.). 406p. 1971. 51.25 (ISBN 0-8089-0672-0). Grune.
A Seminar on Laboratory Management of Hemolysis. 160p. 1979. 18.00 (ISBN 0-914404-44-X). Am Assn Blood.
Weinheimer, Peter. Characterization of Erythrocyte-Reactive Factors of Panulirus Argus: A Contribution to Immunophylogeny. 102p. 1972. 23.00x (ISBN 0-8422-7035-3). Irvington.

HEMOLYTIC DISEASE OF NEWBORN

see Erythroblastosis Fetalis

HEMOPHILIA

Boone, Donna C. Comprehensive Management of Hemophilia. LC 76-18109. 185p. 1976. text ed. 11.95 (ISBN 0-8036-1000-9). Davis Co.
Brinkhous, K. M., ed. Handbook of Hemophilia, 2 vols. LC 74-21851. 1000p. 1975. Set. 207.50 (ISBN 0-444-16709-9, North-Holland). Elsevier.
Committee on Prosthetics Research & Development. Comprehensive Management of Musculoskeletal Disorders in Hemophilia. (Illus.). 200p. 1973. pap. 8.75 (ISBN 0-309-02139-1). Natl Acad Pr.

Congress of the World Federation of Haemophilia, 7th, Teheran 1971. Haemophilia: Proceedings. Ala, F. A. & Denson, K. W., eds. (International Congress Ser.: No. 252). 1973. 55.25 (ISBN 0-444-15090-0, Excerpta Medica). Elsevier.
Driessen, A. P. Arthropaties in Haemophiliacs. 1973. 9.70x (ISBN 90-232-1138-3, Pub by Van Gorcum). Intl Schol Bk Serv.
Egli, H. & Inwood, M. J., eds. The Haemophiliac in the Eighties. (Haemostasis Journal Bks.: Vol. 10, Suppl. 1,1981). (Illus.). xii, 310p. 1981. pap. 57.50 (ISBN 3-8055-2885-X). S Karger.
Green, David, ed. Hemophilia: A Manual of Outpatient Management. (Illus.). 132p. 1973. 12.75 (ISBN 0-398-02853-2). C C Thomas.
Hilgartner. Hemophilia in the Child. Date not set. price not set. Masson Pub.
Hilgartner, Margaret W., ed. Hemophilia in Children. LC 76-3895. (Progress in Pediatric Hematology & Oncology Ser.). 222p. 1976. 22.50 (ISBN 0-88416-138-2). Wright-PSG.
Jones, Peter. Hemophilia Home Therapy. 256p. 1981. text ed. 34.50 (ISBN 0-8391-1660-8). Univ Park.
--Living with Haemophilia. (Illus.). 188p. 1974. text ed. 12.00 (ISBN 0-8036-5060-4). Davis Co.
Katz, Alfred H. Hemophilia: A Study in Hope & Reality. (Illus.). 176p. 1970. text ed. 11.50 (ISBN 0-398-00978-3). C C Thomas.
Kirsh, Catherine A. Are You a Bleeder? (Illus.). 1978. 20.00 (ISBN 0-916750-06-X). Dayton Labs.
Massie, Robert & Massie, Suzanne. Journey. 1975. 12.50 (ISBN 0-394-49018-5). Knopf.
Seligsohn, Uri, et al, eds. Haemophilia. LC 81-42305. 245p. 1981. 48.00 (ISBN 0-8451-3000-5). A R Liss.
Sell, Sarah H. & Karzon, David T., eds. Hemophilus influenzae: Proceedings of a Conference on Antigen-Antibody Systems, Epidemiology, & Immuno/Prophylaxis. LC 73-4557. (Illus.). 325p. 1973. 15.00x (ISBN 0-8265-1185-6). Vanderbilt U Pr.
Ulutin, O., et al, eds. Haemophilia. (International Congress Ser: No. 356). 1975. 59.00 (ISBN 0-444-15175-3, Excerpta Medica). Elsevier.

HEMOPOIESIS
see Hematopoiesis

HEMORRHAGE
see also Bloodletting; Gastrointestinal Hemorrhage; Hemorrhagic Diseases; Hemostasis; Hemostatics
Barsewisch, B. von. Perinatal Retinal Haemorrhages: Morphology, Aetiology & Significanace. (Illus.). 1979. 36.50 (ISBN 0-387-09167-X). Springer-Verlag.
Caprini, Joseph A. Bleeding Problems: Diagnosis & Treatment. (Illus.). 1973. pap. text ed. 3.95x (ISBN 0-06-140625-2, Harper Medical). Harper-Row.
Mammen, E. F., et al, eds. Treatment of Bleeding Disorders with Blood Components. 1980. 39.95 (ISBN 0-915340-01-1). PJD Pubns.
Miescher, Peter A., et al, eds. Disorders of Hemostasis: Current Status. LC 78-166214. (A Seminars in Hematology Reprint). 208p. 1971. 39.50 (ISBN 0-8089-0728-X). Grune.
Smith, R. R. & Robertson, J. T. Subarachnoid Hemorrhage & Cerebrovascular Spasm. (Illus.). 284p. 1975. 33.50 (ISBN 0-398-03230-0). C C Thomas.
Spaet, Theodore H., ed. Progress in Hemostasis & Thrombosis, Vol. I. LC 72-2917. (Illus.). 250p. 1972. 47.75 (ISBN 0-8089-0760-3). Grune.

HEMORRHAGE, CEREBRAL
see Apoplexy

HEMORRHAGE, UTERINE
Robertson, W. B. The Endometrium. (Postgraduate Pathology Ser.). 1981. text ed. 59.95 (ISBN 0-407-00171-9). Butterworth.

HEMORRHAGIC DIATHESIS
see Hemophilia

HEMORRHAGIC DISEASES
Bain, R. V. Hemorrhagic Septicemia. 1963. pap. 4.75 (ISBN 0-685-36303-1, F231, FAO). Unipub.
Hotta, Susumu. Dengue & Related Hemorrhagic Diseases. LC 67-26013. (Illus.). 176p. 1969. 10.75 (ISBN 0-87527-043-3). Green.
Quick, Armand J. The Hemorrhagic Diseases & the Pathology of Hemostasis. (Illus.). 404p. 1974. text ed. 33.50 (ISBN 0-398-02998-9). C C Thomas.
Zieve, Philip D. & Levin, Jack. Disorders of Hemostasis. LC 76-1252. (Major Problems in Internal Medicine Ser.: Vol. 10). 1976. text ed. 14.50 (ISBN 0-7216-9685-6). Saunders.

HEMORRHOIDS
Berkowitz, Stanley. The Lowdown on Hemorrhoids, Piles & Other Lowdown Disorders. (Illus.). 1975. pap. 1.50 (ISBN 0-917746-01-5). A & B Pubs.
Cox, E. Aubrey. Bottoms Up with a Rear Admiral. LC 79-79091. 1969. 7.95 (ISBN 0-87716-004-X, Pub. by Moore Pub Co). F Apple.
Holt, Robert L. Hemorrhoids: A Cure & Preventative. LC 77-86391. (Illus.). 1978. 12.95x (ISBN 0-930926-00-5). Calif Health.
--Hemorrhoids: A Cure & Preventive. rev. ed. LC 79-21792. 1980. pap. 4.95 (ISBN 0-688-08584-9, Quill). Morrow.
--Hemorrhoids: A Cure & Preventive. rev. ed. LC 79-21792. 1980. Repr. of 1977 ed. 8.95 (ISBN 0-688-03584-1). Morrow.
Wood, Clive, ed. Haemorrhoids: Current Concepts on Causation & Management. (Royal Society of Medicine International Congress & Symposium Ser.). 36p. 1979. 13.50 (ISBN 0-8089-1217-8). Grune.

HEMOSTASIS
see also Blood-Coagulation; Hemorrhage; Hemostatics
Blomback, M. & Brakman, P., eds. Synthetic Substrates & Synthetic Inhibitors: The Use of Chromogenic Substrates in Studies of the Haemostatic Mechanism. (Haemostasis: Vol. 7, Nos. 2-3). (Illus.). 1978. pap. 22.75 (ISBN 3-8055-2907-4). S Karger.
Fareed, Jawed, ed. Perspectives in Hemostasis: Proceedings of a Symposium Held 11 May 1979 at Loyola University, Maywood, Ill., U. S. A. (Illus.). 400p. 1981. 50.00 (ISBN 0-08-025092-0). Pergamon.
Harker, Laurence A. Hemostasis Manual. 2nd ed. (Illus.). 86p. 1974. pap. text ed. 2.50 (ISBN 0-8036-4569-4). Davis Co.
Harper, T. A. Laboratory Guide to Disordered Hemostasis. 1970. 14.95 (ISBN 0-407-74250-6). Butterworth.
Hirsh, Jack & Brain, Elizabeth. Hemostasis & Thrombosis: A Conceptual Approach. (Illus.). 1978. pap. text ed. 6.50 (ISBN 0-443-08056-9). Churchill.
Minna, John D., et al. Disseminated Intravascular Coagulation in Man. (Illus.). 212p. 1974. text ed. 23.75 (ISBN 0-398-02992-X). C C Thomas.
Murano, Genesio & Bick, Rodger L., eds. Basic Concepts of Hemostasis & Thrombosis. 304p. 1980. 74.95 (ISBN 0-8493-5393-9). CRC Pr.
Rudowski, Witold J., ed. Disorders of Hemostasis in Surgery. Paryski, Edwin, tr. from Polish. LC 76-47902. (National Library of Medicine). (Illus.). 465p. 1977. text ed. 25.00x (ISBN 0-87451-137-2). U Pr of New Eng.
Serneri, Neri G. G. & Prentice, C. Haemostasis & Thrombosis. LC 78-72545. (Proceedings of the Serono Symposia No. 15). 1980. 93.00 (ISBN 0-12-516150-6). Acad Pr.
Sirridge, Marjorie S. Laboratory Evaluation of Hemostasis. 2nd ed. LC 73-10452. (Medical Technology Ser). (Illus.). 214p. 1974. text ed. 9.75 (ISBN 0-8121-0389-0). Lea & Febiger.
Spaet, Theodore H., ed. Progress in Hemostasis & Thrombosis, Vol. II. LC 72-2917. (Illus.). 384p. 1974. 55.75 (ISBN 0-8089-0816-2). Grune.
--Progress in Hemostasis & Thrombosis, Vol. 5. (Illus.). 320p. 1980. 39.50 (ISBN 0-8089-1220-8). Grune.
--Progress on Hemostasis & Thrombosis, Vol. 4. 432p. 1978. text ed. 43.50 (ISBN 0-8089-1096-5). Grune.
Zoological Society of London - 27th Symposium. Haemostatic Mechanism in Man & Other Animals. MacFarlane, R. G., ed. 39.00 (ISBN 0-12-613327-1). Acad Pr.

HEMOSTATICS
Caprini, Joseph A. Bleeding Problems: Diagnosis & Treatment. (Illus.). 1973. pap. text ed. 3.95x (ISBN 0-06-140625-2, Harper Medical). Harper-Row.
Donati, Maria B., et al, eds. Malignancy & the Hemostatic System. (Monographs of the Mario Negri Institute for Pharmacological Research). 148p. 1981. text ed. 17.00 (ISBN 0-89004-463-5). Raven.
Pia, H. W., et al, eds. Spontaneous Intracerebral Haematomas: Advances in Diagnosis & Therapy. (Illus.). 500p. 1981. 116.90 (ISBN 0-387-10146-2). Springer Verlag.

HEMP
Here are entered works on the description, culture and use of Cannabis sativa as a fiber plant.
see also Cordage; Fibers; Jute; Rope

HEMPHILL, JOHN, 1803-1862
Curtis, Rosalee M. John Hemphill: First Chief Justice of Texas. (Illus.). 1971. 9.50 (ISBN 0-8363-0054-8). Jenkins.

HENDERSON, JOHN, 1747-1785
Pilon, Frederick. Essay on the Character of Hamlet. 2nd ed. LC 73-174202. Repr. of 1777 ed. 21.00 (ISBN 0-404-05048-4). AMS Pr.

HENDRIX, JIMI
Daniels, Richard. Jimi Hendrix: Note for Note. (Orig.). (YA) 1980. pap. 5.95 (ISBN 0-89524-108-0). Cherry Lane.
Henderson, David. Jimi Hendrix: Voodoo Child of the Aquarian Age. LC 76-56299. 1978. 13.95 (ISBN 0-385-07357-7). Doubleday.
--Scuse Me While I Kiss the Sky: Life of Jim Hendrix. 416p. 1981. pap. text ed. 8.95 (ISBN 0-553-01334-3). Bantam.
Welch, Chris. Hendrix. (Illus.). 104p. 1981. pap. 4.95 (ISBN 0-8256-3901-8, Quick Fox). Music Sales.
--Hendrix: A Biography. LC 73-83767. (Illus.). 1972. pap. 5.95 (ISBN 0-8256-3901-8, 030901, Quick Fox). Music Sales.

HENKELS AND MCCOY
Henkels, John B., Jr. American Adventure. LC 65-29146. 1966. 7.50x (ISBN 0-8154-0112-4). Cooper Sq.

HENLEY, WILLIAM ERNEST, 1849-1903
Buckley, Jerome H. William Ernest Henley: A Study in the Counter-Decadence of the Nineties. LC 74-120238. 1971. Repr. lib. bdg. 14.50x (ISBN 0-374-91087-1). Octagon.
Connell, John. W. E. Henley. 1977. Repr. of 1949 ed. lib. bdg. 20.00 (ISBN 0-8492-0441-0). R West.
Cornford, L. William Ernest Henley. 59.95 (ISBN 0-8490-1302-X). Gordon Pr.
Cornford, L. C. William Ernest Henley. LC 72-3679. (English Biography Ser., No. 31). 1972. Repr. of 1913 ed. lib. bdg. 29.95 (ISBN 0-8383-1580-1). Haskell.
--William Ernest Henley. 1973. Repr. of 1913 ed. 19.45 (ISBN 0-8274-1358-0). R West.
Flora, Joseph M. William Ernest Henley. (English Authors Ser.: No. 107). 12.50 (ISBN 0-8057-6750-9). Twayne.
--William Ernest Henley. LC 72-120015. (English Authors Ser.). 1970. lib. bdg. 8.95x (ISBN 0-89197-977-8); pap. text ed. 4.95x (ISBN 0-89197-994-8). Irvington.
Looker, Samuel J. Shelley, Trelawney & Henley. 1950. Repr. 20.00 (ISBN 0-8274-3897-4). R West.
Robertson, John H. William Ernest Henley. 59.95 (ISBN 0-8490-1303-8). Gordon Pr.
Ross, John D., ed. Henley & Burns. LC 77-105828. 1970. Repr. of 1901 ed. 10.00 (ISBN 0-8046-1032-0). Kennikat.
Williamson, Kennedy. W. E. Henley. LC 74-30419. (English Literature Ser., No. 33). 1974. lib. bdg. 53.95 (ISBN 0-8383-1751-0). Haskell.

HENRI 4TH, KING OF FRANCE, 1553-1610
Baird, Henry M. Huguenots & Henry of Navarre, 2 Vols. LC 76-130987. Repr. of 1903 ed. Set. 57.50 (ISBN 0-404-00540-3). Vol. 1 (ISBN 0-404-00541-1). Vol. 2 (ISBN 0-404-00542-X). AMS Pr.
Lee, Maurice, Jr. James First & Henri Fourth: An Essay in English Foreign Policy, 1603-1610. LC 74-100377. (Illus.). 1970. 14.50 (ISBN 0-252-00084-6). U of Ill Pr.
Seward, Desmond. First Bourbon: Henri Fourth, King of France & Navarre. LC 73-167959. (Illus.). 1971. 8.95 (ISBN 0-87645-051-6). Gambit.
Wilkinson, Burke. Helmet of Navarre. (gr. 5 up). 1965. 8.95 (ISBN 0-02-792990-6). Macmillan.
Willert, P. F. Henry of Navarre & the Hugenots in France. 1978. Repr. of 1893 ed. lib. bdg. 40.00 (ISBN 0-8495-5634-1). Arden Lib.
Willert, Paul F. Henry of Navarre & the Huguenots in France. LC 76-149680. (Heroes of the Nations Series). Repr. of 1893 ed. 30.00 (ISBN 0-404-06949-5). AMS Pr.

HENRI 4TH, KING OF FRANCE, 1553-1610–FICTION
Weyman, Stanley J. From the Memoirs of a Minister of France. LC 77-113694. (Short Story Index Reprint Ser.). 1895. 22.00 (ISBN 0-8369-3423-7). Arno.

HENRI, ROBERT, 1865-1929
Century Association, New York. Robert Henri & Five of His Pupils: Loan Exhibition of Paintings, April 5, to June 1, 1946. LC 74-160918. (Biography Index Reprint Ser). Repr. of 1946 ed. 14.00 (ISBN 0-8369-8081-6). Arno.

HENRIETTA MARIE, QUEEN CONSORT OF CHARLES 1ST, 1609-1669
Bone, Quentin. Henrietta Maria, Queen of the Cavaliers. LC 70-172250. (Illus.). 304p. 1972. 18.00 (ISBN 0-252-00198-2). U of Ill Pr.
Maurois, Andre. Trois Portraits de Femme: La Duchesse de Devonshire, la Comtesse D'Albany, Henriette de France. (Coll. les Soirees Du Luxembourg). 11.50 (ISBN 0-685-36965-X). French & Eur.

HENRIQUE, O NAVEGADOR, INFANTE OF PORTUGAL, 1394-1460
Beazley, C. R. Prince Henry the Navigator. (Illus.). 336p. 1968. Repr. of 1923 ed. 27.50x (ISBN 0-7146-1452-1, F Cass Co). Biblio Dist.
Beazley, Charles R. Prince Henry the Navigator, the Hero of Portugal & of Modern Discovery 1394-1460. LC 68-57121. (Research & Source Works Ser: No. 316). (Illus.). 1968. Repr. of 1911 ed. 21.50 (ISBN 0-8337-0210-6). B Franklin.
Major, Richard Henry. Life of Prince Henry of Portugal. 487p. 1967. Repr. of 1868 ed. 29.50x (ISBN 0-7146-1045-3, F Cass Co). Biblio Dist.
Sanceau, Elaine. Henry the Navigator: The Story of a Great Prince & His Times. 1969. Repr. of 1947 ed. 17.50 (ISBN 0-208-00681-8, Archon). Shoe String.

HENRY 2ND, KING OF ENGLAND, 1133-1189
Barber, Richard. Henry Plantagenet: A Biography. (Illus.). 278p. 1972. Repr. of 1964 ed. 15.00x (ISBN 0-87471-062-6). Rowman.
Corfe, T. Archbishop Thomas & King Henry Second. LC 74-14442. (Introduction to the History of Mankind Ser). (Illus.). (gr. 6-11). 1975. pap. text ed. 3.95 (ISBN 0-521-20646-4). Cambridge U Pr.
Salzman, Louis F. Henry Second. LC 66-27144. (Illus.). 1967. Repr. of 1914 ed. 9.00 (ISBN 0-8462-1028-2). Russell.
Warren, W. L. Henry Second. (English Monarchs Ser.). 1973. 36.50x (ISBN 0-520-02282-3); pap. 8.95 (ISBN 0-520-03494-5). U of Cal Pr.

HENRY 4TH, KING OF ENGLAND, 1367-1413–DRAMA
Monarch Notes on Shakespeare's Henry Fourth, Part One. pap. 1.75 (ISBN 0-671-00633-9). Monarch Pr.
Shakespeare, William. Henry Fourth, 2 pts. rev. ed. Kittredge, George L. & Ribner, Irving, eds. 1966. Pt. 1. pap. 4.50x (ISBN 0-471-00513-4); Pt. 2. pap. 3.95x (ISBN 0-471-00518-5). Wiley.
--Henry Fourth, Pt. 1. rev. ed. Sanderson, James L., ed. (Critical Editions Ser). (Annotated). (gr. 9-12). 1969. text ed. 5.00 (ISBN 0-393-04234-0); pap. text ed. 5.95x (ISBN 0-393-09554-1, 9554, NortonC). Norton.
--Henry Fourth, Pt. 1. Quiller-Couch, Arthur, et al, eds. (New Shakespeare Ser). 23.95 (ISBN 0-521-07532-7); pap. 4.50x (ISBN 0-521-09475-5). Cambridge U Pr.
--Henry Fourth, Pt. 1. Mack, Maynard, ed. pap. 1.50 (ISBN 0-451-51327-4, CW1327, Sig Classics). NAL.
--Henry Fourth, Pt. 1. Shaaber, M. A., ed. (Pelican Shakespeare Ser.). (YA) (gr. 9 up). 1957. pap. 1.95 (ISBN 0-14-071407-3, Pelican). Penguin.
--Henry Fourth, Pt. 1. rev. ed. Walter, J. H., ed. (Players' Shakespeare Ser). (YA) (gr. 9 up). 1965. 3.50 (ISBN 0-8238-0111-X). Plays.
--Henry Fourth, Pt. 2. Holland, Norman N., ed. pap. 1.95 (ISBN 0-451-51266-9, CJ1401, Sig Classics). NAL.
--Henry Fourth, Pt. 2. Chester, Alan, ed. (Pelican Shakespeare Ser.). 1957. pap. 1.95 (ISBN 0-14-071408-1, Pelican). Penguin.
--Henry the Fourth, Pt. 1. Wright, Louis B. & LaMar, Virginia A., eds. (gr. 11-12). pap. text ed. 1.95 (ISBN 0-671-48893-7). WSP.

HENRY 5TH, KING OF ENGLAND, 1387-1422
Jarman, Rosemary H. Crispin's Day: The Glory of Agincourt. LC 79-16256. (Illus.). 1979. 15.00 (ISBN 0-316-45783-3). Little.
Kingsford, Charles L. Henry the Fifth: The Typical Mediaeval Hero. LC 73-14452. (Heroes of the Nations Ser.). Repr. of 1901 ed. 30.00 (ISBN 0-404-58269-9). AMS Pr.
Labarge, Margaret W. Henry Fifth: The Cautious Conqueror. LC 75-15238. 1976. 25.00 (ISBN 0-8128-1869-5). Stein & Day.
Taylor, Frank & Roskell, John S., eds. Gesta Henrici Quinti: The Deeds of Henry the Fifth. Taylor, Frank & Roskell, John S., trs. from Latin. (Oxford Medieval Texts Ser.). 242p. 1975. 52.50x (ISBN 0-19-822231-9). Oxford U Pr.
Wylie, James H. Reign of Henry the Fifth, 3 Vols. 1914-1929. Repr. Set. lib. bdg. 77.00x (ISBN 0-8371-0768-7, WYHF). Greenwood.

HENRY 5TH, KING OF ENGLAND, 1387-1422–DRAMA
Famous Victories of Henry the Fifth. LC 79-133664. (Tudor Facsimile Texts. Old English Plays: No. 82). Repr. of 1913 ed. 31.50 (ISBN 0-404-53382-5). AMS Pr.
Monarch Notes on Shakespeare's Henry Fifth. pap. 1.95 (ISBN 0-671-00635-5). Monarch Pr.
Shakespeare, William. Henry Fifth. Wright, Louis B. & LaMar, Virginia A., eds. (Folger Lib. Ser). (gr. 11-12). pap. text ed. 1.75 (ISBN 0-671-48897-X). WSP.
--Henry Fifth. Quiller-Couch, Arthur, et al, eds. (New Shakespeare Ser). 23.95 (ISBN 0-521-07534-3); pap. 4.50x (ISBN 0-521-09477-1). Cambridge U Pr.
--Henry Fifth. Brown, John R., ed. pap. 1.75 (ISBN 0-451-51187-5, CE1314-2, Sig Classics). NAL.
--Henry Fifth. Harbage, Alfred, ed. 1957. pap. 2.50 (ISBN 0-14-071409-X, Pelican). Penguin.
--Henry Fifth. Walter, J. H., ed. (Players' Shakespeare Ser). (YA) (gr. 9 up). 1967. 3.50 (ISBN 0-8238-0112-8). Plays.
--King Henry Fifth. 4th ed. Walter, John H., ed. (Arden Shakespeare Ser.). 1967. Repr. 25.95x (ISBN 0-416-47340-7); pap. 4.50 (ISBN 0-416-47640-6). Methuen Inc.

HENRY 6TH, KING OF ENGLAND, 1421-1471–DRAMA
Gaw, Allison. The Origin & Development of Henry the Sixth in Relation to Shakespeare, Marlowe, Peele, & Greene. LC 74-16121. 1974. Repr. of 1926 ed. lib. bdg. 9.45 (ISBN 0-8414-4564-8). Folcroft.

Griffiths, Ralph A. The Reign of Henry VI. LC 80-53771. (Illus.). 604p. 1981. 35.00 (ISBN 0-520-04356-1). U of Cal Pr.

Shakespeare, William. Henry Sixth, Pt. 1. Quiller-Couch, Arthur, et al, eds. (New Shakespeare Ser). 1968. 23.95 (ISBN 0-521-07535-1); pap. 4.50x (ISBN 0-521-09478-X). Cambridge U Pr.

--Henry Sixth, Pt. 1. Ryan, Lawrence V., ed. pap. 1.95 (ISBN 0-451-51535-8, CJ1535, Sig Classics). NAL.

--Henry Sixth, Pts. 1, 2 & 3. Bevington, D., et al, eds. 1966. Pt. 1. pap. 1.95 (ISBN 0-14-071434-0, Pelican); Pt.2&3. pap. 2.95 (ISBN 0-14-071435-9, Pelican). Penguin.

--Henry Sixth, Pt. 2. Quiller-Couch, Arthur, et al, eds. (New Shakespeare Ser). 1968. 23.95 (ISBN 0-521-07536-X); pap. 4.50x (ISBN 0-521-09479-8). Cambridge U Pr.

--Henry Sixth, Pt. 3. Quiller-Couch, Arthur, et al, eds. (New Shakespeare Ser). 1968. 23.95 (ISBN 0-521-07537-8); pap. 4.50x (ISBN 0-521-09480-1). Cambridge U Pr.

--Henry Sixth, Pt. 3. Crane, Milton, ed. pap. 1.95 (ISBN 0-451-51323-1, CJ1323, Sig Classics). NAL.

--Henry Sixth, Part 2. Wright, Louis B. & LaMar, Virginia A., eds. (Folger Lib. Ser). (gr. 11-12). pap. text ed. 1.95 (ISBN 0-671-48810-4). WSP.

--King Henry Fourth, Pt. 1. rev. 6th ed. Humphresy, Arthur R., ed. (Arden Shakespeare Ser.). 1960. Repr. of 1960 ed. 25.95x (ISBN 0-416-47420-9); pap. 4.50 (ISBN 0-416-47660-0). Methuen Inc.

--King Henry Sixth, Pt. 1. 3rd rev. ed. Cairncross, Andrew S., ed. (Arden Shakespeare Ser.). 1962. 25.95x (ISBN 0-416-47200-1); pap. 5.50 (ISBN 0-416-27840-X). Methuen Inc.

--King Henry Sixth, Pt. 2. 3rd rev. ed. Cairncross, Andrew S., ed. (Arden Shakespeare Ser.). 1957. 25.95x (ISBN 0-416-47210-9); pap. 5.50 (ISBN 0-416-27900-7). Methuen Inc.

--King Henry Sixth, Pt. 3. 3rd rev. ed. Cairncross, Andrew S., ed. (Arden Shakespeare Ser.). 1965. 25.95x (ISBN 0-416-47220-6); pap. 5.50 (ISBN 0-416-27910-4). Methuen Inc.

HENRY 7TH, KING OF ENGLAND, 1457-1509

Chrimes, S. B. Henry VII. LC 72-78947. (English Monarch Ser.). (Illus.). 400p. 1973. 31.50x (ISBN 0-520-02266-1) (ISBN 0-520-04414-2). U of Cal Pr.

Chrimes, S. B., ed. Henry VII. (English Monarch Ser.). 1981. pap. 8.95 cancelled (ISBN 0-520-04414-2, CAL 506). U of Cal Pr.

Gairdner, James. Henry the Seventh. LC 70-112639. Repr. of 1889 ed. 11.50 (ISBN 0-404-02667-2). AMS Pr.

--Henry the Seventh. 1889. 19.00 (ISBN 0-403-00020-3). Scholarly.

Temperley, Gladys. Henry Seventh. LC 75-110871. (Illus.). 1971. Repr. of 1914 ed. lib. bdg. 19.25x (ISBN 0-8371-4550-3, TEHE). Greenwood.

Van Cleave Alexander, Michael. The First of the Tudors: A Study of Henry VII & His Reign. 280p. 1980. 22.50x (ISBN 0-8476-6259-4). Rowman.

HENRY 8TH, KING OF ENGLAND, 1491-1547

Bradshaw, B. The Dissolution of the Religious Orders in Ireland Under Henry Eighth. LC 73-83104. (Illus.). 248p. 1974. 41.50 (ISBN 0-521-20342-2). Cambridge U Pr.

Du Boys, Albert. Catherine of Aragon & the Sources of the English Reformation, 2 vols in 1. Yonge, Charlotte M., ed. 1969. Repr. of 1881 ed. 35.50 (ISBN 0-8337-0931-3). B Franklin.

Erickson, Carolly. Great Harry. LC 79-21868. 1980. 14.95 (ISBN 0-671-40017-7). Summit Bks.

Froude, James A. Divorce of Catherine of Aragon. 2nd ed. LC 68-58379. Repr. of 1891 ed. 31.50 (ISBN 0-404-02626-5). AMS Pr.

Gasquet, Francis A. Henry the Eighth & the English Monasteries, 2 vols. LC 74-39467. (Select Bibliography Reprint Series). 1972. Repr. of 1888 ed. 51.25 (ISBN 0-8369-9905-3). Arno.

Harpsfield, Nicholas. Treatise on the Pretended Divorce Between Henry Eighth & Catharine of Aragon. Pocock, N., ed. 1878. 22.50 (ISBN 0-384-21420-7). Johnson Repr.

Henry VIII. pap. 2.45 (ISBN 0-8277-5603-8). British Bk Ctr.

Henry VIII. A Copy of the Letters, Wherein Kyng Henry the Eyght Made Answere into a Certayn Letter of Martyn Luther. LC 72-204. (English Experince Ser.: No. 322). 100p. 1971. Repr. of 1528 ed. 14.00 (ISBN 90-221-0322-6). Walter J Johnson.

Kelly, Henry A. The Matrimonial Trials of Henry VIII. LC 75-7483. xiv, 314p. 1976. 15.00x (ISBN 0-8047-0895-9). Stanford U Pr.

McKee, Alexander. King Henry Eighth's Mary Rose. LC 73-93035. (Illus.). 338p. 1974. 25.00x (ISBN 0-8128-1656-0). Stein & Day.

Malvern, Gladys. Six Wives of Henry Eighth. LC 71-134678. (Illus.). (gr. 7 up). 1969. 7.95 (ISBN 0-8149-0665-6). Vanguard.

Morrison, N. Brysson. Private Life of Henry the Eighth. LC 63-13796. (Illus.). 1964. 8.95 (ISBN 0-8149-0162-X). Vanguard.

Palmer, M. D. Henry VIII. (Illus.). 1971. pap. text ed. 5.50x (ISBN 0-582-31428-3). Longman.

Scarisbrick, J. J. Henry VIII. LC 68-10995. (English Monarchs Series). (Illus.). 1968. 24.50x (ISBN 0-520-01129-5); pap. 6.95 (ISBN 0-520-01130-9, CAL195). U of Cal Pr.

Smith, Lacey B. Henry Eighth, the Mask of Royalty. (Illus.). 379p. 1973. pap. 4.95 (ISBN 0-586-03820-5, Pub. by Granada England). Academy Chi Ltd.

--Henry Eighth: The Mask of Royalty. (Illus.). 328p. 1980. 17.95 (ISBN 0-224-00523-5, Pub. by Chatto Bodley Jonathan). Merrimack Bk Serv.

Tree, Sir Herbert B. Henry VIII & His Court. 6th ed. LC 77-4446. 1977. lib. bdg. 17.50 (ISBN 0-8414-8545-3). Folcroft.

Waldman, Milton. Some English Dictators. LC 77-112820. 1970. Repr. of 1940 ed. 12.50 (ISBN 0-8046-1087-8). Kennikat.

HENRY 8TH, KING OF ENGLAND, 1491-1547–DRAMA

Dunster, Mark. Surrey: Henry the Eighth, Pt. 6. 1980. pap. 4.00 (ISBN 0-89642-061-2). Linden Pubs.

Rowley, Samuel. When You See Me You Know Me. LC 70-133730. (Tudor Facsimile Texts. Old English Plays: No. 106). Repr. of 1913 ed. 31.50 (ISBN 0-404-53406-6). AMS Pr.

Shakespeare, William. Henry Eighth. Wright, Louis B. & LaMar, Virginia A., eds. (Folger Lib. Ser). (gr. 11-12). 1968. pap. text ed. 1.95 (ISBN 0-671-82660-3). WSP.

--Henry Eighth. Quiller-Couch, Arthur, et al, eds. (New Shakespeare Ser). 1969. pap. 4.50 (ISBN 0-521-09481-X). Cambridge U Pr.

--Henry Eighth. Schoenbaum, Samuel, ed. pap. 1.50 (ISBN 0-451-51246-4, CW1246, Sig Classics). NAL.

--Henry Eighth. Hoeniger, F. D., ed. (Pelican Shakespeare Ser.). 1966. pap. 1.95 (ISBN 0-14-071436-7, Pelican). Penguin.

--Henry VIII. LC 78-24131. (The Shakespeare Plays Ser.). (Illus.). 1979. pap. 2.95 (ISBN 0-8317-4443-X, Mayflower Bks). Smith Pubs.

HENRY 4TH, KING OF GERMANY, 1050-1106

Jaffe, Philipp & Wattenbach, W., trs. from Latin. Historia De Vita Henrici Quarti Imperatoris. xxviii, 56p. Repr. of 1910 ed. pap. 5.50 (ISBN 0-384-23436-4). Johnson Repr.

HENRY, ALEXANDER, 1739-1824

Armour, David A., ed. Attack at Michilimackinac, 1763: Alexander Henry's Travels & Adventures in Canada & the Indian Territories Between the Years 1760 & 1764. (Illus.). 1971. pap. 2.50 (ISBN 0-911872-37-X). Mackinac Island.

HENRY, CHARLES, 1859-1926

Arguelles, Jose A. Charles Henry & the Formation of a Psychophysical Aesthetic. LC 72-189026. 240p. 1972. 12.00x (ISBN 0-226-02757-0). U of Chicago Pr.

--Charles Henry & the Formation of a Psychophysical Aesthetic. LC 72-189026. x, 200p. 1974. pap. 3.25 (ISBN 0-226-02758-9, P596, Phoen). U of Chicago Pr.

Norris, James D. & Shaffer, Arthur H., eds. Politics & Patronage in the Gilded Age: The Correspondence of James A. Garfield & Charles E. Henry. LC 70-629850. (Illus.). 1970. 15.00 (ISBN 0-87020-107-7). State Hist Soc Wis.

HENRY, EDWARD L.

McCausland, Elizabeth. Life & Work of Edward Lamson Henry N. A. LC 74-100614. (Library of American Art Ser.). (Illus.). 1970. Repr. of 1945 ed. lib. bdg. 39.50 (ISBN 0-306-71866-9). Da Capo.

HENRY, JOSEPH, 1797-1878

Crowther, James G. Famous American Men of Science. facs. ed. LC 69-18925. (Essay Index Reprint Ser). 1937. 25.00 (ISBN 0-8369-0040-5). Arno.

Jahns, P. Joseph Henry: Father of American Electronics. (gr. 7-12). 1969. PLB 4.75 (ISBN 0-13-511147-1). P-H.

Molella, Arthur P., et al. A Scientist in American Life: The Essays & Lectures of Joseph Henry. LC 80-19367. (Illus.). 136p. 1981. pap. 6.95 (ISBN 0-87474-641-8). Smithsonian.

The Papers of Joseph Henry: The Princeton Years, January 1838 to 1840, Vol. 4. (Illus.). 432p. 1981. 30.00x (ISBN 0-87474-792-9). Smithsonian.

Reingold, Nathan, ed. The Papers of Joseph Henry. Incl. Volume One: The Albany Years, December 1797-October 1832. LC 72-2005. 496p. 20.00x (ISBN 0-87474-123-8); Volume Two: The Princeton Years, November 1832-December 1835. LC 72-2005. 539p. 30.00x (ISBN 0-87474-164-5). (Illus.). Smithsonian.

--The Papers of Joseph Henry: The Princeton Years, January 1838-1840, Vol. 4. LC 72-2005. (The Papers of Joseph Henry Ser.). (Illus.). 475p. 1981. text ed. 30.00x (ISBN 0-87474-792-9). Smithsonian.

HENRY, PATRICK, 1736-1799

Axelrad, Jacob. Patrick Henry: The Voice of Freedom. LC 75-23310. (Illus.). 318p. 1975. Repr. of 1947 ed. lib. bdg. 18.00x (ISBN 0-8371-8331-6, AXPH). Greenwood.

Campbell, Norine D. Patrick Henry. (Illus.). 1969. 12.50 (ISBN 0-8159-6501-X). Devin.

Fritz, Jean. Where Was Patrick Henry on the 29th of May? (Illus.). 48p. (gr. 3-5). 1975. 6.95 (ISBN 0-698-20307-0). Coward.

Henry, William W. Patrick Henry, Life Correspondence & Speeches, 3 Vols. LC 71-108350. (Research & Source Works Ser.: No. 407). 1970. Repr. of 1891 ed. lib. bdg. 87.00 (ISBN 0-8337-1662-X). B Franklin.

McIlwaine, H. R., ed. The Letters of Patrick Henry. LC 27-2700. (Official Letters of the Governors of the State Virginia Ser: Vol. 1). 1926. 7.50 (ISBN 0-88490-018-5). VA State Lib.

Tyler, M. Patrick Henry. 69.95 (ISBN 0-8490-0806-9). Gordon Pr.

Tyler, Moses C. Patrick Henry. LC 80-18577. (American Statesmen Ser.). 460p. 1980. pap. 6.95 (ISBN 0-87754-190-6). Chelsea Hse.

--Patrick Henry. Morse, John T., Jr., ed. LC 71-128936. (American Statesmen: No. 3). Repr. of 1898 ed. 14.00 (ISBN 0-404-50853-7). AMS Pr.

--Patrick Henry. 1970. Repr. of 1898 ed. text ed. 29.00 (ISBN 0-8337-3587-X). B Franklin.

--Patrick Henry. LC 62-17475. (YA) (gr. 9-12). 1962. pap. 5.95 (ISBN 0-8014-9094-4, CP94). Cornell U Pr.

--Patrick Henry. 1898. Repr. 25.00 (ISBN 0-685-43270-X). Norwood Edns.

Umbreit, Kenneth B. Founding Fathers: Men Who Shaped Our Tradition. LC 68-26228. Repr. of 1941 ed. 13.00 (ISBN 0-8046-0469-X). Kennikat.

Wirt, William. Sketches of the Life & Character of Patrick Henry. facs. ed. LC 72-130568. (Select Bibliographies Reprint Ser). 1836. 21.00 (ISBN 0-8369-5541-2). Arno.

HENRY FREDRICK, PRINCE OF WALES, 1594-1612

Davies, Richard. Chester's Triumph in Honor of Her Prince, As It Was Performed Upon St. George's Day, 1610. 1844. 11.00 (ISBN 0-384-10990-X). Johnson Repr.

HENRY E. HUNTINGTON LIBRARY AND ART GALLERY, SAN MARINO CALIFORNIA BOTANIC GARDENS

Thorpe, James, et al. Founding of the Henry E. Huntington Library & Art Gallery: Four Essays. (Illus.). 1969. 2.50 (ISBN 0-87328-105-5). Huntington Lib.

HENRY FRANCIS DUPONT WINTERTHUR MUSEUM

Winterthur Museum & Gardens. 3rd ed. (Illus.). 1980. pap. 3.00 (ISBN 0-912724-04-8). Winterthur.

The Winterthur Story. (Illus.). 1965. pap. 5.50 (ISBN 0-912724-02-1). Winterthur.

Yuletide at Winterthur: Tastes & Visions of the Season. (Illus.). 1980. pap. 3.50 (ISBN 0-912724-09-9). Winterthur.

HENRYSON, ROBERT, 1430-1506

Kindrick, Robert L. Robert Henryson. (English Authors Ser.: No. 274). 1979. 14.50 (ISBN 0-8057-6758-4). Twayne.

Stearns, Marshall W. Robert Henryson. LC 73-182718. Repr. of 1949 ed. 16.50 (ISBN 0-404-06225-3). AMS Pr.

HENS

see Poultry

HENSEL, LUISE, 1798-1876

Spiecker, F. Luise Hensel Als Dichterin. LC 79-133463. (Northwestern University. Humanities Ser.: No. 3). 1970. Repr. of 1936 ed. 18.00 (ISBN 0-404-50703-4). AMS Pr.

HENSON, JOSIAH, 1789-1883

Cavanah, Frances. The Truth About the Man Behind the Book That Sparked the War Between the States. LC 75-11566. (Illus.). (gr. 3-7). 1975. 7.95 (ISBN 0-664-32572-6). Westminster.

Henson, Josiah. Father Henson's Story of His Own Life. LC 70-99381. (Illus.). vii, 212p. 1972. Repr. of 1858 ed. lib. bdg. 12.50 (ISBN 0-8411-0052-7). Metro Bks.

HENSON, MATTHEW ALEXANDER, 1866-1955

Matthew Henson. (Black History Illustrated: No. 5). (Illus.). 1969. pap. 0.59 (ISBN 0-685-78150-X). Guild Bks.

HEORTOLOGY

see Church Calendar; Church Year; Fasts and Feasts; Saints–Calendar

HEPARIN

Bradshaw, Ralph A. & Wessler, Sanford, eds. Heparin: Structure, Function & Clinical Implications. LC 74-28408. (Advances in Experimental Medicine & Biology Ser.: Vol. 52). 420p. 1975. 37.50 (ISBN 0-306-39052-3, Plenum Pr). Plenum Pub.

Comper, W. D. Heparin (& Related Polysaccharides) Structural & Functional Properties. 1981. write for info. (ISBN 0-677-05040-2). Gordon.

Karkar, Vijay V. & Thomas, Duncan, eds. Heparin: Chemistry & Clinical Usages. 1976. 48.00 (ISBN 0-12-394750-2). Acad Pr.

McDuffie, Norman M., ed. Heparin: Structure, Cellular Functions, & Clinical Applications. LC 78-31254. 1979. 25.50 (ISBN 0-12-484850-8). Acad Pr.

HEPATICAE

see Liverworts

HEPATITIS, INFECTIOUS

Cossart, Yvonne E. Virus Hepatitis & Its Control. (Illus.). 1978. text ed. 23.95 (ISBN 0-02-857420-6). Macmillan.

Gerety, R. J., ed. Non-A, Non-B Hepatitis. 1982. price not set (ISBN 0-12-280680-8). Acad Pr.

Hepatitis: A Technical Workshop. 1981. write for info. (ISBN 0-914404-65-2). Am Assn Blood.

International Symposium on Basic Progress in Blood Transfusion, 6th, Brussels, Feb., 1972. Australia Antigen & Viral Hepatitis: Proceedings. Desmyter, J. & London, W. T., eds. (Vox Sanguinis: Vol. 24). (Illus.). 1973. pap. 11.00 (ISBN 3-8055-1611-8). S Karger.

International Symposium on Problems of Chronic Hepatitis, Montecatini, 1975. Chronic Hepatitis. Gentilini, P., ed. (Illus.). 208p. 1976. 58.75 (ISBN 3-8055-2321-1). S Karger.

Koff, Raymond S. Viral Hepatitis. LC 78-17013. (Clinical Gastroenterology Monographs). 242p. 1978. 28.95 (ISBN 0-471-03695-1, Pub. by Wiley Medical). Wiley.

Krugman, Saul & Gocke, David J. Viral Hepatitis. LC 77-16974. (Major Problems in Internal Medicine Ser.: Vol. 15). (Illus.). 1978. text ed. 19.95 (ISBN 0-7216-5538-6). Saunders.

Oda. Hepatitis Viruses. 1978. 44.50 (ISBN 0-8391-1321-8). Univ Park.

Piazza, Marcello. Experimental Viral Hepatitis. (Illus.). 288p. 1969. photocopy ed. spiral 28.50 (ISBN 0-398-01485-X). C C Thomas.

Sampliner, Richard E. Preventing Viral Hepatitis. 300p. 1981. 22.50 (ISBN 0-87527-229-0). Green.

Symposium Held by European Group for Rapid Virus Diagnosis, London, Jan. 1978. Diagnostic Methods in Viral Hepatitis: Proceedings. Howard, Colin R. & Gardner, P. S., eds. LC 78-20364. (Laboratory & Research Methods in Biology & Medicine: Vol. 2). 104p. 1978. 14.00x (ISBN 0-8451-1651-7). A R Liss.

Symposium on Virus Hepatitis Antigens & Antiobodies, Munich, 1970. Australia Antigen: Hepatitis Associated Antigen & Corresponding Antibodies. Soulier, J. P., ed. (Vox Sanguinis: Vol. 19, Nos. 3-4). 1970. pap. 36.00 (ISBN 3-8055-1088-8). S Karger.

Symposium Organized by the International Association of Biological Standardization, 44th. International Symposium on Viral Hepatitis: Proceedings. Regamey, R. H., et al, eds. (Developments in Biological Standardization: Vol. 30). (Illus.). x, 492p. 1975. 57.50 (ISBN 3-8055-2312-2). S Karger.

Vyas, Girish N., et al, eds. Viral Hepatitis: Etiology, Epidemiology, Pathogenesis & Prevention. LC 78-882. (Clinical Ser). (Illus., Orig.). 1978. 64.50 (ISBN 0-89168-013-6). Franklin Inst Pr.

WHO Meeting. Geneva, 1974. Viral Hepatitis: Report. (Technical Report Ser.: No. 570). (Also avail. in French & Spanish). 1975. pap. 2.80 (ISBN 92-4-120570-9). World Health.

WHO Scientific Group. Geneva, 1972. Viral Hepatitis: Report. (Technical Report Ser.: No. 512). (Also avail. in French & Spanish). 1973. pap. 1.60 (ISBN 92-4-120512-1). World Health.

Zuckerman, A. J. Human-Viral Hepatitis, Hepatitis Associated Antigen & Viruses. 2nd rev. ed. 1975. 58.75 (ISBN 0-444-10849-1, North-Holland). Elsevier.

Zuckerman, Arie & Howard, Colin. Hepatitis Viruses of Man. LC 79-40894. (Experimental Virology Ser.). 1980. 39.00 (ISBN 0-12-782150-3). Acad Pr.

HEPATITIS ASSOCIATED ANTIGEN

International Symposium on Basic Progress in Blood Transfusion, 6th, Brussels, Feb., 1972. Australia Antigen & Viral Hepatitis: Proceedings. Desmyter, J. & London, W. T., eds. (Vox Sanguinis: Vol. 24). (Illus.). 1973. pap. 11.00 (ISBN 3-8055-1611-8). S Karger.

Melnick, J. L. & Maupas, P., eds. Hepatitis B Virus & Primary Liver Cancer. (Progress in Medical Virology Ser.: Vol. 27). (Illus.). viii, 212p. 1981. 75.00 (ISBN 3-8055-1784-X). S Karger.
Prier, J. Australia Antigen. (Illus.). 1974. 24.50 (ISBN 0-8391-0538-X). Univ Park.
Ray, M. B. Hepatitis B Virus Antigens in Tissues. 165p. text ed. 24.95 (ISBN 0-8391-1425-7). Univ Park.
Zuckerman, A. J. Human-Viral Hepatitis, Hepatitis Associated Antigen & Viruses. 2nd rev. ed. 1975. 58.75 (ISBN 0-444-10849-1, North-Holland). Elsevier.

HEPATITIS B ANTIGEN
see Hepatitis Associated Antigen

HEPBURN, KATHERINE, 1909-
Dickens, Homer. The Films of Katharine Hepburn. (Illus.). 256p. 1973. 9.95 (ISBN 0-685-29242-8); pap. 6.95 (ISBN 0-8065-0361-0). Citadel Pr.
Higham, Charles. Kate: The Life of Katharine Hepburn. (Illus.). 244p. 1975. 7.95 (ISBN 0-393-07486-2). Norton.
--Kate: The Life of Katherine Hepburn. updated ed. (Illus.). 1981. pap. 2.95 (ISBN 0-451-11212-1, AE 1212, Sig). NAL.
--Kate: The Life of Katherine Hepburn. (Illus.). (RL 10). 1976. pap. 2.95 (ISBN 0-451-11153-2, AE1153, Sig). NAL.
Marill, Alvin H. Katherine Hepburn. LC 73-90219. (Film Stars Ser.). 5.95 (ISBN 0-88365-166-1). Brown Bk.

HEPPLEWHITE, GEORGE, d. 1786
Edwards, Ralph. Hepplewhite Furniture Designs. 1972. 16.50 (ISBN 0-685-52079-X). Transatlantic.

HERACLITUS
Attridge, Harold W. First-Century Cynicism in the Epistles of Heraclitus. LC 76-20736. (Harvard Theological Review. Harvard Theological Studies: No. 29). 1976. pap. 6.00 (ISBN 0-89130-111-9, 020029). Scholars Pr Ca.
Connor, W. R., ed. Chion of Heraclea. LC 78-18571. (Greek Texts & Commentaries Ser.). 1979. Repr. of 1951 ed. lib. bdg. 12.00x (ISBN 0-405-11415-X). Arno.
Griffith, Gwilym O. Interpreters of Reality: Lao-Tse, Heraclitus & the Christian Faith. 1977. lib. bdg. 59.95 (ISBN 0-8490-2065-4). Gordon Pr.
Heidegger, Martin & Fink, Eugen. Heraclitus Seminar, Nineteen Sixty-Six to Nineteen Sixty-Seven. Seibert, Charles H., tr. 1979. 17.50x (ISBN 0-8173-6628-8). U of Ala Pr.
Kahn, C. H. The Art & Thought of Heraclitus. LC 77-82499. 1980. 38.00 (ISBN 0-521-21883-7). Cambridge U Pr.
Kahn, Charles H., ed. The Art & Thought of Heraclitus: An Edition of the Fragments with Translation & Commentary. LC 77-82499. 368p. Date not set. pap. 15.95 (ISBN 0-521-28645-X). Cambridge U Pr.
Sallis, John & Maly, Kenneth. Heraclitean Fragments: A Companion Volume to the Heidegger-Fink Seminar on Heraclitus. 208p. 1980. 18.50x (ISBN 0-8173-0027-9). U of Ala Pr.

HERALDIC BOOK-PLATES
see Book-Plates

HERALDIC VISITATIONS
see Visitations, Heraldic

HERALDRY
see also Chivalry; Decorations of Honor; Devices; Emblems; Flags; Genealogy; Knights and Knighthood; Mottoes; Nobility; Seals (Numismatics); Titles of Honor and Nobility; Visitations, Heraldic
Bergling, John M. Heraldic Designs & Engravings Manual. rev. ed. Bergling, V. C., ed. LC 66-25383. (Illus.). 1966. 17.50 (ISBN 0-910222-04-5). Gem City Coll.
Berners, Juliana. The Book of Hawking, Hunting & Blasing of Arms. LC 74-25849. (English Experience Ser.: No. 151). 180p. 1969. Repr. of 1486 ed. 42.00 (ISBN 90-221-0151-7). Walter J Johnson.
Bolton, Edmund. The Elements of Armories. LC 73-38160. (English Experience Ser.: No. 363). 356p. 1971. Repr. of 1610 ed. 32.50 (ISBN 90-221-0363-3). Walter J Johnson.
Boutell, Charles. Boutell's Heraldry. rev. ed. LC 73-75030. (Illus.). 368p. 1978. 30.00 (ISBN 0-7232-2096-4). Warne.
Brault, Gerard J. Early Blazon: Heraldic Terminology in the Twelfth & Thirteenth Centuries; with Special Reference to Arthurian Literature. (Illus.). 328p. 1972. text ed. 45.00x (ISBN 0-19-822337-4). Oxford U Pr.
Briggs, Geoffrey, ed. Civic & Corporate Heraldry: A Dictionary of Impersonal Arms of England, Wales, & Northern Ireland. (Illus.). 432p. 1971. 32.00 (ISBN 0-685-29194-4). Gale.
Brook-Little, J. P. An Heraldic Alphabet. LC 72-95468. (Illus.). 240p. 1973. 8.95 (ISBN 0-668-02941-2). Arco.
Cadenas, Vicente de. Diccionario Heraldico. 2nd ed. 304p. (Espn.). 1976. pap. 29.95 (ISBN 84-00-04294-8, S-50107). French & Eur.
Child, Heather. Heraldic Design: A Handbook for Students. LC 66-31918. (Illus.). 1976. Repr. of 1966 ed. 15.00 (ISBN 0-8063-0071-X). Genealog Pub.
Crozier, William A. Crozier's General Armory: A Registry of American Families Entitled to Coat Armor. 2nd ed. LC 66-22143. 1972. Repr. of 1904 ed. 10.00 (ISBN 0-8063-0081-7). Genealog Pub.
Cussans, J. Handbook of Heraldry. 59.95 (ISBN 0-8490-0278-8). Gordon Pr.
Cussans, John E. Handbook of Heraldry. LC 76-132520. 1971. Repr. of 1893 ed. 28.00 (ISBN 0-8103-3012-1). Gale.
De Grandmaison, C. Dictionnaires Heraldique. Migne, J. P., ed. (Nouvelle Encyclopedie Theologique Ser.: Vol. 13). 688p. (Fr.). Date not set. Repr. of 1852 ed. lib. bdg. 90.00x (ISBN 0-89241-262-3). Caratzas Bros.
Eterovich, Adam S. Croatian & Dalmatian Coats of Arms. LC 77-95024. (Illus.). 260p. 1978. pap. 8.00 softcover (ISBN 0-918660-06-8). Ragusan Pr.
Ferne, John. The Blazon of Gentrie. LC 72-5986. (English Experience Ser.: No. 513). (Illus.). 488p. 1973. Repr. of 1586 ed. 70.00 (ISBN 90-221-0513-X). Walter J Johnson.
Filby, P. William. American & British Genealogy & Heraldry: A Selected List of Books. 2nd ed. LC 75-29383. 1976. 25.00 (ISBN 0-8389-0203-0). ALA.
Fox-Davies, Arthur C. Art of Heraldry: An Encyclopaedia of Armory. LC 68-56481. (Illus.). 1968. Repr. of 1904 ed. 60.00 (ISBN 0-405-08530-3, Blom Pubns). Arno.
Fox-Davies, Arthur C., ed. Armorial Families: A Directory of Gentlemen of Coat-Armour, Vol. 1 & 2. LC 76-94029. (Illus.). 1970. Repr. Set. 38.50 (ISBN 0-8048-0721-3). C E Tuttle.
Galbreath, Donald L. Papal Heraldry. 2nd ed. (Illus.). 156p. 1972. 34.00 (ISBN 0-685-29193-6). Gale.
Gatfield, G. Guide to Printed Books & Manuscripts Relating to English & Foreign Heraldry & Genealogy. 59.95 (ISBN 0-8490-0269-9). Gordon Pr.
Gatfield, George. Guide to Printed Books & Manuscripts Relating to English & Foreign Heraldry & Genealogy. 1966. Repr. of 1892 ed. 30.00 (ISBN 0-8103-3121-7). Gale.
Goldsworthy, W. Lansdown. Shakespeare's Heraldic Emblems: Their Origin & Meaning. 1978. Repr. of 1928 ed. lib. bdg. 32.50 (ISBN 0-8414-4618-0). Folcroft.
Gore Roll of Arms. Incl. Positive Pedigrees & Authorized Arms. LC 64-21646. 1964. pap. 5.00 (ISBN 0-8063-0160-0). Genealog Pub.
Gough, H. A Glossary of Terms Used in Heraldry. 59.95 (ISBN 0-8490-0239-7). Gordon Pr.
Gough, Henry & Parker, James. Glossary of Terms Used in Heraldry. (Illus.). 1966. Repr. of 1894 ed. 19.00 (ISBN 0-8103-3126-8). Gale.
Grant, Francis J. The Manual of Heraldry. LC 75-23365. (Illus.). 1976. Repr. of 1929 ed. 19.00 (ISBN 0-8103-4252-9). Gale.
--Manual of Heraldry: A Concise Description of the Several Terms Used, & Containing a Dictionary of Every Description in the Science. rev. ed. LC 78-13922. (Illus.). 1962. Repr. of 1914 ed. 7.50 (ISBN 0-8063-0458-8). Genealog Pub.
Grosswirth, Marvin. The Heraldry Book: A Guide to Designing Your Own Coat of Arms. LC 78-22321. (Illus.). 240p. 1981. 11.95 (ISBN 0-385-14157-2). Doubleday.
Guillim, John. A Display of Heraldrie. LC 79-84115. (English Experience Ser.: No. 934). 308p. 1979. Repr. of 1611 ed. lib. bdg. 46.00 (ISBN 90-221-0934-8). Walter J Johnson.
Heim, Bruno B. Heraldry in the Catholic Church: Its Origin, Customs & Laws. new ed. (Illus.). 1978. text ed. 55.00x (ISBN 0-391-00873-0). Humanities.
Hinton, W. Elmer, Jr. A Manual of Arms, a Practical Guide to the Heraldic Art. LC 79-55379. (Illus., Orig.). Date not set. pap. 4.99 (ISBN 0-935426-00-0). Gamesmasters.
Holden, Edward S. A Primer of Heraldry for Americans. LC 73-2815. (Illus.). 129p. 1973. Repr. of 1898 ed. 19.00 (ISBN 0-8103-3271-X). Gale.
Innes Of Learney, Thomas. Scots Heraldry: A Practical Handbook on the Historical Principles and Modern Application of the Art & Science. 2nd ed. LC 74-152173. (Illus.). 1971. Repr. of 1956 ed. 15.00 (ISBN 0-8063-0478-2). Genealog Pub.
Johnson, David P. The Heraldic Register of America, Vol. 1. LC 80-70042. (Illus.). 151p. 1981. 25.95 (ISBN 0-9605668-1-3); pap. 12.95 spiral bound (ISBN 0-9605668-2-1). Am Coll Heraldry.
--Heraldry: The Armiger's News, 1979-1980. LC 80-70043. (Illus.). 55p. 1980. pap. 9.95 (ISBN 0-9605668-0-5). Am Coll Heraldry.
Johnson, David P., ed. Heraldry: The/Armiger's News, 1979-1980. (Illus.). 55p. 1980. pap. text ed. 9.95 (ISBN 0-9605668-0-5). Am Coll Heraldry.
--Heraldry: The Armiger's News, Vol. 3. (Illus.). 1982. pap. 9.95 (ISBN 0-9605668-3-X). Am Coll Heraldry.
Jones, Evan J., ed. Medieval Heraldry. LC 78-63502. Repr. of 1943 ed. 47.50 (ISBN 0-404-17149-4). AMS Pr.
Louda, Jiri & Maclagan, Michael. Heraldry of the Royal Families of Europe. (Illus.). 352p. 1981. pap. 30.00 (ISBN 0-517-54558-6). Potter.
Lynch-Robinson, Christopher & Lynch-Robinson, Adrian. Intelligible Heraldry. LC 67-28024. (Illus.). 1967. Repr. of 1948 ed. 12.50 (ISBN 0-8063-0216-X). Genealog Pub.
MacKinnon, Charles. Observer's Book of Heraldry. (Observer Bks.). (Illus.). 1977. 3.95 (ISBN 0-684-15216-9, ScribT). Scribner.
Milton, Roger. Heralds & History. LC 78-57631. (Illus.). 1978. 14.95 (ISBN 0-88254-468-3). Hippocrene Bks.
Nason, Arthur H. Heralds & Heraldry in Ben Jonson's Plays: Masques & Entertainments. 1978. Repr. of 1907 ed. lib. bdg. 35.00 (ISBN 0-8495-4004-6). Arden Lib.
Neubecker, Ottfried. A Guide to Heraldry. LC 79-13611. (Illus.). 1980. 9.95 (ISBN 0-07-046312-3). McGraw.
Palliser, Fanny M. Historic Devices, Badges, & War-Cries. LC 68-18030. (Illus.). 1971. Repr. of 1870 ed. 30.00 (ISBN 0-8103-3381-3). Gale.
Planche, James R. The Pursuivant of Arms; or, Heraldry Founded Upon Facts. LC 72-10610. (Illus.). 299p. 1973. Repr. of 1874 ed. 19.00 (ISBN 0-8103-3171-3). Gale.
Preble, George H. The Symbols, Standards, Flags & Banners of Ancient & Modern Nations. 1980. lib. bdg. 12.00 (ISBN 0-8161-8476-3). G K Hall.
Puttock, A. G. Dictionary of Heraldry & Related Subjects. LC 76-137421. (Illus.). 1970. 15.00 (ISBN 0-8063-0449-9). Genealog Pub.
Rietstap, Johannes B. Armorial General, 2 Vols. LC 65-21472. 1972. Repr. of 1884 ed. Set. 75.00 (ISBN 0-8063-0442-1). Genealog Pub.
--Armorial General Precede d'un Dictionnaire des Termes du Blason, Pt. 1. (Fr.). 1934. 135.00 (ISBN 0-686-56594-0, M-7298, Pub. by Olms). French & Eur.
--Armorial General Precede d'un Dictionnaire des Termes du Blason, Pt. 2. (Fr.). 1934. 135.00 (ISBN 0-686-56595-9, M-7299, Pub. by Olms). French & Eur.
Rolland, Victor & Rolland, Henri V. Illustrations to the Armorial General by J. B. Rietstap, 6 Vols. in 3. LC 66-29998. 1967. Repr. of 1926 ed. Set. 150.00 (ISBN 0-8063-0300-X). Genealog Pub.
--Supplement to the Armorial General, 9 vols. LC 75-19156. 1969-71. Repr. of 1954 ed. Set. 185.00 (ISBN 0-8063-0421-9); Vols. 1-3. 70.00 (ISBN 0-685-11730-8); Vols. 4-6. 60.00 (ISBN 0-685-11731-6); Vols. 7-9. 55.00 (ISBN 0-685-11732-4). Genealog Pub.
Rothery, Guy C. Heraldry of Shakespeare. LC 72-194774. 1930. lib. bdg. 15.00 (ISBN 0-8414-7483-4). Folcroft.
St. Louis Public Library. Heraldry Index of the St. Louis Public Library. 1980. lib. bdg. 475.00 (ISBN 0-8161-0311-9). G K Hall.
Scott-Giles, Wilfrid. Civic Heraldry of England & Wales. rev. ed. LC 71-184280. (Illus.). 1972. Repr. of 1953 ed. lib. bdg. 25.00 (ISBN 0-405-08941-4). Arno.
Slade, Richard. Your Book of Heraldry. 4.95 (ISBN 0-685-91533-6). Transatlantic.
Speranov, N. Coats of Arms of Russian Principalities XII-XIX. 1974. 50.00 (ISBN 0-685-86593-2, 569081203). State Mutual Bk.
Von Volborth, Carl A. Heraldry of the World. (Illus.). 251p. 1980. 12.95 (ISBN 0-7137-0647-3, Pub. by Blandford Pr England). Sterling.
Von Volborth, Carl-Alexander. Heraldry Customs & Styles. (Illus.). 1981. 37.50 (ISBN 0-7137-0940-5, Pub. by Blandford Pr England). Sterling.
Wagner, Anthony. Pedigree & Progress: Essays in the Genealogical Interpretation of History. 333p. 1975. 35.00x (ISBN 0-87471-782-5). Rowman.
Zieber, Eugene. Heraldry in America. LC 68-31267. (Reference Ser., No. 44). 1969. lib. bdg. 49.95 (ISBN 0-8383-0322-6). Haskell.
--Heraldry in America. 1973. lib. bdg. 75.00 (ISBN 0-87968-035-0). Gordon Pr.
--Heraldry in America. LC 76-45664. (Illus.). 1977. Repr. of 1909 ed. 17.50 (ISBN 0-8063-0738-2). Genealog Pub.

HERALDRY–JUVENILE LITERATURE
Manning, Rosemary. Heraldry. (Junior Ref. Ser). (Illus.). (gr. 7 up). 1966. 7.95 (ISBN 0-7136-0108-6). Dufour.
Parker, James. Glossary of Terms Used in Heraldry. LC 77-94021. (Illus.). (gr. 9 up). 1970. 12.95 (ISBN 0-8048-0715-9). C E Tuttle.

HERALDRY–CANADA
Massicotte, E. Z. & Roy, Regis. Armorial Du Canada Francais, 2 Vols. in 1. LC 74-113783. (Illus.). 1970. Repr. of 1918 ed. 15.00 (ISBN 0-8063-0402-2). Genealog Pub.
Swan, Conrad. Canada: Symbols of Sovereignty. LC 76-20511. 1977. 35.00x (ISBN 0-8020-5346-7). U of Toronto Pr.

HERALDRY–GREAT BRITAIN
Bossewell, John. Workes of Armorie, 3 bks. LC 72-173. (English Experience Ser.: No. 145). 1969. Repr. of 1572 ed. 39.00 (ISBN 90-221-0145-2). Walter J Johnson.
Brault, Gerard J. Eight Thirteenth-Century Rolls of Arms in French & Anglo-Norman Blazon. LC 72-1065. 148p. 1973. 15.00x (ISBN 0-271-01115-7). Pa St U Pr.
Charles, Nicholas. Visitation of the County of Huntingdon. 1849. 15.50 (ISBN 0-384-08525-3). Johnson Repr.
--Visitation of the County of Huntingdon, Under the Authority of William Camden. Ellis, Henry, ed. LC 17-1223. (Camden Society, London. Publications, First Ser.: No. 43). Repr. of 1849 ed. 14.00 (ISBN 0-404-50143-5). AMS Pr.
Franklin, Charles A. The Bearing of Coat-Armour by Ladies. LC 73-8999. (Illus.). 1973. Repr. of 1923 ed. 10.00 (ISBN 0-8063-0574-6). Genealog Pub.
Gray, Thomas. Scalacronica: A Chronicle of England & Scotland from A.D. 1066 to A. D. 1362. Stevenson, Joseph, ed. LC 70-168186. (Maitland Club. Glasgow. Publications: No. 40). Repr. of 1836 ed. 47.50 (ISBN 0-404-53015-X). AMS Pr.
Hasler, Charles. The Royal Arms: Its Graphic & Decorative Development. 1980. 75.00x (ISBN 0-904041-20-4, Pub. by Jupiter England). State Mutual Bk.
Moule, Thomas. Bibliotheca Heraldica Magnae Britanniae: An Analytical Catalogue of Books on Genealogy, Heraldry, Nobility, Knighthood & Ceremonies. (Illus.). 1966. Repr. of 1822 ed. 25.00 (ISBN 0-685-00429-5). Genealog Pub.
Nason, Arthur H. Heralds & Heraldry in Ben Jonson's Plays, Masques & Entertainments. LC 68-59042. 1968. Repr. of 1907 ed. 8.50 (ISBN 0-87752-076-3). Gordian.
--Heralds & Heraldry in Jonson's Plays. LC 73-12356. 1907. lib. bdg. 7.45 (ISBN 0-8414-6250-X). Folcroft.
Peacham, Henry. The Compleat Gentleman. LC 68-27481. (English Experience Ser.: No. 59). 212p. 1968. Repr. of 1622 ed. 25.00 (ISBN 90-221-0059-6). Walter J Johnson.
Pottinger, Don & Moncreiffe, Iain. Simple Heraldry. new ed. LC 78-23691. (Illus.). 1979. 6.95 (ISBN 0-8317-7799-0, Mayflower Bks). Smith Pubs.
Vinycomb, John. Fictitious & Symbolic Creatures in Art with Special Reference to Their Use in British Heraldry. LC 76-89300. (Illus.). 1969. Repr. of 1906 ed. 22.00 (ISBN 0-8103-3147-0). Gale.
Wagner, Anthony. Heralds & Ancestors. (British Museum Publications). 1978. 15.00 (ISBN 0-374-83298-6); pap. 6.95 (ISBN 0-374-84302-3). FS&G.
--Historic Heraldry of Britain. (Illus.). 118p. 1972. Repr. of 1939 ed. 16.00x (ISBN 0-87471-641-1). Rowman.
Williams, Geoffrey. Heraldry of the Cinque Ports. LC 71-152108. 1971. 6.50 (ISBN 0-8048-0982-8). C E Tuttle.
Woodward, John & Burnett, George. Woodward's, a Treatise on Heraldry, British & Foreign. LC 70-77120. 1969. Repr. 19.25 (ISBN 0-8048-0694-2). C E Tuttle.
Yorke, James. The Union of Honour. LC 72-240. (English Experience Ser.: No. 148). 76p. 1969. Repr. of 1640 ed. 58.00 (ISBN 90-221-0148-7). Walter J Johnson.

HERALDRY–JAPAN
Dower, John. The Elements of Japanese Design: A Handbook of Family Crests, Heraldry & Symbolism. LC 73-139688. (Illus.). 176p. 1971. 20.00 (ISBN 0-8348-0143-4). Weatherhill.
Matsuya Piece-Goods Store. Japanese Design Motifs: 4260 Illustrations of Heraldic Crests. Adachi, Fumie, tr. & illus. 8.50 (ISBN 0-8446-4630-X). Peter Smith.
Matsuya Piece-Goods Store, ed. Japanese Design Motifs: 4260 Illustrations of Heraldic Crests. Adachi, Fumie, tr. from Jap. & intro. by. (Pictorial Archive Ser.). (Illus.). 216p. 1973. pap. 6.00 (ISBN 0-486-22874-6). Dover.

HERALDRY, ORNAMENTAL
Matsuya Piece-Goods Store, ed. Japanese Design Motifs: 4260 Illustrations of Heraldic Crests. Adachi, Fumie, tr. from Jap. & intro. by. (Pictorial Archive Ser.). (Illus.). 216p. 1973. pap. 6.00 (ISBN 0-486-22874-6). Dover.

HERALDRY, SACRED
Drake, M. & Drake, W. Saints & Their Emblems. LC 72-79240. 234p. 1916. Repr. 22.00 (ISBN 0-403-04249-6). Somerset Pub.

HERALDS

Nason, Arthur H. Heralds & Heraldry in Ben Jonson's Plays: Masques & Entertainments. 1978. Repr. of 1907 ed. lib. bdg. 35.00 (ISBN 0-8495-4004-6). Arden Lib.

Stewart, James S. Heralds of God. (James S. Stewart Library). pap. 4.95 (ISBN 0-8010-7976-4). Baker Bk.

HERB GARDENING

Bonar, Ann & MacCarthy, Daphne. How to Grow & Use Herbs. (Orig.). 1980. pap. 6.95x (ISBN 0-8464-1024-9). Beekman Pubs.

Brimer, John. Growing Herbs in Pots. 1978. pap. 3.95 (ISBN 0-671-24207-5, Fireside). S&S.

Garland, Sarah. Complete Book of Herbs & Spices: An Illustrated Guide to Growing & Using Aromatic, Cosmetic, Culinary, & Medicinal Plants. (Illus.). 1979. 25.00 (ISBN 0-670-36866-0, Studio). Viking Pr.

Harvey, Jack. Herbs. (Guidelines Ser.). (Illus.). 96p. 1980. pap. 2.95 (ISBN 0-89542-903-9). Ideals.

Herb Society of America, ed. Herbs for Use & for Delight: An Anthology from The Herbarist. LC 74-80287. (Illus.). 352p. 1974. pap. 4.50 (ISBN 0-486-23104-6). Dover.

Lathrop, Norma J. Herbs. (Orig.). 1981. pap. 7.95 (ISBN 0-89586-077-5). H P Bks.

Loewenfeld, Claire. Herb Gardening. (Illus.). 256p. 1964. 9.95 (ISBN 0-571-06024-2, Pub. by Faber & Faber); pap. 5.50 (ISBN 0-571-09475-9). Merrimack Bk Serv.

Loewenfeld, Claire & Back, Philippa. The Complete Book of Herbs & Spices. 1976. pap. 4.95 (ISBN 0-316-53070-0). Little.

McDonald, Elvin. How to Grow Vegetables & Herbs from Seeds. 1976. 9.95 (ISBN 0-442-80381-8); pap. 5.95 (ISBN 0-442-80403-2). Van Nos Reinhold.

Meltzer, Sol. Herb Gardening in the South. LC 76-52240. (Illus.). 96p. 1977. pap. 3.95 (ISBN 0-88415-366-5). Pacesetter Pr.

Meschter, Joan W. How to Grow Herbs & Salad Greens Indoors. (Illus.). 176p. 1975. pap. 1.50 (ISBN 0-445-03043-7). Popular Lib.

Riggs, Carol. Herbs: Leaves of Magic: The Care, Culture & Cooking of Herbs. Leifield, Timothy J., ed. (Illus.). 1979. pap. 9.95 (ISBN 0-87364-153-1, Sycamore Island). Paladin Ent.

Rohde, Eleanour S. Culinary & Salad Herbs. (Illus.). 128p. 1972. pap. 2.00 (ISBN 0-486-22865-7). Dover.

--Herbs & Herb Gardening. LC 70-180975. (Illus.). 1976. Repr. of 1936 ed. 28.00 (ISBN 0-8103-4303-7). Gale.

Root, Waverly, et al. Herbs & Spices: The Pursuit of Flavor. LC 80-18563. (Illus.). 1980. 19.95 (ISBN 0-07-053591-4). McGraw.

Sanecki, Kay N. The Complete Book of Herbs. (Illus.). 252p. 1974. 12.95 (ISBN 0-02-606890-7). Macmillan.

Simmons, Adelma G. Herb Gardening in Five Seasons. 1977. pap. 6.95 (ISBN 0-8015-3395-3, Hawthorn). Dutton.

--Herb Gardens Delight. 1979. pap. 4.95 (ISBN 0-8015-3403-8, Hawthorn). Dutton.

Verey, Rosemary. The Herb Growing Book. (Illus.). 48p. (gr. 5 up). 1981. 9.95 (ISBN 0-316-89974-7). Little.

HERBAGE

see Grasses

HERBALS

see Botany-Pre-Linnean Works; Botany, Medical; Herbs; Materia Medica-Early Works to 1800; Materia Medica, Vegetable; Medicine, Medieval

HERBARIA

see also Plants-Collection and Preservation

Lasegue, A. Musee Botanique de M. Benjamin Delessert. 1970. Repr. of 1845 ed. 50.00 (ISBN 3-7682-0686-6). Lubrecht & Cramer.

HERBART, JOHANN FRIEDRICH, 1776-1841

Cole, Percival R. Herbart & Froebel: An Attempt at Synthesis. LC 70-176659. (Columbia University. Teachers College. Contributions to Education: No. 14). Repr. of 1907 ed. 17.50 (ISBN 0-404-55014-2). AMS Pr.

De Garmo, Charles. Herbart & Herbartism. Brickman, William W., ed. LC 79-12853. (Educational Ser). Repr. of 1895 ed. 17.50 (ISBN 0-8414-1894-2). Folcroft.

--Herbart & the Herbartians. 1979. Repr. of 1896 ed. lib. bdg. 30.00 (ISBN 0-8414-1894-2). Folcroft.

Dunkel, Harold B. Herbart & Education. 8.00 (ISBN 0-8446-2007-6). Peter Smith.

--Herbart & Education. (Western Educational Tradition Ser). (Orig.). 1969. pap. text ed. 2.85x (ISBN 0-685-19732-8). Phila Bk Co.

--Herbart & Herbartianism: An Educational Ghost Story. LC 77-98126. 1970. 12.50x (ISBN 0-226-17219-8). U of Chicago Pr.

McMurry, Dorothy. Herbartian Contributions to History Instruction in American Elementary Schools. LC 77-177039. (Columbia University. Teachers College. Contributions to Education: No. 920). Repr. of 1946 ed. 17.50 (ISBN 0-404-55920-4). AMS Pr.

Macvannel, John A. The Educational Theories of Herbart & Froebel. LC 72-177043. (Columbia University. Teachers College. Contributions to Education: No. 4). Repr. of 1905 ed. 17.50 (ISBN 0-404-55004-5). AMS Pr.

Mossman, Lois Coffey. Changing Conception Relative to the Planning of Lessons. LC 72-177094. (Columbia University. Teachers College. Contributions to Education: No. 147). Repr. of 1924 ed. 17.50 (ISBN 0-404-55147-5). AMS Pr.

HERBERT, GEORGE, 1593-1633

Asals, Heather A. Equivocal Predication: George Herbert's Way to God. 152p. 1981. 25.00x (ISBN 0-8020-5536-2). U of Toronto Pr.

Bennett, Joan. Five Metaphysical Poets: Donne, Herbert, Vaughan, Crashaw, Marvell. 1964. 27.50 (ISBN 0-521-04156-2); pap. 8.95x (ISBN 0-521-09238-8). Cambridge U Pr.

Beresford, John. Gossip of the Seventeenth & Eighteenth Centuries. facs. ed. LC 68-29191. (Essays Index Reprint Ser). 1968. Repr. of 1924 ed. 15.00 (ISBN 0-8369-0199-1). Arno.

Charles, Amy M. A Life of George Herbert. LC 77-3116. (Illus.). 1977. 20.00x (ISBN 0-8014-1014-2). Cornell U Pr.

Chute, Marchette. Two Gentle Men: The Lives of George Herbert & Robert Herrick. 1959. 6.95 (ISBN 0-525-22528-5). Dutton.

DiCesare, Mario, ed. George Herbert & the Seventeenth Century Religious Poets. (Norton Critical Editions). 401p. 1978. pap. text ed. 5.95 (ISBN 0-393-09254-2). Norton.

Di Cesare, Mario A. & Mignani, Rigo, eds. A Concordance to the Complete Writings of George Herbert. LC 76-56642. (Cornell Concordances Ser.). 1977. 42.50x (ISBN 0-8014-1106-8). Cornell U Pr.

Edgecombe, Rodney. Sweetness Readie Penn'd Imagery, Syntax & Metric in the Poetry of George Herbert. (Elizabethan Studies). 1980. pap. text ed. 25.00x (ISBN 0-391-02185-0). Humanities.

Fish, Stanley E. The Living Temple: George Herbert & Catechizing. LC 73-90664. (Quantum Bks.). 1978. 19.50x (ISBN 0-520-02657-8). U of Cal Pr.

Freer, Coburn. Music for a King: George Herbert's Style & the Metrical Psalms. LC 76-179136. 266p. 1972. 18.50x (ISBN 0-8018-1290-9). Johns Hopkins.

Grant, Patrick. The Transformation of Sin: Studies in Donne, Herbert, Vaughan & Traherne. (Illus.). 1974. 11.95x (ISBN 0-7735-0209-2). McGill-Queens U Pr.

--The Transformation of Sin: Studies in Donne, Herbert, Vaughan & Traherne. LC 73-93174. 308p. 1974. 15.00x (ISBN 0-87023-158-8). U of Mass Pr.

Herbert, George. The English Poems of George Herbert. Patrides, C. A., ed. (Rowman & Littlefield University Library). 247p. 1974. 10.00x (ISBN 0-87471-551-2); pap. 5.00x (ISBN 0-87471-552-0). Rowman.

Higgins, Dick. George Herbert's Pattern Poems: In Their Tradition. 79p. 1977. 19.95 (ISBN 0-914162-23-3); pap. 5.95 (ISBN 0-914162-24-1). Printed Edns.

Mann, Cameron. Concordance to the English Poems of George Herbert. LC 77-4939. 1927. lib. bdg. 19.00 (ISBN 0-8414-6186-4). Folcroft.

Miller, Edmund. Drudgerie Divine: The Rhetoric of God & Man in George Herbert. (SSEL Elizabethan Studies: No. 84). 1980. pap. text ed. 25.00x (ISBN 0-391-01904-X). Humanities.

Palmer, George H. George Herbert Bibliography. LC 73-12942. 1910. lib. bdg. 8.50 (ISBN 0-8414-6708-0). Folcroft.

Roberts, John R. Essential Articles for the Study of George Herbert's Poetry. (Essential Articles Ser.). 600p. 1979. 32.50 (ISBN 0-208-01770-4, Archon). Shoe String.

--George Herbert: An Annotated Bibliography of Modern Criticism, 1905-1974. LC 77-25314. 1978. text ed. 23.00x (ISBN 0-8262-0243-8). U of Mo Pr.

Slights, Camille W. The Casuistical Tradition in Shakespeare, Donne, Herbert, & Milton. LC 80-8576. 352p. 1981. 21.00 (ISBN 0-691-06463-6). Princeton U Pr.

Stein, Arnold. George Herbert's Lyrics. LC 68-12898. 221p. 1968. 15.00x (ISBN 0-8018-0613-5). Johns Hopkins.

Summers, Claude J. & Pebworth, Ted-Larry, eds. Too Rich to Clothe the Sunne: Essays on George Herbert. LC 80-5255. (Illus.). 0278p. 1980. 16.95x (ISBN 0-8229-3421-3). U of Pittsburgh Pr.

Summers, Joseph H. George Herbert: His Religion & Art. 250p. (Orig.). Date not set. 13.95 (ISBN 0-86698-003-2); pap. 5.95 (ISBN 0-86698-008-3). Medieval.

Tuve, Rosemond. Reading of George Herbert. LC 52-44005. 1952. 11.00x (ISBN 0-226-81820-9). U of Chicago Pr.

Wall, John N., ed. George Herbert: The Country Parson & the Temple. LC 81-80287. (Classics of Western Spirituality Ser.). 384p. 11.95 (ISBN 0-8091-0317-6); pap. 7.95 (ISBN 0-8091-2298-7). Paulist Pr.

Walton, Izaak. Lives of John Donne, Sir Henry Wotton, Richard Hooker, George Herbert, & Robert Sanderson. (World's Classics Ser.). 7.95 (ISBN 0-19-250303-0). Oxford U Pr.

HERBERT, HENRY WILLIAM, 1807-1858

Van Winkle, William M. Henry William Herbert, Frank Forester: A Bibliography of His Writings 1832-1858. LC 70-143664. (Bibliography & Reference Ser.: No. 403). 1971. Repr. of 1936 ed. lib. bdg. 19.50 (ISBN 0-8337-3619-1). B Franklin.

HERBERT, VICTOR, 1859-1924

Kaye, Joseph. Victor Herbert. LC 74-109628. (Select Bibliographies Reprint Ser). 1931. 20.00 (ISBN 0-8369-5237-5). Arno.

--Victor Herbert: The Biography of America's Greatest Composer of Romantic Music. 1979. Repr. of 1931 ed. lib. bdg. 30.00 (ISBN 0-8495-3034-2). Arden Lib.

Waters, Edward N. Victor Herbert: A Life in Music. LC 78-9597. (Music Reprint, 1978 Ser.). 1978. Repr. of 1955 ed. lib. bdg. 45.00 (ISBN 0-306-79502-7). Da Capo.

HERBERT HOOVER LIBRARY

Burdick, Charles B. Ralph Lutz & the Hoover Institution. LC 72-87287. (Publications Ser.: No. 131). 185p. 1974. 11.95 (ISBN 0-8179-6311-1). Hoover Inst Pr.

HERBICIDES

Anderson, Wood P. Weed Science: Principles. 1977. text ed. 28.00 (ISBN 0-8299-0084-5). West Pub.

Ashton, Floyd M. & Crafts, Alden S. Mode of Action of Herbicides. 2nd ed. LC 80-23077. 525p. 1981. 42.50 (ISBN 0-471-04847-X, Pub. by Wiley-Interscience). Wiley.

Audus, L. J., ed. Herbicides: Physiology, Biochemistry Ecology. 2nd ed. Vol. 1, 1976. 96.50 (ISBN 0-12-067701-6); Vol. 2, 1977. 89.50 (ISBN 0-12-067702-4). Acad Pr.

Bovey, Rodney W. & Young, Alvin L. The Science of Two, Four, Five-T & Associated Phenoxy Herbicides. 1980. 37.50 (ISBN 0-471-05134-9, Pub. by Wiley-Interscience). Wiley.

Chlorpropham, Propham. (FAO Specifications for Plant Protection Prod. Ser). 9p. 1978. pap. 6.00 (ISBN 92-5-100539-7, F1374, FAO). Unipub.

Critser, James R., Jr. Herbicides. (Ser. 12-77). 1978. 80.00 (ISBN 0-914428-48-9). Lexington Data.

Hance, R. J., ed. Interactions Between Herbicides & the Soil. 1981. 49.50 (ISBN 0-12-323840-4). Acad Pr.

Isotopes in Weed Research. (Illus., Orig.). 1966. pap. 13.00 (ISBN 92-0-010066-X, ISP113, IAEA). Unipub.

Kearney, Philip C. & Kaufman, D., eds. Herbicides: Chemistry, Degradation, & Mode of Action, Vol.1. rev. 2nd ed. 512p. 1975. 58.50 (ISBN 0-8247-6175-8). Dekker.

--Herbicides: Chemistry, Degradation, & Mode of Action, Vol. 2. rev.2nd ed. 1976. 58.50 (ISBN 0-8247-6301-7). Dekker.

Klingman, Glenn C. & Ashton, Floyd M. Weed Science: Principles & Practices. LC 75-8908. 431p. 1975. 24.00 (ISBN 0-471-49171-3, Pub. by Wiley-Interscience). Wiley.

Newton, Michael. Chemicals in the Forest. 160p. 1980. pap. 10.95 (ISBN 0-917304-25-X, Pub. by Timber Pr). Intl Schol Bk Serv.

--Handbook of Weed & Insect Control Chemicals for Forest Resource Management. 160p. 1980. pap. 24.95x (ISBN 0-917304-25-X, Pub. by Timber Pr). Intl Schol Bk Serv.

Page, B. G. & Thomson, W. T. The Nineteen Eighty-One Insecticide, Herbicide, Fungicide Quick Guide. 140p. 1981. pap. 12.00 (ISBN 0-913702-11-0). Thomson Pub Ca.

Pallos, Ferenc M. & Casida, John E., eds. Chemistry & Action of Herbicide Antidotes (Symposium) (MS-REPRO) 1978. 21.00 (ISBN 0-12-544050-2). Acad Pr.

Que Hee, Shane S. & Sutherland, Ronald G. The Phenoxyalkanoic Herbicides: Volume 1 Chemistry, Analysis & Environmental Pollution. 272p. 1981. 84.95 (ISBN 0-8493-5851-5). CRC Pr.

Summers, L. A. The Bipyridinium Herbicides. LC 79-41550. 1980. 79.50 (ISBN 0-12-676450-6). Acad Pr.

Thomson, W. T. Agricultural Chemicals, Book 2: Herbicides. rev. ed. 260p. 1981. pap. 13.50 (ISBN 0-913702-12-9). Thomson Pub Ca.

Weaver, Robert J. Plant Growth Substances in Agriculture. LC 71-166964. (Plant Science Ser.). (Illus.). 1972. text ed. 39.95x (ISBN 0-7167-0824-8). W H Freeman.

HERBIVORA

see also names of herbivorous animals

Paulsen, Gary. The Grass Eaters. LC 76-10313. (Real Animals Ser.). (Illus.). 64p. (gr. 5 up). 1976. PLB 9.85 (ISBN 0-8172-0602-7). Raintree Pubs.

Rosenthal, Gerald A. & Janzen, Daniel, eds. Herbivores: Their Interaction with Secondary Plant Metabolites. LC 79-6944. 1979. 62.50 (ISBN 0-12-597180-X). Acad Pr.

HERBS

see also Botany-Pre-Linnean Works; Botany, Medical; Cookery (Herbs and Spices); Materia Medica, Vegetable; Medicine, Medieval

Abraitys, Vincent. Wayside Simples & Grateful Herbs. LC 76-19236. (Illus.). 1980. pap. 8.95 (ISBN 0-914366-08-4). Columbia Pub.

Althea. Herb for Presents. (ps-2). 1979. pap. 1.45 avail. in 5 pk. (ISBN 0-85122-179-3, Pub. by Dinosaur Pubns). Merrimack Bk Serv.

Anderson, Frank J. An Illustrated History of the Herbals. LC 77-8821. (Illus.). 270p. 1977. 20.00x (ISBN 0-231-04002-4). Columbia U Pr.

Ashin, Deborah. The Herb in Antiquity: A Look into the J. Paul Getty Museum Herb Garden. (Illus.). 1976. pap. text ed. 1.25 (ISBN 0-89236-020-8). J P Getty Mus.

Askham, Anthony. A Little Herball of the Properties of the Herbes. LC 77-6848. (English Experience Ser.: No. 843). 1977. Repr. of 1561 ed. lib. bdg. 11.50 (ISBN 90-221-0843-0). Walter J Johnson.

Back, Philippa. Herbs for Cleaning, Canning & Sundry Household Chores. write for info. Keats.

Bacon, Richard M. The Forgotten Art of Growing, Gardening & Cooking with Herbs. LC 72-91864. (Forgotten Arts Ser.). (Illus.). 128p. (Orig.). 1972. pap. 5.95 (ISBN 0-911658-51-3). Yankee Bks.

Beatty, Virginia L. & Consumer Guide Editors. Consumer Guide Rating & Raising Vegetables: A Practical Guide for Growing Vegetables, Herbs, Fruits & Sprouts. 8.95 (ISBN 0-671-22361-5); pap. 4.95 (ISBN 0-671-22362-3). S&S.

Beckett, Sarah. Herbs for Feminine Ailments. LC 80-53449. (Everybody's Home Herbal Ser.). (Illus.). 63p. (Orig.). 1981. pap. 1.95 (ISBN 0-394-74836-0). Shambhala Pubn.

--Herbs to Soothe Your Nerves. LC 80-53448. (Everybody's Home Herbal Ser.). (Illus.). 64p. (Orig.). 1981. pap. 1.95 (ISBN 0-394-74835-2). Shambhala Pubn.

Bentley, Virginia W. Let Herbs Do It. (Illus.). 1973. pap. 6.95 (ISBN 0-395-15478-2). HM.

Better Homes & Gardens Books Editors, ed. Better Homes & Gardens Vegetables & Herbs You Can Grow. (Illus.). 1978. 5.95 (ISBN 0-696-00295-7). Meredith Corp.

Binding, G. J. Vegetables & Herbs with a Difference. 1980. 19.50x (ISBN 0-85032-178-6, Pub. by Daniel Co England). State Mutual Bk.

Blunt, Wilfrid. The Illustrated Herbal. (Illus.). 1979. 12.98 (ISBN 0-500-01226-1). Thames Hudson.

Brother Aloysius. Comfort to the Sick: A Recipe Book of Medicinal Herbs. 416p. 1981. pap. 8.95 (ISBN 0-87728-525-X). Weiser.

Brownlow, Margaret. Herbs & the Fragrant Garden. 1980. 30.00x (ISBN 0-232-51396-1, Pub. by Darton-Longman-Todd England). State Mutual Bk.

Ceres. Herbs & Fruit for Dieting. LC 80-53452. (Everybodys Home Herbal Ser.). 64p. 1981. pap. 1.95 (ISBN 0-394-74837-9). Shambhala Pubns.

--Herbs for First-Aid & Minor Ailments. LC 80-53453. (Everybodys Home Herbal Ser.). (Illus.). 64p. 1981. pap. 1.95 (ISBN 0-394-74925-1). Shambhala Pubns.

--Herbs for Indigestion. LC 80-53451. (Everybody's Home Herbal Ser.). (Illus.). 63p. (Orig.). 1981. pap. 1.95 (ISBN 0-394-74833-6). Shambhala Pubn.

Challem, Jack & Lewin-Challem, Renate. What Herbs Are All About. LC 80-82913. 150p. (Orig.). 1980. pap. 2.95 (ISBN 0-87983-204-5). Keats.

Clair, Colin. Dictionnaire des Herbes et des Epices. 259p. (Fr.). 1963. pap. 6.95 (ISBN 0-686-56842-7, M-6621). French & Eur.

Clarkson, Rosetta E. The Golden Age of Herbs & Herbalists. (Illus.). 352p. 1972. pap. 5.00 (ISBN 0-486-22869-X). Dover.

--The Golden Age of Herbs & Herbalists. Orig. Title: Green Enchantment. (Illus.). 5.50 (ISBN 0-8446-4623-7). Peter Smith.

--Herbs & Savory Seeds. Orig. Title: Magic Gardens. (Illus.). 6.00 (ISBN 0-8446-4526-5). Peter Smith.

--Herbs, Their Culture & Uses. (Illus.). 1966. 11.95 (ISBN 0-02-526020-0). Macmillan.

Clausen, Jens, et al. Environmental Responses of Climatic Races of Achillea. (Experimental Studies on the Nature of Species, Vol. 3). (Illus.). 132p. 1948. pap. 6.00 (ISBN 0-87279-592-6, 581). Carnegie Inst.

Coats, Alice M. Flowers & Their Histories. 1971. 12.50 (ISBN 0-07-011476-5, GB). McGraw.

Colin. Herbs & Spices. pap. 1.95 (ISBN 0-89437-001-4). Baronet.

Crow, W. B. Occult Properties of Herbs. (Paths to Inner Power Ser). 1980. pap. 2.25 (ISBN 0-87728-097-5). Weiser.

Curtin, L. S. Healing Herbs of the Upper Rio Grande. 12.50 (ISBN 0-686-20686-X). Southwest Mus.
Curtin, L. S. M. Healing Herbs of the Upper Rio Grande. Cortes, Carlos E., ed. LC 76-1226. (Chicano Heritage Ser.). (Illus.). 1976. Repr. of 1947 ed. 19.00x (ISBN 0-405-09499-X). Arno.
Dawson, Adele. Health, Happiness & the Pursuit of Herbs. LC 79-21182. (Illus.). 1980. 12.95 (ISBN 0-8289-0362-X); pap. 7.95 (ISBN 0-8289-0363-8). Greene.
Day, Ivan. Perfumery with Herbs. 1980. 30.00x (ISBN 0-232-51414-3, Pub. by. Darton-Longman-Todd England). State Mutual Bk.
De Bairacli-Levy, Juliette. Common Herbs for Natural Health. LC 73-91335. (Illus.). 198p. 1974. pap. 2.95 (ISBN 0-8052-0436-9). Schocken.
--The Complete Herbal Book for the Dog. LC 72-3339. 1973. 8.95 (ISBN 0-668-02649-9); pap. 3.95 (ISBN 0-668-04181-1). Arco.
De Waal, M. Medicinal Herbs in the Bible. Meijlink, Jane, ed. 96p. 1981. pap. 4.95 (ISBN 0-87728-527-6). Weiser.
Dowden, Anne O. This Noble Harvest: A Chronicle of Herbs. LC 79-12021. (Illus.). 1979. 12.95 (ISBN 0-529-05548-1). Philomel.
Dugdale, Chester B. A Modern American Herbal: Useful Herbaceous Plants, Vol. 2. LC 71-86305. (Illus.). 1978. 20.00 (ISBN 0-498-01908-X). A S Barnes.
Duncan, Thomas. A Taxonomic Study of the Ranunculus hispidus. (U. C. Publications in Botany V Ser.: Vol. 77). 1980. 8.00x (ISBN 0-520-09617-7). U of Cal Pr.
Durrell, Lawrence. The Plant-Magic Man. new ed. (Capra Chapbook Ser.: No. 5). (Illus.). 1973. pap. 2.50 (ISBN 0-912264-51-9). Capra Pr.
Farwell, Edith F. A Book of Herbs. 1980. cancelled (ISBN 0-935720-01-4). Green Hill.
Farwell, Edith F., ed. A Book of Herbs. 1981. pap. 6.95 (ISBN 0-935720-01-4). Caroline Hse.
Fisher, Bonnie. Bonnie Fisher's Way with Herbs Cookbook. LC 80-82326. 140p. (Orig.). 1980. pap. 2.95 (ISBN 0-87983-205-3). Keats.
Fox, H. The Years in My Herb Garden. 1973. pap. 1.95 (ISBN 0-686-66885-5). Macmillan.
Fox, Helen M. Gardening with Herbs for Flavor & Fragrance. (Illus.). 1972. pap. 3.75 (ISBN 0-486-22540-2). Dover.
Freesias. 1981. 15.00x (ISBN 0-686-75415-8, Pub. by Grower Bks). State Mutual Bk.
Frompovich, Catherine J. & Hay, Joanne M. Everyday Herbs for Cooking & Healing. 1980. 100 frame filmstrip, cassette, text 25.00 (ISBN 0-935322-11-6). C J Frompovich.
Gabriel, Ingrid. Herb Identifier & Handbook. LC 74-31698. (Identifier Ser.). (Illus.). 192p. 1975. 9.95 (ISBN 0-8069-3068-3); lib. bdg. 9.89 (ISBN 0-8069-3069-1). Sterling.
Garland, Sarah. Complete Book of Herbs & Spices: An Illustrated Guide to Growing & Using Aromatic, Cosmetic, Culinary, & Medicinal Plants. (Illus.). 1979. 25.00 (ISBN 0-670-36866-0, Studio). Viking Pr.
Genders, Roy. Complete Book of Herbs. LC 79-93206. (Illus.). 160p. 1980. 14.95 (ISBN 0-8069-3928-1); pap. 8.95 (ISBN 0-8069-3930-3). Sterling.
--Growing Herbs As Aromatics. LC 77-86544. (The Living with Herbs Series: Vol. 3). (Illus.). 1977. pap. 2.50 (ISBN 0-87983-155-3). Keats.
Gerard, John. The Herball or General Historie of Plants, 2 vols. LC 74-80179. (English Experience Ser.: Nos. 660a-660b). 1974. Repr. of 1597 ed. Set. 214.00 (ISBN 90-221-0660-8). Walter J Johnson.
Gilbertie, Sal. Herb Gardening at Its Best. LC 77-23678. 1978. 12.95 (ISBN 0-689-10863-X, 255); pap. 6.95, 1980 (ISBN 0-689-70595-6). Atheneum.
Giles, F. A. Herbaceous Perennials. (Illus.). 1980. text ed. 16.95 (ISBN 0-8359-2822-5). Reston.
Gosling, Nalda. Herbs for Colds & Flu. LC 80-53450. (Everybody's Home Herbal Ser.). (Illus.). 64p. (Orig.). 1981. pap. 1.95 (ISBN 0-394-74834-4). Shambhala Pubn.
Grieve, M. Culinary Herbs & Condiments. 5.25 (ISBN 0-8446-0117-9). Peter Smith.
--A Modern Herbal. Leyel, Mrs. C. F., ed. LC 72-169784. (Illus.). 1971. pap. 6.50 ea.; Vol. 1. pap. (ISBN 0-486-22798-7); Vol. 2. pap. (ISBN 0-486-22799-5). Dover.
Grieve, Mrs. M. A Modern Herbal, 2 vols. (Illus.). Set. 22.00 (ISBN 0-8446-0302-3). Peter Smith.
Griffin, LaDean. Herbs to the Rescue. 2.95 (ISBN 0-89557-003-3). Bi World Indus.
--Insulin Vs. Herbs & the Diabetic. 2.00 (ISBN 0-89557-015-7). Bi World Indus.
--No Side Effects: Return to Herbal Medicine. 7.95 (ISBN 0-686-29931-0). Cancer Bk Hse.
--No Side Effects: The Return to Herbal Medicine. 8.95 (ISBN 0-89557-002-5). Bi World Indus.
Grounds, Roger. Growing Vegetables & Herbs. (Orig.). 1980. pap. 6.95x (ISBN 0-8464-1016-8). Beekman Pubs.
Guides. Candlemaking: Old Time Herbs. 1981. 1.95 (ISBN 0-686-30436-5). Cent Hse Americana.
Gutmanis, June. Kahuna La'au Lap'au: The Practice of Hawaiian Herbal Medicine. Kelsey, Theodore, tr. LC 76-1510. (Illus.). 1977. pap. 7.95 (ISBN 0-89610-078-2). Island Her.
Hamilton, Geoff. Herbs: How to Grow Them. 1980. pap. 4.50 (ISBN 0-7153-7897-X). David & Charles.
Harris, Ben C. Better Health with Culinary Herbs. 1971. pap. 3.95 (ISBN 0-517-51723-X). Barre.
--Eat the Weeds. LC 69-12302. 1969. pap. 3.95 (ISBN 0-517-51730-2). Barre.
Harris, Ben C., ed. The Compleat Herbal. LC 77-185615. 243p. (Orig.). 1972. pap. 1.75 (ISBN 0-915962-15-2). Larchmont Bks.
Hayes, Elizabeth S. Spices & Herbs: Lore & Cookery. write for info. (ISBN 0-8446-5772-7). Peter Smith.
--Spices & Herbs: Their Lore & Use. (Illus.). 256p. 1980. pap. 3.50 (ISBN 0-486-24026-6). Dover.
Heffern, Richard. The Herb Buyers Guide. (Orig.). pap. 1.50 (ISBN 0-515-04635-3). Jove Pubns.
Heinerman, John. Science of Herbal Medicine. 15.95 (ISBN 0-686-29743-1). Cancer Bk Hse.
Herb Society of America. Herbs for Use & for Delight: An Anthology from the Herbarist. (Illus.). 6.50 (ISBN 0-8446-5199-0). Peter Smith.
Herb Society of America, ed. Herbs for Use & for Delight: An Anthology from The Herbarist. LC 74-80287. (Illus.). 352p. 1974. pap. 4.50 (ISBN 0-486-23104-6). Dover.
Herbs. 1.95 (ISBN 0-686-21128-6). Bklyn Botanic.
Herbs & Their Ornamental Uses. 1.95 (ISBN 0-686-21160-X). Bklyn Botanic.
Hewer & Senecki. Practical Herb Growing. 13.50x (ISBN 0-392-05980-0, LTB). Sportshelf.
Hiesey, William M., et al. Biosystematics, Genetics, & Physiological Ecology of the Erythranthe Section of Mimulus. LC 40-14859. (Experimental Studies on the Nature of Species: Vol. 5). (Illus.). 219p. 1971. 13.75 (ISBN 0-87279-639-6, 628). Carnegie Inst.
Hills, Lawrence D. Comfrey Report. Rateaver, Bargyla & Rateaver, Gylver, eds. Bd. with Comfrey, the Herbal Healer. LC 75-23178. (Conservation Gardening & Farming Ser: Ser. C). 1975. pap. 6.00 (ISBN 0-9600698-9-5). Rateavers.
Huson, Paul. Mastering Herbalism. LC 73-90704. 1975. pap. 6.95 (ISBN 0-8128-1847-4). Stein & Day.
Hylton, William, ed. The Rodale Herb Book: How to Use, Grow & Buy Nature's Miracle Plants. LC 73-18902. (Illus.). 658p. 1974. 16.95 (ISBN 0-87857-076-4); deluxe ed. 19.95 (ISBN 0-87857-196-5). Rodale Pr Inc.
Jacobs, Betty E. Growing & Using Herbs Successfully. (Illus.). 225p. 1981. pap. 6.95 (ISBN 0-88266-249-X). Garden Way Pub.
--Growing Herbs & Plants for Dyeing. LC 77-77943. (Illus.). 1977. pap. 6.00 (ISBN 0-910458-12-X). Select Bks.
--Growing Herbs for the Kitchen. (Illus.). 1972. 6.95 (ISBN 0-910458-14-6). Select Bks.
Japanese Herbs & Their Uses. 1.95 (ISBN 0-686-21151-0). Bklyn Botanic.
Jones, George. In a Herb Garden. (Illus.). 98p. 1977. 12.95 (ISBN 0-85475-049-5). Dufour.
Kaaiakamanu, D. M. & Akina, J. K. Hawaiian Herbs of Medicinal Value. Akana, Akaiko, tr. LC 76-177367. 1972. pap. 4.75 (ISBN 0-8048-1019-2). C E Tuttle.
Kadans, Joseph. Modern Encyclopedia of Herbs. 1970. 9.95 (ISBN 0-13-593798-1, Reward); pap. 4.95 (ISBN 0-13-593780-9). P-H.
Kadans, Joseph M. Encyclopedia of Medicinal Herbs. LC 79-158469. 256p. 1972. pap. 1.95 (ISBN 0-668-02487-9). Arco.
Kamm, Minnie W. Old Time Herbs for Northern Gardens. (Illus.). 1971. pap. 4.00 (ISBN 0-486-22695-6). Dover.
--Old-Time Herbs for Northern Gardens. (Illus.). 5.50 (ISBN 0-8446-0162-4). Peter Smith.
Keller, Mitzie S. Mysterious Herbs & Roots. LC 78-62301. (Illus.). 402p. 1978. pap. 8.95 (ISBN 0-915238-25-X). Peace Pr.
Kerr, Ralph W. Herbalism Through the Ages. LC 74-96813. 1978. 7.25 (ISBN 0-686-00386-1). AMORC.
Keys, John. Chinese Herbs: Their Botany, Chemistry & Pharmacodynamics. LC 75-35399. 1976. 15.00 (ISBN 0-8048-1179-2). C E Tuttle.
Kirschner, H. E. Nature's Healing Grasses. 3.00 (ISBN 0-686-29771-7). Cancer Bk Hse.
Kloppenburg-Versteegh, J. The Traditional Use of Malay Plants & Herbs. Kaufman, Aileen, tr. from Dutch. LC 79-89939. Orig. Title: Het Gebruik Van Indische Planten. (Illus.). Date not set. price not set (ISBN 0-89793-014-2). Hunter Hse.
Latorre, Dolores L. Cooking & Curing with Herbs in Mexico. (Illus.). 1977. 10.00 (ISBN 0-88426-051-8). Encino Pr.
Lavine, Sigmund A. Wonders of Herbs. LC 75-38356. (Wonders Ser.). (Illus.). (gr. 5 up). 1976. 5.95 (ISBN 0-396-07294-1). Dodd.
Law, Donald. Herb Growing for Health. LC 78-137695. (Illus.). 1969. pap. 1.65 (ISBN 0-668-02418-6). Arco.
Lazow, Alfred & Nelson, Pearl A. The ABC's of Herbs. (Illus.). 1977. 2.50 (ISBN 0-914634-48-8, 7718). DOK Pubs.
Leek, Sybil. Sybil Leek's Book of Herbs. 1980. pap. 3.95 (ISBN 0-346-12435-2). Cornerstone.
--Sybil Leek's Book of Herbs. LC 73-10205. (Illus.). 160p. 1973. 7.95 (ISBN 0-525-66304-5). Elsevier-Nelson.
Leighton, Ann. Early American Gardens: For "Meate & Medicine". (Illus.). 1970. 14.95 (ISBN 0-395-07907-1). HM.
Levy, J. Complete Herbal Book for Dogs. pap. 6.95 (ISBN 0-685-21927-5). Wehman.
Liebman, Malvina W. From Caravan to Casserole: Herbs & Spices in Legend, History & Recipes. (Illus.). 1977. 7.95 (ISBN 0-912458-88-7). E A Seemann.
Loewenfeld, Claire & Back, Philippa. The Complete Book of Herbs & Spices. 1976. pap. 4.95 (ISBN 0-316-53070-0). Little.
Lowenfeld, Claire & Back, Philippa. The Complete Book of Herbs & Spices. (Illus.). 319p. 1980. 19.95 (ISBN 0-7153-7656-X). David & Charles.
Lucas, Richard. Common & Uncommon Uses of Herbs for Healthful Living. LC 74-128898. 1970. pap. 1.95 (ISBN 0-668-02396-1). Arco.
--Magic of Herbs in Daily Living. 1972. 12.95 (ISBN 0-13-544981-2, Parker); pap. 3.95 (ISBN 0-686-66832-4). P-H.
--Secrets of the Chinese Herbalists. 1977. 8.95 (ISBN 0-13-797639-9, Parker). P-H.
Lust, Benedict. Kneipp Herbs & Their Uses. (Illus.), 1968. pap. 1.00 (ISBN 0-87904-009-2). Lust.
Lust, John, ed. The Herb Book. 672p. 1974. pap. 3.95 (ISBN 0-553-20148-4). Bantam.
Lust, John B. The Herb Book. LC 74-75368. (Illus.). 640p. 1974. 12.95 (ISBN 0-87904-007-6). Lust.
Macdonald, Christina. Garden Herbs for Australia & New Zealand. (Illus.). 1969. 8.25 (ISBN 0-589-00066-7, Pub. by Reed Books Australia). C E Tuttle.
Malstrom, Stan. Herbal Remedies II. rev. ed. 2.95 (ISBN 0-89557-004-1). Bi World Indus.
Menzies, Rob. The Herbal Dinner: The Renaissance of Cooking. LC 76-53334. (Illus., Orig.). 1977. pap. 5.95 (ISBN 0-89087-136-1). Celestial Arts.
Menzies, Robert. The Star Herbal. rev. ed. (Illus.). 240p. 1981. pap. 9.95 (ISBN 0-89087-136-1). Celestial Arts.
Meschter, Joan W. How to Grow Herbs & Salad Greens Indoors. (Illus.). 176p. 1975. pap. 1.50 (ISBN 0-445-03043-7). Popular Lib.
Meyer, Joseph E. The Herbalist. (Illus.). 304p. 1981. 11.95 (ISBN 0-8069-3902-8); lib. bdg. 10.79 (ISBN 0-8069-3903-6). Sterling.
--Herbalist. 6.95 (ISBN 0-685-85699-2, Pub. by Meyerbooks). Formur Intl.
Minster, Margaret, ed. Herbs: From Cultivation to Cooking. (Illus.). 228p. 1981. Repr. of 1980 ed. spiral bdg. 8.95 (ISBN 0-88289-288-6). Pelican.
Morton, Julia F. Herbs & Spices. (Golden Guide Ser.). (Illus.). 1977. PLB 10.38 (ISBN 0-307-64364-6, Golden Pr); pap. 1.95 (ISBN 0-307-24364-8). Western Pub.
Moulton, LeArta. Herb Walk, Number One, No. 1. 398p. 1979. 25.00 (ISBN 0-935596-02-X); perfect bd. 25.00 (ISBN 0-935596-03-8). Gluten Co.
Muenscher, Minnie. Minnie Muenscher's Herb Cookbook. LC 77-90908. (Illus.). 246p. (Orig.). 1980. pap. 2.95 (ISBN 0-87983-216-9). Keats.
Muenscher, Walter C. & Rice, Myron A. Garden Spice & Wild Pot-Herbs: An American Herbal. LC 78-56899. (Illus.). 218p. 1978. pap. 8.95 (ISBN 0-8014-9174-6). Comstock.
Neblekopf, Ethan. The Herbal Connection. 1980. 12.95 (ISBN 0-89557-048-3). Bi World Indus.
Null, Gary, et al. Herbs for the Seventies. LC 72-187998. (The Health Library: Vol. 2). 168p. 1972. 5.95 (ISBN 0-8315-0129-4). Speller.
Ortho Books Editorial Staff. The World of Herbs & Spices. LC 78-57892. (Illus.). 1979. pap. 4.95 (ISBN 0-917102-72-X). Ortho.
Owen, Millie. A Cook's Guide to Growing Herbs, Greens, & Aromatics. LC 77-20368. 1978. pap. 6.95 (ISBN 0-394-73454-8). Knopf.
Paterson, Wilma. A Country Cup: Old & New Recipes for Drinks of All Kinds Made from Wild Plants & Herbs. (Illus.). 88p. 1981. 11.95 (ISBN 0-7207-1234-3, Pub. by Michael Joseph). Merrimack Bk Serv.
Pond, Barbara. A Sampler of Wayside Herbs: Rediscovering Old Uses for Familiar Wild Plants. LC 73-89773. (Illus.). 1974. 17.50 (ISBN 0-85699-096-5). Chatham Pr.
Potions, Lotions, Tonics & Teas. LC 76-54817. (Illus.). (gr. 7 up). 1977. 6.95 (ISBN 0-13-686527-5). P-H.
Prenis, John. Herb Grower's Guide: Cooking, Spicing & Lore. (Illus., Orig.). 1974. lib. bdg. 12.90 (ISBN 0-914294-37-7); pap. 3.95 (ISBN 0-914294-07-5). Running Pr.
Rishel, Jonas. The Indian Physician. 132p. 1980. 5.95 (ISBN 0-88215-048-0). Ohio St U Lib.
Rohde, Eleanor S. Culinary & Salad Herbs: Their Cultivation & Food Values with Recipes. (Illus.). 4.50 (ISBN 0-8446-4602-4). Peter Smith.
--The Old English Herbals. (Illus.). 7.00 (ISBN 0-8446-0235-3). Peter Smith.
Rohde, Eleanour S. Culinary & Salad Herbs. (Illus.). 128p. 1972. pap. 2.00 (ISBN 0-486-22865-7). Dover.
--Garden of Herbs. LC 75-81736. 1969. pap. 4.00 (ISBN 0-486-22308-6). Dover.
--Herbs & Herb Gardening. LC 70-180975. (Illus.). 1976. Repr. of 1936 ed. 28.00 (ISBN 0-8103-4303-7). Gale.
Rollins, Reed C. & Shaw, Elizabeth A. Genus Lesquerella (Cruciferae) in North America. LC 72-87777. (Illus.). 385p. 1973. 18.00x (ISBN 0-674-34775-7). Harvard U Pr.
Romanne-James, Constance. Herb-Lore for Housewives. LC 71-180978. (Illus.). 264p. 1974. Repr. of 1938 ed. 22.00 (ISBN 0-8103-3976-5). Gale.
Rose, Jeanne. Herbs & Things: Jeanne Rose's Herbal. 1972. 5.95 (ISBN 0-448-01139-5). G&D.
--Jeanne Rose's Herbal Guide to Inner Health. (Illus.). 1978. pap. 6.95 1980 (ISBN 0-448-14522-7). G&D.
--Kitchen Cosmetics: Using Plants & Herbs in Cosmetics. LC 77-17077. 1978. 8.95 (ISBN 0-915572-25-7); pap. 4.95 (ISBN 0-915572-24-9). Panjandrum.
Rowland, Lorna. Growing Herbs. (Practical Gardening Ser.). (Illus.). 112p. (Orig.). 1979. pap. 10.50 (ISBN 0-589-01244-4, Pub. by Reed Bks Australia). C E Tuttle.
Royal, Penny C. Herbally Yours. 4.95 (ISBN 0-89557-012-2). Bi World Indus.
Rutherford, Meg & Warren-Davis, Ann. A Pattern of Herbs. (Illus.). 150p. 1975. 9.50 (ISBN 0-04-635009-8). Allen Unwin.
Sanderson, Liz. How to Make Your Own Herbal Cosmetics. LC 78-65301. (Illus.). 1979. pap. 4.95 (ISBN 0-87983-190-1). Keats.
Sanecki, Kay N. The Complete Book of Herbs. (Illus.). 252p. 1974. 12.95 (ISBN 0-02-606890-7). Macmillan.
Siegel, Alice & McLoone, Margo. The Herb & Spice Book for Kids. LC 77-26712. (Illus.). 1978. 6.95 (ISBN 0-03-041681-7). HR&W.
Simmons, Adelma G. Herbs to Grow Indoors. 1969. pap. 4.50 (ISBN 0-8015-3416-X, Hawthorn). Dutton.
--A Merry Christmas Herbal. LC 68-56414. (Illus.). 160p. 1968. pap. 5.95 (ISBN 0-688-07080-9). Morrow.
Smith, Alan R. Taxonomy of Thelypteris Subgenus Steiropteris (Including Glaphyropteris) (U. C. Publications in Botany Ser.: Vol. 76). 1980. pap. 7.50 (ISBN 0-520-09602-9). U of Cal Pr.
Smith, W. W., et al. The Genus Primula, 22 pts. in one vol. (Plant Monograph Reprints: No. 11). 1977. lib. bdg. 100.00 (ISBN 3-7682-1118-5). Lubrecht & Cramer.
Stark, Raymond. Guide to Indian Herbs. Campbell, Margaret, ed. (Illus.). 50p. 1981. pap. 3.95 (ISBN 0-87663-628-8, Pub. by Hancock Hse). Universe.
Stracke, J. Richard, ed. The Laud Herbal Glossary. LC 72-93569. 208p. (Orig.). 1976. pap. text ed. 34.25x (ISBN 90-6203-497-7). Humanities.
Sunset Editors. Herbs: How to Grow. LC 73-181520. (Illus.). 80p. (Orig.). 1972. pap. 2.95 (ISBN 0-376-03322-3, Sunset Bks.). Sunset-Lane.
Tanner, Ogden. Herbs. LC 76-51513. (Time-Life Encyclopedia for Gardening Ser.). (Illus.). (gr. 6 up). 1977. pap. text ed. 11.97 (ISBN 0-8094-2551-3, Pub. by Time-Life). Silver.
Thomson, William A. Herbs That Heal. LC 77-72361. (Encore Edition). (Illus.). 1977. pap. 1.95 (ISBN 0-684-16928-2, ScribT). Scribner.
Tierra, Michael. The Way of Herbs. (Illus., Orig.). 1980. pap. 6.95 (ISBN 0-913300-43-8). Unity Pr.
Time-Life Books, ed. Herbs. (The Time-Life Encyclopedia of Gardening Ser.). 1977. 12.95 (ISBN 0-8094-2550-5). Time-Life.
Tisserand, Robert. The Art of Aromatherapy. 1978. pap. 7.95 (ISBN 0-685-62088-3). Weiser.
Twitchell, Paul. Herbs, the Magic Healers. 1971. pap. 2.95 (ISBN 0-914766-10-4). IWP Pub.
--Les Plantes: Guerisseuses Magiques. Lasnier, Denis R., et al, trs. 240p. (Orig., Fr.). 1980. pap. 4.00 (ISBN 0-914766-59-7, 0308). IWP Pub.

Walker, Elizabeth. Making Things with Herbs. LC 77-86543. (The Living with Herbs Series: Vol. 4). (Illus.). 1977. pap. 2.50 (ISBN 0-87983-156-1). Keats.
Weiner, Michael A. Weiner's Herbal. LC 78-26616. (Illus.). 1979. 18.95 (ISBN 0-8128-2586-1); pap. 9.95 (ISBN 0-8128-6023-3). Stein & Day.
Willdenow, Carl L. Herbarium Willdenow - Alphabetical Index. 1972. 32.50x (ISBN 0-8002-1278-9). Intl Pubns Serv.

HERBS-THERAPEUTIC USE
see Botany, Medical; Materia Medica, Vegetable; Medicine, Medieval

HERCULANEUM
Brion, Marcel. Pompeii & Herculaneum: The Glory & the Grief. 1977. 14.95 (ISBN 0-236-30963-3, Pub. by Paul Elek). Merrimack Bk Serv.
Grant, Michael. The Art & Life of Pompeii & Herculaneum. LC 78-65504. (Illus.). 1979. 19.95 (ISBN 0-88225-268-2); pap. 8.95 (ISBN 0-88225-269-0). Newsweek.

HERCULES
Downey, Susan B. The Heracles Sculpture, Part 1, Fascicle 1. LC 43-2669. pap. 22.50 (ISBN 0-685-71741-0). J J Augustin.
Silverthorne, Elizabeth. I, Heracles. LC 78-1811. (Illus.). (gr. 3-7). 1978. 5.95 (ISBN 0-687-18459-2). Abingdon.
Sinatra, Stephen, et al. All About Me, "Hercules the Heart". 1980. cancelled (ISBN 0-8062-1504-6). Carlton.

HERCULES-DRAMA
Colony, Horatio. The Amazon's Hero. 4.75 (ISBN 0-8283-1340-7). Branden.

HERCULES (CONSTELLATION)
see Stars-Clusters

HERCULES CLUB
Stevens, Henry. Thomas Hariot, the Mathematician, the Philosopher & the Scholar. LC 72-82433. 213p. 1972. Repr. of 1900 ed. 19.50 (ISBN 0-8337-3399-0). B Franklin.

HERDER, JOHANN GOTTFRIED VON, 1744-1803
Berlin, Isaiah. Vico & Herder: Two Studies in the History of Ideas. (Giant Ser.). pap. 3.95 (ISBN 0-394-72250-7, V-250, Vin). Random.
--Vico & Herder: Two Studies in the History of Ideas. new ed. LC 75-33299. 216p. 1976. 12.50 (ISBN 0-670-74585-5). Viking Pr.
Ergang, Robert R. Herder & the Foundations of German Nationalism. 1967. lib. bdg. 18.00x (ISBN 0-374-92622-0). Octagon.
Mayo, Robert S. Herder & the Beginnings of Comparative Literature. (Studies in Comparative Literature Ser.: No. 48). 1969. 11.00x (ISBN 0-8078-7048-X). U of NC Pr.
Schick, Edgar B. Metaphorical Organicism in Herder's Early Works: A Study of the Relation of Herder's Literary Idiom to His World-View. LC 74-134546. 135p. 1971. pap. text ed. 16.75x (ISBN 0-686-22489-2). Mouton.

HERDSMEN
see Shepherds

HEREDITARY DISEASES
see Medical Genetics

HEREDITARY METABOLIC DISORDERS
see Metabolism, Inborn Errors of

HEREDITARY SUCCESSION
see Inheritance and Succession

HEREDITY
see also Biometry; Blood Groups; Chromosomes; Consanguinity; Eugenics; Evolution; Hybridization; Genetics; Linkage (Genetics); Man-Constitution; Mendel's Law; Natural Selection; Population Genetics; Prenatal Influences; Variation (Biology)
Brody, Elizabeth G. Genetic Basis at Spontaneous Activity in the Albino Rat. (Comparative Psychology Monographs). 1942. pap. 5.00 (ISBN 0-527-24924-6). Kraus Repr.
Carew, F. A. Heredity. 1978. Repr. of 1929 ed. 12.50 (ISBN 0-8492-3851-X). R West.
Cattell, Raymond B. The Inheritance of Personality & Ability: Research Methods & Findings. (Personality & Psychopathology Ser.). 1981. price not set (ISBN 0-12-164260-7). Acad Pr.
Cold Spring Harbor Symposia on Quantitative Biology: Genes & Chromosomes, Vol. 9. LC 34-8174. (Illus.). 325p. 1941. 30.00 (ISBN 0-87969-008-9). Cold Spring Harbor.
Cold Spring Harbor Symposia on Quantitative Biology: Genes & Mutations, Vol. 16. LC 34-8174. (Illus.). 537p. 1952. 30.00 (ISBN 0-87969-015-1). Cold Spring Harbor.
Cravens, Hamilton. Triumph of Evolution: American Scientists & the Heredity-Environment Controversy, 1900-1941. LC 77-20570. (Illus.). 1978. 22.00x (ISBN 0-8122-7744-9). U of Pa Pr.
Dugdale, Richard L. Jukes: A Study in Crime, Pauperism, Disease, & Heredity. LC 74-112542. (Rise of Urban America). (Illus.). 1970. Repr. of 1877 ed. 13.00 (ISBN 0-405-02451-7). Arno.
Fishman, William H. & Sell, Stewart, eds. Onco-Developmental Gene Expression. 1976. 45.50 (ISBN 0-12-257660-8). Acad Pr.
Fox, L. Raymond & Elliott, Paul R. Heredity & You. LC 76-51113. 1978. pap. text ed. 2.95 (ISBN 0-8403-1691-7). Kendall-Hunt.
Galton, Francis. Natural Inheritance. Bd. with Darwinism. (Contributions to the History of Psychology Ser., Vol. IV, Pt. D: Comparative Psychology). 1978. Repr. of 1889 ed. 30.00 (ISBN 0-89093-173-9). U Pubns Amer.
--Natural Inheritance. LC 72-1633. Repr. of 1889 ed. 22.00 (ISBN 0-404-08129-0). AMS Pr.
Geisert, Paul. Genes & Populations. (EMI Programed Biology Ser). (gr. 9 up). 1967. pap. text ed. 3.95 (ISBN 0-88462-019-0). Ed Methods.
Gillham, Nicholas W. Organelle Heredity. LC 75-43195. 618p. 1978. 53.50 (ISBN 0-89004-102-4). Raven.
Glass, Robert E. Gene Function: E. coli & Its Heritable Elements. 450p. 1980. 60.00x (ISBN 0-686-69929-7, Pub. by Croom Helm England). State Mutual Bk.
Goodwin, Donald. Is Alcoholism Hereditary? LC 75-32346. 1978. pap. 3.95 (ISBN 0-19-502432-X, GB 549, GB). Oxford U Pr.
Greenblatt, Augusta & Greenblatt, I. J. Your Genes & Your Destiny. LC 78-55655. 1978. 8.95 (ISBN 0-672-52302-7). Bobbs.
Hildreth, G. H. Resemblance of Siblings in Intelligence & Achievement. LC 78-176862. (Columbia University. Teachers College. Contributions to Education: No. 186). Repr. of 1925 ed. 17.50 (ISBN 0-404-55186-6). AMS Pr.
Hyatt, Alpheus. Phylogeny of an Acquired Characteristic: Proceedings of American Philosophical Society, Vol.xxxii, No. 143. Gould, Stephen J., ed. LC 79-8333. (The History of Paleontology Ser.). (Illus.). 1980. Repr. of 1893 ed. lib. bdg. 28.00x (ISBN 0-405-12714-6). Arno.
Jacob, Francois. The Logic of Life: A History of Heredity. Spillman, Betty E., tr. from Fr. 1976. pap. 3.95 (ISBN 0-394-71903-4, Vin). Random.
Jennings, H. S., et al. Scientific Aspects of the Race Problem. LC 73-127591. (Essay Index Reprint Ser). 1941. 19.00 (ISBN 0-8369-1774-X). Arno.
Jepsen, Glenn L., et al, eds. Genetics, Paleontology & Evolution. LC 49-9873. (Illus.). 1963. pap. 1.95 (ISBN 0-689-70110-1, 35). Atheneum.
Jinks, J. L. Cytoplasmic Inheritance. rev ed. Head, J. J., ed. LC 77-90233. (Carolina Biology Readers Ser.). (gr. 11 up). 1978. pap. 1.65 (ISBN 0-89278-272-2, 45-9672). Carolina Biological.
Kemp, Roger. Cell Division & Heredity. 1971. text ed. 14.95 (ISBN 0-312-12635-2). St Martin.
Lewin, Benjamin. Gene Expression, Vol. 1: Bacterial Genomes. LC 73-14382. (Illus.). 688p. 1974. 57.75 (ISBN 0-471-53167-7, Pub. by Wiley-Interscience); pap. 23.00 (ISBN 0-471-53168-5). Wiley.
Little, Clarence C. Inheritance of Coat Color in Dogs. LC 67-8658. (Illus.). 1957. 14.95 (ISBN 0-87605-621-4). Howell Bk.
M. D. Anderson Symposia on Fundamental Cancer Research, 33rd. Genes, Chromosomes, & Neoplasia. Arrighi, Frances E., et al, eds. 550p. 1981. 61.50 (ISBN 0-89004-532-1). Raven.
McDevitt, Hugh O., ed. Ir Genes & Ia Antigens (Symposium) (MS-Repro) 1978. 32.00 (ISBN 0-12-483260-1). Acad Pr.
Matsuo, T., ed. Gene Conservation. (Japan International Biological Program Synthetics Ser.: Vol. 5). (Orig.). 1975. pap. 27.50x (ISBN 0-86008-215-6, Pub. by U of Tokyo Pr). Intl Schol Bk Serv.
Mitsuhashi, S., et al, eds. Plasmids: Medical & Theoretical Aspects. (Illus.). 1977. 56.90 (ISBN 0-387-07946-7). Springer-Verlag.
Morrison, Velma F. There's Only One You: The Story of Heredity. LC 78-12659. (Illus.). 64p. (gr. 4-6). 1978. PLB 6.97 (ISBN 0-671-32943-X). Messner.
Nagle, James J. Heredity & Human Affairs. 2nd ed. LC 78-27066. (Illus.). 1979. pap. text ed. 15.95 (ISBN 0-8016-3621-3). Mosby.
Ohno, S. Major Sex-Determining Genes. LC 78-10285. (Monographs on Endocrinology: Vol. 11). (Illus.). 1979. 20.50 (ISBN 0-387-08965-9). Springer-Verlag.
Parker, Gary, et al. Heredity. 2nd ed. (Programed Biology Studies). 1977. 4.95 (ISBN 0-88462-014-X). Ed Methods.
Pettersson, R. F., ed. Expression of Eukaryotic Viral & Cellular Genes. 1981. write for info. (ISBN 0-12-553120-6). Acad Pr.
Ribot, Theodule A. Heredity: A Psychological Study of Its Phenomena, Laws, Causes, & Consequences. R. W., intro. by. LC 78-72821. (Brainedness, Handedness, & Mental Abilities Ser.). Repr. of 1875 ed. 40.00 (ISBN 0-404-60890-6). AMS Pr.
Rosenthal, S., et al, eds. Gene Function: Proceedings of the 12th FEBS Meeting, Dresden, 1978. (Federation of European Biochemical Society Ser.: Vol. 51). (Illus.). 1979. 60.00 (ISBN 0-08-023175-6). Pergamon.
Russell, E. S. Interpretation of Development & Heredity: A Study in Biological Method. LC 70-39699. (Select Bibliographies Reprint Ser.). 312p. 1972. Repr. of 1930 ed. 15.25 (ISBN 0-8369-9943-6). Arno.
Sheppard, Philip M. Natural Selection & Heredity. 4th ed. 1975. text ed. 10.75x (ISBN 0-09-036801-0, Hutchinson U Lib); pap. text ed. 7.50x (ISBN 0-09-036802-9). Humanities.
Steele, E. J. Somatic Selection & Adaptive Evolution: On the Inheritance of Acquired Characters. 2nd ed. 1981. price not set (ISBN 0-226-77163-6, Phoen). U of Chicago Pr.
Taylor, Howard F. The I.Q. Game: A Methodological Inquiry into the Heredity-Environment Controversy. 300p. 1980. 19.50 (ISBN 0-8135-0902-5). Rutgers U Pr.
Traite Philosophique et Physiologique De L'heredite Naturelle D Ans les Etats De Sante et De Maladie Du Systeme Nerveaux. Repr. of 1857 ed. 421.00 (ISBN 0-8287-1422-3). Clearwater Pub.
Wagner, Robert P., ed. Genes & Proteins. LC 75-8851. (Benchmark Papers in Genetics Ser: Vol. 2). 395p. 1975. 47.00 (ISBN 0-12-787710-X). Acad Pr.
Weismann, August, et al. Germ Plasm: A Theory of Heredity. LC 72-1659. Repr. of 1893 ed. 31.00 (ISBN 0-404-08191-6). AMS Pr.
Wiggam, Albert E. The Fruit of the Family Tree. LC 76-46108. (Anti-Movements in America). (Illus.). 1977. Repr. of 1924 ed. lib. bdg. 25.00x (ISBN 0-405-09979-7). Arno.
Winchester, Albert. Heredity, Evolution & Humankind. LC 75-45130. (Illus.). 350p. 1976. text ed. 17.95 (ISBN 0-8299-0106-X). West Pub.
Winterton, Bert W. The Processes of Heredity. 304p. (Orig.). 1980. pap. 10.95 (ISBN 0-8403-2166-X). Kendall-Hunt.

HEREDITY-JUVENILE LITERATURE
Dunbar, Robert E. Heredity. (First Bks.). (Illus.). (gr. 4 up). 1978. PLB 6.90 s&l (ISBN 0-531-01408-8). Watts.
Lipke, Jean C. Heredity. LC 78-104892. (Being Together Books). (Illus.). (gr. 5-11). 1971. PLB 4.95 (ISBN 0-8225-0597-5). Lerner Pubns.
Randal, Judith. All About Heredity. (Allabout Ser.: No. 48). (Illus.). (gr. 5-9). 1963. PLB 5.39 (ISBN 0-394-90248-3). Random.
Showers, Paul. Me & My Family Tree. LC 77-26595. (A Let's-Read-&-Find-Out Science Bk). (Illus.). (gr. k-3). 1978. 8.95 (ISBN 0-690-03886-0, TYC-J); PLB 8.79 (ISBN 0-690-03887-9). Har-Row.

HEREDITY, HUMAN
see also Delinquents; Human Genetics
Alland, Alexander. Human Diversity. LC 79-138293. 203p. 1971. 17.50x (ISBN 0-231-03227-7). Columbia U Pr.
Baltimore Conference, 1975. Human Gene Mapping 3: Proceedings. Bergsma, D., ed. (Cytogenetics & Cell Genetics: Vol. 16, Nos. 1-5). (Illus.). 420p. 1976. pap. 66.00 (ISBN 3-8055-2345-9). S Karger.
Boas, Franz. Materials for the Study of Inheritance in Man. LC 71-82349. (Columbia Univ. Contributions to Anthropology Ser.: No. 6). 1969. Repr. of 1928 ed. 36.50 (ISBN 0-404-50556-2). AMS Pr.
Conklin, Edwin G. Heredity & Environment in the Development of Men. 6th rev. ed. (Illus.). 1930. 23.00 (ISBN 0-384-09755-3). Johnson Repr.
Davenport, Charles B. Heredity in Relation to Eugenics. LC 73-180571. (Medicine & Society in America Ser). (Illus.). 320p. 1972. Repr. of 1911 ed. 16.00 (ISBN 0-405-03946-8). Arno.
Dunn, Leslie C. Heredity & Evolution in Human Populations. rev. ed. LC 65-11617. 1965. pap. text ed. 1.95x (ISBN 0-689-70065-2, 71). Atheneum.
--Heredity & Evolution in Human Populations. rev. ed. LC 65-11617. (Books in Biology Ser: No. 1). (Illus.). 1965. 7.50x (ISBN 0-674-38950-6). Harvard U Pr.
Effect of Radiation on Human Heredity. (Illus.). 168p. (Eng. & Fr.). 1957. 5.60 (ISBN 92-4-156023-1). World Health.
Gove, Walter R. & Carpenter, G. Russell. The Fundamental Connection Between Nature & Nurture: A Review of the Evidence. LC 80-8961. 1981. price not set (ISBN 0-669-04483-0). Lexington Bks.
Haldane, J. B. Heredity & Politics. 1938. 25.00 (ISBN 0-8274-4209-2). R West.
Hubbard, Ruth, et al, eds. Genes & Gender Two: Pitfalls in Research on Sex & Gender. LC 78-50640. 1979. pap. text ed. 6.95 (ISBN 0-87752-219-7). Gordian.
Huntington, Ellsworth. Mainsprings of Civilization. LC 72-4278. (World Affairs Ser.: National & International Viewpoints). 660p. 1972. Repr. of 1945 ed. 30.00 (ISBN 0-405-04572-7). Arno.
Jensen, Arthur R., et al. Environment, Heredity, & Intelligence. (Reprint Ser.: No. 2). 5.95 (ISBN 0-916690-02-4). Harvard Educ Rev.
Koestler, Arthur. The Case of the Midwife Toad. 192p. 1973. pap. 2.45 (ISBN 0-394-71823-2, Vin). Random.
Lidbetter, Ernest J. Heredity & the Social Problem Group. 1977. lib. bdg. 59.95 (ISBN 0-8490-1944-3). Gordon Pr.
Newman, Horatio H., et al. Twins: A Study of Heredity & Environment. LC 37-11639. (Illus.). 1966. 14.00x (ISBN 0-226-57706-6). U of Chicago Pr.
Osborne, Richard H. & De George, Frances V. Genetic Basis of Morphological Variation: An Evaluation & Application of the Twin Study Method. LC 59-15743. (Commonwealth Fund Publications Ser). 1959. 12.50x (ISBN 0-674-34600-9). Harvard U Pr.
Partanen, J., et al. Inheritance of Drinking Behavior. (The Finnish Foundation for Alcohol Studies: Vol. 14). 1966. 5.50x (ISBN 0-685-19936-3). Rutgers Ctr Alcohol.
Scheinfeld, Amram. Your Heredity & Environment. (Illus.). 1965. 20.95 (ISBN 0-397-00406-0, JBL-Med-Nursing). Har-Row.
Sen Gupta, N. N. Heredity in Mental Traits. 207p. 1980. Repr. of 1941 ed. lib. bdg. 50.00 (ISBN 0-89984-409-X). Century Bookbindery.
Stamatoyannopoulos, George & Nienhuis, Arthur W., eds. Organization & Expression of Globin Genes. LC 81-3677. 368p. 1981. 52.00 (ISBN 0-8451-0211-7). A R Liss.
Tobach, Ethel & Rosoff, Betty, eds. Genes & Gender: I. LC 78-50640. 1978. pap. text ed. 5.00 (ISBN 0-87752-215-4). Gordian.
Vale, Jack R. Genes, Environment & Behavior: An Interactionist Approach. (Illus.). 470p. 1980. text ed. 22.50 scp (ISBN 0-06-046758-4, HarpC). Har-Row.
Wiener, Alexander S. & Wexler, Irving B. Heredity of the Blood Groups. 160p. 1958. 33.50 (ISBN 0-8089-0529-5). Grune.
Woodworth, Robert S. Heredity & Environment: A Critical Survey of Recently Published Material on Twins & Foster Children. LC 41-23998. 1941. pap. 2.25 (ISBN 0-527-03279-4). Kraus Repr.

HEREDITY OF DISEASE
see Medical Genetics

HEREFORDSHIRE-DESCRIPTION AND TRAVEL-GUIDEBOOKS
Hammond, Reginald J. & Lowther, Kenneth, eds. Complete Wye Valley, Hereford & Worchester. LC 77-351996. (Red Guide Ser.). (Illus.). 1976. 11.25x (ISBN 0-7063-5134-7). Intl Pubns Serv.

HEREFORDSHIRE-HISTORY
Rowe, Alick. Boy at the Commercial. LC 78-309172. 136p. 1978. 11.95 (ISBN 0-571-10977-2, Pub. by Faber & Faber). Merrimack Bk Serv.

HERESIES AND HERETICS
For general descriptive and historical works. Works on heresy in the abstract are entered under the heading Heresy.
Aldridge, John W. In Search of Heresy: American Literature in an Age of Conformity. LC 74-3618. 208p. 1974. Repr. of 1956 ed. lib. bdg. 15.00 (ISBN 0-8371-7452-X, ALSH). Greenwood.
Barthlet, John. The Pedegrewe of Heretiques. LC 79-76432. (English Experience Ser.: No. 76). 180p. 1969. Repr. of 1566 ed. 21.00 (ISBN 90-221-0076-6). Walter J Johnson.
Batman, Stephen. The Golden Booke of the Leaden Gods, Repr. Of 1577 Ed. Bd. with The Third Part of the Countess of Pembroke's Yvychurch. Fraunce, Abraham. Repr. of 1592 ed; The Fountaine of Ancient Fiction. Lynche, Richard. Repr. of 1599 ed. LC 75-27856. (Renaissance & the Gods Ser.: Vol. 13). (Illus.). 1976. lib. bdg. 73.00 (ISBN 0-8240-2062-6). Garland Pub.
Belloc, Hilaire. Great Heresies. facs. ed. LC 68-16908. (Essay Index Reprint Ser). 1938. 16.00 (ISBN 0-8369-0189-4). Arno.
Chesterton, Gilbert K. Heretics. facs. ed. LC 75-128220. (Essay Index Reprint Ser). 1905. 17.00 (ISBN 0-8369-1869-X). Arno.
Darrow, Clarence. Infidels & Heretics. 69.95 (ISBN 0-87968-240-X). Gordon Pr.
Emery, Richard W. Heresy & Inquisition in Narbonne. LC 75-166031. (Columbia University Studies in the Social Sciences: No. 480). 17.50 (ISBN 0-404-51480-4). AMS Pr.
Heath, Carl. Social & Religious Heretics in Five Centuries. LC 78-147622. (Library of War & Peace; Non-Resis. & Non-Vio.). lib. bdg. 38.00 (ISBN 0-8240-0397-7). Garland Pub.
Hutchinson, Roger. Works. 1842. 25.50 (ISBN 0-384-25120-X). Johnson Repr.
Ingram, Robert T. New Liturgy, Old Heresy. LC 81-52116. (Orig.). 1981. pap. 4.50 (ISBN 0-686-75087-X). St Thomas.
Kelly, Clarence. Conspiracy Against God & Man. LC 73-92438. 280p. 1974. 8.00 (ISBN 0-88279-229-6). Western Islands.

Le Goff, Jacques. Heresies et Societes Dans L'europe Pre-Industrielle 11e-18e Siecles: Communications et Debats Du Colloque De Royaumont. (Civilisations et Societes: No. 10). 1968. pap. 39.50x (ISBN 90-2796-079-8). Mouton.

Metcalfe, J. C. There Must Be Heresies. 1963. pap. 1.25 (ISBN 0-87508-922-4). Chr Lit.

Meyer, Samuel. The Deacon & the Jewess: Adventures in Heresy. LC 80-84734. 1981. 10.00 (ISBN 0-8022-2379-6). Philos Lib.

Nelli, Rene. Dictionnaire Des Heresies Meridionales. 384p. (Fr.). 18.50 (ISBN 0-686-56886-9, F-21110). French & Eur.

Pluquet, F. A. Dictionnaire des Heresies des Erreurs et des Schismes, 2 vols. Migne, J. P., ed. (Encyclopedie Theologique Ser.: Vols. 11-12). 1374p. (Fr.). Date not set. Repr. of 1847 ed. lib. bdg. 175.00x (ISBN 0-89241-235-6). Caratzas Bros.

HERESIES AND HERETICS–EARLY CHURCH, ca. 30-600

see also Gnosticism; Manichaeism

Burton, Edward. An Inquiry into the Heresies of the Apostolic Age. LC 78-63166. (Heresies of the Early Christian & Medieval Era: Second Ser.). Repr. of 1829 ed. 43.50 (ISBN 0-404-16179-0). AMS Pr.

Douais, Celestin. Les Albigeois. 2nd ed. LC 78-63182. (Heresies of the Early Christian & Medieval Era: Second Ser.). Repr. of 1879 ed. 47.50 (ISBN 0-404-16221-5). AMS Pr.

Grant, Robert M., ed. Gnosticism: A Source Book of Heretical Writings from the Early Christian Period. LC 77-85274. Repr. of 1961 ed. 23.50 (ISBN 0-404-16108-1). AMS Pr.

Grobel, Kendrick, tr. The Gospel of Truth. LC 78-63167. (Heresies of the Early Christian & Medieval Era: Second Ser.). Repr. of 1960 ed. 19.50 (ISBN 0-404-16083-2). AMS Pr.

Jones, A. H. Were Ancient Heresies Disguised Social Movements? Lee, Clarence L., ed. LC 66-11534. (Facet Bks.). 1966. pap. 1.00 (ISBN 0-8006-3023-8, 1-3023). Fortress.

Mansel, Henry L. The Gnostic Heresies of the First & Second Centuries. Lightfoot, J. B., ed. LC 78-63170. (Heresies of the Early Christian & Medieval Era: Second Ser.). Repr. of 1875 ed. 26.50 (ISBN 0-404-16185-5). AMS Pr.

Marcion Of Sinope. The Gospel of the Lord. Hill, James H., tr. LC 78-63171. (Heresies of the Early Christian & Medieval Era: Second Ser.). Repr. of 1891 ed. 13.50 (ISBN 0-404-16186-3). AMS Pr.

O'Callaghan, Joseph F., ed. Heresies of the Early Christian & Medieval Era, 67 titles in 92 vols. (An AMS Reprint Ser.). Repr. of 1816 ed. write in info. (ISBN 0-404-16090-5). AMS Pr.

Turner, Henry E. The Pattern of Christian Truth: A Study in the Relations Between Orthodoxy & Heresy in the Early Church. LC 77-84707. (Bampton Lectures: 1954). 1977. Repr. of 1954 ed. 34.50 (ISBN 0-404-16114-6). AMS Pr.

Wand, John W. The Four Great Heresies. LC 78-63174. (Heresies of the Early Christian & Medieval Era: Second Ser.). Repr. of 1955 ed. 20.00 (ISBN 0-404-16189-8). AMS Pr.

Wolfson, Harry A. Philosophy of the Church Fathers: Faith, Trinity, Incarnation. 3rd rev. ed. LC 70-119077. 1970. 25.00x (ISBN 0-674-66551-1). Harvard U Pr.

HERESIES AND HERETICS–MIDDLE AGES, 600-1500

see also Sects, Medieval

Alphandery, Paul. Les Idees Morales Chez les Heterodoxes Latins Au Debut Du Xiii e Siecle. LC 78-63184. (Heresies of the Early Christian & Medieval Era: Second Ser.). Repr. of 1903 ed. 22.50 (ISBN 0-404-16198-7). AMS Pr.

Douais, Celestin. Les Albigeois. 2nd ed. LC 78-63182. (Heresies of the Early Christian & Medieval Era: Second Ser.). Repr. of 1879 ed. 47.50 (ISBN 0-404-16221-5). AMS Pr.

Gebhart, E. Mystics & Heretics in Italy at the End of the Middle Ages. 1977. lib. bdg. 59.95 (ISBN 0-8490-2321-1). Gordon Pr.

Grobel, Kendrick, tr. The Gospel of Truth. LC 78-63167. (Heresies of the Early Christian & Medieval Era: Second Ser.). Repr. of 1960 ed. 19.50 (ISBN 0-404-16083-2). AMS Pr.

Guiraud, Jean. The Medieval Inquisition. Messenger, E. C., tr. LC 78-63181. (Heresies of the Early Christian & Medieval Era: Second Ser.). Repr. of 1929 ed. 21.50 (ISBN 0-404-16222-3). AMS Pr.

Hus, Jan. Mag. Johannis Hus Tractatus Responsiyus. LC 78-63201. (Heresies of the Early Christian & Medieval Era: Second Ser.). Repr. of 1927 ed. 24.50 (ISBN 0-404-16229-0). AMS Pr.

Lambert, Malcolm. Medieval Heresy: Popular Movements from Bogomil to Hus. LC 76-49949. 1977. 45.00x (ISBN 0-8419-0298-4). Holmes & Meier.

Lawler, Thomas, et al, eds. A Dialogue Concerning Heresies: The Yale Edition of the Complete Works of St. Thomas More, Vol. 6, Pts. 1 & 2. LC 63-7949. (Illus.). 910p. 1981. Set. text ed. 80.00x (ISBN 0-300-02211-5). Yale U Pr.

Lerner, Robert E. The Heresy of the Free Spirit in the Later Middle Ages. LC 78-145790. 1972. 24.00x (ISBN 0-520-01908-3). U of Cal Pr.

Marcion Of Sinope. The Gospel of the Lord. Hill, James H., tr. LC 78-63171. (Heresies of the Early Christian & Medieval Era: Second Ser.). Repr. of 1891 ed. 13.50 (ISBN 0-404-16186-3). AMS Pr.

Moore, R. I., ed. The Birth of Popular Heresy. LC 75-32934. (Documents of Medieval History Ser.). 176p. 1976. text ed. 22.95 (ISBN 0-312-08190-1). St Martin.

Nelli, Rene. Spiritualite de l'Heresie: le Catharisme. LC 78-63189. (Heresies of the Early Christian & Medieval Era: Second Ser.). Repr. of 1953 ed. 21.50 (ISBN 0-404-16226-6). AMS Pr.

O'Callaghan, Joseph F., ed. Heresies of the Early Christian & Medieval Era, 67 titles in 92 vols. (An AMS Reprint Ser.). Repr. of 1816 ed. write in info. (ISBN 0-404-16090-5). AMS Pr.

Schmidt, Charles G. Histoire et Doctrine de la Secte des Cathares ou Albigeois, 2 vols. LC 78-63191. (Heresies of the Early Christian & Medieval Era: Second Ser.). 1979. Repr. of 1849 ed. 47.50 set (ISBN 0-404-16180-4). AMS Pr.

Shannon, Albert C. The Popes & Heresy in the Thirteenth Century. LC 78-63192. (Heresies of the Early Christian & Medieval Era: Second Ser.). Repr. of 1949 ed. 21.50 (ISBN 0-404-16228-2). AMS Pr.

Tanner, Norman P., ed. Heresy Trials in the Diocese of Norwich: 1428-31. (Royal Historical Society: Camden Society Fourth Ser.: Vol. 20). 233p. 1977. 20.00x (ISBN 0-8476-3305-5). Rowman.

Wand, John W. The Four Great Heresies. LC 78-63174. (Heresies of the Early Christian & Medieval Era: Second Ser.). Repr. of 1955 ed. 20.00 (ISBN 0-404-16189-8). AMS Pr.

Wilson, Robert S. Marcion. LC 78-63176. (Heresies of the Early Christian & Medieval Era: Second Ser.). Repr. of 1933 ed. 23.00 (ISBN 0-404-16194-4). AMS Pr.

HERESIES AND HERETICS–MODERN PERIOD, 1500-

see also Sects

HERESY

see also Apostasy; Liberty of Speech in the Church; Schism

Boyle, Whiteford. Beyond God & Evil: The Triumph of Herisy in Our Time. Holzgang, David, ed. 1981. 10.00 (ISBN 0-686-75242-2). Wheat Forders.

Kieckhefer, Richard. Repression of Heresy in Medieval Germany. LC 78-65112. (The Middle Ages Ser.). 1979. 16.00x (ISBN 0-8122-7758-9). U of Pa Pr.

Peters, Edward, ed. Heresy & Authority in Medieval Europe. LC 79-5262. (Middle Ages Ser.). 384p. 1980. 25.00x (ISBN 0-8122-7779-1); pap. 11.95x (ISBN 0-8122-1103-0). U of Pa Pr.

Philastrius St. Bishop Of Brescia. Sancti Filastrii Episcopi Brixiensis Diversarum Hereseon Liber. Repr. of 1898 ed. pap. 41.50 (ISBN 0-384-46225-1). Johnson Repr.

HERFF, ADOLPH, 1858-1952

Herff, Ferdinand P. The Doctors Herff: A Three-Generation Memoir, 2 vols. 550p. 1973. text ed. 18.00 boxed set (ISBN 0-911536-40-X). Trinity U Pr.

HERGESHEIMER, JOSEPH, 1880-1954

Jones, Llewellyn. Joseph Hergesheimer. 1920. Repr. 20.00 (ISBN 0-8274-2634-8). R West.

Stappenbeck, Herb, compiled by. A Catalogue of the Joseph Hergesheimer Collection at the University of Texas. LC 78-169267. (Tower Bibliographical Ser.: No. 10). (Illus.). 1974. 12.95 (ISBN 0-87959-043-2). U of Tex Hum Res.

Swire, H. L. Bibliography of the Works of Joseph Hergesheimer. LC 76-42990. 1922. lib. bdg. 15.00 (ISBN 0-8414-7678-0). Folcroft.

HERMANOS PENITENTES

Cortes, Carlos E., ed. The Penitentes of New Mexico. LC 73-14212. (The Mexican American Ser.). (Illus.). 1974. Repr. 30.00x (ISBN 0-405-05686-9). Arno.

Darley, Alex. Passionists of the Southwest: A Revelation of the Penitentes. LC 68-57290. (Beautiful Rio Grande Classics Ser). lib. bdg. 7.00 (ISBN 0-87380-020-6). Rio Grande.

Horka-Follick, Lorayne. Los Hermanos Penitentes. (Great West & Indian Ser: Vol. 38). (Illus.). 1969. 8.95 (ISBN 0-87026-015-4). Westernlore.

HERMAPHRODITISM

see also Bisexuality

Armstrong, C. N. & Marshall, A. J. Intersexuality in Vertebrates Including Man. 1964. 62.00 (ISBN 0-12-063150-4). Acad Pr.

Dewhurst, G. J. & Gordon, R. R. Intersexual Disorders. (Illus.). 1969. text ed. 19.95 (ISBN 0-02-857580-6). Macmillan.

Foucault, Michel, intro. by. Herculine Barbin: Being the Recently Discovered Memoirs of a Nineteenth-Century French Hermaphodite. McDougall, Richard, tr. 1980. 8.95 (ISBN 0-394-50821-1); pap. 4.95 (ISBN 0-394-73862-4). Pantheon.

Jewett, Paul K. Man As Male & Female. 192p. 1975. pap. 3.95 (ISBN 0-8028-1597-9). Eerdmans.

Jirasek, Jan E. Development of the Genital System & Male Pseudohermaphroditism. Cohen, M. Michael, Jr., ed. LC 72-128825. (Illus.). 160p. 1971. 15.00x (ISBN 0-8018-1181-3). Johns Hopkins.

Josso, Nathalie, ed. The Intersex Child. (Pediatric & Adolescent Endocrinology Ser.: Vol. 8). viii, 272p. 1981. pap. 99.00 (ISBN 3-8055-0909-X). S Karger.

Kaplan, Alexandra G., ed. Psychological Androgyny: Further Considerations. LC 79-1647. 1979. 9.95 (ISBN 0-87705-418-5). Human Sci Pr.

Lepori, N. G. Sex Differentiation, Hermaphroditism & Intersexuality in Vertebrates Including Man. (Illus.). 372p. 1980. text ed. 49.50x (ISBN 88-212-0747-1, Pub. by Piccin Italy). J K Burgess.

Reinboth, R. Intersexuality in the Animal Kingdom. (Illus.). 510p. 1975. 53.00 (ISBN 0-387-07118-0). Springer-Verlag.

Van Niekerk, Willem A. True Hermaphroditism. (Illus.). 1974. text ed. 20.00x (ISBN 0-06-142588-5, Harper Medical). Har-Row.

HERMENEUTICS

Bauman, Zygmunt. Hermeneutics & Social Science. LC 78-877. (European Perspectives Ser.). 1978. 17.50x (ISBN 0-231-04546-8). Columbia U Pr.

Birdsong, Robert E. The Challenge of the Aquarian Age. (Aquarian Academy Monograph, Ser. A: Lecture No. 7). 1978. pap. 1.25 (ISBN 0-917108-25-6). Sirius Bks.

Bright, John. The Authority of the Old Testament. (Twin Brooks Ser). 272p. 1975. pap. 4.95 (ISBN 0-8010-0637-6). Baker Bk.

Bryant, Darrol & Foster, Durwood, eds. Hermeneutics & Unification Theology. LC 80-66201. (Conference Ser.: No. 5). (Illus., Orig.). 1980. pap. 7.95 (ISBN 0-932894-05-4). Unif Theol Seminary.

Crowley, Charles B. Universal Mathematics in Aristotelian-Thomistic Philosophy: The Hermeneutics of Aristotelian Texts Relative to Universal Mathematics. LC 79-48093. 239p. 1980. text ed. 18.50 (ISBN 0-8191-1009-4); pap. text ed. 9.50 (ISBN 0-8191-1010-8). U Pr of Amer.

Doyle, Esther M. & Floyd, Virginia H., eds. Studies in Interpretation, No. 2. 375p. 1977. pap. text ed. 25.75x (ISBN 90-6203-070-X). Humanities.

Ellis, E. Earle. Prophecy & Hermeneutic in Early Christianity. 1978. pap. 15.00 (ISBN 0-8028-1689-4). Eerdmans.

Frei, Hans W. The Eclipse of Biblical Narrative: A Study in Eighteenth & Nineteenth Century Hermeneutics. LC 73-86893. 384p. 1974. 25.00x (ISBN 0-300-01623-9); pap. 7.95 (ISBN 0-300-02602-1). Yale U Pr.

Gadamer, Hans-Georg. Essays in Philosophical Hermeneutics. LC 74-30519. (Cal Ser: No. 363). 1977. pap. 5.95 (ISBN 0-520-03475-9). U of Cal Pr.

--Truth & Method. LC 75-2053. 576p. 1975. 24.50 (ISBN 0-8164-9220-4). Continuum.

Hirsch, E. D., Jr. The Aims of Interpretation. LC 75-21269. 1978. pap. 4.50 (ISBN 0-226-34241-7, P767, Phoen). U of Chicago Pr.

Hirsch, Eric D., Jr. Validity in Interpretation. 1973. pap. 5.25x (ISBN 0-300-01692-1, Y259). Yale U Pr.

Ihde, Don. Hermeneutic Phenomenology: The Philosophy of Paul Ricoeur. (Studies in Phenomenology & Existential Philosophy). 1971. 16.95x (ISBN 0-8101-0347-8); pap. 6.95 (ISBN 0-8101-0611-6). Northwestern U Pr.

Kermode, Frank. The Genesis of Secrecy: On the Interpretation of Narrative. LC 78-23403. (Charles Elliot Norton Lectures Ser.). 1979. text ed. 10.00x (ISBN 0-674-34525-8); pap. 3.95 (ISBN 0-674-34525-8). Harvard U Pr.

Lund, A. & Luce, A. Hermeneutica. (Portuguese Bks.). 1979. 1.20 (ISBN 0-8297-0780-8). Life Pubs Intl.

Marriott. The Interpretation of Multiple Observations. 1974. 46.00 (ISBN 0-12-473450-2). Acad Pr.

Muller-Vollmer, Kurt. Hermeneutics Reader. 1981. 20.00 (ISBN 0-916354-88-1); pap. 9.95 (ISBN 0-916354-89-X). Urizen Bks.

O'Hara, Daniel T. Tragic Knowledge: Yeat's Autobiography & Hermeneutics. LC 80-26825. 224p. 1981. 22.50x (ISBN 0-231-05204-9). Columbia U Pr.

Olson, Alan M. Transcendence & Hermeneutics. (Studies in Philosophy & Religion: No. 2). 1979. lib. bdg. 35.00 (ISBN 90-247-2092-3, Pub. by Martinus Nijhoff Netherlands). Kluwer Boston.

Ommen, Thomas B. The Hermeneutic of Dogma. LC 75-29493. (American Academy of Religion. Dissertation Ser.). 1975. pap. 7.50 (ISBN 0-89130-039-2, 010011). Scholars Pr Ca.

Orr, Leonard. De-Structuring the Novel: Essays in Postmodern Hermeneutics. 280p. 1981. 20.00 (ISBN 0-87875-223-4). Whitston Pub.

Outhwaite, William. Understanding Social Life: The Method Called Verstehen. LC 75-26783. 127p. 1976. text ed. 12.00x (ISBN 0-8419-0239-9). Holmes & Meier.

Palmer, Richard E. Hermeneutics: Interpretation Theory in Schleiermacher, Dilthey, Heidegger, & Gadamer. LC 68-54885. (Studies in Phenomenology & Existential Philosophy Ser). 1969. 17.95x (ISBN 0-8101-0027-4); pap. 7.95x (ISBN 0-8101-0459-8). Northwestern U Pr.

Raschke, Carl A. The Alchemy of the Word: Language & the End of Theology. LC 79-15490. (American Academy of Religion, Studies in Religion: No. 20). 1979. 12.00 (ISBN 0-89130-319-7, 010020); pap. 7.50 (ISBN 0-89130-320-0). Scholars Pr Ca.

Ricoeur, Paul. The Conflict of Interpretations: Essays on Hermeneutics. LC 73-91311. (Studies in Phenomenology & Existential Philosophy). 528p. 1974. text ed. 22.95x (ISBN 0-8101-0442-3); pap. 10.95x (ISBN 0-8101-0529-2). Northwestern U Pr.

--Freud & Philosophy: An Essay on Interpretation. Savage, Denis, tr. LC 70-89907. (Terry Lectures Ser). 1970. 35.00x (ISBN 0-300-01165-2); pap. 9.95 (ISBN 0-300-02189-5). Yale U Pr.

--Hermeneutics & the Human Sciences. Thompson, John, ed. LC 80-41546. 280p. Date not set. price not set (ISBN 0-521-23497-2); pap. price not set (ISBN 0-521-28002-8). Cambridge U Pr.

Schleiermacher, Friedrich. Hermeneutics: The Handwritten Manuscripts. Kimmerle, Heinz, ed. Duke, James & Forstman, Jack, trs. from Ger. LC 77-13969. (American Academy of Religion. Text & Translations Ser.: No. 1). 1977. pap. text ed. 7.50x (ISBN 0-89130-186-0, 010201). Scholars Pr Ca.

Seung, T. K. Structuralism & Hermeneutics. 264p. 1982. text ed. 20.00x (ISBN 0-231-05278-2). Columbia U Pr.

Spanos, William V., ed. Martin Heidegger & the Question of Literature: Toward a Postmodern Literary Hermeneutics. LC 79-84261. (Studies in Phenomenology & Existential Philosophy). 352p. 1980. 15.00x (ISBN 0-253-17575-5). Ind U Pr.

Thompson, J. B. Critical Hermeneutics: A Study in the Thought of Paul Ricoeur & Jurgen Habermas. LC 80-41935. 238p. Date not set. price not set (ISBN 0-521-23932-X). Cambridge U Pr.

Traina, Robert A. Methodical Bible Study: A New Approach to Hermeneutics. LC 52-44401. 1952. 6.95x (ISBN 0-9601396-1-3). R A Traina.

Van Til, Cornelius. The New Hermeneutic. pap. 5.95 (ISBN 0-87552-491-5). Presby & Reformed.

--New Hermeneutic. 1974. pap. 5.95 (ISBN 0-8010-9273-6). Baker Bk.

Winquist, Charles E. The Communion of Possibility. LC 75-859. (The Religions Quest Ser: Vol. 2). 160p. 1975. lib. bdg. 17.50x (ISBN 0-914914-05-7); pap. text ed. 6.95x (ISBN 0-914914-04-9). New Horizons.

--Practical Hermeneutics. LC 79-22848. (Scholars Press General Ser.: No. 1). 12.00x (ISBN 0-89130-363-4); pap. 7.50x (ISBN 0-89130-364-2). Scholars Pr CA.

Wolff, Janet. Hermeneutic Philosophy & the Sociology of Art. (International Library of Sociology). 1975. 20.00x (ISBN 0-7100-8048-4). Routledge & Kegan.

--Hermeneutic Philosophy & the Sociology of Art: An Approach to Some of the Epistemological Problems of the Sociology of Art & Literature. (International Library of Sociology). 150p. 1981. pap. 12.50 (ISBN 0-7100-0682-9). Routledge & Kegan.

HERMENEUTICS, BIBLICAL

see Bible–Hermeneutics

HERMETIC ART AND PHILOSOPHY

see Alchemy; Astrology; Magic; Occult Sciences

HERMITAGES

see Hermits; Monasteries

HERMITS

Clay, Rotha M. Hermits & Anchorites of England. LC 68-21759. (Illus.). 1968. Repr. of 1914 ed. 22.00 (ISBN 0-8103-3424-0). Gale.

Fitzell, John. Hermit in German Literature: From Lessing to Eichendorff. LC 74-168033. (North Carolina. University. Studies in the Germanic Languages & Literatures: No. 30). Repr. of 1961 ed. 18.50 (ISBN 0-404-50930-4). AMS Pr.

Jerome. Life of Saint Hilarion. 1976. 1.95 (ISBN 0-686-15462-2). Eastern Orthodox.

Rampa, T. Lobsang. The Hermit. pap. 2.95 (ISBN 0-685-27226-5). Weiser.

Weaver, Charles P. The Hermit in English Literature from the Beginnings to 1660. LC 73-515. 1973. lib. bdg. 15.00 (ISBN 0-8414-1456-4). Folcroft.

HERMOGENES, RHETORICIAN

Burghardt, W. J., et al, eds. Tertullian, the Treatise Against Hermogenes. LC 56-13257. (Ancient Christian Writers Ser.: No. 24). 179p. 1956. 8.95 (ISBN 0-8091-0148-3). Paulist Pr.

Patterson, A. M. Hermogenes & the Renaissance: Seven Ideas of Style. 1970. 17.50x (ISBN 0-691-05182-8). Princeton U Pr.

HERNE, JAMES AHERN, 1839-1901

Perry, John. James A. Herne: The American Ibsen. LC 77-17931. (Illus.). 1978. 18.95x (ISBN 0-88229-265-X); pap. 9.95 (ISBN 0-88229-561-6). Nelson-Hall.

HERNIA

see also Hiatal Hernia

Gahagan, Thomas & Lam, Conrad R. Esophageal Hiatus Hernia: Rationale & Results of Anatomic Repair. (Henry Ford Hospital Surgical Monograph). (Illus.). 208p. 1976. 24.75 (ISBN 0-398-03489-3). C C Thomas.

Kimberly, Robert C. Problems of Recurrent Hernia. (Illus.). 76p. 1975. pap. 9.50 (ISBN 0-398-03374-9). C C Thomas.

Nyhus, Lloyd M. & Condon, Robert. Hernia. (Illus.). 1978. 75.00 (ISBN 0-397-50390-3, JBL-Med-Nursing). Har-Row.

Ponka, Joseph L. Hernias of the Abdominal Wall. LC 77-16965. (Illus.). 644p. 1980. text ed. 57.50 (ISBN 0-7216-7274-4). Saunders.

Ravitch, Mark M. Repair of Hernias. (Illus.). 1969. 26.00 (ISBN 0-8151-7104-8). Year Bk Med.

Rob, C., et al. General Principles & Breast & Hernia. (Operative Surgery Ser.). 1977. 67.95 (ISBN 0-407-00610-9). Butterworth.

Zimmerman, L. M. & Anson, B. J. Anatomy & Surgery of Hernia. 2nd ed. 370p. 1967. 19.50 (ISBN 0-685-54443-5, Pub. by Williams & Wilkins). Krieger.

HERO OF ALEXANDRIA, AUTOMATA

Drachmann, A. G. The Mechanical Technology of Greek & Roman Antiquity. (Illus.). 1963. 7.50 (ISBN 0-934454-61-2). Lubrecht & Cramer.

Martz, Louis B., ed. Hero & Leander. (Facsimiles Ser). 1978. 9.95 (ISBN 0-918016-35-5). Folger Bks.

HERO-WORSHIP

see Heroes

HEROD 1ST, THE GREAT, KING OF JUDEA, d. 4 B.C.

Schalit, Abraham. Koenig Herodes: Der Mann und sein Werk. Amir, Jehoshua, tr. (Studia Judaica, No. 4). (Ger). 1969. 91.75x (ISBN 3-11-001346-0). De Gruyter.

HEROD 1ST, THE GREAT, KING OF JUDEA, d. 4 B.C.-DRAMA

Greenberg, Noah & Smoldon, W. L., eds. Play of Herod: A Twelfth-Century Musical Drama. (Illus.). 1965. pap. 4.25x (ISBN 0-19-385196-2). Oxford U Pr.

Hebbel, Friedrich. Herod & Mariamne. Curts, Paul H., tr. LC 51-895. (North Carolina. University. Studies in the Germanic Languages & Literatures: No. 3). Repr. of 1950 ed. 18.50 (ISBN 0-404-50903-7). AMS Pr.

Valency, Maurice J. Tragedies of Herod & Mariamne. LC 70-8450. Repr. of 1940 ed. 19.50 (ISBN 0-404-06750-6). AMS Pr.

HERODIONES

see also Storks

Bent, Arthur C. Life Histories of North American Marsh Birds. (Illus.). 10.50 (ISBN 0-8446-1639-7). Peter Smith.

--Life Histories of North American Marsh Birds. (Illus.). 1927. pap. 6.50 (ISBN 0-486-21082-0). Dover.

HERODOTUS

Dahlmann, Friedrich C. The Life of Herodotus. Cox, G. Valentine, tr. LC 77-94571. 1979. Repr. of 1845 ed. lib. bdg. 20.00 (ISBN 0-89341-256-2). Longwood Pr.

Fehling, Detlef. Quellenangaben bei Herodot: Studien zur Erzaehlkunst Herodots. (Untersuchungen zur Antiken Literatur und Geschichte, 9). 198p. 1971. 25.90x (ISBN 3-11-003634-7). De Gruyter.

Glover, T. R. Herodotus. LC 70-100515. (BCL Ser.: I). Repr. of 1924 ed. 16.00 (ISBN 0-404-02828-4). AMS Pr.

Glover, Terrot R. Herodotus. LC 70-99661. (Select Bibliographies Reprint Ser). 1924. 19.50 (ISBN 0-8369-5090-9). Arno.

How, Walter W. & Wells, Joseph, eds. Commentary on Herodotus, 2 Vols. 1928. Vol. 1. 39.00x (ISBN 0-19-814128-9); Vol. 2. 37.50x (ISBN 0-19-814129-7). Oxford U Pr.

Hunter, Virginia J. Past & Present in Herodotus & Thucydides. LC 81-47134. 376p. 1982. 27.50x (ISBN 0-691-03556-3). Princeton U Pr.

Immerwahr, Henry R. Form & Thought in Herodotus. LC 66-25319. (American Philological Association Reprint Ser.). 1981. pap. 22.50 (ISBN 0-89130-478-9). Scholars Pr CA.

Wells, Joseph. Studies in Herodotus. facs. ed. LC 77-137388. (Select Bibliographies Reprint Ser). 1923. 15.00 (ISBN 0-8369-5589-7). Arno.

Wood, Henry. The Histories of Herodotus. (De Proprietatibus Litterarum, Ser. Practica: No. 21). 201p. (Orig.). 1972. pap. text ed. 30.00x (ISBN 0-686-22541-4). Mouton.

HEROES

see also Courage; Explorers; Heldensage; Martyrs; Mythology; Saints

also particular civilian and military awards, e.g. Nobel Prizes, Medal of Honor

Bailey, J. D. Some Heroes of the American Revolution. LC 75-44664. 295p. 1976. Repr. of 1924 ed. 10.00 (ISBN 0-89308-002-0). Southern Hist Pr.

Bentley, Eric. The Cult of the Superman. Orig. Title: A Century of Hero Worship. 7.50 (ISBN 0-8446-0486-0). Peter Smith.

Brinton, D. G. American Hero Myths. 59.95 (ISBN 0-87968-602-2). Gordon Pr.

Brinton, Daniel G. American Hero-Myths: A Study in the Native Religions of the Western Continent. LC 15-7574. (American Studies Ser). Repr. of 1882 ed. 14.00 (ISBN 0-384-05860-4). Johnson Repr.

Browne, Ray B., et al, eds. Heroes of Popular Culture. LC 72-88413. 1972. casebound 12.95 (ISBN 0-87972-044-1); pap. 5.95 (ISBN 0-87972-045-X). Bowling Green Univ.

Carlyle, Thomas. On Heroes, Hero-Worship & the Heroic in History. Niemeyer, Carl, ed. LC 66-12130. (Illus.). xxviii, 255p. 1966. pap. 2.95x (ISBN 0-8032-5030-4, BB 334, Bison). U of Nebr Pr.

--On Heroes, Hero-Worship & the Heroic in History. (World's Classics Ser: No. 62). 320p. 1975. 10.95 (ISBN 0-19-250062-7). Oxford U Pr.

--Sartor Resartus. Bd. with On Heroes & Hero Worship. 1954. 8.95x (ISBN 0-460-00278-3, Evman); pap. 3.50x (ISBN 0-460-01278-9, Evman). Dutton.

Chelf, Frank. Young Unsung Heroics. (Illus.). 1976. 4.95 (ISBN 0-914242-14-8). Bookworld Comm.

Daughters of St. Paul. Heroes from Every Walk of Life. 1981. 5.00 (ISBN 0-8198-3303-7); pap. 4.00 (ISBN 0-8198-3304-5). Dghtrs St Paul.

Dumezil, Georges. Destiny of the Warrior. Hiltebeitel, Alf, tr. LC 75-113254. 1971. 9.50x (ISBN 0-226-16970-7). U of Chicago Pr.

Fishwick, Marshall W. American Heroes, Myth & Reality. LC 72-10695. 242p. 1975. Repr. of 1954 ed. lib. bdg. 16.75x (ISBN 0-8371-6610-1, FIAH). Greenwood.

Garmo, Murshed. School of Heroes. (Arabic.). pap. 12.00x (ISBN 0-86685-140-2). Intl Bk Ctr.

Goode, William J. The Celebration of Heroes: Prestige As a Social Control System. LC 77-20322. 1979. 24.50x (ISBN 0-520-03602-6); pap. 8.95x (ISBN 0-520-03811-8). U of Cal Pr.

Grierson, Herbert. Carlyle & Hitler. LC 73-18348. 1930. lib. bdg. 5.00 (ISBN 0-8414-4460-9). Folcroft.

Hadas, Moses & Smith, Morton. Heroes & Gods: Spiritual Biographies in Antiquity. facsimile ed. LC 77-117800. (Essay Index Reprints - Religious Perspectives Ser.: Vol. 13). Repr. of 1965 ed. 17.00 (ISBN 0-8369-1880-0). Arno.

Hamilton, G. R. Hero or Fool. 59.95 (ISBN 0-8490-0297-4). Gordon Pr.

Harnsberger, Caroline T. Gods & Heroes: A Quick Guide to the Occupations, Associations & Experiences of the Greek & Roman Gods & Heroes. LC 76-21470. 1977. 20.00x (ISBN 0-87875-125-4). Whitston Pub.

Hook, Sidney. Hero in History: A Study in Limitation & Possibility. 1955. pap. 5.95x (ISBN 0-8070-5081-4, BP12). Beacon Pr.

Joyce, Mike & Whalen, John. Shoot to Miss. LC 81-50905. 490p. 1981. 12.95 (ISBN 0-86629-031-1). Sunrise MO.

Karsten, Peter. Patriot-Heroes in England & America: Political Symbolism & Changing Values Over Three Centuries. LC 78-53286. (Illus.). 268p. 1978. 25.00 (ISBN 0-299-07500-1). U of Wis Pr.

Kerenyi, C. The Heroes of the Greeks. (Illus.). 1978. pap. 8.95 (ISBN 0-500-27049-X). Thames Hudson.

Lefevre, Raoul. The History of Jason. Munro, John, ed. Caxton, William, tr. (EETS, ES Ser.: No. 111). Repr. of 1913 ed. 12.00 (ISBN 0-527-00314-X). Kraus Repr.

Lehman, B. H. Carlyle's Theory of the Hero. LC 76-181944. Repr. of 1928 ed. 17.25 (ISBN 0-404-03949-9). AMS Pr.

Levy, Alan. So Many Heroes. 1980. 15.95 (ISBN 0-531-07315-7, Pub. by Second Chance Pr). Watts.

Levy, Gertrude R. The Sword from the Rock: An Investigation into the Origins of Epic Literature & the Development of the Hero. LC 76-47642. (Illus.). 1977. Repr. of 1953 ed. lib. bdg. 18.50x (ISBN 0-8371-9300-1, LESFR). Greenwood.

Ouimette, Victor. Reason Aflame: Unamuno & the Heroic Will. (Romantic Studies, Second Ser.: No. 24). 1974. 20.00x (ISBN 0-300-01666-2). Yale U Pr.

Raglan, FitzRoy. The Hero: A Study in Tradition, Myth, & Drama. LC 75-23424. 296p. 1975. Repr. of 1956 ed. lib. bdg. 19.25x (ISBN 0-8371-8138-0, RATH). Greenwood.

Rank, Otto. The Myth of the Birth of the Hero: A Psychological Interpretation of Mythology. (Nervous & Mental Disease Monographs: No. 8). 1914. 15.50 (ISBN 0-384-49570-2). Johnson Repr.

--Myth of the Birth of the Hero & Other Essays. Freund, Philip, ed. 1959. pap. 2.95 (ISBN 0-394-70070-8, Vin). Random.

Rascoe, Burton. Titans & Prometheans, 2 vols. 100.00 (ISBN 0-8490-1216-3). Gordon Pr.

Rosenberg, Bruce A. Custer & the Epic of Defeat: And The Epic of Defent. LC 74-14631. 352p. 1974. 17.95x (ISBN 0-271-01172-6). Pa St U Pr.

Walsh, W. Heroes & Heroines of Fiction, Modern Prose & Poetry. 69.95 (ISBN 0-8490-0299-0). Gordon Pr.

Walsh, William S. Heroes & Heroines of Fiction, 2 vols. LC 66-29782. 1966. Repr. of 1915 ed. 26.00 ea. Vol. 1, Classical (ISBN 0-8103-0167-9). Vol. 2, Modern (ISBN 0-8103-0163-6). Gale.

Wecter, Dixon. The Hero in America: A Chronicle of Hero-Worship. LC 72-1225. 1972. Repr. of 1942 ed. 48.50x (ISBN 0-684-12993-0). Irvington.

Wilson, Bryan. The Noble Savages: An Essay on Charisma-the Rehabilitation of a Concept. LC 74-81444. (Quantum Bk Ser.). 1975. 14.95x (ISBN 0-520-02815-5). U of Cal Pr.

HEROES-JUVENILE LITERATURE

Baldwin, Margaret. The Boys Who Saved the Children. (A Jem Book Ser.). (Illus.). 64p. (Teens reading on a 2-3rd grade level). 1981. PLB 8.29 (ISBN 0-671-43603-1). Messner.

Carlson, Gordon. Get Me Out of Here! Uhlich, Richard, ed. (Bluejeans Paperbacks Ser.). (Illus., Orig.). (gr. 7-12). 1978. pap. text ed. 1.25- (ISBN 0-8374-5005-5). Xerox Ed Pubns.

Fiedler, Jean. Great American Heroes. (gr. 4-9). PLB 6.87 (ISBN 0-87460-182-7). Lion Bks.

Houston, D. Heroes. 1980. pap. 3.95 (ISBN 0-686-77398-5). Starlog.

Mueller, A. C. Bible Heroes. LC 56-1128. (Bible Story Booklet Ser). (Illus.). (gr. 3-5). 1981. pap. 0.69 (ISBN 0-570-06700-6, 56-1128). Concordia.

Pappas, Martha R., ed. Heroes of the American West. (American Character Ser). (Illus.). (gr. 9-12). 1969. pap. text ed. 5.50 (ISBN 0-684-51542-3, SSP21, ScribC). Scribner.

Taylor, L. B., Jr. Rescue: True Stories of Heroism. (Illus.). (gr. 5 up). 1978. PLB 6.90 s&l (ISBN 0-531-02223-4). Watts.

HEROES IN LITERATURE

Aurner, Nellie S. Hengest: A Study in Early English Hero Legend. 1978. lib. bdg. 25.00 (ISBN 0-8495-0044-3). Arden Lib.

Bergonzi, Bernard. Heroes Twilight. 241p. 1980. text ed. 17.50x (ISBN 0-333-28126-8, Pub. by Macmillan England). Humanities.

Burns, Norman T. & Reagan, Christopher J., eds. The Concepts of the Hero in the Middle Ages & the Renaissance. LC 74-34081. (Illus.). 1975. 22.00 (ISBN 0-87395-276-6); microfiche 22.00 (ISBN 0-87395-277-4). State U NY Pr.

Coffin, Tristram P. & Cohen, Hennig, eds. The Parade of Heroes-Legendary Figures in American Lore. LC 77-80881. 1978. 12.50 (ISBN 0-385-09711-5, Anchor Pr). Doubleday.

Folkenflik, Robert, ed. The English Hero, 1660-1800. LC 80-53894. 288p. 1982. 24.00 (ISBN 0-87413-174-X). U Delaware Pr.

Galloway, David. The Absurd Hero in American Fiction: Updike, Styron, Bellow, Salinger. 2nd, rev. ed. 288p. 1981. 22.50 (ISBN 0-292-70356-2); pap. 11.95 (ISBN 0-292-72434-9). U of Tex Pr.

--The Absurd Hero in American Fiction: Updike, Styron, Bellow, Salinger. 2nd, rev. ed. 288p. 1981. text ed. 22.50x (ISBN 0-292-70356-2); pap. text ed. 8.95x (ISBN 0-292-70355-4). U of Tex Pr.

Ide, Richard S. Possessed with Greatness: The Heroic Tragedies of Chapman & Shakespeare. LC 79-25864. xvi, 256p. 1980. 16.50x (ISBN 0-8078-1429-6). U of NC Pr.

Mathewson, Rufus W., Jr. The Positive Hero in Russian Literature. 2nd ed. LC 72-97207. 1975. 17.50x (ISBN 0-8047-0836-3); pap. 6.95 (ISBN 0-8047-0976-9, SP-144). Stanford U Pr.

Moorman, Charles. Kings & Captains: Variations on a Heroic Theme. LC 78-147858. 208p. 1971. 14.00x (ISBN 0-8131-1248-6). U Pr of Ky.

Murray, Albert. The Hero & the Blues. LC 72-97763. (The Paul Anthony Brick Lectures Ser: No. 9). 1973. 5.00x (ISBN 0-8262-0147-4). U of Mo Pr.

Pearson, Carol & Pope, Katherine. The Female Hero in American & British Literature. O'Hare, Joanne, ed. 1981. 29.95 (ISBN 0-8352-1402-8); pap. 16.95 (ISBN 0-8352-1466-4). Bowker.

Rank, Otto. The Myth & Rebirth of the Hero. pap. 2.95 (ISBN 0-394-70070-8, V-70, Vin). Random.

Weinberg, Helen A. New Novel in America: The Kafkan Mode in Contemporary Fiction. LC 70-87011. 1970. 22.50x (ISBN 0-8014-0537-8). Cornell U Pr.

Weinstock, John M. & Rovinsky, Robert T., eds. The Hero in Scandinavian Literature: From Peer Gynt to the Present. LC 74-26815. (Germanic Languages Symposia Ser). (Illus.). 238p. 1975. 14.50x (ISBN 0-292-73001-2). U of Tex Pr.

Welsh, Alexander. Hero of the Waverley Novels. LC 68-9825. 1968. pap. text ed. 2.45x (ISBN 0-689-70203-5, 135). Atheneum.

--Reflections on the Hero As Quixote. LC 80-8584. 256p. 1981. 15.00x (ISBN 0-691-06465-2). Princeton U Pr.

Wisse, Ruth R. The Schlemiel As Modern Hero. LC 72-160841. 1980. pap. 3.95 (ISBN 0-226-90312-5, P881, Phoen). U of Chicago Pr.

Zipes, J. D. The Great Refusal: Studies of the Romantic Hero in German & American Literature. (Ottendorfer Mem. Ser. of Germanic Monographs). 1970. 21.90 (ISBN 3-7610-2002-3). Adler.

HEROIC COUPLET

see Heroic Verse, English

HEROIC POETRY

see Epic Poetry

HEROIC SAGA

see Heldensage

HEROIC VERSE, ENGLISH

Brown, Wallace C. The Triumph of Form. LC 73-13452. 212p. 1973. Repr. of 1948 ed. lib. bdg. 16.50x (ISBN 0-8371-7135-0, BRTF). Greenwood.

Deane, Cecil V. Dramatic Theory & the Rhymed Heroic Play. 1978. Repr. of 1931 ed. lib. bdg. 27.50 (ISBN 0-8495-1019-8). Arden Lib.

Piper, William. An Anthology of Heroic-Couplet Poetry. LC 77-20. 1977. pap. 19.25 (ISBN 0-8357-0198-0, SS-00028). Univ Microfilms.

HEROIN

Agar, Michael. Ripping & Running: A Formal Ethnograph of Urban Heroin Addicts. (Language, Thought & Culture: Advances in the Study of Cognition Ser). 1973. 22.00 (ISBN 0-12-785020-1). Acad Pr.

Ashbrook, Debra L. & Solley, Linda C. Women & Heroin Abuse: A Survey of Sexism in Drug Abuse Administration. LC 78-68461. 1979. perfect bdg. 9.00 (ISBN 0-88247-556-8). R & E Res Assoc.

Bellis, David J. Heroin & Politicians: The Failure of Public Policy to Control Addiction in America. LC 80-21373. (Contributions in Political Science Ser.: No. 58). (Illus.). 256p. 1981. lib. bdg. 27.50 (ISBN 0-313-22557-5, BHP/). Greenwood.

Bourne, Peter G., ed. Addiction. 1974. 36.50 (ISBN 0-12-119535-X). Acad Pr.

Brill, Leon. The De-Addiction Process: Studies in the De-Addiction of Confirmed Heroin Addicts. 180p. 1972. 18.75 (ISBN 0-398-02532-0). C C Thomas.

Bullington, Bruce. Heroin Use in the Barrio. LC 76-40403. 1977. 19.95 (ISBN 0-669-01042-1). Lexington Bks.

Guenther, Gloria M. H As in Heroin. (Contemporary Problems Reading Ser). (Illus.). (gr. 7-12). 1973. pap. 3.25 with tchrs'. guide (ISBN 0-914296-09-4). Activity Rec.

Hughes, Patrick H. Behind the Wall of Respect: Experiments in Heroin Addiction Control in Chicago Neighborhoods. LC 76-25640. 1977. 10.95 (ISBN 0-226-35930-1). U of Chicago Pr.

Hunt, Leon G. Recent Spread of Heroin Use in the United States: Unanswered Questions. LC 74-83625. (Monograph). 1974. 1.25 (ISBN 0-686-09379-8). Drug Abuse.

Kruger, Henrik. The Great Heroin Coup. Meldon, Jerry, tr. 1980. 15.00 (ISBN 0-89608-032-3); pap. 5.50 (ISBN 0-89608-031-5). South End Pr.

Kunnes, Richard. The American Heroin Empire: Power, Profits & Politics. LC 72-3930. 250p. 1973. 5.95 (ISBN 0-396-06697-6). Dodd.

Lidz, Charles W., et al. Heroin, Deviance & Morality. (Sage Library of Social Research: Vol. 112). 274p. 1981. 20.00 (ISBN 0-8039-1549-7); pap. 9.95 (ISBN 0-8039-1550-0). Sage.
McCoy, Alfred W. The Politics of Heroin in Southeast Asia. 325p. 1973. pap. 7.95x (ISBN 0-06-131942-2, TB 1942, Torch). Har-Row.
Meyer, R. E. & Mirin, S. M., eds. The Heroin Stimulus: Implications for a Theory of Addiction. LC 78-13634. (Illus.). 276p. 1979. 22.50 (ISBN 0-306-40104-5, Plenum Pr). Plenum Pub.
Moore. Buy & Bust. LC 73-11665. (Illus.). 1977. 19.95 (ISBN 0-669-88179-1). Lexington Bks.
Platt, Jerome & Labate, Christina. Heroin Addiction: Theory, Research, & Treatment. LC 76-5794. (Personality Processes Ser.). 417p. 1976. 32.95 (ISBN 0-471-69114-3, Pub. by Wiley-Interscience). Wiley.
Robertson, Frank. Triangle of Death: The Inside Story of the Triads--the Chinese Mafia. (Illus.). 1978. 14.95 (ISBN 0-7100-8732-2). Routledge & Kegan.
Rosenbaum, Marsha. Women on Heroin. (Crime, Law & Deviance Ser.). 189p. (Orig.). 1981. 15.00 (ISBN 0-8135-0921-1); pap. 5.95 (ISBN 0-686-76464-1). Rutgers U Pr.
Sowder, Barbara J. & Burt, Marvin R. Children of Heroin Addicts. 200p. 1980. 18.95 (ISBN 0-03-057033-6). Praeger.
Stimson, Gerry V. Heroin & Behaviour. LC 73-174. 246p. 1973. 19.95 (ISBN 0-470-82530-8). Halsted Pr.

HEROINES
see Women; Women in Literature; Women in the Bible

HEROISM
see Courage; Heroes

HERPES SIMPLEX VIRUS
Albert, Daniel M., et al. Herpesvirus: Recent Studies, 3 vols, Vol. 2. LC 73-13558. 1974. 22.50x (ISBN 0-8422-7169-4). Irvington.
Bellanti, Joseph A., et al. Herpesvirus: Recent Studies, 3 vols, Vol. 1. LC 73-13558. 156p. 1974. text ed. 22.50x (ISBN 0-8422-7164-3). Irvington.
Christ College Symposium. Cambridge, England, June 20-25, 1971. Oncogensis & Herpesviruses: Proceedings. Biggs, P. M., et al, eds. (IARC Scientific Pub.: No. 2). 1972. 40.00 (ISBN 0-686-16789-9). World Health.
Gauri, K. K., ed. Anti-Herpesvirus Chemotherapy: Experimental & Clinical Aspects. (Advances in Ophthalmology: Vol. 38). (Illus.). 1979. 89.25 (ISBN 3-8055-2991-0). S Karger.
Gergely, Lajos, et al. Herpesvirus: Recent Studies, 3 vols, Vol. 3. LC 73-13558. 201p. 1974. text ed. 22.50x (ISBN 0-8422-7176-7). Irvington.
Graham, H., et al, eds. Marek's Disease II: Pathogenicity & Immunology. (Herpesvirus-Related Diseases Ser.). 320p. 1974. text ed. 28.50x (ISBN 0-8422-7167-8). Irvington.
Hamilton, Richard. The Herpes Book. 1980. 8.95 (ISBN 0-312-90587-4). St Martin.
--The Herpes Book. LC 79-66691. 216p. 1981. pap. 4.95 (ISBN 0-87477-194-3). J P Tarcher.
Healthworks Medical Group. Stop Your Herpes Now. 52p. (Orig.). 1981. pap. 4.50 (ISBN 0-938480-01-4). Healthworks.
Hinze, Harry C., et al, eds. Animal Models for the Study of Herpes Virus Associated Malignancy, Vol. 2. LC 73-20281. 156p. 1974. text ed. 26.50x (ISBN 0-8422-7180-5). Irvington.
Juretic, Miro, et al. Herpetic Infections of Man. LC 77-75516. (National Library of Medicine Ser.). (Illus.). 202p. 1980. text ed. 13.50x (ISBN 0-87451-151-8). U Pr of New Eng.
Kaplan, A. S. Herpes Simplex & Pseudorabies Viruses. (Virology Monographs: Vol. 5). (Illus.). 1969. 17.20 (ISBN 0-387-80932-5). Springer-Verlag.
Kaplan, Albert S., ed. The Herpesviruses. 1974. 58.50 (ISBN 0-12-397050-4). Acad Pr.
Levy, Jay A., et al. Oncogenesis & Other Pathological Results of Herpesvirus Infection II. Daniel, M. D. & Murphy, Bert L., eds. LC 74-3205. 206p. 1974. text ed. 22.50x (ISBN 0-8422-7156-2). Irvington.
Miller, Daniel, et al. Oncogenesis & Other Pathological Results of Herpesvirus Infection I, Vol. 1. LC 74-3205. 229p. 1974. text ed. 24.50x (ISBN 0-8422-7155-4). Irvington.
Oxford, J. S., et al, eds. Chemotherapy of Herpes Simplex Virus. 1977. 22.50 (ISBN 0-12-531760-3). Acad Pr.
Rapp, Fred, ed. On Cogenic Herpesviruses, Vols. 1 & 2. 1980. Vol. 1, 208 Pgs. 59.95 (ISBN 0-8493-5619-9); Vol. 2, 152 Pgs. 49.95 (ISBN 0-8493-5620-2). CRC Pr.
Symposium. Nuremberg, Germany, Oct. 14-16, 1974. Oncogenesis & Herpesviruses II: Proceedings, 2 pts. De The, G., et al, eds. Incl. Pt. 1. Biochemistry of Viral Replication & in Vitro Transformation. 40.00 (ISBN 0-686-16808-9); Pt. 2. Epidemiology, Host Response & Control. 32.00 (ISBN 0-686-16809-7). (IARC Scientific Pub.: No. 11). 1975. World Health.

HERPETOLOGY
see also Amphibians; Reptiles
Cogger, Harold G. Reptiles & Amphibians of Australia. 2nd ed. (Illus.). 603p. 1980. 49.50 (ISBN 0-88359-012-3). R Curtis Bks.
Girard, Charles. United States Exploring Expedition During the Years 1838, 1839, 1840, 1841, 1842 Under the Command of Charles Wilkes, U.S.N. Herpetology, 2 vols, Vol. 20. Srling, Keir B., ed. LC 77-81095. (Biologists & Their World Ser.). (Illus.). 1978. Repr. of 1858 ed. lib. bdg. 37.00x (ISBN 0-405-10678-5). Arno.
Goin, Coleman J., et al. Introduction to Herpetology. 3rd ed. LC 77-13554. (Illus.). 1978. text ed. 20.95x (ISBN 0-7167-0020-4). W H Freeman.
McKeown, Sean & Honolulu Zoo. Hawaiian Reptiles & Amphibians. 1979. pap. 3.50 (ISBN 0-932596-07-X, Pub. by Oriental). Intl Schol Bk Serv.
Sterling, Keir B., ed. Early Herpetological Studies & Surveys in the Eastern United States: Original Anthology. LC 77-81101. (Biologists & Their World Ser.). (Illus.). 1978. lib. bdg. 40.00x (ISBN 0-405-10685-8). Arno.
--Herpetological Explorations of the Great American West: Original Anthology, 2 vols. LC 77-81100. (Biologists & Their World Ser.). (Illus., Eng. Fr. Ger. & Span.). 1978. Set. lib. bdg. 75.00x (ISBN 0-405-10682-3); lib. bdg. 37.50x ea. Vol. 1 (ISBN 0-405-10683-1). Vol. 2 (ISBN 0-405-10684-X). Arno.

HERRERA, JOSE JOAQUIN DE, PRESIDENT MEXICO, 1792-1854
Cotner, Thomas E. Military & Political Career of Jose Joaquin De Herrera, 1792-1854. LC 69-19007. Repr. of 1949 ed. lib. bdg. 22.75x (ISBN 0-8371-1018-1, TICH). Greenwood.

HERRESHOFF, NATHANAEL GREENE, 1848-1938
Herreshoff, L. F. Capt. Nat Herreshoff: The Wizard of Bristol. LC 80-28519. (Illus.). 350p. 1981. Repr. of 1953 ed. 17.50 (ISBN 0-911378-32-4). Sheridan.

HERRICK, CLARENCE LUTHER, 1858-1904
Herrick, Charles J. Clarence Luther Herrick, Pioneer Naturalist, Teacher & Psychobiologist. LC 55-5431. (Transactions Ser.: Vol. 45, Pt. 1). (Illus.). 1955. pap. 1.50 (ISBN 0-87169-451-4). Am Philos.

HERRICK, ROBERT, 1591-1674
Aiken, Pauline. Influence of the Latin Elegists on English Lyric Poetry 1600-1650. LC 78-91345. 1970. Repr. of 1932 ed. 7.00 (ISBN 0-87753-002-5). Phaeton.
Chute, Marchette. Two Gentle Men: The Lives of George Herbert & Robert Herrick. 1959. 6.95 (ISBN 0-525-22528-5). Dutton.
De Neef, Leigh. This Poetick Liturgie: Robert Herrick's Ceremonial Mode. LC 74-75910. 224p. 1974. 9.75 (ISBN 0-8223-0323-X). Duke.
Macleod, Malcolm L. Concordance to the Poems of Robert Herrick. LC 76-92974. (Studies in Poetry, No. 38). 1970. Repr. of 1936 ed. lib. bdg. 49.95 (ISBN 0-8383-0991-7). Haskell.
--A Concordance to the Poems of Robert Herrick. LC 77-13605. 1977. Repr. lib. bdg. 35.00 (ISBN 0-8414-6219-4). Folcroft.
Musgrove, S. Universe of Robert Herrick. LC 75-20062. 1950. lib. bdg. 7.50 (ISBN 0-8414-6049-3). Folcroft.
Roeckerath, Netty. Der Nachruhm Herricks und Wallers. Repr. of 1931 ed. pap. 7.00 (ISBN 0-384-51630-0). Johnson Repr.
Rollin, Roger B. & Patrick, J. Max, eds. Trust to Good Verses: Herrick Tercentenary Essays. LC 77-74547. (Illus.). 1977. 15.95x (ISBN 0-8229-3353-5). U of Pittsburgh Pr.

HERRICK, ROBERT, 1868-1938
Deming, Robert H. Ceremony & Art: Robert Herrick's Poetry. (De Proprietatibus Litterarum Ser. Practica: No. 64). 1974. pap. text ed. 30.00x (ISBN 90-2792-621-2). Mouton.

HERRING, DAVID WELLS
Jefferies, Susan H. Papa Wore No Halo. LC 63-20783. 1963. 8.95 (ISBN 0-910244-33-2). Blair.

HERRING-GULL
Carrick, Carol. Beach Bird. LC 72-703. (Illus.). 32p. (gr. k-3). 1973. 5.95 (ISBN 0-8037-0886-6); PLB 5.47 (ISBN 0-8037-0885-8). Dial.
Tinbergen, Niko. Herring Gull's World. 1971. pap. 3.95x (ISBN 0-06-131594-X, TB1594, Torch). Har-Row.

HERRIOT, EDOUARD, 1872-1957
Jessner, Sabine. Edouard Herriot & the French Republic. LC 73-20352. (World History Ser., No. 48). 1974. lib. bdg. 22.95 (ISBN 0-8383-1808-8). Haskell.

HERRIOT, JAMES
Herriot, James. All Creatures Great & Small. 1973. Repr. lib. bdg. 13.95 (ISBN 0-8161-6095-3, Large Print Bks). G K Hall.
--All Things Bright & Beautiful. LC 73-87407. 400p. 1974. 12.95 (ISBN 0-312-02030-9). St Martin.
--All Things Wise & Wonderful. LC 77-76640. 1977. 12.95 (ISBN 0-312-02031-7). St Martin.
--If Only They Could Talk. 1977. lib. bdg. 13.95 (ISBN 0-8161-6415-0, Large Print Bks). G K Hall.

HERRNHUT, GERMANY–HISTORY
Gollin, Gillian L. Moravians in Two Worlds: A Study of Changing Communities. LC 67-19653. 302p. 1967. 20.00x (ISBN 0-231-03033-9). Columbia U Pr.

HERRNHUTER
see Bohemian Brethren; Moravians

HERRON, GEORGE DAVIS, 1862-1925
Briggs, Mitchell P. George D. Herron & the European Settlement. LC 71-155607. (Stanford University. Stanford Studies in History, Economics, & Political Science: Vol. 3, No. 2). Repr. of 1932 ed. 12.50 (ISBN 0-404-50965-7). AMS Pr.
--George D. Herron & the European Settlement. LC 71-155607. (Stanford University. Stanford Studies in History, Economics, & Political Science: Vol. 3, No. 2). Repr. of 1932 ed. 12.50 (ISBN 0-404-50965-7). AMS Pr.

HERSCHEL, JOHN FREDERICK WILLIAM, BART., 1792-1871
Leech, James, compiled by. John Herschel & Victorian Science. (Illus., Orig.). 1966. pap. 5.00 (ISBN 0-87959-005-X). U of Tex Hum Res.
Schweber, S. & Cohen, I. Bernard, eds. Aspects of the Life & Thought of Sir John Herschel. LC 80-2110. (Development of Science Ser.). (Illus.). 1981. lib. bdg. 95.00x (ISBN 0-405-13829-6). Arno.

HERSCHEL, WILLIAM, SIR, 1738-1822
Sime, James. William Herschel & His Work. 272p. 1900. text ed. 4.95 (ISBN 0-567-04521-8). Attic Pr.
--William Herschel & His Work. 1978. Repr. of 1900 ed. lib. bdg. 35.00 (ISBN 0-8492-8049-4). R West.

HERSEY, JOHN, 1914-
Sanders, David. John Hersey. (Twayne's United States Authors Ser). 1967. pap. 3.45 (ISBN 0-8084-0184-X, T112, Twayne). Coll & U Pr.
--John Hersey. (U. S. Authors Ser.: No. 112). lib. bdg. 10.95 (ISBN 0-8057-0376-4). Twayne.

HERTER, CHRISTIAN ARCHIBALD, 1865-1910
Noble, G. Bernard. Christian A. Herter. LC 73-122753. (American Secretaries of State & Their Diplomacy, New Ser. 1925-1961: Vol. 18). 1970. 12.50x (ISBN 0-8154-0341-0). Cooper Sq.

HERSKOVITZ, MELVILLE JEAN, 1895-1963
Simpson, George E. Melville J. Herskovitz. (Leaders of Modern Anthropology Ser.). 200p. 1973. 15.00x (ISBN 0-231-03385-0); pap. 6.00x (ISBN 0-231-03396-6). Columbia U Pr.

HERTFORDSHIRE, ENGLAND
Cussans, John E. The History of Hertfordshire, 3 vols. (Classical County Histories). (Illus.). 1972. Repr. of 1870 ed. Set. 165.00x (ISBN 0-87471-312-9). Rowman.
Jones-Baker, Doris. The Folklore of Hertfordshire. (Folklore of the British Isles Ser.). (Illus.). 240p. 1977. 10.00x (ISBN 0-87471-925-9). Rowman.
Morris, John, ed. Hertfordshire. (Domesday Bk). (Illus.). 186p. 1976. 21.00x (ISBN 0-8476-1330-5). Rowman.

HERTZEN, ALEKSANDR IVANOVICH, 1812-1870
Acton, E. Alexander Herzen & the Role of the Intellectual Revolutionary. LC 78-56747. 1979. 22.95 (ISBN 0-521-22166-8). Cambridge U Pr.
Carr, Edward H. The Romantic Exiles. 391p. 1975. Repr. of 1933 ed. lib. bdg. 20.00x (ISBN 0-374-91297-1). Octagon.
Hertzen, Alexander. The Memoirs of Alexander Herzen, Parts I & II. Duff, J. D., tr. from Rus. LC 76-48971. 1977. Repr. of 1923 ed. lib. bdg. 21.75x (ISBN 0-8371-9319-2, HEMH). Greenwood.
Herzen, Alexander. Childhood, Youth & Exile: My Past Thoughts, Pts. I & II. Duff, J. D., tr. (World's Classics Ser.). 1980. pap. 5.95 (ISBN 0-19-281505-9). Oxford U Pr.

HERTZIAN WAVES
see Electric Waves; Microwaves; Radio Waves

HERTZLER, ARTHUR EMANUAL, 1870-1946
Coe, Edith C. Hertzler Heritage. Vandergriff, James, ed. LC 75-32001. (Illus.). 172p. 1975. 7.50x (ISBN 0-686-13109-6); pap. 5.80x (ISBN 0-686-13110-X). Emporia State.

HERVEY, JOHN, 1696-1743
Halsband, Robert. Lord Hervey, Eighteenth Century Courtier. (Illus.). 400p. 1974. 19.95 (ISBN 0-19-501731-5). Oxford U Pr.

HERVIEU, PAUL ERNEST, 1857-1915
Santa Vicca, Edmund F. Four French Dramatists: A Bibliography of Criticism of the Works of Eugene Brieux, Francois De Curel, Emile Fabre, Paul Hervieu. LC 74-7495. (Author Bibliographies Ser.: No. 17). 1974. 10.00 (ISBN 0-8108-0755-6). Scarecrow.

HERVIEUX, LEOPOLD, 1831-1900
Paris, Gaston. Fabulistes Latins. 32p. (Fr.). 1973. Repr. of 1885 ed. lib. bdg. 13.50 (ISBN 0-8337-4310-4). B Franklin.

HERWEGH, GEORG, 1817-1875
Carr, Edward H. The Romantic Exiles. 391p. 1975. Repr. of 1933 ed. lib. bdg. 20.00x (ISBN 0-374-91297-1). Octagon.

HERZL, THEODOR, 1860-1904
Bein, Alex. Theodore Herzl: A Biography of the Founder of Modern Zionism. Samuel, Maurice, tr. from Ger. LC 62-20753. (Temple Bk). 1970. pap. 4.75 (ISBN 0-689-70244-2, T18). Atheneum.
Patai, Raphael, ed. Herzl Year Book: Vol. 5, Studies in the History of Zionism in America. LC 72-117807. (Essay Index Reprint Ser). 1963. 20.00 (ISBN 0-8369-1951-3). Arno.
Weisgal, Meyer W. Theodore Herzl: A Memorial. LC 75-6461. (The Rise of Jewish Nationalism & the Middle East Ser.). 300p. 1976. Repr. of 1929 ed. 39.50 (ISBN 0-88355-346-5). Hyperion Conn.

HERZOG ERNEST (MIDDLE HIGH GERMAN POEM)
Blamires, D. Herzog Ernst & the Otherworld Voyage: A Comparative Study. 128p. 1979. 24.00x (ISBN 0-7190-1292-9, Pub. by Manchester U Pr England). State Mutual Bk.
Lycette, Ronald L. Herzog Notes. 1972. pap. 1.75 (ISBN 0-8220-0591-3). Cliffs.
Rosenfeld, Hans F. Herzog Ernst D. Und Ulrich Von Eschenbach. Repr. of 1929 ed. 21.50 (ISBN 0-384-51980-6); pap. 18.50 (ISBN 0-686-66465-5). Johnson Repr.

HESCHEL, ABRAHAM JOSHUA, 1907-
Kasimow, Harold. Divine-Human Encounter: A Study of Abraham Joshua Heschel. LC 79-63562. 1979. pap. text ed. 7.75 (ISBN 0-8191-0731-X). U Pr of Amer.

HESED (THE WORD)
Glueck, Nelson. Hesed in the Bible. 1968. 10.00x (ISBN 0-87820-104-1, Pub. by Hebrew Union). Ktav.

HESIOD
Better Homes & Gardens Editors, ed. Better Homes & Gardens Homemade Cookies Cook Book. (Illus.). 96p. 1975. 4.95 (ISBN 0-696-00780-0). Meredith Corp.
Burn, Andrew R. World of Hesiod. LC 66-29859. 1966. Repr. of 1936 ed. 15.00 (ISBN 0-405-08332-7, Blom Pubns). Arno.
Hesiod. Work & Days: With Prolegomena & Commentary. West, M. L., ed. 1978. text ed. 52.00x (ISBN 0-19-814005-3). Oxford U Pr.
Lawton, W. C. Successors of Homer. LC 69-17001. Repr. of 1898 ed. 11.00x (ISBN 0-8154-0276-7). Cooper Sq.
Pucci, Pietro. Hesiod & the Language of Poetry. LC 76-234. 160p. 1977. 9.50x (ISBN 0-8018-1787-0). Johns Hopkins.
Solmsen, Friedrich. Hesiod & Aeschylus. 1949. 23.00 (ISBN 0-384-56598-0). Johnson Repr.
Wender, Dorothea, tr. Hesiod & Theognis. (Classics Ser). 1976. pap. 1.95 (ISBN 0-14-044283-9). Penguin.

HESS, HARRY HAMMOND, 1906-1969
Shagam, Reginald, et al, eds. Studies in Earth & Space Sciences: Harry H. Hess Volume. LC 76-190172. (Memoir: No. 132). (Illus.). vii, 688p. 1972. 28.50x (ISBN 0-8137-1132-0). Geol Soc.

HESS, MOSES, 1812-1875
Silberner, Edmund & Blumenberg, Werner. Moses Hess Briefwechsel. (Quellen & Untersuchungen Zur Geschichte der Deutschen & Oesterreichischen Arbeiterbewegung: No. 2). 1959. 75.00x (ISBN 90-2790-151-1). Mouton.

HESS, MYRA, b. 1890
Lassimonne, Denise & Ferguson, Howard, eds. Myra Hess by Her Friends. LC 67-29444. (Illus.). 6.95 (ISBN 0-8149-0140-9). Vanguard.
McKenna, Marian. Myra Hess: A Portrait. (Illus.). 1978. 22.50 (ISBN 0-241-89522-7, Pub. by Hamish Hamilton England). David & Charles.

HESS, RUDOLF, 1894-
Douglas-Hamilton, James. Motive for a Mission: The Story Behind Rudolph Hess's Flight to Britain. 332p. 1981. 35.00x (ISBN 0-906391-05-9, Pub. by Mainstream). State Mutual Bk.
Thomas, W. Hugh. The Murder of Rudolf Hess. LC 79-2237. (Illus.). 1979. 9.95 (ISBN 0-06-014251-0, HarpT). Har-Row.

HESSE, HERMANN, 1877-1962
Baumer, Franz. Hermann Hesse. Conway, John, tr. LC 68-31446. (Modern Literature Ser.). 1969. 10.95 (ISBN 0-8044-2027-0). Ungar.
Boulby, Mark. Hermann Hesse: His Mind & Art. 352p. 1967. 24.50x (ISBN 0-8014-0046-5). Cornell U Pr.
Casebeer, Edwin F. Hermann Hesse. (Writers for the Seventies Ser.). 206p. 1976. 7.95 (ISBN 0-690-01050-8); pap. 2.95 (ISBN 0-690-01051-6, TYC-T). T Y Crowell.
Digan, Kathleen E. Herman Hesse's Narcissus & Goldmund: A Phenomenological Study. 1975. lib. bdg. 59.95 (ISBN 0-87700-238-X). Revisionist Pr.

Field, George W. Hermann Hesse. (World Authors Ser.: Germany: No. 93). lib. bdg. 9.95 (ISBN 0-8057-2424-9). Twayne.
Fleissner, Else M. Herman Hesse: Modern German Poet & Writer. Rahmas, D. Steve, ed. LC 70-190244. (Outstanding Personalities Ser: No. 26). 32p. (Orig.). (gr. 7-9). 1972. lib. bdg. 2.95 incl. catalog cards (ISBN 0-87157-526-4); pap. 1.50 vinyl laminated covers (ISBN 0-87157-026-2). SamHar Pr.
Flubas, John. Monarch Notes on Hesse's Journey to the East. pap. 1.50 (ISBN 0-671-00939-7). Monarch Pr.
Freedman, Ralph. Herman Hesse: Pilgrim of Crisis. LC 78-51795. (Illus.). 1979. 15.00 (ISBN 0-394-41981-2). Pantheon.
--Lyrical Novel: Studies in Hermann Hesse, Andre Gide, & Virginia Woolf. 1963. 19.00 (ISBN 0-691-06071-1); pap. 7.95 (ISBN 0-691-01267-9, 62). Princeton U Pr.
Friedrichsmeyer, E. Monarch Notes on Hesse's Glass Bead Game. pap. 1.50 (ISBN 0-671-00935-4). Monarch Pr.
Glenn, Jerry. Monarch Notes on Hesse's Short Fiction. pap. 1.50 (ISBN 0-671-00942-7). Monarch Pr.
Hesse, Hermann & Rolland, Romain. Hermann Hesse & Romain Rolland Correspondence, Diary: Diary Entries & Reflections 1915-1940. Hesse, M. G., tr. 1978. text ed. 12.75x (ISBN 0-391-00913-3). Humanities.
Liebmann, Judith. Hermann Hesse: A Collection of Criticism. 1977. pap. 2.95 (ISBN 0-07-037822-3, SP). McGraw.
Marcoon, Bruce L. Demian Notes. 62p. (Orig.). 1974. pap. text ed. 1.95 (ISBN 0-8220-0385-6). Cliffs.
Mileck, Joseph. Herman Hesse: Biography & Bibliography, 2 vols. 1977. 80.00x (ISBN 0-520-02756-6). U of Cal Pr.
--Hermann Hesse & His Critics. LC 72-10899. (North Carolina. University. Studies in the Germanic Languages & Literatures: No. 21). Repr. of 1958 ed. 18.50 (ISBN 0-404-50921-5). AMS Pr.
--Hermann Hesse: Life & Art. LC 76-48020. 1978. 16.95 (ISBN 0-520-03351-5); pap. 5.95 (ISBN 0-520-04152-6). U of Cal Pr.
Monarch Notes on Hesse's Demian. pap. 1.50 (ISBN 0-671-00915-X). Monarch Pr.
Monarch Notes on Hesse's Major Works. pap. 1.75 (ISBN 0-671-00908-7). Monarch Pr.
Monarch Notes on Hesse's Narcissus & Goldmund. pap. 1.50 (ISBN 0-671-00916-8). Monarch Pr.
Monarch Notes on Hesse's Siddhartha. pap. 1.50 (ISBN 0-671-00922-2). Monarch Pr.
Monarch Notes on Hesse's Steppenwolf. pap. 1.95 (ISBN 0-671-00917-6). Monarch Pr.
Otten, Anna, ed. Hesse Companion. LC 76-57539. 1977. pap. 6.95x (ISBN 0-8263-0440-0). U of NM Pr.
Rose, Ernst. Faith from the Abyss: Hermann Hesse's Way from Romanticism to Modernity. LC 65-19517. (Gotham Library). 175p. (Orig.). 1965. 12.50x (ISBN 0-8147-0364-X); pap. 9.50x (ISBN 0-8147-0365-8). NYU Pr.
Serrano, Miguel. C. G. Jung & Hermann Hesse: A Record of Two Friendships. MacShane, Frank, tr. LC 66-14085. (Illus.). 1968. 7.00x (ISBN 0-8052-3132-3); pap. 2.95 (ISBN 0-686-66533-3). Schocken.
Sorell, Walter. Hermann Hesse: The Man Who Sought & Found Himself. (Modern German Authors Ser: No. 2). (Illus.). 143p. 1975. text ed. 9.25x (ISBN 0-85496-049-X). Humanities.
Wilson, Colin. Hesse, Reich, Borges: Three Essays. 78p. (Orig.). 1975. pap. 2.45 (ISBN 0-915070-01-4). Leaves of Grass.
Ziolkowski, Theodore. Novels of Hermann Hesse: A Study in Theme & Structure. 1965. 20.00x (ISBN 0-691-06084-3); pap. 5.95 (ISBN 0-691-01272-5). Princeton U Pr.

HESSE–HISTORY

Hesse. (A Panorama in Color Ser.). (Illus.). 87p. 1966. 17.50x (ISBN 3-524-00020-7). Intl Pubns Serv.
White, Dan S. The Splintered Party: National Liberalism in Hessen & the Reich, 1867-1918. LC 75-23213. 445p. 1976. 15.00x (ISBN 0-674-83320-1). Harvard U Pr.

HESSIANS IN THE AMERICAN REVOLUTION

see United States–History–Revolution, 1775-1783–German Mercenaries

HESYCHASM

Jesus Prayer: Selections from the Writings of the Saints. pap. 3.95 (ISBN 0-686-05645-0). Eastern Orthodox.
Maloney, George A. Russian Hesychasm: The Spirituality of Nil Sorskij. (Slavistic Printings & Reprintings: No. 269). 1973. 56.50 (ISBN 0-686-21812-4). Mouton.

HETCH HETCHY AND YOSEMITE VALLEYS RAILWAY COMPANY

Kreig, Allan. Last of the Three Foot Loggers. LC 63-2212. (Illus.). 96p. 15.95 (ISBN 0-87095-014-2). Colden West.

HETCH HETCHY VALLEY, CALIFORNIA

Felzer, Ron. High Sierra Hiking Guide to Hetch Hetchy. Winnett, Thomas, ed. LC 72-89914. (High Sierra Hiking Guide Ser: Vol. 12). (Illus., Orig.). 1973. pap. 4.95 (ISBN 0-911824-24-3). Wilderness.
Muir, John. Rambles of a Botanist Among the Plants & Climates of California. Kimes, William F., intro. by. (Illus.). 44p. 1974. 7.50 (ISBN 0-87093-301-9). Dawsons.

HETEROCERA

see Moths

HETEROCYCLIC COMPOUNDS

Abramovitch, R. A., ed. Chemistry of Hetercyclic Compounds. (A Series of Monographs Pyridine & Its Derivitives: Vol. 14, Pt. 3). 1249p. 1974. 105.00 (ISBN 0-471-37915-8). Krieger.
--Chemistry of Heterocyclic Compounds. (A Series of Monographs Pyridine & Its Derivitives: Vol. 14, Pt. 1). 451p. 1974. 59.00 (ISBN 0-471-37915-8). Krieger.
--Chemistry of Heterocyclic Compounds. (A Series of Monographs Pyridine & Its Derivitives: Vol. 14, Pt. 4). 720p. 1975. 83.50 (ISBN 0-686-76785-3). Krieger.
Acheson, R. M. An Introduction to the Chemistry of Heterocyclic Compounds. 3rd ed. LC 76-21319. 501p. 1976. 40.00 (ISBN 0-471-00268-2, Pub. by Wiley-Interscience). Wiley.
Allcock, H. R. Heteroatom Ring Systems & Polymers. 1967. 57.00 (ISBN 0-12-050550-9). Acad Pr.
Allen, C. F. Six-Membered Heterocyclic Nitrogen Compounds with Three Condensed Rings, Vol. 12. 646p. 1958. 83.50 (ISBN 0-470-37851-4, Pub. by Wiley-Interscience). Wiley.
Ansell, M. F. & Pattenden, G. Saturated Heterocyclic Chemistry, Vols. 2-5. LC 72-83454. Vol. 2 1974. 49.50 (ISBN 0-85186-532-1); Vol. 3 1975. 1973 literature 46.75 (ISBN 0-85186-562-3); Vol. 4 1977. 1974 literature 82.50 (ISBN 0-85186-592-5); Vol. 5 1978. 71.50 (ISBN 0-85186-622-0). Am Chemical.
Armarego, W. L. Stereochemistry of Heterocyclic Compounds: Part II - Oxygen; Sulfur; Mixed N, O, & S; & Phosophorus Heterocycles. LC 76-26023. 512p. 1977. Repr. 66.50 (ISBN 0-471-03322-7). Krieger.
Armarego, W. L. F., ed. Stereochemistry of Heterocyclic Compounds. Incl. Pt. 1. Nitrogen Heterocycles. 1976. 63.50 (ISBN 0-471-01892-9); Pt. 2. Oxygen; Sulfur; Mixed N, D, & S; & Phosphorus Heterocycles. LC 76-26023. (General Heterocyclic Chemistry Ser., Pub. by Wiley-Interscience). Wiley.
Bambas, L. L. Five-Membered Heterocyclic Compounds with Nitrogen & Sulfur or Nitrogen, Sulfur & Oxygen--Except Thrazole, Vol. 4. 416p. 1952. 58.50 (ISBN 0-686-74353-9, Pub. by Wiley-Interscience). Wiley.
Barlin, G. B. The Pyrazines. (The Chemistry of Heterocyclic Compounds Ser.). 968p. 1982. 200.00 (ISBN 0-471-38119-5, Pub. by Wiley-Interscience). Wiley.
Batterham, T. J. NMR Spectra of Simple Heterocycles. LC 80-11724. 560p. 1981. Repr. of 1973 ed. lib. bdg. write for info. (ISBN 0-89874-140-8). Krieger.
Beilstein Institute for Literature of Organic Chemistry. Heterocyclische Verbindungen. Boit, H. G., ed. (Beilsteins Handbuch der Organischen Chemie, 4th Ed., 3rd & 4th Suppl.: Vol. 17, Pt. 6). 868p. 1975. 696.20 (ISBN 0-387-07359-0). Springer-Verlag.
--Heterocyclische Verbindungen. (Beilsteins Handbuch der Orgnaischen Chemie, 4th Ed.,: Vol. 17, Pts. 3-5). 1975. Pt. 3. 710.40 (ISBN 0-387-07084-2); Pt. 4. 918.50 (ISBN 0-387-07220-9); Pt. 5. 627.80 (ISBN 0-387-07310-8). Springer-Verlag.
Berdy, Janos. Heterocyclic Antibiotics. (CRC Handbook of Antibiotic Compounds: Vol. 5). 576p. 1981. 74.95 (ISBN 0-8493-3456-X). CRC Pr.
Breslow, D. S. & Skolnik, H., eds. Multi-Sulfur & Sulfur & Oxygen Five & Six-Membered Heterocycles, Vol. 21, Pt. 1. 610p. 1966. 65.00 (ISBN 0-470-38195-7). Krieger.
--Multi-Sulfur & Sulfur & Oxygen Five & Six-Membered Heterocycles, Vol. 21, Pt. 2. 724p. 1966. 85.00 (ISBN 0-470-38196-5). Krieger.
Chesseman, G. W. & Cookson, R. F. Condensed Pyrannes, Vol. 35. 835p. 1979. 155.00 (ISBN 0-471-38204-3, Pub. by Wiley-Interscience). Wiley.
Coffey, ed. Rodd's Chemistry of Carbon Compounds: Heterocyclic Compounds - 6 Membered Heterocyclic Compounds with a Single Nitrogen Atom from Group V of the Periodic Table, Vol. 4, Pt. G. 1977. 105.00 (ISBN 0-444-41644-7). Elsevier.
Dryhurst, Glenn, ed. Electrochemistry of Biological Molecules: Purines, Pyrimidines, Pteridines, Flavins, Pyrroles, Porphyrins and Pyridines. 1977. 71.50 (ISBN 0-12-222650-X). Acad Pr.
Elguero, J., et al. The Tautomerism of Heterocycles: Supplement I to Advances in Heterocyclic Chemistry. (Serial Publication). 1976. 83.00 (ISBN 0-12-020651-X); lib. ed. 99.00 (ISBN 0-12-020691-9); microfiche 59.50 (ISBN 0-12-020692-7). Acad Pr.
Ellis, G. P. Chromenes, Chromanones, & Chromones: Chemistry of Heterocyclic Compounds-A Series of Monographs. (Vol. 31). 1977. 172.50 (ISBN 0-471-38212-4). Wiley.
Ellis, Gwynn P. & Lockhart, Ian M. Chromans & Tocopherols. LC 80-16902. (The Chemistry of Heterocyclic Compounds: Vol. 36). 1980. 125.00 (ISBN 0-471-03038-4, Pub. by Wiley-Interscience). Wiley.
Finley, K. T. Triazoles. (Chemistry of Heterocyclic Compounds, Series of Monographs: Vol. 39). 368p. 1980. 100.00 (ISBN 0-471-07827-1). Wiley.
Fitton, A. O. & Smalley, R. K. Practical Heterocyclic Chemistry. LC 68-19255. 1968. 23.00 (ISBN 0-12-257850-3). Acad Pr.
Houlihan, William J. The Chemistry of Heterocyclic Compounds: Indoles. LC 76-154323. (Chemistry of Heterocyclic Compounds: Monographs: Vol. 25, Pt. 3). 1979. 105.00 (ISBN 0-471-05132-2, Pub. by Wiley-Interscience). Wiley.
Katrikzky, A. R., ed. Advances in Hetercyclic Chemistry. Incl. Vol. 17. 1974. 63.00 (ISBN 0-12-020617-X); Vol. 18. 1975. 78.00 (ISBN 0-12-020618-8); lib. ed. 96.00 (ISBN 0-12-020674-9); 56.00 (ISBN 0-12-020675-7); Vol. 20. 1976. 54.00 (ISBN 0-12-020620-X); lib. ed. 69.00 (ISBN 0-12-020678-1); 39.00 (ISBN 0-12-020679-X); Vol. 21. 1977. 69.50 (ISBN 0-12-020621-8); lib. ed. 89.00 (ISBN 0-12-020680-3); 49.50 (ISBN 0-12-020681-1). (Serial Publication). Acad Pr.
Katritsky. Physical Methods in Heterocyclic Chemistry, Vol. 6. 1974. 50.00 (ISBN 0-12-401106-3). Acad Pr.
Katritzky, A. R., ed. Advances in Heterocyclic Chemistry, Vols. 1-16, 22-24. Incl. Vol. 1. 1963. 59.00 (ISBN 0-12-020601-3); Vol. 2. 1963. 59.00 (ISBN 0-12-020602-1); Vol. 3. 1964. 59.00 (ISBN 0-12-020603-X); Vol. 4. 1965 (ISBN 0-12-020604-8); Vol. 5. 1965 (ISBN 0-12-020605-6); Vol. 6. Katritzky, A. R. & Boulton, A. J., eds. 1966 (ISBN 0-12-020606-4); Vol. 7. 1966; Vol. 8. 1967 (ISBN 0-12-020608-0); Vol. 9. 1968 (ISBN 0-12-020609-9); Vol. 10. 1969; Vol. 11. 1970 (ISBN 0-12-020611-0); Vol. 12. 1970 (ISBN 0-12-020612-9); Vol. 13. 1971; Vol. 14. 1972 (ISBN 0-12-020614-5); Vol. 15. 1973 (ISBN 0-12-020615-3); Vol. 16. 1974 (ISBN 0-12-020616-1); Vol. 22. 1978. 55.50 (ISBN 0-12-020622-6); lib ed. 71.50 (ISBN 0-12-020682-X); microfiche 40.00 (ISBN 0-12-020683-8); Vol. 23. 60.00 (ISBN 0-12-020623-4); lib ed. 77.00 (ISBN 0-12-020684-6); microfiche 43.00 (ISBN 0-12-020685-4); Vol. 24. 1979. 58.50 (ISBN 0-12-020624-2); lib. ed. 75.00 (ISBN 0-12-020686-2); microfiche 42.00 (ISBN 0-12-020687-0). Vols. 1-16. 59.00 ea. Acad Pr.
--Advances in Heterocyclic Chemistry, Vol. 28. (Serial Publication Ser.). 1981. write for info. (ISBN 0-12-020628-5); lib. ed. (ISBN 0-12-020730-3); microfiche ed. (ISBN 0-12-020731-1). Acad Pr.
Katritzky, A. R & Boulton, A. J., eds. Advances in Heterocyclic Chemistry, Vol. 26. LC 62-13037. 1980. 32.00 (ISBN 0-12-020626-9); lib. ed. 41.50 (ISBN 0-12-020726-5); microfiche ed. 22.50 (ISBN 0-12-020727-3). Acad Pr.
--Advances in Heterocyclic Chemistry, Vol. 27. (Serial Publication). 1981. 49.50 (ISBN 0-12-020627-7); lib. ed. 64.50 (ISBN 0-12-020728-1); microfiche ed. 34.50 (ISBN 0-12-020729-X). Acad Pr.
--Advances in Heterocyclic Chemistry, Vol. 29. (Serial Publication). 1981. price not set (ISBN 0-12-020629-3); price not set lib. ed. (ISBN 0-12-020732-X); price not set microfiche (ISBN 0-12-020733-8). Acad Pr.
Katritzky, Alan R. & Lagowski, J. M., eds. Principles of Heterocyclic Chemistry. 1968. 34.00 (ISBN 0-12-401150-0). Acad Pr.
Meyers, A. I. Heterocycles in Organic Synthesis. (General Heterocyclic Chemistry Ser.). 336p. 1974. 42.00 (ISBN 0-471-60065-2). Wiley.
Mndzhoian, A. L. Synthesis of Heterocyclic Compounds, 4 vols. LC 59-11346. 155p. 1959. Vols. 1 & 2, 1959, 155p. 32.50 (ISBN 0-306-17033-7, Consultants); Vols. 3 & 4, 1961, 156p. 32.50 (ISBN 0-306-17034-5, Consultants). Plenum Pub.
Neunhoeffer, Hans & Wiley, Paul F. Chemistry of One, Two, Three-Triazines & One, Two, Four-Triazines, Tetrazines & Pentazines. LC 77-18932. (Chemistry of Heterocyclic Compounds Ser.: Vol. 33). 1978. Vol. 33. 148.00 (ISBN 0-471-03129-1, Pub. by Wiley-Interscience). Wiley.
Palmer, Michael H. Structure & Reactions of Heterocyclic Compounds. (Illus.). 1967. 21.50 (ISBN 0-312-76790-0). St Martin.
Paquette, L. A. Principles of Modern Heterocyclic Chemistry. 1968. 22.50 (ISBN 0-8053-7726-3, Adv Bk Prog). Benjamin-Cummings.
Penczek, S., et al. Cationic Ring-Opening Polymerization of Heterocyclic Monomers. (Advances in Polymer Science Ser.: Vol. 37). (Illus.). 156p. 1981. 46.00 (ISBN 0-387-10209-4). Springer-Verlag.
Porter, Q. N. & Baides, J. Mass Spectrometry of Heterocyclic Compounds. (General Heterocyclic Chemistry Ser.). 582p. (Orig.). 1971. 39.50 (ISBN 0-471-69504-1). Krieger.
Preston, P. N. Benzimidazoles & Congeneric Tricyclic Compounds, Pt. 1, Vol. 40. LC 80-17383. (Chemistry of Heterocyclic Compounds Ser.). 687p. 1981. 175.00 (ISBN 0-471-03792-3, Pub. by Wiley-Interscience). Wiley.
--Benzimidazoles & Congeneric Tricyclic Compounds, Vol. 40, Pt. 2. LC 80-17383. (Chemistry of Heterocyclic Compounds Ser.). 1200p. 1980. 175.00 (ISBN 0-471-08189-2, Pub. by Wiley-Interscience). Wiley.
Pullman, B. & Bergman, E., eds. Quantum Aspects of Heterocyclic Compounds in Chemistry & Biochemistry: Proceedings. 1970. 60.00 (ISBN 0-12-567050-8). Acad Pr.
Riddell, Frank. The Confromational Analysis of Heterocyclic Compounds. LC 79-41514. 45.50 (ISBN 0-12-588160-6). Acad Pr.
Rosowsky, Andre, ed. Seven-Membered Heterocyclic Compounds Containing Oxygen & Sulfur, Vol. 26. 949p. 1972. 109.00 (ISBN 0-471-38210-8). Krieger.
Schofield, K. Heterocyclic Compounds. (IRS Organic Chemistry Ser. Two: Vol. 4). 1975. 29.95 (ISBN 0-408-70616-3). Butterworth.
Sterochemistry of Heterocyclics Compounds: Part II. (Oxygen; Sulfur; Mixed N,O, & S: And Phosphorus Hetercycles). 512p. Date not set. Repr. of 1977 ed. 66.50 (ISBN 0-471-03322-7). Krieger.
Temple, Carroll. Triazoles, One, Two, Four. LC 80-15637. (Chemistry of Heterocyclic Compounds Ser.). 791p. 1981. 175.00 (ISBN 0-471-04656-6, Pub. by Wiley-Interscience). Wiley.
Van Der Plas, H. C. Ring Transformation of Heterocycles, 2 vols. 1973. Vol. 1. 79.50 (ISBN 0-12-711701-6); Vol. 2. 57.00 (ISBN 0-12-711702-4). Acad Pr.
Weissberger, Arnold & Taylor, Edward C. Special Topics in Heterocyclic Chemistry. LC 76-10672. (Chemistry of Heterocyclic Compounds Ser: Vol.30). 1976. 85.00 (ISBN 0-471-67253-X, Pub. by Wiley-Interscience). Wiley.
Young, D. W. Heterocyclic Chemistry. LC 75-11739. (Illus.). 1976. pap. text ed. 12.50x (ISBN 0-582-44253-2). Longman.

HETEROGENESIS

see Life–Origin; Spontaneous Generation

HETEROPTERA

Slater, James A. & Baranowski, Richard M. How to Know the True Bugs: (Hemiptera: Heteroptera) (Pictured Key Nature Ser). 1978. text ed. 8.95x (ISBN 0-697-04893-4); wire coil 6.95x (ISBN 0-697-04894-2). Wm C Brown.

HETEROSIS

Congress of EUCARPIA, 7th, Budapest, 1974. Heterosis in Plant Breeding: Proceedings. Janossy, A. & Lupton, F. G., eds. 1977. 53.75 (ISBN 0-444-99835-7). Elsevier.
Manwell, Clyde & Baker, C. M. Molecular Biology & the Origin of Species: Heterosis, Protein Polymorphism, & Animal Breeding. LC 70-103299. (Biology Ser). (Illus.). 446p. 1970. 9.95 (ISBN 0-295-95065-X). U of Wash Pr.

HETEROTROPIA

see also Strabismus

Macan, T. T. A Revised Key to the Fritish Water Bugs (Hempitera-Heteroptera) 2nd ed. 1976. 11.00x (ISBN 0-900386-07-X, Pub. by Freshwater Bio). State Mutual Bk.

HETH, HENRY, 1825-1899

Morrison, James L., Jr. Memoirs of Henry Heth. LC 72-820. (Contributions in Military History: No. 6). 1974. lib. bdg. 17.00 (ISBN 0-8371-6389-7, MHH/). Greenwood.

HEVE LANGUAGE

see Eudeve Language

HEWETT, WILLIAM NATHAN WRIGHTE, SIR, 1834-1888

Wylde, Augustus B. Eighty-Three to Eighty-Seven in the Saudan, with an Account of Sir William Hewett's Mission to King John of Abyssinia, 2 Vols. LC 72-82088. (Illus.). Repr. of 1888 ed. 28.00x (ISBN 0-8371-1525-6, Pub. by Negro U Pr). Greenwood.

HEWITT, ABRAM STEVENS, 1822-1903

Nevins, Allan. Abram S. Hewitt: With Some Account of Peter Cooper. 1967. Repr. lib. bdg. 35.00x (ISBN 0-374-96099-2). Octagon.
Post, Louis F. An Account of the George-Hewitt Mayoralty Campaign in the Municipal Election of 1886. LC 75-341. (The Radical Tradition in America Ser). 202p. 1975. Repr. of 1886 ed. 17.50 (ISBN 0-88355-244-2). Hyperion Conn.

HEWLETT, MAURICE HENRI, 1861-1923

Binyon, Laurence, ed. The Letters of Maurice Hewlett to Which Is Added a Diary in Greece, 1914. 294p. lib. bdg. 30.00 (ISBN 0-89984-061-2). Century Bookbindery.

Haworth, Peter. English Hymns & Ballads. 1927. lib. bdg. 15.00 (ISBN 0-8414-4975-9). Folcroft.

Muir, P. H. A Bibliography of the First Editions of Books by Maurice Henry Hewlett. LC 73-14788. 1927. Repr. lib. bdg. 15.00 (ISBN 0-8414-5981-9). Folcroft.

HEXAMETER

Burgi, Richard T. History of the Russian Hexameter. (Foreign Area Studies: No. 2). 1954. 16.50 (ISBN 0-208-00047-X, Archon). Shoe String.

Lawton, W. C. Successors of Homer. LC 69-17001. Repr. of 1898 ed. 11.00x (ISBN 0-8154-0276-7). Cooper Sq.

Tisdall, Fitzgerald. A Theory of the Origins & Development of the Heroic Hexameter. 1889. 25.00 (ISBN 0-8274-3982-2). R West.

Winbolt, Samuel E. Latin Hexametre Verse. Commager, Steele, ed. LC 77-70818. (Latin Poetry Ser.). 1978. lib. bdg. 27.50 (ISBN 0-8240-2982-8). Garland Pub.

HEXAPODA

see Insects

HEYDRICH, REINHARD, 1904-1942

Deschner, Gunther. Reinhard Heydrich. LC 80-6263. 376p. 1981. 16.95 (ISBN 0-8128-2809-7). Stein & Day.

Life & Times of Reinhold Heydrich. 1980. 10.95 (ISBN 0-679-51181-4). McKay.

HEYERDAHL, THOR

Blassingame, Wyatt. Thor Heyerdahl: Viking Scientist. LC 79-1002. (Illus.). (gr. 5 up). 1979. 7.95 (ISBN 0-525-66626-5). Elsevier-Nelson.

Heyerdahl, Thor. FATU-HIVA Back to Nature. (RL 7). 1976. pap. 2.25 (ISBN 0-451-08682-1, E8682, Sig). NAL.

--Kon-Tiki. (Enriched Classics Edition). (gr. 11 up). 1973. pap. 2.95 (ISBN 0-671-83169-0). PB.

Monarch Notes on Heyerdahl's Kon-Tiki, Aku-Aku. (Orig.). pap. 1.50 (ISBN 0-671-00841-2). Monarch Pr.

HEYM, GEORG, 1887-1912

Krispyn, Egbert. Georg Heym: A Reluctant Rebel. LC 68-28871. 1968. 5.00 (ISBN 0-8130-0135-8). U Presses Fla.

HEYSEN, HANS

Thiele, Colin. Heysen of Hahndorf. (Illus.). 1969. 15.00x (ISBN 0-8426-1569-5). Verry.

HEYTESBURY, WILLIAM, fl. 1340

Wilson, Curtis. William Heytesbury: Medieval Logic & the Rise of Mathematical Physics. (Medieval Science Pubns., No. 3). 1956. 20.00x (ISBN 0-299-01350-2). U of Wis Pr.

HEYWARD, DUBOSE, 1885-1940

Allen, Harvey. Du Bose Heyward: A Critical & Biographical Sketch. 1978. lib. bdg. 8.50 (ISBN 0-8495-0043-5). Arden Lib.

--Du Bose Heyward: Critical & Biographical Sketch. LC 73-5974. 1922. lib. bdg. 8.50 (ISBN 0-8414-1731-8). Folcroft.

Slavick, William H. Dubose Heyward. (United States Authors Ser.: No. 392). 1981. lib. bdg. 13.95 (ISBN 0-8057-7342-8). Twayne.

HEYWOOD, JOHN, 1497-1580

Bolwell, Robert W. Life & Works of John Heywood. LC 21-22336. Repr. of 1921 ed. 18.50 (ISBN 0-404-00934-4). AMS Pr.

De La Bere, R. John Heywood: Entertainer. LC 72-188001. 1937. lib. bdg. 20.00 (ISBN 0-8414-2454-3). Folcroft.

Maxwell, Ian C. French Farce & John Heywood. Repr. of 1916 ed. 9.00 (ISBN 0-403-08940-9). Somerset Pub.

Maxwell, Ian R. French Farce & John Heywood. LC 76-42464. 1976. Repr. of 1946 ed. lib. bdg. 25.00 (ISBN 0-8414-6080-9). Folcroft.

Milligan, Burton A., ed. & John Heywood's WORKS & Miscellaneous Short Poems. (Illinois Studies in Language & Literature: Vol. 41). 1977. Repr. of 1956 ed. lib. bdg. 35.00 (ISBN 0-8482-4350-1). Norwood Edns.

HEYWOOD, THOMAS, d. 1641

Boas, Frederick S. Thomas Heywood. Repr. of 1950 ed. 19.00 (ISBN 0-403-02292-4). Somerset Pub.

--Thomas Heywood. LC 74-5032. 1973. lib. bdg. 15.00 (ISBN 0-8414-9938-1). Folcroft.

Clark, Arthur M. Thomas Heywood, Playwright & Miscellanist. LC 67-15999. 1967. Repr. of 1931 ed. 9.00 (ISBN 0-8462-0864-4). Russell.

Cromwell, Otelia. Thomas Heywood: A Study in the Elizabethan Drama of Everyday Life. LC 69-15681. (Yale Studies in English Ser.: No. 78). 1969. Repr. of 1928 ed. 17.50 (ISBN 0-208-00767-9, Archon). Shoe String.

Grivelet, Michel. Thomas Heywood et la Drama Domestique Elizabethan. 1957. Repr. 50.00 (ISBN 0-8274-3612-2). R West.

Heywood, Thomas. The Fair Maid of the West: Pt.I, a Critical Edition. Salomon, Brownell, ed. (Salzburg Studies in English Literature, Jacobean Drama Studies Ser.: No. 36). 209p. 1976. pap. text ed. 25.00x (ISBN 0-391-01408-0). Humanities.

Johnson, Marilyn L. Images of Women in the Works of Thomas Heywood. (Salzburg Studies in English Literature, Jacobean Drama Studies: No. 42). 178p. 1974. pap. text ed. 25.00x (ISBN 0-391-01438-2). Humanities.

Velte, F. Mowbray. Bourgeois Element in the Dramas of Thomas Heywood. LC 65-21092. (Studies in Drama, No. 39). 1969. Repr. of 1922 ed. lib. bdg. 49.95 (ISBN 0-8383-0641-1). Haskell.

HI-FI SYSTEMS

see High-Fidelity Sound Systems

HIATAL HERNIA

Henderson, Robert D. Motor Disorders of the Esophagus. LC 76-13191. 248p. 1976. 26.00 (ISBN 0-683-03947-4). Krieger.

HIAWATHA, IROQUOIS INDIAN

Voight, Virginia F. Adventures of Hiawatha. LC 68-20802. (American Folktales). (Illus.). 48p. (gr. 3-6). 1969. PLB 6.09 (ISBN 0-8116-4011-6). Garrard.

HIBERNATION

see also Animals, Habits and Behavior of; Dormancy in Plants

Bancroft, Henrietta & Van Gelder, Richard G. Animals in Winter. LC 63-17543. (A Let's-Read-&-Find-Out Science Bk). (Illus.). (gr. k-3). 1963. 8.79 (ISBN 0-690-09261-X, TYC-J). Har-Row.

Barker, Will. Winter-Sleeping Wildlife. LC 58-5298. (Illus.). (gr. 5 up). 1958. PLB 8.79 (ISBN 0-06-020391-9, HarpJ). Har-Row.

Mrosovsky, Nicholas. Hibernation & the Hypothalamus. 287p. 1971. 22.50 (ISBN 0-306-50058-2, Plenum Pr). Plenum Pub.

South, F., et al. Hibernation & Hypothermia, Perspectives & Challenges. 1972. 44.00 (ISBN 0-444-41007-4, North Holland). Elsevier.

HICKEY PLOT, 1776

Minutes of a Conspiracy Against the Liberties of America. LC 79-76554. (Eyewitness Accounts of the American Revolution Ser., No. 2). 1969. Repr. of 1865 ed. 9.00 (ISBN 0-405-01145-8). Arno.

HICKOK, JAMES BUTLER, 1837-1876

Buel, J. W. The Life & Wonderful Adventures of Wild Bill. Jones, William R., ed. (Illus.). 1977. pap. 2.95 (ISBN 0-89646-013-4). Outbooks.

Connelley, William E. Wild Bill & His Era: The Life & Adventures of James Butler Hickok. LC 76-187842. (Illus.). xii, 244p. 1972. Repr. of 1933 ed. 10.00x (ISBN 0-8154-0413-1). Cooper Sq.

Secrest, William, ed. I Buried Hickok, the Memoirs of White Eye Anderson. LC 80-65455. 300p. 1980. 17.50 (ISBN 0-932702-07-4); collector's edition 75.00 (ISBN 0-932702-08-2). Creative Texas.

HICKOK, RICHARD EUGENE, 1931-1965

Capote, Truman. In Cold Blood. 1971. pap. 2.95 (ISBN 0-451-09958-3, E9958, Sig). NAL.

--In Cold Blood. 1966. 12.95 (ISBN 0-394-43023-9). Random.

HICKS, EDWARD, 1780-1849

Ford, Alice E. Edward Hicks, Painter of the Peaceable Kingdom. LC 52-13392. (Illus.). 1973. Repr. of 1952 ed. 39.00 (ISBN 0-527-30400-X). Kraus Repr.

Mather, Eleanore P. Edward Hicks, Primitive Quaker. LC 75-110287. (Illus., Orig.). 1970. pap. 0.70x (ISBN 0-87574-170-3). Pendle Hill.

HICKS, JOHN DONALD, 1890-- BIBLIOGRAPHY

Hicks, John D. The American Tradition. LC 72-12311. 135p. 1973. Repr. of 1955 ed. lib. bdg. 15.00 (ISBN 0-8371-6695-0, HIAT). Greenwood.

HIDALGO Y COSTILLA, MIGUEL, 1753-1811

Caruso, J. A. The Liberators of Mexico. (Illus.). 8.75 (ISBN 0-8446-1105-0). Peter Smith.

Father Hidalgo: Mini-Play. (History of Mexico Ser.). (gr. 5 up). 1978. 3.00 (ISBN 0-89550-326-3). RIM.

Noll, Arthur H. & McMahon, A. Philip. The Life & Times of Miguel Hidalgo y Costilla. LC 72-85003. (Illus.). 1973. Repr. of 1910 ed. 12.00 (ISBN 0-8462-1687-6). Russell.

HIDATSA INDIANS

see Indians of North America–The West

HIDATSA LANGUAGE

Lowie, Robert H. Hidatsa Texts. LC 74-7979. Repr. of 1939 ed. 11.50 (ISBN 0-404-11870-4). AMS Pr.

Matthews, Washington. Ethnography & Philology of the Hidatsa Indians: U. S. Geological & Geographical Survey of the Territories, Miscellaneous Publication, No. 7. LC 3-8072. 1971. Repr. of 1877 ed. 19.50 (ISBN 0-384-35892-6). Johnson Repr.

--Ethnography & Philology of the Hidatsa Indians: U. S. Geological & Geographical Survey of the Territories, Miscellaneous Publication, No. 7. LC 3-8072. 1971. Repr. of 1877 ed. 19.50 (ISBN 0-384-35892-6). Johnson Repr.

HIDES AND SKINS

see also Fur; Leather; Tanning

Editors of Time-Life Books. Novel Materials. LC 74-16950. (The Art of Sewing). (Illus.). (gr. 6 up). 1974. PLB 11.97 (ISBN 0-8094-1723-5, Pub. by Time-Life). Silver.

Flaying & Curing of Hides & Skins As a Rural Industry. 1978. pap. 6.75 (ISBN 92-5-100476-5, F 1463, FAO). Unipub.

World Hides, Skins, Leather & Footwear Economy. (Commodity Bulletin Ser.: No. 48). (Orig.). 1971. pap. 6.00 (ISBN 0-685-02927-1, F524, FAO). Unipub.

HIDEYOSHI, 1536-1598

Dening, Walter. Life of Toyotomi Hideyoshi. 3rd ed. LC 79-136391. (BCL Ser. II). Repr. of 1930 ed. 18.50 (ISBN 0-404-02078-X). AMS Pr.

Kuniyoshi. Pictorial Biography of Toyotomi Hideyoshi. 1975. 55.00 (ISBN 0-685-64824-9, 910704-56). Hawley.

HIDING-PLACES (SECRET CHAMBERS, ETC.)

Hjersman, Peter. The Stash Book. LC 78-54343. (Illus.). 1978. pap. 4.95 (ISBN 0-915904-34-9). And-or Pr.

Krotz, David. How to Hide Almost Anything. LC 77-17528. 1978. pap. 3.95 (ISBN 0-02-080590-X, Collier). Macmillan.

Squiers, Granville. Secret Hiding-Places the Origins, Histories & Descriptions of English Secret Hiding-Places Used by Priests, Cavaliers, Jacobites & Smugglers. LC 70-157499. (Tower Bks). (Illus.). 1971. Repr. of 1934 ed. 24.00 (ISBN 0-8103-3920-X). Gale.

HIERATIC INSCRIPTIONS

see Egyptian Language–Inscriptions

HIEROCLES, SOSSIANUS, PROCONSUL OF BITHYNIA, fl. 293-303 A.D.

Philostratus. Life of Apollonius of Tyana. Epistles of Apollonius & the Treatise of Eusebius, 2 vols. (Loeb Classical Library: No. 16-17). 1912. 11.00x ea. Vol. 1 (ISBN 0-674-99018-8). Vol. 2 (ISBN 0-674-99019-6). Harvard U Pr.

HIEROGLYPHIC INSCRIPTIONS

see Inscriptions, Hieroglyphic

HIEROGLYPHICS

see also Alphabet; Egyptian Language–Writing, Hieroglyphic; Writing–History

Dee, John. The Hieroglyphic Monad. 1975. 10.00 (ISBN 0-87728-276-5). Weiser.

Fischer, Henry G. Ancient Egyptian Calligraphy: A Beginner's Guide to Writing Hieroglyphs. (Illus.). 63p. 1979. 10.00 (ISBN 0-87099-198-1). Metro Mus Art.

Gardiner, Alan H. Catalogue of the Egyptian Hieroglyphic Printing Type. 1977. pap. 6.00 (ISBN 0-89005-098-8). Ares.

Gautruche, Pierre. The Poetical Histories, Repr. Of 1671 Ed. D'Assigny, Marius, tr. Bd. with Appendix De Diis et Heroibus Poeticis. Jouvency, Joseph de. Repr. of 1705 ed. LC 75-27877. (Renaissance & the Gods Ser.: Vol. 32). (Illus.). 1976. lib. bdg. 73.00 (ISBN 0-8240-2081-2). Garland Pub.

Griffith, F. L. & Petrie, W. M. Two Hieroglyphic Papyr from Tanis: The Sign Papyrus (a Syllabary) & the Geographical Papyrus (an Almanack) (Illus.). 1976. Repr. of 1889 ed. 19.50x (ISBN 0-85698-039-0, Pub. by Aris & Phillips). Intl Schol Bk Serv.

King, Charles. Hieroglyphs to Alphabets. LC 76-52867. 1977. 12.95x (ISBN 0-8448-1034-7). Crane-Russak Co.

Morley, Sylvanus G. An Introduction to the Study of Maya Hieroglyphs. Repr. of 1915 ed. 27.00 (ISBN 0-403-03615-1). Scholarly.

Valaoritis, Nanos. Hired Hieroglyphs. 1972. pap. 1.50 (ISBN 0-87711-050-6). Kayak.

Von Euw, Eric. Corpus of Maya Hieroglypic Inscriptions: Xultun, Vol. 5, Pt. 1. Condon, Lorna, ed. LC 78-50627. 1978. pap. text ed. 12.00 (ISBN 0-87365-184-7). Peabody Harvard.

HIERONYMUS, SAINT

see Jerome, Saint (Hieronymus, Saint)

HIGGINBOTTOM, SAM

Hess, Gary R. Sam Higginbottom of Allahabad. LC 67-17631. 1967. 7.95x (ISBN 0-8139-0118-9). U Pr of Va.

HIGGINSON, THOMAS WENTWORTH, 1823-1911

Edelstein, Tilden G. Strange Enthusiasm: A Life of Thomas Wentworth Higginson. LC 68-27752. (Illus.). 1968. 30.00x (ISBN 0-300-01072-9). Yale U Pr.

--Strange Enthusiasm: A Life of Thomas Wentworth Higginson, 1823-1911. LC 68-27752. (Studies in American Negro Life). 1970. pap. 3.95 (ISBN 0-689-70241-8, NL25). Atheneum.

Higginson, Mary T. Thomas Wentworth Higginson. LC 70-122657. 1971. Repr. of 1914 ed. 18.00 (ISBN 0-8046-1306-0). Kennikat.

--Thomas Wentworth Higginson: The Story of His Life. facsimile ed. LC 76-37886. (Select Bibliographies Reprint Ser). Repr. of 1914 ed. 25.00 (ISBN 0-8369-6723-2). Arno.

Tuttleton, James W. Thomas Wentworth Higginson. (United States Authors Ser.: No. 313). 1978. lib. bdg. 12.50 (ISBN 0-8057-7236-7). Twayne.

HIGH BLOOD PRESSURE

see Hypertension

HIGH ENERGY FORMING

see also Metals–Extrusion

Bruno, E. J., ed. High-Velocity Forming of Metals. rev. ed. LC 68-23027. (Manufacturing Data Ser). 1968. pap. 10.75x (ISBN 0-87263-009-9). SME.

Ferbel, Thomas, ed. Techniques & Concepts of High-Energy Physics. (NATO Advanced Study Institutes Series B-Physics). 535p. 1981. 65.00 (ISBN 0-306-40721-3, Plenum Pr). Plenum Pub.

Perlmutter, Arnold, et al, eds. High-Energy Physics in the Einstein Centennial Year. (Studies in the Natural Science: Vol. 16). 1979. 55.00 (ISBN 0-306-40297-1, Plenum Pr). Plenum Pub.

HIGH-FIBER DIET

Adams, Ruth & Murray, Frank. High-Fiber Approach Relieving Constipation Naturally. 2.25 (ISBN 0-686-29843-8). Cancer Bk Hse.

Burkitt, D. P. & Trowell, H. C., eds. Refined Carbohydrate Foods & Disease: Some Implications of Dietary Fibre. 1975. 59.50 (ISBN 0-12-144750-2). Acad Pr.

Burkitt, Denis. Eat Right--To Keep Healthy & Enjoy Life More. LC 78-24492. (Positive Health Guides). (Illus.). 1979. 8.95 (ISBN 0-668-04676-7); pap. 5.95 (ISBN 0-668-04682-1). Arco.

Dietary Fiber. (Landmark Ser.). 1979. 22.50x (ISBN 0-8422-4126-4). Irvington.

Fredericks, Carlton. Carlton Frederick's High-Fiber Way to Total Health. 1976. pap. 2.50 (ISBN 0-671-80269-0). PB.

Inglett, George & Falkehag, Ingemar, eds. Dietary Fibers: Chemistry & Nutrition. LC 79-399. 1979. 23.00 (ISBN 0-12-370950-4). Acad Pr.

Jones, Jeanne. Fabulous Fiber Cookbook. rev. ed. LC 77-742. (Illus.). 1979. pap. 5.95 (ISBN 0-89286-155-X). One Hund One Prods.

--The Fabulous Fiber Cookbook. LC 77-742. (Illus.). 1977. 8.95 (ISBN 0-89286-110-X). One Hund One Prods.

Kraus, Barbara. The Barbara Kraus Guide to Fiber in Food. rev. ed. (Orig.). 1981. pap. 2.50 (ISBN 0-451-09976-1, E9976, Sig). NAL.

Moyer, Anne. The Fiber Factor. Prevention Magazine Staff, ed. 1977. pap. 1.50 (ISBN 0-425-03460-7, Medallion). Berkley Pub.

Moyer, Anne & Prevention Magazine Editors. The Fiber Factor. LC 76-18923. 1976. pap. 3.95 (ISBN 0-87857-127-2). Rodale Pr Inc.

Plageman, Karen. Natural Fiber Cooking. LC 76-21472. (Illus.). 1976. pap. 2.50 (ISBN 0-915942-07-0). Owlswood Prods.

Reuben, David. High Fiber Cook Book. 7.95 (ISBN 0-686-29949-3); pap. 1.95 (ISBN 0-686-29950-7). Cancer Bk Hse.

--The Save-Your-Life-Diet. (Special Interest Ser.). 1976. lib. bdg. 9.95 (ISBN 0-8161-6417-7, Large Print Bks). G K Hall.

Reuben, David & Reuben, Barbara. Save-Your-Life-Diet High Fiber Cookbook. 1977. pap. 2.50 (ISBN 0-345-28579-4). Ballantine.

Salmon, Margaret B. A Professional Dietitian's Natural Fiber Diet. (Illus.). 1979. 10.95 (ISBN 0-13-725333-8, Parker). P-H.

Spiller, Gene A. & Amen, Ronald J., eds. Fiber in Human Nutrition. LC 76-20767. 278p. 1976. 24.50 (ISBN 0-306-30919-X, Plenum Pr). Plenum Pub.

Spiller, Gene A. & Kay, Ruth M., eds. Medical Aspects of Dietary Fiber. (Topics in Gastroenterology Ser.). 360p. 1980. 32.50 (ISBN 0-306-40507-5, Plenum Pr). Plenum Pub.

Stanway, Andrew. Taking the Rough with the Smooth: Dietary Fibre & Your Health - a New Medical Breakthrough. 1978. 10.95 (ISBN 0-285-62227-7, Pub. by Souvenir Pr). Intl Schol Bk Serv.

Theander & James. The Analysis of Dietary Fiber in Food. (Basic & Clinical Nutrition Ser.: Vol. 3). 288p. 1981. 35.00 (ISBN 0-8247-1192-0). Dekker.

Wason, Betty. Soup-to-Desert High Fiber Cookbook. pap. 2.50 (ISBN 0-451-09991-5, E9991, Sig). NAL.

HIGH-FIDELITY SOUND SYSTEMS

see also Stereophonic Sound Systems

Audio Equipment. rev. ed. (Illus.). pap. 1.95 (ISBN 0-89552-006-0). DMR Pubns.

Boyce, William F. Hi-Fi Stereo Handbook. 5th ed. LC 78-63121. 1979. pap. 11.95 (ISBN 0-672-21564-0). Sams.

Brown, Clement. Questions & Answers on Hi-Fi. 1978. 3.75 (ISBN 0-408-00151-8, NB 70, Pub. by Newnes-Butterworth). Hayden.

Cameron, Derek. Hi-Fi Stereo Installation Simplified. (Illus.). 1978. 15.95 (ISBN 0-8359-2842-X). Reston.

Cohen, Abraham. Hi-Fi Loudspeakers & Enclosures. 2nd, rev. ed. (Illus.). 1968. 11.60 (ISBN 0-8104-0721-3). Hayden.

Crabbe, John. Hi-Fi in the Home. (Illus.). 1971. 9.95 (ISBN 0-7137-0589-2). Transatlantic.

Davey, Gilbert. Fun with Hi-Fi. Cox, Jack, ed. (Learning with Fun). (Illus.). 64p. 1974. 12.50x (ISBN 0-7182-0083-7, SpS). Sportshelf.

Earl, John. ABC of Hi-Fi. (Illus.). 168p. 1975. 13.50x (ISBN 0-85242-409-4). Intl Pubns Serv.

--Understanding Hi-Fi- Specifications. LC 79-670131. (Illus.). 1978. pap. 8.50x (ISBN 0-85242-582-1). Intl Pubns Serv.

Gayford, M. L. Hi-Fi for the Enthusiast. LC 70-189177. 1972. 6.95 (ISBN 0-8306-2596-8); pap. 3.95 (ISBN 0-8306-1596-2, 596). TAB Bks.

Howard W. Sams Editorial Staff. Dictionary of Audio & Hi-Fi. LC 74-79354. 1975. pap. 5.95 (ISBN 0-672-21084-3). Sams.

Institute of High Fidelity. Official Guide to High Fidelity. 2nd ed. LC 78-54060. 1978. pap. 5.50 (ISBN 0-672-21531-4). Sams.

Johnson, Kenneth W. & Walker, Willard C. Hi-Fidelity: Concepts & Components for Consumers. (Illus.). 1979. pap. 9.95 (ISBN 0-8403-1992-4). Kendall-Hunt.

--The Science of Hi-Fidelity Laboratory Manual. 1978. pap. text ed. 5.95 (ISBN 0-8403-1815-4). Kendall-Hunt.

--Understanding Audio. (Illus.). 256p. 1980. pap. text ed. 5.75 (ISBN 0-8403-2216-X). Kendall-Hunt.

Johnson, Kenneth W., et al. The Science of Hi-Fidelity. LC 81-81012. (Illus.). 1981. pap. text ed. 19.95 (ISBN 0-8403-2297-6). Kendall-Hunt.

King, Gordon J. Master Hi-Fi Installation. (Illus.). (gr. 8 up). 1976. pap. 6.95 (ISBN 0-8104-0840-6). Hayden.

Leon, George D. The ABC Book of Hi-Fi-Audio Projects. (Illus.). 1977. pap. 5.95 (ISBN 0-8306-6921-3, 921). TAB Bks.

Newman, Bernard. Your Future in the High Fidelity Industry. LC 66-12895. (Careers in Depth Ser). (gr. 7 up). PLB 5.97 (ISBN 0-8239-0033-9). Rosen Pr.

Rosenthal, Murray P. How to Select & Use Hi-Fi & Stereo Amplifiers. LC 79-2361. 1979. pap. 6.50 (ISBN 0-8104-0832-5). Hayden.

--How to Select & Use Hi-Fi & Stereo Equipment. 1979. pap. 9.85 (ISBN 0-8104-0424-9). Hayden.

Swearer, Harvey F. Selecting & Improving Your Hi-Fi System. LC 72-87459. (Illus.). 224p. 1973. 7.95 (ISBN 0-8306-2640-9); pap. 4.95 (ISBN 0-8306-1640-3, 640). TAB Bks.

Warring, R. H. Set up Your Own Hi-Fi. (Illus.). 112p. 1974. 7.50x (ISBN 0-7188-1984-5). Intl Pubns Serv.

Wasley, John & Hill, Ron. A Guide to Hi-Fi. 1977. 15.00 (ISBN 0-7207-0906-7). Transatlantic.

Zuckerman, Arthur. Stereo High-Fidelity Speaker Systems. LC 77-93169. 1978. pap. 5.95 (ISBN 0-672-21514-4). Sams.

HIGH-FREQUENCY RADIO

see Radio, Short Wave

HIGH HOLY DAYS

see also Rosh Ha-Shanah; Yom Kippur

Bernards, Solomon S., ed. The Living Heritage of the High Holy Days. 31p. 0.50 (ISBN 0-686-74964-2). ADL.

Freehof, Solomon B. Preaching the Bible. 1974. 15.50x (ISBN 0-87068-244-X). Ktav.

Gordis, Robert. Leave a Little to God. LC 67-22706. 1967. 6.50x (ISBN 0-8197-0087-8). Bloch.

Greenberg, Sidney & Sugarman, Allan. Contemporary High Holiday Service. pap. 7.95x (ISBN 0-685-64876-1). Prayer Bk.

HIGH INTRAOCULAR PRESSURE

see Glaucoma

HIGH JUMPING

see Jumping

HIGH LICENSE

see Liquor Laws; Liquor Problem

HIGH PRESSURE (SCIENCE)

see also Compressibility; High Pressure (Technology); High Pressure Research; Pressure Vessels

Beggerow, O. High-Pressure Properties of Matter. (Landolt-Boernstein Ser.: Group IV, Vol. 4). (Illus.). 1980. 283.20 (ISBN 0-387-09370-2). Springer-Verlag.

Bennett, P. B. & Elliot, D. H., eds. The Physiology & Medicine of Diving & Compressed Air Work. 2nd ed. (Illus.). 1975. text ed. 59.00 (ISBN 0-02-857290-4). Macmillan.

Bradley, C. C. High-Pressure Methods in Solid State Research. 184p. 1969. 15.00 (ISBN 0-306-30693-X, Plenum Pr). Plenum Pub.

Bradley, R. S., ed. High Pressure Physics & Chemistry, 2 Vols. 1963. Vol. 1. 73.00 (ISBN 0-12-124001-0); Vol. 2. 59.50 (ISBN 0-12-124002-9). Acad Pr.

Bridgman, P. W. The Physics of High Pressure. (Illus.). 6.50 (ISBN 0-8446-0039-3). Peter Smith.

Burnham, C. Wayne, et al. Thermodynamic Properties of Water to 1,000 Degrees Centigrade & 10,000 Bars. LC 73-96715. (Special Paper: No. 132). (Illus., Orig.). 1969. pap. 3.00x (ISBN 0-8137-2132-6). Geol Soc.

Caldirola, P. & Knoepfel, H., eds. Physics of High Energy Density. (Italian Physical Society: Course 48). 1971. 54.00 (ISBN 0-12-368848-5). Acad Pr.

International AIRAPT Conference, Le Creuset, France, July 30-Aug. 3, 1979. High Pressure Science & Technology: Proceedings. Vodar, B. & Marteau, P., eds. (Illus.). 1200p. 1980. 230.00 (ISBN 0-08-024774-1). Pergamon.

Tomizuka, Carl & Emrick, Roy, eds. Physics of Solids at High Pressures. 1965. 60.00 (ISBN 0-12-693850-4). Acad Pr.

Ulmer, G. C., ed. Research Techniques for High Pressure & High Temperature. (Illus.). 384p. 1971. 17.60 (ISBN 0-387-05594-0). Springer-Verlag.

Zharkov, V. N. & Kalinin, V. A. Equations of State for Solids at High Pressures & Temperatures. LC 77-120027. 257p. 1971. 37.50 (ISBN 0-306-10852-6, Consultants). Plenum Pub.

HIGH PRESSURE (TECHNOLOGY)

International AIRAPT Conference, Le Creuset, France, July 30-Aug. 3, 1979. High Pressure Science & Technology: Proceedings. Vodar, B. & Marteau, P., eds. (Illus.). 1200p. 1980. 230.00 (ISBN 0-08-024774-1). Pergamon.

Isaacs, Neil S. Liquid Phase High Pressure Chemistry. LC 80-40844. 414p. 1981. 93.00 (ISBN 0-471-27849-1, Pub. by Wiley-Interscience). Wiley.

Johnson, William, et al. Ultra-High Pressure Equipment & Techniques Mainly for Synthesizing Diamond & Cubic Boron Nitride. 101p. 1979. pap. 33.00x (ISBN 0-686-71874-7, Pub. by VDI Verlag Germany). Renouf.

Manning, W. R. & Labrow, S. High Pressure Engineering. 1972. text ed. 37.50x (ISBN 0-7114-3804-8); pap. text ed. 19.95x (ISBN 0-685-83587-1). Intl Ideas.

Sculthorpe, William L. Design of High Pressure Steam & High Temperature Water Plants. LC 79-185992. 112p. 1972. write for info (ISBN 0-8311-1075-9). Krieger.

Spain, Ian L. & Paauwe, Jac. High Pressure Technology: Applications & Processes, Vol. II. 1977. 46.00 (ISBN 0-8247-6591-5). Dekker.

--High Pressure Technology: Equipment Design, Materials & Properties, Vol. I. 1977. 55.00 (ISBN 0-8247-6560-5). Dekker.

Timmerhaus & Barber, eds. Physical Properties & Material Synthesis, 2 vols. (High-Pressure Science & Technology Ser.: 6th AIRAPT Conference Ser.). 1978. Vol. 1. 75.00 (ISBN 0-306-40066-9, Plenum Pr); Vol. 2. 75.00 (ISBN 0-306-40069-3); 140.00set (ISBN 0-686-52341-5). Plenum Pub.

Tsiklis, Daniil S. Handbook of Techniques in High-Pressure Research & Engineering. LC 68-14854. 518p. 1968. 49.50 (ISBN 0-306-30324-8, Consultants). Plenum Pub.

HIGH PRESSURE RESEARCH

Bradley, R. S., ed. Advances in High Pressure Research, 4 vols. Vol. 1 1966. 62.00 (ISBN 0-12-021201-3); Vol. 2 1969. 45.00 (ISBN 0-12-021202-1); Vol. 3 1969. 60.50 (ISBN 0-12-021203-X); Vol. 4 1974. 47.50 (ISBN 0-12-021204-8). Acad Pr.

Manghnani, Merli H. High Pressure Research: Applications to Geophysics. 1977. 48.50 (ISBN 0-12-468750-4). Acad Pr.

Tsiklis, Daniil S. Handbook of Techniques in High-Pressure Research & Engineering. LC 68-14854. 518p. 1968. 49.50 (ISBN 0-306-30324-8, Consultants). Plenum Pub.

Ulmer, G. C., ed. Research Techniques for High Pressure & High Temperature. (Illus.). 384p. 1971. 17.60 (ISBN 0-387-05594-0). Springer-Verlag.

HIGH-RESIDUE DIET

see High-Fiber Diet

HIGH-RISE BUILDINGS

see also Skyscrapers

Fires in High-Rise Buildings. 120p. 1974. pap. 4.75 (ISBN 0-685-58186-1, SPP-25). Natl Fire Prot.

Mendes, Robert F. Fighting High-Rise Building Fires: Tactics & Logistics. Lyons, Paul R., ed. LC 75-13715. (Illus.). 160p. 1975. 12.50 (ISBN 0-87765-037-3). Natl Fire Prot.

HIGH SCHOOL EQUIVALENCY CERTIFICATES

see also Selective Service College Qualification Test

Farley, Eugene J., et al. High School Certification Through the General Educational Development Tests. (Adult Basic Education Ser). (RL 7-8). 1967. pap. text ed. 4.36 (ISBN 0-03-068510-9). HR&W.

Rudman, Jack. California High School Proficiency Examination. (Admission Test Ser.: ATS-39). (Cloth bdg. avail. on request). pap. 7.50 (ISBN 0-8373-5039-5). Natl Learning.

--Nevada Competency-Based High School Diploma Program (CHSD) (Admission Test Ser.: ATS-67). (Cloth bdg. avail. on request). pap. 9.95 (ISBN 0-8373-5167-7). Natl Learning.

HIGH SCHOOL EQUIVALENCY EXAMINATION

see also General Educational Development Tests

Arco Editorial Board. California High School Proficiency Examination. LC 78-4628. 1978. pap. text ed. 6.00 (ISBN 0-668-04412-8, 4412). Arco.

Cerreto, Frank. The Mathematics Test. (Illus.). 1979. pap. 4.95 (ISBN 0-07-010337-2, SP). McGraw.

Del Santo, Louise. Mastering Mathematics. LC 75-2049. (High School Equivalency Prog. Ser.). 205p. (Orig.). (gr. 9-12). 1975. pap. text ed. 5.50 (ISBN 0-913310-38-7). Par Inc.

Farley, Eugene J. Barron's How to Prepare for the High School Equivalency Examination - the Social Studies Test. 1981. pap. text ed. 4.95 (ISBN 0-8120-2056-1). Barron.

--Barron's How to Prepare for the High School Equivalency Examination - the Reading Skills Test: The Reading Skills Test. 1980. pap. text ed. 3.95 (ISBN 0-8120-2057-X). Barron.

--Barron's Preview Examination to Prepare for the High School Equivalency Tests. 2nd, rev. ed. 1979. pap. text ed. 18.00 (ISBN 0-8120-0992-4). Barron.

Farley, Eugene J. & Farley, Alice R. Barron's How to Prepare for the High School Equivalency Examination (GED) The Science Test. (gr. 11-12). 1982. pap. text ed. 4.25 (ISBN 0-8120-2055-3). Barron.

Friedman, I. Edward. How to Prepare for & Pass a High School Equivalency Exam. pap. 3.95 (ISBN 0-385-04537-9). Doubleday.

GED: How to Prepare for the High School Equivalency Examination. 1978. pap. 6.95 (ISBN 0-8092-7498-1). Contemp Bks.

Goodman, Roger & Ince, William. The Reading Test. (Illus.). 1978. pap. 4.95 (ISBN 0-07-023743-3, SP). McGraw.

--The Writing Test. (Illus.). 1979. pap. 4.95 (ISBN 0-07-023742-5, SP). McGraw.

Green, Sharon & Sieman, Michael. Barron's How to Prepare for the California High School Proficiency Examination (CHSPE) LC 77-10521. 1977. pap. 6.50 (ISBN 0-8120-0705-0). Barron.

Gruber, Edward C. Preparation for the New Reading Skills Test: (GED) (Orig.). 1980. pap. 5.95 (ISBN 0-671-09247-2). Monarch Pr.

--Preparation for the New Social Studies Test: (GED) (Orig.). 1980. pap. 5.95 (ISBN 0-671-09246-4). Monarch Pr.

--Preparation for the New Writing Skills Test: (GED) (Orig.). 1980. pap. 5.95 (ISBN 0-671-09244-8). Monarch Pr.

Gruber, Gary R. High School Equivalency Test. (Exam Prep. Ser.). pap. 6.95 (ISBN 0-671-18998-0). Monarch Pr.

Hodges, Raymond W. High School Equivalency Test Guide. LC 75-2181. 95p. (Orig.). (gr. 9-12). 1975. pap. text ed. 5.50 (ISBN 0-913310-13-1). Par Inc.

Irgang, Jacob. The Social Studies Test. (Illus.). 1978. pap. 4.95 (ISBN 0-07-032027-6, SP). McGraw.

Jenkins, C., et al. How to Prepare for the New High School Equivalency Examination. (Illus.). 1978. pap. 5.95 (ISBN 0-07-032350-X, SP). McGraw.

Kahn, Robert & Nestler, Herbert. The Science Test. (Illus.). 1978. pap. 4.95 (ISBN 0-07-033193-6, SP). McGraw.

Lanzano, Susan & Abreu, Rosendo. Preparacion Para el Examen de Equivalencia de la Escuela Superior. 3rd ed. Ringel, Martin & Banks, William K., eds. LC 80-17685. 368p. (Span.). 1981. pap. 6.95 (ISBN 0-668-05095-0, 50950). Arco.

Lloyd, Paul M. Desarrollando Destrezas En Preparacion Para el Examen de Equivalencia De Escuela Superior En Espanol: El Escribir. (Span.). (gr. 9-12). 1982. pap. text ed. 3.75 (ISBN 0-8120-0559-7). Barron.

Lockhart, William E. English Response Sheets & Prescription Sheets. (Michigan Prescriptive Program High School Equivalency-CED). 1975. 2.00x (ISBN 0-89039-164-5). Ann Arbor Pubs.

--English Study Material: High School Equivalency-GED. (Michigan Prescriptive Program Ser.). 1975. pap. text ed. 4.50x (ISBN 0-89039-121-1). Ann Arbor Pubs.

--Mathematics Response Sheets & Prescription Sheets. (Michigan Prescriptive Program,High School Epuivalency-GED Ser.). (gr. 10). 1975. 2.00x (ISBN 0-89039-165-3). Ann Arbor Pubs.

--Mathematics Study Material: High School Equivalency-GED. (Michigan Prescriptive Program Ser.). (gr. 10). 1975. pap. text ed. 8.00x (ISBN 0-89039-120-3). Ann Arbor Pubs.

Long, Jerry & Tenzer, Jeff. The Cambridge Program for the High School Equivalency Examination. Schenk, Brian, ed. (GED Preparation Ser.). (Illus.). 816p. (Orig.). 1981. pap. text ed. price not set (ISBN 0-8428-9385-7). Cambridge Bk.

Nickse, Ruth S. Assessing Life Skills Competence: The New York State External High School Diploma Program. LC 80-82712. (CBE Forum Ser.: Bk. 3). 1980. pap. 9.95 (ISBN 0-8224-0515-6). Pitman Learning.

Potell, Herbert. Barron's How to Prepare for the High School Equivalency Examination: The Writing Skills Test. LC 78-26372. 1979. pap. 5.95 (ISBN 0-8120-0733-6). Barron.

Pryce, Betty H. Mastering English. LC 75-2090. (High School Equivalency Prog. Ser.). 161p. (Orig.). (gr. 9-12). 1975. pap. text ed. 5.50 (ISBN 0-913310-39-5). Par Inc.

Rockowitz, et al. Barron's How to Prepare for the High School Equivalency Exam (GED) rev. 5th ed. (gr. 10-12). 1978. 21.95 (ISBN 0-8120-5306-0); pap. text ed. 6.95 (ISBN 0-8120-0645-3). Barron.

--Basic Tips on the New High School Equivalency Examination (GED) LC 79-26710. 1980. pap. text ed. 2.95 (ISBN 0-8120-2061-8). Barron.

Rockowitz, Murray. Developing Skills for the High School Equivalency Examination in Grammar, Usage, Spelling & Vocabulary. 1972. pap. text ed. 5.50 (ISBN 0-8120-0485-X). Barron.

Rudman, Jack. Examen De Equivalencia Para el Diploma De Escuela Superior (EEE) (Admission Test Ser.: ATS-22). (Cloth bdg. avail. on request). 1977. pap. 11.50 (ISBN 0-8373-5122-7). Natl Learning.

--High School Equivalency Diploma Examination (EE) (Admission Test Ser.: ATS-17). 14.95 (ISBN 0-8373-5117-0); pap. 9.95 (ISBN 0-8373-5017-4). Natl Learning.

Sallese & Dominicis. Desarrollando Destrezas En Preparacion Para el Examen Equivalencia De Escuela Superior En Espanol: Ciencia. Date not set. pap. 3.75 (ISBN 0-8120-0989-4). Barron.

--Desarrollando Destrezas En Preparacion Para el Examen Equivalencia De Escuela Superior En Espanol: Estudios Sociales. Date not set. pap. 3.75 (ISBN 0-8120-0988-6). Barron.

Sallese, Nicolas F., et al. Developing Skills in Reading for the H.S. Equivalency Test (in Spanish) Desarrollando Destrezas En Preparacion Para el Examen Equivalencia De Escuela Superior En Espanol. (gr. 11-12). Date not set. pap. text ed. 2.75 (ISBN 0-8120-0990-8). Barron.

Silvera, T. The McGraw-Hill Guide for Preparing Students for the New High School Equivalency Examination (GED) 1979. 2.50 (ISBN 0-07-057447-2). McGraw.

Turner, David R. High School Entrance & Scholarship Tests. 6th ed. (gr. 8-9). 1967. lib. bdg. 5.50 o. p. (ISBN 0-668-01392-3); pap. 5.00 (ISBN 0-668-00666-8). Arco.

--The New High School Equivalency Diploma Tests. LC 77-20196. 576p. 1978. lib. bdg. 10.00 (ISBN 0-668-04447-0); pap. 5.95 (ISBN 0-668-04451-9). Arco.

--Preliminary Arithmetic for the High School Equivalency Diploma Test. 2nd ed. LC 75-44948. 1976. pap. 5.00 (ISBN 0-668-02165-9). Arco.

--Preliminary Practice for the High School Equivalency Diploma Test. 5th ed. LC 75-34848. (gr. 9-12). 1972. pap. 6.00 (ISBN 0-668-01441-5). Arco.

Vazzana, Nicholas S. Preparing for High School Equivalency Tests. 1979. 36.95 (ISBN 0-89507-001-4); wrkbk 5.50 (ISBN 0-685-49938-3). Multi Dimen.

Williams, Edward. Barron's Getting Ready for the High School Equivaency Examination: Beginning Preparation in Mathematics. LC 76-3662. 1976. pap. 5.95 (ISBN 0-8120-0466-3). Barron.

HIGH SCHOOL GRADUATES

Caldwell, Louis. After the Tassel Is Moved. (Ultra Bks Ser.). 1968. 3.95 (ISBN 0-8010-2332-7). Baker Bk.

Jacobsen, Einar W. Educational Opportunities Provided for Post-Graduate Students in Public High Schools. LC 73-176905. (Columbia University. Teachers College. Contributions to Education: No. 523). Repr. of 1932 ed. 17.50 (ISBN 0-404-55523-3). AMS Pr.

Keyes, Ralph. Is There Life After High School? 240p. 1977. pap. 2.25 (ISBN 0-446-92152-1). Warner Bks.

Lawhead, Steve. After You Graduate. 1978. 9.95 (ISBN 0-310-36960-6); pap. 4.95 (ISBN 0-310-36961-4). Zondervan.

Medved, Michael & Wallechinsky, David. What Really Happened to the Class of '65. 1976. 10.00 (ISBN 0-394-40074-7). Random.

Moore, Margaret. A Study of Young High School Graduates. LC 74-177081. (Columbia University. Teachers College. Contributions to Education: No. 583). Repr. of 1933 ed. 17.50 (ISBN 0-404-55583-7). AMS Pr.

Nolfi, George J., ed. Experiences of Recent High School Graduates. new ed. LC 78-2075. 1978. 19.95 (ISBN 0-669-02264-0). Lexington Bks.

Wildman, Louis. High School Graduation Competencies. 1975. 6.00 (ISBN 0-939630-02-8). Inst Qual Hum Life.

HIGH SCHOOL LIBRARIES

see School Libraries (High School)

HIGH SCHOOL STUDENTS

Ashby, Lloyd W., ed. Student Activism in the Secondary Schools. LC 72-120819. 1970. pap. 2.50x (ISBN 0-8134-1176-9, 1176). Interstate.

Bever, James A. Coming of Age in America: VERCAP, a Guide for High School Students. 1977. pap. 3.00 (ISBN 0-88210-080-7). Natl Assn Principals.

Brown, Marion. Leadership Among High School Pupils. LC 77-176598. (Columbia University. Teachers College. Contributions to Education: No. 559). Repr. of 1933 ed. 17.50 (ISBN 0-404-55559-4). AMS Pr.

Jennings, M. K. High School Seniors Cohort Study, Nineteen Sixty-Five & Nineteen Seventy-Three. 1980. 14.00 (ISBN 0-89138-964-4). ICPSR.

Johnston, Lloyd D., et al. Monitoring the Future: Questionnaire Responses from the Nation's High School Seniors, Annual Vols., 1975, 1976, 1977, 1978, 4 vols. 1980. 15.00 ea.; 1975 (ISBN 0-87944-235-2, 188 PGS.); 1976 (ISBN 0-87944-236-0, 264 PGS.); 1977 (ISBN 0-87944-237-9, 266 PGS.); 1978 (ISBN 0-87944-238-7, 266 PGS.); Set. 45.00 (ISBN 0-87944-241-7). Inst Soc Res.

Jordaan, Jean-Pierre & Hyde, Martha B. Vocational Maturity During the High School Years. LC 78-23973. 1979. text ed. 22.50 (ISBN 0-8077-2453-X). Tchrs Coll.

Larkin, Ralph W. Suburban Youth in Cultural Crisis. LC 78-10742. 1979. text ed. 14.95 (ISBN 0-19-502522-9); pap. text ed. 4.95x (ISBN 0-19-502523-7). Oxford U Pr.

Lawhead, Steve. After You Graduate. 1978. 9.95 (ISBN 0-310-36960-6); pap. 4.95 (ISBN 0-310-36961-4). Zondervan.

McPherson, Andrew & Neave, Guy. The Scottish Sixth. (General Ser.). 170p. 1976. pap. text ed. 14.50x (ISBN 0-85633-093-0, NFER). Humanities.

Responsible Student Involvement. 1975. pap. 4.00 (ISBN 0-88210-062-9). Natl Assn Principals.

Rogness, Alvin N. Today & Tomorrow. LC 77-84095. 1978. pap. 3.95 (ISBN 0-8066-1621-0, 10-6660). Augsburg.

Sterner, Alice P. Radio, Motion Picture & Reading Interests: A Study of High School Pupils. LC 77-177824. (Columbia University. Teachers College. Contributions to Education: No. 932). Repr. of 1947 ed. 17.50 (ISBN 0-404-55932-8). AMS Pr.

Task Force, 1974. The Adolescent, Other Citizens, & Their High Schools. 1975. 8.95 (ISBN 0-07-062918-8, P&RB); pap. 3.95 (ISBN 0-07-062920-X). McGraw.

Tillery, Dale & Kildegaard, Ted. Educational Goals, Attitudes, & Behaviors: A Comparative Study of High School Seniors. LC 73-9573. 288p. 1973. text ed. 16.50 (ISBN 0-88410-151-7). Ballinger Pub.

Who's Who Among American High School Students, 1979-80. 14th ed. (Published in 8 regional vols. annually). 1980. 21.95 ea. (ISBN 0-915130-36-X); Vol. 1. (ISBN 0-915130-37-8); Vol. 2. (ISBN 0-915130-38-6); Vol. 3. (ISBN 0-915130-39-4); Vol. 4. (ISBN 0-915130-40-8); Vol. 5. (ISBN 0-915130-41-6); Vol. 6. (ISBN 0-915130-42-4); Vol. 7. (ISBN 0-915130-43-2); Vol. 8. (ISBN 0-915130-44-0). Educ Comm.

Winkler, Donald R. The Production of Human Capital: A Study of Minority Achievement. Bruchey, Stuart, ed. LC 76-45125. (Nineteen Seventy-Seven Dissertations Ser.). (Illus.). 1977. lib. bdg. 23.00x (ISBN 0-405-09936-3). Arno.

Yeager, Tressa C. An Analysis of Certain Traits of Selected High School Seniors Interested in Teaching. LC 70-177613. (Columbia University. Teachers College. Contributioons to Education: No. 660). Repr. of 1935 ed. 17.50 (ISBN 0-404-55660-4). AMS Pr.

Youth & the Changing Secondary School. (UNESCO Institute for Education). 72p. (Orig.). 1974. pap. 7.50 (ISBN 92-820-1002-3, UNESCO). Unipub.

HIGH SCHOOL TEACHERS

Bryan, Roy C. Pupil Rating of Secondary School Teachers. LC 73-176609. (Columbia University. Teachers College. Contributions to Education: No. 708). Repr. of 1937 ed. 17.50 (ISBN 0-404-55708-2). AMS Pr.

Finley, Charles W. Biology in Secondary Schools & the Training of Biology Teachers. LC 77-176772. (Columbia University. Teachers College. Contributions to Education: No. 199). Repr. of 1926 ed. 17.50 (ISBN 0-404-55199-8). AMS Pr.

Flowers, John G. Content of Student-Teaching Courses Designed for the Training of Secondary Teachers in State Teachers Colleges. LC 77-176780. (Columbia University. Teachers College. Contributions to Education: No. 538). Repr. of 1932 ed. 17.50 (ISBN 0-404-55538-1). AMS Pr.

Keene, Melvin. Beginning Secondary School Teacher's Guide. LC 69-10549. (Orig.). 1969. pap. text ed. 10.95 scp (ISBN 0-06-043593-3, HarpC). Har-Row.

LaBelle, Thomas J. The New Professional in Venezuelan Secondary Education. LC 73-620084. (Latin American Studies Ser.: Vol. 23). 195p. 1973. pap. 7.50 (ISBN 0-87903-023-2). UCLA Lat Am Ctr.

Marshall, John P. Teacher & His Philosophy. LC 72-90382. (Professional Education Ser). 101p. 1973. pap. text ed. 2.75 (ISBN 0-88224-027-7). Cliffs.

Morrisett, Lloyd M. Letters of Recommendation: A Study of Letters of Recommendation As an Instrument in the Selection of Secondary School Teachers. LC 70-177088. (Columbia University. Teachers College. Contributions to Education: No. 641). Repr. of 1935 ed. 17.50 (ISBN 0-404-55641-8). AMS Pr.

Pannell, Henry C. The Preparation & Work of Alabama High School Teachers. LC 77-177142. (Columbia University. Teachers College. Contributions to Education: No. 551). Repr. of 1933 ed. 17.50 (ISBN 0-404-55551-9). AMS Pr.

Smith, James M. Training of High School Teachers in Louisiana. LC 74-177771. (Columbia University. Teachers College. Contributions to Education: No. 247). Repr. of 1926 ed. 17.50 (ISBN 0-404-55247-1). AMS Pr.

Sprague, Harry A. A Decade of Progress in the Preparation of Secondary School Teachers: A Study of Curriculum Requirements in 55 State Teachers Colleges in 1928 and 1938. LC 76-177750. (Columbia University. Teachers College. Contributions to Education: No. 794). Repr. of 1940 ed. 17.50 (ISBN 0-404-55794-5). AMS Pr.

Strebel, Ralph F. The Nature of the Supervision of Student-Teaching in Universities Using Cooperating Public High Schools & Some Conditioning Factors. LC 79-177740. (Columbia University. Teachers College. Contributions to Education: No. 655). Repr. of 1935 ed. 17.50 (ISBN 0-404-55655-8). AMS Pr.

Stuart, Hugh. The Training of Modern Foreign Language Teachers for the Secondary Schools in the United States. LC 70-177738. (Columbia University. Teachers College. Contributions to Education: No. 256). Repr. of 1927 ed. 17.50 (ISBN 0-404-55256-0). AMS Pr.

Sullivan, John C. A Study of the Social Attitudes & Information on Public Problems of Women Teachers in Secondary Schools. LC 72-177733. (Columbia University. Teachers College. Contributions to Education: No. 791). Repr. of 1940 ed. 17.50 (ISBN 0-404-55791-0). AMS Pr.

Van Houten, Lyman H. Length of Service of Pennsylvania High School Teachers. LC 70-177680. (Columbia University. Teachers College. Contributions to Education: No. 522). Repr. of 1932 ed. 17.50 (ISBN 0-404-55522-5). AMS Pr.

HIGH SCHOOL TEACHING

Butterweck, Joseph S. The Problem of Teaching High School Pupils How to Study. LC 75-176620. (Columbia University. Teachers College. Contributions to Education: No. 237). Repr. of 1926 ed. 17.50 (ISBN 0-404-55237-4). AMS Pr.

Hoover, Kenneth H. The Professional Teacher's Handbook: A Guide for Improving Instruction in Today's Middle & Secondary Schools. 2nd abr. ed. 1976. text ed. 18.50 (ISBN 0-205-05582-6, 2255820). Allyn.

Johnson, Joy. Use of Groups in Schools: A Practical Manual for Everyone Who Works in Elementary and Secondary Schools. 137p. 1977. pap. text ed. 7.50 (ISBN 0-8191-0099-4). U Pr of Amer.

Kim, E. C. & Kellough, R. D. Resource Guide for Secondary School Teaching: A Planning for Competence. 1978. pap. 10.95 (ISBN 0-02-363790-0, 36379). Macmillan.

Klein, Thomas, et al. Spinach Is Good for You: A Call for Change in the American School. LC 73-77623. 200p. 1973. pap. 3.95 (ISBN 0-87972-051-4). Bowling Green Univ.

Lorber, Michale A. & Pierce, Walter D. Objectives & Methods for Secondary Teaching. 1977. 16.95 (ISBN 0-13-628958-4). P-H.

Perker, Samuel C. Methods of Teaching in High Schools. 1978. Repr. of 1920 ed. lib. bdg. 20.00 (ISBN 0-89760-703-1, Telegraph). Dynamic Learn Corp.

Sacopulos, Eugenia & Gibson, Marjorie. Teaching Units for Turned-off Teens: Classroom Activities for Secondary School Students. LC 75-44313. (Illus.). 1976. 12.95x (ISBN 0-87628-812-3, C-8123-6). Ctr Appl Res.

HIGH-SCHOOL YEARBOOKS

see School Yearbooks

HIGH SCHOOLS

see also Education, Secondary

Barker, Roger G. & Gump, Paul V. Big School, Small School: High School Size & Student Behavior. 1964. 12.50x (ISBN 0-8047-0195-4). Stanford U Pr.

Belting, Paul E. Development of the Free Public High School in Illinois to 1860. LC 71-89149. (American Education: Its Men, Institutions & Ideas, Ser. 1). 1969. Repr. of 1919 ed. 14.00 (ISBN 0-405-01386-8). Arno.

Bent, R. K. & Dronenberg, D. H. Principles of Secondary Education. 6th ed. 1970. pap. text ed. 15.95 (ISBN 0-07-004810-X, C). McGraw.

Caswell, Hollis L., ed. American High School: Its Responsibility & Opportunity. LC 70-100219. Repr. of 1946 ed. lib. bdg. 15.00x (ISBN 0-8371-3264-9, CAHS). Greenwood.

Chase, Francis S. & Anderson, Harold, eds. High School in a New Era. LC 58-11947. 1958. 14.50x (ISBN 0-226-10170-3). U of Chicago Pr.

Fish, Kenneth L. Conflict & Dissent in American High Schools. 1970. 6.95 (ISBN 0-685-07623-7, 80220). Glencoe.

Fisher, Harwood, ed. Developments in High School Psychology. LC 73-20023. (High School Behavioral Science Ser.: Vol. 1). 308p. 1974. 24.95 (ISBN 0-87705-111-9). Human Sci Pr.

French, Will. Promotional Plans in the High School. LC 72-176787. (Columbia University. Teachers College. Contributions to Education: No. 587). Repr. of 1933 ed. 17.50 (ISBN 0-404-55587-X). AMS Pr.

Garinger, Elmer H. The Administration of Discipline in the High School. LC 72-176795. (Columbia University. Teachers College. Contributions to Education: No. 686). Repr. of 1936 ed. 17.50 (ISBN 0-404-55686-8). AMS Pr.

Garretson, Oliver K. Relationships Between Expressed Preferences & Curricular Abilities of Ninth Grade Boys. LC 76-176976. (Columbia University. Teachers College. Contributions to Education: No. 396). Repr. of 1930 ed. 17.50 (ISBN 0-404-55396-6). AMS Pr.

Gorman, Burton. Secondary Education: The High School America Needs. 1971. text ed. 7.95 (ISBN 0-685-55625-5, 31007). Phila Bk Co.

Greenberg, Cory. How to Start a High School Underground Newspaper. 5th ed. (Illus.). 1977. saddle-stitched 1.50 (ISBN 0-918946-09-3). Youth Lib.

The Greening of the High School. LC 73-76705. (Illus.). 88p. 1973. pap. 2.00 (ISBN 0-89192-055-2). Interbk Inc.

Griffin, Orwin B. Evolution of the Connecticut State School System with Special Reference to the Emergence of the High School. LC 75-176821. (Columbia University. Teachers College. Contributions to Education: No. 293). Repr. of 1928 ed. 17.50 (ISBN 0-404-55293-5). AMS Pr.

Gross, Ronald & Osterman, Paul. High School. LC 71-139623. 1971. 8.95 (ISBN 0-671-20838-1). S&S.

Hamilton, Samuel. High School Ideals. 1978. Repr. of 1922 ed. lib. bdg. 10.00 (ISBN 0-8482-4412-5). Norwood Edns.

Hargreaves, David H. Social Relations in a Secondary School. (International Library of Sociology Ser.). 1967. text ed. 17.50x (ISBN 0-7100-3476-8). Humanities.

Hayes, Wayland J. Some Factors Influencing Participation in Voluntary School Group Activities: Case Study of One High School. LC 73-176850. (Columbia University. Teachers College. Contributions to Education: No. 419). Repr. of 1930 ed. 17.50 (ISBN 0-404-55419-9). AMS Pr.

High School: The Process & the Place. LC 72-187588. 120p. (Orig.). 1972. pap. 3.00 (ISBN 0-88481-216-2). Ed Facilities.

Hutton & Rostron. Comparative Study of Secondary School Building Costs. (Educational Studies & Documents, No. 4). (Illus., Orig.). 1972. pap. 3.50 (ISBN 92-3-100922-2, U96, UNESCO). Unipub.

Inglis, A. J. Rise of the High School in Massachusetts. LC 70-176895. (Columbia University. Teachers College. Contributions to Education: No. 45). Repr. of 1911 ed. 17.50 (ISBN 0-404-55045-2). AMS Pr.

Jones, Faustine C. A Traditional Model of Educational Excellence: Dunbar High School of Little Rock Arkansas. LC 81-6507. 222p. pap. text ed. 6.95 (ISBN 0-88258-099-X). Howard U Pr.

Keller, Franklin J. Comprehensive High School. Repr. of 1955 ed. lib. bdg. 15.00x (ISBN 0-8371-2876-5, KECH). Greenwood.

--Double-Purpose High School: Closing the Gap Between Vocational & Academic Preparation. 1953. lib. bdg. 15.00x (ISBN 0-8371-2875-7, KEDP). Greenwood.

Knapp, Henry & Huser, Mary K., eds. Instructional Innovation in Illinois: Secondary Schools. viii, 152p. 1970. pap. text ed. 3.00x (ISBN 0-8134-1220-X, 1220). Interstate.

Krug, Edward A. Shaping of the American High School, Vol. 1, 1880-1920. LC 64-12801. 504p. 1969. pap. text ed. 8.50 (ISBN 0-299-05165-X). U of Wis Pr.

McDill, Edward L. & Rigsby, Leo C. Structure & Process in Secondary Schools: The Academic Impact of Educational Climates. LC 73-8123. (Illus.). 207p. 1973. 14.00x (ISBN 0-8018-1480-4). Johns Hopkins.

Mayer, Barbara. The High School Survival Guide. 1980. text ed. 6.95 (ISBN 0-686-65117-0, 66701). Natl Textbk.

National Associaton of Secondary School Principals. NASSP Commencement Manual. 7th rev. ed. 1975. pap. 4.00 (ISBN 0-88210-066-1). Natl Assn Principals.

Portenier, Lillian G. Pupils of Low Mentality in High School. LC 76-177158. (Columbia University. Teachers College. Contributions to Education: No. 568). Repr. of 1933 ed. 17.50 (ISBN 0-404-55568-3). AMS Pr.

Propst, Robert. High School: The Process & the Place. LC 72-187588. (Illus.). 120p. 1972. pap. 3.00 (ISBN 0-89192-056-0). Interbk Inc.

Riddle, John I. The Six-Year Rural High School: A Comparative Study of Small & Large Units in Alabama. LC 70-177191. (Columbia University. Teachers College. Contributions to Education: No. 737). Repr. of 1937 ed. 17.50 (ISBN 0-404-55737-6). AMS Pr.

Rufi, John. The Small High School. LC 70-177214. (Columbia University. Teachers College. Contributions to Education: No. 236). Repr. of 1926 ed. 17.50 (ISBN 0-404-55236-6). AMS Pr.

Scott, J. I., ed. Getting the Most Out of High School. 2nd rev. ed. LC 67-26419. (gr. 9 up). 1967. 6.50 (ISBN 0-379-00089-X). Oceana.

Shinn, Duane. I Remember High School Days. (Illus.). 1977. 1.95 (ISBN 0-912732-26-1). Duane Shinn.

Smith, James M. Training of High School Teachers in Louisiana. LC 74-177771. (Columbia University. Teachers College. Contributions to Education: No. 247). Repr. of 1926 ed. 17.50 (ISBN 0-404-55247-1). AMS Pr.

Snyder, Edwin R. Legal Status of Rural High Schools in the United States with Special Reference to the Methods Employed in Extending State Aid to Secondary Education in Rural Communities. LC 77-177761. (Columbia University. Teachers College. Contributions to Education: No. 24). Repr. of 1909 ed. 17.50 (ISBN 0-404-55024-X). AMS Pr.

Spears, Harold. High School for Today. Repr. of 1950 ed. lib. bdg. 14.75x (ISBN 0-8371-2531-6, SPHS). Greenwood.

Stinchcombe, Arthur L. Rebellion in a High School. 256p. 1972. pap. 2.95 (ISBN 0-8129-6097-1, QP211). Times Bks.

Wales, John N. Schools of Democracy: An Englishman's Impressions of Secondary Education in the American Middlewest. xviii, 161p. 1962. 3.95 (ISBN 0-87013-066-8). Mich St U Pr.

HIGH SCHOOLS–ACCOUNTING

see Schools–Accounting

HIGH SCHOOLS–ADMINISTRATION

Ackerly, Robert & Gluckman, Ivan. Reasonable Exercise of Authority, II. 32p. (Orig.). 1976. pap. 3.00 (ISBN 0-88210-070-X). Natl Assn Principals.

Burkhead, Jesse, et al. Input & Output in Large-City High Schools. LC 67-16845. (Education in Large Cities Ser.: No. 2). (Orig.). 1967. pap. 4.95x (ISBN 0-8156-2109-4). Syracuse U Pr.

Corwin, Ronald G. Militant Professionalism: A Study of Organizational Conflict in High Schools. LC 75-98400. 1970. text ed. 20.00x (ISBN 0-89197-303-6); pap. text ed. 7.95x (ISBN 0-89197-304-4). Irvington.

Hughes, M. G., ed. Secondary School Administration: A Management Approach. 2nd ed. LC 74-4453. 1974. text ed. 16.50 (ISBN 0-08-018010-8); pap. text ed. 9.60 (ISBN 0-08-018011-6). Pergamon.

Johnson, Franklin W. The Administration & Supervision of the High School. 402p. 1981. Repr. of 1925 ed. lib. bdg. 25.00 (ISBN 0-89984-262-3). Century Bookbindery.

Jones, J. J., et al. Secondary School Administration. LC 68-30874. (Illus.). 1968. text ed. 16.95 (ISBN 0-07-033010-7, C). McGraw.
Ovard, Glen F. Administration of the Changing Secondary School. 1966. text ed. 13.95x (ISBN 0-685-14568-9). Macmillan.
--Change & Secondary School Administration: A Book of Readings. (Orig.). 1968. pap. text ed. 8.95 (ISBN 0-02-390000-8). Macmillan.
Sargent, James C. Organizational Climate of High Schools. LC 67-21861. 1967. pap. text ed. 1.25x (ISBN 0-8134-0933-0, 933). Interstate.

HIGH SCHOOLS-ALUMNI
see also High School Graduates

HIGH SCHOOLS-CURRICULA
Broudy, Harry S. Democracy & Excellence in American Secondary Education: A Study in Curriculum Theory. LC 76-57660. 310p. 1978. Repr. of 1964 ed. lib. bdg. 14.00 (ISBN 0-88275-513-7). Krieger.
Clark, Leonard H. & Klein, Raymond L. The American Secondary School Curriculum. 2nd ed. (Illus.). 544p. 1972. text ed. 19.95 (ISBN 0-02-322580-7, 32258). Macmillan.
Edelson, Edward. The Secondary School Music Program from Classroom to Concert Hall. (Illus.). 240p. 1972. 13.95 (ISBN 0-13-797555-4, Parker). P-H.
Newmann, Fred M. Education for Citizen Action: Challenge for the Secondary Curriculum. LC 74-30963. 250p. 1975. 16.30 (ISBN 0-8211-1305-4); text ed. 14.70 (ISBN 0-685-52139-7). McCutchan.
Stewart, Hugh H. Comparative Study of the Concentration & Regular Plans of Organization in the Senior High School. LC 72-177820. (Columbia University. Teachers College. Contributions to Education: No. 600). Repr. of 1934 ed. 17.50 (ISBN 0-404-55600-0). AMS Pr.
Stout, John E. Development of High-School Curricula in the North Central States from 1860-1918. LC 77-89240. (American Education: Its Men, Institutions & Ideas, Ser. 1). 1969. Repr. of 1921 ed. 14.00 (ISBN 0-405-01477-5). Arno.
Wilcox, Barbara & Bellamy, G. Thomas. Design of High School Programs for Severely Handicapped Students. 210p. (Orig.). 1981. pap. text ed. 15.95 (ISBN 0-933716-18-4). P H Brookes.

HIGH SCHOOLS-ENTRANCE REQUIREMENTS
Bennett, Leonard S. Review Workbook for High School Entrance Plus Scholarship Examination. pap. 3.95 (ISBN 0-87738-000-7). Youth Ed.
Trends in Allocation Procedures: An NFER Report. 1969. pap. text ed. 2.25x (ISBN 0-901225-05-3, NFER). Humanities.

HIGH SCHOOLS-SCHEDULES
see Schedules, School

HIGH SCHOOLS-GREAT BRITAIN
Taylor, William. Heading for Change: The Management of Innovation in the Large Secondary School. (Orig.). 1973. 11.25x (ISBN 0-7100-7426-3); pap. 6.50 (ISBN 0-7100-7427-1). Routledge & Kegan.
Trends in Allocation Procedures: An NFER Report. 1969. pap. text ed. 2.25x (ISBN 0-901225-05-3, NFER). Humanities.

HIGH SCHOOLS, JUNIOR
see Junior High Schools

HIGH SCHOOLS, RURAL
see Rural Schools

HIGH SEAS, JURISDICTION OVER
see Maritime Law; War, Maritime (International Law)

HIGH SOCIETY
see Upper Classes

HIGH-SPEED AERONAUTICS
see also Aerodynamics, Supersonic; Aerodynamics, Transonic; Aerothermodynamics; Airplanes-Jet Propulsion; Rocket Planes; Rockets (Aeronautics)
Bridgeman, William & Hazard, Jacqueline. The Lonely Sky. Gilbert, James, ed. LC 79-7232. (Flight: Its First Seventy-Five Years Ser.). (Illus.). 1979. Repr. of 1955 ed. lib. bdg. 24.00x (ISBN 0-405-12148-2). Arno.
Cohen, Doris & Jones, Robert T. High Speed Wing Theory. (Aeronautical Paperbacks Ser.: Vol. 6). (Orig.). 1960. pap. 12.00 (ISBN 0-691-07975-7). Princeton U Pr.
Duke, Neville & Lanchbery, Edward. Sound Barrier: The Story of High-Speed Flight. Gilbert, James, ed. LC 79-7248. (Flight: Its First Seventy-Five Years Ser.). (Illus.). 1979. Repr. of 1955 ed. lib. bdg. 12.00x (ISBN 0-405-12160-1). Arno.
Ower, E. & Nayler, J. L. High Speed Flight. 10.00 (ISBN 0-685-28366-6). Philos Lib.

HIGH-SPEED DATA PROCESSING
see Real-Time Data Processing

HIGH SPEED PHOTOGRAPHY
see Photography, High-Speed

HIGH TEMPERATURE MATERIALS
see Heat Resistant Materials

HIGH TEMPERATURE METALLURGY
see Metals at High Temperatures

HIGH TEMPERATURE METALS
see Heat Resistant Alloys

HIGH TEMPERATURES
see also Gases at High Temperatures; Materials at High Temperatures; Metals at High Temperatures; Solar Furnaces
Baulch, D. L., et al. Evaluated Kinetic Data for High Temperature Reactions, Vol. 3. 1977. 99.95 (ISBN 0-408-70787-9). Butterworth.
Burnham, C. Wayne, et al. Thermodynamic Properties of Water to 1,000 Degrees Centigrade & 10,000 Bars. LC 73-96715. (Special Paper: No. 132). (Illus., Orig.). 1969. pap. 3.00x (ISBN 0-8137-2132-6). Geol Soc.
Conference on High-Temperature Systems, 3rd. Proceedings: The Performance of High-Temperature Systems, 2 vols. Bahn, Gilbert S., ed. Incl. Vol. 1. 270p. 1968. 63.25x (ISBN 0-677-10600-9); Vol. 2. 362p. 1969. 81.00x (ISBN 0-677-12960-2). Gordon.
Eyring, LeRoy, ed. Advances in High Temperature Chemistry. Vol. 1. 1967. 56.00 (ISBN 0-12-021501-2); Vol. 2. 1969. 56.00 (ISBN 0-12-021502-0); Vol. 3.1971. 56.00 (ISBN 0-12-021503-9); Vol. 4.1972. 56.00 (ISBN 0-12-021504-7). Acad Pr.
Glaser, Peter E. & Walker, Raymond F. Thermal Imaging Techniques. LC 64-19979. 280p. 1964. 32.50 (ISBN 0-306-30172-5, Plenum Pr). Plenum Pub.
Hastie, John W. High Temperature Vapors: Science & Technology. (Materials Science & Technology Ser.). 1975. 58.50 (ISBN 0-12-331950-1). Acad Pr.
Rouse, C. A., ed. Progress in High Temperature Physics & Chemistry, 5 vols. 1967-1973. Vols. 1 & 5. 62.00 ea.; Vol. 2-4. 58.00 ea. Vol. 1, 1967 (ISBN 0-08-012123-3). Vol. 2, 1968 (ISBN 0-08-012640-5). Vol. 3. 1969 (ISBN 0-08-013959-0). Vol. 4. 1971 (ISBN 0-08-016439-0). Vol. 5. 1973 (ISBN 0-08-017240-7). Pergamon.
Turkdogan, E. T. Physical Chemistry of High Temperature Technology. LC 79-26880. 1980. 49.50 (ISBN 0-12-704650-X). Acad Pr.
Ulmer, G. C., ed. Research Techniques for High Pressure & High Temperature. (Illus.). 384p. 1971. 17.60 (ISBN 0-387-05594-0). Springer-Verlag.
Zemansky, Mark W. Temperatures Very Low & Very High. 144p. 1981. pap. 3.00 (ISBN 0-486-24072-X). Dover.
Zharkov, V. N. & Kalinin, V. A. Equations of State for Solids at High Pressures & Temperatures. LC 77-120027. 257p. 1971. 37.50 (ISBN 0-306-10852-6, Consultants). Plenum Pub.

HIGH TEMPERATURES-MEASUREMENT
see Pyrometers and Pyrometry

HIGH TEMPERATURES-PHYSIOLOGICAL EFFECT
see Heat-Physiological Effect

HIGH TREASON
see Treason

HIGH VACUUM TECHNIQUE
see Vacuum

HIGH VELOCITY FORMING
see High Energy Forming

HIGH-VOLTAGE HIGH-FREQUENCY PHOTOGRAPHY
see Kirlian Photography

HIGHER EDUCATION
see Education, Higher

HIGHER EDUCATION AND STATE
Babbidge, Homer D. & Rosenzweig, Robert M. The Federal Interest in Higher Education. LC 74-25991. 214p. 1975. Repr. of 1962 ed. lib. bdg. 14.00x (ISBN 0-8371-7882-7, BAFI). Greenwood.
Belknap, Robert L. & Kuhns, Richard. Tradition & Innovation: General Education & the Reintegration of the University, a Columbia Report. LC 77-3315. 130p. 1977. 12.00x (ISBN 0-231-04322-8); pap. 4.00x (ISBN 0-231-04323-6). Columbia U Pr.
Berdahl, Robert O. British Universities & the State. Metzger, Walter P., ed. LC 76-55198. (The Academic Profession Ser.). 1977. Repr. of 1959 ed. lib. bdg. 14.00x (ISBN 0-405-10029-9). Arno.
Breneman, David W. & Finn, Chester E., eds. Public Policy & Private Higher Education. (Studies in Higher Education Policy). 1978. 18.95 (ISBN 0-8157-1066-6); pap. 8.95 (ISBN 0-8157-1065-8). Brookings.
Burn, Barbara B. & Karmal, Peter. Federal-State Responsibilities for Postsecondary Education: Australia & the United States. 1977. pap. 2.00 (ISBN 0-89192-237-7). Interbk Inc.
Carnegie Council on Policy Studies in Higher Education. The Federal Role in Postsecondary Education: Unfinished Business, 1975-1980. LC 75-4482. (Carnegie Council Ser). (Illus.). 112p. 1975. 10.95x (ISBN 0-87589-259-0). Jossey-Bass.
--Low or No Tuition: The Feasibility of a National Policy for the First Two Years of College. LC 75-4276. (Carnegie Council Ser). (Illus.). 96p. 1975. 10.95x (ISBN 0-87589-257-4). Jossey-Bass.
--The States & Private Higher Education: Problems & Policies in a New Era. LC 77-90848. (Carnegie Council Ser.). (Illus.). 1977. text ed. 14.95x (ISBN 0-87589-363-5). Jossey-Bass.
Carnegie Foundation for the Advancement of Teaching. The States & Higher Education: A Proud Past & Vital Future. LC 76-11958. (Carnegie Council Ser.). (Illus.). 112p. 1976. 10.95x (ISBN 0-87589-282-5). Jossey-Bass.
Edwards, Harry T. & Nordin, Virginia D. An Introduction to the American Legal System: A Supplement to Higher Education & the Law. LC 80-82033. 76p. (Orig.). 1980. pap. text ed. 5.95x (ISBN 0-934222-02-9). Inst Ed Manage.
--Nineteen Eighty Cumulative Supplement Higher Education & the Law. LC 80-82432. 136p. (Orig.). 1980. pap. text ed. 5.95x (ISBN 0-934222-03-7). Inst Ed Manage.
Furniss, W. Todd & Gardner, David P., eds. Higher Education & Government. 1979. 15.00 (ISBN 0-8268-1327-5). ACE.
Gaffney, Edward M. & Moots, Philip R. Government & Campus: Federal Regulation of Religiously Affiliated Higher Education. LC 80-53164. 210p. 1981. text ed. 15.95 (ISBN 0-268-01003-X); pap. text ed. 8.95 (ISBN 0-268-01005-6). U of Notre Dame Pr.
Gilder, Jamison, ed. Modernizing State Policies: Community Colleges & Lifelong Education. (Orig.). 1981. pap. 7.50 (ISBN 0-87117-107-4). Am Assn Comm Jr Coll.
Hobbs, Walter C., ed. Government Regulation of Higher Education. LC 77-27442. 1978. 15.00 (ISBN 0-88410-183-5). Ballinger Pub.
Hook, Sidney, et al, eds. The University & the State. LC 77-26375. 296p. 1978. 15.95 (ISBN 0-87975-098-7). Prometheus Bks.
Howard, A. E. D. State Aid to Private Higher Education. 1977. 40.00 (ISBN 0-87215-192-1). Michie-Bobbs.
Johns Hopkins University. State Aid to Higher Education: A Series of Addresses Delivered at Johns Hopkins University. LC 78-64263. (Johns Hopkins University. Studies in the Social Sciences. Extra Volumes: 18). Repr. of 1898 ed. 15.00 (ISBN 0-404-61366-7). AMS Pr.
Kagan, Richard L. Students & Society in Early Modern Spain. LC 74-6828. (Illus.). 303p. 1975. 18.00x (ISBN 0-8018-1583-5). Johns Hopkins.
Nowlan, James D. The Politics of Higher Education: Lawmakers & the Academy in Illinois. (Orig.). 1976. pap. 4.95 (ISBN 0-252-00558-9). U of Ill Pr.
O'Neil, Robert M. The Courts, Government, & Higher Education. LC 72-90171. 40p. 1972. pap. 1.00 (ISBN 0-87186-237-9). Comm Econ Dev.
Roche, G. The Balancing Act: Quota Hiring in Higher Education. LC 74-11130. 1974. pap. 2.95 (ISBN 0-87548-305-4). Open Court.
St. John, Edward P. Public Policy & College Management: Title III of the Higher Education Act. 300p. 1981. 27.95 (ISBN 0-03-058454-X). Praeger.
Schuman, David. Policy Analysis, Education & Everyday Life: An Evaluation of Higher Education. 224p. 1981. pap. text ed. 5.95 (ISBN 0-669-04046-0). Heath.
Smithsonian Institution. Educational & Federal Laboratory-University Relationships: Symposium Held at the Museum of History & Technology Smithsonian Institution, October 29-31. LC 78-119595. 1970. 10.00 (ISBN 0-405-00690-X). Arno.
Wiley, Malcolm W. Depression: Recovery & Higher Education. Metzger, Walter P., ed. LC 76-55176. (The Academic Profession Ser.). (Illus.). 1977. Repr. of 1937 ed. lib. bdg. 31.00x (ISBN 0-405-10004-3). Arno.

HIGHER LAW
see Divine Right of Kings; Government, Resistance To

HIGHER PLANE CURVES
see Curves, Plane

HIGHLAND CLANS
see Clans and Clan System

HIGHLAND COUNTY, VIRGINIA
Morton, Oren F. History of Highland County, Virginia. LC 78-88167. (Illus.). 1979. Repr. of 1911 ed. 20.00 (ISBN 0-8063-7963-4). Regional.

HIGHLAND RAILWAY
Vallance, H. A. Highland Railway. 3rd ed. LC 69-12549. (Illus.). 1969. 10.95x (ISBN 0-678-05539-4). Kelley.

HIGHWAY ACCIDENTS
see Traffic Accidents

HIGHWAY COMMUNICATION
see also Electronic Traffic Controls; Traffic Signs and Signals

HIGHWAY ENGINEERING
see Highway Research; Road Construction; Roads; Traffic Engineering

HIGHWAY LAW
see Automobiles-Law and Legislation; Cycling; Traffic Regulations

HIGHWAY PATROLS
see Traffic Police

HIGHWAY RESEARCH
AASHTO Administrative Subcommittee on Computer Technology. Computer Systems Index. 1980. 10.00 (ISBN 0-686-20962-1, CSI). AASHTO.
American Society of Civil Engineers, compiled by. Implementing Highway Safety Improvements. LC 79-93190. 320p. 1980. pap. text ed. 22.50 (ISBN 0-87262-009-3). Am Soc Civil Eng.
--Report on Highway & Bridge Surveys. (Manual & Report on Engineering Practice Ser.: No. 44). 160p. 1962. pap. text ed. 7.50 (ISBN 0-87262-219-3). Am Soc Civil Eng.
Carter, Everett & Homburger, Wolfgang S. Introduction to Transportation Engineering: Highways & Transit. (Illus.). 1978. ref. ed. 21.95 (ISBN 0-87909-388-9). Reston.
Hazardous Road Locations: Identification & Counter Measures. (Road Research Ser.). 1976. 5.00x (ISBN 92-64-11570-6). OECD.
Holiday Traffic. (Round Table Ser.: No. 44). 54p. (Orig.). 1980. pap. 4.50x (ISBN 92-821-1058-3). OECD.
OECD. Bus Lanes & Busway Systems. (Road Research). 124p. (Orig.). 1977. pap. 7.00x (ISBN 92-64-11628-1). OECD.
--Catalog of Road Surface Deficiencies. (Road Research). 60p. (Orig.). pap. 6.50x (ISBN 92-64-01845-X). OECD.
--Cost & Benefits of General Speed Limits. (Round Table No. 37). 93p. (Orig.). 1978. pap. 3.75x (ISBN 0-686-30750-X). OECD.
--Energy Problems & Urban & Suburban Transport. (Road Research). 59p. (Orig.). 1978. pap. 5.00x (ISBN 92-64-11760-1). OECD.
--Geometric Road Design Standards. (Road Research Ser.). 208p. (Orig.). 1977. pap. 8.00x (ISBN 92-64-11640-0). OECD.
--Maintenance Techniques for Road Surfacings. (Road Research Ser.). 212p. (Orig.). 1978. pap. 11.00x (ISBN 92-64-11837-3). OECD.
Oglesby, Clarkson H. & Hicks, Russell G. Highway Engineering. 4th ed. 896p. 1982. text ed. 30.95 (ISBN 0-471-02936-X). Wiley.
Organization for Economic Cooperation & Development. Capacity of at-Grade Junctions. (Road Research Ser.). 119p. 1975. 6.00x (ISBN 92-64-11317-7). OECD.
--Urban Traffic Models: Possibilities for Simplification. (Road Research Ser.). 127p. 1974. 5.00x (ISBN 92-64-11249-9). OECD.
Road Strengthening. (Road Research Ser.). 1976. 6.50x (ISBN 92-64-11557-9). OECD.
Symposium on Frost Action on Roads, Norwegian Road Research Laboratory, Oslo, October 1-3, 1973. Frost Action on Roads: Proceedings. (Road Research Ser.). 229p. 1974. 6.50x (ISBN 92-64-11251-0). OECD.
Wells, G. R. Highway Planning Techniques: The Balance of Cost & Benefit. 150p. 1971. 35.00x (ISBN 0-85264-196-6, Pub. by Griffin England). State Mutual Bk.
Wright, P. H. & Poquette, Radnor J. Highway Engineering. 4th ed. LC 78-13643. 1979. text ed. 33.95 (ISBN 0-471-07260-5); solutions manual avail. (ISBN 0-471-05981-1). Wiley.

HIGHWAY SAFETY
see Traffic Safety

HIGHWAY TRAFFIC NOISE
see Traffic Noise

HIGHWAY TRANSPORT WORKERS
Boyle, David H. How to Succeed in Big Time Trucking. (Orig.). 1979. pap. 6.95 (ISBN 0-913668-97-4). Ten Speed Pr.
Dobbs, Farrell. Teamster Rebellion. LC 78-186690. (Illus.). 192p. 1972. 14.00 (ISBN 0-913460-02-8, Dist. by Path Pr NY); pap. 4.45 (ISBN 0-913460-03-6). Monad Pr.
Educational Research Council of America. Truck Driver. rev. ed. McCabe, Bernard & Marchak, John P., eds. (Real People at Work Ser: C). (Illus.). 1976. pap. text ed. 2.25 (ISBN 0-89247-022-4). Changing Times.
Gilliland, Ken & Millard, J. Trucking: A Truck Driver's Workbook. McFadden, S. Michele, ed. 1981. pap. text ed. 15.00x (ISBN 0-89262-029-3). Career Pub.
--Trucking: Instructor's Guide. McFadden, S. Michele, ed. 1981. pap. text ed. 12.50 (ISBN 0-89262-030-7). Career Pub.
Gilliland, Ken, et al. Trucking: A Truck Driver's Training Handbook. LC 79-90760. (Illus.). 434p. (Orig.). 1981. pap. text ed. 19.50 (ISBN 0-89262-025-0); tchrs' guide avail.; wkbk. avail. Career Pub.
Gousha-Connelley Diesel Fuel & Truck Stop Guide. 5th ed. (Illus.). 1979. pap. 7.95 (ISBN 0-913040-54-1, Gousha Chek-Chart). H M Gousha.

Larned, Phyllis. Kerry Drives a Van. (People Working Today Ser). (Illus.). 40p. (gr. 7-12). 1977. pap. text ed. 1.85 (ISBN 0-915510-18-9). Janus Bks.

Loup-Nory, Jean. The Long Haul: Trucking in America. LC 80-50366. (Illus.). 180p. 1980. 14.95 (ISBN 0-528-81536-9). Rand.

Lynott, John. Loaded & Rollin' Trucks & Their Drivers. rev. ed. (Encore Edition). (Illus.). 1979. pap. 2.95 (ISBN 0-684-16911-8, SL856, ScribT). Scribner.

McDowell, George, ed. Multi-Day Logging. LC 77-93509. 1978. pap. 1.00 (ISBN 0-934674-27-2). J J Keller.

Thomas, James H. The Long Haul: Truckers, Truck Stops, & Trucking. (Illus.). 12.95 (ISBN 0-87870-055-2); pap. 6.95 (ISBN 0-87870-057-9). Memphis St Univ.

Winquist, Henry S. Truck Driving to Glory. 1978. 4.95 (ISBN 0-533-03301-2). Vantage.

Wyckoff, D. Daryl. Truck Drivers in America. LC 78-24793. (Illus.). 1979. 16.95 (ISBN 0-669-02818-5). Lexington Bks.

Wyckoff, D. Daryl & Maister, David H. Owner-Operators: Independent Trucker. LC 74-23978. (Illus.). 1975. 15.95x (ISBN 0-669-96800-5). Lexington Bks.

HIGHWAY TRANSPORT WORKERS–PROGRAMMED INSTRUCTION

Improving Supervisory Skills in Trucking Operations. (Illus.). pap. 5.00 (ISBN 0-686-00454-X). Preston.

HIGHWAY TRANSPORTATION

see Transportation, Automotive

HIGHWAYMEN

see Brigands and Robbers

HIGHWAYS

see Roads

HIJACKING OF AIRCRAFT

Barker, Ralph. Not Here, but in Another Place. (Illus.). 352p. 1980. 13.95 (ISBN 0-312-57961-6). St Martin.

Haas, William & Blair, Ed. Odyssey of Terror. LC 77-72886. (Illus.). 1977. 7.95 (ISBN 0-8054-7908-2). Broadman.

Hubbard, David G. Skyjacker: His Flights of Fancy. Alexandre, Clement, ed. 1971. pap. 1.95 (ISBN 0-02-095920-6). Macmillan.

Joyner, Nancy D. Aerial Hijacking As an International Crime. LC 74-8380. 352p. 1974. lib. bdg. 21.00 (ISBN 0-379-00004-0). Oceana.

Moore, Kenneth C. Airport, Aircraft & Airline Security. LC 76-45104. (Illus.). 1976. 19.95 (ISBN 0-913708-26-7). Butterworth.

HIKING

see also Backpacking; Mountaineering; Orientation; Trails; Walking

Bach, Orville E., Jr. Hiking the Yellowstone Backcountry. LC 72-96121. (Totebook Ser.). (Illus.). 240p. 1973. pap. 7.95 (ISBN 0-87156-078-X). Sierra.

Barnes, F. L. Canyon Country Hiking & Natural History. LC 76-58119. (Canyon Country Ser.). (Illus.). 1977. pap. 3.95 (ISBN 0-915272-07-5). Wasatch Pubs.

Barnsley, Pam, et al. Hiking Trails of the Sunshine Coast. (Illus.). 1979. pap. 4.95 (ISBN 0-913140-41-4). Signpost Bk Pub.

Bluestein, Sheldon. Hiking Trails of Southern Idaho. LC 79-52543. (Illus.). 195p. (Orig.). 1981. pap. 7.95 (ISBN 0-87004-280-7). Caxton.

Boy Scouts Of America. Hiking. LC 19-600. (Illus.). 36p. (gr. 6-12). 1962. pap. 0.70x (ISBN 0-8395-3380-2, 3380). BSA.

Buchanan, James W. Minnesota Walk Book, Vol. 3. (Illus.). 1978. pap. 4.50 (ISBN 0-931714-00-1). Nodin Pr.

--Minnesota Walk Book: A Guide to Hiking & Cross-Country Skiing in the Metroland Region, Vol. 4. (The Minnesota Walk Books). (Illus.). 1979. pap. 4.50 (ISBN 0-931714-03-6). Nodin Pr.

Calder, Jean. Walking: A Guide to Beautiful Walks & Trails in America. (Americans-Discover-America Ser.). 1977. 3.95 (ISBN 0-688-03131-5). Morrow.

Catlett, Cloe. Fifty More Hikes in Maine. LC 79-92571. (Fifty Hikes Ser.). (Illus., Orig.). 1980. pap. 8.95 (ISBN 0-89725-017-6). NH Pub Co.

Chisholm, Craig. Hawaiian Hiking Trails. LC 75-13696. (Illus.). 1975. pap. 7.95 (ISBN 0-911518-35-5). Touchstone Pr Ore.

Dalrymple, Dana & Dalrymple, Helen. Appalachian Trail Guide Southern Pennsylvania to Northern Virginia (Susquehanna River to Shenandoah National Park) 10th rev. ed. (Orig.). 1979. pap. 5.00 (ISBN 0-915746-12-3). Potomac Appalach.

Danielsen, John. Winter Hiking & Camping. 2nd ed. (Illus.). 1977. 6.95 (ISBN 0-935272-04-6). ADK Mtn Club.

Dannen, Donna & Dannen, Kent. Walks with Nature in Rocky Mountain National Park. LC 80-26665. (Illus.). 64p. 1981. pap. 3.95 (ISBN 0-914788-38-8). East Woods.

Dean, John. Hiking the Inland Empire. (Illus.). 1976. pap. 3.95 (ISBN 0-913140-15-5). Signpost Bk Pubns.

DeHaan, Vici. Hiking Trails of the Boulder Mountain Area. (Illus.). 1979. pap. 5.95 (ISBN 0-87108-531-3). Pruett.

Denton, Molly T. Hikers Guide to Wildflowers of the Potomac Appalachians. LC 63-85307. 1979. 2.00 (ISBN 0-915746-11-5). Potomac Appalach.

Doan, Daniel. Fifty More Hikes in New Hampshire. LC 77-94004. (Illus.). 1978. 12.50 (ISBN 0-912274-89-1); pap. 6.95 (ISBN 0-912274-85-9). NH Pub Co.

Duncan, S. Blackwell. How to Make Your Own Camping & Hiking Gear. (Illus.). 1978. pap. 7.95 (ISBN 0-8306-1014-6, 1014). TAB Bks.

Ehling, Bill. Twenty-Five Walks in the Finger Lakes Region of New York. LC 78-71718. (Illus.). 1979. pap. 5.95 (ISBN 0-89725-004-4). NH Pub Co.

Felzer, Ron. High Sierra Hiking Guide to Hetch Hetchy. Winnett, Thomas, ed. LC 72-89914. (High Sierra Hiking Guide Ser: Vol. 12). (Illus., Orig.). 1973. pap. 4.95 (ISBN 0-911824-24-3). Wilderness.

--High Sierra Hiking Guide to Mineral King. 2nd ed. Winnett, Thomas, ed. LC 80-50772. (High Sierra Hiking Guide Ser.: No. 8). (Illus.). 96p. 1981. pap. 4.95 (ISBN 0-89997-008-7). Wilderness.

Felzer, Ron & Winnett, Thomas. High Sierra Hiking Guide to Hetch Hetchy. 2nd ed. LC 81-50771. (High Sierra Hiking Guide Ser.: No. 12). (Illus.). 96p. 1981. pap. 4.95 (ISBN 0-89997-010-9). Wilderness.

Fleming, John. Desert Hiking Guide. (Illus.). 28p. (Orig.). 1979. pap. 2.50 (ISBN 0-937794-01-5). Nature Trails.

Fletcher, Colin. New Complete Walker. LC 73-20763. 512p. 1974. 13.95 (ISBN 0-394-48099-6). Knopf.

Foothills to Mt. Evans: A Trail Guide. Date not set. price not set. Wordsmiths.

Ford, Daniel. The Country Northward: A Hiker's Journal. LC 76-11306. (Illus.). 1976. 12.50 (ISBN 0-912274-60-3); pap. 6.95 (ISBN 0-912274-77-8). NH Pub Co.

Ganci, Dave. Hiking the Desert. 1979. 12.95 (ISBN 0-8092-7617-8); pap. 6.95 (ISBN 0-8092-7615-1). Contemp Bks.

Garvey, Edward B. Appalachian Hiker. LC 70-146063. (Illus.). 397p. 1971. pap. 6.00 (ISBN 0-912660-01-5). Appalachian Bks.

--Hiking Trails in the Mid-Atlantic States. 1976. pap. 6.95 (ISBN 0-8092-7291-1). Contemp Bks.

Geery, Daniel. Wasatch Trails, Vol. 2. (Illus., Orig.). 1977. pap. 2.50 (ISBN 0-915272-10-5). Wasatch Pubs.

Gibson, John. Fifty Hikes in Maine. LC 74-33818. (Illus.). 160p. 1976. pap. 6.95 (ISBN 0-912274-48-4). NH Pub Co.

--Go Light. LC 80-12051. (Illus.). 128p. (Orig.). 1980. pap. 4.95 (ISBN 0-89621-057-X). Thorndike Pr.

Goldmark, Pauline & Hopkins, Marycompiled by. The Gypsy Trail: An Anthology for Campers. rev. & enl. ed. LC 72-460. (Granger Index Reprint Ser.). Repr. of 1914 ed. 19.00 (ISBN 0-8369-6364-4). Arno.

Green, David. A Pacific Crest Odyssey. Winnett, Thomas, ed. (Illus., Orig.). 1980. pap. 7.95 (ISBN 0-911824-91-X). Wilderness.

Grodin, Joseph R., et al. High Sierra Hiking Guide to Silver Lake. 2nd ed. Winnett, Thomas, ed. LC 78-50994. (High Sierra Hiking Guide Ser.: Vol. 17). (Illus., Orig.). 1970. pap. 4.95 (ISBN 0-911824-73-1). Wilderness.

Hagen, Mary. Hiking Trails of Northern Colorado. (Illus.). 1979. pap. 5.95 (ISBN 0-87108-532-1). Pruett.

Hardy, Gerry & Hardy, Sue. Fifty Hikes in Connecticut. LC 77-94006. (Illus.). 1978. 12.50 (ISBN 0-912274-90-5); pap. 6.95 (ISBN 0-912274-86-7). NH Pub Co.

Hart, John. Hiking the Bigfoot Country: Exploring the Wildlands of Northern California & Southern Oregon. LC 75-1149. (Totebook Ser). (Illus.). 398p. 1975. pap. 8.95 (ISBN 0-87156-127-1). Sierra.

--Hiking the Great Basin: Country of California, Oregon, Nevada, & Utah. (Totebooks Ser.). (Illus.). 320p. (Orig.). 1981. pap. 9.95 (ISBN 0-87156-245-6). Sierra.

Henderson, John. Off the Beaten Path: Short Hikes in the White Mountains. LC 76-51803. (Illus., Orig.). 1979. pap. 4.95 (ISBN 0-9602802-0-0). Glen-Bartlett.

Henley, Martin. Orienteering. rev ed. (EP Sport Ser.). (Illus.). 119p. 1978. 12.95 (ISBN 0-8069-9136-4, Pub. by EP Publishing England); pap. 6.95 (ISBN 0-8069-9138-0). Sterling.

Henley, Thomas. Hiking Trails in the Northeast. 1976. pap. 5.95 (ISBN 0-8092-7280-6). Contemp Bks.

Hiking Notes. LC 76-29521. 1976. flexible plastic 2.95 (ISBN 0-916890-45-7). Mountaineers.

Hiking Skill Book. (Illus.). 1977. pap. 0.50x (ISBN 0-8395-6589-5, 6589). BSA.

Hill, Mike. Hikers' & Climbers' Guide to the Sandia Mountains. (Illus.). 1977. pap. 5.95 (ISBN 0-933004-02-8). Adobe Pr.

Hoffman, Carolyn. Fifty Hikes in Eastern Pennsylvania. (Illus., Orig.). Date not set. pap. 7.95 (ISBN 0-89725-018-4). NH Pub Co.

Jenkins, J. C. Self-Propelled in the Southern Sierra, Vol. 1. Winnett, Thomas, ed. LC 74-27689. (Illus., Orig.). 1978. pap. 9.95 (ISBN 0-911824-39-1). Wilderness.

Jenkins, J. C. & Robinson, John W. High Sierra Hiking Guide to Kern Peak-Olancha. 2nd ed. Winnett, Thomas, ed. (High Sierra Hiking Guide Ser.: Vol. 13). (Illus.). 1979. pap. 4.95 (ISBN 0-911824-86-3). Wilderness.

Jones, J. Sydney. Bike & Hike: Sixty Tours Around Great Britain & Ireland. (Illus., Orig.). 1978. pap. 3.95 (ISBN 0-8467-0439-0, Pub. by Two Continents). Hippocrene Bks.

Kelsey, Joe. Climbing & Hiking in the Wind River Mountains: Wyoming. LC 79-23882. (Illus.). 400p. (Totebook). 1980. pap. 8.95 (ISBN 0-87156-267-7). Sierra.

Kelsey, Robert J. Walking in the Wild: Complete Guide to Hiking & Backpacking. (Funk & W Bk.). (Illus.). 384p. 1973. pap. 2.50 (ISBN 0-308-10098-0, F86). T Y Crowell.

Kemsley, William, ed. The Whole Hiker's Handbook. LC 79-88627. (Illus.). 1979. 17.95 (ISBN 0-688-03476-4, Quill); pap. 9.95 (ISBN 0-688-08476-1). Morrow.

Kibling, Mary L. Twenty-Five Walks in the Dartmouth-Lake Sunapee Region of New Hampshire. LC 78-74156. (Illus.). 1979. pap. 4.95 (ISBN 0-89725-003-6). NH Pub Co.

Larson, Randy. Illustrated Backpacking & Hiking Dictionary for Young People. (Treehouse Bks). (Illus.). (gr. 4 up). 1981. pap. 2.50 (ISBN 0-686-72017-2). P-H.

Love, Ken & Love, Ruth. A Guide to the Trails of Badger Creek. rev. ed. (Illus., Orig.) 1980. pap. 4.95 (ISBN 0-913140-38-4). Signpost Bk Pub.

Lowe, Don & Lowe, Roberta. Sixty Two Hiking Trails. 1979. pap. 7.95 (ISBN 0-911518-56-8). Touchstone Pr.

McKinney, John. A Day Hiker's Guide to Southern California. 160p. (Orig.). 1981. pap. 8.95 (ISBN 0-88496-163-X). Capra Pr.

Manning, Harvey. Footsore Four: Walks & Hikes Around Puget Sound. LC 77-23727. (Footsore Ser.). (Illus.). 240p. (Orig.). 1979. pap. 5.95 (ISBN 0-916890-81-3). Mountaineers.

--Footsore One: Walks & Hikes Around Puget Sound. LC 77-23727. (Footsore Ser.). (Illus.). 216p. (Orig.). 1977. pap. 5.95 (ISBN 0-916890-53-8). Mountaineers.

--Footsore Three: Walks & Hikes Around Puget Sound. LC 77-23727. (Footsore Ser.). (Illus.). 232p. (Orig.). 1978. pap. 5.95 (ISBN 0-916890-65-1). Mountaineers.

--Footsore Two: Walks & Hikes Around Puget Sound. LC 77-23727. (Footsore Ser.). (Illus.). 224p. (Orig.). 1978. pap. 5.95 (ISBN 0-916890-54-6). Mountaineers.

Mansfield, Kelly, ed. Best Hiking Trails in the United States. (Illus.). 1977. 6.95 (ISBN 0-8092-7290-3). Contemp Bks.

Mass-Rhode Island Guidebook Committee, ed. AMC Massachusetts-Rhode Island Trail Guide. 4th ed. LC 78-108996. (Illus.). 1978. pap. 9.95 (ISBN 0-910146-11-X). Appalach Mtn.

Maughan, Jackie J. & Puddicombe, Ann. Hiking the Back Country. 240p. (Orig.). 1981. pap. 9.95 (ISBN 0-8117-2170-1). Stackpole.

Merrill, Bill. The Hiker's & Backpacker's Handbook. LC 70-146063. (Illus.). 320p. 1972. pap. 2.95 (ISBN 0-668-02625-1). Arco.

Michigan United Conservation Clubs. Michigan Hiking & Skiing Trails. 1979. 1.75 (ISBN 0-686-65681-4). Mich United Conserv.

Mohn, Peter B. Hiking. LC 75-16088. (Back to Nature Ser.). (gr. 4). 1975. PLB 6.95 (ISBN 0-913940-27-5). Crestwood Hse.

Mohney, Russ. Wintering: The Outdoor Book for Cold Weather Ventures. LC 76-18942. (Packit Ser.). 1976. pap. 2.95 (ISBN 0-8117-2270-8). Stackpole.

Morris, Larry A. Hiking the Grand Canyon & Havasupai. (Illus.). 96p. 1981. pap. 5.95 (ISBN 0-89404-053-7). Aztex.

Mueller, Betty. Packrat Papers, No. 2: Tips on Food (& Other Stuff) for Hikers & Campers. (Illus.). 1977. pap. 3.95 (ISBN 0-913140-20-1). Signpost Bk Pubns.

Nelson, Dick & Nelson, Sharon. Hiker's Guide to Glacier National Park. (Illus.). 112p. (Orig.). 1978. pap. 5.95 (ISBN 0-915030-24-1). Tecolote Pr.

--Hiker's Guide to the Superstition Mountains. (Illus.). 108p. (Orig.). 1978. pap. 4.95 (ISBN 0-915030-21-7). Tecolote Pr.

--Short Hikes & Strolls in Glacier National Park. (Illus.). 48p. (Orig.). (gr. 7-12). 1978. pap. 2.95 (ISBN 0-915030-23-3). Tecolote Pr.

Nolan, Riall, et al. Mountain Walking in Papua New Guinea. new ed. (Illus., Orig.). Date not set. pap. cancelled (ISBN 0-913140-32-5). Signpost Bk Pub.

Olmsted, Nancy. To Walk with a Quiet Mind: Hikes in the Woodlands, Parks & Beaches of the San Francisco Bay Area. LC 75-1053. (Totebook Ser.). (Illus.). 256p. 1975. pap. 6.95 (ISBN 0-87156-125-5). Sierra.

Paulsen, Gary & Morris, John. Hiking & Backpacking. LC 78-14535. (Illus.). 160p. (gr. 7 up). 1978. PLB 7.29 (ISBN 0-671-32899-9). Messner.

Pierce, Robert & Pierce, Margaret. High Sierra Hiking Guide to Merced Peak. Winnett, Thomas, ed. LC 72-89915. (High Sierra Hiking Guide Ser: Vol. 11). (Illus., Orig.). 1973. pap. 4.95 (ISBN 0-911824-23-5). Wilderness.

Pierce, Robert & Pierce, Margaret, eds. High Sierra Hiking Guide to Yosemite. 3rd ed. LC 74-75768. (High Sierra Hiking Guide Ser: Vol. 1). (Illus., Orig.). 1974. pap. 4.95 (ISBN 0-911824-34-0). Wilderness.

Rambling & Youth Hostelling. 1976. pap. 2.50 (ISBN 0-8277-4897-3). British Bk Ctr.

Rathbun, Linda & Ringrose, Linda. Foothills to Mount Evans: A Trail Guide. (Illus.). 80p. (Orig.). 1980. pap. 5.00 (ISBN 0-9606108-0-4). Wordsmiths.

Riley, Michael J. & Cremer, Robert. Basic Orienteering. 1979. 9.95 (ISBN 0-8092-7643-7); pap. 4.95 (ISBN 0-8092-7642-9). Contemp Bks.

Roberts, Harry. Movin' Out: Equipment & Technique for Hikers. rev ed. LC 78-26618. (Illus.). 1979. pap. 5.95 (ISBN 0-913276-29-4). Stone Wall Pr.

Roberts, Harry N. Movin' on: Equipment & Technique of Winter Hikers. LC 77-14740. (Illus.). 1977. pap. 4.95 (ISBN 0-913276-24-3). Stone Wall Pr.

Robinson, John W. High Sierra Hiking Guide to Mt. Goddard. 2nd ed. Winnett, Thomas, ed. (High Sierra Hiking Guide Ser.: Vol. 10). (Illus., Orig.). 1980. pap. 4.95 (ISBN 0-89997-002-8). Wilderness.

Rutstrum, Calvin. Hiking Back to Health. LC 80-19803. (Illus.). 136p. (Orig.). 1980. pap. 5.95 (ISBN 0-934802-06-8). ICS Bks.

Sadlier, Paul & Sadlier, Ruth. Fifty Hikes in Massachusetts. LC 74-33817. (Illus.). 160p. 1975. pap. 7.95 (ISBN 0-912274-47-6). NH Pub Co.

Schad, Jerry. BackCountry Roads & Trails, San Diego County. (Illus.). 1977. pap. 4.95 (ISBN 0-911518-46-0). Touchstone Pr Ore.

Schaffer, Jeffrey P. The Tahoe Sierra. rev. ed. Winnett, Thomas, ed. LC 78-65937. (Trail Guide Ser). (Illus., Orig.). 1979. pap. 9.95 (ISBN 0-911824-75-8). Wilderness.

Schaffer, Jeffrey P., et al. Pacific Crest Trail, Vol. 1: California. rev. ed. LC 76-1354. (Illus., Orig.). 1977. pap. 11.95 (ISBN 0-911824-58-8). Wilderness.

Schneider, Bill. The Hiker's Guide to Montana. LC 79-55480. 208p. (Orig.). 1979. pap. text ed. 6.95 (ISBN 0-934318-01-8). Falcon Pr MT.

Selters, Andrew. High Sierra Hiking Guide to Triple Divide Peak. Winnett, Thomas, ed. LC 79-57596. (High Sierra Hiking Guide Ser.: No. 20). (Illus., Orig.). 1980. pap. 4.95 (ISBN 0-911824-94-4). Wilderness.

Sharp, David. Walking in the Countryside. LC 77-85013. 1978. 7.50 (ISBN 0-7153-7495-8). David & Charles.

Slater, Leslie G. Pocket Compass. (Pocket Hand Book Vol. 1). (Illus.). Date not set. pap. 1.00 (ISBN 0-686-10127-8). Terry Pub.

Smith, Robert. Hiking Hawaii. Winnett, Thomas, ed. LC 79-93247. (Wilderness Press Trail Guide Ser.). (Illus.). 112p. (Orig.). 1981. write for info. (ISBN 0-89997-000-1). Wilderness Pr.

--Hiking Hawaii: The Big Island. 2nd ed. Winnett, Thomas, ed. LC 79-93248. (Wilderness Press Trail Guide Ser.). (Illus.). 112p. 1980. pap. 4.95 (ISBN 0-89997-000-1). Wilderness Pr.

--Hiking Kauai: The Garden Isle. 2nd ed. Winnett, Thomas, ed. LC 79-63922. (Wilderness Press Trail Guide Ser.). (Illus.). 112p. 1979. pap. 4.95 (ISBN 0-911824-89-8). Wilderness Pr.

--Hiking Maui: The Valley Isle. 2nd ed. Winnett, Thomas, ed. LC 79-93159. (Wilderness Press Trail Guide Ser.). (Illus.). 144p. 1980. pap. 4.95 (ISBN 0-911824-99-5). Wilderness Pr.

--Hiking Oahu. 2nd ed. LC 80-53464. 122p. 1980. pap. 4.95 (ISBN 0-89997-006-0). Wilderness Pr.

Spring, Ira & Edwards, Harvey. One Hundred Hikes in the Alps. LC 78-71668. (Illus.). 1979. pap. 7.95 (ISBN 0-916890-72-4). Mountaineers.

Sterling, E. M. Trips & Trails, 1. 2nd ed. LC 67-26501. (Illus.). 216p. 1978. pap. 6.95 (ISBN 0-916890-09-0). Mountaineers.

--Trips & Trails, 2. 2nd ed. LC 67-26501. (Illus.). 224p. 1978. pap. 6.95 (ISBN 0-916890-13-9). Mountaineers.

Sullivan, Jerry & Daniel, Glenda. Hiking Trails in the Midwest. LC 74-173586. (Illus.). 224p. 1974. pap. 6.95 (ISBN 0-8092-7245-8). Contemp Bks.
--Hiking Trails in the Southern Mountains. LC 75-9297. (Illus.). 256p. 1975. pap. 6.95 (ISBN 0-8092-7318-7). Contemp Bks.
Thomas, Lowell J. & Sanderson, Joy L. First Aid for Backpackers & Campers. LC 77-212197. (Illus.). 1979. 7.95 (ISBN 0-03-021106-9); pap. 3.95 (ISBN 0-03-021111-5). HR&W.
Thwaites, Tom. Fifty Hikes in Central Pennsylvania. LC 78-71141. (Illus.). 1979. pap. 6.95 (ISBN 0-89725-002-8). NH Pub Co.
Toner, Mike & Toner, Pat. Florida by Paddle & Pack: Forty-Five Wilderness Trails in Central & South Florida. LC 78-25571. (Illus.). 1979. pap. 6.95 (ISBN 0-916224-37-6). Banyan Bks.
Wadsworth, Bruce. An Adirondack Sampler: Day Hikes for All Seasons. LC 79-55153. (Illus.). 128p. 1979. pap. 5.95 (ISBN 0-935272-00-3). ADK Mtn Club.
Waterman, Laura & Waterman, Guy. Backwoods Ethics: Environmental Concerns for Hikers & Campers. LC 79-16684. (Illus.). 192p. (Orig.). 1979. pap. 6.95 (ISBN 0-913276-28-6). Stone Wall Pr.
Winnett, Thomas. High Sierra Hiking Guide to Mono Craters. LC 72-89916. (High Sierra Hiking Guide Ser: Vol. 15). (Illus., Orig.). 1975. pap. 4.95 (ISBN 0-911824-16-2). Wilderness.
--The John Muir Trail. LC 77-88642. (Trail Guide Ser.). (Illus., Orig.). 1978. pap. 5.95 (ISBN 0-911824-64-2). Wilderness.
Winnett, Thomas & Schaffer, Jeffrey P. High Sierra Hiking Guide to Tuolumne Meadows. 3rd ed. LC 77-70562. (High Sierra Hiking Guide Ser.: No. 4). (Illus., Orig.). 1977. pap. 4.95 (ISBN 0-911824-59-6). Wilderness.
Wood, Amos L. Hiking Trails in the Pacific Northwest. (Illus.). 1977. 5.95 (ISBN 0-8092-7238-5). Contemp Bks.
Woods, Bill & Woods, Erin. Bicycling the Backroads Around Puget Sound. 2nd ed. LC 72-92589. (Illus.). 224p. (Orig.). 1981. pap. 6.95 (ISBN 0-89886-039-3). Mountaineers.
Wuertz-Schaefer, Karin. Hiking Virginia's National Forests. LC 77-70414. (Illus.). 204p. 1977. pap. 6.95 (ISBN 0-914788-05-1). East Woods.
Wyckoff, Jerome. The Adirondack Landscape. LC 67-28445. (Illus.). 1967. pap. 2.25 (ISBN 0-935272-08-9). ADK Mtn Club.

HILARIUS, SAINT, BP. OF POITIERS, d. 367

Geoffroy Saint-Hilaire, Isidore. Vie, Travaux et Doctrine Scientifique D'etienne Geoffroy Sant-Hilaire. Repr. of 1847 ed. 132.00 (ISBN 0-8287-0371-X). Clearwater Pub.

HILBERT ALGEBRAS

see also Functional Analysis; Von Neumann Algebras

Boltyanskiy, Vladimir G. Hilbert's Third Problem. LC 77-19011. (Scripta Mathematics Ser.). 1978. 19.95 (ISBN 0-470-26289-3). Halsted Pr.
Iarrobino, Anthony. Punctual Hilbert Schemes. LC 77-3560. (Memoirs: No. 188). 1977. pap. 11.20 (ISBN 0-8218-2188-1). Am Math.
Kastler, D. C-Algebras & Their Applications of Statistical Mechanics & Quantum Field Theory. 1976. 49.00 (ISBN 0-7204-0449-5, North-Holland). Elsevier.
Sah, C. H. Hilbert's Third Problem. new ed. (Research Notes in Mathematics Ser.). 1979. pap. cancelled (ISBN 0-8224-8426-9). Pitman Learning.
Sah, Chin-Han. Hilbert's Third Problem: Congruence. (Research Notes in Mathematics Ser.: No. 33). 188p. (Orig.). 1979. pap. text ed. 19.95 (ISBN 0-273-08426-7). Pitman Pub MA.

HILBERT SPACE

Akheizer, N. I. Theory of Linear Operators in Hilbert Space, 2 vols. Everitt, N., ed. Dawson, E. R., tr. (Monographs & Studies: No. 10). 1980. Vol. I, 352p. text ed. 79.95 (ISBN 0-273-08495-X); Vol. II, 272p. text ed. 69.95 (ISBN 0-273-08496-8). Pitman Pub MA.
Akhiezer, N. I. & Glazman, I. M. Theory of Linear Operators in Hilbert Space, 2 Vols. Nestell, Merlynd, tr. LC 60-53138. Vol. 1. 12.50 (ISBN 0-8044-4022-0); Vol. 2. 16.50 (ISBN 0-8044-4023-9). Ungar.
Arveson, W. An Invitation to C-Algebras. LC 76-3656. 1976. 17.60 (ISBN 0-387-90176-0). Springer-Verlag.
Aubin, Jean-Pierre. Applied Functional Analysis. LC 78-20896. (Pure & Applied Mathematics: Texts, Monographs & Tracts). 1979. 30.00 (ISBN 0-471-02149-0, Pub. by Wiley-Interscience). Wiley.
Bachar, J. M. & Hadwin, D. W., eds. Hilbert Space Operators: Proceedings, University of California Long Beach, LB CA, June 20-24, 1977. (Lecture Notes in Mathematics: Vol. 693). 1979. pap. 11.30 (ISBN 0-387-09097-5). Springer-Verlag.
Balakrishnan, A. V. Applied Functional Analysis. LC 75-25932. (Applications of Mathematics: Vol. 3). 605p. 1976. 26.00 (ISBN 0-387-90157-4). Springer-Verlag.
Banach, Stefan. Theorie Des Operations Lineaires. 2nd ed. LC 63-21849. (Fr). 9.95 (ISBN 0-8284-0110-1). Chelsea Pub.
Berberian, Sterling K. An Introduction to Hilbert Space. 2nd ed. LC 75-29231. 206p. 1976. text ed. 9.95 (ISBN 0-8284-0287-6). Chelsea Pub.
Brezis, Haim. Operateurs Maximaux Monotones: Et Semi-Groupes de Contractions dans les Espaces de Hilbert. LC 72-95271. (North-Holland Mathematics Studies: No. 5). 132p. 1973. pap. 29.50 (ISBN 0-444-10430-5, North-Holland). Elsevier.
Brodskii, M. S. Triangular & Jordan Representations of Linear Operators. LC 74-162998. (Translations of Mathematical Monographs: Vol. 32). 1972. 28.80 (ISBN 0-8218-1582-2, MMONO-32). Am Math.
De la Harpe, P. Classical Banach-Lie Algebras & Banach-Lie Groups of Operators in Hilbert Space. LC 72-88729. (Lecture Notes in Mathematics: Vol. 285). 160p. 1972. pap. 6.30 (ISBN 0-387-05984-9). Springer-Verlag.
Dirac, P. A. Spinors in Hilbert Space. LC 74-18371. 91p. 1974. 17.50 (ISBN 0-306-30798-7, Plenum Pr). Plenum Pub.
Dolezal, V. Nonlinear Networks. 1977. 39.00 (ISBN 0-444-41571-8). Elsevier.
Friedrichs, K. O. Perturbation of Spectra in Hilbert Space. LC 60-12712. (Lectures in Applied Mathematics Ser.: Vol. 3). 1967. Repr. of 1965 ed. 23.60 (ISBN 0-8218-1103-7, LAM-3). Am Math.
--Spectral Theory of Operators in Hilbert Space. rev. ed. LC 73-13721. (Applied Mathematical Sciences: Vol. 9). x, 246p. 1981. pap. 19.80 (ISBN 0-387-90076-4). Springer-Verlag.
Fuhrmann, Paul A. Linear Systems & Operators in Hilbert Space. 336p. 1981. text ed. 44.95 (ISBN 0-07-022589-3). McGraw.
Gohberg, I. & Goldberg, S. Basic Operator Theory. 350p. 1981. 14.50 (ISBN 3-7643-3028-7). Birkhauser.
Gohberg, I. C. & Krein, M. G. Theory & Applications of Volterra Operators in Hilbert Space. LC 71-120134. (Translations of Mathematical Monographs: Vol. 24). 1970. 54.80 (ISBN 0-8218-1574-1, MMONO-24). Am Math.
Gross, Leonard. Harmonic Analysis on Hilbert Space. LC 52-42839. (Memoirs: No. 46). 1971. pap. 7.20 (ISBN 0-8218-1246-7, MEMO-46). Am Math.
Gudkov, D. A. & Utkin, G. A. Nine Papers on Hilbert's Sixteenth Problem. LC 78-10201. (American Mathematical Society Translations Ser. 2: Vol. 112). 1978. 36.80 (ISBN 0-8218-3062-7, TRANS2-112). Am Math.
Guichardet, A. Symmetric Hilbert Spaces & Related Topics. LC 72-76390. (Lecture Notes in Mathematics: Vol. 261). 102p. 1972. pap. 7.00 (ISBN 0-387-05803-6). Springer-Verlag.
Halmos, P. R. A Hilbert Space Problem Book. LC 74-10673. (Graduate Texts in Mathematics: Vol. 19). 385p. 1974. 20.00 (ISBN 0-387-90090-X). Springer-Verlag.
Halmos, Paul R. Introduction to Hilbert Space. 2nd ed. LC 57-12834. 7.95 (ISBN 0-8284-0082-2). Chelsea Pub.
Hellwig, G. Differential Operators of Mathematical Physics: An Introduction. 1967. 15.50 (ISBN 0-201-02811-5, Adv Bk Prog). A-W.
Helmberg, Gilbert M. Introduction to Spectral Theory in Hilbert Space. (Applied Mathematics & Mechanics Ser: Vol. 6). 1969. 39.00 (ISBN 0-444-10211-6, North-Holland). Elsevier.
Livshits, M. S. & Yantsevich, A. S. Operator Colligations in Hilbert Spaces. (Scripta Series in Math). 1979. 19.95 (ISBN 0-470-26541-8). Halsted Pr.
Moiseiwitsch, Benjamin L. Integral Equations. LC 76-10282. (Longman Mathematical Texts). (Illus.). 1977. pap. text ed. 11.95x (ISBN 0-582-44288-5). Longman.
Murray, Francis J. Introduction to Linear Transformations in Hilbert Space. 1941. pap. 7.00 (ISBN 0-527-02720-0). Kraus Repr.
Nagy, B. Sz. & Foias, C. Harmonic Analysis of Operators on Hilbert Space. LC 78-97933. 1971. 36.75 (ISBN 0-444-10046-6, North-Holland). Elsevier.
Nagy, Bela Sz. Unitary Dilations of Hilbert Space Operators & Related Topics. LC 73-17332. (CBMS Regional Conference Series in Mathematics: No. 19). 54p. 1974. pap. 9.60 (ISBN 0-8218-1669-1, CBMS-19). Am Math.
Nikodym, Otton M. Mathematical Apparatus for Quantum-Theories. (Grundlehren der Mathematischen Wissenschaften: Vol. 129). 1966. 85.50 (ISBN 0-387-03523-0). Springer-Verlag.
Prugovecki, Eduard. Quantum Mechanics in Hilbert Space. 2nd ed. LC 80-534. (Pure & Applied Mathematics Ser.). 1981. 39.50 (ISBN 0-12-566060-X). Acad Pr.
Putnam, Calvin R. Commutation Properties of Hilbert Space Operators & Related Topics. (Ergebnisse der Mathematik und Ihrer Grenzgebiete: Vol. 36). 1967. 22.50 (ISBN 0-387-03778-0). Springer-Verlag.
Radjavi, H. & Rosenthal, P. Invariant Subspaces. LC 73-77570. (Ergebnisse der Mathematik und Ihrer Gremzgebiete: Vol. 77). (Illus.). 230p. 1973. 32.10 (ISBN 0-387-06217-3). Springer-Verlag.
Reid, Constance. Hilbert. LC 76-97989. (Illus.). 1970. 21.770 (ISBN 0-387-04999-1). Springer-Verlag.
Rektorys, Karel. Variational Methods in Mathematics, Sciences & Engineering. new ed. SNTL, ed. LC 74-80530. 1976. lib. bdg. 71.00 (ISBN 90-277-0488-0, Pub. by Reidel Holland). Kluwer Boston.
Sarason, Donald. H-To-The-P Spaces of Annulus. LC 52-42839. (Memoirs: No. 56). 1978. pap. 11.60 (ISBN 0-8218-1256-4, MEMO-56). Am Math.
Schatten, Robert. Norm Ideals of Completely Continuous Operators. (Ergebnisse der Mathematik und Ihrer Grenzebiete: Vol. 27). 1970. Repr. 26.00 (ISBN 0-387-04806-5). Springer-Verlag.
Simon, Barry. Trace Ideals & Their Applications. LC 78-20867. (London Mathematical Society Lecture Notes Ser.: No. 35). 1979. pap. 16.95x (ISBN 0-521-22286-9). Cambridge U Pr.
Skorohod, A. V. Integration in Hilbert Space. Wickwire, T., tr. from Rus. LC 73-82356. (Ergebnisse der Mathematik und Ihrer Grenzgebiete: Vol. 79). 190p. 1974. 28.80 (ISBN 0-387-06322-6). Springer-Verlag.
Soule, J. L. Linear Operators in Hilbert Space. (Notes on Mathematics & Its Applications Ser). (Orig.). 1968. 18.75 (ISBN 0-677-30170-7). Gordon.
--Operateurs Lineaires Dans l'Espace d'Hilbert. (Cours & Documents de Mathematiques & de Physique Ser.). (Orig., Fr). 1967. 18.75x (ISBN 0-677-50170-6). Gordon.
Stone, M. H. Linear Transformations in Hilbert Space & Their Applications to Analysis. LC 33-2746. (Colloquium Pbns. Ser: Vol. 15). 1979. Repr. of 1974 ed. 45.20 (ISBN 0-8218-1015-4, COLL-15). Am Math.
Takesaki, M. Tomita's Theory of Modular Hilbert Algebras & Its Applications. LC 79-117719. (Lecture Notes in Mathematics: Vol. 128). 1970. pap. 10.70 (ISBN 0-387-04917-7). Springer-Verlag.
Weidmann, J. Linear Operators in Hilbert Spaces. Szuecs, J., tr. from Ger. (Graduate Texts in Mathematics: Vol 68). 400p. 1980. 34.00 (ISBN 0-387-90427-1). Springer-Verlag.

HILDEBRAND, ADOLF VON, 1847-1921

Heilmeyer, Alexander. Adolph Hildebrand. 1971. Repr. of 1902 ed. 25.00 (ISBN 0-403-00626-0). Scholarly.

HILDEGARD, SAINT, 1098?-1178

Singer, Charles. From Magic to Science. 1960. 6.00 (ISBN 0-8446-2944-8). Peter Smith.

HILDEMARUS, MONK OF CIVATE, fl. 833

Schroll, Sr. M. Alfred. Benedictine Monasticism As Reflected in the Warnefrid-Hildemar Commentaries on the Rule. LC 77-140026. (Columbia University. Studies in the Social Sciences: No. 478). Repr. of 1941 ed. 20.00 (ISBN 0-404-51478-2). AMS Pr.

HILDRETH RICHARD, 1807-1865

Emerson, Donald E. Richard Hildreth. LC 78-64201. (Johns Hopkins University. Studies in the Social Sciences. Sixty-Fourth Ser. 1946: 2). Repr. of 1946 ed. 18.50 (ISBN 0-404-61307-1). AMS Pr.

HILL, AARON, 1685-1750

Brewster, Dorothy. Aaron Hill: Poet, Dramatist, Projector. LC 13-21690. Repr. of 1913 ed. 9.00 (ISBN 0-404-01076-8). AMS Pr.

HILL, AMBROSE POWELL, 1825-1865

Hassler, William W. A.P. Hill: Lee's Forgotten General. LC 57-13027. 1957. 11.95 (ISBN 0-8078-0973-X). U of NC Pr.

HILL, BENJAMIN HARVEY, 1823-1882

Pearce, Haywood J. Benjamin A. Hill, Secession & Reconstruction. LC 70-97434. Repr. of 1928 ed. 14.50x (ISBN 0-8371-2727-0, Pub. by Negro U Pr). Greenwood.

HILL, DAVID BENNETT

Bass, Herbert J. I Am a Democrat: The Political Career of David Bennett Hill. LC 61-13986. (Illus.). 1961. 12.95x (ISBN 0-8156-0021-6). Syracuse U Pr.

HILL, DAVID JAYNE, 1850-1932

Parkman, Aubrey L. David Jayne Hill & the Problem of World Peace. LC 72-3530. 293p. 1975. 15.00 (ISBN 0-8387-1259-2). Bucknell U Pr.

HILL, JAMES JEROME, 1838-1916

Bruchey, Stuart, ed. Memoirs of Three Railroad Pioneers. LC 80-1293. 1981. lib. bdg. 15.00x (ISBN 0-405-13763-X). Arno.
Comfort, Mildred M. James J. Hill: Young Empire Builder. (Childhood of Famous Americans Ser.). (Illus.). (gr. 3-7). 1968. 3.95 (ISBN 0-672-50083-3). Bobbs.
Martin, Albro. James J. Hill & the Opening of the Northwest. LC 75-46362. (Illus.). 1976. 25.00 (ISBN 0-19-502070-7). Oxford U Pr.
Pyle, Joseph G. The Life of James J. Hill, 2 vols. 16.00 (ISBN 0-8446-1369-X). Peter Smith.

HILL, JOE

see Hillstrom, Joseph, 1879-1915

HILL, STEPHEN DAVIS, MAY 4-AUG. 14, 1971

Hill, Mary V. Angel Children: Those Who Die Before Accountability. LC 73-75397. (Illus.). 70p. (Orig.). 1973. pap. 5.25 (ISBN 0-88290-017-X). Horizon Utah.

HILL FAMILY

Edgar, Betsy J. The McNeel Family Record. (Illus.). 1967. 12.50 (ISBN 0-87012-063-8). B J Edgar.

HILLARY, EDMUND, SIR

Hillary, Edmund. From the Ocean to the Sky. (Illus.). 1979. 12.95 (ISBN 0-670-33172-4). Viking Pr.
Kelly, Robert. For Those in Peril: The Life & Times of Sir William Hillary Founder of the R. N. L. J. 160p. 1979. 25.00x (ISBN 0-904980-27-8, Pub. by Shearwater England). State Mutual Bk.
May, Julian. Hillary & Tenzing: Conquerors of Mt. Everest. LC 72-85045. 40p. (gr. 2-5). 1972. PLB 5.90 (ISBN 0-87191-219-8). Creative Ed.

HILLBILLY MUSICIANS

see Country Musicians

HILLEL, THE ELDER, d. ca. 10

Blumenthal, Aaron H. If I Am Only for Myself: The Story of Hillel. 1973. 3.75x (ISBN 0-8381-0219-0). United Syn Bk.
Buchler, Adolph. Ancient Pious Men: Types of Jewish Palestinian Piety from 70 B. C. E. to 70 C. E. 1922. 15.00x (ISBN 0-87068-030-7). Ktav.

HILLHOUSE, JAMES ABRAHAM, 1789-1841

Hazelrigg, Charles T. American Literary Pioneer: A Biographical Study of James A. Hillhouse. 1978. Repr. of 1953 ed. lib. bdg. 30.00 (ISBN 0-8495-2228-5). Arden Lib.

HILLMAN-MINX (AUTOMOBILE)

see Automobiles, Foreign–Types–Hillman-Minx

HILLQUIT, MORRIS, 1869-1933

Ham, F. Gerald & Warmbrodt, Carole Sue, eds. The Morris Hillquit Papers: Guide to a Microfilm Edition. LC 74-632298. (Guides to Historical Resources Ser.). 1969. pap. 2.00 (ISBN 0-87020-109-3). State Hist Soc Wis.
Pratt, Norma F. Morris Hillquit: A Political History of an American Jewish Socialist. LC 78-55349. (Illus.). 1979. lib. bdg. 18.50x (ISBN 0-313-20526-4, PMH/). Greenwood.

HILLSTROM, JOSEPH, 1879-1915

Foner, Philip S. Case of Joe Hill. LC 65-26742. (Illus.). 1965. pap. 1.95 (ISBN 0-7178-0022-9). Intl Pub Co.

HILTON, JAMES, 1900-1954

Cliff's Notes Editors. Lost Horizon Notes. (Orig.). pap. 1.95 (ISBN 0-8220-0771-1). Cliffs.

HILTON HEAD ISLAND

Daniels, Jonathan. The Gentlemanly Serpent & Other Columns from a Newspaperman in Paradise. Hilton, Ralph, ed. LC 74-22077. 1974. 14.95 (ISBN 0-87249-319-9). U of SC Pr.
Martin, Josephine W., ed. Dear Sister: Letters Written on Hilton Head Island 1867. 1978. 7.95 (ISBN 0-685-27175-7). Beaufort.

HIMA

see Bahima (African People)

HIMALAYA MOUNTAINS

Ali, Salim. Fieldguide to the Birds of the Eastern Himalayas. (Illus.). 1978. 15.95x (ISBN 0-19-560595-0). Oxford U Pr.
Anderson, Emma D. & Campbell, Mary J. In the Shadow of the Himalayas. 1942. 10.00 (ISBN 0-8495-0226-8). Arden Lib.
Armington, Stan. Trekking in the Himalayas. (Illus.). 1979. pap. 5.95 (ISBN 0-908086-06-7). Hippocrene Bks.
Atkinson, E. T. Religion of the Himalayas. 1974. Repr. 15.00x (ISBN 0-8426-0773-0). Verry.
Atkinson, Edwin T., ed. Fauna of the Himalayas Containing Species of Kumaon, Garhwal, Nepal & Tibet. 266p. 1974. Repr. text ed. 22.50x (ISBN 0-8426-0808-7). Verry.
Baume, Louis. Sivalaya: Explorations of the Eight-Thousand Metre Peaks of the Himalaya. LC 79-20964. 348p. 1979. 12.95 (ISBN 0-916890-97-X); pap. 9.95 (ISBN 0-916890-71-6). Mountaineers.
Bernbaum, Edwin. The Way to Shambhala. LC 78-1234. (Illus.). 336p. (Orig.). 1980. pap. 7.95 (ISBN 0-385-12794-4, Anch). Doubleday.
Braham, Trevor. Himalayan Odyssey. 1974. 17.95 (ISBN 0-04-910054-8). Allen Unwin.
Burdsall, Richard L. & Emmons, Arthur B., 3rd. Men Against the Clouds. LC 79-25369. (Illus.). 1980. pap. 9.95 (ISBN 0-916890-93-7). Mountaineers.
Charak, Sukhder S. History & Culture of Himalayan States, Vol. 1. (Himachal Pradesh Ser.: Pt. 1). (Illus.). 1979. text ed. 35.00x (ISBN 0-391-01047-6). Humanities.

Charak, Sukhdev S. History & Culture of the Himalayan States, Vol. 3: Himachal Pradesh, Pt. 3. 385p. 1979. text ed. 35.00x (ISBN 0-391-01747-0). Humanities.

Douglas, William O. Exploring the Himalaya. (World Landmark Ser.: No. 36). (Illus.). (gr. 7-9). 1958. PLB 4.39 (ISBN 0-686-72047-4). Random.

Downs, Hugh R. Rhythms of a Himalayan Village. LC 79-2983. (Illus.). 240p. (Orig.). 1980. pap. 9.95 (ISBN 0-06-250240-9). Har-Row.

Forster, Elizabeth. Himalayan Solo. 220p. 1981. 20.00x (ISBN 0-904614-03-4, Pub. by Nelson Ltd). State Mutual Bk.

Gill, M. S. Himalayan Wonderland: Travels in Lahaul-Spiti. (Illus.). 1979. 11.95x (ISBN 0-7069-0820-1, Pub. by Vikas India). Advent NY.

--Himalayan Wonderland: Travels in Lahul-Spiti. (Illus.). 1974. 7.50x (ISBN 0-7069-0820-1). Intl Bk Dist.

Hara, Hiroshi. The Flora of Eastern Himalaya: Third Report. (Illus.). 450p. 1975. 43.00x (ISBN 0-86008-143-5, Pub. by U of Tokyo Pr). Intl Schol Bk Serv.

Keay, John. The Gilgit Game: The Explorers of the Western Himalayas, 1865-1895. (Illus.). 1979. 17.50 (ISBN 0-208-01774-7, Archon). Shoe String.

--When Men & Mountains Meet: Explorers of the Western Himalayas 1820-75. (Illus.). 1978. 18.50 (ISBN 0-7195-3334-1). Transatlantic.

Khosla, G. G. Himalayan Circuit: The Story of a Journey in the Inner Himalayas. 1956. 12.50 (ISBN 0-8495-3128-4). Arden Lib.

Lall, J. S. & Moddie, A. D., eds. The Himalaya: Aspects of Change. (Illus.). 400p. 1981. 29.95x (ISBN 0-19-561254-X). Oxford U Pr.

MacDonald-Bayne, M. Beyond the Himalayas. 69.95 (ISBN 0-87968-063-6). Gordon Pr.

Matthiessen, Peter. The Snow Leopard. 1979. pap. 3.50 (ISBN 0-553-12343-2). Bantam.

--The Snow Leopard. 1978. 12.95 (ISBN 0-670-65374-8). Viking Pr.

Nicolson, Nigel. The Himalayas. (The World's Wild Places Ser.). (Illus.). 1975. 12.95 (ISBN 0-8094-2021-X). Time-Life.

--The Himalayas. (The World's Wild Places Ser.). (Illus.). 1978. lib. bdg. 11.97 (ISBN 0-686-51019-4). Silver.

Parmar, Y. S. Polyandry in the Himalayas. 1975. 15.00 (ISBN 0-7069-0354-4, Pub. by Vikas India). Advent NY.

Peissel, Michel. Zanskar: The Hidden Kingdom. (Illus.). 1979. 12.95 (ISBN 0-525-24030-6). Dutton.

Rahul, Ram. The Himalaya As a Frontier. 1978. 10.95 (ISBN 0-7069-0564-4, Pub. by Vikas India). Advent NY.

--The Himalaya As a Frontier. 1978. 10.00x (ISBN 0-8364-0208-1). South Asia Bks.

--Himalaya Borderland. 1970. 7.00x (ISBN 0-8426-0010-8). Verry.

Reid, Mayne. The Cliff Climber or the Lone Home in the Himalyas. Repr. of 1889 ed. lib. bdg. 20.00 (ISBN 0-8495-4532-3). Arden Lib.

Rowell, Galen. Many People Come, Looking, Looking. LC 80-19394. (Illus.). 176p. 1980. 30.00 (ISBN 0-916890-86-4). Mountaineers.

Schaller, George B. Stones of Silence: Journeys in the Himalaya. (Illus.). 1980. 15.95 (ISBN 0-670-67140-1). Viking Pr.

Sharma, T. C. & Majumdar, D. N., eds. Eastern Himalayas: A Study on Anthropology & Tribalism. 221p. 1980. 21.00 (ISBN 0-89684-262-2, Pub. by Cosmo Pubns India). Orient Bk Dist.

Shirakawa, Yoshikazu. The Himalayas. (Illus.). 300p. 1973. 125.00 (ISBN 0-8109-0162-5). Abrams.

Skirakawa, Yoshikazu. The Himalayas. concise ed. (Illus.). 1977. 20.00 (ISBN 0-8109-1051-9). Abrams.

Von Furer-Haimendorf, Christoph. Himalayan Traders. LC 75-755. (Illus.). 325p. 1975. 21.50 (ISBN 0-312-37310-4). St Martin.

HIMWICH, HAROLD EDWIN, 1894-- BIBLIOGRAPHY

Himwich, W. A. & Schade, J. P. Horizons in Neuropsychopharmacology. (Progress in Brain Research: Vol. 16). 1965. 73.25 (ISBN 0-444-40287-X, North Holland). Elsevier.

HINDEMITH, PAUL, 1895-1963

Kemp, Ian. Hindemith. (Oxford Studies of Composers: No. 6). (Illus.). 1970. pap. 7.95x (ISBN 0-19-314118-3). Oxford U Pr.

Skelton, Geoffrey. Paul Hindemith: The Man Behind the Music. (Illus.). 1977. 10.00 (ISBN 0-87597-107-5, Crescendo). Taplinger.

HINDENBURG, PAUL VON, PRES. GERMANY, 1847-1934

Goldsmith, Margaret & Voigt, Frederick. Hindenberg. LC 72-1289. (Select Bibliography Reprint Ser.). 1972. Repr. of 1930 ed. 18.00 (ISBN 0-8369-6826-3). Arno.

Kitchen, Martin. The Silent Dictatorship: The Politics of the German High Command Under Hindenburg & Ludendorff, 1916-1918. LC 76-16055. 1976. text ed. 29.50x (ISBN 0-8419-0277-1). Holmes & Meier.

Von Hindenburg, Paul. Out of My Life, 2 vols. in 1. Holt, F. A., tr. from Ger. LC 74-22303. 1979. Repr. of 1921 ed. 23.00 (ISBN 0-86527-146-1). Fertig.

HINDENBURG (AIR-SHIP)

Boning, Richard A. Horror Overhead. (Incredible Ser). (Illus.). (gr. 5-11). 1973. PLB 5.95 (ISBN 0-87966-105-4, Pub. by Dexter & Westbrook). B Loft.

Mooney, Michael M. The Hindenburg. LC 75-184190. (Illus.). 288p. 1972. 8.95 (ISBN 0-396-06502-3). Dodd.

HINDERED ROTATION THEORY

see Molecular Rotation

HINDI LANGUAGE

see also Hindustani Language; Urdu Language

Aggarwal, Narindar K. Bibliography of Studies in Hindi Language & Linguistics. 1978. 14.00x (ISBN 0-8364-0172-7). South Asia Bks.

Bahl, K. C. Studies in the Semantic Structure of Hindi (Synonymous Nouns & Adjectives with Rarana), Vol. 1. 409p. 1974. text ed. 30.00x (ISBN 0-8426-0682-3). Verry.

Bahl, Kali C. Studies in the Semantic Structure of Hindi, Two. 1979. 17.50x (ISBN 0-8364-0513-7). South Asia Bks.

Bahri, Vijal S. & Jagannathan, V. R. Introductory Course in Spoken Hindi. (India Languages & Linguistics Ser.). 280p. 1978. 15.95 (ISBN 0-89684-252-5, Pub. by Bahri Pubns India). Orient Bk Dist.

Bender, Ernest & Riccardi, Theodore, Jr. Introductory Hindi Readings. LC 75-133202. 1971. text ed. 12.00x (ISBN 0-8122-7626-4). U of Pa Pr.

Chandola, Anoop. A Systematic Translation of Hindi-Urdu into English. LC 79-127886. 365p. 1970. pap. 5.95x (ISBN 0-8165-0289-7). U of Ariz Pr.

Chaturvedi, Mahendra & Bhola, Nath T. A Practical Hindi-English Dictionary. 700p. 1974. 12.00x (ISBN 0-88386-380-4). South Asia Bks.

Dasgupta, B. Learn Hindi Yourself. 4.50x (ISBN 0-686-00872-3). Colton Bk.

Dwivedi, S. Hindi on Trial. 250p. 1980. text ed. 25.00x (ISBN 0-7069-1210-1, Pub by Vikas India). Advent NY.

Fairbanks, Gordon H. & Misra, Bal G. Spoken & Written Hindi. 504p. 1966. text ed. 19.50x (ISBN 0-8014-0123-2). Cornell U Pr.

Gaeffke, Peter. Untersuchungen Zur Syntax Des Hindi Disputationes Rheno-Trajectinae, Vol. 2. 1967. pap. 34.50x (ISBN 0-686-21231-2). Mouton.

Harris, Richard M. & Sharma, Rama Nath. Basic Hindi Reader. LC 74-91360. 1969. soft bdg. 19.50x (ISBN 0-8014-0534-3). Cornell U Pr.

Hindi-English Dictionary. 17.50 (ISBN 0-87557-033-X, 034-8); large ed. 22.50 (ISBN 0-685-59369-X). Saphrograph.

Hindi Pocket Dictionary, 2 vols. 10.00 set (ISBN 0-685-30576-7). Heinman.

Hook, Peter E. Hindi Structures: Intermediate Level. LC 79-53527. (Michigan Papers on South & Southeast Asia: No. 16). (Illus.). 336p. (Orig.). 1979. pap. 8.50x (ISBN 0-89148-016-1). Ctr S&SE Asian.

Hook, Peter Edwin. Compound Verb in Hindi. LC 74-82629. (Michigan Series in South & Southeast Asian Languages & Linguistics: No. 1). 318p. 1974. pap. 7.50x (ISBN 0-89148-051-X). Ctr S&SE Asian.

Kachru, Yamuna, ed. Aspects of Hindi Grammar. 1980. 12.50x (ISBN 0-8364-0666-4, Pub. by Manohar India). South Asia Bks.

Kellogg, S. H. Grammar of the Hindi Language. 25.00 (ISBN 0-685-47302-3). Heinman.

Learn Hindi for English Speakers. pap. 8.50 (ISBN 0-87557-035-6, 035-6). Saphrograph.

McGregor, R. S. Exercises in Spoken Hindi. (Illus.). 1970. 32.50 (ISBN 0-521-07487-8); tape 49.50 (ISBN 0-521-07488-6). Cambridge U Pr.

--An Outline of Hindi Grammar. 304p. 1977. 5.95x (ISBN 0-19-560797-X). Oxford U Pr.

Narulla, S. S. Hindi Language-A Scientific History. 1976. 8.50x (ISBN 0-88386-873-3). South Asia Bks.

Ojha, Ashutosh. Hindi Self-Taught. (Orient Paperbacks Ser.). 315p. 1973. pap. 3.95 (ISBN 0-88253-245-6). Ind-US Inc.

Oldenburg, Veena T. Say It in Hindi. (Say It Ser.). 192p. (Orig.). 1981. pap. 3.50 (ISBN 0-486-23959-4). Dover.

Pathak, R. C. Concise Hindi English Dictionary. 1979. 4.50 (ISBN 0-89744-971-1). Auromere.

--Hindi English Dictionary. 1979. 11.00 (ISBN 0-89744-969-X). Auromere.

Platts Dictionary of Urdu, Classical Hindi & English. 1977. Repr. 34.00x (ISBN 0-8364-0445-9). South Asia Bks.

Platts, John T. A Dictionary of Urdu Classical Hindi & English. LC 78-670100. 1977. Repr. of 1884 ed. 37.50x (ISBN 0-8002-0243-0). Intl Pubns Serv.

Pray, Bruce R. Topics in Hindu-Urdu Grammar. (Research Monograph: No. 1). 1970. 10.00 (ISBN 0-686-23622-X, Ctr South & Southeast Asia Studies). Cellar.

Shanney, A. T. Hindi-English Dictionary: With Pronounciations Romanized. 18.50 (ISBN 0-87559-113-2). Shalom.

Suryakanta. Sanskrit-Hindi-English Dictionary. 1976. 27.50x (ISBN 0-8002-1950-3). Intl Pubns Serv.

HINDI LITERATURE-HISTORY AND CRITICISM

Dwivedi, Ram A. Critical Survey of Hindi Literature. 1966. 7.00x (ISBN 0-8426-1245-9). Verry.

Garcin De Tassy, Joseph H. Histoire De la Litterature Hindouie et Hindoustaine, 3 vols. 2nd ed. (Fr). 1968. Repr. of 1871 ed. 84.00 (ISBN 0-8337-1279-9). B Franklin.

Kumar, Shrawan & Machwe, Prabhar, eds. Hindi Short Stories. Kumar, Shrawan & Machwe, Prabhar, trs. 175p. 1970. pap. 1.80 (ISBN 0-88253-053-4). Ind-US Inc.

McGregor, R. S., tr. from Hindi. Nanddas-the Round Dance of Krishna & Uddhav's Message. (Illus.). 135p. 1973. 15.00x (ISBN 0-87471-356-0). Rowman.

Mishra, Jagdish P. Shakespeare's Impact on Hindi Literature. 1971. 8.25x (ISBN 0-8426-0236-4). Verry.

--Shakespeare's Impact on Hindi Literature. 1970. text ed. 6.50x (ISBN 0-391-02049-8). Humanities.

Narulla, S. S. Hindi Language-A Scientific History. 1976. 8.50x (ISBN 0-88386-873-3). South Asia Bks.

Pandey, Indu P. Hindi Literature: Trends & Traits. 10.00x (ISBN 0-88386-521-1). South Asia Bks.

Ratan, Jai, tr. Contemporary Hindi Short Stories. (Writers Workshop Saffronbird Ser.). 180p. 1975. 12.00 (ISBN 0-88253-518-8); pap. text ed. 4.80 (ISBN 0-88253-517-X). Ind-US Inc.

Roadarmel, Gordon C. A Bibliography of English Source Materials for the Study of Modern Hindi Literature. (Occasional Papers Ser.: No. 4). 1969. 10.00 (ISBN 0-686-23629-7, Ctr South & Southeast Asia Studies). Cellar.

Vedalankar, S. Development of Hindi Prose Literature in the Early Nineteenth Century, 1800-1856 A.D. 1969. 9.00x (ISBN 0-8426-0108-2). Verry.

HINDI POETRY

Bryant, Kenneth E. Poems to the Child-God: Structures & Strategies in the Poetry of Surdas. LC 77-80467. (Center for South & Southeast Asian Studies). 1978. 23.75x (ISBN 0-520-03540-2). U of Cal Pr.

Shastri, J. L., ed. Bhagavata Purana: Part 4. (Ancient Indian Tradition & Mythology Ser.: Vol. 10). 1978. text ed. 18.00 (ISBN 0-8426-1079-0). Verry.

White, Charles S., ed. The Caurasi Pad of Sri Hit Harivams: Introduction, Translation, Notes, & Edited Hindi Text. LC 76-54207. (Asian Studies at Hawaii Ser: No. 16). 1977. pap. text ed. 9.50x (ISBN 0-8248-0359-0). U Pr of Hawaii.

HINDU ARCHITECTURE

see Architecture, Hindu

HINDU ART

see Art, Hindu

HINDU CIVILIZATION

see Civilization, Hindu

HINDU CULTUS

see Cultus, Hindu

HINDU ETHICS

Aiyar, P. S. Evolution of Hindu Moral Ideals. 1977. text ed. 15.00x (ISBN 0-8426-1015-4). Verry.

Crawford, S. C. The Evolution of Hindu Ethical Ideals. LC 75-903625. 1975. 14.00 (ISBN 0-88386-558-0). South Asia Bks.

Dasgupta, Subhayu. Hindu Ethos & the Challenge of Change. 2nd ed. 1978. text ed. 15.00 (ISBN 0-8426-1095-2). Verry.

Hindery, Roderick. Comparative Ethics in Hindu & Buddhist Tradition. 1979. 20.00x (ISBN 0-89684-017-4). South Asia Bks.

Hopkins, E. Washburn. Ethics of India. LC 68-15828. 1968. Repr. of 1924 ed. 11.75 (ISBN 0-8046-0215-8). Kennikat.

Krishnamurti, Jiddu. Commentaries on Living, 3 Bks. 3 ser ed. Rajagopal, D., ed. (Ser. 1, LC 67-8405; Ser. 2, LC 67-8407; Ser. 3, LC 67-8416). 1967. pap. 3.95 ser. 1 (ISBN 0-8356-0390-3, Quest); pap. 2.95 ser. 2 (ISBN 0-8356-0415-2); pap. 3.25 ser. 3 (ISBN 0-8356-0402-0). Theos Pub Hse.

Thomas, P. Hindu Religion, Customs & Manners: Describing the Customs & Manners, Religious, Social & Domestic Life, Arts & Science of the Hindus. (Illus.). 155p. 1971. 17.50x (ISBN 0-8002-1494-3). Intl Pubns Serv.

HINDU HYMNS

Griffith, Ralph T., tr. from Sanskrit. Sam-Veda Sanhita. 338p. 1978. Repr. of 1907 ed. 22.00 (ISBN 0-89684-160-X). Orient Bk Dist.

HINDU KUSH MOUNTAINS

Canfield, Robert L. Faction & Conversion in a Plural Society: Religious Alignments in the Hindu Kush. (Anthropological Paper Ser.: No. 50). 1973. 3.00x (ISBN 0-932206-48-4). U Mich Mus Anthro.

HINDU LAW

Kane, Pandurang V. History of Dharmasastra, 5 vols. LC 43-20693. 1973. Set. 175.00x (ISBN 0-8002-0928-1). Intl Pubns Serv.

Kern, H., tr. The Saddharma-Pundarika: Lotus of True Law. lib. bdg. 59.95 (ISBN 0-87968-530-1). Krishna Pr.

Markby, William. An Introduction to Hindu & Mohammedan Law. LC 78-58189. 1978. Repr. of 1906 ed. lib. bdg. 25.00 (ISBN 0-89341-509-X). Longwood Pr.

Virdi, P. K. Grounds for Divorce in Hindu & English Law. 1973. text ed. 9.00x (ISBN 0-8426-0417-0). Verry.

HINDU LEGENDS

see Legends, Hindu

HINDU LITERATURE

see also Hinduism-Sacred Books (Selections: Extracts, etc.)

Alston, A. J. Devotional Poems of Mirabai. 144p. 1980. text ed. 13.50 (ISBN 0-8426-1643-8). Verry.

Arnold, Edwin. Song Celestial. 1971. pap. 1.50 (ISBN 0-8356-0418-7, Quest). Theos Pub Hse.

Bhagavad-Gita. The Song of God. Prabhavananda, Swami & Isherwood, C., trs. pap. 1.50 (ISBN 0-451-61590-5, MW1590, Ment). NAL.

Bhattacharya, Bhabani, ed. Contemporary Indian Short Stories, 2 vols. 1967. Vol. 1. 2.50 (ISBN 0-88253-409-2); Vol. 2. 2.50 (ISBN 0-88253-327-4). Ind-US Inc.

Griffith, R. T., tr. Hymms of the Rgveda. 1974. text ed. 25.00x (ISBN 0-8426-0592-4). Verry.

Naravane, V. S. Premchand: His Life & Work. 280p. 1980. text ed. 18.95x (ISBN 0-7069-1091-5, Pub. by Vikas India). Advent NY.

Nivedita, Sr. Complete Works of Sister Nivedita, 4 vols. Incl. Vol. 1. Our Master & His Message, the Master As I Saw Him, Kali the Mother, Lectures & Articles (ISBN 0-87481-112-0); Vol. 2. The Web of Indian Life, an Indian Study on Love & Death, Studies from an Eastern Home, Lectures & Articles (ISBN 0-87481-113-9); Vol. 3. Indian Art, Cradle Tales of Hinduism, Religion & Dharma (ISBN 0-87481-114-7); Vol. 4. Footfalls of Indian History, Bodh-Gaya, Civic Ideal & Indian Nationality, Hints on National Education in India (ISBN 0-87481-115-5). 32.00x set (ISBN 0-87481-150-3). Vedanta Pr.

--Cradle Tales of Hinduism. (Illus.). 329p. (gr. 3-12). 1972. pap. 3.95 (ISBN 0-87481-131-7). Vedanta Pr.

Panikkar, Raimundo. Mantramanjari: The Vedic Experience. 1977. 37.50 (ISBN 0-520-02854-6). U of Cal Pr.

Prabhavananda, Swami & Isherwood, Christopher, trs. Bhagavad-Gita: Song of God. 3rd ed. LC 46-1825. 1972. 6.95 (ISBN 0-87481-008-6). Vedanta Pr.

Prabhavananda, Swami & Manchester, Frederick, trs. Upanishads: Breath of the Eternal. LC 48-5935. 6.95 (ISBN 0-87481-007-8). Vedanta Pr.

Sastry, P. V. Analysis of Sidhanta Kaumudi of Bhattoji Siksita. 1974. 13.50x (ISBN 0-8426-0582-7). Verry.

Sharma, B. Krishnamurti. The Brahmasutras & Their Principal Commentaries. LC 72-901912. 275p. 1971. Vol 1. 12.50x (ISBN 0-8002-0446-8). Intl Pubns Serv.

Sri Aurobindo. Essays on the Gita. 1976. pap. 6.00 (ISBN 0-89071-222-0). Matagiri.

Talib, Gubachana S. Bani of Sri Guru Amardas. 1979. text ed. 29.50 (ISBN 0-89684-078-6, Pub. by Sterling New Delhi). Orient Bk Dist.

Vimalananda, Swami, tr. Mahanarayanopanisad. (Eng. & Sanskrit.). 6.50 (ISBN 0-87481-419-7). Vedanta Pr.

Vivekananda, Swami. Religion of Love. 114p. pap. 1.95 (ISBN 0-87481-129-5). Vedanta Pr.

--What Religion Is in the Words of Vivekananda. Yale, John, ed. 5.00 (ISBN 0-87481-032-9). Vedanta Pr.

Wade, A. The Ten Principal Upanishads. 75.00 (ISBN 0-8490-1183-3). Gordon Pr.

Zaehner, R. C., ed. & tr. Hindu Scriptures. 1976. 9.95x (ISBN 0-8046-0944-8, Evman); pap. 2.75x (ISBN 0-460-11944-3, Evman). Biblio Dist.

HINDU MATHEMATICS

see Mathematics, Hindu

HINDU MEDICINE

see Medicine, Hindu

HINDU MUSIC

see Music, Indic

HINDU MYSTICISM

see Mysticism-Hinduism

HINDU MYTHOLOGY

see Mythology, Hindu

HINDU NATIONAL CHARACTERISTICS
see National Characteristics, Hindu
HINDU PHILOSOPHY
see Philosophy, Hindu
HINDU SCULPTURE
see Sculpture, Hindu
HINDU SECTS
see also Shaktism; Sahajiya; Vaishnavism

Bhagowalia, Urmila. Vaisnavism & Society in Northern India. 1980. 22.00x (ISBN 0-8364-0664-8, Pub. by Intellectual India). South Asia Bks.

HINDU SOCIOLOGY
see Sociology, Hindu
HINDUISM
see also Advaita; Bhakti; Brahmanism; Caste-India; Civilization, Hindu; Dharma; God (Hinduism); Hindu Hymns; Hindu Sects; Jains; Karma; Maya (Hinduism); Mysticism–Hinduism; Nyaya; Sankhya; Tantrism; Vaisesika; Vedanta; Vedas; Women in Hinduism; Yoga

Akhilananda, Swami. Hindu Psychology: Its Meaning for the West. pap. 3.75 (ISBN 0-8283-1353-9). Branden.

--Hindu Psychology: Its Meaning for the West. 1971. Repr. of 1948 ed. 20.00 (ISBN 0-7100-1006-0). Routledge & Kegan.

--Hindu View of Christ. pap. 3.75 (ISBN 0-8283-1355-5). Branden.

--Mental Health & Hindu Psychology. pap. 3.75 (ISBN 0-8283-1354-7). Branden.

Anand, Balwant S. Guru Tegh Bahadur. 1979. text ed. 11.95 (ISBN 0-89684-076-X, Pub. by Sterling New Delhi). Orient Bk Dist.

Ashby, Philip H. Modern Trends in Hinduism. (Lectures in the History of Religions Ser.: No. 10). 143p. 1974. 16.00x (ISBN 0-231-03768-6). Columbia U Pr.

Baba, Meher. The Everything & the Nothing. 100p. (Orig.). 1963. pap. 3.45 (ISBN 0-940700-00-X). Meher Baba Info.

Babb, Lawrence A. The Divine Hierarchy: Popular Hinduism in Central India. (Illus.). 266p. 1975. 17.50x (ISBN 0-231-03882-8). Columbia U Pr.

Bannerjee, M. Invitation to Hinduism. 1979. pap. 5.95 (ISBN 0-89684-081-6, Pub. by Arnold Heinemann India). Orient Bk Dist.

--Invitation to Hinduism. (Illus.). 1978. text ed. 9.00x (ISBN 0-391-01082-4). Humanities.

Bentley, John. A Historical View of the Hindu Astronomy from the Earliest Dawn of That Science in India to the Present Time. LC 5-29507. 1970. Repr. of 1825 ed. 35.00x (ISBN 3-7648-0107-7). Intl Pubns Serv.

Bergaigne, Abel. Vedic Religion. Paranjpe, V. G., tr. 1978. 25.00 (ISBN 0-89684-006-9, Pub. by Motilal Banarsidass India). Orient Bk Dist.

Berry, Thomas. Religions of India: School Edition. 1971. pap. 5.95 (ISBN 0-02-811100-1). Glencoe.

Bhaktivedanta, A. C. & Sadaputa dasa. Consciousness the Missing Link. (Illus.). 70p. (Orig.). 0.95 (ISBN 0-89213-108-X). Bhaktivedanta.

Bhaktivedanta, Swami A. C. Prahlad, Picture & Story Book. LC 72-2032. (Illus.). (gr. 2-6). 1973. pap. 1.95 (ISBN 0-685-47513-1). Bhaktivedanta.

--Sri Caitanya-Caritamrta: Adi-Lila, 3 vols. (Illus.). 1974. 9.95 ea. Vol. 1 (ISBN 0-912776-50-1). Vol. 2 (ISBN 0-912776-51-X). Vol. 3 (ISBN 0-912776-53-6). Bhaktivedanta.

--Srimad Bhagavatam: First Canto, 3 vols. LC 73-169353. (Illus.). 1972. 9.95 ea. Vol. 1 (ISBN 0-912776-27-7). Vol. 2 (ISBN 0-912776-29-3). Vol. 3 (ISBN 0-912776-34-X). Bhaktivedanta.

--Srimad Bhagavatam: Fourth Canto, 4 vols. LC 73-169353. (Illus.). 1974. 9.95 ea. Vol. 1 (ISBN 0-912776-38-2). Vol. 2 (ISBN 0-912776-47-1). Vol. 3 (ISBN 0-912776-48-X). Vol. 4 (ISBN 0-912776-49-8). Bhaktivedanta.

--Srimad Bhagavatam: Second Canto, 2 vols. LC 73-169353. (Illus.). 1972. 9.95 ea. Vol. 1 (ISBN 0-912776-28-5). Vol. 2 (ISBN 0-912776-35-8). Bhaktivedanta.

--Srimad Bhagavatam: Third Canto, 4 vols. LC 73-169353. (Illus.). 1974. 9.95 ea. Vol. 1 (ISBN 0-912776-37-4). Vol. 2 (ISBN 0-912776-44-7). Vol. 3 (ISBN 0-912776-46-3). Vol. 4 (ISBN 0-912776-75-7). Bhaktivedanta.

--Teachings of Lord Caitanya. LC 75-2060. (Illus.). 1974. 7.95 (ISBN 0-912776-08-0); pap. 2.95 (ISBN 0-912776-07-2). Bhaktivedanta.

Bhaktivedanta, Swami Prabhupada A. C. Teachings of Lord Kapiladeva: The Son of Devahuti. 1977. 9.95 (ISBN 0-685-84743-8). Bhaktivedanta.

Bhatt, Kjmarila. Anthology of Kumarila Bhatt's Works. Sharma, P. S., ed. 96p. 1980. text ed. 9.00x (ISBN 0-8426-1647-0). Verry.

Bijalwan, C. D. Hindu Omens. 176p. 1980. 8.95x (ISBN 0-89955-321-4, Pub. by Interprint India). Intl Schol Bk Serv.

Bloomfield, Maurice. Religion of the Veda. LC 70-94310. (BCL Ser. II). Repr. of 1908 ed. 18.00 (ISBN 0-404-00912-3). AMS Pr.

Bouquet, A. C. Hinduism. 1949. pap. text ed. 5.25x (ISBN 0-09-030672-4, Hutchinson U Lib). Humanities.

Bowes, Pratima. The Hindu Religious Tradition: A Philosophical Approach. 1978. 24.00 (ISBN 0-7100-8668-7). Routledge & Kegan.

Brabazon, Francis. In Dust I Sing. 150p. 1974. 8.95 (ISBN 0-940700-08-5); pap. 4.95 (ISBN 0-940700-07-7). Meher Baba Info.

--The Word at World's End. 88p. 1971. 5.95 (ISBN 0-940700-04-2); pap. 3.45 (ISBN 0-940700-03-4). Meher Baba Info.

Brent, Peter. Godmen of India. LC 73-190123. 1973. 10.00 (ISBN 0-8129-0258-0). Times Bks.

Brockington, J. L. The Sacred Thread: Hinduism in Continuity & Diversity. 192p. 1981. pap. 10.50x (ISBN 0-85224-393-6, Pub. by Edinburgh U Pr Scotland). Columbia U Pr.

Chatterji, Jagadisha C. Hindu Realism: An Introduction to the Metaphysics of the Nyaya Vaisheshika System of Philosophy. LC 75-928123. 1975. Repr. 12.50x (ISBN 0-88386-667-6). South Asia Bks.

Chaudhuri, Nirad C. Hinduism. 1979. 19.95 (ISBN 0-19-520112-4). Oxford U Pr.

--Hinduism: A Religion to Live by. 352p. 1980. pap. 4.95 (ISBN 0-19-520221-X, GB 612). Oxford U Pr.

Chennakesvan, Sarasvati. A Critical Study of Hinduism. 1980. 12.50x (ISBN 0-8364-0614-1). South Asia Bks.

Coomaraswamy, Ananda K. Hinduism & Buddhism. LC 78-138215. 1971. Repr. of 1943 ed. lib. bdg. 15.00x (ISBN 0-8371-5570-3, COHB). Greenwood.

Corlett, William & Moore, John. Questions of Human Existence As Answered by Major World Religions: The Hindu Sound. LC 79-15815. 1980. 8.95 (ISBN 0-87888-151-4). Bradbury Pr.

Crompton, Yorke. Hinduism. LC 76-881370. (Living Religions Ser). (Illus.). 1976. pap. 3.50x (ISBN 0-7062-3598-3). Intl Pubns Serv.

Da Free John. The Eating Gorilla Comes in Peace. LC 75-24582. 1979. pap. 10.95 (ISBN 0-913922-19-6). Dawn Horse Pr.

Das, Venna. Structure & Cognition: Aspects of Hindu Caste & Ritual. 1978. pap. text ed. 8.95x (ISBN 0-19-560889-5). Oxford U Pr.

Dasgupta, Subhayu. Hindu Ethos & the Challenge of Change. 2nd rev. ed. (Illus.). 1977. text ed. 9.00x (ISBN 0-391-01074-3). Humanities.

Dell, David. Guide to Hindu Religion. (Scholarly Reference Publications). 1981. lib. bdg. 39.75 (ISBN 0-8161-7903-4). G K Hall.

Dell, David J. & Knipe, David M. Focus on Hinduism: Audio Visual Resources for Teaching Religion. 2nd, enl. ed. 160p. 1981. text ed. 14.50 (ISBN 0-89012-018-8); pap. text ed. 7.95 (ISBN 0-89012-019-6). Anima Pubns.

The Dharam Shastra: Hindu Religious Codes, 6 vols. Incl. Vol. I. 267p. 1978 (ISBN 0-89684-137-5); Vol. II. 230p. 1979 (ISBN 0-89684-138-3); Vol. III. 309p. 1979 (ISBN 0-89684-139-1); Vol. IV. 187p. 1979 (ISBN 0-89684-140-5); Vol. V. 438p. 1979 (ISBN 0-89684-141-3); Vol. VI. 222p. 1979 (ISBN 0-89684-142-1). Repr. of 1908 ed. 100.00 set (ISBN 0-686-77519-8, Pub. by Cosmo Pubns India). Orient Bk Dist.

Donato, Sri. The Day of Brahma. Morningland Publications, Inc., ed. (Illus.). 377p. 1981. pap. 10.00 (ISBN 0-935146-20-2). Morningland.

Dye, Joseph M. Ways to Shiva: Life & Ritual in Hindu India. LC 80-25113. (Illus.). 94p. (Orig.). 1980. pap. 4.95 (ISBN 0-87633-038-3). Phila Mus Art.

Edmonds, I. G. Hinduism. (First Bks.). (Illus.). (gr. 4 up). 1979. PLB 6.90 s&l (ISBN 0-531-02943-3). Watts.

Eliot, Charles. Hinduism & Buddhism: An Historical Sketch, 3 vols. 1968. Repr. of 1921 ed. Set. 50.00 (ISBN 0-685-36739-8); 18.50 ea. Vol. 1 (ISBN 0-7100-1328-0). Vol. 2 (ISBN 0-7100-1329-9). Vol. 3 (ISBN 0-7100-1330-2). Routledge & Kegan.

Embree, Ainslie T., ed. The Hindu Tradition. 448p. 1972. pap. 2.95 (ISBN 0-394-71702-3, V696, Vin). Random.

Focus on Hinduism: Audio-Visual Resources for Teaching Religion. 122p. 1977. pap. 3.00 (ISBN 0-89192-246-6, Pub. by Foreign Area Materials Ctr). Interbk Inc.

Frazier, Allie M., ed. Readings in Eastern Religious Thought, 3 vols. Incl. Vol. 1. Hinduism. (ISBN 0-664-24846-2); Vol. 2. Buddhism. (ISBN 0-664-24847-0); Vol. 3. Chinese & Japanese Religions. (ISBN 0-664-24848-9). 1969. pap. 3.50 ea. Westminster.

Getty, Alice. Ganesa: A Monograph on the Elephant-Faced God. 2nd ed. LC 72-900721. (Illus.). 126p. 1971. 37.50x (ISBN 0-8002-1447-1). Intl Pubns Serv.

Gupta, Shakti M. Vishnu & His Incarnations. LC 74-901552. (Illus.). 120p. 1974. 12.00x (ISBN 0-8002-0099-3). Intl Pubns Serv.

Hawkridge, Emma. Indian Gods & Kings: The Story of a Living Past. facs. ed. LC 68-24853. (Essay Index Reprint Ser). 1935. 19.50 (ISBN 0-8369-0521-0). Arno.

Hazra, R. C. Studies in the Puranic Records on Hindu Rites & Customs. 2nd ed. 1975. 14.00 (ISBN 0-8426-0965-2). Orient Bk Dist.

Hertel, J. The Panchatranta. lib. bdg. 59.95 (ISBN 0-87968-523-9). Krishna Pr.

Hindery, Roderick. Comparative Ethics in Hindu & Buddhist Traditions. 1978. 14.95 (ISBN 0-89684-017-4, Pub. by Motilal Banarsidass India). Orient Bk Dist.

Hinnells, John R. & Sharpe, Eric J., eds. Hinduism. 1972. cased 13.00 (ISBN 0-85362-116-0, Oriel); pap. 6.50 (ISBN 0-85362-137-3). Routledge & Kegan.

Hobson, John. Hinduism & Its Relation to Christianity. 1977. lib. bdg. 59.95 (ISBN 0-8490-1951-6). Gordon Pr.

Hockings, Paul, ed. Ancient Hindu Refugees: Badaga Social History 1550-1975. (Studies in Anthropology). 1980. text ed. 23.50x (ISBN 90-279-7798-4). Mouton.

Holland, Barron, compiled by. Popular Hinduism & Hindu Mythology: An Annotated Bibliography. LC 79-7188. 1979. lib. bdg. 29.95 (ISBN 0-313-21358-5, HPH/). Greenwood.

Hopkins. Hindu Religious Tradition. LC 74-158118. 1971. pap. 4.95 (ISBN 0-685-04757-1). Duxbury Pr.

Hopkins, Thomas. The Hindu Religious Tradition. (The Religious Life of Man Ser). 1971. pap. text ed. 8.95x (ISBN 0-8221-0022-3). Dickenson.

Isherwood, Christopher. My Guru & His Disciple. 352p. 1981. pap. 4.95 (ISBN 0-14-005837-0). Penguin.

Johnson, Donald & Johnson, Jean. God & Gods in Hinduism. (Illus.). 88p. 1972. text ed. 4.75x (ISBN 0-391-00427-1). Humanities.

Kapoor, O. B. The Philosophy & Religion of Sri Caitanya: The Philosophical Background of the Hare Krishna Movement. 1977. 16.00x (ISBN 0-88386-995-0). South Asia Bks.

Karve, Iravati. Yuganta: The End of an Epoch. 1974. lib. bdg. 4.50x (ISBN 0-8364-0482-3). South Asia Bks.

Keith, Arthur B., ed. The Aitareya Aranyaka. 396p. 1969. Repr. of 1909 ed. text ed. 22.50x (ISBN 0-19-815442-9). Oxford U Pr.

Kinsley, David. Hinduism: A Cultural Perspective. (Illus.). 200p. 1982. 7.50 (ISBN 0-13-388975-0). P-H.

Kinsley, David R. The Divine Player: A Study of KRSNA Lila. 1978. 14.95 (ISBN 0-89684-019-0, Pub. by Motilal Barnarsidass India). Orient Bk Dist.

Kumarappa, B. The Hindu Conception of the Deity. 1979. text ed. 17.50x (ISBN 0-391-01848-5). Humanities.

Mahanarayanopanisad. 1979. pap. 6.50 (ISBN 0-87481-492-8). Vedanta Pr.

Maitra, H. Hinduism: The World Ideal. 34.95 (ISBN 0-8490-0302-4). Gordon Pr.

Mallik, G. N. Philosophy of Vaisnava Religion. 59.95 (ISBN 0-8490-0829-8). Gordon Pr.

Mangalwadi, Vishal. The World of Gurus. 1977. pap. 12.00 (ISBN 0-7069-0523-7). Verry.

Michael, Aloysius. Radhakrishnan on Hindu Moral Life & Action. 1979. text ed. 14.50x (ISBN 0-391-01857-4). Humanities.

Michell, George. The Hindu Temple: An Introduction to Its Meaning & Forms. LC 77-82075. (Icon Editions). (Illus.). 1978. 25.00 (ISBN 0-06-435750-3, HarpT). Har-Row.

Mittal, Kewal K. Role of Materialism in Indian Thought. LC 74-901145. xvi, 328p. 1974. 14.00x (ISBN 0-8364-0461-0). South Asia Bks.

Monier-Williams, M. Hinduism: Non-Christian Religious Systems. lib. bdg. 59.95 (ISBN 0-87968-546-8). Krishna Pr.

Monier-Williams, Monier. Indian Wisdom. 575p. 1978. Repr. of 1893 ed. 21.00 (ISBN 0-89684-105-7, Pub. by Cosmo Pubns India). Orient Bk Dist.

Moor, Edward. Hindu Pantheon. 45.00 (ISBN 0-89314-409-6). Philos Res.

Morgan, Kenneth W., ed. The Religion of the Hindus: Interpreted by Hindus. 1953. 21.50 (ISBN 0-8260-6260-1). Wiley.

Mukerjee, Radhakamal, tr. The Song of the Self Supreme: Astavakra Gita. LC 74-24308. 1981. 7.95 (ISBN 0-913922-14-5). Dawn Horse Pr.

Mukherjee, Prabhat. History of the Chaitanya Faith in Orissa. 1979. 14.00x (ISBN 0-8364-0547-1). South Asia Bks.

Mukherjee, Prabhati. Hindu Women: Normative Models. 1978. 10.00x (ISBN 0-8364-0289-8, Orient Longman). South Asia Bks.

Muktanada, Swami. Satsang with Baba, Vol. 5. (Illus., Orig.). 1978. pap. 5.95 (ISBN 0-914602-33-0). SYDA Found.

Muktananda: Siddha Guru. 1976. pap. 2.50 (ISBN 0-914602-32-2). SYDA Found.

Muktananda, Swami. A Book for the Mind. (Illus., Orig.). 1976. pap. 1.25 (ISBN 0-685-99448-1). SYDA Found.

--God Is with You. (Illus., Orig.). 1978. pap. 1.25 (ISBN 0-914602-57-8). SYDA Found.

Muller, Max, ed. Sacred Book of the East: Vedic Hymns, 2 vols. 250.00 (ISBN 0-87968-438-0). Krishna Pr.

Mutanada, Swami. Sadhana. 1976. pap. 7.95 (ISBN 0-914602-63-2). SYDA Found.

Nandimath, S. C. A Handbook of Virasaivism. 1979. 11.50 (ISBN 0-89684-053-0, Pub. by Motilal Banarsidass India). Orient Bk Dist.

Nikhilananda, Swami. Hinduism: Its Meaning for the Liberation of the Spirit: a Survey of Hinduism. LC 58-6155. 189p. 3.95 (ISBN 0-911206-13-2). Ramakrishna.

Nirvedananda, Swami. Hinduism at a Glance. 3.75 (ISBN 0-87481-153-8). Vedanta Pr.

Nisargadatta Maharaj. I Am That: Conversations with Sri Nisargadatta Maharaj, 2 vols. 2nd ed. Frydman, Maurice, tr. 1979. Repr. of 1976 ed. Set. 17.00 (ISBN 0-85655-406-5, Pub. by Chetana India). Acorn NC.

Obeyesekere, Gananath. Medusa's Hair: An Essay on Personal Symbols & Religious Experiences. LC 80-27372. (Illus.). 252p. 1981. lib. bdg. 22.50x (ISBN 0-226-61600-2). U of Chicago Pr.

O'Malley, Lewis S. Popular Hinduism: The Religion of the Masses. LC 70-142072. 1971. Repr. of 1935 ed. 19.50 (ISBN 0-384-43305-7). Johnson Repr.

O'Neal, L. Thomas. Maya in Sankara: Measuring the Immeasurable. 1980. 16.00x (ISBN 0-8364-0611-7). South Asia Bks.

Organ, Troy W. Hindu Quest for the Perfection of Man. LC 73-81450. x, 439p. 1981. pap. 12.00x (ISBN 0-8214-0575-6). Ohio U Pr.

--Hinduism. LC 73-100676. (Orig.). 1974. pap. text ed. 4.95 (ISBN 0-8120-0500-7). Barron.

Pandey, Raj B. Hindu Sanskaras. 1976. Repr. 12.50 (ISBN 0-8426-0853-2). Orient Bk Dist.

Patel, Satyavrata. Hinduism: Religion & Way of Life. 165p. 1980. text ed. 21.00x (ISBN 0-8426-1661-6). Verry.

Prabhavananda, Swami. Religion in Practice. 6.95 (ISBN 0-87481-016-7). Vedanta Pr.

Prabhu, P. H. Hindu Social Organization: A Study in Socio-Psychological & Ideological Foundations. 6th ed. 389p. 1979. text ed. 18.00 (ISBN 0-8426-1642-X). Verry.

Radhakrishnan. Hindu Moral Life & Action. 1980. text ed. write for info. (ISBN 0-391-02011-0). Humanities.

Radhakrishnan, S. Hindu View of Life. (Unwin Paperbacks Ser.). 92p. 1980. pap. 4.95 (ISBN 0-04-294045-1, 9048). Allen Unwin.

Rammohun Roy, R. The English Works of Raja Ramohun Roy. Ghose, Jogendra C., ed. LC 75-41220. Repr. of 1906 ed. 49.50 (ISBN 0-404-14738-0). AMS Pr.

Rao, K. L. The Concept of Sraddha, in the Brahmanas, Upanisads & the Gita. 1976. text ed. 6.00x (ISBN 0-8426-0894-X). Verry.

Ross, Nancy W. Three Ways of Asian Wisdom: Hinduism, Buddhism, Zen. (Illus.). 1978. pap. 7.95 (ISBN 0-671-24230-X, Touchstone Bks). S&S.

Sarma, Dittakavi S. Essence of Hinduism. LC 72-900416. 128p. 1971. 5.00x (ISBN 0-8002-0625-8). Intl Pubns Serv.

Satsvarupa, Goswamidas. Readings in Vedic Literature: The Tradition Speaks for Itself. LC 76-24941. (Illus.). 1977. pap. 2.95 (ISBN 0-912776-88-9); pap. text ed. 2.95 (ISBN 0-685-70924-8). Bhaktivedanta.

Schweitzer, Albert. Indian Thought & Its Development. 1962. 8.25 (ISBN 0-8446-2893-X). Peter Smith.

Sen, K. M. Hinduism. lib. bdg. 9.00x (ISBN 0-88307-248-3). Gannon.

Sen, Kshitimohan M. Hinduism. (Orig.). 1962. pap. 1.95 (ISBN 0-14-020515-2, Pelican). Penguin.

Sharma, Arbind. Thresholds in Hindu-Buddhist Studies. 1980. 16.50 (ISBN 0-8364-0495-5). South Asia Bks.

Sharma, Arvind. The Hindu Scriptural Value System & the Economic Development of India. x, 113p. 1980. text ed. 15.00x (ISBN 0-86590-004-3). Apt Bks.

Sheth, Surabhi. Religion & Society in the Brahma Purana. 1979. text ed. 30.00x (ISBN 0-8426-1102-9). Verry.

Shourie, Arun. Hinduism: Essence & Consequence. 1980. text ed. 35.00x (ISBN 0-7069-0834-1, Pub. by Vikas India). Advent NY.

Shree Gurudev Ashram. Introduction to Kashmir Shaivism. Swami Tejomayananda, ed. 1975. 2.75 (ISBN 0-685-94391-7). SYDA Found.

Siegel, Lee. Sacred & Profane Dimensions of Love in Indian Traditions As Exemplified in the Gitagovind of Jayadeva. 1978. text ed. 21.00x (ISBN 0-19-560807-0). Oxford U Pr.

Singh, Fauja. Guru Amar Das. 1979. text ed. 9.95 (ISBN 0-89684-080-8, Pub. by Sterling New Delhi). Orient Bk Dist.

Singh, Harbans. Guru Gobind Singh. 1979. text ed. 6.95 (ISBN 0-89684-073-5, Pub. by Sterling New Delhi). Orient Bk Dist.

Smith, F. H. Outline of Hinduism. 59.95 (ISBN 0-8490-0788-7). Gordon Pr.
Spratt, P. Hindu Culture & Personality. 1966. 11.00x (ISBN 0-8188-1142-0). Paragon.
Stein, William B., ed. Two Brahman Sources of Emerson & Thoreau, 1822-1832. LC 67-10340. 1967. 33.00x (ISBN 0-8201-1043-4). Schol Facsimiles.
Stevenson, Margaret S. The Rites of the Twice-Born. LC 72-901002. 500p. 1971. Repr. of 1920 ed. 17.50x (ISBN 0-8002-1928-7). Intl Pubns Serv.
Swami Akhilananda. Hindu Psychology: Its Meaning for the West. LC 75-17493. (God Ser.: No. 153). (Illus.). 1977. 8.50 (ISBN 0-89007-153-5). C Stark.
Swami Muktananda. In the Company of a Siddha: Interviews & Conversations with Swami Muktananda. LC 78-65085. 1978. 4.50 (ISBN 0-685-94386-0). SYDA Found.
--Sadgurunath Maharaj Ki Jay. 1975. 9.95 (ISBN 0-9598216-0-0). SYDA Found.
--Satsang with Baba, Vol. III. 1977. 5.95 (ISBN 0-914602-38-1). SYDA Found.
--Swami Muktananda American Tour 1970. 1974. 2.95 (ISBN 0-914602-25-X). SYDA Found.
Varma, V. P. Studies in Hindu Political Thought & Its Metaphysical Foundations. 3rd ed. 1975. text ed. 18.50x (ISBN 0-8426-0733-1). Verry.
Vasu, Srisa Chandra. A Catechism of Hindu Dharma. 2nd, rev. & enl. ed. Vidyarnava, Srisa Chandra, tr. LC 73-3829. (Sacred Books of the Hindus: No. 3). Repr. of 1919 ed. 14.50 (ISBN 0-404-57847-0). AMS Pr.
--The Daily Practice of the Hindus Containing the Morning & Midday Duties. 3rd, rev. & enl. ed. Vidyarnava, Srisa Chandra, tr. LC 73-3812. (Sacred Books of the Hindus: No. 20). Repr. of 1918 ed. 14.50 (ISBN 0-404-57820-9). AMS Pr.
Vidyarthi, L. P. The Sacred Complex in Hindu Gaya. 2nd ed. 264p. 1980. pap. text ed. 11.25x (ISBN 0-391-02214-8). Humanities.
Vishnu Purana, 2 vols. Wilson, H. H., tr. from Sanskrit. 965p. 1980. 36.00 (ISBN 0-89744-995-9, Pub. by Orient Reprint India). Auromere.
Vivekananda, Swami. Complete Works of Swami Vivekananda, 8 vols. pap. 55.00 (ISBN 0-87481-176-7). Vedanta Pr.
Werner, Karel. Yoga & Indian Philosophy. 1979. 12.50x (ISBN 0-8364-0479-3). South Asia Bks.
Wilkins, W. J. Modern Hinduism. 1975. Repr. 14.00x (ISBN 0-88386-634-X). South Asia Bks.
--Modern Hinduism: An Account of the Religion & Life of the Hindus. 2nd ed. 1975. text ed. 12.50x (ISBN 0-7007-0046-3). Humanities.
Williams, Monier. Indian Wisdom, or Examples of the Religious, Philosophical & Ethical Doctrines of the Hindus. 1974. Repr. of 1875 ed. 30.00x (ISBN 0-8426-0802-8). Verry.
Wilson, H. H. Religion of the Hindus. 416p. 1978. Repr. of 1862 ed. 13.95 (ISBN 0-89684-135-9). Orient Bk Dist.
Wyatt, David K., tr. The Crystal Sands: The Chronicles of Nagara Sri Dharrmaraja. 264p. 1975. 6.50 (ISBN 0-87727-098-8, DP 98). Cornell SE Asia.
Younger, Paul & Younger, Susanna O. Hinduism. (Illus.). 1978. pap. 3.95 (ISBN 0-913592-99-4). Argus Comm.
Zaehner, Robert C. Hinduism. 1962. pap. 6.95 (ISBN 0-19-500383-7, GB172, GB). Oxford U Pr.

HINDUISM–DICTIONARIES

Coward, Harold G. Sphota Theory of Language. 1981. 12.00x (ISBN 0-8364-0692-3). South Asia Bks.
Dowson, John. A Classical Dictionary of Hindu Mythology. 10th ed. 1968. Repr. of 1961 ed. 27.00 (ISBN 0-7100-1302-7). Routledge & Kegan.
--Classical Dictionary of Hindu Mythology, Religion, Geography, History & Literature. 1973. Repr. 15.00x (ISBN 0-8426-0730-7). Verry.
Stutley, M. E. & Stutley, S. J. Harper's Dictionary of Hinduism. LC 76-9999. (Illus.). 1977. 35.00 (ISBN 0-06-067763-5, HarpR). Har-Row.

HINDUISM–RELATIONS–CHRISTIANITY

Akhilananda, Swami. Hindu View of Christ. 2nd ed. LC 75-4134. (God Ser.: No. 152). (Illus.). 291p. 1981. 8.50 (ISBN 0-89007-152-7). C Stark.
Cave, Sydney. Redemption, Hindu & Christian: The Religious Quest of India. facsimile ed. LC 73-102230. (Select Bibliographies Reprint Ser). 1919. 22.00 (ISBN 0-8369-5115-8). Arno.
Devaraja, N. K. Hinduism & Christianity. 1970. 7.25x (ISBN 0-210-98164-4). Asia.
Griffiths, Bede. Vedanta & Christian Faith. LC 73-88179. 1973. pap. 2.95 (ISBN 0-913922-04-8). Dawn Horse Pr.
Luke, P. Y. & Carman, John B. Village Christians & Hindu Culture. (World Studies of Churches in Mission). 1968. pap. 3.95 (ISBN 0-377-82851-3, Pub. by Lutterworth England). Friend Pr.
Satprakashananda, Swami. Hinduism & Christianity: Jesus Christ & His Teachings in the Light of Vedanta. LC 75-32598. 196p. 1975. 7.50 (ISBN 0-916356-53-1). Vedanta Soc St Louis.
Smart, Ninian. Yogi & the Devotee: The Interplay Between the Upanishads & Catholic Theology. 1968. text ed. 5.50x (ISBN 0-391-02072-2). Humanities.

HINDUISM–RELATIONS–ISLAM

Hedayetullah, Muhammad. Kabir: The Apostle of Hindu-Muslim Unity. 1978. 14.95 (ISBN 0-89684-042-5, Pub. by Motilal Banarsidass India). Orient Bk Dist.

HINDUISM–SACRED BOOKS (SELECTIONS: EXTRACTS, ETC.)

Badarayana. Brahma-Sutras (Vedanta-Sutras) Vireswarananda, Swami, tr. (Sanskrit & Eng.). 10.95 (ISBN 0-87481-076-0). Vedanta Pr.
Baman Das Basu, ed. The Sacred Books of the Hindus, 47 vols. Repr. of 1937 ed. 1251.50 (ISBN 0-404-57800-4). AMS Pr.
Bhaktivedanta, A. C. Sri Isopanisad. LC 78-102853. (Illus.). 1969. pap. 2.95 (ISBN 0-912776-04-8). Bhaktivedanta.
Eggeling, Julius, ed. The Satapatha Brahmana, 5 vols. 1974. lib. bdg. 500.00 (ISBN 0-8490-0994-4). Gordon Pr.
Keith, Arthur B., ed. The Aitareya Aranyaka. 396p. 1969. Repr. of 1909 ed. text ed. 22.50x (ISBN 0-19-815442-9). Oxford U Pr.
Kern, H., tr. Saddharma-Pundarika: Or the Lotus of the True Law. (Sacred Books of the East Ser). 8.50 (ISBN 0-8446-2850-6). Peter Smith.
Pinkham, Mildred W. Woman in the Sacred Scriptures of Hinduism. LC 41-7015. Repr. of 1941 ed. 16.50 (ISBN 0-404-05055-7). AMS Pr.
Puranas, Bhagavatapurana. The Bhakti-Ratnavali: With the Commentary of Visnu Puri. LC 73-3794. (Sacred Books of the Hindus: No. 7 Pt.3). Repr. of 1912 ed. 20.00 (ISBN 0-404-57835-7). AMS Pr.
Sastry, P. V. Analysis of Sidhanta Kaumudi of Bhattoji Siksita. 1974. 13.50x (ISBN 0-8426-0582-7). Verry.
Sharma, Arvind. Textual Studies in Hinduism. 1980. lib. bdg. 14.95x (ISBN 0-914914-15-4). New Horizons.
Swami Ambhirananda, tr. from Sanskrit. Aitereya Upanishad. (Upanishads with Shankara's Commentary Ser.). 75p. 1980. pap. 1.25 (ISBN 0-87481-200-3). Vedanta Pr.
Swami Gambhirananda, tr. from Sanskrit. Katha Upanishad. (Upanishads with Shankara's Commentary Ser.). 136p. pap. 2.95 (ISBN 0-87481-201-1). Vedanta Pr.
--Mandukya Upanishad. (Upanishads with Shankara's Commentary Ser.). 240p. 1980. pap. 3.50 (ISBN 0-87481-202-X). Vedanta Pr.
--Mundaka Upanishad with Commentary of Shankara. 100p. pap. 1.25 (ISBN 0-87481-203-8). Vedanta Pr.
--Prasna Upanishad. (Upanishads with Shankara's Commentary Ser.). 104p. 1980. pap. 1.25 (ISBN 0-686-64775-0). Vedanta Pr.
Vijnanananda. The Sri Mad Devi Bhagavatam. LC 73-3819. (The Sacred Books of the Hindus Ser.: No. 26, Bks. 1-12). Repr. of 1921 ed. 79.50 (ISBN 0-404-57826-8). AMS Pr.
Vireswarananda, Swami, tr. from Sanskrit. Srimad Bhagavad-Gita. 381p. (Eng. & Sanskrit., Pocket edition). 1974. pap. 2.50 (ISBN 0-87481-464-2). Vedanta Pr.
Woodroffe, John. The World As Power. new ed. Bd. with Mahamaya: Power As Consciousness. Woodroffe, John & Mukhyopadhyaya, Pramatha N.. 1974. 13.95 (ISBN 0-89744-119-2, Pub. by Ganesh & Co. India). Auromere.

HINDUISM–SECTS

see Hindu Sects

HINDUS

Broomfield, J. H. Elite Conflict in a Plural Society: Twentieth-Century Bengal. LC 68-13822. 1968. 21.50x (ISBN 0-520-00179-6). U of Cal Pr.
Dass, Ram. Miracle of Love: Stories About Neem Karoli Baba. (Illus.). 1979. pap. 9.95 (ISBN 0-525-47611-3). Dutton.
Dayanand. Autobiography of Dayanand Saraswati. Yadav, K. C., ed. LC 76-900170. 1976. Repr. 6.00x (ISBN 0-88386-740-0). South Asia Bks.
Isherwood, Christopher. Ramakrishna & His Disciples. LC 65-17100. 384p. 1980. pap. 8.95 (ISBN 0-87481-037-X). Vedanta Pr.
Jones, Kenneth W. Arya Dharm: Hindu Consciousness in Nineteenth-Century Punjab. LC 74-27290. 350p. 1976. 25.00x (ISBN 0-520-02919-4). U of Cal Pr.
Larus, Joel. Culture & Political-Military Behavior: The Hindus in Pre-Modern India. 1980. 16.50x (ISBN 0-8364-0038-0). South Asia Bks.
Shetty, Sharat. A Hindu Boyhood. LC 76-112304. (Two Worlds Bks.). (Illus.). 64p. (gr. 4 up). 1970. 3.95 (ISBN 0-87131-096-1). M Evans.
Sontheimer, G. D. The Joint Hindu Family: Its Evolution As a Legal Institution. LC 78-670043. 1977. 20.00x (ISBN 0-8002-0241-4). Intl Pubns Serv.
Ward, William. View of the History, Literature, & Mythology of the Hindoos, 3 Vols. LC 71-115207. 1971. Repr. of 1882 ed. Set. 75.00x (ISBN 0-8046-1100-9). Kennikat.
Wilkins, W. J. Modern Hinduism: An Account of the Religion & Life of the Hindus. 2nd ed. 1975. text ed. 12.50x (ISBN 0-7007-0046-3). Humanities.

HINDUS IN AMERICA

Rolland, Romain. La Vie de Vivekananda. 352p. 1978. 16.95 (ISBN 0-686-55280-6). French & Eur.

HINDUS IN NEPAL

Berreman, Gerald D. Hindus of the Himalayas: Ethnography & Change. 2nd ed. LC 73-156468. (Center for South & Southeast Asia Studies, UC Berkeley). 1972. 27.50x (ISBN 0-520-01423-5); pap. 7.95x (ISBN 0-520-02035-9, CAMPUS66). U of Cal Pr.
Caplan, Lionel. Land & Social Change in East Nepal: A Study of Hindu-Tribal Relations. LC 73-81801. 1970. 20.00x (ISBN 0-520-01400-6). U of Cal Pr.

HINDUS IN SOUTH AFRICA

Kuper, Hilda. Indian People in Natal. LC 73-21261. (Illus.). 305p. 1974. Repr. of 1960 ed. lib. bdg. 18.50x (ISBN 0-8371-6096-0, KUIP). Greenwood.

HINDUSTANI LANGUAGE

see also Hindi Language; Urdu Language

Learn Hindustani. pap. 8.50 (ISBN 0-87557-037-2, 037-2). Saphrograph.
Platts, John T. Dictionary of Urdu, Classical Hindi, & English. 1930. 79.00x (ISBN 0-19-864309-8). Oxford U Pr.
Russell, Ralph. A New Course in Hindustani for Learners in Britain, Pt. 2. 1980. pap. 8.50 (ISBN 0-8364-0602-8, Pub. by Sch Orient & African Stud). South Asia Bks.
Tisdall, William. Hindustani Conversation Grammar. 18.50 (ISBN 0-8044-0723-1). Ungar.

HINE, LEWIS WICKES, 1874-1940

International Museum of Photography at George Eastman House. Lewis Wickes Hine's Interpretative Photography: The Six Early Projects. Doherty, Jonathan, compiled by. LC 78-12059. 1978. 6 color fiches incl. 45.00 (ISBN 0-226-69172-1, Chicago Visual Lib). U of Chicago Pr.
Rosenblum, Walter, frwd. by. America & Lewis Hine. (Illus.). 144p. pap. 12.95 (ISBN 0-89381-016-9). Bklyn Mus.
Tractenberg, Alan. America & Lewis Hine. LC 77-70068. 1977. 25.00 (ISBN 0-89381-008-8). Aperture.

HINTIKKA, KAARLO JAAKKO JUHANI, 1929-

Niiniluoto, I. & Tuomela, R. Theoretical Concepts & Hypothetico-Inductive Inference. LC 73-83567. (Synthese Library: No. 53). 1973. lib. bdg. 39.50 (ISBN 90-277-0343-4, Pub. by Reidel Holland). Kluwer Boston.

HIP JOINT

Aho, Arnold J. Materials, Energies & Environmental Design. 1981. lib. bdg. 28.50 (ISBN 0-8240-7178-6). Garland Pub.
Association of Bone & Joint Surgeons. Fractures of the Hip, Vol. 92. Urist, Marshall, ed. (Clinical Orthopaedics & Related Research Ser.). 1973. 15.00 (ISBN 0-685-34613-7, JBL-Med-Nursing). Har-Row.
--Hip Manifestations of Systemic Disease, Vol. 90. Urist, Marshall, ed. (Clinical Orthopaedics & Related Research Ser.). 1973. 15.00 (ISBN 0-685-34611-0, JBL-Med-Nursing). Har-Row.
Bigelow, Henry J. The Mechanism of Dislocations & Fracture of the Hip & Litholapaxy. LC 77-81659. 1977. Repr. of 1900 ed. lib. bdg. 40.00 (ISBN 0-89341-137-X). Longwood Pr.
Bombelli, R. Osteoarthritis of the Hip. (Illus.). 1976. 89.00 (ISBN 0-387-07842-8). Springer-Verlag.
Charnley, J. Low Friction Arthroplasty of the Hip: Theory & Practice. (Illus.). 1979. 52.80 (ISBN 0-387-08893-8). Springer-Verlag.
Chung, Stanley M., ed. Hip Disorders in Infants & Children. LC 81-1549. (Illus.). 396p. 1981. text ed. 40.00 (ISBN 0-8121-0706-3). Lea & Febiger.
Coleman, Sherman S. Congenital Dysplasia & Dislocation of the Hip. LC 78-59669. 1978. 44.50 (ISBN 0-8016-1018-4). Mosby.
Deutman, R. Experience with the McKee-Farrar Total Hip Arthroplasty: A Monograph on Hip Replacement Surgery Today. McKee, G. K., pref. by. (Illus.). xx, 168p. 1975. 40.00x (ISBN 90-232-1241-X, Pub. by Van Gorcum). Intl Schol Bk Serv.
Eftekhar, Nas S. Principles of Total Hip Arthroplasty. new ed. LC 78-18471. (Illus.). 1978. text ed. 68.50 (ISBN 0-8016-1496-1). Mosby.
Epstein, Herman C. Traumatic Dislocations of the Hip. (Illus.). 336p. 1980. lib. bdg. 38.95 (ISBN 0-683-02906-1). Williams & Wilkins.
Freedman, Matthew. Radiology of the Postoperative Hip. LC 79-12411. 1979. 48.00 (ISBN 0-471-04416-4, Pub. by Wiley Medical). Wiley.
Hass, Julius. Congenital Dislocation of the Hip. (Illus.). 416p. 1951. photocopy ed. spiral 37.50 (ISBN 0-398-04272-1). C C Thomas.
Hip Society. The Hip Society: The Hip, 8 vols. Incl. Vol. 1. 1973. text ed. 25.00 (ISBN 0-8016-0019-7); Vol. 2. 1974. text ed. 35.00 (ISBN 0-8016-0020-0); Vol. 3. 332p. 1975. text ed. 39.50 (ISBN 0-8016-0035-9); Vol. 4. Evarts, C. M., ed. 1976. text ed. 32.50 (ISBN 0-8016-0036-7); Vol. 5. 1977. text ed. 35.50 (ISBN 0-8016-0038-3); Vol. 6. 1978. text ed. 34.50 (ISBN 0-8016-0041-3); Vol. 7. 1979. text ed. 45.50 (ISBN 0-8016-0033-2); Vol. 8. 336p. 1980. text ed. 44.50 (ISBN 0-8016-0049-9). LC 73-7515. (Illus.). Mosby.
Lloyd-Roberts, G. C. & Ratliff, A. H. Hip Disorders in Children. (Postgraduate Orthopedics Ser.). 1978. 57.95 (ISBN 0-407-00132-8). Butterworth.
McArdle, J. Functional Morphology of the Hip & Thigh of the Lorisiformes. (Contributions to Primatology Ser.: Vol. 17). (Illus.). 148p. 1981. pap. 19.25 (ISBN 3-8055-1767-X). S Karger.
Muller, M. E. & Ganz, R., eds. Total Hip Prostheses. 1976. ring binder 204.50 (ISBN 0-387-92103-6). Springer-Verlag.
Ninth Open Scientific Meeting, of the Hip Society. The Hip: Proceedings. (Illus.). 336p. 1981. text ed. 34.50 (ISBN 0-8016-0029-4). Mosby.
Pauwels, F. Atlas: The Biomechanics of the Normal & Diseased Hip. Furlong, R. J. & Maguet, P., trs. from Ger. LC 75-31723. (Illus.). 280p. 1976. 212.40 (ISBN 0-387-07428-7). Springer-Verlag.
Schaldach, M. & Hohmann, D., eds. Advances in Artificial Hip & Knee Joint Technology. (Engineering in Medicine Ser: Vol. 2). 1976. 36.00 (ISBN 0-387-07728-6). Springer-Verlag.
Singleton, Mary C. & LeVeau, Barney. The Hip Joint. 1975. pap. 1.00 (ISBN 0-912452-13-7). Am Phys Therapy Assn.
Tachdjian, M. Congenital Dislocation of the Hip. 1982. text ed. price not set (ISBN 0-443-08069-0). Churchill.
Tronzo, Raymond G., ed. Surgery of the Hip Joint. LC 72-79357. (Illus.). 840p. 1973. text ed. 49.50 (ISBN 0-8121-0401-3). Lea & Febiger.

HIPPIES

Bookchin, Murray, et al. Hip Culture: Six Essays on Its Revolutionary Potential. (Orig.). 1971. pap. 1.25 (ISBN 0-87810-010-5). Times Change.
Harland, John. Brave New World: A Different Projection. LC 77-83061. 1978. pap. 2.00 (ISBN 0-914752-08-1). Sovereign Pr.
Kapur, Tribhuwan. Hippies: A Study of Their Drug Habits & Sexual Customs in India. 200p. 1981. text ed. 20.00 (ISBN 0-7069-1368-X, Pub. by Vikas India). Advent NY.
Rather, Lois. Bohemians to Hippies: Waves of Rebellion. (Illus.). 1977. ltd. ed. 20.00 (ISBN 0-686-22962-2). Rather Pr.
Von Hoffman, Nicholas. We Are the People Our Parents Warned Us Against. (Illus.). 256p. (Orig.). (gr. 8 up). 1972. 6.95 (ISBN 0-8129-0078-2). Times Bks.
Wolfe, Tom. The Electric Kool-Aid Acid Test. LC 68-13008. 416p. 1968. 10.00 (ISBN 0-374-14704-3). FS&G.

HIPPOCAMPUS (BRAIN)

Haug, F. M. Sulphide Silver Pattern & Cytoarchitectonics of Parahippocampal Areas in the Rat. (Advances in Anatomy, Embryology & Cell Biology: Vol. 52, Pt. 4). (Illus.). 1976. soft cover 21.30 (ISBN 0-387-07850-9). Springer-Verlag.
Isaacson, Robert L. & Pribram, Karl H., eds. The Hippocampus. Incl. Vol. 1. Structure & Development. 418p. 27.50 (ISBN 0-306-37535-4); Vol. 2. Neurophysiology & Behavior. 445p. 29.50 (ISBN 0-306-37536-2). (Illus.). 1975 (Plenum Pr). Plenum Pub.
O'Keefe, John & Nadel, Lynn. The Hippocampus As a Cognitive Map. (Illus.). 1978. text ed. 45.00x (ISBN 0-19-857206-9). Oxford U Pr.
Ramon Y Cajal, Santiago. Structure of Ammon's Horn. Kraft, Lisbeth M., tr. (Illus.). 100p. 1968. pap. 11.50 photocopy ed. spiral (ISBN 0-398-01543-0). C C Thomas.

HIPPOCRATES

Adams, Francis. The Genuine Works of Hippocrates. 384p. 1972. Repr. of 1939 ed. 19.50 (ISBN 0-88275-002-X). Krieger.
Bulger, Roger, ed. Hippocrates Revisited. 238p. 1973. 12.50 (ISBN 0-685-90279-X, Pub. by W & W). Krieger.
Deichgraeber, Karl. Die Epidemien und das Corpus Hippocraticum: Voruntersuchung zu einer Geschichte der koischen Aerzteschule. 187p. 1971. Repr. 42.50x (ISBN 3-11-003635-5). De Gruyter.

Edelstein, L. The Hippocratic Oath. 90p. 1979. 10.00 (ISBN 0-89005-272-7). Ares.
Fredrich, Carl. Hippokratische Untersuchungen. facsimile ed. LC 75-13264. (History of Ideas in Ancient Greece Ser.). (Ger.). 1976. Repr. of 1899 ed. 14.00x (ISBN 0-405-07306-2). Arno.
Heidel, William A. Hippocratic Medicine. Cohen, I. Bernard, ed. LC 80-2129. (Development of Science Ser.). (Illus.). 1981. lib. bdg. 15.00x (ISBN 0-405-13878-4). Arno.
Hippocrates. L' Ancienne Medecine. Connor, W. R., ed. LC 78-18573. (Greek Texts & Commentaries Ser.). (Illus.). 1979. Repr. of 1948 ed. lib. bdg. 12.00x (ISBN 0-405-11417-6). Arno.
Kibre, Pearl. Hippocrates Latinus: Repertorium of Hipocratic Writings in the Latin Middle Ages, Part VII. 30p. 1981. pap. 4.00 (ISBN 0-8232-0077-9). Fordham.
--Hippocrates Latinus: Repertorium of Hippocratic Writings in the Latin Middle Ages. 1975-81. Pt. 1. pap. 3.50 (ISBN 0-8232-0070-1); Pt. 2. pap. 4.00 (ISBN 0-8232-0071-X); Pt. 3. pap. 4.00 (ISBN 0-8232-0072-8); Pt. 4. pap. 4.00 (ISBN 0-8232-0073-6); Pt. 5. pap. 4.00 (ISBN 0-8232-0074-4); Pt. 6. pap. 4.00 (ISBN 0-8232-0076-0); Pt. 7. pap. 4.00 (ISBN 0-686-77076-5). Fordham.
Moon, Robert O. Hippocrates & His Successors in Relation to the Philosophy of Their Time. LC 75-23745. Repr. of 1923 ed. 18.50 (ISBN 0-404-13351-7). AMS Pr.
Saffron, Morris H. Maurus of Salerno: Twelfth Century "Optimus Physicus" with His Commentary on the Prognostics of Hippocrates. LC 78-184164. (Transactions Ser.: Vol. 62, Pt. 1). 1972. pap. 2.00 (ISBN 0-87169-621-5). Am Philos.
Smith, Wesley D. The Hippocratic Tradition. LC 78-20977. (History of Science Ser.). 1979. 17.50x (ISBN 0-8014-1209-9). Cornell U Pr.

HIPPOLOGY
see Horses

HIPPOLYTUS
Euripides. Hippolytus in Drama & Myth. Sutherland, Donald, tr. LC 60-13112. 1960. pap. 3.50x (ISBN 0-8032-5195-5, BB 103, Bison). U of Nebr Pr.

HIPPOPOTAMUS
Reynolds, S. H. Pleistocene Hippopotamus. Repr. of 1922 ed. pap. 11.50 (ISBN 0-384-50420-5). Johnson Repr.
Trevisick, Charles. Hippos. LC 79-19672. (Animals of the World Ser.). (Illus.). (gr. 4-8). 1980. PLB 11.95 (ISBN 0-8172-1087-3). Raintree Pubs.

HIRE
see also Carriers; Freight Forwarders; Labor Contract; Leases; Master and Servant; Servants
Bullwinkle, Alice & Galloway, Howard P. Finding Summer Staff. 1979. pap. 9.85 (ISBN 0-87874-016-3). Galloway.

HIRE-PURCHASE
see Sales, Conditional

HIRE-PURCHASE PLAN
see Instalment Plan

HIRING HALLS
Larrowe, Charles P. Shape-up & Hiring Hall. LC 75-46614. (Illus.). 250p. 1976. Repr. of 1955 ed. lib. bdg. 15.25x (ISBN 0-8371-8750-8, LASU). Greenwood.

HIROHITO, EMPEROR OF JAPAN, 1901-
Bergamini, David. Japan's Imperial Conspiracy. (Illus.). 1971. 14.95 (ISBN 0-688-01905-6). Morrow.

HIROSHIGE, 1797-1858
Chiba, Reiko, ed. Down the Emperor's Road with Hiroshige. LC 65-18959. (Illus.). 1965. 9.50 (ISBN 0-8048-0143-6). C E Tuttle.
Narazaki, M. Hiroshige: Famous Views. Gage, Richard, tr. LC 68-26557. (Masterpieces of Ukiyo-e Ser.). (Illus.). 1968. pap. 12.95 (ISBN 0-87011-068-3). Kodansha.
--Studies in Nature: Birds & Flowers by Hokusai & Hiroshige. Bester, John, tr. LC 76-82657. (Masterpieces of Ukiyo-e Ser.). (Illus.). 1970. pap. 12.95 (ISBN 0-87011-103-5). Kodansha.

HIROSHIMA
Auxier, John A. Ichiban: Radiation Dosimetry for the Survivors of the Bombings of Hiroshima & Nagasaki. LC 76-30780. (ERDA Critical Review Ser.). 128p. 1977. pap. 4.75 (ISBN 0-686-75824-2); microfiche 3.00 (ISBN 0-686-75825-0). DOE.
Duras, Marguerite, ed. Hiroshima Mon Amour. (Illus.). 7.50 (ISBN 0-8446-5840-5). Peter Smith.
Harris, Jonathan. Hiroshima: A Study in the Science, Politics, & the Ethics of War. Brown, Richard H. & Halsey, Van R., eds. (Amherst Ser). (gr. 10-12). 1970. pap. text ed. 4.52 (ISBN 0-201-02687-2, Sch Div); tchr's manual 1.92 (ISBN 0-201-02689-9). A-W.
Hersey, John. Hiroshima. (gr. 6-12). pap. 2.25 (ISBN 0-553-14569-X). Bantam.
Kurland, Gerald. The Hiroshima Atomic Bomb Blast. Rahmas, D. Steve, ed. LC 73-78401. (Events of Our Times Ser: No. 7). 32p. (Orig.). (gr. 7-12). 1973. lib. bdg. 2.95 incl. catalog cards (ISBN 0-686-05486-5); pap. 1.50 vinyl laminated covers (ISBN 0-87157-209-5). SamHar Pr.
Pacific War Research Society. The Day Man Lost: Hiroshima, 6 August 1945. LC 80-85346. (Illus.). 344p. 1981. pap. 4.95 (ISBN 0-87011-471-9). Kodansha.
--The Day Man Lost: Hiroshima, 6 August 1945. LC 76-174219. (Illus.). 312p. 1972. 10.00x (ISBN 0-87011-174-4). Kodansha.
Thomas, Gordon & Witts, Max M. Enola Gay. LC 76-44343. 1977. 35.00x (ISBN 0-8128-2150-5). Stein & Day.
United States Strategic Bombing Survey. The Effects of the Atomic Bombs on Hiroshima & Nagasaki. LC 73-80704. (Illus.). 53p. 1973. Repr. of 1946 ed. 15.00x (ISBN 0-88307-505-9). Gannon.

HIRSCH, EMIL GUSTAV, 1851-1923
Hirsch, David E. Rabbi Emil G. Hirsch: The Reform Advocate. LC 68-24717. 1968. pap. 3.00x (ISBN 0-87655-502-4). Whitehall Co.
Hirsch, David E., ed. Theology of Emil G. Hirsch. 1977. pap. text ed. 12.50x (ISBN 0-87655-539-3). Whitehall Co.

HIRSCH, MAURICE DE, BARON, 1831-1896
Grunwald, Kurt. Turkenhirsch: A Study of Baron Maurice de Hirsch. 158p. 1966. casebound 9.95 (ISBN 0-87855-182-4). Transaction Bks.

HIRSUTISM
see Hypertrichosis

HIRUDINEA
see Leeches

HIRUNDINIDAE
see Swallows

HISPANIC CIVILIZATION
see Civilization, Hispanic

HISPANIC SOCIETY OF AMERICA
Askins, Arthur. The Hispano-Portuguese Cancionero of the Hispanic Society of America. (Studies in the Romance Languages & Literatures: No. 144). 1974. pap. 13.50x (ISBN 0-8078-9144-4). U of NC Pr.
Garcia-Mazas, Jose. El Poeta y la Escultura: La Espana Que Huntington Conocio. (Illus.). 1962. 2.50 (ISBN 0-87535-097-6). Hispanic Soc.
Hispanic Society Of America. History of the Hispanic Society of America, Museum & Library, 1904-1954, with a Survey of the Collections. (Illus.). 1954. 10.00 (ISBN 0-87535-080-1). Hispanic Soc.
Hispanic Society of America: Handbook of Museum & Library Collections. (Illus.). 1938. 5.00 (ISBN 0-87535-043-7). Hispanic Soc.
Hispanic Society of America, New York. Catalogue of the Library of the Hispanic Society of America, First Supplement, 4 vols. 1970. lib. bdg. 395.00 (ISBN 0-8161-0910-9). G K Hall.
Penny, C. L. Hispanic Society of America: Catalogue of Publications. (Illus.). 1943. 3.50 (ISBN 0-87535-055-0). Hispanic Soc.

HISPANO-AMERICAN WAR, 1898
see United States-History-War of 1898

HISPANOAMERICANISM
see Pan-Hispanism

HISPANOS
see Mexican Americans

HISS, ALGER, 1904-
Chambers, Whittaker. Witness. 1978. pap. 9.95 (ISBN 0-89526-915-5). Regnery-Gateway.
Hiss, Tony. Laughing Last: Alger Hiss. 1977. 8.95 (ISBN 0-395-24899-X). HM.
Rabinowitz, Victor. In Re Alger Hiss, Vol. 2. Tiger, Edith, ed. 1981. pap. 9.95 (ISBN 0-8090-0150-0). Hill & Wang.
Smith, John C. Alger Hiss. LC 75-21462. 1976. 15.00 (ISBN 0-03-013776-4). HR&W.
Tiger, Edith, ed. In Re Alger Hiss. (American Century Ser.). 438p. 1979. pap. 8.95 (ISBN 0-8090-0143-8, AmCen). Hill & Wang.
Weinstein, Allen. Perjury: The Hiss-Chambers Case. LC 78-11048. (Illus.). 1979. pap. 6.95 (ISBN 0-394-72830-0, Vin). Random.
--Perjury: The Hiss-Chambers Case. LC 77-75009. 1978. 15.00 (ISBN 0-394-49546-2). Knopf.

HISTAMINE
Beaven, M. A. Histamine: Its Role in Physiological & Pathological Processes. (Monographs in Allergy: Vol. 13). (Illus.). 1978. pap. 22.75 (ISBN 3-8055-2887-6). S Karger.
International Symposium on Histamaing H2-Receptor Antagonists, 2nd, London, 1976. Cimetidine: Proceedings. Burland, W. L. & Simkins, M. A., eds. (International Congress Ser.: No. 416). 1977. 49.00 (ISBN 90-219-0347-4, Excerpta Medica). Elsevier.
Maslinski, C., ed. Histamine: Mechanisms of Regulation of the Biogenic Amines Level in the Tissues with Special Reference to Histamine. LC 72-95941. 370p. 1974. 42.50 (ISBN 0-12-787052-0). Acad Pr.
Rocha E Silva, M., ed. Histamine & Anti-Histaminics. Incl. Pt. 1: Histamine. (Illus.). xxxvi, 991p. 1966. 99.00 (ISBN 0-387-03535-4); Pt. 2: Anti-Histaminics. (Handbook of Experimental Pharmacology: Vol. 18, Pt. 1). (Eng, Ger, Fr.). Springer-Verlag.
Schachter, M., ed. Histamine & Antihistamines. LC 72-10535. 196p. 1973. text ed. 31.00 (ISBN 0-08-016390-4). Pergamon.
Silva, M. Roche. Histamine 11 & Anti-Histaminics: Chemistry, Metabolism & Physiological & Pharmacological Actions. (Handbook of Experimental Pharmacology: Vol. 18, Pt. 2). 1978. 198.80 (ISBN 0-387-07849-5). Springer-Verlag.

HISTOCHEMISTRY
see also Biological Chemistry; Cytochemistry; Molecular Biology; Physiological Chemistry
Bancroft, J. D. Histochemical Techniques. 2nd ed. 336p. 1975. 39.95 (ISBN 0-407-00033-X). Butterworth.
Brimmer, Frances M. Histological Methods & Terminology. (Orig., In Dictionary Form). 1979. pap. text ed. 14.95x (ISBN 0-934696-00-4). Mosaic Pr.
Chang, Louis W. A Color Atlas & Manual for Applied Histochemistry. (Illus.). 126p. 1979. text ed. 14.75 spiral lexotone (ISBN 0-398-03914-3). C C Thomas.
Chayen, Joseph, et al. Practical Histochemistry. LC 72-8596. 280p. 1973. 29.75 (ISBN 0-471-14950-0, Pub. by Wiley-Interscience). Wiley.
Chouchkov, C. N. Cutaneous Receptors. (Advances in Anatomy, Embryology & Cell Biology Ser.: Vol. 54, Part 5). (Illus.). 1978. pap. 18.50 (ISBN 0-387-08826-1). Springer-Verlag.
Eranko, Olavi, et al, eds. Histochemistry & Cell Biology of Autonomic Neurons: Sif Cells, & Paraneurons. (Advances in Biochemical Psychopharmacology: Vol. 25). 410p. 1980. text ed. 45.00 (ISBN 0-89004-495-3). Raven.
Fujiwara, Motohatsu & Tanaka, Chikako, eds. Amine Fluorescence Histochemistry. (Illus.). 1974. 18.00 (ISBN 0-89640-016-6). Igaku-Shoin.
Garrett, J. R., et al, eds. Histochemistry of Secretory Processes. 340p. 1977. text ed. 39.95x (ISBN 0-412-14870-6, Pub. by Chapman & Hall England). Methuen Inc.
Goldsby, Richard A. Cells & Energy. 2nd ed. 1977. pap. text ed. 8.95 (ISBN 0-02-344300-6, 34430). Macmillan.
Hack, M. H. & Helmy, F. M. An Introduction to Comparative, Correlative Histochemical Principles. (Illus.). 90p. 1974. 24.00 (ISBN 0-685-50594-4). Adler.
Humason, Gretchen L. Animal Tissue Techniques. 4th ed. LC 78-17459. (Illus.). 1979. text ed. 24.95x (ISBN 0-7167-0299-1). W H Freeman.
Lillie, Ralph D. & Fullmer, Hareld M. Histopathologic Technic & Practical Histochemistry. 4th ed. 1976. 48.00 (ISBN 0-07-037862-2, HP). McGraw.
Lojda, Z., et al. Enzyme Histochemistry: A Laboratory Manual. (Illus.). 1979. pap. 43.90 (ISBN 0-387-09269-2). Springer-Verlag.
Pearse, A. G. Histochemistry: Theoretical & Applied, Vol. 1. 4th ed. (Illus.). 439p. 1980. text ed. 62.50 (ISBN 0-443-01998-3). Churchill.
--Histochemistry: Theoretical & Applied, Vol. 2. 3rd ed. (Illus.). 1972. text ed. 60.00 (ISBN 0-443-00865-5). Churchill.
Thompson, Samuel W. Selected Histochemical & Histopathological Methods. (Illus.). 1680p. 1974. text ed. 90.50 (ISBN 0-398-03132-0). C C Thomas.
Troyer, Henry. Principles & Techniques of Histochemistry. LC 80-80592. 1980. text ed. 22.95 (ISBN 0-316-85310-0). Little.
Vacca, Linda L. Laboratory Manual of Histochemistry. 1981. write for info. (ISBN 0-89004-540-2). Raven.
--Laboratory Manual of Histochemistry. 1981. write for info. (ISBN 0-89004-540-2, 649). Raven.
Wied, George. Introduction to Quantitative Cytochemistry. 1966. 71.50 (ISBN 0-12-748850-2). Acad Pr.
Wied, George & Bahr, Gunter F. Introduction to Quantitative Cytochemistry, 2. 1970. 67.50 (ISBN 0-12-748852-9). Acad Pr.

HISTOCOMPATIBILITY
see also Immunological Tolerance
Carpenter, Charles, ed. Clinical Histocompatibility Testing, Vol. 2. (Transplantation Proceedings Reprint). 244p. 1978. 39.00 (ISBN 0-8089-1095-7). Grune.
Carpenter, Charles B., ed. Clinical Histocompatibility Testing, Vol. 4. (Transplantation Proceedings Reprint). 336p. 1980. 32.50 (ISBN 0-8089-1275-5). Grune.
Dick, H. M. & Kissemeyer-Nielsen, F., eds. Histocompatibility Techniques. LC 79-13943. 1979. 44.00 (ISBN 0-444-80132-4, North Holland). Elsevier.
Dorf, Martin E. The Role of the Major Histocompatibility Complex in Immunobiology. LC 80-772. 525p. 1981. lib. bdg. 47.50 (ISBN 0-8240-7129-8). Garland Pub.
Ferrone, Soldano, et al, eds. HLA Antigens in Clinical Medicine & Biology. LC 78-7361. 268p. 1979. lib. bdg. 29.50 (ISBN 0-8240-7051-8). Garland Pub.
Gotz, D., ed. The Major Histocompatibility System in Man & Animals. 1977. 39.60 (ISBN 0-387-08097-X). Springer-Verlag.
International Convocation on Immunology, 7th, Niagra Falls, N. Y., July 1980, et al. Immunbiology of the Major Histocompatibility Complex. Zaleski, M. B. & Kano, K., eds. (Illus.). xii, 396p. 1981. 118.75 (ISBN 3-8055-1896-X). S Karger.
International Symposium on HLA System-New Aspects, Bergamo, Italy, Sept. 25-26, 1976 & Ferrara, G. B. HLA System-New Aspects: Proceedings. LC 76-58403. 1977. 28.00 (ISBN 0-7204-0617-X, North-Holland). Elsevier.
Klein, J. Biology of the Mouse Histocompatibility - 2 Complex: Principles of Immunogenetics Applied to a Single System. LC 74-14843. (Illus.). xiv, 618p. 1975. 54.90 (ISBN 0-387-06733-7). Springer-Verlag.
Reisfeld, Ralph A. & Ferrone, Soldano, eds. Current Trends in Histocompatability, 2 vols. Incl. Vol. 1. Immunogenetic & Molecular Profiles. 565p. 49.50 (ISBN 0-306-40480-X); Vol. 2. Biological & Clinical Concepts. 310p. 2.50 (ISBN 0-306-40481-8). 1981 (Plenum Pr). Plenum Pub.
Snell, George D. & Hildemann, W. H. Cell Surface Antigens: Studies in Mammals Other Than Man. LC 72-13690. (Illus.). 220p. 1973. text ed. 23.00x (ISBN 0-8422-7100-7). Irvington.
Terasaki, Paul I. Histocompatibility Testing Nineteen Eighty, Vol. 1. LC 80-36737. (Illus.). 1980. 59.00 (ISBN 0-9604606-0-8). UCLA Tissue.
Yunis, Edmond J., et al. Tissue Typing & Organ Transplantation. 1973. 42.00 (ISBN 0-12-775160-2). Acad Pr.
Zaleski, M. B., et al, eds. Immunobiology of the Major Histocompatibility Complex. (Illus.). 1981. write for info. (ISBN 3-8055-1896-X). S Karger.

HISTOLOGY
see also Botany-Anatomy; Cells; Histochemistry; Microscope and Microscopy; Tissues; also names of particular tissues or organs, e.g. Muscle, Nerves
Amenta, Peter S. Histology & Embroyology Review. LC 76-44417. 1977. pap. 8.00 (ISBN 0-668-03831-4). Arco.
Amenta, Peter S., ed. Histology. 2nd ed. (Medical Outline Ser.). 1978. spiral bdg. 10.75 (ISBN 0-87488-662-7). Med Exam.
American Registry Of Pathology. Manual of Histologic Staining Methods of the Armed Forces Institute of Pathology. 3rd ed. (Illus.). 1968. 16.95 (ISBN 0-07-001507-4, HP). McGraw.
Arey, Leslie B. Human Histology: A Textbook in Outline Form. 4th ed. LC 73-88256. (Illus.). 338p. 1974. text ed. 19.00 (ISBN 0-7216-1392-6). Saunders.
Bancroft, John D. & Stevens, Alan, eds. Theory & Practice of Histological Techniques. (Illus.). 528p. 1977. text ed. 48.00 (ISBN 0-443-01534-1). Churchill.
Banks, William J. Histology & Comparative Organology: A Text-Atlas. LC 79-24569. 296p. 1980. Repr. of 1974 ed. lib. bdg. 25.50 (ISBN 0-89874-084-3). Krieger.
Bevelander, Gerrit. Outline of Histology. rev. ed. 7th ed. (Illus., Orig.). 1971. text ed. 12.95 (ISBN 0-8016-0680-2). Mosby.
Bevelander, Gerrit & Ramaley, Judith A. Essentials of Histology. 8th ed. LC 78-4847. 1979. text ed. 19.95 (ISBN 0-8016-0669-1). Mosby.
Bhaskar, S. N. Orban's Oral Histology & Embryology. 9th ed. LC 80-11972. (Illus.). 1980. pap. text ed. 29.95 (ISBN 0-8016-4609-X). Mosby.
Bloom, William & Fawcett, Don W. A Textbook of Histology. 10th ed. LC 73-77935. (Illus.). 1040p. 1975. text ed. 38.00 (ISBN 0-7216-1757-3). Saunders.
Borysenko, Myrin, et al. Functional Histology. 1978. text ed. 17.95 (ISBN 0-316-10303-9); pap. text ed. 13.95 (ISBN 0-316-10302-0). Little.
Bourne, Geoffrey H. In Vivo Techniques in Histology. 412p. 1967. 16.50 (ISBN 0-683-00968-0, Pub. by Williams & Wilkins). Krieger.
Bradley, James V. Elementary Microstudies of Human Tissues. (Illus.). 376p. 1972. pap. 36.50 (ISBN 0-398-02240-2). C C Thomas.
Brown, Geoffrey G. An Introduction to Histotechnology: A Manual for the Student, Practicing Technologists, & Resident in Pathology. 2nd ed. (Illus.). 480p. 1978. 24.75 (ISBN 0-8385-4340-5). ACC.

Carleton's Histological Technique. 5th ed. Wallington, E. A. & Wallington, E. A., eds. (Illus.). 592p. 1980. text ed. 59.50 (ISBN 0-19-261310-3). Oxford U Pr.

Carpenter, Charles B. & Miller, William V., eds. Clinical Histocompatibility - Testing, Vol. 1. (Transplantation Proceedings Reprint). 248p. 1977. 39.00 (ISBN 0-8089-1022-1). Grune.

Case, Norman M. Visual Aids for Human Histology. 2nd ed. (Illus.). 96p. 1980. text & slides 275.00 (ISBN 0-683-01468-4). Williams & Wilkins.

Cohen, Annabelle. Handbook of Microscopic Anatomy for the Health Sciences. LC 74-13572. (Illus.). 1975. pap. text ed. 8.95 (ISBN 0-8016-1012-5). Mosby.

Copenhaver, et al. Bailey's Textbook of Histology. 17th ed. 818p. 1978. lib. bdg. 34.50 (ISBN 0-683-02078-1). Williams & Wilkins.

Ehrlich, Paul, et al. The Collected Papers: Index & Bibliography, Vol. 4. Himmelweit, F., et al, eds. write for info. Pergamon.

Elias, Hans, et al. Histology & Human Microanatomy. 4th ed. LC 78-9108. 1978. 31.95 (ISBN 0-471-04929-8, Pub. by Wiley Medical). Wiley.

Feldmann, G., et al. Immunoenzymatic Techniques. LC 76-7438. 1976. 100.00 (ISBN 0-444-11206-5, North-Holland). Elsevier.

Fonts, Alfredo R. Histology & Embryology Notes for Dental Assistants & Dental Hygienists. 1980. pap. text ed. 8.50 (ISBN 0-89669-029-6). Collegium Bk Pubs.

Gabe, M. Histological Techniques. Blackith, R. E. & Kovoor, A., trs. from Fr. (Illus.). 1976. 65.80 (ISBN 0-387-90162-0). Springer-Verlag.

Gardner, Dugald L. & Dodds, T. C. Human Histology. 3rd rev. ed. LC 75-14451. (Illus.). 410p. 1975. text ed. 35.00x (ISBN 0-443-01174-5). Churchill.

Germain, Jocelyn P. & Turvey, David J. Preparatory Techniques in Histology. 1981. text ed. write for info. (ISBN 0-407-16895-8). Butterworth.

Granulocyte Physiology, Function & Dysfunction. 98p. 1979. 9.00 (ISBN 0-914404-50-4). Am Assn Blood.

Ham, Arthur W. & Cormack, David H. Histology. 8th ed. LC 79-13185. 1979. text ed. 43.50 (ISBN 0-397-52089-1, JBL-Med-Nursing). Har-Row.

--Histophysiology of Cartilage, Bone & Joints. 1979. pap. text ed. 8.75 (ISBN 0-397-50460-8, JBL-Med-Nursing). Har-Row.

Hodges, R. D. The Histology of the Fowl. 1974. 100.50 (ISBN 0-12-351350-2). Acad Pr.

Jones, Ruth M. Basic Microscopic Technics. LC 66-20579. 1966. 6.95x (ISBN 0-226-40710-1). U of Chicago Pr.

Junqueira, Luis C. & Carneiro, Jose. Basic Histology. 3rd rev. ed. LC 80-81941. (Illus.). 504p. 1980. lexotone cover 15.50 (ISBN 0-87041-202-7). Lange.

Kiernan, K. A. Histological & Histochemical Methods: Theory & Practice. (Illus.). 400p. Date not set. 70.00 (ISBN 0-08-024936-1); pap. 25.00 (ISBN 0-08-024935-3). Pergamon.

Krause, William J. & Cutts, J. Jarry. Concise Text of Histology. (Illus.). 412p. 1981. soft cover 18.50 (ISBN 0-686-77741-7, 4784-1). Williams & Wilkins.

LaBossiere, Eileen. Histological Processing for the Neural Sciences. (Illus.). 100p. 1976. pap. 10.75 (ISBN 0-398-03516-4). C C Thomas.

--Histological Processing for the Neural Sciences. (Illus.). 100p. 1976. pap. 10.75 (ISBN 0-398-03516-4). C C Thomas.

Lamberg, Stanley L. & Rothstein, Robert. Histology & Cytology: Functional Medical Laboratory Manual. (Illus.). 1978. lab. manual 10.50 (ISBN 0-87055-272-4). AVI.

Leake, Lucy D. Comparative Histology: An Introduction to the Microscopic Structure of Animals. 1976. 112.00 (ISBN 0-12-441050-2). Acad Pr.

Leeson, C. Roland & Leeson, Thomas S. Histology. 3rd ed. LC 74-14783. (Illus.). 605p. 1976. text ed. 19.50 (ISBN 0-7216-5708-7). Saunders.

Leeson, Thomas S. & Leeson, C. Roland. A Brief Atlas of Histology. LC 77-86027. (Illus.). 1979. pap. text ed. 19.50 (ISBN 0-7216-5703-6). Saunders.

--Histology. 1981. text ed. write for info. (ISBN 0-7216-5704-4). Saunders.

Leonhardt, H. Human Histology, Cytology & Microanatomy. 4th ed. (Illus.). 1977. pap. 15.50 (ISBN 0-8151-5375-9). Year Bk Med.

Lovasy, Ernst. Dictionnaire des Termes d'Anatomie, d'Embryologie et d'Histologie. 624p. (Fr.). 1954. 17.50 (ISBN 0-686-57022-7, M-6380). French & Eur.

Majumdar, N. N. A Textbook of Histology. 450p. 1980. text ed. 35.00 (ISBN 0-7069-1012-5, Vikas India). Advent NY.

Pease, Daniel C. Histological Techniques for Electron Microscopy. 2nd ed. 1965. 32.50 (ISBN 0-12-548456-9). Acad Pr.

Poirier, Jacques & Dumas, Jean-Louis R. Review of Medical Histology. Taube, Ursula, tr. LC 76-28944. (Illus.). 1977. pap. text ed. 10.95 (ISBN 0-7216-7273-6). Saunders.

Preece, Ann. Manual for Histologic Technicians. 3rd ed. 300p. 1972. 16.95 (ISBN 0-316-71765-7). Little.

Price, C. J. & Reed, J. E. Histology. (Notes for Students of Animal Husbandry Ser). (Illus.). 109p. (Orig.). 1973. pap. 4.50 (ISBN 0-685-34563-7, F226, FAO). Unipub.

Ralis, H. A., et al. Techniques in Neurohistology. 1973. 14.95 (ISBN 0-407-77400-9). Butterworth.

Recent Advances in Histopathology. (No. 11). (Illus.). pap. text ed. 37.50 (ISBN 0-443-02386-7). Churchill.

Rhodin, Johannes G. Histology: A Text & Atlas. (Illus.). 816p. 1974. text ed. 27.50x (ISBN 0-19-501755-2). Oxford U Pr.

Robertson, W. B. The Endometrium. (Postgraduate Pathology Ser.). 1981. text ed. 59.95 (ISBN 0-407-00171-9). Butterworth.

Roisen, Fred J. & Hsu, Linda. Histology Review. (Basic Science Review Bks.). 1975. spiral bdg. 8.00 (ISBN 0-87488-219-2). Med Exam.

Rudman, Jack. Histology Technician. (Career Examination Ser.: C-2837). (Cloth bdg. avail. on request). 1980. pap. 10.00 (ISBN 0-8373-2837-3). Natl Learning.

Sanders, Charles L. & Schneider, Richard P., eds. Pulmonary Macrophage & Epithelial Cells. LC 77-12024. (ERDA Symposium Ser.). 628p. 1977. pap. 12.50 (ISBN 0-686-75724-6); microfiche 3.00 (ISBN 0-686-75725-4). DOE.

Schwann, Theodor. Microscopical Researches into the Accordance of the Structure & Growth of Animals & Plants. Smith, Henry, tr. LC 7-37464. 1969. Repr. of 1847 ed. 18.00 (ISBN 0-527-80700-1). Kraus Repr.

Sheehan, Denza C. & Hrapchak, Barbara B. Theory & Practice of Histotechnology. 2nd ed. LC 80-11807. 1980. text ed. 30.95 (ISBN 0-8016-4573-5). Mosby.

Smith, Arthur & Bruton, J. W. A Color Atlas of Histological Staining Techniques. (Illus.). 1978. 23.75 (ISBN 0-8151-7847-6). Year Bk Med.

Stolinski, C. & Breathnach, A. S. Freeze - Fracture Replication of Biological Tissue: Techniques, Interpretation & Applications. 1976. 40.00 (ISBN 0-12-672050-9). Acad Pr.

Ten Cate, A. Richard. Oral Histology: Development, Structure & Function. LC 79-18620. (Illus.). 500p. 1980. text ed. 29.95 (ISBN 0-8016-4886-6). Mosby.

Thompson, Samuel W., et al. A Histopathologic & Histologic Coding System for Tissue Collection. (Illus.). 256p. 1961. pap. 25.75 (ISBN 0-398-01922-3). C C Thomas.

Weiss, Leon & Greep, Roy O. Histology. 4th ed. LC 76-42251. (Illus.). 1977. text ed. 35.00 (ISBN 0-07-069091-X, HP). McGraw.

Welsch, Ulrich & Storch, Volker. Comparative Animal Cytology & Histology. rev. ed. LC 75-44254. (Biology Ser). (Illus.). 358p. 1976. 9.95 (ISBN 0-295-95495-7). U of Wash Pr.

Wheater, Paul, et al, eds. Functional Histology: A Text & Colour Atlas. (Illus.). 1979. pap. text ed. 22.00 (ISBN 0-443-01657-7). Churchill.

Windle, William F. Textbook of Histology. 5th ed. 1976. text ed. 18.95 (ISBN 0-07-070977-7, C). McGraw.

Woolf, Neville & Anthony, P. P. Recent Advances in Histopathology, No. 10. (Illus.). 1979. pap. text ed. 32.00 (ISBN 0-443-01783-2). Churchill.

HISTOLOGY–ATLASES

Bergman, Ronald A. & Afifi, Adel K. Atlas of Microscopic Anatomy: A Companion to Histology & Neuroanatomy. LC 72-88844. (Illus.). 426p. 1974. text ed. 26.00 (ISBN 0-7216-1687-9). Saunders.

Bevelander, Gerrit. Atlas of Oral Histology & Embryology. LC 67-29213. (Illus.). 242p. 1967. text ed. 9.75 (ISBN 0-8121-0012-3). Lea & Febiger.

Clara, M. & Herschel, K. Atlas of the Normal Microscopic Anatomy of Man. (Illus., Eng., Ger., Rus., & Span.). 1973. 156.00 (ISBN 0-685-39789-0). Adler.

Craigmyle, M. Color Atlas of Histology. (Year Book Color Atlas Ser.). (Illus.). 320p. 1975. 32.50 (ISBN 0-8151-1888-0). Year Bk Med.

DiFiore, Mariano S. Atlas of Human Histology. 5th ed. LC 81-8164. (Illus.). 231p. 1981. text ed. price not set (ISBN 0-8121-0756-X). Lea & Febiger.

Di Fiore, Mariano S., et al. New Atlas of Histology: Light Microscopy, Histochemistry & Electron Microscopy. 3rd ed. (Illus.). 335p. 1978. text ed. 37.50 (ISBN 0-8121-0736-5). Lea & Febiger.

Freeman, W. H. & Bracegirdle, Brian. An Advanced Atlas of Histology. (Heinemann Biology Atlases Ser.). 1976. text ed. 17.50x (ISBN 0-435-60317-5). Heinemann Ed.

--An Atlas of Histology. 2nd ed. (Heinemann Biology Atlases Ser.). 1967. text ed. 15.50x (ISBN 0-435-60311-6). Heinemann Ed.

Frey, Dorothea, et al. Color Atlas of Pathogenic Fungi. (Illus.). 1979. 42.95 (ISBN 0-8151-3277-8). Year Bk Med.

Graigmyle, M. Atlas a Color De Histologia. 1977. 40.75 (ISBN 0-8151-1890-2). Year Bk Med.

Hammersen, Frithjof, ed. Sobotta-Hammersen: History - A Color Atlas of Cytology, Histology & Microscopic Anatomy. 2nd ed. LC 79-19878. (Illus.). 243p. 1980. text ed. 29.00 (ISBN 0-8067-1742-4). Urban & S.

Kaul, Mohini, et al. Human Histological Atlas. (Illus.). 200p. 1981. text ed. 50.00 (ISBN 0-7069-1055-9, Pub. by Vikas India). Advent NY.

Matthews, James L. & Martin, James H. Atlas of Human Histology & Ultrastructure. LC 72-157470. (Illus.). 382p. 1971. text ed. 12.50 (ISBN 0-8121-0347-5). Lea & Febiger.

Meadows, Robert. Pocket Atlas of Human Histology. (Illus.). 465p. 1981. text ed. 29.50x (ISBN 0-19-261248-4); pap. text ed. 16.95x (ISBN 0-19-261177-1). Oxford U Pr.

Nieuwenhuys, R., et al. The Human Central Nervous System: A Pictorial Survey. (Illus.). 1978. pap. 26.40 (ISBN 0-387-08903-9). Springer-Verlag.

Porter, Keith R. & Bonneville, Mary A. Fine Structure of Cells & Tissues. 4th ed. LC 73-11314. (Illus.). 204p. 1973. text ed. 11.00 (ISBN 0-8121-0430-7). Lea & Febiger.

Reith, Edward J. & Ross, Michael H. Atlas of Descriptive Histology. 3rd ed. 1977. text ed. 18.95 scp (ISBN 0-06-045368-0, HarpC). Har-Row.

Rhodin, Johannes A. An Atlas of Histology. (Illus.). 400p. 1975. text ed. 21.50x (ISBN 0-19-501944-X). Oxford U Pr.

Sandborn, E. B. Light & Electron Microscopy of Cells & Tissues: An Atlas for Students in Biology & Medicine. 1972. text ed. 29.50 (ISBN 0-12-617950-6). Acad Pr.

Thompson, Samuel W., 2nd & Luna, Lee G. An Atlas of Artifacts: Encountered in the Preparation of Microscopic Tissue Sections. (Illus.). 208p. 1978. 27.75 (ISBN 0-398-03624-1). C C Thomas.

Wismar, Beth L. & Ackerman, G. Adolph. Visual Approach to Histology. (Illus.). 1970. text ed. 190.00 (ISBN 0-8036-9480-6); 7 tape cassettes 75.00 (ISBN 0-8036-9482-2); text only 5.00 (ISBN 0-8036-9481-4). Davis Co.

HISTOLOGY–LABORATORY MANUALS

Cook, H. C. Manual of Histological Demonstration Techniques. 1974. 19.95 (ISBN 0-407-74700-1). Butterworth.

A Courthouse Conservation Handbook. LC 76-1039. (Illus.). 1976. pap. 4.95 (ISBN 0-89133-036-4). Preservation Press.

Culling, C. F. Handbook of Histopathological & Histochemical Techniques. 3rd ed. 1974. 53.95 (ISBN 0-407-72901-1). Butterworth.

Gabe, M. Histological Techniques. Blackith, R. E. & Kovoor, A., trs. from Fr. (Illus.). 1976. 65.80 (ISBN 0-387-90162-0). Springer-Verlag.

Humason, Gretchen L. Animal Tissue Techniques. 4th ed. LC 78-17459. (Illus.). 1979. text ed. 24.95x (ISBN 0-7167-0299-1). W H Freeman.

Leeson, C. Roland & Leeson, Thomas S. Practical Histology: A Self-Instructional Laboratory Manual in Filmstrip. 1973. pap. 5.00 (ISBN 0-7216-9831-X); with 4 full-color filmstrips 45.00 (ISBN 0-7216-9838-7). Saunders.

Meyer, David B. Laboratory Guide for Human Histology. LC 78-14519. 1979. 5.95x (ISBN 0-8143-1629-8). Wayne St U Pr.

HISTOLOGY–OUTLINES, SYLLABI, ETC.

Burke, Jack D., et al. Essentials of Histology. LC 75-174346. (Illus.). 176p. (Orig.). 1972. pap. 4.50 (ISBN 0-8120-0439-6). Barron.

Stiles, Karl A. Handbook of Histology. 5th ed. (Illus.). 1968. 14.95 (ISBN 0-07-061426-1, HP). McGraw.

HISTOLOGY, PATHOLOGICAL

Ackerman, A. Bernard. Histologic Diagnosis of Inflammatory Skin Diseases: A Method by Pattern Analysis. LC 76-49437. (Illus.). 1978. text ed. 84.50 (ISBN 0-8121-0581-8). Lea & Febiger.

Bancroft, John D. & Stevens, Alan. Histopathological Stains & Their Diagnostic Uses. LC 74-81753. (Illus.). 224p. 1975. text ed. 23.00 (ISBN 0-443-01226-1). Churchill.

Cohen, Annabelle. Handbook of Microscopic Anatomy for the Health Sciences. LC 74-13572. (Illus.). 1975. pap. text ed. 8.95 (ISBN 0-8016-1012-5). Mosby.

Cook, H. C. Histopathology: Selected Topics. (Illus.). 1972. text ed. 20.95 (ISBN 0-02-857400-1). Macmillan.

Curran, R. C. Color Atlas of Histopathology. 2nd ed. (Illus.). 1972. text ed. 35.00x (ISBN 0-19-519151-X). Oxford U Pr.

Frayer, William C., ed. Lancaster Course in Ophthalmic Histopathology. (Illus.). 325p. 1980. Text, Slides & Fourteen Units With Lectures. 936.00 (ISBN 0-8036-3827-2). Davis Co.

Frey, Dorothea, et al. Color Atlas of Pathogenic Fungi. (Illus.). 1979. 42.95 (ISBN 0-8151-3277-8). Year Bk Med.

Gowing, N. F. Color Atlas of Tumor Histopathology. (Illus.). 240p. 1980. 87.50 (ISBN 0-8151-3837-7). Year Bk Med.

Hamashima, Yoshihiro. Immunohistopathology. LC 76-17451. (Illus.). 1976. 62.00 (ISBN 0-397-58196-3, JBL-Med-Nursing). Har-Row.

Hedinger, C. Histological Typing of Thyroid Tumours. (World Health Organization: International Histological Classification of Tumours Ser.). (Illus.). 1974. 18.50 (ISBN 92-4-176011-7, 70-1-011-20); incl. slides 48.50 (ISBN 0-89189-120-X, 70-1-011-00). Am Soc Clinical.

Histological Typing of Female Genital Tract Tumours. (World Health Organization: International Histological Classification of Tumours Ser.). (Illus.). 1975. 66.00 (ISBN 0-89189-113-7, 70-0-013-20); incl. slides 160.50 (ISBN 92-4-176013-3, 70-0-013-00). Am Soc Clinical.

Histological Typing of Salivary Gland Tumours. (World Health Organization: International Histological Classification of Tumours Ser.). (Illus.). 1972. incl. slides 48.50 (ISBN 0-685-77238-1, 70-1-007-20). Am Soc Clinical.

Histological Typing of Urinary Bladder Tumours. (World Health Organization: International Histological Classification of Tumours Ser.). (Illus.). 1973. 22.50 (ISBN 0-89189-123-4, 70-1-010-20); incl. slides 59.50 (ISBN 0-89189-124-2, 70-1-010-00). Am Soc Clinical.

Kennedy, Alexander. Basic Techniques in Diagnostic Histopathology. LC 77-2362. (Illus.). 1977. text ed. 15.00 (ISBN 0-443-01464-7). Churchill.

Koss, Leopold G. Diagnostic Cytology & It's Histopathologic Bases, 2 vols. 3rd ed. LC 78-24140. 1979. Set. text ed. 137.50x (ISBN 0-397-50402-0, JBL-Med-Nursing). Har-Row.

Lavelle, Christopher L. & Proctor, Donald B. Clinical Pathology of the Oral Mucosa. (Illus.). 1978. text ed. 27.50x (ISBN 0-06-141519-7, Harper Medical). Har-Row.

Law, J. & Oliver, H. J. Glossary of Histopathological Terms. (Illus.). 128p. 1972. text ed. 8.80 (ISBN 0-407-72730-2). Butterworth.

Lever, Walter F. & Schaumburg-Lever, Gundula. Histopathology of the Skin. 5th ed. LC 75-5729. (Illus.). 793p. 1975. 72.50 (ISBN 0-397-52069-7, JBL-Med-Nursing). Har-Row.

McGovern, Vincent J. Malignant Melanoma: Clinical & Histological Diagnosis. LC 76-3793. 1976. 41.95 (ISBN 0-471-58417-7, Pub. by Wiley Medical). Wiley.

Mair, W. G. & Tome, F. M. Atlas of the Ultrastructure of Diseased Human Muscle. (Illus.). 1972. 20.75x (ISBN 0-443-00831-0). Churchill.

Mathe, G. & Rappaport, A. Histological & Cytological Typing of Neoplastic Diseases of Haematopoietic & Lymphoid Tissues. (World Health Organization: International Histological Classification of Tumours Ser.). (Illus.). 1976. 49.50 (ISBN 92-4-176014-1, 70-0-014-20); incl. slides 132.00 (ISBN 0-89189-126-9, 70-1-014-00). Am Soc Clinical.

Moragas, Augusto, et al. Atlas of Neonatal Histopathology. Valdes-Dapena, Antonio & Valdes-Dapena, Marie A., trs. LC 76-45960. (Illus.). 1978. text ed. 62.50 (ISBN 0-7216-6542-X). Saunders.

Papaincolaou, George N. Atlas of Exfoliative Cytology. LC 52-12251. (Commonwealth Fund Publications Ser). (Illus.). 458p. 1954-60. 30.00x (ISBN 0-674-05150-5); 1956 suppl. 1 10.00x (ISBN 0-674-05151-3). Harvard U Pr.

Pindborg, J. J. & Kramer, I. R. Histological Typing of Odontogenic Tumours, Jaw Cysts & Allied Lesions. (World Health Organization: International Histological Classification of Tumours Ser.). (Illus.). 1971. incl. slides 112.50 (ISBN 0-89189-114-5, 70-1-005-00). Am Soc Clinical.

Preece, Ann. Manual for Histologic Technicians. 3rd ed. 300p. 1972. 16.95 (ISBN 0-316-71765-7). Little.

Reed, Richard J. Cutaneous Vasculitides: Immunologic & Histologic Correlations. LC 77-22502. (Illus.). 1978. text ed. 16.00 (ISBN 0-89189-033-5, 16-1-028-00); text & slides 58.00 (ISBN 0-89189-097-1, 15-1-028-00). Am Soc Clinical.

Rossi. Histopathology of Cardiac Arryhthmius. 2nd ed. (Illus.). 299p. 1978. pap. text ed. 54.00 (ISBN 0-8121-0705-5). Lea & Febiger.

Rywlin, Arkadi M. Histopathology of the Bone Marrow. LC 75-41570. (Series in Laboratory Medicine). 229p. 1976. text ed. 22.50 (ISBN 0-316-76369-1). Little.

Sandritter, W., et al. Color Atlas of Histopathology. 6th ed. (Illus.). 1979. 39.95 (ISBN 0-8151-7552-3). Year Bk Med.

Scarff, R. W. & Torloni, H. Histological Typing of Breast Tumours. (World Health Organization: International Histological Classification of Tumours Ser.). (Illus.). 1977. 9.50 (ISBN 0-89189-111-0, 70-1-002-20). Am Soc Clinical.
Schajowicz, F., et al. Histological Typing of Bone Tumours. (World Health Organization: International Histological Classification of Tumours Ser.). (Illus.). 1972. incl. slides 119.00 (ISBN 0-89189-110-2, 70-1-006-00). Am Soc Clinical.
Schumann, G. Berry & Weiss, Mark. Atlas of Renal & Urinary Tract Cytology & Its Histopathologic Bases. (Illus.). 240p. 1981. text ed. 55.00 (ISBN 0-397-50443-8, JBL-Med-Nursing). Har-Row.
Serov, S. F. & Scully, R. F. Histological Typing of Ovarian Tumours. (World Health Organization: International Histological Classification of Tumours Ser.). (Illus.). 1973. 36.50 (ISBN 0-89189-117-X, 70-1-009-20); incl. slides 112.00 (ISBN 0-89189-118-8, 70-1-009-00). Am Soc Clinical.
Ten Seldam, R. E. & Helwig, E. B. Histological Typing of Skin Tumours. (World Health Organization: International Histological Classification of Tumours Ser.). (Illus.). 1977. 70.00 (ISBN 9-2417-6012-5, 70-1-012-20); incl. slides 158.50 (ISBN 0-89189-128-5, 70-1-012-00). Am Soc Clinical.
Thompson, Samuel W., 2nd & Luna, Lee G. An Atlas of Artifacts: Encountered in the Preparation of Microscopic Tissue Sections. (Illus.). 208p. 1978. 27.75 (ISBN 0-398-03624-1). C C Thomas.
Wahl, P. N. Histological Typing of Oral & Oropharyngeal Tumours. (World Health Organization: International Histological Classification of Tumours Ser.). (Illus.). 1971. incl. slides 37.00 (ISBN 0-89189-116-1, 70-1-004-00). Am Soc Clinical.
Weller, R. O. & Navarro, J. Cervos. Pathology of Peripheral Nerves: A Practical Approach. (Postgraduate Pathology Ser.). 1977. 39.95 (ISBN 0-407-00073-9). Butterworth.
Wepler, W. & Wildhirt, E. Clinical Histopathology of the Liver: An Atlas. Lowbeer, Leo, tr. LC 76-182156. 160p. 1972. 62.50 (ISBN 0-8089-0746-8). Grune.
White, David C. An Atlas of Radiation Histopathology. LC 75-17867. 236p. 1975. pap. 7.60 (ISBN 0-686-75692-4); microfiche 3.00 (ISBN 0-686-75693-2). DOE.

HISTOLOGY, VEGETABLE
see Botany–Anatomy

HISTONES

Busch, Harris. Histones & Other Nuclear Proteins. 1965. 43.00 (ISBN 0-12-147656-1). Acad Pr.
Li, Hsueh Jei, ed. Chromatin & Chromosome Structure. 1977. 31.50 (ISBN 0-12-450550-3). Acad Pr.
Philips, D. M., ed. Histones & Nucleohistones. LC 71-161306. 305p. 1971. 35.00 (ISBN 0-306-30456-2, Plenum Pr). Plenum Pub.

HISTOPLASMOSIS

Ajello, Libero E., et al. Histoplasmosis: Proceedings. (American Lecture in Clinical Microbiology Ser.). (Illus.). 540p. 1971. 49.50 (ISBN 0-398-02216-X). C C Thomas.
Schwarz, Jan. Histoplasmosis. (Life Science Ser.). 300p. 1981. 54.50 (ISBN 0-03-058448-5). Praeger.
Sweany, Henry C. Histoplasmosis. (Illus.). 560p. 1960. photocopy ed. spiral 55.75 (ISBN 0-398-01887-1). C C Thomas.

HISTORIANS
see also Archaeologists

Altschuler, Glenn C. Andrew M. White, Educator, Historian, Diplomat. LC 78-58065. (Illus.). 1978. 18.50x (ISBN 0-8014-1156-4). Cornell U Pr.
Antoni, Carlo. From History to Sociology: The Transition in German Historical Thinking. White, Hayden V., tr. from Italian. LC 76-40127. 1976. Repr. of 1959 ed. lib. bdg. 21.50 (ISBN 0-8371-9282-X, ANFH). Greenwood.
Barber, Godfrey L. The Historian Ephorus. LC 76-29429. Repr. of 1935 ed. 18.50 (ISBN 0-404-15343-7). AMS Pr.
Barker, John. The Superhistorians. 480p. Date not set. 17.50 (ISBN 0-684-16664-X, ScribT). Scribner.
Black, John B. The Art of History: A Study of Four Great Historians of the Eighteenth Century. 1976. lib. bdg. 59.95 (ISBN 0-8490-1452-2). Gordon Pr.
Clive, John. Macaulay: The Shaping of the Historian. pap. 4.95 (ISBN 0-394-71507-1, Vin). Random.
Dahlmann, Friedrich C. The Life of Herodotus. Cox, G. Valentine, tr. LC 77-94571. 1979. Repr. of 1845 ed. lib. bdg. 20.00 (ISBN 0-89341-256-2). Longwood Pr.
Dahmus, Joseph. Seven Medieval Historians. 320p. 1981. text ed. 20.95x (ISBN 0-88229-712-0). Nelson-Hall.
Halperin, William S., ed. Essays in Modern European Historiography. LC 79-116920. (Classic European Historians Ser). 1970. pap. text ed. 15.00x (ISBN 0-226-31445-6). U of Chicago Pr.
Hancock, William K. Country & Calling. LC 78-6026. 1978. Repr. of 1954 ed. lib. bdg. 19.25x (ISBN 0-313-20447-0, HACAC). Greenwood.
Hexter, J. H. On Historians. LC 78-16635. 1979. 16.00x (ISBN 0-674-63426-8). Harvard U Pr.
Histoire et Historiens Depuis Cinquante Ans: Methodes, Organisations et Resultats Du Travail Historique De 1876 a 1926, 2 vols in 1. LC 75-156822. 1927-28. 36.50 (ISBN 0-8337-2970-5). B. Franklin.
Holmes, Oliver Wendell. John Lothop Motley: A Memoir. 278p. 1979. Repr. of 1879 ed. lib. bdg. 25.00 (ISBN 0-89984-275-5). Century Bookbindery.
Janssen, E. M. Jacob Burckhardt und die Renaissance. 1970. 20.10x (ISBN 90-232-0808-0, Pub by Van Gorcum). Intl Schol Bk Serv.
Johnson, Charles. The Mechanical Processes of the Historian. 1977. lib. bdg. 59.95 (ISBN 0-8490-2217-7). Gordon Pr.
Kennedy, Patrick. Legendary Fictions of the Irish Celts. LC 69-16321. 1969. Repr. of 1866 ed. 15.00 (ISBN 0-405-08695-4, Blom Pubns). Arno.
Kenner, Charles L. History of New Mexican-Plains Indian Relations. LC 68-31375. (Illus.). 1969. 13.95 (ISBN 0-8061-0829-0). U of Okla Pr.
Kochan, Lionel. The Jew & His History. LC 76-56105. 1977. 15.00x (ISBN 0-8052-3650-3). Schocken.
Krieger, Leonard. Ranke: The Meaning of History. LC 76-25633. 1977. lib. bdg. 26.00x (ISBN 0-226-45349-9). U of Chicago Pr.
Pearson, Lionel. Early Ionian Historians. LC 75-136874. 240p. 1975. Repr. of 1939 ed. lib. bdg. 16.50x (ISBN 0-8371-5314-X, PEIH). Greenwood.
Phillips, Mark. Francesco Guicciardini: The Historian's Craft. LC 76-56341. (Romance Ser). 1977. 22.50x (ISBN 0-8020-5371-8). U of Toronto Pr.
Powicke, Frederick M. Modern Historians & the Study of History: Essays & Papers. LC 75-25496. 1976. Repr. of 1955 ed. lib. bdg. 16.50x (ISBN 0-8371-8428-2, POMH). Greenwood.
Ronan, Charles E. Francisco Javier Clavigero, S. J. (1731-1787) Figure of the Mexican Enlightenment. 1978. pap. 21.00 (ISBN 0-8294-0347-7). Loyola.
Sanders, Jennings B. Historical Interpretations & American Historianship. LC 66-13390. 1966. 6.00x (ISBN 0-87338-070-3). Kent St U Pr.
Schmitt, Hans A., ed. Historians of Modern Europe. LC 71-140961. 1971. 22.50x (ISBN 0-8071-0836-7). La State U Pr.
Sonnichsen, C. L. The Ambidextrous Historian: Historical Writers & Writing in the American West. LC 81-2787. 127p. 1981. 9.95 (ISBN 0-8061-1690-0). U of Okla Pr.
Sterns, Indrikis. The Greater Medieval Historians: An Interpretation & a Bibliography. LC 80-5850. 260p. 1980. lib. bdg. 18.75 (ISBN 0-8191-1327-1); pap. text ed. 10.50 (ISBN 0-8191-1328-X). U Pr of Amer.
Thomas, Lewis H. The Renaissance of Canadian History: A Biography of A. L. Burt. LC 74-79988. 1975. 20.00x (ISBN 0-8020-5304-1). U of Toronto Pr.
Toulmin, H. A. Social Historians. 34.95 (ISBN 0-8490-1065-9). Gordon Pr.
Wilgus, A. Curtis. Historiography of Latin America: A Guide to Historical Writing, 1500-1800. 1975. 18.00 (ISBN 0-8108-0859-5). Scarecrow.
Wilson, A. N. The Laird of Abbotsford: A View of Sir Walter Scott. 214p. 1980. text ed. 24.95x (ISBN 0-19-211756-4). Oxford U Pr.

HISTORIANS–CORRESPONDENCE, REMINISCENCES, ETC.

Alexander, Holmes. Pen & Politics. LC 77-90747. 212p. 1970. 5.50 (ISBN 0-937058-07-6). West Va U Pr.
Bohlen, Charles E. Witness to History. 1973. pap. 6.95x (ISBN 0-393-09287-9, 9287). Norton.
Burckhardt, Jakob. Letters. Dru, Alexander, tr. from Ger. LC 75-8821. (Illus.). 242p. 1975. Repr. of 1955 ed. lib. bdg. 15.00x (ISBN 0-8371-8114-3, BULE). Greenwood.
Carlyle, Thomas. Thomas Carlyle: Letters to His Wife. Bliss, Trudy, ed. 1953. 20.00 (ISBN 0-8274-3603-3). R West.
Clough, Shepard B. The Life I've Lived. LC 80-5503. 297p. 1981. lib. bdg. 19.75 (ISBN 0-8191-1116-3); pap. text ed. 10.75 (ISBN 0-8191-1117-1). U Pr of Amer.
Coulton, G. G. Fourscore Years: An Autobiography. 1944. Repr. 20.00 (ISBN 0-8274-2358-6). R West.
Curtis, George W., ed. The Correspondence of John Lothrop Motley, 2 vols. 1889. Set. 50.00 (ISBN 0-685-43870-8). Norwood Edns.
De Commynes, Philippe. Memoirs of Philippe De Commynes, Vol. 1, Bks 1-5 & Vol. 2, Bks. 6-8. Kinser, Samuel, ed. Cazeaux, Isabelle, tr. from Fr. LC 68-9363. (Illus.). 1969. Vol. 1. 19.50x (ISBN 0-87249-224-9); Vol. 2. 19.50x (ISBN 0-87249-224-9); Set. 37.50x (ISBN 0-87249-199-4). U of SC Pr.
Draper, John W. Thoughts on the Future Civil Policy of America. Incl. Memoir of John William Draper, 1811-1882. Barker, George F. (The Neglected American Economists Ser.). 1974. lib. bdg. 50.00 (ISBN 0-8240-1017-5). Garland Pub.
Evans, J. A. Procopius. (World Authors Ser.: Greece: No. 170). lib. bdg. 10.95 (ISBN 0-8057-2722-1). Twayne.
Hancock, Sir Keith. Professing History. 1977. 10.50x (ISBN 0-424-00024-5, Pub. by Sydney U Pr). Intl Schol Bk Serv.
Holmes, Oliver W. John Lothrop Motley: A Memoir. LC 71-38358. (Select Bibliographies Reprint Ser.). Repr. of 1878 ed. 16.00 (ISBN 0-8369-6775-5). Arno.
Ku, Chieh-Kang. The Autobiography of a Chinese Historian. Hummel, Arthur W., ed. (Perspectives in Asian History Ser: No. 12). 1979. Repr. of 1931 ed. lib. bdg. 15.00x (ISBN 0-87991-077-1). Porcupine Pr.
Lyon, B. & Lyon, M. The Journal de Guerre of Henri Pirenne. new ed. 1976. 31.75 (ISBN 0-444-11150-6, North-Holland). Elsevier.
Moser. Good Maine Food. 1978. pap. 5.95 (ISBN 0-89272-038-7). Down East.
Raleigh, Walter. Selections from His Historie of the World, His Letters, Etc. 1917. Repr. 20.00 (ISBN 0-8274-3357-3). R West.
Trevelyn, George M. Sir George Otto Trevelyan: A Memoir. 1932. Repr. 25.00 (ISBN 0-8274-3424-3). R West.

HISTORIANS–FRANCE

Barthes, Roland. Michelet. (Illus.). 192p. 1954. 6.50 (ISBN 0-686-53937-0). French & Eur.
Bramsen, Michele B. A Portrait of Elie Halevy. 1978. pap. text ed. 28.50x (ISBN 90-6032-100-6). Humanities.
De Tocqueville, Alexis. The Recollections of Alexis De Tocqueville. Mayer, J. P., ed. De Mattos, Alexander, tr. LC 78-13685. 1979. Repr. of 1949 ed. lib. bdg. 20.50x (ISBN 0-313-21052-7, TRRE). Greenwood.
Farmer, Paul. France Reviews Its Revolutionary Origins. 1963. lib. bdg. 13.00x (ISBN 0-374-92698-0). Octagon.
Masson, Gustave. Early Chroniclers of Europe: France. 1879. Repr. lib. bdg. 17.45 (ISBN 0-8414-6450-2). Folcroft.
Ranum, Orest. Artisans of Glory: Writers & Historical Thought in Seventeenth-Century France. LC 79-19248. (Illus.). 1980. 23.00x (ISBN 0-8078-1413-X). U of NC Pr.

HISTORIANS–GREAT BRITAIN

Angus-Butterworth, Lionel M. Ten Master Historians. facs. ed. LC 69-18919. (Essay Index Reprint Ser). 1961. 16.00 (ISBN 0-8369-0000-6). Arno.
Chase, Myrna. Elie Halevy: An Intellectual Biography. LC 79-24314. 1980. text ed. 17.50x (ISBN 0-231-04856-4). Columbia U Pr.
Cockroft, Grace A. The Public Life of George Chalmers. 1972. lib. bdg. 13.00x (ISBN 0-374-91789-2). Octagon.
Colbourn, H. Trevor. Lamp of Experience: Whig History & the Intellectual Origins of the American Revolution. LC 65-23138. (Institute of Early American History & Culture Ser.). 1965. 17.00x (ISBN 0-8078-0958-6). U of NC Pr.
Douglas, David. English Scholars, Sixteen Sixty to Seventeen Thirty. LC 75-3865. (Illus.). 291p. 1975. Repr. of 1951 ed. lib. bdg. 16.25x (ISBN 0-8371-8093-7, DOES). Greenwood.
Eyck, Frank. G. P. Gooch: A Study in History & Politics. 500p. 1981. text ed. 15.00x (ISBN 0-333-30849-2, Pub. by Macmillan England). Humanities.
Gibbon, Edward. Gibbon's Autobiography. Reese, M. M., ed. (Routledge English Texts). 1970. 7.95 (ISBN 0-7100-6923-5); pap. 4.95 (ISBN 0-7100-6925-1). Routledge & Kegan.
Grant, A. J., ed. English Historians. LC 73-118472. 1971. Repr. of 1906 ed. 15.00 (ISBN 0-8046-1221-8). Kennikat.
Hancock, William K. Country & Calling. LC 78-6026. 1978. Repr. of 1954 ed. lib. bdg. 19.25x (ISBN 0-313-20447-0, HACAC). Greenwood.
Llywelyn-Williams, Alun. R. T. Jenkins. (Writers of Wales Ser). 1977. pap. text ed. 6.00x (ISBN 0-7083-0653-5). Verry.
Marsh, Henry. Dark Age Britain: Some Sources of History. (Illus.). 1970. 16.50 (ISBN 0-208-01153-6, Archon). Shoe String.
Miller, Karl. Cockburn's Millenium. 1977. 16.50x (ISBN 0-674-13638-1, MIMC). Harvard U Pr.
Morey, Adrian. David Knowles: A Memoir. 1979. 12.50 (ISBN 0-232-51435-6). Attic Pr.
Morton, S. Fiona, ed. A Bibliography of Arnold J. Toynbee. 300p. 1980. 74.00 (ISBN 0-19-215261-0). Oxford U Pr.
Peardon, Thomas P. Transition in English Historical Writing, 1760-1830. LC 34-967. (Columbia University. Studies in the Social Sciences: No. 390). 24.50 (ISBN 0-404-51390-5). AMS Pr.
Rous, John. The Rous Roll. (Illus.). 144p. 1980. text ed. 31.50x (ISBN 0-904387-43-7). Humanities.
Sansom, Katharine. Sir George Sansom & Japan: A Memoir. LC 78-164855. (Illus.). 183p. 1972. 15.00 (ISBN 0-910512-13-2). Diplomatic Fla.
Stubbs, William. William Stubbs on the English Constitution. Cantor, Norman F., ed. 6.75 (ISBN 0-8446-3030-6). Peter Smith.
Wheeler-Bennett, John. Friends, Enemies & Sovereigns. LC 76-23198. 1977. 8.95 (ISBN 0-312-30555-9). St Martin.
Williams, Eric E. British Historians & the West Indies. LC 72-76470. 238p. 1972. text ed. 21.50x (ISBN 0-8419-0088-4, Africana). Holmes & Meier.
Wormell, Deborah. Sir John Seeley & the Uses of History. LC 79-51832. 303p. 1980. 38.50 (ISBN 0-521-22720-8). Cambridge U Pr.

HISTORIANS–NORWAY

Falnes, Oscar J. National Romanticism in Norway. LC 68-54263. (Columbia University. Studies in the Social Sciences: No. 386). Repr. of 1933 ed. 21.50 (ISBN 0-404-51386-7). AMS Pr.

HISTORIANS–UNITED STATES

Bassett, John S. Middle Group of American Historians. facs. ed. LC 67-22070. (Essay Index Reprint Ser). 1917. 18.00 (ISBN 0-8369-0175-4). Arno.
Cline, Howard F., compiled by. Historians of Latin America in the United States, 1965: Bibliographies of 680 Specialists. LC 66-22589. 1966. 9.00 (ISBN 0-8223-0036-2). Duke.
Cunliffe, Marcus & Winks, Robin W., eds. Pastmasters: Some Essays on American Historians. LC 78-27918. 1979. Repr. of 1969 ed. lib. bdg. 29.75x (ISBN 0-313-20938-3, CUPA). Greenwood.
Cutright, Paul R. & Brodhead, Michael J. Elliott Coues: Naturalist & Frontier Historian. LC 80-12424. (Illus.). 510p. 1981. 28.50 (ISBN 0-252-00802-2). U of Ill Pr.
Dale, Edward E. Frontier Historian: The Life & Work of Edward Everett Dale. Gibson, Arrell M., ed. 300p. 1975. 16.95 (ISBN 0-8061-1305-7). U of Okla Pr.
Durant, Will. Transition: A Mental Autobiography. 1978. pap. 5.95 (ISBN 0-671-24203-2, Touchstone Bks). S&S.
Gay, Peter. A Loss of Mastery: Puritan Historians in Colonial America. LC 67-10969. (Jefferson Memorial Lectures). 1966. 16.75x (ISBN 0-520-00456-6). U of Cal Pr.
Harbert, Earl N. The Force So Much Closer Home: Henry Adams & the Adams Family. LC 76-40744. 1977. 19.50x (ISBN 0-8147-3375-1); pap. 4.95x (ISBN 0-8147-3376-X). NYU Pr.
Hofstadter, Richard. The Progressive Historians: Turner, Beard, Parrington. LC 79-12591. 1979. pap. 7.95 (ISBN 0-226-34818-0, P841, Phoen). U of Chicago Pr.
Holmes, Oliver Wendell. John Lothrop Motley: A Memoir. 278p. 1979. Repr. of 1891 ed. lib. bdg. 25.00 (ISBN 0-8495-2265-X). Arden Lib.
Johns Hopkins University. Herbert B. Adams: Tributes of Friends. LC 78-64268. (Johns Hopkins University. Studies in the Social Sciences. Extra Volumes: 23). Repr. of 1902 ed. 21.00 (ISBN 0-404-61370-5). AMS Pr.
Journey into Another World: The Life Story of Arthur Prudden Coleman, Pioneer American Slavist, 3 pts. 5.00 ea. Alliance Coll.
Langer, William L. In & Out of the Ivory Tower: The Autobiography of William L. Langer. LC 77-20035. 1978. 20.00 (ISBN 0-88202-177-X). N Watson.
Levin, David. History As Romantic Art. LC 70-181945. (Stanford University. Stanford Studies in Language & Literature: No. 20). Repr. of 1959 ed. 21.45 (ISBN 0-404-51830-3). AMS Pr.
Olson, David C. Life on the Upper Michigan Frontier. LC 74-76304. 250p. 1974. 8.95 (ISBN 0-8283-1544-2). Branden.
Perkins, Dexter & Snell, John L. The Education of Historians in the United States. LC 74-25597. 1975. Repr. of 1962 ed. lib. bdg. 15.25x (ISBN 0-8371-7881-9, PEEH). Greenwood.
Robertson, James I., Jr. & McMurry, Richard M., eds. Rank & File: Civil War Essays in Honor of Bell Irvin Wiley. LC 76-48787. (Illus.). 1977. 8.95 (ISBN 0-89141-011-2). Presidio Pr.
Saveth, Edward N. American Historians & European Immigrants, 1875-1925. LC 65-18831. 1965. Repr. of 1948 ed. 8.00 (ISBN 0-8462-0694-3). Russell.
Skotheim, Robert A. American Intellectual Histories & Historian. LC 77-25991. 1978. Repr. of 1966 ed. lib. bdg. 26.00 (ISBN 0-313-20120-X, SKAI). Greenwood.

Stephenson, Wendell H. South Lives in History: Southern Historians & Their Legacy. LC 79-88947. Repr. of 1955 ed. 10.00x (ISBN 0-8371-2219-8). Greenwood.
Sternsher, Bernard. Consensus, Conflict, & American Historians. LC 73-16531. (Illus.). 448p. 1975. pap. 8.95x (ISBN 0-253-28070-2). Ind U Pr.
Stevenson, Elizabeth. Henry Adams: A Biography. LC 76-56793. 1977. Repr. lib. bdg. 25.00x (ISBN 0-374-97624-4). Octagon.
Wrigley, Chris, ed. A J, P. Taylor: A Complete Annotated Bibliography & Guide to His Historical & Other Writings. 608p. 1980. text ed. write for info. (ISBN 0-391-02097-8). Humanities.
Yarwood, A. T. Samuel Marsden: The Great Survivor. 1977. 26.00x (ISBN 0-522-84120-1, Pub. by Melbourne U Pr). Intl Schol Bk Serv.

HISTORIANS, ARAB
Rosenthal, Franz. History of Muslim Historiography. 1968. text ed. 93.50x (ISBN 90-04019-06-5). Humanities.
Wuestenfeld, Heinrich F. Geschichteschreiber Der Araber Und Ihre Werke, 2 Vols. in 1. 1964. Repr. of 1882 ed. 25.50 (ISBN 0-8337-3898-4). B Franklin.

HISTORIANS, GREEK
see Greek Historians

HISTORIANS, LATIN
see Latin Historians

HISTORIC BUILDINGS
see also Hiding-Places (Secret Chambers, etc.); Historic Sites; Historical Markers; Literary Landmarks
also specific kinds of historic buildings according to use, e.g. Churches; Hotels, Taverns, etc.; and subdivision Buildings under names of cities, e.g. New York (city)–Buildings
American Heritage Editors. Historic Houses of America Open to the Public: An American Heritage Guide. Da Costa, Beverley, ed. LC 79-149725. (Illus.). 320p. (Orig.). 1971. pap. 6.95 (ISBN 0-8281-0260-0, BOO3G1-03). Am Heritage.
Burton, Neil. The English Historic Houses Handbook. (Illus.). 668p. 1981. 17.95 (ISBN 0-87196-538-0). Facts on File.
Chase, John. The Sidewalk Companion to Santa Cruz Architecture. rev. ed. Gant, Michael S., ed. LC 79-64876. (Illus.). 367p. (Orig.). 1979. pap. 9.95 (ISBN 0-934136-00-9). Western Tanager.
City House: Commission on Chicago Historical & Architectural Landmarks. (Illus.). 100p. 1979. pap. 4.95 (ISBN 0-934076-00-6). Chicago Review.
Coleman, Laurence V. Historic House Museums. LC 71-175318. (Illus.). xii, 187p. 1973. Repr. of 1933 ed. 24.00 (ISBN 0-8103-3118-7). Gale.
Congdon, Herbert W. Old Vermont Houses, 1763-1850. 1968. pap. 4.95 (ISBN 0-87233-001-X). Bauhan.
Cummings, Abbott L. The Framed Houses of Massachusetts Bay, 1625-1725. LC 78-8390. (Illus.). 1979. 40.00x (ISBN 0-674-31680-0, Belknap Pr). Harvard U Pr.
Daniel, Jean H. & Daniel, Price. Fifty-One Capitols of America & Executive Mansions. LC 71-77604. (Illus.). 290p. 1969. 15.95 (ISBN 0-87294-067-5). Country Beautiful.
Davidson, Marshall B. The American Heritage History of Notable American Houses. LC 75-149724. (Illus.). 384p. 1971. 19.95 (ISBN 0-8281-0258-9, Dist. by Scribner); deluxe ed. 24.95 slipcased (ISBN 0-8281-0259-7, Dist. by Scribner). Am Heritage.
De Rothschild, James. The Rothschilds at Waddesdon Manor. (Illus.). 1979. 20.00 (ISBN 0-670-60854-8, The Vendome Pr.). Viking Pr.
Devlin, Harry. To Grandfather's House We Go: A Roadside Tour of American Homes. LC 80-15294. (Illus.). 48p. (gr. 5 up). 1980. Repr. of 1967 ed. 9.95 (ISBN 0-590-07764-3, Four Winds). Schol Bk Serv.
Drake, Samuel A. Old Landmarks & Historic Personages of Boston. LC 70-157258. (Illus.). 1971. pap. 3.95 (ISBN 0-8048-0993-3). C E Tuttle.
Economic Benefits of Preserving Old Buildings. LC 76-5086. (Illus.). 1976. pap. 7.95 (ISBN 0-89133-037-2). Preservation Pr.
Ervin, Eliza C. & Rudisill, Horace F. Darlingtoniana: A History of People, Places & Events in Darlington County, S.C. LC 76-55771. (Illus.). 1977. Repr. of 1964 ed. 15.00 (ISBN 0-87152-249-7). Reprint.
Favretti, Rudy J. & Favretti, Joy P. Landscapes & Gardens for Historic Buildings: A Handbook for Reproducing & Creating Authentic Landscape Settings. LC 78-17200. (Illus.). 1979. pap. 10.00 (ISBN 0-910050-34-1). AASLH.
Feilden. The Conservation of Historic Buildings. 1981. text ed. price not set (ISBN 0-408-10782-0). Butterworth.
Fitch, James M. Historic Preservation. (Illus.). 448p. 1981. 24.95 (ISBN 0-07-021121-3, P&RB). McGraw.
Goode, James M. Capital Losses: A Cultural History of Washington's Destroyed Buildings. (Illus.). 517p. 1981. pap. 19.95 (ISBN 0-87474-479-2). Smithsonian.
Guide to Stately Homes, Museums, Castles & Gardens (Britain), 1980. (A. A. Guides Ser.). 256p. (Orig.). 1980. pap. 8.95x (ISBN 0-86145-010-8, Pub. by Auto Assn England). Standing Orders.
Historic House Association of America. Historic Property Owner's Handbook. 2nd ed. (Illus.). 128p. (Orig.). 1981. pap. 7.95 (ISBN 0-89133-094-1). Preservation Pr.
Holmes, Knowlton B. The Plymouth Alms House. (Pilgrim Society Notes Ser.: No. 2). 1954. 1.00 (ISBN 0-686-30046-7). Pilgrim Hall.
Ketchum, Richard M. The American Heritage Book of Great Historic Places. LC 57-11274. (Illus.). 288p. 1973. 24.95 (ISBN 0-8281-0280-5, Dist. by Scribner). Am Heritage.
Koblas, John J. F. Scott Fitzgerald in Minnesota: His Homes & Haunts. LC 78-21979. 50p. 1978. pap. 3.75 (ISBN 0-87351-134-4). Minn Hist.
Kraft, Stephanie. No Castles on Main Street: American Authors & Their Homes. LC 79-9816. (Illus.). 1979. 9.95 (ISBN 0-528-81828-7). Rand.
Labine, Clem, ed. The Old-House Journal Compendium. LC 78-4360. (Illus.). 400p. 1980. 19.95 (ISBN 0-87951-080-3). Overlook Pr.
Leiding, Harriette K. Historic Houses of South Carolina. LC 75-1117. (Illus.). 542p. 1975. Repr. of 1921 ed. 25.00 (ISBN 0-87152-197-0). Reprint.
Lovell, Percy & Marcham, William, eds. Parish of St. Pancras, Pt. 2. LC 70-37855. (London County Council. Survey of London: No. 19). Repr. of 1938 ed. 74.50 (ISBN 0-404-51669-6). AMS Pr.
McArdle, Alma De C. & McArdle, Deirdre B. Carpenter Gothic. (Illus.). 1978. 24.50 (ISBN 0-8230-7121-9, Whitney Lib). Watson-Guptill.
May, Antoinette. Haunted Houses & Wandering Ghosts of California. LC 77-92799. (A California Living Book). (Illus.). 1978. pap. 7.95 (ISBN 0-89395-002-5). Cal Living Bks.
Morrison, Jacob H. Historic Preservation Law. LC 65-9187. 198p. 1965. pap. 3.00 (ISBN 0-89133-019-4). Preservation Pr.
National Trust for Historic Preservation. American Landmarks: Properties of the National Trust for Historic Preservation. (Illus.). 72p. (Orig.). 1980. pap. 5.95 (ISBN 0-89133-093-3). Preservation Pr.
National Trust for Historic Preservation, ed. Information: A Preservation Sourcebook. 1979. ring binder 20.00 (ISBN 0-89133-084-4). Preservation Pr.
--The Pope-Leighey House. LC 74-105251. (Illus.). 120p. 1969. pap. 2.50 (ISBN 0-89133-003-8). Preservation Pr.
Newell, Dianne. The Failure to Preserve the Queen City Hotel, Cumberland, Maryland. (Case Studies in Preservation). (Illus.). 36p. 1975. pap. 4.50 (ISBN 0-89133-023-2). Preservation Pr.
Nylander, Jane C. Fabrics for Historic Buildings. 2nd ed. LC 80-18918. (Illus.). 68p. 1980. pap. 6.95 (ISBN 0-89133-081-X). Preservation Pr.
Page, Marian. Historic Houses Restored & Preserved. (Illus.). 1979. pap. 9.95 (ISBN 0-8230-7270-3). Watson-Guptill.
--Historic Houses Restored & Preserved. (Illus., Orig.). 1976. (Whitney). Watson-Guptill.
Perry, E. G. A Trip Around Buzzards Bay Shores. LC 76-3145. (Illus.). 1976. Repr. 15.00 (ISBN 0-88492-013-5). W S Sullwold.
Preservation: Toward an Ethic in the Nineteen Eighties. LC 80-17564. 1980. pap. 8.95 (ISBN 0-89133-079-8). Preservation Pr.
Preserving & Restoring Monuments & Historic Buildings. LC 73-189463. (Museums & Monuments Ser., No. 14). (Illus.). 267p. 1972. 24.75 (ISBN 92-3-100985-0, U479, UNESCO); pap. (U480). Unipub.
Rath, Frederick L., Jr. & O'Connell, Merrilyn R., eds. Historic Preservation: A Bibliography on Historical Organization Practices. LC 75-26770. 182p. 1975. 10.00x (ISBN 0-910050-17-1). AASLH.
Regnery, Dorothy F. An Enduring Heritage: Historic Buildings of the San Francisco Peninsula. LC 76-14272. (Illus.). 1976. 18.95 (ISBN 0-8047-0918-1). Stanford U Pr.
Reynolds, Judith. Appraising Historic Properties. 150p. 1982. text ed. 15.00 (ISBN 0-911780-56-4). Am Inst Real Estate Appraisers.
Rubin, Cynthia & Rubin, Jerome. Guide to Massachusetts Museums, Historic Houses & Points of Interest. new ed. 126p. (Orig.). 1972. pap. 1.95 (ISBN 0-88278-004-2). Emporium Pubns.
Schwartz, Nancy B., compiled by. Historic American Buildings Survey, District of Columbia Catalog. LC 75-9696. (Illus.). 200p. 1976. 9.75x (ISBN 0-8139-0618-0); pap. 3.50x (ISBN 0-8139-0665-2). U Pr of Va.
Scribners. Historic Buildings of Massachusetts. LC 76-12600. 1976. 14.95 (ISBN 0-684-14567-7, ScribT). Scribner.
Seale, William. Recreating the Historic House Interior. LC 78-14361. (Illus.). 1979. text ed. 22.00 (ISBN 0-910050-32-5). AASLH.
Shank, Wesley I., compiled by. The Iowa Catalog: Historic American Buildings Survey. LC 79-11666. (Illus.). 1979. 12.50 (ISBN 0-87745-091-9); pap. 8.95 (ISBN 0-87745-092-7). U of Iowa Pr.
Singleton, Esther, ed. Historic Buildings of America. 341p. 1980. Repr. of 1907 ed. lib. bdg. 40.00 (ISBN 0-8492-8127-X). R West.
Stahls, Paul, Jr. Plantation Homes of the Lafourche Country. LC 76-9802. (Illus.). 1976. 12.95 (ISBN 0-88289-103-0). Pelican.
Tax Incentives for Historic Preservation. rev. ed. LC 79-93052. 240p. 1981. pap. text ed. 12.95 (ISBN 0-89133-096-8). Preservation Pr.
Thorndike, Joseph J., Jr. The Magnificent Builders & Their Dream Houses. LC 78-18371. (Illus.). 352p. 1978. 34.95 (ISBN 0-8281-3064-7, Dist. by Scribner); deluxe ed. 39.95 slipcased (ISBN 0-8281-3072-8). Am Heritage.
Voges, Nettie A. Old Alexandria: Where America's Past Is Present. LC 75-23343. (Illus.). 208p. 1975. pap. 5.95 (ISBN 0-914440-10-1). EPM Pubns.
Ward, Barbara M. & Ward, Gerald W. The John Ward House. LC 76-16902. (Historic House Booklet Ser: No. 1). 1976. 2.00 (ISBN 0-88389-059-3). Essex Inst.
Ward, Barbara M. & Ward, W. R. The Andrew-Safford House. LC 76-16906. (Historic House Booklet Ser: No. 6). 1976. pap. 2.00 (ISBN 0-88389-064-X). Essex Inst.
Ward, Gerald W. The Gardner-Pingree House. LC 76-16907. (Historic House Booklet Ser: No. 5). 1976. 2.00 (ISBN 0-88389-063-1). Essex Inst.
Warner, Raynor, et al. Business & Preservation: A Survey of Business Conservation of Buildings & Neighborhoods. LC 77-90918. (Illus.). 1978. pap. 14.00x (ISBN 0-918780-08-X). Inform.
Waterman, Thomas T. The Dwellings of Colonial America. (Illus.). 1980. pap. 6.95 (ISBN 0-393-00646-8). Norton.
Webster, Richard J. Philadelphia Preserved: Catalog of the Historic American Buildings Survey. LC 76-18669. (Illus.). 1976. 20.00x (ISBN 0-87722-089-1). Temple U Pr.

HISTORIC HOUSES, ETC.
see Historic Buildings

HISTORIC SITES
see also Historic Buildings; Historical Markers; Memorials; Monuments
Alderson, William T. & Low, Shirley P. Interpretation of Historic Sites. LC 75-33292. (Illus.). 1976. pap. 6.95 (ISBN 0-910050-19-8). AASLH.
American Association for State & Local History. One Hundred One Ideas from History News. LC 75-21970. (Illus.). 1975. pap. 5.00 (ISBN 0-910050-18-X). AASLH.
Andrews, Gregory E., ed. Tax Incentives for Historic Preservation. rev. ed. LC 79-93052. (Illus.). 240p. 1981. pap. 12.95 (ISBN 0-89133-096-8). Preservation Pr.
Benson, Elizabeth P. Mesoamerican Sites & World-Views: Conference at Dumbarton Oaks, October 16 & 17, 1976. LC 79-92647. (Illus.). 256p. 1981. 24.00x (ISBN 0-88402-097-5, Ctr Pre-Columbian). Dumbarton Oaks.
Bradford, S. Sydney. Liberty's Road: A Guide to Revolutionary War Sites, 2 vols. Incl. Vol. 1. Conn., Maine, Mass, N.H., N.J., N.Y., Pa., R.I., & Vt. pap. 5.95 (ISBN 0-07-007060-1); Vol. 2. Del., Ga., Md., N.C., S.C., Va., & W. Va. pap. 4.95 (ISBN 0-07-007061-X). LC 75-38695. (Illus.). 1976 (P&RB). McGraw.
Country Beautiful Editors, ed. Four-Hundred Landmarks of America: Where to Go & What to See. LC 74-76835. (Illus.). 296p. 1974. 25.00 (ISBN 0-87294-056-X). Country Beautiful.
Cromie, Alice. Restored Towns & Historic Districts of America: A Tour Guide. (Illus.). 1979. 17.50 (ISBN 0-87690-286-7); pap. 10.95 (ISBN 0-87690-287-5). Dutton.
Crumb, Lawrence N. Historic Preservation in the Pacific Northwest: A Bibliography of Sources, 1947-1978. (CPL Bibliographies: No. 11). 63p. 1979. pap. 7.00 (ISBN 0-86602-011-X). CPL Biblios.
Davidson, Marshall B. The Horizon Book of Great Historic Places of Europe. LC 74-11098. (Illus.). 416p. 1974. 35.00 (ISBN 0-8281-0375-5, Dist. by Scribner). Am Heritage.
Dennis, Stephen N. Recommended Model Provisions for a Preservation Ordinance. 151p. (Orig.). 1980. pap. text ed. 7.95 (ISBN 0-89133-090-9). Preservation Pr.
Fitch, James M. Historic Preservation. (Illus.). 448p. 1981. 24.95 (ISBN 0-07-021121-3, P&RB). McGraw.
Friedlander, Lee. The American Monument. LC 76-6715. 1976. 85.00x (ISBN 0-87130-043-5). Eakins.
Goode, James M. Capital Losses: A Cultural History of Washington's Destroyed Buildings. (Illus.). 517p. 1981. pap. 19.95 (ISBN 0-87474-479-2). Smithsonian.
Haas, Irvin. America's Historic Villages & Restorations. LC 74-77712. (Illus.). 1974. lib. bdg. 8.95 (ISBN 0-668-03354-1). Arco.
Heritage of Canada. (Illus.). 1979. 24.95 (ISBN 0-393-01288-3, Pub. by Reader's Digest). Norton.
Historic Preservation Plans: An Annotated Bibliography. 48p. 1976. pap. 3.95 (ISBN 0-89133-038-0). Preservation Pr.
Horizon Magazine & Hilowitz, Beverley, eds. A Horizon Guide: Great Historic Places of Europe. LC 74-10941. (Illus.). 384p. 1974. 10.00 (ISBN 0-8281-0275-9, Dist. by Scribner). Am Heritage.
Hunt, N. Jane, ed. Brevet's Nebraska Historical Markers- Sites. LC 74-79979. (Historical Markers-Sites Ser). (Illus.). 228p. (Orig.). 1974. pap. 6.95 (ISBN 0-88498-021-9). Brevet Pr.
Ketchum, Richard M. The American Heritage Book of Great Historic Places. LC 57-11274. (Illus.). 288p. 1973. 24.95 (ISBN 0-8281-0280-5, Dist. by Scribner). Am Heritage.
Lord, Suzanne. American Travelers' Treasury: A Guide to the Nation's Heirlooms. (Americans-Discover-America Ser.). 1977. 5.95 (ISBN 0-688-03130-7). Morrow.
Milley, John. Treasures of Independence. (Illus.). 224p. 1980. 25.00 (ISBN 0-8317-8593-4, Mayflower Bks). Smith Pubs.
Morton, Terry B., ed. I Feel I Should Warn You: Historic Preservation Cartoons. LC 75-12480. (Illus.). 1975. 8.95 (ISBN 0-89133-028-3); pap. 5.95 (ISBN 0-89133-027-5). Preservation Pr.
Nord, David P. A Guide to Old Wade House Historical Site. (Illus.). 1978. pap. 1.50 (ISBN 0-87020-169-7). State Hist Soc Wis.
Plucker, Lina S. & Roerick, Kaye L., eds. Brevet's Illinois Historical Markers & Sites. LC 75-253. (Historical Markers-Sites Ser). (Illus.). 300p. (Orig.). 1976. pap. 6.95 (ISBN 0-88498-029-4). Brevet Pr.
Preservation: Toward an Ethic in the Nineteen Eighties. LC 80-17564. 1980. pap. 8.95 (ISBN 0-89133-079-8). Preservation Pr.
Ramati, Racquel & Urban Design Group of the Department of City Planning, New York. How to Save Your Own Street. LC 78-14709. (Illus.). 176p. 1981. pap. 19.95 (ISBN 0-385-14814-3, Dolp). Doubleday.
Rath, Frederick L., Jr. & O'Connell, Merrilyn R., eds. Historic Preservation: A Bibliography on Historical Organization Practices. LC 75-26770. 182p. 1975. 10.00x (ISBN 0-910050-17-1). AASLH.
Robinson, Nicholas A. Historic Preservation Law Nineteen Eighty. LC 80-81531. (Nineteen Eighty-Nineteen Eighty-One Real Estate Law & Practice Course Handbook Ser. Subscription). 840p. 1980. pap. text ed. 25.00 (ISBN 0-686-75082-9, N4-4357). PLI.
Roehrick, Kaye L., ed. Brevet's North Dakota Historical Markers & Sites. LC 74-79978. (Historical Markers-Sites Ser). (Illus.). 176p. 1975. pap. 6.95 (ISBN 0-88498-025-1). Brevet Pr.
Rudman, Jack. Historic Site Manager. (Career Examination Ser.: C-2273). (Cloth bdg. avail. on request). pap. 10.00 (ISBN 0-685-60426-8). Natl Learning.
Schultz, Nancy D. A Guide to Federal Programs for Historic Preservation: 1976 Supplement. LC 75-305235. 56p. 1976. pap. 4.95 (ISBN 0-89133-039-9). Preservation Pr.
Sweeney, James B. Pictorial Guide to the Military Museums, Forts, & Historic Sites of the U. S. 320p. 1981. 19.95 (ISBN 0-517-54481-4). Crown.
Swetnam, George & Smith, Helene. A Guidebook to Historic Western Pennsylvania. LC 75-33421. 1976. 12.95 (ISBN 0-8229-3316-0); pap. 6.95 (ISBN 0-8229-5271-8). U of Pittsburgh Pr.
Talkington, Virginia & Dunsavage, Lyn. The Making of a Historic District, Swiss Avenue, Dallas, Texas. (Case Studies in Preservation). (Illus.). 40p. 1975. pap. 4.50 (ISBN 0-89133-024-0). Preservation Pr.
Walker, E. F. Five Prehistoric Archeological Sites in Los Angeles County, California. (Illus.). 1951. 5.50 (ISBN 0-686-20676-2). Southwest Mus.
Williams, George J., III. The Guide to Bodie & Eastern Sierra Historic Sitos. Dalton, Bill, ed. LC 81-51267. (Illus., Orig.). 1981. pap. 6.95 (ISBN 0-686-73446-7). Tree by River.
Wright, Muriel H., et al. Mark of Heritage. LC 75-40255. 1976. pap. 7.95 (ISBN 0-8061-1356-1). U of Okla Pr.
Wright, Russell, et al. A Guide to Delineating Edges of Historic Districts. LC 76-8747. (Illus.). 96p. 1976. pap. 7.50 (ISBN 0-89133-032-1). Preservation Pr.

HISTORIC WATERS (INTERNATIONAL LAW)
see Territorial Waters

HISTORICAL ART
see History in Art
HISTORICAL ATLASES
see Classical Geography; Geography, Ancient–Maps; Geography, Historical–Maps
HISTORICAL CHRONOLOGY
see Chronology, Historical
HISTORICAL CRITICISM
see Historiography
HISTORICAL DICTIONARIES
see History–Dictionaries
HISTORICAL DRAMA
see also subdivision Drama under names of countries, cities, etc., and under names of historical events and characters
Fleischer, Martha H. The Iconography of the English History Play. (Salzburg Studies in English Literature, Elizabethan & Renaissance Studies: No. 10). 363p. 1974. pap. text ed. 25.00x (ISBN 0-391-01376-9). Humanities.
Lindenberger, Herbert. Historical Drama: The Relationship of Literature & Reality. LC 74-11630. 1978. pap. 3.45 (ISBN 0-226-48240-5, P762, Phoen). U of Chicago Pr.
Lukacs, George. Historical Novel. 1978. Repr. of 1962 ed. text ed. 12.50x (ISBN 0-85036-068-4). Humanities.
Ribner, Irving. The English History Play in the Age of Shakespeare. 1979. Repr. of 1957 ed. lib. bdg. 20.00x (ISBN 0-374-96794-6). Octagon.
Roy, R. N. George Bernard Shaw's Historical Plays. LC 76-901873. 1976. 8.50x (ISBN 0-8364-0407-6). South Asia Bks.
Schelling, Felix E. English Chronicle Play. LC 65-15877. (Studies in Drama, No. 39). 1969. Repr. of 1902 ed. lib. bdg. 37.95 (ISBN 0-8383-0618-7). Haskell.
--English Chronicle Play: A Study in the Popular Historical Literature Environing Shakespeare. (Research & Source Works Ser: No. 180). 1968. Repr. of 1902 ed. 13.50 (ISBN 0-8337-3140-8). B Franklin.
HISTORICAL FICTION
see also subdivision Fiction under names of countries, cities, etc., and under names of historical events and characters
Baker, Ernest A. History in Fiction: Guide to the Best Historical Romances, Sagas, Novels, & Tales. 1977. Repr. of 1907 ed. lib. bdg. 20.00 (ISBN 0-8495-0322-1). Arden Lib.
Butterfield, H. Historical Novel. LC 72-187203. 1924. lib. bdg. 10.00 (ISBN 0-8414-0490-9). Folcroft.
Duggan, Alfred. Historical Fiction. 1957. lib. bdg. 8.50 (ISBN 0-8414-3868-4). Folcroft.
Garner, Arthur G. A Long Road to Eden. (Orig.). 1979. pap. 1.95 (ISBN 0-532-23248-8). Woodhill.
Kaye, James R. Historical Fiction. 1920. Repr. 45.00 (ISBN 0-8274-2497-3). R West.
Lascelles, Mary. The Story-Teller Retrieves the Past: Historical Fiction & Fictitious History in the Art of Scott, Stevenson, Kipling, & Some Others. 116p. 1980. 29.50x (ISBN 0-19-812802-9). Oxford U Pr.
Leisy, Ernest E. American Historical Novel. LC 73-17275. 1923. lib. bdg. 5.50 (ISBN 0-8414-5700-X). Folcroft.
--The American Historical Novel. 1970. Repr. of 1950 ed. 8.95x (ISBN 0-8061-0201-2). U of Okla Pr.
Lively, Robert A. Fiction Fights the Civil War. LC 73-11751. 230p. 1973. Repr. of 1957 ed. lib. bdg. 15.00x (ISBN 0-8371-7084-2, LIFF). Greenwood.
Lukacs, George. Historical Novel. 1978. Repr. of 1962 ed. text ed. 12.50x (ISBN 0-85036-068-4). Humanities.
McGarry, Daniel D. & White, Sarah H. World Historical Fiction Guide: Annotated Chronological, Geographical & Topical List of Selected Historical Novels. 2nd ed. LC 73-4367. 1973. 20.50 (ISBN 0-8108-0616-9). Scarecrow.
Marriott, John. English History in English Fiction. LC 75-105806. 1970. Repr. of 1940 ed. 13.50 (ISBN 0-8046-0961-6). Kennikat.
Matthews, Brander. Historical Novel & Other Essays. LC 68-30586. 1969. Repr. of 1901 ed. 19.00 (ISBN 0-8103-3218-3). Gale.
Read, J. Lloyd. The Mexican Historical Novel,1826-1910. LC 72-85005. iii, 337p. 1973. Repr. of 1939 ed. 18.00 (ISBN 0-8462-1688-4). Russell.
Rutherford, John. Mexican Society During Revolution. 352p. 1971. 29.95x (ISBN 0-19-827183-2). Oxford U Pr.
Sabatini, Rafael. A Century of Historical Stories. 40.00 (ISBN 0-89987-138-0). Darby Bks.
Saintsbury, George E. Historical Novel. LC 72-189860. 1895. lib. bdg. 10.00 (ISBN 0-8414-1087-9). Folcroft.
Sanders, Andrew. Victorian Historical Novel Eighteen Forty to Eighteen Eighty. LC 78-26592. 1979. 18.94x (ISBN 0-312-84293-7). St Martin.
Scott, Sir Walter. The Prefaces to the Waverley Novels. Weinstein, Mark A., ed. LC 78-2710. 1978. 16.95x (ISBN 0-8032-4700-1). U of Nebr Pr.
Sheppard, Alfred T. Art & Practice of Historical Fiction. LC 74-32318. 1930. lib. bdg. 17.50 (ISBN 0-8414-7538-5). Folcroft.
Stone, Irving, et al. Three Views of the Novel. LC 77-7608. 1957. lib. bdg. 8.50 (ISBN 0-8414-7692-6). Folcroft.
Van Wyck Mason, F. Armored Giants: A Novel of the Civil War. 352p. 1980. 13.95 (ISBN 0-316-54922-3). Little.
HISTORICAL FICTION–BIBLIOGRAPHY
Baker, Ernest A. Guide to Historical Fiction. LC 68-9157. 1968. Repr. of 1914 ed. 17.50 (ISBN 0-87266-001-X). Argosy.
--Guide to Historical Fiction. LC 68-58468. (Bibliography & Reference Ser: No. 253). 1969. Repr. of 1914 ed. 23.50 (ISBN 0-8337-0153-3). B Franklin.
Gerhardstein, Virginia B. Dickinson's American Historical Fiction. 4th ed. LC 80-23450. 328p. 1981. 15.00 (ISBN 0-8108-1362-9). Scarecrow.
Hotchkiss, Jeanette K. European Historical Fiction & Biography for Children & Young People. 2nd ed. LC 72-1599. 1972. 10.00 (ISBN 0-8108-0515-4). Scarecrow.
Nield, Jonathan. Guide to the Best Historical Novels & Tales. 5th ed. LC 68-57916. (Bibliography & Reference Ser.: No. 228). 1968. Repr. of 1929 ed. 26.50 (ISBN 0-8337-2509-2). B Franklin.
--A Guide to the Best Historical Novels & Tales. LC 76-27529. 1976. Repr. of 1929 ed. lib. bdg. 45.00 (ISBN 0-89341-051-9). Longwood Pr.
Taylor, W. A. Historical Fiction. LC 73-14838. 1957. lib. bdg. 8.50 (ISBN 0-8414-8531-3). Folcroft.
HISTORICAL GEOGRAPHY
see Geography, Historical
HISTORICAL GEOLOGY
see also Geology, Stratigraphic; Paleontology
Anstey, Robert L. Environments Through Time: A Laboratory Manual in Historical Geology. 2nd ed. 1979. pap. 10.95x (ISBN 0-8087-0050-2). Burgess.
Dott, Robert H. & Batten, Roger L. Evolution of the Earth. 3rd ed. (Illus.). 576p. 1980. text ed. 22.95 (ISBN 0-07-017625-6, C); write for info. McGraw.
Dott, Robert, Jr. & Batten, Roger. Evolution of the Earth. 2nd ed. 1975. text ed. 19.95 (ISBN 0-07-017619-1, C); instructor's manual 3.50 (ISBN 0-07-017620-5). McGraw.
Garrels, Robert M. & Mackenzie, Fred T. Evolution of Sedimentary Rocks. (Illus.). 1971. text ed. 14.95x (ISBN 0-393-09959-8, NortonC). Norton.
Levin, Harold L. The Earth Through Time. LC 77-78573. (Illus.). 1978. 19.95 (ISBN 0-7216-5735-4); study manual 5.50 (ISBN 0-7216-5736-2). Saunders.
Pinet, Paul R., et al. Earth History: An Introduction to the Methods of Historical Geology. (Illus.). 187p. 1980. lab manual 8.95x (ISBN 0-89459-056-1). Hunter NC.
Seyfert, Carl K. & Sirkin, Leslie A. Earth History & Plate Tectonics: An Introduction to Historical Geology. 2nd ed. LC 78-24612. 1979. text ed. 24.50 scp (ISBN 0-06-045921-2, HarpC). Har-Row.
Stokes, William L. Essentials of Earth History: An Introduction to Historical Geology. 3rd ed. (Illus.). 512p. 1973. ref. ed. 22.95 (ISBN 0-13-285932-7). P-H.
HISTORICAL LINGUISTICS
see also Comparative Linguistics; Linguistic Change
Anttila, Raimo A. An Introduction to Historical & Comparative Linguistics. (Illus.). 415p. 1972. text ed. 22.95 (ISBN 0-02-303630-3, 30363). Macmillan.
International Conference on Historical Linguistics, 4th. Papers. Traugott, Elizabeth, ed. 500p. 1980. text ed. 54.25x (ISBN 90-272-3501-5). Humanities.
Jeffers, Robert J. & Lehiste, Ilse. Principles & Methods for Historical Linguistics. (Illus.). 1979. text ed. 13.95x (ISBN 0-262-10020-7). MIT Pr.
HISTORICAL MARKERS
see also Inscriptions
Hunt, N. Jane, ed. Brevet's Nebraska Historical Markers- Sites. LC 74-79979. (Historical Markers-Sites Ser). (Illus.). 228p. (Orig.). 1974. pap. 6.95 (ISBN 0-88498-021-9). Brevet Pr.
Plucker, Lina S. & Roerick, Kaye L., eds. Brevet's Illinois Historical Markers & Sites. LC 75-253. (Historical Markers-Sites Ser). (Illus.). 300p. (Orig.). 1976. pap. 6.95 (ISBN 0-88498-029-4). Brevet Pr.
Roehrick, Kaye L., ed. Brevet's North Dakota Historical Markers & Sites. LC 74-79978. (Historical Markers-Sites Ser). (Illus.). 176p. 1975. pap. 6.95 (ISBN 0-88498-025-1). Brevet Pr.
Scofield, W. M. Washington's Historical Markers. (Illus.). 80p. 1967. pap. 1.95 (ISBN 0-911518-15-0). Touchstone Pr Ore.
HISTORICAL MATERIALISM
Boguslavsky, B. M., et al. A B C of Dialectical & Historical Materialism. 398p. 1976. 3.60 (ISBN 0-8285-0188-2, Pub. by Progress Pubs Russia). Imported Pubns.
Borodulina, T., ed. Marx, Engels & Lenin on Historical Materialism. 751p. 1972. 4.10 (ISBN 0-8285-0034-7, Pub. by Progress Pubs Russia). Imported Pubns.
Corrigan, Philip, et al. For Mao: Essays in Historical Materialism. 1979. text ed. 30.00x (ISBN 0-391-01014-X). Humanities.
Croce, Benedetto. Historical Materialism & the Economics of Karl Marx. LC 78-66239. (Social Science Classics). 225p. 1981. 19.95 (ISBN 0-87855-313-4); pap. text ed. 6.95 (ISBN 0-87855-695-8). Transaction Bks.
Harnacker, Marta. The Basic Concepts of Historical Materialism. (Marxist Theory & Contemporary Capitalism Ser.: No. 23). 1980. text ed. write for info. (ISBN 0-391-01182-0). Humanities.
Jakubowski, Franz. Ideology & Superstructure. LC 75-32930. 144p. 1976. 15.95 (ISBN 0-312-40460-3). St Martin.
Kelle, V. & Kovalson, M. Historical Materialism. 322p. 1975. 16.00x (ISBN 0-8464-0478-8). Beekman Pubs.
McCarthy, Timothy. Marx & the Proletariat: A Study in Social Theory. LC 78-4025. (Contributions in Political Science: No. 18). 1978. lib. bdg. 15.00 (ISBN 0-313-20412-8, MPL/). Greenwood.
Marx, Karl, et al. On Historical Materialism. LC 73-87991. 751p. 1975. 11.00 (ISBN 0-7178-0402-X); pap. 4.25 (ISBN 0-7178-0411-9). Intl Pub Co.
Schimdt, Alfred. History & Structure: An Essay on Hegelian-Marxist & Structuralist Theories of History. Herf, Jeffrey, tr. from Ger. (Sutdies in Contemporary German Social Thought). 128p. 1981. 17.50x (ISBN 0-262-19198-9). MIT Pr.
Sohn-Rethel, Alfred. Intellectual & Manual Labour: A Critique of Epistemology. LC 77-12975. (Critical Social Studies). 1978. text ed. 26.00x (ISBN 0-391-00774-2); pap. text ed. 10.25x (ISBN 0-333-23046-9). Humanities.
Torrance, John. Estrangement, Alienation, & Exploitation: A Sociological Approach to Historical Materialism. LC 77-8246. 1977. 25.00x (ISBN 0-231-04448-8). Columbia U Pr.
Weber, Max. Critique of Stammler. Oakes, Guy, tr. LC 77-72682. 1977. 12.95 (ISBN 0-02-934100-0). Free Pr.
HISTORICAL MONUMENTS
see Monuments
HISTORICAL MUSEUMS
Abbott, Shirley. The National Museum of American History. (Illus.). 496p. 1981. 50.00 (ISBN 0-8109-1363-1). Abrams.
Alexander, Edward P. The Museum: A Living Book of History. LC 59-6904. 1959. pap. 2.00x (ISBN 0-8143-1105-9). Wayne St U Pr.
--Museums in Motion. LC 78-1189. 1978. 12.95 (ISBN 0-910050-39-2); pap. 7.95 (ISBN 0-910050-35-X). AASLH.
American Association for State & Local History. One Hundred One Ideas from History News. LC 75-21970. (Illus.). 1975. pap. 5.00 (ISBN 0-910050-18-X). AASLH.
Guthe, Carl E. Management of Small History Museums. 2nd ed. 1964. pap. 3.00 (ISBN 0-910050-04-X). AASLH.
Lord, Suzanne. American Travelers' Treasury: A Guide to the Nation's Heirlooms. (Americans-Discover-America Ser.). 1977. 5.95 (ISBN 0-688-03130-7). Morrow.
Parker, Arthur C. Manual for History Museums. LC 36-985. Repr. of 1935 ed. write for info. (ISBN 0-404-04887-0). AMS Pr.
Rath, Frederick L., Jr. & O'Connell, Merrilyn R. A Guide to Historic Preservation, Historical Agencies, & Museum Practices: A Selective Bibliography. 12.50 (ISBN 0-686-16046-0). Fenimore Bk.
Reibel, Daniel B. Registration Methods for the Small Museum. (Illus.). 1978. pap. 6.75 (ISBN 0-910050-37-6). AASLH.
Robinson, W. W. The Story of the Southwest Museum. 1.25 (ISBN 0-686-20689-4). Southwest Mus.
HISTORICAL RECORD PRESERVATION
see Archives
HISTORICAL RECORDS SURVEY–BIBLIOGRAPHY
Bauer, Robert. The New Catalogue of Historical Records: 1898 to 1908-09. 2nd ed. LC 48-1665. 494p. Repr. of 1947 ed. lib. bdg. 19.50x (ISBN 0-8371-9104-1, BAHR). Greenwood.
Noggle, Burl. Working with History: The Historical Records Survey in Louisiana & the Nation, 1936-1942. LC 81-5789. 160p. 1981. text ed. 14.95x (ISBN 0-8071-0881-2). La State U Pr.
Rath, Frederick L., Jr. & O'Connell, Merrilyn, eds. Care & Conservation of Collections: A Bibliography on Historical Organization Practices, Vol. 2. LC 75-26770. 1977. 10.00x (ISBN 0-910050-28-7). AASLH.
HISTORICAL RESEARCH
see also Historiography
Allen, Barbara & Montell, William L. From Memory to History: Using Oral Sources in Local Historical Research. (Illus.). 176p. 1981. text ed. 12.50x (ISBN 0-910050-51-1). AASLH.
Bennett, James D. & Harrison, Lowell H. Writing History Papers. (Orig.). 1979. pap. text ed. 2.95x (ISBN 0-88273-105-X). Forum Pr MO.
Bindoff, S. T. & Boulton, James T. Research in Progress in English & History. LC 75-29642. 1976. 15.00 (ISBN 0-312-67690-5). St Martin.
Brewer, E. The Historic Notebook. 59.95 (ISBN 0-8490-0307-5). Gordon Pr.
Brooks, Philip C. Research in Archives: The Use of Unpublished Primary Sources. LC 69-19273. 1969. 7.50x (ISBN 0-226-07575-3). U of Chicago Pr.
Dillard, Tom W. & Thwing, Valerie. Researching Arkansas History: A Beginner's Guide. (Illus.). 64p. 1980. pap. 4.95 (ISBN 0-914546-25-2). Rose Pub.
Dollar, Charles M. & Jensen, Richard J. Historian's Guide to Statistics: Quantitative Analysis & Historical Research. LC 74-12188. 344p. 1974. Repr. of 1971 ed. 13.50 (ISBN 0-88275-197-2). Krieger.
Fussner, F. Smith. The Historical Revolution: English Historical Writing & Thought 1580-1640. LC 75-40916. 1976. Repr. of 1962 ed. lib. bdg. 24.75x (ISBN 0-8371-8684-6, FUHR). Greenwood.
Gabel, Creighton & Bennett, Norman R., eds. Reconstructing African Culture History. LC 67-25932. (Pub. by Boston U Pr). 1967. 9.50x (ISBN 0-8419-8704-1, Africana). Holmes & Meier.
Higham, John. Writing American History: Essays on Modern Scholarship. LC 70-108209. (Midland Bks.: No. 156). 224p. 1970. pap. 2.95x (ISBN 0-253-20156-X). Ind U Pr.
Hockett, Homer C. The Critical Method in Historical Research & Writing. LC 77-13066. 1977. Repr. of 1955 ed. lib. bdg. 25.75 (ISBN 0-8371-9833-X, HOCH). Greenwood.
Leff, Gordon. History & Social Theory. LC 78-76586. 234p. 1969. 16.75x (ISBN 0-8173-6605-9). U of Ala Pr.
McCall, Daniel F. Africa in Time Perspective: A Discussion of Historical Reconstruction from Unwritten Sources. (Illus.). 1969. pap. text ed. 4.95x (ISBN 0-19-500352-7). Oxford U Pr.
McCoy, F. N. Researching & Writing in History: A Practical Handbook for Student. 1974. 14.95x (ISBN 0-520-02447-8); pap. 4.95x (ISBN 0-520-02621-7, CAMPUS 274). U of Cal Pr.
McDermott, John F., ed. Research Opportunities in American Cultural History. LC 77-22111. 1977. Repr. of 1961 ed. lib. bdg. 16.25x (ISBN 0-8371-9754-6, MCRO). Greenwood.
Pitt, D. C. Using Historical Sources in Anthropology & Sociology. LC 70-185789. (Studies in Anthropological Method). 1972. pap. text ed. 5.95 (ISBN 0-03-078785-8, HoltC). HR&W.
Stoffle, Carla & Karter, Simon. Materials & Methods for History Research. LC 79-306. 1979. lib. bdg. 14.95x (ISBN 0-918212-07-3); wkbk. 5 or more 4.95 (ISBN 0-918212-06-5). Neal-Schuman.
Vincent, John M. Aids to Historical Research. facs. ed. LC 70-88035. (Essay Index Reprint Ser). 1934. 15.00 (ISBN 0-8369-1160-1). Arno.
--Historical Research: An Outline of Theory & Practice. LC 73-21817. 360p. 1974. Repr. of 1911 ed. lib. bdg. 23.50 (ISBN 0-8337-5019-4). B Franklin.
Winks, Robin W., ed. Historian As Detective: Essays on Evidence. 1970. pap. 6.95x (ISBN 0-06-131933-3, TB1933, Torch). Har-Row.
HISTORICAL RESEARCH–DATA PROCESSING
Shorter, Edward. The Historian & the Computer: A Practical Guide. (Illus.). 160p. 1975. pap. 2.95x (ISBN 0-393-00732-4). Norton.
HISTORICAL SITES
see Historic Sites
HISTORICAL SOCIETIES
American Association for State & Local History. Directory of Historical Societies & Agencies in the United States & Canada. 11th ed. McDonald, Donna, ed. LC 56-4164. (Illus.). 1978. pap. 24.00x (ISBN 0-910050-36-8). AASLH.
Bickford, Christopher. The Connecticut Historical Society, Eighteen Twenty-Five to Ninteen Seventy-Five: A Brief Illustrated History. (Illus.). 1975. 3.00x (ISBN 0-940748-04-5). Conn Hist Soc.

Bowsher, Alice M. Design Review in Historic Districts. LC 78-61513. (Illus.). 138p. 1978. pap. 6.95 (ISBN 0-89133-080-1). Preservation Pr.

Collections of the New-York Historical Society, Vol. 1. LC 1-16509. (Second Ser.). (Illus.). 20.00x (ISBN 0-685-73881-7). U Pr of Va.

Collections of the New-York Historical Society, Vol. 2, Pt. 1. LC 1-16509. (Second Ser.). 1848. pap. 10.00x (ISBN 0-685-73882-5). U Pr of Va.

Collections of the New-York Historical Society, Vol. 3, Pt. 1. LC 1-16509. (Second Ser.). 1857. 20.00x (ISBN 0-685-73889-2). U Pr of Va.

Collections of the New-York Historical Society: 1882. LC 1-13394. (Illus.). 10.00x (ISBN 0-685-73883-3). U Pr of Va.

Collections of the New-York Historical Society: 1909. LC 1-16508. 5.00x (ISBN 0-685-73885-X). U Pr of Va.

Collections of the New-York Historical Society: 1913. LC 1-16508. 5.00x (ISBN 0-685-73886-8). U Pr of Va.

Collections of the New-York Historical Society: 1912. LC 1-16508. 5.00x (ISBN 0-685-73887-6). U Pr of Va.

Collections of the New-York Historical Society: 1875. LC 1-13394. 10.00x (ISBN 0-685-73888-4). U Pr of Va.

Collections of the New-York Historical Society: 1868. LC 1-16508. 10.00x (ISBN 0-685-73890-6). U Pr of Va.

Collections of the New-York Historical Society: 1869. LC 1-16508. 10.00x (ISBN 0-685-73891-4). U Pr of Va.

Collections of the New-York Historical Society: 1870. LC 1-16508. 5.00x (ISBN 0-685-73892-2). U Pr of Va.

Collections of the New-York Historical Society: 1878, 1879, 1880, 3 vols. LC 1-13394. 10.00x ea. U Pr of Va.

Creigh, Dorothy W. A Primer for Local Historical Societies. LC 76-231. 1976. pap. 6.50 (ISBN 0-910050-20-1). AASLH.

Dunlap, Leslie W. American Historical Societies: 1790-1860. LC 73-16331. (Perspectives in American History Ser.: No. 7). 238p. Repr. of 1944 ed. lib. bdg. 15.00x (ISBN 0-87991-343-6). Porcupine Pr.

Freiberg, Malcolm, ed. Stephen Thomas Riley: The Years of Stewardship. (Illus.). 1976. pap. 10.00 (ISBN 0-686-10136-7). Mass Hist Soc.

French Colonial Historical Society, 5th Meeting. Proceedings. Cooke, James J., ed. LC 80-5683. 125p. lib. bdg. 16.75 (ISBN 0-8191-1146-5); pap. text ed. 7.50 (ISBN 0-8191-1147-3). U Pr of Amer.

Gates, Arnold, ed. Civil War Round Table of New York: Its History, Programs & Membership. 1976. pap. 1.25 (ISBN 0-685-73606-7). Civil War.

Goodyear, Frank H., Jr. American Paintings in the Rhode Island Historical Society. (Illus.). 1974. 10.00 (ISBN 0-685-67651-X). RI Hist Soc.

Halliwell, James O. & Wright, Thomas, eds. Science in England. 310p. 1965. Repr. of 1841 ed. 22.50x (ISBN 0-8464-0817-1). Beekman Pubs.

Hartman, Hedy A. Funding Sources & Technical Assistance for Museums & Historical Agencies. (Orig.). 1979. pap. text ed. 10.00 (ISBN 0-910050-40-6). AASLH.

Maryland Original Research Society of Baltimore. The Maryland Original Research Society of Baltimore. LC 67-28606. 1979. Repr. of 1906 ed. 15.00 (ISBN 0-8063-0546-0). Genealog Pub.

Moody, Eric N., compiled by. An Index to the Publications of the Nevada Historical Society, 1907-1971. 1977. lib. bdg. 12.50 (ISBN 0-686-10437-4). Nevada Hist Soc.

Mulloy, Elizabeth D. The History of the National Trust for Historic Preservation, 1963-1973. LC 65-4705. (Illus.). 192p. 1976. 9.95 (ISBN 0-89133-033-X). Preservation Pr.

National Trust for Historic Preservation. Directory of Private Nonprofit Preservation Organizations: State & Local Levels. 1980. pap. 6.95 (ISBN 0-89133-070-4). Preservation Pr.

Newton, Earle W., compiled by. Index to the Proceedings of the Vermont Historical Society, New Series, Volumes 1-10, 1930-1942. 86p. unbound 3.75x (ISBN 0-934720-09-6). VT Hist Soc.

Papers & Addresses of the Society of Colonial Wars in the State of Connecticut, Vol. 1. 1903. 3.00 (ISBN 0-940748-35-5). Conn Hist Soc.

Pennsylvania Historical Society. Memoirs of the Historical Society of Pennsylvania, 14 vols. Incl. Vol. 1 (ISBN 0-404-11076-2); Vol. 2 (ISBN 0-404-11077-0); Vol. 3 (ISBN 0-404-11078-9); Vol. 4 (ISBN 0-404-11079-7); Vol. 5 (ISBN 0-404-11080-0); Vol. 6 (ISBN 0-404-11081-9); Vol. 7 (ISBN 0-404-11082-7); Vol. 8 (ISBN 0-404-11083-5); Vol. 9 (ISBN 0-404-11084-3); Vol. 10 (ISBN 0-404-11085-1); Vol. 11 (ISBN 0-404-11086-X); Vol. 12 (ISBN 0-404-11087-8); Vol. 13 (ISBN 0-404-11088-6); Vol. 14 (ISBN 0-404-11089-4). LC 72-14378. Repr. of 1826 ed. Set. buckram 400.00 (ISBN 0-404-11075-4); 30.00 ea. AMS Pr.

Rosenberger, Francis C., ed. Records of the Columbia Historical Society of Washington D.C. Incl. 1957-1959. (Illus.). 1961. 15.00x (ISBN 0-8139-0493-5); 1960-1962. (Illus.). 1963. 15.00x (ISBN 0-8139-0494-3); 1963-1965. (Illus.). 1966. 15.00x (ISBN 0-8139-0495-1); 1966-1968. (Illus.). 1969. 15.00x (ISBN 0-8139-0496-X); 1969-1970. LC 1-17677. (Illus.). 1971. 20.00x (ISBN 0-8139-0497-8); 1971-1972. 1973. 20.00x (ISBN 0-8139-0501-X); 1973-74. 1976. 20.00x (ISBN 0-685-38490-X). LC 73-84160. U Pr of Va.

Schiffer, Peter B. The Chester County Historical Society. (Illus.). 70p. 1970. pap. 3.50 (ISBN 0-686-70341-3). Schiffer.

Silvestro, Clement M. Organizing a Local Historical Society. 2nd ed. 1968. pap. 2.25 (ISBN 0-910050-03-1). AASLH.

Tucker, Evelyn A., compiled by. Index to Th Proceedings of the Vermont Historical Society, New Series, Volumes 11-20. 84p. unbound 3.75x (ISBN 0-934720-17-7). VT Hist Soc.

Vail, R. W. Knickerbocker Birthday: A Sesqui-Centennial History of the New-York Historical Society, 1804-1954. LC 54-14828. (Illus.). 1975. 12.50x (ISBN 0-685-73905-8, New York Historical Society). U Pr of Va.

Wainwright, Nicholas B. One Hundred & Fifty Years of Collecting: By the Historical Society of Pennsylvania 1824-1974. 105p. 1974. 10.00 (ISBN 0-910732-09-4). Pa Hist Soc.

Walther, Philipp A. Systematisches Repertorium Ueber Die Schriften Saemmtlicher Historischer Gesellschaften Deutschlands. (Ger). 1969. Repr. of 1845 ed. 35.50 (ISBN 0-8337-3681-7). B Franklin.

Whitehill, Walter M. Independent Historical Societies: An Enquiry into Their Research & Publication Functions & Their Financial Future. LC 63-1190. 1962. 22.50x (ISBN 0-674-44825-1). Harvard U Pr.

--Independent Historical Societies: An Inquiry into Their Research & Publication Functions & Their Financial Future. xviii, 591p. 1962. 15.00 (ISBN 0-934552-21-5). Boston Athenaeum.

HISTORICAL SOCIETIES–BIBLIOGRAPHY

Ericson, Jack T., ed. Shaker Collection of the Western Reserve Historical Society. 77p. 1977. pap. 7.50 (ISBN 0-667-00522-6). Microfilming Corp.

Griffin, A. P. Bibliography of American Historical Societies. 59.95 (ISBN 0-87968-736-3). Gordon Pr.

Griffin, Appleton P. Bibliography of American Historical Societies. 2nd ed. rev. ed. LC 67-480. 1966. Repr. of 1907 ed. 49.00 (ISBN 0-8103-3080-6). Gale.

Rath, Frederick L., Jr. & O'Connell, Merrilyn R. A Guide to Historic Preservation, Historical Agencies, & Museum Practices: A Selective Bibliography. 12.50 (ISBN 0-686-16046-0). Fenimore Bk.

Reese, Rosemary S. & Rath, Frederick L., Jr., eds. Documentation of Collections. (A Bibliography on Historical Organization Practices: Vol. 4). 1979. text ed. 12.50x (ISBN 0-910050-38-4). AASLH.

HISTORICAL SOCIOLOGY

see also Culture; Society, Primitive

Burke, Peter. Sociology & History. (Controversies in Sociology Ser.: No. 10). 128p. (Orig.). 1980. text ed. 14.95x (ISBN 0-04-301114-4); pap. text ed. 5.95x (ISBN 0-04-301115-2). Allen Unwin.

Burrow, J. W. Evolution & Society. 1966. 29.95 (ISBN 0-521-04393-X); pap. 9.95x (ISBN 0-521-09600-6). Cambridge U Pr.

Dahrendorf, Ralf. Life Chances: Approaches to Social & Political Theory. LC 79-18685. 1980. lib. bdg. 15.00x (ISBN 0-226-13408-3). U of Chicago Pr.

Nisbet, Robert A. Social Change & History: Aspects of the Western Theory of Development. 1969. 15.95 (ISBN 0-19-500042-0). Oxford U Pr.

--Social Change & History: Aspects of the Western Theory of Development. LC 69-17772. 1970. pap. 5.95 (ISBN 0-19-500805-7, 313, GB). Oxford U Pr.

--Tradition & Revolt: Essays, Historical, Sociological & Critical. 1968. text ed. 6.95x (ISBN 0-685-77217-9, 0-394-30421). Phila Bk Co.

Richards, A. I. & Kuper, Adam, eds. Councils in Action: Comparative Studies. LC 76-160101. (Cambridge Papers in Social Anthropology: No. 6). (Illus.). 1971. 22.00 (ISBN 0-521-08240-4). Cambridge U Pr.

Rubenstein, Richard. The Cunning of History. 1978. pap. 3.95 (ISBN 0-06-090597-2, CN 597, CN). Har-Row.

Schluchter, Wolfgang. The Rise of Western Rationalism: Max Weber's Developmental History. Roth, Guenther, tr. from Ger. LC 81-2763. 300p. 1981. 16.50x (ISBN 0-520-04060-0). U of Cal Pr.

Stern, Bernhard J. Historical Sociology. 1963. pap. 2.25 (ISBN 0-8065-0128-6, 139). Citadel Pr.

Szacki, Jerzy. History of Sociological Thought. LC 78-67566. (Contributions in Sociology: No. 35). 1979. lib. bdg. 37.50 (ISBN 0-313-20737-2, SZH/). Greenwood.

Vucinich, Alexander. Social Thought in Tsarist Russia: The Quest for a General Science of Society, 1861-1917. LC 75-12229. 304p. 1976. 18.00x (ISBN 0-226-86624-6). U of Chicago Pr.

HISTORIOGRAPHY

see also Diplomatics; Historians; Historical Drama; Historical Research; Local History; Psychohistory;

also subdivision Historiography under names of countries, e.g. United States–History–Historiography

Abbott, Wilbur C. Adventures in Reputation. LC 69-16486. (Essay & General Literature Index Reprint Ser). 1969. Repr. of 1935 ed. 12.50 (ISBN 0-8046-0517-3). Kennikat.

Acton, Lord. Lectures on Modern History. 59.95 (ISBN 0-8490-0496-9). Gordon Pr.

American Psychiatric Association's Task Force on Psychohistory, ed. The Psychiatrist As Psychohistorian. (Task Force Reports: No. 11). 33p. 1976. 5.00 (ISBN 0-685-76790-6, P221-0). Am Psychiatric.

Ausubel, Herman. Historians & Their Craft: A Study of the Presidential Addresses of the American Historical Association, 1884-1945. LC 65-18786. 1965. Repr. of 1950 ed. 8.50 (ISBN 0-8462-0652-8). Russell.

Barnes, H. E. A History of Historical Writing. rev. 2nd ed. 10.00 (ISBN 0-8446-1595-1). Peter Smith.

Barnes, Harry E. The Barnes Trilogy. Brandon, Lewis, ed. 1980. pap. 4.00 (ISBN 0-911038-56-6, 336, Inst Hist Rev). Noontide.

--History & Social Intelligence. 75.00 (ISBN 0-87700-030-1). Revisionist Pr.

--History of Historical Writing. 2nd ed. 1962. pap. 6.00 (ISBN 0-486-20104-X). Dover.

--The New History & the Social Studies. (The Harry Elmer Barnes Ser). (Illus.). 624p. 1972. Repr. of 1925 ed. lib. bdg. 75.00 (ISBN 0-87700-033-6). Revisionist Pr.

Barzun, Jacques & Graff, Henry F. The Modern Researcher. 3rd ed. LC 76-27411. 1977. 12.95 (ISBN 0-15-161480-6, HC); pap. text ed. 11.95 (ISBN 0-15-562511-X). HarBraceJ.

Baumgarten, P. M. Henry Charles Lea's Historical Writings. 69.95 (ISBN 0-87968-262-0). Gordon Pr.

Benham, Benjamin A. Clio & Mr. Croce. LC 74-9707. 1928. lib. bdg. 10.00 (ISBN 0-8414-3117-5). Folcroft.

Berdyaev, Nicolas. The Beginning & the End. 8.00 (ISBN 0-8446-0488-7). Peter Smith.

Birkos, Alexander S. & Tambs, Lewis A. Historiography, Method, History Teaching: A Bibliography of Books & Articles in English, 1965-1973. xi, 130p. (Orig.). 1975. 13.50 (ISBN 0-208-01420-9, Linnet). Shoe String.

Bloch, Marc. Historian's Craft. 1964. pap. 2.95 (ISBN 0-394-70512-2, V512, Vin). Random.

Blundeville, Thomas. The True Order & Method of Wryting & Reading Hystories. LC 79-84088. (English Experience Ser.: No. 908). 68p. (Eng.). 1979. Repr. of 1574 ed. lib. bdg. 7.00 (ISBN 90-221-0908-9). Walter J Johnson.

Braudel, Fernand. On History. Matthews, Sarah, tr. from Fr. LC 80-11201. 1980. lib. bdg. 15.00x (ISBN 0-226-07150-2). U of Chicago Pr.

Burckhardt, Jacob. Reflections on History. LC 78-24385. Orig. Title: Force & Freedom. 1979. 9.00 (ISBN 0-913966-37-1); pap. 4.00 (ISBN 0-913966-38-X). Liberty Fund.

Burke, Peter, ed. Renaissance Sense of the Past. (Documents of Modern History Ser). 1970. 15.95 (ISBN 0-312-67375-2); pap. 4.95 (ISBN 0-312-67340-X). St Martin.

Butterfield, Herbert. Man on His Past. 32.95 (ISBN 0-521-07265-4); pap. 8.50x (ISBN 0-521-09567-0). Cambridge U Pr.

--Whig Interpretation of History. 1965. pap. 3.95 (ISBN 0-393-00318-3, Norton Lib). Norton.

--The Whig Interpretation of History. LC 75-41043. (BCL Ser. II). Repr. of 1931 ed. 16.00 (ISBN 0-404-14515-9). AMS Pr.

Canary, Robert H. & Kozicki, Henry, eds. The Writing of History: Literary Form & Historical Understanding. LC 78-4590. 182p. 1978. 19.50 (ISBN 0-299-07570-2). U of Wis Pr.

Cannon, John, ed. The Historian at Work. 216p. (Orig.). 1980. text ed. 25.00x (ISBN 0-04-901025-5); pap. text ed. 7.50x (ISBN 0-04-901026-3). Allen Unwin.

Cate, James L. & Anderson, E. N. Medieval & Historiographical Essays in Honor of James Westfall Thompson. LC 66-25904. Repr. of 1938 ed. 17.00 (ISBN 0-8046-0072-4). Kennikat.

Chancellor, Valerie E. History for Their Masters. LC 78-129565. 1970. lib. bdg. 12.50x (ISBN 0-678-07768-1). Kelley.

Cochran, Thomas C., et al. Social Sciences in Historical Study. LC 54-9680. 1954. pap. 3.75 (ISBN 0-527-03291-3). Kraus Repr.

Cohen, Morris R. The Meaning of Human History. 2nd ed. LC 61-10174. (The Paul Carus Lectures Ser.). (Illus.). ix, 304p. 1961. 17.50 (ISBN 0-87548-100-0); pap. 6.95 (ISBN 0-87548-101-9). Open Court.

Collingwood, Robin G. Idea of History. Knox, T. M., ed. 1956. pap. 5.95 (ISBN 0-19-500205-9, 1, GB). Oxford U Pr.

Conkin, Paul K. & Stromberg, Roland N. The Heritage & Challenge of History. 1971. pap. text ed. 9.95 scp (ISBN 0-06-041342-5, HarpC). Har-Row.

Croce, Benedetto. History: Its Theory & Practice. Ainslie, Douglas, tr. LC 60-14177. 1960. Repr. of 1920 ed. 16.00 (ISBN 0-8462-0160-7). Russell.

Crook, D., ed. Questioning the Past. 1974. 27.50x (ISBN 0-8448-0738-9). Crane-Russak Co.

Dance, Edward H. History of the Betrayer. LC 73-16869. 162p. 1975. Repr. of 1960 ed. lib. bdg. 15.00x (ISBN 0-8371-7237-3, DAHB). Greenwood.

Daniels, Robert V. Studying History: How & Why. 3rd ed. 128p. 1981. pap. text ed. 5.95 (ISBN 0-13-858738-8). P-H.

Davis, R. H. & Wallace-Hadrill, J. M., eds. The Writing of History in the Middle Ages: Essays Presented to Richard William Southern. (Illus.). 520p. 1981. 66.50 (ISBN 0-19-822556-3). Oxford U Pr.

Downs, Robert B. Books & History. LC 74-620006. (Monograph: No. 13). 83p. 1974. 5.00x (ISBN 0-87845-039-4). U of Ill Lib Info Sci.

Dumoulin, J. & Moisi, D. The Historian Between the Ethnologist & the Futurologist. (New Babylon Studies in the Social Sciences: No. 13). 1973. text ed. 26.25x (ISBN 90-2797-230-3). Mouton.

Ellis, Ann W., et al, eds. Proceedings & Papers of the Georgia Association of Historians 1980. 84p. (Orig.). 1981. pap. 5.00 (ISBN 0-939346-00-1). GA Assn Hist.

Evans, George E. From Mouths of Men. (Illus.). 202p. 1976. 13.95 (ISBN 0-571-10771-0, Pub. by Faber & Faber). Merrimack Bk Serv.

Fehl, Noah E., ed. Sir Herbert Butterfield, Cho Yun Hsu & William H. McNeill on Chinese & World History. 1971. 10.00x (ISBN 0-8002-1978-3). Intl Pubns Serv.

Fisher, Herbert A. Studies in History & Politics. facs. ed. LC 67-26740. (Essay Index Reprint Ser). 1920. 16.00 (ISBN 0-8369-0441-9). Arno.

Fueter, Eduard. Geschichte der Neueren Historiographie. Gerhard, D. & Satler, P., eds. (Ger). 1969. Repr. of 1936 ed. 38.50 (ISBN 0-384-17210-5). Johnson Repr.

Gay, Peter. Style in History. LC 76-25490. (McGraw-Hill Paperbacks). 1976. pap. 3.95 (ISBN 0-07-023063-3, SP). McGraw.

Gilbert, Felix. History: Choice & Commitment. 1977. 25.00x (ISBN 0-674-39656-1, Belknap Pr). Harvard U Pr.

Gooch, G. P. Maria Theresa & Other Studies. 1965. Repr. of 1951 ed. 19.50 (ISBN 0-208-00019-4, Archon). Shoe String.

Gordon, Raoul, ed. Puerto Rican Historiography. 1976. lib. bdg. 59.95 (ISBN 0-8490-0917-0). Gordon Pr.

Gottschalk, Louis, et al. Use of Personal Documents in History, Anthropology, & Sociology. LC 45-2844. 1945. pap. 5.00 (ISBN 0-527-03282-4). Kraus Repr.

Gottschalk, Louis M. Understanding History: A Primer of Historical Method. 1969. pap. 10.95 (ISBN 0-394-30215-X). Knopf.

Grant, A. J., ed. English Historians. LC 73-118472. 1971. Repr. of 1906 ed. 15.00 (ISBN 0-8046-1221-8). Kennikat.

Gray, Wood, et al. Historian's Handbook: A Key to the Study & Writing of History. 2nd ed. (Orig.). 1964. pap. text ed. 3.95 (ISBN 0-395-04537-1, 3-19750). HM.

Gustavson, Carl. The Mansion of History. (McGraw-Hill Paperbacks). 384p. (Orig.). 1976. pap. 4.95 (ISBN 0-07-025276-9, SP). McGraw.

Handlin, Oscar. Truth in History. LC 78-24157. 1979. 20.00x (ISBN 0-674-91025-7, Belknap Pr); pap. 8.95 (ISBN 0-674-91026-5). Harvard U Pr.

Hay, Denys. Annalists & Historians: Western Historiography from the VIII to the XVII Century. 224p. 1977. 19.95x (ISBN 0-416-81180-9); pap. 8.95x (ISBN 0-416-81190-6). Methuen Inc.

Heller, L. G. Communicational Analysis & Methodology for Historians. LC 72-75003. 1972. 15.00x (ISBN 0-8147-3362-X). NYU Pr.

Histoire et Historiens Depuis Cinquante Ans: Methodes, Organisations et Resultats Du Travail Historique De 1876 a 1926, 2 vols in 1. LC 75-156822. 1927-28. 36.50 (ISBN 0-8337-2970-5). B. Franklin.

Hutchins, Robert M. & Adler, Mortimer J., eds. Contemporary Ideas in Historical Perspective. new ed. LC 75-4311. (The Great Ideas Anthologies Ser). (Illus.). 500p. 1976. 15.00x (ISBN 0-405-07174-4). Arno.

Iggers, Georg G. New Directions in European Historiography. LC 75-12665. 240p. 1975. 20.00x (ISBN 0-8195-4084-6, Pub. by Wesleyan U Pr). Columbia U Pr.

Iggers, Georg G. & Parker, Harold T., eds. International Handbook of Historical Studies: Contemporary Research & Theory. LC 79-7061. 1980. lib. bdg. 35.00 (ISBN 0-313-21367-4, ICD/). Greenwood.

Iglesia, Ramon. Columbus, Cortes, & Other Essays. Simpson, Lesley B., tr. LC 69-13727. 1969. 21.75x (ISBN 0-520-01469-3). U of Cal Pr.

International Bibliography of Historical Sciences, 1972, Vol. 41. (International Bibliography of Historical Sciences Ser.). 369p. 70.00 (ISBN 0-686-75628-2, Pub. by K G Saur). Gale.

International Bibliography of Historical Sciences, 1973, Vol. 42. (International Bibliography of Historical Sciences Ser.). 361p. 70.00 (ISBN 0-686-75629-0, Pub. by K G Saur). Gale.

International Bibliography of Historical Sciences, 1968 to 1969, Vol. 37-38. (International Bibliography of Historical Sciences Ser.). 654p. 60.00 (ISBN 0-686-75625-8, Pub. by K G Saur). Gale.

International Bibliography of Historical Sciences, 1970 to 1971, Vol. 39-40. (International Bibliography of Historical Sciences Ser.). 567p. 60.00 (ISBN 0-686-75627-4, Pub. by K G Saur). Gale.

Johnson, Allen. Historian & Historical Evidence. LC 65-14788. Repr. of 1926 ed. 11.50 (ISBN 0-8046-0240-9). Kennikat.

Kahn, S. Jacob. Science & Aesthetic Judgment: A Study in Taine's Critical Method. Repr. of 1953 ed. lib. bdg. 15.00x (ISBN 0-8371-3338-6, KAJU). Greenwood.

Kelley, Donald R. Foundations of Modern Historical Scholarship: Language, Law & History in the French Renaissance. LC 68-8875. 321p. 1970. 20.00x (ISBN 0-231-03141-6). Columbia U Pr.

Kenner, Charles L. History of New Mexican-Plains Indian Relations. LC 68-31375. (Illus.). 1969. 13.95 (ISBN 0-8061-0829-0). U of Okla Pr.

Khalidi, Tarif. Islamic Historiography: The Histories of Masudi. LC 75-5933. 1975. Vol. 1. 17.00 (ISBN 0-87395-282-0); microfiche 17.00 (ISBN 0-87395-283-9). State U NY Pr.

Kracauer, Siegfried. History: The Last Things Before the Last. 1969. text ed. 16.95x (ISBN 0-19-500604-6). Oxford U Pr.

Langlois, Charles V. & Seignobos, Charles. Introduction to the Study of History. Berry, G. G., tr. LC 78-10678. 1979. Repr. of 1906 ed. lib. bdg. 22.50x (ISBN 0-313-20699-6, LAIN). Greenwood.

Leroy-Ladurie, Emmanuel. The Mind & Method of the Historian. Reynolds, Sian & Reynolds, Ben, trs. 224p. 1981. 21.00 (ISBN 0-226-47326-0). U of Chicago Pr.

Levin, David. History As Romantic Art. LC 70-181945. (Stanford University. Stanford Studies in Language & Literature: No. 20). Repr. of 1959 ed. 21.45 (ISBN 0-404-51830-3). AMS Pr.

Lichtman, Allan J. & French, Valerie. Historians & the Living Past: The Theory & Practice of Historical Study. LC 77-86035. 1978. pap. text ed. 9.95x (ISBN 0-88295-773-2). Harlan Davidson.

Lifton, Robert J. & Olson, Eric, eds. Explorations in Psychohistory: The Wellfleet Papers of Erik Erikson, Robert Jay Lifton & Kenneth Kenniston. LC 74-13758. 1975. pap. 3.95 (ISBN 0-671-21849-2). S&S.

Lottinville, Savoie. The Rhetoric of History. LC 75-19418. 256p. 1976. 12.95 (ISBN 0-8061-1330-8). U of Okla Pr.

Mandelbaum, Maurice H. The Problem of Historical Knowledge: An Answer to Relativism. facsimile ed. LC 74-152993. (Select Bibliographies Reprint Ser). Repr. of 1938 ed. 20.00 (ISBN 0-8369-5745-8). Arno.

Marston, Doris. A Guide to Writing History. 1975. 8.50 (ISBN 0-911654-34-8). Writers Digest.

Mazour, Anatole G. Writing of History in the Soviet Union. LC 76-99084. (Publications Ser.: No. 87). 1971. 17.50 (ISBN 0-8179-1871-X). Hoover Inst Pr.

Milburn, Robert L. Early Christian Interpretations of History. LC 79-21671. 1980. Repr. of 1954 ed. lib. bdg. 19.75x (ISBN 0-313-22157-X, MIEA). Greenwood.

Montgomery, John W. The Shape of the Past. LC 75-26651. 400p. 1975. pap. 7.95 (ISBN 0-87123-535-8, 210535). Bethany Hse.

Moss, Peter & Keeton, Joe. Encounters with the Past: Man's Ability to Relive History. LC 79-8010. (Illus.). 1980. 14.00 (ISBN 0-385-15307-4). Doubleday.

Neff, Emery. The Poetry of History: The Contributions of Literature & Literary Scholarship to the Writing of History Since Voltaire. 1979. Repr. of 1947 ed. lib. bdg. 17.00x (ISBN 0-374-96039-9). Octagon.

Neff, Emery E. The Poetry of History: The Contribution of Literature & Literary Scholarship to the Writing of History Since Voltaire. LC 47-30933. 1947. pap. 6.00x (ISBN 0-231-08525-7). Columbia U Pr.

Nordau, Max. The Interpretation of History. 59.95 (ISBN 0-8490-0413-6). Gordon Pr.

Norvell, Theodore J. The Meaning & the Objective of History. (Illus.). 177p. 1980. deluxe ed. 47.65 (ISBN 0-89266-238-7). Am Classical Coll Pr.

Nugent, Walter T. Creative History. 2nd ed. 1973. pap. text ed. 2.95 (ISBN 0-397-47286-2). Har-Row.

Peardon, Thomas P. Transition in English Historical Writing, 1760-1830. LC 34-967. (Columbia University. Studies in the Social Sciences: No. 390). 24.50 (ISBN 0-404-51390-5). AMS Pr.

Phillips, Mark. Francesco Guicciardini: The Historian's Craft. LC 76-56341. (Romance Ser). 1977. 22.50x (ISBN 0-8020-5371-8). U of Toronto Pr.

Rath, Frederick L. & O'Connell, Merrilyn R., eds. Interpretation. LC 75-26770. (A Bibliography on Historical Organization Practices: Vol. 3). 1978. 10.00x (ISBN 0-910050-31-7). AASLH.

Rowse, Alfred L. On History: A Study of Present Tendencies. 1979. Repr. of 1927 ed. lib. bdg. 12.50 (ISBN 0-8495-4618-4). Arden Lib.

Rubenstein, Richard. The Cunning of History. 1978. pap. 3.95 (ISBN 0-06-090597-2, CN 597, CN). Har-Row.

Salmon, Lucy M. Why Is History Rewritten. LC 29-22815. 1929. Repr. 9.50 (ISBN 0-8046-0401-0). Kennikat.

Salvemini, Gaetano. Historian & Scientist. facs. ed. LC 75-80396. (Essay Index Reprint Ser). 1939. 14.75 (ISBN 0-8369-1049-4). Arno.

Saveth, Edward N. American History & the Social Sciences. LC 64-20308. 1964. 15.95 (ISBN 0-02-927750-7). Free Pr.

Schouler, James. Historical Briefs: With a Biography. LC 72-4586. (Essay Index Reprint Ser.). Repr. of 1896 ed. 18.00 (ISBN 0-8369-2974-8). Arno.

Shera, Jesse H. Historians, Books & Libraries. Repr. of 1953 ed. lib. bdg. 15.00 (ISBN 0-8371-2558-8, SHHB). Greenwood.

Shipman, Homer D. Historical Models & the Anticipation of the Future. (Illus.). 1979. deluxe ed. 47.50 (ISBN 0-930008-43-X). Inst Econ Pol.

Shotwell, James T. The Story of Ancient History. LC 39-4448. 1961. pap. 6.00x (ISBN 0-231-08518-4). Columbia U Pr.

Snow, J. H. The Case of Tyler Kent. (Studies in Revisionist Historiography). 1979. lib. bdg. 59.95 (ISBN 0-685-96863-4). Revisionist Pr.

Social Science Research Council - Committee on Historiography. Theory & Practice in Historical Study. LC 46-3597. 1946. pap. 3.75 (ISBN 0-527-03283-2). Kraus Repr.

Stebbing, William. Some Verdicts of History Reviewed: Essay Index Reprint Ser. LC 72-8545. 1972. Repr. of 1887 ed. 22.00 (ISBN 0-8369-7327-5). Arno.

Stephens, Lester D. Historiography: A Bibliography. LC 75-17578. 1975. 11.00 (ISBN 0-8108-0856-0). Scarecrow.

Stone, Lawrence. The Past & the Present. 288p. 1981. 15.95 (ISBN 0-7100-0628-4). Routledge & Kegan.

Taylor, Hugh. History As a Science. LC 70-115331. 1971. Repr. of 1933 ed. 10.00 (ISBN 0-8046-1122-X). Kennikat.

Teggart, Frederick J. Prolegomena to History: The Relation of History to Literature, Philosophy, & Science, Vol. 4. LC 73-14184. (Perspectives in Social Inquiry Ser.). 142p. 1974. Repr. 9.00x (ISBN 0-405-05528-5). Arno.

--Theory & Processes of History. 7.25 (ISBN 0-8446-3057-8). Peter Smith.

Thakurdas, Frank. German Political Idealism. 368p. 1980. text ed. 22.50x (ISBN 0-391-01796-9). Humanities.

Thompson, J. W. A History of Historical Writing, 2 vols. 35.00 (ISBN 0-8446-1448-3). Peter Smith.

Toekei, Ferenc. Essays on the Asiatic Mode of Production. 129p. 1979. 13.50x (ISBN 963-05-1701-9). Intl Pubns Serv.

Urban, G. R., ed. Toynbee on Toynbee: A Conversation Between Arnold J. Toynbee & G. R. Urban. 120p. 1974. 11.95 (ISBN 0-19-501739-0). Oxford U Pr.

Von Ranke, Leopold. The Theory & Practice of History. Iggers, Georg G. & Von Moltke, Konrad, eds. Iggers, Wilma, tr. from Ger. LC 79-167691. 1973. pap. text ed. 16.95x (ISBN 0-672-60920-7). Irvington.

Walsh, Warren B. Perspectives & Patterns: Discourses on History. LC 62-16382. 1962. 11.95x (ISBN 0-8156-0027-5). Syracuse U Pr.

Ware, Caroline F. The Cultural Approach to History. 75.00 (ISBN 0-87968-082-2). Gordon Pr.

White, Hayden. Metahistory: The Historical Imagination in Nineteenth-Century Europe. LC 73-8110. 462p. 1974. 25.00x (ISBN 0-8018-1469-3); pap. 6.95 (ISBN 0-8018-1761-7). Johns Hopkins.

Wilde, Oscar. Rise of Historical Critisism. LC 72-194458. 1905. lib. bdg. 10.00 (ISBN 0-8414-9732-X). Folcroft.

Wilson, Woodrow. On the Writing of History: With Commentaries on Macaulay, Gibbon & Carlyle. (Most Meaningful Classics in World Culture Ser.). 1978. 39.75 (ISBN 0-89266-129-1). Am Classical Coll Pr.

Wiseman, T. P. Clio's Cosmetics: Three Studies in Greco-Roman Literature. 209p. 1979. 27.50x (ISBN 0-8476-6206-3). Rowman.

Young, Louise M. Thomas Carlyle & the Art of History. LC 74-23128. 1939. 20.00 (ISBN 0-8414-9768-0). Folcroft.

HISTORIOGRAPHY–ADDRESSES, ESSAYS, LECTURES

Andrea, Alfred J. & Schmokel, W. The Living Past: Western Historiographical Traditions. 298p. 1981. Repr. of 1975 ed. write for info. (ISBN 0-89874-152-1). Krieger.

Barnes, Harry E. History & Social Intelligence. 75.00 (ISBN 0-87700-030-1). Revisionist Pr.

Becker, Carl L. Detachment & the Writing of History: Essays & Letters of Carl L. Becker. Snyder, Phil L., ed. LC 70-152590. 240p. 1972. Repr. of 1958 ed. lib. bdg. 15.00 (ISBN 0-8371-6023-5, BEWH). Greenwood.

Bremner, Robert H., ed. Essays on History & Literature. LC 66-22733. 1966. 5.00 (ISBN 0-8142-0029-X). Ohio St U Pr.

Geyl, Pieter. Encounters in History. 8.75 (ISBN 0-8446-2125-0). Peter Smith.

Hughes, Henry S., ed. Teachers of History. facs. ed. LC 75-142644. (Essay Index Reprint Ser). 1954. 19.50 (ISBN 0-8369-2164-X). Arno.

Jusserand, Jean J., et al. The Writing of History. LC 73-21924. 160p. 1974. Repr. of 1926 ed. lib. bdg. 18.50 (ISBN 0-8337-5026-7). B Franklin.

Momigliano, Arnaldo. Essays in Ancient & Modern Historiography. LC 76-41484. 1977. lib. bdg. 22.50x (ISBN 0-8195-5010-8, Pub. by Wesleyan U Pr). Columbia U Pr.

Powicke, Frederick M. Modern Historians & the Study of History: Essays & Papers. LC 75-25496. 1976. Repr. of 1955 ed. lib. bdg. 16.50x (ISBN 0-8371-8428-2, POMH). Greenwood.

Stern, Fritz, ed. The Varieties of History: From Voltaire to the Present. 1973. pap. 5.95 (ISBN 0-394-71962-X, Vin). Random.

Waldman, Marilyn R. Toward a Theory of Historical Narrative: A Case Study in Perso-Islamicate Historiography. LC 79-886. 1980. 15.00x (ISBN 0-8142-0297-7). Ohio St U Pr.

HISTORY

Here are entered general works about history, its methods, philosophy, etc. For works on the history of specific places or periods, see World History; History, Ancient; History, modern, etc.
see also Anthropo-Geography; Archaeology; Battles; Biography; Boundaries; Chronology; Church History; Civilization; Constitutional History; Coups d'Etat; Culture; Diplomacy; Diplomatics; Discoveries (In Geography); Ethnology; Genealogy; Geography, Historical; Heraldry; Heroes; Historians; Historic Sites; Historical Drama; Historical Fiction; Historical Research; Historical Sociology; Kings and Rulers; Man-Migrations; Medals; Migrations of Nations; Military History; Naval History; Numismatics; Political Science; Revolutions; Riots; Seals (Numismatics); Social History; Sieges; Society, Primitive; Treaties;
also subdivisions Antiquities, Foreign Relations, History and Politics and Government under names of countries, states, cities, etc.

Annals Index: 1936-1965, Vols 26-55. pap. 6.00 (ISBN 0-89291-143-3). Assn Am Geographers.

Annals of the Bamboo Books: Chu Shu Chi Nien. 88p. 1972. pap. 1.00x (ISBN 0-87291-034-2). Coronado Pr.

Aubin, Francoise, ed. Sung Studies - Etudes Sung: In Memoriam Etienne Balazs. (History & Institutions Ser: No. 3). 296p. 1976. pap. text ed. 13.50x (ISBN 0-686-22620-8). Mouton.

Audet, Louis-Philippe. La Situation Scolaire a la Veille De L'union, 1836-1840. (Le Systeme Scolaire De la Province De Quebec Ser.: Vol. 6). 353p. 1956. pap. 7.50x (ISBN 2-7637-0056-X, Pub by Laval). Intl Schol Bk Serv.

Baring, Maurice. Unreliable History. 1934. 25.00 (ISBN 0-8274-3662-9). R West.

Barnes, Harry E. Blasting the Historical Blackout. 59.95 (ISBN 0-87700-027-1). Revisionist Pr.

--Psychology & History. 59.95 (ISBN 0-87700-034-4). Revisionist Pr.

--The Struggle Against the Historical Blackout. 59.95 (ISBN 0-87700-195-2). Revisionist Pr.

Barnes, Mary S. Studies in Historical Method. 1896. 10.00 (ISBN 0-685-43772-8). Norwood Edns.

Barraclough, Geoffrey. Main Trends in History. LC 79-12662. (Main Trends in the Social & Human Sciences). 1979. pap. text ed. 10.95x (ISBN 0-8419-0505-3). Holmes & Meier.

Bebbington, D. W. Patterns in History. LC 79-3062. 1980. pap. 7.25 (ISBN 0-87784-737-1). Inter-Varsity.

Benjamin, Jules R. A Student's Guide to History. 2nd ed. LC 78-65211. 1979. text ed. 10.95x (ISBN 0-312-77001-4); pap. text ed. 3.95x (ISBN 0-312-77002-2). St Martin.

Benton, Thomas H. Thirty Years' View, 2 vols. LC 72-78644. 1854-1856. 65.00 (ISBN 0-403-02099-9). Somerset Pub.

Beringer, Richard E. Historical Analysis: Contemporary Approaches to Clio's Craft. LC 77-10589. 317p. 1978. pap. text ed. 16.50 (ISBN 0-471-06996-5). Wiley.

Bonkalo, E. Three Centuries. (Winston Mine Editions). 1970. text ed. 3.84 (ISBN 0-685-33409-0); tchr's. guide 5.16 (ISBN 0-685-33410-4). HR&W.

Boochever, Florence & Jackson, Raymond, eds. Writings from the Beaver Trail. (Illus.). 291p. (Orig.). 1979. pap. 5.50 (ISBN 0-9605090-0-3). Albany Pub Lib.

Brown, Stuart E., Jr. Annals of Blackwater & the Land of Canaan, 1746-1880. LC 59-10184. (Illus.). 42p. 1959. 4.25 (ISBN 0-685-65059-6); pap. 1.75 (ISBN 0-685-65060-X). Va Bk.

Cadogan, Edward. Makers of Modern History. LC 75-112797. 1970. Repr. of 1905 ed. 10.50 (ISBN 0-8046-1064-9). Kennikat.

Callcott, M. V. & Peters, Terry, eds. Mr. George, 2 pts. Incl. Pt. 1. In Victorian England; Pt. 2. In Pioneer Texas. (National History Ser.). (Illus.). Date not set. 16.95 (ISBN 0-89482-046-X); ltd. ed. 39.95 (ISBN 0-89482-048-6); pap. 8.95 (ISBN 0-89482-047-8); video cassette of Frank Callcott 165.00 (ISBN 0-89482-022-2). Stevenson Pr.

Calvocoressi, Peter. Top Secret Ultra. (Illus.). 1981. 10.95 (ISBN 0-394-51154-9). Pantheon.

Canning, Albert S. History in Fact & Fiction. 336p. 1980. Repr. of 1897 ed. lib. bdg. 30.00 (ISBN 0-8492-3863-3). R West.

Carney, T. F. The Shape of the Past: Models & Antiquity. (Illus.). 1975. 20.00x (ISBN 0-87291-068-7). Coronado Pr.

Catlin, George E. Science & Method of Politics. 1964. Repr. of 1927 ed. 19.50 (ISBN 0-208-00535-8, Archon). Shoe String.

Caudwell, Christopher, pseud. Men & Nature, a Study in Bourgeois History. 1970. Repr. pap. 1.00 (ISBN 0-88211-004-7). S A Russell.

Childe, Gordon. What Happened in History. lib. bdg. 9.50x (ISBN 0-88307-054-5). Gannon.

Columbia University, Dept. of Philosophy, ed. Studies in the History of Ideas, 3 Vols. LC 79-130993. Repr. of 1935 ed. Set. 90.00 (ISBN 0-404-52670-5). AMS Pr.

Commager, Henry S. Study of History. 1966. pap. text ed. 4.95x (ISBN 0-675-09712-6). Merrill.

Dance, E. H. Place of History in Secondary Teaching: A Comparative Study. (Education in Europe Ser). 1970. 6.00x (ISBN 0-245-59921-5). Intl Pubns Serv.

De Grazia, Alfred. Chaos & Creation: An Introduction to Quantavolution in Human & Natural History. (Quantavolution Ser.). (Illus.). xiii, 336p. 1981. 21.00 (ISBN 0-940268-00-0). Metron Pubns.

Delzell, Charles F., ed. The Future of History: Essays in the Vanderbilt University Centennial Symposium. LC 76-48199. 1977. 13.95x (ISBN 0-8265-1205-4). Vanderbilt U Pr.

Diagram Group. Time Lines. Incl. Science & Inventions (ISBN 0-448-22195-0); World History Through the Ages (ISBN 0-448-22196-9); The Making of America (ISBN 0-448-22197-7); Dinosaurs & Prehistoric Life (ISBN 0-448-22198-5); Artists, Writers, Musicians (ISBN 0-448-22199-3); The Twentieth Century (ISBN 0-448-22200-0). (Illus.). 1978. pap. 2.95 ea. Paddington.

Drake, Michael, ed. Applied Historical Studies. 1979. pap. text ed. 6.95 (ISBN 0-416-79110-7). Methuen Inc.

Dutt, Shoshee C. Historical Studies & Recreations, 2 vols. LC 72-13307. (Essay Index Reprint Ser.). Repr. of 1879 ed. 46.50 (ISBN 0-8369-8155-3). Arno.
Erikson, Erik H. Life History & the Historical Moment. 1975 14.95x, (ISBN 0-393-01103-8, N860, Norton Lib); pap. 3.95 1977 (ISBN 0-393-00860-6). Norton.
Fogg, Walter. One Thousand Sayings of History, Presented As Pictures in Prose. LC 79-143634. 1971. Repr. of 1929 ed. 32.00 (ISBN 0-8103-3779-7). Gale.
Frakes, G. E. & Adams, R. W. From Columbus to Aquarius: An Interpretive History, 2 vols. LC 74-2800. 1976. Vol. 1. pap. text ed. 11.95 (ISBN 0-03-014191-5, HoltC); Vol. 2. pap. text ed. 10.95 (ISBN 0-03-014196-6). HR&W.
Frick, Elizabeth. Library Research Guide to History. (Library Research Guides Ser.: No. 4). 1980. 12.50 (ISBN 0-87650-119-6); pap. 5.95 (ISBN 0-87650-123-4). Pierian.
Gamble, Andrew. The Politics of Decline. (Critical Social Studies). 1980. text ed. write for info. (ISBN 0-391-01179-0); pap. text ed. write for info. (ISBN 0-391-01180-4). Humanities.
Gawronski, Donald V. History: Meaning & Method. 3rd ed. 132p. 1975. pap. 4.95x (ISBN 0-673-07968-6). Scott F.
--Out of the Past: A Topical History of the United States. 2nd ed. 1975. pap. text ed. 9.95x (ISBN 0-02-474410-7, 47441); tchrs' manual free (ISBN 0-02-474420-4). Macmillan.
Gentles, Frederick & Steinfield, Melvin. Hangups from Way Back: Historical Myths & Canons, Vol. 2. 2nd ed. LC 74-1191. 1974. pap. 11.95 scp (ISBN 0-06-382786-7, HarpC). Har-Row.
Geyl, P, et al. The Pattern of the Past: Can We Determine It. LC 68-23291. 126p. 1949. Repr. lib. bdg. 15.00x (ISBN 0-8371-0083-6, GEPP). Greenwood.
Goldenweiser, Alexander. History, Psychology & Culture. 8.00 (ISBN 0-8446-0647-2). Peter Smith.
Gonzalez, D. Resumanes de Historia Universal. 1975. 2.20 (ISBN 0-07-090603-3, W). McGraw.
Gottschalk, Louis, ed. Generalization in the Writing of History. LC 63-13064. (Midway Reprint Ser.). 1980. pap. text ed. 10.00x (ISBN 0-226-30544-9). U of Chicago Pr.
Gregory of Tours, History, Bk. 7. 112p. 1971. pap. 1.65x (ISBN 0-685-65316-1). Coronado Pr.
Gretton, R. H. History. 1979. Repr. lib. bdg. 10.00 (ISBN 0-8495-2037-1). Arden Lib.
--History. 1977. Repr. lib. bdg. 10.00 (ISBN 0-8414-4498-6). Folcroft.
Grombach, John V. The Great Liquidator. LC 77-12862. (Illus.). 1980. 12.95 (ISBN 0-385-13271-9). Doubleday.
Grun, Bernard. The Timetables of History. 1979. 29.95 (ISBN 0-671-24987-8). S&S.
Hewitt, John H. Shadows on the Wall: or, Glimpses of the Past. LC 76-166200. Repr. of 1877 ed. 19.00 (ISBN 0-404-07225-9). AMS Pr.
Hintze, Otto. The Historical Essays of Otto Hintze. Gilbert, Felix, ed. 1975. 25.00x (ISBN 0-19-501819-2); pap. 6.95x (ISBN 0-19-501883-4). Oxford U Pr.
Home, Henry. Sketches of the History of Man, 4 Vols. 1968. Repr. of 1778 ed. 190.00 set (ISBN 0-685-00779-0). Adler.
Hughes, H. Stuart. History As Art & As Science: Twin Vistas on the Past. LC 75-29563. (Midway Reprint Ser). x, 108p. 1975. pap. text ed. 4.95x (ISBN 0-226-35916-6). U of Chicago Pr.
Hulme, Frederick E. History, Principles & Practice of Heraldry. LC 68-25243. (Reference Ser., No. 44). 1969. Repr. of 1892 ed. lib. bdg. 32.95 (ISBN 0-8383-0204-1). Haskell.
Hyams, Edward. Soil & Civilization. 1976. pap. 6.50x (ISBN 0-06-090458-5, TB1962, Torch). Har-Row.
Ireland, William W. The Blot Upon the Brain: Studies in History & Psychology. LC 72-3424. (Essay Index Reprint Ser.). Repr. of 1886 ed. 19.50 (ISBN 0-8369-2909-8). Arno.
Irish Conference of Historians, 6th. Historical Studies, Vol. 5. facsimile ed. McCracken, J. L., ed. LC 79-169941. (Essay Index Reprint Ser). Repr. of 1965 ed. 16.00 (ISBN 0-8369-2458-4). Arno.
Jaspers, Karl. The Origin & Goal of History. Bullock, Michael, tr. from Ger. LC 76-21246. 1976. Repr. of 1953 ed. lib. bdg. 22.00x (ISBN 0-8371-8983-7, JAOG). Greenwood.
Johns Hopkins University. Studies in Historical & Political Science, 1882-1965. Repr. of 1965 ed. Set. 6381.00 (ISBN 0-404-61000-5). AMS Pr.
Kellett, E. E. Aspects of History. 1938. Repr. 10.00 (ISBN 0-685-43048-0). Norwood Edns.
Kiefer, Howard & Munitz, Milton, eds. Mind, Science, & History. LC 69-14642. 1970. 22.00 (ISBN 0-87395-052-6); microfiche 22.00 (ISBN 0-87395-152-2). State U NY Pr.
Kurland, Gerald. Western Civilization, One (to 1500) (Monarch College Outlines). pap. 4.95 (ISBN 0-671-08045-8). Monarch Pr.
Labriola, A. Essais sur la Conception Materialiste de L'Historie. (Reimpressions G & B Ser.). 1970. 29.25x (ISBN 0-677-50415-2). Gordon.
Le Gallienne, Richard. The Romantic Nineties. 1926. Repr. lib. bdg. 25.00 (ISBN 0-8414-5797-2). Folcroft.
Little, G. E. Historical Lights. 59.95 (ISBN 0-8490-0309-1). Gordon Pr.
Locke, Raymond F., ed. The Human Side of History. (Great Adventures of History Ser.). 1970. pap. 1.75 (ISBN 0-87687-004-3, BM004). Mankind Pub.
Lodge, Henry C. Studies in History. LC 70-39132. (Essay Index Reprint Ser.). Repr. of 1884 ed. 23.00 (ISBN 0-8369-2698-6). Arno.
Lyon, Bryce. Origins of the Middle Ages: Pirenne's Challenge to Gibbon. LC 77-163374. 1972. 5.00 (ISBN 0-393-05449-7); pap. 2.95x (ISBN 0-393-09993-8). Norton.
McNeill, William H. The Contemporary World: Nineteen Fourteen to Present. rev. ed. 184p. 1975. pap. 7.95x (ISBN 0-673-07908-2). Scott F.
--Plagues & Peoples. (Illus.). 1977. pap. 4.50 (ISBN 0-385-12122-9, Anch). Doubleday.
Mason, Otis T. The Educational Aspects of the United States National Museum. Bd. with The Study of History in Holland & Belgium. Fredericq, Paul. Leonard, Henrietta, tr. from Fr.. (Johns Hopkins University Studies in Historical & Political Science, Ser. 8: No. 10). Repr. of 1890 ed. pap. 7.00 (ISBN 0-384-16754-3). Johnson Repr.
Mathews, Shailer. The Spiritual Interpretation of History. 1917. Repr. 25.00 (ISBN 0-685-43350-1). Norwood Edns.
Meltzer, Milton. Remember the Days: A Short History of the Jewish American. LC 74-5531. 128p. 1974. 4.95 (ISBN 0-385-05946-9, Zenith); pap. 2.50 (ISBN 0-385-07676-2). Doubleday.
Mikeshin, N. History vs. Anti-History. 197p. 1977. 3.30 (ISBN 0-8285-0477-6, Pub. by Progress Pubs Russia). Imported Pubns.
Miller, Hugh. History & Science: A Study of the Relation of Historical & Theoretical Knowledge. (Historiography, Interdisciplinary Studies: No. 1). Repr. of 1939 ed. lib. bdg. 15.00x (ISBN 0-87991-076-3). Porcupine Pr.
Momjan, K. Landmarks in History. 1980. 4.75 (ISBN 0-8285-1821-1, Pub. by Progress Pubs Russia). Imported Pubns.
Moraze, Charles. The Logic of History. Clough, Wilson, tr. (New Babylon Ser.: No. 11). 260p. 1976. text ed. 36.25x (ISBN 0-686-22616-X). Mouton.
Morrell, Sydney. Spheres of Influence. facs. ed. LC 70-142672. (Essay Index Reprint Ser). 1946. 18.00 (ISBN 0-8369-2197-6). Arno.
Mullins, E. L. Texts & Calendars: An Analytical Guide to Serial Publications. (Royal Historical Society Ser.). 674p. 1958. 18.75x (ISBN 0-8476-1347-X). Rowman.
Navin, Thomas R. Whitin Machine Works Since 1831: A Textile Machinery Company in an Industrial Village. LC 68-15146. (Illus.). 1969. Repr. of 1950 ed. 20.00 (ISBN 0-8462-1207-2). Russell.
Nearing, Scott. Civilization & Beyond: Learning from History. pap. 4.00 (ISBN 0-685-83848-X). Soc Sci Inst.
Nietzsche, Friedrich W. Use & Abuse of History. 2nd ed. Collins, Adrian, tr. LC 57-4499. 1957. pap. 2.50 (ISBN 0-672-60172-9, LLA11). Bobbs.
Ouellet, Fernand. Papineau, Textes Choisis. 2nd ed. (Cahiers De L'histoire: No. 1). (Fr). 1970. pap. 4.50x (ISBN 2-7637-6499-1, Pub. by Laval). Intl Schol Bk Serv.
Pittard, Eugene. Race & History: An Ethnological Introduction to History. Collum, V. C., tr. from Fren. (Historigraphy: Interdisciplinary Studies). xxiii, 505p. Repr. of 1926 ed. lib. bdg. 27.50x (ISBN 0-87991-078-X). Porcupine Pr.
Price, Mary R. & Howell, Margaret. From Barbarism to Chivalry, A.D. 300-1300. 1972. pap. 16.95x (ISBN 0-19-913038-8). Oxford U Pr.
Priestley, Herbert I., ed. The Luna Papers, 2 vols. facsimile ed. LC 75-165803. (Select Bibliographies Reprint Ser). Repr. of 1928 ed. Set. 45.00 (ISBN 0-8369-5959-0). Arno.
Proudhon, Pierre J. What Is Property. 1966. 10.00 (ISBN 0-86527-210-7). Fertig.
Reither, Joseph, ed. Masterworks of History, 3 vols. (Masterworks Ser). 1973. pap. 1.95 ea. (SP). Vol. 1 (ISBN 0-07-040810-6). Vol. 2 (ISBN 0-07-040811-4). Vol. 3 (ISBN 0-07-040812-2). McGraw.
Reports of the XIV International Congress of the Historical Sciences Series. LC 77-81885. 1977. lib. bdg. 125.00 set (ISBN 0-405-10517-7). Arno.
Robertson, J. M. Baconian Heresy: A Confutation. 1971. Repr. of 1913 ed. 32.00 (ISBN 0-403-01181-7). Scholarly.
Robinson, James H. New History. 1965. pap. text ed. 3.50 (ISBN 0-02-926610-6). Free Pr.
Rudman, Jack. History. (Undergraduate Program Field Test Ser.: UPFT-13). (Cloth bdg. avail. on request). pap. 9.95 (ISBN 0-8373-6013-7). Natl Learning.
Rugh, Thomas F. & Silva, Erin R., eds. History As a Tool in Critical Interpretation: A Symposium. LC 78-24729. 1978. pap. 2.50 (ISBN 0-8425-1291-8). Brigham.
Salmon, Lucy M. Why Is History Rewritten. LC 29-22815. 1929. Repr. 9.50 (ISBN 0-8046-0401-0). Kennikat.
Singer, C. Gregg. Christian Approaches: To Philosophy, to History. 1978. pap. 1.00 (ISBN 0-934532-24-9). Presby & Reformed.
Skagestad, Peter. Making Sense of History. 1975. pap. text ed. 10.50x (ISBN 8-200-01460-6, Dist. by Columbia U Pr). Universitet.
Slim, Field-Marshall W. Unoffical History. LC 74-71. (Illus.). 242p. 1974. Repr. of 1962 ed. lib. bdg. 15.00 (ISBN 0-8371-7363-9, SLUH). Greenwood.
Smith, Herbert G. Romance of History. LC 72-5733. (Essay Index Reprint Ser.). Repr. of 1891 ed. 19.00 (ISBN 0-8369-7285-6). Arno.
Snyder, L. L. The Age of Reason. 4.25 (ISBN 0-8446-2965-0). Peter Smith.
Soetbeer, Adolf. Liraturnachweis Ueber Geld-und Muenzwesen Insbesondere Weber der Waehrungsstreit, 1871-1891. LC 72-85106. iv, 322p. 1972. Repr. of 1892 ed. lib. bdg. 32.50 (ISBN 0-8337-3304-4). B Franklin.
Stavrianos, Leften S., et al. A Global History. rev. ed. 1979. text ed. 17.40 (ISBN 0-205-06113-3, 7861133); tchrs'. guide 4.40 (ISBN 0-205-06114-1, 7861141); tests 44.00 (ISBN 0-205-06115-X, 786115X). Allyn.
Stebbing, William. Some Verdicts of History Reviewed. 1887. Repr. 30.00 (ISBN 0-685-43279-3). Norwood Edns.
--Some Verdicts of History Reviewed: Abraham Cowley, Matthew Prior, Benjamin Franklin, William Cobbett. 1978. Repr. of 1887 ed. lib. bdg. 50.00 (ISBN 0-8495-4882-9). Arden Lib.
Sticca, Sanduo, ed. Historical & Literary Perspectives: Essays & Studies in Honor of Albert D. Menut. 234p. 1973. 10.00x (ISBN 0-87291-065-2). Coronado Pr.
Tanselle, G. Thomas. The Editing of Historical Documents. 1978. pap. text ed. 2.50x (ISBN 0-8139-0804-3). U Pr of Va.
Tassin, Myron. The Bacchus. LC 74-20526. (Illus.). 96p. 1975. 15.00 (ISBN 0-88289-061-1). Pelican.
Teggart, Frederick J. Theory & Processes of History. 1977. pap. 7.95x (ISBN 0-520-03176-8, CAMPUS162). U of Cal Pr.
Templer, Victor. The New Art & Science of Historical Prognostication. (Illus.). 137p. 1980. deluxe ed. 59.65 (ISBN 0-89266-259-X). Am Classical Coll Pr.
Tierney, Brian, et al. What Is History. 1968. pap. text ed. 1.95 (ISBN 0-394-32006-9, RanC). Random.
Tierney, Brian, et al, eds. Empire & Papacy: A Search for Right Order in the World? 3rd ed. (Historical Pamphlets). 1977. pap. text ed. 1.95x (ISBN 0-394-32053-0). Random.
--Social Darwinism: Law of Nature or Justification of Repression? 3rd ed. (Historical Pamphlets). 1977. pap. text ed. 1.95x (ISBN 0-394-32059-X). Random.
--What Is History--Fact or Fancy? 3rd ed. (Historical Pamphlets). 1977. pap. text ed. 1.95x (ISBN 0-394-32006-9). Random.
Trompf, G. W. The Idea of Historical Recurrence in Western Thought: From Antiquity to the Reformation. 1979. 27.50x (ISBN 0-520-03479-1). U of Cal Pr.
Tuchman, Barbara. Practicing History. LC 81-47509. 320p. 1981. 16.50 (ISBN 0-394-52086-6). Knopf.
Unstead, R. J. A Pictorial History, 8 vols. Incl. Vol. 1. Invaded Island. LC 78-169914. 1972 (ISBN 0-382-06063-6); Vol. 2. Kings, Barons, & Serfs. LC 71-169915. 1972 (ISBN 0-382-06064-4); Vol. 3. Years of the Sword. LC 75-169916. 1972 (ISBN 0-382-06065-2); Vol. 4. Struggle for Power. LC 72-172430. 1972 (ISBN 0-382-06066-0); Vol. 5. Emerging Empire. LC 76-172431. 1972 (ISBN 0-382-06067-9); Vol. 6. Freedom & Revolution. LC 70-172432. 1972 (ISBN 0-382-06068-7); Vol. 7. Age of Machines. LC 73-172433. 1973 (ISBN 0-382-06069-5); Vol. 8. Incredible Century. LC 77-172434. 1975 (ISBN 0-382-06070-9). (Illus.). (gr. 4 up). lib. bdg. 7.95 (ISBN 0-685-36802-5). Silver.
Von Kahler, Erich. Man the Measure: A New Approach to History. (Historiography: Interdisciplinary Studies: No. 3). 700p. Repr. of 1943 ed. lib. bdg. 35.00x (ISBN 0-87991-102-6). Porcupine Pr.
Wagar, W. W. World Views: A Study in Comparative History. LC 76-55505. 1977. pap. text ed. 9.95 (ISBN 0-03-088043-2, HoltC). HR&W.
Watt, James C. Masters of History: Gibbon, Grote, Macaulay, Motley. lib. bdg. 20.00 (ISBN 0-8414-9680-3). Folcroft.
Webster, John C. Introduction to History. 2nd ed. 1981. 6.00x (ISBN 0-8364-0715-6, Pub. by Macmillan India). South Asia Bks.
Webster, Nesta. The Surrender of an Empire. 75.00 (ISBN 0-8490-1162-0). Gordon Pr.
Webster, Nesta H. Surrender of an Empire. 392p. 1972. pap. 5.00 (ISBN 0-913022-07-1). Angriff Pr.
Wilcox, Donald J. Development of Florentine Humanist Historiography in the Fifteenth Century. LC 76-78526. (Historical Studies: No. 82). 1969. text ed. 12.00x (ISBN 0-674-20026-8). Harvard U Pr.
Williams, William C. A Voyage to Pagany. LC 71-145373. 338p. 1972. Repr. of 1928 ed. 21.00 (ISBN 0-403-01278-3). Scholarly.
Wilson, H. Schutz. Studies in History, Legend & Literature. 1977. Repr. of 1884 ed. lib. bdg. 35.00 (ISBN 0-8492-2884-0). R West.
Wines, Roger, ed. Leopold Von Ranke: The Secret of World History; Selected Writings on the Art & Science of History. LC 80-65600. (Illus.). 240p. 1981. cloth 20.00 (ISBN 0-8232-1050-2); pap. 8.50 (ISBN 0-8232-1051-0). Fordham.
Wright, Jay. Dimensions of History. 80p. 1976. pap. 2.00 (ISBN 0-87711-063-8). Kayak.

HISTORY–ADDRESSES, ESSAYS, LECTURES

Acton, John E. Essays in the Liberal Interpretation of History. McNeill, William H., ed. LC 67-15313. (Classic European Historians Ser). 1967. pap. 4.50 (ISBN 0-226-00342-6, P255, Phoen). U of Chicago Pr.
--Historical Essays & Studies. facs. ed. Figgis, J. N. & Laurence, R. V., eds. LC 67-23171. (Essay Index Reprint Ser). 1907. 22.00 (ISBN 0-8369-0134-7). Arno.
--History of Freedom, & Other Essays. facs. ed. Figgis, J. N. & Laurence, R. V., eds. LC 67-22048. (Essay Index Reprint Ser). 1907. 24.00 (ISBN 0-8369-0135-5). Arno.
Ander, O. Fritiof. The John Hauberg Historical Essays. LC 54-14973. (Augustana College Library Ser.: No. 26). 1954. 4.50 (ISBN 0-910182-21-3). Augustana Coll.
Baring-Gould, Sabine. Freaks of Fanaticism & Other Strange Events. LC 68-21754. 1968. Repr. of 1891 ed. 22.00 (ISBN 0-8103-3503-4). Gale.
Baum, Willa K. Oral History for the Local Historical Society. rev. ed. (Illus.). 1971. pap. 3.00 (ISBN 0-910050-06-6). AASLH.
Buchan, John. Men & Deeds. facs. ed. LC 69-17567. (Essay Index Reprint Ser). 1935. 16.00 (ISBN 0-8369-0065-0). Arno.
Bury, John B. Selected Essays. facs. ed. Temperley, Harold, ed. LC 68-30177. (Essay Index Reprint Ser). 1930. 16.00 (ISBN 0-8369-0267-X). Arno.
Butterfield, Herbert. Whig Interpretation of History. 1965. pap. 3.95 (ISBN 0-393-00318-3, Norton Lib). Norton.
Chislett, William. Moderns & Near-Moderns: Essays on Henry James, Stockton, Shaw & Others. facs. ed. LC 67-30180. (Essay Index Reprint Ser). 1928. 14.00 (ISBN 0-8369-0302-1). Arno.
Creighton, Mandell. Historical Lectures & Addresses. facs. ed. Creighton, L., ed. LC 67-26730. (Essay Index Reprint Ser). 1904. 18.00 (ISBN 0-8369-0350-1). Arno.
Cromer, Evelyn B. Political & Literary Essays: 1st Series. facs. ed. LC 68-8453. (Essay Index Reprint Ser). 1913. 21.25 (ISBN 0-8369-1058-3). Arno.
--Political & Literary Essays: 2nd Series. facsimile ed. LC 73-108636. (Essay Index Reprint Ser). 1914. 18.00 (ISBN 0-8369-1564-X). Arno.
Essays in History Presented to Reginald Lane Poole. facs. ed. LC 67-30186. (Essay Index Reprint Ser). 1927. 20.00 (ISBN 0-8369-0424-9). Arno.
Essays in Intellectual History, Dedicated to James Harvey Robinson. LC 78-126677. Repr. of 1929 ed. 14.00 (ISBN 0-404-05369-6). AMS Pr.
Essays in Intellectual History, Dedicated to James Harvey Robinson by His Former Seminar Students. facs. ed. LC 68-14903. (Essay Index Reprint Ser). 1929. 17.50 (ISBN 0-8369-0425-7). Arno.
Freeman, Edward A. Historical Essays, 4 Vols. 1871-92. Set. 110.00 (ISBN 0-404-02630-3); 27.50 ea. Vol. 1 (ISBN 0-404-02631-1). Vol. 2 (ISBN 0-404-02632-X). Vol. 3 (ISBN 0-404-02633-8). Vol. 4 (ISBN 0-404-02634-6). AMS Pr.
Harrison, Frederic. George Washington & Other American Addresses. LC 71-86758. (Essay Index Reprint Ser). 1901. 16.00 (ISBN 0-8369-1263-2). Arno.
--The Meaning of History & Other Historical Pieces. 482p. 1981. Repr. of 1894 ed. lib. bdg. 30.00 (ISBN 0-89987-376-6). Darby Bks.

Hess, M. Gesellschaftsspiegel: Organ zur Vertretung und zur Beleuchtung der Gesellschaftlichen Zustande der Gegenwart. (Ger.). 1845. text ed. 51.75x (ISBN 90-6090-171-1). Humanities.

Hoffman, Ross. Tradition & Progress, & Other Historical Essays in Culture, Religion & Politics. LC 68-26213. 1968. Repr. of 1938 ed. 12.50 (ISBN 0-8046-0211-5). Kennikat.

Irish Conference Of Historians - 2nd - 1958. Irish Historical Studies: No. 1. 5.95 (ISBN 0-685-09172-4). Dufour.

Irish Conference Of Historians - 3rd - 1959. Irish Historical Studies: No. 2. 5.95 (ISBN 0-685-09173-2). Dufour.

Irish Conference of Historians - 4th. Irish Historical Studies: No. 3. 5.95 (ISBN 0-685-32720-5). Dufour.

Irish Conference Of Historians - 5th - 1963. Irish Historical Studies: No. 4. 5.95 (ISBN 0-685-09174-0). Dufour.

Kurze, Dietrich, ed. Aus Theorie und Praxis der Geschichtswissenschaft: Festschrift fur Hans Herzfeld zum 80, Geburtstag. (Veroeffentlichungen der Historischen Kommission zu Berlin, Band 37). xii, 445p. (Ger.). 1972. 95.75x (ISBN 3-11-003813-7). De Gruyter.

Lang, Andrew. Valet's Tragedy & Other Studies. LC 75-112939. (Illus.). Repr. of 1903 ed. 11.00 (ISBN 0-404-03865-4). AMS Pr.

Leggett, Glen. Years of Turmoil, Years of Change: "Selected Papers of a College President 1965-1975". 1978. pap. 8.95x (ISBN 0-8134-1982-4, 1982). Interstate.

Lightfoot, J. B. Historical Essays. 1979. Repr. of 1895 ed. lib. bdg. 25.00 (ISBN 0-8492-1606-0). R West.

Lyall, Alfred C. Studies in Literature & History. facs. ed. LC 68-29227. (Essay Index Reprint Ser). 1968. Repr. of 1915 ed. 19.50 (ISBN 0-8369-0637-3). Arno.

Macaulay, Thomas. Critical & Historical Essays, Vol. 1. 1961. 8.95x (ISBN 0-460-00225-2, Evman). Biblio Dist.

McIlwain, Charles H. Essays in History & Political Theory in Honor of Charles H. McIlwain. Wittke, Carl, ed. LC 67-18299. 1967. Repr. of 1936 ed. 9.50 (ISBN 0-8462-0944-6). Russell.

McIntire, C. T., ed. God, History, & Historians: An Anthology of Modern Christian Views of History. LC 76-47428. 1977. 22.95 (ISBN 0-19-502203-3). Oxford U Pr.

--God, History & Historians: Modern Christian Views of History. 1977. pap. 6.95 (ISBN 0-19-502204-1, GB496, GB). Oxford U Pr.

Manuel, Frank E. Shapes of Philosophical History. 1965. 10.00x (ISBN 0-8047-0248-9); pap. 2.95 (ISBN 0-8047-0249-7, SP37). Stanford U Pr.

Marcus, John T. Sub Specie Historiae: Essays in the Manifestations of Historical & Moral Consciousness. LC 76-50285. 328p. 1979. 22.50 (ISBN 0-8386-2057-4). Fairleigh Dickinson.

Martin, James J. The Saga of Hog Island & Other Essays in Inconvenient History. LC 76-62654. 1977. pap. 3.95 (ISBN 0-87926-021-1). R Myles.

Morley, John. Notes on Politics & History. LC 70-115326. 1971. Repr. of 1913 ed. 9.75 (ISBN 0-8046-1117-3). Kennikat.

Nevinson, Henry W. In the Dark Backward. LC 72-111854. (Essay Index Reprint Ser). 1934. 16.00 (ISBN 0-8369-1621-2). Arno.

--Visions & Memories. Sharp, Evelyn, ed. 1978. Repr. of 1944 ed. lib. bdg. 20.00 (ISBN 0-89760-600-0, Telegraph). Dynamic Learn Corp.

Newman, John H. Historical Sketches: 3 Vols. 1970. Set. 31.50 (ISBN 0-87061-028-7). Vol. 1 (ISBN 0-87061-025-2). Vol. 2 (ISBN 0-87061-026-0). Vol. 3 (ISBN 0-87061-027-9). Chr Classics.

Oman, Charles W. Unfortunate Colonel Despard & Other Studies. 1922. 22.50 (ISBN 0-8337-2626-9). B Franklin.

Oxford Lectures on History, 1904-1923, 10 Vols in One. facs. ed. LC 67-22107. (Essay Index Reprint Ser). 1924. 18.25 (ISBN 0-8369-1334-5). Arno.

Paetow, Louis J., ed. Crusades & Other Historical Essays, Presented to Dana C. Munro by His Former Students. facs. ed. LC 68-14902. (Essay Index Reprint Ser). 1928. 19.50 (ISBN 0-8369-0354-4). Arno.

Persecution & Liberty: Essays in Honor of George Lincoln Burr. facs. ed. LC 68-26467. (Essay Index Reprint Ser). 1968. Repr. of 1931 ed. 17.50 (ISBN 0-8369-0783-3). Arno.

Rhodes, James F. Historical Essays. LC 66-25938. Repr. of 1909 ed. 12.75 (ISBN 0-8046-0378-2). Kennikat.

Robinson, James H. New History. 1965. pap. text ed. 3.50 (ISBN 0-02-926610-6). Free Pr.

St. John-Stevas, Norman, ed. Bagehot's Historical Essays. 478p. 1966. 15.00x (ISBN 0-8147-7772-4). NYU Pr.

Sked, Alan & Cook, Chris, eds. Crisis & Controversy: Essays in Honor of A. J. P. Taylor. LC 75-42863. 192p. 1976. 18.95 (ISBN 0-312-17290-7). St Martin.

Somervell, David C. Studies in Statesmanship. LC 75-110934. 1970. Repr. of 1923 ed. 17.50 (ISBN 0-8046-0916-0). Kennikat.

Taylor, Charles H., ed. Anniversary Essays in Mediaeval History, by Students of Charles Homer Haskins: Presented on His Completion of Forty Years of Teaching. facs. ed. LC 67-30194. (Essay Index Reprint Ser). 1929. 20.00 (ISBN 0-8369-0155-X). Arno.

Thomson, James A. K. Irony. LC 74-12211. 1974. Repr. of 1927 ed. lib. bdg. 25.00 (ISBN 0-8414-8597-6). Folcroft.

Toth, Charles W. Myth, Reality & History: Selected Essays. LC 76-26548. 1977. pap. 9.00 (ISBN 0-8477-0847-0). U of PR Pr.

Trevelyan, George M. Autobiography & Other Essays. facs. ed. LC 75-142707. (Essay Index Reprint Ser). 1949. 16.00 (ISBN 0-8369-2205-0). Arno.

Trevor-Roper, H. R. Historical Essays. 1966. lib. bdg. 13.50x (ISBN 0-88307-274-2). Gannon.

--Men & Events: Historical Essays. LC 76-44642. 1977. Repr. lib. bdg. 17.50x (ISBN 0-374-97997-9). Octagon.

Wedgwood, C. V. Velvet Studies. 159p. 1980. Repr. of 1946 ed. lib. bdg. 25.00 (ISBN 0-89987-861-X). Darby Bks.

Woodruff, Douglas, ed. For Hilaire Belloc, Essays in Honor of His Seventy-First Birthday. Repr. of 1942 ed. lib. bdg. 15.50x (ISBN 0-8371-2490-5, FOHB). Greenwood.

HISTORY-ANECDOTES

see History-Curiosa and Miscellany

HISTORY-ATLASES

see Classical Geography; Geography, Ancient-Maps; Geography, Historical-Maps

HISTORY-BIBLIOGRAPHY

Brewster, John W. & McLeod, Joseph A. Index to Book Reviews in Historical Periodicals 1972. LC 75-18992. 393p. 1976. 15.50 (ISBN 0-8108-0894-3). Scarecrow.

Brushfield, T. N. The Bibliography of the History of the World & of the Remains of Sir Walter Raleigh. LC 72-10381. 1972. Repr. of 1886 ed. lib. bdg. 8.50 (ISBN 0-8414-0454-2). Folcroft.

California Historical Society. Index to California Historical Society Quarterly, Vol. 1 To 40. 1965. deluxe ed. 15.00 deluxe ed. (ISBN 0-910312-13-3); pap. 10.00 (ISBN 0-910312-12-5). Calif Hist.

Combined Retrospective Indexes to Journals in History, Eighteen Thirty Eight - Nineteen Seventy Four, 11 vols. LC 77-70347. 1977. 1095.00 set (ISBN 0-8408-0175-0). Carrollton Pr.

De Mause, Lloyd, et al. A Bibliography of Psychohistory. LC 75-5140. (Reference Library of Social Science: No. 6). 200p. 1975. lib. bdg. 18.50 (ISBN 0-8240-9999-0). Garland Pub.

Facts on File Master Indexes, 6 vols. LC 42-24704. 1946-50. 70.00 (ISBN 0-87196-065-6); 1951-55. 70.00 (ISBN 0-87196-066-4); 1956-60. 70.00 (ISBN 0-87196-067-2); 1961-65. 70.00 (ISBN 0-87196-068-0); 1966-70 70.00 (ISBN 0-87196-069-9); 1971-75 70.00 (ISBN 0-87196-070-2). Facts on File.

Facts on File's News Reference Service. (Annually). general 329.00 (ISBN 0-685-09367-0). Facts on File.

Francois, Michel, et al, eds. International Bibliography of Historical Sciences: 1976-1977, Vols. 45-46. 492p. 1980. 85.00 (ISBN 3-598-20402-7, Dist. by Gale Research Co.). K G Saur.

Frewer, Louis B. Bibliography of Historical Writings Published in Great Britain & the Empire: Nineteen Forty to Nineteen Forty-Five. LC 74-12628. 346p. 1974. Repr. of 1947 ed. lib. bdg. 19.75x (ISBN 0-8371-7735-9, FRHW). Greenwood.

Great Britain - Her Majesty's Stationery Office, London. Catalogue of the Foreign Office Library, 1926-1968, 8 vols. 6423p. 1973. lib. bdg. 720.00 (ISBN 0-8161-0998-2). G K Hall.

Harvard University Library. General European & World History: Classification Schedule, Author & Title Listing, Chronological Listing. LC 73-128714. (Widener Library Shelflist Ser: No. 32). xiii, 959p. 1970. 50.00x (ISBN 0-674-34420-0). Harvard U Pr.

Higham, Robin. Official Histories: Essays & Bibliographies from Around the World. 1970. 12.00 (ISBN 0-686-20816-1). KSU.

Institute for Contemporary History, Munich. Catalog for the Institute for Contemporary History, 4 vols. Incl. Pt. 1. Alphabetical Catalog, 5 vols. 3458p. Set. 275.00 (ISBN 0-8161-0724-6); Pt. 2. Subject Catalog, 6 vols. 4502p. Set. 390.00 (ISBN 0-8161-0176-0); Pt. 3. Regional Catalog, 2 vols. 1144p. Set. 95.00 (ISBN 0-8161-0177-9); Pt. 4. Biographical Catalog. 764p. 75.00 (ISBN 0-8161-0178-7). 1967. G K Hall.

International Bibliography of Historical Sciences, Vols. 35-44. Incl. Vol. 35. 1966. 1969. pap. 60.00x (ISBN 0-8002-2160-5); Vol. 36. 1967. 1970. 60.00x (ISBN 0-8002-2161-3); Vol. 37-38. 1968-69. 1971. 87.50x (ISBN 0-8002-2162-1); Vol. 39-40. 1970-71. 1974. 87.50x (ISBN 0-8002-2163-X); Vol. 41. 1972. 1975. 87.50x (ISBN 0-8002-2164-8); Vol. 42. 1973. 1976. 87.50x (ISBN 0-8002-2165-6); Vol. 43-44. 1974-75. 1979. 90.00x (ISBN 0-8002-2353-5). Intl Pubns Serv.

Irwin, Leonard B., ed. A Guide to Historical Reading Vol. II: Non-Fiction McKinley Bibliographies. LC 76-7180. 1976. 15.00 (ISBN 0-916882-02-0). Heldref Pubns.

Poulton, Helen J. & Howland, Marguerite S. The Historian's Handbook: A Descriptive Guide to Reference Works. LC 71-165774. 300p. 1972. pap. 8.95x (ISBN 0-8061-1009-0). U of Okla Pr.

HISTORY-CHRONOLOGY

see Chronology, Historical

HISTORY-CRITICISM

see Historiography

HISTORY-CURIOSA AND MISCELLANY

Aurandt, Paul. Paul Harvey's the Rest of the Story. 1978. pap. 2.75 (ISBN 0-553-20227-8). Bantam.

Capes, Bernard. Historical Vignettes. Repr. of 1910 ed. 20.00 (ISBN 0-686-20655-X). Lib Serv Inc.

D'Alembert, Jean. Miscellaneous Pieces in Literature, History, Philosophy. 59.95 (ISBN 0-8490-0642-2). Gordon Pr.

Edwards, Frank. Stranger Than Science. 1959. 4.95 (ISBN 0-8184-0086-2). Lyle Stuart.

Ferguson, Sheila. Projects in History. 1970. 16.95 (ISBN 0-7134-2154-1, Pub. by Batsford England). David & Charles.

Gaddis, Vincent H. Invisible Horizons: True Mysteries of the Sea. LC 65-14893. (Illus.). 239p. (gr. 9 up). 1965. 4.95 (ISBN 0-8019-1407-8). Chilton.

Paxton, John & Fairfield, Sheila. Calendar of Creative Man. (Illus.). 497p. 1980. 27.50 (ISBN 0-87196-470-8). Facts on File.

Pipping, Ella. Soldier of Fortune: The Story of a Nineteenth Century Adventurer. Walford, Naomi, tr. from Swedish. LC 70-107405. 1972. 5.95 (ISBN 0-87645-050-8). Gambit.

Procopius. History of the Wars. Secret History, 7 vols. Incl. Vol. 1, Bks. 1 & 2. Persian War (ISBN 0-674-99054-4); Vol. 2, Bks. 3 & 4. Vandalic War (ISBN 0-674-99090-0); Vols. 3-5, Bks. 5-8. Gothic War. Vol. 3 (ISBN 0-674-99119-2). Vol. 4 (ISBN 0-674-99191-5). Vol. 5 (ISBN 0-674-99239-3); Vol. 6. Anecdota or Secret History (ISBN 0-674-99320-9); Vol. 7. On Buildings; General Index (ISBN 0-674-99378-0). (Loeb Classical Library: No. 48, 81, 107, 173, 217, 290, 343). 11.00x ea. Harvard U Pr.

Queensbury Design Group. The Book of Key Facts: Thirty Thousand Important Events of History Arranged Chronologically & Alphabetically. LC 77-16267. 1978. 10.95 (ISBN 0-448-22896-3). Paddington.

Thibodeau, Lynn, ed. Remember, Remember. LC 77-95171. 1978. 8.95 (ISBN 0-89310-033-1); pap. 3.95 (ISBN 0-89310-034-X). Carillon Bks.

Thirty Famous Front Pages from History. 10.00 (ISBN 0-916822-08-7). Sparks Pr.

Timbs, John. Historic Ninepins. LC 68-22057. 1969. Repr. of 1869 ed. 22.00 (ISBN 0-8103-3539-5). Gale.

Wilkes, Mary & Morrison, Barbara. They Said It Couldn't Be Done. LC 76-24056. (Illus.). (gr. 5). 1976. pap. 2.75 (ISBN 0-87970-140-4). North Plains.

HISTORY-DICTIONARIES

Bayer, Erich. Woerterbuch zur Geschichte. 3rd ed. (Ger.). 1974. pap. 17.50 (ISBN 3-520-28903-2, M-6905). French & Eur.

Bayle, Pierre. Historical & Critical Dictionary: Selections. Popkin, Richard H., tr. LC 64-16703. (Orig.). 1965. pap. 11.50 (ISBN 0-672-60406-X, LLA175). Bobbs.

Brewer, E. Cobham. Historic Note-Book. LC 66-23191. 1966. Repr. of 1891 ed. 45.00 (ISBN 0-8103-0152-0). Gale.

Burickson, Sherwin, ed. Concise Dictionary of Contemporary History. 1959. 4.75 (ISBN 0-8022-0196-2). Philos Lib.

Coler, Christfried. Diccionario por Fechas de Historia Universal. 2nd ed. 480p. (Espn.). 1977. 50.95 (ISBN 84-261-5799-8, S-50366). French & Eur.

Davis, Robert R., Jr. Lexicon of Historical & Political Terms. pap. 1.95 (ISBN 0-671-18706-6, 18706). Monarch Pr.

Encyclopedie Thematique Weber, 9: L'Histoire. (Fr.). 59.95 (ISBN 0-686-57175-4, M-6242). French & Eur.

Harbottle, Thomas B. Dictionary of Historical Allusions. LC 68-23163. 1968. Repr. of 1904 ed. 21.00 (ISBN 0-8103-3088-1). Gale.

Haydn, Joseph T. Haydn's Dictionary of Dates & Universal Information Relating to All Ages & Nations. 1968. Repr. of 1911 ed. 69.00 (ISBN 0-403-00083-1). Scholarly.

Lexikon der Geschicte, 3 vols. (Ger.). 1976. pap. 25.00 (ISBN 3-453-41149-8, M-7255). French & Eur.

Masquet, Georges. Dictionnaire des Grands Evenements de L'histoire. 315p. (Fr.). 1973. pap. 8.95 (ISBN 0-686-56796-X, M-174, Pub. by Hachette). French & Eur.

Mourre, Michel. Dictionnaire Encyclopedique d'Histoire, 8 vols. 5480p. (Fr.). 1978. Set. 495.00 (ISBN 0-686-57054-5, M-6420). French & Eur.

Palmer, Alan. The Penguin Dictionary of Twentieth Century History: Nineteen Hundred to Nineteen Seventy-Eight. (Reference Ser.). 1979. pap. 4.95 (ISBN 0-14-051085-0). Penguin.

Pirenne, Jacques. Les Grands Courants de L'Histoire Universelle, 7 vols. (Fr.). 1944. Set. pap. 195.00 (ISBN 0-686-57081-2, M-6456). French & Eur.

Sachs, Moshe Y. Worldmark Encyclopedia of the Nations, 5 vols. 5th ed. 1976. Set. 99.50 (ISBN 0-471-74833-1, Pub. by Wiley-Interscience). Wiley.

Uden, Grant, ed. Longman Illustrated Companion to World History, 2 vols. LC 75-35742. (Illus.). 1976. 35.00 (ISBN 0-582-20520-4). Longman.

HISTORY-EARLY WORKS TO 1800

see World History-Early Works to 1800

HISTORY-EXAMINATIONS, QUESTIONS, ETC.

Arco Editorial Board. History: Advanced Test for the G.R.E. LC 78-5095. 1979. pap. text ed. 5.95 (ISBN 0-668-04414-4). Arco.

Killikelly, S. H. Curious Questions in History, Literature, Art & Social Life, 3 vols. Set. 300.00 (ISBN 0-87968-979-X). Gordon Pr.

Rudman, Jack. History. (Graduate Record Examination Ser.: GRE-10). 14.95 (ISBN 0-8373-5260-6); pap. 9.95 (ISBN 0-8373-5210-X). Natl Learning.

--Social Sciences & History. (Admission Test Ser.: ATS-9E). (Cloth bdg. avail. on request). pap. 9.95 (ISBN 0-8373-5009-3). Natl Learning.

HISTORY-HISTORIOGRAPHY

see Historiography

HISTORY-JUVENILE LITERATURE

Davies, Penny. Growing up in the Medieval Times. (Growing Up Ser.). 1979. 14.95 (ISBN 0-7134-0483-3, Pub. by Batsford England). David & Charles.

Ferguson, Sheila. Growing up in Victorian Britain. (Growing Up Ser.). 1977. 14.95 (ISBN 0-7134-0281-4, Pub. by Batsford England). David & Charles.

Fyson, Nance L. Growing up in the Eighteenth Century. (Growing Up Ser.). 1977. 14.95 (ISBN 0-7134-0481-7, Pub. by Batsford England). David & Charles.

Jones, Madeline. Growing up in Stuart Times. (Growing Up Ser.). 1979. 14.95 (ISBN 0-7134-0771-9, Pub. by Batsford England). David & Charles.

Lowrey, Janette S. Six Silver Spoons. LC 77-105469. (I Can Read History Books). (Illus.). (ps-2). 1971. PLB 6.89 (ISBN 0-06-024037-7, HarpJ). Har-Row.

Metzner, Seymour. World History in Juvenile Books. 356p. 1973. 12.00 (ISBN 0-8242-0441-7). Wilson.

Morgan, Edmund S. So What About History. LC 69-13533. (Illus.). (gr. 7 up). 1969. PLB 5.95 (ISBN 0-689-20663-1). Atheneum.

Wilkins, Francis. Growing up Between the Wars. (Growing Up Ser.). 1979. 14.95 (ISBN 0-7134-0775-1, Pub. by Batsford England). David & Charles.

HISTORY-METHODOLOGY

see also Oral History

Adams, Herbert B. Methods of Historical Study. LC 78-63742. (Johns Hopkins University. Studies in the Social Sciences. Second Ser. 1884: 1-2). Repr. of 1884 ed. 11.50 (ISBN 0-404-61012-9). AMS Pr.

Albright, William Foxwell. From the Stone Age to Christianity. 2nd ed. 1957. pap. 2.50 (ISBN 0-385-09306-3, A100, Anch). Doubleday.

Aydelotte, William O. Quantification in History. LC 76-150517. (History Ser). 1971. pap. 5.95 (ISBN 0-201-00350-3). A-W.

Barnes, Harry E. The New History & the Social Studies. (The Harry Elmer Barnes Ser). (Illus.). 624p. 1972. Repr. of 1925 ed. lib. bdg. 75.00 (ISBN 0-87700-033-6). Revisionist Pr.

Berkhofer, Robert F., Jr. Behavioral Approach to Historical Analysis. LC 69-11485. (Illus.). 1971. pap. text ed. 6.95 (ISBN 0-02-902960-0). Free Pr.

Bernheim, Ernst. Lehrbuch der Historischen Methode und der Geschichtsphilosophie, 2 vols. in 1. 6th ed. 1960. Repr. of 1914 ed. 44.50 (ISBN 0-8337-0250-5). B Franklin.

Bloch, M. The Historian's Craft. 1954p. 1954. 12.00x (ISBN 0-7190-0664-3, Pub. by Manchester U Pr England). State Mutual Bk.

Bodin, Jean. Method for the Easy Comprehension of History. Reynolds, B., tr. 1966. lib. bdg. 30.00x (ISBN 0-374-96783-0). Octagon.

Brown, John L. Methodus Ad Facilem Historiarum Cognitionem of Jean Bodin: A Critical Study. LC 76-94167. (Catholic University of America Studies in Romance Languages & Literatures Ser: No. 18). Repr. of 1939 ed. 19.00 (ISBN 0-404-50318-7). AMS Pr.

Cochrane, Charles N. Thucydides & the Science of History. LC 65-17885. 1965. Repr. of 1929 ed. 7.50 (ISBN 0-8462-0591-2). Russell.

Crump, Charles G. History & Historical Research. LC 72-21805. 1974. Repr. of 1928 ed. lib. bdg. 20.50 (ISBN 0-8337-5041-0). B Franklin.

Dumoulin, Jerome & Moisi, Dominique, eds. L' Historian Entre L'ethnologue & le Futurologue: Actes Du Seminaire International Organise Sous les Auspices De L'association Internationale Pour la Liberte De la Culture, la Fondation Giovanni Agnelli & la Fondation Giongio Cini, Venice, 2-8 Avril 1971. Actes Du Seminaire International Organise Sous les Auspices De L'association Internationale Pour la Liberte De la Culture, la Fondation Giovanni Agnelli & la Fondation Giorgio Cini, Venice, 2-8 Avril 1971. (Le Savoir Historique: No. 4). 1973. pap. 17.75x (ISBN 90-2797-157-9). Mouton.

Finberg, H. P. Approaches to History. LC 62-52521. 1962. pap. 5.00 (ISBN 0-8020-6107-9). U of Toronto Pr.

Fling, Fred M. Outline of the Historical Method. LC 76-147836. (Research & Source Works Ser.: No. 726). 1971. Repr. of 1899 ed. lib. bdg. 15.00 (ISBN 0-8337-1160-1). B Franklin.

Garraghan, Gilbert J. A Guide to Historical Method. Delanglez, Jean, ed. LC 73-13415. 482p. 1974. Repr. of 1946 ed. lib. bdg. 31.00x (ISBN 0-8371-7132-6, GAIM). Greenwood.

Gilbert, Felix, ed. Historical Studies Today. LC 70-163367. 480p. 1972. pap. 10.95x (ISBN 0-393-09402-2). Norton.

Goldstein, Leon J. Historical Knowing. LC 75-12037. 270p. 1976. 13.50x (ISBN 0-292-73002-0). U of Tex Pr.

Hofstadter, Richard & Lipset, Seymour M., eds. Sociology & History: Methods. LC 68-22327. (Sociology of American History Ser.: Vol. 1). 1968. pap. text ed. 4.75x (ISBN 0-465-07994-6). Basic.

Iggers, Georg G. & Parker, Harold T., eds. International Handbook of Historical Studies: Contemporary Research & Theory. LC 79-7061. 1980. lib. bdg. 35.00 (ISBN 0-313-21367-4, ICD/). Greenwood.

Jones, Tom B. Paths to the Ancient Past. LC 67-12515. 1967. pap. text ed. 6.95 (ISBN 0-02-916630-6). Free Pr.

Leff, Gordon. History & Social Theory. LC 78-76586. 234p. 1969. 16.75x (ISBN 0-8173-6605-9). U of Ala Pr.

McClelland, Peter D. Causal Explanation & Model Building in History, Economics, & the New Economic History. LC 74-25372. (Illus.). 288p. 1975. 20.00x (ISBN 0-8014-0929-2). Cornell U Pr.

Postan, M. M. Fact & Relevance: Essays on Historical Method. 1971. 26.95 (ISBN 0-521-07841-5). Cambridge U Pr.

Quigley, Carroll. The Evolution of Civilizations. LC 79-4091. 1979. 9.00 (ISBN 0-913966-56-8); pap. 4.00 (ISBN 0-913966-57-6). Liberty Fund.

Samaran, Charles. L' Histoire et Ses Methodes. (Historique Ser.). 1792p. 46.95 (ISBN 0-686-56445-6). French & Eur.

Shafer, Robert J., ed. A Guide to Historical Method. 3rd ed. 1980. pap. 10.95x (ISBN 0-256-02313-1). Dorsey.

Small, Melvin, ed. Public Opinion & Historians: Interdisciplinary Perspectives. LC 71-97244. 1970. 9.95x (ISBN 0-8143-1412-0). Wayne St U Pr.

Taylor, Hugh. History As a Science. LC 70-115331. 1971. Repr. of 1933 ed. 10.00 (ISBN 0-8046-1122-X). Kennikat.

Teggart, Frederick J. Prolegomena to History: The Relation of History to Literature, Philosophy, & Science, Vol. 4. LC 73-14184. (Perspectives in Social Inquiry Ser.). 142p. 1974. Repr. 9.00x (ISBN 0-405-05528-5). Arno.

--Theory & Processes of History. 7.25 (ISBN 0-8446-3057-8). Peter Smith.

Todd, William. History As Applied Science. LC 70-165937. 250p. 1972. text ed. 13.95x (ISBN 0-8143-1466-X). Wayne St U Pr.

Topolski, Jerzy. The Methodology of History. new ed. PWN, Polish Scientific Publishers, ed. Wojtasliewicz, O., tr. from Pol. LC 76-25080. (Synthese Library Ser.: No. 88). 1976. lib. bdg. 55.00 (ISBN 90-277-0550-X, Pub. by Reidel Holland). Kluwer Boston.

HISTORY–MUSEUMS

see Historical Museums

HISTORY–OUTLINES, SYLLABI, ETC.

Long, Dwight C. Introduction to the Study of History & Outline of the Growth of Western Civilization from Its Beginnings to About 1648. 1951. 2.25x (ISBN 0-685-21792-2). Wahr.

Perkin, Harold, ed. History: An Introduction for the Intending student. 1970. pap. text ed. 3.50x (ISBN 0-7100-6815-8). Humanities.

Wells, H. G. Outline of History, 4 vols. 1920. Repr. 125.00 (ISBN 0-403-03082-X). Somerset Pub.

HISTORY–PERIODICALS

Brewster, John W. & Gentry, Deborah. Index to Book Reviews in Historical Periodicals 1977. LC 75-18992. 411p. 1979. 22.00 (ISBN 0-8108-1192-8). Scarecrow.

Brewster, John W. & McLeod, Joseph A. Index to Book Reviews in Historical Periodicals, 1973. LC 75-18992. 1976. 18.00 (ISBN 0-8108-0893-5). Scarecrow.

Drew, Katherine F., et al. Studies in History. (Rice University Studies: Vol. 58, No. 4). 155p. 1972. pap. 3.25x (ISBN 0-89263-214-3). Rice Univ.

Katz, Bill, ed. Library Lit Eleven: The Best of 1980. LC 78-154842. 335p. 1981. 13.00 (ISBN 0-8108-1431-5). Scarecrow.

HISTORY–PERIODICALS–BIBLIOGRAPHY

Crouch, Milton & Raum, Hans, eds. Directory of State & Local History Periodicals. LC 77-4396. 1977. pap. 6.00 (ISBN 0-8389-0246-4). ALA.

HISTORY–PHILOSOPHY

see also Church History–Philosophy; Civilization; Demythologization; Historical Materialism; History (Theology);

also subdivision History–Philosophy under names of countries, e.g. United States–History–Philosophy

Acton, John E. History of Freedom, & Other Essays. facs. ed. Figgis, J. N. & Laurence, R. V., eds. LC 67-22048. (Essay Index Reprint Ser). 1907. 24.00 (ISBN 0-8369-0135-5). Arno.

Adams, Brooks. Law of Civilization & Decay: An Essay on History. facsimile ed. LC 71-37125. (Essay Index Reprint Ser). Repr. of 1943 ed. 21.00 (ISBN 0-8369-2478-9). Arno.

--The New Empire: With an Appendix Containing a Chronological Survey from 4000 BC up till 1900. LC 68-27435. 1969. Repr. of 1902 ed. 18.50x (ISBN 0-391-02013-7). Humanities.

Adams, Henry. The Degradation of the Democratic Dogma. 8.00 (ISBN 0-8446-1007-0). Peter Smith.

Albright, William Foxwell. From the Stone Age to Christianity. 2nd ed. 1957. pap. 2.50 (ISBN 0-385-09306-3, A100, Anch). Doubleday.

Antoni, Carlo. From History to Sociology: The Transition in German Historical Thinking. White, Hayden V., tr. from Italian. LC 76-40127. 1976. Repr. of 1959 ed. lib. bdg. 21.50 (ISBN 0-8371-9282-X, ANFH). Greenwood.

Arendt, Hannah. Between Past & Future: Eight Exercises in Political Thought. enl. ed. 1977. pap. 3.95 (ISBN 0-14-004662-3). Penguin.

Aron, Raymond. Introduction to the Philosophy of History: An Essay on the Limits of Historical Objectivity. Irwin, George J., tr. LC 75-17475. 1976. Repr. of 1961 ed. lib. bdg. 24.75 (ISBN 0-8371-8308-1, ARIP). Greenwood.

Atkinson, R. F. Knowledge & Explanation in History: An Introduction to the Philosophy of History. LC 77-90896. 1978. 19.50x (ISBN 0-8014-1116-5); pap. 7.95x (ISBN 0-8014-9171-1). Cornell U Pr.

Atwell, Sterling. The Philosophy of History in Schematic Representations. (Illus.). 1980. deluxe ed. 49.55 (ISBN 0-89266-230-1). Am Classical Coll Pr.

Bagby, Philip. Culture & History. LC 76-3680. (Illus.). 244p. 1976. Repr. of 1963 ed. lib. bdg. 15.75x (ISBN 0-8371-8797-4, BACH). Greenwood.

Barzun, Jacques. Clio & the Doctors: Psycho-History, Quanto-History, & History. LC 74-5723. 192p. 1974. 7.95x (ISBN 0-226-03849-1). U of Chicago Pr.

Becker, Carl L. Everyman His Own Historian: Essays on History & Politics. 1972. pap. 2.95 (ISBN 0-8129-6035-1, QP33). Times Bks.

--Heavenly City of the Eighteenth-Century Philosophers. (Storrs Lectures Ser.). 1932. 15.00x (ISBN 0-300-00297-1); pap. 3.95x (ISBN 0-300-00017-0, Y5). Yale U Pr.

Bernheim, Ernst. Lehrbuch der Historischen Methode und der Geschichtsphilosophie, 2 vols. in 1. 6th ed. 1960. Repr. of 1914 ed. 44.50 (ISBN 0-8337-0250-5). B Franklin.

Bober, Mandell M. Karl Marx's Interpretation of History. 2nd rev. ed. LC 48-8857. (Economic Studies: No. 31). 1948. 18.50x (ISBN 0-674-50150-0). Harvard U Pr.

--Karl Marx's Interpretation of History. 1965. pap. 7.45x (ISBN 0-393-00270-5, Norton Lib). Norton.

Bradley, F. H. The Presuppositions of Critical History. LC 68-26438. 1972. pap. 2.45 (ISBN 0-8129-6057-2, QP108). Times Bks.

Breck, A. D. & Yourgrau, W., eds. Biology, History & Natural Philosophy. LC 70-186262. 355p. 1972. 45.00 (ISBN 0-306-30573-9, Plenum Pr). Plenum Pub.

Breck, Allan D. & Yourgrau, Wolfgang, eds. Biology, History & Natural Philosophy. LC 74-774. 355p. 1974. pap. 6.95 (ISBN 0-306-20009-0, Rosetta). Plenum Pub.

Brown, Norman O. Life Against Death: The Psychoanalytical Meaning of History. LC 59-5369. 1959. 20.00x (ISBN 0-8195-3005-0, Pub. by Wesleyan U Pr); pap. 8.95 (ISBN 0-8195-6010-3). Columbia U Pr.

Bultmann, Rudolf. The Presence of Eternity. LC 75-9540. 170p. 1975. Repr. of 1957 ed. lib. bdg. 15.00x (ISBN 0-8371-8123-2, BUPRE). Greenwood.

Burckhardt, Jacob. Reflections on History. LC 78-24385. Orig. Title: Force & Freedom. 1979. 9.00 (ISBN 0-913966-37-1); pap. 4.00 (ISBN 0-913966-38-X). Liberty Fund.

Cairns, Grace E. Philosophies of History: Meeting of East & West in Cycle-Pattern Theories of History. LC 71-139126. xxiii, 496p. Repr. of 1962 ed. lib. bdg. 23.00 (ISBN 0-8371-5742-0, CAPH). Greenwood.

Carr, Edward H. What Is History. 1967. pap. 2.95 (ISBN 0-394-70391-X, V391, Vin). Random.

Carr, Herbert W. Philosophy of Benedetto Croce: The Problem of Art & History. LC 69-17838. 1969. Repr. of 1917 ed. 8.50 (ISBN 0-8462-1335-4). Russell.

Castro, Americo. An Idea of History: Selected Essays of Americo Castro. Gilman, Stephen & King, Edmund L., eds. LC 76-41762. 1977. 12.50x (ISBN 0-8142-0220-9). Ohio St U Pr.

Catholic Philosophy of History: American Catholic Historical Association. Papers, Vol. 3. facs. ed. LC 67-23190. (Essay Index Reprint Ser). 1936. 13.75 (ISBN 0-8369-0285-8). Arno.

Cebik, L. B. Concepts, Events, & History. LC 78-64825. 1978. pap. text ed. 9.00 (ISBN 0-8191-0639-9). U Pr of Amer.

Chaadayev, Peter Y. Peter Yakovlevich Chaadayev: Philosophical Letters & Apology of a Madman. Zeldin, Mary-Barbara, tr. LC 79-88186. 1970. 11.50x (ISBN 0-87049-102-4). U of Tenn Pr.

Chamberlain, Houston S. Foundations of the Nineteenth Century, 2 vols. LC 67-29735. 1968. Repr. Set. 85.00 (ISBN 0-86527-069-4). Fertig.

Chesneaux, Jean. Pasts & Futures: Or What Is History for? 1978. 10.95 (ISBN 0-500-25062-6). Thames Hudson.

Cohen, Morris R. The Meaning of Human History. 2nd ed. LC 61-10174. (The Paul Carus Lectures Ser.). (Illus.). ix, 304p. 1961. 17.50 (ISBN 0-87548-100-0); pap. 6.95 (ISBN 0-87548-101-9). Open Court.

Cole, Rufus. Human History: The Seventeenth Century & the Stuart Family, 2 Vols. LC 59-8900. 1959. 10.00 set (ISBN 0-87027-042-7); Vol. 1. (ISBN 0-87027-047-8); Vol. 2. (ISBN 0-87027-048-6). Wheelwright.

Collingwood, Robin G. Idea of History. Knox, T. M., ed. 1956. pap. 5.95 (ISBN 0-19-500205-9, 1, GB). Oxford U Pr.

Croce, Benedetto. Philosophy, Poetry, History: An Anthology of Essays. Sprigge, Cecil, tr. 1966. 55.00x (ISBN 0-19-711621-3). Oxford U Pr.

Danielou, Jean. Lord of History. 1958. 6.75x (ISBN 0-8092-8971-7). Contemp Bks.

Danilevskii, Nikolai I. Rossiia I Evropa. 1966. Repr. of 1895 ed. 27.00 (ISBN 0-384-10785-0). Johnson Repr.

Dawson, Christopher H. Progress & Religion, an Historical Enquiry. LC 79-104266. Repr. of 1929 ed. lib. bdg. 15.00x (ISBN 0-8371-3917-1, DAPR). Greenwood.

Dibble, Jerry A. The Pythia's Drunken Song. (International Archives of the History of Ideas, Series Minor: No. 19). 1978. pap. 9.00 (ISBN 90-247-2011-7, Pub. by Martinus Nijhoff Netherlands). Kluwer Boston.

Dray, William. Perspectives on History. 192p. 1980. 20.00x (ISBN 0-7100-0569-5); pap. 10.00 (ISBN 0-7100-0570-9). Routledge & Kegan.

Dray, William H. Laws & Explanation in History. LC 78-25936. 1979. Repr. of 1957 ed. lib. bdg. 18.50x (ISBN 0-313-20790-9, DRLE). Greenwood.

--Philosophy of History. (Orig.). 1964. pap. 7.95x ref. ed. (ISBN 0-13-663849-X). P-H.

Durant, Will & Durant, Ariel. Lessons of History. LC 68-19949. 1968. 9.95 (ISBN 0-671-41333-3). S&S.

Ellmann, Richard & Feidelson, Charles, Jr., eds. Modern Tradition: Backgrounds of Modern Literature. 1965. 25.00 (ISBN 0-19-500542-2). Oxford U Pr.

Fackenheim, Emil L. Metaphysics & Historicity. (Aquinas Lecture). 1961. 6.95 (ISBN 0-87462-126-7). Marquette.

Fain, Haskell. Between Philosophy & History: The Resurrection of Speculative Philosophy of History Within the Analytic Tradition. LC 70-90946. 1970. 20.00x (ISBN 0-691-07158-6). Princeton U Pr.

Federn, Karl. Materialist Conception of History: A Critical Analysis. LC 75-114523. 1971. Repr. of 1939 ed. lib. bdg. 15.00x (ISBN 0-8371-4789-1, FECH). Greenwood.

Feldman, A. Bronson. The Unconscious in History. 1959. 4.75 (ISBN 0-8022-0482-1). Philos Lib.

Fischer, David H. Historians' Fallacies: Toward a Logic of Historical Thought. 1970. pap. 5.95 (ISBN 0-06-131545-1, TB1545 TB, CN). Har-Row.

Flumiani, C. M. The Iron Laws of the Historical Inevitabilities. (Illus.). 1977. 42.75 (ISBN 0-89266-081-3). Am Classical Coll Pr.

--The Laws of History & the Caprice of Men. (Illus.). 1977. 49.75 (ISBN 0-89266-018-X). Am Classical Coll Pr.

Gallie, W. B. Philosophy & the Historical Understanding. 2nd ed. LC 68-26656. 1969. pap. 2.45 (ISBN 0-8052-0187-4). Schocken.

Galston, William A. Kant & the Problem of History. LC 74-11620. xiv, 290p. 1975. 13.50x (ISBN 0-226-28044-6). U of Chicago Pr.

Gangwu, Wang. The Use of History. LC 72-63123. (Papers in International Studies: Southeast Asia: No. 4). 1968. pap. 3.00x (ISBN 0-89680-002-4). Ohio U Ctr Intl.

Gardiner, Patrick. Nature of Historical Explanation. (Oxford Classical & Philosophical Monographs). 1952. pap. 8.95 (ISBN 0-19-824599-8). Oxford U Pr.

Gardiner, Patrick, ed. The Philosophy of History. (Oxford Readings in Philosophy). 230p. 1974. pap. text ed. 5.95x (ISBN 0-19-875031-5). Oxford U Pr.

--Theories of History. LC 58-6481. 1959. text ed. 16.95 (ISBN 0-02-911210-9). Free Pr.

Gay, Peter. Art & Act: On Causes in History - Manet, Gropius, Mondrian. LC 75-12291. (Icon Editions). (Illus.). 320p. 1976. 20.00 (ISBN 0-06-433248-9, HarpT). Har-Row.

--A Loss of Mastery: Puritan Historians in Colonial America. LC 67-10969. (Jefferson Memorial Lectures). 1966. 16.75x (ISBN 0-520-00456-6). U of Cal Pr.

Geyl, Pieter. Debates with Historians. pap. 3.95 (ISBN 0-452-00057-2, F57, Mer). NAL.

--Use & Abuse of History. 1970. Repr. of 1955 ed. 10.50 (ISBN 0-208-00827-6, Archon). Shoe String.

Goel, Dharmendra. Philosophy of History: A Critical Study of Recent Philosophies of History. 1967. 7.00x (ISBN 0-8426-1277-7). Verry.

Graham, Gerald S. & Alexander, John. Secular Abyss: An Interpretation of History & the Human Situation. 1968. pap. 1.95 (ISBN 0-8356-0019-X, Quest). Theos Pub Hse.

Gustavson, Carl G. Preface to History. (YA) (gr. 9-12). 1955. pap. 2.95 (ISBN 0-07-025279-3, SP). McGraw.

Harbison, E. H. Christianity & History: Essays. 1964. 21.00x (ISBN 0-691-07104-7). Princeton U Pr.

Hegel, Georg W. Lectures on the Philosophy of History. Sibree, J., tr. 1956. pap. text ed. 4.50 (ISBN 0-486-20112-0). Dover.

--Philosophy of History. 8.50 (ISBN 0-8446-2232-X). Peter Smith.

--Reason in History: A General Introduction to the Philosophy of History. Hartman, Robert S., tr. LC 53-4476. 1953. pap. 3.95 (ISBN 0-672-60200-8, LLA35). Bobbs.

--The Static & the Dynamic Philosophy of History & the Metaphysics of Reason. 1977. 37.50 (ISBN 0-89266-052-X). Am Classical Coll Pr.

Holmes, Oliver W. Human Reality & the Social World: Ortega's Philosophy of History. LC 74-21238. 224p. 1975. 12.50x (ISBN 0-87023-173-1). U of Mass Pr.

Hook, Sidney. From Hegel to Marx: Studies in the Intellectual Development of Karl Marx. 1962. pap. 4.95 (ISBN 0-472-06066-X, 66, AA). U of Mich Pr.

--Hero in History: A Study in Limitation & Possibility. 1955. pap. 5.95x (ISBN 0-8070-5081-4, BP12). Beacon Pr.

Issawy, Charles. An Arab Philosophy of History. (Wisdom of the East Ser). 4.50 (ISBN 0-7195-0705-7). Paragon.

Jackson, Thomas A. Dialectics: The Logic of Marxism & Its Critics. LC 78-159699. (Research & Source Works Ser.: No. 734). 1971. lib. bdg. 32.00 (ISBN 0-8337-1814-2). B Franklin.

Jaspers, Karl. The Origin & Goal of History. Bullock, Michael, tr. from Ger. LC 76-21246. 1976. Repr. of 1953 ed. lib. bdg. 22.00x (ISBN 0-8371-8983-7, JAOG). Greenwood.

Joyce, Robert. The Esthetic Animal: Man, the Art-Created Art Creator. LC 75-10619. 1975. 7.50 (ISBN 0-682-48300-1, University). Exposition.

Kant, Immanuel. On History. Beck, Lewis W., ed. Beck, L. W., et al, trs. LC 62-22315. (Orig.). 1963. pap. 5.95 (ISBN 0-672-51070-7); pap. 3.95 (ISBN 0-672-60387-X, LLA162). Bobbs.

Kaplan, Morton A. On Historical & Political Knowing: An Inquiry into Some Problems of Universal Law & Human Freedom. LC 79-131879. 1971. 7.50x (ISBN 0-226-42420-0). U of Chicago Pr.

Katz, John. The Will to Civilization: An Inquiry into the Principles of Historic Change. LC 74-25761. (European Sociology Ser.). 358p. 1975. Repr. 20.00x (ISBN 0-405-06515-9). Arno.

Keyes, G. L. Christian Faith & the Interpretation of History: A Study of St. Augustine's Philosophy of History. LC 66-10314. xiv, 206p. 1966. 14.50x (ISBN 0-8032-0091-9). U of Nebr Pr.

Klibansky, R. & Paton, H. J., eds. Philosophy & History. 8.00 (ISBN 0-8446-2387-3). Peter Smith.

Knezevic, Bozidar. History, the Anatomy of Time. Tomashevich, George V. & Wakeman, Sherwood A., trs. from Serbo-Croatian. LC 79-89888. 1980. 15.00 (ISBN 0-8022-2357-5). Philos Lib.

Koht, Halvdan. Driving Forces in History. Haugen, Einar, tr. LC 64-16065. 1968. pap. text ed. 2.25x (ISBN 0-689-70119-5, 121). Atheneum.

--Driving Forces in History. Haygen, E., tr. LC 64-16065. 1964. 12.50x (ISBN 0-674-21650-4, Belknap Pr). Harvard U Pr.

Koselleck, Reinhard. Enlightenment & Hypocrisy: Political Power, Moral Criticism & the Philosophy of History. Date not set. 20.00 (ISBN 0-916354-40-7). Urizen Bks.

Krieger, Leonard. Ranke: The Meaning of History. LC 76-25633. 1977. lib. bdg. 26.00x (ISBN 0-226-45349-9). U of Chicago Pr.

Langley, Ray A. Basic Patterns of Historical Action in the Schematized Analysis of the Philosophy of History. (The Major Currents in Contemporary World History Library). (Illus.). 143p. 1981. 59.25 (ISBN 0-930008-84-7). Inst Econ Pol.

Lavrov, Peter. Historical Letters. Scanlan, James P., tr. LC 67-18900. 1967. 28.50x (ISBN 0-520-01136-8). U of Cal Pr.

Levy, Bernard-Henri. Barbarism with a Human Face. Holoch, George, tr. LC 78-19822. 1980. pap. 3.95 (ISBN 0-06-090745-2, CN 745, CN). Har-Row.

Lewis, Bernard. History - Remembered, Recovered, Invented. 1976. 10.50 (ISBN 0-691-03547-4); pap. 4.95 (ISBN 0-691-00211-8). Princeton U Pr.

Loewenstein, Hubertus Z. Germans in History. LC 78-95395. Repr. of 1945 ed. 34.50 (ISBN 0-404-04008-X). AMS Pr.

Lowith, Karl. Meaning in History: The Theological Implications of the Philosophy of History. LC 57-7900. 1957. pap. 5.50 (ISBN 0-226-49555-8, P16, Phoen). U of Chicago Pr.

Mandelbaum, Maurice. The Anatomy of Historical Knowledge. LC 76-46945. (Illus.). 256p. 1977. 15.00x (ISBN 0-8018-1929-6); pap. 4.95 (ISBN 0-8018-2180-0). Johns Hopkins.

Maritain, Jacques. On the Philosophy of History. LC 73-128059. Repr. of 1957 ed. 12.50x (ISBN 0-678-02760-9). Kelley.

Marsak, L. M., ed. The Nature of Historical Inquiry. LC 74-16092. 220p. 1977. pap. 6.50 (ISBN 0-88275-221-9). Krieger.

Martin, Rex. Historical Explanation. LC 77-3121. (Re-Enactment & Practical Inference). 1977. 19.50x (ISBN 0-8014-1084-3). Cornell U Pr.

Marvin, Francis S., ed. Evolution of World-Peace: Essays. Unity Ser. 4. facs. ed. LC 68-20318. (Essay Index Reprint Ser). 1921. 12.25 (ISBN 0-8369-0682-9). Arno.

--Western Races & the World. Unity Ser. 5. facs. ed. LC 68-22929. (Essay Index Reprint Ser). 1968. Repr. of 1922 ed. 15.00 (ISBN 0-8369-0684-5). Arno.

Masaryk, Thomas G. Masaryk on Thought & Life. LC 78-135840. (Eastern Europe Collection Ser). 1970. Repr. of 1938 ed. 11.00 (ISBN 0-405-02782-6). Arno.

Mathews, Shailer. The Spiritual Interpretation of History. 1977. lib. bdg. 59.95 (ISBN 0-8490-2661-X). Gordon Pr.

Mayer, Jacob, et al. Political Thought. LC 72-134114. (Essay Index Reprint Ser.). 1939. 24.00 (ISBN 0-8369-1932-7). Arno.

Meiland, Jack W. Scepticism & Historical Knowledge. (Orig.). 1965. pap. text ed. 3.95 (ISBN 0-685-19765-4). Phila Bk Co.

Miller, John W. The Philosophy of History with Reflections & Aphorisms. LC 80-29179. 192p. 1981. 17.95 (ISBN 0-393-01464-9). Norton.

Mohan, Robert P. Philosophy of History. 1970. pap. text ed. 4.95 (ISBN 0-02-821250-9). Glencoe.

Montgomery, John W. The Shape of the Past. LC 75-26651. 400p. 1975. pap. 7.95 (ISBN 0-87123-535-8, 210535). Bethany Hse.

Morgan, George W. Human Predicament: Dissolution & Wholeness. LC 68-23791. 360p. 1971. Repr. of 1968 ed. text ed. 15.00x (ISBN 0-87057-111-7, Pub. by Brown U Pr). U Pr of New Eng.

Munz, Peter. The Shapes of Time. LC 77-2459. 1977. lib. bdg. 20.00x (ISBN 0-8195-5017-5, Pub. by Wesleyan U Pr). Columbia U Pr.

Nadel, George H., ed. Studies in the Philosophy of History. 1965. lib. bdg. 13.50x (ISBN 0-88307-212-2). Gannon.

Nadel, George H., et al, eds. History & Theory: Studies in the Philosophy of History. 1977. Set. 363.50 (ISBN 0-685-22179-2). Wesleyan U Pr.

Nash, Ronald, ed. Ideas of History: The Critical Philosophy of History, Vol. 2. 1969. pap. 3.95 (ISBN 0-525-47239-8). Dutton.

Niebuhr, Reinhold. Beyond Tragedy: Essays on the Christian Interpretation of History. facsimile ed. LC 76-167397. (Essay Index Reprint Ser). Repr. of 1937 ed. 18.00 (ISBN 0-8369-2437-1). Arno.

--Faith & History: A Comparison of Christian & Modern Views of History. (Lib. Rep. Ed.). 1949. 17.50x (ISBN 0-684-15318-1, ScribT). Scribner.

Norling, Bernard. Timeless Problems in History. LC 79-105726. 1970. pap. 3.25x (ISBN 0-268-00420-X). U of Notre Dame Pr.

Nota, John H. Phenomenology & History. Grooten, Louis, tr. LC 67-13891. 1967. 2.95 (ISBN 0-8294-0060-5). Loyola.

Olafson, Frederick A. The Dialectic of Action: A Philosophical Interpretation of History & the Humanities. LC 79-10316. 1979. lib. bdg. 22.00x (ISBN 0-226-62564-8). U of Chicago Pr.

Ortega Y Gasset, Jose. History As a System. 1962. pap. 3.95 (ISBN 0-393-00122-9, Norton Lib). Norton.

Partridge, G. E. The Psychology of Nations: A Contribution to the Philosophy of History. 1919. lib. bdg. 30.00 (ISBN 0-8414-9107-0). Folcroft.

Peterson, Forrest H. Philosophy of Man & Society. LC 76-136014. 1970. 8.50 (ISBN 0-8022-2043-6). Philos Lib.

Porter, Dale H. The Emergence of the Past: A Theory of Historical Explanation. LC 80-27165. (Chicago Original Paperback Ser.). 288p. 1981. lib. bdg. 19.00x (ISBN 0-226-67550-5). U of Chicago Pr.

Rader, Melvin. Marx's Interpretation of History. 1979. 14.95x (ISBN 0-19-502474-5); pap. text ed. 5.95x (ISBN 0-19-502475-3). Oxford U Pr.

Randall, John H. Nature & Historical Experience: Essays in Naturalism & the Theory of History. LC 57-11694. 1958. 22.50x (ISBN 0-231-02161-5); pap. 9.00x (ISBN 0-231-08537-0). Columbia U Pr.

Ricoeur, Paul. History & Truth. Kelbley, C. A., tr. (Studies in Phenomenology & Existential Philosophy). 1965. 19.95x (ISBN 0-8101-0207-2); pap. 8.95 (ISBN 0-8101-0598-5). Northwestern U Pr.

Rockwood, Raymond O., ed. Carl Becker's Heavenly City Revisited. 1968. Repr. of 1958 ed. 16.50 (ISBN 0-208-00421-1, Archon). Shoe String.

Ronan, Charles E. Francisco Javier Clavigero, S. J. (1731-1787) Figure of the Mexican Enlightenment. 1978. pap. 21.00 (ISBN 0-8294-0347-7). Loyola.

Rosenberger, Homer T. The Enigma: How Shall History Be Written? LC 78-68731. (Illus.). 453p. 1980. lib. bdg. 12.00 (ISBN 0-917264-02-9). Rose Hill.

Rotenstreich, Nathan. Between Past & Present: An Essay on History. LC 72-85291. 360p. 1973. Repr. of 1958 ed. 15.00 (ISBN 0-8046-1728-7). Kennikat.

Rothblatt, Ben, ed. Changing Perspectives on Man. LC 68-16714. 1968. 9.50x (ISBN 0-226-72906-0). U of Chicago Pr.

Salmon, Lucy M. Why Is History Rewritten? 1972. lib. bdg. 14.50x (ISBN 0-374-97021-1). Octagon.

Savelle, Max. Is Liberalism Dead? & Other Essays. LC 65-23913. 224p. 1967. 10.50 (ISBN 0-295-74004-3). U of Wash Pr.

Schaff, Adam. History & Truth. 230p. 1976. text ed. 27.00 (ISBN 0-08-020579-8). Pergamon.

Schimdt, Alfred. History & Structure: An Essay on Hegelian-Marxist & Structuralist Theories of History. Herf, Jeffrey, tr. from Ger. (Sutdies in Contemporary German Social Thought). 128p. 1981. 17.50x (ISBN 0-262-19198-9). MIT Pr.

Schluchter, Wolfgang. The Rise of Western Rationalism: Max Weber's Developmental History. Roth, Guenther, tr. from Ger. LC 81-2763. 300p. 1981. 16.50x (ISBN 0-520-04060-0). U of Cal Pr.

See, Henri. Economic Interpretation of History. Knight, Melvin M., tr. LC 67-30863. Repr. of 1929 ed. 11.00x (ISBN 0-678-00354-8). Kelley.

See, Henri E. Economic Interpretation of History. Knight, Melvin M., tr. LC 68-56744. (Research & Source Works Ser: No. 225). 1968. Repr. of 1929 ed. 11.50 (ISBN 0-8337-3219-6). B Franklin.

Seligman, Edwin R. Economic Interpretation of History. LC 68-16433. 1966. Repr. of 1961 ed. 7.50 (ISBN 0-87752-099-2). Gordian.

Shaw, William H. Marx's Theory of History. LC 77-76154. 1978. 12.50x (ISBN 0-8047-0960-2); pap. 3.95 (ISBN 0-8047-1059-7, SP-160). Stanford U Pr.

Shine, Hill. Carlyle & the Saint Simonians. LC 71-120666. 1970. Repr. lib. bdg. 13.00x (ISBN 0-374-97360-1). Octagon.

Siebert, Rudolf J. Hegel's Philosophy of History: Theological, Humanistic & Scientific Elements. LC 78-66279. 1979. pap. text ed. 9.00 (ISBN 0-8191-0689-5). U Pr of Amer.

Simmel, Georg. The Problems of the Philosophy of History: An Epistemological Essay. Oakes, Guy, tr. LC 76-51588. 1977. 14.95 (ISBN 0-02-928890-8). Free Pr.

Smith, Goldwin. Lectures on Modern History: Delivered in Oxford, 1859-61. facsimile ed. LC 78-37865. (Essay Index Reprint Ser). Repr. of 1861 ed. 16.00 (ISBN 0-8369-2627-7). Arno.

Smith, Goldwin, ed. The Professor & the Public: The Role of the Scholar in the Modern World. LC 72-2088. (Leo M. Franklin Memorial Lectures in Human Relations Ser: Vol. 20). 128p. 1972. 5.95x (ISBN 0-8143-1477-5). Wayne St U Pr.

Sorokin, Pitirim A. Social & Cultural Dynamics. abr. ed. LC 57-14120. (Extending Horizons Ser). (Illus.). 1970. 10.00 (ISBN 0-87558-029-7). Porter Sargent.

Stephens, Lester D. Historiography: A Bibliography. LC 75-17578. 1975. 11.00 (ISBN 0-8108-0856-0). Scarecrow.

Stover, Robert. Nature of Historical Thinking. 1967. 19.00x (ISBN 0-8078-1030-4). U of NC Pr.

Strayer, J. R. The Interpretation of History. 6.50 (ISBN 0-8446-1427-0). Peter Smith.

Taylor, Henry O. A Layman's View of History. LC 75-41271. Repr. of 1935 ed. 14.00 (ISBN 0-404-14616-3). AMS Pr.

Thompson, William I. From Nation to Emanation. (Illus.). 80p. 1981. pap. 4.95 (ISBN 0-905249-45-3, Pub. by Findhorn-Thule Scotland). Hydra Bk.

Tobey, Jeremy L. The History of Ideas: A Bibliographical Introduction, 2 vols. 320p. 1975-76. Vol. 1 Classical Antiquity. text ed. 26.25 (ISBN 0-87436-143-5, LC 74-83160). ABC-Clio.

Torrance, John. Estrangement, Alienation, & Exploitation: A Sociological Approach to Historical Materialism. LC 77-8246. 1977. 25.00x (ISBN 0-231-04448-8). Columbia U Pr.

Toynbee, Arnold J. A Study of History. abr. ed. Somervell, D. C., ed. Incl. Vols. 1-6. 1947. 15.95 (ISBN 0-19-500198-2); Vols. 7-10. 1957. 15.95 (ISBN 0-19-500199-0). (Royal Institute of International Affairs Ser). Oxford U Pr.

--A Study of History. (Royal Institute of International Affairs). 1954. Vols. 7-10. maroon cloth 60.00 (ISBN 0-19-519689-9); Vols. 11-12 (vol. 11 O.p.) maroon cloth 19.95 (ISBN 0-19-500197-4). Oxford U Pr.

--A Study of History, Vols. 7-10. Incl. Vol. 7. Universal States; Universal Churches. 37.50x (ISBN 0-19-215215-7); Vol. 8. Heroic Ages; Contacts Between Civilization in Space. 38.50x (ISBN 0-19-215216-5); Vol. 9. Contacts Between Civilizations in Time; Law & Freedom in History; the Prospects of the Western Civilization. 29.00x (ISBN 0-19-215217-3); Vol. 10. The Inspirations of Historians. 29.00x (ISBN 0-19-215218-1). (Royal Institute of International Affairs Ser). 1954. Oxford U Pr.

--A Study of History: Introduction the Genesis of Civilization, & the Growth of Civilization, 3 vols. 2nd ed. (Royal Institute of International Affairs Ser.). 1935. Vol. 1. 26.50x (ISBN 0-19-215207-6); Vol. 2. 37.50x (ISBN 0-19-215208-4); Vol. 3. 37.50x (ISBN 0-19-215209-2). Oxford U Pr.

--A Study of History: Reconsideration. 1961. Vol. 12. 37.50x (ISBN 0-19-215225-4). Oxford U Pr.

--A Study of History: The Disintegrations of Civilization. (Royal Institute of International Affairs Ser.). 1939. Vol. 5. 37.50x (ISBN 0-19-215212-2); Vol. 6. 29.95x (ISBN 0-19-215213-0); Vol. 6. 29.95x (ISBN 0-19-215213-0). Oxford U Pr.

Toynbee, Arnold J. & Myers, Edward D. A Study of History: Historical Atlas & Gazetter. 1959. Vol. 11. 36.00x (ISBN 0-19-215223-8). Oxford U Pr.

Ullmann, Richard K. Between God & History: The Human Situation Exemplified in Quaker Thought & Practice. 1959. text ed. 5.25x (ISBN 0-391-01957-0). Humanities.

Urban, G. R., ed. Toynbee on Toynbee: A Conversation Between Arnold J. Toynbee & G. R. Urban. 120p. 1974. 11.95 (ISBN 0-19-501739-0). Oxford U Pr.

Varma, V. P. The Political Philosophy of Sri Aurobindo. 2nd ed. 1976. Repr. of 1960 ed. text ed. 13.50x (ISBN 0-8426-0873-7). Verry.

Viner, Jacob. The Role of Providence in the Social Order: An Essay in Intellectual History. 1976. pap. 5.95 (ISBN 0-691-01990-8). Princeton U Pr.

Volney, C. F. A New Translation of Volney's Ruins, 2 vols. Feldman, Burton & Richardson, Robert D., eds. LC 78-60900. (Myth & Romanticism Ser.: Vol. 25). (Illus.). 1979. Set. lib. bdg. 132.00 (ISBN 0-8240-3574-7); lib. bdg. 66.00 ea. Garland Pub.

Voltaire. Philosophy of History. 1965. pap. 3.45 (ISBN 0-8065-0078-6, 175). Citadel Pr.

--Philosophy of History. LC 65-10662. 1965. 6.00 (ISBN 0-8022-1783-4). Philos Lib.

Von Herder, Johann G. Reflections on the Philosophy of the History of Mankind. abr. ed. LC 68-20412. (Classic European Historians Ser). 1968. 9.00x (ISBN 0-226-32744-2). U of Chicago Pr.

Von Schlegel, Frederick. Philosophy of History: In a Course of Lectures, Delivered in Vienna. Robertson, James B., tr. from Ger. LC 77-145282. 1971. Repr. of 1883 ed. 17.00 (ISBN 0-403-01196-5). Scholarly.

Von Schlegel, Friedrich. The Philosophy of History. LC 72-144683. Repr. of 1873 ed. 18.00 (ISBN 0-404-05606-7). AMS Pr.

Walsh, W. H. An Introduction to the Philosophy of History. 215p. 1976. text ed. 15.00x (ISBN 0-391-00672-X, Pub. by Harvester); pap. text ed. 10.75x (ISBN 0-686-73995-7). Humanities.

Walsh, William H. Introduction to Philosophy of History. 3rd rev. ed. 1967. text ed. 7.50x (ISBN 0-391-00672-X); pap. text ed. 7.50x (ISBN 0-391-02163-X). Humanities.

--Philosophy of History: An Introduction. pap. 3.50x (ISBN 0-06-131020-4, TB1020, Torch). Har-Row.

Weintraub, Karl J. Visions of Culture: Voltaire, Guizot, Burckhardt, Lamprecht, Huizinga, Ortega y Gasset. LC 66-13893. 1966. 9.50x (ISBN 0-226-89088-0). U of Chicago Pr.

--Visions of Culture: Voltaire, Guizot, Burckhardt, Lamprecht, Huizinga, Ortega Y Gasset. LC 66-13893. 1969. pap. 2.95 (ISBN 0-226-89089-9, P340, Phoen). U of Chicago Pr.

Weiss, Paul. History: Written & Lived. LC 62-15006. 254p. 1962. 6.95x (ISBN 0-8093-0067-2). S Ill U Pr.

White, Hayden. Metahistory: The Historical Imagination in Nineteenth-Century Europe. LC 73-8110. 462p. 1974. 25.00x (ISBN 0-8018-1469-3); pap. 6.95 (ISBN 0-8018-1761-7). Johns Hopkins.

Whitehead, Alfred N. Adventures of Ideas. 1967. pap. text ed. 5.95 (ISBN 0-02-935170-7). Free Pr.

--Adventures of Ideas. 1933. 12.95 (ISBN 0-02-627220-2). Macmillan.

Widgery, Alban G. Interpretations of History: Confucius to Toynbee. LC 81-2116. 260p. 1981. Repr. of 1961 ed. lib. bdg. 25.00x (ISBN 0-313-23041-2, WIIN). Greenwood.

Wilkins, Burleigh T. Has History Any Meaning? A Critique of Popper's Philosophy of History. LC 78-58054. 1978. 22.50x (ISBN 0-8014-1187-4). Cornell U Pr.

--Hegel's Philosophy of History. LC 73-16831. 224p. 1974. 16.50x (ISBN 0-8014-0819-9). Cornell U Pr.

Wilson, Edmund. To the Finland Station: A Study in the Writing & Acting of History. LC 53-3591. 1953. pap. 3.95 (ISBN 0-385-09281-4, A6, Anch). Doubleday.

Woodbridge, Frederick J. Purpose of History. LC 65-27115. 1916. Repr. 8.00 (ISBN 0-8046-0513-0). Kennikat.

Wroblewski, Sergius. Prophetic History of the West. 1968. 3.95 (ISBN 0-8189-0120-9). Alba.

Yourgrau, Wolfgang & Breck, Allen D., eds. Physics, Logic, & History. LC 68-32135. 336p. 1970. 29.50 (ISBN 0-306-30360-4, Plenum Pr). Plenum Pub.

Yovel, Irmiahu, ed. Philosophy of History & Action. (Philosophical Studies in Philosophy: No. 11). 1978. lib. bdg. 36.50 (ISBN 90-277-0890-8, Pub. by Reidel Holland). Kluwer Boston.

HISTORY–POETRY

see also Political Ballads and Songs; Poetry of Places; Political Poetry

Flick, Alexander. History in Rhyme & Jingles. 59.95 (ISBN 0-8490-0314-8). Gordon Pr.

Ford, James L. & Ford, Mary K., eds. Every Day in the Year: A Political Epitome of the World's History. LC 68-17941. 1969. Repr. of 1902 ed. 22.00 (ISBN 0-8103-3105-5). Gale.

Holland, Rupert S., ed. Historic Poems & Ballads. facs. ed. LC 75-116406. (Granger Index Reprint Ser). 1912. 17.00 (ISBN 0-8369-6147-1). Arno.

HISTORY–READERS

see Readers–History

HISTORY–RESEARCH

see Historical Research

HISTORY–SATIRE

see History, Comic, Satirical, etc.

HISTORY–SOURCES

see also Archives; Charters; Diplomatics;

also subdivision History-Sources under names of countries, e.g. United States-History-Sources

Calderwood, Ivan. Days of Uncle Dave's Fish House. 1969. 12.50 (ISBN 0-913954-10-1). Courier of Maine.

--The Saga of Hod. 1972. 10.50 (ISBN 0-913954-13-6). Courier of Maine.

--Sequel...Days of Uncle Dave's Fish House. 1972. 12.50 (ISBN 0-685-40636-9). Courier of Maine.

Congressional Quarterly. Historic Documents: Nineteen Seventy-Nine. Congressional Quarterly, ed. 1000p. 1980. 44.00 (ISBN 0-87187-197-1). Congr Quarterly.

Congressional Quaterly Service. Historic Documents, 5 vols. Incl. Vol. 1: 1972. 987p. 1973. 44.00 (ISBN 0-87187-043-6); Vol. 2: 1973. 987p. 1974. 44.00 (ISBN 0-87187-054-1); Vol. 3, 1974. 44.00 (ISBN 0-87187-069-X). LC 72-97888. Congr Quarterly.

Dall, W. H. History, Geography, Resources, Vol. 2. Repr. of 1902 ed. 35.00 (ISBN 0-527-38162-4). Kraus Repr.

Harmatta, J., ed. Prolegomena: To the Sources on the History of Pre-Islamic Central Asia. 339p. (Eng., Fr., Ger.). 1979. 35.00x (ISBN 963-05-1651-9). Intl Pubns Serv.

McNeill, William H. & Sedlar, Jean W. Classical India. (Oxford Readings in World History Ser: Vol. 4). (Orig.). 1969. pap. text ed. 5.95x (ISBN 0-19-500972-X). Oxford U Pr.

--Classical Mediterranean World. (Oxford Readings in World History Ser.: Vol. 3). (Illus., Orig.). 1969. pap. text ed. 5.95x (ISBN 0-19-500971-1). Oxford U Pr.

McNeill, William H. & Sedlar, Jean W., eds. Ancient Near East. (Oxford Readings in World History Ser: Vol. 2). 1968. pap. 4.95x (ISBN 0-19-500970-3). Oxford U Pr.

--Origins of Civilization. (Oxford Readings in World History Ser: Vol. 1). 1968. pap. text ed. 5.95x (ISBN 0-19-500969-X). Oxford U Pr.

Prothero, George W., ed. Peace Handbooks, 25 vols. LC 73-82619. 1973. Repr. of 1920 ed. Set. 875.00 (ISBN 0-8420-1704-6). Scholarly Res Inc.

HISTORY-STATISTICAL METHODS

Aydelotte, William O., et al, eds. Dimensions of Quantitative Research in History. LC 72-736. (Quantitative Studies in History Ser). 420p. 1972. 23.00 (ISBN 0-691-07544-1); pap. 10.50 (ISBN 0-691-10045-4, 45). Princeton U Pr.

Fetter, Bruce, et al. Explorations in Quantitative African History. Smaldone, Joseph P., ed. LC 77-17537. (Foreign & Comparative Studies-African Ser.: No. 27). 190p. 1977. pap. 7.00x (ISBN 0-915984-24-5). Syracuse U Foreign Comp.

HISTORY-STUDY AND TEACHING

see also United States-History-Study and Teaching

Abraham, Henry & Pfeffer, Irwin. Enjoying World History. (gr. 10-12). 1977. text ed. 11.58 (ISBN 0-87720-620-1); pap. text ed. 7.50 (ISBN 0-87720-618-X). AMSCO Sch.

Ballard, Martin, ed. New Movements in the Study & Teaching of History. LC 77-126205. 240p. 1970. 10.00x (ISBN 0-253-34020-9). Ind U Pr.

Block, Jack. Understanding Historical Research: A Search for Truth. (Illus.). 156p. 1971. pap. text ed. 6.00x (ISBN 0-9600478-0-8). Research Pubns.

Bodin, Jean. Method for the Easy Comprehension of History. Reynolds, B., tr. 1966. lib. bdg. 30.00x (ISBN 0-374-96783-0). Octagon.

Botein, Stephen, et al, eds. Experiments in History Teaching. LC 77-148. Date not set. pap. 4.75 (ISBN 0-916704-03-3). Langdon Assocs.

Burston, W. H., et al, eds. Handbook for History Teachers. 2nd ed. 1972. text ed. 35.00x (ISBN 0-423-49060-5). Methuen Inc.

Cairns, Trevor, ed. People Become Civilized. LC 73-20196. (The Cambridge Introduction to History Ser). (Illus.). 104p. (gr. 5-12). 1974. PLB 8.95g (ISBN 0-8225-0801-X). Lerner Pubns.

Cantor, Norman F. & Schneider, Richard I. How to Study History. LC 67-14303. (Orig.). pap. 5.95x (ISBN 0-88295-709-0). Harlan Davidson.

Chaffer, John & Taylor, Lawrence. History & the History Teacher. (Unwin Education Books: Teaching Today Ser.). 1975. text ed. 14.95x (ISBN 0-04-371037-9); pap. text ed. 5.95x (ISBN 0-04-371038-7). Allen Unwin.

Commager, Henry S. & Muessig, Raymond H. The Study & Teaching of History. 2nd ed. (Social Science Seminar, Secondary Education Ser.: No. C28). 136p. 1980. pap. text ed. 6.95 (ISBN 0-675-08317-6). Merrill.

Dance, Edward H. History of the Betrayer. LC 73-16869. 162p. 1975. Repr. of 1960 ed. lib. bdg. 15.00x (ISBN 0-8371-7237-3, DAHB). Greenwood.

Dickinson, A. K., ed. History Teaching & Historical Understanding. Lee, P. J. LC 79-300044. 1978. pap. text ed. 11.00x (ISBN 0-435-80291-7). Heinemann Ed.

Fines, John & Verrier, Raymond. The Drama of History: An Experiment in Cooperative Teaching. 1974. 11.50 (ISBN 0-85157-512-9). Shoe String.

Furay, Conal & Salevouris, Michael J. History: A Workbook of Skill Development. 1979. pap. 6.95 (ISBN 0-531-05620-1). Watts.

Gooch, G. P. Maria Theresa & Other Studies. 1965. Repr. of 1951 ed. 19.50 (ISBN 0-208-00019-4, Archon). Shoe String.

Grau, Brigitha & Spreckelmeyer, Goswin, eds. Fruehmittelalterliche Studien. Jahrbuch Des Instituts Fuer Fruehmittelalterforschung der Universitaet Muenster: Register zu Vol. 1-5. 160p. 1974. 30.00x (ISBN 3-11-004425-0). De Gruyter.

Gunning, Dennis. The Teaching of History. 197p. 1978. 22.00x (ISBN 0-85664-668-7, Pub by Croom Helm Ltd England). Biblio Dist.

Hall, G. Stanley. Methods of Teaching History. Brickman, William W., ed. (Educational Ser). Repr. of 1885 ed. 27.50 (ISBN 0-685-36382-1). Norwood Edns.

Hasluck, Eugene L. The Teaching of History. (Educational Ser.). 1920. Repr. 15.00 (ISBN 0-685-43471-0). Norwood Edns.

Healy, Sean. Ideas for Teaching History. 1974. 14.95 (ISBN 0-7134-2166-5, Pub. by Batsford England). David & Charles.

Heckman, Richard A. Teaching History: Who? What? Why? LC 78-73544. 1979. pap. text ed. 4.95x (ISBN 0-89260-147-7). Hwong Pub.

Hepworth, H. How to Find Out in History. (How to Find Out Series). (Illus.). 1966. 16.00 (ISBN 0-08-011482-2). Pergamon.

Higham, John. Writing American History: Essays on Modern Scholarship. LC 70-108209. (Midland Bks.: No. 156). 224p. 1970. pap. 2.95x (ISBN 0-253-20156-X). Ind U Pr.

Jackson, Martin A. & O'Connor, John E. Teaching History with Film. LC 74-78660. (Discussions on Teaching Ser: No. 2). (Illus.). 60p. 1974. pap. 1.50 (ISBN 0-87229-018-2). Am Hist Assn.

Kochhar, S. K. Teaching of History. 1967. 5.50x (ISBN 0-8426-1337-4). Verry.

Langlois, Charles V. & Seignobos, Charles. Introduction to the Study of History. Berry, G. G., tr. LC 78-10678. 1979. Repr. of 1906 ed. lib. bdg. 22.50x (ISBN 0-313-20699-6, LAIN). Greenwood.

Leinwand, Gerald. The Pageant of World History. new rev. ed. (gr. 9-12). 1977. text ed. 16.80 (ISBN 0-205-05392-0, 7853920); tchrs'. guide 5.40 (ISBN 0-205-05393-9, 7853939); wkbk 60.00 (ISBN 0-205-05657-1, 786571); tests-duplicator masters 48.00 (ISBN 0-205-05658-X, 785658X). Allyn.

--Teaching of World History. LC 77-95099. (Bulletin Ser.: No. 54). (Illus.). 1978. pap. 5.50 (ISBN 0-87986-019-7, 498-15268). Coun Soc Studies.

Lyons, Graham, ed. The Russian Version of the Second World War: The History of the War As Taught to Russian Schoolchildren. (Illus.). 1977. 14.50 (ISBN 0-208-01631-7, Archon). Shoe String.

Nichol, J. & Birt, D. Games & Simulations in History. (Education Today Ser.). (Illus.). 192p. 1975. pap. text ed. 7.50x (ISBN 0-582-36301-2). Longman.

Noel Hume, Ivor. Wells of Williamsburg: Colonial Time Capsules. LC 71-109382. (Archaeological Ser: No. 4). (Illus., Orig.). 1969. pap. 2.25 (ISBN 0-910412-09-X). Williamsburg.

Norling, Bernard. Towards a Better Understanding of History. 157p. 1960. pap. 3.25x (ISBN 0-268-00284-3). U of Notre Dame Pr.

Orwell, George. Homage to Catalonia. LC 52-6442. 1969. pap. 2.45 (ISBN 0-15-642117-8, Harv, Hb162). HarBraceJ.

Perkin, Harold, ed. History: An Outline for the Intending Student. (Outline Ser). 1970. cased 14.95 (ISBN 0-7100-6814-X); pap. 7.95 (ISBN 0-7100-6815-8). Routledge & Kegan.

Perkins, Dexter & Snell, John L. The Education of Historians in the United States. LC 74-25597. 1975. Repr. of 1962 ed. lib. bdg. 15.25x (ISBN 0-8371-7881-9, PEEH). Greenwood.

Pierce, Bessie L. Public Opinion & the Teaching of History in the United States. LC 71-107416. (Civil Liberties in American History Ser.). 1970. Repr. of 1926 ed. lib. bdg. 37.50 (ISBN 0-306-71883-9). Da Capo.

Roucek, Joseph S. Teaching of History. LC 67-11573. 1967. 10.00 (ISBN 0-8022-1396-0). Philos Lib.

Sanderlin, David. Writing the History Paper: The Student Research Guide. LC 74-694. (gr. 10-12). 1975. pap. 2.50 (ISBN 0-8120-0506-6). Barron.

Schlereth, Thomas J. Artifacts & the American Past: Techniques for the Teaching Historian. 300p. 1981. text ed. 13.95 (ISBN 0-910050-47-3). AASLH.

Shafer, Boyd C., et al. Historical Study in the West: France, Western Germany, Great Britain, the United States. LC 68-19485. 1968. 24.00x (ISBN 0-89197-212-9); pap. text ed. 6.95x (ISBN 0-89197-213-7). Irvington.

Shera, Jesse H. Historians, Books & Libraries. Repr. of 1953 ed. lib. bdg. 15.00 (ISBN 0-8371-2558-8, SHHB). Greenwood.

Shropshire, Olive E. The Teaching of History in English Schools. LC 70-177789. (Columbia University. Teachers College. Contributions to Education: No. 617). Repr. of 1936 ed. 17.50 (ISBN 0-404-55671-X). AMS Pr.

Steele, Ian. Developments in History Teaching. (Changing Classroom). 1976. text ed. 9.75x (ISBN 0-7291-0046-4); pap. text ed. 3.75x (ISBN 0-7291-0041-3). Humanities.

Stubbs, William. Seventeen Lectures on the Study of Medieval & Modern History. 1967. 25.00 (ISBN 0-86527-219-0). Fertig.

Success in Twentieth Century World Affairs. (Success Studybooks Ser.). (Illus.). 387p. 1975. pap. 8.95 (ISBN 0-7195-2919-0). Transatlantic.

Swanstrom, Roy. History in the Making: An Introduction to the Study of the Past. LC 78-13881. 1978. pap. text ed. 3.95 (ISBN 0-87784-581-6). Inter-Varsity.

Taylor, Arthur J., ed. The Study of History: A Collection of Inaugural Lectures in Two Volumes. Incl. Vol. 1. Beginnings to Nineteen Forty-Five; Vol. 2. Nineteen Forty-Five to Present. 1981. 30.00x set (ISBN 0-7146-3125-6, F Cass Co). Biblio Dist.

Watts, D. G. The Learning of History. (Students Library of Education). 128p. 1972. 10.00x (ISBN 0-7100-7433-6). Routledge & Kegan.

HISTORY-STUDY AND TEACHING (ELEMENTARY)

Ayer, Adelaide M. Some Difficulties in Elementary School History. LC 72-176527. (Columbia University. Teachers College. Contributions to Education: No. 212). Repr. of 1926 ed. 17.50 (ISBN 0-404-55212-9). AMS Pr.

Klapper, Paul. The Teaching of History: A Manual of Method for Elementary & Junior High Schools. 1979. Repr. of 1926 ed. lib. bdg. 30.00 (ISBN 0-8492-1484-X). R West.

McMurry, Dorothy. Herbartian Contributions to History Instruction in American Elementary Schools. LC 77-177039. (Columbia University. Teachers College. Contributions to Education: No. 920). Repr. of 1946 ed. 17.50 (ISBN 0-404-55920-4). AMS Pr.

Newlun, Chester O. Teaching Children to Summarize in Fifth Grade History. LC 75-177120. (Columbia University. Teachers College. Contributions to Education: No. 404). Repr. of 1930 ed. 17.50 (ISBN 0-404-55404-0). AMS Pr.

HISTORY-STUDY AND TEACHING (HIGHER)

Beck, Earl R. On Teaching History in Colleges & Universities. LC 66-64094. (Florida State Univ. Studies). 1966. 6.95 (ISBN 0-8130-0497-7). U Presses Fla.

Cappuzzello, Paul G. & Schlesinger, Mark A. Recent Trends in History Curricula & Pedagogy: A Bibliographic Study. Woditsch, Gary A., ed. LC 76-22292. (Project Technical Paper Ser.: No. 1). 1976. pap. 4.95 (ISBN 0-89372-000-3). General Stud Res.

Fredericq, Paul. The Study of History in England & Scotland. 1973. pap. 7.00 (ISBN 0-384-16755-1). Johnson Repr.

Klapper, Paul. The Teaching of History: A Manual of Method for Elementary & Junior High Schools. 1979. Repr. of 1926 ed. lib. bdg. 30.00 (ISBN 0-8492-1484-X). R West.

Kuehl, Warren F. Dissertations in History: An Index to Dissertations Completed in History Departments of United States & Canadian Universities, 1837-1960, Vol. 1. LC 65-11832. 264p. 1965. 21.00x (ISBN 0-8131-1111-0). U Pr of Ky.

Ward, Paul L. Elements of Historical Thinking. LC 76-184205. (Discussions on Teaching: No. 1). 1971. pap. text ed. 1.50 (ISBN 0-87229-000-X). Am Hist Assn.

White, A. D. European Schools of History & Politics. Repr. of 1887 ed. pap. 8.00 (ISBN 0-384-68031-3). Johnson Repr.

HISTORY-THEOLOGY

see History (Theology)

HISTORY-YEARBOOKS

Byrne, Janet, ed. Key Issues: Issues & Events of 1979. LC 80-1717. (News in Print Ser.). (Illus.). 1980. lib. bdg. 24.95x (ISBN 0-405-12877-0). Arno.

Epstein, Howard M. & Kanner, Gerald B., eds. News Dictionary: Vol. 5, 1968. annual LC 65-17649. (Illus.). 1969. 14.95 (ISBN 0-87196-087-7). Facts on File.

Facts on File Master Indexes, 6 vols. LC 42-24704. 1946-50. 70.00 (ISBN 0-87196-065-6); 1951-55. 70.00 (ISBN 0-87196-066-4); 1956-60. 70.00 (ISBN 0-87196-067-2); 1961-65. 70.00 (ISBN 0-87196-068-0); 1966-70 70.00 (ISBN 0-87196-069-9); 1971-75 70.00 (ISBN 0-87196-070-2). Facts on File.

Facts on File Staff. FOF Yearbook, 1980. 1200p. 1981. lib. bdg. 65.00 (ISBN 0-87196-039-7). Facts on File.

Facts on File's News Reference Service. (Annually). general 329.00 (ISBN 0-685-09367-0). Facts on File.

Kattleman. Five-Year Index, 1981. 85.00 (ISBN 0-87196-071-0). Facts on File.

Keeton, George W. & Schwarzenberger, Georg, eds. The Year Book of World Affairs, 1981. 285p. 1981. lib. bdg. 41.25 (ISBN 0-86531-150-1). Westview.

Keylin, Arlene, et al, eds. The New York Times Annual Review, 1980. (Illus.). 256p. 1980. lib. bdg. 12.98 (ISBN 0-405-13288-3). Arno.

Lawson, Donald E. & Trier, Marilyn R., eds. World Topics Yearbook. annual ed. LC 56-31513. (Illus.). 8.95 (ISBN 0-87566-011-8). United Ed.

Macadam, I., ed. Annual Register of World Events, 10 vols. Incl. Vol. 1. 1961. 600p; Vol. 3. 1965. 582p; Vol. 4. 1966. 574p; Vol. 5. 1967. 562p. 25.00x (ISBN 0-685-23143-7); Vol. 6. 1968. 600p; Vol. 7. 1969. 600p. (Vol. 2, 1962 o.p.). St Martin.

Paneth, Donald. News Dictionary 1980. 400p. 1981. 14.95 (ISBN 0-87196-111-3). Facts on File.

Pater, Alan F. & Pater, Jason R., eds. What They Said in 1970: The Standard Source Book for the World's Spoken Opinion. LC 74-111080. (Second Annual Vol.). 1971. 17.50 (ISBN 0-9600252-3-5). Monitor.

--What They Said in 1971: The Standard Source Book for the World's Spoken Opinion. LC 74-111080. (Third Annual Vol.). 1972. 17.50 (ISBN 0-9600252-4-3). Monitor.

Postgate, Raymond. Story of a Year: 1848. LC 75-17508. (Illus.). 286p. 1975. Repr. of 1955 ed. lib. bdg. 16.25x (ISBN 0-8371-8249-2, POSY). Greenwood.

Sobel, Lester A., et al. News Dictionary: Vol. 1, 1964. annual LC 65-17649. (Orig.). 1965. 14.95 (ISBN 0-87196-079-6). Facts on File.

Sobel, Lester A., et al, eds. Facts on File Yearbooks: Annual Volumes, 1941 to 1978. LC 42-24704. (Illus.). 57.50 ea. Facts on File.

--News Dictionary: Vol. 2, 1965. annual LC 65-17649. (Orig.). 1966. 14.95 (ISBN 0-87196-081-8). Facts on File.

--News Dictionary: Vol. 3, 1966. annual LC 65-17649. (Orig.). 1967. 14.95 (ISBN 0-87196-083-4). Facts on File.

--News Dictionary: Vol. 4, 1967. annual LC 65-17649. 1968. 14.95 (ISBN 0-87196-085-0). Facts on File.

Trotsky, Judith, ed. News Dictionary 1974, Vol. 11. annual LC 65-17649. 500p. 1975. lib. bdg. 14.95 (ISBN 0-87196-099-0). Facts on File.

HISTORY (THEOLOGY)

see also Time (Theology)

Altizer, Thomas J. Total Presence: The Language of Jesus & the Language of Today. 128p. 1980. 9.95 (ISBN 0-8164-0461-5). Seabury.

Brown, Colin. History, Criticism & Faith. LC 76-12303. 1976. pap. 4.95 (ISBN 0-87784-776-2). Inter-Varsity.

Custance, Arthur C. Noah's Three Sons: Human History in Three Dimensions, Vol. 1. 320p. 1974. 11.95 (ISBN 0-310-22950-2). Zondervan.

Kellett, E. E. A Short History of Religions. 1973. lib. bdg. 30.00 (ISBN 0-8414-5555-4). Folcroft.

Markus, R. A. Saeculum: History & Society in the Theology of St Augustine. LC 71-87136. 1970. 42.00 (ISBN 0-521-07621-8). Cambridge U Pr.

Montgomery, John W. Where Is History Going? LC 69-11659. 1969. 5.95 (ISBN 0-87123-640-0, 210640). Bethany Hse.

Pillai, Joachim. The Apostolic Interpretation of History: A Commentary on Acts 13: 16-41. 1979. 9.00 (ISBN 0-682-49404-6, University). Exposition.

Ratzinger, J. Theology of History According to St. Bonaventure. 12.50 (ISBN 0-8199-0415-5). Franciscan Herald.

Rushdoony, Rousas J. Biblical Philosophy of History. pap. 3.50 (ISBN 0-87552-412-5). Presby & Reformed.

Showers, Renald E. What on Earth Is God Doing? Satan's Conflict with God. LC 73-81551. 1973. pap. 2.10 (ISBN 0-87213-784-8). Loizeaux.

HISTORY, ANCIENT

see also Archaeology; Bible-Chronology; Civilization, Ancient; Classical Dictionaries; Geography, Ancient; Inscriptions; Numismatics; also names of ancient races and peoples, e.g. Indo-Europeans; hittites; Mediterranean Race; and names of countries of antiquity

Abbott, George F. Thucydides: A Study in Historical Reality. LC 79-102462. 1970. Repr. of 1925 ed. 10.00 (ISBN 0-8462-1486-5). Russell.

Africa, Thomas W. Ancient World. (Illus., Orig.). 1969. pap. text ed. 12.50 (ISBN 0-395-04095-7, 3-00250). HM.

Alsop, Joseph W. From the Silent Earth: A Report of the Greek Bronze Age. LC 81-4122. (Illus.). xviii, 296p. 1981. Repr. of 1964 ed. lib. bdg. 39.00x (ISBN 0-313-23014-5, ALFS). Greenwood.

Amichai, Yehuda. Not of This Time, Not of This Place. Katz, Shlomo, tr. from Hebrew. 345p. 1973. 12.50x (ISBN 0-85303-180-0, Pub. by Vallentine Mitchell England). Biblio Dist.

Anderson, J. K. Military Theory & Practice in the Age of Xenophon. LC 74-104010. 1970. 28.50x (ISBN 0-520-01564-9). U of Cal Pr.

The Annals of Tacitus, Books One to Six, Vol. 2. (Cambridge Classical Texts & Commentaries: No. 23). 576p. Date not set. 67.50 (ISBN 0-521-20213-2). Cambridge U Pr.

Austin, Norman, ed. Greek Historians. (Orig.). 1969. pap. text ed. 8.95x (ISBN 0-442-00369-2). Van Nos Reinhold.

Bailkey, Nels, ed. Readings in Ancient History: From Gilgamesh to Diocletian. 2nd ed. 1977. pap. text ed. 9.95x (ISBN 0-669-00249-6). Heath.

Beloch, Julius. Die Bevolkerung der Griechisch-Romischen Welt. Finley, Moses, ed. LC 79-4962. (Ancient Economic History Ser.). (Ger.). 1980. Repr. of 1886 ed. lib. bdg. 38.00x (ISBN 0-405-12349-3). Arno.

Bergier, Jacques. Extraterrestrial Visitations from Prehistoric Times to the Present. 1974. pap. 1.50 (ISBN 0-451-05942-5, W5942, Sig). NAL.

Bickerman, Elias & Smith, Morton. The Ancient History of Western Civilization. (Illus.). 288p. 1976. pap. text ed. 12.50 scp (ISBN 0-06-040668-2, HarpC). Har-Row.

Boardman, John. Pre-Classical. 1978. pap. 4.95 (ISBN 0-14-020807-0, Pelican). Penguin.

Borger, Rykle. Handbuch der Keilschriftliteratur, Vol. 2: Anhang-Zur Kuyunjck-Sammlung. new ed. xxxii, 395p. (Ger.). 1975. 42.50x (ISBN 3-11-002487-X). De Gruyter.

--Handbuch der Keilschriftliteratur, Vol. 3: Inhaltliche Ordnung der sumerischen und akkadischen Texte. viii, 168p. (Ger.). 1975. 24.00x (ISBN 3-11-005960-6). De Gruyter.

Botsford, George W. A History of the Ancient World. 1919. 35.00 (ISBN 0-8274-3932-6). R West.

--A Source Book of Ancient History. 1929. 40.00 (ISBN 0-8274-3934-2). R West.

Bouquet, A. C. Everyday Life in New Testament Times. (Hudson River Editions). (Illus.). 1953. lib. rep. ed. 17.50 (ISBN 0-684-14833-1, ScribT). Scribner.

Bradford, Ernie. The Battle for the West - Thermopylae 480. Date not set. 9.95 (ISBN 0-07-007062-8). McGraw.

Brown, Peter. The Making of Late Antiquity. LC 78-6844. (Carl Newell Jackson Lectures Ser.). 1978. 12.50x (ISBN 0-674-54320-3). Harvard U Pr.

Burstein, Stanley & Okin, Louis, eds. Panhellenica: Essays in Ancient History. 1980. 15.00x (ISBN 0-87291-134-9). Coronado Pr.

Burton, O. E. Study in Creative History. LC 71-105821. (Classics Ser). 1971. Repr. of 1932 ed. 13.50 (ISBN 0-8046-1197-1). Kennikat.

--A Study in Creative History: The Interaction of the Eastern & Western Peoples to 500 B. C. 1977. lib. bdg. 59.95 (ISBN 0-8490-2708-X). Gordon Pr.

Caldwell, W. E. & Gyles, M. F. Ancient World. 3rd ed. LC 66-13290. (gr. 11 up). 1966. text ed. 16.95 (ISBN 0-03-055920-0, HoltC). HR&W.

Capes, W. W. The Age of Antonines. 1897. 10.00 (ISBN 0-8482-7254-4). Norwood Edns.

Chandler, Tertius. Remote Kingdoms. rev. ed. (Illus.). 111p. 1981. pap. 12.00 (ISBN 0-9603872-5-0). Gutenberg.

Clodd, Edward. The Childhood of the World: A Simple Account of Man's Origin & Early History. 1979. Repr. of 1914 ed. lib. bdg. 25.00 (ISBN 0-8492-4035-2). R West.

Connor, W. R., ed. The Acts of the Pagan Martyrs. LC 78-18588. (Greek Texts & Commentaries Ser.). 1979. Repr. of 1954 ed. lib. bdg. 23.00x (ISBN 0-405-11430-3). Arno.

Cootes, R. J. & Snellgrove, L. E. The Ancient World. (Longman Secondary Histories Ser.). (Illus.). 1974. pap. text ed. 6.95x (ISBN 0-582-20503-4). Longman.

Davis, William S. Readings in Ancient History: Greece & the East. 1912. 20.00 (ISBN 0-686-20107-8). Quality Lib.

Delle Colonne, G. Guido De Columnis: Historia Destructionis Troiae. Griffin, Nathanial E., ed. 1936. 16.00 (ISBN 0-527-01696-9). Kraus Repr.

De Romilly, Jacqueline. The Rise & Fall of States According to Greek Authors. LC 75-31056. 1977. 12.50x (ISBN 0-472-08762-2). U of Mich Pr.

Diodorus Siculus. Library of History, 12 vols. Incl. Vol. 1 (ISBN 0-674-99307-1); Vol. 2 (ISBN 0-674-99334-9); Vol. 3 (ISBN 0-674-99375-6); Vol. 4 (ISBN 0-674-99413-2); Vol. 5 (ISBN 0-674-99422-1); Vol. 6 (ISBN 0-674-99439-6); Vol. 7 (ISBN 0-674-99428-0); Vol. 8 (ISBN 0-674-99464-7); Vol. 9 (ISBN 0-674-99415-9); Vol. 10 (ISBN 0-674-99429-9); Vol. 11 (ISBN 0-674-99450-7); Vol. 12 (ISBN 0-674-99465-5). (Loeb Classical Library: No. 279, 303, 340, 375, 377, 384, 389, 390, 399, 409, 422, 423). 11.00x ea. Harvard U Pr.

Drake, W. Raymond. Gods & Spacemen of the Ancient Past. 1974. pap. 1.50 (ISBN 0-451-06140-3, W6140, Sig). NAL.

Drumann, W. Die Arbeiter und Communisten in Griechenland und Rom, Nach den Quellen. (Ger.). 1860. text ed. 30.50x (ISBN 90-6090-101-0). Humanities.

Eadie, John, ed. Early Oriental History: Comprising the Histories of Egypt, Assyria, Persia, Lydia, Phrygia, & Phoenicia. 1852. 20.00 (ISBN 0-685-43866-X). Norwood Edns.

Edwards, I. E., et al, eds. Cambridge Ancient History. Incl. Vol. 1, Pt. 1. Prolegomena & Prehistory. pap. 29.50 (ISBN 0-521-29821-0); Vol. 1, Pts. 2A & 2B. Early History of the Middle East. pap. 34.50 (ISBN 0-521-29822-9); Vol. 2, Pt. 1. The Middle East & the Aegean Region, c 1800-1380 B.C. pap. 29.50 (ISBN 0-521-29823-7); Vol. 2, Pts. 2A & 2B. The Middle East & the Aegean Region, c 1380-1000 B.C. pap. 34.50 (ISBN 0-521-29824-5). LC 75-85719. (Illus.). 1981. Cambridge U Pr.

Ehrenberg, Victor. Aspects of the Ancient World: Essays & Reviews. LC 72-7889. (Greek History Ser.). Repr. of 1946 ed. 15.00 (ISBN 0-405-04785-1). Arno.

--Man, State & Deity: Essays in Ancient History. LC 74-7695. 170p. 1974. pap. 10.95x (ISBN 0-416-79610-9). Methuen Inc.

Evans, J. A., ed. Polis & Imperium: Studies in Honour of Edward Togo Salmon. LC 74-80411. 1974. 15.00 (ISBN 0-88866-526-1). Samuel Stevens.

Finegan, Jack. Light from the Ancient Past, 2 vols. 2nd ed. (Illus.). 1959. Vol. 1 2nd Ed. 35.00 (ISBN 0-691-03550-4); Vol. 1 2nd Edition. pap. 8.95 (ISBN 0-691-00207-X); 25.00 (ISBN 0-691-03551-2); Vol. 2. pap. 8.95 (ISBN 0-691-00208-8); Set. 59.50 (ISBN 0-686-76901-5). Princeton U Pr.

Finley, M. I. Aspects of Antiquity. (Illus.). 1977. pap. 3.95 (ISBN 0-14-021509-3, Pelican). Penguin.

Finley, M. I., ed. Studies in Ancient Society. (Past & Present Ser.). 1978. pap. 6.50 (ISBN 0-7100-8901-5). Routledge & Kegan.

Finley, Moses I., ed. Portable Greek Historians. (Viking Portable Library: No. 65). 1977. pap. 5.95 (ISBN 0-14-015065-X). Penguin.

Garnsey, P. D. & Whittaker, C. R., eds. Imperialism in the Ancient World. LC 77-85699. (Cambridge Classical Studies). (Illus.). 1979. 42.50 (ISBN 0-521-21882-9). Cambridge U Pr.

Gillett, E. H. Historical Patterns of Destruction of Ancient Cities & Empires. (Illus.). 139p. 1982. Repr. of 1867 ed. 79.85 (ISBN 0-89901-039-3). Found Class Reprints.

Glover, Terrot R. The Ancient World: A Beginning. LC 79-11456. 1980. Repr. of 1944 ed. lib. bdg. 25.75x (ISBN 0-313-21459-X, GLAW). Greenwood.

Goguet, Antoine Y. & Fugere, A. C. The Origin of Laws, Arts, & Sciences & Their Progress Among the Most Ancient Nations, 3 vols. LC 72-1630. (Illus.). Repr. of 1761 ed. 87.50 set (ISBN 0-404-08230-0). AMS Pr.

Gray, Basil. The World History of Rashid Al-Din. (Illus.). 76p. 1979. 42.00 (ISBN 0-571-10918-7, Pub. by Faber & Faber). Merrimack Bk Serv.

Gyles, Mary F. & Davis, Eugene W., eds. Laudatores Temporis Acti: Studies in Memory of Wallace Everett Caldwell. (James Sprunt Study in History & Political Science: No. 46). (Orig.). 1964. pap. text ed. 5.00x (ISBN 0-8078-5046-2). U of NC Pr.

Haase, Wolfgang. Aufstieg und Niedergang der Roemischen Welt, Vol. 16, Pts. 1 & 2. 1978. Pt. I. 234.00x (ISBN 3-11-006737-4); Pt. II. 262.00x (ISBN 3-11-007612-8). De Gruyter.

Hahn, I., et al, eds. Oikumene Yearbook of the Economic & Social History of the Ancient World, Vol. 2. 1978. 30.00x (ISBN 963-05-1590-3). Intl Pubns Serv.

Hapgood, Charles H. Maps of the Ancient Sea Kings: Evidence of Advanced Civilization in the Ice Age. (Illus.). 1979. pap. 9.95 (ISBN 0-525-47606-7). Dutton.

Hawkes, Jacquetta. History of Mankind: Cultural & Scientific Development-Vol. 1: Prehistory & the Beginning of Civilization-Part 1. 1963. text ed. 25.00x (ISBN 0-04-913004-8). Allen Unwin.

Herodotus. Famous Hystory of Herodotus. LC 25-8760. (Tudor Translations, Second Series: No. 6). Repr. of 1924 ed. 24.50 (ISBN 0-404-51856-7). AMS Pr.

--Herodotus. LC 75-39478. (Select Bibliographies Reprint Series). 1972. Repr. of 1847 ed. 25.00 (ISBN 0-8369-9913-4). Arno.

--Herodotus, Book 6: Erato. Shuckburgh, E. S., ed. text ed. 9.95x (ISBN 0-521-05248-3). Cambridge U Pr.

--Historiae, 2 Vols. 3rd ed. Hude, Karl, ed. (Oxford Classical Texts Ser). 1927. Vol. 1. 18.95x (ISBN 0-19-814526-8); Vol. 2. 18.95x (ISBN 0-19-814527-6). Oxford U Pr.

--Histories. De Selincourt, Aubrey, tr. (Classics Ser.). (Orig.). 1954. pap. 5.95 (ISBN 0-14-044034-8). Penguin.

--History of Herodotus, 2 Vols. Littlebury, Isaac, tr. LC 76-49907. Repr. of 1737 ed. Set. 75.00 (ISBN 0-404-54140-2); Vol. 1. 25.00 ea. (ISBN 0-404-54141-0). Vol. 2 (ISBN 0-404-54142-9). AMS Pr.

--History of the Persian Wars, 4 Vols. (Loeb Classical Library: No. 117-120). 11.00x ea. Vol. 1 (ISBN 0-674-99130-3). Vol. 2 (ISBN 0-674-99131-1). Vol. 3 (ISBN 0-674-99133-8). Vol. 4 (ISBN 0-674-99134-6). Harvard U Pr.

--Persian Wars. Rawlinson, George, tr. (YA) 1964. pap. 3.95 (ISBN 0-394-30954-5, T54, Mod LibC). Modern Lib.

Hollister, C. Warren. Odysseus to Columbus: A Synopsis of Classical & Medieval History. LC 74-2428. 352p. 1974. pap. text ed. 12.95 (ISBN 0-471-40689-9). Wiley.

--Roots of the Western Tradition: A Short History of the Ancient World. 3rd ed. LC 76-51394. 1977. text ed. 9.95x (ISBN 0-471-40720-8). Wiley.

Jones, A. H. The Decline of the Ancient World. (General History of Europe Ser.). (Illus.). 1975. pap. text ed. 11.95x (ISBN 0-582-48309-3). Longman.

Jones, Tom B. From the Tigris to the Tiber. rev. ed. 1978. pap. text ed. 11.50x (ISBN 0-256-01992-4). Dorsey.

--Paths to the Ancient Past. LC 67-12515. 1967. pap. text ed. 6.95 (ISBN 0-02-916630-6). Free Pr.

Kagan, Donald. Problems in Ancient History, Vol. 2. 2nd ed. (Illus.). 464p. 1975. pap. text ed. 11.95 (ISBN 0-02-361830-2). Macmillan.

Karsten, C. Die Bedeutung der Form Im Obligationenrich. (Ger.). 1878. text ed. 16.50x (ISBN 90-6090-131-2). Humanities.

Keiser, Clarence E. Neo-Sumerian Account Texts from Drehem. LC 76-115373. (Babylonia Inscriptions in the Collection of James B. N. Ser.: No. 3). 1971. 25.00x (ISBN 0-300-01296-9). Yale U Pr.

Lamberg-Karlovsky, C. C. & Sabloff, Jeremy A. Ancient Civilizations: The Near East & Mesoamerica. 1979. pap. text ed. 12.95 (ISBN 0-8053-5672-X). Benjamin-Cummings.

Lepper, F. A. Trajan's Parthian War. LC 79-4519. (Illus.). 1979. Repr. of 1948 ed. lib. bdg. 22.50x (ISBN 0-313-20845-X, LETP). Greenwood.

Leveque, P. Empires et barbaries. (Historie universelle de poche). (Fr). pap. 3.50 (ISBN 0-685-13901-8). Larousse.

Livingstone, Richard, ed. Legacy of Greece. (Legacy Ser). (Illus.). pap. 3.95 (ISBN 0-19-501318-2, GB293, GB). Oxford U Pr.

Lloyd-Jones, Hugh, ed. & intro. by. Tacitus: The Annals & the Histories. text ed. 24.00x (ISBN 0-8290-0208-1). Irvington.

McEvedy, Colin. The Penguin Atlas of Ancient History. (Maps). (YA) (gr. 9 up). 1967. pap. 5.95 (ISBN 0-14-070832-4). Penguin.

Mansfeld, J. Pseudo-Hippocratic Tract & Greek Philosophy. (Philosophy Texts & Studies: No. 20). 1970. text ed. 33.50x (ISBN 9-0232-0701-7). Humanities.

Martin, Ronald. Tacitus. LC 80-28910. 300p. 1981. 30.00x (ISBN 0-520-04427-4). U of Cal Pr.

Maspero, Gaston C. Histoire Ancienne Des Peuples De l'Orient Classique, 3 Vols. Repr. 242.00 set (ISBN 0-384-35780-6). Johnson Repr.

Matthew Of Westminster. Flowers of History, Especially Such As Relate to the Affairs of Britain, 2 Vols. Yonge, C. D., tr. LC 68-57870. (Bohn's Antiquarian Library). Repr. of 1853 ed. Set. 55.00 (ISBN 0-404-50030-7). AMS Pr.

Melko, Matthew & Weigel, Richard D. Peace in the Ancient World. LC 80-20434. 231p. 1981. lib. bdg. 18.95x (ISBN 0-89950-020-X). McFarland & Co.

Milns, R. D. & Ellis, J. R. Spectre of Phillip. (Sources in Ancient History Ser). 1970. pap. 6.50x (ISBN 0-424-06120-1, Pub. by Sydney U Pr). Intl Schol Bk Serv.

Mooney, Richard E. Colony: Earth. LC 73-90698. 304p. 1974. 25.00x (ISBN 0-8128-1658-7). Stein & Day.

--Gods of Air & Darkness. LC 75-8926. 192p. 1975. 25.00 (ISBN 0-8128-1815-6). Stein & Day.

Morgan, Lewis. Ancient Society. 1974. lib. bdg. 105.00 (ISBN 0-87968-630-8). Gordon Pr.

Myers, Philip V. Ancient History. 1978. Repr. of 1904 ed. lib. bdg. 30.00 (ISBN 0-8495-3726-6). Arden Lib.

Pareti, Luigi, et al. History of Mankind: The Ancient World, Vol. 2. 1965. text ed. 25.00x ea. Pt. 1 (ISBN 0-04-931002-X). Pt. 2 (ISBN 0-04-931003-8). Pt. 3 (ISBN 0-04-931004-6). Allen Unwin.

Pergamon: Gesammelte Aufsaetze. (Pergamenische Forschungen Vol. 1). (Illus.). 222p. 1972. 97.50x (ISBN 3-11-001829-2). De Gruyter.

Plutarch. Plutarch's Lives of the Noble Grecians & Romans, 6 Vols. anno ed. North, Thomas, tr. LC 70-158307. (Tudor Translations. First Series: Nos. 7-12). Repr. of 1896 ed. Set. 210.00 (ISBN 0-404-51870-2); 35.00 ea. AMS Pr.

Polybe. Histoire. 1672p. 42.95 (ISBN 0-686-56553-3). French & Eur.

Polybius. The Histories. Badian, E., ed. 1966. text ed. 20.00x (ISBN 0-8290-0196-4). Irvington.

--Histories, 6 Vols. (Loeb Classical Library: No. 128, 137-138, 159-161). 11.00x ea. Vol. 1 (ISBN 0-674-99142-7). Vol. 2 (ISBN 0-674-99152-4). Vol. 3 (ISBN 0-674-99153-2). Vol. 4 (ISBN 0-674-99175-3). Vol. 5 (ISBN 0-674-99176-1). Vol. 6 (ISBN 0-674-99178-8). Harvard U Pr.

Prentice, William K. Ancient Greeks: Studies Toward a Better Understanding of the Ancient World. LC 71-102531. 1970. Repr. of 1940 ed. 11.50 (ISBN 0-8462-1291-9). Russell.

Procopuis. Procopius. LC 67-28144. 351p. 1967. text ed. 20.00x (ISBN 0-8290-0199-9). Irvington.

Psellus, Michael. Fourteen Byzantine Rulers. Sewter, E. R., tr. 1979. pap. 3.95 (ISBN 0-14-044169-7). Penguin.

Rawlinson, George. A Manual of Ancient History. 1975. Repr. of 1881 ed. 50.00 (ISBN 0-8274-4054-5). R West.

Reinaud, Joseph T. Relations Politiques et Commerciales De l'Empire Romain Avec l'Asie Orientale. LC 72-10083. (Illus.). 339p. 1973. Repr. of 1863 ed. 29.00 (ISBN 0-8337-2933-0). B Franklin.

Richardson, Ilona E. Before the World Was. 1979. pap. 4.00 (ISBN 0-682-49358-9). Exposition.

Riche, P. Les Grandes Invasions et empires. (Historie universelle Larousse de poche). (Fr). pap. 3.50 (ISBN 0-685-13932-8). Larousse.

Robinson, Charles A. Ancient History. 2nd, rev. ed. Boegehold, A. L., ed. 1967. text ed. 18.95x (ISBN 0-02-402290-X). Macmillan.

Robinson, Charles A., ed. Selections from Greek & Roman Historians. LC 57-7740. (Rinehart Editions). 1957. pap. text ed. 8.50 (ISBN 0-03-009425-9, HoltC). HR&W.

Roebuck, Carl. World of Ancient Times. (Illus.). 1966. pap. text ed. 14.95x (ISBN 0-684-13726-7, ScribC). Scribner.

Rose, John H. Mediterranean in the Ancient World. Repr. of 1934 ed. lib. bdg. 15.00x (ISBN 0-8371-1933-2, ROME). Greenwood.

Rostovtsev, Mikhail. History of the Ancient World, 2 Vols. Duff, J. D., tr. from Rus. LC 73-109834. 1971. Repr. of 1926 ed. lib. bdg. 55.75x (ISBN 0-8371-4325-X, ROAW). Greenwood.

Rostovtzeff, M. A History of the Ancient World, 2 vols. rev. ed. 1945. Repr. Set. 65.00 (ISBN 0-685-43304-8). Norwood Edns.

Rouche, M. Empires universels. (Historie universelle de poche). (Fr). pap. 3.50 (ISBN 2-03-029108-0). Larousse.

Schwantes, Siegfried J. Short History of the Ancient Near East. (Illus.). 1965. pap. 4.95 (ISBN 0-8010-8026-6). Baker Bk.

Semple, Ellen C. Geography of the Mediterranean Regions. LC 70-137267. Repr. of 1931 ed. 34.50 (ISBN 0-404-05751-9). AMS Pr.

Simpson, William K. Heka-nefer & the Dynastic Material from Toshka & Arminna, Vol. 1. LC 63-21651. 1963. 20.00 (ISBN 0-686-00128-1). Penn-Yale Expedit.

Souttar, Robinson. A Short History of Ancient Peoples. 1979. Repr. of 1904 ed. lib. bdg. 100.00 (ISBN 0-8495-4943-4). Arden Lib.

Starr, Chester G. A History of the Ancient World. 2nd ed. 1974. text ed. 25.00 (ISBN 0-19-501814-1); text ed. 14.95x (ISBN 0-19-501815-X). Oxford U Pr.

Stavrianos, Leften. The World to Fifteen Hundred: A Global History. 2nd ed. (Illus.). 416p. 1975. pap. 15.95 (ISBN 0-13-968198-1). P-H.

Tacitus, Cornelius. Cornelii Taciti Annalium Libri I-IV. Furneaux, H., intro. by. LC 75-41270. 1976. Repr. of 1897 ed. 18.00 (ISBN 0-404-14615-5). AMS Pr.

Talbert, R J. Timoleon & the Revival of Greek Cicily, 344-317 BC. 248p. 1974. 19.95 (ISBN 0-521-20419-4). Cambridge U Pr.

Temporini, Hildegard. Die Frauen am Hofe Trajans. (Illus.). 1979. 66.80x (ISBN 3-11-007822-8). De Gruyter.

Ternaux, Henricus. Historia Reipublicae Massiliensium. 128p. 1974. 10.00 (ISBN 0-89005-038-4). Ares.

Thomas, Gwynne E. H. Political History of the Ancient World. 1981. 7.95 (ISBN 0-8062-1680-8). Carlton.

Thucydides. The Speeches of Pericles. Edinger, H. G., tr. from Gr. LC 78-4304. (Milestones of Thought Ser.). 1979. pap. 3.25 (ISBN 0-8044-6908-3). Ungar.

Tillinghast, William. Epitome of Ancient, Medieval & Modern History. 1883. Repr. 20.00 (ISBN 0-685-43262-9). Norwood Edns.

Tomlinson, R. A. Argos & the Argolid: From the End of the Bronze Age to the Roman Occupation. LC 78-38286. (Illus.). 280p. 1972. 22.50x (ISBN 0-8014-0713-3). Cornell U Pr.

Toynbee, J. M. Roman Historical Portraits. LC 75-38428. (Aspects of Greek & Roman Life). (Illus.). 1978. 45.00x (ISBN 0-8014-1011-8). Cornell U Pr.

Trigger, Bruce G. Late Nubian Settlement at Arminna West, Vol 2. LC 67-26193. 1967. 20.00 (ISBN 0-686-00129-X). Penn-Yale Expedit.

--Meroitic Funerary Inscriptions from Arminna West, Vol. 4. LC 72-123644. 1970. 20.00 (ISBN 0-686-00127-3). Penn-Yale Expedit.

Upadhyaya, B. S. The Ancient World. LC 78-670071. 1976. 12.50x (ISBN 0-8002-0247-3). Intl Pubns Serv.

Van Sickle, Clifton E. Political & Cultural History of the Ancient World from Prehistoric Times to the Dissolution of the Roman Empire in the West, 2 Vols. 1947-1948. Repr. lib. bdg. 53.50x (ISBN 0-8371-2961-3, VAAW). Greenwood.

Vaughan, D. M. Outlines of Ancient History. 1928. Repr. 10.00 (ISBN 0-685-43265-3). Norwood Edns.

Volkmann, Hans. Endoxos Duleia: Kleine Schriften Zur Alten Geschichte. (Illus.). xii, 340p. 1975. 104.75x (ISBN 3-11-005980-0). De Gruyter.

Weeks, Kent R. Classic Christian Townsite at Arminna West, Vol. 3. LC 67-26194. 1967. 20.00 (ISBN 0-686-00130-3). Penn-Yale Expedit.

Weigall, Arthur. Personalities of Antiquity. 235p. 1981. Repr. of 1928 ed. lib. bdg. 35.00 (ISBN 0-89984-508-8). Century Bookbindery.

Weigall, Arthur E. Personalities of Antiquity. facs. ed. LC 77-90672. (Essay Index Reprint Ser.). 1928. 16.00 (ISBN 0-8369-1217-9). Arno.

Welles, H. B. Royal Correspondence in the Hellenistic Period. (Illus.). 510p. 1974. 20.00 (ISBN 0-89005-019-8). Ares.

Wells, Joseph. Studies in Herodotus. facs. ed. LC 77-137388. (Select Bibliographies Reprint Ser). 1923. 15.00 (ISBN 0-8369-5589-7). Arno.

Wheeler, Robert E. Flames Over Persepolis: Turning-Point in History. LC 79-18164. (Illus.). 1979. Repr. of 1968 ed. lib. bdg. 29.50x (ISBN 0-313-22077-8, WHFP). Greenwood.

White, K. D., tr. from Greek & Latin. Country Life in Classical Times. LC 77-74923. (Illus., Eng.). 1977. 22.50x (ISBN 0-8014-1114-9). Cornell U Pr.

Woolley, Leonard. History of Mankind: Cultural & Scientific Development-Vol. 1: Prehistory & the Beginnings of Civilisation-Part 2. 1963. text ed. 27.50x (ISBN 0-04-913008-0). Allen Unwin.

HISTORY, ANCIENT–BIBLIOGRAPHY

Bengtson, Hermann. Introduction to Ancient History. Frank, R. I. & Gilliard, Frank D., trs. LC 78-118685. (California Library Reprint Ser). 1976. 20.00x (ISBN 0-520-03150-4). U of Cal Pr.

Donlan, Walter, intro. by. Classical World Bibliography of Greek & Roman History. LC 76-52511. (Library of Humanities Reference Bks.: No. 94). lib. bdg. 27.00 (ISBN 0-8240-9879-X). Garland Pub.

Harvard University Library. Ancient History: Classification Schedule Author & Title Listing, Chronological Listing. (Widener Library Shelflist Ser.: No. 55). 400p. 1975. 40.00x (ISBN 0-674-03312-4). Harvard U Pr.

Radice, Betty. Who's Who in the Ancient World. (Reference Ser.). (Orig.). 1973. pap. 4.95 (ISBN 0-14-051055-9). Penguin.

HISTORY, ANCIENT–CHRONOLOGY

Bickerman, E. J. Chronology of the Ancient World. 2nd ed. (Aspects of Greek & Roman Life Ser.). (Illus.). 260p. 1980. 18.50x (ISBN 0-8014-1282-X). Cornell U Pr.

Ehrich, Robert W., ed. Chronologies in Old World Archaeology. LC 65-17296. (Illus., Orig.). 1966. 12.00x (ISBN 0-226-19443-4). U of Chicago Pr.

HISTORY, ANCIENT–DICTIONARIES

Cooper, William R. Archaic Dictionary. LC 73-76018. 1969. Repr. of 1876 ed. 47.00 (ISBN 0-8103-3885-8). Gale.

Magill, Frank N., ed. Great Events from History, 3 vols. (Ancient & Medieval Ser.). 1975. 95.00 set (ISBN 0-89356-104-5). Salem Pr.

HISTORY, ANCIENT–JUVENILE LITERATURE

Baer, Ruth. Ancient History, Bk. 1. (gr. 7). 1979. 8.95 (ISBN 0-686-30770-4); tchr's ed. avail. 1.00 (ISBN 0-686-30771-2). Rod & Staff.

Cairns, Trevor, ed. People Become Civilized. LC 73-20196. (The Cambridge Introduction to History Ser). (Illus.). 104p. (gr. 5-12). 1974. PLB 8.95g (ISBN 0-8225-0801-X). Lerner Pubns.

Freebairen-Smith, S. J. & Littlejohn, G. N. Winner Take All: From Trial to Triumph, Vol. 1. 1977. pap. text ed. 6.50x (ISBN 0-435-36320-4). Heinemann Ed.

Freebairn-Smith, S. J. & Littlejohn, G. N. Chief Factors for the Gods: From Trial to Triumph, Vol. 2. 1977. pap. text ed. 6.50x (ISBN 0-435-36321-2). Heinemann Ed.

Unstead, R. J. How They Lived in Cities Long Ago. (Illus.). 80p. (gr. 6 up). 1981. 9.95 (ISBN 0-668-05188-4, 5188). Arco.

--Looking at Ancient History. (Illus.). (gr. 4-6). 1960. 9.95 (ISBN 0-02-790650-7). Macmillan.

HISTORY, ANCIENT–OUTLINES, SYLLABI, ETC.

Cheilik, Michael. Ancient History: From Its Beginnings to the Fall of Rome. LC 79-76467. (Orig.). 1969. pap. 3.95 (ISBN 0-06-460001-7, CO 1, COS). Har-Row.

Marban, Edilberto. Ancient & Medieval History. (Blue Bks.). pap. 1.25 (ISBN 0-671-18102-5). Monarch Pr.

HISTORY, BIBLICAL
see Bible–History of Biblical Events

HISTORY, CHURCH
see Church History

HISTORY, COMIC, SATIRICAL, ETC.
see also United States–History–Humor, Caricatures, Etc.; also subdivision History, Comic, Satirical, etc. under names of other countries

Stewart, Donald O. A Parody Outline of History. 1977. Repr. of 1921 ed. lib. bdg. 15.00 (ISBN 0-8492-2414-4). R West.

HISTORY, CONSTITUTIONAL
see Constitutional History

HISTORY, ECCLESIASTICAL
see Church History

HISTORY, ECONOMIC
see Economic History

HISTORY, JUVENILE
see World History–Juvenile Literature; also subdivision Juvenile Literature, or History, Juvenile under names of countries

HISTORY, LOCAL
see Local History

HISTORY, MEDIEVAL
see Middle Ages–History

HISTORY, MILITARY
see Military History

HISTORY, MODERN
see also Civilization, Modern; Reformation; Renaissance

Acton, Lord. Lectures on Modern History. Golin, E., ed. 8.75 (ISBN 0-8446-1504-8). Peter Smith.

Adams, George B. Medieval & Modern History. 1901. 15.00 (ISBN 0-8482-7276-5). Norwood Edns.

Aurandt, Paul. Paul Harvey's the Rest of the Story. LC 77-75381. 1977. 9.95 (ISBN 0-385-12768-5). Doubleday.

Black, C. E. The Dynamics of Modernization: A Study in Comparative History. 9.00 (ISBN 0-8446-5846-4). Peter Smith.

Bourne, K. & Watt, D. C., eds. Studies in International History, Presented to Professor W. N. Medlicott. 1967. 25.00 (ISBN 0-208-00406-8, Archon). Shoe String.

Bryce, James. Public Opinion in the American Commonwealth. Nisbet, Robert, ed. 1981. 18.95 (ISBN 0-87923-370-2); pap. 8.95 (ISBN 0-87923-371-0). Godine.

Camus, Albert. Neither Victims nor Executioners. MacDonald, Dwight, tr. (Modern Classics of Peace Ser). 1968. pap. 2.95 (ISBN 0-912018-04-6). World Without War.

Chippindale, Peter & Harriman, Ed. Juntas United! 4.95 (ISBN 0-686-73468-8, Pub. by Quartet England). Charles River Bks.

Cowley, Malcolm. Think Back on Us. A Contemporary Chronicle of the 1930s: The Literary Record. Piper, Henry D., ed. LC 72-5606. (Arcturus Books Paperbacks). 210p. (Pt. 2 of the hardbound ed. of Think Back On Us). 1972. pap. 7.95 (ISBN 0-8093-0599-2). S Ill U Pr.

--Think Back on Us. A Contemporary Chronicle of the 1930s: The Social Record. Piper, Henry D., ed. LC 72-5606. (Arcturus Books Paperbacks). 213p. (Pt. 1 of the hardbound ed. of Think Back On Us). 1972. pap. 7.95 (ISBN 0-8093-0598-4). S Ill U Pr.

Dooling, John & Violano, Michael, eds. Great Events As Reported in the New York Times: Program Guide. (Illus.). 101p. (gr. 7-12). 1978. pap. 7.95 wkbk (ISBN 0-667-00604-4). Microfilming Corp.

Fell, Albert, ed. Histories & Historians. (History Today Ser). 1968. 5.00 (ISBN 0-05-001654-7); pap. 3.95 (ISBN 0-685-00927-0). Dufour.

Fuller, John F. War & Western Civilization, 1832-1932. LC 72-102238. (Select Bibliographies Reprint Ser). 1932. 22.00 (ISBN 0-8369-5123-9). Arno.

Gerhardie, William. God's Fifth Column: A Biography of the Age: Eighteen Ninety to Nineteen Forty. Holroyd, Michael & Skidelsky, Robert, eds. 1981. 15.95 (ISBN 0-671-43652-X). S&S.

Gooch, George P. Studies in Modern History. facs. ed. LC 68-16934. (Essay Index Reprint Ser). 1931. 18.00 (ISBN 0-8369-0482-6). Arno.

Holley, I. B. & Goodwin, Craufurd W., eds. Transfer of Ideas: Historical Essays. LC 68-26691. 1968. 9.75 (ISBN 0-8223-0074-5). Duke.

Kim, Han Kyo, ed. Essays on Modern Politics & History. LC 75-91958. xiv, 255p. 1969. 13.95x (ISBN 0-8214-0079-7). Ohio U Pr.

Kohn, Hans. Reflections on Modern History: The Historian & Human Responsibility. LC 77-28495. 1978. Repr. of 1963 ed. lib. bdg. 26.75x (ISBN 0-313-20232-X, KORM). Greenwood.

Kurland, Gerald. Western Civilization, Two (from 1500) (Monarch College Outlines). pap. 4.95 (ISBN 0-671-08050-4). Monarch Pr.

Langer, William L. Explorations in Crisis: Papers on International History. Schorske, Carl E. & Schorske, Elizabeth, eds. LC 69-18036. 1969. 25.00x (ISBN 0-674-27851-8, Belknap Pr). Harvard U Pr.

Laqueur, Walter & Mosse, George L., eds. The New History: Trends in Historical Research & Writing Since World War Two. 1967. lib. bdg. 13.50x (ISBN 0-88307-184-3). Gannon.

McNeill, William H. A World History. 3rd ed. (Illus.). 1979. 24.95 (ISBN 0-19-502554-7); pap. text ed. 12.95x (ISBN 0-19-502555-5). Oxford U Pr.

Mark, Max. Modern Ideologies. 250p. 1973. pap. text ed. 5.95 (ISBN 0-312-54040-X). St Martin.

Namier, Lewis. Personalities & Powers. LC 73-20878. 157p. 1974. Repr. of 1955 ed. lib. bdg. 15.00 (ISBN 0-8371-5780-3, NAPE). Greenwood.

Namier, Lewis B. In the Margin of History. facs. ed. LC 69-18934. (Essay Index Reprint Ser). 1939. 16.00 (ISBN 0-8369-0050-2). Arno.

--Skyscrapers, & Other Essays. facs. ed. LC 68-22113. (Essay Index Reprint Ser). 1931. 12.50 (ISBN 0-8369-0734-5). Arno.

Palmer, Robert R. & Colton, Joel. A History of the Modern World, 2 vols. 5th ed. 1977. one vol. ed. 20.95 (ISBN 0-394-32039-5); 13.95 ea. Vol. 1 (ISBN 0-394-32040-9). Vol. 2 (ISBN 0-394-32041-7). Knopf.

Pares, Richard & Taylor, Alan J., eds. Essays Presented to Sir Lewis Namier. facs. ed. LC 70-134124. (Essay Index Reprint Ser). 1956. 30.00 (ISBN 0-8369-2010-4). Arno.

Parker, Harold T. & Herr, Richard, eds. Ideas in History: Essays Presented to Louis Gottschalk by His Former Students. LC 65-14546. 1965. 14.75 (ISBN 0-8223-0128-8). Duke.

Prescott, Julian K. A History of the Modern Age. 6.50 (ISBN 0-8446-4798-5). Peter Smith.

Romein, Jan. The Watershed of Two Eras: Europe in 1900. Pomerans, Arnold, tr. from Dutch. LC 77-14841. 1978. 30.00x (ISBN 0-8195-5026-4, Pub. by Wesleyan U Pr); pap. 13.00x (ISBN 0-8195-6066-9). Columbia U Pr.

Rush, Gary B. & Denisoff, R. Serge, eds. Social & Political Movements. LC 72-146365. 1971. 38.50x (ISBN 0-89197-411-3). Irvington.

Seldes, George. Even the Gods Can't Change History. 256p. 1976. 10.00 (ISBN 0-8184-0233-4). Lyle Stuart.

Stavrianos, Leften. The World Since Fifteen Hundred: A Global History. 3rd ed. LC 74-30161. (Illus.). 576p. 1975. pap. text ed. 16.95 (ISBN 0-13-968156-6). P-H.

Stubbs, William. Seventeen Lectures on the Study of Medieval & Modern History. 1967. 25.00 (ISBN 0-86527-219-0). Fertig.

Tillinghast, William. Epitome of Ancient, Medieval & Modern History. 1883. Repr. 20.00 (ISBN 0-685-43262-9). Norwood Edns.

Toekei, Ferenc. Essays on the Asiatic Mode of Production. 129p. 1979. 13.50x (ISBN 963-05-1701-9). Intl Pubns Serv.

Vaughan, Henry H. Two Lectures on Modern History. Repr. of 1849 ed. 25.00 (ISBN 0-685-43264-5). Norwood Edns.

Vincitorio, Gaetano, ed. Crisis in the Great Republic: Essays Presented to Ross J. S. Hoffman. LC 70-79567. xxii, 322p. 1969. 30.00 (ISBN 0-8232-0820-6). Fordham.

Wallace, Lillian P. & Askew, William C., eds. Power, Public Opinion, & Diplomacy. facs. ed. LC 68-55861. (Essay Index Reprint Ser). 1959. 18.50 (ISBN 0-8369-0969-0). Arno.

Wallbank, T. Walter, et al. Civilization Past & Present: 1650 to the Present. 5th ed. 1979. Vol. 2. pap. text ed. 13.95x (ISBN 0-673-15247-2). Scott F.

HISTORY, MODERN–CHRONOLOGY
see Chronology, Historical

HISTORY, MODERN–DICTIONARIES

Palmer, Alan W. Dictionary of Modern History. (Reference Ser.). (Orig.). (YA) (gr. 11 up). 1964. pap. 3.95 (ISBN 0-14-051026-5). Penguin.

HISTORY, MODERN–JUVENILE LITERATURE

Cheney, Cora. Vermont: The State with the Storybook Past. 2nd ed. (Illus.). 256p. (gr. 3-6). 1981. pap. 10.95 (ISBN 0-8289-0440-5). Greene.

Foster, Genevieve. Abraham Lincoln's World. (Illus.). (gr. 5-11). 1944. lib. rep. ed. 20.00x (ISBN 0-684-14855-2, ScribJ). Scribner.

Hoobler, Dorothy & Hoobler, Thomas. An Album of the Seventies. (Picture Albums Ser.). (Illus.). 96p. (gr. 5 up). 1981. PLB 8.90 (ISBN 0-531-04322-3). Watts.

HISTORY, MODERN–PERIODICALS
see History–Periodicals

HISTORY, MODERN–PHILOSOPHY
see History–Philosophy

HISTORY, MODERN–SOURCES

The Front Page, 1975. LC 76-1329. (Illus.). 1976. 14.95x (ISBN 0-405-08105-7). Arno.

Heher, J. M., ed. Great Events Two As Reported in the New York Times: Program Guide. 107p. (gr. 7-12). 1980. pap. text ed. 7.95 (ISBN 0-667-00600-1). Microfilming Corp.

Snyder, Louis L. Fifty Major Documents of the Nineteenth Century. LC 78-10792. (Anvil Ser.). 192p. 1979. pap. text ed. 4.95 (ISBN 0-88275-751-2). Krieger.

HISTORY, MODERN–STUDY AND TEACHING
see also Current Events

HISTORY, MODERN–16TH CENTURY
see also Sixteenth Century

Gottschalk, Louis, et al. History of Mankind: Cultural & Scientific Development - Vol. 4: the Foundations of the Modern World, 1300-1775, 2 pts. 1969. Pt. 1. text ed. 30.00x (ISBN 0-04-900007-1); Pt. 2. text ed. 30.00x (ISBN 0-04-900009-8). Allen Unwin.

Munday, Anthony. The English Roman Life. Ayres, Phillip J., ed. (Studies in Tudor & Stewart Literature Ser.). (Illus.). 142p. 1980. 22.00 (ISBN 0-19-812635-2). Oxford U Pr.

HISTORY, MODERN–17TH CENTURY
see also Seventeenth Century

Foster, Genevieve. World of Captain John Smith. LC 59-11853. (Illus.). (gr. 5-11). 1959. lib. rep. ed. 20.00 (ISBN 0-684-15726-8, ScribJ). Scribner.

Gottschalk, Louis, et al. History of Mankind: Cultural & Scientific Development - Vol. 4: the Foundations of the Modern World, 1300-1775, 2 pts. 1969. Pt. 1. text ed. 30.00x (ISBN 0-04-900007-1); Pt. 2. text ed. 30.00x (ISBN 0-04-900009-8). Allen Unwin.

Lievsay, John L. The Seventeenth Century Resolve: A Historical Anthology of a Literary Form. LC 79-4004. 224p. 1980. 15.50x (ISBN 0-8131-1393-8). U Pr of Ky.

HISTORY, MODERN–18TH CENTURY
see also Eighteenth Century

Dawson, Robert L., ed. International Directory of Eighteenth-Century Studies. 404p. 1981. 45.00x (ISBN 0-7294-0258-4, Pub. by Voltaire Found). State Mutual Bk.

Fajn, Max. Le Journal Des Hommes Libres De Tous les Pays 1792-1800. (New Babylon Studies in the Social Sciences: No. 20). (Illus.). 194p. (Orig.). 1976. pap. text ed. 32.50x (ISBN 90-2797-541-8). Mouton.

Foster, Genevieve. Seventeen Seventy-Six: Year of Independence. LC 75-106531. (Illus.). (gr. 2-6). 1970. 5.95 (ISBN 0-684-20822-9, ScribJ). Scribner.

Gottschalk, Louis, et al. History of Mankind: Cultural & Scientific Development - Vol. 4: the Foundations of the Modern World, 1300-1775, 2 pts. 1969. Pt. 1. text ed. 30.00x (ISBN 0-04-900007-1); Pt. 2. text ed. 30.00x (ISBN 0-04-900009-8). Allen Unwin.

Gough, Richard. The History of Myddle. 336p. 1981. pap. 4.95 (ISBN 0-14-005841-9). Penguin.

Payne, Harry C., ed. Studies in Eighteenth Century Culture, Vol. 10. 468p. 1981. 25.00 (ISBN 0-299-08320-9). U of Wis Pr.

Ward, J. T., ed. Age of Change, Seventeen Seventy to Eighteen Seventy. (Ward Documents in Social History Ser). 199p. 1975. text ed. 12.50x (ISBN 0-7136-1576-1). Humanities.

HISTORY, MODERN–19TH CENTURY
see also Nineteenth Century

Adams, Brooks. America's Economic Supremacy. facsimile ed. LC 77-152155. (Essay Index Reprint Ser). Repr. of 1947 ed. 16.00 (ISBN 0-8369-2477-0). Arno.

Birkenhead, Frederick E. Last Essays. facsimile ed. LC 78-104996. (Essay Index Reprint Ser). 1930. 23.00 (ISBN 0-8369-1546-1). Arno.

Cameron, Rondo, ed. Civilization Since Waterloo: A Book of Source Readings. LC 75-108872. 1971. text ed. 14.95x (ISBN 0-88295-778-3); pap. text ed. 9.95x (ISBN 0-88295-779-1). Harlan Davidson.

Chappel, Bernice M. In the Palm of the Mitten: A Memory Book of the Early 1900's. (Illus.). 300p. (Orig.). 1981. pap. 6.95 (ISBN 0-9606400-0-2). G Lakes Bks.

Cruz Monclava, Lidio. Historia Del Ano 1887. 3rd ed. pap. 3.10 (ISBN 0-8477-0809-8). U of PR Pr.

Davis, Richard H. Year from a Reporter's Notebook. LC 70-125691. (American Journalists Ser). (Illus.). 1970. Repr. of 1898 ed. 19.00 (ISBN 0-405-01668-9). Arno.

Educational Research Council. Into the Twentieth Century (1880-1939) (American Adventure Concepts & Inquiry Ser.). (Orig.). (gr. 8). 1977. pap. 9.40 (ISBN 0-205-04631-2, 804631X). Allyn.

Emerson, Edwin. A History of the Nineteenth Century Year by Year, 3 vols. 1980. lib. bdg. 495.00 (ISBN 0-8490-3206-7). Gordon Pr.

--A History of the 19th Century Year by Year, 3 vols. 1977. lib. bdg. 300.00 (ISBN 0-8490-2009-3). Gordon Pr.

Hall & Davis. Course of Europe Since Waterloo, 2 vols. Schmeller, Kurt R., ed. Incl. Vol. 1. From Vienna to Sarajevo (ISBN 0-89197-203-X); Vol. 2. The Twentieth Century (ISBN 0-8290-0379-7). LC 68-15856. (Illus.). 1980. pap. text ed. 14.50x ea. Irvington.

Hall, Walter P. & Beller, Elmer A., eds. Historical Readings in Nineteenth Century Thought. 306p. 1980. lib. bdg. 30.00 (ISBN 0-89760-332-X, Telegraph). Dynamic Learn Corp.

Halstead, John P. & Porcari, Serafinocompiled by. Modern European Imperialism: A Bibliography of Books & Articles, 1815-1972, 2 vols. 1040p. 1974. Set. lib. bdg. 76.00 (ISBN 0-8161-0989-3). G K Hall.

Harrison, Frederic. National & Social Problems. facs. ed. LC 76-142639. (Essay Index Reprint Ser). 1908. 22.00 (ISBN 0-8369-2051-1). Arno.

Loke, Margarett. The World As It Was: A Photographic Portrait 1865 to 1921. LC 80-13031. (Illus.). 220p. 1980. 24.95 (ISBN 0-671-25376-X). Summit Bks.

Maurice, Arthur B. & Cooper, Frederic T. History of the Nineteenth Century in Caricature. LC 73-125160. (Illus.). 1970. Repr. of 1904 ed. 20.00x (ISBN 0-8154-0342-9). Cooper Sq.

Snyder, Louis L. Fifty Major Documents of the Nineteenth Century. LC 78-10792. (Anvil Ser.). 192p. 1979. pap. text ed. 4.95 (ISBN 0-88275-751-2). Krieger.

Snyder, Louis L., ed. Fifty Major Documents of the Twentieth Century. (Orig.). 1955. pap. 5.95x (ISBN 0-442-00005-7, 5, Anv). Van Nos Reinhold.

Sternberger, Dolf. Panorama of the Nineteenth Century. Neugroschel, Joachim, tr. from Ger. (Mole-Editions Ser.). Date not set. pap. cancelled (ISBN 0-916354-25-3). Urizen Bks.

Tilly, Charles, et al. The Rebellious Century: 1830-1930. LC 74-16802. 1975. 20.00x (ISBN 0-674-74955-3); pap. 7.95x (ISBN 0-674-74956-1). Harvard U Pr.

Wilson, Herbert W. Battleships in Action, 2 Vols. 1968. Repr. of 1926 ed. Set. 39.00 (ISBN 0-403-00046-7). Scholarly.

Yeats, W. B. Eighteen Ninety Nine to Nineteen Hundred, 3 vols. in one. Beltaine, ed. 1970. Repr. 35.00x (ISBN 0-7146-2688-0, F Cass Co). Biblio Dist.

HISTORY, MODERN-20TH CENTURY

see also European War, 1914-1918; Twentieth Century; World War, 1939-1945

Barraclough, Geoffrey. Introduction to Contemporary History. (YA) (gr. 9 up). 1968. pap. 3.50 (ISBN 0-14-020827-5, Pelican). Penguin.

--An Introduction to Contemporary History. lib. bdg. 9.50x (ISBN 0-88307-303-X). Gannon.

Birkenhead, Frederick E. Last Essays. facsimile ed. LC 78-104996. (Essay Index Reprint Ser). 1930. 23.00 (ISBN 0-8369-1546-1). Arno.

Cameron, Rondo, ed. Civilization Since Waterloo: A Book of Source Readings. LC 75-108872. 1971. text ed. 14.95x (ISBN 0-88295-778-3); pap. text ed. 9.95x (ISBN 0-88295-779-1). Harlan Davidson.

Chappel, Bernice M. In the Palm of the Mitten: A Memory Book of the Early 1900's. (Illus.). 300p. (Orig.). 1981. pap. 6.95 (ISBN 0-9606400-0-2). G Lakes Bks.

Colton, Joel. Twentieth Century. LC 68-54204. (Great Ages of Man). (Illus.). (gr. 6 up). 1968. PLB 11.97 (ISBN 0-8094-0383-8, Pub. by Time-Life). Silver.

Curti, Merle. The Nineteen Twenties in Historical Perpective. (Cotton Memorial Papers). pap. 3.00 (ISBN 0-685-64637-8). Tex Western.

Dellaquila, William. The Metaphysics of History at the End of the Twentieth Century. (Illus.). 1977. 49.45 (ISBN 0-89266-028-7). Am Classical Coll Pr.

Dos Passos, John. Journeys Between Wars. 394p. 1980. lib. bdg. 22.50x (ISBN 0-374-92251-9). Octagon.

Elton, Oliver. Modern Studies. 1980. Repr. of 1907 ed. lib. bdg. 30.00 (ISBN 0-8492-0799-1). R West.

Ferrara, Grace M., ed. The Disaster File: The Seventies. (Checkmark Ser.). 1979. 17.50x (ISBN 0-87196-155-5). Facts on File.

Gilliam, Laurence, ed. B. B. C. Features. Repr. of 1950 ed. 25.00 (ISBN 0-8492-9950-0). R West.

Goldston, Robert. The Road Between the Wars: 1918-1941. LC 78-51330. (Illus.). (gr. 7 up). 1978. 8.95 (ISBN 0-8037-7467-2). Dial.

Hall & Davis. Course of Europe Since Waterloo, 2 vols. Schmeller, Kurt R., ed. Incl. Vol. 1. From Vienna to Sarajevo (ISBN 0-89197-203-X); Vol. 2. The Twentieth Century (ISBN 0-8290-0379-7). LC 68-15856. (Illus.). 1980. pap. text ed. 14.50x ea. Irvington.

Halle, Louis J. Cold War As History. 1971. pap. 5.95x (ISBN 0-06-131890-6, TB1890, Torch). Har-Row.

Halstead, John P. & Porcari, Serafinocompiled by. Modern European Imperialism: A Bibliography of Books & Articles, 1815-1972, 2 vols. 1040p. 1974. Set. lib. bdg. 76.00 (ISBN 0-8161-0989-3). G K Hall.

Henderson, James L. & Caldwell, Malcolm. Chainless Mind: A Study of Resistance & Liberation. (Twentieth Century Themes Ser). 1968. 7.95 (ISBN 0-241-91337-3). Dufour.

Jenkins, Alan. The Thirties. LC 75-45511. (Illus.). 1976. 35.95x (ISBN 0-8128-1829-6). Stein & Day.

John, Arthur. The Best Years of the Century: Richard Watson Gilder, Scribner's Monthly & the Century Magazine, 1870-1909. LC 80-25841. (Illus.). 250p. 1981. 16.95 (ISBN 0-252-00857-X). U of Ill Pr.

Keylin, Arlene & Barnett, Laurie, eds. The Sixties As Reported by the New York Times. LC 80-84. (Illus.). 256p. 1980. lib. bdg. 9.98 (ISBN 0-405-13085-6). Arno.

Knapp, Wilfrid F. History of War & Peace, 1939-1965. (Royal Institute of Int'l Affairs Ser). 1967. 11.95x (ISBN 0-19-500340-3). Oxford U Pr.

Kohn, Hans. Revolutions & Dictatorships. facs. ed. LC 75-80388. (Essay Index Reprint Ser). 1939. 23.00 (ISBN 0-8369-1145-8). Arno.

Kurland, Gerald, ed. Origins of the Cold War. (Controversial Issues in U. S. History). 176p. (gr. 12). 1975. pap. 2.95 (ISBN 0-671-18736-8). S&S.

Lankevich, George J. & Sokolsky, Wallace. The World & West: Readings in Contemporary History. 2nd ed. (Illus.). 1971. pap. text ed. 6.95 (ISBN 0-89529-152-5). Avery Pub.

McLellan, David S. Cold War in Transition. (Orig.). 1966. pap. text ed. 3.95x (ISBN 0-02-379400-3). Macmillan.

McNeill, William H. Contemporary World: Nineteen Fourteen to Present. (Illus.). 1968. 7.00 (ISBN 0-688-01358-9). Morrow.

Magill, Frank N., ed. Great Events from History, 3 vols. LC 72-86347. (Worldwide Twentieth Century Ser.: No. 4). 1685p. 1980. 95.00 (ISBN 0-89356-116-9). Salem Pr.

Mason, Henry L. Mass Demonstrations Against Foreign Regimes, Vol. 10. 1966. 5.00 (ISBN 0-930598-09-1). Tulane Stud Pol.

Material Progress & World-Wide Problems. (New Cambridge Modern History Ser: Vol. 11). 1962. 59.95 (ISBN 0-521-04549-5); pap. 14.95 (ISBN 0-521-29109-7). Cambridge U Pr.

Merrit, Jeffrey. Day by Day: The Fifties. (Day by Day Ser.). (Illus.). 1979. 65.00x (ISBN 0-87196-383-3). Facts on File.

Namier, Lewis B. Conflicts. LC 73-90667. (Essay Index Reprint Ser). 1942. 16.00 (ISBN 0-8369-1230-6). Arno.

Open University Staff. Understanding the Twentieth Century: A Course Guide. (New Viewpoints-Vision Bks.). 1980. pap. 10.95 (ISBN 0-531-06505-7, EE59). Watts.

Palmer, Alan. Facts on File Dictionary of Twentieth Century History. 403p. 1980. 22.50 (ISBN 0-686-60214-5). Facts on File.

--The Penguin Dictionary of Twentieth Century History: Nineteen Hundred to Nineteen Seventy-Eight. (Reference Ser.). 1979. pap. 4.95 (ISBN 0-14-051085-0). Penguin.

Quigley, Carroll. Tragedy & Hope. 1975. Repr. of 1966 ed. 25.00 (ISBN 0-913022-14-4). Angriff Pr.

Reed, Douglas. The Grand Design. 1977. pap. 2.00x (ISBN 0-911038-49-3). Noontide.

Rodine, Floyd H. Yalta-Responsibility & Response: January-March 1945. 156p. 1974. 6.00x (ISBN 0-87291-049-0). Coronado Pr.

Schneider, Gertrude. Journey into Terror. LC 79-57186. (Illus.). 256p. 1980. 12.95 (ISBN 0-935764-00-3). Ark Hse NY.

Snyder, Louis L. New Nationalism. LC 68-16391. (gr. 11-12). 1968. 25.00x (ISBN 0-8014-0401-0). Cornell U Pr.

--The World in the Twentieth Century. LC 79-10024. (Anvil Ser.). 192p. 1979. pap. 4.95 (ISBN 0-88275-909-4). Krieger.

Sobel, Lester A., ed. News Dictionary: 1973, Vol. 10. annual 500p. 1974. lib. bdg. 14.95 (ISBN 0-87196-097-4). Facts on File.

Spaull, Hebe. World Since Nineteen Forty-Five. 1960. 4.25 (ISBN 0-214-04820-9). Dufour.

Spender, Stephen. The Thirties & After. 1978. 10.00 (ISBN 0-394-50173-X). Random.

Strafford, John L. The Ten Most Momentous Years in the Twentieth Century & Their Significance for the Future of Humanity. (Illus.). 129p. 1980. deluxe ed. 59.85 (ISBN 0-930008-68-5). Inst Econ Pol.

Taylor, Edmond. Awakening from History. LC 69-15947. 1969. 8.95 (ISBN 0-87645-016-8). Gambit.

This Fabulous Century. Incl. Vol. 1. 1900-1910. 1969 (ISBN 0-8094-0121-5); Vol. 2. 1910-1920. 1969 (ISBN 0-8094-0122-3); Vol. 3. 1920-1930. 1969 (ISBN 0-8094-0123-1); Vol. 4. 1930-1940. 1969 (ISBN 0-8094-0124-X); Vol. 5. 1940-1950. 1969 (ISBN 0-8094-1205-5); Vol. 6. 1950-1960. 1970 (ISBN 0-8094-0125-8); Vol. 7. 1960-1970. 1970 (ISBN 0-8094-0126-6); Vol. 8. Prelude 1870-1900. 1970 (ISBN 0-8094-0127-4). (Illus.). 14.95 ea. Time-Life.

Time Editors. Live Them Again. 1953. 1.00 (ISBN 0-671-42700-8). S&S.

Tuchman, Barbara W. Proud Tower. 1966. 16.95 (ISBN 0-02-620300-6). Macmillan.

Urwin, Derek W. Western Europe Since Nineteen Forty-Five: A Short Political History. 1968. text ed. 15.25x (ISBN 0-582-48780-3). Humanities.

Weber, George G. Consummation of History. pap. 8.95 (ISBN 0-8010-9625-1). Baker Bk.

Wilcox, Elliot. The Failure of the Greatest 20th Century Conspiracy for the Economic & Political Restructuring of the World: The Unexpected, Incredible Developments Resulting from Such a Failure. (Illus.). 207p. 1976. 55.00 (ISBN 0-89266-003-1). Am Classical Coll Pr.

Wilson, Herbert W. Battleships in Action, 2 Vols. 1968. Repr. of 1926 ed. Set. 39.00 (ISBN 0-403-00046-7). Scholarly.

Wolf, Eric R. Peasant Wars of the Twentieth Century. 1970. pap. 5.95x (ISBN 0-06-131774-8, TB 1774, Torch). Har-Row.

Yeats, W. B. Nineteen One to Nineteen Eight, Vols. 1-7. Samhain, ed. 324p. 1970. Repr. 35.00x (ISBN 0-7146-2101-3, F Cass Co). Biblio Dist.

Young, Kenneth. Sir Alec Douglas-Home. LC 76-167748. (Illus.). 282p. 1971. 18.00 (ISBN 0-8386-1041-2). Fairleigh Dickinson.

HISTORY, NATURAL

see Natural History

HISTORY, NAVAL

see Naval History

HISTORY, PHILOSOPHY OF

see History–Philosophy

HISTORY, UNIVERSAL

see World History

HISTORY AND LITERATURE

see Literature and History

HISTORY AND SCIENCE

see Science and Civilization

HISTORY AND SEX

see Sex and History

HISTORY IN ART

Krenkel, Roy G. Cities & Scenes from the Ancient World. LC 74-77464. (Illus.). 82p. 1974. 16.00 (ISBN 0-913896-02-0). Owlswick Pr.

Pilgrim Society Collection. History As Art. Date not set. 1.00 (ISBN 0-686-30038-6). Pilgrim Hall.

The Religious & Historical Paintings of Jan Steen. (Illus.). 1977. 42.50 (ISBN 0-8390-0170-3). Allanheld & Schram.

Ziff, Norman D. Paul Delaroche: A Study in 19th Century French History Painting. LC 76-23663. (Outstanding Dissertations in the Fine Arts - 19th Century). (Illus.). 1977. Repr. of 1974 ed. lib. bdg. 56.00 (ISBN 0-8240-2741-8). Garland Pub.

HISTORY, MODERN-YEARBOOKS

see History–Yearbooks

HISTRIONICS

see Acting; Theater

HITCHCOCK, ALFRED JOSEPH, 1899-1980

Durgnat, Raymond. The Strange Case of Alfred Hitchcock, or the Plain Man's Hitchcock. LC 74-7239. 1974. pap. 8.95 (ISBN 0-262-54034-7). MIT Pr.

Haley, Michael. The Alfred Hitchcock Album. 1981. 9.95 (ISBN 0-13-021469-8); pap. 8.95 (ISBN 0-13-021451-5). P-H.

Lasky, Michael & Harris, Robert A. The Films of Alfred Hitchcock. (Illus.). 256p. (YA) 1976. 14.00 (ISBN 0-8065-0509-5). Citadel Pr.

Lasky, Michael S. & Harris, Robert A. The Films of Alfred Hitchcock. (Illus.). pap. 7.95 (ISBN 0-8065-0619-9). Citadel Pr.

Noble, Peter. Alfred Hitchcock. (Film Ser.). 1979. lib. bdg. 69.95 (ISBN 0-8490-2862-0). Gordon Pr.

Rohmer, Eric & Chabrol, Claude. Hitchcock: The First Forty-Four Films. Hochman, Stanley, tr. from Fr. LC 78-20932. (Ungar Film Library). (Illus.). 1979. 11.95 (ISBN 0-8044-2743-7); pap. 5.95 (ISBN 0-8044-6749-8). Ungar.

Spoto, Donald. The Art of Alfred Hitchcock. LC 79-7672. (Illus.). 1979. pap. 9.95 (ISBN 0-385-15569-7, Dolp). Doubleday.

Taylor, John R. Hitch: The Life & Times of Alfred Hitchcock. LC 78-53501. (Illus.). 1978. 10.00 (ISBN 0-394-49996-4). Pantheon.

Truffaut, Francois. Hitchcock. 1969. pap. 9.95 (ISBN 0-671-20346-0, Touchstone Bks). S&S.

Wood, Robin. Hitchcock's Films. 3rd rev. & enlarged ed. 12.00 (ISBN 0-498-01749-4). A S Barnes.

Yacowar, Maurice. Hitchcock's British Films. (Illus.). 1977. 17.50 (ISBN 0-208-01635-X, Archon). Shoe String.

HITCHHIKING

Calder, S. Hitch Hikers Manual: Britain. (Illus.). 144p. 1979. pap. 6.95 (ISBN 0-901205-68-0). Bradt Ent.

DiMaggio, Paul. Hitchhiker's Field Manual. LC 74-188016. (Illus.). 288p. 1974. pap. 1.95 (ISBN 0-02-097380-2). Macmillan.

Jewett, Dick. I'm Going to Hitchhike If It's the Last Thing I Do! (Nugget Ser.). 1977. pap. 0.65 (ISBN 0-8127-0147-X). Review & Herald.

Lobo, Ben & Links, Sara. Side of the Road: A Hitchhiker's Guide to the United States. LC 71-175046. 1972. pap. 1.95 (ISBN 0-671-21236-2, Fireside). S&S.

HITLER, ADOLF, 1889-1945

Abel, Theodore F. Why Hitler Came into Power. LC 78-63647. (Studies in Fascism: Ideology & Practice). Repr. of 1938 ed. 35.00 (ISBN 0-404-16897-3). AMS Pr.

Angebert, Jean-Michel. The Occult & the Third Reich: The Mystical Origins of Nazism & the Search for the Holy Grail. (McGraw-Hill Paperbacks Ser.). 336p. 1975. pap. 3.95 (ISBN 0-07-001850-2, SP). McGraw.

Barnes, James J. & Barnes, Patience P. Hitler's Mein Kampf in Britain & America: A Publishing History, 1930-39. LC 79-54014. 1980. pap. 18.95 (ISBN 0-521-22691-0). Cambridge U Pr.

Bayles, William D. Caesars in Goose Step. LC 68-2622. 1968. Repr. of 1940 ed. 12.50 (ISBN 0-8046-0021-X). Kennikat.

Binion, R. Hitler Among the Germans. 1976. 23.95 (ISBN 0-444-99033-X, Pub. by Elsevier). Greenwood.

Bullock, Alan. Hitler, a Study in Tyranny. abr. ed. 1971. pap. 2.95 (ISBN 0-06-080216-2, P216, PL). Har-Row.

--Hitler, a Study in Tyranny. rev. ed. (Illus.). (YA) 1964. 16.95x (ISBN 0-06-010580-1, HarpT). Har-Row.

--Hitler, a Study in Tyranny. rev. ed. (Illus.). pap. 8.95x (ISBN 0-06-131123-5, TB 1123, Torch). Har-Row.

Carr, William. Hitler: A Study in Personality & Politics. 1979. 18.50x (ISBN 0-312-38818-7). St Martin.

Churchill, Allen. Eyewitness: Hitler. 1979. 15.00 (ISBN 0-8027-0625-8). Walker & Co.

Cohen, Calvin L. The Hitler Myth: Hitler As the Stalking Horse for World Communism. 1980. lib. bdg. 49.50 (ISBN 0-686-59408-8). Revisionist Pr.

Deutsch, Harold C. Conspiracy Against Hitler in the Twilight War. LC 68-22365. 1968. 15.00x (ISBN 0-8166-0473-8); pap. 3.45 (ISBN 0-8166-0550-5). U of Minn Pr.

--Hitler & His Generals: The Hidden Crisis, January-June 1938. LC 73-86627. (Illus.). 1974. 19.50x (ISBN 0-8166-0649-8). U of Minn Pr.

Devaney, John. Hitler: Mad Dictator of World War II. LC 77-21057. (Illus.). (gr. 6-8). 1978. 8.95 (ISBN 0-399-20627-2). Putnam.

Devi, Savitrix. The Lightning & the Sun. (Illus.). 440p. (Orig.). 1960. pap. 12.00 (ISBN 0-911038-84-1, Samisdat). Noontide.

The Diary of Adolf Hitler. 225p. 1980. 14.95 (ISBN 0-9605224-1-7); pap. 8.88 (ISBN 0-9605224-0-9). Ancient Age.

Dolan, Edward F., Jr. Adolf Hitler: A Portrait in Tyranny. (Illus.). 240p. (gr. 7 up). 1981. PLB 8.95 (ISBN 0-396-07982-2). Dodd.

Fest, Joachim C. Hitler. 1975. pap. 6.95 (ISBN 0-394-72023-7, Vin). Random.

Forman, James. The White Crow. LC 76-62530. 240p. (gr. 7 up). 1976. 7.95 (ISBN 0-374-38386-3). FS&G.

Gilbert, Felix, ed. Hitler Directs His War. 1979. pap. 1.95 (ISBN 0-441-33841-0, Pub. by Charter Bks). Ace Bks.

Gisevius, Hans B. To the Bitter End. Winston, Richard & Winston, Clara, trs. from Ger. LC 74-29633. 632p. 1975. Repr. of 1947 ed. lib. bdg. 31.25x (ISBN 0-8371-7983-1, GIBE). Greenwood.

Goering, H. W. Political Testament of Hermann Goering. Blood-Ryan, H. W., tr. LC 71-180403. Repr. of 1939 ed. 21.00 (ISBN 0-404-56127-6). AMS Pr.

Gordon, Harold J., Jr. Hitler & the Beer Hall Putsch. LC 73-166383. 632p. 1972. 37.50x (ISBN 0-691-05189-5); pap. 11.95 (ISBN 0-691-00775-6). Princeton U Pr.

Gray, Ronald. Hitler & the Germans. LC 81-3913. (Cambridge Introduction to the History of Mankind). (Illus.). 32p. Date not set. pap. price not set (ISBN 0-521-22702-X). Cambridge U Pr.

Grierson, Herbert. Carlyle & Hitler. LC 73-18348. 1930. lib. bdg. 5.00 (ISBN 0-8414-4460-9). Folcroft.

Haffner, Sebastian. The Meaning of Hitler. Owers, Ewald, tr. LC 79-927. 1979. 10.95 (ISBN 0-02-547290-9). Macmillan.

Hart, W. E. Hitler's Generals. (Essay Index Reprint Ser.). Repr. of 1944 ed. 18.75 (ISBN 0-518-10165-7). Arno.

Heiden, Konrad. Hitler: A Biography. Ray, Winifred, tr. LC 79-18065. Repr. of 1936 ed. 24.50 (ISBN 0-404-56401-1). AMS Pr.

Heinz, A. Heinz. Germany's Hitler. 288p. Date not set. pap. 5.00 (ISBN 0-913022-36-5). Angriff Pr.

Heinz, Heinz A. Germany's Hitler. (Illus.). 1976. pap. 4.00x (ISBN 0-911038-46-9). Noontide.

Heston, Leonard L. & Heston, Renate. The Medical Casebook of Adolf Hitler: His Illnesses, Doctors & Drugs. (Illus.). 184p. 1980. 12.95 (ISBN 0-8128-2718-X). Stein & Day.

Hiden, John. Germany & Europe, 1919-1939. LC 77-3299. 1978. text ed. 15.00x (ISBN 0-582-48489-8); pap. text ed. 9.50x (ISBN 0-582-48490-1). Longman.

Hills, C. A. The Hitler File. (Leaders Ser.). (Illus.). 96p. (gr. 9-12). 1980. 14.95 (ISBN 0-7134-1919-9, Pub. by Batsford England). David & Charles.

Hitler, Adolf. The Speeches of Adolf Hitler. 1975. lib. bdg. 250.00 (ISBN 0-8490-1107-8). Gordon Pr.

--The Testament of Adolf Hitler. (Illus.). 1978. pap. 3.00x (ISBN 0-911038-44-2). Noontide.

Hitler, Adolph. Hitler's Secret Conversations, 1941-1944. lib. bdg. 37.50x (ISBN 0-374-93919-5). Octagon.

Hitler, Bridget. The Memoirs of Bridget Hitler. Unger, Michael, ed. (Illus.). 1979. 10.95 (ISBN 0-7156-1356-1, Pub. by Duckworth England). Biblio Dist.

Hoffman, Heinrich. Hitler Was My Friend. Stevens, R. H., tr. LC 78-63682. (Studies in Fascism: Ideology & Practice). Repr. of 1955 ed. 24.00 (ISBN 0-404-16947-3). AMS Pr.

Hoffmann, Peter. Hitler's Personal Security. 1979. 15.00 (ISBN 0-262-08099-0). MIT Pr.

Infield, Glenn B. Hitler's Secret Life. LC 79-65109. (Illus.). 1979. 12.95 (ISBN 0-8128-2674-4). Stein & Day.

Irving, David. Hitler's War. 1977. 17.50 (ISBN 0-670-37412-1). Viking Pr.

--The War Path: Hitler's Germany. 1978. 14.95 (ISBN 0-670-74971-0). Viking Pr.

Jackel, Eberhard. Hitler's World View: A Blueprint for Power. LC 80-84740. 144p. 1981. pap. text ed. 4.50x (ISBN 0-674-40425-4). Harvard U Pr.

Jenks, William A. Vienna & the Young Hitler. 252p. 1976. Repr. of 1960 ed. lib. bdg. 17.50x (ISBN 0-374-94206-4). Octagon.

Jetzinger, Franz. Hitler's Youth. Wilson, Lawrence, tr. from German. LC 75-36096. (Illus.). 1976. Repr. of 1958 ed. lib. bdg. 20.75x (ISBN 0-8371-8617-X, JEHY). Greenwood.

Klein, Mina C. & Klein, Arthur H. Hitler's Hang-Ups: An Adventure in Insight. (Illus.). (gr. 7 up). 1976. 9.95 (ISBN 0-525-32052-0). Dutton.

Koenigsberg, Richard A. Hitler's Ideology: A Study in Psychoanalytic Sociology. LC 74-84694. 105p. 1975. 10.00 (ISBN 0-915042-01-0). Lib Soc Sci.

Kubizek, August. The Young Hitler I Knew. Anderson, E. V., tr. LC 75-38385. (Illus.). 1976. Repr. of 1955 ed. lib. bdg. 22.75x (ISBN 0-8371-8664-1, KUYH). Greenwood.

Langer, Walter. Mind of Adolf Hitler. LC 72-86336. 1972. 15.00 (ISBN 0-465-04620-7). Basic.

--The Mind of Adolf Hitler. 1978. pap. 2.25 (ISBN 0-451-61640-5, ME1640, Ment). NAL.

Lewis, Wyndham. Hitler. LC 72-82189. 1972. Repr. of 1931 ed. lib. bdg. 75.00 (ISBN 0-87968-005-9). Gordon Pr.

--The Hitler Cult. LC 72-82187. 1972. Repr. of 1939 ed. lib. bdg. 75.00 (ISBN 0-87968-006-7). Gordon Pr.

--Hitler, the Germans & the Jews, 5 vols. 1522p. 1973. Set. 600.00 (ISBN 0-8490-0366-0). Gordon Pr.

Lichtenberger, Henri. Third Reich. Pinson, Koppel S., tr. LC 73-102249. (Select Bibliographies Reprint Ser). 1937. 29.00 (ISBN 0-8369-5134-4). Arno.

Ludecke, Kurt G. I Knew Hitler: The Story of a Nazi Who Escaped the Blood Purge. LC 78-63687. (Studies in Fascism: Ideology & Practice). Repr. of 1937 ed. 49.50 (ISBN 0-404-16904-X). AMS Pr.

Ludwig, Emil. Three Portraits: Hitler, Mussolini, Stalin. LC 78-63689. (Studies in Fascism: Ideology & Practice). Repr. of 1940 ed. 19.50 (ISBN 0-404-16905-8). AMS Pr.

McKale, Donald M. Hitler: The Survival Myth. LC 80-5405. (Illus.). 264p. 1980. 14.95 (ISBN 0-8128-2724-4). Stein & Day.

McSherry, James E. Stalin, Hitler & Europe. 2 vols. Incl. Origins of World War Two, 1933-1939. Vol. 1. 25.00x (ISBN 0-912162-03-1); Imbalance of Power, 1939-1941. (Illus.). Vol. 2. 28.00x (ISBN 0-912162-04-X). LC 72-79473. 1968-70. Open Door.

Manvell, Roger & Fraenkel, Heinrich. The Hundred Days to Hitler. LC 73-89867. 240p. 1974. 8.95 (ISBN 0-312-40040-3). St Martin.

Mason, Herbert M., Jr. To Kill the Devil: The Attempts on the Life of Adolph Hitler. (Illus.). 1978. 9.95 (ISBN 0-393-05682-1). Norton.

Neilson, Francis. Hitler: The Making of a Tyrant. (Revisionist Historiography Ser.). 1979. lib. bdg. 39.95 (ISBN 0-685-96626-7). Revisionist Pr.

Nicholls, A. J. Weimar & the Rise of Hitler. Thorne, Christopher, ed. LC 68-29506. (Making of the Twentieth Century Ser). (Illus., Orig.). 1969. pap. 5.95 (ISBN 0-312-86065-X, W15701). St Martin.

Nicolas, M. P. From Nietzsche Down to Hitler. LC 70-102579. 1970. Repr. of 1938 ed. 12.50 (ISBN 0-8046-0739-7). Kennikat.

Nobecourt, Jacques. Hitler's Last Gamble. 1980. pap. 2.25 (ISBN 0-505-51474-5). Tower Bks.

O'Donnell, James P. The Bunker. (Illus.). 1979. pap. 2.75 (ISBN 0-553-13248-2). Bantam.

--The Bunker. (Illus.). 1978. 13.95 (ISBN 0-395-25719-0). HM.

Olden, Rudolf. Hitler, the Pawn. LC 78-63702. (Studies in Fascism: Ideology & Practice). Repr. of 1936 ed. 34.50 (ISBN 0-404-16974-0). AMS Pr.

Pauley, Bruce F. Hitler & the Forgotten Nazis. LC 80-17006. 294p. 1981. 19.00 (ISBN 0-8078-1456-3). U of NC Pr.

Payne, Robert. The Life & Death of Adolf Hitler. (Illus.). 1974. pap. 2.95 (ISBN 0-445-08254-2). Popular Lib.

Pearson, Eileen. Hitler's Reich. Yapp, Malcolm & Killingray, Margaret, eds. (World History Ser.). (Illus.). (gr. 10). 1980. Repr. of 1977 ed. lib. bdg. 5.95 (ISBN 0-89908-208-4); pap. text ed. 1.95 (ISBN 0-89908-233-5). Greenhaven.

People's Court, Munich & Hitler, Adolph. Hitler Trial: Before the People's Court in Munich. Freniere, H. Francis, et al, trs. 1976. 130.00 (ISBN 0-89093-050-3). U Pubns Amer.

Phillips, Leona. Hitler: An Annotated Bibliography. 1976. lib. bdg. 69.95 (ISBN 0-8490-1355-0). Gordon Pr.

Pool, James & Pool, Suzanne. Who Financed Hitler? The Secret Funding of Hitler's Rise to Power, 1919-1933. (Illus.). 1979. pap. 7.95 (ISBN 0-8037-8941-6). Dial.

--Who Financed Hitler? The Secret Funding of Hitler's Rise to Power 1919-1933. (Illus.). 1978. 10.95 (ISBN 0-8037-9039-2). Dial.

Price, G. Ward. I Know These Dictators. LC 75-112817. 1970. Repr. of 1937 ed. 12.00 (ISBN 0-8046-1084-3). Kennikat.

Ray, John. Hitler & Mussolini. 1970. pap. text ed. 3.95x (ISBN 0-435-31755-5). Heinemann Ed.

Rich, Norman. Hitler's War Aims: Ideology, the Nazi State, & the Course of Expansion. (Illus., Orig.). 1973. Vol. 1. 12.95x (ISBN 0-393-05454-3). Norton.

--Hitler's War Aims: Ideology, the Nazi State, & the Course of Expansion. 400p. 1976. pap. 7.95 (ISBN 0-393-00802-9, Norton Lib). Norton.

--Hitler's War Aims: The Establishment of the New Order. (Illus.). 548p. 1974. Vol. 2. 14.95x (ISBN 0-393-05509-4). Norton.

Roberts, Stephen. The House That Hitler Built. 75.00 (ISBN 0-87968-338-4). Gordon Pr.

Shirer, William L. Rise & Fall of Adolf Hitler. (World Landmark Ser). (gr. 7-11). 1963. PLB 5.99 (ISBN 0-394-90547-4). Random.

Skipper, G. C. Death of Hitler. (World at War Ser.). (Illus.). 48p. (gr. 3-8). 1980. PLB 8.65 (ISBN 0-516-04783-3); pap. 2.95 (ISBN 0-516-44783-1). Childrens.

Smith, Bradley F. Adolf Hitler: His Family, Childhood, & Youth. LC 66-25727. (Publications Ser.: No. 62). 1967. pap. 6.95 (ISBN 0-8179-1622-9). Hoover Inst Pr.

Snyder, Louis L., ed. Hitler's Third Reich: A Documentary History. LC 81-9512. 640p. 1981. text ed. 33.95x (ISBN 0-88229-705-8); pap. text ed. 16.95x (ISBN 0-88229-793-7). Nelson-Hall.

Speer, Albert. Inside the Third Reich: Memoirs of Albert Speer. (Illus.). 1970. 24.95 (ISBN 0-02-612820-9). Macmillan.

Stachura, Peter D. The Weimar Era & Hitler: A Critical Bibliography, 1918 to 1933. 276p. 1977. text ed. 57.50 (ISBN 0-903450-08-9). ABC-Clio.

Staudinger, Hans. The Inner Nazi: A Critical Analysis of Mein Kampe. Rutkoff, Peter M. & Scott, William B., eds. LC 81-7277. 152p. 1981. text ed. 14.95x (ISBN 0-8071-0882-0). La State U Pr.

Stern, J. P. Hitler: The Fuhrer & the People. (Orig.). 1975. pap. 2.95 (ISBN 0-520-02952-6). U of Cal Pr.

Stone, Norman. Hitler. 1980. 12.50 (ISBN 0-316-81757-0). Little.

Strasser, Otto. Hitler & I. David, Gwenda & Mosbacher, Eric, trs. LC 78-63724. (Studies in Fascism: Ideology & Practice). Repr. of 1940 ed. 24.50 (ISBN 0-404-16997-X). AMS Pr.

Strawson, John. Hitler As Military Commander. (Illus.). 1973. pap. 3.95 (ISBN 0-7221-8209-0). Beachcomber Bks.

Suster, Gerald. Hitler: The Occult Messiah. (Illus.). 272p. 1981. 10.95 (ISBN 0-312-38821-7). St Martin.

Tames, R. Hitler. (Clarendon Biography Ser.). (Illus.). pap. 3.50 (ISBN 0-912728-66-3). Newbury Bks.

Thyssen, Fritz. I Paid Hitler. LC 71-153243. 1971. Repr. of 1941 ed. 14.00 (ISBN 0-8046-1553-5). Kennikat.

Toland, John. Adolf Hitler. 1056p. 1981. pap. 9.95 (ISBN 0-345-29470-X). Ballantine.

--Adolf Hitler. LC 74-25126. 960p. 1976. 14.95 (ISBN 0-385-03724-4). Doubleday.

--Hitler: The Pictorial Documentary of His Life. LC 77-76145. 1978. 14.95 (ISBN 0-385-04546-8). Doubleday.

Trevor-Roper, H. R. The Last Days of Hitler. 1979. Repr. of 1947 ed. lib. bdg. 35.00 (ISBN 0-8495-5146-3). Arden Lib.

Trevor-Roper, Hugh R. Last Days of Hitler. 3rd ed. 1962. pap. 2.95 (ISBN 0-02-038000-3, Collier). Macmillan.

Van Creveld, Martin L. Hitler's Strategy 1940-1941: The Balkan Clue. LC 72-97885. (International Studies). (Illus.). 272p. 1973. 27.50 (ISBN 0-521-20143-8). Cambridge U Pr.

Von Reuter, Florizel. The Master from Afar. 1972. 9.50 (ISBN 0-910476-04-7). Cultural Pr.

Waite, R. Hitler & Nazi Germany. LC 65-19350. 1969. pap. text ed. 8.95 (ISBN 0-03-082797-3, HoltC). HR&W.

Waite, Robert. The Psychopathic God: Adolf Hitler. (Illus.). 1978. pap. 2.95 (ISBN 0-451-08078-5, E8078, Sig). NAL.

Waite, Robert G. Psychopathic God: Adolf Hitler. LC 76-43484. (Illus.). 1977. 13.50 (ISBN 0-465-06743-3). Basic.

Waldman, M. D. Sieg Heil: The Story of Adolf Hitler. LC 62-11854. 1962. 10.00 (ISBN 0-379-00132-2). Oceana.

Weingartner, Thomas. Stalin und der Aufstieg Hitlers: Die Deutschlandpolitik der Kommunistischen Internationale, 1929-1934. (Beitrage zur auswaertigen und international Politik, No. 4). (Ger). 1970. 23.55x (ISBN 3-11-002702-X). De Gruyter.

Wighton, Charles & Peis, Gunter. Hitler's Spies & Saboteurs. 288p. 1979. pap. 1.95 (ISBN 0-441-33845-3, Pub. by Charter Bks). Ace Bks.

Wolfe, Burton H. Hitler & the Nazis. (gr. 7 up). 1970. PLB 5.49 (ISBN 0-399-60261-5). Putnam.

HITLER, ADOLF, 1889-1945–PORTRAITS, CARICATURES, ETC.

Colbert, R. W. & Hyder, William D., eds. Medallic Portraits of Adolf Hitler. (Illus.). 160p. Date not set. 11.00 (ISBN 0-686-73077-1). TAMS.

Hoffmann, Heinrich. Adolf Hitler: Faces of a Dictator. LC 68-24392. 1969. 9.50 (ISBN 0-15-103551-2). HarBraceJ.

HITTI, PHILIP KHURI, 1886-

Kritzeck, James, ed. The World of Islam. LC 79-52558. (Islam Ser.). (Illus.). 1980. Repr. of 1959 ed. lib. bdg. 32.00x (ISBN 0-8369-9265-2). Arno.

HITTITE ART

see Art, Hittite

HITTITE LANGUAGE

Hoffner, Harry A., Jr. An English-Hittite Glossary. 1967. 10.50x (ISBN 0-8002-1398-X). Intl Pubns Serv.

Hoffner, Harry A., Jr. & Guterbock, Hans G., eds. The Hittite Dictionary of the Oriental Institute of the University of Chicago, Vol. 3, Fasc. 1, L. LC 79-53554. 1980. pap. 9.00x (ISBN 0-918986-27-3). Oriental Inst.

Sturtevant, E. H. Hittite Glossary. (Language Monographs: No. 9). 1931. pap. 6.00 (ISBN 0-527-00813-3). Kraus Repr.

Sturtevant, Edgar H. & Hahn, E. A. Comparative Grammar of the Hittite Language. 1951. 45.00x (ISBN 0-686-51357-6). Elliots Bks.

HITTITE LAW

see Law, Hittite

HITTITE MYTHOLOGY

see Mythology, Hittite

HITTITES

Ceram, C. W. Secret of the Hittites. (Illus.). (YA) 1956. 12.50 (ISBN 0-394-44428-0). Knopf.

--The Secret of the Hittites: The Discovery of an Ancient Empire. (Illus.). 362p. 1973. pap. 4.95 (ISBN 0-8052-0397-4). Schocken.

Garstang, John. The Hittite Empire. 1976. lib. bdg. 59.95 (ISBN 0-8490-2014-X). Gordon Pr.

Goetze, Albrecht. Kizzuwatna & the Problem of Hittite Geography. LC 78-63566. (Yale Oriental Ser. Researches: 22). Repr. of 1940 ed. 22.50 (ISBN 0-404-60322-X). AMS Pr.

Gurney, Oliver R. Some Aspects of Hittite Religion. (British Academy - Schweich Lectures). (Illus.). 94p. 1977. text ed. 24.95x (ISBN 0-19-725974-X). Oxford U Pr.

Hempl, George. Mediterranean Studies, 3 pts. in 1 vol. Anderson, Frederick, ed. Incl. Pt. 1, Vol. 1. The Genesis of European Alphabetic Writing; Pt. 1, Vol. 2. Minoan Seals; Pt. 2, Vol. 3. Three Papers on the History & Language of the Hittites; Pt. 3, Vol. 4. Etruscan; Pt. 3, Vol. 5. Venetic. LC 31-33039. Repr. of 1930 ed. 42.50 (ISBN 0-404-51809-5). AMS Pr.

Hicks, James. The Empire Builders. (The Emergence of Man Ser.). (Illus.). 1974. 9.95 (ISBN 0-8094-1320-5); lib. bdg. avail. (ISBN 0-685-48126-3). Time-Life.

Lehmann, Johannes. The Hittites: People of a Thousand Gods. Brownjohn, J. Maxwell, tr. LC 76-49524. 1977. 11.95 (ISBN 0-670-37415-6). Viking Pr.

Osten, Hans Von Der. Explorations in Hittite Asia Minor. LC 69-14025. (Illus.). 1971. Repr. of 1929 ed. lib. bdg. 43.75x (ISBN 0-8371-3880-9, OSEX). Greenwood.

Von Der Osten, Hans H. Discoveries in Anatolia, 1930-31. LC 33-13172. (Oriental Institute Pubns. Ser). (Illus.). 1933. pap. 11.50x (ISBN 0-226-62330-0, OIC14). U of Chicago Pr.

--Explorations in Hittite Asia Minor, Nineteen Twenty-Nine. LC 28-3839. (Oriental Institute Pubns. Ser). (Illus.). 1930. pap. 12.00x (ISBN 0-226-62324-6, OIC8). U of Chicago Pr.

HIWASSEE ISLAND

Lewis, Thomas M. & Kneberg, Madeline. Hiwassee Island: An Archaeological Account of Four Tennessee Indian Peoples. LC 75-130688. (Illus.). 338p. 1970. 15.50 (ISBN 0-87049-123-7). U of Tenn Pr.

HIZB AL-BA'TH AL-ARABI AL ISHTIRAKI

Abu Jaber, Kamel S. Arab Ba'th Socialist Party History, Ideology, & Organization. LC 66-25181. 1966. 11.95x (ISBN 0-8156-0051-8). Syracuse U Pr.

Rabinovitch, Itamar. Syria Under the Ba'th, 1963-1966: Army-Party Symbiosis. 1972. casebound 15.95 (ISBN 0-87855-163-8). Transaction Bks.

HIZB AL-SURI AS-QUAWNI AL IJTIMA'I, AL-

Zuwiyya-Yamak, Labib. Syrian Social Nationalist Party: An Ideological Analysis. LC 66-24812. (Middle Eastern Monographs Ser: No. 14). (Illus.). 1966. pap. 4.50x (ISBN 0-674-86236-8). Harvard U Pr.

HO, CHI MINH, PRES. DEMOCRATIC REPUBLIC OF VIETNAM, 1894-1969

Archer, Jules. Ho Chi Minh: Legend of Hanoi. LC 79-151161. (gr. 7-12). 1971. 7.95 (ISBN 0-02-705630-9, CCPr). Macmillan.

Huyen, N. Khac. Vision Accomplished: The Enigma of Ho Chi Minh. 1971. pap. 2.95 (ISBN 0-02-073590-1, Collier). Macmillan.

HOARE, JOHN, d. 1966

Naydler, Merton. The Penance Way. LC 69-13305. (Illus.). 1969. 5.95 (ISBN 0-688-02282-0). Morrow.

HOAXES

see Impostors and Imposture

HOBBES, THOMAS, 1588-1679

Balz, Albert G. Idea & Essence in the Philosophies of Hobbes & Spinoza. LC 70-161737. Repr. of 1918 ed. 17.00 (ISBN 0-404-00489-X). AMS Pr.

Bowle, John. Hobbes & His Critics: A Study in Seventeenth Century Constitutionalism. 1969. Repr. of 1951 ed. 26.00x (ISBN 0-7146-1548-X, F Cass Co). Biblio Dist.

Bramhall, John. Castigations of Mr. Hobbes. Wellek, Rene, ed. LC 75-11199. (British Philosophers & Theologians of the 17th & 18th Centuries: Vol. 6). 1976. Repr. of 1658 ed. lib. bdg. 42.00 (ISBN 0-8240-1755-2). Garland Pub.

--A Defence of True Liberty from Ante-Cedent & Extrinsical Necessity. an Answer to Hobbes' a Treatise of Liberty & Necessity. Wellek, Rene, ed. LC 75-11200. (British Philosophers & Theologians of the 17th & 18th Centuries: Vol. 7). 1976. Repr. of 1655 ed. lib. bdg. 42.00 (ISBN 0-8240-1756-0). Garland Pub.

Coleman, Frank M. Hobbes & America: Exploring the Constitutional Foundations. LC 76-46434. 1977. 17.50 (ISBN 0-8020-5359-9); pap. 6.50 (ISBN 0-8020-6374-8). U of Toronto Pr.

D'Israeli, Isaac. Quarrels of Authors: Or Some Memoirs for Our Literary History, 3 vols. 1814. Set. 54.00 (ISBN 0-384-11870-4). Johnson Repr.

Eisenach, Eldon J. Two Worlds of Liberalism: Religion & Politics in Hobbes, Locke, & Mill. LC 80-27255. (Chicago Original Paperback Ser.). 272p. 1981. lib. bdg. 20.00x (ISBN 0-226-19533-3). U of Chicago Pr.

Gauthier, David P. Logic of Leviathan: The Moral & Political Theory of Thomas Hobbes. 1969. pap. 11.50x (ISBN 0-19-824616-1). Oxford U Pr.

Goldsmith, M. M. Hobbes's Science of Politics. LC 66-18860. 1966. 17.50x (ISBN 0-231-02803-2); pap. 7.00x (ISBN 0-231-02804-0). Columbia U Pr.

Gooch, G. P. Hobbes. LC 77-5390. 1939. lib. bdg. 5.50 (ISBN 0-8414-4429-3). Folcroft.

Hinnant, Charles H. Thomas Hobbes. (English Authors Ser.: No. 215). 1977. lib. bdg. 9.95 (ISBN 0-8057-6684-7). Twayne.

--Thomas Hobbes: A Reference Guide. (Scholarly Reference Publications). 1980. lib. bdg. 25.00 (ISBN 0-8161-8173-X). G K Hall.

Hobbes, Thomas. Man & Citizen. Gert, Bernard, ed. 8.50 (ISBN 0-8446-4756-X). Peter Smith.

--Thomas White's De Mundo Examined in First English Translation. Jones, H. W., tr. from Lat. (Illus., Eng.). 1976. 39.95x (ISBN 0-8464-0923-2). Beekman Pubs.

James, D. G. The Life of Reason (Hobbes, Locke, Bolingbroke) 1978. Repr. of 1949 ed. lib. bdg. 27.50 (ISBN 0-89760-401-6, Telegraph). Dynamic Learn Corp.

James, David G. Life of Reason: Hobbes, Locke, Bolingbroke. facsimile ed. LC 76-38378. (Biography Index Reprint Ser. - English Augustans: Vol. 1). Repr. of 1949 ed. 17.75 (ISBN 0-8369-8122-7). Arno.

Kang, Sugwon. Monarch Notes on Locke's & Hobbes' Philosophy. (Orig.). pap. 2.25 (ISBN 0-671-00531-6). Monarch Pr.

Laird, John. Hobbes. LC 68-25065. 1968. Repr. of 1934 ed. 17.00 (ISBN 0-8462-1238-2). Russell.

Lemos, Ramon M. Hobbes & Locke: Power & Consent. LC 77-7482. 190p. 1978. 13.50x (ISBN 0-8203-0428-X). U of Ga Pr.

Mace, George. Locke, Hobbes, & the Federalist Papers: An Essay on the Genesis of the American Political Heritage. LC 78-22091. 176p. 1979. 12.50x (ISBN 0-8093-0890-8). S Ill U Pr.

McNeilly, F. A. The Anatomy of Leviathan: A Critical Study of Hobbes's Arguments. 1968. 16.95x (ISBN 0-8464-0133-9). Beekman Pubs.

McNeilly, F. S. Anatomy of Leviathan. LC 68-12304. 1969. 16.95 (ISBN 0-312-03430-X). St Martin.

Macpherson, Crawford B. Political Theory of Possessive Individualism: Hobbes to Locke. (Oxford Paperbacks Ser). 1962. pap. 5.95x (ISBN 0-19-881084-9). Oxford U Pr.

Mintz, Samuel I. Hunting of Leviathan. 1962. 35.50 (ISBN 0-521-05736-1). Cambridge U Pr.

Peters, Richard S. Hobbes. LC 78-26703. 1979. Repr. of 1956 ed. lib. bdg. 20.25x (ISBN 0-313-20799-2, PEHO). Greenwood.

Raphael, D. D. Hobbes. (Political Thinkers Ser.). 1977. text ed. 17.95x (ISBN 0-04-320118-0); pap. text ed. 8.95x (ISBN 0-04-320119-9). Allen Unwin.

Rick, Miriam. The Golden Lands of Thomas Hobbes. LC 77-3594. 1977. text ed. 15.95x (ISBN 0-8143-1574-7). Wayne St U Pr.

Rickaby, Joseph J. Free Will & Four English Philosophers. facs. ed. LC 74-84333. (Essay Index Reprint Ser). 1906. 15.50 (ISBN 0-8369-1103-2). Arno.

Robertson, George C. Hobbes. 1910. Repr. 7.00 (ISBN 0-403-00251-6). Scholarly.

--Hobbes. LC 70-137283. Repr. of 1886 ed. 7.50 (ISBN 0-404-05359-9). AMS Pr.

--Hobbes. LC 70-137283. Repr. of 1886 ed. 7.50 (ISBN 0-404-05359-9). AMS Pr.

Ross, Ralph, et al, eds. Thomas Hobbes in His Time. LC 74-83134. 170p. 1975. 10.00x (ISBN 0-8166-0727-3). U of Minn Pr.

Spragens, Thomas A., Jr. The Politics of Motion: The World of Thomas Hobbes. LC 72-81318. 224p. 1973. 12.00x (ISBN 0-8131-1278-8). U Pr of Ky.

Strauss, Leo. Political Philosophy of Hobbes: Its Basis & Its Genesis. Sinclair, Elsa M., tr. 1963. pap. 3.45 (ISBN 0-226-77696-4, P112, Phoen). U of Chicago Pr.

Taylor, Alfred E. Thomas Hobbes. LC 76-102586. 1970. Repr. of 1908 ed. 10.00 (ISBN 0-8046-0746-X). Kennikat.

Thorpe, Clarence D. Mind of John Keats. LC 64-18603. 1964. Repr. of 1926 ed. 18.00 (ISBN 0-8462-0489-4). Russell.

Von Leyden, W. Hobbes & Locke: The Politics of Freedom & Obligation. 272p. 1981. 22.50x (ISBN 0-312-38824-1). St Martin.

HOBBIES

see also Home Workshops; Music As Recreation

Ambrose, Mike & Walker, Nora S. Captain Mike's Complete Guide to Grunion Hunting. LC 81-1834. (Illus.). 93p. (Orig.). 1981. pap. 3.95 (ISBN 0-916392-70-8). Oak Tree Pubns.

Amidon, Eva V. Easy Quillery: Projects with Paper Coils & Scrolls. (Illus.). (gr. 3-8). 1977. 7.25 (ISBN 0-688-22130-0); PLB 6.96 (ISBN 0-688-32130-5). Morrow.

Armstrong, John. Creative Layout Design. Schafer, Mike, ed. LC 78-71457. 1978. pap. 11.95 (ISBN 0-89024-538-X). Kalmbach.

Beckett, James & Eckes, Dennis W. The Sport Americana Baseball Card Price Guide, No.2. (Illus.). 320p. 1980. 9.95 (ISBN 0-529-05786-7); pap. 7.95 (ISBN 0-529-05785-9). Collins Pubs.

Bender, George A. & Parascandola, John, eds. Historical Hobbies for the Pharmacist. 2nd ed. (Publications Ser.: No. 2). (Illus.). iv, 57p. 1980. pap. 4.00 (ISBN 0-931292-10-7). Am Inst Pharmacy.

Brown, Robert M. & Olsen, Mark. Sixty-Four Hobby Projects for Home & Car. LC 69-14557. (Orig.). 1969. 7.95 (ISBN 0-8306-9487-0). TAB Bks.

Cleaver, Nancy. A Yearround Guide to Family Fun: Games, Crafts, Hobbies & Projects for All Ages. (Illus.). 192p. 1975. 7.95 (ISBN 0-919364-72-1, ADON3524). Pagurian.

Cox, Jack R. Gemcutter's Handbook: Cabochon Cutting. pap. 2.00 (ISBN 0-910652-12-0). Gembooks.

Davis, William. The Best of Everything. 224p. 1981. 9.95 (ISBN 0-312-07713-0). St Martin.

Doering, Henry, ed. The World Almanac Book of Buffs, Masters, Mavens & Uncommon Experts. LC 80-81179. 352p. (Orig.). 1980. pap. 6.95 (ISBN 0-911818-13-8). World Almanac.

Encyclopedie du Bricolage et des Loisirs Manuels, 1, 6 vols. 195p. (Fr.). 1976. 225.00 (ISBN 0-686-56772-2, M-6206). French & Eur.

Estrin, Michael. Treasury of Hobbies & Crafts. pap. 2.00 (ISBN 0-686-00715-8). Key Bks.

Freeman, Larry. Southern Tier Yesterdays: New York & Upstate Cinderella. 1972. pap. 3.50 (ISBN 0-87282-054-8). Century Hse.

Hobbie, Holly. Holly Hobbie's Activity Book. LC 77-81923. (Busybacks Ser.). (Illus.). (gr. k-2). 1977. pap. 1.95 (ISBN 0-448-48001-8). Platt.

Housebook. Hobbies. (Illus.). 1980. 9.95 (ISBN 0-8246-0238-2). Jonathan David.

Lewis, Shari. The Do-It-Better Book. LC 79-3839. (Kids-Only Club Bks.). (Illus.). 96p. (Orig.). (gr. 3-6). 1981. 6.95 (ISBN 0-03-049721-3); pap. 3.95 (ISBN 0-03-049726-4). HR&W.

--Things Kids Collect. LC 79-3838. (Kids-Only Club Bks.). (Illus.). 96p. (Orig.). (gr. 3-6). 1981. 6.95 (ISBN 0-03-049731-0); pap. 3.95 (ISBN 0-03-049736-1). HR&W.

MacDonald, Craig. At Your Leisure. 1980. pap. 4.95 (ISBN 0-89293-012-8). Beta Bk.

Nestrick, William V. Constructional Activities of Adult Males. LC 76-177115. (Columbia University. Teachers College. Contributions to Education: No. 780). Repr. of 1939 ed. 17.50 (ISBN 0-404-55780-5). AMS Pr.

Quinby, E. J. Wilkes-Barre & Hazelton RY. LC 72-87786. 1972. pap. 3.95 (ISBN 0-911868-01-1). Carstens Pubns.

Regensteiner, Else. Art of Weaving. (Illus.). 1970. 15.95 (ISBN 0-442-11442-7); pap. 8.95 (ISBN 0-442-26872-6). Van Nos Reinhold.

Smaridge, Norah. Choosing Your Retirement Hobby. 160p. 1976. 5.95 (ISBN 0-396-07205-4). Dodd.

Smaridge, Norah & Hunter, Hilda. The Teen-Ager's Guide to Hobbies for Here & Now. LC 74-6798. (Illus.). 224p. (gr. 7 up). 1974. 5.95 (ISBN 0-396-06994-0). Dodd.

Wagenvoord, James. Oak Alley, 4 vols. (Illus.). 160p. 1981. 166.80 (ISBN 0-312-58050-9). St Martin.

HOBBIES–BIBLIOGRAPHY

Brown, Robert. CBer's Handybook of Simple Hobby Projects. LC 76-16465. 1976. 6.95 (ISBN 0-8306-6868-3); pap. 3.95 (ISBN 0-8306-5868-8, 868). TAB Bks.

HOBBY ROOMS

see Recreation Rooms

HOBHOUSE, LEONARD TRELAWNEY, 1864-1929

Carter, Hugh. Social Theories of L. T. Hobhouse. LC 67-27609. 1927. Repr. 10.00 (ISBN 0-8046-0070-8). Kennikat.

Collini, Stefan. Liberalism & Sociology: Lt. Hobhouse & Political Argument in English 1880-1914. LC 78-23779. 1979. 32.95 (ISBN 0-521-22304-0). Cambridge U Pr.

Owen, John E. L. T. Hobhouse, Sociologist. LC 74-18457. 1975. 11.00 (ISBN 0-8142-0235-7). Ohio St U Pr.

HOBOES

see Tramps

HOBSON, JOHN ATKINSON, 1858-1940

Allett, John. New Liberalism: The Political Economy of J.A. Hobson. 268p. 1981. 25.00x (ISBN 0-8020-5558-3). U of Toronto Pr.

Homan, Paul T. Contemporary Economic Thought. facs. ed. LC 68-20310. (Essay Index Reprint Ser). 1928. 19.50 (ISBN 0-8369-0546-6). Arno.

Nemmers, Erwin E. Hobson & Underconsumption. LC 73-186784. Repr. of 1956 ed. 12.50x (ISBN 0-678-00672-5). Kelley.

HOBSON, RICHMOND PEARSON, 1870-1937

Brown, W. G. Lower South in American History. LC 68-24973. (American History & Americana Ser., No. 47). 1969. Repr. of 1902 ed. lib. bdg. 33.95 (ISBN 0-8383-0919-4). Haskell.

Brown, William G. Lower South in American History. LC 71-108464. 1970. Repr. of 1902 ed. 19.00 (ISBN 0-403-00446-2). Scholarly.

Disraeli, Benjamin. Lothair. LC 78-115230. 1971. Repr. 14.00x (ISBN 0-403-00458-6). Scholarly.

Pittman, Walter E., Jr. Navalist & Progressive: The Life of Richmond P. Hobson. 1981. pap. 25.00 (ISBN 0-89126-100-1). MA-AH Pub.

HOBSON, RICHMOND PEARSON, 1870-1937–FICTION

Brown, William G. Lower South in American History. LC 69-13843. Repr. of 1902 ed. lib. bdg. 15.00x (ISBN 0-8371-0925-6, BRO&). Greenwood.

HOCHHEIMER (WINE)

see Hock (Wine)

HOCHHUTH, ROLF, 1931-

Taeni, Rainer. Rolf Hochhuth. (Modern German Authors: No. 5). 1977. text ed. 9.25x (ISBN 0-85496-057-0). Humanities.

Thompson, Carlos. The Assassination of Winston Churchill. 1978. text ed. cancelled (ISBN 0-901072-01-X). Humanities.

Ward, Margaret E. Rolf Hochhuth. (World Authors Ser.: No. 463). 1977. lib. bdg. 11.95 (ISBN 0-8057-6300-7). Twayne.

HOCK (WINE)

Simon, Andre L. All About Hock. (All About Wines: Vol. 4). 5.00 (ISBN 0-87559-180-9). Shalom.

HOCKEY

see also Field Hockey

Basic Hockey Strategy. LC 75-32550. (Illus.). 144p. (gr. 6-9). 1976. 5.95a (ISBN 0-385-04891-2); PLB (ISBN 0-385-04951-X). Doubleday.

Brown, Harry. Ice Hockey Skating. (Illus.). (gr. 6-8). 5.95 (ISBN 0-513-01230-3); pap. 3.95 (ISBN 0-513-01228-1). Denison.

Clarke, Trevor. Hockey, Teaching & Playing. 96p. 1980. 9.00x (ISBN 0-86019-020-X, Pub. by Kimpton). State Mutual Bk.

The Complete Book of Soccer - Hockey: New York Times Scrapbook History. 1981. 14.95 (ISBN 0-672-52642-5). Bobbs.

Coombs, Charles. Be a Winner in Ice Hockey. LC 73-10769. (Illus.). 128p. (gr. 5-9). 1974. PLB 6.50 (ISBN 0-688-30099-5); pap. 2.45 (ISBN 0-688-25099-8). Morrow.

Cutler, Mickey. Hockey Masks, & the Great Goalies Who Wear Them. (Illus.). 32p. 1977. pap. 3.95 (ISBN 0-88776-101-1). Tundra Bks.

Deegan, Paul J. Stickhandling & Passing. LC 76-8444. (Sports Instruction Ser.). (Illus.). (gr. 3-9). 1976. PLB 5.95 (ISBN 0-87191-520-0); pap. 2.95 (ISBN 0-686-67437-5). Creative Ed.

Eskenazi, Gerald, et al. Miracle on Ice. 89p. 1980. pap. 2.50 (ISBN 0-553-14034-5). Bantam.

Esposito, Phil & Dew, Dick. Winning Hockey: For Beginners. LC 76-11204. (Winning Ser.). (Illus.). 1976. pap. 5.95 (ISBN 0-8092-8048-5). Contemp Bks.

Esposito, Phil, et al. We Can Teach You to Play Hockey. 1977. 2.95 (ISBN 0-346-12303-8). Cornerstone.

Etter, Les. The Game of Hockey. LC 77-4720. (Sports Ser.). (Illus.). (gr. 3-6). 1977. PLB 6.48 (ISBN 0-8116-6682-4). Garrard.

Fischler, Stan & Fischler, Shirley. Fischlers' Ice Hockey Encyclopedia. LC 79-7640. (Illus.). 1980. pap. 8.95 (ISBN 0-690-01856-8). T Y Crowell.

Fischler, Stan. Heroes of Pro Hockey. (Pro Hockey Library: No. 2). (Illus.). (gr. 5-9). 1971. PLB 3.69 (ISBN 0-394-92146-1, BYR). Random.

--Hockey's Great Rivalries. LC 74-4930. (Pro Hockey Library). (Illus.). 160p. (gr. 5 up). 1974. PLB 3.69 (ISBN 0-394-92830-X, BYR). Random.

--Kings of the Rink. LC 78-7727. (Illus.). (gr. 5 up). 1978. 6.50 (ISBN 0-396-07609-2). Dodd.

--Those Were the Days. LC 75-28233. (Illus.). 1976. 12.50 (ISBN 0-396-07015-9). Dodd.

Foley, Mike. Hockey Play by Play. 1976. pap. 3.95 (ISBN 0-684-14607-X, SL 640, ScribT). Scribner.

Frayne, Trent. Mad Men of Hockey. (Illus.). 1975. 8.95 (ISBN 0-396-07060-4). Dodd.

Fullerton, James H. Ice Hockey! Playing & Coaching. (Illus.). 1978. 10.95 (ISBN 0-8038-3407-1); pap. 5.95 (ISBN 0-8038-3406-3). Hastings.

Gemme, Leila B. Hockey Is Our Game. LC 78-12541. (Illus.). (gr. 4 up). 1979. PLB 9.25 (ISBN 0-516-03492-8); pap. 2.95 (ISBN 0-516-43492-6). Childrens.

Gilbert, Rod & Park, Brad. Playing Hockey the Professional Way. LC 72-79667. 228p. (YA) 1972. 12.95 (ISBN 0-06-011521-1, HarpT). Har-Row.

Gitler, Ira. Ice Hockey A to Z. LC 78-8482. (Illus.). (gr. 4 up). 1978. 7.95 (ISBN 0-688-41842-2); PLB 7.63 (ISBN 0-688-51842-7). Lothrop.

Greenberg, Jay, et al. NHL: The World of Professional Ice Hockey. (Illus.). 256p. 1981. 24.95 (ISBN 0-8317-6370-1, Rutledge Pr). Smith Pubs.

Gutman, Bill. Great Hockey Players, No. 1. 160p. (Orig.). (gr. 5 up). 1974. pap. 0.95 (ISBN 0-448-05711-5, Tempo). Ace Bks.

Hockey Register. 9.00 (ISBN 0-89204-064-5). Sporting News.

Hodge, Ken, et al. Power Hockey. LC 74-77845. (Illus.). (gr. 3-7). 1975. 6.95 (ISBN 0-689-10618-1). Atheneum.

Hollander, Zander. The Complete Handbook of Pro Hockey: 1982 Edition. (Orig.). 1981. pap. 3.50 (ISBN 0-686-77451-5, AE1160, Sig). NAL.

Hollander, Zander, ed. The Complete Handbook of Pro Hockey: 1980 Edition. (Illus., Orig.). (RL 7). 1979. pap. cancelled (ISBN 0-451-08903-0, E8903, Sig). NAL.

--The Complete Handbook of Pro Hockey, 1981. 1980. pap. 2.75 (ISBN 0-451-09470-0, E9470, Sig). NAL.

Ice Skating Institute of America Staff. Olympic Ice Hockey. LC 79-16382. (Olympic Bks.). (Illus.). (gr. 4 up). 1979. lib. bdg. 8.65 (ISBN 0-516-02554-6); pap. 2.50 (ISBN 0-516-42554-4). Childrens.

Isaacs, Neil D. Checking Back: The Story of NHL Hockey. 1977. 9.95 (ISBN 0-393-08788-3). Norton.

Johannson, Ken. Youth Ice Hockey. LC 79-109498. (Sports Techniques Ser.). (Illus.). (gr. 6-12). 1976. pap. 1.95 (ISBN 0-87670-072-5, YIH-SC). Athletic Inst.

Kalb, Jonah. The Easy Hockey Book. (gr. 2-5). 1977. reinforced bdg. 6.95 (ISBN 0-395-25842-1). HM.

Kalchman, Lois. Safe Hockey: How to Survive the Game Intact. 1981. 10.95 (ISBN 0-684-16979-7, ScribT). Scribner.

Liss, Howard. Hockey Talk. (gr. 4-6). pap. 0.95 (ISBN 0-686-68482-6). PB.

--Strange but True Hockey Stories. (Illus.). (gr. 5 up). 1972. (BYR); PLB 4.39 (ISBN 0-394-92463-0). Random.

Lyttle, Richard B. Basic Hockey Strategy. (Illus.). 1978. pap. 2.95 (ISBN 0-346-12367-4). Cornerstone.

McFarlane, Brian. Brian McFarlane's Hockey Quiz. (Illus.). 192p. 7.95 (ISBN 0-919364-81-0, ADON 3531); pap. 3.50 (ISBN 0-919364-82-9, ADON 3532). Pagurian.

--Stanley Cup Fever: The Incredible Story of the Men & the Teams Who Have Fought for Hockey's Most Prized Trophy. 1978. write for info (ISBN 0-525-20956-5). Pagurian.

May, Julian. The Stanley Cup. LC 75-14245. (Sports Classics Ser.). (Illus.). 48p. (gr. 4-6). 1975. PLB 8.95 (ISBN 0-87191-449-2). Creative Ed.

May, Robert. The Hockey Road. (Illus.). (gr. 6-8). PLB 4.95 (ISBN 0-513-00791-1). Denison.

Meeker, Howie. More Hockey Basics from Howie Meeker. 1975. pap. 4.95 (ISBN 0-13-600700-7). P-H.

Mikita, Stan. Inside Hockey. (Inside Sports Ser.). (Illus.). 96p. 1971. pap. 5.95 (ISBN 0-8092-8854-0). Contemp Bks.

Moriarty, Tim & Bereswell, Joe. The Dynamic Islanders: From Cellar to Stanley Cup. (Illus.). 144p. 1981. pap. 9.95 (ISBN 0-385-17489-6). Doubleday.

Morse, Charles & Morse, Ann. Phil & Tony Esposito. LC 74-1461. (Creative's Superstars Ser). 32p. 1974. 5.95 (ISBN 0-87191-344-5). Creative Ed.

Nemchin, Jack. Goalie Album. (Illus.). 50p. 1981. pap. 9.95 (ISBN 0-312-32998-9). St Martin.

Olney, Ross R. This Game Called Hockey. LC 77-16872. (Illus.). (gr. 5 up). 1978. 5.95 (ISBN 0-396-07524-X). Dodd.

Orr, Bobby & Mulvoy, Mark. Bobby Orr: My Game. (A Sports Illustrated Bk). 1974. 9.95 (ISBN 0-316-66490-1). Little.

Orr, Frank. Story of Hockey. (Pro Hockey Library: No. 1). (Illus.). (gr. 5-9). 1971. (BYR); PLB 3.69 (ISBN 0-394-92303-0). Random.

Paulsen, Gary. Facing off, Checking, & Goaltending--Perhaps. LC 78-21079. (Sports on the Light Side Ser.). (Illus.). (gr. 4-6). 1979. PLB 10.65 (ISBN 0-8172-0183-1). Raintree Pubs.

Podesta, Terry. Hockey for Men & Women. (Sports Ser.). (Illus.). 1978. 8.95 (ISBN 0-7158-0578-9). Charles River Bks.

Polnaszek, Frank. Five Hundred Five Hockey Questions Your Friends Can't Answer. 192p. 1980. 9.95 (ISBN 0-8027-0669-X); pap. 5.95 (ISBN 0-8027-7167-X). Walker & Co.

Poole, Geoff. Better Hockey for Boys. LC 73-162785. (Better Sports Ser.). (Illus.). 95p. 1972. 8.50x (ISBN 0-7182-0483-2). Intl Pubns Serv.

Potvin, Denis & Fischler, Stan. Power on Ice. LC 76-9198. (Illus.). (YA) 1977. 9.95 (ISBN 0-06-013387-2, HarpT). Har-Row.

Pro & Amateur Hockey Guide. 7.50 (ISBN 0-89204-063-7). Sporting News.

Professional Hockey Handbook: Official NHL 1974-75 Ed. 160p. 6.95 (ISBN 0-919364-92-6, ADON 3542); pap. 2.95 (ISBN 0-919364-85-3, ADON 3543). Pagurian.

Rainbolt, Richard. Hockey's Top Scorers. LC 74-27471. (Sports Heroes Library). (Illus.). 72p. (gr. 5-11). 1975. PLB 6.95g (ISBN 0-8225-1056-1). Lerner Pubns.

Ray, Jo A. Careers in Hockey. LC 72-7650. (Early Career Bks). (Illus.). 36p. (gr. 2-5). 1973. PLB 4.95 (ISBN 0-8225-0315-8). Lerner Pubns.

Read, Brenda. Better Hockey for Girls. LC 72-171037. (Better Sports Ser.). (Illus.). 96p. 1976. 8.50x (ISBN 0-7182-1445-5). Intl Pubns Serv.

--Better Hockey for Girls. (Better Ser.). (Illus.). text ed. 15.95x (ISBN 0-7182-1445-5, SpS). Sportshelf.

Riley, Jack. Ice Hockey. LC 79-109498. (Sports Technique Ser.). 1973. 3.95 (ISBN 0-87670-014-8); pap. 1.95 (ISBN 0-685-56024-4). Athletic Inst.

Saladino, Tom & Huber, Jim. The Babes of Winter. LC 75-32112. 1975. 7.95 (ISBN 0-87397-092-6). Strode.

Sanderson, Derek & Fischler, Stan. I've Got to Be Me. LC 77-135541. (Illus.). 1970. 5.95 (ISBN 0-396-06255-5). Dodd.

Sloman, Larry. Thin Ice. (Illus.). 1981. price not set (ISBN 0-688-00628-0). Morrow.

Spencer, David & Spencer, Barbara. New Professional Hockey Handbook. (Illus.). 1978. write for info (ISBN 0-525-16605-X); pap. write for info (ISBN 0-525-04025-0). Pagurian.

Sports Illustrated Editors. Sports Illustrated Ice Hockey. LC 78-156366. (Illus.). (gr. 7-9). 1971. 5.95 (ISBN 0-397-00835-X); pap. 2.95 (ISBN 0-397-00836-8). Lippincott.

Stamm, Laura, et al, eds. Power Skating the Hockey Way. LC 76-19759. (Illus.). 1978. pap. 5.95 (ISBN 0-8015-4435-1, Hawthorn). Dutton.

Sullivan, George. Better Ice Hockey for Boys. LC 65-27389. (Better Sports Ser.). (Illus.). 64p. (gr. 5 up). 1976. 5.95 (ISBN 0-396-07359-X). Dodd.

--This Is Pro Hockey. LC 75-38369. (Illus.). 128p. (gr. 5 up). 1976. 5.95 (ISBN 0-396-07318-2). Dodd.

Taylor, Joseph. Lloyd Percival's Total Conditioning for Hockey. LC 78-73728. (Illus.). 1979. 9.95 (ISBN 0-8397-5504-X). Eriksson.

Walker, Henry. Illustrated Hockey Dictionary for Young People. (Treehouse Illustrated Sports Dictionaries Ser.). (Illus.). 1978. pap. 2.50 (ISBN 0-13-451138-7). P-H.

--The Illustrated Hockey Dictionary for Young People. LC 75-34975. (Illustrated Dictionary Ser.). (Illus.). 128p. (gr. 5 up). 1976. PLB 7.29 (ISBN 0-8178-5472-X). Harvey.

Wein, Horst. Science of Hockey. 2nd ed. Belchamber, David, tr. (Illus.). 22.00 (ISBN 0-7207-1149-5). Transatlantic.

Weir, Marie. Woman's Hockey for the '70's. (Illus.). 1974. 15.95x (ISBN 0-7182-0978-8, Sps). Sportshelf.

Wendel, Tim. Going for the Gold. (Illus.). 143p. 1980. 10.00 (ISBN 0-88208-116-0). Lawrence Hill.

Williams, Barbara & Fischler, Shirley. More Power to Your Skating: A Complete Training Program for Ice Hockey Players of All Ages. (Illus.). 1980. 13.95 (ISBN 0-02-629040-5); pap. 7.95 (ISBN 0-02-029940-0). Macmillan.

Woman's Hockey. pap. 2.50 (ISBN 0-8277-4876-0). British Bk Ctr.

Young, Scott. War on Ice: Canada in International Hockey. 1977. pap. 5.95 (ISBN 0-7710-9064-1). McClelland.

HOCKEY-BIOGRAPHY

Burchard, S. H. Sports Star: Brad Park. LC 75-11778. (Sports Star Ser). (Illus.). 64p. (gr. 1-5). 1975. 4.95 (ISBN 0-15-277998-1, HJ). HarBraceJ.

Dolan, Edward F., Jr. & Lyttle, Richard B. Bobby Clarke. LC 76-56280. (gr. 4-7). 1977. 5.95 (ISBN 0-385-12523-2). Doubleday.

Etter, Les. Hockey's Masked Men: Three Great Goalies. LC 75-28413. (Sports Series). (Illus.). 80p. (gr. 3-6). 1976. lib. bdg. 6.48 (ISBN 0-8116-6676-X). Garrard.

Fischler, Stan. Garry Unger & the Battling Blues. LC 76-49993. (Illus.). 1977. 7.95 (ISBN 0-396-07388-3). Dodd.

Frayne, Trent. Famous Hockey Players. LC 73-7095. (Famous Biographies Ser.). (Illus.). 224p. (gr. 7 up). 1973. 5.95 (ISBN 0-396-06848-0). Dodd.

Gilbert, John. An Interview with Bobby Clarke. (Interviews Ser.). (Illus.). (gr. 3-8). 1977. PLB 6.75 (ISBN 0-87191-573-1). Creative Ed.

Gutman, Bill. Modern Hockey Superstars. (High Interest-Low Vocabulary Ser.). (Illus.). (gr. 4-9). 1976. 5.95 (ISBN 0-396-07368-9). Dodd.

Ilowite, Sheldon. On the Wing: Rod Gilbert. LC 76-12547. (Sports Profiles Ser.). (Illus.). 48p. (gr. 4-11). 1976. PLB 9.30 (ISBN 0-8172-0134-3). Raintree Pubs.

Kariher, Harry C. Who's Who in Hockey. 192p. 1973. 7.95 (ISBN 0-87000-221-X). Arlington Hse.

MacPeek, Walt. Hot Shots of Pro Hockey. LC 75-8079. (Pro Hockey Library: No. 9). (Illus.). 160p. (gr. 5 up). 1975. (BYR); PLB 3.69 (ISBN 0-394-93104-1). Random.

Orr, Frank. Great Goalies of Pro Hockey. (Pro Hockey Library: No. 5). (Illus.). (gr. 5 up). 1973. PLB 3.69 (ISBN 0-394-92539-4). Random.

Plimpton, George. Open Net. 300p. 1981. 11.95 (ISBN 0-399-12558-2). Putnam.

Singh, Balbir. The Golden Hat Trick: My Hockey Days. (Illus.). 1977. text ed. 10.50 (ISBN 0-7069-0542-3, Pub. by Vikas India). Advent NY.

Smith, Jay H. Hockey's Legend: Bobby Orr. (The Allstars Ser.). (Illus.). (gr. 2-6). 1977. PLB 5.95 (ISBN 0-87191-590-1). Creative Ed.

Thomas, Linda. Meet the Centers. (Meet the Players: Hockey). (Illus.). (gr. 2-4). 1976. PLB 5.95 (ISBN 0-87191-534-0). Creative Ed.

--Meet the Defensemen. (Meet the Players: Hockey). (Illus.). (gr. 2-4). 1976. PLB 5.95 (ISBN 0-87191-535-9). Creative Ed.

--Meet the Wingmen. (Meet the Players: Hockey). (Illus.). (gr. 2-4). 1976. PLB 5.95 (ISBN 0-87191-536-7). Creative Ed.

Thorne, Ian. The Great Centers. (Stars of the NHL Ser.). (Illus.). (gr. 4-12). 1976. PLB 7.95 (ISBN 0-87191-492-1). Creative Ed.

--The Great Defensemen. (Stars of the NHL Ser.). (Illus.). (gr. 4-12). 1976. PLB 7.95 (ISBN 0-87191-493-X). Creative Ed.

--The Great Goalies. (Stars of the NHL Ser.). (Illus.). (gr. 4-12). 1976. PLB 7.95 (ISBN 0-87191-491-3). Creative Ed.

--The Great Wingmen. (Stars of the NHL Ser.). (Illus.). (gr. 4-12). 1976. PLB 7.95 (ISBN 0-87191-494-8). Creative Ed.

Tretyak, Vladislav & Snegirev, V. The Hockey I Love. Konstantin, Anatole, tr. from Russian. LC 77-9486. (Illus.). 160p. 1977. 7.50 (ISBN 0-88208-080-6). Lawrence Hill.

Wayne, Bennett, ed. Hockey Hotshots. LC 76-47478. (Target). (Illus.). (gr. 3-4). 1977. lib. bdg. 7.29 (ISBN 0-8116-4917-2). Garrard.

Whitehead, Eric. The Patricks: Hockey's Royal Family. LC 79-6879. (Illus.). 288p. 1980. 11.95 (ISBN 0-385-15662-6). Doubleday.

Wright, Jim. Bobby Clarke: Pride of the Team. (Putnam Sports Shelf). (Illus.). (gr. 6-8). 1977. PLB 6.29 (ISBN 0-399-61067-7). Putnam.

HOCKING, WILLIAM ERNEST, 1873-1966

Robinson, Daniel S. Royce & Hocking - American Idealists. 1968. 5.00 (ISBN 0-8158-0178-5). Chris Mass.

Rouner, Leroy S. Within Human Experience: The Philosophy of William Ernest Hocking. LC 71-75433. (Illus.). 1969. text ed. 18.50x (ISBN 0-674-95380-0). Harvard U Pr.

HOCKNEY, DAVID

Hockney, David. David Hockney. Stangos, Nikos, ed. LC 76-11721. (Illus.). 1977. 30.00 (ISBN 0-8109-1058-6). Abrams.

--Paper Pools. Stangos, Nikos, ed. (Illus.). 100p. 1980. 22.50 (ISBN 0-686-62704-0, 1461-1); pap. 14.95 (ISBN 0-686-62705-9, 2229-0). Abrams.

Livingstone, Marco. David Hockney. LC 81-81028. (Illus.). 252p. 1981. 19.95 (ISBN 0-03-059861-3, Owl Bk); pap. 10.95 (ISBN 0-03-059859-1). HR&W.

Seventy-Two Drawings by David Hockney. LC 72-175606. (Illus.). 1979. pap. 5.95 (ISBN 0-224-00655-X, Pub. by Chatto Bodley Jonathan). Merrimack Bk Serv.

HODGE, CHARLES, 1797-1878

Hodge, Archibald A. Life of Charles Hodge, Professor in the Theological Seminary, Princeton, New Jersey. LC 71-83425. (Religion in America, Ser. 1). 1969. Repr. of 1881 ed. 25.00 (ISBN 0-405-00250-5). Arno.

HODGES, EDWARD

Hodges, Faustina H. Edward Hodges, Doctor in Music of Sydney Sussex College, Cambridge. LC 73-135733. Repr. of 1896 ed. 26.50 (ISBN 0-404-03289-3). AMS Pr.

HODGKINS, JOSEPH, 1743-1829

Wade, H. T. & Lively, R. A. This Glorious Cause: The Adventures of Two Company Officers in Washington's Army. 1958. 19.00x (ISBN 0-691-04567-4). Princeton U Pr.

HODGKIN'S DISEASE

Alderson, M. R., et al, eds. Hodgkin's Disease III: Occurence & Diagnosis. LC 73-23030. (Hodgkin's Disease Ser.: Vol. 3). 155p. 1974. text ed. 19.00x (ISBN 0-8422-7195-3). Irvington.

Anglesio, Enrico. Treatment of Hodgkin's Disease. Rentchnick, P., ed. LC 68-56205. (Recent Results in Cancer Research: Vol. 18). 1969. 16.30 (ISBN 0-387-04681-X). Springer-Verlag.

Coltman, Charles A., Jr. & Golomb, Harvey, eds. Hodgkin's & Non-Hodgkin's Lymphomas. (Seminars in Oncology Reprint). 288p. 1980. 29.50 (ISBN 0-8089-1354-9). Grune.

Jacobs, Melville L. Malignant Lymphomas & Their Management. LC 65-6383. (Recent Results in Cancer Research: Vol. 16). (Illus.). 1968. 12.90 (ISBN 0-387-04307-1). Springer-Verlag.

Kaplan, Henry S. Hodgkin's Disease. 2nd, rev. ed. LC 79-16054. (Commonwealth Fund Ser.). (Illus.). 1980. text ed. 50.00x (ISBN 0-674-40485-8). Harvard U Pr.

Katz, David H., et al. Hodgkin's Disease I: Basic Research. LC 73-23030. (Hodgkin's Disease Ser.: Vol. 1). 168p. 1974. text ed. 19.00x (ISBN 0-8422-7193-7). Irvington.

Lacher, Mortimer J. Hodgkin's Disease. LC 75-25644. 508p. 1976. 50.50 (ISBN 0-471-51149-8). Krieger.

Neiman, Richard S., et al, eds. Hodgkin's Disease II: Pathological Considerations. LC 73-23030. (Hodgkin's Disease Ser.: Vol. 2). 141p. 1974. text ed. 19.00x (ISBN 0-8422-7194-5). Irvington.

Taylor, Clive R. Hodgkin's Disease & the Lymphomas, Vol. 1. 1977. 24.00 (ISBN 0-904406-48-2). Eden Med Res.

--Hodgkin's Disease & the Lymphomas, Vol. 2. LC 78-300154. 1978. 28.80 (ISBN 0-88831-015-3). Eden Med Res.

--Hodgkin's Disease & the Lymphomas, Vol. 3. Horrobin, D. F., ed. LC 78-300154. (Annual Research Reviews). 1979. 31.20 (ISBN 0-88831-043-9). Eden Med Res.

--Hodgkin's Disease & the Lymphomas, Vol. 4. Horrobin, D. F., ed. LC 78-300154. (Annual Reviews Ser.). 374p. 1981. 38.00 (ISBN 0-88831-089-7). Eden Med Res.

Variakojis, Daina, et al. Hodgkin's Disease IV: Therapy & Complications. LC 73-23030. (Hodgkin's Disease Ser.: Vol. 4). 187p. 1974. text ed. 19.00x (ISBN 0-685-50111-6). Irvington.

HODGKIN'S DISEASE-PERSONAL NARRATIVES

Lee, Laurel. Signs of Spring. (Illus.). 1980. 7.95 (ISBN 0-525-20428-8, Henry Robbins Book). Dutton.

Sveinson, Kelly. Learning to Live with Cancer. LC 77-76652. 1978. 7.95 (ISBN 0-312-47727-9). St Martin.

HODGSON, FRANCIS, 1781-1852

Hodgson, James T. Memoir of the Rev. Francis Hodgson, B.D., Scholar, Poet, & Divine, 2 vols. LC 75-26864. 1975. Repr. of 1878 ed. lib. bdg. 75.00 (ISBN 0-8414-4804-3). Folcroft.

--Memoirs of the Rev. Francis Hodgson, 2 Vols. LC 76-169470. Repr. of 1878 ed. Set. 57.50 (ISBN 0-404-07374-3). Vol. 1 (ISBN 0-404-07375-1). Vol. 2 (ISBN 0-404-07376-X). AMS Pr.

HODGSON, RALPH, 1871-1962

Sweetser, Wesley D. Ralph Hodgson: A Bibliography. LC 79-7932. (Garland Reference Library of the Humanities). 185p. 1980. lib. bdg. 20.00 (ISBN 0-8240-9524-3). Garland Pub.

HODOGRAPH

Altman, S. P. Orbital Hodograph Analysis. (Science & Technology Ser.: Vol. 3). 1965. 20.00 (ISBN 0-87703-031-6). Am Astronaut.

HOELDERLIN, FRIEDRICH, 1770-1843

Braun, Wilhelm A. Types of Weltschmerz in German Poetry. LC 5-33195. (Columbia University. Germanic Studies, Old Ser.: No. 6). Repr. of 1905 ed. 14.50 (ISBN 0-404-50406-X). AMS Pr.

Fahrner, R. Hoelderlins Begegnung Mit Goethe und Schiller. Repr. of 1925 ed. pap. 7.00 (ISBN 0-384-15080-2). Johnson Repr.

Heidegger, Martin. Existence & Being. 1950. pap. 5.45 (ISBN 0-89526-935-X). Regnery-Gateway.

Pellegrini, Alessandro. Friedrich Hoelderlin: Sein Bild in der Forschung. (Ger). 1965. 52.50x (ISBN 3-11-000338-4). De Gruyter.

Schmidt, Wolfgang. Beitraege Zur Stilistik Von Hoelderlins Tod Des Empedokles. Repr. of 1927 ed. pap. 7.00 (ISBN 0-384-54105-4). Johnson Repr.

Seckel, Dietrich. Holderlins Sprachrhythmus. Repr. of 1937 ed. 29.00 (ISBN 0-384-54661-7); pap. 26.00 (ISBN 0-685-13462-8). Johnson Repr.

Unger, Richard. Holderlin's Major Poetry: The Dialectics of Unity. LC 75-28913. 288p. 1976. 12.50x (ISBN 0-253-32836-5). Ind U Pr.

Van Der Velde, L. Herrschaft und Knechtschaft bein Holderlin. 1973. 18.30x (ISBN 90-232-1092-1, Pub by Van Gorcum). Intl Schol Bk Serv.

HOFFER, ERIC, 1902-

Koerner, James. Hoffer's America. LC 73-82782. 224p. 1973. 9.95 (ISBN 0-912050-45-4, Library Pr). Open Court.

HOFFA, JAMES RIDDLE, 1913-

Ashman, Charles & Sobel, Rebecca. The Strange Disappearance of Jimmy Hoffa. 224p. 1976. pap. 1.50 (ISBN 0-532-15179-8). Woodhill.

Hannibal, Edward & Boris, Robert. Blood Feud. 1979. 10.00 (ISBN 0-345-28100-4). Ballantine.

Hoffa, James R. Hoffa: The Real Story. LC 75-28207. (Illus.). 242p. 1975. 8.95 (ISBN 0-8128-1885-7); pap. 1.95 (ISBN 0-8128-2099-1). Stein & Day.

James Hoffa. (Labor Studies Ser.). (gr. 7 up). 1972. 0.75 (ISBN 0-89550-027-2). RIM.

Kurland, Gerald. James Hoffa, Convicted Leader of the American Teamsters Union. Rahmas, D. Steve, ed. LC 72-89208. (Outstanding Personalities Ser.: No. 44). 32p. (Orig.). (gr. 7-12). 1972. lib. bdg. 2.95 incl. catalog cards (ISBN 0-87157-540-X); pap. 1.50 vinyl laminated covers (ISBN 0-87157-040-8). SamHar Pr.

Moldea, Dan E. The Hoffa Wars. 1979. pap. 2.75 (ISBN 0-441-34010-5, Charter Bks). Ace Bks.

--The Hoffa Wars: Teamsters, Rebels, Politicians & the Mob. LC 78-14286. (Illus.). 1978. 10.95 (ISBN 0-448-22684-7). Paddington.

HOFFMAN, ABBIE

Hoffman, Abbie. Soon to Be a Major Motion Picture. 1980. 13.95 (ISBN 0-686-68806-6, Perigee); pap. 6.95 (ISBN 0-686-68807-4). Putnam.

HOFFMAN, CHARLES FENNO, 1806-1884

Barnes, Homer F. Charles Fenno Hoffman. LC 75-160003. Repr. of 1930 ed. 26.00 (ISBN 0-404-00656-6). AMS Pr.

HOFFMANN, ERNST THEODOR AMADEUS, 1776-1822

Cobb, Palmer. Influence of E. T. A. Hoffman on the Tales of Edgar Allen Poe. (North Carolina. University. Philological Club: Vol. 3). Repr. of 1908 ed. 19.50 (ISBN 0-8337-4967-6). B Franklin.

Harich, Walther. E. T. A. Hoffman, Vols. 1 & 2. LC 71-149660. (Ger.). Repr. of 1922 ed. Set. 52.50 (ISBN 0-404-03116-1). AMS Pr.

Hewett-Thayer, Harvey W. Hoffmann: Author of the Tales. LC 73-120629. 1970. Repr. lib. bdg. 25.00x (ISBN 0-374-93881-4). Octagon.

Ingham, Norman W. E. T. A. Hoffmann's Reception in Russia. 1974. pap. 20.25x (ISBN 3-777-80117-8). Humanities.

Passage, Charles E. Dostoevski the Adapter. (Studies in Comp. Lit.: No. 10). lib. bdg. 14.50x (ISBN 0-8078-7010-2); pap. text ed. 7.00x (ISBN 0-8078-7010-2). U of NC Pr.

Schaeffer, C. Die Bedeutung Des Musikalischen und Akustischen in E. T. A. Hoffmanns Literarischen Schaffen. pap. 7.00 (ISBN 0-384-53480-5). Johnson Repr.

Schafer, R. Murray. E.T.A. Hoffman & Music. LC 73-93502. (Illus.). 224p. 1975. 17.50x (ISBN 0-8020-5310-6). U of Toronto Pr.

Siebert, W. Heinrich Heines Beziehungen Zu E. T. A. Hoffmann. Repr. of 1908 ed. pap. 7.00 (ISBN 0-384-55290-0). Johnson Repr.

Winter, Ilse. Untersuchungen Zum Serapiontischen Prinzip E.T.A. Hoffmans. (De Proprietatibus Litterarum: No. 111). 90p. (Orig.). 1976. pap. text ed. 18.25x (ISBN 90-2793-434-7). Mouton.

HOFMANN, HANS, 1880-

Hofmann, Hans. Hans Hofmann. LC 63-12457. (Contemporary Artist Ser.). 1964. 65.00 (ISBN 0-8109-0185-4). Abrams.

Seitz, William C. Hans Hofmann. LC 79-169314. (Museum of Modern Art Publications in Reprint). (Illus.). 64p. 1972. Repr. of 1963 ed. 14.00 (ISBN 0-405-01572-0). Arno.

HOFMANN, JOSEPH, 1876-1957

Graydon, Nell S. & Sizemore, Margaret D. Amazing Marriage of Marie Eustis & Josef Hofmann. LC 65-28499. (Illus.). 1965. 14.95x (ISBN 0-87249-099-8). U of SC Pr.

HOFMANN, MARIE CLARISSE (EUSTIS) 1866-1956

Graydon, Nell S. & Sizemore, Margaret D. Amazing Marriage of Marie Eustis & Josef Hofmann. LC 65-28499. (Illus.). 1965. 14.95x (ISBN 0-87249-099-8). U of SC Pr.

HOFMANNSTHAL, HUGO HOFMANN, EDLER VON, 1874-1929

Bangerter, Lowell A. Hugo Von Hofmannsthal. LC 76-20408. (Modern Literature Ser.). 1977. 10.95 (ISBN 0-8044-2028-9). Ungar.

Coghlan, Brian. Hofmannsthal's Festival Dramas. 1964. 65.00 (ISBN 0-521-04682-3). Cambridge U Pr.

Daviau, Donald G. & Buelow, George J. The Ariadne Auf Naxos of Hugo von Hofmannsthal & Richard Strauss. (Studies in the Germanic Languages & Literatures: No. 80). 1975. 18.00x (ISBN 0-8078-8080-9). U of NC Pr.

Evans, Arthur R., Jr., ed. On Four Modern Humanists: Hofmannsthal, Gundolf, Curtius, Kantorowicz. LC 76-90945. (Princeton Essays Literature). 1970. 16.00 (ISBN 0-691-06174-2). Princeton U Pr.

Gray, Ronald D. German Tradition in Literature. LC 65-17206. 1966. 48.00 (ISBN 0-521-05133-9); pap. 17.50 (ISBN 0-521-29278-6). Cambridge U Pr.

Hamburger, Michael, ed. Hofmannsthal: Three Essays. (Bollingen Ser.: No. 33). 1970. pap. 5.95 (ISBN 0-691-01767-0). Princeton U Pr.

Hammelmann, Hanns & Osers, Ewald, trs. A Working Friendship: The Correspondence Between Richard Strauss & Hugo Von Hofmannsthal. LC 61-13839. 580p. 1974. pap. 17.50x (ISBN 0-8443-0050-0). Vienna Hse.

Hofmannsthal, Hugo Von. Bibliographie: Werke, Briefe, Gespraeche, Uebersetzungen, Vertonungen. Weber, Horst, ed. (Ger). 1972. 88.00 (ISBN 3-11-003954-0). De Gruyter.

Knaus, Jakob. Hofmannsthals Weg Zur Oper, Die Frau Ohne Schatten: Ruecksichten und Einfluesse auf die Musik. (Quellen und Forschungen zur Sprach-und Kulturgeschichte der germanischen Volker, N. F. 38). (Ger). 1971. 29.40 (ISBN 3-11-001865-9). De Gruyter.

Kobel, Erwin. Hugo Von Hofmannsthal. (Ger). 1970. 24.00x (ISBN 3-11-000551-4). De Gruyter.

Miles, David. Hofmannsthal's Novel Andreas. LC 70-155001. (Princeton Essays in Literature Ser). 1972. 17.50 (ISBN 0-691-06208-0). Princeton U Pr.

Norman, F., ed. Hofmannsthal Studies in Commemoration. 147p. 1963. 50.00x (ISBN 0-85457-018-7, Pub. by Inst Germanic Stud England). State Mutual Bk.

HOG CHOLERA

Eradication of Hog Cholera & Africa Swine Fever. (FAO Animal Production & Health Paper: No. 2). (Illus.). 1978. pap. 7.50 (ISBN 92-5-100182-0, F722, FAO). Unipub.

HOGARTH, WILLIAM, 1697-1764

Bindman, David. Hogarth. (World of Art Ser.). (Illus.). 288p. 1981. 17.95 (ISBN 0-19-520239-2); pap. 9.95 (ISBN 0-19-520240-6). Oxford U Pr.

De Voogd, Peter. Henry Fielding & William Hogarth: The Correspondence of the Arts. 195p. 1981. pap. text ed. 23.00x (ISBN 90-6203-543-4, Pub. by Rodopi Holland). Humanities.

Gaunt, William. The World of William Hogarth. 1978. 10.95 (ISBN 0-224-01445-5, Pub. by Chatto Bodley Jonathan). Merrimack Bk Serv.

Hazlitt, William. Lectures on the English Comic Writers. LC 68-25078. 1969. Repr. of 1819 ed. 10.00 (ISBN 0-8462-1260-9). Russell.

Jarrett, Derek. England in the Age of Hogarth. (Illus.). 223p. 1976. pap. 5.95 (ISBN 0-586-08251-4, Pub. by Granada England). Academy Chi Ltd.

Lindsay, Jack. Hogarth: His Art & His World. LC 78-21289. (Illus.). 1979. 14.95 (ISBN 0-8008-3916-1). Taplinger.

Moore, Robert E. Hogarth's Literary Relationships. LC 70-76001. 1969. Repr. of 1948 ed. lib. bdg. 15.00x (ISBN 0-374-95852-1). Octagon.

Paulson, Ronald. Hogarth, His Life, Art, & Times. abr ed. LC 73-91338. (Illus.). 416p. 1974. 35.00x (ISBN 0-300-01766-9). Yale U Pr.

Rosenthal, Michael. Hogarth. 1981. 27.00x (ISBN 0-686-72291-4, Pub. by Jupiter England). State Mutual Bk.

--Hogarth. (Oresko-Jupiter Art Bks). (Illus.). 96p. 1981. 17.95 (ISBN 0-933516-81-9, Pub. by Oresko-Jupiter England). Hippocrene Bks.

Watson, Ross, intro. by. William Hogarth: Paintings from the Collection of Mr. & Mrs. Paul Mellon. LC 75-148159. (Illus.). pap. 2.50 (ISBN 0-686-16176-9). Natl Gallery Art.

Wensinger, Arthur S. & Coley, William B., trs. Hogarth on High Life: The "Marriage a la Mode" Series from Georg Christoph Lichtenberg's Commentaries. LC 79-82541. (Illus.). 1970. 50.00x (ISBN 0-8195-4009-9, Pub. by Wesleyan U Pr). Columbia U Pr.

Works of William Hogarth. 1978. Repr. of 1825 ed. lib. bdg. 35.00 luxury ed. (ISBN 0-932106-03-X, Pub. by Marathon Pr). S J Durst.

HOGG, JAMES, 1770-1835

Batho, Edith C. Ettrick Shepherd. LC 69-13809. 1969. Repr. of 1927 ed. lib. bdg. 15.00 (ISBN 0-8371-0298-7, BAET). Greenwood.

Carswell, Donald. Scott & His Circle. facsimile ed. LC 72-175692. (Select Bibliographies Reprint Ser). Repr. of 1930 ed. 19.00 (ISBN 0-8369-6607-4). Arno.

Douglas, George. James Hogg. LC 74-9780. 1899. 17.50 (ISBN 0-8414-3762-9). Folcroft.

Scott, Winifred. Jefferson Hogg: Shelley's Biographer. 1973. Repr. of 1951 ed. 22.50 (ISBN 0-8274-0446-8). R West.

Simpson, Louis. James Hogg: A Critical Study. 1977. Repr. of 1962 ed. lib. bdg. 35.00 (ISBN 0-8495-4813-6). Arden Lib.

Smith, Nelson C. James Hogg. (English Authors Ser.: No. 311). 1980. lib. bdg. 11.95 (ISBN 0-8057-6803-3). Twayne.

HOGG, JAMES, 1806-1888

Bonner, William H. De Quincey at Work. LC 73-9715. 1936. lib. bdg. 15.00 (ISBN 0-8414-3162-0). Folcroft.

HOGG, JAMES, 1830-1910

Bonner, William H. De Quincey at Work. LC 73-9715. 1936. lib. bdg. 15.00 (ISBN 0-8414-3162-0). Folcroft.

HOGG, JAMES STEPHEN, 1851-1906

Cotner, Robert C. James Stephen Hogg: A Biography. (Illus.). 643p. 1959. 19.50 (ISBN 0-292-73703-3). U of Tex Pr.

HOGG, THOMAS JEFFERSON, 1792-1862

Hunt, Leigh. Letter on Hogg's Life of Shelley. 1927. lib. bdg. 5.50 (ISBN 0-8414-5232-6). Folcroft.

Norman, Sylva, ed. After Shelley. LC 75-11764. 1934. Repr. lib. bdg. 20.00 (ISBN 0-685-44321-3). Folcroft.

HOGS

see Swine

HOHENZOLLERN, HOUSE OF

Schneider, Reinhold. Hohenzollern: Tragik & Koenigtum. (Suhrkamp Taschenbuecher: No. 590). 218p. 1980. pap. text ed. 5.85 (ISBN 3-518-37090-1, Pub. by Suhrkamp Verlag Germany). Suhrkamp.

HOHOKAM CULTURE

Haury, Emil W. The Hohokam: Desert Farmers & Craftsmen-Excavations at Snaketown, 1964-65. LC 75-31610. 1976. 22.50x (ISBN 0-8165-0445-8). U of Ariz Pr.

Kelly, Isabel, et al. The Hodges Ruin: A Hohokam Community in the Tucson Basin. Hartmann, Gayle H., ed. LC 78-4029. (Anthropological Papers Ser.: No. 30). 1978. pap. 6.95x (ISBN 0-8165-0619-1). U of Ariz Pr.

Wasley, William W. & Johnson, Alfred E. Salvage Archaeology in Painted Rocks Reservoir, Western Arizona. LC 64-63815. (Anthropological Papers: No. 9). 1965. pap. 4.95x (ISBN 0-8165-0273-0). U of Ariz Pr.

Weaver, Donald, et al, eds. Proceedings of the Nineteen Seventy-Three Hohokam Conference, Phoenix, Ariz. 1973. (Contributions to Anthropological Studies: No. 2). (Illus.). 1978. pap. 8.50 (ISBN 0-916552-13-6). Acoma Bks.

HOISTING MACHINERY

see also Conveying Machinery; Cranes, Derricks, etc.; Elevators

Brown, Kermit E. Artificial Lift Methods, Vol. 3A. 1088p. 1980. 75.00 (ISBN 0-87814-031-X). Pennwell Pub.

Hoisting Conference: 1975. 10.50x (ISBN 0-89520-026-0). Soc Mining Eng.

International Committee for Lift Regulations. Code of Practice for the Safe Construction & Installation of Electric Passenger Goods & Service Lifts. 108p. 1972. 4.55 (ISBN 92-2-100159-8). Intl Labour Office.

Karelin, N. T. Mine Transport. 193p. 1981. 10.00x (ISBN 0-86125-796-0, Pub. by Orient Longman India). State Mutual Bk.

Leach, Robert P., Jr. Riggers Bible. 1980. Repr. of 1965 ed. 12.50 (ISBN 0-9600992-1-2). Riggers Bible.

Rossnagel, W. E. Handbook of Rigging: In Construction & Industrial Operations. 3rd ed. 1964. 26.50 (ISBN 0-07-053940-5, P&RB). McGraw.

Rudman, Jack. Hoisting Machine Operator. (Career Examination Ser.: C-2257). (Cloth bdg. avail. on request). 1977. 14.00 (ISBN 0-8373-2257-X). Natl Learning.

HOKKAIDO–DESCRIPTION AND TRAVEL

Landor, Arnold H. Alone with the Hairy Ainu or 3800 Miles on a Pack Saddle in Yezo & a Cruise to the Kurile Islands. Repr. of 1893 ed. 27.00 (ISBN 0-384-31240-3). Johnson Repr.

Lensen, George A. Report from Hokkaido: The Remains of Russian Culture in Northern Japan. LC 73-2878. (Illus.). 216p. 1973. Repr. of 1954 ed. lib. bdg. 15.00x (ISBN 0-8371-6818-X, LERH). Greenwood.

HOKKU

see Haiku

HOKUSAI, KATSUSHIKA, 1760-1849

Bowie, Theodore. The Drawings of Hokusai. LC 78-12135. 1979. Repr. of 1964 ed. lib. bdg. 29.75x (ISBN 0-313-21074-8, BODH). Greenwood.

Michener, James A., ed. Hokusai Sketchbooks: Selections from the Manga. LC 58-9983. (Illus.). 1958. 32.50 (ISBN 0-8048-0252-1). C E Tuttle.

Narazaki, M. Hokusai: Sketches & Paintings. LC 69-16371. (Masterpieces of Ukiyo-e Ser.). (Illus.). 1969. pap. 12.95 (ISBN 0-87011-076-4). Kodansha.

--Studies in Nature: Birds & Flowers by Hokusai & Hiroshige. Bester, John, tr. LC 76-82657. (Masterpieces of Ukiyo-e Ser.). (Illus.). 1970. pap. 12.95 (ISBN 0-87011-103-5). Kodansha.

Strange, Edw. F. Hokusai, the Old Man Mad with Painting. LC 77-357. 1977. Repr. of 1906 ed. lib. bdg. 10.00 (ISBN 0-8414-7753-1). Folcroft.

HOLBACH, PAUL HENRI THIRY, BARON D', 1723-1789

Cushing, M. & Wickwar, W. H. Baron D'Holbach. 59.95 (ISBN 0-87968-707-X). Gordon Pr.

Cushing, Max P. Baron d'Holbach: A Study of Eighteenth Century Radicalism in France. LC 76-166444. (Philosophy Monograph: No. 76). 1971. Repr. of 1914 ed. lib. bdg. 16.50 (ISBN 0-8337-4060-1). B Franklin.

--Baron d'Holbach: A Study of Eighteenth Century Radicalism in France. LC 76-166444. (Philosophy Monograph: No. 76). 1971. Repr. of 1914 ed. lib. bdg. 16.50 (ISBN 0-8337-4060-1). B Franklin.

Plekhanov, G. V. Essays in the History of Materialism. 1968. 25.00 (ISBN 0-86527-061-9). Fertig.

Svitak, Ivan. The Dialectic of Common Sense: The Master Thinkers. LC 78-65849. 1979. pap. text ed. 9.75 (ISBN 0-8191-0675-5). U Pr of Amer.

Wickwar, W. H. Baron D'Holbach. LC 68-22378. Repr. of 1935 ed. 15.00x (ISBN 0-678-00411-0). Kelley.

HOLBEIN, HANS THE YOUNGER, 1497-1543

The Family of Sir Thomas More: Facsimiles of the Drawings by Hans Holbein the Younger in the Royal Library, Windsor Castle. (Illus.). 1977. 65.00 (ISBN 0-685-88559-3). Johnson Repr.

Ford, Ford M. Hans Holbein the Younger: A Critical Monograph. 1980. Repr. lib. bdg. 25.00 (ISBN 0-89341-370-4). Longwood Pr.

Holbein, Hans, illus. Images from the Old Testament. LC 76-3813. (Masterpieces of the Illustrated Book Ser.). (Illus.). 1977. pap. 4.95 (ISBN 0-448-22420-8). Paddington.

Piper, David, ed. Holbein. LC 80-50232. (Every Painting Ser.). (Illus.). 96p. 1980. pap. 5.95 (ISBN 0-8478-0311-2). Rizzoli Intl.

Roberts, Jane. Holbein. 1981. 27.00x (ISBN 0-905368-62-2, Pub. by Jupiter England). State Mutual Bk.

HOLBERG, LUDWIG, BARON, 1684-1754

Campbell, Oscar J. Comedies of Holberg. LC 68-20216. 1968. Repr. of 1914 ed. 16.00 (ISBN 0-405-08339-4, Blom Pubns). Arno.

Jansen, F. J. Ludvig Holberg. LC 74-2171. (World Authors Ser.: Denmark: No. 321). 136p. 1974. lib. bdg. 10.95 (ISBN 0-8057-2431-1). Twayne.

HOLDEN, WILLIAM, 1918-

Quirk, Lawrence J. The Films of William Holden. 256p. 1973. 12.00 (ISBN 0-8065-0375-0); pap. 6.95 (ISBN 0-8065-0517-6). Citadel Pr.

--The Films of William Holden. 256p. 1973. 12.00 (ISBN 0-8065-0375-0); pap. 6.95 (ISBN 0-8065-0517-6). Citadel Pr.

HOLDERLIN, FRIEDRICH

see Hoelderlin, Friedrich, 1770-1843

HOLDING COMPANIES

see also Bank Holding Companies; Trusts, Industrial

Bonbright, James C. & Means, Gardiner C. Holding Company: Its Public Significance & Its Regulation. LC 68-55486. Repr. of 1932 ed. 19.50x (ISBN 0-678-00502-8). Kelley.

Daems, Herman. The Holding Company & Corporate Control. 1978. lib. bdg. 16.00 (ISBN 90-207-0690-X). Kluwer Boston.

Ellmer, R. E. Mechanism of Consolidated Accounts: Accounting for Holding Companies. 1974. 17.95x (ISBN 0-434-90530-5). Intl Ideas.

Mariah, Paul. The Electric Holding Company. 1974. pap. 1.00 (ISBN 0-686-18841-1); pap. 2.00 signed ed. (ISBN 0-686-18842-X). Man-Root.

Ramsay, Marion L. Pyramids of Power: The Story of Roosevelt, Insull & the Utility Wars. (FDR & the Era of the New Deal Ser.). (Illus.). 342p. 1975. Repr. of 1937 ed. lib. bdg. 32.50 (ISBN 0-306-70707-1). Da Capo.

HOLIDAY, BILLIE, 1915-1959

DeVaux, Alexis. Don't Explain (A Song of Billie Holiday) LC 78-19471. (Illus.). 160p. (gr. 7 up). 1980. 8.95 (ISBN 0-06-021629-8, HarpJ); PLB 8.89 (ISBN 0-06-021630-1). Har-Row.

Holiday, Billie & Dufty, William. Lady Sings the Blues. 1979. pap. 2.50 (ISBN 0-380-00491-7, 53173). Avon.

HOLIDAY DECORATIONS

see also Christmas Decorations

Deems, Betty. Easy-to-Make Felt Ornaments for Christmas and Other Occasions. (Dover Needlework Ser). (Illus., Orig.). 1976. pap. 3.00 (ISBN 0-486-23389-8). Dover.

Gerson, Trina. Holiday Crafts. 80p. (ps-7). 1981. pap. text ed. write for info. (ISBN 0-9605878-1-0). Anirt Pr.

Katz, Ruth. Pumpkin Personalities. (Illus.). (gr. k-4). 1979. 5.95 (ISBN 0-8027-6364-2); PLB 5.85 (ISBN 0-8027-6365-0). Walker & Co.

Parish, Peggy. Let's Celebrate: Holiday Decorations You Can Make. LC 76-2726. (Greenwillow Read-Alone Bks.). (Illus.). 56p. (gr. 1-4). 1976. PLB 5.71 (ISBN 0-688-84050-7). Greenwillow.

Sullivan, Eugene T. & Sullivan, Marilynn C., eds. Celebrate! No. V. LC 75-24148. 1978. 12.95 (ISBN 0-912696-14-1). Wilton.

Wagner, Lee. How to Have Fun Making Holiday Decorations. LC 74-112308. (Creative Craft Bks.). (Illus.). 32p. (gr. 2-6). 1974. PLB 5.95 (ISBN 0-87191-362-3). Creative Ed.

Williams, Barbara & Williams, Rosemary. Cookie Craft: No-Bake Designs for Edible Party Decorations. LC 77-3184. (gr. 6 up). 1977. 6.95 (ISBN 0-03-020451-8); pap. 3.50 (ISBN 0-03-048971-7). HR&W.

HOLIDAYS

see also Anniversaries; Arbor Day; Christmas; Fasts and Feasts; Fourth of July; May Day; New Year; Schools–Exercises and Recreations; Sunday Legislation; Thanksgiving Day; Vacations; Washington's Birthday

Aber, William M. A Lenten Zoo. 1973. pap. 3.90 (ISBN 0-89536-127-2). CSS Pub.

Ainsworth, Catherine H. American Calendar Customs, Vol. II. LC 79-55784. (Calender Customs). 105p. (Orig.). 1980. pap. 10.00 (ISBN 0-933190-07-7). Clyde Pr.

Bailey, Carolyn S. Stories for Every Holiday. LC 73-20149. 277p. 1974. Repr. of 1918 ed. 30.00 (ISBN 0-8103-3957-9). Gale.

Betz, Eleanor P., et al. Holiday Eating for a Healthy Heart. 1981. pap. write for info. Rush-Presby-St Lukes.

Brand, John. Observations on the Popular Antiquities of Great Britain, 3 Vols. 3rd ed. Ellis, Henry, ed. LC 71-136368. (Bohn's Antiquarian Library Ser). Repr. of 1849 ed. Set. 37.50 (ISBN 0-404-50005-6); 12.50 ea. Vol. 1 (ISBN 0-404-50011-0). Vol. 2 (ISBN 0-404-50012-9). Vol. 3 (ISBN 0-404-50013-7). AMS Pr.

--Observations on the Popular Antiquities of Great Britain: Chiefly Illustrating the Origin of Our Vulgar & Provincial Customs, Ceremonies & Superstitions. LC 67-23896. 1969. Repr. of 1849 ed. 49.00 (ISBN 0-8103-3256-6). Gale.

Bruno, Giordano. The Ash Wednesday Supper. Jaki, Stanley L., tr. (Illus.). 174p. 1975. text ed. 28.90x (ISBN 90-2797-581-7). Mouton.

Chambers, Robert, ed. Book of Days: A Miscellany of Popular Antiquities in Connection with the Calendar, Including Anecdote, Biography & History, Curiosities of Literature, & Oddities of Human Life & Character, 2 Vols. LC 67-13009. (Illus.). 1967. Repr. of 1862 ed. 74.00 (ISBN 0-8103-3002-4). Gale.

Chavel, Charles. Holidays & Festivals. (Illus.). 1956. 4.00 (ISBN 0-914080-44-X). Shulsinger Sales.

Cordello, Becky S. Celebrations: A Unique Treasury of Holiday Ideas. Brannon, Evelyn, ed. LC 77-89714. (Illus.). 1977. 17.95 (ISBN 0-8329-0209-8). New Century.

Deems, Edward M., ed. Holy-Days & Holidays: A Treasury of Historical Material, Sermons in Full & in Brief, Suggestive Thoughts & Poetry, Relating to Holy Days & Holidays. LC 68-17940. 1968. Repr. of 1902 ed. 40.00 (ISBN 0-8103-3352-X). Gale.

Dobler, Lavinia. National Holidays Around the World. LC 66-16525. (Around the World Ser.). (Illus.). (gr. 7-12). 1968. 7.95 (ISBN 0-8303-0044-9). Fleet.

Dostal, June. Elementary Teacher's September-June Book of Classroom Activities: An Almanac for Every Day in the School Year. 1977. 11.95 (ISBN 0-13-260810-3, Parker). P-H.

DuCharme, Jerome J. The Reader's Guide to Proclamation: For Sundays & Major Feasts in Cycle A. 160p. 1974. pap. 2.95 (ISBN 0-8199-0577-1). Franciscan Herald.

Duddington, John W. Festal Christianity: A Theology of the Mighty Acts. 1977. 10.00 (ISBN 0-533-02802-7). Vantage.

Emmens, Carol A. & Maglione, Harry, eds. An Audio-Visual Guide to American Holidays. LC 78-6230. 1978. lib. bdg. 13.50 (ISBN 0-8108-1140-5). Scarecrow.

Fagg, Christine. All About Caravan Holidays. 1975. 7.95 (ISBN 0-236-30931-5, Pub. by Paul Elek). Merrimack Bk Serv.

Fobel, Jim & Boleach, Jim. The Big Book of Fabulous, Fun'filled Celebrations & Holiday Crafts. LC 78-4698. (Illus.). 1978. 14.95 (ISBN 0-03-040446-0). HR&W.

Gregory, Ruth W. Anniversaries & Holidays. 3rd ed. LC 75-23163. 260p. 1975. text ed. 12.50 (ISBN 0-8389-0200-6). ALA.

--Special Days: The Book of Anniversaries & Holidays. 1978. pap. 5.95 (ISBN 0-8065-0659-8). Citadel Pr.

Greif, Martin. The Holiday Book. LC 77-91924. (Illus.). 1979. 14.95x (ISBN 0-87663-309-2, Main St); pap. 7.95 (ISBN 0-87663-980-5). Universe.

Hatch, Jane M., ed. American Book of Days. 1212p. 1978. 50.00 (ISBN 0-8242-0593-6). Wilson.
Humphrey, Grace. Stories of the World's Holidays. LC 74-3023. 1974. Repr. of 1923 ed. 26.00 (ISBN 0-8103-3660-X). Gale.
--Stories of the World's Holidays. 1978. Repr. of 1923 ed. lib. bdg. 25.00 (ISBN 0-89760-325-7, Telegraph). Dynamic Learn Corp.
Lamm, Norman. Supplement for the Days of Remembrance & Thanksgiving. 1973. 0.85x (ISBN 0-87306-079-2). Feldheim.
Langseth-Christensen, Lillian. Holiday Cook. LC 69-18917. (Illus.). (gr. 5-12). 1969. PLB 8.95 (ISBN 0-87460-087-1). Lion Bks.
Munoz, A. Lopez. Programas Para Dias Especiales Tomo II. 64p. 1980. Repr. of 1977 ed. pap. 1.60 (ISBN 0-311-07006-X). Casa Bautista.
Myers, Robert J. & Hallmark Cards Editors. Celebrations: The Complete Book of American Holidays. LC 77-163086. 288p. 1972. 10.95 (ISBN 0-385-07677-0). Doubleday.
Power, David & Collins, Mary, eds. The Times of Celebration. (Concilium 1981 Ser.: Vol. 142). 128p. (Orig.). 1981. pap. 6.95 (ISBN 0-8164-2309-1). Seabury.
Rice, Sara S., compiled by. Holiday Selections: For Readings & Recitations; Specially Adapted to Christmas, New Year... LC 72-39402. (Granger Reprint Ser.). Repr. of 1892 ed. 16.00 (ISBN 0-8369-6348-2). Arno.
Rice, Wayne & Yaconelli, Mike. Holiday Ideas for Youth Groups. (Ideas for Youth Groups Ser.). 160p. (Orig.). 1981. pap. 5.95 (ISBN 0-310-34991-5). Zondervan.
Rodgers, Edith C. Discussion of Holidays in the Later Middle Ages. LC 41-3851. (Columbia University Studies in the Social Sciences: No. 474). Repr. of 1940 ed. 12.50 (ISBN 0-404-51474-X). AMS Pr.
Schell, Catherine & Kunz, Marilyn. Celebrate the Year. 48p. pap. 1.75 (ISBN 0-89191-191-X, 27730). Cook.
Spicer, Dorothy G. Book of Festivals. LC 75-92667. 1969. Repr. of 1937 ed. 28.00 (ISBN 0-8103-3143-8). Gale.
Sullivan, Eugene T. & Sullivan, Marilynn C., eds. Celebrate! No. V. LC 75-24148. 1978. 12.95 (ISBN 0-912696-14-1). Wilton.
Thomas, Eleanor & Kelty, Mary G. Heroes, Heroines & Holidays. facs. ed. LC 78-148228. (Biography Index Reprint Ser.). 1947. 22.00 (ISBN 0-8369-8075-1). Arno.
Time-Life Editors. Time-Life Holiday Cookbook. LC 76-10075. 1976. lib. bdg. 16.95 (ISBN 0-685-83033-0). Silver.
Valbracht, Louis H. High Days, Holy Days, & Holidaze. 1973. pap. 4.70 (ISBN 0-89536-093-4). CSS Pub.
Walker, Georgiana. The Celebration Book. LC 76-58107. 1977. pap. 3.95 (ISBN 0-8307-0534-1, 54-059-04). Regal.
Watson, Jane W. India Celebrates! LC 72-10743. (Around the World Holiday Ser.). (Illus.). 96p. (gr. 4-7). 1974. PLB 6.48 (ISBN 0-8116-4950-4). Garrard.
Webster, Hutton. Rest Days, the Christian Sunday, the Jewish Sabbath & Their Historical & Anthropological Prototypes. LC 68-58165. 1968. Repr. of 1916 ed. 28.00 (ISBN 0-8103-3342-2). Gale.

HOLIDAYS–DRAMA

Bennett, Rowena. Creative Plays & Programs for Holidays. (gr. 3-6). 1966. 10.95 (ISBN 0-8238-0005-9). Plays.
De Deiros, Norma H. C. Dramatizaciones Infantiles Para Dias Especiales. 1978. pap. 2.10 (ISBN 0-311-07606-8). Casa Bautista.
DuBois, Graham. Plays for Great Occasions. (gr. 7-12). 1951. 10.00 (ISBN 0-8238-0014-8). Plays.
Hark, Mildred & McQueen, Noel. Twenty-Five Plays for Holidays. (gr. 7-12). 1952. 9.95 (ISBN 0-8238-0027-X). Plays.
Kamerman, Sylvia E., ed. Fifty Plays for Holidays. (gr. 3-6). 1975. Repr. 12.00 (ISBN 0-8238-0033-4). Plays.
Munoz, Lopez A. Programas Para Dias Especiales Tomo I. 107p. 1980. pap. 1.60 (ISBN 0-311-07005-1). Casa Bautista.
Newman, Deborah. Holiday Plays for Little Players. (gr. 2-6). 1957. 10.00 (ISBN 0-8238-0053-9). Plays.

HOLIDAYS–JUVENILE LITERATURE

Arthur, Mildred. Holidays of Legend: From New Years to Christmas. LC 73-148110. (Illus.). (gr. 4-7). 1971. PLB 5.87 (ISBN 0-8178-4842-8). Harvey.
Banh Chung Banh Day: The New Year's Rice Cakes. (gr. 2-5). 1972. 1.50x (ISBN 0-686-10279-7). SE Asia Res Ctr.
Behrens, June. Fiesta! Other Lands, Other Places. LC 78-8468. (Illus.). (gr. k-4). 1978. PLB 9.25 (ISBN 0-516-08815-7, Golden Gate). Childrens.
Bennett, Marian. My Book of Special Days. (Illus.). (gr. 4-8). 1977. 4.95 (ISBN 0-87239-156-6, 3049). Standard Pub.
Bornstein, Harry. The Holiday Book. (Signed English Ser.). 48p. 1974. pap. 3.50 (ISBN 0-913580-30-9). Gallaudet Coll.
Burnett, Bernice. The First Book of Holidays. rev. ed. LC 74-3075. (First Bks. Ser.). (Illus.). 72p. (gr. 4-7). 1974. PLB 6.90 (ISBN 0-531-00548-8). Watts.
Cavanah, Frances & Pannell, Lucille. Holiday Roundup. rev. ed. LC 68-18811. (Illus.). (gr. 4-6). 1968. PLB 6.97 (ISBN 0-8255-7041-7). Macrae.
Churchill, E. Richard. Holiday Hullabaloo! Facts, Jokes, & Riddles. (Illus.). (gr. 4 up). 1977. PLB 8.40 (ISBN 0-531-00384-1). Watts.
Cole, Ann, et al. A Pumpkin in a Pear Tree - Creative Ideas for Twelve Months of Holiday Fun. (Illus.). 112p. (gr. 1 up). 1976. 8.95g (ISBN 0-316-15110-6); pap. 5.95 (ISBN 0-316-15111-4). Little.
Dobler, Lavinia. Customs & Holidays Around the World. LC 62-8222. (Around the World Ser.). (Illus.). (gr. 7-12). 1962. 8.95 (ISBN 0-8303-0043-0). Fleet.
Eisner, Vivienne. Quick & Easy Holiday Costumes. LC 77-21987. (Lothrop Craft Ser.). (Illus.). (gr. 1-5). 1977. 9.25 (ISBN 0-688-41809-0); PLB 8.88 (ISBN 0-688-51809-5). Lothrop.
Epstein, Samuel & Epstein, Beryl. Spring Holidays. LC 64-12340. (Holiday Books Ser). (gr. 2-5). 1964. PLB 6.87 (ISBN 0-8116-6553-4). Garrard.
Fenner, Phyllis R., ed. Feasts & Frolics: Special Stories for Special Days. (Illus.). (gr. 3-7). 1949. PLB 5.99 (ISBN 0-394-91152-0). Knopf.
Gaer, Joseph. Holidays Around the World. (Illus.). (gr. 7 up). 1953. 7.95 (ISBN 0-316-30155-8). Little.
Ghinger, Judith. Hooray Days. (Kids Paperback Ser.). (Illus.). 1977. PLB 7.62 (ISBN 0-307-62355-6, Golden Pr); pap. 1.95 (ISBN 0-307-12355-3). Western Pub.
Haas, Carolyn, et al. Backyard Vacation: Outdoor Fun in Your Own Neighborhood. (Illus.). 116p. (gr. 3-6). 1980. 9.95 (ISBN 0-316-33686-6); pap. 5.95 (ISBN 0-316-33685-8). Little.
Hayward, Linda. Sesame Seasons. (Special Ser.). (Illus.). 64p. (ps). 1981. 6.95 (ISBN 0-307-15550-1, Golden Pr); PLB 13.77 (ISBN 0-307-65550-4). Western Pub.
Joy, Margaret. Highdays & Holidays. (Illus.). 128p. (gr. 3 up). 1981. 11.95 (ISBN 0-571-11771-6, Pub. by Faber & Faber). Merrimack Bk Serv.
--Highdays & Holidays. (gr. 3 up). Date not set. 11.95 (ISBN 0-686-31510-3, Pub. by Faber & Faber). Merrimack Bk Serv.
Larrick, Nancy, ed. More Poetry for Holidays. LC 73-6806. (Poetry Ser.). (Illus.). 96p. (gr. 2-5). 1973. PLB 6.09 (ISBN 0-8116-4116-3). Garrard.
Lobel. A Holiday for Mr. Muster. (gr. 2-3). 1980. pap. 3.50 incl. record (ISBN 0-590-24003-X, Schol Pap). Schol Bk Serv.
McSpadden, J. Walker. Book of Holidays. rev. ed. LC 58-12464. (Illus.). (gr. 5 up). 1958. 12.95 (ISBN 0-690-15224-8, TYC-J). Har-Row.
Nelson, Esther L. Holiday Singing & Dancing Games. LC 80-52331. (Illus.). 72p. (gr. k-3). 1980. 8.95 (ISBN 0-8069-4630-X); PLB 8.29 (ISBN 0-8069-4631-8). Sterling.
Olcott, Francis J. Good Stories for Great Holidays. (Illus.). (gr. 4-6). 6.95 (ISBN 0-395-06967-X). HM.
Polette, Nancy & Hamlin, Marjorie. Celebrating with Books. LC 77-3862. (Illus.). 1977. 10.00 (ISBN 0-8108-1032-8). Scarecrow.
Quackenbush, Robert, ed. & illus. The Holiday Song Book. LC 77-5895. (Illus.). (gr. 1 up). 1977. 9.95 (ISBN 0-688-41820-1); PLB 9.55 (ISBN 0-688-51820-6). Lothrop.
Ritchie, Judith & Niggemeyer, Vickie. Holy Days: Holidays. LC 78-23841. (Illus.). (gr. k-6). 1978. 7.95 (ISBN 0-915134-48-9). Mott Media.
Sarnoff, Jane. Light the Candles! Beat the Drums! A Book of Holidays, Occasions, Celebrations, Remembrances, Occurrences, Special Days, Weeks, & Months. LC 79-19529. (Illus.). (gr. 1-5). 1979. 9.95 (ISBN 0-684-16402-7). Scribner.
Sechrist, Elizabeth H. Red Letter Days. rev. ed. (Illus.). (gr. 3-7). 1965. 6.67 (ISBN 0-8255-8162-1); PLB 6.47 (ISBN 0-8255-8163-X). Macrae.
Simond, Ada D. Let's Pretend: Mae Dee & Her Family & the First Wedding of the Year. LC 78-62432. (National History Ser.). (Illus.). (gr. 3 up). 1979. 7.95 (ISBN 0-89482-003-6); softcover 4.95 (ISBN 0-89482-004-4); audio cassettes 5.95 (ISBN 0-89482-016-8). Stevenson Pr.
--Let's Pretend: Mae Dee & Her Family in the Merry, Merry Season. LC 77-88603. (National History Ser.). (Illus.). (gr. 3 up). 1978. 7.95 (ISBN 0-89482-005-2); softcover 4.95 (ISBN 0-89482-006-0); audio cassettes 5.95 (ISBN 0-89482-017-6). Stevenson Pr.
--Let's Pretend: Mae Dee & Her Family on a Weekend in May. LC 77-20629. (National History Ser.). (Illus.). (gr. 3 up). 1977. 7.95 (ISBN 0-89482-010-9); softcover 4.95 (ISBN 0-89482-011-7); audio cassette 5.95 (ISBN 0-89482-018-4). Stevenson Pr.
Tudor, Tasha. A Time to Keep: The Tasha Tudor Book of Holidays. LC 77-9067. (Illus.). (gr. 4-8). 1977. 6.95 (ISBN 0-528-82019-2). Rand.

HOLIDAYS–POETRY

Harrington, Mildred P. & Thomas, Josephine H., eds. Our Holidays in Poetry. 1929. 9.00 (ISBN 0-8242-0039-X). Wilson.
Holiday Poems. 1980. 8.95 (ISBN 0-686-28033-4). Great Nat Soc Poet.
Larrick, Nancy, ed. Poetry for Holidays. LC 66-10724. (Poetry Ser.). (gr. 2-5). 1966. PLB 6.09 (ISBN 0-8116-4100-7). Garrard.
Livingston, Myra C., ed. O Frabjous Day: Poetry for Holidays and Special Occasions. LC 76-28510. 216p. (gr. 7 up). 1977. 8.95 (ISBN 0-689-50076-9, McElderry Bk). Atheneum.
Mother's Day, Father's Day Poems. 110p. 1980. pap. 6.95 (ISBN 0-686-28029-6). Great Nat Soc Poet.
Sechrist, Elizabeth H. Poems for Red Letter Days. (Illus.). (gr. 3-7). 1951. PLB 5.97 (ISBN 0-8255-8155-9). Macrae.

HOLIDAYS–SONGS AND MUSIC

see also Christmas Music; Easter Music

Gerson, Trina. Holiday Songs. 84p. (ps-7). 1981. pap. text ed. write for info. (ISBN 0-9605878-2-9). Anirt Pr.
Munoz, Lopez A. Programas Para Dias Especiales Tomo I. 107p. 1980. pap. 1.60 (ISBN 0-311-07005-1). Casa Bautista.
Quackenbush, Robert, ed. & illus. The Holiday Song Book. LC 77-5895. (Illus.). (gr. 1 up). 1977. 9.95 (ISBN 0-688-41820-1); PLB 9.55 (ISBN 0-688-51820-6). Lothrop.

HOLIDAYS, JEWISH

see Fasts and Feasts–Judaism

HOLINESS

see also Pentecostal Churches; Perfection; Sanctification

Arnoudt, Peter J. The Imitation of the Sacred Heart of Jesus. LC 79-112463. 1974. pap. 7.50 (ISBN 0-89555-012-1, 149). TAN Bks Pubs.
Baker, S. Hidden Manna. pap. 3.50 (ISBN 0-686-12875-3). Schmul Pub Co.
Baldwin, H. A. Holiness & the Human Element. pap. 2.95 (ISBN 0-686-12876-1). Schmul Pub Co.
Baxter, J. Sidlow. His Deeper Work in Us. 256p. 1974. pap. 4.95 (ISBN 0-310-20651-0). Zondervan.
Bray, Gerald L. Holiness & the Will of God: Perspectives on the Theology of Tertullian. LC 79-5211. (New Foundations Theological Library). (Peter Toon & Ralph Martin series editors). 1980. 18.50 (ISBN 0-8042-3705-0). John Knox.
Brengle. Heart Talks on Holiness. pap. 2.95 (ISBN 0-686-12873-7). Schmul Pub Co.
--Helps to Holiness. pap. 2.95 (ISBN 0-686-12874-5). Schmul Pub Co.
--The Way of Holiness. pap. 1.50 (ISBN 0-686-12920-2). Schmul Pub Co.
Bridges, Jerry. The Pursuit of Holiness. LC 78-18109. 1978. pap. 2.95 (ISBN 0-89109-430-X, 14308). NavPress.
Brooks, Noel. Scriptural Holiness. 3.95 (ISBN 0-911866-53-1); pap. 2.95 (ISBN 0-911866-54-X). Advocate.
Bunyan, John. Holy Life: The Beauty of Christianity. pap. 1.95 (ISBN 0-685-19832-4). Reiner.
Cook. New Testament Holiness. 2.95 (ISBN 0-686-12895-8). Schmul Pub Co.
Dieter, Melvin E. The Holiness Revival of the Nineteenth Century. LC 80-17259. (Studies in Evangelicalism: No. 1). 366p. 1980. 17.50 (ISBN 0-8108-1328-9). Scarecrow.
Fenelon, Francois. Christian Perfection. Whiston, Charles F., ed. Stillman, Mildred W., tr. from Fr. LC 75-22545. 224p. 1976. pap. 2.95 (ISBN 0-87123-083-6, 200083). Bethany Hse.
Gillquist, Peter E. Why We Haven't Changed the World. 1981. 8.95 (ISBN 0-8007-1273-0). Revell.
Inskip, J. S. Holiness Essays & Experiences. pap. 2.50 (ISBN 0-686-12877-X). Schmul Pub Co.
Ironside, H. A. Holiness: The False & the True. 4.75 (ISBN 0-87213-364-8); pap. 2.75 (ISBN 0-87213-365-6). Loizeaux.
Jones, Charles E. Guide to the Study of the Holiness Movement. LC 74-659. (ATLA Bibliography Ser.: No. 1). 1974. 35.00 (ISBN 0-8108-0703-3). Scarecrow.
--Perfectionist Persuasion: The Holiness Movement & American Methodism, 1867-1936. LC 74-1376. (ATLA Monograph: No. 5). (Illus.). 1974. 10.00 (ISBN 0-8108-0747-5). Scarecrow.
Lutzer, Erwin. How in This World Can I Be Holy? pap. 4.95 study ed (ISBN 0-8024-3591-2). Moody.
Murray, Andrew. Holy in Christ. 1969. pap. 3.95 (ISBN 0-87123-216-2, 210216). Bethany Hse.
Nicholl, Donald. Holiness. 176p. (Orig.). 1981. pap. 7.95 (ISBN 0-8164-2336-9). Seabury.
Redpath, Alan. Victorious Christian Living: Studies in the Book of Joshua. 1955. 8.95 (ISBN 0-8007-0336-7). Revell.
Ryle, J. C. Holiness. 352p. 1977. Repr. of 1959 ed. 9.50 (ISBN 0-227-67482-0). Attic Pr.
Shelhamer. Holiness: How Obtained & Retained. 2.95 (ISBN 0-686-12878-8). Schmul Pub Co.
Simpson, Albert B. Wholly Sanctified. pap. 2.50 (ISBN 0-87509-043-5). Chr Pubns.
Spurgeon, C. H. Exposition of the Doctrines of Grace. 1.25 (ISBN 0-686-09096-9). Pilgrim Pubns.
--The Saint & His Savior. 3.95 (ISBN 0-686-09087-X). Pilgrim Pubns.

HOLISM

Albright, Peter & Albright, Bets P. Body, Mind & Spirit. 2nd ed. (Illus.). 320p. 1981. pap. 9.95 (ISBN 0-8289-0386-7). Greene.
Albright, Peter & Albright, Bets P., eds. Body, Mind & Spirit. LC 80-12671. (Illus.). 12.95 (ISBN 0-8289-0385-9). Greene.
Allen, David, et al, eds. Whole-Person Medicine. LC 79-2807. 1980. pap. 8.95 (ISBN 0-87784-815-7). Inter-Varsity.
Bach, Edward. The Bach Flower Remedies. LC 79-87679. 1979. 5.95 (ISBN 0-87983-192-8); pap. 4.95 (ISBN 0-87983-193-6). Keats.
Barton, John & Barton, Margaret. Biokinesiology: Vol II Neurovasculars. 3rd ed. (Encyclopedia of Mind & Body: Vol. II). (Illus.). 110p. (Orig.). 1980. pap. 10.00 (ISBN 0-937216-05-4). J&M Barton.
Beierle, Herbert L. Art & Science of Wholeness. 1975. 20.00 (ISBN 0-686-12736-6). U of Healing.
--A Gift from Self to Self. 1981. 10.00 (ISBN 0-686-31155-8). U of Healing.
--Die Kunst und Wissenschaft der Guettlichen Ganzheit. 20.00 (ISBN 0-686-31156-6). U of Healing.
Berkeley Holistic Health Center, compiled by. Holistic Health Lifebook. LC 81-2846. (Illus.). 384p. 1981. pap. 10.95 (ISBN 0-915904-53-5). And-or Pr.
Birch, L. C. & Cobb, J. B. The Liberation of Life: From the Cell to the Community. LC 80-42156. 300p. Date not set. price not set (ISBN 0-521-23787-4). Cambridge U Pr.
Blate, Michael. The Tao of Health. (Illus.). 1978. pap. 6.95 (ISBN 0-916878-05-8). Falkynor Bks.
Blattner, Barbara. Holistic Nursing. (Illus.). 400p. 1981. text ed. 16.95 (ISBN 0-13-392563-3); pap. text ed. 12.95 (ISBN 0-686-68605-5). P-H.
Buess, Lynn M. Synergy Session. LC 80-67932. (Illus.). 113p. (Orig.). 1980. pap. 4.95 (ISBN 0-87516-427-7). De Vorss.
Clark, Linda. Get Well Naturally. 5.95 (ISBN 0-686-29889-6); pap. 1.95 (ISBN 0-686-29890-X). Cancer Bk Hse.
--How to Improve Your Health. LC 78-61329. 1979. 8.95 (ISBN 0-87983-181-2); pap. 4.95 (ISBN 0-87983-180-4). Keats.
Collier, Richard B. Pleneurethic: Way of Life, System of Therapeutics. (Illus.). 1979. 10.00 (ISBN 0-682-49372-4). Exposition.
Daniel, E. J. Any Other Song: A Plea for Holistic Communication. LC 79-24892. 185p. 1980. pap. text ed. 10.95 (ISBN 0-87619-460-9). R J Brady.
Deverell, Dore. How I Healed My Cancer Holistically. 3.95 (ISBN 0-686-29909-4). Cancer Bk Hse.
--How I Healed My Cancer Holistically (& Discovered the Cancer Coverup) Deverell, David, ed. 172p. (Orig.). 1978. 4.95 (ISBN 0-686-30100-5). Psychenutrition.
Duke, William J. Themes of Wholeness. 200p. 1981. pap. write for info. Ideal Pubs.
Flynn, Patricia A. Holistic Health: The Art & Science of Care. (Illus.). 259p. 1980. pap. text ed. 12.95 (ISBN 0-87619-626-1). R J Brady.
Garnet, Eva D. Movement Is Life: A Holistic Approach to Exercise for Older Adults. (Illus.). 150p. (Orig.). 1981. pap. text ed. 12.50 (ISBN 0-916622-19-3). Princeton Bk Co.
Grant, Lillian. The Holistic Revolution. 1978. 7.98 (ISBN 0-517-53814-8, Pub. by Ward Ritchie); pap. 4.95 (ISBN 0-517-53759-1, Pub. by Ward Ritchie). Crown.
Halpern, Ruben & Halpern, Joshua. The Art & Practice of Holistic Healing. 1980. 10.95 (ISBN 0-685-95053-0); pap. 5.95 (ISBN 0-89496-020-2). Ross-Back Roads.
Hames, Carolyn C. & Joseph, Dayle H. Basic Concepts of Helping: A Wholistic Approach. (Illus.). 260p. 1980. pap. text ed. 10.95x (ISBN 0-8385-0558-9). ACC.
Hanna, Thomas. The Body of Life. LC 79-3503. (Illus.). 1980. 9.95 (ISBN 0-394-42383-6). Knopf.
Hastings, Arthur, et al. Health for the Whole Person: The Complete Guide to Holistic Medicine. 672p. 1981. pap. 3.95 (ISBN 0-553-20322-3). Bantam.

Haynes, Una H. Holistic Health Care for Young Children with Developmental Disabilities. 240p. 1981. pap. text ed. 17.95 (ISBN 0-8391-1699-3). Univ Park.
Hillig, Chuck. What Are You Doing in My Universe? 1981. pap. cancelled (ISBN 0-686-72422-4). Vulcan Bks.
Hippchen, Leonard. Holistic Approaches to Offender Rehabilitation. (Illus.). 440p. 1981. 38.75 (ISBN 0-398-04460-0). C C Thomas.
Holism & Ecology. 16p. 1981. pap. 5.00 (ISBN 92-808-0326-3, TUNU141, UNU). Unipub.
Hudson, Thomas J. The Law of Mental Medicine. 1979. pap. 2.50 (ISBN 0-89083-463-6). Zebra.
Jaffe, Dennis T. Healing from Within. LC 79-23831. 1980. 10.95 (ISBN 0-394-41032-7). Knopf.
Johnson, Michael L. Holistic Technology. LC 76-52145. 1977. 9.95 (ISBN 0-87212-070-8). Libra.
Jones, George A. The Possible Vision: Holistic New Age Education. LC 80-52612. 104p. 1981. pap. 5.95 (ISBN 0-917610-02-4). Rookfield.
Kastenbaum, Robert, et al. Holistic Therapy for Geriatric Patients. (Cushing Hospital Ser. on Aging & Terminal Care). write for info. (ISBN 0-88410-717-5). Ballinger Pub.
Khalsa, Rama K. Healing the Healer: A Holistic Transpersonal Approach to Burn-Out Prevention for the Health Professional. LC 78-74168. (Illus.). 1978. pap. 3.95 (ISBN 0-933320-01-9). Center Health.
Kolbe, Nonsignor. The Catholic View of Holism. 1928. 10.00 (ISBN 0-8414-5602-X). Folcroft.
Kushi, Michio. How to See Your Health: The Book of Oriental Diagnosis. LC 79-89346. (Illus.). 208p. (Orig.). 1980. pap. 9.95 (ISBN 0-87040-467-9). Japan Pubns.
LaPatra, Jack. Healing: The Coming Revolution in Holistic Medicine. 1978. 9.95 (ISBN 0-07-036359-5, GB). McGraw.
McGarey, Gladys T. Born to Live: A Holistic Approach to Childbirth. (Illus.). 138p. (Orig.). 1981. pap. 5.95 (ISBN 0-9600882-2-9). Ross-Erikson.
Malone, Marcy. In a Loving Way. 1981. 11.95 (ISBN 0-686-72423-2). Vulcan Bks.
Mehl, Lewis E. Mind & Matter: An Existential Approach to Holistic Health. (Holistic Approaches to Health & Disease Ser.). (Illus.). 1981. pap. price not set (ISBN 0-939508-02-8). Mindbody.
Neev, Elan. Wholistic Healing: How to Harmonize Your Body, Mind & Spirit with Life--for Freedom, Joy, Health, Beauty, Love, Money & Psychic Powers. LC 77-71152. (Illus.). 1977. deluxe ed. 8.95 ltd. ed. (ISBN 0-918482-01-1); pap. 4.95 (ISBN 0-918482-01-1). Ageless Bks.
New Dimensions Foundation, ed. The New Healers. LC 80-12100. 160p. 1980. pap. 5.95 (ISBN 0-915904-49-7). And-Or Pr.
Notes for an Epistemology of Holism. 14p. 1980. pap. 5.00 (ISBN 92-808-0065-5, TUNU 027, UNU). Unipub.
Ouellette, Raymond. Holistic Healing & the Edgar Cayce Readings. LC 80-80446. 384p. 1980. 9.95 (ISBN 0-936450-07-X). Aero Pr.
Peacocke, Christopher A. Holistic Explanation: Action, Space, Interpretation. 1979. 22.50x (ISBN 0-19-824605-6). Oxford U Pr.
Pelletier, Kenneth R. Holistic Medicine. 1980. pap. 5.95 (ISBN 0-440-55288-5, Delta). Dell.
Pelletier, Kenneth R., ed. Holistic Medicine: From Pathology to Optimum Health. (A Merloyd Lawrence Bk.). 1979. 10.00 (ISBN 0-440-05288-2, Sey Lawr). Delacorte.
Phillips, D. C. Holistic Thought in Social Science. LC 76-7688. 1976. 8.50x (ISBN 0-8047-0923-8); pap. 3.75 (ISBN 0-8047-1015-5, SP 156). Stanford U Pr.
Rose-Neil, Sidney. Acupuncture & the Life Energies. 160p. 1981. pap. 8.95 (ISBN 0-88231-121-2). ASI Pubs Inc.
Schuster, Clara & Ashburn, Shirley. The Process of Human Development: A Holistic Approach. LC 79-91938. 1980. text ed. 21.95 (ISBN 0-316-77535-5). Little.
Simon, B. X. The California Directory of Healing Arts, Holistic & Homeopathic Practitioners. (Orig.). 1981. pap. write for info. (ISBN 0-935618-01-5). Rossi Pubns.
Smuts, J. C. Holism & Evolution. LC 72-7967. 362p. 1973. Repr. of 1926 ed. lib. bdg. 22.50 (ISBN 0-8371-6556-3, SMHO). Greenwood.
Sobel, David. Ways of Health: Holistic Approaches to Ancient & Contemporary Medicine. 1979. 14.95 (ISBN 0-15-195308-2). HarBraceJ.
Sobel, David J. Ways of Health: Holistic Approaches to Ancient & Contemporary Medicine. LC 78-14081. 1979. pap. 7.95 (ISBN 0-15-694992-X, Harv). HarBraceJ.
Sonnier, Isidore L. Holistic Education: Teaching-Learning in the Affective Domain. LC 81-80241. 1981. 13.95 (ISBN 0-8022-2389-3). Philos Lib.
Thompson, Carroll J. Holistic Healing. 1979. pap. 4.95 (ISBN 0-89185-195-X). Anthelion Pr.
Van Nuys, Kelvin. A Holist Pilgrimage. LC 80-84738. 400p. 1981. 19.95 (ISBN 0-8022-2383-4). Philos Lib.
Walker, Morton. Total Health: The Holistic Alternative to Traditional Medicine. LC 78-57412. 1979. 9.95 (ISBN 0-89696-010-2). Everest Hse.
Wigmore, Ann. Why Suffer? (Illus.). 173p. pap. text ed. 2.95 (ISBN 0-686-29398-3). Hippocrates.
Woody, Robert H. Bodymind Liberation: Achieving Holistic Health. 172p. 1980. 15.50 (ISBN 0-398-04055-9). C C Thomas.
--The Use of Massage in Facilitating Holistic Health. (Illus.). 136p. 1980. text ed. 12.50 (ISBN 0-398-03954-2). C C Thomas.

HOLLADAY, BENJAMIN, 1819-1887

Lucia, Ellis. Saga of Ben Holladay. 1959. 10.50 (ISBN 0-8038-6641-0). Hastings.

HOLLAND, GEORGE, 1791-1870

Keese, William L. Group of Comedians. LC 71-130104. (Dunlap Society Ser: No. 15). 1970. Repr. of 1901 ed. lib. bdg. 16.50 (ISBN 0-8337-1903-3). B Franklin.

HOLLAND, HENRY RICHARD VASSALL FOX, 1773-1840

Sanders, Lloyd. Holland House Circle. LC 70-82004. (Illus.). Repr. of 1908 ed. 20.00 (ISBN 0-405-08915-5). Arno.

HOLLAND, HENRY SCOTT, 1874-1918

Drew, Mary. Acton, Gladstone & Others. facs. ed. LC 68-20294. (Essay Index Reprint Ser). 1924. 12.00 (ISBN 0-8369-0390-0). Arno.
--Acton, Gladstone & Others. LC 68-16292. 1968. Repr. of 1924 ed. 10.00 (ISBN 0-8046-0118-6). Kennikat.

HOLLAND, JOHN PHILIP, 1841-1914

Morris, Richard K. John P. Holland, 1841 to 1914. LC 79-6120. (Navies & Men Ser.). (Illus.). 1980. Repr. of 1966 ed. lib. bdg. 18.00x (ISBN 0-405-13048-1). Arno.

HOLLAND

see Netherlands

HOLLAND HOUSE

Kriegel, Abraham D., ed. The Holland House Diaries, 1831-1840: The Diary of Henry Richard Vassall Fox, Third Lord Holland. 1976. 42.50x (ISBN 0-7100-8406-4). Routledge & Kegan.
Mitchell, Leslie. Holland House. (Illus.). 320p. 1980. 32.00x (ISBN 0-7156-1116-X, Pub. by Duckworth England). Biblio Dist.
Sanders, Lloyd. Holland House Circle. LC 70-82004. (Illus.). Repr. of 1908 ed. 20.00 (ISBN 0-405-08915-5). Arno.

HOLLAND LAND COMPANY

Chazanof, William. Joseph Ellicott & the Holland Land Company: The Opening of Western New York. 1979. pap. 6.95 (ISBN 0-8156-0161-1). Syracuse U Pr.
Evans, Paul D. Holland Land Company. LC 68-35709. Repr. of 1924 ed. 25.00x (ISBN 0-678-01065-X). Kelley.

HOLLANDER, XAVIERA

Hollander, Xaviera. Xaviera on the Best Part of a Man. (Orig.). 1975. pap. 2.50 (ISBN 0-451-09690-8, E9690, Sig). NAL.

HOLLAR, WENCESLAUS, 1607-1677

Hind, Arthur M. Wenceslaus Holler & His Views of London & Windsor in the Seventeenth Century. LC 68-56500. (Illus.). 1973. Repr. of 1922 ed. lib. bdg. 22.00 (ISBN 0-405-08622-9, Blom Pubns). Arno.
Parthey, G. Wenzel Hollar: Beschreibendes Varzeichniss Seiner Kupferstiche. (Ger.). 1853. pap. text ed. 33.00x (ISBN 90-6041-052-1). Humanities.
Van Eerde, Katherine S. Wenceslaus Hollar: Delineator of His Time. (Special Publications Ser). 1978. 30.00 (ISBN 0-8139-0297-5). Folger Bks.

HOLLIDAY, JOHN HENRY, 1852?-1887?

Churchill, E. Richard. Doc Holliday, Bat Masterson, Wyatt Earp: Their Colorado Careers. 1978. 2.00 (ISBN 0-913488-05-4). Timberline Bks.
Jahns, Pat. The Frontier World of Doc Holliday: Faro Dealer from Dallas to Deadwood. LC 78-26811. xiv, 305p. 1979. pap. 6.50 (ISBN 0-8032-7550-1, BB697, Bison). U of Nebr Pr.
Myers, John M. Doc Holliday. LC 55-5528. 224p. 1973. pap. 3.95 (ISBN 0-8032-5781-3, BB 570, Bison). U of Nebr Pr.

HOLLINS COLLEGE

Niederer, Frances J. Hollins College: An Illustrated History. LC 72-97863. (Illus.). 217p. 1973. 12.50x (ISBN 0-8139-0472-2). U Pr of Va.

HOLLINS (WILLIAM) AND COMPANY, LTD.

Wells, Frederick A. Hollins & Viyella. LC 68-18646. (Illus.). 1968. 12.95x (ISBN 0-678-05646-3). Kelley.

HOLLOW-WARE, SILVER

see Silverware

HOLLY, BUDDY, d. 1959

Goldrosen, John. Buddy Holly. 1979. pap. 7.95 (ISBN 0-8256-3936-0, Quick Fox). Music Sales.

HOLLY

Dallimore. Holly Yew & Box. LC 76-10174. (Illus.). Date not set. Repr. 15.00 (ISBN 0-913728-12-8). Theophrastus.

HOLLYWOOD, CALIFORNIA

Anger, Kenneth. Hollywood Babylon. Date not set. pap. 3.50 (ISBN 0-440-15325-5). Dell.
Bacon, James. Made in Hollywood. (Illus.). 1978. pap. 2.25 (ISBN 0-446-82913-7). Warner Bks.
Balshofer, Fred J. & Miller, Arthur C. One Reel a Week. LC 67-24119. (Illus.). 1968. 19.95 (ISBN 0-520-00073-0). U of Cal Pr.
Buschlen, Jack P. Heil Hollywood. Kupelnick, Bruce S., ed. LC 76-52095. (Classics of Film Literature Ser.). 1978. lib. bdg. 18.00 (ISBN 0-8240-2869-4). Garland Pub.
Carpozi, George, Jr. That's Hollywood: Beautiful & Special People, No. 7. (Orig.). 1980. pap. 1.95 (ISBN 0-532-23281-X). Woodhill.
--That's Hollywood: The Clossal Cowboys, No. 6. (Orig.). 1980. pap. 1.95 (ISBN 0-532-23222-4). Woodhill.
Cini, Zelda, et al. Hollywood: Land & Legend. (Illus.). 192p. 1980. 19.95 (ISBN 0-87000-486-7). Arlington Hse.
Colombo, John R., ed. Popcorn in Paradise: The Wit & Wisdom of Hollywood. LC 79-22186. (Illus.). 192p. 1980. 9.95 (ISBN 0-03-056144-2). HR&W.
Cowie, Peter, ed. Hollywood, 1920-1970. LC 73-18863. (Illus.). 288p. 1976. 25.00 (ISBN 0-498-01400-2). A S Barnes.
David, Saul. The Industry: Life in the Hollywood Fast Lane. Chase, Edward T., ed. LC 80-5783. 288p. 1981. 14.50 (ISBN 0-8129-0971-2). Times Bks.
Davis, Sammy, Jr. Hollywood in a Suitcase. LC 80-14792. (Illus.). 1980. 11.95 (ISBN 0-688-03736-4). Morrow.
Fitzmaurice, Victor. Bel-Heirs. 1981. 9.95 (ISBN 0-533-04875-3). Vantage.
Gow, Gordon. Hollywood in the Fifties. LC 70-141572. (Hollywood Ser). (Illus.). 1971. pap. 4.95 (ISBN 0-498-07859-0). A S Barnes.
Kanin, Garson. Hollywood. 1974. 8.95 (ISBN 0-670-37575-6). Viking Pr.
Lamparski, Richard. Lamparski's Hidden Hollywood: Where the Stars Lived, Loved & Died. 1981. pap. 8.95 (ISBN 0-686-71142-4, Fireside). S&S.
Levin, Martin, ed. Hollywood & the Great Fan Magazines. LC 70-122641. 1971. pap. 5.95 (ISBN 0-87795-006-7). Arbor Hse.
Lewis, Arthur H. It Was Fun While It Lasted. new ed. 1973. 8.95 (ISBN 0-671-27106-7). Trident.
Lockwood, Charles. Dream Palaces: Hollywood "at Home". LC 81-65260. (Illus.). 320p. 1981. 18.95 (ISBN 0-670-28461-0). Viking Pr.
Morrill, Mitch. The Erotic Guide to Hollywood. LC 78-72494. (Illus.). 1979. pap. 5.95 (ISBN 0-89554-006-1). Brasch & Brasch.
Owens, Fred. Making It in Hollywood: An Actor's Guide. 96p. (Orig.). 1980. pap. 5.00 (ISBN 0-936182-01-6). Diamond Heights.
Palmer, Edwin. History of Hollywood. Kupelnick, Bruce S., ed. LC 76-52118. (Classics of Film Literature Ser.). 1978. lib. bdg. 23.00 (ISBN 0-8240-2886-4). Garland Pub.
Samuels, M. Screen Greats: Hollywood Nostalgia. 1980. pap. 2.00 (ISBN 0-931064-30-9). Starlog.
Spatz, Jonas. Hollywood in Fiction: Some Versions of the American Myth. rev. ed. LC 75-75887. (Studies in American Literature: Vol. 22). 1969. text ed. 27.50x (ISBN 90-2790-466-9). Mouton.
Strauss, David P. & Worth, Fred L. Hollywood Trivia. 352p. (Orig.). 1981. pap. 2.75 (ISBN 0-446-95492-6). Warner Bks.
Thomas, Tony & Behlmer, Rudy. Hollywood's Hollywood. 1979. pap. 8.95 (ISBN 0-8065-0680-6). Citadel Pr.
Wallace, Irving. Special People, Special Times. 192p. (Orig.). 1981. pap. 2.25 (ISBN 0-523-48001-6). Pinnacle Bks.

HOLM, HANYA, 1893-

Sorell, Walter. Hanya Holm: The Biography of an Artist. LC 69-17796. 1979. 15.00x (ISBN 0-8195-3096-4, Pub. by Wesleyan U Pr); pap. 8.00x (ISBN 0-8195-6060-X). Columbia U Pr.

HOLMAN, WILLIAM ARTHUR, 1871-1934

Joyner, Conrad. Holman Versus Hughes: Extension of Australian Commonwealth Powers. LC 61-63516. (U of Fla. Social Science Monographs: No. 10). 1961. pap. 3.00 (ISBN 0-8130-0123-4). U Presses Fla.

HOLMES, ERNEST SHURTLEFF

Armor, Reginald. Ernest Holmes: The Man. 1977. pap. 4.95 (ISBN 0-911336-66-4). Sci of Mind.
Holmes, Ernest. Ernest Holmes Seminar Lectures. Maxwell, Georgia, ed. 128p. 1980. pap. 5.95 (ISBN 0-911336-83-4). Sci of Mind.
--Gateway to Life. Kinnear, Willis, ed. 96p. (Orig.). 1974. pap. 4.50 (ISBN 0-911336-59-1). Sci of Mind.

HOLMES, GEORGE FREDERICK, 1820-1897

Gillespie, Neal C. Collapse of Orthodoxy: The Intellectual Ordeal of George Frederick Holmes. LC 70-163978. 1972. 9.95x (ISBN 0-8139-0345-9). U Pr of Va.
Hawkins, Richmond L. Auguste Comte & the United States, 1816-1853. 1936. pap. 9.00 (ISBN 0-527-01109-6). Kraus Repr.

HOLMES, OLIVER WENDELL, 1809-1894

Brown, E. E. Life of Oliver Wendell Holmes. 1903. lib. bdg. 27.50 (ISBN 0-8482-9995-7). Norwood Edns.
Crothers, Samuel M. Oliver Wendell Holmes, the Autocrat & His Fellow-Boarders. facs. ed. LC 72-124231. (Select Bibliographies Reprint Ser). 1909. 10.00 (ISBN 0-8369-5420-3). Arno.
--Oliver Wendell Holmes: The Autocrat & His Fellow Boarders. LC 73-11301. 1973. lib. bdg. 17.50 (ISBN 0-8414-3382-8). Folcroft.
Hayakawa, S. I. & Jones, Howard M., eds. Oliver Wendell Holmes. 472p. 1980. Repr. of 1939 ed. lib. bdg. 40.00 (ISBN 0-8495-2351-6). Arden Lib.
Howe, M. DeWolfe. Holmes of the Breakfast-Table. (Illus.). 172p. Repr. of 1939 ed. 9.00 (ISBN 0-911858-16-4). Appel.
Hoyt, Edwin P. The Improper Bostonian: Dr. Oliver Wendell Holmes. LC 78-21275. (Illus.). 1979. 12.95 (ISBN 0-688-03429-2). Morrow.
Jerrold, Walter. Oliver Wendell Holmes. 1973. Repr. of 1893 ed. 20.00 (ISBN 0-8274-0021-7). R West.
Kennedy, William S. Oliver Wendall Holmes. Repr. of 1883 ed. lib. bdg. 40.00 (ISBN 0-8495-3007-5). Arden Lib.
--Oliver Wendell Holmes. 1973. Repr. of 1883 ed. 35.00 (ISBN 0-8274-0025-X). R West.
--Oliver Wendell Holmes: Poet, Litterateur, Scientist. LC 74-13969. 1974. Repr. of 1883 ed. lib. bdg. 35.00 (ISBN 0-8414-5514-7). Folcroft.
Morse, John T. Life & Letters of Oliver Wendell Holmes, 2 vols. 1897. Repr. 65.00 (ISBN 0-8274-2911-8). R West.
Morse, John T., Jr. Oliver Wendell Holmes, 2 vols. LC 80-21475. (American Men & Women of Letters Ser.). 700p. 1981. Set. pap. 10.95 (ISBN 0-87754-171-X). Chelsea Hse.
Paterson, Helen S. Oliver Wendell Holmes: Soldier, Lawyer, Supreme Court Justice. LC 78-71848. (Illus.). 1979. 7.95 (ISBN 0-914932-03-9). Fox Hills.
Richardson, Dorsey. Constitutional Doctrines of Justice Oliver Wendell Holmes. LC 79-1618. 1980. Repr. of 1924 ed. 11.50 (ISBN 0-88355-921-8). Hyperion Conn.
--Constitutional Doctrines of Justice Oliver Wendell Holmes. LC 78-64115. (Johns Hopkins University. Studies in the Social Sciences. Forty-Second Ser. 1924: 3). Repr. of 1924 ed. 15.00 (ISBN 0-404-61230-X). AMS Pr.
Slicer, Thomas R. From Poet to Premier: The Centennial Cycle, 1809-1909 - Poe, Lincoln, Holmes, Darwin, Tennyson, Gladstone. 1977. Repr. of 1909 ed. lib. bdg. 25.00 (ISBN 0-8495-4820-9). Arden Lib.
Small, Miriam R. Oliver Wendell Holmes. (Twayne's United States Authors Ser). 1962. pap. 3.45 (ISBN 0-8084-0237-4, T29, Twayne). Coll & U Pr.
--Oliver Wendell Holmes. (U. S. Authors Ser.: No. 29). 1962. lib. bdg. 10.95 (ISBN 0-8057-0380-2). Twayne.
Tilton, Eleanor M. Amiable Autocrat: A Biography of Doctor Oliver Wendell Holmes. 1976. Repr. of 1947 ed. lib. bdg. 20.00x (ISBN 0-374-97945-6). Octagon.
Townsend, Lewis W. Oliver Wendell Holmes. LC 74-31155. Repr. of 1895 ed. lib. bdg. 15.00 (ISBN 0-8414-8612-3). Folcroft.

HOLMES, OLIVER WENDELL, 1809-1894-BIBLIOGRAPHY

Currier, Thomas F., compiled by. Bibliography of Oliver Wendell Holmes. Tilton, Eleanor M., ed. LC 70-139916. (Illus.). 1971. Repr. of 1953 ed. 30.00 (ISBN 0-8462-1536-5). Russell.
Ives, George B. Bibliography of Oliver Wendell Holmes. LC 72-193361. 1907. lib. bdg. 25.00 (ISBN 0-8414-5067-6). Folcroft.
--A Bibliography of Oliver Wendell Holmes. LC 77-6175. 1977. Repr. of 1907 ed. lib. bdg. 25.00 (ISBN 0-89341-167-1). Longwood Pr.
Shriver, Harry C. What Justice Holmes Wrote, & What Has Been Written About Him, a Bibliography 1866-1976. LC 77-89073. 1978. 4.00 (ISBN 0-914932-02-0). Fox Hills.

HOLMES, OLIVER WENDELL, 1841-1935

Bander, Edward J., ed. Justice Holmes, Ex Cathedra. 1966. 9.95 (ISBN 0-87215-003-8). Michie-Bobbs.
Bent, Silas. Justice Oliver Wendell Holmes: A Biography. LC 75-98636. (BCL Ser. I). (Illus.). 1969. Repr. of 1932 ed. 28.00 (ISBN 0-404-00751-1). AMS Pr.
Burton, David. Oliver Wendell Holmes, Jr. What Manner of Liberal? LC 78-23645. (American Problem Ser.). 168p. 1979. pap. 5.50 (ISBN 0-88275-793-8). Krieger.

Burton, David H. Oliver Wendell Holmes, Jr. (United States Authors Ser.: No. 375). 1980. lib. bdg. 10.95 (ISBN 0-8057-7262-6). Twayne.
Burton, David H., ed. Progressive Masks: Letters of Oliver Wendell Holmes, Jr., & Franklin Ford. LC 80-54787. 155p. 1982. 16.00 (ISBN 0-87413-188-X). U Delaware Pr.
Holmes, Oliver Wendell. Holmes-Sheehan Correspondence: The Letters of Justice Oliver W. Holmes, Jr. & Canon Patrick Augustine Sheehan. Burton, David H., ed. 1976. 8.95 (ISBN 0-8046-9164-9, National University Pub). Kennikat.
Howe, Mark D. Justice Oliver Wendell Holmes, 2 vols. Incl. Vol. 1. The Shaping Years, 1841-1870. (Illus.). 330p. 1957 (ISBN 0-674-49500-4); Vol. 2. The Proving Years, 1870-1882. (Illus.). 1963. 16.50x ea. (Belknap Pr). Harvard U Pr.
Lief, Alfred, ed. The Dissenting Opinions of Mr. Justice Holmes. xviii, 314p. 1981. Repr. of 1929 ed. lib. bdg. 27.50x (ISBN 0-8377-0811-7). Rothman.
Marke, Julius J., ed. Holmes Reader. rev. ed. LC 55-5961. 1964. pap. 2.50 (ISBN 0-379-11301-5). Oceana.
Schroeder, William L. Oliver Wendell Holmes: An Appreciation. LC 76-5423. 1976. Repr. of 1909 ed. lib. bdg. 17.50 (ISBN 0-8414-7640-3). Folcroft.
Shriver, Harry C. What Gusto: Stories & Anecdotes About Justice Oliver Wendell Holmes. LC 79-132249. (Illus.). 1970. 5.00 (ISBN 0-685-88599-2). Fox Hills.

HOLMES, ROBERT MASTEN, 1844-1864

Dennis, Frank A., ed. Kemper County Rebel: The Civil War Diary of Robert Masten Holmes, C.S.A. LC 72-93645. 128p. 1973. 2.00 (ISBN 0-87805-016-7). U Pr of Miss.

HOLOCAUST, JEWISH (1939-1945)

Alexander, Edward. The Resonance of Dust: Essays on Holocaust Literature & Jewish Fate. LC 79-15515. 1979. 15.00 (ISBN 0-8142-0303-5). Ohio St U Pr.
Altshuler, David A. Hitler's War Against the Jews - the Holocaust: A Young Reader's Version of the War Against the Jews: 1933-1945 by Lucy Dawidowicz. LC 78-5418. (Illus.). 1978. 8.95x (ISBN 0-87441-293-5); pap. 4.95x (ISBN 0-87441-222-6). Behrman.
America & the Holocaust. (American Jewish History Ser.: Vol. 70, Pt. 3). 1981. 6.00 (ISBN 0-911934-20-0). Am Jewish Hist Soc.
America & the Holocaust. (American Jewish History Ser.: Vol. 68, Pt. 3). 1979. 6.00 (ISBN 0-911934-01-4). Am Jewish Hist Soc.
American Jewish Committee. The Jewish Communities of Nazi-Occupied Europe. 400p. 1981. Repr. of 1944 ed. 28.50x (ISBN 0-86527-337-5). Fertig.
--The Jews in Nazi Germany. x, 177p. 1981. Repr. of 1935 ed. 19.50x (ISBN 0-86527-110-0). Fertig.
Apenszlak, Jacob, ed. The Black Book of Polish Jewry: An Account of the Martyrdom of Polish Jewry Under Nazi Occupation. xvi, 343p. 1982. Repr. of 1943 ed. 27.50x (ISBN 0-86527-340-5). Fertig.
Aptecker, George. Beyond Despair. (Illus.). 72p. 1980. 25.00 (ISBN 0-9604286-0-7). Kahn & Kahan.
Arad, Yizhak. Ghetto in Flames: The Struggle & Destruction of the Jews of Vilna. Date not set. price not set. ADL.
Arieti, Silvano. The Parnas. LC 79-1978. 1979. 10.00 (ISBN 0-465-05452-8). Basic.
Aronsfeld, Caesar C. The Ghosts of Fourteen-Ninety-Two. (Conference on Jewish Social Studies Ser.). 1979. 10.00x (ISBN 0-910430-00-4, Pub by Conf Jewish Soc Studies). Columbia U Pr.
Bauer, Yehuda. American Jewry & the Holocaust: The American Jewish Joint Distribution Committee, 1939-1945. 550p. 1981. 25.00 (ISBN 0-8143-1672-7). Wayne St U Pr.
--The Holocaust in Historical Perspective. LC 78-2988. (Samuel & Althea Stroum Lectures in Jewish Studies). 192p. 1978. 10.00 (ISBN 0-295-95606-2). U of Wash Pr.
--The Jewish Emergence from Powerlessness. LC 78-25830. 1979. 10.00x (ISBN 0-8020-2328-2); pap. 6.00 (ISBN 0-8020-6354-3). U of Toronto Pr.
--They Chose Life: Jewish Resistance in the Holocaust. LC 73-89085. (Illus.). 64p. (Orig.). 1973. pap. 1.25 (ISBN 0-87495-000-7). Am Jewish Comm.
Bauer, Yehuda, ed. Guide to Unpublished Materials of the Holocaust Period. (Yad Vashem Archive Material Ser.: Vol. 3, Pt. 1). 413p. 10.00 (ISBN 0-686-74941-3). ADL.
Bauer, Yehuda & Rotenstreich, Nathan, eds. Holocaust As a Historical Experience. 300p. 1981. text ed. 24.50x (ISBN 0-8419-0635-1); pap. text ed. 12.50x (ISBN 0-8419-0636-X). Holmes & Meier.
Berkovits, Eliezer. Faith After the Holocaust. 1973. 10.00x (ISBN 0-685-38388-1). Ktav.
Bilik, Dorothy S. Immigrant-Survivors: Post-Holocaust Consciousness in Recent Jewish-American Literature. 295p. 1981. 15.95x (ISBN 0-8195-5046-9). Wesleyan U Pr.
Blatter, Janet & Milton, Sybil. Art of the Holocaust. 272p. 1981. 29.95 (ISBN 0-8317-0418-7, Rutledge Pr). Smith Pubs.
Braham, Randolph L. The Politics of Genocide: The Holocaust in Hungary, 2 vols. LC 80-11096. (Illus.). 1116p. 1980. Set. 80.00x (ISBN 0-231-04496-8). Columbia U Pr.
Brennan, William. Medical Holocausts I: Exterminative Medicine in Nazi Germany & Contemporary America. LC 80-82305. (The Nordland Series in Contemporary American Social Problems). 392p. 1980. 19.95 (ISBN 0-913124-39-7); pap. 8.95 (ISBN 0-913124-52-4). Nordland Pub.
--Medical Holocausts II: The Language of Exterminative Medicine in Nazi Germany & Contemporary America. LC 80-82305. (The Nordland Series in Contemporary American Social Problems). 320p. 1981. 19.95 (ISBN 0-913124-40-0); pap. 8.95 (ISBN 0-913124-53-2). Nordland Pub.
Brenner, Reeve R. The Faith & Doubt of Holocaust Survivors. LC 79-6764. 1980. 12.95 (ISBN 0-02-904420-0). Free Pr.
Browning, Christopher R. The Final Solution & the German Foreign Office. LC 78-8996. 1978. text ed. 28.00x (ISBN 0-8419-0403-0). Holmes & Meier.
Butz, A. R. The Hoax of the Twentieth Century. LC 77-778964. (Illus.). 1977. 10.00 (ISBN 0-911038-23-X, Inst Hist Rev); pap. 6.00 (ISBN 0-911038-00-0). Noontide.
Butz, Arthur. The Hoax of the Twentieth Century. (Illus.). 315p. Date not set. 12.00 (ISBN 0-911038-23-X); pap. 8.00 (ISBN 0-686-76163-4). Inst Hist Rev.
Cargas, Harry J. A Christian Response to the Holocaust. (Illus.). 203p. 1981. 10.95 (ISBN 0-937050-16-4). Stonehenge Books.
Cargas, Harry J. & Corrigan, John T. The Holocaust: An Annotated Bibliography. 1977. pap. text ed. 4.00 (ISBN 0-87507-005-1). Cath Lib Assn.
Cargas, Henry J., ed. When God & Man Failed: Non-Jewish Views of the Holocaust. 320p. 1981. 16.95 (ISBN 0-02-521300-8). Macmillan.
Central Commission for the Investigation of German Crimes in Poland. German Crimes in Poland, 2 vols. in one. 1981. Repr. of 1947 ed. 29.50x (ISBN 0-86527-336-7). Fertig.
Chaim, Bezalel. A Bio-Bibliographical Dictionary of Holocaust & Anti-Holocaust Authors. 1980. lib. bdg. 49.50 (ISBN 0-686-59401-0). Revisionist Pr.
--A Bio-Bibliographical Dictionary of Notable Jews Who Perished in German Concentration Camps & Ghettos, Etc. 1980. lib. bdg. 49.50 (ISBN 0-686-59563-7). Revisionist Pr.
Chartok, Roselle, ed. The Holocaust Years: Society on Trial. Spencer, Jack. (gr. 9-12). 1978. pap. 2.50 (ISBN 0-553-20129-8). Bantam.
Cohen, Arthur A. The Tremendum: A Theological Interpretation of the Holocaust. 144p. 1981. 9.95 (ISBN 0-8245-0006-7). Crossroad NY.
Committee for Truth in History. The Six Million Reconsidered. Grimstad, William N., ed. (Illus.). 1979. pap. 6.00 (ISBN 0-911038-50-7). Noontide.
Crawford, Fred R. The Seventy-First Came...to Gunskirchen Lager. LC 79-51047. (Witness to the Holocaust: No. 1). (Illus.). 1979. pap. 1.00 (ISBN 0-89937-027-6). Ctr Res Soc Chg.
Czerniakow, Adam. Warsaw Diary of Adam Czerniakow. 1978. 16.95 (ISBN 0-8128-2523-3). Stein & Day.
Dawidowicz, Lucy. Holocaust Reader. LC 75-33740. pap. 6.95x (ISBN 0-87441-236-6). Behrman.
--The Jewish Presence: Essays on Identity & History. LC 78-6236. 1978. pap. 3.95 (ISBN 0-15-646221-4, Harv). HarBraceJ.
Dawidowicz, Lucy S. The Holocaust & the Historians. LC 80-29175. (Illus.). 200p. text ed. 15.00x (ISBN 0-674-40566-8). Harvard U Pr.
--The War Against the Jews: 1933-1945. 640p. 1976. pap. 3.50 (ISBN 0-553-02504-X, 13084-6). Bantam.
Dimensions of the Holocaust: A Series of Lectures Presented at Northwestern University & Coordinated by the Department of History. 64p. 1.95 (ISBN 0-686-74930-8). ADL.
Dimsdale, Joel E., ed. Survivors, Victims, & Perpetrators: Essays on the Nazi Holocaust. LC 79-24834. 474p. 1980. text ed. 19.50 (ISBN 0-89116-145-7). Hemisphere Pub.
Dinur, Ben Z. & Esh, Shaul, eds. Yad Vashem Studies, Vol. I. 183p. 7.50 (ISBN 0-686-74950-2). ADL.
Eisenberg, Azriel. Witness to the Holocaust. LC 80-25961. 649p. 1981. 17.95 (ISBN 0-8298-0432-3). Pilgrim NY.
Epstein, Helen. Children of the Holocaust. 1980. pap. 3.25 (ISBN 0-553-20153-0, G-20153-0). Bantam.
--Children of the Holocaust: Conversations with Sons & Daughters of Survivors. LC 78-23429. 1979. 10.95 (ISBN 0-399-12316-4). Putnam.
Face to Face: An Interreligious Bulletin. 39p. 1.50 (ISBN 0-686-74931-6). ADL.
Fackenheim, Emil L. God's Presence in History: Jewish Affirmations & Philosophical Reflections. LC 79-88135. (Deems Lectureship in Philosophy Ser). 1970. 11.00x (ISBN 0-8147-0142-6). NYU Pr.
--The Jewish Return into History: Reflections in the Age of Auschwitz & a New Jerusalem. LC 77-87861. 312p. 1980. pap. 6.95 (ISBN 0-8052-0649-3). Schocken.
--The Jewish Return into History: Reflections in the Age of Auschwitz & a New Jerusalem. LC 77-87861. 1978. 14.95 (ISBN 0-8052-3677-5). Schocken.
Faurisson, Robert. The Holocaust Debate: Revisionist Historians Versus Six Million Jews. 1980. lib. bdg. 59.95 (ISBN 0-686-62797-0). Revisionist Pr.
Fein, Helen. Accounting for Genocide: National Response & Jewish Victimization During the Holocaust. LC 78-53085. (Illus.). 1979. 15.95 (ISBN 0-02-910220-0). Free Pr.
Feingold, Henry L. The Politics of Rescue: The Roosevelt Administration & the Holocaust, Nineteen Thirty-Eight to Nineteen Forty-Five. expanded & updated ed. LC 80-81713. 432p. 1980. pap. 7.95 (ISBN 0-8052-5019-0, Pub. by Holocaust Library). Schocken.
--The Politics of Rescue: The Roosevelt Administration & the Holocaust, 1938-1945. LC 75-127049. 1970. 25.00 (ISBN 0-8135-0664-6). Rutgers U Pr.
Ferderber-Salz, Bertha. And the Sun Kept Shining. LC 80-81684. (Illus.). 240p. (Orig.). 1980. 12.95 (ISBN 0-89604-015-1); pap. 5.95 (ISBN 0-89604-017-8). Holocaust Lib.
Ferencz, Benjamin B. Less Than Slaves: Jewish Forced Labor & the Quest for Compensation. LC 79-10690. 1979. 15.00x (ISBN 0-674-52525-6). Harvard U Pr.
Fleischner, E., ed. Auschwitz - Beginning of a New Era? Reflections on the Holocaust. 22.50x (ISBN 0-87068-499-X). Ktav.
Flinker, Moshe. Young Moshe's Diary (the Diary of Moshe Flinker) The Spiritual Torment of a Jewish Boy in Nazi Europe. 126p. 6.00 (ISBN 0-686-74948-0). ADL.
Frank, Anne. The Works of Anne Frank. LC 73-16643. (Illus.). 332p. 1974. Repr. of 1959 ed. lib. bdg. 17.75x (ISBN 0-8371-7206-3, FRWO). Greenwood.
Friedlander, Albert H., ed. Out of the Whirlwind: A Reader of Holocaust Literature. LC 75-36488. 544p. 1976. pap. 7.95 (ISBN 0-8052-0517-9). Schocken.
Friedlander, Henry. On the Holocaust: A Critique of the Treatment of the Holocaust in History Textbooks. 31p. 0.75 (ISBN 0-686-74932-4). ADL.
Friedlander, Henry & Milton, Sybil, eds. The Holocaust: Ideology, Bureaucracy & Genocide. LC 80-16913. 1981. lib. bdg. 35.00 (ISBN 0-527-63807-2). Kraus Intl.
Friedlander, Saul. When Memory Comes. Lane, Helen, tr. 192p. 1979. 9.95 (ISBN 0-374-28898-4). FS&G.
Friedman, Philip & Friedman, Ada J., eds. Roads to Extinction: Essays on the Holocaust. 616p. 1980. 27.50 (ISBN 0-8276-0170-0, 446). Jewish Pubn.
Friedman, Saul S. Amcha: An Oral Testament of the Holocaust. LC 79-67054. 1979. pap. text ed. 14.25 (ISBN 0-8191-0867-7). U Pr of Amer.
--No Haven for the Oppressed: United States Policy Toward Jewish Refugees, 1938-1945. LC 72-2271. 275p. 1973. 15.95x (ISBN 0-8143-1474-0). Wayne St U Pr.
Gilbert, Martin. The Final Journey: The Fate of the Jews in Nazi Europe. (Illus.). 1980. 12.50 (ISBN 0-8317-3325-X, Mayflower Bks). Smith Pubs.
--The Holocaust. 64p. 1979. 8.95 (ISBN 0-8090-5511-2); pap. 3.45 (ISBN 0-8090-1389-4). Hill & Wang.
Guide to Unpublished Materials of the Holocaust Period. (Yad Vashem Archive Material Ser.: Vol. 4, Pt. 2). 389p. 10.00 (ISBN 0-686-74942-1). ADL.
Gurdus, Luba K. The Death Train. LC 78-54657. (Illus.). 1979. 10.00 (ISBN 0-89604-005-4, Pub. by Holocaust Library). Schocken.
Gutman, Y. & Zuroff, E., eds. Rescue Attempts During the Holocaust. 22.50x (ISBN 0-87068-345-4). Ktav.
Gutman, Yisrael, ed. The Holocaust in Documents. Date not set. price not set. ADL.
Gutman, Yisrael & Rothkirchen, Livia, eds. The Catastrophe of European Jewry: Antecedents-History-Reflections. 767p. 15.00 (ISBN 0-686-74938-3). ADL.
Harwood, Richard. Six Million Lost & Found. (Illus.). 28p. Date not set. pap. 1.50 (ISBN 0-911038-61-2). Inst Hist Rev.
Heyman, Eva. The Diary of Eva Heyman. 124p. 6.00 (ISBN 0-686-74940-5). ADL.
Hilberg, Raul. The Destruction of European Jews. LC 61-7931. 800p. 1979. pap. 9.50 (ISBN 0-06-090660-X, CN 660, CN). Har-Row.
--The Destruction of the European Jews. 1978. Repr. of 1961 ed. lib. bdg. 48.50x (ISBN 0-374-93888-1). Octagon.
Hilberg, Raul, et al. The Warsaw Diary of Adam Czerniakow. LC 78-9272. (Illus.). 448p. 1981. pap. 9.95 (ISBN 0-8128-6110-8). Stein & Day.
Holocaust & Rebirth: A Symposium. 215p. 4.00 (ISBN 0-686-74943-X). ADL.
Imposed Jewish Governing Bodies Under Nazi Rule: Yivo Colloquium Dec. 2-5, 1967. LC 73-150304. 1972. pap. 5.00 (ISBN 0-914512-03-X). Yivo Inst.
Jackson, Livia. Elli. 1980. 10.95 (ISBN 0-8129-0882-1). Times Bks.
Jaspers, Karl. The Question of German Guilt. LC 78-5401. 1978. Repr. of 1947 ed. lib. bdg. 16.75x (ISBN 0-8371-9305-2, JAQG). Greenwood.
Jewish Resistance During the Holocaust. 562p. 12.00 (ISBN 0-686-74944-8). ADL.
Katz, R. Black Sabbath. 1969. 7.95 (ISBN 0-02-560780-4). Macmillan.
Kielar, Wieslaw. Fifteen Hundred Days in Auschwitz-Birkenau: Fifteen Hundred Days in Auschwitz-Birkenau. Flatauer, Susanne, tr. 352p. 1980. 14.95 (ISBN 0-8129-0921-6). Times Bks.
Klein, Gerda W. Promise of a New Spring: The Holocaust & Renewal. (Illus.). 64p. (gr. 2-5). 1981. 8.95g (ISBN 0-940646-50-1); pap. 4.95 (ISBN 0-940646-51-X). Rossel Bks.
Korczak, Janusz. The Warsaw Ghetto Memoirs of Janusz Korczak. Kulawiec, Edwin P., tr. from Polish. LC 78-63065. 1978. pap. text ed. 8.00 (ISBN 0-8191-0611-9). U Pr of Amer.
Krantz, Morris & Auster, Louis. Hitler's Death March. 1978. pap. 1.95 (ISBN 0-89083-430-X). Zebra.
Kren, George M. & Rappoport, Leon H. Holocaust & the Crisis of Human Behavior. LC 79-23781. 1980. text ed. 19.75x (ISBN 0-8419-0544-4). Holmes & Meier.
Kubovyl, Argeh L. & Kubovy, Aryehl., eds. Yad Vashem Studies, Vol. V. 432p. 10.00 (ISBN 0-686-74951-0). ADL.
Kulka, Erich, compiled by. Collection of Testimonies & Documents on the Participation of Czechoslovak Jews in the Second World War Against Nazi Germany. 83p. 2.50 (ISBN 0-686-74939-1). ADL.
Kuper, Jack. Child of the Holocaust. 1980. pap. 1.95 (ISBN 0-451-09072-1, J9072, Sig). NAL.
Langer, Lawrence L. The Holocaust & the Literary Imagination. LC 75-8443. 336p. 1975. 20.00x (ISBN 0-300-01908-4); pap. 5.95 (ISBN 0-300-02121-6). Yale U Pr.
Laqueur, Walter. The Terrible Secret. 276p. 1980. 12.95 (ISBN 0-316-51474-8). Little.
Lederer, Zdenek. Ghetto Theresienstadt. Weisskopf, K., tr. 275p. 1982. Repr. of 1953 ed. 23.50x (ISBN 0-86527-341-3). Fertig.
Leitner, Isabella. Fragments of Isabella: A Memoir of Auschwitz. Leitner, Irving A., ed. LC 78-4766. 1978. 7.95 (ISBN 0-690-01779-0). T Y Crowell.
Levin, Meyer. Eva: A Novel of the Holocaust. LC 79-14440. 1979. pap. text ed. 5.95x (ISBN 0-87441-283-8). Behrman.
Levin, Nora. The Holocaust: The Destruction of European Jewry, 1933-1945. LC 67-23676. (Illus.). 784p. 1973. pap. 8.95 (ISBN 0-8052-0376-1). Schocken.
Littell, Franklin H. & Locke, Hubert G., eds. The German Church Struggle & the Holocaust. LC 72-9352. 360p. 1974. 15.95x (ISBN 0-8143-1492-9). Wayne St U Pr.
Lorit, Sergius C. The Last Days of Maximilian Kolbe. Moran, Hugh, tr. from Ital. LC 80-82418. Orig. Title: Kolbe: Cronaca Degli Ultimi Giorni. 144p. 1980. pap. 2.95 (ISBN 0-911782-35-4). New City.
McGarry, Michael B. Christology After Auschwitz. LC 77-73977. 128p. 1977. pap. 3.95 (ISBN 0-8091-2024-0). Paulist Pr.
Mallasz, G., ed. Talking with Angels. 432p. 1980. softcover 15.00x (ISBN 0-7224-0174-4, Pub. by Watkins England). State Mutual Bk.
Meltzer, Milton. Never to Forget. 1977. pap. 1.50 (ISBN 0-440-96070-3, LFL). Dell.
--Never to Forget: The Jews of the Holocaust. LC 75-25409. (gr. 7 up). 1976. 10.95 (ISBN 0-06-024174-8, HarpJ); PLB 10.89 (ISBN 0-06-024175-6). Har-Row.
Michelson, Frida. Rumbuli. Goodman, Wolf, tr. from Rus. 224p. 1981. 10.95 (ISBN 0-89604-029-1); pap. 5.95 (ISBN 0-89604-030-5). Holocaust Lib.
Moreas, Elizabeth. Born to Suffer. 1979. 4.75 (ISBN 0-8062-1359-0). Carlton.

Morley, John F. Vatican Diplomacy & the Jews During the Holocaust, Nineteen Thirty-Nine--Nineteen Forty-Three. 1980. 20.00 (ISBN 0-87068-701-8). Ktav.
The Myth of the Six Million. 1973. pap. 3.50 (ISBN 0-911038-05-1). Noontide.
Neusner, Jacob. Stranger at Home: The Holocaust, Zionism, & American Judaism. LC 80-19455. 1981. 15.00 (ISBN 0-226-57628-0). U of Chicago Pr.
Nick, Ann L. A Teachers' Guide to the Holocaust. 39p. 1.00 (ISBN 0-686-74935-9). ADL.
Noar, Gertrud. Teaching the Disadvantaged. 33p. 0.50 (ISBN 0-686-74937-5). ADL.
Novitch, Miriam, ed. Sobibor: Martyrdom & Revolt. LC 79-57354. (Illus.). 168p. (Orig.). 1980. pap. 4.95 (ISBN 0-89604-016-X). Holocaust Lib.
Oliner, S. P. Restless Memories: Recollections-Holocaust. 104p. 1979. pap. 4.95 (ISBN 0-686-27361-3). Magnes Mus.
Parker, Grant. Mayday: The History of a Village Holocaust. LC 80-83408. 260p. 1980. pap. 5.95 (ISBN 0-9604958-0-0). Libty Pr MI.
Pawlikowski, John T. The Challenge of the Holocaust for Christian Theology. 39p. 1.50 (ISBN 0-686-74929-4). ADL.
Perl, William R. The Four Front War: From the Holocaust to the Promised Land. (Illus.). 1979. 12.95 (ISBN 0-517-53837-7). Crown.
Poliakov, Leon. Harvest of Hate: The Nazi Program for the Destruction of the Jews in Europe. LC 74-110836. 1971. Repr. of 1954 ed. lib. bdg. 17.25x (ISBN 0-8371-2635-5, POHH). Greenwood.
--Harvest of Hate: The Nazi Program for the Destruction of the Jews of Europe. rev ed. LC 78-71294. 1979. pap. 4.95 (ISBN 0-89604-006-2, Pub. by Holocaust Library). Schocken.
Quaytman, Wilfred. Holocaust Survivors: Psychological & Social Sequelae. (Special Issue of the Journal of Contemporary Psychotherapy: Vol. 11, No. 1). 1980. pap. 7.95 (ISBN 0-89885-016-9). Human Sci Pr.
Rabinowitz, Dorothy. About the Holocaust: What We Know & How We Know It. LC 79-51801. (Illus.). 1979. pap. 1.50 (ISBN 0-87495-014-7). Am Jewish Comm.
--New Lives: Survivors of the Holocaust Living in America. 1976. 10.95 (ISBN 0-394-48573-4). Knopf.
--New Lives: Survivors of the Holocaust Living in America. 1977. pap. 2.25 (ISBN 0-380-01790-3, 35345). Avon.
Rabinsky, Leatrice & Mann, Gertrude. Journey of Conscience. 1979. pap. 2.95 (ISBN 0-529-05679-8, 5679). Collins Pubs.
Radzivilover, Cantor M. Now or Never: A Time for Survival. LC 78-26200. 192p. 1979. 9.95 (ISBN 0-8119-0314-1). Fell.
Ramati, Alexander. Barbed Wire on the Isle of Man. LC 79-3361. 252p. 1980. 10.95 (ISBN 0-15-256039-4). HarBraceJ.
Rassinier, Paul. The Drama of the European Jews. 3rd ed. (Illus.). 1976. pap. 6.95 (ISBN 0-918184-01-0). Steppingstones.
The Record: The Holocaust in History 1933-1945. (Illus.). 28p. 0.50 (ISBN 0-686-74933-2). ADL.
Rescue Attempts During the Holocaust. 679p. 17.00 (ISBN 0-686-74947-2). ADL.
Robinson, Jacob & Sachs, Henry. The Holocaust: The Nuremberg Evidence, Part I: Documents, Digest, Index & Chronological Tables. (Yad Vashem-Yivo. Joint Documentary Projects). 1976. 30.00 (ISBN 0-914512-37-4). Yivo Inst.
Robinson, Jacob, ed. The Holocaust & After: Sources & Literature in English. 1973. casebound 20.00 (ISBN 0-87855-186-7). Transaction Bks.
Rohtbart, Markus. I Wanted to Live to Tell a Story. 1980. 7.95 (ISBN 0-533-04222-4). Vantage.
Rosenbaum, I. Holocaust & Halakhah. (Library of Jewish Law & Ethics: No. 2). 15.00x (ISBN 0-87068-296-2). Ktav.
Rosenfeld, Alvin H. A Double Dying: Reflections on Holocaust Literature. LC 79-3006. 224p. 1980. 17.50x (ISBN 0-253-13337-8). Ind U Pr.
Rosenfeld, Alvin H. & Greenberg, Irving, eds. Confronting the Holocaust: The Impact of Elie Wiesel. LC 78-15821. (Illus.). 256p. 1979. 12.95x (ISBN 0-253-11290-7). Ind U Pr.
Roskies, Diane. Teaching the Holocaust to Children: A Review & Bibliography. pap. 5.00x (ISBN 0-87068-469-8). Ktav.
Ross, Robert W. So It Was True: The American Protestant Press & the Nazi Persecution of the Jews. LC 80-196. 1980. 20.00x (ISBN 0-8166-0948-9); pap. 9.95x (ISBN 0-8166-0951-9). U of Minn Pr.
Rossel, Seymour. The Holocaust. 160p. (gr. 9 up). 1981. lib. bdg. 9.90 (ISBN 0-531-04351-7). Watts.
Roth, John K. A Consuming Fire: Encounters with Elie Wiesel & the Holocaust. LC 78-52442. 1979. 8.95 (ISBN 0-8042-0812-3). John Knox.
Rothchild, Sylvia, ed. Voices from the Holocaust. 1981. 14.95 (ISBN 0-453-00396-6, H396). NAL.
Rothkirchen, L., ed. Yad Vashem Studies on the European Jewish Catastrophe & Resistance, 14 vols. 180.00 set (ISBN 0-87068-638-0); 15.00x ea. Ktav.
Rothkirchen, Livia, ed. Yad Vashem Studies, Vol. IX. 355p. 10.00 (ISBN 0-686-74952-9). ADL.
--Yad Vashem Studies, Vol. XI. 384p. 12.00 (ISBN 0-686-74953-7). ADL.
--Yad Vashem Studies, Vol. XII. 387p. 12.00 (ISBN 0-686-74954-5). ADL.
Rousset, David. The Other Kingdom. Guthrie, Ramon, tr. from Fr. 173p. 1982. Repr. of 1947 ed. 19.50 (ISBN 0-86527-339-1). Fertig.
Rubenstein, Richard. The Cunning of History: The Holocaust & the American Future. 7.00 (ISBN 0-8446-5860-X). Peter Smith.
Ryan, Michael D., ed. Human Responses to the Holocaust: Perpetrators, Victims, Bystanders & Resisters--Then & Now; Papers of the 1979 Bernhard E. Olson Scholar's Conference on the Church Struggle & the Holocaust Sponsored by the National Conference of Christians & Jews. (Texts & Studies in Religion: Vol. 9). 300p. 1981. soft cover 24.95x (ISBN 0-88946-902-4). E Mellen.
Sandberg, Moshe & Rothkirchen, Livia, eds. My Longest Year. 114p. 6.00 (ISBN 0-686-74945-6). ADL.
Sherwin, Byron & Ament, Susan. Encountering the Holocaust: An Interdisciplinary Survey. LC 79-9126. 502p. 1979. 22.50x (ISBN 0-88482-936-7). Impact Pr IL.
Shur, Irene G. & Littell, Franklin H. Reflection on the Holocaust. Lambert, Richard D., ed. LC 80-66618. (The Annals of the American Academy of Political & Social Science: No. 450). 250p. 1980. pap. 6.00x (ISBN 0-87761-253-6). Am Acad Pol Soc Sci.
Stadtler, Bea. The Holocaust: A History of Courage & Resistance. Bial, Morrison D., ed. LC 74-11469. Orig. Title: The Test. (Illus.). 210p. (gr. 5-7). 1975. pap. text ed. 4.95x (ISBN 0-87441-231-5). Behrman.
Stein, Howard F. The Holocaust, & the Myth of the Past As History. (Studies in Revisionist Historiography). 1981. lib. bdg. 59.95 (ISBN 0-87700-276-2). Revisionist Pr.
Steinitz, Lucy Y. Living After the Holocaust: Reflections by the Post-War Generation in America. Szonyi, David M., ed. LC 76-8322. (Illus.). 1976. 6.95x (ISBN 0-686-77156-7); pap. 4.95 (ISBN 0-8197-0016-9). Bloch.
Szajkowski, Soza. An Illustrated Sourcebook on the Holocaust, 2 vols. Incl. Vol. 1. Prelude to Holocaust: the Jew Must Disappear (ISBN 0-87068-294-6); Vol. 2. The Ghetto & Death Camp Walls Speak (ISBN 0-87068-295-4). 35.00x ea. Ktav.
Szajkowski, Zosa. An Illustrated Sourcebook on the Holocaust, Vol. III. Date not set. 35.00x (ISBN 0-87068-690-9). Ktav.
Thalmann, Rita & Feinermann, Emmanuel. Crystal Night: 9-10 November 1938. Cremonesi, Gilles, tr. from Fr. LC 73-78757. (Illus.). 192p. 1980. pap. 4.95 (ISBN 0-89604-014-3). Holocaust Lib.
Thorne, Leon. Out of the Ashes. 1976. Repr. 6.95 (ISBN 0-8197-0394-X). Bloch.
Toll, Nelly. Without Surrender: Art of the Holocaust. LC 78-14859. (Illus.). lib. bdg. 19.80 (ISBN 0-89471-055-9); pap. 6.95 (ISBN 0-89471-054-0). Running Pr.
Trunk, Isaih. Jewish Responses to Nazi Persecution. LC 78-6378. 384p. 1981. pap. 9.95 (ISBN 0-8128-6103-5). Stein & Day.
Trunk, Isiah. Jewish Responses to Nazi Persecution. 1978. 15.95 (ISBN 0-8128-2500-4). Stein & Day.
The Warsaw Ghetto in Pictures: Illustrated Catalog. LC 79-26657. (Yivo Institute for Jewish Research Guide & Catalogs Ser.: No. 1). (Illus.). 1970. pap. 3.50 (ISBN 0-914512-08-0). Yivo Inst.
Wiesel, Elie, pref. by. Selected & Annotated Resource List of Materials on the Holocaust. 65p. 1.50 (ISBN 0-686-74934-0). ADL.
Wiesel, Elie, et al. Dimensions of the Holocaust. 1978. 11.95x (ISBN 0-8101-0469-5); pap. 4.95x (ISBN 0-8101-0470-9). Northwestern U Pr.
Yad Vashem Studies, Vol. XIII. Date not set. price not set. ADL.
Zimmels, H. J. The Echo of the Nazi Holocaust in Rabbinic Literature. 22.50x (ISBN 0-87068-427-2). Ktav.
Zisenwine, David & Rossel, Seymour, eds. Anti-Semitism in Europe: Sources of the Holocaust. new ed. LC 76-47452. (The Jewish Concepts & Issues Ser.). 128p. (gr. 7-9). 1976. pap. text ed. 2.45x avail discussion guide included (ISBN 0-87441-228-5). Behrman.
Zuroff, Efraim, ed. Yad Vashem Album. (Illus.). 64p. 5.00 (ISBN 0-686-74949-9). ADL.
Zvi. LC 78-56149. 1978. pap. 2.95 (ISBN 0-915540-23-1). Friends Israel-Spearhead Pr.
Zyskind, Sara. Stolen Years. LC 81-1953. (Adult & Young Adult Bks.). 288p. (gr. 6 up). 1981. 11.95 (ISBN 0-8225-0766-8, AACR2). Lerner Pubns.

HOLOGRAPHY

see also Acoustic Holography

Abramson, Nils. The Making & Evaluation of Holograms. 1981. price not set (ISBN 0-12-042820-2). Acad Pr.
Barrekette, E. S., et al, eds. Applications of Holography. LC 76-148415. 396p. 1971. 39.50 (ISBN 0-306-30526-7, Plenum Pr). Plenum Pub.
Berner, Jeff. The Holography Book. 148p. 1980. pap. 5.95 (ISBN 0-380-75267-0, 75267). Avon.
Brcic, V. Application of Holography & Hologram Interferometry to Photoelasticity. 2nd ed. (CISM, International Centre for Mechanical Sciences, Courses & Lectures: Vol. 14). (Illus.). 58p. 1975. pap. 10.00 (ISBN 0-387-81163-X). Springer-Verlag.
Camatini, E., ed. Optical & Acoustical Holography. LC 74-188923. 435p. 1972. 42.50 (ISBN 0-306-30584-4, Plenum Pr). Plenum Pub.
Caulfield, H. J. & Lu, Sun. The Applications of Holography. 138p. 1970. 16.50 (ISBN 0-471-14080-5, Pub. by Wiley). Krieger.
Caulfield, H. J., ed. A Handbook of Optical Holography. LC 79-51672. 1979. 63.00 (ISBN 0-12-165350-1). Acad Pr.
Collier, R., et al, eds. Optical Holography. 2nd ed. 1977. 21.50 (ISBN 0-12-181052-6). Acad Pr.
Collier, Robert J., et al. Optical Holography. 1971. 55.00 (ISBN 0-12-181050-X). Acad Pr.
Dowbenko, George. Homegrown Holography. LC 76-16450. (Illus.). 1978. pap. 8.95 (ISBN 0-8174-2406-7). Amphoto.
Erf, Robert K., ed. Holographic Nondestructive Testing. 1974. 55.00 (ISBN 0-12-241350-4). Acad Pr.
Farhat, Nabil H., ed. Advances in Holography, Vol. 1. 192p. 1975. 29.00 (ISBN 0-8247-6277-0). Dekker.
--Advances in Holography, Vol. 2. 200p. 1976. 34.00 (ISBN 0-8247-6313-0). Dekker.
--Advances in Holography, Vol. 3. 1976. 42.00 (ISBN 0-8247-6389-0). Dekker.
Francon, M. Halography. 1974. 17.00 (ISBN 0-12-265750-0). Acad Pr.
Hildebrand, B. Percy & Brenden, Byron B. An Introduction to Acoustical Holography. 244p. 1974. pap. 6.95 (ISBN 0-306-20005-8, Rosetta). Plenum Pub.
Jones, Ted. Holography: A Source Book to Information. new ed. Jones, Evelyn, ed. (Illus.). 1977. pap. 5.00 (ISBN 0-916928-02-0). New Dimen Studio.
Kallard, T. Laser Art & Optical Transforms. LC 78-70638. (Illus., Orig.). 1979. pap. 12.50 (ISBN 0-87739-009-6). Optosonic Pr.
Kallard, Thomas, ed. Holography, 1971-72. LC 74-160228. (State of the Art Review Ser: Vol. 5). (Illus.). 400p. 1972. pap. 17.50 (ISBN 0-87739-005-3). Optosonic Pr.
Kock, Winston E. Engineering Applications of Lasers & Holography. LC 75-17507. (Optical Physics & Engineering Ser.). (Illus.). 400p. 1975. 29.50 (ISBN 0-306-30849-5, Plenum Pr). Plenum Pub.
--Lasers & Holography: An Introduction to Coherent Optics. rev. ed. (Illus.). 128p. 1981. pap. 3.50 (ISBN 0-486-24041-X). Dover.
Kostelanetz, Richard. On Holography. (Illus.). 1979. 1500.00 (ISBN 0-685-95585-0). RK Edns.
Machade, S., ed. Functional Analysis, Holomorphy, & Approximation Theory: Proceedings. (Lecture Notes in Mathematics Ser.: Vol. 843). 636p. 1981. pap. 36.00 (ISBN 0-387-10560-3). Springer-Verlag.
Menzel. Fingerprint Detection with Lasers. 1980. 19.75 (ISBN 0-8247-6974-0). Dekker.
Noakes, G. R., ed. Sources of Physics Teaching: Atomic Energy. Holography. Electrostatics, Vol. 4. 1970. pap. text ed. 12.95x (ISBN 0-85066-038-6). Intl Ideas.
Okoshi, T. Three-Dimensional Imaginary Techniques. 1976. 30.00 (ISBN 0-12-525250-1). Acad Pr.
Ostrovsky, Y. I., et al. Interferometry by Holography. (Springer Ser. in Optical Sciences: Vol. 20). (Illus.). 280p. 1980. 35.90 (ISBN 0-387-09886-0). Springer-Verlag.
Ostrovsky, Yu. Holography & Its Application. 268p. 1977. 4.25 (ISBN 0-8285-0787-2, Pub. by Mir Pubs Russia). Imported Pubns.
Outwater, Christopher & Hamersveld, Eric Van. Guide to Practical Holography. 2nd ed. LC 74-83824. (Illus.). 1976. 10.00 (ISBN 0-914748-00-9); pap. 8.00 (ISBN 0-914748-01-7). Pentangle Pr.
Saxby, Graham. Holograms: How to Make & Use Them. (Illus.). 184p. 1980. 24.95 (ISBN 0-240-51054-2). Focal Pr.
Schuman, W. & Dubas, M. Holographic Interferometry: From the Scope of Deformation Analysis of Opaque Bodies. (Springer Ser. in Optical Sciences: Vol. 16). (Illus.). 1979. 34.00 (ISBN 0-387-09371-0). Springer-Verlag.
Smith, H. M., ed. Holographic Recording Materials. LC 77-24503. (Topics in Applied Physics: Vol. 20). (Illus.). 1977. 43.50 (ISBN 0-387-08293-X). Springer-Verlag.
Smith, Howard M. Principles of Holography. 2nd ed. LC 75-5631. 279p. 1975. 26.50 (ISBN 0-471-80341-3, Pub. by Wiley-Interscience). Wiley.
Society of Photo-Optical Instrumentation Engineers. Engineering Applications of Holography. 28.00 (ISBN 0-89252-097-3). Photo-Optical.
Soroko, L. M. Holography & Coherent Optics. (Illus.). 650p. 1978. 59.50 (ISBN 0-306-40101-0, Plenum Pr). Plenum Pub.
Stoll, W. Value Distribution of Holomorphic Maps into Compact Complex Manifolds. LC 75-121987. (Lecture Notes in Mathematics: Vol. 135). 1970. pap. 14.70 (ISBN 0-387-04924-X). Springer-Verlag.
Stroke, George W. Introduction to Coherent Optics & Halography. (Illus.). 1969. 34.00 (ISBN 0-12-673956-0). Acad Pr.
Unterseher, Fred, et al. The Holographic Handbook. new ed. (Illus.). 300p. (Orig.). 1980. 21.95 (ISBN 0-89496-018-0); pap. 14.95 (ISBN 0-89496-017-2). Ross Bks.
Vest, Charles M. Holographic Interferometry. LC 78-14883. (Wiley Series in Pure & Applied Optics). 1979. 37.00 (ISBN 0-471-90683-2, Pub. by Wiley-Interscience). Wiley.
Von Bally, G., ed. Holography in Medicine & Biology. (Springer Ser. in Optical Sciences: Vol. 18). (Illus.). 269p. 1980. 39.90 (ISBN 0-387-09793-7). Springer-Verlag.
Wenyon, Michael. Understanding Holography. LC 78-965. (Illus.). 1978. 12.95 (ISBN 0-668-04595-7, 4595). Arco.
Yaroslavskii, L. P. & Merzlyakov, N. S. Methods of Digital Holography. 250p. 1980. 45.00 (ISBN 0-306-10963-8, Consultants). Plenum Pub.

HOLOGRAPHY-BIBLIOGRAPHY

Kallard, Thomas, ed. Holography, 1971-72. LC 74-160228. (State of the Art Review Ser: Vol. 5). (Illus.). 400p. 1972. pap. 17.50 (ISBN 0-87739-005-3). Optosonic Pr.

HOLST, GUSTAV, 1874-1934

Holst, Imogen. Gustav Holst, a Biography. 2nd ed. (Illus.). 1969. 23.50x (ISBN 0-19-315417-X). Oxford U Pr.
--Holst. 2nd. rev. ed. (Great Composers Ser.). (Illus.). 96p. (gr. 7 up). 1981. 14.95 (ISBN 0-571-18032-9, Pub. by Faber & Faber). Merrimack Bk Serv.
--Music of Gustav Holst. 2nd ed. 1968. 5.00x (ISBN 0-19-315416-1). Oxford U Pr.
Rubbra, Edmund. Gustav Holst. LC 78-181241. 48p. 1947. Repr. 19.00 (ISBN 0-403-01666-5). Scholarly.
Short, Michael. Gustav Holst,1874-1934: A Centenary Documentation. 285p. 1974. 45.00x (ISBN 0-8476-1219-8). Rowman.

HOLSTEIN, FRIEDRICH VON, 1837-1909

Rich, Norman. Friedrich Von Holstein: Politics & Diplomacy in the Era of Bismarck & Wilhelm. 1965. 130.00 (ISBN 0-521-06077-X). Cambridge U Pr.

HOLT, HAMILTON, 1872-1951

Kuehl, Warren F. Hamilton Holt: Journalist, Internationalist, Educator. LC 60-15787. (Illus.). 1960. 9.00 (ISBN 0-8130-0137-4). U Presses Fla.

HOLY, THE

see also Theism

Kraft, William F. The Search for the Holy. LC 72-152336. 1971. pap. 3.95 (ISBN 0-664-24923-X). Westminster.
Rouner, Leroy S., ed. Transcendence & the Sacred. LC 81-50456. 256p. 1981. 17.95 (ISBN 0-268-01841-3). U of Notre Dame Pr.
Turner, Harold W. From Temple to Meeting House: The Phenomenology & Theology of Sacred Space. 1979. text ed. 58.00x (ISBN 90-279-7977-4). Mouton.

HOLY ALLIANCE

Knapton, Ernest J. Lady of the Holy Alliance: The Life of Julie De Krudener. LC 39-14081. Repr. of 1939 ed. 22.45 (ISBN 0-404-03732-1). AMS Pr.

HOLY CROSS

Ajijola, A. D. Myth of the Cross. pap. 5.50 (ISBN 0-686-63907-3). Kazi Pubns.
Berna, Kurt. Christ Did Not Perish on the Cross: Christ's Body Buried Alive. 1975. 14.50 (ISBN 0-682-48139-4). Exposition.
Coleman, Bill. Way of the Cross. (Illus.). 24p. 1982. pap. 0.50 (ISBN 0-89622-148-2). Twenty-Third.
Hutchinson, Orion. The Cross in 3-D. 1975. 0.85x (ISBN 0-8358-0320-1). Upper Room.
Joyce, Jon L. Way of the Cross. 1979. pap. 2.45 (ISBN 0-89536-359-3). CSS Pub.

Miller, Calvin. Once Upon a Tree. 1978. pap. 3.95 (ISBN 0-8010-6050-8). Baker Bk.
Morris, Leon. Glory in the Cross. (Canterbury Bks.). pap. 2.50 (ISBN 0-8010-6070-2). Baker Bk.
Olson, Bruce. Por Esta Cruz Te Matare. (Span.). Date not set. 2.25 (ISBN 0-686-76333-5). Life Pubs Intl.
Peelman, Nancy. The Cross. (Illus.). 40p. (Orig.). 1976. pap. 3.25 (ISBN 0-8192-1212-1). Morehouse.
Powell, Richard. Letters About the Cross. (Orig.). 1977. pap. 1.85 (ISBN 0-89536-145-0). CSS Pub.
Prenter, Regin. Luther's Theology of the Cross. Anderson, Charles S., ed. LC 71-152368. (Facet Bks.). 32p. 1971. pap. 1.00 (ISBN 0-8006-3062-9, 1-3062). Fortress.
Quinn, Esther C. Quest of Seth for the Oil of Life. LC 62-18120. (Illus.). 1962. 10.00x (ISBN 0-226-70087-9). U of Chicago Pr.
Stevens, William O. The Cross in the Life & Literature of the Anglo-Saxons. 69.95 (ISBN 0-87968-970-6). Gordon Pr.
Wigram, G. V. The Cross. 5.20x (ISBN 0-686-13049-9). Believers Bkshelf.
Wilikerson, David. La Croix et le Poignard. Date not set. 2.00 (ISBN 0-686-76393-9). Life Pubs Intl.

HOLY GHOST
see Holy Spirit

HOLY GRAIL
see Grail

HOLY HOUR
see Jesus Christ–Passion

HOLY ISLAND
Dunleavy, Gareth W. Colum's Other Island: The Irish at Lindisfarne. (Illus.). 160p. 1960. 11.50x (ISBN 0-299-02120-3). U of Wis Pr.
Lamartine, Alphonse de. A Pilgrimage to the Holy Land. LC 78-14368. 1978. Repr. of 1838 ed. 40.00x (ISBN 0-8201-1323-9). Schol Facsimiles.

HOLY LEAGUE, 1576-1593
see also France–History–Wars of the Huguenots, 1562-1598
Jensen, DeLamar. Diplomacy & Dogmatism: Bernardino De Mendoza & the French Catholic League. LC 63-20769. (Illus.). 1964. 17.50x (ISBN 0-674-20800-5). Harvard U Pr.

HOLY OFFICE
see Inquisition

HOLY OILS
see also Unction

HOLY ORDERS
see Clergy–Office

HOLY ORTHODOX EASTERN CATHOLIC AND APOSTOLIC CHURCH
see Orthodox Eastern Church

HOLY PLACES
see Shrines

HOLY ROMAN EMPIRE
Bryce, James. The Holy Roman Empire. 1978. Repr. of 1911 ed. lib. bdg. 40.00 (ISBN 0-8495-0333-7). Arden Lib.
--The Holy Roman Empire. 1911. 35.00 (ISBN 0-8482-7383-4). Norwood Edns.
Bryce, James B. The Holy Roman Empire. new enl. rev. ed. LC 75-41045. (BCL Ser. II). Repr. of 1913 ed. 28.50 (ISBN 0-404-14516-7). AMS Pr.
Falco, Giorgio. The Holy Roman Republic: A Historic Profile of the Middle Ages. Kent, K. V., tr. from Italian. LC 80-19696. Orig. Title: La Santa Romana Republica. 336p. 1980. Repr. of 1965 ed. lib. bdg. 35.00x (ISBN 0-313-22395-5, FAHR). Greenwood.
Schwarz, Henry F. The Imperial Privy Council in the Seventeenth Century. LC 70-141276. (Illus.). 479p. 1972. Repr. of 1943 ed. lib. bdg. 21.00x (ISBN 0-8371-5886-9, SCPC). Greenwood.
Zeydel, Edwin H. Holy Roman Empire in German Literature. LC 19-1736. Repr. of 1918 ed. 17.50 (ISBN 0-404-50423-X). AMS Pr.

HOLY ROMAN EMPIRE–CONSTITUTIONAL LAW
Walker, Mack. Johann Jakob Moser & the Holy Roman Empire of the German Nation. LC 79-27720. 352p. 1980. 26.00x (ISBN 0-8078-1441-5). U of NC Pr.

HOLY ROMAN EMPIRE–FOREIGN RELATIONS
Bradford, William, ed. Correspondence of the Emperor Charles Fifth. Repr. of 1850 ed. 27.50 (ISBN 0-404-00926-3). AMS Pr.

HOLY ROMAN EMPIRE–HISTORY–843-1273
Besozzi, Cerbonio. Chronik Des Cerbonio Besozzi: 1548-1563. 185p. pap. 19.00 (ISBN 0-384-15678-9). Johnson Repr.
Butler, William F. Lombard Communes. LC 68-25226. (World History Ser., No. 48). 1969. lib. bdg. 62.95 (ISBN 0-8383-0923-2). Haskell.
--Lombard Communes: A History of the Republics of North Italy. LC 69-13847. Repr. of 1906 ed. lib. bdg. 22.75x (ISBN 0-8371-2753-X, BULC). Greenwood.
Chudoba, Bohdan. Spain & the Empire: 1519-1643. LC 71-84177. 1969. Repr. of 1952 ed. lib. bdg. 17.50x (ISBN 0-374-91559-8). Octagon.
Fisher, Herbert A. Medieval Empire, 2 Vols. LC 72-95147. Repr. of 1898 ed. 34.50 (ISBN 0-404-02398-3). AMS Pr.
Gagliardo, John G. Reich & Nation: The Holy Roman Empire As Idea & Reality, 1763-1806. LC 79-2170. 384p. 1980. 25.00x (ISBN 0-253-16773-6). Ind U Pr.
Hampe, Karl. Germany Under the Salian & Hohenstaufen Emperors. rev. ed. Bennett, Ralph F., tr. from Ger. (Illus.). 306p. 1973. 19.50x (ISBN 0-87471-173-8). Rowman.
Hauser, Henri. La Preponderance Espagnole 1559-1660. (Nouvelle Introduction Par Pierre Chaunu Reeditions: No. 11). 1973. 47.75 (ISBN 90-2797-225-7); pap. 43.50x (ISBN 0-686-21234-7). Mouton.
Innocent Third, Pope Register Innocenz' 3rd Uber Die Reichsfrage, 1198-1209. Tangl, Georgine, ed. 1923. pap. 19.00 (ISBN 0-384-07885-0). Johnson Repr.
Kantorowicz, Ernst. Frederick the Second, 1194-1250. Lorimer, E. O., tr. LC 57-9408. (Illus.). 1957. 24.50 (ISBN 0-8044-1468-8). Ungar.
Mathews, Shailer. Select Mediaeval Documents & Other Material Illustrative in the History of Church & Empire, 754 A.D.-1254 A.D. LC 70-178566. (Latin.). Repr. of 1900 ed. 16.75 (ISBN 0-404-56628-6). AMS Pr.
Maximillian. Correspondance De l'Empereur Maximilien Premier et De Marguerite D'Autriche: Emperor of Germany, 2 Vols. Le Glay, M., ed. Set. 71.00 (ISBN 0-384-36006-8); Set. pap. 61.50 (ISBN 0-685-13400-8). Johnson Repr.
Salimbene Ognibene Di Guido Di Adamo. Chronik: Des Salimbene Von Parma Nach der Ausgabe der Monuments Germaniae, 2 Vols. Doren, A., ed. Repr. of 1914 ed. pap. 36.50 set (ISBN 0-384-53125-3). Johnson Repr.
Stubbs, William. Germany in the Later Middle Ages, 1200-1500. LC 77-149675. Repr. of 1908 ed. 16.50 (ISBN 0-404-06301-2). AMS Pr.
--Germany in the Later Middle Ages, 1200-1500. 1908. 7.50 (ISBN 0-86527-084-8). Fertig.
Zophy, Jonathan W., ed. The Holy Roman Empire: A Dictionary Handbook. LC 79-8282. (Illus.). xxvii, 551p. 1980. lib. bdg. 45.00 (ISBN 0-313-21457-3, ZHR/). Greenwood.

HOLY SEE
see Papacy; Popes

HOLY SHROUD
Hoare, Rodney. Testimony of the Shroud. LC 78-4385. (Illus.). 1978. 7.95 (ISBN 0-312-79354-5). St Martin.
O'Connell, Patrick & Carty, Charles. The Holy Shroud & Four Visions: The Holy Shroud New Evidence Compared with the Visions of St. Bridget of Sweden, Maria d'Agrenda, Catherine Emmerick, & Teresa Neumann. (Illus.). 1974. pap. 1.00 (ISBN 0-89555-102-0, 164). TAN Bks Pubs.
Rinaldi, Peter M. It Is the Lord: A Study of the Shroud of Christ. (Illus.). 112p. 1973. pap. 1.50 (ISBN 0-446-88016-7). Warner Bks.
--When Millions Saw the Shroud. LC 79-53065. (Illus.). 1979. 7.95 (ISBN 0-89944-023-1); pap. 2.95 (ISBN 0-89944-024-X). D Bosco Pubns.
Stevenson, Kenneth, ed. Proceedings of the Nineteen Seventy-Seven United States Conference of Research on the Shroud of Turin. (Illus.). 244p. (Orig.). 1980. pap. 10.00 (ISBN 0-9605516-0-3). Shroud of Turin.
Stevenson, Kenneth E. & Habermas, Gary R. Verdict on the Shroud: Evidence for the Death & Resurrection of Jesus Christ. (Illus.). 220p. 1981. 12.95 (ISBN 0-89283-111-1). Servant.
Wilcox, Robert. Shroud. (Illus.). 384p. 1977. 8.95 (ISBN 0-02-628510-X, 62851). Macmillan.
Wilson, Ian. The Shroud of Turin: The Burial Cloth of Jesus Christ. LC 79-1942. (Illus.). 1979. pap. 4.50 (ISBN 0-385-15042-3, Im). Doubleday.
--The Shroud of Turin: The Burial Cloth of Jesus Christ? LC 77-81551. 1978. 10.00 (ISBN 0-385-12736-7). Doubleday.

HOLY SPIRIT
see also Church–Foundation; Gifts, Spiritual; Pentecost; Spirit; Trinity
Alberione, James. The Spirit in My Life. 1977. pap. 0.95 (ISBN 0-8198-0460-6). Dghtrs St Paul.
Alday, Salvador C. Power from on High: The Holy Spirit in the Gospels & the Acts. Mishler, Carolyn, tr. from Sp. 1978. pap. 2.95 (ISBN 0-89283-060-3). Servant.
Arnold, Eberhard. The Inner Land, Vol. 4: Light & Fire & the Holy Spirit. LC 75-16303. 1975. 3.95 (ISBN 0-87486-156-X). Plough.
Augsburger, Myron S. Quench Not the Spirit. LC 62-7330. 178p. 1975. pap. 1.75 (ISBN 0-87983-107-3). Keats.
Barney, Kenneth D. The Fellowship of the Holy Spirit. LC 77-70475. 1977. pap. 1.25 (ISBN 0-88243-515-9, 02-0515). Gospel Pub.
Beall, James L. Strong in the Spirit. new ed. 160p. 1975. pap. 2.95 (ISBN 0-8007-0729-X). Revell.
Bennett, Dennis & Bennett, Rita. El Espiritu Santo y Tu. (Spanish Bks.). (Span.). 1978. 1.95 (ISBN 0-8297-0439-6). Life Pubs Intl.
--Holy Spirit & You Supplement. (To be used with The Holy Spirit & You). 1973. pap. 2.95 (ISBN 0-88270-031-6). Logos.
--Trinity of Man. (Illus.). 1979. text ed. 8.95 (ISBN 0-88270-287-4). Logos.
Bennett, George. In His Healing Steps. LC 76-48507. 1977. pap. 2.95 (ISBN 0-8170-0748-2). Judson.
Berkhof, Hendrikus. Doctrine of the Holy Spirit. LC 64-16279. 1976. pap. 4.50 (ISBN 0-8042-0551-5). John Knox.
Bickersteth, Edward H. Holy Spirit. LC 59-13640. 1976. 4.95 (ISBN 0-8254-2202-7). Kregel.
--Holy Spirit. LC 59-13640. 1976. pap. 3.95 (ISBN 0-8254-2227-2). Kregel.
Black, Garth. The Holy Spirit. rev. ed. (Way of Life Ser: No. 102). 1967. pap. 2.95 (ISBN 0-89112-102-1). Bibl Res Pr.
Boer, Harry R. Pentecost & Missions. LC 61-13664. pap. 4.95 (ISBN 0-8028-1021-7). Eerdmans.
Bogorodskii, N. The Doctrine of St. John Damascene on the Procession of the Holy Spirit. LC 80-2351. Repr. of 1879 ed. 28.50 (ISBN 0-404-18903-2). AMS Pr.
Boles, H. Leo. The Holy Spirit. 8.50 (ISBN 0-89225-102-6). Gospel Advocate.
Brengle, Samuel L. When the Holy Ghost Is Come. 1980. pap. 3.25 (ISBN 0-86544-009-3). Salvation Army.
Bright, Bill. The Holy Spirit: The Key to Supernatural Living. 200p. 1980. 8.95 (ISBN 0-918956-67-6); pap. 4.95 (ISBN 0-918956-66-8). Campus Crusade.
Brown, Dale W. Flamed by the Spirit. 1978. pap. 2.95 (ISBN 0-87178-277-4). Brethren.
Brownville, Gordon. Symbols of the Holy Spirit. 1978. pap. 3.95 (ISBN 0-8423-6698-9). Tyndale.
Bruner, Frederick D. Theology of the Holy Spirit. LC 76-103445. 1970. pap. 5.95 (ISBN 0-8028-1547-2). Eerdmans.
Brunk, George R., ed. Encounter with the Holy Spirit. 1972. pap. 4.95 (ISBN 0-8361-1693-3). Herald Pr.
Buess, Bob. You Can Receive the Holy Ghost Today. pap. 1.50 (ISBN 0-934244-14-6, 316). Sweeter Than Honey.
Buntain, D. N. The Holy Ghost & Fire. 1956. 1.25 (ISBN 0-88243-525-6, 02-0525). Gospel Pub.
Bunyan, John. Holy War. 1975. 12.95 (ISBN 0-685-52819-7). Reiner.
Carroll. Witness of the Spirit. pap. 0.75 (ISBN 0-686-12933-4). Schmul Pub Co.
Carter, Charles W. Person & Ministry of the Holy Spirit: A Wesleyan-Perspective. 1974. pap. 4.95 (ISBN 0-8010-2401-3). Baker Bk.
Carter, Edward. The Spirit Is Present. LC 72-9577. 140p. 1973. pap. 1.25 (ISBN 0-8189-1109-3, Pub. by Alba Bks). Alba.
Carter, Pat H. Vivamos En el Espiritu Cada Dia. 160p. 1979. pap. 2.80 (ISBN 0-311-09089-3). Casa Bautista.
Chadwick, Samuel. Way to Pentecost. 1960. pap. 1.25 (ISBN 0-87508-096-0). Chr Lit.
Chagall, David. The Spieler for the Holy Spirit. Young, Billie, ed. LC 72-79505. 1973. 7.95 (ISBN 0-87949-003-9). Ashley Bks.
Chambers, Oswald. He Shall Glorify Me. 1965. 2.25 (ISBN 0-87508-111-8). Chr Lit.
Chantry, Walter. Signs of the Apostles. 1979. pap. 3.45 (ISBN 0-85151-175-9). Banner of Truth.
The Charismatica. (Illus.). 1979. 6.50 (ISBN 0-911346-03-1). Christianica.
Clark, Glenn. Holy Spirit. pap. 0.50 (ISBN 0-910924-07-4). Macalester.
Conner, W. T. The Work of the Holy Spirit. LC 78-54244. 1978. pap. 3.50 (ISBN 0-8054-1618-8). Broadman.
Coppin, Ezra M. Slain in the Spirit. LC 75-36001. 64p. 1976. pap. 1.95 (ISBN 0-89221-010-9). New Leaf.
Criswell, W. A. The Holy Spirit in Today's World. 192p. 1976. pap. text ed. 5.95 (ISBN 0-310-22852-2). Zondervan.
Cummings, James E. A Handbook on the Holy Spirit. LC 77-79551. 1977. pap. 3.50 (ISBN 0-87123-541-2, 200541). Bethany Hse.
Davis, Susan. The Invisible Gift. (My Church Teaches Ser.). (ps). 1979. pap. 1.25 (ISBN 0-8127-0234-4). Review & Herald.
De Valle, Francisca J. About the Holy Spirit. 120p. 5.00 (ISBN 0-912414-31-6). Lumen Christi.
Dewelt, Don. The Power of the Holy Spirit, Vol. III. pap. 3.95 (ISBN 0-89900-125-4). College Pr Pub.
--Power of the Holy Spirit, Vol. IV. (Orig.). 1976. pap. 5.95 (ISBN 0-89900-126-2). College Pr Pub.
--Power of the Holy Spirit, Vol. II. (Orig.). 1971. pap. 3.95 (ISBN 0-89900-124-6). College Pr Pub.
--Power of the Holy Spirit, Vol. I. (Orig.). 1963. pap. 2.95 (ISBN 0-89900-123-8). College Pr Pub.
Duncan, George B. The Person & Work of the Holy Spirit in the Life of the Believer. LC 74-21900. 87p. 1975. pap. 3.95 (ISBN 0-8042-0681-3). John Knox.
Dunn, James D. Baptism in the Holy Spirit: A Re-Examination of the New Testament Teaching on the Gift of the Spirit in Relation to Pentacostalism Today. LC 77-3995. 1977. pap. 6.95 (ISBN 0-664-24140-9). Westminster.
Eva Of Friedenshort, Sr. The Working of the Holy Spirit in Daily Life. 1974. pap. 1.25 (ISBN 0-87123-647-8, 200647). Bethany Hse.
Fife, Eric S. The Holy Spirit: Common Sense & the Bible. (Orig.). 1979. pap. 4.95 (ISBN 0-310-24341-6). Zondervan.
Fitch, William. The Ministry of the Holy Spirit. 320p. 1974. 7.95 (ISBN 0-310-24380-7, 18320). Zondervan.
Ford, Francis X. Come Holy Spirit. LC 76-20573. 1976. 5.95x (ISBN 0-88344-067-9). Orbis Bks.
Frost, Robert. Set My Spirit Free. LC 73-84475. 234p. 1973. pap. 3.50 (ISBN 0-88270-058-8). Logos.
Frost, Robert C. Overflowing Life: Everyday Living in the Spirit. rev. ed. LC 72-146696. 144p. 1971. pap. 3.95 (ISBN 0-88270-050-2). Logos.
Geissler, Eugene S., compiled by. The Spirit Bible. LC 73-88004. 272p. 1973. pap. 2.25 (ISBN 0-87793-062-7). Ave Maria.
Gelpi, Donald L. Experiencing God: A Theology of Human Emergence. LC 77-14854. 1977. pap. 10.00 (ISBN 0-8091-2061-5). Paulist Pr.
Gesswein, Armin R. With One Accord in One Place. 93p. (Orig.). 1978. pap. 1.50 (ISBN 0-87509-161-X). Chr Pubns.
Gillquist, Peter E. Let's Quit Fighting About the Holy Spirit. 160p. 1974. pap. 3.95 (ISBN 0-310-25001-3). Zondervan.
God's Gift-the Holy Spirit. 1978. 2.95 (ISBN 0-8198-0377-4); pap. 1.95 (ISBN 0-8198-0378-2). Dghtrs St Paul.
Goodwin, Mrs. J. R. & Goodwin, J. R. Entering the Spiritual House. 32p. (Orig.). 1974. pap. 1.00 (ISBN 0-89274-010-8). Harrison Hse.
--The Holy Spirit's Gifts of Reveltion. 31p. (Orig.). 1974. pap. 1.00 (ISBN 0-89274-011-6). Harrison Hse.
--The Holy Spirit's Three Gifts of Power. 31p. (Orig.). 1974. pap. 1.00 (ISBN 0-89274-012-4). Harrison Hse.
--The Holy Spirit's Three Gifts of Utterence. 32p. (Orig.). 1974. pap. 1.00 (ISBN 0-89274-013-2). Harrison Hse.
Goodwin, Thomas. Holy Spirit in Salvation. 1979. 14.95 (ISBN 0-85151-279-8). Banner of Truth.
Gordon, Adoniram J. Holy Spirit in Missions. pap. 2.25 (ISBN 0-87509-094-X). Chr Pubns.
Gordon, Adoniran J. Ministry of the Spirit. 1964. pap. 2.45 (ISBN 0-87123-366-5, 210366). Bethany Hse.
Graham, Billy. El Espiritu Santo. Sipowicz, A. Edwin, tr. from Eng. Orig. Title: The Holy Spirit. 252p. (Span.). 1980. pap. 3.95 (ISBN 0-311-09096-6). Casa Bautista.
--The Holy Spirit. 1978. 7.95 (ISBN 0-8499-0005-0). Word Bks.
--The Holy Spirit. 1979. lib. bdg. 13.95 (ISBN 0-8161-6779-6). G K Hall.
--How to Be Born Again. LC 77-76057. 1977. 6.95 (ISBN 0-8499-0017-4). Word Bks.
Green, Michael. Creo en el Espiritu Santo. Vilela, Ernesto S., tr. from Eng. LC 77-164. (Serie Creo). 267p. (Orig., Span.). 1977. pap. 3.95 (ISBN 0-89922-090-8). Edit Caribe.
--I Believe in the Holy Spirit. (I Believe Ser). 224p. 1975. pap. 3.95 (ISBN 0-8028-1609-6). Eerdmans.
Gunkel, Hermann. The Influence of the Holy Spirit: The Popular View of the Apostolic Age & the Teaching of the Apostle Paul. Harrisville, Roy A. & Quanbeck, Philip A., II, trs. LC 78-20022. 144p. 1979. 10.95 (ISBN 0-8006-0544-6, 1-544). Fortress.
Hall, Manly P. Mystery of Holy Spirit. pap. 1.75 (ISBN 0-89314-333-2). Philos Res.
Hall, Robert B. Receiving the Holy Spirit. 1964. pap. 1.00 (ISBN 0-686-14948-3). Episcopal Ctr.
Harrell, Irene B. Multiplied by Love: Lessons Learned Through the Holy Spirit. LC 76-15370. 112p. 1976. 4.95 (ISBN 0-687-27303-X). Abingdon.
Haughey, John C., S.J. Conspiracy of God: The Holy Spirit in Men. LC 73-80730. 120p. 1976. pap. 1.95 (ISBN 0-385-11558-X, Im). Doubleday.
Heijkoop, H. J. Holy Spirit Is a Divine Person. 4.50 (ISBN 0-686-13170-3); pap. 2.95 (ISBN 0-686-13171-1). Believers Bkshelf.
Hembree, Charles R. Fruto Do Espirito. (Portuguese Bks.). 1979. 1.50 (ISBN 0-8297-0652-6). Life Pubs Intl.
Hession, Roy. Be Filled Now. 1968. pap. 0.50 (ISBN 0-87508-235-1). Chr Lit.

Hicks, Robert & Bewes, Richard. The Holy Spirit. (Understanding Bible Truth Ser.). (Orig.). 1981. pap. 1.50 (ISBN 0-89840-021-X). Heres Life.
Hillis, Dick & Hillis, Don. The Spirit Speaks: Are You Listening? LC 80-50260. 96p. 1980. pap. 2.50 (ISBN 0-8307-0752-2, 5016606). Regal.
Hodges, Melvin. Esp. Santo y Evang. Universal. (Span.). 1981. 1.75 (ISBN 0-686-76368-8). Life Pubs Intl.
Hodges, Melvin L. El Espiritu Santo y el Evangelismo Universal. 149p. (Span.). 1979. pap. 1.75 (ISBN 0-8297-0930-4). Life Pubs Intl.
Holdcroft, Thomas L. The Holy Spirit: A Pentecostal Interpretation. LC 79-54991. (Illus.). 1980. Repr. 5.95 (ISBN 0-88243-554-X, 02-0554). Gospel Pub.
The Holy Spirit. (Aglow Bible Study Bk: No. E-3). (Illus.). 64p. (Orig.). 1980. pap. 1.95 (ISBN 0-930756-57-6, 4220-E3). Women's Aglow.
Horton, Harold. Los Dones Del Espiritu Santo. (Span.). 1981. 2.25 (ISBN 0-686-76362-9). Life Pubs Intl.
Horton, Stanley. Espiritu Santo Revelado... (Span.). 1981. 2.75 (ISBN 0-686-76369-6). Life Pubs Intl.
Horton, Stanley M. El Espiritu Santo Revelado En la Biblia. 216p. (Span.). 1980. pap. 2.35 (ISBN 0-8297-0949-5). Life Pubs Intl.
--What the Bible Says About Holy Spirit. LC 75-43154. 304p. 1976. 7.95 (ISBN 0-88243-640-6, 02-0640); pap. 4.95 (ISBN 0-88243-647-3, 02-0647). Gospel Pub.
Howard, David. By the Power of the Holy Spirit. LC 73-83091. 172p. 1973. pap. 2.50 (ISBN 0-87784-358-9). Inter-Varsity.
Ironside, H. A. Holy Spirit: Mission of, & Praying in. 1950. pap. 2.75 (ISBN 0-87213-366-4). Loizeaux.
Israel, Martin. Smouldering Fire: The Work of the Holy Spirit. LC 81-9794. 192p. 1981. 10.95 (ISBN 0-8245-0072-5). Crossroad NY.
Iverson, Dick. The Holy Spirit Today. (Illus.). 1977. pap. 4.25 (ISBN 0-914936-24-7). Bible Pr.
Jensen, Richard A. Touched by the Spirit: One Man's Struggle to Understand His Experience of the Holy Spirit. LC 75-2838. 160p. 1975. pap. 3.95 (ISBN 0-8066-1484-6, 10-6675). Augsburg.
Jepson, J. W. What You Should Know About the Holy Spirit. pap. 2.95 (ISBN 0-89728-062-8, 669313). Omega Pubns OR.
Kearley, Furman F. God's Indwelling Spirit. 64p. 1974. pap. 2.95x (ISBN 0-88428-035-7). Parchment Pr.
Kelly, W. Lectures on the Doctrine of the Holy Spirit. 4.25 (ISBN 0-686-13129-0). Believers Bkshelf.
Kinghorn, Kenneth C. Fresh Wind of the Spirit. LC 74-7415. 128p. 1975. pap. 4.95 (ISBN 0-687-13495-1). Abingdon.
Kuyper, Abraham. Work of the Holy Spirit. 1956. pap. 7.95 (ISBN 0-8028-8156-4). Eerdmans.
LaHaye, Beverly. Le Femme Dirigee Par l'Esprit. 175p. (Fr. & English.). 1979. pap. 1.85 (ISBN 0-8297-0972-X). Life Pubs Intl.
Lehman, Chester K. Holy Spirit & the Holy Life. (Conrad Grebel Lecture Serv.). 1959. 4.50 (ISBN 0-8361-1375-6). Herald Pr.
Lewis, Warren. Witnesses to the Holy Spirit: An Anthology. LC 78-7546. 1978. softcover 9.95 (ISBN 0-8170-0788-1). Judson.
The Life in the Spirit Seminars Team Manual: Catholic Edition. 1979. pap. 3.50 (ISBN 0-89283-065-4). Servant.
Lindsay, Gordon. Gifts of the Spirit, 4 vols. 2.50 ea. Vol. 1 (ISBN 0-89985-195-9). Vol. 2 (ISBN 0-89985-196-7). Vol. 3 (ISBN 0-89985-197-5). Vol. 4 (ISBN 0-89985-199-1). Christ Nations.
Lindwall, Ted. Poder Espiritual. 1978. Repr. of 1977 ed. 0.65 (ISBN 0-311-46068-2). Casa Bautista.
Linzey, Stanford E. Why I Believe in the Baptism with the Holy Spirit. 1962. pap. 0.50 (ISBN 0-88243-764-X, 02-0764). Gospel Pub.
Lockyer, Herbert. The Holy Spirit of God. 1981. 9.95 (ISBN 0-8407-5234-2). Nelson.
Lovett, C. S. Dealing with the Devil. 1967. pap. 4.45 (ISBN 0-938148-05-2). Personal Christianity.
Lussier, Ernest. God Is Love: According to St. John. LC 76-57254. 1977. 5.95 (ISBN 0-8189-0339-2). Alba.
Macaulay, J. C. Life in Spirit. 1978. pap. 1.95 (ISBN 0-8024-4784-8). Moody.
McBride, Alfred. The Gospel of the Holy Spirit. 1975. pap. 1.50 (ISBN 0-88479-951-4). Arena Lettres.
McConkey, James H. El Triple Secreto Del Espiritu Santo. Agostini, Beatrice, tr. from Eng. Orig. Title: The Three Fold Secret of the Holy Spirit. 106p. (Span.). 1980. pap. 1.80 (ISBN 0-311-09090-7). Casa Bautista.
McConkie, Joseph F. Seeking the Spirit. LC 78-13372. 1978. 5.95 (ISBN 0-87747-721-3). Deseret Bk.
McDonnell, Kilian. The Holy Spirit & Power: The Catholic Charismatic Renewal. LC 74-32573. 192p. 1975. pap. 2.95 (ISBN 0-385-09909-6). Doubleday.
McNair, Jim. Experiencing the Holy Spirit. LC 77-9262. 1977. pap. 3.95 (ISBN 0-87123-135-2, 210135). Bethany Hse.
Mains, David. Getting to Know the Holy Spirit. (Chapel Talks Ser.). 64p. 1.75 (ISBN 0-89191-262-2, 52621). Cook.
Manteau-Bonamy, H. M. Immaculate Conception & the Holy Spirit: The Marian Teachings of Father Kolbe. Geiger, Bernard M., ed. Arnandez, Richard, tr. from Fr. LC 77-93104. (Illus.). 1977. pap. 4.00 (ISBN 0-913382-00-0, 101-20). Prow Bks-Franciscan.
Marsh, F. E. Emblems of the Holy Spirit. LC 63-11465. 1964. 7.95 (ISBN 0-8254-3201-4); pap. 5.95 (ISBN 0-8254-3222-7). Kregel.
Marshall, Catherine. The Helper. 1978. 8.95 (ISBN 0-912376-21-X). Chosen Bks Pub.
Martin, Alfred & Martin, Dorothy. The Holy Spirit. (Personal Bible Study Guide). 64p. 1974. pap. 1.50 (ISBN 0-8024-1104-5). Moody.
Martinez, Luis M. The Sanctifier. 7.50 (ISBN 0-8198-6803-5); pap. 6.00 (ISBN 0-8198-6804-3). Dghtrs St Paul.
Massabki, Charles. Who Is the Holy Spirit? LC 79-15184. 185p. (Orig.). 1979. pap. 6.95 (ISBN 0-8189-0390-2). Alba.
Matheson, George. Voices of the Spirit. (Direction Bks). 1979. pap. 3.45 (ISBN 0-8010-6078-8). Baker Bk.
Montague, George T. The Holy Spirit: Growth of Biblical Tradition. LC 76-4691. 384p. 1976. pap. 8.50 (ISBN 0-8091-1950-1). Paulist Pr.
Moody, Dale. Spirit of the Living God. LC 76-29142. 1977. pap. 3.95 (ISBN 0-8054-1941-1). Broadman.
Mooth, Verla A. The Spirit-Filled Life. 1978. 6.00 (ISBN 0-682-49113-6). Exposition.
Morgan, G. Campbell. The Spirit of God. (Morgan Library). 240p. 1981. pap. 3.95 (ISBN 0-8010-6119-9). Baker Bk.
Moule, C. F. The Holy Spirit. 1979. pap. 3.95 (ISBN 0-8028-1796-3). Eerdmans.
Mozumdar, A. K. The Triumphant Spirit. 1978. pap. 6.50 (ISBN 0-87516-261-4). De Vorss.
Murphy, Roland, et al. Presence of God. LC 78-107214. (Concilium Ser.: Vol. 50). 215p. 6.95 (ISBN 0-8091-0116-5). Paulist Pr.
Newell, Arlo F. Receive the Holy Spirit. (Doctrinal Material of the Church of God: No. 1). 1978. pap. text ed. 3.50 (ISBN 0-87162-207-6, D6430). Warner Pr.
Nystrom, Carolyn. The Holy Spirit in Me. (Children's Bible Ser.). 32p. (ps-2). 1980. pap. 3.25 (ISBN 0-8024-5994-3). Moody.
Oates, Wayne E. Holy Spirit & Contemporary Man. (Source Books for Ministers). 2.45 (ISBN 0-8010-6657-3). Baker Bk.
Opsahl, Paul D. The Holy Spirit in the Life of the Church: From Biblical Times to the Present. LC 77-84099. 1978. pap. 9.95 (ISBN 0-8066-1625-3, 10-3160). Augsburg.
Otis, George. You Shall Receive. pap. 1.50 (ISBN 0-89728-064-4, 533250). Omega Pubns OR.
Otis, George & Walker, Mary. God, the Holy Spirit. pap. 1.25 (ISBN 0-685-60971-5, 532877). Omega Pubns OR.
Owen, John. Holy Spirit, His Gifts & Power. LC 60-16514. 1973. 6.95 (ISBN 0-8254-3404-1); pap. 4.95 (ISBN 0-8254-3413-0). Kregel.
Pache, Rene. Person & Work of the Holy Spirit. 1960. 4.95 (ISBN 0-8024-6471-8). Moody.
Pack, Frank. Tongues & the Holy Spirit. (Way of Life Ser: No. 127). (Orig.). 1972. pap. text ed. 2.95 (ISBN 0-89112-127-7). Bibl Res Pr.
Palma, Anthony D. The Spirit: God in Action. LC 74-75966. 1974. pap. 2.95 (ISBN 0-88243-602-3, 02-0602). Gospel Pub.
Palmer, Edwin H. El Espiritu Santo. 4.75 (ISBN 0-686-12551-7). Banner of Truth.
Pentecost, J. Dwight. Divine Comforter. 1970. pap. 4.95 (ISBN 0-8024-2225-X). Moody.
Petts, David. The Dynamic Difference: How the Holy Spirit Can Add an Exciting New Dimension to Your Life. LC 77-91483. 1978. pap. 0.95 (ISBN 0-88243-484-5, 02-0484, Radiant Bks). Gospel Pub.
Philippe, Thomas. The Fire of Contemplation: A Guide for Inferior Souls. Doran, Verda C., tr. from Fr. LC 81-8099. 128p. (Orig.). 1981. pap. 4.95 (ISBN 0-8189-0414-3, Pub. by Alba Bks). Alba.
Pierson, A. T. Acts of the Holy Spirit. 127p. 1980. pap. 1.95 (ISBN 0-87509-274-8). Chr Pubns.
Pink, Arthur W. Holy Spirit. 1970. pap. 4.95 (ISBN 0-8010-7041-4). Baker Bk.
Pittenger, Norman. The Holy Spirit. LC 74-10839. 128p. 1974. 5.50 (ISBN 0-8298-0284-3). Pilgrim NY.
Poland, Larry W. Spirit Power: All You Need When You Need It! LC 77-91763. (Illus.). 1978. pap. 2.95 (ISBN 0-918956-39-0). Campus Crusade.
Price, Frederick K. The Holy Spirit the Missing Ingredient. 32p. 1978. pap. text ed. 1.25 (ISBN 0-89274-081-7). Harrison Hse.
Prince, Derek. The Baptism in the Holy Spirit. 1966. pap. 1.25 (ISBN 0-934920-07-9, B-19). Derek Prince.
Ramsey, A. Michael, et al. Come Holy Spirit. 128p. (Orig.). 1976. pap. 3.25 (ISBN 0-8192-1186-9). Morehouse.
--The Charismatic Christ. 128p. (Orig.). 1973. pap. 2.50 (ISBN 0-8192-1141-9). Morehouse.
Rayan, Samuel. The Holy Spirit: Heart of the Gospel & Christian Hope. LC 78-2306. 1978. pap. 5.95 (ISBN 0-88344-188-8). Orbis Bks.
Rea, John. A Layman's Commentary on the Holy Spirit: As He Appears in the New Testament. LC 72-92775. 150p. 1972. 5.95 (ISBN 0-912106-22-0); pap. 4.95 (ISBN 0-912106-38-7). Logos.
Riaud, Alexis. The Holy Spirit Acting in Our Souls. Van de Putte, Walter, tr. from Fr. LC 78-31492. 1979. pap. 3.95 (ISBN 0-8189-0381-3). Alba.
Ridout, Samuel. Holy Spirit: Person & Work. pap. 2.95 (ISBN 0-87213-712-0). Loizeaux.
Ryrie, Charles C. El Espiritu Santo. 1978. pap. 2.50 (ISBN 0-8024-2382-5). Moody.
--Holy Spirit. (Bible Doctrine Handbook Ser). (Orig.). 1965. pap. 2.95 (ISBN 0-8024-3565-3); pap. 2.95 leader's guide (ISBN 0-8024-3564-5). Moody.
St. Basil the Great on the Holy Spirit. Anderson, David, tr. from Greek. LC 80-25502. 1980. pap. 3.95 (ISBN 0-913836-74-5). St Vladimirs.
St. Basil The Great. On the Holy Spirit. Anderson, David, tr. from Gr. LC 80-25502. 118p. (Orig.). 1980. pap. 3.95 (ISBN 0-913836-74-5). St Vladimirs.
Sanders, J. Oswald. Holy Spirit & His Gifts. (Contemporary Evangelical Perspectives Ser). kivar 4.95 (ISBN 0-310-32481-5). Zondervan.
Schweizer, Eduard. The Holy Spirit. LC 79-8892. 144p. 1980. 9.95 (ISBN 0-8006-0629-9, 1-629). Fortress.
Seamands, John T. On Tiptoe with Love. (Direction Bk). pap. 1.95 (ISBN 0-8010-7991-8). Baker Bk.
Selby, Thomas G. The Holy Spirit & the Christian Privilege. 1978. Repr. lib. bdg. 20.00 (ISBN 0-8495-4858-6). Arden Lib.
Seven Gifts of the Holy Spirit. 1980. plastic 1.75 (ISBN 0-8198-6807-8); pap. 1.00 (ISBN 0-8198-6808-6). Dghtrs St Paul.
Shevkenek, Alice. Things the Baptism in the Holy Spirit Will Do for You. 1976. pap. 0.75 (ISBN 0-89350-005-4). Fountain Pr.
Shoemaker, Samuel M. With the Holy Spirit & with Fire. 1973. pap. 1.95 (ISBN 0-87680-986-7, 90186). Word Bks.
Simpson, A. B. Holy Spirit. Set. 9.90 (ISBN 0-87509-014-1); Vol. 1. 4.95 (ISBN 0-87509-015-X); Vol. 2. 4.95 (ISBN 0-87509-016-8). Chr Pubns.
Simpson, Albert B. When the Comforter Came. pap. 2.50 (ISBN 0-87509-042-7). Chr Pubns.
Singley, Lloyd. Have You Received the Holy Ghost? 32p. 1977. pap. 1.00 (ISBN 0-89274-070-1). Harrison Hse.
Smeaton, George. Doctrine of the Holy Spirit. 1980. 13.95 (ISBN 0-85151-187-2). Banner of Truth.
Smith, Bertha. How the Spirit Filled My Life. LC 73-87068. 5.95 (ISBN 0-8054-5540-X). Broadman.
Smith, Chuck. The Holy Spirit & the Balanced Life. 1979. pap. cancelled (ISBN 0-89081-185-7, 1857). Harvest Hse.
Spurgeon, C. H. Holy Spirit. 1978. pap. 1.95 (ISBN 0-686-23025-6). Pilgrim Pubns.
--Personality of the Holy Ghost. 1977. pap. 0.50 (ISBN 0-686-23222-4). Pilgrim Pubns.
Stagg, Frank. The Holy Spirit Today. LC 73-85701. 1974. pap. 2.75 (ISBN 0-8054-1919-5). Broadman.
Steinberg, Hardy W. The Church of the Spirit. (Charismatic Bk). 1972. pap. 0.69 (ISBN 0-88243-922-7, 02-0922). Gospel Pub.
Stephens, John F. Spirit Filled Family, No. 11. 48p. (Orig.). 1980. pap. 1.50 (ISBN 0-89841-008-8). Zoe Pubns.
Stephens, W. D. Holy Spirit in the Theology of Martin Bucer. LC 79-96100. Orig. Title: Martin Bucer, a Theologian of the Spirit. 1970. 51.00 (ISBN 0-521-07661-7). Cambridge U Pr.
Stott, John R. Baptism & Fullness: The Work of the Holy Spirit Today. LC 76-21457. 1976. pap. 2.95 (ISBN 0-87784-648-0). Inter-Varsity.
--Sed Llenos del Espiritu Santo. rev. ed. Cook, David A., tr. from Eng. LC 77-162. 112p. (Orig., Span.). 1977. pap. 2.50 (ISBN 0-89922-084-3). Edit Caribe.
Strauss, Lehman. Third Person. 1954. 4.75 (ISBN 0-87213-827-5). Loizeaux.
Stuenkel, Omar. We Are One in the Spirit: How to Receive & Use the Holy Spirit's Gifts. LC 78-66949. 1979. pap. 2.95 (ISBN 0-8066-1693-8, 10-7010). Augsburg.
Surath, Sri. Holy Spirit - the Living Love. 1978. pap. 3.00 (ISBN 0-685-58453-4). Ranney Pubns.
Swails, John W. The Holy Spirit & the Messianic Age. 4.95 (ISBN 0-911866-73-6). Advocate.
Swete, Henry B. Holy Spirit in the New Testament. (Religious Heritage Reprint Library). 1976. 8.95 (ISBN 0-8010-8078-9). Baker Bk.
Tapscott, Betty. Fruit of the Spirit. 1978. pap. 2.95 (ISBN 0-917726-26-X). Hunter Bks.
Taylor, John V. The Go-Between God: The Holy Spirit & the Christian Mission. 1979. pap. 4.95x (ISBN 0-19-520125-6). Oxford U Pr.
Teasley, D. O. The Holy Spirit & Other Spirits. 192p. pap. 1.75 (ISBN 0-686-29150-6). Faith Pub Hse.
Therrien, Vincent. Reaching Out: Together, Through the Holy Spirit. 1978. 6.00 (ISBN 0-682-49162-4, Testament). Exposition.
Torrey, A. Holy Spirit: Who He Is & What He Does. 1927. 10.95 (ISBN 0-8007-0139-9). Revell.
Torrey, R. A. Como Obtener la Plenitud Del Poder. Rivas, Jose G., tr. from Eng. Orig. Title: How to Obtain Fullness of Power. 112p. (Span.). 1980. pap. 1.90 (ISBN 0-311-46083-6). Casa Bautista.
Torrey, Reuben A. Person & Work of the Holy Spirit. 1968. 9.95 (ISBN 0-310-33300-8). Zondervan.
Tozer, A. W. How to Be Filled with the Holy Spirit. 58p. pap. 0.95 (ISBN 0-87509-187-3). Chr Pubns.
Tozer, A. W. & Smith, G. B. When He Is Come. Orig. Title: Tozer Pulpit, Vol. 2: Ten Sermons on the Ministry of the Holy Spirit. 146p. (Orig.). 1980. pap. 2.50 (ISBN 0-87509-221-7). Chr Pubns.
Underwood, B. E. Gifts of the Spirit. 3.95 (ISBN 0-911866-64-7); pap. 2.95 (ISBN 0-911866-65-5). Advocate.
Unger, Merrill F. The Baptism & Gifts of the Holy Spirit. 192p. 1974. pap. text ed. 3.95 (ISBN 0-8024-0467-7). Moody.
Vaughan, C. R. The Gifts of the Holy Spirit. 1975. 11.95 (ISBN 0-85151-222-4). Banner of Truth.
Wagner, C. Peter. Your Spiritual Gifts Can Help Your Church Grow. LC 78-53353. 1979. pap. 4.95 (ISBN 0-8307-0644-5, 54-106-06). Regal.
Walvoord, John F. Holy Spirit. 1958. 11.95 (ISBN 0-310-34060-8). Zondervan.
--The Holy Spirit at Work Today. 64p. 1973. pap. 2.25 (ISBN 0-8024-3566-1). Moody.
Weinrich, William C. Spirit & Martyrdom: A Study of the Work of the Holy Spirit in Contexts of Persecution & Martyrdom in the New Testament & Early Christian Literature. LC 80-5597. 334p. (Orig.). 1981. lib. bdg. 20.75 (ISBN 0-8191-1655-6); pap. text ed. 11.75 (ISBN 0-8191-1656-4). U Pr of Amer.
Wesley, John. The Holy Spirit & Power. Weakley, Clare, ed. 1978. pap. 4.95 (ISBN 0-88270-262-9). Logos.
Wierwille, Victor P. Receiving the Holy Spirit Today. LC 73-176282. 1972. 5.95 (ISBN 0-910068-00-3). Am Christian.
Wilkerson, Ralph. Satellites of the Spirit. Anderson, Bruce & Wilkerson, Allene, eds. LC 78-69963. (Illus.). 1978. pap. 1.45 (ISBN 0-918818-06-0). Melodyland.
Williams, Cyril G. Tongues of the Spirit. 276p. 1981. text ed. 50.00x (ISBN 0-7083-0758-2). Verry.
Williams, John. The Holy Spirit, Lord & Life-Giver: A Biblical Introduction to the Doctrine of the Holy Spirit. LC 79-27891. 1980. 8.50 (ISBN 0-87213-950-6); pap. 5.75 (ISBN 0-87213-951-4); study guide 3.25 (ISBN 0-87213-952-2). Loizeaux.
--The Holy Spirit, Lord & Life-Giver: Study Guide. (Illus.). 1980. pap. text ed. 3.25 (ISBN 0-87213-952-2). Loizeaux.
Windisch, Hans. Spirit-Paraclete in the Fourth Gospel. Reumann, John, ed. Cox, James W., tr. from Ger. LC 68-12330. (Facet Bks.). 64p. (Orig.). 1968. pap. 1.00 (ISBN 0-8006-3046-7, 1-3046). Fortress.
Wood, Leon J. The Holy Spirit in the Old Testament. 192p. 1976. pap. text ed. 3.95 (ISBN 0-310-34751-3). Zondervan.
Yohn, Rick. God's Holy Spirit for Christian Living: A Study Manual. LC 77-71215. 1977. pap. 2.95 (ISBN 0-89081-042-7, 0427). Harvest Hse.
Young, J. Terry. The Spirit Within You. LC 76-47762. 1977. 4.95 (ISBN 0-8054-1945-4). Broadman.

HOLY SPIRIT ASSOCIATON FOR THE UNIFICATION OF WORLD CHRISTIANITY

As Others See Us. pap. 3.00 (ISBN 0-686-13416-8). Unification Church.
Bjornstad, James. The Moon Is Not the Son: A Close Look at the Religion of Rev. Son Myung Moon. LC 76-46208. 1977. pap. 3.50 (ISBN 0-87123-380-0, 200380). Bethany Hse.

Bromley, David G. & Shupe, Anson D., Jr. Moonies in America: Cult, Church, & Crusade. LC 79-16456. (Sage Library of Social Research: Vol. 92). 269p. 1979. 20.00 (ISBN 0-8039-1060-6); pap. 9.95 (ISBN 0-8039-1061-4). Sage.
Bryant, Darrol, ed. Proceedings of the Virgin Islands' Seminar on Unification Theology. LC 80-52594. (Conference Ser.: No. 6). (Illus.). xv, 323p. (Orig.). 1980. pap. text ed. 9.95 (ISBN 0-932894-06-2). Unif Theol Sem.
Bryant, M. Darrol & Richardson, Herbert W. A Time for Consideration: A Scholarly Appraisal of the Unification Church. LC 78-61364. (Symposium Ser.: Vol. 3). xi, 317p. 1978. soft cover 11.95x (ISBN 0-88946-954-7). E Mellen.
Bryant, M. Darrol & Hodges, Susan, eds. Exploring Unification Theology. 2nd ed. LC 78-63274. (Conference Ser.: No. 1). 1978. pap. text ed. 7.95x (ISBN 0-932894-00-3). Unif Theol Seminary.
Communism: A Critique & Counter Proposal. 1975. pap. 2.00 (ISBN 0-686-13413-3). Unification Church.
Communism: A Critique & Counter Proposal, Questions & Answers. pap. 1.50 (ISBN 0-686-13414-1). Unification Church.
Divine Principle. 2nd ed. 10.00 (ISBN 0-686-13402-8); Study Guide, Part 1. pap. (ISBN 0-686-13403-6); Study Guide, Part 2. pap. 3.00 (ISBN 0-686-13404-4). Unification Church.
Durham, Deanna. Life Among the Moonies: Three Years in the Unification Church. (Orig.). 1981. pap. 2.95 (ISBN 0-88270-496-6). Logos.
Elkins, Chris. Heavenly Deception. 1980. pap. 3.95 (ISBN 0-8423-1402-4). Tyndale.
--What Do You Say to a Moonie? 80p. 1981. 2.50 (ISBN 0-686-72552-2). Tyndale.
Johnson, Rose & Ratzlaff, Don. As Angels of Light. (Illus.). 160p. (Orig.). 1980. pap. write for info. (ISBN 0-937364-00-2). Kindred Pr.
Jones, W. Farley, ed. A Prophet Speaks Today. pap. 3.00 (ISBN 0-686-13409-5). Unification Church.
Kemperman, Steve. Lord of the Second Advent. LC 80-54091. 176p. 1981. text ed. 8.95 (ISBN 0-8307-0780-8). Regal.
Kim, Dr. Young Oon. Unification Theology & Christian Thought. pap. 5.00 (ISBN 0-686-13407-9). Unification Church.
Moon, Sun Myung. Christianity in Crisis. pap. 2.00 (ISBN 0-686-13410-9). Unification Church.
--New Future of Christianity. Pak, Bo Hi, ed. pap. 3.00 (ISBN 0-686-13412-5). Unification Church.
--New Hope: Twelve Talks. 2.00 (ISBN 0-686-13411-7). Unification Church.
Quebedeaux, Richard & Sawatsky, Rodney, eds. Evangelical-Unification Dialogue. LC 79-89421. (Conference Ser.: No. 3). (Orig.). 1979. pap. text ed. 7.95 (ISBN 0-932894-02-X). Unif Theol Seminary.
Signs of Presence, Love & More. 4.95 (ISBN 0-686-13417-6). Unification Church.
Tingle, Donald A. & Fordyce, Richard A. Phases & Faces of the Moon: A Critical Evaluation of the Unification Church & Its Principles. 1979. 5.00 (ISBN 0-682-49264-7). Exposition.
Tsirpanlis, Constantine N., ed. Orthodox-Unification Dialogue. LC 80-54586. (Conference Ser.: No. 8). (Illus.). x, 139p. (Orig.). 1981. pap. text ed. 7.95 (ISBN 0-932894-08-9). Unif Theol Seminary.
Unification Thought. 1975. pap. 5.00 (ISBN 0-686-13405-2); Study Guide. pap. text ed. 1.50 (ISBN 0-686-13406-0). Unification Church.
Wilson, Andrew. Communism: Promise & Practice. 1975. pap. 2.00 (ISBN 0-686-13415-X). Unification Church.
Yamamoto, J. Isamu. The Puppet Master: An Inquiry into Sun Myung Moon & the Unification Church. LC 76-55622. 1977. pap. 3.95 (ISBN 0-87784-740-1). Inter-Varsity.

HOLY WEEK
see also Easter; Good Friday
Freeman, Eileen E. The Holy Week Book. new ed. LC 78-73510. 1979. pap. 19.95 (ISBN 0-89390-007-9). Resource Pubns.
Jeske, Richard L. & Barr, Browne. Holy Week. Achtemeier, Elizabeth, et al, eds. LC 79-7377. (Proclamation 2: Aids for Interpreting the Lessons of the Church Year, Ser. A). 64p. (Orig.). 1980. pap. 2.50 (ISBN 0-8006-4094-2, 1-4094). Fortress.
McFadden, William C. & Fuller, Reginald H. Holy Week. LC 74-24932. (Proclamation 1: Aids for Interpreting the Lessons of the Church Year, Ser. B). 64p. 1975. pap. 1.95 (ISBN 0-8006-4074-8, 1-4074). Fortress.
Newhouse, Flower A. Drama of Incarnation. 3rd ed. 1948. 6.50 (ISBN 0-910378-04-5). Christward.
Stendahl, Krister. Holy Week. LC 74-76926. (Proclamation 1: Aids for Interpreting the Lessons of the Church Year, Ser. A). Ser. A). 64p. (Orig.). 1974. pap. 1.95 (ISBN 0-8006-4064-0, 1-4064). Fortress.

HOLY-WEEK SERMONS
Koester, Charles L. Mission Accomplished. 58p. (Orig.). 1975. pap. 3.55 (ISBN 0-89536-158-2). CSS Pub.
Murray, Andrew. Spirit of Christ. 1970. pap. 3.95 (ISBN 0-87508-395-1). Chr Lit.

HOLY WELLS
Hope, Robert C. Legendary Lore of the Holy Wells of England. LC 68-21775. (Illus.). 1968. Repr. of 1893 ed. 19.00 (ISBN 0-8103-3445-3). Gale.
Lane-Davies, A. Holy Wells of Cornwall. pap. 2.45 (ISBN 0-686-22374-8). British Am Bks.
Logan, Patrick. The Holy Wells of Ireland. 170p. 1981. text ed. 15.00x (ISBN 0-686-73234-0, Pub. by Collins Sons England). Humanities.
Masani, Rustom P. Folklore of Wells. LC 77-11936. 1977. Repr. lib. bdg. 20.00 (ISBN 0-8414-6216-X). Folcroft.

HOMANS, GEORGE CASPER, 1910-
Needham, Rodney. Structure & Sentiment: A Test Case in Social Anthropology. LC 62-9738. 1962. 6.50x (ISBN 0-226-56991-8); pap. 1.95 (ISBN 0-226-56992-6). U of Chicago Pr.

HOME
see also Family; Family Life Surveys; Home Economics; Marriage
Alcott, William A. The Young Husband or, Duties of Man in the Marriage Relation. LC 70-169368. (Family in America Ser). (Illus.). 392p. 1972. Repr. of 1841 ed. 19.00 (ISBN 0-405-03844-5). Arno.
Beveridge, Elizabeth. Choosing & Using Home Equipment. 7th ed. (Illus.). 1976. pap. text ed. 5.50x (ISBN 0-8138-0780-8). Iowa St U Pr.
Eisenberg, Azriel & Ain-Globe, Leah, eds. Home at Last. LC 75-4126. 324p. 1976. 7.95 (ISBN 0-8197-0386-9). Bloch.
Jupo, Frank. A Place to Stay: A Man's Home Through the Ages. LC 72-9931. (Illus.). 48p. (gr. 1-4). 1973. PLB 5.95 (ISBN 0-396-06760-3). Dodd.
Loonie, Janice H. New House: A Book of Women. 39p. 2.00 (ISBN 0-685-47011-3). San Marcos.
Morris, Willie. Terrains of the Heart & Other Essays on Home. LC 81-50423. 288p. 1981. 12.95 (ISBN 0-686-72744-4). Yoknapatawpha.
Nickell, Paulena, et al. Management in Family Living. 5th ed. LC 75-41398. 475p. 1976. text ed. 23.95 (ISBN 0-471-63721-1). Wiley.
Talkabout the Home. (Illus.). Arabic 2.50x (ISBN 0-86685-233-6). Intl Bk Ctr.
White House Conference on Child Health & Protection. The Young Child in the Home: A Survey of Three Thousand American Families. LC 71-169371. (Family in America Ser). 446p. 1972. Repr. of 1936 ed. 22.00 (ISBN 0-405-03847-X). Arno.

HOME, DANIEL DUNGLAS, 1833-1886
Adare, Viscount. Experiences in Spiritualism with Mr. D. D. Home. LC 75-36824. (Occult Ser.). 1976. Repr. of 1870 ed. 11.00x (ISBN 0-405-07937-0). Arno.
Edmonds, I. G. D. D. Home: The Man Who Talked with Ghosts. LC 78-7579. (Illus.). 1978. 7.95 (ISBN 0-525-66584-6). Elsevier-Nelson.
Home, Mrs. Douglas. D. D. Home: His Life & Mission. LC 75-36844. (Occult Ser.). 1976. Repr. of 1888 ed. 24.00x (ISBN 0-405-07956-7). Arno.

HOME, HENRY, LORD KAMES, 1696-1782
Edwards, Jonathan. Freedom of the Will. Kaufman, Arnold S. & Frankena, William K., eds. LC 68-22308. 1969. 24.50x (ISBN 0-672-51063-4); pap. text ed. 12.95x (ISBN 0-672-60360-8). Irvington.
Smith, Samuel S. Essay on the Causes of the Variety of Complexion & Figure in the Human Species. Jordan, Winthrop D., ed. LC 65-19831. (The John Harvard Library). 1965. 16.50x (ISBN 0-674-26350-2). Harvard U Pr.
Woodhouselee, Alexander F. Memoirs of the Life & Writings of Henry Home of Kames: Containing Sketches of the Progressof Literature & General Improvement in Scotland During the Greater Part of the Eighteenth Century, 3 vols. 2nd ed. LC 78-67549. Repr. of 1814 ed. 115.00 set (ISBN 0-404-17550-3). AMS Pr.

HOME ACCIDENTS
see also First Aid in Illness and Injury
Backett, E. Maurice. Domestic Accidents. (Public Health Papers Ser: No. 26). 137p. (Eng, Fr, Rus, Span.). 1965. pap. 2.80 (ISBN 92-4-130026-4). World Health.
Berkel, Boyce N. How to Prevent Home Accidents & Handle Emergencies Effectively. LC 79-55195. (Illus.). 1979. pap. 7.50 (ISBN 0-9603184-0-2). B Berkel.
Burman, Sandra & Genn, Hazel, eds. Accidents in the Home. 140p. 1977. 25.00x (ISBN 0-85664-452-8, Pub. by Croom Helm Ltd England). Biblio Dist.
Creese, Angela. Safety for Your Family. (Illus.). 1968. 10.00x (ISBN 0-263-70021-6). Intl Pubns Serv.
Harmon, Murl. A New Vaccine for Child Safety. LC 76-8726. (Illus.). 1976. pap. 7.50 (ISBN 0-917066-00-6). Safety Now.

HOME AIR CONDITIONING
see Dwellings–Air Conditioning

HOME AND SCHOOL
see also Parent-Teacher Relationships; Parents' and Teachers' Associations
Ball, Colin & Ball, Mog. Fit for Work? Youth, School & Unemployment. (Chameleon Education Ser.). 144p. (Orig.). 1981. pap. 5.95 (ISBN 0-686-30858-1). Writers & Readers.
Berger, Eugenia H. Parents As Partners in Education: The School & Home Working Together. LC 80-39691. (Illus.). 424p. 1981. pap. text ed. 11.95 (ISBN 0-8016-0637-3). Mosby.
Brandt, Ronald S., ed. Partners: Parents & Schools. LC 79-90730. 1979. pap. text ed. 4.75 (ISBN 0-87120-096-1, 611-79168). Assn Supervision.
Bush, Catharine S. School & Home Program. 1980. pap. 15.00 (ISBN 0-88450-711-4, 3063-B). Communication Skill.
Clay, Phyllis L. Single Parents & the Public Schools. 77p. 1981. pap. 3.25x (ISBN 0-934460-15-9). NCCE.
Craft, Maurice, et al. Linking Home & School. rev. 2nd ed. 1972. text ed. 6.25x (ISBN 0-582-32472-6); pap. text ed. 3.75x (ISBN 0-582-32470-X). Humanities.
--Linking Home & School. 3rd ed. 1980. text ed. 23.65 (ISBN 0-06-318136-3); pap. text ed. 13.10 (ISBN 0-06-318149-5). Har-Row.
Croft, Doreen J. Parents & Teachers: A Resource Book for Home, School & Community Relations. 1979. pap. text ed. 9.95x (ISBN 0-534-00610-8). Wadsworth Pub.
Dolan, L. J. Home, School & Pupil Attitudes. LC 77-81507. (Illus.). 93p. 1981. pap. 21.00 (ISBN 0-08-027134-0). Pergamon.
Esbensen, Thorwald & Richards, Philip. Family Designed Learning. LC 74-83216. 1976. pap. 5.95 (ISBN 0-8224-2825-3). Pitman Learning.
Fernandez, Happy. Los Padres se organizan para mejorar las escuelas. NCCE, ed. ASPIRA of New York, tr. (Spanish.). 1976. 3.50 (ISBN 0-934460-03-5). NCCE.
Friedman, Robert, ed. Family Roots of School Learning & Behavior Disorders. 360p. 1973. 19.75 (ISBN 0-398-02469-3); pap. 11.50 (ISBN 0-398-02472-3). C C Thomas.
Golick, M. A Parents Guide to Learning Problems. 1970. pap. 1.95x (ISBN 0-88432-009-X). J Norton Pubs.
Goodacre, Elizabeth J. School & Home. 1970. pap. text ed. 5.00x (ISBN 0-391-02083-8, NFER). Humanities.
Hiemstra, Roger. The Educative Community: Linking the Community, School & Family. LC 72-77986. (The Professional Education Ser.). 116p. 1972. pap. 2.25 (ISBN 0-88224-006-4). Cliffs.
Joffe, Carole E. Friendly Intruders: Childcare Professionals & Family Life. LC 74-27281. 1977. 16.95x (ISBN 0-520-02925-9); pap. 3.95 (ISBN 0-520-03934-3). U of Cal Pr.
Kappelman, Murray & Ackerman, Paul. Between Parent & School. 1977. 8.95 (ISBN 0-8037-0544-1, J Wade). Dial.
Kroth, Roger L. & Scholl, Geraldine T. Getting Schools Involved with Parents. 1978. pap. text ed. 5.00 (ISBN 0-86586-035-1). Coun Exc Child.
Kuykendall, Crystal. Developing Leadership for Parent-Citizen Groups. 1976. pap. 3.50 (ISBN 0-934460-02-7). NCCE.
Lightfoot, Sara L. Worlds Apart: Relationships Between Families & Schools. LC 78-54506. 1978. 12.95x (ISBN 0-465-09244-6). Basic.
Litwak, Eugene & Meyer, Henry. School, Family, & Neighborhood. LC 73-17274. 300p. 1974. 17.50x (ISBN 0-231-03354-0). Columbia U Pr.
McWhirter, J. Jeffries. The Learning Disabled Child: A School & Family Concern. LC 77-81300. (Illus.). 1977. text ed. 8.95 (ISBN 0-87822-147-6); pap. text ed. 8.95 (ISBN 0-87822-142-5). Res Press.
Marjoribanks, Kevin. Families & Their Learning Environments. 1979. 22.00x (ISBN 0-7100-0167-3). Routledge & Kegan.
Miller, Mary S. & Baker, Samm S. Straight Talk to Parents: How to Help Your Child Get the Best Out of School. LC 76-6135. 1976. 8.95 (ISBN 0-685-70113-1). Stein & Day.
Monitoring: What Happens to Children Out of School. 1976. 2.00 (ISBN 0-86671-028-0). Comm Coun Great NY.
Morrison, George S. Parent Involvement in the Home, School & Community. (Early Childhood Education Ser.). 1978. pap. text ed. 9.95 (ISBN 0-675-08393-1). Merrill.
Nason, Leslie J. Help Your Child Succeed in School. 1977. pap. 2.95 (ISBN 0-346-12273-2). Cornerstone.
Ramirez, Cesar, tr. from Eng. Los Padres Se Organizan Para Mejorar las Escuelas. rev. ed. 61p. (Span.). 1981. pap. 3.50x (ISBN 0-934460-16-7). NCCE.
Rotter, Paul. A Parent's Program in a School. LC 74-99586. 1977. pap. text ed. 7.50 (ISBN 0-88200-110-8, I5559). Alexander Graham.
Sinclair, Robert L., ed. A Two-Way Street: Home-School Cooperation in Curriculum Decisionmaking. 92p. 1980. pap. 6.00 (ISBN 0-917754-16-6). Inst Responsive.
Stott, D. H. The Parent As Teacher. 1974. pap. 5.95 (ISBN 0-8224-5295-2). Pitman Learning.
Williamson, Darcy. School at Home: An Alternative to the Public School System. LC 79-55830. 100p. (Orig.). 1980. 13.95 (ISBN 0-89288-024-4); pap. 7.95 (ISBN 0-89288-022-8). Maverick.

HOME APPLIANCES
see Household Appliances

HOME BUYING
see House Buying

HOME CARE SERVICES
see also Home Nursing
Laurie, Gini. Housing & Home Services for the Disabled. (Illus.). 1977. 27.50x (ISBN 0-06-141518-9, Harper Medical). Har-Row.
Miller, E. J. A Life Apart. Gwynne, G. V., ed. 1979. pap. 9.95x (ISBN 0-422-75660-1, Pub. by Tavistock England). Methuen Inc.
Rossman, I. J. & Schwartz, Doris R. Family Handbook of Home Nursing & Medical Care. (Illus.). 1968. 8.95 (ISBN 0-87131-059-7). M Evans.
A Systems Analysis of the New York City Home Attendant Program: With Recommendations for a Home Care Service Delivery System. 1977. 4.00 (ISBN 0-86671-040-X). Comm Coun Great NY.
Trager, Brahna. Home Health Care & National Policy. LC 80-15988. (Home Health Care Services Quarterly Monograph: Vol. 1, No. 2). 108p. 1980. text ed. 12.95 (ISBN 0-917724-20-8); pap. text ed. cancelled (ISBN 0-917724-21-6). Haworth Pr.

HOME CONSTRUCTION
see House Construction

HOME DECORATION
see Interior Decoration

HOME DELIVERY OF BOOKS
see Direct Delivery of Books

HOME DESIGN
see Architecture, Domestic

HOME ECONOMICS
see also Consumer Education; Cookery; Cost and Standard of Living; Dairying; Entertaining; Food; Food Service; Fuel; Furniture; Heating; House Furnishings; Household Pests; Housewives; Interior Decoration; Laundry; Laundry and Laundry Industry; Marketing (Home Economics); Mobile Home Living; Needlework; Recipes; Servants; Sewing; Ventilation
Applegate, Dorothy. HHH Helpful Homemaker Hints. Applegate, William G., ed. LC 79-55468. (Illus.). 1979. softcover 2.95 (ISBN 0-9602122-3-X). Apple-Gems.
Arkin, Frieda. Kitchen Wisdom. LC 79-29897. 272p. 1980. pap. 5.95 (ISBN 0-03-056702-5). HR&W.
Aslett, Don. Is There Life After Housework. (Illus.). 109p. (Orig.). 1980. pap. 4.50 (ISBN 0-686-29303-7). Article One.
Aslett, Don A. Is There Life After Housework? (Illus.). 180p. 1981. pap. 6.95 (ISBN 0-89879-067-0). Writers Digest.
Bacon, Richard M. The Forgotten Arts, Bk. 3. LC 75-10770. (Forgotten Arts Ser.). (Illus.). 64p. 1976. pap. 3.95 (ISBN 0-911658-71-8). Yankee Bks.
Barclay, Marion S., et al. Teen Guide to Homemaking. 3rd ed. (gr. 7-9). text ed. 15.20 (ISBN 0-07-003644-6, W); tchr's manual 3.08 (ISBN 0-07-003646-2). McGraw.
Barry, Sheila A., ed. Our New Home. LC 81-8801. 128p. (Orig.). 1981. pap. 4.95 (ISBN 0-8069-7550-4). Sterling.
Beecher, Catharine & Stowe, Harriet B. American Woman's Home: Or, Principles of Domestic Science. LC 77-165703. (American Education Ser, No. 2). 1972. Repr. of 1869 ed. 25.00 (ISBN 0-405-03692-2). Arno.
Beecher, Catharine E. A Treatise on Domestic Economy. 1970. Repr. 16.50 (ISBN 0-685-55668-9). Hacker.
Beecher, Catharine E. & Stowe, Harriet B. American Woman's Home. LC 75-22526. (Library of Victorian Culture). (Illus.). 1975. pap. text ed. 8.00 (ISBN 0-89257-007-5). Am Life Foun.
Beecher, Catharine. A Treatise on Domestic Economy. LC 76-9145. (Illus.). 1977. pap. 4.95 (ISBN 0-8052-0539-X). Schocken.
Beeton, Isabella. Beeton's Book of Household Management. 1112p. 1969. 15.00 (ISBN 0-374-21513-8); pap. 6.95 (ISBN 0-374-51404-6). FS&G.
Beeton, Mrs. Mrs. Beeton's Cookery & Household Management. (Illus.). 59.95x (ISBN 0-8464-0650-0). Beekman Pubs.

Berk, Richard A., et al. Labor & Leisure at Home: Content & Organization of the Household Day. LC 79-13644. (Sage Library of Social Research: No. 87). (Illus.). 280p. 1979. 20.00x (ISBN 0-8039-1101-7); pap. 9.95x (ISBN 0-8039-1102-5). Sage.
Berry, Jo. The Happy Home Handbook. 1976. pap. 7.95 (ISBN 0-8007-0807-5). Revell.
Berthier, Francoise. Guide Trilingue Menager. 320p. (Fr., Span. & Port.). 1972. pap. 12.50 (ISBN 0-686-56916-4, M-6032). French & Eur.
Betters, Paul V. The Bureau of Home Economics: Its History, Activities & Organization. LC 72-3079. (Brookings Institution. Institute for Government Research. Service Monographs of the U.S. Government: No. 62). Repr. of 1930 ed. 18.00 (ISBN 0-404-57162-X). AMS Pr.
Bond, Helen J. Trends & Needs in Home Management: An Analytical Study of Home Management in Higher Institutions, in Order to Ascertain Trends & to Formulate Policies. LC 77-176922. (Columbia University. Teachers College. Contributions to Education: No. 365). Repr. of 1929 ed. 17.50 (ISBN 0-404-55365-6). AMS Pr.
Bonnett, J. Latherow. How to Cut Your Food Costs & Save Kitchen Energy 190 Ways. LC 79-90636. (Illus.). 1979. pap. 3.95 (ISBN 0-935358-00-5). Mini-Word.
Bouma, Mary L. The Creative Homemaker. LC 73-17234. 1973. pap. 2.50 (ISBN 0-87123-078-X, 210508); study guide o.p. 0.95 (ISBN 0-87123-508-0). Bethany Hse.
Brace, Pam & Jones, Peggy. Sidetracked Home Executives: From Pigpen to Paradise. LC 79-56324. (Illus.). 1979. pap. 5.95 (ISBN 0-8323-0355-0). Binford.
Brinkley, J. H., et al. Teen Guide to Homemaking. 4th ed. 1976. 15.20 (ISBN 0-07-007840-8, W); ans. key 2.80 (ISBN 0-07-007841-6). McGraw.
Bromberg, Karen G. & Faulkner, Sarah. Sarah Faulkner's Planning a Home: Projects Manual. 104p. (Orig.). 1980. pap. text ed. write for info. HR&W.
Buckeye Cookery & Practical Housekeeping. LC 72-147780. 464p. 1970. Repr. of 1877 ed. 6.95 (ISBN 0-88319-001-X). Shoal Creek Pub.
Camiel, Reva & Michaelsen, Hila. First Time Out: Skills for Living Away from Home. LC 79-92821. (Illus., Orig.). (gr. 11-12). 1980. pap. 5.95 (ISBN 0-915190-26-5). Jalmar Pr.
Carson, Byrta, et al. How You Plan & Prepare Meals. 3rd ed. (Illus.). 1979. text ed. 14.24 (ISBN 0-07-010162-0); tchr's ed. 3.64 (ISBN 0-07-060992-6). McGraw.
Carson, Byrta R. & Ramee, Marue C. How You Plan & Prepare Meals. 2nd ed. (gr. 7-12). 1968. text ed. 14.24 (ISBN 0-07-010161-2, W). McGraw.
Carver, Jean T. The Extracurricular Homemaker. 1979. 4.00 (ISBN 0-682-49256-6). Exposition.
Catalogs of the Home Economics Library. 1977. lib. bdg. 240.00 (ISBN 0-8161-0054-3). G K Hall.
Center for Science in the Public Interest. Household Pollutant Guide. Fritsch, Al, ed. LC 77-76269. 1978. pap. 3.50 (ISBN 0-385-12494-5, Anch). Doubleday.
--Ninety Nine Ways to a Simple Lifestyle. (Illus.). 320p. 1977. pap. 3.50 (ISBN 0-385-12493-7). Doubleday.
--Ninety-Nine Ways to a Simple Lifestyle. Fritsch, Albert J., et al, eds. LC 77-76831. (Illus.). 400p. 1977. 12.50x (ISBN 0-253-34070-5). Ind U Pr.
Chamberlain, V. Teen Guide to Homemaking. 5th ed. 1981. 18.60 (ISBN 0-07-007843-2); tchr's resource guide 6.72 (ISBN 0-07-007844-0). McGraw.
Chappat, Djenane. Diccionario de la Limpieza. 234p. (Espn.). 1970. pap. 3.50 (ISBN 84-206-1282-0, S-12249). French & Eur.
Child, Lydia M. The American Frugal Housewife: Dedicated to Those Who Are Not Ashamed of Economy. 1977. Repr. 20.00 (ISBN 0-403-07397-9). Scholarly.
Clayton, Nanalee. Young Living. rev. ed. (Illus.). (gr. 7-8). 1970. text ed. 15.36 (ISBN 0-87002-011-0); tchr guide free. Bennett IL.
Coalition Statement: Vocational Home Economics Education. 1979. 1.00 (ISBN 0-686-26996-9, A261-08436). Home Econ Educ.
Cobbett, Anne. The English Housekeeper. 1973. Repr. of 1851 ed. 16.95x (ISBN 0-8464-0378-1). Beekman Pubs.
Cochrun, John W. Avoid Financial Shocks in Your Family's Future. LC 77-77536. (Illus.). 1976. pap. 9.95 (ISBN 0-9601050-0-X). Cochrun.
Compton, Norma & Hall, Olive. Foundations of Home Economics Research: A Human Ecology Approach. LC 72-81810. 1972. pap. text ed. 12.95x (ISBN 0-8087-0338-2). Burgess.
Consumer Guide Editions. Do It Yourself & Save Money. LC 80-7585. (Illus.). 636p. 1980. 14.95 (ISBN 0-06-010861-4, HarpT). Har-Row.
Cooley, Marilyn. Checklist for a Working Wife. LC 78-8205. 1979. pap. 2.50 (ISBN 0-385-14205-6, Dolp). Doubleday.
Cooper, Elizabeth. A Primer of Cooking & Housekeeping. (Illus.). 192p. 1979. 8.95 (ISBN 0-89496-023-7); pap. 4.95 (ISBN 0-89496-015-6). Ross Bks.
Cope, Ann. Hosehold Hints. Reynolds, Maureen, ed. LC 79-92446. (Illus.). 192p. (Orig.). 1980. pap. 4.95 (ISBN 0-911954-54-6). Nitty Gritty.
Coran, Terence. Enciclopedia De la Decoracion. 3rd ed. 343p. (Espn.). 1978. 65.00 (ISBN 84-278-0451-2, S-50463). French & Eur.
Cottrell, Edyth Y. Stretching the Food Dollar Cookbook. LC 80-36894. (Illus., Orig.). 1981. pap. 3.95 (ISBN 0-912800-80-1). Woodbridge Pr.
Cross, Aleene. Introductory Homemaking. 1970. text ed. 12.08 (ISBN 0-397-40169-8); tchrs' manual 1.56 (ISBN 0-397-40170-1). Har-Row.
Davidson, Phyllis. Home Management. 1975. pap. 16.95 (ISBN 0-7134-3047-8, Pub. by Batsford England). David & Charles.
Davis, Melinda. Storage: A House & Garden Book. LC 77-88766. 1979. pap. 6.95 (ISBN 0-394-73464-5). Pantheon.
Delaney, George & Delaney, Sandra. The Number One Home Business Book. 176p. 1981. pap. 4.95 (ISBN 0-89709-022-5). Liberty Pub.
Dennler, Louise. Food Preparation: Study Course. LC 76-146934. (Illus.). 149p. 1971. pap. 9.25x (ISBN 0-8138-0805-7). Iowa St U Pr.
Dernburg, Thomas F., et al. Studies in Household Economic Behavior. 1958. 32.50x (ISBN 0-686-51317-7). Elliots Bks.
De Ropp, Robert S. Eco-Tech. 336p. 1975. pap. 3.45 (ISBN 0-440-54537-4, Delta). Dell.
Dillow, Linda. Priority Planner. rev. ed. 120p. 1980. pap. 5.95 spiral bound (ISBN 0-8407-5719-0). Nelson.
Domestic Goddess Planning Notebook, 1981. 1980. 8.95 (ISBN 0-911094-11-3). Pacific Santa Barbara.
Edman, V. Raymond. Crisis Experiences in the Lives of Noted Christians. 1970. pap. 1.95 (ISBN 0-87123-065-8, 200065). Bethany Hse.
Enciclopedia Carrogio del Hogar, 8 vols. 2nd ed. 1664p. (Espn.). 1976. Set. leather 240.00 (ISBN 84-7254-171-1, S-50548). French & Eur.
Enciclopedia del Hogar, 5 vols. 1625p. (Espn.). 1978. Set. leather 165.00 (ISBN 84-7079-074-9, S-50578). French & Eur.
Enciclopedia del Hogar: Consejos para el Hogar, Consejos de Belleza, el Matrimonia y la Vida Sexual, la Salud de los Hijos, 4 vols. 2nd ed. 640p. (Espn.). Set. 52.00 (ISBN 84-278-0546-2, S-50455). French & Eur.
Enciclopedia Labor de la Mujer y del Hogar: La Mujer, los Hijos, la Casa y la Alimentacion, 4 vols. 2nd ed. 1280p. (Espn.). 1976. Set. 160.00 (ISBN 84-335-0380-4, S-50457). French & Eur.
Enciclopedia Salvat de la Mujer y del Hogar, 12 vols. 2nd ed. 3600p. (Espn.). 1970. Set. 300.00 (ISBN 84-7137-308-4, S-50456). French & Eur.
Enciclopedia Salvat del Bricolaje, 10 vols. 2400p. (Espn.). 1977. Set. 320.00 (ISBN 84-7137-547-8, S-50459). French & Eur.
Enciclopedia Sopena del Hogar, 5 vols. 2900p. (Espn.). Set. 90.00 (ISBN 84-303-0228-X, S-13486). French & Eur.
Everson, Ralph & Everson, Mary. Everson's Best Farm Manual & Helpful Hints. LC 80-68664. (Illus.). 300p. (Orig.). 1980. pap. 9.95 (ISBN 0-89708-027-0). And Bks.
Ewart, Nei. Unsafe As Houses: A Guide to Home Safety. (Illus.). 160p. 1981. 12.50 (ISBN 0-8069-9564-5, Pub. by Blandford Pr England). Sterling.
Feinman, Jeffrey. How to Make Money in Your Kitchen. 1977. 7.95 (ISBN 0-688-03213-3). Morrow.
Firth, Rosemary. Housekeeping Among Malay Peasants. 2nd ed. (Monographs on Social Anthropology: No. 7). 1966. text ed. 18.75x (ISBN 0-485-19507-0, Athlone Pr). Humanities.
Fisher, Polly. Polly's Pointers: One Thousand Eighty-One Helpful Household Hints for Making Everything Last Longer. 1981. 11.95 (ISBN 0-89256-184-X); pap. 7.95 (ISBN 0-89256-197-1). Rawson Wade.
Fleck, H. & Fernandez, L. Exploring Homemaking & Personal Living. 4th ed. 1977. text ed. 11.96x (ISBN 0-13-297051-1). P-H.
Florida Famm Bureau Womens Federation. The Homemakers' Handbook. Perkins, Patsy, ed. 1978. pap. 5.00 (ISBN 0-918544-20-3). Wimmer Bks.
Flynn, Joyce. About the House: New Ideas for Its Easy Management. LC 76-48842. (Illus.). 1977. 6.95 (ISBN 0-916752-08-9). Dorison Hse.
Freed, Dolly. Possum Living. LC 78-52190. 1978. pap. 3.95 (ISBN 0-87663-987-2). Universe.
Gillaspie, Beulah V. Consumer Questions & Their Significance. LC 71-176804. (Columbia University. Teachers College. Contributions to Education: No. 947). Repr. of 1949 ed. 17.50 (ISBN 0-404-55947-6). AMS Pr.
Gilles, Jean, ed. How to Run Your House. LC 72-97091. 1973. 7.95 (ISBN 0-89795-007-0). Farm Journal.
Ginsberg, Linda. Family Financial Survival. LC 80-70436. (Illus.). 192p. (Orig.). 1981. pap. 8.95 (ISBN 0-89087-315-1). Celestial Arts.
Goldfein, Donna. Everywoman's Guide to Time Management. LC 76-54498. 1977. pap. 4.95 (ISBN 0-89087-924-9). Les Femmes Pub.
Goock, Roland. Enciclopedia Del "Hagalo Usted Mismo". 436p. (Espn.). 1975. 41.95 (ISBN 84-239-6599-6, S-50462). French & Eur.
Goodspeed. This Is the Life. (gr. 7-12). 1981. text ed. 11.80 (ISBN 0-87002-342-X). Bennett IL.
Goodyear, Margaret & Klohr, M. C. Managing for Effective Living. 2nd ed. 290p. 1965. text ed. 11.50 (ISBN 0-471-31517-6, Pub. by Wiley). Krieger.
Grady, Tom, ed. The Household Handbook. (Illus.). 170p. (Orig.). 1981. pap. 3.95 (ISBN 0-915658-41-0). Meadowbrook Pr.
Greenblatt, Edwin. Suddenly Single: A Survival Kit for the Single Man. LC 73-79914. 1973. 6.95 (ISBN 0-8129-0369-2). Times Bks.
Greenspan, Nancy B. & Davis, Elaine P. Accent on Home Economics. LC 78-1035. (Messner Career Ser.). (Illus.). 256p. (gr. 7 up). 1978. PLB 8.29 (ISBN 0-671-32898-0). Messner.
Greenwood, B. & Dowell, J. Masculine Focus in Home Economics. LC 75-10815. 1975. pap. 2.50 (ISBN 0-686-14990-4, 261-08422). Home Econ Educ.
Grierson, Alice K. An Army Wife's Cookbook. Williams, Mary L., ed. LC 72-91099. (Popular Ser.: No. 13). 1972. pap. 2.50 (ISBN 0-911408-27-4). SW Pks Mnmts.
Habeeb, Virginia T. The Ladies Home Art Journal of Homemaking: Everything You Need to Know to Run Your Home with Ease & Style. LC 72-90393. 1973. 14.95 (ISBN 0-671-21487-X). S&S.
--Ladies' Home Journal Art of Homemaking. 1978. pap. 6.95 (ISBN 0-671-24210-5, Fireside). S&S.
Halchin, Lilla O. Home Economics for Learners with Special Needs. LC 76-40735. 1976. 3.50 (ISBN 0-686-17285-X, 261-18426). Home Econ Educ.
Hammersmark, Judy. Homemaker's Response to Inflation. (Orig.). 1980. pap. 2.95 (ISBN 0-88270-454-0). Logos.
Harlech, Pamela. Pamela Harlech's Practical Guide to Cooking, Entertaining & Household Management. LC 80-65991. 1981. 16.95 (ISBN 0-689-11108-8). Atheneum.
Hastie, Tom. Home Life. (Past into Present Ser.). 15.00x (ISBN 0-392-05879-0, LTB). Sportshelf.
Hawrylyshyn, Oli. The Economic Value of Household Services: An International Comparison of Empirical Estimates. 1980. cancelled (ISBN 0-03-023211-2). Praeger.
Hazen, Barbara S. You Can't Have Sunbeams Without Little Specks of Dust: Household Hints, Quotes & Anecdotes. (Illus.). 1980. 3.95 (ISBN 0-8378-3101-6). Gibson.
Heasman, Kathleen. Home, Family & Community. 1978. pap. text ed. 7.50x (ISBN 0-04-301087-3). Allen Unwin.
Heloise. Help! from Heloise. LC 80-70543. (Illus.). 500p. 1981. 12.95 (ISBN 0-87795-318-X). Arbor Hse.
--Hints from Heloise. 1981. pap. 6.95 (ISBN 0-380-53066-X, 53066). Avon.
--Hints from Heloise. LC 79-56019. 1980. 12.95 (ISBN 0-87795-260-4). Arbor Hse.
Hickman, Peggy. Jane Austen Household Book. LC 77-89377. 1978. 10.50 (ISBN 0-7153-7324-2). David & Charles.
Home Management & Consumer Education: Latin America. (Nutritional Information Documents Ser: No. 5). 79p. 1976. pap. 7.50 (ISBN 0-685-66337-X, F1049, FAO). Unipub.
Homemaking Tips. LC 77-77305. 1977. 3.50 (ISBN 0-89036-078-2). Hawkes Pub Inc.
Hoole, Daryl. The Joys of Homemaking. LC 75-8031. 118p. 1975. 6.95 (ISBN 0-87747-549-0). Deseret Bk.
Hoole, Daryl V. Art of Homemaking. rev. ed. 7.95 (ISBN 0-87747-011-1). Deseret Bk.
Hostage, Jacqueline. Jackie's Book of Household Charts. LC 80-68361. (Illus.). 112p. (Orig.). 1981. plastic comb bdg. 5.95 (ISBN 0-932620-04-3). Betterway Pubns.
Housework: Slavery or a Labor of Love? 4th ed. 120p. 1982. pap. 4.00 (ISBN 0-9601544-4-2). B Warrior.
Hughes, Martha E., ed. The Woman's Day Book of Household Hints. LC 77-25318. 1978. 7.95 (ISBN 0-688-03283-4); pap. 3.95 (ISBN 0-688-08283-1). Morrow.
Joseph, Marjory & Joseph, William D. Research Fundamentals in Home Economics. LC 79-88756. (The Plycon Home Economics Ser.). 403p. 1979. pap. text ed. 15.95x (ISBN 0-686-75965-6). Burgess.
Joseph, Marjory L. & Joseph, William D. Research Fundamentals in Home Economics. 2nd ed. LC 79-88756. (Illus.). 1979. pap. 15.95x (ISBN 0-916434-33-8). Plycon Pr.
Jurgensen, Barbara. How to Live Better on Less: A Guide for Waste Watchers. LC 74-77677. 144p. (Orig.). 1974. pap. 3.95 (ISBN 0-8066-1427-7, 10-3181). Augsburg.
Keely, Jane. One Thousand One Great Housekeeping Hints. 128p. 1980. pap. 6.95 (ISBN 0-87851-033-8). Hearst Bks.
Kelly & Landers. Today's Teen. (YA) 1977. cancelled (ISBN 0-87002-192-3); tchr's guide 6.60 (ISBN 0-87002-264-4); student guide 3.96 (ISBN 0-87002-268-7). Bennett IL.
Key, Maude D. Grandmother's Amazing Housekeeping Secrets. 2nd ed. 91p. 1968. pap. 3.50 (ISBN 0-917420-01-2). Buck Hill.
Kilmer, Carolyn I. Dollars from Your Discards: The Complete Garage Sale Handbook. LC 80-81565. (Illus.). 56p. (Orig.). 1980. pap. 4.95 (ISBN 0-937028-00-2, 101). Henry John & Co.
Knowles, David H. Consumer Math Series, 7 bks. 1972. pap. 9.00 ea. (ISBN 0-8449-0200-4). Learning Line.
Koff, Richard M. How Does It Work. 304p. (RL 5). 1973. pap. 1.50 (ISBN 0-451-06920-X, W6920, Sig). NAL.
Kohlmann, Eleanore L. Home Economics for Young Men. 214p. 1975. pap. text ed. 9.95x (ISBN 0-8138-0820-0). Iowa St U Pr.
Krakowski, Lili. Starting Out: The Guide I Wish I'd Had When I Left Home. LC 73-79339. 228p. 1973. 25.00x (ISBN 0-8128-1621-8); pap. 2.95 (ISBN 0-8128-1634-X). Stein & Day.
Kramer, Rita. Peanut Butter on My Pillow. 144p. 1980. pap. 3.95 (ISBN 0-8407-5724-7). Nelson.
Kratz, Carole & Lee, Albert. Coupons, Refunds, Rebates. new ed. LC 75-20064. (Illus.). 160p. pap. 2.95 (ISBN 0-911104-62-3). Workman Pub.
Ladies of the American Community in Japan. American Way of Housekeeping. (Jap. & Eng.). 1958. 6.75 (ISBN 0-8048-0020-0). C E Tuttle.
Laird, Jean. Homemaker's Book of Time & Money Savers. 1980. pap. 2.50 (ISBN 0-446-91562-9). Warner Bks.
--The Homemaker's Book of Time & Money Savers. LC 79-11496. 1979. 11.95 (ISBN 0-8289-0345-X). Greene.
Lambert, Regina. Total Woman? I Work. LC 77-81363. 1977. pap. 2.95 (ISBN 0-89221-040-0). New Leaf.
Lewandowski, Stephen, ed. Farmer's & Housekeepers's Cyclopaedia of 1888. Date not set. 16.95 (ISBN 0-912278-91-9); pap. 10.95 (ISBN 0-686-71761-9). Crossing Pr.
Libien, Lois & Strong, Margaret. Super-Economy House Cleaning. 1976. 7.95 (ISBN 0-688-03026-2). Morrow.
Lockerbie, Jeanette W. Salt in My Kitchen. (Quiet Time Books). 1967. pap. 2.25 (ISBN 0-8024-7500-0). Moody.
Longacre, Doris. Living More with Less. LC 80-15461. 296p. 1980. pap. 6.95 (ISBN 0-8361-1930-4). Herald Pr.
Lupton, F. M., ed. The Farm & Home Cyclopedia: A Compendium of Old-Time Knowledge. LC 77-23827. (Illus.). 1977. 11.95 (ISBN 0-912278-90-0); pap. 8.95 (ISBN 0-912278-91-9). Crossing Pr.
McClure, Jon. Jon McClure's Making Ends Meet. (Orig.). 1982. pap. price not set (ISBN 0-440-55442-X, Dell Trade Pbks). Dell.
McCullough, Bonnie R. Bonnie's Household Organizer. 1980. pap. 4.95 (ISBN 0-312-08791-8); prepack 49.50 (ISBN 0-312-08792-6). St Martin.
Mc Dermott, Irene E. & Nicholas, Jeanne L. Homemaking for Teenagers, Bk. 1. new ed. (gr. 7-12). 1975. Bk 1. 19.48 (ISBN 0-87002-070-6). Bennett IL.
Malis, Jody C. Supermarket Cookbook. 1971. pap. 0.95 (ISBN 0-532-95145-X). Woodhill.
Malos, Ellen, ed. The Politics of Housework. 256p. Date not set. 16.00x (ISBN 0-8052-8023-5, Pub. by Allison & Busby England); pap. 7.95 (ISBN 0-8052-8022-7, Pub. by Allison & Busby England). Schocken.
Masnick, George & Bane, Mary Jo. The Nation's Families: 1960-1990. LC 80-20531. (Illus.). 200p. (Orig.). 1980. 17.95 (ISBN 0-86569-050-2); pap. 10.00 (ISBN 0-86569-051-0). Auburn Hse.
Mason, Sheila. Starting a Home. 1976. 3.95x (ISBN 0-521-20739-8). Cambridge U Pr.
Mather, Helen. Light Horsekeeping. (Illus.). 1970. 7.95 (ISBN 0-525-14620-2). Dutton.

Meacham, Esther A. & Sarbaugh, Mabel M., eds. Professional Development. 113p. (Orig.). 1979. pap. text ed. 6.95x (ISBN 0-89894-022-2). Advocate Pub Group.
Mikes, George. How to Run a Stately Home. (Illus.). 125p. 1972. 6.95 (ISBN 0-233-95848-7). Transatlantic.
Miller, Ella M. Hints for Homemakers. LC 73-84237. 1973. pap. 0.95 (ISBN 0-8361-1723-9). Herald Pr.
--Hints for Homemakers. LC 73-84237. 128p. (Orig.). 1973. pap. 1.25 (ISBN 0-87983-063-8). Keats.
--Woman in Her Home. (Orig.). 1968. pap. 1.25 (ISBN 0-8024-9678-4). Moody.
Miller, Vernon E., ed. Handy Devices for Farm & Home. LC 78-55329. (Illus.). 1978. pap. 4.95 (ISBN 0-8487-0487-8). Oxmoor Hse.
Moffitt, William J. The Guide to Home Income. 216p. 1975. pap. 3.00 (ISBN 0-686-11211-3). Arlington Ent.
Moore, Alma C. How to Clean Everything. 1971. pap. 2.95 (ISBN 0-671-20914-0, Fireside). S&S.
Morris, Earl W. & Winter, Mary. Housing, Family, & Society. LC 77-24772. 1978. text ed. 18.95x (ISBN 0-471-61570-6). Wiley.
New Trends in Home Economics Education Series: Teaching of Basic Sciences: Home Economics, Vol. 1. 1979. pap. 9.25 (ISBN 92-3-101622-9, U932, UNESCO). Unipub.
Newman, Cindy C. The Book of Household Hints. (Illus.). pap. 5.95 (ISBN 0-87069-328-X). Wallace-Homestead.
Nickell, Paulena, et al. Management in Family Living. 5th ed. LC 75-41398. 475p. 1976. text ed. 23.95 (ISBN 0-471-63721-1). Wiley.
Nye, Beverly. A Family Raised on Rainbows. 176p. 1981. pap. 6.95 (ISBN 0-553-01331-9). Bantam.
--A Family Raised on Sunshine. 112p. 1981. pap. 5.95 (ISBN 0-553-01332-7). Bantam.
Oakley, Ann. The Sociology of Housework. LC 75-4668. 264p. 1975. pap. 3.95 (ISBN 0-394-73088-7). Pantheon.
Oppenheim, Irene. Management of the Modern Home. 2nd ed. (Illus.). 368p. 1976. text ed. 18.95x (ISBN 0-02-389440-7). Macmillan.
Oppenheimer, Lillian & Epstein, Natalie. Decorative Napkin Folding for Beginners. (Illus.). 1980. pap. 1.75 (ISBN 0-486-23797-4). Dover.
Osgood, William. Wintering in Snow Country. LC 78-58680. (Illus.). 1977. 9.95 (ISBN 0-8289-0319-0); pap. 4.95 (ISBN 0-8289-0320-4). Greene.
Paolucci, Beatrice, et al. Personal Perspectives. 2nd ed. (Illus.). (gr. 9-12). 1978. text ed. 14.64 (ISBN 0-07-048438-4, W); tchr's manual 3.64 (ISBN 0-07-034862-6). McGraw.
Parker, Frances J. Home Economics: An Introduction to a Dynamic Profession. (Illus.). 1980. text ed. 14.95 (ISBN 0-02-391700-8). Macmillan.
Parnell, Frances B. Homemaking: Skills for Everyday Living. LC 81-4156. (Illus.). 464p. 1981. text ed. 15.96 (ISBN 0-87006-324-3). Goodheart.
Pasadena Art Alliance. All Things Wise & Wonderful. 1975. pap. 4.95 (ISBN 0-937042-00-5). Pasadena Art.
Peake, Jacqueline. The Housewife Handyperson. (Illus.). 1978. 8.95 (ISBN 0-8306-7880-8); pap. 4.95 (ISBN 0-8306-6880-2, 880). TAB Bks.
Pearson, James, et al. Hawaii Home Energy Book. LC 77-79935. 1978. pap. 8.95 (ISBN 0-8248-0596-8). U Pr of Hawaii.
Quigley, Eileen E. Introduction to Home Economics. 2nd ed. (Illus.). 1974. text ed. 15.95 (ISBN 0-02-397200-9). Macmillan.
Raines, Margaret. Consumers' Management. rev. ed. Orig. Title: Managing Livingtime. (Illus.). (gr. 9-12). 1973. text ed. 14.32 (ISBN 0-87002-123-0); tchr's guide avail. Bennett IL.
Raintree. The Household Book of Hints & Tips. LC 77-29161. 1979. 13.50 (ISBN 0-8246-0211-0). Jonathan David.
Raintree, Diane, ed. The Household Book of Hints & Tips. 272p. 1980. pap. 2.25 (ISBN 0-345-28927-7). Ballantine.
Reiff, Florence M. Steps in Home Living. rev. ed. (Illus.). (YA) (gr. 7-9). 1971. text ed. 15.96 (ISBN 0-87002-099-4); tchr's guide free. Bennett IL.
Richardson, Lou & Callahan, Genevieve. How to Write for Homemakers. 2nd ed. (Illus.). 1962. 8.95x (ISBN 0-8138-0830-8). Iowa St U Pr.
Rothchild, John & Yergin, Daniel. Stop Burning Your Money: Energy-Saving Guide That You Can Really Believe. LC 80-5271. (Illus.). 1980. 14.95 (ISBN 0-394-51366-5). Random.
Ser-Vo-Tel Institute. Dishwashing Procedures. (Foodservice Career Education Ser.). 1975. pap. 4.95 (ISBN 0-8436-2026-9). CBI Pub.
Seymour, Peter. If a Man's Home Is His Castle, Then How Do You Cook a Moat? A Bachelor's Guide to Cleaning, Cooking, Shopping, Etc. (Illus.). 1980. 3.95 (ISBN 0-8378-3103-2). Gibson.
Shep, R. L. Cleaning & Repairing Books: A Practical Home Manual. LC 80-21244. (Illus.). 112p. 1980. pap. 7.95 (ISBN 0-914046-00-4). R L Shep.
Snyder, Laura. Homemaking Executive. pap. 3.95 (ISBN 0-89036-140-1). Hawkes Pub Inc.
Solomon, Rick & Solomon, Linda. Residential Home Management: A Handbook for Managers of Community-Living Facilities. 1981. 14.95 (ISBN 0-89885-037-1). Human Sci Pr.
Stark, Norman. The Formula Book. 258p. 1975. 10.00 (ISBN 0-8362-0629-0); pap. 5.95 (ISBN 0-8362-0630-4). Andrews & McMeel.
Steidl, Rose E. & Bratton, Esther C. Work in the Home. LC 67-29007. 419p. 1968. 23.95 (ISBN 0-471-82085-7). Wiley.
Strain, Virginia S. A Place of Your Own. (Independent Living Ser.). (Illus.). 1978. pap. text ed. 5.40 (ISBN 0-07-061972-7, G); wkbk. 2.52 (ISBN 0-07-061973-5); tchr's manual 3.30 (ISBN 0-07-061974-3). McGraw.
Swanson. Introduction to Home Management. 1981. 17.95 (ISBN 0-686-72217-5). Macmillan.
Tasso, Torquato. The Householders Philosophie - the True Economia - of Housekeeping - Annexed a Dairie Booke for Huswives. Kyd, T., tr. LC 74-28888. (English Experience Ser.: No. 765). 1975. Repr. of 1588 ed. 8.00 (ISBN 90-221-0765-5). Walter J Johnson.
Torjesen, Hakon. The Househusband: Reflections on a Changing World. 1981. 8.95 (ISBN 0-9602790-6-7). The Garden.
Trow, Ruby L. Home Economics Competencies & Competency Factors. (Orig.). 1979. pap. text ed. 6.95x (ISBN 0-686-65376-9). Plycon Pr.
Tucker, Gina. Science of Housekeeping. 2nd ed. 1973. pap. 11.95 (ISBN 0-8436-0577-4). CBI Pub.
Tusser, Thomas. A Hundreth Good Pointes of Husbandrie. LC 73-7081. (English Experience Ser.: No. 628). 26p. 1973. Repr. of 1557 ed. 3.50 (ISBN 90-221-0628-4). Walter J Johnson.
Wadey, Rosemary, et al. The Pennypincher Householder Handbook. LC 79-52368. (Illus.). 1979. 17.95 (ISBN 0-7153-7844-9). David & Charles.
Walker, Beth. Checklists: A Personal Organizer. 192p. (Orig.). Date not set. leatherette spiral binding 9.95 (ISBN 0-8027-7164-5). Walker & Co.
Walker, C. H. The Abyssinian at Home. LC 70-177876. Repr. of 1933 ed. 18.50 (ISBN 0-404-06806-5). AMS Pr.
Waschek, Carmen & Waschek, Brownlee. Inflation Fighter's Big Book: Beat the High Cost of Operating Your Home. (Illus.). 1979. 13.95 (ISBN 0-8359-3068-8). Reston.
Williams, Adele. Gracious Living: How to Enjoy Being a Woman. LC 76-29227. 1976. 8.95 (ISBN 0-87795-149-7). Arbor Hse.
Wolf, Donald D., ed. One Thousand & One Helpful Family Hints. (Illus.). 256p. (Orig.). 1980. pap. 9.95 (ISBN 0-8326-2246-X, 7030). Delair.
Yost, Lynn. Like New: Cleaning Every Spot, Spill, & Stain in Your Home. (Illus.). 160p. 1981. pap. 4.95 (ISBN 0-8256-3252-8, Quick Fox). Music Sales.

HOME ECONOMICS–ACCOUNTING

Albin, Francis M. Consumer Economics & Personal Money Management. (Illus.). 496p. 1982. 18.95 (ISBN 0-13-169490-1). P-H.
Annual Price Survey - Family Budget Costs. annual 1976. pap. 6.00 mimeo (ISBN 0-86671-030-2). Comm Coun Great NY.
Becker, Gary S. A Treatise on the Family. LC 81-1306. (Illus.). 320p. 1981. text ed. 20.00 (ISBN 0-674-90696-9). Harvard U Pr.
The Budget As a Means to an End. 1970. pap. 1.25 (ISBN 0-686-14997-1, 261-08406). Home Econ Educ.
Cobb, C. G. The Bad Times Primer: A Complete Guide to Survival on a Budget. LC 81-52089. (Illus.). 336p. (Orig.). 1981. pap. 14.95 (ISBN 0-9606608-0-1). Times Pr.
Fairbank, et al. Mathematics for the Consumer. 2nd ed. 1975. text ed. 6.60 (ISBN 0-538-13140-3, M14); problems & drills 2.52 (ISBN 0-538-13141-1); test 0.40 (ISBN 0-538-13143-8). SW Pub.
The Family Budget. 1970. pap. 1.25 (ISBN 0-686-14996-3, 261-08404). Home Econ Educ.
A Family Budget Standard. rev ed. 1971. pap. 4.00 (ISBN 0-86671-008-6). Comm Coun Great NY.
Fortin, Joseph P. Get Out of Debt. 160p. 1980. pap. text ed. 6.95 (ISBN 0-936256-00-1). Omega Pub Co.
Gallagher, Neil. How to Save Money on Almost Everything. LC 78-19113. 1978. pap. 2.95 (ISBN 0-87123-234-0, 210234). Bethany Hse.
Gossett, Donn. What You Say Is What You Get. 1979. pap. 2.50 (ISBN 0-8007-8382-4, Spire Bks). Revell.
Grey, Jonathan. How to Get Out of Debt & Stay Out. 1st ed. LC 67-18355. 120p. (Orig.). 1967. pap. 3.50 (ISBN 0-910610-01-0). Fortuna.
Huber, Roger, ed. Where My Money Is Going: Income & Expense Budget. (Orig.). 1980. pap. 10.00x (ISBN 0-918300-00-2); wkbk. 10.00 (ISBN 0-686-70172-0). Lankey.
Kilgo, Edith F. Money Management: Dollars & Sense for Christian Homemakers. 200p. 1980. pap. 5.95 (ISBN 0-8010-5422-2). Baker Bk.
King, Bill & King, Pat. Money Talks, It Says Good-by. 112p. 1977. 3.45 (ISBN 0-930756-31-2, 4230-K14). Women's Aglow.
Lankford, Francis G., Jr. Consumer Mathematics. (gr. 9-12). 1981. text ed. 13.32 (ISBN 0-205-07190-2, 567906); tchr's guide 14.00 (ISBN 0-205-07191-0); wkbk. 5.12 (ISBN 0-205-07192-9). Allyn.
Lasser Institute. J. K. Lasser's Managing Your Family Finances. 1976. 12.50 (ISBN 0-671-22306-2). S&S.
Lefax Pub. Co. Editors. Family Budgets Simplified. (Lefax Record Bks.: No. 803). looseleaf bdg. 7.00, refills avail (ISBN 0-685-14134-9). Lefax.
McCullough, Bonnie R. Bonnie's Household Budget Book. 64p. 1981. pap. 5.95 (ISBN 0-312-08789-6); prepacks 59.50 (ISBN 0-312-08790-X). St Martin.
Morgan, James. A Panel Study of Income Dynamics: Complete Documentation for Interviewing Years 1968-1979. Incl. Vol. 1. Study Design, Procedures, Available Data. 400p. 1968-72. pap. 8.00 (ISBN 0-87944-141-0); Vol. 2. Tape Codes & Indexes. 1100p. 1968-72. pap. 16.00 (ISBN 0-87944-142-9); 1973 Supplement. 240p. pap. 10.50 (ISBN 0-87944-155-0); 1974 Supplement. 268p. pap. 10.50 (ISBN 0-87944-167-4); 1975 Supplement. 298p. pap. 10.50 (ISBN 0-87944-200-X); 1976 Supplement. 390p. pap. 10.50 (ISBN 0-87944-215-8); pap. 10.50 1977 suppl. 355 pp. (ISBN 0-686-57669-1); pap. 12.00 1978 suppl. 416 pp. (ISBN 0-87944-243-3). Set. 74.00, incl. vols. 1 & 2 & 7 suppls. (ISBN 0-87944-266-2). Inst Soc Res.
Perlman, Robert & Warren, Roland L. Families in the Energy Crisis: Impacts & Implications for Theory & Policy. LC 77-24314. 1977. 17.50 (ISBN 0-88410-068-5). Ballinger Pub.
Pierre, Melvin. How to Manage Your Family Budget During These Troubled Times. rev. ed. 1978. pap. 5.00 (ISBN 0-931664-00-4). RMP Finan Consul.
Raihall, Denis T. Family Finance: Money Management for the Consumer. (Illus.). 458p. 1975. 13.95 (ISBN 0-316-73275-3). Little.
Rogers, Mary & Joyce, Nancy. Women & Money. 1978. 7.95 (ISBN 0-913374-78-4). SF Bk Co.
Saturday Evening Post Editors. The Saturday Evening Post Family Records Book. LC 81-65815. (Illus.). 144p. 1981. padded leatherette with 4-color onlay 15.95 (ISBN 0-89387-055-2). Curtis Pub Co.
Simmons, Dorothy & Howell, Herbert B. Your Family Finances. 1950. pap. 0.95x (ISBN 0-8138-1830-3). Iowa St U Pr.
Sweeney, Karen O. Every Woman's Guide to Family Finances. LC 75-25238. 192p. (Orig.). 1976. pap. 1.25 (ISBN 0-89041-045-3, 3045). Major Bks.
Teacher's Guide to Financial Education. LC 68-20395. 1967. pap. 1.00 (ISBN 0-686-00796-4, 261-08398). Home Econ Educ.
Troelstrup, Arch W. The Consumer in American Society: Personal & Family Finance. 5th ed. (Finance Ser.). (Illus.). 704p. 1974. text ed. 14.95 (ISBN 0-07-065210-4, C). McGraw.
Warmke, et al. Consumer Economic Problems. 8th ed. 1971. text ed. 8.44 (ISBN 0-538-08320-4). SW Pub.
--Consumer Decision Making: Guides to Better Living. 1972. text ed. 7.76 (ISBN 0-538-08330-1, H33). SW Pub.

HOME ECONOMICS–BIBLIOGRAPHY

Rudolph, G. A. The Kansas State University Receipt Book & Household Manual. 1968. 5.00 (ISBN 0-686-20813-7). KSU.

HOME ECONOMICS–EQUIPMENT AND SUPPLIES

see also House Furnishings; Household Appliances

Brasher, Ruth E. & Garrison, Carolyn L. Modern Household Equipment. Date not set. text ed. 22.50 (ISBN 0-02-313540-9). Macmillan.
Nigh, Edward & Stark Research Associates. The Formula Book 3. new ed. (Formula Bks). (Illus.). 1978. 12.00 (ISBN 0-8362-2202-4); pap. 5.95 (ISBN 0-8362-2205-9). Andrews & McMeel.
Peet, Louise J. Science Fundamentals: A Background for Household Equipment. LC 71-137093. (Illus.). 131p. 1972. pap. 4.50x (ISBN 0-8138-0835-9). Iowa St U Pr.
Peet, Louise J. & Pickett, Mary S. Young Homemakers' Equipment Guide. 4th ed. (Illus.). 1974. 7.95x (ISBN 0-8138-1810-9). Iowa St U Pr.
Peet, Louise J., et al. Household Equipment. 8th ed. LC 78-11749. 1979. text ed. 23.50 (ISBN 0-471-02694-8); tchrs. manual avail. (ISBN 0-471-04876-3). Wiley.
Stark, Norman, et al. The Formula Book One, Two, & Three Slipcased Gift Pack. (Formula Ser.). (Illus.). 1979. pap. 17.85 (ISBN 0-8362-2208-3). Andrews & McMeel.
Wilson, Patricia P. Household Equipment: Selection & Management. LC 75-31023. (Illus.). 384p. 1976. text ed. 18.95 (ISBN 0-395-20596-4); resource manual 5.00 (ISBN 0-395-20597-2). HM.

HOME ECONOMICS–EXAMINATIONS, QUESTIONS, ETC.

Rudman, Jack. Domestic Worker. (Career Examination Ser.: C-1258). (Cloth bdg. avail. on request). pap. 6.00 (ISBN 0-8373-1258-2). Natl Learning.
--Home Economics - Jr. H.S. (Teachers License Examination Ser.: T-28). (Cloth bdg. avail. on request). pap. 10.00 (ISBN 0-8373-8028-6). Natl Learning.
--Home Economics - Sr. H.S. (Teachers License Examination Ser.: T-29). (Cloth bdg. avail. on request). pap. 10.00 (ISBN 0-8373-8029-4). Natl Learning.
--Home Economics Education. (National Teachers Examination Ser.: NT-12). (Cloth bdg. avail. on request). pap. 9.95 (ISBN 0-8373-8422-2). Natl Learning.
--Home Economist. (Career Examination Ser.: C-324). (Cloth bdg. avail. on request). pap. 8.00 (ISBN 0-8373-0324-9). Natl Learning.
--Home Economist Trainee. (Career Examination Ser.: C-352). (Cloth bdg. avail. on request). pap. 8.00 (ISBN 0-8373-0352-4). Natl Learning.
--Homemaker. (Career Examination Ser.: C-1303). (Cloth bdg. avail on request). pap. 8.00 (ISBN 0-8373-1303-1). Natl Learning.
--Housekeeper. (Career Examination Ser.: C-330). (Cloth bdg. avail. on request). pap. 8.00 (ISBN 0-8373-0330-3). Natl Learning.
--Senior Housekeeper. (Career Examination Ser.: C-1007). (Cloth bdg. avail. on request). pap. 8.00 (ISBN 0-8373-1007-5). Natl Learning.
--Supervising Housing Teller. (Career Examination Ser.: C-781). (Cloth bdg. avail. on request). pap. 10.00 (ISBN 0-8373-0781-3). Natl Learning.

HOME ECONOMICS–HISTORY

The Complete Country Housewife. LC 76-43179. (Illus.). 1976. 8.95 (ISBN 0-917712-01-3). Longship Pr.
Cooper, Charles. English Table in History & Literature. LC 68-21760. 1968. Repr. of 1929 ed. 19.00 (ISBN 0-8103-3520-4). Gale.
Furnival, Frederick J., ed. Early English Meals & Manners. LC 73-81154. 1969. Repr. of 1868 ed. 39.00 (ISBN 0-8103-3853-X). Gale.
Guillet, Edwin C. Pioneer Arts & Crafts. 2nd ed. LC 72-415879. (Photos). 1968. pap. 3.50 (ISBN 0-8020-6081-1). U of Toronto Pr.
Johnson, Judith M. Victorian House-Keeping: A Combined Study of Restoration & Photography. Smith, Linda H., ed. 1978. pap. 3.95 (ISBN 0-936386-05-3). Creative Learning.

HOME ECONOMICS–JUVENILE LITERATURE

Allen, Eleanor. Home Sweet Home: A History of Housework. (Junior Reference Ser.). (Illus.). 64p. (gr. 7 up). 7.95 (ISBN 0-7136-1927-9). Dufour.
Freeman, Dorothy R., et al. Very Important People in Maintenance Services. LC 75-28386. (Very Important People Ser). (Illus.). (gr. 4-12). 1976. PLB 8.65 (ISBN 0-516-07463-6, Elk Grove Bks). Childrens.
Hautzig, Esther. Life with Working Parents: Practical Hints for Everyday Situations. LC 76-15223. (Illus.). (gr. 5 up). 1976. 8.25 (ISBN 0-02-743500-8, 74350). Macmillan.
McDermott, Irene, et al. Homemaking for Teen-Agers, Bk. 2. rev. ed. (gr. 9-12). 1976. text ed. 18.84 (ISBN 0-87002-171-0). Bennett IL.
Mallon, V. M. First Gear. (Illus.). 1979. pap. text ed. 6.50x (ISBN 0-435-42240-5). Heinemann Ed.

HOME ECONOMICS–STUDY AND TEACHING

Bell, Camille G. & Fallon, Berlie J. Consumer & Homemaking Education. LC 70-147277. xviii, 210p. 1971. pap. text ed. 3.50x (ISBN 0-8134-1234-X, 1234). Interstate.
Beryl, Ruth. Teaching Home Economics in the Integrated Curriculum. 1977. pap. text ed. 2.75x (ISBN 0-435-42268-5). Heinemann Ed.
Blankenship, Martha L. & Moerchen, Barbara D. Home Economics Education. LC 78-69595. (Illus.). 1979. text ed. 16.95 (ISBN 0-395-26700-5); inst. manual 1.80 (ISBN 0-395-26699-8); self instruction module 9.25 (ISBN 0-395-26698-X). HM.
Branegan, Gladys A. Home Economics Teacher Training Under the Smith-Huges Act 1917-1927. LC 76-176587. (Columbia University. Teachers College. Contributions to Education: No. 350). Repr. of 1929 ed. 17.50 (ISBN 0-404-55350-8). AMS Pr.

Callahan, Genevieve & Richardson, Lou. Home Economics Show-How & Showmanship. (Illus.). 1966. 7.95x (ISBN 0-8138-1425-1). Iowa St U Pr.
Chadderdon, H. Determining Effectiveness of Teaching Home Ec. LC 74-78396. 1971. pap. 2.50 (ISBN 0-686-00147-8, 261-08408). Home Econ Educ.
Chamberlain, Valerie & Kelly, Joan. Creative Home Economics Instruction. 2nd ed. O'Neill, Martha, ed. (Illus.). 256p. 1980. pap. text ed. 10.95 (ISBN 0-07-010424-7, W). McGraw.
Chamberlain, Valerie M. & Kelly, Joan. Creative Home Economics Instruction. (Illus.). 272p. 1974. pap. text ed. 10.95 (ISBN 0-07-010423-9, W). McGraw.
Clark, Laura V. A Study of the Relationship Between the Vocational Home Economics Teacher Training Curricula of a Group of Women's Colleges & Expected Responsibilities of Beginning Teachers. LC 72-176649. (Columbia University. Teachers College. Contributions to Education: No. 586). Repr. of 1933 ed. 17.50 (ISBN 0-404-55586-1). AMS Pr.
Compton, Norma & Hall, Olive. Foundations of Home Economics Research: A Human Ecology Approach. LC 72-81810. 1972. pap. text ed. 12.95x (ISBN 0-8087-0338-2). Burgess.
Cross, Aleene. Enjoying Family Living. (Family Living Ser: Bk. 1). (Illus.). (gr. 9-12). 1973. text ed. 12.08 (ISBN 0-397-40199-X). Har-Row.
--Home Economics Evaluation. LC 73-75679. 1973. text ed. 20.95x (ISBN 0-675-08933-6). Merrill.
Dyer, Annie I. Administration of Home Economics in City Schools: A Study of Present & Desired Practices in the Organization of the Home Economics Program. LC 76-176737. (Columbia University. Teachers College. Contributions to Education: No. 318). Repr. of 1928 ed. 17.50 (ISBN 0-404-55318-4). AMS Pr.
Fleck, Henrietta. Toward Better Teaching of Home Economics. 3rd ed. (Illus.). 1980. text ed. 18.95 (ISBN 0-02-338240-6). Macmillan.
Hall, Olive A. & Paolucci, Beatrice. Teaching Home Economics. 2nd ed. LC 73-109432. 1970. text ed. 23.95 (ISBN 0-471-34288-2). Wiley.
Home Economics Teacher Educators. Competencies for Home Economics Teachers. 1978. pap. text ed. 3.95x (ISBN 0-8138-0385-3). Iowa St U Pr.
Iowa State Department of Health. Meal Service: Study Course. 1979. pap. text ed. 5.50x (ISBN 0-8138-0865-0). Iowa St U Pr.
Kent, Druzilla C. Study of the Results of Planning for Home Economics Education in the Southern States As Organized Under the National Acts for Vocational Education. LC 77-176965. (Columbia University. Teachers College. Contributions to Education: No. 689). Repr. of 1936 ed. 17.50 (ISBN 0-404-55689-2). AMS Pr.
Reaching Out to Those We Teach. 1969. pap. 1.00 (ISBN 0-686-00793-X, 261-08308). Home Econ Educ.
Redick, Sharon S. The Physically Handicapped Student in the Regular Home Economics Classrooms: A Guide for Teaching Grooming & Clothing. LC 76-16663. 1976. pap. text ed. 6.75x (ISBN 0-8134-1821-6, 1821). Interstate.
--The Physically Handicapped Student in the Regular Home Economics Classroom: Teaching Nutrition & Foods. LC 76-16663. 1976. pap. text ed. 6.75x (ISBN 0-8134-1822-4, 1822). Interstate.
--The Physically Handicapped Student in the Regular Home Economics Classroom: A Guide for Teaching Housing & Home Care. 1976. pap. text ed. 6.75x (ISBN 0-8134-1823-2, 1823). Interstate.
Rund, Josephine. Handbook on Home & Family Living Through Adult Education. LC 76-24690. 1977. pap. 7.95x (ISBN 0-8134-1824-0, 1824). Interstate.
Ruud, Josephine B. & Hall, Olive A. Adult Education for Home & Family Life. LC 73-15684. 272p. 1974. text ed. 18.95 (ISBN 0-471-74780-7). Wiley.
Spitze, H. Choosing Techniques for Teaching & Learning. 2nd ed. LC 78-68514. 1979. pap. 2.50 (ISBN 0-686-14992-0, 261-08402). Home Econ Educ.
Spitze, H. & Griggs, M. Choosing Evaluation Techniques. LC 75-32848. 1976. pap. 3.50 (ISBN 0-686-15326-X, 261-08424). Home Econ Educ.
Terrass & Comfort. Teaching Occupational Home Economics. 1979. 11.40 (ISBN 0-87002-282-2). Bennett IL.
Training Home Economist for Rural Development. (Economic & Social Development Paper Ser.: No. 6). 1979. pap. 7.50 (ISBN 92-5-100639-3, F1530, FAO). Unipub.
United States Federal Board For Vocational Education. Study of Home-Economics Education in Teacher-Training Institutions for Negroes. LC 75-82094. (Illus.). Repr. of 1923 ed. 13.50x (ISBN 0-8371-2047-0, Pub. by Negro U Pr). Greenwood.
Williamson, Maude & Lyle, Mary S. Homemaking Education in the High School. 4th ed. LC 61-9419. 1961. 18.95x (ISBN 0-89197-556-X). Irvington.

HOME ECONOMICS-VOCATIONAL GUIDANCE

Berger, Gilda. Jobs That Help the Consumer & Homemaker. LC 73-18414. 96p. (gr. 5 up). 1974. 7.25 (ISBN 0-688-75012-5). Lothrop.
Channels, Vera G. & Kupsinel, Penelope E. Career Education in Home Economics. LC 73-77545. (Illus.). 1973. pap. 4.95x (ISBN 0-8134-1573-X, 1573). Interstate.
Christen, Carol A. Career Education & Home Economics. LC 74-11977. (Guidance Monograph). 1975. pap. 2.40 (ISBN 0-395-20050-4). HM.
Educational Research Council of America. Home Economist. rev. ed. Ferris, Theodore N. & Marchak, John P., eds. (Real People at Work Ser: J). (Illus.). 1980. pap. text ed. 2.25 (ISBN 0-89247-073-9). Changing Times.
Hahn, James & Hahn, Lynn. Exploring a Career in Home Economics. (Careers in Depth Ser.). 140p. (gr. 7-12). 1981. lib. bdg. 5.97 (ISBN 0-8239-0530-6). Rosen Pr.
Hall, Olive A. Home Economics: Careers & Homemaking. LC 58-6073. (Illus.). 316p. 1958. text ed. 11.50 (ISBN 0-471-34155-X, Pub. by Wiley). Krieger.
Hoeflin, Ruth, et al. Careers for Professionals: New Perspectives in Home Economics. 224p. 1980. pap. text ed. 8.95 (ISBN 0-8403-2307-7). Kendall-Hunt.
Home Economics Teacher Educators. Instruments for Assessing Selected Professional Competencies for Home Economics Teacher Education. 1978. pap. 13.75x (ISBN 0-8138-0995-9). Iowa St U Pr.
Jacoby, G. Polly. Preparing for a Home Economics Career. Hughes, Ruth P., ed. (Careers in Home Economics Ser.). 1979. pap. text ed. 11.96 (ISBN 0-07-032240-6, G); tchr's manual & key 3.00 (ISBN 0-07-032241-4); wkbk 4.00 (ISBN 0-07-032242-2). McGraw.
Kupsinel, Penelope E. & Channels, Vera G. Home Economics Careers. LC 74-77552. 1974. pap. text ed. 4.95x (ISBN 0-8134-1656-6, 1656). Interstate.
Nelson, Jo. Looking Forward to a Career: Home Economics. 2nd ed. LC 74-26673. (Looking Forward to a Career Ser.). (Illus.). 1974. PLB 6.95 (ISBN 0-87518-107-4). Dillon.
Paris, Jeanne. Your Future As a Home Economist. LC 77-114119. (Career Guidance Ser). 1971. pap. 3.95 (ISBN 0-668-02247-7). Arco.
Rourke, Margaret V. & Gentry, Christine A. So You Want a Successful HERO Program. Simpson, Elizabeth, ed. (Careers in Home Economics Ser.). 1979. pap. text ed. 7.70 (ISBN 0-07-023176-1, G). McGraw.
Tate, Mildred. Home Economics As a Profession. 2nd ed. (Illus.). 320p. 1972. text ed. 14.95 (ISBN 0-07-062916-1, C). McGraw.
Tucker, Gina & Schneider, Madelin S. The Professional Housekeeper. LC 75-29010. (Illus.). 240p. 1976. 24.95 (ISBN 0-8436-0591-X). CBI Pub.
Winn, Charles S. & Baker, M. C. Exploring Occupations in Food Service & Home Economics. (Careers in Focus Ser.). 1975. text ed. 5.32 (ISBN 0-07-071041-4, G); tchr's manual & key 3.30 (ISBN 0-07-071042-2); wksheet bklet 6.08 (ISBN 0-07-071063-5). McGraw.

HOME ECONOMICS CENTERS

Brodshaug, Melvin. Buildings & Equipment for Home Economics in Secondary Schools. LC 75-176592. (Columbia University. Teachers College. Contributions to Education: No. 502). Repr. of 1932 ed. 17.50 (ISBN 0-404-55502-0). AMS Pr.

HOME EDUCATION

see Domestic Education; Self-Culture

HOME FREEZERS

Broughton, Kathleen. Home Freezing from A to Z. 164p. 1975. 9.50x (ISBN 0-7182-1118-9). Intl Pubns Serv.
Dyer, Ceil. Freezer to Oven to Table. LC 75-31075. 224p. 1976. 9.95 (ISBN 0-87795-128-4); pap. 3.95 (ISBN 0-87795-134-9). Arbor Hse.
Ellis, Audrey. All About Home Freezing. 1971. pap. 2.95 (ISBN 0-600-31644-0). Transatlantic.
Nilson, Bee. Deep Freeze Cooking. 1969. 8.25x (ISBN 0-7207-0271-2). Intl Pubns Serv.
Norwak, Mary. Complete Home Freezer. (Illus.). 17.95x (ISBN 0-8464-0266-1). Beekman Pubs.
Williams, Morag. Comprehensive Guide to Deep Freezing. 1972. pap. 2.50 (ISBN 0-600-31799-4). Transatlantic.

HOME FURNISHINGS

see House Furnishings

HOME GAMES

see Indoor Games

HOME HEALTH AGENCIES

see Home Care Services

HOME LABOR

see also Cottage Industries

Behr, Marion & Lazar, Wendy. Women Working Home: The Homebased Business Guide & Directory. (Illus.). 176p. (Orig.). 1981. pap. 12.95 (ISBN 0-939240-00-9). WWH Pr.
Dennis, Virginia & Gillenwater, Susan. Spare Time-Spare Change: Home-Based Employment for the Ingenious Woman. 1981. pap. 6.95 (ISBN 0-686-73312-6). Writers Digest.
Judge. Home Work: The Stay at-Home Money Book. LC 77-7029. 6.95 (ISBN 0-87747-659-4). Deseret Bk.
Lloyd, Cynthia B. & Niemi, Beth T. The Economics of Sex Differentials. LC 79-9569. 1980. 16.50x (ISBN 0-231-04038-5); pap. 10.00x (ISBN 0-231-03751-1). Columbia U Pr.
Steidl, Rose E. & Bratton, Esther C. Work in the Home. LC 67-29007. 419p. 1968. 23.95 (ISBN 0-471-82085-7). Wiley.
Stein, Leon, ed. Suffer the Little Children: Two Children's Bureau Bulletins, Original Anthology. LC 77-70552. (Work Ser.). (Illus.). 1977. lib. bdg. 18.00x (ISBN 0-405-10206-2). Arno.
Tyron, Rolla M. Household Manufacturers in the United States, 1640-1860. Repr. of 1917 ed. 18.50 (ISBN 0-384-61790-5). Johnson Repr.
--Household Manufactures in the United States, 1640-1860. LC 66-23980. Repr. of 1917 ed. 17.50x (ISBN 0-678-00175-8). Kelley.
Woman & Marriage, 5 vols. Incl. Some Reflections Upon Marriage. Astell, Mary. Repr. 9.50 (ISBN 0-442-81056-3); Home: Its Work & Influence. Gilman, Charlotte P. Repr. of 1903 ed. 13.00 (ISBN 0-442-81992-7); Women & Economics. Gilman, Charlotte P. Repr. 15.00 (ISBN 0-442-81081-4); Two Vols. In One. Love, Marriage, & Divorce, & the Sovereignity of the Individual: Bound with Divorce. Greeley, Horace, et al. Repr; Divorce. Greeley, Horace & Owen, Robert D. Repr. 10.50 (ISBN 0-685-37112-3); Law of Baron & Femme, of Parent & Child, Guardian & Ward, Master & Servant, & of the Powers of the Courts of Chancery. 3rd ed. Reeve, Tapping. Repr. 32.50 (ISBN 0-442-81067-9). (Source Library of the Women's Movement). 1970. 80.50 set (ISBN 0-442-81250-7). Hacker.

HOME LIBRARIES

see Libraries, Private

HOME MISSIONS

see Missions, Home

HOME NURSING

see also Practical Nursing

Barnes, Marylou R. & Crutchfield, Carolyn A. The Patient at Home. LC 72-185638. 144p. 1973. 14.95x (ISBN 0-913590-02-9). C B Slack.
Baulch, Evelyn. Home Care. LC 79-55665. 1980. 12.95 (ISBN 0-89087-277-5); pap. 8.95 (ISBN 0-89087-273-2). Celestial Arts.
Bednarski, Mary W. & Florczyk, Sandra E. Nursing Home Care As a Public Policy Issue. (Learning Packages in Policy Issues: No. 4). 62p. (Orig.). 1978. pap. text ed. 1.75 (ISBN 0-936826-13-4). Pol Stud Assocs.
Family Health: Care & Management at Home. 1976. 9.75 (ISBN 0-7207-0889-3). Transatlantic.
Hurtado, Arnold V., et al. Home Care & Extended Care in a Comprehensive Prepayment Plan. LC 72-85388. (Illus.). 127p. 1972. 6.00 (ISBN 0-87914-019-4, 9151). Hosp Res & Educ.
Miller, E. J. A Life Apart. Gwynne, G. V., ed. 1979. pap. 9.95x (ISBN 0-422-75660-1, Pub. by Tavistock England). Methuen Inc.
Prichard, Elizabeth R., et al, eds. Home Care: Living with Dying. LC 78-21983. (Foundation of Thanatology Ser.). 1979. 20.00x (ISBN 0-231-04258-2). Columbia U Pr.
Rosenbaum, Ernest H., et al. Going Home: A Home Care Training Program. (Illus.). 160p. 1980. 12.00 (ISBN 0-686-77635-6); three ring binder 12.00 (ISBN 0-915950-48-0). Bull Pub.
Rossman, I. J. & Schwartz, Doris R. Family Handbook of Home Nursing & Medical Care. (Illus.). 1968. 8.95 (ISBN 0-87131-059-7). M Evans.
Skeet, Muriel & Stroud, Jean. Home Nursing. 1975. 9.95 (ISBN 0-09-122680-5, Pub. by Hutchinson); pap. 4.95 (ISBN 0-09-122681-3). Merrimack Bk Serv.

HOME OWNERSHIP

see also House Buying

Better Homes & Gardens Books Editors, ed. Better Homes & Gardens Energy Saving Projects You Can Build. (You Can Build Ser.). (Illus.). 1979. 5.95 (ISBN 0-696-00485-2). Meredith Corp.
Brady, Constance. Right Where You Live. LC 78-73550. (Illus.). 1979. pap. 9.95 (ISBN 0-89087-242-2). Celestial Arts.
Community Associations Institute. Creating a Community Association: The Developer's Role in Condominium & Homeowners Association. LC 76-56982. 1976. 12.00 (ISBN 0-87420-574-3). Urban Land.
Coons, Alvin E. & Glaze, Bert T. Housing Market Analysis & the Growth of Home Ownership. 1963. 5.00x (ISBN 0-87776-115-9, R115). Ohio St U Admin Sci.
Doyle, John M. The Complete Home Owner's Guide: From Mortgage to Maintenance. (Illus.). 272p. 1975. 9.95 (ISBN 0-87909-154-1). Reston.
Ervin, Thomas & Hart, Don. The Homeowner's Almanac. LC 80-66065. (Illus.). 128p. (Orig.). 1980. pap. write for info. (ISBN 0-936682-00-0). Conquest Corp MI.
Financial Real Estate Handbook No. 512. 256p. 1980. pap. 6.50 (ISBN 0-686-64811-0). Finan Pub.
Fletcher, Connie. How to Buy a Home. 1978. pap. 5.95 (ISBN 0-695-80884-2). New Century.
Greenberg, Dan. How to Love the House You Buy. pap. 1.95 (ISBN 0-9602108-1-4). Modern Mktg.
Kahn, Steve. Homeowner's Record Book. 1979. pap. 9.95 large format (ISBN 0-553-01309-2). Bantam.
Kemeny, Jim. The Myth of Home Qwnership: Private Versus Public Choices in Housing Tenure. 280p. 1981. 20.00 (ISBN 0-7100-0634-9). Routledge & Kegan.
McClintock, Michael. Homeowner's Handbook: What You Need to Know About Buying, Maintaining, Improving, & Running Your Home Successfully. (Illus.). 1980. 14.95 (ISBN 0-684-16145-1, ScribT). Scribner.
Rhodes, Richard. How to Appraise Your Own Home. Cowan, Curt, ed. (Orig.). 1978. pap. 5.95 (ISBN 0-930306-07-4). Delphi Info.
Roy, Robert L. Money-Saving Strategies for the Owner-Builder. LC 81-8843. (Illus.). 160p. (Orig.). 1981. pap. 6.95 (ISBN 0-8069-7548-2). Sterling.
Schuler, Stanley. The Homeowner's Directory. 1978. pap. 7.95x (ISBN 0-671-23016-6). S&S.
--The Homeowner's Minimum-Maintenance Manual. LC 76-122814. (Illus.). 214p. 1971. 6.95 (ISBN 0-87131-058-9). M Evans.
Stacey, William A. Black Home Ownership: A Sociological Case Study of Metropolitan Jacksonville. LC 73-186201. (Special Studies in U.S. Economic, Social & Political Issues). 1972. 29.50x (ISBN 0-275-04810-1). Irvington.
Struyk, Raymond J. Should Government Encourage Homeownership? (An Institute Paper). 85p. 1977. pap. 5.50 (ISBN 0-87766-192-8, 18700). Urban Inst.

HOME PURCHASE

see House Buying

HOME REMODELING

see Dwellings–Remodeling

HOME REPAIRS

see Dwellings–Maintenance and Repair

HOME RULE (IRELAND)

see also Fenians; Irish Question

Balfour, Arthur J., et al. Against Home Rule. Rosenbaum, S., ed. LC 75-102591. (Irish Culture & History Ser). (Illus.). 1970. Repr. of 1912 ed. 14.50 (ISBN 0-8046-0768-0). Kennikat.
MacSwiney, Terence. Principles of Freedom. LC 73-102616. (Irish Culture & History Ser). 1970. Repr. of 1921 ed. 12.50 (ISBN 0-8046-0793-1). Kennikat.
Morgan, J. H., ed. New Irish Constitution. LC 70-118490. 1971. Repr. of 1912 ed. 22.50 (ISBN 0-8046-1367-2). Kennikat.
Nowlan, Kevin B. The Politics of Repeal. LC 75-35339. 248p. 1976. Repr. of 1965 ed. lib. bdg. 15.25x (ISBN 0-8371-8562-9, NOPR). Greenwood.
O'Brien, William. Irish Ideas. LC 79-102620. (Irish Culture & History Ser). 1970. Repr. of 1893 ed. 12.00 (ISBN 0-8046-0797-4). Kennikat.
O'Donnell, F. Hugh. History of the Irish Parliamentary Party, 2 Vols. LC 70-102623. (Irish Culture & History Ser). 1970. Repr. of 1910 ed. Set. 45.00x (ISBN 0-8046-0800-8). Kennikat.
Thornley, David. Isaac Butt & Home Rule. LC 76-11765. 1976. Repr. of 1964 ed. lib. bdg. 24.00x (ISBN 0-8371-8892-X, THIB). Greenwood.

HOME RULE (SCOTLAND)

Keating, Michael & Bleiman, David. Labour & Scottish Nationalism. 1979. text ed. 37.50x (ISBN 0-333-26596-3). Humanities.
McCrone, Gavin. Scotland's Future. LC 71-92501. 1969. 10.00x (ISBN 0-678-06252-8). Kelley.
Mackay, Donald, ed. Scotland Nineteen Eighty: The Economics of Self-Government. 1979. text ed. 18.25x (ISBN 0-905470-03-6). Humanities.

HOME RULE FOR CITIES
see Municipal Home Rule
HOME STORAGE
see Storage in the Home
HOME STUDY COURSES
see Correspondence Schools and Courses; Self-Culture
HOME VISITING (CHURCH WORK)
see Visitations (Church Work)
HOME WORKSHOPS

Adams, Florence. The Woman's Build-It & Fix-It Handbook. LC 75-20817. 320p. 1975. pap. 1.50 (ISBN 0-89041-021-6, 3021). Major Bks.
Bradley, Ian. Beginner's Workshop. (Illus.). 241p. 1975. 10.00x (ISBN 0-85242-428-0). Intl Pubns Serv.
Brann, Donald R. How to Build a Home Workshop. LC 65-19667. 1975. lib. bdg. 5.95 (ISBN 0-87733-077-8); pap. 3.50 (ISBN 0-87733-677-6). Easi-Bild.
--How to Build Workbenches. LC 66-30452. 1979. pap. 5.95 (ISBN 0-87733-672-5). Easi-Bild.
Bruner, Wally. Wally's Workshop. 1974. pap. 3.95 (ISBN 0-671-21908-1, Fireside). S&S.
Burch, Monte. Building & Equipping the Garden & Small Farm Workshop. (Illus.). 1979. pap. 7.95 (ISBN 0-88266-156-6). Garden Way Pub.
Daniels, George. How to Use Hand & Power Tools. 2nd ed. LC 64-13135. (Popular Science Skill Bk.). 1976. pap. 3.95 (ISBN 0-06-010956-4, TD273, HarpT). Har-Row.
Feldstein, Stuart. Home, Inc. LC 81-47700. 256p. 1981. 12.95 (ISBN 0-448-12021-6). G&D.
Geary. How to Design & Build Your Own Workspace-with Plans. 384p. 1981. 16.95 (ISBN 0-8306-9638-5); pap. 9.95 (ISBN 0-8306-1269-6, 1269). TAB Bks.
Gingery, David J. The Milling Machine. LC 80-66142. (Build Your Own Metal Working Shop from Scrap Ser.: Bk. 4). (Illus.). 96p. (Orig.). 1981. pap. 7.95 (ISBN 0-9604330-3-1). D J Gingery.
Gladstone, Bernard. Hints & Tips for the Handyperson. Orig. Title: Hints & Tips for the Handyman. 152p. 1975. pap. 1.95 (ISBN 0-346-12173-6). Cornerstone.
Grennell, Dean A. Home Workshop Digest. 256p. 1981. pap. 7.95 (ISBN 0-910676-14-3). DBI.
Home Workshop Silencers I. (Illus.). 72p. 1980. pap. 12.00 (ISBN 0-87364-193-0). Paladin Ent.
Jackson, Albert & Day, David. Tools & How to Use Them. LC 78-54896. (Illus.). 1978. 17.95 (ISBN 0-394-42657-6); pap. 9.95 (ISBN 0-394-73542-0). Knopf.
Kern, Ken & Kern, Barbara. Ken Kern's Homestead Workshop. (Illus.). 160p. 1981. 14.95 (ISBN 0-684-17015-9, ScribT). Scribner.
Lathrop, Mary Lou & Lathrop, Norman M., eds. Index to How to Do It Information. Incl. 1963-1969 Cumulated Index. pap. 15.00 (ISBN 0-910868-60-3); 1970-1974 Cumulated Index. pap. 15.00 (ISBN 0-910868-59-X); 1975 Index. pap. 7.00 (ISBN 0-910868-75-1); 1976 Index. pap. 7.00 (ISBN 0-910868-76-X); 1977 Index. pap. 10.00 (ISBN 0-910868-77-8); 1978 Index. pap. 10.00x (ISBN 0-910868-78-6); 1979 Index. pap. 12.00x (ISBN 0-910868-79-4). Lathrop.
Manners, David. Planning & Building Your Home Workshop. LC 80-50594. (Illus., Orig.). 1980. pap. 4.95 (ISBN 0-06-090824-6, CN 824, CN). Har-Row.
Manners, David X. How to Plan & Build Your Workshop. LC 77-76854. (Illus.). 1977. 4.95 (ISBN 0-668-04131-5); pap. 2.50 o. p. (ISBN 0-668-04142-0). Arco.
Ruhe-Schoen, Janet. Organizing & Operating Profitable Workshop Classes. LC 80-25466. 1981. pap. 2.50 (ISBN 0-87576-092-9). Pilot Bks.
Scharff, Robert. The Complete Book of Home Workshop Tools. LC 78-14822. (Illus.). 1979. 16.95 (ISBN 0-07-055042-5, P&RB). McGraw.
--Projects for Outdoor Living. 1981. 7.95 (ISBN 0-8359-5698-9). Reston.
--Projects for the Weekend. 1981. 7.95 (ISBN 0-8359-5700-4). Reston.
Seymour, John. Popular Mechanics: The Guide to Self Sufficiency. LC 76-12136. (Illus.). 1976. 16.95 (ISBN 0-910990-66-2); pap. 10.00 (ISBN 0-910990-74-3). Hearst Bks.
Smith, Andrew. Starting a Home Workshop. (Illus.). 185p. (Orig.). 1980. pap. 13.50x (ISBN 0-85242-725-5). Intl Pubns Serv.
Swezey, Kenneth. Formulas, Methods, Tips & Data for Home & Workshop. rev. ed. Scharff, Robert, rev. by. LC 68-54377. (Popular Science Bk.). (Illus.). 1979. 15.95 (ISBN 0-06-014164-6, HarpT). Har-Row.
Time-Life Books Editors. The Home Workshop. (Home Repair & Improvement Ser.). (Illus.). 128p. 1980. 10.95 (ISBN 0-8094-3454-7, Silver Burdett). Time-Life.
Turner, Pearl. Index to Handicrafts, Modelmaking, & Workshop Projects, Fifth Supplement. LC 36-27324. (Useful Reference Ser. of Library Bks: Vol. 102). 1975. lib. bdg. 20.00x (ISBN 0-87305-102-5). Faxon.

HOMEMAKERS
see Housewives
HOMEMAKING CENTERS
see Home Economics Centers
HOMEOPATHY

Anderson, David, et al. Homeopathic Remedies for Physicians, Laymen & Therapists. 1978. pap. 4.95 (ISBN 0-89389-037-5). Himalayan Intl Inst.
Before Calling the Doctor. 1980. 20.00x (ISBN 0-85032-137-9, Pub. by Daniel Co England). State Mutual Bk.
Blackie, Margery G. The Patient, Not the Cure: The Challenge of Homeopathy. LC 78-54659. (Illus.). 1978. pap. 4.95 (ISBN 0-912800-49-6). Woodbridge Pr.
Borland, D. M. Homeopathy in Practice. Priestman, Kathleen, ed. 230p. 1980. 25.00x (ISBN 0-686-69974-2, Pub. by Beaconsfield England). State Mutual Bk.
Boyd, Hamish. Introduction to Homeopathic Medicine. 240p. 1980. 49.00x (ISBN 0-686-69976-9, Pub. by Beaconsfield England). State Mutual Bk.
Clarke, John H. Clinical Repertory. 1980. 25.00x (ISBN 0-85032-179-4, Pub. by Daniel Co England). State Mutual Bk.
--Clinical Repertory. 346p. 1979. text ed. 24.95x (ISBN 0-8464-1000-1). Beekman Pubs.
--A Dictionary of Practical Materia Medica. 1980. 125.00x (ISBN 0-85032-139-5, Pub. by Daniel Co England). State Mutual Bk.
--The Prescriber. 1980. 20.00x (ISBN 0-85032-050-X, Pub. by Daniel Co England). State Mutual Bk.
--The Prescriber. 11th ed. 382p. 1972. 11.95x (ISBN 0-8464-1041-9). Beekman Pubs.
Coulter, Harris. Homoeopathic Science & Modern Medicine: The Physics of Healing with Microdose. 160p. 1981. pap. 4.95 (ISBN 0-913028-84-3). North Atlantic.
Coulter, Harris L. Homoeopathic Influences in Nineteenth-Century Allopathic Therapeutics. LC 73-75139. 1973. pap. 2.50 (ISBN 0-685-64858-3). Formur Intl.
--Homoeopathic Medicine. LC 74-190010. 1972. pap. 1.65 (ISBN 0-89378-072-3). Formur Intl.
A Dictionary of Practical Materia Medica, 3 vols. 2585p. 1980. text ed. 119.95x (ISBN 0-8464-1004-4). Beekman Pubs.
Dictionnaire Homeopatheque d'Urgerce. 11th ed. 765p. (Fr.). 1978. 35.00 (ISBN 0-686-56732-3, M-6461). French & Eur.
Donhoffer, Sz. Homeothermia of the Brain. (Illus.). 140p. (Orig.). 1980. pap. 13.50x (ISBN 963-05-2405-8). Intl Pubns Serv.
Gibson, D. M. First Aid Homoeopathy in Accidents & Ailments. 1975. pap. 3.95 (ISBN 0-685-76564-4, Pub. by British Homoeopathy Assoc.). Formur Intl.
Hamlyn, E. C. Healing Art of Homeopathy. 111p. 1980. 15.00x (ISBN 0-686-69973-4, Pub. by Beaconsfield England). State Mutual Bk.
Hamlyn, Edward. The Healing Art of Homeopathy: The Organon of Samuel Hahnemann. LC 80-82321. (Orig.). 1980. pap. 4.95 (ISBN 0-87983-228-2). Keats.
Henshaw, George R. A Scientific Approach to Homeopathy. 1980. 10.00 (ISBN 0-682-49518-2, University). Exposition.
Homoeopathic Drug Pictures. 1980. 15.75x (ISBN 0-85032-184-0, Pub. by Daniel Co England). State Mutual Bk.
Hubbard-Wright, Elizabeth. A Brief Study Course in Homoeopathy. Naude, Alain, ed. 1977. pap. 2.95 (ISBN 0-89378-071-5). Formur Intl.
Julian, O. A. Materia Medica of New Homeopathic Remedies. rev. ed. Munday, Virginia, tr. from Fr. 637p. 1981. 45.00 (ISBN 0-87983-261-4). Keats.
--Materia Medica of New Homoeopathic Remedies. 637p. 1980. 60.00x (ISBN 0-686-69977-7, Pub. by Beaconsfield England). State Mutual Bk.
Kaufman, Martin. Homeopathy in America: The Rise & Fall of a Medical Heresy. LC 79-149741. 216p. 1971. 15.00x (ISBN 0-8018-1238-0). Johns Hopkins.
Kent, J. T. Repertory of Homoeopathic Materia Medica. 1975. 30.00 (ISBN 0-685-76570-9, Pub. by Harjeet). Formur Intl.
Kent, James T. Lectures in Homeopathic Philosophy. (Fundamental Doctrines of Healing Ser.: Vol. 1). 1979. pap. 5.95 (ISBN 0-913028-61-4). North Atlantic.
--Lectures on Homeopathic Philosophy. 1974. 6.00 (ISBN 0-685-76566-0, Pub. by Harjeet). Formur Intl.
MacLeod, G. The Treatment of Horses by Homoeopathy. 1980. 17.50x (ISBN 0-85032-155-7, Pub. by Daniel Co England). State Mutual Bk.
Maury, E. A. Drainage in Homoeopathy. 1980. text ed. 4.00x (ISBN 0-8464-1007-9). Beekman Pubs.
Mellor, Constance. How to Be Healthy, Wealthy, & Wise. 1980. 18.50x (ISBN 0-85207-137-X, Pub. by Daniel Co England). State Mutual Bk.
Nash, E. B. Leaders in Homeopathic Therapeutics. 493p. 1980. Repr. of 1959 ed. lib. bdg. 40.00 (ISBN 0-89987-623-4). Darby Bks.
--Leaders in Homoeopathic Therapeutics. 1975. 4.50 (ISBN 0-685-76565-2, Pub. by Harjeet). Formur Intl.
The Nelson-Keats Homeopathy Source Book. Date not set. cancelled (ISBN 0-87983-239-8); pap. cancelled (ISBN 0-87983-240-1). Keats.
Panos, Maesimind B. & Heimlich, Jane. Homeopathic Medicine at Home. LC 79-63802. 288p. 1981. 10.95 (ISBN 0-87477-119-6); pap. 5.95 (ISBN 0-87477-195-1). J P Tarcher.
Patersimilias. A Song of Symptoms. 1980. 1.75x (ISBN 0-85032-186-7, Pub. by Daniel Co England). State Mutual Bk.
Perry, Edward L. Luyties Homeopathic Practice. 165p. 1974. pap. 1.65 (ISBN 0-89378-002-2). Formur Intl.
Pratt, Noel. Homoeopathic Prescribing. 96p. 1980. 25.00x (ISBN 0-686-69975-0, Pub. by Beaconsfield England). State Mutual Bk.
The Principles & Art of Cure by Homoeopathy. 1942. 12.00 (ISBN 0-85032-049-6, Pub. by C. W. Daniels). Formur Intl.
Roberts, H. Homeopathic Medicine: Principles & Art of Cure. 1974. lib. bdg. 75.00 (ISBN 0-685-51361-0). Revisionist Pr.
Roberts, Herbert A. The Principles & Art of Cure by Homoeopathy. 1980. 23.75 (ISBN 0-85032-181-6, Pub. by Daniel Co England). State Mutual Bk.
--The Principles & Art of Cure by Homoeopathy. 286p. 1942. 14.95x (ISBN 0-8464-1042-7). Beekman Pubs.
Rusholm, Peter. Country Medicines. 1980. 15.00x (ISBN 0-85032-192-1, Pub. by Daniel Co England). State Mutual Bk.
Shadman, Alonzo J. Who Is Your Doctor & Why? LC 80-82320. 446p. 1980. pap. 3.95 (ISBN 0-87983-227-4). Keats.
Sharma, C. H. & Leland, David. A Manual of Homoeopathy & Natural Medicine: Principles of an Age-Old Practice of Alternative Medicine with Step-by-Step Remedies. 1976. pap. 3.50 (ISBN 0-525-47432-3). Dutton.
Sheperd, Dorothy. Homeopathy for the First Aider. 1980. text ed. 4.75x (ISBN 0-8464-1021-4). Beekman Pubs.
--The Magic of the Minimum Dose. 214p. 1964. text ed. 15.50x (ISBN 0-8464-1030-3). Beekman Pubs.
Shepherd, D. Essentials of Homoeopathic Prescribing. 78p. 1970. pap. 3.00x (ISBN 0-8464-1008-7). Beekman Pubs.
--Homoeopathy in Epidemic Diseases. 1980. 25.00x (ISBN 0-85032-185-9, Pub. by Daniel Co England). State Mutual Bk.
Shepherd, Dorothy. Homoeopathy for the First Aider. 1980. 19.50 (ISBN 0-85032-182-4, Pub. by Daniel Co England). State Mutual Bk.
--Homoeopathy for the First Aider. 1974. pap. 3.95 (ISBN 0-85032-091-7, Pub. by C. W. Daniels). Formur Intl.
--The Magic of the Minimum Dose. 1980. 19.75 (ISBN 0-85032-183-2, Pub. by Daniel Co England). State Mutual Bk.
--Magic of the Minimum Dose. 1964. 12.95 (ISBN 0-85032-112-3, Pub. by C. W. Daniels). Formur Intl.
--More Magic of the Minimum Dose. 1980. text ed. 7.00x (ISBN 0-8464-1033-8). Beekman Pubs.
--More Magic of the Minimum Dose. 1974. 7.00 (ISBN 0-85032-056-9, Pub. by C. W. Daniels). Formur Intl.
Sheppard, K. The Treatment of Cats by Homoeopathy. 1960. pap. 2.95 (ISBN 0-85032-120-4, Pub. by C. W. Daniels). Formur Intl.
--The Treatment of Cats by Homoeopathy. 1980. 17.50x (ISBN 0-85032-187-5, Pub. by Daniel Co England). State Mutual Bk.
--The Treatment of Dogs by Homoeopathy. 1980. 17.50x (ISBN 0-85032-188-3, Pub. by Daniel Co England). State Mutual Bk.
Simon, B. X. The California Directory of Healing Arts, Holistic & Homeopathic Practitioners. (Orig.). 1981. pap. write for info. (ISBN 0-935618-01-5). Rossi Pubns.
Speight, Phyllis. A Comparison of the Chronic Miasma. 1980. 25.00x (ISBN 0-85032-154-9, Pub. by Daniel Co England). State Mutual Bk.
--A Comparison of the Chronic Miasms. 56p. 1977. text ed. 15.50x (ISBN 0-8464-1002-8). Beekman Pubs.
--A Study Course in Homeopathy. 145p. 1979. text ed. 13.95x (ISBN 0-8464-1052-4). Beekman Pubs.
--A Study Course in Homoeopathy. 1980. 17.50x (ISBN 0-85032-164-6, Pub. by Daniel Co England). State Mutual Bk.
Stephenson, James H. A Doctor's Guide to Helping Yourself with Homeopathic Remedies. 1976. 10.95 (ISBN 0-13-216853-7, Parker). P-H.
--A Doctor's Guide to Helping Yourself with Homeopathic Remedies. 1976. 9.95 (ISBN 0-685-72761-0, Pub. by Parker). Formur Intl.
Tyler, M. L. Homoeopathic Drug Pictures. 1970. 20.00 (ISBN 0-85032-021-6, Pub. by C. W. Daniels). Formur Intl.
Tyler, Margaret L. Homeopathic Drug Pictures. 885p. 1952. text ed. 29.95x (ISBN 0-8464-1020-6). Beekman Pubs.
Vithoulkas, George. Homeopathy: Medicine of the New Man. LC 77-29272. 1979. lib. bdg. 7.95 (ISBN 0-668-04577-9, 4577); pap. 3.95 (ISBN 0-668-04581-7). Arco.
--The Science of Homeopathy. LC 79-52056. 1980. 17.50 (ISBN 0-394-50866-1, GP836). Grove.
Wheeler, C. E. & Kenyon, J. D. An Introduction to the Principles & Practice of Homoeopathy. 1980. 25.00 (ISBN 0-85032-180-8, Pub. by Daniel Co England). State Mutual Bk.
Wheeler, Charles E. An Introduction to the Principles & Practices of Homoeopathy. 1971. 12.95 (ISBN 0-85032-062-3, Pub. by C. W. Daniels). Formur Intl.
Whiiler, C. E. & Kenyon, J. D. An Introduction to the Principles & Practice of Homoeopathy. 371p. 1957. 17.95x (ISBN 0-8464-1027-3). Beekman Pubs.
Whitmont, Edward C. Psyche & Substance: Essays on Homeopathy in the Light of Jungian Psychology. (Fundamental Doctrines in Healing Ser.: No. 3). 200p. 1980. 12.95 (ISBN 0-913028-67-3). North Atlantic.
Woods, H. Fergie. Essentials of Homoeopathic Prescribing. 1980. 19.75x (ISBN 0-85032-134-4, Pub. by Daniel Co England). State Mutual Bk.
Young, W. W., et al. Introduction to Homoeotherapeutics. LC 74-82124. 1974. text ed. 15.00 (ISBN 0-685-56930-6, Pub. by American Institute for Homoeopathy). Formur Intl.

HOMEOSTASIS

Biro, Z., et al, eds. Homeostasis in Injury & Shock: Proceedings of a Satellite Symposium of the 28th International Congress of Physiological Sciences, Budapest, Hungary, 1980. LC 80-42104. (Advances in Physiological Sciences: Vol. 26). (Illus.). 360p. 1981. 40.00 (ISBN 0-08-027347-5). Pergamon.
Brenner, Barry M. & Stein, Jay H., eds. Acid Base & Potassium Homeostasis. (Contemporary Issues in Nephrology: Vol. 2). (Illus.). 1978. text ed. 25.00 (ISBN 0-443-08017-8). Churchill.
Darrow, Frank M. Cybernetics Versus Homeostasis. (Illus.). 1977. pap. 2.50 (ISBN 0-685-80843-2). Darrow.
Dilman, Vladimir M. Law of Deviation of Homeostasis & Diseases of Aging. LC 79-21456. (Illus.). 480p. 1981. 39.50 (ISBN 0-88416-250-8). Wright-PSG.
Gardiner, Shelia M. & Bennett, Terence. Cardiovascular Homeostasis: Intrarenal & Extrarenal Mechanisms. (Illus.). 175p. 1981. text ed. 37.50x (ISBN 0-19-261178-X). Oxford U Pr.
Langley, L. L., ed. Homeostasis: Origins of the Concept. LC 72-79805. (Benchmark Papers in Human Physiology Ser). 1973. 43.00 (ISBN 0-12-786916-6). Acad Pr.
Langley, Leroy L. Homeostasis. (Orig.). 1965. pap. text ed. 5.95x (ISBN 0-442-17142-0). Van Nos Reinhold.
Lerner, I. Michael. Genetic Homeostasis. (Illus.). 7.00 (ISBN 0-8446-0772-X). Peter Smith.
Lord, B. I. & Potten, C. S., eds. Stem Cells & Tissue Homeostasis. LC 77-80844. (British Society for Cell Biology Symposium Ser.). (Illus.). 1978. 68.00 (ISBN 0-521-21799-7). Cambridge U Pr.
Talbot, Nathan B., et al. Metabolic Homeostasis: A Syllabus for Those Concerned with the Care of Patients. LC 59-14732. (Commonwealth Fund Publications Ser). 1959. pap. 3.00x (ISBN 0-674-57000-6). Harvard U Pr.
Tuller, Martin A. Acid-Base Homeostasis & Its Disorders. 98p. 1971. spiral bdg. 6.00 (ISBN 0-87488-601-5). Med Exam.

HOMER

Arnold, Matthew. On Translating Homer. LC 78-136411. (BCL Ser.: No. 2). Repr. of 1905 ed. 16.25 (ISBN 0-404-00388-5). AMS Pr.
Atchity, Kenneth J. Homer's Iliad: The Shield of Memory. LC 77-17065. (Literary Structures Ser.). 367p. 1978. 17.50x (ISBN 0-8093-0809-6). S Ill U Pr.
Athanassakis, Apostolos N., tr. from Gr. The Homeric Hymns. LC 75-40305. 128p. 1976. 10.00x (ISBN 0-8018-1791-9); pap. 3.95x (ISBN 0-8018-1792-7). Johns Hopkins.
Austin, Norman. Archery at the Dark of the Moon: Poetic Problems in Homer's Odyssey. LC 73-94442. 300p. 1975. 22.75 (ISBN 0-520-02713-2). U of Cal Pr.
Beye, Charles R. Iliad, the Odyssey & the Epic Tradition. 8.75 (ISBN 0-8446-1674-5). Peter Smith.

--The Iliad, the Odyssey, & the Epic Tradition. LC 76-10726. 276p. 1976. Repr. of 1966 ed. 10.00 (ISBN 0-87752-187-5). Gordian.

Bowra, Sir Cecil M. Tradition & Design in the Iliad. LC 77-3065. 1977. Repr. of 1930 ed. lib. bdg. 22.50x (ISBN 0-8371-9561-6, BOTD). Greenwood.

Boynton, Henry W. World's Leading Poets. facs. ed. LC 68-8439. (Essay Index Reprint Ser). 1912. 18.00 (ISBN 0-8369-0238-6). Arno.

Burn, Andrew R. Minoans, Philistines & Greeks, B. C. 1400-900. LC 74-14350. (Illus.). 273p. 1975. Repr. of 1930 ed. lib. bdg. 21.25x (ISBN 0-8371-7794-4, BUMI). Greenwood.

Butler, Samuel. Authoress of the Odyssey. (Illus.). 1967. 10.00x (ISBN 0-226-08329-2). U of Chicago Pr.

--Authoress of the Odyssey. 1967. pap. 2.45 (ISBN 0-226-08330-6, P289, Phoen). U of Chicago Pr.

Camps, W. A. An Introduction to Homer. 128p. 1980. 17.50x (ISBN 0-19-872099-8); pap. 7.50x (ISBN 0-19-872101-3). Oxford U Pr.

Carpenter, Rhys. Folk Tale, Fiction & Saga in the Homeric Epics. LC 55-7555. (Sather Classical Lectures Ser.: No. 20). 1974. 19.50x (ISBN 0-520-02808-2). U of Cal Pr.

Clarke, Howard. Homer's Readers: A Historical Introduction to the Iliad & the Odyssey. LC 78-66824. 328p. 1980. 26.50 (ISBN 0-87413-150-2). U Delaware Pr.

Codino, Fausto. Einfuehrung in Homer. Enking, Ragna, tr. (Ger). 1970. Repr. of 1965 ed. pap. 15.25x (ISBN 3-11-002819-0). De Gruyter.

Duckworth, George E. Foreshadowing & Suspense. (Studies in Comparative Literature, No. 35). 1970. pap. 12.95 (ISBN 0-8383-0021-9). Haskell.

Dunbar, Henry. Complete Concordance to the Odyssey of Homer. 408p. Repr. of 1880 ed. 73.50 (ISBN 3-4870-4030-1). Adler.

Eberhard, Engelbert. Das Schicksal Als Poetische Idee Bei Homer. 1923. pap. 6.00 (ISBN 0-384-13785-7). Johnson Repr.

Ehnmark, Erland. The Idea of God in Homer. 1980. lib. bdg. 59.95 (ISBN 0-8490-3182-6). Gordon Pr.

Erbse, Hartmut, ed. Scholia Graeca in Homeri Iliadem: Scholia Vetera, 5 vols. Incl. Vol 1. Praefationem et Scholia ad libros A-D continens. 545p. 1969. 124.50x (ISBN 3-11-002558-2); Vol 2. Scholia Ad Libros E - I Continens. 550p. 1971. 154.50x (ISBN 3-11-003882-X); Vol. 3. Scholia Ad Libros K-(Z) Continens. 1974. 237.50x (ISBN 3-11-004641-5); Scholia Ad Libros Y-Continens. 1977. 360.75x (ISBN 3-11-006911-3). De Gruyter.

Farrington, Benjamin. Samuel Butler & the Odyssey. LC 73-21626. (English Literature Ser., No. 33). 1974. lib. bdg. 46.95 (ISBN 0-8383-1777-4). Haskell.

Ferrucci, Franco. The Poetics of Disguise: The Autobiography of the Work in Homer, Dante, & Shakespeare. Dunnigan, Ann, tr. from It. LC 80-11242. 178p. 1980. 13.50x (ISBN 0-8014-1262-5). Cornell U Pr.

Finley, John H., Jr. Homer's Odyssey. LC 78-9308. 1978. 15.00x (ISBN 0-674-40614-1). Harvard U Pr.

Flaxman, John. Flaxman's Illustrations to Homer, Engraved by W. Blake. Essick, R. & Labelle, J., eds. 8.75 (ISBN 0-8446-5575-9). Peter Smith.

Foerster, Donald M. Homer in English Criticism: The Historical Approach in the Eighteenth Century. LC 69-15682. (Yale Studies in English Ser., No. 105). 1969. Repr. of 1947 ed. 13.50 (ISBN 0-208-00772-5, Archon). Shoe String.

Gladstone, W. E. An Enquiry into the Time & Place of Homer. 1876. Repr. 30.00 (ISBN 0-8274-2278-4). R West.

--Studies on Homer & the Homeric Age, 3 vols. LC 77-94580. 1978. Repr. of 1858 ed. lib. bdg. 75.00 (ISBN 0-89341-176-0). Longwood Pr.

Gordon, Cyrus H. Homer & Bible: The Origin & Character of East Mediterranean Literature. 1967. pap. 2.95 (ISBN 0-911566-03-1). Ventnor.

Griffin, Jasper. Homer. (Pastmasters Ser.). 1981. 7.95 (ISBN 0-8090-5523-6); pap. 2.95 (ISBN 0-8090-1413-0). Hill & Wang.

--Homer on Life & Death. 248p. 1980. 37.50x (ISBN 0-19-814016-9). Oxford U Pr.

Hogan, James C. A Guide to the Iliad. LC 78-58757. 1979. pap. 4.95 (ISBN 0-385-14519-5, Anch). Doubleday.

Homer. The Homeric Hymns. 2nd ed. Allen, T. W., et al, eds. LC 76-29451. 1977. Repr. of 1936 ed. 37.50 (ISBN 0-404-15309-7). AMS Pr.

--Opera, Vol. 1: Iliad, I - XII. 3rd ed. Monroe, D. B. & Allen, T. W., eds. 298p. (Greek.). 1920. text ed. 14.95 (ISBN 0-19-814528-4). Oxford U Pr.

--Opera, Vol. 2: Iliad XIII - XXIV. 3rd ed. Monroe, D. B. & Allen, T. W., eds. (OCT Ser.). 314p. (Greek.). 1920. text ed. 14.95 (ISBN 0-19-814529-2). Oxford U Pr.

--Opera, Vol. 3: Odyssey, I - XII. 2nd ed. Allen, T. W., ed. (OCT Ser.). 242p. (Greek.). 1919. text ed. 14.95x (ISBN 0-19-814531-4). Oxford U Pr.

--Opera, Vol. 4: Odyssey, XIII - XXIV. 2nd ed. Allen, T. W., ed. (OCT Ser.). 228p. (Greek.). 1919. text ed. 13.95x (ISBN 0-19-814532-2). Oxford U Pr.

--Opera, Vol. 5: Hymns. Allen, T. W., ed. 294p. (Greek.). 1911. text ed. 16.95 (ISBN 0-19-814534-9). Oxford U Pr.

Jebb, R. C. Homer: An Introduction to the Iliad & the Odyssey. LC 68-26259. 1969. Repr. of 1894 ed. 12.50 (ISBN 0-8046-0237-9). Kennikat.

Kirk, Geoffrey S. Homer & the Epic. abr. ed. Orig. Title: Songs of Homer, Il. pap. 8.50 (ISBN 0-521-09356-2, 356). Cambridge U Pr.

--Songs of Homer. 1962. 55.00 (ISBN 0-521-05890-2). Cambridge U Pr.

Knight, Douglas. Pope & the Heroic Tradition: A Critical Study of His Iliad. LC 69-15686. (Yale Studies in English Ser.: No. 117). 1969. Repr. of 1951 ed. 14.50 (ISBN 0-208-00775-X, Archon). Shoe String.

Lang, Andrew. Homer & His Age. LC 68-59285. Repr. of 1906 ed. 10.00 (ISBN 0-404-03867-0). AMS Pr.

--Homer & the Epic. LC 71-109918. Repr. of 1893 ed. 12.50 (ISBN 0-404-03845-X). AMS Pr.

--World of Homer. LC 68-54281. Repr. of 1910 ed. 10.00 (ISBN 0-404-03870-0). AMS Pr.

Laum, Bernhard. Das Alexandrinische Akzentuationssystem Unter Zugrundelegung der Theoretischen Lehren der Grammatik. Repr. of 1928 ed. pap. 34.00 (ISBN 0-384-31620-4). Johnson Repr.

Lawton, W. C. Successors of Homer. LC 69-17001. Repr. of 1898 ed. 11.00x (ISBN 0-8154-0276-7). Cooper Sq.

Lessing, Erich. Adventures of Ulysses: Homer's Epic in Pictures. LC 71-12865. (Illus.). 1970. 12.50 (ISBN 0-396-06251-2). Dodd.

Michalopoulos, Andre. Homer. (World Authors Ser.: Greece: No. 4). 1966. lib. bdg. 9.95 (ISBN 0-8057-2432-X). Twayne.

--Homer. LC 74-80026. (Griffin Authors Ser.). 217p. 1975. pap. 4.95 (ISBN 0-312-38885-3). St Martin.

Milch, Robert. Iliad Notes. (Orig.). pap. 1.75 (ISBN 0-8220-0645-6). Cliffs.

--Odyssey Notes. (Orig.). pap. 1.95 (ISBN 0-8220-0921-8). Cliffs.

Mireaux, Emile. Daily Life in the Time of Homer. Sells, Iris, tr. 1959. 9.95 (ISBN 0-02-585090-3). Macmillan.

Monarch Notes on Homer's Iliad. (Orig.). pap. 1.75 (ISBN 0-671-00501-4). Monarch Pr.

Monarch Notes on Homer's Odyssey. (Orig.). pap. 1.95 (ISBN 0-671-00502-2). Monarch Pr.

Nagler, Michael. Spontaneity & Tradition: A Study in the Oral Art of Homer. 1975. 22.50x (ISBN 0-520-02244-0). U of Cal Pr.

Nelson, Conny. Homer's Odyssey: A Critical Handbook. 1969. pap. 5.95x (ISBN 0-534-00663-9). Wadsworth Pub.

Nilsson, Martin P. Homer & Mycenae. (Illus.). 1972. pap. 5.95x (ISBN 0-8122-1033-6, Pa. Paperbacks). U of Pa Pr.

--Homer & Mycenae. LC 68-54548. (Illus.). 1968. Repr. of 1933 ed. 13.75x (ISBN 0-8154-0282-1). Cooper Sq.

Owen, William B. & Goodspeed, Edgar J. Homeric Vocabularies: Greek & English Word-Lists for the Study of Homer. LC 68-31669. (Gr, & Eng). (YA) (gr. 9 up). 1969. pap. 2.95x (ISBN 0-8061-0828-2). U of Okla Pr.

Page, Denys L. History & the Homeric Iliad. (Sather Classical Lectures: Vol. 31). (Illus.). 1959. 17.50x (ISBN 0-520-03246-2). U of Cal Pr.

--The Homeric Odyssey. LC 76-39798. (Mary Flexner Lectures Ser., 1954). 1977. Repr. of 1955 ed. lib. bdg. 17.25x (ISBN 0-8371-9308-7, PAHO). Greenwood.

Picard, Barbara L. The Iliad of Homer. (Illus.). 208p. (gr. 6 up). 1980. Repr. of 1960 ed. 14.95 (ISBN 0-19-274517-4). Oxford U Pr.

Redfield, James M. Nature & Culture in the Iliad: The Tragedy of Hector. LC 74-33511. xvi, 288p. 1975. 16.00x (ISBN 0-226-70651-6). U of Chicago Pr.

Reinhold, Meyer. Barron's Simplified Approach to Homer's Iliad. LC 66-30374. 1967. pap. text ed. 1.50 (ISBN 0-8120-0257-1). Barron.

--Barron's Simplified Approach to Homer's Odyssey. LC 66-30373. (Orig.). (YA) 1967. pap. text ed. 1.50 (ISBN 0-8120-0258-X). Barron.

Romer, Adolf. Homerexegese Aristarchs in Ihren Grundzugen. Repr. of 1924 ed. pap. 18.50 (ISBN 0-384-51650-5). Johnson Repr.

Rouse, William H. Homer. LC 77-4736. 1977. Repr. lib. bdg. 20.00 (ISBN 0-8414-7217-3). Folcroft.

Sargent, Thelma, tr. The Homeric Hymns: A Verse Translation. 96p. 1975. pap. 3.95 (ISBN 0-393-00788-X, Norton Lib). Norton.

Scott, John A. Homer & His Influence. LC 63-10272. (Our Debt to Greece & Rome Ser). Repr. of 1930 ed. 7.50x (ISBN 0-8154-0202-3). Cooper Sq.

--Unity of Homer. LC 65-15246. 1921. 10.50x (ISBN 0-8196-0152-7). Biblo.

Seymour, Thomas D. Life in the Homeric Age. LC 63-12451. (Illus.). 1907. 15.00x (ISBN 0-8196-0125-X). Biblo.

Sheppard, J. T. Pattern of the Iliad. LC 68-816. (Studies in Poetry, No. 38). 1969. Repr. of 1922 ed. lib. bdg. 33.95 (ISBN 0-8383-0622-5). Haskell.

Shipp, G. P. Studies in the Language of Homer. 2nd ed. LC 76-149439. (Cambridge Classical Studies). 1972. 42.00 (ISBN 0-521-07706-0). Cambridge U Pr.

Simonsuuri, K. Homer's Original Genius. LC 78-56758. (Illus.). 1979. 32.95 (ISBN 0-521-22198-6). Cambridge U Pr.

Stewart, Douglas J. Disguised Guest: Rank, Role, & Identity in the "Odyssesy". LC 74-18749. 221p. 1976. 12.50 (ISBN 0-8387-1647-4). Bucknell U Pr.

Stubbings, Frank H. & Wace, Alan J. Companion to Homer. 1963. 17.50 (ISBN 0-02-622200-0). Macmillan.

Thomas, C. G. Homer's History: Mycenaean or Dark Age. 5.00 (ISBN 0-8446-0935-8). Peter Smith.

Thomas, Carol G., ed. Homer's History: Mycenaean or Dark Age? LC 77-2546. (European Problem Studies Ser.). 124p. 1977. pap. text ed. 5.50 (ISBN 0-88275-549-8). Krieger.

Trypanis, C. A. The Homeric Epics. Phelps, W. W., tr. 1977. 18.00x (ISBN 0-85668-085-0, Pub. by Aris & Phillips); pap. 10.00x (ISBN 0-85668-086-9, Pub. by Aris & Phillips). Intl Schol Bk Serv.

Tsagarakis, Odysseus. Nature & Background of Major Concepts of Divine Power in Homer. 1977. pap. text ed. 34.25x (ISBN 90-6032-083-2). Humanities.

Van Doorn, Willem. Of the Tribe of Homer. 249p. 1980. Repr. of 1932 ed. lib. bdg. 25.00 (ISBN 0-8495-1125-9). Arden Lib.

--Of the Tribe of Homer: Being an Enquiry into the Theory & Practice of English Narrative Since 1833. LC 76-6164. 1972. Repr. of 1932 ed. lib. bdg. 15.00 (ISBN 0-8414-9155-0). Folcroft.

Vivante, Paolo. The Homeric Imagination: Homer's Poetic Perception of Reality. LC 77-126221. 224p. 1970. 8.50x (ISBN 0-253-13855-8). Ind U Pr.

Weil, Simone. Iliad or the Poem of Force. LC 57-6026. 1956. pap. 1.25x (ISBN 0-87574-091-X). Pendle Hill.

Whitman, Cedric H. Homer & the Heroic Tradition. 1965. pap. 4.95 (ISBN 0-393-00313-2, Norton Lib). Norton.

Willcock, M. M. Commentary on Homer's Iliad Books 1-6. LC 74-108403. 1970. pap. text ed. 8.95 (ISBN 0-312-15225-6). St Martin.

Willcock, M. M., ed. The Iliad of Homer, Bks. 1-12. LC 77-78981. (Illus.). 1978. text ed. 12.95x (ISBN 0-312-40532-4). St Martin.

Willcock, Malcolm M. A Companion to the "Iliad". Lattimore, Richmond, tr. LC 75-20894. (Illus.). 302p. 1976. 16.50x (ISBN 0-226-89854-7). U of Chicago Pr.

Wright, John, ed. Essays on the Iliad: Selected Modern Criticism. LC 77-23634. (Midland Bks: No. 213). 160p. 1978. pap. 3.95x (ISBN 0-253-20213-2). Ind U Pr.

--Essays on the Iliad: Selected Modern Criticism. LC 77-23634. 1978. 10.95x (ISBN 0-253-31990-0). Ind U Pr.

HOMER-BIBLIOGRAPHY

Homerus. Homeric Hymns. Lang, Andrew, tr. LC 72-4249. (Select Bibliography Reprint Ser.). 1972. Repr. of 1899 ed. 20.00 (ISBN 0-8369-6885-9). Arno.

Packard, David W. & Meyers, Tania. A Bibliography of Homeric Scholarship: Preliminary Edition Nineteen Thirty to Nineteen Seventy. LC 74-18918. 1974. pap. 2.50 (ISBN 0-89003-005-7). Undena Pubns.

HOMER-DICTIONARIES

Autenrieth, Georg. Homeric Dictionary for Schools & Colleges. Flagg, Isaac, ed. Keep, Robert P., tr. (Illus.). (YA) (gr. 9 up). 1979. Repr. of 1958 ed. 7.95x (ISBN 0-8061-0394-9). U of Okla Pr.

--A Homeric Dictionary: For Schools & Colleges. Flagg, Isaac & Keep, Robert P., eds. 1976. pap. 5.95x (ISBN 0-8061-1289-1, 1289-1). U of Okla Pr.

Cunliffe, Richard J. A Lexicon of the Homeric Dialect. 1977. pap. 10.95x (ISBN 0-8061-1430-4). U of Okla Pr.

HOMER, LOUISE, 1871-1947

Homer, Sidney. My Wife & I: The Story of Louise & Sidney Homer. LC 77-10561. (Music Reprint Ser.). (Illus.). 1978. Repr. of 1939 ed. lib. bdg. 27.50 (ISBN 0-306-77526-3). Da Capo.

Vermorcken, Elizabeth M. These Too Were Here (Willa Cather) LC 76-30901. 1977. lib. bdg. 15.00 (ISBN 0-8414-6061-2). Folcroft.

HOMER, WINSLOW, 1836-1910

Beam, Philip C. Winslow Homer. (Illus.). 48p. 1975. 17.95 (ISBN 0-07-004215-2, P&RB). McGraw.

--Winslow Homer's Magazine Engravings. LC 78-24825. (Icon Editions). (Illus.). 1979. 25.00 (ISBN 0-06-430381-0, HarpT). Har-Row.

Davis, Melinda D. Winslow Homer: An Annotated Bibliography of Periodical Literature. LC 75-29243. 1975. 10.00 (ISBN 0-8108-0876-5). Scarecrow.

Downes, William H. The Life & Works of Winslow Homer. LC 72-81983. 1974. Repr. of 1911 ed. lib. bdg. 25.50 (ISBN 0-8337-5127-1). B Franklin.

Flexner, James. World of Winslow Homer. (Library of Art). (Illus.). 1966. 15.95 (ISBN 0-8094-0235-1). Time-Life.

--World of Winslow Homer. LC 66-27562. (Library of Art Ser.). (Illus.). (gr. 6 up). 1966. 12.96 (ISBN 0-8094-0264-5, Pub. by Time-Life). Silver.

Gardner, Albert T. Winslow Homer, American Artist: His World & Work. (Illus.). 266p. 1961. 25.00 (ISBN 0-517-03448-4). Crown.

Hendricks, Gordon. The Life & Work of Winslow Homer. LC 79-210. (Illus.). 1979. 55.00 (ISBN 0-8109-1063-2). Abrams.

Hoopes, Donelson F. Winslow Homer Watercolor. (Illus.). 1976. pap. 9.95 (ISBN 0-8230-2326-5). Watson-Guptill.

Hyman, Linda. Winslow Homer: America's Old Master. LC 72-92225. 96p. (gr. 7 up). 1973. PLB 4.95 (ISBN 0-385-07823-4). Doubleday.

Longstreet, Stephen, ed. Drawings of Winslow Homer. (Master Draughtsman Ser). (Illus.). treasure trove bdg. 6.47x (ISBN 0-685-07307-6); pap. 2.95 (ISBN 0-685-07308-4). Borden.

Rogers, Meyric R., et al. Four American Painters: George Caleb Bingham, Winslow Homer, Thomas Eakins, Albert P. Ryder. LC 72-86438. (Museum of Modern Art Publications in Reprint Ser). (Illus.). 1970. Repr. of 1935 ed. 18.00 (ISBN 0-405-01547-X). Arno.

Stepanek, Stephanie. Winslow Homer. 1977. pap. 2.00 (ISBN 0-87846-115-9). Mus Fine Arts Boston.

Tatham, David. Winslow Homer & the New England Poets. (Illus.). 1980. pap. 3.00x (ISBN 0-912296-45-3, Dist. by U Pr of Va). Am Antiquarian.

HOMERIC CIVILIZATION

see Civilization, Homeric

HOMES

see Dwellings

HOMES (INSTITUTIONS)

see Almshouses; Asylums; Charities; Children-Institutional Care; Old Age Homes

HOMES, MOBILE

see Mobile Homes

HOMESTAKE MINING COMPANY

Cash, Joseph H. Working the Homestake. (Illus.). 150p. 1973. 5.95 (ISBN 0-8138-0755-7). Iowa St U Pr.

HOMESTEAD LAW

Churchill, James E. The Homesteader's Handbook. 1975. pap. 2.95 (ISBN 0-394-71346-X). Random.

Circular from the General Land Office: Showing the Manner of Proceeding to Obtain Title to Public Lands Under the Homestead, Desert Land, & Other Laws. LC 72-2838. (Use & Abuse of America's Natural Resources Ser). 332p. 1972. Repr. of 1899 ed. 17.00 (ISBN 0-405-04504-2). Arno.

Lee, Lawrence B. Kansas & the Homestead Act: 1862-1905, 2 vols. in one. Bruchey, Stuart, ed. LC 78-36703. (Management of Public Lands in the U. S. Ser.). (Illus.). 1979. lib. bdg. 40.00x (ISBN 0-405-11341-2). Arno.

Stein, R. Conrad. The Story of the Homestead Act. LC 78-4839. (Cornerstones of Freedom Ser.). (Illus.). (gr. 3-6). 1978. PLB 7.95 (ISBN 0-516-04616-0); pap. 2.50 (ISBN 0-516-44616-9). Childrens.

Tatter, Henry W. The Preferential Treatment of the Actual Settler in the Primary Disposition of the Vacant Lands in the United States to 1841. Bruchey, Stuart, ed. LC 78-53568. (Development of Public Land Law in the U. S. Ser.). 1979. lib. bdg. 28.00x (ISBN 0-405-11367-6). Arno.

HOMESTEAD STRIKE, 1892

Burgoyne, Arthur G. Homestead. LC 68-55495. Repr. of 1893 ed. 15.00x (ISBN 0-678-00872-8). Kelley.

HOMESTEADING

see Agriculture-Handbooks, Manuals, etc.; Frontier and Pioneer Life; Homestead Law

HOMEWORK

Collier, Herbert L. Homework: How to Study & Remember. (Illus.). 144p. 1976. 7.95 (ISBN 0-89019-054-2). O'Sullivan Woodside.

Di Napoli, Peter J. Homework in New York City Elementary Schools. LC 77-176721. (Columbia University. Teachers College. Contributions to Education: No. 719). Repr. of 1937 ed. 17.50 (ISBN 0-404-55719-8). AMS Pr.
Ferguson, Annabelle & Shockley, Robert. The Teenager & Homework. (Personal Guidance & Social Adjustment Ser.). (Illus.). 160p. (gr. 7-12). 1975. PLB 5.97 (ISBN 0-8239-0319-2). Rosen Pr.
Zifferblatt, Steven M. Improving Study & Homework Behaviors. (Illus.). 96p. (Orig.). 1970. pap. 5.95 (ISBN 0-87822-012-7). Res Press.

HOMICIDE
see also Assassination; Euthanasia; Homicide Investigation; Infanticide; Murder; Poisoning; Suicide
Adelson, Lester. The Pathology of Homicide: A Vade Mecum for Pathologist, Prosecutor & Defense Counsel. (Illus.). 992p. 1974. text ed. 67.50 (ISBN 0-398-03000-6). C C Thomas.
Allen, Nancy. Homicide: Perspectives on Prevention. LC 79-11841. 192p. 1979. text ed. 19.95 (ISBN 0-87705-382-0); pap. text ed. 9.95 (ISBN 0-87705-412-6). Human Sci Pr.
Bailey, F. Lee & Rothblatt, Henry B. Crimes of Violence: Rape & Other Sex Crimes. LC 72-97625. (Criminal Law Library). 1973. 47.50 (ISBN 0-686-14500-3). Lawyers Co-Op.
Bensing, Robert C. & Schroeder, Oliver, Jr. Homicide in an Urban Community. (Illus.). 208p. 1960. pap. 19.50 (ISBN 0-398-00133-2). C C Thomas.
Biggs, John, Jr. The Guilty Mind: Psychiatry & the Law of Homicide. LC 55-10812. (Isaac Ray Award Lectures Ser). 248p. (Orig.). 1967. pap. 3.95x (ISBN 0-8018-0070-6). Johns Hopkins.
Brearley, H. C. Homicide in the United States. LC 69-14913. (Criminology, Law Enforcement, & Social Problems Ser.: No. 36). 1969. Repr. of 1932 ed. 15.00 (ISBN 0-87585-036-7). Patterson Smith.
Bromberg, Walter. The Mold of Murder: A Psychiatric Study of Homicide. LC 61-14610. 230p. Repr. of 1961 ed. lib. bdg. 15.00x (ISBN 0-8371-8070-8, BRMM). Greenwood.
Chimbos, Peter D. Marital Violence: A Study of Interspouse Homicide. LC 77-94287. 1978. pap. 12.00 perfect bdg. (ISBN 0-88247-507-X). R & E Res Assoc.
Devine, Philip E. The Ethics of Homicide. LC 78-58055. 1978. 17.50 (ISBN 0-8014-1173-4). Cornell U Pr.
Gagarin, Michael. Drakon & Early Athenian Homicide Law. LC 81-2370. (Classical Monographs). 208p. 1981. text ed. 20.00x (ISBN 0-300-02627-7). Yale U Pr.
Henry, Andrew F. & Short, James F., Jr. Suicide & Homicide: Some Economic, Sociological and Psychological Aspects of Aggression. Kastenbaum, Robert, ed. LC 76-19575. (Death & Dying Ser.). (Illus.). 1977. Repr. of 1954 ed. lib. bdg. 15.00x (ISBN 0-405-09573-2). Arno.
Hughes, Daniel J. Homicide: Investigative Techniques. (Illus.). 376p. 1974. 22.50 (ISBN 0-398-02952-0). C C Thomas.
Lester, David & Lester, Gene. Crime of Passion: Murder & the Murderer. LC 74-20788. 308p. 1975. 17.95x (ISBN 0-88229-139-4). Nelson-Hall.
Macdonald, John M. Homicidal Threats. (Illus.). 136p. 1968. 9.75 (ISBN 0-398-01178-8). C C Thomas.
Palmer, Stuart. The Violent Society. 1972. 6.50x (ISBN 0-8084-0353-2); pap. 2.95 (ISBN 0-8084-0354-0, B60). Coll & U Pr.
Palmer, Stuart, ed. Homicide & Suicide. (Controversy Ser.). Date not set. 9.95x (ISBN 0-88311-210-8); pap. 3.95 (ISBN 0-88311-211-6). Lieber-Atherton.
Reinhardt, James M. The Psychology of Strange Killers. 212p. 1962. photocopy ed. spiral 19.75 (ISBN 0-398-01566-X). C C Thomas.
Revitch, Eugene & Schlesinger, Louis B. Psychopathology of Homicide. (Illus.). 272p. 1981. pap. 27.50 (ISBN 0-398-04178-4). C C Thomas.
Richardson, Lewis F. Statistics of Deadly Quarrels. Wright, Quincy & Lienau, C. C., eds. (Illus.). 1960. 24.00 (ISBN 0-910286-10-8). Boxwood.
Sullivan, Shaun J. Killing in Defense of Private Property: The Development of a Roman Catholic Moral Teaching, Thirteenth to Eighteenth Centuries. LC 75-38843. (American Academy of Religion. Dissertation Ser.). (Illus.). 1976. pap. 7.50 (ISBN 0-89130-067-8, 010115). Scholars Pr Ca.
Sylvester, Sawyer F., et al. Prison Homicide. LC 77-22698. (Sociomedical Science Ser). 1977. 12.00 (ISBN 0-470-99181-X). Halsted Pr.
Thakur, Upendra. Introduction to Homicide in India: Ancient & Early Medieval Period. 1978. 9.50x (ISBN 0-8364-0184-0). South Asia Bks.
Totman, Jane. The Murderess: A Psychosocial Study of Criminal Homicide. LC 77-90373. 1978. pap. 10.00 perfect bdg. (ISBN 0-88247-525-8). R & E Res Assoc.

HOMICIDE–GREAT BRITAIN
Given, James Buchanan. Society & Homicide in Thirteenth-Century England. LC 76-23372. 1977. 12.50x (ISBN 0-8047-0939-4). Stanford U Pr.
Swigert, Victoria & Farrell, Ronald A. Murder, Inequality, & the Law: Differential Treatment & the Legal Process. LC 76-22222. 1976. 15.95 (ISBN 0-669-00881-8). Lexington Bks.

HOMICIDE IN LITERATURE
Davis, David B. Homicide in American Fiction, 1798-1860: A Study in Social Values. 364p. (YA) (gr. 9-12). 1968. pap. 5.95 (ISBN 0-8014-9066-9, CP66). Cornell U Pr.

HOMICIDE INVESTIGATION
Bailey, F. Lee & Rothblatt, Henry B. Crimes of Violence: Homicide & Assault. LC 72-97625. (Criminal Law Library). 543p. 1973. 47.50 (ISBN 0-686-05455-5). Lawyers Co-Op.
Dieckmann, Edward A. Practical Homicide Investigation. 96p. 1961. 10.50 (ISBN 0-398-00450-1). C C Thomas.
Lundsgaarde, Henry. Murder in Space City: A Cultural Analysis of Houston Homicidal Patterns. LC 76-9229. (Illus.). 1977. 12.95 (ISBN 0-19-502100-2). Oxford U Pr.
Snyder, LeMoyne. Homicide Investigation: Practical Information for Coroners, Police Officers, & Other Investigators. 3rd ed. (Illus.). 416p. 1977. 26.75 (ISBN 0-398-03632-2). C C Thomas.
Southwestern Law Enforcement Institute. Homicide Investigaton: Personal Experience Accounts of Professionals & Experts. (Illus.). 144p. 1961. photocopy ed. spiral 14.75 (ISBN 0-398-01814-6). C C Thomas.

HOMICULTURE
see Eugenics

HOMILETICAL ILLUSTRATIONS
see also Bible–Homiletical Use; Exempla; Fables; Legends; Parables; Short Stories; Tales
Cockayne, O., ed. Hali Meidenhad, Alliterative Homily of 13th Century. Repr. of 1922 ed. 6.00 (ISBN 0-527-00020-5). Kraus Repr.
Deems, Edward M., ed. Holy-Days & Holidays: A Treasury of Historical Material, Sermons in Full & in Brief, Suggestive Thoughts & Poetry, Relating to Holy Days & Holidays. LC 68-17940. 1968. Repr. of 1902 ed. 40.00 (ISBN 0-8103-3352-X). Gale.
Fichtner, Joseph. Proclaim His Word: Homiletic Themes for Sundays & Holy Days-Cycle A, Vol. 2. new ed. LC 73-5726. 239p. (Orig.). 1974. pap. 4.95 (ISBN 0-8189-0292-2). Alba.
Kemp, Thomas L. Homilies on the Sunday Gospels. LC 76-675. (Orig.). 1976. 17.95 (ISBN 0-87973-883-9). Our Sunday Visitor.
Knight, Walter B. Knight's Master Book of New Illustrations. 1956. pap. 9.95 (ISBN 0-8028-1699-1). Eerdmans.
Koenig, John. Stories to Learn by. (Illus.). 5.00 (ISBN 0-8198-0333-2); pap. 4.00 (ISBN 0-8198-0334-0). Dghtrs St Paul.
Lee, Robert G. Robert G. Lee's Sourcebook of Five Hundred Illustrations. LC 64-22907. 218p. 1971. pap. 5.95 (ISBN 0-310-27471-0). Zondervan.
Lehman, Louis P. How to Teach with Illustrations. LC 75-12109. 1981. 3.95 (ISBN 0-8254-3112-3). Kregel.
Liptak, David Q. Biblical-Catechetical Homilies for Sundays & Holy Days (a, B & C) Based on the Lectionary & Reflecting the Syllabus of the Pastoral Homiletic Plan. LC 79-27895. 370p. (Orig.). 1980. pap. 10.95 (ISBN 0-8189-0400-3). Alba.
Miller, Charles E., et al. Announcing the Good News: A Cycle Homilies. LC 74-169144. 200p. 1971. pap. 3.95 (ISBN 0-8189-0215-9). Alba.
Moody, Dwight L. Doscientas Anecdotas Y Ilustraciones. (Span). pap. 1.25 (ISBN 0-8024-1490-7). Moody.
Mussner, Franz. Use of Parables in Catechetics. Von Eroes, Maria, tr. (Contemporary Catechetics Ser). (Orig.). 1965. pap. 1.25x (ISBN 0-268-00288-6). U of Notre Dame Pr.
Newman, Louis I., ed. The Hasidic Anthology: Tales & Teachings of the Hasidim. LC 63-11041. 1963. pap. 6.95 (ISBN 0-8052-0046-0). Schocken.
--Maggidim & Hasidim: Their Wisdom. 1962. 6.95 (ISBN 0-8197-0161-0). Bloch.
Nicoll, W. Robertson, ed. Expositor's Dictionary of Texts. 1978. Repr. Set. 59.95 (ISBN 0-8010-6697-2). Baker Bk.
Price, Leo. The Tree That Always Said No. LC 73-90617. (Illus.). 1973. plastic bdg. 2.75 (ISBN 0-8198-0330-8); pap. 1.75 (ISBN 0-8198-0331-6). Dghtrs St Paul.
Smith, James. Handfuls on Purpose, 5 vols. 1943. 69.95 set (ISBN 0-8028-8139-4). Eerdmans.
Spurgeon, C. H. Barbed Arrows. 237p. pap. 2.95 (ISBN 0-87509-049-4). Chr Pubns.
Westphal, Arnold C. Junior Surprise Sermons with Handmade Objects, 2 bks. Set. pap. 6.00 (ISBN 0-686-70924-1); No. 1. pap. 3.00 (ISBN 0-915398-18-4); No. 2. pap. 3.00 (ISBN 0-915398-19-2). Visual Evangels.
Whyte, Alexander & Turnbull, Ralph G., eds. Best of Alexander Whyte. (Best Ser.). 1979. pap. 3.95 (ISBN 0-8010-9628-6). Baker Bk.

HOMILETICS
see Preaching

HOMILIES
see Sermons

HOMING PIGEONS
see Pigeons

HOMOEOPATHY
see Homeopathy

HOMOGENEOUS GROUPING
see Ability Grouping in Education

HOMOGRAFTS
see also Bones–Surgery; Skin-Grafting

HOMOLOGICAL ALGEBRA
see Algebra, Homological

HOMOLOGY THEORY
see also Algebra, Homological; K-Theory; Sheaves, Theory of
Artin, M. & Mazur, B. Etale Homotopy. LC 75-88710. (Lecture Notes in Mathematics: Vol. 100). (Orig.). 1969. pap. 10.70 (ISBN 0-387-04619-4). Springer-Verlag.
Barratt, M. B. & Mahowald, M. E., eds. Geometric Applications of Homotopy Theory II: Proceedings, Evanston, March 21-26, 1977. LC 78-16038. (Lecture Notes in Mathematics: Vol. 658). 1978. pap. 21.30 (ISBN 0-387-08859-8). Springer-Verlag.
Battelle Memorial Institute Conference - Seattle - 1968. Category Theory, Homology Theory & Their Applications, 1: Proceedings. Hilton, P. J., ed. LC 75-75931. (Lecture Notes in Mathematics: Vol. 86). 1969. pap. 14.70 (ISBN 0-387-04605-4). Springer-Verlag.
--Category Theory, Homology Theory & Their Applications, 2: Proceedings. Hilton, Peter J., ed. LC 75-75931. (Lecture Notes in Mathematics: Vol. 92). (Orig.). 1969. pap. 18.30 (ISBN 0-387-04611-9). Springer-Verlag.
--Category Theory, Homology Theory, & Their Applications, 3: Proceedings. Hilton, Peter J., ed. LC 75-75931. (Lecture Notes in Mathematics: Vol. 99). (Orig.). 1969. pap. 21.90 (ISBN 0-387-04618-6). Springer-Verlag.
Berthelot, Pierre & Ogus, Arthur. Notes on Crystalline Coholomology. LC 78-57039. (Mathematical Notes Ser.: No. 21). 1979. 11.00 (ISBN 0-691-08218-9). Princeton U Pr.
Borel, A. Topics in the Homology Theory of Fibre Bundles. (Lecture Notes in Mathematics: Vol. 36). 1967. pap. 10.70 (ISBN 0-387-03907-4). Springer-Verlag.
Borel, A. & Wallach, N. Continuous Cohomology Discrete Subgroups, & Representation of Reductive Groups. LC 79-19858. (Annals of Mathematics Studies: 94). 352p. 1980. 22.50x (ISBN 0-691-08248-0); pap. 10.00x (ISBN 0-691-08249-9). Princeton U Pr.
Bredon, G. E. Equivariant Cohomology Theories. (Lecture Notes in Mathematics: Vol. 34). 1967. pap. 10.70 (ISBN 0-387-03905-8). Springer-Verlag.
Buoncristiano, S., et al. A Geometric Approach to Homology Theory. LC 75-22980. (London Mathematical Society Lecture Note Ser.: No. 18). (Illus.). 216p. 1976. pap. text ed. 17.95x (ISBN 0-521-20940-4). Cambridge U Pr.
Cohen, F. R. The Homology of Iterated Loop Spaces. (Lecture Notes in Mathematics: Vol. 533). 1977. soft cover 20.30 (ISBN 0-387-07984-X). Springer-Verlag.
Conner, Pierre E. & Floyd, E. E. Relation of Corbordism to K-Theories. (Lecture Notes in Mathematics: Vol. 28). 1966. pap. 10.70 (ISBN 0-387-03610-5). Springer-Verlag.
Duskin, J. Simplical Methods & the Interpretation of "Triple" Cohomolgy. LC 75-20008. (Memoirs: No. 163). 1975. pap. 11.20 (ISBN 0-8218-1863-5, MEMO-163). Am Math.
Dyer, E. Cohomology Theories. (Math Lecture Notes Ser.: No. 27). 1969. 17.50 (ISBN 0-8053-2366-X, Adv Bk Prog); pap. 8.50 (ISBN 0-8053-2367-8, Adv Bk Prog). Benjamin-Cummings.
Eilenberg, Samuel & Moore, J. C. Foundations of Relative Homological Algebra. LC 52-42839. (Memoirs: No. 55). 1966. pap. 7.20 (ISBN 0-8218-1255-6, MEMO-55). Am Math.
Epstein, D. B. Cohomology Operations: Lectures by N. E. Steenrod. (Annals of Mathematics Studies: No. 50). 1962. 11.50x (ISBN 0-691-07924-2). Princeton U Pr.
Giblin, P. J. Graphs, Surfaces & Homology: An Introduction to Algebraic Topology. LC 76-48914. 329p. 1977. pap. text ed. 17.95x (ISBN 0-412-21440-7, Pub. by Chapman & Hall). Methuen Inc.
Grothendieck, A. Local Cohomology: A Seminar Given by A. Grothendieck at Harvard University, 1961. Hartshorne, ed. (Lecture Notes in Mathematics: Vol. 41). 1967. pap. 10.70 (ISBN 0-387-03912-0). Springer-Verlag.
Gruenberg, Karl W. Cohomological Topics in Group Theory. LC 70-127042. (Lecture Notes in Mathematics: Vol. 143). 1970. pap. 14.70 (ISBN 0-387-04932-0). Springer-Verlag.
Hartshorne, R. Residues & Duality. (Lecture Notes in Mathematics: Vol. 20). 1966. pap. 21.90 (ISBN 0-387-03603-2). Springer-Verlag.
Hilton, Peter J. General Cohomology Theory & K. Theory. (London Mathematics Society Lecture Note Ser.: No. 1). 1970. text ed. 11.95 (ISBN 0-521-07976-4). Cambridge U Pr.
Hilton, Peter J. & Wylie, Shaun. Homology Theory. 1961. 59.50 (ISBN 0-521-05266-1); pap. 20.50x (ISBN 0-521-09422-4, 422). Cambridge U Pr.
Hochster, Melvin. Topics in the Homological Theory of Modules Over Commutative Rings. LC 75-1325. (CBMS Regional Conference Series in Mathematics: No. 24). 76p. 1977. 8.20 (ISBN 0-8218-1674-8, CBMS-24). Am Math.
Hofmann, K. H. & Mostert, P. S. Cohomology Theories for Compact Abelian Groups. 200p. 1973. 28.50 (ISBN 0-387-05730-7). Springer-Verlag.
Illman, Soren. Equivariant Singular Homology & Cohomology I. (Memoirs: No. 156). 1975. pap. 8.40 (ISBN 0-8218-1856-2, MEMO-156). Am Math.
Johnson, B. E. Cohomology in Banach Algebras. LC 72-4561. (Memoirs: No. 127). 1972. pap. 7.60 (ISBN 0-8218-1827-9, MEMO-127). Am Math.
Kamber, Franz W. & Tondeur, Philippe. Invariant Differential Operators & Cohomology of Lie Algebra Sheaves. LC 52-42839. (Memoirs: No. 113). 1971. pap. 7.20 (ISBN 0-8218-1813-9, MEMO-113). Am Math.
Knutson, D. Algebraic Spaces. (Lecture Notes in Matematics: Vol. 203). 1971. pap. 11.20 (ISBN 0-387-05496-0). Springer-Verlag.
Massey, W. S. Singular Homology Theory. LC 79-23309. (Graduate Texts in Mathematics: Vol. 70). (Illus.). 280p. 1980. 24.80 (ISBN 3-540-90456-5). Springer-Verlag.
Massey, William S. Homology & Cohomology Theory. (Monographs in Pure & Applied Math: Vol. 46). 1978. 36.50 (ISBN 0-8247-6662-8). Dekker.
Milne, J. S. Etale Cohomolgy. LC 79-84003. (Princeton Ser. in Mathematics: 33). 1980. 26.50x (ISBN 0-691-08238-3). Princeton U Pr.
Mostow, Mark A. Continuous Cohomology of Spaces with Two Topologies. LC 76-25187. (Memoirs of the American Mathematical Society: 175). 1976. 12.40 (ISBN 0-8218-2175-X, MEMO 175). Am Math.
Northcott, Douglas G. Introduction to Homological Algebra. 1960. 29.95 (ISBN 0-521-05841-4). Cambridge U Pr.
Sanders, Jack P. The Category of H - Modules Over a Spectrum. LC 73-22409. (Memoirs: No. 141). 1974. 8.80 (ISBN 0-8218-1841-4, MEMO-141). Am Math.
Schwartz, Jacob T. Differential Geometry & Topology. (Notes on Mathematics & Its Applications Ser). 1968. 37.50- (ISBN 0-677-01510-0). Gordon.
Seminar on Triples & Categorical Homology. Proceedings. Eckmann, B., ed. LC 68-59303. (Lecture Notes in Mathematics: Vol. 80). 1969. pap. 18.30 (ISBN 0-387-04601-1). Springer-Verlag.
Shatz, Stephen S. Profinite Groups, Arithmetic, & Geometry. LC 77-126832. (Annals of Mathematics Studies: No. 67). 1971. 16.50x (ISBN 0-691-08017-8). Princeton U Pr.
Stammbach, U. Homology in Group Theory. LC 73-19547. (Lecture Notes in Mathematics: Vol. 359). 183p. 1974. pap. 10.30 (ISBN 0-387-06569-5). Springer-Verlag.
Stong, R. E. Unoriented Bordism & Actions of Finite Groups. LC 52-42839. (Memoirs: No. 103). 1970. pap. 6.40 (ISBN 0-8218-1803-1, MEMO-103). Am Math.
Thomas, Emery. Generalized Pontrjagin Cohomology Operations & Rings with Divided Powers. LC 52-42839. (Memoirs: No. 27). 1968. pap. 7.60 (ISBN 0-8218-1227-0, MEMO-27). Am Math.
Vasconcelos, Wolmer V., ed. The Rings of Dimension II. (Lecture Notes in Pure & Applied Mathematics Ser.: Vol. 22). 1976. 19.50 (ISBN 0-8247-6447-1). Dekker.
Vick, James W. Homology Theory: An Introduction to Algebraic Topology. (Pure & Applied Mathematics Ser., Vol. 54). 1973. text ed. 22.95 (ISBN 0-12-721250-7). Acad Pr.
Weiss, E. Cohomology of Groups. (Pure & Applied Mathematics Ser.: Vol. 34). 1969. 46.50 (ISBN 0-12-742750-3). Acad Pr.
Whitehead, G. Elements of Homotopy Theory. (Graduate Texts in Mathematics Ser.: Vol. 61). (Illus.). 1979. 33.60 (ISBN 0-387-90336-4). Springer-Verlag.

HOMOPTERA
see also Cicada; Scale-Insects
Caldwell, John S. The Jumping Plant-Lice of Ohio (Homoptera: Chermidae) 1938. 1.00 (ISBN 0-686-30307-5). Ohio Bio Survey.
Distant, William L. Synonymic Catalogue of Homoptera, Pt. 1, Cicadidae. 1906. 15.50 (ISBN 0-384-11870-4). Johnson Repr.

Feeding & Multiplication of Three Cereal Aphid Species & Their Effect on Yield of Winter Wheat. (Agricultural Research Reports Ser.: 888). 1979. pap. 10.00 (ISBN 90-220-0694-8, PUDOC). Unipub.
Fennah, R. G. Fulgoroidea of Fiji. 1950. pap. 5.00 (ISBN 0-527-02310-8). Kraus Repr.
Ghauri, M. S. The Morphology & Taxonomy of Male Scale Insects (Homoptera: Coccoidea) (Illus.). vii, 221p. 1962. 21.00x (ISBN 0-565-00580-4, Pub. by British Mus Nat Hist England). Sabbot-Natural Hist Bks.
McKenzie, Howard L. Mealybugs of California: With Taxonomy, Biology, & Control of North American Species. (Illus.). 1968. 65.00x (ISBN 0-520-00844-8). U of Cal Pr.
Mound, L. A. & Halsey, S. H. Whitefly of the World: A Systematic Catalogue of the Aleyrodidoe (Homoptera) with Host Plant & Natural Enemy Data. 1978. 43.75 (ISBN 0-471-99634-3, Pub. by Wiley-Interscience). Wiley.
Osborn, H. Cicadellidae of Hawaii. Repr. of 1935 ed. pap. 6.00 (ISBN 0-527-02240-3). Kraus Repr.
Osborn, Herbert. The Fulgoridae of Ohio. 1938. 1.50 (ISBN 0-686-30308-3). Ohio Bio Survey.
--The Membracidae of Ohio. 1940. 1.00 (ISBN 0-686-30310-5). Ohio Bio Survey.
Watson, S. A. The Miridae of Ohio. 1928. 1.00 (ISBN 0-686-30290-7). Ohio Bio Survey.

HOMOSEXUALITY

see also Bisexuality; Gay Liberation Movement; Lesbianism; Sodomy; Unmarried Couples

Adair, Casey & Adair, Nancy. Word Is Out. 1978. 14.95 (ISBN 0-440-09888-2). Delacorte.
--Word Is Out: Stories of Some of Our Lives. LC 78-9395. (Illus.). 1978. pap. 7.95 (ISBN 0-912078-61-8). New Glide.
Adams, Stephen. The Homosexual As Hero in Contemporary Fiction. (Critical Studies Ser.). 1980. text ed. 23.50x (ISBN 0-06-490018-5). B&N.
Altman, Dennis. Homosexual: Oppression & Liberation. 1973. pap. 1.95 (ISBN 0-686-73844-6, 27425, Discus). Avon.
Alyson, Sasha, ed. Young, Gay & Proud. rev. ed. (Illus., Orig.). (YA) (gr. 9-12). 1980. pap. 2.95 (ISBN 0-932870-01-5). Alyson Pubns.
Baars, Conrad. The Homosexual's Search for Happiness. (Synthesis Ser.). 1977. pap. 0.65 (ISBN 0-8199-0709-X). Franciscan Herald.
Babuscio, Jack. We Speak for Ourselves: Experiences in Homosexual Counselling. LC 77-78623. 160p. 1977. pap. 4.75 (ISBN 0-8006-1264-7, 1-1264). Fortress.
Bahnsen, Greg L. Homosexuality: A Biblical View. LC 78-62911. 1978. pap. 4.95 (ISBN 0-8010-0744-5). Baker Bk.
Bailey, D. Sherwin. Homosexuality & the Western Christian Tradition. xii, 181p. 1975. Repr. of 1955 ed. 14.50 (ISBN 0-208-01492-6, Archon). Shoe String.
Baisden, Major J., Jr. The Dynamics of Homosexuality. LC 75-31. 199p. 1975. 6.95 (ISBN 0-912984-02-3). Allied Res Soc.
Barnett, Walter. Homosexuality & the Bible: An Interpretation. LC 79-84920. 1979. pap. 1.25x (ISBN 0-87574-226-2). Pendle Hill.
Barney, Natalie. Traits et Portraits. LC 75-12303. (Homosexuality: Lesbians & Gay Men in Society, History & Literature Ser.). (French.). 1975. Repr. of 1963 ed. 11.00x (ISBN 0-405-07395-X). Arno.
Baskett, Edward. Entrapped. LC 75-41812. 160p. 1976. 6.50 (ISBN 0-88208-064-4). Lawrence Hill.
Batchelor, Edward, ed. Homosexuality & Ethics. LC 80-10533. 1980. 10.95 (ISBN 0-8298-0392-0). Pilgrim NY.
Bayer, Ronald. Homosexuality & American Psychiatry: The Politics of Diagnosis. LC 80-68182. (Illus.). 224p. 1980. 12.95 (ISBN 0-465-03048-3). Basic.
Bell & Weinber. Homosexualities. 1979. 5.95 (ISBN 0-671-25150-3, Touchstone Bks). S&S.
Bell, Alan P. & Weinberg, Martin S. Homosexualities: A Study of Diversity Among Men & Women. 1978. 12.95 (ISBN 0-671-24212-1). S&S.
Bell, Alan P., et al. Sexual Preference: Its Development in Men & Women. LC 81-47006. (Illus.). 256p. 1981. 15.00x (ISBN 0-253-16673-X); 15.00 (ISBN 0-253-16674-8); Set. 35.00x (ISBN 0-253-16672-1). Ind U Pr.
Berzon, Betty & Leighton, Robert, eds. Positively Gay. LC 78-72287. 1979. pap. 5.95 (ISBN 0-89087-240-6). Celestial Arts.
Bieber, Irving. Homosexuality: A Psychoanalytic Study. 1962. 17.00x (ISBN 0-465-03047-5). Basic.
Brandt, Paul. Sittengeschichte Griechenlands. Lewandowski, Herbert, ed. LC 78-22297. (The Gay Experience). (Illus.). Repr. of 1959 ed. 32.50 (ISBN 0-404-61521-X). AMS Pr.
Brown, James R. & Butwill, N. Religion, Society, & the Homosexual. LC 73-10095. 44p. 1973. pap. 2.95 (ISBN 0-8422-0343-5). Irvington.
Bullogh, Vern L. Homosexuality: A History. LC 79-64736. 200p. 1979. lib. bdg. 14.50 (ISBN 0-8240-7166-2). Garland Pub.
Bullough, Vern & Bullough, Bonnie. Sin, Sickness, & Sanity: A History of Sexual Attitudes. new ed. LC 77-10206. 1977. lib. bdg. 17.50 (ISBN 0-8240-7006-2, Garland STPM Pr). Garland Pub.
Bullough, Vern L. Homosexuality: A History. 1979. pap. 4.95 (ISBN 0-452-00516-7, F516, Mer). NAL.
Bullough, Vern L., et al. An Annotated Bibliography of Homosexuality, 2 vols. LC 75-24106. (Reference Library of Social Science: Vol. 22). 1000p. 1975. Set. lib. bdg. 88.00 (ISBN 0-8240-9959-1). Garland Pub.
Camus, Renaud. Tricks: Twenty-Five Encounters. 252p. 1981. pap. 10.95 (ISBN 0-312-81823-8). St Martin.
Carpenter, Edward. Homogenic Love, & Its Place in a Free Society. LC 78-63984. (The Gay Experience). Repr. of 1894 ed. 11.50 (ISBN 0-404-61523-6). AMS Pr.
--The Intermediate Sex: A Study of Some Transitional Types of Men & Women. 2nd ed. LC 78-22294. (The Gay Experience). Repr. of 1909 ed. 18.00 (ISBN 0-404-61524-4). AMS Pr.
--Intermediate Types Among Primative Folk. LC 75-12308. (Homosexuality). 1975. Repr. of 1919 ed. 15.00x (ISBN 0-405-07352-6). Arno.
Cheseboro, James W., ed. Gayspeak: Gay Male & Lesbian Communication. 448p. 1981. 17.95 (ISBN 0-8298-0472-2); pap. 9.95 (ISBN 0-8298-0456-0). Pilgrim NY.
Christopher Street Magazine. And God Bless Uncle Harry & His Roommate Jack Who We Are Not Supposed to Talk About. 1979. pap. 2.95 (ISBN 0-380-01897-7, 37291). Avon.
Clark, Don. Living Gay. LC 79-50859. 1979. 9.95 (ISBN 0-89087-189-2). Celestial Arts.
--Loving Someone Gay. LC 76-54655. 1979. 9.95 (ISBN 0-89087-190-6). Celestial Arts.
--Loving Someone Gay. LC 76-54655. (Orig.). 1977. pap. 4.95 (ISBN 0-89087-139-6). Celestial Arts.
--Loving Someone Gay. 1978. pap. 2.25 (ISBN 0-451-08593-0, E8593, Sig). NAL.
Clark, Mason A. Nation of Gay Babies: Causing & Curing Homosexuality. (Illus.). 1978. pap. 9.95 (ISBN 0-931400-00-7). Frontal Lobe.
Coleman, Gerald. Homosexuality - an Appraisal. 1978. 0.75 (ISBN 0-685-89391-X). Franciscan Herald.
Coleman, James, Jr. International Homolphilics Institute: A History on Its Fifteenth Anniversary. 1977. pap. 3.95 (ISBN 0-686-17792-4). IHI Pr.
Committee on Homosexual Offences & Prostitution, Home Office, Scottish Home Department. Report. LC 76-24924. (Great Britain Parliament Papers by Command: No. 247). 1976. Repr. of 1968 ed. lib. bdg. 15.00x (ISBN 0-8371-8839-3, RECH). Greenwood.
Cory, Donald W. The Homosexual in America: A Subjective Approach. LC 75-12310. (Homosexuality). 1975. Repr. of 1951 ed. 18.00x (ISBN 0-405-07365-8). Arno.
Craigin, Elisabeth. Either Is Love. LC 75-12311. (Homosexuality). 1975. Repr. of 1937 ed. 9.00x (ISBN 0-405-07379-8). Arno.
Crew, Louie, ed. The Gay Academic. LC 75-37780. 1978. 15.00 (ISBN 0-88280-036-1). ETC Pubns.
Cummings, John. Homophilics: A Doctor's View. 1977. pap. 3.95 (ISBN 0-686-17790-8). IHI Pr.
Davidson, Alex. The Returns of Love: A Christian View of Homosexuality. LC 70-131594. 1977. pap. 2.50 (ISBN 0-87784-698-7). Inter-Varsity.
De Becker, Raymond. The Other Face of Love. 256p. 20.00x (ISBN 0-85435-353-4, Pub. by Spearman England). State Mutual Bk.
Devi, Shakuntala. The World of Homosexuals. 1977. 17.50 (ISBN 0-7069-0478-8, Pub. by Vikas India). Advent NY.
Dey, Richard. A General Ontology of Homophilia. 1977. pap. 15.00 (ISBN 0-686-17787-8). IHI Pr.
--An Introduction to Arcadian Theory. 1977. pap. 3.00 (ISBN 0-686-17789-4). IHI Pr.
--An Introduction to Uranian Theory. 1977. pap. 3.00 (ISBN 0-686-17788-6). IHI Pr.
Dover, K. J. Greek Homosexuality. LC 79-3576. (Illus.). 1980. pap. 5.95 (ISBN 0-394-74224-9, Vin). Random.
--Greek Homosexuality. 1978. 22.50x (ISBN 0-674-36261-6). Harvard U Pr.
Drakeford, John W. A Christian View of Homosexuality. LC 76-41474. 1977. pap. 2.95 (ISBN 0-8054-5620-1). Broadman.
Du Mas, Frank. Gay Is Not Good. 1979. 11.95 (ISBN 0-8407-4076-X). Nelson.
Duncan, Robert, et al. The Male Muse: Gay Poetry Anthology. LC 73-77318. (Crossing Press Ser. of Contemporary Anthologies). 90p. (Orig.). 1973. 8.95 (ISBN 0-912278-35-8); pap. 3.95 (ISBN 0-912278-34-X). Crossing Pr.
Eglington, J. Z. Greek Love. 508p. 25.00x (ISBN 0-85435-343-7, Pub. by Spearman England). State Mutual Bk.
Ellis, Havelock & Symonds, John A. Sexual Inversion. LC 75-12312. (Homosexuality: Lesbians & Gay Men in Society, History & Literature Ser.). 1975. Repr. of 1897 ed. 20.00x (ISBN 0-405-07363-1). Arno.
Emory, Michael. The Gay Picturebook. LC 77-91150. 1978. pap. 8.95 (ISBN 0-8092-7649-6). Contemp Bks.
Eros: An Anthology of Friendship. LC 75-12347. (Homosexuality). 1975. Repr. 20.00x (ISBN 0-405-07393-3). Arno.
Fairchild, Betty & Hayward, Betty. Now That You Know: What Every Parent Should Know About Homosexuality. LC 78-22251. 240p. 1981. 6.95 (ISBN 0-15-667702-4). HarBraceJ.
Feldman, M. P. & Macculloch, M. J. Homosexual Behaviour: Therapy & Assessment. 1971. 55.00 (ISBN 0-08-016244-4). Pergamon.
Fernbach, David. The Spiral Path: A Gay Contribution to Human Survival. 240p. (Orig.). 1981. pap. 6.95 (ISBN 0-932870-12-0). Alyson Pubns.
Fisher, Peter. Gay Mystique. LC 73-186149. 1972. pap. 1.95 (ISBN 0-8128-7005-0). Stein & Day.
Fitzroy, A. T., pseud. Despised & Rejected. LC 75-12314. (Homosexuality). 1975. Repr. of 1917 ed. 15.00x (ISBN 0-405-07389-5). Arno.
Fone, Byrne R., ed. The Gay Experience: Fiction & Non-Fiction from the Homosexual Tradition, 45 vols. Repr. of 1959 ed. write for info. (ISBN 0-404-61500-7). AMS Pr.
--Hidden Heritage: History & the Gay Imagination, an Anthology. 323p. 1979. 18.95 (ISBN 0-686-66021-8); pap. 9.95 (ISBN 0-8290-0401-7). Irvington.
--Hidden Heritage: History & the Gay Imagination. LC 79-55138. 1979. 19.95 (ISBN 0-934200-00-9). Avocation Pubs.
Freedman, Mark. Homosexuality & Psychological Functioning. LC 70-165815. 128p. (Orig.). 1971. pap. text ed. 7.95 (ISBN 0-8185-0023-9). Brooks-Cole.
Fricke, Aaron. Reflections of a Rock Lobster: A Story About Growing up Gay. LC 81-65806. (Illus.). 120p. (Orig.). 1981. pap. 4.95 (ISBN 0-932870-09-0). Alyson Pubns.
Friedlaender, Benedict. Renaissance des Eros Uranios. LC 75-12316. (Homosexuality: Lesbians & Gay Men in Society, History & Literature). (German.). 1975. Repr. of 1904 ed. 27.00x (ISBN 0-405-07362-3). Arno.
Gangel, Kenneth O. The Gospel & the Gay. LC 78-10378. 1978. pap. 3.95 (ISBN 0-8407-5658-5). Nelson.
Garde, Noel I. Jonathan to Gide: The Homosexual in History. LC 64-5339. 1964-69. 10.00 (ISBN 0-685-18955-4). Nosbooks.
Gay, A. Nolder. The View from the Closet: Essays on Gay Life & Liberation, 1973-1977. LC 78-105579. 1978. pap. 3.00 (ISBN 0-9601570-0-X). Union Park.
Gay Left Collective. Homosexuality: Power & Politics. LC 80-40640. 288p. 1980. text ed. 17.95x (ISBN 0-8052-8062-6, Pub. by Allison & Busby England); pap. 7.95 (ISBN 0-8052-8061-8). Schocken.
Gibson, E. Lawrence. Get Off My Ship: Ensign Berg vs. the U.S. Navy. 1978. pap. 4.95 (ISBN 0-380-40071-5, 40071). Avon.
Goldstein, Phillip. Magic Men. 1977. pap. 3.95 (ISBN 0-686-17791-6). IHI Pr.
Goodich, Michael. The Unmentionable Vice: Homosexuality in the Later Medieval Period. LC 78-13276. 164p. 1979. 16.50 (ISBN 0-87436-287-3). ABC-Clio.
Gottlieb, David I. The Gay Tapes: A Candid Discussion About Male Homosexuality. LC 76-57987. 1977. 8.95 (ISBN 0-8128-2262-5); pap. 2.50 (ISBN 0-8128-7021-2). Stein & Day.
Grief, Martin, compiled by. The Gay Engagement Calendar 1981. (Illus.). 128p. 1980. pap. 5.95 (ISBN 0-312-31795-6). St Martin.
Hanckel, Frances & Cunningham, John. A Way of Love, a Way of Life: A Young Person's Introduction to What It Means to Be Gay. LC 79-2424. (Illus.). (gr. 9-12). 1979. 8.50 (ISBN 0-688-41907-0); lib. bdg. 8.16 (ISBN 0-688-51907-5). Lothrop.
Harris, Mervyn. The Dilly Boys. 126p. 1974. Repr. of 1973 ed. 8.50 (ISBN 0-87953-305-6, NP). Inscape Corp.
Harry, Joseph & Devall, William B. The Social Organization of Gay Males. LC 78-8381. (Praeger Special Studies). 1978. 25.95 (ISBN 0-03-044696-1). Praeger.
Harry, Joseph & Das, Man S., eds. Homosexuality in International Perspective. 140p. 1980. text ed. 18.95 (ISBN 0-7069-1090-7, Pub by Vikas India). Advent NY.
Heger, Heinz. The Men with the Pink Triangle. Fernbach, David, tr. LC 80-69205. (Illus.). 120p. (Orig.). 1980. pap. 4.95 (ISBN 0-932870-06-6). Carrier Pigeon.
Henry, George W. Sex Variants: A Study of Homosexual Patterns, 2 vols. LC 78-22292. (The Gay Experience). (Illus.). Repr. of 1941 ed. Set. 75.00 (ISBN 0-404-61525-2). AMS Pr.
Hocquenghem, Guy. Homosexual Desire. Dangoor, Daniella, tr. from Fr. 144p. 1980. 9.95x (ISBN 0-85031-206-X, Pub. by Allison & Busby England); pap. 5.95 (ISBN 0-85031-207-8, Pub. by Allison & Busby England). Schocken.
Hoffman, Martin. Gay World: Male Homosexuality & the Social Creation of Evil. LC 68-54131. 1968. 11.95x (ISBN 0-465-02635-4). Basic.
Humphreys, Laud. Out of the Closets: The Sociology of Homosexual Liberation. 192p. 1972. pap. 2.45 (ISBN 0-13-645317-1, Spec). P-H.
--Tearoom Trade: Impersonal Sex in Public Places. rev. ed. LC 74-22642. 1975. text ed. 18.95x (ISBN 0-202-30282-2); pap. 7.50x (ISBN 0-202-30283-0). Aldine Pub.
Hunt, Morton. Gay: What You Should Know About Homosexuality. 1979. pap. 1.95 (ISBN 0-671-82317-5). PB.
--Gay: What You Should Know About Homosexuality. LC 77-76806. 210p. (gr. 7 up). 1977. 7.95 (ISBN 0-374-38754-0). FS&G.
IHI Staff. Who Was Gay. 1977. pap. 3.00 (ISBN 0-686-17784-3). IHI Pr.
IHI Staff, et al. A Homophilics Workbook. Dey, Richard, ed. 1977. pap. 5.95 (ISBN 0-686-17785-1). IHI Pr.
Jackman, Abraham I. The Paranoid Homosexual Basis of Anti-Semitism. 1979. 8.95 (ISBN 0-533-03340-3). Vantage.
Jay, Karla & Young, Allen. The Gay Report. LC 78-24056. 1979. 14.95 (ISBN 0-671-40013-4). Summit Bks.
Johnston, Gordon. Which Way Out of the Men's Room? LC 76-63542. 1979. 12.95 (ISBN 0-498-02409-1). A S Barnes.
Jones, Clinton R. Homosexuality & Counseling. LC 74-76922. 144p. (Orig.). 1974. pap. 3.95 (ISBN 0-8006-1301-5, 1-1301). Fortress.
Kantrowitz, Arnie. Under the Rainbow: Growing up Gay. LC 76-30442. (Illus.). 1977. 8.95 (ISBN 0-688-03191-9). Morrow.
Katz, Jonathan. Coming Out: A Documentary Play About Gay Life & Liberation in the U.S.A. new ed. LC 75-12327. (Homosexuality). 1975. 15.00x (ISBN 0-405-07399-2). Arno.
--Gay American History: Lesbians & Gay Men in the U.S.A., a Documentary. LC 76-2039. (Illus.). 1976. pap. 9.95 (ISBN 0-690-01165-2, TYC-T). T Y Crowell.
--Gay American History: Lesbians & Gay Men in the U.S.A., a Documentary. LC 76-2039. (Illus.). 1976. pap. 9.95 (ISBN 0-690-01165-2, TYC-T). T Y Crowell.
Katz, Jonathan, ed. Documents of the Homosexual Rights Movement in Germany, 1836-1927. LC 75-12326. (Homosexuality). (German & French.). 1975. 45.00x (ISBN 0-405-07367-4). Arno.
--Gay American History. 1978. pap. 3.95 (ISBN 0-380-40550-4, 40550, Discus). Avon.
--A Gay Bibliography: Eight Bibliographies on Lesbian & Male Homosexuality: an Original Anthology. LC 75-12317. (Homosexuality). (Illus.). 1975. 25.00x (ISBN 0-405-07349-6). Arno.
--A Gay News Chronology, 1969-1975: Index & Abstracts of Articles from the New York Times. LC 75-14265. (Homosexuality). 1975. 12.00x (ISBN 0-405-07409-3). Arno.
--Government Versus Homosexuals: An Original Anthology. LC 75-12320. (Homosexuality). (Illus.). 1975. Repr. 12.00x (ISBN 0-405-07350-X). Arno.
--Government Versus Homosexuals: An Original Anthology. LC 75-12320. (Homosexuality). (Illus.). 1975. Repr. 12.00x (ISBN 0-405-07350-X). Arno.
--A Homosexual Emancipation Miscellany, 1835-1952: An Original Anthology. LC 75-12318. (Homosexuality). (Illus.). 1975. Repr. 15.00x (ISBN 0-405-07370-4). Arno.
--Homosexuality: Lesbians & Gay Men in Society, History & Literature. (Illus.). 1975. 982.00x (ISBN 0-405-07348-8). Arno.
--Lesbianism & Feminism in Germany, 1895-1910: An Original Anthology. LC 75-12332. (Homosexuality). 1975. Repr. 30.00 (ISBN 0-405-07369-0). Arno.
Kleinberg, Seymour. Alienated Affections. 320p. 1981. 13.95 (ISBN 0-312-01857-6). St Martin.
Kopay, David & Young, Perry D. The David Kopay Story. LC 76-29229. 1980. pap. 5.95 (ISBN 0-87795-290-6). Arbor Hse.
--David Kopay Story. LC 76-29229. 1977. 8.95 (ISBN 0-87795-145-4). Arbor Hse.
Koranyi, Erwin K. Transsexuality in the Male: The Spectrum of Gender Dysphoria. (Behavioral Science & Law Ser.). (Illus.). 192p. 1980. text ed. 18.75 (ISBN 0-398-03924-0). C C Thomas.

Kranz, Sheldon, et al. The H Persuasion: How Persons Have Permanently Changed from Homosexuality Through the Study of Aesthetic Realism with Eli Siegel. LC 70-161981. 1971. 4.95 (ISBN 0-910492-14-X); pap. 2.50 (ISBN 0-910492-26-3). Definition.

Krich, Aron M. Homosexuals: As Seen by Themselves & Thirty Authorities. 1962. pap. 2.25 (ISBN 0-8065-0123-5). Citadel Pr.

Kronemeyer, Robert, et al. Overcoming Homosexuality. LC 79-23644. 160p. 1980. 8.95 (ISBN 0-02-566850-1). Macmillan.

LaHaye, Tim. The Unhappy Gays. 1978. pap. 4.95 (ISBN 0-8423-7797-2). Tyndale.

Lane, Erskine. Game Texts. 15.00 (ISBN 0-917342-58-5); pap. 4.95 (ISBN 0-917342-59-3). Gay Sunshine.

Levine, Martin P. Gay Men: The Sociology of Male Homosexuality. LC 78-69628. 1979. pap. 5.95 (ISBN 0-06-090695-2, CN 695, CN). Har-Row.

Leyland, Winston. Gay Sunshine Interviews, Vol I. 15.00 (ISBN 0-917342-60-7); pap. 10.00 (ISBN 0-917342-61-5). Gay Sunshine.

--Now the Volcano: An Anthology of Latin. Lane, Erkine, tr. 20.00 (ISBN 0-917342-66-6); pap. 7.95 (ISBN 0-917342-67-4). Gay Sunshine.

--Orgasms of Light: The Gay Sunshine Anthology. (Poetry, Short Fiction, Graphics). (Illus.). 1977. lib. bdg. 20.00 (ISBN 0-917342-53-4). Gay Sunshine.

Leyland, Winston, ed. Angels of the Lyre: Anthology of Gay Poetry. LC 75-19135. (Illus.). 206p. 1975. 10.00x (ISBN 0-915572-14-1); pap. 5.95 (ISBN 0-915572-13-3). Panjandrum.

Licata, Salvatore J. & Petersen, Robert, eds. Historical Perspectives on Homosexuality. LC 80-6262. 240p. 1981. 14.95 (ISBN 0-8128-2810-0). Stein & Day.

Lind, Earl, et al. Autobiography of an Androgyne. LC 75-12333. (Homosexuality: Lesbians & Gay Men in Society, History & Literature Ser.). 1975. Repr. of 1918 ed. 18.00x (ISBN 0-405-07400-X). Arno.

Loeffler, Donald L. An Analysis of the Treatment of the Homosexual Character in Dramas Produced in the New York Theater from 1950-1968. new ed. LC 75-14262. (Homosexuality). 1975. Repr. 15.00x (ISBN 0-405-07398-4). Arno.

Loraine, J. A., ed. Understanding Homosexuality. 217p. 1974. 16.95 (ISBN 0-444-19519-X). Elsevier.

McNeill, John. The Church & the Homosexual. 1976. 10.00 (ISBN 0-8362-0683-5). Andrews & McMeel.

Marmor, Judd. Homosexual Behavior: A Modern Reappraisal. LC 78-24659. 1980. text ed. 27.50x (ISBN 0-465-03045-9). Basic.

Marotta, Toby. The Politics of Homosexuality. 384p. 1981. 16.95 (ISBN 0-395-29477-0); pap. 9.95 (ISBN 0-395-31338-4). HM.

Masters, William H. & Johnson, Virginia. Homosexuality in Perspective. 1979. 19.95 (ISBN 0-316-54984-3). Little.

Mayne, Xavier. The Intersexes: A History of Similsexualism As a Problem in Social Life. facsimile ed. LC 75-12338. (Homosexuality Ser.). 1975. Repr. of 1908 ed. 40.00x (ISBN 0-405-07364-X). Arno.

Messer, Alfred. When You Are Concerned with Homosexuality. LC 79-55861. (When Books). (Orig.). 1980. pap. 2.45 (ISBN 0-87029-161-0, 20262). Abbey.

Meyers, Jeffrey. Homosexuality & Literature: 1890-1930. 1977. lib. bdg. 13.95x (ISBN 0-7735-0300-5). McGill-Queens U Pr.

Morgan, Patricia & Hoffman, Paul. The Man-Maid Doll. 224p. 1973. 7.95 (ISBN 0-8184-0158-3). Lyle Stuart.

Morris, Paul. Shadow of Sodom. 1978. pap. 3.95 (ISBN 0-8423-5870-6). Tyndale.

Moses, A. Elfin & Hawkins, Robert O., Jr. Counseling Lesbian Women & Gay Men: A Life-Issues Approach. 320p. 1981. pap. text ed. 12.95 (ISBN 0-8016-3563-2). Mosby.

Norton, Rictor H. The Homosexual Literary Tradition. 432p. 1974. 75.00 (ISBN 0-87700-204-5). Revisionist Pr.

Parker, William. Homosexuality Bibliography: Supplement, 1970-1975. LC 77-1114. 1977. 15.00 (ISBN 0-8108-1050-6). Scarecrow.

Plummer, Kenneth, ed. The Making of the Modern Homosexual. 280p. 1981. 22.50x (ISBN 0-389-20159-6). B&N.

Political & Social Action in Homophile Organizations. LC 75-13729. (Homosexuality). 1975. 15.00x (ISBN 0-405-07372-0). Arno.

Raile, pseud. A Defense of Uranian Love. LC 78-22240. (The Gay Experience). Repr. of 1928 ed. 11.50 (ISBN 0-404-61531-7). AMS Pr.

Rechy, John. The Sexual Outlaw: A Documentary. LC 76-54487. 1977. 8.95 (ISBN 0-394-41343-1, GP787). Grove.

Rector, Frank. The Nazi Extermination of Homosexuals. LC 79-3708. (Illus.). 256p. 1980. 12.95 (ISBN 0-8128-2729-5). Stein & Day.

Reynols, Robert. The Homaphile Aristos. 1977. pap. 3.50 (ISBN 0-686-17786-X). IHI Pr.

Richardson, Diane & Hart, John. The Theory & Practice of Homosexuality. 212p. (Orig.). 1981. pap. 11.95 (ISBN 0-7100-0838-4). Routledge & Kegan.

Richmond, Len & Noguera, Gary, eds. The New Gay Liberation Book. LC 78-54081. (Illus.). 1979. 14.00 (ISBN 0-87867-070-X); pap. 5.95 (ISBN 0-87867-071-8). Ramparts.

Rodgers, Bruce. Gay Talk: A (Sometimes Outrageous) Dictionary of Gay Slang. LC 79-13972. 1979. pap. 4.95 (ISBN 0-399-50392-7, Perigee). Putnam.

Rogers, Bruce. Gay Talk. LC 79-13972. 1979. pap. 4.95 (ISBN 0-399-50392-7, Perigee). Putnam.

Rosenfels, Paul. Homosexuality: The Psychology of the Creative Process. LC 78-146467. 1971. 5.95 (ISBN 0-87212-002-3). Libra.

--Homosexuality: The Psychology of the Creative Process. LC 78-146467. 1973. pap. 1.95 (ISBN 0-87212-045-7). Libra.

Rowan, Robert L. & Gillette, Paul G. The Gay Health Guide. (Modern Medicine Ser.). 1978. 9.95 (ISBN 0-316-31356-4). Little.

Ruitenbeek, Hendrik. Homosexuality & Creative Genius. 1965. 20.00 (ISBN 0-8392-1149-X). Astor-Honor.

Ruitenbeek, Hendrik M., ed. Homosexuality a Changing Picture: A Contemporary Study & Interpretation. 1974. text ed. 7.75x (ISBN 0-285-62061-4). Humanities.

Russo, Vito. The Celluloid Closet: Homosexuality in the Movies. LC 79-1682. (Illus.). 256p. 1981. 15.00 (ISBN 0-06-013704-5, HarpT); pap. 7.95 (ISBN 0-06-090871-8, CN871, HarpT). Har-Row.

Saghir, Marcel T. & Robins, Eli. Male & Female Homosexuality: A Comprehensive Investigation. LC 72-91195. 350p. 1973. 17.50 (ISBN 0-683-07490-3). Krieger.

Sanders, Dennis. Gay Source: A Catalog for Men. LC 77-1896. (Illus.). 288p. 1977. pap. 6.95 (ISBN 0-698-10809-4). Coward.

Schofield, M., pseud. A Minority. LC 76-7604. 1976. Repr. of 1960 ed. lib. bdg. 15.50x (ISBN 0-8371-8877-6, SCAMI). Greenwood.

Schur, Edwin M. Crimes Without Victims - Deviant Behavior & Public Policy: Abortion, Homosexuality, Drug Addiction. (Orig.). 1965. pap. 3.95 (ISBN 0-13-192930-5, S111, Spec). P-H.

Silverstein, Charles. A Family Matter: A Parent's Guide to Homosexuality. 1978. 8.95 (ISBN 0-07-057429-4, GB); pap. 3.95 (ISBN 0-07-057452-9). McGraw.

--Man to Man: Gay Couples in America. LC 80-23566. 384p. 1981. 12.95 (ISBN 0-688-00041-X). Morrow.

--Man to Man: Gay Couples in America. LC 80-23566. 384p. 1981. 12.95 (ISBN 0-688-00041-X). Morrow.

Silverstein, Charles & White, Edmund. The Joy of Gay Sex. (Illus.). 1978. pap. 7.95 (ISBN 0-671-24079-X, Fireside). S&S.

Simpson, Ruth. From the Closet to the Courts: The Lesbian Transition. 1977. pap. 2.25 (ISBN 0-14-004353-5). Penguin.

Slater, Don & Copely, Ursula E., eds. Directory of Homosexual Organizations & Publications. rev. ed. (Orig.). 1979. pap. 5.00 (ISBN 0-686-26160-7). Homosexual Info.

Socarides, Charles. Homosexuality. LC 78-13844. 1978. 35.00x (ISBN 0-87668-355-3). Aronson.

Spada, James. Spada Report: The Newest Survey of Gay Male Sexuality. 1979. pap. 2.50 (ISBN 0-451-08660-0, E8660, Sig). NAL.

Stambolian, George & Marks, Elaine, eds. Homosexualities & French Literature: Cultural Contexts, Critical Texts. LC 78-25659. 1979. 24.50x (ISBN 0-8014-1186-6). Cornell U Pr.

Steakley, James D. The Homosexual Emancipation Movement in Germany. LC 75-13728. (Homosexuality). (Illus.). 1975. 12.00x (ISBN 0-405-07366-6). Arno.

Stekel, Wilhelm. Homosexual Neurosis. 8.95 (ISBN 0-87523-029-6). Emerson.

Switzer, David K. & Switzer, Shirley A. Parents of the Homosexual. LC 80-13748. (Christian Care Books). 1980. pap. 5.95 (ISBN 0-664-24327-4). Westminster.

Symonds, John A. Problem in Greek Ethics. LC 71-163126. (Studies in Philosophy, No. 40). 1971. lib. bdg. 31.95 (ISBN 0-8383-1253-5). Haskell.

--A Problem in Modern Ethics. LC 73-173185. Repr. of 1896 ed. 10.75 (ISBN 0-405-09019-6, Pub. by Blom). Arno.

Tarnovskii, Veniamin M. Anthropological Legal, & Medical Studies on Pederasty in Europe. LC 78-22239. (The Gay Experience). Repr. of 1933 ed. 24.50 (ISBN 0-404-61530-9). AMS Pr.

Tiefenbrun, Ruth. Moment of Torment: An Interpretation of Franz Kafka's Short Stories. LC 72-8911. (Crosscurrents-Modern Critiques Ser.). 176p. 1973. 6.95 (ISBN 0-8093-0620-4). S Ill U Pr.

Tobin, Kay & Wicker, Randy. The Gay Crusaders. LC 75-12349. (Homosexuality). (Illus.). 1975. Repr. 12.00x (ISBN 0-405-07374-7). Arno.

Tripp, C. A. Homosexual Matrix. LC 75-6987. 336p. 1975. 10.00 (ISBN 0-07-065201-5, GB). McGraw.

--Homosexual Matrix. 1976. pap. 2.75 (ISBN 0-451-08898-0, E8898, Sig). NAL.

Tsang, Dan, ed. The Age Taboo: Gay Male Sexuality, Power & Consent. 180p. (Orig.). 1981. pap. 5.95 (ISBN 0-932870-13-9). Alyson Pubns.

Twiss, Harold L., ed. Homosexuality & the Christian Faith. LC 77-25112. 1978. pap. 3.95 (ISBN 0-8170-0794-6). Judson.

Vanggaard, Thorkil. Phallos: A Symbol & Its History in the Male World. LC 72-80553. (Illus.). 266p. 1972. text ed. 15.00 (ISBN 0-8236-4135-X); pap. text ed. 4.95 (ISBN 0-8236-8192-0, 024135). Intl Univs Pr.

Vedder, Clyde B. & King, Patricia G. Problems of Homosexuality in Corrections. 80p. 1967. photocopy ed. spiral 9.75 (ISBN 0-398-01976-2). C C Thomas.

Vining, Donald. A Gay Diary, 1954 to 1967. LC 78-71282. (Illus.). 485p. 1981. 14.95 (ISBN 0-9602270-4-0); pap. 9.95 (ISBN 0-9602270-5-9). Pepys Pr.

Vojir, Dan. The Sunny Side of Castro Street. (Illus., Orig.). 1981. pap. 6.95 (ISBN 0-89407-034-7). Strawberry Hill.

Weinberg, George. Society & the Healthy Homosexual. 160p. 1973. pap. 1.95 (ISBN 0-385-05083-6, Anch). Doubleday.

Weinberg, Martin S. & Williams, Colin J. Male Homosexuals: Their Problems & Adaptations. 480p. 1975. pap. 2.95 (ISBN 0-14-004046-3). Penguin.

Weininger, Otto. Physical Attraction & the Theory of Homosexuality. (Illus.). 1979. deluxe ed. 49.85 (ISBN 0-930582-36-5). Gloucester Art.

Weltge, Ralph, ed. Same Sex: An Appraisal of Homosexuality. LC 71-88184. 1969. pap. 3.95 (ISBN 0-8298-0118-9). Pilgrim NY.

West, D. J. Homosexuality Re-Examined. rev. ed. LC 76-51477. 1977. 22.50x (ISBN 0-8166-0812-1). U of Minn Pr.

Westermarck, Edvard A. The Origin & Development of the Moral Ideas, 2 vols. LC 78-22241. (The Gay Experience). Repr. of 1908 ed. Set. 64.50 (ISBN 0-404-61532-5). AMS Pr.

Williams, Don. The Bond That Breaks: Will Homosexuality Split the Church? LC 78-52019. pap. 4.95 (ISBN 0-8307-0668-2, 5411408). Regal.

Woods, Richard. Another Kind of Love. 1977. 8.95 (ISBN 0-88347-075-6). Thomas More.

--Another Kind of Love: Homosexuality & Spirituality. LC 77-27729. 1978. pap. 1.95 (ISBN 0-385-14312-5, Im). Doubleday.

Wright, Stephen. Brief Encyclopedia of Homosexuality. LC 78-62675. 1978. pap. 5.95 (ISBN 0-9601904-0-6). Stephen Wright.

X, Jacobus. Crossways of Sex in Eroto-Pathology, 2 vols. LC 78-22242. (The Gay Experience). Repr. of 1904 ed. Set. 45.00 (ISBN 0-685-91300-7). AMS Pr.

Young, Ian. Male Homosexual in Literature: A Bibliography. LC 75-25611. 1975. 11.00 (ISBN 0-8108-0861-7). Scarecrow.

HOMOSEXUALITY–LAW AND LEGISLATION

Works on the criminal aspects of homosexuality are entered under the heading sodomy.
see also Sodomy

Curry, Hayden & Clifford, Denis. A Legal Guide for Gay & Lesbian Couples. LC 80-18278. 288p. 1980. 10.95 (ISBN 0-201-08307-8). A-W.

Knutson, Donald C., ed. Homosexuality & the Law. LC 79-23673. (Research on Homosexuality Ser. of Journal of Homosexuality: Vol. 5, Nos. 1-2). 1980. text ed. 19.95 (ISBN 0-917724-14-3); pap. text ed. 9.95 (ISBN 0-917724-15-1). Haworth Pr.

Weeks, Jeffrey. Coming Out: Homosexual Politics in Britain from the 19th Century to the Present. 7.95 (ISBN 0-7043-3175-6, Pub. by Quartet England). Charles River Bks.

HOMOSEXUALITY AND CHRISTIANITY

Atkinson, David. Homosexuals in the Christian Fellowship. 128p. (Orig.). 1981. pap. 8.95 (ISBN 0-8028-1890-0). Eerdmans.

Boswell, John. Christianity, Social Tolerance, & Homosexuality: Gay People in Western Europe from the Beginning of the Christian Era to the Fourteenth Century. LC 79-11171. (Illus.). xviii, 424p. 1980. 27.50 (ISBN 0-226-06710-6); pap. 9.95 (ISBN 0-02-260611-4). U of Chicago Pr.

Davidson, Alex. The Returns of Love: A Christian View of Homosexuality. LC 70-131594. 1977. pap. 2.50 (ISBN 0-87784-698-7). Inter-Varsity.

Field, David. The Homosexual Way: A Christian Option? LC 78-13880. 1979. pap. 1.95 (ISBN 0-87784-324-4). Inter-Varsity.

Gangel, Kenneth O. The Gospel & the Gay. LC 78-10378. 1978. pap. 3.95 (ISBN 0-8407-5658-5). Nelson.

Goodich, Michael. The Unmentionable Vice. LC 78-13276. 179p. 1980. pap. 6.95 (ISBN 0-87436-300-4). Ross-Erikson.

Horner, Tom. Homosexuality & the Judeo-Christian Tradition: An Annotated Bibliography. LC 81-889. (ATLA Bibliography Ser.: No. 5). 144p. 1981. 10.00 (ISBN 0-8108-1412-9). Scarecrow.

Keysor, Charles W., ed. What You Should Know About Homosexuality. pap. 6.95 (ISBN 0-310-38231-9). Zondervan.

Linehan, Kevin. Such Were Some of You. LC 79-12178. 1979. pap. 5.95 (ISBN 0-8361-1890-1). Herald Pr.

Malloy, Edward A. Homosexuality & the Christian Way of Life. LC 81-40385. 382p. (Orig.). 1981. lib. bdg. 24.00 (ISBN 0-8191-1794-3); pap. text ed. 13.25 (ISBN 0-8191-1795-1). U Pr of Amer.

Scanzoni, Letha & Mollenkott, Virginia R. Is the Homosexual My Neighbor? Another Christian View. LC 77-20445. 176p. 1980. pap. 5.95 (ISBN 0-06-067076-2, RD 337, HarpR). Har-Row.

Smith, Herbert F. Sexual Inversion: The Questions-with Catholic Answers. 1979. 2.95 (ISBN 0-8198-0612-9); pap. 1.95 (ISBN 0-8198-0613-7). Dghtrs St Paul.

Walker, Mitch. Visionary Love: A Spirit Book of Gay Mythology & Transmutational Faerie. LC 80-51514. (Illus.). 120p. (Orig.). 1980. pap. 6.25 (ISBN 0-9604450-0-5). Treeroots.

Williams, Don. The Bond That Breaks: Will Homosexuality Split the Church? LC 78-52019. pap. 4.95 (ISBN 0-8307-0668-2, 5411408). Regal.

HOMOSEXUALS

The Autobiography of an Englishman P"Y". 176p. 1980. 15.00x (ISBN 0-89771-001-0). State Mutual Bk.

Borhek, Mary V. My Son Eric. LC 79-16161. (Orig.). 1979. 8.95 (ISBN 0-8298-0372-6). Pilgrim NY.

Brown, Howard. Familiar Faces, Hidden Lives: The Story of Homosexual Men in America Today. LC 77-3423. 1977. pap. 2.95 (ISBN 0-15-630120-2, Harv). HarBraceJ.

Dawson, Terry. My Heaven to Hell. 1979. 6.95 (ISBN 0-533-04104-X). Vantage.

Delph, Edward W. The Silent Community: Public Homosexual Encounters. LC 78-629. 1978. 18.95x (ISBN 0-8039-0990-X); pap. 8.95x (ISBN 0-8039-0991-8). Sage.

Denneny, Michael. Lovers: Story of Two Men. 1979. pap. 4.95 (ISBN 0-380-43091-6, 43091). Avon.

Devi, Shakuntala. The World of Homosexuals. 1977. text ed. 10.50 (ISBN 0-7069-0478-8). Verry.

Ebert, Alan. The Homosexuals. 1977. 9.95 (ISBN 0-02-534770-5). Macmillan.

Gay Sunshine Press, compiled by. Meat: How Men Look, Act, Talk, Walk, Dress, Undress, Taste & Smell: True Homosexual Experiences from S.T.H. (Illus.). 192p. (Orig.). 1981. pap. 10.00 (ISBN 0-917342-78-X). Gay Sunshine.

Halloran, Joe. Understanding Homosexual Persons: Straight Answers from Gays. 1979. 6.00 (ISBN 0-682-49468-2). Exposition.

Levine, Martin P., ed. Gay Men: The Sociology of Male Homosexuality. LC 78-69628. 1979. 16.95 (ISBN 0-06-012586-1, HarpT). Har-Row.

Malone, John. Straight Women-Gay Men: A Special Relationship. 1980. 8.95 (ISBN 0-8037-8174-1). Dial.

Mitchell, Pam, ed. Pink Triangles: Radical Perspectives on Gay Liberation. LC 80-67090. 192p. (Orig.). 1980. pap. 4.95 (ISBN 0-932870-03-1). Alyson Pubns.

Rechy, John. The Sexual Outlaw: A Documentary. 1977. pap. 2.25 (ISBN 0-440-17667-0, D17667, Dist. by Dell). Grove.

Rivers, Walter C. Walt Whitman's Anomaly. LC 77-12520. 1977. Repr. lib. bdg. 15.00 (ISBN 0-8414-7357-9). Folcroft.

The Straight or Gay Book. 80p. (Orig.). 1974. pap. 1.25 (ISBN 0-8431-0267-5). Price Stern.

Vining, Donald. A Gay Diary 1933-1946. LC 78-71282. 1979. 14.95 (ISBN 0-9602270-0-8); pap. 9.95 (ISBN 0-9602270-1-6). Pepys Pr.

--A Gay Diary: 1946-1954, Vol. 2. LC 78-71282. (Illus.). 483p. (Orig.). 1980. 14.95 (ISBN 0-9602270-2-4); pap. 9.95 (ISBN 0-9602270-3-2). Pepys Pr.

White, Edmund. States of Desire: Travels in Gay America. 1980. 12.95 (ISBN 0-525-22235-9). Dutton.

Woodman, Natalie J. & Lenna, Harry R. Counseling with Gay Men & Women: A Guide for Facilitating Positive Life-Styles. LC 80-8002. (Social & Behavioral Science Ser.). 1980. text ed. 13.95x (ISBN 0-87589-468-2). Jossey-Bass.

Youth Liberation, ed. Growing up Gay. 2nd ed. (Illus.). 1978. 2.00 (ISBN 0-918946-08-5). Youth Lib.

HOMOTOPY THEORY

Adams, J. Frank. Infinite Loop Spaces. (Annals of Mathematics Studies Ser.: No. 90). 1978. 18.50x (ISBN 0-691-08207-3); pap. 7.50 (ISBN 0-691-08206-5). Princeton U Pr.

--Stable Homotopy Theory. 3rd ed. LC 70-90867. (Lecture Notes in Mathematics: Vol. 3). 1969. pap. 10.70 (ISBN 0-387-04598-8). Springer-Verlag.

Antonelli, P. L., et al. Concordance-Homotopy Groups of Geometric Automorphism Groups. LC 73-171479. (Lecture Notes in Mathematics: Vol. 215). 1971. pap. 8.20 (ISBN 0-387-05560-6). Springer-Verlag.

Arkowitz, M. & Curjel, C. R. Groups of Homotopy Classes: Rank Formualas & Homotopy - Commutativity. 2nd ed. (Lecture Notes in Mathematics: Vol. 4). (Orig.). 1967. pap. 10.70 (ISBN 0-387-03900-7). Springer-Verlag.

Barratt, M. B. & Mahowald, M. E., eds. Geometric Applications of Homotopy Theory I: Proceedings, Evanston, March 21-26, 1977. LC 78-16038. (Lecture Notes in Mathematics: Vol. 657). 1978. pap. 21.30 (ISBN 0-387-08858-X). Springer-Verlag.

Boardman, J. M. & Vogt, R. M. Homotopy Invariant Algebraic Structures on Topological Spaces. LC 73-13427. (Lecture Notes in Mathematics: Vol. 347). pap. 13.40 (ISBN 0-387-06479-6). Springer-Verlag.

Boltyanskii, V. G. & Postnikov, M. M. Two Papers on Homotopy Theory of Continuous Mappings. LC 51-5559. (Translation Ser.: No. 2, Vol. 7). 1957. 24.40 (ISBN 0-8218-1707-8, TRANS 2-7). Am Math.

Bousfield, A. K. & Gugenheim, V. K. On PL DeRham Theory & Rational Homotypy Type. LC 76-44398. (Memoirs: No. 179). 1976. 11.20 (ISBN 0-8218-2179-2). Am Math.

Bousfield, A. K. & Kan, D. M. Homotopy Limits, Completions & Localizations. LC 72-95678. (Lecture Notes in Mathematics: Vol. 304). 348p. 1973. pap. 12.30 (ISBN 0-387-06105-3). Springer-Verlag.

Burghelea, D. & Lashof, R. Groups of Automarphisms of Manifolds. (Lecture Notes in Mathematics Ser.: Vol. 473). 156p. 1975. pap. 10.00 (ISBN 0-387-07182-2). Springer-Verlag.

Cohen, J. M. Stable Homotopy. LC 77-139950. (Lecture Notes in Mathematics: Vol. 165). 1970. pap. 8.20 (ISBN 0-387-05192-9). Springer-Verlag.

Cohen, M. M. A Course in Simple Homotopy Theory. LC 72-93439. (Graduate Texts in Mathematics: Vol. 10). (Illus.). 114p. 1973. text ed. 15.50 (ISBN 0-387-90056-X); pap. text ed. 10.20 (ISBN 0-387-90055-1). Springer-Verlag.

Cohen, Ralph L. Odd Primary Infinite Families in Stable Homotopy Theory. LC 80-28537. (MEMO Ser.: No. 242). Date not set. 5.60 (ISBN 0-8218-2242-X). Am Math.

Edwards, D. A. & Hastings, H. M. Cech & Steenrod Homotopy Theories with Applications to Geometric Topology. (Lecture Notes in Mathematics: Vol. 542). 1976. soft cover 15.30 (ISBN 3-540-07863-0). Springer-Verlag.

Gabriel, Pierre & Zisman, M. Calculus of Fractions & Homotopy Theory. (Ergebnisse der Mathematik und Ihrer Grenzgebiete: Vol. 35). (Illus.). 1967. 26.30 (ISBN 0-387-03777-2). Springer-Verlag.

Gray, Brayton. Homotopy Theory: An Introduction to Algebraic Topology. 1975. 41.50 (ISBN 0-12-296050-5). Acad Pr.

Griffiths, P. A. & Morgan, J. Homotopy Theory & Differential Forms. 1981. text ed. write for info. (ISBN 3-7643-3041-4). Birkhauser.

Hilton, P. Homotopy Theory & Duality. (Notes on Mathematics & Its Applications Ser). 1965. 26.50x (ISBN 0-677-00295-5). Gordon.

Hilton, P. J., ed. Localization in Group Theory & Homotopy Theory & Related Topics. (Lecture Notes in Mathematics: Vol. 418). 185p. 1975. pap. 10.90 (ISBN 0-387-06963-1). Springer-Verlag.

Hilton, Peter J. Introduction to Homotopy Theory. (Cambridge Tracts in Mathematics & Mathematical Physics: No. 43). 1953. 21.50 (ISBN 0-521-05265-3). Cambridge U Pr.

Hu, S. T. Homotopy Theory. (Pure & Applied Mathematics Ser.: Vol. 8). 1959. 50.00 (ISBN 0-12-358450-7). Acad Pr.

Ize, Jorge. Bifurcation Theory for Fredholm Operators. LC 76-25186. (Memoirs of the American Mathematical Society: 174). 1976. 12.00 (ISBN 0-8218-2174-1). Am Math.

Johannson, K. Homotopy Equivalence of Three-Manifolds with Boundaries. (Lecture Notes in Mathematics: Vol. 761). 303p. 1979. pap. 18.90 (ISBN 0-387-09714-7). Springer-Verlag.

Mahowald, Mark. Metastable Homotopy of S-To-The-N. LC 52-42839. (Memoirs: No. 72). 1967. pap. 7.20 (ISBN 0-8218-1272-6, MEMO-72). Am Math.

Milgram, J. Unstable Homotopy from the Stable Point of View. LC 73-2121. (Lecture Notes in Mathematics: Vol. 368). v, 109p. 1974. pap. 8.30 (ISBN 0-387-06655-1). Springer-Verlag.

Milnor, John W. Morse Theory. (Annals of Mathematics Studies: Vol. 51). (Orig.). 1963. pap. 14.00 (ISBN 0-691-08008-9). Princeton U Pr.

Neisendorfer, Joseph. Primary Homotopy Theory. LC 80-12109. (Memoirs of the American Mathematical Society Ser.). 1980. 4.80 (ISBN 0-8218-2232-2, MEMO-232). Am Math.

Quillen, D. G. Homotopical Algebra. (Lecture Notes in Mathematics: Vol. 43). (Orig.). 1967. pap. 10.70 (ISBN 0-387-03914-7). Springer-Verlag.

Switzer, R. M. Algebraic Topology-Homotopy & Homology. (Die Grundlehren der Mathematischen Wissenschaften Ser.: Vol. 212). 526p. 1975. 66.60 (ISBN 0-387-06758-2). Springer-Verlag.

Tierney, Myles. Categorical Constructions in Stable Homotopy Theory. LC 70-77478. (Lecture Notes in Mathematics: Vol. 87). (Orig.). 1969. pap. 10.70 (ISBN 0-387-04606-2). Springer-Verlag.

Whitehead, George W. Recent Advances in Homotopy Theory. LC 79-145639. (CBMS Regional Conference Series in Mathematics: No. 5). iv, 82p. 1970. 8.40 (ISBN 0-8218-1654-3, CBMS-5). Am Math.

HONDA, TOSHIAKI, 1744-1821

Keene, Donald. Japanese Discovery of Europe, 1720-1830. rev. ed. LC 69-13180. (Illus.). 1969. 10.00x (ISBN 0-8047-0668-9); pap. 5.95x (ISBN 0-8047-0669-7). Stanford U Pr.

HONDA–HISTORY–SOURCES

Leonard, Irving A., ed. Spanish Approach to Pensacola 1689-1693. LC 67-24720. (Quivira Society Publications, Vol. 9). 1967. Repr. of 1939 ed. 12.00 (ISBN 0-405-00083-9). Arno.

HONDA AUTOMOBILE

see Automobiles, Foreign–Types–Honda

HONDA MOTORCYCLE

Brotherwood, Clive. Honda Owner's Workshop Manual: One Hundred & One Twenty-Five Singles '70-75. new ed. (Owners Workshop Manuals Ser.: No. 188). 1979. 8.50 (ISBN 0-85696-188-4, Pub. by J H Haynes England). Haynes Pubns.

Chilton's Automotive Ed. Dept. Chilton's Repair & Tune-Up Guide for Honda 350-550, 1972-1977. LC 77-89115. (Chilton's Repair & Tune-up Guides). (Illus., Orig.). 1977. pap. 8.95 (ISBN 0-8019-6603-5, 6603). Chilton.

--Chilton's Repair & Tune-up Guide for Honda 750 1969-1977. LC 76-57321. (Chilton's Repair & Tune-up Guides). (Illus., Orig.). 1977. pap. 8.95 (ISBN 0-8019-6589-6, 6598). Chilton.

Chilton's Automotive Editorial Department. Chilton's Repair & Tune-up Guide for Honda Fours, 1969-1974. 2nd ed. (Illus.). 200p. 1974. 8.95 (ISBN 0-8019-6029-0); pap. 8.95 (ISBN 0-8019-6030-4). Chilton.

--Chilton's Repair & Tune-up Guide for Honda Singles, 1968-1975. (Illus.). 1975. 8.95 (ISBN 0-8019-6033-9); pap. 8.95 (ISBN 0-8019-6034-7). Chilton.

--Chilton's Repair & Tune-up Guide for Honda Twins, 1966-1972. LC 72-7035. (Illus.). 148p. 1972. 8.95 (ISBN 0-8019-5736-2); pap. 8.95 (ISBN 0-8019-5799-0). Chilton.

--Chilton's Repair & Tune-up Guide for Honda 125-200 Twins, 1969-1976. LC 75-38656. (Illus.). 175p. 1975. 8.95 (ISBN 0-8019-6468-7); pap. 8.95 (ISBN 0-8019-6469-5). Chilton.

--Chilton's Repair & Tune-up Guide for Honda 350-360 Twins, 1968-1975. (Illus.). 1975. 8.95 (ISBN 0-8019-6037-1); pap. 8.95 (ISBN 0-8019-6038-X). Chilton.

--Chilton's Repair & Tune-up Guide for Honda 450-500, 1966-1976. LC 75-38676. (Illus.). 175p. (Hardcover ed. avail. to schools & libraries only). 1976. 8.95 (ISBN 0-8019-6450-4); pap. 6.95 (ISBN 0-8019-6451-2). Chilton.

Chilton's Automotive Editorial Dept. Honda Seven-Fifty, 1969-1980. (Illus.). 1980. pap. 8.95 (ISBN 0-8019-6968-9). Chilton.

Chilton's Repair & Tune-up Guide for Honda 350-360, 1968-77: Motorcycle. (Repair & Tune-up Guides Ser.). (Illus.). 1978. pap. 8.95 (ISBN 0-8019-6705-8). Chilton.

Clew, Jeff. Honda Owner's Workshop Manual: Fifty Ohv & Ohc '63-71. new ed. (Owners Workshop Manuals Ser.: No. 114). 1979. 8.50 (ISBN 0-85696-114-0, Pub. by J H Haynes England). Haynes Pubns.

--Honda Owner's Workshop Manual: One Twenty-Five to Two Hundred Twins '64-78. new ed. (Owners Workshop Manuals Ser.: No. 067). 1979. 8.50 (ISBN 0-900550-67-8, Pub. by J H Haynes England). Haynes Pubns.

--Honda Owner's Workshop Manual: Seven-Fifty 4 Cyl '70-79. new ed. (Owners Workshop Manuals Ser.: No. 131). 1979. 8.50 (ISBN 0-85696-131-0, Pub. by J H Haynes England). Haynes Pubns.

--Honda Owner's Workshop Manual: Sixty-Five, Seventy, Ninety Ohv & Ohc '64-73. new ed. (Owners Workshop Manuals Ser.: No. 116). 1979. 8.50 (ISBN 0-85696-116-7, Pub. by J H Haynes England). Haynes Pubns.

--Honda Owner's Workshop Manual: Two Fifty Elsinor '73-75. new ed. (Owners Workshop Manuals Ser.: No. 217). 1979. 8.50 (ISBN 0-85696-217-1, Pub. by J H Haynes England). Haynes Pubns.

--Honda Owner's Workshop Manual: Xl 250, 350 '72-75. new ed. (Owners Workshop Manuals Ser.: No. 209). 1979. 8.50 (ISBN 0-85696-209-0, Pub. by J H Haynes England). Haynes Pubns.

Clymer Publications. Honda Service-Repair Handbook: 750cc Fours, 1969-1978. Jorgensen, Eric, ed. (Illus.). pap. 9.95 (ISBN 0-89287-167-9, M341). Clymer Pubns.

Clymer Publications Staff. Honda Service-Repair Handbook: 250-305cc Twins, All Years. (Illus.). pap. text ed. 9.95 (ISBN 0-89287-010-9, M331). Clymer Pubns.

Collett, George. Honda Owner's Workshop Manual: Four-Fifty Twins '66-78. new ed. (Owners Workshop Manuals Ser.: No. 211). 1979. 8.50 (ISBN 0-85696-211-2, Pub. by J H Haynes England). Haynes Pubns.

Darlington, Mansur. Honda Owner's Workshop Manual: Gold Wing 1000 '75-77. new ed. (Owners Workshop Manuals Ser.: No. 309). 1979. 8.50 (ISBN 0-85696-309-7, Pub. by J H Haynes England). Haynes Pubns.

--Honda Owner's Workshop Manual: One Twenty Five Elsinore, Mr 175 '73-76. new ed. (Owners Workshop Manuals Ser.: No. 312). 1979. 8.50 (ISBN 0-85696-312-7, Pub. by J H Haynes England). Haynes Pubns.

--Honda Owner's Workshop Manual: Three-Sixty Twins '74-78. new ed. (Owners Workshop Manuals Ser.: No. 291). 1979. 8.50 (ISBN 0-85696-291-0, Pub. by J H Haynes England). Haynes Pubns.

Glenn, Harold T. Glenn's Honda Two-Cylinder Repair & Tune-up Guide. 1971. 6.95 (ISBN 0-517-50790-0). Crown.

Haynes, J. H. & Strasman, P. G. Honda Three Sixty; Six Hundred Z Owners Workshop Manual: Thru 1975. (Haynes Owner Workshop Manuals: No. 138). 1974. 9.95 (ISBN 0-85696-138-8, Pub. by J H Haynes England). Haynes Pubns.

Honda Fifty Tune up & Adjustment Instructions. (Illus.). 49p. 1974. pap. 2.35 (ISBN 0-517-50212-7). Crown.

Honda Hawk (Motorcycle) Nineteen Seventy-Seven to Eighty Repair Tune-up Guide: Nineteen Seventy Seven to Eighty Repaair Tune-up Guide. LC 79-3245. (New Automotive Bks.). 192p. 1980. 8.95 (ISBN 0-8019-6868-2). Chilton.

Honda Owner's Workshop Manual: Xr75 '72-76. new ed. (Owners Workshop Manuals Ser.: No. 287). 1979. 8.50 (ISBN 0-85696-287-2, Pub. by J H Haynes England). Haynes Pubns.

Hoy, Ray. Honda ATC-Seventy & ATC Ninety Singles: Service, Repair, Performance, 1970-80. (Illus.). pap. 3.95 (ISBN 0-89287-214-4, M311). Clymer Pubns.

Jorgensen, Eric. Honda Service Repair Handbook: 350-550cc Fours,1972-1978. Robinson, Jeff, ed. (Illus.). pap. 9.95 (ISBN 0-89287-287-X, M332). Clymer Pubns.

--Honda Two-Fifty & Three-Fifty cc Twins, 1964-1974: Service-Repair-Performance. pap. 9.95 (ISBN 0-89287-209-8, M322). Clymer Pubns.

Jorgensen, Eric, ed. Honda CX Five Hundred Twins 1978-1979 Service Repair Maintenance. pap. text ed. 9.95 (ISBN 0-89287-295-0, M335). Clymer Pubns.

--Honda One-Twenty-Five to Two-Fifty Elsinores, 1973-1978: Service, Repair, Performance. (Illus.). pap. 9.95 (ISBN 0-89287-176-8, M317). Clymer Pubns.

--Honda One-Twenty-Five to Two Hundred cc Twins, 1964-1977: Service, Repair, Performance. (Illus.). pap. 9.95 (ISBN 0-89287-208-X, M321). Clymer Pubns.

--Honda Service, Repair Handbook: 50-90cc Singles, 1963-1978. (Illus.). pap. 9.95 (ISBN 0-89287-187-3, M310). Clymer Pubns.

--Honda Three-Fifty - Five-Fifty cc Fours 1972-1978 Service Repair Performance. (Illus.). pap. text ed. 9.95 (ISBN 0-89287-287-X, M332). Clymer Pubns.

--Honda Two-Fifty & Three-Sixty cc Twins, 1974-1977: Service-Repair-Performance. (Illus.). pap. 9.95 (ISBN 0-89287-210-1, M323). Clymer Pubns.

--Honda XR-Seventy Five Singles: Service, Repair, Performance, 1975-78. (Illus.). pap. 9.95 (ISBN 0-89287-215-2, M312). Clymer Pubns.

Reynolds, Mark. Honda Owner's Workshop Manual: Three-Fifty, Five Hundred 4 Cyl Thru '75. new ed. (Owners Workshop Manuals Ser.: No. 132). 1979. 8.50 (ISBN 0-85696-132-9, Pub. by J H Haynes England). Haynes Pubns.

Sanders, Sol. Honda: The Man & His Machines. (Illus.). 1975. 7.95 (ISBN 0-316-77007-8). Little.

Scott, Ed. Honda CB Seven Fifty DOHC Fours: 1979-1980. (Illus.). pap. text ed. 9.95 (ISBN 0-89287-304-3, M337). Clymer Pubns.

Wilkins, Stewart. Honda Owner's Workshop Manual: Two Fifty & Three Fifty Twins Thru '74. new ed. (Owners Workshop Manuals Ser.: No. 133). 1979. 8.50 (ISBN 0-85696-133-7, Pub. by J H Haynes England). Haynes Pubns.

Witcomb, John. Honda Owner's Workshop Manual: Four Hundred, Five-Fifty F 4 Cyl '73-78. new ed. (Owners Workshop Manuals Ser.: No. 262). 1979. 8.50 (ISBN 0-85696-262-7, Pub. by J H Haynes England). Haynes Pubns.

HONDURAS

Adams, Richard N. Cultural Surveys of Panama, Nicaragua, Guatemala, El Salvador, Honduras. LC 76-41776. 1976. Repr. of 1957 ed. 35.00 (ISBN 0-87917-056-5). Blaine Ethridge.

British Honduras Citizens. Defence of the Settlers of Honduras Against the Unjust & Unfounded Representations of Colonel George Arthur, Late Superintendent of That Settlement. LC 70-110007. Repr. of 1824 ed. 11.50x (ISBN 0-8371-4160-5, Pub. by Negro U Pr). Greenwood.

Checchi, Vincent, et al. Honduras: A Problem in Economic Development. LC 76-49911. 1977. Repr. of 1958 ed. lib. bdg. 15.00x (ISBN 0-8371-9393-1, CHHO). Greenwood.

Honduras Information Service & Bennaton, Gwendolyn K. Honduras Economic Outlook & Business Opportunities. 50.00 (ISBN 0-686-27729-5). Honduras Info.

Nance, James. Pre-Spanish Trade in the Bay Islands. (Illus.). 1969. pap. 3.50 (ISBN 0-87651-021-7). Southern U Pr.

Squier, Ephraim G. Honduras. LC 72-128423. Repr. of 1870 ed. 16.00 (ISBN 0-404-06219-9). AMS Pr.

--Notes on Central America. LC 70-172443. (Illus.). Repr. of 1855 ed. 28.50 (ISBN 0-404-06221-0). AMS Pr.

Sterling Publishing Company Editors. Honduras in Pictures. LC 68-8765. (Visual Geography Ser). (Illus., Orig.). (gr. 5-10). 1968. pap. 2.95 (ISBN 0-8069-1100-X). Sterling.

HONDURAS–ANTIQUITIES

Gann, Thomas W. Mystery Cities: Exploration & Adventure in Labaantun. LC 76-44721. 1977. Repr. of 1925 ed. 28.50 (ISBN 0-404-15925-7). AMS Pr.

Gordon, G. B. Hieroglyphic Stairway: Ruins of Copan. Repr. of 1902 ed. pap. 14.00 (ISBN 0-527-01154-1). Kraus Repr.

--Prehistoric Ruins of Copan, Honduras: A Preliminary Report of the Explorations by Museum, 1891-1895. Repr. of 1896 ed. 21.00 (ISBN 0-527-01150-9). Kraus Repr.

--Researches in the Uloa Valley, 1898. Repr. of 1898 ed. pap. 14.00 (ISBN 0-527-01153-3). Kraus Repr.

Stone, Doris. Archaeology of the North Coast of Honduras. Repr. of 1941 ed. pap. 8.00 (ISBN 0-527-01172-X). Kraus Repr.

--Arqueologia de la Costa Norte De Honduras. (Peabody Museum Memoirs: Vol. 9, No. 1). 1975. pap. 12.00 (ISBN 0-87365-678-4). Peabody Harvard.

HONDURAS–DESCRIPTION AND TRAVEL

Discover Honduras Today! 3rd ed. (Illus.). 1980. 7.90 (ISBN 0-686-26261-1). Honduras Info.

Soltera, Maria. Lady's Ride Across Spanish Honduras. Stone, Doris, ed. LC 64-66325. (Latin American Gateway Ser.). (Illus.). 1964. Repr. of 1884 ed. 8.50 (ISBN 0-8130-0215-X). U Presses Fla.

Wilensky, Julius M. Cruising Guide to the Bay Islands of Honduras. Van Ost, John R., ed. LC 79-67057. (Illus., Orig.). 1979. pap. 17.25 (ISBN 0-918752-02-7). Wescott Cove.

HONDURAS–HISTORY

Bolland, O. Nigel. The Formation of a Colonial Society: Belize, from Conquest to Crown Colony. LC 76-47377. (Studies in Atlantic History & Culture). (Illus.). 320p. 1977. 18.00x (ISBN 0-8018-1887-7). Johns Hopkins.

Chamberlain, Robert S. Conquest & Colonization of Honduras, 1502-1550. 1967. lib. bdg. 17.50x (ISBN 0-374-91368-4). Octagon.

Meyer, Harvey K. Historical Dictionary of Honduras. LC 76-4539. (Latin American Historical Dictionaries Ser.: No. 13). 413p. 1976. 18.00 (ISBN 0-8108-0921-4). Scarecrow.

Stokes, William S. Honduras: An Area Study in Government. LC 70-140651. (Illus.). 351p. 1974. Repr. of 1950 ed. lib. bdg. 17.75x (ISBN 0-8371-5813-3, STHO). Greenwood.

Towards a Cultural Policy for Honduras. (Studies & Documents on Cultural Policies). 1979. pap. 5.25 (ISBN 92-3-101520-6, U875, UNESCO). Unipub.

HONDURAS–POLITICS AND GOVERNMENT

Anderson, Thomas P. The War of the Dispossessed: Honduras & El Salvador 1969. LC 80-24080. (Illus.). xiv, 202p. 1981. 15.95x (ISBN 0-8032-1009-4). U of Nebr Pr.

Constitution of Honduras, 1965. 1974. pap. 1.00 (ISBN 0-8270-5415-7). OAS.

Stokes, William S. Honduras: An Area Study in Government. LC 70-140651. (Illus.). 351p. 1974. Repr. of 1950 ed. lib. bdg. 17.75x (ISBN 0-8371-5813-3, STHO). Greenwood.

HONDURAS INTER-OCEANIC RAILWAY

Squier, Ephraim G. Notes on Central America. LC 70-172443. (Illus.). Repr. of 1855 ed. 28.50 (ISBN 0-404-06221-0). AMS Pr.

HONE, WILLIAM, 1780-1842

Hackwood, Frederick W. William Hone: His Life & Times. (Illus.). 1912. 15.00 (ISBN 0-8337-1516-X). B Franklin.

--William Hone: His Life & Times. LC 71-114025. (Illus.). Repr. of 1912 ed. lib. bdg. 14.50x (ISBN 0-678-00640-7). Kelley.

HONECKER, ERICH E., 1912-

Honecker, Erich. From My Life. LC 80-41162. (Leaders of the World Ser.: Vol. 3). (Illus.). 500p. 1980. 24.00 (ISBN 0-08-024532-3). Pergamon.

HONESTY

see also Business Ethics; Truthfulness and Falsehood; Wealth, Ethics Of

Croft, Doreen. Be Honest with Yourself. 1976. pap. text ed. 9.95x (ISBN 0-534-00452-0). Wadsworth Pub.

Furse, Margaret L. Nothing but the Truth: What It Takes to Be Honest. LC 81-3501. 128p. 1981. 7.95 (ISBN 0-687-28130-X). Abingdon.

Hartshorne, Hugh & May, Mark. Studies in the Nature of Character: Studies in Deceit. LC 74-21415. (Classics in Child Development Ser: Vol. 1). 440p. 1975. Repr. 27.00x (ISBN 0-405-06465-9). Arno.

Moncure, Jane B. Honesty. (Values to Live by Ser.). (Illus.). (ps-3). 1981. PLB 8.65 (ISBN 0-516-06523-8). Childrens.

--Honesty. Buerger, Jane, ed. (Illus.). 32p. 1980. 4.95 (ISBN 0-89565-163-7, 4925). Standard Pub.

--Honesty. LC 80-14298. (What Does the Bible Say? Ser.). (Illus.). 32p. (ps-2). 1980. PLB 4.95 (ISBN 0-89565-163-7). Childs World.

--Honesty. rev. ed. LC 80-39571. (What Is It? Ser.). (Illus.). 32p. (gr. k-3). 1981. PLB 5.50 (ISBN 0-89565-203-X). Childs World.

Narot, Joseph R. The Lost Honesty. pap. 1.25 (ISBN 0-686-15804-0). Rostrum Bks.

HONEY

see also Bee Culture; Bees; Cookery (Honey)

Aebi, Harry & Aebi, Ormond. Mastering the Art of Beekeeping. (Illus.). 1980. 14.95 (ISBN 0-913300-42-X); pap. 7.95 (ISBN 0-913300-46-2). Unity Pr.

Bielby, W. B. Home Honey Production. (Invest in Living Ser.). (Illus.). 1977. pap. 7.50x (ISBN 0-7158-0452-9). Intl Pubns Serv.

Crane, Eva, ed. Honey: A Comprehensive Survey. LC 74-14447. 1975. 52.50x (ISBN 0-8448-0062-7). Crane-Russak Co.

Gleanings Staff. Honey Plants Manual. 1977. pap. text ed. 2.25 (ISBN 0-686-20934-6). A I Root.

Gontier, Fernande & Francis, Claude. The Book of Honey. Stiskin, Nahum, ed. LC 78-73469. (Illus.). 1979. pap. 6.95 (ISBN 0-394-73775-X). Autumn Pr.

Gross, Sidney. Honey Marketing: Tips for the Small Producer. 1978. pap. 3.95 (ISBN 0-917234-10-3). Kitchen Harvest.

Mellor, Isha. Honey. (Illus.). 80p. 1981. 6.95 (ISBN 0-312-92306-6). St Martin.

--Honey: A Consideration. (Illus.). 80p. 1981. 6.95 (ISBN 0-312-92306-6). Congdon & Lattes.

Mitgutsch, Ali. From Blossom to Honey. LC 81-80. (Carolrhoda Start to Finish Books Ser.). (Illus.). 24p. (ps-3). 1981. PLB 5.95 (ISBN 0-87614-146-7). Carolrhoda Bks.

Nasi, Andrea, et al. The Honey Handbook. LC 78-57413. (Illus.). 1979. pap. 5.95 (ISBN 0-89696-014-5). Everest Hse.

Norris, P. About Honey: Nature's Elixir for Health. 1980. pap. 1.95 (ISBN 0-87904-043-2). Lust.

Parkhill, Joe. Wonderful World of Honey. 6.95 (ISBN 0-936744-01-4). Green Hill.

Pellett, Frank C. American Honey Plants. LC 75-38346. (Illus.). 467p. 1976. Repr. of 1947 ed. 9.10 (ISBN 0-915698-01-3). Dadant & Sons.

Penner, Lucille R. The Honey Book. (Illus.). (gr. 5 up). 1980. 9.95 (ISBN 0-8038-3054-8). Hastings.

Perlman, Dorothy. The Magic of Honey. 1978. pap. 2.50 (ISBN 0-380-00029-6, 39099). Avon.

Regional Standard for Honey. 1969. pap. 1.50 (ISBN 0-685-36325-2, FAO). Unipub.

Yoirish, N. Curative Properties of Honey & Bee Venom. Danko, Xenia, tr. from Russian. LC 77-12380. 1978. pap. 3.95 (ISBN 0-912078-55-3). New Glide.

HONEYBEES

see Bees

HONGKONG

American Chamber of Commerce in Hong Kong. Living in Hong Kong. 248p. 1977. 14.00 (ISBN 0-686-22824-3). A M Newman.

Elegant, Robert. Hong Kong. Time-Life Books, ed. (The Great Cities Ser.). (Illus.). 1977. 14.95 (ISBN 0-8094-2286-7). Time-Life.

Geiger, Theodore & Geiger, Frances M. Tales of Two City-States: The Development Progress of Hong Kong & Singapore. LC 73-86119. 260p. 1979. 7.00 (ISBN 0-89068-022-1). Natl Planning.

Hayes, J. Y. Hong Kong Region,1850-1911: Institutions & Leadership in Town & Countryside. 1977. 18.50 (ISBN 0-208-01626-0, Archon). Shoe String.

Mitchell, Robert E. Family Life in Urban Hong Kong, 2 vols, Nos. 24-25. (Asian Folklore & Social Life Monograph). 1972. 9.20 (ISBN 0-89986-026-5). E Langstaff.

Osgood, Cornelius. The Chinese: A Study of a Hong Kong Community, 3 vols. LC 74-77207. 1376p. 1975. text ed. 45.00x set (ISBN 0-8165-0418-0). U of Ariz Pr.

Potter, J. M. Capitalism & the Chinese Peasant: Social & Economic Change in a Hong Kong Village. (Center for Chinese Studies, UC Berkeley). 1968. 18.50x (ISBN 0-520-01024-8). U of Cal Pr.

Wong, Aline K. The Kaifong Associations & the Society of Hong Kong, No. 43. (Asian Folklore & Social Life Monograph). 296p. 1972. 5.90 (ISBN 0-89986-042-7). E Langstaff.

Wong, Luke S., ed. Housing in Hong Kong: A Multi-Disciplinary Study. LC 79-670179. 1978. pap. text ed. 14.95x (ISBN 0-686-60438-5, 00108). Heinemann Ed.

Wood, Dianne, ed. Hong Kong Nineteen Eighty: A Review of 1979. 288p. 1980. 12.50x (ISBN 0-8002-2454-X). Intl Pubns Serv.

HONGKONG–DESCRIPTION AND TRAVEL

Bartlett, Magnus, ed. Hong Kong. (China City Guides). 1981. pap. 8.95 (ISBN 0-528-84347-8). Rand.

Davis, S. Hong Kong in Its Geographical Setting. LC 70-179188. (Illus.). Repr. of 1949 ed. 20.00 (ISBN 0-404-54818-0). AMS Pr.

Elegant, Robert. Hong Kong. (The Great Cities Ser.). (Illus.). 1977. lib. bdg. 14.94 (ISBN 0-686-51003-8). Silver.

A Guide to Hong Kong. (China City Guides Ser.). (Illus.). 128p. 1981. pap. 8.95 (ISBN 0-528-84347-8). Rand.

Hoffman, Walter K., ed. A-O-A Hong Kong Guidebook: Official Guidebook Hong Kong Tourist Association. rev. ed. LC 78-3217. (Illus.). 1980. pap. 3.00 (ISBN 0-8048-1301-9). C E Tuttle.

Hong-Kong in Pictures. rev. ed. LC 63-19163. (Illus.). 1979. pap. 2.95 (ISBN 0-8069-1218-9). Sterling.

Lanier, Alison R. Update -- Hong Kong. LC 80-83914. (Country Orientation Ser.). 1980. pap. 25.00x (ISBN 0-933662-38-6). Intercult Pr.

Rabushka, Alvin. The Changing Face of Hong Kong. (AEI-Hoover Policy Studies). 1973. pap. 4.25 (ISBN 0-8447-3104-8). Am Enterprise.

Rand, Christopher. Hong Kong, the Island Between. LC 74-161781. Repr. of 1952 ed. 16.00 (ISBN 0-404-09037-0). AMS Pr.

Smith, Lloyd A. Hong Kong. Repr. of 1962 ed. 20.00 (ISBN 0-89987-018-X). Darby Bks.

HONGKONG–ECONOMIC CONDITIONS

Beazer, William F. The Commercial Future of Hong Kong. LC 76-24343. 1978. 22.95 (ISBN 0-275-23670-6). Praeger.

Factors Which Hinder or Help Productivity Improvement: Country Report--Hong Kong. (APO Basic Research Ser.). 106p. 1981. pap. 7.75 (ISBN 92-833-1466-2, APO 95, APO). Unipub.

Ho, H. C. Y. The Fiscal System of Hong Kong. 182p. 1979. 38.00x (ISBN 0-85664-686-5, Pub by Croom Helm Ltd England). Biblio Dist.

Hopkins, Keith, ed. Hong Kong: The Industrial Colony. 440p. 1971. 15.25x (ISBN 0-19-638137-1). Oxford U Pr.

Hsia, Ronald & Chau, Laurence. Industrialisation, Employment & Income Distribution: A Case Study of Hong Kong. 205p. 1978. 21.50x (ISBN 0-85664-684-9, Pub. by Croom Helm Ltd England). Biblio Dist.

Jao, Y. C. Banking & Currency in Hong Kong: A Study of Postwar Financial Development. 350p. 1975. 37.50x (ISBN 0-8419-5002-4). Holmes & Meier.

Kay, Michele. Doing Business in Hong Kong. (Illus.). 1977. 11.95 (ISBN 0-8120-5196-3). Barron.

Lethbridge, David, ed. The Business Environment of Hong Kong. 320p. 1980. 31.00x (ISBN 0-19-580423-6). Oxford U Pr.

Lin, Tzong-Biau, et al, eds. Hong Kong: Studies in Social, Economic & Political Development. LC 79-88894. 1979. 27.50 (ISBN 0-87332-151-0). M E Sharpe.

Mills, Lennox A. British Rule in Eastern Asia: A Study of Contemporary Government & Economic Development in British Malaya & Hong Kong. LC 76-83863. (Illus.). 1970. Repr. of 1942 ed. 17.50 (ISBN 0-8462-1415-6). Russell.

Rabushka, Alvin. The Changing Face of Hong Kong. (AEI-Hoover Policy Studies). 1973. pap. 4.25 (ISBN 0-8447-3104-8). Am Enterprise.

--Hong Kong: A Study in Economic Freedom. 1979. lib. bdg. 10.00x (ISBN 0-918584-02-7, 70187-5). U of Chicago Pr.

Woronoff, Jon. Hong Kong: Capitalist Paradise. (Orig.). 1981. pap. text ed. 10.95x (ISBN 0-686-72737-1, 00149). Heinemann Ed.

HONGKONG–HISTORY

Cameron, Nigel. Hong Kong: The Cultured Pearl. (Illus.). 1978. text ed. 29.50x (ISBN 0-19-580404-X). Oxford U Pr.

Endacott, G. B. A History of Hong Kong. (Illus.). 351p. 1974. pap. 14.50x (ISBN 0-19-519776-3). Oxford U Pr.

Endacott, G. B. & Hinton, A. Fragrant Harbour: A Short History of Hong Kong. LC 76-57678. 1977. Repr. of 1962 ed. lib. bdg. 16.75x (ISBN 0-8371-9456-3, ENFH). Greenwood.

Endacott, George B. Hong Kong Eclipse. Birch, Alan, ed. (Illus.). 1978. text ed. 22.00x (ISBN 0-19-580374-4). Oxford U Pr.

King, Ambrose & Lee, Rance, eds. Social Life & Development in Hong Kong. 325p. 1981. 25.00 (ISBN 0-295-95877-4). U of Wash Pr.

Lethbridge, Henry J. Hong Kong: Stability & Change: A Collection of Essays. 1979. 26.00x (ISBN 0-19-580402-3). Oxford U Pr.

Lindsay, Oliver. At the Going Down of the Sun: Hong Kong & South East Asia, 1914-45. (Illus.). 250p. 1981. 25.00 (ISBN 0-241-10542-0, Pub. by Hamish Hamilton England). David & Charles.

--The Lasting Honour: The Fall of Hong Kong Nineteen Forty-One. (Illus.). Date not set. cancelled (ISBN 0-241-89946-X). Hippocrene Bks.

Salaff, Janet W. Working Daughters of Hong Kong: Female Piety or Power in the Family? LC 80-23909. (ASA Rose Monographs). (Illus.). 304p. 1981. 24.95 (ISBN 0-521-23679-7); pap. 8.95 (ISBN 0-521-28148-2). Cambridge U Pr.

Warner, John. Fragrant Harbour: Early Photographs of Hong Kong. (Illus.). 192p. 1980. 14.95 (ISBN 962-7015-01-6, Pub. by Warner Pubns Hong Kong). Hippocrene Bks.

HONGKONG–POLITICS AND GOVERNMENT

Collins, Charles H. Public Administration in Hong Kong. LC 70-179180. Repr. of 1952 ed. 17.50 (ISBN 0-404-54810-5). AMS Pr.

Harris, Peter. Hong Kong: A Study in Bureaucratic Politics. 1979. pap. text ed. 8.95x (ISBN 0-686-60437-7, 00106). Heinemann Ed.

Higgins, M. F. Security Regulations in Hong Kong, Nineteen Seventy-Two to Nineteen Seventy-Seven. 192p. 1978. 25.00x (ISBN 90-286-0948-2). Sijthoff & Noordhoff.

Lin, Tzong-Biau, et al, eds. Hong Kong: Studies in Social, Economic & Political Development. LC 79-88894. 1979. 27.50 (ISBN 0-87332-151-0). M E Sharpe.

Miners, Norman. The Government & Politics of Hong Kong. 2nd ed. (East Asian Social Science Monographs). 1977. pap. 16.75x (ISBN 0-19-580371-X). Oxford U Pr.

Rabushka, Alvin. Value for Money: The Hong Kong Budgetary Process. LC 75-27028. (Publications Ser.: No. 152). 152p. 1976. 10.95 (ISBN 0-8179-6521-1). Hoover Inst Pr.

Wesley-Smith, P. The Unequal Treaty Eighteen Ninety-Seven to Nineteen Ninety-Seven. (East Asian Historical Monographs). (Illus.). 296p. 26.00 (ISBN 0-19-580436-8). Oxford U Pr.

HONI HA-MEAGGEL, 1ST CENTURY B.C.

Buchler, Adolph. Ancient Pious Men: Types of Jewish Palestinian Piety from 70 B. C. E. to 70 C. E. 1922. 15.00x (ISBN 0-87068-030-7). Ktav.

Gershator, Phillis. Honi & His Magic Circle. (Illus.). (gr. k-4). 1979. 6.95 (ISBN 0-8276-0167-0). Jewish Pubn.

HONOLULU

Bushnell, O. A. A Walk Through Old Honolulu: An Illustrated Guide. LC 75-25519. (Illus.). 1977. pap. 4.50 (ISBN 0-915870-00-2). Kapa.

Cook, Terri. Family Guide to Honolulu & the Island of Oahu. LC 77-85698. 1977. soft bdg. 2.95 (ISBN 0-930492-00-5). Hawaiian Serv.

Kerr, Jennifer & Sidenstien, Jay. Honolulu Underground Gourmet. pap. 1.95 (ISBN 0-671-21352-0, Fireside). S&S.

Morgan, Roland. Honolulu Then & Now. (Illus., Orig.). 1978. pap. 6.95 (ISBN 0-88875-003-X). Bodima.

Wenkam, Robert. Honolulu Is an Island. LC 78-56260. (Illus.). 1978. 25.00 (ISBN 0-528-81075-8). Rand.

HONOR

see also Business Ethics; Dueling

Pitt-Rivers, J. The Fate of Shechem or the Politics of Sex. LC 76-27913. (Studies in Social Anthropology Ser.: No. 19). (Illus.). 1977. 22.50 (ISBN 0-521-21427-0). Cambridge U Pr.

Wasserman, Paul, ed. Awards, Honors & Prizes: United States & Canada, Vol. 1. 4th ed. LC 78-16691. 1978. 68.00 (ISBN 0-8103-0378-7). Gale.

Watson, Curtis B. Shakespeare & the Renaissance Concept of Honor. LC 75-25499. 1976. Repr. of 1960 ed. lib. bdg. 31.50 (ISBN 0-8371-8424-X, WASH). Greenwood.

HONOR, DECORATIONS OF

see Decorations of Honor

HONOR IN LITERATURE

Barber, C. L. Idea of Honour in the English Drama 1591-1700. LC 72-187097. 1957. lib. bdg. 30.00 (ISBN 0-8414-0616-2). Folcroft.

Jones, George F. Honor in German Literature. LC 60-62591. (North Carolina University. Studies in the Germanic Languages & Literature: No. 25). Repr. of 1959 ed. 18.50 (ISBN 0-404-50925-8), AMS Pr.

Larson, Donald R. The Honor Plays of Lope De Vega. 1977. 15.00x (ISBN 0-674-40628-1). Harvard U Pr.

Shalvi, Alice. The Relationship of Renaissance Concepts of Honour to Shakespeare's Problem Plays. (Salzburg Studies in English Literature, Jacobean Drama Studies: No.7). 1972. pap. text ed. 25.00x (ISBN 0-391-01519-2). Humanities.

Watson, Curtis B. Shakespeare & the Renaissance Concept of Honor. LC 75-25499. 1976. Repr. of 1960 ed. lib. bdg. 31.50 (ISBN 0-8371-8424-X, WASH). Greenwood.

HONOR SYSTEM

see Self-Government (In Education)

HONORARY DEGREES

see Degrees, Academic

HONORARY TITLES

see Titles of Honor and Nobility

HOOD, THOMAS, 1799-1845

Clubbe, John. Victorian Forerunner: The Later Career of Thomas Hood. LC 68-28520. 1968. 12.75 (ISBN 0-8223-0038-9). Duke.

Hood. Memorials of Thomas Hood. 1979. Repr. lib. bdg. 85.00 (ISBN 0-8492-5319-5). R West.

Hood & Hood. Memorials of Thomas Hood, 1 volume ed. 583p. 1981. Repr. lib. bdg. 65.00 (ISBN 0-8495-2427-X). Arden Lib.

Hudson, William H. Quiet Corner in a Library. facs. ed. LC 68-16940. (Essay Index Reprint Ser). 1915. 15.00 (ISBN 0-8369-0550-4). Arno.

Jeffrey, Lloyd N. Thomas Hood. (English Authors Ser.: No. 137). lib. bdg. 10.95 (ISBN 0-8057-1268-2). Twayne.

Jerrold, Walter C. Thomas Hood: His Life & Times. Repr. of 1907 ed. lib. bdg. 17.00x (ISBN 0-8371-1043-2, JETH). Greenwood.

--Thomas Hood: His Life & Times. LC 68-24911. (English Biography Ser., No. 31). (Illus.). 1969. Repr. of 1907 ed. lib. bdg. 49.95 (ISBN 0-8383-0209-2). Haskell.

Oswald, Emil. Thomas Hood und Die Soziale Tendenzdichtung Seiner Zeit. Repr. of 1904 ed. pap. 21.00 (ISBN 0-384-43870-9). Johnson Repr.

HOOD, MOUNT, OREGON

Carey, Robin. Beautiful Mt. Hood. Shangle, Robert D., ed. LC 78-102323. (Illus.). 1977. 14.95 (ISBN 0-915796-27-9); pap. 7.95 (ISBN 0-915796-26-0). Beautiful Am.

Grauer, Jack. Mount Hood: A Complete History. (Illus.). 300p. 1975. pap. 8.00 (ISBN 0-930584-01-5). J Grauer.

Woolley, Ivan. Off to Mt. Hood: An Auto Biography of the Old Road. (Illus.). 109p. 1959. pap. 4.95 (ISBN 0-87595-015-9). Oreg Hist Soc.

HOOD FAMILY

Hood, Dellmann O. Tunis Hood Family: Its Lineage & Traditions. (Illus.). 1960. 25.00 (ISBN 0-8323-0185-X). Binford.

HOODS

see Academic Costume

HOOF-AND-MOUTH DISEASE

see Foot-And-Mouth Disease

HOOFS

Emery, Leslie, et al. Horseshoeing Theory & Hoof Care. LC 76-16742. (Illus.). 271p. 1977. text ed. 15.50 (ISBN 0-8121-0574-5). Lea & Febiger.

Hanauer, Elsie V. No Foot-No Horse. LC 74-81870. 1974. pap. text ed. 7.95x (ISBN -08087-0883-X). Burgess.

Lerner, Marguerite R. Horns, Hoofs, Nails. LC 65-29040. (Medical Bks for Children). (Illus.). (gr. 3-9). 1965. PLB 3.95 (ISBN 0-8225-0015-9). Lerner Pubns.

HOOFT, PIETER CORNELISZOON, 1581-1647

Grierson, Herbert. Essays & Addresses. LC 72-195906. 1940. lib. bdg. 20.00 (ISBN 0-8414-4686-5). Folcroft.

HOOK, THEODORE EDWARD, 1788-1841

Brightfield, Myron F. Theodore Hook & His Novels. 1971. Repr. of 1928 ed. 25.00 (ISBN 0-403-00814-X). Scholarly.

HOOKED RUGS

see Rugs, Hooked

HOOKER, RICHARD, 1553 or 1554-1600

Davies, E. T. Political Ideas of Richard Hooker. LC 75-159177. 1972. Repr. of 1946 ed. lib. bdg. 10.50x (ISBN 0-374-92073-7). Octagon.

D'Entreves, Alexander P. Medieval Contribution to Political Thought: Thomas Aquinas, Marsilius of Padua, Richard Hooker. 1959. Repr. of 1939 ed. text ed. 8.50x (ISBN 0-391-00513-8). Humanities.

Faulkner, Robert K. Richard Hooker & the Politics of a Christian England. LC 79-65776. 195p. 1981. 19.50x (ISBN 0-520-03993-9). U of Cal Pr.

Grislis, Egil & Hill, W. Speed. Richard Hooker: A Selected Bibliography. LC 79-32321. (Bibliographia Tripotamopolitana: No.4). 1971. 5.50 (ISBN 0-931222-03-6). C E Barbour.

Hill, W. Speed, ed. Richard Hooker: A Descriptive Bibliography of the Early Editions, 1593-1724. LC 72-147090. 153p. 1970. pap. 10.00 (ISBN 0-8295-0211-4). UPB.

Munz, Peter. Place of Hooker in the History of Thought. LC 71-137085. 1971. Repr. of 1952 ed. lib. bdg. 15.00x (ISBN 0-8371-5548-7, MUPH). Greenwood.

Shirley, John. Richard Hooker & Contemporary Political Ideas. LC 78-20491. 1980. Repr. of 1949 ed. 22.50 (ISBN 0-88355-868-8). Hyperion Conn.

Walton, Izaak. Lives of John Donne, Sir Henry Wotton, Richard Hooker, George Herbert, & Robert Sanderson. (World's Classics Ser.). 7.95 (ISBN 0-19-250303-0). Oxford U Pr.

HOOKER, THOMAS, 1586-1647

Bush, Sargent, Jr. The Writings of Thomas Hooker: Spiritual Adventure in Two Worlds. LC 79-5404. 256p. 1980. 19.50 (ISBN 0-299-08070-6). U of Wis Pr.

Shuffelton, Frank. Thomas Hooker, 1586-1647. LC 76-45912. 1977. text ed. 25.00 (ISBN 0-691-05249-2). Princeton U Pr.

Walker, George L. Thomas Hooker: Preacher, Founder, Democrat. LC 72-78846. 1891. Repr. 20.00 (ISBN 0-403-02095-6). Somerset Pub.

--Thomas Hooker: Preacher, Founder, Democrat. 1972. Repr. of 1891 ed. lib. bdg. 19.00 (ISBN 0-8422-8120-7). Irvington.

Williams, George H., et al. Thomas Hooker: Writings in England & Holland, Sixteen Twenty-Six to Sixteen Thirty-Three. LC 75-30570. (Harvard Theological Review & Studies). 1975. pap. 12.00 (ISBN 0-89130-310-3, 020028). Scholars Pr Ca.

HOOKING

Beatty, Alice & Sargent, Mary. The Hook Book. LC 77-5852. (Illus.). 160p. 1977. 12.95 (ISBN 0-8117-0820-9). Stackpole.

HOOKWORM DISEASE

Nineteen Twenty to Nineteen Sixty Two. 251p. (Eng. & Fr.). 1965. pap. 5.60 (ISBN 92-4-052001-5). World Health.

HOOLE, WILLIAM STANLEY, 1903-

Hoole, W. Stanley. According to Hoole: The Collected Essays & Tales of a Scholar-Librarian & Literary Maverick. LC 74-148688. 336p. 1973. 19.95x (ISBN 0-8173-7102-8). U of Ala Pr.

HOOPER, JOHNSON JONES (SIMON SUGGS, PSEUD.), 1815-1863

Hoole, William S. Alias Simon Suggs: The Life & Times of Johnson Jones Hooper. Repr. of 1952 ed. lib. bdg. 15.00 (ISBN 0-8371-3367-X, HOAS). Greenwood.

HOOVER, HERBERT CLARK, PRES. U. S., 1874-1964

Best, Gary D. The Politics of American Individualism: Herbert Hoover in Transition, 1918-1921. LC 75-16960. 202p. 1975. lib. bdg. 14.50x (ISBN 0-8371-8160-7, BPA/). Greenwood.

Brandes, Joseph. Herbert Hoover & Economic Diplomacy. LC 75-26622. (Illus.). 237p. 1975. Repr. of 1962 ed. lib. bdg. 15.50x (ISBN 0-8371-8362-6, BRHH). Greenwood.

Burner, David. Herbert Hoover: The Public Life. LC 78-54912. (Illus.). 1978. 17.95 (ISBN 0-394-46134-7). Knopf.

Curry, E. R. Hoover's Dominican Diplomacy & the Origins of the Good Neighbor Policy. Freidel, Frank, ed. LC 78-62379. (Modern American History Ser.: Vol. 5). 1979. lib. bdg. 30.00 (ISBN 0-8240-3629-8). Garland Pub.

De Conde, Alexander. Herbert Hoover's Latin American Policy. 1970. lib. bdg. 12.00x (ISBN 0-374-92085-0). Octagon.

Eckley, Wilton. Herbert Hoover. (United States Authors Ser.: No. 385). 1980. lib. bdg. 10.95 (ISBN 0-8057-7285-5). Twayne.

Fausold, Martin L. & Mazuzan, George T., eds. The Hoover Presidency: A Reappraisal. LC 74-13876. (Illus.). 1974. 17.50 (ISBN 0-87395-280-4); microfiche o.p. 16.00 (ISBN 0-87395-281-2). State U NY Pr.

Gelfand, Lawrence E., ed. Herbert Hoover: The Great War & Its Aftermath, Nineteen Fourteen - Nineteen Twenty-Three. LC 79-10139. (Herbert Hoover Centennial Seminars). (Illus.). 1979. text ed. 17.95x (ISBN 0-87745-095-1). U of Iowa Pr.

Hawley, Ellis W., et al, eds. Herbert Hoover As Secretary of Commerce, 1921-1928: Studies in New Era Thought & Practice. Zieger, Robert & Wilson, Joan H. LC 80-26771. (Herbert Hoover Centennial Seminar Ser.). (Illus.). 272p. 1981. text ed. 19.95x (ISBN 0-87745-109-5). U of Iowa Pr.

Hoover, Herbert. Addresses Upon the American Road: 1955-1960. LC 61-5290. 415p. 1968. 7.50 (ISBN 0-87004-065-0). Caxton.

Huthmacher, J. Joseph & Susman, Warren, eds. Herbert Hoover & the Crisis of American Capitalism. 138p. 1973. 7.95 (ISBN 0-87073-108-4); pap. 4.95 (ISBN 0-87073-109-2). Schenkman.

Joslin, Theodore G. Hoover off the Record. facsimile ed. (Select Bibliographies Reprint Ser). Repr. of 1934 ed. 21.00 (ISBN 0-8369-5953-1). Arno.

Lerski, George J., ed. Herbert Hoover & Poland: A Documentary History of a Friendship. LC 77-72051. (Publication Ser.: No. 174). (Illus.). 144p. 1977. 10.95 (ISBN 0-8179-6741-9). Hoover Inst Pr.

Lisio, Donald J. The President & Protest: Hoover, Conspiracy & the Bonus Riot. LC 73-89489. 368p. 1974. 14.00x (ISBN 0-8262-0158-X). U of Mo Pr.

McLean, Hulda H. Genealogy of the Herbert Hoover Family: Errata & Addenda. (Special Project). 1976. 2.00x (ISBN 0-8179-4112-6). Hoover Inst Pr.

Miller, Walter L. The Life & Accomplishments of Herbert Hoover. LC 78-99300. 1970. 10.95 (ISBN 0-87716-024-4, Pub. by Moore Pub Co). F Apple.

Myers, William S. The Foreign Policies of Herbert Hoover, 1929-1933. Freidel, Frank, ed. LC 78-66558. (The History of the United States Ser.: Vol. 14). 272p. 1979. lib. bdg. 20.00 (ISBN 0-8240-9699-1). Garland Pub.

O'Brien, Francis W. The Hoover-Wilson Wartime Correspondence, Sept, 24, 1914-Nov. 11, 1918. 896p. 1974. 7.95 (ISBN 0-8138-0725-5). Iowa St U Pr.

O'Brien, Francis W., ed. Two Peacemakers in Paris: The Hoover-Wilson Post-Armistice Letters, 1918-1920. LC 77-99273. 304p. 1978. 12.50x (ISBN 0-89096-051-8). Tex A&M Univ Pr.

Rice, A., ed. Herbert Hoover, 1874-1964: Chronology, Documents, Bibliographical Aids. LC 78-111215. (Presidential Chronology Ser). 1971. 8.00 (ISBN 0-379-12071-2). Oceana.

Robinson, Edgar E. & Bornet, Vaughn D. Herbert Hoover: President of the United States. LC 75-18666. (Publications Ser.: No.149). 1975. 14.95 (ISBN 0-8179-6491-6). Hoover Inst Pr.

Romasco, Albert U. Poverty of Abundance: Hoover, the Nation, the Depression. LC 65-26565. 1968. pap. 4.95 (ISBN 0-19-500760-3, 231, GB). Oxford U Pr.

Tracey, Kathleen, compiled by. Herbert Hoover: A Bibliography of His Writings & Addresses. LC 77-77563. (Bibliographical Ser: No. 58). 1977. 15.00 (ISBN 0-8179-2581-3). Hoover Inst Pr.

Warren, Harris G. Herbert Hoover & the Great Depression. LC 80-19603. x, 372p. 1980. Repr. of 1970 ed. lib. bdg. 28.75x (ISBN 0-313-22659-8, WAHO). Greenwood.

Wilson, Joan H. Herbert Hoover: The Forgotten Progressing. (The Library of American Biography). 256p. 1975. pap. text ed. 4.95 (ISBN 0-316-94416-5). Little.

HOOVER, JOHN EDGAR, 1895-1972

Lewis, Eugene. Public Entrepreneurship: Toward a Theory of Bureaucratic Political Power. LC 79-2451. 288p. 1980. 22.50x (ISBN 0-253-17384-1). Ind U Pr.

Nash, Jay R. Citizen Hoover: A Critical Study of the Life & Times of J. Edgar Hoover & His FBI. LC 72-76266. (Illus.). 240p. 1972. 16.95x (ISBN 0-911012-60-5). Nelson-Hall.

HOOVER, LOU (HENRY)

Pryor, Helen B. Lou Henry Hoover, Gallant First Lady. LC 69-16201. (Illus.). (gr. 8 up). 1969. 5.95 (ISBN 0-396-05992-9). Dodd.

HOOVER DAM

Construction of Hoover Dam. LC 77-79677. (Illus.). 1976. Repr. of 1936 ed. 1.00 (ISBN 0-916122-51-4). KC Pubns.

Kleinsorge, Paul. The Boulder Canyon Project: Historical & Economic Aspects. 1941. 36.00x (ISBN 0-8047-1031-7). Stanford U Pr.

Maxon, James C. Lake Mead-Hoover Dam: The Story Behind the Scenery. DenDooven, Gweneth R., ed. LC 79-87573. (Illus.). 1980. 7.95 (ISBN 0-916122-62-X); pap. 3.00 (ISBN 0-916122-61-1). KC Pubns.

HOOVES

see Hoofs

HOP INDUSTRY AND TRADE

see Hops

HOPE, BOB, 1903-

Hope, Bob & Martin, Pete. The Last Christmas Show. (Illus.). 400p. 1981. pap. 10.95 (ISBN 0-385-15752-5, Dolp). Doubleday.

Manchel, Frank. The Box-Office Clowns: Bob Hope, Jerry Lewis, Mel Brooks, Woody Allen. (Illus.). (gr. 7 up). 1979. PLB 7.90 s&l (ISBN 0-531-02881-X). Watts.

Morella, Joe, et al. The Amazing Careers of Bob Hope. (Illus.). 1978. pap. 5.95 (ISBN 0-89508-000-1). Rainbow Bks.

Taylor, Paula. Bob Hope. LC 74-19116. (Illus.). 40p. (gr. 4-8). 1974. PLB 5.95 (ISBN 0-87191-408-5). Creative Ed.

Thompson, Charles. Bob Hope: Portrait of a Superstar. (Illus.). 272p. 1981. 9.95 (ISBN 0-312-08724-1). St Martin.

HOPE, JAMES, 1819-1892

Freeman, Larry. Hope Paintings. LC 60-13415. (Illus.). 1961. deluxe ed. 8.50 (ISBN 0-87282-047-5). Century Hse.

HOPE, JOHN, 1868-1936

Torrence, Ridgely. Story of John Hope. LC 69-18568. (American Negro: His History & Literature, Ser. No. 3). 1970. Repr. of 1948 ed. 19.00 (ISBN 0-405-01939-4). Arno.

HOPE, THOMAS, 1770-1831

Baumgarten, Sandor. Le Crepuscule Neo-Classique Thomas Hope. 1979. Repr. of 1958 ed. lib. bdg. 40.00 (ISBN 0-8495-0503-8). Arden Lib.

Watkins, David. Thomas Hope & the Neo-Classical Idea. 1970. 24.00 (ISBN 0-7195-1819-9). Transatlantic.

HOPE

see also Despair

Blue, Adrianne & Savary, Louis M. Horizons of Hope. (Illus.). 196p. (Orig.). 1969. pap. 3.25 (ISBN 0-88489-020-1). St Marys.

Boros, Ladislaus, S.J. Living in Hope. 120p. 1973. pap. 1.45 (ISBN 0-385-00133-9, Im). Doubleday.

Bridinger, Don. Waiting in Hope. 1973. 3.15 (ISBN 0-89536-253-8). CSS Pub.

Carroll, W. H., et al. Reasons for Hope. 203p. (Orig.). 1978. pap. 5.95 (ISBN 0-931888-01-8, Chris. Coll. Pr.). Christendom Pubns.

Duquoc, Christian, ed. Dimensions of Spirituality. (Concilium Ser.: Religion in the Seventies: Vol. 59). 1970. pap. 4.95 (ISBN 0-8245-0219-1). Crossroad NY.

Galot, Jean. The Mystery of Christian Hope. LC 77-1222. 1977. 4.95 (ISBN 0-8189-0346-5). Alba.

Gardner, Lucille. There Is Hope. LC 76-4615. 208p. 1976. pap. 1.95 (ISBN 0-912692-89-8). Cook.

Getz, Gene A. Measure of a Church. LC 75-17160. (Orig.). 1975. pap. 2.25 (ISBN 0-8307-0398-5, 50-147-00). Regal.

Goff, James & Goff, Margaret. In Every Person Who Hopes... (Orig.). 1980. pap. 3.75 (ISBN 0-377-00096-5). Friend Pr.

Hicks, Roy H. Whatever Happened to Hope. 1978. mini book 0.50 (ISBN 0-89274-074-4). Harrison Hse.

Kline, Harvey S. & Eshbach, Warren M. A Future with Hope. 1978. pap. 2.95 (ISBN 0-87178-298-7). Brethren.

Kuasten, J. & Plumpe, J., eds. St. Augustine, Faith, Hope & Charity. Arand, Louis A., tr. LC 78-62450. (Ancient Christian Writers Ser.: No. 3). 165p. 1947. 8.95 (ISBN 0-8091-0045-2). Paulist Pr.

Marcel, Gabriel. Homo Viator: Introduction to a Metaphysic of Hope. Crauford, Emma, tr. 7.50 (ISBN 0-8446-2529-9). Peter Smith.

Meryman, Richard. Hope: A Loss Survived. 1980. 10.95 (ISBN 0-316-56786-8). Little.

Perl, Susan. Faith, Hope & Charity. (Illus.). 7.95 (ISBN 0-915696-46-0). Determined Prods.

Schuller, Robert H. Your Future Is Your Friend. LC 74-18979. (Pivot Family Reader Ser). 128p. 1974. pap. 1.95 (ISBN 0-87983-099-9). Keats.

Smith, Morton. Hope & History: An Exploration. Anshen, Ruth N., ed. LC 77-3774. (World Perspectives Ser.: Vol. 54). 1980. 12.95 (ISBN 0-06-013991-9, HarpT). Har-Row.

Van Til, Cornelius. The God of Hope. 1978. pap. 9.95 (ISBN 0-87552-486-9). Presby & Reformed.

Warnke, Mike. Hitchhiking on Hope Street. LC 78-73197. 1979. 6.95 (ISBN 0-385-14540-3, Galilee). Doubleday.

HOPE–BIBLICAL TEACHING

Bunyan, John. Israel's Hope Encouraged. pap. 1.95 (ISBN 0-685-19836-7). Reiner.

DeWeese, Paul N. Hope in an Age of Nihilism. 1978. pap. 4.95 (ISBN 0-913550-10-8). Greeno Hadden.

Moule, C. F. Meaning of Hope: A Biblical Exposition with Concordance. Reumann, John, ed. LC 63-17881. (Facet Bks). 80p. (Orig.). 1963. pap. 1.00 (ISBN 0-8006-3001-7, 1-3001). Fortress.

Zimmerli, Walther. Man & His Hope in the Old Testament. (Studies in Biblical Theology, 2nd Ser.: No. 20). 1971. prebound o.p. 9.95x (ISBN 0-8401-4070-3); pap. text ed. 7.45x (ISBN 0-8401-3070-8). Allenson-Breckinridge.

HOPE–SERMONS

Spurgeon, Charles H. Twelve Sermons on Hope. (Charles H. Spurgeon Library Ser.). 1979. pap. 2.95 (ISBN 0-8010-8145-9). Baker Bk.

HOPETOWN REEF

Storr, John F. Ecology & Oceanography of the Coral-Reef Tract, Abaco Island, Bahamas. LC 64-66221. (Special Paper: No. 79). (Illus., Orig.). 1964. pap. 5.50x (ISBN 0-8137-2079-6). Geol Soc.

HOPEWELL CULTURE

McGregor, John C. The Pool & Irving Villages: A Study of Hopewell Occupation in the Illinois River Valley. LC 58-5605. (Illus.). 1958. pap. 7.50 (ISBN 0-252-72610-3). U of Ill Pr.

Moorehead, Warren K. The Hopewell Mound Group of Ohio. LC 76-43782. (Field Museum of Natural History. Publication: 211). (Illus.). Repr. of 1922 ed. 42.50 (ISBN 0-404-15638-X). AMS Pr.

HOPF ALGEBRAS

Abe, E. Hopf Algebras. LC 79-50912. (Cambridge Tracts in Mathematics Ser.: No. 74). 1980. 39.50 (ISBN 0-521-22240-0). Cambridge U Pr.

Chase, U. & Sweedler, M. E. Hopf Algebras & Galois Theory Two. LC 75-84143. (Lecture Notes in Mathematics: Vol. 97). (Orig.). 1969. pap. 10.70 (ISBN 0-387-04616-X). Springer-Verlag.

Harper, J. R. H-Space with Torsion. (Memoirs Ser.: No. 223). 1979. 7.60 (ISBN 0-8218-2223-3). Am Math.

Hassard, D. B., et al. Theory of Applications of Hopf Bifurcation. (London Mathematical Society Lecture Notes Ser.: No. 41). (Illus.). 300p. (Orig.). 1981. 35.00 (ISBN 0-521-23158-2). Cambridge U Pr.

Marsden, J. E. & McCracken, M. The Hopf Bifurcation & Its Applications. LC 76-21727. (Applied Mathematical Sciences Ser: Vol, 19). 1976. soft cover 20.50 (ISBN 0-387-90200-7). Springer-Verlag.

Sweedler, Moss E. Hopf Algebras. (Math Lecture Notes Ser.: No. 44). 1969. 17.50 (ISBN 0-8053-9254-8, Adv Bk Prog); pap. 9.50 (ISBN 0-8053-9255-6, Adv Bk Prog). Benjamin-Cummings.

Yanagihara, H. Theory of Hopf Algebras Attached to Group Schemes. (Lecture Notes in Mathematics: Vol. 614). 1977. pap. text ed. 18.30 (ISBN 0-387-08444-4). Springer-Verlag.

Zabroosky, A. Hopf Spaces. LC 76-54352. (North-Holland Mathematical Studies: Vol. 22). 1976. pap. 22.00 (ISBN 0-7204-0553-X, North-Holland). Elsevier.

HOPI INDIANS

see Indians of North America–Southwest, New

HOPI LANGUAGE–GLOSSARIES, VOCABULARIES, ETC.

Kalectaca, Milo & Langacker, Ronald W. Lessons in Hopi. LC 77-20279. 1978. pap. 5.95x (ISBN 0-8165-0617-5). U of Ariz Pr.

Stephen, Alexander M. Hopi Journal, 2 Vols. Parsons, Elsie C., ed. LC 77-82337. (Columbia University Contributions to Anthropology Ser.: Vol. 23). Repr. of 1936 ed. Set. 95.00 (ISBN 0-404-50573-2); 47.50 ea. Vol. 1 (ISBN 0-404-50594-5). Vol. 2 (ISBN 0-404-50595-3). AMS Pr.

HOPKINS, ERNEST MARTIN, 1877-1964

Widmayer, Charles E. Hopkins of Dartmouth: The Story of Ernest Martin Hopkins & His Presidency of Dartmouth College. LC 77-153864. (Illus.). 320p. 1977. text ed. 18.00x (ISBN 0-87451-145-3). U Pr of New Eng.

HOPKINS, ESEK, 1718-1802

Field, Edward. Esek Hopkins Commander-in-Chief of the Continental Navy During the American Revolution. LC 72-78703. 1898. Repr. 25.00 (ISBN 0-403-08921-2). Somerset Pub.

HOPKINS, GERARD MANLEY, 1844-1889

Bender, Todd K. Gerard Manley Hopkins: The Classical Background and Critical Reception of His Work. 180p. 1966. 12.00x (ISBN 0-8018-0066-8). Johns Hopkins.

Bergonzi, Bernard. Gerard Manley Hopkins. 1977. pap. 4.95 (ISBN 0-02-048590-5, 04859, Collier). Macmillan.

Cohen, Edward H. Works & Criticism of Gerald Manley Hopkins - a Comprehensive Bibliography. 1969. 9.95 (ISBN 0-8132-0253-1); pap. 4.95 (ISBN 0-8132-0533-6). Cath U Pr.

Cotter, James F. Inscape: The Christology & Poetry of Gerard Manley Hopkins. LC 73-189857. 1972. 15.95x (ISBN 0-8229-3247-4). U of Pittsburgh Pr.

Dilligan, Robert J. & Bender, Todd K., eds. Concordance to the English Poetry of Gerard Manley Hopkins. 344p. 1970. 25.00x (ISBN 0-299-05330-X). U of Wis Pr.

Dunne, Tom, compiled by. Gerard Manley Hopkins: A Comprehensive Bibliography. 1976. 55.00x (ISBN 0-19-818158-2). Oxford U Pr.

Fulweiler, Howard W. Letters from the Darkling Plain: Language & the Grounds of Knowledge in the Poetry of Arnold & Hopkins. LC 72-77839. 1972. 12.00x (ISBN 0-8262-0125-3). U of Mo Pr.

Heuser, Alan. Shaping Vision of Gerard Manley Hopkins. 1968. Repr. of 1958 ed. 12.50 (ISBN 0-208-00296-0, Archon). Shoe String.

Holloway, Marcella M. The Prosodic Theory of Gerard Manley Hopkins. 1947. pap. 5.95 (ISBN 0-8132-0257-4). Cath U Pr.

Iyengar, K. Gerard Manley Hopkins: The Man & Poet. 1948. Repr. 20.00 (ISBN 0-8274-3847-8). R West.

Keating, John E. Gerard Manley Hopkins. 149p. 1980. lib. bdg. 15.00 (ISBN 0-686-61627-8). Folcroft.

--The Wreck of the Deutschland. 1979. Repr. of 1963 ed. lib. bdg. 17.50 (ISBN 0-8495-3125-X). Arden Lib.

Kelly, B. Mind & Poetry of Gerard Manly Hopkins. LC 77-119087. (Studies in Poetry, No. 38). 1970. Repr. of 1935 ed. lib. bdg. 24.95 (ISBN 0-8383-1083-4). Haskell.

Kelly, Bernard. Mind & Poetry of Gerard Manley Hopkins. LC 77-8059. 1935. lib. bdg. 8.75 (ISBN 0-8414-5543-0). Folcroft.

Kenyon Critics. Gerard Manley Hopkins. LC 77-28228. 1978. Repr. of 1945 ed. lib. bdg. 15.25x (ISBN 0-313-20255-9, HOKC). Greenwood.

--Gerard Manley Hopkins. LC 72-93975. 160p. 1973. pap. 2.45 (ISBN 0-8112-0479-0, NDP355). New Directions.

Kitchen, Paddy. Gerard Manley Hopkins. LC 78-56337. (Illus.). 1979. 11.95 (ISBN 0-689-10930-X). Atheneum.

Lahey, G. F. Gerard Manley Hopkins. LC 77-120638. 1970. Repr. of 1930 ed. lib. bdg. 14.00x (ISBN 0-374-94709-0). Octagon.

--Gerard Manley Hopkins. LC 72-95435. (Studies in Poetry, No. 38). 1969. Repr. of 1930 ed. lib. bdg. 29.95 (ISBN 0-8383-0986-0). Haskell.

--Gerard Manley Hopkins. 1973. 69.95 (ISBN 0-87968-030-X). Gordon Pr.

Lees, Francis N. Gerard Manley Hopkins. LC 66-26004. (Columbia Essays on Modern Writers, No. 21). 48p. (Orig.). 1966. pap. 2.00 (ISBN 0-231-02832-6). Columbia U Pr.

Mackenzie, Norman H. A Reader's Guide to Gerard Manley Hopkins. LC 80-69275. 256p. 1981. 17.50x (ISBN 0-8014-1349-4); pap. 8.95 (ISBN 0-8014-9221-1). Cornell U Pr.

Mariani, Paul L. Commentary on the Complete Poems of Gerard Manley Hopkins. 372p. 1970. 24.50x (ISBN 0-8014-0553-X). Cornell U Pr.

Milward, Peter S. & Schoder, Raymond S., eds. Milward-Schoder: Readings of the Week. 1976. 5.95 (ISBN 0-8294-0249-7). Loyola.

Morris, David. Poetry of Gerard Manley Hopkins & T. S. Eliot in the Light of the Donne Tradition. LC 72-193009. 1953. lib. bdg. 20.00 (ISBN 0-8414-6649-1). Folcroft.

Peters, W. A. Gerard Manley Hopkins: A Critical Essay Towards the Understanding of His Poetry. (English Literature Ser). 1970. Repr. of 1948 ed. 9.00 (ISBN 0-384-45880-7). Johnson Repr.

Phare, Elsie E. Poetry of Gerard Manley Hopkins: A Survey & Commentary. LC 66-27137. 1967. Repr. of 1933 ed. 10.00 (ISBN 0-8462-0888-1). Russell.

Pick, John. Gerard Manley Hopkins: Priest & Poet. LC 78-14838. 1978. Repr. of 1966 ed. lib. bdg. 20.50x (ISBN 0-313-20589-2, PIGH). Greenwood.

Ritz, Jean-Georges. Le Poete Gerard Manley Hopkins, S. J. (1844-1889) 726p. 1980. Repr. of 1963 ed. lib. bdg. 100.00 (ISBN 0-8492-7748-5). R West.

Robinson, John. In Extremity. LC 77-77725. 176p. 1980. 23.95 (ISBN 0-521-21690-7); pap. 7.95 (ISBN 0-521-29730-3). Cambridge U Pr.

Schneider, Elisabeth. The Dragon in the Gate: Studies in the Poetry of G. M. Hopkins. LC 68-31434. (Perspectives in Criticism: No. 20). 1968. 24.50x (ISBN 0-520-01150-3). U of Cal Pr.

Sprinker, Michael. A Counterpoint of Dissonance: The Aesthetics & Poetry of Gerard Manley Hopkins. LC 80-13585. 160p. 1980. text ed. 10.95 (ISBN 0-8018-2402-8). Johns Hopkins.

Srinivasa, Iengar K. Gerard Manley Hopkins. LC 71-117591. (English Literature Ser., No. 33). 1970. Repr. of 1943 ed. lib. bdg. 49.95 (ISBN 0-8383-1024-9). Haskell.

Srinivasa Iyengar, K. R. Gerard Manley Hopkins: The Man & the Poet. LC 76-29030. 1976. Repr. of 1948 ed. lib. bdg. 20.00 (ISBN 0-8414-5061-7). Folcroft.

Sulloway, Alison G. Gerard Manley Hopkins & the Victorian Temper. 300p. 1972. 17.50x (ISBN 0-231-03645-0). Columbia U Pr.

Walhout, Donald. Send My Roots Rain: A Study of Religious Experience in the Poetry of Gerard Manley Hopkins. LC 80-23549. xii, 203p. 1981. 15.95x (ISBN 0-8214-0565-9). Ohio U Pr.

Weiss, Theodore R. Gerard Manley Hopkins: Realist on Parnassus. LC 76-47472. 1976. Repr. of 1940 ed. lib. bdg. 8.50 (ISBN 0-8414-9453-3). Folcroft.

Weyand, Norman, ed. Immortal Diamond, Studies in Gerard Manley Hopkins. LC 76-86289. 1969. Repr. of 1949 ed. lib. bdg. 27.50x (ISBN 0-374-98379-8). Octagon.

Young, Thomas D., ed. The New Criticism & After. LC 76-6165. 1977. 7.50x (ISBN 0-8139-0672-5). U Pr of Va.

HOPKINS, HARRY LLOYD, 1890-1946

Charles, Searle F. Minister of Relief: Harry Hopkins & the Depression. LC 74-2585. (Illus.). 286p. 1974. Repr. of 1963 ed. lib. bdg. 15.50x (ISBN 0-8371-7407-4, CHMR). Greenwood.

HOPKINS, JOHN HENRY, BISHOP, 1792-1868

Goodwin, Daniel R. Southern Slavery in Its Present Aspects. LC 78-97452. Repr. of 1864 ed. 15.25x (ISBN 0-8371-2687-8, Pub. by Negro U Pr). Greenwood.

HOPKINS, MARK, 1813-1878

Latta, Estelle. Controversial Mark Hopkins. 2nd rev ed. (Illus.). 254p. 1963. 5.00 (ISBN 0-910740-23-2). Holmes.

HOPKINS, SAMUEL, 1721-1803

Conforti, Joseph. Samuel Hopkins & the New Divinity Movement: Calvinism, the Congregational Ministry, & Reform in New England Between the Great Awakenings. 240p. (Orig.). 1981. pap. 16.95 (ISBN 0-8028-1871-4). Eerdmans.

Hopkins, Samuel. Sketches of the Life of the Late Reverend Samuel Hopkins, 2 vols. LC 72-78754. 1805. Repr. 49.00 (ISBN 0-403-08931-X). Somerset Pub.

HOPKINSON, FRANCIS, 1737-1791

Hastings, George E. Life & Works of Francis Hopkinson. LC 68-11334. (Illus.). 1968. Repr. of 1926 ed. 15.00 (ISBN 0-8462-1123-8). Russell.

Sonneck, Oscar G. Francis Hopkinson, the First American Poet-Composer, & James Lyon, Patriot, Preacher, Psalmodist. 2nd ed. LC 65-23393. (Music Ser). 1966. Repr. of 1905 ed. lib. bdg. 19.50 (ISBN 0-306-70918-X). Da Capo.

HOPPED-UP MOTORS

see Automobiles, Racing–Motors

HOPPER, ISAAC T.

Child, Lydia M. Isaac T. Hopper: A True Life. LC 79-88998. Repr. of 1854 ed. 22.00x (ISBN 0-8371-1737-2, Pub. by Negro U Pr). Greenwood.

HOPPER, EDWARD

Century Association, New York. Robert Henri & Five of His Pupils: Loan Exhibition of Paintings, April 5, to June 1, 1946. LC 74-160918. (Biography Index Reprint Ser). Repr. of 1946 ed. 14.00 (ISBN 0-8369-8081-6). Arno.

Goodrich, Lloyd. Edward Hopper. concise ed. LC 76-23494. (Illus.). 1977. 17.50 (ISBN 0-8109-1061-6). Abrams.

Levin, Gail. Edward Hopper As Illustrator. (Illus.). 1979. 24.95 (ISBN 0-393-01243-3). Norton.

--Edward Hopper: The Art & the Artist. (Illus.). 1980. 29.95 (ISBN 0-393-01374-X). Norton.

HOPS

Meeker, E. Hop Culture in the U. S. Repr. of 1883 ed. pap. 16.00 (ISBN 0-8466-6027-X, SJU27). Shorey.

Pearce, Helen R. The Hop Industry in Australia. (Illus.). 1976. 27.50x (ISBN 0-522-84097-3, Pub. by Melbourne U Pr). Intl Schol Bk Serv.

Scot, Reginald. A Perfite Platforme of a Hoppe Garden. LC 73-7079. (English Experience Ser.: No. 620). 56p. 1973. Repr. of 1574 ed. 7.00 (ISBN 90-221-0620-9). Walter J Johnson.

HORACE (QUINTUS HORATIUS FLACCUS)

Aden, John M. Something Like Horace: Studies in the Art & Allusion of Pope's Horatian Satires. LC 71-83208. 1969. 5.00 (ISBN 0-8265-1138-4). Vanderbilt U Pr.

Brink, C. O. On Reading a Horatian Satire: An Interpretation of Sermons II6. 20p. 1965. pap. 2.00x (ISBN 0-424-05100-1, Pub. by Sydney U. Pr). Intl Schol Bk Serv.

Campbell, Archibald Y. Horace, a New Interpretation. LC 70-109714. Repr. of 1924 ed. lib. bdg. 15.25x (ISBN 0-8371-4204-0, CAHO). Greenwood.

Chapman, John B. Horace & His Poetry. LC 70-120975. (Poetry & Life Ser.). Repr. of 1913 ed. 7.25 (ISBN 0-404-52505-9). AMS Pr.

Conway, Robert S. Makers of Europe. Dickinson College, James Henry Morgan Lectures, 1930. facsimile ed. LC 67-28748. (Essay Index Reprint Ser). 1931. 11.00 (ISBN 0-8369-0330-7). Arno.

Costa, C. D., ed. Horace. (Greek & Latin Studies). 176p. 1973. 14.95x (ISBN 0-7100-7597-9). Routledge & Kegan.

Fraenkel, Eduard. Horace. 478p. 1981. pap. 24.00x (ISBN 0-19-814376-1). Oxford U Pr.

--Horace. (Oxford Paperbooks Ser). 1957. 34.00x (ISBN 0-19-814310-9). Oxford U Pr.

Frank, Tenney. Catullus & Horace: Two Poets in Their Environment. LC 65-13941. 1965. Repr. of 1928 ed. 9.50 (ISBN 0-8462-0200-X). Russell.

Fuchs, Jacob, tr. Horace's Satires & Epistles. 1977. 9.95 (ISBN 0-393-04479-3). Norton.

Goad, Caroline. Horace in the English Literature of 18th Century. LC 67-30804. (Studies in Comparative Literature, No. 35). 1969. Repr. of 1918 ed. lib. bdg. 49.95 (ISBN 0-8383-0701-9). Haskell.

Horace. Horace's Satires & Epistles. Fuchs, Jacob, tr. 1980. pap. 3.95 (ISBN 0-393-09093-0). Norton.

Horatius Flaccus, Q. Satires. 1971. Repr. of 1883 ed. 25.00 (ISBN 0-403-01030-6). Scholarly.

Horatius Flaccus, Quintus. Horace His Arte of Poetrie, Pistles, & Satyrs Englished (1567) Drant, Thomas H., tr. from Lat. LC 73-173753. 296p. 1972. Repr. of 1567 ed. 30.00x (ISBN 0-8201-1099-X). Schol Facsimiles.

McKay, A. G. & Shepherd, D. M., eds. Roman Lyric Poetry. 1970. 12.95 (ISBN 0-312-69055-X). St Martin.

Maresca, Thomas E. Pope's Horatian Poems. LC 66-23259. 1966. 5.00 (ISBN 0-8142-0089-3). Ohio St U Pr.

Martin, Theodore. Horace. 1877. Repr. 25.00 (ISBN 0-8274-2537-6). R West.

Naylor, Henry D. Horace, Odes & Epodes: A Study in Poetic Word-Order. (Latin Poetry Ser.: Vol. 9). (LC 77-070832). 1977. Repr. of 1922 ed. lib. bdg. 33.00 (ISBN 0-8240-2958-5). Garland Pub.

Nisbet, Robin G. & Hubbard, Margaret. Commentary on Horace: Odes. Bk. 1 1970. 69.00x (ISBN 0-19-814439-3); Bk. 2 1978. 53.00x (ISBN 0-19-814452-0). Oxford U Pr.

Oates, Whitney. Influence of Simonides of Ceos on Horace. LC 72-122986. (Studies in Comparative Literature, No. 35). 1970. Repr. of 1932 ed. lib. bdg. 29.95 (ISBN 0-8383-1119-9). Haskell.

Perret, Jacques. Horace. Humez, Bertha, tr. LC 64-21812. (Gotham Library). 212p. 1964. pap. 3.95x (ISBN 0-8147-0338-0). NYU Pr.

Pritchard, John P. Return to the Fountains. 1966. lib. bdg. 15.00x (ISBN 0-374-96650-8). Octagon.

Sanders, Henry A., ed. Roman Historical Sources & Institutions. Repr. of 1904 ed. pap. 31.00 (ISBN 0-384-38801-9). Johnson Repr.

Schmidt, Magdalena. Die Komposition Von Vergils Georgica, Mit Vier Beilagen. Repr. of 1930 ed. pap. 15.50 (ISBN 0-384-54070-8). Johnson Repr.

Schweikert, Ernst. Zur Uberlieferung der Horaz-Scholien. Repr. of 1915 ed. pap. 5.50 (ISBN 0-384-54400-2). Johnson Repr.

Sedgwick, Henry D. Horace: A Biography. LC 66-27146. 1967. Repr. of 1947 ed. 7.50 (ISBN 0-8462-0950-0). Russell.

Sellar, William Y. Roman Poets of the Augustan Age. Incl. Bk. 1. Horace & the Elegiac Poets. Lang, Andrew, memoir by. LC 65-23488. (Illus.). xviii, 362p. Repr. of 1892 ed; Bk. 2. Virgil. 3rd ed. LC 65-23489. xiv, 423p. Repr. of 1908 ed. 15.00x (ISBN 0-8196-0162-4). Biblo.

Showerman, Grant. Horace & His Influence. LC 63-10271. (Our Debt to Greece & Rome Ser). Repr. of 1930 ed. 7.50x (ISBN 0-8154-0206-6). Cooper Sq.

Smith, Clement L. The Odes & Epodes of Horace. 1894. Repr. 25.00 (ISBN 0-8274-3055-8). R West.

Thayer, Mary R. Influence of Horace on the Chief English Poets of the Nineteenth Century. LC 67-18297. 1967. Repr. of 1916 ed. 5.75 (ISBN 0-8462-1131-9). Russell.

Tuckwell, W. Horace. 1905. Repr. 30.00 (ISBN 0-8274-2536-8). R West.

Verrall, A. W. Studies Literary & Historical in the Odes of Horace. LC 68-26258. 1969. Repr. of 1884 ed. 10.50 (ISBN 0-8046-0480-0). Kennikat.

Wickham, E. C. Horace for English Readers: Being a Translation of the Poems of Quintus Horatius Flaccus into English Prose. 1903. Repr. 20.00 (ISBN 0-8274-2538-4). R West.

Wilkinson, L. P. Horace & His Lyric Poetry. 1957. pap. 6.95 (ISBN 0-521-09553-0). Cambridge U Pr.

HORAE (BOOKS OF HOURS)

see Hours, Books Of

HORDE

see Nomads

HORGAN, PAUL, 1903-

Horgan, Paul. Approaches to Writing. 352p. 1973. 10.00 (ISBN 0-374-10569-3); pap. 3.25 (ISBN 0-374-51158-6). FS&G.

HORIZONTAL PROPERTY

see Condominium (Housing)

HORMEL (GEORGE A.) AND COMPANY

Blum, Fred H. Toward a Democratic Work Process. LC 73-11840. 229p. 1974. Repr. of 1953 ed. lib. bdg. 15.00x (ISBN 0-8371-7063-X, BLDW). Greenwood.

HORMONAL STEROIDS

see Steroid Hormones

HORMONE RESEARCH

Annual Hormone Research Symposium, 1st, 1974. Hormone Research I: Proceedings. new ed. Norvell, M. & Shellenberger, T., eds. LC 79-114179. (Illus.). 142p. 1976. text ed. 25.00 (ISBN 0-89116-009-4). Hemisphere Pub.

Annual Hormone Research Symposium, 2nd, 1975. Hormone Research II: Proceedings. new ed. Norvell, M. J. & Shellenberger, T. E., eds. LC 79-114179. (Illus.). 1977. text ed. 25.00 (ISBN 0-89116-039-6). Hemisphere Pub.

Annual Hormone Research Symposium, 3rd, 1976. Hormone Research III: Proceedings. new ed. Norvell, M. J. & Shellenberger, T. E., eds. LC 79-114179. (Illus.). 1977. text ed. 25.00 (ISBN 0-89116-070-1). Hemisphere Pub.

Blecher, Melvin & Barr, Robert S. Receptors & Human Disease. (Illus.). 332p. 1981. 39.00 (ISBN 0-686-77753-0, 0609-6). Williams & Wilkins.

Creutzfeldt, W., ed. The Entero-Insular Axis. (Frontiers of Hormone Research: Vol. 7). (Illus.). x, 310p. 1980. 69.00 (ISBN 3-8055-0795-X). S Karger.

Dorfman, Ralph, ed. Methods in Hormone Research: A Multi-Volume Work, 5 vols. Incl. Vol. 3. Steroidal Activity in Experimental Animals & Man: Part a. 1964. 58.00 (ISBN 0-12-221103-0); Vol. 4. Steroidal Activity in Experimental Animals & Man: Part B. 1965. 46.50 (ISBN 0-12-221104-9); Vol. 5. Steroidal Activity in Experimental Animals & Man: Part C. 1966. 46.50 (ISBN 0-12-221105-7); Vol. 1. 2nd ed. 1968. 61.00 (ISBN 0-12-221161-8); Vol. 2a. 2nd ed. 1969. 61.00 (ISBN 0-12-221162-6). Acad Pr.

Edwards, R. G. & Johnson, M. H., eds. Physiological Effects of Immunity Against Reproductive Hormones. LC 75-12470. (Clinical & Experimental Immunoreproduction Ser.: No. 3). (Illus.). 300p. 1976. 42.50 (ISBN 0-521-20914-5). Cambridge U Pr.

Greep, Roy, ed. Recent Progress in Hormone Research, Vol. 37. (Serial Publication). 1981. 65.00 (ISBN 0-12-571137-9). Acad Pr.

Gurpide, E. Tracer Methods in Hormone Research. (Monographs on Endocrinology: Vol. 8). (Illus.). xi, 188p. 1975. 37.50 (ISBN 0-387-07039-7). Springer-Verlag.

Harris, Robert S., et al, eds. Vitamins & Hormones: Advances in Research & Applications. Incl. Vols. 1-8. 1943-50. 48.00 ea. Vol. 1 (ISBN 0-12-709801-1). Vol. 2 (ISBN 0-12-709802-X). Vol. 3 (ISBN 0-12-709803-8). Vol. 4 (ISBN 0-12-709804-6). Vol. 5 (ISBN 0-12-709805-4). Vol. 6 (ISBN 0-12-709806-2). Vol. 7 (ISBN 0-12-709807-0). Vol. 8 (ISBN 0-12-709808-9); Vol. 9. 1951. 48.00 (ISBN 0-12-709809-7); Vol. 10. 1952. 48.00 (ISBN 0-12-709810-0); Vols. 11-16. 1953-58. Vols. 11-12. 48.00 ea.; Vol. 11. (ISBN 0-12-709811-9); Vol. 12. (ISBN 0-12-709812-7); Vols. 13-16. 48.00 ea.; Vol. 13. (ISBN 0-12-709813-5); Vol. 14. (ISBN 0-12-709814-3); Vol. 15. (ISBN 0-12-709815-1); Vol. 16. (ISBN 0-12-709816-X); Vol. 17. Harris, Robert S., ed. 1959. 48.00 ea. (ISBN 0-12-709817-8); Vol. 18. 1960. 48.00 (ISBN 0-12-709818-6); Vol. 19. 1961. 48.00 (ISBN 0-12-709819-4); Vol. 20. Incl. International Symposium on Vitamin E & Metabolism. Wool, I. G. 1962. 48.00 (ISBN 0-12-709820-8); Vol. 21. 1963. 48.00 (ISBN 0-12-709821-6); Vol. 22. Incl. International Symposium on Vitamin B6. 1964. 48.00 (ISBN 0-12-709822-4); Vol. 23. 1965. 48.00 (ISBN 0-12-709823-2); Vol. 24. 1966. 48.00 (ISBN 0-12-709824-0); Vol. 25. 1967. 48.00 (ISBN 0-12-709825-9); Vol. 26. 1968. 48.00 (ISBN 0-12-709826-7); Vol. 27. 1970. 48.00 (ISBN 0-12-709827-5); Vol. 28. Munson, Paul L., ed. 1971. 48.00 (ISBN 0-12-709828-3); Vol. 29. 1971. 48.00 (ISBN 0-12-709829-1); Vol. 30. 1972. 48.00 (ISBN 0-12-709830-5); Vol. 35. Munson, Paul L., et al, eds. 1978. 48.00 (ISBN 0-12-709835-6); Vol. 36. Munson, Paul L., et al, eds. 1979. 59.50 (ISBN 0-12-709836-4). Acad Pr.

Kramer, H. & Krueck, H. J., eds. Natriuretic Hormone. (Illus.). 1978. pap. 18.50 (ISBN 0-387-08795-8). Springer-Verlag.

Laurentian Hormone Conferences. Recent Progress in Hormone Research: Proceedings. Pincus, Gregory, ed. Incl. Vols. 1-5. 1947-50. Set. Vol. 1. 54.50 (ISBN 0-12-571101-8); Vol. 2. 54.00 (ISBN 0-12-571102-6); Vol. 3. 55.50 (ISBN 0-12-571103-4); Vol. 4. 55.50 (ISBN 0-12-571104-2); Vol. 5. 55.50 (ISBN 0-12-571105-0); Vols. 6-11. 1951-55. 55.50 ea.; Vol. 6. (ISBN 0-12-571106-9). Vol. 7 (ISBN 0-12-571107-7). Vol. 8 (ISBN 0-12-571108-5). Vol. 9 (ISBN 0-12-571109-3). Vol. 10 (ISBN 0-12-571110-7). Vol. 11 (ISBN 0-12-571111-5); Vol. 12. 1956. 48.50 (ISBN 0-12-571112-3); Vol. 13. 1957. 48.50 (ISBN 0-12-571113-1); Vols. 14-15. 1958-59. 48.50 ea. Vol. 14 (ISBN 0-12-571114-X). Vol. 15 (ISBN 0-12-571115-8); Vol. 16. 1960. 55.50 (ISBN 0-12-571116-6); Vols. 17-18. 1961-62. 55.50 ea. Vol. 17 (ISBN 0-12-571117-4). Vol. 18 (ISBN 0-12-571118-2); Vol. 19. 1963. 54.00 (ISBN 0-12-571119-0); Vol. 20. 1964. 54.00 (ISBN 0-12-571120-4); Vol. 21. 1965. 62.00 (ISBN 0-12-571121-2); Vol. 22. 1966. 62.00 (ISBN 0-12-571122-0); Vol. 23. 1967. 70.00 (ISBN 0-12-571123-9); Vol. 24. Astwood, E. B., ed. 1968. 70.00 (ISBN 0-12-571124-7); Vol. 25. 1969. 70.00 (ISBN 0-12-571125-5); Vols. 26-27. 1970-71. 70.00 ea. Vol. 26 (ISBN 0-12-571126-3). Vol. 27 (ISBN 0-12-571127-1); Vol. 28. 1972. 58.00 (ISBN 0-12-571128-X); Vol. 29. 1973. 61.00 (ISBN 0-12-571129-8); Vol. 32. Greep, Roy O., ed. 1976. 70.00 (ISBN 0-12-571132-8); Vol. 33. Greep, Roy O., ed. 1977. 60.00 (ISBN 0-12-571133-6); Vol. 34. Greep, Roy O., ed. 1978. 59.00 (ISBN 0-12-571134-4). Acad Pr.

Nieschlag, E., ed. Hormone Assays in Reproductive Medicine. (Hormone Research: Vol. 9, No. 6). (Illus.). 1978. pap. 18.75 (ISBN 3-8055-2975-9). S Karger.

Van Keep, P. A. & Lauritzen, C., eds. Aging & Estrogens. (Frontiers of Normoni Reserach Ser.: Vol. 2). (Illus.). 1973. 27.00 (ISBN 3-8055-1606-1). S Karger.

HORMONE THERAPY

see also Steroid Hormones–Therapeutic Use

Cooper, Wendy. Don't Change: A Biological Revolution for Women. LC 74-26959. 192p. 1975. 7.95 (ISBN 0-8128-1783-4). Stein & Day.

Fanta, D. Hormonal Therapy of Acne. (Illus.). viii, 91p. 1980. pap. 20.10 (ISBN 0-387-81586-4). Springer-Verlag.

Forsling, Mary L. Antidiuretic Hormone, Vol. 4. Horrobin, D. F., ed. (Annual Research Reviews Ser.). 165p. 1980. 26.00 (ISBN 0-88831-072-2). Eden Med Res.

Jern, Helen Z. Hormone Therapy of the Menopause & Aging. (Illus.). 196p. 1973. text ed. 15.75 (ISBN 0-398-02744-7). C C Thomas.

Kielholz, P. A Therapeutic Approach to the Psyche Via the Beta - Adrenergic System. 1978. 24.50 (ISBN 0-8391-1270-X). Univ Park.

Kutsky, Roman J. Handbook of Vitamins, Minerals & Hormones. 1981. text ed. 24.50 (ISBN 0-442-24557-2). Van Nos Reinhold.

Loraine, John A. & Bell, E. Trevor. Hormone Assays & Their Clinical Application. 4th ed. LC 75-38659. (Illus.). 1976. 65.00 (ISBN 0-443-01301-2). Churchill.

Stoll, Basil A., ed. Endocrine Therapy in Malignant Disease. LC 78-188731. (Illus.). 400p. 1972. 23.00 (ISBN 0-7216-8615-X). Saunders.

Tausk, Marius. Pharmacology of Hormones. (Illus.). 1976. pap. 10.95 (ISBN 0-8151-8718-1). Year Bk Med.

Thomas, J. Synopsis of Endocrine Pharmacology. 1973. 19.50 (ISBN 0-8391-0746-3). Univ Park.

Ufer, Joachim. Principles & Practice of Hormone Therapy in Gynaecology & Obstetrics. 1969. 40.00x (ISBN 3-11-000614-6). De Gruyter.

Van Wimersma Greidanus, T. B. & Rees, L. H., eds. ACTH & LPH in Health & Disease. (Frontiers of Hormone Research Ser.: Vol. 8). (Illus.). 200p. 1981. 79.25 (ISBN 3-8055-1977-X). S Karger.

Wilson, Robert A. Feminine Forever. LC 66-11166. (Illus.). 224p. 1966. 8.95 (ISBN 0-87131-049-X). M Evans.

HORMONES

see also Endocrine Glands; Endocrinology; Hormone Research; Hormone Therapy; Hormones, Sex; Peptide Hormones; Plant Hormones; Steroid Hormones; Thyroid Hormones also names of hormones

Agarwal, M. K., ed. Antihormones. 1979. 61.00 (ISBN 0-444-80119-7, Biomedical Pr). Elsevier.

Antoniades, Harry N., ed. Hormones in Human Blood: Detection & Assay. 1976. 49.50x (ISBN 0-674-40635-4, ANHH). Harvard U Pr.

Austin, C. R. & Short, R. V., eds. Mechanisms of Hormone Action. LC 79-16287. (Reproduction in Mammals Ser.: Bk. 7). (Illus.). 1980. 27.50 (ISBN 0-521-22945-6); pap. 7.95x (ISBN 0-521-29737-0). Cambridge U Pr.

Barrington, E. J., ed. Hormones & Evolution. Vol. 1, 1979. 79.50 (ISBN 0-12-079401-2); Vol. 2, 1980. 79.50 (ISBN 0-12-079402-0). Acad Pr.

Barrington, Ernest J. Hormones & Evolution. 164p. 1972. Repr. of 1964 ed. 9.50 (ISBN 0-88275-060-7). Krieger.

Beling, Carl, ed. The LH - Releasing Hormone. (Illus.). 368p. 1979. text ed. 39.50x (ISBN 0-89352-045-4). Masson Pub.

Berde, E. & Eichler, O., eds. Neurohypophysial Hormones & Similar Polypeptides. (Handbook of Experimental Pharmacology: Vol. 23). (Illus.). 1968. 135.70 (ISBN 0-387-04149-4). Springer-Verlag.

Birnbaumer, Lutz & O'Malley, B. W., eds. Receptors & Hormone Action, Vol. 3. 1978. 59.50 (ISBN 0-12-526303-1). Acad Pr.

Blecher, Melvin & Barr, Robert S. Receptors & Human Disease. (Illus.). 332p. 1981. 39.00 (ISBN 0-686-77753-0, 0609-6). Williams & Wilkins.

Bloom, S. R., ed. Gut Hormones. 2nd ed. Polack, J. M. (Illus.). 605p. 1981. text ed. 59.00 (ISBN 0-686-31136-1). Churchill.

Bonfils, S., et al, eds. Hormonal Receptors in Digestive Tract Physiology. (INSERM Symposium: No. 3). 1977. 58.75 (ISBN 0-7204-0618-8, North-Holland). Elsevier.

Boyland, Eric, et al. On Cancer & Hormones: Essays in Experimental Biology. LC 62-13921. (Illus.). 1962. 13.00x (ISBN 0-226-06941-9). U of Chicago Pr.

Brain, Paul F. Hormones & Aggression. Horrobin, D. F., ed. (Hormone Research Review Ser.: Vol. I). 126p. 1980. Repr. of 1977 ed. 19.95 (ISBN 0-87705-963-2). Human Sci Pr.

--Hormones, Drugs & Aggression. (Hormone Research Review Ser.: Vol. III). 173p. 1980. Repr. of 1979 ed. 24.95 (ISBN 0-87705-959-4). Human Sci Pr.

Brandenburg, D., ed. Insulin: Chemistry, Structure & Function of Insulin & Related Hormones. text ed. 112.00 (ISBN 3-11-008156-3). De Gruyter.

Brenner, Barry M. & Stein, Jay H., eds. Hormonal Function & the Kidney. (Contemporary Issues in Nephrology: Vol. 4). (Illus.). 1979. text ed. 29.00 (ISBN 0-443-08039-9). Churchill.

Brooks, Chandler M., et al. Humors, Hormones, & Neurosecretions: The Origins & Development of Man's Present Knowledge of the Humoral Control of Body Functions. LC 61-14336. 1962. 25.50 (ISBN 0-87395-006-2); microfiche 25.50 (ISBN 0-87395-106-9). State U NY Pr.

Buckley, J. P. & Ferrario, C. M. Central Actions of Antiotensin & Related Hormones. 1977. text ed. 60.00 (ISBN 0-08-020933-5). Pergamon.

Burdette, W. J., ed. Invertebrate Endocrinology & Hormonal Heterophylly. (Illus.). 438p. 1974. 32.90 (ISBN 0-387-06594-6). Springer-Verlag.

Butt, W. R. Hormone Chemistry. (Illus.). 1967. 16.95x (ISBN 0-442-01221-7). Van Nos Reinhold.

Butt, Wilfrid R., ed. Topics in Hormone Chemistry, Vol. 1. LC 77-84147. 1978. 60.95 (ISBN 0-470-99310-3). Halsted Pr.

Charyulu, Komanduri & Sudarsanam, Anam, eds. Hormones and Cancer. LC 76-10509. (Illus.). 310p. 1976. 25.00 (ISBN 0-8151-1644-6, Pub. by Symposia Special). Year Bk Med.

Choh Hao Li, ed. Hormonal Proteins & Peptides: Techniques in Protein Chemistry, Vol. 9. LC 80-11061. (Hormonal Proteins & Peptides Ser.). 1980. 35.00 (ISBN 0-12-447209-5). Acad Pr.

Clark, J. H., et al, eds. Hormone & Antihormone, Action at the Target Cell. (Dahlem Workshop Reports Ser.: L.S.R.R. No.3). 1976. pap. 26.50 (ISBN 0-89573-087-1). Verlag Chemie.

--Hormone & Antihormone Action at the Target Cell: Report of the Dahlem Workshop on Hormone & Antihormone Action at the Target Cell. (Illus.). 1976. lib. bdg. 16.50 (ISBN 0-910000-03-4). Dahlem.

Cold Spring Harbor Symposia On Quantitative Biology. Relation of Hormones to Development: Proceedings, Vol. 10. Repr. of 1942 ed. 22.00 (ISBN 0-384-50250-4). Johnson Repr.

Copinschi, G. & Jaquet, P., eds. Lipo-Corticotropic Hormones & Cushing's Disease. (Journal: Hormone Research Ser.: Vol. 13, No. 4-5). (Illus.). 148p. 1981. pap. 39.75 (ISBN 3-8055-3082-X). S Karger.

Csaba, G. The Ontogeny & Phylogeny of Hormone Receptors, Vol. 15. (Monographs in Developmental Biology: Vol. 15). (Illus.). xii, 172p. 1981. 86.25 (ISBN 3-8055-2174-X). S Karger.

De Brux, J., et al, eds. The Endometrium--Hormonal Impacts. 162p. 1981. 29.50 (ISBN 0-306-40749-3, Plenum Pr). Plenum Pub.

Dellman, H. D., et al, eds. Comparative Endocrinology of Prolactin. LC 77-1871. (Advances in Experimental Medicine & Biology: Vol. 80). 215p. 1977. 22.50 (ISBN 0-306-39080-9, Plenum Pr). Plenum Pub.

De Sousa, Maria S., et al. The Effects of Hormones on Immunity, Vol. 2. LC 72-13691. (Illus.). 220p. 1973. text ed. 30.00x (ISBN 0-8422-7098-1). Irvington.

Diamond, Marian C. & Korenbrot, Carol C., eds. Hormonal Contraceptives, Estrogens & Human Welfare. 1978. 18.50 (ISBN 0-12-214750-2). Acad Pr.

The Digestive System & Hormones. (You & Your Body Ser.). (Illus.). 1974. pap. 9.95 (ISBN 0-87618-006-3). R J Brady.

Eisenbach, G. M. & Brod, J., eds. Vasoactive Renal Hormones. (Contributions to Nephrology: Vol. 12). (Illus.). 1978. pap. 40.75 (ISBN 3-8055-2839-6). S Karger.

Eisenbach, G. M. & Brod, Jan, eds. Non-Vasoactive Renal Hormones. (Contributions to Nephrology: Vol. 13). (Illus.). 1978. pap. 40.75 (ISBN 3-8055-2895-7). S Karger.

Eleftheriou, Basil E. & Sprott, Richard L., eds. Hormonal Correlates of Behavior. Incl. Vol. 1 Lifespan View. 439p. 1975. 35.00 (ISBN 0-306-37504-4); Vol. 2, an Organismic View. 366p (ISBN 0-306-37505-2). LC 75-5938. 1975. 35.00 ea. (Plenum Pr). Plenum Pub.

Engle, Earl T. & Pincus, Gregory, eds. Hormones & the Aging Process. 1956. 31.50 (ISBN 0-12-239050-4). Acad Pr.

Euro Inserm Symposium, 3rd, France, 1978. Hormones & Cell Regulation, Vol. 3. Dumont, J & Nunez, J., eds. 1979. 39.00 (ISBN 0-7204-0672-2, North Holland). Elsevier.

Forsling, Mary. Anti-Diuretic Hormone, Vol. 3. Horrobin, D. F., ed. (Annual Research Reviews Ser.). 1979. 26.00 (ISBN 0-88831-044-7). Eden Med Res.

Forsling, Mary L. Anti-Diuretic Hormone, Vol. 1. (Annual Research Reviews Ser.). 1977. 19.20 (ISBN 0-904406-51-2). Eden Med Res.

--Anti-Diuretic Hormone, Vol. 2. LC 78-309279. (Annual Research Reviews). 1978. 24.00 (ISBN 0-88831-016-1). Eden Med Res.

Fotherby, K. & Pal, S. B., eds. Hormones in Normal & Abnormal Human Tissues. 1980. 110.00x (ISBN 3-11-008031-1). De Gruyter.

Franchimont, P. & Burger, H., eds. Human Growth Hormone & Gonadotrophins in Health & Disease. LC 73-86079. 494p. 1975. 78.00 (ISBN 0-444-10594-8, North-Holland). Elsevier.

Gilbert, L. I., ed. Juvenile Hormones. LC 76-21097. 572p. 1976. 45.00 (ISBN 0-306-30959-9, Plenum Pr). Plenum Pub.

Gray, C. H. & James, V. H. T. Hormones in Blood, Vol. 3. 3rd ed. LC 78-73882. 1980. 93.00 (ISBN 0-12-296203-6). Acad Pr.

Gray, C. H. & James, V. H. T., eds. Hormones in Blood, Vol. I. 3rd ed. 1979. 99.50 (ISBN 0-12-296201-X). Acad Pr.

--Hormones in Blood, Vol. 2. 3rd ed. 1979. 81.00 (ISBN 0-12-296202-8). Acad Pr.

Greep, Roy O., ed. Recent Progress in Hormone Research, Vol. 35. 1979. 44.00 (ISBN 0-12-571135-2). Acad Pr.

--Recent Progress in Hormone Research, Vol. 36. (Serial Pub.). 1980. 54.00 (ISBN 0-12-571136-0). Acad Pr.

Gupta, Derek & Voelter, Wolfgang. Hypothalamic Hormones: Chemistry, Physiology & Clinical Applications. (Illus.). 1978. 75.30 (ISBN 3-527-25712-8). Verlag Chemie.

--Hypothalamic Hormones: Structure, Synthesis, & Biological Activity. (Illus.). 1975. 34.20 (ISBN 3-527-25589-3). Verlag Chemie.

Haller, Jurgen. Hormonal Contraception. rev. 2nd ed. Gottfried, Herbert, tr. from Third Ger. Ed. LC 71-188791. (Illus.). 1972. 13.00x (ISBN 0-87672-034-3). Geron-X.

Hamburgh, Max & Barrington, E. J., eds. Hormones in Development. LC 72-116424. 854p. 1971. 59.50 (ISBN 0-306-50028-0, Plenum Pr). Plenum Pub.

Horrobin, David F. Prolactin, Vol. 2. (Annual Research Reviews Ser.). 1974. 19.20 (ISBN 0-85200-120-7). Eden Med Res.

--Prolactin, Vol. 4. (Annual Research Reviews Ser.). 1976. 24.00 (ISBN 0-904406-47-4). Eden Med Res.

--Prolactin, Vol. 5. LC 77-369577. (Annual Research Reviews Ser.). 1977. 24.00 (ISBN 0-88831-009-9). Eden Med Res.

--Prolactin, Vol. 6. (Annual Research Reviews Ser.). 1979. 21.60 (ISBN 0-88831-041-2). Eden Med Res.

--Prolactin, Vol. 8. (Annual Research Reviews Ser.). 152p. 1981. 24.00 (ISBN 0-88831-093-5). Eden Med Res.

Iacobelli, Stefano, et al, eds. Hormones & Cancer. (Progress in Cancer Research & Therapy Ser.). 589p. 1980. text ed. 64.00 (ISBN 0-89004-486-4). Raven.

International Congress On Clinical Chemistry - 7th. Hormones Lipids & Miscellaneous: Proceedings. Felber, J. P. & Scheidegger, J. J., eds. (Clinical Chemistry Ser.: Vol. 3). 1971. 29.50 (ISBN 0-8391-0591-6). Univ Park.

International Seminar on Reproductive Physiology & Sexual Endocrinology, 4th, Brussels, May 1972. Hormones & Antagonists: Proceedings. Hubinont, P. O., et al, eds. (Gynecoiogic Investigation: Vol. 2, Nos. 1-6; Vol. 3, Nos. 1-4). (Illus.). 1973. 67.25 (ISBN 3-8055-1446-8). S Karger.

International Society of Psychoneuroendocrinology-Brooklyn-1970. Influence of Hormones on the Nervous System: Proceedings. Ford, D. H., ed. (Illus.). 1971. 78.50 (ISBN 3-8055-1216-3). S Karger.

International Symposium of MSH Amsterdam 1976. Melanocyte Stimulating Hormone-Control, Chemistry & Effects: Proceedings. Tilders, F. J., et al, eds. (Frontiers of Hormone Research: Vol. 4). 1977. 59.50 (ISBN 3-8055-2635-0). S Karger.

International Symposium on Basic Applications & Clinical Uses of Hypothalamic Hormones, 1st, Madrid, 5-7 May, 1975. Basic Applications & Clinical Uses of Hypothalamic Hormones: Proceedings. Charro Salgado, A. L, et al, eds. LC 75-46593. (International Congres Ser.: No. 374). (Illus.). 1976. 69.75 (ISBN 0-444-15198-2, Excerpta Medica). Elsevier.

Ishii, S., ed. Hormones, Adaptation & Evolution: International Symposium. 300p. 1980. 44.80 (ISBN 0-387-10033-4). Springer-Verlag.

Jaffe, Bernard M. & Behrman, Harold R., eds. Methods of Hormone Radioimmunassay. 2nd ed. 1979. 65.00 (ISBN 0-12-379260-6). Acad Pr.

Jeffcoate, S. L. & Hutchinson, J. S., eds. The Endocrine Hypothalamus. 1979. 67.50 (ISBN 0-12-382150-9). Acad Pr.

Jenkin, P. M. Animal Hormones, Pt. 2: Control of Growth & Metamorphosis. LC 60-8977. 1970. 42.00 (ISBN 0-08-015648-7). Pergamon.

Joss, E. E. Growth Hormone Deficiency in Childhood: Evaluation of Diagnostic Procedures. (Monographs in Paediatrics: Vol. 5). (Illus.). 100p. 1975. 29.50 (ISBN 3-8055-2159-6). S Karger.

Kato, Junzo, et al. Hormone Receptors in the Brain. (Illus.). 220p. 1973. text ed. 26.50x (ISBN 0-8422-7078-7). Irvington.

Kellen, John A. & Hilf, Russell. Influences of Hormones in Tumor Development, 2 vols. 1979. Vol. 1, 192p. 51.95 (ISBN 0-8493-5351-3); Vol. 2, 224p. 54.95 (ISBN 0-8493-5352-1). CRC Pr.

Keller, Paul J. Hormornal Disorders in Gynecology. (Illus.). 113p. 1981. pap. 16.60 (ISBN 0-387-10341-4). Springer-Verlag.

Klachko, et al. Hormones & Energy Metabolism. LC 78-23943. (Advances in Experimental Medicine & Biology Ser.: Vol. 111). 212p. 1979. 25.00 (ISBN 0-306-40070-7, Plenum Pr). Plenum Pub.

Klachko, David M., et al, eds. Hormone Receptors. LC 77-25856. (Advances in Experimental Medicine & Biology Ser.: Vol. 96). 224p. 1978. 27.50 (ISBN 0-306-32696-5, Plenum Pr). Plenum Pub.

Kutsky, Roman J. Handbook of Vitamins & Hormones. 278p. 1973. pap. 7.95 (ISBN 0-442-24550-5). Van Nos Reinhold.

Lamberts, Steven W. & MacLeod, Robert M. Physiological & Pathological Aspects of Prolactin Secretion, Vol. 1. Horrobin, David F., ed. (Annual Research Reviews Ser.). 1978. 19.20 (ISBN 0-88831-034-X). Eden Med Res.

Lazarev, Nikolai I. Dyshormonal Tumors: The Theory of Prophylaxis & Treatment. LC 65-27347. 136p. 1966. 25.00 (ISBN 0-306-10736-8, Consultants). Plenum Pub.

Levey, Gerald S. Hormone Receptor Interaction: Molecular Aspects. (Modern Pharmacology-Toxicology Ser.: Vol. 9). 1976. 65.50 (ISBN 0-8247-6438-2). Dekker.

Levine, Seymour. Hormones & Behavior. 1972. 46.50 (ISBN 0-12-445450-X). Acad Pr.

Li, Choh H., ed. Hormonal Proteins & Peptides, 7 vols. Incl. Vol. 1. 1973. 35.50 (ISBN 0-12-447201-X); Vol. 2. 1973. 43.00 (ISBN 0-12-447202-8); Vol. 3. 1975. 49.50 (ISBN 0-12-447203-6); Vol. 4. 1977. 38.00 (ISBN 0-12-447204-4); Vol. 5. Lipotropin & Related Peptides. 1978. 33.50 (ISBN 0-12-447205-2); Vol. 6. Thyroid Hormones. 1978. 55.50 (ISBN 0-12-447206-0); Vol. 7. Hypothalmic Hormones. 1979. 35.50 (ISBN 0-12-447207-9). LC 78-5444. Acad Pr.

Litwack, G., ed. Biochemical Actions of Hormones, Vol. 8. 1981. 58.00 (ISBN 0-12-452808-2). Acad Pr.

Litwack, Gerald, ed. Biochemical Actions of Hormones, 7 vols. Incl. Vol. 1. 1970. 60.50 (ISBN 0-12-452801-5); Vol. 2. 1972. 60.50 (ISBN 0-12-452802-3); Vol. 3. 1975. 59.00 (ISBN 0-12-452803-1); Vol. 4. 1977. 54.00 (ISBN 0-12-452804-X); Vol. 5. 1978. 48.50 (ISBN 0-12-452805-8); Vol. 6. 1979. 42.50 (ISBN 0-12-452806-6); Vol. 7. 1980. 45.00 (ISBN 0-12-452807-4). LC 70-107567. Acad Pr.

Luckey, T. Thymic Hormones. 1973. 29.50 (ISBN 0-8391-0705-6). Univ Park.

McKerns, K. W. Hormones & Cancer. 1974. 56.00 (ISBN 0-12-485350-1). Acad Pr.
McQuillan, Mary T. Somatostatin, Vol. 1. Horrobin, D. F., ed. (Annual Research Reviews Ser.). 1979. 24.00 (ISBN 0-88831-040-4). Eden Med Res.
Malkinson, A. M. Hormone Action. LC 75-22108. (Outline Studies in Biology). 64p. (Orig.). 1975. pap. text ed. 5.95 (ISBN 0-412-13070-X, Pub. by Chapman & Hall England). Methuen Inc.
Menon, K. M. & Reel, Jerry R., eds. Steroid Hormone Action & Cancer. LC 76-25873. (Current Topics in Molecular Endocrinology Ser.: Vol. 4). 182p. 1976. 29.50 (ISBN 0-306-34004-6, Plenum Pr). Plenum Pub.
Middlebrook, John H. & Kohn, Leonard D., eds. Receptor-Mediated Binding & Internalization of Toxins & Hormones. 1981. 29.00 (ISBN 0-12-494850-2). Acad Pr.
Miller, Jeffrey & Reznikoff, William. The Operon. LC 78-60439. (Monograph Ser.: No. 7). (Illus.). 449p. 1978. 50.00x (ISBN 0-87969-124-7). Cold Spring Harbor.
Mori, K., et al. Synthetic Chemistry of Insect Phermones & Juvenile Hormones. (Recent Developments in the Chemistry of Natural Carbon Compounds: Vol. 9). (Illus.). 420p. 1979. 40.00x (ISBN 963-05-1632-2). Intl Pubns Serv.
Munson, P. L., et al, eds. Vitamins & Hormones, Vol. 38. (Serial Publication Ser.). 1981. 42.00 (ISBN 0-12-709838-0). Acad Pr.
Munson, Paul L., et al, eds. Vitamins & Hormones: Advances in Research & Applications, Vol. 37. LC 43-10535. 1980. 35.00 (ISBN 0-12-709837-2). Acad Pr.
Nieschlag, E., ed. Hormone Assays in Reproductive Medicine. (Hormone Research: Vol. 9, No. 6). (Illus.). 1978. pap. 18.75 (ISBN 3-8055-2975-9). S Karger.
--Immunization with Hormones in Reproduction Research. 250p. 1975. 36.75 (ISBN 0-7204-4518-3, North-Holland). Elsevier.
Nitzan, Menachem, ed. The Influence of Maternal Hormones on the Fetus & Newborn. (Pediatric & Adolescent Endocrinology: Vol. 5). (Illus.). 1979. pap. 59.50 (ISBN 3-8055-2902-3). S Karger.
Nourse, Alan E. Hormones. (Impact Ser.). (Illus.). (gr. 7 up). 1979. PLB 7.45 s&l (ISBN 0-531-02892-5). Watts.
O'Malley, B. W. & Birnbaumer, L., eds. Receptors & Hormone Action, Vol. 1. 1978. 56.00 (ISBN 0-12-526301-5); by subscription 48.50 (ISBN 0-685-79544-6). Acad Pr.
O'Malley, Bert & Means, Anthony, eds. Receptors for Reproductive Hormones. LC 73-81095. (Advances in Experimental Medicine & Biology Ser.: Vol. 36). 460p. 1973. 35.00 (ISBN 0-306-39036-1, Plenum Pr). Plenum Pub.
O'Malley, Bert W., ed. Hormone Action, Vol. 2. 1978. 60.00 (ISBN 0-12-526302-3); by subscription 51.00 (ISBN 0-686-67867-2). Acad Pr.
Pal, S. B., ed. Enzyme Labelled Immunoassay of Hormones & Drugs. 1978. 72.00x (ISBN 3-11007-539-3). De Gruyter.
Palkovic, M. Hormones, Lipoproteins & Atherosclerosis: Proceedings of a Satelite Symposium of the 28th International Congress of Physiological Sciences, Bratislava, Czechoslovakia, 1980. LC 80-41926. (Advances in Physiological Sciences Ser.: Vol. 35). (Illus.). 300p. 1981. 40.00 (ISBN 0-08-027357-2). Pergamon.
Pennington, G. W. & Naik, Sandra. Hormone Analysis: Methodology & Clinical Intrepretation, Vol. 1. 304p. 1981. 83.95 (ISBN 0-8493-5539-7). CRC Pr.
Pincus, Gregory, ed. Hormones & Atherosclerosis: Proceedings. 1959. 44.00 (ISBN 0-12-557050-3). Acad Pr.
Pincus, Gregory & Thimann, Kenneth V., eds. The Hormones: Physiology, Chemistry & Applications, 5 vols. Incl. Vol. 1. 1948. 72.50 (ISBN 0-12-557001-5); Vol. 2. 1950. 72.50 (ISBN 0-12-557002-3); Vol. 3. 1955. 72.50 (ISBN 0-12-557003-1); Vol. 4. Pincus, Gregory, et al, eds. 1964. 72.50 (ISBN 0-12-557004-X); Vol. 5. Pincus, Gregory, et al, eds. 1964. 72.50 (ISBN 0-12-557005-8). Set. 292.50 (ISBN 0-685-23215-8). Acad Pr.
Raabe, Marie. Insect Neurohormones. Marshall, Nissim, tr. 300p. (Fr.). 1982. text ed. price not set (ISBN 0-306-40782-5, Plenum Pr). Plenum Pub.
Radioimmunoassay of Hormones for Clinical Trials of Fertility Regulating Agents in Developing Countries: Report. (Technical Report Ser.: No. 578). (Also avail. in French & Spanish). 1975. pap. 2.00 (ISBN 92-4-120578-4). World Health.
Robyn, C. & Harter, M., eds. Progress in Prolactin Physiology & Pathology: Proceedings of the Intl. Symposium on Prolactin, Nice, France, October 1977. (Developments in Endocrinology: Vol. 2). 1978. 59.00 (ISBN 0-444-80038-7, Biomedical Pr). Elsevier.
Rosner, Martic C. Hormones & Hyacinths. LC 79-82087. 1980. 5.95 (ISBN 0-87212-126-7). Libra.
Rosselin, G., et al, eds. Hormone Receptors in Digestion & Nutrition: Proceedings of the 2nd Int'l Symposium, France 797. 520p. 1979. 66.00 (ISBN 0-444-80155-3, North Holland). Elsevier.
Sachar, Edward J., ed. Hormones, Behavior, & Psychopathology. LC 75-16660. (American Psychopathological Association Ser.). 325p. 1976. 32.00 (ISBN 0-89004-094-X). Raven.
Sato, Gordon & Ross, Russell, eds. Hormones & Cell Culture, 2 bk. set. LC 79-16328. (Cold Spring Harbor Conferences on Cell Proliferation Ser.: Vol. 6). (Illus.). 982p. 1979. 105.00 (ISBN 0-87969-125-5). Cold Spring Harbor.
Sawin, Clark T. The Hormones: Endocrine Physiology. (Illus.). 308p. 1969. 15.95 (ISBN 0-316-77170-8). Little.
Schulster, D. & Levitzki, A. Cellular Receptors for Hormones & Neurotransmitters. 412p. 1980. 77.00 (ISBN 0-471-27682-0, Pub. by Wiley-Interscience). Wiley.
Seaman, Barbara & Seaman, Gideon. Women & the Crisis in Sex Hormones. 1978. pap. 3.95 (ISBN 0-553-14871-0). Bantam.
Selye, H. Hormones & Resistance, 2 vols. LC 78-155342. (Illus.). 1971. Set. 98.20 (ISBN 0-387-05411-1). Springer-Verlag.
Sereno Research Foundation Conference, Acapulco, July 1972. Hypothalamic Hypophysiotropic Hormones - Physiological & Clinical Studies: Proceedings. Gual, Carlos & Rosemberg, Eugenia, eds. (International Congress Ser.: No. 263). 450p. 1973. 61.00 (ISBN 0-444-15026-9, Excerpta Medica). Elsevier.
Shire, John G. Genetic Variation in Hormone Systems, 2 vols. 1979. Vol. 1, 208p. 54.95 (ISBN 0-8493-5283-5); Vol. 2, 192p. 49.95 (ISBN 0-8493-5284-3). CRC Pr.
Silverberg, Steven G. & Major, Francis J. Estrogens & Cancer. LC 78-17275. 1978. 37.95 (ISBN 0-471-04172-6, Pub. by Wiley Medical). Wiley.
Silverstein, Alvin & Silverstein, Virginia B. Endocrine System: Hormones in the Living World. LC 70-135648. (Systems of the Body Ser.: Vol. 7). (Illus.). (gr. 3-7). 1971. PLB 6.95 (ISBN 0-13-277152-7). P-H.
Swiss Juvenile Hormone Symposium. Proceedings. Schneider, Fritz, ed. (Mitteilungen der Schweizer Entomologischen Gesellschaft Ser: Vol. 44). (Illus.). 207p. 1971. pap. 35.00x (ISBN 0-8002-1876-0). Intl Pubns Serv.
Symposium on Hormones & Cell Regulation (INSERM), 1st, le Bischenberg, Bischoffsheim, France Sept. 27-30, 1976. Hormones & Cell Regulation: Proceedings, Proceedings. Dumont, J. & Nunez, J., eds. 1977. Vol. 1. 30.25 (ISBN 0-7204-0622-6, North-Holland); Vol. 2. 47.00 (ISBN 0-7204-0658-7). Elsevier.
Tausk, Marius. Pharmacology of Hormones. (Illus.). 1976. pap. 10.95 (ISBN 0-8151-8718-1). Year Bk Med.
Thomas, J. Molecular Mechanisms of Gonadal Hormone Action. 1976. 37.50 (ISBN 0-8391-0775-7). Univ Park.
Tribe, M. A. & Eraut, M. R. Hormones Book. LC 77-87396. (Basic Biology Course Ser.: Bk. 11). 1979. 35.50 (ISBN 0-521-21371-1); pap. 11.95x (ISBN 0-521-21370-3); film strip 19.95x (ISBN 0-521-22956-1). Cambridge U Pr.
VanBekkum, D. W., ed. The Biological Activity of Thymic Hormones. LC 75-17617. 1975. 39.95 (ISBN 0-470-89835-6). Halsted Pr.
Van Keep, Peter A. Hormones & the Brain. 352p. text ed. 34.50 (ISBN 0-8391-1645-4). Univ Park.
Verandakis, A. Hormones in Development & Aging. 600p. 1981. text ed. 54.00 (ISBN 0-89335-140-7). Spectrum Pub.
Voitkevick, A. A. Feather & Plumage of Birds. 1966. 9.75 (ISBN 0-8079-0050-8). October.
Wade, Carlson. Natural Hormones: Secret of Youthful Health. 3.45 (ISBN 0-686-29984-1). Cancer Bk Hse.
--Natural Hormones: The Secret of Youthful Health. 1972. 9.95 (ISBN 0-13-609941-6, Reward); pap. 3.45 (ISBN 0-13-609958-0). P-H.
Weaver, Robert J. Plant Growth Substances in Agriculture. LC 71-166964. (Plant Science Ser.). (Illus.). 1972. text ed. 39.95x (ISBN 0-7167-0824-8). W H Freeman.
Weisbart, Melvin, et al. Isolation & Purification of Hormones. (Illus.). 220p. 1973. text ed. 20.00x (ISBN 0-8422-7107-4). Irvington.
Wigglesworth, V. B. Insect Hormones. rev. ed. Head, J. J., ed. LC 76-62977. (Carolina Biology Readers Ser.). (Illus.). (gr. 11 up). 1980. pap. 2.00 (ISBN 0-89278-270-6, 45-9670). Carolina Biological.
--Insect Hormones. (Illus.). 1970. text ed. 11.95x (ISBN 0-7167-0688-1). W H Freeman.
Wigglesworth, Vincent B. Control of Growth & Form: A Study of the Epidermal Cell in an Insect. (Illus.). 1959. 22.50x (ISBN 0-8014-0450-9). Cornell U Pr.
Wolff, E., ed. Hormones et Differenciation Sexuelle Chez les Invertebres. (Cours & Documents De Biologie Ser.). (Fr.). 1972. 52.75 (ISBN 0-677-50430-6). Gordon.
Workshop Conference, Basel 1971, et al. Thyrotrophin Releasing Hormone: Proceedings. Marois, M. & Werner, I., eds. (Frontiers of Hormone Research: Vol. 1). (Illus.). 196p. 1972. 31.25 (ISBN 3-8055-1288-0). S Karger.
Yoshida, Sho, et al, eds. Antidiuretic Hormone. 307p. 1981. text ed. 49.50 (ISBN 0-8391-1642-X). Univ Park.

HORMONES (PLANTS)

see Plant Hormones

HORMONES, SEX

see also names of hormones, e.g. Androgens, Testosterone

Alcaraz, Manuel, et al. Sexual Hormones: Influence on the Electrophysiology of the Brain. LC 74-4137. 223p. 1974. text ed. 28.00x (ISBN 0-8422-7214-3). Irvington.
--Sexual Hormones: Influence on the Electrophysiology of the Brain. LC 74-4137. 223p. 1974. text ed. 28.00x (ISBN 0-8422-7214-3). Irvington.
Austin, C. R. & Short, R. V., eds. Hormones in Reproduction. LC 73-178279. (Reproduction in Mammals Ser.: Bk. 3). (Illus.). 1972. 24.50 (ISBN 0-521-08438-5); pap. 6.50x (ISBN 0-521-09696-0). Cambridge U Pr.
Baulieu, E. E. Etude sur le Mode D'Action des Hormones Steroides Sexuelles: Metabolisme Au Niveau des Organes Cibles et Liaison a Des Proteines Specifiques. LC 74-185798. (Cours & Documents de Biologie Ser.). (Illus.). 150p. 1974. 41.25x (ISBN 0-677-50650-3). Gordon.
Brotherton, J. Sex Hormone Pharmacology. 1977. 78.00 (ISBN 0-12-137250-2). Acad Pr.
CIBA Foundation. Sex, Hormones & Behaviour. (CIBA Foundation Symposium: No. 62). 1979. 41.00 (ISBN 0-444-90045-4). Elsevier.
Clark, J. H. & Peck, E. J. Female Sex Steroids: Receptors & Function. (Monographs on Endocrinology: Vol. 14). (Illus.). 1979. 44.80 (ISBN 0-387-09375-3). Springer-Verlag.
Corner, George W. Hormones in Human Reproduction. LC 42-51440. (Illus.). 1963. pap. 1.65 (ISBN 0-689-70051-2, 16). Atheneum.
Dorner, G. Hormones & Brain Differentiation. 1976. 62.00 (ISBN 0-444-41477-0, North Holland). Elsevier.
Dorner, G. & Kawakami, M., eds. Hormones & Brain Development. LC 78-25863. (Developments in Endocrinology Ser.: Vol. 3). 1979. 70.25 (ISBN 0-444-80091-3, Biomedical Pr). Elsevier.
Dufau, Maria & Means, Anthony, eds. Hormone Binding & Target Cell Activation in the Testis. LC 74-23709. (Current Topics in Molecular Endocrinology: Vol. 1). 371p. 1974. 32.50 (ISBN 0-306-34001-1, Plenum Pr). Plenum Pub.
French, Frank S., et al, eds. Hormonal Regulation of Spermatogenesis. LC 75-32541. (Current Topics in Molecular Endocrinology Ser.: Vol. 2). 526p. 1975. 45.00 (ISBN 0-306-34002-X, Plenum Pr). Plenum Pub.
Hafez, E. S. & Peluso, J. J., eds. Sexual Maturity: Physiological & Clinical Parameters. LC 76-22248. (Perspectives in Human Reproduction: Vol. 3). 1976. 24.00 (ISBN 0-250-40112-6). Ann Arbor Science.
Holmes, R. L. & Fox, C. A. Control of Human Reproduction. (Monographs for Students of Medicine Ser.). 1979. 13.00 (ISBN 0-12-353450-X). Acad Pr.
International Seminar on Reproductive Physiology & Sexual Endocrinology, 3rd, Brussels, 1970. Basic Actions of Sex Steroids on Target Organs: Proceedings. Hubinont, P. O., et al, eds. 1971. 34.25 (ISBN 3-8055-1156-6). S Karger.
James, V. H. T., et al, eds. Endocrine Function of the Human Ovary. 1976. 65.00 (ISBN 0-686-74509-4). Acad Pr.
Lisk, R. D., et al. Neonatal Hormone Treatment & Adult Sexual Behavior in Rodents. (Biology of Sex Ser.). 230p. 1974. text ed. 25.50x (ISBN 0-8422-7125-2). Irvington.
O'Malley, Bert & Means, Anthony, eds. Receptors for Reproductive Hormones. LC 73-81095. (Advances in Experimental Medicine & Biology Ser.: Vol. 36). 460p. 1973. 35.00 (ISBN 0-306-39036-1, Plenum Pr). Plenum Pub.
Salhanick, Hilton A., et al. Metabolic Effects of Gonadal Hormones & Contraceptive Steroids. LC 71-89792. 762p. 1969. 49.50 (ISBN 0-306-30422-8, Plenum Pr). Plenum Pub.
Silver, Rae, intro. by. Hormones & Reproductive Behavior: Readings from Scientific American. LC 79-1192. (Illus.). 1979. text ed. 16.95x (ISBN 0-7167-1093-5); pap. text ed. 8.95x (ISBN 0-7167-1094-3). W H Freeman.
Slater. Sex Hormones & Behavior. (Studies in Biology: No. 103). 1979. 5.95 (ISBN 0-8391-0253-4). Univ Park.
Thomas, J. Regulatory Mechanisms Affecting Gonadal Hormone Action: Advances in Sex Hormone Research, Vol. 3. 1976. 37.50 (ISBN 0-8391-0777-3). Univ Park.
Thomas, John A., ed. Advances in Sex Hormone Research, Vol. 4. Singhal, Radhey L. LC 79-25717. (Illus.). 1980. text ed. 32.50 (ISBN 0-8067-1914-1). Urban & S.
Wolff, E., ed. Hormones et Differenciation Sexuelle Chez les Invertebres. (Cours & Documents De Biologie Ser.). (Fr.). 1972. 52.75 (ISBN 0-677-50430-6). Gordon.

HORN, TOM, 1860-1903

Horn, Tom. The Life of Tom Horn, Government Scout & Interpreter. LC 76-49944. (Beautiful Rio Grande Classics Ser). 1976. lib. bdg. 15.00 (ISBN 0-87380-144-X). Rio Grande.

HORN (MUSICAL INSTRUMENT)

Barbour, J. Murray. Trumpets, Horns & Music. 1964. 10.00 (ISBN 0-87013-079-X). Mich St U Pr.
Boydell, Barra. The Crumhorn. 1981. write for info. (ISBN 90-6027-176-9, Pub. by Frits Knuf Netherlands). Pendragon NY.
Morley-Pegge, R. The French Horn. 2nd ed. (Illus.). 222p. 1973. 13.95x (ISBN 0-393-02171-8). Norton.
Plenckers, L. J. Hoorn-En Trompetachtige Blaasinstrumenten. (Haags Gemeente-Museum Ser.). (Illus.). 20.00 (ISBN 90-6027-322-2, Pub. by Frits Knuf Netherlands). Pendragon NY.
Schuller, Gunther. Horn Technique. (YA) (gr. 9 up). 1962. 7.75 (ISBN 0-19-318701-9). Oxford U Pr.

HORN MUSIC-BIBLIOGRAPHY

Schuller, Gunther. Horn Technique. (YA) (gr. 9 up). 1962. 7.75 (ISBN 0-19-318701-9). Oxford U Pr.

HORNADAY, WILLIAM TEMPLE, 1854-1937

Forbes, John R. In the Steps of the Great American Zoologist, William Temple Hornaday. (In the Step S of the Great American Naturalists Ser.). (Illus.). 1976. Repr. of 1966 ed. 3.95 (ISBN 0-916544-09-5). Natural Sci Youth.

HORNBLOWER, HORATIO (FICTITIOUS CHARACTER)

Forester, C. S. The Hornblower Companion. 192p. 1980. pap. 1.95 (ISBN 0-523-25440-7). Pinnacle Bks.

HORNBOOKS

Folmsbee, Beulah. Little History of the Horn-Book. LC 42-36336. (Illus.). 1942. 7.50 (ISBN 0-87675-085-4). Horn Bk.
Tuer, Andrew W. History of the Horn Book. LC 68-58921. (Illus.). 1968. Repr. of 1897 ed. 24.00 (ISBN 0-405-09035-8, Pub. by Blom). Arno.
Tuer, J. History of the Horn Book, 2 vols. 1976. lib. bdg. 150.00 (ISBN 0-8490-1999-0). Gordon Pr.

HORNBY, ENGLAND (LANCASHIRE)

Chippindall, W. H. Sixteenth Century Survey & Year's Account of the Estates of Hornby Castles, Lancashire. 1939. 13.00 (ISBN 0-384-08905-4). Johnson Repr.

HORNE, LENA

Howard, Brett. Lena Horne. (Orig.). 1980. pap. 2.00 (ISBN 0-87067-675-X). Holloway.

HORNED POUT

see Brown Bullhead

HORNED TOADS

Sherbrook, Wade C. Horned Lizards, Unique Reptiles of Western North America. Jackson, Earl, ed. LC 81-51078. (Popular Ser.: No. 31). (Illus.). 48p. 1981. pap. 8.95 (ISBN 0-911408-59-2). SW Pks Mnmts.

HORNEY, KAREN, 1885-1952

Horney, Karen. The Adolescent Diaries of Karen Horney. LC 80-50552. (Illus.). 271p. 1980. 12.95 (ISBN 0-465-00055-X). Basic.
Kelman, Harold. Helping People: Karen Horney's Psychoanalytic Approach. LC 75-140098. 1971. 35.00x (ISBN 0-87668-039-2, 75-140098). Aronson.
Kelman, Harold, ed. New Perspectives in Psychoanalysis. 1965. 5.00 (ISBN 0-393-01028-7). Norton.

HORNS-JUVENILE LITERATURE

Lerner, Marguerite R. Horns, Hoofs, Nails. LC 65-29040. (Medical Bks for Children). (Illus.). (gr. 3-9). 1965. PLB 3.95 (ISBN 0-8225-0015-9). Lerner Pubns.

HORNS (IN RELIGION, FOLK-LORE, ETC.)

see also Religion, Primitive

Mellinkoff, Ruth. The Horned Moses in Medieval Art & Thought. LC 77-85450. (California Studies in the History of Art: No. XIV). (Illus.). 1970. 35.00x (ISBN 0-520-01705-6). U of Cal Pr.

HOROLOGY
see also Chronometer; Clocks and Watches; Days; Sun-Dials; Time
Britten, F. W. Horological Hints & Helps. (Illus.). 1977. 21.50 (ISBN 0-902028-64-2). Apollo.
Bromley, John, ed. The Clockmakers' Library: The Catalogue of the Books & Manuscripts in the Library of the Worshipful Company of Clockmakers. (Illus.). 136p. 1977. 52.50x (ISBN 0-85667-033-2, Pub. by Sotheby Parke Bernet England). Biblio Dist.
Daniels, George. The Art of Breguet. (Illus.). 412p. 1975. 132.50 (ISBN 0-85667-004-9, Pub. by Sotheby Park Bernet England). Biblio Dist.
Haswell, J. Eric. Horology. (Illus.). 1976. 25.00 (ISBN 0-7158-1146-0). Charles River Bks.
HOROSCOPES
American AstroAnalysts Institute. Astroanalysis. Incl. Aries. pap. (ISBN 0-448-12556-0); Taurus. pap. (ISBN 0-448-12557-9); Gemini. pap. (ISBN 0-448-12558-7); Cancer. pap. (ISBN 0-448-12559-5); Leo. pap. (ISBN 0-448-12560-9); Virgo. pap. (ISBN 0-448-12561-7); Libra. pap. (ISBN 0-448-12562-5); Scorpio. pap. (ISBN 0-448-12563-3); Sagittarius. pap. (ISBN 0-448-12564-1); Capricorn. pap. (ISBN 0-448-12565-X); Aquarius. pap. (ISBN 0-448-12566-8); Pisces. pap. (ISBN 0-448-12567-6). 1977. pap. 8.95 ea. G&D.
Aries Press Table of Houses. (Illus., Orig.). 1940. pap. 4.50 (ISBN 0-933646-00-3). Aries Pr.
Brightfield, Rick & Orser, Mary. Predicting with Astrology. 1977. pap. 5.95 (ISBN 0-06-090572-7, CN572, CN). Har-Row.
Buchan, Vivian. Cat Sun Signs. LC 79-65117. (Illus.). 156p. 1981. pap. 5.95 (ISBN 0-8128-6097-7). Stein & Day.
Carpenter, Garth. Southern Hemisphere Horoscopes. 12 bks. 112p. price not set (Pub. by Reed Books Australia). C E Tuttle.
Cattano, Vincent. A to Z Personal Guidance. 40p. 1956. pap. 1.00x (ISBN 0-87542-101-6). Llewellyn Pubns.
Davison, Ronald. The Synastry, Astrology of Human Relationships. LC 76-28731. (Illus.). 1977. 15.95 (ISBN 0-88231-016-X). ASI Pubs Inc.
Dixon, Jeane. Horoscopes for Dogs. 1979. 5.95 (ISBN 0-395-27453-2). HM.
Donchess, Barbara. How to Cope with His Horoscope. LC 77-73679. 1978. pap. 4.00 (ISBN 0-914350-27-7). Vulcan Bks.
--In Other Women's Houses. LC 77-92680. 1978. pap. 3.50 (ISBN 0-914350-28-5). Vulcan Bks.
Folino, Joseph. Contemporary World Horoscopes, No. 1. Date not set. pap. cancelled (ISBN 0-88231-061-5). ASI Pubs Inc.
Gauquelin, Michael. The Gauquelin Book of American Charts. 320p. (Orig.). 1981. pap. 15.95 (ISBN 0-686-73157-3, Pub. by Astro Comp Serv). Para Res.
George, Llewellyn. The A to Z Horoscope Maker & Delineator. 13th, rev. ed. Bytheriver, Marylee, ed. (Illus.). 600p. (Orig.). 1981. 17.95 (ISBN 0-87542-263-2). Llewellyn Pubns.
Goodman, Linda. Linda Goodman's Love Signs: A New Approach to the Human Heart. (Illus.). 1981. pap. 7.95 (ISBN 0-449-90043-6, Columbine). Fawcett.
--Linda Goodman's Sun Signs. 512p. 1981. pap. 3.95 (ISBN 0-553-20229-4). Bantam.
--Linda Goodman's Sun Signs. 1979. pap. 7.95 (ISBN 0-553-01291-6). Bantam.
Hand, Robert. Planets in Youth: Patterns of Early Development. (Planets Ser.). 1981. pap. 13.95 (ISBN 0-914918-26-5). Para Res.
The Hero in the Horoscope: The Dynamics of Transpersonal Astrology. 1982. pap. 11.50 (ISBN 0-914350-23-4). Vulcan Bks.
Holleran, Peter L. Horoscopes of Saints & Sages. LC 76-26805. 1982. pap. 9.95 (ISBN 0-914350-16-1). Vulcan Bks.
Jay, Michael. Gay Love Signs. (Orig.). 1980. pap. 6.95 (ISBN 0-345-28774-6). Ballantine.
Jones, Marc E. Guide to Horoscope Interpretation. LC 73-12102. pap. 2.75 (ISBN 0-8356-0442-X, Quest). Theos Pub Hse.
Koval, Barbara. The Lively Circle. 200p. (Orig.). 1981. pap. 9.95 (ISBN 0-917086-29-5, Pub. by Astro Comp Serv). Para Res.
Laskowski, Jerzy, tr. from Pol. Casanova's Book of Numbers & the Daily Horoscope. rev. ed. LC 74-76808. 1975. pap. 4.25 (ISBN 0-914350-05-6). Vulcan Bks.
Lau, Theodora. The Handbook of Chinese Horoscopes. LC 77-11814. (Illus.). 1980. pap. 4.95 (ISBN 0-06-090752-5, CN 752, CN). Har-Row.
--Handbook of Chinese Horoscopes. LC 77-11814. (Illus.). 1979. 12.95 (ISBN 0-06-012521-7, HarpT). Har-Row.
Lee, Fleming. Your Hidden Horoscope. 1976. pap. 1.75 (ISBN 0-89041-104-2, 3104). Major Bks.
Leo, Alan. Casting the Horoscope. (Astrologer's Library). 1979. pap. 6.95 (ISBN 0-89281-176-5). Inner Tradit.
--The Progressed Horoscope. 1978. pap. 6.95 (ISBN 0-685-62087-5). Weiser.
Lewis, Ursula. Chart Your Own Horoscope. (Illus.). 1979. pap. 2.50 (ISBN 0-523-40651-7). Pinnacle Bks.
Llewellyn's Moon Sign Book 1981. 512p. (Orig.). 1980. pap. 3.95 (ISBN 0-686-72993-5). Bantam.
Moore, Moon, ed. The Book of World Horoscopes: The Astrological Gazateer of the Modern Geopolitical World. (Illus.). 336p. (Orig.). 1980. pap. 15.00 (ISBN 0-930706-04-8). Seek-It Pubns.
Morey, Robert A. Horoscopes & the Christian. 64p. (Orig.). 1981. pap. 1.95 (ISBN 0-87123-202-2). Bethany Hse.
Morley, Evan. Tempo Day-by-Day Horoscopes 1982: Aquarius. (Tempo Day-by-Day Horoscopes Ser.). 192p. (Orig.). 1981. pap. 1.95 (ISBN 0-448-16234-2). Ace Bks.
--Tempo Day-by-Day Horoscopes 1982: Aries. (Tempo Day-by-Day Horoscopes Ser.). 192p. 1981. pap. 1.95 (ISBN 0-448-16224-5). Ace Bks.
--Tempo Day-by-Day Horoscopes 1982: Cancer. (Tempo Day-by-Day Horoscopes Ser.). 192p. (Orig.). 1981. pap. 1.95 (ISBN 0-448-16227-X). Ace Bks.
--Tempo Day-by-Day Horoscopes 1982: Capricorn. (Tempo Day-by-Day Horoscopes Ser.). 192p. (Orig.). 1981. pap. 1.95 (ISBN 0-448-16233-4). Ace Bks.
--Tempo Day-by-Day Horoscopes 1982: Gemini. (Tempo Day-by-Day Horoscopes Ser.). 192p. (Orig.). 1981. pap. 1.95 (ISBN 0-448-16226-1). Ace Bks.
--Tempo Day-by-Day Horoscopes 1982: Leo. (Tempo Day-by-Day Horoscopes Ser.). 192p. (Orig.). 1981. pap. 1.95 (ISBN 0-448-16228-8). Ace Bks.
--Tempo Day-by-Day Horoscopes 1982: Libra. (Tempo Day-by-Day Horoscopes Ser.). 192p. (Orig.). 1981. pap. 1.95 (ISBN 0-448-16230-X). Ace Bks.
--Tempo Day-by-Day Horoscopes 1982: Pisces. (Tempo Day-by-Day Horoscopes Ser.). 192p. (Orig.). 1981. pap. 1.95 (ISBN 0-686-71797-X). Ace Bks.
--Tempo Day-by-Day Horoscopes 1982: Sagittarius. (Tempo Day-by-Day Horoscopes Ser.). 192p. (Orig.). 1981. pap. 1.95 (ISBN 0-448-16232-6). Ace Bks.
--Tempo Day-by-Day Horoscopes 1982: Scorpio. (Tempo Day-by-Day Horoscopes Ser.). 192p. (Orig.). 1981. pap. 1.95 (ISBN 0-448-16231-8). Ace Bks.
--Tempo Day-by-Day Horoscopes 1982: Taurus. (Tempo Day-by-Day Horoscopes Ser.). 192p. (Orig.). 1981. pap. 1.95 (ISBN 0-448-16225-3). Ace Bks.
Neugebauer, Otto & Van Hoesen, Henry B. Greek Horoscopes. LC 78-7352. (Memoirs: Vol. 48). 1978. pap. 21.00 (ISBN 0-8357-0314-2, ST-00006, Pub by Am Philos). Univ Microfilms.
Noel, Tyl. Horoscope As Identity. LC 73-20069. 1977. Repr. of 1977 ed. 10.00 (ISBN 0-87542-799-5). Llewellyn Pubns.
Parker, Julia. Aquarius. (Pocket Guides to Astrology 1982 Ser.). (Orig.). 1981. pap. 4.95 (ISBN 0-671-43444-6). S&S.
--Aries. (Pocket Guides to Astrology 1982 Ser.). (Orig.). 1981. pap. 4.95 (ISBN 0-671-43442-X). S&S.
--Cancer. (Pocket Guide to Astrology Ser.). (Orig.). 1981. pap. 4.95 (ISBN 0-671-43439-X). S&S.
--Capricorn. (Orig.). 1981. pap. 4.95 (ISBN 0-671-43433-0). S&S.
--Gemini. (Orig.). 1981. pap. 4.95 (ISBN 0-671-43440-3). S&S.
--Leo. (Orig.). 1981. pap. 4.95 (ISBN 0-671-43434-9). S&S.
--Libra. (Orig.). 1980. pap. 4.95 (ISBN 0-671-25554-1). S&S.
--Pisces. (Orig.). 1981. pap. 4.95 (ISBN 0-671-25558-4). S&S.
--Sagittarius. (Orig.). 1981. pap. 4.95 (ISBN 0-671-25556-8). S&S.
--Scorpio. (Orig.). 1981. pap. 4.95 (ISBN 0-671-43435-7). S&S.
--Taurus. (Pocket Guides to Astrology 1982 Ser.). (Orig.). 1981. pap. 4.95 (ISBN 0-671-43441-1). S&S.
--Virgo. (Pocket Guides to Astrology 1982 Ser.). (Orig.). 1981. pap. 4.95 (ISBN 0-671-25549-5). S&S.
Paul, Helen & O'Toole, Bridget M. The Yod & Other Points in Your Horoscope. 1977. pap. 5.55 (ISBN 0-914350-17-X). Vulcan Bks.
Penfield, Marc. America: Its Cities & States: An Astrological Portrait. LC 75-20922. 1976. 14.95 (ISBN 0-914350-14-5). Vulcan Bks.
--An Astrological Who's Who. 541p. 1972. 10.00 (ISBN 0-912240-08-3). Arcane Pubns.
--Two Thousand & One: The Penfield Collection. LC 79-83867. 1979. kivar 9.95 (ISBN 0-914350-34-X). Vulcan Bks.
The Progressed Horoscope. (Astrologer's Library). 1978. pap. 6.95 (ISBN 0-89281-180-3). Inner Tradit.
Puotinen, C. J. Computing Horoscopes with Your Electronic Calculator. (Illus.). 1978. pap. 4.95 (ISBN 0-930840-07-0). Ninth Sign.
Robertson, Arlene & Wilson, Margaret. The Complete Book on the Power of Pluto. 258p. 1979. pap. 7.95 (ISBN 0-930706-02-1). Seek-It Pubns.
Schulman, Martin. Celestial Harmony: A Guide to Horoscope Interpretation. 1980. pap. 7.95 (ISBN 0-87728-495-4). Weiser.
Super Horoscopes, 1982: Aquarius. (Illus., Orig.). 1981. pap. 2.95 (ISBN 0-448-14239-2). G&D.
Super Horoscopes, 1982: Aries. (Illus., Orig.). 1981. pap. 2.95 (ISBN 0-448-14229-5). G&D.
Super Horoscopes, 1982: Cancer. (Illus., Orig.). 1981. pap. 2.95 (ISBN 0-448-14232-5). G&D.
Super Horoscopes, 1982: Capricorn. (Illus., Orig.). 1981. pap. 2.95 (ISBN 0-448-14238-4). G&D.
Super Horoscopes, 1982: Gemini. (Illus., Orig.). 1981. pap. 2.95 (ISBN 0-448-14231-7). G&D.
Super Horoscopes, 1982: Leo. (Illus., Orig.). 1981. pap. 2.95 (ISBN 0-448-14233-3). G&D.
Super Horoscopes, 1982: Libra. (Illus., Orig.). 1981. pap. 2.95 (ISBN 0-448-14235-X). G&D.
Super Horoscopes, 1982: Pisces. (Illus., Orig.). 1981. pap. 2.95 (ISBN 0-448-14240-6). G&D.
Super Horoscopes, 1982: Sagittarius. (Illus., Orig.). 1981. pap. 2.95 (ISBN 0-448-14237-6). G&D.
Super Horoscopes, 1982: Scorpio. (Illus., Orig.). 1981. pap. 2.95 (ISBN 0-448-14236-8). G&D.
Super Horoscopes, 1982: Taurus. (Illus., Orig.). 1981. pap. 2.95 (ISBN 0-448-14230-9). G&D.
Super Horoscopes, 1982: Virgo. (Illus., Orig.). 1981. pap. 2.95 (ISBN 0-448-14234-1). G&D.
Sydney Omarr's Weekly Astrological Guide for 1982, 12 vols. Incl. Aries (ISBN 0-451-00991-6, W9916); Taurus (ISBN 0-451-09917-6, W9917); Gemini (ISBN 0-451-09918-4, W9918); Cancer (ISBN 0-451-09919-2, W9919); Leo (ISBN 0-451-09920-6, W9920); Virgo (ISBN 0-451-09921-4, W9921); Libra (ISBN 0-451-09922-2, Y9922); Scorpio (ISBN 0-451-09923-0, W9923); Sagitarius (ISBN 0-451-09924-9, W9924); Capricorn (ISBN 0-451-09925-7, W9925); Aquarius (ISBN 0-451-09926-5, W9926); Pisces (ISBN 0-451-09927-3, W9927). 1980. pap. 1.50 ea. (ISBN 0-451-11110-9, Sig). NAL.
Townley, John. Planets in Love: Exploring Your Emotional & Sexual Needs. Anderson, Margaret E., ed. (Planets Ser.). 1979. pap. 12.95 (ISBN 0-914918-21-4). Para Res.
Tyl, Noel. Horoscope Construction. (Principles & Practice of Astrology Ser.: Vol. 1). 200p. 1973. pap. 3.95 (ISBN 0-87542-800-2). Llewellyn Pubns.
--Special Horoscope Dimensions. LC 73-19910. (Principles & Practice of Astrology Ser.: Vol. 9). (Illus., Orig.). 1975. pap. 3.95 (ISBN 0-87542-808-8). Llewellyn Pubns.
Wagman, Naomi. Sun & Daughter Signs. 1974. 12.95 (ISBN 0-685-42361-1). Assoc Bk.
Warren, David. Your Best Place: Astrological Relocation Techniques. rev. ed. 1978. pap. 4.95 (ISBN 0-930840-06-2). Ninth Sign.
White, Thelma. What the Stars Reveal About the Men in Your Life. 1980. pap. 3.00 (ISBN 0-87980-378-9). Wilshire.
Wilhelm, Hans. Your Chinese Hororscope. 208p. 1980. pap. 4.95 (ISBN 0-380-75275-1, 75275). Avon.
Your Day by Day Horoscope. Incl. Aries (ISBN 0-448-16212-1); Taurus (ISBN 0-448-16201-6); Gemini (ISBN 0-448-16214-8); Cancer (ISBN 0-448-16215-6); Leo (ISBN 0-448-16216-4); Virgo (ISBN 0-448-16217-2); Libra (ISBN 0-448-16218-0); Scorpio (ISBN 0-448-16219-9); Sagittarius (ISBN 0-448-16220-2); Capricorn (ISBN 0-448-16221-0); Aquarius (ISBN 0-448-16222-9); Pisces (ISBN 0-448-16223-7). (Illus.). 1979. pap. 1.50 ea. (Tempo). Ace Bks.
Your Personal Forecase 1982: Pisces. 1981. pap. 1.95 (ISBN 0-441-66183-1). Ace Bks.
Your Personal Forecast 1982: Aquarius. 1981. pap. 1.95 (ISBN 0-441-66182-3). Ace Bks.
Your Personal Forecast 1982: Aries. 1981. pap. 1.95 (ISBN 0-441-66172-6). Ace Bks.
Your Personal Forecast 1982: Cancer. 1981. pap. 1.95 (ISBN 0-441-66175-0). Ace Bks.
Your Personal Forecast 1982: Capricorn. 1981. pap. 1.95 (ISBN 0-441-66181-5). Ace Bks.
Your Personal Forecast 1982: Gemini. 1981. pap. 1.95 (ISBN 0-441-66174-2). Ace Bks.
Your Personal Forecast 1982: Leo. 1981. pap. 1.95 (ISBN 0-441-66176-9). Ace Bks.
Your Personal Forecast 1982: Libra. 1981. pap. 1.95 (ISBN 0-441-66178-5). Ace Bks.
Your Personal Forecast 1982: Sagittarius. 1981. pap. 1.95 (ISBN 0-441-66180-7). Ace Bks.
Your Personal Forecast 1982: Scorpio. 1981. pap. 1.95 (ISBN 0-441-66179-3). Ace Bks.
Your Personal Forecast 1982: Taurus. 1981. pap. 1.95 (ISBN 0-441-66173-4). Ace Bks.
Your Personal Forecast 1982: Virgo. 1981. pap. 1.95 (ISBN 0-441-66177-7). Ace Bks.
Zolar's Horoscope & Lucky Number Dream Book. 544p. 1981. 7.95 (ISBN 0-686-31179-5, 2900). Playmore & Prestige.
HOROSCOPY
see Astrology
HORROR
see also Fear
Wright, Elizabeth. E. T. A. Hoffman & the Rhetoric of Terror. 307p. 1981. 40.00x (ISBN 0-85457-087-X, Pub. by Inst Germanic Stud England). State Mutual Bk.
HORROR FILMS
Adkinson, A. Wyle & Fry, N., eds. The House of Horror: The Story of Hammer Films. LC 74-76299. 1974. 6.95 (ISBN 0-89388-163-5). Okpaku Communications.
Aylesworth, Thomas G. Movie Monsters. LC 75-12997. (Illus.). 80p. (gr. 1-3). 1975. 8.95 (ISBN 0-397-31639-9, JBL-J); pap. 2.95 (ISBN 0-397-31640-2, LSC-42). Har-Row.
Bedford, Michael & Dettman, B. The Horror Factory: Universal Pictures & the Horror Film, 1925-1950. 1975. lib. bdg. 69.95 (ISBN 0-87968-443-7). Gordon Pr.
Brosnan, John. The Horror People. (Illus.). (RL 8). 1977. pap. 3.95 (ISBN 0-452-25160-5, Z5160, Plume). NAL.
Butler, Ivan. Horror in the Cinema. 3rd ed. LC 77-84787. (Illus.). 1979. 15.00 (ISBN 0-498-02137-8). A S Barnes.
Derry, Charles. Dark Dreams: The Horror Film from Psycho to Jaws. LC 76-10879. (Illus.). 1977. 15.00 (ISBN 0-498-01915-2). A S Barnes.
Everson, William K. Classics of the Horror Film. (Illus.). 256p. 1974. 14.00 (ISBN 0-8065-0437-4). Citadel Pr.
--Classics of the Horror Film. 1977. pap. 6.95 (ISBN 0-8065-0595-8). Citadel Pr.
Friedman, F. Louis. Great Horror Movies on TV. (gr. 7-12). 1974. pap. 1.25 (ISBN 0-590-02291-1). Schol Bk Serv.
Glut, Donald F. Classic Movie Monsters. LC 77-16014. (Illus.). 1978. 18.00 (ISBN 0-8108-1049-2). Scarecrow.
Hogan, David J. Who's Who of Horrors. LC 79-17606. 1980. 19.95 (ISBN 0-498-02475-X). A S Barnes.
Lee, Walt, ed. Reference Guide to Fantastic Films, Science Fiction, Fantasy, & Horror, 3 vols. LC 72-88775. (Illus.). 1974. pap. 47.85 set (ISBN 0-913974-04-8). Chelsea-Lee Bks.
McCarty, John. Splatter Movies: Breaking the Last Taboo. LC 81-65111. (Illus.). 160p. (Orig.). 1981. pap. 8.95 (ISBN 0-938782-01-0). Fantaco.
Pattison, Barrie. The Seal of Dracula. (Illus.). 128p. 1975. pap. 2.95 (ISBN 0-517-52153-9). Crown.
Pitts, Michael R. Horror Film Stars. LC 80-11241. (Illus.). 333p. 1981. lib. bdg. 16.95x (ISBN 0-89950-003-X); pap. 12.95x (ISBN 0-89950-004-8). McFarland & Co.
Soren, David. The Rise & Fall of the Horror Film. 1977. perfect bdg. 5.50x (ISBN 0-87543-136-4). Lucas.
Stanley, John. The Creature Features Movie Guide or An A to Z Encyclopedia to Fantastic Films or Is There a Mad Doctor in the House? (Illus.). 200p. (Orig.). (gr. 8 up). 1981. pap. 8.95 (ISBN 0-940064-00-6). Creatures at Large.
Turner, George E. & Price, Michael H. Forgotten Horrors: Early Talkie Chillers from Poverty Row. LC 78-69636. (Illus.). 1979. 19.95 (ISBN 0-498-02136-X). A S Barnes.
Zambrano, A. L. Horror: Film & Literature, 2 vols. 600p. 1975. lib. bdg. 250.00 (ISBN 0-87968-444-5). Gordon Pr.
HORROR TALES
see also Ghost Stories
Ashley, Mike. Who's Who in Horror & Fantasy Fiction. LC 77-4608. 1978. pap. 4.95 (ISBN 0-8008-8278-4). Taplinger.
Century of Creepy Stories. facsimile ed. LC 74-37261. (Short Story Index Reprint Ser.). Repr. of 1934 ed. 40.25 (ISBN 0-8369-4072-5). Arno.
Collins, Wilkie. Tales of Terror & the Supernatural. Van Thal, Herbert, ed. 5.50 (ISBN 0-8446-4725-X). Peter Smith.
Fairclough, Peter, ed. Three Gothic Novels. Incl. Castle of Otronto. Walpole, Horace; Vathek. Bockford, William; Frankenstein. Shelley, Mary W. (English Library Ser.). (Orig.). 1968. pap. 2.50 (ISBN 0-14-043036-9). Penguin.
Goldberg, Gerry, et al, eds. Nighttouch. LC 77-9177. (Illus.). pap. 5.95 (ISBN 0-312-57348-0). St Martin.
Haining, Peter, ed. Christopher Lee's New Chamber of Horrors. (Illus.). 1977. 9.50 (ISBN 0-285-62152-1, Pub. by Souvenir Pr). Intl Schol Bk Serv.
--Clans of Darkness: Scottish Stories of Fantasy & Horror. LC 74-162964. 1971. 7.50 (ISBN 0-8008-1621-8). Taplinger.
--Gothic Tales of Terror: Classic Horror Stories from Great Britain, Europe & the United States 1765-1840. LC 78-158841. 1972. 11.95 (ISBN 0-8008-3590-5). Taplinger.

--Hollywood Nightmare: Tales of Fantasy & Horror from the Film World. 1971. 7.95 (ISBN 0-8008-3921-8). Taplinger.
--Hollywood Nightmare: Tales of Fantasy & Horror from the Film World. 1971. 7.95 (ISBN 0-8008-3921-8). Taplinger.
--The Lucifer Society: Macabre Tales by Great Modern Writers. LC 70-179949. 256p. 1972. 8.95 (ISBN 0-8008-5042-4). Taplinger.
--Nightfrights: Occult Stories for All Ages. LC 72-7793. (Illus.). 256p. 1973. 7.95 (ISBN 0-8008-5556-6). Taplinger.
Hoke, Helen. Horrors, Horrors, Horrors. LC 78-2350. (Terrific Triple Titles Ser.). (Illus.). 1978. lib. bdg. 8.40 s&l (ISBN 0-531-02211-0). Watts.
Hoke, Helen, ed. A Chilling Collection. LC 79-18864. (gr. 6 up). 1980. 7.95 (ISBN 0-525-66662-1). Elsevier-Nelson.
--Demons Within: And Other Disturbing Tales. LC 77-76473. 1977. 8.95 (ISBN 0-8008-2156-4). Taplinger.
--Mysterious, Menacing & Macabre. 160p. (gr. 7 up). 1981. 12.00 (ISBN 0-525-66748-2, 01117-330). Elsevier-Nelson.
Lamb, Hugh, ed. The Taste of Fear: Thirteen Eerie Tales of Horror. LC 76-8997. (YA) (gr. 9 up). 1976. 8.95 (ISBN 0-8008-7549-4). Taplinger.
--Terror by Gaslight: More Victorian Tales of Terror. LC 75-27980. 222p. 1976. 8.95 (ISBN 0-8008-7559-1). Taplinger.
--The Thrill of Horror: Twenty-Two Terrifying Tales. LC 75-8200. 222p. 1975. 8.50 (ISBN 0-8008-7683-0). Taplinger.
--Victorian Nightmares. LC 76-55901. 1977. 8.95 (ISBN 0-8008-7984-8). Taplinger.
--Victorian Tales of Terror. LC 74-20217. 288p. 1975. 8.50 (ISBN 0-8008-7986-4). Taplinger.
Liebman, Arthur. Tales of Horror & the Supernatural. (Masterworks of Mystery Ser.). 190p. (gr. 7-12). 1975. PLB 7.97 (ISBN 0-8239-0299-4); tchr's manual 1.50 (ISBN 0-686-67049-3). Rosen Pr.
Lines, Kathleen, ed. House of the Nighmare & Other Eerie Tales. LC 68-23749. 256p. (gr. 7 up). 1968. 5.95 (ISBN 0-374-33432-3). FS&G.
Lovecraft, H. P., et al. Horror in the Museum & Other Revisions. Derleth, August, ed. 1970. 10.00 (ISBN 0-87054-031-9). Arkham.
Parry, Michel, ed. Beware of the Cat: Stories of Feline Fantasy & Horror. LC 72-75664. (Illus.). 192p. 1972. 7.50 (ISBN 0-8008-0730-8). Taplinger.
Pearce, Philippa. The Shadow Cage & Other Tales of the Supernatural. LC 77-3174. (Illus.). (gr. 3-7). 1977. 8.95 (ISBN 0-690-01396-5, TYC-J). Har-Row.
Protter, Eric, ed. A Harvest of Horrors: Classic Tales of the Macabre. LC 79-56028. (Illus.). 286p. 1980. 12.50 (ISBN 0-8149-0755-5). Vanguard.
--Monster Festival: Classic Tales of the Macabre. LC 79-56028. (Illus.). (gr. 7 up). 10.00 (ISBN 0-8149-0377-0). Vanguard.
Schiff, Stuart, ed. Whispers Two. LC 78-22542. (Illus.). 1979. 8.95 (ISBN 0-385-14967-0). Doubleday.
Shepard, Leslie, ed. The Dracula Book of Great Vampire Stories. 1977. 10.00 (ISBN 0-8065-0565-6). Citadel Pr.
--The Dracula Book of Great Vampire Stories. 1979. pap. 5.95 (ISBN 0-8065-0704-7). Citadel Pr.
Snow, Edward R. Ghost, Gales & Gold. LC 72-3936. (Illus.). 288p. 1972. 6.95 (ISBN 0-396-06658-5). Dodd.
Sullivan, Jack. Elegant Nightmares: The English Ghost Story from le Fanu to Blackwood. LC 77-92258. 155p. 1978. 12.95x (ISBN 0-8214-0374-5). Ohio U Pr.
Wheatley, Dennis, ed. A Century of Horror Stories. facsimile ed. LC 71-160952. (Short Story Index Reprint Ser.). Repr. of 1935 ed. 40.00 (ISBN 0-8369-3931-X). Arno.
Wolf, Leonard. Wolf's Complete Book of Terror. 1979. 16.95 (ISBN 0-517-53634-X, Dist. by Crown); pap. 8.95 (ISBN 0-517-53635-8). Potter.

HORROR TALES–HISTORY AND CRITICISM

Haining, Peter, ed. Monster Makers: Creators & Creations of Fantasy & Horror. LC 74-1961. 1974. 8.50 (ISBN 0-8008-5324-5). Taplinger.
St. John Barclay, Glen. Anatomy of Horror: The Masters of Occult Fiction. LC 78-70899. 1979. 8.95 (ISBN 0-312-03408-3). St Martin.
Tymn, Marshall B. Horror Literature. 520p. 1981. 32.95 (ISBN 0-8352-1341-2). Bowker.
Zambrano, A. L. Horror: Film & Literature, 2 vols. 600p. 1975. lib. bdg. 250.00 (ISBN 0-87968-444-5). Gordon Pr.

HORS D'OEUVRES

see Cookery (Appetizers); Cookery (Relishes)

HORSE

see Horses

HORSE-BREAKING

see Horse-Training

HORSE BREEDING

see also Horse Breeds

Bierschwal, C. J. & DeBois, C. H. The Technique of Fetotomy in Large Animals. (Illus.). 1972. soft bdg. 8.75 (ISBN 0-935078-05-3, VM 16). Veterinary Med.
Blakely, James. Horses & Horse Sense: The Practical Science of Horse Husbandry. 1981. 23.95 (ISBN 0-8359-2887-X); instr's. manual free (ISBN 0-8359-2888-8). Reston.
Blood-Horse, ed. Sires of Runners of 1979. (Annual Supplement). 1980. lib. bdg. 20.00 (ISBN 0-936032-19-7); pap. 10.00 (ISBN 0-936032-20-0). Thoroughbred Own & Breed.
Blood Horse, ed. Stallion Register, 1981. (Illus.). 900p. 1980. 20.00 (ISBN 0-936032-33-2); pap. 10.00 (ISBN 0-936032-34-0). Thoroughbred Own & Breed.
Blood-Horse-Thoroughbred Owners & Breeders Assn., ed. The Breeder's Guide for 1979. (Bound Supplements of the Blood-Horse). 1980. 51.75 (ISBN 0-936032-01-4). Thoroughbred Own & Breed.
The Breeders Guide, 1978. 46.75 (ISBN 0-936032-00-6). Thoroughbred Own and Breed.
Buckle, Esme. Dams of National Hunt Winners: 1973-1975. 17.50 (ISBN 0-85131-340-X). J A Allen.
Campbell, Judith. Police Horses. pap. 2.00 (ISBN 0-87980-199-9). Wilshire.
Conn, George H. Horse Selection & Care for Beginners. pap. 4.00 (ISBN 0-87980-193-X). Wilshire.
Dossenbach, Monique, et al. Great Stud Farms of the World. LC 78-51034. (Illus.). 1978. 35.00 (ISBN 0-688-03326-1). Morrow.
Edwards, Elwyn H., ed. A Standard Guide to Horse & Pony Breeds. LC 79-23921. (Illus.). 352p. 1980. 24.95 (ISBN 0-07-019035-6). McGraw.
Feeding the Horse. 1974. lib. bdg. 10.75 (ISBN 0-936032-04-9). Thoroughbred Own & Breed.
Finney, Humphrey S. A Stud Farm Diary. 5.25 (ISBN 0-85131-194-6, Dist. by Sporting Book Center). J A Allen.
Gill, James. Bloodstock: Breeding Winners in Europe & America. LC 77-8671. (Illus.). 1977. 25.00 (ISBN 0-668-04139-0). Arco.
Griffith, Rubye & Griffith, Frank. Fun of Raising a Colt. pap. 3.00 (ISBN 0-87980-190-5). Wilshire.
Hardman, A. Leighton. The Amateur Horse Breeder. 2nd ed. (Illus.). 240p. 1980. cancelled (ISBN 0-7207-1177-0). Transatlantic.
--Amateur Horse Breeder. pap. 3.00 (ISBN 0-87980-181-6). Wilshire.
Hardman, Ann C. The Amateur Horse Breeder. LC 72-132207. (Illus.). 1970. 6.95 (ISBN 0-668-02743-6). Arco.
Hardman, Ann L. Young Horse Management. 176p. 1976. 11.95 (ISBN 0-7207-0904-0, Pub. by Michael Joseph). Merrimack Bk Serv.
Horse & Pony Breeding Explained. LC 78-9001. (Horseman's Handbook Ser.). (Illus.). 1979. 7.95 (ISBN 0-668-04580-9); pap. 3.95 (ISBN 0-668-04584-1). Arco.
Jones, William E. Genetics & Horsebreeding. LC 81-6059. (Illus.). 400p. 1982. text ed. price not set (ISBN 0-8121-0721-7). Lea & Febiger.
Lesh, Donald. Treatise on Thoroughbred Selection. new ed. 12.25 (ISBN 0-85131-296-9, Dist. by Sporting Book Center). J A Allen.
Lorch. An Amateur's Guide to Foaling. (Illus.). 1978. 4.37 (ISBN 0-85131-302-7, Dist. by Sporting Book Center). J A Allen.
McLean, Malcolm. Fine Texas Horses, Their Pedigrees & Performance: 1830-1845. LC 66-29218. (History & Culture Monograph Ser. No.1). 1966. 4.50 (ISBN 0-912646-11-X). Tex Christian.
Napier, Miles. Breeding a Racehorse. pap. 4.50 (ISBN 0-85131-224-1, Dist. by Sporting Book Center). J A Allen.
O'Sullivan, Bernard J., compiled by. Bloodstock Sales Analysis, 1962. 1.75 (ISBN 0-85131-058-3, Dist. by Sporting Book Center). J A Allen.
Pittenger, Peggy J. The Back-Yard Foal. LC 72-95504. 1965. 7.50 (ISBN 0-668-02748-7). Arco.
Rabinowitz, Sandy. What's Happening to Daisy? LC 76-24313. (ps-3). 1977. (HarpJ); PLB 6.79 (ISBN 0-06-024835-1). Har-Row.
Rosedale, Peter. Horse Breeding. (Illus.). 320p. 1981. 45.00 (ISBN 0-7153-7987-9). David & Charles.
Rossdale, P. D. & Ricketts, S. W. The Practice of Equine Stud Medicine. 2nd ed. (Illus.). 425p. 1980. text ed. write for info. (ISBN 0-8121-0750-0). Lea & Febiger.
Sasse, F. Theme on a Pipe Dream. 1970. 10.00 (ISBN 0-87556-309-0). Saifer.
Schockemohle, Alwin & Kaiser, Ulrich. Alwin Schockemohle. 1978. 7.95 (ISBN 0-8120-5186-6). Barron.
Self, Margaret C. Horses - Their Selection, Care & Handling. pap. 3.00 (ISBN 0-87980-195-6). Wilshire.
Split Pedigree Book. ring bdg 13.00 (ISBN 0-85131-259-4, Dist. by Sporting Book Center). J A Allen.
Sutcliffe, Anne. Breeding & Training a Horse or Pony. (Illus.). 165p. 1981. 17.95 (ISBN 0-7153-7953-4). David & Charles.
Tesio, Frederico. Breeding the Racehorse. Spinola, Edward, ed. & tr. (Illus.). 13.10 (ISBN 0-85131-028-1, Dist. by Sporting Book Center). J A Allen.
The Blood-Horse Staff, ed. Stallion Register - 1982. (Annual Supplement to the Blood-Horse). (Illus.). 900p. 1981. 20.00 (ISBN 0-936032-44-8); pap. 10.00 (ISBN 0-936032-45-6). Thoroughbred Own & Breed.
Thomas, Heather S. Horses: Their Breeding, Care & Training. LC 72-5176. (Illus.). 400p. 1975. 17.50 (ISBN 0-498-01072-4). A S Barnes.
Thoroughbred Owners & Breeders Association. The Breeder's Guide for 1980. 1981. 57.50 (ISBN 0-936032-41-3). Thoroughbred O.
Thoroughbred Owners & Breeders Assn., ed. Thoroughbred Broodmare Records, 1979: Annual. 1980. leather 77.75 (ISBN 0-936032-32-4); text ed. 66.75 (ISBN 0-936032-31-6). Thoroughbred Own & Breed.
Thoroughbred Owners & Breeders Association. Thoroughbred Broodmare Records, 1980. 1981. text ed. 86.75 (ISBN 0-936032-42-1); leather bdg. 101.75 (ISBN 0-936032-43-X). Thoroughbred O.
Thrall, Ellen. American Tarpan Studbook, Vol. 1. (Illus.). 1975. 12.50 (ISBN 0-912830-32-8). Printed Horse.
Von Oettingen, Burchard. Horse Breeding in Theory & Practice. 1978. Repr. of 1909 ed. lib. bdg. 100.00 (ISBN 0-89760-925-5, Telegraph). Dynamic Learn Corp.
Wharton, Mary E. & Bowen, Edward L. The Horse World of the Bluegrass, Vol. 1. Denbo, Bruce F. & Wharton, Mary E., eds. 246p. 1980. 30.00 (ISBN 0-934554-00-5). Host Assoc.
Willis, Larryann C. The Horse-Breeding Farm. LC 72-5179. (Illus.). 480p. 1973. 17.50 (ISBN 0-498-01164-X); pap. 9.95 (ISBN 0-498-01977-2). A S Barnes.
Wynmalen, Henry. Horse Breeding & Stud Management. (Illus.). 20.10 (ISBN 0-85131-139-3, Dist. by Sporting Book Center). J A Allen.

HORSE BREEDS

see also names of specific breeds

Baker, Jennifer. Horses & Ponies. LC 73-91685. (Source Book Ser.). (Illus.). 1973. 5.00x (ISBN 0-7063-1493-X). Intl Pubns Serv.
Berry, Barbara J. The Standardbreds. LC 78-69680. (Illus.). 1979. 14.50 (ISBN 0-498-02251-X). A S Barnes.
Buckle, E., ed. Dams of National Hunt Winners, 1955-60. pap. 3.60 (ISBN 0-85131-076-1, Dist. by Sporting Book Center). J A Allen.
Buckle, E., compiled by. Dams of National Hunt Winners, 1966-73. (Illus.). pap. 18.35 (ISBN 0-85131-237-3, Dist. by Sporting Book Center). J A Allen.
Chivers, Keith. The Shire Horse. (Illus.). 45.00 (ISBN 0-85131-245-4, Dist. by Sporting Book Center). J A Allen.
Dent, Anthony. Cleveland Bay Horses. (Illus.). 1978. 7.85 (ISBN 0-85131-283-7, Dist. by Sporting Book Center). J A Allen.
Edwards, Elwyn H. The Larousse Guide to Horses & Ponies of the World. LC 77-71167. (The Larousse Guide Bks.). (Illus.). 1979. 15.95 (ISBN 0-88332-120-3); pap. 7.95 (ISBN 0-88332-121-1). Larousse.
Edwards, Elwyn H., ed. A Standard Guide to Horse & Pony Breeds. LC 79-23921. (Illus.). 352p. 1980. 24.95 (ISBN 0-07-019035-6). McGraw.
--A Standard Guide to Horse & Pony Breeds. LC 79-23921. (Illus.). 352p. 1980. 24.95 (ISBN 0-07-019035-6). McGraw.
Haines, Francis. Appaloosa: The Spotted Horse in Art & History. 2nd ed. (Illus.). 1972. 15.95 (ISBN 0-912830-18-2). Printed Horse.
Hayes, M. Horace. Points of the Horse. rev. ed. LC 69-10649. 1969. 15.00 (ISBN 0-668-01811-9). Arco.
Haynes, Glynn W. The American Paint Horse. LC 75-9645. (Illus.). 375p. 1976. 17.95 (ISBN 0-8061-1293-X). U of Okla Pr.
Hill, Marie. Single G: The Horse That Time Forgot. LC 68-11568. (Illus.). 1968. 4.95 (ISBN 0-668-02820-3). Arco.
McCarr, Ken. The Kentucky Harness Horse. LC 75-3548. (Kentucky Bicentennial Bookshelf Ser.). (Illus.). 152p. 1978. 6.95 (ISBN 0-8131-0213-8). U Pr of Ky.
MacClintock, Dorcas. Horses As I See Them. LC 78-31778. (Illus.). 96p. (gr. 3 up). 1979. 9.95 (ISBN 0-684-16116-8, ScribT). Scribner.
Mann, Gerhard. Holstein Horses. (Breed Ser.). 1977. pap. 1.95 (ISBN 0-88376-017-7). Dreenan Pr.
Montgomery, E. S. The Thoroughbred. LC 72-93791. (Illus.). 1971. 15.00 (ISBN 0-668-02824-6). Arco.
Rudofsky, Herbert. Trakehnen Horses. (Breed Ser.). 1977. pap. 1.95 (ISBN 0-88376-011-8). Dreenan Pr.
Sterling Editors. Horse Identifier. LC 80-50439. (Illus.). 128p. 1980. 7.95 (ISBN 0-8069-3742-4); lib. bdg. 7.49 (ISBN 0-8069-3743-2). Sterling.
Thompson, Neil. A Closer Look at Horses. (Closer Look at Ser.). (Illus.). (gr. 4 up). 1978. PLB 7.45 (ISBN 0-531-01428-2); pap. 1.95 (ISBN 0-531-02486-5). Watts.

HORSE-DRAWN VEHICLE DRIVING

see Driving of Horse-Drawn Vehicles

HORSE RACE BETTING

see also Book-Making (Betting)

Ader, Paul. How to Make a Million at the Track. LC 77-91196. 1978. pap. 6.95 (ISBN 0-8092-7531-7). Contemp Bks.
Ainslie, Tom. Ainslie's Complete Guide to Thoroughbred Racing. LC 68-18312. (Illus.). 1968. 12.95 (ISBN 0-671-01469-2). Trident.
--Compleat Horseplayer. 1966. 5.95 (ISBN 0-671-15525-3). Trident.
--Handicapper's Handbook. LC 69-13515. (Illus.). 1969. 9.95 (ISBN 0-671-27015-X). Trident.
Bacon, Robert L. Secrets of Professional Turf Betting. 1965. 10.00 (ISBN 0-685-13752-X). Landau.
Badone, Chuck. Class in Thoroughbred Racing. 128p. (Orig.). 1979. pap. 3.95 (ISBN 0-89650-650-9). Gamblers.
--Secrets of a Successful Race Handicapper. LC 77-84924. 1977. pap. text ed. 11.95 (ISBN 0-916852-02-4). Pay Day Pr.
Barr, David. Making Money at the Races. pap. 3.00 (ISBN 0-87980-268-5). Wilshire.
Bauman, William. Smart Handicapping Made Easy. pap. 3.00 (ISBN 0-87980-270-7). Wilshire.
Beyer, Andrew. My Fifty Thousand Dollar Year at the Races. LC 79-24212. 176p. 1980. pap. 3.95 (ISBN 0-15-662327-7, Harv). HarBraceJ.
--Picking Winners: A Horse Players Guide. LC 74-34311. 288p. 1975. 8.95 (ISBN 0-395-20424-0). HM.
--Picking Winners: A Horseplayer's Guide. 1978. pap. 4.95 (ISBN 0-395-25942-8). HM.
Bomze, Henry D. Treasury of American Turf. 1967. 10.00 (ISBN 0-685-13754-6). Landau.
Brecher, Steven L. Beating the Races with a Computer. LC 80-11311. 105p. (Orig.). 1980. pap. 14.95 (ISBN 0-9603792-0-7). Software Supply.
Buck, Fred S. Horse Race Betting. 3rd ed. LC 76-48227. (Illus.). 1977. pap. 5.95 (ISBN 0-668-02477-1). Arco.
Cohen, Ira S. Scientific Handicapping: Tested Way to Win at the Race Track. (Illus., Orig.). 1966. pap. 3.95 (ISBN 0-13-795880-3). P-H.
Cole, Edward W. Racing Maxims & Methods of Pittsburg Phil. 64p. 1965. pap. 2.95 (ISBN 0-89650-506-5). Gamblers.
Conklin, Les. Betting Horses to Win. pap. 3.00 (ISBN 0-87980-265-0). Wilshire.
--Payday at the Races. pap. 3.00 (ISBN 0-87980-269-3). Wilshire.
Crist, Steven. Offtrack: Bets & Pieces. LC 79-6662. 168p. 1981. 9.95 (ISBN 0-385-15215-9). Doubleday.
Davidowitz, Steven. Betting Thoroughbreds: Professional's Guide for the Horseplayer. (Illus.). 1977. pap. 5.95 (ISBN 0-525-47620-2). Dutton.
Dorgan, H. M. Horse Racing: The Method. 3.95 (ISBN 0-685-22041-9). Wehman.
Dowst, R. S. Winners: How to Select Them. 2.95 (ISBN 0-685-21980-1). Wehman.
Doyle, Douglas J. The Ghost Horse. 1978. 4.95 (ISBN 0-533-03210-5). Vantage.
Emerson, Elliot. Bet & Win at Harness Racing. 1966. pap. 0.75 (ISBN 0-911996-24-9). Gamblers.
Flohr, Scott. Handicapping to Win. LC 71-108665. (Illus.). 1969. softcover 5.95 (ISBN 0-87067-801-9, BH802, Melrose Sq). Holloway.
Gambling Times Guide to Harness Race Tracks. (Illus.). 1982. pap. text ed. 2.95 (ISBN 0-89746-002-2). Gambling Times.
Gambling Times Guide to Legal Off-Track Betting Establishments. 1983. pap. text ed. 2.95 (ISBN 0-89746-007-3). Gambling Times.
Gambling Times Guide to Quarter Horse, Appaloosa & Fair Racing. (Illus.). 1983. pap. text ed. 2.95 (ISBN 0-89746-008-1). Gambling Times.
Gambling Times Guide to Thoroughbred Race Tracks. 1983. pap. 2.95 (ISBN 0-89746-009-X). Gambling Times.
GBC Editorial Staff, ed. More Blue Ribbon Systems. (Gambler's Book Shelf). 64p. (Orig.). 1979. pap. 2.95 (ISBN 0-911996-84-2). Gamblers.
--One Hundred Fifty Blue Ribbon Systems. (Gambler's Book Shelf). (Orig.). 1979. pap. 2.95 (ISBN 0-89650-813-7). Gamblers.
Geer, Dan. Pro Rated Longshots: A Proven Method for Selecting Longshot Winners. 1975. 20.00 (ISBN 0-13-731554-6). P-H.
Gibson, Walter B. How to Bet the Harness Races. (Gambler's Book Shelf). 72p. 1975. pap. 2.95 (ISBN 0-911996-57-5). Gamblers.

--Winning the Two-Dollar Bet. (Gambler's Book Shelf). 80p. 1975. pap. 2.95 (ISBN 0-911996-56-7). Gamblers.
Goodwon, Katcha. Rate the Contenders: Secrets of Longshot Handicapping. 29p. (Orig.). 1981. price not set (ISBN 0-932896-04-9). Westcliff Pubns.
--Thinking Man's Guide to Handicapping. rev. enl. ed. 1980. pap. text ed. 11.00 (ISBN 0-932896-02-2). Westcliff Pubns.
--A Thinking Man's Guide to Handicapping. 1979. pap. text ed. 10.00 (ISBN 0-932896-01-4). Westcliff Pubns.
Haskins, Jim. Gambling: Who Really Wins? (First Bks.). (Illus.). (gr. 4 up). 1979. PLB 6.90 (ISBN 0-531-02942-5). Watts.
Hillis, James. Pari Mutuel Betting. (Gambler's Book Shelf). (Illus.). 69p. 1972. pap. 2.95 (ISBN 0-911996-27-3). Gamblers.
Illich, Albert G. Al Illich's How to Pick Winners. LC 72-161211. (Illus.). 224p. (Orig.). 1971. pap. 6.00 (ISBN 0-668-02472-0). Arco.
Kaplan & Loughrey. Ins & Outs of On-Track & Off-Track Horse Race Betting. 1971. 5.00x (ISBN 0-87526-084-5). Gould.
McKinght, Bob. How to Pick Winning Horses. pap. 3.00 (ISBN 0-87980-266-9). Wilshire.
McKnight, Bob. Eliminate the Losers: A Tested Method for Successful Handicapping. 1968. 3.95 (ISBN 0-8065-0165-0). Citadel Pr.
Mahl, Huey. Beating the Bookie. (Gambler's Book Shelf Ser.). 1975. pap. 2.95 (ISBN 0-89650-547-2). Gamblers.
Meadow, Barry. Success at the Harness Races. 1970. 4.95 (ISBN 0-685-08136-2); pap. 2.45 (ISBN 0-8065-0005-0). Citadel Pr.
Mellen, Mark. Horse Racing 'Hot Tips' 3.95 (ISBN 0-685-21974-7). Wehman.
Mozan. Mozan's Racing Numerology. (Gambler's Book Shelf). 72p. 1972. pap. 2.95 (ISBN 0-911996-36-2). Gamblers.
National Turf Review Editors. Race Track Profits: Turf Review. 1.95 (ISBN 0-685-22083-4). Wehman.
Perlmutter, Nate. How to Win Money at the Races. updated ed. (Illus.). 1979. pap. 3.95 (ISBN 0-02-081090-3, Collier). Macmillan.
Perry, Rufus. Play the Horses & Win. pap. 2.00 (ISBN 0-686-00711-5). Key Bks.
--Play the Trotters & Win. pap. 1.00 (ISBN 0-686-00712-3). Key Bks.
Phifer, Kate G. Track Talk: An Introduction to Thoroughbred Horse Racing. LC 77-94198. (Illus.). 1978. 12.00 (ISBN 0-88331-098-8). Luce.
Quirin, William L. Winning at the Races: Computer Discoveries in Thoroughbred Handicapping. LC 79-1271. (Tom Ainslie--Winner's Circle Book). (Illus.). 1979. 19.95 (ISBN 0-688-03400-4). Morrow.
Reynolds, Randolph. Complete Handicapper's Manual: A Scientific Guide to Making Money at the Races. 1978. pap. write for info (ISBN 0-525-03185-5). Pagurian.
--The New Handicapper's Manual: A Guide to Making Money at the Races. (Illus.). 144p. 1975. 6.95 (ISBN 0-919364-84-5, ADON3528). Pagurian.
Rust, Shirley J., ed. Consolidated Handicapper's. 1979. 9.95 (ISBN 0-89260-133-7). Hwong Pub.
Sasuly, Richard. The Search for the Winning Horse. LC 78-14189. 1979. 9.95 (ISBN 0-03-047441-8). HR&W.
Schneider, Dick. The Harness Horse & Strategic Win Betting. LC 76-44186. 1977. 10.00 (ISBN 0-682-48693-0, Banner). Exposition.
Steward, John S. The Game Plan for Handicapping Harness Races. 15.00 (ISBN 0-533-01730-0). Vantage.
Taulbet, Ray. Thoroughbred Horse Racing. 1965. 10.00 (ISBN 0-685-13753-8). Landau.
Thacker, Ron. Dowst Revisited. (Gambler's Book Shelf). 1976. pap. 2.95 (ISBN 0-911996-72-9). Gamblers.

HORSE-RACING

see also Harness Racing; Horse Race Betting; Jockeys; Race Horses; Steeplechasing

Abbey, Donald S. To Take the Money. LC 80-65745. 326p. 1980. 10.00 (ISBN 0-9604228-0-3). Allowance.
Ainslie, Tom. Ainslie on Jockeys. rev. ed. LC 74-32023. 160p. 1975. 9.95 (ISBN 0-671-22068-3). S&S.
--Ainslie's Complete Guide to Thoroughbred Racing. rev. ed. 1979. 17.95 (ISBN 0-671-24632-1). S&S.
--Ainslie's Complete Guide to Thoroughbred Racing. LC 68-18312. (Illus.). 1968. 12.95 (ISBN 0-671-01469-2). Trident.
--Ainslie's Encyclopedia of Thoroughbred Handicapping. LC 78-9755. 1978. o.p. 19.95 (ISBN 0-688-03345-8); pap. 10.95 (ISBN 0-688-00466-0). Morrow.
Alcock, Anne. They're Off. (Illus.). 1979. 15.75 (ISBN 0-85131-299-3, Dist. by Sporting Book Center). J A Allen.
Blood-Horse, ed. Principal•Winners Abroad of 1979. (Annual Supplement, the Blood-Horse). (Orig.). 1980. pap. 10.00 (ISBN 0-936032-07-3). Thoroughbred Own & Breed.
--Sires of Runners of 1979. (Annual Supplement). 1980. lib. bdg. 20.00 (ISBN 0-936032-19-7); pap. 10.00 (ISBN 0-936032-20-0). Thoroughbred Own & Breed.
--Stakes Winners of 1979. (Annual Supplement, the Blood-Horse). 1980. lib. bdg. 20.00 (ISBN 0-936032-23-5); pap. 10.00 (ISBN 0-936032-24-3). Thoroughbred Own & Breed.
Blood-Horse Editors. Principal Winners Abroad of 1980. (Annual Supplement of the Blood-Horse). (Orig.). 1981. pap. 10.00 (ISBN 0-936032-38-3). Thoroughbred Own & Breed.
--Sires of Runners, 1980. 1981. pap. 10.00 (ISBN 0-936032-37-5). Thoroughbred Own & Breed.
--Stakes Winners of 1980. (Annual Supplement of the Blood-Horse). 1981. lib. bdg. 20.00 (ISBN 0-936032-39-1); pap. 10.00 (ISBN 0-936032-40-5). Thoroughbred Own & Breed.
Blood-Horse-Thoroughbred Owners & Breeders Assn., ed. The Breeder's Guide for 1979. (Bound Supplements of the Blood-Horse). 1980. 51.75 (ISBN 0-936032-01-4). Thoroughbred Own & Breed.
Buess, Bob. The Triple Crown. 1980. pap. 1.95 (ISBN 0-934244-13-8). Sweeter Than Honey.
Carroll, Theodus. Firsts Under the Wire: The World's Fastest Horses (1900-1950) LC 78-11476. (Famous Firsts Ser.). (Illus.). 1978. lib. bdg. 7.35 (ISBN 0-686-51108-5). Silver.
Churchill, Peter. Horse Racing. (Illus.). 168p. 1981. 12.95 (ISBN 0-8069-9442-8, Pub. by Blandford Pr England); pap. 6.95 (ISBN 0-8069-9428-2). Sterling.
Cohen, Ira S. Scientific Handicapping: Tested Way to Win at the Race Track. (Illus., Orig.). 1966. pap. 3.95 (ISBN 0-13-795880-3). P-H.
The Complete Book of Horse - Auto Racing: New York Times Scrapbook History. 1981. 14.95 (ISBN 0-672-52647-6). Bobbs.
Davidson, Joseph B. Inside Horseracing. (Illus.). 282p. (Orig.). 1974. pap. 6.00 (ISBN 0-668-03332-0). Arco.
Fairfax-Blakeborough, Noel, ed. Jack Fairfax-Blakeborough: Memoirs. 1978. 17.35 (ISBN 0-85131-269-1, Dist. by Sporting Book Center). J A Allen.
Foote, John T. Look of Eagles: Racing Story. 1970. 10.00x (ISBN 0-87556-090-3). Saifer.
Foulds, Jervis. The Lady Dudley Challenge Cup. (Illus.). 1978. 17.50 (ISBN 0-85131-294-2, Dist. by Sporting Book Center). J A Allen.
Gaines, Milt. The Tote Board Is Alive and Well. 182p. (Orig.). 1981. pap. 9.95 (ISBN 0-89650-943-5). Gamblers.
Goodwon, Katcha. Rate All the Contenders: Secrets of Longshot Handicapping. Date not set. pap. 12.95 (ISBN 0-932896-04-9). Westcliff Pubns.
Gould, Bernard. The Horseplayer's Guide to Picking Winners. 1977. pap. 5.95 (ISBN 0-679-50639-X). McKay.
Hartigan, Joe. To Become a Racehorse Trainer. 7.00 (ISBN 0-85131-234-9, Dist. by Sporting Book Center). J A Allen.
--To Own a Racehorse. pap. 5.75 (ISBN 0-85131-233-0, Dist. by Sporting Book Center). J A Allen.
Hislop, J. From Start to Finish. (Illus.). 1978. 24.35 (ISBN 0-85131-265-9, Dist. by Sporting Book Center). J A Allen.
Irving, John B. The South Carolina Jockey Club. LC 75-1143. (Illus.). 262p. 1975. Repr. of 1857 ed. 16.50 (ISBN 0-87152-194-6). Reprint.
Johnson, Virginia W. & Johnson, Thula. Distance Riding from Start to Finish. 1976. 8.95 (ISBN 0-395-24773-X). HM.
Jones, Michael W. The Derby: A Celebration of the World's Most Famous Horse Race. (Illus.). 206p. 1979. 21.00x (ISBN 0-85664-884-1, Pub. by Croom Helm Ltd England). Biblio Dist.
Lee, Harry. Race Horse Handicapping. 1978. pap. 2.95 (ISBN 0-346-12317-8). Cornerstone.
Lewin, Sam. How to Win at the Races. pap. 3.00 (ISBN 0-87980-244-8). Wilshire.
Mahl, Huey. How They Ran - S. A. Seventy Five. (Gambler's Book Shelf). 64p. 1975. pap. 2.95 (ISBN 0-911996-67-2). Gamblers.
May, Julian. The Triple Crown of Horseracing. LC 76-13189. (Sports Classics Ser.). (Illus.). (gr. 4-12). 1976. PLB 8.95 (ISBN 0-87191-527-8). Creative Ed.
Messick, Hank. The Politics of Prosecution: Jim Thompson, Richard Nixon, Marje Everett, & the Trial of Otto Kerner. LC 77-15915. (Illus.). 1978. 10.95 (ISBN 0-916054-64-0, Caroline Hse Inc). Green Hill.
Murray, William. Horse Fever. LC 76-12532. 1976. 7.95 (ISBN 0-396-07336-0). Dodd.
Napier, Miles. The Racing Men of TV. new ed. 1978. pap. 8.75 (ISBN 0-85131-301-9, Dist. by Sporting Book Center). J A Allen.
Nye, Nelson C. Great Moments in Quarter Racing History. LC 81-3442. (Illus.). 224p. 1981. 11.95 (ISBN 0-668-05304-6, 5304). Arco.
Peddie, James. Racing for Gold: Or, Incidents in the Life of a Turf Commissioner with Examples of the Most Successful Systems of Speculating on the Turf & in Games of Chance. 1979. Repr. of 1891 ed. lib. bdg. 50.00 (ISBN 0-8495-4333-9). Arden Lib.
Phifer, Kate G. Track Talk: An Introduction to Thoroughbred Horse Racing. LC 77-94198. (Illus.). 1978. 12.00 (ISBN 0-88331-098-8). Luce.
Principal Winners Abroad of 1978. 10.00 (ISBN 0-936032-06-5). Thoroughbred Own and Breed.
Quinn, James. Handicapper's Condition Book. 192p. (Orig.). 1981. pap. 9.95 (ISBN 0-89650-733-5). Gamblers.
Ramsden, Caroline. Racing Without Tears. (Illus.). pap. 4.35 (ISBN 0-85131-004-4, Dist. by Sporting Book Center). J A Allen.
--Racing Without Tears: Horses. (Illus.). 3.00x (ISBN 0-87556-247-7). Saifer.
Roblin, Ronald. The Bettor's Guide to Harness Racing: A New Guide to Successful Handicapping. 1979. 9.95 (ISBN 0-8065-0645-8). Citadel Pr.
Rowe, Howard A. Aqueduct & Santa Anita on One Hundred & Five Dollars a Day. 1970. 4.95 (ISBN 0-671-27057-5). Trident.
Rudman, Jack. Pari-Mutuel Examiner. (Career Examination Ser.: C-644). (Cloth bdg. avail. on request). pap. 8.00 (ISBN 0-8373-0644-2). Natl Learning.
St. John Williams, Guy & Hyland, Francis. The Irish Derby: Eighteen Sixty-Six to Nineteen Seventy-Nine. (Illus.). 432p. 1980. 40.00 (ISBN 0-85131-358-2). J A Allen.
Sasse, F. Theme on a Pipe Dream. 1970. 10.00 (ISBN 0-87556-309-0). Saifer.
Savitt, Sam. One Horse, One Hundred Miles, One Day: The Story of the Tevis Cup Endurance Ride. LC 80-2777. (Illus.). 96p. (gr. 7 up). 1981. PLB 7.95 (ISBN 0-396-07935-0). Dodd.
Schorsch, L. M. & Schorsch, W. T., Jr. The Common Sense Guide to Handicapping. LC 78-115079. (Illus.). cancelled (ISBN 0-686-26458-4). Com Sense Ltd.
Scott, Alexander. Turf Memories of Sixty Years. Collins, W. J., ed. 1979. Repr. lib. bdg. 35.00 (ISBN 0-8495-4903-5). Arden Lib.
Scullin, Joseph D. Horseracing from A to Z. 1965. pap. 2.00 (ISBN 0-685-13751-1). Landau.
A Second Quarter Century of American Racing. 1967. 27.25 (ISBN 0-936032-08-1). Thoroughbred Own & Breed.
Shaefer, Jack. Great Endurance Horse Race. (Illus.). 112p. (Orig.). 1981. pap. 6.95 (ISBN 0-88496-165-6). Capra Pr.
Sires & Dams of Stakes Winners, 1928-1978. 82.50 (ISBN 0-936032-10-3). Thoroughbred Own and Breed.
Stewart, Kenneth. A Background to Racing. (Illus.). 12.25 (ISBN 0-85131-221-7, Dist. by Sporting Book Center). J A Allen.
Thorne, Jean W. Horse & Rider. LC 76-5642. (Winners Circle Ser.). (gr. 4-5). 1976. PLB 6.95 (ISBN 0-913940-41-0). Crestwood Hse.
Thoroughbred Owners & Breeders Assn., ed. Thoroughbred Broodmare Records, 1979: Annual. 1980. leather 77.75 (ISBN 0-936032-32-4); text ed. 66.75 (ISBN 0-936032-31-6). Thoroughbred Own & Breed.
Tobin, Thomas. Drugs & the Performance Horse. (Illus.). 512p. 1981. 44.75 (ISBN 0-398-04446-5). C C Thomas.
Varola, Franco. Typology of the Racehorse. (Illus.). 29.75 (ISBN 0-85131-196-2, Dist. by Sporting Book Center). J A Allen.
Von Hoelscher, Baron. Professional Handicappers Handbook. (Orig.). 1980. pap. 5.95 (ISBN 0-934064-00-8). Publishers Media.

HORSE-RACING–BIBLIOGRAPHY

Herbert, Ivor, ed. Horse Racing. (Illus.). 256p. 1981. 40.00 (ISBN 0-312-39190-0). St Martin.

HORSE-RACING–LAW AND LEGISLATION

Greene, Edward H. The Law & Your Horse. pap. 5.00 (ISBN 0-87980-202-2). Wilshire.
Tobin, Thomas. Drugs & the Performance Horse. (Illus.). 512p. 1981. 44.75 (ISBN 0-398-04446-5). C C Thomas.

HORSE-RACING–MISCELLANEA

Forbis, Judith E. Hoofbeats Along the Tigris. (Illus.). 14.00 (ISBN 0-85131-018-4, Dist. by Sporting Book Center). J A Allen.
Hirsch, Joe. Treasury of Questions & Answers from the Morning Telegraph & Daily Racing Form. LC 69-18266. (Illus.). 1969. 5.95 (ISBN 0-671-27031-1). Trident.
Leach, Jack. Sods I Have Cut on the Turf. (Illus.). 4.50 (ISBN 0-85131-190-3, Dist. by Sporting Book Center). J A Allen.

HORSE-RACING–GREAT BRITAIN

Ayres, Michael & Newbond, Gary. Over the Sticks: The Sport of National Hunt Racing. LC 79-171921. (Illus.). 216p. 1972. 7.95 (ISBN 0-8453-1060-7). Assoc Univ Prs.
Campbell, Barry. Horse Racing in Britain. 248p. 1977. 19.50 (ISBN 0-7181-1427-2, Pub. by Michael Joseph). Merrimack Bk Serv.
Curling, Bill. All the Queen's Horses. LC 79-302909. (Illus.). 1979. 25.00 (ISBN 0-7011-2310-9, Pub. by Chatto Bodley Jonathan). Merrimack Bk Serv.
Famous Horses of the British Turf, 10 vols. Incl. Vol. 2. An Illustrated Review of Racing in Great Britain in 1924. Repr. of 1925 ed; Vol. 3. An Illustrated Review of Racing in Great Britain in 1925. Repr. of 1926 ed; Vol. 4. An Illustrated Review of Racing in Great Britain in 1926. Repr. of 1927 ed; Vol. 5. An Illustrated Review of Racing in Great Britain in 1927. Repr. of 1928 ed; Vol. 6. An Illustrated Review of Racing in Great Britain in 1928. Repr. of 1929 ed; Vol. 7. An Illustrated Review of Racing in Great Britain in 1929. 1930; Vol. 8. An Illustrated Review of Racing in Great Britain in 1930. Repr. of 1931 ed; Vol. 9. An Illustrated Review of Racing in Great Britain in 1931. Repr. of 1932 ed; Vol. 10. An Illlustrated Review of Racing in Great Britain in 1932. Repr. of 1933 ed. (Illus.). Set. 400.00 (ISBN 0-686-20666-5). Lib Serv Inc.
Gilbey, Quintin. Fun Was My Living. 1970. 12.50 (ISBN 0-392-00259-0, LTB). Sportshelf.
Mortimer, Roger. The Flat: Flat Racing in Britain Since 1939. (Illus.). 1979. 35.00 (ISBN 0-04-798002-8). Allen Unwin.

HORSE SENSE

see Common Sense

HORSESHOE BEND, BATTLE OF

Brantley, W. H., ed. Battle of Horseshoe Bend. 1955. pap. 3.50 (ISBN 0-87651-205-8). Southern U Pr.

HORSE-SHOWS

see also Jockeys; Rodeos

Abbey, Harlan C. Horses & Horse Shows. LC 78-55449. (Illus.). 1980. 14.95 (ISBN 0-498-02247-1). A S Barnes.
--Showing Your Horse. LC 72-96963. (Illus.). 1970. 9.95 (ISBN 0-668-02818-1). Arco.
Abbey, Harlan C., et al. Showing Your Horse. LC 72-96963. (Illus.). 1979. pap. 4.95 (ISBN 0-668-04792-5). Arco.
Ansell, Mike. Riding High. LC 77-74116. (Illus.). 1978. 9.95 (ISBN 0-498-02100-9). A S Barnes.
Blood-Horse Editors. Auctions of 1980. (Annual Supplement of the Blood-Horse). (Illus.). 190p. (Orig.). 1981. pap. 10.00 (ISBN 0-936032-36-7). Thoroughbred Own & Breed.
Bloom, Lynda. Fitting & Showing the Halter Horse. LC 79-13615. (Illus.). 1980. 9.95 (ISBN 0-668-04431-4). Arco.
Bullen, Anne. Showing Ponies. (Illus.). 48p. pap. 1.75 (ISBN 0-85131-106-7, Dist. by Sporting Book Center). J A Allen.
Burt, Don. Western Division. Rich, Ray, ed. LC 73-87741. (As the Judge Sees It Ser). (Illus.). 81p. 1973. pap. 2.95 (ISBN 0-686-11800-6). Rich Pub.
Cooper, L. C. Horse Show Organization. (Illus.). 15.00 (ISBN 0-87556-621-9). Saifer.
--Horseshow Organization. new ed. 1978. 15.75 (ISBN 0-85131-310-8, Dist. by Sporting Book Center). J A Allen.
Ganton, Doris L. Drive on: Training & Showing the Advanced Driving Horse. LC 78-69658. (Illus.). 1979. 12.00 (ISBN 0-498-02255-2). A S Barnes.
Haley, Neale. Training Your Horse to Show. LC 74-30731. (Illus.). 1976. 12.00 (ISBN 0-498-01554-8). A S Barnes.
--Training Your Horse to Show. 1977. pap. 3.00 (ISBN 0-87980-335-5). Wilshire.
Hart, Edward. The Care & Showing of the Heavy Horse. (Illus.). 144p. 1981. 25.50 (ISBN 0-686-73585-4, Pub. by Batsford England). David & Charles.
Jousseaume, Andre. Progressive Dressage. Vigneron, Jeanette, tr. from Fr. pap. 8.75 (ISBN 0-85131-231-4). J A Allen.
Kauffman, Sandra, ed. Rider's Digest. LC 76-28792. 1977. 12.00 (ISBN 0-668-04115-3). Arco.
Phillips, A. Horse Shows: How to Organize & Run Them. 1956. 5.00 (ISBN 0-910294-09-7). Brown Bk.
Self, Margaret C. At the Horse Show. pap. 3.00 (ISBN 0-87980-184-0). Wilshire.
--At the Horse Show. LC 72-92310. (Illus.). 1966. 8.95 (ISBN 0-668-02747-9). Arco.
Spector, David A. So You're Showing Your Horse. LC 72-3338. (Illus.). 128p. 1973. 5.95 (ISBN 0-668-02650-2). Arco.
Spooner, Glenda. The Handbook of Showing. (Illus.). pap. 9.65 (ISBN 0-85131-240-3, Dist. by Sporting Book Center). J A Allen.
Thompson, Bill. Constructing Cross-Country Obstacles. (Illus.). 17.35 (ISBN 0-85131-140-7, Dist. by Sporting Book Center). J A Allen.
Willcox, Sheila. The Event Horse. LC 73-5923. (Illus.). 160p. 1973. 9.95 (ISBN 0-397-01000-1). Lippincott.
Williams, Michael. Show Jumping in Britain. Date not set. 4.50x (ISBN 0-392-09530-0, SpS). Sportshelf.

Wright, Gordon. Learning to Ride, Hunt & Show. rev. ed. LC 66-17404. 8.95 (ISBN 0-385-05182-4). Doubleday.

HORSE TRAILS

see Trails

HORSE-TRAINING

Amaral, Anthony. How to Train Your Horse. (Illus.). 1977. 10.95 (ISBN 0-87691-193-9). Winchester Pr.
--Movie Horses: The Fascinating Techniques of Training. pap. 2.00 (ISBN 0-87980-274-X). Wilshire.
--Movie Horses: Their Treatment & Training. (gr. 5-7). 5.50 (ISBN 0-672-50388-3). Bobbs.
Ansell, Mike. Riding High. LC 77-74116. (Illus.). 1978. 9.95 (ISBN 0-498-02100-9). A S Barnes.
British Horse Society & Pony Club. Basic Training for Young Horses & Ponies. LC 76-54933. 1977. pap. 1.95 (ISBN 0-8120-0757-3). Barron.
--Training the Young Horse & Pony. LC 76-41140. 1977. text ed. 4.95 (ISBN 0-8120-5106-8). Barron.
Brooke, Geoffrey. Training Your Horses to Jump. 1978. Repr. of 1913 ed. 35.00 (ISBN 0-8492-3566-9). R West.
Burch. Training Thoroughbred Horses. 2nd rev. ed. 1973. lib. bdg. 10.75 (ISBN 0-936032-29-4). Thoroughbred Own & Breed.
Chamberlain, Harry D. Training Hunters, Jumpers & Hacks. (Illus.). 336p. 1972. 9.95 (ISBN 0-668-02620-0). Arco.
Condax, Kate D. Horse Sense: The Cause & Correction of Problems. (Illus.). 140p. 1980. 10.95 (ISBN 0-87691-300-1). Winchester Pr.
Crossley, Anthony. Training the Young Horse: The First Two Years. LC 78-16769. (Illus.). 1979. 9.95 (ISBN 0-668-04696-1). Arco.
Dickerson, Jan. Training Your Own Young Horse. LC 74-9444. 1978. 10.95 (ISBN 0-385-02222-0). Doubleday.
Dwyer, Francis. On Seats & Saddles, Bits & Bitting, and the Prevention & Cure of Restiveness in Horses. reprint ed. LC 77-3336. (Illus.). 1977. Repr. of 1869 ed. 20.00 (ISBN 0-88427-027-0). North River.
Essary, Don. Training Quarter Horses. LC 77-84565. (Illus.). 1980. 12.00 (ISBN 0-498-02160-2). A S Barnes.
Fackelman, G. E. & Nunamaker, D. M. A Manual of Internal Fixation in the Horse. (Illus.). 110p. 1981. 52.00 (ISBN 0-387-10096-2). Springer-Verlag.
Faudel-Phillips, H. Breaking & Schooling Horses. 5.00x (ISBN 0-87556-237-X). Saifer.
Fillis, James. Breaking & Riding. (Illus.). 1975. 10.95 (ISBN 0-912830-18-2). Printed Horse.
Fiske, Jeanna C. How Horses Learn. LC 79-17752. (Illus.). 1979. 9.95 (ISBN 0-8289-0355-7). Greene.
Froissard, Jean. Jumping: Learning & Teaching. pap. 3.00 (ISBN 0-87980-197-2). Wilshire.
Froud, W. J. Teaching Your Horse to Jump. pap. 2.00 (ISBN 0-87980-227-8). Wilshire.
Fusco, Patricia S. & Fusco, Marina. Marina & Ruby: Training a Filly with Love. LC 77-80233. (Illus.). 1979. pap. 8.95 (ISBN 0-688-08229-7). Morrow.
Ganton, Doris. Breaking & Training the Driving Horse. pap. 2.00 (ISBN 0-87980-272-3). Wilshire.
Ganton, Doris L. Drive on: Training & Showing the Advanced Driving Horse. LC 78-69658. (Illus.). 1979. 12.00 (ISBN 0-498-02255-2). A S Barnes.
Gorman, John A. Western Horse. LC 66-12997. (Illus.). (gr. 9-12). 1967. 14.60 (ISBN 0-8134-0126-7). Interstate.
Green, Carol. Training Explained. (Illus.). 1977. 6.95 (ISBN 0-668-04110-2); pap. 3.95 (ISBN 0-668-04090-4). Arco.
Haley, Neal. Training Your Horse to Show. pap. 3.00 (ISBN 0-685-85591-0). Borden.
Haley, Neale. Training Your Horse to Show. LC 74-30731. (Illus.). 1976. 12.00 (ISBN 0-498-01554-8). A S Barnes.
--Training Your Horse to Show. 1977. pap. 3.00 (ISBN 0-87980-335-5). Wilshire.
Hayes, M. H. Illustrated Horse Training. pap. 5.00 (ISBN 0-87980-240-5). Wilshire.
Hayhew, E. Illustrated Horse Management. pap. 6.00 (ISBN 0-87980-210-3). Wilshire.
Jones, Dave. Practical Western Training. LC 72-485. (Illus.). 176p. 1968. 6.95 (ISBN 0-668-02537-9). Arco.
--The Western Trainer. LC 73-92075. (Illus.). 1979. pap. 5.95 (ISBN 0-668-04791-7, 4791). Arco.
--The Western Trainer. LC 73-92075. (Illus.). 1976. 8.95 (ISBN 0-668-03443-2). Arco.
Lambton, George. Men & Horses I Have Known. (Illus.). 9.75 (ISBN 0-85131-031-1, Dist. by Sporting Book Center). J A Allen.
Leighton-Hardman, A. C. Stallion Management. 1975. pap. 3.00 (ISBN 0-87980-297-9). Wilshire.
Levings, H. Patricia. Training the Quarter Horse Jumper. LC 68-10750. (Illus.). 1968. 8.50 (ISBN 0-668-02826-2). Arco.
Littauer, Vladimir S. Schooling Your Horse. LC 56-11756. (Illus.). 177p. 1956. 6.95 (ISBN 0-668-02536-0). Arco.
McCrary, Emma J. Influencing Horses. (Illus.). 1973. 8.95 (ISBN 0-912830-15-8). Printed Horse.
Miller, Robert W. Western Horse Behavior & Training. 336p. 1975. 6.95 (ISBN 0-385-08181-2, Dolp). Doubleday.
Murray, Robbie. The Gentle Art of Horsebreaking. LC 78-55450. (Illus.). 1978. 9.95 (ISBN 0-498-02233-1). A S Barnes.
Parsons, Derrick. Do Your Own Horse. (Illus.). 12.25 (ISBN 0-85131-280-2). J A Allen.
Patent, Peter. The Adventures of Arthur Artfully. (Illus.). pap. 4.50 (ISBN 0-85131-232-2, Dist. by Sporting Book Center). J A Allen.
Phinny, Peter & Brainard, Jack. Training the Reined Horse. LC 75-38441. (Illus.). 1976. 8.95 (ISBN 0-498-01874-1). A S Barnes.
Pittenger, Peggy J. Reschooling the Thoroughbred. pap. 3.00 (ISBN 0-87980-225-1). Wilshire.
Podhajsky, Alois. Complete Training of Horse & Rider in the Principles of Classical Horsemanship. LC 67-11157. 1967. 9.95 (ISBN 0-385-07872-2). Doubleday.
Prince, Eleanor F., illus. Basic Training for Horses--English & Western. LC 76-42383. (Illus.). 1979. 14.95 (ISBN 0-385-03244-7). Doubleday.
Rabinowitz, Sandy. How I Trained My Colt. LC 79-3162. (Reading-on-My-Own Bk.). (Illus.). 64p. (gr. 2). 1981. 4.95a (ISBN 0-385-15423-2); PLB (ISBN 0-385-15424-0). Doubleday.
Ricci, A. James. Understanding & Training Horses. LC 64-14466. (Illus.). (gr. 10 up). 1964. 10.95 (ISBN 0-397-00356-0). Har-Row.
Sandall, Tony. Horse Breaking. (Illus.). 72p. 1964. 3.75x (ISBN 0-7233-0223-5). Intl Pubns Serv.
Sasse, F. H. Theme on a Pipedream. 7.35 (ISBN 0-85131-027-3, Dist. by Sporting Book Center). J A Allen.
Sautter, Frederic J. & Glover, John A. Behavior, Development & Training of the Horse: A Primer of Equine Psychology. LC 80-23654. 160p. 1980. 9.95 (ISBN 0-668-04809-3, 4809). Arco.
Self, Margaret C. The Problem Horse & the Problem Horseman. LC 75-38952. (Illus.). 1977. 8.50 (ISBN 0-668-03934-5). Arco.
Seunig, Waldemar. Horsemanship. rev. ed. LC 56-5594. 1961. 12.95 (ISBN 0-385-01015-X). Doubleday.
Silver, Caroline. Classic Lives: The Education of a Racehorse. LC 72-93148. 1973. 7.50 (ISBN 0-15-118130-6). HarBraceJ.
Small, Howard I. Monty's Pal. (Illus.). viii, 120p. 1979. 8.95 (ISBN 0-931474-08-6). TBW Bks.
Smythe, Heather. Basic Horse Training: A Practical Guide. LC 80-51684. (Illus.). 144p. 1980. 12.95 (ISBN 0-8128-2748-1). Stein & Day.
Sordillo, Darlene. Training & Showing the Western Trail Horse. LC 74-27438. 1975. 7.95 (ISBN 0-668-03757-1). Arco.
Spaulding, Jackie. The Family Horse. (Illus.). 1980. cancelled (ISBN 0-88930-050-X, Pub. by Cloudburst Canada); pap. cancelled (ISBN 0-88930-049-6). Madrona Pubs.
Stewart, Dwight. Western Horsemanship & Equitation. LC 76-45386. (Illus.). 1977. 14.95 (ISBN 0-668-04044-0). Arco.
Summerhays, Reginald S. Problem Horse. rev. ed. LC 76-40487. (Illus.). 1977. 4.95 (ISBN 0-668-04125-0). Arco.
--Problem Horses - Tested Guide for Curing Most Common & Serious Horse Behavior Habits. pap. 3.00 (ISBN 0-87980-200-6). Wilshire.
Sumner, W. Dayton. Breaking Your Horse's Bad Habits. LC 74-30971. (Illus.). 1976. 9.95 (ISBN 0-498-01695-1). A S Barnes.
--Breaking Your Horse's Bad Habits. 1977. pap. 3.00 (ISBN 0-87980-334-7). Wilshire.
Sutcliffe, Anne. Breeding & Training a Horse or Pony. (Illus.). 165p. 1981. 17.95 (ISBN 0-7153-7953-4). David & Charles.
Thompson, Terry & O'Malley, Jeanne. Training the Performance Horse. 1979. 7.95 (ISBN 0-685-99719-7). Lippincott.
Tuke, Diana. Getting Your Horse Fit. (Illus.). pap. 5.10 (ISBN 0-85131-255-1, Dist. by Sporting Book Center). J A Allen.
Wheatley, George. Schooling a Young Horse. LC 68-29868. (Illus.). 1968. 4.95 (ISBN 0-668-02816-5). Arco.
--Schooling Your Young Horse. pap. 2.00 (ISBN 0-87980-201-4). Wilshire.
Williamson, Charles O. Breaking & Training the Stock Horse. 6th rev. ed. LC 62-22012. (Illus.). 1968. 12.50 (ISBN 0-9600144-1-1). Williamson Sch.
Wright, Gordon, ed. Cavalry Manual of Horsemanship & Horsemastership. LC 62-8914. 6.95 (ISBN 0-385-01647-6). Doubleday.
Young, John R. Schooling for Young Riders: A Handbook for the Horseman of Tomorrow. (Illus.). 1977. Repr. of 1970 ed. 13.50 (ISBN 0-8061-0890-8). U of Okla Pr.
--The Schooling of the Western Horse. rev. ed. (Illus.). 12.50 (ISBN 0-8061-0306-X). U of Okla Pr.
Young, Richard. Schooling of the Western Horse. (Illus.). 15.75 (ISBN 0-85131-182-2). J A Allen.

HORSEMANSHIP

see also Coaching; Driving of Horse-Drawn Vehicles; Horsemen; Rodeos

Abbey, Harlan C., et al. Showing Your Horse. LC 72-96963. (Illus.). 1979. pap. 4.95 (ISBN 0-668-04792-5). Arco.
Albright, Verne. The Peruvian Paso: And His Classic Equitation. (Illus.). 1975. 15.95 (ISBN 0-912830-13-1). Printed Horse.
American Alliance for Health, Physical Education, & Recreation. Riding Selected Articles. 1969. pap. 0.60x (ISBN 0-685-05101-3, 243-080.3). AAHPERD.
Anderson, C. W. Complete Book of Horses & Horsemanship. 1973. pap. 2.95 (ISBN 0-02-041460-9, Collier). Macmillan.
Anderson, J. K. Ancient Greek Horsemanship. LC 61-6780. (Illus.). 1961. 30.00x (ISBN 0-520-00023-4). U of Cal Pr.
Ansell, Mike. Riding High. LC 77-74116. (Illus.). 1978. 9.95 (ISBN 0-498-02100-9). A S Barnes.
Arnold & Luke. Riders of the Range. Date not set. 6.95 (ISBN 0-392-09348-0, SpS). Sportshelf.
Astley, John. The Art of Riding: Set Forthe in a Breefe Treatise. LC 68-54610. (English Experience Ser.: No. 10). 80p. 1968. Repr. of 1584 ed. 13.00 (ISBN 90-221-0010-3). Walter J Johnson.
Baird, Eric. Illustrated Guide to Riding. LC 75-41871. 1976. 11.95 (ISBN 0-8289-0265-8). Greene.
Balch, Glen. Western Horseback Riding. 1974. pap. 3.00 (ISBN 0-87980-285-5). Wilshire.
Ball, Charles E. Saddle Up: The Farm Journal Book of Western Horsemanship. LC 71-11065. (Illus.). 1970. 9.95 (ISBN 0-397-00668-3); pap. 5.95 (ISBN 0-397-00990-9). Har-Row.
Basic Riding Techniques. (Illus.). 96p. 1979. pap. 2.95 (ISBN 0-87857-284-8). Rodale Pr Inc.
Batchelor, Vivien. Observer's Book of Show Jumping & Eventing. (Observer Bks.). (Illus.). 1977. 2.95 (ISBN 0-684-15211-8, ScribT). Scribner.
Beach, Belle. Riding & Driving for Women. LC 77-3505. (Illus.). 1978. Repr. of 1912 ed. 25.00 (ISBN 0-88427-028-9, Dist. by Caroline Hse). North River.
Becher, Rolf. Schooling by the Natural Method. (Illus.). 8.75 (ISBN 0-85131-105-9, Dist. by Sporting Book Center). J A Allen.
Bell, Glenys. Our Own Riding Stables. (Illus.). 1975. 7.50 (ISBN 0-589-00943-5, Pub. by Reed Books Australia). C E Tuttle.
Best, Heidi. How to Book of Riding & Horse Care. (How to Bks). (Illus.). 96p. (Orig.). 1981. pap. 3.95 (ISBN 0-7137-1057-8, Pub. by Blandford Pr England). Sterling.
Black, Harold. Manual of Horsemanship: Instructions from Mexico's Renowned Escuela Ecuestre. LC 73-19083. (Illus.). 250p. 1974. 8.95 (ISBN 0-396-06916-9). Dodd.
--Manual Of Horsemanship. 1978. pap. 5.00 (ISBN 0-87980-359-2). Wilshire.
Blake, Neil F. The World of Show Jumping. 1973. Repr. 13.95 (ISBN 0-912830-29-8). Printed Horse.
Blazer, Don. Natural Western Riding. 1979. 9.95 (ISBN 0-395-28476-7). HM.
--Training the Western Show Horse. 1978. 9.95 (ISBN 0-498-01964-0). A S Barnes.
Bloodgood, Lida. Saddle of the Queens. (Illus.). 12.50x (ISBN 0-87556-028-8). Saifer.
Bloom, Lynda. The Horse of Course! Guide to Winning at Western Trail Riding. LC 78-13541. (Illus.). 1981. 12.95 (ISBN 0-668-04569-8, 4569). Arco.
Blundeville, Thomas. A Newe Booke, Containing the Arte of Ryding. LC 75-25640. (English Experience Ser.: No. 118). (Illus.). 232p. 1969. Repr. of 1560 ed. 35.00 (ISBN 90-221-0118-5). Walter J Johnson.
Bradley, Melvin. Practical & Scientific Horsemanship. (Illus.). 1980. text ed. 16.00 (ISBN 0-07-007065-2). McGraw.
Brandl, Albert. Improve Your Riding: Dressage, Jumping, Cross-Country. 116p. 1980. 12.95 (ISBN 0-8069-9120-8, Pub. by EP Publishing England). Sterling.
--Modern Riding. (EP Sports Ser.). (Illus.). 142p. 1981. 12.95 (ISBN 0-8069-9133-X, Pub. by EP Publishing England). Sterling.
--Modern Riding: Walk, Trot, Canter Gallop. (EP Sports Ser.). (Illus.). 1973. 6.95 (ISBN 0-7158-0580-0). Charles River Bks.
British Horse Society & Pony Club. Aids & Their Application. 1976. pap. 3.25 (ISBN 0-8120-0760-3). Barron.
--The Instructors' Handbook. LC 76-55317. 1977. 5.75 (ISBN 0-8120-5125-4). Barron.
--The Manual of Horsemanship. LC 76-8050. (Illus.). 1976. Repr. of 1950 ed. text ed. 5.95 (ISBN 0-8120-5105-X). Barron.
--Mounted Games & Gymkhanas. LC 76-56448. 1977. 5.75 (ISBN 0-8120-5124-6). Barron.
Burn, Barbara. Complete Guide to Riding People's Horses. (Illus.). 256p. 1981. pap. 5.95 (ISBN 0-312-15746-0). St Martin.
--The Horseless Rider. LC 78-19394. (Illus.). 1979. 9.95 (ISBN 0-312-39213-3). St Martin.
Canning, George. The Occasional Horseman. (Illus.). 8.05 (ISBN 0-85131-188-1, Dist. by Sporting Book Center). J A Allen.
Carden, Karen W. Western Rider's Handbook. LC 75-5171. (Illus.). 224p. 1976. 9.95 (ISBN 0-498-01631-5). A S Barnes.
Chamberlain, Lyle B. You Can Break Your Own Horse. (Illus.). 1970. 4.00 (ISBN 0-914208-07-1). Longhorn Pr.
Childs, Marilyn C. Training Your Colt to Ride & Drive. (Illus.). 136p. (YA) 1972. 8.95 (ISBN 0-668-02610-3). Arco.
Churchill, Peter. Riding from A to Z: A Practical Manual of Horsemanship. LC 77-88451. (Illus.). 1978. 9.95 (ISBN 0-8008-6796-3). Taplinger.
Coen, Sue H. Horseback Riding Made Easy & Fun. pap. 4.00 (ISBN 0-87980-194-8). Wilshire.
--Let's Ride. LC 68-27242. (Illus.). 1969. 8.50 (ISBN 0-668-02793-2). Arco.
Coffin, Bobbi. Rider or Horseman? LC 77-663. 1978. lib. bdg. 8.95 (ISBN 0-668-04257-5, 4257). Arco.
Coggins, Jack. Horseman's Bible. LC 66-17921. pap. 3.50 (ISBN 0-385-03167-X). Doubleday.
Coldrey, C. Courses for Horses. new ed. 1978. 20.10 (ISBN 0-85131-305-1, Dist. by Sporting Book Center). J A Allen.
Condax, Kate D. Horse Sense: The Cause & Correction of Problems. (Illus.). 140p. 1980. 10.95 (ISBN 0-87691-300-1). Winchester Pr.
Connell, Ed C. Hackamore Reinsman. (Illus.). 1952. 4.00 (ISBN 0-914208-03-9). Longhorn Pr.
Coombs, Charles. Be a Winner in Horsemanship. LC 76-17118. (Illus.). 128p. (gr. 5-9). 1976. 7.25 (ISBN 0-688-22080-0); PLB 6.96 (ISBN 0-688-32080-5). Morrow.
Copper, Marcia S. The Horseman's Etiquette Book. LC 76-880. (Encore Edition). (Illus.). 160p. 1976. 2.95 (ISBN 0-684-16187-7, ScribT). Scribner.
Crabtree, Helen K. Saddle Seat Equitation. LC 79-97656. 1970. 9.95 (ISBN 0-385-03170-X). Doubleday.
Crossley, Anthony. Training the Young Horse: The First Two Years. LC 78-16769. (Illus.). 1979. 9.95 (ISBN 0-668-04696-1). Arco.
Deacon, Alan. Horse Sense: A Complete Guide to Riding & Care. pap. 4.00 (ISBN 0-87980-209-X). Wilshire.
Decarpentery. Piaffer & Passage. Galvin, Patricia, tr. LC 74-17395. (Illus.). 80p. 1975. 10.00 (ISBN 0-668-03676-1). Arco.
Decarpentry. Academic Equitation. Bartle, Nicole, tr. from Fr. (Illus.). Repr. of 1949 ed. pap. 5.25 (ISBN 0-85131-036-2, Dist. by Sporting Book Center). J A Allen.
De Kunffy, Charles. Creative Horsemanship. LC 73-10517. (Illus.). 256p. 1975. 12.00 (ISBN 0-498-01386-3). A S Barnes.
De Romaszkan, Gregor. Riding Problems: Basic Elements of Modern Riding Tech. LC 69-11343. (Illus.). 1969. 4.95 (ISBN 0-8289-0085-X). Greene.
Devereux, Frederick L., Jr., ed. The Cavalry Manual of Horse Management. LC 76-50183. (Illus.). 1979. 17.50 (ISBN 0-498-01947-0); pap. 8.95 (ISBN 0-498-02371-0). A S Barnes.
Dillon, Jane M. Form Over Fences. LC 72-479. (Illus.). 132p. 1972. 6.95 (ISBN 0-668-02604-9). Arco.
--School for Young Riders. (Illus.). (YA) 8.95 (ISBN 0-668-02605-7). Arco.
Disston, Harry. Elementary Dressage. LC 79-107111. (Illus.). 1970. 6.50 (ISBN 0-668-02758-4). Arco.
Dressage: Begin the Right Way. LC 75-6. 1978. 10.95 (ISBN 0-8120-5230-7). Barron.
Dwyer, Francis. On Seats & Saddles, Bits & Bitting, and the Prevention & Cure of Restiveness in Horses. reprint ed. LC 77-3336. (Illus.). 1977. Repr. of 1869 ed. 20.00 (ISBN 0-88427-027-0). North River.
Ensminger, M. E. Horses & Horsemanship. 5th ed. LC 76-45238. (Illus.). 1977. 23.35 (ISBN 0-8134-1888-7). Interstate.
Evans, J. Warren. Horses: A Guide to Selection, Care, & Enjoyment. LC 80-29070. (Illus.). 1981. text ed. 20.95x (ISBN 0-7167-1253-9). W H Freeman.
Farshler, Earl R. Riding & Training. (Illus.). 320p. 1972. 7.95 (ISBN 0-668-02603-0). Arco.
Faudel-Phillips, H. The Driving Book. pap. 5.25 (ISBN 0-85131-032-X, Dist. by Sporting Book Center). J A Allen.
Felton, Sidney. Masters of Equitation. (Illus.). 7.50x (ISBN 0-87556-088-1). Saifer.
Felton, W. Sidney. Masters of Equitation. (Illus.). 7.35 (ISBN 0-85131-091-5, Dist. by Sporting Book Center). J A Allen.

Ffrench Blake, R. L. Dressage for Beginners. 1976. pap. 5.95 (ISBN 0-395-24399-8). HM.
--Intermediate Dressage: Work at Second & Third Levels. 1977. pap. 4.95 (ISBN 0-395-25406-X). HM.
Fife, Alta & Fife, Austin. Heaven on Horseback. (Western Text Society Ser.: Vol. 1, No. 1). (Illus.). 114p. (Orig.). 1970. pap. 3.00 (ISBN 0-87421-044-5). Utah St U Pr.
Flandorffer, Tamas & Hajas, Jozsef. The Horse & Horsemanship. Kortvelyessy, Eniko, tr. (Illus.). 184p. 1979. 12.50x (ISBN 963-13-3701-4). Intl Pubns Serv.
Frank, Dean. The Complete Book of Trick & Fancy Riding. LC 60-13312. (Illus.). 1975. boxed 14.95 (ISBN 0-87004-240-8). Caxton.
Fredericson, Ingvar. Horses & Jumping. LC 75-18876. (Illus.). 120p. 1975. 10.00 (ISBN 0-668-03862-4). Arco.
Frederiksen, A. K. Finer Points of Riding. (Illus.). 1970. 10.00x (ISBN 0-87556-094-6). Saifer.
--The Finer Points of Riding. rev. ed. (Illus.). pap. 8.75 (ISBN 0-85131-323-X, Dist. by Sporting Book Center). J A Allen.
Freeman, G. W., ed. The Masters of Eventing. LC 78-3772. 1978. 25.00 (ISBN 0-668-04639-2, 4639). Arco.
Froissard, Jean. Basic Dressage. pap. 2.00 (ISBN 0-87980-219-7). Wilshire.
--Equitation. pap. 4.00 (ISBN 0-87980-188-3). Wilshire.
--Equitation: Learning & Teaching. LC 66-16928. 1967. 10.00 (ISBN 0-668-02760-6). Arco.
--Lipizzaners & the Spanish Riding School. pap. 2.50 (ISBN 0-87980-198-0). Wilshire.
Froud, Bill. Better Riding. LC 73-5148. (Illus.). 96p. 1973. 6.95 (ISBN 0-684-13561-2, ScribT). Scribner.
--Better Riding. LC 74-597496. (Better Sports Ser.). (Illus.). 95p. 1971. 8.50x (ISBN 0-7182-0159-0). Intl Pubns Serv.
Fry, Joan & Denby-Wrightson, Kathryn. The Beginning Dressage Book: A Guide to the Basics for Horse & Rider. LC 80-16950. (Illus.). 240p. 1981. 12.95 (ISBN 0-668-04969-3, 4969). Arco.
Fry, Patricia L. Hints for the Backyard Rider. LC 77-84568. (Illus.). 1979. 7.95 (ISBN 0-498-02166-1); pap. 4.95 (ISBN 0-498-02305-2). A S Barnes.
Gordon, Sally. The Rider's Handbook. (Illus.). 224p. 1980. 9.95 (ISBN 0-399-12556-6). Putnam.
Gray, Patsey. Show & Tell. LC 74-30727. (Illus.). 192p. 1976. 8.95 (ISBN 0-498-01644-7). A S Barnes.
Green, Carol. Dressage Explained. LC 76-43067. (Illus.). 1977. 6.95 (ISBN 0-668-04137-4); pap. 3.95 (ISBN 0-668-04143-9). Arco.
--Eventing Explained. (Horseman's Handbooks). 1978. 6.95 (ISBN 0-668-04383-0); pap. 3.95 (ISBN 0-668-04390-3). Arco.
--Jumping Explained. LC 76-26622. (Illus.). 1977. 6.95 (ISBN 0-668-04116-1); pap. 3.95 (ISBN 0-668-04085-8). Arco.
--Tack Explained. (Horseman's Handbooks). 1977. 6.95 (ISBN 0-668-04385-7); pap. 3.95 (ISBN 0-668-04393-8). Arco.
Halely, Neale. How to Teach Group Riding. LC 72-114288. (Illus.). 1970. 7.95 (ISBN 0-668-02787-8). Arco.
Harrison, James C. Care & Training of the Trotter & Pacer. Date not set. 7.50 (ISBN 0-686-20618-5). US Trotting.
Haworth, Josephine. Riding from Scratch. (Illus.). 87p. 1980. 6.95 (ISBN 0-312-68230-1). St Martin.
Healey, Pepper M. You & Your Pony. 1978. pap. 6.00 (ISBN 0-87980-360-6). Wilshire.
Heath, Veronica. Beginner's Guide to Riding. 1971. 8.50 (ISBN 0-7207-0440-5). Transatlantic.
--Come Pony Trekking with Me. (Illus.). 9.50 (ISBN 0-392-02609-0, SpS). Sportshelf.
Henschel, Georgie. Basic Riding Explained. LC 80-253. (Horseman's Handbooks Ser.). (Illus.). 96p. 1980. 8.95 (ISBN 0-668-04950-2); pap. 4.95 (ISBN 0-668-04961-8). Arco.
Holmelund, Paul. Ride Gently - Ride Well. LC 78-107119. (Illus.). 1970. 5.95 (ISBN 0-668-02808-4). Arco.
Holmes, Edward. Horse & Pony Care in Pictures. (Illus.). (gr. 7-11). 1977. pap. 4.95 (ISBN 0-668-04079-3). Arco.
Houblon, Doreen A. Side-Saddle. (Illus.). 18.00 (ISBN 0-85131-143-1, Dist. by Sporting Book Center). J A Allen.
Hundt, Sheila W. Invitation to Riding. (Illus.). 320p. 1976. 12.95 (ISBN 0-671-22239-2). S&S.
Hurley, Cynthia G. & Willmeroth, Doreen. Teach Yourself to Ride a Horse: A Complete Illustrated Guide from Beginner to Advanced Lessons. 1978. 16.95 (ISBN 0-13-896704-0, Spec); pap. 8.95 (ISBN 0-13-896696-6, Spec). P-H.
Hutchins, James S. Horse Equipment & Cavalry Accoutrements. LC 87-130398. (Illus.). 11.00 (ISBN 0-87026-042-1). Westernlore.
Hyland, Ann. Endurance Riding. LC 75-17774. (Illus.). 1976. 9.95 (ISBN 0-397-01082-6). Har-Row.
--Endurance Riding. 1976. pap. 2.00 (ISBN 0-87980-316-9). Wilshire.
Improve Your Riding. (Sports Ser.). (Illus.). 1978. 8.95 (ISBN 0-7158-0588-6). Charles River Bks.
Inderwick, Sheila. Lungeing the Horse & Rider. LC 77-76095. 1977. 15.95 (ISBN 0-7153-7370-6). David & Charles.
Ingram, Patricia & Hollander, Lewis. Successful Endurance Riding: The Ultimate Test of Horsemanship. 192p. 1981. 11.95 (ISBN 0-8289-0423-5). Greene.
Jackson, Noel. Effective Horsemanship. (Illus.). 328p. (YA) 1972. 15.00 (ISBN 0-668-02613-8). Arco.
Jacobs, Donald T. Ride & Tie: The Challenge of Running & Riding. LC 78-365. (Illus.). 207p. 1978. 6.95 (ISBN 0-89037-099-0). Anderson World.
Johnson, Dorothy. All About Riding. 1969. pap. 1.95 (ISBN 0-09-098750-0, Pub. by Hutchinson). Merrimack Bk Serv.
Jones, Susan Norton. Art of Western Riding. pap. 3.00 (ISBN 0-87980-273-1). Wilshire.
Jousseaume, Andre. Progressive Dressage. Vigneron, Jeanette, tr. from Fr. pap. 8.75 (ISBN 0-85131-231-4). J A Allen.
Kauffman, Sandra. Kauffmans Manual of Riding Safety. (Illus.). 1978. 7.95 (ISBN 0-517-53293-X). Potter.
Kauffman, Sandra, ed. Rider's Digest. LC 76-28792. 1977. 12.00 (ISBN 0-668-04115-3). Arco.
Kelly, J. F. Pony Riding. (Illus.). 8.50 (ISBN 0-392-04229-0, SpS). Sportshelf.
Kenoyer, Natlee. Beginner's Guide to the Western Horse. pap. 2.00 (ISBN 0-87980-271-5). Wilshire.
Kidd, Jane. Horsemanship in Europe. (Illus.). 17.35 (ISBN 0-85131-243-8, Dist. by Sporting Book Center). J A Allen.
Klimke, Reiner. Cavalletti. Goodall, Daphne M., tr. (Illus.). pap. 7.85 (ISBN 0-85131-192-X, Dist. by Sporting Book Center). J A Allen.
Knight, C. Morley. Hints on Driving. (Illus.). 12.25 (ISBN 0-85131-040-0, Dist. by Sporting Book Center). J A Allen.
Kulesza, Severyn R. Modern Riding. LC 66-13062. (Illus.). 202p. 1975. pap. 2.50 (ISBN 0-668-03682-6). Arco.
Kydd, Rachael. Long Distance Riding Explained. LC 78-8998. (Horseman's Handbook Ser.). (Illus.). 1979. 7.95 (ISBN 0-668-04579-5); pap. 3.95 (ISBN 0-668-04583-3). Arco.
Ladendorf, Janice M. Practical Dressage for Amateur Trainers. LC 73-149. 192p. 1973. 8.95 (ISBN 0-498-01285-9). A S Barnes.
Lee, Hollis. The Pleasure Horse. (Country Home & Small Farm Guides). 96p. 1981. 5.95 (ISBN 0-442-27235-9); pap. 2.95 (ISBN 0-442-27234-0). Van Nos Reinhold.
Lewis, Anne. A Guide to Basic Riding Instruction. (Illus.). pap. 4.35 (ISBN 0-85131-218-7, Dist. by Sporting Book Center). J A Allen.
Lewis, Benjamin. Riding. 1958. 7.95 (ISBN 0-448-01299-5). G&D.
Licart, Jean. Basic Equitation. (Illus.). pap. 6.10 (ISBN 0-85131-202-0, Dist. by Sporting Book Center). J A Allen.
--Start Riding Right. LC 79-175249. (Illus.). 125p. 1966. 4.95 (ISBN 0-668-02535-2). Arco.
Littauer, Vladimir S. Commonsense Horsemanship. 2nd ed. (Illus.). 384p. 1972. 8.95 (ISBN 0-668-02602-2). Arco.
Lyne, Michael. A Parson's Son. (Illus.). signed ed 87.50 (ISBN 0-85131-176-8, Dist. by Sporting Book Center). J A Allen.
McArthur, J. Wayne. Training for Western Riders. (Illus., Orig.). 1979. pap. text ed. 6.95 (ISBN 0-89832-003-8). Brighton Pub Co.
MacDonald, Janet & Francis, Valerie. Riding Side Saddle. (Pelham Horsemaster Ser.). (Illus.). 1979. 14.00 (ISBN 0-7207-1100-2). Transatlantic.
Mellin, Jeanne. Illustrated Horseback Riding for Beginners. pap. 2.00 (ISBN 0-87980-196-4). Wilshire.
Merrill, Bill. Vacationing with Saddle & Packhorse. (Illus.). 1977. pap. 3.95 (ISBN 0-668-03487-4). Arco.
Molesworth, Roger. Knowing Horses. LC 62-13447. (Illus.). 1962. 6.95 (ISBN 0-668-00882-2). Arco.
Money, Keith. Horseman in Our Midst. 10.00 (ISBN 0-392-03291-0, SpS). Sportshelf.
Morris, George H. Hunter Seat Equitation. rev. ed. LC 79-7071. (Illus.). 1979. 12.95 (ISBN 0-385-15253-1). Doubleday.
Mortimer, Monty. The Riding Instructor's Handbook. (Illus.). 160p. 1981. 19.95 (ISBN 0-7153-8102-4). David & Charles.
Muller, Hanns. Pocket Dictionary of Horseman's Terms in English, German, French & Spanish. (Fr.). 1971. 5.25 (ISBN 0-685-00343-4). Transatlantic.
Museler, Wilhelm. Riding Logic. LC 76-768. 1976. pap. 5.95 (ISBN 0-668-03960-4). Arco.
Muslim Horsemanship. 1981. pap. 6.00x (ISBN 0-904654-12-5, Pub. by Brit Lib England). State Mutual Bk.
Nye, Nelson C. Your Western Horse. LC 63-9372. (Illus.). 1963. 7.50 (ISBN 0-668-02834-3). Arco.
O'Conner, Sally, et al. Bruce Davidson: World Champion of Eventing. 1980. 25.00 (ISBN 0-395-29117-8). HM.
Oliveira, Nuno. Reflections on Equestrian Art. Fields, Phyllis, tr. from Portuguese. (Illus.). 12.25 (ISBN 0-85131-257-8, Dist. by Sporting Book Center). J A Allen.
Owen, Robert. Horses: Care, Riding, Jumping for All Ages. LC 78-50719. (Illus.). 1978. 6.95 (ISBN 0-668-04606-6, 4606). Arco.
--Learning to Ride. LC 80-12781. (Illus.). 112p. 1980. 9.95 (ISBN 0-668-04976-6, 4976-6). Arco.
Pinch, Dorothy H. Happy Horsemanship. LC 66-27522. (Illus.). 1966. pap. 3.25 (ISBN 0-668-03605-2). Arco.
Podhajsky, Alois. The Art of Dressage. LC 75-21241. 192p. 1976. 8.95 (ISBN 0-385-01552-6). Doubleday.
--Complete Training of Horse & Rider. pap. 4.00 (ISBN 0-87980-235-9). Wilshire.
--Complete Training of Horse & Rider in the Principles of Classical Horsemanship. LC 67-11157. 1967. 9.95 (ISBN 0-385-07872-2). Doubleday.
Posey, Jeanne K. The Rider's Handbook. LC 75-15135. (Illus.). 1977. 9.95 (ISBN 0-668-03854-3). Arco.
Price, Steven D. Teaching Riding at Summer Camps. rev. ed. LC 78-162633. (Illus.). 1971. pap. 2.95 (ISBN 0-8289-0136-8). Greene.
Prince, Eleanor F., illus. Basic Horsemanship-English & Western: A Complete Guide for Riders & Instructors. LC 71-144289. 384p. 1974. 12.95 (ISBN 0-385-06587-6). Doubleday.
Richards, Lockie. Dressage: Begin the Right Way. LC 75-6. (Illus.). 96p. 1975. 12.95 (ISBN 0-7153-6926-1). David & Charles.
Richardson, Julie. Horse Tack: The Complete Equipment Guide for Riding & Driving. LC 80-85251. (Illus.). 192p. 1981. 25.00 (ISBN 0-688-00563-2). Morrow.
Richter, Judy. Horse & Rider: From Basics to Show Competition. LC 78-11735. (Illus.). 1979. 9.95 (ISBN 0-671-18369-9). Sovereign Bks.
Riding. 1975. pap. 2.50 (ISBN 0-8277-4168-5). British Bk Ctr.
Riding Standards 1978-79. rev. ed. 1978. 3.00 (ISBN 0-685-67026-0, 243-26216). AAHPERD.
Roberts, Pamela. Teaching the Child Rider. 5.50x (ISBN 0-87556-302-3). Saifer.
--Teaching the Child Rider. (Illus.). pap. 4.55 (ISBN 0-85131-195-4, Dist. by Sporting Book Center). J A Allen.
Russel, Valerie. Judging Horses & Ponies. (Pelham Horsemaster Ser.). (Illus.). 1979. 14.00 (ISBN 0-7207-1099-5). Transatlantic.
Sager, Floyd C. & Toby, Milton C. Colonel Sager, Practitioner. (Illus.). 150p. 1980. 10.75 (ISBN 0-936032-35-9). Thoroughbred Own & Breed.
Saunders, George C. Your First Horse. pap. 3.00 (ISBN 0-87980-251-0). Wilshire.
Saurel, E. Le Cheval: Equitation et sports hippiques. (La Vie active). (Illus., Fr.). 25.50x (ISBN 0-685-13827-5). Larousse.
Scott, Rosemary. You Can Be a Trick Rider. new ed. (Illus.). 88p. 1973. 5.00x (ISBN 0-914208-06-3); pap. 4.00x (ISBN 0-685-31948-2). Longhorn Pr.
Self, Charles R. Western Horsemanship. (Illus.). 1979. 11.95 (ISBN 0-87691-291-9). Winchester Pr.
Self, Margaret C. Complete Book of Horses & Ponies. (Illus.). (gr. 6 up). 1963. 7.95 (ISBN 0-07-056109-5, GB). McGraw.
--Fun on Horseback. pap. 4.00 (ISBN 0-87980-191-3). Wilshire.
--Fun on Horseback. LC 64-20093. 1964. 6.95 (ISBN 0-668-02764-9). Arco.
--Horsemastership. (Illus.). 1952. 12.95 (ISBN 0-668-02778-9). Arco.
--The Problem Horse & the Problem Horseman. LC 75-38952. (Illus.). 1977. 8.50 (ISBN 0-668-03934-5). Arco.
--Young Rider & His First Pony. LC 69-14892. (Illus.). 178p. 1974. pap. 2.95 (ISBN 0-668-03408-4). Arco.
Selvidge, James N. Hold Your Horses. 2nd ed. (Illus.). 176p. 1976. pap. 6.95 (ISBN 0-915700-01-8). Jacada Pubns.
Seunig, Waldemar. Horsemanship. rev. ed. LC 56-5594. 1961. 12.95 (ISBN 0-385-01015-X). Doubleday.
Shapiro, Neal & Lehrman, Steve. The World of Horseback Riding. LC 76-13244. 1976. 6.95 (ISBN 0-689-10752-8). Atheneum.
Sherred, Alison, et al. Showing & Ringcraft Explained. LC 77-17185. (Horseman's Handbook Ser.). 1978. 6.95 (ISBN 0-668-04405-5); pap. 3.95 (ISBN 0-668-04410-1). Arco.
Sholinsky, Jane. In the Saddle. Horseback Riding for Girls & Boys. LC 76-52388. (Illus.). 80p. (gr. 3-6). 1977. PLB 6.97 (ISBN 0-671-32825-5). Messner.
Silver, Caroline. Eventing. LC 76-28058. 1977. 15.95 (ISBN 0-312-27090-9). St Martin.
Skelton, Betty. Horses & Riding. 1974. 8.95 (ISBN 0-09-118290-5, Pub. by Hutchinson). Merrimack Bk Serv.
--Pictorial Encyclopedia of Horses & Riding. LC 77-82259. (Illus.). 1978. 14.95 (ISBN 0-528-81065-0). Rand.
Smith, Eph. Riding to Win. (Illus.). 10.00x (ISBN 0-392-04411-0, SpS). Sportshelf.
Smith, Myron J., Jr. Equestrian Studies: The Salem College Guide to Sources in English, 1950-1980. LC 81-2002. 372p. 1981. 17.50 (ISBN 0-8108-1423-4). Scarecrow.
Solomon, Diane S. Teaching Riding: Step-by-Step Schooling for Horse & Rider. LC 81-40281. (Illus.). 321p. 1981. 15.95 (ISBN 0-8061-1580-7). U of Okla Pr.
Spooner, Glenda. Instructions in Ponymastership. (Illus.). 1977. 9.10 (ISBN 0-85131-241-1, Dist. by Sporting Book Center). J A Allen.
--Pony Trekking. (Illus.). pap. 4.35 (ISBN 0-85131-246-2, Dist. by Sporting Book Center). J A Allen.
Sports Illustrated Editors. Sports Illustrated Horseback Riding. LC 74-161580. (Illus.). (gr. 7-9). 1971. 5.95 (ISBN 0-397-00736-1); pap. 2.95 (ISBN 0-397-00735-3, LP55). Lippincott.
Springfield Museum of Fine Arts. Glorious Horseman: Equestrian Art in Europe, 1500-1800. (Illus.). 1981. write for info. (ISBN 0-916746-04-6). Springfield Lib & Mus.
Stanier, Sylvia. The Art of Long Reining. (Illus.). pap. 2.25 (ISBN 0-85131-181-4, Dist. by Sporting Book Center). J A Allen.
--The Art of Lungeing. (Illus.). pap. 3.75 (ISBN 0-85131-252-7, Dist. by Sporting Book Center). J A Allen.
Starkey, Jane, ed. Horse Sense: Buying & Looking After Your First Horse. LC 81-50021. (Illus.). 128p. 1981. 9.95 (ISBN 0-8069-3746-7); lib. bdg. 9.29 (ISBN 0-8069-3747-5). Sterling.
Stecken, Fritz. Training the Horse & Rider. LC 72-2706. (Illus.). 1976. 6.95 (ISBN 0-668-03786-5). Arco.
Stedwell, Paki. Vaulting: Gymnastics on Horseback. 1979. pap. cancelled (ISBN 0-671-33063-2). Wanderer Bks.
Steinkraus, William. Riding & Jumping. new ed. LC 79-91104. 1969. 7.95 (ISBN 0-385-04816-5). Doubleday.
Steinkraus, William, ed. The U.S. Equestrian Team Book of Riding. 1976. 14.95 (ISBN 0-671-22371-2). S&S.
Stull, Sally. What You Can Do with a Horse. 9.95 (ISBN 0-498-01786-9). A S Barnes.
Talbot-Ponsonby, J. Harmony in Horsemanship. (Illus.). 10.50 (ISBN 0-85131-169-5, Dist. by Sporting Book Center). J A Allen.
Taylor, Louis. Bits-Their History, Use & Misuse. pap. 3.00 (ISBN 0-87980-231-6). Wilshire.
--Horseback Riding for Beginners. pap. 4.00 (ISBN 0-87980-229-4). Wilshire.
--Ride Western. pap. 3.00 (ISBN 0-87980-252-9). Wilshire.
Tellington, Wentworth & Tellington-Jones, Linda. Endurance & Competitive Trail Riding. LC 78-18568. 1979. 10.95 (ISBN 0-385-14277-3). Doubleday.
Tinker, Edward L. Centaurs of Many Lands. (Illus.). 5.25 (ISBN 0-85131-072-9, Dist. by Sporting Book Center). J A Allen.
Tuke, Diana. The Rider's Handbook. (Illus.). pap. 4.55 (ISBN 0-85131-258-6). J A Allen.
Ulmer, Donald E. & Juergenson, E. M. Approved Practices in Raising & Handling Horses. LC 73-80303. 1974. 14.00 (ISBN 0-8134-1594-2, 1594). Interstate.
Vezzoli, Gary C. Superior Horsemanship: Learning & Teaching the English Hunt Seat. LC 76-10889. (Illus.). 1978. 17.50 (ISBN 0-498-01922-5). A S Barnes.
Vischer, Peter, ed. Horse & Horseman. LC 67-27976. 1975. 14.95 (ISBN 0-668-02619-7). Arco.
Von Blixen-Finecke, Hans. The Art of Riding. (Illus.). pap. 5.25 (ISBN 0-85131-253-5, Dist. by Sporting Book Center). J A Allen.
Von Rokitansky, Friederike. Horses & Riders. (Breed Ser.). 1977. pap. 1.95 (ISBN 0-88376-013-4). Dreenan Pr.
Von Walter, Ella. Learn to Ride. 1976. text ed. 9.95 (ISBN 0-8120-5112-2). Barron.
Wall, Sheila. Beginner's Guide to Horseback Riding. 1974. pap. 2.00 (ISBN 0-87980-284-7). Wilshire.
Walrond, Sallie. Driving Horses. pap. 3.00 (ISBN 0-87980-242-1). Wilshire.
Watjen, Richard L. Dressage Riding. (Illus.). 1978. Repr. 10.35 (ISBN 0-85131-275-6, Dist. by Sporting Book Center). J A Allen.

Watney, Marylian & Kenward, William. Show Driving Explained. LC 77-24620. (Horseman's Handbooks). 1978. 6.95 (ISBN 0-668-04384-9); pap. 3.95 (ISBN 0-668-04391-1). Arco.
Wheatley, George. Pony Riders Book. 1970. 10.00x (ISBN 0-87556-407-0). Saifer.
Wilde, Louise M. Guide to Dressage. LC 81-3612. (Illus.). 288p. 1981. 12.95 (ISBN 0-498-02440-7). A S Barnes.
Williams, Dorian. Equestrianism. (Illus.). 237p. 1980. 19.95 (ISBN 0-8069-9228-X, Pub by Guinness Superlatives England). Sterling.
Williams, V. D. Riding. Date not set. 7.50 (ISBN 0-392-09544-0, SpS). Sportshelf.
--Riding. LC 76-54799. 1977. pap. 3.25 (ISBN 0-8120-0732-8). Barron.
Williamson, Charles O. Breaking & Training the Stock Horse. 6th rev. ed. LC 62-22012. (Illus.). 1968. 12.50 (ISBN 0-9600144-1-1). Williamson Sch.
Wright, Gordon. Cavalry Manual of Horsemanship. pap. 3.00 (ISBN 0-87980-222-7). Wilshire.
--Learning to Ride, Hunt & Show. rev. ed. LC 66-17404. 8.95 (ISBN 0-385-05182-4). Doubleday.
Wright, Gordon & Kelley, Michael. The Riding Instructor's Manual. LC 74-12719. 144p. 1975. 7.95 (ISBN 0-385-04457-7). Doubleday.
Wright, Gordon, ed. Cavalry Manual of Horsemanship & Horsemastership. LC 62-8914. 6.95 (ISBN 0-385-01647-6). Doubleday.
Wynmalen, Henry. Dressage. LC 74-29443. (Illus.). 1975. 7.95 (ISBN 0-668-02757-6). Arco.
--Dressage - a Study of the Finer Points in Riding. pap. 4.00 (ISBN 0-87980-187-5). Wilshire.
--Equitation. (Illus.). 21.85 (ISBN 0-85131-138-5, Dist. by Sporting Book Center). J A Allen.
Young, John R. Schooling for Young Riders: A Handbook for the Horseman of Tomorrow. (Illus.). 1977. Repr. of 1970 ed. 13.50 (ISBN 0-8061-0890-8). U of Okla Pr.

HORSEMANSHIP-DICTIONARIES

Baranowski, Zdzislaw. Woerterbuch Pferd und Reiter. (Eng., Fr. & Ger., Dictionary of Horses and Horsemanship). 1977. 15.00 (ISBN 0-273-00937-0, M-6910). French & Eur.
Cassart, C. & Moirant, R. Dictionnaire du Cheval et du Chevalier. 288p. (Fr.). 1979. 49.95 (ISBN 0-686-56942-3, M-6064). French & Eur.
Saint-Riquier, Marc de. Lexique De L'homme a Cheval. (Fr.). 25.00 (ISBN 0-686-57287-4, M-4669). French & Eur.
Self, Margaret C. The Horseman's Encyclopedia. LC 63-9365. (Illus.). 1963. 9.95 (ISBN 0-668-02777-0). Arco.
Taylor, Louis. Harper's Encyclopedia for Horsemen: The Complete Book of the Horse. LC 72-79697. (Illus.). 572p. 1973. 24.95 (ISBN 0-06-014226-X, HarpT). Har-Row.
Vansteenwyk, E. Illustrated Horseback Riding Dictionary for Young People. 1980. pap. 2.50 (ISBN 0-13-450908-0). P-H.
Wells, Ellen B., ed. Horsemanship: A Guide to Information Sources. LC 79-16046. (Sports, Games, & Pastimes Information Guide Ser.: Vol. 4). 1979. 36.00 (ISBN 0-8103-1444-4). Gale.

HORSEMANSHIP-JUVENILE LITERATURE

Boy Scouts Of America. Horsemanship. LC 19-600. (Illus.). 56p. (gr. 6-12). 1974. pap. 0.70x (ISBN 0-8395-3298-9, 3298). BSA.
Clemens, Virginia P. A Horse in Your Backyard? LC 77-7394. (Illus.). (gr. 7-10). 1977. 8.50 (ISBN 0-664-32616-1). Westminster.
Devereux, Frederick L., Jr. Jump Your Horse Right. LC 78-7734. (Illus.). (gr. 7 up). 1978. 6.50 (ISBN 0-396-07611-4). Dodd.
--Ride Your Pony Right. LC 74-3780. (Illus.). 160p. (gr. 7 up). 1974. 5.95 (ISBN 0-396-06977-0). Dodd.
Frond, Bill. Better Riding. (Better Bks.). (Illus.). (gr. 7 up). 15.95x (ISBN 0-7182-0159-0, SpS). Sportshelf.
Galbraith, Thistle. Outline for the Young Rider. 1971. 3.50 (ISBN 0-600-43346-3). Transatlantic.
Haley, Neale. Teach Yourself To Ride. LC 73-141. (Illus.). 224p. 1974. 9.95 (ISBN 0-498-01271-9). A S Barnes.
Holmes, Edward. Horse & Pony Care in Pictures. (Illus.). (gr. 7-11). 1977. pap. 4.95 (ISBN 0-668-04079-3). Arco.
Pervier, Evelyn. The Beginning Rider: A Common Sense Approach. LC 80-17821. (Illus.). 192p. (gr. 7 up). 1980. PLB 8.79 (ISBN 0-671-34068-9). Messner.
Sholinsky, Jane. In the Saddle. Horseback Riding for Girls & Boys. LC 76-52388. (Illus.). 80p. (gr. 3-6). 1977. PLB 6.97 (ISBN 0-671-32825-5). Messner.
Stedwell, Paki. Vaulting: Gymnastics on Horseback. LC 79-11556. (Illus.). 128p. (gr. 7 up). 1980. PLB 7.79 (ISBN 0-671-34023-9). Messner.
Sullivan, George. Better Horseback Riding for Boys & Girls. LC 75-88071. (Better Sports Ser.). (Illus.). (gr. 3 up). 1969. PLB 5.95 (ISBN 0-396-06404-3). Dodd.
Thomas, Art & Blackburn, Emily. Horseback Riding Is for Me. LC 80-13081. (Sports for Me Bks.). (Illus.). (gr. 2-5). 1981. PLB 5.95 (ISBN 0-8225-1092-8). Lerner Pubns.
Thompson, Christine-Pullein. Good Riding. (YA) (gr. 7-12). 1979. pap. 1.25 (ISBN 0-590-05741-3, Schol Pap). Schol Bk Serv.
Van Steenwyk, Elizabeth. Illustrated Riding Dictionary for Young People. LC 80-81789. (Illustrated Dictionaries Ser.). (Illus.). 128p. (gr. 5 up). 1981. PLB 7.29 (ISBN 0-8178-0015-8). Harvey.
Wheatley, George. The Young Rider's Companion. LC 81-27509. (Adult & Young Adult Bks.). (Illus.). 120p. (gr. 4 up). 1981. PLB 14.95 (ISBN 0-8225-0767-6, *A*A*C*R1). Lerner Pubns.
Wilding, Suzanne & Savitt, Sam. Ups & Downs: A Basic Guide to Riding & Horsemanship. (Illus.). 160p. 1973. 7.95 (ISBN 0-312-83405-5). St Martin.
Winter, Ginny L. Riding Book. (Illus.). (gr. k-3). 1963. 4.50 (ISBN 0-8392-3031-1). Astor-Honor.

HORSEMEN

see also Cowboys; Jockeys

Bennett, Alan. Horsewoman: Louie Dingwall. 200p. 40.00 (ISBN 0-686-75651-7, Pub by Dorset). State Mutual Bk.
Hull, Robert C. The Search for Adele Parker. LC 74-82751. (Illus.). 1975. 6.95 (ISBN 0-87212-046-5). Libra.
Quicke, Kenneth. Immortal Henry: The Story of a Lipizzaner Stallion. (Illus.). 1978. 9.95 (ISBN 0-236-40096-7, Pub. by Paul Elek). Merrimack Bk Serv.
Smythe, R. H. Healers on Horseback. pap. 8.75 (ISBN 0-85131-282-9). J A Allen.
Steiner, Stan. Dark & Dashing Horsemen. LC 81-47420. (Illus.). 192p. 1981. 13.50 (ISBN 0-06-250850-4, HarpR). Har-Row.
Tinker, Edward L. Centaurs of Many Lands. (Illus.). 1964. 7.50 (ISBN 0-87959-065-3). U of Tex Hum Res.
Trippet, Frank. The First Horsemen. (Emergence of Man Ser.). (Illus.). 1974. 9.95 (ISBN 0-8094-1278-0); lib. bdg. avail. (ISBN 0-685-50286-4). Time-Life.
Vernam, Glenn R. Man on Horseback: The Story of the Mounted Man from the Scythians to the American Cowboy. LC 64-20544. (Illus.). xii, 436p. 1972. pap. 4.95 (ISBN 0-8032-5770-8, BB 561, Bison). U of Nebr Pr.

HORSEMEN-CORRESPONDENCE, REMINISCENCES, ETC.

Albright, Verne. Horseback Across Three Americas. (Illus.). 204p. 1974. 10.00 (ISBN 0-912830-17-4). Printed Horse.
Gibson, Francis. Gibby: The Memoirs Of a Horsey Man. 1978. pap. 8.75 (ISBN 0-85131-277-2). J A Allen.
Martin, Ann. The Equestrian Woman. LC 78-24241. (Illus.). 1979. 8.95 (ISBN 0-448-22686-3). Paddington.

HORSEPOWER (MECHANICS)

Advani, L. T. Horsepower Tables for Agitator Impellers. (Illus.). 175p. 1976. 18.95x (ISBN 0-87201-368-5). Gulf Pub.
Lessiter, Frank D. Horsepower. LC 76-45044. 1977. 11.95 (ISBN 0-89821-018-6). Reiman Assocs.
Veinott, Cyril G. Fractional & Subfractional Horsepower Electric Motors. 3rd ed. LC 79-85117. (Illus.). 1970. 34.00 (ISBN 0-07-067390-X, P&RB). McGraw.

HORSES

see also Draft Horses; Hoofs; Horse Breeds; Horsemen; Mustang; Ponies; Quarter Horse; Race Horses

Abbey, Harlan C. Horses & Horse Shows. LC 78-55449. (Illus.). 1980. 14.95 (ISBN 0-498-02247-1). A S Barnes.
Ainslie, Tom & Ledbetter, Bonnie. The Body Language of Horses: Revealing the Nature of Equine Needs, Wishes & Emotions & How Horses Communicate Them--for Owners, Breeders, Trainers, Riders & All Other Horse Lovers--Including Handicappers. LC 79-26995. (Illus.). 224p. 1980. 10.95 (ISBN 0-688-03620-1). Morrow.
Alexander, A. S. Horse Secrets. (Illus.). 68p. pap. 7.75 (ISBN 0-8466-6024-5, SJU24). Shorey.
Anderson, Clarence W. C. W. Anderson's Complete Book of Horses & Horsemanship. (gr. 5 up). 1963. 6.95g (ISBN 0-02-703340-6). Macmillan.
Andrist, Friedrich. Mares, Foals & Foaling. Dent, A., tr. pap. 3.35 (ISBN 0-85131-053-2, Dist. by Sporting Book Center). J A Allen.
Arab Horse Society. The Arab Horse Stud Book: Containing the Entries of Arab Stallions & Mares, 6 vols. 1976. lib. bdg. 634.95 (ISBN 0-8490-1445-X). Gordon Pr.
Auction Yearlings of 1978. pap. 10.00 (ISBN 0-936032-02-2). Thoroughbred Own and Breed.
Back, Joe. Horses, Hitches & Rocky Trails. 1959. 8.00 (ISBN 0-933472-06-4). Johnson Bks.
Baird, Eric. Horse Care. (Illus.). 1979. 11.95 (ISBN 0-87691-296-X). Winchester Pr.
Baker, Jennifer. Horses & Ponies. LC 73-91685. (Source Book Ser.). (Illus.). 1973. 5.00x (ISBN 0-7063-1493-X). Intl Pubns Serv.
Barbalace, Roberta C. An Introduction to Light Horse Management. LC 74-18651. 1974. text ed. 14.95x (ISBN 0-8087-2823-7). Burgess.
Best, Heidi. How to Book of Riding & Horse Care. (How to Bks). (Illus.). 96p. (Orig.). 1981. pap. 3.95 (ISBN 0-7137-1057-8, Pub. by Blandford Pr England). Sterling.
Blake, Henry. Talking with Horses. Date not set. pap. cancelled (ISBN 0-553-10076-9). Bantam.
Blakely, James. Horses & Horse Sense: The Practical Science of Horse Husbandry. 1981. 23.95 (ISBN 0-8359-2887-X); instr's. manual free (ISBN 0-8359-2888-8). Reston.
Blazer, Don. Horses Don't Care About Women's Lib. LC 78-53437. 1978. 9.95 (ISBN 0-89325-010-4). Joyce Pr.
--Training the Western Show Horse. 1978. 9.95 (ISBN 0-498-01964-0). A S Barnes.
Blood-Horse, ed. Principal Winners Abroad of 1979. (Annual Supplement, the Blood-Horse). (Orig.). 1980. pap. 10.00 (ISBN 0-936032-07-3). Thoroughbred Own & Breed.
Blood-Horse Editors. Auctions of 1980. (Annual Supplement of the Blood-Horse). (Illus.). 190p. (Orig.). 1981. pap. 10.00 (ISBN 0-936032-36-7). Thoroughbred Own & Breed.
Bowen. Thoroughbreds of 1976. 1979. 46.25 (ISBN 0-936032-14-6). Thoroughbred Own & Breed.
--Thoroughbreds of 1978. 1979. 36.25 (ISBN 0-936032-15-4). Thoroughbred Own & Breed.
Bradley, Melvin. Horses: A Practical & Scientific Approach. (Illus.). 560p. 1980. text ed. 19.95x (ISBN 0-07-007065-2). McGraw.
Brady, Irene. America's Horses & Ponies. LC 70-86298. (Illus.). (gr. 4 up). 1969. 12.95 (ISBN 0-395-06659-X). HM.
British Horse Society & Pony Club. A Guide to the Purchase of Children's Ponies. 1979. pap. 1.95 (ISBN 0-8120-0786-7). Barron.
Bullock, John. Care of the Horse. LC 80-12671. 112p. 1980. 9.95 (ISBN 0-668-04977-4, 4977-4). Arco.
Burt, Olive W. Horse in America. LC 73-6187. (Illus.). (gr. 7-12). 1975. 8.95 (ISBN 0-381-99630-1, JD-J). Har-Row.
Carne, Barbara & Mills, Bruce. A Basic Guide to Horse Care & Management. LC 78-12794. (Illus.). 1979. 9.95 (ISBN 0-668-04498-5, 4498). Arco.
Cernik, Sheridan L. Preventative Medicine & Management for the Horse. LC 76-50192. (Illus.). 1978. 12.00 (ISBN 0-498-01925-X). A S Barnes.
Clay, Patrice A. Your Own Horse: A Beginner's Guide to Horse Care. (Illus.). 1977. 7.95 (ISBN 0-399-20538-1). Putnam.
Codrington, W. S. Know Your Horse. (Illus.). 14.75 (ISBN 0-85131-207-1, Dist. by Sporting Book Center); pap. 9.75 (ISBN 0-85131-208-X). J A Allen.
Coggins, Jack. Horseman's Bible. LC 66-17921. pap. 3.50 (ISBN 0-385-03167-X). Doubleday.
The Complete Book of Horse - Auto Racing: New York Times Scrapbook History. 1981. 14.95 (ISBN 0-672-52647-6). Bobbs.
Conn, George H. How to Get a Horse & Live with It. LC 69-15783. (Illus.). 1969. 10.00 (ISBN 0-668-02782-7). Arco.
Cunha, Tony J. Horse Feeding & Nutrition. LC 80-531. (Animal Feeding & Nutrition Ser.). 1980. 26.50 (ISBN 0-12-196560-0). Acad Pr.
Devereux, Frederick L., Jr. Famous American Horses. LC 75-13347. (Illus.). 128p. 1975. 10.00 (ISBN 0-8159-5512-X). Devin.
Disston, Harry. Know All About Horses. 1975. pap. 3.00 (ISBN 0-87980-294-4). Wilshire.
Dossenbach, Monique & Dossenbach, Hans. Irish Horses. (Illus.). 1978. 22.00x (ISBN 0-8464-0532-6). Beekman Pubs.
Dougall, Neil. Horses & Ponies on Small Areas. (Illus.). pap. 2.65 (ISBN 0-85131-273-X, Dist. by Sporting Book Center). J A Allen.
--Stallions: Their Management & Handling. pap. 4.50 (ISBN 0-85131-256-X, Dist. by Sporting Book Center). J A Allen.
Duggan, Moira. Horses. (Golden Leisure Library). (Illus.). (gr. 7 up). 1974. PLB 10.38 (ISBN 0-307-64346-8, Golden Pr). Western Pub.
Dyke, Bill & Jones, Bill. The Horse Business: An Investor's Guide. (Illus.). 1974. 10.00 (ISBN 0-912830-22-0). Printed Horse.
Edwards, E. Hartley. All About Horses & Ponies. 1976. 7.95 (ISBN 0-491-01726-X). Transatlantic.
Edwards, Elwyn H. & Geddes, Candida, eds. The Complete Book of the Horse. LC 73-80764. (Illus.). 320p. 1974. 16.95 (ISBN 0-668-03335-5). Arco.
Ensminger, M. E. Horses & Horsemanship. 5th ed. LC 76-45238. (Illus.). 1977. 23.35 (ISBN 0-8134-1888-7). Interstate.
--Horses & Tack. 1977. 18.50 (ISBN 0-395-24766-7). HM.
Evans, J. Warren. Horses: A Guide to Selection, Care, & Enjoyment. LC 80-29070. (Illus.). 1981. text ed. 20.95x (ISBN 0-7167-1253-9). W H Freeman.
Evans, J. Warren, et al. The Horse. LC 76-22686. (Animal Science Ser.). (Illus.). 1977. 27.95x (ISBN 0-7167-0491-9). W H Freeman.
Ewers, John C. The Horse in Blackfoot Indian Culture. LC 55-60591. (Classics in Smithsonian Anthropology Ser.: No. 3). (Illus.). 374p. 1980. pap. text ed. 9.95x (ISBN 0-87474-419-9). Smithsonian.
Farley, Walter. Walter Farley's How to Stay Out of Trouble with Your Horse: Some Basic Safety Rules to Help You Enjoy Riding. LC 79-8922. (Illus.). 80p. (gr. 4-8). 1981. 7.95a (ISBN 0-385-15480-1); lib. bdg. (ISBN 0-385-15481-X). Doubleday.
Feeding the Horse. 1974. lib. bdg. 10.75 (ISBN 0-936032-04-9). Thoroughbred Own & Breed.
Ferris, Bill. Ray Lum: Mule Trader -- an Essay. Friedman, Jack, ed. LC 76-53834. (Illus.). 1977. 2.50 (ISBN 0-89267-003-7); film transcript 2.50 (ISBN 0-89267-001-0); record transcript 2.50 (ISBN 0-89267-002-9). Ctr South Folklore.
Field, Walter L. Tale of the Horse. 50p. 1978. 5.95 (ISBN 0-8143-1607-7). Wayne St U Pr.
Flandorffer, Tamas & Hajas, Jozsef. The Horse & Horsemanship. Kortvelyessy, Eniko, tr. (Illus.). 184p. 1979. 12.50x (ISBN 963-13-3701-4). Intl Pubns Serv.
Flower, William H. The Horse: A Study in Natural History. 1978. Repr. of 1892 ed. lib. bdg. 25.00 (ISBN 0-8482-0824-2). Norwood Edns.
Garland, James A. The Private Stable. LC 75-44371. (Illus.). 1976. Repr. of 1903 ed. 50.00 (ISBN 0-88427-018-1, Dist. by Caroline Hse Pubs). North River.
Goldsmith, Don. Horsin' Around Again. (Illus.). 180p. 1981. 12.95 (ISBN 0-931722-13-6); pap. 7.95 (ISBN 0-931722-14-4). Corona Pub.
Goodall, Daphne M. Horses of the World. rev. ed. LC 73-7480. (Illus.). 272p. 1974. 14.95 (ISBN 0-02-544650-9). Macmillan.
Gorman, John A. Western Horse. LC 66-12997. (Illus.). (gr. 9-12). 1967. 14.60 (ISBN 0-8134-0126-7). Interstate.
Green, Ben K. The Color of Horses. LC 74-79459. (Illus.). 120p. 1974. 25.00 (ISBN 0-87358-131-8). Northland.
--Horse Conformation: As to Soundness & Performance. LC 74-82362. (Illus.). 1974. Repr. 6.95 (ISBN 0-87358-135-0). Northland.
Green, Carol. Stable Management Explained. LC 77-4932. (Horseman's Handbooks Ser.). (Illus.). 1978. 6.95 (ISBN 0-668-04326-1); pap. 3.95 (ISBN 0-668-04332-6). Arco.
--Tack Explained. (Horseman's Handbooks). 1977. 6.95 (ISBN 0-668-04385-7); pap. 3.95 (ISBN 0-668-04393-8). Arco.
Greene, Edward H. The Law & Your Horse. LC 70-124201. 1971. 8.50 (ISBN 0-668-02792-4). Arco.
Griffith, Frank B. & Griffith, Rubye M. How to Live with a Horse. LC 67-17383. (Illus.). 1967. 4.95 (ISBN 0-668-02783-5). Arco.
Grimshaw, Anne. A Bibliographic Social History of the Horse. (Illus.). 372p. 1981. text ed. price not set (ISBN 0-85365-533-2, Pub. by Lib Assn England). Oryx Pr.
Groves, Colin P. Horses, Asses & Zebras in the Wild. LC 74-79610. (Illus.). 191p. 1974. 10.00 (ISBN 0-88359-008-5). R Curtis Bks.
Haley, Neale. Grooming Your Horse. LC 73-143. 224p. 1973. 9.95 (ISBN 0-498-01280-8). A S Barnes.
Haley, Mrs. Neale. How to Have Fun with a Horse. 1972. 8.95 (ISBN 0-668-02842-4). Arco.
Hanauer, Elsie. The Science of Equine Feeding. LC 72-5190. (Illus.). 80p. 1973. 6.95 (ISBN 0-498-01183-6). A S Barnes.
Hanauer, Elsie V. Horse Owner's Concise Guide. pap. 2.00 (ISBN 0-87980-192-1). Wilshire.
--The Horse Owner's Concise Guide. LC 69-14880. (Illus.). 1978. pap. 3.50 (ISBN 0-668-04661-9, 4661). Arco.
--No Foot-No Horse. LC 74-81870. 1974. pap. text ed. 7.95x (ISBN -08087-0883-X). Burgess.
Hardman, A. C. Equine Nutrition. (Illus.). 128p. 1981. 17.95 (ISBN 0-7207-1244-0, Pub. by Michael Joseph). Merrimack Bk Serv.
Hardman, Ann L. A Guide to Feeding Horses & Ponies. (Illus.). 164p. 1978. 10.95 (ISBN 0-7207-0944-X, Pub. by Michael Joseph). Merrimack Bk Serv.
--Young Horse Management. 176p. 1976. 11.95 (ISBN 0-7207-0904-0, Pub. by Michael Joseph). Merrimack Bk Serv.
Harris, Susan E. Grooming to Win: How to Groom, Trim, Braid, & Prepare Your Horse for Show. LC 76-50591. (Illus.). 1977. 12.50 (ISBN 0-684-14859-5, ScribT). Scribner.
Harrison, James C. Care & Training of the Trotter & Pacer. Date not set. 7.50 (ISBN 0-686-20618-5). US Trotting.

Hartigan, Joe. Your First Point to'Point Horse. pap. 5.25 (ISBN 0-85131-212-8, Dist. by Sporting Book Center). J A Allen.
Hayes, M. Horace. Points of the Horse. rev. ed. LC 69-10649. 1969. 15.00 (ISBN 0-668-01811-9). Arco.
Henschel, Georgie. The Illustrated Guide to Horses & Ponies. LC 81-68189. 192p. 1982. 16.95 (ISBN 0-668-05353-4, 5353). Arco.
Holmes, Edward. Horse & Pony Care in Pictures. (Illus.). (gr. 7-11). 1977. pap. 4.95 (ISBN 0-668-04079-3). Arco.
The Horse from Conception to Maturity. 22.50 (ISBN 0-8277-2634-1). British Bk Ctr.
Horses & Ponies. LC 79-710. (Spotter's Guides Ser.). (Illus.). 1979. 3.95 (ISBN 0-8317-4579-7, Mayflower Bks); pap. 1.95 (ISBN 0-8317-4580-0). Smith Pubs.
Hyland, Ann. Foal to Five Years. LC 80-11310. 128p. 1980. 12.95 (ISBN 0-668-04952-9, 4952-9). Arco.
The Illustrated Glossary of Horse Equipment. LC 74-83421. (Illus.). 1977. pap. 3.95 (ISBN 0-668-03835-7). Arco.
Jacobson, Patricia & Hayes, Marcia. A Horse Around the House. rev. ed. (Illus.). 1978. 10.00 (ISBN 0-517-53166-6). Crown.
Jepsen, Stanley M. The Coach Horse: Servant with Style. LC 75-20612. (Illus.). 1977. 9.95 (ISBN 0-498-01789-3). A S Barnes.
Johnson, Elizabeth. All Color Book of Horses. (Bounty Bks.). (Illus.). 72p. 1974. pap. 2.95 (ISBN 0-517-51409-5). Crown.
Jones, Dave. The Western Horse: Advice & Training. LC 73-7422. (Illus.). 200p. 1974. 9.95 (ISBN 0-8061-1130-5). U of Okla Pr.
Jones, Howard A. Hooked on Horses. (Illus.). 256p. 1981. 12.50 (ISBN 0-682-49791-6). Exposition.
Jones, William E., ed. Basic First Aid for Horses. (Horse Health & Care Ser.). (Illus.). 1973. pap. 2.95 (ISBN 0-912830-04-2). Printed Horse.
--A Descriptive Bibliography of One Thousand One Horse Books. 128p. 1972. pap. 4.95 (ISBN 0-912830-10-7). Printed Horse.
Kays, John M. The Horse. LC 68-27248. (Illus.). 1977. 12.95 (ISBN 0-668-02770-3). Arco.
Keegan, Terry. The Heavy Horse: Its Harness & Harness Decoration. LC 73-15040. (Illus.). 217p. 1974. 9.95 (ISBN 0-498-01472-X). A S Barnes.
Kenrick, Vivienne. Horses in Japan. (Illus.). 5.25 (ISBN 0-85131-084-2, Dist. by Sporting Book Center). J A Allen.
Kidd, Jane. An Illustrated Guide to Horses & Pony Care. LC 81-68162. 240p. 1982. 9.95 (ISBN 0-668-05368-2, 5368). Arco.
Lee, Hollis. The Pleasure Horse. (Country Home & Small Farm Guides Ser.). (Illus.). 1978. pap. 2.95 (ISBN 0-88453-004-3). Barrington.
Leech, Jay. How to Care for Your Horse. LC 78-69635. (Illus.). 1979. 12.00 (ISBN 0-498-02235-8). A S Barnes.
Lewis, Lon D. Feeding & Care of the Horse. LC 81-8137. (Illus.). 175p. 1982. text ed. price not set (ISBN 0-8121-0803-5). Lea & Febiger.
Lose, M. Phyllis. Blessed Are the Brood Mares. (Illus.). 1978. 15.95 (ISBN 0-02-575250-2). Macmillan.
Macgregor-Morris, Pamela, ed. The Book of the Horse. LC 79-84551. (Illus.). 1979. 20.00 (ISBN 0-399-12424-1). Putnam.
McTaggart, M. F. A Handbook for Horse Owners. 1979. Repr. of 1935 ed. lib. bdg. 35.00 (ISBN 0-8414-6342-5). Folcroft.
Magner, D. Classic Encyclopedia of the Horse. (Illus.). Repr. 6.98 (ISBN 0-517-32168-8). Bonanza.
Magnusson, Sigurdur A. Stallion of the North: The Unique Story of the Iceland Horse. LC 78-67094. (Illus.). 1979. 12.95 (ISBN 0-917712-06-4). Longship Pr.
Martin, George A. The Family Horse. 12.50 (ISBN 0-88427-020-3). Green Hill.
--The Family Horse: Its Stabling, Care, and Feeding. LC 77-3503. (Illus.). 1977. Repr. of 1895 ed. 12.50 (ISBN 0-88427-020-3, Dist. by Caroline House Pubs). North River.
Melcher, Carol R. Horse Care from A to Z. LC 75-20599. (Illus.). 224p. 1976. 12.95 (ISBN 0-498-01691-9). A S Barnes.
Mellin, Jeanne. The Morgan Horse Handbook. LC 72-91799. 256p. 1980. pap. 8.95 (ISBN 0-8289-0390-5). Greene.
Midwest Plan Service Personnel. Horse Housing & Equipment Handbook. (Illus.). 1971. pap. 4.00 (ISBN 0-89373-009-2, MWPS-15). Midwest Plan Serv.
Miller, Jane. Birth of a Foal. LC 76-5402. 1977. 6.95 (ISBN 0-397-31702-6, JBL-J). Har-Row.
Mohr, Erna. The Asiatic Wild Horse. Goodall, Daphne M., tr. (Illus.). 7.50 (ISBN 0-85131-013-3, Dist. by Sporting Book Center). J A Allen.
Money, Keith. Salute the Horse. (Illus.). 10.00 (ISBN 0-392-04473-0, SpS). Sportshelf.
Morris, Dean. Horses. LC 77-8243. (Read About Animals Ser.). (Illus.). (gr. k-3). 1977. PLB 11.15 (ISBN 0-8393-0008-5). Raintree Child.
Morrow, Harvie. New Zealand Wild Horses. (Illus.). 78p. 1975. 12.25x (ISBN 0-8002-1753-5). Intl Pubns Serv.
Mulder. Imported Foundation Stock of North American Arabian Horses, Vol. 2. 15.00 (ISBN 0-685-27810-7). Borden.
Mutch, Ronnie. Mutch About Horses. LC 77-17352. (Illus.). 1978. 7.95 (ISBN 0-668-04387-3). Arco.
Naviaux, James L. Horses in Health & Disease. rev. ed. LC 75-34594. (Illus.). 1976. 10.00 (ISBN 0-668-03930-2). Arco.
Nutrient Requirements of Horses. 1978. 3.75 (ISBN 0-309-02760-8). Natl Acad Pr.
Nye, Nelson C. Your Western Horse. pap. 2.00 (ISBN 0-87980-205-7). Wilshire.
Oaksey, John. Pride of the Shires: The Story of the Whitebread Horses. (Illus.). 1979. 12.95 (ISBN 0-09-136240-7, Pub. by Hutchinson). Merrimack Bk Serv.
Owen, Robert. Horses: Care, Riding, Jumping for All Ages. LC 78-50719. (Illus.). 1978. 6.95 (ISBN 0-668-04606-6, 4606). Arco.
Patent, Dorothy H. Horses of America. (Illus.). 80p. (gr. 3-7). 1981. reinforced bdg 10.95 (ISBN 0-8234-0399-8). Holiday.
Perrin, Blanche. Horses. (Illus.). 24p. (ps-4). 1962. PLB 5.00 (ISBN 0-307-60459-4, Golden Pr). Western Pub.
Phillips, Lance. The Saddle Horse. LC 64-14315. (Illus.). 1964. 8.95 (ISBN 0-668-02814-9). Arco.
Pittenger, Peggy J. The Back-Yard Horse. LC 72-92312. (Illus.). 1964. 7.50 (ISBN 0-668-02749-5). Arco.
Pittinger, Peggy J. Back Yard Foal. pap. 3.00 (ISBN 0-87980-185-9). Wilshire.
--Back Yard Horse. pap. 3.00 (ISBN 0-87980-186-7). Wilshire.
Posey, Jeanne. How to Buy a Better Horse & Sell the Horse You Own. 1974. pap. 3.00 (ISBN 0-87980-279-0). Wilshire.
Posey, Jeanne K. The Horsekeeper's Handbook. LC 75-6971. (Illus.). 288p. 1975. pap. 3.95 (ISBN 0-02-063550-8, 06355, Collier). Macmillan.
Potter, Murray A. Four Essays. 1917. pap. 8.00 (ISBN 0-527-01101-0). Kraus Repr.
Power, Elaine. Horse in New Zealand. 1976. 21.85x (ISBN 0-8002-0464-6). Intl Pubns Serv.
Practical Horse Psychology. pap. 3.00 (ISBN 0-87980-247-2). Wilshire.
Price, Steven D. Practical Guide to Owning Your Own Horse. 1974. pap. 2.00 (ISBN 0-87980-292-8). Wilshire.
--Practical Guide to Owning Your Own Horse. pap. 2.00 (ISBN 0-685-64542-8). Borden.
Price, Steven D., et al, eds. The Whole Horse Catalog. (Illus.). 1977. pap. 6.95 (ISBN 0-671-22692-4). S&S.
Rayner, Nick & Chivers, Keith. The Heavy Horse Manual. LC 80-85501. (Illus.). 224p. 1981. 38.00 (ISBN 0-7153-8057-5). David & Charles.
Register of Thoroughbred Stallions. 25.00x (ISBN 0-8277-0249-3). British Bk Ctr.
Reynolds, James. A World of Horses. 1979. Repr. of 1947 ed. lib. bdg. 35.00 (ISBN 0-8492-2397-0). R West.
Rossdale, P. D. Das Pferd. Fortpflanzung und Entwicklung. Gerber, H., ed. (Illus.). 120p. 1975. 28.75 (ISBN 3-8055-2030-1). S Karger.
Rossdale, Peter. The Horse. (Illus.). 20.00 (ISBN 0-87556-609-X). Saifer.
--Seeing Equine Practice. (Illus.). 1976. pap. 14.95 (ISBN 0-397-58208-0, Heinemann). Har-Row.
Rossdale, Peter D. The Horse: From Conception to Maturity. 21.00 (ISBN 0-85131-198-9, Dist. by Sporting Book Center). J A Allen.
Rossdale, Peter D. & Wreford, Susan M. Horses' Health A to Z. LC 73-89678. 256p. 1974. 19.95 (ISBN 0-668-03414-9). Arco.
Rudofsky, Herbert. Young Horses. (Breed Ser.). 1977. pap. 1.95 (ISBN 0-88376-009-6). Dreenan Pr.
Rudofsky, Hubert. Horses. (Breed Ser.). 1977. pap. 1.95 (ISBN 0-88376-015-0). Dreenan Pr.
Ryden, Hope. America's Last Wild Horses. (Illus.). 1978. pap. 5.95 (ISBN 0-525-47505-2). Dutton.
Saiga Editors, ed. Heavy Horses. 1981. 10.00x (ISBN 0-86230-025-8, Pub. by Saiga Pub). State Mutual Bk.
Sanchis, Frank E. American Architecture: Westchester County, New York: Colonial to Contemporary. LC 77-21642. (Illus.). 1977. 30.00 (ISBN 0-88427-026-2, Dist. by Caroline House Pubs). North River.
Saurel, E. Le Cheval: Equitation et sports hippiques. (La Vie active). (Illus., Fr.). 25.50x (ISBN 0-685-13827-5). Larousse.
Savitt, Sam. Sam Savitt's True Horse Stories. LC 70-123500. (gr. 5 up). 1977. 5.95 (ISBN 0-396-06204-0). Dodd.
Self, Margaret C. Complete Book of Horses & Ponies. (Illus.). (gr. 6 up). 1963. 7.95 (ISBN 0-07-056109-5, GB). McGraw.
--Horses: Their Selection, Care & Handling. 1943. 5.95 (ISBN 0-668-02779-7). Arco.
--The Nature of the Horse. LC 73-77840. (Illus.). 224p. 1974. 8.95 (ISBN 0-668-02993-5). Arco.
--The Problem Horse & the Problem Horseman. LC 75-38952. (Illus.). 1977. 8.50 (ISBN 0-668-03934-5). Arco.
Shafer, Michael. The Language of the Horse. LC 74-24802. (Illus.). 1975. 15.00 (ISBN 0-668-03762-8). Arco.
Silver, Caroline. Guide to Horses of the World. (Illustrated Natural History Guides). (Illus.). 1977. pap. 4.95 (ISBN 0-8467-0365-3, Pub. by Two Continents). Hippocrene Bks.
Silvester, Hans. Horses of the Camargue. 1979. pap. 12.95 (ISBN 0-14-005360-3). Penguin.
Simmons, Sue, ed. The Sporting Horse. LC 75-29901. (Illus.). 128p. 1976. 8.95 (ISBN 0-668-03925-6). Arco.
Sires & Dams of Stakes Winners, 1928-1978. 82.50 (ISBN 0-936032-10-3). Thoroughbred Own and Breed.
Skelton, Betty. Pictorial Encyclopedia of Horses & Riding. LC 77-82259. (Illus.). 1978. 14.95 (ISBN 0-528-81065-0). Rand.
Sloan, Earl S. Treatise on the Horse. (Illus.). 1980. Repr. of 1897 ed. softcover 5.00 (ISBN 0-686-64453-0). S J Durst.
Small, Howard I. Monty's Pal. (Illus.). viii, 120p. 1979. 8.95 (ISBN 0-931474-08-6). TBW Bks.
--Monty's Pal. (Illus.). viii, 120p. 1979. 8.95 (ISBN 0-931474-08-6). TBW Bks.
Smith, Jean F. Horse Markings & Coloration. LC 75-20604. (Illus.). 1977. 9.95 (ISBN 0-498-01751-6). A S Barnes.
Smythe, R. H. The Horse: Structure & Movement. 2nd ed. (Illus.). pap. 10.50 (ISBN 0-85131-242-X, Dist. by Sporting Book Center). J A Allen.
--The Mind of the Horse. (Illus.). 10.50 (ISBN 0-85131-150-4, Dist. by Sporting Book Center). J A Allen.
Smythe, Reginald H. Mind of the Horse. LC 65-22225. 1965. 7.95 (ISBN 0-8289-0042-6). Greene.
Spaulding, Jackie. The Family Horse. (Illus.). 1980. cancelled (ISBN 0-88930-050-X, Pub. by Cloudburst Canada); pap. cancelled (ISBN 0-88930-049-6). Madrona Pubs.
Stallion Register, 1980. 1979. lib. bdg. 20.00 (ISBN 0-936032-27-8); pap. 10.00 (ISBN 0-936032-28-6). Thoroughbred Own & Breed.
Steinkraus, William & Savitt, Sam. Great Horses of the U. S. Equestrian Team. LC 76-53434. (Illus.). (gr. 5 up). 1977. 6.95 (ISBN 0-396-07432-4). Dodd.
STIS Inc., compiled by. Horsedom One. Hodinar, Dagmar, ed. (Pet & Hobby Animal Annual Reference Books & Directories: Horsedom). (Illus., Orig.). 1979. pap. write for info (ISBN 0-931994-11-X). PHIP Inc.
Stoneridge, M. A. A Horse of Your Own. rev. ed. LC 78-22369. (Illus.). 560p. 1980. 15.95 (ISBN 0-385-14617-5). Doubleday.
Streeter, Carol. My Kingdom for a Horse: A Owner's Manual. LC 78-69643. (Illus.). 128p. 1980. 9.95 (ISBN 0-498-02226-9). A S Barnes.
Stull, Sally. What You Can Do with a Horse. 9.95 (ISBN 0-498-01786-9). A S Barnes.
Suares, Jean Clande & Stephens, Charles. The Illustrated Horse. 1979. 12.95 (ISBN 0-517-53632-3); pap. 6.95 (ISBN 0-517-53633-1). Crown.
Summerhays, R. S. The Observer's Book of Horses & Ponies. (Illus.). 1977. 3.95 (ISBN 0-684-14945-1, ScribT). Scribner.
--The Problem Horse. (Illus.). pap. 6.10 (ISBN 0-85131-225-X, Dist. by Sporting Book Center). J A Allen.
Summerhays, R. S. & Walker, Stella A. The Controversial Horse. (Illus.). 8.75 (ISBN 0-85131-075-3, Dist. by Sporting Book Center). J A Allen.
Sumner, W. Dayton. Breaking Your Horse's Bad Habits. LC 74-30971. (Illus.). 1976. 9.95 (ISBN 0-498-01695-1). A S Barnes.
Tait, M. E. Horses & Ponies: Their Care & Management for Owners & Riders. LC 73-91685. (Illus.). 1974. 4.95 (ISBN 0-668-03439-4); pap. 2.50 (ISBN 0-686-66999-1). Arco.
Taylor, Joyce. Horses in Suburbia. (Illus.). 5.25 (ISBN 0-85131-085-0, Dist. by Sporting Book Center). J A Allen.
Thomas, Heather S. The Wild Horse Controversy. LC 77-84588. (Illus.). 1979. 19.95 (ISBN 0-498-02191-2). A S Barnes.
Thoroughbred Broodmare Records, Nineteen Seventy-Eight. 1979. text ed. 66.75 (ISBN 0-936032-11-1). Thoroughbred Own & Breed.
Thoroughbred Owner & Breeder Directory, 1976. 1977. 97.50 (ISBN 0-936032-12-X). Thoroughbred Own & Breed.
Thoroughbred Owner & Breeder Directory, 1978. 1979. 27.50 (ISBN 0-936032-13-8). Thoroughbred Own & Breed.
Tovey, Doreen. Making the Horse Laugh. (Illus.). 184p. 1974. 6.95 (ISBN 0-393-08703-4). Norton.
Trahan, Ronald. Careers for Horse Lovers. (Illus.). 288p. 1981. 12.95 (ISBN 0-395-31331-7). HM.
Tuke, Diana R. Bit by Bit. (Illus.). 13.85 (ISBN 0-85131-033-8). J A Allen.
--Horse by Horse. (Illus.). 19.25 (ISBN 0-85131-203-9, Dist. by Sporting Book Center); pap. 12.25 (ISBN 0-685-85287-3). J A Allen.
Tuke, Diane R. Feeding Your Horse. (Illus.). 104p. (Orig.). 1980. pap. 13.10 (ISBN 0-85131-334-5). J A Allen.
Vasiloff, Mary Jean. Alone with Your Horse. LC 76-5532. (Illus.). 1978. 19.95 (ISBN 0-06-014499-8, HarpT). Har-Row.
Vavra, Robert. Such Is the Real Nature of Horses. LC 79-52901. (Illus.). 1979. 39.95 (ISBN 0-688-03504-3). Morrow.
Villiers, Guy. The British Heavy Horse. (Illus.). 1978. 12.00 (ISBN 0-214-20095-7). Transatlantic.
Weatherley, Lee. Great Horses of Britain. 1981. 50.00x (ISBN 0-904558-34-7, Pub. by Saiga Pub). State Mutual Bk.
Weber, Philip & Jepsen, Stanley M. Heroes in Harness. LC 77-84593. (Illus.). 1979. 12.00 (ISBN 0-498-02118-1). A S Barnes.
Weikel, Bill, ed. Farnam Horse Library Ser. Incl. Understanding Horse Psychology; How to Become a Better Rider; Know Practical Horse Feeding; How to Break & Train the Western Horse; Know the American Horse; How to Recognize Horse Health Problems; Know the Anatomy of a Horse; Riding the Show Ring Hunter; Know Practical Horse Breeding; How to Shoe Your Horse; Know the Arabian Horse; How to Buy the Right Horse; Know First Aid for Your Horse; Riding the Gymkana Winner; Know the English Equitation & Training; How to Correct the Problem Horse; Know All About Tack; How to Show Your Horse & Win; Know Stable Design & Management; Know All About Trail Riding; How to Raise a Foal; How to Train the Roping Horse; Know the Appaloosa Horse; How to Train the Reining Horse; Between Mare & Foal. Coen, Sue; Book of Bad Habits. Jones, Dave; The Save Your Horse Handbook: Care & Treatment of Sick Horses. Bailey, Nevajac; Hapiness Is a Well Trained Horse. Gray, Patsy; Winning Through Grooming. Self, Charles. (Illus.). pap. 1.95 ea. Borden.
Wheatley, George. Stable Management for the Owner-Groom. LC 75-37954. (Illus.). 262p. 1973. 7.95 (ISBN 0-498-01137-2). A S Barnes.
Wiederhold, Hermann. Your Pony Book. pap. 2.00 (ISBN 0-87980-331-2). Wilshire.
Williams, Dorian. Book of Horses. LC 70-164017. (Illus.). 1971. 8.95 (ISBN 0-397-00888-0). Lippincott.
--Book of Horses. LC 70-164017. (Illus.). 1971. 8.95 (ISBN 0-397-00888-0). Lippincott.
--Equestrianism. (Illus.). 237p. 1980. 19.95 (ISBN 0-8069-9228-X, Pub by Guinness Superlatives England). Sterling.
--The Horseman's Companion. 574p. 1980. 15.00 (ISBN 0-312-39217-6). St Martin.
Williams, M. Horse Psychology. 1978. 10.00 (ISBN 0-87556-616-2). Saifer.
Williams, Moyra. Breed of Horses. LC 75-134731. 1971. text ed. 15.00 (ISBN 0-08-007123-6). Pergamon.
--Horse Psychology. (Illus.). pap. 7.50 (ISBN 0-85131-238-1, Dist. by Sporting Book Center). J A Allen.
Willoughby, David P. Growth & Nutrition in the Horse. LC 74-9276. (Illus.). 160p. 1975. 9.95 (ISBN 0-498-01427-4). A S Barnes.
Wonder Book of Horses. (gr. k-3). 0.79 (ISBN 0-448-00857-2). Wonder.
Wright, Gordon, ed. Cavalry Manual of Horsemanship & Horsemastership. LC 62-8914. 6.95 (ISBN 0-385-01647-6). Doubleday.
Wyman, Walker D. Wild Horse of the West. LC 66-17457. (Illus.). 1962. pap. 2.45 (ISBN 0-8032-5223-4, BB 144, Bison). U of Nebr Pr.
Wynne, Michael. Hoofmarks. LC 80-51728. 270p. Date not set. pap. 7.95 (ISBN 0-89526-673-3). Regnery-Gateway.
Young, Richard. Schooling of the Western Horse. (Illus.). 15.75 (ISBN 0-85131-182-2). J A Allen.

HORSES–ANATOMY

Bradley, Melvin. Horses: A Practical & Scientific Approach. (Illus.). 560p. 1980. text ed. 19.95x (ISBN 0-07-007065-2). McGraw.
Devlin, C. B. Duke. The Horseman's Dictionary: Medical & General. LC 73-10518. 200p. 1974. 8.95 (ISBN 0-498-01416-9). A S Barnes.
Edwards, Gladys B. Anatomy & Conformation of the Horse. LC 73-77060. 224p. 1973. pap. 5.95 (ISBN 0-88376-025-8). Dreenan Pr.
Geurts, Reiner. Hair Colour in the Horse. Dent, Anthony, tr. from Dutch. (Illus.). pap. 8.75 (ISBN 0-85131-290-X). J A Allen.
Goody, Peter. Horse Anatomy. (Illus.). 17.50 (ISBN 0-85131-230-6, Dist. by Sporting Book Center). J A Allen.
Goody, Peter C. Horse Anatomy. 1978. 25.00 (ISBN 0-87556-610-3). Saifer.
Jones, William E., ed. Anatomy of the Horse. (Horse Health & Care Ser.). (Illus.). 1973. pap. 6.95 (ISBN 0-912830-07-7). Printed Horse.
--Teeth of the Horse. (Horse Health & Care Ser.). (Illus.). 1973. pap. 2.95 (ISBN 0-912830-15-8). Printed Horse.

Rooney, James R. Autopsy of the Horse: Technique & Interpretation. LC 75-11887. 164p. 1976. Repr. of 1970 ed. 14.95 (ISBN 0-88275-329-0). Krieger.
Smythe, R. H. The Horse; Structure & Movement. 12.50x (ISBN 0-87556-321-X). Saifer.
Stubbs, George. Anatomy of the Horse. 1979. 100.00x (ISBN 0-87556-328-7). Saifer.
--The Anatomy of the Horse. McCunn, J. C. & Ottaway, C. W., eds. LC 76-17945. (Illus.). 128p. 1977. pap. 6.00 (ISBN 0-486-23402-9). Dover.
--The Anatomy of the Horse. 15.00 (ISBN 0-8446-5663-1). Peter Smith.
Way, Robert F. Horse Anatomy. LC 73-77063. (Illus.). 1973. pap. 3.95 (ISBN 0-88376-007-X). Dreenan Pr.
Way, Robert F. & Lee, Donald G. The Anatomy of the Horse. LC 64-7778. (Illus.). 214p. 1965. text ed. 17.50 (ISBN 0-397-50142-0). Har-Row.

HORSES–BREEDING
see Horse Breeding

HORSES–BREEDS
see Horse Breeds

HORSES–DICTIONARIES
Baranowski, Zdzislaw. The International Horseman's Dictionary. (Illus.). 9.10 (ISBN 0-85131-262-4, Dist. by Sporting Book Center). J A Allen.
--Woerterbuch Pferd und Reiter. (Eng., Fr. & Ger., Dictionary of Horses and Horsemanship). 1977. 15.00 (ISBN 0-273-00937-0, M-6910). French & Eur.
Blood Horse, ed. Stallion Register, 1981. (Illus.). 900p. 1980. 20.00 (ISBN 0-936032-33-2); pap. 10.00 (ISBN 0-936032-34-0). Thoroughbred Own & Breed.
Cassart, C. & Moirant, R. Dictionnaire du Cheval et du Chevalier. 288p. (Fr.). 1979. 49.95 (ISBN 0-686-56942-3, M-6064). French & Eur.
Ensminger, M. E. The Complete Encyclopedia of Horses. LC 74-9282. (Illus.). 720p. 1977. 29.50 (ISBN 0-498-01508-4). A S Barnes.
Lexikon Fuer Pferdefreunde. (Ger.). 1976. 25.00 (ISBN 3-7658-0221-2, M-7197). French & Eur.
Marcenac, Louis N. & Aublet, Henri. Encyclopedie Du Cheval. 3rd ed. 1244p. (Fr.). 1974. 125.00 (ISBN 0-686-57037-5, M-6397). French & Eur.
Rousselet-Blanc, Pierre, ed. Larousse du cheval. new ed. (Larousse des animaux familiers). (Illus.). 260p. (Fr.). 1975. 43.95x (ISBN 2-03-014855-5). Larousse.
--Larousse Du Chevel. (Fr.). 1976. 47.50 (ISBN 0-686-56997-0, M-6337). French & Eur.
Taylor, Louis. Harper's Encyclopedia for Horsemen: The Complete Book of the Horse. LC 72-79697. (Illus.). 572p. 1973. 24.95 (ISBN 0-06-014226-X, HarpT). Har-Row.
Webber, Toni. Know Your Horses. LC 77-76211. (Illus.). (gr. 6-9). 1977. pap. 1.95 (ISBN 0-528-87023-8). Rand.

HORSES–DISEASES
see also Veterinary Surgery
Adams, O. R. Lameness in Horses. 3rd ed. LC 73-16030. (Illus.). 566p. 1974. text ed. 22.50 (ISBN 0-8121-0474-9). Lea & Febiger.
Beaver, Bonnie V. Your Horse's Health: A Handbook for Owners & Trainers. LC 78-75297. (Illus.). 1980. 9.95 (ISBN 0-498-02338-9). A S Barnes.
Belschner, H. G. Horse Diseases. 1975. pap. 4.00 (ISBN 0-87980-302-9). Wilshire.
Blood, D. C., et al. Veterinary Medicine: A Textbook of the Diseases of Cattle, Sheep, Pigs & Horses. 5th ed. 1135p. 1979. text ed. 46.00 (ISBN 0-8121-0649-0). Lea & Febiger.
Bostock, D. E. Neoplasia in the Cat, Dog & Horse. (Illus.). 1975. 55.00 (ISBN 0-8151-1079-0). Year Bk Med.
Cernik, Sheridan L. Preventative Medicine & Management for the Horse. LC 76-50192. (Illus.). 1978. 12.00 (ISBN 0-498-01925-X). A S Barnes.
Conn, George H. Treating Common Diseases of Your Horse. pap. 3.00 (ISBN 0-87980-255-3). Wilshire.
Davidson, Joseph B. Inside Horseracing. (Illus.). 282p. (Orig.). 1974. pap. 6.00 (ISBN 0-668-03332-0). Arco.
Denning, Charles H., Jr. First Aid for Horses. (Orig.). pap. 2.00 (ISBN 0-87980-189-1). Wilshire.
Devlin, C. B. Duke. The Horseman's Dictionary: Medical & General. LC 73-10518. 200p. 1974. 8.95 (ISBN 0-498-01416-9). A S Barnes.
Hanauer, Elsie. Disorders of the Horse. LC 73-6364. (Illus.). 110p. 1973. 6.95 (ISBN 0-498-01256-5). A S Barnes.
--Disorders of the Horse & What to Do About It. 1974. pap. 3.00 (ISBN 0-87980-281-2). Wilshire.
Hayes, Horace M. Veterinary Notes for Horse Owners. 15th ed. Tutt, J. F., ed. LC 64-12209. (Illus.). 1964. 17.95 (ISBN 0-668-00656-0). Arco.
International Conference on Equine Infectious Diseases, 2nd, Paris, 1969. Equine Infectious Diseases II: Proceedings. Bryans, J. T. & Gerber, H., eds. 1970. 45.00 (ISBN 3-8055-0825-5). S Karger.
International Conference on Equine Infectious Diseases, 3rd. Equine Infectious Diseases III: Proceedings. Bryans, J. T. & Gerber, H., eds. 1973. 74.25 (ISBN 3-8055-1392-5). S Karger.
Loomis, Edmond C., et al. The Common Parasites of Horses. 1975. pap. 4.00x (ISBN 0-931876-07-9, 4006). Ag Sci Pubns.
McKibbin, Lloyd S. Horse Owner's Handbook. LC 75-44652. 1977. pap. text ed. 19.95 (ISBN 0-7216-5920-9). Saunders.
MacLeod, G. The Treatment of Horses by Homoeopathy. 1980. 17.50x (ISBN 0-85032-155-7, Pub. by Daniel Co England). State Mutual Bk.
Magner, D. Classic Encyclopedia of the Horse. (Illus.). Repr. 6.98 (ISBN 0-517-32168-8). Bonanza.
Marlin, Herb & Savitt, Sam. How to Take Care of Your Horse Until the Vet Comes. LC 75-11727. (Illus.). 96p. (gr. 5 up). 1975. 5.95 (ISBN 0-396-07145-7). Dodd.
Montes & Vaughn. Atlas of Skin Diseases of the Horse. (Illus.). 240p. 1980. text ed. write for info. (ISBN 0-7216-6436-9). Saunders.
Naviaux, James L. Horses in Health & Disease. rev. ed. LC 75-34594. (Illus.). 1976. 10.00 (ISBN 0-668-03930-2). Arco.
Rooney, James R. Biomechanics of Lameness in Horses. LC 76-18771. (Illus.). 272p. 1977. Repr. of 1969 ed. 17.50 (ISBN 0-88275-447-5). Krieger.
--The Lame Horse: Causes, Symptoms & Treatment. LC 73-121. (Illus.). 288p. 1973. 13.50 (ISBN 0-498-01278-6). A S Barnes.
--Lame Horses - Causes, Symptoms & Treatment. 1975. pap. 4.00 (ISBN 0-87980-308-8). Wilshire.
--Mechanics of the Horse. LC 78-8774. 104p. 1980. lib. bdg. 12.50 (ISBN 0-88275-693-1). Krieger.
--The Sick Horse: Causes, Symptoms, & Treatment. LC 75-22565. (Illus.). 224p. 1976. 12.00 (ISBN 0-498-01827-X). A S Barnes.
Rossdale, Peter. Horse Ailments Explained. LC 78-8941. (Horseman's Handbook Ser.). (Illus.). 1979. 7.95 (ISBN 0-668-04582-5); pap. 3.95 (ISBN 0-668-04586-8). Arco.
Serth, G. W. Treating Horse Ailments. pap. 2.00 (ISBN 0-87980-230-8). Wilshire.
Sevelius, Pritz, et al. Keeping Your Horse Healthy: The Prevention & Cure of Illness. (Illus.). 176p. 1981. Repr. of 1978 ed. 19.95 (ISBN 0-7153-7638-1). David & Charles.
Straiton, E. C. The Horse Owner's Vet Book. rev. & updated ed. 1979. 12.95 (ISBN 0-685-99717-0). Lippincott.
--The Horse Owner's Vet Book. LC 72-11708. (Illus.). 192p. 1973. 10.95 (ISBN 0-397-00915-1). Lippincott.
Strong, Charles L. Horses' Injuries. LC 72-97583. (Illus.). 118p. 1973. 11.95 (ISBN 0-668-02959-5). Arco.
Turner, Diane E. Understanding Your Horse's Lameness. LC 79-12687. (Illus.). 1980. 8.95 (ISBN 0-668-04769-0). Arco.
Westermayer, Erwin. The Treatment of Horses by Acupuncture. 1980. 25.00x (ISBN 0-85032-161-1, Pub. by Daniel Co England). State Mutual Bk.
Wiseman, Robert F. The Complete Horseshoeing Guide. rev. ed. LC 72-9279. (Illus.). 160p. 1973. 7.95 (ISBN 0-8061-1049-X). U of Okla Pr.

HORSES–EXHIBITIONS
see Horse-Shows

HORSES–HISTORY
Anderson, J. K. Ancient Greek Horsemanship. LC 61-6780. (Illus.). 1961. 30.00x (ISBN 0-520-00023-4). U of Cal Pr.
Baker, Jennifer. Horses & Ponies. LC 73-91685. (Source Book Ser.). (Illus.). 1973. 5.00x (ISBN 0-7063-1493-X). Intl Pubns Serv.
Brereton, J. M. The Horse in War. LC 76-866. (Illus.). 1976. 12.95 (ISBN 0-668-03959-0). Arco.
Clabby, John. The Natural History of the Horse. LC 75-33426. (Illus.). 144p. 1976. 9.95 (ISBN 0-8008-5467-5). Taplinger.
Denhardt, Robert M. The Horse of the Americas. LC 74-5955. (Illus.). 343p. 1981. pap. 8.95 (ISBN 0-8061-1724-9). U of Okla Pr.
Evans, George E. Horse Power & Magic. (Illus.). 240p. 1979. 17.95 (ISBN 0-686-25059-1, Pub. by Faber & Faber). Merrimack Bk Serv.
Gordon, W. J. The Horse World of London. (Illus.). 7.00 (ISBN 0-85131-144-X, Dist. by Sporting Book Center). J A Allen.
Grimshaw, A. A Bibliographic Social History of the Horse. 1981. 88.50 (ISBN 0-85365-533-2). Oryx Pr.
Grimshaw, Anne. A Bibliographic Social History of the Horse. (Illus.). 372p. 1981. text ed. price not set (ISBN 0-85365-533-2, Pub. by Lib Assn England). Oryx Pr.
Hart, Edward. The Heavy Horse at Work. (Illus.). 64p. 1981. pap. 5.95 (ISBN 0-7134-3805-3, Pub. by Batsford England). David & Charles.
--Heavy Horses Past & Present. LC 75-31325. (Illus.). 112p. 1976. 16.95 (ISBN 0-7153-7146-0). David & Charles.
Keith, Thomas B. The Horse Interlude. LC 76-46792. 1976. 10.95 (ISBN 0-89301-036-7). U Pr of Idaho.
Kennett, David. Victorian & Edwardian Horses from Historic Photographs. LC 79-56443. (Illus.). 120p. 1980. 19.95 (ISBN 0-7134-1569-X, Pub. by Batsford England). David & Charles.
Law, Robin. The Horse in West African History: The Role of the Horse in the Societies of Pre-Colonial West Africa. (IAI Ser.). (Illus.). 240p. 1980. 37.50x (ISBN 0-19-724206-5). Oxford U Pr.
MacClintock, Dorcas. Horses As I See Them. LC 78-31778. (Illus.). 96p. (gr. 3 up). 1979. 9.95 (ISBN 0-684-16116-8, ScribT). Scribner.
Poska, Valentine J. Miniature Horses. (Illus.). 48p. 1981. 24.00 (ISBN 0-686-76456-0). Mosaic Pr.
Ridgeway, William. The Origin & Influence of the Thoroughbred Horse. LC 73-174446. (Illus.). Repr. of 1905 ed. 25.00 (ISBN 0-405-08890-6, Blom Pubns). Arno.
Seth-Smith, Michael. The Horse. (Illus.). 1980. 35.00 (ISBN 0-7064-1024-6, Mayflower Bks). Smith Pubs.
Seth-Smith, Michael, ed. The Horse in Art & History. (Illus.). 1978. 12.95 (ISBN 0-8317-4550-9, Mayflower Bks). Smith Pubs.
Vernon, Arthur. The History & Romance of the Horse. LC 70-185379. (Illus.). xviii, 525p. 1975. Repr. of 1939 ed. 26.00 (ISBN 0-8103-3982-X). Gale.
Wallace, John H. The Horse in America in His Derivation, History, & Development. LC 72-89083. (Rural America Ser.). 1973. Repr. of 1897 ed. 28.00 (ISBN 0-8420-1502-7). Scholarly Res Inc.

HORSES–JUVENILE LITERATURE
see also Horses–Legends and Stories
Anderson, John K. Horses & Riding. 48p. (gr. 7-9). 1979. pap. 2.50 (ISBN 0-88388-066-0). Bellerophon Bks.
Balch, Glenn. Book of Horses. (Illus.). 96p. (gr. 3-7). 1967. 8.95 (ISBN 0-590-07048-7, Four Winds). Schol Bk Serv.
--The Book of Horses. (Illus.). (gr. 4-6). 1972. pap. 1.50 (ISBN 0-590-01457-9, Schol Pap). Schol Bk Serv.
Brady, Irene. America's Horses & Ponies. (Illus.). 202p. (gr. 5-12). 1976. pap. 6.95 (ISBN 0-395-24050-6, Sandpiper). HM.
Brown, Fern. Behind the Scenes at the Horse Hospital. Tucker, Kathleen, ed. (Behind the Scenes Ser.). (Illus.). 48p. (gr. 3-9). 1981. 8.25 (ISBN 0-8075-0610-9). A Whitman.
Chase, Edward L. Big Book of Horses. (Illus.). (gr. 4-6). 1970. 1.95 (ISBN 0-448-02241-9). G&D.
Clay, Patrice. We Work with Horses. (Illus.). 160p. (YA) (gr. 7-12). 1980. 8.95 (ISBN 0-399-20735-X). Putnam.
Clemens, Virginia P. A Horse in Your Backyard? LC 77-7394. (Illus.). (gr. 7-10). 1977. 8.50 (ISBN 0-664-32616-1). Westminster.
Cole, Joanna. A Horse's Body. LC 80-28147. (Illus.). 48p. (gr. k-3). 1981. 6.95 (ISBN 0-688-00362-1); PLB 6.67 (ISBN 0-688-00363-X). Morrow.
Copper, Marcia. Take Care of Your Horse. (Illus.). (gr. 7 up). 1974. pap. 3.95 (ISBN 0-684-15375-0, SL759, ScribT). Scribner.
Darling, Lois & Darling, Louis. Sixty Million Years of Horses. (Illus.). (gr. 3-7). 1960. PLB 6.48 (ISBN 0-688-31000-1). Morrow.
Davidson, Margaret. Five True Horse Stories. (gr. 2-6). 1979. pap. 1.25 (ISBN 0-590-05737-5, Schol Pap). Schol Bk Serv.
Dumas, Philippe. The Lippizaners: And the Spanish Riding School of Vienna. (gr. 3-7). 1981. 8.95 (ISBN 0-686-72003-2). P-H.
Farley, Walter. The Black Stallion & the Girl. (gr. 4 up). 1971. (BYR); PLB 6.99 (ISBN 0-394-92145-3); pap. 1.95 (ISBN 0-394-83614-6). Random.
Hapgood, Ruth. First Horse: Basic Horse Care Illustrated. LC 72-76929. (Illus.). 160p. 1972. 6.95 (ISBN 0-87701-015-3). Chronicle Bks.
Harris, Richard. I Can Read About Horses. LC 72-96960. (Illus.). (gr. 2-4). 1973. pap. 1.25 (ISBN 0-89375-054-9). Troll Assocs.
Henry, Marguerite. Album of Horses. LC 51-14002. (Illus.). (gr. 5-12). 1951. 8.95 (ISBN 0-528-82050-8); PLB 6.79 (ISBN 0-528-80155-4). Rand.
--All About Horses. (Allabout Ser.: No. 43). (Illus.). (gr. 5-9). 1962. 4.95 (ISBN 0-394-80243-8, BYR). Random.
--Marguerite Henry's All About Horses. (gr. 4-8). 1967. deluxe ed. 6.95 (ISBN 0-394-81699-4, BYR); PLB 6.99 (ISBN 0-394-91699-9). Random.
Hofsinde, Robert. The Indian & His Horse. (Illus.). (gr. 3-7). 1960. PLB 6.48 (ISBN 0-688-31421-X). Morrow.
Holmes, Edward. Horse & Pony Care in Pictures. (Illus.). (gr. 7-11). 1977. pap. 4.95 (ISBN 0-668-04079-3). Arco.
Hopkins, Lee B., et al, eds. My Mane Catches the Wind: Poems About Horses. LC 79-87518. (Illus.). (gr. 4 up). 1979. 8.95 (ISBN 0-15-256343-1, HJ). HarBraceJ.
Isenbart, Hans-Heinrich. A Foal Is Born. LC 76-2605. (Illus.). 48p. (gr. k-5). 1976. 5.95 (ISBN 0-399-20517-9). Putnam.
Jeffers, Susan. All the Pretty Horses. (gr. k-3). 1977. pap. 1.95 (ISBN 0-590-00184-1, Schol Pap). Schol Bk Serv.
--If Wishes Were Horses: Mother Goose Rhymes. LC 79-9986. (Illus.). (ps-3). 1979. 9.95 (ISBN 0-525-32531-X). Dutton.
Johnson, Pat. Story of Horses. LC 68-23675. (Gateway Ser.: No. 49). (Illus.). (gr. 3-6). 1968. 2.95 (ISBN 0-394-80149-0, BYR); PLB 5.99 (ISBN 0-394-90149-5). Random.
Kirst, Werner & Diekmeyer, Ulrich. Horses. 1977. 7.95x (ISBN 0-8464-0489-3). Beekman Pubs.
Krementz, Jill. A Very Young Rider. LC 77-74996. (gr. 5 up). 1977. 10.95 (ISBN 0-394-41092-0). Knopf.
Lavine, Sigmund A. & Casey, Brigid. Wonders of the World of Horses. (Wonders Ser.). (Illus.). (gr. 5 up). 1972. 5.95 (ISBN 0-396-06617-8). Dodd.
McCreight, Ruby E. Horses. (Illus.). 32p. (ps-4). 1981. 6.75 (ISBN 0-525-66743-1, 0655-200). Elsevier-Nelson.
Miller, Jane. Birth of a Foal. (gr. k-3). 1978. pap. 1.25 (ISBN 0-590-05361-2, Schol Pap). Schol Bk Serv.
--Birth of a Foal. LC 76-5402. 1977. 6.95 (ISBN 0-397-31702-6, JBL-J). Har-Row.
O'Connor, Karen. Working with Horses: A Roundup of Careers. LC 79-6636. (Illus.). (gr. 5 up). 1980. 6.95 (ISBN 0-396-07812-5). Dodd.
Patent, Dorothy H. Horses & Their Wild Relatives. LC 80-23559. (Illus.). 128p. (gr. 5 up). 1981. 8.95 (ISBN 0-8234-0383-1). Holiday.
Pluckrose, Henry, ed. Small World of Horses. (Small World Ser.). (Illus.). (gr. 5-8). 1979. 2.95 (ISBN 0-531-03427-5). Watts.
--Small World of Horses. (Small Worlds Ser.). (Illus.). (gr. k-3). 1979. PLB 6.45 s&l (ISBN 0-531-03405-4). Watts.
Posell, Elsa. Horses. (The New True Bks.). (Illus.). (gr. k-4). 1981. PLB 9.25 (ISBN 0-516-01623-7). Childrens.
Rabinowich, Ellen. Horses & Foals. (Easy-Read Fact Bk.). (Illus.). (gr. 2-4). 1979. PLB 6.90 s&l (ISBN 0-531-02272-2). Watts.
Rabinowitz, Sandy. What's Happening to Daisy? LC 76-24313. (ps-3). 1977. (HarpJ); PLB 6.79 (ISBN 0-06-024835-1). Har-Row.
Radlauer, Ed & Radlauer, Ruth. Horse Mania. LC 80-21550. (Mania Bks). (Illus.). 32p. (gr. k-5). 1981. PLB 9.25 (ISBN 0-516-07784-8, Elk Grove Bks); pap. 2.95 (ISBN 0-686-77714-X, Elk Grove Bks). Childrens.
Robertson, Alden. The Wild Horse Gatherers. LC 77-17512. (Sierra Club-Scribner Juvenile Ser.). (Illus.). (gr. 7 up). 1978. pap. 6.95 (ISBN 0-684-15591-5). Sierra.
Rounds, Glen. Wild Horses of the Red Desert. (Illus.). (gr. 4-6). 1969. reinforced bdg. 7.95 (ISBN 0-8234-0146-4). Holiday.
Scott, Jack D. & Sweet, Ozzie. Island of Wild Horses. LC 78-17380. (Illus.). (gr. 6-8). 1978. 8.95 (ISBN 0-399-20648-5). Putnam.
Selsam, Millicent. Questions & Answers About Horses. LC 73-88073. (Illus.). 64p. (gr. k-3). 1974. 6.95 (ISBN 0-590-07352-4, Four Winds). Schol Bk Serv.
Selsam, Millicent E. Questions & Answers About Horses. (gr. k-3). 1976. pap. 1.25 (ISBN 0-590-03278-X, Schol Pap). Schol Bk Serv.
Smith, Beatrice S. Proudest Horse on the Prairie. LC 74-128804. (Real Life Bks). (gr. 4-9). 1971. PLB 3.95 (ISBN 0-8225-0702-1). Lerner Pubns.
Steinberg, Phil. You & Your Pet: Horses. LC 78-54355. (You & Your Pet Bks). (Illus.). (gr. 4 up). PLB 5.95 (ISBN 0-8225-1257-2). Lerner Pubns.
Steiner, Alexis. All My Horses. LC 64-8402. (Foreign Land Bks). (gr. k-5). 1965. PLB 4.95g (ISBN 0-8225-0353-0). Lerner Pubns.
Sutton, Felix. Horses of America. (Illus.). (gr. 5-9). 1964. PLB 5.69 (ISBN 0-399-60265-8). Putnam.
Thelwell, Norman. Pony Birthday Book. (Illus.). 192p. 1979. 6.95 (ISBN 0-684-16235-0). Scribner.
Thomas, David, ed. Horse Stories. (gr. 5-7). 1978. pap. 1.50 (ISBN 0-671-29925-5). Archway.
Thompson, Neil. A Closer Look at Horses. (Closer Look at Ser.). (Illus.). (gr. 4 up). 1978. PLB 7.45 (ISBN 0-531-01428-2); pap. 1.95 (ISBN 0-531-02486-5). Watts.
Weeks, Morris. The Last Wild Horse. LC 77-13392. (gr. 7 up). 1977. 6.95 (ISBN 0-395-25838-3). HM.

Wilding, Suzanne & Savitt, Sam. Ups & Downs: A Basic Guide to Riding & Horsemanship. (Illus.). 160p. 1973. 7.95 (ISBN 0-312-83405-5). St Martin.

HORSES–LEGENDS AND STORIES

Amaral, Anthony. Mustang: Life & Legends of Nevada's Wild Horses. LC 76-53821. (Lancehead Ser.). (Illus.). xiv, 156p. 1977. 9.00 (ISBN 0-87417-046-X). U of Nev Pr.

Anderson, Clarence W. High Courage. (Illus.). (gr. 7 up). 1968. 6.95 (ISBN 0-02-704280-4). Macmillan.

--Twenty Gallant Horses. (gr. 5 up). 1965. 8.95 (ISBN 0-02-705530-2). Macmillan.

Barrett, Lawrence. Twinkle, the Baby Colt. (Illus.). (gr. k-3). 1945. PLB 4.69 (ISBN 0-394-91780-4). Knopf.

Blassingame, Wyatt. His Kingdom for a Horse. facs. ed. LC 75-81263. (Short Story Index Reprint Ser). 1957. 15.00 (ISBN 0-8369-3015-0). Arno.

Braun, P. C., ed. Big Book of Favorite Horse Stories. (Illus.). (YA) (gr. 7 up). 1965. 5.95 (ISBN 0-448-42641-2). Platt.

Davidson, Margaret. Seven True Horse Stories. (Illus.). (gr. 2-5). 1979. 6.95g (ISBN 0-8038-6760-3). Hastings.

Dobie, J. Frank, et al, eds. Mustangs & Cow Horses. 2nd ed. LC 65-3030. (Texas Folklore Society Publications: No. 16). (Illus.). 1965. Repr. of 1940 ed. 10.00 (ISBN 0-87074-047-4). SMU Press.

Gilbert, Miriam. Rosie: The Oldest Horse in St. Augustine. LC 67-30409. (Illus., Eng., Fr. & Spain.). (gr. k-6). 1974. pap. 1.95 (ISBN 0-87208-007-2). Island Pr.

Green, Ben K. Horse Tradin' (Illus.). (YA) 1967. 11.95 (ISBN 0-394-42929-X). Knopf.

--Some More Horse Tradin' (Illus.). (YA) 1972. 11.95 (ISBN 0-394-46123-1). Knopf.

Henry, Marguerite. Justin Morgan Had a Horse. LC 54-8903. (Illus.). (gr. 2-9). 1954. 6.95 (ISBN 0-528-82255-1); pap. 2.95 (ISBN 0-528-87682-1). Rand.

--The Little Fellow. LC 75-6828. (Illus.). 48p. (gr. 2-5). 1975. 4.95 (ISBN 0-528-82142-3); pap. 3.95 (ISBN 0-528-87147-1). Rand.

James, Will. Scorpion: A Good Bad Horse. LC 36-23527. (Illus.). vi, 312p. 1975. pap. 5.95 (ISBN 0-8032-5822-4, BB 604, Bison). U of Nebr Pr.

--Smoky. (gr. 7-11). 1926. willow leaf ed. 8.95 (ISBN 0-684-12875-6, ScribT). Scribner.

Licata, Anthony. A Horse Called Ringo. 1981. 4.75 (ISBN 0-8062-1758-8). Carlton.

Rounds, Glen. Blind Colt. (Illus.). 78p. (gr. 4-6). 1960. 8.95 (ISBN 0-8234-0010-7). Holiday.

Ryan, Dixie. Stories of Champions: And the National Arabian Shows, Vol. 1. (Illus.). 1975. 12.95 (ISBN 0-912830-25-5). Printed Horse.

Self, Margaret C., ed. A Treasury of Horse Stories. new ed. LC 72-92321. 1977. pap. 5.95 (ISBN 0-668-04205-2). Arco.

Small, Howard I. Monty's Pal. (Illus.). viii, 120p. 1979. 8.95 (ISBN 0-931474-08-6). TBW Bks.

Welsch, Roger L., ed. Mister, You Got Yourself a Horse: Tales of Old-Time Horse Trading. LC 81-436. (Illus.). xii, 208p. 1981. 14.95 (ISBN 0-8032-4711-7). U of Nebr Pr.

Wilding, Suzanne, ed. Horse Tales. LC 76-13052. (Illus.). (YA) 1976. 7.95 (ISBN 0-312-39200-1). St Martin.

Woodhouse, Barbara. Talking to Animals. LC 73-90700. 1975. pap. 1.95 (ISBN 0-8128-1863-6). Stein & Day.

HORSES–PICTORIAL WORKS

see also Horses in Art

Ciechanowska, Paola. Le Pur-Sang Francais. (Illus.). 18.35 (ISBN 0-85131-003-6, Dist. by Sporting Book Center). J A Allen.

Clifford, Timothy. The Stable of Don Juan of Austria. LC 78-53628. (Illus.). 39.50 (ISBN 0-913870-75-7). Abaris Bks.

Green, Ben K. The Color of Horses. LC 74-79459. (Illus.). 120p. 1974. 25.00 (ISBN 0-87358-131-8). Northland.

Hemzo, Karoly. Hoofbeats: Au Galop. (Illus.). 1978. 9.50x (ISBN 963-13-3722-7). Intl Pubns Serv.

Henry, Marguerite. Album of Horses. LC 51-14002. (Illus.). (gr. 5-12). 1951. 8.95 (ISBN 0-528-82050-8); PLB 6.79 (ISBN 0-528-80155-4). Rand.

Kennett, David. Victorian & Edwardian Horses from Historic Photographs. LC 79-56443. (Illus.). 120p. 1980. 19.95 (ISBN 0-7134-1569-X, Pub. by Batsford England). David & Charles.

MacClintock, Dorcas. Horses As I See Them. LC 78-31778. (Illus.). 96p. (gr. 3 up). 1979. 9.95 (ISBN 0-684-16116-8, ScribT). Scribner.

Neiman, LeRoy. Horses. (Illus.). 1979. 100.00 (ISBN 0-8109-1070-5). Abrams.

Reddick, Kate. Horses. (Knowledge Through Color Ser.). 160p. (YA) (gr. 6 up). 1976. pap. 3.50 (ISBN 0-553-14875-3). Bantam.

Robertson, Alden. The Wild Horse Gatherers. LC 77-17512. (Sierra Club-Scribner Juvenile Ser.). (Illus.). (gr. 7 up). 1978. pap. 6.95 (ISBN 0-684-15591-5). Sierra.

Scott, Jack D. & Sweet, Ozzie. Island of Wild Horses. LC 78-17380. (Illus.). (gr. 6-8). 1978. 8.95 (ISBN 0-399-20648-5). Putnam.

Self, Margaret C. American Quarter Horse in Pictures. pap. 3.00 (ISBN 0-87980-237-5). Wilshire.

--Morgan Horse in Pictures. pap. 2.00 (ISBN 0-87980-236-7). Wilshire.

Sidney, S. Illustrated Book of the Horse. pap. 10.00 (ISBN 0-87980-241-3). Wilshire.

Vavra, Robert. Equus: The Creation of a Horse. LC 77-78061. (Illus.). 1977. 29.95 (ISBN 0-688-03239-7). Morrow.

Welsh, Peter C. Track & Road: The American Trotting Horse. LC 67-29351. (Illus.). 174p. 1967. 15.00 (ISBN 0-87474-097-5). Smithsonian.

HORSES–TRAINING

see Horse-Training

HORSES (IN RELIGION, FOLK-LORE, ETC.)

Cawte, E. C. Ritual Animal Disguise. (Folklore Society Mistletoe Ser.). (Illus.). 293p. 1978. 17.50x (ISBN 0-8476-6005-2). Rowman.

Mayo, Margaret. The Book of Magical Horses. (Illus.). (gr. 4-7). 1977. 6.95g (ISBN 0-8038-0778-3). Hastings.

Welsch, Roger L., ed. Mister, You Got Yourself a Horse: Tales of Old-Time Horse Trading. LC 81-436. (Illus.). xii, 208p. 1981. 14.95 (ISBN 0-8032-4711-7). U of Nebr Pr.

HORSES IN ART

Baskett, John. The Horse in Art. 156p. 1980. 70.00 (ISBN 0-8212-0757-1, 373753). NYGS.

Benson, J. L. Horse, Bird, & Man: The Origins of Greek Painting. LC 70-95787. (Illus.). 1970. 20.00x (ISBN 0-87023-053-0). U of Mass Pr.

Bolognese, Don. Drawing Horses & Foals. (How to Draw Ser.). (gr. 4-6). 1977. PLB 7.60 (ISBN 0-531-00379-5). Watts.

Brown, Paul. Drawing the Horse: His Gaits, Points, & Conformation. 1981. pap. 4.95 (ISBN 0-442-26317-1). Van Nos Reinhold.

Cook, Gladys E. & Perard, Victor. Drawing Horses. (Grosset Art Instruction Ser.: Vol. 16). 1966. pap. 2.95 (ISBN 0-448-00525-5). G&D.

Haddelsey, Vincent & Silver, Caroline. Haddelsey's Horses. LC 78-438. (Illus.). 1978. 10.00 (ISBN 0-312-35642-0). St Martin.

Hogeboom, Amy. Horses & How to Draw Them. (gr. 1-5). 1948. 4.95 (ISBN 0-8149-0321-5). Vanguard.

Longstreet, Stephen, ed. Horse in Art. (Master Draughtsman Ser). (Illus., Orig.). 1965. treasure trove bdg. 5.97 (ISBN 0-685-07333-5); pap. 2.95 (ISBN 0-685-07334-3). Borden.

Markman, Sidney D. Horse in Greek Art. LC 72-88057. (Illus.). 1969. Repr. of 1943 ed. 17.50x (ISBN 0-8196-0247-7). Biblo.

Parker, Constance-Anne. Mr. Stubbs: Horsepainter. (Illus.). 24.50 (ISBN 0-85131-123-7, Dist. by Sporting Book Center). J A Allen.

Schmalenbach, Werner. Noble Horse, Equestrian Art. (Illus.). 5.50x (ISBN 0-87556-311-2). Saifer.

Seth-Smith, Michael, ed. The Horse in Art & History. (Illus.). 1978. 12.95 (ISBN 0-8317-4550-9, Mayflower Bks). Smith Pubs.

Urquhart, Fred, ed. Book of Horses. LC 81-82551. (Illus.). 288p. 1981. 29.95 (ISBN 0-688-00419-9). Morrow.

Zuelke, Ruth. Horse in Art. LC 64-22378. (Fine Art Books). (Illus.). (gr. 5-11). 1965. PLB 4.95 (ISBN 0-8225-0151-1). Lerner Pubns.

HORSES IN LITERATURE

Conn, George H., ed. The Arabian Horse in Fact, Fantasy & Fiction. LC 72-92309. (Illus.). 1959. 7.50 (ISBN 0-668-02746-0). Arco.

Edwards, Eleanor M., compiled by. Great Stories About Horses. new ed. LC 63-18759. (Illus.). 160p. (YA) 1972. PLB 6.98 (ISBN 0-87460-202-5); pap. 1.95 (ISBN 0-87460-203-3). Lion Bks.

Fetros, John G. Dictionary of Factual & Fictional Riders & Their Horses. 1979. 10.00 (ISBN 0-682-49417-8). Exposition.

Oldfield, Howey M. The Horse in Magic & Myth. 1979. Repr. of 1923 ed. lib. bdg. 30.00 (ISBN 0-8414-4972-4). Folcroft.

Urquhart, Fred, ed. Book of Horses. LC 81-82551. (Illus.). 288p. 1981. 29.95 (ISBN 0-688-00419-9). Morrow.

HORSESHOEING

Adams, O. R. Lameness in Horses. 3rd ed. LC 73-16030. (Illus.). 566p. 1974. text ed. 22.50 (ISBN 0-8121-0474-9). Lea & Febiger.

British Horse Society & Pony Club. The Foot & Shoeing. LC 76-55015. 1976. pap. 1.95 (ISBN 0-8120-0758-1). Barron.

Butler, Doug. The Principles of Horseshoeing. LC 73-88039. (Illus.). 428p. 1974. 19.95 (ISBN 0-916992-01-2). Doug Butler.

DeHaven, William. Horseshoeing Technology Illustrated. (Illus.). 1978. 27.50 (ISBN 0-930430-01-8). Harbor Hse Pub.

Emery, Leslie, et al. Horseshoeing Theory & Hoof Care. LC 76-16742. (Illus.). 271p. 1977. text ed. 15.50 (ISBN 0-8121-0574-5). Lea & Febiger.

Getz, Andrew L. Shoe Your Own Horse: An Illustrated Guide. LC 75-34900. (Illus.). 1976. 6.95 (ISBN 0-668-03931-0). Arco.

Hickman, J. Farriery. (Illus.). 1976. 29.75 (ISBN 0-85131-228-4, Dist. by Sporting Book Center). J A Allen.

Jones, William E., ed. Horseshoeing. (Horse Health & Care Ser.). (Illus.). 1973. pap. 2.95 (ISBN 0-912830-03-4). Printed Horse.

Manwill, Marion C. How to Shoe a Horse. LC 68-11397. (Illus.). 1968. 5.95 (ISBN 0-668-02785-1). Arco.

Practical Guide to Horseshoeing. pap. 3.00 (ISBN 0-87980-239-1). Wilshire.

Springhall, J. A. Elements of Horseshoeing. 2nd ed. (Illus.). 1975. 7.95x (ISBN 0-7022-1026-9). U of Queensland Pr.

Wiseman, Robert F. The Complete Horseshoeing Guide. rev. ed. LC 72-9279. (Illus.). 160p. 1973. 7.95 (ISBN 0-8061-1049-X). U of Okla Pr.

HORSEWOMEN

see Horsemen

HORTICULTURAL EXHIBITIONS

see also Flower Shows

HORTICULTURE

see also Agricultural Pests; Bulbs; Floriculture; Forcing (Plants); Frost Protection; Fruit-Culture; Grafting; Greenhouses; Horticulturists; Hydroponics; Insects, Injurious and Beneficial; Landscape Gardening; Mulching; Mushroom Culture; Nurseries (Horticulture); Organic Farming; Plant Propagation; Plants, Potted; Pruning; Truck Farming; Vegetable Gardening

Adriance, Guy W. & Brison, Fred R. Propagation of Horticultural Plants. 2nd ed. LC 79-9753. 308p. 1979. Repr. of 1955 ed. lib. bdg. 19.50 (ISBN 0-88275-965-5). Krieger.

Arthey, V. D. Quality of Horticultural Products. 228p. 1975. 24.95 (ISBN 0-470-03425-4). Halsted Pr.

Bailey, Liberty H. Cyclopedia of American Horticulture, 6 vols. Set. lib. bdg. 600.00 (ISBN 0-87968-247-7). Gordon Pr.

--Hortus Third: A Concise Dictionary of Plants Cultivated in the United States & Canada. (Illus.). 1976. 99.50 (ISBN 0-02-505470-8). Macmillan.

Ballard, Edward B., et al, eds. A Technical Glossary of Horticultural & Landscape Terminology. LC 78-165521. 1971 (ISBN 0-686-26652-8). text ed. 9.95 (ISBN 0-935336-00-1); tchrs' ed. 6.00 (ISBN 0-935336-00-1). Horticult Research.

Baudendistel. Horticulture: A Basic Awareness. 2nd ed. 368p. 1982. pap. text ed. 15.95 (ISBN 0-8359-2895-0); instr's. manual free (ISBN 0-8359-2896-9). Reston.

Baudendistel, Robert F. Horticulture: A Basic Awareness. (Illus.). 1978. pap. 15.95 ref. ed. (ISBN 0-8359-2891-8); instrs'. manual avail. Reston.

Beard, James B. & DiPaola, Joseph M. Introduction to Turfgrass Science & Culture Laboratory Exercises. 1979. pap. text ed. 10.95x (ISBN 0-8087-2894-6). Burgess.

Bienz, D. R. The Why & How of Home Horticulture. LC 79-19915. (Illus.). 1980. text ed. 17.95x (ISBN 0-7167-1078-1). W H Freeman.

Bleasdale, J. K. Plant Physiology in Relation to Horticulture. 1978. text ed. 12.00 (ISBN 0-87055-239-2). AVI.

Christopher, Everett P. Introductory Horticulture. (Agricultural Sciences Ser.). 1958. text ed. 18.95 (ISBN 0-07-010795-5, C). McGraw.

Cole, John N. The Amaranth: From the Past for the Future. (Illus.). 1979. 12.95 (ISBN 0-87857-240-6). Rodale Pr Inc.

Commercial Applications of NFT. 1979. pap. 6.95 (ISBN 0-89955-218-8, Pub. by Grower Books England). Intl Schol Bk Serv.

Couch, Houston B. Diseases of Turfgrasses. 2nd ed. LC 73-80742. 376p. 1976. Repr. of 1962 ed. 27.00 (ISBN 0-88275-062-3). Krieger.

Cowell, F. R. The Garden As Fine Art. 1978. 20.00 (ISBN 0-395-27065-0). HM.

Daubert, James R. & Rothert, Eugene A., Jr. Horticultural Therapy at a Psychiatric Hospital. (Illus.). 128p. (Orig.). 1981. pap. 10.00 (ISBN 0-939914-03-4). Chi Horticult.

--Horticultural Therapy for the Mentally Handicapped. (Illus.). 128p. 1981. pap. 10.00 (ISBN 0-939914-04-2). Chi Horticult.

Dawson, Oliver. Shrubs & How to Use Them. LC 78-511210. (Illus.). 1969. 8.75x (ISBN 0-434-17930-2). Intl Pubns Serv.

Denisen, Ervin L. Principles of Horticulture. 2nd ed. (Illus.). 1979. text ed. 18.95x (ISBN 0-02-328380-7); instrs'. manual avail. (ISBN 0-685-96773-5). Macmillan.

Denisen, Ervin L. & Nichols, Harry E. Laboratory Manual in Horticulture. 4th ed. (Illus.). 1962. pap. 4.50x (ISBN 0-8138-0770-0). Iowa St U Pr.

Edmond, J. B., et al. Fundamentals of Horticulture. 4th ed. (Illus.). 576p. 1975. text ed. 19.95 (ISBN 0-07-018985-4, C). McGraw.

Fisher, T. Richard. Workbook & Manual Introduction to Horticulture. 2nd ed. 1979. pap. text ed. 7.50x (ISBN 0-89917-006-4). TIS Inc.

Gardner, V. R. Principles of Horticultural Production. 583p. 1966. text ed. 18.50x (ISBN 0-87013-095-1). Mich St U Pr.

Geiser, Samuel W. Horticulture & Horticulturists in Early Texas. LC 46-161. 1945. pap. 1.00 (ISBN 0-87074-058-X). SMU Press.

Halfacre, Gordon & Barden, John A. Horticulture. (Illus.). 1979. text ed. 19.95 (ISBN 0-07-025573-3, C). McGraw.

Hemp, Paul E. Fifty Laboratory Exercises for Vocational Ornamental Horticulture Students. (Illus.). 1968. text ed. 4.95x spiral bdg (ISBN 0-8134-1039-8, 1039). Interstate.

--Ornamental Horticulture Experience Program Planning Guide & Record Bk. 1970. pap. text ed. 2.50x (ISBN 0-8134-1200-5, 1200). Interstate.

--Ornamental Horticulture Source Units for Vocational Teachers. LC 68-56066. (Illus.). 1968. pap. text ed. 4.95x (ISBN 0-8134-1048-7, 1048). Interstate.

Horticultural Research International Directory of Horticultural Research Institutes & Their Activities in 54 Countries. 1972. pap. 48.00 (ISBN 90-220-0415-5, PUDOC). Unipub.

Horticulture in the Mediterranean Area: Outlook for Production & Trade. (Commodity Bulletin Ser: No. 42). 1968. pap. 17.00 (ISBN 0-685-09388-3, F232, FAO). Unipub.

Hutchinson, William A. Plant Propagation & Cultivation. (Illus.). 1980. pap. text ed. 18.00 (ISBN 0-87055-340-2). AVI.

Janick, Jules. Horticultural Reviews, Vol. 2. (Illus.). 1980. lib. bdg. 33.00 (ISBN 0-87055-352-6). AVI.

--Horticultural Science. 3rd ed. LC 78-13053. (Illus.). 1979. text ed. 21.95x (ISBN 0-7167-1031-5). W H Freeman.

Janick, Jules, ed. Horticultural Reviews, Vol. 1. 1979. lib. bdg. 33.00 (ISBN 0-87055-314-3). AVI.

--Horticultural Reviews, Vol 3. (Illus.). 1981. lib. bdg. 33.00 (ISBN 0-87055-383-6). AVI.

McDaniel, Gary M. Ornamental Horticulture. (Illus.). 1979. 18.50 (ISBN 0-8359-5346-7); instrs'. manual avail. (ISBN 0-8359-5347-5). Reston.

Mollison, Bill & Holmgren, David. Permaculture One: A Perennial Agriculture for Human Settlements. (Illus.). 136p. 1981. pap. 9.95 (ISBN 0-938240-00-5). Intl Tree Crops.

Moore, Stanley B. Ornamental Horticulture As a Vocation. (gr. 11 up). 1969. text ed. 8.00x (ISBN 0-912178-01-9). Mor-Mac.

Nijdam, J. & Ministry Of Agriculture & Fisheries - Netherlands, eds. Elsevier's Dictionary of Horticulture. 1970. 85.50 (ISBN 0-444-40812-6). Elsevier.

Nitrogen-15 in Soil-Plant Studies. (Illus., Orig.). 1971. pap. 19.50 (ISBN 92-0-111171-1, ISP 278, IAEA). Unipub.

North, C. Plant Breeding & Genetics in Horticulture. LC 79-10436. 1980. pap. 18.95 (ISBN 0-470-26661-9). Halsted Pr.

Poincelot, R. Horticulture: Principles & Practical Applications. 1980. 21.95 (ISBN 0-13-394809-9). P-H.

Poulter, Nick. Growing Vines. 1973. pap. 2.25 (ISBN 0-8277-2214-1). British Bk Ctr.

Reiley, H. Edward & Shry, Carroll L. Introductory Horticulture. 1979. 22.50 (ISBN 0-442-26946-3). Van Nos Reinhold.

Reiley, H. Edward & Shry, Carroll L., Jr. Introductory Horticulture. LC 77-81006. 1979. pap. text ed. 22.00 (ISBN 0-8273-1893-6); instructor's guide 1.60 (ISBN 0-8273-1645-3). Delmar.

Richardson, William B. & Moore, Gary. Working in Horticulture. (Career Preparations for Agricultural-Agribusiness Ser.). (Illus.). 1980. text ed. 14.56 (ISBN 0-07-052285-5); tchr's. manual & key 3.00 (ISBN 0-07-052287-1); activity guide 4.60 (ISBN 0-07-052286-3). McGraw.

Rodgers, Andrew D., 3rd. Liberty Hyde Bailey: A Story of American Plant Sciences. (Illus.). 1965. Repr. of 1949 ed. 13.95 (ISBN 0-02-851100-X). Hafner.

Rothert, Eugene A. & Daubert, James R. Horticultural Therapy at a Physical Rehabilitation Facility. (Illus.). 140p. (Orig.). 1981. pap. 10.00 (ISBN 0-939914-02-6). Chi Horticult.

Rothert, Eugene A., Jr. & Daubert, James R. Horticultural Therapy for Nursing Homes, Senior Centers, & Retirement Living. (Illus.). 140p. (Orig.). 1981. pap. 10.00 (ISBN 0-939914-01-8). Chi Horticult.

Rudman, Jack. Horticultural Inspector. (Career Examination Ser.: C-1304). (Cloth bdg. avail. on request). pap. 8.00 (ISBN 0-8373-1304-X). Natl Learning.

--Horticulturist. (Career Examination Ser.: C-1305). (Cloth bdg. avail. on request). text ed. 8.00 (ISBN 0-8373-1305-8). Natl Learning.

Schuler, Stanley. How to Grow Almost Everything. LC 65-13249. (Illus.). 256p. 1965. 6.95 (ISBN 0-87131-061-9); pap. 4.95 (ISBN 0-87131-257-3). M Evans.
Schumann, Donna N. Living with Plants: A Guide to the Practical Application of Botany. (Illus.). 328p. (Orig.). 1980. pap. 14.45 (ISBN 0-916422-20-8). Mad River.
Smith, Joanna. Farm Your Garden. (Illus.). 1977. 14.95x (ISBN 0-8464-0405-2). Beekman Pubs.
White, Gilbert. The Garden Kalendar 1751-1771. facsimile ed. 470p. 1975. Repr. 16.95 (ISBN 0-85967-215-8, Pub. by Scolar Pr England). Biblio Dist.
Whitehead, George. Growing for Showing. (Illus.). 176p. 1978. 9.95 (ISBN 0-571-11206-4, Pub. by Faber & Faber). Merrimack Bk Serv.
Wood, Henry. Pelargoniums: A Complete Guide to Their Cultivation. 170p. (Orig.). 1981. pap. 14.95x (ISBN 0-89955-343-5, Pub. by Henry Wood England). Intl Schol Bk Serv.

HORTICULTURE–BIBLIOGRAPHY

Everett, T. H. The New York Botanical Garden Illustrated Encyclopedia of Horticulture, 10 vols. 1980. Set. lib. bdg. 525.00 (ISBN 0-8240-7222-7). Garland Pub.
Horticulture: A Select Bibliography. (Plant & Protection Papers Ser: No. 1). 1977. pap. 7.50 (ISBN 92-5-100184-7, F1065, FAO). Unipub.
Massachusetts Horticultural Society, Boston. Dictionary Catalog of the Library of the Massachusetts Horticultural Society, 3 Vols. 1963. Set. lib. bdg. 195.00 (ISBN 0-8161-0648-7). G K Hall.
--Dictionary Catalog of the Library of the Massachusetts Horticultural Society, First Supplement. 465p. 1972. lib. bdg. 60.00 (ISBN 0-8161-1038-7). G K Hall.

HORTICULTURE–VOCATIONAL GUIDANCE

Educational Research Council of America. Horticulturist. Ferris, Theodore N. & Marchak, John P., eds. (Real People at Work Ser.: R). (Illus.). 36p. 1977. 2.25 (ISBN 0-89247-133-6). Changing Times.
Hemp, Paul E. Fifty Laboratory Exercises for Vocational Ornamental Horticulture Students. (Illus.). 1968. text ed. 4.95x spiral bdg (ISBN 0-8134-1039-8, 1039). Interstate.
McDaniel, Gary M. Ornamental Horticulture. (Illus.). 1979. 18.50 (ISBN 0-8359-5346-7); instrs'. manual avail. (ISBN 0-8359-5347-5). Reston.
Pinney, John J. Your Future in the Nursery Industry. LC 67-10084. (Careers in Depth Ser). (Illus.). (gr. 7 up). 1978. PLB 5.97 (ISBN 0-8239-0331-1). Rosen Pr.
Rudman, Jack. Assistant Gardener. (Career Examination Ser.: C-40). (Cloth bdg. avail. on request). pap. 6.00 (ISBN 0-8373-0040-1). Natl Learning.
--Ornamental Horticulture. (Occupational Competency Examination Ser.: OCE-28). (Cloth bdg. avail. on request). pap. 9.95 (ISBN 0-8373-5728-4). Natl Learning.

HORTICULTURISTS

see also Horticulture–Vocational Guidance

Desmond, Ray. Dictionary of British & Irish Botanists & Horticulturists: Including Plant Collectors & Botanical Artists. 3rd ed. 747p. 1977. 99.50x (ISBN 0-8476-1392-5). Rowman.
Hadfield, Miles, et al, eds. British Gardeners: A Biographical Dictionary. 233p. 1980. 60.00x (ISBN 0-302-00541-2, Pub. by Wright Pub Scotland). State Mutual Bk.

HORTON, AFRICANUS, 1835-1883

Fyfe, Christopher. Africanus Horton, Eighteen Thirty-Five to Eighteen Eighty-Three. 225p. 1972. pap. 4.95x (ISBN 0-19-501500-2). Oxford U Pr.
Nicol, Davidson, ed. Africanus Horton: The Dawn of Nationalism in Modern Africa - Extracts from the Political, Educational & Scientific Writings of J. A. B. Horton M.D. 1835-1883. (Illus.). 1969. pap. text ed. 3.50x (ISBN 0-582-64051-2). Longman.

HORTON, GEORGE MOSES, 1797-1883?

Richmond, M. A. Bid the Vassal Soar: Interpretive Essays on the Life & Poetry of Phillis Wheatley & George Moses Horton. LC 73-85493. 1974. 8.95x (ISBN 0-88258-001-9). Howard U Pr.

HORTON, LESTER, 1906-1953

Warren, Larry. Lester Horton: Modern Dance Pioneer. 1977. 13.75 (ISBN 0-8247-6503-6). Dekker.

HORY, ELMYR DE

Irving, Clifford. Fake: The Story of Elmer De Hory, the Greatest Art Forger of Our Time. 1969. 7.95 (ISBN 0-07-032047-0, GB). McGraw.

HOSEA, THE PROPHET

Beacon Bible Commentary. Hosea-Malachi, Vol. V. 9.95 (ISBN 0-8010-0692-9). Baker Bk.
Cohen, Gary G. & Vandermey, H. Ronald, eds. Hosea-Amos. (Everyman's Bible Commentary). 128p. 1981. pap. 2.95 (ISBN 0-8024-2028-1). Moody.
Rand, Howard B. Study in Hosea. 1955. 2.50 (ISBN 0-685-08815-4). Destiny.

HOSIERY AND HOSIERY INDUSTRY

Fairchild Market Research Division. Men's & Women's Hosiery & Legwear. (Fact File Ser). 1978. pap. 10.00 (ISBN 0-87005-223-3). Fairchild.
Felkin, William. History of the Machine-Wrought Hosiery & Lace Manufactures. (Illus.). 1967. Repr. of 1867 ed. 23.50 (ISBN 0-8337-1104-0). B Franklin.
--History of the Machine-Wrought Hosiery & Lace Manufactures. LC 67-89041. Repr. of 1867 ed. 16.50x (ISBN 0-678-05685-4). Kelley.
Wignall, H. Hosiery Technology. 12.50 (ISBN 0-87245-382-0). Textile Bk.

HOSKING, ERIC JOHN

Hosking, Eric. A Passion for Birds: Fifty Years of Photographing Wildlife. LC 79-10943. 1979. 25.00 (ISBN 0-698-11002-1). Coward.

HOSKYNS, JOHN, 1566-1638

Osborn, Louise B. The Life, Letters & Writings of John Hoskyns, 1566-1638. (Yale Studies in English Ser.: No. 87). 321p. 1973. Repr. of 1937 ed. 19.50 (ISBN 0-208-01132-3, Archon). Shoe String.

HOSPICES (TERMINAL CARE)

see Terminal Care Facilities

HOSPITAL ADMINISTRATION

see Hospitals–Administration

HOSPITAL ATTENDANTS

see Hospitals–Staff

HOSPITAL CARE

see also Coronary Care Units; Intensive Care Units; Monitoring (Hospital Care)

Accreditation Manual for Hospitals: 1981 Ed. 218p. pap. 20.00 (ISBN 0-86688-005-4). Joint Comm Hosp.
Accreditation Manual for Long Term Care Facilities: 1980 Ed. 86p. pap. 12.50 (ISBN 0-86688-031-3). Joint Comm Hosp.
Accreditation Self-Assessment Checklist for Long-Term Care Facilities: 1980 Ed. rev. ed. 94p. pap. 10.00 (ISBN 0-86688-032-1). Joint Comm Hosp.
Alexander, Edythe L. Nursing Administration in the Hospital Health Care System. 2nd ed. LC 77-18114. (Illus.). 1978. text ed. 16.95 (ISBN 0-8016-0110-X). Mosby.
American College of Emergency Physicians. Emergency Department Organization & Management. 2nd ed. Jenkins, A. L. & Van De Leuv, John H., eds. LC 78-13594. (Illus.). 1978. text ed. 27.50 (ISBN 0-8016-0122-3). Mosby.
American Hospital Association. The Extended Care Unit in a General Hospital: A Guide to Planning, Organization, & Management. rev. ed. LC 73-80342. (Illus.). 60p. 1973. pap. 7.50 (ISBN 0-87258-131-4, 1570). Am Hospital.
--Hospital Literature Index: 1978, Vol. 34. 350p. 75.00 (ISBN 0-87258-346-5, 1389). Am Hospital.
--Hospital Literature Index: 1979, Vol. 35. Dunlap, Alice, et al, eds. 736p. 1980. 75.00 (ISBN 0-87258-346-5, 1388). Am Hospital.
--Implementing Patient Education in the Hospital. LC 79-4292. (Illus.). 316p. 1979. pap. 34.25 (ISBN 0-87258-274-4, 1488). Am Hospital.
Blanken, Gary E. Surgical Operations in Short-Stay Hospitals, U. S. 1971. LC 74-6259. (Data from the Hospital Discharge Survey Ser. 13: No. 18). 62p. 1974. pap. text ed. 1.10 (ISBN 0-8406-0017-8). Natl Ctr Health Stats.
Brown, Esther L. Newer Dimensions of Patient Care, 3 pts. Incl. Pt. 1. The Use of the Physical & Social Environment of the General Hospital for Therapeutic Purposes. LC 61-13217. 159p. 1961 (ISBN 0-87154-183-1); Pt. 2. Improving Staff Motivation & Competence in the General Hospital. LC 62-18147. 194p. 1962 (ISBN 0-87154-184-X); Pt. 3. Patients As People. LC 64-17897. 1964 (ISBN 0-87154-185-8). pap. 4.95 ea.; Three Vol. Set. (ISBN 0-87154-182-3). Russell Sage.
Carroll, Walter J., ed. Hospital-Health Care Training Media Profiles, Vol. 8. 1981. 85.00 (ISBN 0-88367-208-1). Olympic Media.
Chartridge Symposium on Real-Time Computing in Patient Management, 1975. Proceedings. Date not set. 28.50 (ISBN 0-901223-88-3, Pub. by Peregrinus England). Inst Elect Eng.
Chartridge Symposium on the Management of the Acutely Ill, 1976. Proceedings. Date not set. 29.50 (ISBN 0-901223-92-1, Pub. by Peregrinus England). Inst Elect Eng.
Cherry, William. Whom the Gods Would Destroy. 1980. 5.95 (ISBN 0-533-04378-6). Vantage.
David, J. H., et al. Guidelines for Discharge Planning. 59p. 1973. 9.00 (ISBN 0-913590-15-0). C B Slack.
DePaul & Mount St. Vincent Center Staffs. Administrative Manual of Policies & Procedures for Long Term Care Facilities. LC 75-21141. (Orig.). 1976. pap. 10.00 (ISBN 0-87125-028-4). Cath Health.
Dunlap, Alice, et al, eds. Hospital Literature Index: 1980 Cumulative Annual, Vol. 36. 704p. 1981. 90.00 (ISBN 0-87258-348-1, 1389). Am Hospital.
Egdahl, Richard H. & Gertman, Paul M., eds. Quality Assurance in Health Care. LC 76-15770. 372p. 1976. 28.95 (ISBN 0-912862-23-8). Aspen Systems.
Evaluation & Quality Assurance in Long Term Care System (EQALS) Program. 199p. Date not set. pap. 25.00 (ISBN 0-86688-033-X). Joint Comm Hosp.
Fahlberg, W. J. & Groschal, D., eds. Occurrance Diagnoses & Sources of Hospital-Associated Diseases. (Hospital Associated Disease Ser.: Vol. 3). 1978. 23.50 (ISBN 0-8247-6724-1). Dekker.
Geist, Harold & Hawkins, C. F. Adults Going to the Hospital. LC 66-22695. (Illus.). 31p. 1966. pap. 4.10x (ISBN 0-87424-203-7); pap. 3.75x ea. 2 or more copies. Western Psych.
Gekas, Alexandra B. & Countryman, Kathleen M. Development & Implementation of a Patient's Bill of Rights in Hospitals. LC 80-11366. 24p. 1980. pap. 7.50 (ISBN 0-87258-306-6, 1580). Am Hospital.
Hardy, Robert C. Sick: How People Feel About Being Sick & What They Think of Those Who Care for Them. LC 77-90162. 1978. 18.95 (ISBN 0-931028-05-1); pap. 14.95 (ISBN 0-931028-04-3). Teach'em.
Haupt, Barbara J. Utilization of Short-Stay Hospitals, Series 13, No. 46: Annual Summary for the United States 1978. Cox, Klaudia, ed. 50p. 1980. pap. text ed. 1.50 (ISBN 0-8406-0185-9). Natl Ctr Health Stats.
Hitchcock, Edward & Massan, Alastair. Management of the Unconscious Patient. 1st ed. (Illus.). 96p. 1970. 3.50 (ISBN 0-632-07860-X, Blackwell Scientific). Mosby.
Infection Control & Drug & Antibiotic Review: QRB Special Edition. 80p. Date not set. pap. 25.00 (ISBN 0-86688-039-9). Joint Comm Hosp.
International Symposium on Critical Care, 3rd, Rio de Janeiro, November, 1974. Current Topics in Critical Care Medicine: Proceedings. Shoemaker, W. C., et al, eds. (Current Topics in Critical Care Medicine: Vol. 1). (Illus.). 200p. 1976. 53.50 (ISBN 3-8055-2211-8). S Karger.
Jacobs, Charles M., et al. Measuring the Quality of Patient Care: The Rationale for Outcome Audit. LC 75-29234. 1976. 19.50 (ISBN 0-88410-128-2). Ballinger Pub.
Kruse, Christine G. Patient Centered Audit. (Illus.). 180p. (Orig.). 1981. 14.50 (ISBN 0-87527-247-9). Green.
Laufman, Harold. Hospital Special Care Facilities: Planning for User Needs. LC 80-68552. (Clinical Engineering Ser.). 1981. 49.50 (ISBN 0-12-437740-8). Acad Pr.
Lewis, Frank. Average Length of Stay on Short-Stay Hospitals United States, 1977. Shipp, Audrey, ed. (Ser. 13-50). 50p. 1980. pap. text ed. 1.75 (ISBN 0-8406-0198-0). Natl Ctr Health Stats.
Luber, R. F., ed. Partial Hospitalization: A Current Perspective. (Illus.). 205p. 1979. 23.50 (ISBN 0-306-40201-7, Plenum Pr). Plenum Pub.
Model Screening Criteria for Hospital Admissions in Obstetrics & Gynecology. 2.50 (ISBN 0-686-24126-6). Am Coll Obstetric.
Multidisciplinary Audit: QRB Special Edition. 104p. Date not set. pap. 25.00 (ISBN 0-86688-037-2). Joint Comm Hosp.
National Society of Patient Representatives of the American Hospital Association. Assessing the Patient Representative Program. LC 80-28949. (Illus., Orig.). 1981. pap. 8.00 (ISBN 0-87258-334-1, 1082). Am Hospital.
Nicholson, J. P., ed. Scientific Aids in Hospital Diagnosis. 288p. 1976. 35.00 (ISBN 0-306-30938-6, Plenum Pr). Plenum Pub.
Nicosia, Joan & Petro, Jane. A Manual for Burn Patient Management. 1981. text ed. price not set (ISBN 0-89004-644-1). Raven.
OCHE & Madnick, Myra E. Consumer Health Education: A Guide to Hospital-Based Programs. LC 79-90381. 239p. 1980. text ed. 17.95 (ISBN 0-913654-61-2). Nursing Res.
Orlikoff, James E., et al. Malpractice Prevention & Liability Control for Hospitals. Greeley, Hugh P., ed. (Orig.). 1981. price not set (ISBN 0-87258-359-7, 1467). Am Hospital.
Payne, Beverly C. The Quality of Medical Care: Evaluation & Improvement. LC 75-27157. 1976. 8.00 (ISBN 0-87914-029-1, 9153). Hosp Res & Educ.
Physician-Oriented Review: Criteria Development & Analysis of Patient Care: QRB Special Edition. 64p. 1981. pap. 20.00 (ISBN 0-86688-049-6). Joint Comm Hosp.
Price, Elmina. Staffing for Patient Care: A Guide for Nursing Service. LC 76-111051. 1970. pap. text ed. 6.95 (ISBN 0-8261-1111-4). Springer Pub.
Rantz, Marilyn & Courtial, Donald C. Lifting, Moving & Transferring Patients: A Manual. 2nd ed. LC 80-26567. (Illus.). 182p. 1981. pap. text ed. 9.95 (ISBN 0-8016-4087-3). Mosby.
Ratliff, Bascom W. Leaving the Hospital: Discharge Planning for Total Patient Care. 204p. 1981. 19.75 (ISBN 0-398-04146-6). C C Thomas.
Redman, Barbara K., ed. Patient Teaching. LC 78-53461. 87p. 1978. pap. text ed. 6.95 (ISBN 0-913654-43-4). Nursing Res.
Robinson, Geoffrey C. & Clarke, Heather F. The Hospital Care of Children: A Review of Contemporary Issues. 288p. 1980. 18.95x (ISBN 0-19-502673-X). Oxford U Pr.
Rosenbaum, Ernest H. The Cancer Patient's Guide to Social Services & Hospital Procedure. (Orig.). 1980. pap. 4.95 (ISBN 0-915950-40-5). Bull Pub.
Rosenthal, Carolyn J., et al. Nurses, Patients, & Families: Care & Control in the Hospital. 176p. 1980. text ed. 13.50 (ISBN 0-8261-3470-X). Springer Pub.
Rudman, Jack. Principal Hospital Care Investigator. (Career Examination Ser.: C-612). (Cloth bdg. avail. on request). pap. 10.00 (ISBN 0-8373-0612-4). Natl Learning.
Skillicorn, Stanley A. Quality & Accountability: A New Era in American Hospitals. (Illus.). 143p. 1980. 14.00 (ISBN 0-917636-03-1). Edit Consult.
Society of Patient Representatives of the American Hospital Association. Essentials of Patient Representative Programs in Hospitals. LC 78-26889. 1978. pap. 8.75 (ISBN 0-87258-255-8, 1251). Am Hospital.
Support Services Review: Problem Identification & Analysis of Patient Care: QRB Special Edition. 80p. 1981. pap. 20.00 (ISBN 0-86688-048-8). Joint Comm Hosp.
Thompson, Richard A. & Stanford, Gene. Child Life in Hospitals: Theory & Practice. 286p. 1981. 24.75 (ISBN 0-398-04445-7); pap. 18.75 (ISBN 0-398-04456-2). C C Thomas.
Turner, Glenn O. The Cardiovascular Care Unit: A Guide for Planning & Operation. LC 77-14215. 512p. (Orig.). 1978. 29.50 (ISBN 0-471-03022-8). Krieger.
Vernon, David T., et al. The Psychological Responses of Children to Hospitalization & Illness: A Review of Literature. 208p. 1965. photocopy ed. spiral 19.75 (ISBN 0-398-01980-0). C C Thomas.
Vogel, Morris J. The Invention of the Modern Hospital: Boston, 1870-1930. LC 79-26052. (Illus.). 1980. lib. bdg. 15.50x (ISBN 0-226-86240-2). U of Chicago Pr.
Walraven, Gail. Manual of Advanced Prehospital Care. (Illus.). 430p. 1978. pap. text ed. 14.95 (ISBN 0-87618-995-8). R J Brady.
Wentzel, Kenneth B. To Those Who Need It Most, Hospice Means Hope. 1980. 5.95 (ISBN 0-89182-020-5); pap. text ed. 4.95 (ISBN 0-89182-030-2). Charles River Bks.
Willner, Robert F. Criteria for Long Term Care Placement: Referral Guidelines for the Clergy. LC 78-26278. 1979. pap. 1.50 (ISBN 0-87125-048-9). Cath Health.
Yanda, Roman L. Doctors As Managers of Health Teams: A Career Guide for Hospital Based Physicians. LC 76-54735. 1977. 15.95 (ISBN 0-8144-5432-1). Am Mgmt.

HOSPITAL CARE, COST OF

see Hospitals–Rates

HOSPITAL CHARGES

see Hospitals–Rates

HOSPITAL DIETARY DEPARTMENT

see Hospitals–Food Service

HOSPITAL EMPLOYEES

see Hospitals–Staff

HOSPITAL ENDOWMENTS

see Endowments

HOSPITAL HOUSE STAFF

see Interns (Medicine)

HOSPITAL HOUSEKEEPING

American Hospital Association. Hospital Housekeeping Handbook. 2nd ed. Orig. Title: Housekeeping Manual for Health Care. (Illus.). 1980. 18.75 (ISBN 0-87258-273-6, 2086). Am Hospital.
Blount, Raymond N. Housekeeping Procedures for the Small Hospital. 152p. 1978. 14.00 (ISBN 0-398-03693-4). C C Thomas.
Hospital Research & Educational Trust of the AHA. Being a Housekeeping Aide. (Illus.). 1968. pap. 9.95 (ISBN 0-87618-048-9). R J Brady.
--Training the Housekeeping Aide. (Illus.). 1968. pap. 9.95 (ISBN 0-87618-049-7). R J Brady.
Miller, Charles B. How to Organize & Maintain an Efficient Hospital Housekeeping Department. (Illus.). 142p. (Orig.). 1980. pap. 18.75 (ISBN 0-87258-290-6, 1440). Am Hospital.

Training Programs for Health Care Workers: Housekeeping Aides. Incl. Being a Housekeeping Aide. 320p. student manual 9.95 (ISBN 0-87914-009-7, 9785, 9660); Training the Housekeeping Aide. 271p. instructor's guide 9.95 (ISBN 0-87914-010-0, 9786). 1967. Hosp Res & Educ.

HOSPITAL INTERNS
see Interns (Medicine)

HOSPITAL LIBRARIES
see also Bibliotherapy

Gardner, Frank & Lewis, Joy, eds. Reading Round the World: A Set of International Reading Lists Compiled by the International Federation of Library Associates. 1969. 16.50 (ISBN 0-208-00865-9, Archon). Shoe String.

Going, M. E. Hospital Libraries & Work with the Disabled in the Community. 1981. 28.75 (ISBN 0-686-75531-6). Oryx Pr.

Going, Mona E., ed. Hospital Libraries & Work with the Disabled in the Community. 311p. 1981. lib. bdg. 28.75x (ISBN 0-686-73903-5, Pub. by Lib Assn England). Oryx Pr.

Phinney, Eleanor, ed. Librarian & the Patient. LC 76-45178. 1977. text ed. 20.00 (ISBN 0-8389-0227-8). ALA.

HOSPITAL MANAGEMENT
see Hospitals–Administration

HOSPITAL MEDICAL RECORDS
see Medical Records

HOSPITAL PERSONNEL
see Hospitals–Staff

HOSPITAL PHARMACIES

American Society of Hospital Pharmacists, ed. Sourcebook on Unit Dose Drug Distribution Systems. (Illus.). 1978. pap. 25.00 (ISBN 0-930530-06-3). Am Soc Hosp Pharm.

Hassan, William E., Jr. Hospital Pharmacy. 4th ed. LC 80-20700. (Illus.). 588p. 1981. text ed. 29.50 (ISBN 0-8121-0772-1). Lea & Febiger.

Idsvoog, Peter B. Manual for Hospital Pharmacy Technicians: A Progammed Course in Basic Skills. LC 77-15359. 1977. pap. 12.50 (ISBN 0-930530-05-5). Am Soc Hosp Pharm.

Lew, Marvin I. Hospital Pharmacy Journal Articles. 3rd ed. 1977. spiral bdg. 15.50 (ISBN 0-87488-799-2). Med Exam.

Model Quality Assurance Program for Hospital Pharmacies. 2nd ed. 1980. pap. text ed. 25.00 (ISBN 0-930530-16-0). Am Soc Hosp Pharm.

Pharmaceutical Services in the Long Term Care Facility. 57th ed. 1975. 3.00 (ISBN 0-917330-01-3). Am Pharm Assn.

Smith, Mickey & Brown, Thomas. Handbook of Institutional Pharmacy Practice. (Illus.). 718p. 1979. 28.95 (ISBN 0-683-07884-4). Williams & Wilkins.

HOSPITAL RATES
see Hospitals–Rates

HOSPITAL RECORDS
see also Medical Records

American Hospital Association. ICD-Nine-CM Coding Handbook for Entry-Level Coders. 348p. 1979. 19.25 (ISBN 0-87258-263-9, 2062); with answers 23.75 (ISBN 0-87258-264-7, 2061). Am Hospital.

--Medical Record Departments in Hospitals: Guide to Organization. 100p. 1972. pap. 10.00 (ISBN 0-87258-089-X, 2345). Am Hospital.

Hayt, Emanuel. Medicolegal Aspects of Hospital Records. 1977. 19.80 (ISBN 0-917036-13-1). Physicians Rec.

HOSPITAL SERVICE (WAR)
see Red Cross

HOSPITAL SOCIAL WORK
see Medical Social Work

HOSPITAL SUPPLIES
see Hospitals–Furniture, Equipment, Etc.; Medical Supplies

HOSPITAL TRAINING SCHOOLS
see Nursing Schools

HOSPITAL WORKERS
see Hospitals–Staff

HOSPITALERS

Bedford, William K. The Order or the Hospital of St. John of Jerusalem. LC 76-29831. Repr. of 1902 ed. 25.00 (ISBN 0-404-15412-3). AMS Pr.

Gervers, Michael, ed. The Cartulary of the Order of St. John of Jerusalem (Hospitalers) in England. (Records of Social & Economic History Ser.). 618p. 1981. 125.00 (ISBN 0-19-725996-0). Oxford U Pr.

King, Edwin J. The Grand Priory of the Order of the Hospital of St. John of Jerusalem in England: A Short History. LC 76-29826. Repr. of 1924 ed. 20.00 (ISBN 0-404-15420-4). AMS Pr.

Philippus De Thame. Knights Hospitallers in England: Being the Report of Prior Phillip De Thame to the Grand Master Elyan De Villanova for A. D. 1338. Larking, Lambert B., ed. (Camden Society, London. Publications, First Ser.: No. 65). Repr. of 1857 ed. 28.00 (ISBN 0-404-50165-6). AMS Pr.

HOSPITALS
see also Almshouses; Children–Hospitals; Clinics; Hospital Care; Hospital Libraries; Hospital Pharmacies; Hospitalers; Medical Centers; Medicine, Clinical; Nurses and Nursing; Nursing Homes; Operating Rooms; Psychiatric Hospitals; Public Relations–Hospitals; Terminal Care Facilities; Volunteer Workers in Hospitals; also subdivision Hospitals under names of cities, e.g. New York (City)–Hospitals

American Association Of Hospital Consultants. Functional Planning of General Hospitals. Mills, Alden, ed. (Illus.). 1969. 30.00 (ISBN 0-07-001273-3, HP). McGraw.

American Hospital Association. Capital Financing for Hospitals. LC 73-87100. (Financial Management Ser.). 60p. (Orig.). 1974. pap. 8.75 (ISBN 0-87258-139-X, 1175). Am Hospital.

--Cumulative Index of Hospital Literature: 1965-1969. 864p. 1970. 62.50 (ISBN 0-87258-055-5, 1384). Am Hospital.

--Cumulative Index of Hospital Literature: 1970-1974. 1004p. 1976. casebound 93.75 (ISBN 0-87258-192-6, 1385). Am Hospital.

--Directory of Multihospital Systems, 1981 Edition. (Illus.). 90p. (Orig.). 1981. pap. 37.50 (ISBN 0-87258-355-4, 1218). Am Hospital.

--Directory of Shared Services Organizations for Health Care Institutions, 1981. 186p. (Orig.). 1981. write for info. (ISBN 0-87258-354-6, 1208). Am Hospital.

--The Hospital Admitting Department. LC 76-54284. (Illus.). 100p. (Orig.). 1977. pap. 13.75 (ISBN 0-87258-200-0, 1855). Am Hospital.

--Hospital Statistics: Data from the American Hospital Association 1979 Annual Survey. 256p. 1980. pap. 18.75 (ISBN 0-87258-282-5, 2452). Am Hospital.

--Hospital Statistics: Data from the American Hospital Association 1978 Annual Survey. (Illus.). 244p. 1979. pap. 15.00 (ISBN 0-87258-257-4, 2451). Am Hospital.

--Hospital Statistics: Data from the American Hospital Association 1977 Annual Survey. (Illus.). 1978. pap. 12.50 (ISBN 0-87258-224-8, 2450). Am Hospital.

--Hospital Statistics: Data from the American Hospital Association 1972 Annual Survey. (Illus.). 224p. 1973. pap. 9.50 (ISBN 0-87258-127-6, 2445). Am Hospital.

--Hospital Statistics: Data from the American Hospital Association 1973 Annual Survey. (Illus.). 225p. 1974. pap. 9.50 (ISBN 0-87258-158-6, 2446). Am Hospital.

--Hospital Statistics: Data from the American Hospital Association 1974 Annual Survey. (Illus.). 230p. 1975. pap. 9.50 (ISBN 0-87258-167-5, 2447). Am Hospital.

--Hospital Statistics: Data from the American Hospital Association 1975 Annual Survey. (Illus.). 232p. 1976. pap. 9.50 (ISBN 0-87258-185-3, 2448). Am Hospital.

--Hospital Statistics: Data from the American Hospital Association 1976 Annual Survey. (Illus.). 246p. 1977. pap. 12.50 (ISBN 0-87258-204-3, 2449). Am Hospital.

--Hospitals in the 1980s: Nine Views. LC 77-11065. 240p. 1977. 23.25 (ISBN 0-87258-223-X, 1752). Am Hospital.

--Volunteer in Long-Term Care. LC 68-3723. 60p. 1968. pap. 7.50 (ISBN 0-87258-043-1, 2855). Am Hospital.

Appert, B. Rapport sur l'Etat Actuel des Prisons, des Hospices des Ecoles, Etc. (Conditions of the 19th Century French Working Class Ser.). 168p. (Fr.). 1974. Repr. of 1824 ed. lib. bdg. 50.00x (ISBN 0-8287-0035-4, 1080). Clearwater Pub.

Barocci, Thomas A. Non-Profit Hospitals: Their Structure, Human Resources, & Economic Importance. LC 80-22075. 232p. 1981. 19.95 (ISBN 0-86569-054-5). Auburn Hse.

Blanken, Ann J. Hospital Discharges & Length of Stay: Short-Stay Hospitals, U. S., 1972. LC 75-619408. (Ser. 10: No. 107). 52p. 1976. pap. text ed. 1.25 (ISBN 0-8406-0063-1). Natl Ctr Health Stats.

Bloom, Samuel W. Doctor & His Patient: A Sociological Interpretation. LC 66-1994. 1965. pap. text ed. 4.95 (ISBN 0-02-903890-1). Free Pr.

Bridgeman, R. F. Hospital Utilization: An International Study. (Illus.). 1979. text ed. 37.50x (ISBN 0-19-261158-5). Oxford U Pr.

Brown, Vernon K. A Cathedral of Healing. (Illus.). 288p. 1981. 12.00 (ISBN 0-9605996-1-4). Northwest Memorial.

Cadmus, Robert R. Hospitals Are Us. 184p. (Orig.). 1979. 15.95 (ISBN 0-931028-12-4); pap. 12.95 (ISBN 0-931028-11-6). Teach'em.

Champion, J. M. General Hospital: A Model. (Illus.). 1976. 16.50 (ISBN 0-8391-0927-X). Univ Park.

Cross, Frank L. & Noble, George. Handbook on Hospital Solid Waste Management. LC 72-86164. (Illus.). 114p. (Orig.). 1973. pap. 15.00 (ISBN 0-87762-096-2). Technomic.

Cunningham, Robert M., Jr. Asking & Giving: A Report on Hospital Philanthropy. LC 79-28315. 148p. (Orig.). 1980. pap. 12.50 (ISBN 0-87258-300-7, 1030). Am Hospital.

Dain, Norman. Disordered Minds: The First Century of Eastern State Hospital in Williamsburg, Virginia, 1766-1866. LC 76-125913. (Williamsburg in America Ser.). (Illus.). 216p. 1971. 5.95x (ISBN 0-8139-0317-3). U Pr of Va.

De La Chapelle, Clarence E. & Jensen, Frode. A Mission in Action: The Story of The Regional Hospital Plan of New York University. LC 64-22262. 1964. 8.50x (ISBN 0-8147-0115-9). NYU Pr.

De Winter, E. R. Health Services in a District Hospital. 1972. 20.90x (ISBN 90-232-0991-5, Pub by Van Gorcum). Intl Schol Bk Serv.

Distribution of Physicians in the U. S. 1973. pap. 6.00 (ISBN 0-89970-039-X, OP-399). AMA.

Douglas, D. M. Surgical Departments in Hospitals: The Surgeon's View. 1972. 8.95 (ISBN 0-407-40340-X). Butterworth.

Fallon, Edward B. Hospital Days. 138p. 1981. text ed. 14.95 (ISBN 0-935976-03-5). Midland Pub Co.

Freidson, Eliot, ed. Hospital in Modern Society. LC 63-10648. (Illus.). 1963. 19.95 (ISBN 0-02-910690-7). Free Pr.

Gold, Don. Bellvue. 1982. pap. price not set. Dell.

Goldsmith, Jeff C. Can Hospitals Survive? 250p. 1981. 16.95 (ISBN 0-87094-248-4). Dow Jones-Irwin.

Groschel. Hospital Associated Infections in the General Hospital Populations & Specific Measures of Control. (Handbook on Hospital-Associated Infections Ser.: Vol. 3). 1979. 29.50 (ISBN 0-8247-6815-9). Dekker.

Hamill, Charlotte M. The Day Hospital: Organization & Management. LC 80-607802. 192p. 1981. text ed. write for info. (ISBN 0-8261-3040-2). Springer Pub.

Harris, W. Kenneth & Hoffman, Keith L. Quality Control in the Hospital Discharge Survey. Stevenson, Taloria, ed. LC 75-619242. (Data Evaluation & Methods Research Ser 2: No.68). 1976. pap. text ed. 1.50 (ISBN 0-8406-0050-X). Natl Ctr Health Stats.

Haupt, Barbara J. Utilization of Short-Stay Hospitals: Annual Summary for the United States, 1979. Cox, Klaudia, ed. (Series 13: No. 60). 50p. 1981. pap. text ed. 1.75 (ISBN 0-8406-0231-6). Natl Ctr Health Stats.

Herkimer, Allen G. Understanding Hospital Financial Management. LC 78-12182. 360p. 1978. text ed. 25.95 (ISBN 0-89443-047-5). Aspen Systems.

Hess, Irene, et al. Probability Sampling of Hospitals & Patients. 2nd ed. LC 75-20990. 204p. 1976. 9.75 (ISBN 0-914904-10-8). Health Admin Pr.

Hospital Phone Book 1980-81. 1980. 17.95 (ISBN 0-916524-16-7). US Direct Serv.

Kitzinger, Sheila & Davis, John A., eds. The Place of Birth. (Illus.). 1978. text ed. 29.50x (ISBN 0-19-261125-9); pap. text ed. 15.95x (ISBN 0-19-261238-7). Oxford U Pr.

Knowles, John H., ed. Teaching Hospital: Evolution & Contemporary Issues. LC 66-21338. 1966. 8.95x (ISBN 0-674-86955-9). Harvard U Pr.

Kozak, Lola J. The Status of Hospital Discharge Data in Six Countries. Olmstead, Mary, ed. (Ser. 2: No. 80). 50p. 1980. pap. 1.75 (ISBN 0-8406-0186-7). Natl Ctr Health Stats.

Lewis, D. Sclater. Royal Victoria Hospital 1887-1947. 352p. 1969. 10.00 (ISBN 0-7735-9073-0). McGill-Queens U Pr.

Lewis, W. Frank. Utilization of Short-Stay Hospitals, Summary of Nonmedical Statistics, U. S., 1973. (Ser. 13: No. 23). 55p. 1976. pap. text ed. 1.25 (ISBN 0-8406-0065-8). Natl Ctr Health Stats.

Little, Nina F. Early Years of the McLean Hospital, Recorded in the Journal of George William Folsom, Apothecary at the Asylum in Charlestown. LC 72-181085. (Illus.). 176p. 1972. 8.95 (ISBN 0-686-05704-X). F A Countway.

Lowry, Cynthia. Hospital: Biography of Benedictine. LC 76-18936. (Illus.). 188p. 1976. text ed. 10.00 (ISBN 0-912526-19-X). Lib Res.

Martin, Helen E. History of the Los Angeles County Hospital (1878-1968) & the Los Angeles County University of Southern California Medical Center (1968 - 1978) text ed. 20.00 (ISBN 0-88474-100-1). U of S Cal Pr.

Maryland Hospital Education Institute. Controlling Hospital Liability: A Systems Approach. (Illus., Orig.). 1976. pap. 7.50 (ISBN 0-87258-199-3, 2662). Am Hospital.

Maynard, Aubre D. Surgeons to the Poor: The Harlem Hospital Story. 1978. 16.50 (ISBN 0-8385-8720-8). ACC.

Minnesota Hospital Association, compiled by. The Changing Role of the Hospital: Options for the Future. 324p. (Orig.). 1980. pap. 35.00 (ISBN 0-87258-310-4, 1186). Am Hospital.

Morton, Thomas G. The History of the Pennsylvania Hospital, 1751-1895. LC 73-2408. (Mental Illness & Social Policy; the American Experience Ser.). Repr. of 1895 ed. 33.00 (ISBN 0-405-05218-9). Arno.

Nierenberg, Judith & Janovic, Florence. The Hospital Experience: A Complete Guide to Understanding & Participating in Your Own Care. LC 78-55658. (Illus.). 1978. 12.95 (ISBN 0-672-52372-8); pap. 9.95 (ISBN 0-672-52373-6). Bobbs.

Nightingale, Florence. Notes on Hospitals. 1976. lib. bdg. 59.45 (ISBN 0-8490-2357-2). Gordon Pr.

Obrecht, J. B. & Dubach, U. C., eds. Medizinische Universitaets Poliklinik Basel, 100 Jahre. (Illus.). 100p. 1975. 18.00 (ISBN 3-8055-2280-0). S Karger.

Paine, Leslie & British Hospital Journal Staff. Know Your Hospital. 1972. pap. 9.95x (ISBN 0-685-83617-7). Intl Ideas.

Peters, Joseph P. A Guide to Strategic Planning for Hospitals. LC 79-10063. 148p. (Orig.). 1979. 16.00 (ISBN 0-87258-259-0, 1200). Am Hospital.

Peth, C. F., et al. Application Design Manual for a Hospital Admitting System. 1977. 6.00 (ISBN 0-918118-13-1). MUMPS.

Phillip, P. Joseph & Dombrosk, Stephen J. Seasonal Patterns of Hospital Activity. LC 79-1752. 160p. 1979. 15.95 (ISBN 0-669-02926-2). Lexington Bks.

Pottle, Frederick A. Stretchers: The Story of a Hospital Unit on the Western Front. 1929. 34.50x (ISBN 0-685-89785-0). Elliots Bks.

Ranofsky, Abraham L. Inpatient Utilization of Short-Stay Hospitals, by Diagnosis, U. S., 1971. LC 74-2270. (Data from the Hospital Discharge Survey Ser. 13: No. 16). 54p. 1974. pap. text ed. 1.50 (ISBN 0-8406-0002-X). Natl Ctr Health Stats.

--Utilization of Short-Stay Hospitals: Annual Summary for the United States, 1976. Stevenson, Taloria, ed. (Ser. 13: No. 37). 1978. pap. text ed. 1.75 (ISBN 0-8406-0129-8). Natl Ctr Health Stats.

Readings on Public-General Hospitals. LC 78-7454. (Illus.). 1978. pap. text ed. 15.00 (ISBN 0-87914-049-6, 9093). Hosp Res & Educ.

Research Staff of the F&S Press with Ekaterinin Siafeca. Investor Owned Hospitals & Their Role in the Changing U. S. Health Care System. 224p. 1981. prof. ref. 32.95 (ISBN 0-86621-000-8). Ballinger Pub.

Rudman, Jack. Hospital Care Investigator. (Career Examination Ser.: C-326). (Cloth bdg. avail. on request). pap. 8.00 (ISBN 0-8373-0326-5). Natl Learning.

--Hospital Care Investigator Trainee. (Career Examination Ser.: C-327). (Cloth bdg. avail. on request). pap. 8.00 (ISBN 0-8373-0327-3). Natl Learning.

--Senior Hospital Care Investigator. (Career Examination Ser.: C-715). (Cloth bdg. avail. on request). pap. 10.00 (ISBN 0-8373-0715-5). Natl Learning.

--Supervising Hospital Care Investigator. (Career Examination Ser.: C-779). (Cloth bdg. avail. on request). pap. 10.00 (ISBN 0-8373-0779-1). Natl Learning.

Safar, Peter. Public Health Aspects of Critical Care Medicine & Anesthesiology. (Illus.). 378p. 1974. text ed. 20.00 (ISBN 0-8036-7718-9). Davis Co.

Shaffer, Alice, et al. The Indiana Poor Law: Its Development & Administration with Special Reference to the Provision of State Care for the Sick Poor. LC 75-17242. (Social Problems & Social Policy Ser.). 1976. Repr. of 1936 ed. 22.00x (ISBN 0-405-07513-8). Arno.

Shannon, R. H., ed. Hospital Information Systems. LC 79-15608. 405p. 1979. 58.75 (ISBN 0-444-85341-3, North Holland). Elsevier.

Shipp, Audrey, ed. Utilization of Short-Stay Hospitals: Annual Summary for the United States, 1975. (Series 13: No. 31). 1977. pap. 1.95 (ISBN 0-8406-0092-5). Natl Ctr Health Stats.

Shonick, William. Elements of Planning for Area-Wide Personal Health Services. LC 76-6445. (Issues & Problems in Health Care Ser.). (Illus.). 288p. 1976. pap. text ed. 8.50 (ISBN 0-8016-4592-1). Mosby.

Siafaca, Ekaterini. Investor-Owned Hospitals & Their Role in the Changing U. S. Health Care System. (Health Care Economics & Technology Ser.). 192p. 1981. 32.95x (ISBN 0-86621-000-8). F&S Pr.

Skillicorn, Stanley A. Quality & Accountability: A New Era in American Hospitals. (Illus.). 143p. 1980. 14.00 (ISBN 0-917636-03-1). Edit Consult.

Sloan, Frank A. & Steinwald, Bruce. Insurance, Regulation, & Hospital Costs. LC 79-3752. (Illus.). 288p. 1980. 25.95x (ISBN 0-669-03472-X). Lexington Bks.

Snook, Donald. Hospitals: What They Are & How They Work. LC 80-26956. 275p. 1981. text ed. 21.00 (ISBN 0-89443-339-3). Aspen Systems.

Starkweather, David. Hospital Mergers in the Making. (Illus.). 1981. text ed. write for info. (ISBN 0-914904-54-X). Health Admin Pr.

Summers, H. J. They Crossed the River. (Illus.). 1979. 20.00x (ISBN 0-7022-1357-8). U of Queensland Pr.

Thompson, John D. & Goldin, Grace. The Hospital: A Social & Architectural History. LC 74-19574. (Illus.). 320p. 1975. 30.00x (ISBN 0-300-01829-0). Yale U Pr.

Universitaets-Klinik und Poliklinik fuer Hals -, Nasen- und Ohren-Krankheiten Basel 1876-1976. 1976. 11.50 (ISBN 3-8055-2405-6). S Karger.

Warren, David G. Problems in Hospital Law. 3rd. ed. LC 78-15865. 339p. 1978. text ed. 21.50 (ISBN 0-89443-045-9). Aspen Systems.

Wastell, Christopher & Lance, Peter, eds. Cimetidine: The Westminster Hospital Symposium. (Illus.). 1978. text ed. 37.50 (ISBN 0-443-01882-0). Churchill.

Wheeler, E. Todd. Hospital Modernization & Expansion. 1971. 39.50 (ISBN 0-07-069520-2, P&RB). McGraw.

Wilder, Mary H. & Moy, Claudia S. Persons Hospitalized by Number of Episodes & Days Hospitalized in a Year: United States, 1972. Stevenson, Taloria, ed. (Ser. 10, No. 116). 1977. pap. text ed. 1.50 (ISBN 0-8406-0104-2). Natl Ctr Health Stats.

Wilson-Barnett, Jenifer. Stress in Hospital. (Illus.). 136p. 1980. pap. text ed. 10.50x (ISBN 0-443-01879-0). Churchill.

Woodward, John. To Do the Sick No Harm: A Study of the British Voluntary Hospital System to 1875. (International Library of Social Policy Ser.). 1978. pap. 8.95 (ISBN 0-7100-8911-2). Routledge & Kegan.

HOSPITALS–ACCOUNTING

Allcorn, Seth. Internal Auditing for Hospitals. LC 79-20072. 212p. 1979. text ed. 29.00 (ISBN 0-89443-163-3). Aspen Systems.

American Hospital Association. Capital Financing for Hospitals. LC 73-87100. (Financial Management Ser.). 60p. (Orig.). 1974. pap. 8.75 (ISBN 0-87258-139-X, 1175). Am Hospital.

--Internal Control, Internal Auditing, & Operations Auditing for Hospitals. LC 79-15042. (Financial Management Ser). (Illus.). 1979. pap. 15.00 (ISBN 0-87258-272-8, 1450). Am Hospital.

--Managerial Cost Accounting for Hospitals. LC 79-29708. (Financial Management Ser.). (Illus.). 144p. 1980. 20.00 (ISBN 0-87258-296-5, 1333). Am Hospital.

American Medical Record Association. Glossary of Hospital Terms. 2nd rev. ed. 128p. 1974. 5.75 (ISBN 0-686-68577-6, 14911). Hospital Finan.

AUPHA Task Force on Financial Management. Financial Management of Health Care Organizations: A Referenced Outline & Annotated Bibliography. 237p. 1978. 8.00 (ISBN 0-686-68588-1, 14921). Hospital Finan.

Berman, Howard W. & Weeks, Lewis E. The Financial Management of Hospitals. 3rd ed. (Illus.). 585p. 1976. 17.50 (ISBN 0-686-68573-3, 1496). Hospital Finan.

Bolandis, Jerry. Hospital Finance: A Comprehensive Case Approach. 400p. 1981. text ed. price not set (ISBN 0-89443-377-6). Aspen Systems.

Bower, James B., et al. Hospital Income Flow: A Study of the Effects of Source of Payment on Hospital Income. (Monograph: No. 2). (Orig.). 1970. pap. 3.00x (ISBN 0-912084-06-5). Mimir.

Budgeting Procedures for Hospitals. 88p. 1971. 8.25 (ISBN 0-686-68590-3, 1130). Hospital Finan.

Chart of Accounts for Hospitals. 157p. 1976. 10.75 (ISBN 0-686-68594-6, 2830). Hospital Finan.

Chart of Accounts for Hospitals. LC 76-6469. (Financial Management Ser.). (Illus.). 168p. (Orig.). 1976. 20.00 (ISBN 0-87258-176-4, 2830). Am Hospital.

Cleverley, William O. Financial Management of Health Care Facilities. 394p. 1976. 18.75 (ISBN 0-686-68581-4, 14915). Hospital Finan.

Flesher, Dale L. Operations Auditing in Hospitals. LC 75-29936. 128p. 1976. 16.95 (ISBN 0-669-00363-8). Lexington Bks.

Frank, C. W. Maximizing Hospital Cash Resources. LC 78-14271. (Illus.). 250p. 1978. text ed. 25.95 (ISBN 0-89443-076-9). Aspen Systems.

Garrett, Raymond. Hospital Computer Systems & Procedures: Vol. 1, Accounting Systems. 310p. 1976. 16.95x (ISBN 0-442-80326-5). Van Nos Reinhold.

H. F. M. A. Staff. Patient Account Management Techniques. 1976. 8.50 (ISBN 0-930228-01-4, 1443). Hospital Finan.

Hall, B. T. Auditing the Modern Hospital. 256p. 1977. 32.95 (ISBN 0-686-68587-3, 14920). Hospital Finan.

Hospital Audit Guide. (Industry Audit Guides). 1972. pap. 7.00 (ISBN 0-685-58489-5). Am Inst CPA.

Internal Control & Internal Auditing for Hospitals. 66p. 1969. 8.00 (ISBN 0-686-68592-X, 2025). Hospital Finan.

Katz, L. William. Manchester Community Hospital: Case Study in Hospital Financial Management. (Illus.). 1978. instructor's manual 2.00 (ISBN 0-87914-047-X, 9051). Hosp Res & Educ.

--Manchester Community Hospital: Case Study in Hospital Financial Management. rev ed. (Illus.). 1977. student manual 4.00 (ISBN 0-87914-044-5, 9050). Hosp Res & Educ.

Kinzer, David M. Health Controls Out of Control. 194p. 9.75 (ISBN 0-686-68584-9, 14918). Hospital Finan.

Lipson, Stephen H. & Hensel, Mary D. Hospital Manpower Budget Preparation Manual. 200p. 1975. 12.00 (ISBN 0-686-68583-0, 14917). Hospital Finan.

Maher & Mehta. Hospital Accounting Systems & Controls. 1976. 32.95 (ISBN 0-13-394791-2). P-H.

Martin, T. Leroy. Hospital Accounting Principles & Practice. 1958. 5.75 (ISBN 0-917036-08-5). Physicians Rec.

Mehta, Nitin H. & Maher, Donald J. Hospital Accounting Systems & Controls. 272p. 1977. 32.95 (ISBN 0-686-68586-5, 14919). Hospital Finan.

Rudman, Jack. Medical Facilities Auditor. (Career Examination Ser.: C-2058). (Cloth bdg. avail. on request). 1977. pap. 10.00 (ISBN 0-8373-2058-5). Natl Learning.

Safeguarding the Hospital's Assets. 2nd ed. LC 78-67106. (Illus.). 1978. 9.00 (ISBN 0-930228-09-X). Hospital Finan.

Salkever, David & Bice, Thomas. Hospital Certificate-of-Need Controls: Impact on Investment, Costs, & Use. 1979. pap. 5.25 (ISBN 0-8447-3325-3). Am Enterprise.

Seawell, L. Vann. Hospital Financial Accounting Theory & Practice. LC 74-27241. (Illus.). 569p. 1975. text ed. 19.95x (ISBN 0-930228-00-6, 1454); instr's manual 39.90 (ISBN 0-686-77079-X). Hospital Finan.

--Introduction to Hospital Accounting. rev. ed. LC 77-74543. (Illus.). 508p. 1977. text ed. 14.95x (ISBN 0-930228-05-7); Practice Set (1978) 7.00 (ISBN 0-930228-08-1); Solutions Manual (1977) 29.90 (ISBN 0-930228-06-5). Hospital Finan.

Silvers, John B. & Prahalad, C. K. Financial Management of Health Institutions. 339p. 1974. 17.95 (ISBN 0-686-68576-8, 14910). Hospital Finan.

Sloan, Frank A. & Steinwald, Bruce. Insurance, Regulation, & Hospital Costs. LC 79-3752. (Illus.). 288p. 1980. 25.95x (ISBN 0-669-03472-X). Lexington Bks.

Suver, James D. & Neumann, Bruce R. Management Accounting for Health Care Organizations. (Illus.). 300p. 1981. text ed. 27.50 (ISBN 0-930228-16-2). Hospital Finan.

Umbdenstock, Richard J. So You're on the Hospital Board! 1981. pap. 5.75 (ISBN 0-87258-351-1, 1505). Am Hospital.

HOSPITALS–ADMINISTRATION

see also Hospital Housekeeping

Abernathy, William J., et al, eds. The Management of Health Care: A Technology Perspective. LC 74-14771. 192p. 1975. text ed. 22.50 (ISBN 0-88410-110-X). Ballinger Pub.

Abrahamson, Lee M. How to Develop & Administer an Effective Personnel Policy Program in Hospitals & Health Care Facilities. 170p. 1981. 59.90 (ISBN 0-938726-03-X). Omega Ctr.

Accreditation Manual for Hospitals: 1982 Ed. 218p. 1981. pap. 20.00 (ISBN 0-86688-044-5). Joint Comm Hosp.

Administrator's Collection. LC 77-23776. 72p. 1978. pap. 6.25 (ISBN 0-87258-238-8, 1088). Am Hospital.

Allen, Rex W. & Von Karolyi, Ilona. Hospital Planning Handbook. LC 75-30599. 272p. 1976. text ed. 27.50 (ISBN 0-471-02319-1, Pub. by Wiley-Interscience). Wiley.

American Hospital Association. Budgeting Procedures for Hospitals. (Financial Management Ser.). (Illus.). 96p. 1971. pap. 8.25 (ISBN 0-87258-066-0, 1130). Am Hospital.

--Cost Finding & Rate Setting for Hospitals. (Financial Management Ser.). (Illus.). 112p. 1968. pap. 15.00 (ISBN 0-87258-036-9, 1365). Am Hospital.

--Developing Policies & Procedures for Long-Term Care Institutions. LC 68-3673. 1975. pap. 7.50 (ISBN 0-87258-191-8, 3170). Am Hospital.

--The Extended Care Unit in a General Hospital: A Guide to Planning, Organization, & Management. rev. ed. LC 73-80342. (Illus.). 60p. 1973. pap. 7.50 (ISBN 0-87258-131-4, 1570). Am Hospital.

--Food Service Manual for Health Care Institutions. LC 75-188855. 328p. 1972. 15.00 (ISBN 0-87258-086-5, 1845). Am Hospital.

--Guide for Preparation of Constitution & Bylaws for General Hospitals. rev. ed. LC 81-2788. 32p. 1981. pap. text ed. 12.50 (ISBN 0-87258-123-3, 2430). Am Hospital.

--Hospital Computer Systems Planning: Preparation of Request for Proposal. LC 80-18002. 124p. 1980. 25.00 (ISBN 0-87258-295-7, 1445). Am Hospital.

--Hospital Cost Containment Through Operations Management, 2 pts. (Illus.). 1980. Instructor's Manual. loose-leaf 37.50 (ISBN 0-87258-304-X, 2435, 206 PAGES); Participant's Manual. loose-leaf 10.00 (ISBN 0-87258-305-8, 2436, 2434, 264 PAGES). Am Hospital.

--The Hospital Trustee Reader: Selections from Trustee Magazine. LC 75-19443. 216p. 1975. pap. 13.75 (ISBN 0-87258-169-1, 1915). Am Hospital.

--Improving Work Methods in Small Hospitals. LC 75-32509. (Illus.). 88p. 1975. pap. 12.50 (ISBN 0-87258-165-9, 1910). Am Hospital.

--Multihospital Arrangements: Public Policy Implications. Mason, Scott A., ed. LC 79-14654. (Illus.). 176p. (Orig.). 1979. pap. 11.50 (ISBN 0-87258-258-2, 1161). Am Hospital.

--Organizing a Cost Containment Committee in the Hospital. LC 76-26173. 104p. 1979. 15.00 (ISBN 0-87258-272-8, 1450). Am Hospital.

--Readings in Hospital Central Service. LC 75-2358. 172p. 1975. pap. 25.00 (ISBN 0-87258-164-0, 2590). Am Hospital.

--Readings in Hospital Risk Management. 64p. 1979. pap. 7.50 (ISBN 0-87258-284-1, 1360). Am Hospital.

American Hospital Association of the Hospital Management Systems Society. Selection & Employment of Management Consultants for Health Care. LC 78-4971. (Illus.). 64p. 1978. pap. 12.00 (ISBN 0-87258-233-7, 1062). Am Hospital.

American Society for Hospital Food Service Administrators. Hospital Food Service Management Review. LC 80-11834. 80p. (Orig.). 1980. 10.00 (ISBN 0-87258-323-6, 1410). Am Hospital.

American Society for Hospital Food Service Administrators of the American Hospital Association. Preparation of a Hospital Food Service Department Budget. LC 78-24399. 56p. 1978. pap. 9.50 (ISBN 0-87258-254-X, 1615). Am Hospital.

Austin, Charles J. Information Systems for Hospital Administration. LC 79-5408. (Illus.). 1979. text ed. 25.00 (ISBN 0-914904-30-2). Health Admin Pr.

Barrett, Diana. Multihospital Systems: The Process of Development. LC 79-26111. 200p. 1980. text ed. 25.00 (ISBN 0-89946-011-9). Oelgeschlager.

Bean, Joseph J., Jr. & Laliberty, Rene. Understanding Hospital Labor Relations: An Orientation for Supervisors. LC 76-20014. 110p. 1977. pap. text ed. 8.95 (ISBN 0-201-00496-8). A-W.

Bean, Joseph, Jr. & Laliberty, Rene. Decentralizing Hospital Management: A Manual for Supervisors. 1980. pap. text ed. 8.95 (ISBN 0-201-00556-5). A-W.

Beck, Donald R. Basic Hospital Financial Management. LC 80-19598. 300p. 1980. text ed. 24.00 (ISBN 0-89443-329-6). Aspen Systems.

Bennett, Addison C. Improving Management Performance in Health Care Institutions: A Total Systems Approach. LC 78-8010. (Illus.). 256p. (Orig.). 1978. casebound 26.00 (ISBN 0-87258-246-9, 1066); pap. 25.00 (ISBN 0-87258-229-9, 1056). Am Hospital.

--Managing Hospital Costs Effectively As a System: A Primer for Hospital Administration. (Illus.). 72p. (Orig.). 1980. pap. 18.75 (ISBN 0-87258-327-9, 1404). Am Hospital.

Berkeley, A. Eliot & Barnes, Ann, eds. Labor Relations in Hospitals & Health Care Facilities. LC 75-45236. 110p. 1976. 10.00 (ISBN 0-87179-229-X). BNA.

Berman, Howard J. & Weeks, Lewis E. The Financial Management of Hospitals. 4th ed. LC 79-16947. (Illus.). 1979. text ed. 29.50 (ISBN 0-914904-33-7). Health Admin Pr.

Block, Lee F., ed. Marketing for Hospitals in Hard Times. 200p. 1981. text ed. 17.95 (ISBN 0-931028-16-7); pap. 13.95 (ISBN 0-931028-15-9). Teach'em.

Bowers, Warner F. Interpersonal Relationships in the Hospital. 136p. 1960. ed. spiral bdg. 14.75photocopy (ISBN 0-398-00203-7). C C Thomas.

Branson, Joan C. & Lennox, Margaret. Hotel, Hostel & Hospital Housekeeping. 3rd ed. (Illus.). 1976. pap. 12.95x (ISBN 0-7131-1974-8). Intl Ideas.

Bridgman, R. F. Rural Hospital: Its Structure & Organization. (Monograph Ser: No. 21). (Illus.). 162p. (Eng. & Fr.). 1970. 8.00 (ISBN 92-4-140021-8). World Health.

Brown, Bernard L. Risk Management for Hospitals: A Practical Approach. LC 78-31925. 216p. 1979. text ed. 28.00 (ISBN 0-89443-090-4). Aspen Systems.

Brown, Montague & Lewis, Howard L. Hospital Management Systems: Multi-Unit Organization & Delivery of Health Care. LC 76-15769. 305p. 1976. 25.95 (ISBN 0-912862-22-X). Aspen Systems.

Brown, Montague & McCool, Barbara P. Multihospital Systems: Strategies for Organization & Management. LC 79-23439. (Illus.). 564p. 1979. text ed. 36.00 (ISBN 0-89443-169-2). Aspen Systems.

Broyles, Robert. The Management of Working Capital in Hospitals. LC 80-26802. 499p. 1981. text ed. 42.00 (ISBN 0-89443-335-0). Aspen Systems.

Chaney, Warren H. & Beech, Thomas R. The Union Epidemic: A Prescription for Supervisors. LC 76-24132. 180p. 1976. 24.00 (ISBN 0-912862-28-9). Aspen Systems.

Christman, Luther & Counte, Michael A. Hospital Organization & Health Care Delivery. (Behavioral Science for Health Care Professionals Ser.). 128p. 1981. lib. bdg. 15.00 (ISBN 0-86531-006-8); pap. 6.75 (ISBN 0-86531-007-6). Westview.

Cleverley, William O. Essentials of Hospital Finance. LC 78-7447. (Illus.). 225p. 1978. text ed. 21.95 (ISBN 0-89443-035-1). Aspen Systems.

Colling, Russell L. Hospital Security. LC 75-46098. (Illus.). 384p. 1976. 19.95 (ISBN 0-913708-22-4). Butterworth.

Craig, C. Departmental Procedures for Infection Control Programs. 1977. pap. 29.95 (ISBN 0-87489-139-6); pap. 10.00 suppl. (ISBN 0-87489-186-8). Med Economics.

Cunningham, Robert, Jr. Governing Hospitals: Trustees & the New Accountabilities. LC 75-44127. 1976. pap. 12.50 (ISBN 0-87258-182-9, 1665). Am Hospital.

Deegan, Arthur X., 2nd. Management by Objectives for Hospitals. LC 76-45523. 1977. 24.95 (ISBN 0-912862-33-5). Aspen Systems.

Dixon, Nancy, et al. Quality, Trending, & Management for the Eighties (QTM-80) 236p. 1980. pap. 40.00 (ISBN 0-87258-345-7, 1377). Am Hospital.

Donnelly, Paul R. Guide for Developing a Hospital Administrative Policy Manual. LC 74-82196. (Orig.). 1974. pap. 4.00 (ISBN 0-87125-017-9). Cath Health.

Douglass, Merrill E. & Goodwin, Phillip H. Successful Time Management for Hospital Administrators. 160p. 1980. 16.95 (ISBN 0-8144-5602-2). Am Mgmt.

Dowling, William L. Hospital Production: A Linear Programming Approach. LC 74-14408. (Illus.). 1976. 17.95 (ISBN 0-669-93187-X). Lexington Bks.

Engstrom, Karen M. Consent Manual: Policies, Laws, Procedures. 100p. 1981. pap. 10.00 (ISBN 0-87125-062-4). Cath Health.

Evaluative Criteria for Catholic Health Care Facilities. 70p. 1980. pap. 8.50 (ISBN 0-87125-064-0). Cath Health.

Flesher, Dale L. Operations Auditing in Hospitals. LC 75-29936. 128p. 1976. 16.95 (ISBN 0-669-00363-8). Lexington Bks.

Flexner, William, et al. Strategic Planning in Health Care Management. (Illus.). 450p. 1981. text ed. 31.50 (ISBN 0-89443-298-2). Aspen Systems.

Frank, C. W. Maximizing Hospital Cash Resources. LC 78-14271. (Illus.). 250p. 1978. text ed. 25.95 (ISBN 0-89443-076-9). Aspen Systems.

Garber, A. Brent & Sparks, Leroy. Hospital Crisis Management: A Casebook. LC 79-25691. 180p. 1978. text ed. 27.00 (ISBN 0-89443-079-3). Aspen Systems.

Gardocki, Gloria J. & Pokras, Robert. Utilization of Short-Stay Hospitals by Persons with Heart Disease & Malignant Neoplasms. Shipp, Audrey, ed. (Ser. Thirteen: No. 52). 50p. 1981. pap. 1.75 (ISBN 0-8406-0214-6). Natl Ctr Health Stats.

Garrett, Raymond. Hospitals: A Systems Approach. 224p. 1973. 16.95x (ISBN 0-442-80238-2). Van Nos Reinhold.

Glickman, Linda. Inpatient Utilization of Short-Stay Hospitals by Diagnosis: United States, 1975. Stevenson, Taloria, ed. (Ser. 13: No. 35). 1978. pap. 1.75 (ISBN 0-8406-0123-9). Natl Ctr Health Stats.

Grant, Colin. Hospital Management. 272p. 1972. pap. text ed. write for info. (ISBN 0-443-01677-1). Churchill.

Grant, Dean E. How to Negotiate Physician Contracts. 254p. (Orig.). 1979. text ed. 25.95 (ISBN 0-931028-17-5); pap. text ed. 22.95 (ISBN 0-931028-10-8). Teach'em.

Greenblatt, Milton, et al. Dynamics of Institutional Change: The Hospital in Transition. LC 79-139597. (Contemporary Community Health Ser). 1971. 12.95 (ISBN 0-8229-3222-9). U of Pittsburgh Pr.

Griffith, John R. Quantitative Techniques for Hospital Planning & Control. LC 72-3550. (Illus.). 308p. 1972. 18.95 (ISBN 0-669-84087-4). Lexington Bks.

Grubb, Reba D. Hospital Manuals: A Guide to Development & Maintenance. 250p. 1981. text ed. write for info. (ISBN 0-89443-366-0). Aspen Systems.

Guide to the Retention & Preservation of Records with Destruction Schedules. 6th ed. 1981. pap. 25.00 (ISBN 0-930228-15-4). Hospital Finan.

Guidelines on Roles & Relationships of Board, Chief Executive Officer, & Medical Staff of Catholic Hospital & Long Term Care Facilities. LC 74-84787. 28p. (Orig.). 1974. pap. 2.00 (ISBN 0-87125-020-9). Cath Health.

Guidelines on the Responsibilities, Functions, & Selections Criteria for Hospital Boards of Trustees. LC 73-115340. 1974. pap. 1.25 (ISBN 0-87125-053-5). Cath Health.

Haimann, Theo. Supervisory Management for Health Care Institutions. LC 72-92380. 1973. 13.00 (ISBN 0-87125-004-7). Cath Health.

Hardy, Owen B. & Lammers, Lawrence P. Hospitals: The Planning & Design Process. LC 77-76922. 276p. 1977. 38.50 (ISBN 0-912862-44-0). Aspen Systems.

Health Law Center. Hospital Law Manual: Administrator's Set, 3 vols. (Updated quarterly). 1974. loose-leaf metal binding 295.00 (ISBN 0-912862-06-8). Aspen Systems.

Hohman, Jo. Taft-Hartley Amendments: Implications for the Health Care Field. LC 76-29662. 136p. (Orig.). 1976. pap. 13.50 (ISBN 0-87258-181-0, 1875). Am Hospital.

The Hospital Admitting Department. 90p. 1977. 9.50 (ISBN 0-87258-200-0, 1855). Hospital Finan.

Hospital Costs Containment Operations Management. 201p. 1979. 37.50 (ISBN 0-686-68595-4, 2435). Hospital Finan.

Hospital Financial Management Association. Cost Effectiveness Notebook. 1978. loose leaf 7.50 (ISBN 0-930228-10-3). Hospital Finan.

--Cost Effectiveness Notebook: Nineteen Eighty Update. 1980. write for info. (ISBN 0-930228-14-6). Hospital Finan.

--Cost Effectiveness Notebook: Nineteen Seventy-Nine Update. 1979. looseleaf 4.00 (ISBN 0-930228-12-X). Hospital Finan.

--Departmental Method Handbook. LC 79-88945. 70p. 1979. pap. 10.00 (ISBN 0-930228-11-1, 14411). Hospital Finan.

Hospital Survey Profile: 1981 Ed. 232p. pap. 12.50 (ISBN 0-86688-006-2). Joint Comm Hosp.

Hospital Survey Profile: 1982 Ed. 232p. 1981. pap. 12.50 (ISBN 0-86688-045-3). Joint Comm Hosp.

Hospital Trustee Development Program. LC 79-26280. 1979. 13.75 (ISBN 0-87258-253-1, 1710). Am Hospital.

Hospital Trustee Development Program, Vol. 2. LC 78-26280. 176p. 1981. price not set (ISBN 0-87258-361-9, 1740). Am Hospital.

Housley, Charles E. Hospital Material Management. LC 78-14526. (Illus.). 1978. text ed. 32.95 (ISBN 0-89443-046-7). Aspen Systems.

Hunter, B. The Administration of Hospital Wards. 80p. 1972. 21.00x (ISBN 0-7190-0525-6, Pub. by Manchester U Pr England). State Mutual Bk.

Improving the Effectiveness of Hospital Management. pap. 14.00 (ISBN 0-686-02546-6). Preston.

Integration Issues in Quality Assurance: QRB Special Edition. 96p. Date not set. pap. 25.00 (ISBN 0-86688-041-0). Joint Comm Hosp.

Johannides, David F. Cost Containment Through Systems Engineering: A Guide for Hospitals. LC 79-15217. 326p. 1979. text ed. 31.00 (ISBN 0-89443-098-X). Aspen Systems.

John R. Zabka Associated, Inc. Hospital Salary Survey Report 1981-82: 11th Annual Report. 200p. 1981. 90.00 (ISBN 0-939326-01-9). Hosp Compensation.

Johnson, A. P. Organization & Management of Hospital Laboratories. (Illus.). 1969. 6.95 (ISBN 0-407-34650-3). Butterworth.

Johnson, Everett A. & Johnson, Richard L. Contemporary Hospital Trusteeship. LC 75-40898. 1975. pap. 12.95 (ISBN 0-931028-00-0). Teach'em.

Kaplan, Karen O. & Hopkins, Julie M. The QA Guide: A Resource for Hospital Quality Assurance. Shanahan, Maryanne, ed. 213p. Date not set. pap. 30.00 (ISBN 0-86688-007-0). Joint Comm Hosp.

Katz, L. William. Manchester Community Hospital: Case Study in Hospital Financial Management. (Illus.). 1978. instructor's manual 2.00 (ISBN 0-87914-047-X, 9051). Hosp Res & Educ.

Koza, Russell C. Mathematical & Operations Research Techniques in Health Administration. LC 72-96158. (Illus.). 319p. 1973. text ed. 13.50x (ISBN 0-87081-051-0). Colo Assoc.

Kozak, Lola J. The Status of Hospital Discharge Data, in Denmark, Scotland, West Germany, & the United States. Cox, Klaudia, ed. (Ser. Two: No. 88). 55p. 1981. pap. 1.75 (ISBN 0-8406-0211-1). Natl Ctr Health Stats.

Larson, Gene F. The Unforgettable. rev. ed. 1978. 10.00 (ISBN 0-686-68574-1, 1491). Hospital Finan.

Lebowitz, Gordon. Exploring Health Careers Ser., Bk. 4: Careers in Hospital Administration, Maintenance, & Medical Secretarial Services. (Illus.). 128p. (gr. 7-12). 1975. pap. text ed. 3.00 (ISBN 0-87005-127-X); tchrs' guide 1.50 (ISBN 0-87005-132-6). Fairchild.

Levey, S. & Loomba, N. Paul. Long-Term Care Administration: A Managerial Perspective I, 2 vols. (Health System Management Ser.). 1977. Vol. 1. 17.95x (ISBN 0-470-99111-9); Vol. 2. 17.95x (ISBN 0-470-99110-0). Halsted Pr.

Levey, Samuel & Loomba, Narendra P., eds. Health Care Administration: A Managerial Perspective. LC 72-10830. 603p. 1973. 23.50 (ISBN 0-397-52059-X, JBL-Med-Nursing). Har-Row.

Lindsay, Cotton M. Veterans Administration Hospitals: An Economic Analysis of Government Enterprise. LC 75-29828. 1975. pap. 4.25 (ISBN 0-8447-3185-4). Am Enterprise.

Linton, Corrine B. & Truelove, James W. Hospital-Based Education. LC 79-4273. 1979. pap. text ed. 10.00 (ISBN 0-668-04776-3). Arco.

Llewelyn-Davies, R. & Macaulay, H. M. Hospital Planning & Administration. (Monograph Ser: No. 54). (Illus.). 215p. (Eng, Fr, Rus, & Span.). 1966. 12.80 (ISBN 92-4-140054-4). World Health.

Long, Hugh W. Upton University Hospital: Case Study in Hospital Financial Management. 1973. student manual 4.00 (ISBN 0-87914-034-8, 9170); instructor's guide 2.00 (ISBN 0-87914-035-6, 9175). Hosp Res & Educ.

Longest, Beaufort B., Jr. Administrative Coordination in General Hospitals. LC 74-621513. (Research Monograph: No. 55). (Illus.). 1973. spiral bdg. 25.00 (ISBN 0-88406-018-7). Ga St U Busn Pub.

--Principles of Hospital Business Office Management. 1975. 11.75 (ISBN 0-930228-02-2); instr's manual 23.50 (ISBN 0-686-77078-1, 1448). Hospital Finan.

McCarthy, Eileen. Inpatient Utilization of Short-Stay Hospitals by Diagnosis United States, 1978. Shipp, Audrey, ed. (Ser. Thirteen: No. 55). 50p. 1981. pap. text ed. 1.75 (ISBN 0-8406-0220-0). Natl Ctr Health Stats.

McFarland, Dalton E. Managerial Innovation & Change in the Metropolitan Hospital. LC 79-14557. (Praeger Special Studies Ser.). 336p. 1979. 28.95 (ISBN 0-03-051341-3). Praeger.

McGibony, John R. Principles of Hospital Administration. 2nd ed. (Illus.). 1969. 12.95m (ISBN 0-399-40033-8). Putnam.

McMillan, Norman H. Planning for Survival: A Handbook for Hospital Trustees. LC 78-2281. 128p. (Orig.). 1978. pap. 12.50 (ISBN 0-87258-221-3, 1073). Am Hospital.

Malsky, Stanley J. Hospital Administration for Middle Management: A Practical Approach. 320p. 1981. 27.50 (ISBN 0-87527-170-7). Green.

Malvey, Mari. Simple Systems, Complex Environments: Hospital Financial Information Systems. LC 80-29597. (Managing Information Ser.: Vol. 2). (Illus.). 185p. 1981. 17.50 (ISBN 0-8039-1541-1). Sage.

Massachusetts General Hospital. Clinical Anesthesia Procedures of the Massachusetts General Hospital. Lebowitz, Philip W., ed. 1978. pap. text ed. 11.95 (ISBN 0-316-54957-6). Little.

Mathieu, Robert P. Hospital & Nursing Home Management: An Instructional & Administrative Manual. LC 76-158401. (Illus.). 1971. 9.75x (ISBN 0-7216-6188-2). Saunders.

Medical Group Management Assocation. The Best of MGM: Nineteen Fifty to Nineteen Eighty. 1981. pap. cancelled (ISBN 0-686-30453-5). Med Group Mgmt.

Methods Improvement in Hospitals. pap. 10.00 (ISBN 0-686-02544-X). Preston.

Minnesota Hospital Association, compiled by. The Changing Role of the Hospital: Options for the Future. 324p. (Orig.). 1980. pap. 35.00 (ISBN 0-87258-310-4, 1186). Am Hospital.

Modern Hospital: International Planning Practices. (Illus.). 682p. 1980. text ed. 69.95 (ISBN 0-85324-141-4). Aspen Systems.

Moien, Mary. Inpatient Utilization of Short Stay Hospitals: U.S. 1972. Rutherford, Margaret, ed. LC 75-619178. (Data from the Hospital Discharge Survey Ser 13: No. 20). 50p. 1976. pap. text ed. 1.25 (ISBN 0-8406-0045-3). Natl Ctr Health Stats.

Moien, Mary & Stevenson, Taloria. Inpatient Utilization of Short-Stay Hospitals by Diagnosis, United States, 1973. (No. 12). 65p. 1976. pap. 1.75 (ISBN 0-8406-0072-0). Natl Ctr Health Stats.

Morgan, James A. & Seidlitz, Paul. OSHA & the Hospital Manager. LC 75-21371. 32p. 1975. pap. 2.50 (ISBN 0-87125-029-2). Cath Health.

Murphy, Frank D. Administrative Manual Guidelines for Hospitals. (Medical Bks.). 1980. lib. bdg. 49.95 (ISBN 0-8161-2198-2, Hall Medical). G K Hall.

--Cost Management Techniques for Hospitals. (Medical Bks.). 1980. lib. bdg. 29.95 (ISBN 0-8161-2200-8, Hall Medical). G K Hall.

National Society of Patient Representatives of the American Hospital Association. Assessing the Patient Representative Program. LC 80-28949. (Illus., Orig.). 1981. pap. 8.00 (ISBN 0-87258-334-1, 1082). Am Hospital.

Needles, Belverd, Jr. Bonnington Community Hospital: Case Study in Hospital Financial Management. 1971. 4.00 (ISBN 0-87914-030-5, 9040); instructor's guide 2.00 (ISBN 0-87914-031-3, 9045). Hosp Res & Educ.

Orlikoff, James E., et al. Malpractice Prevention & Liability Control for Hospitals. Greeley, Hugh P., ed. (Orig.). 1981. price not set (ISBN 0-87258-359-7, 1467). Am Hospital.

Packer, Clinton L. Preparing Hospital Management for Labor Contract Negotiations. LC 75-11826. (Illus.). 40p. (Orig.). 1975. pap. 7.50 (ISBN 0-87258-161-6, 2361). Am Hospital.

Parslow, R. D. & Green, R. Elliot, eds. Computer Graphics in Medical Research & Hospital Administration. LC 77-137741. 100p. 1971. 25.00 (ISBN 0-306-30518-6, Plenum Pr). Plenum Pub.

Perlin, Martin S. Managing Institutional Planning: Health Facilities & PL93-641. LC 76-29788. 168p. 1976. 24.75 (ISBN 0-912862-31-9). Aspen Systems.

Peterson, John E., et al. Enhancing Hospital Efficiency: A Guide to Expanding Beds Without Bricks. (Illus.). 1980. text ed. 15.00 (ISBN 0-914904-45-0). Health Admin Pr.

Phillip, P. Joseph & Dombrosk, Stephen J. Seasonal Patterns of Hospital Activity. LC 79-1752. 160p. 1979. 15.95 (ISBN 0-669-02926-2). Lexington Bks.

Physician-Oriented Review: Criteria Development & Analysis of Patient Care: QRB Special Edition. 64p. 1981. pap. 20.00 (ISBN 0-86688-049-6). Joint Comm Hosp.

The Practice of Planning in Health Care Institutions. 100p. 1973. 11.25 (ISBN 0-686-68593-8, 2765). Hospital Finan.

The Practice of Planning in Health Care Institutions. LC 73-77589. 112p. 1973. pap. 15.00 (ISBN 0-87258-120-9, 2765). Am Hospital.

Program on Hospital Accreditation Standards (PHAS) Manual: 1982 Ed. 750p. 1981. pap. 45.00 (ISBN 0-86688-042-9). Joint Comm Hosp.

Pugh. The Hospital Plot. 224p. (Orig.). 1980. pap. 2.25 (ISBN 0-87067-005-0). Holloway.

Rausch, Erwin & Wohlking, Wallace. Handling Conflict in Hospital Management: Conflict Among Peers (Game I) (Simulation Game Ser.). 1973. pap. 24.90 (ISBN 0-89401-036-0); pap. 21.50 two or more (ISBN 0-685-78117-8). Didactic Syst.

--Handling Conflict in Hospital Management: Superior - Subordinate Conflict (Game III) (Simulation Game Ser.). 1974. pap. 24.90 (ISBN 0-89401-043-3); pap. 21.50 two or more (ISBN 0-685-78123-2). Didactic Syst.

Rea, John, et al. Building a Hospital: A Primer for Administrators. LC 77-18854. 88p. (Orig.). 1978. pap. 15.00 (ISBN 0-87258-210-8, 2373). Am Hospital.

Reisman, Arnold. Systems Analysis in Health-Care Delivery. LC 79-3907. 336p. 1979. 24.95 (ISBN 0-669-02855-X). Lexington Bks.

Rothman, William A. A Bibliography of Collective Bargaining in Hospitals & Related Facilities, 2 vols. Incl. Vol. 1. 1959-1968. LC 71-630131. 6.95x (ISBN 0-87736-301-3); Vol. 2. 1969-1971. LC 72-619673. 7.95x (ISBN 0-87736-320-X). 1970. U of Mich Inst Labor.

Rowe, R. G. & Brewer, W. Hospital Activity Analysis. (Computers in Medicine Ser.). (Illus.). 112p. 1972. 15.95 (ISBN 0-407-55000-3). Butterworth.

Rudman, Jack. Assistant Hospital Administrator. (Career Examination Ser.: C-1107). (Cloth bdg. avail. on request). pap. 8.00 (ISBN 0-8373-1107-1). Natl Learning.

--Junior Hospital Administrator. (Career Examination Ser.: C-400). (Cloth bdg. avail. on request). pap. 8.00 (ISBN 0-8373-0400-8). Natl Learning.

--Supervising Hospital Care Investigator. (Career Examination Ser.: C-779). (Cloth bdg. avail. on request). pap. 10.00 (ISBN 0-8373-0779-1). Natl Learning.

St. Johns Hospital Staff. The Administrative Manual of Saint Johns Hospital: Springfield, Illinois. LC 75-1931. 1975. pap. 10.00 (ISBN 0-87125-026-8). Cath Health.

Salkever, David & Bice, Thomas. Hospital Certificate-of-Need Controls: Impact on Investment, Costs, & Use. 1979. pap. 5.25 (ISBN 0-8447-3325-3). Am Enterprise.

Sanderson, Edward D. Hospital Purchasing & Inventory Management. 275p. 1981. text ed. price not set (ISBN 0-89443-389-X). Aspen Systems.

Savage, P. E. Disasters: Hospital Planning. 1979. 28.00 (ISBN 0-08-024914-0); pap. 12.75 (ISBN 0-08-024913-2). Pergamon.

Schulz, R. & Johnson, A. C. Management of Hospitals. 1975. 15.95 (ISBN 0-07-055651-2, HP). McGraw.

Seawell, L. Vann. Hospital Financial Accounting Theory & Practice. LC 74-27241. (Illus.). 569p. 1975. text ed. 19.95x (ISBN 0-930228-00-6, 1454); instr's manual 39.90 (ISBN 0-686-77079-X). Hospital Finan.

Selbst, Paul L. Modern Health Care Forms. 1976. 46.50 (ISBN 0-88262-114-9). Warren.

Shuffstall, Richard M. & Hemmaplardh, Brecharr. The Hospital Laboratory: Modern Concepts of Management, Operations, & Finance. LC 78-11877. (Illus.). 1979. 16.95 (ISBN 0-8016-4620-0). Mosby.

Skoler, Martin E., ed. Health Care Labor Manual, 3 vols. (Updated bimonthly). 1974. loose-leaf metal binding 275.00 (ISBN 0-912862-11-4). Aspen Systems.

Smalley, Harold E. Hospital Management Engineering: A Guide to the Improvement of Hospital Management Systems. (Illus.). 480p. 1982. 27.95 (ISBN 0-13-394775-0). P-H.

Society for Hospital Planning of the American Hospital Association. Compendium of Resources for Strategic Planning in Hospitals. LC 80-28585. 132p. (Orig.). 1981. pap. 13.75 (ISBN 0-87258-326-0, 1188). Am Hospital.

Society for Hospital Social Work Directors of the American Hospital Association. Cost Accountability for Hospital Social Work. LC 80-12334. 48p. (Orig.). 1980. pap. 10.00 (ISBN 0-87258-278-7, 1330). Am Hospital.

--Reporting System for Hospital Social Work. LC 78-5696. 32p. 1978. pap. 8.75 (ISBN 0-87258-237-X, 1562). Am Hospital.

Stimson, David H. & Stimson, Ruth H. Operations Research in Hospitals: Diagnosis & Prognosis. LC 72-85387. 110p. 1972. 7.00 (ISBN 0-87914-018-6, 9180). Hosp Res & Educ.

Sudnow, David. Passing On: The Social Organization of Dying. (Orig.). 1967. pap. 8.95 (ISBN 0-13-652719-1). P-H.

Support Services Review: Problem Identification & Analysis of Patient Care: QRB Special Edition. 80p. 1981. pap. 20.00 (ISBN 0-86688-048-8). Joint Comm Hosp.

Tew, Raya E. How Not to Kill a Cockroach. 1978. 10.95 (ISBN 0-533-03179-6). Vantage.

Thompson, Richard E. Helping Hospital Trustees Understand Physicians. LC 79-21428. 96p. (Orig.). 1979. pap. 11.25 (ISBN 0-87258-287-6, 1347). Am Hospital.

Wanat, John A. Hospital Security Guard Training Manual. (Illus.). 192p. 1977. 21.75 (ISBN 0-398-03656-X). C C Thomas.

Warner, D. Michael & Griffith, John R. Exercises in Quantitative Techniques for Hospital Planning & Control. LC 74-28899. 150p. 1974. pap. text ed. 10.00 (ISBN 0-914904-07-8). Health Admin Pr.

Weaver, Jerry L. Conflict & Control in Health Care Administration. LC 74-82998. (Sage Library of Social Research: Vol. 14). 197p. 1975. 20.00 (ISBN 0-8039-0448-7); pap. 9.95 (ISBN 0-8039-0447-9). Sage.

White, Donald K. Continuing Education in Management for Health Care Personnel. LC 75-27158. 1975. 5.00 (ISBN 0-87914-028-3, 9152). Hosp Res & Educ.

Withersty, David J., ed. Communication & Compliance in a Hospital Setting. (Illus.). 208p. 1980. 18.50 (ISBN 0-398-03996-8). C C Thomas.

HOSPITALS–ADMINISTRATION–VOCATIONAL GUIDANCE

Rudman, Jack. Director of Patient Services. (Career Examination Ser.: C-2724). (Cloth bdg. avail. on request). 1980. pap. 18.00 (ISBN 0-8373-2724-5). Natl Learning.

--Hospital Administration Consultant. (Career Examination Ser.: C-2768). (Cloth bdg. avail. on request). 1980. pap. 12.00 (ISBN 0-8373-2768-7). Natl Learning.

--Hospital Administration Intern. (Career Examination Ser.: C-1967). (Cloth bdg. avail. on request). pap. 8.00 (ISBN 0-8373-1967-6). Natl Learning.

--Hospital Administrator. (Career Examination Ser.: C-1743). (Cloth bdg. avail. on request). 1977. pap. 10.00 (ISBN 0-685-78613-7). Natl Learning.

--Hospital Controller. (Career Examination Ser.: C-1760). (Cloth bdg. avail. on request). 1977. pap. 10.00 (ISBN 0-8373-1760-6). Natl Learning.

--Senior Hospital Administration Consultant. (Career Examination Ser.: C-2769). (Cloth bdg. avail. on request). 1980. pap. 14.00 (ISBN 0-8373-2769-5). Natl Learning.

HOSPITALS–ATTENDANTS

see Hospitals–Staff

HOSPITALS–CHARGES

see Hospitals–Rates

HOSPITALS–CLEANING

see Hospital Housekeeping

HOSPITALS–DESIGN AND CONSTRUCTION

Aloi, R. & Bassi, C. Hospitals (Architecture) (Illus.). 1972. 50.00 (ISBN 0-685-30577-5). Heinman.

American Hospital Association. Hospital Design Checklist. 48p. 1965. 8.75 (ISBN 0-87258-016-4, 3310). Am Hospital.

American Society for Hospital Engineering. Hospital Engineering Handbook. 3rd ed. (Illus.). 348p. 1980. casebound 31.25 (ISBN 0-87258-311-2, 1820). Am Hospital.

Cammock, Ruth. Primary Health Care Buildings. (Illus.). 96p. 1981. 25.00 (ISBN 0-85139-962-2). Nichols Pub.

Hardy, Owen B. & Lammers, Lawrence P. Hospitals: The Planning & Design Process. LC 77-76922. 276p. 1977. 38.50 (ISBN 0-912862-44-0). Aspen Systems.

Hospitals, Clinics, & Health Centers. LC 70-142928. (An Architectural Record Book). (Illus.). viii, 264p. Repr. of 1960 ed. lib. bdg. 29.50x (ISBN 0-8371-5930-X, ARHC). Greenwood.

Howe, Eunice D. The Hospital of Santo Spirito & Pope Sixtus IV. (Outstanding Dissertations in the Fine Arts Ser.). (Illus.). 1978. lib. bdg. 43.00x (ISBN 0-8240-3230-6). Garland Pub.

Hudenburg, Roy. Planning the Community Hospital. LC 76-51415. (Illus.). 448p. 1977. Repr. of 1967 ed. lib. bdg. 20.50 (ISBN 0-88275-511-0). Krieger.

Lave, Judith & Lave, Lester. The Hospital Construction Act: An Evaluation of the Hill-Burton Program, 1948-1973. 1974. pap. 4.25 (ISBN 0-8447-3129-3). Am Enterprise.

Millard, Graham. Commissioning Hospital Buildings. (King Edward's Hospital Fund Ser.). 1975. pap. text ed. 14.95x (ISBN 0-8464-0260-2). Beekman Pubs.

Miller, C. Eugene. Water Technology for the Hospital Engineer. 1978. lib. bdg. 35.00 (ISBN 0-8240-7008-9, Garland STPM Pr). Garland Pub.

Porter, David. Hospital Architecture: Guidelines for Design & Renovation. (Illus.). 450p. text ed. write for info. (ISBN 0-914904-53-1); pap. text ed. write for info. Health Admin Pr.

Porter, David R. Hospital Architecture: Guidelines for Design & Renovation. rev. ed. (Illus.). 450p. 1981. price not set (ISBN 0-914904-53-1). Health Admin Pr.

Rosenfield, Isadore & Rosenfield, Zachary. Hospital Architecture & Beyond. (Illus.). 1969. 29.95x (ISBN 0-442-15619-7). Van Nos Reinhold.

Sarkissian, Wendy, et al. The Design of Medical Environments for Children & Adolescents: An Annotated Bibliography. (Archtecture Ser.: Bibliography A-261). 65p. 1980. pap. 7.00 (ISBN 0-686-29050-X). Vance Biblios.

Stewart, Clifford D., et al, eds. Comprogram: Hospital Space Allocation, 2 vols. LC 73-158290. 1973. 58.00 (ISBN 0-915250-02-0). Environ Design.

Stone, Peter, ed. British Hospitals & Health-Care Buildings: Designs & Appraisals. (Illus.). 1980. 80.00 (ISBN 0-89397-072-7). Nichols Pub.

Wheeler, E. Todd. Hospital Design & Function. 1964. 32.50 (ISBN 0-07-069505-9, P&RB). McGraw.

HOSPITALS–EMPLOYEES

see Hospitals–Staff

HOSPITALS–FOOD SERVICE

American Society for Hospital Food Service Administrators. Determination & Allocation of Food Service Costs. 24p. 1975. pap. 7.00 (ISBN 0-87258-316-3, 1495). Am Hospital.

Downs, Rose G. Dietary Policy & Procedure Manual. new ed. 1979. pap. 9.00 (ISBN 0-87125-058-6). Cath Health.

Gordon A. Friesen International, Inc. The Ready Foods Systems for Health Care Facilities. LC 72-95360. 1973. 14.95 (ISBN 0-8436-0562-6). CBI Pub.

Hohman, Jo. Shared Food Services in Health Care Institutions. LC 76-13193. (Illus.). 100p. (Orig.). 1976. pap. 10.75 (ISBN 0-87258-178-0, 2636). Am Hospital.

Hospital Research & Educational Trust of the AHA. Being a Food Service Worker. (Illus.). 1967. pap. 9.95 (ISBN 0-87618-046-2). R J Brady.

--Training the Food Service Worker. (Illus.). 1967. pap. 9.95 (ISBN 0-87618-047-0). R J Brady.

Mahaffey, Mary J. & Mennes, Mary E. Food Service Manual for Health Care Institutions. (Illus.). 376p. 1981. pap. text ed. 25.00 (ISBN 0-87258-330-9). Am Hospital.

On-the-Job Training: A Practical Guide for Food Service Supervisors. 1975. 8.95 (ISBN 0-87914-026-7, 9778). Hosp Res & Educ.

Rice, John. Better Food for Patients: New Menus, Cooking, & Ward Service for Hospital Patients, 3 vols. (King Endward's Hospital Fund Ser.). 1975. folder 20.00x (ISBN 0-8464-0191-6). Beekman Pubs.

Training Programs for Health Care Workers: Food Service Workers. Incl. Being a Food Service Worker. 276p. student manual 9.95 (ISBN 0-87914-007-0, 9775, 9655); Training the Food Service Worker. 155p. instructor's guide 9.95 (ISBN 0-87914-008-9). 1967. Hosp Res & Educ.

HOSPITALS–FURNITURE, EQUIPMENT, ETC.

see also Hospitals–Food Service

American Hospital Association. American Society for Hospital Engineering. Medical Equipment Management in Hospitals. LC 78-1041. (Illus.). 528p. (Orig.). 1978. pap. 45.00 (ISBN 0-87258-241-8, 1272). Am Hospital.

Ammer, Dean S. Purchasing & Materials Management for Health Care Institutions. LC 74-11416. (Illus.). 1975. 16.95 (ISBN 0-669-95604-X). Lexington Bks.

Distribution of Physicians, Hospitals & Hospital Beds in the U.S., 1966 Ed, 2 vols. 1967. Set. pap. 2.00 set (ISBN 0-89970-036-5, OP-151). AMA.

Distribution of Physicians, Hospitals & Hospital Beds in the U.S., 1968 Ed. 1970. pap. 5.00 (ISBN 0-89970-037-3, OP-241). AMA.

Distribution of Physicians, Hospitals & Hospital Beds in the U.S., 1969 Ed, 2 vols. 1970. Set. pap. 5.00 set (ISBN 0-89970-038-1, OP-269). AMA.

England, Roger, compiled by. How to Make Basic Hospital Equipment. (Illus.). 86p. (Orig.). 1979. pap. 6.50 (ISBN 0-903031-60-4, Pub. by Intermediate Tech England). Intermediate Tech.

Housley, Charles E. Hospital Material Management. LC 78-14526. (Illus.). 1978. text ed. 32.95 (ISBN 0-89443-046-7). Aspen Systems.

Housley, Charles E., ed. Aspen Hospital Purchasing Price Index. 20p. Date not set. text ed. 150.00 (ISBN 0-686-74613-9). Aspen Systems.

Keithwood Directory of Hospital & Surgical Supply Dealers. 302p. 1980. 45.00 (ISBN 0-686-27082-7). Keithwood.

Probst, Calvin, ed. Hospital Purchasing Guide: Nieteen Eighty Two. 6th ed. (Annual Ser.). 1982. pap. text ed. 95.00 (ISBN 0-933916-06-X). IMS Comm.

Smith, E. J., ed. Hospital Consumables: Reference for Medical Surgical Products. LC 80-14970. (Illus.). 702p. 1981. loose-leaf 192.00 (ISBN 0-87619-925-2). R J Brady.

Wright, Nadean E. Central Supply Procedure Manual. 3rd ed. LC 78-26237. 1979. pap. 8.00 (ISBN 0-87125-046-2). Cath Health.

HOSPITALS–HOUSE STAFF

see Interns (Medicine)

HOSPITALS–HYGIENE

Castle, M. Hospital Infection Control: Principles & Practices. LC 80-13424. 1980. 18.95 (ISBN 0-471-05395-3). Wiley.

Craig, C. Departmental Procedures for Infection Control Programs. 1977. pap. 29.95 (ISBN 0-87489-139-6); pap. 10.00 suppl. (ISBN 0-87489-186-8). Med Economics.

Dubay, Elaine C. & Grubb, Reba D. Infection: Prevention & Control. 2nd ed. LC 77-9512. (Illus.). 1978. 11.50 (ISBN 0-8016-1463-5). Mosby.

Lowbury, E. J., et al. Control of Hospital Infection: A Practical Handbook. LC 75-16119. 306p. 1975. text ed. 28.95x (ISBN 0-412-13530-2, Pub by Chapman & Hall England). Methuen Inc.

Murphy, Frank D. Model Department Safety, Environmental & Infection Control Policies for Hospitals. (Medical Bks.). 1980. lib. bdg. 39.95 (ISBN 0-8161-2201-6, Hall Medical). G K Hall.

--Review & Update of Department Safety, Environmental & Infection Control Policies for Hospitals. (Medical Bks.). 1980. lib. bdg. 29.95 (ISBN 0-8161-2202-4, Hall Medical). G K Hall.

Newsom, S. W. & Caldwell, A. D., eds. Problems in the Control of Hospital Infection. (Royal Society of Medicine International Congress & Symposium Ser.: No. 23). 116p. 1980. pap. 20.50 (ISBN 0-8089-1257-7). Grune.

HOSPITALS–JUVENILE LITERATURE

Clark, Bettina & Coleman, Lester L. Going to the Hospital. (Illus.). (gr. k-3). 1971. 4.95 (ISBN 0-394-82160-2). Random.

Coleman, William L. My Hospital Book. (Illus.). 128p. (Orig.). (gr. 2-7). 1981. pap. 3.50 (ISBN 0-87123-354-1). Bethany Hse.

Deegan, Paul & Larson, Bruce. Hospital: Life in a Medical Center. LC 76-156064. (gr. 5-9). 1970. PLB 6.95 (ISBN 0-87191-052-7). Creative Ed.

Fisher, Leonard E. The Hospitals. LC 79-22357. (Nineteenth Century America Bk.). (Illus.). 64p. (gr. 5 up). 1980. PLB 7.95 (ISBN 0-8234-0405-6). Holiday.

Holmes, Burnham. Early Morning Rounds: A Portrait of a Hospital. LC 80-69995. (Illus.). 96p. (gr. 7 up). 1981. 9.95 (ISBN 0-590-07611-6, Four Winds). Schol Bk Serv.

Howe, James. The Hospital Book. (Illus.). 96p. (gr. 2-4). 1981. 10.95 (ISBN 0-517-54168-8); pap. 4.95 (ISBN 0-517-54235-8). Crown.

Marino, Barbara. Eric Needs Stitches. LC 78-31694. (gr. k-3). 1979. PLB 6.95 (ISBN 0-201-04401-3, A-W Childrens). A-W.

Schaleben-Lewis, Joy. Careers in a Hospital. LC 76-12487. (Whole Works Ser.). (Illus.). 48p. (gr. 3-7). 1976. PLB 10.65 (ISBN 0-8172-0709-0). Raintree Pubs.

Steedman, Julie. Emergency Room: An ABC Tour. LC 74-18335. (Illus.). (gr. k-3). 1975. pap. 3.95 (ISBN 0-914440-05-5). EPM Pubns.

Stein, Sarah B. A Hospital Story. LC 73-15269. (Open Family Ser). (Illus.). 48p. (gr. 1 up). 1974. 7.95 (ISBN 0-8027-6173-9). Walker & Co.

Visit to the Hospital. (gr. k-3). 0.79 (ISBN 0-448-00690-1). Wonder.

Ward, Bryan. Hospital. LC 78-61228. (Careers Ser.). (Illus.). 1978. lib. bdg. 7.95 (ISBN 0-686-51120-4). Silver.

HOSPITALS–MANAGEMENT AND REGULATION

see Hospitals–Administration

HOSPITALS–NURSES

see Hospitals–Staff; Nurses and Nursing

HOSPITALS–OUTPATIENT SERVICES

Access to Home Care. 1980. 3.00 (ISBN 0-86671-063-9). Comm Coun Great NY.

Accreditation Manual for Ambulatory Health Care. 1978. 7.50 (ISBN 0-86688-034-8, AHC-501). Joint Comm Hosp.

Alderman, Michael H., ed. Hypertension: The Nurse's Role in Ambulatory Care. LC 77-22259. (Illus.). 1977. text ed. 12.50 (ISBN 0-8261-2370-8). Springer Pub.

Aledort, L. M., et al. Outpatient Medicine. LC 78-51280. 1979. text ed. 10.50 (ISBN 0-89004-354-X). Raven.

Ambulatory ECG Monitoring, First National Conference. Proceedings. Jacobsen, Nancy & Yarnall, Stephen, eds. (Illus.). 150p. 1975. 16.50 (ISBN 0-917054-08-3). Med Communications.

Batalden, Paul B. & O'Conner, J. Paul. Quality Assurance in Ambulatory Care. LC 79-24700. 1980. text ed. 55.00 loose-leaf 3-ring binder (ISBN 0-89443-165-X). Aspen Systems.

--Quality Assurance in Ambulatory Care. LC 79-24700. 1980. text ed. 55.00 loose-leaf 3-ring binder (ISBN 0-89443-165-X). Aspen Systems.

Chung, E. K. Ambulatory Electrocardiography: Holter Monitor Electrocardiography. (Illus.). 1979. 26.20 (ISBN 0-387-90360-7). Springer-Verlag.

Cohen, David D. & Dillon, John B. Anesthesia for Outpatient Surgery. (Illus.). 84p. 1970. 11.75 (ISBN 0-398-00324-6). C C Thomas.

Coleman, J. R. & Kaminsky, F. C. Ambulatory Care Systems, Vol. 4: Designing Medical Services for Health Maintenance Organizations. LC 76-55865. (Illus.). 1977. 27.95 (ISBN 0-669-01327-7). Lexington Bks.

DeLozier, James E. & Gagnon, Raymond O. National Ambulatory Medical Care Survey 1973 Summary, U. S. May 1973 - April 1974. Stevenson, Taloria, ed. LC 75-35700. (Ser. 13: No. 21). 73p. 1976. pap. text ed. 1.75 (ISBN 0-8406-0057-7). Natl Ctr Health Stats.

Fleming, Rita A., ed. Primary Care Techniques: Laboratory Tests in Ambulatory Facilities. 1st ed. LC 79-20295. (Illus.). 1980. pap. text ed. 9.50 (ISBN 0-8016-1592-5). Mosby.

Giglio, Richard. Ambulatory Care Systems, Vol. 2: Location, Layout, & Information Systems for Efficient Operations. LC 76-55865. 1977. 19.50 (ISBN 0-669-01324-2). Lexington Bks.

Goldsmith, Seth B. Ambulatory Care: Theory & Practice. LC 77-10315. 135p. 1977. 21.50 (ISBN 0-912862-46-7). Aspen Systems.

Jacobsen, Nancy K., ed. Clinical & Research Uses of Ambulatory Monitoring. 1976. pap. 17.50 (ISBN 0-917054-13-X). Med Communications.

Jonas, Steven. Quality Control of Ambulatory Care: A Task for Health Departments. LC 77-24502. (Health Care & Society Ser.: Vol. 1). 1977. text ed. 12.50 (ISBN 0-8261-2240-X). Springer Pub.

Klippel, Allen P. & Anderson, Charles B. Manual of Outpatient & Emergency Surgical Techniques. (Washington University Dept. of Surgery Spiral Manual Ser.). 1979. 13.95 (ISBN 0-316-49868-8). Little.

O'Donovan, Thomas R., ed. Ambulatory Surgical Centers: Development & Management. LC 76-15767. 348p. 1976. 27.00 (ISBN 0-912862-21-1). Aspen Systems.

Reidel, Ruth L. & Reidel, Donald C. Practice & Performance: An Assessment of Ambulatory Care. LC 78-31776. (Illus.). 1979. text ed. 25.00 (ISBN 0-914904-29-9). Health Admin Pr.

Rising, Edward. Ambulatory Care Systems, Vol. 1: Design of Ambulatory Care Systems for Improved Patient Flow. LC 76-55865. 1977. 16.95 (ISBN 0-669-01323-4). Lexington Bks.

Rosenbaum, Ernest H., et al. Going Home: A Home Care Training Program. (Illus.). 160p. 1980. 12.00 (ISBN 0-686-77635-6); three ring binder 12.00 (ISBN 0-915950-48-0). Bull Pub.

Schneider, Don, et al. A Reason for Visit Classification for Ambulatory Care. Stevenson, Taloria, ed. (Ser. 2: No. 78). 40p. 1978. pap. 1.50 (ISBN 0-8406-0145-X). Natl Ctr Health Stats.

Spencer, James H., et al. The Hospital Emergency Department. (Illus.). 388p. 1972. 29.75 (ISBN 0-398-02482-0). C C Thomas.

Vorzimer, Jefferson J. Coordinated Ambulatory Care: the POMR. (Illus.). 128p. 1976. pap. text ed. 14.50 (ISBN 0-8385-1203-8). ACC.

HOSPITALS–PHARMACEUTICAL SERVICES

see Hospital Pharmacies

HOSPITALS–PHARMACY DEPARTMENTS

see Hospital Pharmacies

HOSPITALS–PSYCHIATRIC SERVICES

see Psychiatric Hospitals

HOSPITALS–RATES

Abernethy, David S. & Pearson, David A. Regulating Hospital Costs: The Development of Public Policy. LC 79-9227. (Illus.). 1979. text ed. 22.00 (ISBN 0-914904-36-1); pap. text ed. 13.95 (ISBN 0-914904-37-X). Health Admin Pr.

American Hospital Assn. Digest of Hospital Cost Containment Projects. 3rd ed. LC 79-27674. 132p. (Orig.). 1980. pap. 6.25 (ISBN 0-87258-299-X, 1020). Am Hospital.

American Hospital Association. Organizing a Cost Containment Committee in the Hospital. LC 76-26173. 104p. 1979. 15.00 (ISBN 0-87258-272-8, 1450). Am Hospital.

Carson, Clayborne. In Struggle: SNCC & the Black Awakening of the Nineteen Sixties. LC 80-16540. (Illus.). 384p. 1981. text ed. 22.00 (ISBN 0-674-44725-5). Harvard U Pr.

Cost Finding & Rate Setting for Hospitals. 103p. 1968. 9.25 (ISBN 0-686-68591-1, 1365). Hospital Finan.

Drummond, M. F. Studies in Economic Appraisal in Health Care. 240p. 1981. text ed. 32.50x (ISBN 0-19-261274-3). Oxford U Pr.

Erlich, David, ed. The Health Care Cost Explosion: Which Way Now? 250p. 1975. pap. 18.25 (ISBN 0-683-02789-1, Pub. by W & W). Krieger.

Feldstein, Martin S. The Rising Cost of Hospital Care. LC 72-171922. (Illus.). 88p. 1971. pap. text ed. 7.50 (ISBN 0-87815-004-8). Info Resources.

Griffith, John R., et al. Cost Control in Hospitals. LC 75-28579. 375p. 1976. text ed. 17.50x (ISBN 0-914904-12-4). Health Admin Pr.

Hospital Costs Containment Operations Management. 201p. 1979. 37.50 (ISBN 0-686-68595-4, 2435). Hospital Finan.

Hospital Financial Management Association. Cost Effectiveness Notebook: Nineteen Seventy-Nine Update. 1979. looseleaf 4.00 (ISBN 0-930228-12-X). Hospital Finan.

Hospital Regulation Through State Rate Review: Mandated Interference or a Noble Intrusion. 116p. 1978. 7.90 (ISBN 0-686-68585-7, 14922). Hospital Finan.

Hughes, Edward F. X. Hospital Cost Containment Programs: A Policy Analysis. LC 78-13793. 1978. 19.50 (ISBN 0-88410-705-1). Ballinger Pub.

Ingbar, Mary L. & Taylor, Lester D. Hospital Costs in Massachusetts: An Econometric Study. LC 68-14258. (Wertheim Publications in Industrial Relations Ser). (Illus.). 1968. 12.50x (ISBN 0-674-40700-8). Harvard U Pr.

Joskow, Paul L. Controlling Hospital Costs: The Role of Government Regulation. (Health & Public Policy). 224p. 1981. 25.00x (ISBN 0-262-10024-X). MIT Pr.

Lewis, W. Frank. Utilization of Short-Stay Hospitals: Summary of Non-Medical Statistics, U.S., 1971. LC 74-2233. (Data from the Hospital Discharge Survey Ser. 13: No. 19). 51p. 1974. pap. text ed. 1.50 (ISBN 0-8406-0036-4). Natl Ctr Health Stats.

Moien, Mary. Patient Charges in Short-Stay Hospitals, United States, 1968-1970. LC 74-3217. (Data from the Hospital Discharge Survey Ser. 13: No. 15). 55p. 1974. pap. text ed. 1.50 (ISBN 0-8406-0001-1). Natl Ctr Health Stats.

Salkever, David. Hospital Sector Inflation. (Illus.). 208p. 1979. 22.95 (ISBN 0-669-00704-8). Lexington Bks.

Ward, Richard A. The Economics of Health Resources. 150p. 1975. 10.25 (ISBN 0-686-68580-6, 14914). Hospital Finan.

Weeks, Lewis E., et al. Financing of Health Care - An Inquiry Anthology. LC 79-13436. (Illus.). 1979. pap. text ed. 14.00 (ISBN 0-914904-34-5); pap. text ed. 17.00 (ISBN 0-914904-35-3). Health Admin Pr.

HOSPITALS-SAFETY MEASURES

American Hospital Association. Fire Safety Training in Health Care Institutions. LC 75-20295. (Illus.). 60p. 1975. pap. 10.00 (ISBN 0-87258-163-2, 1595). Am Hospital.

American Hospital Association & National Safety Council. Safety Guide for Health Care Institutions. LC 72-81003. (Illus.). 248p. (Orig.). 1972. pap. 5.50 (ISBN 0-87258-106-3, 1975). Am Hospital.

American Hospital Association, et al. Sharing Responsibility for Patient Safety. 1979. 5.75 (ISBN 0-87258-248-5, 1152). Am Hospital.

Buchsbaum, W. H. & Goldsmith, B. Electrical Safety in the Hospital. 1975. pap. 5.95 (ISBN 0-87489-056-X). Med Economics.

Buchsbaum, Walter H. & Goldsmith, Bonnie. Electrical Safety in the Hospital. 1975. 5.95 (ISBN 0-442-84047-0). Van Nos Reinhold.

Camplin, C. Roger & Bartels, Robert. Safety Clinic One Handbook. 149p. Date not set. pap. 20.00 (ISBN 0-86688-025-9). Joint Comm Hosp.

Colling, Russell L. Hospital Security. 2nd ed. 1981. text ed. 25.95 (ISBN 0-686-31756-4). Butterworth.

Curran, William J., et al. Electrical Safety & Hazards in Hospitals. 205p. 1974. text ed. 19.50x (ISBN 0-8422-7135-X). Irvington.

Health Care Safety: Basic Library, 12 bks. 1300p. 27.90 (ISBN 0-685-58052-0, HCSL-A). Natl Fire Prot.

Health Care Safety: Fire Protection Systems Library, 13 bks. 1000p. 29.00 (ISBN 0-685-58051-2, HCSL-C). Natl Fire Prot.

Health Care Safety: Private Fire Brigades Library, 13 bks. 1000p. 37.00 (ISBN 0-685-58048-2, HCSL-FB). Natl Fire Prot.

Health Care Safety Reports & Articles. LC 75-27108. (Illus.). 129p. 1975. pap. 5.50 (ISBN 0-87765-056-X, SPP-32). Natl Fire Prot.

Health Care Safety: Supplemental Library, 13 bks. 1270p. 28.50 (ISBN 0-685-58050-4, HCSL-B). Natl Fire Prot.

High-Frequency Electrical Equipment in Hospitals. (Seventy Ser). 1970. pap. 2.00 (ISBN 0-685-58147-0, 76CM). Natl Fire Prot.

Hyperbaric Facilities. (Fifty Ser). 1970. pap. 2.00 (ISBN 0-685-58086-5, 56D). Natl Fire Prot.

Hypobaric Facilities. (Fifty Ser). 1972. pap. 2.00 (ISBN 0-685-58085-7, 56E). Natl Fire Prot.

Infection Control in the Hospital. 4th ed. LC 79-9862. (Illus.). 256p. 1980. pap. 16.25 (ISBN 0-87258-262-0, 2117). Am Hospital.

Luciano, J. R. Air Contamination Control in Hospitals. LC 76-39993. 479p. 1977. 39.50 (ISBN 0-306-30984-X, Plenum Pr). Plenum Pub.

McGrath, Robert. Emergency Removal of Patients & First Aid Fire Fighting in Hospitals. 3rd ed. (Illus.). 1974. pap. 4.15 (ISBN 0-87912-101-7, 12959). Natl Safety Coun.

Nonflammable Medical Gas Systems. (Fifty Ser). 1974. pap. 2.50 (ISBN 0-685-58084-9, 56F). Natl Fire Prot.

Pascal, A. Michael. Hospital Security & Safety. LC 77-14083. 177p. 1977. text ed. 28.00 (ISBN 0-89443-029-7). Aspen Systems.

Roth, Herbert H., et al. Electrical Safety in Health Care Facilities. (Clinical Engineering Ser.). 1975. 39.50 (ISBN 0-12-599050-2). Acad Pr.

Safety Clinic Two Handbook. 116p. 1981. pap. text ed. 20.00 (ISBN 0-86688-026-7). Joint Comm Hosp.

Spooner, Robert B. Hospital Electrical Safety Simplified. LC 79-66144. 144p. 1980. pap. text ed. 7.95 (ISBN 0-87664-431-0). Instru Soc.

Stanley, Paul E., ed. Handbook of Hospital Safety. 416p. 1981. 64.95 (ISBN 0-8493-0751-1). CRC Pr.

Teague, Paul E. Firesafety in Hospitals. LC 77-72080. (Illus.). 1977. pap. text ed. 58.50 (ISBN 0-87765-092-6, SL-24). Natl Fire Prot.

Theodore, Louis. Air Pollution Control for Hospitals & Medical Facilities. LC 80-19352. 332p. 1981. lib. bdg. 32.50 (ISBN 0-8240-7132-8). Garland Pub.

Turner, David R. Hospital Security Officer. (Orig.). 1976. pap. 6.00 (ISBN 0-668-03866-7). Arco.

HOSPITALS-SOCIOLOGICAL ASPECTS

see also Social Medicine

American Hospital Association. Essentials of Social Work Programs in Hospitals. 48p. 1971. pap. 5.00 (ISBN 0-87258-073-3, 1565). Am Hospital.

Bassett, S. Denton. Public Religious Services in the Hospital. (Illus.). 80p. 1976. 12.75 (ISBN 0-398-03563-6). C C Thomas.

Beuf, Ann H. Biting off the Bracelet: A Study of Children in Hospitals. LC 79-5047. 1979. 12.00 (ISBN 0-8122-7766-X). U of Pa Pr.

Fagerhaugh, Shizuko & Strauss, Anselm. Politics of Pain Management: Staff-Patient Interaction. LC 77-75114. 1977. pap. text ed. 16.95 (ISBN 0-201-06909-1, Med-Nurse). A-W.

Fox, Renee C. Experiment Perilous. LC 59-6816. 264p. 1974. pap. 6.50x (ISBN 0-8122-1040-9). U of Pa Pr.

Graham, James. So! You're Going to the Hospital! LC 68-20945. 178p. 1968. 5.00 (ISBN 0-87527-013-1); pap. 3.50 (ISBN 0-87527-038-7). Green.

Kirkpatrick, Joanna. The Sociology of an Indian Hospital Ward. 1980. 14.00x (ISBN 0-8364-0588-9). South Asia Bks.

Roberts, Cecilia M. Doctor & Patient in the Teaching Hospital: A Tale of Two Life-Worlds. LC 75-40629. 1977. 16.95 (ISBN 0-669-00453-7). Lexington Bks.

Scaria, K. S. There Is a Reason. 1980. 7.95 (ISBN 0-533-04443-X). Vantage.

HOSPITALS-STAFF

American Hospital Association. Auxiliary: New Concepts, New Directions. LC 74-22174. 244p. (Orig.). 1974. pap. 16.25 (ISBN 0-87258-160-8, 1075). Am Hospital.

--Fire Safety Training in Health Care Institutions. LC 75-20295. (Illus.). 60p. 1975. pap. 10.00 (ISBN 0-87258-163-2, 1595). Am Hospital.

--Technology Evaluation & Acquisition Methods (TEAM) for Hospitals. LC 79-21859. (Illus.). 212p. 1979. 200.00 (ISBN 0-87258-293-0, 1288). Am Hospital.

--The Volunteer Services Department in a Health Care Institution. LC 73-77522. 72p. 1973. pap. 7.50 (ISBN 0-87258-124-1, 2865). Am Hospital.

Ayres, Stephen. Medical Resident's Manual. 4th ed. 512p. 1981. 15.00 (ISBN 0-8385-6253-1). ACC.

Bean, Joseph, Jr. & Laliberty, Rene. Decentralizing Hospital Management: A Manual for Supervisors. 1980. pap. text ed. 8.95 (ISBN 0-201-00556-5). A-W.

Berkeley, A. Eliot & Barnes, Ann, eds. Labor Relations in Hospitals & Health Care Facilities. LC 75-45236. 110p. 1976. 10.00 (ISBN 0-87179-229-X). BNA.

Brill, Ernie. I Looked Over Jordan & Other Stories. LC 80-51042. 344p. (Orig.). 1980. 15.00 (ISBN 0-89608-118-4); pap. 6.00 (ISBN 0-89608-117-6). South End Pr.

Brockbank, W. The Honorary Medical Staff of the Manchester Royal Infirmary 1830 to 1948. 254p. 1965. 24.00x (ISBN 0-7190-1220-1, Pub. by Manchester U Pr England). State Mutual Bk.

Carey, Raymond G. Hospital Chaplains: Who Needs Them? 1974. pap. 7.00 (ISBN 0-87125-054-3). Cath Health.

Carrenno, Josephine & Larson, Diane. Spanish for Hospital Personnel. 1974. spiral bdg. 3.50 (ISBN 0-87488-722-4). Med Exam.

Diekelmann, Nancy & Broadwell, Martin M. The New Hospital Supervisor. (Illus.). 1977. pap. text ed. 8.95 (ISBN 0-201-00773-8). A-W.

Fagerhaugh, Shizuko & Strauss, Anselm. Politics of Pain Management: Staff-Patient Interaction. LC 77-75114. 1977. pap. text ed. 16.95 (ISBN 0-201-06909-1, Med-Nurse). A-W.

Fottler, Myron D. Manpower Substitution in the Hospital Industry: A Study of New York City Voluntary & Municipal Hospital Systems. LC 73-173280. (Special Studies in U.S. Economic, Social & Political Issues). 1972. 32.50x (ISBN 0-275-06150-7). Irvington.

Goldstein, Harold M. & Horowitz, Morris A. Utilization of Health Personnel: A Five Hospital Study. LC 78-12011. 180p. 1978. text ed. 22.00 (ISBN 0-89443-080-7). Aspen Systems.

Hospital Research & Educational Trust of the AHA. Being a Ward Clerk. (Illus.). 1967. pap. 9.95 (ISBN 0-87618-052-7). R J Brady.

--Training the Ward Clerk. (Illus.). 1967. pap. 9.95 (ISBN 0-87618-053-5). R J Brady.

How to Train Employees in Hospitals & Health Care Institutions. pap. 9.00 (ISBN 0-686-02542-3). Preston.

Isler, Charlotte. The Nurses' Aide. 2nd ed. LC 73-77723. 1973. pap. text ed. 5.95 (ISBN 0-8261-0913-6). Springer Pub.

John R. Zabka Associated, Inc. Compensation Report on Hospital-Based Physicians 1981-82: 6th Annual Report. 220p. 1981. 90.00 (ISBN 0-939326-02-7). Hosp Compensation.

--Hospital Salary Survey Report 1981-82: 11th Annual Report. 200p. 1981. 90.00 (ISBN 0-939326-01-9). Hosp Compensation.

Lee, Mary P. The Team That Runs Your Hospital. LC 80-36762. 1980. 9.50 (ISBN 0-664-32669-2). Westminster.

Lipson, Stephen H. & Hensel, Mary D. Hospital Manpower Budget Preparation Manual. LC 75-20992. 200p. 1975. pap. text ed. 15.00 (ISBN 0-914904-11-6). Health Admin Pr.

Lunn, J. A. Health of Staff in Hospitals. 1975. pap. 10.00x (ISBN 0-433-19905-9). Intl Ideas.

Massachusetts General Hospital Department of Nursing, et al, eds. Manual of Nursing Procedures. 1980. text ed. write for info. (ISBN 0-316-54958-4); pap. text ed. write for info. (ISBN 0-316-54958-4). Little.

Miller, Richard U. Hospital Labor Relations. (Wisconsin Business Monographs: No. 11). (Illus.). 104p. 1980. 7.50 (ISBN 0-86603-003-4). Bureau Busn Res U Wis.

Miller, Richard V., et al. The Impact of Collective Bargaining on Hospitals. 1979. 26.50 (ISBN 0-03-051346-4). Praeger.

Munk, Robert J. & Lovett, Marc. Hospitalwide Education & Training. LC 77-13675. (Illus.). 1977. casebound 8.00 (ISBN 0-87914-045-3, 9615). Hosp Res & Educ.

Payne, Beverly C. The Quality of Medical Care: Evaluation & Improvement. LC 75-27157. 1976. 8.00 (ISBN 0-87914-029-1, 9153). Hosp Res & Educ.

Rambo, B. J. Ward Clerk Skills. LC 77-1819. (Nursing & Allied Health Ser.). 1977. pap. text ed. 5.95 (ISBN 0-07-051176-4, G); teacher's manual & key 2.75 (ISBN 0-07-051177-2). McGraw.

Record, Jane C. Staffing Primary Care in Nineteen Ninety: Physician Replacement & Cost Savings. (Health Care & Society Ser.: No. 6). 1981. text ed. 23.50 (ISBN 0-8261-3370-3); pap. text ed. cancelled (ISBN 0-8261-3371-1). Springer Pub.

Rudman, Jack. Hospital Attendant. (Career Examination Ser.: C-325). (Cloth bdg. avail. on request). 6.00 (ISBN 0-8373-0325-7). Natl Learning.

--Hospital Clerk. (Career Examination Ser.: C-328). (Cloth bdg. avail. on request). pap. 8.00 (ISBN 0-8373-0328-1). Natl Learning.

--Hospital Security Officer. (Career Examination Ser.: C-353). (Cloth bdg. avail. on request). pap. 8.00 (ISBN 0-8373-0353-2). Natl Learning.

Sloan, Frank A. & Steinwald, Bruce. Hospital Labor Markets: Analysis of Wages & Work Force Composition. LC 79-5324. (Illus.). 208p. 1980. 22.95x (ISBN 0-669-03385-5). Lexington Bks.

Smith, D. N. A Forgotten Sector: The Training of Ancillary Staff in Hospitals. 1969. text ed. 22.00 (ISBN 0-08-013379-7); pap. text ed. 10.75 (ISBN 0-08-013378-9). Pergamon.

Society for Hospital Social Work Directors of the American Hospital Association. Social Work Staff Development for Health Care. LC 76-41793. 36p. 1976. pap. 7.25 (ISBN 0-87258-322-8, 2550). Am Hospital.

Stevens, Rosemary, et al. Alien Doctors: Foreign Medical Graduates in American Hospitals. LC 77-12934. (Health, Medicine & Society Ser.). 365p. 1978. 29.95 (ISBN 0-471-82455-0, Pub. by Wiley-Interscience). Wiley.

Teters, Dolly G. Ward Clerk Manual. 1978. 4.95 (ISBN 0-533-03388-8). Vantage.

Yanda, Roman L. Doctors As Managers of Health Teams: A Career Guide for Hospital Based Physicians. LC 76-54735. 1977. 15.95 (ISBN 0-8144-5432-1). Am Mgmt.

Zerubavel, Eviatar. Patterns of Time in Hospital Life: A Sociological Perspective. LC 78-11385. (Illus.). 1979. lib. bdg. 13.50x (ISBN 0-226-98160-6). U of Chicago Pr.

HOSPITALS-STAFF-PROGRAMMED INSTRUCTION

Dunkel, Patty L. Curriculum for Educators in Health Care Institutions: Proceedings & Recommendations of an Invitational Conference. LC 77-26933. (Illus.). 1978. pap. 10.00 (ISBN 0-87914-046-1, 9620). Hosp Res & Educ.

HOSPITALS-VOCATIONAL GUIDANCE

Bloom, Gretchen. The Language of Hospital Services in English. (English for Careers Ser.). (Illus.). (gr. 10 up). 1976. pap. 3.50 (ISBN 0-88345-270-7). Regents Pub.

Carlson, Richard O. Orderly Career Opportunities. LC 79-54079. 1979. 4.95 (ISBN 0-936276-09-6). Ctr Educ Policy Mgmt.

John, Hughes. Janet the Hospital Helper. (People Working Today Ser). (Illus.). 40p. 1975. pap. 1.85 (ISBN 0-915510-02-2). Janus Bks.

Kirk, Richard. Aim for a Job in a Hospital. LC 68-10138. (Aim High Vocational Guidance Ser.). (Illus., Photos). (gr. 7 up). 1968. PLB 5.97 (ISBN 0-8239-0096-7). Rosen Pr.

Kirk, W. Richard. Aim for a Job in Hospital Work. LC 74-114137. (Career Guidance Ser.). 124p. 1971. pap. 3.95 (ISBN 0-668-02230-2). Arco.

--Aim for a Job in Hospital Work. LC 74-114137. (Career Guidance Ser.). 124p. 1971. pap. 3.95 (ISBN 0-668-02230-2). Arco.

Murphy, Frank D. Model & Department Policy Statement with Job Descriptions for Hospitals. (Medical Bks.). 1980. lib. bdg. 64.95 (ISBN 0-8161-2199-0, Hall Medical). G K Hall.

Smith, D. N. A Forgotten Sector: The Training of Ancillary Staff in Hospitals. 1969. text ed. 22.00 (ISBN 0-08-013379-7); pap. text ed. 10.75 (ISBN 0-08-013378-9). Pergamon.

HOSPITALS-CANADA

Agnew, G. Harvey. Canadian Hospitals, Nineteen Twenty to Nineteen Seventy: A Dramatic Half Century. LC 73-78942. (Illus.). 1974. 25.00x (ISBN 0-8020-1994-3). U of Toronto Pr.

American Hospital Association. Directory of Shared Services Organizations for Health Care Institutions, 1981. 186p. (Orig.). 1981. write for info. (ISBN 0-87258-354-6, 1208). Am Hospital.

HOSPITALS-GREAT BRITAIN

Ayers, Gwendoline M. England's First State Hospitals & the Metropolitan Asylums Board 1867-1930. LC 75-126766. (Wellcome Institute of the History of Medicine). (Illus.). 1971. 34.50x (ISBN 0-520-01792-7). U of Cal Pr.

Clay, R. M. Mediaeval Hospitals of England. new ed. 357p. 1966. 25.00x (ISBN 0-7146-1292-8, F Cass Co). Biblio Dist.

Norton, D. Hospitals & the Long-Stay Patient. 1967. 21.00 (ISBN 0-08-011053-3); pap. 9.75 (ISBN 0-08-011052-5). Pergamon.

Sell's Hospital & Surgical in Great Britain, 1975. rev. ed. 1975. pap. 10.50x (ISBN 0-8277-2614-7). British Bk Ctr.

Wellman, Frank & Palmer, Paul. London Specialist Postgraduate Hospitals. (King Edward's Hospital Fund Ser.). 1975. pap. 15.00x (ISBN 0-8464-0577-6). Beekman Pubs.

Woodward, John. To Do the Sick No Harm: A Study of the British Voluntary Hospital System to 1875. (International Library of Social Policy). 1974. 20.00x (ISBN 0-7100-7970-2). Routledge & Kegan.

HOSPITALS, CONVALESCENT

see also Convalescence

Pharmaceutical Services in the Long Term Care Facility. 57th ed. 1975. 3.00 (ISBN 0-917330-01-3). Am Pharm Assn.

HOSPITALS, FIELD

see Medicine, Military

HOSPITALS, INSANE

see Psychiatric Hospitals

HOSPITALS, PSYCHIATRIC

see Psychiatric Hospitals

HOST-PARASITE RELATIONSHIPS

see also Host-Virus Relationships

Andrews, Michael. The Life That Lives on Man. LC 76-53299. (Illus.). 1978. pap. 4.95 (ISBN 0-8008-4820-9). Taplinger.

Annual Oholo Biological Conference, 21st, Israel, March 1976. Host-Parasite Relationships in Systemic Mycoses: Proceedings. Beemer, A. M., et al, eds. Incl. Methodology, Pathology & Immunology, Pt. I. (Contributions to Microbiology & Immunology: Vol. 3) (ISBN 3-8055-2443-9); Specific Diseases & Therapy, Pt. II. (Contributions to Microbiology & Immunology: Vol. 4) (ISBN 3-8055-2444-7). (Illus.). 1978. pap. 46.75 ea. S Karger.

Bossche, H. Van Den. Biochemistry of Parasites & Host-Parasite Relationships. 1977. 66.00 (ISBN 0-7204-0592-0, North-Holland). Elsevier.

Braun, W. & Ungar, J., eds. Non-Specific Factors Influencing Host Resistance: A Reexamination. (Illus.). 1973. 80.25 (ISBN 3-8055-1598-7). S Karger.

Daly, J. M. Recognition & Specificity in Plant Host-Parasite Interactions. 355p. text ed. 49.50 (ISBN 0-8391-1440-0). Univ Park.

Day, Peter R. Genetics of Host-Parasite Interaction. LC 73-17054. (Illus.). 1974. text ed. 23.95x (ISBN 0-7167-0844-2). W H Freeman.

Dickinson, C. H. & Lucas, J. A. Plant Pathology & Plant Pathogens. LC 77-8689. (Basic Microbiology Ser.: Vol. 6). 1977. pap. 13.95 (ISBN 0-470-99212-3). Halsted Pr.

Fallis, A. M., ed. Ecology & Physiology of Parasites: A Symposium. LC 70-151365. 1971. 25.00x (ISBN 0-8020-1730-4). U of Toronto Pr.

Gaafar, S. M., et al, eds. Pathology of Parasitic Diseases. LC 72-108014. (Illus.). 1971. 15.00 (ISBN 0-911198-28-8). Purdue.

Gallin, John I. & Fauci, Anthony S., eds. Advances in Host Defense Mechanisms, Vol. 1. 1981. text ed. 32.00 (ISBN 0-89004-574-7). Raven.

Grieco, Michael H., ed. Infections in the Abnormal Host. LC 79-65400. (Illus.). 1980. 75.00 (ISBN 0-914316-18-4). Yorke Med.

Heitefuss, R. & Willaims, P. H., eds. Physiological Plant Pathology. (Encyclopedia of Plant Physiology: Vol. 4). 1976. 100.70 (ISBN 0-387-07557-7). Springer-Verlag.

Kennedy, C. R., ed. Ecological Aspects of Parasitology. 1976. 85.50 (ISBN 0-7204-0602-1, North-Holland). Elsevier.

McKelvey, John J., Jr., et al, eds. Vectors of Disease Agents: Interactions with Plants, Animals, & Men. 350p. 1981. 37.50 (ISBN 0-03-056887-0). Praeger.

Muller, Paul, ed. Verhandlungen der Gesellschaft Fur Okologie, Gottingen 1976. 1977. pap. 60.50 (ISBN 90-6193-568-7, Pub. by Junk Pubs Netherlands). Kluwer Boston.

Nickol, Brent B., ed. Host-Parasite Interfaces. 1979. 16.00 (ISBN 0-12-518750-5). Acad Pr.
O'Grady, Francis & Smith, H., eds. Microbial Perturbation of Host Defenses. LC 81-66700. (The Beecham Colloquia). 1981. price not set (ISBN 0-12-524750-8). Acad Pr.
Papavero, N. The World Oestridae (Diptera), Mammals & Continental Drift. (Series Entomologica: No. 14). 1977. lib. bdg. 45.00 (ISBN 90-6193-124-X, Pub. by Junk Pubs Netherlands). Kluwer Boston.
Rodger, Frederick C., ed. Onchocerciasis in Zaire. 1977. text ed. 50.00 (ISBN 0-08-020619-0). Pergamon.
Schlessinger, David, ed. Microbiology 1974. LC 74-33538. (Annual Microbiology Ser.). 1975. 22.00 (ISBN 0-914826-02-6). Am Soc Microbio.
Soulsby, E. J., ed. Pathophysiology of Parasitic Infections. 1976. 26.00 (ISBN 0-12-655365-3). Acad Pr.
Street, Philip. Animal Partners & Parasites. LC 72-6630. (Illus.). 220p. 1975. 10.95 (ISBN 0-8008-0255-1). Taplinger.
Zuckerman, A., ed. Dynamic Aspects of Host-Parasite Relationships, Vol. 2. LC 70-189940. 225p. 1976. 46.95 (ISBN 0-470-98430-9). Halsted Pr.
Zuckerman, Avivah & Weiss, David W., eds. Dynamic Aspects of Host Parasite Relationships, Vol.1. 1973. 35.50 (ISBN 0-12-782001-9). Acad Pr.

HOST-VIRUS RELATIONSHIPS

Andrews, Michael. The Life That Lives on Man. LC 76-53299. (Illus.). 1978. pap. 4.95 (ISBN 0-8008-4820-9). Taplinger.
Beam, T. R., ed. Antibiotics, Hosts & Host Defences Innosocomial Infections. 20.00 (ISBN 0-915340-07-0). PJD Pubns.
Chakravorty, M., ed. Molecular Basis of Host-Virus Interaction. LC 77-16743. (Illus.). 1979. lib. bdg. 65.00 (ISBN 0-89500-009-1). Sci Pr.
Esau, Katherine. Viruses in Plant Hosts: Form, Distribution, & Pathologic Effects. LC 68-9831. (Illus.). 1968. 25.00x (ISBN 0-299-05110-2). U of Wis Pr.
Fraenkel-Conrat, H. & Wagner, R. R., eds. Comprehensive Virology, Vol. 10: Regulation & Genetics - Viral Gene Expression & Integeration. (Illus.). 496p. 1977. 39.50 (ISBN 0-306-35150-1, Plenum Pr). Plenum Pub.
Grieco, Michael H., ed. Infections in the Abnormal Host. LC 79-65400. (Illus.). 1980. 75.00 (ISBN 0-914316-18-4). Yorke Med.
Juhasz, Stephen E. & Plummer, Gordon. Host-Virus Relationships in Mycobacterium, Nocardia & Actinomyces: Proceedings. (Illus.). 248p. 1970. photocopy ed. spiral 24.75 (ISBN 0-398-00953-8). C C Thomas.
Kolber, Alan, ed. Tumor Virus - Host Cell Interaction. LC 75-16203. (NATO Advanced Study Institutes Ser.--Series A: Life Sciences: Vol. 5). 460p. 1975. 42.50 (ISBN 0-306-35605-8, Plenum Pr). Plenum Pub.
Mahy, B. W. & Barry, R. D., eds. Negative Strand Viruses & the Host Cell. 1978. 92.50 (ISBN 0-12-465350-2). Acad Pr.
Poste, G. & Nicholson, G., eds. Virus Infection & the Cell Surface. (Cell Surface Reviews: Vol. 2). 1977. 67.00 (ISBN 0-7204-0598-X, North-Holland). Elsevier.
Shugar, D. & Shugar, D., eds. Virus-Cell Interaction & Viral Antimetabolites, Vol. 22. 1972. 37.00 (ISBN 0-12-640866-1). Acad Pr.
Smith, Kenneth M. Virus-Insect Relationships. (Illus.). 1977. text ed. 30.00x (ISBN 0-582-46612-1). Longman.
Solheim, B. Cell Wall Biochemistry Related to Specificity in Host-Plant Pathogen Interactions. 1977. pap. 43.00x (ISBN 82-00-05141-2, Dist. by Columbia U Pr). Universitet.

HOSTILITIES

see War; War (International Law); War, Maritime (International Law)

HOSTILITY (PSYCHOLOGY)

see also Fighting (Psychology)

Gottschalk, Louis A., et al. Manual of Instructions for Using the Gottschalk-Gleser Content Analysis Scales: Anxiety, Hostility, Social Alienation - Personal Disorganization. 1979. Repr. of 1969 ed. 14.00x (ISBN 0-520-03814-2). U of Cal Pr.
Layden, Milton. Escaping the Hostility Trap: The One Sure Way to Deal with Impossible People. LC 76-54672. 1977. pap. 3.95 (ISBN 0-13-283606-8). P-H.
--Escaping the Hostility Trap: The One Sure Way to Deal with Impossible People. LC 76-54672. 1977. 7.95 (ISBN 0-13-283580-0). P-H.
Stoller, Robert J. Perversion. 1976. pap. 3.45 (ISBN 0-440-56907-9, Delta). Dell.
Sumrall, Lester. Hostility. 1981. pap. 3.95 (ISBN 0-8407-5765-4). Nelson.
Zillman, Dolf. Hostility & Aggression. LC 79-18641. (Candidate for Social Psychology Ser.). 1979. 24.95x (ISBN 0-470-26832-8). Halsted Pr.

HOT CAKES

see Pancakes, Waffles, etc.

HOT-HOUSES

see Greenhouses

HOT RODS

see Automobiles, Racing; Automobiles, Racing-Motors

HOT SPRINGS

see Springs

HOT WATER DISCHARGES INTO RIVERS, LAKES, ETC.

see Thermal Pollution of Rivers, Lakes, etc.

HOT-WATER HEATERS

see Water Heaters

HOT-WATER HEATING

Building Research Advisory Board - Federal Construction Council. High-Temperature Water for Heating & Light Process Loads. 1960. pap. 3.00 (ISBN 0-309-00753-4). Natl Acad Pr.

HOT WATER SUPPLY

see also Water Heaters

Kut, D. Heating & Hot Water Services in Buildings. 1968. 32.00 (ISBN 0-08-012218-3). Pergamon.
Shaw, E. W. Heating & Hot Water Services. 1979. 32.95 (ISBN 0-8464-0048-0); pap. 18.95 (ISBN 0-8464-0049-9). Beekman Pubs.
--Heating & Hot-Water Services: Selected Subjects with Worked Examples in SI Units. 4th ed. 241p. pap. text ed. 22.75x (ISBN 0-246-11229-8, Pub. by Granada England). Renouf.
Sussman, Art & Frazier, Richard. Handmade Hot Water Systems. LC 78-71915. pap. 4.95 (ISBN 0-932708-00-5). Garcia River.

HOTCHKISS, JEDEDIAH, 1828-1899

McDonald, Archie P., ed. Make Me a Map of the Valley: The Civil War Journal of Stonewall Jackson's Topographer. LC 73-82036. (Bicentennial Series in American Studies: No. 1). (Illus.). 1980. Repr. of 1973 ed. 15.00 (ISBN 0-87074-137-3). SMU Press.

HOTEL ADMINISTRATION

see Hotel Management

HOTEL MANAGEMENT

see also Stewards

Almarode, Richard L. Guidelines for Hospitality Education in Junior Colleges. 1967. pap. 2.50 (ISBN 0-87117-020-5). Am Assn Comm Jr Coll.
Argiry, George P. Catch the Sticky Fingers: Guide to Bar Management & Mixed Drinks. 1977. pap. 5.00 (ISBN 0-931868-00-9). Beninda.
Axler, Bruce H. Increasing Lodging Revenues & Restaurant Checks. 1974. pap. 3.95 (ISBN 0-672-96121-0). Bobbs.
--Room Care for Hotels & Motels. 1974. pap. 3.95 (ISBN 0-672-96125-3). Bobbs.
--Security for Hotels, Motels, & Restaurants. 1974. pap. 3.95 (ISBN 0-672-96123-7). Bobbs.
Berkman, Frank W., et al. Convention Management & Service. (Illus.). 238p. 1979. 18.95x (ISBN 0-86612-002-5). Educ Inst Am Hotel.
Binham, Philip, et al. Hotel English. LC 80-42264. (Illus.). 128p. 1981. pap. 4.95 (ISBN 0-08-025340-7). Pergamon.
Borsenik, Frank D. The Management of Maintenance & Engineering Systems in Hospitality Industries. LC 78-13677. (Service Management Ser.). 1979. text ed. 24.95 (ISBN 0-471-03213-1). Wiley.
Branson, Joan C. & Lennox, Margaret. Hotel, Hostel & Hospital Housekeeping. 3rd ed. (Illus.). 1976. pap. 12.95x (ISBN 0-7131-1974-8). Intl Ideas.
Burstein. Management of Hotel & Motel Security. (Occupational Safety & Health Ser.: Vol. 5). 216p. 1980. 26.50 (ISBN 0-8247-1002-9). Dekker.
Buzby, Walter J. & Paine, David. Hotel & Motel Security Management. LC 76-12555. 256p. 1976. 17.95 (ISBN 0-913708-24-0). Butterworth.
Coffman, C. DeWitt. Hospitality for Sale: Techniques of Promoting Business for Hospitality Establishments. LC 79-28567. (Illus.). 339p. 1980. 17.56x (ISBN 0-86612-000-9); text ed. 21.95 (ISBN 0-686-28892-0). Educ Inst Am Hotel.
Dukas, Peter. Hotel Front Office Management & Operation. 3rd ed. 186p. 1970. text ed. write for info. (ISBN 0-697-08400-0); solutions manual avail. (ISBN 0-686-66349-7). Wm C Brown.
Eyster, James J. The Negotiation & Administration of Hotel Management Contracts. 2nd, rev. ed. (Illus.). 209p. 1980. text ed. 22.95 (ISBN 0-937056-04-9). Cornell U Sch Hotel.
Gray, William S. & Liquori, Salvatore C. Hotel & Motel Management & Operations. (Illus.). 1980. text ed. 19.95 (ISBN 0-13-394908-7). P-H.
Green, Eric F., et al. Profitable Food & Beverage Management: Operations. 1978. text ed. 21.95 (ISBN 0-8104-9466-3). Hayden.
Gunnar, Peter M. & Burkhart, Judith A. The Management of Hotel & Motel Condominiums. (Illus.). 1978. text ed. 17.50 (ISBN 0-937056-01-4, A&F16). Cornell U Sch Hotel.
Hertzson, Seymour. Hospitality Industry Cooperative Training. LC 75-142506. 1971. pap. text ed. 13.95 (ISBN 0-672-96098-2); tchr's manual 6.67 (ISBN 0-672-96099-0). Bobbs.
Kalt, Nathan. Introduction to the Hospitality Industry. LC 71-142505. 1971. text ed. 13.50 (ISBN 0-672-96086-9); tchr's manual 6.67 (ISBN 0-672-96088-5); wkbk. 6.50 (ISBN 0-672-96087-7). Bobbs.
--Legal Aspects of Hotel, Motel, & Restaurant Operation. 1st ed. LC 78-142504. 1971. 19.95 (ISBN 0-672-96089-3); tchrs' manual 6.67 (ISBN 0-672-96091-5); wkbk. 9.95 (ISBN 0-672-96090-7). Bobbs.
Keiser, James. Principles & Practice of Management in the Hospitality Industry. LC 80-12866. 1980. text ed. 18.95 (ISBN 0-8436-2182-6). CBI Pub.
Kreck, Lothar A. Operational Problem Solving for the Hotel & Restaurant Industry. LC 78-15134. 1978. pap. 12.95 (ISBN 0-8436-2132-X). CBI Pub.
Kreck, Lothar A. & McConnell, Jon P. Hospitality Management: Avoiding Legal Pitfalls. 1976. 17.95 (ISBN 0-8436-2064-1). CBI Pub.
Kreck, Lothar A. & McCracken, John W., eds. Dimensions of Hospitality Management: (an Industry Performance in Seven Acts, 2 vols. LC 75-15701. 824p. 1975. 17.95 ea. Vol. 1. Vol. Ii (ISBN 0-8436-2085-4). Set (ISBN 0-8436-2085-4). CBI Pub.
Lattin, Gerald W. Modern Hotel & Motel Management. 3rd ed. LC 77-10007. (Illus.). 1977. text ed. 16.95x (ISBN 0-7167-0483-8). W H Freeman.
Laughton, Tom. Pavillions by the Sea: Memoirs of a Hotel Keeper. (Illus.). 1977. 12.50 (ISBN 0-7011-2205-6). Transatlantic.
Lundberg, Donald E. & Armatas, James P. The Management of People in Hotels, Restaurants, & Clubs. 4th ed. 350p. 1980. write for info. (ISBN 0-697-08410-8). Wm C Brown.
Lyda, Harold. Motel-Hotel Management Directory. 1977. looseleaf 29.95 (ISBN 0-915260-06-9). Atcom.
Molina Aranda, Fernando. Diccionario Tecnico Hostelero. 245p. (Espn.). 1972. pap. 12.25 (ISBN 84-85087-02-X, S-50021). French & Eur.
Morgan, William J., Jr. Hospitality Personnel Management. LC 78-22031. 1979. text ed. 15.95 (ISBN 0-8436-2138-9). CBI Pub.
Powers, Thomas F. Introduction to Management in the Hospitality Industry. LC 78-23205. (Service Management Ser.). 1979. text ed. 19.95 (ISBN 0-471-03128-3); tchrs. manual (ISBN 0-471-05355-4). Wiley.
Quest, Miles. How to Buy Your Own Hotel. 236p. 1981. 25.00x (ISBN 0-7198-2764-7, Pub. by Northwood Bks). State Mutual Bk.
Renner, Peter F. Basic Hotel Front Office Procedures. LC 80-17905. 295p. 1980. pap. text ed. 13.95 (ISBN 0-8436-2190-7). CBI Pub.
Sapienza, D., et al. Readings on Managing Hotels-Restaurants-Institutions. 1977. pap. text ed. 13.95x (ISBN 0-8104-9469-8); net instructor's manual 1.95 (ISBN 0-8104-9473-6). Hayden.
Sell's Hotel, Restaurant & Canteen Supplies in Great Britain, 1975. rev. ed. 1975. pap. 10.95x (ISBN 0-8277-2613-9). British Bk Ctr.
Stefanelli, John M. Selection & Procurement for the Hospitality Industry. LC 80-20604. (Wiley Service Management Ser.). 502p. 1981. text ed. 19.95 (ISBN 0-471-04538-1). Wiley.
Stevenson, W. C. Making & Managing a Pub. LC 79-51101. (Making & Managing Ser.). (Illus.). 1980. 17.95 (ISBN 0-7153-7801-5). David & Charles.
Stokes, Arch. The Collective Bargaining Handbook for Hotels, Restaurants & Institutions. (The Stokes Employee Relations Ser.). 352p. 1981. spiral bdg. 54.95 (ISBN 0-8436-2149-4). CBI Pub.
--The Wage & Hour Handbook for Hotels, Restaurants, & Institutions. LC 78-9278. 1978. 15.95 (ISBN 0-8436-2133-8). CBI Pub.
Vallen, J., et al. The Art & Science of Managing Hotels-Restaurants-Institutions. Orig. Title: The Art & Science of Modern Innkeeping. 1978. 14.25x (ISBN 0-8104-9470-1). Hayden.
White, Paul B. & Beckley, Helen. Hotel Reception. 3rd ed. (Illus.). 1978. pap. 12.95x (ISBN 0-7131-0191-1). Intl Ideas.
Witzky, Herbert K. Modern Hotel-Motel Management Methods. rev.,2nd ed. 1976. text ed. 15.25x (ISBN 0-8104-9467-1). Hayden.
Worsdall, V. Special English for Hotel Personnel, Bk. 2: Bar & Restaurant Employees. 1972. pap. 2.75 (ISBN 0-02-976030-5); 4 tapes 65.00 (ISBN 0-02-985260-9). Macmillan.

HOTEL MANAGEMENT-VOCATIONAL GUIDANCE

Brymer, Robert A. Introduction to Hotel & Restaurant Management: A Book of Readings. 2nd ed. 1979. pap. text ed. 12.95 (ISBN 0-8403-2478-2, 40247801). Kendall-Hunt.
Keister, Douglas C. & Wilson, Ralph D. Selected Readings for an Introduction to Hotel & Restaurant Management. 2nd ed. 454p. 1971. pap. 6.95x (ISBN 0-8211-1013-6); text ed. 5.56 10 or more copies (ISBN 0-686-66702-6). McCutchan.
Sonnabend, Roger P. Your Future in Hotel Management. LC 64-10199. (Careers in Depth Ser). (gr. 7 up). 1975. PLB 5.97 (ISBN 0-8239-0036-3). Rosen Pr.

HOTELLING, HAROLD, 1895-

Olkin, Ingram, et al, eds. Contributions to Probability & Statistics: Essays in Honor of Harold Hotelling. 1960. 15.00x (ISBN 0-8047-0596-8). Stanford U Pr.

HOTELS, TAVERNS, ETC.

see also Coffee Houses; Hotel Management; Motels; Music-Halls (Variety-Theaters, Cabarets, etc.); Restaurants, Lunchrooms, etc.; Tourist Camps, Hostels, etc.;
also names of individual hotels and restaurants

Ade, George. The Old-Time Saloon: Not Wet--Not Dry, Just History. LC 77-181797. (Illus.). xii, 176p. 1975. Repr. of 1931 ed. 22.00 (ISBN 0-8103-4076-3). Gale.
Aloi, G. Hotel-Motel (Architecture) (Illus.). 1970. 40.00 (ISBN 0-685-12023-6). Heinman.
Axler, Bruce H. Building Care for Hospitality Operations. 1974. pap. 3.95 (ISBN 0-672-96124-5). Bobbs.
Borsenik, Frank D. Maintenance & Engineering for Lodging & Foodservice Facilities. rev. ed. (Illus.). 279p. 1977. Repr. of 1975 ed. 18.95x (ISBN 0-86612-004-1). Educ Inst Am Hotel.
Brown, Robert L. Saloons of the American West. (Illus.). 144p. 16.50 (ISBN 0-913582-24-7). Sundance.
Burstein, Harvey. Hotel Security Management. LC 74-14039. 138p. 1975. text ed. 22.95 (ISBN 0-275-09820-6). Praeger.
Busk, Fred & Andrews, Peter. Country Inns of America: Pacific Northwest. LC 81-1617. (Illus.). 96p. 1981. pap. 8.95 (ISBN 0-03-059181-3, Owl Bk). HR&W.
Calkins, Raymond. Substitutes for the Saloon: An Investigation Originally Made for the Committee of Fifty. LC 75-137181. (Poverty U.S.A. Historical Record Ser). 1971. Repr. of 1919 ed. 19.00 (ISBN 0-405-03119-X). Arno.
Christopher, Robert & Christopher, Ellen. America's Favorite Restaurants & Inns: From Budget to Luxury. 1024p. 1980. pap. 11.95 (ISBN 0-930570-01-4, Dist. by Morrow). Travel Discover.
Coplin, Maxine. A National Guide to Guest Homes. (Illus., Orig.). 1981. pap. 4.95 (ISBN 0-686-29699-0, 0-96057804). Home on Arrange.
Country Inns: California & the West, 1981-1982. 1981. 4.95 (ISBN 0-89102-234-1). B Franklin.
Country Inns: Mid Atlantic, 1981-1982. 1981. 4.95 (ISBN 0-89102-233-3). B Franklin.
Country Inns: Mid-West & Rocky Mountains, 1981-1982. 1981. 4.95 (ISBN 0-89102-210-4). B Franklin.
Country Inns of Great Britain. 1979. pap. 4.95 (ISBN 0-89102-162-0). B Franklin.
Country Inns: 1981-1982. 1981. 4.95 (ISBN 0-89102-235-X). B Franklin.
Country New England Inns: 1981-1982. 1981. 4.95 (ISBN 0-89102-232-5). B Franklin.
Crawford, H. W. & McDowell, Milton C. Math Workbook for Foodservice-Lodging. 1980. pap. 12.95 (ISBN 0-8436-2197-4); o. p. 11.95 (ISBN 0-8436-0534-0); answer bk. o. p. 1.95 (ISBN 0-8436-0538-3). CBI Pub.
Crawford, Mary C. Little Pilgrimages Among Old New England Inns: Being an Account of Little Journeys to Various Quaint Inns & Hostelries of Colonial New England. LC 76-107629. (Illus.). 1970. Repr. of 1907 ed. 22.00 (ISBN 0-8103-3536-0). Gale.
Crosette, Barbara, ed. America's Wonderful Little Hotels & Inns. 1980. 13.95 (ISBN 0-525-05370-0, Thomas Congdon Book); pap. 6.95 (ISBN 0-525-03005-0, Thomas Congdon Book). Dutton.
Crossette, Barbara. America's Wonderful Little Hotels & Inns. (Illus.). 400p. 1981. 14.95 (ISBN 0-312-92016-4); pap. 8.95 (ISBN 0-312-92017-2). St Martin.
Dallas, Sandra. No More Than Five in a Bed: Colorado Hotels in the Old Days. (Illus.). 1967. 9.95 (ISBN 0-8061-0742-1). U of Okla Pr.
Dickerman, Pat. Farm, Ranch, & Country Vacations. (Illus.). 1981. pap. 7.95 (ISBN 0-913214-03-5). Farm & Ranch.
Earle, A. M. Stage-Coach & Tavern Days. LC 68-26351. (American History & Americana Ser., No. 47). (Illus.). 1969. Repr. of 1900 ed. lib. bdg. 58.95 (ISBN 0-8383-0280-7). Haskell.

Earle, Alice M. Stage Coach & Tavern Days. LC 70-81558. (Illus.). Repr. of 1900 ed. 25.00 (ISBN 0-405-08476-5, Blom Pubns). Arno.

--Stage-Coach & Tavern Days. LC 68-17962. (Illus.). 1968. Repr. of 1900 ed. 24.00 (ISBN 0-8103-3431-3). Gale.

End, Henry. Interiors: Second Book of Hotels. (Illus.). 1978. 26.50 (ISBN 0-8230-7281-9, Whitney Lib). Watson-Guptill.

Endell, Fritz A. Old Tavern Signs: An Excursion into the History of Hospitality. LC 68-26572. (Illus.). 1968. Repr. of 1916 ed. 22.00 (ISBN 0-8103-3505-0). Gale.

Etsell, Karen & Brennan, Elaine. How to Open a Country Inn. (Illus.). 166p. 1981. pap. 6.95 (ISBN 0-912944-69-2). Berkshire Traveller.

Fales, John T. Functional Housekeeping in Hotels & Motels. LC 72-142508. 1971. text ed. 14.50 (ISBN 0-672-96080-X); tchr's manual 6.67 (ISBN 0-672-96082-6); wkbk. 6.50 (ISBN 0-672-96081-8). Bobbs.

Gardner, Roberta H. Country Inns of America: The Great Lakes. LC 81-1618. (Illus.). 96p. 1981. pap. 8.95 (ISBN 0-03-059159-7, Owl Bk). HR&W.

Harris, Peter & Hazzard, Peter. Accounting & Financial Measurement in the Hotel & Catering Industry, 2 vols. 2nd ed. 1977. 29.95x (ISBN 0-686-31785-8). Vol. 1 (ISBN 0-7198-2543-1). Vol. 2 (ISBN 0-7198-2553-9). Intl Ideas.

Hertzson, David. Hotel-Motel Marketing. LC 76-142509. 1971. text ed. 14.50 (ISBN 0-672-96083-4); tchr's manual 6.67 (ISBN 0-672-96085-0); wkbk. 6.95 (ISBN 0-672-96084-2). Bobbs.

Hitchcock, Anthony & Lindgren, Jean. The Compleat Traveler's Guide to Inns & Guesthouses of Country New England. (Illus.). pap. 4.95 (ISBN 0-89102-135-3). B Franklin.

--Country Inns of Canada. 1979. pap. 5.95 (ISBN 0-686-58474-0) (ISBN 0-89102-161-2). B Franklin.

--Country Inns of the Middle Atlantic States. 1979. pap. 4.95 (ISBN 0-89102-157-4). B Franklin.

--Country Inns of the Middle Atlantic States. 1979. pap. 4.95 (ISBN 0-89102-157-4). B Franklin.

--Country Inns of the Midwest & Rocky Mountain States. 1979. pap. 4.95 (ISBN 0-89102-159-0). B Franklin.

--Country Inns of the West & Southwest. 1979. pap. 4.95 (ISBN 0-89102-160-4). B Franklin.

Horowitz, Morris A. New York Hotel Industry: A Labor Relations Study. LC 60-7992. (Wertheim Publications in Industrial Relations Ser). (Illus.). 1960. 14.00x (ISBN 0-674-61900-5). Harvard U Pr.

International Hotel Assn., ed. International Hotel Guide 1981. 34th ed. LC 52-16324. 455p. 1981. pap. 30.00x (ISBN 0-8002-2798-0). Intl Pubns Serv.

Kasavana, Michael L. Hotel Information Systems: A Contemporary Approach to Front Office Procedures. LC 78-9310. 1978. text ed. 17.95 (ISBN 0-8436-2131-1). CBI Pub.

Keown, Ian M. Lover's Guide to America. (Illus.). 384p. 1974. 8.95 (ISBN 0-02-562300-1). Macmillan.

--Lovers' Guide to America. 1975. pap. 3.95 (ISBN 0-02-097800-6, Collier). Macmillan.

Kramer, J. J. The Last of the Grand Hotels. 1978. 24.95 (ISBN 0-442-20819-7). Van Nos Reinhold.

Lathrop, Elise L. Early American Inns & Taverns. LC 68-20234. (Illus.). 1968. Repr. of 1935 ed. 17.50 (ISBN 0-405-08734-9, Blom Pubns). Arno.

Lawson, Fred. Hotels, Motels & Condominiums: Design, Planning & Maintenance. (Illus.). 1976. 54.95 (ISBN 0-8436-2109-5). CBI Pub.

Lecler, Rene. The Three Hundred Best Hotels in the World. (Illus.). 224p. (Orig.). Date not set. pap. 7.95 (ISBN 0-8317-8745-7, Pub. by Mayflower Bks). Smith Pubs.

Lecler, Rene, ed. The Three Hundred Best Hotels in the World. (Illus.). 1981. pap. 7.95 (ISBN 0-8317-8745-7, Rutledge Pr). Smith Pubs.

Limerick, Jeffrey, et al. America's Grand Resort Hotels. LC 79-1885. 1979. 20.00 (ISBN 0-394-50107-1). Pantheon.

Lundberg, Donald E. The Hotel & Restaurant Business. 3rd ed. LC 79-207. 1979. text ed. 16.95 o. p. (ISBN 0-8436-2142-7); pap. text ed. 15.95 (ISBN 0-8436-2175-3). CBI Pub.

Matthew, Christopher. A Different World: Stories of Great Hotels. (Illus.). 12.98 (ISBN 0-686-74651-1). Bookthrift.

--A Different World: Stories of Great Hotels. LC 76-3802. (Illus.). 1976. 19.95 (ISBN 0-8467-0135-9). Paddington.

Melcher, Joan. Watering Hole: A User's Guide to Montana Bars. 128p. 1980. pap. text ed. 6.95 (ISBN 0-938314-00-9). MT Mag.

Mooney, Sean & Green, George. Sean Mooney's Practical Guide to Running a Pub. LC 78-27436. 1979. 15.95x (ISBN 0-88229-400-8); pap. 8.95 (ISBN 0-88229-681-7). Nelson-Hall.

Motels, Hotels, Restaurants, & Bars. 2nd ed. LC 73-142929. (Architectural Record Book). (Illus.). v, 327p. Repr. of 1960 ed. lib. bdg. 28.00x (ISBN 0-8371-5931-8, ARMH). Greenwood.

Neuer, Kathleen. The Inn Book: A Field Guide to Old Inns & Good Food in New York, New Jersey, Eastern Pennsylvania, Delaware & Connecticut. 1976. pap. 4.95 (ISBN 0-394-71446-6, Vin). Random.

Powell, Walbridge J. Hawaiian Hotels & Condominiums. 1979. 2.50 (ISBN 0-686-24240-8). Searchers Pubns.

Ranger, C. Gray's Inn Journal. 1978. 50.00 (ISBN 0-379-20369-3). Oceana.

Ross, Corinne M. The Southern Guest House Book. LC 80-70777. (Illus.). 192p. 1981. pap. 6.95 (ISBN 0-914788-35-3). East Woods.

Rushmore, Stephen. The Valuation of Hotels & Motels. 1978. 18.00 (ISBN 0-911780-44-0). Am Inst Real Estate Appraisers.

Schneider. Guide to New England Country Inns. 3.75 (ISBN 0-915248-36-0). Vermont Crossroads.

School of Hotel Administration, Cornell University. Subject Catalog of the Library of the Cornell University School of Hotel Administration. (Library Catalogs-Supplements Ser.). Date not set. lib. bdg. 200.00 (ISBN 0-8161-0421-2). G K Hall.

Schuhholz, Annaliese & Dieckmann, Jens. Romantik Hotels & Restaurants. (Illus.). 160p. 1981. pap. 4.98 (ISBN 0-912944-66-8). Berkshire Traveller.

Sherry, John H. The Laws of Innkeepers: For Hotels, Motels, Restaurants & Clubs. LC 76-37780. 528p. 1972. 25.00x (ISBN 0-8014-0702-8). Cornell U Pr.

Signpost Ltd. Signpost: Colour Hotel Guide 1978. 1978. pap. 12.50x (ISBN 0-8464-0848-1). Beekman Pubs.

Simpson, Norman T. Bed & Breakfast American Style. (Illus.). 200p. (Orig.). 1981. pap. 6.95 (ISBN 0-912944-68-4). Berkshire Traveller.

--Country Inns & Back Roads, North America. 16th ed. (Illus.). 450p. (Orig.). 1981. pap. 7.95 (ISBN 0-912944-65-X). Berkshire Traveller.

Smith, Douglas. Hotel & Restaurant Design. 137p. 1979. 23.00 (ISBN 0-435-86501-3, Pub. by Design Council Pub). Intl Schol Bk Serv.

Steadman. One Hundred Country Inns of Maine. 1979. pap. 6.95 (ISBN 0-89272-061-1). Down East.

Stuart, Sandra L. The Pink Palace: Behind Closed Doors at the Beverly Hills Hotel. 1978. 10.00 (ISBN 0-8184-0246-6). Lyle Stuart.

Sulzby, James F., Jr. Historic Alabama Hotels & Resorts. (Illus.). 294p. 1960. 13.50 (ISBN 0-8173-5309-7). U of Ala Pr.

Tolf, Robert W. Country Inns of the Old South. LC 78-11262. (Illus.). 1978. pap. 4.95 (ISBN 0-89286-144-4). One Hund One Prods.

West, Elliott. The Saloon on the Rocky Mountain Mining Frontier. LC 78-24090. (Illus.). 1979. 14.50 (ISBN 0-8032-4704-4). U of Nebr Pr.

White, Arthur. Palaces of the People: A Social History of Commercial Hospitality. LC 70-107011. 1970. 5.50 (ISBN 0-8008-6207-4). Taplinger.

Williamson, Jefferson. The American Hotel: An Anecdotal History. facsimile ed. LC 75-1873. (Leisure Class in America Ser.). (Illus.). 1975. Repr. of 1930 ed. 22.00x (ISBN 0-405-06939-1). Arno.

Winberg, Ellie & Wilson, Tom. Single Rooms: Stories of an Urban Subculture. 192p. 1981. text ed. 14.50 (ISBN 0-87073-495-4); pap. text ed. 7.95 (ISBN 0-87073-496-2). Schenkman.

Wright, Carol. Hotel. LC 78-61229. (Careers Ser.). (Illus.). 1979. lib. bdg. 7.95 (ISBN 0-686-51121-2). Silver.

Wrigley's Hotel Directory, 1980. 70th ed. 272p. (Orig.). 1980. vinyl cover 19.00x (ISBN 0-8002-2698-4). Intl Pubns Serv.

Wykes, Alan. Ale & Hearty. 144p. 1981. 19.00x (ISBN 0-906379-20-2, Pub. by Jupiter England). State Mutual Bk.

HOTELS, TAVERNS, ETC.-ACCOUNTING

Coltman, Michael M. Financial Management for the Hospitality Industry. LC 79-378. 1979. text ed. 17.95 (ISBN 0-8436-2141-9). CBI Pub.

--Hospitality Management Accounting. LC 77-16670. (Illus.). 1978. 16.95 (ISBN 0-8436-2170-2); paper student wkbk. 6.95 (ISBN 0-8436-2180-X). CBI Pub.

Crawford, Hollie & McDowell, Milton C. Metric Workbook for Food Service & Lodging. LC 76-22181. 224p. 1976. pap. 12.95 (ISBN 0-8436-2103-6); answer book 1.95 (ISBN 0-8436-2168-0). CBI Pub.

Dittmer, Paul. Accounting Practices for Hotels, Motels, & Restaurants. LC 79-142507. 1971. text ed. 17.95 (ISBN 0-672-96062-1); tchr's manual 5.00 (ISBN 0-672-26064-6); wkbk., 1972 9.95 (ISBN 0-672-96063-X). Bobbs.

Dukas, Peter. Planning Profits in the Food and Lodging Industry. 180p. 1976. 14.95 (ISBN 0-8436-2080-3). CBI Pub.

Fay, Clifford T., Jr., et al. Managerial Accounting for the Hospitality Service Industries. 2nd ed. 616p. 1976. pap. text ed. write for info (ISBN 0-697-08406-X); instrs.' manual avail. (ISBN 0-686-67396-4). Wm C Brown.

--Financial Accounting in the Hospitality Service Industries. rev. ed. 1981. price not set (ISBN 0-86612-010-6); text ed. price not set (ISBN 0-86612-010-6). Educ Inst Am Hotel.

Horwath, Ernest B., et al. Hotel Accounting. 4th ed. LC 77-79169. 1978. 29.95 (ISBN 0-471-07247-8, Pub. by Wiley-Interscience). Wiley.

Kotas, Richard & Kreul, L. Management Accounting for Hotels & Restaurants. (gr. 10 up). 1979. text ed. 15.50x (ISBN 0-8104-9472-8). Hayden.

Tarr, Stanley B. & Fay, Clifford T., Jr. Basic Bookkeeping for the Hospitality Industry. (Illus.). 152p. 1975. text ed. 14.95x (ISBN 0-86612-006-8). Educ Inst Am Hotel.

The American Hotel & Motel Association. Uniform System of Accounts & Expense Dictionary for Small Hotels & Motels. (Illus.). 157p. 1981. Repr. 11.00x (ISBN 0-86612-001-7). Educ Inst Am Hotel.

HOTELS, TAVERNS, ETC.-EMPLOYEES

see also Waiters and Waitresses

Henderson, John P. Labor Market Institutions & Wages in the Lodging Industry. LC 65-63958. 1965. 7.50 (ISBN 0-87744-040-9). Mich St U Busn.

International Labour Office. Employment in the Hotel & Catering Industry. (Hotel & Tourism Management Ser.: No. 4). ii, 76p. (Orig.). 1980. pap. 7.15 (ISBN 92-2-102462-8). Intl Labour Office.

John, Hughes. Jester the Bellhop. (People Working Today Ser). (Illus.). 40p. (gr. 7-12). 1975. pap. 1.85 (ISBN 0-915510-05-7). Janus Bks.

Mars, G., et al. Manpower Problems in the Hotel & Catering Industry. 180p. 1979. text ed. 28.25x (ISBN 0-566-00214-0, Pub. by Gower Pub Co England). Renouf.

Morgan, William J., Jr. Instructor's Manual for Hospitality Personnel Management. 1979. write for info. (ISBN 0-8436-2143-5). CBI Pub.

Pfeiffer, William B. & Voegele, Walter O. Correct Maid for Hotels & Motels. rev. 2nd ed. (Illus., Orig.). 1965. pap. 3.50 (ISBN 0-8104-9456-6). Hayden.

Stokes, Arch. The Equal Opportunity Handbook for Hotels, Restaurants & Institutions. LC 79-859. 1979. 15.95 (ISBN 0-8436-2148-6). CBI Pub.

Tourism Education Corp. A Hospitality Industry Guide for Writing & Using Task Unit Job Descriptions. 1976. pap. 14.50 (ISBN 0-8436-2118-4). CBI Pub.

Witzky, Herbert K. The Labor-Management Relations Handbook: For Hotels, Motels, Restaurants & Institutions. LC 75-37532. 224p. 1976. 15.95 (ISBN 0-8436-2083-8). CBI Pub.

HOTELS, TAVERNS, ETC.-LAW

Cournoyer. Hotel, Restaurant & Travel Law. LC 77-16429. 1978. 16.95 (ISBN 0-87872-143-6). Duxbury Pr.

Couroyner, Norman C. Hotel, Restaurant & Travel Law. 544p. 1978. 17.95 (ISBN 0-87872-143-6). CBI Pub.

Sherry, John E. The Laws of Innkeepers: For Hotels, Motels, Restaurants & Clubs. rev. ed. LC 81-67174. 784p. 1981. 39.50x (ISBN 0-8014-1421-0). Cornell U Pr.

Sherry, John H. The Laws of Innkeepers: For Hotels, Motels, Restaurants & Clubs. LC 76-37780. 528p. 1972. 25.00x (ISBN 0-8014-0702-8). Cornell U Pr.

Stokes, Arch. The Equal Opportunity Handbook for Hotels, Restaurants & Institutions. LC 79-859. 1979. 15.95 (ISBN 0-8436-2148-6). CBI Pub.

--The Wage & Hour Handbook for Hotels, Restaurants, & Institutions. LC 78-9278. 1978. 15.95 (ISBN 0-8436-2133-8). CBI Pub.

HOTELS, TAVERNS, ETC.-MANAGEMENT

see Hotel Management

HOTELS, TAVERNS, ETC.-VOCATIONAL GUIDANCE

Clark, D. C. Bartending Made Simple. (Illus.). 65p. (Orig.). spiral bound 4.50 (ISBN 0-940144-00-X). Self-Motiv Careers.

Hall, Eugene J. The Language of Hotels in English. (English for Careers Ser.). (Illus.). (gr. 10 up). 1976. pap. text ed. 3.50 (ISBN 0-88345-273-1). Regents Pub.

Henkin, Shepard. Opportunities in Hotel & Motel Management. rev. ed. LC 78-51256. (gr. 8 up). 1978. PLB 6.60 (ISBN 0-8442-6577-2); pap. 4.95 (ISBN 0-8442-6578-0). Natl Textbk.

International Labour Office. Tasks to Jobs: Developing a Modular System of Training for Hotel Occupations. (Hotel & Tourism Management Ser.: No. 3). 302p. 1979. text ed. 17.10 (ISBN 9-22-102148-3). Intl Labour Office.

Lerner, Mark. Careers in Hotels & Motels. LC 78-21171. (Early Career Books). (Illus.). (gr. 2-5). 1979. PLB 4.95 (ISBN 0-8225-0335-2). Lerner Pubns.

Ser-Vol-Tel Institute. Busing Attendant. (Foodservice Career Education Ser.). 1974. pap. 4.95 (ISBN 0-8436-2018-8). CBI Pub.

--Counter Service. (Food Service Career Education Ser.). 1974. pap. 4.95 (ISBN 0-8436-2020-X). CBI Pub.

HOTELS, TAVERNS, ETC.-CANADA

Country Inns: Canada. 1981. 5.95 (ISBN 0-89102-161-2). B Franklin.

Simpson, Norman T. Country Inns & Back Roads, North America. 16th ed. (Illus.). 450p. (Orig.). 1981. pap. 7.95 (ISBN 0-912944-65-X). Berkshire Traveller.

HOTELS, TAVERNS, ETC.-EUROPE

Brown, Karen A. French Country Inns & Chateau Hotels. LC 77-82024. (Illus., Orig.). 1977. pap. 7.95 (ISBN 0-930328-01-9). Travel Pr.

Fielding, Dodge. Fielding's Favorites: Hotels & Inns, Europe 1982. (Illus.). 480p. 1981. 5.95 (ISBN 0-688-00659-0). Morrow.

Firebaugh, W. C. The Inns of Greece & Rome. LC 76-175878. (Illus.). Repr. of 1928 ed. 18.00 (ISBN 0-405-08515-X, Blom Pubns). Arno.

Long, Robert P. Castle Hotels of Europe. 5th ed. 1977. pap. 4.95 (ISBN 0-9600064-1-9); 1981 suppl. update incl. R P Long.

Michelin Green Travel Guide: Portugal. annual (Illus., Fr. & Eng.). 4.95 (ISBN 0-685-11408-2). French & Eur.

Michelin Red Travel Guide: Benelux. annual (Illus., Fr.). 1968. 4.95 (ISBN 0-685-11387-6). French & Eur.

Michelin Red Travel Guide: Espana - Portugal. annual (Illus., Fr.). 1968. 8.95 (ISBN 0-685-11393-0). French & Eur.

Michelin Red Travel Guide: France. annual (Illus.). 1968. 10.95 (ISBN 0-685-11388-4). French & Eur.

Michelin Red Travel Guide: Paris & Environs. annual 1.95 (ISBN 0-685-11391-4). French & Eur.

Rubenstein, Hilary. Europe's Wonderful Little Hotels & Inns. (Illus.). 512p. 1981. 12.95 (ISBN 0-312-92188-8); pap. 8.95 (ISBN 0-312-92189-6). St Martin.

Rubinstein, Hilary, ed. Europe's Wonderful Little Hotels & Inns. 3rd rev. ed. (Illus.). 512p. 1981. pap. 9.95 (ISBN 0-686-77669-0). Congdon & Lattes.

Zellers, Margaret. The Inn Way...Switzerland. rev. ed. 1980. pap. 4.95 (ISBN 0-912944-61-7). Berkshire Traveller.

HOTELS, TAVERNS, ETC.-GREAT BRITAIN

Akerman, John Y. Tradesmen's Tokens, Current in London & Its Vicinity Between the Years 1648-1672. (Illus.). 1969. Repr. of 1849 ed. 22.50 (ISBN 0-8337-0029-4). B Franklin.

Automobile Association. AA Hotels & Restaurants in Britain. rev. ed. (Illus.). 600p. 1981. pap. 12.95 (ISBN 0-86145-040-X, Pub. by Auto Assn-British Tourist Authority England). Merrimack Bk Serv.

Automobile Association & British Tourist Authority. London: Hotels & Restaurants Including Budget Accomodations. rev. ed. (Illus.). 146p. 1981. pap. 3.50 (ISBN 0-7095-0576-0, Pub. by Auto Assn-British Tourist Authority England). Merrimack Bk Serv.

Automobile Association (Britain) Hotels & Restaurants in Britain 1981. LC 52-21171. 600p. 1981. 10.00 (ISBN 0-7095-0579-5). Intl Pubns Serv.

Borer, Mary C. The British Hotel Through the Ages. (Illus.). 264p. 1973. 12.00x (ISBN 0-7188-1860-1). Intl Pubns Serv.

Britain: Commended Country Hotels. rev. ed. 102p. 1980. pap. 2.50 (ISBN 0-85630-872-2, Pub. by B T A). Merrimack Bk Serv.

Burke, John. The English Inn. LC 81-4292. (Illus.). 240p. 1981. 24.50x (ISBN 0-8419-0706-4). Holmes & Meier.

Country Inns: Britain. 1981. 5.95 (ISBN 0-89102-162-0). B Franklin.

Courtenay, Ashley. Nineteen Eighty-Two Let's Halt Awhile in Great Britain Hotel Guide. (Orig.). 1982. pap. 14.95 (ISBN 0-8038-4339-9). Hastings.

Davis, Ben. The Traditional English Pub: A Way of Drinking. (Illus.). 170p. 1981. 31.50x (ISBN 0-85139-055-2). Nichols Pub.

Egon Ronay's Pub Guide. (Illus.). 1977. pap. 11.95 (ISBN 0-8277-5300-4). British Bk Ctr.

Guide to Guesthouses, Farmhouses & Inns in Britain, 1980. (A. A. Guides Ser.). 256p. 1980. pap. 8.95x (ISBN 0-86145-008-6, Pub. by Auto Assn England). Standing Orders.

Guide to Hotels & Restaurants in Britain, 1980. (A. A. Guides Ser.). 576p. (Orig.). 1980. pap. 10.95x (ISBN 0-86145-006-X, Pub. by Auto Assn England). Standing Orders.

Guide to Hotels & Restaurants, 1978: Great Britain & Ireland. (A.A. Guides Ser.). (Illus.). 1978. pap. 8.95x (ISBN 0-09-132001-1). Standing Orders.

Guide to Self-Catering in Britain, 1980. (A. A. Guides Ser.). (Orig.). 1980. pap. 7.95x (ISBN 0-86145-009-4, Pub. by Auto Assn England). Standing Orders.
Hogg, Garry. The English Country Inn. (Illus.). 1975. 10.95 (ISBN 0-8038-1921-8). Hastings.
Richardson, A. E. The Old Inns of England. LC 72-80704. (Illus.). 1972. Repr. of 1934 ed. lib. bdg. 16.00 (ISBN 0-405-08886-8, Pub. by Blom). Arno.
Richardson, A. E. & Eberlein, H. Donaldson. English Inn Past & Present. LC 68-56499. (Illus.). Repr. of 1925 ed. 22.00 (ISBN 0-405-08887-6, Pub. by Blom). Arno.
Ronay, Egon. Egon Ronay's Nineteen Eighty-One Pub Guide. rev. ed. (Illus.). 1981. pap. 5.95 3-copy minimum order (ISBN 0-14-005813-3, Pub. by Auto Assn-British Tourist Authority England). Merrimack Bk Serv.
Russell, Ronald. Waterside Pubs: Pubs of the (British) Inland Waterways. LC 74-81057. 1975. 10.50 (ISBN 0-7153-6743-9). David & Charles.
Scottish Tourist Board. Scotland: Bed & Breakfast. rev. ed. (Illus.). 252p. 1981. pap. 4.95 3-copy minimum order (ISBN 0-85419-170-4, Pub. by Auto Assn-British Tourist Authority England). Merrimack Bk Serv.
--Scotland: Hotels & Guesthouses. rev. ed. (Illus.). 328p. 1981. pap. 4.95 3-copy minimum order (ISBN 0-85419-169-0, Pub. by Auto Assn-British Tourist Authority England). Merrimack Bk Serv.
Taylor, John. The Carriers Cosmographie; or a Briefe Relation of the Innes in & Neere London. LC 74-80229. (English Experience Ser.: No. 698). 1974. Repr. of 1637 ed. 3.50 (ISBN 90-221-0698-5). Walter J Johnson.

HOTELS, TAVERNS, ETC.–IRELAND

Country Inns: Ireland. 1981. 5.95 (ISBN 0-89102-208-2). B Franklin.
Guide to Hotels & Restaurants, 1978: Great Britain & Ireland. (A.A. Guides Ser.). (Illus.). 1978. pap. 8.95x (ISBN 0-09-132001-1). Standing Orders.

HOTELS, TAVERNS, ETC.–NEW ZEALAND

Lawlor, Pat. Old Wellington Hotels. (Illus.). 96p. 1974. 12.50x (ISBN 0-8002-0878-1). Intl Pubns Serv.

HOTLINES (PSYCHIATRY)

see Crisis Intervention (Psychiatry)

HOTMAN, FRANCOIS, SIEUR DE VILLIERS, SAINT PAUL, 1524-1590

Kelley, Donald R. Francois Hotman: A Revolutionary's Ordeal. LC 72-735. 358p. 1973. 25.00 (ISBN 0-691-05206-9). Princeton U Pr.
Reynolds, Beatrice. Proponents of Limited Monarchy in Sixteenth Century France. LC 68-58616. (Columbia University. Studies in the Social Sciences: No. 334). Repr. of 1931 ed. 18.50 (ISBN 0-404-51334-4). AMS Pr.

HOTTENTOTS

see also Bushmen

Hagman, Roy S. Nama Hottentot Grammar. (Language Science Monographs: No. 15). 1977. pap. text ed. 15.00x (ISBN 0-87750-212-9). Res Ctr Lang Semiotic.
Hahn, Theophilus. Tsuni-llgoam. facsimile ed. LC 70-164388. (Black Heritage Library Collection). Repr. of 1880 ed. 16.00 (ISBN 0-8369-8847-7). Arno.
Kolb, Peter. The Present State of the Cape of Good-Hope: Or, a Particular Account of the Several Nations of the Hottentots, 2 vols. (Anthropology Ser.). 1969. Repr. of 1731 ed. Vol. 1. 27.00 (ISBN 0-384-30100-2); Vol. 2. 34.50 (ISBN 0-685-13553-5). Johnson Repr.
Leguat, Francois. Voyage et Aventures de Fr. Leguat en Deux Isles Desertes des Indes Orientales, 2 vols. (Bibliotheque Africaine Ser.). 472p. (Fr.). 1974. Repr. of 1708 ed. lib. bdg. 130.00x (ISBN 0-8287-0524-0, 72-2114). Clearwater Pub.
Schapera, Isaac. Khoisan Peoples of South Africa. 1930. text ed. 39.00x (ISBN 0-7100-2081-3). Humanities.
Schapera, Isaac, ed. Early Cape Hottentots. Farrington, B., tr. LC 79-107485. Repr. of 1933 ed. 17.00x (ISBN 0-8371-3787-X, Pub. by Negro U Pr). Greenwood.
Sutherland, John. Original Matter Contained in Lieutenant Colonel Sutherland's Memoir on the Kaffers, Hottentots, & Bosjemans of South Africa, Heads 1st & 2nd. LC 74-155412. Repr. of 1847 ed. 26.50x (ISBN 0-8371-6109-6). Greenwood.
Theal, George M. Yellow & Dark-Skinned People of Africa, South of the Zambesi. LC 77-82081. (Illus.). Repr. of 1910 ed. 21.25x (ISBN 0-8371-1557-4). Greenwood.

HOUCK, LOUIS, 1840-1925

Doherty, William T., Jr. Louis Houck: Missouri Historian & Entrepreneur. LC 60-15511. 1960. 10.00x (ISBN 0-8262-0542-9). U of Mo Pr.

HOUDINI, HARRY, 1874-1926

Brandreth, Gyles & Morley, John. The Magic of Houdini. (Illus.). 1979. 18.00 (ISBN 0-7207-1114-2). Transatlantic.
Cannell, J. Secrets of Houdini. 2.95 (ISBN 0-685-47573-5). Wehman.
Cannell, J. C. Secrets of Houdini. LC 74-10523. (Illus.). 1974. Repr. of 1931 ed. 28.00 (ISBN 0-8103-3725-8). Gale.
--The Secrets of Houdini. LC 72-93609. (Illus.). 288p. 1973. pap. 4.00 (ISBN 0-486-22913-0). Dover.
--The Secrets of Houdini. (Illus.). 6.50 (ISBN 0-8446-4719-5). Peter Smith.
Christopher, Milbourne. Houdini: A Pictorial Life. (Illus.). 1976. 14.95 (ISBN 0-690-01152-0). T Y Crowell.
Dunninger. One Hundred Classic Houdini Tricks You Can Do. LC 74-14200. (Illus.). 144p. 1975. pap. 3.50 (ISBN 0-668-03617-6). Arco.
Edwards, Anne. The Great Houdini. LC 76-8472. (See & Read Biographies). (Illus.). (gr. k-3). 1977. PLB 5.99 (ISBN 0-399-61020-0). Putnam.
Ernst, Bernard M. & Carrington, Hereward. Houdini & Conan Doyle: The Story of a Strange Friendship. LC 72-174861. Repr. of 1933 ed. 15.00 (ISBN 0-405-08490-0, Blom Pubns). Arno.
Ernst, J. Escape King: The Story of Harry Houdini. (Illus.). (gr. 2-8). 1975. 5.95 (ISBN 0-13-283416-2); pap. 1.50 (ISBN 0-13-283424-3). P-H.
Fago, John N. & Toan, Debbie. Houdini - Walt Disney. (Pendulum Illustrated Biography Ser.). (Illus.). (gr. 4-12). 1979. text ed. 5.00 (ISBN 0-88301-362-2); pap. text ed. 1.95 (ISBN 0-88301-350-9); wkbk 1.25 (ISBN 0-88301-374-6). Pendulum Pr.
Gibson, Walter. Houdini on Magic. 2.50 (ISBN 0-685-21975-5). Wehman.
Gresham, William L. Houdini. (Illus.). 1975. pap. 1.50 (ISBN 0-532-15166-6). Woodhill.
Henning, Doug & Reynolds, Charles. Houdini: His Legend & His Magic. 1978. pap. 8.95 (ISBN 0-446-87328-4). Warner Bks.
--Houdini: His Legend & His Magic. LC 76-52817. 1977. 14.95 (ISBN 0-8129-0686-1). Times Bks.
Kendall, Lace. Houdini: Master of Escape. (gr. 7-9). 1960. 6.50 (ISBN 0-8255-5075-0). Macrae.
Kraske, Robert. Daredevils Do Amazing Things. LC 77-90194. (Step-up Bks.: No. 26). (gr. 3-6). 1978. 3.95 (ISBN 0-394-83623-5, BYR); PLB 4.99 (ISBN 0-394-93623-X). Random.
--Harry Houdini: Master of Magic. LC 72-3446. (Americans All Ser.). (Illus.). 96p. (gr. 3-6). 1973. PLB 6.48 (ISBN 0-8116-4578-9). Garrard.
--Harry Houdini, Master of Magic. (gr. k-3). 1978. pap. 1.25 (ISBN 0-590-05374-4, Schol Pap). Schol Bk Serv.
Warren, David. The Great Escaper. LC 78-26629. (Raintree Great Adventures). (Illus.). (gr. 3-6). 1979. PLB 10.25 (ISBN 0-8393-0152-9). Raintree Child.
Wayne, Bennett, ed. & commentary by. The Super Showmen. LC 74-2282. (Target Bks). (Illus.). 168p. (gr. 5-12). 1974. PLB 7.29 (ISBN 0-8116-4909-1). Garrard.
White, Florence M. Escape: The Life of Harry Houdini. LC 78-26248. (Illus.). 112p. (gr. 4-6). 1979. PLB 7.79 (ISBN 0-671-32937-5). Messner.

HOUGH, EMERSON, 1857-1923

Wylder, Delbert E. Emerson Hough. (U. S. Authors Ser.: No. 397). 13.95 (ISBN 0-8057-7328-2). Twayne.

HOUGH, HENRY BEETLE, 1896-

Hough, Henry B. Mostly on Martha's Vineyard: A Personal Record. LC 74-22494. 298p. 1975. 7.95 (ISBN 0-15-106800-3). HarBraceJ.
--Soundings at Sea Level. 1980. 10.95 (ISBN 0-395-29165-8). HM.
--To the Harbor Light. 1976. Repr. lib. bdg. 10.95 (ISBN 0-8161-6435-5, Large Print Bks). G K Hall.

HOUGHTON, RICHARD MONCKTON MILDES, 1ST BARON, 1809-1885

Ince, Richard B. Calverley & Some Cambridge Wits of the Nineteenth Century. LC 74-28333. 1929. lib. bdg. 17.50 (ISBN 0-8414-0887-4). Folcroft.
Reid, Wemyss T. The Life, Letters & Friendships of Richard Monckton Milnes, First Lord Houghton, 2 vols. LC 77-88581. 1977. Repr. of 1891 ed. lib. bdg. 55.00 (ISBN 0-89341-463-8). Longwood Pr.

HOUGHTON-MIFFLIN COMPANY

Ballou, Ellen B. Building of the House: Houghton Mifflin's First Half Century. LC 69-15006. (Illus.). 1970. 12.50 (ISBN 0-395-07383-9). HM.

HOUNDS

see also Dogs–Breeds–Russian Wolfhound

De Vezins, Elie. Hounds for a Pack. Woolner, Lionel R., tr. (Illus.). 7.00 (ISBN 0-85131-210-1, Dist. by Sporting Book Center). J A Allen.
Johnston, George & Ericson, Maria. Hounds of France. 1981. 50.00x (ISBN 0-904558-43-6, Pub. by Saiga Pub). State Mutual Bk.
Salmon, H. M. Gazehounds & Coursing. (Illus.). 1977. 18.50 (ISBN 0-87839-024-3). North Star.
Scott, C. M., rev. by. Hounds in Old Days. 1981. 30.00x (ISBN 0-904558-35-5, Pub. by Saiga Pub). State Mutual Bk.

HOURS (TIME)

see Chronology; Days; Sun-Dials; Time

HOURS, BOOKS OF

De Vinck, Catherine. Readings: John at Patmos & A Book of Hours. LC 78-55341. 1978. 5.75 (ISBN 0-911726-32-2); pap. 3.75 (ISBN 0-911726-33-0). Alleluia Pr.
Fouquet, Jean. The Hours of Etienne Chevalier. (Illus.). 128p. slipcased 30.00 (ISBN 0-8076-0618-9). Braziller.
Knapp, Elsie M. Horary Art & It's Synthesis. 1974. 5.00x (ISBN 0-686-17210-8). Sandollar Pr.
The Liturgy of the Hours, 4 vols. Incl. Vol. 1. Advent & Christmas. 19.95 (ISBN 0-686-14344-2, 401/08); Vol. 2. Lent & Easter. 21.50 (ISBN 0-686-14345-0, 402/08); Vol. 3. Ordinary Time-Weeks 1 to 17. 19.95 (ISBN 0-686-14346-9, 403/08); Vol. 4. Ordinary Time-Weeks 18 to 34. 19.95 (ISBN 0-686-14347-7, 404/08). Boxed. gift set 82.50 (ISBN 0-686-14341-8); St. Joseph guide for 1978 1.25 (ISBN 0-686-14342-6, 400-G). Blue (401C). Red (402C). Brown (403C). Green (404C). Catholic Bk Pub.
Meiss, Millard. The Tres Riches Heures of Jean, Duke of Berry. (Illus.). 290p. (Gold slipcased). slipcase 60.00 (ISBN 0-8076-0512-3). Braziller.
Miller, Charles E. Making Holy the Day: A Commentary in the Liturgy of the Hours. red flexible bdg. 0.95 (ISBN 0-686-14286-1, 410/04). Catholic Bk Pub.
Plummer, John. Book of Hours of Catherine of Cleves. (Illus.). 1964. pap. 5.00 (ISBN 0-87598-011-2). Pierpont Morgan.
Plummer, John, intro. by. The Hours of Catherine of Cleves. LC 66-23096. (Illus.). 360p. 1975. 30.00 (ISBN 0-8076-0379-1). Braziller.
Smith, Webster. The Farnese Hours. LC 76-4041. (Library of Illuminated Manuscripts). (Illus.). 168p. 1976. slipcase 30.00 (ISBN 0-8076-0856-4). Braziller.
Thomas, Marcel, ed. The Grandes Heures of Jean, Duke of Berry. LC 75-167761. (Illus.). 192p. 1971. 70.00 (ISBN 0-8076-0613-8). Braziller.

HOURS OF LABOR

see also Children–Employment; Holidays; Shift Systems; Sunday Legislation

Allenspach, Heinz. Flexible Working Hours. 2nd ed. 1978. 8.75 (ISBN 92-2-101198-4). Intl Labour Office.
The Battle for the Ten Hour Day Continues: 1837-1843. LC 72-2519. (British Labour Struggles Before 1850 Ser). 1972. Repr. 12.00 (ISBN 0-405-04412-7). Arno.
Baum, Stephen J. A Practical Guide to Flexible Working Hours. 190p. 1973. 16.50x (ISBN 0-85038-014-6). Intl Pubns Serv.
Branch & Swann. The Wage & Hour Law Handbook for the Lodging & Food Service Industry. LC 80-65115. 1980. 29.95 (ISBN 0-912016-86-8). Lebhar Friedman.
Brandeis, Louis D. & Goldmark, Josephine. Women in Industry. LC 73-89720. (American Labor, from Conspiracy to Collective Bargaining Ser., No. 1). 121p. 1969. Repr. of 1907 ed. 10.00 (ISBN 0-405-02106-2). Arno.
Cahill, Marion C. Shorter Hours: A Study of the Movement Since the Civil War. LC 68-54258. (Columbia University Studies in the Social Sciences: No. 380). 1971. Repr. of 1932 ed. 17.50 (ISBN 0-404-51380-8). AMS Pr.
Calkins, Robert G. Distribution of Labor: The Illuminators of the Hours of Catherine of Cleves & Their Workshop. LC 79-51537. (Transactions Ser.: Vol. 69, Pt. 5). 1979. 10.00 (ISBN 0-87169-695-9). Am Philos.
Dahlberg, Arthur A. Jobs, Machines & Capitalism. LC 70-91296. (BCL Ser. I). Repr. of 1932 ed. 16.50 (ISBN 0-404-01917-X). AMS Pr.
Dankert, Clyde E., et al, eds. Hours of Work. LC 78-27581. (Industrial Relations Research Association Publication: No. 32). 1979. Repr. of 1965 ed. lib. bdg. 17.75x (ISBN 0-313-20903-0, DAHW). Greenwood.
Demands for Early Closing Hours: 1843. LC 72-2523. (British Labour Struggles Before 1850 Ser). (3 pamphlets). 1972. Repr. 10.00 (ISBN 0-405-04416-X). Arno.
Ehrenberg, Ronald G. & Schumann, Paul L. Longer Hours or More Jobs? An Investigation of Amending Hours Legislation to Create Unemployment. (Cornell Studies in Industrial & Labor Relations: No. 22). 160p. 1981. write for info. (ISBN 0-87546-090-9); pap. write for info. (ISBN 0-87546-091-7). NY Sch Indus Rel.
Evans, Archibald A. Hours of Work in Industrialised Countries. xiv, 164p. 1975. 11.40 (ISBN 92-2-101296-4). Intl Labour Office.
Goldmark, Josephine & Hopkins, Mary D. Comparison of an Eight-Hour Plant & a Ten-Hour Plant: U.S. Public Health Bulletin, No. 106. Stein, Leon, ed. LC 77-70495. (Work Ser.). 1977. Repr. of 1920 ed. lib. bdg. 15.00x (ISBN 0-405-10168-6). Arno.
Gunton, George. Wealth & Progress. facs. ed. LC 71-130549. (Select Bibliographies Reprint Ser). 1887. 19.00 (ISBN 0-8369-5522-6). Arno.
--Wealth & Progress; A Critical Examination of the Labor Problem; The Natural Basis for Industrial Reform; or, How to Increase Wages Without Reducing Profits or Lowering Rents: The Economic Philosophy of the Eight Hour Movement. LC 77-88507. xxiii, 382p. Repr. of 1887 ed. lib. bdg. 16.75x (ISBN 0-8371-4971-1, GUWP). Greenwood.
Keracher, John. Wages & the Working Day. 1946. pap. 1.00 (ISBN 0-88286-039-9). C H Kerr.
Lafargue, Paul. The Right to Be Lazy. 69.95 (ISBN 0-87968-039-3). Gordon Pr.
Maklan, David M. The Four-Day Work Week: Blue Collar Adjustment to a Nonconventional Arrangement of Work & Leisure Time. LC 77-14308. (Praeger Special Studies). 1977. 23.95 (ISBN 0-03-039916-5). Praeger.
Meany, George, et al. Shorter Work Week. 1957. pap. 2.50 (ISBN 0-8183-0207-0). Pub Aff Pr.
Nollen, Stanley D. & Martin, Virginia H. Alternative Work Schedules, Pt. 1: Flexitime. LC 78-5932. 1978. 10.00 (ISBN 0-8144-3132-1). Am Mgmt.
--Alternative Work Schedules, Pts. 2 & 3: Permanent Part-Time & the Compressed Workweek. LC 78-17323. 1978. pap. 10.00 (ISBN 0-8144-3134-8). Am Mgmt.
Owen. Working Hours: An Economic Analysis. LC 78-22287. (Illus.). 1979. 21.95 (ISBN 0-669-02740-5). Lexington Bks.
Prelude to Victory of the Ten Hour Movement: 1844. LC 72-2536. (British Labour Struggles Before 1850 Ser). (4 pamphlets). 1972. 10.00 (ISBN 0-405-04429-1). Arno.
Robison, David. Alternative Work Patterns: Changing Approaches to Work Scheduling. LC 76-42369. 1976. pap. text ed. 5.00 (ISBN 0-89361-001-1). Work in Amer.
Ronen, Simcha. The Flexible Work Schedule: An Innovation in the Quality of Work Life. (Illus.). 352p. 1980. 18.95 (ISBN 0-07-053607-4). McGraw.
Silverstein, Pam & Srb, Jozetta H. Flexitime: Where, When, & How? LC 79-88670. (Key Issues Ser.: No. 24). 1979. pap. 3.50 (ISBN 0-87546-074-7). NY Sch Indus Rel.
Smigel, Edwin O., ed. Work & Leisure: A Contemporary Social Problem. (Orig.). 1963. 6.00 (ISBN 0-8084-0334-6). Coll & U Pr.
Technical Guide, Vol. II: Employment, Unemployment, Hours of Work, Wages. 416p. 1981. pap. 17.50 (ISBN 92-2-102286-2, ILO 168, ILO). Unipub.
The Ten Hours Movement in 1831 & 1832. LC 72-2548. (British Labour Struggles Before 1850 Ser). (7 pamphlets). 1972. 12.00 (ISBN 0-405-04439-9). Arno.
Teper, Lazare. Hours of Labor. LC 78-64144. (Johns Hopkins University. Studies in the Social Sciences. Fiftieth Ser. 1932: 1). Repr. of 1932 ed. 14.50 (ISBN 0-404-61255-5). AMS Pr.

HOUSATONIC RIVER AND VALLEY

Cawley, James & Cawley, Margaret. Exploring the Housatonic River & Valley. LC 76-50184. (Illus.). 1978. 7.95 (ISBN 0-498-02022-3). A S Barnes.

HOUSE, EDWARD MANDELL, 1858-1938

George, Alexander L. & George, Juliette L. Woodrow Wilson & Colonel House: A Personality Study. 1956. pap. 4.00 (ISBN 0-486-21144-4). Dover.
Smith, A. D. Mr. House of Texas. PLB 59.95 (ISBN 0-8490-0644-9). Gordon Pr.
--The Real Col. House. PLB 59.95 (ISBN 0-8490-0931-6). Gordon Pr.
Viereck, George S. The Strangest Friendship in History. LC 75-26222. 1976. Repr. of 1932 ed. lib. bdg. 26.25 (ISBN 0-8371-8413-4, VISF). Greenwood.

HOUSE BOATS

Anderson, Eugene N. Essays on South China's Boat People, No. 29. (Asian Folklore & Social Life Monograph). 1972. 4.60 (ISBN 0-89986-029-X). E Langstaff.
Ashbery, John. Houseboat Days. 1977. pap. 2.95 (ISBN 0-14-042202-1). Penguin.
Dennis, Ben & Case, Betsy. Houseboat: Reflections of North America's Floating Homes...History, Architecture, & Lifestyles. new ed. 1977. 14.95 (ISBN 0-918484-00-6); pap. 9.95 (ISBN 0-918484-01-4). Smugglers.
Gabor, Mark. Houseboats. (Illus.). 1979. 17.95 (ISBN 0-345-27312-5); pap. 8.95 (ISBN 0-345-28117-9). Ballantine.
Neumeyer, Ken. Sailing the Farm: Independence on 30 Feet - a Survival Guide to Homesteading the Ocean. 192p. (Orig.). 1981. pap. 7.95 (ISBN 0-89815-051-5). Ten Speed Pr.

HOUSE BUYING

see also Home Ownership

Anosike, Benji O. How to Buy or Sell Your Own Home Without a Lawyer or Broker. 120p. (Orig.). 1981. pap. text ed. 8.95x (ISBN 0-932704-09-3). Do-It-Yourself Pubs.

Beasley, M. Robert. Fell's Guide to Buying, Building & Financing a Home. LC 63-21657. 1963. 9.95 (ISBN 0-8119-0039-8). Fell.

Bjelland, Harley. How to Buy the Right Home. 1980. pap. 3.95 (ISBN 0-346-12438-7). Cornerstone.

Bowman, Thomas F., et al. Finding Your Best Place to Live in America. LC 81-51506. (Illus.). 352p. (Orig.). 1981. pap. 9.95 (ISBN 0-940162-00-8). Red Lion.

Brady, Constance. Right Where You Live. LC 78-73550. (Illus.). 1979. pap. 9.95 (ISBN 0-89087-242-2). Celestial Arts.

Braunstein, Michael. House Fever: Buying, Selling, Remodeling, Decorating & Agonizing Over Your Home. LC 79-2959. 1980. 6.95 (ISBN 0-15-142182-X). HarBraceJ.

Cobb, H. & Schwartz, Robert. Complete Homeowner. 1965. 5.95 (ISBN 0-02-607730-2). Macmillan.

Cobb, Hubbard. How to Buy & Remodel the Older House. 1972. pap. 8.95 (ISBN 0-02-079300-6, Collier). Macmillan.

Curran, June. Profile Your Lifestyle: Questions to Ask Yourself Before Building, Buying or Remodeling a Home. Wilbur, Shay & Weine, Ruth, eds. LC 78-72187. 1979. pap. 7.95 (ISBN 0-932370-00-4). Brooks Pub Co.

Davis, Joseph C. & Walker, Claxton. Buying Your House: A Complete Guide to Inspection & Evaluation. LC 75-5477. (Illus.). 252p. 1975. 9.95 (ISBN 0-87523-184-5). Emerson.

Davis, Joseph C. & Walker, Clayton. Buying Your House. 1978. pap. 4.95 (ISBN 0-425-03853-X, Windhover). Berkley Pub.

Doyle, John M. The Complete Home Owner's Guide: From Mortgage to Maintenance. (Illus.). 272p. 1975. 9.95 (ISBN 0-87909-154-1). Reston.

Etter, Robert A. Homes, Buy Right-Sell Right or How to Avoid the Ripoff When Buying or Selling Your Home. 1976. pap. 4.95 (ISBN 0-930628-00-4). Patchwork Pubns.

Financial Real Estate Handbook No. 512. 256p. 1980. pap. 6.50 (ISBN 0-686-64811-0). Finan Pub.

Fletcher, Connie. How to Buy a Home. 1978. pap. 5.95 (ISBN 0-695-80884-2). New Century.

Gaines, George, Jr. & Coleman, David S. How to Decide...Which Home to Buy. LC 78-12774. (Illus.). 1978. pap. 5.95 (ISBN 0-9602004-0-1). G&C Learn.

Grebler, Leo & Mittelbach, Frank G. The Inflation of House Prices: Its Extent, Causes & Consequences. LC 78-20272. (Special Ser. in Real Estate & Urban Land Economics). 1979. 25.95 (ISBN 0-669-02708-1). Lexington Bks.

Green, Michael. A Roof Over My Head. 1969. 5.95 (ISBN 0-09-100280-X, Pub. by Hutchinson). Merrimack Bk Serv.

Gritz, Robert D. The Complete Home Buying Guide. LC 81-87212. 170p. (Orig.). 1981. 9.95 (ISBN 0-940708-00-0); pap. write for info. (ISBN 0-940708-01-9). KAY Pub.

Hammond, David. The Home Ownership Game & How to Win It. LC 80-68693. (Illus.). 112p. 1981. 14.95 (ISBN 0-7153-7710-8). David & Charles.

Harrison, Henry S. & Leonard, Margery B. Home Buying: The Complete Illustrated Guide. (Illus.). 768p. 1981. 14.95 (ISBN 0-684-17304-2, ScribT). Scribner.

--Home Buying: The Complete Illustrated Guide. (Illus.). 625p. (Orig.). 1980. pap. 15.00 (ISBN 0-913652-18-0, BK128). Realtors Natl.

Hess, Nancy R. The Home Buyer's Guide. (Illus.). 224p. 1981. pap. 9.95 (ISBN 0-13-392647-8, Spec). P-H.

Hoffman, George. Saucelito: Sausalito. LC 76-716. 256p. 1976. pap. 2.95 (ISBN 0-916028-02-X). Woodward Bks.

Howell, Yvonne & Miller, Harry. Selling the Solar Home-California Edition. 93p. 1980. pap. 15.00 (ISBN 0-89934-081-4, R.005). Solar Energy Info.

Hunter, Steven. Home Inspection Workbook. (Illus., Orig.). 1980. pap. 5.95 (ISBN 0-8437-3345-4). Hammond Inc.

Irwin, Robert. How to Buy a Home at a Reasonable Price. LC 78-23828. (Illus.). 1979. 13.50 (ISBN 0-07-032060-8, P&RB). McGraw.

--Protect Yourself in Real Estate. 1977. 18.95 (ISBN 0-07-032064-0, P&RB). McGraw.

Jacobe, Dennis & Kendall, James N. How to Get the Money to Buy Your New Home. LC 81-65476. 200p. 1981. 11.95 (ISBN 0-87094-258-1). Dow Jones-Irwin.

Janik, Carolyn. The House Hunt Game: A Guide to Winning. 1979. 6.95 (ISBN 0-02-558970-9). Macmillan.

Johnson, Nancy B. A Place to Live. new ed. Gall, Morris, ed. (Consumer Education Ser). (Illus.). 88p. (Orig.). (gr. 7-12). 1973. pap. text ed. 1.45 (ISBN 0-88301-114-X). Pendulum Pr.

Kiev, Phyllis. The Woman's Guide to Buying Houses, Co-Ops & Condominiums. 352p. 1981. pap. 7.95 (ISBN 0-345-27496-2). Ballantine.

Koch, James H. Profits from Country Property: How to Select, Buy, Improve & Maintain Your Country Property. (Illus.). 320p. 1981. 12.95 (ISBN 0-07-035248-8, P&RB). McGraw.

Kravitol, R. Buying, Owning & Selling a Home in the Nineteen Eighties. 1981. 17.95 (ISBN 0-13-109512-9); pap. 9.95 (ISBN 0-13-109504-8). P-H.

Lank, Edith. Home Buying. 48p. (Orig.). 1980. pap. 1.95 (ISBN 0-88462-369-6). Real Estate Ed Co.

Lee, James S. Buyer's Handbook for the Single Family House. 1979. pap. text ed. 7.95 (ISBN 0-442-23291-8). Van Nos Reinhold.

Lee, Ralph E. Nine Ways to Buy a House. 100p. (Orig.). 1981. pap. 6.95 (ISBN 0-686-30983-9). R E Lee.

Lee, Steven J. Buyer's Handbook for Cooperatives & Condominiums. 1978. 15.95 (ISBN 0-442-23284-5); pap. 9.95 (ISBN 0-442-23285-3). Van Nos Reinhold.

McNeill, Joseph G. Homeowner's Guide to Buying, Evaluating & Maintaining Your Home. 1979. 14.95 (ISBN 0-442-23607-7). Van Nos Reinhold.

Moger, Byron J. How to Buy a House. LC 69-10635. 1969. 4.95 (ISBN 0-8184-0040-4). Lyle Stuart.

Morris, David J., Jr. The Wizard's Structural & Mechanical Guide to Buying Your Own Home. Date not set. pap. 5.95 (ISBN 0-933528-03-5). ANKH.

Murphy, Michael C. How to Buy a Home While You Can Still Afford to. LC 79-91390. (Illus.). 160p. 1981. 10.95 (ISBN 0-8069-7154-1); lib. bdg. 9.89 (ISBN 0-8069-7155-X); pap. 5.95 (ISBN 0-8069-8912-2). Sterling.

Murray, Robert, Jr. How to Buy the Right House at the Right Price. (Orig.). 1965. pap. 1.95 (ISBN 0-02-080900-X, Collier). Macmillan.

National Association of Home Builders. Condominium Buyers Guide. 31p. 1980. 7.50 (ISBN 0-86718-016-1). Natl Assn Home Builders.

--Profile of the Condominium Buyer. (Illus.). 133p. 1979. pap. 20.00 (ISBN 0-86718-030-7). Natl Assn Home Builders.

Nielsen, Jens & Nielson, Jackie. How to Save or Make Thousands When You Buy or Sell Your House. LC 78-62635. 1979. Repr. of 1971 ed. 6.95 (ISBN 0-385-13522-X, Dolp). Doubleday.

O'Neill, Richard W. The Homebuyer's Guide for the 80's: A Complete Guide to Every Step You Need to Take for the Biggest & Best Investment You'll Ever Make. LC 79-56187. 1980. pap. 7.95 (ISBN 0-448-16182-6). G&D.

Padgett, Douglas J. How to Buy a House During a Recession. LC 80-52062. (Illus.). 143p. (Orig.). 1980. pap. 5.95 (ISBN 0-9604598-0-4). Regal Pub Co.

Phelon, Sheldon, & Marsar, Inc., ed. Sheldon's Retail & Phelon's Resident Buyers Book. 97th ed. 1981. pap. 70.00 (ISBN 0-686-28951-X). P S & M Inc.

Philbin, Tom. Buyer's Guide to Manufactured Homes. LC 79-84667. (Illus.). 1980. 22.50 (ISBN 0-8015-0984-X, Hawthorn). Dutton.

Phipps, Antony A. & Moseley, Norma F. The Homebuying Guide. LC 78-72888. (Illus.). 1978. 12.50 (ISBN 0-89011-528-1); pap. 7.95 (ISBN 0-89011-527-3). Abt Assoc.

Pomeroy, Ruth. Redbook's Guide to Buying Your First Home. 1980. pap. 4.95 (ISBN 0-686-60934-4, 24716, Fireside, 25385). S&S.

Previews Staff. The New Previews' Dream House Catalog. rev., 3rd ed. (Illus.). 192p. 1980. pap. 10.95 (ISBN 0-517-54083-5, Harmony). Crown.

--Previews Book of Dream Houses. (Illus.). (Harmony); pap. 8.95 (ISBN 0-517-53342-1). Crown.

Scher, Les. Finding & Buying Your Place in the Country. LC 72-12959. (Illus.). 196p. 1974. pap. 5.95 (ISBN 0-02-089200-4, Collier). Macmillan.

Schram, Joseph F. Finding & Fixing the Older Home. LC 76-25112. (Illus.). 1976. 13.95 (ISBN 0-912336-32-3); pap. 6.95 (ISBN 0-912336-33-1). Structures Pub.

Schwartz, Robert. Home Owner's Legal Guide. 1969. pap. 2.95 (ISBN 0-02-081980-3, Collier). Macmillan.

Stamm, Martha & Stanforth, Deidre. Buying & Renovating a House in the City: A Practical Guide. 1972. pap. 6.95 (ISBN 0-394-70759-1). Knopf.

Stewart, Ronald E. Do It Yourself Real Estate Kit. rev. ed. (Illus., Orig.). 1979. pap. 7.95 (ISBN 0-686-28572-7). Thunderchief.

Sumichrast, Michael. Profile of the New Home Buyer: 1979 Survey of New Home Owners. (Illus.). 1979. pap. 20.00 (ISBN 0-86718-029-3). Natl Assn Home Builders.

Sumichrast, Michael & Shafer, Ronald G. The Complete Book of Home Buying: A Consumer's Guide to Housing in the 80's. rev. ed. LC 80-11100. 366p. 1980. 14.95 (ISBN 0-87128-589-4). Dow Jones-Irwin.

Talbot, Janet M. Isn't Hindsight Wonderful: How to Save Money, Make Your Best Deal, & Come Out Smelling Like a Rose, When Buying or Selling a Home, Choosing a Financial Representative, Signing Legal Contracts. LC 81-47416. (Illus.). 180p. 1981. 12.95 (ISBN 0-86707-001-3, 001); pap. 10.00 (ISBN 0-86707-000-5). MJT Intl Pubns.

Tammany, T. V. Home Buying Made Easy. 180p. 1981. 10.95 (ISBN 0-89182-037-X); pap. 5.95 (ISBN 0-89182-031-0). Charles River Bks.

TruesDell, Clarence C. How to Buy a Home in Florida: Without Getting Cheated. LC 79-56404. (Illus.). 64p. (Orig.). 1980. pap. 2.95 (ISBN 0-89317-031-3). Windward Pub.

Tuck, Curt, ed. The Fannie Mae Guide to Buying, Financing & Selling Your Home. rev. ed. LC 78-1017. 1978. pap. 5.95 (ISBN 0-385-14382-6, Dolp). Doubleday.

Watkins, A. M. How to Judge a House. 1972. pap. 3.50 (ISBN 0-8015-3732-0, Hawthorn). Dutton.

Watkins, Art. How to Avoid the Ten Biggest Home Buying Traps. 1979. pap. 5.50 (ISBN 0-8015-3895-5, Hawthorn). Dutton.

Wilkes, Joy & Wilkes, Paul. You Don't Have to Be Rich to Own a Brownstone. LC 72-90452. 224p. 1973. 6.95 (ISBN 0-8129-0336-6). Times Bks.

HOUSE CONSTRUCTION

see also Drainage, House; Dwellings–Maintenance and Repair; Dwellings–Remodeling; House Painting

Allen, Edward B., ed. The Responsive House. LC 74-23518. 320p. 1974. 22.50x (ISBN 0-262-01040-2); pap. 9.95 (ISBN 0-262-51012-X). MIT Pr.

Anderson, L. O. How to Build a Wood-Frame House. Orig. Title: Wood-Frame House Construction. (Illus.). 233p. 1970. pap. 4.25 (ISBN 0-486-22954-8). Dover.

--How to Build a Wood-Frame House. LC 73-77635. 1973. lib. bdg. 12.50x (ISBN 0-88307-541-5). Gannon.

Anderson, L. O. & Zornig, Harold F. Build Your Own Low Cost Home. 200p. 1972. pap. 6.95 (ISBN 0-486-21525-3). Dover.

Anderson, L. O. & Winslow, Taylor F., illus. Wood-Frame House Construction. rev. ed. (Illus.). 1976. pap. 5.00 (ISBN 0-910460-20-5). Craftsman.

Associated Press. One Hundred One Select Dream Houses. Lang, Andy, ed. (Illus.). 224p. 1972. 9.95 (ISBN 0-8437-3240-7); pap. 8.95 (ISBN 0-8437-3242-3). Hammond Inc.

Badzinski, Stanley. Home Construction & Estimating. (Illus.). 1979. ref. 16.95 (ISBN 0-13-392654-0). P-H.

Badzinski, Stanley, Jr. House Construction: A Guide to Buying, Building, & Evaluating. 256p. 1975. 19.95 (ISBN 0-685-61371-2); text ed. 14.95 (ISBN 0-13-394767-X). P-H.

Barton, Byron. Building a House. LC 80-22674. (Illus.). 32p. (ps-1). 1981. 7.95 (ISBN 0-688-80291-5); PLB 7.63 (ISBN 0-688-84291-7). Greenwillow.

Benson, Tedd & Gruber, James. Building the Timber Frame House. (Illus.). 1980. 17.95 (ISBN 0-684-16446-9, ScribT). Scribner.

Blackburn, Graham. Illustrated Housebuilding. LC 73-87998. (Illus.). 160p. 1974. 10.00 (ISBN 0-87951-020-X). Overlook Pr.

--Illustrated Housebuilding. LC 73-87998. (Illus.). 160p. 1977. pap. 4.95 (ISBN 0-87951-054-4). Overlook Pr.

Blustin, Lewis. How to Subcontract Your House: Building-Remodeling. LC 75-41734. (Illus.). 196p. 1976. 9.95 (ISBN 0-8306-6744-X); pap. 5.95 (ISBN 0-8306-5744-4, 744). TAB Bks.

Boericke, Art & Shapiro, Barry. Handmade Houses. 1975. pap. 6.95 (ISBN 0-89104-001-3). A & W Pubs.

Brann, Donald R. Forms, Footings, Foundations, Framings, Stair, Building, Bk. 697. rev. ed. LC 70-105687. (Illus.). 210p. 1980. pap. 5.95 (ISBN 0-87733-697-0). Easi-Bild.

--How to Build a Vacation or Retirement House. rev ed. LC 68-54905. 1975. lib. bdg. 6.95 (ISBN 0-87733-032-8); pap. 5.95 (ISBN 0-87733-632-6). Easi-Bild.

--How to Transform a Garage into Living Space, Bk. 684. LC 72-92125. (Illus.). 128p. 1974. lib. bdg. 5.95 (ISBN 0-87733-084-0); pap. 5.95 (ISBN 0-87733-684-9). Easi-Bild.

Browne, Dan. Multiply Your Living Space: How to Put an Addition on Your Home at a Cost You Can Afford. (Illus.). 1978. 12.95 (ISBN 0-07-008485-8, GB). McGraw.

Building Research Establishment. Energy, Heating & Thermal Comfort. (Building Research Ser.: Vol. 4). 1979. text ed. 38.00x (ISBN 0-904406-99-7). Longman.

Building the Hewn Log House. Date not set. 13.95 (ISBN 0-685-54509-1); pap. 8.95 (ISBN 0-685-54510-5). Mountain Pub Servs.

Burbank, Nelson L. & Romney, Arnold B. House Construction Details. 7th ed. 1981. 22.50 (ISBN 0-684-16824-3, ScribT). Scribner.

Bureau of Naval Personnel. Basic Construction Techniques for Houses & Small Buildings Simply Explained. (Illus.). 11.50 (ISBN 0-8446-4506-0). Peter Smith.

Cambell, Stu. The Illustrated Guide to Building Your House. 1979. o. p. 14.95 (ISBN 0-88266-154-X); pap. 9.95 (ISBN 0-88266-153-1). Garden Way Pub.

Charney, Len. Build a Yurt. LC 74-513. (The Low-Cost Mongolian Round House Ser.). (Illus.). 144p. (Orig.). 1981. pap. 6.95 (ISBN 0-8069-7518-0). Sterling.

Ching, Francis D. Building Construction Illustrated. 1975. 18.95 (ISBN 0-442-21533-9); pap. 11.95 (ISBN 0-442-21532-0). Van Nos Reinhold.

Chirgotis, William G. One Hundred & Seventy-Five Multi-Level Home Plans for Today's Living. Lurie, Anne, ed. LC 79-54251. (Illus.). 1979. 0.12.95 (ISBN 0-932944-05-1); pap. 6.95 (ISBN 0-932944-04-3). Creative Homeowner.

--Two Hundred & Fifty Home Plans for Today's Living. Birnbaum, Allan R. & Drate, Stanley, eds. LC 78-65787. (Illus.). 1979. 11.95 (ISBN 0-932944-03-5); pap. 6.95 (ISBN 0-932944-01-9). Creative Homeowner.

Churchill, James E. The Backyard Building Book. LC 76-17609. (Illus.). 192p. 1976. pap. 6.95 (ISBN 0-8117-2105-1). Stackpole.

Clark, Sam. Designing & Building Your Own House Your Own Way. 1978. 16.95 (ISBN 0-395-25486-8); pap. 8.95 (ISBN 0-395-26685-8). HM.

Cole, John & Wing, Charles. From the Ground Up: The Shelter Institute Guide to Building Your Own House. 1976. pap. 9.95 (ISBN 0-316-15112-2, Pub. by Atlantic Monthly Pr). Little.

Crowdis, Kay & Crowdis, David. Designing & Building Your Own Home. (Illus.). 240p. 1980. text ed. 14.95 (ISBN 0-8359-1272-8). Reston.

Curran, June. Profile Your Lifestyle: Questions to Ask Yourself Before Building, Buying or Remodeling a Home. Wilbur, Shay & Weine, Ruth, eds. LC 78-72187. 1979. pap. 7.95 (ISBN 0-932370-00-4). Brooks Pub Co.

Cutler, Laurence S. & Cutler, Sherrie S. Handbook of Housing Systems for Designers & Developers. LC 73-7629. Date not set. Repr. of 1974 ed. pap. text ed. 19.95 (ISBN 0-442-21820-6). Krieger.

DiDonno, Lupe & Sperling, Phyllis. How to Design & Build Your Own House. (Illus.). 1978. 17.95 (ISBN 0-394-40228-6); pap. 10.95 (ISBN 0-394-73416-5). Knopf.

Dietz, Albert G. Dwelling House Construction. rev., 4th ed. (Illus.). 528p. 1974. 22.50x (ISBN 0-262-04044-1); pap. text ed. 8.95 (ISBN 0-262-54033-9). MIT Pr.

Duce, Richard & Ziegler, Olive. The Washington Supplement for Modern Real Estate Practice. 1978. pap. 7.95 (ISBN 0-88462-331-9). Real Estate Ed Co.

Duncan, S. Blackwell. The Dream House Think Book. (Illus.). 1977. 7.95 (ISBN 0-8306-7990-1); pap. 4.95 (ISBN 0-8306-6990-6, 990). TAB Bks.

Elliott, Stewart. Timber Frame Planning Book. 1979. 25.00 (ISBN 0-8092-7340-3); pap. 15.00 o. p. (ISBN 0-8092-7341-1). Contemp Bks.

Falcone, Joseph D. How to Design, Build, Remodel & Maintain Your Home. 1980. pap. write for info. (Fireside). S&S.

Farmer, W. D. Homes for Pleasant Living. 35th ed. (Illus., Orig.). 1980. pap. 2.50 (ISBN 0-931518-12-1). W D Farmer.

--Homes for Pleasant Living. 36th ed. (Illus.). 72p. (Orig.). 1980. pap. 3.50 (ISBN 0-931518-13-X). W D Farmer.

Feldheym, Len. Pole House Construction. (Orig.). 1982. pap. 15.75 (ISBN 0-910460-85-X). Craftsman.

Galbraith, Anne & Evans, Robert. Revision Notes on Building Law. (Revision Notes Ser.). (Illus.). 1979. pap. text ed. 4.95 (ISBN 0-408-00329-4). Butterworth.

Garvy, Helen. I Built Myself a House. (Illus.). 128p. pap. 2.50 (ISBN 0-918828-02-3). Crossing Pr.

--I Built Myself a House. rev. ed. LC 77-5597. (Illus.). 1977. pap. 2.50 (ISBN 0-918828-02-3). Shire Pr.

Hackenberg, Larry M. The Green Wood House: How to Build & Own a Beautiful,Inexpensive House. rev. ed. LC 75-33166. 1978. 9.75x (ISBN 0-8139-0646-6). U Pr of Va.

Harrison, Henry S. Houses: The Illustrated Guide to Construction, Design & Systems. rev. ed. LC 73-84029. 1976. 12.00 (ISBN 0-913652-05-9); wkbk. 6.00 (ISBN 0-913652-09-1). Realtors Natl.

Hasenau, J. James. Build Your Own Home: A Guide for Subcontracting the Easy Way, a System to Save Time & Money. (Illus.). 1976. 11.95 (ISBN 0-913042-03-X); pap. 6.95 (ISBN 0-913042-09-9). Holland Hse Pr.

Hasenav, J. James. Building Consultant: The Owner's Guide to Understanding Construction of His Home, What You Should Know About Building Specifications. (Illus.). 11.95 (ISBN 0-913042-08-0). Holland Hse Pr.

Heldman, Carl. Be Your Own House Contractor. (Illus.). 144p. 1981. pap. 6.95 (ISBN 0-88266-256-2). Garden Way Pub.

Higson, James D. The Home Builder's Guide. rev. ed. (Illus.). 1977. pap. 7.00 (ISBN 0-910460-50-7). Craftsman.

Hoffman, George. How to Inspect a House. (Illus.). 1979. 8.95 (ISBN 0-440-04366-2, Sey Lawr). Delacorte.

--How to Inspect a House. 1979. pap. 4.95 (ISBN 0-440-53331-7, Delta). Dell.

Home & Homebuilding 1981. 4th. ed. 234p. 1981. 15.00 (ISBN 0-86718-055-2). Natl Assn Home.

Home Planners, Inc. Two Hundred & Fifty Homes: One Story Designs Under 2,000 Square Feet. (Design Category Ser.: Vol. 3). (Illus.). pap. 3.00 (ISBN 0-918894-02-6). Home Planners.

Hotton, Peter. So You Want to Build a House. 256p. (Orig.). 1976. pap. 7.95 (ISBN 0-316-37386-9). Little.

Hunt, Don J. How to Build Your Own House & Save Money. (Illus.). 160p. 1981. pap. 9.95 (ISBN 0-934750-16-5). Jalamap.

Isaacs, Ken. How to Build Your Own Living Structures. (Illus.). 144p. 1974. 9.95 (ISBN 0-517-50562-2); spiral bound 4.95 (ISBN 0-517-50559-2). Crown.

Kahn, Lloyd, ed. Shelter II. LC 78-57133. (Illus.). 224p. (Orig.). 1978. 15.00 (ISBN 0-394-50219-1); pap. 9.50 (ISBN 0-394-73611-7). Shelter Pubns.

Kahn, Lloyd, Jr., ed. Shelter Two. LC 78-57133. (Illus.). 1978. 15.00 (ISBN 0-394-50219-1); pap. 9.50 (ISBN 0-394-73611-7). Random.

Kern & Magers. Fireplaces. 200p. 7.95 (ISBN 0-686-31218-X). Owner-Builder.

Kern & Turner. The Work Book. 316p. 7.95 (ISBN 0-686-31217-1). Owner-Builder.

Kern, et al. Stone Masonry. 192p. 10.95 (ISBN 0-686-31221-X). Owner-Builder.

--The Owner-Builder & the Code. 192p. 5.00 (ISBN 0-686-31223-6). Owner-Builder.

Kern, Barbara & Kern, Ken. The Owner-Built Homestead. 400p. 9.20 (ISBN 0-686-31219-8). Owner-Builder.

--The Owner Built Homestead. LC 77-4032. (Illus.). 1977. pap. 7.95 (ISBN 0-684-14926-5, ScribT). Scribner.

--The Pole Frame House. 1981. 16.95 (ISBN 0-686-31224-4). Owner-Builder.

Kern, Ken. The Healthy House. 180p. 5.75 (ISBN 0-686-31222-8). Owner-Builder.

--The Owner-Built Home. 375p. 9.20 (ISBN 0-686-31220-1). Owner-Builder.

--The Owner-Built Home. LC 75-5653. 1975. pap. 7.95 (ISBN 0-684-14223-6, ScribT, SL582, ScribT). Scribner.

Kravitol, R. Buying, Owning & Selling a Home in the Nineteen Eighties. 1981. 17.95 (ISBN 0-13-109512-9); pap. 9.95 (ISBN 0-13-109504-8). P-H.

Krieger, Morris. Homeowner's Encyclopedia of House Construction. (Illus.). 1978. 19.95 (ISBN 0-07-035497-9, P&RB). McGraw.

Lefax Pub. Co. Editors. Handi-Fax. (Lefax Technical Manuals.: No. 852). (Illus.). looseleaf bdg. 9.50 (ISBN 0-685-14140-3). Lefax.

Mc Clain, Harry W. Beat the Building Cost Boom: How to Build Your Own Home for 1/10th the Cost of Conventional Construction. (Illus.). 1978. pap. text ed. 12.95 (ISBN 0-933608-00-4). Mountain View.

McGrath, Ed. The Superinsulated House: A Working Guide for Owner-Builders & Architects. (Illus.). 128p. 1981. 13.95 (ISBN 0-918270-11-1); pap. 9.95 (ISBN 0-918270-12-X). That New Pub.

McLaughlin, Jack. The Housebuilding Experience. LC 80-24670. 224p. 1981. write for info. (ISBN 0-442-25398-2). Van Nos Reinhold.

McNellis, Cathy & McNellis, Bob. You Can Still Own a Home: A Strategy for Stretching Your Housing Dollar. 1978. 7.00 (ISBN 0-682-49030-X). Exposition.

Maguire, Byron W. Carpentry in Residential Construction. (Illus.). 416p. 1975. 18.95 (ISBN 0-87909-118-5). Reston.

Manley, Deborah. A New House. LC 78-31914. (Ready, Set, Look Ser.). (Illus.). (gr. k-3). 1979. PLB 10.65 (ISBN 0-8172-1306-6). Raintree Pubs.

Martindale, David. Earth Shelters. (Illus.). 160p. 1981. 18.50 (ISBN 0-525-93199-6, 01796-540); pap. 10.25 (ISBN 0-525-93200-3, 0995-300). Dutton.

Mayer, Martin. The Builders: Houses, People, Neighborhoods, Government, Money. 1978. 17.50 (ISBN 0-393-08796-4). Norton.

Montgomery, Clarence. The Book of Beautiful Homes with Building Instructions. (A Promotion of the Arts Library Bk.). (Illus.). 1979. 39.75 (ISBN 0-89266-194-1). Am Classical Coll Pr.

Myller, Rolf. From Idea into House. LC 73-84832. (Illus.). 64p. (gr. 4 up). 1974. 7.95 (ISBN 0-689-30144-8). Atheneum.

Neal, Charles D. Do-It-Yourself Housebuilding Step-by-Step. LC 72-91256. 1977. pap. 10.95 (ISBN 0-8128-2188-2). Stein & Day.

Neigoff, Anne. New House, New Town. LC 72-13352. (Career Awareness-Community Helpers Ser.). (Illus.). 32p. (gr. k-2). 1973. 5.25g (ISBN 0-8075-5570-3). A. Whitman.

Norris, Henry D. The Plans Book. LC 77-86203. 1977. pap. 12.50 (ISBN 0-930560-01-9, Pub. by Two Continents). Hippocrene Bks.

O'Mara, W. P., et al. Residential Development Handbook. LC 77-930497. (Community Builders Handbook Ser.). (Illus.). 350p. 1978. 34.00 (ISBN 0-87420-580-8). Urban Land.

Patton, W. Construction Materials. 1976. 19.95 (ISBN 0-13-168724-7). P-H.

Powell, M. J. V., ed. House Builders Reference Book. (Illus.). 1979. text ed. 84.95 (ISBN 0-408-00337-5). Butterworth.

Reidelbach, J. A., Jr. Modular Housing '72, Statistics & Specifics. LC 72-94628. 236p. 1972. 24.50 (ISBN 0-89047-002-2). Herman Pub.

Reif, Rita. Home - It Takes More Than Money. LC 74-77953. (Illus.). 288p. 1976. pap. 6.95 (ISBN 0-8129-6269-9). Times Bks.

--Home: It Takes More Than Money. LC 74-77953. (Illus.). 288p. 1975. 9.95 (ISBN 0-8129-0493-1). Times Bks.

Reiner, Laurence E. Methods & Materials of Residential Construction. (Illus.). 336p. 1981. text ed. 24.95 (ISBN 0-13-578864-1). P-H.

Reschke, Robert C. Successful How to Build Your Own Home. 2nd ed. LC 79-91999. (Successful Ser.). (Illus.). 1979. 15.95 (ISBN 0-912336-93-5); pap. 9.95 (ISBN 0-912336-94-3). Structures Pub.

Roebuck, Alan D. How to Put up Your Own Post-Frame House & Cabin. (Illus.). 1979. pap. 8.95 (ISBN 0-8306-1154-1, 1154). TAB Bks.

Rosen, Kenneth. A Regional Model of Residential Construction. 220p. Date not set. 18.00 (ISBN 0-88410-618-7). Ballinger Pub.

Roy, Robert L. Cordwood Masonry Houses: A Practical Guide for the Owner-Builder. LC 80-52325. (Illus.). 168p. 1980. 14.95 (ISBN 0-8069-5418-3); lib. bdg. 13.29 (ISBN 0-8069-5419-1); pap. 7.95 (ISBN 0-8069-8944-0). Sterling.

--Money-Saving Strategies for the Owner-Builder. LC 81-8843. (Illus.). 160p. (Orig.). 1981. pap. 6.95 (ISBN 0-8069-7548-2). Sterling.

Schuler, Stanley. All Your Home Building & Remodeling Questions Answered. Roberts, Ray, ed. LC 72-97760. 1971. 13.95 (ISBN 0-02-607470-2). Macmillan.

Schwenke, Karl & Schwenke, Sue. Build Your Own Stone House: Using the Easy Slipform Method. LC 75-16831. (Illus.). 156p. 1975. 10.95 (ISBN 0-88266-071-3); pap. 5.95 (ISBN 0-88266-069-1). Garden Way Pub.

Self, Charles R. Building Your Own Home. (Illus.). 1978. 16.95 (ISBN 0-87909-098-7). Reston.

Sobol, Harriet L. Pete's House. LC 77-12564. (Illus.). (gr. 3-6). 1978. 8.95 (ISBN 0-02-785980-0, 78598). Macmillan.

Spikins, Joe. How to Save Twenty-Five Thousand Dollars Building Your House. (Illus.). 1982. 18.95 (ISBN 0-9602442-1-2); pap. 16.95 (ISBN 0-686-30555-8). Consumer Assoc.

Stickley, Gustav. The Best of Craftsman Homes. (Illus.). 1979. pap. 9.95 (ISBN 0-87905-058-6). Peregrine Smith.

Stillman, Richard J. Do-It-Yourself Contracting to Build Your Own Home. LC 74-2297. 176p. 1974. 10.95 (ISBN 0-8019-5937-3). Chilton.

Summers, Lydia B., et al. Researching the Old House. (Illus.). 1981. pap. 3.95 (ISBN 0-686-73779-2). Greater Portland.

TAB Editorial Staff. Practical Home Construction-Carpentry Handbook. LC 76-1552. 448p. 1976. pap. 5.95 (ISBN 0-8306-5900-5, 900). TAB Bks.

Tuttle, Edward X. With Benefit of Architect. LC 68-19826. (Illus.). 1968. 7.95 (ISBN 0-02-620750-8). Macmillan.

Ural, Oktay. Construction of Lower-Cost Housing. LC 79-15561. (Practical Construction Guides Ser.). 1980. 28.50 (ISBN 0-471-89643-8, Pub. by Wiley-Interscience). Wiley.

U.S. Dept. of Agriculture. Vacation Homes & Cabins: Sixteen Complete Plans. (USDA Material Ser.). (Illus.). 1978. pap. 3.00 (ISBN 0-486-23631-5). Dover.

Van Orman, Halsey. Illustrated Handbook of Home Construction. (Illus.). 350p. 1981. text ed. price not set (ISBN 0-442-25887-9); pap. text ed. price not set (ISBN 0-442-25886-0). Van Nos Reinhold.

Ventolo, William. Residential Construction. 1979. pap. 19.95 (ISBN 0-88462-356-4). Real Estate Ed Co.

Vila, Robert & Stephen, George. Bob Vila's This Old House. 1981. 21.00 (ISBN 0-525-93192-9); pap. 13.50 (ISBN 0-525-47670-9). Dutton.

Wade, Alex. A Design & Construction Handbook for Energy Saving Houses. (Illus.). 1980. 19.95 (ISBN 0-87857-275-9); pap. 14.95 (ISBN 0-87857-274-0). Rodale Pr Inc.

Walker, Les. Housebuilding for Children. LC 76-47220. (Illus.). 176p. 1977. 11.95 (ISBN 0-87951-059-5). Overlook Pr.

Walker, Mabel. The House Is Built. 1979. 10.95 (ISBN 0-533-03158-3). Vantage.

Wampler, Jan. All Their Own: People & the Places They Build. (Illus.). 1978. pap. 10.95 (ISBN 0-19-520028-4, GB539, GB). Oxford U Pr.

Wass, Alonzo. Estimating Residential Construction. (Illus.). 1980. text ed. 21.95 (ISBN 0-13-289942-6). P-H.

--Methods & Materials of Residential Construction. 2nd ed. LC 76-39990. 1977. ref. ed. 19.95 (ISBN 0-87909-488-5); text ed. 14.95 (ISBN 0-686-66263-6). Reston.

Wass, Alonzo & Sanders, Gordon. Materials & Procedures for Residential Construction. (Illus.). text ed. 19.95 (ISBN 0-8359-4284-8). Reston.

Webber, Joan. How Old Is Your House? A Guide to Research. LC 77-88359. (Illus.). 1978. pap. 4.95 (ISBN 0-87106-092-2). Globe Pequot.

Wilson, J. Douglas. Practical House Carpentry: Simplified Methods for Building. 3rd ed. (Illus.). 1979. pap. 4.95 (ISBN 0-07-070889-4, SP). McGraw.

Woodframe Houses: Construction & Maintenance. LC 81-50025. (Illus.). 223p. 1981. pap. 7.95 (ISBN 0-8069-7512-1). Sterling.

Yeck, Fred. Building Your Own Home. rev. ed. LC 78-3419. (Illus.). 1979. pap. 4.95 (ISBN 0-668-04637-6, 4637). Arco.

Zink, William. How to Build a House Simply for One-Third Cost. 2nd ed. LC 75-46405. (Illus.). 1977. 7.50 (ISBN 0-916666-02-6); pap. 4.95 (ISBN 0-916666-01-8). Jay Pubns.

HOUSE DECORATION
see Interior Decoration

HOUSE DRAINAGE
see Drainage, House; Plumbing; Sanitation; Sewerage

HOUSE FITTINGS
see Building Fittings

HOUSE-FLIES
see Flies

HOUSE FURNISHINGS
see also Candlesticks; Carpets; Clocks and Watches; Furniture; Glassware; Household Appliances; Interior Decoration; Kitchen Utensils; Lamps; Pottery; Rugs; Silverwork

Alexander, Patsy R. Textile Products: Selection, Use & Care. LC 76-11955. (Illus.). 416p. 1977. text ed. 15.50 (ISBN 0-395-20358-9); inst. manual 1.50 (ISBN 0-395-20357-0). HM.

Allen, Phyllis S. The Young Decorator. LC 74-23449. (Illus.). 220p. (gr. 10-12). 1975. pap. text ed. 12.95x (ISBN 0-8425-0062-6). Brigham.

Avery, James R. & Null, Roberta L. Environmental Design Laboratory Guide. 3rd ed. (Illus.). 1978. pap. text ed. 6.95 (ISBN 0-8403-1077-3). Kendall-Hunt.

Beecher, Catharine E. & Stowe, Harriet B. The American Woman's Home. LC 75-22526. (Illus.). 1975. pap. 6.95 (ISBN 0-917482-04-2). Stowe-Day.

Bingham, Joan & Riccio, Dolores. Make It Yourself. LC 77-14689. (Illus.). 1978. 12.95 (ISBN 0-8019-6672-8); pap. 8.95 (ISBN 0-8019-6673-6). Chilton.

Collins, Peggie & Collins, Shirley. Putting It All Together, A Consumer's Guide to Home Furnishings. LC 77-1885. (Illus.). 1977. 10.00 (ISBN 0-684-14883-8, ScribT); (ScribT). Scribner.

Cummings, A. L. & Fales, D. A., Jr. The Crowninshield-Bentley House. LC 76-16905. (Historic House Booklet Ser: No. 2). 1976. 2.00 (ISBN 0-88389-060-7). Essex Inst.

De Wolfe, Elsie. The House in Good Taste. fascimile ed. LC 75-1839. (Leisure Class in America Ser.). (Illus.). 1975. Repr. of 1913 ed. 19.00x (ISBN 0-405-06908-1). Arno.

Do-It-Yourself & Home Improvement Markets. 1981. 250.00x (ISBN 0-686-71951-4, Pub. by Euromonitor). State Mutual Bk.

Frey, Iris I. Staple It. 1979. 12.95 (ISBN 0-517-53254-9); pap. 8.95 (ISBN 0-517-53255-7). Crown.

Gallick, Sarah & Gallick, Mary. Furnish-Your-Home-by-Mail Catalogue. 1981. pap. 9.95 (ISBN 0-452-25291-1, Z5291, Plume). NAL.

Gump, Richard. Good Taste Costs No More. 1970. pap. 1.95 (ISBN 0-02-080170-X, Collier). Macmillan.

Halliday, Anne. Decorating with Crochet. LC 75-15893. (Illus.). 176p. 1975. 16.95 (ISBN 0-395-20992-7). HM.

Hoffman, Emanuel. Fairchild's Dictionary of Home Furnishings: Furniture, Accessories, Curtains & Draperies, Fabrics, Floor Coverings. new ed. Buck, Babs F. & Small, Verna, eds. LC 70-180155. (Illus.). 384p. 1974. lib. bdg. 25.00 (ISBN 0-87005-106-7). Fairchild.

Kaplan, Barbara. Home Furnishings. LC 74-19485. 1975. pap. text ed. 9.50 (ISBN 0-672-96412-0); tchr's manual 6.67 (ISBN 0-672-96832-0). Bobbs.

Louie, Elaine. The Manhattan Home Furnishings Shopping Guide. 1979. pap. 5.95 (ISBN 0-02-080730-9, Collier). Macmillan.

McCall's Magazine Editors. McCall's Sewing for Your Home. 1977. 12.50 (ISBN 0-671-22372-0). S&S.

McMillan, Patricia H. & Gilbert, Rose B. Decorating Country-Style: The Look & How to Have It. LC 78-68324. (Illus.). 1980. 17.95 (ISBN 0-385-14086-X). Doubleday.

Mademoiselle Magazine Editors. Make It with Mademoiselle. 1977. pap. 5.95 (ISBN 0-517-52865-7, Harmony). Crown.

Prior, Joanne. Soft Furnishing. (Leisure Time Bks). (Illus.). pap. 11.75x (ISBN 0-7135-1589-9, LTB). Sportshelf.

Roy, Doreen. Champagne Decorating on a Beer Budget. LC 76-55704. (Illus.). 1977. 10.95 (ISBN 0-8128-2202-1); pap. 6.95 (ISBN 0-8128-2203-X). Stein & Day.

Sieber, Roy. African Furniture & Household Objects. LC 79-5340. (Illus.). 280p. 1980. 37.50x (ISBN 0-253-11927-8); pap. 20.00x (ISBN 0-253-28242-X). Ind U Pr.

Small, HyDee. The Complete Bed Building Book. (Illus.). 1979. pap. 7.95 (ISBN 0-8306-1124-X, 1124). TAB Bks.

Stepat-Devan, Dorothy, et al. Introduction to Home Furnishings. 3rd ed. (Illus.). 1980. text ed. 18.95 (ISBN 0-02-417090-9). Macmillan.

Wilson, Jose & Leaman, Arthur. The First Complete Home Decorating Catalogue. LC 75-5474. (Illus.). 256p. 1976. 10.00 (ISBN 0-685-58403-8); pap. 5.95 (ISBN 0-03-014646-1). HR&W.

HOUSE FURNISHINGS INDUSTRY AND TRADE–DIRECTORIES

Directory of the Furnishing Trade 1979. (Benn Directories Ser.). 1979. 70.00 (ISBN 0-686-60655-8, Pub by Benn Pubns). Nichols Pub.

HOUSE MOTHERS
see Housemothers

HOUSE ORGANS
see also Employees' Magazines, Handbooks, etc.

Darrow, Ralph C. House Journal Editing. LC 73-93505. x, 249p. 1974. pap. text ed. 5.95 (ISBN 0-8134-1628-0, 1628). Interstate.

Hazzlewood, John W. House Journals. (Facts of Print Ser). 1967. Repr. of 1963 ed. 8.95 (ISBN 0-289-27810-4). Dufour.

Mann, Charles. Editing for Industry: The Production of House Journals. LC 75-302619. (Illus.). 208p. 1974. 10.00x (ISBN 0-434-91200-X). Intl Pubns Serv.

Nanfria, Linda. How to Publish an Organization Newsletter. 1976. pap. 3.30 (ISBN 0-88409-040-X). Creative Bk Co.

HOUSE PAINTING
see also Painting, Industrial; Texture Painting

Banov, Abel & Lytle, Marie-Jeanne. Book of Successful Painting. LC 74-21836. (Illus.). 114p. 1975. 12.00 (ISBN 0-912336-11-0); pap. 4.95 (ISBN 0-912336-12-9). Structures Pub.

Brushwell, William, ed. Painting & Decorating Encyclopedia. LC 72-90782. (Illus.). 272p. 1973. text ed. 10.00 (ISBN 0-87006-160-7). Goodheart.

Demske, Dick. Painting, Paneling, & Wallpapering. Wolf, Donald D. & Wolf, Margot L., eds. LC 76-8373. (Adventures in Home Repair Ser.). (Illus.). 1977. pap. 3.95 (ISBN 0-8326-2212-5, 7702). Delair.

Geary, Donald. Interior & Exterior Painting. (Illus.). 1979. 11.95 (ISBN 0-8359-3126-9). Reston.

Goodier, J. H. Dictionary of Painting & Decorating. 308p. 1974. 39.50x (ISBN 0-85264-224-5, Pub. by Griffin England). State Mutual Bk.

--Painting & Decorating: A Guide for Houseowner & Decorator. (Illus.). 1977. 17.95x (ISBN 0-7114-4612-1). Intl Ideas.

Gundrey, Elizabeth. Painting & Decorating. (Orig.). 1980. pap. 8.95x (ISBN 0-8464-1036-2). Beekman Pubs.

How to Paint Interiors. (Home Care Guides Ser.). (Illus.). 1981. pap. 2.50 (ISBN 0-686-71128-9). S&S.

Hurst, A. E. & Goodier, J. M. Painting & Decorating. 620p. 1980. 75.00x (ISBN 0-85264-243-1, Pub. by Griffin England). State Mutual Bk.

Rudman, Jack. House Painter. (Career Examination Ser.: C-354). (Cloth bdg. avail. on request). pap. 8.00 (ISBN 0-8373-0354-0). Natl Learning.
Schultz, Morton. Painting & Wallpapering. LC 77-90416. (Practical Workshop Library Ser). (Illus.). 1969. lib. bdg. 4.95 (ISBN 0-668-02059-8). Arco.
Sunset Editors. Paneling, Painting & Wallpapering. LC 75-26493. (Illus.). 80p. 1976. pap. 3.95 (ISBN 0-376-01393-1, Sunset Bks.). Sunset-Lane.
Time Life Books, ed. Paint & Wallpaper. LC 76-3377. (Home Repair & Improvement). (Illus.). (gr. 7 up). 1976. PLB 11.97 (ISBN 0-8094-2355-3, Pub. by Time-Life). Silver.

HOUSE PLANS

see Architecture, Domestic–Designs and Plans

HOUSE PLANTS

see also Artificial Light Gardening; Gardens, Miniature; Hanging Plants; Plants, Potted; Window-Gardening;
also names of plants or classes of plants used as house plants, e.g., African Violets; Cactus; Succulent Plants

Abraham, George. Green Thumb Book of Indoor Gardening: A Complete Guide. LC 67-19294. 1967. 7.95 (ISBN 0-13-365163-0). P-H.
Bagnasco, John J. Plants for the Home, Vol. 1. 1978. pap. 3.95 (ISBN 0-918134-02-1). Nature Life.
--Plants for the Home, Vol. 1. 1975. 15.00 (ISBN 0-918134-01-3). Nature Life.
Baines, Jocelyn & Key, Katherine. A B C of Indoor Plants. 1973. 14.95 (ISBN 0-394-48774-5). Knopf.
Bauske, Robert J. Home Horticulture. LC 76-2733. (Illus.). 200p. 1976. text ed. 15.95 (ISBN 0-8299-0112-4). West Pub.
Baylis, Maggie. House Plants for the Purple Thumb. LC 72-94894. (Illus.). 192p. (Orig.). 1973. 4.95 (ISBN 0-912238-33-X); pap. 4.95 (ISBN 0-912238-32-1). One Hund One Prods.
--Practicing Plant Parenthood. LC 75-22361. (Illus.). 192p. (Orig.). 1975. 4.95 (ISBN 0-912238-62-3); pap. 4.95 (ISBN 0-912238-61-5). One Hund One Prods.
Beatty, Virginia & Consumer Guide Editors. Rating & Raising Indoor Plants. 1975. 8.95 (ISBN 0-671-22050-0); pap. 4.95 (ISBN 0-671-22051-9). S&S.
Bechtel, Helmut. House Plant Identifier. LC 72-95203. (Identifier Bks.). (Illus.). 256p. (gr. 6 up). 1973. 6.95 (ISBN 0-8069-3056-X); PLB 6.69 (ISBN 0-8069-3057-8). Sterling.
Better Homes & Gardens Books, ed. Better Homes & Gardens Favorite Houseplants. 1976. 5.95 (ISBN 0-696-00065-2). Meredith Corp.
Blashfield, Jean F. Apartment Greenery: Growing Plants in Unpromising Places. LC 75-2310. (Orig.). 1975. pap. 4.95 (ISBN 0-316-09954-6). Little.
--The Healthy House Plant: A Guide to the Prevention, Detection, & Cure of Pests & Diseases. 1980. 12.95 (ISBN 0-316-09955-4). Little.
Bracken, John. Great Plants for Cool Places. LC 80-5406. (Illus.). 192p. (Orig.). 1980. 12.95 (ISBN 0-8128-2721-X); pap. 6.95 (ISBN 0-8128-6064-0). Stein & Day.
Brandon, Dorothy & Scheider, Alfred F. Max Schling Book of Indoor Gardening. (Illus.). 1963. 12.00 (ISBN 0-8392-1065-5). Astor-Honor.
Breeding Plants for Home & Garden. 1.95 (ISBN 0-686-21167-7). Bklyn Botanic.
Canaday, John. The Artful Avocado. 1975. pap. 1.95 (ISBN 0-346-12179-5). Cornerstone.
Compton, Joan. House Plants No. 44. (Knowledge Through Color Ser). 160p. 1973. pap. 1.95 (ISBN 0-553-07994-8). Bantam.
Consumer Guide: Rating & Raising Indoor Plants. 1976. pap. 2.25 (ISBN 0-451-07160-3, E7160, Sig). NAL.
Crayson, Suzanne. Plants from Plants: How to Grow New Houseplants for Next to Nothing. LC 76-12559. (Illus.). 1976. pap. 6.95 (ISBN 0-397-01175-X). Har-Row.
Crockett, James U. Flowering House Plants. (Encyclopedia of Gardening Ser). (Illus.). 1971. 12.95 (ISBN 0-8094-1097-4); lib. bdg. avail. (ISBN 0-685-00195-4). Time-Life.
--Flowering House Plants. LC 78-140420. (Time-Life Encyclopedia of Gardening). (Illus.). 1971. lib. bdg. 11.97 (ISBN 0-8094-1098-2, Pub. by Time-Life). Silver.
--Foliage House Plants. (Encyclopedia of Gardening Ser). (Illus.). 1972. 12.95 (ISBN 0-8094-1121-0); lib. bdg. avail. (ISBN 0-685-25145-4). Time-Life.
Crockett, James V. Foliage House Plants. LC 78-140420. (Time-Life Encyclopedia of Gardening). (Illus.). (gr. 6 up). 1972. lib. bdg. 11.97 (ISBN 0-8094-1123-7, Pub. by Time-Life). Silver.
Davidson, William. Woman's Own Book of House Plants. LC 71-481686. (Illus.). 1969. 7.50x (ISBN 0-600-40350-5). Intl Pubns Serv.
Dworkin, Stan & Dworkin, Floss. The Apartment Gardener. 280p. (Orig.). 1974. pap. 1.75 (ISBN 0-451-08414-4, E8414, Sig). NAL.
Efraimsson, Ralf. Sixty-Five Houseplants from Seeds, Pits & Kernels. LC 77-7173. Orig. Title: Satte En Karna. (Illus.). 1977. pap. 4.95 (ISBN 0-912800-40-2). Woodbridge Pr.
Eley, Geoffrey. One Hundred & One Wild Plants for the Kitchen. (Invest in Living Ser.). (Illus.). 1977. pap. 5.00x (ISBN 0-7158-0489-8). Intl Pubns Serv.
Evans, Charles M. New Plants from Old: Pruning & Propagating for the Indoor Gardener. 1977. lib. bdg. 10.95 (ISBN 0-8161-6514-9, Large Print Bks). G K Hall.
Evans, Charles M. & Pliner, Roberta L. Rx for Ailing House Plants. 1978. lib. bdg. 10.95 (ISBN 0-8161-6567-X, Large Print Bks). G K Hall.
--Rx for Ailing House Plants. 1974. 7.95 (ISBN 0-394-48683-8). Random.
Evans, Hazel & Kumm, Alan. Woman's Own Pot Plant Doctor - a Guide to Coping with Pot Plant Ailments. (Illus.). 1978. pap. 4.95 (ISBN 0-600-37150-6). Transatlantic.
Faust, Joan L. The New York Times Book of House Plants. (Illus.). 1973. 9.95 (ISBN 0-8129-0309-9). Times Bks.
--New York Times Book of House Plants. 1975. pap. 6.95 (ISBN 0-89104-002-1). A & W Pubs.
Fell, Dereck. House Plants & Crafts: For Fun & Profit. (Fun & Profit Ser.). (Illus.). 1978. 9.95 (ISBN 0-916302-16-4); pap. 5.50 (ISBN 0-916302-04-0). Bookworm Pub.
Fenten, D. X. Easy to Make House Plants. LC 81-80075. (Easy to Make Ser.). (Illus.). 48p. (gr. 3-6). 1981. PLB 5.79 (ISBN 0-8178-0024-7). Harvey.
Finkle-Strauss, Linda. House Plants: How to Keep 'em Fat & Happy. LC 76-16104. 1977. 12.95 (ISBN 0-07-021007-1, GB); pap. 6.95 (ISBN 0-07-021008-X). McGraw.
Fitch, Charles M. The Complete Book of Houseplants. (Illus.). 320p. 1980. pap. 7.95 (ISBN 0-8015-1660-9, Hawthorn). Dutton.
Free, Montague & Dietz, Marjorie J. All About House Plants. rev. ed. LC 78-1197. (Illus.). 1980. 12.95 (ISBN 0-385-13532-7). Doubleday.
Gorer, Richard & Rochford, Thomas. The Rochford Book of House Plants. 3rd ed. (Illus.). 302p. 1973. 11.95 (ISBN 0-571-04807-2, Pub. by Faber & Faber). Merrimack Bk Serv.
--Rochford's House-Plants for Everyone. (Illus.). 112p. (Orig.). 1978. pap. 4.95 (ISBN 0-571-08827-9, Pub. by Faber & Faber). Merrimack Bk Serv.
Graf, Alfred B. Exotic House Plants. 10th ed. LC 72-97182. (Illus.). 1976. 8.95 (ISBN 0-911266-10-0). Roehrs.
--Exotic House Plants Illustrated. 10th ed. (Illus.). 8.95 (ISBN 0-911266-10-0, ScribT). Scribner.
--Exotic Plant Manual: Exotic Plants to Live with. 5th ed. LC 74-75310. (Illus.). 1978. 37.50 (ISBN 0-911266-13-5). Roehrs.
--Exotica Series Three: Pictorial Cyclopedia of Exotic Plants. 10th, rev. ed. LC 72-90669. (Illus.). 1980. 78.00 (ISBN 0-911266-15-1). Roehrs.
Gramenz, Gisela. Indoor Gardens & Window Boxes. (Practical Knowledge Ser.). (Illus.). 96p. 1971. 5.00x (ISBN 0-7188-1783-4). Intl Pubns Serv.
Greenfingers, G. & Bicknell, Andrew. Dr. Greenfingers' Rx for Healthy, Vigorous Houseplants. (Illus.). 160p. 1980. 12.95 (ISBN 0-517-53821-0, Michelman Bks); pap. 6.95 (ISBN 0-517-53822-9). Crown.
Grounds, Roger. House Plants. LC 77-700394. (Illus.). (gr. 11-12). 1977. pap. 3.95 (ISBN 0-8120-0796-4). Barron.
Halpin, Anne M., ed. Rodale's Encyclopedia of Indoor Gardening. (Illus.). 912p. 1980. 29.95 (ISBN 0-87857-319-4). Rodale Pr Inc.
Hardigree, Peggy. The Edible Indoor Garden. 320p. 1981. 16.95 (ISBN 0-312-23689-1); pap. 7.95 (ISBN 0-312-23690-5). St Martin.
Hawkey, William S. Living with Plants: A Book of Home Decorating & Plant Care. (Illus.). 216p. 1974. 15.95 (ISBN 0-688-00277-3). Morrow.
Hay, Roy, et al. Diccionario Ilustrado en Color De Plantas De Interior. 231p. (Espn.). 1976. 48.00 (ISBN 84-252-0892-0, S-50277). French & Eur.
Helmer, M. Jane. Foliage Plants for Modern Living. 2nd rev. ed. (Modern Living Ser.). (Illus.). 80p. 1977. pap. 2.95 (ISBN 0-89484-009-6, 10101). Merchants Pub Co.
Herda, D. J. Growing Trees Indoors. LC 78-37164. 1979. 16.95x (ISBN 0-88229-346-X); pap. 8.95 (ISBN 0-686-66163-X). Nelson-Hall.
Hersey, Jean D. Woman's Day Book of House Plants. (Illus.). 1965. 8.95 (ISBN 0-671-82535-6). S&S.
Herwig, Bob & Schubert, Margot. A Treasury of Houseplants. (Illus.). 1979. pap. 9.95 (ISBN 0-02-063120-0, Collier). Macmillan.
Herwig, Rob. How to Grow Healthy Houseplants. LC 79-84701. (Illus.). 1979. pap. 5.95 (ISBN 0-89586-026-0). H P Bks.
--One Hundred & Twenty Eight More Houseplants You Can Grow: Domestic Reprint Edition. 1974. pap. 1.95 (ISBN 0-02-065420-0, Collier); pap. 39.00 pre-pack (ISBN 0-02-065440-5). Macmillan.
--Two Hundred & One Houseplants in Color. Powell, Marian, tr. (Illus.). 1976. pap. 4.95 (ISBN 0-02-063050-6, Collier). Macmillan.
Hessayon, D. G. Be Your Own House Plant Expert. 35p. 1976. pap. 1.95 (ISBN 0-8119-0356-7). Fell.
--Be Your Own House Plant Spotter. 35p. 1977. 1.95 (ISBN 0-8119-0357-5). Fell.
Hessayon, David. The House Plant Expert. 128p. (Orig.). 1981. pap. 7.95 (ISBN 0-684-17163-5, ScribT). Scribner.
Hirsch, Doris F. Indoor Plants: Comprehensive Care & Culture. LC 76-57249. 1977. 15.00 (ISBN 0-8019-6489-X). Chilton.
--Indoor Plants: Comprehensive Care & Culture. LC 76-57249. 1977. 15.00 (ISBN 0-8019-6489-X). Chilton.
House Plant Primer. 1.95 (ISBN 0-686-21162-6). Bklyn Botanic.
House Plants. 1.95 (ISBN 0-686-21135-9). Bklyn Botanic.
House Plants Indoors - Outdoors. (Illus.). 1977. pap. 3.98 (ISBN 0-917102-03-7). Ortho.
Johnson, Deborah. A Blooming Success. (Illus.). 1978. pap. 7.95 (ISBN 0-88453-019-1). Barrington.
Kohler, Julilly H. Plants & Flowers to Decorate Your Home. (Illus.). 1977. 12.95 (ISBN 0-307-49335-0, Golden Pr); pap. 5.95 (ISBN 0-307-49254-0). Western Pub.
Kramer, Jack. Bromeliads: Colorful House Plants. 1976. pap. 4.95 (ISBN 0-442-24518-1). Van Nos Reinhold.
--Drip System Watering for Bigger & Better Plants. (Illus.). 1980. 12.95 (ISBN 0-393-01299-9). Norton.
--Flowering Houseplants. 160p. 1981. 6.95 (ISBN 0-8317-4854-0, Rutledge Pr). Smith Pubs.
--Growing Beautiful Flowers Indoors. (Illus.). 1980. 24.95 (ISBN 0-312-35120-8). St Martin.
--Indoor Trees. 1980. 25.00x (ISBN 0-232-51399-6, Pub. by Darton-Longman-Todd England). State Mutual Bk.
--Once-a-Week Indoor Gardening Guide. (Orig.). pap. 1.75 (ISBN 0-515-04475-X). Jove Pubns.
--One Thousand Beautiful House Plants & How to Grow Them. LC 69-12554. (Illus.). 1969. 15.00 (ISBN 0-688-02843-8). Morrow.
--Picture Encyclopedia of Small Plants. 1978. 11.95 (ISBN 0-8128-2497-0). Stein & Day.
--Plant Language: What Your Plants Tell About You. 1979. pap. 1.95 (ISBN 0-440-16932-1). Dell.
Kromdijk, G. Two-Hundred House Plants in Color. (Illus.). 1972. 9.95 (ISBN 0-07-073280-9, GB). McGraw.
Kurtz, Regina & Van Gieson, Susan. Interior Planting Line Art. LC 80-7578. (Illus.). 1980. pap. text ed. 25.00 (ISBN 0-918436-13-3). Environ Des VA.
Langer, Richard W. Grow It Indoors. (Illus.). 384p. 1976. pap. 4.95 (ISBN 0-446-80054-6). Warner Bks.
--Grow It Indoors. (Illus.). 1976. pap. 2.50 (ISBN 0-446-91022-8). Warner Bks.
Lester, Lee. The Absolute Beginners Book of House Plants. (Illus.). 192p. 1975. 8.95 (ISBN 0-8065-0473-0). Citadel Pr.
Loewer, H. Peter. Bringing the Outdoors in: How to Do Wonders with Vines, Wildflowers, Ferns, Moses, Bulbs, Grasses, & Dozens of Other Plants Most People Overlook. LC 73-83863. (Illus.). 1974. 12.50 (ISBN 0-8027-0436-0). Walker & Co.
Longman, David. The Instant Guide to Successful Houseplants. (Illus.). 1980. 15.95 (ISBN 0-686-65926-0). Times Bks.
McDonald, Elvin. House Plants to Grow If You Have No Sun. 192p. 1975. pap. 1.50 (ISBN 0-445-03082-8). Popular Lib.
--How to Grow House Plants from Seeds. (How to Grow Plants from Seed Ser.). (Illus.). 224p. 1976. 8.95 (ISBN 0-442-80352-4); pap. 5.95 (ISBN 0-442-80400-8). Van Nos Reinhold.
--The World Book of House Plants. 320p. 1981. pap. 2.50 (ISBN 0-445-03152-2). Popular Lib.
Maldaver, Alice. Easy Ways to Multiply Your House Plants. LC 78-53073. 1978. pap. 4.50 (ISBN 0-931970-00-8). Elica Bks.
Manakar, George H. Interior Plantscapes: Installation Maintenance & Management. 1981. 19.95 (ISBN 0-686-72657-X). P-H.
Minnich, Jerry. No Time for Houseplants: A Busy Person's Guide to Indoor Gardening. LC 78-58102. (Illus.). 1979. pap. 5.95 (ISBN 0-8061-1499-1). U of Okla Pr.
Minton, Penny & Minton, Cronan. How to Grow Trees Indoors. LC 76-23782. 1978. pap. 4.95 (ISBN 0-385-11475-3). Doubleday.
Mott, Russell. Total Book of House Plants. 208p. 1975. 16.95 (ISBN 0-440-08584-5). Delacorte.
Muller-Idzerda, A. C. One Hundred Indoor Plants. (Illus.). 1959. 5.95 (ISBN 0-87523-114-4). Emerson.
Muller-Idzerda, A. C, & De Lestreux, Elisabeth. Living Color: Decorating Your Home with Plants. LC 81-1357. (Illus.). 144p. 1981. 19.95 (ISBN 0-668-05257-0, 5257). Arco.
Nehrling, Arno & Nehrling, Irene. Propagating House Plants: New - How to Grow Herbs & Vegetables Indoors. LC 70-151460. (Illus.). 1971. 7.95 (ISBN 0-8208-0020-1). Hearthside.
Nicholls, Richard E. The Plant Buyer's Handbook: A Consumer's Guide to Buying House Plants. LC 76-41669. (Illus.). 128p. (Orig.). 1977. lib. bdg. 12.90 (ISBN 0-914294-57-1); pap. 3.95 (ISBN 0-914294-58-X). Running Pr.
Nicolaisen, Age. Pocket Encyclopaedia of Indoor Plants. (Illus.). 272p. (Orig.). 1981. pap. 6.95 (ISBN 0-7137-1172-8, Pub. by Blandford Pr England). Sterling.
--Pocket Encyclopedia of Indoor Plants in Color. Goren, Richard, ed. LC 77-91385. 1970. 9.95 (ISBN 0-02-589500-1). Macmillan.
Olson, Craig. Craig Olson's Decorating with Plants. Grooms, Kathe, ed. (Illus.). 110p. 1981. pap. 2.95 (ISBN 0-915658-31-3). Meadowbrook Pr.
Orans, Muriel. Houseplants & Indooor Landscaping. (Illus.). 1973. pap. 4.95 (ISBN 0-88453-000-0). Countryside Bks.
Paul, Aileen. Kids Gardening. LC 73-177239. 96p. (gr. 3-7). 1972. 5.95 (ISBN 0-385-02492-4). Doubleday.
Pautz, Phyllis. Decorating with Plant Crafts & Natural Material. LC 70-150912. 1971. 9.95 (ISBN 0-385-08327-0). Doubleday.
Perper, Hazel. Citrus Seed Grower's Indoor How-to Book. LC 73-179694. (Illus.). 1971. 4.50 (ISBN 0-396-06434-5). Dodd.
Perry, Frances. Beautiful Leaved Plants. LC 79-90555. (Illus.). 160p. 1980. 17.95 (ISBN 0-87923-316-8). Godine.
Poincelot, Raymond. Gardening Indoors with House Plants. LC 74-16238. (Illus.). 272p. 1974. 9.95 (ISBN 0-87857-085-3); pap. 4.95 (ISBN 0-87857-108-6). Rodale Pr Inc.
Portugal, Nancy & Main, Jody. Potted Plant Organic Care. 3rd ed. LC 79-22173. (Living on This Planet Ser.). (Illus.). 1980. pap. 4.50 (ISBN 0-9601088-7-4). Wide World-Tetra.
Proudley, Brian & Proudley, Valerie. Indoor Plants: A Popular Guide. (Illus.). 176p. 1981. 14.95 (ISBN 0-7137-1003-9, Pub. by Blandford Pr England). Sterling.
Robinette, Gary O. Planting Details. LC 80-70576. 249p. 1980. pap. text ed. 20.00 (ISBN 0-918436-14-1). Environ Des VA.
Roca, Nancy. House Plants: A New Primer for Dumb Thumb. rev. ed. (Orig.). 1979. pap. 4.95 (ISBN 0-89815-006-X). Ten Speed Pr.
Ross, Shirley. Plant Consciousness, Plant Care. LC 73-79931. (Illus.). 194p. 1973. 7.95 (ISBN 0-8129-0394-3). Times Bks.
Roth, Ernest, ed. Plants for the Home. LC 77-82737. (Illus.). 1977. 7.95 (ISBN 0-8467-0370-X, Pub. by Two Continents). Hippocrene Bks.
Scrivens, Steven. Interior Planting in Large Buildings: A Handbook for Architects Interior Designers & Horticulturists. LC 80-23565. 129p. 1981. 44.95 (ISBN 0-470-27067-5). Halsted Pr.
Seddon, George. The Best Plant Book Ever. LC 76-51529. (Illus.). 1977. 12.50 (ISBN 0-528-81799-X); pap. 8.95 (ISBN 0-528-88196-5). Rand.
--The Pocket Guide to Indoor Plants. (Illus.). 1980. pap. 4.95 (ISBN 0-671-25249-6). S&S.
Selsam, Millicent & Peterson, Deborah. The Don't-Throw-It Grow-It Book of Houseplants. 1977. pap. 3.95 (ISBN 0-394-73308-8). Random.
Skelsey, Alice & Mooney, Cecile. Every Room a Garden. LC 75-20176. (Illus.). 1976. pap. 6.95 (ISBN 0-911104-91-7). Workman Pub.
Steffek, Edwin, ed. The Complete Book of Houseplants & Indoor Gardening. (Illus.). 1976. 16.95 (ISBN 0-517-52614-X). Crown.
Stevenson, Violet. Indoor Plants. LC 80-80743. (Arco Fact Guides in Color Ser.). (Illus.). 128p. 1980. 7.95 (ISBN 0-668-04942-1, 4942-1). Arco.
Stewart, Bonnie E. One Hundred One Trouble Free Houseplants for Modern Living. Wilson, Helen V., ed. (Modern Living Ser.). (Illus.). 80p. (Orig.). 1978. pap. 2.95 (ISBN 0-89484-010-X, 10107). Merchants Pub Co.
Stuckey, Martha & Hoffman-Biskar, Ethel. Green Plants for Gray Days. (Illus.). 1975. pap. 4.95 (ISBN 0-918480-00-0). Victoria Hse.
Sunset Editors. House Plants: How to Grow. 3rd ed. LC 76-7660. (Illus.). 80p. 1976. pap. 3.95 (ISBN 0-376-03335-5, Sunset Bks). Sunset-Lane.
Sweningson, Sally. Indoor Gardening. LC 74-33528. (Early Craft Bks.). (Illus.). 32p. (gr. 1-4). 1975. PLB 3.95g (ISBN 0-8225-0871-0). Lerner Pubns.

Taloumis, George. House Plants for Five Exposures. 1975. pap. 1.50 (ISBN 0-451-06374-0, W6374, Sig). NAL.
Tenenbaum, Frances. Plants from Nine to Five: Gardening Where You Work. LC 76-43062. (Illus.). 1977. Encore Ed. pap. 7.95 (ISBN 0-684-16377-2, SL732, ScribT). Scribner.
Thompson, H. C. & Bonnie, Fred. House Plants. LC 75-12123. (Family Guidebooks Ser.). (Illus.). 96p. 1975. pap. 2.95 (ISBN 0-8487-0384-7). Oxmoor Hse.
Time-Life Books & Time Life Books Editors, eds. Decorating with Plants. (Encyclopedia of Gardening Ser.). (Illus.). 1978. 12.95 (ISBN 0-8094-2579-3). Time-Life.
Van Alphen, Corry. Effective Use of House Plants. (Illus.). 1959. 5.95 (ISBN 0-87523-112-8). Emerson.
Vermiglio, Maria & Henkin, Bill. The Plant Book. LC 77-73862. (Illus.). 1977. 11.95 (ISBN 0-03-022096-3). HR&W.
Wallach, Carla. Interior Decorating with Plants. (Illus.). 224p. 1976. 14.95 (ISBN 0-02-623140-9). Macmillan.
Walzer, Michael. Political Action: A Practical Guide to Movement Politics. LC 79-143571. 120p. (Orig.). 1971. pap. 1.95 (ISBN 0-8129-6142-0). Times Bks.
Warren, Ann. Modern Guide to House Plants. (Illus.). 128p. 1974. pap. 1.50 (ISBN 0-87131-158-5). M Evans.
Weston, Marybeth L. Decorating with Plants. LC 77-88777. 1978. 12.95 (ISBN 0-394-42680-0). Pantheon.
Wheeler, Esther & Lasker, Anabel C. Flowers & Plants for Interior Decoration. 1969. 10.00 (ISBN 0-8208-0065-1). Hearthside.
Whitehead, Stanley B. The Observer's Book of House Plants. (Illus.). 1977. 2.95 (ISBN 0-684-14943-5, ScribT). Scribner.
Whitman, John. Starting from Scratch: A Guide to Indoor Gardening. LC 75-37371. (Illus.). 256p. 1976. 8.95 (ISBN 0-8129-0631-4). Times Bks.
--Starting from Scratch: A Guide to Indoor Gardening. (Illus.). 1978. pap. 1.95 (ISBN 0-451-08024-6, J8024, Sig). NAL.
Wilson, Helen Van Pelt. Houseplants Are for Pleasure: How to Grow Healthy Plants for Home Decoration. LC 72-97260. 192p. 1973. 7.95 (ISBN 0-385-06708-9). Doubleday.
Wright, Michael, ed. Plantes et jardins d'interieur. Derssenbrock, El, et al, trs. from Eng. Orig. Title: The Complete Indoor Gardener. (Illus.). 255p. (Fr.). 1975. 31.00x (ISBN 2-03-018150-1). Larousse.
Wright, Michael & Brown, Dennis, eds. Complete Indoor Gardner. (Pan Bk Ser). (Illus.). 1975. pap. 7.95 (ISBN 0-394-73045-3). Random.

HOUSE PURCHASING
see House Buying

HOUSE SANITATION
see Sanitation, Household

HOUSE SELLING
Anosike, Benji O. How to Buy or Sell Your Own Home Without a Lawyer or Broker. 120p. (Orig.). 1981. pap. text ed. 8.95x (ISBN 0-932704-09-3). Do-It-Yourself Pubs.
Bjelland, Harley. How to Sell Your Own House: Without a Broker! 1979. pap. 4.95 (ISBN 0-346-12381-X). Cornerstone.
Eldred, Gary W. House for Sale. LC 76-11440. (Orig.). 1976. 7.95 (ISBN 0-917254-01-5); pap. 4.95 (ISBN 0-917254-02-3). Harbour Hse.
Etter, Robert A. Homes, Buy Right-Sell Right or How to Avoid the Ripoff When Buying or Selling Your Home. 1976. pap. 4.95 (ISBN 0-930628-00-4). Patchwork Pubns.
Gilmore, Louis. For Sale by Owner. 1979. pap. 4.95 (ISBN 0-671-25120-1, Fireside). S&S.
--For Sale by Owner. 1974. 4.95 (ISBN 0-671-21690-2, Fireside). S&S.
Hasenau, J. James. Real Estate by Yourself. (Illus.). pap. 8.95 (ISBN 0-913042-12-9). Holland Hse Pr.
Hunter, Steven. Home Inspection Workbook. (Illus., Orig.). 1980. pap. 5.95 (ISBN 0-8437-3345-4). Hammond Inc.
Irwin, Robert. Protect Yourself in Real Estate. 1977. 18.95 (ISBN 0-07-032064-0, P&RB). McGraw.
Janik, Carolyn. Selling Your Home: A Guide to Getting the Best Price with or Without a Broker. 1981. 8.95 (ISBN 0-02-558920-2); pap. 4.95 (ISBN 0-02-008350-5). Macmillan.
--The Woman's Guide to Selling Residential Real Estate Successfully. 288p. Date not set. 10.95 (ISBN 0-686-30966-9). Everest Hse.
Joyner, Glenn P. How to Save Thousands When You Sell Your Home. LC 78-55272. 1978. pap. text ed. 7.95 (ISBN 0-932800-00-9). Ginseng Pr.
Kavanaugh, Kam. You Don't Need That Damn Broker: A Complete Guide to Selling Your Own Home. LC 81-90038. 96p. 1981. pap. 7.95 (ISBN 0-9605742-0-4). Kambrina.
Kosnar, Carl J. How to Sell Your Home Without a Real Estate Broker. 208p. 1975. 16.50 (ISBN 0-07-035364-6, P&RB). McGraw.
Kravitol, R. Buying, Owning & Selling a Home in the Nineteen Eighties. 1981. 17.95 (ISBN 0-13-109512-9); pap. 9.95 (ISBN 0-13-109504-8). P-H.
Lank, Edith. How to Sell Your Home with an Agent. 1982. pap. 9.95 (ISBN 0-8359-2975-2). Reston.
Pennington, Jerry. How to Sell Your House for More Than It's Worth. LC 76-17637. 1977. pap. 1.95 (ISBN 0-87216-615-5). Playboy Pbks.
Price, Irving. How to Get Top Dollar for Your Home. 256p. 1980. 9.95 (ISBN 0-8129-0901-1). Times Bks.
Steiner, Gerald M. Home for Sale by Owner. Ritter, Michael, ed. (Illus.). 1977. 14.95 (ISBN 0-916946-01-0). Ana-Doug Pub.
--Home for Sale by Owner. LC 77-85358. (Illus.). 1978. pap. 8.95 (ISBN 0-8015-3529-8, Hawthorn). Dutton.
Stewart, Ronald E. Do It Yourself Real Estate Kit. rev. ed. (Illus., Orig.). 1979. pap. 7.95 (ISBN 0-686-28572-7). Thunderchief.
Stone, Dave. How to Sell New Homes & Condominiums. 1975. 19.95 (ISBN 0-915742-01-2, Architectural Res Bks). McGraw.
Stone, David. How to Sell New Homes & Condominiums. LC 75-15546. 1977. 26.00 (ISBN 0-07-061735-X). McGraw.
Tuck, Curt, ed. The Fannie Mae Guide to Buying, Financing & Selling Your Home. rev. ed. LC 78-1017. 1978. pap. 5.95 (ISBN 0-385-14382-6, Dolp). Doubleday.
Weir, Sam & Weir, Mary. How We Made a Million Dollars Recycling Great Old Houses. 1980. pap. 6.95 (ISBN 0-8092-7426-4). Contemp Bks.
Williamson, Cynthia. For Sale by Owner Guide. (Orig.). 1980. pap. 3.95 (ISBN 0-930306-02-3). Delphi Info.

HOUSE STYLE
see Industrial Design Coordination

HOUSE-TO-HOUSE FIGHTING
see Street Fighting (Military Science)

HOUSE-TREE-PERSON TECHNIQUE
Buck, John N. House-Tree-Person Technique: Manual. rev. ed. LC 65-28468. (Illus.). 350p. 1970. 27.50x (ISBN 0-87424-301-7). Western Psych.
Hammer, Emanuel F. House-Tree-Person (H-T-P) Clinical Research Manual. 47p. (Orig.). 1964. pap. 6.90x (ISBN 0-87424-016-6). Western Psych.

HOUSEBOATS
see House Boats

HOUSEHOLD APPLIANCES
see also Home Economics–Equipment and Supplies
Advice About Household Appliances, Cooking, Entertaining. (Home Adviser Ser.). 80p. (Orig.). 1981. pap. 1.95 (ISBN 0-8326-2403-9, 7052). Delair.
BCC Staff. New Markets for Kitchen Appliances Gb-047. 1979. text ed. 650.00 (ISBN 0-89336-171-2). BCC.
Brasher, Ruth E. & Garrison, Carolyn L. Modern Household Equipment. Date not set. text ed. 22.50 (ISBN 0-02-313540-9). Macmillan.
Campbell, Edward A. How to Repair Home Appliances. LC 57-3885. (Illus.). 1957. lib. bdg. 3.95 (ISBN 0-668-00609-9). Arco.
De Haan, David. Antique Household Gadgets & Appliances. LC 77-88895. 1978. 5.95 (ISBN 0-8120-5261-7). Barron.
Fairchild Market Research Division. Major Appliances & Electrical Housewares. (Fairchild Fact Files Ser.). (Illus.). 64p. 1981. pap. text ed. 10.00 (ISBN 0-87005-396-5). Fairchild.
Idleman, H. K. Housing, Furniture & Appliances. (Contemporary Consumer Ser.). 1974. text ed. 4.24 (ISBN 0-07-031701-1, G); tchr's manual & key 4.95 (ISBN 0-07-031702-X). McGraw.
Lemons, Wayne & Montgomery, Glen. Small Appliance Repair Guide, Vol. 1. LC 76-105971. 1970. pap. 5.95 (ISBN 0-8306-9515-X, 515). TAB Bks.
Pearsall, Ronald. Collecting Mechanical Antiques. LC 73-76415. (Illus.). 197p. 1973. 7.95 (ISBN 0-668-02967-6). Arco.
Powell, Evan & Stevenson, Robert P. Complete Guide to Home Appliance Repair. LC 73-92403. (Popular Science Book). (Illus.). 478p. (YA) 1974. 12.95 (ISBN 0-06-013426-7, HarpT). Har-Row.

HOUSEHOLD APPLIANCES–MAINTENANCE AND REPAIR
Caprio, Dennis. Appliance Repair. (Illus.). 1979. 18.95 (ISBN 0-8359-0244-7). Reston.
Castellano, Carmine C. & Seitz, Clifford P. You Fix It: Clothes Dryers (Electric & Gas) LC 73-93616. (Illus.). 1975. pap. 4.95 (ISBN 0-668-03464-5). Arco.
Darr, Jack. The Home Appliance Clinic: Controls, Cycle Timers, Wiring & Repair. LC 74-14324. (Illus.). 196p. (YA) 1974. 7.95 (ISBN 0-8306-4745-7); pap. 4.95 (ISBN 0-8306-3745-1, 745). TAB Bks.
Drake, George R. The Repair & Servicing of Small Appliances. (Illus.). 528p. 1977. ref. ed. 19.95 (ISBN 0-87909-727-2); text ed. 16.95 (ISBN 0-686-67656-4); instructor's manual free (ISBN 0-87909-726-4). Reston.
Harris, R. Emerson & Castellano, Carmine C. You Fix It: Small Appliances. LC 73-93615. (Illus.). 1979. pap. 4.95 (ISBN 0-668-03463-7, 3463). Arco.
Heiserman, D. L. Handbook of Major Appliance Trouble-Shooting & Repair. LC 76-10684. (Illus.). 1977. 18.95 (ISBN 0-13-380295-7). P-H.
Home Appliance Repair Manual. (Illus.). Date not set. cancelled (ISBN 0-686-73605-2). Hearst Bks.
Meyerink, George. Appliance Service Handbook. (Illus.). 464p. 1973. ref. ed. 21.95x (ISBN 0-13-038844-0). P-H.
Palmore, Phyllis & Andre, Nevin. Small Appliance Repair. Schuler, Charles A., ed. LC 79-19186. (Basic Skills in Electricity & Electronics Ser.). (Illus.). 192p. (gr. 9-12). 1980. 11.60 (ISBN 0-07-048361-2, G); tchrs. manual 2.00 (ISBN 0-07-048363-9); activities manual 5.96 (ISBN 0-07-048362-0). McGraw.
Popular Mechanics Home Appliance Repair Manual. LC 80-29670. (Illus.). 320p. 1981. 22.95 (ISBN 0-910990-75-1). Hearst Bks.
Sands, Leo G. Small Appliance Repair Guide, Vol. 2. LC 76-105971. (Illus.). 196p. 1974. pap. 4.95 (ISBN 0-8306-3715-X). TAB Bks.
Scharff, B. Basics of Electric Appliance Servicing. 1976. 12.95 (ISBN 0-07-055141-3, P&RB). McGraw.
--Major Appliance Servicing: Laundry, Washing, Pumping & Waste Disposal Equipment. 1976. 13.95 (ISBN 0-07-055143-X, P&RB). McGraw.

HOUSEHOLD EXPENSES
see Cost and Standard of Living; Home Economics–Accounting

HOUSEHOLD GOODS
see House Furnishings; Household Appliances; Kitchen Utensils

HOUSEHOLD MANAGEMENT
see Home Economics

HOUSEHOLD MOVING
see Moving, Household

HOUSEHOLD PESTS
see also specific pests, e.g. Flies
Bateman, Peter. Household Pests: A Guide to the Identification & Control of Insect, Rodent Damp & Fungoid Problems in the Home. (Illus.). 1979. 14.95 (ISBN 0-7137-0915-4, Pub by Blandford Pr England). Sterling.
Von Frisch, Karl. Twelve Little Housemates. Sugar, A. T., tr. LC 78-40341. 1978. text ed. 15.75 (ISBN 0-08-021959-4); pap. text ed. 7.75 (ISBN 0-08-021958-6). Pergamon.

HOUSEHOLD SANITATION
see Sanitation, Household

HOUSEHOLD UTENSILS
see Implements, Utensils, etc.; Kitchen Utensils

HOUSEHOLD WORKERS
see Servants

HOUSEKEEPING
see Home Economics

HOUSEKEEPING, INDUSTRIAL
see Industrial Housekeeping

HOUSEMAIDS
see Servants

HOUSEMOTHERS
Burmeister, Eva E. The Professional Houseparent. LC 60-6548. 244p. 1960. 20.00x (ISBN 0-231-02370-7). Columbia U Pr.
Hammersmark, Judy. Occupation: Nestbuilder. LC 78-74203. 1979. pap. 2.95 (ISBN 0-89636-020-2). Accent Bks.
Reich, Helen. College Housemother. LC 68-21256. 1968. pap. text ed. 3.50x (ISBN 0-8134-0157-7, 157). Interstate.
Rudman, Jack. Housemother. (Career Examination Ser.: C-1306). (Cloth bdg. avail. on request). pap. 6.00 (ISBN 0-8373-1306-6). Natl Learning.

HOUSES
see Architecture, Domestic; Dwellings

HOUSES, APARTMENT
see Apartment Houses

HOUSES, DEMOUNTABLE
see Buildings, Prefabricated

HOUSES, PREFABRICATED
see Buildings, Prefabricated

HOUSES, SOD
see Sod Houses

HOUSEWIVES
see also Mothers; Wives
Andre, Rae. Homemakers: The Forgotten Workers. LC 80-21258. 320p. 1981. 15.00 (ISBN 0-226-01993-4). U of Chicago Pr.
Baker, Nancy. New Lives for Former Wives: Displaced Homemakers. LC 79-6093. (Illus.). 288p. 1980. 9.95 (ISBN 0-385-14979-4, Anchor Pr). Doubleday.
Berk, Sarah F., ed. Women & Household Labor. LC 79-23003. (Sage Yearbooks in Women's Policy Studies: Vol. 5). (Illus.). 295p. 1980. 22.50 (ISBN 0-8039-1211-0); pap. 9.95 (ISBN 0-8039-1212-9). Sage.
Carlson, Harriet. New Horizons for the Housewife. LC 75-85822. (Orig.). 1969. pap. 2.00 (ISBN 0-87576-024-4). Pilot Bks.
Coyle, Neva. Living Free. 160p. 1981. pap. 3.95 (ISBN 0-87123-346-0, 210346). Bethany Hse.
Florida Famm Bureau Womens Federation. The Homemakers' Handbook. Perkins, Patsy, ed. 1978. pap. 5.00 (ISBN 0-918544-20-3). Wimmer Bks.
Hekker, Terry. Ever Since Adam and Eve: Memoirs of an Endangered Species. LC 79-363. (Illus.). 1979. 7.95 (ISBN 0-688-03442-X). Morrow.
Lopata, Helena Z. Occupation: Housewife. LC 80-23658. (Illus.). xvi, 387p. 1980. Repr. of 1971 ed. lib. bdg. 25.00x (ISBN 0-313-22697-0, LOOH). Greenwood.
Myerson, Abraham. The Nervous Housewife. LC 72-2616. (American Women Ser: Images & Realities). 278p. 1972. Repr. of 1927 ed. 14.00 (ISBN 0-405-04470-4). Arno.
Oakley, Ann. Woman's Work: A History of the Housewife. LC 74-4765. 320p. 1975. 8.95 (ISBN 0-394-46097-9). Pantheon.
--Woman's Work: The Housewife, Past & Present. 1976. pap. 2.95 (ISBN 0-394-71960-3, Vin). Random.
Rutledge, Sarah. The Carolina Housewife. 1979. 9.95x (ISBN 0-87249-383-0); pap. 5.95x (ISBN 0-87249-258-3). U of SC Pr.
Shields, Laurie. Displaced Homemakers: Organizing for a New Life. (McGraw-Hill Paperback Ser.). 256p. (Orig.). 1980. pap. 5.95 (ISBN 0-07-056802-2). McGraw.
Thibodeau, Lynn, ed. The Happy Housewife. LC 77-89089. 1977. 6.95 (ISBN 0-89310-024-2); pap. 3.95 (ISBN 0-89310-050-1). Carillon Bks.
Worthington, Robin. Beyond the Kitchen Sink. (Orig.). 1979. pap. 1.95 (ISBN 0-912228-52-0). St Anthony Mess Pr.

HOUSING
see also Aged–Dwellings; Discrimination in Housing; Garden Cities; Home Ownership; Housing, Rural; Housing Management; Mobile Homes; Public Housing; Real Estate Management; Relocation (Housing); Second Homes; Slums; Tenement Houses
Aaron, Henry J. Shelter & Subsidies: Who Benefits from Federal Housing Policies? (Studies in Social Economics). 200p. 1972. 11.95 (ISBN 0-8157-0018-0); pap. 4.95 (ISBN 0-8157-0017-2). Brookings.
Architectural Record Editors. Affordable Houses Designed by Architects. (Illus.). 1979. 18.95 (ISBN 0-07-002341-7, P&RB). McGraw.
Association for the Improvement of the Conditions of the Poor. Housing Conditions in Baltimore: Report of a Special Committee of the Assoc. for the Improvement of the Condition of the Poor and the Charity Organization Society. LC 73-11915. (Metropolitan America Ser.). (Illus.). 104p. 1974. Repr. of 1907 ed. 10.00 (ISBN 0-405-05384-3). Arno.
Baird, Charles. Rent Control: The Perennial Folly. LC 80-16317. (Cato Public Policy Research Cato Monograph: No. 2). 110p. (Orig.). 1980. pap. 5.00x (ISBN 0-932790-22-4). Cato Inst.
Balchin, Paul N. Housing Improvement & Social Inequality. 1979. text ed. 36.25x (ISBN 0-566-00274-4, Pub. by Gower Pub Co England). Renouf.
Bassett, Keith & Short, John R. Housing & Residential Structure, Alternative Approaches. 1980. 25.00x (ISBN 0-7100-0439-7); pap. 13.50 (ISBN 0-7100-0440-0). Routledge & Kegan.
Bauer, Catherine. Modern Housing. LC 73-11908. (Metropolitan America Ser.). (Illus.). 380p. 1974. Repr. 19.00x (ISBN 0-405-05386-X). Arno.
Becker, Franklin D. Housing Messages. LC 76-21267. (Community Development Ser: Vol. 30). (Illus.). 1979. 21.50 (ISBN 0-87933-259-X). Hutchinson Ross.
Black, J. Thomas, et al. Private Market Housing Renovation in Older Urban Areas. LC 77-80214. (ULI Research Report: No. 26). (Illus.). 40p. 1977. pap. text ed. 9.75 (ISBN 0-87420-326-0). Urban Land.
Blake, Peter. Our Housing Mess... & What Can Be Done About It. LC 74-78497. (Institute of Human Relations Press Paperback Ser.). 80p. (Orig.). 1974. pap. 1.25 (ISBN 0-87495-002-3). Am Jewish Comm.
Bloch, Stuart M. & Ingersoll, William B. Timesharing. LC 77-88799. (Illus.). 136p. 1977. pap. text ed. 19.50 (ISBN 0-87420-575-1). Urban Land.
Bourne, Larry S. Geography of Housing. LC 80-19908. (Scripta Series in Geography). 288p. 1981. 37.95 (ISBN 0-470-27058-6); pap. 19.95 (ISBN 0-470-27059-4). Halsted Pr.
Bourne, Larry S. & Hitchcock, John R., eds. Urban Housing Markets: Recent Directions in Research & Policy. (Orig.). 1979. pap. 15.00x (ISBN 0-8020-2339-8). U of Toronto Pr.

Buckley, Robert H., et al, eds. Capital Markets & the Housing Sector: Perspectives on Financial Reform. LC 77-5117. 1977. 20.00 (ISBN 0-88410-658-6). Ballinger Pub.

Burby, Raymond J. & Marsden, Mary E., eds. Energy & Housing: Consumer & Builder Perspectives. LC 79-26662. 288p. 1980. text ed. 30.00 (ISBN 0-89946-030-5). Oelgeschlager.

Bureau of the Census, U.S. Department of Commerce. Housing Construction Statistics, 1889 to 1964. LC 75-22865. (America in Two Centuries Ser). 1976. Repr. of 1966 ed. 51.00x (ISBN 0-405-07731-9). Arno.

Burns, L. S. & Grebler, L. The Housing of Nations: Analysis & Policy in a Comparative Framework. LC 76-43023. 1977. 32.95 (ISBN 0-470-98970-X). Halsted Pr.

Carlson, David B. & Heinberg, John D. How Housing Allowances Work: Integrated Findings to Date from the Experimental Housing Allowance Program. (An Institute Paper). 95p. 1978. pap. 4.00 (ISBN 0-87766-215-0, 21300). Urban Inst.

Chung, Hyung C. The Economics of Residential Rehabilitation: Social Life of Housing in Harlem. LC 73-5167. (Special Studies in Economic, Social, & Political Issues). 1973. 27.50x (ISBN 0-275-07180-4). Irvington.

Compendium of Housing Statistics Nineteen Seventy-Five to Nineteen Seventy-Seven. 354p. 1980. pap. 31.00 (ISBN 0-686-70039-2, UN80/17/4, UN). Unipub.

Conference on Economic Progress Staff & Conference on Economic Progress Staff. The Coming Crisis in Housing. (Illus.). 1972. 1.00 (ISBN 0-685-41557-0). Conf Econ Prog.

Coolidge, John P. Mill & Mansion: A Study of Architecture & Society in Lowell, Massachusetts, 1820-1865. LC 66-27058. (Illus.). 1967. Repr. of 1942 ed. 27.00 (ISBN 0-8462-0866-0). Russell.

Dakhil, Fahd, et al. Housing Problems in Developing Countries: Proceedings of IAHS International Conference 1978, 2 vols. LC 78-65357. 1979. Set. 174.50 (ISBN 0-471-27561-1); 79.25 ea. Vol. 1 (ISBN 0-471-27558-1). Vol. 2 (ISBN 0-471-27559-X, Pub. by Wiley-Interscience). Wiley.

Danielson, Michael N. The Politics of Exclusion. LC 76-7609. 443p. 1976. 22.50x (ISBN 0-231-03697-3); pap. 10.00x (ISBN 0-231-08342-4). Columbia U Pr.

Davies, Joseph E. Fundamentals of Housing Study: A Determination of Factors Basic to an Understanding of American Housing Problems. LC 74-176715. (Columbia University. Teachers College. Contributions to Education: No. 759). Repr. of 1938 ed. 20.00 (ISBN 0-404-55759-7). AMS Pr.

Davies, Richard O. Housing Reform During the Truman Administration. LC 65-25641. 1966. 12.00x (ISBN 0-8262-0046-X). U of Mo Pr.

Davis, Sam. The Form of Housing. (Illus.). 1977. text ed. 24.50x (ISBN 0-442-22007-3). Van Nos Reinhold.

Dennis, Michael & Fish, Susan. Programs in Search of a Policy. (Illus.). 392p. 1972. pap. 5.95 (ISBN 0-88866-521-0). Samuel Stevens.

Design Bulletins. Housing the Family. 1974. 21.50 (ISBN 0-8436-0129-9). CBI Pub.

Dietz, Albert G. & Cutler, Laurence S., eds. Industrialized Building Systems for Housing. 1971. 25.00x (ISBN 0-262-04034-4). MIT Pr.

Doxiadis, C. I. Action for Human Settlements. (Illus.). 1977. 12.95x (ISBN 0-393-08361-6). Norton.

Drakakis-Smith, David. Urbanization, Housing & the Development Process. 256p. 1980. write for info. (ISBN 0-312-83519-1). St Martin.

Dwyer, D. J. People & Housing in Third World Cities. LC 74-84346. (Illus.). 30p. 1979. pap. text ed. 13.95x (ISBN 0-582-49017-0). Longman.

Education, Health & Housing. 1979. text ed. 28.25x (ISBN 0-566-00298-1, Pub. by Gower Pub Co England). Renouf.

Educational Research Council of America. Housing Consultant. Ferris, Theodore N. & Marchak, John P., eds. (Real People at Work Ser.: S). (Illus.). 36p. 1977. 2.25 (ISBN 0-89247-147-6). Changing Times.

Egan, John, et al. Housing & Public Policy: A Role for Mediating Structures. 160p. 1981. 17.50 (ISBN 0-88410-827-9). Ballinger Pub.

Engels, Friedrich. The Housing Question. 109p. 1979. pap. 1.25 (ISBN 0-8285-0029-0, Pub. by Progress Pubs Russia). Imported Pubns.

Evans, Barry. Housing Rehabilitation Handbook. (Illus.). 1980. 52.50 (ISBN 0-85139-293-8, Pub. by Architectural Pr). Nichols Pub.

Fareed, A. & El-Hifnawi, M. Industrial Housing Systems, an Evaluation: Proceedings of the IAHS Cairo Workshop, 1976. (Illus.). 1979. text ed. 60.00 (ISBN 0-08-024236-7). Pergamon.

Fathy, Hassan. Architecture for the Poor. LC 72-95133. 1973. 15.00x (ISBN 0-226-23915-2). U of Chicago Pr.

Fish, Gertrude S., ed. The Story of Housing. (Illus.). 1979. text ed. 20.95 (ISBN 0-02-337920-0). Macmillan.

Fisher, Robert M. Twenty Years of Public Housing. LC 75-29075. (Illus.). 303p. 1975. Repr. of 1959 ed. lib. bdg. 19.00x (ISBN 0-8371-8411-8, FIPH). Greenwood.

Ford, James. Slums & Housing, with Special Reference to New York City. LC 76-142935. (Illus.). 1972. Repr. of 1936 ed. 64.00x (ISBN 0-8371-5936-9). Greenwood.

Fredland, J. Eric & Macrae, C. Duncan. Econometric Models of the Housing Sector: A Policy-Oriented Survey. (An Institute Paper). 109p. 1978. pap. 5.00 (ISBN 0-87766-232-0, 23600). Urban Inst.

Friedman, L. M. Government & Slum Housing: A Century of Frustrations. LC 77-74941. (American Federalism,the Urban Dimension Ser.). 1978. Repr. of 1968 ed. lib. bdg. 15.00x (ISBN 0-405-10488-X). Arno.

Fuller, Millard & Scott, Diane. Love in the Mortar Joints: The Story of Habitat for Humanity. 150p. 1980. pap. 4.95 (ISBN 0-8329-1444-4, Assn Pr). New Century.

Goederf, Jeanne E. Generalizing from the Experimental Housing Allowance Program: An Assessment of Site Characteristics. (An Institute Paper). 67p. 1978. pap. 4.50 (ISBN 0-87766-224-X, 22900). Urban Inst.

Goedert, Jeanne E. & Goodman, John L., Jr. Indicators of the Quality of U. S. Housing. (An Institute Paper). 55p. 1977. pap. 5.50 (ISBN 0-87766-204-5, 20200). Urban Inst.

Golany, Gideon. Housing in Arid Lands Design & Planning. LC 80-41108. 257p. 1980. 115.95 (ISBN 0-470-27055-1). Halsted Pr.

Goodman, Robert. After the Planners. LC 74-154100. 1973. pap. 4.95 (ISBN 0-671-21530-2, Touchstone Bks). S&S.

Goromosov, M. S. Physiological Basis of Health Standards for Dwellings. (Public Health Papers Ser: No. 33). 99p. 1968. pap. 2.80 (ISBN 92-4-130033-7, 761). World Health.

Greater London Council Department of Architecture & Civic Design. Introduction to Housing Layout. 1978. 25.00x (ISBN 0-85365-058-6). Nichols Pub.

Grigsby, William G. & Rosenburg, Louis. Urban Housing Policy. 350p. 1975. 15.00 (ISBN 0-87855-117-4). Transaction Bks.

Groak, S. & Koenigsberger, O. H., eds. Housing. 140p. 1980. pap. 32.00 (ISBN 0-08-026082-9). Pergamon.

Gropius, Walter. New Architecture & the Bauhaus. (Illus.). 1965. pap. 4.95 (ISBN 0-262-57006-8). MIT Pr.

Grubb, C. A. & Phares, M. I. Industrialization: A New Concept for Housing. LC 75-143972. (Special Studies in U.S. Economic, Social & Political Issues). 1972. 32.50x (ISBN 0-89197-794-5). Irvington.

Hai, Tan Soo & Sendut, Hamzah, eds. Public & Private Housing in Malaysia. 1979. text ed. 27.50x (ISBN 0-686-26358-8, 00109). Heinemann Ed.

Hartman, Chester. Housing & Social Policy. (Ser. in Social Policy). 176p. 1975. ref. ed. 11.95 (ISBN 0-13-394999-0). P-H.

Headey, Bruce. Housing Policy in the Developed Economy: UK, USA, & Sweden. LC 78-9404. (Illus.). 1978. 21.95x (ISBN 0-312-39353-9). St Martin.

Heilbrun, James. Real Estate Taxes & Urban Housing. LC 66-20489. 1966. 15.00x (ISBN 0-231-02821-0). Columbia U Pr.

Hinman, Albert G. Population Growth & Its Demands Upon Land for Housing in Evanston, Illinois. LC 73-2904. (Metropolitan America Ser.). (Illus.). 132p. 1974. Repr. 10.00x (ISBN 0-405-05395-9). Arno.

House, J. D. Contemporary Entrepreneurs: The Sociology of Residential Real Estate Agents. LC 76-52329. (Contributions in Sociology: No. 25). 1977. lib. bdg. 15.95x (ISBN 0-8371-9533-0, HCE/). Greenwood.

Hunter, Robert. Tenement Conditions in Chicago: Report by the Investigating Committee of the City Homes Association. 1972. Repr. of 1901 ed. lib. bdg. 29.00 (ISBN 0-8422-8182-7). Irvington.

Ingram, Gregory K. Residential Location & Urban Housing Markets. (Studies in Income & Wealth Ser.: No. 43). 1978. 20.00 (ISBN 0-88410-479-6). Ballinger Pub.

Ingram, Gregory K., ed. Residental Location & Urban Housing Markets. LC 77-10831. (National Bureau of Economic Research, Studies in Income & Wealth: Vol. 43). 1977. 20.00 (ISBN 0-88410-479-6). Ballinger Pub.

International Conference on Housing, Planning, Financing, Construction, 2-7 December, 1979, Miami Beach, Florida. Housing As Human Habitat: Proceedings, 2 vols. Ural, Oktay, ed. (Pergamon Policy Studies Ser.). 1200p. 1980. Set. 165.00 (ISBN 0-08-025592-2). Pergamon.

Jackson, Anthony. A Place Called Home: A History of Low Cost Housing in Manhattan. LC 76-17659. 1976. 20.00x (ISBN 0-262-10017-7). MIT Pr.

Jensen, David. Zero Lot Line Housing. (Illus.). 150p. 1981. pap. 22.00 (ISBN 0-87420-600-6). Urban Land.

Johnson, M. Bruce, ed. Resolving the Housing Crisis. (Pacific Institute on Public Policy Research Ser.). Date not set. price not set professional reference (ISBN 0-88410-381-1). Ballinger Pub.

Kantrowitz, Nathan. Ethnic & Racial Segregation Patterns in the New York City Metropolis: Residential Patterns Among White Ethnic Groups, Blacks & Puerto Ricans. LC 72-86840. (Special Studies in U.S. Economic, Social & Political Issues). 1973. 29.50x (ISBN 0-275-06550-2). Irvington.

Keiser, Marjorie B. Housing: An Environment for Living. (Illus.). text ed. 19.95 (ISBN 0-02-362230-X). Macmillan.

Keith, Nathaniel S. Politics & the Housing Crisis Since 1930. LC 73-85852. 232p. 1974. 10.00x (ISBN 0-87663-201-0); pap. 3.50x (ISBN 0-87663-912-0). Universe.

Keyes, Langley C. Boston Rehabilitation Program: An Independent Analysis. LC 70-127881. 1968. pap. 4.75x (ISBN 0-674-07990-6). Harvard U Pr.

Kirchenmann, Jorg C. & Muschalek, Christian. Residential Districts. (Illus.). 192p. 1980. 32.50 (ISBN 0-8230-7491-9). Watson-Guptill.

Koenigsberger, O. H., et al, eds. Work of Charles Abrams: Housing & Urban Renewal in the U. S. A. & the Third World. (Illus.). 264p. 1981. 60.00 (ISBN 0-08-026111-6). Pergamon.

Kraemer, Karl. One-Family Houses in Groups-Einfamilienhauser in der Gruppe: A Collection of Examples. LC 67-80524. 1966. 30.00x (ISBN 3-7667-0233-5). Intl Pubns Serv.

Krapfenbauer, Robert & Ural, Oktay, eds. Housing: the Impact of Economy & Technology: Proceedings of the International Congress on Housing, Vienna, Austria, November 15-19, 1981. (Pergamon Policy Studies on Urban & Regional Affairs). 1095p. 1981. 130.00 (ISBN 0-08-028066-8); prepub. 100.00 pre-Dec. (ISBN 0-686-75666-5). Pergamon.

Lansing, John B., et al. New Homes & Poor People: A Study of Chains of Moves. LC 70-625278. 136p. 1969. pap. 5.50 (ISBN 0-87944-065-1). Inst Soc Res.

--Planned Residential Environments. LC 76-632967. 283p. 1970. 14.00 (ISBN 0-87944-088-0). Inst Soc Res.

Laurenti, Luigi. Property Values & Race: Studies in Seven Cities. LC 76-5437. (Illus.). 256p. 1976. Repr. of 1961 ed. lib. bdg. 16.50x (ISBN 0-8371-8795-8, LAPV). Greenwood.

Leeuw, Frank de, et al. The Web of Urban Housing. 240p. 1975. 10.00 (ISBN 0-87766-151-0, 12900); pap. 4.95 (ISBN 0-87766-151-0, 12700). Urban Inst.

Lewis, Evelyn L. Housing Decisions. LC 80-19068. 1980. text ed. 13.20 (ISBN 0-87006-302-2). Goodheart.

Lindamood, Suzanne & Hanna, Sherman D. Housing, Society & Consumers: An Introduction. (Illus.). 1979. text ed. 20.95 (ISBN 0-8299-0230-9). West Pub.

Lockwood, Charles. Bricks & Brownstones. Rawl, Walton, ed. 262p. 1981. pap. 16.95 (ISBN 0-89659-228-6). Abbeville Pr.

Lord, Tom F. Decent Housing: A Promise to Keep. LC 76-26714. 176p. 1977. text ed. 15.00x (ISBN 0-87073-491-1). Schenkman.

McClellan, Grant S., ed. Crisis in Urban Housing. (Reference Shelf Ser.). 1974. 6.25 (ISBN 0-8242-0509-X). Wilson.

McConnell, Stephen R. & Usher, Carolyn E. Intergenerational House-Sharing. LC 80-67436. (Andrus Papers). 52p. 1980. pap. 3.25 (ISBN 0-88474-098-6). USC Andrus Geron.

McDonald, John F. Economic Analysis of an Urban Housing Market. LC 79-20969. (Studies in Urban Economics). 1979. 22.50 (ISBN 0-12-483360-8). Acad Pr.

McFarland, M. Carter. The Federal Government & Urban Problems: HUD: Successes, Failures, & the Fate of Our Cities. LC 77-26301. 1978. lib. bdg. 29.25x (ISBN 0-89158-085-9). Westview.

McGuire, Chester C. International Housing Policies: A Comparative Analysis. LC 80-8815. 272p. 1981. 25.95x (ISBN 0-669-04385-0). Lexington Bks.

McKay, David. Housing & Race in Industrial Society: Civil Rights & Urban Policy in Britain & the United States. 193p. 1977. 16.50x (ISBN 0-87471-946-1). Rowman.

Mackey, David. Multiple Family Housing. (Illus.). 1977. 32.50 (ISBN 0-8038-0164-5). Architectural.

McKie, Robert. Housing & the Whitehall Bulldozer. (Institute of Economic Affairs, Hobart Papers Ser.: No. 52). 1972. pap. 2.50 (ISBN 0-255-36011-8). Transatlantic.

Macsai, John. Housing. 2nd ed. 600p. 1981. 40.00 (ISBN 0-471-08126-4, Pub. by Wiley-Interscience). Wiley.

Macsai, John, et al. Housing. LC 75-38736. 1976. 48.50 (ISBN 0-471-56312-9, Pub. by Wiley-Interscience). Wiley.

Major Trends in Housing Policy in ECE Countries. 77p. 1980. pap. 7.00 (ISBN 0-686-72713-4, UN80/2E12, UN). Unipub.

Mandelker. Housing Subsidies in the United States & England. 1973. 13.50 (ISBN 0-672-81871-X, Bobbs-Merrill Law). Michie-Bobbs.

Mandelker & Montgomery. Housing in America: Problems & Perspectives. LC 73-7689. 1973. pap. 18.10 (ISBN 0-672-61346-8). Bobbs.

Mandelker, Daniel R. & Montgomery, Roger. Housing in America: Problems & Perspectives. 2nd ed. 600p. pap. 19.50 (ISBN 0-672-83699-8). Bobbs.

Marshall, Dale & Montgomery, Roger, eds. Housing Policy for the Eighties. 1979. pap. 5.00 (ISBN 0-918592-36-4). Policy Studies.

Martin, A. E., et al. Housing, the Housing Environment & Health. (Offset Pub.: No. 27). (Also avail. in French). 1976. pap. 7.20 (ISBN 92-4-170027-0). World Health.

Meeks, Carol B. Housing. (Illus.). 1980. text ed. 16.95 (ISBN 0-13-394981-8). P-H.

Mendelson, Robert E. & Quinn, Michael A., eds. The Politics of Housing in Older Urban Areas. LC 75-23984. (Special Studies). 1976. text ed. 32.50 (ISBN 0-275-56120-8). Praeger.

Meyerson, Martin & Banfield, Edward C. Politics, Planning & the Public Interest. LC 55-7335. 1964. pap. text ed. 5.95 (ISBN 0-02-921230-8). Free Pr.

Meyerson, Martin, et al. Housing, People, & Cities. (Action Ser.). (Illus.). 1962. text ed. 17.50 (ISBN 0-07-041760-1, P&RB). McGraw.

Moore, Eric G., ed. Models of Residential Location & Relocation in the Cities. (Studies in Geography: No. 20). 1973. pap. 4.95x (ISBN 0-8101-0444-X). Northwestern U Pr.

Mumford, Lewis. From the Ground Up: Observations on Contemporary Architecture, Housing, Highway Building, & Civic Design. LC 56-13736. (Orig.). 1956. pap. 3.50 (ISBN 0-15-634019-4, HB13, Harv). HarBraceJ.

Murison, Hamish S. & Lea, John P. Housing in Third World Countries: Perspectives on Policy & Practice. LC 79-20565. 1980. 27.50x (ISBN 0-312-39350-4). St Martin.

Muth, Richard F. Cities & Housing: The Spatial Pattern of Urban Residential Land Use. LC 69-13201. (Studies in Business & Society Ser). (Illus.). 1969. 19.00x (ISBN 0-226-55413-9). U of Chicago Pr.

National Association of Home Builders. Housing Fact Book: Housing & Housing Related Statistics. (Illus.). 163p. 1979. pap. 22.00 (ISBN 0-86718-056-0). Natl Assn Home Builders.

--Planning for Housing: Development Alternatives. (Illus.). 106p. 1980. 28.00 (ISBN 0-86718-074-9). Natl Assn Home Builders.

Nattrass, Karen & Morrison, Bonnie M. Human Needs in Housing: An Ecological Approach. 1977. pap. text ed. 9.00 (ISBN 0-8191-0094-3). U Pr of Amer.

Nelson-Walker, Roberta. Planning, Creating & Financing Housing for Handicapped People. (Illus.). 240p. 1981. 24.50 (ISBN 0-398-04485-6). C C Thomas.

Newman, Oscar. Community of Interest. (Illus.). 368p. 1981. pap. 8.95 (ISBN 0-385-11124-X, Anch). Doubleday.

Newmark, Norma L. & Thompson, Patrica J. Self, Space & Shelter. 1977. text ed. 18.95 scp (ISBN 0-06-453512-6, HarpC). Har-Row.

Nivola, Pietro S. The Urban Service Problem: A Study of Housing Inspection. LC 78-21444. 192p. 1979. 19.95 (ISBN 0-669-02801-0). Lexington Bks.

Northwest Regional Educational Laboratory. Housing: Buying a House, Buying a Mobile Home. (Illus.). 1980. pap. text ed. cancelled (ISBN 0-07-047302-1, G). McGraw.

--Housing: Moving on Getting Utilities & Using Them Wisely. (Illus.). 1980. pap. text ed. cancelled (ISBN 0-07-047303-X, G). McGraw.

--Housing: What Are Your Needs, Renting a Place to Live. 1980. pap. text ed. cancelled (ISBN 0-07-047301-3, G). McGraw.

O'Mara, W. P., et al. Residential Development Handbook. LC 77-930497. (Community Builders Handbook Ser.). (Illus.). 350p. 1978. 34.00 (ISBN 0-87420-580-8). Urban Land.

Pawley, Martin. Garbage Housing. 120p. 1975. 17.95 (ISBN 0-85139-240-7). Krieger.

Perloff, Harvey S. A National Program of Research in Housing & Urban Development: The Major Requirements & a Suggested Approach. LC 77-86406. (A Resources for the Future Staff Study). Repr. of 1961 ed. 12.00 (ISBN 0-404-60341-6). AMS Pr.

Phares, Donald, ed. A Decent Home & Environment: Housing Urban America. LC 77-2780. 1977. 16.50 (ISBN 0-88410-357-9). Ballinger Pub.

Pink, Louis H. The New Day in Housing. LC 73-11941. (Metropolitan America Ser.). (Illus.). 262p. 1974. Repr. 14.00 (ISBN 0-405-05410-6). Arno.

Plesums, Guntis. Townframe: Environments for Adaptive Housing. (Community Development Ser.: Vol. 38). (Illus.). 1978. 35.00 (ISBN 0-87933-303-0). Hutchinson Ross.

Plunz, Richard, ed. Housing Form & Public Policy in the United States. LC 77-22686. 264p. 1980. 29.95 (ISBN 0-03-056839-0). Praeger.

Polikoff, Alexander. Housing the Poor: The Case for Heroism. LC 77-11869. 1977. 15.00 (ISBN 0-88410-665-9). Ballinger Pub.

Pollakowski, Henry O. Urban Housing Markets & Residential Location. LC 78-20609. 1981. price not set (ISBN 0-669-02773-1). Lexington Bks.

Previews Staff. Previews Book of Dream Houses. (Illus.). (Harmony); pap. 8.95 (ISBN 0-517-53342-1). Crown.

Principles & Recommendations for Population & Housing Censuses. (Statistical Papers Ser.: No. 67). 330p. 1980. pap. 20.00 (ISBN 0-686-70040-6, UN80/17/8, UN). Unipub.

Pugh, Cedric. Housing in Capitalist Societies. 300p. 1980. lib. bdg. 44.00 (ISBN 0-566-00336-8, Pub. by Gower Pub Co England). Renouf.

Pynoos, Jon, et al, eds. Housing Urban America. 2nd ed. LC 80-12108. 1980. text ed. 37.95 (ISBN 0-202-32010-3); pap. text ed. 15.95 (ISBN 0-202-32011-1). Aldine Pub.

Rad, P. F. I A H S International Symposium on Housing Problems, 1976: Proceedings, 2 vols. Rad, P. F., et al, eds. 1977. pap. 76.00 (ISBN 0-08-022121-1). Pergamon.

Reidelbach, J. A., Jr. Housing Compendiums, Vol. 1. LC 72-835111. 320p. 1972. 19.75 (ISBN 0-89047-003-0). Herman Pub.

Research Group on Living & Surviving. Inhabiting the Earth As a Finite World. 1979. lib. bdg. 28.00 (ISBN 0-89838-018-9, Pub. by Martinus Nijhoff Netherlands). Kluwer Boston.

Rice Center. The Cost of Delay Due to Government Regulation in the Houston Housing Market. LC 79-65687. (ULI Research Report Ser.: No. 28). (Illus.). 92p. 1979. pap. text ed. 9.75 (ISBN 0-87420-328-7). Urban Land.

Robinson, Ray. Housing Economics & Public Policy. LC 79-18974. 1979. text ed. 26.50x (ISBN 0-8419-5059-8). Holmes & Meier.

Rose, Edgar & Bozeat, Nicholas. Communal Facilities in Sheltered Housing. 1980. text ed. 29.50x (ISBN 0-566-00354-6, Pub. by Gower Pub Co England). Renouf.

Rosen, Kenneth. Seasonal Cycles in the Housing Market: Patterns, Costs & Policies. (Illus.). 1979. text ed. 20.00x (ISBN 0-262-18091-X). MIT Pr.

Rouse, John E., Jr., ed. Urban Housing--Public & Private: A Guide to Information Sources. LC 79-100279. (Urban Studies Information Guide Ser.: Vol. 5). 1978. 36.00 (ISBN 0-8103-1398-7). Gale.

Rubinowitz, Leonard S. Low-Income Housing: Suburban Strategies. LC 74-1182. 192p. 1974. text ed. 17.50 (ISBN 0-88410-407-9). Ballinger Pub.

Salins, Peter D. The Ecology of Housing Destruction: Economic Effects of Public Intervention in the Housing Market. LC 79-3845. 176p. 1980. 12.50x (ISBN 0-8147-7811-9); pap. 7.50x (ISBN 0-8147-7812-7). NYU Pr.

Saltman, Juliet. Open Housing. LC 78-19464. 1978. 31.95 (ISBN 0-03-022376-8). Praeger.

Sands, Gary. Land-Office Business: Land & Housing Prices in Rapidly Growing Metropolitan Areas. 1981. price not set (ISBN 0-669-04859-3). Lexington Bks.

Sands, Gary & Bower, Lewis L. Housing Turnover & Housing Policy: Case Studies of Vacancy Chains in New York State. LC 76-12619. (Special Studies). (Illus.). 1976. text ed. 23.95 (ISBN 0-275-56690-0). Praeger.

Schultz, Robert E. Life Insurance Housing Projects. 1956. 6.50x (ISBN 0-256-00678-4). Irwin.

Schussheim, Morton J. Toward a New Housing Policy: The Legacy of the Sixties. LC 70-88027. 76p. 1969. pap. 1.50 (ISBN 0-87186-229-8). Comm Econ Dev.

Schwab, Gerhard. Differentiated Housing Estates. 1975. 24.95x (ISBN 0-442-80006-1). Van Nos Reinhold.

Schwartz, Sidney. Housing Careers. (Home Economics Careers Ser.). (gr. 10-12). 1977. 6.36 (ISBN 0-13-392811-X); pap. text ed. 5.12 (ISBN 0-13-392803-9). P-H.

Shin, Kilman. Inflation, Stock Price, & Housing Cost: Empirical Studies. LC 77-84026. 1978. text ed. 20.00 (ISBN 0-686-12043-4). Ctr Econ Analysis.

Smith, Wallace F. Housing: The Social & Economic Elements. LC 71-86372. (California Studies in Urbanization & Environmental Design). (Illus.). 1970. 21.75x (ISBN 0-520-01561-4). U of Cal Pr.

Social Science Panel. Freedom of Choice in Housing. 80p. 1972. pap. 3.00 (ISBN 0-309-02025-5). Natl Acad Pr.

Solomon, Arthur P. Housing the Urban Poor: A Critical Analysis of Federal Housing Policy. (Joint Center for Urban Studies). 300p. 1974. 17.00x (ISBN 0-262-19120-2); pap. 4.95 (ISBN 0-262-69058-6). MIT Pr.

Soules, Gordon. The Housing Crisis: Causes, Effects, Solutions. LC 75-38486. 500p. 1976. 75.00 (ISBN 0-919574-09-2). Gordon Soules Econ.

Starr, Roger. America's Housing Challenge: What It Is & How to Meet It. pap. 3.95 (ISBN 0-8090-0128-4, AmCen). Hill & Wang.

--America's Housing Challenge: What It Is & How to Meet It. 1977. 8.95 (ISBN 0-8090-2592-2); pap. 3.95 (ISBN 0-8090-0128-4). Hill & Wang.

Stegman, Michael A. & Sumka, Howard J. Nonmetropolitan Urban Housing: An Economic Analysis of Problems & Policies. LC 76-17023. 1976. 19.00 (ISBN 0-88410-581-4). Ballinger Pub.

Sternlieb, George & Hughes, James W., eds. America's Housing: Prospects & Problems. LC 80-10700. 480p. 1980. text ed. 20.00 (ISBN 0-88285-063-6). Ctr Urban Pol Res.

Sternlieb, George, et al, eds. Housing: An AMS Anthology, Vols. 1-3. 1972-76. Set. 90.00 (ISBN 0-404-10400-2); Vol. 1. 30.00 (ISBN 0-404-10401-0); Vol. 2. 30.00 (ISBN 0-404-10402-9); Vol. 3. 30.00 (ISBN 0-404-10403-7); Vol. 1. pap. 9.95 (ISBN 0-404-10451-7); Vol. 2. pap. 9.95 (ISBN 0-404-10452-5); Vol. 3. pap. 9.95 (ISBN 0-404-10453-3); AMS Pr.

Strassmann, W. Paul. Housing & Building Technology in Developing Countries. LC 78-620029. 1978. pap. 8.00 (ISBN 0-87744-152-9). Mich St U Busn.

Straszheim, Mahlon. An Econometric Analysis of the Urban Housing Market. (Urban & Regional Studies: No. 2). 1975. 12.50 (ISBN 0-87014-512-6, Dist. by Columbia U Pr). Natl Bur Econ Res.

Straus, Nathan. The Seven Myths of Housing. LC 73-11910. (Metropolitan America Ser.). (Illus.). 362p. 1974. Repr. 19.00x (ISBN 0-405-05426-2). Arno.

Struyk, Raymond J., et al. Housing Policies for the Urban Poor. 153p. 1978. pap. 7.50 (ISBN 0-87766-230-4, 23500). Urban Inst.

Stryk, Raymond J. & Bendick, Mark, Jr., eds. Housing Vouchers for the Poor: Lessons from a National Experiment. 1981. 25.00 (ISBN 0-87766-280-0). Urban Inst.

Taylor, Graham R. Satellite Cities: A Study of Industrial Suburbs. LC 70-112576. (Rise of Urban America). (Illus.). 1970. Repr. of 1915 ed. 18.00 (ISBN 0-405-02478-9). Arno.

Taylor, Robert, et al. Boulder Housing Study. 230p. 1979. 25.00 (ISBN 0-686-64174-4). U CO Busn Res Div.

Turner, John. Housing by People: Toward Autonomy in Building Environments. (Illus.). 1977. 10.00 (ISBN 0-394-40902-7); pap. 3.95 (ISBN 0-394-73258-8). Pantheon.

Turner, John F. & Fichter, Robert, eds. Freedom to Build: Housing for & by the People. (Illus.). 288p. 1972. pap. 2.95 (ISBN 0-02-089690-5). Macmillan.

ULI Research Division. Effects of Regulations on Housing Costs: Two Case Studies. LC 77-82249. (ULI Research Report Ser.: No. 27). (Illus.). 34p. 1977. pap. 11.75 (ISBN 0-87420-327-9). Urban Land.

--New Opportunities, for Residential Development in Central Cities. (Research Report Ser.: No. 25). 1976. pap. 6.00 (ISBN 0-87420-325-2). Urban Land.

United Nations Economic Commission for Europe. Housing for Special Groups: Proceedings. 1977. pap. text ed. 34.00 (ISBN 0-08-021985-3). Pergamon.

U. S. Federal Housing Administration. The Structure & Growth of Residential Neighborhoods in American Cities. Hoyt, Homer, ed. LC 75-115283. (Illus.). 190p. 1972. Repr. of 1939 ed. 27.00 (ISBN 0-403-00266-4). Scholarly.

U.S. Senate Select Committee on Reconstruction & Production. The Federal Government & the Housing Problem, 2 vols. LC 77-74969. (American Federalism-the Urban Dimension). (Illus.). 1978. Repr. of 1921 ed. Set. lib. bdg. 78.00x (ISBN 0-405-10511-8); lib. bdg. 39.00x ea. Vol. 1 (ISBN 0-405-10513-4). Vol. 2 (ISBN 0-405-10514-2). Arno.

Vanski, Jean & Ozanne, Larry. Simulating the Housing Allowance Program in Green Bay & South Bend: A Comparison of the Urban Institute Housing Model with the Supply Experiment. (An Institute Paper). 93p. 1978. pap. 6.50 (ISBN 0-87766-236-3, 23800). Urban Inst.

Watson, Frank. Housing Problems & Possibilities in the United States. 100p. 1981. Repr. of 1935 ed. lib. bdg. 20.00 (ISBN 0-8495-5834-4). Arden Lib.

Wedin, Carol & Nygren, Gertrude L. Housing Perspectives: Individuals & Families. 2nd ed. LC 79-83677. 291p. (Orig.). 1979. pap. text ed. 13.95x (ISBN 0-8087-2387-1, Feffer & Simons). Burgess.

Wegelin, E. A. Urban Low-Income Housing & Development: A Case Study in Peninsular Malaysia. 1978. lib. bdg. 23.00 (ISBN 90-207-0729-9, Pub. by Martinus Nijhoff Netherlands). Kluwer Boston.

Welfeld, Irving H. America's Housing Problem: An Approach to Its Solution. 1973. pap. 4.25 (ISBN 0-8447-3111-0). Am Enterprise.

Wikstrom, Walter S. Corporate Response to Employees' Housing Needs. LC 75-42501. (Report Ser.: No. 676). (Illus.). 55p. 1975. pap. 15.00 (ISBN 0-8237-0110-7). Conference Bd.

Wilbur, D. Elliott, Jr. Housing: Expectations & Realities. 115p. 1971. pap. 8.50 (ISBN 0-87659-405-4). Gryphon Hse.

Winnick, Louis & Shilling, Ned. American Housing & Its Use: The Demand for Shelter Space. LC 73-86730. (Census Monograph). (Illus.). xiv, 143p. 1975. Repr. of 1957 ed. 13.00 (ISBN 0-8462-1768-6). Russell.

Working Paper 2: A Reader for American Public Housing. (Working Paper Ser). (Illus.). 1977. pap. 15.00 (ISBN 0-685-86432-4). Jaap Rietman.

Zeitz. Private Urban Renewal: A Different Residential Trend. LC 78-19568. (Illus.). 1979. 15.95 (ISBN 0-669-02627-1). Lexington Bks.

HOUSING–BIBLIOGRAPHY

Ansley, Robert E., Jr. Discrimination in Housing. (CPL Bibliographies: No. 13). 75p. 1979. pap. 10.00 (ISBN 0-86602-013-6). CPL Biblios.

Dowall, David E. & Mingilton, Jesse. Effects of Environmental Regulations on Housing Costs. (CPL Bibliographies: No. 6). 67p. 1979. pap. 7.00 (ISBN 0-86602-006-3). CPL Biblios.

Housing & Urban Affairs: A Bibliographic Guide to the 1978 Documents Update. 1981. pap. 25.00 (ISBN 0-667-00574-9). Microfilming Corp.

Paulus, Virginia, ed. Housing: A Bibliography, 1960-72. LC 73-15863. (AMS Studies in Modern Society, Social & Political Issues: No. 4). 1974. 37.00 (ISBN 0-404-10537-8). AMS Pr.

Rengers, Rosemary. Design & Social Planning in Housing for the Elderly, 1975-1977: An Annotated Bibliography. (Architecture Ser.: A 13). 1978. pap. 12.50 (ISBN 0-686-24281-5). Vance Biblios.

Tilton, Doreen B., ed. Housing & Urban Affairs, Nineteen Sixty-Five to Nineteen Seventy-Six: A Bibliographic Guide to the Microform Collection. 342p. 1978. 50.00 (ISBN 0-667-00519-6). Microfilming Corp.

United Nations Statistical Office, compiled by. United Nations Conference on Human Settlements, Vancouver, B. C., 1976: Human Settlements Factbook Statistical Annex, 2 vols. 1976. text ed. 165.00 (ISBN 0-08-021045-7). Pergamon.

Vance, Mary. Housing: A Selective Bibliography. (Architecture Ser.: Bibliography A-93). 1979. pap. 6.50 (ISBN 0-686-26363-4). Vance Biblios.

HOUSING–FINANCE

see also Mortgages

Armfield, W. A., Jr. Investment in Subsidized Housing: Opportunities & Risks. LC 78-15544. 1979. pap. 10.00 (ISBN 0-87576-072-4). Pilot Bks.

Barrett, David, et al. Financing the Solar Home. LC 77-3858. 1977. 22.95 (ISBN 0-669-01684-5). Lexington Bks.

Betnun, Nathan S. Housing Finance Agencies: A Comparison Between State Agencies & Hud. LC 76-2899. 1976. text ed. 32.95 (ISBN 0-275-56660-9). Praeger.

Black, J. Thomas. Prospects for Rental Housing Production Under Rent: A Case Study of Washington, D.C. (Research Report Ser.: No. 24). 1976. pap. 3.75 (ISBN 0-87420-324-4). Urban Land.

Boswell, Kenneth W. A Guide to Buying Your Home. 1981. 7.95 (ISBN 0-8062-1769-3). Carlton.

Bradbury, Katharine L. & Downs, Anthony, eds. Do Housing Allowances Work? LC 81-6689. (Studies in Social Experimentation). 430p. 1981. 26.95 (ISBN 0-8157-1052-6); pap. 10.95 (ISBN 0-8157-1051-8). Brookings.

Carlson, David B. & Heinberg, John D. How Housing Allowances Work: Integrated Findings to Date from the Experimental Housing Allowance Program. (An Institute Paper). 95p. 1978. pap. 4.00 (ISBN 0-87766-215-0, 21300). Urban Inst.

Committee for Economic Development. Financing the Nation's Housing Needs. LC 73-77093. 69p. 1973. pap. 1.50 (ISBN 0-87186-050-3). Comm Econ Dev.

Connolly, William G. The New York Times Guide to Buying or Building a Home. LC 77-87819. 1978. 12.50 (ISBN 0-8129-0755-8). Times Bks.

Dennis, Michael & Fish, Susan. Programs in Search of a Policy. (Illus.). 392p. 1972. pap. 5.95 (ISBN 0-88866-521-0). Samuel Stevens.

Fredland, J. Eric & Macrae, C. Duncan. Econometric Models of the Housing Sector: A Policy-Oriented Survey. (An Institute Paper). 109p. 1978. pap. 5.00 (ISBN 0-87766-232-0, 23600). Urban Inst.

Hamilton, William L. A Social Experiment in Program Administration: The Housing Allowance Administrative Agency Experiment. LC 79-87501. 1979. text ed. 30.00 (ISBN 0-89011-533-8). Abt Assoc.

Hendershott, Patric H. & Villani, Kevin H. Regulation & Reform of the Housing Finance System. 1978. pap. 5.25 (ISBN 0-8447-3312-1). Am Enterprise.

Institute of Real Estate Management. Income - Expense Analysis: Apartments, 1981 Edition. Anderson, Kenneth R., ed. 220p. 1981. pap. text ed. 49.00 (ISBN 0-912104-55-4). Inst Real Estate.

Kain, John F. & Quigley, John M. Housing Markets & Racial Discrimination: A Microeconomic Analysis. (Urban & Regional Studies: No. 3). 1975. 17.50 (ISBN 0-87014-270-4, Dist. by Columbia U Pr). Natl Bur Econ Res.

Lefcoe, George. Land Finance Law. (Contemporary Legal Education Ser). 1969. 18.00 (ISBN 0-672-80999-0, Bobbs-Merrill Law). Michie-Bobbs.

McConnell, Stephen R. & Usher, Carolyn E. Intergenerational House-Sharing. LC 80-67436. (Andrus Papers). 52p. 1980. pap. 3.25 (ISBN 0-88474-098-6). USC Andrus Geron.

Organization for Economic Cooperation & Development. Housing Finance: Present Problems. 1974. 4.50x (ISBN 92-64-11277-4). OECD.

Phillips, Kenneth F. & Teitz, Michael B. Housing Conservation in Older Urban Areas: A Mortgage Insurance Approach. LC 78-181. (Research Report Ser.: No. 78-2). 39p. 1978. pap. 3.50x (ISBN 0-87772-254-4). Inst Gov Stud Berk.

Roberts, Joseph M. O.S.H.A. Compliance Manual. (Illus.). 272p. 1976. 18.95 (ISBN 0-87909-599-7). Reston.

Starr, Roger. Housing & the Money Market. LC 73-91083. 1975. 12.50x (ISBN 0-465-03072-6). Basic.

Stegman, Michael. Housing Investment in the Inner City: The Dynamics of Decline: a Study of Baltimore Maryland, 1968-1970. 320p. 1972. 18.00x (ISBN 0-262-19103-2). MIT Pr.

Tuck, Curt, ed. The Fannie Mae Guide to Buying, Financing & Selling Your Home. rev. ed. LC 78-1017. 1978. pap. 5.95 (ISBN 0-385-14382-6, Dolp). Doubleday.

HOUSING–LAW AND LEGISLATION

Carlson, David B. & Heinberg, John D. How Housing Allowances Work: Integrated Findings to Date from the Experimental Housing Allowance Program. (An Institute Paper). 95p. 1978. pap. 4.00 (ISBN 0-87766-215-0, 21300). Urban Inst.

Carothers, L. The Public Accommodations Law of 1964: Arguments, Issues, & Attitudes in a Legal Debate. LC 67-21036. (Edwin H. Land Prize Essays). 1968. 2.00 (ISBN 0-87391-003-6). Smith Coll.

Everett, Robinson O. & Johnston, John D., Jr., eds. Housing. LC 68-54245. (Law & Contemporary Problems Ser.: No. 9). 1968. Repr. of 1967 ed. 20.00 (ISBN 0-379-11509-3). Oceana.

Fishman, Richard, ed. Housing for All Under Law: New Directions in Housing, Land Use & Planning Law. LC 77-810. 1977. 25.00 (ISBN 0-88410-751-5). Ballinger Pub.

Heilbrun, James, ed. Rent Control: Its Effect on Housing Availability & Assessed Values. 1977. pap. text ed. 1.00 (ISBN 0-686-20038-1). Lincoln Inst Land.

Jacobs, Barry, et al. Housing & Development Desk Guide. Date not set. write for info. (ISBN 0-87179-275-3). BNA.

Little, James T. The Impact of Housing Codes & Occupancy Controls on the Neighborhood Succession Process. Date not set. pap. 4.00 (ISBN 0-686-15723-0). Inst for Urban & Regional.

Mandelker, Daniel R., et al. Housing & Community Development. (Contemporary Legal Education). 900p. 1981. 26.00 (ISBN 0-672-84385-4). Bobbs.

Montgomery, Roger & Marshall, Dale R., eds. Housing Policy for the Nineteen Eighties. LC 79-3278. (A Policy Studies Organization Bk.). 272p. 1980. 23.95x (ISBN 0-669-03443-6). Lexington Bks.

National Housing Law Project. HUD Housing Programs: Tenants' Rights. 475p. (Orig.). 1981. pap. 75.00 (ISBN 0-9606098-0-6). Natl Housing Law.

Nelkin, Dorothy. The Politics of Housing Innovation: The Fate of the Civilian Industrial Technology Program. LC 79-161308. 6.50 (ISBN 0-8076-0720-7, Orig. Pub. by Cornell U. Pr.); pap. 1.95 (ISBN 0-8076-0721-5). Braziller.

Rice Center. The Cost of Delay Due to Government Regulation in the Houston Housing Market. LC 79-65687. (ULI Research Report Ser.: No. 28). (Illus.). 92p. 1979. pap. text ed. 9.75 (ISBN 0-87420-328-7). Urban Land.

Selesnick, Herbert L. Rent Control: A Case for. LC 75-312990. 1976. 15.95 (ISBN 0-669-00338-7). Lexington Bks.

Stevens, Joseph L. Impact of Federal Legislation & Programs on Private Land in Urban & Metropolitan Development. LC 73-5229. (Special Studies in U.S. Economic, Social & Political Issues). 1973. 28.50x (ISBN 0-275-28728-9). Irvington.

Stewart, Ann. Housing Action in an Industrial Suburb. (Law, State & Society). 1981. write for info. (ISBN 0-12-669250-5). Acad Pr.

Trutko, John, et al. A Comparison of the Experimental Housing Allowance Program & Great Britain's Rent Allowance Program. (An Institute Paper). 52p. 1978. pap. 5.00 (ISBN 0-87766-222-3, 22500). Urban Inst.

ULI Research Division. Effects of Regulations on Housing Costs: Two Case Studies. LC 77-82249. (ULI Research Report Ser.: No. 27). (Illus.). 34p. 1977. pap. 11.75 (ISBN 0-87420-327-9). Urban Land.

Weicher, John C. Housing: Federal Policies & Programs. 1980. pap. 6.25 (ISBN 0-8447-3378-4). Am Enterprise.

HOUSING–MANAGEMENT

see Housing Management

HOUSING–AFRICA

Andrew, Paul & Japha, Derek. Low Income Housing Alternatives for the Western Cape. (Illus.). 165p. 1978. pap. 14.50x (ISBN 0-8476-2400-5). Rowman.

Dewar, David & Ellis, George. Low Income Housing Policy in South Africa: With Particular Reference to the Western Cape. (Illus.). 244p. 1979. pap. 15.00x (ISBN 0-8476-3285-7). Rowman.

Dewar, David, et al. Housing: A Comparative Evaluation of Urbanism in Cape Town. (Illus.). 207p. 1976. 24.00x (ISBN 0-8476-2399-8). Rowman.

Granelli, Roger. Urban Black Housing: A Review of Existing Conditions in the Cape Peninsula with Some Guidelines for Change. (Illus.). 79p. 1977. pap. 10.00x (ISBN 0-8476-2401-3). Rowman.

Gutkind, Peter C., ed. Housing the Urban Poor. (Foreign & Comparative Studies, African Ser.: No. 37). (Orig.). 1981. pap. text ed. price not set (ISBN 0-915984-61-X). Syracuse U Foreign Comp.

Kenya National Housing Corporation. Homes for Kenya. 108p. 1969. 5.00x (ISBN 0-8002-0571-5). Intl Pubns Serv.

Lewin, A. C. Housing Cooperatives in Developing Countries: A Manual for Self-Help in Low Cost Housing Schemes. LC 80-40500. 170p. 1981. 35.25 (ISBN 0-471-27820-3, Pub. by Wiley-Intrscience); pap. write for info. (ISBN 0-471-27819-X). Wiley.

Marris, Peter. Family & Social Change in an African City: A Study of Rehousing in Lagos. (African Studies Ser.: No. 8). (Illus.). 1962. 9.95x (ISBN 0-8101-0156-4). Northwestern U Pr.

Pietermaritzburg - University Of Natal - Department Of Economics. Durban Housing Survey: A Study of Housing in a Multi-Racial Community. LC 75-100274. Repr. of 1952 ed. 27.50x (ISBN 0-8371-2931-1, Pub. by Negro U Pr). Greenwood.

Schwerdtfeger, Friedrich W. Traditional Housing in African Cities: A Comparative Study of Houses in Zaria, Ibadan & Marrakech. LC 80-41693. 1982. write for info. (ISBN 0-471-27953-6, Pub. by Wiley-Interscience). Wiley.

Simon, Joan C. Housing in Ghana. (Public Administration Ser.: P 221). 1979. pap. 5.50 (ISBN 0-686-24729-9). Vance Biblios.

Stren, Richard E. Urban Inequality & Housing Policy in Tanzania: The Problem of Squatting. LC 75-620118. (Research Ser.: No. 24). (Illus.). 128p. 1975. pap. 2.95x (ISBN 0-87725-124-X). U of Cal Intl St.

HOUSING–ASIA

Housing Asia's Millions: Problems, Policies, & Prospects for Low-Cost Housing in Southeast Asia. 1979. 12.00 (ISBN 0-88936-163-0, IDRC104, IDRC). Unipub.

HOUSING–AUSTRALIA

Heppell, Michael, ed. Black Reality, White Imposition: Remote Aboriginal Housing. (AIAS New Ser.). (Illus.). 1979. pap. text ed. 13.00x (ISBN 0-85575-089-8). Humanities.

Hill, Malcolm R. Housing Finance in Australia, 1945-1956. 1959. 11.50x (ISBN 0-522-83634-8, Pub. by Melbourne U Pr). Intl Schol Bk Serv.

Jones, M. A. Housing & Poverty in Australia. (Illus.). 254p. 1972. 20.00x (ISBN 0-522-84022-1, Pub. by Melbourne U Pr). Intl Schol Bk Serv.

McKay, Ian, et al. Living & Partly Living: Housing in Australia. (Illus.). 195p. 1972. 25.00x (ISBN 0-17-001908-X). Verry.

Rennison, Audrey & Claxton, Monica. Housing the People: State Housing in Australia. LC 78-54875. 1979. text ed. 17.95 (ISBN 0-909465-77-0, 5032). Bks Australia.

Wilson, Paul R. Public Housing for Australia. (Illus.). 1976. 15.00x (ISBN 0-7022-1363-2); pap. 9.95x (ISBN 0-7022-1363-2). U of Queensland Pr.

HOUSING–CANADA

Auld, John W. Canadian Housing References, Nineteen Seventy-Five to Nineteen Seventy-Seven. (Public Administration Ser.: P 11). 1978. pap. 12.50 (ISBN 0-686-24279-3). Vance Biblios.

Bland, John & Schoenauer, Norbert. University Housing in Canada. (Illus.). 1966. pap. 5.00 (ISBN 0-7735-0040-5). McGill-Queens U Pr.

Fallis, George. Housing Programs & Income Distribution in Canada. (Ontario Economic Council Research Studies). 184p. 1980. pap. 10.00x (ISBN 0-8020-3366-0). U of Toronto Pr.

HOUSING–CHINA

Mitchell, Robert E. Housing, Urban Growth & Economic Development, No. 31. (Asian Folklore & Social Life Monograph). 1972. 6.60 (ISBN 0-89986-031-1). E Langstaff.

HOUSING–EUROPE

Bardet, Jean-Pierre, et al, eds. Le Batiment: Enquete D'histoire Economidue XIVe-XIXe Siecles, Tome 1. (Maisons Rurales et Urbaines Dans la France Traditionnello Industrite et Artisanat: No. 6). 1971. pap. 51.20x (ISBN 90-2796-880-2). Mouton.

Becker, Hans J. New Housing in Finland-Neuer Wohnbau in Finnland. 2nd ed. LC 66-39433. 1964. 32.50x (ISBN 3-7828-0401-5). Intl Pubns Serv.

Goldenberg, Leon & Weese, Harry. Housing for the Elderly: New Trends in Europe. 1981. lib. bdg. 29.50 (ISBN 0-8240-7139-5). Garland Pub.

Hardy, Charles O. The Housing Program of the City of Vienna. 1934. 10.00 (ISBN 0-686-17733-9). Quest Edns.

Headey, Bruce. Housing Policy in the Developed Economy: UK, USA, & Sweden. LC 78-9404. (Illus.). 1978. 21.95x (ISBN 0-312-39353-9). St Martin.

Organization for Economic Cooperation & Development. Housing Finance: Present Problems. 1974. 4.50x (ISBN 92-64-11277-4). OECD.

Topalov, Christian. Les Promoteurs Immobiliers: Contribution a L'analyse De la Production Capitaliste Du Logement En France. (La Recherche Urbaine: No. 4). (Illus.). 1974. pap. 22.75x (ISBN 90-2797-283-4). Mouton.

HOUSING–FRANCE

Duclaud-Williams, Roger H. The Politics of Housing in Britain & France. LC 78-323819. (Centre for Environmental Studies). 1978. text ed. 40.00x (ISBN 0-435-85222-1). Heinemann Ed.

Prefontaine, Chevalier De. Maison rustique a l'usage des habitans de la partie de la France equinoxiale connue sous le nom de Cayenne. 213p. 1981. Repr. of 1763 ed. lib. bdg. 90.00 (ISBN 0-8287-1581-5). Clearwater Pub.

HOUSING–GREAT BRITAIN

Burke, Gill. Housing & Social Justice. LC 79-42624. 240p. 1981. pap. text ed. 11.95x (ISBN 0-582-29514-9). Longman.

Carmichael, John. Vacant Possessions. (Institute of Economic Affairs, Hobart Papers Ser.: No. 28). (Illus., Orig.). 1969. pap. 2.50 (ISBN 0-255-69578-0). Transatlantic.

Chapman, Stanley D., ed. History of Working-Class Housing: A Symposium. (Illus.). 307p. 1971. 19.75x (ISBN 0-87471-040-5). Rowman.

Cornford, A. J. The Market for Owned Houses in England & Wales Since Ninteen Forty-Five. 1979. text ed. 33.25x (ISBN 0-566-00195-0, Pub. by Gower Pub Co England). Renouf.

Cullingworth, J. B. Essays on Housing Policy: The British Scene. 1979. text ed. 19.95x (ISBN 0-04-350054-4); pap. text ed. 8.95x (ISBN 0-04-350055-2). Allen Unwin.

Duclaud-Williams, Roger H. The Politics of Housing in Britain & France. LC 78-323819. (Centre for Environmental Studies). 1978. text ed. 40.00x (ISBN 0-435-85222-1). Heinemann Ed.

Dunleavy, Patrick. The Politics of Mass Housing in Britain, 1945-1975: A Study of Corporate Power & Professional Influence in the Welfare State. (Illus.). 320p. 1981. 49.95 (ISBN 0-19-827426-2). Oxford U Pr.

Girouard, Mark. Life in the English Country House: A Social & Architectural History. LC 78-9088. (Illus.). 1978. 29.95x (ISBN 0-300-02273-5). Yale U Pr.

Gittus, Elizabeth. Flats, Families & the Under-Fives. (International Library of Social Policy). 1976. 20.00 (ISBN 0-7100-8284-3). Routledge & Kegan.

Gray, Hamish. Cost of Council Housing. (Institute of Economic Affairs, Research Monographs: No. 18). (Orig.). pap. 2.50 (ISBN 0-255-69639-6). Transatlantic.

Headey, Bruce. Housing Policy in the Developed Economy: UK, USA, & Sweden. LC 78-9404. (Illus.). 1978. 21.95x (ISBN 0-312-39353-9). St Martin.

Jacobs, Sidney. The Right to a Decent House. (Direct Editions Ser.). (Orig.). 1976. 14.00x (ISBN 0-7100-8305-X). Routledge & Kegan.

Kirby, D. A. Slum Housing & Residential Renewal: The Case in Urban Britain. (Topics in Applied Geography). (Illus.). 1979. pap. text ed. 9.50x (ISBN 0-582-48691-2). Longman.

Lansley, Stewart. Housing & Public Policy. 246p. 1979. 32.00x (ISBN 0-7099-0052-X, Pub. by Croom Helm Ltd England). Biblio Dist.

McKay, David. Housing & Race in Industrial Society: Civil Rights & Urban Policy in Britain & the United States. 193p. 1977. 16.50x (ISBN 0-87471-946-1). Rowman.

Mayes, David G. The Property Boom: The Effects of Building Society Behaviour on House Prices. 146p. 1979. 30.50x (ISBN 0-85520-296-3, Pub by Martin Robertson England). Biblio Dist.

Mearns, Andrew, et al. Bitter Cry of Outcast London. Wohl, Anthony S., ed. (Victorian Library). 1970. Repr. of 1883 ed. text ed. 8.00x (ISBN 0-7185-5003-X, Leicester). Humanities.

Melling, Joseph, ed. Housing, Social Policy & the State. 233p. 1980. 26.50x (ISBN 0-85664-918-X, Pub. by Croom Helm Ltd England). Biblio Dist.

Merrett, Stephen. State Housing in Britain. (Illus.). 1979. 34.00x (ISBN 0-7100-0264-5). Routledge & Kegan.

Niven, Douglas. The Development of Housing in Scotland. (Illus.). 136p. 1979. 19.00x (ISBN 0-7099-0159-3, Pub. by Croom Helm Lgtd England). Biblio Dist.

Pepper, Simon. Housing Improvement: Goals & Strategy. (Architectural Association Papers Ser: Vol. 8). (Illus., Orig.,). 1971. pap. 15.00x (ISBN 0-8150-0180-0). Wittenborn.

Pritchard, R. M. Housing & the Spatial Structure of the City. LC 75-3859. (Cambridge Geographical Studies). (Illus.). 403p. 1976. 41.50 (ISBN 0-521-20882-3). Cambridge U Pr.

Rex, John & Moore, Robert. Race, Community, & Conflict: A Study of Sparkbrook. 1967. pap. 6.50x (ISBN 0-19-218162-9). Oxford U Pr.

Sabatino, Richard A. Housing in Great Britain, Nineteen Forty-Five to Nineteen Forty-Nine. LC 55-12082. (Arnold Foundation Studies: New Ser., No. 6). 1956. 3.00 (ISBN 0-87074-102-0); pap. 2.00 (ISBN 0-87074-103-9). SMU Press.

Simpson, M. A. & Lloyd, T. H., eds. Middle Class Housing in Britain. (Illus.). 1977. 17.50 (ISBN 0-208-01606-6, Archon). Shoe String.

Stafford, D. C. The Economics of Housing Policy. 163p. 1978. 22.00x (ISBN 0-85664-159-6, Pub. by Croom Helm Ltd England). Biblio Dist.

Stone, P. A. Urban Development in Britain: Measurement of Consumer's Expenditure in the United Kingdom, 1920-38. Vol. 1. 42.00 (ISBN 0-521-06932-7); Vol. 2. 50.50 (ISBN 0-521-06558-5). Cambridge U Pr.

Trutko, John, et al. A Comparison of the Experimental Housing Allowance Program & Great Britain's Rent Allowance Program. (An Institute Paper). 52p. 1978. pap. 5.00 (ISBN 0-87766-222-3, 22500). Urban Inst.

White, Jerry. Rothschild Buildings: Life in an East End Tenement Block 1887-1920. (History Workshop Ser.). 1980. 30.00 (ISBN 0-7100-0429-X); pap. 15.00 (ISBN 0-686-65998-8). Routledge & Kegan.

Young, Ken. Strategy & Conflict in Metropolitan Housing: Suburbia Versus the Greater London Council, 1965-1975. LC 79-301254. (Centre for Environmental Studies Ser.). 1978. text ed. 47.00x (ISBN 0-435-85924-2). Heinemann Ed.

HOUSING–LATIN AMERICA

Gonzalez, Nancie L. Black Carib Household Structure: A Study of Migration & Modernization. LC 77-93024. (Illus.). 188p. 1980. pap. text ed. 7.50 (ISBN 0-295-95733-6). U of Wash Pr.

HOUSING–MEXICO

Oldman, Oliver, et al. Financing Urban Development in Mexico City: A Case Study of Property Tax, Land Use, Housing, & Urban Planning. Herrmann, Lawrence M. & Lee, Laurence D., eds. LC 67-20878. (Harvard Law School International Tax Program Ser). 1967. 17.50x (ISBN 0-674-30150-1). Harvard U Pr.

HOUSING–NEAR EAST

Al-Alak, B. & Ford, J. D. The Housebuilding Market in the Middle East. 164p. 1979. 121.00x (ISBN 0-86010-153-3, Pub. by Graham & Trotman England). State Mutual Bk.

Hardoy, Jorge E. & Satterthwaite, David. Shelter - Need & Response: Housing, Land & Settlement Policies in Seventeen Third World Nations. LC 80-41417. 1981. 48.00 (ISBN 0-471-27919-6, Pub. by Wiley-Interscience). Wiley.

HOUSING–NIGERIA

Schwerdtfeger, Freidrich W. Traditional Housing in African Cities: A Comparative Study of Houses in Zaria, Ibadan & Marrakech. LC 80-41693. 1982. write for info. (ISBN 0-471-27953-6, Pub. by Wiley-Interscience). Wiley.

HOUSING–PUERTO RICO

Back, Kurt W. Slums, Projects & People. LC 73-19572. 123p. 1974. Repr. of 1962 ed. lib. bdg. 15.00 (ISBN 0-8371-7289-6, BASL). Greenwood.

Roberts, Lydia J. & Stefani, Rosa L. Patterns of Living in Puerto Rican Families. LC 74-14247. (A Puerto Rican Experience Ser). (Illus.). 440p. 1975. Repr. of 1949 ed. 24.00x (ISBN 0-405-06233-8). Arno.

HOUSING, AFRO-AMERICAN

see Afro-Americans–Housing

HOUSING, COOPERATIVE

Anderson, Kenneth, ed. Expense Analysis: Condominiums, Cooperatives, & Planned Unit Developments. 1980. lib. bdg. 30.00 (ISBN 0-912104-41-4). Inst Real Estate.

Clurman, David & Hebard, Edna L. Condominiums & Cooperatives. LC 73-106012. (Real Estate for Professional Practitioners Ser.). 1970. 35.95 (ISBN 0-471-16130-6, Pub. by Wiley-Interscience). Wiley.

Digby, Margaret. Co-Operative Housing. 253p. 1978. 25.00x (ISBN 0-85042-019-9, Pub. by Plunkett Found England). State Mutual Bk.

Institute of Real Estate Management. Expense Analysis: Condominiums, Cooperatives, & Planned Unit Developments - 1981 Edition. Anderson, Kenneth R., ed. 125p. 1981. pap. text ed. 30.00 (ISBN 0-912104-57-0). Inst Real Estate.

The Insuring of Condominiums & Cooperatives. 8.00 (ISBN 0-686-31019-5, 26628). Rough Notes.

Kehoe, Patrick E. Cooperative & Condominiums. LC 74-8270. 128p. 1974. lib. bdg. 5.95 (ISBN 0-379-11091-1). Oceana.

Kiev, Phyllis. The Woman's Guide to Buying Houses, Co-Ops & Condominiums. 352p. 1981. pap. 7.95 (ISBN 0-345-27496-2). Ballantine.

Liblit, Jerome. Housing the Cooperative Way: Selected Readings. 10.95 (ISBN 0-685-60130-7, Pub by Twyane). Cyrco Pr.

Readings in Co-Operative Housing. LC 75-907260. (International Co-Operative Alliance Ser). 161p. 1973. 6.50x (ISBN 0-8002-1898-1). Intl Pubns Serv.

HOUSING, DISCRIMINATION IN

see Discrimination in Housing

HOUSING, RURAL

see also Cottages; Country Homes; Farm Buildings

Beyer, Glenn H. & Rose, J. Hugh. Farm Housing. LC 73-86719. (Census Monograph). (Illus.). xii, 194p. Date not set. Repr. of 1957 ed. cancelled (ISBN 0-8462-1762-7). Russell.

Jones, Alwyn. Rural Housing. 76p. 1975. pap. text ed. 5.00x (ISBN 0-7135-1887-1, Pub. by Bedford England). Renouf.

HOUSING, STUDENT

see Student Housing

HOUSING FOR THE AGED

see Aged–Dwellings

HOUSING MANAGEMENT

see also Landlord and Tenant

Abrams, Edwin D & Blackman, Edward B. Managing Low & Moderate Income Housing. LC 72-14209. (Special Studies in U.S. Economic, Social & Political Issues). 1973. 29.50x (ISBN 0-275-28816-1). Irvington.

Andrzejewski, A., et al. Housing Programmes: The Role of Public Health Agencies. (Public Health Papers Ser: No. 25). 197p. (Eng, Fr, Rus, & Span.). 1964. pap. 3.60 (ISBN 92-4-130025-6). World Health.

Arco Editorial Board. Housing Assistant. 3rd ed. LC 57-14659. (Orig.). 1968. pap. 5.00 (ISBN 0-668-00054-6). Arco.

--Housing Inspector. 2nd ed. LC 67-23003. (Orig.). 1968. lib. bdg. 7.50 (ISBN 0-668-01804-6); pap. 5.00 (ISBN 0-668-00055-4). Arco.

--Housing Manager--Assistant Housing Manager. 2nd ed. LC 67-16545. (Orig.). 1969. lib. bdg. 7.50 (ISBN 0-668-02091-1); pap. 5.00 (ISBN 0-668-00813-X). Arco.

--Housing Patrolman. 4th ed. LC 57-14650. Orig. Title: Housing Officer. (Orig.). 1969. pap. 5.00 (ISBN 0-668-00192-5). Arco.

--Resident Building Superintendent. 3rd ed. LC 64-24940. (Orig.). 1968. lib. bdg. 7.50 (ISBN 0-668-01930-1); pap. 5.00 (ISBN 0-668-00068-6). Arco.

Basile, Frank M. Beyond the Basics. Basile, Marianne G., ed. (Illus.). 76p. (Orig.). 1980. pap. 10.00 (ISBN 0-937008-02-8). Charisma Pubns.

Becker, William E. Marketing Checklist for the Development of a Single Family Residential Community. 31p. 1976. 7.00 (ISBN 0-86718-047-1). Natl Assn Home Builders.

Community Management Corporation. Financial Management of Condominium & Homeowner's Associations. LC 76-21960. (Special Report Ser.). 1976. 14.50 (ISBN 0-87420-569-7). Urban Land.

Ellington, C. D. Complaint Handling for Resident Managers. 70p. 1981. 7.00 (ISBN 0-86718-119-2). Natl Assn Home.

Expert Committee on the Public Health Aspects of Housing, 1st, Geneva, 1961. Report. (Technical Report Ser: No. 225). 60p. (Eng, Fr, Span.). 1961. pap. 1.20 (ISBN 92-4-120225-4). World Health.

Festinger, Leon, et al. Social Pressures in Informal Groups: A Study of Human Factors in Housing. 1950. 10.00x (ISBN 0-8047-0173-3); pap. 2.75 (ISBN 0-8047-0174-1, SP57). Stanford U Pr.

Goetze, Rolf. Building Neighborhood Confidence: A Humanistic Strategy for Urban Housing. LC 76-7469. 128p. 1976. text ed. 16.00 (ISBN 0-88410-442-7). Ballinger Pub.

Gower Publications, ed. Managing Buildings & Building Services in Great Britain. 1973. 19.95x (ISBN 0-8464-0595-4). Beekman Pubs.

Holt, Mary M. Guide to Apartment House Management. LC 70-159493. 1971. 6.00 (ISBN 0-682-47269-7, Banner). Exposition.

Institute of Real Estate Management Staff. How To Write an Operations Manual: A Guide for Apartment Management. Kirk, Nancye J., ed. LC 78-61862. 1978. pap. text ed. 18.95 (ISBN 0-912104-35-X). Inst Real Estate.

Kelley, Edward N. Practical Apartment Management. 2nd ed. Kirk, Nancye J., ed. LC 81-80947. 360p. 1981. 18.95 (ISBN 0-912104-49-X). Inst Real Estate.

Kirk, Nancye J., ed. Forms for Apartment Management. LC 78-61861. 1978. 35.00 (ISBN 0-912104-30-9). Inst Real Estate.

Lindeman, Bruce. Low Income Housing Subsidies & the Housing Market: An Economic Analysis. LC 73-630597. 1969. pap. 3.95 (ISBN 0-88406-010-1). Ga St U Busn Pub.

Merritt Company Staff. OSHA Reference Manual. 1981. 197.00 (ISBN 0-930868-03-X). Merritt Co.

Ozanne, Larry & Struyk, Raymond J. Housing from the Existing Stock: Comparative, Economic Analyses of Owner-Occupants & Landlords. (An Institute Paper). 196p. 1976. pap. 5.50 (ISBN 0-87766-168-5, 14900). Urban Inst.

Rudman, Jack. Administrative Housing Manager. (Career Examination Ser.: C-1799). (Cloth bdg. avail. on request). pap. 10.00 (ISBN 0-8373-1799-1). Natl Learning.

--Administrative Housing Superintendent. (Career Examination Ser.: C-1800). (Cloth bdg. avail. on request). pap. 10.00 (ISBN 0-8373-1800-9). Natl Learning.

--Assistant Housing Manager. (Career Examination Ser.: C-41). (Cloth bdg. avail. on request). pap. 8.00 (ISBN 0-8373-0041-X). Natl Learning.

--Assistant Resident Buildings Superintendent. (Career Examination Ser.: C-1058). (Cloth bdg. avail. on request). pap. 8.00 (ISBN 0-8373-1058-X). Natl Learning.

--Building Manager. (Career Examination Ser.: C-1149). (Cloth bdg. avail. on request). pap. 10.00 (ISBN 0-8373-1149-7). Natl Learning.

--Foreman of Housing Caretakers. (Career Examination Ser.: C-269). (Cloth bdg. avail. on request). pap. 8.00 (ISBN 0-8373-0269-2). Natl Learning.

--Housing Assistant. (Career Examination Ser.: C-331). (Cloth bdg. avail. on request). pap. 8.00 (ISBN 0-685-17935-4). Natl Learning.

--Housing Captain. (Career Examination Ser.: C-332). (Cloth bdg. avail. on request). pap. 10.00 (ISBN 0-8373-0332-X). Natl Learning.

--Housing Community Activities Coordinator. (Career Examination Ser.: C-334). (Cloth bdg. avail. on request). pap. 8.00 (ISBN 0-8373-0334-6). Natl Learning.

--Housing Fireman. (Career Examination Ser.: C-336). (Cloth bdg. avail. on request). pap. 8.00 (ISBN 0-8373-0336-2). Natl Learning.

--Housing Groundsman. (Career Examination Ser.: C-337). (Cloth bdg. avail. on request). pap. 8.00 (ISBN 0-8373-0337-0). Natl Learning.

--Housing Guard. (Career Examination Ser.: C-338). (Cloth bdg. avail. on request). pap. 8.00 (ISBN 0-8373-0338-9). Natl Learning.

--Housing Inspector. (Career Examination Ser.: C-339). (Cloth bdg. avail. on request). pap. 10.00 (ISBN 0-8373-0339-7). Natl Learning.

--Housing Lieutenant. (Career Examination Ser.: C-340). (Cloth bdg. avail. on request). pap. 10.00 (ISBN 0-8373-0340-0). Natl Learning.

--Housing Maintenance Helper. (Career Examination Ser.: C-355). (Cloth bdg. avail. on request). pap. 8.00 (ISBN 0-8373-0355-9). Natl Learning.

--Housing Management Assistant. (Career Examination Ser.: C-2290). (Cloth bdg. avail. on request). 1977. pap. 10.00 (ISBN 0-8373-2290-1). Natl Learning.

--Housing Management Representative. (Career Examination Ser.: C-2291). (Cloth bdg. avail. on request). 1977. 10.00 (ISBN 0-8373-2291-X). Natl Learning.

--Housing Manager. (Career Examination Ser.: C-341). (Cloth bdg. avail. on request). pap. 10.00 (ISBN 0-8373-0341-9). Natl Learning.

--Housing Patrolman. (Career Examination Ser.: C-342). (Cloth bdg. avail. on request). 8.00 (ISBN 0-8373-0342-7). Natl Learning.

--Housing Supplyman. (Career Examination Ser.: C-345). (Cloth bdg. avail. on request). pap. 8.00 (ISBN 0-8373-0345-1). Natl Learning.

--Housing Teller. (Career Examination Ser.: C-346). (Cloth bdg. avail. on request). pap. 8.00 (ISBN 0-8373-0346-X). Natl Learning.

--Leasing Agent. (Career Examination Ser.: C-1992). (Cloth bng. avail. on request). pap. 10.00 (ISBN 0-8373-1992-7). Natl Learning.

--Principal Nursing Inspector. (Career Examination Ser.: C-1426). (Cloth bdg. avail. on request). pap. 8.00 (ISBN 0-8373-1426-7). Natl Learning.

--Senior Housing Inspector. (Career Examination Ser.: C-792). (Cloth bdg. avail. on request). pap. 10.00 (ISBN 0-8373-0792-9). Natl Learning.

--Senior Housing Management Assistant. (Career Examination Ser.: C-2538). (Cloth bdg. avail. on request). pap. 12.00 (ISBN 0-8373-2538-2). Natl Learning.

--Senior Housing Management Representative. (Career Examination Ser.: C-2540). (Cloth bdg. avail. on request). pap. 12.00 (ISBN 0-8373-2540-4). Natl Learning.

--Senior Housing Teller. (Career Examination Ser.: C-714). (Cloth bdg. avail. on request). pap. 10.00 (ISBN 0-8373-0714-7). Natl Learning.

--Supervising Housing Groundsman. (Career Examination Ser.: C-780). (Cloth bdg. avail. on request). pap. 10.00 (ISBN 0-8373-0780-5). Natl Learning.

--Supervising Housing Inspector. (Career Examination Ser.: C-1045). (Cloth bdg. avail. on request). pap. 10.00 (ISBN 0-8373-1045-8). Natl Learning.

--Supervising Housing Sergeant. (Career Examination Ser.: C-1667). (Cloth bdg. avail. on request). pap. 10.00 (ISBN 0-8373-1667-7). Natl Learning.

--Supervising Housing Teller. (Career Examination Ser.: C-781). (Cloth bdg. avail. on request). pap. 10.00 (ISBN 0-8373-0781-3). Natl Learning.

Ward, Colin, ed. Tenants Take Over. LC 75-302140. (Illus.). 160p. 1974. pap. 8.25x (ISBN 0-85139-630-5). Intl Pubns Serv.

WHO Expert Committee, Geneva, 1966. Appraisal of the Hygiene Quality of Housing & Its Environment: A Report. (Technical Report Ser: No. 353). 54p. (Eng, Fr, Rus, & Span.). 1967. pap. 2.00 (ISBN 92-4-120353-6). World Health.

HOUSING PROJECTS, GOVERNMENT

see Public Housing

HOUSING SECURITY

see Burglary Protection

HOUSMAN, ALFRED EDWARD, 1859-1936

Aldington, Richard. A. E. Housman & W. B. Yeats. LC 73-3175. 1955. lib. bdg. 8.50 (ISBN 0-8414-1716-4). Folcroft.

--A. E. Housman & W. B. Yeats. 1978. 28.50 (ISBN 0-685-65704-3). Porter.

Clemens, Cyril. An Evening with A.E. Housman. LC 77-3670. 1937. lib. bdg. 6.50 (ISBN 0-8414-3594-4). Folcroft.

Gow, A. S. A. E. Housman. LC 72-699. (English Literature, No. 33). 1972. Repr. of 1936 ed. lib. bdg. 32.95 (ISBN 0-8383-1423-6). Haskell.

Graves, Perceval. A. E. Housman: The Scholar-Poet. 15.95 (ISBN 0-684-16106-0). Scribner.

Haber, Tom B. A. E. Housman. (English Authors Ser.: No. 46). 1967. lib. bdg. 10.95 (ISBN 0-8057-1272-0). Twayne.

--The Making of "A Shropshire Lad". A Manuscript Variorum. LC 65-23917. 336p. 1966. 13.50 (ISBN 0-295-95211-3). U of Wash Pr.

Hamilton, Robert. Housman the Poet. LC 72-187522. 1953. lib. bdg. 7.50 (ISBN 0-8414-2062-9). Folcroft.

Housman, Laurence. My Brother: A. E. Housman. LC 68-8214. 1969. Repr. of 1938 ed. 12.50 (ISBN 0-8046-0217-4). Kennikat.

Leggett, B. J. The Poetic Art of A. E. Housman: Theory & Practice. LC 77-15792. 1978. 11.50x (ISBN 0-8032-0969-X). U of Nebr Pr.

Maas, Henry. The Letters of A. E. Housman. 488p. 1980. text ed. 14.50x (ISBN 0-246-64007-3). Humanities.

Maas, Henry, ed. A. E. Houseman Letters. 488p. 1980. 13.75x (ISBN 0-246-64007-3). Humanities.

Richards, Grant. Housman, Eighteen Ninety-Seven - Nineteen Thirty-Six. 1972. lib. bdg. 27.50x (ISBN 0-374-96799-7). Octagon.

Ricks, Christopher, ed. A. E. Housman: A Collection of Critical Essays. (Twentieth Century Views Ser). 1968. 10.05 (ISBN 0-13-395913-9, Spec); pap. 1.95 (ISBN 0-13-395905-8, STC83, Spec). P-H.

Robb, Nesca A. Four in Exile: Critical Essays on Leopardi, Hans Christian Anderson, Christina Rossetti & A. E. Housman. LC 68-26275. 1968. Repr. of 1948 ed. 10.00 (ISBN 0-8046-0384-7). Kennikat.

Skutsch, Otto. Alfred Edward Housman. 1973. Repr. of 1960 ed. 6.50 (ISBN 0-8274-0454-9). R West.

Watson, George L. A. E. Housman: A Divided Life. 1979. Repr. of 1957 ed. lib. bdg. 25.00 (ISBN 0-8482-6994-2). Norwood Edns.

Withers, Percy. A Buried Life: Personal Recollections of A. E. Housman. 59.95 (ISBN 0-87968-805-X). Gordon Pr.

HOUSTON, JEANNE WAKATSUKI

Houston, Jeanne W. & Houston, James D. Farewell to Manzanar. (San Francisco Book Co. Bk.). 1973. 8.95 (ISBN 0-395-17215-2). HM.

--Farewell to Manzanar. 160p. (gr. 7 up). 1974. pap. 1.95 (ISBN 0-553-13529-5, Y13529-5). Bantam.

HOUSTON, SAMUEL, 1793-1863

Crane, William C. Life & Select Literary Remains of Sam Houston of Texas, 2 vols in 1. LC 74-38348. (Select Bibliographies Reprint Ser.). Repr. of 1884 ed. 31.00 (ISBN 0-8369-6765-8). Arno.

Ever Thine Truly: Love Letters from Sam Houston to Anna Raguet. (Illus.). 19.50 (ISBN 0-89063-002-X, Pub. by Jenkins Garrett Press); limited ed. 75.00 (ISBN 0-685-83959-1). Jenkins.

Friend, Llerena. Sam Houston: The Great Designer. LC 54-13252. (Illus.). 408p. 1954. pap. 7.95x (ISBN 0-292-78422-8). U of Tex Pr.

Gregory, Jack & Strickland, Rennard. Sam Houston with the Cherokees, 1829-1833. (Illus.). 226p. 1967. pap. 4.95 (ISBN 0-292-77526-1). U of Tex Pr.

Hiatt, D. B. Sam Houston: Mid Muddle & Mud. (Illus.). 200p. 1980. 8.95 (ISBN 0-89015-276-4). Eakin Pubns.

Houston, Fred F. Sam Houston's Navy. LC 76-5597. (Illus.). 240p. 1976. lib. bdg. 5.95 (ISBN 0-685-68333-8); pap. 2.25 (ISBN 0-685-68334-6). Grossmont Pr.

Houston, Samuel. The Autobiography of Sam Houston. Day, Donald & Ullom, Harry H., eds. LC 80-18864. (Illus.). xviii, 298p. 1980. Repr. of 1954 ed. lib. bdg. 29.95x (ISBN 0-313-22704-7, HOAUS). Greenwood.

James, Marquis. The Raven. 1981. pap. 2.50 (ISBN 0-89176-022-9, 6022). Mockingbird Bks.

--The Raven: A Biography of Sam Houston. LC 29-22644. (Maps, Photos). 1970. pap. 25.00 (ISBN 0-910220-15-8). Larlin Corp.

Kennedy, John F. Sam Houston & the Senate. Smitherman, Larry, ed. LC 79-14422. 12.50 (ISBN 0-8363-0087-4). Jenkins.

Lester, Charles E. The Life of Sam Houston: The Only Authentic Memoir of Him Ever Published. LC 70-38360. (Select Bibliographies Reprint Ser.). Repr. of 1855 ed. 21.00 (ISBN 0-8369-6777-1). Arno.

Toepperwein, Herman. Sam Houston. pap. 1.50 (ISBN 0-910722-09-9). Highland Pr.

HOUSTON, SAMUEL, 1793-1863–JUVENILE LITERATURE

Grant, Matthew G. Sam Houston. LC 73-18080. 1974. PLB 5.95 (ISBN 0-87191-299-6). Creative Ed.

HOUSTON, TEXAS

Abbott, Rona & Criswell, Ann. Dining in Houston, Vol. I. (Dining in Ser.). (Orig.). 1979. pap. 7.95 (ISBN 0-89716-019-3). Peanut Butter.

Bloom, Joel & Bloom, Peggy. Five Hundred Things to Do in Houston for Free. 140p. 1981. pap. 3.95 (ISBN 0-8329-1563-7). New Century.

Buchanan, J. E. Houston: A Chronological & Documentary History 1519-1970. LC 74-30380. 160p. 1975. 8.50 (ISBN 0-379-00615-4). Oceana.

Federal Writers' Project. Houston: A History & Guide. (American Guidebook Ser.). 1980. Repr. of 1942 ed. lib. bdg. 45.00 (ISBN 0-686-30668-6). Somerset Pub.

Frantz, Joe B. Houston. LC 70-76316. 1971. pap. 2.95 (ISBN 0-8077-1384-8). Tchrs Coll.

Fuermann, George. Houston: The Once & Future City. LC 73-150578. (Illus.). 1971. deluxe ed. 25.00 (ISBN 0-385-00715-9). Doubleday.

Gaylord, Elizabeth B. & Abercrombie, V. T. Places to Take a Crowd: Three to Three Thousand. LC 79-66213. (Orig.). 1979. pap. 5.95 (ISBN 0-933988-01-X). Brown Rabbit.

Haynes, Robert V. A Night of Violence: The Houston Riot of 1917. LC 75-18041. 344p. 1976. 22.50x (ISBN 0-8071-0172-9). La State U Pr.

Lundsgaarde, Henry P. Murder in Space City: A Cultural Analysis of Houston Homicide Patterns. (Illus.). 288p. 1981. pap. text ed. 6.95x (ISBN 0-19-502984-4). Oxford U Pr.

McComb, David G. Houston: A History. rev. ed. 320p. 1981. 25.00 (ISBN 0-292-73018-7); pap. 8.95 (ISBN 0-292-73020-9). U of Tex Pr.

Marchiafava, Louis J. The Houston Police, 1878-1948. LC 77-81468. (Rice University Studies: Vol. 63, No. 2). (Illus.). 119p. (Orig.). 1977. pap. 4.25x (ISBN 0-89263-232-1). Rice Univ.

Sibley, Marilyn M. The Port of Houston: A History. (Illus.). 262p. 1968. 15.00 (ISBN 0-292-73619-3). U of Tex Pr.

Thurston, Amy M., ed. Lodestar: The Guiding Light to the Good Life in Houston. 180p. (Orig.). 1981. pap. 8.95 (ISBN 0-9604796-0-0). Bartlett Pubns.

Unibook, ed. Houston: City of Destiny. 176p. 1980. 19.95 (ISBN 0-02-620900-4). Macmillan.

Untermeyer, Chase. Houston Survival Handbook. LC 79-57381. (Illus.). 144p. (Orig.). 1980. pap. 5.95 (ISBN 0-934018-10-3, Houston Home-Garden Mag). Bayland Pub.

Wilson, Ann Q. Houston: A Pictorial History. Friedman, Donna R., ed. LC 80-27644. (Illus.). 205p. 1981. pap. 12.95 (ISBN 0-89865-087-9). Donning Co.

HOUSTON FAMILY

Tune, Bernice. The Golden Heritage & Silver Tongue of Temple Lea Houston. (Illus.). 192p. 1981. 12.95 (ISBN 0-89015-282-9). Eakin Pubns.

HOUSTON FOOTBALL CLUB (AMERICAN LEAGUE)

Rothaus, Jim. Houston Oilers. (NFL Today Ser.). (gr. 3-12). 1980. PLB 6.45 (ISBN 0-87191-796-3); pap. 2.95 (ISBN 0-89812-248-1). Creative Ed.

HOUWALD, ERNST CHRISTOPH, FREIHERR VON, 1778-1845

Schmidtborn, O. Christoph Ernst Frhr Von Houwald Als Dramatiker. Repr. of 1909 ed. pap. 7.00 (ISBN 0-384-54115-1). Johnson Repr.

HOVERCRAFT

see Ground-Effect Machines

HOVEY, RICHARD, 1864-1900

Linneman, William R. Richard Hovey. (U. S. Authors Ser.: No. 263). 1976. lib. bdg. 10.95 (ISBN 0-8057-7162-X). Twayne.

Macdonald, Allan H. Richard Hovey, Man & Craftsman. LC 68-29745. (Illus.). 1968. Repr. of 1957 ed. lib. bdg. 14.50x (ISBN 0-8371-0157-3, MARH). Greenwood.

HOWAR, BARBARA

Howar, Barbara. Laughing All the Way. 1977. pap. 2.50 (ISBN 0-449-23145-3, Crest). Fawcett.

HOWARD, EBENEZER, SIR, 1850-1928

Eccardt, J. M. Ebenezer Howard. (Clarendon Biography Ser.). (Illus.). 1973. pap. 3.50 (ISBN 0-912728-67-1). Newbury Bks.

MacFadyen, Dugald. Sir Ebenezer Howard & the Town Planning Movement. 1970. 16.00x (ISBN 0-262-13066-1). MIT Pr.

MacFayden, D. Sir Ebenezer Howard & the Town Planning Movement. 210p. 1933. 30.00 (ISBN 0-7190-0409-8, Pub. by Manchester U Pr England). State Mutual Bk.

HOWARD, CHARLES, 1ST EARL OF NOTTINGHAM, 1536-1624

Kenny, Robert W. Elizabeth's Admiral: The Political Career of Charles Howard, Earl of Nottingham, 1536-1624. LC 76-101459. 365p. 1970. 25.00x (ISBN 0-8018-1105-8). Johns Hopkins.

HOWARD, FRANK, 1936–JUVENILE LITERATURE

Hirshberg, Al. Frank Howard, the Gentle Giant. new ed. (Putnam Sports Shelf). 192p. (gr. 5 up). 1973. PLB 6.29 (ISBN 0-399-60803-6). Putnam.

HOWARD, JOHN, 1726?-1790

Brown, James Baldwin. Memoirs of Howard, Compiled from His Diary. LC 73-156007. Repr. of 1831 ed. 18.50 (ISBN 0-404-09107-5). AMS Pr.

HOWARD, ROBERT, SIR, 1626-1698

Lord, Glenn. Robert R. Howard: The Last Celt. 1977. pap. 5.95 (ISBN 0-425-03630-8, Windhover). Berkley Pub.

Oliver, Harold J. Sir Robert Howard, 1626-1698: A Critical Biography. LC 63-17327. 1963. 14.75 (ISBN 0-8223-0124-5). Duke.

Thurber, Carryl N. Sir Robert Howard's Comedy "The Committee". 1978. Repr. of 1921 ed. lib. bdg. 35.00 (ISBN 0-89760-877-1, Telegraph). Dynamic Learn Corp.
Weinberg, Robert. Annotated Guide to Robert E. Howard's Sword & Sorcery. LC 76-16708. 1976. 7.95 (ISBN 0-916732-00-2). Starmont Hse.

HOWARD UNIVERSITY
Lamb, Daniel S., ed. Howard University Medical Department, Washington, D. C. facsimile ed. LC 78-37309. (Black Heritage Library Collection). Repr. of 1900 ed. 36.00 (ISBN 0-8369-8946-5). Arno.
Logan, Rayford W. Howard University: The First Hundred Years, 1867-1967. LC 68-24658. 1969. 20.00x (ISBN 0-8147-0263-5). NYU Pr.

HOWE, EDGAR WATSON, 1853-1937
Bucco, Martin. E. W. Howe. LC 77-76322. (Western Writers Ser.: No. 26). 1977. pap. 2.00 (ISBN 0-88430-050-1). Boise St Univ.
Sackett, S. J. Edgar Watson Howe. (U. S. Authors Ser.: No. 195). lib. bdg. 10.95 (ISBN 0-8057-0383-7). Twayne.

HOWE, GORDIE, 1928-
Batson, Larry. Gordie Howe. LC 74-895. (Creative's Superstars Ser). 32p. 1974. 5.95 (ISBN 0-87191-347-X). Creative Ed.
--Gordie Howe. LC 74-895. (Creative's Superstars Ser). 32p. 1974. 5.95 (ISBN 0-87191-347-X). Creative Ed.

HOWE, JULIA (WARD) 1819-1910
Clifford, Deborah. Mine Eyes Have Seen the Glory: A Biography of Julia Ward Howe. 15.00 (ISBN 0-316-14747-8). Little.
Hall, Florence H. The Story of the Battle Hymn of the Republic. facsimile ed. LC 71-178474. (Black Heritage Library Collection). Repr. of 1916 ed. 13.25 (ISBN 0-8369-8923-6). Arno.
Richards, Laura E. & Elliott, Maude H. Julia Ward Howe, 2 Vols in One. LC 16-694. 1970. lib. bdg. 40.00 (ISBN 0-910220-24-7). Larlin Corp.

HOWE, MARK ANTONY DE WOLFE, 1864-1960
Howe, Helen H. Gentle Americans, Eighteen Sixty-Four to Nineteen Sixty: Biography of a Breed. LC 78-24027. (Illus.). 1979. Repr. of 1965 ed. lib. bdg. 29.75x (ISBN 0-313-20826-3, HOGA). Greenwood.

HOWE, RICHARD, EARL, 1726-1779
Anderson, Troyer S. Command of the Howe Brothers During the Amercan Revolution. LC 77-144861. 1971. Repr. of 1936 ed. 40.00 (ISBN 0-403-00816-6). Scholarly.
--The Command of the Howe Brothers During the American Revolution. LC 72-4221. vii, 368p. 1972. Repr. of 1936 ed. lib. bdg. 20.00x (ISBN 0-374-90198-8). Octagon.
Gruber, Ira D. The Howe Brothers & the American Revolution. (Illus.). 416p. 1975. pap. 4.45x (ISBN 0-393-00756-1, Norton Lib). Norton.
O'Beirne, Thomas. Candid - Impartial Narrative of the Transactions of the Fleet Under the Command of Lord Howe. LC 75-77108. (Eyewitness Accounts of the American Revolution Ser., No. 2). 1969. Repr. of 1779 ed. 9.50 (ISBN 0-405-01170-9). Arno.

HOWE, SAMUEL GRIDLEY, 1801-1876
Schwartz, Harold. Samuel Gridley Howe: Social Reformer, 1801-1876. LC 56-11286. (Historical Studies: No. 67). 1956. 16.50x (ISBN 0-674-78721-8). Harvard U Pr.

HOWE, WILLIAM HOWE, 5TH VISCOUNT, 1729-1814
Anderson, Troyer S. Command of the Howe Brothers During the Amercan Revolution. LC 77-144861. 1971. Repr. of 1936 ed. 40.00 (ISBN 0-403-00816-6). Scholarly.
--The Command of the Howe Brothers During the American Revolution. LC 72-4221. vii, 368p. 1972. Repr. of 1936 ed. lib. bdg. 20.00x (ISBN 0-374-90198-8). Octagon.
Gruber, Ira D. The Howe Brothers & the American Revolution. (Institute of Early American History & Culture Ser.). 396p. 1972. 24.50x (ISBN 0-8078-1229-3). U of NC Pr.
--The Howe Brothers & the American Revolution. (Illus.). 416p. 1975. pap. 4.45x (ISBN 0-393-00756-1, Norton Lib). Norton.

HOWELL, CHARLES AUGUSTUS
Angeli, Helen R. Pre-Raphaelite Twilight: The Story of Charles Augustus Howell. LC 72-158494. (Illus.). 1971. Repr. of 1954 ed. 25.00 (ISBN 0-403-01312-7). Scholarly.

HOWELL, CHARLES JAMES, b. 1870
Ford, Clellan S. Smoke from Their Fires: The Life of a Kwakiutl Chief. (Illus.). 1968. Repr. of 1941 ed. 15.00 (ISBN 0-208-00336-3, Archon). Shoe String.
Howell, James. Certain Letters of James Howell. 1978. Repr. of 1928 ed. lib. bdg. 40.00 (ISBN 0-89760-327-3, Telegraph). Dynamic Learn Corp.

HOWELLS, REES
Grubb, Norman P. Rees Howells: Intercessor. 1964-1967. pap. 3.95 (ISBN 0-87508-219-X). Chr Lit.

HOWELLS, WILLIAM DEAN, 1837-1920
Arms, George, ed. Selected Letters of W. D. Howells, Vol. 2: 1873-1881. (Critical Editions Program Ser.). 30.00 (ISBN 0-686-75277-5). Twayne.
Bennett, George N. The Realism of William Dean Howells, 1889-1920. LC 72-1345. 256p. 1973. 11.95 (ISBN 0-8265-1180-5). Vanderbilt U Pr.
Bishop, W. H. Mr. Howells in Beacon Street, Boston, in "Authors at Home," Edited by J. L. & J. B. Gilder. 1888. Repr. 35.00 (ISBN 0-8274-2768-9). R West.
Brenni, Vito J. William Dean Howells: A Bibliography. LC 73-4855. (Author Bibliographies Ser.: No. 9). 1973. 10.00 (ISBN 0-8108-0620-7). Scarecrow.
Cady, Edwin H., ed. W. D. Howells a Critic. (Routledge Critic Ser). 510p. 1973. 30.00x (ISBN 0-7100-7676-2). Routledge & Kegan.
Carrington, George C., Jr. Immense Complex Drama: The World & Art of the Howells Novel. LC 66-16764. 1966. 6.25 (ISBN 0-8142-0036-2). Ohio St U Pr.
Carrington, George C., Jr. & Carrington, Ildiko. Plots & Characters in the Fiction of William Dean Howells. (Plots & Characters Ser.). 336p. 1976. 19.50 (ISBN 0-208-01461-6, Archon). Shoe String.
Cooke, Delmar G. William Dean Howells: A Critical Study. LC 73-10412. 1922. lib. bdg. 25.00 (ISBN 0-8414-3380-1). Folcroft.
--William Dean Howells: A Critical Study. 1978. Repr. of 1922 ed. lib. bdg. 30.00 (ISBN 0-8495-0833-9). Arden Lib.
Eble, Kenneth E., ed. Howells: A Century of Criticism. LC 62-13275. 1962. 5.95 (ISBN 0-87074-050-4). SMU Press.
Eichelberger, Clayton L. Published Comment on William Dean Howells Through 1920: A Research Bibliography. (Ser. Seventy). 1976. lib. bdg. 23.00 (ISBN 0-8161-1078-6). G K Hall.
Eschholz, Paul A., ed. Critics on Willian Dean Howells. LC 74-11430. (Readings in Literary Criticism Ser: No. 23). 128p. 1975. 5.95x (ISBN 0-87024-271-7). U of Miami Pr.
Firkins, Oscar W. William Dean Howells: A Study. LC 63-11030. (Illus.). 1963. Repr. of 1924 ed. 8.50 (ISBN 0-8462-0346-4). Russell.
Fryckstedt, Olov W. In Quest of America: A Study of Howells' Early Development As a Novelist. LC 79-139921. 1971. Repr. of 1958 ed. 14.00 (ISBN 0-8462-1557-8). Russell.
--In Quest of America, Study of Howell's Early Development As a Novelist. LC 76-23434. 1945. lib. bdg. 13.95 (ISBN 0-8414-4176-6). Folcroft.
Garlin, Sender. William Dean Howells & the Haymarket Era. (Occasional Paper Ser.). 1979. pap. 1.75 (ISBN 0-89977-025-8). Am Inst Marxist.
Gibson, William M. William D. Howells. (Pamphlets on American Writers Ser: No. 63). (Orig.). 1967. pap. 1.25 (ISBN 0-8166-0436-3, MPAW63). U of Minn Pr.
Gibson, William M. & Arms, George. A Bibliography of William Dean Howells. 182p. 1980. Repr. of 1948 ed. lib. bdg. 17.50 (ISBN 0-8495-1951-9). Arden Lib.
Gibson, William M. & Arms, George A. Bibliography of William Dean Howells. 1971. Repr. of 1948 ed. lib. bdg. 17.50 (ISBN 0-8414-4648-2). Folcroft.
Gibson, William M. & Arms, George, eds. Bibliography of William Dean Howells. LC 71-137708. (New York Public Library Publications in Reprint Ser). 1971. Repr. of 1948 ed. 12.00 (ISBN 0-405-01743-X). Arno.
Harvey, Alexander. William Dean Howells. LC 73-4378. 1917. lib. bdg. 12.50 (ISBN 0-8414-2081-5). Folcroft.
--William Dean Howells. LC 72-697. (American Literature Ser., No. 49). 267p. 1972. Repr. of 1917 ed. lib. bdg. 33.95 (ISBN 0-8383-1379-5). Haskell.
--William Dean Howells: A Study of the Achievement of a Literary Artist. 1978. Repr. of 1917 ed. lib. bdg. 23.50 (ISBN 0-8495-2310-9). Arden Lib.
Hough, Robert L. Quiet Rebel: William Dean Howells As Social Commentator. 1968. Repr. of 1959 ed. 15.00 (ISBN 0-208-00688-5, Archon). Shoe String.
Howells, W. D. Selected Letters of W. D. Howells: 1852-1872, Vol. 1. Arms, George, et al, eds. (Critical Editions Programs Ser.). 1979. lib. bdg. 30.00 (ISBN 0-8057-8527-2). Twayne.
--Years of My Youth & Three Essays. Nordloh, David J., ed. & intro. by. LC 78-166119. (A Selected Edition of W. D. Howells: Center for Editions of American Authors: Vol. 29). 448p. 1975. 20.00x (ISBN 0-253-36850-2). Ind U Pr.
Howitt, Mary B. Mary Howitt: An Autobiography, 2 vols. Howitt, Margaret, ed. LC 70-37697. Repr. of 1889 ed. 27.25 ea.; Set. 54.50 (ISBN 0-404-56754-1). AMS Pr.
Keating, Patrick. Rise of Silas Lapham Notes. (Orig.). pap. 1.95 (ISBN 0-8220-1147-6). Cliffs.
Kirk, Rudolf & Kirk, Clara M. William Dean Howells. (Twayne's United States Authors Ser). 1962. pap. 3.45 (ISBN 0-8084-0324-9, T16, Twayne). Coll & U Pr.
Leitz, Robert C., et al, eds. The Selected Letters of W. D. Howells: Volume 3: 1882-1891. (Critical Editions Program Ser.). 1980. lib. bdg. 27.50 (ISBN 0-8057-8529-9). Twayne.
McMurray, William. Literary Realism of William Dean Howells. LC 67-10283. (Crosscurrents-Modern Critiques Ser.). 157p. 1967. 6.95 (ISBN 0-8093-0237-3). S Ill U Pr.
Monteiro, George & Murphy, Brenda, eds. John Hay-Howells Letters: The Correspondence of John Milton Hay & William Dean Howells. (American Literary Manuscripts Ser.). 1981. lib. bdg. 17.50 (ISBN 0-8057-9652-5). Twayne.
Montiero, George & Murphy, Brenda, eds. Correspondence of John Hay & William Dean Howells. (American Literature Manuscripts Ser.). 1980. 17.50 (ISBN 0-8057-9652-5). Twayne.
Wagenknecht, Edward C. William Dean Howells: The Friendly Eye. LC 70-83055. 1969. 13.95 (ISBN 0-19-500649-6). Oxford U Pr.
Woodress, James L. Howells & Italy. Repr. of 1952 ed. lib. bdg. 15.00x (ISBN 0-8371-2393-3, WOHI). Greenwood.
Wortham, Thomas, et al, eds. Selected Letters of W. D. Howells, Vol. 4: 1892-19: Voloume 4: 1892-1901. (Critical Editions Program Ser.). 1981. lib. bdg. 30.00 (ISBN 0-8057-8530-2). Twayne.

HROSWITHA OF GANDERSHEIM
see Roswitha of Gandersheim, 935-1000

HSIANG CHI (GAME)
see Chinese Chess

HSIN-HSING, FORMOSA (CHANG-HUA DISTRICT)
Gallin, Bernard. Hsin Hsing, Taiwan: A Chinese Village in Change. LC 66-14734. 1966. 23.75x (ISBN 0-520-00451-5). U of Cal Pr.

HSUAN-TSANG, 596?-664
Hwuy-Le. The Life of Hiuen-Tsiang. Beal, Samuel, tr. from Chinese. & intro. by. LC 73-880. (China Studies: from Confucius to Mao Ser). xlvii, 218p. 1973. Repr. of 1911 ed. 19.50 (ISBN 0-88355-074-1). Hyperion Conn.
Watters, Thomas. On Yuan Chwang's Travels in India 629-645 A. D. LC 74-158213. Repr. of 1905 ed. Set. 20.00 (ISBN 0-404-06878-2). AMS Pr.

HSUAN-TSANG, 596?-664-FICTION
Wu Ch'Eng-En. Monkey. Waley, Arthur, tr. from Chinese. & pref. by. 1958. pap. 4.95 (ISBN 0-394-17211-6, E112, Ever). Grove.

HU, SHIH, 1891-1962
Hu Shih. My Mother's Betrothal. Rouse, Mary, ed. 2.00 (ISBN 0-686-15213-1). Far Eastern Pubns.

HUA KUO FENG
Ting, Wang. Chairman Hua: Leader of the Chinese Communists. (Illus.). 181p. 1980. 19.95 (ISBN 0-686-76139-1). McGill-Queens U Pr.
Ting Wing. Chairman Hua: The New Leader of the Chinese Communists. 200p. 1980. 19.95x (ISBN 0-7735-0524-5); pap. 9.95 (ISBN 0-7735-0525-3). McGill-Queens U Pr.

HUALAPAI INDIANS
see Indians of North America-Southwest, New

HUALCANA, PERU
Stein, William W. Hualcan: Life in the Highlands of Peru. LC 75-26221. (Cornell Studies in Anthropology). (Illus.). 383p. 1976. Repr. of 1961 ed. lib. bdg. 21.25x (ISBN 0-8371-8406-1, STHU). Greenwood.

HUANG, HSING, 1874-1916
Hsueh, Chun-tu. Huang Hsing & the Chinese Revolution. 1961. 10.00x (ISBN 0-8047-0031-1). Stanford U Pr.

HUBBARD, ELBERT, 1856-1915
Hamilton, Charles F. As Bees in Honey Drown: Elbert Hubbard & the Roycrofters. LC 77-37811. (Illus.). 1973. 10.00 (ISBN 0-498-01052-X). A S Barnes.
Hubbard, Elbert. Hubbard-Rebel with Reverence: Granddaughter's Biography. LC 75-21057. 1975. 4.95 (ISBN 0-87282-076-9). Century Hse.

HUBBARDTON, BATTLE OF 1777
Fletcher, Ebenezer. Narrative of a Soldier of the Revolution. facs. ed. LC 72-117874. (Select Bibliographies Reprint Ser). 1827. 11.00 (ISBN 0-8369-5327-4). Arno.

HUBMAIER, BALTHASAR, d. 1528
Bergsten, Torsten. Balthasar Hubmaier: Anabaptist Theologian & Martyr. Estep, W. R., Jr., ed. LC 78-2683. 1978. 19.95 (ISBN 0-8170-0793-8). Judson.
Vedder, Henry C. Baltahsar Hubmaier: The Leader of the Anabaptists. LC 79-149670. Repr. of 1905 ed. 24.50 (ISBN 0-404-06755-7). AMS Pr.

HUCKSTERS
see Peddlers and Peddling

HUDSON, DAVID ROCK-JUVENILE LITERATURE
Kirk, Ruth. David, Young Chief of the Quileutes: An American Indian Today. LC 67-10206. (Illus.). (gr. 3-5). 1967. 5.95 (ISBN 0-15-222498-X, HJ). HarBraceJ.

HUDSON, HENRY, d. 1611
Asher, George M., ed. Henry Hudson the Navigator. (Hakluyt Soc. First Ser.: No. 27). (Illus.). 1964. Repr. of 1613 ed. 32.00 (ISBN 0-8337-0098-7). B Franklin.
Harley, Ruth. Henry Hudson. new ed. LC 78-18053. (Illus.). 48p. (gr. 4-7). 1979. PLB 5.89 (ISBN 0-89375-171-5); pap. 1.75 (ISBN 0-89375-163-4). Troll Assocs.
Henry Hudson. (gr. 1). 1974. pap. text ed. 2.08 (ISBN 0-205-03872-7, 8038724); tchrs. guide 8.80 (ISBN 0-205-03866-2, 803866X). Allyn.
Murphy, Henry C. Henry Hudson in Holland: An Inquiry into the Origin & Objects of the Voyage Which Led to the Discovery of the Hudson River. LC 72-85105. xii, 150p. 1972. Repr. of 1909 ed. lib. bdg. 17.50 (ISBN 0-8337-2489-4). B Franklin.
O'Connell, Richard. Hudson's Fourth Voyage. 1978. pap. 4.50 (ISBN 0-685-87717-5). Atlantis Edns.

HUDSON, WILLIAM HENRY, 1841-1922
Hamilton, Robert. W. H. Hudson: The Vision of Earth. LC 76-113336. 1970. Repr. of 1946 ed. 12.00 (ISBN 0-8046-1019-3). Kennikat.
Hudson, W. H. Far Away & Long Ago. 350p. 1981. 14.95 (ISBN 0-8180-0251-4). Horizon.
--Letters from W. H. Hudson to Edward Garnett. 1925. 30.00 (ISBN 0-932062-87-3). Sharon Hill.
Klibbe, Lawrence H. Green Mansions Notes. (Orig.). 1970. pap. 1.75 (ISBN 0-8220-0565-4). Cliffs.
Payne, John R. W. H. Hudson: A Bibliography. LC 76-30003. 248p. 1977. 22.50x (ISBN 0-7129-0750-5, Pub. by St. Pauls Biblios England) (ISBN 0-208-01647-3). U Pr of Va.
--W. H. Hudson: A Bibliography. LC 76-30003. 248p. 1977. 22.50x (ISBN 0-7129-0750-5, Pub. by St. Pauls Biblios England). U Pr of Va.
Roberts, Morley. W. H. Hudson. 1924. Repr. 40.00 (ISBN 0-8274-3684-X). R West.
Tomalin, Ruth. W. H. Hudson. Repr. of 1954 ed. lib. bdg. 15.00x (ISBN 0-8371-2097-7, TOWH). Greenwood.
Wilson, G. F. A Bibliography of the Writings of W. H. Hudson. LC 72-3094. (English Literature Ser., No. 33). 1972. Repr. of 1922 ed. lib. bdg. 45.95 (ISBN 0-8383-1510-0). Haskell.

HUDSON BAY
Coats, William S. Geography of Hudson's Bay: Being the Remarks of Captain W. Coats in Many Voyages to That Locality Between the Years 1727-51. Barrow, John, ed. (Hakluyt Society. First Ser.: No. 11). 1964. 24.50 (ISBN 0-8337-0180-0). B Franklin.
Ellis, Henry. Voyage to Hudson's Bay, by the Dobbs Galley & California, in the Years 1746 & 1747, for Discovering a North West Passage. 1748. 23.00 (ISBN 0-384-14200-1). Johnson Repr.
Fleming, Howard A. Canada's Artic Outlet: A History of the Hudson Bay Railway. LC 78-5665. (Illus.). 129p. 1978. Repr. of 1957 ed. lib. bdg. 17.00x (ISBN 0-313-20392-X, FLCA). Greenwood.
Miller, Sheila. My Book About Hudson. 1975. pap. 1.20 (ISBN 0-85363-101-8). OMF Bks.
Tyrrell, Joseph B., ed. Documents Relating to the Early History of Hudson Bay. LC 68-28606. 1968. Repr. of 1931 ed. lib. bdg. 34.50x (ISBN 0-8371-5056-6, TYDR). Greenwood.

HUDSON RIVER AND VALLEY
Adams, Arthur G. The Hudson: A Guidebook to the River. LC 79-14846. (Illus.). 424p. 1981. 14.95 (ISBN 0-87395-406-8). State U NY Pr.
Boyle, Robert H. The Hudson River: A Natural & Unnatural History. LC 68-10877. (Illus.). 1969 7.95 (ISBN 0-393-05379-2, N844, Norton Lib); pap. 4.95 1979 (ISBN 0-393-00844-4). Norton.
Bruce, Wallace. Along the Hudson with Washington Irving. LC 77-776. 1913. lib. bdg. 20.00 (ISBN 0-8414-9880-6). Folcroft.
Burmeister, Walter F. Appalachian Waters 2: The Hudson River & Its Tributaries. LC 74-80983. 1974. pap. 7.50 (ISBN 0-912660-20-1). Appalachian Bks.
Burroughs, John. A River View & Other Hudson Valley Essays. (Illus.). 224p. 1981. 9.95 (ISBN 0-88427-049-1). North River.
Elting, Irving. Dutch Village Communities on the Hudson River. pap. 7.00 (ISBN 0-384-14288-5). Johnson Repr.
Hudson River Ecology: Fourth Symposium. 1976. pap. text ed. 11.50x (ISBN 0-89062-090-3, Pub by Hres). Pub Ctr Cult Res.
Kenney, Alice P. Stubborn for Liberty: The Dutch in New York. (New York State Studies). (Illus.). 320p. 1975. 10.00x (ISBN 0-8156-0113-1). Syracuse U Pr.

Lossing, Benson J. The Hudson: From the Wilderness to the Sea. LC 72-86787. (Empire State Historical Publications Ser., No. 99). 1972. Repr. of 1866 ed. 22.00 (ISBN 0-8046-8099-X). Kennikat.
--The Hudson: From the Wilderness to the Sea. LC 72-86787. (Empire State Historical Publications Ser., No. 99). 1972. Repr. of 1866 ed. 22.00 (ISBN 0-8046-8099-X). Kennikat.
McNeer, May. The Hudson: River of History. LC 62-15313. (Rivers of the World Ser.). (Illus.). (gr. 4-7). 1962. PLB 3.68 (ISBN 0-8116-6356-6). Garrard.
Mayborn, Mitch, ed. Hudson: The Hudson, Essex, Terraplane Story. rev., 2nd ed. (Highland Ser. 3: Bk. 3). (Illus.). 1975. pap. 2.98 (ISBN 0-913490-11-3). Highland Ent.
Milbert, Jacques. Picturesque Itinerary of the Hudson River & Peripheral Parts of North America. LC 67-29606. (American Environmental Studies). 1968. Repr. of 1928 ed. 20.00 (ISBN 0-405-02678-1). Arno.
O'Brien, Raymond J. American Sublime: Landscape & Scenery of the Lower Hudson Valley. (Illus.). 336p. 1981. 19.95 (ISBN 0-231-04778-9). Columbia U Pr.
Reynolds, Helen W. Dutch Houses in the Hudson Valley Before 1776. (Illus.). 12.50 (ISBN 0-8446-2796-8). Peter Smith.
Richardson, Ralph W. The Hudson River Basin, Vol. 2. 1979. 25.00 (ISBN 0-12-588402-8). Acad Pr.
--The Hudson River Basin: Environmental Problems & Instititional Response, Vol. 1. 1979. 25.00 (ISBN 0-12-588401-X). Acad Pr.
Roels, Oswald A., ed. Hudson River Colloquium, Vol. 250. (Annals of the New York Academy of Sciences). 185p. 1974. 27.00x (ISBN 0-89072-764-3). NY Acad Sci.
Shear, W. G. Panorama of the Hudson: 200 Photos Showing Both Sides of the River from New York to Albany. 1977. lib. bdg. 200.00 (ISBN 0-8490-2405-6). Gordon Pr.
Simpson, Jeffrey. The Hudson River Eighteen Fifty to Nineteen Eighteen: A Photographic Portrait. LC 81-8743. (Illus.). 208p. 1981. 29.95 (ISBN 0-912882-44-1). Sleepy Hollow.
Van Zandt, Roland. Chronicles of the Hudson: Three Centuries of Travelers' Accounts. 1971. 22.50 (ISBN 0-8135-0693-X). Rutgers U Pr.
Whitson, Skip, compiled by. Hudson River: One Hundred Years Ago. (Sun Historical Ser). 40p. (YA) 1975. pap. 3.50 (ISBN 0-89540-012-X, SB-012). Sun Pub.
Wyckoff, Jerome. Rock Scenery of the Hudson Highlands & Palisades. LC 79-173287. (Illus.). 1971. pap. 3.00 (ISBN 0-935272-09-7). ADK Mtn Club.

HUDSON RIVER AND VALLEY-HISTORIC HOUSES, ETC.

Keller, Allan. Life Along the Hudson. LC 75-7155. (Illus.). (YA) 1976. 10.00 (ISBN 0-912882-20-4). Sleepy Hollow.
Reynolds, Helen W. Dutch Houses in the Hudson Valley Before 1776. (Illus.). 1965. pap. 6.95 (ISBN 0-486-21469-9). Dover.
Whitefield, Edwin. Hudson River Houses: Edwin Whitefield's the Hudson River & Railroad Illustrated. 1980. 14.95 (ISBN 0-88427-043-2). Caroline Hse.

HUDSON RIVER DAY LINE

Ringwald, Donald C. Hudson River Day Line. LC 65-18744. (Illus.). 1965. 9.50 (ISBN 0-8310-7050-1). Howell-North.

HUDSON'S BAY COMPANY

Bryce, George. The Hudson's Bay Company, 2 vols. 1910. Set. 65.00 (ISBN 0-8482-7385-0). Norwood Edns.
--Remarkable History of the Hudson's Bay Company: Induding That of the French Traders of Northwestern Canada, & of the Astor Fur Companies. (Research & Source Works Ser.: No. 171). (Illus.). 1968. 29.50 (ISBN 0-8337-0407-9). B Franklin.
Cline, Gloria G. Peter Skene Ogden & the Hudson's Bay Company. LC 72-9266. (American Exploration & Travel Ser.: Vol. 64). (Illus.). 1974. 14.95 (ISBN 0-8061-1073-2). U of Okla Pr.
Davidson, Gordon C. North West Company. LC 66-27059. (Illus.). 1967. Repr. of 1918 ed. 30.00 (ISBN 0-8462-0894-6). Russell.
Dillon, Richard. The Siskiyou Trail: The Hudson's Bay Company Route to California. LC 74-23553. 416p. 1975. 9.95 (ISBN 0-07-016980-2, GB). McGraw.
Galbraith, John S. The Hudson's Bay Company As an Imperial Factory. 1977. 27.50x (ISBN 0-374-92974-2). Octagon.
Hargrave, James. Hargrave Correspondence, 1821-1843. Glazebrook, G. P., ed. LC 68-28612. 1968. Repr. of 1938 ed. lib. bdg. 32.50x (ISBN 0-8371-5062-0, HAHC). Greenwood.
Hargrave, Letitia M. Letters of Letitia Hargrave. Macleod, Margaret A., ed. LC 69-14502. 1968. Repr. of 1947 ed. lib. bdg. 24.50x (ISBN 0-8371-5065-5, HALE). Greenwood.
Hearne, Samuel. Journals of Samuel Hearne & Philip Turnor. Tyrrell, J. B., ed. LC 68-28609. 1968. Repr. of 1934 ed. lib. bdg. 44.25x (ISBN 0-8371-5059-0, HEJH). Greenwood.
MacKay, Douglas. Honourable Company. facs. ed. LC 73-124242. (Select Bibliographies Reprint Ser). 1936. 23.00 (ISBN 0-8369-5430-0). Arno.
McLean, John. Notes of a Twenty-Five Years' Service in the Hudson's Bay Territory. Wallace, W. S., ed. LC 68-28607. 1968. Repr. of 1932 ed. lib. bdg. 29.50x (ISBN 0-8371-5057-4, MCNS). Greenwood.
Morton, Arthur S. History of the Canadian West to 1870-71. 2nd ed. Thomas, Lewis G., ed. LC 72-97150. (Illus.). 1973. 35.00x (ISBN 0-8020-4033-0). U of Toronto Pr.
Ray, Arthur J. & Freeman, Donald. Give Us Good Measure: An Economic Analysis of Relations Between the Indians & the Hudson's Bay Company Before 1763. 1978. 20.00x (ISBN 0-8020-5418-8); pap. 6.50 (ISBN 0-8020-6334-9). U of Toronto Pr.
Robson, Joseph. An Account of Six Years Residence in Hudson's Bay: From 1733 to 1736, & 1744 to 1747. Repr. of 1757 ed. 13.00 (ISBN 0-384-51580-0). Johnson Repr.
Sampson, William R., ed. John McLoughlin's Business Correspondence, 1847-48. LC 73-8747. (Illus.). 232p. 1973. 16.50 (ISBN 0-295-95299-7). U of Wash Pr.
Simpson, George. Fur Trade & Empire: George Simpson's Journal, 1824-1825. rev. ed. Merk, Frederick, ed. LC 68-15646. 1968. 20.00x (ISBN 0-674-33500-7, Belknap Pr). Harvard U Pr.
Thompson, David. David Thompson's Narrative of His Explorations in Western America, 1784-1812. Tyrrell, J. B., ed. LC 68-28603. Repr. of 1916 ed. lib. bdg. 50.00x (ISBN 0-8371-3879-5, THNE). Greenwood.
Woodcock, George. Hudson's Bay Company. LC 78-109444. (gr. 9-12). 1970. 8.95 (ISBN 0-02-793260-5, CCPr). Macmillan.
Work, John. The Snake Country Expedition of 1830-1831: John Work's Field Journal. Haines, Francis D., Jr., ed. (American Exploration & Travel Ser.: No. 59). (Illus.). 224p. 1971. 11.95 (ISBN 0-8061-0947-5). U of Okla Pr.
Young, Frank G., ed. The Correspondence & Journals of Captain Nathaniel J. Wyeth, 1831-6. LC 72-9474. (The Far Western Frontier Ser.). (Illus.). 288p. 1973. Repr. of 1899 ed. 17.00 (ISBN 0-405-05001-1). Arno.

HUECORIO

Belshaw, Michael H. A Village Economy: Land & People of Huecorio. LC 66-28489. (Institute of Latin American Studies). (Illus.). 421p. 1967. 22.50x (ISBN 0-231-02928-4). Columbia U Pr.

HUEGEL, FRIEDRICH, FRIEHERR VON, 1852-1925

Barmann, Lawrence F. Baron Friedrich Von Hugel & the Modernist Crisis in England. LC 77-153014. 1972. 39.00 (ISBN 0-521-08178-5). Cambridge U Pr.
Whelan, Joseph P. Spirituality of Friedrich Von Hugel. LC 72-75631. 320p. 1972. 8.95 (ISBN 0-8091-0166-1). Paulist Pr.

HUET, GEDEON BUSKEN, 1860-1921, ED.

Gautier De Dargies. Chansons et Descorts De Gautier De Dargies. 20.00 (ISBN 0-384-17770-0); pap. 15.50 (ISBN 0-384-17775-1). Johnson Repr.

HUGEL, FRIEDRICH, FREIHERR VON, 1852-1925

see Huegel, Friedrich, Frieherr Von, 1852-1925

HUGHES, CHARLES EVANS, 1862-1948

Hendel, Samuel. Charles Evans Hughes & the Supreme Court. LC 68-10926. 1968. Repr. of 1951 ed. 11.50 (ISBN 0-8462-1092-4). Russell.
Perkins, Dexter. Charles Evans Hughes & American Democratic Statesmanship. Handlin, Oscar, ed. LC 78-5919. (The Library of American Biography Ser.). 1978. Repr. of 1956 ed. lib. bdg. 18.00x (ISBN 0-313-20463-2, PECH). Greenwood.
Wesser, Robert F. Charles Evans Hughes: Politics & Reform in New York, 1905-1910. (Illus.). 366p. 25.00x (ISBN 0-8014-0446-0). Cornell U Pr.

HUGHES, HOWARD ROBARD, 1905-1976

Barlett, Donald L. & Steele, James B. Empire: The Life, Legend, & Madness of Howard Hughes. (Illus.). 1981. pap. 6.95 (ISBN 0-393-00025-7). Norton.
--Empire: The Life, Legend & Madness of Howard Hughes. (Illus.). 1979. 17.50 (ISBN 0-393-07513-3). Norton.
Barton, Charles. Howard Hughes & His Flying Boat. 304p. 1981. 19.95 (ISBN 0-8168-6457-8); pap. 14.95 (ISBN 0-8168-6456-X). Aero.
Bell, Jerry. Howard Hughes. 1977. pap. 4.50 (ISBN 0-89036-069-3). Hawkes Pub Inc.
Davenport, Joe & Lawson, Todd. The Empire of Howard Hughes. LC 75-16010. 1975. pap. 2.95 (ISBN 0-914024-22-1). SF Arts & Letters.
Drosnin, Michael, ed. Citizen Hughes. Date not set. 10.00 (ISBN 0-03-041846-1). HR&W.
Finke, Blythe F. Howard R. Hughes, Twentieth Century Multi-Millionaire & Recluse. Rahmas, D. Steve, ed. (Outstanding Personalities Ser.: No. 69). 32p. (Orig.). (gr. 7-12). 1974. lib. bdg. 2.95 incl. catalog cards (ISBN 0-686-05488-1); pap. 1.50 vinyl laminated covers (ISBN 0-87157-069-6). SamHar Pr.
Garrison, Omar V. Howard Hughes in Las Vegas. LC 69-17955. (Illus.). 1970. 5.95 (ISBN 0-8184-0038-2). Lyle Stuart.
Hatfield, David D. Howard Hughes H-Four Hercules Airplane. 1974. pap. 4.95 (ISBN 0-911721-21-5, Pub. by Hist Airplanes). Aviation.
Irving, Clifford. The Hoax. LC 80-85344. 380p. 1981. 14.95 (ISBN 0-932966-14-4). Permanent Pr.
Phelan, James. Howard Hughes: The Hidden Years. 1977. 7.95 (ISBN 0-394-41042-4). Random.
--Howard Hughes: The Hidden Years. (Illus.). 1977. pap. 2.50 (ISBN 0-446-91223-9). Warner Bks.
Rhoden, Harold. High Stakes: The Gamble for the Howard Hughes Will. 416p. 1980. 12.95 (ISBN 0-517-54067-3). Crown.
Winokur, Lou & Winokur, Alice. Joy in the Mountains. LC 77-365501. (Illus.). 1980. pap. 4.95 (ISBN 0-9601758-0-6). Joy Pub Co.

HUGHES, LANGSTON, 1902-1967

Cobb, Martha. Harlem, Haiti, & Havana: A Comparative Critical Study of Langston Hughes, Jacques Roumain, & Nicolas Guillen. LC 78-19962. (Illus.). 1979. 15.00 (ISBN 0-914478-90-7); pap. 8.00 (ISBN 0-914478-91-5). Three Continents.
Dickinson, Donald C. A Bio-Bibliography of Langston Hughes, 1902-1967. 2nd ed. LC 70-181877. 273p. 1972. 19.50 (ISBN 0-208-01269-9, Archon). Shoe String.
Dunham, Montrew. Langston Hughes: Young Black Poet. LC 72-81622. (Childhood of Famous Americans Ser). 1972. 3.95 (ISBN 0-672-51755-8). Bobbs.
Emanuel, James A. Langston Hughes. (Twayne's United States Authors Ser). 1967. pap. 3.45 (ISBN 0-8084-0004-5, T123, Twayne). Coll & U Pr.
--Langston Hughes. (U. S. Authors Ser.: No. 123). 1967. lib. bdg. 9.95 (ISBN 0-8057-0388-8). Twayne.
Hughes, Langston. The Big Sea. 1963. pap. 7.50 (ISBN 0-8090-0065-2, AmCen). Hill & Wang.
--I Wonder As I Wander. 415p. 1974. Repr. lib. bdg. 24.00x (ISBN 0-374-94031-2). Octagon.
Jemie, Onwuchekwa. Langston Hughes: An Introduction to the Poetry. LC 76-18219. (Columbia Introductions to Twentieth Century American Poetry Ser.). 234p. 1977. 15.00x (ISBN 0-231-03780-5). Columbia U Pr.
Larson, Norita D. Langston Hughes, Poet of Harlem. Redpath, Ann, ed. (People to Remember Ser.). (Illus.). 32p. (gr. 5-9). 1981. PLB 5.95 (ISBN 0-87191-798-X). Creative Ed.
Mandelik, Peter & Schatt, Stanley, eds. Concordance to the Poetry of Langston Hughes. LC 74-11251. (Illus.). 296p. 1975. 65.00 (ISBN 0-8103-1011-2). Gale.
Meltzer, Milton. Langston Hughes: A Biography. LC 68-21952. (gr. 7 up). 1968. 8.95 (ISBN 0-690-48525-5, TYC-J). Har-Row.
Mullen, Edward J. Langston Hughes in the Hispanic World & Haiti. 1977. 16.50 (ISBN 0-208-01634-1, Archon). Shoe String.
Myers, Elisabeth P. Langston Hughes. (gr. k-6). 1981. pap. 1.50 (ISBN 0-440-44723-2, YB). Dell.
Walker, Alice. Langston Hughes, American Poet. LC 73-9565. (Biography Ser). (Illus.). 40p. (gr. 2-5). 1974. PLB 8.79 (ISBN 0-690-00219-X, TYC-J). Har-Row.

HUGHES, TED

Roberts, Neil & Gifford, Terry. Ted Hughes: A Critical Study. 288p. 1981. 27.00 (ISBN 0-571-11701-5, Pub. by Faber & Faber). Merrimack Bk Serv.

HUGHES, WILLIAM, fl. 1585-1595

Douglas, Alfred. True History of Shakespeare's Sonnets. LC 70-113364. 1970. Repr. of 1933 ed. 12.00 (ISBN 0-8046-1014-2). Kennikat.

HUGHES, WILLIAM MORRIS, 1864-1952

Joyner, Conrad. Holman Versus Hughes: Extension of Australian Commonwealth Powers. LC 61-63516. (U of Fla. Social Science Monographs: No. 10). 1961. pap. 3.00 (ISBN 0-8130-0123-4). U Presses Fla.

HUGO, OF SAINT VICTOR, 1096 or 7-1141

Baron, Roger. Hugh of St. Victor. (Mediaeval Studies Ser.: No. 20). 1966. 12.95x (ISBN 0-268-00121-9). U of Notre Dame Pr.

HUGO, VICTOR MARIE, COMTE, 1802-1885

Affron, Charles. Stage for Poets: Studies in the Theatre of Hugo & Musset. LC 75-153847. (Princeton Essays in Literature Ser.). 1972. 18.00 (ISBN 0-691-06201-3). Princeton U Pr.
Barbou, Alfred. Victor Hugo & His Time. 59.95 (ISBN 0-8490-1259-7). Gordon Pr.
Brown, Nathalie B. Hugo & Dostoevsky. 1978. 15.00x (ISBN 0-88233-268-6); pap. 5.00 (ISBN 0-88233-273-2). Ardis Pubs.
Deamicis, Edmondo. Studies of Paris: (Victor Hugo, Emile Zola) 276p. 1981. Repr. of 1882 ed. lib. bdg. 35.00 (ISBN 0-8495-1062-7). Arden Lib.
Doyle, Ruth L., compiled by. Victor Hugo's Drama: An Annotated Bibliography, 1900 to 1980. LC 80-29680. x, 217p. 1981. lib. bdg. 35.00 (ISBN 0-313-22884-1, DVH/). Greenwood.
Duclaux, Mary. Victor Hugo. LC 70-153903. 1971. Repr. of 1921 ed. 12.50 (ISBN 0-8046-1594-2). Kennikat.
Escholier, Raymond. Victor Hugo. Galantiere, Lewis, tr. 1973. Repr. of 1930 ed. 25.00 (ISBN 0-8274-0413-1). R West.
Giese, William F. Victor Hugo: The Man & the Poet. Repr. 30.00 (ISBN 0-8274-3671-8). R West.
Gladden, Washington. Witnesses of the Light. facs. ed. LC 77-84307. (Essay Index Reprint Ser). 1903. 15.75 (ISBN 0-8369-1081-8). Arno.
Grant, Elliott M. Career of Victor Hugo. (Harvard Studies in Romance Languages). 1945. pap. 22.00 (ISBN 0-527-01119-3). Kraus Repr.
Grant, Richard B. Perilous Quest: Image, Myth & Prophecy in the Narratives of Victor Hugo. LC 68-20494. 1968. 12.75 (ISBN 0-8223-0076-1). Duke.
Haggard, Andrew C. Victor Hugo, His Work & Love. Repr. 30.00 (ISBN 0-8274-3672-6). R West.
--Victor Hugo: His Work & Love. 1979. Repr. of 1923 ed. lib. bdg. 35.00 (ISBN 0-8495-2326-5). Arden Lib.
Hooker, Kenneth W. Fortunes of Victor Hugo in England. LC 39-3325. Repr. of 1938 ed. 12.50 (ISBN 0-404-03328-8). AMS Pr.
--The Fortunes of Victor Hugo in England. 1973. Repr. of 1938 ed. 12.00 (ISBN 0-8274-0045-4). R West.
Houston, John P. Victor Hugo. LC 74-8729. (World Authors Ser.: France: No. 312). 1974. lib. bdg. 9.95 (ISBN 0-8057-2443-5). Twayne.
Hudson, William H. Victor Hugo & His Poetry. LC 70-120967. (Poetry & Life Ser.). Repr. of 1918 ed. 7.25 (ISBN 0-404-52514-8). AMS Pr.
Hugo, Victor. Carnets Intimes, 1870-1871. (Illus.). 304p. 1953. 5.95 (ISBN 0-686-54058-1). French & Eur.
--Chatiments. Yarrow, P. J., ed. (French Poets Ser). 312p. 1975. text ed. 22.50x (ISBN 0-485-14707-6, Athlone Pr); pap. text ed. 9.00x (ISBN 0-485-12707-5). Humanities.
--Journal 1830-1848. 304p. 1954. 5.95 (ISBN 0-686-54075-1). French & Eur.
--Poesies choisies de Victor Hugo. new ed. (Documentation thematique). (Illus.). 168p. (Orig., Fr.). 1975. pap. 2.95 (ISBN 0-685-60916-2, 129). Larousse.
--Prefaces de Cromwell et autres prefaces dramatiques. (Documentation thematique). (Fr). pap. 2.95 (ISBN 0-685-14057-1, 124). Larousse.
--Souvenirs Personnels, 1848-1851. 328p. 1952. 5.95 (ISBN 0-686-54042-5). French & Eur.
Klin, George & Marsland, Amy L. Les Miserables Notes. (Orig.). 1968. pap. 2.25 (ISBN 0-8220-0735-5). Cliffs.
Marzials, Frank T. Life of Victor Hugo. 1973. Repr. of 1888 ed. 20.00 (ISBN 0-8274-1032-8). R West.
Maurois, Andre. Olympio ou La Vie de Victor Hugo. 18.50 (ISBN 0-685-36951-X). French & Eur.
Mehlman, Jeffrey. Revolution & Repetition: Marx-Hugo-Balzac. LC 76-24589. (Quantum Ser.). 1977. 14.00x (ISBN 0-520-03111-3); pap. 2.45 (ISBN 0-520-03531-3). U of Cal Pr.
Monarch Notes on Hugo's Les Miserables. (Orig.). pap. 2.25 (ISBN 0-671-00844-7). Monarch Pr.
Nash, S. Les Contemplations of Victor Hugo: An Allegory of the Creative Process. 1975. 17.50 (ISBN 0-691-06313-3). Princeton U Pr.
Nichol, J. Pringle. Victor Hugo. 1973. Repr. of 1893 ed. 20.00 (ISBN 0-8274-1006-9). R West.
O'Connor, Mary I. Study of the Sources of Han D'Islande & Their Significance in the Literary Development of Victor Hugo. LC 76-115357. (Catholic University Romance Languages Ser: No. 24). Repr. of 1942 ed. 14.50 (ISBN 0-404-50324-1). AMS Pr.
Olivier, Juste. Paris en 1830: Journal de Juste Olivier. Delattre, Andre & Denkinger, Marc, eds. (Studies in the Romance Languages & Literatures: No. 19). 1951. pap. 17.00x (ISBN 0-8078-9019-7). U of NC Pr.
Peguy, Charles. Notre Patrie. 12p. 1915. 2.95 (ISBN 0-686-54861-2). French & Eur.
--Victor-Marie, Comte Hugo. pap. 5.95 (ISBN 0-685-37047-X). French & Eur.
Peyre, Henri. Victor Hugo: Philosophy & Poetry. Roberts, Roda P., tr. from Fr. LC 79-9876. 176p. 1980. 12.75x (ISBN 0-8173-0017-1). U of Ala Pr.

Richardson, Joanna. Victor Hugo. LC 76-10564. (Illus.). 1977. 14.95 (ISBN 0-312-84035-7). St Martin.
Saltus, Edgar. Victor Hugo & Golgotha: Two Essays. LC 68-54295. Repr. of 1925 ed. 17.50 (ISBN 0-404-05551-6). AMS Pr.
Swinburne, Algernon. A Study of Victor Hugo. LC 76-25888. 1976. Repr. of 1866 ed. lib. bdg. 17.50 (ISBN 0-8414-7781-7). Folcroft.
Swinburne, Algernon C. Study of Victor Hugo. LC 78-113323. 1970. Repr. of 1886 ed. 10.00 (ISBN 0-8046-1000-2). Kennikat.
Van Tieghem, Philippe. Dictionnaire de Victor Hugo. (Dictionnaires de l'homme du vingtieme siecle). (Orig., Fr). 1970. pap. 8.50 (ISBN 0-685-13864-X, 3722). Larousse.
Ward, Patricia A. The Medievalism of Victor Hugo. LC 74-28421. (Penn State Studies: No. 39). 148p. 1975. pap. 3.95x (ISBN 0-271-01182-3). Pa St U Pr.

HUGO, VICTOR MARIE, COMTE, 1802-1885–BIBLIOGRAPHY

Dubois, Pierre. Bio-Bibliographie De Victor Hugo De 1802 a 1825. 1971. Repr. of 1913 ed. lib. bdg. 22.50 (ISBN 0-8337-0929-1). B Franklin.

HUGO VON TRIMBERG, fl. 1260-1309

Behrendt, Leo. Ethical Teaching of Hugo of Trimberg. LC 77-140042. (Catholic University of America. Studies in German: No. 1). Repr. of 1926 ed. 14.50 (ISBN 0-404-50221-0). AMS Pr.
Rapp, Catherine. Burgher & Peasant. LC 75-140039. (Catholic University Studies in German Ser.: No. 7). Repr. of 1936 ed. 17.00 (ISBN 0-404-50227-X). AMS Pr.

HUGUENOT WARS

see France–History–Wars of the Huguenots, 1562-1598

HUGUENOTS

Baird, Henry M. History of the Rise of the Huguenots of France, 2 Vols. LC 79-130236. Repr. of 1879 ed. Set. 90.00 (ISBN 0-404-00520-9); 45.00 ea. Vol. 1 (ISBN 0-404-00521-7). Vol. 2 (ISBN 0-404-00522-5). AMS Pr.
Dodge, Guy H. The Political Theory of the Huguenots of the Dispersion. LC 79-159178. ix, 287p. 1971. Repr. of 1947 ed. lib. bdg. 15.50x (ISBN 0-374-92213-6). Octagon.
Grant, Arthur J. Huguenots. 1969. Repr. of 1934 ed. 17.50 (ISBN 0-208-00745-8, Archon). Shoe String.
Hayward, J. F. Huguenot Silver in England, 1688-1727. 206p. 1959. 26.00 (ISBN 0-571-04551-0, Pub. by Faber & Faber). Merrimack Bk Serv.
Reaman, George E. Trail of the Huguenots in Europe, the United States, South Africa & Canada. LC 65-21923. 1972. Repr. of 1963 ed. 15.00 (ISBN 0-8063-0290-9). Genealog Pub.
Rothrock, George A. The Huguenots: A Biography of a Minority. LC 78-23476. (Illus.). 1979. 18.95x (ISBN 0-88229-277-3). Nelson-Hall.
Schwartz, Hillel. Knaves, Fools, Madmen & That Subtile Effluvium: A Study of the Opposition to the French Prophets in England, 1706-1710. LC 78-1692. (U of Fla. Social Science Monographs: No. 62). 1978. pap. 5.50 (ISBN 0-8130-0505-1). U Presses Fla.

HUGUENOTS–GENEALOGY

Fontaine, James. Memoirs of a Huguenot Family & Other Family Manuscripts. Maury, Ann, ed. LC 67-22179. (Illus.). 1973. Repr. of 1853 ed. 18.50 (ISBN 0-8063-0553-3). Genealog Pub.
Lart, Charles E. Huguenot Pedigrees, 2 vols. in 1. LC 67-28595. 1973. Repr. of 1928 ed. 17.50 (ISBN 0-8063-0207-0). Genealog Pub.
Morand, Julia P. Catalogue or Bibliography of the Library of the Huguenot Society of America. 2nd ed. LC 72-141421. 1971. Repr. of 1920 ed. 16.50 (ISBN 0-8063-0475-8). Genealog Pub.

HUGUENOTS IN FOREIGN COUNTRIES

Baird, Charles W. History of the Huguenot Emigration to America, 2 vols in 1. LC 66-29569. (Illus.). 1973. Repr. of 1885 ed. 25.00 (ISBN 0-8063-0554-1). Genealog Pub.
Brock, Robert A., compiled by. Documents, Chiefly Unpublished, Relating to the Huguenot Emigration to Virginia & the Settlement at Manakin-Town. LC 72-14424. (Virginia Historical Society. Collections, New Ser.: No. 5). Repr. of 1886 ed. 17.50 (ISBN 0-404-57655-9). AMS Pr.
Cooper, William D., ed. List of Foreign Protestants, & Aliens, Resident in England, 1618-1688. 1862. 15.50 (ISBN 0-384-09795-2). Johnson Repr.
--Lists of Foreign Protestants & Aliens Resident in England 1618-1688. Repr. of 1862 ed. 14.00 (ISBN 0-404-50182-6). AMS Pr.
Hirsch, Arthur H. Huguenots of Colonial South Carolina. (Illus.). 1973. Repr. of 1928 ed. 19.50 (ISBN 0-208-00467-X, Archon). Shoe String.
Lee, Hannah F. The Huguenots in France & America, 2 vols. in 1. LC 72-10564. 1973. Repr. of 1843 ed. 18.50 (ISBN 0-8063-0531-2). Genealog Pub.
Potter, Elisha R. Memoir Concerning the French Settlements & French Settlers in the Colony of Rhode Island. LC 68-27007. (Rhode Island Historical Tracts Ser: No. 5). 1968. Repr. of 1879 ed. 12.50 (ISBN 0-8063-0280-1). Genealog Pub.
Rupp, Israel D. A Collection of Upwards of Thirty Thousand Names of German, Swiss, Dutch, French & Other Immigrants in Pennsylvania from 1727 to 1776. 2nd ed. LC 65-26916. (Illus.). 583p. 1980. Repr. of 1876 ed. 20.00 (ISBN 0-8063-0302-6). Genealog Pub.
Schwartz, Hillel. The French Prophets: The History of a Millenarian Group in Eighteenth-Century England. LC 78-65459. (Illus.). 1980. 31.50x (ISBN 0-520-03815-0). U of Cal Pr.
Smiles, Samuel. The Huguenots: Their Settlements, Churches & Industries in England & Ireland. LC 72-39366. 448p. 1972. Repr. of 1868 ed. 17.50 (ISBN 0-8063-0497-9). Genealog Pub.

HUGUENOTS IN FRANCE

see also Edict of Nantes; France–History–Wars of the Huguenots, 1562-1598; Holy League, 1576-1593

Baird, Henry M. History of the Rise of the Huguenots of France, 2 Vols. LC 79-130236. Repr. of 1879 ed. Set. 90.00 (ISBN 0-404-00520-9); 45.00 ea. Vol. 1 (ISBN 0-404-00521-7). Vol. 2 (ISBN 0-404-00522-5). AMS Pr.
--Huguenots & Henry of Navarre, 2 Vols. LC 76-130987. Repr. of 1903 ed. Set. 57.50 (ISBN 0-404-00540-3). Vol. 1 (ISBN 0-404-00541-1). Vol. 2 (ISBN 0-404-00542-X). AMS Pr.
--The Huguenots & the Revocation of the Edict of Nantes, 2 vols. LC 76-161752. Repr. of 1895 ed. Set. 74.50 (ISBN 0-404-08003-0). AMS Pr.
--The Huguenots & the Revocation of the Edict of Nantes, 2 vols. 1977. lib. bdg. 250.00 (ISBN 0-8490-2025-5). Gordon Pr.
Bien, David D. The Calas Affair: Persecution, Toleration, & Heresy in Eighteenth-Century Toulouse. LC 78-12393. 1979. Repr. of 1960 ed. lib. bdg. 16.00x (ISBN 0-313-21206-6, BICA). Greenwood.
Grant, Arthur J. Huguenots. 1969. Repr. of 1934 ed. 17.50 (ISBN 0-208-00745-8, Archon). Shoe String.
Gray, Janet G. The French Huguenots. 200p. (Orig.). 1981. pap. 6.95 (ISBN 0-8010-3758-1). Baker Bk.
Lee, Hannah F. The Huguenots in France & America, 2 vols. in 1. LC 72-10564. 1973. Repr. of 1843 ed. 18.50 (ISBN 0-8063-0531-2). Genealog Pub.
Schwartz, Hillel. The French Prophets: The History of a Millenarian Group in Eighteenth-Century England. LC 78-65459. (Illus.). 1980. 31.50x (ISBN 0-520-03815-0). U of Cal Pr.
Sutherland, N. M. The Huguenot Struggle for Recognition. LC 79-64070. 1980. text ed. 30.00 (ISBN 0-300-02328-6). Yale U Pr.

HUIA

Hawkins, Clifford W. Log of the Huia. 3rd ed. (Illus.). 147p. 1973. 9.60x (ISBN 0-8002-0085-3). Intl Pubns Serv.

HUKBONG MAPAGPALAYA NG BAYAN (PHILIPPINE ISLANDS)

Taruc, Luis. Born of the People. (Illus.). 286p. 1973. Repr. of 1953 ed. lib. bdg. 15.00x (ISBN 0-8371-6669-1, TABP). Greenwood.

HULA LANGUAGE

Roes, Carol. Children's Christmas Hulas. 1965. pap. 4.50 with record (ISBN 0-930932-18-8). M Loke.
--Children's Hulas from Hawaii, Bk. 5. (Illus.). 13p. 1966. pap. 4.50 with record (ISBN 0-930932-10-2). M Loke.
--Hulas from Hawaii. (Hulas from Hawaii Ser.: Book No. 7). 15p. 1978. pap. 4.50 with record (ISBN 0-930932-03-X). M Loke.
--Introduction to the Hula. (Illus.). 12p. (gr. 1-3). 1961. pap. 1.50 (ISBN 0-930932-07-2). M Loke.
Roes, Carol & Kaiulani. Children's Hulas for Song Stories, Bk. 3. (Illus.). 24p. 1963. pap. 4.50 with record (ISBN 0-930932-08-0). M Loke.
--Hulas for 4 Songs. (Hula Book Ser.: Bk. 4). 18p. 1963. pap. 4.50 with record (ISBN 0-930932-09-9). M Loke.

HULI (PAPUAN PEOPLE)

Glasse, Robert M. Huli of Papua: A Cognatic Descent System. (Cahiers de l'Homme, Nouvelle Ser.: No. 8). (Illus., Orig.). 1968. pap. text ed. 21.75x (ISBN 90-2796-067-4). Mouton.

HULL, JOSEPHINE (SHERWOOD)

Carson, William G. Dear Josephine: The Theatrical Career of Josephine Hull. (Illus.). 1963. 15.95x (ISBN 0-8061-0558-5). U of Okla Pr.

HULL, ROBERT MARVIN

Zalewski, Ted. Bobby Hull. LC 73-10282. (Creative Superstars Ser.). 1974. PLB 5.95 (ISBN 0-87191-264-3). Creative Ed.

HULL, WILLIAM, 1753-1825

Campbell, Maria, ed. Revolutionary Services & Civil Life of General William Hull. 1972. Repr. of 1848 ed. lib. bdg. 29.50x (ISBN 0-8422-8022-7). Irvington.

HULL, ENGLAND

Gillett, Edward & MacMahon, Kenneth A., eds. A History of Hull. (Illus.). 448p. 1980. 45.00x (ISBN 0-19-713436-X). Oxford U Pr.

HULL HOUSE, CHICAGO

Addams, Jane. Twenty Years at Hull-House. pap. 1.95 (ISBN 0-451-51284-7, CJ1284, Sig Classics). NAL.
Hull House Residents. Hull-House Maps & Papers: A Presentation of Nationalities & Wages in a Congested District of Chicago. LC 78-112519. (Rise of Urban America). (Illus.). 1970. Repr. of 1895 ed. lib. bdg. 13.00 (ISBN 0-405-02457-6). Arno.

HULLS (NAVAL ARCHITECTURE)

Geen, Fox. Fitting Out a Moulded Hull. (Illus.). 176p. 1976. pap. 10.95 (ISBN 0-685-69131-4). Transatlantic.
Tucker, Robert. Fitting Out Ferrocement Hulls. (Illus.). 1979. 19.95 (ISBN 0-229-11512-8, ScribT). Scribner.
Verney, Michael. Care & Repair of Hulls. (Illus.). 1979. 9.95 (ISBN 0-229-11577-2, ScribT). Scribner.

HULME, THOMAS ERNEST, 1883-1917

Ghose, Zulfikar. Hulme's Investigations into the Bogart Script. 1981. 9.95 (ISBN 0-931604-03-6); pap. 4.95 (ISBN 0-931604-03-6). Curbstone Pub.
Jones, Alun R. The Life & Opinions of T. E. Hulme. LC 78-64036. (Des Imagistes: Literature of the Imagist Movement). Repr. of 1960 ed. 20.00 (ISBN 0-404-17117-6). AMS Pr.
Riding, Laura. Contemporaries & Snobs. LC 71-131818. 1971. Repr. of 1928 ed. 24.50 (ISBN 0-403-00705-4). Scholarly.
Roberts, Michael. T. E. Hulme. LC 72-169106. (English Biography Ser., No. 31). 1971. Repr. of 1938 ed. lib. bdg. 37.95 (ISBN 0-8383-1342-6). Haskell.

HULMECAS

see Olmecs

HUMA

see Bahima (African People)

HUMAN ABNORMALITIES

see Abnormalities, Human

HUMAN ACTS

see also Free Will and Determinism; Sin; Virtue and Virtues

Brand, Myles, ed. Action Theory: Proceedings. LC 76-6882. (Synthese Library: No. 97). 1976. PLB 55.00 (ISBN 90-277-0671-9, Pub. by Reidel Holland). Kluwer Boston.
Gauld & Shotter. Human Action & Its Psychological Investigation. 1977. 16.00 (ISBN 0-7100-8568-0). Routledge & Kegan.
More, Paul E. On Being Human. 1978. Repr. of 1936 ed. lib. bdg. 25.00 (ISBN 0-8414-2308-3). Folcroft.

HUMAN ANATOMY

see Anatomy, Human

HUMAN BEHAVIOR

see also Behavior Modification; Electronic Behavior Control; Psychobiology; Psychology, Comparative

Alberti, Robert & Emmons, Michael L. Your Perfect Right: A Guide to Assertive Behavior. 3rd ed. LC 78-6059. 1978. 7.95 (ISBN 0-915166-04-6); pap. 5.95 (ISBN 0-915166-03-8). Impact Pubs Cal.
Alexander, Richard D. Darwinism & Human Affairs. LC 78-65829. (Jessie & John Danz Lecture Ser.). (Illus.). 342p. 1980. 14.95 (ISBN 0-295-95641-0). U of Wash Pr.
Altman, Irwin & Wohlwill, J. F., eds. Human Behavior & Environment: Advances in Theory & Research, Vol. 2. (Illus.). 358p. 1977. 18.95 (ISBN 0-306-33302-3, Plenum Pr). Plenum Pub.
Altman, Irwin, et al, eds. Transportation & Behavior. (Human Behavior & Environment - Advances in Theory & Research Ser.: Vol. 5). 290p. 1981. text ed. price not set (ISBN 0-306-40773-6, Plenum Pr). Plenum Pub.
Altschule, M. D. Origins in Concepts in Human Behavior: Social & Cultural Factors. 1977. 17.95 (ISBN 0-470-99001-5). Halsted Pr.
Altschule, Mark D. Origins of Concepts in Human Behavior: Social & Cultural Factors. LC 76-46320. 204p. 1977. 17.95 (ISBN 0-470-99001-5, Pub. by Wiley). Krieger.
American Psychological Association. Natural Behavior in Humans & Animals. (Human Behavior Curriculum Project Ser.). 64p. (Orig.). 1981. pap. text ed. 3.95x (ISBN 0-8077-2613-3); tchrs. manual & duplication masters 9.95 (ISBN 0-8077-2614-1). Tchrs Coll.
--School Life & Organizational Psychology. (Human Behavior Curriculum Project Ser.). 64p. (Orig.). 1981. pap. text ed. 3.95x (ISBN 0-8077-2617-6); 9.95 (ISBN 0-8077-2618-4). Tchrs Coll.
American Psychological Association, et al. States of Consciousness. (Human Behavior Curriculum Project Ser.). 64p. 1981. pap. text ed. 3.95x (ISBN 0-8077-2615-X); tchrs. manual & duplication masters 9.95x (ISBN 0-8077-2616-8). Tchrs Coll.
Amory, Cleveland. Man Kind? 1.75 (ISBN 0-686-29858-6). Cancer Bk Hse.
Anderson, Ralph E. & Carter, Irl. Human Behavior in the Social Environment. 2nd ed. LC 77-95322. 1978. text ed. 19.95x (ISBN 0-202-36021-0); pap. text ed. 8.50x (ISBN 0-202-36022-9). Aldine Pub.
Andreassi, John L. Psychophysiology: Human Behavior & Physiological Response. 1980. text ed. 9.95x (ISBN 0-19-502581-4); pap. text ed. 7.00x (ISBN 0-19-502582-2). Oxford U Pr.
Anisman, H. & Bignami, G., eds. Psychopharmacology of Aversively Motivated Behavior. (Illus.). 564p. 1978. 35.00 (ISBN 0-306-31055-4, Plenum Pr). Plenum Pub.
Ardrey, Robert. Social Contract. 1971. pap. 2.65 (ISBN 0-440-57896-5, Delta). Dell.
--Territorial Imperative. 1968. pap. 3.25 (ISBN 0-440-58619-4, Delta). Dell.
--The Territorial Imperative: A Personal Inquiry into the Animal Origins of Property & Nations. LC 66-23572. (Illus.). 1966. 10.95 (ISBN 0-689-10015-9). Atheneum.
Atkinson, Rita L., intro. by. Mind & Behavior: Readings from Scientific American. LC 80-15307. (Illus.). 1980. text ed. 19.95x (ISBN 0-7167-1215-6); pap. text ed. 9.95x (ISBN 0-7167-1216-4). W H Freeman.
Auger, J. Behavioral Systems & Nursing. (Illus.). 224p. 1976. ref. ed. 13.95x (ISBN 0-13-074484-0). P-H.
Bakker, Cornelis & Bakker-Rabdau, Marianne. No Trespassing! Explorations in Human Territoriality. LC 73-7326. 284p. 1973. pap. 5.95 (ISBN 0-88316-528-7). Chandler & Sharp.
Barash, David. The Whisperings Within: Evolution & the Origin of Human Nature. LC 78-20155. 1979. 12.50 (ISBN 0-06-010341-8, HarpT). Har-Row.
Barker, Roger G., ed. Stream of Behavior: Explorations of Its Structure & Content. LC 62-18400. (Century Psychology Ser.). (Illus.). 1963. 18.95x (ISBN 0-89197-427-X); pap. text ed. 8.95x (ISBN 0-89197-428-8). Irvington.
Baron, R. A. Human Aggression. LC 77-24567. (Perspectives in Social Psychology Ser.). (Illus.). 298p. 1977. 14.95 (ISBN 0-306-31050-3, Plenum Pr). Plenum Pub.
Barraclough, Norman. Preology: The Scientific Study of the Planning of Human Development. LC 80-40600. 265p. 1981. pap. 14.25 (ISBN 0-08-026083-7). Pergamon.
Bar-Tal, D. Prosocial Behavior, Theory & Research. LC 75-43624. 1976. 12.50 (ISBN 0-470-15223-0). Halsted Pr.
Bartz, Albert E. Descriptive Statistics for Education & the Behavioral Sciences. 5th ed. LC 77-91504. Orig. Title: Basic Descriptive Statistics for Education & the Behavioral Sciences. 1979. pap. 7.95x (ISBN 0-8087-2853-9). Burgess.
Bateson, P. P. & Klopfer, Peter H., eds. Perspectives in Ethology, 3 vols. Incl. Vol. 1. 336p. 1973. 27.50 (ISBN 0-306-36601-0); Vol. 2. 340p. 1976. 27.50 (ISBN 0-306-36602-9); Vol. 3: Social Behavior. 277p. 1978. 22.50 (ISBN 0-306-36603-7). (Illus., Plenum Pr). Plenum Pub.
--Perspectives in Ethology: Advantages of Diversity, Vol. 4. 230p. 1980. 25.00 (ISBN 0-306-40511-3, Plenum Pr). Plenum Pub.
Becker, Ernest. Birth & Death of Meaning. 2nd ed. LC 62-15359. 1971. 9.95 (ISBN 0-02-902170-7); pap. 5.95 (ISBN 0-02-902190-1). Free Pr.
Becker, Gary S. The Economic Approach to Human Behavior. LC 75-43240. 1978. pap. 6.95 (ISBN 0-226-04112-3, P803, Phoen). U of Chicago Pr.
Beckman, A. L., ed. The Neural Basis of Behavior. (Illus.). 447p. 1981. text ed. 35.00 (ISBN 0-89335-132-6). SP Med & Sci Bks.
Benjamin, Alfred. Behavior in Small Groups. LC 77-73213. 1977. pap. text ed. 6.25 (ISBN 0-395-25447-7). HM.
Berger, Robert & Federico, Ron. Human Behavior. 1982. pap. text ed. 9.95x tent. (ISBN 0-582-28180-6). Longman.
Birdsong, Robert E. Positive Behavior Patterns. (Aquarian Academy Monography: Suppl. Lecture No. 2). 1978. pap. text ed. 1.00 (ISBN 0-917108-21-3). Sirius Bks.
Birnbaumer, Niels, et al. Self Regulation of the Brain & Behavior: Cortical Potentials, Behavior & Psychopathology. 1982. price not set. Urban & S.
Bock, Kenneth. Human Nature & History: A Response to Sociobiology. 192p. 1980. 18.95 (ISBN 0-231-05078-X). Columbia U Pr.

Brandt, Richard M. Studying Behavior in Natural Settings. LC 81-40189. (Illus.). 416p. 1981. lib. bdg. 25.25 (ISBN 0-8191-1829-X); pap. text ed. 14.75 (ISBN 0-8191-1830-3). U Pr of Amer.
Braunstein, Jonathan J. & Toister, Richard P. Medical Applications of the Behavioral Sciences. (Illus.). 634p. Date not set. price not set (ISBN 0-8151-1194-0). Year Bk Med.
Brayer, Herbert O. Teaching for Responsible Behavior: A Comprehensive Values-Oriented Approach to High-Risk Behavior. Date not set. pap. price not set (ISBN 0-913458-15-5). Pennant Pr.
Brim, Orville G., Jr. & Kagan, Jerome, eds. Constancy & Change in Human Development. (Illus.). 760p. 1980. 27.50x (ISBN 0-674-16625-6). Harvard U Pr.
Brown, Hugh. Brain & Behavior: A Textbook of Physiological Psychology. (Illus.). 400p. 1976. text ed. 13.95x (ISBN 0-19-501945-8). Oxford U Pr.
Bruner, Jerome S. & Garton, Alison, eds. Human Growth & Development: The Wolfson College Lectures, 1976. (Illus.). 1978. pap. text ed. 8.95x (ISBN 0-19-857518-1). Oxford U Pr.
Bufford, Rodger K. The Human Reflex: Behavioral Psychology in Biblical Perspective. LC 80-8900. (Illus.). 256p. 1981. 12.95 (ISBN 0-06-061165-0, HarpR). Har-Row.
Burns, R. B. The Self Concept: Theory, Measurement, Development & Behaviour. (Illus.). 1979. pap. text ed. 12.95x (ISBN 0-582-48951-2). Longman.
Burr, H. S. The Neural Basis of Human Behavior. 272p. 1960. pap. 19.75 photocopy ed. spiral (ISBN 0-398-00264-9). C C Thomas.
Campbell, Frank & Sinaer, George. Brain & Behaviour: Psychobiology of Everyday Life. (Illus.). 168p. 1980. 22.50 (ISBN 0-08-024788-1); pap. 11.25 (ISBN 0-08-024787-3). Pergamon.
Cantril, Hadley. Pattern of Human Concerns Data, 1957-1963. 1977. codebk. 28.00 (ISBN 0-89138-115-5). ICPSR.
Carver, C. S. & Scheier, M. F. Attention & Self Regulation: A Control-Theory Approach to Human Behavior. (Springer Series in Social Psychology). (Illus.). 403p. 1981. 29.90 (ISBN 0-686-72582-4). Springer-Verlag.
Catania, A. Charles & Brigham, T. A., eds. Handbook of Applied Behavior Analysis: Social & Instructional Processes. (Century Psychology Ser.). 1979. 39.50 (ISBN 0-470-99347-2). Halsted Pr.
Centore, F. F. Persons: A Comparative Account of the Six Possible Theories. LC 78-74653. (Contributions in Philosophy: No. 13). 1979. lib. bdg. 25.00 (ISBN 0-313-20817-4, CPE/). Greenwood.
Chalmers, Neil, et al, eds. Biological Bases of Behavior. 1971. pap. text ed. 8.40 (ISBN 0-06-318007-3, IntlDept). Har-Row.
Charron, C., et al. Behavior: A Guide for Managers. 1977. 14.95 (ISBN 0-87909-078-2). Reston.
Chorover, Stephan. From Genesis to Genocide: The Meaning of Human Nature & the Power of Behavior Control. 256p. 1980. pap. 5.95 (ISBN 0-262-53039-2). MIT Pr.
CIBA Foundation. Sex, Hormones & Behaviour. (CIBA Foundation Symposium: No. 62). 1979. 41.00 (ISBN 0-444-90045-4). Elsevier.
Cohen, Marilyn & Gross, Pamela. The Developmental Resource: A Behavioral Resource for Assessment & Programming, 2 vols. 1978. Vol. 1, 224pps. 19.25 (ISBN 0-8089-1122-8); Vol. 2, 256pps. 20.25 (ISBN 0-8089-1157-0). Grune.
Cole, Jim. The Facade: A View of Our Behavior. (Illus.). 64p. 1970. pap. 2.50 (ISBN 0-88310-003-7). Publishers Consult.
--The Facade-a View of Our Behavior. 1970. pap. 2.50 (ISBN 0-9601200-1-7). J Cole.
Coleman, James C. Contemporary Psychology & Effective Behavior. 4th ed. 1979. text ed. 17.95x (ISBN 0-673-15202-2); student's guide 5.95x (ISBN 0-673-15203-0). Scott F.
Counte, Michael A. & Christman, Luther. Interpersonal Behavior & Health Care. (Behavioral Sciences for the Health Care Professional Ser.). 128p. (Orig.). 1981. lib. bdg. 15.00x (ISBN 0-86531-008-4); pap. text ed. 6.75x (ISBN 0-86531-009-2). Westview.
Craig, Grace J. Human Development. 2nd ed. (Illus.). 1980. text ed. 19.95 (ISBN 0-13-444984-3); study guide 6.95 (ISBN 0-13-445015-9). P-H.
Cranach, Mario, ed. Methods of Inference from Animal to Human Behavior: Proceedings of the Conference on "the Logic of Inference from Animal to Human Behavior" Held in Muren, Switzerland, in March 1973. (Maison Des Sciences Del'homme: Publications No. 3). 1976. 37.25x (ISBN 90-2797-763-1). Mouton.
Crook, John H. The Evolution of Human Consciousness. (Illus.). 462p. 1980. 39.00x (ISBN 0-19-857174-7). Oxford U Pr.
Cross, Gary P., et al. Conflict & Human Interaction. 1979. pap. text ed. 9.95 (ISBN 0-8403-1990-8). Kendall-Hunt.
Crouch, Robert L. Human Behavior: An Economic Approach. LC 78-10391. (Illus.). 1979. pap. text ed. 8.95 (ISBN 0-87872-205-X). Duxbury Pr.
Cullen, Joseph, ed. Legacies in the Study of Behavior: The Wisdom & Experience of Many. (American Lectures in Objective Psychiatry Ser.). (Illus.). 288p. 1975. text ed. 24.50 (ISBN 0-398-03147-9). C C Thomas.
Cushman, Donald P. & McPhee, Robert D., eds. Message-Attitude-Behavior Relationship: Theory, Methodology & Application. LC 80-529. (Human Communications Research Ser.). 1980. 27.00 (ISBN 0-12-199760-X). Acad Pr.
Davis, Flora. Inside Intuition: What We Know About Nonverbal Communication. 240p. 1975. pap. 1.95 (ISBN 0-451-07831-4, J7831, Sig). NAL.
Davis, Keith. Human Behavior at Work. 6th ed. (Management Ser.). (Illus.). 576p. 1981. text ed. 18.95x (ISBN 0-07-015516-X, C); instr's. manual & test file 15.00 (ISBN 0-07-015517-8); study guide avail. (ISBN 0-07-015535-6). McGraw.
Davis, Keith & Newstrom, John. Organizational Behavior: Readings & Exercises. 6th ed. (Management Ser.). (Illus.). 468p. 1981. text ed. 11.95 (ISBN 0-07-015500-3, C). McGraw.
DeFeudis, F. & DeFeudis, P. Elements of the Behavioral Code. 1978. 61.50 (ISBN 0-12-208760-7). Acad Pr.
Deibert, Alvin N. & Harmon, Alice J. New Tools for Changing Behavior. LC 72-75094. (Illus.). 136p. (Orig.). 1973. pap. 6.95 (ISBN 0-87822-115-8). Res Press.
Denenberg, V. H. Statistics & Experimental Design for Behavioral & Biological Researchers: An Introduction. LC 76-21841. 1976. text ed. 17.50 (ISBN 0-470-15202-8). Halsted Pr.
Denison, J. H. The Enlargement of Personality: Behavior Patterns & Their Formation. 1930. 30.00 (ISBN 0-8495-6271-6). Arden Lib.
Denny, Ray & Davis, Robert. Understanding Behavior: Foundations & Applications. 1981. 16.95 (ISBN 0-88252-113-6). Paladin Hse.
Derber, Charles. The Pursuit of Attention: Power & Individualism in Everyday Life. 120p. 1979. pap. text ed. 6.95 (ISBN 0-87073-885-2). Schenkman.
Derlega, Valerian & Grzelak, Janusz, eds. Cooperation & Helping Behavior: Theories & Research. 1981. price not set (ISBN 0-12-210820-5). Acad Pr.
Desiraju, T. Mechanisms in Transmission of Signals for Conscious Behavior. 1976. 78.00 (ISBN 0-444-41397-9, North Holland). Elsevier.
Dodge, Raymond. Conditions & Consequences of Human Variability. 1931. 32.50x (ISBN 0-685-69812-2). Elliots Bks.
Dorsey, George A. Why We Behave Like Human Beings. 1978. Repr. of 1925 ed. lib. bdg. 25.00 (ISBN 0-8495-1009-0). Arden Lib.
Earnest, Franklin, III. Transitional Man: The Anatomy of a Miracle. 96p. 1981. pap. 5.95 (ISBN 0-914480-06-5). Far West Edns.
Eccles, J. The Human Psyche. (Illus.). 300p. 1980. 25.00 (ISBN 0-387-09954-9). Springer-Verlag.
Edlund, Calvin V. How Human Behavior Is Learned: A Handbook for Parents & Professional Workers with Children. LC 79-170092. (Orig.). 1972. pap. 5.00x (ISBN 0-87562-033-7). Spec Child.
Edman, Irwin. Human Traits & Their Social Significance. 1978. Repr. of 1919 ed. lib. bdg. 30.00 (ISBN 0-8495-1307-3). Arden Lib.
Ehrmann, Lee & Omenn, Gilbert S., eds. Genetics, Environment & Behavior: Implications for Educational Policy. 1972. 43.00 (ISBN 0-12-233450-7). Acad Pr.
Ellenson, Ann. Human Relations. 2nd ed. (Illus.). 352p. 1982. text ed. 18.95 (ISBN 0-13-445650-5). P-H.
Endleman, Robert. Psyche & Society: Explorations of Human Nature, Sex & Aggression, Deviation & Psychopathology. 448p. 1981. 30.00 (ISBN 0-231-04992-7). Columbia U Pr.
Evans, Robert L. The Fall & Rise of Man, If... LC 72-97467. 259p. 1973. 6.95 (ISBN 0-9606698-0-9); pap. 3.95 (ISBN 0-9606698-1-7). R L Evans.
Eysenck, H. J. & Rachman, S., eds. Advances in Behaviour Research & Therapy, Vol. 1, Pt. 1. 1977. pap. 19.50 (ISBN 0-08-022257-9). Pergamon.
Favell, Judith E. & Greene, James W. How to Treat Self-Injurious Behavior. 1981. 4.00 (ISBN 0-89079-055-8). H & H Ent.
Fedigan, Linda M. Primate Paradigms: Sex Roles & Social Bonds. (Illus.). 1981. (ISBN 0-920792-03-0); pap. write for info. EPWP.
Ferster, Charles & Culbertson, Stuart A. Behavior Principles. 3rd ed. (Illus.). 384p. 1982. reference 20.95 (ISBN 0-13-072520-X). P-H.
Forbes, Jean & Ross, James. Communications & Networks. (Place & People Ser.: No. 3). (Illus.). 1977. pap. text ed. 4.95x (ISBN 0-435-34694-6). Heinemann Ed.
Foreyt, J. P. & Rathjen, D. P. Cognitive-Behavior Therapy. LC 78-15948. (Illus.). 279p. 1978. 18.95 (ISBN 0-306-31145-3, Plenum Pr). Plenum Pub.
Fourth Banff International Conference on Behavior Modification, et al. Behavior Change: Methodology, Concepts, & Practice. 1973. pap. text ed. 10.95 (ISBN 0-87822-089-5). Res Press.
Fox, M. W. Concepts in Ethology: Animal & Human Behavior. LC 73-93834. (Wesley W. Spink Lectures on Comparative Medicine Ser: Vol. 2). (Illus.). 160p. 1974. 8.50x (ISBN 0-8166-0723-0). U of Minn Pr.
Friedman, Herbert. Understanding & Improving Behavior. rev. ed. LC 75-22951. 1980. text ed. 3.50 (ISBN 0-686-17339-2). CAPP Bks.
Friedman, Myles. Rational Behavior: An Explanation of Behavior That Is Especially Human. LC 75-2416. 200p. 1975. 14.95x (ISBN 0-87249-325-3). U of SC Pr.
Friedman, Richard, et al, eds. Sex Differences in Behavior. LC 78-15815. 512p. 1978. Repr. of 1974 ed. lib. bdg. 32.50 (ISBN 0-88275-720-2). Krieger.
Frisancho, A. Roberto. Human Adaptation: A Functional Interpretation. LC 78-31913. (Illus.). 1979. text ed. 14.95 (ISBN 0-8016-1693-X). Mosby.
Gallistel, C. R. The Organization of Action: A New Synthesis. 432p. 1980. 29.95x (ISBN 0-470-26912-X). Halsted Pr.
Garfinkel, Alan. Forms of Explanation: Rethinking the Questions in Social Theory. LC 80-23341. 192p. 1981. 16.00x (ISBN 0-300-02136-4). Yale U Pr.
Gauld & Shotter. Human Action & Its Psychological Investigation. 1977. 16.00 (ISBN 0-7100-8568-0). Routledge & Kegan.
Gaylin, Willard. Caring. 1979. pap. 2.25 (ISBN 0-380-44693-6, 44693). Avon.
Gehring, Robert E. Basic Behavioral Statistics. LC 77-78447. (Illus.). 1978. text ed. 19.95 (ISBN 0-395-24684-9); study guide 6.95 (ISBN 0-395-24683-0); inst. manual 0.65 (ISBN 0-395-25511-2). HM.
Genoves, Santiago. The Acali Experiment: Six Women & Five Men on a Raft Across the Atlantic. LC 79-51447. (Illus.). 1979. 15.00 (ISBN 0-8129-0855-4, Dist. by Har-Row). Times Bks.
Gesell, Arnold. Atlas of Infant Behavior, Vol. 2. (Illus.). 1934. 125.00x (ISBN 0-685-69821-1). Elliots Bks.
Gillette, Frank, ed. Between Paradigms: The Mood & Its Purpose. (Social Change Ser.). 1973. 35.75x (ISBN 0-677-15060-1). Gordon.
Glaros, Alan. Maladaptive Behavior: Study Guide. 1980. pap. text ed. 5.95x (ISBN 0-673-15152-2). Scott F.
Goldfried, M. & Merbaum, M. Behavior Change Through Self-Control. LC 72-84063. 1973. pap. text ed. 9.95 (ISBN 0-03-086046-6, HoltC). HR&W.
Goldman, Alvin I. Theory of Human Action. 1977. 16.00 (ISBN 0-691-07216-7); pap. 5.95 (ISBN 0-691-01974-6). Princeton U Pr.
Goodstein, Leonard D. & Lanyon, Richard I. Adjustment, Behavior, & Personality. 2nd ed. LC 78-62553. (Illus.). 1979. text ed. 17.95 (ISBN 0-201-02455-1); wkbk. 6.50 (ISBN 0-201-02456-X). A-W.
Goslee, Catherine L. Handling "Problem" Employees. Reilly, Harry A., ed. 76p. 1981. pap. 125.00 (ISBN 0-89290-142-X, SMP-214); pap. text ed. 45.00 participants manual (ISBN 0-89290-143-8). Soc for Visual.
Gottschalk, Louis A., ed. The Content Analysis of Verbal Behavior: Further Studies. 1979. 45.00 (ISBN 0-470-26367-9). Halsted Pr.
Gottsegen, Gloria B., ed. Group Behavior: A Guide to Information Sources. LC 79-63744. (Psychology Information Guide Ser.: Vol. 2). 1979. 36.00 (ISBN 0-8103-1439-8). Gale.
Gould, James L. Ethology: The Mechanisms & Evolution of Behavior. 1981. text ed. 18.95x (ISBN 0-686-73558-7). Norton.
Grant, Igor. Behavioral Disorders: Clinical Psychopathology for Health Sciences Students. LC 78-15309. (Illus.). 318p. 1979. text ed. 14.95 (ISBN 0-89335-061-3). Spectrum Pub.
Gregory, Michael S., et al, eds. Sociobiology & Human Nature: An Interdisciplinary Critique & Defense. LC 78-62559. (Social & Behavioral Science Ser.). (Illus.). 1978. text ed. 17.95x (ISBN 0-87589-384-8). Jossey-Bass.
Grey, Arnold. The Choice of Life: A New Perspective on Human Nature and Inhuman Events. LC 76-57338. (Illus.). 1977. pap. 3.95 (ISBN 0-89476-101-3). Emet Bks.
Gutsch, Kenneth U. & Thornton, Larry L. Insights into Human Development: Commentaries. LC 77-17020. 1978. 9.95x (ISBN 0-87805-043-4); pap. 4.95x (ISBN 0-87805-044-2). U Pr of Miss.
Haber, Bernard & Aprison, M. H., eds. Neuropharmacology & Behavior. LC 77-14178. (Illus.). 225p. 1978. 24.50 (ISBN 0-306-31056-2, Plenum Pr). Plenum Pub.
Hall-Quest, Alfred L. It's Not Our Fault: Why We Can't Be Good! Repr. of 1929 ed. 10.00 (ISBN 0-89987-054-6). Darby Bks.
Halsey, A. H., ed. Heredity & Environment. LC 77-2530. 1977. 13.95 (ISBN 0-02-913670-9). Free Pr.
Hamel, Frank. Human Animals. 75.00 (ISBN 0-87968-098-9). Gordon Pr.
Handy, Rollo. Value Theory & the Behavioral Sciences. (American Lecture Philosophy). 212p. 1969. photocopy ed. spiral 19.75 (ISBN 0-398-00770-5). C C Thomas.
Handy, Rollo & Harwood, E. C. A Current Appraisal of the Behavioral Sciences. 2nd. rev. ed. LC 73-79255. 1973. 10.00x (ISBN 0-913610-01-1). Behavioral Mass.
Hansell, Norris. The Person-in-Distress: On the Biosocial Dynamics of Adaptation. LC 74-8096. 252p. 1976. text ed. 24.95 (ISBN 0-87705-213-1). Human Sci Pr.
Harding, Robert S., ed. Omnivorous Primates: Gathering & Hunting in Human Evolution. Teleki, Geza P. LC 80-23726. (Illus.). 912p. 1981. 40.00x (ISBN 0-231-04024-5). Columbia U Pr.
Harris, Dale B., ed. The Concept of Development: An Issue in the Study of Human Behavior. 1957. pap. 5.95x (ISBN 0-8166-0447-9). U of Minn Pr.
Harrison, Albert A. Individuals & Groups: Understanding Social Behavior. LC 75-25147. (Core Books in Psychology Ser.). (Illus.). 1976. text ed. 18.95 (ISBN 0-8185-0176-6); test items avail. (ISBN 0-685-61934-6). Brooks-Cole.
Harrison, Paul D. The Truth of Human Nature. (Illus.). 300p. (Orig.). Date not set. 14.95 (ISBN 0-938058-25-8); pap. 11.95 (ISBN 0-938058-26-6). Wrightwill Pub.
Hayes, Harold. Three Levels of Time. LC 80-22963. 1981. 13.50 (ISBN 0-525-21853-X). Dutton.
Haynes, Stephen N. Principles of Behavioral Assessment. LC 77-19134. 1978. 24.95 (ISBN 0-470-26292-3). Halsted Pr.
Haynes, Stephen N. & Wilson, C. Chrisman. Behavioral Assessment: Recent Advances in Methods, Concepts, & Applications. LC 79-88775. (Social & Behavioral Science Ser.). 1980. text ed. 22.95x (ISBN 0-87589-439-9). Jossey-Bass.
Hazelbauer, G., ed. Taxis & Behavior. (Receptors & Recognition Series B: Vol. 5). 1978. 47.95x (ISBN 0-412-14880-3, Pub. by Chapman & Hall). Methuen Inc.
Hersen, Michel & Bellack, Alan S., eds. Behavioral Assessment: A Practical Handbook. 2nd ed. (Pergamon General Psychology Ser.: No. 65). 614p. 1981. 45.00 (ISBN 0-08-025956-1); pap. 19.50 (ISBN 0-08-025955-3). Pergamon.
Hervath, S. M., et al, eds. Comparative Studies on Human Adaptability of Japanese, Caucasians & Japanese Americans. (Japan International Biological Program Synthetics Ser.). 1975. pap. 22.00x (ISBN 0-86008-211-3, Pub. by U of Tokyo Pr). Intl Schol Bk Serv.
Hinde, Robert A. Biological Bases of Human Social Behavior. (Illus.). 416p. 1974. text ed. 19.00 (ISBN 0-07-028932-8, C); pap. text ed. 14.95 (ISBN 0-07-028931-X). McGraw.
Hobbs, Albert H. Man Is Moral Choice. 1979. 12.95 (ISBN 0-87000-433-6). Arlington Hse.
Hofer, Myron. The Roots of Human Behavior: An Introduction to the Psychobiology of Early Development. LC 80-28377. (Psychology Ser.). (Illus.). 1981. text ed. 22.50x (ISBN 0-7167-1277-6); pap. text ed. 11.50x (ISBN 0-7167-1278-4). W H Freeman.
Holahan, C. J. Environment & Behavior: A Dynamical Perspective. LC 77-25400. (Plenum Social Ecology Ser.). (Illus.). 206p. 1977. 14.95 (ISBN 0-306-31086-4, Plenum Pr). Plenum Pub.
Holland, James & Skinner, B. F. Analysis of Behavior: A Program for Self-Instruction. 1961. pap. text ed. 10.50 (ISBN 0-07-029565-4, C). McGraw.
Hooton, Earnest A. Why Men Behave Like Apes & Vice Versa (or, Body & Behavior) (Psychology Ser). 1968. Repr. of 1940 ed. 15.50 (ISBN 0-384-24235-9). Johnson Repr.
Human Aspects of Medical Sciences, Medical Technology, & the Responsibility of the Physician. 8p. 1981. pap. 5.00 (ISBN 92-808-0180-5, TUNU 122, UNU). Unipub.
Hume, David. Treatise of Human Nature, 2 vols. in 1. 1978. 12.95x (ISBN 0-460-00548-0, Evman). Biblio Dist.
--A Treatise on Human Nature, 3 vols. LC 78-67528. (Scottish Enlightenment Ser.). Repr. of 1740 ed. Set. 97.50 (ISBN 0-404-17653-4). Vol. 1 (ISBN 0-404-17654-2). Vol. 2 (ISBN 0-404-17655-0). V0l. 3 (ISBN 0-404-17656-9). AMS Pr.

Hunt, Chester L. & Walker, Lewis. Ethnic Dynamics: Patterns of Intergroup Relations in Various Societies. 2nd ed. LC 78-73117. 1979. text ed. 15.95x (ISBN 0-918452-16-3). Learning Pubns.
Hunter, Marvinia & White, Howard. Writing Behavioral Objectives: The Process & the Argument. 1974. 6.00 (ISBN 0-939630-09-5). Inst Qual Hum Life.
Hutt, S. J. & Hutt, C. Behaviour Studies in Psychiatry. 1970. 17.25 (ISBN 0-08-015780-7). Pergamon.
Hyman, Herbert H. The Psychology of Status. Zuckerman, Harriet & Merton, Robert K., eds. LC 79-9005. (Dissertations on Sociology Ser.). 1980. lib. bdg. 10.00x (ISBN 0-405-12974-2). Arno.
Il'yuchenok, R. Pharmacology of Behavior & Memory. LC 76-11831. 1976. 22.50 (ISBN 0-470-15116-1). Halsted Pr.
Jackins, Harvey. The Human Side of Human Beings: Japanese Translation. Sullivan, Anna Hirata, tr. 1979. pap. 3.00 (ISBN 0-911214-67-4). Rational Isl.
--O Lado Humano Dos Seres Humanos. Cordeiro, Aquiles, tr. 1979. pap. 3.00 (ISBN 0-911214-66-6). Rational Isl.
Jakle, John A., et al. Human Spatial Behavior. LC 75-11278. 1976. text ed. 13.95x (ISBN 0-87872-098-7). Duxbury Pr.
Johnston, James M. Behavior Research & Technology in Higher Education. (Illus.). 536p. 1975. 27.50 (ISBN 0-398-03315-3). C C Thomas.
Johnston, James M. & Pennypacker, H. S. Strategies & Tactics of Human Behavioral Research. LC 80-22612. 496p. 1980. text ed. 24.95x (ISBN 0-89859-030-2). L Erlbaum Assocs.
Joseph, N. R. Physicochemical Anthropology, Part II: Comparative Morphology & Behavior. 1979. 58.75 (ISBN 3-8055-2951-1). S Karger.
Kalat, James W. & Norton, Thomas J., eds. From Brains to Behavior. 1973. 39.50x (ISBN 0-8422-5115-4). Irvington.
Kaufmann, Harry. Introduction to the Study of Human Behavior. 1976. 3.95 (ISBN 0-685-74219-9). Plantagenet Pr.
Kazdin, Alan E. & Esveldt-Dawson, Karen. How to Maintain Behavior. 1981. 3.25 (ISBN 0-89079-054-X). H & H Ent.
Kelman, Herbert C., ed. International Behavior: A Social-Psychological Analysis. 1980. text ed. 38.50x (ISBN 0-8290-0027-5); pap. text ed. 18.50x (ISBN 0-8290-0028-3). Irvington.
Kennedy, Eugene. Free to Be Human. 1980. pap. 2.95 (ISBN 0-346-12431-X). Cornerstone.
Kerlinger, F. N. Multiple Regression in Behavioral Research. LC 73-3936. 1973. text ed. 24.95 (ISBN 0-03-086211-6, HoltC). HR&W.
Kerlinger, Fred N. Scientific Behavioral Research: A Conceptual Primer. new ed. LC 78-16793. 1979. text ed. 18.95 (ISBN 0-03-013331-9, HoltC). HR&W.
Kierkegaard, Soren A. Internal Development of Man in Dynamic Representational Expressions. Karlweiss, Joseph R., ed. (Illus.). 107p. 1981. 49.75 (ISBN 0-89266-273-5). Am Classical Coll Pr.
Kiernan, Chris & Jones, Malcolm. Behaviour Assessment Battery. (General Ser.). 1977. pap. text ed. 19.25x (ISBN 0-685-05810-7, NFER). Humanities.
Klapp, Orrin E. Currents of Unrest: An Introduction to Collective Behavior. LC 76-189252. 1972. 28.00x (ISBN 0-03-085305-2); pap. text ed. 14.95x (ISBN 0-89197-717-1). Irvington.
Kolaja, Jiri T. Social System & Time & Space: An Introduction to the Theory of Recurrent Behavior. LC 79-25635. (Illus.). viii, 113p. 1980. Repr. of 1969 ed. lib. bdg. 15.50x (ISBN 0-313-22278-9, KOSS). Greenwood.
Krasner, L. & Ullmann, L. P. Behavior Influence & Personality. LC 72-9583. 1973. text ed. 16.95 (ISBN 0-03-056155-8, HoltC). HR&W.
Krebs, John R. & Davies, Nicholas B. An Introduction to Behavioural Ecology. LC 80-25843. (Illus.). 300p. 1981. text ed. 39.60x (ISBN 0-87893-431-6); pap. text ed. 16.50x (ISBN 0-87893-432-4). Sinauer Assoc.
Lake, Dale. Perceiving & Behaving. LC 72-77891. (Illus.). 1970. text ed. 10.50x (ISBN 0-8077-1658-8). Tchrs Coll.
Lehrman, D. S., et al, eds. Advances in the Study of Behavior, Vols. 1-9. Incl. Vol. 1. 1965. 38.50 (ISBN 0-12-004501-X); Vol. 2. 1969. 38.50 (ISBN 0-12-004502-8); Vol. 3. 1970. 38.50 (ISBN 0-12-004503-6); Vol. 4. 1972. 38.50 (ISBN 0-12-004504-4); Vol. 5. 1974. 38.50 (ISBN 0-12-004505-2); Vol. 6. 1976. 38.50 (ISBN 0-12-004506-0); Vol. 7. 1976. 43.00 (ISBN 0-12-004507-9); Vol. 8. 1978. 28.00 (ISBN 0-12-004508-7); Vol. 9. 1979. 31.00 (ISBN 0-12-004509-5). Acad Pr.
Lerner, Richard & Busch-Rossnagel, Nancy, eds. Individuals As Producers of Their Development: A Life-Span Perspectives. 1981. write for info. (ISBN 0-12-444550-0). Acad Pr.
Levinson, David & Malone, Martin. Toward Explaining Human Culture: A Critical Review of the Findings of Worldwide Cross-Cultural Research. LC 80-83324. (Comparative Studies Ser.). 400p. 1981. 25.00 (ISBN 0-87536-339-3); pap. 15.00 (ISBN 0-87536-340-7). HRAFP.
Lewis, M. & Rosenblum, L. A. Origins of Behavior, 4 vols. Incl. Vol. 1. The Effect of the Infant on Its Caregiver. 1974. 28.95 (ISBN 0-471-53202-9); Vol. 3. Structure & Transformation: Developmental & Historical Aspects. Riegel, K. F. & Rosenwald, G. C., eds. LC 75-15659. 1975. 27.95 (ISBN 0-471-72140-9); Vol. 4. Friendship & Peer Relations. LC 75-20181. 1975. 31.95 (ISBN 0-471-53345-9). LC 73-12804 (Pub. by Wiley-Interscience). Wiley.
Lewis, M. & Rosenblum, L. A., eds. The Development of Affect. LC 77-19209. (Genesis of Human Behavior Ser.: Vol. 1). (Illus.). 438p. 1978. 22.50 (ISBN 0-306-34341-X, Plenum Pr). Plenum Pub.
Lindzey, Gardner, ed. Assessment of Human Motives. LC 79-4248. 1979. Repr. of 1958 ed. lib. bdg. 23.25x (ISBN 0-313-21247-3, LIAS). Greenwood.
Lisitzky, Gene. Four Ways of Being Human. 1976. pap. 3.50 (ISBN 0-14-004391-8). Penguin.
Liska, A. E., ed. The Consistency Controversy: Readings on the Impact of Attitude on Behavior. 277p. 1975. pap. 5.95x (ISBN 0-470-54123-7). Halsted Pr.
Lombardi, Thomas P. Career Adaptive Behavior Inventory Activity Book. Preston, J. B., ed. 88p. (Orig.). 1980. pap. text ed. 10.00x (ISBN 0-87562-066-3). Spec Child.
Lorenz, K. & Leyhausen, P. Motivation of Human & Animal Behavior. 1973. 22.50x (ISBN 0-442-24885-7). Van Nos Reinhold.
Lorenz, Konrad. Studies in Animal & Human Behaviour, 2 vols. LC 75-11087. 390p. Vol. 2. 1971. 20.00x (ISBN 0-674-84631-1). Harvard U Pr.
Lowen, Alexander. Fear of Life. 224p. 1980. 10.95 (ISBN 0-02-575880-2). Macmillan.
Lubar, Joel. Readings on Biological Foundations of Behavior. 1975. text ed. 5.95 (ISBN 0-88429-004-2). Collegiate Pub.
Lubar, Joel F. Biological Foundations of Behavior. 1976. 4.95 (ISBN 0-685-62879-5). Collegiate Pub.
McConnell, James V. Understanding Human Behavior. 3rd ed. LC 79-24039. 799p. 1980. text ed. 20.95 (ISBN 0-03-044411-X, HoltC); student manual 6.95 (ISBN 0-03-044456-X); instr's. manual avail. (ISBN 0-03-044461-6). computerized test bank avail. (ISBN 0-03-044486-1); test bank avail. (ISBN 0-03-044481-0); study guide 7.95 (ISBN 0-03-058267-9). HR&W.
McGuigan, F. J. Biological Basis of Behavior: A Program. (Illus.). 1963. pap. text ed. 8.95x (ISBN 0-8290-0383-5). Irvington.
Malmberg, Torsten. Human Teritoriality: A Survey on the Behavioral Territories of Man with Preliminary Analysis & Discussion of Meaning. 1979. pap. 40.00x (ISBN 90-279-7948-0). Mouton.
Mason, Russell E. SET, H.E.S.T-a: Humanistic Endeavor & Surgent Train-Ascendance. 1975. pap. 3.00 (ISBN 0-89533-028-8). F I Comm.
Masserman, Jules H. Behavior & Neurosis: An Experimental Psychoanalytic Approach to Psychobiologic Principles. 1964. Repr. of 1943 ed. 13.75 (ISBN 0-02-848840-7). Hafner.
--The Biodynamic Roots of Human Behavior. 132p. 1968. photocopy ed. spiral 12.75 (ISBN 0-398-01232-6). C C Thomas.
Masserman, Jules H. & Schwab, John J. Man for Humanity: On Concordence vs Discord in Human Behavior. (Illus.). 384p. 1972. photocopy ed. spiral 37.50 (ISBN 0-398-02354-9). C C Thomas.
Mazur, Allan & Robertson, Leon S. Biology & Social Behavior. LC 72-169236. 1972. 12.95 (ISBN 0-02-920450-X); pap. text ed. 3.00 (ISBN 0-02-920410-0). Free Pr.
Mehrabian, Albert. Tactics of Social Influence. 1970. pap. text ed. 9.95 (ISBN 0-13-882159-3). P-H.
Merikangas, James R. Brain-Behavior Relationships. LC 79-2075. 240p. 1981. 23.95x (ISBN 0-669-03082-1). Lexington Bks.
Merleau-Ponty, Maurice. Structure of Behavior. 1963. pap. 4.95x (ISBN 0-8070-2987-4, BP266). Beacon Pr.
--Struktur des Verhaltens. (Phaenomenologisch-Psychologische Forschungen: Vol. 13). xxvi, 278p. 1976. text ed. 48.75x (ISBN 3-11-004469-2). De Gruyter.
Merton, Robert K., ed. Factors Determining Human Behavior. LC 73-14153. (Perspectives in Social Inquiry Ser.). 186p. 1974. Repr. 10.00x (ISBN 0-405-05500-5). Arno.
Meyer, Eugene & Brady, Joseph V. Research in the Psychobiology of Human Behavior. LC 78-24710. 1979. text ed. 14.00x (ISBN 0-8018-2238-6). Johns Hopkins.
Meyers, Lawrence S. & Grossen, Neal E. Behavioral Research: Theory, Procedure, & Design. 2nd ed. LC 78-2212. (Psychology Ser.). (Illus.). 1978. text ed. 17.95x (ISBN 0-7167-0049-2). W H Freeman.
Michael, Richard P. & Crook, John H., eds. Comparative Ecology & Behaviour of Primates. 1973. 93.00 (ISBN 0-12-493450-1). Acad Pr.
Midgley, Mary. Beast & Man: The Roots of Human Nature. 1980. pap. 5.95 (ISBN 0-452-00529-9, F529, Mer). NAL.
--Beast & Man: The Roots of Human Nature. LC 78-58021. 1978. 17.50x (ISBN 0-8014-1032-0). Cornell U Pr.
Millenson, J. R. & Leslie, Julian C. Principles of Behavioral Analysis. 2nd ed. 1978. text ed. 19.95 (ISBN 0-02-381280-X). Macmillan.
Miller, L. Keith. Everyday Behavior Analysis. 1976. pap. text ed. 14.95 (ISBN 0-8185-0200-2); instructor's manual avail. (ISBN 0-685-67245-X). Brooks-Cole.
Milliken, Mary E. Understanding Human Behavior. LC 80-51266. (Practical Nursing Ser.). 256p. 1981. 9.20 (ISBN 0-8273-1968-1); pap. 6.80 (ISBN 0-8273-1439-6); instr's. guide 1.70 (ISBN 0-8273-1445-0). Delmar.
Milton, Charles R. Human Behavior in Organizations. (Illus.). 432p. 1981. text ed. 20.95 (ISBN 0-13-444596-1). P-H.
Miron, Nathan B. Winning the Games People Play: How to Master the Art of Changing People's Behavior. LC 76-52149. (Illus.). 1977. 12.95 (ISBN 0-918418-01-1); pap. 7.95 (ISBN 0-918418-02-X). Mission Pr CA.
Moore, John. Zeluco: Various Views of Human Nature Taken from Life and Manners, Foreign and Domestic, 2 vols. in 1. LC 80-2492. Repr. of 1789 ed. 89.50 (ISBN 0-404-19126-6). AMS Pr.
Morris, Desmond. Human Zoo. 1970. pap. 2.75 (ISBN 0-440-53912-9, Delta). Dell.
--Manwatching: A Field Guide to Human Behavior. (Illus.). 1979. pap. 14.95 (ISBN 0-8109-2184-7). Abrams.
--Manwatching: A Field Guide to Human Behavior. (Illus.). 1977. 25.00 (ISBN 0-8109-1310-0). Abrams.
Morrison, Denton E. & Hornback, Kenneth E. Collective Behavior: A Bibliography. LC 75-24098. (Reference Library of Social Science: Vol. 15). 534p. 1975. lib. bdg. 55.00 (ISBN 0-8240-9975-3). Garland Pub.
Mule, S. Joseph, ed. Behavior in Excess: An Examination of the Volitional Disorders. LC 81-65506. (Illus.). 480p. 1981. 25.00 (ISBN 0-02-922220-6). Free Pr.
Mussen, Paul & Eisenberg-Berg, Nancy. Roots of Caring, Sharing, & Helping: The Development of Prosocial Behavior in Children. LC 77-22750. (Psychology Ser.). (Illus.). 1977. text ed. 16.95x (ISBN 0-7167-0045-X); pap. text ed. 7.95x (ISBN 0-7167-0044-1). W H Freeman.
Neale, John M. & Liebert, Robert M. Science & Behavior: An Introduction to the Methods of Research. 2nd ed. (Ser. in Social Learning Theory). (Illus.). 1980. text ed. 17.95 (ISBN 0-13-795195-7). P-H.
Newell, Clarence A. Human Behavior in Educational Administration: A Behavioral Science Interpretation. (Illus.). 1978. ref. ed. 17.95 (ISBN 0-13-444638-0). P-H.
Nicolson, Harold. Good Behavior: Being a Study of Certain Types of Civility. 7.50 (ISBN 0-8446-0822-X). Peter Smith.
Notterman, Joseph M. Behavior, a Systematic Approach. pap. text ed. 8.50x (ISBN 0-394-30423-3). Phila Bk Co.
Notterman, Joseph M., ed. Laboratory Manual for Behavior. 1970. pap. 2.95x (ISBN 0-685-38352-0). Phila Bk Co.
Odahl, Charles M. Catilinarian Conspiracy. 1972. 6.00x (ISBN 0-8084-0032-0); pap. 2.95 (ISBN 0-8084-0033-9, H3). Coll & U Pr.
Omark, Donald, et al. Dominance Relations: An Ethological View of Human Conflict and Social Interactions. LC 79-14352. 528p. 1980. lib. bdg. 37.50 (ISBN 0-8240-7048-8). Garland Pub.
Ostwald, Peter F., ed. Communication & Social Interaction: Clinical & Therapeutic Aspects of Human Behavior. 384p. 1978. 37.25 (ISBN 0-8089-1049-3). Grune.
Otto, Herbert A. Explorations in Human Potentialities. (Illus.). 580p. 1966. photocopy ed. spiral 49.75 (ISBN 0-686-71892-5). C C Thomas.
Perkins, Hugh V. Human Development. 1975. text ed. 15.95x (ISBN 0-534-00383-4). Wadsworth Pub.
Perry, Joseph B., Jr. & Pugh, Meredith. Collective Behavior: Response to Social Stress. (Illus.). 1978. text ed. 13.50 (ISBN 0-8299-0158-2). West Pub.
Persinger, Michael A. Weather Matrix & Human Behavior. LC 80-18422. 300p. 1980. 27.95 (ISBN 0-03-057731-4). Praeger.
Peter, Laurence J. Peter's People. LC 79-12906. (Illus.). 1979. lib. bdg. 8.95 (ISBN 0-688-03488-8). Morrow.
Plessner, Helmuth. Laughing & Crying: A Study of the Limits of Human Behavior. Churchill, James S. & Grene, Marjorie, trs. from Ger. LC 70-123611. (Studies in Phenomenology & Existential Philosophy). 1970. text ed. 11.95x (ISBN 0-8101-0321-4). Northwestern U Pr.
Powers, Richard & Osborne, James G. Fundamentals of Behavior. LC 75-40098. (Illus.). 200p. 1976. pap. text ed. 13.95 (ISBN 0-8299-0073-X). West Pub.
Powers, William T. Behavior: The Control of Perception. LC 73-75697. 320p. 1973. text ed. 19.95x (ISBN 0-202-25113-6). Aldine Pub.
Pugh, Meredith D. Collective Behavior: A Source Book. 1980. pap. 12.50 (ISBN 0-8299-0317-8). West Pub.
Puligandla, R. Fact & Fiction in B. F. Skinner's Science & Utopia. LC 73-21001. 114p. 1974. 10.00 (ISBN 0-87527-130-8). Green.
Rachlin, Howard. Behavior & Learning. LC 76-2068. (Psychology Ser.). (Illus.). 1976. text ed. 21.95x (ISBN 0-7167-0568-0). W H Freeman.
Radzinski, John M. Masks of Moscow: A History of Russian Behavior Patterns. 2nd ed. 1981. Repr. of 1957 ed. 10.95 (ISBN 0-686-76741-1). Regent House.
Readings in Human Development 76-77. rev. ed. LC 72-91973. (Annual Editions Ser.). 320p. (Orig.). 1976. pap. text ed. 5.95 (ISBN 0-87967-147-5). Dushkin Pub.
Reese, Ellen P., et al. Human Behavior: Analysis & Application. 2nd ed. 280p. 1978. pap. text ed. write for info. (ISBN 0-697-06622-3). Wm C Brown.
Reynolds, Peter C. On the Evolution of Human Behavior. 1980. 9.95 (ISBN 0-8302-2762-8). Goodyear.
--On the Evolution of Human Behavior: The Argument from Animals to Man. LC 80-6056. 265p. 1981. 17.50x (ISBN 0-520-04294-8); pap. 8.95 (ISBN 0-520-04416-9, CAL 513). U of Cal Pr.
Reynolds, Vernon. The Biology of Human Action. 2nd ed. LC 80-11856. (Illus.). 1980. text ed. 19.95x (ISBN 0-7167-1239-3); pap. text ed. 10.95x (ISBN 0-7167-1240-7). W H Freeman.
Riklan & Levita. Subcortical Correlates of Human Behavior. 356p. 1969. 19.00 (ISBN 0-683-07264-1, Pub. by Williams & Wilkins). Krieger.
Riley, Sue. Help! LC 77-16030. (What Does It Mean Ser.). (Illus.). (ps-2). 1978. PLB 5.50 (ISBN 0-89565-012-6). Childs World.
Roberts, Sharon L. Behavioral Concepts & Nursing Throughout the Lifespan. 1978. ref. 16.95x (ISBN 0-13-074559-6); pap. text ed. 12.95x (ISBN 0-13-074567-7). P-H.
Robinson, John. How Americans Use Time: A Social-Psychological Analysis of Everyday Behavior. LC 76-58838. (Special Studies). 1977. text ed. 24.95 (ISBN 0-275-24200-5). Praeger.
Rosenblatt, Jay S., et al, eds. Advances in the Study of Behavior, Vol. 10. LC 64-8031. 1979. 33.50 (ISBN 0-12-004510-9). Acad Pr.
--Advances in the Study of Behavior, Vol. 11. 1980. 35.00 (ISBN 0-12-004511-7). Acad Pr.
Rosenthal, Robert. Experimenter Effects in Behavior Research. enlarged ed. LC 75-37669. (Century Psychology Ser.). 1976. 15.95 (ISBN 0-470-01391-5). Halsted Pr.
Ross, Lewis. Extra-Marital Relationships. (Topics in Human Behavior Ser.). 1978. pap. text ed. 5.95 (ISBN 0-8403-1853-7). Kendall-Hunt.
Ross, Robert R. & McKay, Hugh B. Self-Mutilation. (Illus.). 1979. 21.00 (ISBN 0-669-02116-4). Lexington Bks.
Rudman, Jack. Behavioral Sciences for Nurses. (College Level Examination Ser.: CLEP-39). (Cloth bdg. avail. on request). 1977. pap. 9.95 (ISBN 0-8373-5389-0). Natl Learning.
Russell, Hugh & Black, Kenneth. Understanding & Influencing Human Behavior. (Illus.). 240p. 1981. text ed. 12.95 (ISBN 0-13-936674-1, Spec). P-H.
Rutter, Michael, et al, eds. Education, Health & Behaviour. 496p. 1981. Repr. of 1970 ed. text ed. 19.50 (ISBN 0-89874-268-4). Krieger.
St. John, Bob. Sand Castles. 190p. 1981. price not set (ISBN 0-88319-058-3). Shoal Creek Pubs.
Scandura, M. N. Structural-Process Models of Complex Human Behavior, No. 26. (NATO Advanced Study Applied Science Ser.). 620p. 1978. 49.00x (ISBN 9-0286-0578-9). Sijthoff & Noordhoff.
Schechner, Richard & Schuman, Mady, eds. Ritual, Play, & Performance: Readings in the Social Sciences-Theatre. 1976. 14.95 (ISBN 0-8164-9285-9). Continuum.
Scheibe, Karl E. Mirrors, Masks, Lies, Secrets & the Limits of Human Predictability. LC 78-19791. 192p. 1979. 19.95 (ISBN 0-03-046661-X). Praeger.

Schelling, Thomas C. Micromotives & Macrobehavior. (Illus.). 1978. 19.95 (ISBN 0-393-05701-1); pap. 3.95x (ISBN 0-393-09009-4). Norton.
Schoedinger, Andrew B. Wants, Decisions & Human Action: A Praxeological Investigation. LC 78-62705. 1978. pap. text ed. 9.50 (ISBN 0-8191-0591-0). U Pr of Amer.
Schoen, Max. Human Nature: A First Book in Psychology. 1979. Repr. of 1930 ed. lib. bdg. 35.00 (ISBN 0-8495-4925-6). Arden Lib.
--Human Nature in the Making. Repr. of 1913 ed. 20.00 (ISBN 0-89987-076-7). Darby Bks.
Schulman, Jerome L., et al. Brain Damage & Behavior: A Clinical-Experimental Study. (Illus.). 176p. 1965. pap. 17.50 (ISBN 0-398-01691-7). C C Thomas.
Schur, Max, ed. Drives, Affects, Behavior, Vol. 2: Essays in Memory of Marie Bonaparte. LC 53-11056. 1965. text ed. 25.00 (ISBN 0-8236-1500-6). Intl Univs Pr.
Seagrim, G. N. & Lendon, R. J. Furnishing the Mind-Aboriginal & White: A Report on the Hemannsburg Project. (Behavioral Development: a Series of Monographs). 1981. 38.50 (ISBN 0-12-634340-3). Acad Pr.
Sells, S. B., et al. Human Functioning in Longitudinal Perspective: Studies of Normal & Psychopathic Populations. 305p. 1980. lib. bdg. 25.00 (ISBN 0-683-07628-0). Williams & Wilkins.
Shain, Merle. When Lovers Are Friends. 1978. 6.95 (ISBN 0-397-01265-9). Lippincott.
Sherman, Mandel & Sherman, Irene C. The Process of Human Behavior. 1978. Repr. of 1929 ed. lib. bdg. 27.50 (ISBN 0-89760-805-4, Telegraph). Dynamic Learn Corp.
Shye, Samuel, ed. Theory Construction & Data Analysis in the Behavioral Sciences. LC 78-62554. (Social & Behavioral Science Ser.). (Illus.). 1978. text ed. 25.95x (ISBN 0-87589-379-1). Jossey-Bass.
Sierles, Frederick. Clinical Behavioral Science. 1981. text ed. write for info. (ISBN 0-89335-131-8). Spectrum Pub.
Simmons, Richard C. Understanding Human Behavior in Health & Illness. 2nd ed. 733p. 1981. 29.95 (ISBN 0-686-76612-1). Williams & Wilkins.
Singleton, W. T., et al, eds. The Analysis of Social Skill. (NATO Conference Ser., Series III, Human Factors: Vol. II). 350p. 1980. 35.00 (ISBN 0-306-40337-4). Plenum Pub.
Smith, Bruce D. Prehistoric Patterns of Human Behavior: A Case Study in the Mississippi Valley. (Studies in Archeology Ser.). 1978. 27.50 (ISBN 0-12-650650-7). Acad Pr.
Starr, Bernard D. & Goldstein, Harris A. Human Development & Behavior: Psychology in Nursing. LC 73-92205. 1975. text ed. 15.50 (ISBN 0-8261-1550-0). Springer Pub.
Statt, D. Dictionary of Human Behavior. 1981. text ed. 15.50 (ISBN 0-686-69149-0, Pub. by Har-Row Ltd England). Har-Row.
Staub, Ervin. Positive Social Behavior & Morality, 2 vols. Incl. Vol. 1. Social & Personal Influences. 21.00 (ISBN 0-12-663101-8); Vol. 2. Socialization & Development. 16.00 (ISBN 0-12-663102-6). 1978-79. Acad Pr.
Steele, F. I. Physical Settings & Organization Development. LC 70-172802. 1973. pap. text ed. 6.50 (ISBN 0-201-07211-4). A-W.
Stein, R. Incest & Human Love. LC 73-82641. 1973. 8.95 (ISBN 0-89388-090-6). Okpaku Communications.
Steinberg, Rafael. Man & the Organization. (Human Behavior Ser). 176p. 1975. 9.95 (ISBN 0-8094-1912-2); lib. bdg. avail. (ISBN 0-685-52490-6). Time-Life.
Sterman, M. B., et al. Brain Development & Behavior. 1971. 56.50 (ISBN 0-12-666350-5). Acad Pr.
Stevenson, Leslie, ed. The Study of Human Nature. 352p. 1981. pap. text ed. 7.95x (ISBN 0-19-502827-9). Oxford U Pr.
Streufert, Siegfried & Streufert, Susan C. Behavior in the Complex Environment. (Scripta Personality & Social Psychology Ser.). 1978. 18.75x (ISBN 0-470-26335-0). Halsted Pr.
Stuart, Richard B., ed. Behavioral Self-Management. LC 77-23501. 1977. 20.00 (ISBN 0-87630-148-0). Brunner-Mazel.
Sudnow, David. Ways of the Hand: The Organization of Improvised Conduct. (Illus.). 1978. 12.50x (ISBN 0-674-94833-5). Harvard U Pr.
Sulzer, B. & Mayer, R. G. Procedures & Behavioral Modification for School Personnel. LC 75-172794. 1972. text ed. 10.95 (ISBN 0-686-66283-0, HoltC). HR&W.
Swift, Morrison I. Human Submission. 1977. lib. bdg. 59.95 (ISBN 0-8490-2027-1). Gordon Pr.
Thalberg, Irving. Perception, Emotion & Action: A Component Approach. LC 76-52340. 1977. 12.50x (ISBN 0-300-02129-1). Yale U Pr.
Thomas, Edwin J., ed. Behavior Modification Procedure: A Sourcebook. LC 73-89513. 368p. 1974. text ed. 24.95x (ISBN 0-202-36018-0); pap. text ed. 12.95x (ISBN 0-202-36019-9). Aldine Pub.
Tullar, Richard M. The Human Species: Its Nature, Evolution & Ecology. (Illus.). 1976. pap. text ed. 15.95 (ISBN 0-07-065423-9, C); instructor's manual 5.50 (ISBN 0-07-065424-7). McGraw.
Turner, A. N. & Lombard, G. F. Interpersonal Behavior and Administration. LC 69-11486. 1969. text ed. 16.95 (ISBN 0-02-932760-1). Free Pr.
Ulrich, Roger E., et al. Control of Human Behavior, Vol. 1: Expanding the Behavioral Laboratory. 1966. pap. 8.95x (ISBN 0-673-05484-5). Scott F.
--Control of Human Behavior, Vol. 3: Behavior Modification in Education. 448p. 1974. pap. 8.95x (ISBN 0-673-07621-0). Scott F.
Vale, Jack R. Genes, Environment & Behavior: An Interactionist Approach. (Illus.). 470p. 1980. text ed. 22.50 scp (ISBN 0-06-046758-4, HarpC). Har-Row.
Van Den Berghe, P. Man in Society: A Biosocial View. 1978. pap. 8.50 (ISBN 0-444-99045-3). Elsevier.
Vaughn, James A. & Deep, Samuel D. Program of Exercises for Management & Organizational Behavior. 1975. pap. text ed. 6.95x (ISBN 0-02-479440-6); tchrs' manual free (ISBN 0-02-479450-3). Macmillan.
Von Cranach, Mario, ed. Methods of Inference from Animal to Human Behaviour. 1977. 24.50x (ISBN 0-202-02020-7). Beresford Bk Serv.
Wachtel, Paul, ed. Resistance: Problematic Patient Behavior in Psychodynamic & Behavior Therapies. 230p. 1982. text ed. 22.50 (ISBN 0-306-40769-8, Plenum Pr). Plenum Pub.
Walker, Nigel. Behavior & Misbehavior: Explanations & Non-Explanations. LC 77-75252. 1977. 12.95x (ISBN 0-465-00585-3). Basic.
Walsh, Anthony. Human Nature & Love: Biological, Intrapsychic & Social-Behavioral Perspectives. LC 80-6176. 342p. 1981. lib. bdg. 20.50 (ISBN 0-8191-1532-0); pap. text ed. 11.75 (ISBN 0-8191-1533-9). U Pr of Amer.
Warden, Carl J. The Evolution of Human Behavior. 248p. 1981. Repr. of 1932 ed. lib. bdg. 45.00 (ISBN 0-8495-5658-9). Arden Lib.
--The Evolution of Human Behavior. 1932. lib. bdg. 30.00 (ISBN 0-8414-9654-4). Folcroft.
Warmington, C., et al. Organizational Behavior & Performance. 1978. 14.95 (ISBN 0-87909-594-6). Reston.
Weisberg, Robert W. Memory, Thought, & Behavior. LC 79-56. (Illus.). 1979. text ed. 16.95x (ISBN 0-19-502583-0). Oxford U Pr.
Weiss, Mark L. & Mann, Alan E. Human Biology & Behavior: An Anthropological Perspective. 2nd ed. 252p. 1978. text ed. 15.95 (ISBN 0-316-92890-9). Little.
Weller, Carol & Strawser, Sherri. Secondary Scale: Weller-Strawser Scales of Adaptive Behavior. 2nd ed. 6p. 1981. pap. 6.00 (ISBN 0-87879-260-0). Acad Therapy.
White, Burton L., et al. The Origins of Human Competence. LC 77-81793. 1979. 19.95 (ISBN 0-669-01943-7). Lexington Bks.
Whitman, R. Douglas. Adjustment: The Development & Organization of Human Behavior. (Illus.). 1980. text ed. 15.95x (ISBN 0-19-502590-3); write for info inst. manual (ISBN 0-19-502714-0). Oxford U Pr.
Widroe, Harvey J. Human Behavior & Brain Function. (Illus.). 132p. 1975. 10.75 (ISBN 0-398-03271-8). C C Thomas.
Wildman, Louis. Post Behavioral Objective Strategies. 1974. 3.00 (ISBN 0-939630-01-X). Inst Qual Hum Life.
Willemes, W. A. Constitution: Types in Delinquency. 266p. 1980. Repr. of 1932 ed. lib. bdg. 40.00 (ISBN 0-89984-501-0). Century Bookbindery.
Williams, Terrell G. Consumer Behavior: Concepts & Strategies. 600p. 1982. pap. text ed. 20.95 (ISBN 0-8299-0420-4). West Pub.
Williamson, G. Scott & Pearse, Innes H. Science, Synthesis, & Sanity. 352p. 1980. pap. 13.00x (ISBN 0-7073-0259-5, Pub. by Scottish Academic Pr Scotland). Columbia U Pr.
Wills, Richard H. The Institutionalized Severely Retarded: A Study of Activity & Interaction. (Illus.). 208p. 1973. 13.75 (ISBN 0-398-02755-2). C C Thomas.
Wilson, Edward O. On Human Nature. 1979. pap. 3.95 (ISBN 0-553-12943-0). Bantam.
Wilson, Howard. Changing Behavior. 1978. pap. 1.50 (ISBN 0-910022-19-4). ARA.
Wohlwill, J. F. & Weisman, G. D. The Physical Environment & Behavior: An Annotated Bibliography & Guide to the Literature. 474p. 1981. 45.00 (ISBN 0-306-40739-6, Plenum Pr). Plenum Pub.
Wright, Nicolas & Joiner, Susan, eds. Understanding Human Behavior: An Illustrated Guide to Human Relationships, 24 vols. LC 77-21477. (Illus.). 1977. Repr. of 1974 ed. Set. lib. bdg. 199.50 (ISBN 0-8393-6006-1). Purnell Ref Bks.
Wrightsman, Lawrence S., et al. Psychology: A Scientific Study of Human Behavior. 5th ed. LC 78-59674. (Illus.). 1979. text ed. 18.95 (ISBN 0-8185-0280-0). Brooks-Cole.
Zeiler, Michael D. & Harzem, Peter. Advances in Analysis of Behaviour: Reinforcement & the Organisation of Behaviour, Vol. 1. LC 78-31697. (Wiley Series on Advances in Analysis of Behaviour). 1980. 60.50 (ISBN 0-471-27573-5, Pub. by Wiley-Interscience). Wiley.
Zimbardo, Philip G., et al. Influencing Attitudes & Changing Behavior: An Introduction to Method, Theory & Applications of Social Control & Personal Power. (Topics in Social Psychology). 1977. pap. text ed. 7.95 (ISBN 0-201-08796-0). A-W.

HUMAN BEHAVIOR–MATHEMATICAL MODELS

Darlington, Richard B. Radicals & Squares: Statistical Methods for the Behavioral Sciences. 1975. 12.50 (ISBN 0-918610-01-X); autotutorial wrkbk. & supplementary chapters 6.25 (ISBN 0-918610-02-8); instrs'. manual avail. (ISBN 0-685-83160-4). Logan Hill.
Dubin, Robert. Theory Building. rev. ed. LC 77-90010. (Illus.). 1978. text ed. 15.95 (ISBN 0-02-907620-X). Free Pr.
Horton, Raymond L. The General Linear Model: Data Analysis in the Social & Behavioral Sciences. (Illus.). 1978. text ed. 30.50x (ISBN 0-07-030418-1). McGraw.
Maxwell, A. E. Multivariate Analysis in Behavioral Research: For Medical & Social Science Students. 2nd ed. 1978. 13.95x (ISBN 0-412-15580-X, Pub. by Chapman & Hall). Methuen Inc.
Nowakowska, Maria. Language of Motivation & Language of Actions. LC 72-94491. (Janua Linguarum, Ser. Major: No. 67). (Illus.). 272p. 1973. text ed. 55.00x (ISBN 0-686-22550-3). Mouton.
Pfeiffer, Kenneth & Olson, James N. Basic Statistics for the Behavioral Sciences. LC 80-22778. 1981. text ed. 19.95 (ISBN 0-03-049866-X, HoltC); wkbk. 5.95 (ISBN 0-03-049876-7). HR&W.
Stopher, Peter R. & Mevburg, Arnim H., eds. Behavioral Travel-Demand Models. LC 76-14666. 1976. 27.95 (ISBN 0-669-00734-X). Lexington Bks.
Young, Robert K. & Veldman, Donald J. Introductory Statistics for the Behavioral Sciences. LC 80-26006. 1981. text ed. 19.95 (ISBN 0-03-043051-8, HoltC). HR&W.

HUMAN BEINGS ON OTHER PLANETS

see Life on Other Planets

HUMAN BIOLOGY

see also Physical Anthropology

Barnett, S. A. The Human Species: The Biology of Man. (Illus.). 8.50 (ISBN 0-8446-0477-1). Peter Smith.
Bates, Marston. Gluttons & Libertines: Human Problems of Being Natural. LC 66-11978. 1971. pap. 2.45 (ISBN 0-394-71267-6, V-267, Vin). Random.
Bliss. Bliss Bibliography, Second Class H: Anthropology, Human Biology & Health Sciences. 1981. 64.95 (ISBN 0-408-70828-X). Butterworth.
Blurton-Jones, N. & Reynolds, V., eds. Human Behavior & Adaptation, Vol. 18. (Symposium of the Society for the Study of Human Biology). 1979. 39.95x (ISBN 0-470-26578-7). Halsted Pr.
Borek, Ernest. The Atoms Within Us. rev. ed. LC 80-19010. 272p. 1980. 20.00x (ISBN 0-231-04386-4); pap. 8.00x (ISBN 0-231-04387-2). Columbia U Pr.
Bowers, John Z. & Purcell, Elizabeth F., eds. Teaching the Basic Medical Sciences: Human Biology. LC 74-82069. (Illus.). 1974. pap. 7.50 (ISBN 0-914362-14-3). J Macy Foun.
British Museum Natural History. Human Biology-an Exhibition of Ourselves. LC 76-53266. (Illus.). 1977. 18.95 (ISBN 0-521-21589-7); pap. 5.95 (ISBN 0-521-29193-3). Cambridge U Pr.
Carter, Nicholas, ed. Development, Growth & Aging. 169p. 1980. 27.50x (ISBN 0-85664-861-2, Pub. by Croom Helm Ltd England). Biblio Dist.
Chiarenza, Loretta & Burkart, John, eds. Readings in Human Biology. 2nd ed. 104p. 1981. pap. text ed. 6.50 (ISBN 0-89529-134-7). Avery Pub.
Conn, H. W. The Story of the Living Machine: A Review of the Conclusions of Modern Biology in Regard to the Mechanism Which Controls the Phenomena of Living Activity. 1979. Repr. of 1904 ed. lib. bdg. 20.00 (ISBN 0-8495-0775-8). Arden Lib.
Damon, Albert. Human Biology & Ecology. LC 77-559. (Illus.). 1977. pap. text ed. 8.95x (ISBN 0-393-09103-1). Norton.
East, Edward M., ed. Biology in Human Affairs. 399p. 1980. Repr. of 1931 ed. lib. bdg. 30.00 (ISBN 0-8495-1348-0). Arden Lib.
Edwards, R. G. Conception in the Human Female. LC 80-40423. 1980. 116.50 (ISBN 0-12-232450-1). Acad Pr.
Ewington, E. J. & Moore, D. F. Human Biology & Hygiene: Biology, Bk. 2. (Secondary Science Ser). (Illus., Orig.). (gr. 8-11). 1980. pap. 6.95 (ISBN 0-7100-7079-9). Routledge & Kegan.
Farish, Donald J. Biology: The Human Perspective. (Illus.). 1978. text ed. 20.95 scp (ISBN 0-06-041995-4, HarpC); inst. manual avail. (ISBN 0-06-361976-8); scp study guide 8.95 (ISBN 0-06-041992-X). Har-Row.
Fitch, Kenneth & Johnson, Perry. Human Life Science. LC 76-46987. 1977. text ed. 22.95 (ISBN 0-03-018876-8, HoltC). HR&W.
Gibson, John R. Human Biology. 3rd ed. 216p. 1979. pap. 7.50 (ISBN 0-571-04974-5, Pub. by Faber & Faber). Merrimack Bk Serv.
Harrison, G. A., et al. Human Biology: An Introduction to Human Evolution, Variation, Growth, & Ecology. 2nd ed. (Illus.). 1977. text ed. 36.50x (ISBN 0-19-857164-X); pap. text ed. 12.95x (ISBN 0-19-857165-8). Oxford U Pr.
Ho, B. T., et al, eds. Drug Discrimination & State Dependent Learning. 1978. 37.50 (ISBN 0-12-350250-0). Acad Pr.
Inglis, J. K. A Textbook of Human Biology. 2nd rev. ed. LC 73-21696. 1974. text ed. 14.50 (ISBN 0-08-017846-4); pap. text ed. 6.75 (ISBN 0-08-017847-2). Pergamon.
Kellogg, Vernon. Human Life As the Biologist Sees It. 1922. 20.00 (ISBN 0-8274-4227-0). R West.
Kimball, John W. Man & Nature: Principles of Human & Environmental Biology. LC 74-19694. 480p. 1975. text ed. 18.95 (ISBN 0-201-03688-6). A-W.
Kirk, R. L., ed. The Human Biology of Aborigines in Cape York. (AIAS Human Biology Ser.: No. 5). (Illus., Orig.). 1973. pap. text ed. 10.00x (ISBN 0-85575-028-6). Humanities.
Levine, Louis. Biology for a Modern Society. LC 76-46318. (Illus.). 1977. pap. 11.95 (ISBN 0-8016-2990-X). Mosby.
Lugo, James O. & Hershey, Gerald L. Human Development: A Psychological, Biological, & Sociological Approach to the Life Span. 2nd ed. 1979. text ed. 17.95 (ISBN 0-02-372320-3); instrs'. manual avail. (ISBN 0-685-96772-7). Macmillan.
Metchnikoff, Elie. The Nature of Man: Studies in Optimistic Philosophy. Kastenbaum, Robert, ed. Mitchell, P. Chalmers, tr. LC 76-19582. (Death & Dying Ser.). (Illus.). 1977. Repr. of 1910 ed. lib. bdg. 21.00x (ISBN 0-405-09578-3). Arno.
Nilsson, Lennart. Behold Man. 1974. pap. 9.95 (ISBN 0-316-60752-5). Little.
Papalia, Diane E. & Olds, Sally. Human Development. (Illus.). 1977. text ed. 16.95 (ISBN 0-07-048427-9, C); instructor's guide 5.95 (ISBN 0-07-048428-7); study guide 6.95 (ISBN 0-07-048429-5). McGraw.
Readings in Human Development 77-78. new ed. LC 72-91973. (Annual Editions Ser). (Illus., Orig.). 1977. write for info. (ISBN 0-87967-173-4). Dushkin Pub.
Santos, Miguel A., ed. Readings in Biology & Man. LC 73-12020. 1974. 29.00x (ISBN 0-8422-5048-4); pap. text ed. 9.75x (ISBN 0-8422-0334-6). Irvington.
Schoeninger, Margaret J. Dietary Reconstruction at Chalcatzingo, a Formative Period Site in Morelos, Mexico. (Technical Reports Ser.: No. 9). (Illus., Orig., Contribution 2 in contributions in human biology). 1979. pap. 3.50x (ISBN 0-932206-78-6). U Mich Mus Anthro.
Schulz, Charles M. Charlie Brown's Super Book of Questions & Answers About All Kinds of Animals from Snails to People. LC 75-39340. (Illus.). (gr. 3-6). 1976. 7.95 (ISBN 0-394-83249-3, BYR); PLB 8.99 (ISBN 0-394-93249-8). Random.
Shapiro, Mark. The Sociobiology of Homo Sapiens. LC 78-60932. 1978. 9.95 (ISBN 0-9601858-0-1). Pinecrest Fund.
Shephard, R. J. Human Physiological Work Capacity. LC 77-80847. (International Biological Programme Ser.: No. 15). (Illus.). 1978. 68.00 (ISBN 0-521-21781-4). Cambridge U Pr.
Singer, Sam & Hilgard, Henry R. The Biology of People. LC 77-17893. (Biology Ser.). (Illus.). 1978. text ed. 21.95x (ISBN 0-7167-0026-3); tchr's resource bk. 2.95x (ISBN 0-686-77342-X). W H Freeman.
Spencer, F. Introduction to Human & Molecular Biology. 235p. 1970. 9.95 (ISBN 0-407-55900-0). Butterworth.
Vorster, D. J., ed. Human Biology of Environmental Change. 1972. pap. text ed. 14.95x (ISBN 0-89563-007-9). Intl Ideas.
Weiner, J. S. & Lourie, J. A. Practical Human Biology. LC 81-66372. 1981. write for info. (ISBN 0-12-741960-8). Acad Pr.
Weiner, J. S. & Weiner, J. S., eds. Physiological Variation & Its Genetic Basis: Proceedings, Vol. 17. (Society for the Study of Human Biology, Symposia). 1977. 27.95 (ISBN 0-470-99314-6). Halsted Pr.

Weiss & Mann. Human Biology & Behavior. 3rd ed. 1981. text ed. 16.95 (ISBN 0-316-92891-7); training manual free (ISBN 0-316-92892-5). Little.

Wever, R. A. The Circadian System of Man: Results of Experiments Under Temporal Isolation. Schaefer, K. E., ed. (Topics in Environmental Physiology & Medicine Ser.). (Illus.). 1979. 51.40 (ISBN 0-387-90338-0). Springer-Verlag.

Wittman, Karl S. Basic Sciences for Health Careers. 1976. text ed. 14.25 (ISBN 0-07-071195-X, G); tchr's manual & key 4.00 (ISBN 0-07-071197-6); activities & projects 6.95 (ISBN 0-07-071196-8). McGraw.

Wunderli, J. Biologie des Menschen. 3rd ed. (Illus.). 200p. 1976. 11.75 (ISBN 3-8055-2331-9). S Karger.

Yura, Helen & Walsh, Mary B., eds. Human Needs & the Nursing Process. LC 78-16148. (Illus.). 330p. 1978. pap. 12.50 (ISBN 0-8385-3941-6). ACC.

HUMAN BODY

see Body, Human

HUMAN CAPITAL

see also Labor Supply

Becker, Gary S. Human Capital: A Theoretical & Empirical Analysis, with Special Reference to Education. rev. ed. LC 80-14068. 288p. 1980. pap. 7.50 (ISBN 0-226-04110-7, P905, Phoen). U of Chicago Pr.

Dhesi, Autar S. Human Capital Formation & Its Utilization. (Illus.). 291p. 1979. 17.50x (ISBN 0-8002-1002-6). Intl Pubns Serv.

Huq, Muhammad S. Education, Manpower, & Development in South & Southeast Asia. LC 74-19336. (Special Studies). (Illus.). 240p. 1975. 18.95 (ISBN 0-275-09120-1). Praeger.

Olson, Mancur & Landsberg, Hans H., eds. The No-Growth Society. 259p. 1974. 10.00 (ISBN 0-393-01111-9); pap. text ed. 4.95x (ISBN 0-393-09260-7). Norton.

Sirageldin, Ismail, ed. Research in Human Capital & Development: An Annual Compilation of Research, Vol. 1. 1979. lib. bdg. 34.50 (ISBN 0-89232-019-2). Jai Pr.

--Research in Human Capital & Development, Vol. 2. 325p. 1981. 34.50 (ISBN 0-89232-098-2). Jai Pr.

Yudin, Elinor B. Human Capital Migration, Direct Investment & the Transfer of Technology: An Examination of Americans Privately Employed Overseas. Bruchey, Stuart & Bruchey, Eleanor, eds. LC 76-5045. (American Business Abroad Ser.). (Illus.). 1976. 18.00x (ISBN 0-405-09310-1). Arno.

HUMAN CHROMOSOMES

Berg, Kare, ed. Genetic Damage in Man Caused by Environmental Agents. LC 79-414. 1979. 27.00 (ISBN 0-12-089550-1). Acad Pr.

Bergsma, Daniel, ed. Cytogenetics, Environmental Malformation Syndromes. LC 76-20510. (Alan R. Liss., Inc. Ser.: Vol 12, No. 5). 1976. 30.00 (ISBN 0-686-18079-8). March of Dimes.

Boyce, A. J. Chromosome Variation in Human Evolution: Symposia of the Institute of Biology Ser, Vol. 14. 131p. 1975. 24.95 (ISBN 0-470-09330-7). Wiley.

Buckton, K. E. & Evans, H. J. Methods for the Analysis of Human Chromosome Aberrations. (Also avail. in French & Russian). 1973. 4.80 (ISBN 92-4-154031-1). World Health.

De Grouchy, Jean & Turleau, Catherine. Clinical Atlas of Human Chromosomes. LC 77-2282. 1977. 57.50 (ISBN 0-471-01704-3, Pub. by Wiley Medical). Wiley.

Giannelli, F. Human Chromosomes DNA Synthesis. Beckman, L. & Hauge, M., eds. (Monographs in Human Genetics: Vol. 5). 1970. 28.25 (ISBN 3-8055-0448-9). S Karger.

Priest, Jean H. Medical Cytogenetics & Cell Culture. 2nd ed. LC 76-7402. (Illus.). 344p. 1977. text ed. 19.50 (ISBN 0-8121-0556-7). Lea & Febiger.

Valentine, G. H. Chromosome Disorders: An Introduction for Clinicians. 3rd ed. (Illus.). 1975. 15.00 (ISBN 0-397-58185-8). Lippincott.

Yunis, G. J. New Chromosomal Syndromes. 1977. 46.50 (ISBN 0-12-775165-3). Acad Pr.

Yunis, Jorge, ed. Molecular Structure of Human Chromosomes. 1977. 39.50 (ISBN 0-12-775168-8). Acad Pr.

Yunis, Jorge J., ed. Human Chromosome Methodology. 2nd ed. 1974. 38.50 (ISBN 0-12-775155-6). Acad Pr.

--Human Chromosome Methodology. 2nd ed. 1974. 38.50 (ISBN 0-12-775155-6). Acad Pr.

HUMAN COLD STORAGE

see Cryonics

HUMAN DISSECTION

see also Anatomy, Human-Laboratory Manuals; Autopsy

Finley, Claudette. The Dissector's Guide: A Detailed Investigation of Musculoskeletal Anatomy. (Illus.). 176p. 1975. vinyl cover 16.50 (ISBN 0-398-03084-7). C C Thomas.

Lassek, Arthur M. Human Dissection: Its Drama & Struggle. (Illus.). 320p. 1958. photocopy ed. spiral 29.75 (ISBN 0-398-01083-8). C C Thomas.

Mausolf, F. The Anatomy of the Ocular Adnexa: Guide to Orbital Dissection. (Illus.). 66p. 1975. pap. 8.75 (ISBN 0-398-03172-X). C C Thomas.

Romanes, G. J., ed. Cunningham's Manual of Practical Anatomy: Head & Neck & Brain, Vol. 3. 14th ed. (Illus.). 1979. pap. text ed. 10.95x (ISBN 0-19-263205-1). Oxford U Pr.

Sauerland, E. K. & Sauerland, B. A. Human Anatomical Dissections: Laboratory Exercises for the Health Professions. (Illus.). 152p. 1980. pap. 14.95 (ISBN 0-683-07558-6). Williams & Wilkins.

Sauerland, Eberhardt K. Grant's Dissector. 8th ed. (Illus.). 192p. 1978. pap. 18.00 (ISBN 0-683-07559-4). Williams & Wilkins.

Tobin, Charles E. & Jacobs, John J. Shearer's Manual of Human Dissection. 6th ed. (Illus.). 352p. 1981. pap. text ed. 16.95 (ISBN 0-07-064926-X). McGraw.

HUMAN ECOLOGY

see also Anthropo-Geography; Community Life; Environmental Policy; Man-Influence of Environment; Man-Influence on Nature; Population; Social Psychology; Sociology

Adams, Robert M., et al. The Fitness of Man's Environment. LC 68-20988. (Smithsonian Annual, No. 2). 250p. 1968. 17.50x (ISBN 0-87474-058-4). Smithsonian.

Alihan, Milla A. Social Ecology, a Critical Analysis. LC 64-24804. 267p. Repr. of 1938 ed. 11.00x (ISBN 0-8154-0008-X). Cooper Sq.

Altman, Irwin & Wehlwill, J. F., eds. Human Behavior & Environment: Advances in Theory & Research, Vol. 1. (Illus.). 1976. 25.00 (ISBN 0-306-33301-5, Plenum Pr). Plenum Pub.

Altman, Irwin & Wohlwill, J. F., eds. Human Behavior & Environment: Children & the Environment. (Advances in Theory & Environment Ser.: Vol. 3). (Illus.). 316p. 1978. 18.95 (ISBN 0-306-40090-1, Plenum Pr). Plenum Pub.

Anderson, Walter. A Place of Power: The American Episode in Human Evolution. LC 76-12809. 1976. text ed. 15.95 (ISBN 0-87620-080-3); pap. text ed. 11.95 (ISBN 0-87620-079-X). Goodyear.

Armstrong, R. W. & Lewis, H. T., eds. Human Ecology: North Kohala Studies. (Social Science & Linguistics Institute Special Publications). (Illus.). 144p. 1972. pap. 5.00x (ISBN 0-8248-0247-0). U Pr of Hawaii.

Asimov, Isaac. Earth: Our Crowded Spaceship. LC 74-8967. (Illus.). (gr. 7-9). 1974. 8.95 (ISBN 0-381-99625-5, JD-J). Har-Row.

Barker, Roger G., et al. Habitats, Enviroments, & Human Behavior: Studies in Ecological Psychology & Eco-Behavioral Science. LC 77-82912. (Social & Behavioral Science Ser). 1978. text ed. 17.95x (ISBN 0-87589-356-2). Jossey-Bass.

Bates, Marston. Jungle in the House: Essays in Natural & Unnatural History. LC 70-103375. 1970. 7.50 (ISBN 0-8027-0159-0). Walker & Co.

Baum, Andrew & Epstein, Yakov M., eds. Human Response to Crowding. LC 78-6875. (Environmental Psychology Ser.). 1978. 24.95 (ISBN 0-470-26374-1). Halsted Pr.

Bayliss-Smith, Timothy & Feachem, Richard, eds. Subsistence & Survival: Rural Ecology in the Pacific. 1978. 68.00 (ISBN 0-12-083250-X). Acad Pr.

Bean, Lowell J. Mukat's People: The Cahuilla Indians of Southern California. LC 78-145782. (Illus.). 300p. 1972. 15.95x (ISBN 0-520-01912-1); pap. 5.75x (ISBN 0-520-02627-6). U of Cal Pr.

Bellak, Leopold. Overload: The New Human Condition. LC 74-19052. 224p. 1975. 19.95 (ISBN 0-87705-245-X). Human Sci Pr.

Bennett, John W. The Ecological Transition. 1976. text ed. 27.00 (ISBN 0-08-017867-7); pap. text ed. 16.00 (ISBN 0-08-017868-5). Pergamon.

Benoit, Emile. Progress & Survival: An Essay on the the Future of Mankind. Gohn, Jack B., ed. 144p. 1980. 17.95 (ISBN 0-03-056911-7). Praeger.

Bergeret, et al. Nourrir En Harmonie Avec L'environment. 1977. 21.75x (ISBN 90-279-7684-8). Mouton.

Berglund, Berndt. Wilderness Survival. LC 72-2767. 1975. pap. 4.95 (ISBN 0-684-13814-X, SL 532, ScribT). Scribner.

Bews, John W. Human Ecology, with an Introduction by Jan C. Smuts. LC 72-84979. 312p. 1973. Repr. of 1935 ed. 18.00 (ISBN 0-8462-1671-X). Russell.

Bham, Thamsanqa E. The Will to Live. LC 79-66395. 115p. 1980. 6.95 (ISBN 0-533-04383-2). Vantage.

Bilsky, Lester J., ed. Historical Ecology: Essays on Environment & Social Change. (National University Pubns.). 1980. 13.50 (ISBN 0-8046-9247-5). Kennikat.

Blurton-Jones, N. & Reynolds, V., eds. Human Behavior & Adaptation, Vol. 18. (Symposium of the Society for the Study of Human Biology). 1979. 39.95x (ISBN 0-470-26578-7). Halsted Pr.

Bodley, John H. Anthropology & Contemporary Human Problems. LC 75-39332. 1976. pap. 8.95 (ISBN 0-8465-0544-4). Benjamin-Cummings.

Bookchin, Murray. Our Synthetic Environment. rev. ed. 6.50 (ISBN 0-8446-5162-1). Peter Smith.

Boughey, Arthur S. Man & the Environment. 2nd ed. (Illus.). 480p. pap. text ed. 13.95 (ISBN 0-02-312770-8, 31277). Macmillan.

--Readings in Man, the Environment, & Human Ecology. (Illus.). 576p. 1973. text ed. 12.95 (ISBN 0-02-312720-1, 31272). Macmillan.

Braun & Collingridge. Technology & Survival. (Siscon Ser.). 1977. 3.95 (ISBN 0-408-71301-1). Butterworth.

Brierley, John. A Natural History of Man. 184p. 1970. 10.00 (ISBN 0-8386-7819-X). Fairleigh Dickinson.

Bronfenbrenner, Urie. Reality & Research in the Ecology of Human Development. (Master Lectures on Developmental Psychology: Manuscript No. 1333). 4.00x (ISBN 0-912704-30-6). Am Psychol.

Brubaker, Sterling. To Live on Earth: Man & His Environment in Perspective. LC 75-185514. (Resources for the Future Ser.). 218p. 1972. 14.00x (ISBN 0-8018-1378-6). Johns Hopkins.

Butzer, Karl & Freeman, Leslie G., eds. Early Hydraulic Civilization in Egypt. LC 75-36398. (Prehistoric Archaelogy & Ecology Ser). (Illus.). 1976. 9.00x (ISBN 0-226-08634-8); pap. 3.25x (ISBN 0-226-08635-6). U of Chicago Pr.

Calabrese, Edward J. Pollutants & High Risk Groups: The Biological Basis of Increased Human Susceptibility to Environmental & Occupational Pollutants. LC 77-13957. (Environmental Science & Technology: Wiley-Interscience Series of Texts & Monographs). 1977. 27.00 (ISBN 0-471-02940-8, Pub. by Wiley-Inerscience). Wiley.

Canter, David, ed. Environmental Interaction. LC 75-37077. 1976. 22.50 (ISBN 0-8236-1685-1). Intl Univs Pr.

Carr, Donald E. Energy & the Earth Machine. 288p. 1976. 10.00 (ISBN 0-393-06407-7). Norton.

Carter, Vernon G. & Dale, Tom. Topsoil & Civilization. rev. ed. (Illus.). 240p. 1974. pap. 6.95x (ISBN 0-8061-1107-0). U of Okla Pr.

Catton, William R., Jr. Overshoot: The Ecological Basis of Revolutionary Change. LC 80-13443. (Illus.). 250p. 1980. 16.50 (ISBN 0-252-00818-9). U of Ill Pr.

Chapman, Graham P. Human & Environmental Systems: A Geographer's Appraisal. 1978. 67.00 (ISBN 0-12-168650-7). Acad Pr.

Chen, Kan & Lagler, Karl F., eds. Growth Policy: Population, Environment, & Beyond. LC 72-94760. 250p. 1974. 12.95 (ISBN 0-472-22000-4); pap. 2.95x (ISBN 0-472-08209-4). U of Mich Pr.

Clapham, W. B., Jr. Human Ecosystems. 1981. pap. 12.95 (ISBN 0-02-322510-6). Macmillan.

Cody, Martin L. & Diamond, Jared M., eds. Ecology & Evolution of Communities. LC 74-27749. (Illus.). 838p. 1975. text ed. 35.00x (ISBN 0-674-22444-2, Belknap Pr); pap. 12.50x (ISBN 0-674-22446-9). Harvard U Pr.

Collier, George A. Fields of the Tzotzil: The Ecological Bases of Tradition in Highland Chiapas. LC 75-12840. (Texas Pan American Ser.). (Illus.). 270p. 1975. 15.00x (ISBN 0-292-72412-8). U of Tex Pr.

Colloque Sur L'ecologie Pyreneenne & Prepyreneenne, Auvillar (France), 12, 13, 14 Juin 1973. Premiere Partie Des Actes Du Colloque Cahiers D'anthropologie & D'ecologie Humaine, Nos. II-3,4. (Illus.). 1975. pap. 55.50x (ISBN 0-686-21254-1). Mouton.

Commission on Critical Choices for Americans: Qualities of Life, Vol. VII. LC 75-44725. (Critical Choices for Americans Ser.). 1976. 23.95 (ISBN 0-669-00417-0). Lexington Bks.

Committee on the Alaska Earthquake. Great Alaska Earthquake of 1964: Human Ecology. 1970. 29.50 (ISBN 0-309-01607-X). Natl Acad Pr.

Conference on Population Genetics & Ecology, Israel, 1973. Population Genetics & Ecology: Proceedings. Karlin, Samuel, et al, eds. 1976. 47.00 (ISBN 0-12-398560-9). Acad Pr.

Conference on the Human Environment, Founex, Switzerland, June 4-12, 1971. Development & Environment: Proceedings. Strong, Maurice F., ed. LC 72-75446. (Illus.). 225p. (Orig.). 1973. pap. text ed. 17.75x (ISBN 90-2796-990-6). Mouton.

Conseil International De la Langue Francaise. Glossary of the Environment. LC 76-19547. 1977. 21.95 (ISBN 0-275-23760-5). Praeger.

Conservation Education Association. Critical Index of Films on Man & His Environment. LC 65-23951. 32p. 1972. pap. text ed. 1.25x (ISBN 0-8134-1374-5, 1374). Interstate.

Damon, Albert. Human Biology & Ecology. LC 77-559. (Illus.). 1977. pap. text ed. 8.95x (ISBN 0-393-09103-1). Norton.

Dansereau, Pierre, ed. Challenge for Survival: Land, Air, & Water for Man in Megalopolis. LC 78-98397. 235p. 1970. 16.00x (ISBN 0-231-03267-6); pap. 7.50x (ISBN 0-231-08638-5). Columbia U Pr.

Darnell, Rezneat. Ecology & Man. 1973. pap. text ed. 2.95x (ISBN 0-697-04521-8). Wm C Brown.

Dasmann, Raymond F. Different Kind of Country. (gr. 8 up). 1970. pap. 1.95 (ISBN 0-02-072810-7, Collier). Macmillan.

Detweiler, Robert, et al. Environmental Decay in Its Historical Context. 140p. 1973. pap. 4.95x (ISBN 0-673-07678-4). Scott F.

Dice, Lee R. Man's Nature & Nature's Man: The Ecology of Human Communities. LC 72-9607. 329p. 1973. Repr. of 1955 ed. lib. bdg. 18.75x (ISBN 0-8371-6594-6, DIMN). Greenwood.

Dogan, Mattei & Rokkan, Stein, eds. Social Ecology. 458p. (Paperback edition of Quantitative Ecological Analysis in the Social Sciences). 1974. pap. 6.95x (ISBN 0-262-54022-3). MIT Pr.

Doxiadis, C. I. Action for Human Settlements. (Illus.). 1977. 12.95x (ISBN 0-393-08361-6). Norton.

Dubos, Rene. A God Within. LC 76-37224. 1972. text ed. 24.50x (ISBN 0-684-12768-7). Irvington.

--So Human an Animal. LC 68-27794. 1968. pap. 3.95 (ISBN 0-684-71753-0, SL195, ScribT). Scribner.

Eckholm, E. P. Losing Ground: Environmental Stress & World Food Prospects. 1978. text ed. 27.00 (ISBN 0-08-021496-7); pap. text ed. 11.25 (ISBN 0-08-021495-9). Pergamon.

Ehrlich, Paul R., et al. Human Ecology: Problems & Solutions. LC 72-12828. (Illus.). 1973. pap. 10.95x (ISBN 0-7167-0595-8). W H Freeman.

Eiseley, Loren. The Innocent Assassins. LC 73-5182. 1975. pap. 3.95 (ISBN 0-684-14437-9, SL608, ScribT); encore edition 3.95 (ISBN 0-684-14970-2, ScribT). Scribner.

Ellison, Vivian. Chemical Invasion: The Body Breakers. new ed. Eblen, William, ed. LC 72-79108. (Illus.). 64p. (Orig.). (gr. 7-12). 1972. pap. 1.45 (ISBN 0-88301-037-2). Pendulum Pr.

Emery, F. E. & Trist, E. L. Towards a Social Ecology: Contextual Appreciation of the Future in the Present. LC 70-178778. 239p. 1973. 22.50 (ISBN 0-306-30563-1, Plenum Pr). Plenum Pub.

Emery, Frederick E. & Trist, E. L. Towards a Social Ecology. LC 74-26842. 239p. 1975. pap. 5.95 (ISBN 0-306-20015-5, Rosetta). Plenum Pub.

English, Paul W. & Mayfield, Robert C., eds. Man, Space & Environment: Concepts in Contemporary Human Geography. (Orig.). 1972. text ed. 9.95x (ISBN 0-19-501441-3). Oxford U Pr.

Enthoven, Alain C. & Freeman, A. Myrick, 3rd, eds. Pollution, Resources & the Environment. new ed. 1973. pap. 7.95x (ISBN 0-393-09933-4). Norton.

Environmental Changes on the Coasts of Indonesia. 52p. 1981. pap. 10.00 (ISBN 92-808-0197-X, TUNU 128, UNU). Unipub.

Eriksen. Human Services Today. 1977. text ed. 12.95 (ISBN 0-87909-336-6). Reston.

Evans, Robert L. The Fall & Rise of Man, If... LC 72-97467. 259p. 1973. 6.95 (ISBN 0-9606698-0-9); pap. 3.95 (ISBN 0-9606698-1-7). R L Evans.

Fear, Gene. Teaching with Survival Graphics No. Three. (G.I.J. Ser). (Illus.). 1975. pap. 3.00 (ISBN 0-913724-13-0). Survival Ed Assoc.

--Teaching with Survival Graphics No. Two. (D.E.F. Ser). (Illus.). 1975. pap. 3.00 (ISBN 0-913724-12-2). Survival Ed Assoc.

Fiennes, R. N. The Environment of Man. LC 77-26881. (Biology & Environment Ser.). 1978. 16.95x (ISBN 0-312-25699-X). St Martin.

Finsterbusch, Gail W. Man & Earth: Their Changing Relationship. LC 76-26914. (Studies in Sociology). (gr. 12). 1976. pap. 3.50 (ISBN 0-672-61325-5). Bobbs.

Freedman. Deterministic Mathematical Models in Population Ecology. (Pure & Applied Math. Ser.: Vol. 57). 264p. 1980. 29.75 (ISBN 0-8247-6653-9). Dekker.

Freedman, Daniel G. Human Sociobiology: A Holistic Approach. LC 78-73025. (Illus.). 1979. 12.95 (ISBN 0-02-910660-5). Free Pr.

Friendly Shared Powers for Life on Earth: Practicing Wise Habits & Group Genius for Local & Global Communities. LC 78-78317. 1979. pap. 5.00 (ISBN 0-9602388-1-6). Clear Marks.

Garlick, J. P. & Keay, R.. Human Ecology in the Tropics: Symposia of the Society for the Study of Human Biology, Vol. 16. LC 76-18781. 1977. 17.95 (ISBN 0-470-15165-X). Halsted Pr.
George, Carl J. & McKinley, Daniel. Urban Ecology: In Search of an Asphalt Rose. new ed. (Population Biology Ser.). (Illus.). 168p. 1974. pap. text ed. 9.95 (ISBN 0-07-023086-2, C). McGraw.
George, F. H. Cybernetics & the Environment. 1978. 7.95 (ISBN 0-236-40021-5, Pub by Paul Elek). Merrimack Bk Serv.
Glacken, Clarence J. Traces on the Rhodian Shore: Nature & Culture in Western Thought from Ancient Times to the End of the Eighteenth Century. LC 67-10970. 1967. pap. 12.95x (ISBN 0-520-03216-0, CAMPUS 170). U of Cal Pr.
Golden-Wolfe, Malka. Malka - A Total Celebration (a survival manual) LC 80-53000. (Illus., Orig.). 1980. pap. 5.85 (ISBN 0-937946-00-1). Univ Goddess.
Goldman, Charles R., et al, eds. Environmental Quality & Water Development. LC 72-83739. (Illus.). 1973. 34.95x (ISBN 0-7167-0256-8). W H Freeman.
Goodman, Percival. The Double E. LC 76-50873. 1977. pap. 3.50 (ISBN 0-385-12868-1, Anch). Doubleday.
Goodwin, Gary C. Cherokees in Transition: A Study of Changing Culture & Environment Prior to 1775. LC 77-2709. (Research Papers). (Illus.). 1977. pap. 8.00 (ISBN 0-89065-088-8). U Chicago Dept Geog.
Goyal, Bhagwat S. The Strategy of Survival. 185p. 1975. text ed. 15.00 (ISBN 0-686-75684-3, Pub. by UBS India). Humanities.
Graham, Ada & Graham, Frank, Jr. The Careless Animal. LC 73-14222. 112p. (gr. 3-5). 1975. PLB 4.95 (ISBN 0-385-01828-2). Doubleday.
Greenwood, Ned J. & Edwards, J. M. Human Environments & Natural Systems. 2nd ed. LC 78-13082. (Illus.). 1979. 15.95 (ISBN 0-87872-168-1). Duxbury Pr.
Grunfeld, Joseph, ed. Growth in a Finite World. LC 78-27457. (Illus.). 1979. pap. 7.95 (ISBN 0-89168-022-5). Franklin Inst Pr.
Guha, A. Evolutionary Theory of Economic Growth. 128p. 1981. 22.00 (ISBN 0-19-828431-4). Oxford U Pr.
Gunn, Angus M. Habitat: Human Settlements in an Urban Age. 1978. text ed. 27.00 (ISBN 0-08-021487-8); pap. 15.00 (ISBN 0-08-021486-X). Pergamon.
Gyorgy, P. & Kline, O. L., eds. Malnutrition Is a Problem of Ecology. (Bibliotheca Nutritio et Dieta: No. 14). 1970. pap. 20.50 (ISBN 3-8055-0164-1). S Karger.
Hansen, Niles M., ed. Human Settlement Systems: International Perspectives on Structure Change & Public Policy. LC 77-9964. 1977. 20.00 (ISBN 0-88410-176-2). Ballinger Pub.
Hardin, Garrett. Exploring New Ethics for Survival: The Voyage of the Spaceship Beagle. 320p. 1972. 10.95 (ISBN 0-670-30268-6). Viking Pr.
Harris, D. R. Human Ecology in Savanna Environments. LC 80-40210. 1980. 57.50 (ISBN 0-12-326550-9). Acad Pr.
Haupt, et al. Surviving. (Human Condition Ser.). (gr. 9-12). 1977. pap. text ed. 3.96 (ISBN 0-88343-330-3); tchrs'. manual 1.80 (ISBN 0-88343-331-1). McDougal-Littell.
Hayes, Harold. Three Levels of Time. LC 80-22963. 1981. 13.50 (ISBN 0-525-21853-X). Dutton.
--Three Levels of Time. LC 80-22963. 1981. 13.50 (ISBN 0-525-21853-X). Dutton.
Hazen, William E. Readings in Population & Community Ecology. 3rd ed. LC 74-17755. (Illus.). 445p. 1975. pap. text ed. 10.95 (ISBN 0-7216-4607-7). HR&W.
Henderson, M. A. The Survival Resource Book. (Illus.). 180p. 1981. pap. 8.95 (ISBN 0-312-77951-8). St Martin.
Herndon, James. How to Survive in Your Native Land. 1977. pap. 4.95 (ISBN 0-671-23027-1, Touchstone Bks). S&S.
Herzlich, Claudine. Sante et Maladie: Analyse d'une Representation Sociale. Moscovici, Serge, pref. by. (Interaction: L'homme et Son Environment Social Ser.: No. 5). 210p. 1975. pap. text ed. 22.25x (ISBN 90-2797-805-0). Mouton.
Hewitt, K. & Hare, F. K. Man & Environment. LC 72-90876. (CCG Resource Papers Ser.: No. 20). (Illus.). 1973. pap. text ed. 4.00 (ISBN 0-89291-067-4). Assn Am Geographers.
Hill, James E. & Kedar, Ervin Y. Ecology-Environment Handbook. LC 78-57574. 1978. pap. text ed. 6.75 (ISBN 0-8191-0525-2). U Pr of Amer.
Hobbs, Fredric. Eat Your House: Art Eco Guide to Self Sufficiency. (Illus.). 120p. (Orig.). 1980. pap. 9.95 (ISBN 0-9604566-0-0). VA City Rest.
Hoffman, Norman S. A New World of Health. (Illus.). 1976. pap. text ed. 10.95 (ISBN 0-07-029203-5, C); instructor's manual 3.95 (ISBN 0-07-029204-3). McGraw.
Holahan, C. J. Environment & Behavior: A Dynamical Perspective. LC 77-25400. (Plenum Social Ecology Ser.). (Illus.). 206p. 1977. 14.95 (ISBN 0-306-31086-4, Plenum Pr). Plenum Pub.
Hoyt, Joseph B. Man & the Earth. 3rd ed. (Illus.). 512p. 1973. text ed. 21.95 (ISBN 0-13-550947-5). P-H.
Human Population Problems in the Biosphere: Some Research Strategies & Designs. (MAB Technical Notes: No. 3). (Illus.). 1977. pap. 6.25 (ISBN 92-3-201482-3, U288, UNESCO). Unipub.
Inger, Robert F., et al, eds. Man in the Living Environment. 312p. 1972. 20.00 (ISBN 0-299-06050-0); pap. 5.95 (ISBN 0-299-06054-3). U of Wis Pr.
Institute of Environmental Sciences, 17th Annual Meeting, los Angeles, 1971. Living in Our Environment: Proceedings. LC 62-38584. (Illus.). 1971. pap. text ed. 20.00 (ISBN 0-915414-11-2). Inst Environ Sci.
Institute of Environmental Sciences, 15th Annual Meeting, Anaheim, 1969. Man in His Environment: Proceedings. (Illus.). 1969. pap. text ed. 18.00 (ISBN 0-915414-09-0). Inst Environ Sci.
Jackson, Wes. Man & the Environment. 3rd ed. 450p. 1979. pap. text ed. write for info. (ISBN 0-697-04704-0). Wm C Brown.
Jensen, Arthur R., et al. Environment, Heredity, & Intelligence. (Reprint Ser.: No. 2). 5.95 (ISBN 0-916690-02-4). Harvard Educ Rev.
Jochim, Michael. Strategies for Survival: Cultural Behavior in an Ecological Context. 1981. write for info. (ISBN 0-12-385460-1). Acad Pr.
Johnson, Warren. Muddling Toward Frugality. LC 78-8595. 1978. 7.95 (ISBN 0-87156-214-6). Sierra.
Jones, J. Owen & Rogers, Paul, eds. Human Ecology & the Development of Settlements. LC 76-10301. (Frontiers in Human Ecology Ser.: Vol. 3). 146p. 1976. 24.50 (ISBN 0-306-30941-6, Plenum Pr). Plenum Pub.
Jones, James C. Plan to Survive: Programs for Individual & Group Survival. (Illus.). 1977. pap. text ed. 4.00 (ISBN 0-686-20040-3). Live Free.
Jones, Orville E. & Swan, Malcolm D. Discovering Your Environment. 1971. text ed. 9.25x (ISBN 0-8134-1169-6, 1169). Interstate.
Jones, Owen J. Index of Human Ecology. LC 73-90302. 150p. 1974. 16.00x (ISBN 0-900362-66-9). Intl Pubns Serv.
Jorgensen, S. E., ed. Handbook of Environmental Data & Ecological Parameters. rev. ed. LC 78-41207. (Enviromental Sciences & Applications Ser.: Vol. 6). (Illus.). 1100p. 1979. 225.00 (ISBN 0-08-023436-4). Pergamon.
Kabbe, Frederick & Kabbe, Lois. Chemistry, Energy, & Human Ecology. LC 75-27126. (Illus.). 464p. 1976. pap. text ed. 16.95 (ISBN 0-395-19833-X); instr. manual 1.00 (ISBN 0-395-19831-3); slides o.p. 11.25 (ISBN 0-395-19832-1). HM.
Kallen, Horace M. Toward a Philosophy of the Seas. LC 72-97788. 70p. 1973. pap. 1.50x (ISBN 0-8139-0487-0). U Pr of Va.
Kaplan, S. J. & Kivy-Rosenberg, E. Ecology & the Quality of Life. (Illus.). 308p. 1973. 23.75 (ISBN 0-398-02828-1). C C Thomas.
Kaplan, Stephen & Kaplan, Rachel. Humanscape: Environments for People. LC 77-27531. 1978. pap. text ed. 8.95 (ISBN 0-87872-163-0). Duxbury Pr.
Keppes, Gyorgy, ed. Arts of the Environment. (Vision & Value Ser). (Illus.). 244p. 1972. 17.50 (ISBN 0-8076-0620-0). Braziller.
King, Grace E., ed. Conflict & Harmony: A Source-Book of Man in His Environment. 450p. 1972. 12.50x (ISBN 0-540-00953-9). Intl Pubns Serv.
--Conflict & Harmony: A Source-Book of Man in His Environment. 450p. 1972. 15.95x (ISBN 0-8464-0274-2). Beekman Pubs.
Kneese, Allen V. & Bower, Blair T., eds. Environmental Quality Analysis: Theory & Method in the Social Sciences. LC 78-181556. (Resources for the Future Ser). (Illus.). 408p. 1972. 24.00x (ISBN 0-8018-1332-8). Johns Hopkins.
Kornhauser, D. H. Urban Japan: Its Foundations & Growth. LC 75-17907. (World's Landscapes). 1976. pap. text ed. 9.95x (ISBN 0-582-48176-7). Longman.
Krebs, John R. & Davies, Nicholas B. An Introduction to Behavioural Ecology. LC 80-25843. (Illus.). 300p. 1981. text ed. 39.60x (ISBN 0-87893-431-6); pap. text ed. 16.50x (ISBN 0-87893-432-4). Sinauer Assoc.
Laconte, P., ed. The Environments of Human Settlement: Proceedings, 2 vols. 322p. 1977. Set. text ed. 75.00 (ISBN 0-08-021857-1). Pergamon.
Langbein, Laura I. & Lichtman, Allan J. Ecological Inference. LC 77-93283. (University Papers Ser.: Quantitative Applications in the Social Sciences, No. 10). 70p. 1978. pap. 4.00 (ISBN 0-8039-0941-1). Sage.
Laptev, I. The Planet of Reason: A Sociological Study of the Interrelation of Society & Nature. (Current Problems Ser.). 1977. 3.50 (ISBN 0-8285-3327-X, Pub. by Progress Pubs Russia). Imported Pubns.
Lehmann, Dietrich & Callaway, Enoch, eds. Human Evoked Potentials: Applications & Problems. LC 79-4320. (NATO Conference Ser., Series III: Human Factors: Vol. 9). 511p. 1979. 39.50 (ISBN 0-306-40160-6, Plenum Pr). Plenum Pub.
Leonaites, Joseph. New Genesis and the Technoid Movement. (Illus.). 1977. pap. write for info (ISBN 0-9601272-1-6). Leonaitis.
Levy, Leo & Rowitz, Louis. The Ecology of Mental Disorder. LC 73-6767. (Illus.). 164p. 1973. text ed. 19.95 (ISBN 0-87705-034-1). Human Sci Pr.
Lillard, Richard. Eden in Jeopardy: Man's Prodigal Meddling with His Environment-the Southern California Experience. LC 76-1842. (Illus.). 1977. Repr. of 1966 ed. lib. bdg. 22.75x (ISBN 0-8371-8181-X, LIEJ). Greenwood.
Llewellyn-Jones, Derek. People Populating. 384p. 1976. 18.00 (ISBN 0-571-09943-2). Transatlantic.
McClary, Andrew. Biology & Society: The Evolution of Man & His Technology. (Illus.). 352p. 1975. pap. text ed. 9.95 (ISBN 0-685-51085-9). Macmillan.
McGurk, H., ed. Ecological Factors in Human Development. LC 76-30321. (Illus.). 1977. 22.00 (ISBN 0-7204-0488-6, North-Holland). Elsevier.
McHale, John. The Ecological Context. new ed. LC 77-132200. 1970. 7.95 (ISBN 0-8076-0562-X). Braziller.
McHarg, Ian L. Design with Nature. LC 76-77344. 1971. 17.95 (ISBN 0-385-02142-9); pap. 6.95 (ISBN 0-385-05509-9). Natural Hist.
McKenzie, Roderick D. Roderick D. McKenzie on Human Ecology. Hawley, Amos H., ed. LC 68-9728. (Heritage of Sociology Ser). 1968. 15.00x (ISBN 0-226-31981-4). U of Chicago Pr.
--Roderick D. McKenzie on Human Ecology. Hawley, Amos H., ed. LC 68-9728. (Heritage of Sociology Ser). 1969. pap. 3.45 (ISBN 0-226-31982-2, P326, Phoen). U of Chicago Pr.
Maddox, John. The Doomsday Syndrome. LC 72-3844. 336p. 1972. 8.95 (ISBN 0-07-039428-8, GB). McGraw.
Manshard, W. & Fischnich, O. E. Man & Environment. 108p. 1975. pap. text ed. 24.00 (ISBN 0-08-019673-X). Pergamon.
Marden, P. G. & Hodgson, D., eds. Population, Environment & the Quality of Life. LC 74-579. 328p. 1975. pap. 10.95 (ISBN 0-470-56868-2). Halsted Pr.
Margenau, Henry & Sellon, Emily B., eds. Nature, Man & Society. 1976. 16.00 (ISBN 0-89254-005-2). Nicolas-Hays.
Marois, Maurice, ed. Towards a Plan of Actions for Mankind, 5 vols. Incl. Vol. 1. Long Range Mineral Resources & Growth. text ed. 60.00 (ISBN 0-08-021445-2); Vol. 2. Long Range Energetic Resources & Growth. text ed. 40.00 (ISBN 0-08-021446-0); Vol. 3. Biological Balance & Thermal Modification. text ed. 60.00 (ISBN 0-08-021447-9); Vol. 4. Design of Global System Models & Their Limitations. text ed. 55.00 (ISBN 0-08-021448-7); Vol. 5. Conclusions & Perspectives. text ed. 100.00 (ISBN 0-08-021449-5). 1977. Set. 445.00 (ISBN 0-08-021850-4). Pergamon.
Maxwell, Kenneth E. Environment of Life. 3rd ed. LC 79-18690. 1980. text ed. 14.95 (ISBN 0-8185-0355-6). Brooks-Cole.
Medvedkov, Yuri, ed. Amelioration of the Human Environment: IGU Congress, Moscow, 1976, Proceedings, Pt. 1. 1977. pap. text ed. 19.50 (ISBN 0-08-021322-7). Pergamon.
Meeker, Joseph W. Comedy of Survival. LC 79-54815. 1980. pap. 7.95 (ISBN 0-89615-048-8). Guild of Tutors.
Metress, James, ed. Man in Ecological Perspective. 1972. 29.50x (ISBN 0-8422-5022-0); pap. text ed. 12.50x (ISBN 0-8422-0125-4). Irvington.
Miller, G. Tyler. Replenish the Earth: A Primer in Human Ecology. 96p. 1972. pap. 8.95x (ISBN 0-534-00203-X). Wadsworth Pub.
Mohtadi, M. F., ed. Man & His Environment, Vol. 2: Proceedings of the Second Banff Conference. 216p. 1976. text ed. 37.00 (ISBN 0-08-019922-4). Pergamon.
Montgomery, David. Imperial Science & National Survival. LC 80-70692. 1981. 2.50x (ISBN 0-87081-094-4). Colo Assoc.
Moore, Gary T. & Golledge, R. G., eds. Environmental Knowing: Theories, Research & Methods. (Community Development Ser.: Vol. 23). 416p. 1976. 21.50 (ISBN 0-87933-297-2). Hutchinson Ross.
Moos, Rudolf & Brownstein, Robert. Environment & Utopia: A Synthesis. LC 77-23275. (Plenum Social Ecology Ser.). 284p. 1977. 19.50 (ISBN 0-306-30985-8, Plenum Pr). Plenum Pub.
Moos, Rudolf H. The Human Context: Environmental Determinants of Behavior. LC 75-26870. 444p. 1976. 31.95 (ISBN 0-471-61504-8, Pub. by Wiley-Interscience). Wiley.
Moran, Emilio F. Human Adaptability: An Introduction to Ecological Anthropology. 1979. 13.95 (ISBN 0-87872-192-4). Duxbury Pr.
Moran, Joseph M., et al. An Introduction to Environmental Sciences. 464p. 1973. text ed. 14.95 (ISBN 0-316-58218-2); instructor's manual free (ISBN 0-316-58204-2). Little.
Morris, Desmond. The Human Zoo. 1970. pap. 2.25 (ISBN 0-440-33913-8). Dell.
Moser, Leo J. The Technology Trap. LC 78-26034. 1979. 17.95x (ISBN 0-88229-419-9); pap. 8.95 (ISBN 0-88229-669-8). Nelson-Hall.
Nag, Moni, ed. Population & Social Organization. (Mouton World Anthropology Ser.). 376p. 1975. 20.00x (ISBN 0-202-01148-8). Beresford Bk Serv.
National Geographic Society, ed. As We Live & Breathe: The Challenge of Our Environment. LC 74-151945. (Special Publications Ser.). (Illus.). 1971. 5.75, avail. only from Natl Geog (ISBN 0-87044-097-7). Natl Geog.
National Research Council. Earth & Human Affairs. 1972. pap. text ed. 8.95 scp (ISBN 0-06-385490-2, HarpC). Har-Row.
Netting, Robert M. Balancing on an Alp: Ecological Change & Continuity in a Swiss Mountain Community. LC 81-358. (Illus.). 436p. Date not set. price not set (ISBN 0-521-23743-2); pap. price not set (ISBN 0-521-28197-0). Cambridge U Pr.
Norwine, Jim. Climate & Human Ecology. LC 78-52975. (Illus.). 1978. pap. 9.95 (ISBN 0-918464-19-6). D Armstrong.
Odum, Howard T. Environment Power & Society. LC 78-129660. (Environmental Science & Technology Ser). 331p. 1971. pap. text ed. 9.95x (ISBN 0-471-65275-X, Pub. by Wiley-Interscience). Wiley.
Odum, Howard T. & Odum, Elisabeth C. Energy Basis for Man & Nature. 2nd ed. (Illus.). 352p. 1981. text ed. 19.50 (ISBN 0-07-047511-3, C); pap. text ed. 12.95 (ISBN 0-07-047510-5, C); instr's. manual 6.00 (ISBN 0-07-047512-1). McGraw.
Olson, Mancur & Landsberg, Hans H., eds. The No-Growth Society. 259p. 1974. 10.00 (ISBN 0-393-01111-9); pap. text ed. 4.95x (ISBN 0-393-09260-7). Norton.
Orr, David W. & Soroos, Marvin S., eds. The Global Predicament: Ecological Perspectives on World Order. LC 78-10207. 1979. 19.00 (ISBN 0-8078-1346-X); pap. 9.00x (ISBN 0-8078-1349-4). U of NC Pr.
Owen, D. F. Man in Tropical Africa: Human Ecology in Tropical Africa. 220p. 1973. 12.95x (ISBN 0-19-519746-1). Oxford U Pr.
Passmore, John. Man's Responsibility for Nature: Ecological Problems & Western Traditions. LC 73-19273. 1974. 7.95 (ISBN 0-684-13815-8, ScribC); pap. text ed. 7.95x (ISBN 0-684-15600-8, ScribC). Scribner.
Peter, Laurence J. The Peter Plan: A Proposal for Survival. LC 75-22327. (Illus.). 224p. 1976. 6.95 (ISBN 0-688-02972-8). Morrow.
Pewe, Troy L., ed. The Periglacial Environment: Past & Present. 1969. 25.00x (ISBN 0-7735-0042-1). McGill-Queens U Pr.
Piburne, Michael. The Environment: A Human Crisis. (American Values Ser). 160p. (gr. 9-12). 1974. pap. text ed. 4.00x (ISBN 0-8104-5905-1). Hayden.
Polgar, Steven, ed. Culture & Population: A Collection of Current Studies. LC 80-20070. (Carolina Population Center, Monograph: 9). vi, 195p. 1980. Repr. of 1971 ed. lib. bdg. 19.75x (ISBN 0-313-22620-2, POCP). Greenwood.
--Population, Ecology, & Social Evolution. (World Anthropology Ser.). (Illus.). 320p. 1975. 23.00x (ISBN 0-202-90013-4). Beresford Bk Serv.
Pregel, Boris, et al, eds. World Priorities. LC 75-29389. 277p. 1977. pap. text ed. 4.95x (ISBN 0-87855-633-8). Transaction Bks.
Pursell, Margaret S. A Look at the Environment. LC 75-38465. (Lerner Awareness Bks.). (Illus.). 36p. (gr. 3-6). 1976. PLB 4.95 (ISBN 0-8225-1302-1). Lerner Pubns.
Quinn, James A. Human Ecology. LC 72-143887. (Illus.). 1971. Repr. of 1950 ed. 25.00 (ISBN 0-208-01151-X, Archon). Shoe String.
Randolph, Theron G. Human Ecology & Susceptibility to the Chemical Environment. (Illus.). 160p. 1978. 12.50 (ISBN 0-398-01548-1). C C Thomas.

Rapoport, Amos, ed. The Mutual Interaction of People & Their Built Environment. (World Anthropology Ser.). 1977. 38.00x (ISBN 0-202-90042-8). Beresford Bk Serv.
Reed, C. B. Fuels, Minerals & Human Survival. LC 74-21575. 1978. softcover 12.50 (ISBN 0-250-40256-4). Ann Arbor Science.
Robertson, Thomas. Human Ecology, 2 vols. 560p. 1973. 200.00 (ISBN 0-87968-340-6). Gordon Pr.
Rogers, Dorothy. Life-Span Human Development. LC 80-25158. 512p. 1981. text ed. 17.95 (ISBN 0-8185-0389-0). Brooks-Cole.
Rose, J. & Weidener, E. W., eds. Westview Environmental Studies, 3 vols. Incl. Vol. 1. Pesticides: Boon or Bane? Green, M. B. LC 76-5881. 18.00x (ISBN 0-89158-610-5); Vol. 2. Climate & the Environment: The Atmospheric Impact on Man. Griffiths, John F. LC 76-5801. pap. text ed. 11.00x (ISBN 0-236-40022-3); Vol. 3. Electromagnetism, Man & the Environment. Battocletti, Joseph H. LC 76-7905. 17.50x (ISBN 0-89158-612-1). 1976. Westview.
Roszak, Theodore. Person Planet: The Creative Disintegration of Industrial Society. LC 75-6165. 1979. pap. 5.95 (ISBN 0-385-00082-0, Anch). Doubleday.
Savage, N. E. & Wood, R. S. Man & His Environment: General Science, Bk. 2. (Secondary Science Ser). (Illus., Orig.). (gr. 8-11). 1972. pap. text ed. 5.75 (ISBN 0-7100-7209-0). Routledge & Kegan.
Schaeffer, Francis. Pollution & the Death of Man. pap. 2.95 (ISBN 0-8423-4840-9). Tyndale.
Scherer, Donald. Personal Values & Environmental Issues. 256p. 1978. pap. 6.95 (ISBN 0-89104-256-3). A & W Pubs.
Schneider, Steven & Mestrow, L. E. Genesis Strategy. 1977. pap. 4.95 (ISBN 0-440-52792-9, Delta). Dell.
Scott, Allan & Lorraine, John, eds. Here Today... World Outlooks from the Centre of Human Ecology. 120p. 1979. 30.00x (ISBN 0-904919-34-X, Pub. by Polygon Bks Scotland). State Mutual Bk.
Shaler, Nathaniel S. Man & the Earth. Repr. of 1905 ed. 14.50 (ISBN 0-384-54960-8). Johnson Repr.
Shepard, Paul & McKinley, Daniel, eds. Subversive Science: Essays Toward an Ecology of Man. LC 69-15029. (Illus., Orig.). 1969. pap. text ed. 11.50 (ISBN 0-395-05399-4). HM.
Sherman, Anthony C. Land & Trash: Our Wounded Land. new ed. Eblen, William, ed. LC 72-79107. (Illus.). 64p. (Orig.). (gr. 7-12). 1972. pap. 1.45 (ISBN 0-88301-043-7). Pendulum Pr.
Simmons, Ian. The Ecology of Natural Resources. LC 74-4812. 424p. 1974. pap. text ed. 14.95 (ISBN 0-470-79194-2). Halsted Pr.
Sims, John H. & Baumann, Duane D., eds. Human Behavior & the Environment Interactions Between Man & His Physical World. LC 73-89450. (Maaroufa Press Geography Ser.). (Illus.). 354p. 1974. pap. text ed. 5.95x (ISBN 0-88425-002-4). Maaroufa Pr.
Smith, Robert L., ed. The Ecology of Man: An Ecosystem Approach. 2nd ed. 448p. 1976. pap. text ed. 14.95 scp (ISBN 0-06-046338-4, HarpC). Har-Row.
Smole, William J. The Yanoama Indians: A Cultural Geography. (Texas Pan American Ser.). (Illus.). 286p. 1976. 17.50x (ISBN 0-292-71019-4). U of Tex Pr.
Society for Human Ecology. Proceedings of the International Meeting on Human Ecology, 2 vols. Knotig, Helmut, ed. (Illus.). 1977. Set. pap. 85.00x (ISBN 2-604-00027-X). Renouf.
Soleri, Paolo. The Bridge Between Matter & Spirit Is Matter Becoming Spirit. LC 72-87501. 280p. 1973. pap. 2.95 (ISBN 0-385-02361-8, Anch). Doubleday.
Sorokin, P. A. Reconstruction of Humanity. Repr. of 1948 ed. 16.00 (ISBN 0-527-84826-3). Kraus Repr.
SPR Charter. Man on Earth: A Preliminary Evaluation of the Ecology of Man. LC 78-75232. 1979. text ed. 8.00 (ISBN 0-89615-007-0); pap. 10.95 (ISBN 0-89615-051-8). Guild of Tutors.
Spradlin, W. W. & Porterfield, P. B. Human Biosociology: From Cell to Culture. (Heidelberg Science Library). (Illus.). 1979. pap. 10.30 (ISBN 0-387-90350-X). Springer-Verlag.
Stanley, N. F. & Alpers, M. Man Made Lakes & Human Health. 1975. 78.50 (ISBN 0-12-663550-1). Acad Pr.
Stapp, William B. & Liston, Mary D., eds. Environmental Education: A Guide to Information Sources. LC 73-17542. (Man & the Environment Information Guide Ser.: Vol. 1). 350p. 1975. 36.00 (ISBN 0-8103-1337-5). Gale.
Steiner, Stan. The Vanishing White Man. 1977. pap. 3.95 (ISBN 0-06-090574-3, CN 574, CN). Har-Row.
Strong, Maurice, ed. Who Speaks for Earth? 160p. 1973. 6.95 (ISBN 0-393-06392-5); pap. 1.95x (ISBN 0-393-09341-7). Norton.
Swift, Morrison I. Can Mankind Survive? 1977. lib. bdg. 59.95 (ISBN 0-8490-1565-0). Gordon Pr.
Sychev, Yu. V. The Individual & the Micro-Environment. Judelson, Katherine, tr. from Rus. 1978. 4.80 (ISBN 0-8285-3302-4, Pub. by Progress Pubs Russia). Imported Pubns.
Tappan, Mel. Tappan on Survival. 1981. 8.95 (ISBN 0-916172-04-X). Janus Pr.
Taylor, Griffith. Environment, Race & Migration: Fundamentals of Human Distribution, with Special Sections on Racial Classification, & Settlement in Canada & Australia. LC 38-9816. (Illus.). 1937. 45.00x (ISBN 0-8020-7043-4). U of Toronto Pr.
Tinker, Irene & Buvinic, Mayra, eds. The Many Facets of Human Settlement: Science & Society. LC 77-6307. 1977. text ed. 125.00 (ISBN 0-08-021994-2). Pergamon.
Treshow, Michael. The Human Environment. (Population Biology Ser.). 1976. text ed. 10.95 (ISBN 0-07-065136-1, C). McGraw.
Triandis, Harry C., ed. Variations in Black & White Perceptions of the Social Environment. LC 75-29056. 235p. 1976. 17.50 (ISBN 0-252-00515-5). U of Ill Pr.
Tullar, Richard M. The Human Species: Its Nature, Evolution & Ecology. (Illus.). 1976. pap. text ed. 15.95 (ISBN 0-07-065423-9, C); instructor's manual 5.50 (ISBN 0-07-065424-7). McGraw.
Tybout, Richard A., ed. Environmental Quality & Society. LC 75-2244. (Illus., Orig.). 1975. pap. 7.50x (ISBN 0-8142-0214-4). Ohio St U Pr.
United Nations Statistical Office, compiled by. United Nations Conference on Human Settlements, Vancouver, B. C., 1976: Human Settlements Factbook Statistical Annex, 2 vols. 1976. text ed. 165.00 (ISBN 0-08-021045-7). Pergamon.
Vale, Jack R. Genes, Environment & Behavior: An Interactionist Approach. (Illus.). 470p. 1980. text ed. 22.50 scp (ISBN 0-06-046758-4, HarpC). Har-Row.
Vann, Anthony & Rogers, Paul, eds. Human Ecology & World Development. (Frontiers in Human Ecology Ser: Vol. 1). 180p. 1974. 25.00 (ISBN 0-306-30794-4, Plenum Pr). Plenum Pub.
Vayda, Andrew P. War in Ecological Perspective. LC 75-40272. (Illus.). 129p. 1976. 19.50 (ISBN 0-306-30876-2, Plenum Pr). Plenum Pub.
Volpe, Peter E. Man, Nature, & Society: An Introduction to Biology. 2nd ed. 650p. 1979. text ed. write for info. (ISBN 0-697-04568-4); instr's manual avail. (ISBN 0-685-91873-4); lab. manual avail. (ISBN 0-697-04569-2); study guide avail. (ISBN 0-697-04571-4). Wm C Brown.
Waddington, C. H. The Man-Made Future. LC 77-29043. 1978. 19.95x (ISBN 0-312-51045-4). St Martin.
Wagner, Philip L. Human Use of the Earth. LC 60-7092. 1964. pap. text ed. 3.00 (ISBN 0-02-933570-1). Free Pr.
Wagner, Richard H. Environment & Man. 3rd ed. 606p. 1978. text ed. 19.95x (ISBN 0-393-09066-3). Norton.
Wapner, Seymour, et al, eds. Experiencing the Environment. (Illus.). 240p. 1976. 19.50 (ISBN 0-306-30873-8, Plenum Pr). Plenum Pub.
Ward, Barbara & Dubos, Rene. Only One Earth: The Care & Maintenance of a Small Planet. 1972. 13.95 (ISBN 0-393-06391-7). Norton.
Waterman, Laura & Waterman, Guy. Backwoods Ethics: Environmental Concerns for Hikers & Campers. LC 79-16684. (Illus.). 192p. (Orig.). 1979. pap. 6.95 (ISBN 0-913276-28-6). Stone Wall Pr.
Watt, Kenneth E. Principles of Environmental Science. (Illus.). 1972. text ed. 21.00 (ISBN 0-07-068575-4, C). McGraw.
Williams, Duncan. To Be or Not to Be: A Question of Survival. (International Library Ser.). 1975. pap. text ed. 8.25 (ISBN 0-08-019934-8). Pergamon.
Wilson, Edward O., intro. by. Ecology, Evolution, & Population Biology: Readings from Scientific American. LC 73-17448. (Illus.). 1974. text ed. 19.95x (ISBN 0-7167-0888-4); pap. text ed. 9.95x (ISBN 0-7167-0887-6). W H Freeman.
Witters, Weldon L. & Jones-Witters, Patricia. Environmental Biology: The Human Factor. 2nd ed. LC 75-35412. 1978. perfect bdg. 7.95 (ISBN 0-8403-8000-3). Kendall Hunt.
Wittman, James S., ed. Selected Articles in Social Ecology. LC 73-609. 295p. 1973. text ed. 34.50x (ISBN 0-8422-5086-7); pap. text ed. 12.50x (ISBN 0-8422-0293-5). Irvington.
Wolf, Eric R., ed. The Valley of Mexico: Studies in Pre-Hispanic Ecology & Society. LC 75-21184. (School of American Research Advanced Seminar Ser.). 337p. 1976. 20.00x (ISBN 0-8263-0398-6). U of NM Pr.
Woodbury, Angus M. Notes on the Human Ecology of Glen Canyon. (Glen Canyon Ser.: No. 26). Repr. of 1965 ed. 20.00 (ISBN 0-404-60674-1). AMS Pr.
Yi-Fu Tuan. Man & Nature. LC 71-182310. (CCG Resource Papers Ser.: No. 10). (Illus.). 1971. pap. text ed. 4.00 (ISBN 0-89291-057-7). Assn Am Geographers.

HUMAN ECOLOGY–BIBLIOGRAPHY

Berry, Peter S., ed. Sourcebook for Environmental Studies. 1975. pap. text ed. 11.00x (ISBN 0-8464-0865-1). Beekman Pubs.
Burke, John G. & Reddig, Jill S. Guide to Ecology Information & Organizations. 1976. 12.50 (ISBN 0-8242-0567-7). Wilson.
Chicorel, Marietta, ed. Chicorel Index to Environment & Ecology, Vols. 16 & 16A. LC 75-306805. (Index Ser.). 1000p. 1974. Set. 170.00 (ISBN 0-934598-21-5). Am Lib Pub Co.
Garwood Wolff & Co. Environmental Information Sources Handbook. 1973. text ed. 25.00 (ISBN 0-671-18711-2). Monarch Pr.
Hammond, Kenneth A., et al. Sourcebook on the Environment: A Guide to the Literature. LC 77-17407. 1978. lib. bdg. 22.00x (ISBN 0-226-31522-3). U of Chicago Pr.
Lee, Kaiman, ed. Bibliography of the Computer in Environmental Design, 3 vols. 2nd ed. LC 73-158197. 600p. 1973. 110.00 (ISBN 0-915250-03-9). Environ Design.
Owings, Loren C., ed. Environmental Values, 1860-1972: A Guide to Information Sources. LC 73-17539. (Man & the Environment Information Guide Ser.: Vol. 4). 593p. 1976. 36.00 (ISBN 0-8103-1343-X). Gale.
Sargent, Frederick, II, ed. Human Ecology: A Guide to Information Sources. (Health Affairs Information Guide Series, Gale Information Guide Library: Vol. 10). 300p. 1982. 36.00 (ISBN 0-8103-1504-1). Gale.
Young, Gerald L. Human Ecology As an Interdisciplinary Domain: An Epistemological Bibliography. (Public Administration Ser.: P 72). 1978. pap. 7.00 (ISBN 0-686-24284-X). Vance Biblios.

HUMAN ECOLOGY–MORAL AND RELIGIOUS ASPECTS

Barbour, Ian G., ed. Western Man & Environmental Ethics. LC 72-1936. 1973. pap. text ed. 6.50 (ISBN 0-201-00387-2). A-W.
Blackstone, William T., ed. Philosophy & Environmental Crisis. LC 73-90842. 147p. 1974. pap. 5.50x (ISBN 0-8203-0343-7). U of Ga Pr.
Scherer, Donald. Personal Values & Environmental Issues. 256p. 1978. pap. 6.95 (ISBN 0-89104-256-3). A & W Pubs.

HUMAN ECOLOGY–PUBLIC OPINION

Murch, Arvin W., ed. Environmental Concern: Personal Attitudes & Behavior Toward Environmental Problems. 378p. 1974. text ed. 29.50x (ISBN 0-8422-5169-3); pap. text ed. 11.00x (ISBN 0-8422-0410-5). Irvington.
Tuan Yi-Fu. Topophilia: A Study of Environmental Perception, Attitudes & Values. (Illus.). 272p. 1974. pap. text ed. 9.95 (ISBN 0-13-925230-4). P-H.
Whisenhunt, Donald W. The Environment & the American Experience: A Historian Looks at the Ecological Crisis. LC 74-80068. (National University Publications). 1974. 12.95 (ISBN 0-8046-9071-5). Kennikat.

HUMAN ECOLOGY–STUDY AND TEACHING

see also Nature Study

Biological Science Curriculum Study. Investigating Your Environment Ser. Incl. Bk. 1. The Environment: Some Viewpoints. pap. text ed. 4.52 (ISBN 0-201-00933-1); Bk. 2. The Price of Progress. pap. text ed. 4.52 (ISBN 0-201-00934-X); Bk. 3. Food for Humanity. pap. text ed. 4.52 (ISBN 0-201-00935-8); Bk. 4. Human Population. pap. text ed. 4.52 (ISBN 0-201-00936-6); Bk. 5. Solid Waste. pap. text ed. 4.52 (ISBN 0-201-00937-4); Bk. 6. Pesticides. pap. text ed. 4.52 (ISBN 0-201-00938-2); Bk. 7. Land Use. pap. text ed. 4.52 (ISBN 0-201-00939-0); Bk. 8. Water Quality. pap. text ed. 4.52 (ISBN 0-201-00940-4). (gr. 10-12). 1975. pap. text ed. 8.80 student hndbk. (ISBN 0-201-00931-5, Sch Div); tchr's hndbk. 8.00 (ISBN 0-201-00932-3). A-W.
Hughes-Evans, ed. Environmental Education - Key Issues of the Future: Proceedings of the Conference Held at the College of Technology, Farnborough, England. LC 77-827. 1977. pap. text ed. 12.00 (ISBN 0-08-021490-8). Pergamon.
Ittelson, W. Introduction to Environmental Psychology. LC 73-21953. 1974. text ed. 16.95 (ISBN 0-03-001346-1, HoltC). HR&W.
Stapp, William B. & Liston, Mary D., eds. Environmental Education: A Guide to Information Sources. LC 73-17542. (Man & the Environment Information Guide Ser.: Vol. 1). 350p. 1975. 36.00 (ISBN 0-8103-1337-5). Gale.
Terry, Mark & Witt, Paul. Energy & Order. LC 76-19208. 41p. 1976. pap. text ed. 3.00 (ISBN 0-913890-14-6). Friends Earth.
Wang, J. Y., et al. Exploring Man's Environment. 1973. pap. text ed. 10.95 (ISBN 0-8465-3051-1). Benjamin-Cummings.

HUMAN EMBRYOLOGY

see Embryology, Human

HUMAN ENGINEERING

see also Human Information Processing; Man-Machine Systems

Bootzin, David & Muffley, Harry C., eds. Biomechanics. LC 69-16519. 185p. 1969. 25.00 (ISBN 0-306-30392-2, Plenum Pr). Plenum Pub.
Chapanis, Alphonse, ed. Ethnic Variables in Human Factors Engineering. LC 74-24393. 310p. 1975. 20.00x (ISBN 0-8018-1668-8). Johns Hopkins.
Damon, Albert, et al. Human Body in Equipment Design. LC 65-22067. (Illus.). 1966. 20.00x (ISBN 0-674-41450-0). Harvard U Pr.
DECHEMA, Deutsche Gesellschaft Fuer Chemisches Apparatewesen E. V., ed. Biotechnology: Proceedings of the First European Congress on Biotechnology. (Dechema Monographs: Vol. 82). 304p. 1979. pap. text ed. 37.50 (ISBN 3-527-10765-7). Verlag Chemie.
Dreyfuss, Henry. Measure of Man. rev & enl ed. (Illus.). 1967. 19.95 (ISBN 0-8230-7370-X, Whitney Lib). Watson-Guptill.
Elison, Craig, ed. Modifying Man: Implications & Ethics. 11.25 (ISBN 0-8191-0302-0). U Pr of Amer.
Ergonomic Principles in the Design of Hand Tools. (Occupational Safety & Health Ser.: No. 44). 93p. 1981. pap. 9.50 (ISBN 92-2-102356-7, ILO 155, ILO). Unipub.
Floyd, W. F. & Welford, A. T., eds. Symposium on Fatigue & Symposium on Human Factors in Equipment Design, 2 vols. in one. LC 77-70494. (Work Ser.). (Illus.). 1977. Repr. of 1954 ed. lib. bdg. 25.00x (ISBN 0-405-10165-1). Arno.
Grandjean, Etienne. Ergonomics of the Home. LC 73-13221. (Illus.). 344p. 1973. 31.95x (ISBN 0-85066-067-X). Intl Pubns Serv.
--Fitting the Task to the Man: An Ergonomic Approach. 3rd ed. LC 77-447838. 379p. 1980. 35.00 (ISBN 0-85066-192-7); pap. 22.50 (ISBN 0-8002-2225-3). Intl Pubns Serv.
Hammond, John. Understanding Human Engineering: An Introduction to Ergonomics. 1979. 14.95 (ISBN 0-7153-7670-5). David & Charles.
International Ergonomics Association - 2nd - Dortmund - 1964. Ergonomics: Proceedings. (Illus.). 1966. 30.00x (ISBN 0-85066-005-X). Intl Pubns Serv.
International Union of Pure & Applied Chemistry. Chemical Control of the Human Environment: Proceedings of an International Symposium, Johannesburg, 1969. 148p. 1976. 25.00 (ISBN 0-08-020733-2). Pergamon.
Lenihan, John. Human Engineering: The Body Re-Examined. LC 74-25318. 212p. 1975. 7.95 (ISBN 0-8076-0782-7). Braziller.
Lovell, K. & Elkind, David. An Introduction to Human Development. 1971. pap. 4.95x (ISBN 0-673-07583-4). Scott F.
McCormick, E. J. Human Factors in Engineering & Design. 4th ed. 1975. text ed. 25.00 (ISBN 0-07-044886-8, C). McGraw.
McCue, Gerald M., et al. Creating the Human Environment. LC 73-110423. (Illus.). 1971. pap. 7.95 (ISBN 0-252-00119-2). U of Ill Pr.
Marsh, George P. The Earth As Modified by Human Action. (American Environmental Studies). Repr. of 1876 ed. 27.00 (ISBN 0-405-02677-3). Arno.
Maule, H. G. & Weiner, J. S., eds. Design for Work & Use: Case Studies in Ergonomic Practice. 150p. 1981. 27.50 (ISBN 0-85066-208-7). Intl Pubns Serv.
--Human Factors in Work Design & Production. 138p. 1977. 29.95 (ISBN 0-470-99074-0). Halsted Pr.
Meister, David. Human Factors: Theory & Practice. LC 77-148505. (Human Factors Ser). 1971. 39.50 (ISBN 0-471-59190-4, Pub. by Wiley-Interscience). Wiley.
Moo-Young. Advances in Biotechnology: Fermentation & Yeasts--Proceedings of the 6th International Fermentation Symposium-5th International Symposium on Yeasts, London, Canada, July 20-25, 1980, 4 vols. (Illus.). 2900p. 1981. Set. 350.00 (ISBN 0-686-72857-2); Vol. 1. 100.00 (ISBN 0-686-72858-0); Vol. 2. 100.00 (ISBN 0-686-72859-9); Vol. 3. 100.00 (ISBN 0-686-72860-2); Vol. 4. 95.00 (ISBN 0-686-72861-0). Pergamon.
Moraal, J. & Kraiss, F., eds. Manned Systems Design: Methods, Equipment, & Applications. (NATO Conference Series (III - Human Factors) Ser.: Vol. 17). 487p. 1981. text ed. 35.00 (ISBN 0-306-40804-X, Plenum Pr). Plenum Pub.
Packard, Vance. The People Shapers. 1977. 12.50 (ISBN 0-316-68750-2). Little.

Reeve, E. G. Validation of Selection Boards; & Procedures As Exemplified in a Study of the War Office Selection Boards. Murrell, K. H., ed. (Ergonomics: Studies of Man & His Work Ser). 1972. 48.50 (ISBN 0-12-585750-0). Acad Pr.

Rudman, Jack. Human Resources Specialist. (Career Examination Ser.: C-356). (Cloth bdg. avail. on request). pap. 8.00 (ISBN 0-8373-0356-7). Natl Learning.

--Supervising Human Resources Specialist. (Career Examination Ser.: C-1046). (Cloth bdg. avail. on request). pap. 10.00 (ISBN 0-8373-1046-6). Natl Learning.

Shephard, Roy J. Men at Work: Applications of Ergonomics to Performance & Design. (Illus.). 408p. 1974. 32.75 (ISBN 0-398-02965-2). C C Thomas.

Sinaiko, H. Wallace, ed. Selected Papers on Human Factors in the Design & Use of Control Systems. 8.75 (ISBN 0-8446-2943-X). Peter Smith.

--Selected Papers on Human Factors in the Design & Use of Control Systems. (Illus., Orig.). 1961. pap. text ed. 6.00 (ISBN 0-486-60140-4). Dover.

Singleton, W. T. Introduction to Ergonomics. 145p. 1972. pap. 8.00 (ISBN 92-4-156038-X, 1243). World Health.

Symposium on Psychophysiological Aspects of Space Flight, Brooks Air Force Base, Texas, 1960. Proceedings. Flaherty, Bernard E., ed. LC 60-15809. 1961. 22.50x (ISBN 0-231-02456-8). Columbia U Pr.

Tichauer, E. R. The Biochemical Basis of Ergonomics: Anatomy Applied to the Design of Work Situations. LC 77-28807. 99p. 1978. 15.00 (ISBN 0-471-03644-7, Pub. by Wiley-Interscience). Wiley.

Woodson, Wesley E. Human Factors Design Handbook: Information & Guidelines for the Design of Systems, Facilities, Equipment, & Products for Human Use. LC 80-13299. (Illus.). 1049p. 1981. 75.00 (ISBN 0-07-071765-6). McGraw.

Woodson, Wesley E. & Conover, Donald W. Human Engineering Guide for Equipment Designers. 2nd rev ed. (Illus.). 1965. 35.75x (ISBN 0-520-01363-8). U of Cal Pr.

HUMAN ENVIRONMENT

see Human Ecology

HUMAN EVOLUTION

see also Fossil Man; Sociobiology

Adams, Fred T. Way to Modern Man: An Introduction to Human Evolution. LC 68-28011. (Illus.). 1968. text ed. 10.25x (ISBN 0-8077-1001-6); pap. text ed. 6.50x (ISBN 0-8077-1003-2). Tchrs Coll.

Alfonseca, Manuel. Human Cultures & Evolution. 1978. 6.95 (ISBN 0-533-03747-6). Vantage.

Alsberg, P. In Quest of Man. 1970. text ed. 14.50 (ISBN 0-08-015680-0). Pergamon.

Ardrey, Robert. The Hunting Hypothesis: A Personal Conclusion Concerning the Evolutionary Nature of Man. LC 75-37781. 256p. 1976. 10.00 (ISBN 0-689-10672-6). Atheneum.

--Social Contract. 1971. pap. 2.65 (ISBN 0-440-57896-5, Delta). Dell.

Ashley Montagu. On Being Human. (gr. 9-12). 1967. (Hawthorn); pap. 3.50 (ISBN 0-8015-5514-0, Hawthorn). Dutton.

Bajema, Carl J., ed. Natural Selection in Human Populations: The Measurement of Ongoing Genetic Evolution in Contemporary Societies. LC 76-50639. (Illus.). 416p. 1977. Repr. of 1971 ed. lib. bdg. 13.50 (ISBN 0-88275-476-9). Krieger.

Bleibtreu, Hermann K. & Downs, James F. Human Variation. (gr. 4-9). 1971. pap. text ed. 7.95x (ISBN 0-02-473200-1). Macmillan.

Bodmer, W. F. & Cavalli-Sforza, L. L. Genetics, Evolution, & Man. LC 75-33990. (Illus.). 1976. 23.95x (ISBN 0-7167-0573-7). W H Freeman.

Boughey, Arthur S. Man & the Environment. 2nd ed. (Illus.). 480p. pap. text ed. 13.95 (ISBN 0-02-312770-8, 31277). Macmillan.

Boyce, A. J. Chromosome Variation in Human Evolution: Symposia of the Institute of Biology Ser, Vol. 14. 131p. 1975. 24.95 (ISBN 0-470-09330-7). Wiley.

Brierley, John. A Natural History of Man. 184p. 1970. 10.00 (ISBN 0-8386-7819-X). Fairleigh Dickinson.

Bronfenbrenner, Urie. The Ecology of Human Development: Experiments by Nature & Design. LC 78-27232. 1979. text ed. 18.50x (ISBN 0-674-22456-6). Harvard U Pr.

Campbell, Bernard. Human Evolution: An Introduction to Man's Adaptations. 2nd ed. LC 72-140006. 404p. 1974. lib. bdg. 37.95x (ISBN 0-202-02012-6); pap. text ed. 13.95x (ISBN 0-202-02013-4). Aldine Pub.

--Sexual Selection & the Descent of Man. LC 70-169510. 1972. 34.95x (ISBN 0-202-02005-3). Aldine Pub.

Clark, W. E. The Fossil Evidence for Human Evolution: An Introduction to the Study of Paleoanthropology. 3rd rev. ed. Campbell, Bernard G., ed. LC 78-529. (Illus.). 1979. 16.00x (ISBN 0-226-10937-2); pap. 4.95 (ISBN 0-226-10938-0, P502, Phoen). U of Chicago Pr.

Cold Spring Harbor Symposia on Quantitative Biology: Origin & Evolution of Man, Vol. 15. LC 34-8174. (Illus.). 437p. 1951. 30.00 (ISBN 0-87969-014-3). Cold Spring Harbor.

Darwin, Charles. The Descent of Man & Selection in Relation to Sex. LC 80-8679. (Illus.). 935p. 1981. 30.00x (ISBN 0-691-08278-2); pap. 8.95 (ISBN 0-691-02369-7). Princeton U Pr.

Darwin, Charles R. The Descent of Man & Selection in Relation to Sex, 2 vols. 916p. 1971. Repr. of 1871 ed. Set. 87.50x (ISBN 0-8002-0149-3). Intl Pubns Serv.

Dickinson, George. The Dynamic Principle of Historical Growth. (Illus.). 1978. 49.95 (ISBN 0-89266-089-9). Am Classical Coll Pr.

Dobzhansky, Theodosius. Mankind Evolving: The Evolution of the Human Species. (Silliman Memorial Lectures Ser.). (Illus.). 1962. 25.00x (ISBN 0-300-00427-3); pap. 6.95x 1964 (ISBN 0-300-00070-7, Y116). Yale U Pr.

Downs, James F. & Bleibtreu, Hermann. Human Variation: An Introduction to Physical Anthropology. 2nd ed. 1972. text ed. 10.95x (ISBN 0-02-474490-5, 47449). Macmillan.

Dunn, Leslie C. Heredity & Evolution in Human Populations. rev. ed. LC 65-11617. 1965. pap. text ed. 1.95x (ISBN 0-689-70065-2, 71). Atheneum.

--Heredity & Evolution in Human Populations. rev. ed. LC 65-11617. (Books in Biology Ser: No. 1). (Illus.). 1965. 7.50x (ISBN 0-674-38950-6). Harvard U Pr.

Edey, Maitland A. The Missing Link. (The Emergence of Man Ser.). (Illus.). 160p. 1972. 9.95 (ISBN 0-8094-1255-1); lib. bdg. avail. (ISBN 0-685-28517-0). Time-Life.

Edwards, R. G. Beginnings of Human Life. Head, J. J., ed. LC 79-208. (Carolina Biology Reader Ser.). 16p. (gr. 11 up). 1981. pap. 1.65 (ISBN 0-89278-217-X, 45-9735). Carolina Biological.

Engels, Friedrich. The Part Played by Labour in the Transition from Ape to Man. 16p. 1972. pap. 0.50 (ISBN 0-8285-0044-4, Pub. by Progress Pubs Russia). Imported Pubns.

Garn, Stanley M., ed. Culture & the Direction of Human Evolution. LC 64-16088. (Publications on Human Evolution Ser). 1964. 5.95x (ISBN 0-8143-1230-6). Wayne St U Pr.

Geist, V. Life Strategies, Human Evolution, Environmental Design: Toward a Biological Theory of Health, Vol. I. LC 78-10807. (Illus.). 1979. 31.30 (ISBN 0-387-90363-1). Springer-Verlag.

Gooch, Stan. The Secret Life of Humans. 1981. 18.95x (ISBN 0-460-04527-X, Pub. by J M Dent England). Biblio Dist.

Grau, Joseph A. Morality & the Human Future in the Thought of Teilhard De Chardin: A Critical Study. LC 74-4976. 389p. 1976. 19.50 (ISBN 0-8386-1579-1). Fairleigh Dickinson.

Haviland, William A. Human Evolution & Prehistory. LC 78-14737. 1979. pap. text ed. 14.95 (ISBN 0-03-044761-5, HoltC); inst. manual avail. (ISBN 0-03-044766-6). HR&W.

Higham, Charles. Life in the Old Stone Age. 2nd ed. (Introduction to the History of Mankind Ser). (Illus.). (gr. 4-9). 1971. 3.95 (ISBN 0-521-21869-1). Cambridge U Pr.

--Life in the Old Stone Age. LC 76-22442. (Cambridge Topic Bks). (Illus.). (gr. 5-10). 1977. PLB 5.95 (ISBN 0-8225-1206-8). Lerner Pubns.

Hooton, Earnest A. Apes, Men & Morons. LC 76-134095. (Essay Index Reprint Ser). 1937. 19.50 (ISBN 0-8369-1956-4). Arno.

Howells, William. Evolution of the Genus Homo. 1973. pap. text ed. 5.95 (ISBN 0-8461-1633-2). Benjamin-Cummings.

Huntington, Ellsworth. The Character of Races: Influenced by Physical Environment, Natural Selection & Historical Development. Grob, Gerald, ed. LC 76-46082. (Anti-Movements in America). 1977. lib. bdg. 23.00x (ISBN 0-405-09955-X). Arno.

Isaac, G. & McCown, E. Human Evolution: Louis Leakey & the East African Experience. 1976. pap. 13.95 (ISBN 0-8053-9942-9). Benjamin-Cummings.

Isaac, Glynn, intro. by. Human Ancestors: Readings from Scientific American. LC 79-4486. (Illus.). 1979. text ed. 15.95x (ISBN 0-7167-1100-1); pap. text ed. 7.95x (ISBN 0-7167-1101-X). W H Freeman.

Johnston, Francis E. Microevolution of Human Populations. (Illus.). 160p. 1973. pap. 9.95 ref. ed. (ISBN 0-13-581512-6). P-H.

Kierkegaard, Soren A. Internal Development of Man in Dynamic Representational Expressions. Karlweiss, Joseph R., ed. (Illus.). 107p. 1981. 49.75 (ISBN 0-89266-273-5). Am Classical Coll Pr.

Korn, N. Human Evolution: Readings for Physical Anthropology. 4th ed. LC 77-27086. 1978. pap. 9.95 (ISBN 0-03-019321-4, HoltC). HR&W.

Kurten, Bjorn. Not from the Apes: A History of Man's Origin & Evolution. LC 72-154018. (Illus.). 1972. 24.00x (ISBN 0-394-47123-7). Irvington.

Lancaster, J. B. Primate Behavior & the Emergence of Human Culture. LC 74-22256. (Basic Anthropology Units Ser). 1975. pap. text ed. 5.95 (ISBN 0-03-091311-X, HoltC). HR&W.

Leakey, Richard & Lewin, Roger. Origins: What New Discoveries Reveal About the Emergence of Our Species & Its Possible Future. 1977. 17.95 (ISBN 0-525-17194-0); pap. 8.95 (ISBN 0-525-47572-9). Dutton.

Lerner, I. Michael & Libby, William J. Heredity, Evolution, & Society. 2nd ed. LC 75-33968. (Illus.). 1976. text ed. 22.95x (ISBN 0-7167-0576-1); tchr's manual avail. W H Freeman.

Lewis, John. Uniqueness of Man. 1974. pap. 7.95x (ISBN 0-8464-0948-8). Beekman Pubs.

Linden, Millicent. Preparing Your Body to Fly, Vol. 1. (Tx 112-882). 1977. pap. 7.00 (ISBN 0-912628-05-7). M Linden NY.

MacCurdy, George G. Human Origins: A Manual of Prehistory, 2 vols. 1978. Repr. of 1924 ed. lib. bdg. 65.00 (ISBN 0-8482-1724-1). Norwood Edns.

Meier, Robert, et al, eds. Evolutionary Models & Studies in Human Diversity. (World Anthropology Ser.). 1978. 36.75 (ISBN 0-202-90091-6). Beresford Bk Serv.

Mother & Satprem. Mother's Agenda - 1962, Vol. 3. LC 80-472990. Orig. Title: L'Agenda De Mere-1962. 540p. (Orig.). 1981. pap. text ed. 9.95 (ISBN 0-938710-02-8). Inst Evolutionary.

Oxnard, Charles. Form & Pattern in Human Evolution. 256p. 1973. 14.00x (ISBN 0-226-64251-8). U of Chicago Pr.

--Uniqueness & Diversity in Human Evolution: Morphometric Studies of Australopithecines. LC 74-16689. viii, 134p. 1975. text ed. 17.50x (ISBN 0-226-64253-4). U of Chicago Pr.

Pfeiffer, John E. The Emergence of Man. 3rd ed. (Illus.). 1978. pap. text ed. 14.95 scp (ISBN 0-06-045196-3, HarpC); inst. manual free (ISBN 0-06-365188-2). Har-Row.

Pilbeam, David. The Ascent of Man: An Introduction to Human Evolution. (Illus.). 224p. 1972. pap. text ed. 11.95 (ISBN 0-02-395270-9). Macmillan.

Poirier, Frank E. Fossil Evidence: The Human Evolutionary Journey. 2nd ed. LC 76-17110. (Illus.). 1977. pap. 11.95 (ISBN 0-8016-3951-4). Mosby.

Pringle, J. W., ed. Biology & the Human Sciences. 1972. pap. 3.50x (ISBN 0-19-857122-4). Oxford U Pr.

Rensch, Bernhard. Homo Sapiens: From Man to DemiGod. LC 72-80482. 1972. 17.50x (ISBN 0-231-03683-3). Columbia U Pr.

Ronen, Avraham. Introducing Prehistory: Digging up the Past. LC 72-10803. (Lerner Archaeology Ser.: Digging up the Past). (Illus.). (gr. 5 up). 1976. PLB 7.95 (ISBN 0-8225-0833-8). Lerner Pubns.

Schrodinger, Erwin. What Is Life? Bd. with Mind & Matter. pap. 8.95x (ISBN 0-521-09397-X). Cambridge U Pr.

Sigmon, Becky A. & Cybulski, Jerome S., eds. Homo erectus: Essays in Honor of Davidson Black. 336p. 1981. 30.00x (ISBN 0-8020-5511-7). U of Toronto Pr.

Simons, Elwyn L. Primate Evolution: An Introduction to Man's Place in Nature. (Illus.). 352p. 1972. pap. text ed. 11.95x (ISBN 0-02-410680-1). Macmillan.

Smith, G. E. Evolution of Man. 2nd ed. Repr. of 1927 ed. 18.00 (ISBN 0-527-84020-3). Kraus Repr.

Steele, E. J. Somatic Selection & Adaptive Evolution. 100p. 1980. 30.00x (ISBN 0-686-69937-8, Pub. by Croom Helm England). State Mutual Bk.

Stuart, Friend. The Fifth Kingdom. 98p. 1970. pap. 4.95 (ISBN 0-912132-03-5). Dominion Pr.

--Fifth Kingdom Messenger. 1972. pap. 4.95 (ISBN 0-912132-07-8). Dominion Pr.

Tanner, Nancy M. Becoming Human. LC 80-21526. (Illus.). 370p. 1981. 29.95 (ISBN 0-521-23554-5); pap. write for info. (ISBN 0-521-28028-1). Cambridge U Pr.

Tattersall, Ian. Man's Ancestors: An Introduction to Primate & Human Evolution. (Illus.). 1971. pap. 7.50 (ISBN 0-7195-2188-2). Transatlantic.

Teilhard De Chardin, Pierre. Phenomenon of Man. pap. 4.95 (ISBN 0-06-090495-X, CN495, CN). Har-Row.

Tuttle, Russell H., ed. Primate Functional Morphology & Evolution. (World Anthropology Ser.). (Illus.). 448p. 1975. 47.50x (ISBN 0-202-90016-9). Beresford Bk Serv.

Underwood, Jane H. Human Variation & Human Microevolution. (Illus.). 1979. pap. 10.95 (ISBN 0-13-447573-9). P-H.

Weidenreich, Franz. Apes, Giants & Man. (Illus.). 1946. 5.75x (ISBN 0-226-88147-4). U of Chicago Pr.

White, Edmund. The First Men. (The Emergence of Man Ser.). (Illus.). 1973. 9.95 (ISBN 0-8094-1259-4); lib. bdg. avail. (ISBN 0-685-28794-7). Time-Life.

Wilber, Ken. Up from Eden: A Transpersonal View of Human Evolution. (Illus.). 336p. 1981. 15.95 (ISBN 0-385-17363-6, Anchor Pr). Doubleday.

Wilder-Smith, A. W. Man's Origin, Man's Destiny. LC 74-28508. 320p. 1975. pap. 6.95 (ISBN 0-87123-356-8, 210356). Bethany Hse.

Williams, B. J. Evolution & Human Origins: An Introduction to Physical Anthropology. 2nd ed. (Illus.). 1979. text ed. 15.95 scp (ISBN 0-06-047121-2, HarpC). Har-Row.

Wolsky, M. I. & Wolsky, A. The Mechanism of Evolution: A New Look at Old Ideas. (Contributions to Human Development: Vol. 4). (Illus.). 160p. 1976. 26.50 (ISBN 3-8055-2347-5). S Karger.

Wood, B. A. Human Evolution. LC 77-29099. (Outline Studies in Biology). 80p. 1978. pap. text ed. 5.95x (ISBN 0-412-15600-8, Pub. by Chapman & Hall England). Methuen Inc.

Young, Louise B., ed. Evolution of Man. (Orig.). 1970. text ed. 12.95x (ISBN 0-19-501107-4). Oxford U Pr.

HUMAN EXPERIMENTATION IN MEDICINE

Annas, George J., et al. Informed Consent to Human Experimentation: The Subject's Dilemma. LC 77-2266. 1977. 25.00 (ISBN 0-88410-147-9). Ballinger Pub.

Barber, Bernard, et al. Research on Human Subjects: Problems of Social Control in Medical Experimentation. LC 78-55938. 263p. 1979. pap. text ed. 4.95 (ISBN 0-87855-649-4). Transaction Bks.

--Research on Human Subjects: Problems of Social Control in Medical Experimentation. LC 70-83831. 1973. 10.50 (ISBN 0-87154-090-8). Russell Sage.

Beecher, Henry K. Experimentation in Man. (American Lecture Medicine). 88p. 1957. pap. 9.75 (ISBN 0-398-00124-3). C C Thomas.

Davis, Anne J. & Krueger, Janelle C., eds. Patients, Nurses, Ethics. LC 80-57573. 245p. 1980. pap. text ed. 9.95 (ISBN 0-937126-84-5). Am Journal Nurse.

Finkel, Marion J. Factors Influencing Clinical Research Success. LC 76-27229. (Principles & Techniques of Human Research & Therapeutics: Vol.11). 1976. 15.50 (ISBN 0-87993-082-9). Futura Pub.

Finland, Maxwell & McCabe, William R., eds. Contemporary Standards for Antimicrobial Usage. LC 76-27216. (Principles & Techniques of Human Research & Therapeutics: Vol. 13). (Illus.). 1977. monograph 13.50 (ISBN 0-87993-085-3). Futura Pub.

Freund, Paul A., ed. Experimentation with Human Subjects. LC 70-107776. (Daedalus Library Ser). 1970. pap. 3.50 (ISBN 0-8076-0542-5). Braziller.

Gallant, Donald M. & Force, Robert, eds. Legal & Ethical Issues in Human Research & Treatment: Psychopharmacologic Considerations. 1978. 15.00 (ISBN 0-470-26354-7). Halsted Pr.

Gray, Bradford H. Human Subjects in Medical Experimentation: A Sociological Study of the Conduct & Regulation of Clinical Research. LC 80-11612. 406p. 1981. Repr. of 1975 ed. lib. bdg. write for info. (ISBN 0-89874-134-3). Krieger.

Jones, James H. Bad Blood: The Tuskegee Syphilis Experiment. LC 80-69281. (Illus.). 1981. 14.95 (ISBN 0-02-916670-5). Free Pr.

Katz, Jay. Experimentation with Human Beings: The Authority of Investigator, Subject, Professions, & State in the Human Experimentation Process. LC 70-188394. 1200p. 1972. 22.50 (ISBN 0-87154-438-5). Russell Sage.

Meyer, Peter B. Drug Experiments on Prisoners. LC 75-13307. 144p. 1976. 16.95 (ISBN 0-669-00047-7). Lexington Bks.

Ryan, J. Corboy. Fail-Safe Human Research Protocols. LC 80-24690. 146p. 1981. 19.95 (ISBN 0-89874-292-7). Krieger.

Van Eys, Jan, ed. Research on Children: Medical Imperatives, Ethical Quandaries & Legal Constraints. LC 77-25235. 1977. pap. 9.75 (ISBN 0-8391-1191-6). Univ Park.

Wells, S. H., et al. Pharmacological Testing in a Correctional Institution. 76p. 1975. 11.75 (ISBN 0-398-03202-5). C C Thomas.

HUMAN FERTILIZATION IN VITRO

see Fertilization in Vitro, Human

HUMAN FIGURE IN ART

see also Action in Art; Anatomy, Artistic; Figure Drawing; Figure Painting; Hand in Art; Head in Art; Nude in Art; Photography of the Nude; Women in Art

Benson, J. L. Horse, Bird, & Man: The Origins of Greek Painting. LC 70-95787. (Illus.). 1970. 20.00x (ISBN 0-87023-053-0). U of Mass Pr.

Bieber, Margarete. Laocoon: The Influence of the Group Since Its Rediscovery. 2nd ed. LC 67-16850. (Illus.). 1967. 7.95x (ISBN 0-8143-1323-X). Wayne St U Pr.

Durer, Albrecht. Human Figure: Dresden Sketchbook. Strauss, Walter L., ed. & tr. 1972. pap. 7.95 (ISBN 0-486-21042-1). Dover.

Elsen, Albert E. The Partial Figure in Modern Sculpture, from Rodin to 1969. LC 73-106903. (Illus.). 1969. pap. 9.00 (ISBN 0-912298-03-0); pap. 6.50 (ISBN 0-912298-04-9). Baltimore Mus.

Gordon, Louise. How to Draw the Human Figure. (Illus.). 1979. 12.95 (ISBN 0-670-38329-5, Studio). Viking Pr.

Hale, Robert B. Drawing Lessons from the Great Masters. (Illus.). 1964. 17.95 (ISBN 0-8230-1400-2). Watson-Guptill.

Hatton, Richard G. Figure Drawing. (Illus.). 8.50 (ISBN 0-8446-2220-6). Peter Smith.

--Figure Drawing. (Illus., Orig). pap. 4.00 (ISBN 0-486-21377-3). Dover.

Hollander, Anne. Seeing Through Clothes. (Illus.). 1978. 25.00 (ISBN 0-670-63174-4). Viking Pr.

Kelley, Ramon & Nelson, Mary C. Ramon Kelley Paints Portraits & Figures. (Illus.). 1977. 18.95 (ISBN 0-8230-4505-6). Watson-Guptill.

Knox, Robert. Great Artists & Great Anatomists: A Biographical & Philosophical Study. LC 75-23734. Repr. of 1852 ed. 18.00 (ISBN 0-404-13291-X). AMS Pr.

Laidman, Hugh. Figures-Faces: A Sketcher's Handbook. (Illus.). 1979. 12.95 (ISBN 0-670-31319-X, Studio). Viking Pr.

Longstreet, Stephen, ed. Figure in Art. (Master Draughtsman Ser). (Illus., Orig.). treasure trove bdg. 6.47x (ISBN 0-685-07315-7); pap. 2.95 (ISBN 0-685-07316-5). Borden.

Loomis, Andrew. Figure Drawing for All It's Worth. (Illus.). (YA) (gr. 9 up). 1943. 16.95 (ISBN 0-670-31255-X). Viking Pr.

McElhaney, Mark. Clinical Psychological Assessment of the Human Figure Drawing. (Illus.). 268p. 1969. pap. 25.75 (ISBN 0-398-01250-4). C C Thomas.

Martindale, David E. The Human Figure As an Art Object. (Illus.). 1980. deluxe ed. 45.85 (ISBN 0-930582-52-7). Gloucester Art.

Richardson, Bessie E. Old Age Among the Ancient Greeks. LC 74-93775. (Illus.). Repr. of 1933 ed. 21.50 (ISBN 0-404-05289-4). AMS Pr.

--Old Age Among the Ancient Greeks: The Greek Portrayal of Old Age in Literature, Art & Inscriptions. Repr. of 1933 ed. lib. bdg. 23.50x (ISBN 0-8371-0637-0, RIOA). Greenwood.

Selz, Peter. New Images of Man. LC 59-14221. (Museum of Modern Art Publications in Reprint Ser). (Illus.). 1970. Repr. of 1959 ed. 22.50 (ISBN 0-405-01549-6). Arno.

Vanderpoel, John H. The Human Figure. LC 57-14883. 1958. lib. bdg. 10.50x (ISBN 0-88307-547-4). Gannon.

Wentinck, Charles. Human Figure in Art from Prehistoric Times to the Present Day. Cooper, Eva, tr. from Fr. LC 72-167747. (Illus.). 1971. 18.50 (ISBN 0-87098-037-8). Livingston.

Zaidenberg, Arthur. Anyone Can Draw. 1947. 10.95 (ISBN 0-385-00294-7). Doubleday.

--How to Draw People: A Book for Beginners. (Illus.). (gr. 7-9). 1952. 5.95 (ISBN 0-8149-0445-9). Vanguard.

HUMAN FIGURE IN LITERATURE

Hall, Manly P. Man, the Grand Symbol of the Mysteries. 12.50 (ISBN 0-89314-513-0); pap. 8.95 (ISBN 0-89314-389-8). Philos Res.

HUMAN GENETICS

see also Genetic Counseling; Genetic Psychology; Genetics; Human Chromosomes

Ananthakrishnan, R., et al. Human Biochemical Genetics. LC 73-645. 147p. 1973. text ed. 22.50x (ISBN 0-8422-7095-7). Irvington.

Anderson, Bruce L. Let Us Make Man. (Orig.). 1980. pap. 4.95 (ISBN 0-88270-430-3). Logos.

Armendares, S. & Lisker, R. Human Genetics. (International Congress Ser.: No. 411). 1978. 85.50 (ISBN 0-444-15252-0, Excerpta Medica). Elsevier.

Bajema, Carl J., ed. Natural Selection in Human Populations: The Measurement of Ongoing Genetic Evolution in Contemporary Societies. LC 76-50639. (Illus.). 416p. 1977. Repr. of 1971 ed. lib. bdg. 13.50 (ISBN 0-88275-476-9). Krieger.

Baltimore Conference, 1975. Human Gene Mapping 3: Proceedings. Bergsma, D., ed. (Cytogenetics & Cell Genetics: Vol. 16, Nos. 1-5). (Illus.). 420p. 1976. pap. 66.00 (ISBN 3-8055-2345-9). S Karger.

Bendick, Jeanne. Super People: Who Will They Be? Date not set. 7.95 (ISBN 0-07-004503-8). McGraw.

Bergsma, D., ed. Winnipeg Conference, 4th International Workshop on Human Gene Mapping, Winnipeg, August 1977. (Human Gene Mapping: No. 4). (Illus.). 1979. pap. 49.25 (ISBN 3-8055-3052-8). S Karger.

Bergsma, Daniel, ed. Ethical, Social & Legal Dimensions of Screening for Human Genetic Disease. (Symposia Ser.: Vol. 10, No. 6). 13.95 (ISBN 0-686-10018-2). March of Dimes.

--Human Gene Mapping III. LC 76-2955. (S. Karger Ser: Vol. 12, No. 7). 1976. 42.50 (ISBN 0-686-18084-4). March of Dimes.

--Human Gene Mapping 4, Vol. 4. LC 78-61294. (S. Karger Ser.: Vol. 14, No. 4). 1978. 50.00 (ISBN 0-686-29472-6). March of Dimes.

--An International System for Human Cytogenetic Namenclature. LC 78-61295. (S. Karger Ser.: Vol. 14, No. 8). 1978. 10.00 (ISBN 0-686-29473-4). March of Dimes.

Blank, Robert H. The Political Implications of Human Genetic Technology. (Special Studies in Science, Technology, & Public Policy). 209p. (Orig.). 1981. lib. bdg. 25.25x (ISBN 0-89158-975-9); pap. text ed. 12.00x (ISBN 0-86531-193-5). Westview.

Bond, Austin D. An Experiment in the Teaching of Genetics with Special Reference to the Objectives of General Education. LC 71-176575. (Columbia University. Teachers College. Contributions to Education: No. 797). Repr. of 1940 ed. 17.50 (ISBN 0-404-55797-X). AMS Pr.

Brierly, John. The Thinking Machine. LC 72-14220. 195p. 1973. 10.00 (ISBN 0-8386-1364-0). Fairleigh Dickinson.

Brock, D. J. & Mayo, O., eds. The Biochemical Genetics of Man. 2nd ed. 1979. 76.00 (ISBN 0-12-134760-5). Acad Pr.

Burns, George W. & Tullis, James E. Solutions Manual for Burns: The Science of Genetics-an Inttroduction to Heredity. 4th ed. 1980. 0.95 (ISBN 0-02-317150-2). Macmillan.

Capron, Alexander M., et al, eds. Genetic Counseling: Fact, Values & Norms. LC 79-1736. (Alan R. Liss Ser.: Vol. 15, No. 2). 1979. write for info. (ISBN 0-8451-1025-X). March of Dimes.

Cavalli-Sforza, L. L. Elements of Human Genetics. 2nd ed. LC 76-58969. 1977. pap. text ed. 8.95 (ISBN 0-8053-1874-7). Benjamin-Cummings.

Cavalli-Sforza, L. L. & Bodmer, Walter F. The Genetics of Human Populations. LC 79-120302. (Biology Ser.). (Illus.). 1978. pap. text ed. 21.95x (ISBN 0-7167-1018-8). W H Freeman.

Clarke, C. A. Human Genetics & Medicine. (Studies in Biology Ser). 1971. 13.95 (ISBN 0-312-39935-9). St Martin.

Crispens, Charles G., Jr. Essentials of Medical Genetics. (Illus.). 1971. text ed. 11.50x (ISBN 0-06-140669-4, Harper Medical). Har-Row.

Dausset, Jean & Svejgaard, Arne. HLA & Disease. 332p. 1977. 39.95 (ISBN 0-686-74089-0). Krieger.

Davis, Bernard D. & Flaherty, Patricia, eds. Human Diversity: Its Causes and Social Significance. LC 76-7002. (American Academy of Arts and Sciences Ser.). 192p. 1976. text ed. 16.50 (ISBN 0-88410-047-2). Ballinger Pub.

Desnick, Robert J., ed. Enzyme Therapy in Genetic Diseases: Proceedings, No. 2. 2nd ed. LC 79-48026. (Birth Defects: Original Article Ser.: Vol. XVI, No. 1). 568p. 1980. 64.00 (ISBN 0-8451-1035-7). A R Liss.

Dobzhansky, Theodosius. Mankind Evolving: The Evolution of the Human Species. (Silliman Memorial Lectures Ser.). (Illus.). 1962. 25.00x (ISBN 0-300-00427-3); pap. 6.95x 1964 (ISBN 0-300-00070-7, Y116). Yale U Pr.

Ebon, Martin. Cloning of Man: A Brave New Hope---or Horror? (Orig.). 1978. pap. 1.95 (ISBN 0-451-08526-4, J8526, Sig). NAL.

Edwards, J. H. Human Genetics. LC 77-21582. (Outline Studies in Biology). 80p. 1978. pap. 5.95x (ISBN 0-412-13170-6, Pub. by Chapman & Hall England). Methuen Inc.

Emery. Modern Trends in Human Genetics, Vol. 2. 1975. 54.95 (ISBN 0-407-00028-3). Butterworth.

Epstein, Charles J., ed. Risk, Communication, & Decision Making in Genetic Counseling. LC 79-5120. (Alan R. Liss Ser.: Vol. 15, No. 5c). 1979. 36.00 (ISBN 0-8451-1030-6). March of Dimes.

Fraser, F. Clarke & Nora, James J. Genetics of Man. LC 75-4743. (Illus.). 270p. 1975. text ed. 14.50 (ISBN 0-8121-0484-6). Lea & Febiger.

Friedlaender, Jonathan S. Patterns of Human Variation: The Demography, Genetics, & Phenetics of the Bougainville Islanders. LC 74-17858. (Illus.). 288p. 1975. text ed. 20.00x (ISBN 0-674-65855-8). Harvard U Pr.

Green, M. M. Human Genetics Notes. LC 74-28814. (Illus.). 240p. 1975. text ed. 8.95 (ISBN 0-201-02599-X). A-W.

Gropp, A., ed. Developmental Biology & Pathology. LC 56-49162. (Current Topics in Pathology: Vol. 62). (Illus.). 1976. 52.40 (ISBN 0-387-07881-9). Springer-Verlag.

Halacy, D. S., Jr. Genetic Revolution: Shaping Life for Tomorrow. LC 73-4085. 224p. (YA) 1974. 10.95 (ISBN 0-06-011713-3, HarpT). Har-Row.

Halsey, A. H., ed. Heredity & Environment. LC 77-2530. 1977. 13.95 (ISBN 0-02-913670-9). Free Pr.

Harris, H. & Hopkinson, D. A. Handbook of Enzyme Electrophoresis in Human Genetics: 1977 Supplement. 1978. write for info. (ISBN 0-444-11203-0, North-Holland). Elsevier.

Harris, H., ed. Principles of Human Biochemical Genetics. 2nd rev. ed. LC 75-108280. (Frontiers of Biology Ser.: Vol. 19). 477p. 1975. 78.00 (ISBN 0-444-10012-1, North-Holland); pap. 24.00 (ISBN 0-444-10656-1). Elsevier.

Harris, Harry & Hirschhorn, Kurt, eds. Advances in Human Genetics. Incl. Vol. 1. 339p. 1970 (ISBN 0-306-39601-7); Vol. 2. 317p. 1971 (ISBN 0-306-39602-5); Vol. 3. 446p. 1972 (ISBN 0-306-39603-3); Vol. 4. 410p. 1974 (ISBN 0-306-39604-1); Vol. 5. 385p. 1975 (ISBN 0-306-39605-X); Vol. 6. 382p. 1976 (ISBN 0-306-39606-8); Vol. 7. 261p. 1976 (ISBN 0-306-39607-6); Vol. 8. 445p. 1977 (ISBN 0-306-39608-4); Vol. 9. 393p. 1979 (ISBN 0-306-40219-X); Vol. 10. 380p. 1980 (ISBN 0-306-40386-2). LC 77-84583. (Illus.). Vols 1-8. 37.50 ea. (Plenum Pr); Vol. 9 & 10. 35.00 ea. Plenum Pub.

--Advances in Human Genetics, Vol. 11. 320p. 1981. 35.00 (ISBN 0-306-40688-8). Plenum Pub.

Harrison, G. A. & Boyce, A. J., eds. The Structure of Human Populations. (Illus.). 463p. 1972. 24.00x (ISBN 0-19-857117-8); pap. 15.50x (ISBN 0-19-857120-8). Oxford U Pr.

Hartl, Daniel L. Our Uncertain Heritage: Genetics & Human Diversity. LC 76-30509. 1977. text ed. 20.50 scp (ISBN 0-397-47366-4, HarpC); scp study guide 6.50 (ISBN 0-397-47367-2). Har-Row.

Hauser, Stuart T. & Kasendorf, E. Black & White Identity Formation. rev. ed. 1981. write for info. (ISBN 0-89874-055-X). Krieger.

Hilton, Bruce, et al, eds. Ethical Issues in Human Genetics: Genetic Counseling & the Use of Genetic Knowledge. LC 72-93443. 445p. 1973. 25.00 (ISBN 0-306-30715-4, Plenum Pr). Plenum Pub.

Hoagland, Mahlon B. The Roots of Life: A Layman's Guide to Genes, Evolution, & the Ways of Cells. 1978. 7.95 (ISBN 0-395-25811-1). HM.

International Symposium on Inborn Errors of Metabolism in Man, Tel Aviv, 1977. Abstracts. Sperling, O., ed. (Human Heredity: Vol. 27, No. 3). 1977. 22.25 (ISBN 3-8055-2710-1). S Karger.

International Symposium on Inborn Errors of Metabolism in Man, Tel Aviv, June 1977. Proceedings: Part I. Beckman, L. & Hauge, M., eds. (Monographs in Human Genetics: Vol. 9). (Illus.). 1978. 53.50 (ISBN 3-8055-2836-1). S Karger.

--Proceedings: Part II. Beckman, L. & Hauge, M., eds. (Monographs in Human Genetics: Vol. 10). (Illus.). 1978. 47.50 (ISBN 3-8055-2835-3). S Karger.

Jewett, Frances G. The Next Generation: A Study in the Physiology of Inheritance. 1914. 15.00 (ISBN 0-8274-4224-6). R West.

Johnston, Francis E. Microevolution of Human Populations. (Illus.). 160p. 1973. pap. 9.95 ref. ed. (ISBN 0-13-581512-6). P-H.

Kaplan, Arnold R. Human Behavior Genetics. (Illus.). 496p. 1976. 85.75 (ISBN 0-398-03378-1). C C Thomas.

Karlin, S. Equilibrium Behavior of Population Genetic Models with Non-Random Mating. 1969. 44.00x (ISBN 0-677-61910-3). Gordon.

Karlsson, John L. Inheritance of Creative Intelligence. LC 77-19297. 1978. text ed. 18.95x (ISBN 0-88229-391-5); pap. text ed. 9.95x (ISBN 0-88229-607-8). Nelson-Hall.

Lenz, Widukind. Medical Genetics. Lanzl, Elizabeth F., tr. LC 63-11399. (Illus.). 1963. 10.00x (ISBN 0-226-47212-4). U of Chicago Pr.

Levitan, Max & Montagu, Ashley. Textbook of Human Genetics. 2nd ed. (Illus.). 1977. text ed. 22.95x (ISBN 0-19-502101-0). Oxford U Pr.

Lisker, Ruben, ed. Human Genetics: Proceedings of the 5th International Congress of Human Genetics. (Intl Congress Ser.: No. 397). 1976. 27.00 (ISBN 0-444-15236-9, Excerpta Medica). Elsevier.

Ludmerer, Kenneth M. Genetics & American Society. LC 72-4227. 224p. 1972. 16.00x (ISBN 0-8018-1357-3). Johns Hopkins.

McKusick, Victor. Human Genetics. 2nd ed. (Foundations of Modern Genetics Ser). 1969. pap. 11.95x ref. ed. (ISBN 0-13-445106-6). P-H.

McKusick, Victor A. Mendelian Inheritance in Man: Catalogs of Autosomal Dominant, Autosomal Recessive, & X-Linked Phenotypes. 5th ed. LC 77-17248. (Illus.). 918p. 1975. 29.50x (ISBN 0-8018-2087-1). Johns Hopkins.

Mendlewicz, J., ed. Genetics & Psychopharmacology. (Modern Problems of Pharmacopsychiatry: Vol. 10). viii, 132p. 1975. 34.75 (ISBN 3-8055-2117-0). S Karger.

Mertens, Thomas R. Human Genetics: Readings on the Implications of Genetic Engineering. LC 74-30471. 320p. 1975. text ed. 12.50x (ISBN 0-471-59628-0). Wiley.

Ohta, T. Evolution & Variation of Multigene Families. (Lecture Notes in Biomathematics: Vol. 37). 131p. 1980. pap. 9.80 (ISBN 0-387-09998-0). Springer-Verlag.

Osborne, R. T., et al, eds. Human Variation: The Biopsychology of Age, Race, & Sex. 1978. 28.00 (ISBN 0-12-529050-0). Acad Pr.

Packard, Vance. The People Shapers. 1977. 12.50 (ISBN 0-316-68750-2). Little.

Ramsey, Paul. Fabricated Man: The Ethics of Genetic Control. LC 78-123395. 1970. 15.00x (ISBN 0-300-01373-6); pap. 3.95x (ISBN 0-300-01374-4, YF6). Yale U Pr.

Reed, Sheldon, ed. Counseling in Medical Genetics. LC 80-22266. 246p. 1980. 26.00 (ISBN 0-8451-0208-7). A R Liss.

Reid, Russell M. Human Population Genetics. LC 77-74167. 1978. pap. 2.95x (ISBN 0-8087-1844-4). Burgess.

Rogers, F. E. Illustrations in Applied Network Theory. LC 72-75949. 1973. 17.50x (ISBN 0-8448-0165-8). Crane-Russak Co.

Rothwell, Norman V. Human Genetics. (Illus.). 1977. text ed. 20.95 (ISBN 0-13-445080-9). P-H.

Rotterdam Conference, 1974. Human Gene Mapping 2: Proceedings. Bergsma, D., ed. (Cytogenetics & Cell Genetics: Vol. 14, Nos. 3-6). (Illus.). 332p. 1975. pap. 47.50 (ISBN 3-8055-2251-7). S Karger.

Rotterdam Conference, 2nd 1974. Human Gene Mapping. Bergsma, Daniel, ed. LC 75-8204. (S. Karger Ser.: Vol. 11, No. 3). 1976. 30.50 (ISBN 0-686-14571-2). March of Dimes.

Scheinfeld, Amram. Heredity in Humans. rev. ed. (Illus.). 1972. 9.95 (ISBN 0-397-00820-1, JBL-Med-Nursing). Har-Row.

Shine, I. Serendipity in St. Helena. 1970. 34.00 (ISBN 0-08-012794-0). Pergamon.

Singer, Sam. Human Genetics: An Introduction to the Principles of Heredity. LC 78-82. (Biology Ser.). (Illus.). 1978. pap. text ed. 7.95x (ISBN 0-7167-0054-9); tchr's resource bk. 2.95x (ISBN 0-686-77350-0). W H Freeman.

Steinberg, Arthur G. & Cook, Charles E. The Distribution of the Human Immunoglobulin Allotypes. (Illus.). 272p. 1981. text ed. 69.50x (ISBN 0-19-261181-X). Oxford U Pr.

Stern, Curt. Principles of Human Genetics. 3rd ed. LC 72-4357. (Illus.). 1973. text ed. 25.95x (ISBN 0-7167-0597-4); answers to problems avail. W H Freeman.

Stockton, William. Altered Destinies. LC 78-73196. 1979. 9.95 (ISBN 0-385-14011-8). Doubleday.

Svejgaard, A. The HLA System: An Introductory Survey. Beckman, L., ed. Hauge, M. (Monographs in Human Genetics: Vol. 7). (Illus.). 120p. 1976. 22.75 (ISBN 3-8055-2304-1). S Karger.

Svejgaard, A., et al. The HLA System: An Introductory Survey. 2nd ed. (Monographs in Human Genetics: Vol. 7). (Illus.). 1979. pap. 21.75 (ISBN 3-8055-3049-8). S Karger.

Temtamy, Samia A. & McKusick, Victor A. The Genetics of Hand Malformation. LC 77-27829. (Birth Defects Original Article Ser.: Vol. 14, No. 3). 620p. 1978. 104.00 (ISBN 0-8451-1017-9). A R Liss.

Thompson, E. A. Human Evolutionary Trees. LC 75-2739. (Illus.). 160p. (Orig.). 1975. pap. 23.95x (ISBN 0-521-09945-5). Cambridge U Pr.

Underwood, Jane H. Human Variation & Human Microevolution. (Illus.). 1979. pap. 10.95 (ISBN 0-13-447573-9). P-H.

Vogel, F. & Motulsky, A. G. Human Genetics: Problems & Approaches. (Illus.). 1979. 52.00 (ISBN 0-387-09459-8). Springer-Verlag.

WHO Scientific Group, Geneva, 1968. Genetic Disorders-Prevention, Treatment & Rehabilitation: Report. (Technical Report Ser.: No. 497). (Also avail. in French, Russian & Spanish). 1972. pap. 1.40 (ISBN 92-4-120497-4). World Health.

WHO Scientific Group. Geneva, 1970. Methodology for Family Studies of Genetic Factors: Report. (Technical Report Ser.: No. 466). (Also avail. in French, Russian & Spanish). 1971. pap. 2.00 (ISBN 92-4-120466-4). World Health.

Williams, Roger J. Biochemical Individuality: The Basis for the Genetotrophic Concept. LC 56-12578. (Illus.). 1969. pap. 4.95x (ISBN 0-292-70022-9). U of Tex Pr.

Yunis, Jorge J., ed. Human Chromosome Methodology. 2nd ed. 1974. 38.50 (ISBN 0-12-775155-6). Acad Pr.

HUMAN GENETICS–MORAL AND RELIGIOUS ASPECTS

Birch, C. & Albrecht, P., eds. Genetics & the Quality of Life. 1976. text ed. 32.00 (ISBN 0-08-018210-0); pap. text ed. 16.50 (ISBN 0-08-019861-9). Pergamon.

Hilton, Bruce, et al, eds. Ethical Issues in Human Genetics: Genetic Counseling & the Use of Genetic Knowledge. LC 72-93443. 445p. 1973. 25.00 (ISBN 0-306-30715-4, Plenum Pr). Plenum Pub.

Langone, John. Human Engineering: Marvel or Menace? (gr. 7 up). 1978. 6.95 (ISBN 0-316-51427-6). Little.

Mertens, Thomas R. Human Genetics: Readings on the Implications of Genetic Engineering. LC 74-30471. 320p. 1975. text ed. 12.50x (ISBN 0-471-59628-0). Wiley.

HUMAN GENETICS–SOCIAL ASPECTS

Baer, Adela S. Heredity & Society: Readings in Social Genetics. 2nd ed. 352p. 1977. pap. text ed. 10.95 (ISBN 0-02-305160-4, 30516). Macmillan.

Birch, C. & Albrecht, P., eds. Genetics & the Quality of Life. 1976. text ed. 32.00 (ISBN 0-08-018210-0); pap. text ed. 16.50 (ISBN 0-08-019861-9). Pergamon.

Bodmer, W. F. & Cavalli-Sforza, L. L. Genetics, Evolution, & Man. LC 75-33990. (Illus.). 1976. 23.95x (ISBN 0-7167-0573-7). W H Freeman.

Bresler, J., ed. Genetics & Society. LC 72-2650. 1973. pap. text ed. 7.95 (ISBN 0-201-00600-6). A-W.

Halacy, D. S., Jr. Genetic Revolution: Shaping Life for Tomorrow. LC 73-4085. 224p. (YA) 1974. 10.95 (ISBN 0-06-011713-3, HarpT). Har-Row.

Hilton, Bruce, et al, eds. Ethical Issues in Human Genetics: Genetic Counseling & the Use of Genetic Knowledge. LC 72-93443. 445p. 1973. 25.00 (ISBN 0-306-30715-4, Plenum Pr). Plenum Pub.

Lerner, I. Michael & Libby, William J. Heredity, Evolution, & Society. 2nd ed. LC 75-33968. (Illus.). 1976. text ed. 22.95x (ISBN 0-7167-0576-1); tchr's manual avail. W H Freeman.

Mertens, Thomas & Robinson, Sandra K., eds. Human Genetics & Social Problems. 212p. 1973. text ed. 29.00x (ISBN 0-8422-5090-5); pap. text ed. 9.95x (ISBN 0-8422-0230-7). Irvington.

Mertens, Thomas R. Human Genetics: Readings on the Implications of Genetic Engineering. LC 74-30471. 320p. 1975. text ed. 12.50x (ISBN 0-471-59628-0). Wiley.

Muller, Hermann J. Man's Future Birthright: Essays on Science & Humanity. Carlson, Elof A., ed. LC 79-171215. 200p. 1973. 12.00 (ISBN 0-87395-097-6); microfiche 12.00 (ISBN 0-87395-197-2). State U NY Pr.

Newmann, Sr. Marguerite. The Tricentennial People: Human Applications of the New Genetics. 1978. pap. text ed. 4.75 (ISBN 0-8138-1650-5). Iowa St U Pr.

Reilly, Philip. Genetics, Law, & Social Policy. 1977. 15.00x (ISBN 0-674-34657-2). Harvard U Pr.

Smith, Anthony. The Human Pedigree. (McGraw-Hill Paperback). 320p. 1976. pap. 3.95 (ISBN 0-07-059045-1, SP). McGraw.

Symposium of the Birth Defects Institute of the New York State Dept. of Health, Second, October, 1971. Heredity & Society. Porter, Ian H., et al, eds. 1973. 30.00 (ISBN 0-12-562850-1). Acad Pr.

HUMAN GEOGRAPHY

see Anthropo-Geography

HUMAN IN VITRO FERTILIZATION

see Fertilization in Vitro, Human

HUMAN INFORMATION PROCESSING

Bott, Ross, et al. Human Information Processing: Study Guide. 2nd ed. Lindsay, Norman, ed. 1977. 6.95 (ISBN 0-12-450962-2). Acad Pr.

Cassel, Don & Jackson, Martin. Introduction to Computers & Information Processing: Language Free Editon. 1981. text ed. 17.95 (ISBN 0-8359-3155-2); study guide 7.95 (ISBN 0-8359-3157-9); instrs'. manual avail. (ISBN 0-8359-3156-0). Reston.

Conrad & Magar, eds. Physical Principles of Neuronal & Organismic Behavior. 1973. 46.25x (ISBN 0-677-12290-X). Gordon.

Dodd & White. Cognition: Mental Structures & Processes. 500p. 1980. text ed. 18.95 (ISBN 0-205-06930-4, 7969309). Allyn.

Farnham-Diggory, Sylvia, ed. Information Processing in Children. 1972. 23.50 (ISBN 0-12-249550-0). Acad Pr.

Goldberg, Robert & Lorin, Harold. The Economics of Information Processing: Vol. 1, Management Perspectives. 300p. 1981. 35.00 (ISBN 0-471-09206-1, Pub. by Wiley Interscience). Wiley.

Hamilton, Vernon & Warburton, David M. Human Stress & Cognition: An Information Processing Approach. LC 78-31691. 1979. 68.25x (ISBN 0-471-27572-7, Pub. by Wiley-Interscience). Wiley.

Howell, William C. & Fleishman, Edwin A., eds. Information Processing & Decision Making. (Human Performance & Productivity Ser.: Vol. 2). 192p. 1981. text ed. 19.95 (ISBN 0-89859-090-6). L Erlbaum Assocs.

Kantowitz, Barry H., ed. Human Information Processing: Tutorials in Performance & Cognition. LC 74-19028. (Experimental Psychology Ser.). 365p. 1974. 19.95 (ISBN 0-470-45674-4). Halsted Pr.

Kardos, L., ed. Problems of Information Processing & Perceptual Organization. 1978. casebound 7.00 (ISBN 0-9960009-6-8, 99600-096-8, Pub. by Kiado Hungary). Heyden.

Lindsay, Peter H. & Norman, Donald A. Human Information Processing: An Introduction to Psychology. 2nd ed. 1977. 18.95 (ISBN 0-12-450960-6); test bklet. avail. Acad Pr.

Madey, J., ed. Information Conference on Information Processing: Ifip-Infopol-Warsaw, 1976. 1977. 61.00 (ISBN 0-7204-0555-6, North-Holland). Elsevier.

Marteniuk, R. G. Information Processing in Motor Skills. LC 75-43982. 1976. text ed. 20.95 (ISBN 0-03-006091-5, HoltC). HR&W.

Newell, Allen & Simon, Herbert. Human Problem Solving. LC 79-152528. (Illus.). 1972. 28.95 (ISBN 0-13-445403-0). P-H.

Ornstein, Robert E. The Psychology of Consciousness. 1975. pap. 2.95 (ISBN 0-14-021679-0, Pelican). Penguin.

Pavlidis, Theo. Algorithms for Graphics & Image Processing. (Illus.). 1981. text ed. 24.95 (ISBN 0-914894-65-X). Computer Sci.

Pick, Herbert L., Jr. & Saltzman, Elliot, eds. Modes of Perceiving & Processing Information. LC 77-21025. 1977. 14.95 (ISBN 0-470-99342-1). Halsted Pr.

Powers, William T. Behavior: The Control of Perception. LC 73-75697. 320p. 1973. text ed. 19.95x (ISBN 0-202-25113-6). Aldine Pub.

Reed, Stephen K. Psychological Processes in Pattern Recognition. (Cognition & Perception Ser.). 1973. 31.000 (ISBN 0-12-585350-5). Acad Pr.

Simon. Models of Thought. LC 78-31744. 1979. text ed. 50.00 (ISBN 0-300-02347-2); pap. 17.95x (ISBN 0-300-02432-0, Y-352). Yale U Pr.

Solso, Robert L, ed. Information Processing & Cognition: The Loyola Symposium. LC 75-14324. 438p. 1975. 19.95 (ISBN 0-470-81230-3). Halsted Pr.

Underwood, Geoffrey, ed. Strategies of Information Processing. 1979. 58.50 (ISBN 0-12-708950-0). Acad Pr.

Van Der Heijden, A. H. Short-Term Visual Information Forgetting. (International Library of Psychology). 224p. 1981. price not set (ISBN 0-7100-0851-1). Routledge & Kegan.

Vdinsky, B. Flavian, et al. Evaluation Resource Handbook: Gathering, Analyzing, Reporting Data. LC 81-65479. 1981. 9.95 (ISBN 0-912736-24-0). EDITS Pubs.

HUMAN INTERACTION

see Social Interaction

HUMAN LEOPARDS

see Leopard Men

HUMAN LOCOMOTION

see also Action in Art; Man–Attitude and Movement; Running; Swimming; Walking

Davis, Martha, ed. Body Movement: Perspectives in Research, 10 vols. (Illus.). 1975. Set. 84.00x (ISBN 0-405-06197-8). Arno.

Dickinson, John. Proprioceptive Control of Human Movement. (Illus.). 221p. 1976. text ed. 10.50x (ISBN 0-86019-002-1). Princeton Bk Co.

Hay, James G. & Reid, J. Gavin. The Anatomical & Mechanical Bases of Human Motion. (Illus.). 432p. 1982. text ed. 17.95 (ISBN 0-13-035139-3). P-H.

Herman, Robert H., et al, eds. Neural Control of Locomotion. LC 76-18949. (Advances in Behavioral Biology: Vol. 18). 822p. 1976. 55.00 (ISBN 0-306-37918-X, Plenum Pr). Plenum Pub.

Higgins, Joseph R. Human Movement: An Integrated Approach. LC 76-57714. (Illus.). 1977. pap. text ed. 9.45 (ISBN 0-8016-2181-X). Mosby.

Levangie, Pamela & Norkin, Cynthia. Structure & Function: Elements of Movement. (Illus.). 550p. 1982. price not set (ISBN 0-8036-5586-X). Davis Co.

Muybridge, Eadweard. Muybridge's Complete Human & Animal Locomotion: All 781 Plates from the 1887 Animal Locomotion, 3 vols. Incl. Vol. 1 (ISBN 0-486-23792-3); Vol. 2 (ISBN 0-486-23793-1); Vol. 3 (ISBN 0-486-23794-X). (Illus.). 1979. Repr. of 1887 ed. Set. 33.33 ea. (ISBN 0-685-92659-1). Dover.

Stein, R. B., et al, eds. Control of Posture & Locomotion. LC 73-19634. (Advances in Behavioral Biology Ser.: Vol. 7). 635p. 1974. 45.00 (ISBN 0-306-37907-4, Plenum Pr). Plenum Pub.

HUMAN MAGNETISM

see Animal Magnetism

HUMAN MECHANICS

see also Human Locomotion; Kinesiology

Barham, Jerry N. & Wooten, Edna L. Structural Kinesiology. (Illus.). 448p. 1973. text ed. 19.95 (ISBN 0-02-306000-X, 30600). Macmillan.

Barrow, Harold M. Man & Movement: Principles of Physical Education. 2nd ed. LC 77-22989. 396p. 1977. text ed. 14.00 (ISBN 0-8121-0599-0). Lea & Febiger.

Bleustein, Jeffrey L., ed. Mechanics & Sport AMD, Vol. 4. 318p. 1973. pap. text ed. 25.00 (ISBN 0-685-41497-3, H00007). ASME.

Bootzin, David & Muffley, Harry C., eds. Biomechanics. LC 69-16519. 185p. 1969. 25.00 (ISBN 0-306-30392-2, Plenum Pr). Plenum Pub.

Cerquiglini, S., et al, eds. Biomechanics III. (Illus.). 1973. 49.50 (ISBN 0-8391-0531-2). Univ Park.

Cooper, John M. & Glassow, Ruth B. Kinesiology. rev. 4th ed. LC 75-33991. (Illus.). 1976. 13.95 (ISBN 0-8016-1048-6). Mosby.

Davis, Martha, ed. Anthropological Perspectives of Movement: An Original Anthology. LC 74-9162. (Body Movement Perspectives in Research). (Illus.). 203p. 1975. Repr. text ed. 19.00x (ISBN 0-405-06201-X). Arno.

Dickinson, John. Proprioceptive Control of Human Movement. 209p. 1980. 12.00x (ISBN 0-86019-002-1, Pub. by Kimpton). State Mutual Bk.

Dyson, Geoffrey H. The Mechanics of Athletics. 7th rev. ed. LC 77-3430. (Illus.). 1978. text ed. 28.50x (ISBN 0-8419-0309-3); pap. text ed. 16.00x (ISBN 0-8419-0310-7). Holmes & Meier.

Esch, Dortha & Lepley, Marvin. Musculoskeletal Function: An Anatomy & Kinesiology Laboratory Manual. LC 73-93577. (Illus.). 112p. 1974. text ed. 6.50x (ISBN 0-8166-0716-8). U of Minn Pr.

Fenton, Jack V. Practical Movement Control. LC 73-1572. Orig. Title: Choice of Habit. 1973. 7.95 (ISBN 0-8238-0145-4). Plays.

Fink, B. Raymond & Demarest, Robert J. Laryngeal Biomechanics. LC 77-26937. (Commonwealth Fund Ser.). 1978. 30.00x (ISBN 0-674-51085-2). Harvard U Pr.

Fisher, John. Body Magic. 1979. 10.00 (ISBN 0-8128-2330-3). Stein & Day.

Frankel, Victor H. & Nordin, Margareta, eds. Basic Biomechanics of the Skeletal System. LC 79-24593. (Illus.). 303p. 1980. text ed. 20.00 (ISBN 0-8121-0708-X). Lea & Febiger.

Ghista, D. N. & Roaf, R., eds. Orthopaedic Mechanics: Procedures & Devices. 1979. 51.50 (ISBN 0-12-281650-1). Acad Pr.

Gowitzke, Barbara & Milner, Morris. Understanding the Scientific Bases of Human Movement. 2nd ed. (Illus.). 376p. 1980. pap. 28.50 (ISBN 0-683-03592-4). Williams & Wilkins.

Gozna, Eric R. & Harrington, Ian J. Biomechanics of Musculoskeletal Injury. 150p. 1981. lib. bdg. 19.95 (ISBN 0-683-03728-5). Williams & Wilkins.

Granit, Ragnar. Basis of Motor Control. 1970. 55.00 (ISBN 0-12-295350-9). Acad Pr.

Grieve, D. W. Techniques for the Analysis of Human Movement. 177p. 1980. 18.00x (ISBN 0-86019-006-4, Pub. by Kimpton). State Mutual Bk.

Hay, James G. & Reid, J. Gavin. The Anatomical & Mechanical Bases of Human Motion. (Illus.). 432p. 1982. text ed. 17.95 (ISBN 0-13-035139-3). P-H.

Hertel, Heinrich. Structure, Form & Movement. 264p. 1966. 21.50 (ISBN 0-442-15057-1, Pub. by Van Nos Reinhold). Krieger.

Higgins, Joseph R. Human Movement: An Integrated Approach. LC 76-57714. (Illus.). 1977. pap. text ed. 9.45 (ISBN 0-8016-2181-X). Mosby.

Kelley, David L. Kinesiology: Fundamentals of Motion Description. LC 79-144098. (Physical Education Ser). 1971. text ed. 18.50 (ISBN 0-13-516260-2). P-H.

Maquet, P. G. Biomechanics of the Knee: With Application to the Pathogenesis & the Surgical Treatment of Osteoarthritis. (Illus.). 1976. 91.60 (ISBN 0-387-07882-7). Springer-Verlag.

Margaria, R. Biomechanics & Energetics of Muscular Exercise. (Illus.). 1976. text ed. 19.50x (ISBN 0-19-857397-9). Oxford U Pr.

Maser, Jack D., ed. Efferent Organization & the Integration of Behavior. 1973. 43.00 (ISBN 0-12-476950-0). Acad Pr.

Miller, Doris I. & Nelson, Richard C. Biomechanics of Sport. LC 73-3173. (Health Education, Physical Education & Recreation Ser). (Illus.). 265p. 1973. text ed. 12.00 (ISBN 0-8121-0431-5). Lea & Febiger.

Penrod, James. Movement for the Performing Artist. LC 73-93344. Orig. Title: Stage Movement. 194p. 1974. pap. text ed. 8.95 (ISBN 0-87484-234-4). Mayfield Pub.

Radin, E. L., et al. Practical Biomechanics for the Orthopedic Surgeon. 168p. 1979. 24.50 (ISBN 0-686-74422-5, Pub. by Wiley Med). Wiley.

Sharkey, Brian J. Physiology & Physical Activity. (Scientific Perspectives of Physical Education Ser.). 220p. 1975. pap. text ed. 10.95 scp (ISBN 0-06-045965-4, HarpC). Har-Row.

Swanson, S. A. & Freeman, M. A., eds. The Scientific Basis of Joint Replacement. LC 76-51524. 182p. 1977. 45.00 (ISBN 0-471-03012-0, Pub. by Wiley Medical). Wiley.

Sweigard, Lulu E. Human Movement Potential: Its Ideokinetic Facilitation. 352p. 1974. text ed. 18.50 scp (ISBN 0-06-046521-2, HarpC). Har-Row.

Todd, Mabel E. Thinking Body: A Study of Balancing Forces of Dynamic Man. LC 68-28048. (Illus.). 1968. pap. 8.25 (ISBN 0-87127-014-5). Dance Horiz.

Vredenbregt, J. & Wartenweiler, J., eds. Biomechanics II. (Medicine & Sport Ser.: Vol. 6). (Illus.). 1971. 29.50 (ISBN 0-8391-0530-4, Pub by Karger). Univ Park.

Walker, Peter S. Human Joints & Their Artificial Replacements. (Illus.). 528p. 1978. 64.75 (ISBN 0-398-03615-2). C C Thomas.

Whiting, H. T. & Whiting, Marilyn G., eds. Journal of Human Movement Studies. 1980. 35.00x (ISBN 0-686-71771-6, Pub. by Kimpton). State Mutual Bk.

Yahr, Melvin D. & Purpura, Dominick P., eds. Neurophysiological Basis of Normal & Abnormal Motor Activities. LC 67-28247. 512p. 1967. 37.50 (ISBN 0-911216-04-9). Raven.

HUMAN OPERATORS (SYSTEMS ENGINEERING)

see Man-Machine Systems

HUMAN PALEONTOLOGY

see Fossil Man

HUMAN PARASITOLOGY

see Medical Parasitology

HUMAN RELATIONS

see Interpersonal Relations

HUMAN RESOURCE DEVELOPMENT

see Manpower Policy

HUMAN RIGHTS

see Civil Rights; Civil Rights (International Law)

HUMAN SACRIFICE

see Sacrifice, Human

HUMAN SCIENCE

see Anthroposophy

HUMAN SUBSYSTEMS (SYSTEMS ENGINEERING)

see Man-Machine Systems

HUMANE SOCIETIES

see Animals, Treatment Of; Child Welfare

HUMANE TREATMENT OF ANIMALS

see Animals, Treatment of

HUMANISM

see also Civilization; Classical Education; Classical Philology; Culture; Hellenism; Humanistic Ethics; Humanities; Learning and Scholarship; Philosophical Anthropology; Renaissance

Abel, Reuben E., ed. Humanistic Pragmatism: The Philosophy of F. C. S. Schiller. (Orig.). 1966. pap. text ed. 4.95 (ISBN 0-02-900120-X). Free Pr.

Abelard, Peter. Historia Calamitatum: Story of My Misfortunes. 59.95 (ISBN 0-8490-0305-9). Gordon Pr.

Alexander, Edward. Matthew Arnold & John Stuart Mill. LC 65-14321. 313p. 1965. 16.00x (ISBN 0-231-02786-9). Columbia U Pr.

Anderson, Walt. Politics & the New Humanism. LC 72-96311. 176p. 1973. pap. text ed. 8.95 (ISBN 0-87620-661-5). Goodyear.

Baker, Herschel. The Wars of Truth: Studies in the Decay of Christian Humanism in the Earlier 17th Century. 8.00 (ISBN 0-8446-0472-0). Peter Smith.

Baron, Hans. Crisis of the Early Italian Renaissance: Civic Humanism & Republican Liberty in an Age of Classicism & Tyranny. rev. ed. 1966. 30.00 (ISBN 0-691-05114-3); pap. 9.95 (ISBN 0-691-00752-7). Princeton U Pr.

--From Petrarch to Leonardo Bruni: Studies in Humanistic & Political Literature. LC 68-16686. 1968. 12.00x (ISBN 0-226-03801-7); pap. 3.25 (ISBN 0-226-03802-5). U of Chicago Pr.

Berkowitz, William. Conversations with... LC 75-5487. 300p. 1976. 8.95 (ISBN 0-8197-0380-X). Bloch.

Blackham, H. J. Humanism. 2nd rev. ed. LC 75-30604. 225p. 1976. 11.25x (ISBN 0-8002-0162-0). Intl Pubns Serv.

Blackham, H. J., et al. Objections to Humanism. LC 73-16796. 128p. 1974. Repr. of 1963 ed. lib. bdg. 15.00x (ISBN 0-8371-7235-7, BLOH). Greenwood.

Boase, Alan M. Fortunes of Montaigne: A History of the Essays in France, 1580-1669. 1970. Repr. lib. bdg. 25.00 (ISBN 0-374-90725-0). Octagon.

Braunthal, Alfred. Salvation & the Perfect Society: The Eternal Quest. LC 79-4705. 1979. lib. bdg. 25.00x (ISBN 0-87023-273-8). U of Mass Pr.

Breen, Quirinus. John Calvin: A Study in French Humanism. 2nd ed. 1968. 16.50 (ISBN 0-208-00463-7, Archon). Shoe String.

Brown, Harcourt, ed. Science & the Creative Spirit: Essays on Humanistic Aspects of Science. LC 58-1232. 1971. 15.00x (ISBN 0-8020-7012-4). U of Toronto Pr.
Brown, Patricia. Humanism in Education. 70p. 1981. pap. 2.00 (ISBN 0-913098-39-6). Myrin Institute.
Burnet, John. Essays & Addresses. facs. ed. LC 68-54335. (Essay Index Reprint Ser). 1968. Repr. of 1930 ed. 16.00 (ISBN 0-8369-0265-3). Arno.
Bush, Douglas. Renaissance & English Humanism. LC 40-11006. 1939. pap. 4.00 (ISBN 0-8020-6008-0). U of Toronto Pr.
Cantore, Enrico. Scientific Man: The Humanistic Significance of Science. LC 76-28439. 1977. 20.00 (ISBN 0-917392-01-9). Intl Schol Bk Serv.
Champigny, Robert. Humanism & Human Racism: A Critical Study of Essays by Sartre & Camus. LC 77-189701. (De Proprietatibus Litterarum, Ser. Practica: No. 41). 82p. (Orig.). 1973. pap. text ed. 16.75x (ISBN 90-2792-373-6). Mouton.
Coates, W. H. & White, H. V. Ordeal of Liberal Humanism: An Intellectual History of Western Europe Since the French Revolution, Vol 2. 1969. pap. text ed. 10.50 (ISBN 0-07-011464-1, C). McGraw.
Cohen, Arthur A., et al, eds. Humanistic Education & Western Civilization: Essays for Robert M. Hutchins. LC 72-13226. (Essay Index Reprint Ser.). Repr. of 1964 ed. 13.00 (ISBN 0-8369-8150-2). Arno.
Dobson, Russell, et al. Staff Development: A Humanistic Approach. LC 80-67254. 175p. 1980. pap. text ed. 8.50 (ISBN 0-8191-1131-7). U Pr of Amer.
Doran, Madeleine. Something About Swans: Essays by Madeleine Doran. 134p. 1973. 5.00 (ISBN 0-299-06170-1). U of Wis Pr.
Drerup, Engelbert. Der Humanismus in Seiner Geschichte. 1934. pap. 9.50 (ISBN 0-384-12815-7). Johnson Repr.
Eaker, Helen L., ed. Giovanni Di Conversino Da Ravenna, Dragmalogia De Eligibili Vite Genere. LC 75-39111. 296p. 1980. 24.50 (ISBN 0-8387-1897-3). Bucknell U Pr.
Ehrenfeld, David. The Arrogance of Humanism. (A Galaxy Bk.: No. 637). 304p. 1981. pap. 5.95 (ISBN 0-19-502890-2). Oxford U Pr.
Einstein, Albert. Essays in Humanism. 0.95 (ISBN 0-8022-0435-X). Philos Lib.
Emerton, Ephraim. Humanism & Tyranny: Studies in the Italian Trecento. 7.50 (ISBN 0-8446-5871-5). Peter Smith.
Fairfield, Roy P., ed. Humanistic Frontiers in American Education. LC 79-166138. 260p. 1971. 7.95 (ISBN 0-87975-054-5). Prometheus Bks.
Fiero, Gloria K. The Humanistic Tradition: Chapters in the History of Culture to 1650. LC 81-40631. (Illus.). 510p. (Orig.). 1981. lib. bdg. 27.25 (ISBN 0-8191-1755-2); pap. text ed. 17.75 (ISBN 0-8191-1756-0). U Pr of Amer.
Flynn, James R. Humanism & Ideology: An Aristotelian View. (Studies in Ethics & the Philosophy of Religion). 1973. 14.00x (ISBN 0-7100-7442-5). Routledge & Kegan.
--Humanism & Ideology: An Aristotelian View. 1978. pap. 6.00 (ISBN 0-7100-8907-4). Routledge & Kegan.
Foerster, Norman. Toward Standards. LC 66-13476. 1928. 9.00x (ISBN 0-8196-0166-7). Biblo.
Foerster, Norman, ed. Humanism & America: Essays on the Outlook of Modern Civilization. LC 67-27598. 1967. Repr. of 1930 ed. 12.50 (ISBN 0-8046-0154-2). Kennikat.
Gilmore, David B. The Essence & the Vocation of Man. (Illus.). 123p. 1980. deluxe ed. 37.50 (ISBN 0-89920-009-5). Am Inst Psych.
Gilmore, Myron P. World of Humanism, 1453-1517. (Rise of Modern Europe Ser). pap. 4.95x (ISBN 0-06-133003-5, TB 3003, Torch). Har-Row.
Goode, Stephen H., ed. American Humanities Index for 1980. 465p. 1981. 89.50 (ISBN 0-87875-209-9). Whitston Pub.
Goodsell, Willystine. Conflict of Naturalism & Humanism. LC 74-176814. (Columbia University. Teachers College. Contributions to Education: No. 33). Repr. of 1910 ed. 17.50 (ISBN 0-404-55033-9). AMS Pr.
Gragg, Florence A., ed. The Latin Writings of the Italian Humanists. (College Classical Ser.). xxxvi, 434p. (gr. 11-12). Date not set. pap. text ed. 17.50x (ISBN 0-89241-110-4). Caratzas Bros.
Grassi, Ernesto. Rhetoric As Philosophy: The Humanist Tradition. LC 79-25276. 1980. text ed. 14.95x (ISBN 0-271-00256-5). Pa St U Pr.
Gundersheimer, Werner L. French Humanism: 1470-1600. 6.75 (ISBN 0-8446-4749-7). Peter Smith.
Hadas, Moses. The Greek Ideal & Its Survival. 1960. lib. bdg. 11.50x (ISBN 0-88307-122-3). Gannon.
--Humanism: The Greek Ideal & Its Survival. 6.25 (ISBN 0-8446-4011-5). Peter Smith.
Hamburgh, Max. The New Humanism. LC 75-3783. 210p. 1975. 9.75 (ISBN 0-8022-2167-X). Philos Lib.
Hassan, Ihab, ed. Liberations: New Essays on the Humanities in Revolution. LC 77-142729. 1971. (Pub. by Wesleyan U Pr); pap. 5.95 (ISBN 0-8195-6025-1). Columbia U Pr.
Heller, Agnes. Renaissance Man. Allen, Richard E., tr. 1978. 45.00x (ISBN 0-7100-8881-7). Routledge & Kegan.
Hirsch, Rudolf. The Printed Word: Its Impact & Diffusion (Primarily in the 15th & 16th Centuries) 338p. 1980. 70.00x (ISBN 0-86078-026-0, Pub. by Variorum England). State Mutual Bk.
Hodges, Donald C. Socialist Humanism. LC 73-96983. 384p. 1974. 19.75 (ISBN 0-87527-042-5). Fireside Bks.
--Socialist Humanism: The Outcome of Classical European Morality. LC 73-96983. 384p. 1974. 19.75 (ISBN 0-87527-042-5). Green.
Horoscz, William. The Promise & Peril of Human Purpose. LC 71-93793. 350p. 1970. 15.00 (ISBN 0-87527-018-2). Fireside Bks.
Hulme, T. E. Speculations: Essays on Humanism & the Philosophy of Art. Read, Herbert, ed. (International Library of Philosophy, Psychology & Scientific Method Ser.). 1977. Repr. of 1936 ed. 14.95x (ISBN 0-7100-3014-2). Routledge & Kegan.
Hulme, Thomas E. Speculations. LC 78-64034. (Des Imagistes: Literature of the Imagist Movement). Repr. of 1924 ed. 24.00 (ISBN 0-404-17115-X). AMS Pr.
Hume, David. Natural Religion & the Posthumous Essays: Understanding & Other Posthumous Works. Popkin, Richard H., ed. LC 79-25349. 1980. lib. bdg. 12.50 (ISBN 0-915144-46-8); pap. text ed. 2.75 (ISBN 0-915144-45-X). Hackett Pub.
Jackins, Harvey. Die Menschliche Seite der Menschen. (Ger.). 1975. 3.00 (ISBN 0-911214-36-4). Rational Isl.
Jaeger, Werner. Humanism & Theology. (Aquinas Lecture). 1943. 6.95 (ISBN 0-87462-107-0). Marquette.
Janaro, R. P. Human Worth. LC 72-91162. 1973. text ed. 10.95 (ISBN 0-03-086591-3, HoltC). HR&W.
Jones, Howard M. American Humanism: Its Meaning for World Survival. LC 72-1852. 108p. 1957. Repr. lib. bdg. 15.00x (ISBN 0-8371-5540-1, JOAH). Greenwood.
Kaplan, Abraham. Love...& Death: Talks on Contemporary & Perennial Themes. LC 72-93402. (Illus.). 112p. 1973. 5.95 (ISBN 0-472-50465-7). U of Mich Pr.
Kaplan, Harold. Democratic Humanism & American Literature. LC 71-184508. 1972. 18.00x (ISBN 0-226-42422-7). U of Chicago Pr.
Kisch, Guido. Gestalten und Probleme aus Humanismus und Jurisprudenz: Neue Studien und Texte. (Ger). 1969. 40.00x (ISBN 3-11-002566-3). De Gruyter.
Klingberg, Frank J. Anglican Humanitarianism in Colonial New York. facsimile ed. LC 71-164612. (Select Bibliographies Reprint Ser). Repr. of 1940 ed. 19.00 (ISBN 0-8369-5896-9). Arno.
Kohl, Benjamin G. & Witt, Ronald G. The Earthly Republic: Italian Humanists on Government & Society. LC 78-53335. 1978. 22.00x (ISBN 0-8122-7752-X); pap. 9.95x (ISBN 0-8122-1097-2). U of Pa Pr.
Kristeller, Paul. Renaissance Thought, Vol. 1. pap. 3.25x (ISBN 0-06-131048-4, TB1048, Torch). Har-Row.
Kristeller, Paul O. Renaissance Thought: The Classic, Scholastic & Humanistic Strains, Vol. 1. 8.00 (ISBN 0-8446-2405-5). Peter Smith.
Kurtz, Paul, intro. by. Humanist Manifestos One & Two. 32p. 1973. pap. 1.95 (ISBN 0-87975-031-6). Prometheus Bks.
Labadie, Laurance. Humanism & Morality. (Men & Movements in the History & Philosophy of Anarchism Ser.). 1979. lib. bdg. 59.95 (ISBN 0-685-96397-7). Revisionist Pr.
Lamont, Corliss. The Independent Mind. 2.75 (ISBN 0-8180-1306-0). Horizon.
--Philosophy of Humanism. 5th ed. LC 65-16612. 10.50 (ISBN 0-8044-5595-3); pap. 5.95 (ISBN 0-8044-6378-6). Ungar.
McCloy, J. Humanitarianism in 18th Century. LC 72-5476. (World History Ser., No. 48). 1972. Repr. of 1956 ed. lib. bdg. 51.95 (ISBN 0-8383-1600-X). Haskell.
Mackail, John W. Studies in Humanism. facs. ed. LC 73-84322. (Essay Index Reprint Ser). 1938. 15.75 (ISBN 0-8369-1092-3). Arno.
MacKenzie, John S. Lectures on Humanism, with Special Reference to Its Bearings on Sociology. LC 74-157161. (Research & Source Works Ser: No. 89). 252p. (Philosophy Monographs No. 89). 1972. Repr. of 1907 ed. lib. bdg. 21.00 (ISBN 0-8337-2166-6). B Franklin.
Mahoney, Edward P., ed. Philosophy & Humanism: Renaissance Essays in Honor of Paul Oskar Kristeller. LC 75-42285. 624p. 1976. 50.00x (ISBN 0-231-03904-2). Columbia U Pr.
Mahood, M. M. Poetry & Humanism. 1970. pap. 2.45x (ISBN 0-393-00533-X, Norton Lib). Norton.
Mandrou, Robert. From Humanism to Science: 1480 to 1700. Pearce, Brian, tr. 1979. pap. 3.95 (ISBN 0-14-022079-8, Pelican). Penguin.
Maritain, Jacques. Freedom & the Modern World. O'Sullivan, Richard, tr. LC 77-150414. 1971. Repr. of 1936 ed. text ed. 9.00 (ISBN 0-87752-147-6). Gordian.
--True Humanism. Adamson, M. R., tr. LC 71-114888. (Select Bibliographies Reprint Ser). 1938. 20.00 (ISBN 0-8369-5292-8). Arno.
--True Humanism. 3rd ed. Adamson, Margot, tr. Repr. of 1941 ed. lib. bdg. 15.00 (ISBN 0-8371-2902-8, MAHU). Greenwood.
Masaryk, Thomas G. Ideals of Humanity, & How to Work. LC 79-90663. (Essay Index Reprint Ser). 1938. 15.00 (ISBN 0-8369-1306-X). Arno.
--Ideals of Humanity & How to Work: Lectures Delivered in 1898 at the University of Prague. LC 72-135844. (Eastern Europe Collection Ser). 1970. Repr. of 1938 ed. 9.50 (ISBN 0-405-02786-9). Arno.
Mitchell, Basil. Morality-Religious & Secular: The Dilemma of the Traditional Conscience. 180p. 1980. 22.50 (ISBN 0-19-824537-8). Oxford U Pr.
Moller, Mary E. Thoreau in the Human Community. LC 79-22549. (New England Writers Ser.). 1980. lib. bdg. 14.00x (ISBN 0-87023-293-2). U of Mass Pr.
Moravia, Alberto. Man As an End, a Defense of Humanism: Literary, Social & Political Essays. Wall, Bernard, tr. from It. LC 75-391. 254p. 1976. Repr. of 1966 ed. lib. bdg. 15.75x (ISBN 0-8371-8019-8, PIME). Greenwood.
Morison, Richard. Humanist Scholarship & Public Order: Two Tracts Against the Pilgrimage of Grace, & a Collection of Related Contemporary Documents. Berkowitz, David S., ed. LC 79-89983. 1979. text ed. 14.95 (ISBN 0-918016-01-0). Folger Bks.
Murray, Gilbert. Humanist Essays. (Unwin Bks.). 1965. pap. 2.95 (ISBN 0-04-824004-4). Allen Unwin.
Mwaipaya, Paul A. African Humanism & National Development: A Critical Analysis of the Fundamental Theoretical Principle of Zambian Humanism. LC 80-68980. 62p. (Orig.). 1981. pap. text ed. 6.75 (ISBN 0-8191-1754-4). U Pr of Amer.
Novack, George. Humanism & Socialism. LC 73-77559. 160p. 1973. 12.00- (ISBN 0-87348-308-1); pap. 3.45 (ISBN 0-87348-309-X). Path Pr NY.
Ofman, William V. Affirmation & Reality: Fundamentals of Humanistic Existential Therapy & Counseling. LC 76-46878. 203p. 1976. 19.70x (ISBN 0-87424-304-1). Western Psych.
Ouden, Bernard D. The Fusion of Naturalism & Humanism. LC 79-5348. 1979. pap. text ed. 9.00 (ISBN 0-8191-0869-3). U Pr of Amer.
Panofsky, Erwin. Studies in Iconology: Humanistic Themes in the Art of the Renaissance. 11.50 (ISBN 0-8446-2696-1). Peter Smith.
Pellegrino, Edmund D. Humanism & the Physician. LC 78-23174. 1979. 16.50x (ISBN 0-87049-218-7); pap. 7.50x (ISBN 0-87049-311-6). U of Tenn Pr.
Petrosyan, M. Humanism: Its Philosophical, Ethical & Sociological Aspects. 307p. 1972. 3.25 (ISBN 0-8285-0196-3, Pub. by Progress Pubs Russia). Imported Pubns.
Reiser, Oliver. Cosmic Humanism & World Unity. new ed. LC 73-86468. (World Institute Creative Findings Ser.). (Illus.). 286p. 1975. 29.75x (ISBN 0-677-03870-4); pap. 14.25x (ISBN 0-677-03875-5). Gordon.
Robertson, C. Grant, et al. Humanism & Technology & Other Essays. facs. ed. LC 68-22099. (Essay Index Reprint Ser). 1924. 12.00 (ISBN 0-8369-0553-9). Arno.
Robertson, John M. Pioneer Humanists. LC 77-2881. 1977. Repr. of 1907 ed. lib. bdg. 35.00 (ISBN 0-8414-7202-5). Folcroft.
Rothman, David, et al. Humanitarianism or Control? A Symposium on Nineteenth-Century Social Reform in Britain & America. Wiener, Martin, ed. (Rice University Studies: Vol. 67, No. 1). 84p. (Orig.). 1981. pap. 5.50x (ISBN 0-89263-248-8). Rice Univ.
Saintsbury, G. The Earlier Renaissance. LC 68-9660. 1968. Repr. of 1901 ed. 22.50 (ISBN 0-86527-047-3). Fertig.
Schevill, Ferdinand. First Century of Italian Humanism. (World History Ser., No. 48). 1970. pap. 12.95 (ISBN 0-8383-0100-2). Haskell.
--First Century of Italian Humanism. LC 66-27145. 1967. Repr. of 1928 ed. 5.00 (ISBN 0-8462-1029-0). Russell.
Schiller, F. C. Studies in Humanism. 1907. 35.00 (ISBN 0-89984-239-9). Century Bookbindery.
Schiller, Ferdinand C. Humanism. facs. ed. LC 79-75514. (Select Bibliographies Reprint Ser). 1903. 22.00 (ISBN 0-8369-5016-X). Arno.
--Humanism: Philosophical Essays. Repr. of 1912 ed. lib. bdg. 15.50x (ISBN 0-8371-2837-4, SCHU). Greenwood.
--Riddles of the Sphinx. facs. ed. LC 70-126254. (Select Bibliographies Reprint Ser). 1910. 22.00 (ISBN 0-8369-5481-5). Arno.
--Riddles of the Sphinx: A Study in the Philosophy of Humanism. rev. ed. LC 68-21331. 1968. Repr. of 1912 ed. lib. bdg. 20.00x (ISBN 0-8371-0212-X, SCRS). Greenwood.
--Studies in Humanism. facsimile ed. LC 76-102255. (Select Bibliographies Reprint Ser). 1907. 30.00 (ISBN 0-8369-5140-9). Arno.
--Studies in Humanism. Repr. of 1912 ed. lib. bdg. 17.75x (ISBN 0-8371-2812-9, SCSH). Greenwood.
Schuller, Peter M., ed. Progress & Human Value. (Orig.). 1979. 12.50x (ISBN 0-89894-007-9); pap. 8.95 (ISBN 0-89894-008-7). Advocate Pub Group.
Schultz, H. Milton & Forbidden Knowledge. 1955. pap. 15.00 (ISBN 0-527-80600-5). Kraus Repr.
Sher, Gerson, ed. Marxist Humanism & Praxis. LC 77-26377. 183p. 1978. 14.95 (ISBN 0-87975-097-9). Prometheus Bks.
Shinn, Roger L. New Directions in Theology Today. (Vol. 6). 1968. pap. 2.85 (ISBN 0-664-24812-8). Westminster.
Smoker, Barbara. Humanism. LC 74-155698. (Living Religions Series). (Illus.). 1976. pap. 3.50x (ISBN 0-7062-3146-5). Intl Pubns Serv.
Stahl, William H. Martianus Capella & the Seven Liberal Arts, Vol. 1. LC 76-121876. (Records of Civilization, Sources & Studies). 1971. 17.50x (ISBN 0-231-03254-4). Columbia U Pr.
Stirner, Max. False Principle of Our Education, Or, Humanism & Realism. (Libertarian Broadsides Ser: No. 1). 1967. pap. 0.60 (ISBN 0-87926-001-7). R Myles.
Streebing, Cecilian. Devout Humanism As a Style. LC 70-128930. (Catholic University. Romance Literature: No. 50). Repr. of 1954 ed. 17.50 (ISBN 0-404-50350-0). AMS Pr.
Symonds, John A. The Renaissance in Italy, 3 vols. Incl. Fine Arts (ISBN 0-8446-1494-7); Revival of Learning (ISBN 0-8446-1495-5); Age of the Despots (ISBN 0-8446-1496-3). (Illus.). Set. 22.50 (ISBN 0-8446-1433-5); 8.50 ea. Peter Smith.
Thorndike, Lynn. Science & Thought in the Fifteenth Century. (Illus.). 1967. Repr. of 1929 ed. 14.95 (ISBN 0-02-853480-8). Hafner.
Trinkaus, Charles. Adversity's Noblemen. rev. ed. 1965. lib. bdg. 11.50x (ISBN 0-374-97999-5). Octagon.
Tripp, Raymond P., Jr. Beyond Canterbury: Chaucer, Humanism, & Literature. 1977. pap. 7.00 (ISBN 0-905019-03-2). Soc New Lang Study.
Ullman, Walter. Medieval Foundations of Renaissance Humanism. LC 77-278. 1977. 19.50x (ISBN 0-8014-1110-6). Cornell U Pr.
Vasconcellos, John. A Liberating Vision: Politics for Growing Humans. LC 79-16778. 1979. pap. 6.95 (ISBN 0-915166-16-X). Impact Pubs Cal.
Versenyi, Lazslo. Socratic Humanism. LC 78-23762. 1979. Repr. of 1963 ed. lib. bdg. 16.75x (ISBN 0-313-20716-X, VESH). Greenwood.
Von Blum, Paul. The Art of Social Conscience. LC 76-2127. (Illus.). 256p. 1976. 12.50x (ISBN 0-87663-228-2); pap. 5.95x (ISBN 0-87663-934-1). Universe.
Washington, R. O. Program Evaluation in the Human Services. LC 80-5479. 283p. 1980. lib. bdg. 18.50 (ISBN 0-8191-1105-8); pap. text ed. 10.75 (ISBN 0-8191-1106-6). U Pr of Amer.
Watkins, Renee N., ed. Humanism & Liberty: Writings on Freedom from Fifteenth-Century Florence. LC 78-6588. 1978. lib. bdg. 14.95x (ISBN 0-87249-360-1). U of SC Pr.
Weiss, Roberto. Dawn of Humanism in Italy. LC 78-99169. (World History, Ser. No. 48). 1970. Repr. of 1947 ed. lib. bdg. 18.95 (ISBN 0-8383-0336-6). Haskell.
Whener, Walter L. Humanism & the Aesthetic Experience: Eduaction of the Sensibilities. 1977. pap. text ed. 7.50 (ISBN 0-8191-0311-X). U Pr of Amer.
Whitfield, J. H. Petrarch & the Renascence. LC 68-1761. (Studies in Italian Literature, No. 46). 1969. Repr. of 1943 ed. lib. bdg. 33.95 (ISBN 0-8383-0687-X). Haskell.
Whitfield, John H. Petrarch & the Renascence. LC 66-13176. 1965. Repr. of 1943 ed. 7.50 (ISBN 0-8462-0713-3). Russell.
Wigner, Eugene P. Symmetries & Reflections. LC 79-89843. 1979. pap. text ed. 9.50 (ISBN 0-918024-16-1). Ox Bow.

Wittenberg, Charles A. The Cultural Fraud of Secular Humanism. (Illus.). 129p. 1981. 41.75 (ISBN 0-89266-314-6). Am Classical Coll Pr.

Zimenko, V. The Humanism of Art. 1976. 6.50 (ISBN 0-8285-0874-7, Pub. by Progress Pubs Russia). Imported Pubns.

HUMANISM–20TH CENTURY

Balfour, A. J. Theism & Humanism. Repr. of 1915 ed. 20.00 (ISBN 0-527-04810-0). Kraus Repr.

Binkley, Luther J. Conflict of Ideals: Changing Values in Western Society. 1969. pap. text ed. 10.95x (ISBN 0-442-00765-5). Van Nos Reinhold.

Boynton, Percy H. Challenge of Modern Criticism. LC 73-15611. 1931. lib. bdg. 12.50 (ISBN 0-8414-3276-7). Folcroft.

Burkhardt, Frederick H., ed. Cleavage in Our Culture. facsimile ed. LC 74-90619. (Essay Index Reprint Ser). 1952. 18.00 (ISBN 0-8369-1396-5). Arno.

Conrad, David R. Education for Transformation: Implications in Lewis Mumford's Ecohumanism. LC 75-25867. 1976. 10.00 (ISBN 0-88280-030-2). ETC Pubns.

Ehrenfeld, David W. The Arrogance of Humanism. LC 78-1664. 1978. 11.95 (ISBN 0-19-502415-X). Oxford U Pr.

Grattan, C. Hartley, ed. Critique of Humanism. LC 68-26241. 1968. Repr. of 1930 ed. 13.50 (ISBN 0-8046-0177-1). Kennikat.

Grattan, Clinton H., ed. Critique of Humanism: A Symposium. facs. ed. LC 68-20303. (Essay Index Reprint Ser). 1930. 18.00 (ISBN 0-8369-0493-1). Arno.

Hoeveler, J. David, Jr. The New Humanism: A Critique of Modern America, 1900-1940. LC 76-25168. 1977. 13.95x (ISBN 0-8139-0658-X). U Pr of Va.

Humanitas - Journal of the Institute of Man, 12 vols. Repr. Set. 330.00 (ISBN 0-686-76929-5); 27.50 ea. AMS Pr.

Hyde, Lawrence. Prospects of Humanism. LC 77-94273. (Select Bibliographies Reprint Ser). 1931. 20.00 (ISBN 0-8369-5047-X). Arno.

--Prospects of Humanism. Repr. of 1931 ed. lib. bdg. 15.00x (ISBN 0-8371-2966-4, HYPH). Greenwood.

--Prospects of Humanism. LC 71-102574. 1970. Repr. of 1931 ed. 10.75 (ISBN 0-8046-0734-6). Kennikat.

--Prospects of Humanism. 1931. Repr. 25.00 (ISBN 0-8274-3218-6). R West.

Kovaly, Pavel. Rehumanization or Dehumanization: Essays on Alexander Solzhenitsyn, Arnost Kolman, Gyorgy Lukacs, Adam Schaff. 260p. 1974. 8.75 (ISBN 0-8283-1536-1). Branden.

Kurtz, Paul, ed. The Humanist Alternative: Some Definitions of Humanism. 190p. 1973. 8.95 (ISBN 0-87975-013-8); pap. 5.95 (ISBN 0-87975-018-9). Prometheus Bks.

Kurtz, Paul & Stojanovic, Svetozar, eds. Tolerance & Revolution. 167p. 1970. pap. 4.95 (ISBN 0-87975-001-4). Prometheus Bks.

Masaryk, Thomas. Humanistic Ideals. Warren, W. Preston, tr. LC 79-124100. 132p. 1971. 12.00 (ISBN 0-8387-7664-7). Bucknell U Pr.

Miller, R. Baxter, ed. Black American Literature & Humanism. LC 80-5179. 128p. 1981. 9.00 (ISBN 0-8131-1436-5). U Pr of Ky.

Munson, Gorham. The Dilemma of the Liberated: An Interpretation of 20th Century Humanism. 1979. Repr. of 1930 ed. lib. bdg. 25.00 (ISBN 0-8482-5087-7). Norwood Edns.

Munson, Gorham B. The Dilemma of the Liberated: An Interpretation of Twentieth Century Humanism. LC 66-25933. 1967. Repr. of 1930 ed. 12.50 (ISBN 0-8046-0329-4). Kennikat.

Ney, Albert C. Seeing into Life: Sociological Essays. 1969. 5.50 (ISBN 0-87164-008-2). William-F.

Perry, Ralph B. Humanity of Man. 1956. 4.50 (ISBN 0-8076-0028-8). Braziller.

Prophet, Elizabeth C., ed. Ich Dien. LC 74-20377. (Illus.). 234p. (Orig.). 1975. pap. 3.95 (ISBN 0-916766-11-X). Summit Univ.

Reiser, Oliver. Integration of Human Knowledge. (Extending Horizons Ser). (Illus.). 1958. 8.00 (ISBN 0-87558-031-9). Porter Sargent.

Santayana, George. The Genteel Tradition at Bay. LC 76-30569. (American Literature Ser, No. 49). 1977. lib. bdg. 49.95 (ISBN 0-8383-2154-2). Haskell.

HUMANISM, RELIGIOUS

Baker, Derek, ed. Religion & Humanism. (Studies in Church History: Vol. 17). 500p. 1981. 36.00x (ISBN 0-631-18050-8, Pub. by Basil Blackwell). Biblio Dist.

Chambers, Claire. The Siecus Circle. LC 75-41650. 1977. pap. 6.95 (ISBN 0-88279-119-2). Western Islands.

Eggenschwiler, David. The Christian Humanism of Flannery O'Connor. LC 79-179560. 156p. 1972. 9.95x (ISBN 0-8143-1463-5). Wayne St U Pr.

Erasmus. Christian Humanism & the Reformation: Selected Writings with the Life of Erasmus by Beatus Rhenanus. Olin, John C., ed. 7.50 (ISBN 0-8446-2035-1). Peter Smith.

Friedman, Maurice. The Human Way. (Religion & Human Experience Ser.). 168p. 1981. 13.95 (ISBN 0-89012-025-0). Anima Pubns.

Irish Bishop's Pastoral. Human Life Is Sacred. 1977. pap. 1.50 (ISBN 0-8198-0416-9). Dghtrs St Paul.

McShane, Philip. The Shaping of the Foundations: Being at Home in the Transcendental Method. 9.50 (ISBN 0-8191-0209-1). U Pr of Amer.

Molnar, Thomas. Christian Humanism, a Critique of the Secular City & Its Ideology. 1978. 7.95 (ISBN 0-8199-0694-8). Franciscan Herald.

Olds, Mason. Religious Humanism in America: Dietrich, Reese & Potter. 1977. 10.00 (ISBN 0-8191-0267-9). U Pr of Amer.

Phelps, William L. Human Nature & the Gospel. 1977. Repr. of 1925 ed. lib. bdg. 30.00 (ISBN 0-8414-6807-9). Folcroft.

Rice, Charles E. Secular Humanism. 1978. cancelled (ISBN 0-685-89389-8). Franciscan Herald.

Sheldon, William H. Prometheus Revisited. 225p. 1974. 11.25x (ISBN 0-87073-808-9). Schenkman.

Yonker, Nicolas. God, Man & the Planetary Age: Preface for a Theistic Humanism. LC 78-4233. 1978. 10.00 (ISBN 0-87071-322-1); pap. 5.75 (ISBN 0-87071-326-4). Oreg St U Pr.

HUMANIST ETHICS

see Humanistic Ethics

HUMANISTIC EDUCATION

see Education, Humanistic

HUMANISTIC ETHICS

Janaro, R. P. Human Worth. LC 72-91162. 1973. text ed. 10.95 (ISBN 0-03-086591-3, HoltC). HR&W.

Kerstan, Reinhold. Blood & Honor. LC 79-57520. 1980. pap. 3.95 (ISBN 0-89191-192-8). Cook.

Koopman, LeRoy. Beauty Care for the Tongue. (Illus.). 96p. (Orig.). 1974. pap. 2.25 (ISBN 0-310-26842-7). Zondervan.

Kurtz, Paul, ed. Moral Problems in Contemporary Society: Essays in Humanistic Ethics. 2nd ed. 310p. 1973. pap. 5.95 (ISBN 0-87975-022-7). Prometheus Bks.

Rudman, Jack. Human Resources Aide. (Career Examination Ser.: C-1785). (Cloth bdg. avail. on request). pap. 8.00 (ISBN 0-8373-1785-1). Natl Learning.

Spetter, Matthew I. Man the Reluctant Brother. 1967. 7.50 (ISBN 0-912166-01-0). Fieldston.

Storer, Morris B., ed. Humanist Ethics. LC 80-7456. (Impact Ser.). 313p. 1980. 17.95 (ISBN 0-87975-117-7); pap. 9.95 (ISBN 0-87975-118-5). Prometheus Bks.

HUMANISTIC PSYCHOLOGY

Anderson, Walt. Politics & the New Humanism. LC 72-96311. 176p. 1973. pap. text ed. 8.95 (ISBN 0-87620-661-5). Goodyear.

Brammer, Lawrence M. The Helping Relationship: Process & Skills. 2nd ed. (P-H Ser. in Counseling & Human Development). (Illus.). 1979. ref. ed. 15.95 (ISBN 0-13-386268-2); pap. 9.95 ref. ed. (ISBN 0-13-386250-X). P-H.

Buhler, Charlotte & Allen, Melanie. Introduction to Humanistic Psychology. LC 72-77603. (Orig.). 1972. pap. text ed. 7.95 (ISBN 0-8185-0032-8). Brooks-Cole.

Child, Irvin L. Humanistic Psychology & the Research Tradition: Their Several Virtues. 220p. 1981. Repr. of 1973 ed. text ed. 11.50 (ISBN 0-89874-277-3). Krieger.

Combs, Arthur W., et al. Helping Relationships: Basic Concepts for the Helping Professions. 2nd ed. 1978. pap. text ed. 11.50 (ISBN 0-205-05959-7). Allyn.

--Perceptual Psychology: A Humanistic Approach to the Study of Persons. 492p. 1976. pap. text ed. 16.95 scp (ISBN 0-06-041346-8, HarpC). Har-Row.

Covin, Theron M., ed. Readings in Human Development: A Humanist Approach. 197p. 1974. pap. text ed. 6.95x (ISBN 0-8422-0439-3). Irvington.

Daniels & Horowitz. Being & Caring. LC 75-43975. 1976. 10.95 (ISBN 0-913374-29-6). SF Bk Co.

Daniels, Victor & Horowitz, Laurence J. Being & Caring: A Journey to Self. 1976. pap. text ed. 10.95 (ISBN 0-87484-374-X). Mayfield Pub.

Davis, Bruce. The Magical Child Within You. LC 76-55831. (Illus., Orig.). 1977. pap. 4.95 (ISBN 0-89087-167-1). Celestial Arts.

Eglash, Albert. How to Be a Decent Human Being: Humanistic Communication--Sharing, Caring, Trusting. LC 79-54711. (Beyond Assertion Training Ser.: No. 1). (Illus., Orig.). 1980. pap. 15.00 (ISBN 0-935320-11-3). Quest Pr.

Fubin, Zick & McNeil, Elton B. The Psychology of Being Human. 3rd ed. 656p. 1981. text ed. 20.95 scp (ISBN 0-06-044383-9, HarpC); scp study guide 6.50 (ISBN 0-686-77444-2); scp activities manual 9.50 (ISBN 0-06-042471-0); instrs' manual avail. (ISBN 0-06-364211-5); test item avail. (ISBN 0-06-364211-5); instrs' manual test & activity manual avail. (ISBN 0-06-362480-X). Har-Row.

Gale, Raymond F. Explorations into Humanness. 1977. 4.95 (ISBN 0-8158-0346-X). Chris Mass.

Gauld, Alan & Shotter, John. Human Action & Its Psychological Investigation. 248p. 1980. pap. 12.95 (ISBN 0-7100-0589-X). Routledge & Kegan.

Gottsegen, Gloria B. & Gottsegen, Abby J., eds. Humanistic Psychology: A Guide to Information Sources. (Psychology Information Guide Ser.: Vol. 6). 175p. 1980. 36.00 (ISBN 0-8103-1462-2). Gale.

Heitner, Jack. The Search for the Real Self: Humanistic Psychology & Literature. LC 78-62174. 1978. pap. text ed. 8.75 (ISBN 0-8191-0474-4). U Pr of Amer.

Johnson, Richard E. In Quest of a New Psychology: Toward a Redefinition of Humanism. LC 74-9529. 320p. 1975. text ed. 19.95 (ISBN 0-87705-212-3). Human Sci Pr.

Kirschenbaum, Howard. On Becoming Carl Rogers. 1978. 12.95 (ISBN 0-440-06707-3). Delacorte.

Lombardi, Donald. Search for Significance. LC 75-17676. (Illus.). 144p. 1975. 13.95x (ISBN 0-88229-109-2). Nelson-Hall.

Mahrer, Alvin R. Experiencing: A Humanistic Theory of Psychology & Psychiatry. LC 77-27269. 1978. 30.00 (ISBN 0-87630-159-6). Brunner-Mazel.

Matson, Floyd W. Without-Within: Behaviorism & Humanism. LC 73-75563. (Orig.). 1973. pap. text ed. 5.95 (ISBN 0-8185-0094-8). Brooks-Cole.

Misiak, Henryk & Sexton, Virginia S. Phenomenological, Existential & Humanistic Psychologies: A Historical Survey. LC 73-6973. 176p. 1973. pap. text ed. 14.00 (ISBN 0-8089-0814-6). Grune.

Nevill, D. D., ed. Humanistic Psychology: New Frontiers. LC 77-23369. 1977. 18.95 (ISBN 0-470-99165-8). Halsted Pr.

Nikelly, Arthur G. Achieving Competence & Fulfillment. LC 76-46477. 1977. text ed. 14.95 (ISBN 0-8185-0199-5). Brooks-Cole.

Nye, Robert D. Three Views of Man: Perspectives from Sigmund Freud, B. F. Skinner, & Carl Rogers. LC 74-27872. 1975. pap. text ed. 7.95 (ISBN 0-685-52380-2). Brooks-Cole.

Pollio, Howard. Behavior & Existence: An Introduction to Empirical Humanistic Psychology. 512p. 1981. text ed. 18.95 (ISBN 0-8185-0425-0). Brooks-Cole.

Reeves, Clement. The Psychology of Rollo May: A Study in Existential Theory & Psychotherapy. LC 76-50708. (Social & Behavioral Science Ser.). 352p. 1977. text ed. 17.95x (ISBN 0-87589-303-1). Jossey-Bass.

Richards, Fred & Welch, I. David, eds. Sightings: Essays in Humanistic Psychology. LC 72-96552. 228p. 1973. pap. 4.95 (ISBN 0-88310-002-9). Publishers Consult.

Rogers, Carl. Carl Rogers on Personal Power. 1978. pap. 4.95 (ISBN 0-440-51530-0, Delta). Dell.

--Carl Rogers on Personal Power. 1977. 10.00 (ISBN 0-440-00980-4). Delacorte.

Rowan, John. Ordinary Ecstasy: Humanistic Psychology in Action. (Orig.). 1976. pap. 10.00 (ISBN 0-7100-8344-0). Routledge & Kegan.

Royce, Joseph R. & Mos, Leendert P., eds. Humanistic Psychology: Concepts & Criticisms. (PATH in Psychology Ser.). 295p. 1981. 27.50 (ISBN 0-306-40596-2). Plenum Pub.

Rychlak, Joseph F. The Psychology of Rigorous Humanism. LC 76-54838. 1977. 31.95 (ISBN 0-471-74796-3, Pub. by Wiley-Interscience). Wiley.

Schultz, Duane. Growth Psychology: Models of the Healthy Personality. 1977. 8.95 (ISBN 0-442-27443-2); pap. 7.95x (ISBN 0-442-27434-3). Van Nos Reinhold.

Severin, Frank T. Discovering Man in Psychology. 2nd ed. Orig. Title: Humanistic Viewpoints in Psychology. (Illus.). 420p. 1973. pap. text ed. 8.95 (ISBN 0-07-056340-3, C). McGraw.

Shaffer, John B. Humanistic Psychology. LC 77-15044. (Foundations of Modern Psychology Ser.). (Illus.). 1978. ref. ed. 16.95 (ISBN 0-13-447698-0); pap. text ed. 11.95 (ISBN 0-13-447680-8). P-H.

Simon, Sidney B. & O'Rourke, Robert. Developing Values with Exceptional Children. (Illus.). 160p. 1977. pap. text ed. 10.95 (ISBN 0-13-205310-1). P-H.

Vasconcellos, John. A Liberating Vision: Politics for Growing Humans. LC 79-16778. 1979. pap. 6.95 (ISBN 0-915166-16-X). Impact Pubs Cal.

Waldrop, Stanley. Closeness & Creativity. LC 77-84984. 1977. 6.95 (ISBN 0-9603364-0-0). Waldrop Pubns.

Walkenstein, Eileen. Don't Shrink to Fit! A Confrontation with Dehumanization in Psychiatry & Psychology. LC 76-17473. 1976. pap. 3.95 (ISBN 0-394-17004-0, E689, Ever). Grove.

Wandersman, Abraham, et al. Humanism & Behaviorism: Dialogue & Growth. 400p. 1976. text ed. 42.00 (ISBN 0-08-019589-X); pap. text ed. 12.75 (ISBN 0-08-019588-1). Pergamon.

Welch, I. David, et al, eds. Humanistic Psychology. LC 77-90497. 448p. 1978. 16.95 (ISBN 0-87975-103-7); pap. 9.95 (ISBN 0-87975-104-5). Prometheus Bks.

HUMANISTS

Agresto, John & Riesenberg, Peter, eds. The Humanist As Citizen. 300p. 1981. 19.50x (ISBN 0-8078-1450-4). U of NC Pr.

Cosenza, Mario E., compiled by. Checklist of the Non-Italian Humanists, 1300-1800. 1969. lib. bdg. 75.00 (ISBN 0-8161-0839-0). G K Hall.

Eaker, Helen L., ed. Giovanni Di Conversino Da Ravenna, Dragmalogia De Eligibili Vite Genere. LC 75-39111. 296p. 1980. 24.50 (ISBN 0-8387-1897-3). Bucknell U Pr.

Hendrick, George. Henry Salt: Humanitarian Reformer & Man of Letters. LC 77-5142. 1977. 15.50 (ISBN 0-252-00611-9). U of Ill Pr.

Katz, M. Barry. Leon Battista Alberti & the Humanist Theory of the Arts. 1977. pap. text ed. 6.75 (ISBN 0-8191-0279-2). U Pr of Amer.

Kurtz, Paul. A Secular Humanist Declaration. 40p. 1981. pap. 1.95 (ISBN 0-87975-149-5). Prometheus Bks.

Lamont, Corliss. A Humanist Wedding Service. 32p. pap. 2.95 saddle bdg. (ISBN 0-87975-000-6). Prometheus Bks.

Lennon, Colm. Richard Stanihurst the Dubliner Fifteen Forty-Seven-Sixteen Eighteen. 200p. 1981. 27.50x (ISBN 0-686-28963-3, Pub. by Irish Academic Pr Ireland). Biblio Dist.

May, Ernest & Blaney, D. Careers for Humanists. 1981. price not set (ISBN 0-12-480620-1). Acad Pr.

Mirandola, Pico D. & Francesco, Giovanni. Here Is Coteyned the Lyfe of Joan Picus Erle of Myrandula. More, T., tr. LC 77-7421. (English Experience Ser.: No. 884). 1977. Repr. of 1510 ed. lib. bdg. 9.50 (ISBN 90-221-0884-8). Walter J Johnson.

Rabil, Albert, Jr. Laura Cerata: Quattrocento Humanist. (Medieval & Renaissance Texts & Studies: 3). 190p. (Orig.). 1981. 13.95 (ISBN 0-686-73527-7); pap. 6.95 (ISBN 0-86698-007-5). Medieval.

Robertson, J. Modern Humanists Reconsidered. 59.95 (ISBN 0-8490-0649-X). Gordon Pr.

Scimecca, Joseph A. Society & Freedom: An Introduction to Humanist Sociology. 250p. 1981. text ed. 14.95x (ISBN 0-312-73806-4); pap. text ed. 7.95x (ISBN 0-686-71653-1). St Martin.

HUMANISTS–BIBLIOGRAPHY

Cosenza, Mario E., compiled by. Biographical & Bibliographical Dictionary of the Italian Humanists & of the World of Classical Scholarship in Italy, 1300-1800, 5 Vols. 1962. Set. 420.00 (ISBN 0-8161-0626-6); Vol. 6. suppl. (1967) 40.00 (ISBN 0-8161-0765-3). G K Hall.

HUMANITARIANISM (RELIGION)

see Humanism–20th Century; Jesus Christ–Divinity; Positivism; Socinianism; Trinity; Unitarianism

HUMANITIES

see also Classical Education; Education, Humanistic; Science and the Humanities

Agard, William R. Humanities for Our Time. facsimile ed. LC 68-29218. (Essay Index Reprint Ser: Univ. of Kansas Lectures in the Humanities). Repr. of 1949 ed. 15.00 (ISBN 0-8369-0554-7). Arno.

American Council Of Learned Societies Devoted To Humanistic Studies - Conference Of Secretaries. Studies in the History of Culture. facs. ed. LC 70-86728. (Essay Index Reprint Ser). 1942. 23.00 (ISBN 0-8369-1170-9). Arno.

American Humanities Index: 1977 Annual Cumulation, 2 vols. 1977. Set. 89.50 (ISBN 0-87875-143-2). Whitston Pub.

American Humanities Index: 1978 Annual Cumulation. 377p. 1979. 89.50 (ISBN 0-87875-158-0). Whitston Pub.

Armogathe, J. R. Theologia Cartesiana. (International Archives of the History of Ideas Ser: No. 84). 1977. lib. bdg. 42.00 (ISBN 90-247-1869-4, Pub. by Martinus Nijhoff Netherlands). Kluwer Boston.

Arthos, John. The Status of the Humanities. LC 80-84732. 256p. 1981. 12.50 (ISBN 0-8022-2377-X). Philos Lib.

Australian Academy of the Humanities Proceedings, 1973. new ed. 96p. 1974. 10.00x (ISBN 0-424-06770-6, Pub. by Sydney U Pr). Intl Schol Bk Serv.
Australian Academy of the Humanities, 1977. Proceedings. 1978. 14.00x (ISBN 0-424-00045-8, Pub. by Sydney U Pr). Intl Schol Bk Serv.
Australian Academy of the Humanities, 1974. Proceedings. 1975. 10.00 (ISBN 0-424-06980-6, Pub by Sydney U Pr). Intl Schol Bk Serv.
Australian Academy of the Humanities, 1978. Proceedings, Vol. 9. LC 78-150721. 1979. 20.00x (ISBN 0-424-00059-8, Pub. by Sydney U Pr). Intl Schol Bk Serv.
Australian Academy of the Humanities. Proceedings Nineteen Seventy-Nine. LC 78-150721. (Illus.). 1980. 20.00x (ISBN 0-424-00073-3, Pub. by Sydney U Pr). Intl Schol Bk Serv.
Australian Humanities Research Council Publications: Annual Reports. Incl. No. 1. 16p. 1956-57. pap. 2.00x (ISBN 0-686-01324-7); No. 6. 28p. 1961-62; No. 7. 28p. 1962-63. pap. 2.00x (ISBN 0-686-01326-3); No. 8. 72p. 1963-64. pap. 2.00x (ISBN 0-686-01327-1); No. 9. 64p. 1964-65. pap. 2.00x (ISBN 0-686-01328-X); No. 10. 68p. 1965-66. pap. 2.25x (ISBN 0-686-01329-8); No. 11. 68p. 1966-67. pap. 2.25x (ISBN 0-686-01330-1); No. 12. 96p. 1967-68. pap. 3.00x (ISBN 0-686-01331-X); No. 13. 96p. 1968-69. pap. 6.50x (ISBN 0-686-01332-8). Pub. by Sydney U Pr). Intl Schol Bk Serv.
Bibb, Clifford & Ely, Robert. The Humanities: A Cross-Cultural Approach. (Orig.). 1979. pap. text ed. 15.95 (ISBN 0-8403-2097-3). Kendall-Hunt.
Bird, Otto. Cultures in Conflict. LC 76-638. 1978. pap. text ed. 4.95 (ISBN 0-268-00724-1, 85-07246). U of Notre Dame Pr.
Blizek, William L., ed. The Humanities & Public Life. 1978. pap. 4.95 (ISBN 0-918626-50-1, Pied Pubns). Word Serv.
Blok, Alexander. The Spirit of Music. Freiman, I., tr. from Rus. LC 72-14050. (Soviet Literature in English Translation Ser.). (Illus.). 70p. 1973. Repr. of 1946 ed. 8.50 (ISBN 0-88355-001-6). Hyperion Conn.
Cecchettini, Philip A. CLEP: Introduction to Humanities. 1979. text ed. 5.95 (ISBN 0-07-010307-0, C). McGraw.
Chatterji, Sunjti K. Selected Writings, Vol. I. 1978. text ed. 25.00 (ISBN 0-7069-0533-4, RS 85, Pub. by Vikas India). Advent NY.
Commission on the Humanities. The Humanities in American Life: Report of the Commission on the Humanities. LC 80-14084. 1980. 14.50 (ISBN 0-520-04183-6); pap. 4.50 (ISBN 0-520-04208-5). U of Cal Pr.
Crane, Ronald S. Idea of the Humanities, & Other Essays Critical & Historical, 2 Vols. LC 66-30214. 1967. 17.50x (ISBN 0-226-11825-8). U of Chicago Pr.
Cross, Neal M., et al. The Search for Personal Freedom, 2 vols, Vol. 1. 6th ed. 500p. 1981. pap. text ed. write for info. (ISBN 0-697-03121-7). Vol. 2 (ISBN 0-697-03122-5). instrs.' manual avail. (ISBN 0-697-03123-3). Wm C Brown.
Dudley, Louise, et al. The Humanities. 6th ed. (Illus.). 1978. text ed. 18.95 (ISBN 0-07-017971-9, C); instructor's manual 4.95 (ISBN 0-07-017972-7); study guide 6.95 (ISBN 0-07-017973-5). McGraw.
Elwood, Douglas J., ed. The Humanities in Christian Higher Education in Asia: Ethical & Religious Perspectives. 1978. pap. text ed. 6.75x (ISBN 0-686-23913-X, Pub. by New Day Pub). Cellar.
Essays in the Humanities. (Rice University Studies: Vol. 57, No. 1). 85p. 1971. pap. 3.25x (ISBN 0-89263-207-0). Rice Univ.
Foerster, Norman, ed. Humanities After the War, by Wendell L. Willkie. facs. ed. LC 77-76898. (Essay Index Reprint Ser). 1944. 11.50 (ISBN 0-8369-1035-4). Arno.
Frazier, Robert C., et al. The Humanities: An American Experience. LC 77-77928. 1977. pap. text ed. 9.95 (ISBN 0-8403-1687-9). Kendall-Hunt.
--The Humanities: Ideas & Values. 1976. pap. text ed. 8.50 (ISBN 0-8403-1539-2). Kendall-Hunt.
Garvin, Harry R. New Dimensions in the Humanities & Social Sciences. LC 76-27914. (Bucknell Review, Spring 1977). 186p. 1977. 12.00 (ISBN 0-8387-1966-X). Bucknell U Pr.
Gelfand, Morris A. & Colby, Robert A. Access to Knowledge & Information in the Social Sciences & Humanities: Conference Proceedings. 1974. pap. 12.50 (ISBN 0-930146-06-9). Queens Coll Pr.
Gibson, A. Works of Literature & Work in Philosophy. (Australian Humanities Research Council Publication). 1963. pap. 2.00x (ISBN 0-424-04459-5, Pub. by Sydney U Pr). Intl Schol Bk Serv.
Greene, Theodore M., ed. Meaning of the Humanities. LC 73-86020. (Essay & General Literature Index Reprint Ser). 1969. Repr. of 1938 ed. 12.50 (ISBN 0-8046-0562-9). Kennikat.
Hancock, K., et al. Postgraduate Studies in the Humanities in Australia: Three Essays. 1967. pap. 3.00x (ISBN 0-424-05600-3, Pub. by Sydney U Pr). Intl Schol Bk Serv.
Harris, Julian, ed. Humanities: An Appraisal. 190p. 1950. pap. 4.25x (ISBN 0-299-00634-4). U of Wis Pr.
Harzfeld, Lois A. Periodical Indexes in the Social Sciences & Humanities: A Subject Guide. LC 78-5230. 1978. lib. bdg. 10.00 (ISBN 0-8108-1133-2). Scarecrow.
Hassan, Ihab, ed. Liberations: New Essays on the Humanities in Revolution. LC 77-142729. 1971. (Pub. by Wesleyan U Pr); pap. 5.95 (ISBN 0-8195-6025-1). Columbia U Pr.
Hockey, Susan. A Guide to Computer Applications in the Humanities. LC 79-3378. 1980. text ed. 16.95x (ISBN 0-8018-2346-3). Johns Hopkins.
Humanities Index. (Sold on service basis). 1974. Vols. 1-5. write for info. (ISBN 0-685-48364-9). Wilson.
Hutchins, Robert M. & Adler, Mortimer J., eds. The Humanities Today. LC 75-4298. (The Great Ideas Anthologies Ser). (Illus.). 562p. 1976. 15.00x (ISBN 0-405-07172-8). Arno.
Janaro, Richard P. & Altshuler, Thelma. The Art of Being Human: The Humanities As a Technique for Living. 1979. text ed. 17.50 scp (ISBN 0-06-044427-4, HarpC); instr's. manual free (ISBN 0-06-364425-8); scp study guide 9.50 (ISBN 0-06-044428-2). Har-Row.
Langridge, D. W. Classification & Indexing in the Humanities. 224p. 1976. 13.95 (ISBN 0-408-70777-1). Butterworth.
Lienhard, M. The Origins & Characteristics of Anabaptism. (International Archives of the History of Ideas Ser: No. 87). 1977. lib. bdg. 53.00 (ISBN 90-247-1896-1, Pub. by Martinus Nijhoff Netherlands). Kluwer Boston.
MacCarthy, Desmond. Humanities (T. S. Eliot, Isben, Chekhov, Swinburne, Leigh Bunt, Katherine Mansfield, Vernon Lee) LC 77-4860. 1973. lib. bdg. 20.00 (ISBN 0-8414-6225-9). Folcroft.
McManners, J. & Crawford, R. Future of the Humanities in the Australian Universities. 1965. pap. 2.00x (ISBN 0-424-05570-8, Pub. by Sydney U Pr). Intl Schol Bk Serv.
Maegraith, Brian. One World. (Heath Clark Lectures 1970). 250p. 1973. text ed. 23.50x (ISBN 0-485-26323-8, Athlone Pr). Humanities.
Melanges Sur les Humanites. (Fr). 1954. pap. 4.95x (ISBN 2-7637-0123-X, Pub. by Laval). Intl Schol Bk Serv.
Moore, David S. Statistics: Concepts & Controversies. LC 78-12740. (Illus.). 1979. text ed. 18.95x (ISBN 0-7167-1022-6); pap. text ed. 8.95x (ISBN 0-7167-1021-8); instrs.' guide avail. W H Freeman.
Natanson, Maurice, ed. Phenomenology & the Social Sciences, Vols. I & II. LC 79-91001. (Studies in Phenomenology Existential Philosophy). 1082p. 1973. Vol. I. text ed. 21.95x (ISBN 0-8101-0400-8); Vol. 1. pap. 10.95x (ISBN 0-8101-0616-7) (ISBN 0-8101-0401-6). pap. 11.95 (ISBN 0-8101-0617-5). Northwestern U Pr.
Norena. Studies in Spanish Renaissance Thought. (International Archives of the History of Ideas Ser: No. 82). 1975. lib. bdg. 50.00 (ISBN 90-247-1727-2, Pub. by Martinus Nijhoff Netherlands). Kluwer Boston.
Olafson, Frederick A. The Dialectic of Action: A Philosophical Interpretation of History & the Humanities. LC 79-10316. 1979. lib. bdg. 22.00x (ISBN 0-226-62564-8). U of Chicago Pr.
Patton, Peter C. & Holoien, Renee A., eds. Computing in the Humanities. LC 79-3185. 416p. 1981. 29.95x (ISBN 0-669-03397-9). Lexington Bks.
Raben, Joseph. Computer Assisted Research in the Humanities: A Directory of Scholars Active, 1966-1972. LC 75-16447. 1977. text ed. 69.50 (ISBN 0-08-019870-8). Pergamon.
Rademaker, C. S. Life & Work of Gerardus Joannes Vossius (1577-1659) (Respublica Literaria Neerlandica). 472p. 1980. text ed. 48.50x (ISBN 90-232-1785-3). Humanities.
Roberts, Charles, et al. Mirrors of Mind: Commitment & Creativity in the Twentieth Century. LC 79-67863. (Illus.). 284p. 1980. pap. text ed. 12.95x (ISBN 0-89459-072-3). Hunter NC.
Rudman, Jack. Humanities. (Graduate Record Area Examination Ser.: GRE-42). 16.50 (ISBN 0-8373-5292-4); pap. 11.50 (ISBN 0-8373-5242-8). Natl Learning.
--Humanities. (Admission Test Ser.: ATS-9B). 14.95 (ISBN 0-8373-5109-X); pap. 9.95 (ISBN 0-8373-5009-3). Natl Learning.
SantaVicca, Edmund F. Reference Work in the Humanities. LC 80-18783. 173p. 1980. 10.00 (ISBN 0-8108-1342-4). Scarecrow.
Shoemaker, F. Aesthetic Experience & the Humanities. LC 70-176013. Repr. of 1943 ed. 21.00 (ISBN 0-404-05987-2). AMS Pr.
Slavens. Questions in the Humanities & the Social Sciences. (Library Science & Information Ser.). 136p. 1981. price not set (ISBN 0-8247-1542-X). Dekker.
Stevens, David H. Changing Humanities. LC 70-90682. (Essay Index Reprint Ser). 1953. 18.00 (ISBN 0-8369-1482-1). Arno.
Stroup, Thomas B., ed. The Humanities & the Understanding of Reality. LC 66-21647. 96p. 1966. 5.50 (ISBN 0-8131-1121-8). U Pr of Ky.
Stuart, B. Traite Sur L'art De la Guerre. (International Archives of the History of Ideas Ser: No. 85). 1977. pap. 26.00 (ISBN 90-247-1871-6, Pub. by Martinus Nijhoff Netherlands). Kluwer Boston.
Studer, Ginny L., et al. Humanities in Physical Education. Kneer, Marian, ed. (Basic Stuff Ser.: No. I, 5 of 6). (Orig.). 1981. pap. text ed. 5.95 (ISBN 0-686-30219-2). AAHPERD.
Thomas, Sidney, ed. Images of Man: Selected Readings in Arts & Ideas in Western Civilization. LC 78-94895. 1978. pap. text ed. 8.95x (ISBN 0-685-77813-4). Irvington.
Thomson, Phillip, ed. Index to Book Reviews in the Humanities, Vol. 19. LC 62-21757. 1979. 20.00x (ISBN 0-911504-19-2). Thomson.
Thomson, Phillip, compiled by. An Index to Book Reviews in the Humanities, Vol. 21. LC 62-21757. 414p. 1981. 20.00x (ISBN 0-911504-21-4). Thomson.
U R T A-A T A Humanities & the Theatre, 2 vols. Set. 5.00x (ISBN 0-686-29495-5). Am Theatre Assoc.
University of North Carolina Division of the Humanities. State University Surveys the Humanities. MacKinney, L. C., ed. LC 72-3386. (Essay Index Reprint Ser.). Repr. of 1945 ed. 17.00 (ISBN 0-8369-2916-0). Arno.
Van De Bogart, Doris. Introduction to the Humanities: Painting, Sculpture, Architecture, Music & Literature. LC 67-29656. (Orig.). 1968. pap. 4.95 (ISBN 0-06-463277-6, EH 277, EH). Har-Row.
--Introduction to the Humanities: Painting, Sculpture, Architecture, Music & Literature. LC 67-29656. (Illus.). 1968. 13.50x (ISBN 0-06-480910-2). B&N.
Wagner, Maria & Ainsworth, Jeanette, eds. Basic Concepts in the Humanities. LC 77-85175. 1977. pap. 18.25 (ISBN 0-8357-0271-5, SS-00042). Univ Microfilms.
White, Howard B. Antiquity Forgot. (Archives Internationales D'Historie Des Idees: Vol. 90). 1978. lib. bdg. 31.50 (ISBN 90-247-1971-2, Pub. by Martinus Nijhoff Netherlands). Kluwer Boston.
Wilson. A Medievalist in the Eighteenth Century. (International Archives of the History of Ideas Ser: No. 83). 1976. lib. bdg. 60.50 (ISBN 90-247-1782-5, Pub. by Martinus Nijhoff Netherlands). Kluwer Boston.
Witt, Mary A., et al. The Humanities: Cultural Roots & Continuities. 1980. Vol. 1. pap. text ed. 11.95x (ISBN 0-669-01450-8); Vol. 2. 0.11.95 (ISBN 0-669-01451-6); 11.95 (ISBN 0-669-02825-8). Heath.
Woods, John & Coward, Harold G., eds. Humanities in the Present Day. 107p. 1979. text ed. 8.75 (ISBN 0-88920-076-9, Pub. by Laurier U Pr Canada). Humanities.

HUMANITIES–BIBLIOGRAPHY

American Humanities Index: Annual Cumulation. 410p. 1980. 89.50 (ISBN 0-87875-193-9). Whitston Pub.
American Humanities Index: 1975 Annual Cumulation, 2 vols. 1976. 89.50 set (ISBN 0-87875-089-4). Whitston Pub.
Library Association (London), ed. British Humanities Index 1978. LC 63-24940. 802p. 1979. 175.00x (ISBN 0-85365-901-X). Intl Pubns Serv.
Library Assoociation (London) British Humanities Index 1979. LC 63-24940. 744p. 1980. 190.00x (ISBN 0-85365-583-9). Intl Pubns Serv.
Magill, Frank N., ed. Magill Books Index. LC 80-53597. 800p. 1980. 35.00 (ISBN 0-89356-200-9). Salem Pr.
OAS General Secretariat. Revista Interamericana De Bibliografia, Vol. 31, No. 1. 196p. (Fr., Span., Portuguese.). 1981. pap. 3.00 (ISBN 0-686-75080-2). OAS.
Rogers, A. Robert. The Humanities: A Selective Guide to Information Sources. 2nd ed. LC 79-25335. (Library Science Text Ser.). 1980. lib. bdg. 25.00 (ISBN 0-87287-206-8); pap. text ed. 14.50 (ISBN 0-87287-222-X). Libs Unl.
Social Sciences & Humanities Index. 1965-74. 30.00 (ISBN 0-685-22255-1). Wilson.
Southwestern Library Association. Guide to Humanities Resources in the Southwest. 1978. text ed. 24.50 (ISBN 0-918212-04-9, Dist. by ABC-CLIO). Neal-Schuman.
Thomson, Phillip, ed. Index to Book Reviews in the Humanities. Incl. Vol. 1, Cumulation. 1978. 25.00x (ISBN 0-911504-01-X); Vols. 2-5, 7-10. 20.00x ea. Vol. 2 (ISBN 0-911504-02-8). Vol. 3 (ISBN 0-911504-03-6). Vol. 4 (ISBN 0-911504-04-4). Vol. 5 (ISBN 0-911504-05-2). Vol. 7 (ISBN 0-911504-07-9). Vol. 8 (ISBN 0-911504-08-7). Vol. 9 (ISBN 0-911504-09-5). Vol. 10 (ISBN 0-911504-10-9); Vols. 11-18. 20.00x ea. Vol. 11 (ISBN 0-911504-11-7). Vol. 12 (ISBN 0-911504-12-5). Vol. 13 (ISBN 0-911504-13-3). Vol. 14 (ISBN 0-911504-14-1). Vol. 15 (ISBN 0-911504-15-X). Vol. 16 (ISBN 0-911504-16-8). Vol. 17 (ISBN 0-911504-17-6). Vol. 18 (ISBN 0-911504-18-4). LC 62-21757. Thomson.
Thomson, Phillip, compiled by. An Index to Book Reviews in the Humanities, Vol. 20. LC 62-21757. 400p. 1980. 20.00x (ISBN 0-911504-20-6). Thomson.

HUMANITIES–METHODOLOGY

Brown, R. H. A Poetics for Sociology. LC 75-35454. (Illus.). 1977. 34.50 (ISBN 0-521-21121-2); pap. 8.95x (ISBN 0-521-29391-X). Cambridge U Pr.
Gadamer, Hans-Georg. Truth & Method. LC 75-2053. 576p. 1975. 24.50 (ISBN 0-8164-9220-4). Continuum.
Mechling, Jay, et al. Morning Work: A Trialogue on Issues of Knowledge & Freedom in Doing American Culture Studies. LC 78-52592. (Ailanthus Ser.). (Illus.). 1979. pap. text ed. 8.00x (ISBN 0-930474-01-5). Connect Pr.
Pawlowski, Tadeusz. Concept Formation in the Humanities & the Social Sciences. (Synthese Library: No. 144). 233p. 1980. lib. bdg. 36.50 (ISBN 90-277-1096-1, Pub. by Reidel Holland). Kluwer Boston.

HUMANITIES–STUDY AND TEACHING

Bayerl, Elizabeth. Interdisciplinary Studies in the Humanities: A Directory. LC 77-22960. 1977. 40.00 (ISBN 0-8108-1076-X). Scarecrow.
Bushman, John H. & Jones, Sandra. Teaching English & the Humanities Through Thematic Units. LC 79-52998. 1979. pap. text ed. 4.50x (ISBN 0-87543-148-8). Lucas.
Drake, Sandra & Lynch, Mary Jo. Community Colleges, Public Libraries, & the Humanities. 1978. 6.00 (ISBN 0-87117-055-8). Am Assn Comm Jr Coll.
Hutchison, John A. Paths of Faith. 2nd ed. 1974. text ed. 17.00 (ISBN 0-07-031531-0, C). McGraw.
Lane, Robert E. Liberties of Wit, Humanism, Criticism & the Civic Mind. LC 74-113017. 1970. Repr. of 1961 ed. 14.50 (ISBN 0-208-00823-3, Archon). Shoe String.
Merlan, Philip. A Syllabus in the Humanities. 128p. 1973. text ed. 6.50 (ISBN 0-8158-0288-9). Chris Mass.
Spann, Sylvia & Culp, Mary B., eds. Thematic Units in Teaching English & the Humanities. 3rd ed. (Orig.). (gr. 6-12). 1980. pap. text ed. 6.00 (ISBN 0-8141-5376-3). NCTE.
--Themetic Units in Teaching English & the Humanities. LC 75-37626. 1975. loose leaf bdg 11.20 (ISBN 0-8141-5372-0); 3 hole punch, no binder 7.00 (ISBN 0-8141-5373-9). NCTE.
Trzyna, Thomas N., et al, eds. Careers for Humanities - Liberal Arts Majors: A Guide to Programs & Resources. LC 80-50352. 188p. (Orig.). 1980. pap. 22.50x (ISBN 0-9604078-0-4). Weatherford.
Yarrington, Roger, ed. Strengthening Humanities in Community Colleges. (Orig.). 1980. pap. 5.00 (ISBN 0-87117-094-9). Am Assn Comm Jr Coll.

HUMANITIES AND SCIENCE

see Science and the Humanities

HUMANITY

see also Charity; Kindness; Sympathy

Heywood, Philip. Planning & Human Need. 192p. 1976. 6.50 (ISBN 0-7153-6315-8). David & Charles.
Rudinger, Joel. The Human Condition. (Anthology of the Arts Ser.). 1976. pap. 3.00 (ISBN 0-918342-00-7). Cambric.
Van Eys, Jan. Humanity & Personhood: Personal Reaction to a World in Which Children Can Die. 126p. 1981. pap. 14.75 (ISBN 0-398-00467-8). C C Thomas.
Winston Press Editorial Staff. Humans Kind. (Infinity Ser.: No. 16). 1972. text ed. 2.50 (ISBN 0-03-004031-0, 257); tchr's. guide by Marian Nesset 1.15 (ISBN 0-03-004036-1, 258). Winston Pr.

HUMBLEBEES

see Bumblebees

HUMBOLDT, ALEXANDER, FREIHERR VON, 1769-1859

De Terra, Helmut. Humboldt: The Life & Times of Alexander Humboldt. LC 78-27653. 386p. 1979. Repr. of 1955 ed. lib. bdg. 26.50x (ISBN 0-374-92134-2). Octagon.

HUMBOLDT, WILHELM VON, 1767-1835

Brown, Roger L. Wilhelm Von Humboldt's Conception of Linguistic Relativity. LC 67-30542. (Janua Linguarum, Ser. Minor: No. 65). (Orig.). 1967. pap. text ed. 20.00x (ISBN 90-2790-593-2). Mouton.

Humboldt, Wilhelm Von. Gesammelte Schriften (Werke, 17vols. Preussische Akademie der Wissenschaften, ed. (Ger). 1967-68. Repr. of 1936 ed. Set. 958.00x (ISBN 3-11-005158-3). De Gruyter.
Sweet, Paul R. Wilhelm von Humboldt: A Biography, 1767-1808, Vol. 1. LC 77-26654. (Illus.). 1978. 18.50 (ISBN 0-8142-0278-0). Ohio St U Pr.

HUMBOLDT BAY, CALIFORNIA

Lewis, Oscar, frwd. by. The Quest for Qual-a-wa-loo (Humboldt Bay) (Illus.). 190p. 1966. 10.00 (ISBN 0-910740-06-2). Holmes.

HUMBOLDT COUNTY, CALIFORNIA

Chase, Don. They Came This Way: The Humboldt Valley, Highroad to the Gold Rush. ltd. ed. (Illus.). 1973. velo-bind 3.50 (ISBN 0-918634-31-8); pap. 3.00 limited ed. (ISBN 0-918634-33-4). D M Chase.
Chase, Don M. He Opened the West: Jedediah Strong Smith. (Illus.). 40p. 1968. pap. 2.00 (ISBN 0-918634-26-1). D M Chase.
Lewis, Oscar, frwd. by. The Quest for Qual-a-wa-loo (Humboldt Bay) (Illus.). 190p. 1966. 10.00 (ISBN 0-910740-06-2). Holmes.

HUMBOLDT RIVER, NEVADA

Morgan, Dale L. Humboldt, Highroad of the West. facs. ed. LC 70-146867. (Select Bibliographies Reprint Ser). 1943. 22.00 (ISBN 0-8369-5634-6). Arno.

HUMBUG

see Impostors and Imposture; Swindlers and Swindling

HUME, DAVID, 1711-1776

Anderson, Robert F. Hume's First Principles. LC 65-18415. xvi, 189p. 1966. 14.50x (ISBN 0-8032-0000-5). U of Nebr Pr.
Ayer, A. J. Hume. 108p. 1980. 7.95 (ISBN 0-8090-5615-1); pap. 2.95 (ISBN 0-8090-1409-2). Hill & Wang.
Ayer, Alfred J. Probability & Evidence. LC 71-185572. (John Dewey Lecture Ser). 144p. 1979. 12.50x (ISBN 0-231-03650-7); pap. 6.00x (ISBN 0-231-04767-3). Columbia U Pr.
Basson, A. H. David Hume. LC 78-26704. 183p. 1981. Repr. of 1958 ed. lib. bdg. 19.75x (ISBN 0-313-20668-6, BADH). Greenwood.
Beauchamp, Tom L. & Rosenberg, Alexander. Hume & the Problem of Causation. 352p. 1981. 23.50 (ISBN 0-19-520236-8). Oxford U Pr.
Botwinick, Aryeh. Ethics, Politics & Epistemology: A Study in the Unity of Hume's Thought. LC 80-5809. 197p. 1980. lib. bdg. 17.50 (ISBN 0-8191-1288-7); pap. text ed. 9.00 (ISBN 0-8191-1289-5). U Pr of Amer.
Bricke, John. Hume's Philosophy of Mind. LC 79-48025. 200p. 1980. 18.50 (ISBN 0-691-07255-8). Princeton U Pr.
Burton, John H. Life & Correspondence of David Hume, 2 Vols. 1967. Repr. of 1846 ed. Set. 39.50 (ISBN 0-8337-0433-8). B Franklin.
--Life & Correspondence of David Hume, 2 vols. 1035p. 1969. Repr. of 1846 ed. Set. 65.00x (ISBN 0-8002-1296-7). Intl Pubns Serv.
Calderwood, Henry. David Hume. 158p. 1980. Repr. of 1898 ed. lib. bdg. 22.50 (ISBN 0-8492-3862-5). R West.
--David Hume. LC 77-973. 1977. lib. bdg. 22.50 (ISBN 0-8414-3571-5). Folcroft.
Capaldi, Nicholas. Monarch Notes on Hume's Philosophy. (Orig.). pap. 1.95 (ISBN 0-671-00529-4). Monarch Pr.
Chakraborty, Tapan K. Hume's Theory of Causality. 1979. 8.50x (ISBN 0-8364-0560-9, Pub. by Minerva Associates). South Asia Bks.
Chappell, V. C., ed. Hume: A Collection of Critical Essays. 1968. 10.95x (ISBN 0-268-00124-3). U of Notre Dame Pr.
Church, Ralph W. Hume's Theory of the Understanding. LC 79-55608. 238p. 1980. Repr. of 1935 ed. lib. bdg. 19.75x (ISBN 0-313-20651-1, CHHU). Greenwood.
Collins, James. British Empiricists: Locke, Berkeley, Hume. (Orig.). 1967. pap. 3.50 (ISBN 0-02-813460-5). Glencoe.
Flew, Antony G. Hume's Philosophy of Belief. (International Library of Philosophy & Scientific Method). 1961. pap. text ed. 26.25x (ISBN 0-7100-1370-1). Humanities.
Forbes, D. Hume's Philosophical Politics. LC 75-9282. 400p. 1975. 47.95 (ISBN 0-521-20754-1). Cambridge U Pr.
Gaskin, J. C. A. Hume's Philosophy of Religion. LC 77-22633. (Library of Philosophy & Religion Ser). 1978. text ed. 23.50x (ISBN 0-06-492327-4). B&N.
Glathe, Alfred B. Hume's Theory of the Passions & of Morals: A Study of Books 2 & 3 of the Treatise. (Publications in Philosophy Ser: Vol. 24). Repr. of 1950 ed. pap. 18.50 (ISBN 0-384-18905-9). Johnson Repr.
Green, Thomas H. Hume & Locke. 6.00 (ISBN 0-8446-2161-7). Peter Smith.
Hall, Roland. Fifty Years of Hume Scholarship. 100p. 1979. 11.50x (ISBN 0-85224-337-5, Pub. by Edinburgh U Pr Scotland). Columbia U Pr.
Harre, Romano & Madden, E. H. Causal Powers: A Theory of Natural Necessity. 191p. 1975. 18.50x (ISBN 0-87471-624-1). Rowman.
Harrison, J. Hume's Moral Epistemology. 144p. 1976. 10.95x (ISBN 0-19-824566-1); pap. 7.95x (ISBN 0-19-875037-4). Oxford U Pr.
Harrison, Jonathan. Hume's Theory of Justice. 320p. 1981. 49.50x (ISBN 0-19-824619-6). Oxford U Pr.
Hume, David. A Treatise of Human Nature. Selby-Bigge, L. A. & Nidditch, P. H., eds. 1978. text ed. 24.95x (ISBN 0-19-824587-4); pap. text ed. 5.50x (ISBN 0-19-824588-2). Oxford U Pr.
Huxley, Thomas H. David Hume. Morley, John, ed. LC 68-58382. (English Men of Letters). Repr. of 1887 ed. lib. bdg. 12.50 (ISBN 0-404-51714-5). AMS Pr.
--David Hume. 1973. Repr. of 1887 ed. 12.00 (ISBN 0-8274-1352-1). R West.
Knight, William. Hume. LC 72-103199. 1970. Repr. of 1886 ed. 12.50 (ISBN 0-8046-0836-9). Kennikat.
Laing, Bertram M. David Hume. LC 68-15134. 1968. Repr. of 1932 ed. 8.00 (ISBN 0-8462-1237-4). Russell.
Laird, John. Hume's Philosophy of Human Nature. 1967. Repr. of 1932 ed. 19.50 (ISBN 0-208-00096-8, Archon). Shoe String.
Leroy, Andre L. David Hume. Mayer, J. P., ed. LC 78-67413. (European Political Thought Ser.). (Fr.). 1979. Repr. of 1953 ed. lib. bdg. 22.00x (ISBN 0-405-11713-2). Arno.
Livingston, Donald & King, James T., eds. Hume: A Re-Evaluation. LC 76-13968. 1976. 27.50 (ISBN 0-8232-1007-3); pap. 12.00 (ISBN 0-8232-1008-1). Fordham.
Mackie, J. L. Hume's Moral Theory. (International Library of Philosophy & Scientific Method). 1980. 25.00x (ISBN 0-7100-0524-5); pap. 12.50 (ISBN 0-7100-0525-3). Routledge & Kegan.
Maund, Constance. Hume's Theory of Knowledge: A Critical Examination. LC 74-184234. xxiii, 310p. 1972. Repr. of 1937 ed. 18.00 (ISBN 0-8462-1645-0). Russell.
Merrill, Kenneth R. & Shahan, Robert W., eds. David Hume: Many-Sided Genius. LC 76-18499. 1976. pap. 5.95 (ISBN 0-8061-1387-1). U of Okla Pr.
Morice, G. P., ed. David Hume: Bicentenary Papers. LC 77-81915. 1977. 12.50x (ISBN 0-292-71515-3). U of Tex Pr.
Morris, Charles R. Locke, Berkeley, Hume. LC 79-17847. 1979. Repr. of 1931 ed. lib. bdg. 16.50x (ISBN 0-313-22091-3, MOLO). Greenwood.
Mossner, Ernest C. Forgotten Hume, Le Bon David. LC 43-1705. Repr. of 1943 ed. 10.00 (ISBN 0-404-04506-5). AMS Pr.
--The Life of David Hume. 2nd ed. LC 78-41137. 1980. 55.00x (ISBN 0-19-824381-2). Oxford U Pr.
Murphy, Richard T. Hume & Husserl: Towards Radical Subjectivism. 156p. 1980. lib. bdg. 34.00 (ISBN 90-247-2172-5, Pub. by Martinus Nijhoff Netherlands). Kluwer Boston.
Neu, Jerome. Emotion, Thought,& Therapy: A Study of Hume & Spinoza & the Relationship of Philosophical Theories of the Emotions to Psychological Theories of Therapy. LC 76-20010. 1977. 21.50x (ISBN 0-520-03288-8). U of Cal Pr.
Norton, D. F. & Capaldi, N., eds. McGill Hume Studies. LC 78-10398. (Studies in Hume & Scottish Philosophy). 1980. 22.50x (ISBN 0-89690-000-2); pap. 8.95 (ISBN 0-89690-001-0). Austin Hill Pr.
Norton, David F. David Hume: Common-Sense Moralist, Sceptical Metaphysician. Date not set. 25.00 (ISBN 0-686-76570-2). Princeton U Pr.
Noxon, James. Hume's Philosophical Development: A Study of His Methods. 1973. 24.95x (ISBN 0-19-824398-7). Oxford U Pr.
Passmore, John. Hume's Intentions. 3rd ed. 180p. 1980. 26.50x (ISBN 0-7156-0918-1, Pub. by Duckworth England). Biblio Dist.
Penelhum, Terence. Hume. LC 75-2951. (Philosophers in Perspective Ser.). 200p. 1975. text ed. 15.95 (ISBN 0-312-40005-5). St Martin.
Phillips, D. Z. Religion Without Explanation. 200p. 1976. 18.50x (ISBN 0-631-17100-2, Pub. by Basil Blackwell). Biblio Dist.
Popkin, Richard H. The High Road to Pyrrhonism. Watson, R. A. & Force, J. E., eds. LC 78-10493. (Studies in Hume & Scottish Philosophy). 1979. 25.00x (ISBN 0-89690-002-9); pap. 10.00x (ISBN 0-89690-003-7). Austin Hill Pr.
Price, Henry H. Hume's Theory of the External World. LC 80-25734. 231p. 1981. Repr. of 1940 ed. lib. bdg. 25.00x (ISBN 0-313-22707-1, PRTE). Greenwood.
Price, John V. David Hume. LC 68-24287. (English Authors Ser.: No. 77). 1969. lib. bdg. 10.95 (ISBN 0-8057-1280-1). Twayne.
Rickaby, Joseph J. Free Will & Four English Philosophers. facs. ed. LC 74-84333. (Essay Index Reprint Ser). 1906. 15.50 (ISBN 0-8369-1103-2). Arno.
Ross, W. Gordon. Human Nature & Utility in Hume's Social Philosophy. LC 73-86726. xvi, 107p. (With a new preface). Date not set. Repr. of 1942 ed. cancelled (ISBN 0-8462-1753-8). Russell.
Rotwein, Eugene, ed. David Hume: Writings on Economics. LC 55-12064. 1955. pap. 7.95 (ISBN 0-299-01324-3). U of Wis Pr.
Schatz, Albert. L' Oeuvre Economique de David Hume. (Research & Source Work Ser). 303p. (Fr.). 1972. Repr. of 1902 ed. lib. bdg. 21.00 (ISBN 0-8337-3139-4). B Franklin.
Seth Pringle Pattison, Andrew. Scottish Philosophy: A Comparison of the Scottish & German Answers to Hume. 1971. Repr. of 1890 ed. lib. bdg. 20.50 (ISBN 0-8337-3237-4). B Franklin.
Soghoian, Richard J. The Ethics of G. E. Moore & David Hume: The Treatise As a Response to Moore's Refutation of Ethical Naturalism. LC 79-88306. 1979. pap. text ed. 7.50 (ISBN 0-8191-0774-3). U Pr of Amer.
Stewart, John B. The Moral & Political Philosophy of David Hume. 422p. 1973. Repr. of 1963 ed. lib. bdg. 24.25x (ISBN 0-8371-6488-5, STDH). Greenwood.
Stove, D. C. Probability & Hume's Inductive Scepticism. 146p. 1973. 26.00x (ISBN 0-19-824501-7). Oxford U Pr.
Stroud, Barry. Hume. (Arguments of the Philosophers Ser.). 292p. 1981. pap. 10.00 (ISBN 0-7100-0667-5). Routledge & Kegan.
--Hume. (The Arguments of the Philosophers Ser.). 1977. 22.00x (ISBN 0-7100-8601-6). Routledge & Kegan.
Talmor, Ezra. Descartes & Hume. LC 79-41748. 188p. 1980. 19.75 (ISBN 0-08-024274-X). Pergamon.
Taylor, A. E. David Hume & the Miraculous. LC 72-191241. 1927. lib. bdg. 8.50 (ISBN 0-8414-0845-9). Folcroft.
Taylor, W. L. Francis Hutcheson & David Hume As Predecessors of Adam Smith. LC 65-20591. (Illus.). 1965. 12.75 (ISBN 0-8223-0172-5). Duke.
Todd, William B., ed. Hume & the Enlightenment: Essays Presented to Ernest Campbell Mossner. LC 74-84713. 1974. 12.95 (ISBN 0-87959-003-3). U of Tex Hum Res.
Vesey, Godfrey. Personal Identity. LC 76-41208. (Problems of Philosophy, Cornell Paperback Ser.). 1977. pap. 4.95 (ISBN 0-8014-9162-2). Cornell U Pr.
Wexler, Victor. David Hume & "The History of England". LC 78-68423. (Memoirs Ser.: Vol. 131). 1979. 8.00 (ISBN 0-87169-131-0). Am Philos.
Wilbur, James B., ed. The Worlds of Hume & Kant. rev. ed. Allen, Harold J. 196p. 1981. pap. text ed. 7.95 (ISBN 0-87975-163-0). Prometheus Bks.

HUMIDITY

see also Moisture

Povoledo, D. & Golterman, H., eds. Humic Substances: Their Structure & Function in the Biosphere. 300p. 1975. pap. 60.00 (ISBN 90-220-0552-6, Pub. by PUDOC). Unipub.
Wexler, Arnold, ed. Humidity & Moisture: Measurement & Control in Science & Industry, Vols. 1, 3 & 4. 1964-65. Vol. 1, 704 Pgs. 34.50 (ISBN 0-685-36922-6, Pub. by UNR); Vol. 3, 1977 576 Pgs. 32.50 (ISBN 0-88275-941-8, Pub. by UNR); Vol. 4, 347 Pgs. 26.00 (ISBN 0-685-36924-2). Krieger.

HUMILIATI

see also Waldenses

HUMILITY

Leo, Pope The Practice of Humility. O'Conor, John F., tr. 1980. lib. bdg. 59.95 (ISBN 0-8490-3177-X). Gordon Pr.
--The Practice of Humility. O'Connor, John F., tr. 1976. lib. bdg. 59.95 (ISBN 0-8490-2462-5). Gordon Pr.
Martin, Francis P. Relative Humility One Hundred Percent. 1.95 (ISBN 0-89274-093-0). Harrison Hse.
Mary da Bergamo, Cajetan. Humility of Heart. Vaughan, Herbert C., tr. 240p. 1978. pap. 3.00 (ISBN 0-89555-067-9, 117). Tan Bks Pubs.
Olson, E. E. A Day of Humility. 1973. 2.05 (ISBN 0-89536-051-9). CSS Pub.
Practice of Humilty. 1978. 2.50 (ISBN 0-8198-0546-7); pap. 1.50 (ISBN 0-8198-0547-5). Dghtrs St Paul.

HUMMING-BIRDS

Gans, Roma. Hummingbirds in the Garden. LC 69-11083. (A Let's Read- & Find-Out Science Bk). (Illus.). (gr. k-3). 1969. PLB 8.79 (ISBN 0-690-42562-7, TYC-J). Har-Row.
Grant, Karen A. & Grant, Verne. Hummingbirds & Their Flowers. LC 68-23462. (Illus.). 1968. 20.00x (ISBN 0-231-03126-2). Columbia U Pr.
McClung, Robert M. Ruby Throat: The Story of a Hummingbird. (Illus.). (gr. 1-5). 1950. PLB 6.96 (ISBN 0-688-31538-0); pap. 3.80 pkg. of 4 (ISBN 0-688-35012-7); pap. 9.75 pkg. of 4 with cassette (ISBN 0-688-35011-9). Morrow.
Muir, John. The Hummingbird of the California Waterfalls. Jones, William R., ed. (Illus.). 24p. 1977. Repr. of 1878 ed. pap. 2.00 (ISBN 0-89646-019-3). Outbooks.
Simon, Hilda. Wonders of Hummingbirds. LC 64-22916. (Wonders Ser.). (Illus.). (gr. 3-7). 1964. PLB 5.95 (ISBN 0-396-06882-0). Dodd.
Skutch, Alexander F. The Life of the Hummingbird. (Illus.). 96p. 1980. 15.95 (ISBN 0-517-50572-X). Crown.

HUMOR

see Wit and Humor

HUMORISTS

see also Satirists

Beckett, Arthur W. Recollections of a Humourist. Repr. of 1907 ed. 15.00 (ISBN 0-8274-4145-2). R West.
Besant, Walter. The French Humorists: From the Twelfth to the Ninteenth Century. Date not set. Repr. of 1873 ed. lib. bdg. 40.00 (ISBN 0-8495-0378-7). Arden Lib.
Campbell, C. W. Will Rogers. LC 79-4058. (Story of an American Indian Ser.). (Illus.). (gr. 5 up). 1979. PLB 6.95 (ISBN 0-87518-177-5). Dillon.
Hogarth, William, illus. English Humorists of the Eighteenth Century: Sir Richard Steele, Joseph Addison, Laurence Sterne, Oliver Goldsmith. Repr. of 1906 ed. lib. bdg. 35.00 (ISBN 0-8492-0078-4). R West.
How, Frederick D. Clerical Humor of Olden Times. 1978. Repr. of 1908 ed. lib. bdg. 40.00 (ISBN 0-8492-5315-2). R West.
Jerrold, Walter. A Book of Famous Wits. 1975. Repr. of 1912 ed. 17.50 (ISBN 0-8274-4073-1). R West.
Johnson, Malcolm. David Claypool Johnston, American Graphic Humorist, 1798-1865. (Illus.). 1970. 4.00 (ISBN 0-89073-028-8); pap. 2.00 (ISBN 0-685-72185-X). Boston Public Lib.
Kesterson, David B. Bill Nye. LC 76-45132. (Western Writers Ser.: No. 22). 1970. pap. 2.00 (ISBN 0-88430-021-8). Boise St Univ.
Masson, Thomas L. Our American Humorists. facsimile ed. LC 67-23245. (Essay Index Reprint Ser). 1931. 21.75 (ISBN 0-8369-0692-6). Arno.
Meryman, Richard. Mank: The Wit, World, & Life of Herman Mankiewicz. LC 78-8276. (Illus.). 1978. 12.95 (ISBN 0-688-03356-3). Morrow.
Mikes, George. Eight Humorists. 1977. Repr. of 1954 ed. lib. bdg. 20.00 (ISBN 0-8495-3703-7). Arden Lib.
Nutt, Grady. So Good, So Far. LC 79-90248. 152p. 1981. pap. 4.95 (ISBN 0-914850-68-7). Impact Tenn.
Nye, Bill. Bill Nye, His Own Life Story. facsimile ed. LC 78-124246. (Select Bibliographies Reprint Ser). Repr. of 1926 ed. 22.00 (ISBN 0-8369-5434-3). Arno.
Patterson, Becky C. Hondo: My Father. (Illus.). 268p. 1979. 12.50 (ISBN 0-88319-044-3). Shoal Creek Pub.
Spofford, A. R. English Humorists of the Eighteeth Century: Sir Richard Steele; Joseph Addison; Laurence Sterne; Oliver Goldsmith. 1977. Repr. of 1906 ed. lib. bdg. 40.00 (ISBN 0-8495-4804-7). Arden Lib.
Timbs, John. Lives of Wits & Humourists, 2 vols. 1862. 65.00set (ISBN 0-8495-6279-1). Arden Lib.
Urwin, G. C., ed. Humorists of the Eighteenth Century. (gr. 9-12). 1969. 3.50 (ISBN 0-7195-1432-0). Transatlantic.
Yates, Norris W. American Humorist: Conscience of the Twentieth Century. facsimile ed. 1964. pap. 14.50x (ISBN 0-8138-2205-X). Iowa St U Pr.

HUMOROUS ILLUSTRATIONS

see Caricatures and Cartoons; Wit and Humor, Pictorial

HUMOROUS RECITATIONS

Barton, Jerome, ed. Barton's Comic Recitations: And Humorous Dialogues... facsimile ed. LC 79-167474. (Granger Index Reprint Ser.). Repr. of 1871 ed. 12.00 (ISBN 0-8369-6279-6). Arno.
Brown, Charles W., ed. Comic Recitations & Readings. facs. ed. LC 72-139756. (Granger Index Reprint Ser). 1902. 15.00 (ISBN 0-8369-6210-9). Arno.
McGee, Shelagh. Smile Please. LC 77-27880. (Illus.). (gr. 3 up). 1978. 3.95g (ISBN 0-13-814558-X). P-H.
Pearson, Paul M., ed. The Humourous Speaker: A Book of Humourous Selections for Reading & Speaking. facsimile ed. LC 77-167479. (Granger Index Reprint Ser.). Repr. of 1928 ed. 19.00 (ISBN 0-8369-6284-2). Arno.
Thomas, Gary. Best of the Little Books. LC 79-56010. (Little Book Ser.). (Illus.). 96p. (gr. 1-4). 1980. PLB 5.99 (ISBN 0-8178-5170-4). Harvey.

Wood, Henry F. Good Humor. facs. ed. LC 71-133078. (Granger Index Reprint Ser). 1893. 13.00 (ISBN 0-8369-6208-7). Arno.

HUMOROUS SONGS

Silverman, Jerry. The Dirty Song Book. LC 80-6205. (Illus.). 176p. 1981. 15.95 (ISBN 0-8128-2800-3); pap. 8.95 (ISBN 0-8128-6118-3). Stein & Day.

HUMPHREY, HUBERT HORATIO, 1911-1978

Cohen, Dan. Undefeated: The Life of Hubert H. Humphrey. LC 78-53933. (Adult & Young Adult Bks.). (Illus.). 1978. 25.00 (ISBN 0-8225-9953-8). Lerner Pubns.

Eisele, Albert. Almost to the Presidency. LC 76-187432. 1972. 15.00 (ISBN 0-87832-005-9). Piper.

Engelmayer, Sheldon D. & Wagman, Robert J. Hubert Humphrey: The Man & His Dream. 1979. pap. text ed. 1.95 (ISBN 0-89559-151-0). Dale Books Inc.

HUMPHREY, WILLIAM

Humphrey, William. Farther off from Heaven. 1977. 10.95 (ISBN 0-394-41188-9). Knopf.

HUMPHREYS, DAVID, 1752-1818

Humphreys, Frank L. Life & Times of David Humphreys, Soldier-Stateman-Poet, Belov'd of Washington. LC 73-145099. (Illus.). 1971. Repr. of 1917 ed. 55.00 (ISBN 0-403-01036-5). Scholarly.

HUMUS

see also Compost; Forest Soils

Darwin, Charles. Darwin on Earthworms: The Formation of Vegetable Mould Through the Action of Worms. Orig. Title: Darwin on Humus & the Earthworm. (Illus.). 160p. 1976. 7.95 (ISBN 0-916302-10-5); pap. 3.95 (ISBN 0-916302-06-7). Bookworm Pub.

--Darwin on Humus & the Earthworm: The Formation of Vegetable Mould. 4th ed. 1966. text ed. 5.00x (ISBN 0-571-06778-6). Humanities.

Darwin, Charles R. The Formation of Vegetable Mould, Through the Action of Worms. LC 79-464270. 336p. 1969. Repr. of 1881 ed. 30.00x (ISBN 0-8002-0811-0). Intl Pubns Serv.

Gjessing, Egil T. Physical & Chemical Characteristics of Aquatic Humus. LC 75-36278. (Illus.). 1976. 20.00 (ISBN 0-250-40115-0). Ann Arbor Science.

Isotopes & Radiation in Soil Organic-Matter Studies. (Illus., Orig., Eng. , Fr. , Rus. & Span.). 1968. pap. 36.75 (ISBN 92-0-010368-5, ISP190, IAEA). Unipub.

Organic Materials & Soil Productivity. (FAO Soils Bulletin Ser: No. 35). 1978. pap. 8.50 (ISBN 92-5-100510-9, F1404, FAO). Unipub.

Organic Matter & Soils. (Discovering Soils Ser.: No. 7). 51p. 1979. pap. 6.00 (ISBN 0-686-71837-2, CO 47, CSIRO). Unipub.

Overcash, Michael R. Decomposition of Toxic & Non-Toxic Organic Compounds in Soil. Pal, Dhiraj, ed. 1981. text ed. write for info. Ann Arbor Science.

Soil Organic Matter Studies, Vol. 1. (Illus.). 1977. pap. 44.25 (ISBN 92-0-010077-5, ISP438-1, IAEA). Unipub.

Soil Organic Matter Studies, Vol. 2. 1978. pap. 42.25 (ISBN 92-0-010177-1, ISP 438-2, IAEA). Unipub.

Stevenson, F. J. Humus Chemistry: Genesis, Composition Reactions. 425p. 1982. 35.00 (ISBN 0-471-09299-1, Pub. by Wiley-Interscience). Wiley.

HUNDRED ROLLS

Cam, Helen. Hundred & the Hundred Rolls: An Outline of Local Government in Medieval England. 1960. Repr. of 1930 ed. 21.50 (ISBN 0-8337-0455-9). B Franklin.

HUNDRED YEARS' WAR, 1339-1453

see also Agincourt, Battle Of, 1415

Barnie, John. War in Medieval English Society: Social Values & the Hundred Years War 1337-99. LC 74-2687. 204p. 1974. 16.50x (ISBN 0-8014-0865-2). Cornell U Pr.

The Boke of Noblesse: Addressed to King Edward the Fourth on His Invasion of France in 1475. LC 73-80201. 95p. 1972. Repr. of 1860 ed. lib. bdg. 25.50 (ISBN 0-8337-2524-6). B Franklin.

Burne, Alfred H. The Agincourt War. LC 75-17190. 1976. Repr. of 1956 ed. lib. bdg. 25.25x (ISBN 0-8371-8300-6, BUAW). Greenwood.

--The Crecy War: A Military History of the Hundred Years War from 1337 to the Peace of Bretigny, 1360. LC 75-17195. (Illus.). 1976. Repr. of 1955 ed. lib. bdg. 29.75x (ISBN 0-8371-8301-4, BUCW). Greenwood.

Chandos, Herald. Life of the Black Prince. LC 74-178519. Repr. of 1910 ed. 25.00 (ISBN 0-404-56532-8). AMS Pr.

De Monstrelet, Enguerrend. Chronique D'Enguerrand De Monstrelet, 6 Vols. Douet D'Arcq, L., ed. 1857-62. Set. 212.50 (ISBN 0-384-39781-6); Set. pap. 185.00 (ISBN 0-384-39780-8). Johnson Repr.

D'Escouchy, Mathieu. Chronique De Mathieu D'Escouchy, 3 Vols. 1863-1864. Set. 106.00 (ISBN 0-384-14650-3); Set. pap. 92.50 (ISBN 0-384-14651-1). Johnson Repr.

Edwards, Goronwy. The Second Century of the English Parliament. 1978. 22.50x (ISBN 0-19-822479-6). Oxford U Pr.

Froissart. Chronicles. Brereton, Geoffrey, tr. from Fr. (Classics Ser). 1978. pap. 3.95 (ISBN 0-14-044200-6). Penguin.

Froissart, Jean. Chronicle of Froissart, 6 Vols. Bourchier, John, tr. LC 70-168064. (Tudor Translations. First Ser.: Nos. 27-32). Repr. of 1903 ed. Set. 147.00 (ISBN 0-404-51930-X); 24.50 ea. Vol. 1 (ISBN 0-404-51931-8). Vol. 2 (ISBN 0-404-51932-6). Vol. 3 (ISBN 0-404-51933-4). Vol. 4 (ISBN 0-404-51934-2). Vol. 5 (ISBN 0-404-51935-0). Vol. 6 (ISBN 0-404-51936-9). AMS Pr.

--Here Begynneth the First Volum of Sir J. Froyssart. Bourchier, J., tr. LC 72-26004. (English Experience Ser.: No. 257). 644p. 1970. Repr. of 1523 ed. 104.00 (ISBN 90-221-0257-2). Walter J Johnson.

Harvey, John. The Black Prince & His Age. (Illus.). 184p. 1976. 16.00x (ISBN 0-87471-818-X). Rowman.

Lucas, Henry S. The Low Countries & the Hundred Years' War 1326-1347. LC 76-13150. (Perspectives in European Hist. Ser.: No. 9). Repr. of 1929 ed. lib. bdg. 35.00x (ISBN 0-87991-615-X). Porcupine Pr.

Luce, Simeon, ed. Chronique Du Mont-Saint-Michel 1343-1468, 2 Vols. 1879-83. Set. 55.50 (ISBN 0-384-09010-9); Set. pap. 46.00 (ISBN 0-384-09011-7). Johnson Repr.

Newhall, Richard A. English Conquest of Normandy, 1416-1424: A Study in Fifteenth Century Warfare. LC 71-151553. (Illus.). 1971. Repr. of 1924 ed. 16.00 (ISBN 0-8462-1599-3). Russell.

Seward, Desmond. The Hundred Years War. LC 78-55424. (Illus.). 1978. 11.95 (ISBN 0-689-10919-9). Atheneum.

HUNEKER, JAMES G., 1860-1921

De Casseres, Benjamin. James Gibbons Huneker. 62p. 1980. Repr. of 1925 ed. lib. bdg. 15.00 (ISBN 0-8492-4215-0). R West.

--James Gibbons Huneker. 59.95 (ISBN 0-8490-0433-0). Gordon Pr.

--James Gibbons Huneker. LC 77-17168. 1977. lib. bdg. 15.00 (ISBN 0-8414-1895-0). Folcroft.

Huneker, Josephine. Intimate Letters of James Gibbons Huneker. 1973. Repr. of 1924 ed. 25.00 (ISBN 0-8274-0050-0). R West.

--Letters of James Gibbons Huneker. 1973. Repr. of 1922 ed. 25.00 (ISBN 0-8274-0051-9). R West.

Schwab, Arnold T. James Gibbons Huneker: Critic of the Seven Arts. (Illus.). 1963. 12.50x (ISBN 0-8047-0156-3). Stanford U Pr.

HUNG MEN

Schlegel, Gustave. Thian Ti Hwui: The Hung-League. LC 73-12558. (Illus.). Repr. of 1866 ed. 26.00 (ISBN 0-404-11222-6). AMS Pr.

HUNGARIAN ART

see Art, Hungarian

HUNGARIAN BALLADS AND SONGS–HISTORY AND CRITICISM

Leader, Ninon A. Hungarian Classical Ballads & Their Folklore. 1967. 72.00 (ISBN 0-521-05526-1). Cambridge U Pr.

HUNGARIAN FICTION

see also Short Stories, Hungarian

HUNGARIAN LANGUAGE

Andras, M. Hungarian: How to Say It in. 6th ed. 1979. 4.00x (ISBN 9-6317-4194-X, H275). Vanous.

Andres, P. & Murai, T. How to Say It in Hungarian. 238p. 1980. 10.00x (ISBN 0-569-00222-2, Pub. by Collet's). State Mutual Bk.

Banhidi, Zoltan, et al. Learn Hungarian. 1965. text ed. 22.00x (ISBN 963-17-0971-X). Intl Learn Syst.

Benko, Lorand & Imre, Samu, eds. The Hungarian Language. (Janua Linguarum, Ser. Practica: No. 134). (Illus.). 377p. (Orig.). 1972. pap. text ed. 64.70x (ISBN 90-2792-075-3). Mouton.

Fishman, Joshua A. Hungarian Language Maintenance in the United States. LC 66-63012. (Uralic & Altaic Ser: Vol. 62). (Orig.). 1966. pap. text ed. 5.00x (ISBN 0-87750-021-5). Res Ctr Lang Semiotic.

Foreign Service Institute. Hungarian, Vol. 1. 266p. 1980. plus 24 audio-cassettes 160.00 (ISBN 0-88432-046-4, U500). J Norton Pubs.

Gyarmathi, Samuel. Affinitas Linguae Hungaricae Cum Linguis Fennicae Originis, Grammatice Demonstrata, 1799. (Uralic & Altaic Ser: Vol. 95). (Lat). 1968. pap. text ed. 11.00x (ISBN 0-87750-040-1). Res Ctr Lang Semiotic.

Kakuk, Suzanne. Recherches Sur L'histoire De la Langue Osmanlie Des XVIe et XV11e Siecles: Les Elements Osmanlis De la Langue Hongroise. (Near & Middle East Monographs: No. 17). 1974. 113.75 (ISBN 90-2792-626-3). Mouton.

Kalman, B. The World of Names: A Study in Hungarian Onomatologyl. 1978. 14.50 (ISBN 0-9960009-5-X, Pub. by Kaido Hungary). Heyden.

Keresztes, Kalman. Morphemic & Semantic Analysis of the Word Families: Finnish ETE- & Hungarian EL- 'fore' LC 64-64194. (Uralic & Altaic Ser: Vol. 41). (Orig.). 1964. pap. text ed. 4.00x (ISBN 0-87750-010-X). Res Ctr Lang Semiotic.

Kiefer, Ferenc. On Emphasis & Word Order in Hungarian. LC 66-64930. (Uralic & Altaic Ser: Vol. 76). 1967. pap. text ed. 8.50x (ISBN 0-87750-027-4). Res Ctr Lang Semiotic.

Koski, Augustus A. & Mihalyfy, Ilona. FSI Hungarian Basic Course, Units 1-12. 1963. pap. text ed. 8.75x (ISBN 0-686-10732-2); 24 cassettes 144.00x (ISBN 0-686-10733-0). Intl Learn Syst.

--FSI Hungarian Basic Course, Units 13-24. 1964. pap. text ed. 4.50x (ISBN 0-686-10734-9); 26 cassettes 156.00x (ISBN 0-686-10735-7). Intl Learn Syst.

--FSI Hungarian Graded Reader. 1968. pap. text ed. 9.25x (ISBN 0-686-10736-5); 16 cassettes 96.00x (ISBN 0-686-10737-3). Intl Learn Syst.

Kovacs, Ferenc. Linguistic Structures & Linguistic Laws. Simon, Sandor, tr. from Hungarian. 1971. text ed. 42.75x (ISBN 90-6032-492-7). Humanities.

Magdics, Klara. Studies in the Acoustic Characteristics of Hungarian Speech Sounds. LC 68-65314. (Uralic & Altaic Ser: Vol. 97). (Illus.). 1969. pap. text ed. 7.00x (ISBN 0-87750-041-X). Res Ctr Lang Semiotic.

Tamas, Lajos. Etymologisch-Historisches Worterbuch der Ungarisch Elemente Im Rumanischen: Unter Berucksichtigung der Mundartworter. (Uralic & Altaic Ser.: No. 83). 938p. 1967. text ed. 92.50x (ISBN 0-686-27748-1). Mouton.

Tamas, Magay. Hungarian Dictionary for Tourists: Hungarian. 4th ed. (Orig., English-hungarian-english). 1980. 6.00x (ISBN 9-63205-069-X, H300). Vanous.

Vago, Robert M. The Sound Pattern of Hungarian. 150p. 1980. pap. text ed. 7.95 (ISBN 0-87840-177-6). Georgetown U Pr.

Whitney, Arthur H. Colloquial Hungarian. 2nd ed. (Trubner's Colloquial Manuals). (Illus.). 1977. pap. 7.95 (ISBN 0-7100-8550-8). Routledge & Kegan.

Zsilka, Janos. System of the Hungarian Sentence Patterns. (Uralic & Altaic Ser: Vol. 67). 1967. pap. text ed. 7.00x (ISBN 0-87750-023-1). Res Ctr Lang Semiotic.

HUNGARIAN LANGUAGE–DIALECTS

Arany, A. Laszlo. Phonological System of a Hungarian Dialect: An Introduction to Structural Dialectology. LC 67-63039. (Uralic & Altaic Ser: Vol. 85). (Hun). 1967. pap. text ed. 7.00x (ISBN 0-87750-034-7). Res Ctr Lang Semiotic.

HUNGARIAN LANGUAGE–DICTIONARIES

Budenz, Jozsef. Comparative Dictionary of the Finno-Ugric Elements in the Hungarian Vocabulary. LC 66-64927. (Uralic & Altaic Ser: Vol. 78). (Repr. of 1881 ed). 1966. pap. text ed. 22.00x (ISBN 0-87750-029-0). Res Ctr Lang Semiotic.

Hungarian Little Dictionary, 2 vols. 12th ed. Set. 15.00 (ISBN 0-685-12024-4). Vol. 1, Hungarian-English (ISBN 9-6305-2019-2). Vol. 2, English-Hungarian (ISBN 9-6305-2018-4). Heinman.

Laszlo, Orszagh. English-Hungarian Dictionary. 10th ed. LC 70-250364. 1973. 5.00x (ISBN 0-8002-1399-8). Intl Pubns Serv.

Lee-Delisle, Dora. English-Hungarian, Hungarian-English Medical Dictionary. 18.00 (ISBN 0-87557-040-2, 042-2X). Saphrograph.

Nagy, E. & Klar, J., eds. English-Hungarian Technical Dictionary. 792p. 1980. 70.00x (ISBN 0-686-72096-2, Pub. by Collet's). State Mutual Bk.

Nagy, T. Hungarian-English Technical Dictionary. 752p. 1980. 70.00x (ISBN 0-569-00731-3, Pub. by Collet's). State Mutual Bk.

Orszagh. Hungarian Deluxe Dictionary: English-Hungarian, 2 vols. 4th ed. 1974. 60.00x (ISBN 963-05-0554-1, H-331). Vanous.

--Hungarian Deluxe Dictionary: Hungarian-English, 2 vols. 4th ed. 1974. 60.00x (ISBN 0-686-15319-7, H-330). Vanous.

Orszagh, I. Pocket English-Hungarian Dictionary. 1980. 10.00x (ISBN 0-569-00408-X, Pub. by Collet's). State Mutual Bk.

--Pocket Hungarian-English Dictionary. 1980. 10.00x (ISBN 0-569-00344-X, Pub. by Collet's). State Mutual Bk.

Orszagh, L. English Hungarian Dictionary. 19.50 (ISBN 0-686-65153-7, 043-7). Saphrograph.

--Hungarian-English Dictionary, 2 vols. 24.00 (ISBN 0-87557-042-9, 042-9). Saphrograph.

--Hungarian-English, English-Hungarian Concise Dictionary (1976-79, 2 vols. 45.00 set (ISBN 0-685-29277-0). Vol. 1, Hungarian-English (ISBN 963-05-0612-2). Vol. 2, English-Hungarian (ISBN 9-6305-1883-X). Heinman.

Orszagh, L., ed. Magyar-Angol Szotar Hungarian-English Dictionary. rev. ed. 24.00 (ISBN 0-87557-042-9, 042-9). Saphrograph.

Orszagh, Laszlo. Hungarian Concise Dictionary: English-Hungarian. 9th ed. 1979. 20.00x (ISBN 963-05-1883-X, H-269). Vanous.

--Hungarian-English: English Hungarian (Little) Dictionary, 2 vols. 12th rev. ed. Set. 15.00x (ISBN 963-05-2019-2). Heinman.

--Hungarian Pocket Dictionary: Hungarian-English, Vol. 2. 12th ed. 462p. 1979. 6.00x (ISBN 9-6305-0546-0, H273). Vanous.

Orszagh, V. A Concise English-Hungarian Dictionary. 1091p. 1980. 30.00 (ISBN 0-569-00407-1, Pub. by Collet's). State Mutual Bk.

--A Concise Hungarian-English Dictionary. 1180p. 1980. 25.00x (ISBN 0-569-00343-1, Pub. by Collet's). State Mutual Bk.

--English-Hungarian Dictionary, 2 vols. 2336p. 1980. 99.00x (ISBN 0-569-00359-8, Pub. by Collet's). State Mutual Bk.

--Hungarian-English Dictionary, 2 vols. 2160p. 1980. 125.00x (ISBN 0-569-00409-8, Pub. by Collet's). State Mutual Bk.

Orszagn, L. Angol-Magyar Szotar English-Hungarian Dictionary. 791p. 19.50 (ISBN 0-87557-043-7, 043-7). Saphrograph.

Willerfest, Biro. English-Hungarian, Hungarian-English Dictionary - Angol-Magyar-Angol Szotar. 16.00 (ISBN 0-87557-039-9, 042-2). Saphrograph.

HUNGARIAN LANGUAGE–GRAMMAR

Hall, Robert A. Analytical Grammar of the Hungarian Language. 1938. pap. 6.00 (ISBN 0-527-00822-2). Kraus Repr.

--Hungarian Grammar. 1944. pap. 6.00 (ISBN 0-527-00825-7). Kraus Repr.

Pannonius, Ionnas S. Grammatica Hungaro-Latina. LC 68-65313. (Uralic & Altaic Ser: Vol. 55). (Lat). 1968. pap. text ed. 6.00x (ISBN 0-87750-019-3). Res Ctr Lang Semiotic.

Rice, Lester A. Hungarian Morphological Irregularities. 1970. soft cover 3.95 (ISBN 0-89357-005-2). Slavica.

Sajnovics, Joannis. Demonstratio Idioma Ungarorum & Lapponum Idem Esse. (Uralic & Altaic Ser: Vol. 91). 1967. pap. text ed. 8.00x (ISBN 0-87750-037-1). Res Ctr Lang Semiotic.

Szenciensis, Albertus M. Nova Grammatica Ungarica. LC 68-65315. (Uralic & Altaic Ser: Vol. 98). (Latin). 1969. pap. text ed. 9.50x (ISBN 0-87750-042-8). Res Ctr Lang Semiotic.

Tompa, Jozsef. Ungarische Grammatik. (Janua Linguarum, Series Practica: No. 96). 1968. 77.50x (ISBN 90-2790-674-2). Mouton.

Whitney, A. H. Learn Hungarian for English Speakers. 264p. pap. 7.50 (ISBN 0-87557-044-5, 044-5). Saphrograph.

HUNGARIAN LEGENDS

see Legends, Hungarian

HUNGARIAN LITERATURE (COLLECTIONS)

Csicsery-Ronay, Istvan, ed. Koltok Forradalma, Antologia, 1953-1956. (Hung). 1956. pap. 6.00 (ISBN 0-911050-06-X). Occidental.

Kessler, Jascha, intro. by. The Face of Creation. LC 79-12089. 1980. 8.95 (ISBN 0-89807-011-2); pap. 4.95 (ISBN 0-89807-010-4). Illuminati.

Somogyi, Ferenc. Szajrol Szajra. (Reference Books of Hungarian Self Knowledge). 1978. 12.00 (ISBN 0-918570-02-6). Karpat.

HUNGARIAN LITERATURE–BIO-BIBLIOGRAPHY

Harvard University Library. Hungarian History & Literature: Classification Schedule, Author & Title Listing, Chronological Listing. LC 72-83390. (Widener Library Shelflist Ser: No. 44). 1973. 25.00x (ISBN 0-674-42700-9). Harvard U Pr.

Tezla, Albert. Hungarian Authors: A Bibliographical Handbook. LC 74-88813. 1970. 35.00x (ISBN 0-674-42650-9, Belknap Pr). Harvard U Pr.

HUNGARIAN LITERATURE–HISTORY AND CRITICISM

Cushing, G. F., ed. Hungarian Prose & Verse. (London East European Ser.). 1956. text ed. 15.50x (ISBN 0-485-17501-0, Athlone Pr). Humanities.

Katona, Anna B. Mihaly Vitez Csokonai. (World Authors Ser.: No. 579). 1980. lib. bdg. 13.50 (ISBN 0-8057-6421-6). Twayne.

Klaniaczay, Tibor. History of Hungarian Literature. Date not set. 14.95 (ISBN 0-392-13237-0, SpS). Sportshelf.

Konnyu, Leslie. History of American Hungarian Literature. LC 62-16881. 1962-1963. 4.00 (ISBN 0-685-12523-8); pap. 3.25 (ISBN 0-911862-03-X). Hungarian Rev.

Nyerges, Anton N. Babits & Psychoanalysis Christiana. 112p. (Orig.). 1981. pap. 12.00 (ISBN 0-9600954-2-X). Nyerges.

--Gyula Juhasz the Beard Sunner. 117p. (Orig.). 1980. pap. 12.00 (ISBN 0-9600954-0-3). Nyerges.

Reich, Emil. Hungarian Literature: Historical & Critical Survey. LC 72-80503. Repr. of 1898 ed. 12.50 (ISBN 0-405-08876-0). Arno.

Riech, Emil. Hungarian Literature: An Historical & Critical Survey. 1977. lib. bdg. 69.95 (ISBN 0-8490-2028-X). Gordon Pr.
Riedl, F. A History of Hungarian Literature. 69.95 (ISBN 0-8490-0330-X). Gordon Pr.
Riedl, Frederick. History of Hungarian Literature. Ginever, C. A., tr. LC 68-26602. 1968. Repr. of 1906 ed. 22.00 (ISBN 0-8103-3221-3). Gale.
Scheer, Steven C. Kalman Mikszath. (World Authors Ser.: Hungary: No. 462). 1977. lib. bdg. 11.95 (ISBN 0-8057-6299-X). Twayne.
Tezla, Albert. Introductory Bibliography to the Study of Hungarian Literature. LC 64-19586. 1964. 15.00x (ISBN 0-674-46350-1). Harvard U Pr.
Tezla, Albert, ed. Ocean at the Window: Hungarian Prose & Poetry Since Nineteen Forty Five. 450p. 1980. 25.00x (ISBN 0-8166-0992-6). U of Minn Pr.

HUNGARIAN MUSIC
see Music, Hungarian

HUNGARIAN MYTHOLOGY
see Mythology, Finno-Ugrian

HUNGARIAN PAINTING
see Painting, Hungarian

HUNGARIAN PAINTINGS
see Paintings, Hungarian

HUNGARIAN POTTERY
see Pottery, Hungarian

HUNGARIAN SCULPTURE
see Sculpture–Hungary

HUNGARIAN TALES
see Tales, Hungarian

HUNGARIANS
see also Magyars

HUNGARIANS IN FOREIGN COUNTRIES
Bognar, Desi K. Hungarians in America. LC 72-97113. (East-European Biographies & Studies Ser.: No. 3). 240p. 1972. 8.50x (ISBN 0-912460-01-6). AFI Pubns.
Bognar, Desi K., ed. Hungarians in America: A Biographical Directory of Professionals of Hungarian Origin. rev. ed. LC 79-53801. (East Central European Biographies & Studies Ser.: Nos. 4 & 5). 1979. 25.00 (ISBN 0-685-71858-1). AFI Pubns.
Chaszar, Edward. Decision in Vienna. 1978. 10.00 (ISBN 0-87934-018-5). Danubian.
Fishman, Joshua A. Hungarian Language Maintenance in the United States. LC 66-63012. (Uralic & Altaic Ser: Vol. 62). (Orig.). 1966. pap. text ed. 5.00x (ISBN 0-87750-021-5). Res Ctr Lang Semiotic.
Florescu, Radu R. Magyar Culture in Socialist Romania. (Ethnology Ser.: No. 1). (Illus.). 1976. pap. 2.50 (ISBN 0-89304-005-3, CCC103). Cross Cult.
Konnyu, Leslie. Acacias: Hungarians of the Mississippi Valley. LC 76-6789. 1976. pap. text ed. 4.50 (ISBN 0-685-68332-X). Hungarian Rev.
Lengyel, Emil. Americans from Hungary. LC 72-12628. 319p. 1975. Repr. of 1948 ed. lib. bdg. 15.25x (ISBN 0-8371-6678-0, LEAH). Greenwood.
Nanay, Julia. Transylvania: The Hungarian Minority in Romania. LC 76-19730. (Behind the Iron Curtain Ser.: No. 11). 1976. pap. 5.00 (ISBN 0-87934-014-2). Danubian.
Rezsoe Gracza & Gracza, Margaret. Hungarians in America. LC 68-31503. (In America Bks.). (Illus.). (gr. 5-11). 1969. PLB 6.95g (ISBN 0-8225-0216-X). Lerner Pubns.
Szeplaki, Joseph. The Hungarians in America 1583-1974: A Chronology & Fact Book. LC 75-11505. (Ethnic Chronology Ser.). 160p. 1975. text ed. 8.50 (ISBN 0-379-00514-X). Oceana.
Wass, Albert. Our Hungarian Heritage. 74p. 1975. pap. 3.00 (ISBN 0-87934-013-4). Danubian.

HUNGARY
Antalffy, Gyula. A Short Geography of Hungary. LC 78-304815. (Illus.). 47p. 1977. pap. 3.00x (ISBN 963-13-0238-5). Intl Pubns Serv.
Bartok, Bela. Hungarian Folk Music. Calvocoressi, M. D., tr. LC 77-87537. Repr. of 1931 ed. 37.00 (ISBN 0-404-16600-8). AMS Pr.
Csizmadia, Erno. Socialist Agriculture in Hungary. LC 77-376499. 1977. 15.00x (ISBN 963-05-1184-3). Intl Pubns Serv.
Friss, Istvan, ed. Essays on Economic Policy & Planning in Hungary. (Illus.). 279p. (Orig.). 1978. pap. 7.50x (ISBN 963-13-0156-7). Intl Pubns Serv.
Gaborjan, Alice. Hungarian Peasant Costumes. (Illus.). 1969. 4.00x (ISBN 0-8002-1521-4). Intl Pubns Serv.
Gardos, Miklos, ed. Hungary Seventy Eight. 13th ed. LC 67-32021. (Illus.). 1978. pap. 10.50x (ISBN 0-8002-2182-6). Intl Pubns Serv.
Halasz, Zoltan, ed. Hungary: A Guide with a Difference. (Illus.). 474p. 1978. 15.00x (ISBN 963-13-3007-9). Intl Pubns Serv.
Helmreich, Ernst C., ed. Hungary. LC 72-12328. (Illus.). 466p. 1973. Repr. of 1957 ed. lib. bdg. 21.75x (ISBN 0-8371-6725-6, HEHU). Greenwood.
Hungary Today. 250p. 1974. 15.00x (ISBN 0-8002-1524-9). Intl Pubns Serv.
Konnyu, L. One-Hundred Five Ev Tamasiban: 105 Years in Tamasi. LC 80-65905. (Illus.). 124p. 6.00 (ISBN 0-686-63834-4). Hungarian Rev.
Konnyu, Leslie. Condensed Geography of Hungary. LC 74-156069. 1971. text ed. 6.25 (ISBN 0-685-01022-8); pap. text ed. 4.25 (ISBN 0-911862-19-6). Hungarian Rev.
Lengyel, Emil. The Land & People of Hungary. rev. ed. LC 72-37763. (Portraits of the Nations Ser.). (Illus.). (gr. 6 up). 1972. 8.79 (ISBN 0-397-31545-7, JBL-J). Har-Row.
Manga, Janos. Herdsmen's Art in Hungary. 1972. 4.50x (ISBN 0-8002-0833-1). Intl Pubns Serv.
Sinor, Denis, ed. Modern Hungary: Readings from the New Hungarian Quarterly. LC 77-74441. 448p. 1978. 17.50x (ISBN 0-253-33862-X). Ind U Pr.
Statistical Pocketbook: Hungary. annual 10.00x (ISBN 0-89918-274-7, H-274). Vanous.
Statistical Yearbook, Hungarian. (Yearly). pap. 27.50x (ISBN 0-89918-288-7, H288). Vanous.
Szanto, Miklos, ed. Ways of Life: Hungarian Sociological Studies. Szente, Peter & Saunders, Penelope, trs. from Hungarian. 406p. (Orig.). 1977. pap. 7.50x (ISBN 963-13-3028-1). Intl Pubns Serv.
Volgyes, Ivan. Hungary: A Profile. (Nations of Contemporary Eastern Europe). (Illus.). 128p. 1981. lib. bdg. 16.50x (ISBN 0-89158-929-5). Westview.

HUNGARY–ANTIQUITIES
Ecsedy, Istvan. The People of the Pit-Grave Kurgans in Eastern Hungary. Ecsedy, Judit, et al, trs. (Fontes Archaeoligici Hungariae Ser.). (Illus.). 148p. (Orig.). 1979. pap. 30.00x (ISBN 963-05-1733-7). Intl Pubns Serv.
Foltiny, Stephen. Hungarian Archaeological Collection of the American Museum of Natural History in New York. LC 67-66165. (Uralic & Altaic Ser: Vol. 77). (Illus.). 1969. pap. text ed. 9.00x (ISBN 0-87750-028-2). Res Ctr Lang Semiotic.
Kedves. Paleogene Fossil Sporomorphus of the Bokony Mountains, Vol. I. 1973. 8.75 (ISBN 0-9960001-5-1, Pub. by Kaido Hungary). Heyden.
--Paleogene Fossil Sporomorphus of the Bokony Mountains, Vol. II. 1974. 8.00 (ISBN 0-9960001-6-X, Pub. by Kaido Hungary). Heyden.
--Paleogene Fossil Sporomorphus of the Bokony Mountains, Vol. III. 1979. 11.50 (ISBN 0-9960012-8-X, Pub. by Kaido Hungary). Heyden.

HUNGARY–BIBLIOGRAPHY
Bako, Elemer. Guide to Hungarian Studies, 2 vols. LC 79-152422. (Bibliographical Ser.: No. 52). 1218p. 1973. PLB 45.00 (ISBN 0-8179-2521-X). Hoover Inst Pr.
Kabdebo, Thomas. Hungary. (World Bibliographical Ser.: No. 15). 236p. 1980. 34.75 (ISBN 0-903450-28-3). ABC-Clio.
Volgyes, Ivan. Hungarian Soviet Republic, 1919: An Evaluation & a Bibliography. LC 70-108958. (Bibliographical Ser.: No. 43). 1970. 8.95 (ISBN 0-8179-2431-0). Hoover Inst Pr.

HUNGARY–DESCRIPTION AND TRAVEL
Enyedi, Gyorgy & Meszaros, Julia, eds. Development of Settlement Systems. (Studies in Geography in Hungary: 15). (Illus.). 265p. 1980. 27.50x (ISBN 963-05-1898-8). Intl Pubns Serv.
Gink, K. Hungary Towns & Countryside. 18.50 (ISBN 0-912729-12-0). Newbury Bks Inc.
Granasztoi, Pal. Beautiful Hungarian Towns: Through the Eyes of an Architect. (Illus.). 1978. 12.50x (ISBN 963-13-0231-8). Intl Pubns Serv.
Halasz, Zoltan. Hungary. Beres, Z. & Sollosy, J. B., trs. from Hungarian. Orig. Title: Halasz Zoltan: Szines Magyarorszag. (Illus.). 212p. 1981. 27.50x (ISBN 963-13-0860-X). Intl Pubns Serv.
Hejj, Miklos. The Royal Palace of Visegrad. LC 78-670094. (Illus.). 1977. pap. 5.00x (ISBN 963-13-0026-9). Intl Pubns Serv.
Hungarian State Folk Ensemble. LC 75-329067. (Illus.). 100p. 1975. 12.50x (ISBN 0-8002-1523-0). Intl Pubns Serv.
Kapocsy, Gyorgy. Hortobagy (National Park) Varga, Margaret, tr. from Hungarian. (Illus.). 1980. 11.25x (ISBN 963-13-1103-1). Intl Pubns Serv.
McNair-Wilson, Diana. Hungary. 1976. 22.50 (ISBN 0-7134-3199-7). David & Charles.
Nagel Travel Guide to Hungary. 304p. 1974. 38.00 (ISBN 2-8263-0527-1). Hippocrene Bks.
Nagel's Encyclopedia Guide: Hungary. (Illus.). 304p. 1974. 38.00 (ISBN 2-8263-0527-1). Masson Pub.
Nemeth, Gyula, ed. Hungary: A Comprehensive Guide. (Illus.). 326p. 1981. 12.50x (ISBN 963-13-0975-4). Intl Pubns Serv.
Paget, John. Hungary & Transylvania: With Remarks on Their Social, Political & Economical Condition. LC 79-135827. (Eastern Europe Collection Ser). 1970. Repr. of 1850 ed. 45.00 (ISBN 0-405-02769-9). Arno.
Papp, Antal. Hungary: Guidebook. rev., 2nd ed. Ravasz, Karoly, tr. (Illus.). 1976. Repr. of 1971 ed. 10.00x (ISBN 9-6313-6605-7). Intl Pubns Serv.
Racz, Endre. Tihany. (Illus.). 1978. 12.50x (ISBN 963-13-0433-7). Intl Pubns Serv.
Szabo, Zoltan. Szerelmes Foldrajz. 2nd ed. LC 63-14466. (Hungarian). 1964. 6.00 (ISBN 0-911050-20-5). Occidental.

HUNGARY–ECONOMIC CONDITIONS
Berend, Ivan T. & Ranki, Gyorgy. Underdevelopment & Economic Growth: Studies in Hungarian Social & Economic History. (Illus.). 299p. 1979. 30.00x (ISBN 963-05-1745-0). Intl Pubns Serv.
Enyedi, G., ed. Rural Transformation in Hungary. (Illus.). 1977. 8.50x (ISBN 963-05-1025-1). Intl Pubns Serv.
Enyedi, Gyorgy. Hungary: An Economic Geography. Fischer-Galati, Stephen, ed. LC 76-3742. (Special Studies on Contemporary Eastern Europe Ser). 1976. 32.75x (ISBN 0-89158-030-1). Westview.
Fischer, Lewis A. & Uren, Philip E. The New Hungarian Agriculture. (Illus.). 168p. 1974. 10.00x (ISBN 0-7735-0136-3). McGill-Queen's U Pr.
Friss, Istvan. Reform of the Economic Mechanism in Hungary. LC 77-290601. 1971. Repr. of 1969 ed. 12.50x (ISBN 0-8002-1910-4). Intl Pubns Serv.
Friss, Istvan, ed. Essays on Economic Policy & Planning in Hungary. (Illus.). 279p. (Orig.). 1978. pap. 7.50x (ISBN 963-13-0156-7). Intl Pubns Serv.
Gado, Otto. Reform of the Economic Mechanism in Hungary: Development 1968-71. 314p. 1972. 14.50x (ISBN 0-8002-1909-0). Intl Pubns Serv.
Haraszti, Miklos. A Worker in a Worker's State. Wright, Michael, tr. LC 77-88841. 1978. 10.00x (ISBN 0-87663-307-6). Universe.
Hare, Paul, et al, eds. Hungary: A Decade of Economic Reform. (Illus.). 272p. 1981. text ed. 29.95x (ISBN 0-04-339021-8). Allen Unwin.
Held, Joseph, ed. The Modernization of Agriculture: Rural Transformation in Hungary, 1848-1975. (East European Monographs: No. 67). 1980. 25.00x (ISBN 0-914710-60-5). East Eur Quarterly.
Horchler, Gabriel F., compiled by. Hungarian Economic Reforms: A Selective, Partially Annotated Bibliography. LC 77-7876. (Hungarian Reference Shelf Ser.: No. 3). 1977. 8.95 (ISBN 0-686-23405-7); pap. 4.95 (ISBN 0-686-23406-5). Am Hungarian Foun.
Kornai, Janos. Mathematical Planning of Structural Decisions. 2nd ed. (Contributions to Economic Analysis). 644p. 1975. 58.75 (ISBN 0-444-10734-7, North-Holland). Elsevier.
Vajda, Imre & Simai, M., eds. Foreign Trade in a Planned Economy. LC 74-149433. 1971. 38.50 (ISBN 0-521-08153-X). Cambridge U Pr.
Zsoldos, Laszlo. The Economic Integration of Hungary into the Soviet Bloc: Foreign Trade Experience, 1950-1960. (Illus.). 149p. 1963. 5.00x (ISBN 0-87776-109-4, R-109). Ohio St U Admin Sci.

HUNGARY–FOREIGN RELATIONS
Bogo, Rozalia & Hungarian Academy of Sciences, Institute for World Economics. Hungary & the Developing Countries: A Historical Analysis of Hungary's Foreign Trade with the Developing Countries. (Studies on Developing Countries: No. 100). (Illus.). 73p. (Orig.). 1979. pap. 7.50x (ISBN 963-301-056-X). Intl Pubns Serv.
Juhasz. Hungarian Foreign Policy Nineteen Nineteen to Nineteen Forty-Five. 1979. 29.00 (ISBN 0-9960013-7-9, Pub. by Kaido Hungary). Heyden.
Juhasz, Gyula. Hungarian Foreign Policy, 1919-1945. rev. ed. Simon, Sandor, tr. from Hungarian. LC 80-468278. Orig. Title: Magyarorszag Kulpolitikaja, 1919-1945. 356p. 1979. 30.00x (ISBN 963-05-1882-1). Intl Pubns Serv.
Kertesz, Stephen D. Diplomacy in a Whirlpool. LC 74-7431. (Illus.). 273p. 1974. Repr. of 1953 ed. lib. bdg. 16.50x (ISBN 0-8371-7540-2, KEDW). Greenwood.
Lindberg. Hungary & Sweden, Early Contacts, Early Sources. 1975. 7.50 (ISBN 0-9960005-8-5, Pub. by Kaido Hungary). Heyden.
Major, Mark. American Hungarian Relations, Nineteen Eighteen-Nineteen Forty-Four. LC 74-80001. 288p. 1974. 10.00 (ISBN 0-87934-036-3). Danubian.
Spira, Thomas. German-Hungarian Relations & the Swabian Problem. (East European Monographs: No. 25). 1977. 18.50x (ISBN 0-914710-18-4). East Eur Quarterly.
Urbansky, Andrew B. Byzantium & the Danube Frontier. LC 68-17232. 174p. 1968. text ed. 24.50x (ISBN 0-8290-0158-1); pap. text ed. 9.95x (ISBN 0-8290-0159-X). Irvington.

HUNGARY–HISTORY
Ady, Endre. The Explosive Country: A Selection of Articles & Studies 1898-1916. Cushing, G. F., tr. from Hungarian. 1977. pap. 8.50x (ISBN 963-13-0188-5). Intl Pubns Serv.
Ahmad, I. Letters from the Great Turke. LC 72-164. (English Experience Ser.: No. 292). 16p. Repr. of 1606 ed. 7.00 (ISBN 90-221-0292-0). Walter J Johnson.
Bak, Janos & Kiraly, Bela K., eds. War & Society in Cast Central Europe: Vol. 3, from Hunyadi to Rakoczi: War & Society in Late Medieval & Early Modern Hungary. 600p. 1981. 30.00x (ISBN 0-686-74802-6). Brooklyn Coll Pr.
Bako, Elemer. Guide to Hungarian Studies, 2 vols. LC 79-152422. (Bibliographical Ser.: No. 52). 1218p. 1973. PLB 45.00 (ISBN 0-8179-2521-X). Hoover Inst Pr.
Baress, Gabor. Hungary & Hitler. 1971. pap. 4.00 (ISBN 0-685-03435-6). Danubian.
Bartha. Hungarian Society in the Ninth & Tenth Centuries. 1975. 10.00 (ISBN 0-9960005-7-7, Pub. by Kaido Hungary). Heyden.
Bartha, Antal. Hungarian Society in the Ninth & Tenth Centuries. 147p. 1975. 12.50x (ISBN 963-05-0308-5). Intl Pubns Serv.
Bayerle, Gustav. Ottoman Tributes in Hungary According to Sixteenth Century Tapu Registers of Novigrad. (Near & Middle East Monographs: No. 8). 1973. text ed. 62.50x (ISBN 90-2792-437-6). Mouton.
Berend, Ivan T & Ranki, Gyorgy. Underdevelopment & Economic Growth: Studies in Hungarian Social & Economic History. (Illus.). 299p. 1979. 30.00x (ISBN 963-05-1745-0). Intl Pubns Serv.
Braham, Randolph L. The Hungarian Labor Service System, 1939-1945. (East European Monographs: No. 31). 1977. 11.00x (ISBN 0-914710-24-9). East Eur Quarterly.
Deak, Istvan. The Lawful Revolution: Louis Kossuth & the Hungarians, 1848-1849. LC 78-22063. Orig. Title: Reluctant Rebels. (Illus.). 416p. 1979. 20.00x (ISBN 0-231-04602-2). Columbia U Pr.
Deme, Lazlo & Deme, Laszlo. The Radical Left in the Hungarian Revolution of 1848. (East European Monographs: No. 19). 1976. 12.00x (ISBN 0-914710-12-5). East Eur Quarterly.
Dercsenyi, Dezso. Historical Monuments in Hungary, Restoration & Preservation. LC 70-13941. (Illus.). 180p. 1969. 16.00x (ISBN 0-8002-1497-8). Intl Pubns Serv.
Dienes, Istvan. The Hungarians Cross the Carpathians. Balogh, Barna & Aston, Paul, trs. from Hungarian. (Illus.). 144p. 1972. pap. 7.50x (ISBN 0-8002-0495-6). Intl Pubns Serv.
Eszterhas, Istvan. Szamuzott a Szabadsag Igajaban. 1978. perfect bdg. 10.00 (ISBN 0-912404-10-8). Alpha Pubns.
Halasz, Z. Hungary: A Short History. 1975. 8.75x (ISBN 0-89918-360-3, H-360). Vanous.
Hidas, Peter I. The Metamorphosis of a Social Class in Hungary During the Reign of Young Franz Joseph. (East European Monographs: No. 26). 1977. 12.00x (ISBN 0-914710-19-2). East Eur Quarterly.
Horthy, Nicholas. Admiral Horthy Memoirs. 6.00 (ISBN 0-8315-0062-X). Speller.
Hungarian Historical Research Society. Secret Historical Facts: Events of October 15, 1944; Record of Evidence of Interrogations at Sopronkohida, Hungary. LC 77-95241. Orig. Title: Titkos Tortenelmi Adatok Az 1944 Oktober 15.-I Esemenyek Sopronkohidai Kihallhatasok. 422p. 1978. pap. 15.95 (ISBN 0-935484-02-7). Universe Pub Co.
--Secrete Correspondences of the Leaders of Governments in the Year Nineteen Forty-Four & Earlier Years. LC 80-65046. Orig. Title: Allamvezetok Titkos Levelei Az 1944 Ev Elotti Es Az 1944 Evbol. 110p. 1980. pap. 7.95 (ISBN 0-935484-04-3). Universe Pub Co.
Hungarian Historical Society. Reports of Ministers on the Secrete Meeting of the So Called "Chroncommittee" of the Government of Szalasi. LC 77-85228. 194p. 1980. pap. 11.95 (ISBN 0-935484-05-1). Universe Pub Co.
Ives, Margaret C. Enlightenment & National Revival: Patterns of Interplay & Paradox in Late 18th Century Hungary. LC 79-15155. 1979. 21.75 (ISBN 0-8357-0418-1, SS-00094). Univ Microfilms.
Kabdebo, Thomas. Diplomat in Exile: Francis Pulszky's Political Activities in England, 1849-1860. (East European Monographs: No. 56). 1979. 13.00x (ISBN 0-914710-47-8). East Eur Quarterly.
Kallai, Gyula. The People's Front Movement in Hungary. Gulyas, Gyula, tr. from Hungarian. 304p. (Orig.). 1979. pap. 7.50 (ISBN 963-13-0839-1). Intl Pubns Serv.
Kiraly, Bela. Ferenc Deak. Brown, Arthur W., et al, eds. (World Leaders Ser.: No. 39). 1975. lib. bdg. 10.95 (ISBN 0-8057-3030-3). Twayne.
Kiraly, Bela K. Hungary in the Late Eighteenth Century. LC 69-19459. (East Central European Studies). (Illus.). 274p. 1969. 20.00x (ISBN 0-231-03223-4). Columbia U Pr.

Knatchbull-Hugessen, C. M. Political Evolution of the Hungarian Nation. LC 79-135843. (Eastern Europe Collection Ser). 1970. Repr. of 1908 ed. 30.00 (ISBN 0-405-02785-0). Arno.
Konnyu, Laszlo L. Tamasi Monografiaja. LC 78-74527. (A Monograph of the Hungarian Town of Tamasi). (Illus.). 1979. pap. 5.00 (ISBN 0-685-67251-4). Hungarian Rev.
Kosary, Dominic G. History of Hungary. LC 77-135813. (Eastern Europe Collection Ser). 1970. Repr. of 1941 ed. 24.00 (ISBN 0-405-02755-9). Arno.
Kosztolnyik, Z. J. Five Eleventh Century Hungarian Kings: Their Policies & Their Relations with Rome. (East European Monographs: No. 79). 288p. 1981. text ed. 20.00x (ISBN 0-914710-73-7). East Eur Quarterly.
Kovacs, Tibor. The Bronze Age in Hungary. LC 78-312848. (Illus.). 1977. pap. 8.50x (ISBN 963-13-4490-8). Intl Pubns Serv.
Lukinich, Imre. History of Hungary in Biographical Sketches. facs. ed. LC 68-20314. (Essay Index Reprint Ser). 1937. 15.00 (ISBN 0-8369-0635-7). Arno.
Marczali, Henry. Hungary in the Eighteenth Century. LC 75-135818. (Eastern Europe Collection Ser). 1970. Repr. of 1910 ed. 18.00 (ISBN 0-405-02760-5). Arno.
Pastor, Peter. Hungary Between Wilson & Lenin: The Hungarian Revolution of 1918-1919 & the Big Three. 1976. 13.00x (ISBN 0-914710-13-3). East Eur Quarterly.
Roster of Officers & Similar Assigned Persons, Listed by Ranks, in the Hungarian Armed Forces, 3 vols. LC 76-17260. Orig. Title: A Mkirhonyedseg Csendorseg Tisztjeinek Es Hasonla Allasuaknak Rangsorolasa. 1340p. 1976. Set (ISBN 0-935484-01-9). Vols. 1 & 2. 20.00 ea.; Vol. 3. 50.00 (ISBN 0-686-61485-2). Universe Pub Co.
Sakmyster, Thomas L. Hungary, the Great Powers, & the Danubian Crisis, 1936-1939. LC 78-23678. 298p. 1980. 20.00 (ISBN 0-8203-0469-7). U of Ga Pr.
Sarfalvi, Bela, ed. Changing Face of the Great Hungarian Plain. 1971. 10.00x (ISBN 0-8002-0291-0). Intl Pubns Serv.
Seton-Watson, Hugh & Seton-Watson, Christopher. The Making of a New Europe: R. W. Seton-Watson & the Last Years of Austria-Hungary. 528p. 1981. 50.00 (ISBN 0-295-95792-1). U of Wash Pr.
Seton-Watson, R. W. Racial Problems in Hungary. 540p. 1973. Repr. of 1908 ed. 29.50 (ISBN 0-86527-163-1). Fertig.
Sinor, Denis. History of Hungary. LC 76-26674. 1976. Repr. of 1959 ed. lib. bdg. 19.00x (ISBN 0-8371-9024-X, SIHH). Greenwood.
Somogyi, Ferenc. Kuldetes: A Magyarsag Tortenete. 3rd ed. (Reference Books of Hungarian Self-Knowledge). 1978. 12.50 (ISBN 0-918570-01-8). Karpat.
Sozan, Michael. The History of Hungarian Ethnography. 437p. 1978. pap. text ed. 14.00 (ISBN 0-8191-0361-6). U Pr of Amer.
Spira, Gyorgy. Hungarian Count in the Revolution of 1848. LC 75-323188. (Illus.). 346p. 1974. 17.50x (ISBN 963-05-0326-3). Intl Pubns Serv.
Stroup, Edsel W. Hungary in Early Eighteen Forty Eight: The Constitutional Struggle Against Absolutism in Contemporary Eyes. LC 75-46400. (History Ser.). (Illus.). 1977. 8.80 (ISBN 0-914648-07-1). Hungarian Cultural.
Szabo, Miklos. The Celtic Heritage in Hungary. (Illus.). 90p. 1971. 6.00x (ISBN 0-8002-0720-3). Intl Pubns Serv.
Szemak, J. Living History of Hungary. pap. 2.00 (ISBN 0-685-03436-4). Danubian.
Taylor, A. J. The Habsburg Monarchy, 1809-1918: A History of the Austrian Empire & Austria-Hungary. 1976. pap. 5.50x (ISBN 0-226-79145-9, P683, Phoen). U of Chicago Pr.
Teleki, Paul. Evolution of Hungary & Its Place in European History. (Central & East European Ser.: No. 20). 1975. Repr. of 1923 ed. 15.00 (ISBN 0-87569-059-9). Academic Intl.
Vambery, Arminius. The Story of Hungary. 1886. Repr. 40.00 (ISBN 0-685-43269-6). Norwood Edns.
Vambery, Arminius & Heilprin, Louis. Hungary: In Ancient, Mediaeval & Modern Times. LC 71-39706. (Select Bibliographies Reprint Ser). 1972. Repr. of 1886 ed. 25.25 (ISBN 0-8369-9947-9). Arno.
Vardy, Steven B. Hungarian Historiography & the Geistesgeschichte School. 96p. 1974. 4.00 (ISBN 0-914648-06-3). Hungarian Cultural.
--Modern Hungarian Historiography. (East European Monographs: No. 16). 268p. 1976. 16.50x (ISBN 0-914710-08-7). East Eur Quarterly.
Vass, Henrik, ed. Studies on the History of the Hungarian Working Class Movement: 1867-1966. 429p. 1976. 30.00x (ISBN 963-05-0484-7). Intl Pubns Serv.
Visy, Zsolt. Intercisa: Dunaujvaros in the Roman Period. (Illus.). 1977. pap. 5.00x (ISBN 963-13-4591-2). Intl Pubns Serv.
Volgyes, Ivan. Hungarian Soviet Republic, 1919: An Evaluation & a Bibliography. LC 70-108958. (Bibliographical Ser.: No. 43). 1970. 8.95 (ISBN 0-8179-2431-0). Hoover Inst Pr.
Wagner, Francis. Hungarian Contribution to World Civilisation. exp. ed. 1977. casebound 15.00 (ISBN 0-685-82332-6). Alpha Pubns.
Zarek, Otto. Kossuth. Hudson, Lynton, tr. LC 78-112823. 1970. Repr. of 1937 ed. 12.50 (ISBN 0-8046-1090-8). Kennikat.
Zinner, Paul E. Revolution in Hungary. LC 74-39215. (Select Bibliographies Reprint Ser). Repr. of 1962 ed. 21.00 (ISBN 0-8369-6817-4). Arno.

HUNGARY-HISTORY-REVOLUTION, 1918-1919

Bandholtz, Harry H. Undiplomatic Diary. LC 77-160009. Repr. of 1933 ed. 27.50 (ISBN 0-404-00494-6). AMS Pr.
De Daruvar, Ives. The Tragic Fate of Hungary: A Country Carved up Alive at Trianon. (Illus., Eng.). casebound 10.00 (ISBN 0-912404-03-5). Alpha Pubns.
Hajdu, Tibor. The Hungarian Soviet Republic. De Laczay, Etelka & Fischer, Rudolph, trs. from Hungarian. LC 80-468236. (Studia Historica Academiae Scientiarum Hungaricae Ser.: No. 131). (Illus.). 172p. 1979. 20.00x (ISBN 963-05-1990-9). Intl Pubns Serv.
Janos, Andrew C. & Slottman, William B., eds. Revolution in Perspective: Essays on the Hungarian Soviet Republic. LC 74-138510. 1971. 25.00x (ISBN 0-520-01920-2). U of Cal Pr.
Jaszi, Oscar. Revolution & Counter-Revolution in Hungary. LC 68-9595. 1969. Repr. of 1924 ed. 22.50 (ISBN 0-86527-168-2). Fertig.
Szilassy, Sander. Revolutionary Hungary: 1918-1921. (Behind the Iron Curtain Ser.: No. 9). 1971. pap. 4.00 (ISBN 0-87934-005-3). Danubian.
Volgyes, Ivan, ed. Hungary in Revolution, 1918-19: Nine Essays. LC 71-125855. 1971. 12.50x (ISBN 0-8032-0788-3). U of Nebr Pr.

HUNGARY-HISTORY-REVOLUTION, 1956

Anderson, Andy. Hungary Nineteen Fifty-Six. 1976. pap. 1.90 (ISBN 0-934868-01-8). Black & Red.
Barber, Noel. Seven Days of Freedom. LC 74-78536. 1975. pap. 2.95 (ISBN 0-8128-1861-X). Stein & Day.
--Seven Days of Freedom: The Hungarian Uprising, 1956. LC 74-78536. (Illus.). 280p. 1974. 25.00x (ISBN 0-8128-1730-3). Stein & Day.
James, C. L., et al. Facing Reality. (Illus.). 174p. 1974. pap. 3.00 (ISBN 0-935590-05-6). Bewick Edns.
Kecskemeti, Paul. The Unexpected Revolution: Social Forces in the Hungarian Uprising. 1961. 12.50x (ISBN 0-8047-0085-0). Stanford U Pr.
Kiraly, Bela K. & Jonas, Paul. The Hungarian Revolution of 1956 in Retrospect. (Eastern European Monographs: No. 40). 1978. 11.00x (ISBN 0-914710-33-8). East Eur Quarterly.
Kurland, Gerald. The Hungarian Rebellion of 1956. (Events of Our Times Ser.: No. 17). 32p. (Orig.). (gr. 7-12). 1974. lib. bdg. 2.95 incl. catalog cards (ISBN 0-686-07230-8); pap. 1.50 vinyl laminated covers (ISBN 0-686-07231-6). SamHar Pr.
Laping, Francis & Knight, Hans. Remember Hungary 1956: A Pictorial History of the Hungarian Revolution in 1956. 300p. (YA) 1975. 30.00 (ISBN 0-912404-01-9). Alpha Pubns.
Lasky, Melvin J., ed. The Hungarian Revolution: A White Book. facsimile ed. LC 70-119936. (Select Bibliographies Reprint Ser). Repr. of 1957 ed. 26.00 (ISBN 0-8369-5379-7). Arno.
Lomax, Bill. Hungay Nineteen Fifty-Six. LC 76-41633. (Motive Ser.). 1977. 17.95 (ISBN 0-312-40145-0). St Martin.
Michener, James A. Bridge at Andau. (gr. 10 up). 1957. 12.95 (ISBN 0-394-41778-X). Random.
Radvanyi, Janos. Hungary & the Superpowers: The 1956 Revolution & Realpolitik. LC 71-17028. (Publications Ser.: No. 111). 197p. 1972. 9.95 (ISBN 0-8179-6111-9). Hoover Inst Pr.

HUNGARY-INTELLECTUAL LIFE

Aczel, Tamas & Meray, Tibor. The Revolt of the Mind. LC 74-20275. 449p. 1975. Repr. of 1960 ed. lib. bdg. 24.00x (ISBN 0-8371-7851-7, ACRM). Greenwood.
Cultural Policy in Hungary. (Studies & Documents on Cultural Policies). (Illus.). 79p. (Orig.). 1974. pap. 5.00 (ISBN 92-3-101169-3, U123, UNESCO). Unipub.
Erdy-Gruz, Tibor. Science & Scholarship in Hungary. 2nd ed. 417p. 1976. 11.75x (ISBN 963-13-3006-0). Intl Pubns Serv.

HUNGARY-JUVENILE LITERATURE

Gidal, Sonia. My Village in Hungary. LC 74-152. (Illus.). 96p. (gr. 4-8). 1974. PLB 5.69 (ISBN 0-394-92127-5). Pantheon.
Norris, Marianna. Young Hungary. LC 70-102729. (Illus.). (gr. 3 up). 1970. 4.50 (ISBN 0-396-07168-6). Dodd.
Seredy, Kate. Good Master. (Illus.). (gr. 4-6). 1935. 5.95 (ISBN 0-670-34592-X). Viking Pr.

HUNGARY-POLITICS AND GOVERNMENT

Aczel, Tamas & Meray, Tibor. The Revolt of the Mind. LC 74-20275. 449p. 1975. Repr. of 1960 ed. lib. bdg. 24.00x (ISBN 0-8371-7851-7, ACRM). Greenwood.
Aptheker, Herbert. The Truth About Hungary. LC 57-2931. 1976. Repr. of 1957 ed. 17.00 (ISBN 0-527-03001-5). Kraus Repr.
Berend, Ivan T. & Ranki, Gyorgy. Underdevelopment & Economic Growth: Studies in Hungarian Social & Economic History. (Illus.). 299p. 1979. 30.00x (ISBN 963-05-1745-0). Intl Pubns Serv.
Dubcek, Alexander. Dubcek's Blueprint for Freedom. Lunghi, Hugh, intro. by. 352p. 1969. 10.00x (ISBN 0-7183-0231-1). Intl Pubns Serv.
Gombos, Gyula, ed. Szabo Dezso Es a Magyar Miniszterelnokok. (Hungarian.). 1975. 6.00 (ISBN 0-911050-43-4). Occidental.
Graham, M. W., Jr. New Governments of Eastern Europe. LC 27-20024. (Illus.). 1969. Repr. of 1927 ed. 33.00 (ISBN 0-527-35250-0). Kraus Repr.
Hadju. The Hungarian Soviet Republic. 1979. 17.50 (ISBN 0-9960013-6-0, Pub. by Kaido Hungary). Heyden.
Huszar, Tibor, et al, eds. Hungarian Society & Marxist Sociology in the Nineteen Seventies. Dienes, G., tr. from Hungarian. LC 81-457176. 280p. (Orig.). 1978. pap. 7.50x (ISBN 963-13-0378-0). Intl Pubns Serv.
Kadar, Janos. For a Socialist Hungary. LC 76-357871. 404p. 1974. 10.00x (ISBN 0-8002-0812-9). Intl Pubns Serv.
Kallai, Gyula. The People's Front Movement in Hungary. Gulyas, Gyula, tr. from Hungarian. 304p. (Orig.). 1979. pap. 7.50 (ISBN 963-13-0839-1). Intl Pubns Serv.
Kallay, Miklos. Hungarian Premier: A Personal Account of a Nation's Struggle in the Second World War. Repr. of 1954 ed. lib. bdg. 23.25x (ISBN 0-8371-3965-1, KAHP). Greenwood.
Knatchbull-Hugessen, C. M. Political Evolution of the Hungarian Nation. LC 79-135843. (Eastern Europe Collection Ser). 1970. Repr. of 1908 ed. 30.00 (ISBN 0-405-02785-0). Arno.
Kovrig, Bennett. The Hungarian People's Republic. LC 72-101458. (Integration & Community Building in Eastern Europe Ser: No. 7). (Illus.). 206p. 1970. 14.00x (ISBN 0-8018-1126-0); pap. 2.95x (ISBN 0-8018-1128-7). Johns Hopkins.
Malyusz, Edith C. The Theatre & National Awakening. Szendrey, Thomas, tr. LC 79-89134. 349p. 1980. write for info. (ISBN 0-914648-10-1). Hungarian Cultural.
Marczali, Henry. Hungary in the Eighteenth Century. LC 75-135818. (Eastern Europe Collection Ser). 1970. Repr. of 1910 ed. 18.00 (ISBN 0-405-02760-5). Arno.
Mezerik, Avrahm G., ed. Hungary & UN. 1958. pap. 15.00 (ISBN 0-685-13199-8, 40). Intl Review.
Nemes, Dezso. History of the Revolutionary Workers Movement in Hungary, 1944-1962. 387p. 1973. 12.50x (ISBN 0-8002-0831-5). Intl Pubns Serv.
Seton-Watson, R. W. Racial Problems in Hungary. 540p. 1973. Repr. of 1908 ed. 29.50 (ISBN 0-86527-163-1). Fertig.
Spira, Thomas. German-Hungarian Relations & the Swabian Problem. (East European Monographs: No. 25). 1977. 18.50x (ISBN 0-914710-18-4). East Eur Quarterly.
Szabad. Hungarian Political Trends Between the Revolution & the Compromise (1849 to 1867) 1977. 12.50 (ISBN 0-9960005-6-9, Pub. by Kaido Hungary). Heyden.
Szabod, Segy. Hungarian Political Trends Between the Revolution & the Compromise (1849-1867) 1977. 14.00x (ISBN 963-05-1221-1). Intl Pubns Serv.
Tilkovzky, L. Pal Teleki. 70p. 1974. 6.50x (ISBN 963-05-0371-9). Intl Pubns Serv.
Toma, Peter A. & Volgyes, Ivan. Politics in Hungary. LC 76-29613. (Illus.). 1977. text ed. 17.95x (ISBN 0-7167-0557-5). W H Freeman.
Zarek, Otto. Kossuth. Hudson, Lynton, tr. LC 78-112823. 1970. Repr. of 1937 ed. 12.50 (ISBN 0-8046-1090-8). Kennikat.

HUNGER

see also Appetite

Archer, Jules. Hunger on Planet Earth. LC 76-3603. (Illus.). (gr. 8 up). 1977. 10.00 (ISBN 0-690-01126-1, TYC-J). Har-Row.
Ball, Nicole. World Hunger: A Guide to the Economic & Political Dimensions. Burns, Richard D., ed. (War-Peace Bibliography Ser.: No. 15). (Illus.). 1981. lib. bdg. 46.50 (ISBN 0-87436-308-X). ABC-Clio.
Bigman, David. Coping with Hunger: Toward a System of Food Security & Price Stabilization. Date not set. write for info. (ISBN 0-88410-371-4). Ballinger Pub.
Bobo, Kimberley A., ed. World Food-Hunger Studies. 1977. pap. write for info. Inst World Order.
Booth, D. A., ed. Hunger Models: Computable Theory of Feeding Control. 1978. 76.00 (ISBN 0-12-115950-7). Acad Pr.
Cesaretti, Charles, et al. To Care Enough: For Christians Concerned About the Hungry. 1979. Kit. pap. text ed. 7.95 (ISBN 0-03-049511-3). Winston Pr.
Coles, Robert. Still Hungry in America. (Illus.). 128p. 1973. pap. 3.95 (ISBN 0-452-25142-7, Z5142, Plume). NAL.
Crouch, Tim & Dessem, Ralph. Hunger Workbook. (Orig.). 1977. pap. text ed. 4.05 (ISBN 0-89536-099-3). CSS Pub.
DeCastro, Josue. The Geopolitics of Hunger. rev. & enl. ed. LC 52-5012. 1977. 18.50 (ISBN 0-85345-357-8, CL-3578); pap. 7.50 (ISBN 0-85345-456-6, PB4566). Monthly Rev.
Dumont, Rene & Cohen, Nicholas. The Growth of Hunger: Concerning a New Politics of Agriculture. (Ideas in Progress). 240p. 1980. 15.00 (ISBN 0-7145-2641-X, Pub. by M Boyars); pap. 7.95 (ISBN 0-7145-2642-8). Merrimack Bk Serv.
Ensminger, Douglas & Bomani, Paul. Conquest of World Hunger & Poverty. (Illus.). 140p. 1980. text ed. 7.50 (ISBN 0-8138-1140-6). Iowa St U Pr.
Hessel, Dieter & Hissel, Dieter, eds. The Agricultural Mission of Churches & Land-Grant Universities: Papers. 1979. pap. text ed. 7.50 (ISBN 0-8138-0920-7). Iowa St U Pr.
Holden, Frances. Study of the Effect of Starvation Upon Behavior by Means of the Obstruction Method. LC 27-998. 1926. pap. 5.00 (ISBN 0-527-24852-5). Kraus Repr.
The Hunger Problematique & a Critique of Research. 72p. 1981. pap. 5.00 (ISBN 92-808-0163-5, TUNU 131, UNU). Unipub.
Linowitz, Sol M. World Hunger: A Challenge to American Policy. LC 80-85486. (Headline Ser.: No. 252). (Illus.). 64p. 1980. pap. 2.00 (ISBN 0-87124-065-3). Foreign Policy.
Lord Walston. Dealing with Hunger. 1977. 10.00 (ISBN 0-370-10464-1). Transatlantic.
Novin, D., et al, eds. Hunger: Basic Mechanisms & Clinical Implications. LC 75-14563. 510p. 1976. 39.00 (ISBN 0-89004-059-1). Raven.
Pettepiece, Thomas G. Visions of a World Hungry: Study, Prayer, & Action. LC 79-63097. 1979. pap. text ed. 3.95x (ISBN 0-8358-0371-6). Upper Room.
Pike, Morris D. Your Need for Bread Is Mine. (Orig.). 1977. pap. 2.45 (ISBN 0-377-00067-1). Friend Pr.
A Record of Experience: FFHC-Action for Development. 1978. pap. 7.50 (ISBN 92-5-100316-5, F1361, FAO). Unipub.
Sorokin, Pitirim A. Hunger As a Factor in Human Affairs. Smith, T. Lynn, ed. Sorokin, Elena P., tr. LC 75-11850. (Illus.). 1975. 12.50 (ISBN 0-8130-0519-1). U Presses Fla.
Stakman, E. C., et al. Campaigns Against Hunger. LC 67-20882. (Illus.). 1967. 16.50x (ISBN 0-674-09150-7, Belknap Pr). Harvard U Pr.
Sugar, Maurice. Ford Hunger March. LC 80-81137. (Studies in Law & Social Change: No.1). 1980. pap. 5.00 (ISBN 0-913876-15-1). Meiklejohn Civil Lib.
Sumner, William G. Earth-Hunger & Other Essays. 404p. 1980. text ed. 19.95 (ISBN 0-87855-323-1); pap. text ed. 6.95 (ISBN 0-87855-705-9). Transaction Bks.
Turner, Ewart. Feed My Sheep: Sermons for an Awareness of World Hunger. (Orig.). 1977. pap. 3.50 (ISBN 0-89536-073-X). CSS Pub.
Woito, Robert, ed. World Hunger Crisis Kit. 1975. pap. 1.50 (ISBN 0-912018-19-4). World Without War.

HUNS

Maenchen-Helfen, Otto J. The World of the Huns: Studies in Their History & Culture. Knight, Max, ed. LC 79-94985. 1973. 35.00x (ISBN 0-520-01596-7). U of Cal Pr.
Thompson, E. A. A History of Attila & the Huns. LC 74-9320. 228p. 1975. Repr. of 1948 ed. lib. bdg. 19.75x (ISBN 0-8371-7640-9, THAH). Greenwood.

HUNT, H. L.

Hurt, Harry, III. Texas Rich: The Hunt Dynasty from the Early Oil Days Through the Silver Crash. (Illus.). 1981. 16.95 (ISBN 0-393-01391-X). Norton.

HUNT, JAMES HENRY LEIGH, 1784-1859

Blunden, Edmund. Leigh Hunt's "Examiner" Examined. xiii, 263p. 1967. Repr. of 1928 ed. 18.50 (ISBN 0-208-00258-8, Archon). Shoe String.
Blunden, Edmund C. Leigh Hunt's Examiner Examined: Comprising Some Accounts of That Celebrated Newspaper's Contents. 1973. Repr. of 1928 ed. 6.95 (ISBN 0-8274-1349-1). R West.
Brewer, L. Leigh Hunt & Charles Dickens: The Skimpole Caricature. LC 72-160466. (English Literature Ser., No. 33). 1971. Repr. of 1930 ed. lib. bdg. 54.95 (ISBN 0-8383-1301-9). Haskell.

Brewer, Luther A. Leigh Hunt & Charles Dickens: The Skimpole Caricature. LC 74-7385. 1930. lib. bdg. 6.75 (ISBN 0-8414-3169-8). Folcroft.
--Some Lamb & Browning Letters to Leigh Hunt. LC 72-196923. 1924. lib. bdg. 6.50 (ISBN 0-8414-2541-8). Folcroft.
Brewer, Luther A. & Iowa University Library, eds. My Leigh Hunt Library, Vol. 1: The First Editions. 1970. Repr. of 1932 ed. 25.50 (ISBN 0-8337-0369-2). B Franklin.
--My Leigh Hunt Library, Vol. 2: The Holograph Letters. 1967. Repr. of 1938 ed. 29.50 (ISBN 0-8337-0370-6). B Franklin.
Green, David B. & Wilson, Edwin G., eds. Keats, Shelley, Byron, Hunt & Their Circles: A Bibliography, July 1, 1950-June 30, 1962. LC 64-15181. 1964. 15.00x (ISBN 0-8032-0059-5). U of Nebr Pr.
Harper, Howard. Byron's Malach Hamoves: A Commentary of Leigh Hunt's Work Entitled, Lord Byron & Some of His Contemporaries. rev. ed. LC 72-14285. 1933. lib. bdg. 15.00 (ISBN 0-8414-1350-9). Folcroft.
Hunt, Leigh. Autobiography of Leigh Hunt, 2 Vols. LC 25-25547. Repr. of 1850 ed. Set. 37.50 (ISBN 0-404-03415-2). Vol. 1 (ISBN 0-404-03416-0). Vol. 2 (ISBN 0-404-03417-9). AMS Pr.
--Leigh Hunt's Autobiography: The Earliest Sketches. Fogle, Stephen F., ed. LC 59-63812. (U Fo Fla. Humanities Monographs: No. 2). 1959. pap. 3.00 (ISBN 0-8130-0117-X). U Presses Fla.
Hunt, Vincent. Letters to Leigh Hunt from His Son Vincent. Mumby, A. N., ed. LC 76-45785. 1976. Repr. of 1934 ed. lib. bdg. 10.00 (ISBN 0-8414-6053-1). Folcroft.
Ireland, Alexander. List of the Writings of William Hazlitt, Leigh Hunt & Charles Lamb. LC 70-102856. (Bibliography & Reference Ser: No. 299). 1970. Repr. of 1868 ed. lib. bdg. 13.00 (ISBN 0-8337-1806-1). B Franklin.
Johnson, R. B. Shelley-Leigh Hunt: How Friendship Made History. LC 72-3431. (Studies in Shelley, No. 25). 1972. Repr. of 1929 ed. lib. bdg. 56.95 (ISBN 0-8383-1536-4). Haskell.
Johnson, R. Brimley, ed. Leigh Hunt. LC 73-115182. (English Literature Ser., No. 33). 1970. Repr. of 1896 ed. lib. bdg. 45.95 (ISBN 0-8383-1010-9). Haskell.
Keats-Shelley Memorial House, Rome. Catalog of Books & Manuscripts at the Keats-Shelley Memorial House in Rome. 1969. lib. bdg. 50.00 (ISBN 0-8161-0856-0). G K Hall.
Kent, Charles. Leigh Hunt As Poet & Essayist. 1973. Repr. of 1889 ed. 25.00 (ISBN 0-8274-0026-8). R West.
Law, Marie H. English Familiar Essay in the Early Nineteenth Century: The Elements Old & New Which Went into Its Making, As Exemplified in the Writings of Hunt, Hazlitt & Lamb. LC 65-17906. 1965. Repr. of 1934 ed. 7.50 (ISBN 0-8462-0580-7). Russell.
Miller, Barnett. Leigh Hunt's Relations with Byron, Shelley & Keats. LC 72-194452. 1910. lib. bdg. 17.50 (ISBN 0-8414-6616-5). Folcroft.
Mitchell, Alexander. A Bibliography of the Writings of Leigh Hunt with Critical Notes. LC 73-14762. 1927. Repr. lib. bdg. 10.00 (ISBN 0-8414-5985-1). Folcroft.

HUNT, RICHARD MORRIS

Baker, Paul R. Richard Morris Hunt. (Illus.). 1980. 39.95x (ISBN 0-262-02139-0). MIT Pr.

HUNT, WILLIAM HOLMAN, 1827-1910

Kerr, Robert. Correspondence, 2 vols. LC 78-171062. (Bannatyne Club, Edinburgh. Publications). Repr. of 1875 ed. Set. 62.00 (ISBN 0-404-52896-1). AMS Pr.
Landow, George. William Holman Hunt & Typological Symbolism. LC 77-91017. 1979. 35.00x (ISBN 0-300-02196-8). Yale U Pr.

HUNT, WILLIAM MORRIS, 1824-1879

Hoppin, Martha J. & Adam, Henry S. William Morris Hunt: A Memorial Exhibition. LC 79-2475. (Illus.). 1979. pap. 6.95 (ISBN 0-87846-138-8). Mus Fine Arts Boston.
Ruskin, John. The Art of England: Lectures Given in Oxford by John Ruskin During His Second Tenure of the Slade Professorship. Freedberg, Sydney J., ed. LC 77-25769. (Connossseurship, Criticism, & Art History Ser.: Vol. 23). 292p. 1979. lib. bdg. 21.00 (ISBN 0-8240-3281-0). Garland Pub.

HUNT FAMILY

Lockley, Fred. To Oregon by Ox Team in '47. facs. ed. 16p. Repr. pap. 3.75 (ISBN 0-8466-0145-1, SJS145). Shorey.

HUNTER, CATFISH

Deegan, Paul. Catfish Hunter. (Sports Superstars Ser.). (Illus.). (gr. 3-9). 1979. PLB 5.95 (ISBN 0-87191-720-3); pap. 2.95 (ISBN 0-89812-159-0). Creative Ed.

HUNTER COLLEGE, NEW YORK

Bildersee, A. State Scholarship Students at Hunter College of the City of New York. LC 77-176563. (Columbia University. Teachers College. Contributions to Education: No. 540). Repr. of 1932 ed. 17.50 (ISBN 0-404-55540-3). AMS Pr.

HUNTERDON MEDICAL CENTER

Curry, et al. Twenty Years of Community Medicine: A Hunterdon Medical Center Symposium. LC 74-80237. (Illus.). 192p. 1974. 15.00 (ISBN 0-914366-01-7). Columbia Pub.

HUNTERS' LODGES (SECRET SOCIETIES)

Corey, Albert B. Crisis of Eighteen Thirty to Eighteen Forty-Two in Canadian - American Relations. LC 77-102483. (Relations of Canada & the U. S. Ser). (Illus.). 203p. 1970. Repr. of 1941 ed. 11.00 (ISBN 0-8462-1356-7). Russell.

HUNTING

see also Big Game Hunting; Bird Dogs; Camping; Decoys (Hunting); Falconry; Fowling; Game and Game-Birds; Dogs; Hunting with Bow and Arrow; Trapping;
also headings beginning with names of animals and birds hunted, e.g. Deer Hunting, Duck Shooting, Fox Hunting, Moose Hunting

Acerrano, Anthony J. The Practical Hunter's Handbook. (Illus.). 1978. 9.95 (ISBN 0-87691-342-7). Winchester Pr.
Amory, Cleveland. Man Kind? Our Incredible War on Wildlife. LC 76-181605. 352p. (YA) 1974. 12.50 (ISBN 0-06-010092-3, HarpT). Har-Row.
Anderson, Luther A. Hunting the Woodlands for Small & Big Game. LC 78-75295. (Illus.). 1980. 12.00 (ISBN 0-498-02348-6). A S Barnes.
Bashline, L. James, ed. The Eastern Trail. (Illus.). 320p. 1972. 8.95 (ISBN 0-88395-014-6). Freshet Pr.
Bauer, Erwin A., ed. Hunter's Digest. 2nd ed. (Illus.). 288p. pap. 7.95 (ISBN 0-695-81314-5). DBI.
Berners, Juliana. The Boke of Saint Albans Containing Treatises on Hawking, Hunting & Cote Armour. 1976. Repr. of 1881 ed. 25.00 (ISBN 0-403-06683-2, Regency). Scholarly.
--The Book of Hawking, Hunting & Blasing of Arms. LC 74-25849. (English Experience Ser.: No. 151). 180p. 1969. Repr. of 1486 ed. 42.00 (ISBN 90-221-0151-7). Walter J Johnson.
Bourjaily, Vance. Country Matters: Collected Reports from the Fields & Streams of Iowa & Other Places. 352p. 1973. 8.95 (ISBN 0-8037-1627-3). Dial.
Bowring, Dave. How to Hunt. (Illus.). 1978. 10.95 (ISBN 0-87691-251-X). Winchester Pr.
Brakefield, Tom. Small Game Hunting. (Illus.). 1978. 10.00 (ISBN 0-397-01318-3). Har-Row.
Brister, Bob. Shotgunning: The Art & the Science. 1976. 12.95 (ISBN 0-87691-184-X). Winchester Pr.
Bucher, Ruth & Gelb, Norman. The Book of Hunting. LC 77-5031. (Illus.). 1977. 60.00 (ISBN 0-448-22185-3). Paddington.
Cadman, Arthur. A Guide to Rough Shooting. LC 74-15791. (Illus.). 144p. 1975. 11.95 (ISBN 0-7153-6637-8). David & Charles.
Cartier, John O., ed. Twenty Great Trophy Hunts. 1980. 17.95 (ISBN 0-679-51379-5). McKay.
Clarke, H. Edwardes. The Waterloo Cup: (1922-1977) 1981. 60.00x (ISBN 0-904558-40-1, Pub. by Saiga Pub). State Mutual Bk.
Danziger, Jeff & Davis, Tom. Unofficial Hunting Rules. (Illus.). 64p. (Orig.). 1980. pap. 3.95 (ISBN 0-9603900-5-7). Lanser Pr.
De Ruttie, Andrew. Hunting on a Budget -- for Food & Profit. LC 75-13183. 192p. (Orig.). 1975. pap. 1.25 (ISBN 0-89041-039-9, 3039). Major Bks.
Dickey, Charley. Charley Dickey's Bobwhite Quail Hunting. LC 74-79232. (Family Guide Book Ser). (Illus.). 1974. pap. 3.95 (ISBN 0-8487-0362-6). Oxmoor Hse.
Eggert, Richard. Fish & Hunt the Backcountry. LC 78-17135. (Illus.). 224p. 1978. 9.95 (ISBN 0-8117-0191-3). Stackpole.
Elliott, William. Carolina Sports by Land & Water: Incidents of Devil-Fishing, Wild-Cat, Deer & Bear Hunting. (Illus.). 1978. Repr. of 1859 ed. 10.00 (ISBN 0-87921-040-0). Attic Pr.
Elman, Robert. One Thousand One Hunting Tips. (Illus.). 1978. 15.95 (ISBN 0-87691-266-8). Winchester Pr.
Elman, Robert, ed. The Complete Book of Hunting. LC 80-21486. (Illus.). 320p. 1981. 49.95 (ISBN 0-89659-174-3). Abbeville Pr.
Fadala, Sam. Blackpowder Hunting. LC 78-17940. (Illus.). 256p. 1978. 10.95 (ISBN 0-8117-0251-0). Stackpole.
Ferber, Steve, ed. All About Rifle Hunting & Shooting in America. 1977. 12.95 (ISBN 0-87691-244-7). Winchester Pr.
Field & Stream. Field & Stream Reader. facs. ed. LC 77-128242. (Essay Index Reprint Ser). 1946. 19.50 (ISBN 0-8369-1875-4). Arno.
Fischl, Josef & Lee, Leonard, III. After Your Deer Is Down. 160p. 1981. pap. 9.95 (ISBN 0-87691-353-2). Winchester Pr.
Frankenstein, Alfred. After the Hunt. LC 68-31417. (Illus.). 1975. 48.50 (ISBN 0-520-02936-4). U of Cal Pr.
Gilsvik, Bob. All Season Hunting. 1976. 11.95 (ISBN 0-87691-181-5). Winchester Pr.
--The Guide to Good Cheap Hunting. LC 77-8759. (Illus.). 1979. pap. 5.95 (ISBN 0-8128-6031-4). Stein & Day.
Gooch, Bob. Conveys & Singles. LC 78-75306. (Illus.). 192p. 1980. 10.95 (ISBN 0-498-02342-7). A S Barnes.
--Land You Can Hunt. LC 78-75307. (Illus.). 1980. 12.00 (ISBN 0-498-02390-7). A S Barnes.
Grinnell, George B. & Sheldon, Charles, eds. Hunting & Conservation. LC 71-125741. (American Environmental Studies). 1970. Repr. of 1925 ed. 25.00 (ISBN 0-405-02666-8). Arno.
Gryndall, William. Hawking, Hunting, Fouling & Fishing; Newly Corrected by W. Gryndall Faulkener. LC 70-38194. (English Experience Ser.: No. 463). 88p. 1972. Repr. of 1596 ed. 13.00 (ISBN 90-221-0463-X). Walter J Johnson.
Hacker, Rick. The Muzzleloading Hunter. 224p. 1981. 14.95 (ISBN 0-87691-354-0). Winchester Pr.
Hagel, Bob. Game Loads & Practical Ballistics for the American Hunter. LC 77-21053. (Illus.). 1978. 12.95 (ISBN 0-394-40397-5). Knopf.
Hall, Marty & Penfold, Pam. One Stride Ahead. 288p. 1981. 15.95 (ISBN 0-87691-331-1). Winchester Pr.
Hammond, Samuel H. Wild Northern Scene or Sporting Adventures with Rifle & the Rod. (Illus.). 1979. Repr. of 1857 ed. 12.50 (ISBN 0-916346-33-1). Harbor Hill Bks.
Hastings, Macdonald. Churchill's Gameshooting. 254p. 1974. 19.95 (ISBN 0-7181-0962-7, Pub. by Michael Joseph). Merrimack Bk Serv.
Heacox, Cecil E. & Heacox, Dorothy. The Gallant Grouse: All About the Hunting & Natural History of Old Ruff. (Illus.). 1980. 14.95 (ISBN 0-679-51052-4). McKay.
Hill, Gene. A Hunter's Fireside Book: Tales of Dogs, Ducks, Birds & Guns. (Illus.). 1972. 11.95 (ISBN 0-87691-076-2). Winchester Pr.
--Mostly Tailfeathers. 192p. 1975. 11.95 (ISBN 0-87691-167-X). Winchester Pr.
Holden, Philip. Hunter by Profession. LC 73-179799. (Illus.). 179p. 1973. 9.90x (ISBN 0-340-17740-3). Intl Pubns Serv.
Hunting Magazine Eds. Hunting Annual 1982. (Illus.). 288p. (Orig.). 1981. pap. 6.95 (ISBN 0-8227-3018-9). Petersen Pub.
James, David & Stephens, Wilson, eds. In Praise of Hunting. (Illus.). 1961. 10.00 (ISBN 0-8159-5806-4). Devin.
Janes, E. C. A Boy & His Gun. (Illus.). (gr. 7-9). 1951. 6.95 (ISBN 0-498-08305-5). A S Barnes.
--Ringneck! Pheasants & Pheasant Hunting. (Sportsmen's Classics Ser.). (Illus.). 215p. (YA) 1975. 8.95 (ISBN 0-517-52321-3). Crown.
Johnson, et al. Outdoor Tips: A Remington Sportsmen's Library Bk. pap. 2.95 (ISBN 0-87502-905-1). Benjamin Co.
Knap, Jerome J. Complete Hunter's Almanac: A Guide to Everything the Hunter Needs to Know About Guns, Game, Tracking & Gear with a Special Section on Hunting Locations in North America. (Illus.). 1978. write for info (ISBN 0-525-08368-5). Pagurian.
Laycock, George. Shotgunner's Bible. LC 69-15216. 1969. pap. 2.95 (ISBN 0-385-00978-X). Doubleday.
Lindner, Kurt, commentary by. The Second Hunting Book of Wolfgang Birkner. LC 77-98938. (Illus.). 1976. ltd. ed. (250 copies) 175.00 (ISBN 0-87691-000-2). Arma Pr.
Lingertwood, Kenneth. Huntsman of Our Time. 15.00x (ISBN 0-392-07938-0, SpS). Sportshelf.
Lockard, John R. Bee Hunting. 72p. pap. 1.50 (ISBN 0-936622-00-8). A R Harding Pub.
Lovell, Mary S. A Hunting Pageant. 1981. 50.00x (ISBN 0-904558-77-0, Pub. by Saiga Pub). State Mutual Bk.
McCristal, Vic. Top End Safari. 14.95x (ISBN 0-392-05008-0, ABC). Sportshelf.
McNair, Paul C. The Sportsman's Crafts Book. 1978. 12.95 (ISBN 0-87691-263-3). Winchester Pr.
Madden, D. H. Chapter of Mediaeval History. LC 74-91048. 1969. Repr. of 1924 ed. 15.00 (ISBN 0-8046-0658-7). Kennikat.
Madden, Dodgson H. Diary of Master William Silence: A Study of Shakespeare & Elizabethan Sport. LC 71-95440. (Studies in Shakespeare, No. 24). 1970. Repr. of 1897 ed. lib. bdg. 51.95 (ISBN 0-8383-0993-3). Haskell.
Merrill, William K. Hunter's Bible. 1968. 3.50 (ISBN 0-385-01533-X). Doubleday.
Mosher, John A. The Shooter's Workbench. (Illus.). 1977. 12.95 (ISBN 0-87691-199-8). Winchester Pr.
Nonte, George C., Jr. & Jurras, Lee E. Handgun Hunting. (Illus.). 1975. 10.95 (ISBN 0-87691-211-0). Winchester Pr.
O'Connor, Jack. The Shotgun Book. LC 77-92795. (Illus.). 1978. 15.00 (ISBN 0-394-50138-1); pap. 8.95 (ISBN 0-394-73562-5). Knopf.
Ormond, Clyde. Outdoorsman's Handbook. 1975. pap. 1.95 (ISBN 0-425-02893-3, Windhover). Berkley Pub.
Petzal, David E., ed. Experts' Book of the Shooting Sports. 9.95 (ISBN 0-671-21328-8). S&S.
Pollard, Jack. Straight Shooting. 17.50 (ISBN 0-392-04781-0, ABC). Sportshelf.
Rees, Clair & Wixom, Hartt. The Penny-Pinching Guide to Bigger Fish & Better Hunting. (Illus.). 160p. 1980. 9.95 (ISBN 0-87691-319-2). Winchester Pr.
Scharff, Robert. Hunter's Game, Gun & Dog Guide. (Quick & Easy Ser). (Orig.). 1967. pap. 1.95 (ISBN 0-02-081570-0, Collier). Macmillan.
Schwenk, Sigrid, et al, eds. Et Multum et Multa: Beitraege zur Literatur, Geschichte und Kultur der Jagd. (Illus.). 435p. 1971. 75.00x (ISBN 3-11-004034-4). De Gruyter.
Scott, Robert F., ed. Shooter's Bible 1982, No. 73. 576p. 1981. pap. 10.95 (ISBN 0-88317-105-8). Stoeger Pub Co.
Stehsel, Donald L. Hunting the California Black Bear. LC 65-19814. (Illus.). 194p. 1965. pap. 6.95 (ISBN 0-686-09158-2); pap. 6.00 ea. 3 or more copies. Stehsel.
Strung, Norman. Complete Hunter's Catalog. LC 77-23867. (Illus.). 1977. Lippincott.
Washburn, O. A. General Red. (Illus.). 160p. 5.50 (ISBN 0-8363-0035-1). Jenkins.
Whisker, James B. The Right to Hunt. LC 81-1524. 192p. 1981. 8.95 (ISBN 0-88427-042-4, Dist. by Caroline Hse). North River.
--The Right to Hunt. 1980. 8.95 (ISBN 0-88427-042-4). Caroline Hse.
Willett, Roderick. Gun Safety. LC 78-412108. (Illus.). 1967. 5.25x (ISBN 0-85140-185-6). Intl Pubns Serv.
Wilson, Loring D. The Handy Sportsman. 1976. 12.95 (ISBN 0-87691-213-7). Winchester Pr.
Woodcock, E. N. Fifty Years a Hunter & Trapper. 318p. pap. 3.00 (ISBN 0-936622-05-9). A R Harding Pub.
Young, Ralph W. Grizzlies Don't Come Easy. (Illus.). 176p. 1981. 13.95 (ISBN 0-87691-349-4). Winchester Pr.
Zumbo, Jim. Hunting America's Male Deer. 272p. 1981. 14.95 (ISBN 0-87691-344-3). Winchester Pr.
Zutz, Don. Handloading for Hunters. 1977. pap. 9.95 (ISBN 0-87691-346-X). Winchester Pr.

HUNTING–ANECDOTES, FACETIAE, SATIRE, ETC.

see Hunting Stories

HUNTING–BIBLIOGRAPHY

Glogan, Joseph. Sportsmans Book of U.S. Records. (Illus.). 96p. (Orig.). 1980. pap. text ed. 2.50 (ISBN 0-937328-00-6). NY Hunting.
Taylor, Archer. Problems in German Literary History of the Fifteenth & Sixteenth Centuries. 1939. pap. 13.00 (ISBN 0-527-89056-1). Kraus Repr.

HUNTING–DICTIONARIES

Burnand, Tony. Dictionnaire chasse. (Dictionnaires de l'homme du vingtieme siecle). (Fr). 1970. 8.50 (ISBN 0-685-13859-3, 3711). Larousse.
--Dictionnaire De la Chasse. 250p. (Fr.). 1970. pap. 7.50 (ISBN 0-686-56817-6, M-6595, Pub. by Larousse). French & Eur.
Frevert, W. Woerterbuch der Jaegerei. 4th ed. (Ger.). 1975. 12.00 (ISBN 3-490-05612-4, M-6990). French & Eur.
Kehrein, Franz. Woerterbuch der Weidmannssprache. (Ger.). 1969. 36.00 (ISBN 3-500-26250-3, M-6943). French & Eur.
Kirchoff, Anne. Woerterbuch der Jagel. (Ger., Eng. & Fr., Dictionary of Hunting). 1976. 27.50 (ISBN 3-405-11571-X, M-6989). French & Eur.
Wisconsin Hunting Encyclopedia. 1976. pap. 2.95 (ISBN 0-932558-06-2). Wisconsin Sptm.

HUNTING–HISTORY

Allison, Colin. The Trophy Hunters. (Illus.). 240p. 1981. 19.95 (ISBN 0-8117-1744-5). Stackpole.
Butler, Alfred J. Sport in Classic Times. LC 74-12191. (Illus.). 213p. 1975. 11.95 (ISBN 0-913232-13-0). W Kaufmann.
Cheney, Roberta & Erskine, Clyde. Music, Saddles & Flapjacks: Dudes at the Oto Ranch. LC 78-13774. (Illus.). 115p. 1978. 12.95 (ISBN 0-87842-074-6). Mountain Pr.
Danielsson, Bror, ed. William Twiti's the Art of Hunting, Vol. 1. (Mediaeval English Hunt: Cynegetics Anglica Ser.: No. 1). (Illus.). 1977. pap. text ed. 31.50x (ISBN 91-22-00084-4). Humanities.
Greene, Robert. The Thirde & Last Part of Conny-Catching. 1923. 12.50 (ISBN 0-8495-6284-8). Arden Lib.

Harding, Robert S., ed. Omnivorous Primates: Gathering & Hunting in Human Evolution. Teleki, Geza P. LC 80-23726. (Illus.). 912p. 1981. 40.00x (ISBN 0-231-04024-5). Columbia U Pr.

Hobusch, Erich. Fair Game: A History of Hunting, Shooting & Animal Conservation. Michaelis-Jena, Ruth & Murray, Patrick, trs. from Ger. LC 80-19008. (Illus.). 280p. 1981. 29.95 (ISBN 0-668-05101-9, 5101). Arco.

Petersen, Eugene T. Hunters' Heritage: A History of Hunting in Michigan. Lowe, Kenneth S., ed. (Illus.). 1979. lib. bdg. 4.65 (ISBN 0-933112-01-7). Mich United Conserv.

Rick, John W. Prehistoric Hunters of the High Andes. LC 79-28090. (Studies in Archaeology Ser.). 1980. 27.50 (ISBN 0-12-587760-9). Acad Pr.

Spiess, Arthur E. Reindeer & Caribou Hunters: An Archaeological Study. LC 79-17697. (Studies in Archaeology Ser.). 1979. 30.00 (ISBN 0-12-657950-4). Acad Pr.

HUNTING–JUVENILE LITERATURE

Forester, Frank. The Complete Manual for Young Sportsmen. LC 74-15739. (Popular Culture in America Ser.). (Illus.). 1975. Repr. 27.00x (ISBN 0-405-06374-1). Arno.

HUNTING–AFRICA

Capstick, Peter H. Death in the Long Grass. LC 77-9224. (Illus.). 1978. 10.95 (ISBN 0-312-18613-4). St Martin.

Cloudsley-Thompson, J. L. Animal Twilight, Man & Game in Eastern Africa. (Illus.). 1967. 10.50 (ISBN 0-85429-062-1). Dufour.

Findlay, Frederick R. N. & Cronwright-Schreiner, S. C. Big Game Shooting and Travel in Southeast Africa: Account of Shooting in the Cheringoma & Gorongoza Divisions of Portuguese South-East Africa & in Zululand. LC 72-4362. (Black Heritage Library Collection Ser.). Repr. of 1903 ed. 40.25 (ISBN 0-8369-9095-1). Arno.

Gillmore, Parker. Days & Nights by the Desert. LC 72-3982. (Black Heritage Library Collection Ser.). Repr. of 1888 ed. 20.50 (ISBN 0-8369-9097-8). Arno.

Haardt, Georges M. & Audouin-Dubreuil, Louis. Black Journey: Across Central Africa with the Citroen Expedition. LC 78-91258. (Illus.). Repr. of 1927 ed. 20.25x (ISBN 0-8371-2061-6, Pub. by Negro U Pr). Greenwood.

Hemingway, Ernest. Green Hills of Africa. 1935. Hudson River Edition. 17.50x (ISBN 0-684-16481-7); pap. 4.95 (ISBN 0-684-71799-9, SL50, ScribT). Scribner.

Herne, Brian. Ugandi Safaris. 1980. 12.95 (ISBN 0-87691-316-8). Winchester Pr.

Holub, Emil. Seven Years in South Africa, 2 Vols. 1881. Set. 45.00 (ISBN 0-403-00390-3). Scholarly.

--Seven Years in South Africa: Travels, Researches, & Hunting Adventures, Between the Diamond-Fields & the Zambesi, 1827-79, 2 Vols. LC 2-14174. 1971. Repr. of 1881 ed. Set. 57.00 (ISBN 0-384-24073-9, L158). Johnson Repr.

MacQueen, Peter. In Wildest Africa. 1909. 29.00 (ISBN 0-403-00353-9). Scholarly.

Nassau, Robert H. In an Elephant Corral: And Other Tales of West African Experiences. LC 70-78771. Repr. of 1912 ed. 10.00x (ISBN 0-8371-1402-0, Pub. by Negro U Pr). Greenwood.

HUNTING–ALASKA

Alaska Magazine Editors, ed. Selected Alaska Hunting & Fishing Tales, Vol. 4. LC 72-92077. 1976. pap. 4.95 (ISBN 0-88240-068-1). Alaska Northwest.

Hubback, T. R. Ten Thousand Miles to Alaska for Moose & Sheep, facs. ed. 19p. Repr. of 1921 ed. pap. 2.25 (ISBN 0-8466-0131-1, SJS131). Shorey.

Joll, Gary. To Alaska to Hunt. (Illus.). 1978. pap. 8.50x (ISBN 0-908565-80-1). Intl Pubns Serv.

Keim, Charles J. Alaska Game Trails with a Master Guide. LC 76-50576. (Illus.). 1977. pap. 6.95 (ISBN 0-88240-031-2). Alaska Northwest.

Waugh, Hal & Keim, Charles J. Fair Chase with Alaskan Guides. LC 72-83636. (Illus.). 206p. 1972. pap. 3.95 (ISBN 0-88240-010-X). Alaska Northwest.

HUNTING–ARCTIC REGIONS

Stefansson, Vilhjalmur. Hunters of the Great North. LC 74-5878. Repr. of 1922 ed. 22.00 (ISBN 0-404-11686-8). AMS Pr.

HUNTING–ASIA

Ferge, Zsusza, tr. from Hungarian. A Society in the Making: Hungarian Social & Societal Policy 1945-75. LC 80-80116. 1980. 22.50 (ISBN 0-87332-155-3). M E Sharpe.

HUNTING–AUSTRALIA

Stewart, Allan. The Green Eyes Are Buffalos. (gr. 9 up). 17.50x (ISBN 0-392-00097-0, SpS). Sportshelf.

HUNTING–BRITISH COLUMBIA

Shaughnessy, Patrick & Swingle, Diane. Hard Hunting. 1978. 11.95 (ISBN 0-87691-270-6). Winchester Pr.

HUNTING–GREAT BRITAIN

Danielsson, Bror, ed. William Twiti's the Art of Hunting, Vol. 1. (Mediaeval English Hunt: Cynegetics Anglica Ser.: No. 1). (Illus.). 1977. pap. text ed. 31.50x (ISBN 91-22-00084-4). Humanities.

Edward of Norwich. Master of Game: Oldest English Book on Hunting. Baillie-Grohman, William A. & Baillie-Grohman, F., eds. LC 78-178528. (Illus.). Repr. of 1909 ed. 45.00 (ISBN 0-404-56541-7). AMS Pr.

Hands, Rachel, ed. English Hawking & Hunting in the Boke of St. Albans. facsimile ed. (Oxford English Monographs). (Illus.). 264p. 1975. 55.00x (ISBN 0-19-811715-9). Oxford U Pr.

Jefferies, Richard. The Gamekeeper at Home & the Amateur Poacher. 1978. pap. 5.95 (ISBN 0-19-281240-8). Oxford U Pr.

Thomas, William B. Hunting England: A Survey of the Sport, & of Its Chief Grounds. 1978. Repr. of 1936 ed. lib. bdg. 30.00 (ISBN 0-8492-2737-2). R West.

Watson, J. N. British & Irish Hunts & Huntsmen: Vols. I & II. (Illus.). 192p. 1981. Set. 49.95 (ISBN 0-686-73584-6, Pub. by Batsford England). Vol. 1 (ISBN 0-7134-2169-X). Vol. 2 (ISBN 0-7134-2093-6). David & Charles.

HUNTING–GREECE

Butler, Alfred J. Sport in Classic Times. LC 74-12191. (Illus.). 213p. 1975. 11.95 (ISBN 0-913232-13-0). W Kaufmann.

HUNTING–INDIA

Jaipal. Great Hunt. 1980. 9.50 (ISBN 0-8062-1511-9). Carlton.

HUNTING–NEW ZEALAND

Joll, Gary. Big Game Hunting in New Zealand. LC 68-119869. (Illus.). 258p. 1968. 9.00x (ISBN 0-7233-0142-5). Intl Pubns Serv.

HUNTING–NORTH AMERICA

Cadbury, Warder, frwd. by. Journal of a Hunting Excursion to Louis Lake, 1851. (Illus.). 80p. 1961. 4.95 (ISBN 0-686-74832-8). Adirondack Mus.

Knap, Jerome. Where to Fish & Hunt in North America: A Complete Sportsman's Guide. (Illus.). 192p. 8.95 (ISBN 0-919364-78-0, ADON 3513). Pagurian.

Leopold, Luna B., ed. Round River: From the Journals of Aldo Leopold. (Illus.). 188p. 1972. pap. 3.95 (ISBN 0-19-501563-0, 372, GB). Oxford U Pr.

Smith. The One-Eyed Poacher & the Maine Woods. 1975. Repr. 4.50 (ISBN 0-89272-023-9). Down East.

HUNTING–UNITED STATES

Abbott, Henry. Birch Bark Books of Henry Abbott: Sporting Adventures & Nature Observations in the Adirondacks in the Early 1900s. LC 80-11071. (Illus., Repr. of 1914 & 1932 eds.). 1980. 19.95 (ISBN 0-916346-40-4). Harbor Hill Bks.

Baily's Hunting Directory 78-79. (Illus.). 1978. 36.00 (ISBN 0-85131-272-1, Dist. by Sporting Book Center). J A Allen.

Barsness, John. Hunting the Great Plains. LC 79-22096. (Illus.). 164p. 1979. pap. 6.95 (ISBN 0-87842-117-3). Mountain Pr.

Cadbury, Warder, intro. by. Journal of a Hunting Excursion to Louis Lake, 1851. (Illus.). 1961. 8.95 (ISBN 0-8156-8029-5, Pub. by Adirondack Museum). Syracuse U Pr.

Cory, Charles B. Hunting & Fishing in Florida, Including a Key to the Water Birds. LC 75-125734. (American Environmental Studies). 1970. Repr. of 1896 ed. 14.00 (ISBN 0-405-02657-9). Arno.

Elman, Robert, ed. All About Deer Hunting in America. 1976. 13.95 (ISBN 0-87691-176-9). Winchester Pr.

Kaplan, Meyer A. Varmint Hunting. (Monarch Illustrated Guide Ser.). 1977. pap. 2.95 (ISBN 0-671-18766-X). Monarch Pr.

Lang, Varley. Follow the Water. LC 61-16637. (Illus.). 1961. 6.95 (ISBN 0-910244-24-3). Blair.

McTeer, Ed. Adventures in the Woods & Waters of the Low Country. LC 72-91815. 5.95 (ISBN 0-685-30849-9). Beaufort.

Mitchell, John G. The Hunt. 256p. 1981. pap. 4.95 (ISBN 0-14-005981-4). Penguin.

--The Hunt. LC 80-7621. 320p. 1980. 11.95 (ISBN 0-394-50684-7). Knopf.

Murray, William H. Adventures in the Wilderness. Verner, William K., ed. (Illus.). 1970. Repr. 10.50 (ISBN 0-8156-0071-2, Co-Pub. by Adirondack Museum). Syracuse U Pr.

Palliser, John. Solitary Rambles & Adventures of a Hunter in the Prairies. LC 69-13511. (Illus.). 1969. Repr. of 1853 ed. 5.00 (ISBN 0-8048-0534-2). C E Tuttle.

Rearden, Jim, ed. Alaska Magazine's Alaska Hunting Guide. (Illus.). 1979. pap. 5.95 (ISBN 0-88240-127-0). Alaska Northwest.

Richardson, Larry. A Guide to Hunting in Tennessee. (Illus.). Date not set. cancelled (ISBN 0-89732-004-2). Thomas Pr.

Roosevelt, Theodore. Hunting Trips of a Ranchman. LC 75-104553. Repr. of 1885 ed. lib. bdg. 17.50x (ISBN 0-8398-1763-0). Irvington.

--Outdoor Pastimes of an American Hunter. LC 70-25762. (American Environmental Studies). 1970. Repr. of 1905 ed. 24.00 (ISBN 0-405-02687-0). Arno.

--Ranch Life & the Hunting Trail. LC 76-125761. (American Environmental Studies). 1970. Repr. of 1901 ed. 12.00 (ISBN 0-405-02688-9). Arno.

--Theodore Roosevelt's America: American Naturalists Ser. Wiley, Farida, ed. (Illus.). 1955. 10.00 (ISBN 0-8159-6714-4). Devin.

--The Wilderness Hunter. LC 72-104555. Repr. of 1900 ed. lib. bdg. 16.00x (ISBN 0-8398-1765-7). Irvington.

Sandoz, Mari. The Buffalo Hunters: The Story of the Hide Men. LC 77-14079. 1978. pap. 4.50 (ISBN 0-8032-5883-6, BB 659, Bison). U of Nebr Pr.

Tillet, Paul. Doe Day: The Antlerless Deer Controversy in New Jersey. 1963. pap. 3.25 (ISBN 0-8135-0419-8). Rutgers U Pr.

Tome, Philip. Pioneer Life or Thirty Years a Hunter: Being Scenes & Adventures in the Life of Philip Tome. LC 78-146424. (First American Frontier Ser). (Illus.). 1971. Repr. of 1854 ed. 15.00 (ISBN 0-405-02893-8). Arno.

Wootters, John. A Guide to Hunting in Texas. LC 79-19642. 128p. 1979. pap. 5.95 (ISBN 0-88415-369-X). Pacesetter Pr.

HUNTING, PRIMITIVE

see also Indians of North America–Hunting and Fishing

Clark, Grahame. Stone Age Hunters. (Library of the Early Civilizations Ser). (gr. 9-12). 1967. pap. 2.95 (ISBN 0-07-011146-4, SP). McGraw.

Frison, George C. Prehistoric Hunters of the High Plains. 1978. 29.50 (ISBN 0-12-268560-1). Acad Pr.

Gerstacker, Friedrich. Wild Sports in the Far West. Steeves, Edna L. & Steeves, Harrison R., eds. LC 68-16624. 1968. 14.75 (ISBN 0-686-67566-5). Duke.

Lee, Richard B. & De Vore, Irven, eds. Man the Hunter. LC 67-17603. 1968. pap. 12.95x (ISBN 0-202-33032-X). Aldine Pub.

Marks, Stuart A. Large Mammals & a Brave People: Subsistence Hunters in Zambia. LC 75-26945. (Illus.). 274p. 1976. 16.00 (ISBN 0-295-95447-7). U of Wash Pr.

Sergeant, R. B. South Arabian Hunt. 1976. text ed. 20.00x (ISBN 0-7189-0172-X). Verry.

HUNTING DOGS

see also Bird Dogs; Retrievers;
also particular breeds of hunting dogs

Baily's Hunting Directory 1975-1976. 1976. 22.50 (ISBN 0-8277-5215-6). British Bk Ctr.

Bernard, Art. Dog Days. LC 69-12374. 1969. 5.95 (ISBN 0-87004-126-6). Caxton.

Brown, William F. Field Trials. LC 74-30716. (Illus.). 1977. 12.00 (ISBN 0-498-01693-5). A S Barnes.

Drabble, Phil. Of Pedigree Unknown: Sporting and Working Dogs. (Illus.). 1977. 8.75 (ISBN 0-7181-1447-7). Transatlantic.

Duffey, Dave. Hunting Dog Know-How. (Illus.). 1972. 9.95 (ISBN 0-87691-081-9). Winchester Pr.

Duffey, David M. Expert Advice on Gun Dog Training. 1977. 11.95 (ISBN 0-87691-195-5). Winchester Pr.

Falk, John R. Practical Hunter's Dog Book. (Illus.). 1971. 10.95 (ISBN 0-87691-037-1). Winchester Pr.

Goodall, Charles. How to Train Your Own Gun Dog. LC 77-92420. (Illus.). 1978. 9.95 (ISBN 0-87605-561-7). Howell Bk.

Hartley, Oliver. Hunting Dogs. 251p. pap. 3.00 (ISBN 0-936622-13-X). A R Harding Pub.

Henschel, Stan. How to Raise & Train a Coonhound. (Orig.). pap. 2.00 (ISBN 0-87666-274-2, DS1057). TFH Pubns.

Irving, Joe. Training Spaniels. (Illus.). 230p. 1980. 19.95 (ISBN 0-7153-8008-7). David & Charles.

Lent, Patricia A. Sport with Terriers. LC 73-85940. (Illus.). 1973. 8.95 (ISBN 0-914124-01-3). Arner Pubns.

Moxon, Peter. Gundogs: Questions & Answers. (Illus.). 96p. (Orig.). 1980. pap. 7.50x (ISBN 0-85242-734-4). Intl Pubns Serv.

Russell, Joanna. All About Gazehounds. (Illus.). 160p. 1976. 9.95 (ISBN 0-7207-0926-1, Pub. by Michael Joseph). Merrimack Bk Serv.

Salmon, H. M. Gazehounds & Coursing. (Illus.). 1977. 18.50 (ISBN 0-87839-024-3). North Star.

Smith, Guy N. Sporting & Working Dogs. 1981. 40.00x (ISBN 0-904558-47-9, Pub. by Saiga Pub). State Mutual Bk.

Stetson, Joe. Handbook of Gundogs. (Sportsman's Library of Gun Dogs, Vol. 1). (Orig.). 1965. pap. 2.00 (ISBN 0-87666-315-3, DS1139). TFH Pubns.

--Hunting with Flushing Dogs. (Sportsman's Library of Gun Dogs, Vol. 2). (Orig.). 1965. pap. 2.00 (ISBN 0-87666-293-9, DS1137). TFH Pubns.

Tarrant, Bill. Best Way to Train Your Gun Dog: The Delmar Smith Method. 1977. 10.95 (ISBN 0-679-50750-7). McKay.

Wehle, Robert G. Wing & Shot. 1964. 12.00 (ISBN 0-686-65297-5). Country Pr NY.

Whitney, Leon F. & Underwood, Acil B. Coon Hunter's Handbook. Hart, Ernest, ed. (Illus.). 1952. 5.95 (ISBN 0-03-028235-7). HR&W.

Wolters, Richard A. Gun Dog. Revolutionary Rapid Training Method. (Illus.). 1961. 11.95 (ISBN 0-525-12005-X). Dutton.

HUNTING IN LITERATURE

Darton, F. Harvey. From Surtees to Sassoon: Some English Contrasts 1838-1928. LC 77-6713. 1931. lib. bdg. 20.00 (ISBN 0-8414-3822-6). Folcroft.

Fontenrose, Joseph. Orion: The Myth of the Hunter & the Huntress. (U. C. Publications in Classical Studies: Vol. 23). 230p. 1981. 14.50x (ISBN 0-520-09632-0). U of Cal Pr.

Madden, Dodgson H. Diary of Master William Silence: A Study of Shakespeare & of Elizabethan Sport. Repr. of 1897 ed. lib. bdg. 15.00x (ISBN 0-8371-2322-4, MAMS). Greenwood.

HUNTING LEOPARDS

see Cheetahs

HUNTING RECORDS

see Hunting Trophies

HUNTING STORIES

see also American Wit and Humor–Sports and Games

Bear, Fred. Fred Bear's Field Notes. LC 76-2752. 1976. 11.95 (ISBN 0-385-11690-X). Doubleday.

Hill, Gene. Hill Country: Stories About Hunting & Fishing & Dogs & Guns & Such. 1978. 11.95 (ISBN 0-87690-297-2). Dutton.

Holden, Philip. Backblocks. LC 75-305803. (Illus.). 1974. 9.25x (ISBN 0-340-18981-9). Intl Pubns Serv.

Linkert, Lo. Hunter's Fisherman & Other Liars. 2nd ed. (Illus.). 1980. 5.95 (ISBN 0-686-75269-4). Jolex.

McManus, Patrick. They Shoot Canoes, Don't They? 228p. 1981. 10.95 (ISBN 0-03-058646-1). HR&W.

MacQuarrie, Gordon. Stories of the Old Duck Hunters. 1979. pap. 5.95 (ISBN 0-932558-10-0). Willow Creek.

HUNTING TROPHIES

Brakefield, Tom. The Sportsman's Complete Book of Trophy & Meat Care. LC 75-17712. (Illus.). 224p. 1975. 8.95 (ISBN 0-8117-1685-6). Stackpole.

Elliott, Charles. Care of Game Meat & Trophies. LC 74-33570. (Funk & W Bk.). (Illus.). 160p. 1975. 7.50 (ISBN 0-308-10206-1); pap. 4.50 (ISBN 0-308-10207-X, TYC-T). T Y Crowell.

Trense, Werner, et al, eds. The Game Trophies of the World - Les Trophees de Chasse du Monde - Die Jagdtrophaen der Welt. (Illus.). 216p. (Orig., Eng., Fr., Ger.). 1981. pap. 29.00 (ISBN 3-490-44012-9). Parey Sci Pubs.

HUNTING WITH BOW AND ARROW

Adams, Chuck. Bowhunter's Digest. 2nd ed. LC 73-91589. (Illus.). 288p. 1981. pap. 8.95 (ISBN 0-910676-29-1, 7426). DBI.

--The Complete Book of Bowhunting. (Illus.). 1978. 14.95 (ISBN 0-87691-271-4). Winchester Pr.

Bear, Fred. The Archer's Bible. rev. ed. LC 79-7485. (Outdoor Bible Ser.). (Illus.). 1980. pap. 3.95 (ISBN 0-385-15155-1). Doubleday.

Conatser, Dean. Bowhunting the White Deer. (Illus.). 1977. 12.95 (ISBN 0-87691-192-0). Winchester Pr.

Helgeland, G. Archery World's Complete Guide to Bow Hunting. 1975. pap. 5.95 (ISBN 0-13-044016-7). P-H.

James, M. R. Bowhunting: For Whitetail & Mule Deer. new ed. LC 73-20851. 224p. 1976. 10.95 (ISBN 0-685-69916-1); pap. 6.96 (ISBN 0-89149-019-1). Jolex.

Kittredge, Doug & Wambold, H. R. Bowhunting for Deer. rev. ed. LC 64-21466. (Illus.). 160p. 1978. 10.95 (ISBN 0-8117-0304-5). Stackpole.

Lewis, Jack, ed. Archer's Digest. 2nd ed. (Illus.). 320p. 1977. pap. 7.95 (ISBN 0-695-80718-8). DBI.

Schuyler, Keith C. Bowhunting for Big Game. LC 74-6276. (Illus.). 224p. 1977. pap. 5.95 (ISBN 0-8117-2071-3). Stackpole.

Smythe, John & Barwick, Humphrey. Bow Vs. Gun. 1976. Repr. 15.00x (ISBN 0-85409-881-X). Charles River Bks.

HUNTINGDON, ENGLAND–GENEALOGIES

Charles, Nicholas. Visitation of the County of Huntingdon. 1849. 15.50 (ISBN 0-384-08525-3). Johnson Repr.

HUNTINGDONSHIRE, ENGLAND–DESCRIPTION AND TRAVEL

Harvey, Sally, ed. Huntingdonshire. (The Domesday Book Ser). (Illus.). 74p. 1976. 15.00x (ISBN 0-8476-1269-4). Rowman.

HUNTINGTON, MRS. ANNA VAUGHAN (HYATT), B.1876
Garcia-Mazas, Jose. El Poeta y la Escultura: La Espana Que Huntington Conocio. (Illus.). 1962. 2.50 (ISBN 0-87535-097-6). Hispanic Soc.
Proske, Beatrice G. Anna Hyatt Huntington Eighteen Seventy-Six to Nineteen Seventy-Three: Small Bronzes & Sketches. (Illus.). 16p. 1974. pap. text ed. 0.75 (ISBN 0-686-74463-2). Hispanic Soc.
HUNTINGTON, ARCHER MILTON, 1870-1955
Garcia-Mazas, Jose. El Poeta y la Escultura: La Espana Que Huntington Conocio. (Illus.). 1962. 2.50 (ISBN 0-87535-097-6). Hispanic Soc.
HUNTINGTON, COLLIS POTTER, 1821-1900
Collis P. Huntington Papers, 1856-1901. 56p. 1979. pap. 50.00 (ISBN 0-667-00570-6). Microfilming Corp.
Evans, Cerinda W. Collis Potter Huntington, 2 vols. (Mariners Museum). (Illus.). 775p. 1954. Set. 12.50x (ISBN 0-8139-0376-9). U Pr of Va.
Lewis, Oscar. The Big Four: The Story of Huntington, Stanford, Hopkins, & Crocker, & of the Building of the Central Pacific. Bruchey, Stuart, ed. LC 80-1324. (Railroads Ser.). (Illus.). 1981. Repr. of 1938 ed. lib. bdg. 40.00x (ISBN 0-405-13799-0). Arno.
HUNTINGTON, ELLSWORTH, 1876-1947
Martin, Geoffrey J. Ellsworth Huntington: His Life & Thought. (Illus.). xx, 315p. 1973. 25.00 (ISBN 0-208-01347-4, Archon). Shoe String.
HUNTINGTON, HENRY EDWARDS, 1850-1927
Crump, Spencer. Henry Huntington - the Pacific Electric: A Pictorial Album. 2nd revised ed. 10.00 (ISBN 0-87046-048-X). Trans-Anglo.
HUNTINGTON, MOUNT
Roberts, David. Mountain of My Fear. LC 68-20393. (Illus.). (gr. 7-12). 1968. 8.95 (ISBN 0-8149-0192-1). Vanguard.
HUNTSVILLE, ALABAMA
Betts, Edward C. Historic Huntsville: Eighteen Four to Eighteen Seventy. (Illus.). 1966. pap. 5.95 (ISBN 0-87651-011-X). Southern U Pr.
Brantley, William H. Three Capitals: A Book About the First Three Capitals of Alabama-St. Stephens, Huntsville, & Cahawba, 1818-1826. LC 76-28483. (A Bicentennial Bk.). (Illus.). 1976. Repr. of 1947 ed. 10.75 (ISBN 0-8173-5231-7). U of Ala Pr.
Huntsville Directory: City Guide & Business Mirror 1859-60. Repr. 6.00 (ISBN 0-87397-035-7). Strode.
HUNZA
Taylor, Renee. Hunza Health Secrets for Long Life & Happiness. LC 63-19916. 1978. pap. 4.95 (ISBN 0-87983-189-8). Keats.
HURD, PETER, 1904-
Horgan, Paul. Peter Hurd: A Portrait Sketch from Life. (Illus.). 68p. 1965. pap. 8.95 (ISBN 0-292-76437-5). U of Tex Pr.
Hurd, Peter. Peter Hurd-the Lithographs. 2nd ed. Meigs, John, ed. LC 68-9683. (Illus.). 1969. 15.00 (ISBN 0-912196-00-9). Baker Gallery.
HURD, RICHARD, BP. OF WORCESTER, 1720-1808
Smith, Audley L. Richard Hurd's Letters on Chivalry & Romance. 1939. lib. bdg. 8.50 (ISBN 0-8414-7540-7). Folcroft.
HURLEY, PATRICK JAY, 1883-1963
Buhite, Russell D. Patrick J. Hurley & American Foreign Policy. 342p. 1973. 22.50x (ISBN 0-8014-0751-6). Cornell U Pr.
HURON LANGUAGE
see also Iroquoian Languages
HURRIANS
Gelb, Ignace. Hurrians & Subarians. 1944. 7.00x (ISBN 0-226-62393-9, SAOC22). U of Chicago Pr.
HURRICANE (FIGHTER PLANES)
Allward, Maurice. Hurricane Special. LC 76-352409. (Illus.). 64p. 1975. 10.25x (ISBN 0-7110-0541-9). Intl Pubns Serv.
Bowyer, Chaz. Hurricane at War. (Illus.). 1978. 14.95 (ISBN 0-684-15969-4, ScribT). Scribner.
Bruce, J. M., intro. by. Hurricane Two Manual. LC 76-391. (RAF Museum Ser: Vol. 2). (Illus.). 448p. 1976. 17.50 (ISBN 0-88254-377-6). Hippocrene Bks.
Shores, Christopher F. Battle of Britain. Cooksey, Peter G. & Ward, Richard, eds. LC 77-93935. (Aircam Aviation Ser). (Illus., Orig.). 1969. pap. 2.95 (ISBN 0-668-02119-5). Arco.
Ward, Richard & Shores, Christopher. Hawker Hurricane Mk. 1-4. (Arco-Aircam Aviation Ser., No. 33). (Illus.). 46p. 1972. pap. 3.25 (ISBN 0-668-02316-3). Arco.
HURRICANE PROTECTION
see also Agricultural Credit; Building Laws; Flood Control; Hydraulic Engineering; Public Works; Shore Protection; Zoning
Regional Association IV (North & Central America) Hurricane Operational Plan. 1979. pap. 23.00 (ISBN 92-63-10524-3, W429, WMO). Unipub.

HURRICANES
Here are entered mainly works on storms in the neighborhood of the West Indies.
see also Disaster Relief; Storms; Typhoons
Allen, Everett S. A Wind to Shake the World: The Story of the 1938 Hurricane. (Illus.). 1976. 11.95 (ISBN 0-316-03426-6). Little.
Bixby, William. Hurricanes. (Illus.). (gr. 4-7). 1979. 6.95 (ISBN 0-679-20678-7). McKay.
Chantz, N. E. Just Pick a Murricane? 1.25 (ISBN 0-902675-11-7). Oleander Pr.
Chesapeake Research Consortium. Effects of Tropical Storm Agnes on the Chesapeake Bay Estuarine System. LC 76-47392. 1977. text ed. 35.00x (ISBN 0-8018-1945-8). Johns Hopkins.
Cory, George. Head-on with Hurricane Camille. LC 79-21323. (Quest, Adventure, Survival Ser.). (Illus.). (gr. 4-8). 1980. PLB 11.15 (ISBN 0-8172-1565-4). Raintree Pubs.
Douglas, Marjory S. Hurricane. rev. abr. ed. LC 58-5205. (Illus.). 1976. pap. 2.95 (ISBN 0-89176-015-6, 6015). Mockingbird Bks.
Gordon, Bernard L., ed. Hurricane in Southern New England: An Analysis of the Great Storm of 1938. LC 75-38912. (Illus.). 64p. 1976. pap. 4.00 (ISBN 0-910258-05-8). Book & Tackle.
Kotsch, William J. & Harding, Edwin T. Heavy Weather Guide. LC 64-25388. (Illus.). 1965. 9.50x (ISBN 0-87021-262-1). Naval Inst Pr.
Mason, Herbert M., Jr. Death from the Sea: Our Greatest Natural Disaster, the Galveston Hurricane of 1900. (Illus.). 1972. 7.95 (ISBN 0-8037-1824-1). Dial.
Simpson, Robert H. & Riehl, Herbert. The Hurricane & Its Impact. LC 80-13911. (Illus.). 448p. 1981. 20.00x (ISBN 0-8071-0688-7). La State U Pr.
Tannehill, Ivan R. Hurricane Hunters. LC 55-9480. (Illus.). (gr. 9 up). 1955. 4.50 (ISBN 0-396-03789-5). Dodd.
--Hurricanes, Their Nature & History, Particularly Those of the West Indies & the Southern Coasts of the United States. Repr. of 1938 ed. lib. bdg. 15.00x (ISBN 0-8371-2316-X, TAHU). Greenwood.
HUS, JOHN, 1369-1415
Denis, Ernest. Huss et les guerres hussites. LC 77-8424. Repr. of 1930 ed. 34.00 (ISBN 0-404-16126-X). AMS Pr.
Gillett, Ezra H. The Life & Times of John Huss: The Bohemian Reformation of the Fifteenth Century, 2 vols. LC 77-85271. Repr. of 1863 ed. Set. 82.00 (ISBN 0-404-16150-2). AMS Pr.
Kitts, Eustace J. Pope John Twenty-Third & Master John Hus of Bohemia. LC 77-84726. Repr. of 1910 ed. 32.50 (ISBN 0-404-16127-8). AMS Pr.
Loserth, Johann. Wiclif & Hus. Evans, M. J., tr. LC 78-63198. (Heresies of the Early Christian & Medieval Era: Second Ser.). 1979. Repr. of 1884 ed. 35.00 (ISBN 0-404-16236-3). AMS Pr.
Lutzow, Franz. The Life & Times of Master John Hus. LC 77-84728. (Illus.). Repr. of 1909 ed. 28.50 (ISBN 0-404-16128-6). AMS Pr.
Schaff, D. S. John Huss. 59.95 (ISBN 0-8490-0451-9). Gordon Pr.
Spinka, Matthew. John Hus: A Biography. LC 78-14366. (Illus.). 1978. Repr. of 1968 ed. lib. bdg. 25.75 (ISBN 0-313-21050-0, SPJH). Greenwood.
--John Hus & the Czech Reform. 1966. Repr. of 1941 ed. 11.50 (ISBN 0-208-00138-7, Archon). Shoe String.
Spinka, Matthew, tr. John Hus at the Council of Constance. LC 65-11019. (Records of Civilzation, Sources & Studies: No. 73). 1965. 20.00x (ISBN 0-231-02742-7). Columbia U Pr.
Spinka, Matthew, tr. from Czech. The Letters of John Hus. 233p. 1973. 15.00x (ISBN 0-87471-021-9). Rowman.
HUSAIN, MAQBOOL FIDA
Ali, S. V. Husain the Savior of Islam. LC 81-51900. 252p. 1981. 5.95 (ISBN 0-940368-05-6); pap. 3.95 (ISBN 0-940368-03-X). Tahrike Tarsile Quran.
HUSBAND AND WIFE
see also Community Property; Divorce; Marriage Law; Separation (Law); Support (Domestic Relations)
Ashley, Paul P. Oh Promise Me, but Put It in Writing: Living Together Arrangements Without, During & After Marriage. (Illus.). 1978. 9.95 (ISBN 0-07-002409-X, P&RB). McGraw.
Baxter, Ian F. Marital Property. LC 72-97627. (American Family Law Library). 640p. 1973. 47.50 (ISBN 0-686-05456-3). Lawyers Co-Op.
Bryson, Jeff B. & Bryson, Rebecca B., eds. Dual-Career Couples. LC 77-89983. 120p. 1978. 9.95x (ISBN 0-87705-371-5). Human Sci Pr.
Campion, Michael & Zehr, Wilmer. Especially for Husbands. (When Was the Last Time Ser.). (Illus.). 1978. pap. 5.95 (ISBN 0-87123-136-0, 210136). Bethany Hse.
Carlinsky, Dan. Do You Know Your Husband? (Illus., Orig.). 1979. pap. 1.50 (ISBN 0-8431-0495-3). Price Stern.
--Do You Know Your Wife? (Illus., Orig.). 1979. pap. 1.50 (ISBN 0-8431-0496-1). Price Stern.
Chapman, Jane R. & Gates, Margaret, eds. Women into Wives: The Legal & Economic Impact of Marriage. LC 76-47070. (Sage Yearbooks in Women's Policy Studies: Vol. 2). 320p. 1977. 22.50 (ISBN 0-8039-0700-1); pap. 9.95 (ISBN 0-8039-0701-X). Sage.
Coble, Harold H. Man: Responsible & Caring. LC 77-75765. 1977. 5.95 (ISBN 0-8054-5625-2). Broadman.
Cothren, Paige. Let None Deal Treacherously. 224p. (Orig.). 1981. pap. 4.95 (ISBN 0-937778-03-6). Fulness Hse.
Dobson, James. What Wives Wish Their Husbands Knew About Women. 1977. pap. 3.95 (ISBN 0-8423-7889-8). Tyndale.
Durkin, Henry P. Forty-Four Hours to Change Your Life: Marriage Encounter. (Orig.). pap. 1.25 (ISBN 0-89129-139-3). Jove Pubns.
Exel, G. W. Live Happily with the Woman You Love. 1977. pap. 2.95 (ISBN 0-8024-4900-X). Moody.
Exley, Richard & Exley, Helen, eds. What Is a Husband? LC 78-4012. (Illus.). 1979. 5.95 (ISBN 0-312-86599-6). St Martin.
Fast, Julius. Incompatability of Men & Women: And How to Overcome It. 192p. 1972. pap. 1.75 (ISBN 0-380-01300-2, 25320). Avon.
Groves, Harold M. Federal Tax Treatment of the Family. LC 76-55946. (Brookings Institution, Studies of Government Finance Ser). 1977. Repr. of 1963 ed. lib. bdg. 15.00x (ISBN 0-8371-9425-3, GRFT). Greenwood.
Huber, Charles H. & Baruth, Leroy G. Coping with Marital Conflict: An Adlerian Approach to Succeeding in Marriage. 160p. 1981. pap. text ed. 5.00x (ISBN 0-87563-201-7). Stipes.
Jewett, Dick. Why Do I Shout at My Wife? (Uplook Ser.). 1978. pap. 0.75 (ISBN 0-8163-0300-2, 23617-4). Pacific Pr Pub Assn.
Johnson, Cynthia, compiled by. To My Husband, with Love. 1979. pap. 4.50 (ISBN 0-8378-5027-4). Gibson.
Loeb, Isidor. Legal Property Relations of Married Parties: A Study in Comparative Legislation. LC 68-56668. (Columbia University, Studies in the Social Sciences Ser.: No. 34). Repr. of 1900 ed. 18.00 (ISBN 0-404-51034-5). AMS Pr.
Martin, J. P., ed. Violence & the Family. LC 77-21846. 1978. 43.75 (ISBN 0-471-99576-2, Pub. by Wiley-Interscience). Wiley.
Merrill, Dean. Manual Del Esposo. (Spanish Bks.). (Span.). 1979. 1.90 (ISBN 0-8297-0891-X). Life Pubs Intl.
Myra, Harold. Love Notes to Jeanette. 1979. pap. 3.95 (ISBN 0-88207-638-8). Victor Bks.
Pietropinto, Anthony & Simenauer, Jacqueline. Husbands & Wives. 496p. 1981. pap. 3.50 (ISBN 0-425-04701-6). Berkley Pub.
Renich, Fred. The Christian Husband. 1978. pap. 4.95 (ISBN 0-8423-0237-9). Tyndale.
Rowatt, G. Wade, Jr. & Rowatt, Mary Jo. The Two-Career Marriage. LC 79-28408. (Christian Care Books). 1980. pap. 5.95 (ISBN 0-664-24298-7). Westminster.
Scanzoni, John. Sexual Bargaining: Power Politics in the American Marriage. 1972. pap. 2.95 (ISBN 0-13-807453-4, Spec). P-H.
Shaevitz, Morton H. & Shaevitz, Marjorie H. Making It Together: As a Career Couple. 1979. 8.95 (ISBN 0-395-28592-5). HM.
Shedd, Charlie. The Best Dad Is a Good Lover. 1977. 5.95 (ISBN 0-8362-0660-6). Andrews & McMeel.
Shivanandan, Mary. When Your Wife Wants to Work. LC 79-51278. (When Bks). (Illus.). 1980. pap. 2.45 (ISBN 0-87029-151-3, 20237). Abbey.
Smith, Ruth. Wifie & Hubby: Incidents in the Life of a New York Couple. LC 76-49356. 1976. 3.50 (ISBN 0-9601182-1-7). R Smith.
Stanley, Charles F. A Man's Touch. 1977. pap. 3.50 (ISBN 0-88207-753-8). Victor Bks.
Straus, Murray A., ed. The Social Causes of Husband-Wife Violence. Hotaling, Gerald T. LC 79-27071. (Illus.). 1980. text ed. 20.00x (ISBN 0-8166-0886-5); pap. text ed. 8.95x (ISBN 0-8166-0955-1). U of Minn Pr.
Strodtback, Fred L. A Study of Husband-Wife Interaction in Three Cultures. Zuckerman, Harriet & Merton, Robert K., eds. LC 79-9032. (Dissertation on Sociology Ser.). 1980. lib. bdg. 46.00x (ISBN 0-405-12998-X). Arno.
Torjesen, Hakon. The Househusband's World: Reflections of a Former Diplomat-- at Home. 1979. pap. 3.95 (ISBN 0-9602790-0-8). The Garden.
Vernon, Bob & Carlson, Carole. The Married Man. 1980. 6.95 (ISBN 0-8007-1117-3). Revell.
Williams, Patti. Husbands. LC 75-7477. 1976. 4.95 (ISBN 0-88270-147-9); pap. 3.95 (ISBN 0-88270-148-7). Logos.
HUSBANDRY
see Agriculture
HUSBANDRY, PATRONS OF
see Patrons of Husbandry

HUSKISSON, WILLIAM, 1770-1830
Brady, Alexander. William Huskisson & Liberal Reform. 2nd ed. 177p. 1967. 25.00x (ISBN 0-7146-1456-4, F Cass Co). Biblio Dist.
HUSSERL, EDMUND, 1859-1938
Bachelard, Suzanne. Study of Husserl's Formal & Transcendental Logic. Embree, Lester E., tr. LC 68-15330. (Studies in Phenomenology & Existential Philosophy Ser). 1968. 12.95 (ISBN 0-8101-0028-2). Northwestern U Pr.
Bauman, Zygmunt. Towards a Critical Sociology: An Essay on Commonsense & Emancipation. (Direct Edition Ser.). 1976. pap. 10.50 (ISBN 0-7100-8306-8). Routledge & Kegan.
Berger, Gaston. The Cogito in Husserl's Philosophy. McLaughlin, Kathleen, tr. (Studies in Phenomenology & Existential Philosophy). 1972. 11.95 (ISBN 0-8101-0375-3). Northwestern U Pr.
Boer, Theodore De. The Development of Husserl's Thought. Plantinga, Theodore, tr. (Phaenomenologica: No. 76). 1978. lib. bdg. 79.00 (ISBN 9-0247-2039-7, Pub. by Martinus Nijhoff Netherlands); pap. 45.00 (ISBN 9-0247-2124-5, Pub. by Martinus Nijhoff Netherlands). Kluwer Boston.
Cairns. Guide for Translating Husserl. (Phaenomenologica Ser: No. 55). 1973. pap. 18.50 (ISBN 90-247-1452-4, Pub. by Martinus Nijhoff Netherlands). Kluwer Boston.
Claesges. Edmund Husserls Theorie der Raumkonstition. (Phaenomenologica Ser: No. 19). 1964. lib. bdg. 18.50 (ISBN 90-247-0251-8, Pub. by Martinus Nijhoff Netherlands). Kluwer Boston.
Cunningham, S. Language & the Phenomenological Reductions of E. Husserl. (Phaenomenologica Ser: No. 70). 1976. pap. 18.50 (ISBN 90-247-1823-6, Pub. by Martinus Nijhoff Netherlands). Kluwer Boston.
De Muralt, Andre. The Idea of Phenomenology: Husserlian Exemplarism. Breckon, Garry L., tr. from Fr. LC 73-94433. (Studies in Phenomenology & Existential Philosophy). 1974. text ed. 20.95x (ISBN 0-8101-0448-2). Northwestern U Pr.
Derrida, Jacques. Edmund Husserl's The Origin of Geometry: An Introduction. Leavey, John P., tr. from Fr. LC 77-13723. 1977. 12.95 (ISBN 0-89254-006-0). Nicolas-Hays.
--Speech and Phenomena: And Other Essays on Husserl's Theory of Signs. Allison, David B., tr. from Ger. LC 72-80565. (Studies in Phenomenology & Existential Philosophy). 1973. text ed. 15.95x (ISBN 0-8101-0397-4); pap. 5.95x (ISBN 0-8101-0590-X). Northwestern U Pr.
Dreyfus. Husserl. Date not set. price not set (ISBN 0-262-04065-4, Pub. by Bradford). MIT Pr.
Dreyfus, Hubert L. & Hall, Harrison, eds. Husserl, Intentionality & Cognitive Science. 1982. text ed. price not set (ISBN 0-262-52072-9, Pub. by Bradford). MIT Pr.
Eighteen Fifty-Nine to Nineteen Fifty-Nine Edmund Husserl. (Phaenomenologica Ser: No. 4). 1959. lib. bdg. 31.50 (ISBN 90-247-0237-2, Pub. by Martinus Nijhoff Netherlands). Kluwer Boston.
Eley. Die Krise Des Apriori in der Transzendentalen Phanomenologie Edmund Husserls. (Phaenomenologica Ser: No. 10). 1962. lib. bdg. 21.00 (ISBN 90-247-0244-5, Pub. by Martinus Nijhoff Netherlands). Kluwer Boston.
Elliston, Frederick & McCormick, Peter, eds. Husserl: Expositions & Appraisals. LC 75-19882. 370p. 1976. text ed. 18.95x (ISBN 0-268-01063-3). U of Notre Dame Pr.
--Husserl: Expositions & Appraisals. LC 75-19882. 1978. pap. 7.95x (ISBN 0-268-01064-1). U of Notre Dame Pr.
Farber, Marvin. Foundation of Phenomenology: Edmund Husserl & the Quest for a Rigorous Science of Philosophy. 3rd ed. LC 67-25983. 1967. 36.00 (ISBN 0-87395-023-2); pap. 12.00 (ISBN 0-87395-037-2); microfiche 36.00 (ISBN 0-87395-123-9). State U NY Pr.
Gurwitsch, Aron. Phenomenology & the Theory of Science. Embree, Lester, ed. LC 78-25738. (Studies in Phenomenology & Existential Philosophy). 1978. pap. 23.75 (ISBN 0-8357-0346-0, ST-00023, Pub. by Northwestern U Pr). Univ Microfilms.
--Studies in Phenomenology & Psychology. (Studies in Phenomenology & Existential Philosophy Ser). 1966. 21.95x (ISBN 0-8101-0110-6); pap. 10.95x (ISBN 0-8101-0592-6). Northwestern U Pr.
Hines, Thomas J. The Later Poetry of Wallace Stevens: Phenomenological Parallels with Husserl & Heidegger. LC 74-6773. 298p. 1975. 18.50 (ISBN 0-8387-1613-X). Bucknell U Pr.
Husserl. Erste Philosophie (1923-24) (Husserliana Ser.: No. 8). 1959. lib. bdg. 68.50 (ISBN 90-247-0225-9, Pub. by Martinus Nijhoff Netherlands). Kluwer Boston.

--Die Idee der Phanomenologie. 2nd ed. (Husserliana Ser: No. 2). 1973. lib. bdg. 16.00 (ISBN 90-247-5139-X, Pub. by Martinus Nijhoff Netherlands). Kluwer Boston.
--Die Krises der Europaischen Wissenschaften und Die Transzendentale Phanomenol. (Husserliana Ser: No. 6). 1976. lib. bdg. 60.50 (ISBN 90-247-0221-6, Pub. by Martinus Nijhoff Netherlands). Kluwer Boston.
--Par-Fifteen Lectures. 1975. 13.00 (ISBN 90-247-5133-0, Pub. by Martinus Nijhoff Netherlands). Kluwer Boston.
--Phanomenologische Psychologie. 2nd ed. (Husserliana Ser: No. 9). 1968. lib. bdg. 68.50 (ISBN 90-247-0226-7, Pub. by Martinus Nijhoff Netherlands). Kluwer Boston.
--Philosophie der Arithmetik. (Husserliana Ser: No. 12). 1970. lib. bdg. 50.00 (ISBN 90-247-0230-5, Pub. by Martinus Nijhoff Netherlands). Kluwer Boston.
--Zur Phanomenologie Des Inneren Zeitbewustseins: (1893-1917) (Husserliana Ser: No. 10). 1966. lib. bdg. 53.00 (ISBN 90-247-0227-5, Pub. by Martinus Nijhoff Netherlands). Kluwer Boston.
Ingarden. On the Motives Which Led Husserl to Transcedental Idealism. (Phaenomenologica Ser: No. 64). 1975. pap. 16.00 (ISBN 90-247-1751-5, Pub. by Martinus Nijhoff Netherlands). Kluwer Boston.
Kockelmans, Joseph J. Edmund Husserl's Phenomenological Psychology. (Psychology Ser.: No. 4). 1978. Repr. of 1967 ed. text ed. 15.00x (ISBN 0-391-00875-7). Humanities.
Kohak, Erazim. Idea & Experience: Edmund Husserl's Project of Phenomenology in Ideas I. LC 78-661. 1978. lib. bdg. 18.50x (ISBN 0-226-45019-8). U of Chicago Pr.
Kolakowski, Leszek. Husserl & the Search for Certitude. LC 74-29724. (Cassirer Lectures). 96p. 1975. text ed. 10.00x (ISBN 0-300-01858-4). Yale U Pr.
Landgrebe, Ludwig. The Phenomenology of Edmund Husserl: Six Essays. Welton, Donn, ed. 1981. 19.50x (ISBN 0-8014-1177-7). Cornell U Pr.
Lapointe, Francois. Edmund Husserl & His Critics: An International Bibliography (1894-1979) (Bibliographies of Famous Philosophers: Vol. 4). 352p. 1980. 27.50 (ISBN 0-912632-42-9). Philos Document.
Levin, David M. Reason & Evidence in Husserl's Phenomenology. (Studies in Phenomenology & Existential Philosophy). 1970. 19.95x (ISBN 0-8101-0298-6). Northwestern U Pr.
Levinas, Emmanuel. The Theory of Intuition in Husserl's Phenomenology. Orianne, Andre, tr. from Fr. (Studies in Phenomenology & Existential Philosophy). 165p. 1973. 11.95x (ISBN 0-8101-0413-X). Northwestern U Pr.
McCormick, Peter & Elliston, Frederick A., eds. Husserl: Shorter Works. LC 80-53178. 440p. 1981. text ed. 26.00 (ISBN 0-268-01703-4); pap. text ed. 10.95 (ISBN 0-268-01077-3). U of Notre Dame Pr.
Marbach. Das Problem Des Ich in der Phan. Husserls. (Phaenomenologica Ser). 1974. lib. bdg. 47.50 (ISBN 90-247-1587-3, Pub. by Martinus Nijhoff Netherlands). Kluwer Boston.
Mohanty, J. N. Edmund Husserl's Theory of Meaning. 3rd enl. ed. (Phaenomenologica Ser: No. 14). 1976. lib. bdg. 24.00 (ISBN 90-247-0247-X, Pub. by Martinus Nijhoff Netherlands). Kluwer Boston.
Mohanty, J. N., ed. Readings on Edmund Hysserl's Logical Investigations. 1977. lib. bdg. 28.00 (ISBN 90-247-1928-3, Pub. by Martinus Nijhoff Netherlands). Kluwer Boston.
Natanson, Maurice. Edmund Husserl: Philosopher of Infinite Tasks. (Studies in Phenomenology & Existential Philosophy). 1973. 16.95x (ISBN 0-8101-0425-3); pap. 6.95x (ISBN 0-8101-0456-3). Northwestern U Pr.
Paci, Enzo. The Function of the Sciences & the Meaning of Man. Piccone, Paul & Hansen, James, trs. (Studies in Phenomenology & Existential Philosophy). 1972. 21.95x (ISBN 0-8101-0378-8); pap. 10.95 (ISBN 0-8101-0618-3). Northwestern U Pr.
Ricoeur, Paul. Husserl: An Analysis of His Phenomenology. Ballard, Edward G & Embree, Lester, trs. (Studies in Phenomenology & Existential Philosophy Ser). 1967. 16.95x (ISBN 0-8101-0209-9); pap. 6.95 (ISBN 0-8101-0530-6). Northwestern UPr.
Roth. Husserls Ethische Untersuchungen Dargestellt Anhand Seiner Vorlesungsmanuskripte. (Phaenomenologica Ser: No. 7). 1960. lib. bdg. 21.00 (ISBN 90-247-0241-0, Pub. by Martinus Nijhoff Netherlands). Kluwer Boston.
Saraiva, L' Imagination Selon Husserl. (Phaenomenologica Ser: No. 34). 1970. lib. bdg. 24.00 (ISBN 90-247-0273-9, Pub. by Martinus Nijhoff Netherlands). Kluwer Boston.
Schumann, K. Husserl-Chronik: Denk und Lebensweg E. Husserls. (Husserliana Ser: Doc. 1). 1977. lib. bdg. 97.50 (ISBN 90-247-1972-0, Pub. by Martinus Nijhoff Netherlands). Kluwer Boston.
Sokolowski, Robert. The Formation of Husserl's Concept of Constitution. (Phaenomenologica Ser: No. 18). 1970. lib. bdg. 26.00 (ISBN 90-247-5086-5, Pub. by Martinus Nijhoff Netherlands). Kluwer Boston.
--Husserlian Meditations: How Words Present Things. LC 73-91312. (Studies in Phenomenology & Existential Philosophy). 315p. 1974. 18.95x (ISBN 0-8101-0440-7); pap. 8.95 (ISBN 0-8101-0623-X). Northwestern U Pr.
Stevens. James und Husserl. (Phaernomenologica Ser: No. 60). 1974. lib. bdg. 26.00 (ISBN 90-247-1631-4, Pub. by Martinus Nijhoff Netherlands). Kluwer Boston.
Vanbreda & Taminiaux, eds. Husserl et la Pensee Moderne. (Phaenomenologica Ser: No. 2). 1959. lib. bdg. 26.00 (ISBN 90-247-0235-6, Pub. by Martinus Nijhoff Netherlands). Kluwer Boston.
Welch, E. Parl. Edmund Husserl's Phenomenology. 1939. pap. 17.50x (ISBN 0-686-51375-4). Elliots Bks.
--Philosophy of Edmund Husserl. 1965. lib. bdg. 12.50x (ISBN 0-374-98341-0). Octagon.
Williams, Robert R. Schleiermacher the Theologian: The Construction of the Doctrine of God. LC 77-78650. 316p. 1978. 11.95 (ISBN 0-8006-0513-6, 1-513). Fortress.

HUSSEY, THOMAS, BP., 1741-1803

Bemis, Samuel F. The Hussey-Cumberland Mission & American Independence: An Essay in the Diplomacy of the American Revolution. 7.50 (ISBN 0-8446-1069-0). Peter Smith.

HUSSITES

see also Moravians

Kaminsky, Howard. A History of the Hussite Revolution. LC 67-12608. 1967. 32.50x (ISBN 0-520-00625-9). U of Cal Pr.
Kaminsky, Howard, et al. Master Nicholas of Dresden: Old Color & the New. LC 64-25396. (Transactions Ser.: Vol. 55, Pt. 1). (Illus.). 1965. pap. 1.00 (ISBN 0-87169-551-0). Am Philos.
Kautsky, Karl. Communism in Central Europe in the Time of the Reformation. Mulliken, J. L. & Mulliken, E. G., trs. LC 66-22631. Repr. of 1897 ed. 15.00x (ISBN 0-678-00193-6). Kelley.
Klassen, John M. The Nobility & the Making of the Hussite Revolution. (East European Monographs: No. 47). 1978. 12.00x (ISBN 0-914710-40-0). East Eur Quarterly.
Macek, Josef. The Hussite Movement in Bohemia. Fried, Vilem & Milner, Ian, trs. LC 78-63207. (Heresies of the Early Christian & Medieval Era: Second Ser.). Repr. of 1958 ed. 27.50 (ISBN 0-404-16237-1). AMS Pr.
Zeman, Jarold K. The Hussite Movement & the Reformation in Bohemia, Moravia & Slovakia, 1350-1650: A Bibliographic Study Guide. 1977. 9.50 (ISBN 0-930042-00-X). Mich Slavic Pubns.

HUSTLER (BOMBERS)

see B-Fifty-Eight Bomber

HUSTON, JOHN, 1906-

Huston, John. An Open Book. 447p. 1981. pap. 3.95 (ISBN 0-345-25444-9). Ballantine.
--An Open Book. LC 80-7619. (Illus.). 400p. 1980. 15.00 (ISBN 0-394-40465-3). Knopf.
Kaminsky, Stuart M. John Huston: Maker of Magic. LC 77-17017. 1978. 10.95 (ISBN 0-395-25716-6). HM.
Pratley, Gerald. The Cinema of John Huston. LC 73-13192. (Illus.). 192p. 1976. 12.00 (ISBN 0-498-01443-6). A S Barnes.

HUTCHESON, FRANCIS, 1694-1746

Kivy, Peter. The Seventh Sense: A Study of Francis Hutcheson's Aesthetics & Its Influence in Eighteenth Century Britain. 241p. 1976. lib. bdg. 19.95 (ISBN 0-89102-044-6). B Franklin.
Scott, William R. Francis Hutcheson: His Life, Teaching & Position in the History of Philosophy. LC 65-26380. Repr. of 1900 ed. 15.00x (ISBN 0-678-00155-3). Kelley.

HUTCHINSON, ANNE (MARBURY), 1590-1643

Adams, Charles F., ed. Antionomianism in the Colony of Massachusetts Bay, 1636-38, Including the Short Story & Documents. 1966. 26.00 (ISBN 0-8337-0010-3). B Franklin.
Battis, Emery. Saints & Sectaries. (Institute of Early American History & Culture Ser.). 1962. 25.00x (ISBN 0-8078-0863-6). U of NC Pr.
Bremer, Francis J., ed. Anne Hutchison: Troubler of the Puritan Zion. new ed. LC 80-13218. (American Problem Studies Ser.). 180p. (Orig.). 1981. pap. text ed. 5.50 (ISBN 0-89874-063-0). Krieger.
Fowler, James W. & Lovin, Robin W. Trajectories in Faith: Five Life Stories. LC 79-20485. 1980. pap. 6.50 (ISBN 0-687-42480-1). Abingdon.
Rugg, Winnifred K. Unafraid. facsimile ed. LC 73-114891. (Select Bibliographies Reprint Ser). 1930. 17.00 (ISBN 0-8369-5295-2). Arno.
Williams, Selma R. Divine Rebel: The Life of Anne Marbury Hutchinson. LC 80-20109. 256p. 1981. 12.95 (ISBN 0-03-055846-8). HR&W.

HUTCHINSON, JOHN, 1615-1664

Hutchinson, Lucy. Memoirs of the Life of Colonel Hutchinson. 1965. pap. 3.25x (ISBN 0-460-01317-3, Evman). Biblio Dist.

HUTCHINSON, SARA, 1775-1835

Coburn, Kathleen, ed. The Letters of Sara Hutchinson from 1800-1835. 1979. Repr. of 1954 ed. lib. bdg. 45.00 (ISBN 0-8495-0920-3). Arden Lib.
Whalley, George. Coleridge & Sara Hutchinson & the Asra Poems. LC 55-2481. 1955. 15.00x (ISBN 0-8020-5039-5). U of Toronto Pr.

HUTCHINSON, THOMAS, 1711-1780

Bailyn, Bernard. The Ordeal of Thomas Hutchinson. LC 73-76379. 458p. 1974. 17.50x (ISBN 0-674-64160-4, Belknap Pr); pap. 5.95x (ISBN 0-674-64161-2). Harvard U Pr.
Hosmer, James K. The Life of Thomas Hutchinson: Royal Governor of the Province of Massachusetts Bay. LC 70-124926. (American Scene Ser). (Illus.). 454p. 1972. Repr. of 1896 ed. lib. bdg. 42.50 (ISBN 0-306-71038-2). Da Capo.
Thomas Hutchinson & His Contemporaries. (Massachusetts Historical Society Picture Books Ser.). 1974. 2.50 (ISBN 0-686-21444-7). Mass Hist Soc.

HUTCHINSON FAMILY

Hutchinson, John Wallace. Story of the Hutchinsons, 2 vols. Mann, Charles E., ed. LC 76-58562. (Music Reprint Series). 1977. Repr. of 1896 ed. lib. bdg. 65.00 set (ISBN 0-306-70864-7). Da Capo.
Hutchinson, Thomas. Diary & Letters of Thomas Hutchinson, 2 vols. Hutchinson, Peter O., compiled by. 1971. Repr. of 1883 ed. Set. lib. bdg. 55.50 (ISBN 0-8337-1783-9). B Franklin.

HUTTEN, ULRICH VON, 1488-1523

Holborn, Hajo. Ulrich Von Hutten & the German Reformation. Bainton, Roland H., tr. LC 77-25067. (Yale Historical Publications Studies: No. XI). (Illus.). 1978. Repr. of 1937 ed. lib. bdg. 18.50x (ISBN 0-313-20125-0, HOUV). Greenwood.
Kalkoff, Paul. Ulrich Von Hutten und Die Reformation: Eine Kritische Geschichte Seiner Wichtigsten Lebenszeit und der Entscheidungsjahre der Reformation, 1517-1523. (Ger). Repr. of 1920 ed. 53.00 (ISBN 0-384-28511-2); pap. 46.00 (ISBN 0-685-92696-6). Johnson Repr.
Strauss, David F. Ulrich Von Hutten. Sturge, Mrs. G., tr. from Ger. LC 77-130624. Repr. of 1874 ed. 27.50 (ISBN 0-404-06296-2). AMS Pr.

HUTTERITE BRETHREN

Arnold, Eberhard. Foundation & Orders of Sannerz & the Rhon Bruderhof: Introductory History: the Basis for Our Orders, Vol. 1. LC 76-5856. 1976. pap. 3.25 (ISBN 0-87486-162-4). Plough.
--Why We Live in Community. 1976. pap. 2.00 (ISBN 0-87486-168-3). Plough.
Arnold, Emmy. Ein Inneres Wort Fur Jeden Tag Des Jahres. LC 76-10987. 192p. 1976. 4.25 (ISBN 0-87486-166-7). Plough.
Bennett, John W. Hutterian Brethren: The Agricultural Economy & Social Organization of a Communal People. (Illus.). 1967. 15.00x (ISBN 0-8047-0329-9). Stanford U Pr.
Blumhardt, Johann C. & Blumhardt, Christoph. Now Is Eternity. LC 76-10251. 1976. 4.95 (ISBN 0-87486-209-4); pap. 3.95 (ISBN 0-87486-219-1). Plough.
Deets, Lee E. The Hutterities: A Study in Social Cohesion. LC 74-26737. (The American Utopian Adventure Ser.). 89p. Repr. of 1939 ed. lib. bdg. 8.50x (ISBN 0-87991-029-1). Porcupine Pr.
Ehrenpreis, Andreas & Felbinger, Claus. Brotherly Community, the Highest Command of Love: Two Anabaptist Documents of 1650 & 1560. LC 78-21065. 1979. pap. 4.50 (ISBN 0-87486-190-X). Plough.
Gross, Leonard. The Golden Years of the Hutterites. LC 80-10711. (Studies in Anabaptist & Mennonite History Ser.: Vol. 23). 1980. 12.95x (ISBN 0-8361-1227-X). Herald Pr.
Horsch, John. Hutterian Brethren. 1931. 9.95x (ISBN 0-8361-1188-5). Herald Pr.
Horst, Irvin B. The Radical Brethren. 1972. 39.50x (ISBN 0-8361-1193-1). Herald Pr.
Hostetler, John & Huntington, Gertrude. The Hutterites in North America. LC 79-19718. 141p. 1980. pap. text ed. 6.95 (ISBN 0-03-045391-7, HoltC). HR&W.
Hostetler, John A. Hutterite Life. (Illus., Orig.). 1965. pap. 1.10 (ISBN 0-8361-1524-4). Herald Pr.
--Hutterite Society. LC 74-6827. (Illus.). 420p. 1974. 20.00x (ISBN 0-8018-1584-3); pap. 5.95 (ISBN 0-8018-1956-3). Johns Hopkins.
Howells, W. W. & Bleibtreu, Hermann K. Hutterite Age Differences in Body Measurements. LC 78-115048. (Museum Papers: Vol. 57, No. 2). (Orig.). 1970. pap. text ed. 10.00 (ISBN 0-87365-168-5). Peabody Harvard.
Peters, Victor. All Things Common: The Hutterian Way of Life. LC 65-28661. (Illus.). 1966. 11.95x (ISBN 0-8166-0371-5). U of Minn Pr.
Smucker, Donovan E., ed. The Sociology of Canadian Mennonites, Hutterites & Amish: A Bibliography with Annotations. 232p. 1977. text ed. 11.00 (ISBN 0-88920-052-1, Pub. by Laurier U Pr Canada). Humanities.

HUTTON, BARBARA

Van Rensselaer, Phillip. A Million Dollar Baby: The Life Story of Barbara Hutton. 1979. 10.95 (ISBN 0-399-12366-0). Putnam.

HUTTON, JAMES, 1726-1797

Donovan, Arthur & Prentiss, Joseph. James Hutton's Medical Dissertation. LC 80-65850. (Transaction Ser.: Vol. 70). 1980. 8.00 (ISBN 0-87169-706-8). Am Philos.
Playfair, John. Illustrations of the Huttonian Theory of the Earth. 8.50 (ISBN 0-8446-2746-1). Peter Smith.
--Illustrations of the Huttonian Theory of the Earth. 1956. pap. 5.00 (ISBN 0-486-61168-X). Dover.

HUWA-FUTAYYIH CAVE

McBurney, C. B. Haua Fteah & the Stone Age of the South-East Mediterranean. 1968. 99.00 (ISBN 0-521-06915-7). Cambridge U Pr.

HUXLEY, ALDOUS LEONARD, 1894-1963

Bedford, Sybille. Aldous Huxley. 1974. 17.50 (ISBN 0-394-46587-3, 46587). Knopf.
Birnbaum, Milton. Aldous Huxley's Quest for Values. LC 71-142146. 1971. 12.50x (ISBN 0-87049-127-X). U of Tenn Pr.
--Aldous Huxley's Quest for Values. LC 71-142146. 1971. 12.50x (ISBN 0-87049-127-X). U of Tenn Pr.
Calder, J. Huxley: Brave New World, Orwell. (Studies in English Literature Ser.). 1976. pap. text ed. 3.95x (ISBN 0-7131-5920-0). Dynamic Learn Corp.
Chatterjee, Sisir. Aldous Huxley. 1955. lib. bdg. 12.50 (ISBN 0-8414-3483-2). Folcroft.
Clodd, Edward. Pioneers of Evolution: From Thales to Huxley; with an Intermediate Chapter on the Causes of Arrest of the Movement. facsimile ed. LC 74-37470. (Essay Index Reprint Ser). Repr. of 1897 ed. 17.00 (ISBN 0-8369-2540-8). Arno.
Cockshott, Gerald. Music & Nature: A Study of Aldous Huxley. (Salzburger Studien: No. 11). 1980. pap. text ed. 39.00x (ISBN 0-391-02158-3). Humanities.
Ferns, C. S. Aldous Huxley: Novelist. 1980. text ed. 35.00x (ISBN 0-485-11194-2, Athlone Pr). Humanities.
Gandhi, Kishore. Aldous Huxley: Vedantic & Buddhistic Influences. 256p. 1980. text ed. 12.50x (ISBN 0-391-02024-2). Humanities.
Gannon, Paul. Monarch Notes on Huxley's Brave New World, Point Counter Point & Other Works. (Orig.). pap. 1.95 (ISBN 0-671-00714-9). Monarch Pr.
Henderson, Alexander. Aldous Huxley. LC 64-20668. 1964. Repr. of 1936 ed. 8.00 (ISBN 0-8462-0501-7). Russell.
Holmes, Charles M. Aldous Huxley & the Way to Reality. LC 77-16216. (Illus.). 1978. Repr. of 1970 ed. lib. bdg. 23.00 (ISBN 0-313-20016-5, HOAH). Greenwood.
Huxley, Laura. This Timeless Moment: A Personal View of Aldous Huxley. LC 74-32396. (Illus.). 1975. pap. 4.95 (ISBN 0-89087-022-5). Celestial Arts.
Jog, Dattatreya V. Aldous Huxley: The Novelist. LC 77-18731. 1965. 20.00 (ISBN 0-8414-5271-7). Folcroft.
Krishnan, Bharathi. Aspects of Structure, Technique & Quest in Aldous Huxley's Major Novels. (Studia Anglistica Upsaliensia: No. 33). 1977. pap. text ed. 19.75x (ISBN 91-554-0669-6). Humanities.
Kuehn, Robert E., ed. Aldous Huxley: A Collection of Critical Essays. (Twentieth Century Views Ser.). 192p. 1974. 10.95 (ISBN 0-13-448514-9, Spec); (Spec). P-H.
Leighton, Gerald. Huxley: His Life & Work. 94p. 1980. Repr. lib. bdg. 15.00 (ISBN 0-8492-1649-4). R West.
May, Keith M. Aldous Huxley. 1972. text ed. 15.50x (ISBN 0-236-17682-X). Humanities.
Paradis, James G. T. H. Huxley: Man's Place in Nature. LC 78-5492. 1978. 16.50x (ISBN 0-8032-0917-7). U of Nebr Pr.
Paul, Warren. Brave New World Notes. Bd. with Brave New World Revisited Notes. (Orig.). pap. 2.25 (ISBN 0-8220-0256-6). Cliffs.
Ramamurty, Bhaskara K. Aldous Huxley: A Study of His Novels. 200p. 1975. lib. bdg. 10.00x (ISBN 0-210-22346-4). Asia.
Savage, D. S. Mysticism & Aldous Huxley. LC 77-23247. 1947. lib. bdg. 7.50 (ISBN 0-8414-7805-8). Folcroft.

Scales, D. Aldous Huxley & French Literature. (Australian Humanities Research Council Monograph: No. 13). 1969. pap. 6.50x (ISBN 0-424-05900-2, Pub by Sydney U Pr). Intl Schol Bk Serv.
Watt, Donald, ed. Aldous Huxley: The Critical Heritage. (The Critical Heritage Ser.). 1975. 30.00x (ISBN 0-7100-8114-6). Routledge & Kegan.
Watts, Harold H. Aldous Huxley. LC 68-24289. (English Authors Ser.: No. 79). 1969. lib. bdg. 9.95 (ISBN 0-8057-1284-4). Twayne.
Woodcock, George. Dawn & the Darkest Hour: A Study of Aldous Huxley. 296p. 1972. 9.95 (ISBN 0-571-08939-9, Pub. by Faber & Faber). Merrimack Bk Serv.

HUXLEY, ALDOUS LEONARD, 1894-1963–BIBLIOGRAPHY

Bass, Eben E. Aldous Huxley: An Annotated Bibliography. LC 79-7907. (Garland Reference Library of Humanities). 275p. 1981. 30.00 (ISBN 0-8240-9525-1). Garland Pub.
Duval, Hanson R. Aldous Huxley: A Bibliography. LC 72-190714. 1939. lib. bdg. 25.00 (ISBN 0-8414-0812-2). Folcroft.
Eschelbach, Claire J. & Shober, Joyce L. Aldous Huxley: A Bibliography Nineteen Sixteen to Nineteen Fifty-Nine. 1979. Repr. 12.50x (ISBN 0-374-92626-3). Octagon.
Muir, P. H. & Van Thal, B. Bibliographies of the First Editions of Books by Aldous Huxley & T. F. Powys. LC 76-27300. 1927. lib. bdg. 15.00 (ISBN 0-8414-6011-6). Folcroft.

HUXLEY, JULIAN SORELL, 1887-

Julian Huxley: Scientist & World Citizen, 1887-1975. 1979. pap. 7.00 (ISBN 92-3-101461-7, U894, UNESCO). Unipub.

HUXLEY, THOMAS HENRY, 1825-1895

Ainsworth-Davis, James R. Thomas H. Huxley. LC 70-158236. (English Men of Science: No. 2). Repr. of 1907 ed. 21.50 (ISBN 0-404-07892-3). AMS Pr.
Clodd, Edward. Thomas Henry Huxley. LC 74-2491. 1902. lib. bdg. 15.00 (ISBN 0-685-45595-5). Folcroft.
--Thomas Henry Huxley. LC 75-30018. Repr. of 1902 ed. 14.50 (ISBN 0-404-14023-8). AMS Pr.
Huxley, Leonard. Life & Letters of Thomas Henry Huxley, 2 vols. LC 75-41152. (BCL Ser. II). Repr. of 1900 ed. 67.50 set (ISBN 0-404-14980-4). AMS Pr.
--Life & Letters of Thomas Henry Huxley, 2 vols. 1979. Repr. of 1901 ed. Set. lib. bdg. 75.00 (ISBN 0-8492-5317-9). R West.
--Thomas Henry Huxley. LC 76-102247. (Select Bibliographies Reprint Ser). 1920. 16.00 (ISBN 0-8369-5132-8). Arno.
Marshall, A. J. Darwin & Huxley in Australia. (Illus.). 1971. 11.00x (ISBN 0-340-12639-6). Verry.
Peterson, Houston. Huxley, Prophet of Science. LC 75-30039. Repr. of 1932 ed. 26.00 (ISBN 0-404-14040-8). AMS Pr.

HUYGENS, CHRISTIAAN, 1629-1695

Panofsky, Erwin. Codex Huygens & Leonardo Da Vinci's Art Theory. LC 79-109814. (Illus.). 1971. Repr. of 1940 ed. lib. bdg. 16.75 (ISBN 0-8371-4306-3, PACH). Greenwood.
Symposium on the Life and Work of Christiaan Huygens, Amsterdam, 22-25 August 1979. Studies on Christiean Huygens: Invited Papers. Bos, H. J., et al, eds. 1980. text ed. 34.25 (ISBN 90-265-0333-4, Pub. by Swets Pub Serv Holland). Swets North Am.

HUYGENS, CONSTANTIJN, HEER VAN ZUILICHEM, 1596-1687

Bachrach, A. G. Sir Constantine Huygens & Britain: 1597-1619, Vol. 1. (Publications of the Sir Thomas Browne Institute Ser: No. 1). 1962. pap. 26.00 (ISBN 90-6021-059-X, Pub. by Leiden Univ Holland). Kluwer Boston.

HUYSMANS, JORIS KARL, 1848-1907

Cervasco, G. A. J. K. Huysman: A Reference Guide. 1980. lib. bdg. 24.50 (ISBN 0-686-61017-2). G K Hall.
Huysman, Joris-Karl. Lettres Inedites a Arif Prins, 1885-1907. 415p. 1977. 60.00 (ISBN 0-686-54178-2). French & Eur.

HUZVARESH

see Pahlavi Language

HYBRID COMPUTERS

see also Digital-To-Analogue Converters; Electronic Analog Computers; Electronic Digital Computers

Hyndman, D. E. Analog & Hybrid Computing. LC 75-120691. 1970. 25.00 (ISBN 0-08-015573-1); pap. 13.25 (ISBN 0-08-015572-3). Pergamon.
Korn, Granino A. & Korn, Theresa M. Electronic Analog & Hybrid Computers. 2nd ed. LC 70-170174. (Illus.). 448p. 1972. 39.50 (ISBN 0-07-035363-8, P&RB). McGraw.
Reliability Analysis Center. Hybrid Microcircuit Reliability Compiled by IIT Research Institute, Chicago. 200p. 1976. pap. text ed. 94.00 (ISBN 0-08-020535-6). Pergamon.

HYBRID VIGOR

see Heterosis

HYBRIDITY OF RACES

see Miscegenation

HYBRIDIZATION

see also Genetics; Heterosis; Mendel's Law

Ephrussi, Boris. Hybridization of Somatic Cells. LC 79-39783. (Illus.). 192p. 1972. 14.50x (ISBN 0-691-08114-X); pap. 6.50 (ISBN 0-691-08117-4). Princeton U Pr.
Knobloch, Irving W. A Check List of Crosses in the Gramineae. 1968. pap. 10.00 (ISBN 0-934454-22-1). Lubrecht & Cramer.
Protides of the Biological Fluids, Colloquium 28: Proceedings of the 28th Colloquium on Protides of the Biological Fluids, Brussels, 5-8 May 1980. LC 58-5908. (Illus.). 600p. 1980. 120.00 (ISBN 0-08-026370-4). Pergamon.
Stace, C. A., ed. Hybridization & the Flora of the British Isles. 1975. 96.50 (ISBN 0-12-661650-7). Acad Pr.

HYBRIDIZATION, VEGETABLE

De Vries, H. Mutation Theory, 2 Vols. in 1. Farmer, J. B. & Darbishire, trs. 1909-1910. 48.00 (ISBN 0-527-93470-4). Kraus Repr.
Fehr, W. R. & Hadley, H. H., eds. Hybridization of Crop Plants. (Illus.). 1980. 25.00 (ISBN 0-89118-034-6). Am Soc Agron.
Herbert, William. Amaryllidacea...and...a Treatise on Cross-Bred Vegetables. (Illus.). 1970. 80.00 (ISBN 3-7682-0672-6). Lubrecht & Cramer.
Mendel, G. Versuche Ueber Pflanzenhybriden. 1966. Repr. of 1866 ed. pap. 5.00 (ISBN 3-7682-0013-2). Lubrecht & Cramer.
Mendel, Gregor. Experiments in Plant-Hybridisation. LC 67-9611. 1965. pap. 1.95x (ISBN 0-674-27800-3). Harvard U Pr.
Roberts, Herbert F. Plant Hybridization Before Mendel. (Illus.). 1965. Repr. of 1929 ed. 13.95 (ISBN 0-02-851000-3). Hafner.
Watts, Leslie. Flower & Vegetable Plant Breeding. 179p. 1981. 40.00x (ISBN 0-686-75413-1, Pub. by Grower Bks). State Mutual Bk.

HYDATID DISEASE

see Echinococcosis

HYDATIFORM MOLE

Borell, Ulf, et al. The Diagnosis of Hydatidiform Mole, Malignant Hydatiform Mole & Choriocarcinoma with Special Reference to the Diagnosti Value of Pelvic Arteriography. (Illus.). 128p. 1966. ed. spiral bdg. 14.50photocopy (ISBN 0-398-00190-1). C C Thomas.

HYDE, CHARLES MCEWEN, 1832-1899

Kent, Harold W. Dr. Hyde & Mr. Stevenson. LC 72-83673. 1973. 10.00 (ISBN 0-8048-1062-1). C E Tuttle.

HYDE, DOUGLAS, 1860-1949

Daly, Dominic. The Young Douglas Hyde: The Dawn of the Irish Revolution & Renaissance, 1874-1893. 232p. 1974. 15.00x (ISBN 0-87471-478-8). Rowman.
Dunleavy, Gareth. Douglas Hyde. (Irish Writers Ser.). 92p. 1974. 4.50 (ISBN 0-8387-7883-6); pap. 1.95 (ISBN 0-8387-7975-1). Bucknell U Pr.

HYDE, EDWARD, 1ST EARL OF CLARENDON, 1609-1674

Wormald, B. H. Claredon: Politics, History, & Religion 1640-1660. LC 75-35494. (Midway Reprint Ser). 1976. pap. text ed. 12.00x (ISBN 0-226-90738-4). U of Chicago Pr.

HYDERABAD, INDIA (STATE)

Alam, S. Manzoor & Khan, Waheeduddin. Metropolitan Hyderabad & Its Region: A Strategy for Development. (Illus.). 316p. 1973. 12.50x (ISBN 0-210-22344-8). Asia.
Husain, Yusuf H. First Nizam. 1964. 9.25x (ISBN 0-210-34081-9). Asia.
Lynton, Harriet R. & Rajan, Mohini. The Days of the Beloved. 1974. 18.95 (ISBN 0-520-02442-7); pap. 5.95 (ISBN 0-520-03939-4). U of Cal Pr.
Munshi, K. M. End of an Era-Hyderabad Memories. 1957. 6.75x (ISBN 0-8426-0032-9). Verry.

HYDNUM

Coker, W. C. & Beers, A. H. The Stipitate Hydnums of the Eastern U.S. (Illus.). 1970. Repr. of 1951 ed. 32.00 (ISBN 3-7682-0695-5). Lubrecht & Cramer.

HYDRA

Burnett, Allison L., ed. Biology of Hydra. 1973. 60.00 (ISBN 0-12-145950-0). Acad Pr.
Lenhoff, Howard M. & Loomis, W. Farnsworth, eds. Biology of Hydra & of Some Other Coelenterates. LC 61-18157. 1961. 9.95x (ISBN 0-87024-010-2). U of Miami Pr.
Shostak, Stanley. Hydra: A Photomicrographic Book. LC 77-9875. (Illus.). (gr. 6-8). 1978. PLB 5.99 (ISBN 0-698-30671-6). Coward.

HYDRATION

Taylor, R. E., ed. Advances in Obsidian Glass Studies: Archaeological & Geochemical Perspectives. LC 76-43192. (Illus.). 1977. 32.00 (ISBN 0-8155-5050-2, NP). Noyes.

HYDRAULIC CEMENT

see Cement

HYDRAULIC CONTROL

Dransfield, P. Hydraulic Control Systems: Design & Analysis of the Dynamics. (Lecture Notes in Control & Information Sciences Ser.: Vol. 33). 227p. 1981. pap. 13.40 (ISBN 0-387-10890-4). Springer-Verlag.
Fluidics Quarterly, Vol. 1. (Illus.). 1968-69. 85.00 (ISBN 0-88232-001-7). Delbridge Pub Co.
Fluidics Quarterly, Vol. 2. (Illus.). 1970. 125.00 (ISBN 0-88232-006-8). Delbridge Pub Co.
Fluidics Quarterly, Vol. 3. (Illus.). 1971. 100.00 (ISBN 0-88232-012-2). Delbridge Pub Co.
Fluidics Quarterly, Vol. 9. (Illus.). 1977. 115.00 (ISBN 0-88232-042-4). Delbridge Pub Co.
Merritt, Herbert E. Hydraulic Control Systems. LC 66-28759. 1967. 41.50 (ISBN 0-471-59617-5, Pub. by Wiley-Interscience). Wiley.

HYDRAULIC CONVEYING

International Technical Conference on Slurry Transportation, 2nd. Proceedings. Linderman, Charles W., ed. LC 77-81416. (Illus.). 152p. 1977. pap. 40.00 (ISBN 0-932066-02-X). Slurry Transport.
Round, Gilbert F., ed. Solid-Liquid Flow Abstracts, 3 Vols. 1969. Set. 222.75x (ISBN 0-677-40120-5); Vol. 1. 99.50x (ISBN 0-677-40080-2); Vol. 2. 102.25 (ISBN 0-677-40090-X); Vol. 3. 48.50x (ISBN 0-677-40100-0). Gordon.
Stepanoff, Alexely. Gravity Flow & Transportation of Solids in Suspension. (Materials Handling & Packaging Ser). 1969. text ed. 11.25 (ISBN 0-471-82202-7, Pub. by Wiley). Krieger.
Stephens, H. S. & Gittins, L., eds. Hydrotransport Seven: Papers Presented at the Seventh International Conference on the Hydraulic Transport of Solids in Pipes. (Illus., Orig.). 1980. pap. 112.00 (ISBN 0-906085-46-2). BHRA Fluid.

HYDRAULIC ENGINEERING

see also Boring; Channels (Hydraulic Engineering); Drainage; Flood Control; Hydraulic Machinery; Hydraulic Measurements; Hydraulic Mining; Hydraulic Structures; Hydraulics; Hydrodynamics; Hydrostatics; Irrigation; Offshore Structures; Pumping Machinery; Reclamation of Land; Rivers; Shore Protection; Stream Measurements; Underwater Drilling; Water-Supply Engineering; Wells

American Society of Civil Engineers, compiled by. Hydraulic Engineering & the Environment. 480p. 1973. pap. text ed. 12.50 (ISBN 0-87262-054-9). Am Soc Civil Eng.
--Verification of Mathematical & Physical Models in Hydraulic Engineering. 904p. 1978. pap. text ed. 40.00 (ISBN 0-87262-131-6). Am Soc Civil Eng.
ASCE Conference, Hydraulics Division, 1980. Computer & Physical Models in Hydraulic Engineering: Proceedings. Ashton, George, ed. LC 80-67878. 504p. 1980. pap. text ed. 36.00 (ISBN 0-87262-252-5). Am Soc Civil Eng.
Bretschneider, Charles L., ed. Topics in Ocean Engineering. Incl. Vol. 1. (Illus.). 428p. 1969. (ISBN 0-87201-598-X); Vol. 2. (Illus.). 229p. 1970 (ISBN 0-87201-599-8). 26.50x ea. Gulf Pub.
Brown, J. Guthrie, ed. Hydro-Electric Engineering Practice: Mechanical & Electrical Engineering, Vol. 2. 2nd ed. (Illus.). 1970. 95.00x (ISBN 0-216-89056-X). Intl Ideas.
Cunge, J. A. & Holley, F. M. Practical Aspects of Computational River Hydraulics. (Water Resources Engineering Ser.). 420p. 1981. text ed. 69.95 (ISBN 0-273-08442-9). Pitman Pub MA.
Davis, Calvin V. & Sorensen, K. E. Handbook of Applied Hydraulics. 3rd ed. (Illus.). 1968. 56.50 (ISBN 0-07-015538-0, P&RB). McGraw.
The Efficient Use of Water in the Manufacturing Industries: Proceedings, No. 52, Leeds, September 1977. 208p. 1981. 80.00x (ISBN 0-85295-105-1, Pub. by Inst Chem Eng England). State Mutual Bk.
Fawcett, J. R. Hydraulic Circuits & Control Systems. 240p. 1979. 36.00x (ISBN 0-85461-078-2). State Mutual Bks.
Fifth International Conference on the Hydraulic Transport of Solids in Pipes. Proceedings, 2 vols. Stephens, H. S. & Gittins, L., eds. (Illus.). 1979. Set. pap. text ed. 86.00 (ISBN 0-900983-82-5, Dist by Air Science Co.). BHRA Fluid.
Greenberg, P., ed. Hydraulic Engineering Transactions, Vol. 95, 1971. Wald, A., tr. from Rus. (Transactions of the Vedeneev All-Union Scientific Research Institute of Hydraulic Engineering). (Illus.). 332p. 1974. 30.00x (ISBN 0-7065-1474-2, Pub. by IPST). Intl Schol Bk Serv.
Gyorke, Olivier. European Hydraulics Laboratories: A Survey. (Illus.). 128p. (Orig.). 1974. pap. 6.25 (ISBN 92-3-101064-6, U217, UNESCO). Unipub.
Hwang, Ned H. Fundamentals of Hydraulic Systems. (P-H Ser. in Environmental Sciences). (Illus.). 352p. 1981. text ed. 28.95 (ISBN 0-13-340000-X). P-H.
Hydraulic Engineering: Transactions of the Vedeneev Institute. 2144p. 1971. Vol. 87. 22.50x (ISBN 0-7065-1174-3, Pub. by IPST); Vol. 88. 22.50x (ISBN 0-7065-1175-1); Vol. 89. 22.50x (ISBN 0-7065-1176-X); Vol. 90. 25.00x (ISBN 0-7065-1202-2); Vol. 91. 25.00x (ISBN 0-7065-1203-0); Vol. 92. 30.00x (ISBN 0-7065-1219-7). Intl Schol Bk Serv.
Hydraulic System Cleanliness. 1971. pap. 4.50 (ISBN 0-8031-0005-1, 04-491000-12). ASTM.
Institute for Power System. Hydraulic Handbook. 7th ed. 850p. 1979. 100.00x (ISBN 0-85461-074-X). State Mutual Bks.
International Conference on the Hydraulic Transport of Solids in Pipes, 6th. Hydrotransport Six: Proceedings, 2 vols. Stephens, H. S., ed. 400p. 1979. Set. pap. 112.00 lib. ed. (ISBN 0-906085-21-7, Dist. by Air Science Co.). BHRA Fluid.
Jaeger, Charles. Fluid Transients in Hydro-Electric Engineering Practice. (Illus.). 1977. 68.50x (ISBN 0-216-90225-8). Intl Ideas.
Jansen, P. P., et al. Principles of River Engineering: The Non-Tidal Alluvial River. (Water Resources Engineering Ser.). 509p. 1979. text ed. 119.95 (ISBN 0-686-31210-4). Pitman Pub MA.
Kinori, B. Z. Manual of Surface Drainage Engineering, Vol. 1. 1970. 41.50 (ISBN 0-444-40851-7). Elsevier.
Lajos, Ivicsics. Hydraulic Models. 1980. write for info. WRP.
Lefax Pub. Co. Editors. Hydraulic Engineering Handbook. (Lefax Technical Manuals: No. 789). (Illus.). looseleaf bdg. 8.00 (ISBN 0-685-14145-4). Lefax.
Leliavsky, S. Irrigation & Hydraulic Design, Vol. 3. 765p. 1960. text ed. 49.95x (ISBN 0-412-05120-6, Pub. by Chapman & Hall England). Methuen Inc.
Linsley, Ray K. & Franzini, Joseph. Water Resources Engineering. 3rd ed. (Water Resources & Environmental Engineering Ser.). (Illus.). 1979. text ed. 26.50 (ISBN 0-07-037965-3); solutions manual 8.50 (ISBN 0-07-037966-1). McGraw.
Lyapichev, P. A. River Runoff Regulation & Water Management Calculations. 304p. 1975. 33.50 (ISBN 0-7065-1498-X, Pub. by IPST). Intl Schol Bk Serv.
Maass, Arthur. Muddy Waters: The Army Engineers & the Nation's Rivers. LC 73-20238. (FDR & the Era of the New Deal Ser). 306p. 1974. Repr. of 1951 ed. lib. bdg. 29.50 (ISBN 0-306-70607-5). Da Capo.
Maass, Arthur, et al. Design of Water-Resource Systems: New Techniques for Relating Economic Objectives, Engineering Analysis, & Governmental Planning. LC 62-8181. (Illus.). 1962. 30.00x (ISBN 0-674-19950-2). Harvard U Pr.
Morris, Henry M. & Wiggert, James M. Applied Hydraulics in Engineering. 2nd ed. 600p. 1972. 27.95 (ISBN 0-471-06669-9); instr's solution avail. (ISBN 0-471-07503-5). Wiley.
National Association of Home Builders, et al. Residential Storm Water Management: Objectives, Principles, & Design Considerations. LC 75-34759. 1975. pap. 7.50 (ISBN 0-87420-564-6). Urban Land.
Naudascher, E. & Rockwell, D., eds. Practical Experiences with Flow-Induced Vibrations: Symposium Proceedings. (International Association for Hydraulic Research - International Union of Theoretical & Applied Mechanics). (Illus.). 850p. 1980. 82.60 (ISBN 0-387-10314-7). Springer-Verlag.
Neill, C. R. Guide to Bridge Hydraulics. LC 72-95811. (Illus.). 1975. 17.50x (ISBN 0-8020-1961-7). U of Toronto Pr.
Novak, P. & Cabelka, J. Models in Hydraulic Engineering. (Water Resources Engineering). 480p. 1981. text ed. 85.00 (ISBN 0-273-08436-4). Pitman Pub MA.
Pippenger, John H. & Hicks, Tyler G. Industrial Hydraulics. 2nd ed. 1970. text ed. 19.95 (ISBN 0-07-050064-9, G). McGraw.
Robb, Louis A. Engineers' Dictionary, Spanish-English, English-Spanish. 2nd ed. 1949. 41.00 (ISBN 0-471-72501-3, Pub. by Wiley-Interscience). Wiley.
Rudman, Jack. Hydraulic Engineer. (Career Examination Ser.: C-357). (Cloth bdg. avail. on request). pap. 10.00 (ISBN 0-8373-0357-5). Natl Learning.
Schwab, G. O., et al. Elementary Soil & Water Engineering. 2nd ed. LC 76-132224. 1978. 23.95x (ISBN 0-471-76526-0); Arabic Translation 7.95 (ISBN 0-471-04504-7). Wiley.
Shen, Hsieh W. Modeling of Rivers. LC 79-3913. 1979. 49.00 (ISBN 0-471-05474-7, Pub. by Wiley-Interscience). Wiley.
Studien Zur Hydronymie des Savesystems: Woerterbuch der Gewaessernamen, Auswertung. 2nd ed. (Ger.). 1966. pap. 32.50 (ISBN 3-533-00810-X, M-7629, Pub. by Carl Winter). French & Eur.

Thorma, Jean. Modern Oil: Hydraulic Engineering. 350p. 1971. lib. bdg. 40.00x (ISBN 0-85461-043-X, Pub by Trade & Tech England). Renouf.

Threlfall, A. J. Design Charts for Water Retaining Structures: BS 5337. (Viewpoint Publication Ser). (Illus.). 1978. pap. text ed. 15.00 (ISBN 0-7210-1104-7). Scholium Intl.

Trade & Technical Press Ltd, ed. Hydraulic Technical Data, Vol. 4. 21.00x (ISBN 0-85461-066-9). Intl Ideas.

U. S. Dept. of Agriculture-Soil Conservation Service & Forest Service. Headwaters Control & Use: A Summary of Fundamental Principles & Their Application in the Conservation & Utilization of Waters & Soils Throughout Headwater Areas. LC 72-2871. (Use & Abuse of America's Natural Resources Ser). (Illus.). 290p. 1972. Repr. of 1937 ed. 20.00 (ISBN 0-405-04539-5). Arno.

HYDRAULIC ENGINEERING–PROBLEMS, EXERCISES, ETC.

Shames, Irving H. Mechanics of Fluids. 1962. text ed. 24.50 (ISBN 0-07-056390-X, C); solutions manual 4.95 (ISBN 0-07-056391-8). McGraw.

HYDRAULIC FLUIDS

see also Petroleum Products

Tourret. Performance Testing of Hydraulic Fluids. 1979. 72.00 (ISBN 0-85501-317-6). Heyden.

Trade & Technical Press Editors. Fluids for Power Systems. 250p. 1970. 35.00x (ISBN 0-85461-040-5, Pub by Trade & Tech England). Renouf.

Zandi, I., ed. Advances in Solid-Liquid Flow in Pipes & Its Application. LC 77-120000. 1971. 50.00 (ISBN 0-08-015767-X). Pergamon.

HYDRAULIC MACHINERY

see also Centrifugal Pumps; Hydraulic Control; Hydraulic Servomechanisms; Oil Hydraulic Machinery; Pumping Machinery; Turbines

Elonka, Stephen M. & Johnson, O. H. Standard Industrial Hydraulics Questions & Answers. (Illus.). 1967. 25.00 (ISBN 0-07-019280-4, P&RB). McGraw.

Helfman, Elizabeth S. Wheels, Scoops, & Buckets: How People Lift Water for Their Fields. LC 68-27709. (Illus.). (gr. 4-6). 1968. 6.75 (ISBN 0-688-41154-1). Lothrop.

Institute for Power System. Some Aspects of Hydraulics in Mechanical Handling & Mobile Equipment. 120p. 1979. 30.00x (ISBN 0-85461-006-5). State Mutual Bks.

Manohar, M. & Krishnamachar, P. Hydraulic Machinery & Advanced Hydraulics. 600p. Date not set. text ed. 37.50 (ISBN 0-7069-1194-6, Pub. by Vikas India). Advent NY.

Mataix, Claudio. Mecanica De Fluidos y Maquinas Hidraulicas. (Span). 1970. pap. text ed. 13.80 (ISBN 0-06-315590-7, IntlDept). Har-Row.

Mishra, C. B. Hydraulic Machines Through Theory & Examples. x, 318p. (Orig.). 1980. pap. text ed. 10.00x (ISBN 0-210-33860-1). Asia.

Pippenger, John H. & Hicks, Tyler G. Industrial Hydraulics. 2nd ed. 1970. text ed. 19.95 (ISBN 0-07-050064-9, G). McGraw.

Prokes, J. Hydraulic Mechanisms in Automation. 1977. 48.00 (ISBN 0-444-99829-2). Elsevier.

Society of Automotive Engineers. Topics on Contamination in Hydraulic Systems. 1979. 15.00 (ISBN 0-89883-218-7). SAE.

Some Aspects of Hydraulics in Mechanical Handling & Mobile Equipment. (Illus.). 1970. 27.50x (ISBN 0-85461-006-5). Intl Ideas.

HYDRAULIC MEASUREMENTS

see also Flow Meters; Hydrometer; Stream Measurements; Water-Meters

Herschy, R. W. Hydrometry: Principles & Practices. LC 78-4101. 1978. 89.00 (ISBN 0-471-99649-1, Pub. by Wiley-Interscience). Wiley.

Kolupaila, Steponas. Bibliography of Hydrometry. 1961. 15.00x (ISBN 0-268-00021-2). U of Notre Dame Pr.

Modern Developments in Hydrometry: Proceedings, Vol. 1. (Illus.). 71p. 1975. pap. 16.00 (ISBN 92-63-10427-1, WMO). Unipub.

Swinney, H. L. & Gollup, J. P., eds. Hydrodynamic Instabilities & the Transition to Turbulence. (Topics in Applied Physics Ser.: Vol. 45). (Illus.). 320p. 1981. 56.60 (ISBN 0-387-10390-2). Springer-Verlag.

HYDRAULIC MINING

see also Gold Mines and Mining; Manganese Mines and Mining, Submarine

Evans, Taliesin. Hydraulic Mining in California in Eighteen Eighty-Three. Jones, William R., ed. (Illus.). 1981. pap. 2.00 (ISBN 0-89646-052-5). Outbooks.

Hill, Mary. Diving & Digging for Gold. rev ed. LC 73-22389. (Illus.). 48p. 1973. pap. 2.50 (ISBN 0-87961-005-0). Naturegraph.

LeGaye, E. S. Gold: ABC's of Panning! new rev. 3rd ed. LC 74-128599. (Illus.). 1975. pap. 4.95 (ISBN 0-685-70348-7). Western Her Texas.

--Gold: ABC's of Panning! rev. 2nd ed. LC 74-128599. (Illus.). 1970. pap. 3.00 (ISBN 0-685-70349-5). Western Her Texas.

May, Philip R. Origins of Hydraulic Mining in California. limited ed. (Illus.). 88p. 1970. octavo 6.95 (ISBN 0-910740-17-8). Holmes.

Wilson, Eldred D. Arizona Gold Placers & Placering. (Illus.). 148p. 1980. pap. 5.95 (ISBN 0-89632-003-0). Del Oeste.

HYDRAULIC POWER PLANTS

see Water-Power; Water-Power Electric Plants

HYDRAULIC PRESSES

Mueller, E. Hydraulic Forging Presses. 3rd ed. (Illus.). 1968. 49.80 (ISBN 0-387-04286-5). Springer-Verlag.

Oehler, Gerhard. Hydraulic Presses. Minden, F., tr. 393p. 1968. 37.50x (ISBN 0-8448-0095-3). Crane-Russak Co.

HYDRAULIC SERVOMECHANISMS

Fawcett, J. R. Hydraulic Servo-Mechanisms & Their Applications. 130p. 1979. 25.00x (ISBN 0-85461-026-X). State Mutual Bks.

--Hydraulic Servo Mechanisms & Their Applications. (Illus.). 1970. 24.95x (ISBN 0-85461-026-X). Intl Ideas.

HYDRAULIC STRUCTURES

see also Aqueducts; Canals; Coffer-Dams; Dams; Docks; Flood Dams and Reservoirs; Fountains; Harbors; Lighthouses; Piers; Pipe Lines; Reservoirs; Sea-Walls; Sewerage; Structural Engineering; Tunnels and Tunneling; Wharves

McCormick, Michael E. Ocean Engineering Wave Mechanics. LC 72-12756. (Ocean Engineering Ser.). 192p. 1973. 29.50 (ISBN 0-471-58177-1, Pub. by Wiley-Interscience). Wiley.

Muga, Bruce J. & Wilson, James F. Dynamic Analysis of Ocean Structures. LC 77-122021. (Ocean Technology Ser.). 377p. 1970. 35.00 (ISBN 0-306-30483-X, Plenum Pr). Plenum Pub.

Small Hydraulic Structures, 2 vols. (Irrigation & Drainagepaper, No. 26). (Illus.). 293p. 1975. pap. 26.00 (ISBN 0-685-54184-3, F995, FAO). Vol. 1 (F995). Vol. 2. pap. 20.00 (ISBN 0-686-77065-X, 26/1). Unipub.

Wiegel, Robert L. Oceanographical Engineering. 1964. ref. ed. 34.95 (ISBN 0-13-629600-9). P-H.

HYDRAULIC TRANSMISSION

see Oil Hydraulic Machinery

HYDRAULICS

see also Channels (Hydraulic Engineering); Fire Extinction; Fluids; Hydraulic Engineering; Hydraulic Measurements; Hydrostatics; Seepage; Water Hammer

Abbott, M. B. Computational Hydraulics: Elements of the Theory of Free Surface Flows. (Water Resources Engineering Ser.). 324p. 1979. text ed. 52.00 (ISBN 0-273-01140-5). Pitman Pub MA.

American Institute of Physics. Hydraulic Devices. (Physics of Technology Project Ser.). (Illus.). 64p. (Orig.). 1975. pap. text ed. 4.00 (ISBN 0-07-001724-7, G). McGraw.

American Society of Civil Engineers, compiled by. Hydraulics in the Coastal Zone. 376p. 1977. pap. text ed. 19.75 (ISBN 0-87262-085-9). Am Soc Civil Eng.

--A List of Translations of Foreign Literature on Hydraulics. (ASCE Manual & Report on Energy Practice Ser.: No. 35). 144p. 1968. pap. text ed. 6.00 (ISBN 0-87262-212-6). Am Soc Civil Eng.

--Symposium on Rearation Research. 376p. 1979. pap. text ed. 26.00 (ISBN 0-87262-142-1). Am Soc Civil Eng.

ASCE Conference, Hydraulics Division, 1980. Urban Stormwater Management in Coastal Areas: Proceedings. Kuo, Chin Y., ed. LC 80-66949. 448p. 1980. pap. text ed. 32.00 (ISBN 0-87262-247-9). Am Soc Civil Eng.

Aviation Maintenance Foundation. Aircraft Hydraulics Systems. Crane, Dale, ed. (Aviation Technician Training Ser.). (Illus.). 52p. 1977. pap. text ed. 4.95 (ISBN 0-89100-058-5). Aviation Maint.

Azevedo, J. M. Manual De Hidraulica. (Span.). 1976. pap. text ed. 15.00 (ISBN 0-06-310007-X, IntlDept). Har-Row.

Binder, Raymond C. Fluid Mechanics. 5th ed. (Illus.). 448p. 1973. ref. ed. 25.95x (ISBN 0-13-322594-1). P-H.

Brater, E. F. Handbook of Hydraulics. 6th ed. (Handbook Ser.). 1976. 31.50 (ISBN 0-07-007243-4, P&RB). McGraw.

Chaudhry, M. Hanif. Applied Hydraulic Transients. 1979. text ed. 22.50x (ISBN 0-442-21517-7). Van Nos Reinhold.

Chernov, A. & Bessrebrennikov, N. Fundamentals of Heat Engineering & Hydraulics. Troitsky, A., tr. from Rus. (Illus.). 407p. 1969. 17.00x (ISBN 0-8464-0437-0). Beekman Pubs.

Chow Ven Te, ed. Advances in Hydroscience, 12 vols. Incl. Vol. 1. 1964. 55.00 (ISBN 0-12-021801-1); Vol. 2. 1966. 55.00 (ISBN 0-12-021802-X); Vol. 3. 1967. 55.00 (ISBN 0-12-021803-8); Vol. 4. 1968. 55.00 (ISBN 0-12-021804-6); Vol. 5. 1969. 55.00 (ISBN 0-12-021805-4); Vol. 6. 1970. 55.00 (ISBN 0-12-021806-2); Vol. 7. 1971. 55.00 (ISBN 0-12-021807-0); Vol. 8. 1972. 55.00 (ISBN 0-12-021808-9); Vol. 9. 1973. 50.00 (ISBN 0-12-021809-7); Vol. 10. 1975. 63.00 (ISBN 0-12-021810-0); lib. ed. 81.00 (ISBN 0-12-021874-7); microfiche 45.50 (ISBN 0-12-021875-5); Vol. 11. 1978. 55.00 (ISBN 0-12-021811-9); lib ed. 70.50 (ISBN 0-12-021876-3); microfiche 39.50 (ISBN 0-12-021877-1); Vol. 12. 1978. 51.00 (ISBN 0-12-021812-7); 66.50 (ISBN 0-12-021878-X); 36.00 (ISBN 0-12-021879-8). Acad Pr.

Daugherty, Robert L. & Franzini, Joseph B. Fluid Mechanics: With Engineering Applications. 7th ed. (Illus.). 1977. text ed. 22.50 (ISBN 0-07-015427-9, C); solutions manual 9.95 (ISBN 0-07-015428-7). McGraw.

Davis, Calvin V. & Sorensen, K. E. Handbook of Applied Hydraulics. 3rd ed. (Illus.). 1968. 56.50 (ISBN 0-07-015538-0, P&RB). McGraw.

De Vore, R. William & Wood, Don J., eds. Proceedings - 1981 International Symposium on Urban Hydrology, Hydraulics & Sediment Control. LC 81-82243. (Illus.). 473p. (Orig.). 1981. pap. 33.50 (ISBN 0-89779-047-2, UKY BU125); microfiche 4.50 (ISBN 0-89779-048-0). OES Pubns.

DeWiest, Roger J. Geohydrology. (Illus.). 1965. 29.95 (ISBN 0-471-20410-2). Wiley.

Drago, John J. Hydraulics: A New Approach. LC 78-67464. (Illus.). 1978. pap. 3.00 (ISBN 0-89368-301-9). Davis Pub Co.

Erven, Lawrence. Techniques of Fire Hydraulics. (Fire Science Ser). 1972. text ed. 17.95 (ISBN 0-02-473000-9, 47300). Macmillan.

Essery, I. T. S. Revision Notes on Hydraulics. 1971. text ed. 4.95 (ISBN 0-408-00068-6). Butterworth.

Ewbank, Thomas. A Descriptive & Historical Account of Hydraulic & Other Machines for Raising Water, Ancient & Modern. LC 72-5048. (Technology & Society Ser.). 598p. 1972. Repr. of 1842 ed. 27.00 (ISBN 0-405-04700-2). Arno.

Fawcett, J. R. Applied Hydraulics & Pneumatics in Industry. (Illus.). 1968. 35.00x (ISBN 0-686-31716-5). Intl Ideas.

Giles, Ronald V. Fluid Mechanics & Hydraulics. (Schaum's Outline Ser). (Orig.). 1962. pap. 6.95 (ISBN 0-07-023234-2, SP). McGraw.

Glover, Robert E. Transient Ground Water Hydraulics. 1978. 18.00 (ISBN 0-918334-24-1). WRP.

Hjorth, Peder, et al, eds. Hydraulic Problems Solved by Stochastic Methods. LC 77-78941. 1977. 28.00 (ISBN 0-918334-22-5). WRP.

Institute for Power System. Applied Hydraulics & Pneumatics in Industry. 260p. 1979. 36.00x (ISBN 0-686-77475-2). State Mutual Bks.

--Hydraulic Standards, Lexicon & Data. 200p. 1979. 35.00x (ISBN 0-85461-005-7). State Mutual Bks.

--Hydraulic Technical Data, Vol. 3. 117p. 1979. 25.00x (ISBN 0-85461-047-2). State Mutual Bks.

--Hydraulic Technical Data, Vol. 4. 120p. 1979. 25.00x (ISBN 0-85461-066-9). State Mutual Bks.

--Principles of Hydraulics. 150p. 1979. 25.00x (ISBN 0-85461-002-2). State Mutual Bks.

Interafrican Committee for Hydraulic Studies. Catalog of the Documentation Center Interafrican Committee for Hydraulic Studies. 1977. lib. bdg. 160.00 (ISBN 0-8161-0091-8). G K Hall.

International Conference on Hydraulics, Pneumatics & Fluidics in Control & Automation. Proceedings. 1977. text ed. 65.00 (ISBN 0-900983-53-1, Dist. by Air Science Co.). BHRA Fluid.

Isman, Warren E. Fire Service Pumps & Hydraulics. LC 76-3943. 1977. pap. 8.40 (ISBN 0-8273-0591-5). Delmar.

King, Horace W., et al. Hydraulics. 5th ed. LC 79-25379. 364p. 1980. Repr. of 1941 ed. 19.50 (ISBN 0-89874-106-8). Krieger.

Lefax Pub. Co. Editors. Hydraulics. (Lefax Data Bks.: No. 612). (Illus.). looseleaf bdg. 3.00 (ISBN 0-685-14146-2). Lefax.

Lomax, W. R. & Saul, A. J. Laboratory Work in Hydraulics. 264p. 1979. pap. text ed. 22.75x (ISBN 0-258-97088-X, Pub. by Granada England). Renouf.

McWhorter, David B. & Sunada, Daniel K. Ground Water Hydrology & Hydraulics. LC 77-74259. 1981. 27.00 (ISBN 0-918334-18-7). WRP.

Manohar, M. & Krishnamachar, P. Hydraulic Machinery & Advanced Hydraulics. 600p. Date not set. text ed. 37.50 (ISBN 0-7069-1194-6, Pub. by Vikas India). Advent NY.

Mariotte, Edme. The Motion of Water & Other Fluids: Being a Treatise of Hydrostaticks. Albritton, Claude C., ed. Desaguliers, J. T., tr. (History of Geology Ser.). (Illus.). 1978. Repr. of 1718 ed. lib. bdg. 20.00x (ISBN 0-405-10449-9). Arno.

Muirwood, A. M. & Fleming, C. A. Coastal Hydraulics. 2nd ed. LC 81-2992. 288p. 1981. 49.95 (ISBN 0-470-27198-1). Halsted Pr.

National Fire Protection Association. Hydraulics for the Fire Service: Hydraulic Field Equations, Vol. VI. Lyons, Paul R., ed. LC 78-50007. (Illus.). 72p. (Orig.). 1980. pap. text ed. 42.50 (ISBN 0-87765-171-X, SL-60). Natl Fire Prot.

--Hydraulics for the Fire Sevice: Operating the Pumper, Vol. V. Lyons, Paul R., ed. LC 78-50007. (Illus.). 88p. 1979. text ed. 42.50 (ISBN 0-87765-157-4, SL-51). Natl Fire Prot.

Neubert, Gunter. Dictionary of Hydraulics & Pneumatics. 226p. 1980. 40.00x (ISBN 0-569-08523-3, Pub. by Collet's). State Mutual Bk.

Nichil, P. Lexique Francais-Anglais et Anglais-Francais des Termes d'usage Courant En Hydraulique et Pneumatique. 42p. (Fr. -Eng., French-English, English-French Lexicon of Commonly Used Terms in Hydraulics and Pneumatics). 1974. pap. 8.95 (ISBN 0-686-56790-0, M-6426). French & Eur.

Pippenger, John & Hicks, Tyler. Industrial Hydraulics. 3rd ed. (Illus.). 1979. text ed. 19.95 (ISBN 0-07-050140-8, G). McGraw.

Polubarinova-Kochina, P. Theory of Ground Water Movement. De Wiest, R., tr. 1962. 45.00 (ISBN 0-691-08048-8). Princeton U Pr.

Purington, Robert C. Fire Fighting Hydraulics. Cleverdon, Ardelle, ed. (Illus.). 416p. (Orig.). 1974. pap. text ed. 15.95 (ISBN 0-07-050957-3, G); instructor's guide 3.00 (ISBN 0-07-050958-1). McGraw.

Purington, Robert G. Hydraulics for the Fire Service: Pumps & Pumpers, Unit 4. Lyons, Paul R., ed. LC 78-50007. (Illus.). 1979. pap. text ed. 42.50 (ISBN 0-87765-148-5). Natl Fire Prot.

--Hydraulics for the Fire Service: Unit I-Characteristics of Water. Lyons, Paul R., ed. LC 78-50007. (Illus.). 1978. pap. text ed. 42.50 (ISBN 0-87765-117-5, SL-27). Natl Fire Prot.

--Hydraulics for the Fire Service: Unit II - Water Flow, Friction Loss, Engine Pressure. Lyons, Paul R., ed. LC 78-50007. (Illus.). 1978. pap. text ed. 42.50 (ISBN 0-685-63021-8, SL-28). Natl Fire Prot.

Purington, Robert G., et al. Hydraulics for the Fire Service Unit III, Multiple Lines, Unequal Layouts. Lyons, Paul R., ed. LC 78-50007. (Illus.). 1979. pap. 42.50 (ISBN 0-87765-132-9, SL-33). Natl Fire Prot.

Rouse, Hunter, ed. Engineering Hydraulics. 1950. 59.95 (ISBN 0-471-74283-X, Pub. by Wiley-Interscience). Wiley.

Sharp, J. J. Hydraulic Modelling: Theory & Practice. 1981. text ed. write for info. (ISBN 0-408-00482-7, Newnes-Butterworth). Butterworth.

Simon, Andrew L. Basic Hydraulics. LC 80-15341. 226p. 1981. text ed. 19.95 (ISBN 0-471-07965-0). Wiley.

--Practical Hydraulics. 2nd ed. LC 79-27270. 403p. 1981. text ed. 19.95 (ISBN 0-471-05381-3); tchrs.' ed. avail. (ISBN 0-471-07783-6). Wiley.

Stewart, Harry L. Hydraulics for off-the Road Equipment. LC 77-93790. 1978. 8.95 (ISBN 0-672-23306-1). Audel.

--Pneumatics & Hydraulics. 3rd ed. LC 75-36658. (Illus.). 1976. 10.95 (ISBN 0-672-23237-5, 23237). Audel.

Stoker, James J. Water Waves. LC 56-8228. (Pure & Applied Mathematics Ser.). (Illus.). 595p. 1957. 46.50 (ISBN 0-470-82863-3, Pub. by Wiley-Interscience). Wiley.

Trade & Techinical Press Editors. Applied Hydraulics & Pneumatics in Industry. 260p. 1968. 32.50x (ISBN 0-85461-077-4, Pub by Trade & Tech England). Renouf.

Trade & Technical Press Editors. Principles of Hydraulics. 150p. 1963. 25.00x (ISBN 0-85461-002-2, Pub by Trade & Tech England). Renouf.

--Some Aspects of Hydraulics in Mechanical Handling & Mobile Equipment. 120p. 1970. 20.00x (ISBN 0-85461-006-5, Pub by Trade & Tech England). Renouf.

Trade & Technical Press Ltd, ed. Principles of Hydraulics. (Illus.). 24.00x (ISBN 0-89563-015-X). Intl Ideas.

Vollmer, Ernst. Encyclopaedia of Hydraulics, Soil & Foundation Engineering. 1967. 73.25 (ISBN 0-444-40615-8). Elsevier.

HYDRAZENE

Malone, H. E. The Determination of Hydrazine-Hydrazide Groups. 1970. 46.00 (ISBN 0-08-015871-4). Pergamon.

HYDRIDES
Andresen, A. F. & Maeland, A., eds. Hydrides for Energy Storage: Proceedings of an International Symposium Held in Norway, Aug. 1977. 1978. text ed. 90.00 (ISBN 0-08-022715-5). Pergamon.
Bau, Robert, ed. Transition Metal Hydrides. LC 78-7327. (Advances in Chemistry Ser.: No. 167). 1978. 42.00 (ISBN 0-8412-0390-3). Am Chemical.
Gaylord, Norman G. Reduction with Complex Metal Hydrides. (Illus.). 1062p. 1956. text ed. 34.00 (ISBN 0-470-29436-1, Pub. by Wiley). Krieger.
Hajos, A. Complex Hydrides & Related Reducing Agents in Organic Synthesis. LC 78-14524. (Studies in Organic Chemistry: Vol. 1). 1979. 76.00 (ISBN 0-444-99791-1). Elsevier.
Malone, H. E. The Determination of Hydrazine-Hydrazide Groups. 1970. 46.00 (ISBN 0-08-015871-4). Pergamon.
Shaw, B. L. Inorganic Hydrides. 1967. pap. 9.75 (ISBN 0-08-012109-8). Pergamon.
Wiberg, E. & Amberger, E. Hydrides: The Elements of Main Groups, 1-4. 1971. 141.50 (ISBN 0-444-40807-X). Elsevier.

HYDROAIRPLANES
see Seaplanes

HYDROBIIDAE
Thompson, Fred G. Aquatic Snails of the Family Hydrobiidae of Peninsular Florida. LC 68-9707. 1968. 9.00 (ISBN 0-8130-0273-7). U Presses Fla.

HYDROBIOLOGY
see Fresh-Water Biology; Marine Biology

HYDROBORATION
Lane, Clinton F. & Kabalka, George W. A New Hydroboration Reagent. 1976. pap. text ed. 12.75 (ISBN 0-08-021330-8). Pergamon.

HYDROBOTANY
see Aquatic Plants

HYDROCARBON RESEARCH
Nicholson, William J. & Moore, John A., eds. Health Effects of Halogenated Aromatic Hydrocarbons. LC 79-12253. (Annals of the New York Academy of Sciences: Vol. 320). 730p. 1979. 115.00x (ISBN 0-89766-008-0). NY Acad Sci.
Pucknat, A. W., ed. Health Impacts of Polynuclear Aromatic Hydrocarbons. LC 80-28039. (Environmental Health Review Ser.: No. 5). (Illus.). 271p. 1981. 39.00 (ISBN 0-8155-0840-9). Noyes.

HYDROCARBONS
see also Alkylation; Cracking Process; Hydrocarbon Research; Mineral Oils; Petroleum Products
Afghan, B. K. & Mackay, D., eds. Hydrocarbons & Halogenated Hydrocarbons in the Aquatic Environment. LC 79-26462. (Environmental Science Research Ser.: Vol. 16). 602p. 1980. 59.50 (ISBN 0-306-40329-3, Plenum Pr). Plenum Pub.
Andrew, William G. & Williams, H. B. Applied Instrumentation in the Process Industries: Engineering Data & Resource Material, Vol. 3. 2nd ed. (Illus.). 520p. 1981. 39.95x (ISBN 0-87201-384-7). Gulf Pub.
Applied Science Publishers Ltd London, ed. Metabolism of Hydrocarbons, Oils, Fuels & Lubricants. (Illus.). 1976. 50.40x (ISBN 0-85334-703-4). Intl Ideas.
Baker, Bernard S., ed. Hydrocarbon Fuel Cell Technology: A Symposium. (Illus.). 1966. 74.50 (ISBN 0-12-074250-0). Acad Pr.
Bingham, R. C. & Von Schleyer, P. R. Chemistry of Adamantanes: Recent Developments in the Chemistry of Adamantane & Related Polycyclic Hydrocarbons. (Topics in Current Chemistry: Vol. 18). (Illus.). 1971. pap. 32.50 (ISBN 0-387-05387-5). Springer-Verlag.
Bjorseth, Alf & Dennis, Anthony J., eds. Polynuclear Aromatic Hydrocarbons: Chemistry & Biological Effects. (Illus.). 1128p. 1980. 49.95 (ISBN 0-935470-05-0). Battelle.
Compressor Handbook for the Hydrocarbon Processing Industries. (Illus.). 264p. 1979. pap. 15.95x (ISBN 0-87201-131-3). Gulf Pub.
Cooke, Marcus & Dennis, Anthony J., eds. Analytical Chemistry & Biological Fate: Polynuclear Aromatic Hydrocarbons. (Internaional Symposium on Polynuclear Aromatic Hydrocarbons). 800p. 1981. 59.95 (ISBN 0-935470-09-3). Battelle.
Edmister, Wayne C. Applied Hydrocarbon Thermodynamics, Vol. 2. (Illus.). 298p. 1974. 29.95x (ISBN 0-87201-857-1). Gulf Pub.
Emanuel, N. M., et al. Liquid-Phase Oxidation of Hydrocarbons. LC 66-12888. 350p. 1967. 39.50 (ISBN 0-306-30292-6, Plenum Pr). Plenum Pub.
Environmental Studies Board. Polychlorinated Biphenyls. 1979. pap. 7.25 (ISBN 0-309-02885-X). Natl Acad Pr.
Ferris, Seymour W. Handbook of Hydrocarbons. 1955. 40.50 (ISBN 0-12-254050-6). Acad Pr.
Freudenthal, Ralph I. & Jones, Peter, eds. Polynuclear Aromatic Hydrocarbons: Chemistry, Metabolism, & Carcinogenesis. LC 75-43194. 465p. 1976. 48.00 (ISBN 0-89004-103-2). Raven.
Gajewski, Joseph J. Hydrocarbon Thermal Isomerizations. LC 80-70594. 1981. price not set (ISBN 0-12-273350-9). Acad Pr.
Gallant, Robert W. Physical Properties of Hydrocarbons, Vol. 1. LC 68-9302. (Illus.). 234p. 1968. 23.95x (ISBN 0-87201-688-9). Gulf Pub.
Gallant, Robert W. & Railey, Jay M. Physical Properties of Hydrocarbons, Vol. 2. 2nd ed. 1981. 21.95 (ISBN 0-87201-690-0). Gulf Pub.
Garrett, William & Smagin, V. M. Determination of the Atmospheric Contribution of Petroleum Hydrocarbons to the Oceans. (Special Environmental Report Ser: No. 6). (Illus.). 27p. 1977. pap. 16.00 (ISBN 92-63-10440-9, WMO). Unipub.
Gaumann, T. & Hoigne, J., eds. Aspects of Hydrocarbon Radiolysis. LC 68-19261. 1968. 44.00 (ISBN 0-12-277650-X). Acad Pr.
Germain, J. E. Catalytic Conversion of Hydrocarbons. 1969. 51.00 (ISBN 0-12-280850-9). Acad Pr.
Green, M. L. Aspects of Hydrocarbon Activation by Transition Metals. cancelled (ISBN 0-08-020468-6). Pergamon.
Harrison. Hydrocarbons in Biotechnology. 1980. 40.50 (ISBN 0-85501-325-7). Heyden.
Hatch, Lewis F. & Matar, Sami. From Hydrocarbons to Petrochemicals. (Illus.). 230p. 1981. 24.95x (ISBN 0-87201-374-X). Gulf Pub.
Hucknall, D. J. Selective Oxidation of Hydrocarbons. 1974. 36.00 (ISBN 0-12-358950-9). Acad Pr.
Jacobs, Peter A. Carboniogenic Activity of Zeolites. LC 77-1788. 1977. 39.00 (ISBN 0-444-41556-4). Elsevier.
Jagannath, S. Calculator Programs for the Hydrocarbon Processing Industries, Vol. 1. (Illus.). 230p. 1980. 19.95 (ISBN 0-87201-091-0). Gulf Pub.
--Calculator Programs for the Hydrocarbon Processing Industries, Vol. 2. 200p. 1981. 19.95 (ISBN 0-87201-092-9). Gulf Pub.
Jones, Peter W. & Leber, Philip, eds. Polynuclear Aromatic Hydrocarbons: Third International Symposium on Chemistry & Biology, Carcinogenesis & Methodology. LC 79-642622. (Illus.). 1979. 49.95 (ISBN 0-250-40317-X). Ann Arbor Science.
Kugler, Edwin L. & Steffgen, F. W., eds. Hydrocarbon Synthesis from Carbon Monoxide & Hydrogen. LC 79-18286. (Advances in Chemistry Ser.: No. 178). 1979. 26.50 (ISBN 0-8412-0453-5). Am Chemical.
McKervey, A. The Chemistry of Diamondoid Hydrocarbons. cancelled (ISBN 0-08-020473-2). Pergamon.
Manual on Hydrocarbon Analysis. 1977. pap. 26.00 (ISBN 0-686-52072-6, 03-332030-12). ASTM.
Marta, F. & Kallo, D., eds. Mechanisms of Hydrocarbon Reactions: Proceedings. 1975. 85.50 (ISBN 0-444-99862-4). Elsevier.
Maxwell, J. B. Data Book on Hydrocarbons: Application to Process Engineering. LC 74-30163. 268p. 1975. Repr. of 1950 ed. text ed. 15.00 (ISBN 0-88275-257-X). Krieger.
Norwegian Petroleum Society. Large Scale Flow Measurement of Hydrocarbon Fluids. 173p. 1980. 75.00x (ISBN 82-7270-003-4, Pub. by Norwegian Info Norway). State Mutual Bk.
Oblad, Alex, et al, eds. Thermal Hydrocarbon Chemistry. LC 79-22817. (Advances in Chemistry Ser.: No. 183). 1979. 39.50 (ISBN 0-8412-0468-3). Am Chemical.
Paruit, Bernard. Pictorial Translator for the Process Industries. (Illus.). 400p. (Eng., Fr., Span.). 1981. 36.95x (ISBN 0-87201-691-9). Gulf Pub.
Pechuro, N. S., ed. Organic Reactions in Electrical Discharges. LC 68-28093. (Illus.). 135p. 1968. 25.00 (ISBN 0-306-10809-7, Consultants). Plenum Pub.
Photoelectric Spectrometry Group, England & Institut fuer Spektrochemie und Angewandte Spektroskopie, Germany. U V Atlas of Organic Compounds, 5 vols. 1966-71. Set. 275.00 (ISBN 0-306-68300-8); 65.00 ea. Vol. 1 (ISBN 0-306-68301-6). Vol. 2 (ISBN 0-306-68302-4). Vol. 3 (ISBN 0-306-68303-2). Vol. 4 (ISBN 0-306-68304-0). Vol. 5 (ISBN 0-306-68305-9). IFI Plenum.
Physical Constants of Hydrocarbons C Subscript 1 to C Subscript 10. 1971. pap. 4.00 (ISBN 0-8031-0009-4, 05-004010-12). ASTM.
Pines, Herman. The Chemistry of Catalytic Hydrocarbon Conversions. 1981. 35.00 (ISBN 0-12-557160-7). Acad Pr.
Polycyclic Aromatic Hydrocarbons: Colloquium Hanover 1979. 422p. 1980. pap. 123.00x (ISBN 3-18-090358-9, Pub. by VDI Verlag Germany). Renouf.
Preston, S. T., ed. Analysis of Hydrocarbons by Chromatographic Methods. new ed. 1976. 25.00 (ISBN 0-912474-10-6). Preston Pubns.
Preston, S. T., Jr. A Guide to the Analysis of Hydro-Carbons by Gas Chromatography. 2nd ed. 1976. spiral bdg 30.00 (ISBN 0-913106-02-X). PolyScience.
Pucknat, A. W., ed. Health Impacts of Polynuclear Aromatic Hydrocarbons. LC 80-28039. (Environmental Health Review Ser.: No. 5). (Illus.). 271p. 1981. 39.00 (ISBN 0-8155-0840-9). Noyes.
Rider, Don K. Energy: Hydrocarbon Fuels & Chemical Resources. LC 81-196. 493p. 1981. 34.95 (ISBN 0-471-05915-3, Pub. by Wiley-Interscience). Wiley.
Thomas, Gordon W. Principles of Hydrocarbon Reservoir Simulation. 2nd ed. LC 81-82011. (Illus.). 224p. 1981. text ed. 42.00 (ISBN 0-934634-11-4). Intl Human Res.
Tsang, Wing-Sum & Griffin, Gary W. Metabolic Activation of Polynuclear Aromatic Hydrocarbons. (Illus.). 1979. 37.00 (ISBN 0-08-023835-1). Pergamon.
Wall, James D., ed. Environmental Management Handbook for Hydrocarbon Processing Industries. (Illus.). 224p. (Orig.). 1980. pap. 16.95 (ISBN 0-87201-265-4). Gulf Pub.
Watkinson, R. J., ed. Developments in Biodegradation of Hydrocarbons, Vol. 1. (Illus.). 1978. text ed. 45.50x (ISBN 0-85334-751-4, Pub. by Applied Science). Burgess-Intl Ideas.
Wolfe, Douglas A., ed. Fate & Effects of Petroleum Hydrocarbons in Marine Organisms & Ecosystems. LC 77-76464. 1977. text ed. 67.00 (ISBN 0-08-021613-7). Pergamon.

HYDROCARBONS–SPECTRA
Chamberlain, Nugent F. The Practice of NMR Spectroscopy: With Spectra-Structure Correlations for Hydrogen-One. LC 74-11479. (Illus.). 430p. 1974. 39.50 (ISBN 0-306-30766-9, Plenum Pr). Plenum Pub.
Sterin, K. E., et al. Raman Spectra of Hydrocarbons: A Data Handbook. LC 79-42704. 360p. 1980. 80.00 (ISBN 0-08-023596-4). Pergamon.

HYDROCEPHALUS
Grote, W., et al, eds. Surgery of Cervical Myelopathy Infantile Hydrocephalus: Long Term Results. (Advances in Neurosurgery Ser.: Vol. 8). (Illus.). 456p. 1980. pap. 54.30 (ISBN 0-387-09949-2). Springer-Verlag.
Harbert, John C., ed. Cisternography & Hydrocephalus: A Symposium. (Illus.). 670p. 1972. 58.75 (ISBN 0-398-02308-5). C C Thomas.
Milhorat, Thomas H. Hydrocephalus & the Cerebrospinal Fluid. 238p. 1972. 23.50 (ISBN 0-683-05989-0). Krieger.
Patterson, Katheryn. No Time for Tears. 1965. 3.95 (ISBN 0-87485-016-9). Johnson Chi.
Wuellenweber, R., et al, eds. Treatment of Hydrocephalus: Computer Tomography. (Advances in Neurosurgery: Vol. 6). (Illus.). 1978. pap. 40.70 (ISBN 0-387-09031-2). Springer-Verlag.

HYDROCHLORIC ACID
Division of Medical Sciences, Assembly of Life Sciences, National Research Council. Chlorine & Hydrogen Chloride. LC 76-39940. (Medical & Biological Effects of Environmental Pollutants Ser.). 1976. pap. 10.00 (ISBN 0-309-02519-2). Natl Acad Pr.

HYDROCYCLONES
see Separators (Machines)

HYDRODYNAMIC WEATHER FORECASTING
see also Numerical Weather Forecasting

HYDRODYNAMICS
see also Cavitation; Channels (Hydraulic Engineering); Hydraulics; Hydrostatics; Magnetohydrodynamics; Mixing; Rotating Masses of Fluid; Turbulence; Viscosity; Water Hammer; Waves
Bisshopp, F., et al, eds. Problems of Hydrodynamics & Continuum Mechanics. (Illus.). 1969. text ed. 42.50 (ISBN 0-686-24253-X). Soc Indus-Appl Math.
Boon, Jean P. & Yip, Sidney. Molecular Hydrodynamics. (Illus.). 440p. 1980. text ed. 49.95 (ISBN 0-07-006560-8). McGraw.
Bretschneider, Charles L., ed. Topics in Ocean Engineering. Incl. Vol. 1. (Illus.). 428p. 1969. (ISBN 0-87201-598-X); Vol. 2. (Illus.). 229p. 1970 (ISBN 0-87201-599-8). 26.50x ea. Gulf Pub.
Bruun, P. & Mehta, A. J. Stability of Tidal Inlets. (Developments in Geotechnical Engineering Ser.: Vol. 23). 1978. 63.50 (ISBN 0-444-41728-1). Elsevier.
Chandrasekhar, S. Hydrodynamic & Hydromagnetic Stability. (Illus.). 704p. pap. 10.95 (ISBN 0-486-64071-X). Dover.
Chirgwin, B. & Plumpton, C. A. Elementary Classical Hydrodynamics. 1968. 19.50 (ISBN 0-08-012406-2); pap. 10.75 (ISBN 0-08-012405-4). Pergamon.
Drazin, P. & Reid, W. Hydrodynamic Stability. LC 80-40273. (Cambridge Monographs on Mechanics & Applied Mathematics). (Illus.). 600p. 1981. 77.00 (ISBN 0-521-22798-4). Cambridge U Pr.
Fisher, John S. & Dolan, Robert, eds. Beach Processes & Coastal Hydrodynamics. (Benchmark Papers in Geology Ser.: Vol. 39). 1977. 43.00 (ISBN 0-12-786471-7). Acad Pr.
Graf, W. H. & Mortimer, C. H., eds. Hydrodynamics of Lakes: Proceeding of the Symposium, Switzerland, Oct. 1978. LC 79-17492. (Developments in Water Science Ser.: Vol. 11). 360p. 1979. 61.00 (ISBN 0-444-41827-X). Elsevier.
Happel, J. & Brenner, H., eds. Low Reynolds Number Hydrodynamics. (Mechanics of Fluid Transport Ser.). 556p. 1977. Repr. of 1975 ed. 45.00x (ISBN 90-01-37115-9). Sijthoff & Noordhoff.
Ippen, A. T. Estuary & Coastline Hydrodynamics. (Engineering Societies Monographs). 1966. text ed. 38.00 (ISBN 0-07-032015-2, C). McGraw.
Kamenkovich, J. M. Fundamentals of Ocean Dynamics. (Elsevier Oceanography Ser.: 16). 1977. 63.50 (ISBN 0-444-41546-7). Elsevier.
Ladyzhenskaya, O. A. The Mathematical Theory of Viscous Incompressible Flow. 2nd ed. (Mathematics & Its Applications Ser.). (Illus.). 1969. 51.25x (ISBN 0-677-20760-3). Gordon.
Lamb, Horace. Hydrodynamics. 6th ed. (Illus.). 1932. pap. text ed. 10.50 (ISBN 0-486-60256-7). Dover.
Le Mehante, B. An Introduction to Hydrodynamics & Water Waves. LC 75-18631. (Illus.). 512p. 1975. text ed. 31.40 (ISBN 0-387-07232-2). Springer-Verlag.
Levich, V. Physiochemical Hydrodynamics. 1962. ref. ed. 39.95 (ISBN 0-13-674440-0). P-H.
McDowell, D. M. & O'Connor, B. A. Hydraulic Behaviour of Estuaries. 1977. 34.95x (ISBN 0-470-98922-X). Halsted Pr.
March, N. H. & Tosi, M. P. Atomic Dynamics in Liquids. LC 76-16040. 330p. 1977. 65.95 (ISBN 0-470-15145-5). Halsted Pr.
Moiseyev, N. N. & Rumyantsev, V. V. Dynamic Stability of Bodies Containing Fluid. LC 68-22688. (Applied Physics & Engineering Ser.: Vol. 6). (Illus.). 1968. 43.50 (ISBN 0-387-04052-8). Springer-Verlag.
Monin, A. S., et al. Variability of the Oceans. LC 77-826. 1977. 39.50 (ISBN 0-471-61328-2, Pub. by Wiley-Interscience). Wiley.
Nihoul, J. C., ed. Marine Forecasting. Predictability & Modelling in Ocean Hydrodynamics. (Elsevier Oceanography Ser.: Vol. 25). 1979. 63.50 (ISBN 0-444-41797-4). Elsevier.
Pickford, J. Analysis of Water Surge. 1969. 45.25x (ISBN 0-677-61670-8). Gordon.
Pomraning, G. C. Radiation Hydrodynamics. 304p. 1973. text ed. 50.00 (ISBN 0-08-016893-0). Pergamon.
Pomraning, G. C., et al. Theoretical & Computational Radiation Hydrodynamics: Vol. 1, Radiation-Hydrodynamics Theoretical Considerations. LC 70-135085. 228p. 1969. 29.50 (ISBN 0-686-01966-0). Mgmt Info Serv.
Shaw, T. L., ed. Mechanics of Wave-Induced Forces on Cylinders. new ed. (Illus.). 1979. cancelled (ISBN 0-8224-8433-1). Pitman Learning.
Simeons, Charles. Hydro-Power: The Use of Water As an Alternative Source. (Illus.). 560p. 1980. 89.00 (ISBN 0-08-023269-8). Pergamon.
Skolbel'tsyn, D. V., ed. Quantum Field Theory & Hydrodynamics. LC 66-12629. (P. N. Lebedev Physics Institute Ser.: Vol. 29). 271p. 1967. 32.50 (ISBN 0-306-10768-6, Consultants). Plenum Pub.
Stern, Melvin E. Ocean Circulation Physics. (International Geophysics Ser.). 1975. 36.50 (ISBN 0-12-666750-0). Acad Pr.
Stoker, James J. Water Waves. LC 56-8228. (Pure & Applied Mathematics Ser.). (Illus.). 595p. 1957. 46.50 (ISBN 0-470-82863-3, Pub. by Wiley-Interscience). Wiley.
Stokes, George G. Mathematical & Physical Papers, 5 Vols. 2nd ed. Repr. of 1905 ed. Set. 115.50 (ISBN 0-384-58370-9). Johnson Repr.
Symposium on Naval Hydrodynamics, 12th, Naval Studies Board. Naval Hydrodynamics: Proceedings. 1979. 18.75 (ISBN 0-309-02896-5). Natl Acad Pr.
Thackston, Edward L. & Eckenfielder, W. W., eds. Process Design in Water Quality Engineering: New Concepts & Development. (Illus.). 15.00 (ISBN 0-8363-0079-3). Jenkins.

HYDRO-ELECTRIC PLANTS
see Water-Power Electric Plants

HYDROFOIL BOATS
McLeavy, Roy & Wood, John W. Hovercraft & Hydrofoils. LC 76-27703. (Arco Color Books). (Illus.). 1977. 7.95 (ISBN 0-668-04105-6, 4105); pap. 5.95 (ISBN 0-668-04254-0, 4254). Arco.

HYDROFOILS (VESSELS)
see Hydrofoil Boats

HYDROGEN
see also Liquid Hydrogen
Alefeld, G. & Voelkl, J., eds. Hydrogen in Metals I: Basic Properties. (Topics in Applied Physics Ser.: Vol. 28). (Illus.). 1978. 56.70 (ISBN 0-387-08705-2). Springer-Verlag.
--Hydrogens in Metals II: Application - Oriented Properties. LC 78-4487. (Topics in Applied Physics: Vol. 29). (Illus.). 1978. 45.80 (ISBN 0-387-08883-0). Springer-Verlag.
Andersen, Hans H. & Ziegler, James F., eds. Hydrogen Stopping Powers & Ranges in All Elements. LC 77-3068. 1977. text ed. 40.00 (ISBN 0-08-021605-6). Pergamon.
Bahn, Gilbert S., ed. Reaction Rate Compilation for the H-O-N System. LC 68-20396. 1968. Repr. of 1967 ed. 57.75x (ISBN 0-677-12750-2). Gordon.
BCC Staff. What About Hydrogen As a Fuel? E-002. rev. ed. 1978. 600.00 (ISBN 0-89336-102-X). BCC.
Dickson, Edward M., et al. The Hydrogen Energy Economy: A Realistic Appraisal of Prospects & Impacts. LC 76-56807. (Special Studies). 1977. text ed. 31.95 (ISBN 0-275-24290-0). Praeger.
Gaseous Hydrogen Systems at Consumer Sites. (Fifty Ser). 1973. pap. 2.00 (ISBN 0-685-58093-8, 50A). Natl Fire Prot.
Hoffman, Peter. The Forever Fuel: The Story of Hydrogen. 250p. 1981. 16.00x (ISBN 0-89158-581-8). Westview.
Hydrogen Fuels: A Bibliography, Supplement 1. 1981. write for info. DOE.
Hydrogen Fuels: A Bibliograpy, Nineteen Thirty to January Nineteen Seventy-Six. 1976. write for info. DOE.
International Association for Hydrogen Energy. Directory of Hydrogen Energy Products & Services Nineteen Eighty to Nineteen Eighty-One. 32p. 1981. pap. 10.00 (ISBN 0-08-027326-2). Pergamon.
International Seminar, Brussels, Feb. 12-14, 1980. Hydrogen As an Energy Vector: Proceedings. Strub, A. S. & Imarisio, G., eds. 704p. 1980. lib. bdg. 50.00 (ISBN 90-277-1124-0, Pub. by Reidel Holland). Kluwer Boston.
Kermode, R. I., et al. Hydrogen: Its Technology & Implications: Hydrogen Production Technology, Vol. I. Cox, K. E. & Williamson, K. D., eds. 200p. 1977. 59.95 (ISBN 0-8493-5121-9). CRC Pr.
McAuliffe, Charles A. Hydrogen & Energy. 112p. 1980. 10.95 (ISBN 0-87201-372-3). Gulf Pub.
Ohta, T., ed. Solar-Hydrogen Energy System: An Authoritative Review of Water-Splitting Systems by Solar Beam & Solar Heat; Hydrogen Production, Storage & Utilisation. LC 79-40694. (Illus.). 1979. 48.00 (ISBN 0-08-022713-9). Pergamon.
Resonancia Magnetica Nuclear De Hidrogeno. (Serie De Quimica: No. 9). (Span.). 1973. pap. 1.25 (ISBN 0-8270-6365-2). OAS.
Santangelo, J. G. & Smith, W. Novis, eds. Hydrogen: Production & Marketing. LC 80-386. (ACS Symposium Ser.: No. 116). 1980. 36.50 (ISBN 0-8412-0522-1). Am Chemical.
Veziroglu, Nejat, ed. Hydrogen Energy, Pts. A & B. LC 74-34483. 1369p. 1975. Set. 95.00 (ISBN 0-306-34301-0, Plenum Pr). Plenum Pub.
Veziroglu, T. Nejat, ed. Proceedings of the Clean Energy Research Institute, 1st, Miami Beach, 1976. 1977. pap. text ed. 225.00 (ISBN 0-08-021561-0). Pergamon.
Wilhelm, E. & Young, C. L. Hydrogen, Deuterium, Fluorine & Chlorine: Gas Solubilities. (Solubility Data Ser.). Date not set. 100.01 (ISBN 0-08-023927-7). Pergamon.
Williams, L. O. Hydrogen Power: An Introduction to Hydrogen Energy & Its Applications. LC 80-40434. (Illus.). 200p. 1980. 27.00 (ISBN 0-08-024783-0); pap. 11.00 (ISBN 0-08-025422-5). Pergamon.
World Hydrogen Energy Conference, 2nd, Zurich, Aug. 1978. Hydrogen Energy System: Proceedings, 4 vols. Veziroglu, T. N. & Seifritz, W., eds. LC 78-40507. 1979. Set. text ed. 410.00 (ISBN 0-08-023224-8). Pergamon.
World Hydrogen Energy Conference, 3rd, Tokyo, Japan 23-26 June 1980, et al. Hydrogen Energy Progress: Proceedings, 4 vols. Veziroglu, T. N., et al, eds. LC 80-40559. (Advances in Hydrogen Energy: 2). (Illus.). 2500p. 1981. 385.00 set (ISBN 0-08-024729-6). Pergamon.
Young, C. L. Hydrogen & Deuterium, 2 vols. (IUPAC Solubility Data Series: Vol. 5 & 6). 670p. 1981. Vol. 1. 200.00 (ISBN 0-08-023927-7); Vol. 2. 260.00 (ISBN 0-08-023964-1). Pergamon.

HYDROGEN-ISOTOPES
see also Deuterium
Rae, Howard K., ed. Separation of Hydrogen Isotopes. LC 78-760. (ACS Symposium Ser.: No. 68). 1978. 19.00 (ISBN 0-8412-0420-9). Am Chemical.
Shatenshtein, A. I. Isotopic Exchange & the Replacement of Hydrogen in Organic Compounds. LC 62-12859. 308p. 1962. 35.00 (ISBN 0-306-10547-0, Consultants). Plenum Pub.

HYDROGEN BOMB
see also Atomic Bomb; Radioactive Fallout
De Volpi, A., et al. Born Secret: The H-Bomb, the "Progressive" Case & National Security. (Illus.). 320p. 1981. 17.50 (ISBN 0-08-025995-2). Pergamon.
Shepley, James R. & Blair, Clay. Hydrogen Bomb: The Men, the Menace, the Mechanism. LC 70-136085. 1971. Repr. of 1954 ed. lib. bdg. 15.00 (ISBN 0-8371-5235-6, SHHY). Greenwood.
--Hydrogen Bomb: The Men, the Menace, the Mechanism. LC 70-136085. 1971. Repr. of 1954 ed. lib. bdg. 15.00 (ISBN 0-8371-5235-6, SHHY). Greenwood.

HYDROGEN BONDING
Green, R. D. Hydrogen Bonding by C-H Groups. LC 74-11310. 207p. 1974. 43.95 (ISBN 0-470-32478-3). Halsted Pr.
Joesten, Melvin D. & Schaad, L. Hydrogen Bonding. 632p. 1974. 65.00 (ISBN 0-8247-6211-8). Dekker.
Schuster, Peter, et al. The Hydrogen Bond: Recent Developments in Theory & Experiments, 3 vols. new ed. LC 76-373671. (Illus.). 1976. 219.50 (ISBN 0-444-10805-X, North-Holland). Elsevier.

HYDROGEN-ION CONCENTRATION
see also Ionization
Bates, Roger G. Determination of pH: Theory & Practice. 2nd ed. LC 72-8779. 510p. 1973. 38.50 (ISBN 0-471-05647-2, Pub. by Wiley-Interscience). Wiley.
Behrendt, Hans & Green, Marvin. Patterns of Skin PH from Birth Through Adolesence: With a Synopsis on Skin Growth. (Illus.). 116p. 1971. 14.75 (ISBN 0-398-00125-1). C C Thomas.
Kasbekar, Dinkar K., et al, eds. Gastric Hydrogen Ion Secretion. (Nutrition & Clinical Nutrition Ser.: Vol. 3). 1976. 49.75 (ISBN 0-8247-6432-3). Dekker.
Perrin, D. D. & Dempsey, B. Buffers for pH & Metal Ion Control. LC 74-2779. 176p. 1974. text ed. 15.95x (ISBN 0-412-11700-2, Pub. by Chapman & Hall England); pap. 12.95x (ISBN 0-412-21890-9). Methuen Inc.
Ricci, John E. Hydrogen Ion Concentration. 1952. 31.00 (ISBN 0-691-07981-1). Princeton U Pr.

HYDROGEN NUCLEUS
see Protons

HYDROGEN PEROXIDE
Ardon, Michael. Oxygen: Elementary Forms & Hydrogen Peroxide. 1965. 12.50 (ISBN 0-8053-0270-0, Adv Bk Prog). Benjamin-Cummings.

HYDROGENATION
Augustine, R. L. Catalytic Hydrogenation. (Techniques & Applications in Organic Synthesis Ser: Vol. 1). 1965. 26.50 (ISBN 0-8247-1020-7). Dekker.
Freifelder, Morris. Catalytic Hydrogenation in Organic Synthesis: Procedures & Commentary. LC 78-9458. 1978. 25.00 (ISBN 0-471-02945-9, Pub. by Wiley-Interscience). Wiley.
James, Brian R. Homogeneous Hydrogenation. LC 72-11804. 512p. 1973. 56.00 (ISBN 0-471-43915-0, Pub. by Wiley-Interscience). Wiley.
McQuillin, F. J., ed. Homogeneous Hydrogenation in Organic Chemistry. LC 75-37874. (Homogeneous Catalysis in Organic & Inorganic Chemistry: No. 1). vi, 146p. 1976. lib. bdg. 26.00 (ISBN 90-277-0646-8, Pub. by Reidel Holland). Kluwer Boston.
Peterson, R. J. Hydrogenation Catalysts. LC 77-71929. (Chemical Technology Review Ser.: No. 94). (Illus.). 1977. 36.00 (ISBN 0-8155-0666-X). Noyes.
Rylander, Paul N. Catalytic Hydrogenation Over Platinum Metals. 1967. 63.50 (ISBN 0-12-605350-2). Acad Pr.
Ward, John W. & Qader, Shaik A., eds. Hydrocracking & Hydrotreating. LC 75-33727. (ACS Symposium Ser.: No. 20). 1975. 19.00 (ISBN 0-8412-0303-2). Am Chemical.
Whitehurst, D. D., ed. Coal Liquefaction Fundamentals. LC 80-20585. (ACS Symposium Ser.: No. 139). 1980. 38.00 (ISBN 0-8412-0587-6). Am Chemical.
Whitehurst, D. D., et al. Coal Liquefaction: The Chemistry & Technology of Thermal Process. 1980. 19.50 (ISBN 0-12-747080-8). Acad Pr.

HYDROGEOLOGY
Cermak, V. & Rybach, L., eds. Terrestrial Heat Flow in Europe. (Illus.). 1979. 51.50 (ISBN 0-387-09440-7). Springer-Verlag.
De Vries, Johannes J. Groundwater Flow Systems & Stream Nets in the Netherlands: A Groundwater-Hydrological Approach to the Functional Relationship Between the Drainage System & the Geological & Climatical Conditions in a Quaternary Accumulation Area. LC 74-79527. (Amsterdam Hydrology Ser: No. 1). 226p. (Orig.). 1974. pap. text ed. 29.00x (ISBN 90-6203-248-6). Humanities.
Fetter, Charles W., Jr. Applied Hydrogeology. (Physics & Physical Science Ser.). 448p. 1980. text ed. 31.50 (ISBN 0-675-08126-2). Merrill.
Gheorghe, Alexandru. Processing & Synthesis of Hydrogeological Data. (Illus.). 1978. 43.50 (ISBN 0-85626-107-6, Pub. by Abacus Pr). Intl Schol Bk Serv.
Hydrogeological Investigations of the Peel Region & Its Environs. (Agricultural Research Reports Ser.: 684). 1967. pap. 9.75 (ISBN 0-686-51208-1, PUDOC). Unipub.
Lamarck, Jean B. Hydrogeology. Carozzi, Albert V., tr. from Fr. LC 64-12253. (Illus.). 1964. 10.00 (ISBN 0-252-72468-2). U of Ill Pr.
Legends for Geohydrochemical Maps. (Technical Papers in Hydrology Ser.). (Illus.). 61p. 1976. pap. 6.00 (ISBN 92-3-001207-6, U351, UNESCO). Unipub.
Milanovic, Petar J. Karst Hydrogeology. 1981. 29.00 (ISBN 0-918334-36-5). WRP.
Pfannkuch, Hans-Olaf. Elsevier's Dictionary of Hydrogeology. 1969. 36.75 (ISBN 0-444-40717-0). Elsevier.
Tolson, J. S. & Doyle, F. L., eds. Karst Hydrogeology. (Illus., Eng. & Fr.). 1977. 15.00 (ISBN 0-933958-03-X). UAH Pr.
Van der Leeden, Frits, ed. Ground Water: A Selected Bibliography. 2nd ed. LC 74-82279. 1974. 18.00 (ISBN 0-912394-11-0). Water Info.

HYDROGRAPHIC CHARTS
see Nautical Charts

HYDROGRAPHIC SURVEYING
see also Hydrography; Navigation
Ingham, A. E. Sea Surveying. LC 74-3066. 1975. 103.25 (ISBN 0-471-42729-2, Pub. by Wiley-Interscience). Wiley.
Milne, P. H. Underwater Surveying. (Illus.). 400p. 1980. 49.95x (ISBN 0-87201-884-9). Gulf Pub.
Morris, Byron F. & Schroeder, Elizabeth. Hydrographic Observations in the Sargasso Sea off Bermuda: 1967-1973. (Bermuda Biological Station Special Pubn.: No. 12). 105p. 1973. pap. 3.00 (ISBN 0-917642-12-0). Bermuda Bio.
Norwegian Petroleum Society. Offshore Seismic Data Acquisition & Quality Control. 287p. 1980. 100.00x (ISBN 82-7270-001-8, Pub. by Norwegian Info Norway). State Mutual Bk.

HYDROGRAPHY
see also Coastwise Navigation; Harbors; Hydrographic Surveying; Hydrology; Inland Navigation; Lakes; Navigation; Ocean Currents; Rivers; Stream Measurements; Submarine Topography; Tides
De Cardonda, Nicolas. Geographic & Hydrographic Descriptions, Sixteen Thirty-Two. Mathes, Michael, ed. & tr. (Baja California Travels Ser.: No. 35). 1974. 18.00 (ISBN 0-87093-235-7). Dawsons.
Galtsoff, P. S. Pearl & Hermes Reef, Hawaii, Hydrographical & Biographical Observations. Repr. of 1933 ed. pap. 6.00 (ISBN 0-527-02213-6). Kraus Repr.
Hubbs, Carl L., et al. Memoir VIII: Hydrographic History & Relict Fishes of the North-Central Great Basin. Kessel, Edward L., ed. (Memoirs of the California Academy of Sciences Ser.). (Illus.). 259p. (Orig.). 1974. pap. 15.00 (ISBN 0-940228-11-4). Calif Acad Sci.
Morel-Seytoux, Hubert J., et al, eds. Modeling Hydrologic Processes. LC 78-68497. 1979. 28.00 (ISBN 0-918334-27-6). WRP.
--Surface & Subsurface Hydrology. LC 78-68497. 1979. 28.00 (ISBN 0-918334-28-4). WRP.

HYDROIDEA
see Hydrozoa

HYDROLOGIC CYCLE
see also Energy Budget (Geophysics)
Bartlett, Margaret F. Where Does All the Rain Go? (Science Is What & Why Ser.). (Illus.). 48p. (gr. k-3). 1974. PLB 5.99 (ISBN 0-698-30509-4). Coward.
Green, Ivah. Splash & Trickle. (Illus.). (gr. 2-3). 1978. pap. 1.25 (ISBN 0-89508-062-1). Rainbow Bks.
Reidel, Marlene. From Ice to Rain. LC 81-19. (Carolrhoda Start to Finish Bks.). Orig. Title: Vom Eis Zum Regen. (Illus.). 24p. (ps-3). 1981. PLB 5.95 (ISBN 0-87614-157-2). Carolrhoda Bks.
Tuan, Yi-Fu. The Hydrologic Cycle & the Wisdom of God: A Theme in Geoteleology. 1980. Repr. of 1968 ed. 22.50x (ISBN 0-8020-7112-0). U of Toronto Pr.
Wendt, Charles. Water Transfer from Soil to the Atmosphere As Related to Climate & Soil Properties. LC 73-136103. 101p. 1970. 12.00 (ISBN 0-686-01915-6). Mgmt Info Serv.

HYDROLOGY
see also Hydrogeology; Hydrography; Oceanography; Radioisotopes in Hydrology; Water;
also headings beginning with the word Water
Abridged Final Report of the Sixth Session Commission for Hydrology. 129p. 1981. pap. 25.00 (ISBN 0-686-73317-7, W489, WMO). Unipub.
Advisory Group Meeting, Vienna, Jan. 27-31, 1975. Interpretation of Environmental Isotope and Hydrochemcal Data in Groundwater Hydrology: Proceedings. (Panel Proceedings Ser.). (Illus., Orig.). 1976. pap. 22.79 (ISBN 92-0-141076-X, ISP429, IAEA). Unipub.
Applications of Remote Sensing to Hydrology. (Operational Hydrology Report: No. 12). 52p. 1980. pap. 10.00 (ISBN 92-63-10513-8, WMO 453, WMO). Unipub.
Applied Modeling of Hydrologic Time Series. 1981. 32.00 (ISBN 0-918334-37-3). WRP.
Arid-Zone Hydrology: Investigations with Isotope Techniques. 265p. 1981. pap. 34.25 (ISBN 92-0-141180-4, ISP 547, IAEA). Unipub.
Automatic Collection & Transmission of Hydrological Observations. (Operational Hydrology Report Ser.: No. 2). (Illus.). 69p. 1973. pap. 15.00 (ISBN 0-685-39016-0, 337, WMO). Unipub.
Balek, Jaroslav. Hydrology & Water Resources in Tropical Africa. 1977. 58.75 (ISBN 0-444-99814-4). Elsevier.
Beukeboom, Th. J. The Hydrology of the Frisian Islands. (Amsterdam Hydrology: No. 2). 1976. pap. text ed. 17.25x (ISBN 90-6203-419-5). Humanities.
Bilateral U.S.-Japan Seminar in Hydrology, 1st, Honolulu, Jan. 11-17, 1971. Systems Approach to Hydrology: Proceedings. Yevjevich, Vujica, ed. LC 71-168496. 1971. 21.00 (ISBN 0-918334-02-0). WRP.
Biswas, Asit K. History of Hydrology. 2nd ed. (Water Development, Supply & Management). Date not set. write for info. (ISBN 0-08-022433-4). Pergamon.
Boegli, A. Karst Hydrology & Physical Speleology & Physical Speleology. (Illus.). 300p. 1980. 38.00 (ISBN 0-387-10098-9). Springer-Verlag.
Bouwer, Herman. Groundwater Hydrology. (Environment Water & Resources Ser). (Illus.). 1978. text ed. 27.50x (ISBN 0-07-006715-5, C); solution manual 2.50 (ISBN 0-07-006716-3). McGraw.
Branson, Farrell A., et al. Rangeland Hydrology. 2nd ed. 352p. 1981. pap. text ed. 15.00 (ISBN 0-8403-2408-1). Kendall-Hunt.
Casebook of Examples of Organization & Operation of Hydrological Services. (Operational Hydrology Report: No. 9). 1978. pap. 22.00 (ISBN 92-63-10461-1, WMO 461, WMO). Unipub.
Casebook of Methods of Computation of Quantitative Changes in the Hydrological Regime of River Basins Due to Human Activities. (Studies & Reports in Hydrology: No. 28). 330p. 1980. pap. 24.25 (ISBN 92-3-101798-5, U1037, UNESCO). Unipub.
Chorley, Richard J., ed. Introduction to Geographical Hydrology. (Illus.). 1971. pap. 8.50x (ISBN 0-416-68830-6). Methuen Inc.
--Introduction to Physical Hydrology. 1971. pap. 10.95x (ISBN 0-416-68810-1). Methuen Inc.
Chow Ven-Te. Handbook of Applied Hydrology: A Compendium of Water Resources Technology. 1964. 57.50 (ISBN 0-07-010774-2, P&RB). McGraw.
Chow Ven Te, ed. Advances in Hydroscience, 12 vols. Incl. Vol. 1. 1964. 55.00 (ISBN 0-12-021801-1); Vol. 2. 1966. 55.00 (ISBN 0-12-021802-X); Vol. 3. 1967. 55.00 (ISBN 0-12-021803-8); Vol. 4. 1968. 55.00 (ISBN 0-12-021804-6); Vol. 5. 1969. 55.00 (ISBN 0-12-021805-4); Vol. 6. 1970. 55.00 (ISBN 0-12-021806-2); Vol. 7. 1971. 55.00 (ISBN 0-12-021807-0); Vol. 8. 1972. 55.00 (ISBN 0-12-021808-9); Vol. 9. 1973. 50.00 (ISBN 0-12-021809-7); Vol. 10. 1975. 63.00 (ISBN 0-12-021810-0); lib. ed. 81.00 (ISBN 0-12-021874-7); microfiche 45.50 (ISBN 0-12-021875-5); Vol. 11. 1978. 55.00 (ISBN 0-12-021811-9); lib ed. 70.50 (ISBN 0-12-021876-3); microfiche 39.50 (ISBN 0-12-021877-1); Vol. 12. 1978. 51.00 (ISBN 0-12-021812-7); 66.50 (ISBN 0-12-021878-X); 36.00 (ISBN 0-12-021879-8). Acad Pr.
Ciriani, Tito A., ed. Mathematical Models for Surface Water Hydrology: Proceedings of the Workshop Held at the IBM Scientific Center, Pisa Italy. LC 76-13457. 1977. 80.25 (ISBN 0-471-99400-6, Pub. by Wiley-Interscience). Wiley.
Combined Heat, Ice & Water Balances at Selected Glacier Basins, Pt. 2: Specifications, Standards & Data Exchange. (Technical Papers in Hydrology Ser.). (Illus.). 32p. (Orig.). 1973. pap. 2.50 (ISBN 92-3-101050-6, #U738, UNESCO). Unipub.

Commission for Hydrology: Abridged Final Report of the 5th Session. (WMO Ser: No. 453). 1977. pap. 25.00 (ISBN 92-63-10453-0, WMO). Unipub.
Compendium of Meteorology: General Hydrology, Vol. II, Pt. 1. (WMO Ser: No. 364). (Illus.). 42p. 1978. pap. 10.00 (ISBN 0-685-86542-8, W359, WMO). Unipub.
Compendium of Training Facilities in Environmental Problems Related to Meteorological & Operational Hydrology. (Illus.). 1978. pap. 22.00 (ISBN 92-63-10489-1, WMO 489, WMO). Unipub.
Cummings, Ronald G. Interbasin Water Transfers: A Case Study in Mexico. LC 74-6819. (Resources for the Future Research Report Ser). (Illus.). 128p. 1974. 8.50x (ISBN 0-8018-1648-3). Johns Hopkins.
Curricula & Syllabi in Hydrology. LC 72-89904. (Technical Papers in Hydrology). 74p. (Orig.). 1973. pap. 6.75 (ISBN 92-3-100964-8, U147, UNESCO). Unipub.
Cushman, R. M., et al. Sourcebook of Hydrologic & Ecological Features: Water Resource Regions of the Conterminous United States. LC 79-56108. (Illus.). 1980. 24.00 (ISBN 0-250-40355-2). Ann Arbor Science.
Deju, Raul A. Regional Hydrology Fundamentals. (Illus.). 222p. 1971. 45.25x (ISBN 0-677-03860-7). Gordon.
--Regional Hydrology Fundamentals. (Illus.). 222p. 1971. 45.25x (ISBN 0-677-03860-7). Gordon.
De Vries, J. J. Inleiding Tot De Hydrologie Van Nederland. (Chemie En Technick Ser.: No. 2). (Illus.). 78p. (Ger.). 1976. pap. text ed. 6.00x (ISBN 90-6203-149-8). Humanities.
Discharge of Selected Rivers of the World. Incl. Vol. 1. General & Regime Characteristics of Stations Selected. 70p. 1969. pap. 9.25 (ISBN 0-685-48299-5, U165); Vol. 2. Monthly & Annual Discharges Recorded at Various Selected Stations (from Start of Observations up to 1964) 194p. 1971. pap. 12.50 (ISBN 92-3-000847-8, U166); Vol. 3. Mean Monthly & Extreme Discharges (1965-1969) 98p. 1971. pap. 12.25 (ISBN 92-3-000919-9, U167). (Studies & Reports in Hydrology Ser.). (Orig., UNESCO). Unipub.
Discharge of Selected Rivers of the World, Vol.3 Pt. 3. (Studies & Reports in Hydrology: No. 5). 1979. pap. 9.25 (ISBN 92-3-001569-5, U916, UNESCO). Unipub.
Discharge of Selected Rivers of the World, Vol. 3, Pt. 2: Mean Monthly & Extreme Discharges (1969-1972) (Studies & Reports in Hydrology). 124p. 1975. pap. 13.25 (ISBN 92-3-001178-9, U168, UNESCO). Unipub.
Dubreuil, P. Recueil Quadrilingue de Mots Usuels en Hydrologie. 113p. (Quadrilingual Collection of Commonly Used Words in Hydrology). 1969. pap. 9.95 (ISBN 0-686-56767-6, M-6176). French & Eur.
Eagleson, P. Dynamic Hydrology. 1970. text ed. 25.50 (ISBN 0-07-018596-4, C). McGraw.
Engelen, G. B. Aqua-Vua: A Catalogue of Hydrological Research Projects Over the Period 1966-1972 in the Hydrology Program of the Inst. of Earth Sciences, Amsterdam, No. 2. (Communication of the Institute of Earth Sciences, Ser. A: No. 2). 35p. 1976. pap. text ed. 4.75x (ISBN 0-685-66839-8). Humanities.
Engelen, G. B. & Van Lissa, R. V. Aqua-Vu Three: Hydrological Surveys in the Algarve, Portugal, Part I. (Communications of the Institute of Earth Sciences, Ser A: No. 3). 1979. pap. text ed. write for info (ISBN 90-6203-009-2). Humanities.
Engineering Foundation Conference, 1979. Improved Hydrologic Forecasting: Why & How, Proceedings. 464p. 1980. pap. text ed. 32.50 (ISBN 0-87262-203-7). Am Soc Civil Eng.
Eschner, Arthur R. & Black, Peter E., eds. Readings in Forest Hydrology. (Illus.). 293p. 1975. text ed. 24.50x (ISBN 0-8422-5228-2). Irvington.
Fleming, George. Computer Simulation Techniques in Hydrology. (Environmental Science Ser.). 352p. 1975. 30.00 (ISBN 0-444-00157-3). Elsevier.
Fox, Cyril S. Water. LC 75-138233. (Illus.). 148p. 1972. Repr. of 1951 ed. lib. bdg. 15.00x (ISBN 0-8371-5590-8, FOWA). Greenwood.
Freeze, R. Allan & Cherry, John A. Groundwater. (Illus.). 1979. text ed. 31.95 (ISBN 0-13-365312-9). P-H.
Gillman, K. & Newson, M. D. Soil Pipes & Pipeflow. (Bgrg Research Monography Ser.). 1980. pap. 9.90x (ISBN 0-686-27388-5, Pub. by GEO Abstracts England). State Mutual Bk.
Glossaire International d'Hydrologie. 393p. (Fr.). 1974. pap. 29.95 (ISBN 0-686-57304-8, M-6281). French & Eur.
Gray, D. M., ed. Handbook on the Principles of Hydrology. LC 73-82157. (Illus.). 720p. 1973. pap. text ed. 20.00 (ISBN 0-912394-07-2). Water Info.
Guide to Hydrological Practices. 3rd ed. (Illus.). 1975. pap. 55.00 (ISBN 0-685-61958-3, WMO). Unipub.
Guide to World Inventory of Sea, Lake & River Ice. (Technical Papers in Hydrology Ser). (Illus.). 52p. (Orig.). 1973. pap. 5.25 (ISBN 92-3-100958-3, U276, UNESCO). Unipub.
Guidelines for the Education & Training of Personnel in Meteorology & Operational Hydrology. (WMO Ser: No. 258). (Illus.). 1978. pap. 20.00 (ISBN 0-685-87431-1, W-373, WMO). Unipub.
Haan, C. T. Statistical Methods in Hydrology. 1977. text ed. 14.50 (ISBN 0-8138-1510-X). Iowa St U Pr.
Hammer, Mark J. & Mackichan, Kenneth A. Hydrology & Quality of Water Resources. LC 80-209. 486p. 1981. text ed. 20.95 (ISBN 0-471-02681-6). Wiley.
Heintze, Carl. The Biosphere: Earth, Air, Fire, & Water. LC 76-51231. (Illus.). (gr. 8 up). 1977. Repr. 7.95 (ISBN 0-525-66498-X). Elsevier-Nelson.
Henry, C. D. & Gluck, J. K. A Preliminary Assessment of the Geological Setting, Hydrology, & Geochemistry of the Hueco Tanks Geothermal Area, Texas & New Mexico. (Geological Circular Ser.: No. 81-1). (Illus.). 49p. 1981. write for info. U of Tex Econ Geology.
Hewlett, John D. & Nutter, Wade L. Outline of Forest Hydrology. 1969. pap. 4.95x (ISBN 0-8203-0325-9). U of Ga Pr.
Hjelmfelt, A. T., Jr. & Cassidy, J. J. Hydrology for Engineers & Planners. (Illus.). 1975. text ed. 13.50x (ISBN 0-8138-0795-6). Iowa St U Pr.
Huckstedt, Guido. Water Chemistry for Advanced Hobbyist. (Illus.). 1973. pap. 4.95 (ISBN 0-87666-166-5, PS-300). TFH Pubns.
Hydrological Application of Atmospheric Vapour-Flux Analyses. (WMO Ser: No. 476). (Illus.). 1978. pap. 10.00 (ISBN 92-63-10476-X, WMO). Unipub.
Hydrological Effects of Urbanization. (Studies & Reports in Hydrology, No. 18). (Illus.). 280p. 1975. pap. 35.75 (ISBN 92-3-101223-1, U290, UNESCO). Unipub.
Hydrological Forecasting Practices. (Operational Hydrology Report Ser.: No. 6). (Illus.). 134p. 1976. pap. 21.00 (ISBN 92-63-10425-5, WMO). Unipub.
Hydrological Maps: A Contribution to the International Hydrological Decade. (Studies & Reports in Hydrology: No. 20). (Illus.). 1977. pap. 22.50 (ISBN 92-3-101260-6, U292, UNESCO). Unipub.
Hydrological Problems Arising from the Development of Energy. (Technical Papers in Hydrology: No. 17). 1979. pap. 3.25 (ISBN 92-3-101685-7, U912, UNESCO). Unipub.
Hydrology of Deltas, 2 vols. (Studies & Reports in Hydrology Ser). (Illus., Orig.). 1971. Set. pap. 93.00 (ISBN 92-3-000836-2, UNESCO). Unipub.
Hydrology of Marsh-Ridden Areas. (Studies and Reports in Hydrology: No. 19). (Illus.). 562p. 1975. pap. 37.50 (ISBN 0-685-65018-9, 92-3-101264-9, UNESCO). Unipub.
Institute of Civil Engineers, UK. Engineering Hydrology Today. 152p. 1980. 65.00x (ISBN 0-7277-0012-X, Pub. by Telford England). State Mutual Bk.
Intercomparison of Conceptual Models Used in Operational Hydrological Forecasting: Operational Hydrology Report No. Seven. (WMO Ser.: No. 429). (Illus.). 172p. pap. 22.00 (ISBN 92-63-10429-8, WMO). Unipub.
International Glossary of Hydrology. 1976. pap. 24.00 (ISBN 0-685-55840-1, U328, UNESCO). Unipub.
International Hydrological Programme (IHP) Third Session of the Intergovernmental Council Final Report IHP-IC-III. 72p. 1981. pap. 10.00 (ISBN 0-686-69436-8, UNI 1051, UNESCO). Unipub.
International Symposium in Hydrology, 2nd, Colorado State Univ., Sep. 11-13, 1972. Decision with Inadequate Hydrologic Data: Proceedings. Woolhiser, David A., ed. LC 73-80677. 1973. 14.00 (ISBN 0-918334-04-7). WRP.
Isotope Hydrology, 1978, 2 vols. 1979. Vol. 1. pap. 54.50 (ISBN 92-0-040079-5, ISP 493-1, IAEA); Vol. 2. pap. 66.75 (ISBN 92-0-040179-1, ISP 493-2, IAEA). Unipub.
Isotope Techniques in Groundwater Hydrology, 1974, 2 vols. (Illus.). 1003p. (Orig.). 1975. Set. pap. 78.00 (ISBN 0-685-52196-6, ISP373, IAEA); 39.00 ea. Vol. 1 (ISP373-1). Vol. 2 (ISP373-2). Unipub.
Isotopes in Hydrology. (Illus., Orig., Eng. , Fr. & Rus.). 1967. pap. 44.00 (ISBN 92-0-040067-1, ISP141, IAEA). Unipub.
Kazmann, Raphael G. Modern Hydrology. 2nd ed. (Goescience Ser). (Illus.). 352p. 1972. text ed. 32.50 scp (ISBN 0-06-043571-2, HarpC). Har-Row.
Kirkby, M. J., ed. Hillslope Hydrology. LC 77-2669. (Landscape Systems-A Ser. in Geomorphology). 389p. 1978. 70.50 (ISBN 0-471-99510-X, Pub. by Wiley-Interscience). Wiley.
Kite, G. W. Frequency & Risk Analyses in Hydrology. 1977. 15.00 (ISBN 0-918334-23-3). WRP.
Knapp, B. J. Elements of Geographical Hydrology. (Illus.). 1978. pap, text ed. 6.95x (ISBN 0-04-551030-X). Allen Unwin.
Kohler, Max A. Design of Hydrological Networks. (Technical Note Ser.). 1967. pap. 10.00 (ISBN 0-685-22300-0, WMO 82, WMO). Unipub.
Kovacs, G., et al. Subterranean Hydrology. LC 80-54120. 1981. 49.00 (ISBN 0-918334-35-7). WRP.
Kunkle, S. H. & Thames, J. L., eds. Hydrological Techniques for Upstream Conservation. (FAO Conservation Guide: No. 2). 1977. pap. 9.75 (ISBN 92-5-100115-4, F742, FAO). Unipub.
Lal, R. & Russell, E. W. Tropical Agricultural Hydrology: Watershed Management & Land Use. LC 80-41590. 448p. 1981. 69.00 (ISBN 0-471-27931-5, Pub. by Wiley-Interscience). Wiley.
Lazaro, Timothy. Urban Hydrology: A Multidisciplinary Perspective. LC 79-55149. 1979. 24.00 (ISBN 0-250-40330-7). Ann Arbor Science.
Lexique Trilingue des Termes de l'Eau. 224p. (Trilingual Lexicon of Water Terminology). 1975. pap. 29.95 (ISBN 0-686-56724-2, M-6372). French & Eur.
Linsley, Ray K., et al. Hydrology for Engineers. 2nd ed. (Environmental Engineering & Water Resources Ser.). 1974. text ed. 24.95 (ISBN 0-07-037967-X, C); solutions manual 2.50 (ISBN 0-07-037969-6). McGraw.
--Hydrology for Engineers. 3rd ed. (Water Resources & Environmental Engineering Ser.). (Illus.). 496p. 1981. price not set (ISBN 0-07-037956-4). McGraw.
List of International Hydrological Decade Stations of the World. (Studies & Reports in Hydrology, No. 6). (Illus., Orig.). 1969. pap. 18.75 (ISBN 92-3-000761-7, U357, UNESCO). Unipub.
McCuen, Richard H. A Guide to Hydrologic Analysis Using SCS Methods. (Illus.). 160p. 1982. 22.95 (ISBN 0-13-370205-7). P-H.
McWhorter, David B. & Sunada, Daniel K. Ground Water Hydrology & Hydraulics. LC 77-74259. 1981. 27.00 (ISBN 0-918334-18-7). WRP.
Miller, D. H. Water at the Surface of the Earth: An Introduction to Ecosystem Hydrodynamics. 1977. 65.00 (ISBN 0-12-496750-7). Acad Pr.
Modern Developments in Hydrometry II. (Illus.). 1977. pap. 16.00 (ISBN 92-63-10427-1, WMO). Unipub.
Neal, James T., ed. Playas & Dried Lakes: Occurrence & Development. LC 74-31134. (Benchmark Papers in Geology Ser: No. 20). 411p. 1975. 52.50 (ISBN 0-12-787110-1). Acad Pr.
Nuclear Well Logging in Hydrology. (Technical Reports: No. 126). (Illus., Orig.). 1971. pap. 9.75 (ISBN 92-0-145071-0, IDC126, IAEA). Unipub.
Patry, Andre. Regime Des Cours D'Eau Internationaux. (Fr). 1960. pap. 1.95x (ISBN 0-7746-0112-4, Pub. by Laval). Intl Schol Bk Serv.
Perrault, Pierre. On the Origin of Springs. La Rocque, Aurele, tr. (Illus.). 1967. 20.25 (ISBN 0-02-850200-0). Hafner.
Pinder, G. F. & Gray, W. G. Finite Element Simulation in Surface & Subsurface Hydrology. 1977. 43.00 (ISBN 0-12-556950-5). Acad Pr.
Pitty, A. F. A Geographical Approach to Fluvial Processes. 300p. 1980. text ed. 29.50x (ISBN 0-86094-027-6, Pub. by GEO Abstracts England); pap. text ed. 15.55 (ISBN 0-86094-026-8, Pub. by GEO Abstracts England). State Mutual Bk.
Predicting Effects of Power Plant One-Through Cooling on Aquatic Systems. (Technical Papers in Hydrology: No. 20). 1979. pap. 17.00 (ISBN 92-3-101704-7, U939, UNESCO). Unipub.
Raudkivi, A. J. Hydrology. 1979. 68.00 (ISBN 0-08-024261-8). Pergamon.
Research of Urban Hydrology: State of the Arts Reports from Australia, Canada, U. S. S. R., United Kingdom, U. S. A. (Technical Papers in Hydrology: No. 15). (Illus.). 1978. pap. 13.75 (ISBN 92-3-101488-9, U763, UNESCO). Unipub.
Research on Urban Hydrology, Vol. 2. (Technical Papers in Hydrology Ser.: No. 16). 1978. pap. 13.75 (ISBN 92-3-101555-9, U849, UNESCO). Unipub.
Rodda, J. C., et al. Systematic Hydrology. 1976. 49.95 (ISBN 0-408-00234-4). Butterworth.
Rodda, John C. Facets of Hydrology. LC 75-26568. 1976. 86.75 (ISBN 0-471-01359-5, Pub. by Wiley-Interscience). Wiley.
Rodier, J. Bibliography of African Hydrology. 1963. 11.50 (ISBN 92-3-000541-X, U47, UNESCO). Unipub.
The Role of Ice & Snow in Hydrology, 2 vols. (Illus.). 1484p. (Orig.). 1974. Set. pap. 31.00 (ISBN 92-3-001146-0, WMO). Unipub.
Schulz, E. F. Problems in Applied Hydrology. 1974. 25.00 (ISBN 0-918334-07-1). WRP.
Simeons, Charles. Hydro-Power: The Use of Water As an Alternative Source. (Illus.). 560p. 1980. 89.00 (ISBN 0-08-023269-8). Pergamon.
Smith, D. I. & Stopp, P. The River Basin. LC 77-85688. (Topics in Geography Ser.). (Illus.). 1979. 17.95 (ISBN 0-521-21900-0); pap. 7.95x (ISBN 0-521-29307-3). Cambridge U Pr.
Socio-Economic Aspects of Urban Hydrology. (Studies & Reports in Hydrology: No. 27). 85p. 1980. pap. 10.00 (ISBN 0-686-60292-7, U965, UNESCO). Unipub.
Sokolov, A. A., et al. Floodflow Computation. (Studies & Reports in Hydrology: No. 22). (Illus.). 1977. pap. 26.50 (ISBN 92-3-101350-5, U248, UNESCO). Unipub.
Statistical Information on Activities in Operational Hydrology. (Operational Hydrology Report: No. 10). (Illus.). 1977. pap. 22.00 (ISBN 92-63-10464-6, WMO). Unipub.
Svanidze, G. G. Mathematical Modeling of Hydrologic Series. LC 79-57578. 1980. 28.00 (ISBN 0-918334-32-2). WRP.
Symposium on Karst Hydrology & Water Resources, Dubrovnik, Yugo., Jun 2-7, 1975. Karst Hydrology & Water Resources: Proceedings, 2 vols. Yevjevich, V., ed. LC 76-12972. 1976. Set. 34.00 (ISBN 0-686-67935-0); Vol. 1. (ISBN 0-918334-15-2); Vol. 2. (ISBN 0-918334-16-0). WRP.
Technical Conference of Hydrological & Meteorological Services, Geneva, 1970. Scientific Papers. (Illus.). 123p. (Orig.). 1972. pap. 10.00 (ISBN 0-685-24966-2, 304, WMO). Unipub.
Technical Regulations, 2 vols. (Basic Documents Ser.: No. 49). (Vol. I, 95 p.; Vol. II, 45 p.). 1980. Set. sheets in binder 40.00 (ISBN 0-686-61622-7, WMO). Vol. I, General. Vol. II, Hydrology. Unipub.
Textbooks on Hydrology, Vol. 2: Analyses of Selected Textbooks. (Technical Papers in Hydrology No. 6). 223p. (Orig.). 1974. pap. 17.75 (ISBN 92-3-101148-0, UNESCO). Unipub.
Thompson, Betty F. The Shaping of America's Heartland: The Landscape of the Middle West. (Naturalist's America Ser.: Vol. 4). 1977. 11.95 (ISBN 0-395-24760-8). HM.
Todd, David K. Groundwater Hydrology. 2nd ed. LC 80-11831. 535p. 1980. 28.95 (ISBN 0-471-87616-X). Wiley.
Toebes, C. & Ouryvaer, V., eds. Representative & Experimental Basins. (Studies & Reports in Hydrology Ser., No. 4). (Illus., Orig.). 1970. 24.25 (ISBN 92-3-100808-0, U551, UNESCO). Unipub.
Urban Hydrological Modeling & Catchment Research: International Summary. (Technical Papers in Hydrology Ser.: No. 18). 48p. 1979. pap. 4.75 (ISBN 0-685-95367-X, U896, UNESCO). Unipub.
Use of WWW Facilities for Hydrology. (World Weather Watch Planning Report Ser: No. 35). (Illus.). 34p. 1977. pap. 10.00 (ISBN 92-63-10451-4, WMO). Unipub.
Van der Leeden, Fritz. Water Resources of the World. LC 75-20952. (Illus.). 1975. 45.00 (ISBN 0-912394-14-5). Water Info.
Verstraten, J. M. Water-Rock Interactions. (Bgrg Research Monograph Ser.). 1980. pap. 9.90x (ISBN 0-686-27389-3, Pub. by GEO Abstracts England). State Mutual Bk.
Viessman, Warren, et al. Introduction to Hydrology. 2nd ed. 1977. text ed. 31.50 scp (ISBN 0-7002-2497-1, HarpC). Har-Row.
Whetstone, G. W. & Grigoriev, V. J., eds. Hydrologic Information Systems. LC 72-90686. (Studies & Reports in Hydrology). (Illus.). 72p. (Orig.). 1973. pap. 9.25 (ISBN 92-3-100957-5, U289, UNESCO). Unipub.
World Catalogue of Very Large Floods. (Studies and Reports in Hydrology). (Illus.). 1977. pap. 37.25 (ISBN 92-3-001310-2, UNESCO). Unipub.
Yevjevich, Vujica. Probability & Statistics in Hydrology. LC 74-168494. 1972. 25.00 (ISBN 0-918334-00-4). WRP.
--Stochastic Processes in Hydrology. LC 78-168495. 25.00 (ISBN 0-918334-01-2). WRP.

HYDROLOGY–DATA PROCESSING

Hydrological Network Design & Information Transfer. (WMO Operatinal Hydrology Report: No. 8). (Illus.). 185p. 1976. pap. 30.00 (ISBN 92-63-10433-6, WMO). Unipub.
Pinder, G. F. & Gray, W. G. Finite Element Simulation in Surface & Subsurface Hydrology. 1977. 43.00 (ISBN 0-12-556950-5). Acad Pr.
Technical Regulations Hydrology & International Codes. 129p. 1981. pap. 20.00 (ISBN 92-63-10555-3, W477, WMO). Unipub.

Use of Analog & Digital Computers in Hydrology, 2 Vols. (Studies & Reports in Hydrology Ser). (Illus.). 1969. Set. 46.25 (ISBN 92-3-000734-X, UNESCO). Unipub.

HYDROLYSIS

see also Lysosomes

Deslongchamps, Pierre. Stereoelectronic Control in the Cleavage of Tetrahedral Intermediates in the Hydrolysis of Esters & Amides. Barton, et al, eds. 1976. pap. text ed. 12.75 (ISBN 0-08-020480-5). Pergamon.

Fishman, William H., ed. Metabolic Conjugation & Metabolic Hydrolysis, 3 vols. LC 79-107556. 1970-73. Vol. 1. 64.00 (ISBN 0-12-257601-2); Vol. 2. 87.50 (ISBN 0-12-257602-0); Vol. 3. 62.50 (ISBN 0-12-257603-9); Set. 173.50 (ISBN 0-685-03086-5). Acad Pr.

HYDROMAGNETIC WAVES

see Magnetohydrodynamics

HYDROMECHANICS

see Fluid Mechanics

HYDROMEDUSA

see also Hydrozoa; Siphonophora

Hydromedusae of British Columbia & Puget Sound. (Canadian Bulletin of Fisheries & Aquatic Sciences Ser.: No. 204). 192p. 1981. pap. 24.25 (ISBN 0-660-10494-6, SSC 152, SSC). Unipub.

HYDROMETALLURGY

Habashi, Fathi. Hydrometallurgy. (Principles of Extractive Metallurgy Ser.: Vol. 2). 468p. 1970. 70.00 (ISBN 0-677-01780-4). Gordon.

Society of Mining Engineers of AIME, 1973. Hydrometallurgy: Proceedings. LC 72-88874. 28.00x (ISBN 0-89520-017-1). Soc Mining Eng.

HYDROMETEOROLOGY

Bonin, Serge. Le Traitement Graphique D'une Information Hydrometeorologique Relative a L'espace Maritime Du Nord Sovietique, 2 vols. Incl. Vol. 1. Les Documents Graphiques. (Illus.); Vol. 2. Analyses et Commentaires. 2200p. (Contributions Du Centre D' Etudes Antiques: No. 11). (Illus., Fr.). 1974. Set. pap. text ed. 48.50x (ISBN 0-686-22587-2). Mouton.

Bruce, J. P. & Clark, R. H. Introduction to Hydrometeorology. 1966. 25.00 (ISBN 0-08-011715-5); pap. 12.00 (ISBN 0-08-011714-7). Pergamon.

Commission on Hydrometeorology, 1972. Report. pap. 20.00 (ISBN 0-685-57278-1, 330, WMO). Unipub.

Hydrological Forecasting. (Technical Note Ser.: No. 92). (Illus., Orig.). 1969. pap. 60.00 (ISBN 0-685-22307-8, WMO). Unipub.

Hydrometeorological Instruments, Observations & Networks in Africa. (Illus., Orig.). 1970. pap. 12.00 (ISBN 0-685-04914-0, WMO). Unipub.

Manual for Estimation of Probable Maximum Precipitation. (Operational Hydrology Report Ser.: No. 1). (Illus.). 190p. 1973. pap. 15.00 (ISBN 0-685-39012-8, 332, WMO). Unipub.

Technical Conference of Hydrological & Meteorological Services. Abridged Final Report. 1970. pap. 8.00 (ISBN 0-685-02478-4, 282, W95, WMO). Unipub.

World Meteorological Organization. Manual for Depth-Area-Duration Analysis of Storm Precipitation. 1969. pap. 20.00 (ISBN 0-685-22315-9, WMO). Unipub.

--Weather & Water. 1966. pap. 2.00 (ISBN 0-685-22348-5, WMO). Unipub.

HYDROMETER

Kolupaila, Steponas. Bibliography of Hydrometry. 1961. 15.00x (ISBN 0-268-00021-2). U of Notre Dame Pr.

HYDROMETRY

see Hydraulic Measurements

HYDROPATHY

see Hydrotherapy

HYDROPERITONEUM

see Ascites

HYDROPHOBIA

see Rabies

HYDROPHYTES

see Algae; Fresh-Water Biology; Fresh-Water Flora; Marine Flora

HYDROPLANES

see also Seaplanes

Stone, Jane. Challenge! The Big Thunderboats. new ed. LC 75-23408. (Illus.). 32p. (gr. 5-10). 1976. PLB 6.89 (ISBN 0-89375-003-4); pap. 2.50 (ISBN 0-89375-019-0). Troll Assocs.

HYDROPONICS

Brenizer, Sherman. Hydro-Story, Hydroponic Gardening at Home. 1977. pap. 4.95 (ISBN 0-917316-13-4). Nolo Pr.

Bridwell, Raymond. Hydroponic Gardening: The Magic of Hydroponics for the Home Gardener. LC 72-86151. (Illus.). 224p. 1972. 8.95 (ISBN 0-912800-00-3); pap. 5.95 (ISBN 0-912800-09-7). Woodbridge Pr.

Cooper, Allen. The ABC of NFT. 1979. pap. 16.00x (ISBN 0-901361-22-4, Pub. by Grower Books England). Intl Schol Bk Serv.

Dickerman, Alexandra & Dickerman, John. Discovering Hydroponic Gardening: Beginner's Guide to the Pleasures of Soil-Less Gardening. LC 75-17274. (Illus.). 160p. (Orig.). 1975. pap. 3.95 (ISBN 0-912800-19-4). Woodbridge Pr.

Douglas, J. Sholto. Hydroponics: The Bengal System with Notes on Other Methods of Soil Cultivation. 5th ed. 206p. 1975. 5.95x (ISBN 0-19-560566-7). Oxford U Pr.

Douglas, James S. Advanced Guide to Hydroponics. (Illus.). 333p. 1980. 19.95 (ISBN 0-7207-0830-3, Pub. by Michael Joseph). Merrimack Bk Serv.

--Beginner's Guide to Hydroponics. LC 73-5941. (Illus.). 146p. 1979. pap. 4.95 (ISBN 0-8069-8158-X). Sterling.

--Beginner's Guide to Hydroponics (Soiless Gardening) 156p. 1972. 8.50 (ISBN 0-7207-0572-X, Pub. by Michael Joseph). Merrimack Bk Serv.

Harris, Dudley. Hydroponics: Growing Without Soil. rev. ed. (Illus.). 160p. 1975. 22.50 (ISBN 0-7153-6397-2). David & Charles.

Johnsen, Jan. Gardening Without Soil. LC 78-11898. (Illus.). (gr. 3-6). 1979. 7.95 (ISBN 0-397-31729-8, JBL-J); PLB 7.89 (ISBN 0-397-31868-5). Har-Row.

Jones, Lem & Beardsley, Paul. Home Hydrophonics...How to Do It! (Illus.). 1977. pap. 5.95 (ISBN 0-517-53760-5, Pub. by Ward Ritchie). Crown.

Kenyon, Stewart. Hydroponics for the Home Gardener: An Easy to Follow Step-by-Step Guide for Growing Healthy Vegetables, Herbs & House Plants Without Soil. 158p. 1980. pap. 6.95 (ISBN 0-442-29702-5). Van Nos Reinhold.

Nicholls, Richard E. Beginning Hydroponics: Soiless Gardening - A Beginner's Guide to Growing Vegetables, House Plants, Flowers & Herbs Without Soil. LC 77-13770. (Illus.). 1977. lib. bdg. 12.90 (ISBN 0-89471-009-5); pap. 4.95 (ISBN 0-89471-008-7). Running Pr.

Resh, Howard M. Hydroponic Food Production: A Definitive Guide to Soilless Culture. rev. ed. LC 81-10405. (Illus.). 1981. text ed. 17.95 (ISBN 0-912800-93-3). Woodbridge Pr.

Riedman, Sarah R. Gardening Without Soil. LC 78-13088. (First Bks.). (Illus.). (gr. 4-6). 1979. PLB 6.90 s&l (ISBN 0-531-02256-0). Watts.

Schwarz, Meir. A Guide to Commercial Hydroponics. (Illus.). 148p. 1968. 10.00 (ISBN 0-7065-0060-1, Pub. by IPST). Intl Schol Bk Serv.

Sherman, Ed. How to Build a Bigger Hydropanic Garden. 1978. pap. 3.95 (ISBN 0-917316-18-5). Nolo Pr.

Sullivan, George. Understanding Hydroponics. LC 75-32639. (Understanding Ser.). (Illus.). 96p. (gr. 5 up). 1976. 6.95 (ISBN 0-7232-6036-2). Warne.

Ticquet, C. E. Successful Gardening Without Soil. (Illus.). 1956. 15.00 (ISBN 0-8206-0124-1). Chem Pub.

Watlington, Frank. How to Build & Use Low Cost Hydrophones. (Illus.). 1979. 8.95 (ISBN 0-8306-9846-9); pap. 4.95 (ISBN 0-8306-1079-0, 1079). TAB Bks.

HYDROPS ABDOMINIS

see Ascites

HYDROSTATICS

see also Compressibility; Floating Bodies; Fluids; Gases; Hydrometer; Rotating Masses of Fluid; Soil Percolation; Specific Gravity

Korn, J. Hydrostatic Transmission Systems. 1970. pap. 10.00 (ISBN 0-7002-0189-0). Transatlantic.

McKenzie, Arthur E. Physics. 4th ed. 1970. 17.95x (ISBN 0-521-07698-6). Cambridge U Pr.

Mariotte, Edme. The Motion of Water & Other Fluids: Being a Treatise of Hydrostaticks. Albritton, Claude C., ed. Desaguliers, J. T., tr. (History of Geology Ser.). (Illus.). 1978. Repr. of 1718 ed. lib. bdg. 20.00x (ISBN 0-405-10449-9). Arno.

Pascal, Blaise. Extraits des Traites de l'Equilibre des Liqueurs et de la Pesanteur de la Masse de l'A Ir. 64p. 1963. 5.95 (ISBN 0-686-54846-9). French & Eur.

--Physical Treatises of Pascal. Barry, Frederick, ed. 1969. lib. bdg. 18.00x (ISBN 0-374-90418-9). Octagon.

--Traite de l'Equilibre des Liqueurs et de la Pesanteur de la Masse de l'Aire. 106p. 1956. 22.50 (ISBN 0-686-54853-1). French & Eur.

Thoma, Jean. Hydrostatic Power Transmission. 185p. 1979. 30.00x (ISBN 0-85461-080-4). State Mutual Bks.

HYDROTHERAPY

see also Baths; Health Resorts, Watering-Places, etc.

Buchman, Dian D. The Complete Book of Water Therapy: Five Hundred Ways to Use Our Oldest & Safest Medicine. 1979. 12.95 (ISBN 0-525-93092-2); pap. 8.95 (ISBN 0-525-93093-0). Dutton.

Claridge, R. T. Hydropathy, or, the Cold Water Cure. LC 74-29286. Repr. of 1843 ed. 17.00 (ISBN 0-404-13406-8). AMS Pr.

Finnerty, Gertrude B. & Corbitt, Theodore. Hydrotherapy. LC 60-6593. (Illus.). 1960. 13.50 (ISBN 0-8044-4236-3). Ungar.

Lee, Terri. Aquacises: Water Exercises for Fitness & Figure Beauty. (Illus.). 1969. 5.95x (ISBN 0-9602332-0-2). T Lee.

Lust, John B. Kneipp's My Water Cure. 1978. 12.95 (ISBN 0-87904-022-X). Lust.

Nichols, Thomas L. Esoteric Anthropology: The Mysteries of Man. LC 75-180585. (Medicine & Society in America Ser). (Illus.). 350p. 1972. Repr. of 1853 ed. 16.00x (ISBN 0-405-03962-X). Arno.

Ramacharaka, Yogi. Hindu-Yogi Practical Water Cure. leatherette 2.50 (ISBN 0-911662-12-X). Yoga.

Rhodes, Helen. Doctor, What Can I Do? (Horizon Ser.). 128p. 1981. pap. write for info. (ISBN 0-8127-0327-8). Review & Herald.

HYDROXYL GROUP

Biochemical Society Symposium, 34th. Biological Hydroxylation Mechanisms: Proceedings. Boyd, G. S. & Smellie, R. M., eds. 1973. 40.00 (ISBN 0-12-121850-3). Acad Pr.

Dryhurst, G. Periodate Oxidation of Diol & Other Functional Groups. LC 72-101490. 1970. 25.00 (ISBN 0-08-006877-4). Pergamon.

Veibel, S. The Determination of Hydroxyl Groups. (The Analysis of Organic Materials & International Series of Monographs, No. 1). 1972. 30.00 (ISBN 0-12-715250-4). Acad Pr.

HYDROXYSTEROID DEHYDROGENASE

Baillie, A. H., et al. Developments in Steroid Histochemistry. 1966. 29.50 (ISBN 0-12-073550-4). Acad Pr.

HYDROXYTRYPTAMINE

see Serotonin

HYDROZOA

see also Siphonophora

Fraser, C. McLean. Hydroids of the Pacific Coast of Canada & the United States. LC 38-8455. 1937. 25.00x (ISBN 0-8020-7035-3). U of Toronto Pr.

HYER, ROBERT STEWART

Brown, Ray H. Robert Stewart Hyer, the Man I Knew. (Illus.). 1957. 8.00 (ISBN 0-685-05005-X). A Jones.

HYGIENE

Here are entered works on personal body care and cleanliness. Works on optimal physical, mental, and social well-being, as well as how to achieve and preserve it, are entered under Health.

see also Health; Mental Health;

also subdivision Care and hygiene under parts of the body, and under age groups dependent on the assistance of others, e.g. Eye-Care and hygiene; Infants-Care and hygiene; and subdivision Health and hygiene under classes of persons or ethnic groups, e.g. Students-Health and hygiene; Afro-Americans-Health and hygiene

Abrahamson, E. M. & Pezet, A. W. Body, Mind & Sugar. 1977. pap. 3.95 (ISBN 0-380-00903-X, 47415). Avon.

Allen, Eleanor. Wash & Br ..h up. (Junior Reference Ser.). (Illus.). 64p. (gr. 7 up). 7.95 (ISBN 0-7136-1639-3). Dufour.

Bhatia, B. L. & Suri, P. N. Elementary Hygiene. 134p. 1981. 10.00x (ISBN 0-86125-781-2, Pub. by Orient Longman India). State Mutual Bk.

Bragg, Paul C. & Bragg, Patricia. Shocking Truth About Water. 22nd ed. LC 77-101348. pap. 2.95 (ISBN 0-87790-000-0). Health Sci.

Corsaro, Maria & Korzeniowsky, Carole. STD: A Common Sense Guide. 1980. 9.95 (ISBN 0-312-69644-2). St Martin.

Dalet, Roger. How to Safeguard Your Health & Beauty with the Simple Pressure of a Finger. LC 80-5497. (Illus.). 160p. 1981. 10.95 (ISBN 0-8128-2742-2). Stein & Day.

Diagram Group. The Healthy Body: A Maintenance Manual. 1981. pap. 6.95 (ISBN 0-452-25294-6, Z5294, Plume). NAL.

Galenus, Claudius. A Translation of Galen's Hygiene (De Sanitate Tuenda) Green, Robert M., tr. (Historia Medicinae Ser.). (Illus.). xxvi, 277p. Repr. of 1951 ed. lib. bdg. 20.00x (ISBN 0-87991-119-0). Porcupine Pr.

Green, Robert M. A Translation of Galen's Hygiene (De Sanitate Tuenda) 304p. 1952. photocopy ed. spiral 27.50 (ISBN 0-398-00723-3). C C Thomas.

Haas, Elson. Staying Healthy with the Seasons. LC 80-69469. (Illus.). 192p. (Orig.). 1981. pap. 9.95 (ISBN 0-89087-306-2). Celestial Arts.

Johnson, G. Timothy & Goldfinger, Stephen E., eds. The Harvard Medical School Health Letter Book. LC 80-27215. (Illus.). 460p. 1981. 15.95 (ISBN 0-686-71097-5). Harvard U Pr.

Koopman, Leroy. Beauty Care for the Ears. 1980. pap. 2.50 (ISBN 0-310-26872-9). Zondervan.

Kozuszek, Jane E. Hygiene. (First Bks.). (Illus.). (gr. 4 up). 1978. PLB 6.90 s&l (ISBN 0-531-01410-X). Watts.

Odor, Ruth. What's a Body to Do? Buerger, Jane, ed. (Illus.). 112p. 1980. 5.95 (ISBN 0-686-77526-0, 4933). Standard Pub.

Parkinson, Virginia. Cleanliness. (Pointers for Little Persons Ser). (Illus.). (gr. k-3). 1961. PLB 5.99 (ISBN 0-8178-5012-0). Harvey.

Stephan, Peter. Growing up Young. 224p. 1980. 11.95 (ISBN 0-906071-34-8). Proteus Pub NY.

Watch Your Line. pap. 5.00x (ISBN 0-392-06112-0, SpS). Sportshelf.

HYGIENE-ECONOMIC ASPECTS

see Medical Economics

HYGIENE, DENTAL

see Teeth-Care and Hygiene

HYGIENE, PERSONAL

Beckett, Sarah. Herbs for Clearing the Skin. LC 80-50748. (Everybody's Home Herbal Ser.). (Illus.). 64p. (Orig.). 1980. pap. 1.95 (ISBN 0-394-73942-6). Shambhala Pubns.

Broccoletti, Pete. Thirty-Five & Holding: Complete Conditioning for the Adult Male. (Illus.). 1981. 16.95 (ISBN 0-89651-778-0); pap. 10.95 (ISBN 0-89651-779-9). Icarus.

Miller, Donald. Bodymind: The Whole Person Health Book. LC 73-20280. (Illus.). 224p. 1974. pap. 4.50 (ISBN 0-13-079616-6). P-H.

Saffon, M. J. The Fifteen Minute-a-Day Natural Face Lift. 112p. 1981. pap. 3.95 (ISBN 0-446-97788-8). Warner Bks.

HYGIENE, PUBLIC

see Public Health

HYGIENE, RURAL

see Health, Rural

HYGIENE, SEXUAL

see also Birth Control; Contraception; Prostitution; Sex Instruction; Sexual Ethics; Venereal Diseases

Busby, Trent. Be Good to Your Body. 1977. 8.95 (ISBN 0-8065-0558-3). Citadel Pr.

Bush, Patricia J. Drugs, Alcohol, & Sex. 352p. 1980. 12.95 (ISBN 0-399-90080-2). Marek.

Butterfield, Oliver M. Sex Life in Marriage. (Illus.). 7.95 (ISBN 0-87523-035-0). Emerson.

--Sexual Harmony in Marriage. (Illus.). pap. 1.95 (ISBN 0-87523-092-X). Emerson.

Comfort, Alex. Barbarism & Sexual Freedom. LC 76-30586. (Anarchy & Anarchism: No. 99). 1977. lib. bdg. 24.95 (ISBN 0-8383-2147-X). Haskell.

Cooke, Nicholas F. Satan in Society. LC 73-20617. (Sex, Marriage & Society Ser.). 412p. 1974. Repr. of 1876 ed. 23.00x (ISBN 0-405-05796-2). Arno.

DeMoya, Armando & DeMoya, Dorothy. Sex & Health: A Practical Encyclopedia of Sexual Medicine. LC 80-5799. 304p. 1981. 16.95 (ISBN 0-8128-2794-5). Stein & Day.

Dunbar, Robert E. A Doctor Discusses a Man's Sexual Health. (Illus.). 1979. pap. 2.50 (ISBN 0-685-64313-1). Budlong.

Ellis, Havelock. Sex & Marriage: Eros in Contemporary Life. LC 77-7264. 1977. Repr. of 1952 ed. lib. bdg. 20.25 (ISBN 0-8371-9667-1, ELSM). Greenwood.

--The Task of Social Hygiene. 414p. 1980. Repr. lib. bdg. 25.00 (ISBN 0-8495-1340-5). Arden Lib.

Gardner, Augustus K. Conjugal Sins Against the Laws of Life & Health: Their Effects Upon the Father, Mother & Child. LC 73-20624. (Sex, Marriage & Society Ser.). 244p. 1974. Repr. of 1870 ed. 15.00x (ISBN 0-405-05800-4). Arno.

Groves, Ernest R., et al. Sex Fulfillment in Marriage. (Illus.). 8.95 (ISBN 0-87523-065-2). Emerson.

Howe, Joseph W. Excessive Venery, Masturbation & Continence. LC 73-20629. (Sex, Marriage & Society Ser.). 298p. 1974. Repr. 17.00x (ISBN 0-405-05805-5). Arno.

Hutton, Isabel E. Sex Technique in Marriage. rev. enl. ed. (Illus.). 1961. 7.95 (ISBN 0-87523-001-6). Emerson.

Hyde, Janet. Understanding Human Sexuality. (Illus.). 1978. text ed. 14.95 (ISBN 0-07-031558-2, C); instructor's manual 4.50 (ISBN 0-07-031559-0). McGraw.

Kellogg, J. H. Plain Facts for Old & Young: Natural History & Hygiene of Organic Life. LC 73-20633. (Sex, Marriage & Society Ser.). 648p. 1974. Repr. 33.00x (ISBN 0-405-05808-X). Arno.

Kennel, Arthur & Kennel, Lois. Your Body & You: For Young People in the Early & Middle Teens. (Family Life Ser.). (Orig.). (YA) (gr. 9 up). 1964. pap. 0.60 (ISBN 0-8361-1490-6). Herald Pr.

McCary, James L. Human Sexuality. 3rd ed. (Illus.). 1978. text ed. 16.95 (ISBN 0-442-25237-4); instructors' manual 3.50x (ISBN 0-442-25241-2); study guide 4.95x (ISBN 0-442-25244-7). D Van Nostrand.

--Human Sexuality. brief ed. 1979. pap. text ed. 9.95 (ISBN 0-442-25236-6). D Van Nostrand.

Rapp, Clyde E., Jr. & Calderone, Mary S., eds. Sexual Health Services for Academic Communities. new ed. LC 76-21129. (Illus.). 1976. pap. text ed. 4.50x (ISBN 0-89313-000-1). G F Stickley Co.

Sex for the Common Man. LC 73-20654. 222p. 1974. Repr. 13.00x (ISBN 0-405-05819-5). Arno.

Stone, Hannah & Stone, Abraham. Marriage Manual. rev. & enl. ed. Aitken, Gloria S. & Sobrero, Acquiles, eds. (Illus.). 1968. 8.95 (ISBN 0-671-45101-4). S&S.

Tyrer, Alfred H. Sex Satisfaction & Happy Marriage. (Illus.). 1951. 6.95 (ISBN 0-87523-039-3). Emerson.

Van De Velde, T. A. Ideal Marriage: Its Physiology & Technique. 400p. 1975. pap. 2.25 (ISBN 0-345-25841-X). Ballantine.

Wright, Henry C. Marriage & Parentage. LC 73-20651. (Sex, Marriage & Society Ser.). 330p. 1974. Repr. 17.00x (ISBN 0-405-05823-3). Arno.

Zales, Michael R. Eating, Sleeping & Sexuality: Recent Advances in Basic Life Functions. 320p. 1981. 25.00 (ISBN 0-87630-288-6). Brunner-Mazel.

HYGIENE, SOCIAL

see Hygiene, Sexual; Prostitution; Public Health; Venereal Diseases

HYGIENE, TROPICAL

see Tropical Medicine

HYGIENE, VETERINARY

see Veterinary Hygiene

HYGROMETRY

Lambert, Jean-Henri. Essais D'hygrometrie. Repr. of 1769 ed. 32.00 (ISBN 0-8287-0496-1). Clearwater Pub.

HYGROPHORUS

Hesler, L. R. & Smith, Alexander H. North American Species of Hygrophorus. LC 62-20535. (Illus.). 1963. 21.50x (ISBN 0-87049-039-7). U of Tenn Pr.

HYLOMORPHISM

McMullin, Ernan, ed. Concept of Matter in Greek & Mediaeval Philosophy. 1965. pap. 4.95x (ISBN 0-268-00055-7). U of Notre Dame Pr.

HYLOZOISM

see also Animism

HYMENOMYCETES

Bourdot, H. & Galzin, A. Hymenomycetes De France: Heterobasidies-Homobasidies Gymnocarpes. (Biblio. Myco. Ser.: No.23). 1969. Repr. of 1927 ed. 60.00 (ISBN 3-7682-0655-6). Lubrecht & Cramer.

Donk, M. A. The Generic Names Proposed for Hymenomycetes 1-9,12,13. 1966. pap. 25.00 (ISBN 3-7682-0347-6). Lubrecht & Cramer.

Fries, Elias. Hymenomycetes Europei, Seu Epicriseos Systematis Mycologici. 2nd ed. 1963. Repr. of 1874 ed. 45.00 (ISBN 90-6123-066-7). Lubrecht & Cramer.

--Monographia Hymenomycetum Sueciae: 1857-62, 2 vols. in 1. 1963. 50.00 (ISBN 90-6123-067-5). Lubrecht & Cramer.

Fries, Elias M. Epicrisis Systematis Mycologici, Seu Synopsis Hymenomycetum. 1965. Repr. of 1838 ed. 38.50 (ISBN 0-384-16950-3). Johnson Repr.

Patouillard, Narcisse-Theophile. Essai Taxonomique Sur les Familles et les Genres Des Hymenomycetes. 1963. Repr. of 1900 ed. 19.20 (ISBN 90-6123-119-1). Lubrecht & Cramer.

Soehner, E. Die Gattung Hymenogaster Vitt. 1962. pap. 20.00 (ISBN 3-7682-5402-X). Lubrecht & Cramer.

Symposium Lausanne, Switzerland Aug. 16 to 20 1976. Species Concept Hymenomycetes: Proceedings. Clemencon, H., ed. (Bibliotheca Mycologica: No. 61). (Illus.). 1978. pap. text ed. 60.00 (ISBN 3-7682-1173-8). Lubrecht & Cramer.

HYMENOPTERA

see also Ants; Bees; Wasps

Cameron, P. Monograph of the British Phytophagous Hymenoptera, 4 Vols. 1882-1893. Set. 77.00 (ISBN 0-384-07240-2). Johnson Repr.

Copeland, E. B. Hymenophyllum. Bd. with Trichomanes; Genera Hymenophyllacearum. (Illus.). 460p. (Repr. of 1933-38 eds.). 1975. lib. bdg. 80.00x (ISBN 3-87429-079-4). Lubrecht & Cramer.

Dasch. Neotropic Mesochorinae - Hymenoptera, Ichneumonidae. (Memoirs Ser: No. 22). (Illus.). 509p. 1974. 30.00 (ISBN 0-686-17149-7). Am Entom Inst.

The Hymenopterist's Handbook. 160p. 1969. 30.00x (ISBN 0-686-75583-9, Pub. by Amateur Entomol Soc). State Mutual Bk.

Linsley, E. G. & MacSwain, J. W. Nesting Biology & Associates of Melitoma (Hymenoptera, Anthrophoridae) (U. C. Publications in Entomolgy: Vol. 90). 1980. pap. 7.50 (ISBN 0-520-09618-5). U of Cal Pr.

Timberlake, P. H. Review of the Species of Exomalopsis Occurring in North America (Hymenoptera, Anthophoridae) (Publications in Entomology Ser.: Vol. 86). 164p. 1980. 18.50x (ISBN 0-520-09606-1). U of Cal Pr.

--Supplementary Studies on the Systematics of the Genus Perdita (Hymenoptera, Andrenidae, Part II. (U. C. Publications in Entomology Ser.: Vol. 85). 1980. pap. 10.00 (ISBN 0-520-09605-3). U of Cal Pr.

Townes, Henry & Chiu, Shui-Chen. The Indo-Australian Species of Xanthopimpla - Ichneumonidae. (Memoirs Ser: No. 14). (Illus.). 372p. 1970. 25.00 (ISBN 0-686-17147-0). Am Entom Inst.

Townes, Henry & Townes, Marjorie. A Revision of the Serphidge (Hymensptera) (Memoir Ser.: No. 32). (Illus.). 541p. 48.00 (ISBN 0-686-30277-X). Am Entom Inst.

Wharton, Robert. Review of the Nearctic Alysiini (Hymenoptera, Braconidae) (U. C. Publications in Entomology Ser.: Vol. 88). 122p. 1980. 15.00x (ISBN 0-520-09611-8). U of Cal Pr.

HYMN FESTIVALS

Prewitt, Vivian. Praise Him! Inspiring Song Services. 100p. 1976. pap. 3.75 (ISBN 0-89536-180-9). CSS Pub.

HYMN PLAYING

see Hymns-Accompaniment

HYMN TUNES

see also Chorale; Tune-Books

Breed, David R. The History & Use of Hymns & Hymn Tunes. LC 76-39525. Repr. of 1903 ed. 20.00 (ISBN 0-404-09906-8). AMS Pr.

Butterworth, Hezekiah. Story of Hymns & Tunes. 1981. Repr. lib. bdg. 49.00 (ISBN 0-403-00107-2). Scholarly.

Hays, Henry B. Swayed Pines Song Book. x, 88p. 1981. wirebound 7.95 (ISBN 0-8146-1238-5). Liturgical Pr.

Lyon, James. Urania: A Choice Collection of Psalm-Tunes, Anthems & Hymns. LC 69-11667. (Music Reprint Ser.). 198p. 1974. Repr. of 1761 ed. lib. bdg. 27.50 (ISBN 0-306-71198-2). Da Capo.

Mason, H. Lowell. Hymn-Tunes of Lowell Mason. LC 74-24144. Repr. of 1944 ed. 15.00 (ISBN 0-404-13035-6). AMS Pr.

HYMN WRITERS

Goodenough, Caroline L. High Lights on Hymnists & Their Hymns. LC 72-1626. Repr. of 1931 ed. 32.50 (ISBN 0-404-08310-2). AMS Pr.

Hatfield, Edwin F. Poets of the Church: A Series of Biographical Sketches of Hymn-Writers, with Notes on Their Hymns. 1979. Repr. of 1884 ed. 74.00 (ISBN 0-8103-4291-X). Gale.

Reynolds, William J. Hymns of Our Faith. LC 64-14049. 1964. 12.95 (ISBN 0-8054-6805-6). Broadman.

Ruffin, Bernard. Fanny Crosby. LC 75-45273. 264p. 1976. 8.00 (ISBN 0-8298-0290-8). Pilgrim NY.

Stebbins, George C. Reminiscences & Gospel Hymn Stories. LC 74-144689. Repr. of 1924 ed. 24.50 (ISBN 0-404-07203-8). AMS Pr.

HYMNOLOGY

see Hymns

HYMNS

see also Carols; Children's Hymns; Church Music; Gospel Music; Hymn Festivals; Hymn Tunes; Psalmody; Religious Poetry; Sunday-Schools-Hymns; Tune-Books

Aitken, John. Compilations of Litanies & Vesper Hymns. 10.00x (ISBN 0-87556-004-0). Saifer.

Andrews, Edward D. Gift to Be Simple. (Illus.). 1940. pap. 2.50 (ISBN 0-486-20022-1). Dover.

--Gift to Be Simple: Songs, Dances & Rituals of the American Shakers. (Illus.). 6.50 (ISBN 0-8446-1536-6). Peter Smith.

Bacon, Dolores, ed. Hymns That Every Child Should Know. 203p. 1980. Repr. of 1907 ed. lib. bdg. 25.00 (ISBN 0-89984-063-9). Century Bookbindery.

Banks, Louis A. Immortal Hymns & Their Story. LC 77-75198. 1977. Repr. of 1899 ed. lib. bdg. 30.00 (ISBN 0-89341-088-8). Longwood Pr.

Bausch, Michael & Duck, Ruth. Everflowing Streams. LC 81-701. 96p. (Orig.). 1981. pap. 3.95 (ISBN 0-8298-0428-5). Pilgrim NY.

Bay, Bill. Mel Bay's Deluxe Guitar Praise Book. 64p. (Orig.). 1973. pap. 1.95 (ISBN 0-89228-007-7). Impact Bks MO.

--Mel Bay's Guitar Hymnal. 80p. (Orig.). 1972. pap. 1.95 (ISBN 0-89228-009-3). Impact Bks MO.

Beckwith, Paul. Sounds. LC 73-84595. 72p. 1973. pap. 1.25 (ISBN 0-87784-551-4). Inter-Varsity.

Beckwith, Paul, et al, eds. Hymns II. LC 76-47503. 1976. text ed. 7.95 (ISBN 0-87784-898-X); pap. text ed. 6.95 (ISBN 0-87784-783-5); pap. text ed. 5.95 spiral text (ISBN 0-87784-750-9). Inter-Varsity.

Beierle, Herbert L. Song of the Spirit. 1978. 20.00 (ISBN 0-686-12735-8). U of Healing.

Bennett, Marian, ed. Songs for Preschool Children. LC 80-25091. 96p. 1981. pap. 5.95 (ISBN 0-87239-429-8, 5754). Standard Pub.

Blair, Mark & Blair, Carol. Best Loved Hymns Arranged for the Appalachian Dulcimer. LC 76-51465. (American Music Ser.). (Illus.). 1976. pap. 4.95 (ISBN 0-89461-001-5). Comm Pr Inc.

--Christmas & Easter Hymns Arranged for Appalachian Dulcimer. LC 79-53227. (American Music Ser.). (Illus.). 1979. pap. 4.95 (ISBN 0-89461-005-8). Comm Pr Inc.

Blattner, Elsie & Walker, Luisa, trs. Bosquejos Homileticos. (Spanish Bks.). 1979. 1.75 (ISBN 0-8297-0511-2). Life Pubs Intl.

Bly, Tacey, compiled by. Poems & Hymns of Christ's Sweet Singer: Frances Ridley Havergal. LC 77-86549. 1977. 7.95 (ISBN 0-87983-163-4); pap. 3.95 (ISBN 0-87983-164-2). Keats.

Bock, Fred & Leech, Bryan J., eds. The Hymnal Companion. 1979. 12.95 (ISBN 0-89477-004-7). Paragon Assocs.

--Hymns for the Family of God. 1976. 6.95 (ISBN 0-89477-000-4, Dist. by Alexandria House); looseleaf 5.00 (ISBN 0-89477-002-0); pap. 5.00 (ISBN 0-89477-001-2). Paragon Assocs.

Boring, Holland, ed. Songs of Hope. 1979. pap. 2.25 (ISBN 0-686-25230-6). Firm Foun Pub.

British Broadcasting Corporation. B B C Hymn Book. 1951. words & music 9.95x (ISBN 0-19-231301-0). Oxford U Pr.

Brunk, J. D., ed. Church & Sunday School Hymnal with Supplement. (532 hymns & songs, & 50 german songs, words only, 1902; supplement 1911). 1902. 5.50x (ISBN 0-8361-1110-9). Herald Pr.

Calvin, John. Six Psalms of John Calvin. Battles, Ford L., tr. 1977. pap. 1.95 (ISBN 0-8010-2400-5). Baker Bk.

Cantate Domino: An Ecumenical Hymn Book. full music ed. 376p. 1980. 19.50x (ISBN 0-19-143371-3). Oxford U Pr.

Carr, Sam, ed. Hymns As Poetry. 1980. 17.95 (ISBN 0-7134-3447-3). David & Charles.

Catholic Hymnal And Service Book Editorial Committee & Doherty, John T. Catholic Hymnal. (Orig.). 1966. pap. 1.50 (ISBN 0-02-640300-5, 64030). Glencoe.

Chapel Hymnal. 1944. 1.75 (ISBN 0-570-01017-9, 3-1004). Concordia.

Children's Hymnal. LC 55-1001. (gr. 3-6). 1955. 4.95 (ISBN 0-570-01002-0, 3-1052). Concordia.

Christian Hymns: No. 3. 3.00 (ISBN 0-89225-063-1). Gospel Advocate.

Christ-Janer, Albert, et al, eds. American Hymns Old & New: Notes on the Hymns & Biographies of the Authors & Composers, 2 vols. LC 79-4630. (Illus.). 1454p. 1980. 55.00 (ISBN 0-231-05148-4). Columbia U Pr.

The Church Hymnary: With Music. 3rd ed. 1055p. 1973. 18.50x (ISBN 0-19-146605-0). Oxford U Pr.

Cirou, Joseph, et al. The Johannine Hymnal. LC 75-14542. (Melody ed). 1970. 3.95 (ISBN 0-915866-00-5). Am Cath Pr.

Coffman, S. F., ed. Life Songs No. 2. (With Responsive Readings). 1938. 4.95x (ISBN 0-8361-1116-8). Herald Pr.

Cokesbury Worship Hymnal. 288p. 1976. 3.95 (ISBN 0-687-08863-1); pap. 1.95 (ISBN 0-687-08865-8); accompanist ed. 3.95 (ISBN 0-687-08866-6). Abingdon.

Davisson, A., ed. Kentucky Harmony: A Collection of Psalms, Tunes, Hymns & Anthems. 1976. 8.50 (ISBN 0-8066-1546-X, 11-9249). Augsburg.

Dearmer, Percy. Songs of Praise. Vaughan Williams, Ralph & Shaw, Martin, eds. Incl. Music Ed. rev. & enl. ed. 1932. 18.95x (ISBN 0-19-231207-3); enl. ed. 1931. 3.50x (ISBN 0-19-231205-7). Oxford U Pr.

De Lacey & O'Leary, trs. from Coptic. Fragmentary Coptic Hymns from the Wadi N Natrum: Part One Translation. 1973. pap. 4.00 (ISBN 0-686-08835-2). British Am Bks.

Dell'Isola, Frank. Moments with God: Hymns of Praise & Thanksgiving from the Bible. 1979. pap. 3.95 (ISBN 0-529-05668-2, FT5668). Collins Pubs.

Diehl, Katharine S. Hymns & Tunes: An Index. LC 66-13743. 1242p. 1979. lib. bdg. 45.00 (ISBN 0-8108-0062-4). Scarecrow.

Drillock, David, et al. Holy Week. (Music Ser.: Vol. I). 186p. (Orig.). 1980. 18.00 (ISBN 0-913836-67-2); pap. 14.00 (ISBN 0-913836-66-4). St Vladimirs.

Emurian, Ernest K. Living Stories of Famous Hymns. (Interlude Bks). 1971. pap. 3.45 (ISBN 0-8010-3260-1). Baker Bk.

English Hymnal. 1933. 18.50 (ISBN 0-19-231111-5); words only 7.95x (ISBN 0-19-231108-5). Oxford U Pr.

English Hymnal Service Book. 1962. 14.50x (ISBN 0-19-231120-4); words only 5.50x (ISBN 0-19-231121-2). Oxford U Pr.

English Praise: A Supplement to the English Hymnal, Full Music Edition. 1976. pap. 3.95x (ISBN 0-19-231126-3). Oxford U Pr.

Evening Light Songs. 512p. 4.50 (ISBN 0-686-29108-5). Faith Pub Hse.

Faber, Fredrick W. Hymns. 1977. Repr. of 1881 ed. 20.00 (ISBN 0-8274-4295-5). R West.

Favorite Hymns for Senior Adults. LC 77-80939. 1977. pap. 2.95 (ISBN 0-8054-3303-1). Broadman.

Ferntheil, Carol, ed. Songs of Cheer. (Illus.). 16p. (Orig.). 1979. pap. 0.85 (ISBN 0-87239-345-3, 7948). Standard Pub.

Foster, Stephen C. Biography, Songs, & Musical Compositions of Stephen C. Foster. LC 74-24086. Repr. of 1896 ed. 40.00 (ISBN 0-404-12915-3). AMS Pr.

Frost, Marjorie, ed. The Gift of Hymns. 1979. pap. 1.95 (ISBN 0-916642-12-7). Hope Pub.

Grieve, Nichol. The Scottish Metrical Psalter (1650) A Revision. 183p. pap. text ed. 3.75 (ISBN 0-567-02127-0). Attic Pr.

Hall, Frederick. Know Your Hymns Quiz Book. (Quiz & Puzzle Bks.). 1972. pap. 1.95 (ISBN 0-8010-4062-0). Baker Bk.

Hall, Roger L. The Stoughton Musical Society's Centennial Collection of Sacred Music. (Earlier American Music Ser.: No. 23). 304p. 1980. Repr. of 1878 ed. lib. bdg. 25.00 (ISBN 0-306-79618-X). Da Capo.

Harlow, Louis K. The World's Best Hymns. Churchill, J. W., ed. 1978. Repr. of 1893 ed. lib. bdg. 25.00 (ISBN 0-8495-2323-0). Arden Lib.

Harper, Jeanne & Pulkingham, Betty. The Sound of Living Waters: A Charismatic Hymnal. 1974. 6.95 (ISBN 0-8028-1581-2). Eerdmans.

Harvard University. Harvard University Hymn Book. LC 64-23297. 1964. 14.00x (ISBN 0-674-38000-2). Harvard U Pr.

Heaton, Charles H., ed. Hymnbook for Christian Worship. 1970. Red. 4.95x (ISBN 0-8272-8020-3). Blue (ISBN 0-8272-8021-1). Beige (ISBN 0-8272-8024-6). black leather pulpit ed. 17.50x (ISBN 0-8272-8023-8); spiral organist ed. 5.95x (ISBN 0-8272-8022-X); brown gift 6.50x (ISBN 0-8272-8027-0). Bethany Pr.

Henry, Victor. La Magie dans L'Inde Antique: Paris, 1904. LC 78-74261. (Oriental Religions Ser.: Vol. 5). 325p. 1980. lib. bdg. 33.00 (ISBN 0-8240-3903-3). Garland Pub.

Herron, Mike, et al. Psalms, Hymns & Spiritual Songs. 155p. 1980. pap. 8.75 (ISBN 0-914936-45-X). Bible Pr.

Himnos De Gloria y Triunfo. (Spanish Bks.). 1977. 3.75 (ISBN 0-8297-0567-8). Life Pubs Intl.

Himnos De Gloria y Triunfo; Sin Musica. (Spanish Bks.). 1977. 1.40 (ISBN 0-8297-0568-6). Life Pubs Intl.

Hogrogian, Nonny, illus. The Pearl: Hymn of the Robe of Glory. LC 79-66092. (Illus.). 1979. 7.95 (ISBN 0-89756-002-7). Two Rivers.

Hostetler, Lester & Yoder, Walter E., eds. Mennonite Hymnal. LC 69-18131. 1969. 6.95x (ISBN 0-87303-515-1). Faith & Life.

Hume, Alexander. Hymns & Sacred Songs. Repr. of 1599 ed. 15.50 (ISBN 0-384-24880-2). Johnson Repr.

Huntington, F. D. Hymns of the Ages, 3 vols. 1977. 300.00 (ISBN 0-8490-2031-X). Gordon Pr.

Hymn Book. 1981. vinyl bound 5.95 (ISBN 0-687-39120-2). Aberigdow.

Hymnal. 6.50 (ISBN 0-664-10033-3). Westminster.

Hymnal for Juniors in Worship & Study. 2.25 (ISBN 0-664-10082-1). Westminster.

Hymnbook for Christian Worship. red 4.95 (ISBN 0-8170-9018-5); blue 4.95 (ISBN 0-8170-9019-3); beige 4.95 (ISBN 0-8170-9020-7); per 100 (red,blue or beige) 425.00 (ISBN 0-686-76887-6); leather binding 12.50 (ISBN 0-8170-9022-3); organ ed. 4.95 (ISBN 0-8170-9021-5). Judson.

The Hymnbook: The Johannine Hymnal: Organ Ed. rev. ed. (Illus.). 1978. 24.95 (ISBN 0-915866-08-0). Am Cath Pr.

Hymnos De Gloria; Sin Musica. (Spanish Bks.). 1977. 1.10 (ISBN 0-8297-0566-X). Life Pubs Intl.

Hymnos De Gloria y Triunfo; Sin Musica. (Spanish Bks.). 1977. pap. 1.75 (ISBN 0-8297-0569-4). Life Pubs Intl.

Hymnos De Gloria y Triunfo; Sin Musica. (Spanish Bks.). 1977. 2.60 (ISBN 0-8297-0726-3). Life Pubs Intl.

Hymns & Songs of the Spirit. 1.95 (ISBN 0-8170-9017-7); 165.00, per hundred (ISBN 0-685-13646-9). Judson.

Hymns & Songs of the Spirit. 1966. 2.50 (ISBN 0-8272-8017-3). Bethany Pr.

Hymns for Creative Living. 2.50 (ISBN 0-8170-9009-6). Judson.

Hymns for Worship. 5.95 (ISBN 0-686-12671-8, BE-30); organist copy 15.00 (ISBN 0-686-12672-6). Evangel Indiana.

Hymns of Grace & Glory. 128p. (Orig.). 1976. pap. 3.95 (ISBN 0-687-18128-3). Abingdon.

Hymns of Grace & Truth. 3.75 (ISBN 0-87213-342-7); pap. 0.25 abr. word ed. (ISBN 0-87213-343-5). Loizeaux.

Hymns of the Christian Life. 698p. 1978. 8.95 (ISBN 0-87509-278-0). Chr Pubns.

Hyneman, Charles S., ed. Hymns Ancient & Modern for Use in the Services of the Church, with Accompanying Tunes. LC 74-24123. (Illus.). Repr. of 1909 ed. 150.00 (ISBN 0-404-12981-1). AMS Pr.

Jasper, Tony, ed. The Illustrated Family Hymn Book. (Illus.). 192p. 1980. 19.50 (ISBN 0-8164-0143-8); pap. 9.95 (ISBN 0-8164-2051-3). Seabury.
Lemmons, Reuel, ed. Hymns of Praise. 1978. pap. 4.25x (ISBN 0-686-25519-4). Firm Foun Pub.
--The Majestic Hymnal. 1959. 2.75x (ISBN 0-686-21485-4). Firm Foun Pub.
Leupold, Ulrich S. & Lehmann, Helmut T., eds. Luther's Works: Liturgy & Hymns, Vol. 53. LC 55-9893. 1965. 12.95 (ISBN 0-8006-0353-2, 1-353). Fortress.
Lodge, Ann, ed. Creation Sings. 1980. pap. 1.25 ea. (ISBN 0-664-10091-0); pkg. of 24 30.00 (ISBN 0-686-65966-X). Westminster.
Lund, Lynn S. Songs of Eternal Faith. LC 81-80954. 56p. (Orig.). 1981. pap. 5.95 (ISBN 0-88290-184-2, 2901). Horizon Utah.
Lyon, Lawrence A. Choral Settings for Six Lds Hymns. 56p. (Orig.). 1975. pap. 2.50 (ISBN 0-87747-605-5). Deseret Bk.
McNeil, Margaret C. Come Sing with Me. (ps). 1971. pap. 2.95 (ISBN 0-8170-0535-8); bk. & record o.p. 5.95 (ISBN 0-685-01111-9). Judson.
Mahadevan, T. M. The Hymns of Sankaras. (Illus.). 188p. 1980. text ed. 16.50 (ISBN 0-8426-1652-7). Verry.
Mennonite Youth Fellowship. Singing Together. rev. ed. 1966. pap. 0.60x (ISBN 0-8361-1127-3). Herald Pr.
Miller, Max B. & Drew, Louise C., eds. Sing of Life & Faith. LC 68-22233. (Illus.). (gr. k-6). 1969. 5.95 (ISBN 0-8298-0123-5). Pilgrim NY.
Mudditt, B. Howard, ed. Christian Worship (Hymns) 716p. 1976. Repr. text ed. 15.00x (ISBN 0-85364-194-3). Attic Pr.
New Baptist Hymnal. 3.50 (ISBN 0-8170-9011-8); 315.00, per hundred (ISBN 0-685-13648-5). Judson.
The New Saint Joseph Sunday Missal & Hymnal. complete ed. (Illus., References, Calendar,Bold Sense-Lines, Two Color Ordinary, Perpetual). red flexible vinyl 7.25 (ISBN 0-686-14305-1, 820/09); green cloth, colored edges 9.25 (ISBN 0-686-14306-X, 820/22-GN); black cloth hard bdg. 9.25 (ISBN 0-686-14307-8, 820/22-B); brown flexible bdg., colored edges 9.95 (ISBN 0-686-14308-6, 820/10-BN). Catholic Bk Pub.
Norton, Henry. Words & Music: People & Faith. 1978. 8.95 (ISBN 0-685-61607-X); pap. 5.95 (ISBN 0-685-61608-8). Maverick.
Olson, Nat. Hymns of Faith. Kuse, James A., ed. (Illus.). 1979. pap. 3.95 (ISBN 0-89542-066-X). Ideals.
Olson, Ruth L., ed. Hymns & Songs for Church Schools. LC 62-13898. (Illus.). 1962. 2.25 ea. (12-1500); 10-49 2.10 ea.; 50 or more 2.00 ea. Augsburg.
Osbeck, Kenneth W. One Hundred & One Hymn Stories. 288p. 1981. pap. 6.95 (ISBN 0-8254-3416-5). Kregel.
--Singing with Understanding: Including 101 Beloved Hymn Backgrounds. LC 78-19960. 1979. 11.95 (ISBN 0-8254-3414-9). Kregel.
--Teen-Age Praise. (Orig.). 1970. pap. 1.50 (ISBN 0-8254-3401-7). Kregel.
Pilgrim Hymnal. LC 58-1015. 1958. 6.00x (ISBN 0-8298-0107-3). Pilgrim NY.
Polack, W. G. The Handbook to the Lutheran Hymnal. 3rd rev. ed. 1975. Repr. of 1942 ed. lib. bdg. 13.95 (ISBN 0-8100-0003-2, 03-0700). Northwest Pub.
Porter, Ethel & Porter, Hugh. Pilgrim Hymnal. organist's ed. 596p. 8.00 (ISBN 0-686-70697-8). Pilgrim Pr.
Porter, Ethel & Porter, Hugh, eds. Pilgrim Hymnal. 596p. 1931. 6.50 (ISBN 0-8298-0107-3). Pilgrim Pr.
Poteat, Hubert M. Practical Hymnology. LC 72-1693. Repr. of 1921 ed. 14.50 (ISBN 0-404-09912-2). AMS Pr.
Reeves, J. B. The Hymn As Literature. 59.95 (ISBN 0-8490-0378-4). Gordon Pr.
Reynolds, William J. & Price, Milburn. A Joyful Sound: Christian Hymnody. 2nd ed. LC 77-12048. 1978. 19.95 (ISBN 0-03-040831-8, HoltC). HR&W.
Rizk, Helen S. Stories of the Christian Hymns. 64p. 1974. pap. 1.25 (ISBN 0-687-39614-X). Abingdon.
Rodeheaver, Homer A. Hymnal Handbook for Standard Hymns & Gospel Songs. LC 72-1686. Repr. of 1931 ed. 17.50 (ISBN 0-404-09913-0). AMS Pr.
Romero, Juan. Los Himnos De Juan Romero. (Spanish Bks.). (Span.). 1978. 1.95 (ISBN 0-8297-0878-2). Life Pubs Intl.
Ross, Joe. NESFA Hymnal. 2nd ed. pap. 6.00 (ISBN 0-915368-69-2). Nesfa Pr.
Sandford, Frank W., intro. by. Warrior Songs for the White Cavalry. 4th ed. 1979. 7.50 (ISBN 0-910840-14-8). Kingdom.
Schmidt, Orlando. Sing & Rejoice! LC 79-84367. 1979. 4.95x (ISBN 0-8361-1210-5); pap. 3.95x (ISBN 0-8361-1211-3). Herald Pr.
Shakers. A Collection of Millennial Hymns Adapted to the Present Order of the Church. LC 72-2991. (Communal Societies in America Ser). Repr. of 1847 ed. 17.00 (ISBN 0-404-10753-2). AMS Pr.
Sheppard, W. J. Great Hymns & Their Stories. lib. bdg. 69.95 (ISBN 0-87968-350-3). Gordon Pr.
Shiplett, Gary R. Worship & Hymnody. (Illus.). 122p. (Orig.). 1980. pap. text ed. 8.95 (ISBN 0-916260-08-9). A Meriwether.
Shull, Eva & Shull, Russell. CFO Songs. 1972. pap. 2.50 (ISBN 0-910924-53-8); pap. 3.95 spiral bdg. (ISBN 0-910924-54-6). Macalester.
Sievers, Eduard. Murbacher Hymnen, nach den Handschriften Herausgegeben. Repr. of 1874 ed. 23.00 (ISBN 0-384-55359-1). Johnson Repr.
Sizer, Sandra S. Gospel Hymns & Social Religion: The Rhetoric of Nineteenth-Century Revivalism. Davis, Allen F., ed. LC 78-10165. (American Civilization Ser.). 1978. lib. bdg. 19.50x (ISBN 0-87722-142-1). Temple U Pr.
Spiritual Life Songs. 0.95 (ISBN 0-687-39228-4). Abingdon.
Spurgeon, C. H. Spurgeon's Our Own Hymnbook. 1976. pap. 3.25 (ISBN 0-686-16839-9). Pilgrim Pubns.
Stauffer, J. Mark, ed. Our Hymns of Praise. (Illus.). (gr. 1-6). 1958. 3.75x (ISBN 0-8361-1126-5). Herald Pr.
Stevenson, Arthur L. Story of Southern Hymnology. LC 72-1676. Repr. of 1931 ed. 17.50 (ISBN 0-404-08334-X). AMS Pr.
Symeon. Hymns of Divine Love. Maloney, George, ed. 6.95 (ISBN 0-87193-061-7). Dimension Bks.
Szoverffy, Joseph. Iberian Hymnody: No. 1. 10.50 (ISBN 0-686-23379-4). Classical Folia.
--Peter Abelard's Hymnarius Paraclitensis: No. 2. 14.60 (ISBN 0-686-23380-8). Classical Folia.
Teddlie, Tillit S. Great Christian Hymnal. 1965. 3.00 (ISBN 0-89137-600-3). Quality Pubns.
Unity School of Christianity. Unity Song Selections. 1975. 2.95 (ISBN 0-87159-163-4). Unity Bks.
Wake, Arthur N. Companion to Hymnbook for Christian Worship. 1970. 8.95 (ISBN 0-8272-8025-4). Bethany Pr.
Willcocks, David, ed. Hymns for Choirs. 1976. pap. 5.00 (ISBN 0-19-353556-4). Oxford U Pr.
Winkworth, Catherine. The Choral Hymn Book for England. 59.95 (ISBN 0-87968-859-9). Gordon Pr.
Wither, George. Hymnes & Songs of the Church. (1623, 1881 Reprint 1967). 54.00 (ISBN 0-8337-3937-9). B Franklin.
World Church Congregational Music Committee. Hymns of the Saints. text ed. 9.50 (ISBN 0-8309-0326-7). Herald Hse.
Yoder, Walter E., ed. Junior Hymns. (149 hymns). 1947. 2.00x (ISBN 0-8361-1115-X). Herald Pr.
--Songs of the Church: Hymns & Sacred Songs. (274 songs). 1953. 4.95x (ISBN 0-8361-1129-X). Herald Pr.
Young, Carlton R., ed. Supplement to the Book of Hymns. 160p. (Orig.). 1981. pap. 3.95 (ISBN 0-687-03757-3); pap. 5.95 accompanist ed. (ISBN 0-687-03758-1). Abingdon.
Young, Carlton R., et al, eds. Ecumenical Praise. 1977. 12.95x (ISBN 0-916642-07-0). Hope Pub.

HYMNS–ACCOMPANIMENT

Now Songs: Contemporary Gospel Songs with Guitar Chords. Orig. Title: Gospel Song Book. 1969. pap. 2.50 (ISBN 0-687-28211-X). Abingdon.
Schoenhals, Lawrence R. Companion to Hymns of Faith & Life. (Orig.). 1980. pap. 9.95 (ISBN 0-89367-040-5). Light & Life.

HYMNS–BIBLIOGRAPHY

Dearmer, Percy. A Subject Index of Hymns in the English Hymnal & Songs of Praise. 59.95 (ISBN 0-8490-1159-0). Gordon Pr.
Hatfield, Edwin F. Poets of the Church: A Series of Biographical Sketches of Hymn-Writers, with Notes on Their Hymns. 1979. Repr. of 1884 ed. 74.00 (ISBN 0-8103-4291-X). Gale.
Metcalf, Frank J. American Psalmody. 2nd ed. LC 68-13274. (Music Reprint Ser). (Illus.). 1968. Repr. of 1917 ed. lib. bdg. 12.50 (ISBN 0-306-71132-X). Da Capo.
Warrington, James. Short Titles of Books Relating to or Illustrating the History & Practice of Psalmody in the U. S., 1620-1820. LC 77-178095. (American Classics in History & Social Science Ser.: No. 218). 102p. 1972. Repr. of 1898 ed. lib. bdg. 19.00 (ISBN 0-8337-5357-6). B Franklin.

HYMNS–CONCORDANCES

McDormand, Thomas B., et al. Judson Concordance to Hymns. 1975. 7.50 (ISBN 0-8170-0337-1). Judson.
Ronander, Albert C. & Porter, Ethel K. Guide to the Pilgrim Hymnal. LC 65-26448. 456p. 1966. 10.95 (ISBN 0-8298-0055-7). Pilgrim Pr.
Sheppard, W. L. Great Hymns & Their Stories. 1979. pap. 2.95 (ISBN 0-87508-492-3). Chr Lit.

HYMNS–DICTIONARIES, INDEXES, ETC.

Hustad, Donald P. & Shorney, George H, Jr. Dictionary-Handbook to Hymns for the Living Church. LC 77-75916. 1978. 12.95 (ISBN 0-916642-09-7). Hope Pub.
Julian, J., ed. A Dictionary of Hymnology: Origin & History of Christian Hymns, 4 vols. 1977. Set. lib. bdg. 600.00 (ISBN 0-8490-1719-X). Gordon Pr.
Julian, John. Dictionary of Hymnology, 2 vols. 1982. 120.00 (ISBN 0-8254-2960-9). Kregel.
Richardson, Alice M. Index to Stories of Hymns. LC 72-1690. Repr. of 1929 ed. 11.50 (ISBN 0-404-09911-4). AMS Pr.
Ross, Joe. NESFA Hymnal. 2nd ed. pap. 6.00 (ISBN 0-915368-69-2). Nesfa Pr.
Shaw, John M. The Poetry of Sacred Song. 1972. 3.00 (ISBN 0-686-27709-0). Friends Fla St.

HYMNS–HISTORY AND CRITICISM

see also Church Music; Hymn Writers

Athanassakis, Apostolos N., ed. The Orphic Hymns. LC 76-54179. (Society of Biblical Literature. Texts & Translation - Graeco-Roman Religion Ser.). (Illus.). 1977. pap. text ed. 7.50 (ISBN 0-89130-119-4, 060212). Scholars Pr Ca.
Bonner, Clint. Hymn Is Born. LC 59-9694. 1959. 7.95 (ISBN 0-8054-6801-3). Broadman.
Breed, David R. The History & Use of Hymns & Hymn Tunes. 59.95 (ISBN 0-8490-0313-X). Gordon Pr.
--The History & Use of Hymns & Hymn Tunes. LC 76-39525. Repr. of 1903 ed. 20.00 (ISBN 0-404-09906-8). AMS Pr.
Brock, Earl E. Devotional Interpretation of Familiar Hymns. facsimile ed. LC 72-93319. (Essay Index Reprint Ser). 1947. 12.00 (ISBN 0-8369-1395-7). Arno.
Butterworth, H. The Story of the Hymns. 59.95 (ISBN 0-8490-1139-6). Gordon Pr.
Butterworth, Hezekiah. Story of Hymns & Tunes. 1981. Repr. lib. bdg. 49.00 (ISBN 0-403-00107-2). Scholarly.
Cobb, Buell E., Jr. The Sacred Harp: A Tradition & Its Music. LC 76-12680. 248p. 1978. 12.50x (ISBN 0-8203-0426-3). U of Ga Pr.
Colquhoun, Frank. Hymns That Live. LC 81-1458. 320p. 1981. pap. 6.95 (ISBN 0-87784-473-9). Inter Varsity.
Dahle, John, ed. Library of Christian Hymns, 3 vols. in 2. LC 72-1649. Repr. of 1928 ed. 67.50 set (ISBN 0-404-13202-2). AMS Pr.
Dircks, Henry. Naturalistic Poetry, Selected from Psalms & Hymns of the Last Three Centuries: In Four Essays, Developing the Progress of Nature-Study, in Connection with Sacred Song. 1979. Repr. of 1872 ed. lib. bdg. 20.00 (ISBN 0-8482-0622-3). Norwood Edns.
Duffield, Samuel W. English Hymns: Their Authors & History. 1980. Repr. of 1886 ed. lib. bdg. 60.00 (ISBN 0-89341-441-7). Longwood Pr.
Egge, Mandus A. & Moede, Janet, eds. Hymns, How to Sing Them. (Orig.). 1966. pap. 1.75 (ISBN 0-8066-0634-7, 11-9204). Augsburg.
Emurian, Ernest K. Famous Stories of Inspiring Hymns. (Interlude Books). 186p. 1975. pap. 4.45 (ISBN 0-8010-3317-9). Baker Bk.
--Hymn Stories for Programs. (Paperback Program Ser). (gr. k-3). 1969. pap. 3.95 (ISBN 0-8010-3274-1). Baker Bk.
--Living Stories of Famous Hymns. (Interlude Bks). 1971. pap. 3.45 (ISBN 0-8010-3260-1). Baker Bk.
--Stories of Christmas Carols. (Paperback Program Ser). 1969. pap. 3.45 (ISBN 0-8010-3265-2). Baker Bk.
England, Martha W. & Sparrow, John. Hymns Unbidden: Donne, Herbert, Blake, Emily Dickinson & the Hymnographers. LC 66-28617. 1966. 8.00 (ISBN 0-87104-092-1). NY Pub Lib.
Foote, Henry W. Three Centuries of American Hymnody. 1968. Repr. of 1940 ed. 20.00 (ISBN 0-208-00576-5, Archon). Shoe String.
Frost, Maurice. English & Scottish Psalm & Hymn Tunes from Circa Fifteen Forty-Three to Sixteen Seventy-Seven. LC 72-181158. 531p. 1953. Repr. 35.00 (ISBN 0-403-01560-X). Scholarly.
George, Emery. Holderlin's "Ars Poetica". A Part-Rigorous Analysis of Information Structure in the Late Hymns. (De Proprietatibu Litterarum Ser. Practica: No. 32). text ed. 96.00x (ISBN 90-2792-381-7). Mouton.
Goodenough, Caroline L. High Lights on Hymnists & Their Hymns. LC 72-1626. Repr. of 1931 ed. 32.50 (ISBN 0-404-08310-2). AMS Pr.
Haworth, Peter. English Hymns & Ballads. 1927. lib. bdg. 15.00 (ISBN 0-8414-4975-9). Folcroft.
The History of Hymn Singing As Told Through One Hundred & One Famous Hymns. LC 79-65287. (Illus.). 224p. 1981. 14.95 (ISBN 0-87319-016-5). C Hallberg.
Horn, Dorothy D. Sing to Me of Heaven: A Study of Folk & Early American Materials in Three Old Harp Books. LC 74-99212. (Illus.). 1970. 10.00 (ISBN 0-8130-0293-1). U Presses Fla.
Idle, Christopher. Stories of Our Favorite Hymns. (Illus.). 80p. 1980. 10.95 (ISBN 0-8028-3535-X). Eerdmans.
Jackson, George P. White & Negro Spirituals, Their Life Span & Kinship. (Music Reprint Ser). (Illus.). xii, 349p. 1975. Repr. of 1944 ed. lib. bdg. 32.50 (ISBN 0-306-70667-9). Da Capo.
Jackson, George P., ed. Spiritual Folk-Songs of Early America. 8.50 (ISBN 0-8446-2297-4). Peter Smith.
Jones, F. A. Famous Hymns & Their Authors. 59.95 (ISBN 0-8490-0154-4). Gordon Pr.
Mc Cutchan, Robert G. Hymn Tune Names: Their Sources & Significance. Repr. of 1957 ed. 19.00 (ISBN 0-403-03608-9). Scholarly.
Metcalf, Frank J. American Writers & Compilers of Sacred Music. LC 66-24731. (Illus.). 1967. Repr. of 1925 ed. 10.00 (ISBN 0-8462-0876-8). Russell.
Ninde, Edward S. The Story of the American Hymn. LC 72-1708. (Illus.). Repr. of 1921 ed. 29.75 (ISBN 0-404-09914-9). AMS Pr.
Osbeck, Kenneth W. One Hundred & One Hymn Stories. 288p. 1981. pap. 6.95 (ISBN 0-8254-3416-5). Kregel.
Patterson, Daniel W. The Shaker Spiritual. LC 77-85557. (Illus.). 1979. text ed. 65.00 (ISBN 0-691-09124-2). Princeton U Pr.
Phelps, Austin, et al. Hymns & Choirs. LC 78-144671. Repr. of 1860 ed. 29.50 (ISBN 0-404-07207-0). AMS Pr.
Poling, David. Songs of Faith-Signs of Hope. LC 75-36184. 1976. 5.95 (ISBN 0-87680-408-3). Word Bks.
Pratt, Waldo S. Musical Ministries in the Church. LC 74-24193. Repr. of 1923 ed. 18.75 (ISBN 0-404-13095-X). AMS Pr.
Rest, Friedrich O. The Cross in Hymns. 1969. bds. 4.95 (ISBN 0-8170-0419-X). Judson.
Reynolds, William J. Hymns of Our Faith. LC 64-14049. 1964. 12.95 (ISBN 0-8054-6805-6). Broadman.
Reynolds, William J. & Price, Milburn. A Joyful Sound: Christian Hymnody. 2nd ed. LC 77-12048. 1978. 19.95 (ISBN 0-03-040831-8, HoltC). HR&W.
Routley, Erik. The English Carol. LC 73-9129. (Illus.). 272p. 1973. Repr. of 1959 ed. lib. bdg. 22.25x (ISBN 0-8371-6989-5, ROEC). Greenwood.
Sankey, Ira D. My Life & the Story of the Gospel Hymns & of Sacred Songs & Solos. LC 72-1682. Repr. of 1907 ed. 15.00 (ISBN 0-404-08332-3). AMS Pr.
Schroeder, M. J. Mary-Verse in "Meistergesang". (Catholic University Studies in German: No. 16). 1970. Repr. of 1942 ed. 23.50 (ISBN 0-404-50236-9). AMS Pr.
Spencer, Donald A. Hymn & Scripture Selection Guide. LC 76-48529. 1977. text ed. 7.95 (ISBN 0-8170-0705-9). Judson.
Tamke, Susan S. Make a Joyful Noise Unto the Lord: Hymns As a Reflection of Victorian Social Attitudes. LC 76-51693. 209p. 1978. 12.00x (ISBN 0-8214-0371-0); pap. text ed. 5.00x (ISBN 0-8214-0382-6). Ohio U Pr.
Wells, Amos R. Treasure of Hymns. facs. ed. LC 70-128330. (Essay Index Reprint Ser). 1945. 19.50 (ISBN 0-8369-2096-1). Arno.

HYMNS–JUVENILE LITERATURE

Bunyan, John. A Book for Boys & Girls: Or Country Rhymes for Children. Lurie, Alison & Sciller, Justin G., eds. Incl. Divine Songs. Watts, Isaac; Moral Songs Composed for the Use of Children. Foxton, Thomas. LC 75-32136. (Classics of Children's Literature Ser., 1621-1932). 1978. PLB 38.00 (ISBN 0-8240-2253-X). Garland Pub.
Ford, Bud & Ford, Donna. The Dulcimer Hymn Book. 72p. 1979. wkbk 4.95 (ISBN 0-89228-054-9). Impact Bks MO.
Griffin, Steve. Children's Guitar Hymnal. 32p. 1978. wkbk 1.95 (ISBN 0-89228-052-2). Impact Bks MO.
Peterson, Meg. Hymns for Auto Harp. 56p. 1978. wkbk 3.95 (ISBN 0-89228-053-0). Impact Bks MO.

HYMNS, ASSYRO-BABYLONIAN

Clay, Albert T. Epics, Hymns, Omens & Other Texts. LC 78-63519. (Babylonian Records in the Library of J. Pierpont Morgan: 4). Repr. of 1923 ed. 30.00 (ISBN 0-404-60124-3). AMS Pr.
Schollmeyer, Anastasius, ed. Sumerisch - Babylonische Hymnen und Gebete an Samas. Repr. of 1912 ed. pap. 9.50 (ISBN 0-384-54240-9). Johnson Repr.

HYMNS, ASSYRO-BABYLONIAN–HISTORY AND CRITICISM

Cumming, Charles G. Assyrian & Hebrew Hymns of Praise. LC 34-3318. (Columbia University. Oriental Studies: No. 12). Repr. of 1934 ed. 16.50 (ISBN 0-404-50502-3). AMS Pr.

HYMNS, BYZANTINE

see Hymns, Greek

HYMNS, GERMAN

see also Chorale; Chorales

Gesangbuch: Seven-Hundred Thirty German Songs Without Notes, No. 105. 1918. painted edge 8.95x (ISBN 0-8361-1145-1, 105). Herald Pr.

Liedersammlung, 2 vols. Incl. Vol. B. Collection of 148 German Hymns Without Notes. 1917. 2.95x (ISBN 0-8361-1144-3); Vol. G. Collection of 317 German Hymns Without Notes. 3.50x (ISBN 0-8361-1163-X). Repr. of 1928 ed. Herald Pr.

Seipt, A. A. Schwenkfelder Hymnology. LC 77-134414. Repr. of 1909 ed. 14.50 (ISBN 0-404-09908-4). AMS Pr.

HYMNS, GREEK

Kambylis, Athanasios, ed. Symeon Neos Theologos, Hymnen Einleitung und kritischer Text. (Supplementa Byzantina, Vol. 3). 1976. 309.00x (ISBN 3-11-004888-4). De Gruyter.

Schwartz, Benjamin & Athanassakis, Apostolos N., eds. The Judaeo-Greek Hymns of Jannina. Schwartz, Benjamin & Athanassakis, Apostolos N., trs. Date not set. price not set (ISBN 0-918618-06-1). Pella Pub.

Tillyard, Henry J. Byzantine Music & Hymnography. LC 74-24242. Repr. of 1923 ed. 11.50 (ISBN 0-404-13116-6). AMS Pr.

Wellesz, Egon. History of Byzantine Music & Hymnography. 2nd ed. 1961. 49.95x (ISBN 0-19-816111-5). Oxford U Pr.

Ziehn, Bernhard. The Doric Hymns of Mesomedes. 1979. pap. 1.75 (ISBN 0-686-66047-1). Newberry.

HYMNS, HINDU

see Hindu Hymns

HYMNS, LATIN

Analecta Hymnica Medii Aevi, Vols. 1-55. 1886-1922. Set. 2750.00 (ISBN 0-685-13342-7). Johnson Repr.

Blume, Clemens, ed. Hymnodia Gotica. Repr. of 1909 ed. 50.00 ea. Vol. 1. (ISBN 0-384-04766-1); Vol. 2. (ISBN 0-384-04767-X). Johnson Repr.

--Thesauri Hymnologica Hymnarium, 2 Vols. Repr. of 1909 ed. 50.00 ea. Johnson Repr.

--Thesauri Hymnologica Prosarium, 2 Vols in 3. (Illus.). Repr. of 1922 ed. 50.00 ea. Johnson Repr.

Boncore Di Santa Vittoria. Boncore Di Santa Victoria Novus Liber Hymnorum Ac Orationum. Repr. of 1903 ed. 50.00 (ISBN 0-384-12867-X). Johnson Repr.

Dreves, Guido M., ed. Cantiones Bohemicae. 1886. 50.00 (ISBN 0-384-12860-2). Johnson Repr.

--Cantiones et Muteti, 3 vols. (Illus.). 1895-1904. 50.00 ea. (ISBN 0-384-12865-3). Johnson Repr.

--Historiae Rhythmicae, 8 Vols. 1889-1904. 50.00 ea. (ISBN 0-384-12880-7). Johnson Repr.

--Hymni Inediti, 7 Vols. 1888-1903. 50.00 ea. Johnson Repr.

--Hymnodia Hiberica: Liturgische Reimofficien, Aus Spanischen Brevieren. (Illus.). 1894. 50.00 (ISBN 0-384-12915-3). Johnson Repr.

--Hymnodia Hiberica: Spanische Hymnen Des Mittelalters. 1894. 50.00 (ISBN 0-384-12920-X). Johnson Repr.

--Pia Dictamina, 7 Vols. 1893-1905. 50.00 ea. (ISBN 0-384-12950-1). Johnson Repr.

--Psalteria Rhythmica, 2 Vols. 1900-01. 50.00 ea. Johnson Repr.

Moissac France Benedictine Abbey. Hymnarius Moissiancensis. 1888. 50.00 (ISBN 0-384-39520-1). Johnson Repr.

Stocklin, Ulrich V. Psalteria Wessofontana. Dreves, Guido M., ed. Repr. of 1902 ed. 50.00 (ISBN 0-384-58320-2). Johnson Repr.

--Udalricus Wessofontanus. Dreves, Guido M., ed. Repr. of 1889 ed. 50.00 (ISBN 0-384-58330-X). Johnson Repr.

HYMNS, LATIN-HISTORY AND CRITICISM

Duffield, Samuel W. The Latin Hymn-Writers & Their Hymns. 1980. Repr. of 1889 ed. lib. bdg. 50.00 (ISBN 0-89341-440-9). Longwood Pr.

Messenger, Ruth E. Ethical Teachings in the Latin Hymns of Medieval England. LC 30-20975. (Columbia University. Studies in the Social Sciences: No. 321). Repr. of 1930 ed. 18.50 (ISBN 0-404-51321-2). AMS Pr.

HYMNS, SANSKRIT

Advaita Ashrama Staff, ed. Altar Flowers: A Bouquet of Choicest Sanskrit Hymns. (Eng. & Sanskrit). 1974. pap. 2.95 (ISBN 0-87481-101-5). Vedanta Pr.

Le Mee, Jean, tr. Hymns from the Rig-Veda. 1975. pap. 5.95 (ISBN 0-394-73055-0). Knopf.

Sanskrit Mantras. 1977. 10.00x (ISBN 0-930736-03-6); cassett tape recording incl. (ISBN 0-685-32618-7). E W Cultural Ctr.

SYDA Foundation, ed. El Nectar Del Canto: Transliteration of Sanskrit Chants. (Illus.). 1981. 5.95 (ISBN 0-686-73883-7). SYDA Found.

S.Y.D.A. Foundation, ed. Nectar of Chanting: Transliteration of Sanskrit Chants. (Illus.). 138p. 1978. text ed. 5.25 (ISBN 0-914602-16-0); pap. text ed. 3.75 (ISBN 0-914602-10-1). SYDA Found.

HYMNS, SIKH

see Sikh Hymns

HYMNS, SPANISH

see also Alabados

Eck, Ellen, tr. from Eng. Himnos de la Vida Cristiana. 1980. write for info. (ISBN 0-87509-277-2); pap. write for info. (ISBN 0-87509-275-6). Chr Pubns.

Himnario Cristiano. (Span.). 5.95x (ISBN 0-8361-1198-2). Herald Pr.

Himnos De Gloria. 150p. pap. 0.75 (ISBN 0-686-29116-6). Faith Pub Hse.

McConnell, Cecil. Conozcamos Nuestro Himnario. 1980. pap. 2.95 (ISBN 0-311-32432-0). Casa Bautista.

Szoverffy, Joseph. Iberian Hymnody: No. 1. 10.50 (ISBN 0-686-23379-4). Classical Folia.

HYMNS, SUMERIAN

Cohen, Mark E. Sumerian Hymnology: The Ersemma. Date not set. 18.75x (ISBN 0-87820-601-9). Ktav.

Klein, Jacob. Royal Hymns of Shulgi, King of Ur: Man's Quest for Immortal Fame. LC 81-65929. (Transactions Ser.: Vol. 71, Pt. 7.). 1981. 6.00 (ISBN 0-87169-717-3). Am Philos.

Schollmeyer, Anastasius, ed. Sumerisch - Babylonische Hymnen und Gebete an Samas. Repr. of 1912 ed. pap. 9.50 (ISBN 0-384-54240-9). Johnson Repr.

Sjoberg, A. W. & Bergmann, E. Sumerian Hymns to Temples. LC 66-25697. 20.00 (ISBN 0-685-71733-X). J J Augustin.

Vanderburgh, Frederick A., ed. Sumerian Hymns from Cuneiform Texts in the British Museum. LC 68-23118. (Columbia University. Contributions to Oriential History & Philology: No. 1). Repr. of 1908 ed. 14.00 (ISBN 0-404-50531-7). AMS Pr.

HYMNS, SUMERIAN-HISTORY AND CRITICISM

Stummer, Friedrich. Summerisch - Akkadische Parallelen Zum Aufbau Alttestamentlicher Psalmen. Repr. of 1922 ed. pap. 12.50 (ISBN 0-384-58710-0). Johnson Repr.

HYMNS, YIDDISH

Union Hymnal: Songs & Prayers for Jewish Worship, Pt. 2. 1964. Repr. 3.50 (ISBN 0-916694-15-1). Central Conf.

HYPERACTIVITY

see Hyperkinesia

HYPERBARIC OXYGENATION

Innes, G. S., ed. The Production & Hazards of a Hyperbaric Oxygen Environment: Proceedings. 1970. 19.50 (ISBN 0-08-006767-0). Pergamon.

International Conference On Hyperbaric Medicine - 3rd - Durham - N. C. - 1965. Proceedings. Brown, Ivan W. & Cox, Barbara G., eds. 1966. 16.00 (ISBN 0-309-01404-2). Natl Acad Pr.

Pittinger, Charls B. Hyperbaric Oxygenation. (American Lecture Anesthesiology). (Illus.). 128p. 1966. photocopy ed. spiral 12.75 (ISBN 0-398-01493-0). C C Thomas.

HYPERBOLIC FUNCTIONS

see Functions, Exponential

HYPERBOLIC GEOMETRY

see Geometry, Hyperbolic

HYPERBOREAN LANGUAGES

see also Eskimo Language

Bogoraz, Vladimir G. Koryak Texts. LC 73-3540. (American Ethnological Society. Publications: No. 5). Repr. of 1917 ed. 16.75 (ISBN 0-404-58155-2). AMS Pr.

HYPERBOREANS

see Arctic Races

HYPERCINESIA

see Hyperkinesia

HYPERDULIA

see Mary, Virgin-Cultus

HYPERFINE INTERACTIONS

Deutch, B. I., et al, eds. Hyperfine Interactions. 1977. 68.50 (ISBN 0-7204-0452-5, North-Holland). Elsevier.

Freeman, Arthur J. & Frankel, Richard B. Hyperfine Interactions. 1967. 55.50 (ISBN 0-12-266750-6). Acad Pr.

Goldring, Gvirol & Kalish, Rafael. Hyper Interactions of Excited Nuclei. 4 vols. LC 78-127883. (Illus.). 1378p. 1971. Set. 297.50x (ISBN 0-677-14600-0); 83.75x ea. Vol. 1 (ISBN 0-677-15120-9). Vol. 2 (ISBN 0-677-15130-6). Vol. 3 (ISBN 0-677-15140-3). Vol. 4 (ISBN 0-677-15150-0). Gordon.

Raghavan, R. S. & Murnick, D. E., eds. Hyperfine Interactions IV: Proceedings of the Fourth International Conference on Hyperfine Interactions, Madison, N.J., U.S.A. June 1977. 1978. 50.00 (ISBN 0-444-85151-8, North-Holland). Elsevier.

HYPERGAMMAGLOBULINEMIA

Waldenstrom, Jan G. Monoclonal & Polyclonal Hypergammaglobulinemia: Clinical & Biological Significance. LC 67-12380. (Abraham Flexner Lectures in Medicine for 1965, No. 15). (Illus.). 1968. 6.95x (ISBN 0-8265-1111-2, Co-Pub. by Cambridge U Pr). Vanderbilt U Pr.

HYPERGEOMETRIC FUNCTIONS

see Functions, Hypergeometric

HYPERION (RACE HORSE)

Graham, Clive. Hyperion, Classic Race Horse Sire. (Illus.). 25.00x (ISBN 0-87556-107-1). Saifer.

HYPERKINESIA

Alabiso, Frank P. & Hansen, James C. The Hyperactive Child in the Classroom. 336p. 1977. ed. spiral bdg. 24.75photocopy (ISBN 0-398-03550-4). C C Thomas.

Barkley, Russell. Hyperactive Children: A Handbook for Diagnosis & Treatment. LC 81-1382. 500p. 1981. 25.00 (ISBN 0-89862-609-9). Guilford Pr.

Bittinger, Marvin L., ed. Living with Our Hyperactive Children: Parents' Own Stories. (Illus.). 1977. 8.95 (ISBN 0-8467-0275-4, Pub. by Two Continents). Hippocrene Bks.

Bosco, James J. & Robin, Stanley S. The Hyperactive Child & Stimulant Drugs. LC 76-57934. 1977. 12.00x (ISBN 0-226-06661-4). U of Chicago Pr.

Connors, C. Keith. Food Additives for Hyperactive Children. 180p. 1980. 18.50 (ISBN 0-306-40400-1, Plenum Pr). Plenum Pub.

Cratty, Bryant J. Remedial Motor Activity for Children. LC 74-26973. (Illus.). 327p. 1975. text ed. 13.50 (ISBN 0-8121-0513-3). Lea & Febiger.

Cruickshank, William. A Teaching Method for Brain-Injured & Hyperactive Children: A Demonstration-Pilot Study. LC 81-6255. (Syracuse University Special Education & Rehabilitation Monograph: No. 6). (Illus.). xxi, 576p. 1981. Repr. of 1961 ed. lib. bdg. 45.00x (ISBN 0-313-23071-4, CRTC). Greenwood.

Feingold, Ben. Why Your Child Is Hyperactive. 8.95 (ISBN 0-686-29919-1). Cancer Bk Hse.

Feingold, Ben F. Why Your Child Is Hyperactive. LC 74-9078. 1974. 9.95 (ISBN 0-394-49343-5, Co-Pub by Bookworks). Random.

Feingold, Helene & Feingold, Ben. The Feingold Cookbook for Hyperactive Children & Others with Problems Associated with Food Additives & Salicylates. 1979. 10.95 (ISBN 0-394-41232-X); pap. 5.95 (ISBN 0-394-73664-8). Random.

Fine, M. J. Intervention with Hyperactive Children: A Case Study Approach. (Illus.). 215p. 1980. 20.00 (ISBN 0-89335-113-X). Spectrum Pub.

Fine, Marvin J. Principles & Techniques of Intervention with Hyperactive Children. (Illus.). 328p. 1977. 29.50 (ISBN 0-398-03570-9). C C Thomas.

Gadow, Kenneth D. & Loney, Jan, eds. Psychosocial Aspects of Drug Treatment for Hyperactivity. (AAAS Selected Symposium: No. 44). 460p. 1981. lib. bdg. 30.00x (ISBN 0-89158-834-5). Westview.

Gittelman, Martin, ed. Strategic Intervention for Hyperactive Children. 224p. 1981. 20.00 (ISBN 0-87332-202-9). M E Sharpe.

Heiting, Kenneth. When Your Child Is Hyperactive. LC 78-73015. (When Bks). (Illus., Orig.). 1979. pap. 2.45 (ISBN 0-87029-142-4, 20227). Abbey.

Lahey, Benjamin B., ed. Behavior Therapy with Hyperactive & Learning Disabled Children. (Illus.). 1979. text ed. 16.95x (ISBN 0-19-502478-8); pap. text ed. 8.95x (ISBN 0-19-502479-6). Oxford U Pr.

Millicap, J. Gordon. The Hyperactive Child with Minimal Brain Dysfunction. (Illus.). 1975. 16.95 (ISBN 0-8151-5911-0). Year Bk Med.

Minde, K. A Parent's Guide to Hyperactivity. 1972. pap. 1.95x (ISBN 0-88432-011-1). J Norton Pubs.

Piazza, Robert, ed. Readings in Hyperactivity. (Special Education Ser.). (Illus.). 1979. pap. text ed. 10.95 (ISBN 0-89568-107-2). Spec Learn Corp.

Renshaw, Domeena C. The Hyperactive Child. LC 73-86936. 1974. 15.95x (ISBN 0-911012-76-1). Nelson-Hall.

--The Hyperactive Child. 1975. pap. 3.95 (ISBN 0-316-74030-6). Little.

Robin, Stanley S. & Bosco, James J. Parent, Teacher & Physician in the Life of the Hyperactive Child: The Coherence of the Social Environment. 164p. 1981. 16.75 (ISBN 0-398-04528-3). C C Thomas.

Ross, Dorothea M. & Ross, Sheila A. Hyperactivity: Research, Theory & Action. LC 76-5227. (Personality Processes Ser.). 480p. 1976. 32.95 (ISBN 0-471-73678-3, Pub. by Wiley-Interscience). Wiley.

Roth, June. Cooking for Your Hyperactive Child. 1978. pap. 6.95 (ISBN 0-8092-7408-6). Contemp Bks.

Safer, Daniel J. & Allen, Richard P. Hyperactive Children: Diagnosis & Management. (Illus.). 1976. 12.95 (ISBN 0-8391-0757-9). Univ Park.

Schrag & Divoky. The Myth of the Hyperactive Child. 1976. pap. 2.25 (ISBN 0-440-36194-X, LE). Dell.

Stevens, Laura J. & Stevens, George E. How to Feed Your Hyperactive Child. LC 76-23799. 1977. 7.95 (ISBN 0-385-12465-1). Doubleday.

Stewart, Mark A. & Olds, Sally W. Raising a Hyperactive Child. LC 72-79696. (Illus.). 312p. 1973. 12.95 (ISBN 0-06-014121-2, HarpT). Har-Row.

Sugarman, Gerald I. & Stone, Margaret. Your Hyperactive Child. 168p. 1976. pap. 4.95 (ISBN 0-8092-8058-2). Contemp Bks.

Taylor, John F. The Hyperactive Child & the Family: The Complete What-to-Do Handbook. LC 79-56871. 256p. 1980. 12.95 (ISBN 0-89696-080-3). Everest Hse.

Trites, R. Hyperactivity in Children. 1979. 24.50 (ISBN 0-8391-1400-1). Univ Park.

Walker, Sydney, 3rd. Help for the Hyperactive Child. 1978. 8.95 (ISBN 0-395-25722-0). HM.

Wender, Paul & Wender, Estelle. The Hyperactive Child & the Learning Disabled Child. 1978. 6.95 (ISBN 0-517-53473-8). Crown.

Whalen, Carol K. & Henker, Barbara, eds. Hyperactive Children: The Social Ecology of Identification & Treatment. LC 80-324. 1980. 25.00 (ISBN 0-12-745950-2). Acad Pr.

Winchell, Carol A., compiled by. The Hyperkinetic Child: An Annotated Bibliography, 1974 to 1979. LC 81-6200. (Contemporary Problems of Childhood Ser.: No.4). (Illus.). 488p. 1981. lib. bdg. 35.00 (ISBN 0-313-21452-2, WHCS/). Greenwood.

Winchell, Carol Ann. The Hyperkinetic Child. LC 74-28527. 178p. 1975. lib. bdg. 15.00 (ISBN 0-8371-7813-4, WMC/). Greenwood.

HYPERLIPEMIA

Buchwald, Henry, et al. Surgical Treatment of Hyperlipidemia. 35p. 1974. 1.00 (ISBN 0-87493-037-5, 73-314A). Am Heart.

Casdorph, Herman R. Treatment of the Hyperlipidemic States. (Illus.). 464p. 1971. ed. spiral bdg. 44.50photocopy (ISBN 0-398-02255-0). C C Thomas.

Fumagalli, Remo, et al, eds. Human Hyperlipoproteinemias: Principles & Methods. LC 73-16295. (Advances in Experimental Medicine & Biology Ser.: Vol. 38). 292p. 1973. 29.50 (ISBN 0-306-39038-8, Plenum Pr). Plenum Pub.

Paoletti, Rodolfo, ed. Therapeutic Selectivity & Risk-Benefit Assessment of Hypolipidemic Drugs. 1981. text ed. 31.00 (ISBN 0-89004-649-2). Raven.

Rifkind, Basil M. & Levy, Robert I., eds. Hyperlipidemia: Diagnosis & Therapy. (Clinical Cardiology Monographs). (Illus.). 416p. 1977. 57.00 (ISBN 0-8089-1006-X). Grune.

HYPERNASALITY

Massengill, Raymond, Jr. Hypernasality: Considerations in Causes & Treatment Procedures. (Illus.). 152p. 1972. photocopy ed. spiral 13.75 (ISBN 0-398-02353-0). C C Thomas.

HYPERPARATHYROIDISM

Bruining. Surgical Treatment of Hyperparathyroidism. 1971. 13.00x (ISBN 90-232-0908-7, Pub by Van Gorcum). Intl Schol Bk Serv.

Johnston, D. A. Surgical Aspects of Hyperparathyroidism. (Illus.). 1977. text ed. write for info (ISBN 0-7216-5190-9). Saunders.

Paloyan, Edward, et al. Hyperparathyroidism. LC 73-8626. (Modern Surgical Monographs). (Illus.). 232p. 1973. 41.00 (ISBN 0-8089-0705-0). Grune.

HYPERSENSITIVITY, CONTACT

see Contact Dermatitis

HYPERSONIC AERODYNAMICS

see Aerodynamics, Hypersonic

HYPERSPACE

see also Hilbert Space; Polytopes; Spaces, Generalized

Eckhart, Ludwig. Four-Dimensional Space. Bigelow, Arthur L. & Slaby, Steve M., trs. LC 68-27343. (Illus.). 96p. 1968. 7.50x (ISBN 0-253-32435-1). Ind U Pr.

Gelfand, I. M., et al. Coordinate Method. (Pocket Mathematical Library Ser.). 1968. 18.75x (ISBN 0-677-20640-2). Gordon.

Hinton, Charles H. Speculations on the Fourth Dimension: Selected Writings of C. H. Hinton. Rucker, Rudolf V., ed. (Illus.). 1980. pap. 4.00 (ISBN 0-486-23916-0). Dover.

Nadler, Sam B. Hyperspace of Sets: A Text with Research Questions. (Pure & Applied Ser.: Vol. 49). 1978. 55.00 (ISBN 0-8247-6768-3). Dekker.

Rucker, Rudolf v. B. Geometry, Relativity & the Fourth Dimension. LC 76-22240. 1977. lib. bdg. 9.50x (ISBN 0-88307-584-9). Gannon.

HYPERSUSCEPTIBILITY

see Anaphylaxis

HYPERTENSION

see also Portal Hypertension; Renal Hypertension

Abboud, Francois M., ed. Mechanics of Hypertension. (Hypertension Ser: Vol. 18). pap. 5.00 (ISBN 0-87493-001-4, 73-209A). Am Heart.

Advice About First Aid, High Blood Pressure, Heart Attack. (Home Adviser Ser.). 80p. (Orig.). 1981. pap. 1.95 (ISBN 0-8326-2404-7, 7054). Delair.

Alderman, Michael H., ed. Hypertension: The Nurse's Role in Ambulatory Care. LC 77-22259. (Illus.). 1977. text ed. 12.50 (ISBN 0-8261-2370-8). Springer Pub.

Auer, L. The Pathogenesis of Hypertensive Encephalography. (Acta Neurochirurgica: Supplementum 27). (Illus.). 1978. pap. 44.90 (ISBN 0-387-81490-6). Springer-Verlag.

Babayan, E. A., et al, eds. Modern Approaches to the Treatment of Hypertension. 1976. 15.00 (ISBN 3-8055-2400-5). S Karger.

Beller, Fritz & MacGillivray, Ian, eds. Hypertensive Disorders in Pregnancy. LC 78-24680. (Illus.). 108p. 1979. text ed. 18.50 (ISBN 0-88416-262-1). Wright-PSG.

Benson, Herbert & Klipper, Miriam Z. The Relaxation Response. 1976. pap. 2.50 (ISBN 0-380-00676-6, 50955). Avon.

Bianchi, G. The Kidney in Arterial Hypertension. 181p. pap. text ed. 24.50 (ISBN 0-8391-1482-6). Univ Park.

Birkenhager, W. H. & Schalekamp, M. A. Control Mechanisms in Essential Hypertension. 1976. 43.00 (ISBN 0-444-41452-5). Elsevier.

Blaufox, M. Donald & Bianchi, Claudio, eds. Secondary Forms of Hypertension: Current Diagnosis & Management. (Illus.). 341p. 1981. 20.00 (ISBN 0-8089-1384-0, 790614). Grune.

Bonnar, J. Pregnancy Hypertension. 597p. text ed. 49.50 (ISBN 0-686-72923-4). Univ Park.

Brams, William A. Living with Your High Blood Pressure. LC 72-85751. (Illus.). pap. 1.75 (ISBN 0-668-04286-9, 4286). Arco.

Brunner & Gravas. Clinical Hypertension & Hypotension. (Kidney Disease Ser.: Vol. 2). 1982. price not set (ISBN 0-8247-1279-X). Dekker.

Buckley, Joseph P. & Ferrario, Carlos, eds. Central Nervous System Mechanisms in Hypertension. (Perspectives in Cardiovascular Research Ser.: Vol. 6). 432p. 1981. 38.50 (ISBN 0-89004-545-3). Raven.

Caplan, Robert D., et al. Adhering to Medical Regimens: Pilot Experiments in Patient Education & Social Support. LC 76-620035. 284p. 1976. pap. 10.00 (ISBN 0-87944-207-7). Inst Soc Res.

Case, David, et al, eds. Captopril & Hypertension. (Topics in Cardiovascular Disease Ser.). 230p. 1980. 23.50 (ISBN 0-306-40532-6, Plenum Pr). Plenum Pub.

Chaithiraphan, S. Current Concept in the Therapy of Hypertension with Beta-Blockers. (Journal: Cardiology Ser.: Vol. 66, Suppl. 1). (Illus.). vi, 62p. 1980. pap. 19.50 (ISBN 3-8055-0912-X). S Karger.

Chan, James C., ed. Hypertension, Steroid & Mineral Metabolsim: Festschrift to Frederic C. Bartter. (Nephron: Vol. 23, No. 2). (Illus.). 1979. pap. 22.25 (ISBN 3-8055-3001-3). S Karger.

Chewning, Betty. Staff Manual for Teaching Patients About Hypertension. LC 78-27337. (Illus.). 340p. 1979. pap. 37.75 (ISBN 0-87258-251-5, 1319). Am Hospital.

Clinical Research Institute of Montreal Symposium. Hypertension Nineteen Seventy Two: Proceedings. Genest, J. & Koiw, E., eds. (Illus.). 635p. 1972. pap. 64.90 (ISBN 0-387-05755-2). Springer-Verlag.

Cohn, Jay N., ed. Hypertension: Neural, Vascular & Hormonal Factors. LC 66-7606. (Hypertension Ser.: Vol. 24). 1976. pap. 3.00 (ISBN 0-87493-048-0, 73-215A). Am Heart.

--Hypertension XXV: Hypertension - Experimental & Clinical Studies. LC 77-76010. (Circulation Research Journal Suppl.: Vol. 40, No. 5). 1977. pap. 4.00 (ISBN 0-87493-053-7, 73-216A). Am Heart.

--Hypertension XXVI. (AHA Monograph: No. 58). 1978. 5.00 (ISBN 0-87493-024-3, 73-044-A). Am Heart.

Council for High Blood Pressure. Hypertension in Man & Animals. Hunt, James C., ed. (Hypertension Ser.: Vol. 21). 1973. pap. 5.00 (ISBN 0-87493-034-0, 73-212A). Am Heart.

Council for High Blood Research, 1972. Blood Pressure - Regulation & Control: Proceedings. Hunt, James C., ed. (Hypertension Ser.: Vol. 20). 1972. pap. 5.00 (ISBN 0-87493-026-X, 73-211A). Am Heart.

Council on High Blood Pressure Research - American Heart Association Cleveland, Oct. 19, 20, 1973. Hypertension: Peptides, Lipids, Electrolytes & Hypertension. Hunt, James C., ed. 225p. 1974. 5.00 (ISBN 0-87493-038-3, 73-213A). Am Heart.

Cruickshank, J. M., et al, eds. Atenolol & Renal Function. (Royal Society of Medicine International Congress & Symposium Ser.: No. 19). 112p. 1980. pap. 18.50 (ISBN 0-8089-1237-2). Grune.

Davis, James O. & Laragh, John H., eds. Hypertension: Mechanisms, Diagnosis & Management. (Illus.). 288p. 1977. text ed. 18.95 (ISBN 0-913800-07-4). HP Pub Co.

D'Cruz, Fvan C. All About High Blood Pressure. 224p. 1979. 15.00x (ISBN 0-86125-006-0, Pub. by Orient Longman India). State Mutual Bk.

De Jong, W., ed. Hypertension & Brain Mechanisms. 1977. 69.50 (ISBN 0-444-41534-3, North Holland). Elsevier.

Detecting & Controlling Hypertension. 1976. 3.00 (ISBN 0-917330-13-7). Am Pharm Assn.

Doyle, Austin. Pharmacological & Therapeutic Aspects of Hypertension, Vol. III. LC 78-27898. 1980. cancelled (ISBN 0-8493-5387-4). CRC Pr.

Doyle, Austin E. Pharmacological & Therapeutic Aspects of Hypertension. LC 78-27898. 232p. 1980. Vol. 1, 224p. 64.95 (ISBN 0-8493-5385-8); Vol. 2, 256p. 69.95 (ISBN 0-8493-5386-6). CRC Pr.

Elias, Merrill F. & Streeten, David H., eds. Hypertension & Cognitive Processes. LC 80-22618. 165p. 1980. 20.00 (ISBN 0-933786-04-2); pap. text ed. 10.00 (ISBN 0-933786-03-4). Beech Hill.

Engelhardt, Edward L., ed. Antihypertensive Agents. LC 76-15416. (ACS Symposium Ser: No. 27). 1976. 15.50 (ISBN 0-8412-0333-4). Am Chemical.

Foote, Andrea E. & Erfurt, John C. Development & Dissemination of Model Systems for Hypertension Control in Organizational Settings. 1974. 3.50x (ISBN 0-87736-322-6). U of Mich Inst Labor.

Freis. Treatment of Hypertension. 1978. 19.95 (ISBN 0-8391-1316-1). Univ Park.

Freis, Edward C. Introduction to Nature & Management of Hypertension. (Illus.). 1974. pap. 16.95 (ISBN 0-87618-030-6). R J Brady.

Freis, Edward D. & Kolata, Gina B. The High Blood Pressure Book: A Guide for Patients & Their Families. 1979. 12.95 (ISBN 0-525-12472-1, Painter-Hopkins). Dutton.

Friedman, E. A. & Neff, R. K. Pregnancy Hypertension: A Systematic Evaluation of Clinical Diagnostic Criteria. LC 76-45951. 268p. 1977. 29.50 (ISBN 0-88416-185-4). Wright-PSG.

Fuchs, Ulrich. Submicroscopy of the Arterial Vascular Wall: Observations in the State of Hypertension & Arteiosclerosis. (Experimental Pathology Ser.). (Illus.). 1977. 25.00x (ISBN 0-8002-0372-0). Intl Pubns Serv.

Galletti, P. M., ed. Pharmacokinetics & Clinical Pharmacology of Beta-Blockers in Hypertension. (Cardiology: Vol. 64, Suppl. 1). (Illus.). 1979. pap. 19.75 (ISBN 3-8055-3061-7). S Karger.

Galton, Lawrence. The Silent Disease. 192p. 1973. 6.95 (ISBN 0-517-50357-3). Crown.

--The Silent Disease: Hypertension. 1974. pap. 2.50 (ISBN 0-451-09853-6, E9853, Sig). NAL.

Gant, Norman F. & Worley, Richard. Hypertensions in Pregnancy. (Illus.). 224p. 1980. 22.50x (ISBN 0-8385-4002-3). ACC.

Genest, et al. Hypertension: Physiopathology & Treatment. 1st ed. (Illus.). 1977. 49.00 (ISBN 0-07-023060-9, HP). McGraw.

Gerrick, David J. High Blood Pressure in Teenagers. (Illus.). 1978. 20.00 (ISBN 0-916750-27-2). Dayton Labs.

Giovannelli, G., et al, eds. Hypertension in Children & Adolescents. 368p. 1981. text ed. 39.00 (ISBN 0-89004-523-2). Raven.

Haft, Jacob I. & Bailey, Charles P., eds. Therapeutics, Hypertension & Aspects of Echocardiography. LC 78-52967. (Advances in the Management of Clinical Heart Disease Ser.: Vol. III). (Illus.). 1978. medical monograph 19.75 (ISBN 0-87993-111-6). Futura Pub.

Hart, Julian T. Hypertension. (Library of General Practice Ser.). 296p. 1980. text ed. 18.75x (ISBN 0-443-01665-8). Churchill.

Hutchinson, James C. Hypertension: A Practitioner's Guide to Therapy. 1975. spiral bdg. 13.00 (ISBN 0-87488-709-7). Med Exam.

Hyptertension: Salt, Hormones & Hypertension. (Hypertension Ser.: Vol. 19). 5.00 (ISBN 0-87493-020-0, 73-210A). Am Heart.

International Symposium on Pulmonary Circulation 2, Prague, June 1974. Pulmonary Hypertension: Proceedings. Widimsky, J., ed. (Progress in Respiration Research: Vol. 9). (Illus.). 320p. 1975. 106.75 (ISBN 3-8055-2171-5). S Karger.

Julius, Stevo & Esler, Murray D. The Nervous System in Arterial Hypertension. (American Lectures in Circulation Ser.). (Illus.). 496p. 1976. 47.50 (ISBN 0-398-03377-3). C C Thomas.

Kaplan, Norman M. Kaplan's Hypertension Self-Assessment. (Medcom Ser.). 94p. 1973. pap. 11.50 (ISBN 0-686-65353-X). Krieger.

--Your Blood Pressure: The Most Deadly High. LC 76-28706. 198p. 1976. Repr. of 1974 ed. 8.50 (ISBN 0-88275-455-6). Krieger.

Kaplan, Norman M., ed. Hypertension: Hypertension Research, 1974: Clinical & Experimental. (Hypertension Ser.: Vol. 23). 1975. pap. 6.00 (ISBN 0-87493-043-X, 73-214A). Am Heart.

Kezdi, P., ed. Baroreceptors & Hypertension. 1967. 67.00 (ISBN 0-08-012488-7). Pergamon.

Kochar, Mahendra S. & Daniels, Linda M. Hypertension Control: For Nurses & Other Health Professionals. LC 78-3750. 1978. pap. text ed. 11.95 (ISBN 0-8016-2717-6). Mosby.

Langford, Herbert G. & Watson, Robert. Preventing Hypertension. 280p. 1981. 22.50 (ISBN 0-87527-185-5). Green.

Laragh, John H. Hypertension. Incl. Mechanisms. LC 74-21661. (Illus.). pap. 12.50 (ISBN 0-914316-01-X); Methods. LC 74-21662. (Illus.). 124p. pap. 7.50 (ISBN 0-914316-02-8); Renin System, Drug Therapy & Diet. LC 74-21663. 108p. 1974. pap. 7.50 (ISBN 0-914316-03-6). (Illus.). 1975. Set. pap. 25.00 (ISBN 0-685-64471-5). Yorke Med.

Laragh, John H., ed. Frontiers in Hypertension Research. (Illus.). 628p. 1981. 39.80 (ISBN 0-387-90557-X). Springer-Verlag.

--Topics in Hypertension. LC 80-52799. (Illus.). 644p. 1980. 49.00 (ISBN 0-914316-20-6). Yorke Med.

Liebau, H., ed. Mechanisms & Recent Advances in Therapy of Hypertension. (Contributions to Nephrology: Vol. 8). (Illus.). 1977. 49.75 (ISBN 3-8055-2671-4). S Karger.

Lindheimer, Marshall D. & Katz, Adrian I. Kidney Function & Disease in Pregnancy. LC 76-30312. (Illus.). 241p. 1977. text ed. 15.00 (ISBN 0-8121-0593-1). Lea & Febiger.

McDonald. Clinical Kidney Disease & Hypertension. LC 80-14107. 1980. 32.00 (ISBN 0-913258-91-1). Thieme Stratton.

McMahon, F. Gilbert. Management of Essential Hypertension. LC 77-99164. (Illus.). 1978. 18.50 (ISBN 0-87993-108-6). Futura Pub.

Magnani, Bruno, ed. Beta-Adrenergic Blocking Agents in the Management of Hypertension & Angina Pectoris. LC 74-15629. 202p. 1974. 19.50 (ISBN 0-89004-013-3). Raven.

Marks, Charles, ed. Surgical Management of Systematic Hypertension. (Illus.). 250p. 1981. write for info. (ISBN 0-87993-156-6). Futura Pub.

Marshall, Andrew J. Hypertensive Patient. 517p. text ed. 49.50 (ISBN 0-272-79537-2). Univ Park.

Mendlowitz, Milton. Systemic Arterial Hypertension. (Illus.). 208p. 1974. 16.75 (ISBN 0-398-02884-2). C C Thomas.

Meyer, Philippe. Hypertension: Mechanisms & Clinical & Therapeutic Aspects. (Illus.). 208p. 1980. text ed. 25.00x (ISBN 0-19-261240-9). Oxford U Pr.

Moss, Abigail J. & Scott, Geraldine. Characteristics of Persons with Hypertension United States, 1974. Stevenson, Taloria, ed. (Ser. 10: No. 121). 1978. pap. text ed. 1.75 (ISBN 0-8406-0127-1). Natl Ctr Health Stats.

Mulrow, Patrick J. Experimental Hypertension. (Hypertension Ser.: Vol. 17). 1969. pap. text ed. 4.00x (ISBN 0-87493-007-3, 73-208A). Am Heart.

Murray, Frank. Program Your Heart for Health. 368p. (Orig.). 1977. pap. 2.95 (ISBN 0-915962-20-9). Larchmont Bks.

Neural Control of Arterial Pressure. (Hypertension Ser.: Vol. 16). 5.00 (ISBN 0-87493-021-9, 73-207A). Am Heart.

Neuro Humoral Mechanisms & Vascular Smooth Muscle. (Hypertension Ser: Vol. 14). 5.00 (ISBN 0-87493-022-7, 73-206A). Am Heart.

New, Maria & Levine, Lenore, eds. Juvenile Hypertension. LC 76-51556. 244p. 1977. 20.00 (ISBN 0-89004-145-8). Raven.

Onesti, Gaddo & Brest, Albert N. Hypertension: Mechanisms, Diagnosis & Treatment. LC 77-25888. (Cardiovascular Clinics Ser.: Vol. 9, No. 1). (Illus.). 333p. 1978. text ed. 35.00 (ISBN 0-8036-6630-6). Davis Co.

Onesti, Gaddo & Kim, Kwan E., eds. Hypertension in the Young & the Old. (The Sixth Hahnemann International Symposium on Hypertension Ser.). (Illus.). 356p. 1981. 39.50 (ISBN 0-8089-1319-0). Grune.

--Hypertension: Mechanisms & Management. (The Twenty-Sixth Hahnemann Symposium Ser.). (Illus.). 848p. 1973. 87.75 (ISBN 0-8089-0790-5). Grune.

Onesti, Gaddo & Klimt, Christian R., eds. Hypertension: Determinants, Complications & Intervention: Fifth Hahnemann International Symposium on Hypertension. 480p. 1978. 45.50 (ISBN 0-8089-1108-2). Grune.

Page, I. H. & Bumpus, F. M., eds. Angiotensin. LC 73-78809. (Handbook of Experimental Pharmacology: Vol. 37). (Illus.). xviii, 660p. 1973. 125.70 (ISBN 0-387-06276-9). Springer-Verlag.

Paul, Oglesby, ed. Epidemiology & Control of Hypertension. LC 74-27863. (Illus.). 694p. 1975. text ed. 35.00 (ISBN 0-8151-6652-4, Pub. by Symposia Special). Year Bk Med.

Philip, T. & Distler, A., eds. Hypertension: Mechanisms & Management. 279p. 1981. pap. 42.00 (ISBN 0-387-10171-3). Springer-Verlag.

Pickering, George. Hypertension. 2nd ed. LC 73-88900. 152p. 1974. pap. text ed. 9.75x (ISBN 0-443-01124-9). Churchill.

Radzialowski. Hypertension Research: Methods & Models. (Modern Pharmacology-Toxicology Ser.: Vol. 19). 1981. price not set (ISBN 0-8247-1344-3). Dekker.

Reader, Ralph, ed. Hypertensive Mechanisms. (AHA Monograph Ser: Vol. 32). pap. 6.00 (ISBN 0-87493-002-2, 73-023A). Am Heart.

Rees, Michael K. The Complete Family Guide to Living with High Blood Pressure. LC 80-18767. 1980. 9.95 (ISBN 0-13-160432-5). P-H.

Roberts, Jean & Maurer, Kurt. Blood Pressure Levels of Persons 6-74 Years, United States, 1971-1974. Stevenson, Taloria, ed. (Ser. II: No. 203). 1977. pap. 1.75 (ISBN 0-8406-0087-9). Natl Ctr Health Stats.

Robertson, J. I. & Caldwell, A. D., eds. Left Ventricular Hypertrophy in Hypertension. (Royal Society of Medicine International Congress & Symposium Ser.: No. 9). 114p. 1979. pap. 16.00 (ISBN 0-8089-1190-2). Grune.

Robertson, J. I., et al, eds. The Therapeutics of Hypertension. (Royal Society of Medicine International Congress & Symposium Ser.: No. 26). 288p. 1981. pap. 29.00 (ISBN 0-8089-1277-1). Grune.

Rorvik, David M. & Heyns, O. S. Decompression Babies. new ed. LC 73-7487. (Illus.). 160p. 1973. 5.95 (ISBN 0-396-06836-7). Dodd.

Rosenvold, Lloyd. Drop Your Blood Pressure. 176p. (Orig.). 1980. pap. 2.50 (ISBN 0-515-05721-5). Jove Pubns.

Rowland, Michael. Hypertension of Adults Twenty-Five to Seventy-Four Years of Age: United States, 1971-1975. Shipp, Audrey, ed. (Ser. 11, No. 221). 50p. Date not set. text ed. 1.75 (ISBN 0-8406-0207-3). Natl Ctr Health Stats.

Ruskin, Arthur. Classics in Arterial Hypertension. (American Lectures Classics in Science & Medicine). (Illus.). 400p. 1956. photocopy ed. spiral 39.50 (ISBN 0-398-01633-X). C C Thomas.

Sambhi, M. Mechanisms of Hypertension. (International Congress Ser.: No. 302). 1974. 94.25 (ISBN 0-444-15079-X, Excerpta Medica). Elsevier.

Sambhi, Mohinder P., ed. Systemic Effects of Antihypertensive Agents. LC 76-14018. (Illus.). 1976. text ed. 37.50 (ISBN 0-8151-7530-2, Pub. by Symposia Special). Year Bk Med.

Schlittler, Emil, ed. Antihypertensive Agents. (Medicinal Chemistry: Vol. 7). 1967. 63.50 (ISBN 0-12-625650-0). Acad Pr.

Scriabine, A., ed. New Antihypertensive Drugs: A. N. Richards Symposium. Sweet, C. S. LC 76-20746. (Monographs of the Physiological Society of Philadelphia). 1976. 40.00 (ISBN 0-470-15181-1). Halsted Pr.

Scriabine, Alexander, ed. The Pharmacology of Antihypertensive Drugs. 472p. 1980. text ed. 39.50 (ISBN 0-89004-329-9). Raven.

Sleight, Peter, ed. Arterial Baroreceptors & Hypertension. (Illus.). 380p. 1981. text ed. 69.50x (ISBN 0-19-261259-X). Oxford U Pr.

Snider, Arthur J. & Oparil, Suzanne. A Doctor Discusses Hypertension. (Illus.). 1981. pap. 2.50 (ISBN 0-685-79070-3). Budlong.

Stamler, Jeremiah, et al, eds. Epidemiology of Hypertension: Proceedings of an International Symposium. LC 66-25407. (Illus.). 484p. 1967. 69.00 (ISBN 0-8089-0471-X). Grune.

Strauer, B. E. Hypertensive Heart Disease. (Illus.). 106p. 1980. pap. 16.60 (ISBN 0-387-10041-5). Springer-Verlag.

Strauer, B. E., ed. Heart in Hypertension: Symposium. (International Boehringer Mannheim Symposia Ser.). (Illus.). 484p. 1981. pap. 48.40 (ISBN 0-387-10496-8). Springer-Verlag.

Swales, J. D. Clinical Hypertension. (Illus.). 1980. 31.00 (ISBN 0-8151-8620-7). Year Bk Med.

Thomas, Pat. High Blood Pressure Review. Hull, Nancy R., ed. (Illus., Orig.). (gr. 8-10). 1981. pap. text ed. 3.75 (ISBN 0-939838-01-X). Pritchett & Hull.

Thurm, Richard H., ed. Essential Hypertension. (Illus.). 1979. 42.50 (ISBN 0-8151-8803-X). Year Bk Med.

Villarreal, Herman. Hypertension. LC 81-4952. (Becker-Perspectives in Nephrology & Hypertension Ser.). 448p. 1981. 35.00 (ISBN 0-471-07900-6, Pub. by Wiley Med). Wiley.

Wade, Carlson. Fact-Book on Hypertension, High Blood Pressure & Your Diet. LC 74-31668. (Pivot Original Health Book Ser). (Illus.). 128p. (Orig.). 1975. pap. 1.95 (ISBN 0-87983-095-6). Keats.
Weinstein, Milton & Stason, William. Hypertension: A Policy Perspective. 1976. 15.00x (ISBN 0-674-43900-7, WEHP). Harvard U Pr.
WHO Meeting. Geneva, Oct. 15-17, 1973. Primary Pulmonary Hypertension: Report. Hatano, S. & Strasser, T., eds. 1975. 4.00 (ISBN 92-4-156044-4). World Health.
WHO Meeting. Tokyo Mar. 11-13, 1974. Hypertension & Stroke Control in the Community: Proceedings. Hatano, S., et al, eds. (Illus., Also avail. in French). 1976. 12.00 (ISBN 92-4-156052-5). World Health.
Wolff, Hanns P. Speaking of: High Blood Pressure. Steinberg, Jean, tr. from Ger. LC 78-72873. (Medical Adviser Ser.). (Illus.). 1979. pap. 3.95 (ISBN 0-8326-2235-4, 7454). Delair.
Yamori, Yukio, et al. Prophylactic Approach to Hypertensive Disease: Symposium. (Perspectives in Cardiovascular Research Ser.: Vol. 4). 624p. 1979. 58.50 (ISBN 0-89004-339-6). Raven.
Zanchetti, Alberto. Methyldopa in Hypertension. LC 78-68086. 1978. 3.00 (ISBN 0-911910-96-4). Merck-Sharp-Dohme.

HYPERTHERMIA

see Heat-Physiological Effect

HYPERTHYROIDISM

Hamburger, Joel I. Hyperthyroidism: Concept & Controversy. (Illus.). 212p. 1972. 12.00 (ISBN 0-398-02304-2). C C Thomas.

HYPERTRICHOSIS

Mauvais-Jarvis, P., et al. Hirsutism. (Monographs on Endocrinology: Vol. 19). (Illus.). 110p. 1981. 40.20 (ISBN 0-387-10509-3). Springer-Verlag.

HYPERVENTILATION

Lowry, Thomas P. Hyperventilation & Hysteria: The Physiology & Psychology of Overbreathing & Its Realationship to the Mind-Body Problem. (Illus.). 208p. 1967. photocopy ed. spiral 19.75 (ISBN 0-398-01156-7). C C Thomas.

HYPHOMYCETES

see Moniliales

HYPNOPAEDIA

see Sleep Learning

HYPNOSIS

see Hypnotism

HYPNOTIC SUSCEPTIBILITY

Hilgard, Ernest R. Experience of Hypnosis. LC 68-25372. (Shorter Version of Hypnotic Susceptibility). 1968. pap. 3.45 (ISBN 0-15-629552-0, H065, Hbgr). HarBraceJ.
--Hypnotic Susceptibility. 1965. text ed. 17.95 (ISBN 0-15-540523-3, HC). HarBraceJ.

HYPNOTISM

see also Animal Magnetism; Crystal-Gazing; Hypnotic Susceptibility; Hypnotism and Crime; Mental Suggestion; Mesmerism; Mind and Body; Personality, Disorders of; Psychoanalysis; Rigidity (Psychology); Subconsciousness; Therapeutics, Suggestive

Adams, Paul. New Self-Hypnosis. pap. 4.00 (ISBN 0-87980-233-2). Wilshire.
Anderson-Evangelista, Anita. Hypnosis: A Journey into the Mind. LC 79-27817. (Illus.). 256p. 1980. 10.95 (ISBN 0-668-04908-1, 4908-1). Arco.
Arons. Best & Easiest Disguised Method of Inducing Hypnosis: Indirect Method. pap. 1.00 (ISBN 0-685-02587-X, Power). Borden.
--Seven Best Techniques for Deepening Hypnosis. pap. 1.00 (ISBN 0-685-02590-X, Power). Borden.
Arons, Harry. The Fait Accompli Technique. pap. 1.25 (ISBN 0-685-57713-9). Borden.
--Handbook of Self-Hypnosis. rev. ed. pap. 4.95 (ISBN 0-685-07330-0). Borden.
--How to Formulate Suggestions for Hypnosis and Self Hypnosis. 1978. pap. 1.00 (ISBN 0-685-57712-0). Borden.
--How to Present an Ethical Lecture-Demonstration in Scientific Hypnosis. pap. 1.25 (ISBN 0-685-64532-0). Borden.
--Hypnosis for Speeding up the Learning Process. pap. 1.00 (ISBN 0-685-07341-6, Power). Borden.
--Hypnosis in Criminal Investigation. pap. 9.00 (ISBN 0-685-57706-6). Borden.
--New Master Course in Hypnotism. 14.00 (ISBN 0-685-07392-0). Borden.
--Prize-Winning Methods of Hypnosis. pap. 4.00 (ISBN 0-685-07397-1). Borden.
--Speed Hypnosis. pap. 3.00 (ISBN 0-685-07408-0). Borden.
Arons, Harry & Bubeck, Marne F. H. Handbook of Professional Hypnosis. 1976. 15.00 (ISBN 0-685-71395-4). Borden.
Atkinson, William W. Mental Influence. pap. 1.00 (ISBN 0-911662-42-1). Yoga.
Bandler, Richard & Grinder, John. Patterns of Hypnotic Techniques of Milton H. Erickson, M. D. LC 75-24584. 1975. pap. 6.95x (ISBN 0-916990-01-X). Meta Pubns.
Barabasz, Arreed F. New Techniques in Behavior Therapy & Hypnosis: Including Advanced Techniques in Sex Therapy. 15.50 (ISBN 0-685-57679-5). Borden.
Barber, Theodore X. LSD, Marijuana, Yoga, & Hypnosis. LC 73-115935. 1970. 24.95x (ISBN 0-202-25004-0). Aldine Pub.
Bernheim, H. Hypnosis & Suggestion in Psychotherapy: The Nature & Uses of Hypnotism. LC 73-15303. 438p. 1974. Repr. 30.00x (ISBN 0-87668-110-0). Aronson.
Biddle, W. Earl. Hypnosis in the Psychoses. 152p. 1967. pap. 12.75 photocopy ed. spiral (ISBN 0-398-00152-9). C C Thomas.
Bjornstrom, Fredik J. Hypnotism, Its History & Present Development. 1976. Repr. of 1889 ed. 25.00 (ISBN 0-685-71309-1, Regency). Scholarly.
Blythe, Peter. Hypnotism: Its Power & Practice. LC 70-155092. 1971. 5.95 (ISBN 0-8008-4045-3). Taplinger.
Bordas, Carl W. Premeditated Success Through Hypnotism. 168p. (Orig.). 1981. pap. 4.50x (ISBN 0-935648-07-0). Halldin Pub.
Braid, James. Magic, Witchcraft, Animal Magnetism, Hypnotism, & Electro-Biology. 1976. Repr. 25.00 (ISBN 0-685-71981-2, Regency). Scholarly.
--Neurypnology. LC 75-16688. (Classics in Psychiatry Ser.). 1976. Repr. of 1843 ed. 15.00x (ISBN 0-405-07418-2). Arno.
Brandler, Richard, et al. Patterns of Hypnotic Techniques of Milton H. Erickson M. D, Vol. 2. LC 75-24584. 1977. 17.95 (ISBN 0-916990-02-8). Meta Pubns.
Burrows, G. D., et al, eds. Hypnosis Nineteen Hundred Seventy-Nine. LC 79-16095. 354p. 1979. 58.75 (ISBN 0-444-80142-1, North Holland). Elsevier.
Caprio, Frank S. & Berger, Joseph R. Helping Yourself with Self-Hypnosis. 1971. pap. 2.50 (ISBN 0-446-31073-5). Warner Bks.
--Helping Yourself with Self-Hypnosis. LC 63-10671. 1963. pap. 3.95 (ISBN 0-13-386623-8, Reward). P-H.
Chambers, Bradford. How to Hypnotize. LC 57-6582. (Illus.). 1957. 8.95 (ISBN 0-87396-004-1). Stravon.
Chastenet de Puysegur, A. M. Du Magnetisme Animal: Considere Dans Ses Rapports Avec Diverses Brances De la Physique Generale. 483p. (Fr.). Repr. of 1807 ed. text ed. 35.00x (ISBN 0-8290-0285-5). Irvington.
Chertok, Leon. Sense & Nonsense in Psychotherapy: The Challenge of Hypnosis. LC 80-41755. (Illus.). 260p. 1981. 36.00 (ISBN 0-08-026793-9); pap. 18.00 (ISBN 0-08-026813-7). Pergamon.
Clark, Cline. Self-Programming Self-Hypnosis. (Orig.). 1980. pap. text ed. 17.95 (ISBN 0-937798-00-2). Packard Pub.
Cooke, Charles E. & Van Vogt, A. E. Hypnotism Handbook. 12.00 (ISBN 0-685-07342-4). Borden.
Cooper, Linn F. & Erickson, Milton H. Time Distortion in Hypnosis. (Illus.). 1981. Repr. of 1954 ed. text ed. 22.50x (ISBN 0-89197-967-0). Irvington.
Copeland, Rachel. How to Hypnotize Yourself & Others. LC 80-70951. 240p. 1981. 10.95 (ISBN 0-8119-0418-0). Fell.
Dauven, Jean. The Powers of Hypnosis. (Illus.). 254p. 1980. pap. 5.95 (ISBN 0-8128-1391-X). Stein & Day.
Edmonston, William E. Hypnosis & Relaxation: Modern Verification of an Old Equation. LC 80-22506. (Personality Processes Ser.). 255p. 1981. 24.50 (ISBN 0-471-05903-X, Pub. by Wiley Interscience). Wiley.
Edmonston, William E., Jr., ed. Conceptual & Investigative Approaches to Hypnosis & Hypnotic Phenomena, Vol. 296. (Annals of the New York Academy of Sciences). 619p. 1977. 22.00x (ISBN 0-89072-042-8). NY Acad Sci.
Edmunds, Simeon. Hypnotism & Psychic Phenomena. pap. 3.00 (ISBN 0-87980-077-1). Wilshire.
--Psychic Powers of Hypnosis. (Paths to Inner Power Ser). 1968. pap. 1.25 (ISBN 0-87728-095-9). Weiser.
Erickson, Milton H. & Rossi, Ernest, eds. Hypnotic Alteration of Sensory, Perceptual & Psychophysical Processes. LC 79-15940. (Papers of Milton H. Erickson on Hypnosis: Vol. 2). 1980. 29.95 (ISBN 0-470-26722-4). Halsted Pr.
--Hypnotic Investigation of Psychodynamic Processes. LC 79-15939. (Collected Papers of Milton H. Erickson on Hypnosis: Vol. 3). 1980. 29.95x (ISBN 0-470-26723-2). Halsted Pr.
--Innovative Hypnotherapy. (Collected Papers of Milton H. Erickson on Hypnosis: Vol. 4). 1980. 34.95 (ISBN 0-470-26724-0). Halsted Pr.
--The Nature of Hypnosis & Suggestion. LC 79-15942. (Collected Papers of Milton H. Erickson on Hypnosis: Vol. 1). 1980. 34.95x (ISBN 0-470-26721-6). Halsted Pr.
Erickson, Milton H., et al. Hypnotic Realities: The Induction of Clinical Hypnosis & Forms of Indirect Suggestion. LC 76-20636. 1976. 24.95x (ISBN 0-8290-0112-3). Irvington.
Estabrooks, George H. Hypnotism. rev. ed. 1959. pap. 3.95 (ISBN 0-525-47038-7). Dutton.
Forel, August. Hypnotism Suggestion. 9.95 (ISBN 0-685-21984-4). Wehman.
Frankel, F. H. & Zamansky, H., eds. Hypnosis at Its Bicentennial: Selected Papers. LC 78-16605. 320p. 1978. 27.50 (ISBN 0-306-40029-4, Plenum Pr). Plenum Pub.
Frankel, Fred H., ed. Hypnosis: Trance As a Coping Mechanism. 185p. 1976. 18.50 (ISBN 0-306-30932-7, Plenum Pr). Plenum Pub.
Fromm, Erika & Shor, Ronald E. Hypnosis: Developments in Research & New Perspectives. 2nd ed. LC 79-89279. (Illus.). 1979. 47.50 (ISBN 0-202-26085-2). Aldine Pub.
Fross. Handbook of Hypnotic Techniques. pap. 4.50 (ISBN 0-685-07329-7). Borden.
Furst, Arnold. How to Prepare & Administer Hypnotic Prescriptions. 1980. 6.95 (ISBN 0-915926-13-X). Magic Ltd.
--Post Hypnotic Instructions. pap. 3.00 (ISBN 0-87980-119-0). Wilshire.
Gardner, G. Gail & Olness, Karen. Hypnosis & Hypnptherapy with Children. 1981. price not set (ISBN 0-8089-1413-8). Grune.
Gibbons, D. E. Applied Hypnosis & Hyperempiria. LC 79-20879. 227p. 1979. 18.50 (ISBN 0-306-40271-8, Plenum Pr). Plenum Pub.
Gibson, H. B. Hypnosis: Its Nature & Therapeutic Uses. LC 77-92821. 1980. pap. 4.95 (ISBN 0-8008-4043-7). Taplinger.
--Hypnosis: Its Nature & Therapeutic Uses. LC 77-92821. (Illus.). 1978. 8.95 (ISBN 0-8008-4044-5). Taplinger.
Gibson, Walter B. Key to Hypnotism. pap. 1.00 (ISBN 0-686-00703-4). Key Bks.
Gill, Merton M. & Brenman, Margaret. Hypnosis & Related States. LC 59-9821. 1959. text ed. 20.00 (ISBN 0-8236-2400-5). Intl Univs Pr.
Gindes, B. New Concepts in Hypnosis. 4.00 (ISBN 0-685-22059-1). Wehman.
Gindes, Bernard C. New Concepts of Hypnosis. pap. 4.00 (ISBN 0-87980-108-5). Wilshire.
Gray & Hidalgo. How to Hypnotize. 2.00 (ISBN 0-685-27807-7). Borden.
Grinder, John & Bandler, Richard. Trance-Formations: Neuro-Linguistic Programming & the Structure of Hypnosis. Andreas, Connirae, ed. 275p. (Orig.). 1981. 9.00 (ISBN 0-911226-22-2); pap. 5.50 (ISBN 0-911226-23-0). Real People.
Grossach, Martin. Hypnosis & Self-Hypnosis. pap. 2.50 (ISBN 0-8283-1526-4). Inst Rat Liv.
Grossi, Ralph. Reliving Reincarnation Through Hypnosis. 1975. 7.00 (ISBN 0-682-48286-2, Banner). Exposition.
Haley, Jay, ed. Advanced Techniques of Hypnosis & Therapy: Selected Papers of Milton H. Erickson, M. D. LC 67-23991. (Illus.). 368p. 1967. 52.00 (ISBN 0-8089-0169-9). Grune.
Hibbard, Whitney & Worring, Raymond. Forensic Hypnosis: The Practical Application of Hypnosis in Criminal Investigations. (Illus.). 400p. 1981. text ed. 34.75 (ISBN 0-398-04098-2). C C Thomas.
Hilgard, Josephine R. Personality & Hypnosis: A Study of Imaginative Involvement. 2nd ed. LC 79-13387. 1979. lib. bdg. 19.50x (ISBN 0-226-33443-0); pap. 5.95 (ISBN 0-226-33442-2, P852). U of Chicago Pr.
Hoke, James H. I Would If I Could & I Can. LC 80-51606. 180p. 1981. pap. 5.95 (ISBN 0-8128-6135-3). Stein & Day.
Hollander, Bernard. Hypnosis & Self-Hypnosis. pap. 3.00 (ISBN 0-87980-075-5). Wilshire.
Hull, Clark L. Hypnosis & Suggestibility: An Experimental Approach. LC 33-30268. (Century Psychology Ser.). (Illus.). 1933. pap. text ed. 12.95x (ISBN 0-89197-223-4). Irvington.
Hypnosis for Salesmen. Date not set. pap. 3.00 (ISBN 0-685-55921-1). Borden.
International Brain Research Organization. Psychophysiological Mechanisms of Hypnosis: Proceedings. Chertok, L., ed. (Illus.). 1969. 29.00 (ISBN 0-387-04678-X). Springer-Verlag.
Johns, Alfred E. Scientific Autosuggestion. 1957. 2.95 (ISBN 0-685-06594-4). Assoc Bk.
Katz, Leandro. Self Hypnosis. (Viper's Tongue Books Ser.). 1975. 5.00 (ISBN 0-931106-11-7). TVRT.
Kettelkamp, Larry. Hypnosis: the Wakeful Sleep. LC 75-17605. (Illus.). 96p. (gr. 5-9). 1975. 7.25 (ISBN 0-688-22045-2); PLB 6.96 (ISBN 0-688-32045-7). Morrow.
Kroger, William S. Clinical & Experimental Hypnosis in Medicine, Dentistry, & Psychology. 2nd ed. LC 77-10320. 1977. 29.00 (ISBN 0-397-50377-6, JBL-Med-Nursing). Lippincott.
Kroger, William S. & Fezler, William D. Hypnosis & Behavior Modification: Imagery Conditioning. LC 76-20586. 1976. 27.50 (ISBN 0-397-50362-8, JBL-Med-Nursing). Har-Row.
Kuhn, Lesley & Russo, Salvatore. Modern Hypnosis. pap. 5.00 (ISBN 0-87980-100-X). Wilshire.
LeCron, Leslie & Bordeaux, Jean. Hypnotism Today. pap. 4.00 (ISBN 0-87980-081-X). Wilshire.
LeCron, Leslie M. The Complete Guide to Hypnosis. 240p. 1976. pap. 2.95 (ISBN 0-06-465069-3, BN 5000, BN). Har-Row.
--How to Stop Smoking Thru Self-Hypnosis. pap. 3.00 (ISBN 0-87980-065-8). Wilshire.
--Self Hypnotism: The Technique & Its Use in Daily Living. 1970. pap. 2.50 (ISBN 0-451-09824-2, E9824, Sig). NAL.
Le Cron, M. Self-Hypnotism: The Technique & Its Use in Daily Living. pap. 3.95 (ISBN 0-13-803486-9, Reward). P-H.
Leonidas. Secrets of Stage Hypnotism. LC 80-19741. 149p. 1980. Repr. of 1975 ed. lib. bdg. 9.95x (ISBN 0-89370-629-9). Borgo Pr.
Leonidas, Professor. Secrets of Stage Hypnotism. new ed. LC 74-23500. Orig. Title: Stage Hypnotism. 149p. 1975. pap. 2.95 (ISBN 0-87877-029-1, P-29). Newcastle Pub.
Lindner, Robert M. Rebel Without a Cause. 309p. 1944. 34.75 (ISBN 0-8089-0265-2). Grune.
Long, Max F. Self-Suggestion & the New Huna Theory of Mesmerism & Hypnosis. 1958. pap. 3.95 (ISBN 0-87516-048-4). De Vorss.
McGill, Ormond. The Art of Stage Hypnosis. 1975. 17.50 (ISBN 0-915926-10-5). Magic Ltd.
--The Art of Stage Hypnotism. Date not set. 17.50 (ISBN 0-685-55926-2). Borden.
--Hypnotism & Mysticism of India. 2nd ed. (Illus.). Date not set. Repr. of 1977 ed. text ed. 10.00 (ISBN 0-930298-01-2). Westwood Pub Co.
--Professional Stage Hypnotism. (Illus.). 1978. 15.00x (ISBN 0-685-59907-8). Westwood Pub Co.
Magonet, Philip. Practical Hypnotism. pap. 3.00 (ISBN 0-87980-123-9). Wilshire.
Marcuse, F. L. Hypnosis Throughout the World. (Illus.). 324p. 1964. photocopy ed. spiral 29.75 (ISBN 0-398-01214-8). C C Thomas.
Meares, Ainslie. A System of Medical Hypnosis. LC 61-5108. 484p. 1972. Repr. of 1960 ed. 15.00 (ISBN 0-517-52771-5). Crown.
Michaluk, Wladyslaw, ed. Understanding Hypnosis: A Brief Guide. LC 81-80438. 86p. (Orig.). 1981. pap. 4.95 (ISBN 0-939628-00-7). Hypnos Pr.
Morris, Freda. Hypnosis with Friends & Lovers. LC 78-360. (Orig.). 1979. pap. 5.95 (ISBN 0-06-250600-5, RD 286, HarpR). Har-Row.
--Self Hypnosis in Two Days. 1975. pap. 3.50 (ISBN 0-525-47403-X). Dutton.
Oakley, Gilbert. Self Hypnosis Explained. 244p. 1978. pap. 4.95 (ISBN 0-8119-0396-6). Fell.
Orton, Louis. Hypnotism Made Practical. pap. 3.00 (ISBN 0-87980-079-8). Wilshire.
Ousby, William J. Self-Hypnosis & Scientific Self-Suggestion. 1969. pap. 1.75 (ISBN 0-668-01815-1). Arco.
--Theory & Practice of Hypnotism. LC 68-20505. (Orig.). 1968. pap. 1.50 (ISBN 0-668-01735-X). Arco.
--The Theory & Practice of Hypnotism. LC 68-20505. 1968. 4.50 (ISBN 0-668-01734-1). Arco.
Powers, Melvin. Advanced Techniques of Hypnosis. pap. 2.00 (ISBN 0-87980-002-X). Wilshire.
--Hypnotism Revealed. pap. 2.00 (ISBN 0-87980-080-1). Wilshire.
--Practical Guide to Self-Hypnosis. (Orig.). 1960. pap. 3.00 (ISBN 0-87980-122-0). Wilshire.
--Self-Hypnosis: Its Theory, Technique & Application. pap. 3.00 (ISBN 0-87980-138-7). Wilshire.
Pratt, George J., et al. A Clinical Hypnosis Primer. LC 79-92665. 1980. 14.95 (ISBN 0-930626-07-9). Psych & Consul Assocs.
Professional Hypnotism Manual: Introducting Physical & Emotional Suggestibility & Sexuality. rev. ed. 1978. pap. 12.50 (ISBN 0-686-57995-X). Borden.
Reiff, Robert & Scheerer, Martin. Memory & Hypnotic Age Regression: Developmental Aspects of Cognitive Function Explored Through Hypnosis. LC 59-13120. 1970. text ed. 17.50 (ISBN 0-8236-3340-3); pap. text ed. 5.95 (ISBN 0-8236-8150-5, 023340). Intl Univs Pr.
Rhodes, Raphael H. Hypnosis: Theory, Practice & Application. 1960. pap. 2.95 (ISBN 0-8065-0117-0). Citadel Pr.
Rodney, Jonathan. Explorations of a Hypnotist. 4.00 (ISBN 0-685-06554-5). Assoc Bk.
Sackett, Patrick L. The Power of Autosuggestion & How to Master It. (Illus.). 1979. deluxe ed. 39.85 (ISBN 0-930582-61-6). Gloucester Art.

Salter, Andrew. What Is Hypnosis? 106p. 1973. pap. 3.95 (ISBN 0-374-51038-5, N439). FS&G.
Sandor, Richard S., tr. Bernheim's New Studies in Hypnotism. 1980. 27.50 (ISBN 0-8236-0496-9). Intl Univs Pr.
Sarbin, Theodore R. & Coe, William C. Hypnosis: A Social Psychological Analysis of Influence Communication. LC 72-185784. 1981. Repr. of 1972 ed. 22.00x (ISBN 0-8290-0388-6). Irvington.
Schilder, Paul. The Nature of Hypnosis. 1956. text ed. 12.00 (ISBN 0-8236-3500-7); pap. text ed. 4.95 (ISBN 0-8236-8156-4, 023500). Intl Univs Pr.
Segall. The Questions They Ask About Hypnosis. pap. 1.50 (ISBN 0-685-64539-8). Borden.
Sextus, Carl. Hypnotism. pap. 5.00 (ISBN 0-87980-076-3). Wilshire.
Shaftesbury, Edmund. Universal Magnetism, Vol. 2. 9.95 (ISBN 0-685-22150-4). Wehman.
Shames, Richard & Sterin, Chuck. Healing with Mind Power. 1980. 8.95 (ISBN 0-87857-210-4); pap. 6.95 (ISBN 0-87857-293-7). Rodale Pr Inc.
Sheehan, P. W. & Perry, C. W. Methodologies of Hypnosis: A Critical Appraisal of Contemporary Paradigms of Hypnosis. LC 76-3543. 1976. 18.00 (ISBN 0-470-15028-9). Halsted Pr.
Shor, R. E. & Orne, M. T., eds. The Nature of Hypnosis: Selected Basic Readings. 1981. Repr. of 1965 ed. 18.95x (ISBN 0-03-050965-3). Irvington.
Simmons, Charles M. Your Subconscious Power. pap. 4.00 (ISBN 0-87980-178-6). Wilshire.
Sparks, L. Self-Hypnosis: A Conditioned Response Technique. LC 61-18529. (Illus.). 270p. 1962. 29.00 (ISBN 0-8089-0444-2). Grune.
Sparks, Laurence. Self-Hypnosis: A Conditioned - Response Technique. pap. 4.00 (ISBN 0-87980-139-5). Wilshire.
Sutphen, Dick. Past Life Hypnotic Regression Course. 1977. 24.95 (ISBN 0-911842-13-6). Valley Sun.
Teitelbaum, Myron. Hypnosis Induction Techniques. 200p. 1980. 12.50 (ISBN 0-398-01907-X). C C Thomas.
Tinterow, Maurice M. Foundations of Hypnosis: From Mesmer to Freud. (Illus.). 620p. 1970. 59.75 (ISBN 0-398-01928-2). C C Thomas.
Udolf, Roy. Handbook of Hypnosis for Professionals. 384p. 1981. text ed. 24.50 (ISBN 0-442-28881-6). Van Nos Reinhold.
Van Pelt, Sydney J. Modern Hypnotism, Key to the Mind. 1956. 2.50 (ISBN 0-685-06581-2); pap. 1.00 (ISBN 0-685-06582-0). Assoc Bk.
--Secrets of Hypnotism. 3.00 (ISBN 0-685-22102-4). Wehman.
--Secrets of Hypnotism. pap. 3.00 (ISBN 0-87980-135-2). Wilshire.
Wallace, Benjamin. Applied Hypnosis. LC 79-65. 144p. 1979. 15.95x (ISBN 0-88229-415-6). Nelson-Hall.
Wambach, Helen. Reliving Past Lives: The Evidence Under Hypnosis. LC 77-11805. (Illus.). 1978. 9.95 (ISBN 0-06-014513-7, HarpT). Har-Row.
Weisman, Alan. We, Immortals: The Dick Sutphen Past Life Seminars. LC 77-71545. 1977. 3.95 (ISBN 0-911842-17-9). Valley Sun.
Weitzenhoffer, Andre M. General Techniques of Hypnotism. (Illus.). 476p. 1967. 44.00 (ISBN 0-8089-0523-6). Grune.
Williams, Robert L. & Karacan, Ismet, eds. Pharmacology of Sleep. LC 76-55167. 368p. 1976. 48.95 (ISBN 0-471-94856-X). Krieger.
Winn, Ralph. Hypnotism Made Easy. pap. 3.00 (ISBN 0-87980-078-X). Wilshire.
Wittkofski, Joseph. The Pastoral Use of Hypnotic Technique. 128p. 1971. photocopy ed. spiral 12.75 (ISBN 0-398-02101-5). C C Thomas.
Wolberg, Lewis R. Hypnoanalysis. 2nd ed. LC 64-20777. 446p. 1964. 37.75 (ISBN 0-8089-0534-1). Grune.
Zolar. Everything You Want to Know About Hypnotism, Psychic Powers, Telepathy, E.S.P., Sex & Hypnosis. LC 72-3139. (Zolar's Everything You Want to Know Ser.). 224p. 1972. pap. 0.95 (ISBN 0-668-02662-6). Arco.

HYPNOTISM–MORAL AND RELIGIOUS ASPECTS

Francuch, Peter D. Principles of Spiritual Hypnosis. LC 81-50059. 240p. 1981. 20.00 (ISBN 0-939386-00-3). Spiritual Advisory.

HYPNOTISM–THERAPEUTIC USE

Ambrose, G. & Newbold, G. A Handbook of Medical Hypnosis. 4th ed. 1980. text ed. 25.95 (ISBN 0-02-857110-X). Macmillan.
Anderson-Evangelista, Anita. Hypnosis: A Journey into the Mind. LC 79-27817. (Illus.). 256p. 1980. 10.95 (ISBN 0-668-04908-1, 4908-1). Arco.
Barber, Theodore X., et al. Hypnosis, Imagination & Human Potentialities. LC 73-19539. 1974. 23.00 (ISBN 0-08-017932-0). Pergamon.
Barnett, Edgar A. Unlock Your Mind & Be Free: A Practical Approach to Hypnotherapy. LC 79-87715. 155p. 7.95 (ISBN 0-89882-002-2). Lane & Assoc.
Beahrs, John O. Unity & Multiplicity: Multilevel Consciousness of Self in Hypnosis, Psychiatric Disorder & Mental Health. 200p. 1981. 17.50 (ISBN 0-87630-273-8). Brunner-Mazel.
Beigel, Hugo G. & Johnson, Warren R. Application of Hypnosis in Sex Therapy. 352p. 1980. 29.75 (ISBN 0-398-03965-8). C C Thomas.
Bernhardt, Roger & Martin, David. Self-Mastery Through Self-Hypnosis. 1978. pap. 1.95 (ISBN 0-451-08352-0, J8352, Sig). NAL.
Bernheim, Hippolyte. Suggestive Therapeutics. 1957. 5.95 (ISBN 0-685-06601-0). Assoc Bk.
Bordas, Carl W. Premeditated Success Through Hypnotism. 168p. (Orig.). 1981. pap. 4.50x (ISBN 0-935648-07-0). Halldin Pub.
Brenman, Margaret & Gill, Merton M. Hypnotherapy: A Survey of the Literature. (Menninger Foundation Monograph Ser.: No. 5). 303p. 1971. text ed. 17.50 (ISBN 0-8236-2420-X); pap. text ed. 5.95 (ISBN 0-8236-8073-8, 022420). Intl Univs Pr.
Cheek, David B. & LeCron, Leslie M. Clinical Hypnotherapy. LC 68-16304. 256p. 1968. 29.00 (ISBN 0-8089-0097-8). Grune.
Copeland, Rachel. How to Hypnotize Yourself & Others. 240p. 1982. pap. text ed. 5.05 (ISBN 0-06-463554-6, EH 554, BN). Har-Row.
Crasilneck, Harold B. & Hall, James A. Clinical Hypnosis: Principles & Applications. LC 75-23325. (Illus.). 364p. 1975. 39.00 (ISBN 0-8089-0907-X). Grune.
Dengrove, Edward. Hypnosis & Behavior Therapy. (Illus.). 428p. 1976. 36.75 (ISBN 0-398-03336-6). C C Thomas.
Edelstien, M. Gerald. Trauma, Trance & Transformation: A Clinical Guide to Hypnotherapy. 150p. 1981. 15.00 (ISBN 0-87630-278-9). Brunner-Mazel.
Elman, Dave. Hypnotherapy. 1977. deluxe ed. 17.50x (ISBN 0-685-59058-5). Westwood Pub Co.
Erickson, Milton H. & Rossi, Ernest L. Experiencing Hypnosis: Theraputic Aproaches to Altered States. 300p. 1981. text ed. 34.50x incl. two audio cassette (ISBN 0-8290-0246-4). Irvington.
--Hypnotherapy: An Exploratory Casebook. LC 78-23839. 512p. (Orig.). 1980. text ed. 34.50x incl. audio cassette (ISBN 0-8290-0347-9). Irvington.
Furst, Arnold. How to Prepare & Administer Hypnotic Prescriptions. 10.00 (ISBN 0-685-07338-6). Borden.
Gardner, G. Gail & Olness, Karen. Hypnosis & Hypnptherapy with Children. 1981. price not set (ISBN 0-8089-1413-8). Grune.
Gibson, H. B. Hypnosis: Its Nature & Therapeutic Uses. LC 77-92821. 1980. pap. 4.95 (ISBN 0-8008-4043-7). Taplinger.
Gill, Merton M. & Brenman, Margaret. Hypnosis & Related States. LC 59-9821. 1959. text ed. 20.00 (ISBN 0-8236-2400-5). Intl Univs Pr.
Greenberg, Ira A., ed. Group Hypnotherapy & Hypnodrama. LC 76-17012. 320p. 1977. 20.95x (ISBN 0-88229-256-0). Nelson-Hall.
Group for the Advancement of Psychiatry. Medical Uses of Hypnosis, Vol. 4. (Symposium No. 8). 1962. pap. 1.00 (ISBN 0-87318-069-0, Pub. by Adv Psychiatry). Mental Health.
Gurman, Alan S., ed. Questions & Answers in the Practice of Family Therapy. LC 80-22460. 544p. 1981. 25.00 (ISBN 0-87630-246-0). Brunner-Mazel.
Haley, Jay. Uncommon Therapy: The Psychiatric Techniques of Milton H. Erickson, M. D. 1977. Repr. of 1973 ed. 10.00x (ISBN 0-393-01100-3, Norton Lib); pap. 3.95 (ISBN 0-393-00846-0). Norton.
Hartland, J. Medical & Dental Hypnosis & Its Clinical Application. 2nd ed. 1971. pap. text ed. 26.95 (ISBN 0-02-858010-9). Macmillan.
Hartman, B. J. A System of Hypnotherapy. 1980. 21.95x (ISBN 0-88229-449-0). Nelson-Hall.
Heron, William T. Clinical Applications of Suggestion & Hypnosis. 3rd ed. 184p. 1959. photocopy ed. spiral 18.50 (ISBN 0-398-04279-9). C C Thomas.
Hilgard, E. R. & Hilgard, J. R. Hypnosis in the Relief of Pain. LC 75-19490. (Illus.). 272p. 1975. 14.95 (ISBN 0-913232-16-5). W Kaufmann.
International Congress for Hypnosis & Psychosomatic Medicine, Paris, 1965. Proceedings. Lassner, J., ed. (Illus., Eng, Fr & Ger.). 1967. 50.80 (ISBN 0-387-03879-5). Springer-Verlag.
Klemperer, Edith. Past Ego States Emerging in Hypoanalysis. 292p. 1968. photocopy ed. spiral 29.50 (ISBN 0-398-01026-9). C C Thomas.
Kline, Milton V. Clinical Correlations of Experimental Hypnosis. (Illus.). 540p. 1963. photocopy ed. spiral 40.50 (ISBN 0-398-01027-7). C C Thomas.
--Psychodynamics & Hypnosis: New Contributions to the Practice & Theory of Hypnotherapy. (Illus.). 208p. 1966. photocopy ed. spiral 19.50 (ISBN 0-398-01028-5). C C Thomas.
Kroger, William S. Clinical & Experimental Hypnosis in Medicine, Dentistry, & Psychology. 2nd ed. LC 77-10320. 1977. 29.00 (ISBN 0-397-50377-6, JBL-Med-Nursing). Lippincott.
LeCron, Leslie M. & Bordeaux, Jean. Hypnotism Today. LC 47-1654. 287p. 1947. 30.75 (ISBN 0-8089-0259-8). Grune.
Magonet, A. P. Introduction to Psychotherapy by Hypnosis. 1970. 8.95 (ISBN 0-407-57050-0). Butterworth.
Meares, Ainslie. Hypnography: A Study in the Therapeutic Use of Hypnotic Painting. (Illus.). 288p. 1957. photocopy ed. spiral 27.50 (ISBN 0-398-01274-1). C C Thomas.
Miller, Michael. Therapeutic Hypnosis. LC 78-10405. 1979. 29.95 (ISBN 0-87705-341-3). Human Sci Pr.
Moodie, William. Hypnosis in Treatment. 1960. 8.95 (ISBN 0-87523-121-7). Emerson.
Moss, C. Scott. Dreams, Images, & Fantasy: A Semantic Differential Casebook. LC 79-105543. (Illus.). 1970. 17.50 (ISBN 0-252-00102-8). U of Ill Pr.
Moss, C. Scott & James, Pauline. Black Rover, Come Over: The Hypnosymbolic Treatment of a Phobia. LC 76-110421. (Illus.). 1970. pap. 3.95 (ISBN 0-252-00109-5); incl. audio tape cassette 12.50 (ISBN 0-252-00110-9). U of Ill Pr.
Netherton, Morris & Shiffrin, Nancy. Past Lives Therapy. 1979. pap. 2.25 (ISBN 0-441-65245-X). Ace Bks.
O'Hara, Monica. New Hope Through Hypnotherapy: The Joe Keeton Phenomenon. 150p. 1980. 13.50x (ISBN 0-85626-194-7, Pub. by Abacus Pr England); pap. 7.95x (ISBN 0-85626-194-7). Intl Schol Bk Serv.
Rhoades, Raphael H., ed. Therapy Through Hypnosis. pap. 4.00 (ISBN 0-87980-162-X). Wilshire.
Scott, Michael J. Hypnosis in Skin & Allergic Diseases. (Illus.). 164p. 1960. photocopy ed. spiral 16.50 (ISBN 0-398-01703-4). C C Thomas.
Shaw, H. Laurence. Hypnosis in Practice: Its Application in Stress & Disease. 1978. pap. text ed. 10.95 (ISBN 0-02-859200-X). Macmillan.
Spiegel, Herbert & Speigel, David. Trance & Treatment: Clinical Uses of Hypnosis. LC 77-20420. 1978. text ed. 18.50x (ISBN 0-465-08687-X). Basic.
Tebbets, Charles. Self Hypnosis & Other Mind Expanding Techniques. 1977. 7.95x (ISBN 0-930298-00-4). Westwood Pub Co.
Wain. Hypnosis in Clinical Medicine. 1980. 32.75 (ISBN 0-8151-9067-0). Year Bk Med.
Watkins, John G. & Watkins, Helen H. Ego-States & Hidden Observers & the Women in Black & the Lady in White. (Sound Seminars Ser.). 1980. transcript & tapes 29.50x (ISBN 0-88432-065-0, 29400-29401). J Norton Pubs.
Wolberg, Lewis R. Medical Hypnosis, 2 vols. Incl. Vol. I. Principles of Hypnotherapy. 460p. 39.50 (ISBN 0-8089-0536-8); Vol. II. Practice of Hypnotherapy. 520p. 39.50 (ISBN 0-8089-0537-6). LC 48-2929. 1948. Grune.
Zeig, Jeffrey K., ed. International Congress on Ericksonian Approaches to Hypnosis & Psychotherapy: Proceedings. 1981. 30.00 (ISBN 0-87630-276-2). Brunner-Mazel.
Zelvelder. Therapeutic Evaluation of Hypnotics. 1971. 18.55x (ISBN 90-232-0889-7, Pub by Van Gorcum). Intl Schol Bk Serv.

HYPNOTISM AND CRIME

Monoghan, Frank J. Hypnosis in Criminal Investigation. (Orig.). 1980. pap. text ed. 6.95 (ISBN 0-8403-2132-5). Kendall-Hunt.
Reiser, Martin. Handbook of Investigative Hypnosis. LC 79-53215. 1980. 24.95 (ISBN 0-934486-00-X). LEHI Pub Co.

HYPNOTISM IN DENTISTRY

Shaw, H. Laurence. Hypnosis in Practice: Its Application in Stress & Disease. 1978. pap. text ed. 10.95 (ISBN 0-02-859200-X). Macmillan.

HYPNOTISM IN OBSTETRICS

Arons, Harry. Hypnotic Conditioning for Childbirth. pap. 1.00 (ISBN 0-685-02588-8, Power). Borden.
Shaw, H. Laurence. Hypnosis in Practice: Its Application in Stress & Disease. 1978. pap. text ed. 10.95 (ISBN 0-02-859200-X). Macmillan.

HYPNOTISM IN SURGERY

European Congress of Anaesthesiology of the World Federation of Societies of Anaesthesiologists, 1st, Vienna, 1962. Hypnosis in Anaesthesiology: Proceedings. Lassner, J., ed. (Anaesthesiology & Resuscitation Ser.: Vol. 2). 1964. pap. 14.20 (ISBN 0-387-03166-9). Springer-Verlag.

HYPOACOUSTIC CHILDREN

see Children, Deaf

HYPOCHONDRIA

Boswell, James. Hypochondriack, 2 Vols. Bailey, Margery, ed. LC 78-39512. Repr. of 1928 ed. Set. 32.50 (ISBN 0-404-07654-8); 16.50 ea. Vol. 1 (ISBN 0-404-07655-6). Vol. 2 (ISBN 0-404-07656-4). AMS Pr.
De Mandeville, Bernard. A Treatise of the Hypochondriack & Hysterick Passions. LC 75-16717. (Classics in Psychiatry Ser.). 1976. Repr. of 1711 ed. 17.00x (ISBN 0-405-07445-X). Arno.
Ehrlich, Richard. Hypochondria: Everyone's Illness. LC 79-23810. 1980. 11.95 (ISBN 0-448-22242-6). Paddington.
Mandeville, Bernard. A Treatise of the Hypochondriack & Hysterick Diseases. LC 76-45623. 1976. Repr. of 1732 ed. 43.00x (ISBN 0-8201-1277-1). Schol Facsimiles.
Meister, Robert. Hypochondria: Toward a Better Understanding. LC 79-8700. 1980. 12.95 (ISBN 0-8008-4044-5). Taplinger.

HYPOCHROMIC ANEMIA

see also Iron Deficiency Anemia

HYPODERMIC INJECTIONS

see Injections, Hypodermic

HYPOFERRIC ANEMIA

see Iron Deficiency Anemia

HYPOGLYCEMIA

Abrahamson, E. M. & Pezet, A. W. Body, Mind & Sugar. 1951. 5.95 (ISBN 0-03-026555-X). HR&W.
Adams, Ruth & Murray, Frank. Is Blood Sugar Making You a Nutritional Cripple? rev. ed. 174p. (Orig.). 1975. pap. 2.25 (ISBN 0-915962-11-X). Larchmont Bks.
Airola, Paavo. Hypoglycemia. 4.95 (ISBN 0-686-29853-5). Cancer Bk Hse.
--Hypoglycemia: A Better Approach. 1977. 5.95 (ISBN 0-932090-01-X). Health Plus.
Andreani, Domeinco, et al, eds. Second European Symposium on Hypoglycemia. (Serono Symposia Ser.). 1980. 65.00 (ISBN 0-12-058680-0). Acad Pr.
Andreani, Dominico, et al, eds. Current Views on Hypoglycemia & Glucagon: Proceedings. LC 79-41558. (Serono Symposia: No. 30). 1980. 65.00 (ISBN 0-12-058680-0). Acad Pr.
Barnes, Broda. Hope: Hypoglycemia. 4.00 (ISBN 0-686-29861-6). Cancer Bk Hse.
Bolton, Ralph. Aggression & Hypoglycemia in Qolla Society. (LC 76-052698). Date not set. lib. bdg. 18.00 (ISBN 0-8240-9867-6, Garland STPM Pr). Garland Pub.
Brennan, R. O. Nutrigenetics: New Concepts for Relieving Hypoglycemia. 1977. pap. 1.95 (ISBN 0-451-07746-6, J7746, Sig). NAL.
Brennan, R. O. & Mulligan, William C. Nutrigenetics: New Concepts for Relieving Hypoglycemia: Case Studies. LC 75-23063. (Illus.). 264p. 1976. 8.95 (ISBN 0-87131-187-9). M Evans.
Brennen, R. O. Nutrigenetics: Relieving Hypoglycemia. 8.95 (ISBN 0-686-29875-6). Cancer Bk Hse.
Dannett, Sylvia G. & McCabe, Maureen. The Low Blood Sugar Gourmet Cookbook. 176p. 1975. pap. 3.50 (ISBN 0-06-463428-0, EH 428, EH). Har-Row.
Danowski, T. S. Hypoglycemia Syndromes. 1978. pap. 9.95 (ISBN 0-683-02346-2). Williams & Wilkins.
Fredericks, Carlton. Low Blood Sugar & You. 2.25 (ISBN 0-686-29923-X). Cancer Bk Hse.
Fredericks, Carlton & Goodman, Herman. Low Blood Sugar & You. 1969. pap. 4.95 (ISBN 0-448-12246-4, Today Press). G&D.
Griffin, LaDean. Hyper & Hypo-Glycemia. 2.00 (ISBN 0-89557-008-4). Bi World Indus.
Hofeldt, Fred D. Preventing Reactive Hypoglycemia. 300p. 1981. 27.50 (ISBN 0-87527-214-2). Green.
Hurdle, J. Frank. Low Blood Sugar: A Doctor's Guide to Its Effective Control. Orig. Title: Low Blood Sugar: How to Control This Hidden Menace to Your Health & Vitality. 1969. 12.95 (ISBN 0-13-541086-X, Parker). P-H.
--Low Blood Sugar: A Doctor's Guide to Its Effective Control. Orig. Title: Low Blood Sugar: How to Control This Hidden Menace to Your Health & Vitality. 1969. 12.95 (ISBN 0-13-541086-X, Reward); pap. 3.95 (ISBN 0-13-541078-9). P-H.
Martin, Clement G. Low Blood Sugar: The Hidden Menace of Hypoglycemia. LC 74-112735. Orig. Title: Low Blood Sugar & Your Health: Eat Your Way Out of Fatigue. 1970. pap. 1.75 (ISBN 0-668-02286-8). Arco.
Saunders, Jeraldine & Ross, Harvey. Hypoglycemia: The Disease Your Doctor Won't Treat. 256p. (Orig.). 1980. pap. 2.95 (ISBN 0-523-41053-0). Pinnacle Bks.
Steincrohn, Peter J. Low Blood Sugar. 1973. pap. 1.95 (ISBN 0-451-09750-5, J9750, Sig). NAL.
Symposium, Kingston, Jamaica. Hypoglycin: Proceedings. Kean, Eccleston A., ed. (PAABS Symposium Ser.). 1976. 38.50 (ISBN 0-12-404150-7). Acad Pr.

Weller, Charles & Boylan, Brian R. How to Live with Hypoglycemia. 1977. pap. 2.25 (ISBN 0-515-05979-X). Jove Pubns.

HYPOPHYSIS CEREBRI

see Pituitary Body

HYPOSTATIC UNION

Chemnitz, Martin. Two Natures in Christ. Preus, J. A., tr. LC 74-115465. Orig. Title: De Duabus Naturis in Christo. 1970. 19.95 (ISBN 0-570-03210-5, 15-2109). Concordia.

HYPOTENSION

see also Blood Pressure

Brunner & Gravas. Clinical Hypertension & Hypotension. (Kidney Disease Ser.: Vol. 2). 1982. price not set (ISBN 0-8247-1279-X). Dekker.

Gross. Mild Hypertension. 1980. 35.00 (ISBN 0-8151-4005-3). Year Bk Med.

Hatch & Sumner. Neonatal Anesthesia. (Current Topics Anesthesia: Vol. 5). Date not set. 27.95 (ISBN 0-8151-4191-2). Year Bk Med.

HYPOTENSIVE AGENTS

see also Kinins

De Jong, W., ed. Hypertension & Brain Mechanisms. 1977. 69.50 (ISBN 0-444-41534-3, North Holland). Elsevier.

Scriabine, A., ed. New Antihypertensive Drugs: A. N. Richards Symposium. Sweet, C. S. LC 76-20746. (Monographs of the Physiological Society of Philadelphia). 1976. 40.00 (ISBN 0-470-15181-1). Halsted Pr.

HYPOTHALAMUS

Cox. Pharmacology of the Hypothalamus. 1978. 39.50 (ISBN 0-8391-1299-8). Univ Park.

Cushing, Harvey. Papers Relating to the Pituitary Body, Hypothalamus & Parasympathetic Nervous System. (Illus.). 234p. 1932. ed. spiral bdg. 24.75photocopy (ISBN 0-398-04237-3). C C Thomas.

Everitt, Arthur V. & Burgess, John A. Hypothalamus, Pituitary & Aging. (Illus.). 808p. 1976. 67.50 (ISBN 0-398-03346-3). C C Thomas.

Gellhorn, Ernst. Autonomic Imbalance & the Hypothalamus: Implications for Physiology, Medicine, Psychology & Neuropsychiatry. LC 57-8919. (Illus.). 1957. 15.00x (ISBN 0-8166-0141-0). U of Minn Pr.

Gupta, Derek & Voelter, Wolfgang. Hypothalamic Hormones: Chemistry, Physiology & Clinical Applications. (Illus.). 1978. 75.30 (ISBN 3-527-25712-8). Verlag Chemie.

--Hypothalamic Hormones: Structure, Synthesis, & Biological Activity. (Illus.). 1975. 34.20 (ISBN 3-527-25589-3). Verlag Chemie.

Hafez, E. S. & Reel, J. R., eds. Hypothalamic Hormones, Vol. 1. LC 74-28654. (Perspectives in Human Reproduction Ser.). (Illus.). 1975. 24.00 (ISBN 0-250-40089-8). Ann Arbor Science.

Haymaker, Webb, et al. Hypothalamus. (Illus.). 820p. 1969. text ed. 57.00 (ISBN 0-398-00810-8). C C Thomas.

Jeffcoate, S. L. & Hutchinson, J. S., eds. The Endocrine Hypothalamus. 1979. 67.50 (ISBN 0-12-382150-9). Acad Pr.

Labrie, Fernand, et al, eds. Hypothalamus & Endocrine Functions. LC 76-13912. (Current Topics in Molecular Endocrinology Ser.: Vol. 3). 508p. 1976. 42.50 (ISBN 0-306-34003-8, Plenum Pr). Plenum Pub.

Lederis, K. & Veale, W. L., eds. Current Studies of Hypothalamic Function 1978. Incl. Part I: Hormones. 49.00 (ISBN 3-8055-2860-4); Part II: Metabolism & Behaviour. 49.00 (ISBN 3-8055-2861-2). (Illus.). 1978. 88.00 set (ISBN 3-8055-2969-4). S Karger.

Locke, William & Schally, Andrew V., eds. The Hypothalamus & Pituitary in Health & Disease. (Illus.). 624p. 1972. 41.75 (ISBN 0-398-02526-6). C C Thomas.

Martini, L. & Meites, J., eds. Neurochemical Aspects of Hypothalmic Function. 1971. 25.00 (ISBN 0-12-475560-7). Acad Pr.

Martini, L., et al, eds. Hypothalamus. 1971. 28.50 (ISBN 0-12-475550-X). Acad Pr.

Meites, J. Hypophysiotropic Hormones of Hypothalamus: Assay & Chemistry. 348p. 1970. 25.00 (ISBN 0-683-05910-6, Pub. by Williams & Wilkins). Krieger.

Morgane & Panksepp. Handbook of the Hypothalmus, Vol. 3, Pt. A. (Behavioral Studies of the Hypothalmus). 472p. 1980. 93.50 (ISBN 0-8247-6904-X). Dekker.

--Physiology of the Hypothalamus, Pt. A: Handbook of the Hypothalamus, Vol. 3. 512p. 1980. 145.00 (ISBN 0-8247-6881-7). Dekker.

Morgane & Panskepp. Physiology of the Hypothalmus: Handbook of the Hypothalamus, Vol. 2. 688p. 1980. 145.00 (ISBN 0-8247-6881-7). Dekker.

Morgane & Panksepp, eds. Anatomy of the Hypothalmus. (Handbook of the Hypothalmus Ser.: Vol. 1). 145.00 (ISBN 0-8247-6834-5). Dekker.

Morgane, P. & Panksepp, J. Handbook of the Hypothalmus, Vol. 1. 1979. 145.00 (ISBN 0-8247-6834-5). Dekker.

Morgane, Panksepp. Behavioral Studies of the Hypothalmus, Part B. 480p. 1981. 93.50 (ISBN 0-8247-6905-8). Dekker.

Motta, M., et al. Hypothalamic Hormones: Chemistry, Physiology, Pharmacology & Clinical Uses. (Serono Symposia Ser.). 1976. 56.00 (ISBN 0-12-509150-8). Acad Pr.

Mrosovsky, Nicholas. Hibernation & the Hypothalamus. 287p. 1971. 22.50 (ISBN 0-306-50058-2, Plenum Pr). Plenum Pub.

Olds, James. Drives & Reinforcements: Behavioral Studies of Hypothalamic Functions. LC 75-31480. 148p. 1977. pap. 10.50 (ISBN 0-89004-087-7). Raven.

Reichlin, Seymour, et al, eds. The Hypothalamus, Vol. 56. LC 77-83691. (Association for Research in Nervous & Mental Disease Research Publications). 504p. 1978. 43.50 (ISBN 0-89004-167-9). Raven.

Sulman, F. G. Hypothalamic Control of Lactation. LC 70-125281. (Monographs on Endocrinology: Vol. 3). (Illus.). 1970. 34.40 (ISBN 0-387-04973-8). Springer-Verlag.

Symposium, Calgary, Alberta, May, 1973. Recent Studies of Hypothalamic Function: Proceedings. Lederis, K. & Cooper, K. E., eds. (Illus.). 450p. 1974. 34.75 (ISBN 3-8055-1694-0). S Karger.

Watkins, Wayne. Hypothalamic Releasing Factors, Vol. 1. 1977. 19.20 (ISBN 0-88831-002-1). Eden Med Res.

--Hypothalamic Releasing Factors, Vol. 3. Horrobin, D. F., ed. (Annual Research Reviews Ser.). 1979. 20.00 (ISBN 0-88831-046-3). Eden Med Res.

Watkins, Wayne B. Hypothalamic Releasing Factors, Vol. 2. Horrobin, David F., ed. (Annual Research Reviews Ser.). 1978. 21.60 (ISBN 0-88831-033-1). Eden Med Res.

Zimmermann, E. & George, R., eds. Narcotics & the Hypothalamus. LC 74-83453. 286p. 1974. 27.00 (ISBN 0-911216-87-1). Raven.

HYPOTHECATION

see Liens; Mortgages

HYPOTHERMIA

Adam, James M. Hypothermia - Ashore & Afloat: Proceedings of 3rd International " Action for Disaster " Conference, Aberdeen 1979. (Illus.). 216p. 1981. 45.00 (ISBN 0-08-025750-X). Pergamon.

Boba, Antonio. Hypothermia for the Neurosugical Patient. (Illus.). 132p. 1960. ed. spiral bdg. 12.75photocopy (ISBN 0-398-00182-0). C C Thomas.

Forgey, William W. Hypothermia. (Illus.). 52p. (Orig.). 1981. pap. 1.95 (ISBN 0-934802-10-6). ICS Bks.

Negovskii, V. A. Acute Problems of Resuscitation & Artificial Hypothermia. LC 62-2189. 1962. 40.00 (ISBN 0-306-10598-5, Consultants). Plenum Pub.

Negovskii, V. A., ed. Acute Problems in Resuscitation & Hypothermia. LC 65-20214. 91p. 1965. 32.50 (ISBN 0-306-10705-8, Consultants). Plenum Pub.

Wicks, Malcolm. Old & Cold. LC 78-321889. (Studies in Social Policy & Welfare). 1978. text ed. 31.95x (ISBN 0-435-82939-4). Heinemann Ed.

HYPOTHESIS

see also Statistical Hypothesis Testing

Barker, S. F. Induction & Hypothesis: A Study of the Logic of Confirmation. (Contemporary Philosophy Ser.). 203p. 1957. 17.50x (ISBN 0-8014-0027-9). Cornell U Pr.

Harris, Errol E. Hypothesis & Perception: The Roots of Scientific Method. (Muirhead Library of Philosophy). 1970. text ed. 16.50x (ISBN 0-391-00014-4). Humanities.

Levine, Martin. A Cognitive Theory of Learning: Research on Hypotheses Testing. (Experimental Psychology Ser.). 1975. text ed. 16.50 (ISBN 0-470-53126-6). Halsted Pr.

Poincare, H. Science & Hypothesis. LC 53-13673. 1952. lib. bdg. 11.50 (ISBN 0-88307-235-1). Gannon.

HYPOTHESIS TESTING (STATISTICS)

see Statistical Hypothesis Testing

HYPOXIA

see Anoxemia

HYSTERECTOMY

Baggish, Michael S. Atlas of Contact Hysteroscopy. 1982. price not set. Urban & S.

Gitsch, Eduard & Palmrich, Adolf. Gynecological Operative Anatomy: The Simple & Radical Hysterectomy Atlas. (Illus.). 1977. 123.00x (ISBN 3-11-006691-2). De Gruyter.

Gray, Laman A. Vaginal Hysterectomy: Indications, Technique & Complications. 2nd ed. (American Lectures in Gynecology & Obstetrics Ser.). (Illus.). 240p. 1963. 14.75 (ISBN 0-398-00721-7). C C Thomas.

Guistini, F. G. & Keefer, F. J. Understanding Hysterectomy: A Woman's Guide. (Illus.). 1979. 12.95 (ISBN 0-8027-0633-9); pap. 7.95 (ISBN 0-8027-7150-5). Walker & Co.

Hirsch, H. A., ed. Vaginale Hysterektomie und Inkontinenz-Operationen. (Gynaekologische Rundschau, 1979: Supplement 1, Vol. 19). (Illus.). 1979. 25.25 (ISBN 3-8055-3072-2). S Karger.

HYSTERIA

see also Demoniac Possession; Ecstasy; Trance; Witchcraft

De Mandeville, Bernard. A Treatise of the Hypochondriack & Hysterick Passions. LC 75-16717. (Classics in Psychiatry Ser.). 1976. Repr. of 1711 ed. 17.00x (ISBN 0-405-07445-X). Arno.

Detmar, Bernhard. Nervous Disorders & Hysteria. 1955. 1.50 (ISBN 0-685-06585-5). Assoc Bk.

Freud, Sigmund. Selected Papers on Hysteria & Other Psychoneuroses. Brill, A. A., tr. (Nervous & Mental Disease Monographs: No. 4). Repr. of 1912 ed. 15.50 (ISBN 0-384-16810-8). Johnson Repr.

Horowitz, Mardi J. Hysterical Personality. LC 77-73100. 1977. 25.00x (ISBN 0-87668-264-6). Aronson.

Janet, P. Major Symptoms of Hysteria. 2nd ed. 1965. Repr. of 1929 ed. 13.00 (ISBN 0-02-847170-9). Hafner.

Janet, Pierre. The Major Symptoms of Hysteria. 345p. 1980. Repr. of 1920 ed. lib. bdg. 40.00 (ISBN 0-8492-1367-3). R West.

--Mental State of Hystericals. (Contributions to the History of Psychology Ser.: Pt. 2, Medical Psychology). 1978. Repr. of 1901 ed. 30.00 (ISBN 0-89093-166-6). U Pubns Amer.

Jorden, Edward. A Briefe Discourse of a Disease Called the Suffocation of the Mother. LC 77-171768. (English Experience Ser.: No. 392). 58p. 1971. Repr. of 1603 ed. 7.00 (ISBN 90-221-0392-7). Walter J Johnson.

Kretschmer, Ernst. Hysteria, Reflex, & Instinct. Baskin, Vlasta & Baskin, Wade, trs. from Ger. LC 76-139138. 1971. Repr. of 1960 ed. lib. bdg. 15.00x (ISBN 0-8371-5754-4, KRHR). Greenwood.

Lowry, Thomas P. Hyperventilation & Hysteria: The Physiology & Psychology of Overbreathing & Its Realationship to the Mind-Body Problem. (Illus.). 208p. 1967. photocopy ed. spiral 19.75 (ISBN 0-398-01156-7). C C Thomas.

Mandeville, Bernard. A Treatise of the Hypochondriack & Hysterick Diseases. LC 76-45623. 1976. Repr. of 1732 ed. 43.00x (ISBN 0-8201-1277-1). Schol Facsimiles.

Merskey, Harold. The Analysis of Hysteria. 1979. text ed. 26.50 (ISBN 0-02-858490-2). Macmillan.

Veith, Ilza. Hysteria: The History of a Disease. LC 65-24429. (Illus.). 1970. pap. 3.25 (ISBN 0-226-85253-9, P351, Phoen). U of Chicago Pr.

Wesley, George R. A History of Hysteria. LC 79-51464. 1979. pap. text ed. 9.00 (ISBN 0-8191-0751-4). U Pr of Amer.

HYSTERIA (SOCIAL PSYCHOLOGY)

Abse, D. W. Hysteria & Related Mental Disorders. (Illus.). 1966. 18.95 (ISBN 0-8151-0005-1). Year Bk Med.

Eysenck, H. J. The Dynamics of Anxiety & Hysteria: An Experimental Application of Modern Learning Theory to Psychiatry. (Illus.). 1967. Repr. of 1957 ed. 30.00x (ISBN 0-7100-1354-X). Routledge & Kegan.

Krohn, Alan. Hysteria: The Elusive Neurosis. LC 76-45546. (Psychological Issues Monograph: Nos. 45/46). 1978. text ed. 25.00 (ISBN 0-8236-2426-9); pap. text ed. 16.50 (ISBN 0-8236-2425-0). Intl Univs Pr.

Levin, Murray B. Political Hysteria in America: The Democratic Capacity for Repression. LC 71-174826. 1972. 12.50x (ISBN 0-465-05898-1). Basic.

Murray, Robert K. Red Scare: A Study in National Hysteria, 1919-1920. 1955. pap. 3.95 (ISBN 0-07-044075-1, SP). McGraw.

HYSTERIA, EPIDEMIC

see also Chorea, Epidemic

I

I CHING

Albertson, Edward. The Complete I Ching. 1969. 2.50 (ISBN 0-8202-0011-5). Sherbourne.

Anthony, Carol K. A Guide to the I Ching. LC 79-93376. 184p. (Orig.). 1980. pap. 5.95 (ISBN 0-9603832-0-4). Anthony Pub Co.

Culling, L. T. Incredible I Ching. LC 79-18011. pap. 1.25 (ISBN 0-87728-054-1). Weiser.

Da Liu. I Ching Numerology. LC 77-20459. (Illus.). 1979. pap. 4.95 (ISBN 0-06-061668-7, RD 262, HarpR). Har-Row.

Govinda, Lama Anagarika. The Inner Structure of the I Ching: The Book of Transformations. (Illus.). 224p. 1981. 17.95 (ISBN 0-8348-0165-5). Weatherhill.

Hook, Diana F. The I Ching & Its Associations. (Illus.). 1980. 15.95 (ISBN 0-7100-0506-7); pap. 7.95 (ISBN 0-7100-0507-5). Routledge & Kegan.

--I Ching & Mankind. 1975. 12.95 (ISBN 0-7100-8058-1). Routledge & Kegan.

--I Ching & You. 1973. pap. 4.25 (ISBN 0-525-47343-2). Dutton.

Hwuy-Le. The Life of Hiuen-Tsiang. Beal, Samuel, tr. from Chinese. & intro. by. LC 73-880. (China Studies: from Confucius to Mao Ser). xlvii, 218p. 1973. Repr. of 1911 ed. 19.50 (ISBN 0-88355-074-1). Hyperion Conn.

I Ching. I Ching: The Book of Changes. Legge, James, tr. (Sacred Books of the East Ser.). 8.75 (ISBN 0-8446-2291-5). Peter Smith.

I Ching: Book of Changes. 1971. 2.95 (ISBN 0-442-82261-8). Peter Pauper.

I Ching Cards; a Visual Introduction. 6.00 (ISBN 0-8216-0096-6). Univ Bks.

Kegan, Frank R. I Ching Primer: An Introduction to Relevant Process, Perspective Upon the Occult in General & the Flux Tome. (Illus.). 1979. pap. 5.00 (ISBN 0-933646-03-8). Aries Pr.

--Oracle Book: An Explanation of the Powers & Uses of Oracles Particularly the I Ching in Modern American Perspective. (Illus.). 1981. pap. 7.50 (ISBN 0-933646-10-0). Aries Pr.

Lee, Jung Y. The I Ching & Modern Man. LC 74-28541. 1975. 8.95 (ISBN 0-8216-0253-5). Univ Bks.

--Principle of Changes: Understanding the I Ching. 1971. 10.00 (ISBN 0-8216-0139-3). Univ Bks.

Legge, James. I Ching: Book of Changes. 450p. 1974. pap. 4.95 (ISBN 0-8065-0458-7). Citadel Pr.

Li, H. Y. & Morrill, Sibley S., eds. I Ching Games of Duke Tan of Chou & C. C. T'ung. LC 73-168424. (Illus.). 138p. 1971. pap. 5.95 (ISBN 0-9600310-2-2). Cadleon Pr.

Melyan, Gary G. & Chu, Wen-Kaung. I-Ching: The Hexagrams Revealed. LC 76-6029. 1976. 8.75 (ISBN 0-8048-1182-2). C E Tuttle.

Murphy. Secrets of the I Ching. pap. 3.95 (ISBN 0-13-798694-7). P-H.

Murphy, Joseph. Secrets of the I Ching. LC 78-113173. (Illus.). 1970. 8.95 (ISBN 0-13-798702-1, Parker). P-H.

Oshiro, Hide. The Graphic I Ching. (Illus.). 1979. 9.95 (ISBN 0-932284-10-8); collector ed. 200.00 (ISBN 0-932284-09-4). Turtle Island.

Post, James N. Sixty-Four Keys: An Introductory Guide to the I Ching. LC 78-52145. 2.50 (ISBN 0-89861-008-7). Esoteric Pubns.

Reifler, Sam. I Ching: A New Interpretation for Modern Times. 288p. (Orig.). 1974. pap. 3.50 (ISBN 0-553-14932-6). Bantam.

Schoenholtz, Larry. New Directions in the I Ching: The Yellow River Legacy. LC 74-28540. 1975. 7.95 (ISBN 0-8216-0255-1). Univ Bks.

Shchutskii, Iulien. Researches on the I Ching. Macdonald, William L., et al, trs. Hasegawa, Tsuyoshi & Wilhelm, Hellmut, eds. LC 78-63600. (Bollingen Ser.: No. 62). 1979. text ed. 14.50 (ISBN 0-691-09939-1). Princeton U Pr.

Sherril, W. A., ed. The Astrology of I Ching. Chu, W. K., tr. 1976. pap. 9.95 (ISBN 0-87728-492-X). Weiser.

Sherrill, W. A. & Chu, W. K. An Anthology of I Ching. 1978. 22.00 (ISBN 0-7100-8590-7). Routledge & Kegan.

Siu, R. G. The Portable Dragon: The Western Man's Guide to the I Ching. LC 68-18242. 1968. pap. 8.95 (ISBN 0-262-69030-6). MIT Pr.

Spaulding, Ken & Richards, Lois. Simple I Ching. 1978. 4.95 (ISBN 0-533-03281-4). Vantage.

Sung, Z. D. Symbols of Yi King, or the Symbols of the Chinese Logic of Changes. LC 73-77389. (Illus.). 1969. Repr. of 1934 ed. 9.00 (ISBN 0-8188-0086-0). Paragon.

Van Over, Raymond, ed. I Ching. rev ed. (Orig.). 1971. pap. 1.95 (ISBN 0-451-61524-7, MJ1524, Ment). NAL.

Wilhelm, Hellmut. The Book of Changes in the Western Tradition: A Selective Bibliography. LC 76-7802. (Parerga Ser.: No. 2). 30p. 1976. pap. 2.75 (ISBN 0-295-95481-7). U of Wash Pr.

--Change: Eight Lectures on the I Ching. Baynes, C. F., tr. (Bollingen Series, Vol. 62). 115p. 1960. 11.00 (ISBN 0-691-09714-3); pap. 3.95 (ISBN 0-691-01787-5). Princeton U Pr.

--Heaven, Earth, & Man in the Book of Changes: Seven Eranos Lectures. LC 76-7801. (Publications on Asia of the School of International Studies: No. 28). 248p. 1977. 15.00 (ISBN 0-295-95516-3); pap. 8.95 (ISBN 0-295-95692-5). U of Wash Pr.

Wilhelm, Richard. Lectures on the I Ching: Constancy & Change. Eber, Irene, ed. LC 79-84027. (Bollingen Ser. 19: 2). 1979. 9.75 (ISBN 0-691-09902-2). Princeton U Pr.

Wing, R. L. The I Ching Workbook. LC 77-15142. 1979. pap. 7.95 (ISBN 0-385-12838-X). Doubleday.

I-LI HA-SA-KO TZU CHIH CHOU
Moseley, George. Sino-Soviet Cultural Frontier: The Ili Kazakh Autonomous Chou. LC 67-827. (East Asian Monographs Ser: No. 22). 1966. pap. 9.00x (ISBN 0-674-80925-4). Harvard U Pr.

IAMBIC TETRAMETER
Bailey, James. Towards a Statistical Analysis of English Verse: The Iambic Tetrameter of Ten Poets. (English Metrics). 1975. pap. text ed. 7.00x (ISBN 90-316-0004-0). Humanities.

IATMULS
Bateson, Gregory. Naven. 2nd ed. (Illus.). 1958. 17.50x (ISBN 0-8047-0519-4); pap. 6.95x (ISBN 0-8047-0520-8). Stanford U Pr.

IATROGENIC DISEASES
D'Arcy, P. F. Latrogenic Diseases. 2nd ed. (Illus.). 1980. text ed. 67.50x (ISBN 0-19-264179-4). Oxford U Pr.
D'Arcy, P. F. & Griffin, J. P. Iatrogenic Diseases: Annual Update 1981. 2nd ed. (Illus.). 200p. 1981. text ed. 46.50x (ISBN 0-19-261263-8). Oxford U Pr.
Illich, Ivan. Medical Nemesis: The Expropriation of Health. 1977. pap. 2.75 (ISBN 0-553-10596-5, 13371-3). Bantam.
Lambert, Edward C. Modern Medical Mistakes. LC 77-15214. 192p. 1978. 10.95x (ISBN 0-253-15425-1). Ind U Pr.
Meyers, M. A. & Ghahremani, G. G., eds. Iatrogenic Gastrointestinal Complications. (Radiology of Iatrogenic Disorders Ser.). (Illus.). 307p. 1981. 49.00 (ISBN 0-387-90505-7). Springer-Verlag.
Moser, Roberth. Diseases of Medical Progress: A Study of Iatrogenic Disease: a Contemporary Analysis of Illness Produced by Drugs & Other Therapeutic Procedures. 3rd ed. (Illus.). 967p. 1969. ed. spiral bdg. 97.50photocopy (ISBN 0-398-01356-X). C C Thomas.
Schwartz, E. E. The Radiology of Complications in Medical Practice. (Illus.). 480p. 1981. lib. bdg. 48.00 (ISBN 0-683-07571-3). Williams & Wilkins.

IBADAN, NIGERIA
Afigbo, A. E. The Warrant Chiefs: Indirect Rule in Southeastern Nigeria, 1891-1929. (Ibadan History Ser.). 320p. 1972. text ed. 13.25x (ISBN 0-391-00215-5). Humanities.
Aronson, Dan R. The City Is Our Farm: Seven Migrant Ijebu Yoruba Families. 2nd ed. 224p. 1978. pap. text ed. 7.95 (ISBN 0-87073-563-2). Schenkman.
Oloruntimehin, B. O. Segu Tukulor Empire. (Ibadan History Ser.). (Illus.). 357p. 1972. text ed. 14.00x (ISBN 0-391-00206-6). Humanities.
Parrinder, Geoffrey. Religion in an African City. LC 74-142921. (Illus.). Repr. of 1953 ed. 13.25x (ISBN 0-8371-5947-4). Greenwood.

IBADAN, NIGERIA-UNIVERSITY COLLEGE
Ibadan University Library -(Ibadan - Nigeria) Africana Catalogue of the Ibadan University Library, 2 vols. 1973. Set. 145.00 (ISBN 0-8161-0941-9). G K Hall.

IBARA, FRANCISCO DE, 1538-1575
Mecham, John L. Francisco De Ibarra & Nueva Vizcaya. LC 68-23315. (Illus.). 1968. Repr. of 1927 ed. lib. bdg. 17.50x (ISBN 0-8371-0168-9, MEFI). Greenwood.

IBATAN LANGUAGE
see Batan Language

IBERIANS
see also Basques
Carver, Norman. Iberian Villages: Spain & Portugal. 1981. 26.95 (ISBN 0-932076-02-5); pap. 17.95 (ISBN 0-932076-03-3). Morgan.
Hanson, Carl A. Dissertations on Iberian & Latin American History. LC 74-97478. 400p. 1975. 20.00 (ISBN 0-87875-073-8). Whitston Pub.
Index to Leaders of Iberian Christianity. 1.00 (ISBN 0-686-23370-0). Classical Folia.
Marique, J. M., ed. Leaders of Iberian Christianity. 5.00 (ISBN 0-686-23369-7). Classical Folia.
Zyla, Wolodymyr T. & Aycock, Wendell M., eds. Ibero-American Letters in a Comparative Perspective: Proceedings of the Comparative Literature Symposium. LC 78-52067. (Vol. X). (Illus.). 1978. 8.00 (ISBN 0-89672-061-6). Tex Tech Pr.

IBERO-INSULAR RACE
see Mediterranean Race

IBIBIOS
Andreski, Iris, ed. Old Wives' Tales: Life-Stories of African Women. LC 77-107613. (Sourcebooks in Negro History Ser). 1971. 8.00x (ISBN 0-8052-3342-3). Schocken.
Talbot, D. A. Woman's Mysteries of a Primitive People: Ibibios of Southern Nigeria. (Illus.). 252p. (Orig.). 1968. 27.50x (ISBN 0-686-11427-2, F Cass Co). Biblio Dist.

IBIZA-DESCRIPTION AND TRAVEL
Foss, Arthur. Ibiza & Minorca. (Illus.). 210p. 1978. 15.95 (ISBN 0-571-10487-8, Pub. by Faber & Faber); pap. 7.95 (ISBN 0-571-11220-X). Merrimack Bk Serv.
Llopis, Arturo. Iviza. (Spanish Guide Ser). (Illus.). 1964. 4.50x (ISBN 0-8002-1602-4). Intl Pubns Serv.
Thurson, Hazel. The Balearic Islands: Majorca, Minorca, Ibiza & Formentera. 1977. 19.95 (ISBN 0-7134-0882-0). David & Charles.

IBM APERTURE CARD SYSTEMS
see Microfilm Aperture Card Systems

IBM 360 (COMPUTER)
Ashby, Gordon P. & Heilman, Robert L. Introduction to I-O Concepts & Job Control Language for the IBM Operating System 360. 1971. pap. 13.95x (ISBN 0-8221-0004-5). Dickenson.
Basic PL-1 for IBM System-360, Bks. 1 & 2. 1969-70. PL-1, Bk. 1. pap. text ed. 8.95 (ISBN 0-574-16099-X, 15-0021); notebook for bk. 1 1.20 (ISBN 0-574-16101-5); PL-1, Bk. 2. pap. text ed. 8.95 (ISBN 0-574-16100-7, 15-0022); notebook for bk. 2 3.50 (ISBN 0-686-67711-0, 15-0024); guide 1.75 (ISBN 0-686-67712-9, 15-0025). SRA.
Batten, William T. Understanding the IBM Three-Sixty & Three-Seventy Computer with Machine Language Programming. (Illus.). 480p. 1974. 19.95 (ISBN 0-13-936096-4). P-H.
Brooks, Frederick P., Jr. The Mythical Man-Month: Essays on Software Engineering. (Illus.). 200p. 1974. pap. text ed. 9.95 (ISBN 0-201-00650-2). A-W.
Brown, Gary D. System-360 Job-Control Language. 1970. pap. 18.50 (ISBN 0-471-10870-7, Pub. by Wiley-Interscience). Wiley.
Cashman, Thomas J. & Shelly, Gary B. IBM 360 & Assembler Language Work Book. LC 75-23969. (Illus.). 1973. pap. text ed. 6.95x (ISBN 0-88236-051-5). Anaheim Pub Co.
--Introduction to Computer Programming IBM System-360 Assembler Language. LC 75-4790. 250p. pap. text ed. 12.95x (ISBN 0-88236-050-7). Anaheim Pub Co.
Chapin, Ned. Three-Sixty - Three-Seventy Programming in Assembly Language. 1973. text ed. 22.95 (ISBN 0-07-010552-9, C). McGraw.
Computer Usage Company Inc. & Weiss, E. A. Computer Usage - Three Sixty Fortran Programming. 1969. pap. text ed. 15.95 (ISBN 0-07-012381-0, C). McGraw.
Essick, Edward L. RPG for System 360 & System 370. (Orig.). 1973. pap. text ed. 16.95 scp (ISBN 0-06-382625-9, HarpC). Har-Row.
Feingold, Carl. Introduction to Assembler Language Programming. 427p. 1978. pap. text ed. write for info. (ISBN 0-697-08124-9); instrs.' manual avail. (ISBN 0-686-67946-6). Wm C Brown.
FORTRAN for IBM System-360. 1968. pap. text ed. 10.95 (ISBN 0-574-16104-X, 15-0600); guide 2.25 (ISBN 0-574-16105-8, 15-0601). SRA.
Hannula, Reino. Computers & Programming: A System 360-370 Assembler Language Approach. 400p. 1974. text ed. 22.50 (ISBN 0-395-16796-5). HM.
--System 360-370 Job Control Language & the Access Methods. LC 76-23986. (Illus.). 1977. pap. text ed. 11.95 (ISBN 0-201-02755-0). A-W.
Kapur, Gopal K. IBM 360 Assembler Language Programming. LC 76-12572. 560p. 1971. 25.95 (ISBN 0-471-45840-6). Wiley.
Laurie, Edward J. Modern Computer Concepts. 1970. text ed. 11.45 (ISBN 0-538-10200-4). SW Pub.
Loschetter, Richard F. RPG for IBM Systems-360, 370 & System 3. (Illus.). 448p. 1975. ref. ed. 25.95 (ISBN 0-13-773713-0). P-H.
Murach, Mike. System-Three-Sixty RPG. LC 70-178830. (Illus.). 297p. 1972. pap. text ed. 15.95 (ISBN 0-574-16097-3, 13-1415); instr's guide avail. (ISBN 0-574-16128-7, 13-1416); transparency masters 29.95 (ISBN 0-574-16129-5, 13-1417). SRA.
Rattenbury, Judith. Introduction to the IBM 360 Computer & OS-JCL (Job Control Language) rev. ed. LC 73-620248. 103p. 1974. 8.00 (ISBN 0-87944-011-2). Inst Soc Res.
Rindfleisch. Debugging System 360-370 Programs Using OS & VS Storage Dumps. 1976. 24.95 (ISBN 0-13-197632-X). P-H.
Rudd, Walter G. Assembly Language Programming & the IBM 360 & 370 Computers. 1976. 21.95 (ISBN 0-13-049536-0); wkbk. 6.95 (ISBN 0-13-049510-7). P-H.
Schriber, T. J. Simulation Using GPSS. LC 73-21896. 608p. 1974. 32.95 (ISBN 0-471-76310-1). Wiley.
Shelly, Gary B. & Cashman, Thomas J. IBM 360 Assembler Language Disk-Tape Advanced Concepts. LC 78-22880. 300p. pap. text ed. 14.95x (ISBN 0-88236-060-4). Anaheim Pub Co.
Smillie, Keith W. APL-360 with Statistical Examples. 1974. text ed. 11.95 (ISBN 0-201-07069-3). A-W.
Stabley, Don. Logical Programming with System 360. LC 75-96047. 579p. 1970. 33.95 (ISBN 0-471-81945-X). Wiley.
--System 360 Assembler Language. LC 67-30037. 129p. 1967. pap. 15.95 (ISBN 0-471-81950-6, Pub. by Wiley-Interscience). Wiley.
Stark, Richard & Dearholt, Donald W. Computer Concepts & Assembler Programming: 360-370 Systems. 1975. text ed. 20.95 (ISBN 0-12-664550-7); instr's manual 3.00 (ISBN 0-12-664552-3). Acad Pr.
Struble, George W. Assembler Language Programming: The IBM System 360. 2nd ed. 496p. 1975. text ed. 20.95 (ISBN 0-201-07322-6). A-W.

IBM 370 (COMPUTER)
Batten, William T. Understanding the IBM Three-Sixty & Three-Seventy Computer with Machine Language Programming. (Illus.). 480p. 1974. 19.95 (ISBN 0-13-936096-4). P-H.
Brown, Gary D. System-370 Job Control Language. LC 77-24901. 1977. 17.25 (ISBN 0-471-03155-0, Pub. by Wiley-Interscience). Wiley.
Feingold, Carl. Introduction to Assembler Language Programming. 427p. 1978. pap. text ed. write for info. (ISBN 0-697-08124-9); instrs.' manual avail. (ISBN 0-686-67946-6). Wm C Brown.
Hannula, Reino. Computers & Programming: A System 360-370 Assembler Language Approach. 400p. 1974. text ed. 22.50 (ISBN 0-395-16796-5). HM.
--System 360-370 Job Control Language & the Access Methods. LC 76-23986. (Illus.). 1977. pap. text ed. 11.95 (ISBN 0-201-02755-0). A-W.
Rindfleisch. Debugging System 360-370 Programs Using OS & VS Storage Dumps. 1976. 24.95 (ISBN 0-13-197632-X). P-H.
Rudd, Walter G. Assembly Language Programming & the IBM 360 & 370 Computers. 1976. 21.95 (ISBN 0-13-049536-0); wkbk. 6.95 (ISBN 0-13-049510-7). P-H.
Stark, Richard & Dearholt, Donald W. Computer Concepts & Assembler Programming: 360-370 Systems. 1975. text ed. 20.95 (ISBN 0-12-664550-7); instr's manual 3.00 (ISBN 0-12-664552-3). Acad Pr.

IBM 1130 (COMPUTER)
Hughes, Joan. Programming the IBM 1130. LC 69-16045. 1969. 26.95x (ISBN 0-471-42040-9). Wiley.
Jamison, Robert V. Fortran IV Programming: Based on the IBM System 1130. LC 70-96241. (Illus.). 1970. text ed. 17.95 (ISBN 0-07-032270-8, G); instructor's manual 2.95 (ISBN 0-07-032274-0). McGraw.
Louden, Robert K. & Ledin, George. Programming the IBM 1130. 2nd ed. (Illus.). 448p. 1972. pap. 17.95 ref. ed. (ISBN 0-13-730275-4). P-H.

IBM 1620 (COMPUTER)
Andree, Richard V. Computer Programming & Related Mathematics. 284p. 1967. text ed. 14.00x (ISBN 0-471-02920-3, Pub. by Wiley). Krieger.
Stuart, Frederick. Introductory Computer Programming. 155p. 1966. text ed. 8.50 (ISBN 0-471-83475-0, Pub. by Wiley). Krieger.

IBN AL-ARABI, 1165-1240
Affifi, Abul E. The Mystical Philosophy of Muhyid Din-Ibnul 'arabi. LC 77-180312. (Mid-East Studies). Repr. of 1939 ed. 12.00 (ISBN 0-404-56205-1). AMS Pr.
Corbin, Henry. Creative Imagination in the Sufism of Ibn'Arabi. Manheim, R., tr. (Bollingen Ser.: Vol. 91). 1969. 25.00 (ISBN 0-691-09852-2). Princeton U Pr.
Husaini. Ibn-Al-Arabi. pap. 1.50 (ISBN 0-686-18320-7). Kazi Pubns.
Husaini, S. A. The Pantheistic Monism of Ibn Al-Arabi. 1970. 8.60x (ISBN 0-87902-164-0). Orientalia.
Nasr, Seyyed H. Three Muslim Sages. LC 75-14430. 192p. 1976. pap. text ed. 8.00x (ISBN 0-88206-500-9). Caravan Bks.

IBN AL-KHATIB
Al-Maqqari, Ahmed, ed. History of the Mohammedan Dynasties in Spain, 2 Vols. De Gayangos, P., tr. 1969. Repr. of 1840 ed. Set. 146.50 (ISBN 0-384-35253-7). Johnson Repr.

IBN-BATUTA
see Muhammad Ibn-'Abdullah Ibn-Battutah, 1304-1377

IBN KHALDUN, 1332-1406
Ednan, M. A. Life of Ibn Khaldun & His Work. 4.95 (ISBN 0-686-18317-7). Kazi Pubns.
Fischel, Walter J. Ibn Khaldun in Egypt: His Public Functions & His Historical Research, (1382-1406); A Study in Islamic Historiography. LC 67-11200. 1967. 21.50x (ISBN 0-520-00414-0). U of Cal Pr.
Ibn Khaldun: His Life & Works. 1970. 6.50x (ISBN 0-87902-165-9). Orientalia.
Mahdi, Muhsin. Ibn Khaldun's Philosophy of History. (Orig.). 1964. pap. 4.25 (ISBN 0-226-50183-3, P167, Phoen). U of Chicago Pr.
Schmidt, Nathaniel. Ibn Khaldun: Historian, Sociologist & Philosopher. LC 30-28858. Repr. of 1930 ed. 11.50 (ISBN 0-404-05609-1). AMS Pr.

IBN SAUD, KING OF SAUDI ARABIA, 1880-1953
Philby, H. St. John. The Heart of Arabia, 2 vols. 1981. Repr. Set. 55.00x (ISBN 0-7146-3072-1, F Cass Co). Biblio Dist.
Philby, Harry. Sa'udi Arabia. LC 72-4289. (World Affairs Ser.: National & International Viewpoints). (Illus.). 422p. 1972. Repr. of 1955 ed. 20.00 (ISBN 0-405-04581-6). Arno.

IBO LANGUAGE
Abraham, Roy C. The Principles of IBO. 127p. 1967. 12.50x (ISBN 0-8002-1836-1). Intl Pubns Serv.
Njoku, John E. A Dictionary of Igbo Names, Culture & Proverbs. LC 78-66416. 1978. pap. text ed. 6.50 (ISBN 0-8191-0134-6). U Pr of Amer.
Thomas, Northcote W. Anthropological Report on the Edo-Speaking Peoples of Nigeria, 2 vols. LC 70-82082. (Illus.). Repr. of 1910 ed. Set. 28.00x (ISBN 0-8371-3807-8, Pub. by Negro U Pr). Greenwood.
--Anthropological Reports on the Ibo-Speaking Peoples of Nigeria, 6 Vols. LC 72-79277. (Illus.). 1913-14. Repr. Set. 75.00x (ISBN 0-8371-1458-6, Pub. by Negro U Pr). Greenwood.
Vahid, Syed A. Studies in Iqbal. 364p. (Orig.). 1981. pap. 9.50 (ISBN 0-88004-000-9). Sunwise Turn.

IBO TRIBE
Basden, G. T. Among the Ibos of Nigeria. new ed. 352p. 1966. 26.00x (ISBN 0-7146-1633-8, F Cass Co). Biblio Dist.
Henderson, Richard N. The King in Every Man: Evolutionary Trends in Onitsha Ibo Society & Culture. LC 77-151576. 592p. 1972. 40.00x (ISBN 0-300-01292-6). Yale U Pr.
Isichei, Elizabeth. A History of the Igbo People. LC 75-14713. 200p. 1976. text ed. 21.50 (ISBN 0-312-37975-7). St Martin.
--Igbo Worlds: An Anthology of Oral Histories & Historical Descriptions. LC 76-56170. (Illus.). 1978. text ed. 22.00x (ISBN 0-915980-62-2). Inst Study Human.
Nwabara. Iboland: A Century of Conflict with Britain 1860-1960. (Illus.). 1978. pap. text ed. 14.50x (ISBN 0-391-00552-9). Humanities.
Nzimiro, Ikenna. Studies in Ibo Political Systems: Chieftaincy & Politics in Four Niger States. (Illus.). 282p. 1972. 27.50x (ISBN 0-7146-1705-9, F Cass Co). Biblio Dist.
Samaan, Sadek H. & Samaan, Anne J. Fears & Worries of Nigerian Igbo Secondary School Students: An Empirical Psychocultural Study. LC 76-620061. (Papers in International Studies: Africa: No. 30). (Illus.). 1976. pap. 6.00 (ISBN 0-89680-062-8). Ohio U Ctr Intl.
Shaw, Thurston. Unearthing Igbo-Ukwu. (Illus.). 1977. pap. 12.50x (ISBN 0-19-575251-1). Oxford U Pr.
Thomas, Northcote W. Anthropological Report on the Edo-Speaking Peoples of Nigeria, 2 vols. LC 70-82082. (Illus.). Repr. of 1910 ed. Set. 28.00x (ISBN 0-8371-3807-8, Pub. by Negro U Pr). Greenwood.
--Anthropological Reports on the Ibo-Speaking Peoples of Nigeria, 6 Vols. LC 72-79277. (Illus.). 1913-14. Repr. Set. 75.00x (ISBN 0-8371-1458-6, Pub. by Negro U Pr). Greenwood.
Uchendu, Victor C. Igbo of Southeast Nigeria. LC 65-20597. (Case Studies in Cultural Anthropology). 1965. pap. text ed. 6.95 (ISBN 0-03-052475-X, HoltC). HR&W.

IBRAHIM PACHA, 1494-1536
Jenkins, Hester D. Ibrahim Pasha: Grand Vizir of Suleiman the Magnificent. LC 70-120210. (Columbia University. Studies in the Social Sciences: No. 115). Repr. of 1911 ed. 12.50 (ISBN 0-404-51115-5). AMS Pr.

IBSEN, HENRIK, 1828-1906
Acker, Helen. Four Sons of Norway. facsimile ed. LC 72-117318. (Biography Index Reprint Ser). 1948. 20.00 (ISBN 0-8369-8010-7). Arno.
Allphin, Clela. Women in the Plays of Henrik Ibsen. 1974. lib. bdg. 69.95 (ISBN 0-87700-211-8). Revisionist Pr.
Anstensen, Ansten. Proverb in Ibsen: Proverbial Sayings & Citations As Elements in His Style. LC 74-158264. (Columbia University. Germanic Studies, New Ser.: No. 1). Repr. of 1936 ed. 27.00 (ISBN 0-404-50451-5). AMS Pr.
Barranger, Milly S. Barron's Simplified Approach to Ibsen's Ghosts, the Wild Duck, & Hedda Gabler. LC 73-78047. 1969. pap. text ed. 1.50 (ISBN 0-8120-0376-4). Barron.
--Barron's Simplified Approach to Ibsen's Peer Gynt, a Doll's House, & an Enemy of the People. LC 72-75838. 1969. pap. text ed. 1.50 (ISBN 0-8120-0375-6). Barron.
Bernstein, Alice & Thompson, Rebecca. About Hedda Gabler: On Playing Hedda Gabler & a Short History of Criticism. 1970. 1.00x (ISBN 0-911492-13-5). Aesthetic Realism.
Beyer, Edward. Ibsen: The Man & His Work. LC 79-1917. (Illus.). 1980. 10.95 (ISBN 0-8008-4055-0); pap. 5.95 (ISBN 0-8008-4056-9). Taplinger.

Boyesen, Hjalmar H. A Commentary on the Works of Henrik Ibsen. LC 71-173514. iii, 317p. 1973. Repr. of 1894 ed. 16.00 (ISBN 0-8462-1681-7). Russell.

Brandes, Georg. Henrik Ibsen. LC 64-14698. 1899. 14.00 (ISBN 0-405-08302-5, Blom Pubns). Arno.

Bull, Francis. Ibsen: The Man & the Dramatist. LC 73-11340. 1973. lib. bdg. 8.50 (ISBN 0-8414-3216-3). Folcroft.

Byrnes, Edward. Monarch Notes on Ibsen's Plays. (Orig.). pap. 1.75 (ISBN 0-671-00562-6). Monarch Pr.

Clurman, Harold. Ibsen. (Masters of World Literature). 1977. 12.95 (ISBN 0-02-526420-6). Macmillan.

--Ibsen. (Master of World Literature Ser.). 1977. pap. 4.95 (ISBN 0-02-049650-8, Collier). Macmillan.

Downs, Brian W. Ibsen: The Intellectual Background. LC 74-86275. 1969. Repr. of 1946 ed. lib. bdg. 13.00x (ISBN 0-374-92261-6). Octagon.

--A Study of Six Plays by Ibsen. LC 72-5255. xii, 212p. 1972. Repr. of 1950 ed. lib. bdg. 14.00x (ISBN 0-374-92262-4). Octagon.

Dukore, Bernard F. Money & Politics in Ibsen, Shaw, & Brecht. LC 79-5380. 1980. text ed. 15.95x (ISBN 0-8262-0294-2). U of Mo Pr.

Durbach, Errol. Ibsen the Romantic: Analogues of Paradise in the Later Plays. 192p. 1981. lib. bdg. 19.00x (ISBN 0-8203-0554-5). U of Ga Pr.

Durbach, Errol, ed. Ibsen & the Theatre: The Dramatist in Production. LC 79-47995. 1980. 25.00x (ISBN 0-8147-1773-X). NYU Pr.

Egan, Michael, ed. Henry James: The Ibsen Years. 154p. 1972. text ed. 8.00x (ISBN 0-85478-242-7). Humanities.

--Ibsen: The Critical Heritage. (Critical Heritage Ser). 1972. 38.50 (ISBN 0-7100-7255-4). Routledge & Kegan.

Eikeland, Peter J. Ibsen Studies. LC 76-117595. (Studies in European Literature, No. 56). 1970. Repr. of 1934 ed. lib. bdg. 29.95 (ISBN 0-8383-1028-1). Haskell.

Eller, W. Ibsen in Germany. 59.95 (ISBN 0-8490-0381-4). Gordon Pr.

Ellis, Havelock. New Spirit. LC 39-224. 1969. Repr. of 1935 ed. 12.00 (ISBN 0-527-26920-4). Kraus Repr.

Ewbank, Inga-Stina & Hall, Peter. Henrik Ibsen: John Gabriel Borkman, an English Version. 96p. 1975. pap. text ed. 4.50x (ISBN 0-485-12100-X, Athlone Pr). Humanities.

Firkins, Ina T. Henrik Ibsen: A Bibliography of Criticism & Biography, with an Index to Characters. LC 72-191605. 1973. lib. bdg. 10.00 (ISBN 0-8414-0816-5). Folcroft.

Franc, Miriam A. Ibsen in England. LC 72-192404. 1919. lib. bdg. 15.00 (ISBN 0-8414-4277-0). Folcroft.

Gosse, Edmund. Northern Studies. LC 75-103225. 1970. Repr. of 1890 ed. 11.50 (ISBN 0-8046-0862-8). Kennikat.

Gosse, Edmund W. Henrik Ibsen. LC 77-51434. 1977. Repr. of 1907 ed. lib. bdg. 25.00 (ISBN 0-8414-4417-X). Folcroft.

Gray, R. Ibsen: A Dissenting View. LC 77-5653. 1980. pap. 8.50 (ISBN 0-521-29835-0). Cambridge U Pr.

--Ibsen: A Dissenting View. LC 77-5653. 1977. 28.50 (ISBN 0-521-21702-4). Cambridge U Pr.

Gregersen, H. Ibsen & Spain: A Study in Comparative Drama. 1936. pap. 14.00 (ISBN 0-527-01108-8). Kraus Repr.

Grene, David. Reality & the Heroic Pattern: Last Plays of Ibsen, Shakespeare & Sophocles. LC 67-25519. 1970. pap. 1.95 (ISBN 0-226-30789-1, P349, Phoen). U of Chicago Pr.

--Reality & the Heroic Pattern: Last Plays of Ibsen, Shakespeare, & Sophocles. LC 67-25519. 1967. 7.00x (ISBN 0-226-30788-3). U of Chicago Pr.

Haakonsen, Daniel. Contemporary Approaches to Ibsen, Vol. II. (Ibsen Yearbook). 210p. 1980. 22.00x (ISBN 82-00-01937-3). Universitet.

Haugen, Einar. Ibsen's Drama: Author to Audience. 1979. 15.00x (ISBN 0-8166-0893-8); pap. 6.95x (ISBN 0-8166-0896-2). U of Minn Pr.

Heiberg, Hans. Ibsen: A Portrait of the Artist. Tate, Joan, tr. LC 71-124089. 1969. 14.95x (ISBN 0-87024-156-7). U of Miami Pr.

Herrmann, Oscar. Living Dramatists: Pinero, Ibsen & D'annunzio. 1977. lib. bdg. 59.95 (ISBN 0-8490-2176-6). Gordon Pr.

Hornby, Richard. Patterns in Ibsen's Middle Plays. LC 80-67969. 192p. 1981. 19.50 (ISBN 0-8387-5014-1). Bucknell U Pr.

Hurt, James. Catiline's Dream: An Essay on Ibsen's Plays. LC 79-186346. 224p. 1972. 14.50 (ISBN 0-252-00238-5). U of Ill Pr.

Ibsen, Henrik. Peer Gynt. Jurgensen, Kai & Schenkkan, Robert, eds. Jurgensen, Kai & Schenkkan, Robert, trs. LC 66-22189. (Crofts Classics Ser). 1966. pap. 1.25x (ISBN 0-88295-045-2). Harlan Davidson.

--Speeches & New Letters. LC 71-184646. (Studies in European Literature, No. 56). 222p. 1972. Repr. of 1910 ed. lib. bdg. 33.95 (ISBN 0-8383-1377-9). Haskell.

--Wild Duck. Jurgensen, Kai & Schenkkan, Robert, eds. Jurgensen, Kai & Schenkkan, Robert, trs. LC 66-21588. 1966. pap. text ed. 2.95x (ISBN 0-88295-046-0). Harlan Davidson.

Jaeger, H. Henrik Ibsen: A Critical Biography. LC 72-567. (Studies in Scandinavian Life & Literature, No. 18). 320p. 1972. Repr. of 1901 ed. lib. bdg. 38.95 (ISBN 0-8383-1414-7). Haskell.

Jaeger, Henrik. Henrik Ibsen: A Critical Biography. LC 70-180033. Repr. of 1890 ed. 15.00 (ISBN 0-405-08664-4, Pub. by Blom). Arno.

James, Henry. Most Unholy Trade, Being Letters on the Drama. LC 74-28389. 1923. lib. bdg. 12.50 (ISBN 0-8414-5349-7). Folcroft.

Johnston, Brian. To the Third Empire: Ibsen's Early Drama. 1980. 20.00x (ISBN 0-8166-0902-0). U of Minn Pr.

Jorgenson, Theodore. Henrik Ibsen: A Study in Art and Personality. LC 77-28153. 1978. Repr. of 1945 ed. lib. bdg. 33.75x (ISBN 0-313-20209-5, JOHE). Greenwood.

Koht, Halvdan. Life of Ibsen. Haugen, Einar & Santaniello, A. E., eds. LC 69-16322. (Illus.). 1971. 25.00 (ISBN 0-405-08715-2). Arno.

Kroner, Johanna. The Technik Des Realistischen Dramas Bei Ibsen und Galsworthy. Repr. of 1935 ed. pap. 6.00 (ISBN 0-384-30490-7). Johnson Repr.

Lavrin, Janko. Ibsen: An Approach. LC 68-27071. (Illus.). 1969. Repr. of 1950 ed. 7.50 (ISBN 0-8462-1204-8). Russell.

Lee, Jeanette. The Ibsen Secret. LC 75-30877. (Studies in Scandinavian Literature, No. 18). 1975. lib. bdg. 33.95 (ISBN 0-8383-2092-9). Haskell.

Lee, Jennette. The Ibsen Secret. LC 74-9747. 1907. 15.00 (ISBN 0-8414-5729-8). Folcroft.

Logeman, Henri. Commentary, Critical, & Explanatory, on the Norwegian Text of Henrik Ibsen's Peer Gynt: Its Language, Literary Association & Folklore. Repr. of 1917 ed. lib. bdg. 17.75x (ISBN 0-8371-3027-1, LOIP). Greenwood.

Lyons, Charles R. Henrik Ibsen: The Divided Consciousness. LC 71-179593. (Crosscurrents-Modern Critiques Ser.). 222p. 1972. 7.95 (ISBN 0-8093-0550-X). S Ill U Pr.

MacFall, Haldane. Ibsen: The Man, His Art & His Significance. LC 76-17001. 1976. Repr. of 1907 ed. lib. bdg. 27.50 (ISBN 0-8414-6003-5). Folcroft.

McFarlane, James W. Ibsen & the Temper of Norwegian Literature. 1979. Repr. of 1960 ed. lib. bdg. 15.00x (ISBN 0-374-95479-8). Octagon.

Meyer, Michael, ed. Henrik Ibsen, Vol. 1: The Making of a Dramatist, 1864-1882. 260p. 1980. text ed. 9.25x (ISBN 0-246-64457-5). Humanities.

--Henrik Ibsen, Vol. 2: The Farewell to Poetry, 1864-1882. 344p. 1980. text ed. 13.00x (ISBN 0-246-64001-4). Humanities.

--Henrik Ibsen, Vol. 3: The Top of a Cold Mountain 1883-1906. 368p. 1980. text ed. 14.50x (ISBN 0-246-64040-5). Humanities.

Munoz, V. Henrik Ibsen: A Chronology. Johnson, W. Scott, tr. (Libertarian & Anarchist Chronology Ser.). 1979. lib. bdg. 59.95 (ISBN 0-8490-3031-5). Gordon Pr.

Northam, J. Ibsen: A Critical Study. LC 72-80297. (Major European Authors Ser.). 240p. 1973. 38.50 (ISBN 0-521-08682-5); pap. 11.50x (ISBN 0-521-09733-9). Cambridge U Pr.

Plekhanov, George V. Art & Society. LC 74-79551. 188p. 1974. 10.00 (ISBN 0-88211-069-1). S A Russell.

Reich, Wilhelm. Ibsen's Peer Gynt. 74p. 1975. 10.00 (ISBN 0-374-17416-4). FS&G.

Roberts, R. E. Henrik Ibsen: A Critical Study. LC 73-21628. (Studies in Ibsen, No. 63). 1974. lib. bdg. 49.95 (ISBN 0-8383-1834-7). Haskell.

Roberts, Richard E. Henrik Ibsen: A Critical Study. 59.95 (ISBN 0-8490-0292-3). Gordon Pr.

--Henrik Ibsen: A Critical Study. LC 76-13162. 1976. Repr. of 1912 ed. lib. bdg. 23.50 (ISBN 0-8414-7216-5). Folcroft.

Robins, E. Ibsen & the Actress. LC 73-10253. (Studies in Drama, No. 39). 1973. Repr. lib. bdg. 49.95 (ISBN 0-8383-1718-9). Haskell.

Rose, Henry. Henrik Ibsen: Poet, Mystic & Moralist. LC 72-1323. (Studies in Scandinavian Life & Literature, No. 18). 1972. Repr. of 1913 ed. lib. bdg. 31.95 (ISBN 0-8383-1428-7). Haskell.

Russell, Edward R. & Standing, P. C. Ibsen on His Merits. LC 79-181000. (Studies in European Literature, No. 56). 1972. Repr. of 1897 ed. lib. bdg. 32.95 (ISBN 0-8383-1370-1). Haskell.

Russell, Edward R. & Standing, Percy C. Ibsen on His Merits. LC 71-160778. 1971. Repr. of 1897 ed. 11.50 (ISBN 0-8046-1610-8). Kennikat.

Setterquist, Jan. Ibsen & the Beginnings of Anglo-Irish Drama. Liljegren, S. B., ed. Incl. John Millington Synge. (Irish Language & Literature Institute). 92p. Repr. of 1952 ed (ISBN 0-88211-045-4); Edward Martyn. (Upsala Irish Studies). 116p. Repr. of 1960 ed (ISBN 0-88211-048-9). LC 73-80308. 1973. Repr. 7.50 ea. S A Russell.

--Ibsen & the Beginnings of Anglo-Irish Drama, 2 vols. in 1. LC 73-22357. 210p. 1974. Repr. of 1951 ed. 10.00 (ISBN 0-87752-170-0). Gordian.

Shaw, George B. Major Critical Essays. LC 74-145292. 1971. Repr. of 1932 ed. 29.00 (ISBN 0-403-01205-8). Scholarly.

--The Quintessence of Ibsenism. 188p. 1959. pap. 3.95 (ISBN 0-8090-0509-3, Drama). Hill & Wang.

Sturman, Marianne. Ibsen's Plays Notes, 2 vols. Incl. Vol. 1, Pt. 1. A Doll's House Notes; Vol. 1, Pt. 2. Hedda Gabler Notes; Vol. 2, Pt. 1. Ghosts Notes; Vol. 2, Pt. 2. The Enemy of the People Notes; Vol. 2, Pt. 3. Wild Ducks. (Orig.). Vol. 1. pap. 1.75 (ISBN 0-8220-0614-6); Vol. 2. pap. 1.75 (ISBN 0-8220-0617-0). Cliffs.

Tammany, Jane E. Henrik Ibsen's Theatre Aesthetic & Dramatic Art. LC 79-92436. (Illus.). 380p. 1980. 22.50 (ISBN 0-8022-2365-6). Philos Lib.

--Ibsen's Theatre Aesthetic & Dramatic Art. LC 79-92436. 1980. 19.95 (ISBN 0-8022-2365-6). Philos Lib.

Tennant, P. F. Ibsen's Dramatic Technique. 1965. Repr. of 1948 ed. text ed. 10.00x (ISBN 0-391-00471-9). Humanities.

Thalmann, M. Henrik Ibsen, Ein Erlebnis der Deutschen. Repr. of 1928 ed. pap. 7.00 (ISBN 0-384-59975-3). Johnson Repr.

Turnbull, H. G. Shakespeare & Ibsen. LC 72-117586. (Studies in Comparative Literature, No. 35). 1970. Repr. of 1926 ed. lib. bdg. 24.95 (ISBN 0-8383-1019-2). Haskell.

Valency, Maurice. The Flower & the Castle: An Introduction to Modern Drama. vii, 460p. 1976. Repr. of 1963 ed. lib. bdg. 22.50x (ISBN 0-374-98066-7). Octagon.

Weigand, Hermann J. The Modern Ibsen: A Reconsideration. facs. ed. LC 73-126263. (Select Bibliographies Reprint Ser.). Repr. of 1953 ed. 22.00 (ISBN 0-8369-5490-4). Arno.

Wicksteed, Philip H. Four Lectures on Henrik Ibsen: Dealing Chiefly with His Metrical Works. LC 68-26255. 1969. Repr. of 1892 ed. 8.00 (ISBN 0-8046-0501-7). Kennikat.

Wisenthal, J. L. Shaw & Ibsen: Bernard Shaw's 'The Quintessence of Ibsenism' & Related Writings. LC 79-14858. 1979. 22.50x (ISBN 0-8020-5454-4). U of Toronto Pr.

Zucker, Adolf. Ibsen: The Master Builder. LC 73-4670. x, 312p. 1973. Repr. of 1929 ed. lib. bdg. 16.00x (ISBN 0-374-98910-9). Octagon.

IBURG, GERMANY–BENEDICTINE ABBEY

Norbert. Das Leben des Bischofs Benno der Zweiter von Osnabruck. Bd. with Ausfuehrliches Namenregister und Sachregister Mit Genauem Inhalsverzeichnis der Seither Erschienene Baende 1-90. (Die Geschichtschreiber der Deutschen Vorzeit Ser: Vol. 91). (Ger.). pap. 10.00 (ISBN 0-384-41895-3). Johnson Repr.

ICA, PERU (DEPT.)

Hammel, Eugene A. Wealth, Authority & Prestige in the Ica Valley, Peru. LC 62-62641. (Anthropology Ser.: No. 10). 1962. pap. 2.00x (ISBN 0-8263-0108-8). U of NM Pr.

Menzel, D. Paraccas Pottery of Ica a Study in Style & Time. Repr. of 1964 ed. pap. 28.00 (ISBN 0-527-01406-0). Kraus Repr.

ICARIA

Cabet, Etienne. History & Constitution of the Icarian Community. LC 72-2962. (Communal Societies of America Ser). Repr. of 1917 ed. 11.50 (ISBN 0-404-10726-5). AMS Pr.

--Voyage En Icarie. LC 69-16857. Repr. of 1848 ed. 25.00x (ISBN 0-678-00923-6). Kelley.

Ross, Marie. Child of Icaria. LC 75-343. (The Radical Tradition in America Ser). 147p. 1975. Repr. of 1938 ed. 16.00 (ISBN 0-88355-246-9). Hyperion Conn.

Shaw, Albert. Icaria: A Chapter in the History of Communism. LC 78-187462. (The American Utopian Adventure Ser.). x, 219p. Repr. of 1884 ed. lib. bdg. 12.50x (ISBN 0-87991-016-X). Porcupine Pr.

--Icaria, a Chapter in the History of Communism. LC 72-2966. Repr. of 1884 ed. 19.00 (ISBN 0-685-32620-9). AMS Pr.

ICE

see also Glaciers; Icebergs

Bogorodskii, V. V. The Physics of Ice. 164p. 1971. 14.50x (ISBN 0-7065-1197-2, Pub. by IPST). Intl Schol Bk Serv.

Colbeck, Samuel C. Dynamics of Snow & Ice Masses. LC 79-17949. 1980. 55.00 (ISBN 0-12-179450-4). Acad Pr.

Elementary Science Study. Ice Cubes. 1975. tchr's. guide 9.48 (ISBN 0-07-018522-0, W). McGraw.

Fletcher, Neville H. Chemical Physics of Ice. LC 74-75825. (Monographs on Physics). (Illus.). 1970. 41.95 (ISBN 0-521-07597-1). Cambridge U Pr.

Hobbs, Peter V. Ice Physics. (Illus.). 782p. 1975. 105.00x (ISBN 0-19-851936-2). Oxford U Pr.

Ice in Fisheries. (FAO Fisheries Reports: No. 59, Revision 1). (Illus.). 57p. 1975. pap. 7.50 (ISBN 0-685-55203-9, F779, FAO). Unipub.

Shumski, P. A. Principles of Structural Glaciology. Kraus, tr. (Illus.). 8.75 (ISBN 0-8446-2935-9). Peter Smith.

Symposium Copenhagen, Technical University of Denmark, August 6-10, 1979. Physics & Mechanics of Ice: Proceedings. Tryde, P., ed. (IUTAM Ser.). (Illus.). 378p. 1980. 43.70 (ISBN 3-540-09906-9). Springer-Verlag.

U. S. National Committee for the International Hydrological Decade. Advanced Concepts & Techniques in the Study of Snow & Ice Resources. Santeford, H. & Smith, J., eds. x, 789p. 1974. pap. 15.25 (ISBN 0-309-02235-5). Natl Acad Pr.

Yakovlev, G. N., ed. Studies in Ice Physics & Ice Engineering. Hardin, R., tr. from Rus. (Israel Program for Scientific Translations Ser). (Illus.). vi, 194p. 1974. 19.50 (ISBN 0-7065-1275-8, Pub. by IPST). Intl Schol Bk Serv.

ICE–MANUFACTURE

see Refrigeration and Refrigerating Machinery

ICE AGE

see Glacial Epoch

ICE-BOATS

Andresen, Jack. Sailing on Ice. LC 73-101. (Illus.). 224p. 1974. 9.95 (ISBN 0-498-01241-7). A S Barnes.

ICE CARNIVALS

see Winter Sports

ICE CARVING

Amendola, J. Ice Carving Made Easy. (Illus.). pap. 14.00x (ISBN 0-685-47434-8). Corner.

Durocher, Joseph F. Practical Ice Carving. 112p. 1981. pap. text ed. 9.95 (ISBN 0-8436-2206-7). CBI Pub.

Hasegawa, Hideo. Ice Carving. Athey, Jackie, ed. LC 77-83288. (Illus.). 1978. text ed. 35.00 (ISBN 0-916096-11-4). Continental CA.

ICE CREAM, ICES, ETC.

see also Confectionery; Desserts

Arbuckle, W. S. Ice Cream Service Handbook. (Illus.). 1976. pap. text ed. 7.50 (ISBN 0-87055-211-2). AVI.

Arbuckle, Wendell S. Ice Cream. 3rd ed. (Illus.). 1977. lib. bdg. 32.00 (ISBN 0-87055-256-2). AVI.

Baldwin, Jo G. Let's Make Ice Cream. 1977. 2.00 (ISBN 0-914208-02-0). Longhorn Pr.

Cameron, Sheila M. Homemade Ice Cream & Sherbet. LC 69-16175. (Illus.). (gr. 9 up). 1969. pap. 3.50 (ISBN 0-8048-0258-0). C E Tuttle.

De Gouy, Louis P. Ice Cream & Ice Cream Desserts: 470 Recipes. 4.50 (ISBN 0-8446-5026-9). Peter Smith.

--Ice Cream & Ice Cream Desserts: 470 Tested Recipes for Ice Creams, Coupes, Bombes, Frappes, Ices, Mousses, Parfaits, Sherbets, Etc. LC 73-88333. 281p. 1974. pap. 3.00 (ISBN 0-486-22999-8). Dover.

Dickson, Paul. The Great American Ice Cream Book. LC 72-78284. (Illus.). 1978. pap. 4.95 (ISBN 0-689-70572-7, 240). Atheneum.

Goldman, Earl. Ice Cream Cookbook. LC 70-21243. (Illus., Orig.). 1970. pap. 4.95 (ISBN 0-911954-09-0). Nitty Gritty.

Hendrichs, G. & Leavenworth, C. Cool & Creamy: The Ice Cream & Frozen Yogurt Book. 1979. 10.95 (ISBN 0-13-171975-0, Spec); pap. 4.95 (ISBN 0-13-171967-X, Spec). P-H.

Herrel, Stephen & Schonbach, Michael. Steve's Ice Cream Book. LC 79-56530. (Illus.). 224p. (Orig.). 1981. pap. 5.95 (ISBN 0-89480-080-9). Workman Pub.

Hoffman, Mable & Hoffman, Gar. Ice Cream. 1981. pap. 5.95 (ISBN 0-89586-040-6). H P Bks.

LeBar, Mary. How God Gives Us Ice Cream. (A Happy Day Book). (Illus.). 24p. (gr. k-5). 1979. 0.98 (ISBN 0-87239-358-5, 3628). Standard Pub.

Lenotre, Gaston. Lenotre's Ice Cream & Candies. Hyman, Philip & Hyman, Mary, trs. (Illus.). 1979. 18.95 (ISBN 0-8120-5334-6). Barron.

Marshall, A. B. Ices, Plain & Fancy: A Reprint of Book of Ices by A. B. Marshall. LC 76-18215. (Illus.). 1976. 6.95 (ISBN 0-87099-150-7). Metro Mus Art.

Mitgutsch, Ali. From Milk to Ice Cream. LC 81-81. (Carolrhoda Start to Finish Bks.). Orig. Title: Von der Milch zum Speiseeis. (Illus.). 24p. (ps-3). 1981. PLB 5.95 (ISBN 0-87614-158-0). Carolrhoda Bks.

Nilson, Bee. Making Ice-Cream & Other Cold Sweets. 1973. 7.95 (ISBN 0-7207-0612-2, Pub. by Michael Joseph). Merrimack Bk Serv.

O'Roarke, Mary A. The Baskin-Robbins Book of Ice Cream, Fun & Entertaining. 1980. 5.95 (ISBN 0-671-24751-4, 24751). S&S.
Ray, Elizabeth. Homemade Ice Cream. 1978. pap. 2.95 (ISBN 0-09-131961-7, Pub. by Hutchinson). Merrimack Bk Serv.
Spagnola, Elena. Making Ice Cream. Lyceum Editorial Staff, ed. (Illus.). 1978. 8.95 (ISBN 0-915336-25-1). Lyceum Bks.

ICE CRYSTALS
see also Snow Crystals
Fletcher, Neville H. Chemical Physics of Ice. LC 74-75825. (Monographs on Physics). (Illus.). 1970. 41.95 (ISBN 0-521-07597-1). Cambridge U Pr.
Lavrov, V. V. Deformation & Strength of Ice. 170p. 1971. 14.00x (ISBN 0-7065-1098-4, Pub. by IPST). Intl Schol Bk Serv.
Riehl, N., et al, eds. Physics of Ice. LC 72-81281. 642p. 1969. 49.50 (ISBN 0-306-30412-0, Plenum Pr). Plenum Pub.

ICE FISHING
Little, Gene. Ice Fishing. LC 75-13230. (Illus.). 224p. 1975. pap. 4.95 (ISBN 0-8092-8219-4). Contemp Bks.

ICE HOCKEY
see Hockey

ICE ON RIVERS, LAKES, ETC.
Pivovarov, A. A. Thermal Conditions in Freezing Lakes & Rivers. LC 73-12269. 136p. 1973. 21.95 (ISBN 0-470-69103-4, Pub. by Wiley). Krieger.
--Thermal Conditions in Freezing Lakes & Rivers. Vilim, E., tr. from Rus. LC 73-12269. 136p. 1973. 36.95 (ISBN 0-470-69103-4). Halsted Pr.

ICE SKATING
see Skating

ICE SPORTS
see Winter Sports

ICE-WEDGE POLYGONS
Lachenbruch, Arthur H. Mechanics of Thermal Contraction Cracks & Ice-Wedge Polygons in Permafrost. LC 63-31. (Special Paper: No. 70). (Illus., Orig.). 1962. pap. 3.50x (ISBN 0-8137-2070-2). Geol Soc.

ICEBERGS
Anderson, Madelyn K. Iceberg Alley. LC 76-28234. (Illus.). 64p. (gr. 4-6). 1976. PLB 6.97 (ISBN 0-671-32804-2). Messner.
Gans, Roma. Icebergs. LC 64-18163. (A Let's-Read-&-Find-Out Science Bk). (Illus.). (gr. k-3). 1964. PLB 8.79 (ISBN 0-690-42775-1, TYC-J). Har-Row.
Husseiny. Icebergs. 350p. Date not set. text ed. price not set (ISBN 0-08-023911-0). Pergamon.
Husseiny, A. A., ed. Iceberg Utilization: Proceedings of the First International Iceberg Utilization Conference, Ames, Iowa. LC 78-5119. (Illus.). 780p. 1978. 73.00 (ISBN 0-08-022916-6); pap. 44.00 (ISBN 0-08-022915-8). Pergamon.
Lauber, Patricia. Icebergs & Glaciers. LC 61-9738. (Junior Science Ser.). (gr. 2-5). 1961. PLB 5.49 (ISBN 0-8116-6158-X). Garrard.
Poole, Lynn & Poole, Gray. Danger, Iceberg Ahead. (Illus.). (gr. 1-4). 1961. PLB 4.39 (ISBN 0-394-90121-5). Random.
Schultz, Gwen. Icebergs & Their Voyages. LC 75-9958. (Illus.). 96p. (gr. 7-9). 1975. PLB 6.96 (ISBN 0-688-32047-3). Morrow.

ICELAND
Foged, Neils. Freshwater Diatoms in Iceland. (Bibliotheca Phycologia). (Illus.). 1977. pap. 20.00x (ISBN 3-7682-0938-5, Pub. by J. Cramer). Intl Schol Bk Serv.
Iceland. (Panorama Bks.). (Illus., Fr.). 3.95 (ISBN 0-685-11241-1). French & Eur.
Magnusson, Sigurdur A. Stallion of the North: The Unique Story of the Iceland Horse. LC 78-67094. (Illus.). 1979. 12.95 (ISBN 0-917712-06-4). Longship Pr.
Samivel. Golden Iceland. (Illus.). 308p. 1970. 15.00 (ISBN 0-87131-018-X). M Evans.
Scherman, Katharine. Daughter of Fire: A Portrait of Iceland. (Illus.). 1976. 12.50 (ISBN 0-316-77325-5). Little.
Stefansson, Vilhjalmur. Iceland: The First American Republic. LC 70-138131. 1971. Repr. of 1939 ed. lib. bdg. 16.00x (ISBN 0-8371-5167-8, STIF). Greenwood.
Thule Press Editors, ed. Iceland: Surprising Island of the Atlantic. 1981. 16.50 (ISBN 0-906191-70-X, Pub. by Findhorn-Thule Scotland). Hydra Bk.
Von Linden, Franz-Karl & Wyer, Helfried. Iceland. LC 78-53349. (Illus.). 1978. 35.00 (ISBN 0-89674-001-3). J J Binns.

ICELAND-BIBLIOGRAPHY
Hermannsson, Halldor. Bibliographical Notes. LC 43-13095. (Islandica, Vol. 29). 1942. pap. 9.00 (ISBN 0-527-00359-X). Kraus Repr.
--Icelandic Books of the Seventeenth Century. LC 22-23992. (Islandica Ser.: Vol. 14). 1922. pap. 10.00 (ISBN 0-527-00344-1). Kraus Repr.
--Icelandic Books of the Sixteenth Century. (Islandica Ser.: Vol. 9). 1916. pap. 8.00 (ISBN 0-527-00339-5). Kraus Repr.

ICELAND-CIVILIZATION
Erlingsson, Thorsteinn. Ruins of the Saga-Time in Iceland. LC 76-43951. (Viking Society for Northern Research: Extra Ser.: Vol. 2). Repr. of 1899 ed. 27.00 (ISBN 0-404-60022-0). AMS Pr.
Sveinsson, Einar O. Age of the Sturlungs. (Islandia Ser.: Vol. 36). 1953. pap. 14.00 (ISBN 0-527-00366-2). Kraus Repr.

ICELAND-DESCRIPTION AND TRAVEL
Auden, W. H. & MacNeice, Louis. Letters from Iceland. 1969. 13.95 (ISBN 0-394-40375-4). Random.
Coles, John. Summer Travelling in Iceland. LC 80-1978. Repr. of 1882 ed. 47.00 (ISBN 0-404-18631-9). AMS Pr.
Hermannsson, Halldor. Sir Joseph Banks & Iceland. LC 28-11080. (Islandica Ser.: Vol. 18). 1928. pap. 12.00 (ISBN 0-527-00348-4). Kraus Repr.
Linden, F. von & Weyer, H. Iceland. (Illus.). 1974. 58.50x (ISBN 3-405-11044-0). Intl Pubns Serv.
Metcalfe, Frederick. The Oxonian in Iceland: Or, Notes of Travel in That Island in the Summer of 1860. LC 77-87702. Repr. of 1861 ed. 32.50 (ISBN 0-404-16496-X). AMS Pr.
Nagel Travel Guide to Iceland. (Illus.). 1974. 22.00 (ISBN 2-8263-0363-5). Hippocrene Bks.
Oddsson, Gisli. Annalium in Islandia Farrago, & De Mirabilibus Islandiae. Hermannsson, Halldor, ed. (Islandica Ser.: Vol. 10). 1917. pap. 8.00 (ISBN 0-527-00340-9). Kraus Repr.
Purkis, John A. The Icelandic Jaunt: A Study of the Expeditions Made by Morris to Iceland in 1871 & 1873. LC 77-8166. 1977. Repr. of 1962 ed. lib. bdg. 10.00 (ISBN 0-8414-6792-7). Folcroft.
Ruins of the Saga Time. LC 76-43951. (Viking Society for Northern Research, Extra Ser.: No. 2). Repr. of 1899 ed. 27.00 (ISBN 0-404-60022-0). AMS Pr.

ICELAND-DESCRIPTION AND TRAVEL-MAPS
Hermannsson, Halldor. Cartography of Iceland. LC 32-4391. (Islandica Ser.: Vol. 21). 1931. pap. 14.00 (ISBN 0-527-00351-4). Kraus Repr.
--Two Cartographers: Gudbrandur Thorlaksson & Thordur Thorlaksson. LC 27-13445. (Islandica Ser.: Vol. 17). 1926. pap. 14.00 (ISBN 0-527-00347-6). Kraus Repr.

ICELAND-ECONOMIC CONDITIONS
Business Directory of Iceland: Vidskipti Og Pjonusta, 1978-79. (Illus.). 1979. pap. 55.00x (ISBN 0-8002-0402-6). Intl Pubns Serv.
Chamberlin, William C. Economic Development of Iceland Through World War Two. LC 73-76653. (Columbia University Studies in the Social Sciences: No. 531). Repr. of 1947 ed. 15.00 (ISBN 0-404-51531-2). AMS Pr.

ICELAND-FOREIGN RELATIONS
Nuechterlein, Donald E. Iceland: Reluctant Ally. LC 75-3868. (Illus.). 213p. 1975. lib. bdg. 15.00 (ISBN 0-8371-8096-1, NUIC). Greenwood.

ICELAND-HISTORY
Boyer, Regis, notes by. Livre De la Colonisation De L'islande (Landnamabok), le. (Contributions Du Centre D'etudes Arctiques: No. 10). 1973. pap. 19.50x (ISBN 90-279-2690-5). Mouton.
Conybeare, Charles A. Place of Iceland in the History of European Institutions, Being the Lothian Prize Essay, 1877. Repr. of 1877 ed. 15.00 (ISBN 0-404-01696-0). AMS Pr.
Gelsinger, Bruce E. Icelandic Enterprise: Economy & Commerce in the Middle Ages. LC 80-26116. (Illus.). 400p. 1981. text ed. 19.50 (ISBN 0-87249-405-5). U of SC Pr.
Gudmundsson, J. Jon Gudmundsson & His Natural History of Iceland. (Islandica: Vol. 15). Repr. of 1924 ed. pap. 6.00 (ISBN 0-527-00345-X). Kraus Repr.
Guthmundsson, Barthi. The Origin of the Icelanders. Hollander, Lee M., tr. LC 66-19275. 1967. 12.95x (ISBN 0-8032-0063-3). U of Nebr Pr.
Hermannsson, Halldor. Saemund Sigfusson & the Oddaverjar. LC 33-5652. (Islandica Ser.: Vol. 22). 1932. pap. 6.00 (ISBN 0-527-00352-2). Kraus Repr.
Hood, John C. Icelandic Church Saga. LC 79-8720. (Illus.). xii, 241p. 1981. Repr. of 1946 ed. lib. bdg. 27.50x (ISBN 0-313-22194-4, HOIC). Greenwood.
Magnusson, Sigurdur A. Northern Sphinx: Iceland & the Icelanders from the Settlement to the Present Day. 1977. lib. bdg. 13.00x (ISBN 0-7735-0277-7). McGill-Queens U Pr.
Oddsson, Gisli. Annalium in Islandia Farrago, & De Mirabilibus Islandiae. Hermannsson, Halldor, ed. (Islandica Ser.: Vol. 10). 1917. pap. 8.00 (ISBN 0-527-00340-9). Kraus Repr.
Sveinsson, Einar O. Age of the Sturlungs. (Islandia Ser.: Vol. 36). 1953. pap. 14.00 (ISBN 0-527-00366-2). Kraus Repr.
Tomasson, Richard F. Iceland: The First New Society. (Illus.). 1980. 17.50x (ISBN 0-8166-0913-6). U of Minn Pr.
Vigfusson, Gudbrandur & Powell, F. York, eds. Origines Islandicae, 2 vols. LC 5-33562. 1976. Repr. of 1905 ed. Set. 59.00 (ISBN 0-527-93160-8). Kraus Repr.
Whitelock, Peter. Nations in Trial: Conflict in Palestine 1945-1969 & Ireland 1910-1949. (Illus.). 72p. 1975. 4.50x (ISBN 0-8002-1745-4). Intl Pubns Serv.

ICELAND-JUVENILE LITERATURE
Berry, Erick. The Land & People of Iceland. new rev. ed. LC 72-1569. (Portraits of the Nations Ser.). (Illus.). (gr. 6 up). 1972. lib. bdg. 8.79 (ISBN 0-397-31401-9, JBL-J). Har-Row.

ICELAND-POLITICS AND GOVERNMENT
Nuechterlein, Donald E. Iceland: Reluctant Ally. LC 75-3868. (Illus.). 213p. 1975. lib. bdg. 15.00 (ISBN 0-8371-8096-1, NUIC). Greenwood.

ICELAND-RELIGION
Van Woerkom, Dorothy. The Lands of Fire & Ice. (gr. 2-5). 1979. 4.95 (ISBN 0-570-03472-8, 56-1338). Concordia.

ICELANDERS
Ari, Thorgilsson. Book of the Icelanders. (Islandica Ser: Vol. 20). Repr. of 1930 ed. pap. 8.00 (ISBN 0-527-00350-6). Kraus Repr.

ICELANDERS IN THE UNITED STATES
Walters, Thorstina. Modern Sagas. LC 54-8826. (Illus.). 229p. 1953. 3.75 (ISBN 0-911042-01-6). N Dak Inst.

ICELANDIC AND OLD NORSE LANGUAGES
see also Norwegian Language; Scandinavian Philology
Buchanan, C. D. Substantivized Adjectives in Old Norse. Repr. of 1933 ed. pap. 6.00 (ISBN 0-527-00761-7). Kraus Repr.
Chapman, Kenneth G. Graded Readings & Exercises in Old Icelandic. LC 64-23903. 1970. pap. 9.75x (ISBN 0-520-00221-0, CAMPUS25). U of Cal Pr.
Flom, George T. The Language of the Konungs Skuggsja Speculum Regale, 2 Vols. 1921-1923. Vol. 7. 9.50 ea. (ISBN 0-384-16060-3); Vol. 8. (ISBN 0-384-16070-0). Johnson Repr.
Gordon, Eric V. Introduction to Old Norse. 2nd ed. Taylor, A. R., ed. 1957. 17.95x (ISBN 0-19-811105-3). Oxford U Pr.
Haugen, Einar, ed. First Grammatical Treatise: The Earliest Germanic Phonology. 2nd, rev. ed. (Classics of Linguistics Ser). (Illus.). 112p. 1973. text ed. 15.00x (ISBN 0-582-52491-1). Longman.
Homiliubok. Codex AM 619 Quarto. 15.50 (ISBN 0-384-24130-1). Johnson Repr.
Noreen, Adolf. Altnordische Grammatik I. 2nd ed. LC 72-130813. (Alabama Linguistic & Philological Ser: Vol. 19). 496p. 1971. 27.50x (ISBN 0-8173-0354-5). U of Ala Pr.
Rask, Rasmus K. A Grammar of the Icelandic or Old Norse Tongue. Dasent, Sir George W., tr. viii, 273p. 1976. 32.00 (ISBN 90-272-0873-5, ACL 2). Benjamins North Am.

ICELANDIC AND OLD NORSE LANGUAGES-DICTIONARIES
Cleasby, Richard & Vigfusson, Gudbrand, eds. Icelandic-English Dictionary. 2nd ed. 1957. 74.00x (ISBN 0-19-863103-0). Oxford U Pr.
Sigurdsson, A. Icelandic-English Dictionary. 3rd ed. 80.00 (ISBN 0-686-64772-6). Heinman.
Sigurdsson, Arngrimur. Icelandic English Dictionary. 42.50 (ISBN 0-87559-166-3). Shalom.
Zoega, Geir T. Concise Dictionary of Old Icelandic. 1910. 39.00x (ISBN 0-19-863108-1). Oxford U Pr.

ICELANDIC AND OLD NORSE LITERATURE
see also Eddas; Norwegian Literature; Sagas; Scalds and Scaldic Poetry; Scandinavian Philology
Anderson, R. B. Norse Mythology or the Religion of Our Forefathers. LC 77-6879. 1977. Repr. of 1891 ed. lib. bdg. 25.00 (ISBN 0-89341-147-7). Longwood Pr.
Frank, Roberta. Old Norse Court Poetry: The Drottkvaett Stanza. LC 77-90904. (Islandica Ser.: XLII). 1978. 24.50x (ISBN 0-8014-1060-6). Cornell U Pr.
Hollander, Lee M. Skalds: A Selection of Their Poems. (Orig.). 1968. pap. 1.95 (ISBN 0-472-06135-6, 135, AA). U of Mich Pr.
--Skalds: A Selection of Their Poems with Introduction & Notes. 1968. Repr. 4.40 (ISBN 0-472-09135-2). U of Mich Pr.
Koht, H. Old Norse Sagas. (Lowell Institute Lectures Ser). Repr. of 1931 ed. 14.00 (ISBN 0-527-52400-X). Kraus Repr.
Palsson, Herman & Edwards, Paul, trs. Orkneyinga Saga: The History of the Earls of Orkney. 1978. 14.95 (ISBN 0-7012-0431-1, Pub. by Chatto Bodley Jonathan). Merrimack Bk Serv.
Phillpotts, Bertha S. Edda & Saga. LC 73-14914. 1931. Repr. lib. bdg. 25.00 (ISBN 0-8414-6736-6). Folcroft.
Schlauch, Margaret, tr. The Saga of the Volsungs, the Saga of Ragnar Lodbrook, Together with the Lay of Kraka. LC 75-41284. Repr. of 1930 ed. 21.50 (ISBN 0-404-14704-6). AMS Pr.
Snorra, S. Snnorra Sagas of Norse Kings. 1973. 32.50x (ISBN 82-09-00752-1, N-393). Vanous.
Snorri Sturluson. Heimskringla: Sagas of the Norse Kings. Laing, Samuel, tr. LC 75-41259. Repr. of 1930 ed. 30.00 (ISBN 0-404-14607-4). AMS Pr.
Vigfusson, Guthbrandr & Powell, Frederick Y. An Icelandic Prose Reader. LC 80-1940. Repr. of 1879 ed. 64.00 (ISBN 0-404-18729-3). AMS Pr.

ICELANDIC AND OLD NORSE LITERATURE-BIBLIOGRAPHY
Bekker-Nielsen, Hans. Old Norse-Icelandic Studies: A Select Bibliography. LC 68-75888. 1967. pap. 7.50x (ISBN 0-8020-1465-8). U of Toronto Pr.
Fry, Donald K., compiled by. Norse Sagas Translated into English: A Bibliography. LC 79-8632. (AMS Studies in the Middle Ages: No. 3). 1980. 16.50 (ISBN 0-404-18016-7). AMS Pr.
Hermannsson, Halldor. Bibliographical Notes. LC 43-13095. (Islandica, Vol. 29). 1942. pap. 9.00 (ISBN 0-527-00359-X). Kraus Repr.
--Bibliography of the Icelandic Sagas & Minor Tales. LC 8-19528. (Islandica Ser.: Vol. 1). 1908. pap. 8.00 (ISBN 0-527-00331-X). Kraus Repr.
--Bibliography of the Sagas of the Kings of Norway & Related Sagas & Tales. LC 10-10613. (Islandica Ser.: Vol. 3). 1910. pap. 6.00 (ISBN 0-527-00333-6). Kraus Repr.
--Old Icelandic Literature, a Bibliographical Essay. LC 34-1071. (Islandica Ser.: Vol. 23). 1933. pap. 6.00 (ISBN 0-527-00353-0). Kraus Repr.
--Sagas of Icelanders. (Islandica Ser.: Vol. 24). 1935. pap. 6.00 (ISBN 0-527-00354-9). Kraus Repr.
--Sagas of the Kings & the Mythical-Heroic Sagas. LC 38-32451. (Islandica Ser.: Vol. 26). 1937. pap. 6.00 (ISBN 0-527-00356-5). Kraus Repr.

ICELANDIC AND OLD NORSE LITERATURE-HISTORY AND CRITICISM
Craigie, William A. The Icelandic Sagas. LC 73-6948. 1913. lib. bdg. 12.50 (ISBN 0-8414-3368-2). Folcroft.
Einarsson, Stefan. A History of Icelandic Literature. 426p. 1957. 20.00x (ISBN 0-8018-0186-9). Johns Hopkins.
--History of Icelandic Literature. 1957. 20.00x (ISBN 0-89067-033-1). Am Scandinavian.
Ellis, Hilda R. Road to Hel: A Study of the Conception of the Dead in Old Norse Literature. LC 68-23286. (Illus.). 1968. Repr. of 1943 ed. lib. bdg. 15.00 (ISBN 0-8371-0070-4, ELRH). Greenwood.
Frank, Roberta. Old Norse Court Poetry: The Drottkvaett Stanza. LC 77-90904. (Islandica Ser.: XLII). 1978. 24.50x (ISBN 0-8014-1060-6). Cornell U Pr.
Hollander, Lee M. Skalds: A Selection of Their Poems. (Orig.). 1968. pap. 1.95 (ISBN 0-472-06135-6, 135, AA). U of Mich Pr.
--Skalds: A Selection of Their Poems with Introduction & Notes. 1968. Repr. 4.40 (ISBN 0-472-09135-2). U of Mich Pr.
Kelchner, Georgia D. Dreams in Old Norse Literature & Their Affinities in Folklore. 154p. 1980. Repr. of 1935 ed. lib. bdg. 30.00 (ISBN 0-8492-1496-3). R West.
--Dreams in Old Norse Literature & Their Affinities in Folklore. LC 77-2928. 1977. Repr. of 1935 ed. lib. bdg. 27.50 (ISBN 0-8414-5538-4). Folcroft.
Mitchell, P. M. Halldor Hermannsson. LC 77-14665. (Islandica Ser.: XLI). (Illus.). 1978. 24.50x (ISBN 0-8014-1085-1). Cornell U Pr.
Turville-Petre, Gabriel. Origins of Icelandic Literature. 1953. 24.95x (ISBN 0-19-811114-2). Oxford U Pr.

ICELANDIC AND OLD NORSE LITERATURE-TRANSLATIONS INTO ENGLISH
Bayerschmidt, Carl F. & Hollander, Lee M., trs. from Old Icelandic. Njal's Saga. LC 54-11996. (Library of Scandinavian Literature: Vol. 3). 1955. 7.00x (ISBN 0-89067-011-0). Am Scandinavian.
Green, W. C., ed. & tr. Translations from the Icelandic. 1976. lib. bdg. 59.95 (ISBN 0-8490-2757-8). Gordon Pr.
Green, William C., ed. Translations from the Icelandic. LC 66-30733. (Medieval Library). Repr. of 1926 ed. 8.50x (ISBN 0-8154-0089-6). Cooper Sq.
Hollander, Lee M. Skalds: A Selection of Their Poems. (Orig.). 1968. pap. 1.95 (ISBN 0-472-06135-6, 135, AA). U of Mich Pr.
--Skalds: A Selection of Their Poems with Introduction & Notes. 1968. Repr. 4.40 (ISBN 0-472-09135-2). U of Mich Pr.
Jones, Gwyn, tr. Egil's Saga. LC 59-15243. (Library of Scandinavian Literature: Vol. 8). (Old Icelandic.). 1960. 7.00x (ISBN 0-89067-012-9). Am Scandinavian.

McGrew, Julia H., tr. from Old Icelandic. Sturlunga Saga, Vol. I. LC 71-120536. (Library of Scandinavian Literature: Vol. 9). 1970. 10.50x (ISBN 0-89067-020-X). Am Scandinavian.

ICELANDIC AND OLD NORSE POETRY

see also Eddas; Scalds and Scaldic Poetry

Anderson, George K., tr. The Saga of the Volsungs. LC 80-65685. 200p. 1981. 18.00 (ISBN 0-87413-172-3). U Delaware Pr.

Hallberg, Peter. Old Icelandic Poetry: Eddic Lay & Skaldic Verse. Schach, Paul & Lindgrenson, Sonja, trs. LC 74-27186. (Illus.). xii, 219p. 1975. 19.95x (ISBN 0-8032-0855-3). U of Nebr Pr.

ICELANDIC AUTHORS

see Authors, Icelandic

ICELANDIC DRAMA

Haugen, Einar, ed. Fire & Ice: Three Icelandic Plays. Incl. The Wish. Sigurjonsson, Johann. Haugen, Einar, tr; The Golden Gate. Stefansson, David. Hardy, G. Gathorne, tr; Atoms & Madams. Thoroarson, Agnar. Haugen, Einar, tr. (Nordic Translation Ser). 1967. 15.00 (ISBN 0-299-04481-5); pap. 6.00 (ISBN 0-299-04484-X). U of Wis Pr.

ICELANDIC LANGUAGE

see Icelandic and Old Norse Languages; Icelandic Language, Modern

ICELANDIC LANGUAGE, MODERN

Einarsson, Stefan. Icelandic Grammar, Text & Glossary. 2nd ed. 538p. 1949. 22.00x (ISBN 0-8018-0187-7). Johns Hopkins.

Glendening, P. J. Teach Yourself Icelandic. (Teach Yourself Ser.). pap. 4.95 (ISBN 0-679-10181-0). McKay.

Hermannsson, Halldor. Modern Icelandic: An Essay. LC 20-7699. (Islandica Ser.: Vol. 12). 1919. pap. 6.00 (ISBN 0-527-00342-5). Kraus Repr.

Icelandic Pocket Dictionary. 11.50 (ISBN 0-685-36175-6). Heinman.

Johannesson, Alex. Islaendisches Etymologisches Woerterbuch. 1406p. (Ice.-Ger.). 1956. 232.00 (ISBN 3-7720-0429-6, M-7485, Pub. by Francke). French & Eur.

ICELANDIC LITERATURE

see Icelandic and Old Norse Literature; Icelandic Literature, Modern (Collections)

ICELANDIC LITERATURE, MODERN (COLLECTIONS)

Iceland Review Library, ed. Short Stories of Today. 1981. pap. 4.95 (ISBN 0-906191-77-7, Pub. by Findhorn-Thule Scotland). Hydra Bk.

ICELANDIC LITERATURE, MODERN–BIBLIOGRAPHY

Hermannsson, Halldor. Icelandic Authors of to-Day. LC 13-24270. (Islandica Ser.: Vol. 6). 1913. pap. 6.00 (ISBN 0-527-00336-0). Kraus Repr.

--Icelandic Books of the Seventeenth Century. LC 22-23992. (Islandica Ser.: Vol. 14). 1922. pap. 10.00 (ISBN 0-527-00344-1). Kraus Repr.

--Icelandic Books of the Sixteenth Century. (Islandica Ser.: Vol. 9). 1916. pap. 8.00 (ISBN 0-527-00339-5). Kraus Repr.

Mitchell, P. M. & Ober, Kenneth H., eds. Bibliography of Modern Icelandic Literature in Translation. LC 74-19751. (Islandica). 324p. 1975. Vol. 40. 48.50x (ISBN 0-8014-0897-0). Cornell U Pr.

ICELANDIC LITERATURE, MODERN–HISTORY AND CRITICISM

Beck, Richard. History of Icelandic Poets, Eighteen Hundred to Nineteen-Forty. (Islandica: Vol. 34). 1950. pap. 16.00 (ISBN 0-527-00364-6). Kraus Repr.

Einarsson, Stefan. A History of Icelandic Literature. 426p. 1957. 20.00x (ISBN 0-8018-0186-9). Johns Hopkins.

--History of Icelandic Prose Writers. (Islandica Ser.: Vols. 32 - 23). 1800-1940. pap. 16.00 (ISBN 0-527-00363-8). Kraus Repr.

ICELANDIC LITERATURE, MODERN–TRANSLATIONS INTO ENGLISH

Beck, Richard, ed. Icelandic Poems & Stories. facsimile ed. LC 68-57059. (Short Story Index Reprint Ser.). 1943. 18.00 (ISBN 0-8369-6001-7). Arno.

ICELANDIC PERIODICALS–BIBLIOGRAPHY

Hermannsson, Halldor. Periodical Literature of Iceland Down to Year 1874, an Historical Sketch. LC 19-7907. (Islandica Ser.: Vol. 11). 1918. pap. 8.00 (ISBN 0-527-00341-7). Kraus Repr.

ICELANDIC TALES

see Tales, Icelandic

ICES

see Ice Cream, Ices, etc.

ICHNEUMONIDAE

Dasch, Clement E. Ichneumonidae of America North of Mexico: Subfamily Diplazontinae. (Memoirs Ser: No. 3). (Illus.). 1964. 20.00 (ISBN 0-686-00422-1). Am Entom Inst.

--Ichneumonidae of America North of Mexico: Subfamily Mesochorinae. (Memoirs Ser: No. 16). (Illus.). 376p. 1971. 30.00 (ISBN 0-686-01269-0). Am Entom Inst.

Short, John. The Final Larval Instars of the Ichneumonidae. (Memoir Ser.: No. 25). (Illus.). 508p. 1978. 35.00 (ISBN 0-686-26663-3). Am Entom Inst.

Townes, Henry. The Genera of Ichneumonidae, Pt. 1, Ephialtinae To Agriotypinae. (Memoirs Ser: No. 11). (Illus.). 300p. 1969. 20.00 (ISBN 0-686-00418-3). Am Entom Inst.

--The Genera of Ichneumonidae, Pt. 2, Gelinae. (Memoirs Ser: No. 12). (Illus.). 537p. 1970. 35.00 (ISBN 0-686-00419-1). Am Entom Inst.

--The Genera of Ichneumonidae, Pt. 3, Lycorininae To Porizontinae. (Memoirs Ser: No. 13). (Illus.). 307p. 1970. 20.00 (ISBN 0-686-00420-5). Am Entom Inst.

--Genera of Ichneumonidae, Pt. 4, Cremastinae To Diplazontinae. (Memoirs Ser: No. 17). (Illus.). 372p. 1971. 28.00x (ISBN 0-686-01268-2). Am Entom Inst.

Townes, Henry & Gupta, Virendra K. Ichneumonidae of America North of Mexico: Subfamily Gelinae, Tribe Hemigasterini. (Memoirs Ser: No. 2). (Illus.). 20.00 (ISBN 0-686-00421-3). Am Entom Inst.

Townes, Henry & Townes, Marjorie. Catalogue & Reclassification of the Neotropic Ichneumonidae. (Memoirs Ser: No. 8). 1966. 25.00 (ISBN 0-686-00416-7). Am Entom Inst.

Townes, Henry, et al. Catalogue & Reclassification of the Eastern Palearctic Ichneumonidae. (Memoirs Ser.: No. 5). 661p. 1965. 40.00 (ISBN 0-686-00414-0). Am Entom Inst.

--Catalogue & Reclassification of the Indo-Australian Ichneumonidae. (Memoirs Ser: No. 1). 522p. 1961. 33.00 (ISBN 0-686-00415-9). Am Entom Inst.

ICHTHYOLOGY

see Fishes

ICHTHYS

see Fish (In Religion, Folk-Lore, etc.)

ICINGS, CAKE

see also Cake Decorating

Guertner, Beryl. Cake Icing & Decorating for All Occasions. LC 67-19283. 1967. 8.95 (ISBN 0-8008-1151-8). Taplinger.

Holding, Audrey. The Art of Royal Icing. (Illus.). xviii, 176p. 1980. pap. 16.25x (ISBN 0-85334-860-X, Pub. by Applied Science). Burgess-Intl Ideas.

McNamara. Magic in Frosting: The Ultimate in Cake Decorating. pap. 10.95 (ISBN 0-685-27814-X). Borden.

ICKES, HAROLD LE CLAIRE, 1874-1952

Ickes, Harold L. The Secret Diary of Harold L. Ickes, 3 vols. LC 73-21721. (FDR & the Era of the New Deal Ser.). 1974. Repr. of 1954 ed. Set. lib. bdg. 125.00 (ISBN 0-306-70626-1); lib. bdg. 47.50 ea. Vol. 1, The First Thousand Days, 1933-1936 (ISBN 0-306-70627-X). Vol. 2, The Inside Struggle, 1936-1939 (ISBN 0-306-70628-8). Vol. 3, The Lowering Clouds, 1939-1941 (ISBN 0-306-70629-6). Da Capo.

ICONOCLASM

Brandon, S. G. Man & God in Art & Ritual: A Study of Iconography, Architecture & Ritual Action As Primary Evidence of Religious Belief & Practice. (Illus.). 514p. 14.95 (ISBN 0-686-74480-2). Scribner.

Brehier, Louis. La Querelle des images huitieme-neuvieme siecle. 1969. 14.00 (ISBN 0-8337-0362-5). B Franklin.

Gutmann, Joseph, ed. The Image & the Word. LC 77-23470. (American Academy of Religion & Society of Biblical Literature. Religion & the Arts Ser.: Vol. 4). 1977. write for info. (ISBN 0-89130-142-9, 090104); pap. write for info. (ISBN 0-89130-143-7). Scholars Pr Ca.

Hubbard, Harlan. Payne Hollow: Life on the Fringe of Society. LC 75-34720. (Illus.). 168p. 1976. pap. 3.95 (ISBN 0-690-01024-9, TYC-T). T Y Crowell.

Joannes, Damascenus. On Holy Images. Allies, Mary H., tr. from Greek. 1977. pap. 2.95 (ISBN 0-686-19232-X). Eastern Orthodox.

Landow, George P. Images of Crisis: Literary Iconology, 1750 to the Present. 200p. 1981. write for info. (ISBN 0-7100-0818-X). Routledge & Kegan.

Martin, Edward J. A History of the Iconclastic Controversy. LC 77-84711. Repr. of 1930 ed. 23.50 (ISBN 0-404-16117-0). AMS Pr.

ICONOGRAPHY

see Art; Christian Art and Symbolism; Idols and Images; Portraits

ICONS

Brehier, L. L' Art Chretien, son Developement Iconographique des Origines a nos Jours. 2nd ed. (Illus.). 480p. (Fr.). 1981. Repr. of 1928 ed. lib. bdg. 125.00 (ISBN 0-89241-138-4). Caratzas Bros.

Browne. Icons of America. LC 77-84917. 1978. 14.95 (ISBN 0-87972-090-5); pap. 6.95 (ISBN 0-87972-091-3). Bowling Green Univ.

Dabovich, Sebastian. Holy Orthodox Church: Its Ritual, Services, & Sacraments. 1898. pap. 1.50 (ISBN 0-686-00253-9). Eastern Orthodox.

Davis, Peggy. New Icons. 16p. 1980. pap. 2.00 (ISBN 0-913198-15-3, Lucky Heart Books). Salt Lick.

Iconmakers' Handbook of the Stroganov School of Icon Painting. 1974. 8.50 (ISBN 0-686-10192-8). Eastern Orthodox.

Icons in the Eastern Orthodox Church, a Brief Theological Introduction: Jeremiah, Patriarch of Constantinople & St. John of Damascus. pap. 0.25 (ISBN 0-686-01294-1). Eastern Orthodox.

Irimie, Cornel & Focsa, Marcela. Romanian Icons Painted on Glass. (Illus.). 1971. 75.00 (ISBN 0-393-04309-6). Norton.

John Of Damascus, St. Veneration of Icons. pap. 0.25 (ISBN 0-686-05666-3). Eastern Orthodox.

Laurina, Vera & Pushkariov, Vasily, eds. Novgorod Icons 12th - 17th Century. Cook, Kathleen, et al, trs. 1981. 45.00 (ISBN 0-89893-077-4). CDP.

Lazarer, V. N. Novgorodian Icon-Painting. (Illus.). 38.00 (ISBN 0-912729-00-7). Newbury Bks Inc.

Lazarev, Viktor N., compiled by. Pages from the History of Novgorodian Painting. Strelkova, G. V., tr. Date not set. 12.50 (ISBN 0-89893-042-1). CDP.

Ouspensky, Leonid. Theology of the Icon. Meyendorff, Elizabeth, tr. from Fr. LC 77-11882. (Illus.). 232p. 1978. pap. 7.95 (ISBN 0-913836-42-7). St Vladimirs.

Radojoio, S., et al. Icons. (Alpine Fine Art Collection Ser.). (Illus.). Date not set. 50.00 (ISBN 0-933516-07-X). Alpine Bk Co.

Rice, David & Rice, Tamara T. Icons & Their History. LC 74-78136. (Illus.). 192p. 1974. 45.00 (ISBN 0-87951-021-8). Overlook Pr.

Stroganov School of Iconpainting. Iconpainters Handbook of the Stroganov School of Iconpainting. (Illus.). 1974. Repr. of 1869 ed. 12.50 (ISBN 0-686-10201-0). Eastern Orthodox.

Stuart, John. Ikons. 274p. 1975. 48.00 (ISBN 0-571-08846-5, Pub. by Faber & Faber). Merrimack Bk Serv.

Taylor, John. Icon Painting. LC 78-25925. (The Mayflower Gallery Ser.). (Illus.). 1979. 12.50 (ISBN 0-8317-4813-3, Mayflower Bks); pap. 6.95 (ISBN 0-8317-4814-1). Smith Pubs.

Trubetskoi, Eugene. Icons: Theology in Color. (Illus.). 1973. pap. write for info. (ISBN 0-913836-09-5). St Vladimirs.

Uspensky, Boris. The Semiotics of the Russian Icon. Rudy, Stephen, ed. Reed, P. A., tr. (PdR Press Publications in Semiotics of Art Ser.: No. 3). 101p. 1976. pap. text ed. 8.75x (ISBN 903-1600-78-4). Humanities.

Verdier, Philippe. Russian Art, Icons & Decorative Arts from the Origin to the 20th Century. (Illus.). 1959. pap. 5.00 (ISBN 0-685-21833-3). Walters Art.

Weitzman, Kurt. The Icon: Holy Images 6th to 14th Century. (Magnificant Paperback Art Ser.). 136p. 1978. 24.95 (ISBN 0-8076-0892-0); pap. 11.95 (ISBN 0-8076-0893-9). Braziller.

Weitzmann, Kurt. The Monastery of Saint Catherine at Mount Sinai: The Icons I - from the Sixth to the Tenth Century. LC 75-3482. 276p. 1976. 140.00x (ISBN 0-691-03543-1). Princeton U Pr.

Wild, Doris. Holy Icons: In the Religious Art of the Eastern Church. (World in Color Ser.). (Illus.). 50p. 1976. 3.95 (ISBN 0-88254-386-5). Hippocrene Bks.

ICTERUS (PATHOLOGY)

see Jaundice

ID (PSYCHOLOGY)

Schur, Max. Id & the Regulatory Principles of Mental Functioning. LC 66-20144. (Journal of the American Psychoanalytic Association Monograph Ser.: No. 4). 1966. text ed. 15.00 (ISBN 0-8236-2440-4). Intl Univs Pr.

IDAHO

see also Names of Cities, counties, etc. in Idaho

Bailey, Bernadine. Picture Book of Idaho. rev. ed. LC 62-10660. (Illus.). (gr. 3-5). 1967. 5.50g (ISBN 0-8075-9514-4). A Whitman.

Bailey, William A., et al. Bill Bailey Came Home. 183p. 1973. 6.00 (ISBN 0-87421-061-5); pap. 4.00 (ISBN 0-87421-092-5). Utah St U Pr.

Beatty, Robert O. Idaho: A Pictorial Overview. LC 74-11819. (Illus.). 1975. 50.00 (ISBN 0-9600776-1-8). R O Beatty Assoc.

Bjork, Philip R. Carnivora of the Hagerman Local Fauna: Late Pliocene of Southwestern Idaho. LC 70-131553. (Transactions Ser.: Vol. 60, Pt. 7). (Illus.). 1970. pap. 1.00 (ISBN 0-87169-607-X). Am Philos.

Blank, Robert H. Regional Diversity of Political Values: Idaho Political Culture. LC 78-62742. 1978. pap. text ed. 8.75 (ISBN 0-8191-0590-2). U Pr of Amer.

Carpenter, Allan. Idaho. new ed. LC 79-9804. (New Enchantment of America State Bks.). (Illus.). (gr. 4 up). 1979. PLB 10.60 (ISBN 0-516-04112-6). Childrens.

D'Easum, Dick. Sawtooth Tales. LC 76-24379. (Illus.). 1977. pap. 7.95 (ISBN 0-87004-259-9). Caxton.

Donaldson, Thomas C. Idaho of Yesterday. LC 70-104218. Repr. of 1941 ed. lib. bdg. 25.00x (ISBN 0-8371-3335-1, DOID). Greenwood.

Duncombe, H. Sydney, et al. Idaho Election Statistics. Incl. 1972. 3.00 (ISBN 0-89301-011-1); 1974. 3.00 (ISBN 0-89301-026-X); 1976. 3.00 (ISBN 0-89301-048-0). Set. 10.00 (ISBN 0-686-77202-4). U Pr of Idaho.

Duncombe, S., et al, eds. Idaho Tomorrow Book. 1975. 1.95 (ISBN 0-89301-024-3). U Pr of Idaho.

Duncombe, Sydney, et al. Idaho State & Local Government. LC 77-155358. (Illus.). 1971. 3.00 (ISBN 0-87004-224-6). Caxton.

Federal Writers' Project, Idaho. Idaho Lore. LC 73-3612. (American Guide Ser). Repr. of 1939 ed. 21.50 (ISBN 0-404-57915-9). AMS Pr.

Forbush, Zebina. The Co-Opolitan: A Story of the Co-Operative Commonwealth of Idaho. LC 76-42804. Repr. of 1898 ed. 21.50 (ISBN 0-404-60066-2). AMS Pr.

Fradin, Dennis. Idaho: In Words & Pictures. LC 80-14660. (Young People's Stories of Our States Ser.). (Illus.). (gr. 2-5). 1980. PLB 9.25 (ISBN 0-516-03914-8). Childrens.

Frederickson, Lars. History of Weston, Idaho. Simmonds, A. J., ed. (Western Text Society Ser.: No. 5). (Illus.). 78p. 1972. pap. 4.00 (ISBN 0-87421-051-8). Utah St U Pr.

Gittins, H. Leigh. Idaho's Gold Road. LC 76-46791. 1976. 6.95 (ISBN 0-89301-035-9). U Pr of Idaho.

Idaho. 23.00 (ISBN 0-89770-088-0). Curriculum Info Ctr.

Idaho Manufacturing Directory: 1982-83. rev. ed. 1982. 30.00x (ISBN 0-686-05494-6). Ctr Bus Devel.

Idaho Session Laws. Incl. Nineteen Forty-Seven. 6.00 (ISBN 0-87004-185-1); Nineteen Fifty-Five. 6.00 (ISBN 0-87004-186-X); Nineteen Fifty-Nine. 8.50 (ISBN 0-87004-187-8); Nineteen Sixty-One. 10.00 (ISBN 0-87004-188-6); Nineteen Sixty-Three. 11.00 (ISBN 0-87004-189-4); Nineteen Sixty-Five. 11.00 (ISBN 0-87004-190-8); Nineteen Sixty-Seven, 2 vols. Set. 14.25 (ISBN 0-87004-191-6); Nineteen Sixty-Nine, 2 vols. Set. 14.50 (ISBN 0-87004-197-5); Nineteen Seventy. 14.50 (ISBN 0-87004-211-4); Nineteen Seventy-One, 2 vols. Set. 15.90 (ISBN 0-87004-268-8); Nineteen Seventy-Two. 14.50 (ISBN 0-87004-269-6); Nineteen Seventy-Three. 14.50 (ISBN 0-87004-270-X); Nineteen Seventy-Four, 2 vols. 15.90 (ISBN 0-87004-271-8). Caxton; Nineteen Seventy-Five. 14.50 (ISBN 0-87004-272-6); Nineteen Seventy-Six. 14.50 (ISBN 0-87004-273-4); Nineteen Seventy-Seven. 18.50 (ISBN 0-87004-274-2); Nineteen Seventy-Eight. 18.50 (ISBN 0-87004-277-7); Nineteen Seventy-Nine. 1980. 18.50 (ISBN 0-87004-279-3). Caxton.

Koelsch, Clay. Idaho Reports, Volume 62. 3.50 (ISBN 0-87004-192-4). Caxton.

--Idaho Reports, Volume 63. 3.50 (ISBN 0-87004-193-2). Caxton.

Larrison, Earl J. & Johnson, Donald R. Mammals of Idaho. LC 80-51876. (GEM Bks-Natural History Ser.). (Illus.). 200p. 1981. pap. 6.95 (ISBN 0-89301-070-7). U Pr of Idaho.

Malone, Michael P. C. Ben Ross & the New Deal in Idaho. LC 69-14207. (Illus.). 217p. 1970. 10.50 (ISBN 0-295-95060-9). U of Wash Pr.

Martin, Boyd. Idaho Voting Trends: Eighteen Ninety-Nineteen Seventy Four. 1975. 6.00 (ISBN 0-89301-025-1). U Pr of Idaho.

Murray, Alberta. These Are My Children. 1977. 9.95 (ISBN 0-87770-194-6). Ye Galleon.

Oppenheimer, Doug & Poore, Jim. Sun Valley: A Biography. LC 76-27113. (Illus.). 1976. 12.95 (ISBN 0-916238-04-0); pap. 7.95 (ISBN 0-916238-02-4). R O Beatty Assocs.

Peterson, F. Ross. Idaho: A Bicentennial History. (State & the Nation Ser.). 1976. 12.95 (ISBN 0-393-05600-7, Co-Pub by AASLH). Norton.

Preston, Ralph N. Early Idaho Atlas. LC 78-57018. (Illus.). 1978. pap. 6.50 (ISBN 0-8323-0312-7). Binford.

Rees, John. Idaho, Chronology, Nomenclature & Bibliography. Repr. of 1918 ed. pap. 14.00 (ISBN 0-8466-0104-4, SJS104). Shorey.

Rouyer, Alwyn R., et al. Economic, Social & Voting Characteristics of Idaho's Precincts. 1972. 3.00 (ISBN 0-89301-013-8). U Pr of Idaho.

Simpson, James C. & Wallace, Richard L. Fishes of Idaho. LC 78-65345. 1978. 6.50 (ISBN 0-89301-058-8). U Pr of Idaho.

Sparling, Wayne. Southern Idaho Ghost Towns. LC 73-156484. (Illus., Orig.). 1974. pap. 5.95 (ISBN 0-87004-229-7). Caxton.

Taylor, Lee. Pend Oreille Profiles. 1977. 14.95 (ISBN 0-87770-185-7). Ye Galleon.

Webbert, Charles A. Scottiana Idahoensis. LC 78-51147. 1978. 2.95 (ISBN 0-89301-052-9). U Pr of Idaho.

Young, Virgil M. & Young, Katherine A. Story of Idaho Teacher's Aid Booklet. rev. ed. LC 80-51706. 1980. 15.00 (ISBN 0-89301-055-3). U Pr of Idaho.

IDAHO-DESCRIPTION AND TRAVEL

Angelo, C. Aubrey. Idaho: A Descriptive Tour. 1971. Repr. 7.50 (ISBN 0-87770-030-3). Ye Galleon.

Beatty, Robert O. Idaho: A Pictorial Overview. LC 74-11819. (Illus.). 1975. 50.00 (ISBN 0-9600776-1-8). R O Beatty Assoc.

Bluestein, Sheldon. Hiking Trails of Southern Idaho. LC 79-52543. (Illus.). 195p. (Orig.). 1981. pap. 7.95 (ISBN 0-87004-280-7). Caxton.

Federal Writers Project. Idaho: A Guide in Word & Picture. 2nd ed. (American Guide Ser). 1950. 14.95 (ISBN 0-19-500589-9). Oxford U Pr.

Federal Writers' Project. Idaho: A Guide in Word & Picture. 1937. Repr. 45.00 (ISBN 0-403-02163-4). Somerset Pub.

Fuller, Margaret. Trails of the Sawtooth & White Cloud Mountains. new ed. LC 78-68661. (Illus., Orig.). 1979. pap. 7.95 (ISBN 0-913140-29-5). Signpost Bk Pub.

Hart, Herbert M. Tour Guide to Old Forts of Oregon, Idaho, Washington, California, Vol. 3. (Illus.). 65p. (Orig.). 1981. pap. 3.95 (ISBN 0-87108-582-8). Pruett.

Jensen, Dwight W. Visiting Boise: A Personal Guide. LC 80-27098. (Illus.). 145p. 1981. pap. 7.95 (ISBN 0-87004-290-4). Caxton.

Kelner, Alexis & Hanscom, David. Wasatch Tours. LC 76-28112. 1976. pap. 4.95 (ISBN 0-915272-06-7). Wasatch Pubs.

Lewis, Paul M. Beautiful Idaho. Shangle, Robert D., ed. LC 79-779. 72p. 1979. 14.95 (ISBN 0-915796-93-7); pap. 7.95 (ISBN 0-915796-92-9). Beautiful Am.

--Beautiful North Idaho. LC 79-4546. 72p. 1979. 14.95 (ISBN 0-915796-95-3); pap. 7.95 (ISBN 0-915796-94-5). Beautiful Am.

Linkhart, Luther. The Sawtooth National Recreation Area. Winnett, Thomas, ed. LC 79-57594. (Illus., Orig.). 1981. pap. 12.95 (ISBN 0-911824-96-0). Wilderness.

Mitchell, Ron. Fifty Eastern Idaho Hiking Trails. (Illus.). 1979. pap. 5.95 (ISBN 0-87108-551-8). Pruett.

Russell, Bert. Swiftwater People. LC 79-92395. 1979. pap. 7.95 (ISBN 0-930344-02-2). Lacon Pubs.

Wolf, Elliott. Sun Valley Epicure. (Epicure Ser.). (Orig.). 1981. pap. 2.50 (ISBN 0-89716-077-0). Peanut Butter.

Wolf, James R. Guide to the Continental Divide Trail: Southern Montana & Idaho, Vol. 2. LC 76-17632. (Guide to the Continental Divide Trail Ser.). (Illus.). 1979. pap. 8.95 (ISBN 0-934326-02-9). Continent Divide.

Wright, Bank. Sun Valley: A Mountain Guide. LC 75-30387. 1976. 4.95 (ISBN 0-686-16323-0). Mntn & Sea.

IDAHO-HISTORY

Bischoff, William N. The Coeur D'alene County, 1805-1892: An Historical Sketch. 33.00 (ISBN 0-8287-1005-8). Clearwater Pub.

Byers, Roland O. To the Sundown Side: The Mountain Man in Idaho. LC 79-65601. (GEM Books-Historical). (Illus.). 214p. (Orig.). 1979. pap. 8.95 (ISBN 0-89301-063-4). U Pr of Idaho.

Cohen, Stan B. & Miller, Donald C. Big Burn: Big Burn: the Northwest's Forest Fire of Nineteen Ten. LC 78-51507. (Illus.). 96p. 1978. pap. 4.95 (ISBN 0-933126-04-2). Pictorial Hist.

Gibbs, Rafe. Beckoning the Bold. LC 76-16212. 1976. 5.95 (ISBN 0-89301-031-6). U Pr of Idaho.

Jensen, Dwight W. Discovering Idaho, a History. LC 77-24010. (Illus.). 1977. text ed. 11.95x (ISBN 0-87004-261-0); wkbk. 3.00x (ISBN 0-87004-262-9). Caxton.

Simpson, Claude C. & Simpson, Catherine. North of the Narrows: Story of Priest Lake Country. LC 80-51781. (GEM Bks-Historical Ser.). (Illus.). 332p. (Orig.). 1981. pap. 11.95 (ISBN 0-89301-069-3). U Pr of Idaho.

Taylor, Dorice. Sun Valley. (Illus.). 264p. 1980. 20.00 (ISBN 0-9605212-0-8). Ex Libris ID.

Vance, Mary. Historical Society Architectural Publications: Georgia, Hawaii, Idaho, Illinois & Indiana. (Architecture Ser.: Bibliography A-157). 54p. 1980. pap. 6.00 (ISBN 0-686-26906-3). Vance Biblios.

Vexler, R. I. Idaho Chronology & Factbook, Vol. 12. 1978. 8.50 (ISBN 0-379-16137-0). Oceana.

Young, Virgil M. The Story of Idaho. LC 76-58667. (gr. 4-7). 1977. 9.95 (ISBN 0-89301-041-3). U Pr of Idaho.

IDAHO-IMPRINTS

Historical Records Survey: Check List of Idaho Imprints, 1839-1890. 1939. pap. 6.00 (ISBN 0-527-01910-0). Kraus Repr.

IDEA (PHILOSOPHY)

Aristotelian Society For The Systematic Study Of Philosophy. Knowledge & Foreknowledge: Proceedings, Supplementary Vol. 16. Repr. of 1937 ed. 14.00 (ISBN 0-384-29990-3); pap. 9.00 (ISBN 0-384-29991-1). Johnson Repr.

Cournot, Antoine A. Considerations Sur la Marche Des Idees et Des Evenements Dans les Temps Modernes. 1971. Repr. of 1872 ed. lib. bdg. 40.50 (ISBN 0-8337-0700-0). B Franklin.

Hammond, Albert L. Ideas About Substance. LC 69-13537. (Seminars in the History of Ideas). 160p. (Orig.). 1969. 10.00x (ISBN 0-8018-1012-4); pap. 3.45x (ISBN 0-8018-1013-2). Johns Hopkins.

Nakamura, Hajime. Parallel Developments: A Comparative History of Ideas. LC 75-24947. 567p. 1975. 34.50x (ISBN 0-87011-272-4). Kodansha.

Schopenhauer, Arthur, et al. The World As Will & Idea, 3 vols. Haldane, R. B. & Kemp, J., trs. from Ger. LC 75-41243. Repr. of 1896 ed. 87.50 set (ISBN 0-404-15060-8). AMS Pr.

Stewart, John A. Plato's Doctrine of Ideas. LC 77-23824. 1977. lib. bdg. 25.00 (ISBN 0-8414-7930-5). Folcroft.

Stich, Stephen P., ed. Innate Ideas. 1975. 22.75x (ISBN 0-520-02822-8); pap. 6.95x (ISBN 0-520-02961-5). U of Cal Pr.

University Of California Philosophical Union - 1925. Nature of Ideas: Lectures. (Publications in Philosophy Ser: Vol. 8). 1926. pap. 17.00 (ISBN 0-685-13525-X). Johnson Repr.

Vickers, John M. Belief & Probability. new ed. (Synthese Library: No. 104). 1976. lib. bdg. 31.50 (ISBN 90-277-0744-8, Pub. by Reidel Holland). Kluwer Boston.

Weinberg, Julius R. Ideas & Concept. (Aquinas Lectures Ser). 1970. 6.95 (ISBN 0-87462-135-6). Marquette.

Wiener, Philip P., ed. Dictionary of the History of Ideas. 1980. pap. 100.00 5-volume boxed edition (ISBN 0-686-61145-4). Scribner.

IDEAL STATES

see Utopias

IDEALISM

see also Dualism; Form (Philosophy); Materialism; Pragmatism; Realism; Transcendentalism

Adams, George P. Idealism & the Modern Age. LC 75-3015. Repr. of 1919 ed. 18.00 (ISBN 0-404-59009-8). AMS Pr.

Barrett, Clifford, ed. Contemporary Idealism in America. LC 64-11850. 1964. Repr. of 1932 ed. 8.50 (ISBN 0-8462-0444-4). Russell.

Berkeley, George. Three Dialogues Between Hylas & Philonous. Turbayne, Colin M., ed. 1954. pap. 3.95 (ISBN 0-672-60206-7, LLA39). Bobbs.

--Three Dialogues Between Hylas & Philonous. McCormack, Thomas J., ed. vi, 136p. 1969. 9.95 (ISBN 0-87548-068-3); pap. 3.95 (ISBN 0-87548-069-1). Open Court.

--Treatise Concerning the Principles of Human Knowledge. Turbayne, Colin M., ed. LC 57-1290. 1957. pap. 3.50 (ISBN 0-672-60225-3, LLA53). Bobbs.

--A Treatise Concerning the Principles of Human Knowledge. McCormack, Thomas J., ed. & pref. by. xv, 128p. 1963. 9.95 (ISBN 0-87548-071-3); pap. 3.95 (ISBN 0-87548-072-1). Open Court.

Brown, Rollo W. Creative Spirit: An Inquiry into American Life. LC 70-85999. 1970. Repr. of 1925 ed. 12.50 (ISBN 0-8046-0604-8). Kennikat.

Butler, J. Donald. Four Philosophies & Their Practice in Education & Religion. 3rd ed. 1968. text ed. 22.50 scp (ISBN 0-06-041108-2, HarpC). Har-Row.

Cunningham, Gustavus W. Idealistic Argument in Recent British & American Philosophy. facs. ed. LC 67-23200. (Essay Index Reprint Ser). 1933. 25.00 (ISBN 0-8369-0356-0). Arno.

--Idealistic Argument in Recent British & American Philosophy. LC 76-98750. Repr. of 1933 ed. lib. bdg. 19.00x (ISBN 0-8371-2833-1, CUBA). Greenwood.

Dasgupta, Surendranath. Indian Idealism. 1962. 26.95 (ISBN 0-521-04783-8); pap. 7.95x (ISBN 0-521-09194-2, 194). Cambridge U Pr.

Dilthey, Wilthelm. Philosophy of Existence: Introduction to Weltanschauugslehre. LC 78-5673. 1978. Repr. of 1957 ed. lib. bdg. 15.00x (ISBN 0-313-20460-8, DIPH). Greenwood.

Dockhorn, Klaus. Die Staatsphilosophie Des Englischen Idealismus. 1937. pap. 17.00 (ISBN 0-384-12065-2). Johnson Repr.

Ekirch, Arthur A., Jr. Ideologies & Utopias. pap. text ed. 2.95x (ISBN 0-8290-0342-8). Irvington.

Esposito, Joseph L. Schelling's Idealism & Philosophy of Nature. 294p. 1978. 16.50 (ISBN 0-8387-1904-X). Bucknell U Pr.

Ewing, A. C. Idealism: A Critical Survey. 454p. 1974. Repr. of 1934 ed. text ed. 19.50x (ISBN 0-416-80950-2). Methuen Inc.

Fausset, Hugh L. Studies in Idealism. LC 65-18603. Repr. of 1923 ed. 12.00 (ISBN 0-8046-0140-2). Kennikat.

Hammond, Phillip E. The Role of Ideology in Church Participation. Zuckerman, Harriet & Merton, Robert K., eds. LC 79-9003. (Dissertations on Sociology Ser.). 1980. lib. bdg. 24.00x (ISBN 0-405-12972-6). Arno.

Hoernle, R. F. Idealism, As a Philosophical Doctrine. 1979. Repr. of 1924 ed. lib. bdg. 25.00 (ISBN 0-8495-2281-1). Arden Lib.

Howard, Claud. Coleridge's Idealism. LC 72-191125. 1924. lib. bdg. 17.50 (ISBN 0-8414-5131-1). Folcroft.

Howie, John & Buford, Thomas O., eds. Contemporary Studies in Philosophical Idealism. LC 74-76007. (Philosophy Ser.: No. 601). 285p. 1976. 15.00 (ISBN 0-89007-601-4). C Stark.

Howison, George H. George Holmes Howison, Philosopher & Teacher. Buckham, J. W. & Stratton, G. M., eds. 1934. 16.00 (ISBN 0-527-42800-0). Kraus Repr.

Hunt, John. Pantheism & Christianity. LC 78-102573. 1970. Repr. of 1884 ed. 15.00 (ISBN 0-8046-0733-8). Kennikat.

Jackson, Holbrook. Dreamers of Dreams: The Rise & Fall of 19th Century Idealism. LC 78-15808. 1978. Repr. of 1948 ed. lib. bdg. 35.00 (ISBN 0-8414-5410-8). Folcroft.

--Rise & Fall of Nineteenth Century Idealsim. 1969. pap. 2.45 (ISBN 0-8065-0016-6). Citadel Pr.

Knappen, Marshall M. Tudor Puritanism. 1963. 7.50 (ISBN 0-8446-1267-7). Peter Smith.

--Tudor Puritanism: A Chapter in the History of Idealism. LC 39-10082. 1965. pap. 3.45 (ISBN 0-226-44627-1, P194, Phoen). U of Chicago Pr.

Lloyd, Alfred H. Dynamic Idealism. LC 75-3243. Repr. of 1898 ed. 17.00 (ISBN 0-404-59233-3). AMS Pr.

Marsh, Daniel L. Unto the Generations. LC 68-27392. 7.95 (ISBN 0-912806-25-7). Long Hse.

Morris, Charles R. Idealistic Logic. LC 76-102578. 1970. Repr. of 1933 ed. 14.00 (ISBN 0-8046-0738-9). Kennikat.

Muirhead, John H. Platonic Tradition in Anglo-Saxon Philosophy. (Muirhead Library of Philosophy). 1965. Repr. of 1931 ed. text ed. 12.00x (ISBN 0-04-141003-3). Humanities.

Orsini, Gian N. Coleridge & German Idealism: A Study in the History of Philosophy. with Unpublished Material from Coleridge's Manuscripts. LC 69-11512. 320p. 1969. 10.00x (ISBN 0-8093-0363-9). S Ill U Pr.

Otto, Max C. Things & Ideals. 1924. 15.00 (ISBN 0-527-68800-2). Kraus Repr.

Panofsky, Erwin. Idea: A Concept in Art Theory. Peake, Joseph J., tr. LC 67-29380. (Illus.). 1968. 14.95x (ISBN 0-87249-117-X). U of SC Pr.

Radhakrishnan, Sarvepalli. An Idealist View of Life. LC 77-27145. (Hibbert Lectures: 1929). Repr. of 1932 ed. 37.00 (ISBN 0-404-60425-0). AMS Pr.

Rescher, Nicholas. Conceptual Idealism. 204p. 1973. 25.00x (ISBN 0-631-14950-3, Pub. by Basil Blackwell). Biblio Dist.

Shortt, S. E. The Search for an Ideal: Six Canadian Intellectuals & Their Convictions in an Age of Transition, 1890-1930. 1976. 17.50x (ISBN 0-8020-5350-5); pap. 7.50 (ISBN 0-8020-6285-7). U of Toronto Pr.

Solomon, Robert C. Introducing the German Idealists. (Philosophical Dialogue Ser.). 80p. 1981. lib. bdg. 9.50 (ISBN 0-915145-02-2); pap. text ed. 2.50 (ISBN 0-915145-03-0). Hackett Pub.

Stackelberg, Roderick. Idealism Debased: From Volkisch Ideology to National Socialism. LC 80-84663. (Illus.). 220p. 1981. 18.00x (ISBN 0-87338-252-8). Kent St U Pr.

Van Sickle, John V. Freedom in Jeopardy: The Tyranny of Idealism. LC 68-54126. (Principles of Freedom Ser.). 204p. 1969. 9.95 (ISBN 0-89617-045-4). Inst Humane.

--Freedom in Jeopardy: The Tyranny of Idealism. (Principles of Freedom Ser.). 204p. 1980. text ed. 7.50x (ISBN 0-391-02086-2). Humanities.

Webb, Thomas E. Veil of Isis: A Series of Essays on Idealism. LC 72-8522. (Essay Index Reprint Ser.). 1972. Repr. of 1885 ed. 21.00 (ISBN 0-8369-7337-2). Arno.

Wolandt, Gerd. Idealismus und Faktizitaet. 287p. 1971. 41.75x (ISBN 3-11-002375-X). De Gruyter.

IDEALISM IN ART

see also Naturalism in Art; Realism in Art; Romanticism in Art

Sheldon, George W. Recent Ideals of American Art. LC 75-28882. (Art Experience in Late 19th Century America Ser.: Vol. 16). (Illus.). 1976. Repr. of 1890 ed. lib. bdg. 87.00 (ISBN 0-8240-2240-8). Garland Pub.

Young, Howard T. The Line in the Margin: Juan Ramon Jimenez & His Readings in Blake, Shelley, & Yeats. LC 79-3963. 242p. 1980. 22.50 (ISBN 0-299-07950-3). U of Wis Pr.

IDEALISM IN LITERATURE

see also Naturalism in Literature; Realism in Literature; Romanticism

Goetz, Sr. Mary P. Concept of Nobility in German Didactic Literature of the Thirteenth Century. LC 79-140021. (Catholic University Studies in German Ser.: No. 5). Repr. of 1935 ed. 16.00 (ISBN 0-404-50225-3). AMS Pr.

Jackson, Holbrook. Dreamers of Dreams: The Rise & Fall of 19th Century Idealism. LC 70-158496. 1971. Repr. of 1948 ed. 18.00 (ISBN 0-403-01314-3). Scholarly.

Lucas, Frank L. The Decline & Fall of the Romantic Ideal. 1978. Repr. of 1936 ed. lib. bdg. 25.00 (ISBN 0-8495-3229-9). Arden Lib.

IDEALS (ALGEBRA)

Burton, D. M. First Course in Rings & Ideals. LC 73-100855. 1970. text ed. 13.50 (ISBN 0-201-00731-2, Adv Bk Prog). A-W.

Gilmer, R. W. Multiplicative Ideal Theory. (Pure & Applied Mathematics Ser: Vol. 12). 614p. 1972. 37.75 (ISBN 0-8247-1242-0). Dekker.

Jategaonkar, A. V. Left Principal Ideal Rings. LC 74-114015. (Lecture Notes in Mathematics: Vol. 123). 1970. pap. 10.70 (ISBN 0-387-04912-6). Springer-Verlag.

Kaplansky, Irving. Commutative Rings. rev. ed. LC 74-5732. 192p. 1974. text ed. 12.00x (ISBN 0-226-42454-5). U of Chicago Pr.

Larsen, Max D. & McCarthy, Paul J. Multiplicative Theory of Ideals. (Pure & Applied Mathematics Ser.: Vol. 43). 1971. 49.50 (ISBN 0-12-436850-6). Acad Pr.

Reiner, I. Maximal Orders. (London Mathematical Society Monographs). 1975. 61.00 (ISBN 0-12-586650-X). Acad Pr.

Simon, Barry. Trace Ideals & Their Applications. LC 78-20867. (London Mathematical Society Lecture Notes Ser.: No. 35). 1979. pap. 16.95x (ISBN 0-521-22286-9). Cambridge U Pr.

Steinfeld, Otto. Quasi-Ideals in Rings & Semi-Groups. LC 79-308570. (Illus.). 154p. 1978. 17.50x (ISBN 963-05-1696-9). Intl Pubns Serv.

IDEALS (PSYCHOLOGY)

see also Influence (Psychology)

Wilson, John. Ideals. LC 74-80383. (Illus.). 96p. 1974. pap. 3.25 (ISBN 0-8192-1172-9). Morehouse.

IDEAS, ASSOCIATION OF

see Association of Ideas

IDENTIFICATION

see also Fingerprints; Medical Jurisprudence

Clifford, Brian & Bull, Ray. The Psychology of Person Identification. 1978. 22.50 (ISBN 0-7100-8867-1). Routledge & Kegan.

Eykhoff, P., ed. Trends & Progress in System Identification. LC 80-41994. (IFAC Ser. for Graduate, Research Workers & Practicing Engineers: Vol. 1). (Illus.). 410p. 1981. 70.00 (ISBN 0-08-025683-X). Pergamon.

Isermann, R., ed. System Identification Tutorials. (Illus.). 88p. 1981. 12.50 (ISBN 0-08-027583-4); pap. 7.00 (ISBN 0-08-027302-5). Pergamon.

Kolb, Patricia A. H.I.T. A Manual for the Classification, Filing, & Retrieval of Palmprints. (Illus.). 112p. 1979. text ed. 16.50 spiral bdg. (ISBN 0-398-03855-4). C C Thomas.

Rudman, Jack. Identification Officer. (Career Examination Ser.: C-1986). (Cloth bdg. avail. on request). pap. 8.00 (ISBN 0-8373-1986-2). Natl Learning.

--Identification Specialist. (Career Examination Ser.: C-2294). (Cloth bdg. avail. on request). 1977. pap. 8.00 (ISBN 0-8373-2294-4). Natl Learning.

--Senior Identification Clerk. (Career Examination Ser.: C-2293). (Cloth bdg. avail. on request). pap. 10.00 (ISBN 0-8373-2293-6). Natl Learning.

--Senior Identification Officer. (Career Examination Ser.: C-1987). (Cloth bdg. avail. on request). pap. 10.00 (ISBN 0-8373-1987-0). Natl Learning.

--Senior Identification Specialist. (Career Examination Ser.: C-2512). (Cloth bdg. avail. on request). pap. 10.00 (ISBN 0-8373-2512-9). Natl Learning.

--Supervising Identification Specialist. (Career Examination Ser.: C-2513). (Cloth bdg. avail. on request). pap. 10.00 (ISBN 0-8373-2513-7). Natl Learning.

Sobel, Nathan R. Eye-Witness Identification. LC 72-85036. 1972. 25.00 (ISBN 0-87632-083-3); 1979 supplement incl. (ISBN 0-685-99205-5). Boardman.

Warfel, George H. Identification Technologies: Computer, Optical, & Chemical Aids to Personal ID. (Illus.). 200p. 1979. text ed. 19.50 (ISBN 0-398-03889-9). C C Thomas.

Zavala, Albert & Paley, James J., eds. Personal Appearance Identification. (Illus.). 352p. 1972. pap. 23.75 (ISBN 0-398-02447-2). C C Thomas.

IDENTIFICATION (PSYCHOLOGY)

see also Reference Groups

Sears, Robert R., et al. Identification & Child Rearing. 1965. 17.50x (ISBN 0-8047-0261-6). Stanford U Pr.

Wheelis, Allen. Quest for Identity. 1966. pap. 3.95 (ISBN 0-393-00745-6). Norton.

IDENTIFICATION (RELIGION)

Balokovic, Joyce B. Towards the Center. 1956. 3.95 (ISBN 0-910664-23-4). Gotham.

Bhaktivedanta, Swami. The Science of Self Realization. (Illus.). 1977. 9.95 (ISBN 0-89213-101-2). Bhaktivedanta.

Boom, Corrie T. A Prisoner & Yet. (Orig.). pap. 1.95 (ISBN 0-515-05334-1). Jove Pubns.

Cooper, Norman W. Finding Your Self. new ed. 96p. 1974. pap. 3.00 (ISBN 0-87516-183-9). De Vorss.

Dolby, James R. Dare to Be You. Orig. Title: I, Too, Am Man. 1977. pap. 1.50 (ISBN 0-89129-207-1). Jove Pubns.

Freeman, David. Know Your Self. 1976. pap. 3.95 (ISBN 0-934532-11-7). Presby & Reformed.

Frei, Hans W. The Identity of Jesus Christ: The Hermeneutical Bases of Dogmatic Theology. LC 74-80422. 192p. 1975. 8.95 (ISBN 0-8006-0292-7, 1-292). Fortress.

Goldsmith, Joel S. Man Was Not Born to Cry. 1977. pap. 4.95 (ISBN 0-8065-0569-9). Citadel Pr.

Haught, John F. Religion & Self-Acceptance: A Study of the Relationship Between Belief in God & the Desire to Know. LC 80-5872. 195p. 1980. lib. bdg. 17.00 (ISBN 0-8191-1296-8); pap. text ed. 8.75 (ISBN 0-8191-1297-6). U Pr of Amer.

Mata, Sri Daya. Only Love. LC 75-44633. Orig. Title: Qualities of a Devotee. (Illus.). 1976. 6.50 (ISBN 0-87612-215-2). Self Realization.

O'Flaherty, Vincent M. Who...Me? A Study in Identification by Seeking the Will of God. 200p. 1974. 4.95 (ISBN 0-8199-0540-2). Franciscan Herald.

Raymond, M. You: The Surprising Answer to the Question Who Are You? LC 57-13414. 312p. 1972. pap. 1.45 (ISBN 0-8189-1108-5, Pub. by Alba Bks). Alba.

Steere, Daniel C. I Am, I Can. 1976. pap. 1.25 (ISBN 0-89129-216-0). Jove Pubns.

IDENTIFICATION OF CRIMINALS

see Crime and Criminals–Identification

IDENTIFICATION OF DOCUMENTS

see Legal Documents

IDENTIFICATION OF FIREARMS

see Firearms–Identification

IDENTIFICATION OF HANDWRITING

see Writing–Identification

IDENTIFICATION OF PLANTS

see Plants–Identification

IDENTITY

see also Reference Groups

Agus, Jacob B. Jewish Identity in an Age of Ideologies. LC 76-14230. 1978. 20.00 (ISBN 0-8044-5018-8). Ungar.

Borst, C. V., ed. Mind-Brain Identity Theory. LC 70-106388. (Controversies in Philosophy Ser). 1970. pap. text ed. 7.50 (ISBN 0-312-53305-5). St Martin.

Butchvarov, Panayot. Being Qua Being: A Theory of Identity, Existence & Predication. LC 78-13812. 288p. 1979. 15.00x (ISBN 0-253-13700-4). Ind U Pr.

Care, Norman S. & Grimm, Robert H., eds. Perception & Personal Identity: Proceedings of the 1967 Oberlin Colloquium in Philosophy. LC 68-9427. (Oberlin Colloquia in Philosophy Ser). 1969. 15.00 (ISBN 0-8295-0145-2). UPB.

Dupreez, Peter. The Politics of Identity. 1980. 25.00 (ISBN 0-312-62697-5). St Martin.

Gerstner, Herbert B. Mankind's Quest for Identity. 309p. 1981. text ed. 22.50 (ISBN 0-930376-23-4). Pathotox Pubs.

Hardison, O. B., Jr. Entering the Maze: Identity & Change in Modern Culture. 320p. 1981. 17.95 (ISBN 0-19-502953-4). Oxford U Pr.

Kakar, Sudhir. Identity & Adulthood. 148p. 1979. text ed. 6.95x (ISBN 0-19-561119-5). Oxford U Pr.

Kaplan, Morton A. Alienation & Identification. LC 76-8146. 1976. 14.95 (ISBN 0-02-916790-6). Free Pr.

Mackenzie, W. J. Political Identity. LC 77-26851. 1978. 14.95 (ISBN 0-312-62308-9). St Martin.

Munitz, Milton K., ed. Identity & Individuation. LC 73-124530. (Studies in Contemporary Philosophy). 1971. o.p. 9.50x (ISBN 0-8147-5352-3); pap. 7.00x (ISBN 0-8147-5375-2). NYU Pr.

Noonan, Harold W. Objects & Identity: An Examination of the Relative Identity Thesis & Its Consequences. (Melbourne International Philosophy Ser.: Vol. 6). 192p. 1980. lib. bdg. 31.50 (ISBN 90-247-2292-6, Pub. by Martinus Nijhoff Netherlands). Kluwer Boston.

Redman, Lenn. What Am I? (Illus.). 72p. 1980. pap. 4.95 (ISBN 0-9606258-0-1). Victor Pub Co.

Tapscott, Bangs L. Elementary Applied Symbolic Logic. (Illus.). 512p. 1976. text ed. 17.50 (ISBN 0-13-252940-8). P-H.

IDENTITY (PSYCHOLOGY)

Ballard, Martin. Who Am I? 1971. pap. 3.95 (ISBN 0-09-109161-6, Pub. by Hutchinson). Merrimack Bk Serv.

Benson, L. Images, Heroes & Self Perceptions: The Struggle for Identity from Maskwearing to Authenticity. 1974. 18.95 (ISBN 0-13-451187-5). P-H.

Botheroyd, Paul F. Ich und Er: First & Third-Person Self-Reference & Problems of Identity in Three Contemporary German-Language Novels. (De Proprietatibus Litterarum Series Practica: No.67). 143p. (Orig.). 1976. pap. text ed. 28.25x (ISBN 90-2793-214-X). Mouton.

Crisp, Quentin & Carroll, Donald. Doing It with Style. 185p. 1981. 10.95 (ISBN 0-531-09852-4). Watts.

Damrell, Joseph. Search for Identity: Youth, Religion, & Culture. LC 78-5887. (Sage Library of Social Research: No. 64). 232p. 20.00 (ISBN 0-8039-0987-X); pap. 9.95 (ISBN 0-8039-0988-8). Sage.

Erikson, Erik H. Identity & the Life Cycle: Selected Papers. (Psychological Issues Monograph: No. 1, Vol. 1, No. 1). (Orig.). 1967. write for info. avail. (ISBN 0-8236-2460-9). Intl Univs Pr.

--Identity: Youth & Crisis. 1968. 12.95 (ISBN 0-393-01069-4); pap. 5.95x (ISBN 0-393-09786-2). Norton.

Glasser, William. Identity Society. rev. ed. 1976. pap. 2.95 (ISBN 0-06-080359-2, P359, PL). Har-Row.

Grotstein, James S. Splitting & Projective Identification. LC 79-51928. 1980. 25.00x (ISBN 0-87668-348-0). Aronson.

Haupt, et al. Becoming Me. (Human Condition Ser.), (gr. 9-12). 1977. pap. text ed. 3.96 (ISBN 0-88343-325-7); tchrs'. manual 1.80 (ISBN 0-88343-326-5). McDougal-Littell.

Heinz, Lichtenstein. The Dilemma of Human Identity. LC 77-87146. 1977. 25.00x (ISBN 0-87668-269-7). Aronson.

Hoehn, Robert G. Illustrated Treasury of General Science Activities: The Struggle for Identity from Mask-Wearing to Authenticity. LC 73-17134. (Illus.). 512p. 1974. ref. ed. 13.95x (ISBN 0-685-38854-9). P-H.

Identity. (Winston Mine Editions). 1972. text ed. 2.50 (ISBN 0-685-26903-5, HoltC); tchr's guide 1.00 (ISBN 0-685-26904-3). HR&W.

Identity. (Being & Becoming Ser.: Bk. 2). 2.22 (ISBN 0-02-810590-7); group leader's manual 2.82 (ISBN 0-02-810600-8). Benziger Pub Co.

Kane, Thomas A. Who Controls Me? A Psychotheological Reflection. LC 74-22261. 1974. 4.50 (ISBN 0-682-48186-6). Exposition.

Kilpatrick, William K. Identity & Intimacy. 272p. 1975. pap. 4.95 (ISBN 0-440-54576-5, Delta). Dell.

LaTorre, Ronald A. Sexual Identity: Implications for Mental Health. LC 78-26442. 1979. 17.95x (ISBN 0-88229-360-5). Nelson-Hall.

Macdonald, G. F., intro. by. Perception & Identity: Essays Presented to A. J. Ayer with His Responses. LC 79-52503. (Illus.). 1979. 35.00x (ISBN 0-8014-1265-X). Cornell U Pr.

Money, John. Differentiation of Gender Identity. (Master Lectures on Physiological Psychology: Manuscript No. 1330). 4.00x (ISBN 0-912704-22-5). Am Psychol.

Nelson, Marie C. & Ikenberry, Jean, eds. Psychosexual Imperatives: Their Role in Identity Formation, Vol. II. LC 78-17739. (Self-in-Process Ser.). 1979. 29.95 (ISBN 0-87705-302-2). Human Sci Pr.

Paranjpe, A. C. In Search of Identity. LC 75-257. 1976. 19.95 (ISBN 0-470-65856-8). Halsted Pr.

Perry, John, ed. Personal Identity. 246p. 1975. pap. 5.95x (ISBN 0-520-02960-7). U of Cal Pr.

Rorty, Amelie O., ed. The Identities of Persons. LC 75-13156. (Topics in Philosophy: Vol. 3). 1976. pap. 6.95x (ISBN 0-520-03309-4, CAMPUS 180). U of Cal Pr.

Spacks, Patricia M. Imagining a Self. 1976. 18.50x (ISBN 0-674-44005-6). Harvard U Pr.

Strauss, Anselm. Mirrors & Masks. LC 78-300956. 1970. pap. 7.00 (ISBN 0-686-24891-0). Sociology Pr.

Valentine, P. F. The Psychology of Personality. 1936. 30.00 (ISBN 0-8495-6259-7). Arden Lib.

IDENTITY, PERSONAL

see Personality

IDEOGRAPHY

see Chinese Language–Writing

IDEOLOGY

Adlam, Diana, et al, eds. Ideology & Consciousness: Governing the Present, Vol. 6. 128p. 1979. pap. text ed. 3.50x (ISBN 0-686-72927-7, Pub. by I & C England). Humanities.

Aiken, Henry D., ed. Age of Ideology. facs. ed. LC 77-117748. (Essay Index Reprint Ser). 1956. 17.00 (ISBN 0-8369-1821-5). Arno.

--Age of Ideology: The Nineteenth Century Philosophers. (Orig.). pap. 1.95 (ISBN 0-451-61797-5, MJ1797, Ment). NAL.

Aldam, Diana, et al, eds. Ideology & Consciousness Autumn 1978, No. 4. 1978. pap. text ed. 2.75x (ISBN 0-391-01214-2). Humanities.

Baradat, Leon P. Political Ideologies: Their Origins & Impact. (Illus.). 1979. pap. 11.50 ref. (ISBN 0-13-684985-7). P-H.

Barnett, Steve & Silverman, Martin G. Ideology & Everyday Life: Anthropology, Neomarxist Thought, & the Problem of Ideology & the Social Whole. 192p. 1979. pap. 5.95x (ISBN 0-472-02704-2). U of Mich Pr.

Barth, Hans. Truth & Ideology. LC 74-81430. Orig. Title: Wahrheit und Ideologie. 1977. 21.75x (ISBN 0-520-02820-1). U of Cal Pr.

Beardsley, Philip L. Redefining Rigor: Ideology & Statistics in Political Inquiry. (Sage Library of Social Research: Vol. 104). (Illus.). 199p. 1980. 20.00x (ISBN 0-8039-1472-5); pap. 9.95x (ISBN 0-8039-1473-3). Sage.

Belyaev, A. The Ideological Struggle & Literature. 308p. 1978. 6.60 (ISBN 0-8285-1083-0, Pub. by Progress Pubs Russia). Imported Pubns.

Ben-David, Joseph & Clark, Terry N. Culture & Its Creators. LC 76-610. 1977. 17.00x (ISBN 0-226-04222-7). U of Chicago Pr.

Benewick, Robert, et al, eds. Knowledge & Belief in Politics: The Problems of Ideology. LC 73-85266. 320p. 1973. 18.95 (ISBN 0-312-45885-1). St Martin.

Bhaskar, Roy. Philosophical Idealogies. Date not set. text ed. price not set (ISBN 0-391-01773-X). Humanities.

Burchell, Graham. Ideology & Consciousness: Power & Desire - Diagrams of the Social, Vol. 8. 124p. 1981. pap. text ed. 3.50x (ISBN 0-686-75682-7, Pub. by I & C England). Humanities.

Carlsnaes, Walter. The Concept of Ideology & Political Analysis: A Critical Examination of Its Usage by Marx, Lenin, & Mannheim. LC 80-1202. (Contributions in Philosophy Ser.: No. 17). xii, 274p. 1981. lib. bdg. 32.50 (ISBN 0-313-22267-3, CCI/). Greenwood.

Carroll, John. Break-Out from the Crystal Palace: The Anarcho-Psychological Critique-Stirner, Nietzsche, Dostoevsky. (International Library of Sociology). 1974. 18.00x (ISBN 0-7100-7750-5). Routledge & Kegan.

Christenson, Reo M., et al. Ideologies & Modern Politics. 3rd ed. 288p. 1981. pap. 10.50 scp (ISBN 0-06-041273-9, HarpC). Har-Row.

Colletti, Lucio. From Rousseau to Lenin: Studies in Ideology & Society. Merringer, John, tr. from H. LC 72-92035. 1975. pap. 5.95 (ISBN 0-85345-350-0, PB-3500). Monthly Rev.

Coughlin, Richard M. Ideology, Public Opinion, & Welfare Policy: Attitudes Toward Taxes & Spending in Industrialized Societies. LC 79-22894. (Research Ser.: No. 42). 1980. pap. 6.50x (ISBN 0-87725-142-8). U of Cal Intl St.

De Crespigny, Anthony, ed. Ideologies of Politics. 1976. pap. 6.95x (ISBN 0-19-570070-8). Oxford U Pr.

Dilthey, Wilthelm. Philosophy of Existence: Introduction to Weltanschauugslehre. LC 78-5673. 1978. Repr. of 1957 ed. lib. bdg. 15.00x (ISBN 0-313-20460-8, DIPH). Greenwood.

Dittberner, Job L. End of Ideology & American Social Thought: 1930 to 1960. Berkhofer, Edward, ed. (Studies in American History & Culture: No. 1). 1979. 29.95x (ISBN 0-8357-0972-8, Pub. by UMI Res Pr). Univ Microfilms.

Earle, William. Public Sorrows & Private Pleasures. LC 75-28911. (Studies in Phenomenology & Existential Philosophy). 192p. 1976. 10.95x (ISBN 0-253-34678-9). Ind U Pr.

Eysenck, H. J. & Wilson, G. D., eds. The Psychological Basis of Ideology. 1978. 29.50 (ISBN 0-8391-1221-1). Univ Park.

Flakser, David. Marxism Ideology & Myths. LC 70-164908. 1971. 6.75 (ISBN 0-8022-2059-2). Philos Lib.

Flynn, James R. Humanism & Ideology: An Aristotelian View. 1978. pap. 6.00 (ISBN 0-7100-8907-4). Routledge & Kegan.

Gould, James A. & Truitt, Willis H. Political Ideologies. 576p. 1973. pap. text ed. 11.95 (ISBN 0-02-345470-9, 34547). Macmillan.

Gross, Felix. European Ideologies. 1955. 12.00 (ISBN 0-8022-0633-6). Philos Lib.

Groth, Alexander J. Major Ideologies: An Interpretative Survey of Democracy, Socialism & Nationalism. LC 74-168636. 244p. 1971. pap. 9.50 (ISBN 0-471-32895-2). Krieger.

Grundy, Kenneth W. & Weinstein, Michael A. Ideologies of Violence. LC 73-91055. 1974. pap. 6.95x (ISBN 0-675-08835-6). Merrill.

Halle, Louis J. Ideological Imagination. LC 70-152093. 256p. 1972. 6.95 (ISBN 0-8129-0195-9). Times Bks.

Hibbin, Sally, ed. Politics, Ideology & the State: Papers from the Communist University of London. 1978. pap. text ed. 6.50x (ISBN 0-85315-462-7). Humanities.

Hirst, Paul. On Law & Ideology. 1979. text ed. 20.00x (ISBN 0-391-00970-2); pap. 10.25x (ISBN 0-391-01009-3). Humanities.

Howe, J. R., Jr., ed. The Role of Ideology in the American Revolution. LC 76-3777. (American Problem Studies). 132p. 1976. Repr. of 1970 ed. 5.50 (ISBN 0-88275-406-8). Krieger.

Huer, Jon H. Ideology & Social Character. LC 78-56917. 1978. pap. 9.50 (ISBN 0-8191-0522-8). U Pr of Amer.

Jung, Hwa Y. Crisis of Political Understanding: A Phenomenological Perspective in the Conduct of Political Inquiry. LC 78-26938. 1979. text ed. 18.00x (ISBN 0-391-00861-7). Duquesne.

Kaplan, Morton A. On Historical & Political Knowing: An Inquiry into Some Problems of Universal Law & Human Freedom. LC 79-131879. 1971. 7.50x (ISBN 0-226-42420-0). U of Chicago Pr.

Kinloch, Graham C. Ideology & Contemporary Sociological Theory. (P-H Ser. in Sociology). (Illus.). 208p. 1981. text ed. 18.95 (ISBN 0-13-450601-4). P-H.

Larrain, Jorge. The Concept of Ideology. LC 79-53386. 250p. 1980. 18.00x (ISBN 0-8203-0490-5). U of Ga Pr.

Lasswell, Harold D. & Lerner, Daniel, eds. World Revolutionary Elites: Studies in Coercive Ideological Movements. LC 80-21600. xi, 478p. 1980. Repr. of 1965 ed. lib. bdg. 39.75x (ISBN 0-313-22572-9, LAWE). Greenwood.

Loye, David. The Leadership Passion: A Psychology of Ideology. LC 76-45481. (Social & Behavioral Science Ser.). (Illus.). 1977. 16.95x (ISBN 0-87589-302-3). Jossey-Bass.

MacIntyre, Alasdair. Against the Self-Images of the Age: Essays on Ideology & Philosophy. LC 78-1571. 1978. text ed. 12.95 (ISBN 0-268-00586-9); pap. text ed. 4.95 (ISBN 0-268-00587-7). U of Notre Dame Pr.

Mafeje, Archie. Science Ideology & Development-Three Essays on Development Theory. 1978. pap. text ed. 9.50x (ISBN 0-8419-9731-4). Holmes & Meier.

Mannheim, Karl. Ideology & Utopia: An Introduction to the Sociology of Knowledge. LC 68-77694. 1955. pap. 3.95 (ISBN 0-15-643955-7, HB3, Harv). HarBraceJ.

Manning, D. J., ed. The Form of Iceology. 1980. text ed. 19.50x (ISBN 0-04-320138-5); pap. text ed. 8.95x (ISBN 0-04-320139-3). Allen Unwin.

Mark, Max. Modern Ideologies. 250p. 1973. pap. text ed. 5.95 (ISBN 0-312-54040-X). St Martin.

Martin, William O. Metaphysics & Ideology. (Aquinas Lecture). 1959. 6.95 (ISBN 0-87462-124-0). Marquette.

Miller, K. Bruce. Ideology & Moral Philosophy: The Relation of Moral Ideology to Dynamic Moral Philosophy. 1971. text ed. 7.50x (ISBN 0-391-00011-X). Humanities.

Moskvichov, L. N. The End of Ideology Theory: Illusions & Reality. 191p. 1974. 2.75 (ISBN 0-8285-0225-0, Pub. by Progress Pubs Russia). Imported Pubns.

Ney, Albert C. Seeing into Life: Sociological Essays. 1969. 5.50 (ISBN 0-87164-008-2). William-F.

Rejai, Mostafa. Decline of Ideology? (Controversy Ser). 325p. 1971. text ed. 9.95x (ISBN 0-202-24094-0); pap. text ed. 3.95x (ISBN 0-202-24095-9). Lieber-Atherton.

Rude, George. Ideology & Popular Protest. 1980. 10.95 (ISBN 0-394-51372-X); pap. 4.95 (ISBN 0-394-73966-3). Pantheon.

Schneider, Jerrold E. Ideological Coalitions in Congress. LC 78-4019. (Contributions in Political Science Ser.: No. 16). (Illus.). 1978. lib. bdg. 22.50x (ISBN 0-313-20410-1, SID/). Greenwood.

Seliger, M. The Marxist Conception of Ideology. LC 76-11092. (International Studies). 1977. 29.50 (ISBN 0-521-21229-4); pap. 10.50x (ISBN 0-521-29625-0). Cambridge U Pr.

Seliger, Martin. Ideology & Politics. LC 75-15430. 1976. 14.95 (ISBN 0-02-928360-4). Free Pr.

Therborn, Goran. The Ideology of Power & the Power of Ideology. 144p. 1981. 12.50x (ISBN 0-8052-7095-7, Pub. by NLB England); pap. 5.50 (ISBN 0-8052-7094-9). Schocken.

Whitehead, Alfred N. Adventures of Ideas. 1933. 12.95 (ISBN 0-02-627220-2). Macmillan.

Wisdom, J. O. Philosophy & Its Place in Our Culture. new ed. (Current Topics of Contemporary Thought Ser.). 280p. 1975. 29.25x (ISBN 0-677-05150-6). Gordon.

Zeitlin, Irving M. Ideology & the Development of Sociological Theory. 2nd ed. (P-H Ser. in Sociology). (Illus.). 336p. 1981. text ed. 19.95 (ISBN 0-13-449769-4). P-H.

IDIOCY

see also Amaurotic Family Idiocy; Cretinism; Insanity

Howe, Samuel G. On the Causes of Idiocy. LC 79-180578. (Medicine & Society in America Ser). 100p. 1972. Repr. of 1858 ed. 15.00 (ISBN 0-405-03955-7). Arno.

Seguin, Edward. Idiocy & Its Treatment by the Physiological Method. LC 79-12541. Repr. of 1866 ed. 19.50x (ISBN 0-678-00731-4). Kelley.

IDIOPATHIC HEMORRHAGIC SARCOMA

see Kaposi's Sarcoma

IDOLATRY

see Idols and Images

IDOLS AND IMAGES

see also Gods in Art; Iconoclasm

Barfield, Owen. Saving the Appearances: A Study in Idolatry. LC 65-23538. 1965. pap. text ed. 3.50 (ISBN 0-15-679490-X, Harv). HarBraceJ.
Bevan, Edwyn R. Holy Images: An Inquiry into Idolatry & Image-Worship in Ancient Paganism & in Christianity. LC 77-27191. (Gifford Lectures: 1933). Repr. of 1940 ed. 18.00 (ISBN 0-404-60489-7). AMS Pr.
Boehn, Max. Dolls. 1972. pap. 4.00 (ISBN 0-486-22847-9). Dover.
Brehier, Louis. La Querelle des images huitieme-neuvieme siecle. 1969. 14.00 (ISBN 0-8337-0362-5). B Franklin.
Cousteau, Pierre. Pegmes: The Renaissance & the Gods. Orgel, Stephen, ed. LC 78-68181. (Philosophy of Images Ser.). (Illus.). 1980. lib. bdg. 66.00 (ISBN 0-8240-3677-8). Garland Pub.
De Montault, X. Barbier. Traite d'Iconographie Chretienne. (Illus.). 972p. (Fr.). 1981. Repr. of 1890 ed. lib. bdg. 200.00x (ISBN 0-89241-137-6). Caratzas Bros.
Heroldt, Johann. Heydenweldt und Ihrer Gotter: The Renaissance & the Gods. Orgel, Stephen, ed. LC 78-68202. (The Philosophy of Images Ser.). 1980. lib. bdg. 66.00 (ISBN 0-8240-3676-X). Garland Pub.
Huggins, William H. & Entwisle, Doris R. Iconic Communication: An Annotated Bibliography. LC 73-8130. (Illus.). 184p. 1974. 14.00x (ISBN 0-8018-1528-2). Johns Hopkins.
Hurley, William P. An Analysis of Effigy Mound Complexes in Wisconsin. (Anthropological Papers: No. 59). (Illus.). pap. 8.00x (ISBN 0-932206-57-3). U Mich Mus Anthro.
L'Orange, H. P. Studies in the Iconography of Cosmic Kingship in the Ancient World. (Illus.). 206p. 1981. Repr. of 1953 ed. lib. bdg. 45.00x (ISBN 0-89241-150-3). Caratzas Bros.
Menestrier, Claude. La Philosophie des Images, 2 vols. Orgel, Stephen, ed. LC 78-68189. (The Renaissance & the Gods: the Philosophy of Images Ser.). 1980. lib. bdg. 66.00 (ISBN 0-8240-3691-3). Garland Pub.
Menestrier, Claude F. L' Art Des Emblemes. Orgel, Stephen, ed. LC 78-68185. (Philosophy of Images Ser.: Vol. 15). (Illus.). 1979. lib. bdg. 66.00 (ISBN 0-8240-3689-1). Garland Pub.
Pasztory, Esther. The Iconography of the Teotihuacan Tlaloc. LC 74-16543. (Studies in Pre-Columbian Art & Archaeology: No. 15). (Illus.). 22p. 1974. pap. 3.00x (ISBN 0-88402-059-2, Ctr Pre-Columbian). Dumbarton Oaks.
Pignoria, Lorenzo & Orgel, Stephen, eds. Vere e Nove Imagini de gli Dei delli Antichi. LC 78-68193. (The Renaissance & the Gods: the Philosophy of Images Ser.). (Illus.). 1980. lib. bdg. 66.00 (ISBN 0-8240-3686-7). Garland Pub.
Schellhas, P. Representation of Deities of the Maya Manuscripts. (Illus.). 1904. pap. 4.00 (ISBN 0-527-01198-3). Kraus Repr.
Simard, Jean. Une Iconographie Du Clerge Francais Au XVIIe Siecle: Les Devotins De L'ecole Francaise et les Sources De L'imagerie Religience En France. (Illus.). 1977. pap. 15.50x (ISBN 2-7637-6768-0, Pub. by Laval). Intl Schol Bk Serv.
Spencer. The Image Maker. 1975. 19.95 (ISBN 0-07-060150-X, I); pap. 9.95 (ISBN 0-07-060151-8). McGraw.
Van de Pusse, Crispin. Metamorphoseon Ovidianarum. LC 78-68195. (The Philosophy of Images Ser.). (Illus.). 1980. lib. bdg. 66.00 (ISBN 0-8240-3682-4). Garland Pub.
Von Boehn, Max. Dolls & Puppets. Nicoll, Josephine, tr. (Illus.). 1966. Repr. of 1932 ed. 25.00x (ISBN 0-8154-0026-8). Cooper Sq.

IDYLLIC POETRY
see Pastoral Poetry

IFA
Abimbola, Wande. Ifa: An Exposition of Ifa Literary Corpus. (Illus.). 1977. 7.50x (ISBN 0-19-575325-9). Oxford U Pr.
Bascom, William. Ifa Divination: Communication Between Gods & Men in West Africa. LC 69-10349. (Illus.). 604p. 1969. 35.00x (ISBN 0-253-32890-X). Ind U Pr.

IFALIK ATOLL
Burrows, Edwin G. Atoll Culture: Ethnology of Ifaluk in the Central Carolines. LC 79-11044. Repr. of 1953 ed. lib. bdg. 21.50x (ISBN 0-8371-4426-4, BUAT). Greenwood.
Tracey, J. I., Jr., et al. Natural History of Ifaluk Atoll. (BMB Ser.: No. 222). 1961. pap. 9.00 (ISBN 0-527-02330-2). Kraus Repr.

IFUGAOS
Barton, R. F. Religion of the Ifugaos. LC 48-3664. (American Anthropological Association Memoirs Ser). Repr. of 1946 ed. pap. 14.00 (ISBN 0-527-00564-9). Kraus Repr.
Barton, Roy F. Ifugao Law. LC 78-76334. (Illus.). 1969. Repr. of 1919 ed. 16.75x (ISBN 0-520-01427-8). U of Cal Pr.
--Philippine Pagans: The Autobiographies of Three Ifugaos. LC 76-44686. Repr. of 1938 ed. 24.50 (ISBN 0-404-15903-6). AMS Pr.
Conklin, Harold C. Ethnographic Atlas of Ifugao. LC 79-689774. (Illus.). 124p. 1980. text ed. 75.00x (ISBN 0-300-02529-7). Yale U Pr.
--Ifugao Bibliography. (Bibliography Ser.: No. 11). vi, 75p. 1968. 4.00 (ISBN 0-686-30907-3). Yale U SE Asia.
Dumia, Mariano A. The Ifugao World. Edades, Jean, ed. (Illus.). 1979. pap. 6.75x (ISBN 0-686-24953-4, Pub. by New Day Pub). Cellar.

IGARA (AFRICAN TRIBE)
see also Ethnology–Nigeria

IGBO LANGUAGE
see Ibo Language

IGNATIEV, NIKOLAY PAVLOVICH, 1832-1908
Meininger, Thomas A. Ignatiev & the Establishment of the Bulgarian Exarchate, 1864-1872: A Study in Personal Diplomacy. LC 70-630135. 1970. 3.25 (ISBN 0-87020-137-9, Logmark Eds). State Hist Soc Wis.

IGNATIUS, SAINT, BP. OF ANTIOCH, 1ST CENTURY
Brown, Milton P., Jr. Authentic Writings of Ignatius: A Study of Linguistic Criteria. LC 63-19458. 1963. 11.75 (ISBN 0-8223-0030-3). Duke.
Ignatius, Saint Epistles of St. Ignatius. Lightfoot, J. D., tr. pap. 0.95 (ISBN 0-686-25549-6). Eastern Orthodox.
Richardson, Cyril C. Christianity of Ignatius of Antioch. LC 35-7948. Repr. of 1935 ed. 14.50 (ISBN 0-404-05297-5). AMS Pr.

IGNATIUS OF LOYOLA, SAINT
see Loyola, Ignacio De, Saint, 1491-1556

IGNEOUS ROCKS
see Rocks, Igneous

IGNITION DEVICES
see Automobiles–Ignition

IGO (GAME)
see Go (Game)

IGUANAS
see Lizards

IK (AFRICAN PEOPLE)
Turnbull, Colin M. Mountain People. 1972. 8.95 (ISBN 0-671-21320-2); pap. 4.95 (ISBN 0-671-21724-0). S&S.

IKEBANA
see Flower Arrangement, Japanese

IKHNATON
see Amenhetep 4th, King of Egypt, 1388-1358 B.C.

IKONS
see Icons

IL FIORE
Ramacciotti, Sr. Mary D. Syntax of Il Fiore & of Dante's Inferno As Evidence in the Question of the Authorship of Il Fiore. LC 72-115356. (Catholic University of America. Studies in Romance Languages & Literatures: No. 12). Repr. of 1936 ed. 18.00 (ISBN 0-685-05985-5). AMS Pr.

ILA (BANTU TRIBE)
Smith, Edwin W. & Dale, A. M. Ila-Speaking Peoples of Northern Rhodesia, 2 Vols. 1966. 20.00 (ISBN 0-8216-0097-4). Univ Bks.

ILEITIS
see Ileum–Diseases

ILEUM–DISEASES
Atlee, H. B. Acute & Chronic Iliac Pain in Women: A Problem in Diagnosis. 2nd ed. (Illus.). 208p. 1966. photocopy spiral ed. 16.75 (ISBN 0-398-00067-0). C C Thomas.
Children's Hospital Medical Center, the Health Education Department, Boston, Mass. Your Child & Ilael Conduit Surgery: A Guidebook for Parents. (Illus.). 120p. 1970. pap. 11.75 (ISBN 0-398-00305-X). C C Thomas.
Michele, Arthur A. Iliopsoas: Development of Anomalies in Man. (Illus.). 572p. 1962. pap. 54.75 (ISBN 0-398-01305-5). C C Thomas.
Mullen, Barbara D. & McGinn, Kerry A. The Ostomy Book: Living Comfortably with Colostomies, Ileostomies, & Urostomies. (Illus., Orig.). 1980. pap. 7.95 (ISBN 0-915950-41-3). Bull Pub.
Sparberg, Marshall. Ileostomy Care. (Illus.). 176p. 1971. 14.50 (ISBN 0-398-02620-3). C C Thomas.
Weterman, I. T., et al, eds. Crohn's Disease Diagnosis & Treatment: Proc. Workshop. (International Congress Ser.: No. 386). 1976. pap. 58.75 (ISBN 90-219-0317-2, Excerpta Medica). Elsevier.

ILEUS
see Intestines–Obstructions

ILFIELD (CHARLES) COMPANY
Parish, William J. Charles Ilfeld Company: A Study in the Rise & Decline of Mercantile Capitalism in New Mexico. LC 61-9687. (Studies in Business History: No. 20). (Illus.). 1961. 20.00x (ISBN 0-674-11075-7). Harvard U Pr.

ILLEGAL LITERATURE
see Underground Literature

ILLEGALITY
Ermann, M. David & Lundman, Richard J., eds. Corporate & Governmental Deviance: Problems of Organizational Behavior in Contemporary Society. 1978. pap. text ed. 4.95x (ISBN 0-19-502324-2). Oxford U Pr.

ILLEGITIMACY
see also Unmarried Fathers; Unmarried Mothers
Abbott, Grace, ed. Child & State: Select Documents, 2 Vols. LC 68-57587. (Illus.). 1968. Repr. of 1938 ed. Set. lib. bdg. 53.75x (ISBN 0-8371-0279-0, ABCS). Greenwood.
Austen, Alfred. Bastard Without Portfolio: The Story of a Forgotten Bastard. 217p. 1982. 10.00 (ISBN 0-533-04813-3). Vantage.
A Briefe Declaration for What Manner of Speciall Nusance Man May Have His Remedy by Assise. LC 76-38169. (English Experience Ser.: No. 446). 1972. Repr. of 1636 ed. 7.00 (ISBN 90-221-0446-X). Walter J Johnson.
Brydall, John. Lex Spuriorum; or the Law Relating to Bastardy, Collected from the Common, Civil & Ecclesiastical Laws. LC 77-86581. (Classics of English Legal History in the Modern Era Ser.: Vol. 17). 1978. Repr. of 1703 ed. lib. bdg. 55.00 (ISBN 0-8240-3064-8). Garland Pub.
Gill, Derek. Illegitimacy, Sexuality & the Status of Women. 362p. 1977. 36.00x (ISBN 0-631-17020-0, Pub. by Basil Blackwell). Biblio Dist.
Hartley, Shirley F. Illegitimacy. LC 73-83057. 1975. 18.50x (ISBN 0-520-02533-4). U of Cal Pr.
Kammerer, Percy G. Unmarried Mother: A Study of 500 Cases. LC 69-14935. (Criminology, Law Enforcement, & Social Problems Ser.: No. 58). 1969. Repr. of 1918 ed. 15.00 (ISBN 0-87585-058-8). Patterson Smith.
Laslett, Peter. Family Life & Illicit Love in Earlier Generations. 1977. 47.50 (ISBN 0-521-21408-4); pap. 12.95x (ISBN 0-521-29221-2). Cambridge U Pr.
Laslett, Peter, et al, eds. Bastardy & Its Comparative History: Studies in the History of Illegitimacy & Martial Nonconformism. (Studies in Social & Demographic History). (Illus.). 446p. 1980. 35.00x (ISBN 0-674-06338-4). Harvard U Pr.
Leffingwell, Albert. Illegitimacy & the Influence of Seasons Upon Conduct: Two Studies in Demography. LC 75-38134. (Demography Ser.). (Illus.). 1976. Repr. of 1892 ed. 13.00x (ISBN 0-405-07987-7). Arno.
Lundberg, Emma O. & Lenrott, Katherine F. Illegitimacy As a Child-Welfare Problem. LC 74-1713. (Children & Youth Ser.: Pts. 1 & 2). 1974. 28.00x (ISBN 0-405-05972-8). Arno.
Reed, Ruth. The Illegitimate Family in New York City. LC 72-152395. 385p. 1972. Repr. of 1934 ed. 16.25x (ISBN 0-8371-6056-1, Pub. by Negro U Pr). Greenwood.
--The Illegitimate Family in New York City: Its Treatment by Social & Health Agencies. LC 78-169397. (Family in America Ser). 408p. 1972. Repr. of 1934 ed. 17.00 (ISBN 0-405-03874-7). Arno.
--Negro Illegitimacy in New York City. LC 68-57577. (Columbia University. Studies in the Social Sciences: No. 277). Repr. of 1926 ed. 12.50 (ISBN 0-404-51277-1). AMS Pr.
Young, Leontine. Out of Wedlock: A Study of the Problems of the Unmarried Mother & Her Child. 1964. pap. 2.95 (ISBN 0-07-072556-X, SP). McGraw.
--Out of Wedlock: A Study of the Problems of the Unmarried Mother & Her Child. LC 78-16486. 1978. Repr. of 1954 ed. lib. bdg. 24.00x (ISBN 0-313-20604-X, YOWE). Greenwood.

ILLICIT COINING
see Counterfeits and Counterfeiting

ILLICIT DISTILLING
see Distilling, Illicit

ILLINOIS
see also names of cities, counties, etc. in Illinois
Bailey, Bernadine. Picture Book of Illinois. rev. ed. LC 66-5264. (Illus.). (gr. 3-5). 1967. 5.50g (ISBN 0-8075-9515-2). A Whitman.
Beck, Lewis C. A Gazetteer of the States of Illinois & Missouri. fascimile ed. LC 75-84. (Mid-American Frontier Ser.). 1975. Repr. of 1823 ed. 28.00x (ISBN 0-405-06853-0). Arno.
Carpenter, Allan. Illinois. LC 78-32064. (New Enchantment of America State Bks.). (Illus.). (gr. 4 up). 1979. PLB 10.60 (ISBN 0-516-04113-4). Childrens.
Clayton, John, ed. Illinois Fact Book & Historical Almanac, 1673-1968. LC 68-21417. (Illus.). 576p. 1970. 15.00x (ISBN 0-8093-0380-9). S Ill U Pr.
Faux, William. Memorable Days in America. LC 71-95144. Repr. of 1823 ed. 33.50 (ISBN 0-404-02371-1). AMS Pr.
Fleming, Thomas. Living Land of Lincoln. 1980. 20.00 (ISBN 0-07-021297-X). Readers Digest Pr.
Garson, Bill. The Knight on Broadway. LC 78-64865. (Illus.). 1978. pap. 7.50 (ISBN 0-9602150-1-8). City Bank-Rockford.
Hinman, Albert G. Population Growth & Its Demands Upon Land for Housing in Evanston, Illinois. LC 73-2904. (Metropolitan America Ser.). (Illus.). 132p. 1974. Repr. 10.00x (ISBN 0-405-05395-9). Arno.
Horrell, C. W., et al. Land Between the Rivers: The Southern Illinois Country. LC 71-156777. (Illus.). 207p. 1973. 24.95 (ISBN 0-8093-0566-6). S Ill U Pr.
Illinois. 33.00 (ISBN 0-89770-089-9). Curriculum Info Ctr.
Illinois: A Discriptive & Historical Guide. rev. ed. (American Guide Ser.). (Illus.). 1974. 14.95 (ISBN 0-8038-3381-4). Hastings.
Mikkelsen, M. A. The Bishop Hill Colony: A Religious, Communistic Settlement in Henry County, Illinois. LC 72-187466. (The American Utopian Adventure Ser.). Repr. of 1892 ed. lib. bdg. 13.50x (ISBN 0-87991-014-3). Porcupine Pr.
--The Bishop Hill Colony, a Religious Communistic Settlement in Henry County, Illinois. pap. 7.00 (ISBN 0-384-38850-7). Johnson Repr.
Perica, Esther. They Took the Challenge: The Story of Rolling Meadows. LC 79-14803. (Illus.). 167p. 1980. 9.75 (ISBN 0-9602782-0-6). Rolling Meadows.
Sandburg, Carl. Prairie-Town Boy. LC 77-4647. (Illus.). (gr. 9-12). 1977. pap. 1.75 (ISBN 0-15-263331-6, VoyB). HarBraceJ.
Stringham, Paul & Wallin, Richard. Chicago & Illinois Midland. (Illus.). 224p. 32.50 (ISBN 0-87095-077-0). Golden West.

ILLINOIS–ANTIQUITIES
Cole, Fay-Cooper & Deuel, Thorne. Rediscovering Illinois: Archaeological Explorations in & Around Fulton County. (Midway Reprint Ser.). (Illus.). xvi, 296p. 1975. pap. text ed. 12.50x (ISBN 0-226-11336-1). U of Chicago Pr.
Keiser, John H. The Union Miners Cemetery at Mt. Olive, Illinois. 40p. 1980. pap. 2.50 (ISBN 0-916884-09-0). Ill Labor Hist Soc.
Roper, Donna C. Archaeological Survey & Settlement Pattern Models in Central Illinois. LC 79-4539. (MCJA Special Papers). 1979. pap. 4.50x (ISBN 0-87338-230-7, Pub. for Illinois State Museum). Kent St U Pr.

ILLINOIS–BIBLIOGRAPHY
Adams, James N., compiled by. Cumulative Index, Journal of the Illinois State Historical Society, Vols. 26-50. 710p. 1968. 20.00 (ISBN 0-912154-17-9). Ill St Hist Lib.
--General Index to Journal of the Illinois State Historical Society, Vols. 1-25. 714p. 1949. 20.00 (ISBN 0-912154-15-2). Ill St Hist Lib.
Smith, Cynthia H., compiled by. Cumulative Index, Journal of the Illinois State Historical Society, Vol. 51-60. 220p. 1971. 8.00 (ISBN 0-912154-21-7). Ill St Hist Lib.
Vexler, R. I. Illinois Chronology & Factbook, Vol. 13. 1978. 8.50 (ISBN 0-379-16138-9). Oceana.

ILLINOIS–DESCRIPTION AND TRAVEL
Benton, Chris. Chicagoland Nature Trails. LC 77-91183. 1978. pap. 7.95 (ISBN 0-8092-7662-3). Contemp Bks.
Birkbeck, Morris. Letters from Illinois. LC 68-8685. (American Scene Ser). 1970. Repr. of 1818 ed. lib. bdg. 19.50 (ISBN 0-306-71170-2). Da Capo.
--Letters from Illinois & Notes of a Journey in America. 3rd ed. LC 71-119545. Repr. of 1818 ed. 17.50x (ISBN 0-678-00686-5). Kelley.
Brown, William T. Architecture Evolving: An Illinois Saga. Hasbrouck, Marilyn, ed. LC 76-45690. (Illus.). 1976. 25.00x (ISBN 0-931028-02-7); pap. 15.00x (ISBN 0-931028-01-9). Teach'em.
Buck, Solon J. Illinois in 1818. LC 67-14657. (Illus.). 1967. Repr. of 1918 ed. 19.95 (ISBN 0-252-72508-5). U of Ill Pr.
Catherwood, Mary H. Lower Illinois Valley Local Sketches of Long Ago. 55p. 1980. Repr. 3.00 (ISBN 0-686-27587-X). E S Cunningham.
Drury, John. Old Illinois Houses. (Illus.). 1977. pap. 3.95 (ISBN 0-226-16552-3). U of Chicago Pr.
Farnham, Eliza W. Life in Prairie Land. LC 72-2601. (American Women Ser: Images & Realities). 412p. 1972. Repr. of 1846 ed. 18.00 (ISBN 0-405-04457-7). Arno.
Faux, William. Memorable Days in America. LC 71-95144. Repr. of 1823 ed. 33.50 (ISBN 0-404-02371-1). AMS Pr.
Federal Writers Project. Illinois: A Descriptive & Historical Guide. LC 72-145010. (Illus.). 1971. Repr. of 1947 ed. 59.00 (ISBN 0-403-01292-9). Somerset Pub.
Flower, George. The Errors of Emigrants. facsimile ed. LC 75-100. (Mid-American Frontier Ser.). 1975. Repr. of 1841 ed. 9.50x (ISBN 0-405-06868-9). Arno.
Kennet, Andrea. Beautiful Illinois. Shangle, Robert D., ed. LC 80-18774. (Illus.). 72p. 1980. 14.95 (ISBN 0-915796-73-2); pap. 7.95 (ISBN 0-915796-72-4). Beautiful Am.
Koeper, Frederick. Illinois Architecture from Territorial Times to the Present. LC 68-16700. (Illus.). 1968. 11.00x (ISBN 0-226-44993-9); pap. 3.25 (ISBN 0-226-44994-7). U of Chicago Pr.
Lower Illinois Valley Book of White Hall. 252p. 1978. Repr. 6.00 (ISBN 0-686-27590-X). E S Cunningham.
May, George W. Down Illinois Rivers. (Illus.). 400p. 1981. 16.00x (ISBN 0-9605566-5-6). G W May.

Nelson, Ronald E., ed. Illinois: Land & Life in the Prairie State. (Regional Geography Ser.). (Illus.). 1978. pap. text ed. 12.95 (ISBN 0-8403-1831-6). Kendall-Hunt.

Thias, Edward J., ed. Pencil Sketches of Illinois. LC 81-50902. (Illus.). 159p. 1981. 14.95 (ISBN 0-86629-034-6). Sunrise MO.

ILLINOIS–ECONOMIC CONDITIONS

Alvord, Clarence W. & Carter, Clarence E., eds. Invitation Serieuse Aux Habitants Des Illinois Byun Habitant Des Kaskaskias. Repr. of 1908 ed. 16.50 (ISBN 0-8337-0038-3). B Franklin.

Chicago, Cook County & Illinois Industrial Directory. 1981. 85.00 (ISBN 0-686-21882-5). Registry Pubns.

Commerce Clearing House. Guidebook to Illinois Taxes: 1982. 1982. 10.00 (ISBN 0-686-76126-X). Commerce.

Fishbane, Joyce O. & Fisher, Glenn W. Politics of the Purse: Revenue & Finance in the Sixth Illinois Constitutional Convention. (Studies in Illinois Constitution Making Ser.). 215p. 1974. pap. 5.95 (ISBN 0-252-00455-8). U of Ill Pr.

Keiser, John H. Building for the Centuries: Illinois, 1865-1898. LC 77-1764. 402p. 1977. 12.50 (ISBN 0-252-00617-8). U of Ill Pr.

Lloyd, Henry D. A Strike of Millionaires Against Miners: The Story of Spring Valley. 2nd rev. & enl. ed. LC 7-29952. 1971. Repr. of 1890 ed. 18.50 (ISBN 0-384-33183-1). Johnson Repr.

ILLINOIS–GENEALOGY

Jackson, Ronald V. & Teeples, Gary R. Illinois Census Index 1820. LC 77-85916. (Illus.). lib. bdg. 20.00 (ISBN 0-89593-032-3). Accelerated Index.

--Illinois Census Index 1830. LC 77-85917. (Illus.). lib. bdg. 22.00 (ISBN 0-89593-033-1). Accelerated Index.

--Illinois Census Index 1840. LC 77-85919. (Illus.). lib. bdg. 44.00 (ISBN 0-89593-034-X). Accelerated Index.

--Illinois Census Index 1850. LC 77-85920. (Illus.). lib. bdg. 60.00 (ISBN 0-89593-035-8). Accelerated Index.

Norton, Margaret C. Illinois Census Returns, 1810 & 1818. LC 70-75351. (Collections of the Illinois State Historical Library Ser: Vol. 2). 1969. Repr. of 1935 ed. 17.50 (ISBN 0-8063-0261-5). Genealog Pub.

--Illinois Census Returns, 1820. LC 77-75350. (Collections of the Illinois State Historical Library Ser: Vol. 3). 1969. Repr. of 1934 ed. 20.00 (ISBN 0-8063-0262-3). Genealog Pub.

Walker, Harriet J. Revolutionary Soldiers Buried in Illinois. LC 67-28602. 1967. Repr. of 1917 ed. 12.00 (ISBN 0-8063-0370-0). Genealog Pub.

ILLINOIS–HISTORY

Allen, John W. It Happened in Southern Illinois. 1973. 6.00 (ISBN 0-686-11834-0). Univ Graphics.

Alvord, C. W. & Carter, C. E., eds. Trade & Politics: 1767-1769. (Illinois Historical Collections Ser.: Vol. 16). 1921. 7.50 (ISBN 0-912154-04-7). Ill St Hist Lib.

Alvord, Clarence W. The Illinois Country Sixteen Seventy-Three to Eighteen Eighteen. (The American West Ser.). 1965. 7.00 (ISBN 0-8294-0000-1). Loyola.

Bain, Donald. War in Illinois. LC 78-17562. 1979. 9.95 (ISBN 0-13-944272-3). P-H.

Baldwin, Carl R. Echoes of Their Voices. 400p. 1978. 10.95 (ISBN 0-86629-003-6). Sunrise MO.

Birkbeck, Morris. Letters from Illinois. LC 68-8685. (American Scene Ser). 1970. Repr. of 1818 ed. lib. bdg. 19.50 (ISBN 0-306-71170-2). Da Capo.

Boggess, Arthur C. Settlement of Illinois, 1778-1830. facs. ed. LC 71-128873. (Select Bibliographies Reprint Ser). 1908. 16.00 (ISBN 0-8369-5493-9). Arno.

Bogue, Margaret B. Patterns from the Sod: Land Use & Tenure in the Grand Prairie, 1850-1900. (Illinois Historical Collections Ser.: Vol. 34). 1959. 2.50 (ISBN 0-912154-14-4). Ill St Hist Lib.

Bradshaw, Charles. Patriot Souvenir Edition-Eighteen Ninety-Six. 76p. 1976. 3.00 (ISBN 0-686-27518-7). E S Cunningham.

Brown, Margaret K. & Dean, Lawrie, eds. The Village of Chartres in Colonial Illinois: 1720-1765. 1977. 30.00x (ISBN 0-686-09340-2). Polyanthos.

Burman, Ian D. Lobbying at the Illinois Constitutional Convention. LC 72-95000. (Studies in Illinois Constitution Making Ser). 130p. 1973. pap. 5.95 (ISBN 0-252-00336-5). U of Ill Pr.

Calkins, Earnest E. They Broke the Prairie: Being Some Account of the Settlement of the Upper Mississippi Valley by Religious & Educational Pioneers, Told in Terms of One City, Galesburg, & of One College, Knox. LC 75-138103. 1971. Repr. of 1937 ed. lib. bdg. 19.50x (ISBN 0-8371-5679-3, CABP). Greenwood.

Carter, Clarence E. Great Britain & the Illinois Country, 1763-1774. LC 73-120870. (American Bicentennial Ser). 1970. Repr. of 1910 ed. 12.00 (ISBN 0-8046-1263-3). Kennikat.

Cavanagh, Helen M. Funk of Funk's Grove. 1968. 5.50 (ISBN 0-912226-10-2). Ill St Hist Soc.

Clayton, John, ed. Illinois Fact Book & Historical Almanac, 1673-1968. LC 68-21417. (Illus.). 576p. 1970. 15.00x (ISBN 0-8093-0380-9). S Ill U Pr.

Cole, Arthur C., ed. The Constitutional Debates of 1847. (Illinois Historical Collections Ser.: Vol. 14). 1919. 10.00 (ISBN 0-912154-25-X). Ill St Hist Lib.

Cornelius, Janet. Constitution Making in Illinois, 1818 to 1970. LC 72-76864. (Studies in Illinois Constitution Making Ser.). 224p. 1972. pap. 5.95 (ISBN 0-252-00251-2). U of Ill Pr.

Cunningham, Eileen S. Lower Illinois Valley, Greene County 1821, Containment: Morgan to 1823, Scott to 1823, Macoupin to 1829, Jersey to 1839. 1980. 98.40 (ISBN 0-686-29479-3, AU00128); pap. 88.40 (ISBN 0-686-29480-7). E S Cunningham.

--Lower Illinois Valley Limestone Houses. 1976. pap. 3.00 (ISBN 0-686-31826-9) (ISBN 0-686-29476-9). E S Cunningham.

Doyle, Don H. The Social Order of a Frontier Community: Jacksonville, Illinois, 1825-70. LC 78-5287. 1978. 15.00 (ISBN 0-252-00685-2). U of Ill Pr.

Drown, Simeon DeWitt. The Peoria Directory for 1844. 1978. Repr. of 1844 ed. 6.95x (ISBN 0-930358-02-3). Spoon River.

Edwards, Ninian W. History of Illinois, from 1778 to 1833: And Life & Times of Ninian Edwards. facsimile ed. LC 75-97. (Mid-American Frontierser.). 1975. Repr. of 1870 ed. 31.00x (ISBN 0-405-06863-8). Arno.

Federal Writers Project. Illinois: A Descriptive & Historical Guide. LC 72-145010. (Illus.). 1971. Repr. of 1947 ed. 59.00 (ISBN 0-403-01292-9). Somerset Pub.

Federal Writers' Project. Illinois. Galena Guide. LC 73-3615. Repr. of 1937 ed. 14.00 (ISBN 0-404-57918-3). AMS Pr.

Foster, Olive S. Illinois. LC 68-9184. (Localized History Ser). 1968. pap. 2.95 (ISBN 0-8077-1380-5). Tchrs Coll.

Fradin, Dennis. Illinois: In Words & Pictures. LC 76-7389. (Young People's Stories of Our States). (Illus.). (gr. 2-5). 1976. PLB 9.25 (ISBN 0-516-03911-3). Childrens.

Gates, Paul W. The Illinois Central Railroad & Its Colonization Work. (American Economy Ser). 1969. Repr. of 1934 ed. 23.00 (ISBN 0-384-17710-7). Johnson Repr.

Grant, H. Roger, ed. An Icarian Communist in Nauvoo: Commentary by Emile Vallet. 79p. 1971. pap. 2.00 (ISBN 0-912226-06-4). Ill St Hist Soc.

Harris, Mark. City of Discontent: An Interpretive Biography of Vachel Lindsay, Being Also the Story of Springfield, Illinois, USA. 403p. 1975. Repr. of 1952 ed. lib. bdg. 20.00x (ISBN 0-374-93676-5). Octagon.

Howard, Robert P. Illinois: A History of the Prairie State. 512p. 1972. 15.95 (ISBN 0-8028-7025-2). Eerdmans.

Jensen, Richard J. Illinois: A History. (States & the Nation Ser.). (Illus.). 1978. 12.95 (ISBN 0-393-05596-5, Co-Pub by AASLH). Norton.

John Francis Snyder: Selected Writings. Walton, Clyde C., ed. 1962. 15.00 (ISBN 0-912226-03-X). Ill St Hist Soc.

Keiser, John H. Building for the Centuries: Illinois, 1865-1898. LC 77-1764. 402p. 1977. 12.50 (ISBN 0-252-00617-8). U of Ill Pr.

McCarthy, Mary J. Elk Grove: The Peony Village. Wagner, Roswita M., ed. (Illus.). 160p. 1981. pap. write for info. (ISBN 0-9605940-0-0). Elk Grove Vill.

Nelson, Ronald E., ed. Illinois: Land & Life in the Prairie State. (Regional Geography Ser.). (Illus.). 1978. pap. text ed. 12.95 (ISBN 0-8403-1831-6). Kendall-Hunt.

Patton, Dave, et al. As It Was Told to Me. LC 77-95394. (Illus.). 1978. pap. 6.95 (ISBN 0-685-63527-9). Elysian Fields.

Pease, T. C., ed. Illinois Election Returns: 1818-1848. (Illinois Historical Collections Ser: Vol. 18). 1923. 10.00 (ISBN 0-912154-06-3). Ill St Hist Lib.

Pease, Theodore C. Story of Illinois. 3rd ed. Pease, Marguerite J., ed. LC 65-17299. (Illus.). 1965. 12.00x (ISBN 0-226-65156-8). U of Chicago Pr.

--The Story of Illinois. 3rd rev. ed. LC 65-17299. (Illus.). xvi, 332p. 1975. pap. 3.95 (ISBN 0-226-65157-6). U of Chicago Pr.

Pease, Theodore C. & Pease, Marguerite J. George Rogers Clark & the Revolution in Illinois, Seventeen Sixty-Three to Seventeen Eighty-Seven. 1929. 3.00 (ISBN 0-912226-12-9). Ill St Hist So.

Perica, Esther. They Took the Challenge: The Story of Rolling Meadows. LC 79-14803. (Illus.), 167p. 1980. 9.75 (ISBN 0-9602782-0-6). Rolling Meadows.

Philbrick, F. S., ed. The Laws of Illinois Territory: 1809-1818. (Illinois Historical Collections Ser.: Vol. 25). 1950. 2.50 (ISBN 0-912154-11-X). Ill St Hist Lib.

Pierce, Bess. Moline: A Pictorial History. Friedman, Donna R., ed. LC 80-22905. (Illus.). 208p. 1981. pap. 12.95 (ISBN 0-89865-095-X). Donning Co.

Plucker, Lina S. & Roerick, Kaye L., eds. Brevet's Illinois Historical Markers & Sites. LC 75-253. (Historical Markers-Sites Ser). (Illus.). 300p. (Orig.). 1976. pap. 6.95 (ISBN 0-88498-029-4). Brevet Pr.

Savelle, Max. George Morgan: Colony Builder. LC 32-30652. Repr. of 1932 ed. 14.00 (ISBN 0-404-05567-2). AMS Pr.

Schoen, Elin. Tales of an All-Night Town. LC 79-1841. 1979. 9.95 (ISBN 0-15-184993-5). HarBraceJ.

Seineke, Katherine W., ed. Guide to the Microfilm Publication of the Pierre Menard Collection in the Illinois State Historical Library. 138p. 1972. pap. 2.00 (ISBN 0-912226-04-8). Ill St Hist Soc.

Smeal, Lee. Illinois Historical & Biographical Index. LC 78-53693. (Illus.). Date not set. lib. bdg. price not set (ISBN 0-89593-178-8). Accelerated Index.

The Territory of Illinois, 1809-1814. (The Territorial Papers of the United States: Vol. 16). Repr. of 1948 ed. 69.50 (ISBN 0-404-01466-6). AMS Pr.

The Territory of Illinois, 1814-1818. (The Territorial Papers of the United States: Vol. 17). Repr. of 1950 ed. 69.50 (ISBN 0-404-01467-4). AMS Pr.

Tingley, Donald F. The Structuring of a State: The History of Illinois, 1899-1928. LC 79-14964. (Sesquicentenniel History of Illinois Ser.: Vol. 5). (Illus.). 452p. 1980. 20.00 (ISBN 0-252-00736-0). U of Ill Pr.

Tingley, Donald F., ed. Essays in Illinois History in Honor of Glenn Huron Seymour. LC 68-11650. 179p. 1968. 6.95x (ISBN 0-8093-0284-5). S Ill U Pr.

Tomcsanyi, Linda, illus. Color Me Greene. (Illus.). 1980. 3.00 (ISBN 0-686-26237-9). E S Cunningham.

Trutter, John T. & Trutter, Edith E. The Governor Takes a Bride: The Celebrated Marriage of Cora English & John R. Tanner, Governor of Illinois, 1897-1901. LC 77-7643. (Illus.). 82p. 1977. pap. 3.95x (ISBN 0-8093-0825-8). S Ill U Pr.

Vance, Mary. Historical Society Architectural Publications: Georgia, Hawaii, Idaho, Illinois & Indiana. (Architecture Ser.: Bibliography A-157). 54p. 1980. pap. 6.00 (ISBN 0-686-26906-3). Vance Biblios.

Vexler, R. I. Illinois Chronology & Factbook, Vol. 13. 1978. 8.50 (ISBN 0-379-16138-9). Oceana.

Watters, Mary. Illinois in the Second World War: Vol. 1 Operation Home Front, Vol. 1. 1951. 5.00 (ISBN 0-912154-18-7). Ill St Hist Lib.

--Illinois in the Second World War: Vol. 2, The Production Front. 1952. 5.00 (ISBN 0-912154-19-5). Ill St Hist Lib.

Whitson, Skip, compiled by. Illinois-One Hundred Years Ago. (Sun Historical Ser). (Illus., Orig.). 1976. pap. 3.50 (ISBN 0-89540-028-6, SB028). Sun Pub.

ILLINOIS–HISTORY–BLACK HAWK WAR, 1832

see Black Hawk War, 1832

ILLINOIS–HISTORY–FICTION

Allen, John W. Legends & Lore of Southern Illinois. 1973. 6.00 (ISBN 0-686-11835-9). Univ Graphics.

ILLINOIS–IMPRINTS

Byrd, Cecil K. Bibliography of Illinois Imprints, Eighteen Fourteen to Eighteen Fifty-Eight. LC 65-24423. 1966. 25.00x (ISBN 0-226-08789-1). U of Chicago Pr.

ILLINOIS–POLITICS AND GOVERNMENT

Altgeld, John P. Mind & Spirit of John Peter Altgeld. facs. ed. Christman, Henry M., ed. LC 70-128200. (Essay Index Reprint Ser). 1960. 15.00 (ISBN 0-8369-1860-6). Arno.

Blair, George S. Cumulative Voting. LC 75-10210. (Illinois Studies in the Social Sciences: Vol. 45). (Illus.). 145p. 1975. Repr. of 1960 ed. lib. bdg. 15.00x (ISBN 0-8371-8174-7, BLCV). Greenwood.

Christman, Henry M., ed. The Mind & Spirit of John Peter Altgeld. LC 60-5349. 1965. pap. 3.95 (ISBN 0-252-72549-2). U of Ill Pr.

Cleary, Edward W. & Graham, Michael H. Handbook of Illinois Evidence: 1981 Supplement. LC 79-89121. 96p. 1981. pap. 10.00 (ISBN 0-316-14721-4). Little.

Cohn, Rubin G. To Judge with Justice: History & Politics of Illinois Judicial Reform. LC 72-95002. (Studies in Illinois Constitution Making Ser). 180p. 1973. pap. 5.95 (ISBN 0-252-00332-2). U of Ill Pr.

Cornelius, Janet. Constitution Making in Illinois, 1818 to 1970. LC 72-76864. (Studies in Illinois Constitution Making Ser.). 224p. 1972. pap. 5.95 (ISBN 0-252-00251-2). U of Ill Pr.

Cullom, Shelby. Fifty Years of Public Service: Personal Recollections of Shelby M. Cullom. LC 75-87504. (American Public Figures Ser). Repr. of 1911 ed. lib. bdg. 45.00 (ISBN 0-306-71410-8). Da Capo.

Fishbane, Joyce O. & Fisher, Glenn W. Politics of the Purse: Revenue & Finance in the Sixth Illinois Constitutional Convention. (Studies in Illinois Constitution Making Ser.). 215p. 1974. pap. 5.95 (ISBN 0-252-00455-8). U of Ill Pr.

Gertz, Elmer & Pisciotte, Joe. Charter for a New Age: An Inside View of the Sixth Illinois Constitutional Convention. LC 80-10837. (Studies in Illinois Constitution Making Ser.). 368p. 1980. 15.00 (ISBN 0-252-00820-0). U of Ill Pr.

Gould Editorial Staff. Criminal Laws of Illinois. (Annual). 1981. text ed. 9.95x (ISBN 0-87526-199-X). Gould.

Gove, Samuel K., et al. Illinois Legislature: Structure & Process. LC 76-21238. 208p. 1976. pap. 5.95 (ISBN 0-252-00621-6). U of Ill Pr.

Gratch, Alan S. & Ubik, Virginia H. Ballots for Change: New Suffrage & Amending Articles for Illinois. LC 73-16472. (Studies in Illinois Constitution Making Ser). 1974. pap. 5.95 (ISBN 0-252-00433-7). U of Ill Pr.

Horsley, Jack C. Illinois Civil Practice & Procedure. 1970. text ed. 15.00 (ISBN 0-87473-051-1). A Smith Co.

Keiser, John H. Building for the Centuries: Illinois, 1865-1898. LC 77-1764. 402p. 1977. 12.50 (ISBN 0-252-00617-8). U of Ill Pr.

Kenney, David. Basic Illinois Government: A Systematic Explanation. rev. ed. LC 74-115118. 453p. 1974. pap. 8.95x (ISBN 0-8093-0470-8). S Ill U Pr.

Kenney, David, et al. Roll Call. Patterns of Voting in the Sixth Illinois Constitutional Convention. LC 74-32337. (Studies in Illinois Constitution Making Ser). 112p. 1975. pap. 5.95 (ISBN 0-252-00524-4). U of Ill Pr.

McGriggs, Lee A. Black Legislative Politics in Illinois. 1977. pap. text ed. 11.25 (ISBN 0-8191-0336-5). U Pr of Amer.

Messick, Hank. The Politics of Prosecution: Jim Thompson, Richard Nixon, Marje Everett, & the Trial of Otto Kerner. LC 77-15915. (Illus.). 1978. 10.95 (ISBN 0-916054-64-0, Caroline Hse Inc). Green Hill.

Moore, Blaine F. The History of Cumulative Voting & Minority Representation in Illinois, 1870-1919. rev. ed. (Illinois Studies in the Social Sciences Ser.: Vol. 8, No. 2). pap. 6.00 (ISBN 0-384-39955-X). Johnson Repr.

Rothman, Rozann. The Great Society at the Grass Roots. 1980. 18.50x (ISBN 965-20-0017-5, Pub. by Turtledove Pub Ltd Israel). Intl Schol Bk Serv.

Schuyler, Robert L. Transition in Illinois from British to American Government. Repr. of 1909 ed. 16.00 (ISBN 0-404-05627-X). AMS Pr.

Simon, Paul. Lincoln's Preparation for Greatness: The Illinois Legislative Years. LC 65-24195. (Illus.). 1971. pap. 2.95 (ISBN 0-252-00203-2). U of Ill Pr.

Tarr, Joel A. Study in Boss Politics: William Lorimer of Chicago. LC 72-133945. (Illus.). 387p. 1971. 22.50 (ISBN 0-252-00139-7). U of Ill Pr.

Thompson, Charles M. The Illinois Whigs Before 1846. Repr. of 1915 ed. 9.50 (ISBN 0-384-60230-4). Johnson Repr.

Waller, Robert A. Rainey of Illinois: A Political Biography, 1903-34. LC 77-23859. (Illnois Studies in Social Sciences: No. 60). 1977. 12.50 (ISBN 0-252-00647-X). U of Ill Pr.

Watson, JoAnna M. Electing a Constitution: The Illinois Citizen & the Nineteen Seventy Constitution. LC 79-26224. (Studies in Illinois Constitution Making: Vol. 9). 150p. (Orig.). 1980. pap. 5.95 (ISBN 0-252-00458-2). U of Ill Pr.

Wooddy, Carroll H. The Case of Frank L. Smith: Study of Representative Government. LC 73-19187. (Politics & People Ser.). (Illus.). 404p. 1974. Repr. 21.00x (ISBN 0-405-05907-8). Arno.

ILLINOIS–SOCIAL LIFE AND CUSTOMS

Farnham, Eliza W. Life in Prairie Land. LC 72-2601. (American Women Ser: Images & Realities). 412p. 1972. Repr. of 1846 ed. 18.00 (ISBN 0-405-04457-7). Arno.

King, Willard L. Lincoln's Manager, David Davis. (Midway Reprint Ser.). 1960. pap. 12.00x (ISBN 0-226-43699-3). U of Chicago Pr.

Schoen, Elin. Tales of an All-Night Town. LC 79-1841. 1979. 9.95 (ISBN 0-15-184993-5). HarBraceJ.

ILLINOIS, DEPARTMENT OF PUBLIC WELFARE, DIVISION OF PARDONS AND PAROLES

Bruce, Andrew A., et al. Workings of the Indeterminate-Sentence Law & the Parole System in Illinois. LC 68-19466. (Criminology, Law Enforcement, & Social Problems Ser.: No. 5). 1968. Repr. of 1928 ed. 15.00 (ISBN 0-87585-005-7). Patterson Smith.

ILLINOIS, SOUTHERN UNIVERSITY OF, CARBONDALE

Plochmann, Carolyn G. University Portrait: Nine Paintings. 1959. 6.95x (ISBN 0-8093-0022-2). S Ill U Pr.

Plochmann, George K. Ordeal of Southern Illinois University. LC 59-7379. (Illus.). 1959. 693pp. 10.00x (ISBN 0-8093-0020-6); 2 vols. set boxed 704pp. 15.00x (ISBN 0-8093-0021-4). S Ill U Pr.

ILLINOIS, UNIVERSITY OF

The Dictionary Catalog of the Applied Life Studies Library, University of Illinois at Urbana-Champaign, 4 vols. 1976. 300.00 (ISBN 0-8161-0047-0). G K Hall.

Eubanks, Lon. University of Illinois Football. LC 76-7853. (College Sports Ser.). 1976. 9.95 (ISBN 0-87397-065-9). Strode.

Hatch, Richard A., compiled by. Some Founding Papers of the University of Illinois. LC 66-21365. 1967. 10.00 (ISBN 0-252-74515-9). U of Ill Pr.

Johnson, Henry C., Jr. & Johanningmeier, E. V. Teachers for the Prairie: The University of Illinois & the Schools, 1868-1945. LC 75-157889. 512p. 1972. 29.95 (ISBN 0-252-00183-4). U of Ill Pr.

Kersey, Harry A., Jr. John Milton Gregory & the University of Illinois. LC 67-21854. 1968. 16.50 (ISBN 0-252-72563-8). U of Ill Pr.

Moores, Richard G. Fields of Rich Toil: The Development of the University of Illinois College of Agriculture. LC 78-100378. (Illus.). 1970. 15.00 (ISBN 0-252-00094-3). U of Ill Pr.

Rosen, George. Decision Making Chicago-Style: The Genesis of a University of Illinois Campus. LC 79-25643. (Illus.). 224p. 1980. 15.00 (ISBN 0-252-00803-0). U of Ill Pr.

ILLINOIS AND VALLEY-ANTIQUITIES

McGregor, John C. The Pool & Irving Villages: A Study of Hopewell Occupation in the Illinois River Valley. LC 58-5605. (Illus.). 1958. pap. 7.50 (ISBN 0-252-72610-3). U of Ill Pr.

ILLINOIS CENTRAL RAILROAD

Brownson, Howard G. History of the Illinois Central Railroad to 1870. 1915. 12.50 (ISBN 0-384-06025-0). Johnson Repr.

Gates, Paul W. The Illinois Central Railroad & Its Colonization Work. (American Economy Ser). 1969. Repr. of 1934 ed. 23.00 (ISBN 0-384-17710-7). Johnson Repr.

Lightner, David L. Labor on the Illinois Central Railroad, 1852-1900: The Evolution of an Industrial Environment. Bruchey, Stuart, ed. LC 76-39834. (Nineteen Seventy-Seven Dissertations Ser.). (Illus.). 1977. lib. bdg. 27.00x (ISBN 0-405-09914-2). Arno.

Person, Carl E. The Lizard's Trail. LC 74-22755. (The Labor Movement in Fiction & Non-Fiction). Repr. of 1918 ed. 31.00 (ISBN 0-404-58508-6). AMS Pr.

Sutton, Robert M. The Illinois Central Railroad in Peace & War, 1858-1868. Bruchey, Stuart, ed. LC 80-1290. (Railroads Ser.). 1981. lib. bdg. 25.00x (ISBN 0-405-13761-3). Arno.

ILLINOIS INFANTRY, 96TH REGT., 1862-1865

Snetsinger, Robert J. Kiss Clara for Me. LC 69-17409. (Illus.). 180p. 1969. 7.50 (ISBN 0-87601-002-8). Carnation.

ILLINOIS MILITARY TRACT

Carlson, Theodore L. The Illinois Military Tract. Bruchey, Stuart, ed. LC 78-56707. (Management of Public Lands in the U. S. Ser.). (Illus.). 1979. Repr. of 1951 ed. lib. bdg. 15.00 (ISBN 0-405-11322-6). Arno.

ILLINOIS RIVER AND VALLEY

Kofoid, C. A. The Plankton of the Illinois River 1894-1899. (Bibliotheca Phycologica: Band 29). (Illus.). 1978. Repr. of 1903 ed. 60.00x (ISBN 3-7682-1104-5, Pub. by J Cramer). Intl Schol Bk Serv.

ILLINOIS TEST OF PSYCHOLINGUISTIC ABILITIES

Kirk, Samuel A. & Paraskevopoulos, John N. The Development & Psychometric Characteristics of the Revised Illinois Test of Psycholinguistic Abilities. LC 69-19511. (Illus.). 1969. pap. 10.00 (ISBN 0-252-00007-2). U of Ill Pr.

Kirk, Winifred D. Aids & Precautions in Administering the Illinois Test of Psycholinguistic Abilities. LC 74-4876. 119p. 1974. pap. 2.95 (ISBN 0-252-00445-0). U of Ill Pr.

ILLITERACY

see also Education and Crime; Libraries and New Literates; New Literates, Writing For

Adamson, John W. Illiterate Anglo-Saxon & Other Essays on Education, Medieval & Modern. LC 74-1485. 1946. lib. bdg. 15.00 (ISBN 0-8414-2956-1). Folcroft.

Bataille, Leon, ed. A Turning Point for Literacy-Adult Education for Development-Spirit & Declaration of Persepolis: Proceedings of the International Symposium for Literacy, Iran, 1975. LC 76-46206. 1976. text ed. 29.00 (ISBN 0-08-021385-5); pap. text ed. 16.00 (ISBN 0-08-021386-3). Pergamon.

Carroll, John B. & Chall, Jeanne, eds. Toward a Literate Society: A Report from the National Academy of Education. 352p. 1975. 18.50 (ISBN 0-07-010130-2, P&RB). McGraw.

Conference Held on the Campus of Lenoir-Rhyne College, Hickory, North Carolina, October, 1978. Culture & Literacy: The Problems & the Promise, Proceedings. Tucker, Edward F., ed. LC 79-13796. (Orig.). 1979. pap. 11.75 (ISBN 0-8357-0415-7, SS-00093). Univ Microfilms.

Cook, Wanda D. Adult Literacy Education in the United States. LC 76-58957. 1977. pap. 4.50 (ISBN 0-87207-934-1). Intl Reading.

Copperman, Paul. The Literacy Hoax: The Decline of Reading, Writing, & Learning in the Public Schools & What We Can Do About It. LC 78-18703. 1979. pap. 5.95 (ISBN 0-688-08353-6, Quill). Morrow.

--The Literacy Hoax: The Decline of Reading, Writing & Learning in the Public Schools & What We Can Do About It. LC 78-18703. 1978. 10.95 (ISBN 0-688-03353-9). Morrow.

Cressy, David. Literacy & the Social Order. (Illus.). 250p. 1980. 29.50 (ISBN 0-521-22514-0). Cambridge U Pr.

Documents from the Experimental World Literacy Programme. 88p. 1980. pap. 4.50 (ISBN 92-3-001728-0, U957, Pub. by UNESCO). Unipub.

Dumont, Bernard. Functional Literacy in Mali: Training for Development. LC 73-77353. (Educational Studies & Documents, No. 10). (Illus.). 67p. (Orig.). 1973. pap. 2.50 (ISBN 92-3-101113-8, U257, UNESCO). Unipub.

The Evaluation of Literacy Programmes: A Practical Guide. 1979. pap. 9.00 (ISBN 92-3-101580-X, U911, UNESCO). Unipub.

The Experimental World Literacy Programme: A Critical Assessment. 198p. 1976. pap. 9.25 (ISBN 92-3-101314-9, U232, UNESCO). Unipub.

Furter, Pierre. Possibilities & Limitations of Functional Literacy: The Iranian Experiment. LC 73-781021. (Educational Studies & Documents, No. 9). (Illus.). 59p. (Orig.). 1973. pap. 2.50 (ISBN 92-3-101075-1, U472, UNESCO). Unipub.

Giorgianni, Frank. The Functioning Illiterate in Modern Times. LC 81-80145. (Illus.). 64p. (Orig.). 1981. pap. 5.95 (ISBN 0-86666-002-X). GWP.

Goldberg, Samuel. Army Training of Illiterates in World War Two. LC 74-176810. (Columbia University. Teachers College. Contributions to Education: No. 966). Repr. of 1951 ed. 17.50 (ISBN 0-404-55966-2). AMS Pr.

Goody, J. The Domestication of the Savage Mind. (Themes in the Social Sciences Ser.). (Illus.). 1977. 24.95 (ISBN 0-521-21726-1); pap. 6.95x (ISBN 0-521-29242-5). Cambridge U Pr.

Goody, Jack R., ed. Literacy in Traditional Societies. LC 69-10427. 1969. pap. 11.95x (ISBN 0-521-29005-8). Cambridge U Pr.

Gordon, Donald. New Literacy. LC 71-163816. 1971. pap. 6.00 (ISBN 0-8020-6120-6). U of Toronto Pr.

Graff, Harvey J. Literacy in History: An Interdisciplinary Research Bibliography. 1981. lib. bdg. 30.00 (ISBN 0-8240-9460-3). Garland Pub.

Graff, Harvey L. The Literacy Myth: Literacy & Social Structure in the Nineteenth Century City. LC 79-51702. (Studies in Social Discontinuity). 1979. 27.50 (ISBN 0-12-294520-4). Acad Pr.

Grundin, Elizabeth H. Literacy. 1979. text ed. 14.25 (ISBN 0-06-318128-2, IntlDept); pap. text ed. 9.25 (ISBN 0-06-318140-1). Har-Row.

Gudschinsky, Sarah C. A Manual of Literacy for Preliterate Peoples. x, 180p. 1973. pap. 4.00x (ISBN 0-7263-0054-3); microfiche 1.60 (ISBN 0-88312-354-1). Summer Inst Ling.

Hargreaves, David. Adult Literacy & Broadcasting: The BBC's Experience. 220p. 1980. 25.00 (ISBN 0-89397-089-1). Nichols Pub.

Hay, W., ed. Adult Literacy in Britain: An Annotated Bibliography. 1978. 12.25x (ISBN 0-85365-811-0, Pub. by Lib Assn England). Oryx Pr.

Hoyles, Martin, ed. The Politics of Literacy. (Education Ser.). 216p. 1980. 14.00 (ISBN 0-904613-47-X); pap. 3.95 (ISBN 0-904613-28-3). Writers & Readers.

Hunter, Carman S. Adult Illiteracy in the United States. (Illus.). 1979. 10.95 (ISBN 0-07-031380-6, P&RB). McGraw.

Isenberg, Irwin, ed. Drive Against Illiteracy. (Reference Shelf Ser.: Vol. 36, No. 5). 1964. 6.25 (ISBN 0-8242-0082-9). Wilson.

Jacomy. Dictionnaire des Savants et des Ignorants, 2 vols. Migne, J. P., ed. (Troisieme et Derniere Encyclopedie Theologique Ser.: Vols. 46-47). 1248p. (Fr.). Date not set. Repr. of 1859 ed. lib. bdg. 160.00x (ISBN 0-89241-320-4). Caratzas Bros.

Judy, Stephen N. The ABC's of Literacy: A Guide for Parents & Educators. 380p. 1981. pap. 6.95 (ISBN 0-19-502988-7, GB 651, GB). Oxford U Pr.

Kozol, Jonathan. Prisoners of Silence: Breaking the Bonds of Adult Illiteracy in the United States. 128p. 1980. 8.95 (ISBN 0-8164-9004-X). Continuum.

Literacy & Society, 3 pts. Incl. Pt. 1. The Rise & Dissolution of Infidel Societies in This Metropolis (1800; Pt. 2. James Watson, a Memoir (1880; Pt. 3. Appendix-Catalogue of James Watson's Publications. LC 70-78980. (Social History of Education). 218p. 1971. 18.00x (ISBN 0-678-08462-9). Kelley.

Literacy in Asia: A Continuing Challenge. 1978. pap. 13.75 (ISBN 0-685-59479-3, UB63, UNESCO). Unipub.

Literacy Nineteen Seventy-Two to Nineteen Seventy-Six. 83p. 1980. pap. 4.75 (ISBN 92-3-101731-4, U 1010, UNESCO). Unipub.

Mackie, Robert, ed. Literacy & Revolution: The Pedagogy of Paulo Freire. 172p. 1981. pap. 7.95 (ISBN 0-8264-0055-8). Continuum.

Motta, J. & Riley, K. Breakthrough to Literacy, 3 bks. 1981. pap. write for info. Bk. 1 (ISBN 0-201-05310-1). Bk. 2 (ISBN 0-201-05313-6). Bk. 3 (ISBN 0-201-05316-0). write for info. instr's manuals. Bk. 1 (ISBN 0-201-05311-X). Bk. 2 (ISBN 0-201-05314-4). Bk. 3 (ISBN 0-201-05317-9). A-W.

Murphy, James J., et al. Rhetorical Essays & Modern Writing: Essays Toward the Re-Marriage of Literature & Literacy. 300p. 1982. 14.50x (ISBN 0-87352-097-1); pap. 8.50x (ISBN 0-87352-098-X). Modern Lang.

Neuberg, Victor E., ed. Literacy & Society, 2 vols in 1. (The Social History of Education Ser.: 2nd Ser., No. 5). 1971. Repr. of 1800 ed. Set. 24.00x (ISBN 0-7130-0014-7, Woburn Pr England). Biblio Dist.

The Operational Seminar: A Pioneering Method of Training for Development. (Educational Studies & Documents: No. 20). (Illus.). 59p. 1976. pap. 3.25 (ISBN 92-3-101323-8, U435, UNESCO). Unipub.

Owen, Robert. Revolution in the Mind & Practice of the Human Race. LC 74-183620. Repr. of 1849 ed. 17.50x (ISBN 0-678-00892-2). Kelley.

Oxenham, John. Literacy: Writing, Reading & Social Organisation. (Studies in Language & Society). 128p. 1980. 17.50x (ISBN 0-7100-0584-9); pap. 10.00 (ISBN 0-7100-0619-5). Routledge & Kegan.

Paulsen, Vic. English Illiteracy: Deification of Decadence. LC 80-54844. 66p. 1981. pap. 3.95 (ISBN 0-913048-03-8). Torskript Pubs.

Practical Guide to Functional Literacy: A Method of Training for Development. LC 73-75104. (Illus.). 173p. (Orig.). 1973. pap. 4.00 (ISBN 92-3-101054-9, U474, UNESCO). Unipub.

Rogers, Will. The Illiterate Digest. LC 77-145720. (Illus.). 351p. 1975. Repr. of 1924 ed. 28.00 (ISBN 0-8103-3975-7). Gale.

Roy, Prodipto. The Retention of Literacy. LC 75-902217. 1975. 8.50x (ISBN 0-8364-0458-0). South Asia Bks.

Simon, John. Paradigms Lost: Essays on Literacy & Its Decline. (Illus.). 224p. 1980. 12.95 (ISBN 0-517-54034-7). Potter.

Soltow, Lee & Stevens, Edward. The Rise of Literacy & the Common School in the United States: A Socioeconomic Analysis to 1870. LC 81-7464. 1981. price not set (ISBN 0-226-76812-0, Phoen). U of Chicago Pr.

Stubbs, Michael. Language & Literacy: The Sociolinguistics of Reading & Writing. (Education Bks.). 1980. 25.00x (ISBN 0-7100-0426-5); pap. 12.50 (ISBN 0-7100-0499-0). Routledge & Kegan.

Tests of Functional Adult Literacy. 1975. 7.50 (ISBN 0-89354-825-1). Northwest Regional.

UNESCO. World Illiteracy at Mid-Century, a Statistical Study. Repr. of 1957 ed. lib. bdg. 15.00x (ISBN 0-8371-3405-6, UNWI). Greenwood.

Viscusi, Margo. Literacy for Working: Functional Literacy in Rural Tanzania. (Educational Studies & Documents, No. 5). (Illus.). 57p. (Orig.). 1972. pap. 2.50 (ISBN 92-3-100905-2, U360, UNESCO). Unipub.

Wheeler, Thomas C. The Great American Writing Block: Causes & Cures of the New Illiteracy. 224p. 1980. pap. 3.95 (ISBN 0-14-004693-3). Penguin.

The World of Literacy: Policy, Research & Action. 1979. pap. 9.00 (ISBN 0-88936-193-2, IDRC 117, IDRC). Unipub.

ILLUMINATI

see also Enlightenment

Robison, John. Proofs of a Conspiracy. 1967. pap. 3.95 (ISBN 0-88279-121-4). Western Islands.

Stauffer, Vernon. New England & the Bavarian Illuminati. LC 66-27153. 1967. Repr. of 1918 ed. 8.50 (ISBN 0-8462-0953-5). Russell.

ILLUMINATION

see Lighting

ILLUMINATION OF BOOKS AND MANUSCRIPTS

see also Alphabets; Hours, Books Of; Initials; Miniature Painting; Paleography

Alexander, J. J., ed. Insular Manuscripts from the 6th Century to the 9th Century. (A Survey of Manuscripts Illuminated in the British Isles: Vol. 1). (Illus.). 95.00 (ISBN 0-905203-01-1, Pub. by H Miller England). Heyden.

--Italian Renaissance Illuminations. LC 77-2841. (Magnificent Paperback Ser.). (Illus.). 1977. 19.95 (ISBN 0-8076-0863-7); pap. 9.95 (ISBN 0-8076-0864-5). Braziller.

Arnold, Thomas W. Painting in Islam. (Illus.). 11.00 (ISBN 0-8446-1553-6). Peter Smith.

--Painting in Islam: A Study of the Place of Pictorial Art in Muslim Culture. (Illus.). 1928. pap. 6.00 (ISBN 0-486-21310-2). Dover.

Berenson, Bernard. Studies in Medieval Painting. LC 73-153884. (Graphic Art Ser.). (Illus.). 148p. 1971. Repr. of 1930 ed. lib. bdg. 35.00 (ISBN 0-306-70292-4). Da Capo.

Binyon, L, et al. Persian Miniature Painting. (Illus.). 10.00 (ISBN 0-8446-0031-8). Peter Smith.

Brown, Peter. The Book of Kells: A Selection from the Irish Medieval Manuscripts. LC 80-7973. (Illus.). 96p. 1980. pap. 10.95 (ISBN 0-394-73960-4). Knopf.

Carder, James N. Art Historical Problems of a Roman Land. LC 77-94730. (Outstanding Dissertations in the Fine Arts Ser.). 1979. lib. bdg. 33.00x (ISBN 0-8240-3218-7). Garland Pub.

Cockerell, Sydney C. & Plummer, John. Old Testament Miniatures. LC 75-82000. (K). 1969. 60.00 (ISBN 0-8076-0513-1). Braziller.

Crane, Walter. Of the Decorative Illustration of Books Old & New. LC 68-30611. 1968. Repr. of 1905 ed. 28.00 (ISBN 0-8103-3299-X). Gale.

Delaisse, L. M. A Century of Dutch Manuscript Illumination. (California Studies in the History of Art: No. VI). (Illus.). 1968. 58.50x (ISBN 0-520-00315-2). U of Cal Pr.

Dominguez-Bordona, Jesus. Spanish Illumination, 2 Vols. in 1. LC 77-78360. (Illus.). 1969. Repr. of 1929 ed. 60.00 (ISBN 0-87817-028-6). Hacker.

Dynes, Wayne. The Illuminations of the Stavelot Bible. LC 77-94693. (Outstanding Dissertations in the Fine Arts Ser.). (Illus.). 1979. lib. bdg. 36.00 (ISBN 0-8240-3225-X). Garland Pub.

Folda, Jaroslav. Crusader Manuscript Illumination at Saint-Jean D'acre, 1275-1291. LC 75-2991. (Illus.). 646p. 1976. 47.50x (ISBN 0-691-03907-0). Princeton U Pr.

Hatch, William H. Greek & Syrian Miniatures in Jerusalem. (Illus.). 1931. 15.00 (ISBN 0-910956-04-9). Medieval Acad.

Henry, Francoise, ed. The Book of Kells. 1974. 65.00 (ISBN 0-394-49475-X). Knopf.

Herbert, John A. Illuminated Manuscripts. (Illus.). 1911. 24.50 (ISBN 0-8337-1667-0). B Franklin.

Hermannsson, Halldor. Illuminated Manuscripts of the Jonsbok. LC 42-7225. (Islandica Ser.: Vol. 28). 1940. pap. 9.00 (ISBN 0-527-00358-1). Kraus Repr.

Hilliard, Nicholas. A Treatise Concerning the Arte of Limning. LC 77-94584. 1979. Repr. of 1912 ed. lib. bdg. 15.00 (ISBN 0-89341-242-2). Longwood Pr.

Hindman, Sandra. Text & Image in Fifteenth-Century Illustrated Dutch Bibles (1977) (Corpus Sacrae Scripturae Neerlandicae Medii Aevi Ser.: Miscellanea: Vol. 1). (Illus.). 35.00 (ISBN 90-04-04901-0). Heinman.

Johnston, Edward. Writing & Illuminating & Lettering. 1977. pap. 10.95 (ISBN 0-8008-8731-X, Pentalic). Taplinger.

Kauffmann, C. M. Romanesque Manuscripts 1066-1190. (A Survey of Manuscripts Illuminated in the British Isles: Vol. 3). (Illus.). 95.00 (ISBN 0-85602-017-6, Pub. by H Miller England). Heyden.

Lehman-Haupt, Hellmut. The Gottingen Model Book. LC 78-62289. (Text in German & English). 1979. text ed. 35.00x (ISBN 0-8262-0261-6). U of Mo Pr.

Leveen, Jacob. The Hebrew Bible in Art. LC 74-78239. (Illus.). 208p. 1974. Repr. 14.50 (ISBN 0-87203-045-8). Hermon.

Lichten, Frances. Fraktur: The Illuminated Manuscripts of the Pennsylvania Dutch. 1958. wrappers 1.00 (ISBN 0-911132-10-4). Phila Free Lib.

Loomis, Roger S. & Hibbard, L. Arthurian Legends in Medieval Art. (MLA Monograph: No. 9). 1938. 41.00 (ISBN 0-527-58300-6). Kraus Repr.

Meiss, Millard. The Tres Riches Heures of Jean, Duke of Berry. (Illus.). 290p. (Gold slipcased). slipcase 60.00 (ISBN 0-8076-0512-3). Braziller.
Mercier, Jacques. Ethiopian Magic Scrolls. Molinaro, Ursule, tr. from Fr. LC 78-9330. (Illus.). 1979. 24.95 (ISBN 0-8076-0896-3); pap. 11.95 (ISBN 0-8076-0897-1). Braziller.
Nordenfalk, Carl, ed. Medieval & Renaissance Miniatures from the National Gallery of Art. LC 74-28397. (Illus.). pap. 8.95 (ISBN 0-686-16181-5). Natl Gallery Art.
Orcutt, William D. In Quest of the Perfect Book. LC 79-86577. (Essay & General Literature Index Reprint Ser). (Illus.). 1969. Repr. of 1926 ed. 18.50 (ISBN 0-8046-0582-3). Kennikat.
Pacht, Otto & Alexander, J. J. Illuminated Manuscripts in the Bodleian Library Vol. 2: Italian Schools. 1970. 25.75x (ISBN 0-19-817169-2). Oxford U Pr.
Pinder-Wilson, R., ed. Paintings from Islamic Lands. LC 69-17154. (Oriental Studies: No. 4). (Illus.). 1969. 19.50x (ISBN 0-87249-138-2). U of SC Pr.
Plummer, John. Book of Hours of Catherine of Cleves. (Illus.). 1964. pap. 5.00 (ISBN 0-87598-011-2). Pierpont Morgan.
Plummer, John, intro. by. The Hours of Catherine of Cleves. LC 66-23096. (Illus.). 360p. 1975. 30.00 (ISBN 0-8076-0379-1). Braziller.
Randall, Lilian M. Images in the Margins of Gothic Manuscripts. (California Studies in the History of Art: No. IV). 1966. 67.50x (ISBN 0-520-01047-7). U of Cal Pr.
Seguy, Marie-Rose. The Miraculous Journey of Mahomet. LC 77-5140. (Library of Illuminated Manuscripts). (Illus.). 1977. 40.00 (ISBN 0-8076-0868-8). Braziller.
Simpson, Marianna S. The Illustration of an Epic: The Earliest Shahnama Manuscripts. LC 78-74379. (Outstanding Dissertations in the Fine Arts, Fourth Ser.). (Illus.). 1979. lib. bdg. 47.00 (ISBN 0-8240-3966-1). Garland Pub.
Temple, E. Anglo-Saxon Manuscripts 900-1066. Alexander, J. J., ed. (A Survey of Manuscripts Illuminated in the British Isles: Vol. 2). (Illus.). 95.00 (ISBN 0-85602-016-8, Pub. by H Miller England). Heyden.
Thomas, Marcel, ed. The Grandes Heures of Jean, Duke of Berry. LC 75-167761. (Illus.). 192p. 1971. 70.00 (ISBN 0-8076-0613-8). Braziller.
Toda, Kenji. Japanese Scroll Painting. LC 35-4632. (Illus.). 1969. Repr. of 1935 ed. lib. bdg. 24.25x (ISBN 0-8371-1883-2, TOSP). Greenwood.
Watson, Ernest W. Forty Illustrators - How They Work. LC 76-121510. (Essay Index Reprint Ser). 1946. 75.00 (ISBN 0-8369-1899-1). Arno.
Weitzmann, Kurt & Loerke, W. Illustrations in Roll & Codex. (Studies in Manuscript Illumination,: Vol. 2). 1970. 40.00x (ISBN 0-691-03865-1). Princeton U Pr.
Welch, Anthony. Artists for the Shah: Late Sixteenth-Century Painting at the Imperial Court of Iran. LC 75-18188. (Illus.). 1976. 30.00x (ISBN 0-300-01915-7). Yale U Pr.
Welch, Stuart C. Imperial Mughal Painting. LC 77-4049. (Magnificent Paperback Art Ser.). (Illus.). 1978. 19.95 (ISBN 0-8076-0870-X); pap. 9.95 (ISBN 0-8076-0871-8). Braziller.

ILLUMINATION OF BOOKS AND MANUSCRIPTS–CATALOGS

Kup, Karl. Christmas Story in Medieval & Renaissance Manuscripts from the Spencer Collection, the New York Public Library. LC 70-98680. (Illus.). 1969. 12.00 (ISBN 0-87104-052-2); pap. 8.50 (ISBN 0-87104-053-0). NY Pub Lib.
New York Public Library, Research Libraries. Dictionary Catalog & Shelf List of the Spencer Collection of Illustrated Books & Manuscripts & Fine Bindings, 2 vols. 1970. Set. lib. bdg. 170.00 (ISBN 0-8161-0862-5). G K Hall.
Ohlgren, Thomas. Illuminated Manuscripts & Books in the Bodleian Library: A Supplemental Index. LC 76-52689. (Reference Library of the Humanities: Vol. 123). 1980. lib. bdg. 85.00 (ISBN 0-8240-9820-X). Garland Pub.
Ohlgren, Thomas C. Illuminated Manuscripts: An Index to Selected Bodleian Library Color Reproductions. (Reference Library of the Humanities: Vol. 89). (LC 76-052689). 1977. lib. bdg. 85.00 (ISBN 0-8240-9884-6). Garland Pub.
Pacht, Otto & Alexander, J. G. Illuminated Manuscripts of the Bodleian Library, Vol. 3: British, Irish, & Icelandic Schools. (Illus.). 182p. 1973. 37.00x (ISBN 0-19-817185-4). Oxford U Pr.
Wolf, Edwin, 2nd, ed. Descriptive Catalogue of the John Frederick Lewis Collection of European Manuscripts. (Illus.). 1937. 15.00 (ISBN 0-911132-04-X). Phila Free Lib.

ILLUMINATION OF BOOKS AND MANUSCRIPTS–EXHIBITIONS

see also Bibliographical Exhibitions

Binney, Edwin. Turkish Miniature Paintings & Manuscripts from the Collection of Edwin Binney, Third. LC 73-11016. (Illus.). 140p. 1973. pap. 3.50 (ISBN 0-87099-077-2). Metro Mus Art.
Binyon, Laurence, et al. Persian Miniature Painting: Including a Critical & Descriptive Catalogue of the Miniatures Exhibited at Burlington House, January Through March, 1931. 1967. pap. 6.00 (ISBN 0-486-22054-0). Dover.
Early Gothic Illuminated Manuscripts in England. 1981. pap. 6.00x (ISBN 0-904654-32-X, Pub. by Brit Lib England). State Mutual Bk.
Romanesque Illuminated Manuscripts in the British Museum. 1981. pap. 6.00x (ISBN 0-7141-0449-3, Pub. by Brit Lib England). State Mutual Bk.
Vikan, Gary, ed. Illuminated Greek Manuscripts from American Collections: An Exhibition in Honor of Kurt Weitzmann. LC 72-92151. (Publication of the Art Museum, Princeton University Ser.). (Illus.). 200p. 1973. 30.00x (ISBN 0-691-03889-9). Princeton U Pr.

ILLUMINATION OF BOOKS AND MANUSCRIPTS–HISTORY

Avril, Francois. Manuscript Painting at the Court of France. (Magnificent Paperback Ser.). (Illus.). 1978. 19.95 (ISBN 0-8076-0878-5); pap. 9.95 (ISBN 0-8076-0879-3). Braziller.
Avril, Francois, ed. Manuscripts Illumination at the Court of France: The Fourteenth Century. LC 77-78721. (Illus.). 1978. 19.95 (ISBN 0-8076-0878-5); pap. 9.95 (ISBN 0-8076-0879-3). Braziller.
Hatch, William H. Greek & Syrian Miniatures in Jerusalem. (Illus.). 1931. 15.00 (ISBN 0-910956-04-9). Medieval Acad.
Kondakov, Nikodim P. Histoire De l'Art Byzantin, Considere Pincipalement dans les Minatures. LC 74-117975. (Research & Source Works Ser: No. 464). 1970. Repr. of 1886 ed. lib. bdg. 50.50 (ISBN 0-8337-1947-5). B Franklin.
Lacaze, Charlotte. The Vie De St. Denis Manuscript. LC 78-74369. (Fine Arts Dissertations, Fourth Ser.). (Illus.). 1980. lib. bdg. 50.00 (ISBN 0-8240-3957-2). Garland Pub.
Morgan. A Survey of Manuscripts Illuminated in the British Isles: Early Gothic Manuscripts 1190-1285, Vol. 4. write for info. (ISBN 0-905203-02-X, Pub. by H Miller England). Heyden.
Simon, Howard. Five Hundred Years of Art in Illustrations: From Albrecht Durer to Rockwell Kent. LC 77-73730. (Illus.). 1978. Repr. of 1942 ed. lib. bdg. 45.00 (ISBN 0-87817-212-2). Hacker.
Weitzmann, Kurt. Studies in Classical & Byzantine Manuscript Illumination. Kessler, Herbert L., ed. LC 76-117623. (Illus.). 1971. 25.00x (ISBN 0-226-89246-8). U of Chicago Pr.
Williams, John. Early Spanish Manuscript Illumination. LC 77-4042. (Magnificent Paperback Art Ser.). (Illus.). 1977. 19.95. (ISBN 0-8076-0866-1); pap. 9.95 (ISBN 0-8076-0867-X). Braziller.

ILLUMINATION OF BOOKS AND MANUSCRIPTS–SPECIMENS, REPRODUCTIONS, ETC.

Brieger, Peter & Meiss, M. Illuminated Manuscripts of the Divine Comedy, 2 Vols. LC 68-20867. (Bollingen Ser., No. 81). (Illus.). 1969. Set. boxed 70.00 (ISBN 0-691-09850-6). Princeton U Pr.
Browne, Edward G. Literary History of Persia, 4 Vols. 1928. 62.00 ea. Vol. 1 (ISBN 0-521-04344-1). Vol. 2 (ISBN 0-521-04345-X). Vol. 3 (ISBN 0-521-04346-8). Vol. 4. Cambridge U Pr.
Buchthal, Hugo & Belting, Hans. Patronage in Thirteenth-Century Constantinople. An Atelier of Late Byzantine Book Illumination & Calligraphy. LC 77-99269. (Dumbarton Oaks Studies: Vol. 16). (Illus.). 124p. 1978. 35.00x (ISBN 0-88402-076-2, Ctr Byzantine). Dumbarton Oaks.
The Cloisters Apocalypse: A Fourteenth-Century Manuscript in Facsimile. LC 77-162342. (Illus.). 1971. 18.75 (ISBN 0-87099-110-8). Metro Mus Art.
Goodspeed, Edgar J., et al, eds. Rockefeller McCormick New Testament, 3 Vols. LC 32-30657. (Illus.). 1932. Set. 100.00x (ISBN 0-226-30379-9). U of Chicago Pr.
Hatch, William H. Greek & Syrian Miniatures in Jerusalem. (Illus.). 1931. 15.00 (ISBN 0-910956-04-9). Medieval Acad.
Introduction to Armenian Manuscript Illumination: A Picture Book. (Illus., Orig.). 1974. pap. 4.00 (ISBN 0-685-48624-9). Walters Art.
Jonsdottir, Selma. Illuminations in a Manuscript of Stjorn. (Illus.). 1980. 11.50 (ISBN 0-906191-74-2, Pub. by Findhorn-Thule Scotland). Hydra Bk.
Kadar. Survivals of Greek Zoological Illuminations in Byzantine Manuscripts. 1979. 63.00 (ISBN 0-9960003-1-3, Pub. by Kaido Hungary). Heyden.
Kadar, Zoltan. Survivals of Greek Zoological Illuminations in Byzantine Manuscripts. (Illus.). 1978. 60.00x (ISBN 963-05-1187-8). Intl Pubns Serv.
Loomis, Roger S. Mirror of Chaucer's World. 1965. 25.00 (ISBN 0-691-06079-7); pap. 9.95 (ISBN 0-691-01349-7). Princeton U Pr.
Narkiss, Bezalel. Hebrew Illuminated Manuscripts in the British Isles: A Catalogue Raisonne, Vol. I; Spanish & Portugese Manuscripts. (Illus.). 492p. 1981. 125.00 (ISBN 0-686-69114-8) (ISBN 0-19-725977-4). Oxford U Pr.
Pelekanidis, S. M., et al. The Treasures of Mount Athos: Illuminated Manuscripts, Vol. 1. (Patriarchal Institute for Patristic Studies Ser.). (Illus.). 500p. 1975. 120.00 (ISBN 0-89241-003-5). Caratzas Bros.
Rickert, Edith, ed. Ancient English Christmans Carols. LC 66-25700. (Medieval Library). (Illus.). Repr. of 1926 ed. 10.00x (ISBN 0-8154-0190-6). Cooper Sq.
--Early English Romances of Friendship. LC 66-30608. (Medieval Library). (Illus.). Repr. of 1926 ed. 7.50x (ISBN 0-8154-0191-4). Cooper Sq.
--Early English Romances of Love. LC 66-30732. (Medieval Library). (Illus.). Repr. of 1926 ed. 8.50x (ISBN 0-8154-0192-2). Cooper Sq.
Simms, G. O. The Book of Kells: A Selection of Pages Reproduced with a Description & Notes. 1976. Repr. of 1961 ed. pap. text ed. 3.75x (ISBN 0-391-00608-8, Dolmen Pr). Humanities.
Spalding, Frances. Mudejar Ornament in Manuscripts. 1953. 4.50 (ISBN 0-87535-078-X). Hispanic Soc.
Thomas, Marcel. The Golden Age: Manuscript Painting at the Time of Jean, Duke of Berry. (Magnificent Paperback Maunscript Ser.). (Illus.). 120p. 1979. 24.95 (ISBN 0-8076-0923-4); pap. 11.95 (ISBN 0-8076-0924-2). Braziller.

ILLUSIONS

see Hallucinations and Illusions

ILLUSIONS, OPTICAL

see Optical Illusions

ILLUSTRATED BOOKS

see also Hours, Books Of; Illumination of Books and Manuscripts–Specimens, Reproductions, etc.

Class of 1926 Memorial Committee. Sampler from the Class of 1926 Memorial Collection of Illustrated Books Published in New England, 1769-1869. LC 77-125188. (Illus.). 36p. 1970. text ed. 10.00x (ISBN 0-87451-995-0); pap. text ed. 5.00x (ISBN 0-87451-994-2). U Pr of New Eng.
Crane, Walter. Of the Decorative Illustration of Books Old & New. LC 68-30611. 1968. Repr. of 1905 ed. 28.00 (ISBN 0-8103-3299-X). Gale.
Davies, Hugh W. Catalog of Early French & German Books in the Library of C. Fairfax Murray, 4 Vols. 280.00x (ISBN 0-87556-065-2); Set. fr. 150.00x (ISBN 0-87556-066-0); Set. ger. 150.00x (ISBN 0-87556-067-9). Saifer.
Flaxman, John. Flaxman's Illustrations to Homer. Essick, Robert & La Belle, Jenijoy, eds. LC 76-62809. 1977. pap. 4.50 (ISBN 0-486-23477-0). Dover.
Freeman, Rosemary. English Emblem Books. 1966. lib. bdg. 15.00x (ISBN 0-374-92888-6). Octagon.
Garvey, Eleanor M. & Wick, Peter A. Arts of the French Book, Nineteen Hundred to Nineteen Sixty-Five: Illustrated Books of the School of Paris. LC 67-16782. (Illus., Orig.). 1967. 12.50 (ISBN 0-87074-056-3); pap. 5.00 (ISBN 0-87074-057-1). SMU Press.
Grabar, Oleg & Blair, Sheila. Epic Images & Contemporary History: The Illustrations of the Great Mongol Shahnama. LC 80-305. 1980. lib. bdg. 27.50x (ISBN 0-226-30585-6). U of Chicago Pr.
Harthan, John. The History of the Illustrated Book: The Western Tradition. (Illus.). 1981. 60.00 (ISBN 0-500-23316-0). Thames Hudson.
Holloway, Owen E. French Rococo Book Illustration. (Illus.). 1969. 15.00 (ISBN 0-85458-140-5). Transatlantic.
Ivins, William M., Jr. Prints & Books. LC 76-75295. (Graphic Art Ser). 1969. Repr. of 1927 ed. lib. bdg. 32.50 (ISBN 0-306-71288-1). Da Capo.
Kent, Rockwell. Illustrations of Rockwell Kent. Johnson, Fridolf, ed. LC 75-28786. (Illus.). 144p. (Orig.). 1976. pap. 5.00 (ISBN 0-486-23305-7). Dover.
Lang, Andrew. Library. LC 68-59288. Repr. of 1881 ed. 14.00 (ISBN 0-404-03816-6). AMS Pr.
Lang, Lothar. Expressionist Book Illustration in Germany, 1907-1927. LC 74-21732. (Illus.). 248p. 1976. 35.00 (ISBN 0-8212-0617-6, 258504). NYGS.
Munce, Howard, ed. Magic & Other Realism. (Library of American Illustration: Vol. 2). (Illus.). 1980. 19.50 (ISBN 0-8038-4721-1). Hastings.
Pollard, Alfred W. Early Illustrated Books. LC 68-26366. (Bibliophile Ser., No. 83). 1969. Repr. of 1893 ed. lib. bdg. 49.95 (ISBN 0-8383-0278-5). Haskell.
--Italian Book Illustrations. LC 73-3363. 1973. Repr. of 1905 ed. lib. bdg. 20.50 (ISBN 0-8337-4328-7). B Franklin.
--Old Picture Books with Other Essays on Bookish Subjects. 1902. 24.50 (ISBN 0-8337-2797-4). B Franklin.
Sketchley, Rose E. English Book-Illustration of To-Day: Appreciations of the Work of Living English Illustrators with Lists of Their Books. LC 78-179655. (Illus.). xxx, 175p. 1974. Repr. of 1903 ed. 29.00 (ISBN 0-8103-4052-6). Gale.
Strachan, W. J. Artist & the Book in France. LC 68-29813. (Illus.). 1969. 45.00 (ISBN 0-8150-0122-3). Wittenborn.
Tooley, Ronald V. Some English Books with Coloured Plates. LC 75-162521. 1971. Repr. of 1935 ed. 25.00 (ISBN 0-8103-3762-2). Gale.
Wofsy, Alan. Prints & Illustrated Books. (Catalogue No. 4 Ser.). (Illus.). 1976. pap. 2.50 (ISBN 0-915346-13-3). A Wofsy Fine Arts.

ILLUSTRATED BOOKS–BIBLIOGRAPHY

Ellis, Jessie C. Index to Illustrations. LC 66-11619. (The Useful Reference Ser. of Library Bks: Vol. 95). 1966. lib. bdg. 13.00x (ISBN 0-87305-095-9). Faxon.
Hind, Arthur M. Introduction to a History of Woodcut, 2 Vols. (Illus.). 10.00 ea. (ISBN 0-8446-2257-5). Peter Smith.
--Introduction to a History of Woodcut with a Detailed Survey of Work Done in the 15th Century, 2 Vols. (Illus.). 1935. pap. 6.00 ea.; Vol. 1. pap. (ISBN 0-486-20952-0); Vol. 2. pap. (ISBN 0-486-20953-9). Dover.
Kristeller, Paul. Early Florentine Woodcuts. 1897. 45.00x (ISBN 0-87556-141-1). Saifer.
New York Public Library, Research Libraries. Dictionary Catalog & Shelf List of the Spencer Collection of Illustrated Books & Manuscripts & Fine Bindings, 2 vols. 1970. Set. lib. bdg. 170.00 (ISBN 0-8161-0862-5). G K Hall.
Olmsted, John C. & Welch, Jeffrey. Victorian Novel Illustration: A Selected Checklist 1900-1976. LC 78-68248. (Reference Library of Humanities Ser.). 1979. lib. bdg. 18.00 (ISBN 0-8240-9773-4). Garland Pub.
Shaw, Renata V., compiled by. Picture Searching: Tools & Techniques. LC 72-13234. (Bibliography Ser.: No. 6). 1973. pap. 3.25 (ISBN 0-87111-207-8). SLA.
Sketchley, Rose E. English Book-Illustration of To-Day: Appreciations of the Work of Living English Illustrators with Lists of Their Books. LC 78-179655. (Illus.). xxx, 175p. 1974. Repr. of 1903 ed. 29.00 (ISBN 0-8103-4052-6). Gale.
Slater, John H. Illustrated Sporting Books. LC 71-75800. 1969. Repr. of 1899 ed. 19.00 (ISBN 0-8103-3889-0). Gale.
Wakeman, Geoffrey. Victorian Book Illustration. LC 72-14042. (Illus.). 200p. 1973. 26.00 (ISBN 0-8103-2008-8). Gale.

ILLUSTRATED BOOKS, CHILDREN'S

see also Caldecott Medal Books; Picture-Books for Children

Andersen, Hans C. Kate Greenaway's Original Drawings for the Snow Queen. Boner, Charles, tr. LC 81-40406. (Illus.). 64p. 1981. 12.95 (ISBN 0-8052-3776-3). Schocken.
Bader, Barbara. American Picturebooks from Noah's Ark to the Beast Within. LC 72-93304. (Illus.). 624p. 1976. 45.00 (ISBN 0-02-708080-3, 70808). Macmillan.
Cianciolo, Patricia J. Illustrations in Childrens Books. 2nd ed. (Children's Literature Ser.). 224p. 1976. pap. text ed. write for info. (ISBN 0-697-06208-2). Wm C Brown.
Freeman, R. S. Children's Picture Books. LC 66-29514. (Victorian Culture Series). (Illus.). 1967. 15.00 (ISBN 0-87282-063-7); pap. 7.50 (ISBN 0-87282-107-2). Century Hse.
Gottlieb, G. Early Children's Books & Their Illustration. (Illus.). 1975. 35.00 (ISBN 0-87598-051-1). Pierpont Morgan.
Kingman, Lee, et al, eds. Illustrators of Children's Books: 1967-1976, Vol. 4. LC 78-13759. (Illus.). 1978. 35.00 (ISBN 0-87675-018-8). Horn Bk.
Klemin, Diana. Art of Art for Children's Books. (Illus.). 1966. 6.95 (ISBN 0-517-02438-1). Potter.
Larkin, David, ed. The Art of Nancy Ekholm Burkert. LC 76-54103. (Illus.). (YA) 1977. 15.00 (ISBN 0-06-023699-X, HarpJ). Har-Row.
Ovenden, Graham. Nymphets & Fairies: Three Victorian Children's Illustrators. LC 76-44580. 1977. pap. 3.95 (ISBN 0-312-58047-9). St Martin.

Poctarnees, Welleran. All Mirrors Are Magic Mirrors. (Illus.). 1981. 16.95 (ISBN 0-914676-30-X, Star & Elephant Bk); pap. 9.95 (ISBN 0-914676-33-4). Star & Elephant.
Urblikova, Anna, ed. Biennial of Illustrations Bratislava '71, '73. (Illus.). 288p. 1976. 20.00 (ISBN 0-87675-277-6). Horn Bk.
Whalley, Joyce I. Cobwebs to Catch Flies: Illustrated Books for the Nursery & Schoolroom 1700-1900. (Illus.). 1975. 19.95 (ISBN 0-520-02931-3). U of Cal Pr.

ILLUSTRATED BOOKS, CHILDREN'S–BIBLIOGRAPHY

Gumuchian & Cie. Les Livres De L'enfance Du Quinzieme Au Dix-Neuvieme Siecle. (Illus.). Repr. 160.00x (ISBN 0-87556-117-9). Saifer.
Kingman, Lee, et al, eds. Illustrators of Children's Books: 1957-1966, Vol. 3. LC 47-31264. (Illus.). 1968. 28.00 (ISBN 0-87675-017-X). Horn Bk.
Mahony, Bertha E., et al, eds. Illustrators of Children's Books: 1744-1945, Vol. 1. (Illus.). 1947. 28.00x (ISBN 0-87675-015-3). Horn Bk.
Miller, et al. Illustrators of Children's Books: 1946-1956, Vol. 2. LC 57-31264. (Illus.). 1958. 28.00 (ISBN 0-87675-016-1). Horn Bk.

ILLUSTRATED CHILDREN'S BOOKS

see Illustrated Books, Children's

ILLUSTRATION, BIOLOGICAL

see Biological Illustration

ILLUSTRATION, MEDICAL

see Medical Illustration

ILLUSTRATION, SCIENTIFIC

see Scientific Illustration

ILLUSTRATION, TECHNICAL

see Technical Illustration

ILLUSTRATION OF BOOKS

see also Caricature; Drawing; Engraving; Illumination of Books and Manuscripts; Illustrated Books; Photomechanical Processes; Scientific Illustration; Technical Illustration;
also subdivisions illustrations or pictures, illustrations, etc. under specific subjects, e.g. Bible–Pictures, eillustrations, etc.; Shakespeare, William–Illustrations

Appel, Marsha C. Illustration Index. 4th ed. LC 79-26091. 468p. 1980. lib. bdg. 22.50 (ISBN 0-8108-1273-8). Scarecrow.
Art of the Book in Central Asia. 314p. 1980. 130.00 (ISBN 92-3-101677-6, U 968, UNESCO). Unipub.
The Association of Illustrators' Third Annual. (Illus.). 1979. 29.95 (ISBN 0-8317-4861-3, Mayflower Bks). Smith Pubs.
Banderly, Mark B. Name It! (Illus.). 128p. (Orig.). 1980. pap. 7.95 (ISBN 0-89104-145-1). A & W Pubs.
Blake, William. William Blake's Design for Edward Young's Night Thoughts: Complete, Vols. 1 & 2. Grant, John E. & Rose, Edward J., eds. (Illus., Vol. 1 382, vol. 2 584). 1980. Set. 365.00x (ISBN 0-19-817312-1). Oxford U Pr.
Blumenthal, Joseph. Art of the Printed Book, Fourteen Fifty-Five to Nineteen Fifty-Five. LC 73-82830. (Illus.). 212p. 1973. 30.00x (ISBN 0-87923-082-7). Godine.
Brenni, Vito J., compiled by. Book Illustration & Decoration: A Guide to Research. LC 80-1701. (Art Reference Collection Ser.: No. 1). viii, 191p. 1980. lib. bdg. 27.50 (ISBN 0-313-22340-8, BBI/). Greenwood.
Butsch, Albert F. Handbook of Renaissance Ornament: 1290 Designs from Decorated Books. Werner, Alfred, ed. LC 68-13685. Orig. Title: Die Bucherornamentik Der Renaissance. (Illus.). 1970. pap. 6.95 (ISBN 0-486-21998-4). Dover.
Chibbett, D. G. The History of Japanese Printing & Book Illustration. LC 76-9362. (Illus.). 264p. 1977. 55.00 (ISBN 0-87011-288-0). Kodansha.
Corbett, Margery & Lightbown, R. W. The Comely Frontispiece: The Emblematic Title-Page in England, 1550-1660. (Illus.). 1979. 35.00x (ISBN 0-7100-8554-0). Routledge & Kegan.
Crane, Walter. Of the Decorative Illustration of Books Old & New. LC 68-30611. 1968. Repr. of 1905 ed. 28.00 (ISBN 0-8103-3299-X). Gale.
Dalley, Terence, ed. The Complete Guide to Illustration & Design: Techniques & Materials. LC 79-13326. (Illus.). Date not set. 19.95 (ISBN 0-8317-1612-6, Mayflower Bks). Smith Pubs.
Dore, Gustave. The Dore Illustrations for Dante's Devine Comedy. LC 75-17176. 1976. lib. bdg. 12.50x (ISBN 0-88307-605-5). Gannon.
Everitt, Graham. English Caricaturists & Graphic Humourists of the Nineteenth Century: How They Illustrated & Interpreted Their Times. fascimile ed. LC 77-37523. (Essay Index Reprint Ser). Repr. of 1885 ed. 17.00 (ISBN 0-8369-2547-5). Arno.
Greer, Roger C. Illustration Index. 3rd ed. LC 72-10918. 1973. 10.00 (ISBN 0-8108-0568-5). Scarecrow.
Hart, Harold, compiled by. The Illustrator's Handbook. (Illus.). 368p. 1981. pap. 10.95 (ISBN 0-89104-278-4). A & W Pubs.
Head, Barclay V. The Illustrations of the Historia Numorum. (Illus.). 1976. 10.00 (ISBN 0-89005-100-3). Ares.
Heck, J. G. Encyclopedia of Source Illustrations, 2 vols. Baird, Spencer F., ed. & tr. (Illus.). 301p. 1972. boxed set 60.00 (ISBN 0-87100-026-1). pap. 36.00 set (ISBN 0-87100-148-9). Morgan.
Henry, Marguerite. The Illustrated Marguerite Henry. LC 80-52017. (Illus.). 128p. (gr. 3-7). 1980. 9.95 (ISBN 0-528-82301-9); PLB 9.97 (ISBN 0-528-80072-8). Rand.
Hill, Mary & Cochran, Wendell. Into Print: A Practical Guide to Writing, Illustrating & Publishing. LC 77-4083. (Illus.). 188p. 1977. 12.00 (ISBN 0-913232-43-2); pap. 6.95 (ISBN 0-913232-44-0). W Kaufmann.
Hodnett, Edward. Aesop in England. LC 78-15268. (Illus.). 1979. 20.00x (ISBN 0-8139-0772-1). U Pr of Va.
--Francis Barlow: First Master of English Book Illustration. LC 76-55570. 1978. 47.50x (ISBN 0-520-03409-0). U of Cal Pr.
Hofer, Philip. Baroque Book Illustration: A Short Survey. LC 51-14003. (Illus.). 1970. 12.50x (ISBN 0-674-06175-6). Harvard U Pr.
Holloway, Owen E. French Rococo Book Illustration. (Illus.). 1969. 15.00 (ISBN 0-85458-140-5). Transatlantic.
Jackson, Arlene M. Illustration & the Novels of Thomas Hardy. (Illus.). 168p. 1981. 25.00x (ISBN 0-8476-6275-6). Rowman.
Jackson, Mason. Pictorial Press: Its Origin & Progress. (Illus.). 1969. 13.00 (ISBN 0-8337-1815-0). B Franklin.
--Pictorial Press, Its Origin & Progress. LC 68-21776. (Illus.). 1968. Repr. of 1885 ed. 19.00 (ISBN 0-8103-3355-4). Gale.
Johnson, Diana L. & Landow, George P. Fantastic Illustration & Design in Britain, Eighteen Fifty to Nineteen Thirty. LC 78-70652. (Illus.). 1979. 25.00 (ISBN 0-686-25091-5); pap. 12.00 (ISBN 0-686-26247-6). Mus of Art RI.
Kingman, Lee, ed. The Illustrator's Notebook. LC 77-20028. (Illus.). 1978. 28.00 (ISBN 0-87675-013-7). Horn Bk.
Kitton, Frederic G. Dickens & His Illustrators. LC 78-148804. (Illus.). Repr. of 1899 ed. 32.50 (ISBN 0-404-08872-4). AMS Pr.
Lyell, James P. Early Book Illustration in Spain. LC 70-143357. (Illus.). 1976. Repr. of 1926 ed. lib. bdg. 45.00 (ISBN 0-87817-076-6). Hacker.
McConnell, Gerald, ed. Illustrators Twenty-One: The Twenty-First Annual of American Illustration. new ed. (Illus.). 368p. 1980. 35.00 (ISBN 0-8038-3427-6, Visual Communication). Hastings.
--Illustrators-Twenty: The Twentieth Annual of American Illustration. (Illus.). 1979. 29.50 (ISBN 0-8038-3420-9). Hastings.
Mahony, Bertha E., et al, eds. Illustrators of Children's Books: 1744-1945, Vol. 1. (Illus.). 1947. 28.00x (ISBN 0-87675-015-3). Horn Bk.
Ovenden, Graham. Nymphets & Fairies: Three Victorian Children's Illustrators. LC 76-44580. 1977. pap. 3.95 (ISBN 0-312-58047-9). St Martin.
Pennell, Joseph. The Illustration of Books. 59.95 (ISBN 0-8490-0384-9). Gordon Pr.
--Illustration of Books: A Manual for the Use of Students. LC 78-146921. 1971. Repr. of 1896 ed. 22.00 (ISBN 0-8103-3641-3). Gale.
Perlman, Bernard B. F. R. Gruger & His Circle: The Golden Age of American Illustration. LC 77-99224. (Illus.). 1978. 14.95 (ISBN 0-89134-011-4, Pub. by Van Nostrand Reinhold). North Light Pub.
Pollard, A. W. Italian Book Illustrations. LC 73-11341. 1894. Repr. lib. bdg. 20.00 (ISBN 0-8414-2481-0). Folcroft.
Ray, Gordon N. The Illustrator & the Book in England, 1790-1914. 1976. 65.00 (ISBN 0-19-519883-2). Oxford U Pr.
Reid, Forrest. Illustrators of the Eighteen Sixties: An Illustrated Survey of the Work of 58 Artists. 8.00 (ISBN 0-8446-5237-7). Peter Smith.
Sainton, Roger. Art Nouveau Posters & Graphics. LC 76-51472. (Illus.). 1977. pap. 12.50 (ISBN 0-8478-0085-7). Rizzoli Intl.
Salaman, Malcolm C. British Book Illustration Yesterday & Today, with Commentary. Holme, Geoffrey, ed. LC 73-175758. (Illus.). viii, 175p. 1974. Repr. of 1923 ed. 30.00 (ISBN 0-8103-3977-3). Gale.
Schapiro, Meyer. Words & Pictures: On the Literal & the Symbolic in the Illustrations of a Text. 1973. pap. text ed. 18.75x (ISBN 0-686-22563-5). Mouton.
Shimizu, Yutaka. Nara Picture Books. Zumwinkle, Richard, tr. from Japanese. 1960. pap. 4.75 (ISBN 0-87093-045-1). Dawsons.
Strachan, W. J. Artist & the Book in France. LC 68-29813. (Illus.). 1969. 45.00 (ISBN 0-8150-0122-3). Wittenborn.
Strauss, Walter L., ed. Bartsch 80: German Book Illustration. 432p. 120.00 (ISBN 0-913870-50-1). Abaris Bks.
--Bartsch 81: German Book Illustrations. (Illus.). 320p. 1981. 120.00 (ISBN 0-89835-052-2). Abaris Bks.
--Bartsch 82: German Book Illustrations. (Illus.). 276p. 1981. 120.00 (ISBN 0-89835-054-9). Abaris Bks.
Sutphen, Dick. The Early Illustrators. LC 76-27145. (Illus.). 1976. 19.50 (ISBN 0-910158-21-5). Art Dir.
Thomas, Payne E. Guide for Authors: Manuscript, Proof & Illustration. 2nd ed. (Illus.). 96p. 1980. pap. 5.25 (ISBN 0-398-03443-5). C C Thomas.
Whalley, Joyce I. Cobwebs to Catch Flies: Illustrated Books for the Nursery & Schoolroom 1700-1900. (Illus.). 1975. 19.95 (ISBN 0-520-02931-3). U of Cal Pr.
White, Gleeson. English Illustration, Eighteen Fifty-Five to Nineteen Seventy. 12.00x (ISBN 0-87556-528-X). Saifer.

ILLUSTRATION OF BOOKS–EXHIBITIONS

see also Bibliographical Exhibitions

Garvey, Eleanor M. & Wick, Peter A. Arts of the French Book, Nineteen Hundred to Nineteen Sixty-Five: Illustrated Books of the School of Paris. LC 67-16782. (Illus., Orig.). 1967. 12.50 (ISBN 0-87074-056-3); pap. 5.00 (ISBN 0-87074-057-1). SMU Press.
Ivins, William M., Jr. Notes on Prints. 1969. pap. 4.95 (ISBN 0-262-59003-4). MIT Pr.
--Notes on Prints. LC 67-25544. (Graphic Art Ser). 1967. Repr. of 1930 ed. lib. bdg. 27.50 (ISBN 0-306-70957-0). Da Capo.
Szladits, Lola L. & Simmonds, Harvey. Pen & Brush: The Author As Artist: An Exhibition in the Berg Collection. LC 71-92623. (Illus.). 1969. pap. 5.00 (ISBN 0-87104-142-1). NY Pub Lib.

ILLUSTRATIONS, HOMILETICAL

see Homiletical Illustrations

ILLUSTRATIONS, HUMOROUS

see Caricatures and Cartoons; Wit and Humor, Pictorial

ILLUSTRATORS

see also Pen Drawing

Appelbaum, Stanley & Kelly, Richard, eds. Great Drawings & Illustrations from Punch Eighteen Forty-One to Nineteen Hundred-One: One Hundred Ninety-Two Works by Leech, Keene, du Maurier, May & 21 Others. (Illus.). 144p. (Orig.). 1981. pap. 6.00 (ISBN 0-486-24110-6). Dover.
Arwas, Victor. Alastair: Illustrator of Decadence. (Illus.). 1979. pap. 8.95 (ISBN 0-500-27152-6). Thames Hudson.
Blegvad, Erik. Self-Portrait: Erik Blegvad. LC 78-23765. (Self-Portrait Collection). (Illus.). 1979. PLB 7.95 (ISBN 0-201-00498-4, A-W Childrens). A-W.
Booth-Clibborn, Edward, ed. European Illustration Seventy-Nine to Eighty: The Sixth Annual of European Editorial, Book, Advertising, Television, Cinema, & Design Art. (Illus.). 1980. 50.00 (ISBN 0-8038-1956-0). Hastings.
Buchanan-Brown, John. Phiz!: Illustrator of Dickens' World. (Encore Editions). (Illus.). 1978. 4.95 (ISBN 0-684-16675-5, ScribT). Scribner.
Commire, Anne, ed. Something About the Author, Vol. 22. LC 72-27107. (Illus.). 375p. 1981. 42.00 (ISBN 0-8103-0085-0). Gale.
Dance, S. Peter. The Art of Natural History: Animal Illustrators & Their Work. LC 78-56076. (Illus.). 224p. 1978. 75.00 (ISBN 0-87951-077-3). Overlook Pr.
De La Ree, Gerry, ed. The Sixth Book of Virgil Finlay. (Illus.). 1980. 15.75 (ISBN 0-938192-06-X). De La Ree.
Dykes, Jeff C. Fifty Great Western Illustrators. LC 73-79780. (Illus.). 550p. 1974. 35.00 (ISBN 0-87358-114-8). Northland.
Engen, Rodney. Randolph Caldecott. 1981. 27.00x (ISBN 0-905368-02-9, Pub. by Jupiter England). State Mutual Bk.
Fisher, Jay M. Theodore Chasseriau: Illustrations for Othello. LC 79-67570. 1980. pap. 13.50 (ISBN 0-912298-50-2). Baltimore Mus.
Freas, Frank K. Frank Kelly Freas: The Art of Science Fiction. LC 77-8644. (Illus.). 1977. pap. 7.95 (ISBN 0-915442-37-X). Donning Co.
Fuller, Muriel, ed. More Junior Authors. (Illus.). 1963. 10.00 (ISBN 0-8242-0036-5). Wilson.
Guerin, Marcel. Forain Aquafortiste. rev. ed. (Illus.). 336p. (Fr.). 1980. 100.00 (ISBN 0-915346-38-9). A Wofsy Fine Arts.
Heneage, Simon & Ford, Henry. Sidney Sime: Master of the Mysterious. 1980. pap. 8.95 (ISBN 0-500-27154-2). Thames Hudson.
Hodnett, Edward. Francis Barlow: First Master of English Book Illustration. LC 76-55570. 1978. 47.50x (ISBN 0-520-03409-0). U of Cal Pr.
Hoffman, Miriam S. & Samuels, Eva A. Authors & Illustrators of Children's Books: Writings on Their Lives & Works. LC 76-38607. 471p. 1972. 17.95 (ISBN 0-8352-0523-1). Bowker.
Hogarth, Paul. The World of Arthur Boyd Houghton. 160p. 1981. 110.00x (ISBN 0-900406-75-5, Pub. by Fraser Bks). State Mutual Bk.
Houfe, Simon, ed. Dictionary of British Book Illustrators & Caricaturists, Eighteen Hundred to Nineteen Fourteen. (Illus.). 520p. 1978. 105.00 (ISBN 0-902028-73-1, Pub. by Antique Collectors Club England). Gale.
Hutchins, Michael, ed. Yours Pictorially. LC 76-2923. (Illus.). 1977. 15.00 (ISBN 0-7232-1981-8). Warne.
Illustrator Illustrated: Art Directors Index to Illustrators. (Illustrator Illustrated Ser.: No. 2). (Illus.). 1981. 55.00 (ISBN 2-88046-004-2, Pub. by Roto-Vision). Norton.
Illustrator Illustrated No. 2: North American Edition. (Illus.). 1981. pap. 12.95 (ISBN 2-88046-007-7). Norton.
Illustrators Annual of American Illustrators, No. 22. Date not set. 37.50 (ISBN 0-686-73835-7). Hastings.
Jessie Willcox Smith (1863-1935) Childhood's Great Illustrator. Freeman, Ruth S., ed. LC 77-82463. (Illus.). 1977. pap. text ed. 4.95x (ISBN 0-87282-105-6). Century Hse.
Johnson, Fridolf, ed. Rockwell Kent. LC 81-47477. (Illus.). 352p. 1981. 45.00 (ISBN 0-394-41771-2). Knopf.
Jones, Cornelia & Way, Olivia R. British Children's Authors. LC 76-44494. 1976. text ed. 10.00 (ISBN 0-8389-0224-3). ALA.
Jones, Helen L. Robert Lawson: Illustrator. (Illus.). 128p. 1972. 7.95 (ISBN 0-316-47281-6). Little.
Kent, Rockwell. It's Me, O Lord: The Autobiography of Rockwell Kent. LC 77-5590. (Graphic Arts Ser.). (Illus.). 1977. Repr. of 1955 ed. lib. bdg. 50.00 (ISBN 0-306-77412-7). Da Capo.
Kingman, Lee, ed. The Illustrator's Notebook. LC 77-20028. (Illus.). 1978. 28.00 (ISBN 0-87675-013-7). Horn Bk.
Kingman, Lee, et al, eds. Illustrators of Children's Books: 1957-1966, Vol. 3. LC 47-31264. (Illus.). 1968. 28.00 (ISBN 0-87675-017-X). Horn Bk.
--Illustrators of Children's Books: 1967-1976, Vol. 4. LC 78-13759. (Illus.). 1978. 35.00 (ISBN 0-87675-018-8). Horn Bk.
Kitton, Frederic G. Dickens & His Illustrators. LC 78-148804. (Illus.). Repr. of 1899 ed. 32.50 (ISBN 0-404-08872-4). AMS Pr.
Klemin, Diana. Art of Art for Children's Books. (Illus.). 1966. 6.95 (ISBN 0-517-02438-1). Potter.
Kunitz, Stanley J. & Haycraft, Howard, eds. Junior Book of Authors. 2nd rev. ed. (Illus.). 1951. 12.00 (ISBN 0-8242-0028-4). Wilson.
Lanes, Selma G. The Art of Maurice Sendak. (Illus.). 264p. 1980. 45.00 (ISBN 0-8109-1600-2, 1600-2). Abrams.
Leach, Bernard, ed. Michael Cardew. (Illus., Orig.). 1976. 9.95 (ISBN 0-8230-0563-1). Watson-Guptill.
McConnell, Gerald, ed. Illustrators: A Visual Communication Book. 35.00 (ISBN 0-8038-3427-6). Hastings.
Mackie, George. Lynton Lamb: Illustrator. (Illus.). 128p. 1979. 17.95x (ISBN 0-85967-473-8, Pub. by Scolar Pr England). Biblio Dist.
Mahoney, Bertha & Whitney, Elinor. Contemporary Illustrators of Children's Books. LC 79-185381. (Illus.). 1978. Repr. of 1930 ed. 38.00 (ISBN 0-8103-4308-8). Gale.
Mahony, Bertha E., et al, eds. Illustrators of Children's Books: 1744-1945, Vol. 1. (Illus.). 1947. 28.00x (ISBN 0-87675-015-3). Horn Bk.
Meyer, Susan E. America's Great Illustrators. LC 77-12715. (Illus.). 1978. 45.00 (ISBN 0-8109-0680-5). Abrams.
Miller, et al. Illustrators of Children's Books: 1946-1956, Vol. 2. LC 57-31264. (Illus.). 1958. 28.00 (ISBN 0-87675-016-1). Horn Bk.
Mitchell, Eugene F. The Subject Was Children: Jessie Willcox Smith. (Illus.). 1980. 19.95 (ISBN 0-525-21185-3); pap. 10.95 (ISBN 0-525-47601-6). Dutton.
Nuzzi, Christina. Umberto Brunelleschi: Fashion Stylist, Illustrator, Stage & Costume Designer. LC 79-88271. (Illus.). 1979. pap. 12.50 (ISBN 0-8478-0225-6). Rizzoli Intl.
Ovenden, Graham. The Illustrators of Alice in Wonderland. 1980. pap. 4.95 (ISBN 0-312-40846-3). St Martin.
--Nymphets & Fairies: Three Victorian Children's Illustrators. LC 76-44580. 1977. pap. 3.95 (ISBN 0-312-58047-9). St Martin.
Peppin, Brigid. Dictionary of Book Illustrators, 1800-1970. (Illus.). 544p. Date not set. 30.00 (ISBN 0-668-04366-0). Arco.
Perlman, Bernard B. F. R. Gruger & His Circle: The Golden Age of American Illustration. LC 77-99224. (Illus.). 1978. 14.95 (ISBN 0-89134-011-4, Pub. by Van Nostrand Reinhold). North Light Pub.
Reed, Walt. Great American Illustrators. LC 79-5378. 156p. 1980. 17.95 (ISBN 0-89659-075-5). Abbeville Pr.

--The Magic Pen of Joseph Clement Coll. LC 77-99225. (Illus.). 1978. pap. 8.95 (ISBN 0-89134-009-2, Pub. by Van Nostrand Reinhold). North Light Pub.

Reid, Forrest. Illustrators of the Eighteen Sixties. LC 74-12539. Orig. Title: Illustrators of the Sixties. 352p. 1975. pap. 5.00 (ISBN 0-486-23121-6). Dover.

--Illustrators of the Eighteen Sixties: An Illustrated Survey of the Work of 58 Artists. 8.00 (ISBN 0-8446-5237-7). Peter Smith.

Rudman, Jack. Illustrator. (Career Examination Ser.: C-379). (Cloth bdg. avail. on request). pap. 8.00 (ISBN 0-8373-0379-6). Natl Learning.

Salaman, Malcolm C. British Book Illustration Yesterday & Today, with Commentary. Holme, Geoffrey, ed. LC 73-175758. (Illus.). viii, 175p. 1974. Repr. of 1923 ed. 30.00 (ISBN 0-8103-3977-3). Gale.

Tinkleman, Murray. The Illustrations of Murray Tinkelman. (Illus.). 111p. 15.00 (ISBN 0-910158-59-2); pap. 8.95 (ISBN 0-686-65838-8). Art Dir.

Ward, Martha E. & Marquardt, Dorothy A. Illustrators of Books for Young People. 2nd ed. LC 75-9880. 223p. 1975. 10.00 (ISBN 0-8108-0819-6). Scarecrow.

Watson, Ernest W. Forty Illustrators - How They Work. LC 76-121510. (Essay Index Reprint Ser). 1946. 75.00 (ISBN 0-8369-1899-1). Arno.

Weithas, Art, ed. Twenty Years of Award Winners from the Society of Illustrators. (Illus.). 352p. 1981. 65.00 (ISBN 0-8038-7224-0, Visual Communication). Hastings.

White, Gabriel. Edward Ardizzone. LC 80-16213. (Illus.). 200p. 1980. 22.50 (ISBN 0-8052-3754-2). Schocken.

Witty, Ken. A Day in the Life of an Illustrator. LC 80-54100. (Illus.). 32p. (gr. 4 up). 1981. PLB 6.89 (ISBN 0-89375-448-X); pap. 2.50 (ISBN 0-89375-449-8). Troll Assocs.

Woolsey, Raymond H. & Anderson, Ruth. Harry Anderson: The Man Behind the Paintings. LC 76-15700. (Illus.). 1976. 7.95 (ISBN 0-8280-0047-6). Review & Herald.

Zemach, Margot. Self-Portrait: Margot Zemach. LC 78-17140. (Self-Portrait Collection). (Illus.). 1978. PLB 7.95 (ISBN 0-201-09096-1, A-W Childrens). A-W.

ILLYES, GYULA

Gara, Laszlo. Az Ismeretlen Illyes. 2nd ed. LC 65-28178. (Hungarian). 1969. 6.00 (ISBN 0-911050-34-5). Occidental.

Illyes, Gyula. Tribute to Gyula Illyes: Poems. Kabdebo, Thomas & Tabori, Paul, eds. Watkins, Vernon, et al, trs. LC 68-58722. 1968. 8.00 (ISBN 0-911050-32-9). Occidental.

ILLYRIAN LANGUAGE (SLAVIC)

see Serbo-Croatian Language

ILLYRIANS

Stipcevic, Aleksander, ed. The Illyrians. Burton, Stojana C., tr. from Yugoslavian. LC 77-150. (History & Culture Ser.). (Illus.). 1977. 24.00 (ISBN 0-8155-5052-9, NP). Noyes.

ILOKANOS

Bernabe, Emma, et al. Ilokano Lessons. McKaughan, Howard P., ed. (PALI Language Texts: Philippines). (Orig.). 1971. pap. text ed. 8.00x (ISBN 0-87022-074-8). U Pr of Hawaii.

Constantino, Ernesto. Ilokano Dictionary. McKaughan, Howard P., ed. (PALI Language Texts: Philippines). (Orig.). 1971. pap. text ed. 7.00x (ISBN 0-87022-152-3). U Pr of Hawaii.

IMAGE, BODY

see Body Image

IMAGE CONVERTERS

Aggarwal, J. K., et al, eds. Computer Methods in Image Analysis. LC 76-50335. 1977. 39.95 (ISBN 0-87942-089-8). Inst Electrical.

Bolc, L. & Kulpa, Z., eds. Digital Image Processing Systems: Proceedings. (Lecture Notes in Computer Science Ser.: Vol. 109). 353p. 1981. pap. 20.00 (ISBN 0-387-10705-3). Springer-Verlag.

Fu, K. S. & Pavlidis, T., eds. Biomedical Pattern Recognition & Image Processing. (Dahlem Workshop Reports-Life Sciences Reseach Report Ser.: No. 15). 1979. 33.80 (ISBN 0-89573-097-9). Verlag Chemie.

Herman, G. T., ed. Image Reconstruction from Projections Implementation & Applications. LC 79-13823. (Topics in Applied Physics Ser.: Vol. 32). (Illus.). 1979. 51.50 (ISBN 0-387-09417-2). Springer-Verlag.

IMAGE INTENSIFIERS

see also Electron Microscope; Image Converters; Television Picture Tubes

Jacobson, K. I. & Jacobson, R. E. Imaging Systems: Mechanism & Applications of Established & New Photosensitive Processes. LC 76-23144. 1976. 38.95 (ISBN 0-470-98905-X). Halsted Pr.

Machine-Aided Image Analysis Nineteen Seventy-Eight: Oxford. (Institute of Physics Conference Ser.: No. 44). 1979. 75.00 (ISBN 0-9960032-4-X, Pub. by Inst Physics England). Heyden.

Machine Perception of Patterns & Pictures: 1972. (Institute of Physics Conference Ser.: No. 13). 1972. 45.00 (ISBN 0-9960029-2-8, Pub. by Inst Physics England). Heyden.

Misell, D. L. Image Analysis, Enhancement & Interpretation. (Practical Methods in Electron Microscopy: Vol. 7). 1979. pap. 31.75 (ISBN 0-7204-0666-8, North Nolland). Elsevier.

Watson, B. W., ed. Medical Imaging Techniques. (IEE Medical Electronics Monographs: No. 6). (Illus.). 1979. 47.00 (ISBN 0-906048-20-6). Inst Elect Eng.

IMAGE TUBES

see Image Converters

IMAGERY (PSYCHOLOGY)

see also Eidetic Imagery

Block, Ned J., ed. Imagery. LC 81-24732. 192p. 1981. text ed. 15.00x (ISBN 0-262-02168-4, Pub. by Bradford); pap. text ed. 7.50x (ISBN 0-262-52072-9). MIT Pr.

Blom, Dorothea. Art Imagery & the Mythic Process. LC 77-91636. (Illus.). 31p. (Orig.). 1977. pap. 0.95x (ISBN 0-87574-215-7). Pendle Hill.

Bugelski, B. R. Principles of Learning & Memory. LC 78-19760. 1979. 21.95 (ISBN 0-03-046596-6). Præger.

Dainty, J. C. & Shaw, R. Image Science: Principles, Analysis, & Evaluation of Picture-Imaging Processes. 1975. 67.00 (ISBN 0-12-200850-2). Acad Pr.

Epstein, Gerald. Waking Dream Therapy: Dream Process As Imagination. 240p. 1981. 19.95 (ISBN 0-89885-018-5). Human Sci Pr.

Kaufman, Geir. Imagery, Language & Cognition. 1979. 19.00x (ISBN 82-00-01961-6). Universitet.

King, Donald L. Conditioning: An Image Approach. LC 78-7268. 1979. 27.95 (ISBN 0-470-26386-5). Halsted Pr.

Kosslyn, Stephen M. Image & Mind. LC 80-10329. (Illus.). 515p. 1980. text ed. 20.00x (ISBN 0-674-44365-9). Harvard U Pr.

Nicholas, John M., ed. Images, Perception & Knowledge. (Western Ontario Ser: No. 8). 1977. lib. bdg. 50.00 (ISBN 90-277-0782-0, Pub. by Reidel Holland). Kluwer Boston.

Nimmo, Dan & Savage, Robert L. Candidates & Their Images: Concepts, Methods & Findings. LC 75-21173. 288p. 1976. pap. text ed. 9.95 (ISBN 0-87620-154-0). Goodyear.

Paivio, Allan. Imagery & Verbal Processes. LC 73-150787. 608p. 1979. text ed. 29.95x (ISBN 0-89859-069-8). L Erlbaum Assocs.

Piaget, Jean & Inhelder, Barbel. Mental Imagery in the Child: A Study of the Development of Imaginal Representation. LC 79-150811. 1971. 13.50x (ISBN 0-465-04498-0). Basic.

Shepard. Mental Images. Date not set. 22.50x (ISBN 0-686-31120-5, Pub. by Bradford). MIT Pr.

Shepard, Roger N. & Cooper, Lynn A. Mental Images & Their Transformations. (Illus.). 1982. text ed. 22.50x (ISBN 0-262-19200-4, Pub. by Bradford). MIT Pr.

Shorr, Joseph B., et al, eds. Imagery: Its Many Demensions & Applications. 405p. 1980. 32.50 (ISBN 0-306-40456-7, Plenum Pr). Plenum Pub.

Singer, Jerome L. Imagery & Daydream Methods in Psychotherapy & Behavior Modification. 1974. 32.50 (ISBN 0-12-646665-3). Acad Pr.

Spencer, Harold. The Image Maker. LC 74-13116. (Illus.). 1975. encore ed. o.p. 6.95 (ISBN 0-684-15263-0, ScribC); (ScribC). Scribner.

IMAGERY, EIDETIC

see Eidetic Imagery

IMAGES AND IDOLS

see Idols and Images

IMAGINARY ANIMALS

see Animal Lore; Animals, Mythical

IMAGINARY BATTLES

see Imaginary Wars and Battles

IMAGINARY CITIES

see Geographical Myths

IMAGINARY CONVERSATIONS

Landor, Walter S. Selected Imaginary Conversations of Literary Men & Statesmen. Proudfit, Charles L., ed. LC 69-10272. xx, 270p. 1969. 17.50x (ISBN 0-8032-0097-8). U of Nebr Pr.

IMAGINARY IMPRINTS

see Imprints (In Books), Fictitious

IMAGINARY ISLANDS

see Geographical Myths

IMAGINARY QUANTITIES

see Numbers, Complex

IMAGINARY VOYAGES

see Voyages, Imaginary

IMAGINARY WARS AND BATTLES

Colomb, P., et al. The Great War of 189- A Forecast. LC 74-16390. (Science Fiction Ser). (Illus.). 320p. 1975. Repr. of 1893 ed. 20.00x (ISBN 0-685-51336-X). Arno.

Siecke, Ernst. Drachenkampfe: Untersuchungen Sagenkunde, Vol. 1-pt. 1. Bolle, Kees W., ed. LC 77-79155. (Mythology Ser.). (Ger.). 1978. Repr. of 1907 ed. lib. bdg. 12.00x (ISBN 0-405-10564-9). Arno.

IMAGINATION

see also Creative Ability; Eidetic Imagery; Fantasy; Imagery (Psychology)

Alkema, Chester J. Alkema's Complete Guide to Creative Art for Young People. LC 70-167654. (Illus.). 1971. 16.95 (ISBN 0-8069-5188-5); PLB 14.99 (ISBN 0-8069-5189-3). Sterling.

Avens, Robert. Imagination Is Reality. rev. ed. Severson, Bedford A., ed. 128p. 1979. pap. 7.00 (ISBN 0-88214-311-5). Spring Pubns.

Avens, Roberts. Imagination: A Way Toward Western Nirvana. LC 78-68693. 1979. pap. text ed. 8.25 (ISBN 0-8191-0697-6). U Pr of Amer.

Bachelard, Gaston. On Poetic Imagination & Reverie: Selections from the Works of Gaston Bachelard. Gaudin, C., ed. LC 73-148015. (Library of Liberal Arts Ser). 1971. pap. 3.95 (ISBN 0-672-61187-2). Bobbs.

--Poetics of Space. Joles, Maria, tr. 1969. pap. 5.95 (ISBN 0-8070-6439-4, BP330). Beacon Pr.

--The Poetics of Space. Jolas, Maria, tr. from Fr. 1964. 7.50 (ISBN 0-670-56269-6, Grossman). Viking Pr.

Baker, James V. Sacred River: Coleridge's Theory of the Imagination. LC 73-90466. Repr. of 1957 ed. lib. bdg. 15.00 (ISBN 0-8371-2205-8, BASR). Greenwood.

Bakhtin, M. M. The Dialogic Imagination: Four Essays. Holquist, Micheal, ed. Emerson, Caryl, tr. (University of Texas Press Slavic Ser.: No. 1). 477p. 1981. 25.00 (ISBN 0-292-71527-7). U of Tex Pr.

Berenbaum, Linda B. The Gothic Imagination: Expansion in Gothic Literature & Art. LC 80-67035. (Illus.). 140p. 1981. 15.00 (ISBN 0-8386-3068-5). Fairleigh Dickinson.

Betts, George H. The Distribution & Functions of Mental Imagery. LC 76-176560. (Columbia University. Teachers College. Contributions to Education: No. 26). Repr. of 1909 ed. 17.50 (ISBN 0-404-55026-6). AMS Pr.

Bodkin, Maud. Archetypal Patterns in Poetry: Psychological Studies of Imagination. (Oxford Paperbacks Ser). pap. 8.95x (ISBN 0-19-281018-9). Oxford U Pr.

Brett, R. L. Fancy & Imagination. (Critical Idiom Ser.: Vol. 6). 1969. pap. 5.50 (ISBN 0-416-15820-X). Methuen Inc.

Bronowski, Jacob. The Origins of Knowledge & Imagination. LC 77-13209. (Silliman Lectures Ser.). 1978. 12.50 (ISBN 0-300-02192-5); pap. 3.95 (ISBN 0-300-02409-6). Yale U Pr.

Bundy, Murray W. Theory of Imagination in Classical & Mediaeval Thought. LC 76-40267. 1927. lib. bdg. 25.00 (ISBN 0-8414-1795-4). Folcroft.

Casey, Edward S. Imagining: A Phenomenological Study. LC 76-12370. (Studies in Phenomenology & Existential Philosophy). 256p. 1976. 12.50x (ISBN 0-253-32912-4); pap. text ed. 6.95x (ISBN 0-253-20228-0). Ind U Pr.

Centeno, Augusto, ed. Intent of the Artist, by Sherwood Anderson, Thornton Wilder, Roger Sessions, & William Lescaze. LC 71-81455. 1970. Repr. of 1941 ed. 8.50 (ISBN 0-8462-1358-3). Russell.

Chiari, Joseph. Realism & Imagination. LC 74-131248. 1970. Repr. of 1960 ed. text ed. 9.00 (ISBN 0-87752-019-4). Gordian.

Cobb, Edith. The Ecology of Imagination in Childhood. LC 77-361. 139p. 1977. 10.00x (ISBN 0-231-03870-4). Columbia U Pr.

Copland, Aaron. Music & Imagination. LC 52-9385. (Charles Eliot Norton Lectures Ser: 1951-1952). 1952. pap. 2.95 (ISBN 0-674-58915-7). Harvard U Pr.

Corbin, Henri. Avicenna & the Visionary Recital. Task, Willard R., tr. from French. 320p. 1980. pap. text ed. 13.50 (ISBN 0-88214-213-5). Spring Pubns.

Davenport, Guy. The Geography of the Imagination. LC 80-23870. 400p. 1981. 20.00 (ISBN 0-86547-000-6); pap. 10.00 (ISBN 0-86547-001-4). N Point Pr.

De Fer, Hugo. The Metaphysics of Inventiveness. (Illus.). 200p. 1976. 34.15 (ISBN 0-913314-72-2). Am Classical Coll Pr.

Dekker, Julian. How to Master the Forces of Your Imagination for the Pursuit of Your Scientific Objectives. (Illus.). 1978. deluxe ed. 37.50 (ISBN 0-930582-07-1). Gloucester Art.

Demille, Robert. Put Your Mother on the Ceiling. 1976. pap. 3.95 (ISBN 0-14-004379-9). Penguin.

Donoghue, Denis. The Sovereign Ghost: Studies in Imagination. LC 75-27923. 1977. 15.95x (ISBN 0-520-03134-2). U of Cal Pr.

Durr, Robert A. Poetic Vision & the Psychedelic Experience. LC 78-112038. 1970. 14.95x (ISBN 0-8156-0067-4). Syracuse U Pr.

Ehrenzweig, Anton. The Hidden Order of Art: A Study in the Psychology of Artistic Imagination. LC 67-20443. (California Library Reprint Ser). 1976. 24.50x (ISBN 0-520-03181-4, CAL 418); pap. 6.95 (ISBN 0-520-03845-2). U of Cal Pr.

Engell, James. The Creative Imagination: Enlightenment to Romanticism. LC 80-20265. 435p. 1981. text ed. 16.00x (ISBN 0-674-17572-7). Harvard U Pr.

Epstein, Gerald. Waking Dream Therapy: Dream Process As Imagination. 240p. 1981. 19.95 (ISBN 0-89885-018-5). Human Sci Pr.

Griffiths, Ruth. Study of Imagination in Early Childhood & Its Function in Mental Development. Repr. of 1935 ed. lib. bdg. 16.75x (ISBN 0-8371-3427-7, GRIM). Greenwood.

Griffiths, Ruth & Harvey, Nathan A. A Study of Imagination in Early Childhood & Its Function in Mental Development: Imaginary Playmates & Other Mental Phenomena of Children. LC 74-21411. (Classics in Child Development Ser). 390p. 1975. Repr. 28.00x (ISBN 0-405-06463-2). Arno.

Guerin, Dominique. La Politique de l'Imaginaire. (Archontes Ser.: No. 1). 140p. (Fr.). 1975. pap. text ed. 23.75x (ISBN 90-2797-795-X). Mouton.

Hamilton, G. Rostrevor. Guides & Marshals: An Essay on Words & Imaginative Order. 1956. lib. bdg. 20.00 (ISBN 0-8482-9971-X). Norwood Edns.

Hannah, Barbara. Encounters with the Soul: Active Imagination As Developed by C. G. Jung. LC 81-5316. 264p. 1981. 15.00 (ISBN 0-938434-04-7); pap. 9.50 (ISBN 0-938434-02-0). Sigo Pr.

Hill, John S., ed. Imagination in Coleridge. 232p. 1978. 20.00x (ISBN 0-8476-6026-5). Rowman.

How to Stimulate the Force of Your Imagination for the Development of a Creative Mentality. (YA) 28.55 (ISBN 0-89266-037-6). Am Classical Coll Pr.

Inglis, F. Ideology & Imagination. LC 74-82220. 240p. 1975. 27.50 (ISBN 0-521-20540-9); pap. 8.95x (ISBN 0-521-09886-6). Cambridge U Pr.

Kennedy, Wilma L. English Heritage of Coloridge of Bristol, Seventeen Ninety-Eight; The Basis in Eighteenth Century English Thought for His Distinction Between Imagination & Fancy. LC 69-15685. (Yale Studies in English Ser.: No. 104). 1969. Repr. of 1947 ed. 13.50 (ISBN 0-208-00771-7, Archon). Shoe String.

Kubat, D. Paths of Sociological Imagination. 1971. 63.75 (ISBN 0-685-99244-6). Gordon.

Lynch, William F. Images of Hope: Imagination As Healer of the Hopeless. LC 85-5364. 320p. 1974. 10.95x (ISBN 0-268-00536-2); pap. 4.95 (ISBN 0-268-00537-0). U of Notre Dame Pr.

MacBeth, John W. The Might & Mirth of Literature: A Treatise on Figurative Language. 1875. 45.00 (ISBN 0-8495-6257-0). Arden Lib.

Markey, Frances V. Imaginative Behavior of Preschool Children. LC 75-35075. (Studies in Play & Games). 1976. Repr. 10.00x (ISBN 0-405-07925-7). Arno.

Moore, Marvin. How to Handle Your Imagination. LC 78-13660. (Flame Ser.). 1979. pap. 0.95 (ISBN 0-8127-0195-X). Review & Herald.

Needham, Rodney. Primordial Characters. LC 78-17230. (Illus.). 1978. 7.95x (ISBN 0-8139-0774-8). U Pr of Va.

Osborn, Alex F. Your Creative Power. (Lib. Rep. Ed.). 1972. 20.00x (ISBN 0-684-15314-9, ScribT). Scribner.

Pico della Mirandola, Giovanni. On the Imagination. Caplan, Harry, tr. & notes by. LC 72-113063. ix, 102p. (Lat. & Eng.). Repr. of 1930 ed. lib. bdg. 15.00x (ISBN 0-8371-4703-4, PIOI). Greenwood.

Reguerio, Helen. The Limits of Imagination: Wordsworth, Yeats, & Stevens. LC 76-13663. 1976. 17.50x (ISBN 0-8014-0994-2). Cornell U Pr.

Ribot, Theodule A. Essay on the Creative Imagination. LC 73-2987. (Classics in Psychology Ser.). Repr. of 1906 ed. 18.00 (ISBN 0-405-05159-X). Arno.

Rycroft, Charles. Imagination & Reality. 1968. text ed. 20.00 (ISBN 0-8236-2520-6). Intl Univs Pr.

Sartre. Psychology of Imagination. pap. 4.95 (ISBN 0-8065-0305-X). Citadel Pr.

Sartre, Jean-Paul. L' Imaginaire. new ed. 384p. 1970. 4.50 (ISBN 0-686-54980-5). French & Eur.

--L' Imagination. (Nouveau Coll. Scientifique). pap. 11.50 (ISBN 0-685-36562-X). French & Eur.

--Imagination: A Psychological Critique. Williams, Forrest, tr. from Fr. 1972. pap. 5.95 (ISBN 0-472-06185-2, 185, AA). U of Mich Pr.

--Psychology of Imagination. 1980. pap. 4.95 (ISBN 0-8065-0305-X). Lyle Stuart.

Sartre, Jean Paul. The Psychology of Imagination. LC 78-6632. 1978. lib. bdg. 25.75x (ISBN 0-313-20498-5, SAPI). Greenwood.

Sawyers, Phyllis & Henry, Frances L. Song of the Coyote: Freeing the Imagination Through the Arts. (Illus.). 173p. (Orig.). 1980. pap. text ed. 21.95x (ISBN 0-686-63063-7). American Pr.

Sheikh, A. A. & Shaffer, John T. The Potential of Fantasy & Imagination. LC 79-88092. 1979. lib. bdg. 15.00 (ISBN 0-913412-31-7). Brandon Hse.

Singer, Jerome L. The Child's World of Make-Believe: Experimental Studies of Imaginative Play. (Child Psychology Series: Experimental & Theoretical Analyses of Child Behavior). 1973. 25.50 (ISBN 0-12-646660-2). Acad Pr.

Singer, K. S. & Pope, J. L., eds. The Power of Human Imagination. LC 78-15392. (Emotions, Personality, & Psychotherapy Ser.). (Illus.). 425p. 1978. 25.00 (ISBN 0-306-31140-2, Plenum Pr). Plenum Pub.

Slosson, Edwin E. & Downey, J. Plots & Personalities: A New Method of Testing & Training the Creative Imagination. 1922. Repr. 20.00 (ISBN 0-8274-3145-7). R West.

Sprigge, L. S. Facts, Words & Beliefs. (International Library of Philosophy & Scientific Method). 1970. text ed. 15.00x (ISBN 0-391-00069-1). Humanities.

Tarbox, Todd. Imagine & Make up Your Own Book. (Illus.). 1976. 4.95 (ISBN 0-89297-016-2); pap. 3.50 (ISBN 0-89297-003-0). Todd Tarbox.

Thompson, Vernon. Reading Imaginative Literature. LC 74-24533. 1975. pap. 5.00x (ISBN 0-912112-06-9). Everett-Edward.

Tuveson, Ernest L. Imagination As a Means of Grace. LC 73-21543. 218p. 1973. Repr. of 1960 ed. 10.00 (ISBN 0-87752-173-5). Gordian.

Tyndall, John. The Art of Physical Investigation & the Scientific Use of Man's Imagination. (Illus.). 1979. Repr. of 1898 ed. 47.75 (ISBN 0-89901-001-6). Found Class Reprints.

Wakayama, Shizuko. Out for a Walk. (Fun Time Ser.). (Illus.). 22p. (ps-1). 1981. 2.95 (ISBN 0-89346-196-2). Heian Intl.

Warnock, Mary. Imagination. LC 75-22663. 1976. 24.75x (ISBN 0-520-03724-3); pap. 3.95 (ISBN 0-520-03115-6). U of Cal Pr.

Willey, Basil. Coleridge on Imagination. 1977. 16.50 (ISBN 0-685-86327-1). Porter.

Wilner, Eleanor R. Gathering the Winds: Visionary Imagination & Radical Transformation of Self & Society. LC 75-9846. (Illus.). 208p. 1975. 13.50x (ISBN 0-8018-1670-X). Johns Hopkins.

Wilson, Colin. The Strength to Dream: Literature & the Imagination. LC 73-2876. 277p. 1973. Repr. of 1962 ed. lib. bdg. 19.75x (ISBN 0-8371-6819-8, WISD). Greenwood.

Wlecke, Albert O. Wordsworth & the Sublime: An Essay on Romantic Self-Consciousness. (Perspectives in Criticism: No. 23). 1973. 19.50x (ISBN 0-520-02233-5). U of Cal Pr.

IMAGING SYSTEMS

Alais, Pierre & Metherell, Alexander F., eds. Acoustical Imaging, Vol. 10. 842p. 1981. 85.00 (ISBN 0-306-40725-6, Plenum Pr). Plenum Pub.

Amelinckx, S., et al, eds. Diffraction & Imaging Techniques in Materials Science: Vol. 1, Electron Microscopy. rev. ed. 1978. 61.00 (ISBN 0-444-85128-3, North Holland). Elsevier.

--Diffraction & Imaging Techniques in Materials Science: Vol. 2, Imaging & Diffraction Techniques. rev. ed. 1978. 61.00 (ISBN 0-444-85129-1, North Holland). Elsevier.

Castleman, Kenneth R. Digital Image Processing. LC 78-27578. (Illus.). 1979. text ed. 34.00 (ISBN 0-13-212365-7). P-H.

Chang, Ning-San. Image Analysis & Image Database Management. Stone, Harold S., ed. LC 81-10406. (Computer Science: Artificial Intelligence Ser.: No. 9). 1981. write for info. (ISBN 0-8357-1217-6, Pub. by UMI Res Pr). Univ Microfilms.

Clifton, Nancy A. & Simmons, Pamela J. Basic Imaging Procedures in Nuclear Medicine. 159p. 1981. pap. 13.95 (ISBN 0-8385-0578-3). ACC.

Coulam, Craig M., ed. Physical Basis of Medical Imaging. (Illus.). 354p. 1981. 49.50 (ISBN 0-8385-7844-6). ACC.

Duff, M. J. & Leviadi, S., eds. Languages & Architectures for Image Processing. 1981. price not set (ISBN 0-12-223320-4). Acad Pr.

Huang, T. S., ed. Picture Processing & Digital Filtering. (Topics in Applied Physics: Vol. 6). (Illus., Second & updated edition). 1979. pap. 20.80 (ISBN 0-387-09339-7). Springer-Verlag.

International Conference Under the Headings of Phenomenological Aspects, Optical System Design, Components, Techniques, Application, 2nd. Low Light & Thermal Imaging: Proceedings. (IEE Conference Publications Ser.: No. 173). 1979. soft bdg. 24.00 (ISBN 0-85296-201-0). Inst Elect Eng.

Klinger, E., ed. Imagery, Vol. 2: Concepts, Results, & Applications. 399p. 1981. 35.00 (ISBN 0-686-73236-7, Plenum Pr). Plenum Pub.

Lalli. Tailored Urologic Imaging. 1981. 39.95 (ISBN 0-8151-5276-0). Year Bk Med.

Mycardial Imaging. (Landmark Ser.). 1979. 22.50x (ISBN 0-8422-4107-8). Irvington.

Onoe, Morio, et al, eds. Real-Time-Parallel Computing: Imaging Analysis. 397p. 1981. 45.00 (ISBN 0-306-40639-X, Plenum Pr). Plenum Pub.

Preston, Kendall, et al, eds. Medical Imaging Techniques: A Comparison. LC 79-4424. 396p. 1979. 37.50 (ISBN 0-306-40161-4, Plenum Pr). Plenum Pub.

Putman, Charles E., ed. Pulmonary Diagnosis: Imaging & Other Techniques. 320p. 1981. 46.50 (ISBN 0-8385-8058-0). ACC.

Rosenfeld, Azriel, ed. Image Modeling. 1981. write for info. (ISBN 0-12-597320-9). Acad Pr.

Sodee, D. B., ed. Correlations in Diagnostic Imaging: Nuclear Medicine, Ultrasound & Computed Tomography in Medical Practice. (Illus.). 165p. 1979. 22.00 (ISBN 0-8385-1234-8). ACC.

Stucki, ed. Advances in Digital Image Processing: Theory, Application, Implementation. (IBM Research Symposia Ser.). 1979. 37.50 (ISBN 0-306-40314-5, Plenum Pr). Plenum Pub.

Sutton, David. Textbook of Radiology & Imaging, 2 vols. 3rd ed. 1981. Vol. 1 Set. text ed. 149.00 (ISBN 0-443-01700-X); Vol. 2 Set. text ed. 175.00 (ISBN 0-443-02371-9). Churchill.

Tanimoto, S. & Klinger, A., eds. Structured Computer Vision: Machine Perception Through Hierarchical Computation Structures. LC 80-14878. 1980. 21.00 (ISBN 0-12-683280-3). Acad Pr.

Wade, Kent. Alternative Photographic Processes. LC 77-83836. 1978. pap. 11.95 (ISBN 0-87100-136-5). Morgan.

IMAGIST POETRY

see also Free Verse

Monroe, Harriet. The New Poetry: An Anthology. LC 78-64048. (Des Imagistes: Literature of the Imagist Movement). Repr. of 1917 ed. 33.50 (ISBN 0-404-17080-3). AMS Pr.

Some Imagist Poets, an Anthology, 3 vols in one. 1915-1917. 14.00 (ISBN 0-527-84700-3). Kraus Repr.

IMAGIST POETRY–HISTORY AND CRITICISM

A Catalogue of the Imagist Poets. LC 81-3601. (Des Imagistes: Literature of the Imagist Movement). 72p. Repr. of 1966 ed. 16.50 (ISBN 0-404-17079-X). AMS Pr.

Coffman, Stanley K. Imagism, a Chapter in the History of Modern Poetry. LC 72-4262. xii, 236p. 1972. Repr. of 1951 ed. lib. bdg. 16.00x (ISBN 0-374-91793-0). Octagon.

De Chasca, Edmund S. John Gould Fletcher & Imagism. LC 77-10795. 1978. 15.50x (ISBN 0-8262-0229-2). U of Mo Pr.

Des Imagistes. LC 78-64017. (Des Imagistes: Literature of the Imagist Movement). Repr. of 1914 ed. 11.50 (ISBN 0-404-17089-7). AMS Pr.

The Egoist: Special Imagist Number. LC 78-64018. (Des Imagistes: Literature of the Imagist Movement). Repr. of 1915 ed. 11.00 (ISBN 0-404-17093-5). AMS Pr.

Gould, Jean. Amy: The World of Amy Lowell & the Imagist Movement. LC 75-11563. 350p. 1975. 12.50 (ISBN 0-396-07022-1). Dodd.

Macneice, Louis. Modern Poetry: A Personal Essay. LC 77-95439. (Studies in Poetry, No. 38). 1969. Repr. of 1938 ed. lib. bdg. 28.95 (ISBN 0-8383-0992-5). Haskell.

Pratt, William, ed. Imagist Poem: Modern Poetry in Miniature. pap. 2.25 (ISBN 0-525-47126-X). Dutton.

Stead, Christian K. The New Poetic. LC 78-64053. (Des Imagistes: Literature of the Imagist Movement). 200p. Repr. of 1964 ed. 24.50 (ISBN 0-404-17103-6). AMS Pr.

Vildrac, Charles & Duhamel, Georges. Notes sur la technique poetique. LC 78-64057. (Des Imagistes: Literature of the Imagist Movement). Repr. of 1910 ed. 12.50 (ISBN 0-404-17111-7). AMS Pr.

Visan, Tancrede De. L' Attitude du Lyrisme Contemporain. LC 78-64058. (Des Imagistes: Literature of the Imagist Movement). Repr. of 1911 ed. 35.00 (ISBN 0-404-17112-5). AMS Pr.

IMAMITES

see Shiites

IMBECILITY

see Mentally Handicapped

IMBEDDINGS, TOPOLOGICAL

see Topological Imbeddings

IMHOTEP

Hurry, J. B. Imhotep: The Egyptian God of Medicine. (Illus.). 1978. 12.50 (ISBN 0-89005-239-5). Ares.

Hurry, Jamieson B. Imhotep, the Vizier & Physician of King Zoser & Afterwards the Egyptian God of Medicine. 2nd rev. ed. LC 75-23727. Repr. of 1928 ed. 19.00 (ISBN 0-404-13285-5). AMS Pr.

IMIDOYL HALIDES

Ulrich, Henri. Chemistry of Imidoyl Halides. LC 68-26773. 238p. 1968. 35.00 (ISBN 0-306-30353-1, Plenum Pr). Plenum Pub.

IMINES

see also Polyamines

Patai, Saul. The Chemistry of Amidines & Imidates. LC 75-6913. (Chemistry of Functional Groups Ser.). 677p. 1976. 107.95 (ISBN 0-471-66923-7, Pub by Wiley-Interscience). Wiley.

IMITATION

see also Influence (Psychology)

Boyd, John D. The Function of Mimesis & Its Decline. 2nd ed. LC 68-28691. 1980. pap. 8.00 (ISBN 0-8232-1046-4). Fordham.

Dunn, Edgar S., Jr. Economic & Social Development: A Process of Social Learning. LC 70-134691. (Resources for the Future Ser). 342p. 1971. 20.00x (ISBN 0-8018-1198-8). Johns Hopkins.

Guillaume, Paul. Imitation in Children. Halperin, Elaine P., tr. from Fr. LC 77-135742. xviii, 214p. 1971. 8.75x (ISBN 0-226-31045-0). U of Chicago Pr.

--Imitation in Children. Halperin, Elaine P., tr. from Fr. LC 77-135742. xviii, 214p. 1973. pap. 2.95 (ISBN 0-226-31046-9, P423, Phoen). U of Chicago Pr.

Miller, Neal E. & Dollard, John. Social Learning & Imitation. LC 78-23728. (Illus.). 1979. Repr. of 1962 ed. lib. bdg. 21.50x (ISBN 0-313-20714-3, MISL). Greenwood.

Piaget, Jean. Play, Dreams & Imitation in Childhood. 1962. pap. 4.95 (ISBN 0-393-00171-7, Norton Lib). Norton.

Tarde, Gabriel. The Laws of Imitation. 9.00 (ISBN 0-8446-1442-4). Peter Smith.

Yando, Regina, et al. Imitation: A Developmental Perspective. 1978. 14.95 (ISBN 0-470-26358-X). Halsted Pr.

IMITATION (IN LITERATURE)

see also Plagiarism

Fiske, George C. Lucilius & Horace, a Study in Classical Theory of Imitation. LC 78-109732. 524p. Repr. of 1920 ed. lib. bdg. 20.25x (ISBN 0-8371-4222-9, FILH). Greenwood.

Girard, Rene. To Double Business Bound: Essays on Literature, Mimesis & Anthropology. LC 7-8418. 256p. 1978. text ed. 16.50x (ISBN 0-8018-2114-2). Johns Hopkins.

White, Harold O. Plagiarism & Imitation During the English Renaissance. 1965. lib. bdg. 13.50x (ISBN 0-374-98436-0). Octagon.

IMMACULATE CONCEPTION

see also Mary, Virgin; Virgin Birth

Brown, Raymond. The Virginal Conception & Bodily Resurrection of Jesus. LC 72-97399. 1973. pap. 2.95 (ISBN 0-8091-1768-1). Paulist Pr.

Clasen, Souphronius, ed. Henrici De Werla, O. F. M. Opera Omnia: Tractatus De Immaculata Conceptione Beatae Mariae Virginis. (Text Ser). 1955. 5.00 (ISBN 0-686-11555-4). Franciscan Inst.

Manteau-Bonamy, H. M. Immaculate Conception & the Holy Spirit: The Marian Teachings of Father Kolbe. Geiger, Bernard M., ed. Arnandez, Richard, tr. from Fr. LC 77-93104. (Illus.). 1977. pap. 4.00 (ISBN 0-913382-00-0, 101-20). Prow Bks-Franciscan.

Mary in the Seraphic Order. (Franciscan Educational Conferences). 1954. pap. 6.00 (ISBN 0-685-77541-0). Franciscan Herald.

IMMANENCE OF GOD

see also Jesus Christ–Mystical Body; Mystical Union; Mysticism; Transcendence of God

Bontrager, Ida B. Under God's Arrest. 1974. 9.40 (ISBN 0-87813-508-1). Christian Light.

Bowne, Borden P. The Immanence of God. LC 75-3071. Repr. of 1905 ed. 18.50 (ISBN 0-404-59070-5). AMS Pr.

Capps, Charles. God's Creative Power Will Work for You. 27p. 1977. 0.60 (ISBN 0-89274-024-8). Harrison Hse.

Daly, Gabriel. Transcendence & Immanence: A Study in Catholic Modernism & Integralism. 266p. 1980. 37.50x (ISBN 0-19-826652-9). Oxford U Pr.

Hunter, Charles & Hunter, Frances. Don't Limit God. 1976. pap. 2.25 (ISBN 0-917726-04-9). Hunter Bks.

Steed, Ernest H. J. Two Be One. pap. 2.95 (ISBN 0-88270-313-7, P313-7). Logos.

IMMERMAN, KARL LEBRECHT, 1796-1840

Jahn, Kurt. Immermanns Merlin. Repr. of 1899 ed. 14.00 (ISBN 0-384-26715-7); pap. 11.00 (ISBN 0-685-02271-4). Johnson Repr.

Porterfield, Allen W. Karl Lebrecht Immermann: A Study in German Romanticism. 1977. lib. bdg. 59.95 (ISBN 0-8490-2112-X). Gordon Pr.

--Karl Lebrecht Immermann: A Study of German Romanticism. LC 11-6169. (Columbia University. Germanic Studies, Old Ser.: No. 13). Repr. of 1911 ed. 27.00 (ISBN 0-404-50413-2). AMS Pr.

Szymanzig, M. Immermanns Tristan und Isolde. Repr. of 1911 ed. pap. 15.50 (ISBN 0-384-59390-9). Johnson Repr.

IMMERSION, BAPTISMAL

see Baptism

IMMIGRANT LABOR

see Alien Labor

IMMIGRATION

see Emigration and Immigration

IMMIGRATION LAW

see Emigration and Immigration Law

IMMORAL LITERATURE

see Literature, Immoral

IMMORTALISM

Here are entered works on the concept of living indefinitely in the flesh. For works on the concept of the survival of the soul after death, see Immortality.

see also Cryonics; Immortality

Orr, Leonard. Physical Immortality. pap. 10.00 (ISBN 0-686-27685-X). L Orr.

Otto, A. S., ed. Comprehensive Immortalist Primer. 1970-1975. vinyl 24.95 (ISBN 0-912132-06-X). Dominion Pr.

Stuart, Friend. How to Conquer Physical Death. 1968. vinyl 24.95 (ISBN 0-912132-02-7). Dominion Pr.

IMMORTALITY

Here are entered works on the concept of the survival of the soul after death. For works on the concept of living indefinitely in the flesh, see Immortalism.

see also Eschatology; Future Life; Soul

Altasen, J., et al. Immortality. 733p. 1978. 6.00 (ISBN 0-8285-0939-5, Pub. by Progress Pubs Russia). Imported Pubns.

Augustine, St. Immortality of the Soul. (Fathers of the Church Ser.: Vol. 4). 24.00 (ISBN 0-8132-0004-0). Cath U Pr.

Balaramiah, V. The Art of Deathlessness. (Illus.). 128p. 1980. pap. 4.95 (ISBN 0-937698-01-6). Golden Mean.

Banerji, Barenya K. Towards Quiescence & Immortality. LC 80-81693. 140p. 1981. 10.00 (ISBN 0-8022-2366-4). Philos Lib.

Benoit, Pierre & Murphy, Roland, eds. Immortality & Resurrection. LC 71-129759. (Concilium Ser.: Religion in the Seventies: Vol. 60). 1970. pap. 4.95 (ISBN 0-8245-0220-5). Crossroad NY.

Birdsong, Robert E. Way of the Immortal Threefold Self: The Straight Path. (Aquarian Academy Monograph: Ser. E, No. 4). 1980. pap. 1.45 (ISBN 0-917108-29-9). Sirius Bks.

--Way of the Soul: The "Heart Path" to Human Perfection. (Aquarian Academy Monograph: Ser. D, No. 2). 1980. pap. 1.45 (ISBN 0-917108-28-0). Sirius Bks.

--Way of the Spirit: The "Head Path" to Human Perfection, Ser. C, No. 2. (Aquarian Academy Monograph). 1980. pap. 1.45 (ISBN 0-917108-27-2). Sirius Bks.

Bixler, Julius S. Immortality & the Present Mood. LC 75-3047. Repr. of 1931 ed. 16.00 (ISBN 0-404-59044-6). AMS Pr.

Brown, Stuart, ed. Reason & Religion. LC 77-3115. 1977. 22.50x (ISBN 0-8014-1025-8); pap. 7.95 (ISBN 0-8014-9166-5). Cornell U Pr.

Burns, Norman T. Christian Mortalism from Tyndale to Milton. LC 72-75406. 224p. 1972. 12.50x (ISBN 0-674-12875-3). Harvard U Pr.

Carrington, Hereward. Death: The Causes & Phenomena with Special Reference to Immortality. Kastenbaum, Robert, ed. LC 76-19563. (Death & Dying Ser.). 1977. lib. bdg. 20.00 (ISBN 0-405-09559-7). Arno.

Clymer, R. Swinburne. Philosophy of Immortality. 1960. 4.95 (ISBN 0-686-05885-2). Philos Pub.

--Way to Life & Immortality. 1948. 4.95 (ISBN 0-686-00832-4). Philos Pub.

Compton, Arthur H. Man's Destiny in Eternity. LC 75-117821. (Essay Index Reprint Ser). 1949. 17.00 (ISBN 0-8369-1762-6). Arno.

Daily, Starr. Wellsprings of Immortality. pap. 1.95 (ISBN 0-910924-24-4). Macalester.

Davis, Roy E. Conscious Immortality. 150p. 1978. pap. 2.95 (ISBN 0-87707-216-7). CSA Pr.

De Unamuno, Miguel. Tragic Sense of Life. 8.50 (ISBN 0-8446-3100-0). Peter Smith.

Ducasse, C. J. Critical Examination of the Belief in a Life After Death. (American Lecture Philosophy Ser). 336p. 1974. pap. 12.75 (ISBN 0-398-03037-5). C C Thomas.

Fechner, Gustav T. The Little Book of Life After Death. Kastenbaum, Robert, ed. LC 76-19570. (Death & Dying Ser.). 1977. Repr. of 1904 ed. lib. bdg. 12.00x (ISBN 0-405-09565-1). Arno.

Garfield, Samuel. The Immortality of the Soul & the Perfectibility of Man. (Illus.). 1977. 35.00 (ISBN 0-89266-026-0). Am Classical Coll Pr.

Hall, Manly P. Science & Immortality. pap. 1.75 (ISBN 0-89314-351-0). Philos Res.

Harrington, Alan. The Immortalist. rev ed. LC 76-56899. 1977. pap. 5.95 (ISBN 0-89087-135-3). Celestial Arts.

Hickok, Laurens P. Humanity Immortal: Or, Man Tried, Fallen & Redeemed. LC 75-3180. Repr. of 1872 ed. 25.00 (ISBN 0-404-59183-3). AMS Pr.

Hirsch, W. Rabbinic Psychology. LC 73-2208. (The Jewish People; History, Religion, Literature Ser.). Repr. of 1947 ed. 18.00 (ISBN 0-405-05272-3). Arno.

Hyslop, James H. Psychical Research & the Nature of Life After Death. (Illus.). 124p. 1980. deluxe ed. 66.35 (ISBN 0-89920-017-6). Am Inst Psych.
James, William. The Will to Believe & Human Immortality. pap. 5.00 (ISBN 0-486-20291-7). Dover.
--Will to Believe & Other Essays in Popular Philosophy & Human Immortality. 8.50 (ISBN 0-8446-2313-X). Peter Smith.
Johnson, Charles W., Jr. Fasting, Longevity, & Immortality. (Illus.). 213p. (Orig.). pap. 3.00 (ISBN 0-686-27081-9). Survival CT.
Kennedy, David. A Venture in Immortality. LC 74-186547. (Illus.). 202p. 1973. 10.00x (ISBN 0-900675-79-9). Intl Pubns Serv.
Lamont, Corliss. Illusion of Immortality. 4th ed. LC 65-25140. 1965. pap. 4.95 (ISBN 0-8044-6377-8). Ungar.
McBride, Alfred. Death Shall Have No Dominion. 208p. 1979. pap. write for info. (ISBN 0-697-01700-1); tchr's manual avail. (ISBN 0-697-01707-9); pap. text ed. write for info. Wm C Brown.
McConnell, S. D. The Evolution of Immortality. 1978. Repr. of 1901 ed. lib. bdg. 25.00 (ISBN 0-8495-3508-5). Arden Lib.
McTaggart, John. Human Immortality & Pre-Existence. Repr. of 1916 ed. 14.00 (ISBN 0-527-59950-6). Kraus Repr.
--Some Dogmas of Religion. LC 68-57622. (Illus.). 1969. Repr. of 1906 ed. lib. bdg. 15.50x (ISBN 0-8371-0587-0, MCDR). Greenwood.
--Some Dogmas of Religion. LC 7-7484. 1968. Repr. of 1906 ed. 14.00 (ISBN 0-527-60000-8). Kraus Repr.
Maududi, A. A. Life After Death. pap. 0.95 (ISBN 0-686-18469-6). Kazi Pubns.
Mendelssohn, Moses. Phaedon; or, the Death of Socrates. LC 73-2219. (The Jewish People; History, Religion, Literature Ser.). Repr. of 1789 ed. 18.00 (ISBN 0-405-05282-0). Arno.
Montagu, Henry. Contemplatio Mortis et Immortalitatis. LC 72-218. (English Experience Ser.: No. 337). 148p. 1971. Repr. of 1631 ed. 11.50 (ISBN 90-221-0337-4). Walter J Johnson.
Moore, Clifford H. Ancient Beliefs in the Immortality of the Soul. LC 63-10283. (Our Debt to Greece & Rome Ser). 183p. 1963. Repr. of 1930 ed. 18.50x (ISBN 0-8154-0154-X). Cooper Sq.
Myers, Frederic W. Human Personality & Its Survival of Bodily Death, 2 vols. LC 75-7391. (Perspectives in Psychical Research Ser.). 1975. Repr. of 1954 ed. 80.00x (ISBN 0-405-07038-1). Arno.
Osler, William. Science and Immortality. Kastenbaum, Robert, ed. LC 76-19586. (Death & Dying Ser.). 1977. Repr. of 1904 ed. lib. bdg. 10.00x (ISBN 0-405-09581-3). Arno.
Paramananda, Swami. Reincarnation & Immortality. 2nd ed. 1961. 3.00 (ISBN 0-911564-05-5). Vedanta Ctr.
Pattison, A. Seth. Idea of Immortality. Repr. of 1922 ed. 11.00 (ISBN 0-527-81506-3). Kraus Repr.
Pelikan, Jaroslav J. The Shape of Death: Life, Death, & Immortality in the Early Fathers. LC 78-6030. 1978. Repr. of 1961 ed. lib. bdg. 16.75x (ISBN 0-313-20458-6, PESD). Greenwood.
Perry, John R. A Dialogue on Personal Identity & Immortality. LC 78-52943. 1978. lib. bdg. 12.50 (ISBN 0-915144-91-3); pap. text ed. 2.25x (ISBN 0-915144-53-0). Hackett Pub.
Phillips, D. Z. Death & Immortality. LC 71-124953. (New Studies in the Philosophy of Religion). 1971. pap. text ed. 4.50 (ISBN 0-312-18865-X). St Martin.
Plato. Phaedo. Church, F. J., tr. LC 51-10496. 1951. pap. 2.95 (ISBN 0-672-60192-3, LLA30). Bobbs.
--Phaedo. new ed. Grube, G. M., tr. LC 76-40412. 1977. pap. 2.25x (ISBN 0-915144-18-2). Hackett Pub.
--Phaedo. Burnet, John, ed. 1979. pap. 11.95x (ISBN 0-19-814014-2). Oxford U Pr.
--Plato's Phaedo. Bluck, R. S., tr. 1955. pap. 5.50 (ISBN 0-672-60308-X, LLA110). Bobbs.
Reesman, Richard T. Contributions of the Major Philosophers into the Problem of Body Resurrection & Personal Immortality. (Illus.). 117p. 1981. 41.85 (ISBN 0-89920-021-4). Am Inst Psych.
Rosin, Jacob. In God's Image. LC 75-86507. 1969. 4.00 (ISBN 0-8022-2299-4). Philos Lib.
Royce, Josiah. Conception of Immortality. 1968. Repr. of 1900 ed. lib. bdg. 15.00x (ISBN 0-8371-0207-3, ROCI). Greenwood.
--Conception of Immortality. 1900. Repr. 5.00 (ISBN 0-403-00308-3). Scholarly.
Schmahl, Phillip. Logic of Faith. LC 65-20327. 1965. 3.50 (ISBN 0-8022-1503-3). Philos Lib.
Silverstein, Alvin. Conquest of Death. (Illus.). 1979. 9.95 (ISBN 0-02-610930-1). Macmillan.
Steiner, Rudolf. Reincarnation & Immortality. LC 79-3592. (Harper Library of Spiritual Wisdom). 208p. 1980. pap. 5.95 (ISBN 0-06-067571-3, RD 404). Har-Row.
Stendahl, Krister, ed. Immortality & Resurrection: Ingersoll Lectures. (Orig.). 1965. pap. 1.95x (ISBN 0-02-089520-8). Macmillan.
Strauss, Lehman. We Live Forever. pap. 2.50 (ISBN 0-87213-830-5). Loizeaux.
Streeter, Burnett H., et al. Immortality: An Essay in Discovery, Co-Ordinating Scientific, Physical, & Biblical Research. 1977. Repr. of 1917 ed. lib. bdg. 27.50 (ISBN 0-8492-2418-7). R West.
Transformation-Night, Immortality-Dawn. 1975. 2.00 (ISBN 0-88497-111-2). Aum Pubns.
Unamuno, Miguel. Tragic Sense of Life. Flitch, J. Crawford, tr. 1921. pap. 4.50 (ISBN 0-486-20257-7). Dover.
Weatherhead, Leslie D. After-World of the Poets. LC 71-105848. 1970. Repr. of 1929 ed. 11.00 (ISBN 0-8046-1058-4). Kennikat.
Wilson, Everett L. Jesus & the End-Time. 1977. pap. 3.95 (ISBN 0-910452-32-6). Covenant.

IMMORTELLE
see Everlasting Flowers

IMMUNE COMPLEX DISEASES

Branca, Margherita, et al. Immune Complexes & Their Role in the Pathogenesis of Various Diseases. LC 72-10434. (Illus.). 220p. 1973. text ed. 23.50x (ISBN 0-8422-7058-2). Irvington.
Turk, J. L. Drugs & Immune Responsiveness. 254p. text ed. 44.50 (ISBN 0-8391-1360-9). Univ Park.
Williams, Ralph C., Jr. Immune Complexes in Clinical & Experimental Medicine. LC 79-21448. (Commonwealth Fund Ser.). 1980. text ed. 50.00x (ISBN 0-674-44438-8). Harvard U Pr.

IMMUNE COMPLEXES

Branca, Margherita, et al. Immune Complexes & Their Role in the Pathogenesis of Various Diseases. LC 72-10434. (Illus.). 220p. 1973. text ed. 23.50x (ISBN 0-8422-7058-2). Irvington.
Williams, Ralph C., Jr. Immune Complexes in Clinical & Experimental Medicine. LC 79-21448. (Commonwealth Fund Ser.). 1980. text ed. 50.00x (ISBN 0-674-44438-8). Harvard U Pr.

IMMUNE SERUM GLOBULIN
see Immunoglobulins

IMMUNITIES AND PRIVILEGES
see Privileges and Immunities

IMMUNITIES OF FOREIGN STATES
see also Diplomatic Privileges and Immunities; Exterritoriality

IMMUNITY
see also Allergy; Anaphylaxis; Antigens; Communicable Diseases; Complements (Immunity); Hemolysis and Hemolysins; Immunochemistry; Serumtherapy; Toxins and Antitoxins; Vaccination;
also subdivision Preventive Innoculations under certain diseases, e.g. Tuberculosis–Preventive Innoculations

Battisto, Jack R. & Streilein, Wayne. Immuno-Aspects of the Spleen. 1976. 61.00 (ISBN 0-7204-0593-9, North-Holland). Elsevier.
Biggar, W. D., et al. Thymus Involvement in Immunity & Disease. new ed. LC 72-13558. (Illus.). 220p. 1973. text ed. 24.50x (ISBN 0-8422-7068-X). Irvington.
Blasecki. Mechanisms of Immunity to Virus-Induced Tumors. (Immunology Ser.: Vol. 12). 376p. 1981. 49.50 (ISBN 0-8247-1162-9). Dekker.
Borek, Felix, ed. Immunogenicity. (Frontiers of Biology Ser. Vol. 25). 1972. 131.75 (ISBN 0-444-10104-7, North-Holland). Elsevier.
Brain, et al. Respiratory Defense Mechanisms, Pt. 1. (Lung Biology in Health & Disease: Vol. 5). 1977. 49.75 (ISBN 0-8247-6381-5). Dekker.
Burnet, F. Macfarlane & White, D. O. Natural History of Infectious Disease. 4th ed. LC 74-174264. (Illus.). 400p. 1972. 38.50 (ISBN 0-521-08389-3); pap. 12.95x (ISBN 0-521-09688-X). Cambridge U Pr.
Burnet, Frank M. Integrity of the Body. LC 62-8180. (Illus.). 1966. pap. 1.75 (ISBN 0-689-70029-6, 85). Atheneum.
--Integrity of the Body: A Discussion of Modern Immunological Ideas. LC 62-8180. (Books in Biology Ser: No. 3). (Illus.). 1962. 10.00x (ISBN 0-674-45650-5). Harvard U Pr.
Catsimpoolas, Nicholas. Immunological Aspects of Food. (Illus.). 1977. lib. bdg. 42.00 (ISBN 0-87055-203-1). AVI.
Chandra, R. K. & Newberne, P. M. Nutrition, Immunity & Infection: Mechanisms of Interaction. (Illus.). 262p. 1977. 22.50 (ISBN 0-306-31058-9, Plenum Pr). Plenum Pub.
Ciba Foundation. Ontogeny of Acquired Immunity. (CIBA Foundation Symposium Ser.: No. 5). 1972. 20.50 (ISBN 0-444-10381-3, Excerpta Medica). Elsevier.
Constantinides, P., et al. Immunity and Atherosclerosis. (Serono Symposia: No.24). 1980. 38.50 (ISBN 0-12-186250-X). Acad Pr.
Cooper, M. D., et al, eds. Immune Deficiency. (Illus.). 1979. pap. 23.30 (ISBN 0-387-09490-3). Springer-Verlag.
Cudkowitz, Gustavo, et al, eds. Natural Resistance Systems Against Foreign Cells, Tumors & Microbes. (Perspectives in Immunology Ser.: Vol. 7). 1978. 20.50 (ISBN 0-12-199735-9). Acad Pr.
Dau, P. C. Plasmapheresis & the Immunobiology of Myasthemia Gravis. 371p. 1979. 50.00 (ISBN 0-471-09477-3, Pub. by Wiley Med). Wiley.
Davies, A. J. & Carter, R. L., eds. Contemporary Topics in Immunobiology: Vol. 2, Thymus Dependency. LC 78-165398. (Illus.). 361p. 1973. 32.50 (ISBN 0-306-37802-7, Plenum Pr). Plenum Pub.
De Sousa, Maria S., et al. The Effects of Hormones on Immunity, Vol. 2. LC 72-13691. (Illus.). 220p. 1973. text ed. 30.00x (ISBN 0-8422-7098-1). Irvington.
Di Luzio, N. R. & Flemming, K., eds. The Reticuloendothelial System & Immune Phenomena. LC 70-163288. (Advances in Experimental Medicine & Biology Ser.: Vol. 15). 441p. 1971. 42.50 (ISBN 0-306-39015-9, Plenum Pr). Plenum Pub.
Doria, G. & Eshkol, A. The Immune System: Functions and Therapy of Dysfunction. LC 79-41519. (Serono Symposia: No.27). 1980. 40.00 (ISBN 0-12-220550-2). Acad Pr.
Edelman, Gerald M., ed. Cellular Selection & Regulation in the Immune Response. LC 73-93857. (Society of General Physiologists Ser.: Vol. 29). 299p. 1974. 34.50 (ISBN 0-911216-71-5). Raven.
Fiore-Donati, L. & Hanna, M. G. Lymphatic Tissue & Germinal Centers in Immune Response. LC 75-82374. (Advances in Experimental Medicine & Biology Ser.: Vol. 5). 529p. 1969. 42.50 (ISBN 0-306-39005-1, Plenum Pr). Plenum Pub.
Friedman. Infection, Immunity & Genetics. 1978. 16.50 (ISBN 0-8391-1292-0). Univ Park.
Friedman, Herman, ed. Subcellular Factors Immunity. LC 79-24875. (Annals of the New York Academy of Sciences: Vol. 332). 625p. 1979. 110.00x (ISBN 0-89766-035-8). NY Acad Sci.
--Thymus Factors in Immunity. (Annals of the New York Academy of Sciences: Vol. 249). 547p. 1975. 63.00x (ISBN 0-89072-003-7). NY Acad Sci.
Gadebusch, Hans H. Phagocytes & Cellular Immunity. 176p. 1979. 59.95 (ISBN 0-8493-5349-1). CRC Pr.
Gelfand, Erwin W. & Dosch, Hans-Michael, eds. Biological Basis of Immunodeficiency. 334p. 1979. text ed. 35.50 (ISBN 0-89004-361-2). Raven.
Gottlieb, Arthur A., et al, eds. Developments in Lymphoid Cell Biology. new ed. LC 74-77918. (Uniscience Ser.). 176p. 1974. 42.50 (ISBN 0-87819-056-2). CRC Pr.
Guttler, F. Inborn Errors of Immunity & Phagocytosis. 391p. text ed. 32.50 (ISBN 0-83391-1363-3). Univ Park.
Ham, Arthur W., et al. Blood Cell Formation & the Cellular Basis of Immune Responses. (Illus.). 1979. pap. text ed. 10.95 (ISBN 0-397-50461-6, JBL-Med-Nursing). Har-Row.
Hare, Ronald & Cooke, Mary. Bacteriology & Immunity for Nurses. 5th ed. (Churchill Livingstone Nursing Texts). 1979. pap. text ed. 11.25 (ISBN 0-443-01757-3). Churchill.
International Symposium of the American Society of Zoologists, Toronto, December 27-30, 1977. Animal Models of Comparative & Developmental Aspects of Immunity & Disease: Proceedings. Gershwin, M. Eric & Cooper, Edwin L., eds. LC 78-15022. 1978. text ed. 43.00 (ISBN 0-08-022648-5). Pergamon.
Jankovic, B. D. & Isakovic, K., eds. Microenvironmental Aspects of Immunity. LC 72-89487. (Advances in Experimental Medicine & Biology Ser.: Vol. 29). 726p. 1973. 55.00 (ISBN 0-306-39029-9, Plenum Pr). Plenum Pub.
Kahn, Reuben L. Tissue Immunity. (Illus.). 707p. 1936. pap. 68.75 (ISBN 0-398-04301-9). C C Thomas.
Knight, David C. Your Body's Defenses. LC 74-11083. (Illus.). 64p. (gr. 5-8). 1975. PLB 7.95 (ISBN 0-07-035105-8, GB). McGraw.
Kohn, A. & Klingberg, M. A., eds. Immunity in Viral & Rickettsial Diseases. LC 72-93347. (Advances in Experimental Medicine & Biology Ser.: Vol. 31). 275p. 1972. 32.50 (ISBN 0-306-39031-0, Plenum Pr). Plenum Pub.
Lawrence, H. S. & Landy, M., eds. Mediators of Cellular Immunity. (Perspectives in Immunology Ser). 1969. 38.00 (ISBN 0-12-439350-0). Acad Pr.
Lefkovitz, Ivan & Waldmann, Hermann. Limiting Dilution Analysis of Cells in the Immune System. LC 77-82502. (Illus.). 1980. 43.50 (ISBN 0-521-22771-2). Cambridge U Pr.
Leukocyte Culture Conference, 9th. Immune Recognition: Proceedings. Rosenthal, Alan S., ed. 1975. 50.00 (ISBN 0-12-597850-2). Acad Pr.
Litwin, Stephen D., et al, eds. Clinical Evaluation of Immune Function in Man. LC 76-48408. 256p. 1976. 24.25 (ISBN 0-8089-0971-1). Grune.
Lobuglio, A. E. Clinical Immunotherapy. (Immunology Ser.: Vol. 11). 1980. 39.50 (ISBN 0-8247-6942-2). Dekker.
Lucas, D. O., ed. Regulatory Mechanism in Lymphocyte Activation. 1977. 60.00 (ISBN 0-12-458050-5). Acad Pr.
Lurie, Max B. Resistance to Tuberculosis: Experimental Studies in Native & Acquired Defense Mechanisms. LC 64-25055. (Commonwealth Fund Publications Ser). (Illus.). 1965. 20.00x (ISBN 0-674-76516-8). Harvard U Pr.
McGhee, J. R., et al, eds. Secretory Immunity & Infection. LC 78-18927. (Advances in Experimental Medicine & Biology Ser.: Vol. 107). 927p. 1978. 75.00 (ISBN 0-306-40027-8, Plenum Pr). Plenum Pub.
Makinodan, T., et al. Aging & the Immune Function. 227p. 1974. text ed. 28.50x (ISBN 0-8422-7228-3). Irvington.
Manning, M. J. & Turner, R. J. Comparative Immunobiology. LC 75-42363. (Teritiary Level Biology Ser.). 184p. 1976. pap. 10.95 (ISBN 0-470-14995-7). Halsted Pr.
Maramorosch, Karl, ed. Invertebrate Immunity: Mechanisms of Invertebrate Vector-Parasite Relations. 1975. 34.00 (ISBN 0-12-470265-1). Acad Pr.
Metchnikoff, Elie. Immunity in Infective Diseases. Binnie, F. G., tr. (Sources of Science Ser: No. 61). 1969. Repr. 38.50 (ISBN 0-384-38390-4). Johnson Repr.
Moss, Gordon E. Illness, Immunity & Social Interaction. 298p. 1981. Repr. of 1973 ed. text ed. write for info. (ISBN 0-89874-266-8). Krieger.
Neumann, Hans H. Foreign Travel & Immunization Guide 1981. 10th ed. (A Medical Economics Book). 1981. pap. 5.50 (ISBN 0-686-71547-0). Van Nos Reinhold.
New York State Department of Health Birth Defects Symposium, 9th. Inborn Errors of Specific Immunity: Proceedings. Pollara, Bernard, et al, eds. LC 79-23179. (Birth Defects Institute Ser.). 1980. 34.00 (ISBN 0-12-559650-2). Acad Pr.
Nossal, G. J. Antibodies & Immunity. rev. ed. LC 77-76472. 1978. 14.95 (ISBN 0-465-00361-3). Basic.
Sell, Stewart. Immunology, Immunopathology & Immunity. 3rd ed. (Illus.). 600p. 1980. pap. text ed. 27.00 (ISBN 0-06-142369-6, Harper Medical). Har-Row.
Sercarz, Eli, ed. Regulatory Genetics of the Immune System. 1977. 43.50 (ISBN 0-12-637160-1). Acad Pr.
Steinberg, C. M. & Lefkovits, I., eds. The Immune System: Festschrift in Honor of Niels Kaj Jerne, on the Occasion of His 70th Birthday, Vol. 1. (Illus.). x, 390p. 1981. 118.75 (ISBN 3-8055-3407-8). S Karger.
--The Immune System: Festschrift in Honor of Niels Kaj Jerne, on the Occasion of His 70th Birthday, 2 vols, Vols. 1 & 2. (Illus.). xx, 780p. 1981. 237.50 set (ISBN 3-8055-3409-4). S Karger.
--The Immune System: Festschrift in Honor of Neils Kaj Jerne, on the Occasion of His 70th Birthday, Vol. 2. (Illus.). x, 390p. 1981. 118.75 (ISBN 3-8055-3408-6). S Karger.
Stewart, F. S. & Beswick, S. L. Bacteriology, Virology, & Immunity for Students of Medicine. 10th ed. 1978. pap. text ed. 27.50 (ISBN 0-02-859400-2). Macmillan.
Strober, Warren & Hanson, Lars A., eds. Mechanisms in Mucosal Immunity. 1981. write for info. (ISBN 0-89004-642-5). Raven.
Summitt, Robert & Bergsma, Daniel, eds. Cell Surface Factors Immune Deficiencies Twin Studies. (Alan R. Liss, Inc. Ser.: Vol. 14 No. 6A). 1978. 24.00 (ISBN 0-686-23949-0). March of Dimes.
Thomas, Lewis, et al. International Symposium of Injury, Inflammation & Immunity. 422p. 1964. 19.50 (ISBN 0-685-91061-X, Pub. by W & W). Krieger.
Walford, R. L., et al. The Relation of Aging to Immunity. (Illus.). 220p. 1973. text ed. 29.75x (ISBN 0-8422-7106-6). Irvington.
Watson, James, et al. Effects of Hormones on Immunity, Vol. 1. 1973. 30.00x (ISBN 0-8422-7113-9). Irvington.
WHO Scientific Group. Geneva, 1972. Cell-Mediated Immunity & Resistance to Infection: Report. (Technical Report Ser.: No. 519). (Also avail. in French & Spanish). 1973. pap. 2.00 (ISBN 92-4-120519-9). World Health.
Wilson, G. S. & Miles, A. A., eds. Topley & Wilson's Principles of Bacteriology & Immunity, 2 vols. 6th ed. (Illus.). 1975. Set. 225.00 (ISBN 0-683-08378-3). Williams & Wilkins.

IMMUNITY (EXEMPTION)
see Privileges and Immunities
IMMUNITY (PLANTS)
see Plants-Disease and Pest Resistance
IMMUNITY FROM SELF-INCRIMINATION
see Self-Incrimination
IMMUNOCHEMISTRY

Acton, Ronald T. Immunobiological & Immunochemical Studies of the Oyster, Crassptrea Virginica. 144p. 1972. text ed. 29.50x (ISBN 0-8422-7034-5). Irvington.

Atassi, M. Z., ed. Immunochemistry of Proteins, 3 vols. LC 76-2596. (Illus.). 1979. Vol. 1, 485p, 1977. 44.50 (ISBN 0-306-36221-X, Plenum Pr); Vol. 2, 438p, 1977. 44.50 (ISBN 0-306-36222-8); Vol. 3, 339p, 1979. 35.00 (ISBN 0-306-40131-2). Plenum Pub.

Clausen, J. Immunochemical Techniques for the Identification & Estimation of Macromolecules. (Lab Techiques in Biochemistry & Molecular Biology Vol. 1, Pt. 3). 1969. pap. 12.25 (ISBN 0-444-10160-8, North-Holland). Elsevier.

Day, Eugene D. Advanced Immunochemistry. 447p. 1972. 22.00 (ISBN 0-683-02416-7). Krieger.

--Foundations of Immunochemistry. 200p. 1966. pap. 7.25 (ISBN 0-683-02405-1, Pub. by Williams & Wilkins). Krieger.

Glynn, L. E. & Steward, M. W. Immunochemistry: An Advanced Textbook. LC 77-1630. 628p. 1977. 110.50x (ISBN 0-471-99508-8, Pub. by Wiley-Interscience). Wiley.

Inman, F. P. Contemporary Topics in Molecular Immunology, Vol. 1. LC 73-186260. 230p. 1972. 25.00 (ISBN 0-306-36101-9, Plenum Pr). Plenum Pub.

Kabat, Elvin A. Blood Group Substances: Their Chemistry & Immunochemistry. 1956. 51.50 (ISBN 0-12-392850-8). Acad Pr.

--Experimental Immunochemistry. 2nd ed. (Illus.). 920p. 1971. 89.50 (ISBN 0-398-00956-2). C C Thomas.

Katz, David & Benacerraf, Baruj, eds. Immunological Tolerance: Mechanisms & Potential Therapeutic Applications. 1974. 46.00 (ISBN 0-12-401650-2). Acad Pr.

Kwapinski, George. The Methodology of Investigative & Clinical Immunology. LC 78-26882. 1981. Repr. of 1972 ed. text ed. price not set (ISBN 0-88275-828-4). Krieger.

Kwapinski, J. B., ed. Research in Immunochemistry & Immunobiology, Vol. 1. (Illus.). 1972. 34.50 (ISBN 0-8391-0651-3). Univ Park.

--Research in Immunochemistry & Immunobiology, Vol. 2. (Illus.). 1972. 34.50 (ISBN 0-8391-0652-1). Univ Park.

--Research in Immunochemistry & Immunobiology, Vol. 3. (Illus.). 1973. 34.50 (ISBN 0-8391-0653-X). Univ Park.

Nowotny, A. Basic Exercises in Immunochemistry: A Laboratory Manual. 2nd ed. LC 79-14029. (Illus.). 1979. pap. 17.80 (ISBN 0-387-09453-9). Springer-Verlag.

Porter, R. R. Chemical Aspects of Immunology. Head, J. J., ed. LC 76-28269. (Carolina Biology Readers Ser.). (Illus.). (gr. 11-12). 1976. pap. 1.65 (ISBN 0-89278-285-4, 45-9685). Carolina Biological.

Sela, Michael, ed. The Antigens. 1974. Vol. 1. 60.00 (ISBN 0-12-635501-0). Acad Pr.

Smith, Richard T. & Landy, Maurice, eds. Immunobiology of the Tumor-Host Relationship: Proceedings. (Perspectives in Immunology Ser.). 1975. 43.00 (ISBN 0-12-652260-X). Acad Pr.

Steward, M. W. Immunochemistry. (Outline Studies in Biology Ser.). 1974. pap. 5.95x (ISBN 0-412-12450-5, Pub. by Chapman & Hall). Methuen Inc.

Ward, A. Milford. Immunochemistry in Clinical Laboratory Medicine. 247p. text ed. 37.50 (ISBN 0-8391-1348-X). Univ Park.

Williams, Curtis A. & Chase, Merrill W., eds. Methods in Immunology & Immunochemistry, 5 vols. Vol. 1. 1968. 56.00, subscription 48.50 (ISBN 0-12-754401-1); Vol. 2. 1968. 56.50, subscription 48.50 (ISBN 0-12-754402-X); Vol. 3. 1971. 56.50, by subscription 48.50 (ISBN 0-12-754403-8); Vol. 4 1977. 56.50, subscription 48.50 (ISBN 0-12-754404-6); Vol. 5 1976. 56.50, subscription 48.50 (ISBN 0-12-754405-4). Acad Pr.

Williams, M. A., ed. Practical Methods in Electron Microscopy: Autoradiography & Immunocytochemistry, Vol. 6, Pt. 1. 1978. 31.75 (ISBN 0-7204-0637-4, North-Holland). Elsevier.

IMMUNODIFFUSION

Crowle, Alfred J. Immunodiffusion. 2nd ed. 1973. 55.00 (ISBN 0-12-198156-8). Acad Pr.

IMMUNOELECTROPHORESIS

Arquembourg, P. C. Immunoelectrophoresis Theory, Methods, Identification, Interpretation. 2nd rev. ed. (Illus.). ix, 104p. 1975. 36.75 (ISBN 3-8055-2136-7). S Karger.

Axelson, Nils H., ed. Quantitative Immunoelectrophoresis: New Developments & Applications. (Illus.). 1975. 29.50 (ISBN 0-685-71643-0). Univ Park.

Cawley, Leo P., et al. Electrophoresis & Immunochemical Reactions in Gels: Techniques & Interpretation. LC 77-93631. (Illus.). 1978. pap. text ed. 20.00 (ISBN 0-89189-038-6, 45-2-035-00). Am Soc Clinical.

Laurell, C. B. Electrophoretic & Electro-Immuno-Chemical Analysis of Proteins. (Illus.). 1977. 34.50 (ISBN 0-8391-0990-3). Univ Park.

Penn, Gerald M. & Batya, Judith. Interpretation of Immunoelectrophoretic Patterns. LC 77-93640. (Atlas Ser.). (Illus.). 1978. text ed. 30.00 (ISBN 0-89189-036-X, 16-A-001-00); incl. slides 140.00 (ISBN 0-89189-098-X, 15-A-001-00). Am Soc Clinical.

IMMUNOFLUORESCENCE
see also Fluorescence Microscopy; Fluorescent Antibody Technique; Immunology-Technique

Hijams, Willy & Schaeffer, Morris, eds. International Conference on Immunofluorescence & Related Staining Techniques, 5th. (Annals of the New York Academy of Sciences Ser.: Vol. 254). 627p. 1975. 72.00x (ISBN 0-89072-008-8). NY Acad Sci.

Nairn, R. C. Fluorescent Protein Tracing. 4th ed. LC 74-29062. (Illus.). 650p. 1975. text ed. 65.00 (ISBN 0-443-01273-3). Churchill.

IMMUNOGENETICS

Balner, Hans & Van Rood, J. J., eds. Transplantation Genetics of Primates. LC 72-1131. (Illus.). 148p. 1972. 39.00 (ISBN 0-8089-0770-0). Grune.

Benacerraf. Immunogenetics & Immunodeficiency. (Illus.). 288p. 1975. 34.50 (ISBN 0-8391-0835-4). Univ Park.

Bergsma, Daniel, ed. Immunodeficiency in Man & Animals. LC 74-81132. (Robert E. Krieger: Vol. 11, No. 1). 1976. 40.00 (ISBN 0-686-14569-0). March of Dimes.

Borek, Felix, ed. Immunogenicity. (Frontiers of Biology Ser. Vol. 25). 1972. 131.75 (ISBN 0-444-10104-7, North-Holland). Elsevier.

Dorf, Martin E. The Role of the Major Histocompatibility Complex in Immunobiology. LC 80-772. 525p. 1981. lib. bdg. 47.50 (ISBN 0-8240-7129-8). Garland Pub.

Fudenberg, H. Hugh, et al. Basic Immunogenetics. 2nd ed. (Illus.). 1978. text ed. 16.95x (ISBN 0-19-502054-5); pap. text ed. 11.95x (ISBN 0-19-502055-3). Oxford U Pr.

Hildemann, William H. Immunogenetics. LC 72-95293. 1970. 16.95x (ISBN 0-8162-3810-3). Holden-Day.

Lengerova, A. Immunogenetics of Tissue Transplantation. (Frontiers of Biology Ser.: Vol. 16). 1970. 26.50 (ISBN 0-444-10230-2, North-Holland). Elsevier.

McDevitt, Hugh O. & Landy, Maurice, eds. Genetic Control of Immune Responsiveness: Relationship to Disease Susceptibility. (Perspectives in Immunology Ser). 1973. 46.50 (ISBN 0-12-483250-4). Acad Pr.

Symposium, Liblice-Prague - 1970. Immunogenetics of the H-2 System: Proceedings. Lengerova, Alena & Vojtiskova, Marta, eds. 1971. 66.00 (ISBN 3-8055-1236-8). S Karger.

IMMUNOGLOBULINS
see also Adjuvants, Immunological; Antigen-Antibody Reactions; Antigens; Fluorescent Antibody Technique; Gamma Globulin; Immunofluorescence

Bach, Michael K., ed. Immediate Hypersensitivity: Modern Concepts & Developments. (Immunology Ser.: Vol. 7). 1978. 65.00 (ISBN 0-8247-6602-4). Dekker.

Cinader, Bernhard. Regulation of the Antibody Response. 2nd ed. (Illus.). 417p. 1971. ed. spiral bdg. 34.00photocopy (ISBN 0-398-00309-2). C C Thomas.

Clinically Significant & Insignificant Antibodies. 70p. 1979. 9.00 (ISBN 0-914404-49-0). Am Assn Blood.

Cold Spring Harbor Symposia on Quantitative Biology: Antibodies, Vol. 32. LC 34-8174. (Illus.). 638p. 1968. 30.00 (ISBN 0-87969-031-3). Cold Spring Harbor.

Cunningham, A. J., ed. The Generation of Antibody Diversity: A New Look. 1976. 32.00 (ISBN 0-12-199850-9). Acad Pr.

Dienstfrey. Protides of the Biological Fluids: Proceedings, Colloquium on Protides of the Biological Fluids, 25th. LC 58-5908. 1978. text ed. 150.00 (ISBN 0-08-021524-6). Pergamon.

Fauci, Anthony S. & Ballieux, Rudy, eds. Antibody Production in Man: In Vitro Synthesis & Clinical Implications. LC 79-928. 1979. 21.00 (ISBN 0-12-249950-6). Acad Pr.

FEBS Meeting, 8th, et al. Immunoglobulins-Cell Bound Receptors & Humoral Antibodies: Proceedings, Vol. 26. Ballieux, R., ed. 1973. 11.00 (ISBN 0-444-10421-6, North-Holland). Elsevier.

Fellows, Robert & Eisenbarth, George, eds. Monoclonal Antibodies in Endocrine Research. 208p. 1981. text ed. 23.00 (ISBN 0-89004-687-5). Raven.

Glynn, I. E. & Stewart, M. W. Antibody Production. 231p. 1981. 53.25 (ISBN 0-471-27916-1, Pub. by Wiley-Interscience). Wiley.

Glynn, L. E. Structure & Fuction of Antibodies. Steward, M. W., ed. LC 80-41379. 306p. 1981. pap. 13.25 (ISBN 0-471-27917-X, Pub. by Wiley-Interscience). Wiley.

Glynn, L. E. & Steward, M. W. Structure & Function of Antibodies. 306p. 1981. 13.25 (ISBN 0-471-27917-X, Pub. by Wiley-Interscience). Wiley.

Glynn, L. E. & Steward, M. W., eds. Antibody Production. LC 80-41378. 231p. 1981. 13.25 (ISBN 0-471-27916-1, Pub. by Wiley-Interscience). Wiley.

Grubb, R. Genetic Markers of Human Immunoglobulins. LC 72-121989. (Molecular Biology, Biochemistry & Biophysics Ser.: Vol. 9). (Illus.). 1970. 26.30 (ISBN 0-387-05211-9). Springer-Verlag.

Haber, Edgar & Krause, Richard M., eds. Antibodies in Human Diagnosis & Therapy. LC 75-32089. (Royal Society of Medicine Foundation Ser.). 431p. 1977. 34.50 (ISBN 0-89004-089-3). Raven.

Hemmings, W. A., ed. Materno Foetal Transmission of Immunoglobulins. LC 75-2721. (Clinical & Experimental Immunoreproduction: No. 2). (Illus.). 400p. 1975. 57.50 (ISBN 0-521-20747-9). Cambridge U Pr.

Hybridomas & Monoclonal Antibodies. 1981. write for info. (ISBN 0-914404-69-5). Am Assn Blood.

Immunoglobulins: Biologic Aspects & Clinical Uses. (Illus.). 1971. 10.25 (ISBN 0-309-01850-1). Natl Acad Pr.

Kennett, Roger H., et al, eds. Monoclonal Antibodies. (Illus.). 375p. 1980. 29.50 (ISBN 0-306-40408-7, Plenum Pr). Plenum Pub.

Melchers, F. & Potter, M., eds. Lymphocyte Hybridomas: Second Workshop on "Functional Properties of Tumors of T & B Lymphocytes" Sponsored by the National Cancer Institute (NIH) April 3-5, 1978, Bethesda, MD, USA. (Current Topics in Microbiology & Immunology: Vol. 81). (Illus.). 1978. 30.50 (ISBN 0-387-08810-5). Springer-Verlag.

Mestecky, Jiri & Lawton, Alexander R., III, eds. The Immunoglobulin A System. LC 74-8720. (Advances in Experimental Medicine & Biology Ser.: Vol. 45). 550p. 1974. 39.50 (ISBN 0-306-39045-0, Plenum Pr). Plenum Pub.

Nezlin, R. S. Biochemistry of Antibodies. LC 69-12534. 381p. 1970. 39.50 (ISBN 0-306-30430-9, Plenum Pr). Plenum Pub.

Nezlin, R. S., ed. Structure & Biosynthesis of Antibodies. (Illus.). 367p. 1977. 42.50 (ISBN 0-306-10921-2, Consultants). Plenum Pub.

Nossal, G. J. Antibodies & Immunity. rev. ed. LC 77-76472. 1978. 14.95 (ISBN 0-465-00361-3). Basic.

Penn, Gerald M., ed. Identification of Myeloma Proteins. Davis, Ted. Davis, Ted, ed. LC 75-10803. (Illus.). 1975. pap. text ed. 17.00 perfect bdg. (ISBN 0-89189-027-0, 45-A-002-00). Am Soc Clinical.

Pernis, Benvenuto & Vogel, Henry J., eds. Cells of Immunoglobulin Synthesis. LC 78-20000. (P. & S. Biomedical Sciences Symposia Ser.). 1979. 51.50 (ISBN 0-12-551850-1). Acad Pr.

Salton, Milton R., ed. Immunochemistry of Enzymes & Their Antibodies. 240p. 1981. Repr. of 1977 ed. lib. bdg. write for info. (ISBN 0-89874-165-3). Krieger.

Shugar, D. & Franek, F., eds. Gammaglobulins, Structure & Biosynthesis. 1969. 39.00 (ISBN 0-12-640850-5). Acad Pr.

Smith, George P. The Variation & Adaptive Expression of Antibodies. LC 72-95186. 192p. 1973. text ed. 12.00x (ISBN 0-674-93205-6). Harvard U Pr.

Sox, Harold C., Jr., et al, eds. Carbohydrate Moieties of Immunoglobulin. LC 74-3461. 187p. 1974. text ed. 24.00x (ISBN 0-8422-7213-5). Irvington.

Steinberg, Arthur G. & Cook, Charles E. The Distribution of the Human Immunoglobulin Allotypes. (Illus.). 272p. 1981. text ed. 69.50x (ISBN 0-19-261181-X). Oxford U Pr.

Sterzl, J. & Riha, I., eds. Developmental Aspects of Antibody Formation & Structure: Proceedings, Vols. 1 & 2. 1971. Vol. 1. 59.00 (ISBN 0-12-667901-0); Vol. 2. 59.00 (ISBN 0-12-667902-9). Acad Pr.

Zaimis, Eleanor, ed. Nerve Growth Factor & Its Antiserum. (Illus.). 384p. 1972. text ed. 25.00x (ISBN 0-485-11132-2, Athlone Pr). Humanities.

IMMUNOHEMATOLOGY
see also Immunoelectrophoresis

Bryant, Neville J. An Introduction to Immunohematology. LC 75-25269. (Illus.). 320p. 1976. text ed. 14.95 (ISBN 0-7216-2170-8). Saunders.

Davidsohn, Israel & Stern, Kurt. Problem Solving in Immunohematology. 2nd ed. LC 77-93058. 1978. pap. text ed. 20.00 (ISBN 0-89189-035-1, 45-6-012-00). Am Soc Clinical.

Rudman, Jack. Immunohematology & Blood Banking. (College Level Examination Ser.: CLEP-34). 14.95 (ISBN 0-8373-5384-X); pap. 9.95 (ISBN 0-8373-5334-3). Natl Learning.

Simmons, Arthur. Problem Solving in Immunohematology. 1978. 19.95 (ISBN 0-8151-7654-6). Year Bk Med.

WHO Scientific Group. Geneva, 1970. Prevention of Rh Sensitization: Report. (Technical Report Ser.: No. 468). (Also avail. French & Spanish). 1971. pap. 2.00 (ISBN 92-4-120468-0). World Health.

Zmijewski. Immunohematology. 3rd ed. (Illus.). 1978. 19.75 (ISBN 0-8385-4290-5). ACC.

IMMUNOLOGICAL ADJUVANTS
see Adjuvants, Immunological
IMMUNOLOGICAL DISEASES
see Immunopathology

Williams, Ralph C., Jr., ed. Lymphocytes & Their Interactions. 240p. 1975. text ed. 18.00 (ISBN 0-89004-052-4). Raven.

IMMUNOLOGICAL TOLERANCE
see also Histocompatibility

Balner, Hans & Van Rood, J. J., eds. Transplantation Genetics of Primates. LC 72-1131. (Illus.). 148p. 1972. 39.00 (ISBN 0-8089-0770-0). Grune.

Borek, Felix, ed. Immunogenicity. (Frontiers of Biology Ser. Vol. 25). 1972. 131.75 (ISBN 0-444-10104-7, North-Holland). Elsevier.

Fleischmajer, P. & Billingham, R. Epithelial Mesenchymal Interactions. 340p. 1968. 17.50 (ISBN 0-683-03260-7, Pub. by Williams & Wilkins). Krieger.

Haller, O., ed. Natural Resistance to Tumors & Viruses. (Current Topics in Microbiology & Immunology Ser.: Vol. 92). (Illus.). 200p. 1981. 57.20 (ISBN 0-387-10732-0). Springer-Verlag.

Hasek, Milan, et al, eds. Mechanisms of Immunological Tolerance: Proceedings. 1963. 56.00 (ISBN 0-12-330250-1). Acad Pr.

International Convocation on Immunology, 7th, Niagra Falls, N. Y., July 1980, et al. Immunbiology of the Major Histocompatibility Complex. Zaleski, M. B. & Kano, K., eds. (Illus.). xii, 396p. 1981. 118.75 (ISBN 3-8055-1896-X). S Karger.

Katz, David & Benacerraf, Baruj, eds. Immunological Tolerance: Mechanisms & Potential Therapeutic Applications. 1974. 46.00 (ISBN 0-12-401650-2). Acad Pr.

--Immunological Tolerance: Mechanisms & Potential Therapeutic Applications. 1974. 46.00 (ISBN 0-12-401650-2). Acad Pr.

Landy, Maurice & Braun, W., eds. Immunological Tolerance. (Perspectives in Immunology Ser). 1969. 33.50 (ISBN 0-12-435650-8). Acad Pr.

Lawrence, H. S. & Landy, M., eds. Mediators of Cellular Immunity. (Perspectives in Immunology Ser). 1969. 38.00 (ISBN 0-12-439350-0). Acad Pr.

Rapaport, Felix T. & Dausset, Jean, eds. Tissue Typing Today. LC 74-170194. 160p. 1971. 39.00 (ISBN 0-8089-0738-7). Grune.

Sigel, M. Michael & Good, Robert A. Tolerance, Autoimmunity & Aging. (American Lectures Geriatrics & Gerontology). (Illus.). 196p. 1972. photocopy ed. spiral 21.75 (ISBN 0-398-02413-8). C C Thomas.

Spreafico, F. & Arnon, R., eds. Tumor Associated Antigens & Their Specific Immune Responses. (Serono Symposium Ser.). 1979. 40.00 (ISBN 0-12-658350-1). Acad Pr.

Stuart. Immunological Tolerance & Enhancement. 1979. 29.50 (ISBN 0-8391-1170-3). Univ Park.

Thorsby, E., et al. Genetics of Human Histocompatibility Antigens & Their Relation to Disease. (Illus.). 220p. 1973. text ed. 29.50x (ISBN 0-8422-7062-0). Irvington.

Turk, J. L. Delayed Hypersensitivity. 2nd rev. ed. Neuberger, A. & Tatum, E. L., eds. (Frontiers of Biology Ser.: Vol. 4). 1975. 56.00 (ISBN 0-444-10814-9, North-Holland). Elsevier.

Zaleski, M. B., et al, eds. Immunobiology of the Major Histocompatibility Complex. (Illus.). 1981. write for info. (ISBN 3-8055-1896-X). S Karger.

IMMUNOLOGY
see also Antigen-Antibody Reactions; Immunity; Immunodiffusion; Immunogenetics; Immunohematology; Immunological Tolerance; Immunopathology; Radiation Immunology; Veterinary Immunology

Abbott, David. New Life for Old: Therapeutic Immunology. 176p. 1981. 40.00x (ISBN 0-584-10399-9, Pub. by Muller Ltd). State Mutual Bk.

Ablin, Richard J. Immunobiology of the Prostate. 320p. 1982. 27.50 (ISBN 0-87527-178-2). Green.

Acton, Ronald T. Immunobiological & Immunochemical Studies of the Oyster, Crassptrea Virginica. 144p. 1972. text ed. 29.50x (ISBN 0-8422-7034-5). Irvington.

Ada, G. L., ed. Contemporary Topics in Molecular Immunology, Vol. 3. LC 73-186260. (Illus.). 260p. 1974. 25.00 (ISBN 0-306-36103-5, Plenum Pr). Plenum Pub.
Adinolfi, Matteo, ed. Developmental Immunology. (Clinics in Developmental Medicine Ser.: Vol. 34). 187p. 1969. 19.50 (ISBN 0-685-59041-0, JBL-Med Nursing). Lippincott.
--Immunology & Development. (Illus.). 1970. 18.95x (ISBN 0-685-83591-X). Intl Ideas.
Alder, William H. & Nordin, Albert A. Immunological Techniques Applied to Aging Research. 240p. 1981. 62.95 (ISBN 0-8493-5809-4). CRC Pr.
Alexander, J. Wesley & Good, Robert. Fundamentals of Clinical Immunology. LC 77-75530. (Illus.). 1977. pap. text ed. 14.50 (ISBN 0-7216-1101-X). Saunders.
Allansmith, Mathea R. The Eye & Immunology. (Illus.). 200p. 1981. text ed. 29.50 (ISBN 0-8016-0117-7). Mosby.
Aloisi, Ralph M. Principles of Immunodiagnostics. (Illus.). 1979. pap. text ed. 15.95 (ISBN 0-8016-0118-5). Mosby.
Amos, Bernard, ed. Progress in Immunology. 1971. 111.50 (ISBN 0-12-057550-7). Acad Pr.
Amos, D. Bernard, et al, eds. Immune Mechanisms & Disease. LC 79-19241. 1979. 25.00 (ISBN 0-12-055850-5). Acad Pr.
Amos, W. M. Basic Immunology. 210p. 1981. text ed. price not set. Butterworth.
Annual Chicago Symposium, 4th Chicago, 1975. Neoplasm Immunity: Mechanisms: Proceedings. Crispen, Ray G., ed. LC 76-8600. (Neoplasm Immunity Ser.). 1977. 18.00 (ISBN 0-915314-03-7). Inst Tuberculosis.
Antoni, F. & Staub, Maria, eds. Tonsils Structure Immunology & Biochemistry. 1978. 17.50x (ISBN 963-05-1562-8). Intl Pubns Serv.
Arber, W., ed. Current Topics in Microbiology & Immunology, Vol. 72. LC 15-12910. (Illus.). 200p. 1976. 44.80 (ISBN 0-387-07564-X). Springer-Verlag.
--Current Topics in Microbiology & Immunology, Vol. 78. LC 15-12910. (Illus.). 1977. 50.40 (ISBN 0-387-08499-1). Springer-Verlag.
Arber, W., et al. Current Topics in Microbiology & Immunology, Vol. 75. LC 15-12910. (Illus.). 1976. 48.10 (ISBN 3-540-08013-9). Springer-Verlag.
--Current Topics in Microbiology & Immunology, Vol. 79. LC 15-12910. 1978. 56.70 (ISBN 0-387-08587-4). Springer-Verlag.
Arber, W., et al, eds. Current Topics in Microbiology & Immunology, Vols. 40-55. Incl. Vols. 40-50 & 52-55. Chronic Infections Neuropathic Agents & Other Slow Virsus Infections. Brody, J. A., et al, eds. (Illus.). vii, 74p. 1967. 22.90 (ISBN 0-387-03754-3); Vol. 41. (Illus.). iv, 183p. 1967. 49.00 (ISBN 0-387-03755-1); Vol. 42. Insect Viruses. Maramorosch, K., ed. (Illus.). viii, 192p. 1968. 26.70 (ISBN 0-387-04071-4); Vol. 43. (Illus.). iii, 233p. (Incl. 32 pp. in German). 1968. 52.00 (ISBN 0-387-04072-2); Vol. 44. (Illus.). iii, 175p. 1968. 52.00 (ISBN 0-387-04073-0); Vol. 45. (Illus.). iii, 237p. (Incl. 61 pp. in German). 1968. 52.00 (ISBN 0-387-04074-9); Vol. 46. (Illus.). iii, 203p. (Incl. 90 pp. in German). 1968. 57.90 (ISBN 0-387-04075-7); Vol. 47. (Illus.). iii, 222p. (Incl. 29 pp. in German). 1969. 55.50 (ISBN 0-387-04445-0); Vol. 48. (Illus.). iii, 206p. 1969. 55.50 (ISBN 0-387-04446-9); Vol. 49. (Illus.). iii, 250p. 1969. 55.50 (ISBN 0-387-04447-7); Vol. 50. (Illus.). iii, 238p. 1969. 55.50 (ISBN 0-387-04448-5); Vol. 52. (Illus.). iv, 197p. 1970. 55.50 (ISBN 0-387-04787-5); Vol. 53. (Illus.). 236p. 1970. 58.50 (ISBN 0-387-05069-8); Vol. 54. (Illus.). 230p. 1971. 58.50 (ISBN 0-387-05289-5); Vol. 55. Arthropod Cell Cultures & Their Application to the Study of Viruses: Arthropod Cell Cultures & Their Application to the Study of Viruses. Weiss, E., ed. (Illus.). 340p. 1971. 49.10 (ISBN 0-387-05451-0). (Illus., Eng. & Ger.). Springer-Verlag.
--Current Topics in Microbiology & Immunology, Vol. 62. LC 73-17985. (Illus.). 170p. 1974. 35.90 (ISBN 0-387-06598-9). Springer-Verlag.
--Current Topics in Microbiology & Immunology, Vol. 63. LC 73-20915. (Illus.). 230p. 1974. 44.00 (ISBN 0-387-06599-7). Springer-Verlag.
--Current Topics in Microbiology & Immunology, Vol. 64. LC 74-3541. (Illus.). 190p. 1974. 42.20 (ISBN 0-387-06713-2). Springer-Verlag.
--Current Topics in Microbiology & Immunology, Vol. 65. LC 15-12910. (Illus.). 165p. 1974. 41.30 (ISBN 0-387-06774-4). Springer-Verlag.
--Current Topics in Microbiology & Immunology, Vol. 66. LC 15-12910. (Illus.). 130p. 1974. 31.40 (ISBN 3-540-06831-7). Springer-Verlag.
--Current Topics in Microbiology & Immunology, Vol. 67. LC 15-12910. (Illus.). iv, 162p. 1975. 42.20 (ISBN 3-540-06838-4). Springer-Verlag.
--Current Topics in Microbiology & Immunology, Vol. 76. LC 15-12910. (Illus.). 1977. 48.10 (ISBN 3-540-08238-7). Springer-Verlag.
--Current Topics in Microbiology & Immunology, Vol. 77. LC 15-12910. (Illus.). 1977. 45.70 (ISBN 0-387-08401-0). Springer-Verlag.
--Current Topics in Microbiology & Immunology, Vol. 82. LC 15-12910. (Illus.). 1978. 37.50 (ISBN 0-387-08981-0). Springer-Verlag.
--Current Topics in Microbiology & Immunology, Vol. 83. LC 15-12910. (Illus.). 1978. 39.30 (ISBN 0-387-09034-7). Springer-Verlag.
--Current Topics in Microbiology & Immunology, Vol. 85. (Illus.). 1979. 50.80 (ISBN 0-387-09410-5). Springer-Verlag.
--Current Topics in Microbiology & Immunology, Vols. 86-87. (Illus.). 1980. Vol. 86. 39.30 (ISBN 0-387-09432-6); Vol. 87. 37.40 (ISBN 0-387-09433-4). Springer-Verlag.
--Current Topics in Microbiology & Immunology, Vol. 90. (Illus.). 147p. 1980. 51.90 (ISBN 0-387-10181-0). Springer-Verlag.
--Current Topics in Microbiology & Immunology, Vol. 91. (Illus.). 250p. 37.20 (ISBN 0-387-10722-3). Springer-Verlag.
Arnason, Barry G. W. Clinical Immunology of the Nervous System. (Clinical Neurology & Neurosurgery Monographs). (Illus.). 1982. text ed. pns (ISBN 0-443-08002-X). Churchill.
Azzolina, L. S., ed. Comparative Immunology: Proceedings of the Verona Workshop, 16-17 July 1980, Verona, Italy. (Illus.). 180p. 1981. pap. 25.00 (ISBN 0-08-028019-6). Pergamon.
Bach, Fritz H., ed. Clinical Immunobiology, Vol. 4. 1980. 19.50 (ISBN 0-12-070004-2). Acad Pr.
Bach, Fritz H. & Good, Robert A., eds. Clinical Immunobiology. (Illus.). Vol. 1 1972. 32.00 (ISBN 0-12-070001-8); Vol. 2 1974. 32.00 (ISBN 0-12-070002-6); Vol. 3 1976. 46.00 (ISBN 0-12-070003-4). Acad Pr.
Bach, J. F., ed. The Mode of Action of Immunosuppressive Agents. LC 74-18772. (Frontiers of Biology Ser.: Vol. 41). 400p. 1975. 58.75 (ISBN 0-444-10808-4, North-Holland). Elsevier.
Bach, Jean F., ed. Immunology. 2nd ed. 950p. 1981. 70.00 (ISBN 0-471-08044-6, Pub. by Wiley Med). Wiley.
Bach, Jean-Francois, ed. Immunology. LC 77-12139. 1978. 63.50 (ISBN 0-471-01760-4, Pub. by Wiley Medical). Wiley.
Banker, D. D. Modern Practice in Immunization. rev. 3rd ed. xii, 384p. 1980. pap. text ed. 12.95 (ISBN 0-86590-007-8, Pub. by Popular Prakashan India). Apt Bks.
Barber, H. R. Immunobiology for the Clinician. LC 76-23386. 310p. 1977. 38.95 (ISBN 0-471-04785-6). Wiley.
Barrett, James T. Basic Immunology & Its Medical Application. 2nd ed. LC 80-14328. (Illus.). 304p. 1980. pap. text ed. 17.50 (ISBN 0-8016-0495-8). Mosby.
--Textbook of Immunology: An Introduction to Immunochemistry & Immunobiology. 3rd ed. LC 77-16208. (Illus.). 1978. text ed. 19.95 (ISBN 0-8016-0500-8). Mosby.
Barriga, Omar O. Immunology of Parasitic Infections. 368p. (Orig.). 1981. pap. text ed. 24.95 (ISBN 0-8391-1621-7). Univ Park.
Baumgarten, Alexander & Richards, Frank F. Handbook Series in Clinical Laboratory Science, CRC: Section F, Immunology, 2 pts, Vol. 1. 1978-79. Pt. 1. 63.95 (ISBN 0-8493-7021-3); Pt. 2, 480p. 62.95 (ISBN 0-8493-7022-1). CRC Pr.
Beers, Roland F., Jr. & Bassett, Edward G., eds. The Role of Immunological Factors in Infectious, Allergic, & Autoimmune Processes. LC 75-25109. (Miles International Symposium Ser: No. 8). 1976. 45.00 (ISBN 0-89004-073-7). Raven.
Beers, Roland F., Jr. & Tilghman, R. Carmichael, eds. The Role of Immunological Factors in Viral & Oncogenic Processes 5th: Seventh Miles International Symposium on Molecular Biology. LC 73-19346. (Medical Journal Supplement: No. 3). (Illus.). 512p. 1974. 34.00x (ISBN 0-8018-1599-1). Johns Hopkins.
Bell, George, et al, eds. Theoretical Immunology. (Immunology Ser.: Vol. 8). 1978. 55.00 (ISBN 0-8247-6618-0). Dekker.
Bellanti, Joseph A. Immunology: Basic Process. new ed. LC 79-3947. (Illus.). 1979. pap. text ed. 11.95 (ISBN 0-7216-1677-1). Saunders.
--Immunology II. LC 77-72808. (Illus.). 1978. text ed. 27.50 (ISBN 0-7216-1681-X). Saunders.
Benacerraf, Baruj. Textbook of Immunology. (Illus.). 1979. pap. 13.95 (ISBN 0-683-00527-8). Williams & Wilkins.
Benedict, A. A., ed. Avian Immunology. LC 77-2732. (Advances in Experimental Medicine & Biology: Vol. 88). 407p. 1977. 39.50 (ISBN 0-306-32688-4, Plenum Pr). Plenum Pub.
Bier, O. G., et al. Fundamentals of Immunology. (Illus.). 442p. 1981. pap. 24.00 (ISBN 0-387-90529-4). Springer-Verlag.
Bigley, Nancy J. Immunologic Fundamentals. 1980. 15.50 (ISBN 0-8151-0801-X). Year Bk Med.
Blake, Patricia J. & Perez, Rosanne C. Applied Immunological Concepts. (Illus.). 176p. 1978. pap. 8.95 (ISBN 0-8385-0240-7). ACC.
Bloom, Barry R. & Glade, Philip R., eds. In Vitro Methods in Cell-Mediated Immunity. 1971. 43.00 (ISBN 0-12-107750-0). Acad Pr.
Blough, H. A., et al. Current Topics in Microbiology & Immunology, Vol. 70. LC 75-12910. (Illus.). 140p. 1975. 35.10 (ISBN 0-387-07223-3). Springer-Verlag.
Bona, Constantin. Idiotypes & Lymphocytes. (Immunology: an International Ser. of Monographs & Treatise). 1981. price not set (ISBN 0-12-112950-0). Acad Pr.
Bowry, T. R. Immunology Simplified. (Illus.). 1978. pap. text ed. 8.95x (ISBN 0-19-261148-8). Oxford U Pr.
Boyd, William C. Fundamentals of Immunology. 4th ed. LC 66-20389. 1967. 45.00 (ISBN 0-470-09342-0, Pub. by Wiley-Interscience). Wiley.
Brooks, G. F., et al, eds. Immunobiology of Neisseria Gonorrhoeae. (Illus.). 1978. text ed. 15.00 (ISBN 0-914826-18-2). Am Soc Microbio.
Bruni, C., ed. Systems Theory in Immunology. (Lecture Notes in Biomathematics: Vol. 32). 273p. 1980. pap. 16.00 (ISBN 0-387-09728-7). Springer-Verlag.
Burnet, F. M. Immunology, Aging, & Cancer. LC 76-16166. (Illus.). 1976. pap. text ed. 8.95x (ISBN 0-7167-0489-7). W H Freeman.
Burnet, F. M., intro. by. Immunology: Readings from Scientific American. LC 75-19356. (Illus.). 1976. text ed. 19.95x (ISBN 0-7167-0525-7); pap. text ed. 9.95x (ISBN 0-7167-0524-9). W H Freeman.
Burnet, F. Macfarlane. Cellular Immunology, 2 bks. in 1. LC 69-12162. (Illus.). 1969. 74.50 (ISBN 0-521-07217-4). Cambridge U Pr.
--Self & Not Self: Cellular Immunology, Bk. 1. (Illus.). 1969. 32.50 (ISBN 0-521-07521-1); pap. 14.50x (ISBN 0-521-09558-1, 558). Cambridge U Pr.
Burrell, Robert. Experimental Immunology. 5th ed. 1979. spiral bdg. 9.95x (ISBN 0-8087-2876-8). Burgess.
Calne, R. Y. Organ Grafts. (Current Topics in Immunology: Vol. 4). (Illus.). 1978. pap. 12.95 (ISBN 0-8151-1415-X). Year Bk Med.
Castro, J. E., ed. Immunology for Surgeons. 1976. 39.50 (ISBN 0-8391-0932-6). Univ Park.
Chandra. Immunology of Nutritional Diseases. (Current Topics Immunology Ser.: Vol. 12). 1980. 23.75 (ISBN 0-8151-1640-3). Year Bk Med.
Chedid, L., ed. Immunostimulation. (Illus.). 236p. 1981. 22.50 (ISBN 0-387-10354-6). Springer-Verlag.
Clark, William R. The Experimental Foundations of Modern Immunology. LC 80-13565. 372p. 1980. text ed. 22.50 (ISBN 0-471-04088-6). Wiley.
Cohen, Alan S., ed. Rheumatology & Immunology. (The Science & Practice of Clinical Medicine Ser.). 464p. 1979. 37.00 (ISBN 0-8089-1118-X). Grune.
Cohen, Edward P. & Kohler, Heinz, eds. Membranes, Receptors, & the Immune Response: Eighty Years After Ehrich's Side Chain Theory. LC 80-7811. (Progress in Clinical & Biological Research Ser.: Vol. 42). 404p. 1980. 34.00 (ISBN 0-8451-0042-4). A R Liss.
Colloquium of the Workshop for Biological Chemistry, April 29 - May 1, 1976, Mosbach-Baden. The Immune System: Proceedings. Melchers, F., ed. (Illus.). 1976. 40.30 (ISBN 0-387-07976-9). Springer-Verlag.
Cooper, E. L. General Immunology. LC 80-42218. (Illus.). 300p. 1981. 60.00 (ISBN 0-08-026368-2); pap. 21.00 (ISBN 0-08-026369-0). Pergamon.
Cooper, Edward L. Comparative Immunology. (Foundations of Immunology Ser.). (Illus.). 480p. 1976. 23.95x (ISBN 0-13-153429-7). P-H.
Cooper, Edwin L., ed. Contemporary Topics in Immunobiology: Vol. 4, Invertebrate Immunology. LC 78-165398. (Illus.). 299p. 1974. 25.00 (ISBN 0-306-37804-3, Plenum Pr). Plenum Pub.
Cooper, M., et al, eds. B Lymphocytes in the Immune Response. (Developments in Immunology: Vol. 3). 1979. 45.00 (ISBN 0-444-00319-3, North Holland). Elsevier.
Cooper, Max D. & Dayton, Delbert H., eds. Development of Host Defenses. LC 76-51866. 320p. 1977. 31.50 (ISBN 0-89004-117-2). Raven.
Cooper, Max D. & Warner, Noel L., eds. Contemporary Topics in Immunobiology, Vol. 3. LC 68-26769. (Illus.). 263p. 1974. 25.00 (ISBN 0-306-37803-5, Plenum Pr). Plenum Pub.
Criep, Leo H. Allergy & Clinical Immunology: With Addenda. LC 76-14352. (Illus.). 1980. 59.50 (ISBN 0-8089-0823-5). Grune.
--Clinical Immunology & Allergy. 2nd ed. LC 68-20165. (Illus.). 976p. 1969. 81.00 (ISBN 0-8089-0105-2). Grune.
Current Topics in Microbiology & Immunology, Vol. 71. LC 15-12910. (Illus.). 1975. 39.00 (ISBN 0-387-07369-8). Springer-Verlag.
Current Topics in Microbiology & Immunology, Vol. 80. LC 15-12910. (Illus.). 1978. 39.30 (ISBN 0-387-08781-8). Springer-Verlag.
Current Topics in Microbiology & Immunology, Vol. 88. (Illus.). 142p. 1980. 35.20 (ISBN 0-387-09415-6). Springer-Verlag.
Curtis, A. S., ed. Cell-Cell Recognition. LC 77-28646. (Society for Experimental Biology: Symposia No. 32). (Illus.). 1978. 72.50 (ISBN 0-521-22020-3). Cambridge U Pr.
Dahl. Clinical Immunodermatology. 1981. 27.50 (ISBN 0-8151-2246-2). Year Bk Med.
Day, N. K. & Good, R. A., eds. Biological Amplification Systems in Immunology. LC 76-56828. (Comprehensive Immunology: Vol. 2). (Illus.). 325p. 1977. 29.50 (ISBN 0-306-33102-0, Plenum Pr). Plenum Pub.
Dodd, Barbara E. Blood Group Topics. (Current Topics in Immunology: Vol. 3). (Illus.). 1978. pap. 17.50 (ISBN 0-8151-2710-3). Year Bk Med.
Dubin, N. A Stochastic Model for Immunological Feedback in Carcinogenesis: Analysis & Approximations. (Lecture Notes in Biomathematics: Vol. 9). 1976. soft cover 11.00 (ISBN 0-387-07786-3). Springer-Verlag.
Eisen, H. N. & Reisfeld, R. A., eds. Contemporary Topics in Molecular Immunology, Vol. 5. (Illus.). 234p. 1976. 32.50 (ISBN 0-306-36105-1, Plenum Pr). Plenum Pub.
Eisen, Herman N. Immunology. 2nd ed. (Illus.). 259p. 1980. text ed. 18.00 (ISBN 0-06-140781-X, Harper Medical). Har-Row.
Emerson, S. U., et al. Current Topics in Microbiology & Immunology, Vol. 73. LC 15-12910. 1976. 43.60 (ISBN 0-387-07593-3). Springer-Verlag.
Escobar, M. R. & Friedman, H., eds. Macrophages & Lymphocytes: Nature, Functions, & Interaction, Pt. A. LC 79-9566. (Advances in Experimental Medicine & Biology Ser.: Vol. 121A). 660p. 1980. 59.50 (ISBN 0-306-40285-8, Plenum Pr). Plenum Pub.
European Immunology Meeting, 4th, Budapest, Hungary, April 12-14, 1978. Immunology 1978. Gergely, J., et al, eds. 1978. 48.30 (ISBN 963-05-1562-8, 996001158). Heyden.
Feldmann, G., et al. Immunoenzymatic Techniques. LC 76-7438. 1976. 100.00 (ISBN 0-444-11206-5, North-Holland). Elsevier.
Ferrone, Soldano, et al, eds. Current Trends in Immunology. LC 78-31911. (Illus.). 400p. 1979. lib. bdg. 37.50 (ISBN 0-8240-7065-8). Garland Pub.
Festenstein & Demant. HLA & H2. (Current Topics Immunology Ser.: Vol. 9). 1979. 19.95 (ISBN 0-8151-3217-4). Year Bk Med.
Fougereau, M. & Dausset, J., eds. Immunology Eighty: Fourth International Congress of Immunology. 1981. 110.00 (ISBN 0-686-74510-8). Acad Pr.
--Immunology Eighty: Progress in Immunology IV (Fourth International Congress of Immunology) 1500p. pap. 110.00 (ISBN 0-12-262940-X). Acad Pr.
Fougereau, M. & Daussett, J., eds. Immunology, 80. LC 80-49682. 1981. Vol. 1. 60.00 (ISBN 0-12-262901-9); Vol. 2. 60.00 (ISBN 0-12-262902-7); Vol. 3. 60.00 (ISBN 0-12-262903-5). Acad Pr.
Fraenkel-Conrat, H. & Wagner, R. R., eds. Comprehensive Virology, Vol. 15: Virus - Host Interactions - Immunity to Viruses. LC 79-26533. (Illus.). 309p. 1979. 29.50 (ISBN 0-306-40262-9, Plenum Pr). Plenum Pub.
Franklin, E. C., ed. Clinical Immunology Update: Reviews for Physicians. 1979. 24.95 (ISBN 0-444-00312-6). Elsevier.
Franklin, T. J. & Snow, G. A. Biochemistry of Antimicrobial Action. 2nd ed. LC 75-8549. 224p. 1975. text ed. 27.50x (ISBN 0-412-12900-0, Pub. by Chapman & Hall). Methuen Inc.
Frazer, A. C., et al. Current Topics in Microbiology & Immunology, Vol. 69. (Illus.). 200p. 1975. 42.60 (ISBN 0-387-07195-4). Springer-Verlag.
Freedman, Samuel O. & Gold, Phil. Clinical Immunology. 2nd ed. (Illus.). 1976. 37.00x (ISBN 0-06-140834-4, Harper Medical). Har-Row.
Fudenberg, H. Hugh, et al, eds. Basic & Clinical Immunology. 3rd ed. LC 80-82159. (Illus.). 782p. 1980. lexotone cover 17.50 (ISBN 0-87041-222-1). Lange.
Fudenberg, Hugh H. & Graber, Charles D. Microbiology & Immunology: A Positive Statement Manual. 1977. spiral bddg. 9.75 (ISBN 0-87488-242-7). Med Exam.

Fulginiti, Vincent A. Immunology: Theory & Practice. (Illus.). 192p. 1981. pap. text ed. price not set (ISBN 0-397-50539-6, JBL-Med-Nursing). Har-Row.
Galbraith, Robert M. Immunological Aspects of Diabetes Mellitus. 96p. 1979. 29.95 (ISBN 0-8493-5365-3). CRC Pr.
Gale, R. P. & Opelz, Gerhard, eds. Immunobiology of Bone Marrow Transplantation, Vol. 2. (Transplantation Proceedings). 288p. 1978. 39.00 (ISBN 0-8089-1116-3). Grune.
Gergely, J., ed. Immunology 1978. (Illus.). 532p. 1978. 45.00x (ISBN 963-05-1878-3). Intl Pubns Serv.
Glasser, Ronald J. The Body Is the Hero. 1976. 8.95 (ISBN 0-394-40013-5). Random.
Golub, E. S., ed. Immunology, 2 pts. (Benchmark Papers in Microbiology Ser.). 1981. 72.00 set (ISBN 0-686-76207-X); Pt. 1: Cell Interactions. 46.00 (ISBN 0-12-786546-2); Pt. 2: Regulation. 34.00 (ISBN 0-12-786547-0). Acad Pr.
Golub, Edward S. The Cellular Basis of the Immune Response. rev. & 2nd ed. LC 80-28080. (Illus.). 325p. 1981. pap. text ed. 14.00x (ISBN 0-87893-212-7). Sinauer Assoc.
Goodman, Joel M., et al. Phylogenetic Development of Vertebrate Immunity, No. 2. new ed. (Illus.). 220p. 1972. text ed. 28.50x (ISBN 0-8422-7057-4). Irvington.
Gowans, J. L. Cellular Immunology. Head, J. J., ed. LC 76-29374. (Carolina Biology Readers Ser.). (Illus.). (gr. 11 up). 1977. pap. 1.65 (ISBN 0-89278-287-0, 45-9687). Carolina Biological.
Graham, H., et al, eds. Marek's Disease II: Pathogenicity & Immunology. (Herpesvirus-Related Diseases Ser.). 320p. 1974. text ed. 28.50x (ISBN 0-8422-7167-8). Irvington.
Guttmann, R., ed. Immunology. 103p. 1972. pap. 9.95 (ISBN 0-685-90283-8, Pub. by W & W). Krieger.
Hadden, J., et al. Advances in Immunopharmacology: Proceedings of the First International Conference on Immunopharmacology, 29 July-1 August 1980, Brighton. (Illus.). 538p. 1981. 80.00 (ISBN 0-08-026384-4); pap. 35.00 (ISBN 0-08-027974-0). Pergamon.
Hadden, J. W., et al, eds. Comprehensive Immunology: Vol. 3, Immunopharmacology. LC 77-23915. (Illus.). 423p. 1977. 35.00 (ISBN 0-306-33103-9, Plenum Pr). Plenum Pub.
Halliday, W. J. Glossary of Immunological Terms. 102p. 1971. 9.95 (ISBN 0-407-72740-X). Butterworth.
Hanna, M. G., Jr., ed. Contemporary Topics in Immunobiology, Vol. 1. LC 68-26769. 188p. 1972. 25.00 (ISBN 0-306-37801-9, Plenum Pr). Plenum Pub.
Hanna, Michael G., Jr. & Rapp, Fred, eds. Contemporary Tonics in Immunology: Immunology of Oncogenic Viruses. (Illus.). 289p. 1977. 27.50 (ISBN 0-306-37806-X, Plenum Pr). Plenum Pub.
Hare, Ronald & Cooke, Mary. Bacteriology & Immunity for Nurses. 5th ed. (Churchill Livingstone Nursing Texts). 1979. pap. text ed. 11.25 (ISBN 0-443-01757-3). Churchill.
Heden, Carl-Goran & Illeni, Tibor, eds. Automation in Microbiology & Immunology. LC 74-12082. 610p. 1975. 50.00 (ISBN 0-471-36745-1, Pub. by Wiley). Krieger.
Hennessen, W. & Huygelen, C., eds. Immunization: Benefit Versus Risk Factors. (Developments in Biological Standardization: Vol. 43). (Illus.). 1979. pap. 60.00 (ISBN 3-8055-2816-7). S Karger.
Hildemann, W. H. & Benedict, A. A., eds. Immunologic Phylogeny. LC 75-35524. (Advances in Experimental Medicine & Biology Ser.: Vol. 64). 478p. 1975. 37.50 (ISBN 0-306-39064-7, Plenum Pr). Plenum Pub.
Holborow, E. J. & Reeves, W. G., eds. Immunology in Medicine: A Comprehensive Guide to Clinical Immunology. 1174p. 1977. 65.50 (ISBN 0-8089-1028-0). Grune.
Hood, Leroy, et al. Immunology. 1978. 15.95 (ISBN 0-8053-4405-5). Benjamin-Cummings.
Hudson, Leslie & Hay, Frank C. Practical Immunology. (Blackwell Scientific Pubns.). (Illus.). 1976. softcover 16.25 (ISBN 0-632-00353-7). Mosby.
Hyde, R. M. & Patnode, Robert. Immunology. (Illus.). 1978. text ed. 13.95 (ISBN 0-87909-385-4); pap. text ed. 11.95 (ISBN 0-8359-3853-0); instrs'. manual avail. Reston.
Immunology & Parasitic Diseases. (Technical Report Ser: No. 315). 64p. (Eng, Fr, Rus, & Span.). 1965. pap. 2.00 (ISBN 92-4-120315-3). World Health.
Immunology & the Skin. LC 75-133174. (Advances in Biology of Skin Ser.: Vol. 11). 396p. 1971. 32.50 (ISBN 0-306-50055-8, Plenum Pr). Plenum Pub.
Immunology of the Gut. (Ciba Foundation Symposium Ser: No. 46). 1977. 34.25 (ISBN 90-219-4052-3, Excerpta Medica). Elsevier.
Inderbitzin, T. M., ed. Prophylaxis of Infectious & Other Diseases by Means of Vaccination & the Use of Immunoglobulins. (Monographs in Allergy: Vol. 9). (Illus.). 300p. 1975. 45.50 (ISBN 3-8055-1779-3). S Karger.
Inman, F. P. Contemporary Topics in Molecular Immunology, Vol. 4. LC 73-648513. (Illus.). 245p. 1975. 27.50 (ISBN 0-306-36104-3, Plenum Pr). Plenum Pub.
Inman, F. P. & Mandy, W. J., eds. Contemporary Topics in Molecular Immunology, Vol. 8. 226p. 1981. 32.50 (ISBN 0-306-40661-6, Plenum Pr). Plenum Pub.
International Co-Ordination Committee for the Immunology of Reproduction, 1st Symposium. Immunology & Reproduction: Proceedings. Edwards, R. G., ed. LC 70-449061. (Illus.). 1969. 18.50x (ISBN 0-900924-06-3). Intl Pubns Serv.
International Conference, Duesseldorf, November 14-15, 1977 & Chicago, December 5-6, 1977. New Developments in Immunoassays. Schoenfeld, H., ed. (Antibiotics & Chemotherapy: Vol. 26). (Illus.). 1979. 58.75 (ISBN 3-8055-2882-5). S Karger.
International Congress of Allergology, 10th, Jerusalem, Israel, Nov. 1979. Advances in Allergology & Applied Immunology: Proceedings. Oehling, A., et al, eds. (Illus.). 680p. 1980. 145.00 (ISBN 0-08-025519-1). Pergamon.
International Congress of Allergology, 9th, Buenos Aires, 24-30 Oct. 1976. Allergy & Clinical Immunology: Proceedings. Mathov & Sindo, eds. (International Congress Ser.: No. 414). 1977. 124.00 (ISBN 0-444-15253-9, Excerpta Medica). Elsevier.
International Convocation in Immunology, 2nd, Buffalo, 1970. Cellular Interactions in the Immune Response. Cohen, S., et al, eds. 1971. 59.25 (ISBN 3-8055-1202-3). S Karger.
International Convocation on Immunology, 4th, Buffalo, Jun 1974. The Immune System & Infectious Diseases: Proceedings. Milgrom, F. & Neter, E., eds. (Illus.). xii, 549p. 1975. 99.00 (ISBN 3-8055-2177-4). S Karger.
International Convocation on Immunology, 3rd, Buffalo, 1972. Specific Receptors of Antibodies, Antigens & Cells: Proceedings. Rose, N. R., et al. ed. 300p. 1973. 92.25 (ISBN 3-8055-1372-0). S Karger.
International Society for Cell Biology. Differentiation & Immunology. Warren, Katherine B., ed. (Proceedings: Vol. 7). 1969. 56.00 (ISBN 0-12-611907-4). Acad Pr.
International Symposium, Montpellier, March 1974. Immunological Aspects of Rheumatoid Arthritis: Proceedings. Clot, J., ed. (Rheumatology: Vol. 6). 250p. 1975. 84.00 (ISBN 3-8055-2116-2). S Karger.
International Symposium on Brucellosis, 24th, Tunise, 1968. Brucellosis: Standardization & Control of Vaccines & Reagents. Proceedings. Permanent Section of Microbiological Standardization, Bourse Du Travail, ed. (Immunobiological Standardization: Vol. 12). 1970. 36.00 (ISBN 3-8055-0634-1). S Karger.
International Symposium on Rabies, 40th, Lyon, December 9-11, 1972. Proceedings. (Symposia Series in Immunobiological Standardization: Vol. 21). 336p. 1975. 54.00 (ISBN 3-8055-1649-5). S Karger.
International Symposium on Smallpox Vaccine, 37th, Bilthoven, October 1972. Proceedings. Regamey, R. H., et al, eds. (Symposia Series in Immunobiologucal Standardization: Vol. 19). 365p. 1973. 45.00 (ISBN 3-8055-1773-4). S Karger.
International Symposium on Yersinia, 3rd, Montreal, September 1977. Yersinia enterocolitica. Carter, Philip B., et al, eds. (Contributions to Microbiology & Immunology: Vol. 5). (Illus.). 1979. 93.00 (ISBN 3-8055-2927-9). S Karger.
International Symposium on Yersinia, Pasteurella & Francisella, Malmoe, April 1972. Yersinia, Pasteurella & Francisella: Proceedings. Winblad, ed. (Contributions to Microbiology & Immunology: Vol. 2). 1973. 45.00 (ISBN 3-8055-1636-3). S Karger.
Irvine, W. James, ed. Medical Immunology. (Illus.). 506p. 1980. pap. text ed. 25.00x (ISBN 0-07-032049-7, HP). McGraw.
Jirsch, D. W., ed. Immunological Engineering. 1978. 34.50 (ISBN 0-8391-1225-4). Univ Park.
Kahan, Barry D. & Reisfeld, Ralph A., eds. Markers of Biological Individuality: The Transplantation Antigens Immunology. (Immunology Ser, Vol. 2). 1972. 63.50 (ISBN 0-12-394350-7). Acad Pr.
Karcher, D., et al, eds. Humoral Immunity in Neurological Diseases. LC 79-15096. (Nato Advanced Study Institutes Ser. A: Life Sciences: Vol. 24). 684p. 1979. 59.50 (ISBN 0-306-40195-9, Plenum Pr). Plenum Pub.
Khan, Amanullah, et al, eds. Immune Regulators in Transfer Factor. LC 79-1464. 1979. 38.00 (ISBN 0-12-406060-9). Acad Pr.
Kunkel, Henry & Dixon, Frank, eds. Advances in Immunology, Vol. 31. (Serial Publication Ser.). 1981. price not set (ISBN 0-12-022431-3). Acad Pr.
Kwapinski, George. The Methodology of Investigative & Clinical Immunology. LC 78-26882. 1981. Repr. of 1972 ed. text ed. price not set (ISBN 0-88275-828-4). Krieger.
--The Methodology of Investigative & Clinical Immunology: Based Upon Methods of Immunochemical & Immunological Research. LC 78-26882. Date not set. price not set (ISBN 0-88275-828-4). Krieger.
Kwapinski, J. B., ed. Research in Immunochemistry & Immunobiology, Vol. 1. (Illus.). 1972. 34.50 (ISBN 0-8391-0651-3). Univ Park.
--Research in Immunochemistry & Immunobiology, Vol. 2. (Illus.). 1972. 34.50 (ISBN 0-8391-0652-1). Univ Park.
--Research in Immunochemistry & Immunobiology, Vol. 3. (Illus.). 1973. 34.50 (ISBN 0-8391-0653-X). Univ Park.
LaDu, Bert. Immunopharmacology: New York Heart Association Symposium. 220p. 1973. 16.75 (ISBN 0-683-04857-0, Pub. by Williams & Wilkins). Krieger.
Lambert, H. P. & Wood, C. B., eds. Immunological Aspects of Infection in the Fetus & New Born. (Beecham Colloquia Ser.). 1981. 39.50 (ISBN 0-12-434660-X). Acad Pr.
Larralde, Carlos, et al, eds. Molecules, Cells & Parasites in Immunology. 1980. 19.50 (ISBN 0-12-436840-9). Acad Pr.
Lawlor, Glenn J. & Fischer, Thomas J. Manual of Allerfy & Immunology: Diagnosis & Therapy. (SPIRAL TM Manual Ser.). 1981. pap. text ed. price not set (ISBN 0-316-51665-1). Little.
Lawlor, Glenn J., Jr. & Fischer, Thomas J. Manual of Allergy & Immunology. (Little, Brown Spiral Manual Ser.). 1981. pap. text ed. write for info. Little.
Lawrence, H. S. & Landy, M., eds. Mediators of Cellular Immunity. (Perspectives in Immunology Ser). 1969. 38.00 (ISBN 0-12-439350-0). Acad Pr.
Lefkovits, Ivan, ed. Immunological Methods, Vol. 2. LC 78-3342. 1981. 35.00 (ISBN 0-12-442702-2). Acad Pr.
Lefkovits, Ivan & Pernis, Benvenuto, eds. Immunological Methods. LC 78-3342. 1979. 44.50 (ISBN 0-12-442750-2). Acad Pr.
Lindahl-Kiessling, K., et al, eds. Morphological & Functional Aspects of Immunity. LC 75-148822. (Advances in Experimental Medicine & Biology Ser.: Vol. 12). 694p. 1971. 45.00 (ISBN 0-306-39012-4, Plenum Pr). Plenum Pub.
Linscott, William D. Linscott's Directory of Immunological & Biological Reagents. 2nd ed. 120p. 1981. 25.00x (ISBN 0-9604920-1-1). W D Linscott.
Litman, Gary W. & Good, Robert A., eds. Comprehensive Immunology, Vol. 5: Immunoglobulins. LC 78-1439. (Illus.). 401p. 1978. 29.50 (ISBN 0-306-33105-5, Plenum Pr). Plenum Pub.
Litton Bionetics. Biological Relevance of Immune Suppression As Induced by Genetic, Therapeutic & Environmental Factors. (Litton Bionetics Workshop Ser.). 384p. 1981. text ed. 27.50 (ISBN 0-442-24429-0). Van Nos Reinhold.
Lockey, Richard F., ed. Allergy & Clinical Immunology. LC 78-62073. 1979. 42.50 (ISBN 0-87488-665-1). Med Exam.
Loke, Y. W. Immunology & Immunopathology of the Human Foetal-Maternal Interaction. 1978. 70.75 (ISBN 0-444-80055-7, Biomedical Pr). Elsevier.
Luderer, Albert A. & Weetall, Howard H., eds. Clinical Cellular Immunology. (Contemporary Immunology Ser.). (Illus.). 1981. 49.50 (ISBN 0-89603-011-3). Humana.
McGardy, Pat. New Immunology. 3.00 (ISBN 0-686-29802-0). Cancer Bk Hse.
McGovern, John P., et al. Chronobiology in Allergy & Immunology. (Illus.). 308p. 1977. 27.75 (ISBN 0-398-03583-0). C C Thomas.
Maggio, Edward T. Enzyme Immunoassay. 304p. 1980. 69.95 (ISBN 0-8493-5617-2). CRC Pr.
Makela, O., et al. Cell Interactions & Receptor Antibodies in Immune Responses. 472p. 1971. 75.00 (ISBN 0-12-466050-9). Acad Pr.
Makinodan, T. & Yunis, Edmond, eds. Comprehensive Immunology: Vol. 1, Immunology & Aging. LC 76-53755. (Illus.). 208p. 1977. 22.50 (ISBN 0-306-33101-2, Plenum Pr). Plenum Pub.
Makinodan, Takashi & Kay, Marguerite M., eds. CRC Handbook of Immunology of Aging. (CRC Ser. in Aging). 352p. 1981. 59.95 (ISBN 0-8493-3144-7). CRC Pr.
Malone, Fred. Bees Don't Get Arthritis. (Illus.). 1979. 8.95 (ISBN 0-525-06240-8, Thomas Congdon Book). Dutton.
Mandel, T. E., et al, eds. Progress in Immunology: Proceedings of the 3rd Intl. Congress of Immunology, Sydney Australia, July 1977, Vol. III. 1978. 116.75 (ISBN 0-444-80004-2, Biomedical Pr). Elsevier.
Marchalonis, J. J., ed. Comparative Immunology. LC 76-18782. 470p. 1976. 54.95 (ISBN 0-470-15160-9). Halsted Pr.
Marchalonis, John J. & Cohen, Nicholas, eds. Contemporary Topics in Immunobiology, Vol. 9: Self-Non Self Discrimination. LC 79-179761. (Illus.). 309p. 1980. 29.50 (ISBN 0-306-40263-7, Plenum Pr). Plenum Pub.
Marshall, Wallace. Immunologic Psychology & Psychiatry. LC 75-8713. 240p. 1977. 16.75x (ISBN 0-8173-2703-7). U of Ala Pr.
Mathieu, Alix & Kahan, Barry D., eds. Immunological Aspects of Anesthetic & Surgical Practice. LC 75-15889. 352p. 1975. 54.50 (ISBN 0-8089-0874-X). Grune.
Meeting of the Midwest Autumn Immunology Conference, 7th, Michigan, Nov. 1978. Immunologic Tolerance & Macrophage Function: Proceedings. Baram, R., et al, eds. LC 79-243. (Developments in Immunology Ser.: Vol. 4). 1979. 40.00 (ISBN 0-444-00316-9, North Holland). Elsevier.
Milgrom, et al, eds. Principles of Immunological Diagnosis in Medicine. LC 80-20724. (Illus.). 520p. 1981. text ed. write for info. (ISBN 0-8121-0720-9). Lea & Febiger.
Miller, Michael E. Host Defenses in the Human Neonate. (Monographs in Neonatology). 144p. 1978. text ed. 20.25 (ISBN 0-8089-1094-9). Grune.
Mishell, Barbara B. & Shiigi, Stanley M., eds. Selected Methods in Cellular Immunology. LC 79-19990. (Illus.). 1980. text ed. 31.95x (ISBN 0-7167-1106-0). W H Freeman.
Mitchison, N. Avrion, ed. Manipulation of the Immune Response in Cancer. (Perspectives in Immunology Ser.). 1979. 34.50 (ISBN 0-12-500250-5). Acad Pr.
Mitsuhashi, S., ed. Drug Action & Drug Resistance in Bacteria - Vol. 1: Macrolide Antibiotics & Lincomycin. (Illus.). 1971. 49.50 (ISBN 0-8391-0642-4). Univ Park.
Mizuno, D. Host Defense Against Cancer & Its Potentiation. (Illus.). 1976. 49.50 (ISBN 0-8391-0854-0). Univ Park.
Morell, A., et al. IgG-Subklassen der Menschlichen Immunglobuline: Immunochemische genetische, biologische Ud klinische Aspekte. (Illus.). 88p. 1975. pap. 17.50 (ISBN 3-8055-2153-7). S Karger.
Muller-Ruchholtz, Wolfgang & Muller-Hermelink, Hans K., eds. Function & Structure of the Immune System: Physiological and Pathological Patterns. LC 79-4272. (Advances in Experimental Medicine and Biology Ser.: Vol. 114). 872p. 1979. 75.00 (ISBN 0-306-40158-4, Plenum Pr). Plenum Pub.
Munster, Andrew M., ed. Surgical Immunology. LC 76-14341. (Illus.). 336p. 1976. 44.00 (ISBN 0-8089-0943-6). Grune.
Nahmias, Andre J. & O'Reilly, Richard, eds. Immunology of Human Infection. Incl. Pt. 1, Bacteria, Mycoplasmae, Chlamydiae, & Fungi. 49.50 (ISBN 0-306-40257-2); Pt. 2, Viruses & Parasites Immunodiagnosis & Presentation of Infectious Disease. 45.00 (ISBN 0-306-40258-0). (Comprehensive Immunology Ser.: Vols. 8 & 9). 1981 (Plenum Pr). Plenum Pub.
Nakamura, R.., et al, eds. Immunoassays: Clinical Laboratory Techniques for the 1980's. LC 80-21230. (Laboratory & Research Methods in Biology & Medicine: Vol. 4). 482p. 1980. 58.00 (ISBN 0-8451-1653-3). A R Liss.
Nakamura, R. M., et al, eds. Immunoassays in the Clinical Laboratory: Proceedings of the First Annual Conference on Immunoassays in the Clinical Laboratory, La Jolla, Calif., Mar.-Apr. 1978. LC 79-1649. (Laboratory & Research Methods in Biology & Medicine: Vol. 3). 394p. 1979. 40.00x (ISBN 0-8451-1652-5). A R Liss.
Neidermeier, William, et al. Phylogenetic Development of Vertebrate Immunity, No. 1. (Illus.). 206p. 1973. text ed. 28.50x (ISBN 0-8422-7056-6). Irvington.
Neubauer, Russell H. Naturally Occuring Biological Immunosuppresive Factors & Their Relationship to Disease. 304p. 1979. 69.95 (ISBN 0-8493-5243-6). CRC Pr.
Notkins, Abner L., ed. Viral Immunology & Immunopathology. 1975. 27.50 (ISBN 0-12-522050-2). Acad Pr.
Parker, Charles W., ed. Clinical Immunology, 2 vols. LC 79-63406. (Illus.). 1438p. 1980. Set. text ed. 80.00 (ISBN 0-7216-7075-X); Vol. 1. 40.00 (ISBN 0-7216-7073-3); Vol. 2. 40.00 (ISBN 0-7216-7074-1). Saunders.
Permanent Section of Microbiological Standardization, 31st Symposium, Omstotite of Child Health, Ondon, 1969. Interferon & Interferon Inducers. Perkins, F. T. & Regamey, R. H., eds. (Immunobiological Standardization: Vol. 14). 1970. 36.00 (ISBN 3-8055-0637-6). S Karger.

Pilapil, Frediswinda & Studva, Kathleen V. Programmed Instruction: Immunology, No. 3. 72p. 1981. 6.50 (ISBN 0-89352-150-7). Masson Pub.
Pilapil, Frediswinda & Studva, Kathleen V., eds. Programmed Instruction: Immunology. 72p. 1981. pap. text ed. 6.50 (ISBN 0-89352-150-7). Seiden.
Porter, R. R. & Ada, G. L., eds. Contemporary Topics in Molecular Immunology, Vol. 6. (Illus.). 252p. 1977. 29.50 (ISBN 0-306-36106-X, Plenum Pr). Plenum Pub.
Profitt, M. R., ed. Virus-Lymphocyte Interactions: Implications for Disease. LC 79-19984. (Developments in Immunology: Vol. 7). 319p. 1979. 40.00 (ISBN 0-444-00348-7, North Holland). Elsevier.
Quinn, Loyd Y. Immunological Concepts. (Illus.). 1968. 7.95x (ISBN 0-8138-1114-7). Iowa St U Pr.
Rapid Methods & Automation in Microbiology & Immunology: A Bibliography. 250p. 24.00 (ISBN 0-904147-07-X). Info Retrieval.
Ray, ed. Immunobiology & Transplantation, Cancer & Pregnancy. 500p. Date not set. text ed. price not set (ISBN 0-08-025994-4). Pergamon.
Reisfeld, R. A. & Inman, F. P., eds. Contemporary Topics in Molecular Immunology, Vol. 7. 447p. 1978. 39.50 (ISBN 0-306-40081-2, Plenum Pr). Plenum Pub.
Reisfeld, R. A. & Mandy, W. J., eds. Contemporary Topics in Molecular Immunology, Vol. 2. LC 73-186260. (Illus.). 271p. 1973. 25.00 (ISBN 0-306-36102-7, Plenum Pr). Plenum Pub.
Research in Immunology: Report of 5 Scientific Groups Convened by the Director-General of the World Health Organization, Geneva, 1962. (Technical Report Ser: No. 286). 97p. (Eng, Fr, Rus, & Span.). 1964. pap. 2.80 (ISBN 92-4-120286-6). World Health.
Richter, Maxwell. Physician's Guide to Clinical Immunology. 2nd. ed. (Illus.). 360p. 1981. lib. bdg. 14.95 (ISBN 0-683-07255-2). Williams & Wilkins.
Rimon, A., et al. Current Topics in Microbiology & Immunology, Vol. 74. LC 15-12910. 1976. 42.50 (ISBN 0-387-07657-3). Springer-Verlag.
Ritchie, Robert F., ed. Automated Immunoanalyses, Pt. 2. (Clinical Chemistry & Biochemical Analysis Ser.: Vol. 7). 1978. 34.50 (ISBN 0-8247-6679-2). Dekker.
--Automated Immunoanalysis, Pt. 1. (Clinical Chemistry & Biochemical Analysis Ser.). 1978. 42.50 (ISBN 0-8247-6678-4). Dekker.
Roesel, Catherine E. Immunology: A Self-Instructional Approach. 1978. pap. text ed. 10.95 (ISBN 0-07-053411-X, HP). McGraw.
Rose, Noel & Bigazzi, Pierluigi E. Methods in Immunodiagnosis. 2nd ed. LC 80-15273. (Techniques in Pure & Applied Microbiology). 269p. 1980. 21.50 (ISBN 0-471-02208-X, Pub. by Wiley Med). Wiley.
Rose, Noel R. & Friedman, Herman, eds. Manual of Clinical Immunology. LC 76-17595. (Illus.). 1976. 20.00 (ISBN 0-914826-09-3); flexible 16.00 (ISBN 0-914826-10-7). Am Soc Microbio.
Rose, Noel R. & Milgrom, Felix, eds. Principles of Immunology. 2nd ed. (Illus.). 1979. pap. text ed. 14.95 (ISBN 0-02-403610-2). Macmillan.
Rose, Noel R., et al, eds. International Convocation on Immunology. 1969. 72.00 (ISBN 3-8055-0888-3). S Karger.
Rothfield, Lawrence I. & Ward, Peter A. Microbiology & Immunology Review. 2nd ed. LC 79-23991. (Arco Medical Review Ser.). (Illus.). 159p. 1981. pap. text ed. 10.00 (ISBN 0-668-04882-4, 4882). Arco.
Rotstein, J., ed. Immunosuppression Systematic Lupus Erythematosus. (Rheumatology: Vol. 5). (Illus.). 1974. 69.00 (ISBN 3-8055-1540-5). S Karger.
Rudbach, B. & Baker, R., eds. Immunology of Bacterial Polysaccharides. LC 78-31961. (Developments in Immunology Ser.: Vol. 2). 1979. 24.00 (ISBN 0-444-00315-0, North Holland). Elsevier.
Safai, Bijan & Good, Robert A., eds. Immunodermatology. (Comprehensive Immunology Ser.: Vol. 7). (Illus.). 625p. 1981. 49.50 (ISBN 0-306-40380-3, Plenum Pr). Plenum Pub.
Sandler, S. Gerald & Nusbacher, Jacob, eds. Immunobiology of the Erythrocyte. LC 80-81465. (Progress in Clinical & Biological Research Ser.: Vol. 43). 360p. 1980. 40.00 (ISBN 0-8451-0043-2). A R Liss.
Sarma, P. S., et al. Current Topics in Microbiology & Immunology, Vol. 68. LC 75-12910. (Illus.). 180p. 1975. 40.50 (ISBN 0-387-07074-5). Springer-Verlag.
Sartorelli, A. C. & Johns, D. G., eds. Antineoplastic & Immunosurpressive Agents, Pt. 2. LC 73-10507. (Handbook of Experimental Pharmacology: Vol. 38). (Illus.). 1975. 189.80 (ISBN 0-387-06633-0). Springer-Verlag.
Schmeck, Harold M., Jr. Immunology: The Many-Edged Sword. new ed. LC 73-80335. (Illus.). 128p. 1974. pap. 3.95 (ISBN 0-8076-0712-6). Braziller.
Schmidtke, Jon R. & Ferguson, Ronald M., eds. Immunology for the Practicing Physician. LC 77-2170. 160p. 1977. 25.00 (ISBN 0-306-31035-X, Plenum Pr). Plenum Pub.
Schuppli, R. Immunbiologie: Einfuehrung in die allergologischen und immunologischen Grundlagen der klinischen Medizin. (Ueberarbeitete Auflage). (Illus.). 1979. pap. 15.00 (ISBN 3-8055-3000-5). S Karger.
Schwartz, Lazar. Compendium of Immunology, Vol. 2. 2nd ed. 672p. 1981. text ed. price not set (ISBN 0-442-26708-8). Van Nos Reinhold.
Schwartz, Lazar M. Compendium of Immunology. 2nd ed. 560p. 1979. text ed. 34.50 (ISBN 0-442-27472-6). Van Nos Reinhold.
Schwartz, Lazar M. & Schwartz, Paula. An Excersise Manual in Immunology. LC 75-14774. 324p. 1975. pap. 15.00 (ISBN 0-686-65368-8). Krieger.
Schwartz, Lazarm. Compendium of Immunology. LC 77-83914. (Medical Pocketbook Library). 1977. pap. 5.00 (ISBN 0-930728-01-7). Educ Medical.
Schwartz, Robert S., ed. Progress in Clinical Immunology, Vol. IV. 288p. 1980. 23.50 (ISBN 0-8089-1239-9). Grune.
--Progress in Clinical Immunology, Vol. II. 244p. 1974. 44.00 (ISBN 0-8089-0850-2). Grune.
--Progress in Clinical Immunology, Vol. III. (Illus.). 224p. 1977. 35.75 (ISBN 0-8089-0997-5). Grune.
Sela, M. & Prywes, M., eds. Topics in Basic Immunology. 1969. 37.50 (ISBN 0-12-635550-9). Acad Pr.
Sell, Stewart. Immunologia Inmunopatologia. (Span.). 1981. pap. text ed. 16.50 (ISBN 0-06-317151-1, Pub. by HarLA Mexico). Har-Row.
--Immunology, Immunopathology & Immunity. 3rd ed. (Illus.). 600p. 1980. pap. text ed. 27.00 (ISBN 0-06-142369-6, Harper Medical). Har-Row.
Sercarz, Eli, et al, eds. The Immune System: Genes, Receptors, Signals. 1974. 41.50 (ISBN 0-12-637150-4). Acad Pr.
Sercarz, Eli E. & Cunningham, Alastair J., eds. Strategies of Immune Regulation. LC 79-28392. 1980. 39.50 (ISBN 0-12-637140-7). Acad Pr.
Sharma, R. P., ed. Immunologic Considerations in Toxicology, Vols. I & II. 1981. Vol. I, 192p. 59.95 (ISBN 0-8493-5271-1); Vol. II, 192p. 59.95 (ISBN 0-8493-5272-X). CRC Pr.
Singhal, S. K., et al, eds. Aging & Immunity. (Developments in Immunology Ser.: Vol. 5). 350p. 1979. 40.00 (ISBN 0-444-00346-0, North Holland). Elsevier.
Siskind, Gregory W., ed. Developmental Immunobiology. 272p. 1979. 21.25 (ISBN 0-8089-1191-0). Grune.
Skamene, Emil, ed. Genetic Control of Natural Resistance to Infection & Malignancy. (Perspectives in Immunology Ser.). 1980. 33.00 (ISBN 0-12-647680-2). Acad Pr.
Smith, E. E. & Ribbons, D. W., eds. Molecular Approaches to Immunology. (Miami Winter Symposia Ser.). 1975. 34.00 (ISBN 0-12-651050-4). Acad Pr.
Smith, Richard T. & Landy, Maurice, eds. Immune Surveillance. LC 73-138439. (Perspectives in Immunology Ser). 1971. 43.00 (ISBN 0-12-652250-2). Acad Pr.
Smith, Richard T., et al, eds. Ontogeny of Immunity. LC 66-29457. (Illus.). 1967. 15.00 (ISBN 0-8130-0207-9). U Presses Fla.
Smolensky, M. H. & Reinberg, A., eds. Recent Advances of the Chronobiology of Allergy & Immunology: Symposium on Chronobiology in Allergy & Immunology, Israel, 1979. LC 80-41028. (Illus.). 350p. 1980. 65.00 (ISBN 0-08-025891-3). Pergamon.
Smolin, Gilbert & O'Connor, G. Richard. Ocular Immunology. LC 81-8218. (Illus.). 250p. 1981. text ed. price not set (ISBN 0-8121-0688-1). Lea & Febiger.
Soloman, J. B., ed. Developmental & Comparative Immunology I: First Congress of Developmental & Comparative Immunology, 27 July-1 August 1980, Aberdeen. (Illus.). 580p. 1981. 110.00 (ISBN 0-08-025922-7). Pergamon.
Solomon, J. B. Foetal & Neonatal Immunology. 1971. 38.00 (ISBN 0-444-10066-0, North-Holland). Elsevier.
Solomon, J. B. & Horton, J. D., eds. Developmental Immunobiology: Proceedings of the Symposia on Developmental Immunobiology, Aberdeen, U.K., Sept. 1977. 1978. 74.25 (ISBN 0-444-80034-4, Biomedical Pr). Elsevier.
Stansfield. Serology & Immunology. 1981. 20.95 (ISBN 0-686-71604-3). Macmillan.
Sternberger, Ludwig A. Immunocytochemistry. 2nd ed. LC 78-13263. (Basic & Clinical Immunology Ser.). 354p. 1979. 40.95 (ISBN 0-471-03386-3, Pub. by Wiley Medical). Wiley.
Stewart, Alice, et al. Burkitt's Disease: Immunological Aspects, Vol. 1. LC 73-16381. 1974. 19.00x (ISBN 0-8422-7173-2). Irvington.
Stiehm, E. Richard & Fulginiti, Vincent A. Immunologic Disorders in Infants & Children. 2nd ed. LC 79-66045. (Illus.). 817p. 1980. text ed. 50.00 (ISBN 0-7216-8603-6). Saunders.
--Immunologic Disorders in Infants & Children. LC 72-90730. (Illus.). 637p. 1973. pap. text ed. 27.75 (ISBN 0-7216-8602-8). Saunders.
Stiehm, E. Richard, et al. Immunotherapy: Cellular Transplants & Immunostimulation. LC 74-591. 233p. 1974. text ed. 23.50x (ISBN 0-8422-7199-6). Irvington.
Stiller, Calvin R., et al, eds. Immunologic Monitoring of the Transplant Patient. LC 78-7173. (Transplantation Proceedings Reprint). 384p. 1978. 53.50 (ISBN 0-8089-1124-4). Grune.
Streilein, Wayne J. & Hughes, John D. Immunology: A Programmed Text. 1977. pap. text ed. 11.95 (ISBN 0-316-81919-0, Little Med Div). Little.
Studer, A. & Cottier, H., eds. Immune Reactions. (Handbuch der Allgemeinen Pathologie: Vol. 7/3). (Illus.). 1970. 224.20 (ISBN 0-387-05129-5). Springer-Verlag.
Suskind, Robert M., ed. Malnutrition & the Immune Response. LC 75-14589. 1977. 43.50 (ISBN 0-89004-060-5). Raven.
Symposium On Germinal Centers In Immune Responses - University Of Bern-Switzerland - 1966. Proceedings. Cottier, H., et al, eds. (Illus.). 1967. 59.80 (ISBN 0-387-03807-8). Springer-Verlag.
Taliaferro, W. H. & Humphrey, J. H., eds. Advances in Immunology, Vols. 1-30. Incl. Vol. 1. 1961. (ISBN 0-12-022401-1); Vol. 2. 1963 (ISBN 0-12-022402-X); Vol. 3. Dixon, F. J., Jr. & Humphrey, J. H., eds. 1963 (ISBN 0-12-022403-8); Vol. 4. 1964 (ISBN 0-12-022404-6); Vol. 5. 1966 (ISBN 0-12-022405-4); Vol. 6. 1967 (ISBN 0-12-022406-2); Vol. 7. Dixon, F. J., Jr. & Kunkel, Henry G., eds. 1967. (ISBN 0-12-022407-0); Vol. 8. 1968 (ISBN 0-12-022408-9); Vol. 9. 1968 (ISBN 0-12-022409-7); Vol. 10. 1969 (ISBN 0-12-022410-0); Vol. 11. 1969. (ISBN 0-12-022411-9); Vol. 12. 1970 (ISBN 0-12-022412-7); Vol. 13. 1971 (ISBN 0-12-022413-5); Vol. 14. 1971 (ISBN 0-12-022414-3); Vol. 15. 1972 (ISBN 0-12-022415-1); Vol. 16. 1973 (ISBN 0-12-022416-X); Vol. 17. 1973 (ISBN 0-12-022417-8); Vol. 18. 1974 (ISBN 0-12-022418-6); Vol. 19. 1974 (ISBN 0-12-022419-4); Vol. 20. 1975 (ISBN 0-12-022420-8); Vol. 21. 1975 (ISBN 0-12-022421-6); Vol. 22. 1976 (ISBN 0-12-022422-4); Vol. 23. 1976 (ISBN 0-12-022423-2); Vol. 24. 1976 (ISBN 0-12-022424-0); Vol. 25. 1978. 36.50 (ISBN 0-12-022425-9); Vol. 26. Kunkel, Henry G. & Dixon, E. J., eds. 1978. 40.00 (ISBN 0-12-022426-7); Vol. 27. 1979. 37.50 (ISBN 0-12-022427-5); Vol. 28. 1980. 43.00 (ISBN 0-12-022428-3); Vol. 29. 1980. 35.00 (ISBN 0-12-022429-1). LC 61-17057. Vol. 1-24. 50.00 (ISBN 0-686-66773-5). Acad Pr.
Taylor, G. Immunology in Medical Practice. LC 74-4592. (Illus.). 390p. 1975. text ed. 29.75 (ISBN 0-7216-8767-9). Saunders.
Terry, W. D. & Yamamura, Y., eds. Immunobiology & Immunotherapy of Cancer. LC 79-19197. (Developments in Immunobiology Ser.: Vol. 6). 432p. 1980. 45.00 (ISBN 0-444-00356-8, North Holland). Elsevier.
Thaler, Malcolm S & Klausner, Richard D. Medical Immunology. LC 77-3656. 22.50 (ISBN 0-397-52081-6). Lippincott.
Thompson, R. A., ed. Recent Advances in Clinical Immunology, No. 1. LC 77-30129. (Recent Advances in Clinical Immunology Ser.). (Illus.). 1977. text ed. 32.50 (ISBN 0-443-01388-8). Churchill.
--Recent Advances in Clinical Immunology, No. 2. (Recent Advances Ser.). (Illus.). 361p. 1980. text ed. 49.00x (ISBN 0-443-01963-0). Churchill.
Thomson, R. A. The Practice of Clinical Immunology. 2nd ed. (Current Topics in Immunology: Vol. 1). (Illus.). 1979. pap. 22.95 (ISBN 0-8151-8784-X). Year Bk Med.
Touraine, J. L., et al, eds. Transplantation & Clinical Immunology, Vol. X. (International Congress Ser.: No. 447). 1979. 61.00 (ISBN 0-444-90042-X, Excerpta Medica). Elsevier.
Turk, J. L. Immunology in Clinical Medicine. 3rd ed. 268p. 1978. pap. 17.50 (ISBN 0-8385-4303-0). ACC.
Twomey, J. J. & Good, R. A., eds. Comprehensive Immunology: Volume 4, Immunopathology of Lymphoreticular Neoplasms. LC 77-27315. (Illus.). 781p. 1978. 45.00 (ISBN 0-306-33104-7, Plenum Pr). Plenum Pub.
Uhr, Jonathan W. & Landy, Maurice, eds. Immunologic Intervention. (Perspectives in Immunology Ser.). 1972. 43.00 (ISBN 0-12-706950-X). Acad Pr.
Voller, A. & Bartlett, A., eds. Immunoassays for the Eighties. 500p. 1981. text ed. 34.50 (ISBN 0-8391-1672-1). Univ Park.
Waksman, Byron H. Atlas of Experimental Immunobiology & Immunopathology. LC 73-81434. (Illus.). 1970. 50.00x (ISBN 0-300-01154-7). Yale U Pr.
Waldman. Immunology. (Clinical Concepts in Medicine Ser.). (Illus.). 260p. 1979. 23.00 (ISBN 0-683-08656-1). Williams & Wilkins.
Warner & Cooper, eds. Contemporary Topics in Immunobiology, Vol. 8. (Illus.). 286p. 1978. 27.50 (ISBN 0-306-37808-6, Plenum Pr). Plenum Pub.
Warner, Noel L., ed. Contemporary Topics in Immunobiology, Vol. 11. (Illus.). 390p. 1980. 32.50 (ISBN 0-306-40419-2, Plenum Pr). Plenum Pub.
Weigle, William O., ed. Contemporary Topics in Immunobiology, Vol. 5. 341p. 1976. 35.00 (ISBN 0-306-37805-1, Plenum Pr). Plenum Pub.
Weir. Handbook of Experimental Immunology: Application of Immunological Methods, Vol. 3. 3rd ed. 1978. pap. 45.25 (ISBN 0-632-00186-0, Blackwell Scientific). Mosby.
Weir, D. M., ed. Handbook of Experimental Immunology: Cellular Immunology, Vol. 2. 3rd ed. 1978. pap. 45.25 (ISBN 0-632-00176-3, Blackwell Scientific). Mosby.
Weir, Donald M. Immunology: An Outline for Students of Medicine & Biology. 4th ed. LC 77-30004. (Churchill Livingstone Medical Texts). (Illus.). 1977. pap. text ed. 4.00 (ISBN 0-443-01522-8). Churchill.
Weiss, D. W., ed. Immunological Parameters of Host - Tumor Relationships, Vol. 4. 1977. 38.00 (ISBN 0-12-743554-9). Acad Pr.
Weiss, Leon. Cells & Tissues of the Immune System: Structure, Functions, Interactions. (Foundations of Immunology Ser). (Illus.). 1972. ref. ed. 23.95x (ISBN 0-13-121772-0). P-H.
Weissman, Irving, compiled by. Annual Reviews Reprints: Immunology, 1977-1979. (Illus.). 1980. soft cover 12.00 (ISBN 0-8243-2502-8). Annual Reviews.
Weissman, Irving, et al. Essential Concepts in Immunology. LC 78-57262. 1978. 10.95 (ISBN 0-8053-4406-3). Benjamin-Cummings.
Weksler, Marc E., et al. Immune Effector Mechanisms in Disease. 272p. 1978. 23.50 (ISBN 0-8089-1069-8). Grune.
WHO Sceintific Group, Geneva, 1968. Cell-Mediated Immune Responses: A Report. (Technical Report Ser: No. 423). 61p. 1969. pap. 2.00 (ISBN 92-4-120423-0, 396). World Health.
WHO Scientific Group. Clinical Immunology. (Technical Report Ser: No. 496). 50p. 1972. pap. 1.60 (ISBN 92-4-120496-6, 78). World Health.
WHO Scientific Group, Geneva, 1967. Genetics of the Immune Response: A Report. (Technical Report Ser: No. 402). 52p. 1968. pap. 2.00 (ISBN 92-4-120402-8, 698). World Health.
WHO Scientific Group, Geneva, 1969. Factor Regulating the Immune Response: A Report. (Technical Report Ser: No. 448). 88p. 1970. pap. 2.80 (ISBN 92-4-120448-6, 766). World Health.
WHO Scientific Group. Geneva, 1975. Developments in Malaria Immunology: Report. (Technical Report Ser.: No. 579). (Also avail. in French & Spanish). 1975. pap. 2.80 (ISBN 92-4-120579-2). World Health.
WHO Seminar, Kumasi, Ghana 1974, 1st. Expansion of the Use of Immunization in Developing Countries. (Offset Pub.: No. 16). (Also avail. in French). 1975. pap. 4.80 (ISBN 92-4-170016-5). World Health.
Wilkinson, A. W., ed. The Immunology of Infant Feeding. (Ettore Majorana International Science Series - Life Sciences: Vol. 8). 144p. 1981. text ed. write for info. (ISBN 0-306-40816-3, Plenum Pr). Plenum Pub.
Williams, Curtis A. & Chase, Merrill W., eds. Methods in Immunology & Immunochemistry, 5 vols. Vol. 1. 1968. 56.00, subscription 48.50 (ISBN 0-12-754401-1); Vol. 2. 1968. 56.50, subscription 48.50 (ISBN 0-12-754402-X); Vol. 3. 1971. 56.50, by subscription 48.50 (ISBN 0-12-754403-8); Vol. 4 1977. 56.50, subscription 48.50 (ISBN 0-12-754404-6); Vol. 5 1976. 56.50, subscription 48.50 (ISBN 0-12-754405-4). Acad Pr.
Williams, Harriet B., ed. Serology, Immunology & Blood Banking. (Functional Mdical Laboratory Manual). (Illus.). 1978. pap. text ed. 10.00 (ISBN 0-87055-266-X). AVI.
Wilson, J. D. Diagnostic Immunology & Serology: A Clinician's Guide. Simpson, Sandra I., ed. 161p. 1980. pap. text ed. 14.95x (ISBN 0-909337-01-2). ADIS Pr.
Wright, C. A., ed. Biochemical & Immunological Taxonomy of Animals. 1975. 76.00 (ISBN 0-12-765350-3). Acad Pr.

Yoshitsugi, Hokama & Nakamura, Robert M. Immunology & Immunopathology: Basic Concepts. 1981. price not set (ISBN 0-316-36932-2). Little.

IMMUNOLOGY–BIBLIOGRAPHY

Breuel, Hans-Peter, ed. Documentation of Literature - Literatur Dokumentation, Ser., 4: Local Immunization with Non-Living Microorganisms or Their Antigens 1891-1968. 370p. (Eng. & Ger.). 1969. 35.00x (ISBN 3-437-10030-0). Intl Pubns Serv.

IMMUNOLOGY–LABORATORY MANUALS

Peacock, Julia E. & Tomar, Russell H. Manual of Laboratory Immunology. LC 80-16716. (Illus.). 228p. 1980. pap. 17.00 (ISBN 0-8121-0719-5). Lea & Febiger.

Rose, N. R. & Friedman, H., eds. Manual of Clinical Immunology. 2nd ed. (Illus.). 1980. 25.00 (ISBN 0-914826-25-5); flexible binding 21.00 (ISBN 0-914826-27-1). Am Soc Microbio.

IMMUNOLOGY–STANDARDS

International Symposium on Antilymphocyte Serum, 26th. Antilymphocyte Serum: Proceedings. Regamey, R. H., et al, eds. (Immunrobiological Standardization Symposia Ser.: Vol.16). 1970. 36.00 (ISBN 3-8055-0638-4). S Karger.

International Symposium on BCG Vaccine, 32nd, Frankfurt, 1970. Proceedings. Regamey, R. H., et al, eds. (Immunobiological Standardization: Vol. 17). 1971. 36.00 (ISBN 3-8055-1256-2). S Karger.

International Symposium on Enterobacterial Vaccines, 27th, Bern, 1969. Enterobacterial Vaccines: Proceedings. Regamey, R. H., et al, eds. (Immunobiological Standardization: Vol. 15). 1971. 36.00 (ISBN 3-8055-1143-4). S Karger.

IMMUNOLOGY–TECHNIQUE

see also Immunofluorescence

Garvey, Justine S., et al. Methods in Immunology: A Laboratory Text for Instruction & Research. 3rd rev. & enl. ed. LC 77-11998. (Illus.). 1977. text ed. 29.50 (ISBN 0-8053-3125-5, Adv Bk Prog). A-W.

McGiven, A. R., ed. Immunological Investigation of Renal Disease. (Practical Methods in Clinical Immunology Ser.: Vol. 1). (Illus.). 160p. 1980. text ed. 39.50 (ISBN 0-443-01899-5). Churchill.

Mayer, R. J. & Walker, J. H. Immunological Methods in the Biological Sciences: Enzymes and Proteins. 1980. 29.50 (ISBN 0-12-480750-X). Acad Pr.

Olitzki, A. Immunological Methods in Brucellosis Research: Procedures, Pt. 2, Vol. 9. (Bibliotheca Microbiologica: Vol 9). 1970. pap. 63.50 (ISBN 3-8055-0149-8). S Karger.

IMMUNOPATHOLOGY

see also Allergy; Autoimmune Diseases

Bach, Fritz H. & Good, Robert A., eds. Clinical Immunobiology. (Illus.). Vol. 1 1972. 32.00 (ISBN 0-12-070001-8); Vol. 2 1974. 32.00 (ISBN 0-12-070002-6); Vol. 3 1976. 46.00 (ISBN 0-12-070003-4). Acad Pr.

Cohen, S., et al. Mechanisms of Immunopathology. LC 78-18290. (Basic & Clinical Immunologies Ser.). 1979. 37.95 (ISBN 0-471-16429-1, Pub. by Wiley Medical). Wiley.

Cohen, Sydney & Sadun, Elvio H. Immunology of Parasitic Infections. (Blackwell Scientific Pubns.). (Illus.). 1976. 48.75 (ISBN 0-632-00097-X). Mosby.

Conference on Membranes, Viruses & Immune Mechanisms in Experimental & Clinical Diseases, University of Minnesota, June, 1972. Membranes & Viruses in Immunopathology: Proceedings. Day, Stacey B. & Good, Robert A., eds. 1973. 47.00 (ISBN 0-12-207250-2). Acad Pr.

Dick, George. Immunological Aspects of Infectious Diseases. 524p. text ed. 29.50 (ISBN 0-8391-1373-0). Univ Park.

Dixon, Frank & Fisher, David W. Immunopathology. 1980. text ed. write for info. HP Pub Co.

Edelson, Paul J., et al. Immunological Deficiency Syndromes. LC 73-13446. (Illus.). 220p. 1972. text ed. 24.50x (ISBN 0-8422-7082-5). Irvington.

Federlin, K. Immunopathology of Insulin: Clinical & Experimental Studies. LC 71-154799. (Monographs on Endocrinology: Vol. 6). (Illus.). 1971. 32.70 (ISBN 0-387-05408-1). Springer-Verlag.

Friedman, Herman. Immunoserology in the Diagnosis of Infectious Diseases. 193p. text ed. 22.50 (ISBN 0-8391-1342-0). Univ Park.

Gershwin, M. E. & Merchant, B., eds. Immunologic Defects in Laboratory Animals, 2 vols. (Vol. 1 357 pp.;vol. 2 379 pp.). 1981. Vol. 1. 37.50 (ISBN 0-306-40668-3, Plenum Pr); Vol. 2. 42.50 (ISBN 0-306-40673-X); Set. 72.50 (ISBN 0-686-73235-9). Plenum Pub.

Goodwin, James S. Suppressor Cells in Human Disease. (Immunology Ser: Vol. 14). (Illus.). 376p. 1981. 39.75 (ISBN 0-8247-1290-0). Dekker.

Grabar, Pierre & Miescher, Peter A., eds. Immunopathology of Malignacy: Fourth International Symposium on Immunopathology. (Illus.). 468p. 1966. 79.50 (ISBN 0-8089-0626-7). Grune.

Hayward, A. Immunodeficiency. (Current Topics in Immunology Ser.: Vol. 6). (Illus.). 1978. pap. 15.95 (ISBN 0-8151-4217-X). Year Bk Med.

International Congress of Allergology, 7th, Florence, 1970. New Concepts in Allergy & Clinic Immunology. Serafini, U., et al, eds. (International Congress Ser.: No. 232). 1971. 77.75 (ISBN 9-0219-0141-2, Excerpta Medica). Elsevier.

International Congress on Neuro-Genetics & Neuro-Ophthalmology, 3rd, Brussels, 1970. Aminoacidopathies, Immunoglobinopathies Neuro-Genetics & Neuro-Ophthalmology: Proceedings. Francois. J., ed. (Monographs in Human Genetics: Vol. 6). (Illus.). 1972. 39.00 (ISBN 3-8055-1280-5). S Karger.

International Convocation on Immunology, 6th. Immunopathology. Milgrom, F. & Albini, B., eds. (Illus.). 1979. 89.25 (ISBN 3-8055-2971-6). S Karger.

International Symposium on Immunopathology 3rd. Immunopathology: Proceedings. Miescher, Peter A. & Graham, Pierre, eds. (Illus.). 392p. 1964. 74.00 (ISBN 0-8089-0625-9). Grune.

Koprowski, Claude & Koprowski, Hilary. Viruses & Immunity: Toward Understanding Viral Immunology & Immunopathology. 1975. 21.00 (ISBN 0-12-420350-7). Acad Pr.

Litwin, Stephen D., et al, eds. Clinical Evaluation of Immune Function in Man. LC 76-48408. 256p. 1976. 24.25 (ISBN 0-8089-0971-1). Grune.

Loke, Y. W. Immunology & Immunopathology of the Human Foetal-Maternal Interaction. 1978. 70.75 (ISBN 0-444-80055-7, Biomedical Pr). Elsevier.

Miescher, Peter A., ed. Immunopathology: Seventh International Symposium on Immunopathology. 432p. 1977. 73.25 (ISBN 0-8089-1034-5). Grune.

Miescher, Peter A. & Miecher, Peter A., eds. Antigen Cell Interaction & Control of Antibody Synthesis: Sixth International Symposium on Immunopathology. 448p. 1972. 70.50 (ISBN 0-8089-0732-8). Grune.

Miescher, Peter A. & Mueller-Eberhard, Hans J., eds. Textbook of Immunopathology, 2 vols. 2nd ed. LC 76-155406. (Illus.). 544p. 1976. 70.75 ea. Vol. I (ISBN 0-8089-0931-2). Vol. II (ISBN 0-8089-0932-0). Set. 123.00 (ISBN 0-686-67367-0). Grune.

Munster, Andrew M., ed. Surgical Immunology. LC 76-14341. (Illus.). 336p. 1976. 44.00 (ISBN 0-8089-0943-6). Grune.

Nakamura, Robert M. Immunopathology: Clinical Laboratory Concepts & Methods. LC 73-2031. (Series in Laboratory Medicine). 600p. 1974. text ed. 38.50 (ISBN 0-316-59678-7). Little.

Neuwelt, Edward A. & Clark, W. Kemp. Clinical Aspects of Neuroimmunology. LC 78-2213. 292p. 1978. 29.50 (ISBN 0-683-06437-1). Krieger.

Notkins, Abner L., ed. Viral Immunology & Immunopathology. 1975. 27.50 (ISBN 0-12-522050-2). Acad Pr.

O'Connor, Richard C., ed. Immunologic Diseases of the Mucous Membranes: Pathology, Diagnosis, & Treatment. LC 80-82050. (Illus.). 176p. 1980. 29.50x (ISBN 0-89352-102-7). Masson Pub.

Perper, R. J., ed. Mechanisms of Tissue Injury with Reference to Rheumatoid Arthritis. (Annals of the New York Academy of Sciences Ser.: Vol. 256). 450p. 1975. 52.50x (ISBN 0-89072-010-X). NY Acad Sci.

Pollard, Morris, ed. Virus-Induced Immunopathology. (Perspectives in Virology: Vol. 6). 1969. 43.00 (ISBN 0-12-560556-0). Acad Pr.

Salaman, John & Sampson, Derek, eds. Clinical Immunosuppression. 1980. 28.50 (ISBN 0-8089-1335-2). Grune.

Schwartz, Robert S., ed. Progress in Clinical Immunology, Vol. I. LC 72-5124. 192p. 1972. 41.50 (ISBN 0-8089-0761-1). Grune.

Sell, Stewart. Immunologia Inmunopatologia. (Span.). 1981. pap. text ed. 16.50 (ISBN 0-06-317151-1, Pub. by HarLA Mexico). Har-Row.

--Immunology, Immunopathology & Immunity. 3rd ed. (Illus.). 600p. 1980. pap. text ed. 27.00 (ISBN 0-06-142369-6, Harper Medical). Har-Row.

Semenov, B., et al. Immunopathology of Viral Diseases: Experimental & Clinical. (Illus.). 1978. 43.00 (ISBN 0-685-87207-6). Adler.

Sparrow, Stephen, ed. Immunodeficient Animals for Cancer Research. (Illus.). 230p. 1980. text ed. 39.50 (ISBN 0-19-520220-1). Oxford U Pr.

Streilein, Jacob W., et al, eds. Hamster Immune Responses in Infectious & Oncologic Diseases. (Advances in Experimental Medicine & Biology Ser.: Vol. 134). 474p. 1981. 55.00 (ISBN 0-306-40642-X, Plenum Pr). Plenum Pub.

Symposium on Cyclic AMP, Cell Growth, & the Immune Response, Marco Island, Fla., 1973. Proceedings. Braun, W., et al, eds. (Illus.). 432p. 1974. 33.50 (ISBN 0-387-06654-3). Springer-Verlag.

Thaler, Malcolm S & Klausner, Richard D. Medical Immunology. LC 77-3656. 22.50 (ISBN 0-397-52081-6). Lippincott.

Thivolet, Jean & Schmitt, Daniel, eds. Cutaneous Immopathology. 506p. 1978. pap. text ed. 19.50 (ISBN 2-85598-175-1). Masson Pub.

Twomey, Jeremiah J. The Pathophysiology of Human Immunologic Disorders. 1982. price not set. Urban & S.

Uhr, Jonathan W. & Landy, Maurice, eds. Immunologic Intervention. (Perspectives in Immunology Ser.). 1972. 43.00 (ISBN 0-12-706950-X). Acad Pr.

Vyas, G., et al, eds. Laboratory Diagnosis of Immunologic Disorders. Brecher, G. & Stites, P. LC 75-6967. (Illus.). 320p. 1975. 41.75 (ISBN 0-8089-0869-3). Grune.

Waksman, Byron H. Atlas of Experimental Immunobiology & Immunopathology. LC 73-81434. (Illus.). 1970. 50.00x (ISBN 0-300-01154-7). Yale U Pr.

Waldman. Immunology. (Clinical Concepts in Medicine Ser.). (Illus.). 260p. 1979. 23.00 (ISBN 0-683-08656-1). Williams & Wilkins.

Wittig, Heinz J., et al. A Primer on Immunologic Disorders. (Illus.). 132p. 1970. photocopy ed. spiral 13.50 (ISBN 0-398-02100-7). C C Thomas.

Yoshitsugi, Hokama & Nakamura, Robert M. Immunology & Immunopathology: Basic Concepts. 1981. price not set (ISBN 0-316-36932-2). Little.

Zacharia, Theodore P. & Breese, S., Jr., eds. Immunopathology: Methods & Techniques. (Immunology Ser: Vol. 2). 276p. 1973. 39.50 (ISBN 0-8247-6115-4). Dekker.

IMMUNOPOTENTIATION

see Adjuvants, Immunological

IMPACT

see also Crash Injuries; Elasticity; Shock (Mechanics); Structural Dynamics

Afanas' ev, G. T. & Bobolev, V. K. Initiation of Solid Explosives by Impact. 124p. 1970. 15.00x (ISBN 0-7065-1051-8, Pub. by IPST). Intl Schol Bk Serv.

Instrumented Impacted Testing. 1974. 21.75 (ISBN 0-686-52049-1, 04-563000-23). ASTM.

King, W. F. & Mertz, H. J., eds. Human Impact Response: Measurement & Simulation. LC 73-80138. (General Motors Symposia Ser.). 406p. 1973. 39.50 (ISBN 0-306-30745-6, Plenum Pr). Plenum Pub.

Kinslow, R., ed. High-Velocity Impact Phenomena. 1970. 74.50 (ISBN 0-12-408950-X). Acad Pr.

Lyons, W. James. Impact Phenomena in Textiles. (Press Research Monographs: No. 19). 1963. 14.00x (ISBN 0-262-12008-9). MIT Pr.

Symposium on Planetary Cratering Mechanics, Flagstaff, Ariz., 1976. Impact & Explosion Cratering--Planetary & Terrestrial Implications: Proceedings. Roddy, D. J., et al, eds. LC 77-24753. 900p. 1978. 150.00 (ISBN 0-08-022050-9). Pergamon.

Zukas, Jonas A. & Nicholas, Theodore. Impact Dynamics. 575p. 1982. 60.00 (ISBN 0-471-08677-0, Pub. by Wiley-Interscience). Wiley.

IMPACT, ION

see Ion Bombardment

IMPACT PHENOMENA (NUCLEAR PHYSICS)

see Collisions (Nuclear Physics)

IMPEACHMENTS

see also Privileges and Immunities; Recall

Barth, Alan. Presidential Impeachment. 1974. pap. 4.50 (ISBN 0-8183-0134-1). Pub Aff Pr.

Berger, Raoul. Impeachment: The Constitutional Problems. LC 72-75428. (Studies in Legal History). 360p. 1973. 16.00 (ISBN 0-674-44475-2); pap. 5.95x (ISBN 0-674-44476-0). Harvard U Pr.

Black, Charles L. Impeachment: A Handbook. LC 74-82692. (Illus.). 90p. 1974. 10.00x (ISBN 0-300-01818-5); pap. 3.45x (ISBN 0-300-01819-3). Yale U Pr.

Brant, Irving. Impeachment: Trials & Errors. (gr. 9 up). 1972. 6.95 (ISBN 0-394-47326-4). Knopf.

Chase, Samuel. Trial of Samuel Chase, an Associate Justice of the Supreme Court Impeached by the House of Representatives, 2 Vols. LC 69-11324. (Law, Politics, & History Ser). Repr. of 1805 ed. 59.50 (ISBN 0-306-71181-8). Da Capo.

Dewitt, David M. The Impeachment & Trial of Andrew Johnson, Seventeenth President of the U.S. 1977. Repr. 55.00 (ISBN 0-403-08179-3). Scholarly.

Impeachment Inquiry Staff of the House Judiciary Committee. Constitutional Grounds for Impeachment. 1.00 (ISBN 0-8183-0129-5). Pub Aff Pr.

Johnson, Andrew. Trial of Andrew Johnson. LC 69-11326. (Law, Politics, & History Ser). 1970. Repr. of 1868 ed. lib. bdg. 95.00 (ISBN 0-306-71184-2). Da Capo.

Labovitz, John R. Presidential Inpeachment. LC 77-76300. 1978. 20.00x (ISBN 0-300-02213-1). Yale U Pr.

IMPEDANCE (ELECTRICITY)

Thomas, Robert L. A Practical Introduction to Impedance Matching. LC 75-31378. (Modern Frontiers in Applied Science). (Illus.). 180p. 1976. 24.00 (ISBN 0-89006-050-9). Artech Hse.

Turner, Rufus. Impedance. LC 75-41733. (Illus.). 196p. 1976. 11.95 (ISBN 0-8306-6829-2); pap. 5.95 (ISBN 0-8306-5829-7, 829). TAB Bks.

IMPEDIMENTS TO MARRIAGE

see also Abduction; Adoption; Adultery; Consanguinity

IMPEDIMENTS TO MARRIAGE (CANON LAW)

see also Marriage, Mixed

IMPELLERS

Advani, L. T. Horsepower Tables for Agitator Impellers. (Illus.). 175p. 1976. 18.95x (ISBN 0-87201-368-5). Gulf Pub.

Elam, Houston G. & Paley, Norton. Marketing for the Non-Marketing Executive. (Illus.). 1978. 15.95 (ISBN 0-8144-5465-8). Am Mgmt.

IMPENNES

see also Penguins

IMPERIAL FEDERATION

see also Commonwealth of Nations

Barker, Ernest. Ideas & Ideals of the British Empire. LC 69-13807. Repr. of 1951 ed. lib. bdg. 15.00 (ISBN 0-8371-0970-1, BABE). Greenwood.

Berger, Carl, ed. Imperial Relations in the Age of Laurier. LC 23-16213. (Canadian Historical Readings Ser.: No. 6). 1969. pap. 2.00x (ISBN 0-8020-1616-2). U of Toronto Pr.

Brassey, Thomas A. Problems of Empire. 2nd ed. LC 75-118478. 1971. Repr. of 1913 ed. 12.50 (ISBN 0-8046-1227-7). Kennikat.

Cheng, Seymour C. Schemes for the Federation of the British Empire. LC 68-59048. (Columbia University Studies in the Social Sciences: No. 335). Repr. of 1931 ed. 24.50 (ISBN 0-404-51335-2). AMS Pr.

Hancock, W. K. Survey of British Commonwealth Affairs, 2 vols. LC 76-56781. (Illus., Includes color map on microfiche). 1977. Repr. of 1937 ed. lib. bdg. 72.75x (ISBN 0-8371-9414-8, HABCA). Greenwood.

Hobson, John A. Imperialism. 1965. pap. 5.95 (ISBN 0-472-06103-8, 103, AA). U of Mich Pr.

Jennings, William I. The British Commonwealth of Nations. LC 78-14363. 1978. Repr. of 1961 ed. lib. bdg. 20.00x (ISBN 0-8371-9357-5, JEBC). Greenwood.

Knaplund, Paul. British Empire, Eighteen Fifteen to Nineteen Thirty. LC 68-9617. (Illus.). 1970. Repr. 29.50 (ISBN 0-86527-017-1). Fertig.

Latham, Richard T. Law & the Commonwealth. Repr. of 1949 ed. lib. bdg. 16.75x (ISBN 0-8371-3974-0, LALC). Greenwood.

Mahan, Alfred T. Retrospect & Prospect. LC 68-15831. 1968. Repr. of 1902 ed. 12.50 (ISBN 0-8046-0294-8). Kennikat.

Mansergh, Nicholas, ed. Commonwealth Perspectives. LC 58-1138. (Commonwealth Studies Center: No. 8). 1958. 12.50 (ISBN 0-8223-0113-X). Duke.

Nimocks, Walter. Milner's Young Men: The Kindergarten in Edwardian Imperial Affairs. LC 68-8588. 1968. 12.50 (ISBN 0-8223-0122-9). Duke.

Penlington, Norman. Canada & Imperialism, Eighteen Ninety-Six to Ninety-Nine. 1965. 17.50x (ISBN 0-8020-5148-0). U of Toronto Pr.

Silburn, P. A. Governance of Empire. LC 70-118502. 1971. Repr. of 1910 ed. 14.00 (ISBN 0-8046-1250-1). Kennikat.

IMPERIALISM

see also Imperial Federation; Militarism also subdivision Foreign Relations under names of countries

Amey, Peter. Imperialism. Yapp, Malcolm, et al, eds. (World History Ser.). (Illus.). (gr. 10). 1980. Repr. of 1977 ed. lib. bdg. 5.95 (ISBN 0-89908-226-2); pap. text ed. 1.95 (ISBN 0-89908-201-7). Greenhaven.

Amin, Samir. Imperialism & Unequal Development. LC 77-76169. 1979. pap. 5.00 (ISBN 0-85345-499-X, PB-499X). Monthly Rev.

Arendt, Hannah. Imperialism. LC 66-22273. Orig. Title: Origins of Totalitarianism Pt. 2. (2). 1968. pap. 4.95 (ISBN 0-15-644200-0, HB132, Harv). HarBraceJ.

Arrighi, Giovanni. The Geometry of Imperialism. (Illus.). 1978. 14.50 (ISBN 0-86091-004-0, Pub by NLB). Schocken.

Badian, E. Roman Imperialism in the Late Republic. 2nd ed. 1969. 8.50x (ISBN 0-8014-0024-4); pap. 3.95 (ISBN 0-8014-9109-6, CP109). Cornell U Pr.

Berard, Victor. British Imperialism & Commercial Supremacy. LC 70-80613. 298p. 1973. Repr. of 1906 ed. 24.00 (ISBN 0-86527-018-X). Fertig.

Betts, Raymond F. The False Dawn: European Imperialism in the Nineteenth Century. Shafer, Boyd C., ed. LC 75-14683. (Europe & the World in the Age of Expansion: Vol. VI). (Illus.). 1975. 15.00x (ISBN 0-8166-0762-4). U of Minn Pr.

--The False Dawn: European Imperialism in the 19th Century. LC 75-14683. (Europe & the World in the Age of Expansion Ser). 1978. pap. 3.45x (ISBN 0-8166-0852-0). U of Minn Pr.

Billington, Ray A. & Ridge, Martin. Westward Expansion. 5th ed. 1982. text ed. 19.95 (ISBN 0-686-75059-4). Macmillan.

Boulding, Kenneth E. & Mukerjee, Tapan, eds. Economic Imperialism: A Book of Readings. LC 74-146490. 1972. 10.00 (ISBN 0-472-16830-4); pap. 4.95x (ISBN 0-472-08170-5). U of Mich Pr.

Boyko, P. America Latina: Expansion Del Imperialismo y Crisis De la Via Capitalista De Desarrollo. 259p. (Span.). 4.00 (ISBN 0-8285-1412-7, Pub. by Progress Pubs Russia). Imported Pubns.

Brewer, Anthony. Marxist Theories of Imperialism. 304p. 1980. 35.00 (ISBN 0-7100-0531-8); pap. 16.50 (ISBN 0-7100-0621-7). Routledge & Kegan.

British Imperialism: Three Documents. LC 70-141119. (Research Library of Colonial Americana). 1972. Repr. of 1720 ed. 17.00 (ISBN 0-405-03330-3). Arno.

Brown, Michael B. Essays on Imperialism. (Illus.). 1972. pap. text ed. 5.25x (ISBN 0-85124-110-7). Humanities.

Brun, Henry J. Social Studies Student Investigates the Retreat from Imperialism. (YA) 1978. PLB 7.97 (ISBN 0-8239-0414-8). Rosen Pr.

Buffinton, Thomas. Imperialism & the Dilemma of Power. Brown, Richard H. & Halsey, Van R., eds. (Amherst Ser). (gr. 9-12). 1975. pap. text ed. 4.52 (ISBN 0-201-00757-6, Sch Div); tchr's. manual 1.92 (ISBN 0-201-00772-X). A-W.

Bukharin, Nicolai. Imperialism & World Economy. 1966. 18.50 (ISBN 0-86527-102-X). Fertig.

Bukharin, Nikolai. Imperialism & World Economy. LC 72-93461. (Modern Reader Paperbacks). (Illus.). 176p. 1973. pap. 3.95 (ISBN 0-85345-290-3, PB-2903). Monthly Rev.

Chattopadhyay, Baudhayan, ed. Imperialism in the Modern Phase, Vol. 1: Papers of the International Seminar on Imperialism, Independence, & Social Transformation in the Contemporary World, 2 pts. Pt. 1. 1974 7.50x (ISBN 0-8364-0417-3); Pt. 2. 1977 8.50x (ISBN 0-8364-0418-1). South Asia Bks.

Clark, Grover. Balance Sheets of Imperialism: Facts & Figures on Colonies. LC 66-27052. 1967. Repr. of 1936 ed. 10.00 (ISBN 0-8462-0839-3). Russell.

Cogan, Morton. Imperialism & Religion: Assyria, Judah and Israel in the Eighth and Seventh Centuries B.C.E. LC 73-83723. (Society of Biblical Literature. Monograph). 1974. 9.00 (ISBN 0-89130-330-8, 060019); pap. 7.50 (ISBN 0-89130-331-6). Scholars Pr Ca.

Cohen, Benjamin J. The Question of Imperialism: The Political Economy of Dominance & Dependence. LC 73-81036. (Illus.). 245p. 1973. text ed. 8.95x (ISBN 0-465-06780-8). Basic.

Collotti-Pischel, Enrica & Robertazzi, Chiara. L'Internationale Communiste et les Problemes Coloniaux, 1919-1935. (Materiaux Pour L'histoire Du Socialisme International, Essais Bibliographiques: No. 2). 1968. pap. 55.50x (ISBN 90-2796-149-2). Mouton.

Deutsch, Harold C. The Genesis of Napoleonic Imperialism. LC 75-25811. (Perspectives in European Hist. Ser.: No. 4). 460p. Repr. of 1938 ed. lib. bdg. 25.00x (ISBN 0-87991-611-7). Porcupine Pr.

Diamond, Solomon. Roots of Psychology: Psychology Recollected. LC 72-76919. (Illus.). 800p. 1973. text ed. 25.95x (ISBN 0-465-07137-6). Basic.

Eckhardt, William & Young, Christopher. Governments Under Fire: Civil Conflict & Imperialism. LC 76-51701. (Comparative Studies). xxi, 379p. 1977. 16.00x (ISBN 0-87536-335-0); pap. 8.00x (ISBN 0-87536-336-9). HRAFP.

Enteen, George M., et al. Soviet Historians & the Study of Russian Imperialism. LC 78-27563. (Penn State Studies: No. 45). 1979. pap. text ed. 3.00x (ISBN 0-271-00211-5). Pa St U Pr.

Fann, K. T. & Hodges, Donald C., eds. Readings in U. S. Imperialism. LC 78-133507. (Extending Horizons Ser). 1971. pap. 4.95 (ISBN 0-87558-054-8). Porter Sargent.

Ferguson, William S. Greek Imperialism. LC 63-18045. 1941. 10.50x (ISBN 0-8196-0127-6). Biblo.

Garnsey, P. D. & Whittaker, C. R., eds. Imperialism in the Ancient World. LC 77-85699. (Cambridge Classical Studies). (Illus.). 1979. 42.50 (ISBN 0-521-21882-9). Cambridge U Pr.

Girvan, Norman. Corporate Imperialism: Conflict & Expropriation. Transnational Corporations & Economic Nationalism in the Third World. LC 78-1141. 1978. pap. 6.95 (ISBN 0-85345-472-8, PB4728). Monthly Rev.

Gladwin, Thomas & Saidin, Ahmad. Slaves of the White Myth: The Psychology of Neocolonialism. LC 80-14939. 1981. text ed. 12.50x (ISBN 0-391-01936-8). Humanities.

Gollwitzer, Heinz. Europe in the Age of Imperialism, Eighteen Eighty to Nineteen Fourteen. (Library of World Civilization). 1979. pap. 5.95x (ISBN 0-393-95104-9). Norton.

Greene, Felix. The Enemy: What Every American Should Know About Imperialism. 1971. pap. 3.95 (ISBN 0-394-71457-1, Vin). Random.

Guiraud, Paul. Etudes Economiques Sur l'Antiquite. LC 77-126394. (Research & Source Ser.: No. 501). (Fr). 1970. Repr. of 1905 ed. 22.50 (ISBN 0-8337-1488-0). B Franklin.

Harris, William V. War & Imperialism in Republican Rome, 327-70 B.C. 1979. 45.00x (ISBN 0-19-814827-5). Oxford U Pr.

Harrison, Frederic. National & Social Problems. facs. ed. LC 76-142639. (Essay Index Reprint Ser). 1908. 22.00 (ISBN 0-8369-2051-1). Arno.

Headrick, Daniel R. The Tools of Empire: Technology & European Imperialism in the Nineteenth Century. 224p. 1981. text ed. 14.95x (ISBN 0-19-502831-7); pap. text ed. 6.95x (ISBN 0-19-502832-5). Oxford U Pr.

Healy, David. U. S. Expansionism: The Imperialist Urge in the 1890's. LC 71-121769. (Illus.). 1970. 25.00 (ISBN 0-299-05851-4). U of Wis Pr.

--U. S. Expansionism: The Imperialist Urge in the 1890s. 326p. 1970. pap. text ed. 7.95 (ISBN 0-299-05854-9). U of Wis Pr.

Hobson, J. A. Imperialism. 75.00 (ISBN 0-87968-237-X). Gordon Pr.

Hobson, John A. Imperialism. 1965. pap. 5.95 (ISBN 0-472-06103-8, 103, AA). U of Mich Pr.

Hodgart, Alan. The Economics of European Imperialism. (Foundations of Modern History Ser.). 1978. 7.95 (ISBN 0-393-05667-8); pap. 4.95x (ISBN 0-393-09061-2). Norton.

Hoskins, Halford L. European Imperialism in Africa. LC 66-27103. 1967. Repr. of 1930 ed. 6.50 (ISBN 0-8462-0937-3). Russell.

Hoxha, Enver. Imperialism & the Revolution. new ed. LC 79-84364. 1979. pap. 5.95 (ISBN 0-933774-00-1). World View Pubns.

Huttenback, Robert A. The British Imperial Experience. LC 75-31434. (Illus.). 225p. 1976. Repr. of 1966 ed. lib. bdg. 18.00x (ISBN 0-8371-8505-X, HUBI). Greenwood.

Jalee, Pierre. Imperialism in the Seventies. Sokolov, Raymond & Sokolov, Margaret, trs. LC 71-162957. 240p. 1971. 8.95 (ISBN 0-89388-012-4). Okpaku Communications.

--Imperialism in the Seventies. Sokolov, Raymond & Sokolov, Margaret, trs. from Fr. LC 71-162957. 240p. 1973. pap. 5.95 (ISBN 0-89388-013-2). Okpaku Communications.

--Pillage of the Third World. LC 68-13069. 1968. pap. 2.95 (ISBN 0-85345-118-4, PB-1184). Monthly Rev.

Kiernan, V. G. America: The New Imperialism. 306p. 1981. 19.00 (ISBN 0-905762-18-5, Pub. by Zed Pr. England); pap. 9.95 (ISBN 0-905762-76-2). Lawrence Hill.

Kohn, Hans. Nationalism & Imperialism in the Hither East. 1932. 25.00 (ISBN 0-86527-139-9). Fertig.

Kolchkovsky, L. L. Economic Neocolonialism. 309p. 1975. 4.10 (ISBN 0-8285-0358-3, Pub. by Progress Pubs Russia). Imported Pubns.

Krooth, Richard. Arms & Empire: Imperial Patterns Before World War II. 1980. pap. 5.95 (ISBN 0-939074-07-9). Harvest Pubns.

Kubicek, Robert V. The Administration of Imperialism: Joseph Chamberlain at the Colonial Office. LC 72-89874. 1969. 11.50 (ISBN 0-8223-0216-0). Duke.

--Economic Imperialism in Theory & Practice: The Case of South African Gold Mining Finance, 1886-1914. LC 78-52488. (Illus.). 1979. 14.75 (ISBN 0-8223-0409-0). Duke.

LaFeber, Walter. New Empire: An Interpretation of American Expansion, 1860-1898. (Beveridge Award Books Ser.). 444p. pap. 8.95 (ISBN 0-8014-9048-0, CP48). Cornell U Pr.

Lenin, V. I. Against Imperialistic War. 365p. 1974. pap. text ed. 2.50 (ISBN 0-8285-0067-3, Pub. by Progress Pubs Russia). Imported Pubns.

--Imperialism & the Split in Socialism. 22p. 1979. pap. 0.50 (ISBN 0-8285-0131-9, Pub. by Progress Pubs Russia). Imported Pubns.

--Imperialism, the Highest Stage of Capitalism. 128p. 1975. pap. 1.00 (ISBN 0-8285-0130-0, Pub. by Progress Pubs Russia). Imported Pubns.

--Selected Works, 1-vol. ed. LC 75-175177. 800p. 1971. pap. 5.75 (ISBN 0-7178-0300-7). Intl Pub Co.

Lenin, Vladimir I. Contra la Guerra Imperialista. 394p. (Span.). 1967. 1.95 (ISBN 0-8285-1368-6, Pub. by Progress Pubs Russia). Imported Pubns.

--Imperialism. 1965. pap. 1.95 (ISBN 0-8351-0113-4). China Bks.

--Imperialism: The Highest Stage of Capitalism. new ed. 1969. pap. 1.25 (ISBN 0-7178-0098-9). Intl Pub Co.

--Lenin on the National & Colonial Questions. 1967. pap. 0.75 (ISBN 0-8351-0129-0). China Bks.

Liska, George. Career of Empire: America & Imperial Expansion Over Land & Sea. LC 78-4576. 1978. text ed. 19.50x (ISBN 0-8018-2057-X). Johns Hopkins.

--Imperial America: The International Politics of Primacy. LC 67-21584. (Studies in International Affairs: No. 2). 115p. (Orig.). 1967. pap. 2.95x (ISBN 0-8018-0379-9). Johns Hopkins.

Louis, William R. Imperialism at Bay: The United States & the Decolonization of the British Empire, 1941-1945. 1978. 22.50x (ISBN 0-19-821125-2). Oxford U Pr.

Low, Donald A. Lion Rampant: Essays in the Study of British Imperialism. 232p. 1973. 24.00x (ISBN 0-7146-2986-3, F Cass Co). Biblio Dist.

--Lion Rampant: Essays in the Study of British Imperialism. 232p. 1975. pap. 9.95x (ISBN 0-7146-4010-7, F Cass Co). Biblio Dist.

Luxemburg, Rosa. Accumulation of Capital. LC 64-16176. 1964. pap. 7.50 (ISBN 0-85345-059-5, PB0595). Monthly Rev.

Luxemburg, Rosa & Bukharin, Nikolai. The Accumulation of Capital--an Anti-Critique & Imperialism & the Accumulation of Capital. Tarbuck, Kenneth J., ed. Wichmann, Rudolf, tr. from Ger. LC 72-81768. 304p. 1973 (CL2652). pap. 5.95 (ISBN 0-85345-291-1, PB2911). Monthly Rev.

Mack, Andrew, et al, eds. Imperialism, Intervention & Development. 393p. 1979. 32.00x (ISBN 0-686-28574-3, Pub. by Croom Helm Ltd England). Biblio Dist.

Magdoff, Harry. Imperialism: From the Colonial Age to the Present. LC 77-76167. 1979. pap. 5.00 (ISBN 0-85345-498-1, PB4981). Monthly Rev.

--Imperialism: From the Colonial Age to the Present. LC 76-76167. 1978. 12.50 (ISBN 0-85345-426-4). Monthly Rev.

Marburg, Theodore. Expansion. LC 70-147734. (Library of War & Peace; the Political Economy of War). lib. bdg. 38.00 (ISBN 0-8240-0485-X). Garland Pub.

Marx, Karl & Engels, Friedrich. On Colonialism. 383p. 1974. 2.50 (ISBN 0-8285-0035-5, Pub. by Progress Pubs Russia). Imported Pubns.

Marxist-Leninist Party, USA. No to U. S. Imperialist War Preparations. National Executive Committee of the MLP, USA, ed. (Illus.). 1980. pap. 1.00 (ISBN 0-86714-003-8). Marxist-Leninist.

Merk, Frederick. Manifest Destiny & Mission in American History. 1966. pap. 2.95 (ISBN 0-394-70318-9, Vin). Random.

Michel, Marc. La Mission Marchand, 1895-1899. (Le Monde D'outre-Mer Passe et Present, Etudes: No. 36). (Illus.). 1972. pap. 25.50x (ISBN 90-2797-153-6). Mouton.

Mommsen, Wolfgang J. Theories of Imperialism. Falla, P. S., tr. LC 80-5279. 156p. 1981. 9.95 (ISBN 0-394-50932-3). Random.

Moon, Parker T. Imperialism & World Politics. LC 75-147502. (Library of War & Peace; the Political Economy of War). lib. bdg. 38.00 (ISBN 0-8240-0296-2). Garland Pub.

Morgan, Howard W. America's Road to Empire: The War with Spain & Overseas Expansion. LC 64-8714. (America in Crisis Ser.). 124p. 1965. pap. text ed. 9.95 (ISBN 0-471-61520-X). Wiley.

Morris, Bernard S. Imperialism & Revolution: An Essay for Radicals. LC 73-81164. (Midland Bks.: No. 170). 96p. 1973. pap. 1.95x (ISBN 0-253-20170-5). Ind U Pr.

Nabudere, Wadada D. Essays on the Theory & Practice of Imperialism. 192p. 1980. text ed. 22.25x (ISBN 0-906383-02-1); pap. text ed. 9.25x (ISBN 0-906383-03-X). Humanities.

Nearing, Scott & Freeman, Joseph. Dollar Diplomacy: A Study in American Imperialism. LC 74-111703. (American Imperialism: Viewpoints of United States Foreign Policy, 1898-1941). 1970. Repr. of 1926 ed. 17.00 (ISBN 0-405-02040-6). Arno.

Owen, R. & Sutcliffe, R., eds. Studies in the Theory of Imperialism. (Illus.). 390p. 1972. pap. text ed. 14.95x (ISBN 0-582-48753-6). Longman.

Parry, John H. Spanish Theory of Empire in the Sixteenth Century. LC 73-447. 1940. lib. bdg. 9.50 (ISBN 0-8414-1471-8). Folcroft.

Peffer, Nathaniel. The White Man's Dilemma: Climax of the Age of Imperialism. LC 72-4288. (World Affairs Ser.: National & International Viewpoints). 320p. 1972. Repr. of 1927 ed. 15.00 (ISBN 0-405-04580-8). Arno.

Penrose, Ernest Francis. European Imperialism & the Partition of Africa. 180p. 1975. 27.50x (ISBN 0-7146-3058-6, F Cass Co). Biblio Dist.

Perimbam, Marie. Holy Violence in the Thought of Frantz Fanon. LC 81-51664. 224p. (Orig.). 1981. 22.00x (ISBN 0-89410-175-7); pap. 8.00x (ISBN 0-89410-176-5). Three Continents.

Petras, James. Critical Perspectives on Imperialism & Social Class in the Third World. LC 78-13915. 1980. pap. 5.95 (ISBN 0-85345-529-5, PB5295). Monthly Rev.

Petras, James & Morley, Morris. The United States & Chile: Imperialism & the Overthrow of the Allende Government. LC 74-21474. (Modern Reader Paperback Ser). 240p. 1976. pap. 6.00 (ISBN 0-85345-388-8, PB3888). Monthly Rev.

Power, Thomas F., Jr. Jules Ferry & the Renaissance of French Imperialism. 1966. lib. bdg. 15.00x (ISBN 0-374-96555-2). Octagon.

Rahman, A., et al. Imperialism in the Modern Phase, Vol. 2. 1977. 12.50x (ISBN 0-88386-986-1). South Asia Bks.

Rhodes, Robert I., ed. Imperialism & Underdevelopment: A Reader. LC 70-112736. 1971. pap. 6.50 (ISBN 0-85345-155-9, PB-1559). Monthly Rev.

Rothschild, Eric, ed. The Rise of Big Business & Imperialism, Eightteen Seventy-Eight to Eighteen Ninety-Nine. (The New York Times School Microfilm Collection: Guide No. 3). 100p. (gr. 7-12). 1978. pap. 5.50 wkbk (ISBN 0-667-00552-8). Microfilming Corp.

Rudin, Harry R. Germans in the Cameroons, Eighteen Eighty-Four to Nineteen Fourteen: A Case Study in Modern Imperialism. (Illus.). 1968. Repr. of 1938 ed. 22.50 (ISBN 0-208-00680-X, Archon). Shoe String.

Said, Edward W. Orientalism. LC 78-51803. 1978. 15.00 (ISBN 0-394-42814-5). Pantheon.

Sau, Ranjit. Unequal Exchange, Imperialism & Underdevelopment. (Illus.). 1978. 15.95x (ISBN 0-19-560895-X). Oxford U Pr.

Schumpeter, Joseph A. Imperialism & Social Classes. Sweezy, Paul M., ed. Norden, Heinz, tr. LC 51-4379. Repr. of 1951 ed. 15.00x (ISBN 0-678-00020-4). Kelley.

Seeley, John R. Expansion of England. Gross, John, ed. LC 73-152225. (Classics of British Historical Literature Ser). 1971. 12.50x (ISBN 0-226-74428-0). U of Chicago Pr.

Semmel, Bernard. Rise of Free Trade Imperialism. LC 71-112473. 1970. 41.50 (ISBN 0-521-07725-7). Cambridge U Pr.

Sexton, William T. Soldiers in the Son: an Adventure in Imperialism. facsimile ed. LC 70-146872. (Select Bibliographies Reprint Ser). Repr. of 1939 ed. 18.00 (ISBN 0-8369-5638-9). Arno.

Smal-Stocki, Roman & Sokolnicki, Alfred J., eds. Russian & Communist Imperialism in Action, 2 vols. (Marquette Slavic Ser.). Vol. 1. pap. 9.95 (ISBN 0-87462-306-5); Vol. 2. pap. 12.95 (ISBN 0-87462-307-3). Marquette.

Smith, Tony. The Pattern of Imperialism: The United States, Great Britain & the Late-Industrializing World Since 1815. LC 80-39676. (Illus.). 240p. Date not set. price not set (ISBN 0-521-23619-3); pap. price not set (ISBN 0-521-28076-1). Cambridge U Pr.

Snyder, Louis B., ed. The Imperialism Reader: Documents & Readings on Modern Expansionism. LC 72-85293. 640p. 1973. Repr. of 1962 ed. 27.50x (ISBN 0-8046-1722-8). Kennikat.

Sprietsma, Cargill. We Imperialists: Notes on Ernest Seilliere's "Philosophy of Imperialism". LC 70-176005. Repr. of 1931 ed. 16.50 (ISBN 0-404-06198-2). AMS Pr.

Steel, Ronald. Pax Americana. rev. ed. 1977. pap. 4.50 (ISBN 0-14-004664-X). Penguin.

Stenson, M. M. & Stenson, M. R. Imperialism Eighteen Seventy to Nineteen Fourteen. (Orig.). 1972. pap. text ed. 4.50 (ISBN 0-435-00545-6). Heinemann Ed.

Swift, Morrison I. Imperialism & Liberty. 1976. lib. bdg. 59.95 (ISBN 0-8490-2041-7). Gordon Pr.

Tarabrin, E. A., ed. Neocolonialism & Africa in the Nineteen Seventies. 335p. 1978. 5.00 (ISBN 0-8285-3330-X, Pub. by Progress Pubs Russia). Imported Pubns.

Thornton, A. P. Imperialism in the Twentieth Century. LC 77-81211. xii, 363p. 1980. pap. 10.95x (ISBN 0-8166-0993-4). U of Minn Pr.

--Imperialism in the Twentieth Century. LC 77-81211. 1978. 22.50x (ISBN 0-8166-0820-2). U of Minn Pr.

Tierney, Brian, et al. Origins of Modern Imperialism. 1968. pap. text ed. 1.95 (ISBN 0-394-30878-6, RanC). Random.
Vakhrushev, V. Neocolonialism: Methods & Manoeuvres. 372p. 1973. 4.25 (ISBN 0-8285-0309-5, Pub. by Progress Pubs Russia). Imported Pubns.
Van Alstyne, Richard W. The Rising American Empire. (Illus.). 240p. 1974. pap. 3.95 (ISBN 0-393-00750-2). Norton.
Van Campen, S. I. The Imperator: Consequences of Frustrated Expansion. 162p. 1978. 22.50x (ISBN 90-286-0328-X). Sijthoff & Noordhoff.
Warren, Bill. Imperialism: Pioneer of Capitalism. 296p. 1981. 19.50x (ISBN 0-8052-7089-2, Pub. by NLB England); pap. 8.50 (ISBN 0-8052-7088-4). Schocken.
Welch, Richard E., Jr., ed. Imperialists Vs Anti-Imperialists: The Debate Over Expansionism in the 1890's. LC 79-174162. (AHM Primary Sources in American History Ser.). 1972. text ed. 9.95x (ISBN 0-88295-792-9); pap. text ed. 4.95x (ISBN 0-88295-793-7). Harlan Davidson.
Wesson, Robert G. The Imperial Order. 1967. 37.50x (ISBN 0-520-01325-5). U of Cal Pr.
Williams, William A. Empire As a Way of Life: An Essay on the Causes & Character of America's Present Predicament, Along with a Few Thoughts About an Alternative. 208p. 1980. 14.95 (ISBN 0-19-502766-3). Oxford U Pr.
Winslow, Earle M. The Pattern of Imperialism: A Study in the Theories of Power. LC 78-159238. xii, 278p. 1971. Repr. lib. bdg. 15.00x (ISBN 0-374-98685-1). Octagon.
Wright, Harrison M., ed. New Imperialism: Analysis of Late Nineteenth Century Expansion. 2nd ed. (Problems in European Civilization Ser.). 1975. pap. text ed. 4.95x (ISBN 0-669-96008-X). Heath.
Zahar, Renate. Frantz Fanon: Colonialism & Alienation. Feuser, Willfried F., tr. from Ger. LC 74-7783. (Modern Reader Paperback Ser). 144p. 1976. pap. 5.00 (ISBN 0-85345-374-8, PB-3748). Monthly Rev.

IMPERSONAL JUDGMENT
see Judgment (Logic)
IMPERSONATION
see also Impersonators, Female; Transvestism
IMPERSONATION IN LITERATURE
Freeburg, Victor O. Disguise Plots in Elizabethan Drama. LC 65-19616. 1965. Repr. of 1915 ed. 15.00 (ISBN 0-405-08532-X, Blom Pubns). Arno.
IMPERSONATORS, FEMALE
Newton, Esther. Mother Camp: Female Impersonators in America. LC 76-37634. 1979. pap. 3.95 (ISBN 0-226-57760-0, P807, Phoen). U of Chicago Pr.
IMPLANTATION, ION
see Ion Implantation
IMPLANTATION OF OVUM
see Ovum Implantation
IMPLEMENTS, UTENSILS, ETC.
see also Agricultural Implements; Agricultural Machinery; Kitchen Utensils; Stone Implements; Tools;
also subdivision Implements under Indians, Mound-builders and similar headings; names of particular implements, e.g. Knives, Scythes
Brasher, Ruth E. & Garrison, Carolyn L. Modern Household Equipment. Date not set. text ed. 22.50 (ISBN 0-02-313540-9). Macmillan.
Carelman, Jacques. Thingumajigs. MacDonald, Sandy, tr. LC 81-66776. (Illus., Fr.). 1981. pap. 4.95 (ISBN 0-914398-34-2). Autumn Pr.
Cripps, Ann, ed. Countryman Rescuing the Past. (Countryman Ser.). (Illus.). 1975. 5.50 (ISBN 0-7153-6071-X). David & Charles.
De Haan, David. Antique Household Gadgets & Appliances. LC 77-88895. 1978. 5.95 (ISBN 0-8120-5261-7). Barron.
Drepperd, Carl W. Pioneer America: Its First Three Centuries. LC 71-190546. (Illus.). vi, 311p. 1972. Repr. of 1949 ed. lib. bdg. 16.50x (ISBN 0-8154-0415-8). Cooper Sq.
Gould, Mary E. Antique Tin & Tole Ware: Its History & Romance. LC 57-8796. (Illus.). 1957. 27.50 (ISBN 0-8048-0026-X). C E Tuttle.
--Early American Wooden Ware. LC 69-13499. (Illus.). 1962. 15.00 (ISBN 0-8048-0153-3). C E Tuttle.
Graf, Rudolf F. & Whalen, George J. How It Works Illustrated: Every Day Devices & Mechanisms. LC 73-80716. (A Popular Science Bk.). (Illus.). 192p. 1974. 11.95 (ISBN 0-06-011589-0, HarpT). Har-Row.
Lindsay, J. Seymour. Iron & Brass Implements of the English & American House. rev. & enl. ed. (Illus.). 248p. 1964. 27.50 (ISBN 0-85458-999-6). Herman Pub.
Nutting, Wallace. Furniture Treasury, 3 Vols. (Illus.). Vols. 1 & 2 In 1. 29.95 (ISBN 0-02-590980-0); Vol. 3. 24.95 (ISBN 0-02-591040-X). Macmillan.
Oakley, Kenneth P. Man the Tool-Maker. 6th ed. LC 50-13440. viii, 102p. 1976. pap. 1.95 (ISBN 0-226-61270-8, P20, Phoen). U of Chicago Pr.
Russell, Loris. Handy Things to Have Around the House: Old-Time Domestic Appliances of Canada & the United States. (Illus.). 1979. 19.95 (ISBN 0-07-082781-8). McGraw.
Shuldiner, Herbert & Heyn, Ernest V. Book of Gadgets: The Latest Time, Energy, & Work Savers. (Illus.). 256p. 1981. 19.95 (ISBN 0-517-54280-3); pap. 10.95 (ISBN 0-517-54443-1). Crown.
Sloane, Eric. A B C Book of Early Americana. LC 63-18657. (gr. 1 up). 1963. 7.95a (ISBN 0-385-04663-4). Doubleday.
Tinkham, Sandra S., ed. Catalog of Domestic Utensils. (Index of American Design Ser.: Pt. 5). (Orig.). 1979. pap. 25.00x (ISBN 0-914146-71-8); incl. color microfiche 495.00x (ISBN 0-914146-70-X). Somerset Hse.
Van Rippen, B. Notes on Some Bushman Implements. LC 19-15013. 1918. pap. 5.00 (ISBN 0-527-00522-3). Kraus Repr.

IMPLIED POWERS (CONSTITUTIONAL LAW)
see also Executive Power; Judicial Power; Legislative Power; War and Emergency Powers
IMPORT AND EXPORT CONTROLS
see Foreign Trade Regulation
IMPORT CONTROLS
see Tariff
IMPORT QUOTAS
Destler, I. M., et al. The Textile Wrangle: Conflict in Japanese-American Relations, 1969-1971. LC 78-14429. 1979. 25.00x (ISBN 0-8014-1120-3). Cornell U Pr.
Olnek, Jay I. The Invisible Hand: How Free Trade Is Choking the Life Out of America. 1981. 15.00 (ISBN 0-938538-00-4). N Stonington.
The President's Trade Reform Proposal. (Legislative Analyses). 1973. pap. 2.00 (ISBN 0-8447-0153-X). Am Enterprise.
IMPORT RESTRICTIONS
see Foreign Trade Regulation; Import Quotas
IMPORTS
see Commerce; Tariff
IMPOSTORS AND IMPOSTURE
see also Fraud; Quacks and Quackery; Swindlers and Swindling
Barnum, Phineas T. Humbugs of the World. LC 68-21755. 1970. Repr. of 1865 ed. 19.00 (ISBN 0-8103-3580-8). Gale.
Bay, Timothy. Fake Giants & Other Great Hoaxes. LC 80-21132. (Monsters & Mysteries Ser.). (gr. 4-10). 1980. pap. 1.95 (ISBN 0-88436-766-5). EMC.
Blum, Richard H. Deceivers & Deceived: Observations on Confidence Men & Their Victims, Informants & Their Quarry, Political & Industrial Spies & Ordinary Citizens. (Illus.). 340p. 1972. 24.50 (ISBN 0-398-02235-6). C C Thomas.
De Francesco, Grete. The Power of the Charlatan. Beard, Miriam, tr. from Ger. LC 79-8609. Repr. of 1939 ed. 31.50 (ISBN 0-404-18471-5). AMS Pr.
Elkanah, Settle. The Compleat Memoirs of the Life of That Notorious Imposter Will Morrell, Alias Bowyer, Alias Wickham,Etc, LC 80-2498. Repr. of 1694 ed. 47.50 (ISBN 0-404-19134-7). AMS Pr.
Felderer, Ditlieb. Anne Frank's Diary: A Hoax. (Illus.). 100p. (Orig.). 1980. pap. 5.00 (ISBN 0-911038-57-4, 335, Dist. by Inst Hist Rev.). Noontide.
MacDougall, Curtis. Hoaxes. 2nd ed. 1958. pap. 4.50 (ISBN 0-486-20465-0). Dover.
Matthews, Ronald. English Messiahs: Studies of Six English Religious Pretenders, 1656-1927. LC 76-172553. Repr. of 1936 ed. 12.75 (ISBN 0-405-08783-7, Pub. by Blom). Arno.
Roberts, David. Great Exploration Hoaxes. Michaelman, Herbert, ed. 192p. 1981. 10.95 (ISBN 0-517-54075-4, Michaelman Books). Crown.
Thomas, Fred W. Masters of Deception. pap. 3.95 (ISBN 0-8010-8779-1). Baker Bk.
Thompson, C. J. Mysteries of History, with Accounts of Some Remarkable Characters & Charlatans. LC 76-164056. (Tower Bks). 1971. Repr. of 1928 ed. 22.00 (ISBN 0-8103-3908-0). Gale.
IMPOTENCE
Brooks, Marvin B. & Brooks, Sally W. Lifelong Sexual Vigor: How to Avoid & Overcome Impotence. LC 81-43115. 288p. 1981. 12.95 (ISBN 0-385-17712-7). Doubleday.
Carlton, Eric. Sexual Anxiety: A Study of Male Impotence. 197p. 1980. 22.50x (ISBN 0-06-490960-3). B&N.
Fellman, Sheldon & Fellman, Sheldon. The Virile Man: Sixty Minutes to Greater Potency. LC 76-16275. 1976. 8.95 (ISBN 0-685-70123-9). Stein & Day.
Hammond, William A. Sexual Impotence in the Male & Female. LC 73-20626. (Sex, Marriage & Society Ser.). 310p. 1974. Repr. 18.00x (ISBN 0-405-05802-0). Arno.
Hirsch, Edwin W. Impotence & Frigidity. pap. 3.00 (ISBN 0-87980-084-4). Wilshire.
Stekel, Wilhelm. Impotence in the Male, 2 Vols. rev. ed. LC 78-149627. 1959. 14.95x (ISBN 0-87140-842-2); pap. 3.95 (ISBN 0-87140-050-2). Liveright.
Wagner, Gorm & Green, Richard. Impotence (Erectile Failure) Physiological, Psychological, & Surgical Diagnosis & Treatment. (Perspectives in Sexuality Ser.). 215p. 1981. text ed. 24.50 (ISBN 0-306-40719-1, Plenum Pr). Plenum Pub.
Zorgniotti, A. W. & Rossi, G. Vasculogenic Impotence. (Illus.). 344p. 1980. 39.75 (ISBN 0-398-03982-8). C C Thomas.
IMPRECATION
see Blessing and Cursing
IMPREGNATION, ARTIFICIAL
see Artificial Insemination
IMPRESARIOS
see also Theatrical Agencies
Bing, Rudolf. A Knight at the Opera. (Illus.). 1981. 14.95 (ISBN 0-399-12653-8). Putnam.
Haskell, Arnold & Nouvel, Walter W. Diaghileff: His Artistic & Private Life. LC 78-9314. (Ser. in Dance). 1977. Repr. of 1935 ed. lib. bdg. 25.00 (ISBN 0-306-70869-8); pap. 6.95 (ISBN 0-306-80085-3). Da Capo.
Hurok, Solomon & Goode, Ruth. Impresario, a Memoir. LC 75-8838. (Illus.). 1975. Repr. of 1946 ed. lib. bdg. 18.50x (ISBN 0-8371-8125-9, HUIM). Greenwood.
Moses, Montrose J. The Life of Heinrich Conried. Farkas, Andrew, ed. LC 76-29959. (Opera Biographies). (Illus.). 1977. Repr. of 1916 ed. lib. bdg. 25.00x (ISBN 0-405-09699-2). Arno.
Wagner, Charles L. Seeing Stars. Farkas, Andrew, ed. LC 76-29976. (Opera Biographies). (Illus.). 1977. Repr. of 1940 ed. lib. bdg. 24.00x (ISBN 0-405-09714-X). Arno.
IMPRESSIONISM (ART)
see also Post-Impressionism (Art)
Bellony-Rewald, Alice. The Lost World of the Impressionists. LC 76-10096. (Illus.). 1976. 32.50 (ISBN 0-8212-0687-7, 533513). NYGS.
Blunden, Godfrey & Blunden, Maria. Impressionists & Impressionism. (Illus.). 1980. pap. 14.95 (ISBN 0-686-68748-5). Rizzoli Intl.
--Impressionists & Impressionism. LC 76-12315. (Illus.). 1976. 65.00 (ISBN 0-8478-0047-4). Rizzoli Intl.
Boyle, Richard J. American Impressionism. LC 73-89951. (Illus.). 224p. 1974. 32.50 (ISBN 0-8212-0597-8, 036730). NYGS.
Chatelet, Albert. Impressionist Painting. (Color Slide Program of Art Enjoyment Ser.). (Illus.). 1962. 17.95 (ISBN 0-07-010710-6, P&RB). McGraw.
Clark, Eliot. Theodore Robinson: His Life & Art. LC 79-91552. (Illus.). 78p. (Orig.). 1979. 25.00 (ISBN 0-940114-11-9); pap. 16.00 (ISBN 0-940114-10-0). Love Galleries.
Cognia, Raymond & Elgar, Frank. Illustrated Dictionary of Impressionism. (Pocket Art Ser.). (Illus.). (gr. 10-12). 1979. pap. 3.95 (ISBN 0-8120-0986-X). Barron.
Cogniat, Raymond. The Century of the Impressionists. (Illus.). 1968. 12.98 (ISBN 0-517-01320-7). Crown.
Courthion, Pierre. Impressionism. LC 79-142740. (Illus.). 206p. 1971. 37.50 (ISBN 0-8109-0202-8). Abrams.
--Impressionism. concise ed. Shepley, John, tr. (Illus.). 1977. 17.50 (ISBN 0-8109-1112-4); pap. 7.95 (ISBN 0-8109-2067-0). Abrams.
De Forges, Maria T. Impressionist Painters: From Cezanne to Toulouse-Lautrec. Graig, Marjorie G., tr. (World in Color Ser.). (Illus.). 50p. 1976. 3.95 (ISBN 0-88254-389-X). Hippocrene Bks.
De Forges, Marie-Therese. Impressionist Painters: From Manet to Sisley. Craig, Marjorie, tr. (World in Color Ser.). (Illus.). 50p. 1976. 3.95 (ISBN 0-88254-388-1). Hippocrene Bks.
Denvir, B. Impressionism. LC 77-80177. (Modern Movements in Art Ser.). 1978. pap. 1.95 (ISBN 0-8120-0879-0). Barron.
Dunstan, Bernard. Painting Methods of the Impressionists. (Illus., Orig.). 1976. 21.95 (ISBN 0-8230-3710-X). Watson-Guptill.
Duret, Theodore. Manet & the French Impressionists. facsimile ed. Crawford Flitch, J. E., tr. (Select Bibliographies Reprint Ser). Repr. of 1910 ed. 24.00 (ISBN 0-8369-6687-2). Arno.
Everitt, A. Abstract Expressionism. LC 77-80188. (Modern Movements in Art Ser.). 1978. pap. 1.95 (ISBN 0-8120-0880-4). Barron.
Gerdts, William H. American Impressionism. (Illus.). 1980. 35.00 (ISBN 0-935558-00-4); pap. 22.00 (ISBN 0-935558-01-2). Henry Art.
Getlein, Frank. Twenty Five Impressionist Masterpieces. (Illus.). 64p. 1981. 12.95 (ISBN 0-8109-2247-9). Abrams.
Kelder, Diane. French Impressionists. LC 79-57411. (Abbeville Library of Art: No. 2). (Illus.). 112p. 1980. pap. 4.95 (ISBN 0-89659-093-3). Abbeville Pr.
--The Great Book of French Impressionism. LC 80-66527. (Illus.). 448p. 1980. 100.00 (ISBN 0-89659-151-4). Abbeville Pr.
--Great Masters of French Impressionism. (Illus.). 1978. 17.95 (ISBN 0-517-53447-9). Crown.
Keller, Horst. The Great Book of French Impressionism. Brown, Alexis, tr. from Ger. LC 80-13206. (Illus.). 272p. 1980. 50.00 (ISBN 0-933920-11-3). Hudson Hills.
Kronegger, Maria E. James Joyce & Associated Image Makers. 1968. 6.00x (ISBN 0-8084-0169-6); pap. 2.95 (ISBN 0-8084-0170-X, L20). Coll & U Pr.
Leaders of American Impressionism: Mary Cassatt, Childe Hassam, John H. Twachtman & J. Alden Weit. LC 75-128385. (Brooklyn Museum Pulbications in Reprint Ser). (Illus.). 70p. Repr. of 1937 ed. 6.50 (ISBN 0-405-00876-7). Arno.
Love, Richard H. Harriet Randall Lumis (1870-1953) An American Impressionist. LC 77-90984. (Illus.). 64p. (Orig.). 1977. 12.00 (ISBN 0-940114-07-0); pap. 6.00 (ISBN 0-940114-06-2). Love Galleries.
--Walter Griffin: American Impressionist (1861-1935) (Illus.). 25p. 1975. pap. 5.00 (ISBN 0-940114-01-1). Love Galleries.
--William Chadwick (Eighteen Seventy-Nine to Nineteen Sixty-Two) An American Impressionist. LC 78-61711. (Illus.). 110p. (Orig.). 1978. 15.00 (ISBN 0-940114-09-7); pap. 7.50 (ISBN 0-940114-08-9). Love Galleries.
Marandel, J. Patrice & Daulte, Francois. Frederic Bazille & Early Impressionism. LC 78-53512. (Illus.). 227p. (Orig.). 1978. pap. 9.95 (ISBN 0-86559-028-1). Art Inst Chi.
Moffet, Charles S., intro. by. Monet's Years at Giverny: Beyond Impressionism. LC 78-328. (Illus.). 1978. 12.50 (ISBN 0-87099-175-2); pap. 6.95 (ISBN 0-87099-174-4). Metro Mus Art.
Nochlin, L. Impressionism & Post-Impressionism, 1874-1904: Sources in Documents. 1966. pap. 11.95 (ISBN 0-13-452003-3). P-H.
Paret, Peter. The Berlin Secession: Modernism & Its Enemies in Imperial Germany. LC 80-15117. 1980. text ed. 17.50x (ISBN 0-674-06773-8). Harvard U Pr.
Pool, Phoebe. Impressionism. (World of Art Ser.). (Illus.). 1967. pap. 9.95 (ISBN 0-19-519930-8). Oxford U Pr.
Powell-Jones, Mark. Impressionist Painting. LC 78-25565. (Gallery Ser.). (Illus.). 1979. 12.50 (ISBN 0-8317-4893-1, Mayflower Bks); pap. 6.95 (ISBN 0-8317-4894-X). Smith Pubs.
Reff, Theodore, ed. Exhibitions of Impressionist Art, Bk. I. (Modern Art in Paris 1855 to 1900 Ser.). 356p. 1981. lib. bdg. 44.00 (ISBN 0-8240-4741-9). Garland Pub.
--Exhibitions of Impressionist Art, Bk. II. (Modern Art in Paris 1855 to 1900 Ser.). 259p. 1981. lib. bdg. 44.00 (ISBN 0-8240-4742-7). Garland Pub.
--Impressionist Group Exhibitions. (Modern Art in Paris 1855 to 1900 Ser.). 157p. 1981. lib. bdg. 44.00 (ISBN 0-8240-4723-0). Garland Pub.
Rewald, John. The History of Impressionism. LC 68-17468. (Illus.). 672p. 1980. 40.00 (ISBN 0-87070-369-2, 365149, Pub. by Museum Mod Art); pap. 19.95 (ISBN 0-87070-369-2). NYGS.
--History of Impressionism. LC 68-17468. (Illus.). 672p. 1973. 32.50 (ISBN 0-87070-360-9, Pub. by Museum Mod Art). NYGS.
Rothenstein, John K. Nineteenth-Century Painting: A Study in Conflict. facs. ed. LC 67-28739. (Essay Index Reprint Ser). 1932. 16.00 (ISBN 0-8369-0838-4). Arno.
Serullaz, Maurice. Lexikon des Impressionismus. (Ger.). 1975. 25.00 (ISBN 3-8046-0011-5, M-7208). French & Eur.
Serulllaz, Maurice, et al. Encyclopedie De L'impressionnisme. 288p. (Fr.). 1976. 35.00 (ISBN 0-686-57220-3, M-6515). French & Eur.
Slocombe, George. Rebels of Art: Manet to Matisse. LC 68-8229. (Illus.). 1969. Repr. of 1939 ed. 14.50 (ISBN 0-8046-0425-8). Kennikat.
Strauss, Michel, ed. Impressionism & Modern Art: The Season at Sotheby Parke Bernet 1973-74. (Illus.). 288p. 1974. 40.00x (ISBN 0-85667-008-1, Pub. by Sotheby Parke Bernet England). Biblio Dist.
Venturi, Lionello. Impressionists & Symbolists. (Illus.). 244p. 1973. Repr. of 1950 ed. lib. bdg. 22.50x (ISBN 0-8154-0459-X). Cooper Sq.
Venturi, Lionello, ed. Archives de l'Impressionisme, Lettres De Renoir, Monet, Pissarro, Sisley & Autres, Memoires De Paul Durand-Ruel, 2 Vols. LC 69-19035. (Illus., Fr.). 1969. Repr. of 1939 ed. 61.50 (ISBN 0-8337-3629-9). B Franklin.
Warshawsky, Abel G. The Memories of an American Impressionist. Bassham, Ben L., ed. LC 80-82203. (Illus.). 259p. 1980. 17.50 (ISBN 0-87338-249-8). Kent St U Pr.

Wildenstein, Daniel. Monet's Years at Giverny: Beyond Impressionism. LC 78-328. (Illus.). 1978. 22.50 (ISBN 0-8109-1336-4); pap. 9.95 (ISBN 0-8109-2183-9). Abrams.

IMPRESSIONISM (MUSIC)

Palmer, Christopher. Impressionism in Music. 248p. 1980. pap. text ed. 8.50x (ISBN 0-09-115141-4, Hutchinson U Lib). Humanities.

IMPRESSMENT

Zimmerman, James F. Impressment of American Seamen. LC 65-27121. Repr. of 1925 ed. 10.50 (ISBN 0-8046-0516-5). Kennikat.

IMPRINTING (PSYCHOLOGY)

Hess, Eckhard H. & Petrovich, S. B., eds. Imprinting. (Benchmark Papers in Animal Behavior: Vol. 5). 1977. 42.50 (ISBN 0-12-786658-2). Acad Pr.

IMPRINTS (IN BOOKS)

see also Colophons

Annenberg, Maurice, compiled by. A Typographical Journey Through the Inland Printer. LC 77-89269. 1977. write for info. Maran Pub.

Bruntjen, Scott & Bruntjen, Carol R., eds. A Checklist of American Imprints for 1832. LC 64-11784. (Checklist of American Imprints Ser.: Vol. 1832). 1977. 22.50 (ISBN 0-8108-1019-0). Scarecrow.

Cotton, Henry. The Typographical Gazetteer. LC 76-159922. 1975. Repr. of 1825 ed. 22.00 (ISBN 0-8103-4121-2). Gale.

Echols, John M. Preliminary Checklist of Indonesian Imprints During the Japanese Period: March 1962 - August 1945. 1963. pap. 1.50 (ISBN 0-686-62725-3). Cornell Mod Indo.

Grenoble Catalog of Printed Books to 1900, 12 vols. (Illus.). 12000p. (Fr.). 1981. Set. 2400.00 (ISBN 3-598-10160-0, Pub. by K G Saur). Gale.

Hargrett, Lester. The Gilcrease-Hargrett Catalogue of Imprints. LC 72-859. (Illus.). 450p. 1972. 24.95 (ISBN 0-8061-1020-1). U of Okla Pr.

Library of Congress, Washington, D. C. Far Eastern Languages Catalog, 22 vols. 1972. Set. lib. bdg. 2175.00 (ISBN 0-8161-0980-X). G K Hall.

Peddie, Robert A. Place-Names in Imprints: An Index to the Latin & Other Forms Used on Title-Pages. LC 68-30594. 1968. Repr. of 1932 ed. 19.00 (ISBN 0-8103-3239-6). Gale.

IMPRINTS (IN BOOKS), FICTITIOUS

see also Literary Forgeries and Mystifications

Brunet, Gustave. Imprimeurs imaginaires et librairies supposes. 1962. Repr. of 1866 ed. 23.50 (ISBN 0-8337-0404-4). B Franklin.

IMPRISONMENT

see also Arrest; Debt, Imprisonment for; Juvenile Detention Homes; Penal Colonies; Prisons; Reformatories

Brandon, Ruth & Davies, Christie. Wrongful Imprisonment, Mistaken Convictions & Their Consequences. 296p. 1973. 19.50 (ISBN 0-208-01337-7, Archon). Shoe String.

Hawkins, Gordon. The Prison: Policy & Practice. LC 75-20892. (Studies in Crime & Justice Ser.). 224p. 1976. 12.50x (ISBN 0-226-31999-7). U of Chicago Pr.

--The Prison: Policy & Practice. LC 75-20892. (Studies in Crime & Justice). 1977. pap. 4.95 (ISBN 0-226-32000-6, P749, Phoen). U of Chicago Pr.

McConville, S. The Use of Imprisonment: Essays in the Changing State of English Penal Policy. (Direct Edition Ser.). (Orig.). 1975. pap. 8.25 (ISBN 0-7100-8309-2). Routledge & Kegan.

Miller, Robert & Basten, Fred. Gringo. LC 14-251. 1980. 10.95 (ISBN 0-9603490-0-6). Noble Hse.

Morris, Norval. The Future of Imprisonment. LC 74-13920. (Studies in Crime & Justice Ser). xiv, 144p. 1974. 10.00x (ISBN 0-226-53905-9). U of Chicago Pr.

--The Future of Imprisonment. LC 74-13920. (Studies in Crime & Justice). 1977. pap. 3.95 (ISBN 0-226-53906-7, P736, Phoen). U of Chicago Pr.

Pugh, Ralph B. Imprisonment in Medieval England. LC 68-12061. (Illus.). 54.50 (ISBN 0-521-06005-2). Cambridge U Pr.

Sherman, Michael & Hawkins, Gordon. Imprisonment in America: Choosing the Future. LC 81-10453. 1981. price not set (ISBN 0-226-75279-8). U of Chicago Pr.

Sleffel, Linda. The Law & the Dangerous Criminal. LC 77-287. (Dangerous Offender Project Ser.). 1977. 17.95 (ISBN 0-669-01481-8). Lexington Bks.

Sommer, Robert. The End of Imprisonment. LC 75-38097. 192p. 1976. 12.95 (ISBN 0-19-502045-6). Oxford U Pr.

Tomasic, R. & Dobinson, I. The Failure of Imprisonment. LC 79-62900. (Law & Society Ser.: No. 3). 1979. text ed. 15.95x (ISBN 0-86861-089-5); pap. text ed. 8.50x (ISBN 0-86861-097-6). Allen Unwin.

Wooden, Kenneth. Weeping in the Playtime of Others: The Plight of Incarcerated Children. 1976. 8.95 (ISBN 0-07-071642-0, GB); pap. 4.95 (ISBN 0-07-071643-9). McGraw.

IMPRISONMENT FOR DEBT

see Debt, Imprisonment for

IMPROMPTU THEATER

see Improvisation (Acting)

IMPROPER INTEGRALS

see Integrals, Improper

IMPROPRIATION

see Secularization

IMPROVISATION (ACTING)

see also Commedia Dell'Arte

Johnstone, Keith. Impro: Improvisation & the Theatre. 1979. 12.95 (ISBN 0-87830-163-1). Theatre Arts.

Spolin, Viola. Improvisation for the Theater: A Handbook of Teaching & Directing Techniques. 1963. text ed. 12.50x (ISBN 0-8101-0249-8). Northwestern U Pr.

Sweet, Jeffrey. Something Wonderful Right Away. 1978. pap. 2.95 (ISBN 0-380-01884-5, 37119, Discus). Avon.

IMPROVISATION (MUSIC)

see also Harmony, Keyboard

Bailey, Derek. Improvisation: Its Nature & Practice in Music. 160p. 1981. 25.00x (ISBN 0-903485-73-7, Pub. by Moorland). State Mutual Bk.

Berkowitz, Sol. Improvisation Through Keyboard Harmony. (Illus.). 288p. 1975. pap. 14.50 (ISBN 0-13-453472-7). P-H.

Conely, James. A Guide to Improvisation: An Introductory Handbook for Church Organists. LC 74-26945. 64p. 1975. pap. 2.95 (ISBN 0-687-16287-4). Abingdon.

Green Note Music Publications Staff. Electric Blues Guitar. (Contemporary Guitar Styles Ser). (Illus.). 96p. (Orig., Prog. Bk.). 1977. pap. 8.95 (ISBN 0-912910-05-4). Green Note Music.

Harris, Howard C., Jr. & Fielder, William. The Complete Book of Improvisation - Composition & Funk Techniques: Essentials & Augmentations for the Vital Self-Instrument in Jazz Music - Theory, Practices & Life Parallels. (Illus.). 181p. (Orig.). Date not set. price not set spiral bound (ISBN 0-940026-00-7). DeMos Music.

Hunt, Reginald. Extemporization for Music Students. (YA) (gr. 9 up). 1968. pap. 10.00 (ISBN 0-19-321380-X). Oxford U Pr.

Konowitz, Bert. Music Improvisation As a Classroom Method. LC 72-96015. 100p. 1973. pap. text ed. 6.95 (ISBN 0-88284-003-7). Alfred Pub.

Krapf, Gerhard. Organ Improvisation. 1967. pap. 5.25 (ISBN 0-8066-0727-0, 11-9310). Augsburg.

Mack, Glenn. Adventures in Improvisation at the Keyboard. 64p. 1970. pap. text ed. 7.65 (ISBN 0-87487-076-3). Summy.

Mehegan, John. Jazz Improvisation, 4 vols. Incl. Vol. 1. Tonal & Rhythmic Principles. Bernstein, Leonard, intro. by. 1959 (ISBN 0-8256-4157-8); Vol. 2. Jazz Rhythm & the Improvised Line. Arlen, Harold, intro. by. 1962 (ISBN 0-8256-4158-6); Vol. 3. Swing & Early Progressive Piano Styles. Silver, Horace, intro. by. 1964 (ISBN 0-8256-4159-4); Vol. 4. Contemporary Piano Styles. 1965 (ISBN 0-8256-4160-8). LC 58-13525. (Orig.). pap. 9.95 ea. (Consolidated). Music Sales.

Pelz, William. Basic Keyboard Skills: An Introduction to Accompaniment Improvisation, Transposition & Modulation, with an Appendix on Sight Reading. LC 80-22820. vii, 173p. 1981. Repr. of 1963 ed. PLB 23.50x (ISBN 0-313-22882-5, PEBK). Greenwood.

Tobin, Joseph R. How to Improvise Piano Accompaniments. 1956. 7.50 (ISBN 0-19-321800-3). Oxford U Pr.

Wollner, Gertrude P. Improvisation in Music. 9.50 (ISBN 0-8283-1422-5). Branden.

IMPULSE

see also Inhibition

Kipnis, David. Character Structure & Impulsiveness. LC 76-127687. (Personality & Psychopathology Ser.). 1971. 21.00 (ISBN 0-12-409450-3). Acad Pr.

Wisnie, H. A. The Impulsive Personality. LC 77-23464. (Illus.). 208p. 1977. 18.95 (ISBN 0-306-30973-4, Plenum Pr). Plenum Pub.

IN FORMA PAUPERIS

see also Legal Aid; Public Defenders

Comer, John P. Forging of the Federal Indigent Code. 1966. 6.00 (ISBN 0-911536-07-8). Trinity U Pr.

IN-LINE DATA PROCESSING

see on-Line Data Processing

IN-SERVICE TRAINING

see Employees, Training Of

INAUDIBLE SOUND

see Ultrasonics

INAYAT KHAN, 1882-1926

Khan, Pir V. The Message in Our Time: The Life & Teachings of the Sufi Master, Hazrat Inayat Khan. LC 78-4751. (Illus.). 1979. 15.95 (ISBN 0-06-064237-8, HarpR). Har-Row.

INBORN ERRORS OF METABOLISM

see Metabolism, Inborn Errors of

INBREEDING

see also Consanguinity; Miscegenation

INCA LANGUAGE

see Quechua Language

INCA LAW

see Law, Inca

INCA MUSIC

see Incas-Music

INCANDESCENT LAMPS

see Electric Lamps

INCANTATIONS

see also Blessing and Cursing

Biggs, Robert. Sa. Zi. Ga. Ancient Mesopotamian Potency Incantations. LC 66-25697. 8.00 (ISBN 0-685-71734-8). J J Augustin.

Burns, Gerald. A Book of Spells First Third. (Lucky Heart Bks.). 1979. pap. 2.00 (ISBN 0-913198-12-9). Salt Lick.

Kilpatrick, Jack F. & Kilpatrick, Anna G. Run Toward the Nightland: Magic of the Oklahoma Cherokees. LC 67-19814. (Illus.). 1967. pap. 6.95 (ISBN 0-87074-165-9). SMU Press.

McCullough, W. S. Jewish & Mandaean Incantation Bowls in the Royal Ontario Museum. LC 67-101762. (Illus.). 1967. 12.50x (ISBN 0-8020-5184-7). U of Toronto Pr.

Maple, Eric. Incantations & Words of Power. (Paths to Inner Power Ser). 1974. pap. 1.25 (ISBN 0-87728-234-X). Weiser.

Thompson, Reginald C. The Devils & Evil Spirits of Babylonia, 2 vols. LC 73-18855. (Luzac's Semitic Text & Translation Ser.: Nos. 14-15). (Illus.). Repr. of 1904 ed. 34.50 set (ISBN 0-404-11353-2). AMS Pr.

Yamauchi, Edwin M. Mandaic Incantation Texts. (American Oriental Ser.: Vol. 49). 1967. 9.00x (ISBN 0-940490-49-8). Am Orient Soc.

INCAPACITY, ESTIMATION OF

see Disability Evaluation

INCARNATION

see also Theophanies

Anderson, Norman. The Mystery of the Incarnation. LC 79-13879. 1979. pap. 3.95 (ISBN 0-87784-530-1). Inter-Varsity.

Andrews, Samuel J. & Gifford, E. H. Man & the Incarnation: The Study of Philippians 2 & Psalm 110. 1981. lib. bdg. 15.00 (ISBN 0-86524-078-7). Klock & Klock.

Athanasius, Saint On the Incarnation of the Word. pap. 1.95 (ISBN 0-686-25556-9). Eastern Orthodox.

Blackwood, Andrew W., Jr. When God Came Down. (Pocket Paperback Library Ser.). 1978. pap. 1.45 (ISBN 0-8010-0753-4). Baker Bk.

Gorodetzky, Nadejda. Humiliated Christ in Modern Russian Thought. LC 79-168159. Repr. of 1938 ed. 18.75 (ISBN 0-404-02883-7). AMS Pr.

Goulder, Michael, ed. Incarnation & Myth: The Debate Continued. LC 79-16509. 1979. pap. 5.95 (ISBN 0-8028-1199-X). Eerdmans.

Hick, John, ed. The Myth of God Incarnate. 1978. pap. 6.95 (ISBN 0-664-24178-6). Westminster.

Lewis, C. S., intro. by. St. Athanasius on the Incarnation: The Treatise De Incarnationi Verbi Dei. 126p. 1981. pap. 3.95 (ISBN 0-02-083200-1). Macmillan.

St. Anthanasius. St. Athanasius on the Incarnation. 120p. 1977. pap. 3.95 (ISBN 0-913836-40-0). St Vladimirs.

Schlitzer, Albert L. Our Life in Christ. (University Theology Ser.: Vols. 1 & 2). 1962. Set. 9.95x (ISBN 0-268-00201-0). U of Notre Dame Pr.

Spurgeon, C. H. Christ's Incarnation-"Good Tidings of Great Joy". 1978. pap. 2.25 (ISBN 0-686-00498-1). Pilgrim Pubns.

Surath, Sri. God Is Now Here. 1976. 5.00 (ISBN 0-685-58439-9). Ranney Pubns.

Torrance, Thomas F. Space, Time & Incarnation. 1978. pap. 2.95 (ISBN 0-19-520082-9, GB562, GB). Oxford U Pr.

Wolfson, Harry A. Philosophy of the Church Fathers: Faith, Trinity, Incarnation. 3rd rev. ed. LC 70-119077. 1970. 25.00x (ISBN 0-674-66551-1). Harvard U Pr.

Zodhiates, Spiros. The Perfect Gift. (Illus.). 1973. pap. 1.75 (ISBN 0-89957-511-0). AMG Pubs.

INCAS

see also Indians of South America; Peru-Antiquities; Peru-History-To 1548

Baudin, Louis. Daily Life in Peru Under the Last Incas. Bradford, Winifred, tr. (Illus.). 1962. 10.95 (ISBN 0-02-507870-4). Macmillan.

Bingham, Hiram. Lost City of the Incas. LC 48-9227. (Illus.). 1963. pap. text ed. 3.95x (ISBN 0-689-70014-8, 33). Atheneum.

Blassingame, Wyatt. The Incas & the Spanish Conquest. LC 80-10931. (Illus.). 192p. (gr. 7 up). 1980. PLB 8.29 (ISBN 0-671-33031-4). Messner.

Brundage, Burr C. Empire of the Inca. (Civilization of the American Indian Ser.: No. 69). (Illus.). 1974. Repr. of 1963 ed. 19.95 (ISBN 0-8061-0573-9). U of Okla Pr.

Cobo, Bernabe. History of the Inca Empire. Hamilton, Roland, tr. from Sp. (Texas Pan American Ser.). 301p. 1979. text ed. 17.95x (ISBN 0-292-73008-X). U of Tex Pr.

De La Vega, Garcilasco. Incas. 1964. pap. 3.50 (ISBN 0-380-01269-3, 45542, Discus). Avon.

De Leon, Cieza. The Incas of Pedro De Cieza De Leon. Von Hagen, Victor W., ed. (Civilization of the American Indian Ser: No. 53). 1976. 24.95 (ISBN 0-8061-0433-3); pap. 9.95 (ISBN 0-8061-1355-3). U of Okla Pr.

Garcilaso de la Vega. Royal Commentaries of the Incas & General History of Peru, 2 Vols. Livermore, Harold V., tr. (Texas Pan American Ser.). 1965. Set. 75.00x (ISBN 0-292-73358-5). U of Tex Pr.

--Royal Commentaries of the Yncas, 2 vols. Markham, Clements R., ed. & tr. (Hakluyt Society, First Ser.: Nos. 41 & 45). Repr. of 1869 ed. 63.00 (ISBN 0-8337-2233-6). B Franklin.

Gasparini, Graziano & Margolies, Luise. Inca Architecture. Lyon, Patricia J., tr. from Sp. LC 79-3005. (Illus.). 368p. 1980. 32.50x (ISBN 0-253-30443-1). Ind U Pr.

Gibson, Charles. Inca Concept of Sovereignty & the Spanish Administration in Peru. LC 69-19004. Repr. of 1948 ed. lib. bdg. 14.25x (ISBN 0-8371-1021-1, TLGI). Greenwood.

Guidoni, Enrico & Magni, Roberto. The Andes. Mondadori, tr. from Ital. LC 74-3643. (Monuments of Civilization Ser.). Orig. Title: Civilta Andine Grandi Monumenti. (Illus.). 1977. 25.00 (ISBN 0-448-02025-4). G&D.

Hanstein, Otfrid Von. The World of the Incas: A Socialist State of the Past. 1976. lib. bdg. 59.95 (ISBN 0-8490-2846-9). Gordon Pr.

Hemming, John. The Conquest of the Incas. LC 73-4616. (Illus.). 641p. 1973. pap. 6.95 (ISBN 0-15-622300-7, HB258, Harv). HarBraceJ.

--Machu Picchu. Bayrd, Edwin, ed. LC 80-82066. (Illus.). 1981. 16.95 (ISBN 0-88225-302-6). Newsweek.

Karsten, Rafael. Totalitarian State of the Past. LC 79-86027. 1969. Repr. of 1949 ed. 15.00 (ISBN 0-8046-0617-X). Kennikat.

Kendall, Anne. Everyday Life of the Incas. 1978. pap. 14.95 (ISBN 0-7134-1072-8, Pub. by Batsford England). David & Charles.

Kubler, George. The Indian Caste of Peru 1795-1940. LC 78-119552. (Illus.). 71p. 1973. Repr. of 1952 ed. lib. bdg. 15.00x (ISBN 0-8371-5085-X, SMIP). Greenwood.

Lothrop, S. K. Inca Treasure As Depicted by Spanish Historians. (Illus.). 1938. 5.00 (ISBN 0-686-20672-X). Southwest Mus.

Markham, Clements. Incas of Peru. LC 79-84877. (Illus.). Repr. of 1910 ed. 28.75 (ISBN 0-404-04188-4). AMS Pr.

Markham, Clements R., ed. & tr. Narratives of the Rites & Laws of the Yncas. (Hakluyt Society First Ser: No. 48). (Illus.). 1964. Repr. of 1873 ed. 26.50 (ISBN 0-8337-2232-8). B Franklin.

Mason, J. Alden. Ancient Civilizations of Peru. rev. ed. (Illus., Orig.). 1957. pap. 4.95 (ISBN 0-14-020395-8, Pelican). Penguin.

Means, Philip A. Ancient Civilization of the Andes. LC 64-8175. 1964. Repr. of 1931 ed. 18.50 (ISBN 0-87752-072-0). Gordian.

--Fall of the Inca Empire & the Spanish Rule in Peru, 1530-1780. LC 64-8176. (Illus.). 1964. Repr. of 1931 ed. 15.00 (ISBN 0-87752-073-9). Gordian.

Meisch, Lynn. A Traveler's Guide to El Dorado & the Inca Empire. 1977. pap. 8.95 (ISBN 0-14-046280-5). Penguin.

Metraux, Alfred. History of the Incas. Ordish, George, tr. LC 68-20890. (Illus., Fr.). 1969. 7.95 (ISBN 0-394-42894-3, 2894). Pantheon.

--The History of the Incas. Ordish, George, tr. LC 68-20890. (Illus., Fr). 1970. pap. 4.95 (ISBN 0-8052-0248-X). Schocken.

Moore, Sally F. Power & Property in Inca Peru. LC 72-5456. 190p. 1973. Repr. of 1958 ed. lib. bdg. 14.50x (ISBN 0-8371-6441-9, MOPO). Greenwood.

Moseley, Michael E. Peru's Golden Treasures. Willimas, P. M., ed. LC 77-93483. (Illus.). 1978. pap. 6.00 (ISBN 0-914868-03-9). Field Mus.

Murra, John V. The Economic Organization of the Inka State. Dalton, George, ed. (Research in Economic Anthropology Supplement Ser.: No. 1). 214p. 1980. 37.50 (ISBN 0-89232-118-0). Jai Pr.

National Geographic Society, ed. The Incredible Incas & Their Timeless Land. LC 74-28805. (Special Publications Ser). (Illus.). 200p. 1975. 6.95, avail. only from natl. geog. (ISBN 0-87044-177-9). Natl Geog.

Philip. Secret of the Andes. 1976. pap. 5.95 (ISBN 0-915070-02-2). Leaves of Grass.

Prescott, William H. The Conquest of Mexico. Bd. with The Conquest of Peru. 1931. 5.95 (ISBN 0-394-60729-5, G29). Modern Lib.

--Conquest of Peru. abr ed. Von Hagen, Victor W., ed. pap. 1.50 (ISBN 0-451-61495-X, MW1495, Ment). NAL.
Silvester, Hans, photos by. The Route of the Incas. (Studio Bk). (Illus.). 1977. 35.00 (ISBN 0-670-60916-1). Viking Pr.
Stierlin, Henri. The Pre-Colombian Civilizations: The World of the Maya, Aztecs & Incas. (Illus.). Date not set. 7.98 (ISBN 0-8317-7116-X, Pub. by Mayflower Bks). Smith Pubs.
Von Hagen, Victor W. Realm of the Incas. pap. 1.95 (ISBN 0-451-61715-0, MJ1715, Ment). NAL.
Von Hanstein, Otfrid. The World of the Incas: A Socialistic State of the Past. facsimile ed. Barwell, Anna, tr. LC 75-165811. (Select Bibliographies Reprint Ser.). Repr. of 1925 ed. 15.00 (ISBN 0-8369-5968-X). Arno.

INCAS–JUVENILE LITERATURE

Appel, Benjamin. Shepherd of the Sun. (Illus.). (gr. 5 up). 1961. 4.95 (ISBN 0-8392-3033-8). Astor-Honor.
Beals, Carleton. Incredible Incas: Yesterday & Today. LC 72-2077. (Illus.). 192p. (gr. 7 up). 1973. 8.95 (ISBN 0-200-71901-7, AbS-J). Har-Row.
Bierhorst, John, ed. & tr. Black Rainbow: Legends of the Incas & Myths of Ancient Peru. LC 76-19092. 176p. (gr. 7 up). 1976. 9.95 (ISBN 0-374-30829-2). FS&G.
Bleeker, Sonia. The Inca: Indians of the Andes. (Illus.). (gr. 3-6). 1960. PLB 6.67 (ISBN 0-688-31417-1). Morrow.
Burland, Cottie. The Incas. LC 78-61225. (Peoples of the Past Ser.). (Illus.). 1979. lib. bdg. 7.95 (ISBN 0-686-51158-1). Silver.
Burland, Cottie A. Inca Peru. (Great Civilization Ser). (Illus.). (gr. 4-8). 1962. 5.75 (ISBN 0-7175-0017-9). Dufour.
Gemming, Elizabeth. Lost City in the Clouds: The Discovery of Machu Picchu. LC 78-31877. (Science Dicovery Ser.). (Illus.). (gr. 3-7). 1980. PLB 5.99 (ISBN 0-698-30698-8). Coward.
Lewis, Brenda R. Growing up in Inca Times. (Growing up Ser.). (Illus.). 72p. (gr. 7-9). 1981. 14.95 (ISBN 0-7134-2736-1, Pub. by Batsford England). David & Charles.
Millard, Anne. The Incas. (Warwick Press Ser.). (gr. 5 up). 1980. PLB 7.60 (ISBN 0-531-09171-6, F23). Watts.
Pine, Tillie S. & Levine, Joseph. Incas Knew. (Illus.). (gr. k-3). 1967. PLB 7.95 (ISBN 0-07-050078-9, GB). McGraw.

INCAS–MUSIC

Stevenson, Robert. Music in Aztec & Inca Territory. (California Library Reprint Ser.: No. 64). 1977. Repr. of 1968 ed. 38.50x (ISBN 0-520-03169-5). UCDLA.

INCENDIARISM

see Arson

INCENSE

Groom, N. S. Frankincense & Myrrh: A Study of the Arabian Incense Trade. (Arab Background Ser.). (Illus.). 328p. 1980. text ed. 37.00x (ISBN 0-582-76476-9). Longman.

INCENTIVE (PSYCHOLOGY)

see also Reinforcement (Psychology); Rewards and Punishments in Education

Woshinsky, Oliver H. The French Deputy. LC 73-7960. 233p. 1980. Repr. of 1973 ed. text ed. 9.95x (ISBN 0-686-64208-2). Lytton Pub.

INCENTIVES IN EDUCATION

see Rewards and Punishments in Education

INCENTIVES IN INDUSTRY

see also Bonus System; Employee Ownership; Profit-Sharing; Rewards (Prizes, etc.); Wages

Barry, John W. & Henry, Porter J. Effective Sales Incentive Compensation. (Illus.). 192p. 1980. write for info. (ISBN 0-07-003860-0, P&RB). McGraw.
Hoffmann, Charles. Work Incentive Practices & Policies in the People's Republic of China, 1953-1965. LC 67-28936. 1967. 10.00 (ISBN 0-87395-028-3); microfiche 10.00 (ISBN 0-87395-128-X). State U NY Pr.
Jewell, Donald O. & Manners, George E., Jr. Dynamic Incentive Systems. LC 75-9562. (Research Monograph: No. 60). 76p. 1975. spiral bdg. 7.00 (ISBN 0-88406-092-6). Ga St U Busn Pub.
Strumpel, Burkhard, et al. Economic Incentives, Values & Subjective Well-Being, 1971-1974. 1976. codebk. 26.00 (ISBN 0-87944-187-9). ICPSR.
Torrence, George W. Motivation & Measurement of Performance. LC 67-17106. 102p. 1967. spiral bdg. 12.50 (ISBN 0-87179-092-0). BNA.

INCEST

see also Crimes without Victims

Allen, Charlotte V. Daddy's Girl. 1980. 10.95 (ISBN 0-671-61024-4, Wyndham). S&S.
Brady, Katherine. Father's Days: A True Story of Incest. LC 79-4878. 1979. 9.95 (ISBN 0-87223-539-4, Dist. by Har-Row). Seaview Bks.
Butler, Sandra. Conspiracy of Silence: The Trauma of Incest. LC 78-1975. 1978. 10.00 (ISBN 0-912078-56-1). New Glide.
Forward, Susan & Buck, Craig. Betrayal of Innocence: Incest & Its Devastation. 1979. pap. 3.95 (ISBN 0-14-005264-X). Penguin.
--Betrayal of Innocence: Incest & Its Devastation. new ed. LC 77-91388. 1977. 8.95 (ISBN 0-87477-073-4). J P Tarcher.
Fox, Robin. The Red Lamp of Incest: What the Taboo Can Tell Us About Who We Are & How We Got That Way. (Illus.). 288p. 1980. 12.95 (ISBN 0-525-18943-2). Dutton.
Herman, Judith. Father-Daughter Incest. LC 81-2534. (Illus.). 285p. 1981. 15.95 (ISBN 0-674-29505-6). Harvard U Pr.
Justice, Blair & Justice, Rita. Broken Taboo: Sex in the Family. 304p. 1981. pap. 7.95 (ISBN 0-87705-482-7). Human Sci Pr.
--The Broken Taboo: Sex in the Family. LC 78-23720. 1979. 16.95 (ISBN 0-87705-389-8). Human Sci Pr.
Meiselman, Karin C. Incest: A Psychological Study of Causes & Effects with Treatment Recommendations. LC 78-62557. (Social & Behavioral Science Ser.). (Illus.). 1978. text ed. 16.95x (ISBN 0-87589-380-5). Jossey-Bass.
Santiago, Luciano P. The Children of Oedipus: Brother & Sister Incest in Psychiatry, Literature, History & Mythology. LC 73-79773. 1973. 6.95 (ISBN 0-87212-028-7). Libra.
Shepher, Joseph. Incest: A Biosocial View. 1981. lib. bdg. 19.50 (ISBN 0-686-73099-2). Garland Pub.
Weinberg, Kirson S. Incest Behavior. 1976. pap. 4.95 (ISBN 0-8065-0533-8). Citadel Pr.
Woodbury, John & Schwartz, Elroy. Silent Sin. (Orig.). 1971. pap. 1.75 (ISBN 0-451-07927-2, E7927, Sig). NAL.

INCINERATION

see Cremation

INCINERATORS

Brunner, Calvin. Design of Sewage Sludge Incineration Systems. LC 80-21916. (Pollution Technology Review: No. 71). (Illus.). 380p. 1981. 48.00 (ISBN 0-8155-0825-5). Noyes.
Combustion Fundamentals for Waste Incineration. 212p. 1974. 30.00 (ISBN 0-685-48047-X, H00087). ASME.
Federal Housing Administration - Building Research Advisory Board. Apartment House Incinerators: Flue-Fed. 1965. pap. 3.00 (ISBN 0-309-01280-5). Natl Acad Pr.
Hooper, G. V., ed. Offshore Ship & Platform Incineration of Hazardous Wastes. LC 81-38372. (Pollution Tech. Rev. 79). (Illus.). 468p. 1981. 42.00 (ISBN 0-8155-0854-9). Noyes.
Incinerators, Rubbish Handling. (Eighty-Ninety Ser). 1972. pap. 2.00 (ISBN 0-685-58144-6, 82). Natl Fire Prot.
National Incinerator Conference, New York City, June, 1972. Proceedings. LC 70-124402. 353p. 1972. pap. 28.00 (ISBN 0-685-25546-8, I00081). ASME.
National Incinerator Conference - 1970. Proceedings. pap. 25.00 (ISBN 0-685-06529-4, I00070). ASME.
National Materials Advisory Board, National Research Council. Materials of Construction for Shipboard Waste Incinerators. 1977. pap. 8.75 (ISBN 0-309-02606-7). Natl Acad Pr.
Neissen, Walter R. Combustion & Incineration. (Pollution Engineering & Technology Ser.: Vol. 13). 1978. 42.50 (ISBN 0-8247-6656-3). Dekker.
Resource Recovery from Incinerator Residue. (Special Reports Ser: No. 33). (Illus.). 35p. 1970. 5.00 (ISBN 0-917084-20-9). Am Public Works.
Rubel, Fred N. Incineration of Solid Wastes. LC 74-77723. (Pollution Technology Review Ser: No. 13). (Illus.). 246p. 1975. 24.00 (ISBN 0-8155-0551-5). Noyes.
Rudman, Jack. Incinerator Plant Foreman. (Career Examination Ser.: C-2163). (Cloth bdg. avail. on request). 1976. pap. 8.00 (ISBN 0-8373-0362-1). Natl Learning.
--Incinerator Plant Maintenance Foreman. (Career Examination Ser.: C-2773). (Cloth bdg. avail. on request). 1980. pap. 12.00 (ISBN 0-8373-2773-3). Natl Learning.
--Incinerator Plant Supervisor. (Career Examination Ser.: C-2164). (Cloth bdg. avail. on request). 1976. pap. 8.00 (ISBN 0-8373-2164-6). Natl Learning.
Sittig, Marshall. Incineration of Industrial Hazardous Wastes & Sludges. LC 79-21252. (Pollution Technology Review: No. 63). (Illus.). 1980. 48.00 (ISBN 0-8155-0774-7). Noyes.
Stephenson, J. W., et al, eds. Incinerator & Solid Waste Technology, 1962-1975. 415p. 1975. pap. text ed. 60.00 (ISBN 0-685-62568-0, I00092). ASME.

INCIPITS

Thornidike, Lynn & Kibre, Pearl, eds. Catalogue of Incipits of Mediaeval Scientific Writings in Latin. rev. & enl. ed. 1963. 35.00 (ISBN 0-910956-11-1). Medieval Acad.

INCLOSURES

see also Waste Lands

Ault, Warren O. Open-Field Husbandry & the Village Community: A Study of Agrarian By-Laws in Medieval England. LC 65-27426. (Transactions Ser.: Vol. 55, Pt. 7). 1965. pap. 1.00 (ISBN 0-87169-557-X). Am Philos.
Bradley, Harriet. Enclosures in England: An Economic Reconstruction. LC 70-76715. (Columbia University Studies in the Social Sciences: No. 186). Repr. of 1918 ed. 12.50 (ISBN 0-404-51186-4). AMS Pr.
Gonner, E. C. Common Land & Inclosure. rev. ed. 461p. 1966. 32.50x (ISBN 0-7146-1311-8, F Cass Co). Biblio Dist.
Gonner, Edward C. Common Land & Inclosure. 2nd ed. (Illus.). Repr. of 1912 ed. 27.50 (ISBN 0-678-05050-3). Kelley.
Johnson, A. H. The Disappearance of the Small Landowner. LC 79-14625. (Illus.). 1979. Repr. of 1909 ed. lib. bdg. 13.50 (ISBN 0-678-08077-1). Kelly.
Mingay, G. E. Enclosure & the Small Farmer in the Age of the Industrial Revolution. (Studies in Economic & Social History). (Illus.). 1968. pap. text ed. 3.25x (ISBN 0-333-03909-2). Humanities.
Scrutton, Thomas E. Commons & Common Fields: The History & Policy of the Laws Relating to Commons & Enclosures in England. LC 73-143654. (Research & Source Works Ser.: No. 614). 1971. Repr. lib. bdg. 20.50 (ISBN 0-8337-3216-1). B Franklin.
Slater, Gilbert. English Peasantry & the Enclosure of Common Fields. LC 68-27295. (Illus.). Repr. of 1907 ed. 17.50x (ISBN 0-678-00401-3). Kelley.
Young, Arthur. General Report on Enclosures, Drawn up by Order of the Board of Agriculture. LC 72-120417. 1970. Repr. of 1808 ed. 20.00x (ISBN 0-678-00702-0). Kelley.

INCOME

see also Capital; Consumption (Economics); Guaranteed Annual Income; Gross National Product; Profit; Purchasing Power; Retirement Income

Abramovitz, Moses, et al. The Allocation of Economic Resources. LC 59-7420. 1959. pap. 4.85x (ISBN 0-8047-0569-0). Stanford U Pr.
Adleman, Irma & Robinson, Sherman. Income Distribution Policy in Developing Countries: A Case Study of Korea. LC 76-14269. 1978. 12.50x (ISBN 0-8047-0925-4). Stanford U Pr.
Alexander, Sidney S., et al. Five Monographs on Business Income. LC 73-84377. 1973. Repr. of 1950 ed. text ed. 13.00 (ISBN 0-914348-00-0). Scholars Bk.
American Economic Association Committee, compiled by. Readings in the Theory of Income Distribution. LC 76-29414. (BCL II Ser.). Repr. of 1946 ed. 45.00 (ISBN 0-404-15332-1). AMS Pr.
Atkinson, A. B., ed. Personal Distribution of Incomes. (Illus.). 1977. pap. text ed. 25.00x (ISBN 0-04-332065-1). Allen Unwin.
Bender, Stephen O., et al. Issues in Income Distribution. Soligo, Ronald & Von der Mehden, Fred R., eds. (Rice University Studies: Vol. 61, No. 4). (Illus.). 176p. (Orig.). 1976. pap. 4.25x (ISBN 0-89263-226-7). Rice Univ.
Berry, Albert & Urrutia, Miguel. Income Distribution in Colombia. LC 75-18164. (Illus.). 288p. 1976. 25.00 (ISBN 0-300-01874-6). Yale U Pr.
Blinder, Alan S. Toward an Economic Theory of Income Distribution. LC 74-5417. 1975. 17.50x (ISBN 0-262-02114-5). MIT Pr.
Bliss. Capital Theory & the Distribution of Income. LC 74-30938. (Advanced Textbooks in Economics: Vol. 4). 378p. 1975. 29.50 (ISBN 0-444-10782-7, North-Holland); pap. 18.00 (ISBN 0-444-10865-3). Elsevier.
Boot, John C. Common Globe or Global Commons: Population Regulation & Income Distribution. (Business Economics & Finance Ser.: Vol. 1). 160p. 1974. 19.50 (ISBN 0-8247-6231-2). Dekker.
Brittan, Samuel & Lilley, Peter. Delusion of Incomes Policy. 1977. text ed. 13.50x (ISBN 0-8419-6900-0). Holmes & Meier.
Bronfenbrenner, Martin. Income Distribution Theory. LC 77-131045. (Treatises in Modern Economics Ser). 1971. 36.95x (ISBN 0-202-06037-3). Aldine Pub.
Brundage, Percival F. Changing Concepts of Business Income. LC 75-21163. 1975. Repr. of 1952 ed. text ed. 10.00 (ISBN 0-914348-18-3). Scholars Bk.
Cain, Glen G. & Watts, Harold W., eds. Income Maintenance & Labor Supply. 1973. 22.50 (ISBN 0-12-154950-X). Acad Pr.
Campbell, Colin D., ed. Income Redistribution: Proceedings of a Conference Held in Washington, May 1976. 1977. 15.25 (ISBN 0-8447-2099-2); pap. 7.25 (ISBN 0-8447-2098-4). Am Enterprise.
Chambers, Edward J., et al. National Income Analysis & Forecasting. 406p. 1975. text ed. 14.95x (ISBN 0-673-05134-X). Scott F.
Chipman, John S. The Theory of Inter-Sectoral Money Flows & Income Formation. LC 78-64212. (Johns Hopkins University. Studies in the Social Sciences. Sixty-Eighth Ser. 1950: 2). Repr. of 1851 ed. 18.00 (ISBN 0-404-61317-9). AMS Pr.
Chiswick, Barry R. Income Inequality: Regional Analyses Within a Human Capital Framework. (Studies in Human Behavior & Social Institutions: No. 4). 1974. 15.00 (ISBN 0-87014-264-X, Dist. by Columbia U Pr). Natl Bur Econ Res.
Chiswick, Barry R. & O'Neill, June, eds. Human Resources & Income Distribution. 1977. 12.50 (ISBN 0-393-05623-6); pap. 5.95x (ISBN 0-393-09131-7). Norton.
Collard, David, et al. Income Distribution: The Limits to Redistribution. 267p. 1981. 34.95 (ISBN 0-470-27099-3). Halsted Pr.
Committee on National Statistics, National Research Council. Estimating Population & Income of Small Areas. 1980. pap. text ed. 13.75 (ISBN 0-309-03096-X). Natl Acad Pr.
Coppedge, Robert O. & Davis, Carlton G., eds. Rural Poverty & Policy Crisis. 1977. text ed. 9.50x (ISBN 0-8138-1220-8). Iowa St U Pr.
Cramer, J. S., ed. Relevance & Precision. 1976. 33.50 (ISBN 0-7204-0534-3, North-Holland). Elsevier.
Craven, John. Distribution of the Product. (Studies in Economics). (Illus., Orig.). 1979. text ed. 21.50x (ISBN 0-04-339014-5); pap. text ed. 10.50x (ISBN 0-04-339015-3). Allen Unwin.
Duesenberry, James S. Income, Saving & the Theory of Consumer Behavior. LC 49-50134. (Economic Studies: No. 87). (Illus.). 1949. 6.95x (ISBN 0-674-44750-6). Harvard U Pr.
Duncan, Greg J. & Morgan, James N., eds. Five Thousand American Families: Patterns of Economic Progess, Vol. VIII: Analyses of the First Eleven Years of the Study of Income Dynamics. LC 74-62002. (Five Thousand American Families Ser.). (Illus.). 464p. 1980. 16.00 (ISBN 0-87944-250-6). Inst Soc Res.
Edwards, Edgar O. & Bell, Philip W. The Theory & Measurement of Business Income. 1961. 15.75x (ISBN 0-520-00376-4). U of Cal Pr.
Fallick, J. L. & Elliot, R. F., eds. Incomes Policies, Inflation & Relative Pay. (Illus.). 304p. 1981. text ed. 29.95x (ISBN 0-04-331077-X); pap. text ed. 12.50x (ISBN 0-04-331078-8). Allen Unwin.
Fallis, George. Housing Programs & Income Distribution in Canada. (Ontario Economic Council Research Studies). 184p. 1980. pap. 10.00x (ISBN 0-8020-3366-0). U of Toronto Pr.
Feinschreiber, Robert, ed. Earnings & Profits: The International Aspects. LC 79-52908. 192p. 1979. 35.00 (ISBN 0-916592-30-8). Panel Pubs.
Fields, Gary S. Poverty, Inequality, & Development. LC 79-21017. (Illus.). 256p. 1980. 29.50 (ISBN 0-521-22572-8); pap. 7.95 (ISBN 0-521-29852-0). Cambridge U Pr.
Fisher, Irving. Nature of Capital & Income. LC 65-20921. Repr. of 1906 ed. 19.50x (ISBN 0-678-00112-X). Kelley.
Focus on Earning Money, Bk. 1. (Handy Math Ser.). 1981. 6.25 (ISBN 0-88488-212-8, 10617). Creative Pubns.
Foxley, A., ed. Income Distribution in Latin America. LC 75-20835. 1976. 35.50 (ISBN 0-521-21029-1). Cambridge U Pr.
Garvy, G. An Appraisal of the Nineteen-Fifty Census Income Data. (National Bureau of Economic Research: F.23). 1958. 28.00 (ISBN 0-691-04102-4). Princeton U Pr.
Grimaldi, Paul L. Supplemental Security Income: New Federal Program Aged, Blind, & Disabled. 1980. pap. 5.25 (ISBN 0-8447-3356-3). Am Enterprise.
Hacche, John. Economics of Money & Income. LC 77-555712. (Illus.). 1970. 11.25x (ISBN 0-435-84396-6). Intl Pubns Serv.
Hamberg, Daniel. Economic Growth & Instability: A Study in the Problem of Capital Accumulation, Employment, & the Business Cycle. LC 77-18876. (Illus.). 1978. Repr. of 1956 ed. lib. bdg. 25.75x (ISBN 0-313-20215-X, HAEG). Greenwood.
Hansen, W. Lee, ed. Education, Income, & Human Capital. (Studies in Income & Wealth: No. 35). (Illus.). 1970. text ed. 15.00x (ISBN 0-87014-218-6, Dist. by Columbia U Pr). Natl Bur Econ Res.
Harris, Donald J. Capital Accumulation & Income Distribution. LC 76-54097. 1978. 15.00x (ISBN 0-8047-0947-5). Stanford U Pr.
Hartog, Joop. Personal Income Distribution: A Multicapability Theory. 208p. 1980. lib. bdg. 22.00 (ISBN 0-89838-047-2, Pub. by Martinus Nijhoff Netherlands). Kluwer Boston.
Hashimi, Rasool M. Studies in Functional Income Distribution. LC 60-63392. 1960. pap. 2.50 (ISBN 0-87744-065-4). Mich St U Busn.

Herzlinger, Regina & Kane, Nancy M. A Managerial Analysis of Federal Income Distribution Mechanisms: The Government As Factory, Insurance Company & Bank. LC 79-14524. (Illus.). 1979. 24.50 (ISBN 0-88410-368-4). Ballinger Pub.

Hirsch, Fred. Social Limits to Growth. (Twentieth Century Fund Study). 1976. 12.50x (ISBN 0-674-81365-0); pap. 4.95x (ISBN 0-674-81366-9). Harvard U Pr.

Hochman, Harold M. & Peterson, George E. Redistribution Through Public Choice. LC 73-19748. 1974. 20.00x (ISBN 0-231-03775-9). Columbia U Pr.

Horowitz, Irving L., ed. Equity, Income, & Policy: Comparative Studies in Three Worlds of Development. LC 76-2904. (Special Studies). 1977. text ed. 32.95 (ISBN 0-275-56570-X). Praeger.

Howard, Michael C. Modern Theories of Income Distribution. LC 79-13523. 1979. 25.00x (ISBN 0-312-54244-5). St Martin.

Hubbard, Joshua C. Creation of Income by Taxation. Repr. of 1950 ed. lib. bdg. 15.00x (ISBN 0-8371-0110-7, HUCI). Greenwood.

Juster, F. Thomas, ed. The Distribution of Economic Well-Being: NBER Studies in Income & Wealth. LC 76-58909. (Vol. 41). 1978. 22.50 (ISBN 0-88410-478-8). Ballinger Pub.

Kakwani, Nanak. Income Inequality & Poverty: Methods of Estimation & Policy Applications. (World Bank Research Publications). (Illus.). 1980. pap. 8.95x (ISBN 0-19-520227-9). Oxford U Pr.

Kalecki, Michal. Essays in the Theory of Economic Fluctuations. LC 70-173538. (Illus.). 1972. Repr. of 1939 ed. 18.00 (ISBN 0-8462-1629-9). Russell.

King, Willford I. Wealth & Income of the People of the United States. 1969. Repr. of 1915 ed. 15.50 (ISBN 0-384-29435-9). Johnson Repr.

Kleene, Gustav A. Profit & Wages: A Study in the Distribution of Income. Repr. of 1916 ed. lib. bdg. 15.00x (ISBN 0-87991-803-9). Porcupine Pr.

Kravis, Irving B., et al. A System of International Comparisons of Gross Product & Purchasing Power. LC 73-19352. (World Bank Ser). (Illus.). 308p. 1975. 25.00x (ISBN 0-8018-1606-8); pap. 7.50x (ISBN 0-8018-1669-6). Johns Hopkins.

Kreps, Juanita M. Lifetime Allocation of Work & Income: Essays in the Economics of Aging. LC 74-161355. 1971. 12.50 (ISBN 0-8223-0249-7). Duke.

Kristol, Irving & Bauer, Peter T. Two Essays on Income Distibution & the Open Society. 1977. pap. cancelled (ISBN 0-916054-44-6, Caroline Hse Inc). Green Hill.

Kuznets, Simon. Growth, Population, & Income Distribution: Selected Essays. 1980. text ed. 19.95x (ISBN 0-393-95061-1). Norton.

Lampman, Robert J. Ends & Means of Reducing Income Poverty. 1971. 14.00 (ISBN 0-12-435250-2). Acad Pr.

Lankford, Philip M. Regional Incomes in the United States 1929-1967: Level, Distribution, Stability & Growth. LC 72-91224. (Research Papers Ser.: No. 145). (Illus.). 137p. 1973. pap. 8.00 (ISBN 0-89065-052-7). U Chicago Dept Geog.

Lawrence, William J. & Leeds, Stephen. An Inventory of State & Local Income Transfer Programs: Fiscal Year 1977. LC 80-82153. 1980. 12.00 (ISBN 0-915312-09-3). Inst Socioecon.

Lee, T. A. Income & Value Measurement. 2nd ed. 205p. 1980. pap. text ed. 14.95 (ISBN 0-8391-4129-7). Univ Park.

Lee, Thomas A. Income & Value Measurement: Theory & Practice. (Illus.). 160p. 1976. 12.50 (ISBN 0-8391-0808-7). Univ Park.

Leibenstein, Harvey. Inflation, Income Distribution & X-Efficiency Theory: A Study Prepared for the International Labour Office Within the Framework of the World Employment Programme. 122p. 1980. 23.50x (ISBN 0-389-20003-4). B&N.

Lydall, Harold. A Theory of Income Distribution. (Illus.). 1979. 45.00x (ISBN 0-19-828415-2). Oxford U Pr.

McCormick, Robert E. & Tollison, Robert D. Politicians, Legislation, & the Economy: An Inquiry into the Interest-Group Theory of Government. (Rochester Economics & Public Policy Issue Studies). 160p. 1981. lib. bdg. 20.00 (ISBN 0-89838-058-8, Pub. by Martinus Nijhoff). Kluwer Boston.

Marschak, Jacob. Income, Employment, & the Price Level. LC 65-25861. Repr. of 1951 ed. 10.00x (ISBN 0-678-00117-0). Kelley.

Masters, S. Black-White Income Differentials: Empirical Studies & Policy. 1975. 16.50 (ISBN 0-12-479050-X). Acad Pr.

Mera, Koichi. Income Distribution & Regional Development. 254p. 1976. 19.50x (ISBN 0-86008-140-0, Pub. by U of Tokyo Pr). Intl Schol Bk Serv.

Metcalf, C. E. An Econometric Model of Income Distribution. 1972. 17.50 (ISBN 0-12-492450-6). Acad Pr.

Millikan, Max F., ed. Income Stabilization for a Developing Democracy. 1953. 75.00x (ISBN 0-685-69843-2). Elliots Bks.

Moon, M. L. & Smolensky, Eugene, eds. Augmenting Economic Measures of Well-Being. 1977. 21.00 (ISBN 0-12-504640-5). Acad Pr.

Moroney, John R. Income Inequality: Trends & International Comparisons. LC 79-4726. 192p. 1979. 20.95 (ISBN 0-669-03058-9). Lexington Bks.

Orr, Larry L., et al. Income Maintenance: Interdiciplinary Approaches to Research. 1971. 17.50 (ISBN 0-12-528450-0). Acad Pr.

Paish, F. W. & Henessy, Josselyn. Rise & Fall of Incomes Policy. (Institute of Economic Affairs, Hobart Papers Ser.: No. 47). (Orig.). pap. 2.75 (ISBN 0-255-36016-9). Transatlantic.

Parker, R. H. & Harcourt, G. C., eds. Readings in the Concept & Measurement of Income. LC 75-87137. (Illus.). 1969. 47.50 (ISBN 0-521-07463-0). Cambridge U Pr.

Peterson, Wallace C. Income, Employment & Economic Growth. 4th ed. Incl. Macroeconomics: Problems, Concepts & Self Tests. Williams, Harold R. 1978. pap. text ed. 9.95x wkbk. (ISBN 0-393-09058-2). 1978. text ed. 17.95x (ISBN 0-393-09069-8). Norton.

Pigou, Arthur C. Income: An Introduction to Economics. LC 78-21487. 1979. Repr. of 1966 ed. lib. bdg. 14.75x (ISBN 0-313-20665-1, PIIN). Greenwood.

--The Veil of Money. LC 78-10214. 1979. Repr. of 1949 ed. lib. bdg. 17.50x (ISBN 0-313-20742-9, PIVM). Greenwood.

Ranadive, K. R. Income Distribution: The Unsolved Puzzle. 1978. 11.50x (ISBN 0-19-560805-4). Oxford U Pr.

Ritzen, J. J. Education, Economic Growth & Income Distribution. (Contributions to Economic Analysis: Vol. 112). 1977. text ed. 34.25 (ISBN 0-7204-0720-6, North-Holland). Elsevier.

Rudman, Jack. Clerk (Income Maintenance) (Career Examination Ser.: C-1642). (Cloth bdg. avail. on request). 1976. pap. 8.00 (ISBN 0-8373-1642-1). Natl Learning.

Sawhill, Isabel V., et al. Income Transfers & Family Structure. (An Institute Paper). 211p. 1975. pap. 8.50 (ISBN 0-87766-156-1, 13100). Urban Inst.

Schiff, Eric. Incomes Policies Abroad Part I. United Kingdom, Sweden, The Netherlands, Canada. 42p. 1971. pap. 3.25 (ISBN 0-8447-1049-0). Am Enterprise.

Smith, James D., ed. The Personal Distribution of Income & Wealth. (Studies in Income & Wealth: No. 39). 1975. 17.50 (ISBN 0-87014-268-2, Dist. by Columbia U Pr). Natl Bur Econ Res.

Soltow, Lee, ed. Six Papers on the Size Distribution of Wealth & Income. (Studies in Income & Wealth: No. 33). 1969. 15.00x (ISBN 0-87014-488-X, Dist. by Columbia U Pr). Natl Bur Econ Res.

Stewart, Frances, ed. Employment Income Distribution & Development. 192p. 1975. 26.00x (ISBN 0-7146-3057-8, F Cass Co). Biblio Dist.

Studenski, Paul. The Income of Nations: Part 1: History. LC 57-6376. 185p. 1958. pap. 4.95x (ISBN 0-8147-0406-9). NYU Pr.

Taubman, Paul. Income Distribution & Redistribution. (A-W Ser. in Economics). (Illus.). 1978. text ed. 6.95 (ISBN 0-201-08362-0). A-W.

Tinbergen, J. Income Differences. (Professor Dr. F. De Vries Lectures). 1976. 19.50 (ISBN 0-444-11054-2, North-Holland). Elsevier.

--Income Distribution. LC 74-30921. 170p. 1975. 22.00 (ISBN 0-444-10832-7, North-Holland). Elsevier.

Vaitsos, Constantine V. Intercountry Income Distribution & Transnational Enterprises. 192p. 1974. 33.00x (ISBN 0-19-828195-1). Oxford U Pr.

Webb, Adrian L. Income Redistribution & the Welfare State. 125p. 1971. pap. text ed. 6.25x (ISBN 0-7135-1806-5, Pub. by Bedford England). Renouf.

Wedgwood, Josiah. Economics of Inheritance. LC 74-137966. (Economic Thought, History & Challenge Ser). 1971. Repr. of 1939 ed. 14.50 (ISBN 0-8046-1467-9). Kennikat.

Weintraub, Sidney. An Approach to the Theory of Income Distribution. LC 72-2572. (Illus.). 214p. 1958. Repr. lib. bdg. 15.00 (ISBN 0-8371-6420-6, WEID). Greenwood.

--A General Theory of the Price Level, Output, Income Distribution, & Economic Growth. LC 72-2574. (Illus.). 123p. 1959. Repr. lib. bdg. 15.00 (ISBN 0-8371-6422-2, WEPL). Greenwood.

--Price Theory. LC 69-10169. 1969. Repr. of 1949 ed. lib. bdg. 22.00x (ISBN 0-8371-0744-X, WEPT). Greenwood.

Weintraub, Sidney & Lambert, Richard D., eds. Income Inequality. LC 73-78959. (Annals of the American Academy of Political & Social Science: No. 409). 300p. 1973. 7.50 (ISBN 0-87761-169-6); pap. 6.00 (ISBN 0-87761-168-8). Am Acad Pol Soc Sci.

Wiles. Distribution of Income: East & West. LC 74-76883. (De Vries Lectures). 136p. 1975. pap. 22.00 (ISBN 0-444-10683-9, North-Holland). Elsevier.

Wright, Erik O. Class Structure & Income Determination. (Institute for Research on Poverty Monograph). 1979. 21.00 (ISBN 0-12-764950-6). Acad Pr.

INCOME–ACCOUNTING

see Income Accounting

INCOME–MATHEMATICAL MODELS

Miyazawa, K. Input-Output Analysis & the Structure of Income Distribution. (Lecture Notes in Economics & Math Systems: Vol. 116). 150p. 1976. pap. 9.90 (ISBN 0-387-07613-1). Springer-Verlag.

Nikaido, Hukukane. Monopolistic Competition & Effective Demand. (Studies in Mathematical Economics, No. 6). 160p. 1975. 13.50 (ISBN 0-691-04206-3). Princeton U Pr.

INCOME–PROGRAMMED INSTRUCTION

Entelek Inc. Theory of Income Determination. 1963. pap. text ed. 3.95x (ISBN 0-02-333670-6, 33367). Macmillan.

INCOME–AUSTRALIA

Kerr, Alex. State & Regional Income Estimation: Theory & Pratice. 1963. 10.00x (ISBN 0-85564-015-4, Pub. by U of W Austral Pr). Intl Schol Bk Serv.

Tulloch, Patricia. Poor Policies: Australian Income Security Nineteen Seventy-Two to Seventy-Seven. 191p. 1979. 24.00x (ISBN 0-85664-901-5, Pub. by Croom Helm Ltd England). Biblio Dist.

INCOME–CHINA

Eckstein, Alexander. The National Income of Communist China. 1962. 8.95 (ISBN 0-02-908810-0). Free Pr.

Roll, Charles R., Jr. The Distribution of Rural Incomes in China: A Comparison of the 1930's & 1950's. LC 78-74301. (The Modern Chinese Economy Ser.: Vol. 13). 223p. 1980. lib. bdg. 22.00 (ISBN 0-8240-4288-3). Garland Pub.

INCOME– EUROPE

Schiff, Eric. Incomes Policies Abroad Part I. United Kingdom, Sweden, The Netherlands, Canada. 42p. 1971. pap. 3.25 (ISBN 0-8447-1049-0). Am Enterprise.

--Incomes Policies Abroad, Part Two: France, West Germany, Austria, Denmark. 1972. pap. 4.25 (ISBN 0-8447-1071-7). Am Enterprise.

INCOME–FRANCE

Marker, Gordon A. Internal Migration & Economic Opportunity: France, 1872-1911. Bruchey, Stuart, ed. LC 80-2815. (Dissertations in European Economic History II). (Illus.). 1981. lib. bdg. 25.00x (ISBN 0-405-13999-3). Arno.

INCOME–GREAT BRITAIN

Atkinson, A. B. Poverty in Britain & the Reform of Social Security. LC 76-85711. (Department of Applied Economic, Occasional Papers Ser). 1969. 15.95 (ISBN 0-521-07522-X); pap. 8.50 (ISBN 0-521-09607-3, 607). Cambridge U Pr.

Cartter, Allan M. The Redistribution of Income in Postwar Britain. LC 72-86540. 256p. 1973. Repr. of 1955 ed. 14.50 (ISBN 0-8046-1750-3). Kennikat.

Stamp, Josiah. Wealth & Taxable Capacity. facsimile ed. LC 79-150200. (Select Bibliographies Reprint Ser.). Repr. of 1922 ed. 16.00 (ISBN 0-8369-5713-X). Arno.

Stark, Thomas. Distribution of Personal Income in the United Kingdom, 1949-1963. LC 72-160099. (Illus.). 1972. 34.50 (ISBN 0-521-08258-7). Cambridge U Pr.

INCOME–INDIA

Sinha, R., et al. Income Distribution, Growth & Basic Needs in India. 175p. 1979. 24.00x (ISBN 0-85664-968-6, Pub. by Croom Helm Ltd England). Biblio Dist.

INCOME–LATIN AMERICA

Carnoy, Martin, et al. Can Educational Policy Equalise Income Distribution in Latin America. 1979. text ed. 22.00x (ISBN 0-566-00255-8, Pub. by Gower Pub Co England). Renouf.

Foxley, A., ed. Income Distribution in Latin America. LC 75-20835. 1976. 35.50 (ISBN 0-521-21029-1). Cambridge U Pr.

Webb, Richard C. Government Policy & the Distribution of Income in Peru, 1963-1973. (Economic Studies: No. 147). (Illus.). 1977. 15.00x (ISBN 0-674-35830-9). Harvard U Pr.

INCOME–RUSSIA

Mehta, Vinod. Soviet Economic Policy: Income Differentials in the USSR. LC 77-70009. 1977. text ed. 8.50x (ISBN 0-391-00750-5). Humanities.

INCOME–SINGAPORE

Bhanoji Rao, V. V. & Ramakrishnan, M. K. Income Inequality in Singapore, 1966-1975: Impact of Economic Growth & Structural Change. 1981. 20.00 (ISBN 9971-69-010-1, Pub. by Singapore U Pr); pap. 10.00 (ISBN 9971-69-018-7, Pub. by Singapore U Pr). Ohio U Pr.

INCOME–UNITED STATES

Anderson, Terry L. The Economic Growth of Seventeenth Century New England: A Measurement of Regional Income. LC 75-2574. (Dissertations in American Economic History). (Illus.). 1975. 16.00x (ISBN 0-405-07255-4). Arno.

Annual Research Conference, 14th, UCLA, 1972. National Incomes Policy & Manpower Problems: Proceedings. 2.00 (ISBN 0-89215-032-7). U Cal LA Indus Rel.

Bianchi, Suzanne M. Household Composition & Racial Inequality. 192p. 1981. 16.00 (ISBN 0-8135-0913-0). Rutgers U Pr.

Budd, Edward C., ed. Inequality & Poverty. (Problems of the Modern Economy Series). (Orig.). 1967. pap. 2.95x (ISBN 0-393-09502-9, NortonC). Norton.

Claudon, Michael P. & Cornwall, Richard. Incomes Policy for the United States: New Approaches. 240p. 1980. lib. bdg. 18.00 (ISBN 0-89838-048-0, Pub. by Martinus Nijhoff Netherlands). Kluwer Boston.

Conference on Income Support Policies for the Aging-University of Chicago. Income Support Policies for the Aged. Tolley, George S. & Burkhauser, Richard V., eds. LC 77-4155. 1977. 16.50 (ISBN 0-88410-359-5). Ballinger Pub.

Curtin, Richard T. Income Equity Among U. S. Workers: The Bases & Consequences of Deprivation. LC 76-24349. (Praeger Special Studies). 1977. 22.95 (ISBN 0-275-23780-X). Praeger.

Doctoral Dissertation, University of California, Berkley, 1964 & Campbell, Carl. Economic Growth, Capital Gains & Income Distribution: 1897-1956. LC 76-39824. (Illus.). 1977. lib. bdg. 37.00x (ISBN 0-405-09904-5). Arno.

Garvy, G., ed. Appraisal of the 1950 Census Income Data. (Studies in Income & Wealth Ser.: No. 23). 1958. 19.50 (ISBN 0-691-04102-4, Dist. by Princeton U Pr). Natl Bur Econ Res.

Gillard, Quentin. Incomes & Accessibility: Metropolitan Labor Force Participation, Commuting, Income Differentials in the United States, 1960-1970. (Research Papers Ser: No. 175). 1977. 8.00 (ISBN 0-89065-082-9). U Chicago Dept Geog.

Golloday, Frederick L. & Haveman, Robert H. The Economic Impacts of Tax-Transfer Policy: Regional & Distributional Effects. 1976. 18.50 (ISBN 0-12-288850-2). Acad Pr.

Green, Christopher. Negative Taxes & the Poverty Problem. (Studies of Government Finance). 1967. 11.95 (ISBN 0-8157-3264-3); pap. 4.95 (ISBN 0-8157-3263-5). Brookings.

Hochman, Harold M. & Peterson, George E. Redistribution Through Public Choice. LC 73-19748. 1974. 20.00x (ISBN 0-231-03775-9). Columbia U Pr.

Hochwald, Werner, ed. Design of Regional Accounts. (Resources for the Future Ser). 281p. 1961. 19.50x (ISBN 0-8018-0277-6). Johns Hopkins.

Income Maintenance Policy: An Analysis of Historical & Legislative Precedents. LC 78-6190. (Policy Research Project Report: No. 28, Vol. 2). 1978. 3.00 (ISBN 0-89940-622-X). LBJ Sch Public Affairs.

International Institute of Public Finance, 35th Congress, 1979. Reforms of Tax Systems: Proceedings. Roskamp, Karl W. & Forte, Francesco, eds. 1981. 30.00 (ISBN 0-8143-1675-1). Wayne St U Pr.

Kahn, C. H. Business & Professional Income Under Personal Income Tax. (National Bureau of Economic Research, D, 8). 1964. 15.00 (ISBN 0-691-04107-5). Princeton U Pr.

Katona, George & Mueller, Eva. Consumer Response to Income Increases. LC 80-17. (Brookings Institution, National Committee on Government Finance, Studies of Government Finance). (Illus.). xviii, 244p. 1980. Repr. of 1968 ed. lib. bdg. 22.25x (ISBN 0-313-22298-3, KACR). Greenwood.

Lebergott, Stanley. The American Economy: Income, Wealth, & Want. LC 75-4661. 364p. 1975. 28.00 (ISBN 0-691-04210-1). Princeton U Pr.

--Wealth & Want. LC 75-4460. 188p. 1975. 15.00 (ISBN 0-691-04211-X). Princeton U Pr.

Lindert, Peter H. Fertility & Scarcity in America. LC 77-71991. 1978. text ed. 28.50 (ISBN 0-691-04217-9). Princeton U Pr.

Marmor, Theodore R., ed. Poverty Policy: A Compendium of Cash Transfer Proposals. LC 71-140011. 1971. 19.95x (ISBN 0-202-32004-9). Aldine Pub.

Mendershausen, Horst. Changes in Income Distribution During the Great Depression. LC 75-19726. (National Bureau of Economic Research Ser.). (Illus.). 1975. Repr. 13.00x (ISBN 0-405-07604-5). Arno.
Miller, Herman P. Income of the American People. LC 73-86724. (Census Monograph). (Illus.). xvi, 206p. Date not set. Repr. of 1955 ed. cancelled (ISBN 0-8462-1766-X). Russell.
--Rich Man, Poor Man. (Illus.). 1971. 8.95 (ISBN 0-690-70039-3). T Y Crowell.
Mitchell, Wesley C., et al. Income in the United States: Its Amount & Distribution 1909-1919, Vol. 1. Incl. Vol. 2. LC 75-19733. 25.00x (ISBN 0-405-07610-X). LC 75-19731. (National Bureau of Economic Research Ser.). (Illus.). 1975. Repr. 9.00x (ISBN 0-405-07609-6). Arno.
Morgan, James N. & Duncan, Greg J. Five Thousand American Families: Patterns of Economic Progress, 8 vols. Incl. Vol. 1. An Analyses of the First Five Years of the Panel Study of Income Dynamics; Vol. 2. Special Studies of the First Five Years of the Panel Study of Income Dynamics. 376p. 1974. Set Vols. 1 & 2. 15.00 (ISBN 0-87944-154-2); Set Vols. 1 & 2. pap. 9.50 (ISBN 0-87944-153-4); Vol. 3. Analyses of the First Six Years of the Panel Study of Income Dynamics. 490p. 1975. 12.50 (ISBN 0-87944-176-3); pap. 7.50 (ISBN 0-87944-175-5); Vol. 4. Family Composition Change & Other Analyses of the First Seven Years of the Panel Study of Income Dynamics. 520p. 1976. 12.50 (ISBN 0-87944-197-6); pap. 7.50 (ISBN 0-87944-196-8); Vol. 5. Components of Change in Family Well-Being & Other Analyses of the First Eight Years of the Panel Study of Income Dynamics. 536p. 1977. 12.50 (ISBN 0-87944-212-3); pap. 7.50 (ISBN 0-87944-211-5); Vol. 6. Accounting for Race & Sex Differences in Earnings & Other Analyses of the First Nine Years of the Panel Study of Income Dynamics. 392p. 1978. 16.00 (ISBN 0-87944-223-9); Vol. 7, Analyses Of The First Ten Years Of The Panel Study Of Income Dynamics, 1979. 16.00 (ISBN 0-87944-234-4). Set. 74.00 (ISBN 0-87944-249-2). Inst Soc. Res.
Niemi, Albert W., Jr. Gross State Product & Productivity in the Southeast. LC 74-14923. (Illus.). 136p. 1975. 14.00x (ISBN 0-8078-1238-2). U of NC Pr.
Orr, Larry L. Income, Employment & Urban Residential Location. (Institute for Research on Poverty Monograph Ser). 1975. 12.00 (ISBN 0-12-528440-3). Acad Pr.
Parker, Richard. The Myth of the Middle Class: Notes on Affluence & Equality. LC 76-167291. (Illus.). 288p. 1972. 7.95 (ISBN 0-87140-539-3). Liveright.
Reynolds, M. & Smolensky, E., eds. Public Expenditures, Taxes & the Distribution of Income: The U.S. 1950, 1961, 1970. 1977. 16.00 (ISBN 0-12-586550-3). Acad Pr.
Romans, J. Thomas. Capital Exports & Growth Among U.S. Regions. LC 65-21131. (New England Research Ser: No. 1). 1965. 17.50x (ISBN 0-8195-8009-0, Pub. by Wesleyan U Pr). Columbia U Pr.
Schaffer, Richard L. Income Flows in Poverty Areas. LC 72-12562. (Illus.). 128p. 1973. 13.50 (ISBN 0-669-85779-3). Lexington Bks.
Schorr, Alvin L., ed. Jubilee for Our Times: A Practical Program for Income Equality. LC 76-41824. 1977. 17.50x (ISBN 0-231-04056-3). Columbia U Pr.
Streightoff, Frank H. Distribution of Incomes in the United States. LC 68-56688. (Columbia University. Studies in the Social Sciences: No. 129). Repr. of 1912 ed. 16.50 (ISBN 0-404-51129-5). AMS Pr.
Taubman. Sources of Inequality in Earnings. LC 75-23117. (Contributions to Economic Analysis: Vol. 96). 273p. 1976. 39.00 (ISBN 0-444-10965-X, North-Holland). Elsevier.
Terleckyj, Nestor J. Household Production & Consumption. (Studies in Income & Wealth: No. 40). 1976. 20.00 (ISBN 0-87014-515-0, Dist. by Columbia U Pr). Natl Bur Econ Res.
Thurow, Lester C. Generating Inequality: Mechanisms of Distribution in the U. S. Economy. LC 75-7264. 1975. 10.95x (ISBN 0-465-02670-2); pap. 5.95x (ISBN 0-465-02668-0). Basic.
Turner, Jonathan H. & Starnes, Charles E. Inequality: Privilege & Poverty in America. LC 75-20583. (Goodyear Series in American Society). 200p. 1976. text ed. 11.95 (ISBN 0-87620-419-1); pap. text ed. 9.95 (ISBN 0-87620-418-3). Goodyear.
United States National Resources Committee. Consumer Incomes in the United States. LC 75-174476. (FDR & the Era of the New Deal Ser). 104p. 1972. Repr. of 1938 ed. lib. bdg. 20.00 (ISBN 0-306-70386-6). Da Capo.
Watts, Harold W. & Rees, Albert, eds. The New Jersey Income Maintenance Experiment. (Institute for Research on Poverty Monograph Ser.: Vols. 2 & 3). 1977. Vol. 2. 28.50 (ISBN 0-12-738502-9); Vol. 3. 29.50 (ISBN 0-12-738503-7). Acad Pr.
Weintraub, Sidney & Lambert, Richard D., eds. Income Inequality. LC 73-78959. (Annals of the American Academy of Political & Social Science: No. 409). 300p. 1973. 7.50 (ISBN 0-87761-169-6); pap. 6.00 (ISBN 0-87761-168-8). Am Acad Pol Soc Sci.
Wilder, C. S. Income Protection for Time Lost from Work, United States, 1974. Shipp, Audrey, ed. (Ser. 10: No. 123). 1978. pap. text ed. 1.75 (ISBN 0-8406-0128-X). Natl Ctr Health Stats.

INCOME ACCOUNTING

see also National Income–Accounting

Accounting for Income Taxes: An Interpretation of APB Opinion No. 11. 1969. pap. 4.50 (ISBN 0-685-03111-X). Am Inst CPA.
Bedford. Income Determination Theory: An Accounting Framework. 1976. 17.95 (ISBN 0-201-00460-7). A-W.
Brown, Clifford D. Emergence of Income Reporting: An Historical Study. LC 71-634897. 1971. pap. 4.25 (ISBN 0-87744-106-5). Mich St U Busn.
Eckstein, Otto, ed. Studies in the Economics of Income Maintenance. LC 77-592. (Brookings Institution Studies of Government Finance). 1977. Repr. of 1967 ed. lib. bdg. 19.75x (ISBN 0-8371-9488-1, ECTE). Greenwood.
Gambling, Trevor. Societal Accounting. 1974. text ed. 17.95x (ISBN 0-04-330242-4). Allen Unwin.
Huber, Roger, ed. Where My Money Is Going: Income & Expense Budget. (Orig.). 1980. pap. 10.00x (ISBN 0-918300-00-2); wkbk. 10.00 (ISBN 0-686-70172-0). Lankey.
James, Simon & Nobes, Christopher. Workbook for the Economics of Taxation. 72p. 1978. pap. 3.00x (ISBN 0-86003-608-1, Pub. by Allan Pubs England). State Mutual Bk.
Lewis, John P. & Turner, R. C. Business Conditions Analysis. 2nd ed. 1967. 17.95 (ISBN 0-07-037600-X, C). McGraw.
Livingstone, J. Leslie & Burns, Thomas J., eds. Income Theory & Rate of Return. 389p. 1971. pap. text ed. 6.00x (ISBN 0-87776-402-6, S-2). Ohio St U Admin Sci.
Parker, R. H. & Harcourt, G. C., eds. Readings in the Concept & Measurement of Income. LC 75-87137. (Illus.). 1969. 47.50 (ISBN 0-521-07463-0). Cambridge U Pr.
Ronen, Joshua & Sadan, Simcha. Smoothing Income Numbers: Objectives, Means & Implications. LC 80-21350. (Paperback Series of Accounting). 1981. pap. text ed. 5.95 (ISBN 0-201-06347-6). A-W.
Sterling, Robert R., ed. Asset Valuation & Income Determination: A Consideration of the Alternatives. LC 73-160580. 1971. text ed. 10.00 (ISBN 0-914348-11-6). Scholars Bk.
Vives-Amengual, Evangelina. A Present Value Approach for the Determination of the Accounting Income & Wealth of the Firm. pap. 5.00 (ISBN 0-8477-2621-5). U of PR Pr.
Warner, James C., ed. Bradley CPA Review Taxation. rev ed. LC 78-65093. 1980. pap. 9.00 (ISBN 0-932788-04-1). Bradley CPA.

INCOME DISTRIBUTION

see Income

INCOME STATEMENTS

see Financial Statements

INCOME TAX

see also Capital Gains Tax; Dividends; Excess Profits Tax; Real Property and Taxation; Undistributed Profits Tax; Wages–Taxation; Withholding Tax

Aaron, Henry J., ed. Inflation & the Income Tax. LC 76-28669. (Studies of Government Finance). 1976. 15.95 (ISBN 0-8157-0024-5); pap. 6.95 (ISBN 0-8157-0023-7). Brookings.
Andrews, William. Basic Federal Income Taxation: 1981 Supplement. 1981. 25.00 (ISBN 0-686-77416-7). Little.
Andrews, William D. Basic Federal Income Taxation. 1979. text ed. 25.00 (ISBN 0-316-04213-7). Little.
Armstrong, Robert. Personal Income Tax Practice Set. 1976. 4.50x (ISBN 0-916060-02-0). Math Alternatives.
Bhagwati, Jagdish, ed. The Brain Drain & Income Taxation. 1977. pap. text ed. 13.50 (ISBN 0-08-020600-X). Pergamon.
Bischel, Jon E., ed. Income Tax Treaties. LC 78-58373. 1978. text ed. 30.00 (ISBN 0-685-65701-9, J3-1412). PLI.
Bittker, Boris & Stone, Lawrence. Federal Income Taxation 1981 Supplement. LC 79-89122. 90p. 1981. write for info. case book suppl. (ISBN 0-316-09688-1, Law Division). Little.
Bittker, Boris I. & Eustice, James S. Federal Income Taxation of Corporations & Shareholders. 4th. ed. 1979. 68.00 (ISBN 0-88262-288-9, 79-63336); pap. text ed. 22.50 (ISBN 0-88262-288-9). Warren.
Black, Duncan. Incidence of Income Taxes. 136p. 1965. Repr. of 1939 ed. 25.00x (ISBN 0-7146-1207-3, F Cass Co). Biblio Dist.
Brown, C. V. Taxation & the Incentive to Work. (Illus.). 128p. 1980. 29.95x (ISBN 0-19-877134-7); pap. 11.95x (ISBN 0-19-877135-5). Oxford U Pr.
Business Taxation Symposium. Effects of the Corporation Income Tax: Papers Presented at the Symposium on Business Taxation. Krzyzaniak, Marian, ed. LC 65-24513. 1966. 13.95x (ISBN 0-8143-1277-2). Wayne St U Pr.
Carson, Gerald. The Golden Egg: The Personal Income Tax, Where It Came from, How It Grew. 1977. 10.00 (ISBN 0-395-25177-X). HM.
Chodorov, Frank. Income Tax: The Root of All Evil. rev. ed. 1959. 4.95 (ISBN 0-8159-5809-9). Devin.
Diamond, Walter H. & Barrett, Charles F. Comparative State Income Tax Guide with Forms, 3 vols, Vol 1. LC 76-57809. (1979 supplement). 1977. looseleaf set 225.00 (ISBN 0-379-10120-3). Oceana.
Editorial Board. Federal Income Taxation of Banks & Financial Institutions. 5th ed. 1978. 96.00 (ISBN 0-88262-161-0, 77-29550). Warren.
Edwards, James W. Effects of Federal Income Taxes on Capital Budgeting. 5.95 (ISBN 0-686-09782-3, 6946). Natl Assn Accts.
Elgers, Pieter T. & Clark, John J. The Lease-Buy Decision: A Simplified Guide to Maximizing Financial & Tax Advantages in the 1980's. LC 80-66131. (Illus.). 1980. 16.95 (ISBN 0-02-909470-4). Free Pr.
Fry. The I.R.S. Code Made Understandable. 1977. 10.00 (ISBN 0-686-17822-X). Tax Info Ctr.
Fry, Phillip. How to Disinherit the Internal Revenue. 1978. 15.00 (ISBN 0-686-18233-2). Tax Info Ctr.
--Pay No More Income Taxes Without Going to Jail. new ed. 1978. 10.00 (ISBN 0-686-18232-4). Tax Info Ctr.
Gaffney, D. J. & Skadden, D. H. Principles of Federal Income Taxation. 1982. price not set (ISBN 0-07-057781-1); price not set instr's manual (ISBN 0-07-057782-X). McGraw.
Green, Michael L., ed. Nineteen Eighty U. S. Income Tax Guide. (Buyer's Guide Ser.). 1979. pap. 2.25 (ISBN 0-89552-064-8). DMR Pubns.
--Nineteen Eighty U. S. Income Tax Guide. (Buyer's Guide Ser.). 1979. pap. 2.25 (ISBN 0-89552-064-8). DMR Pubns.
H&R Block Income Tax Workbook, 1982. 224p. 1981. wrkbk. 4.95 (ISBN 0-02-511820-X, Collier); 18-copy counter display 89.10 (ISBN 0-02-511910-9); 48-copy floor stand 237.60 (ISBN 0-02-511880-3). Macmillan.
Hanlon, R. Brendan. A Guide to Taxes & Record Keeping for Performers, Designers & Directors. rev. ed. LC 79-25783. (Illus.). 96p. 1980. pap. text ed. 4.95x (ISBN 0-89676-032-4). Drama Bk.
Holzman, Robert S. Tax-Free Reorganizations (After the Pension Reform Act of 1974) rev. ed. LC 75-7574. 350p. 1977. 24.95 (ISBN 0-910580-09-X). Farnswth Pub.
Howell, John C. Citizens Legal Guide for Avoiding Income Taxes. (Howell Legal Guides Ser.). 160p. 1981. pap. 7.95 (ISBN 0-89648-092-5). Hamilton Pr.
Lasser, Jacob K., ed. Handbook of Tax Accounting Methods. LC 78-106722. xii, 897p. Repr. of 1951 ed. lib. bdg. 33.00x (ISBN 0-8371-3547-8, LATA). Greenwood.
Lasser, S. Jay. Everyone's Income Tax Guide. rev. ed. 192p. 1980. write for info. (ISBN 0-937782-00-9). Hilltop Pubns.
Leibowitz, Arleen A., ed. Wealth Redistribution & the Income Tax. LC 77-18652. 1978. 15.95 (ISBN 0-669-01506-7). Lexington Bks.
Lein, Charles F., Jr. How Farmers Can Beat the Tax Ripoff. 1977. 9.95 (ISBN 0-87000-385-2). Arlington Hse.
McLure, Charles E., Jr. Must Corporate Income Be Taxed Twice? LC 78-27905. (Studies of Government Finance). 1979. 14.95 (ISBN 0-8157-5620-8); pap. 5.95 (ISBN 0-8157-5619-4). Brookings.
Malone, Midas. How to Do Business Tax Free. rev. ed. LC 75-45877. 1980. pap. 4.95 (ISBN 0-913864-45-5). Enterprise Del.
OECD. Model Double Taxation Convention on Income & on Capital. 216p. (Orig.). 1977. pap. 12.50x (ISBN 92-64-11693-1). OECD.
Price Waterhouse & Co., ed. Abingdon Clergy Income Tax Guide, 1982: Edition for 1981 Returns. rev. ed. (Illus.). 1981. price not set. Abingdon.
Raby, William L. Income Tax & Business Decisions: An Introductory Tax Text. 4th ed. LC 77-25840. (Illus.). 1978. ref. ed. 21.00 (ISBN 0-13-454363-7). P-H.
Rossi, Peter H. & Lyall, Katharine C. Reforming Public Welfare: A Critique of the Negative Income Tax Experiment. 1976. text ed. 11.95 (ISBN 0-87154-754-6). Russell Sage.
Sandford, C. T., et al. An Annual Wealth Tax. 353p. 1975. 24.00x (ISBN 0-8419-5301-5). Holmes & Meier.
Schafer, Grant C., et al. Elements of Income Tax: Individual. new ed. Visse, Richard H. & Hanberry, Glyn W., eds. 260p. 1978. pap. 10.95x (ISBN 0-686-10189-8). Guffey Bks.
Seidman, J. Seidman's Legislative History of Federal Income & Excess Profits Tax Laws: 1939-1953, 2 vols. 1959. 50.00 (ISBN 0-13-799742-6). P-H.
--Seidman's Legislative History of Federal Income Tax Laws: 1851-1938. 25.00 (ISBN 0-13-799767-1). P-H.
Seligman, Edwin R. Income Tax. 2nd rev. ed. LC 68-58012. Repr. of 1914 ed. 25.00x (ISBN 0-678-00746-2). Kelley.
Simons, Henry C. Personal Income Taxation: The Definition of Income As a Problem of Fiscal Policy. LC 79-21225. (Midway Reprint Ser.). 1980. pap. text ed. 13.00x (ISBN 0-226-75893-1). U of Chicago Pr.
Sloan, Irving J. Income & Estate Tax Planning. LC 79-27001. 118p. 1980. lib. bdg. 5.95 (ISBN 0-379-11123-3). Oceana.
Sneed, Joseph T. Configurations of Gross Income. LC 67-63164. (Law Forum Ser.: No. 5). 1967. 7.00 (ISBN 0-8142-0113-X). Ohio St U Pr.
Tanzi, Vito. The Individual Income Tax & Economic Growth: An International Comparison, France, Germany, Italy, Japan, United Kingdom, United States. LC 69-11243. (Illus.). 136p. 1969. 10.00x (ISBN 0-8018-1024-8). Johns Hopkins.
--Inflation & Personal Income Tax. LC 79-52667. 1980. 27.50 (ISBN 0-521-22987-1). Cambridge U Pr.
Visse, Richard, et al. Elements of Income Tax--Individual. 1979. pap. text ed. 16.95 (ISBN 0-87620-293-8). Goodyear.

INCOME TAX–AUDITING

see Tax Auditing

INCOME TAX–FOREIGN INCOME

see also Taxation, Double

Brownlee, Oswald H. Taxing the Income from U. S. Corporate Investment Abroad. 1979. pap. 3.25 (ISBN 0-8447-3367-9). Am Enterprise.
Feinschreiber, Robert. Tax Incentives for U. S. Exports. LC 74-23774. 400p. 1975. lib. bdg. 26.00 (ISBN 0-379-00235-3). Oceana.
Huston, John. The Income Tax Treaty Between the U. S. & Japan. 1982. price not set. U of Wash Pr.
International Fiscal Assoc., ed. The Dialogue Between the Tax Administration & the Taxpayer up to the Filing of the Tax Return: Rules Determining Income & Expenses As Domestic or Foreign, 2 pts, Vol. LXV. 1980. pap. 37.00 ea. (Pub. by Kluwer Law Netherlands). Vol. LXVa, 550p (ISBN 90-200-0603-7). Vol. LXVb, 650p (ISBN 90-200-0604-5). Kluwer Boston.
League of Nations. Taxation of Foreign & National Enterprises, 5 vols. in 4. 1933. 100.00 (ISBN 0-379-20875-X). Oceana.
Lynn, James T. Keep "Deferral". US Shareholders Should Not Be Taxed on Foreign Corporation Income Before They Receive It. 1978. pap. 4.00 (ISBN 0-89834-000-4, 5880). Chamber Comm US.
O'Connor, Walter F. An Inquiry into the Foreign Tax Burdens If U. S. Based Multinational Corporations. Bruchey, Stuart, ed. LC 80-586. (Multinational Corporations Ser.). 1980. lib. bdg. 39.00x (ISBN 0-405-13377-4). Arno.
Owens, Elisabeth A. The Foreign Tax Credit: A Study of the Credit for Foreign Taxes Under United States Income Tax Law. LC 60-15260. (Illus.). 666p. 1961. 25.00x (ISBN 0-915506-02-5). Harvard Law Intl Tax.
--International Aspects of U. S. Income Taxation: Cases & Materials, Vol. III, Parts Four & Five. LC 80-18605. 512p. 1980. pap. text ed. 12.50x (ISBN 0-915506-24-6). Harvard Law Intl Tax.
Owens, Elisabeth A. & Hovemeyer, Gretchen A. Bibliography on Taxation of Foreign Operations & Foreigners. LC 76-14456. (Orig.). 1976. pap. 7.50x (ISBN 0-915506-21-1). Harvard Law Intl Tax.
Storck, A. Auslandische Betriebsstatten Im Ertragsund Vermogensteuerrecht: Taxation of Foreign Permanent Establishments. 458p. (Ger.). 1980. pap. 38.00 (ISBN 90-200-0612-6, Pub. by Kluwer Law Netherlands). Kluwer Boston.

INCOME TAX–LAW

Broenner, Herbert. Berlin Promotion Law in Its Version of Februrary 18, 1976 Including a Brief Commentary. 2nd ed. pap. 11.25x (ISBN 3-11-007037-5). De Gruyter.
Chirelstein, Marvin A., et al. Taxation in the United States, As of April 1, 1963 with 1964 Suppl. LC 63-20788. 1963. 27.50 (ISBN 0-685-08542-2, 4487). Commerce.
E R C Editorial Staff. Executive's Tax Desk Manual. 1971. 79.50 (ISBN 0-13-294561-4). P-H.

Ferguson, M. Carr, et al. Federal Income Taxation of Estates & Beneficiaries. 749p. (Orig.). 1970. text ed. 40.00 (ISBN 0-316-27889-0); text ed. 12.50 1979 supplement (ISBN 0-316-27899-8). 1980 supplement 13.95 (ISBN 0-316-27900-5). Little.
Gunn, Alan. Cases & Other Materials on Federal Income Taxation. (American Casebook Ser.). 142p. 1981. write for info. tchr's manual (ISBN 0-314-63144-5). West Pub.
Holzman, Robert S. A Survival Kit for Taxpayers: How to Deal with the I.R.S. 1981. 8.95 (ISBN 0-02-553510-2); pap. 4.95 (ISBN 0-02-008270-3). Macmillan.
Yudkin, Leon. A Legal Structure for Effective Income Tax Administration. LC 78-172244. (Tax Technique Handbook Ser). 124p. (Orig.). 1971. pap. 5.00x (ISBN 0-915506-13-0). Harvard Law Intl Tax.

INCOME TAX–AFRICA

Ola, C. S. Income Tax Law & Practice in Nigeria. 1977. pap. text ed. 50.00x (ISBN 0-435-89671-7). Heinemann Ed.
Schwab, Peter. Decision-Making in Ethiopia: A Study of the Political Process. LC 72-419. 201p. 1972. 16.50 (ISBN 0-8386-1153-2). Fairleigh Dickinson.

INCOME TAX–CANADA

Commerce Clearing House. Canadian Master Tax Guide. 35th ed. 1980. 14.75 (ISBN 0-685-79423-7). Commerce.

INCOME TAX–GREAT BRITAIN

Barr, N. A., et al. Self-Assessment for Income Tax. 1977. text ed. 30.00x (ISBN 0-435-84060-6). Heinemann Ed.

INCOME TAX–INDIA

Kapoor, M. C. & Prasad, Bhagwati. Fundamentals of Income-Tax. 6th ed. (Illus.). 420p. 1973. 4.50x (ISBN 0-8002-0627-4). Intl Pubns Serv.
Lal, B. B. Elements of Income Tax. 2nd rev. ed. 1980. text ed. 35.00x (ISBN 0-7069-0701-9, Pub. by Vikas India). Advent NY.
--Income-Tax Law & Practice. 2nd rev. ed. 1980. text ed. 35.00x (ISBN 0-7069-0702-7, Pub. by Vikas India). Advent NY.

INCOME TAX–UNITED STATES

American Institute of Certified Public Accountants. Tax Research Techniques. (Study in Federal Taxation: No. 5). 1976. 8.50 (ISBN 0-685-65552-0). Am Inst CPA.
Arch, John C. Income Tax Guide for Teachers: NEA Federal. 1980. pap. write for info. (1386-7-06). NEA.
Aronsohn, Alan J. Partnership Income Taxes. 7th ed. LC 77-93944. 1978. text ed. 25.00 (ISBN 0-685-86797-8, J1-1420). PLI.
Bittker, Boris & Stone, Lawrence M. Federal Income Taxation. 5th ed. 1196p. 1980. text ed. 25.00 (ISBN 0-316-09679-2). Little.
Bittker, Boris I. Federal Taxation of Income, Estates & Gifts, 4 vols. LC 80-50773. 1981. 295.00 set (ISBN 0-88262-460-1). Warren.
Block, H. & Block, R. H&R Block Income Tax Workbook 1981. 1980. 3.95 (ISBN 0-02-511820-X); prepack avail. (ISBN 0-02-511840-4). Macmillan.
Bower, James B. & Langenderfer, Harold Q. Income Tax Procedure. 1973. pap. text ed. 9.36 (ISBN 0-538-01410-5, A41). SW Pub.
Bower, James B & Langenderfer, Harold Q. Income Tax Procedure. rev. ed. pap. text ed. 9.36 (ISBN 0-538-01416-4). SW Pub.
Brownlee, W. Elliot, Jr. Progressivism & Economic Growth: The Wisconsin Income Tax, 1911-1929. LC 74-80065. 1974. 13.50 (ISBN 0-8046-9091-X, Natl U). Kennikat.
Buckley, John W. Income Tax Allocation: An Inquiry into Problems of Methodology & Estimation. LC 72-87212. 1972. 9.75 (ISBN 0-910586-04-7). Finan Exec.
Cain, Eulalia. The ABC's of Taxes: A Poor Man's Primer. 1978. pap. 7.75 (ISBN 0-89420-051-8, 481000); cassette recordings 22.75 (ISBN 0-89420-197-2, 481004). Natl Book.
Cheeks, James. How Proper Planning Can Reduce Your Income Taxes. LC 73-16036. 1971. 2.00 (ISBN 0-87576-034-1). Pilot Bks.
Davis, P. Michael & Whiteside, Frederick W. A Practical Guide to Preparing a Fiduciary Income Tax Return. 7th ed. 1978. pap. 8.50 (ISBN 0-88450-059-4, 1706-B). Lawyers & Judges.
Edelson. Federal Income Tax. 1982 ed. 1982. text ed. 11.95 (ISBN 0-8359-1875-0); instr's. manual free (ISBN 0-8359-1876-9). Reston.
Edelson, et al. Federal Income Tax: Nineteen Eighty-One Edition. 250p. (Orig.). 1981. pap. text ed. 10.95 (ISBN 0-8359-1873-4); instrs. manual avail. (ISBN 0-8359-1874-2). Reston.
Fiore, Ernest D., Jr. & Ornstein, Melvin. How to Save Time & Taxes Preparing the Federal Partnership Return. 38.50 (ISBN 0-685-02519-5). Bender.
Freeman, Roger A. Tax Loopholes: the Legend & the Reality. (AEI-Hoover Policy Studies). 1973. pap. 4.25 (ISBN 0-8447-3102-1). Am Enterprise.
Frisch, Nathan. Your Income Tax Organizer. 1976. pap. 4.95 (ISBN 0-517-52748-0). Crown.
Fry, Phillip. Blood Taxes at Harvest Time. 1978. 15.00 (ISBN 0-686-09544-8). Tax Info Ctr.
Galvin, Charles O. & Bittker, Boris I. The Income Tax: How Progressive Should It Be. 14.25 (ISBN 0-8447-2013-5). Am Enterprise.
Goode, Richard. The Individual Income Tax. rev. ed. (Studies of Government Finance). 1976. 15.95 (ISBN 0-8157-3198-1); pap. 6.95 (ISBN 0-8157-3197-3). Brookings.
Green, Michael L., ed. Nineteen Seventy Nine US Income Tax Guide. (Buyer's Guide Reports Ser.). 1978. pap. 1.95 (ISBN 0-89552-054-0). DMR Pubns.
--U. S. Income Tax Guide, 1981. rev. ed. (Buyer's Guide Ser.). 80p. (Orig.). Date not set. pap. 2.50 (ISBN 0-89552-074-5). DMR Pubns.
Greene, Bill. Win Your Personal Tax Revolt. (Illus.). 192p. 1981. 14.00 (ISBN 0-936602-10-4). Harbor Pub CA.
Groves, Harold M. Federal Tax Treatment of the Family. LC 76-55946. (Brookings Institution, Studies of Government Finance Ser). 1977. Repr. of 1963 ed. lib. bdg. 15.00x (ISBN 0-8371-9425-3, GRFT). Greenwood.
Hansen, George & Anderson, Larry. How the IRS Seizes Your Dollars & How to Fight Back. 1981. pap. 5.95 (ISBN 0-671-42795-4, Fireside). S&S.
Heller, Kenneth H. The Impact of U. S. Income Taxation on the Financing & Earnings Remittance Decisions of U. S.-Based Multinational Firms with Controlled Foreign Corporations. Bruchey, Stuart, ed. LC 80-575. (Multinational Corporations Ser.). (Illus.). 1980. lib. bdg. 35.00x (ISBN 0-405-13368-5). Arno.
Internal Revenue Service, ed. Nineteen Seventy-Eight U. S. Income Tax Guide. rev. ed. (Illus.). 1977. pap. 1.95 (ISBN 0-89552-010-9). DMR Pubns.
J. K. Lasser's Professional Income Tax Guide, 1980. 1979. pap. 3.95 (ISBN 0-671-25334-4, Fireside). S&S.
J. K. Lasser's Your Income Tax 1980. 1979. pap. 3.95 (ISBN 0-671-25145-7, Fireside). S&S.
Jensen, John L. Teachers Income Tax Guide. LC 72-185181. 72p. pap. 4.50 (ISBN 0-686-66083-8). Teachers Tax.
Kahn, C. H. Business & Professional Income Under Personal Income Tax. (National Bureau of Economic Research, D, 8). 1964. 15.00 (ISBN 0-691-04107-5). Princeton U Pr.
Kahn, Douglas. Federal Income Tax. 6th ed. (Sum & Substance Ser.). 1979. 13.95 (ISBN 0-686-27113-0). Center Creative Ed.
Kragen, Adrian A. & McNulty, John K. Cases & Materials on Federal Income Taxation: Taxation of Individuals, Vol. 1. 3rd ed. LC 79-16910. (American Casebook Ser.). 1236p. 1979. text ed. 24.95 (ISBN 0-8299-2058-7). West Pub.
Larson, Martin. How You Can Save Money on Your Taxes This Year. 4.95 (ISBN 0-686-24160-6). Liberty Lobby.
--A Manual on How to Establish a Trust & Reduce Taxation. 195.00 (ISBN 0-935036-01-6). Liberty Lobby.
Larson, Martin A. The Continuing Tax Rebellion: What Millions of Americans Are Doing to Restore Constitutional Government. rev. ed. LC 79-89020. 1979. pap. 5.95 (ISBN 0-8159-5220-1). Devin.
Lasser. Professional Edition of Your Income Tax 1975. 1981. 20.95 (ISBN 0-671-41230-2). S&S.
Lasser, A. Jay. Everyone's Income Tax Guide, 1980. LC 58-3391. 1980. pap. 2.95 (ISBN 0-399-50402-8, Perigee). Putnam.
Lasser Institute. Your Income Tax 1976. 1982. pap. 4.95 (ISBN 0-671-22164-7). S&S.
Lasser, J. K. J. K. Lasser's Your Income Tax, 1981. 1980. pap. 5.95 (ISBN 0-686-72557-3, Fireside). S&S.
McCartney, Clarence, et al. The Federal Income Tax, 1981 Edition: Its Sources & Applications. (Illus.). 912p. 1980. text ed. 21.95 (ISBN 0-13-309005-1). P-H.
McNulty, John K. Federal Income Taxation of Individuals in a Nutshell. 2nd ed. LC 78-6218. (Nutshell Ser.). 422p. 1978. pap. text ed. 6.95 (ISBN 0-8299-2005-6). West Pub.
Miller. Miller's Oil & Gas Federal Income Taxation. 19th ed. 712p. (Includes three suppls.). 1981. 22.50 (ISBN 0-686-75937-0). Commerce.
Minkow, Rosalie & Minkow, Howard. The Complete List of IRS Tax Deductions. LC 80-82660. 272p. (Orig.). 1981. pap. 2.50 (ISBN 0-87216-775-5). Playboy Pbks.
Nardone, M. A. Income Tax Nineteen Seventy-Nine - Nineteen Eighty. 192p. 1980. 19.75x (ISBN 0-906501-08-3, Pub. by Keenan England). State Mutual Bk.
Niemann, John O., et al. The Bank Income Tax Return Manual with Specimen Filled-in Returns. 1978. 48.00 (ISBN 0-88262-564-0, 80-54680). Warren.
Norwood, F. & Chisholm, S. Federal Income Taxes: Research & Planning. 1962. 11.95 (ISBN 0-13-308759-X). P-H.
Ott, Attiat F. & Dittrich, Ludwig O. Federal Income Tax Burden on Households. 1981. pap. 3.25 (ISBN 0-8447-3429-2). Am Enterprise.
Owens, Elisabeth A. & Ball, Gerald T. Indirect Credit: A Study of Various Foreign Tax Credits Granted to Domestic Shareholders Under U.S. Income Tax Law, Vol. 1. LC 75-14037. (Illus.). 497p. 1975. 40.00x (ISBN 0-915506-17-3). Harvard Law Intl Tax.
Pechman, Joseph A. Comprehensive Income Taxation. LC 77-24246. (Studies of Government Finance). 1977. 14.95 (ISBN 0-8157-6982-2); pap. 5.95 (ISBN 0-8157-6981-4). Brookings.
Phillips, Lawrence C. & Hoffman, William H. West's Federal Taxation: 1979 Annual: Individual Incomes Taxes. new rev. ed. 1978. text ed. 17.95 (ISBN 0-8299-0178-7); solutions manual avail. (ISBN 0-8299-0567-7). West Pub.
Porter, Sylvia. Sylvia Porter's Nineteen Eighty-Two Income Tax Book. 184p. (Orig.). 1981. pap. 3.95 (ISBN 0-380-77925-0). Avon.
Prentice-Hall Tax Editorial Staff. Ten-Forty Handbook. 1979. 18.50 (ISBN 0-13-903393-9). P-H.
Reese, Thomas J. The Politics of Taxation. LC 79-8413. (Illus.). xxv, 237p. 1980. lib. bdg. 25.00 (ISBN 0-89930-003-0, RPT/, Quorum Bks). Greenwood.
Research Institute of America, compiled by. Federal Income Tax Guide 1982. 1981. 3.95 (ISBN 0-441-55188-2). Ace Bks.
Rice, Ralph S. & Solomon, Lewis D. Problems & Materials in Federal Income Taxation. 3rd ed. LC 79-14315. 670p. 1979. text ed. 17.95 (ISBN 0-8299-2049-8). West Pub.
Rounds, Stowell & O'Connell, Joseph J. How to Save Time & Taxes Preparing Fiduciary Income Tax Returns Federal & State. 38.50 (ISBN 0-685-02525-X). Bender.
Simon, William E. Reforming the Income Tax System. 1981. pap. 4.25 (ISBN 0-8447-3437-3). Am Enterprise.
Smith, R. Stafford. Local Income Taxes: Economic Effects & Equity. LC 77-633802. (Illus.). 220p. (Orig.). 1972. pap. 4.50x (ISBN 0-87772-076-2). Inst Gov Stud Berk.
Strassels, Paul N. & Wool, Robert. All You Need to Know About the IRS: A Taxpayers Guide. 10.95 (ISBN 0-394-50747-9). Random.
--All You Need to Know About the IRS: A Taxpayer's Guide, 1981 Edition. 1981. 11.95 (ISBN 0-394-51675-3). Random.
Surrey, Stanley S. Pathways to Tax Reform. LC 73-87686. 440p. 1973. text ed. 18.50x (ISBN 0-674-65789-6). Harvard U Pr.
U. S. Office Of Business Economics. Personal Income by States Since 1929: A Supplement to the Survey of Current Business. Schwartz, Charles F. & Graham, Robert E., Jr., eds. Repr. of 1956 ed. lib. bdg. 18.75x (ISBN 0-8371-2492-1, PEIS). Greenwood.
Visse & Hanbery. Elements of Income Tax, 1981. 400p. 1981. pap. text ed. 14.95 (ISBN 0-8302-2435-1). Goodyear.
Walker, Charls E. & Reuss, Henry S. Major Tax Reform: Urgent Necessity or Not? 1973. 11.25 (ISBN 0-8447-2037-2). Am Enterprise.
Waltman, Jerold. Copying Other Nations' Policies: Two American Case Studies. LC 80-12083. 110p. 1981. text ed. 13.25x (ISBN 0-87073-832-1). Schenkman.
White, Melvin I. Personal Income Tax Reduction in a Business Contraction. LC 68-58638. (Columbia University. Studies Social Sciences: No. 564). Repr. of 1951 ed. 15.00 (ISBN 0-404-51564-9). AMS Pr.
Wittenbach & Milani. Plaid for Federal Income Tax. 3rd ed. 1979. 6.95 (ISBN 0-256-02254-2, 01-1177-03). Learning Syst.

INCOME TAX–UNITED STATES–LAW

Claudon, Michael P. & Cornwall, Richard. Incomes Policy for the United States: New Approaches. 240p. 1980. lib. bdg. 18.00 (ISBN 0-89838-048-0, Pub. by Martinus Nijhoff Netherlands). Kluwer Boston.
Collins, Adrian A. Federal Income Taxation of Employee Benefits. LC 76-163722. 770p. 1971. looseleaf with 1978 rev. pages & suppl. 47.50 (ISBN 0-87632-077-9). Boardman.
Commerce Clearing House. Income Tax Regulations, As of March 15, 1981. 1981. 25.00 (ISBN 0-686-75936-2). Commerce.
Freeland, James J., et al. Fundamentals of Federal Income Taxation Cases & Materials. 3rd ed. LC 81-2818. (University Casebook Ser.). 979p. 1981. text ed. write for info. (ISBN 0-88277-028-4). Foundation Pr.
Gunn, Alan. Cases & Other Materials on Federal Income Taxation. LC 81-1502. (American Casebook Ser.). 822p. 1981. text ed. write for info. West Pub.
Halstead, Harry M., et al. Federal Taxation of Agriculture. 416p. 40.00 (ISBN 0-686-61148-9, B276). Am Law Inst.
Kragen, Adrian A. & McNulty, John K. Cases & Materials on Federal Income Taxation: Taxation of Corporations, Shareholders, Partnerships & Partners, Vol. II. LC 79-16910. (American Casebook Ser.). 1106p. 1981. text ed. 24.95 (ISBN 0-8299-2133-8). West Pub.
Langenderfer, Harold Q. The Federal Income Tax, 1861 to 1872. Brief, Richard P., ed. LC 80-1500. (Dimensions of Accounting Theory & Practice Ser.). 1981. lib. bdg. 70.00x (ISBN 0-405-13493-2). Arno.
Lawyers Medical Cyclopedia of Personal Injuries & Allied Specialties: 1980 Supplementary Service. 1979. 45.00 (ISBN 0-686-60285-4). A Smith Co.
Norwood, Fred W., et al. Federal Taxation: Research Planning & Procedures. 2nd ed. LC 78-27524. (Illus.). 1979. text ed. 31.95 (ISBN 0-13-308775-1). P-H.
O'Byrne, John C. Farm Income Tax Manual: 1980 Supplement for Use in 1981. 1980. 20.25 (ISBN 0-686-60284-6). A Smith Co.
Owens, Elisabeth A. International Aspects of U. S. Income Taxation: Cases & Materials, Vol. III, Parts Four & Five. LC 80-18605. 512p. 1980. pap. text ed. 12.50x (ISBN 0-915506-24-6). Harvard Law Intl Tax.
Parker & Leimburg. Federal Income Tax Law. 1980. 24.50 (ISBN 0-686-60983-2, 80-5077); student ed. 19.25 (ISBN 0-88262-450-4). Warren.
Prentice-Hall Editorial Staff & Rubin, A. Federal Tax Course, 1979. students ed. 1979. 16.95 (ISBN 0-13-312413-4). P-H.
Stanley, Joyce & Kilcullen, Richard. Federal Income Tax Law. 6th ed. Parker, Allan J., ed. 1974. 38.50 (ISBN 0-88262-033-9). Warren.
Surrey, Stanley S. Pathways to Tax Reform. LC 73-87686. 440p. 1973. text ed. 18.50x (ISBN 0-674-65789-6). Harvard U Pr.
Westphal, William H. Accountant's Tax Practice Handbook. 1978. 32.95 (ISBN 0-13-001263-7, Busn). P-H.
Worth, B. J. Income Tax Law for Ministers & Religious Workers: 1982 Ed. for Preparing 1981 Tax Returns. (Orig.). 1981. pap. 2.95 (ISBN 0-8010-9649-9). Baker Bk.

INCOME TAX–UNITED STATES–STATES

Comstock, Alzada. State Taxation of Personal Incomes. LC 74-78007. (Columbia University Studies in the Social Sciences: No. 229). Repr. of 1921 ed. 20.00 (ISBN 0-404-51229-1). AMS Pr.
Hanna, Frank A. State Income Differentials, 1919-1954. LC 76-39841. 1977. Repr. of 1959 ed. lib. bdg. 20.00x (ISBN 0-8371-9352-4, HASD). Greenwood.
Penniman, Clara. State Income Taxation. LC 79-20081. 1980. 22.50x (ISBN 0-8018-2290-4). Johns Hopkins.
Phares, Donald. Who Pays State & Local Taxes? LC 80-15454. 240p. 1980. text ed. 22.50 (ISBN 0-89946-026-7). Oelgeschlager.
Taylor, Milton & Peppard, Donald. The Easy Case for Progressive Income Taxation in Michigan. 1973. 2.50 (ISBN 0-686-16216-1). MSU-Inst Comm Devel.

INCOME TAX, MUNICIPAL

Academy of Political Science. Municipal Income Taxes: Proceedings, Vol. 28, No. 4. Connery, R. H., ed. 6.00 (ISBN 0-8446-1887-X). Peter Smith.
Phares, Donald. Who Pays State & Local Taxes? LC 80-15454. 240p. 1980. text ed. 22.50 (ISBN 0-89946-026-7). Oelgeschlager.

INCOMPATIBILITY OF OFFICES

see also Conflict of Interests (Public Office)

IMCOMPLETE BOOKS

see Unfinished Books

INCOMPLETE SENTENCE TEST

see Sentence Completion Test

INCORPORATED FARMS

see Farm Corporations

INCORPORATION

see also Charters

Fry, Phillip. How to Cut Your Taxes in Half by Incorporating Your Job or Business. 1978. 50.00 (ISBN 0-686-17659-6). Tax Info Ctr.
Hess, Robert P. Desk Book for Setting up the Closely - Held Corporation. 1979. 39.50 (ISBN 0-87624-113-5). Inst Busn Plan.
Incorporating a Closely Held Business. (Study in Federal Taxation: No. 1). 1978. pap. 13.50 (ISBN 0-685-58512-3). Am Inst CPA.
Nader, Ralph & Green, Mark. Taming the Giant Corporation. 1976. 10.50 (ISBN 0-393-08753-0, N872, Norton Lib); pap. 3.95 (ISBN 0-393-00872-X). Norton.
Ray, George. Incorporating the Professional Practice. 2nd ed. (Illus.). 1978. 32.95 (ISBN 0-13-455923-1, Busn). P-H.
Vaughan, Grinyer & Vaughan, Birley. Newly Floated Public Companies. 1980. cased 30.00 (ISBN 0-685-77760-X). State Mutual Bk.

INCUNABULA

see also Bibliography–Rare Books; Colophons; Incipits; Printers' Marks; Printing–History

Boyd, Beverly. Chaucer & the Medieval Book. LC 73-77021. (Illus.). 1973. 12.50 (ISBN 0-87328-060-1). Huntington Lib.

Fifty Five Books Printed Before Fifteen Hundred Twenty Five: Representing the Works of England's First Painters. (Illus.). viii, 62p. 1968. 10.50x (ISBN 0-8139-0451-X, Dist. by U Pr of Va). Grolier Club.

Haebler, K. Study of Incunabula. Osborne, Lucy E., tr. Repr. of 1933 ed. 30.00 (ISBN 0-527-37100-9). Kraus Repr.

Hellinger, Wytze & Hellinger, Lotte, eds. Henry Bradshaw's Correspondence on incunabula with J. W. Holtrop: 1864-84, 2 vols. 1978. 70.00 set (ISBN 0-8390-0244-0). Allanheld & Schram.

Morison, Stanley. Germam Incunabula in the British Museum. LC 73-143358. (Illus.). 1975. Repr. of 1928 ed. 150.00 (ISBN 0-87817-077-4). Hacker.

Plimpton, George A. Education of Chaucer. LC 74-160453. Repr. of 1935 ed. 17.50 (ISBN 0-404-05064-6). AMS Pr.

Pollard, Alfred W. Early Illustrated Books. LC 68-26366. (Bibliophile Ser., No. 83). 1969. Repr. of 1893 ed. lib. bdg. 49.95 (ISBN 0-8383-0278-5). Haskell.

Proctor, Robert G. Bibliographical Essays. LC 68-58470. (Bibliography & Reference Ser.: No. 60). (Illus.). 1969. Repr. of 1905 ed. 22.50 (ISBN 0-8337-2865-2). B Franklin.

Stillwell, Margaret B. Incunabula & Americana Fourteen Fifty to Eighteen Hundred. LC 61-13271. (Illus.). 1968. Repr. of 1930 ed. 23.50x (ISBN 0-8154-0219-8). Cooper Sq.

INCUNABULA-BIBLIOGRAPHY

see also Bibliography-Rare Books; Incipits; Printers' Marks; Printing-History

Besterman, Theodore. Early Printed Books to the End of the Sixteenth Century: A Bibliography of Bibliographies. 2nd rev. & enl. ed. 344p. 1969. 21.50x (ISBN 0-87471-008-1). Rowman.

Cambridge University Library. Early English Printed Books in the University Library, 4 Vols. Repr. of 1907 ed. Set. 138.50 (ISBN 0-384-07221-6); Vols. 1-2. 31.00 ea.; Vols. 3-4. 31.00 ea. Johnson Repr.

Cardenas, Anthony, et al. Bibliography of Old Spanish Texts. 2nd, rev., enl. ed. (Literary texts). 1977. 9.50x (ISBN 0-686-16324-9); pap. 7.50x (ISBN 0-686-16325-7). Hispanic Seminary.

Charles Louis De Bourbon. Bibliotheque liturgique, 2 vols. in 1. Ales, Anatole, ed. LC 72-130592. (Fr). 1970. Repr. of 1898 ed. lib. bdg. 40.50 (ISBN 0-8337-0036-7). B Franklin.

Davies, Hugh W. Catalog of Early French & German Books in the Library of C. Fairfax Murray, 4 Vols. 280.00x (ISBN 0-87556-065-2); Set. fr. 150.00x (ISBN 0-87556-066-0); Set. ger. 150.00x (ISBN 0-87556-067-9). Saifer.

De Rothschild, James E. Catalogue Des Livres Composant la Bibliotheque De Feu M. le Baron Rothschild, 5 Vols. Picot, Emile, ed. Repr. of 1884 ed. 215.00 (ISBN 0-8337-3070-3). B Franklin.

Dublin University. Catalogue of Fifteenth Century Books in the Library of Trinity College, Dublin, & in Marsh's Library, Dublin, with a Few from Other Collections. Abbott, T. K., ed. LC 70-128846. (Bibliography & Reference Ser.: No. 360). 1970. Repr. of 1905 ed. lib. bdg. 21.00 (ISBN 0-8337-0001-4). B Franklin.

Duff, E. Gordon. Early Printed Books. LC 68-25309. (Bibliophile Ser., No. 83). (Illus.). 1968. Repr. of 1843 ed. lib. bdg. 51.95 (ISBN 0-8383-0936-4). Haskell.

Faye, Christopher U. Fifteenth-Century Printed Books at the University of Illinois. 1949. 12.50 (ISBN 0-252-72412-7). U of Ill Pr.

Gerulaitis, Leonardas V. Printing & Publishing in Fifteenth Century Venice. 1976. text ed. 25.00 (ISBN 0-8389-0126-3). ALA.

Goff, Frederick R. Incunabula in American Libraries: A Supplement to the Third Census of Fifteenth-Century Books Recorded in North American Collections. 104p. 1972. 75.00 (ISBN 0-686-31068-3). Biblio Soc Am.

--Incunabula in American Libraries: A Supplement to the Third Census of Fifteenth-Century Books Recorded in North American Collections (1964) LC 72-76024. 1972. 10.00x (ISBN 0-685-73901-5, Bibliographical Society of America). U Pr of Va.

--Incunabula in American Libraries: A Third Census of 15th Century Books Recorded in North American Collections. LC 72-10463. 1973. 75.00 (ISBN 0-527-34200-9). Kraus Intl.

Goldschmidt, E. P. Medieval Texts & Their First Appearance in Print. LC 68-54232. 1969. Repr. of 1943 ed. 9.50x (ISBN 0-8196-0226-4). Biblo.

Haebler, Konrad. Bibliografia Iberica Del Siglo Quince, 2 Vols. 1903-1917. 50.50 (ISBN 0-8337-1520-8). B Franklin.

Harman, Marian, ed. Incunabula in the University of Illinois Library at Urbana-Champaign. LC 79-17355. (Robert B. Downs Publication Fund Ser.: No. 5). 251p. 1979. 25.00 (ISBN 0-252-00789-1). U of Ill Lib Info Sci.

Hoskins, Janina W, compiled by. Early & Rare Polonica of the 15th-17th Centuries in American Libraries: A Bibliographic Survey. (Ser Seventy). 200p. 1973. lib. bdg. 19.50 (ISBN 0-8161-1002-6). G K Hall.

Kingston, Caxton. Early English Printed Books in the University Library Cambridge, 4 vols. 1979. Repr. of 1900 ed. Set. lib. bdg. 200.00 (ISBN 0-8492-1483-1). R West.

Paris Universite Bibliotheque. Catalogue Des Incunables De la Bibliotheque De l'Universite De Paris, 2 vols in 1. LC 76-168920. (Bibliography & Reference Ser.: No. 427). 26.50 (ISBN 0-8337-0548-2). B Franklin.

Peddie, Robert A. Fifteenth Century Books: A Guide to Their Identification. LC 73-101990. (Bibliography & Reference Ser.: No. 294). 1970. Repr. of 1913 ed. lib. bdg. 19.50 (ISBN 0-8337-2705-2). B Franklin.

Penney, Clara L. Printed Books, 1468-1700, in the Hispanic Society of America. (Illus.). 1965. 15.00 (ISBN 0-87535-102-6). Hispanic Soc.

Prime, Wendell. Fifteenth Century Bibles. LC 77-85626. 1977. Repr. of 1888 ed. lib. bdg. 15.00 (ISBN 0-89341-320-8). Longwood Pr.

Proctor, Robert. Index to Early Printed Books in the British Museum: With Notes on Those in the Bodlean Library. 65.00 (ISBN 0-87556-242-6). Saifer.

--An Index to the Early Printed Books in the British Museum from the Invention of Printing to the Year 1500: With Notes of Those in the Bodleian Library. 975p. 1960. Repr. of 1902 ed. 75.00 (ISBN 0-900470-72-0). Oak Knoll.

Stillwell, Margaret B. The Beginning of the World of Books, 1450 to 1470. 112p. 1972. 10.00 (ISBN 0-686-31062-4). Biblio Soc Am.

INCUNABULA-FACSIMILES

Berners, Juliana. The Book of Hawking, Hunting & Blasing of Arms. LC 74-25849. (English Experience Ser.: No. 151). 180p. 1969. Repr. of 1486 ed. 42.00 (ISBN 90-221-0151-7). Walter J Johnson.

Hieronymus, Von Braunschweig. The Noble Experyence of the Vertuous Handy Warke of Surgeri. LC 76-60044. (English Experience Ser.: No. 531). 156p. 1973. Repr. of 1525 ed. 30.00 (ISBN 90-221-0531-8). Walter J Johnson.

Meres, Francis. Palladis Tamia. LC 72-9751. Repr. of 1598 ed. 35.00 (ISBN 0-404-04309-7). AMS Pr.

INCURABLE DISEASES

Bircher-Brenner, M. The Prevention of Incurable Disease. LC 78-61330. 1978. pap. 3.95 (ISBN 0-87983-186-3). Keats.

The Healing Art of Clara Walter. 64p. (Orig.). 1981. pap. 2.95 (ISBN 0-932870-08-2). Alyson Pubns.

Saunders, Cicely M., ed. The Management of Terminal Disease. (Management of Malignant Diseases: Vol. 1). (Illus.). 1979. 26.50 (ISBN 0-8151-7536-1). Year Bk Med.

INDEMNITY INSURANCE

see Insurance, Liability

INDENTURED SERVANTS

Alderman, Clifford L. Colonists for Sale: The Story of Indentured Servants in America. 192p. (gr. 5-9). 1975. 8.95 (ISBN 0-02-700220-9, 70022). Macmillan.

Ballagh, J. C. White Servitude in the Colony of Virginia: A Study of the System of Indentured Labor in the American Colonies. pap. 8.50 (ISBN 0-384-03146-3). Johnson Repr.

Ballagh, James C. White Servitude in the Colony of Virginia. LC 71-101987. 1970. Repr. of 1898 ed. 15.00 (ISBN 0-8337-0158-4). B Franklin.

Cordasco, Francesco & Pitkin, Thomas M. The White Slave Trade & the Immigrants: A Chapter in American Social History. LC 80-25556. 1981. 16.50 (ISBN 0-87917-077-8); pap. 6.95 (ISBN 0-87917-076-X). Blaine Ethridge.

Dunham, William H., Jr. Lord Hastings' Indentured Retainers, 1461-1483: The Lawfulness of Livery & Retaining Under the Yorkists & Tudors. (Connecticut Academy of Arts & Sciences Transactions: Vol. 39). 1970. Repr. of 1955 ed. 15.00 (ISBN 0-208-00989-2, Archon). Shoe String.

Geiser, Karl F. Redemptioners & Indentured Servants in the Colony & Commonwealth of Pennsylvania. 1901. 47.50x (ISBN 0-686-51298-7). Elliots Bks.

Heavner, Robert O. Economic Aspects of Indentured Servitude in Colonial Pennsylvania, 1771-1773. LC 77-14753. (Dissertations in American Economic History Ser.). 1978. 15.00 (ISBN 0-405-11038-3). Arno.

Herrick, Cheesman A. White Servitude in Pennsylvania: Indentured & Redemption Labor in Colony & Commonwealth. LC 70-99480. Repr. of 1926 ed. 15.75x (ISBN 0-8371-2373-9). Greenwood.

Philadelphia Office of Mayor. Record of Indentures (1771-1773) Excerpted from the Pennsylvania-German Society Proceedings and Addresses 16. LC 72-10671. 364p. 1973. Repr. of 1907 ed. 17.50 (ISBN 0-8063-0540-1). Genealog Pub.

Smith, Abbot E. Colonists in Bondage: White Servitude & Convict Labor in America, 1607-1776. 1971. pap. 5.95x (ISBN 0-393-00592-5, Norton Lib). Norton.

Smith, Warren B. White Servitude in Colonial South Carolina. LC 60-53017. (Illus.). 1961. 9.95x (ISBN 0-87249-078-5); pap. 2.25x (ISBN 0-87249-177-3). U of SC Pr.

INDENTURES

see Deeds; Trust Indentures

INDEPENDENCE

see Autonomy

INDEPENDENCE DAY (U. S.)

see Fourth of July

INDEPENDENCY (CHURCH POLITY)

see Congregationalism

INDEPENDENT ADMINISTRATIVE AGENCIES

see Independent Regulatory Commissions

INDEPENDENT CONTRACTORS

see Agency (Law); Employers' Liability; Labor Contract; Liability (Law); Master and Servant

INDEPENDENT LABOUR PARTY (GREAT BRITAIN)

Middlemas, Robert K. Clydesiders. LC 66-2916. (Illus.). 1965. 15.00x (ISBN 0-678-08040-2). Kelley.

INDEPENDENT REGULATORY COMMISSIONS

see also Public Service Commissions

Anderson, Douglas D. Regulatory Politics & Electric Utilities. LC 80-26943. 191p. 1981. 19.95 (ISBN 0-86569-058-8). Auburn Hse.

Baldwin, John R. The Regulatory Agency & the Public Corporation: The Canadian Air Transport Industry. LC 75-8916. 256p. 1975. 19.50 (ISBN 0-88410-262-9). Ballinger Pub.

Bernstein, Marver H. Regulating Business by Independent Commission. LC 77-2985. 1977. Repr. of 1955 ed. lib. bdg. 23.50x (ISBN 0-8371-9563-2, BERB). Greenwood.

Carron, Andrew S. & MacAvoy, Paul W. Decline of Service in the Regulated Industries. 1980. pap. 4.25 (ISBN 0-8447-3417-9). Am Enterprise.

Congressional Quarterly. Federal Regulatory Directory. (Annual Ser.). 1979. 25.00 (ISBN 0-87187-186-6). Congr Quarterly.

Cushman, Robert E. The Independent Regulatory Commissions. LC 71-159176. xiv, 780p. 1972. Repr. of 1941 ed. lib. bdg. 40.00x (ISBN 0-374-92019-2). Octagon.

--The Independent Regulatory Commissions. LC 71-159176. xiv, 780p. 1972. Repr. of 1941 ed. lib. bdg. 40.00x (ISBN 0-374-92019-2). Octagon.

Fain, Tyrus G., et al, eds. Federal Reorganization: The Executive Branch. LC 77-23444. (Public Documents Ser.). 1977. 38.50 (ISBN 0-8352-0981-4). Bowker.

How Federal Regulatory Agencies Work. 1980. pap. 4.95 (ISBN 0-917386-88-4). Exec Ent.

Kagan, Robert A. Regulatory Justice. LC 77-72498. 1978. text ed. 11.95 (ISBN 0-87154-425-3). Russell Sage.

MacAvoy, Paul W., ed. Crisis of the Regulatory Commissions. LC 75-98888. (Problems of the Modern Economy Ser.). 1970. pap. 5.95x (ISBN 0-393-09897-4). Norton.

Noll, Roger G. Reforming Regulation: An Evaluation of the Ash Council Proposals. LC 75-179326. (Studies in the Regulation of Economic Activity). 1971. pap. 4.95 (ISBN 0-8157-6107-4). Brookings.

Welborn, David M. Governance of Federal Regulatory Agencies. LC 77-8012. 1977. 11.50x (ISBN 0-87049-216-0). U of Tenn Pr.

Woll, Peter. American Bureaucracy. 8.75 (ISBN 0-8446-3206-6). Peter Smith.

--American Bureaucracy. (Orig.). 1963. pap. 2.95x (ISBN 0-393-09595-9, NortonC). Norton.

--American Bureaucracy. 2nd ed. 1977. pap. 5.95x (ISBN 0-393-09141-4). Norton.

INDEPENDENT SCHOOLS

see Private Schools

INDEPENDENT STUDY

Atwood, Beth S. Building Independent Learning Skills. LC 74-16807. (Learning Handbooks Ser.). 1974. pap. 4.95 (ISBN 0-8224-1973-4). Pitman Learning.

Cline, Starr. A Practical Guide to Independent Study: Instructional Manuals for Students & Teachers. 75p. 12.00 (ISBN 0-89824-013-1). Trillium Pr.

Ericksen, Stanford C. Motivation for Learning: A Guide for the Teacher of the Young Adult. LC 73-90885. (Illus.). 1974. text ed. 9.50x (ISBN 0-472-08313-9). U of Mich Pr.

Far West Laboratory for Educational Research & Development. Minicourse Fifteen: Organizing Independent Learning-Intermediate Level. 1972. pap. 3.90 coordinators' hndbk. (ISBN 0-02-274170-4); pap. 3.90 tchr's hndbk (ISBN 0-02-274180-1); films & pap. bks. 1140.00 (ISBN 0-02-274150-X). Macmillan.

Gomez, Thelma J. & Simpson, Elizabeth, eds. Independent Activities for Learning Centers. 1971. pap. 4.75x (ISBN 0-8422-0145-9). Irvington.

The Guide to Independent Study Through Correspondence Instruction. 1977. pap. 2.00 (ISBN 0-87866-086-0). Natl Univ Ext.

Holland, J. L. College Degrees Through Independent Studies: An Alternative Approach. LC 78-67669. 1978. 5.98x (ISBN 0-932700-00-4). Centaur Pubn VA.

Hunter, Joan, ed. Guide to Independent Study Through Correspondence Instruction 1980-82. 1980. pap. 4.50 (ISBN 0-87866-120-4). Petersons Guides.

Knowles, Malcolm S. Self-Directed Learning: A Guide for Learners & Teachers. 128p. 1975. 4.95 (ISBN 0-8096-1902-4, Assn Pr). New Century.

Powell, James D. & Kelley, C. Aron. Students Resource Manual: Hicks-Gullett Management of Organization. th ed. 368p. Date not set. text ed. price not set (ISBN 0-07-028777-5). McGraw.

Rossman, Michael. Learning Without a Teacher. LC 74-83883. (Fastback Ser.: No. 45). (Orig.). 1974. pap. 0.75 (ISBN 0-87367-045-0). Phi Delta Kappa.

INDEPENDENT TREASURY

Kinley, David. History, Organization & Influence of the Independent Treasury of the United States. LC 68-28637. 1968. Repr. of 1893 ed. lib. bdg. 20.25x (ISBN 0-8371-0514-5, KIHO). Greenwood.

--Independent Treasury of the United States & Its Relation to the Banks of the Country. LC 74-81508. Repr. of 1910 ed. 17.50x (ISBN 0-678-00545-1). Kelley.

INDEPENDENT UNIONS

Shostak, Arthur B. America's Forgotten Labor Organization. LC 73-10583. 141p. 1973. Repr. of 1962 ed. lib. bdg. 15.00 (ISBN 0-8371-7014-1, SHLO). Greenwood.

INDETERMINATE ANALYSIS

see Diophantine Analysis

INDETERMINATE SENTENCE

see also Probation

Wheeler, Gerald R. Counterdeterrence: A Report on Juvenile Sentencing & Effects of Prisonization. LC 77-26975. 208p. 1978. 17.95x (ISBN 0-88229-315-X). Nelson-Hall.

INDETERMINISM

see Free Will and Determinism

INDEX LIBRORUM PROHIBITORUM

see also Censorship

INDEX NUMBERS (ECONOMICS)

see also Price Indexes

Allen, R. G. D. Index Numbers in Theory & Practice. LC 75-7612. 304p. 1975. 42.95x (ISBN 0-202-06071-3). Aldine Pub.

Cowden, Dudley J. Measures of Exports of the United States. LC 68-58561. (Columbia University Studies in the Social Sciences: No. 356). 14.50 (ISBN 0-404-51356-5). AMS Pr.

Fisher, Irving. Making of Index Numbers. 3rd ed. LC 67-28291. Repr. of 1927 ed. 19.50x (ISBN 0-678-00319-X). Kelley.

Kuznets, Simon. Seasonal Variations in Industry & Trade. LC 75-19723. (National Bureau of Economic Research Ser.). (Illus.). 1975. Repr. 27.00x (ISBN 0-405-07602-9). Arno.

Loomis, Arthur K. The Techniques of Estimating School Equipment Costs. LC 70-177010. (Columbia University. Teachers College. Contributions to Education: No. 208). Repr. of 1926 ed. 17.50 (ISBN 0-404-55208-0). AMS Pr.

Mitchell, Wesley C. Making & Using of Index Numbers. LC 65-19653. Repr. of 1938 ed. 12.50x (ISBN 0-678-00098-0). Kelley.

Stone, Richard. Quantity & Price Indexes in National Accounts. 124p. 1956. 1.50x (ISBN 0-686-14788-X). OECD.

INDEX NUMBERS (ECONOMICS)-BIBLIOGRAPHY

Cole, Arthur H. Measures of Business Change. LC 72-7502. 444p. 1974. Repr. of 1952 ed. lib. bdg. 20.50x (ISBN 0-8371-6513-X, COBC). Greenwood.

Davenport, Donald H. Index to Business Indices. LC 70-153015. 1971. Repr. of 1937 ed. 22.00 (ISBN 0-8103-3706-1). Gale.

Indice Analitico: No. 3, Enero-Diciembre, Vol. 4-12. Incl. Vol. 4. 1963 (ISBN 0-8270-0130-4); Vol. 5. 1964 (ISBN 0-8270-0135-5); Vol. 6. 1965 (ISBN 0-8270-0140-1); Vol. 7. 1966 (ISBN 0-8270-0145-2); Vol. 8. 1967 (ISBN 0-8270-0150-9); Vol. 9. 1968 (ISBN 0-8270-0155-X); Vol. 10. 1969 (ISBN 0-8270-0160-6); Vol. 11. 1970. 178p. 1970 (ISBN 0-8270-0165-7); Vol. 12. 1971 (ISBN 0-8270-0170-3). (Documentos Officiales Ser.). (Span.). Vol. 1-9 & 11-12. pap. 2.00 ea.; Vol. 10. pap. 1.00 (ISBN 0-686-65025-5). OAS.

INDEX OF AMERICAN DESIGN

Christensen, Erwin O. Index of American Design. (Illus.). 1950. 19.95 (ISBN 0-02-525240-2). Macmillan.

INDEXES

see also Abstracting and Indexing Services; Periodicals–Indexes; Subject Headings; also subdivision Indexes or Dictionaries, Indexes, etc. under specific subjects, e.g. Biography–Dictionaries, Indexes, etc.

American Geographical Society-Map Department-New York. Index to Maps in Books & Periodicals, First Supplement. 1971. lib. bdg. 105.00 (ISBN 0-8161-0806-4). G K Hall.

American Humanities Index: 1976 Annual Cumulation, 3 vols. Set. 89.50 (ISBN 0-87875-116-5). Whitston Pub.

Chicorel, Marietta, ed. Chicorel Theater Index to Plays in Anthologies, Periodicals, Discs & Tapes, Vol. 2. LC 71-106198. 1971. 85.00 (ISBN 0-934598-70-3). Am Lib Pub Co.

Dadson, Theresa. Index to the Legon Observer: Volumes Two Through Nine, Nineteen Sixty-Seven to Nineteen Seventy-Four, Vols. 2-9. 1979. lib. bdg. 30.00 (ISBN 0-8161-8294-9). G K Hall.

Falk, Byron A., Jr. & Falk, Valerie R. Personal Name Index to the New York Times Index: Eighteen Fifty-One to Nineteen Seventy-Four, Vol. 18. 600p. 1981. lib. bdg. 57.50 (ISBN 0-89902-118-2). Roxbury Data.

Index Translationum, Vol. 24. 995p. (Orig.). 1974. 83.00 (ISBN 92-3-001105-3, U308, UNESCO). Unipub.

Indexes, Nineteen Seventy-Four to Nineteen Eighty, 7 vols. 1981. price not set (ISBN 0-8379-1411-6). Marquis.

Mohapatra, R. P. Udayagiri & Khandagiri Caves. (Illus.). 270p. 1981. text ed. 84.50x (ISBN 0-391-02263-6, Pub. by Concept India). Humanities.

Molnar, John E. Author-Title Index to Joseph Sabin's Dictionary of Books Relating to America, 3 vols. LC 74-6291. 1974. Set. 135.00 (ISBN 0-8108-0652-5). Scarecrow.

Murray, Janet H. & Clark, Anna K., eds. The Englishwoman's Review of Social & Industrial Questions: An Index. 1981. lib. bdg. 40.00 (ISBN 0-8240-3765-0). Garland Pub.

National Agricultural Library Catalog: Indexes for 1971-1975, 2 vols. 1978. Set. 115.00x (ISBN 0-8476-6093-1). Rowman.

Pearson, J. D., compiled by. Index Islamicus, Fourth Supplement, 1971-1975. LC 59-23014. (Index Islmaicus Ser.). 1978. lib. bdg. 42.00 (ISBN 0-7201-0639-7, Pub. by Mansell England). Merrimack Bk Serv.

Penrose, Maryly B., compiled by. Heads of Families Index: 1850 Federal Census, City of Philadelphia. LC 74-84454. 378p. 1974. 37.00 (ISBN 0-918940-01-X); softcover 32.00 (ISBN 0-918940-02-8). Libty Bell Assoc.

Reuter, Margaret. Two Thousand Plus Index & Glossary. (gr. k-3). 1977. PLB 7.30 (ISBN 0-8172-1025-3). Raintree Pubs.

Ross & Tukey. Index to Statistics & Probability: Locations & Authors, Vol. 5. LC 72-86075. 1973. 94.00 (ISBN 0-88274-004-0). R & D Pr.

--Index to Statistics & Probability: Permuted Titles, Vols. 3 & 4. LC 72-86075. 1975. Set. 137.00 (ISBN 0-686-15779-6). R & D Pr.

Sokol, Irene & Krzyzanowski, Ludwik, eds. Index to the Polish Review 1956-1966. 66p. 1967. pap. 2.00 (ISBN 0-686-09125-6). Polish Inst Arts.

Sokol, Irene, et al, eds. Index to the Polish Review 1967-1970. 39p. 1971. pap. 1.00 (ISBN 0-686-09126-4). Polish Inst Arts.

Spurgeon, C. H. Textual & Subject Indexes of C. H. Spurgeon's Sermons. (Key to the Metropolitan Tabernacle Pulpit set). 2.95 (ISBN 0-686-09095-0). Pilgrim Pubns.

Tukey. Index to Statistics & Probability: Index to Minimum Abbreviations, Vol. 6. LC 72-86075. 1979. 60.00 (ISBN 0-88274-005-9). R & D Pr.

Van Patten, Nathan. Index to Bibliographies & Bibliographical Contributions Relating to the Work of American & British Authors, 1923-32. 1934. 21.00 (ISBN 0-8337-3617-5). B Franklin.

--Index to Bibliographies & Bibliographical Contributions Relating to the Work of American & British Authors, 1923-1932. (English Literary Reference Ser). 1969. Repr. of 1934 ed. 23.00 (ISBN 0-384-63930-5). Johnson Repr.

Vasu, Nagendranath. The Archaeological Survey of Mayurabhanja. (Illus.). 160p. 1981. Repr. text ed. 56.25x (ISBN 0-391-02262-8, Pub. by Concept India). Humanities.

Wasserman, Paul & Herman, Esther, eds. Library Bibliographies & Indexes: A Subject Guide to Resource Material Available from Libraries, Information Centers, Library Schools, & Library Associations in the U. S. & Canada. LC 74-26741. xii, 301p. 1975. 65.00 (ISBN 0-8103-0390-6). Gale.

Williams, William P. Index to the Stationers' Register, 1640-1708. 68p. 1980. lib. bdg. 20.00x (ISBN 0-910938-85-7). McGilvery.

INDEXES, CARD

see Catalogs, Card; Files and Filing (Documents)

INDEXING

see also Automatic Indexing; Cataloging; Files and Filing (Documents); Punched Card Systems

Anderson, Mrs. M. D. Book Indexing. (Authors' & Printers' Guides Ser.: No. 8). 1971. 4.50 (ISBN 0-521-08202-1). Cambridge U Pr.

Automated Education Center. Studies in Indexing & Cataloging. LC 78-120543. 29.00 (ISBN 0-686-01959-8). Mgmt Info Serv.

Bakewell, K. G. Classification & Indexing Practice. 1978. 16.50 (ISBN 0-208-01671-6, Linnet). Shoe String.

--Classification for Information Retrieval. 1968. 12.50 (ISBN 0-208-00850-0, Linnet). Shoe String.

Borko, Harold & Bernier, Charles L. Indexing Concepts & Methods. (Library & Information Science). 1978. 14.50 (ISBN 0-12-118660-1). Acad Pr.

Brown, A. G., et al. An Introduction to Subject Indexing: Volume 2: UDC & Chain Procedure in Subject Cataloguing. (Programmed Texts in Library & Information Science Ser.). 144p. (Orig.). 1976. 13.50 (ISBN 0-208-01529-9, Linnet). Shoe String.

--An Introduction to Subject Indexing, Vol. 1: Subject Analysis & Practical Classification. (Programmed Texts in Library & Information Science Ser.). 144p. (Orig.). 1976. 13.50 (ISBN 0-208-01524-8, Linnet). Shoe String.

Buchanan, Brian W. Glossary of Indexing Terms. 144p. (Orig.). 1976. 14.00 (ISBN 0-208-01377-6, Linnet). Shoe String.

Foskett, D. Classification for a General Indexing Language. 1970. pap. 7.00x (ISBN 0-85365-032-2, Pub. by Lib Assn England). Oryx Pr.

Garfield, Eugene. Citation Indexing: Its Theory & Application in Science, Technology & Humanities. LC 78-9713. (Information Science Ser.). 1979. 21.95x (ISBN 0-471-02559-3, Pub. by Wiley-Interscience). Wiley.

Guthrie. Alphabetic Indexing. 3rd ed. (Combined ed. text & wkbk.). (gr. 9-12). 1964. text ed. 1.44 (ISBN 0-538-11530-0). SW Pub.

Indexation of Financial Assets: Further Material on Problems & Experiences. 1976. 5.50x (ISBN 92-64-11417-3). OECD.

Indexers on Indexing: Selections from the Indexer 1958-1977. 1978. 25.00 (ISBN 0-8352-1099-5). Bowker.

Kahn, Gilbert, et al. Filing Systems & Records Management. 2nd ed. 1971. text ed. 10.95 (ISBN 0-07-033231-2, G); tests 2.56 (ISBN 0-07-033238-X); practice materials 7.95 (ISBN 0-07-033232-0); instructors guide & key 6.70 (ISBN 0-07-033241-X). McGraw.

--Progressive Filing. 8th ed. 1968. text ed. 9.04 (ISBN 0-07-033225-8, G); tchr's manual 5.35 (ISBN 0-07-033227-4); tests 1.36 (ISBN 0-07-033226-6); supplies pad 2.96 (ISBN 0-07-033220-7). McGraw.

--Progressive Filing. 7th ed. 1961. text ed. 9.04 (ISBN 0-07-033210-X, G); tchr's. manual & key 5.35 (ISBN 0-07-033211-8). McGraw.

Knight, G. Norman. The Art of Indexing. 1979. text ed. 22.50x (ISBN 0-04-029002-6). Allen Unwin.

Miller, Howard L. & Woodin, Ralph J. AGDEX: A System for Classifying, Indexing, & Filing Agricultural Publications. (Illus.). 50p. tchrs ed. 10.00 (ISBN 0-89514-030-6, 01081). Am Voc Assn.

NFAIS-UNESCO Indexing in Perspective Education Kit. 1979. 30.00 (ISBN 0-686-28393-7); 18.00 set. twenty transparencies (ISBN 0-686-28394-5). NFAIS.

Perica, Esther. Newspaper Indexing for Historical Societies, Colleges & High Schools. LC 74-20822. 60p. 1975. pap. 2.45 (ISBN 0-912526-15-7). Lib Res.

Ramsden, Michael. An Introduction to Index Language Construction. (Programmed Texts in Lib. & Info. Science Ser.). 1974. 13.50 (ISBN 0-208-01187-0, Linnet). Shoe String.

Smith, R. M. Coordinated Indexing. 1981. spiral 46.00 (ISBN 0-85365-933-8). Oryx Pr.

Smith, Richard M. Articulated Subject Indexing: A Cobol Computer System for the Generation of Low-Cost Indexes. 84p. 1981. spiral bd. 57.50x (ISBN 0-85365-923-0, Pub. by Lib Assn England). Oryx Pr.

Soergel, Dagobert. Indexing Languages & Thesauri: Construction & Maintenance. LC 73-20301. (Information Sciences Ser.). 800p. 1974. 51.50 (ISBN 0-471-81047-9, Pub. by Wiley-Interscience). Wiley.

Spiker, Sina K. Indexing Your Book: A Practical Guide for Authors. 2nd ed. 1954. pap. 2.50x (ISBN 0-299-01173-9). U of Wis Pr.

Walsh, John W. Indexing of Books & Periodicals. 1980. lib. bdg. 59.95 (ISBN 0-8490-3184-2). Gordon Pr.

INDEXING, AUTOMATIC

see Automatic Indexing

INDEXING AND ABSTRACTING SERVICES

see Abstracting and Indexing Services

INDEXING VOCABULARIES

see Subject Headings

INDIA

see also names of cities, villages and geographic areas in India

Arachi, J. X. Pictorial Presentation of Indian Flora. (Illus.). 1968. 14.00x (ISBN 0-8002-1799-3). Intl Pubns Serv.

B. N. Pande for Festschrift Committee, ed. The Spirit of India, 2 vols. (Indira Gandhi Festschrift Ser.). (Illus.). 1976. lib. bdg. 100.00x set (ISBN 0-685-68908-5). Vol. 1 (ISBN 0-210-40560-0). Vol. 2 (ISBN 0-210-40561-9). Asia.

Baark, Erik & Sigurdson, Jon, eds. India-China Comparative Research: Technology & Science for Development. (Studies on Asian Topics: No. 3). 180p. 1980. pap. text ed. 10.50x (ISBN 0-7007-0138-9). Humanities.

Bayley, Emily & Metcalfe, Thomas. The Golden Calm. Kaye, M. M., ed. LC 80-5361. 224p. 1980. 25.00 (ISBN 0-670-34400-1, Studio). Viking Pr.

Berreman, Gerald D. Hindus of the Himalayas: Ethnography & Change. 2nd ed. LC 73-156468. (Center for South & Southeast Asia Studies, UC Berkeley). 1972. 27.50x (ISBN 0-520-01423-5); pap. 7.95x (ISBN 0-520-02035-9, CAMPUS66). U of Cal Pr.

Bhattacharjee, Arun. Dateline Mujibnagar. 1973. 9.00 (ISBN 0-686-20210-4). Intl Bk Dist.

Birla Institute of Scientific Research, Economic Research Div. India Two Thousand One. 1978. text ed. 6.00x (ISBN 0-8426-1082-0). Verry.

Bromwell, C. David. India Emerges. (Asia Emerges Ser.). 1975. pap. 4.80 (ISBN 0-02-648230-4, 64823); tchr's guide 1.36 (ISBN 0-02-648240-1, 64824). Glencoe.

Chopra, Pran. India's Second Liberation. (Illus.). 1973. 7.50 (ISBN 0-7069-0259-9). Intl Bk Dist.

Chopra, S. N. India: An Area Study. (Illus.). 237p. 1977. 20.00x (ISBN 0-7069-0494-X). Intl Pubns Serv.

--India: An Area Study. 237p. 1977. 26.00x (ISBN 0-7069-0494-X, Pub by Croom Helm Ltd. England). Biblio Dist.

Chopra, Surendranath. India: An Area Study. 1977. text ed. 22.50x (ISBN 0-7069-0494-X). Verry.

Coomaraswamy, Ananda K. Yaksas, 2 pts. in 1 vol. 1971. 20.00x (ISBN 0-8002-0979-6). Intl Pubns Serv.

Das, A. C. Rgvedic India, 2 vols. 1971. Repr. of 1971 ed. Set. 29.50 (ISBN 0-686-77263-6). Vol. I (ISBN 0-89684-267-3). Vol. II (ISBN 0-89684-306-8). Orient Bk Dist.

Das, Sukla. Socio-Economic Life of Northern India. 1980. 22.50 (ISBN 0-8364-0609-5, Abhina India). South Asia Bks.

Devi, Gayatri. One Life's Pilgrimage. 1977. pap. 4.95 (ISBN 0-911564-27-6). Vedanta Ctr.

Dikshit, S. R, ed. All India Booksellers & Publishers Directory: 1970. 680p. 1970. 10.00x (ISBN 0-8002-0432-8). Intl Pubns Serv.

Dube, S. C. Contemporary India & Its Modernization. 1974. 7.50 (ISBN 0-686-20207-4). Intl Bk Dist.

Franda, Marcus F. Bangladesh & India: Population, Politics, & Resources in a Global Environment. Spitzer, Manon, ed. 1976. spiral bdg. 6.50 (ISBN 0-88333-000-8). Am U Field.

--India in an Emergency. Spitzer, Manon, ed. 1976. spiral bdg. 7.50 (ISBN 0-88333-001-6). Am U Field.

--India in the Seventies. Spitzer, Manon, ed. 1976. spiral bdg. 8.50 (ISBN 0-88333-002-4). Am U Field.

Gerber, William, ed. The Mind of India. LC 76-27668. (Arcturus Books Paperbacks). 288p. 1977. pap. 3.95 (ISBN 0-8093-0804-5). S Ill U Pr.

Godden, Jon & Godden, Rumer. Shiva's Pigeons: An Experience of India. (Illus.). 384p. 1972. 17.95 (ISBN 0-670-64055-7, Studio). Viking Pr.

Gopal, Ram. India, China, Tibet Triangle. 1966. pap. 2.00 (ISBN 0-88253-139-5). Ind-US Inc.

Harris, Nigel. India-China-Underdevelopment & Revolution. 1974. 13.50 (ISBN 0-7069-0312-9). Intl Bk Dist.

Harrison, Barbara J., ed. Learning About India: An Annotated Guide for Nonspecialists. (Occasional Publications Ser.: No. 24). 364p. 1977. pap. 3.95 (ISBN 0-89192-234-2). Interbk Inc.

Hunter, William W. Indian Empire: Its Peoples, History & Products. LC 71-181076. Repr. of 1893 ed. 27.50 (ISBN 0-404-03461-6). AMS Pr.

Hurlimann, Martin. India. (Illus.). 1975. 35.00 (ISBN 0-686-20247-3). Intl Bk Dist.

India. (gr. 6-8). Complete Pack. pap. text ed. 60.00x (ISBN 0-435-31505-6); Folder A-D. 6.50 ea. Folder A: Food (ISBN 0-435-31506-4). Folder B: Work (ISBN 0-435-31507-2). Folder C: Family (ISBN 0-435-31508-0). Folder D: Village (ISBN 0-435-31509-9). Heinemann Ed.

Indian Institute of Advanced Study. Transactions. Incl. No. 1. Religion & Society. (Illus.). 445p. 1965. 10.00x (ISBN 0-8002-2095-1); No. 2. Indian Aesthetics & Art Activity. 343p. 1968. 15.00x (ISBN 0-8002-2096-X); No. 4. Sikhism & Indian Society. 344p. 1967. 14.00x (ISBN 0-8002-2097-8); No. 5. Modernity & Contemporary Indian Literature. 443p. 1968. 18.00x (ISBN 0-8002-2098-6); No. 7. Trends of Socio-Economic Change in India 1871-1961. Chaudhuri, M. K., ed. (Illus.). 811p. 1969. 30.00x (ISBN 0-8002-2099-4); No. 8. Language & Society in India. 601p. 1969. 22.00x (ISBN 0-8002-2100-1); No. 10. Urgent Research in Social Anthropology. Abbi, Behari L. & Saberwal, Satish, eds. 235p. 1969. 11.00x (ISBN 0-8002-2101-X); No. 11. Ghandi: Theory & Practice, Social Impact & Contemporary Relevance. Biswas, S. C., ed. 635p. 1969. 22.00x (ISBN 0-8002-2102-8). Intl Pubns Serv.

INFA Press & Advertisers Yearbook 1980. 18th ed. LC 63-2244. 326p. 1980. 25.00x (ISBN 0-8002-2811-1). Intl Pubns Serv.

Kenworthy, Leonard. Studying India. LC 74-23809. 1975. pap. text ed. 4.25x (ISBN 0-8077-2457-2). Tchrs Coll.

Kumar, Virendra. Committees & Commissions in India, Vol. 3. 1977. 27.50x (ISBN 0-685-58422-4). South Asia Bks.

--Committees & Commissions in India, Vol. 6. 1978. 30.00x (ISBN 0-8364-0279-0). South Asia Bks.

Lacy, Creighton. Indian Insights: Public Issues in Private Perspective. 1972. 12.50 (ISBN 0-8046-8815-X). Kennikat.

Madan, G. R. India of Tomorrow. 1975. 11.00x (ISBN 0-88386-588-2). South Asia Bks.

Mason, Philip, ed. India & Ceylon: Unity & Diversity: A Symposium. 1967. pap. 5.95x (ISBN 0-19-500351-9). Oxford U Pr.

Mehta, D. S. Mass Communication & Journalism in India. LC 80-5314. 332p. 1981. 12.95 (ISBN 0-8039-1488-1). Sage.

Mellor, John W. India: A Rising Middle Power. (Special Studies on South & Southeast Asia). 1979. lib. bdg. 28.75x (ISBN 0-89158-298-3). Westview.

Michell, J. F. North-East Frontier of India. 1973. 24.00x (ISBN 0-8426-0623-8). Verry.

Ministry of Education & Social Welfare. India (Republic). the Gazetteers Unit. The Gazetteer of India; Indian Union. Incl. Vol. 1. Country & People. (Illus.). 652p. 17.50x (ISBN 0-8002-1448-X); Vol. 2. History & Culture. (Illus.). 807p. 1973. 25.00x (ISBN 0-8002-1449-8); Vol. 3. 1975. 45.00x (ISBN 0-8002-1450-1). 1974. Repr. of 1965 ed. Intl Pubns Serv.

Ministry of Information & Broadcasting (India) India: A Reference Annual, 1980. 26th ed. LC 54-2074. (Illus.). 580p. 1980. 17.50x (ISBN 0-8002-2761-1). Intl Pubns Serv.

Misra, R. P. & Sundaram, K. V., eds. Rural Area Development: Perspectives & Approaches. (Illus.). 427p. 1979. 17.50x (ISBN 0-8002-0997-4). Intl Pubns Serv.

Naipaul, V. S. India: A Wounded Civilization. 1977. 10.00 (ISBN 0-394-40291-X). Knopf.

Nakagawa, Tsuyoshi. India. LC 72-90227. (This Beautiful World Ser.: Vol. 39). (Illus.). 1973. pap. 4.95 (ISBN 0-87011-188-4). Kodansha.

Narayana Rao, K. V. The Emergence of Andhra Pradesh. 350p. 1974. lib. bdg. 12.50 (ISBN 0-88253-472-6). Ind-US Inc.

Nath, R. The Art of Khajuraho. 1980. 90.00x (ISBN 0-8364-0608-7, Pub. by Abhina India). South Asia Bks.

Nayar, Kuldip. Distant Neighbours: Tale of the Subcontinent. 1972. 6.00 (ISBN 0-686-20213-9). Intl Bk Dist.

Noon, Firozkhan. India. 1941. 12.50 (ISBN 0-8495-4027-5). Arden Lib.

Operations Research Group. India in Perspective: Development Issues, Vol. 1. Basu, D. N., ed. 1978. text ed. 15.00x (ISBN 0-8426-1089-8). Verry.

Operations Research Group & Nagarajan, R. India in Perspective: Development Issues, Vol. 2. 1978. text ed. 15.00x (ISBN 0-8426-1088-X). Verry.

Ramachandran, H. Village Clusters & Rural Development. 140p. 1980. text ed. 12.50 (ISBN 0-391-02138-9). Humanities.
Raman, T. A. India. rev. ed. LC 78-54252. (World Cultures Ser). (Illus.). (gr. 6 up). 1980. 1-4 copies 9.95 (ISBN 0-88296-127-6); 5 or more 7.96 (ISBN 0-685-14487-9); tchrs'. guide 8.94 (ISBN 0-88296-369-4). Fideler.
Ramroop, Govinda V. The Voices of India. 1980. 4.95 (ISBN 0-533-03273-3). Vantage.
Saberwal, Satish, ed. Towards a Cultural Policy. 1974. 15.00 (ISBN 0-686-20320-8). Intl Bk Dist.
Sengupta, Syamalkanti. Applied Anthropology, Meaning & Necessity (India) 1977. 8.00x (ISBN 0-88386-065-1). South Asia Bks.
Sethi, J. D. India in Crisis. 1974. 10.50 (ISBN 0-686-20250-3). Intl Bk Dist.
Shah, Giri R. India Rediscovered. LC 75-903828. 1975. 9.50x (ISBN 0-88386-076-7). South Asia Bks.
Singh, Karan. Towards a New India. 1974. 7.50 (ISBN 0-686-20321-6). Intl Bk Dist.
Singh, Yogendra. Essays on Modernization in India. 1978. 10.00x (ISBN 0-8364-0264-2). South Asia Bks.
Singha, H. S. Modern Educational Testing. 235p. 1974. text ed. 10.50x (ISBN 0-8426-0650-5). Verry.
Sitwell, Constance. Flowers & Elephants. 1979. Repr. of 1927 ed. lib. bdg. 20.00 (ISBN 0-8495-5026-2). Arden Lib.
Subramanian, C. India of My Dreams. 1972. 12.50 (ISBN 0-8046-8831-1). Kennikat.
The Times of India Directory & Yearbook, Including Who's Who 1980-81. 57th ed. (Illus.). 956p. 1980. 45.00x (ISBN 0-8002-2800-6). Intl Pubns Serv.
Towards Understanding India. 3rd ed. 1967. pap. 2.00 (ISBN 0-88253-398-3). Ind-US Inc.
Twain, Mark, pseud. Following the Equator. LC 77-12690. 1897. 32.50 (ISBN 0-404-01577-8). AMS Pr.
Varma, Satyakam. Studies in Indology. 320p. 1976. lib. bdg. 17.50 (ISBN 0-210-40584-8). Asia.
Venkataramani, M. S. & Srivastava, B. K. Quit India: The American Response to the Nineteen Forty-Two Struggle. 1979. 25.00x (ISBN 0-7069-0693-4, Pub. by Vikas India). Advent NY.
Venugopal Reddy, Y. Multilevel Planning in India. (Illus.). 1979. text ed. 17.50x (ISBN 0-7069-0761-2, Pub. by Vikas India). Advent NY.
Warfel, A. & Duckwitz, M., eds. German Scholars on India, Vol. 2. 1976. 18.00 (ISBN 0-89684-208-8). Orient Bk Dist.
Wheeler, Post. India Against the Storm. Repr. of 1944 ed. 15.00 (ISBN 0-89987-030-9). Darby Bks.
Wirsing, Giselher. The Indian Experiment: Key to Asia's Future. 1972. 12.50 (ISBN 0-8046-8838-9). Kennikat.
Zimand, Savel. Living India. LC 72-19. (Select Bibliographies Reprint Ser). 1972. Repr. of 1928 ed. 18.75 (ISBN 0-8369-9974-6). Arno.

INDIA–ANTIQUITIES

Agarwal, Rajesh K. & Nangia, Sudesh. Economic & Employment Potential of Archaeological Monuments in India. (Illus.). 90p. 1974. 5.95x (ISBN 0-210-40553-8). Asia.
Agrawal, D. & Chakravarti, D., eds. Essays in Indian Protohistory. 1980. text ed. 42.00x (ISBN 0-391-01866-3). Humanities.
Agrawal, D. P. The Archaeology of India. (Scandinavian Institute of Asian Studies Monograph). (Illus.). 320p. 1981. pap. text ed. 23.50 (ISBN 0-7007-0140-0). Humanities.
Agrawal, D. R. Ecology & Archaeology of Western India. 1978. 26.00x (ISBN 0-8364-0152-2). South Asia Bks.
Asthana, Shashi P. History & Archeology of India's Contacts with Other Countries from the Earliest Times to 300 B.C. LC 76-903130. 1976. 27.00x (ISBN 0-88386-787-7). South Asia Bks.
Barnett, L. D. Antiquities of India: An Account of the History & Culture of Ancient Hindustan. (Illus.). 1964. 9.50x (ISBN 0-8426-1143-6). Verry.
Bernier, Ronald M. The Temples of Nepal. 1979. 17.00x (ISBN 0-8364-0326-6). South Asia Bks.
Betancourt, Philip P. Vasilike Ware, One Hundred, Vol. LVI. (Studies in Mediterranean Archaeology). 1979. text ed. 28.00x (ISBN 91-85058-88-2). Humanities.
Burgess, James. The Temples of Palitana in Kathiawad. 1977. 65.00x (ISBN 0-8364-0021-6). South Asia Bks.
Chandra, Jagdish, compiled by. Bibliography of Indian Art, History & Archaeology: Dr. Anand K. Coomanaswamy Memorial Volume, Vol. 1. 1978. text ed. 62.50x (ISBN 0-391-01072-7). Humanities.
Chopra, S. R., ed. Early Man in North-West India. 1979. 10.00x (ISBN 0-8364-0451-3). South Asia Bks.
Cousens, Henry. The Antiquities of Sind: With Historical Outline, Archaeological Survey of India. (Imperial Ser.: Vol. 46). (Illus.). 308p. 1975. 21.25x (ISBN 0-19-577197-4). Oxford U Pr.
Fairservis, Walter A., Jr. The Roots of Ancient India: The Archaeology of Early Indian Civilization. 2nd. rev ed. LC 74-33510. xxxiv, 480p. 1975. pap. 7.95 (ISBN 0-226-23429-0, P636, Phoen). U of Chicago Pr.
Foote, R. B. Prehistory & Protohistoric Antiquities of India. 1979. text ed. 21.50x (ISBN 0-391-01865-5). Humanities.
Gordon, Douglas H. The Pre-Historic Background of Indian Culture. Barrett, D. & Madhuri, Desai, eds. LC 75-31825. (Illus.). 199p. 1976. lib. bdg. 20.00x (ISBN 0-8371-8440-1, GOIC). Greenwood.
Gupta, S. P. Archaeology of Central Asia & the Indian Border Lands, 2 vols. 1979. text ed. 41.00 ea. Vol. 1 (ISBN 0-391-01855-8). Vol. 2 (ISBN 0-391-02092-7). Humanities.
Jain, P. C. Labour in Ancient India: From the Vedic Age up to the Gupta Period. 302p. 1971. 12.50x (ISBN 0-8426-0284-4). Verry.
Lal Dey, Nando. The Geographical Dictionary of Ancient & Medieval India. 262p. 1979. Repr. of 1927 ed. 27.50 (ISBN 0-89684-150-2). Orient Bk Dist.
MacKay, Ernest J., et al. Further Excavations at Mohenjo-Daro: Being an Official Account of Archaeological Excavations at Mohenjo-Daro Carried Out by the Gov't of India Between 1927 & 1931, 2 vols. LC 77-87006. Repr. of 1938 ed. 127.00 set (ISBN 0-404-16670-9). AMS Pr.
Masson, Emilia. Etude De Vingt-Six Boules D'argile Inscrites Trouvees a Enkomi et Hala Sultan Tekke Chypre. (Studies in Mediterranean Archaeology: No. 31, 1). (Illus.). 1979. pap. text ed. 14.00x (ISBN 91-85058-42-4). Humanities.
Mitra, Debala. Bronzes from Achutrajpur Orissa. 1978. 50.00x (ISBN 0-8364-0136-0). South Asia Bks.
Prakash, S. & Rawat, N. S. Chemical Study of Some Indian Antiquities. pap. 3.75x (ISBN 0-210-22656-0). Asia.
Rajan, K. V. Megalithic Architecture in Southern India. Feldman, Lawrence H., ed. LC 76-352339. (Museum Brief Ser.: No. 12). (Illus.). ii, 14p. 1975. pap. 2.50x (ISBN 0-913134-97-X). Mus Anthro Mo.
Ramaswami, N. S. Indian Monuments. 1979. text ed. 20.00 (ISBN 0-89684-091-3, Pub. by Abhinay New Delhi). Orient Bk Dist.
Sircar, D. C. Some Epigraphical Records of the Medieval Period from Eastern India. 1979. 22.00x (ISBN 0-8364-0349-5). South Asia Bks.
Taddei, Maurizio. India. Hogarth, James, tr. from It. (Archaeologia Mundi Ser.). (Illus.). 264p. 1970. 29.50 (ISBN 0-88254-142-0). Hippocrene Bks.
Terra, Hellmut D. & Paterson, Thomas T. Studies on the Ice Age in India & Associated Human Cultures. LC 76-44795. (Carnegie Institution of Washington Publication: No. 493). Repr. of 1939 ed. 39.00 (ISBN 0-404-15881-1). AMS Pr.
Tripathy, K. C. Lithic Industries in India: A Study of South Western Orissa. 190p. 1980. text ed. 12.50x (ISBN 0-391-02139-7). Humanities.
Vatuk, Sylvia, ed. American Studies in the Anthropology of India. 1979. 11.50x (ISBN 0-8364-0319-3). South Asia Bks.
Wheeler, Mortimer. Indus Civilization. 3rd ed. LC 22-11272. (Illus.). 1968. 32.50 (ISBN 0-521-06958-0); pap. 8.50x (ISBN 0-521-09538-7). Cambridge U Pr.
Winstead, Richard, ed. Indian Art. (Illus.). 1967. 5.95 (ISBN 0-8079-0067-2); pap. 2.95 (ISBN 0-8079-0068-0). October.

INDIA–ARMED FORCES

Chaturvedi, M. S. History of the Indian Air Force. (Illus.). 1978. text ed. 16.50 (ISBN 0-7069-0620-9, Pub. by Vikas India). Advent NY.
Naib, V. P. The Land Army. 1978. 12.50 (ISBN 0-7069-0695-0, Pub. by Vikas India). Advent NY.
Singh, Pushpindar. Aircraft of the Indian Air Force, 1933-73. LC 74-903552. (Illus.). 186p. 1974. 21.00x (ISBN 0-8002-0433-6). Intl Pubns Serv.

INDIA–BIBLIOGRAPHY

Bose, Ashish. Bibliography on Urbanization in India, Nineteen Forty-Seven to Seventy-Six. 1977. 12.00x (ISBN 0-8364-0385-1). South Asia Bks.
Chirol, Valentine. India. LC 72-2561. (Select Bibliographies Reprint Ser.). 1972. Repr. of 1926 ed. 20.00 (ISBN 0-8369-6851-4). Arno.
Commonwealth Relations Office, Great Britain. Catalogue of European Printed Books, India Office Library, 10 Vols. 1964. Set. 800.00 (ISBN 0-8161-0671-1). G K Hall.
Fazal-E-Rab, Syed. The JP Movement & Emergence of Janata Party: A Select Bibliography, Vol. 1: Pre-Emergency. 1977. 12.50x (ISBN 0-8364-0097-6). South Asia Bks.
Field, T. W. An Essay Towards an Indian Bibliography. 59.95 (ISBN 0-8490-0125-0). Gordon Pr.
Gidwani, N. N. & Navalani, K. A Guide to Reference Materials in India, 2 vols. LC 74-901997. 1974. Set. 75.00x (ISBN 0-88386-578-5). South Asia Bks.
Jafar, S. M. Student Unrest in India: A Select Bibliography. 1977. 12.50x (ISBN 0-8364-0095-X). South Asia Bks.
Kaul, H. K., ed. Early Writing on India: A Union Catalogue of Books on India in the English Language Published up to 1900 & Available in Delhi Libraries. 324p. 1975. 22.50x (ISBN 0-87471-770-1). Rowman.
Kaul, T. N. Diplomacy in Peace & War. 1979. text ed. 15.00x (ISBN 0-7069-0749-3, Pub. by Vikas India). Advent NY.
Mahar, J. Michael. India: A Critical Bibliography. rev. ed. Date not set. price not set (ISBN 0-8165-0635-3). U of Ariz Pr.
Perkins, David L., et al, eds. India & Its People: A Bibliography. LC 80-14774. 474p. 1980. 28.50 (ISBN 0-8357-0555-2, IS-00113, Pub. by Santa Susana). Univ Microfilms.
Satyaprakash. Gandhiana, 1962-76: A Bibliography. 1977. 12.50 (ISBN 0-88386-977-2). South Asia Bks.
--Indian Science Index, 1976. 1978. 32.50x (ISBN 0-8364-0421-1). South Asia Bks.
Satyaprakash, ed. Andhra Pradesh: A Bibliography. LC 76-904271. 1976. 11.00x (ISBN 0-88386-450-9). South Asia Bks.
--Gujarat: A Select Bibliography. 1977. 9.50x (ISBN 0-8364-0408-4). South Asia Bks.
--Karnataka: A Select Bibliography. 1978. 15.00x (ISBN 0-8364-0221-9). South Asia Bks.
Sharma, J. S. Fundamentals of Bibliography with Special Reference to India. 1977. text ed. 7.50x (ISBN 0-8426-1012-X). Verry.
Warikoo, J., ed. Jammu, Kashmir & Ladakh: A Classified & Comprehensive Bibliography. 1977. text ed. 30.00x (ISBN 0-8426-1001-4). Verry.

INDIA–BIOGRAPHY

Abbott, Justin E. Life of Eknath. 1981. 12.00x (ISBN 0-8364-0746-6, Pub. by Motilal Banarsidass). South Asia Bks.
Abbott, Justin E., tr. from Sanskrit. Life of Tukaram. 346p. 1980. pap. text ed. 6.95 (ISBN 0-89684-251-7, Pub. by Motilal Banarsidass India). Orient Bk Dist.
Abdulla, Ramjoo. Ramjoo's Diaries, Nineteen Twenty-Two to Nineteen Twenty-Nine. Deitrick, Ira G., intro. by. LC 78-32145. (Illus.). 1979. 13.95 (ISBN 0-915828-14-6). Sufism Reoriented.
Alfassa, Mira. Glimpses of the Mothers Life, Vol. 1. Das, Nilima, ed. 259p. 1978. 9.50 (ISBN 0-89071-247-6). Matagiri.
--The Mother on Herself. 84p. 1977. pap. 1.85 (ISBN 0-89071-248-4). Matagiri.
Armstrong, Robert C. Just Before the Dawn: Life & Work of Ninomiya Sontoku. LC 78-72370. Repr. of 1912 ed. 32.50 (ISBN 0-404-17217-2). AMS Pr.
Azad, Abul K. India Wins Freedom. 1978. 8.50x (ISBN 0-8364-0288-X). South Asia Bks.
Basu, S. N. Jagadis Chandra Bose. (National Biography Ser.). (Orig.). 1979. pap. 2.50 (ISBN 0-89744-205-9). Auromere.
Bhattacharjea, Ajit. Jayaprakash Narayan: A Political Biography. rev. ed. 1978. 8.00x (ISBN 0-8364-0115-8). South Asia Bks.
Borthwick, Meredith. Keshub Chunder Sen: A Search for Cultural Synthesis in India. 1978. 13.50x (ISBN 0-88386-904-7). South Asia Bks.
Boxer, C. R. Joao De Barros. (XCHR Studies Ser.: No. 1). 159p. 1981. text ed. 13.50x (ISBN 0-686-73708-3, Pub. by Concept India). Humanities.
Brata, Sasthi. Traitor to India. 1977. 10.95 (ISBN 0-236-40039-8, Pub. by Paul Elek). Merrimack Bk Serv.
Brijbhushan, Jamila. Kamaladevi Chattopadhyaya: Portrait of a Rebel. LC 76-900583. 1976. 11.00x (ISBN 0-88386-784-2). South Asia Bks.
Brooke, Tal. Sai Baba: Lord of the Air. 1979. 15.00x (ISBN 0-7069-0792-2, Pub. by Vikas India). Advent NY.
Buckland, C. E. Dictionary of Indian Biography. LC 68-26350. (Reference Ser. No. 44). 1969. Repr. of 1906 ed. lib. bdg. 59.95 (ISBN 0-8383-0277-7). Haskell.
Buckland, Charles E. Dictionary of Indian Biography. LC 68-23140. 1968. Repr. of 1906 ed. 41.00 (ISBN 0-8103-3156-X). Gale.
--Dictionary of Indian Biography. LC 69-13845. Repr. of 1906 ed. lib. bdg. 21.00x (ISBN 0-8371-0331-2, BUIB). Greenwood.
Chagla, M. C. Roses in December: An Autobiography. LC 73-907500. (Illus.). 1974. 7.50x (ISBN 0-8002-1941-4). Intl Pubns Serv.
Chatterjee, Santimay & Chatterjee, Enakshi. Satyendra Nath Bose. (National Biography Ser.). 1979. pap. 2.25 (ISBN 0-89744-196-6). Auromere.
Chatterjee, Vera. All This Is Ended: The Life & Times of Her Highness Begum Sumroo. 1979. 12.00x (ISBN 0-7069-0719-1, Pub. by Vikas India). Advent NY.
Chaudhuri, J. N. An Autobiography. 1978. 14.00 (ISBN 0-7069-0655-1, Pub. by Vikas India). Advent NY.
Clark, Chris. Record-Breaking Sunil Gavaskar. LC 80-66423. (Illus.). 1980. 16.95 (ISBN 0-7153-8001-X). David & Charles.
Dattaray, Rajatbaran. A Critical Survey of the Life & Works of Ksemendra. 1974. 9.00 (ISBN 0-88386-574-2). South Asia Bks.
Deshmukh, Chintaman D. The Course of My Life. LC 75-900454. 1974. 12.50 (ISBN 0-8364-0485-8, Orient Longman). South Asia Bks.
Engle, Jon. Servants of God: The Lives of the 10 Gurus of the Sikhs. LC 79-63457. (Illus.). 1980. pap. 6.00 (ISBN 0-89142-035-5). Sant Bani Ash.
Freeman, James M. Untouchable: An Indian Life History. LC 78-55319. (Illus.). 1979. 18.95x (ISBN 0-8047-1001-5); pap. 8.95 (ISBN 0-8047-1103-8, SP40). Stanford U Pr.
Gandhi, Rajmohan. The Rajaji Story: Warrior from the South. 1979. 12.50x (ISBN 0-8364-0562-5, Pub. by Bharathan India): South Asia Bks.
Ghosh, A. Chanakya. (Illus.). (gr. 1-8). 1979. pap. 2.00 (ISBN 0-89744-152-4). Auromere.
Giri, V. V. My Life & Times, Vol. 1. 1976. 15.00x (ISBN 0-8002-1741-1). Intl Pubns Serv.
Gopal, Madan. Sir Chhotu Ram: A Political Biography. 1977. 9.00x (ISBN 0-88386-946-2). South Asia Bks.
Gupta, Bhagwan Das. Life & Times of Maharaja Chhatrasal Bundela. 178p. 1980. text ed. 10.00x (ISBN 0-391-01771-3). Humanities.
Husain, A. M. Tughluq Dynasty. (Illus.). 1976. Repr. of 1935 ed. 30.00x (ISBN 0-8002-0250-3). Intl Pubns Serv.
Hwui-Li, Shaman. The Life of Hiuen-Tsiang. Beal, Samuel, tr. LC 73-880. (Illus.). 317p. 1973. Repr. of 1884 ed. 12.75x (ISBN 0-8002-0916-8). Intl Pubns Serv.
Iyengar, K. R. On the Mother: A Chronicle of a Manifestation & a Ministry, 2 vols. 847p. 1978. pap. 18.75 (ISBN 0-89071-277-8). Matagiri.
Khosla, G. D. The Murder of the Mahatma & Other Cases from a Judge's Notebook. 276p. 1965. pap. 3.00 (ISBN 0-88253-051-8). Ind-US Inc.
Kriyananda, Swami. Stories of Mukunda. LC 76-5748. (Illus.). 110p. 1976. pap. 4.95 (ISBN 0-916124-09-6). Ananda.
Kumar, Shanta. A Chief Minister's Prison Diary. 1979. 12.00x (ISBN 0-7069-0760-4, Pub. by Vikas India). Advent NY.
Lai, Muni. Akbar. 380p. 1980. text ed. 17.95x (ISBN 0-7069-1076-1, Pub. by Vikas India). Advent NY.
Lal, Muni. Humayun. 1978. 14.00x (ISBN 0-7069-0645-4, Pub. by Croom Helm Ltd. England). Biblio Dist.
--Profile of a Chief Minister. 1978. text ed. 9.00 (ISBN 0-7069-0364-1, Pub. by Vikas India). Advent NY.
Langley, G. H. Sri Aurobindo. 59.95 (ISBN 0-8490-1119-1). Gordon Pr.
Lewis, Primila. Reason Wounded: An Experience of India's Emergency. 1979. 13.95 (ISBN 0-04-301096-2). Allen Unwin.
Malik, Hafeez. Sir Sayyid Ahmad Khan & Muslim Modernization in India & Pakistan. LC 80-13905. (Illus.). 288p. 1980. 25.00x (ISBN 0-231-04970-6). Columbia U Pr.
Masani, M. R. Against the Tide. (Illus.). 350p. 1981. text ed. 25.00 (ISBN 0-7069-1205-5, Pub. by Vikas India). Advent NY.
Mathai, M. O. My Days with Nehru. 1979. 15.00x (ISBN 0-7069-0823-6, Pub. by Vikas India). Advent NY.
Max Mueller, F. Keshub Chunder Sen. rev. ed. Mookerjee, Nanda, ed. 1976. 6.00x (ISBN 0-88386-862-8). South Asia Bks.
Mukerji, Dhan G. The Face of Silence. 1979. pap. 3.50 (ISBN 90-6077-460-4, Pub. by Servire BV Netherlands). Hunter Hse.
Nanda, B. R. Gokhale, Gandhi & the Nehrus: Studies in Indian Nationalism. LC 74-76991. 200p. 1974. 19.95 (ISBN 0-312-33145-2). St Martin.
Nandakumar, Prema. The Mother of Sri Aurobindo Ashram. (National Biography Ser.). 1979. pap. 2.25 (ISBN 0-89744-198-2). Auromere.
Naravane, V. S. Introduction to Rabindranath Tagore. 1978. 11.00x (ISBN 0-8364-0130-1). South Asia Bks.
--Sarat Chandra Chatterji. 1976. 11.00x (ISBN 0-8364-0465-3). South Asia Bks.
Nirodbaran. The Mother: Sweetness & Light. (Illus.). 212p. 1978. pap. 5.00 (ISBN 0-89071-280-8). Matagiri.

Prasad, Rajendra. Portrait of a President: Letters of Dr. Rajendra Prasad, Vol. I. Darbar, Gyanwati, ed. write for info. (ISBN 0-7069-0289-0, Pub. by Vikas India). Advent NY.
Pritam, Amrita. The Revenue Stamp: Autobiography. 1977. 9.00x (ISBN 0-88386-932-2). South Asia Bks.
Pugh, B. M. The Story of a Tribal: An Auto-Biography. 1976. text ed. 7.50x (ISBN 0-88386-619-6, Orient Longman). South Asia Bks.
Ramakrisnananda, Swami. Life of Sri Ranauja. 1979. pap. 6.75 (ISBN 0-87481-446-4). Vedanta Pr.
Ravindra. The White Lotus: At the Feet of the Mother. (Illus.). 1978. 8.50x (ISBN 0-8002-0369-0). Intl Pubns Serv.
Rawlinson, Hugh G. Makers of India. facsimile ed. LC 77-134126. (Essay Index Reprints - Living Names Ser.). Repr. of 1942 ed. 10.00 (ISBN 0-8369-2251-4). Arno.
Roy-Chaudhury, P. C. Gandhi & His Contemporaries. 336p. 1972. 11.25x (ISBN 0-8002-1442-0). Intl Pubns Serv.
Saraswati, Dayanand. Yadav: Autobiography of Dayanand Saraswati. rev. ed. Yadav, K. C., ed. 1979. 10.00x (ISBN 0-8364-0372-X). South Asia Bks.
Satsvarupa dasa Goswami. A Lifetime in Preparation: Srila Prabhupada-lilamrta, Vol. 1. (Illus.). 357p. 1980. 9.95 (ISBN 0-686-71685-X). Bhaktivedanta.
Satyajit. India Who's Who 1980-81. 12th ed. LC 73-90638. 522p. 1980. 35.00x (ISBN 0-8002-2799-9). Intl Pubns Serv.
Sen, S. P., ed. Dictionary of National Biography, 4 vols. LC 72-906859. 1972. Set. 120.00x (ISBN 0-88386-030-9). South Asia Bks.
Sethna, H. D. The Mind's Journey. 1979. text ed. 7.50 (ISBN 0-8426-1630-6). Verry.
Sharma, Jagdish S. The National Biographical Dictionary of India. LC 72-901576. 288p. 1972. 13.50x (ISBN 0-8002-0943-5). Intl Pubns Serv.
Singh, Hajinder. Birth of an Air Force: Memoirs of Air Vice Marshal Harjinder Singh. 1977. 15.00 (ISBN 0-8364-0107-7). South Asia Bks.
Singh, Harbans. Bhai Vir Singh. LC 73-902536. 1972. 5.75x (ISBN 0-88386-268-9). South Asia Bks.
Spear, Percival & Spear, Margaret. India Remembered. 1981. 19.00x (ISBN 0-86131-264-3, Orient Longman). South Asia Bks.
Sreenivasan, Kasthuri. Climbing the Coconut Tree: A Partial Autobiography. (Illus.). 178p. 1980. 13.95x (ISBN 0-19-561242-6). Oxford U Pr.
Stracey, Erik. Odd Man in: My Years in the Indian Police, 1943-79. 300p. 1980. text ed. 20.00x (ISBN 0-7069-1206-3, Pub. by Vikas India). Advent NY.
Swami Aseshananda. Glimpses of a Great Soul: Reminiscences & Teachings of Swami Saradanada, Direct Disciple to SriRamakrishna & His Definitive Biographer. LC 74-20572. (God Ser.: No. 107). (Illus.). 300p. 1981. 12.00 (ISBN 0-89007-107-1). C Stark.
Talib, Gurbachan Singh & Singh, Attar. Bhai Vir Singh: Life, Times & Works. 320p. 1974. 8.00x (ISBN 0-88386-420-7). South Asia Bks.
Trotter, L. J. Warren Hastings: Volume Six of Rulers of India. Hunter, William W., ed. LC 70-39407. (Select Bibliographies Reprint Series). 1972. Repr. of 1890 ed. 15.00 (ISBN 0-8369-9922-3). Arno.
Yajnik, Indulal K. Life of Ranchoddas Bhavan Lotvala. (Great Men of India Ser.). 1980. lib. bdg. 69.95 (ISBN 0-8490-3080-3). Gordon Pr.

INDIA–BOUNDARIES

Bajpai, S. C. The Northern Frontier of India. (Illus.). 223p. 1970. 7.00x (ISBN 0-8188-1157-9). Paragon.
Lamb, Alastair. The Sino-Indian Border in Ladakh. LC 73-19964. (Asian Publications Ser.: No. 3). (Illus.). 114p. 1975. 14.95x (ISBN 0-87249-300-8). U of SC Pr.
Mehra, Parshotam. The McMahon Line & After. LC 76-6251. 1976. 19.00x (ISBN 0-88386-616-1). South Asia Bks.
Perti, P. K. South Asia Frontier Policies, Administrative Problems & Lord Lansdowne. 1976. 12.50x (ISBN 0-88386-847-4). South Asia Bks.
Sharma, Surya P. India's Boundary & Territorial Disputes. 1971. 6.75 (ISBN 0-686-20252-X). Intl Bk Dist.

INDIA–CENTRAL BOARD OF REVENUE–OFFICIALS AND EMPLOYEES

Chettur, S. K. Steel Frame & I: Life in the Indian Civil Service. 1963. 4.50x (ISBN 0-210-34087-8). Asia.

INDIA–CHURCH HISTORY

Appadurai, Arjun. Worship & Conflict Under Colonial Rule: A South India Case. (Cambridge South Asian Studies: No. 27). (Illus.). 282p. 1981. 34.95 (ISBN 0-521-23122-1). Cambridge U Pr.
Lillie, Arthur. India in Primitive Christianity. 2nd ed. 299p. 1981. Repr. of 1893 ed. text ed. 25.00x (ISBN 0-391-02336-5, Pub. by Concept India). Humanities.

INDIA–CIVILIZATION

Ali, Abdullah Yusuf. A Cultural History of India During the British Period. LC 75-41006. Repr. of 1940 ed. 25.50 (ISBN 0-404-14723-2). AMS Pr.
Basham, A. L. Aspects of Ancient Indian Culture. 1981. pap. 2.00x (ISBN 0-210-22664-1). Asia.
Basham, A. L., ed. A Cultural History of India. (Illus.). 642p. 1975. 34.00x (ISBN 0-19-821914-8). Oxford U Pr.
Beck, Brenda E., ed. Perspectives on a Regional Culture: Essays About the Coimbatore Area of South India. 211p. 1979. 18.00x (ISBN 0-7069-0723-X, Pub. by Croom Helm Ltd England). Biblio Dist.
Bhattacharyya, et al, eds. The Cultural Heritage of India, 4 vols. Incl. Vol. 1. Early Phases. Radhakrishnan, S., intro. by. (ISBN 0-87481-560-6); Vol. 2. Itihasas, Puranas, Dharma & Other Shastras (ISBN 0-87481-561-4); Vol. 3. The Philosophies (ISBN 0-87481-562-2); Vol. 4. The Religions (ISBN 0-87481-563-0). (Illus.). 30.00x ea.; Set. 150.00x (ISBN 0-87481-558-4). Vedanta Pr.
Brown, W. Norman. India & Indology. Rocher, Rosane, ed. (Illus.). 1978. 43.50 (ISBN 0-89684-066-2). Orient Bk Dist.
Davids, Thomas W. Buddhist India. LC 78-38349. (Select Bibliographies Reprint Ser). Repr. of 1903 ed. 28.00 (ISBN 0-8369-6766-6). Arno.
Deshpande, Madhav M. & Hook, Peter E., eds. Aryan & Non-Aryan in India. LC 78-60016. (Michigan Papers on South & Southeast Asia: No. 14). 350p. 1979. 16.50x (ISBN 0-89720-012-8); pap. 12.50x (ISBN 0-89148-014-5). Ctr S&SE Asian.
Drekmeier, Charles. Kingship & Community in Early India. LC 62-9565. 1962. 19.50x (ISBN 0-8047-0114-8). Stanford U Pr.
Dumont, Louis. Religion, Politics & History in India: Collected Papers in Indian Sociology. (Le Monde D'outre Mer Passe et Present Etudes: No.34). 1970. text ed. 15.50x (ISBN 90-2791-571-7). Mouton.
Dunbar, George. History of India from Earliest Times to 1939, 2 vols. 1949. Set. 13.00x (ISBN 0-391-01989-9). Humanities.
Dutt, Romesh C. A History of Civilisation in Ancient India, 2 vols. 789p. 1972. Repr. of 1888 ed. Set. 29.50x (ISBN 0-8002-0900-1). Intl Pubns Serv.
Fabri, Charles. Indian Dress. 1977. Repr. of 1960 ed. 4.00x (ISBN 0-8364-0114-X). South Asia Bks.
Fairservis, Walter A., Jr. The Roots of Ancient India: The Archaeology of Early Indian Civilization. 2nd. rev ed. LC 74-33510. xxxiv, 480p. 1975. pap. 7.95 (ISBN 0-226-23429-0, P636, Phoen). U of Chicago Pr.
Ghosh, O. K. The Changing Indian Civilization, Vol. 1, 2. LC 76-52201. 1976. 17.00x ea.; Vol. 1. (ISBN 0-88386-502-5); Vol. 2. (ISBN 0-88386-805-9). South Asia Bks.
Ghurye, G. S. Vedic India. 1979. 44.00x (ISBN 0-8364-0455-6). South Asia Bks.
Gordon, Leonard A. & Miller, Barbara S. A Syllabus of Indian Civilization. LC 70-168868. (Companions to Asian Studies). 182p. 1971. pap. 7.50x (ISBN 0-231-03560-8). Columbia U Pr.
Hawkes, Jacquetta. First Great Civilizations. 1973. 15.95 (ISBN 0-394-46161-4). Knopf.
Isaacs, Harold R. Scratches on Our Minds: American Images of China & India. LC 73-9211. (Illus.). 416p. 1973. Repr. of 1958 ed. lib. bdg. 22.75x (ISBN 0-8371-6983-6, ISSM). Greenwood.
Jha, Akhileshwar. Sexual Designs in Indian Culture. LC 79-901853. 185p. 1979. 12.50x (ISBN 0-7069-0744-2). Intl Pubns Serv.
Joshi, N. P. Iconography of Balarama. 1979. 16.50x (ISBN 0-8364-0538-2). South Asia Bks.
Kanitkar, Helen & Kanitkar, Hemant. Asoka & Indian Civilization. Yapp, Malcolm, et al, eds. (World History Ser.). (Illus.). 32p. (gr. 10). 1980. Repr. lib. bdg. 5.95 (ISBN 0-89908-035-9); pap. text ed. 1.95 (ISBN 0-89908-010-3). Greenhaven.
Kublin, Hyman. India: Selected Readings. rev. ed. LC 72-7637. 230p. (gr. 9-12). 1973. pap. text ed. 6.60 (ISBN 0-395-13929-5, 2-31040). HM.
Lalwani, K. C. The Burden of the Past. LC 75-903169. 1974. 8.50x (ISBN 0-88386-472-X). South Asia Bks.
Levai, Blaise. Ask an Indian About India. (Orig.). 1972. pap. 1.75 (ISBN 0-377-12101-0). Friend Pr.
Lorenzen, David N. The Kapalikas & Kalamukhas: Two Lost Saivite Sects. 1972. 8.25x (ISBN 0-8426-0363-8). Verry.
Macdonell, Arthur A. India's Past: A Survey of Her Literatures, Religions, Languages & Antiquities. LC 78-20481. 1979. Repr. of 1927 ed. text ed. 26.50 (ISBN 0-88355-858-0). Hyperion Conn.
MacRitchie, David, ed. Accounts of the Gypsies of India. LC 75-3461. (Illus.). Repr. of 1886 ed. 24.00 (ISBN 0-404-16893-0). AMS Pr.
Mill, James. The History of British India. Thomas, William, ed. LC 74-11632. (Classics of British Historical Literature Ser). 1975. lib. bdg. 20.00x (ISBN 0-226-52555-4). U of Chicago Pr.
Mook, Jane D. The Secret of the Drumstick Tree. (Orig.). (gr. 1-3). 1972. pap. 1.95 (ISBN 0-377-12701-9). Friend Pr.
Murthy, H. V. & Kamath, S. U. Studies in Indian Culture. (Illus.). 184p. 1973. pap. text ed. 3.75 (ISBN 0-210-22391-X). Asia.
Naipaul, V. S. India: A Wounded Civilization. 1978. pap. 2.95 (ISBN 0-394-72463-1, Vin). Random.
Possehl, Gregory L. Indus Civilization in Saurashtra. 264p. 1981. text ed. 45.00x (ISBN 0-391-02260-1, Pub. by Concept India). Humanities.
Puri, Baij N. India Under the Kushanas. (Illus.). 1965. 7.50x (ISBN 0-685-19319-5). Paragon.
Radhakrishnan, Sarvepalli. Our Heritage. (Orient Paperback Ser.). 156p. (Orig.). 1973. pap. 2.35 (ISBN 0-88253-249-9). Ind-US Inc.
Reiniche, M. L. Les Dieux & les Hommes: Etudes Des Cultes D'un Village Du Tiruneiveli, Inde Du Sud. (Cahiers De L'homme, Nouvelle Serie: No. 18). 1979. pap. text ed. 29.00x (ISBN 2-7193-0460-3). Mouton.
Rice, Edward. Mother India's Children. (Illus.). 1972. pap. 2.95 (ISBN 0-377-12111-8). Friend Pr.
Rolland, Romain. Inde Journal 1915-1943. 628p. 1960. 9.95 (ISBN 0-686-55254-7). French & Eur.
Roy, Girish C. Indian Culture. 1977. write for info. (ISBN 0-686-22664-X). Intl Bk Dist.
Saraswati, Baidyanath. Pottery-Making Cultures & Indian Civilization. 1979. 27.50x (ISBN 0-8364-0321-5). South Asia Bks.
Sharma, R. N. Culture & Civilization As Revealed in the Srauta Sutras. 1977. 14.95 (ISBN 0-89684-191-X). Orient Bk Dist.
Sherwani, H. K. Cultural Trends in Medieval India: Architecture, Painting, Literature, Language. 4.50x (ISBN 0-210-98143-1). Asia.
Singer, Milton, ed. Traditional India: Structure & Change. (American Folklore Society Bibliographical & Special Ser.: No. 10). 356p. 1959. pap. 9.95x (ISBN 0-292-73504-9). U of Tex Pr.
Singhal, D. P. India & World Civilization, Vols. 1 & 2. LC 68-29146. (Illus.). 1969. 25.00 (ISBN 0-87013-143-5). Mich St U Pr.
Symposium on Dravidian Civilization. Papers. Sjoberg, Andree F., ed. LC 72-169898. 1971. 7.50 (ISBN 0-8363-0091-2). Jenkins.
Taddei, Maurizio. India. Hogarth, James, tr. from It. (Archaeologia Mundi Ser.). (Illus.). 264p. 1970. 29.50 (ISBN 0-88254-142-0). Hippocrene Bks.
--India. LC 74-3645. (Monuments of Civilization). (Illus.). 1978. 25.00 (ISBN 0-448-02024-6). G&D.
Terra, Hellmut D. & Paterson, Thomas T. Studies on the Ice Age in India & Associated Human Cultures. LC 76-44795. (Carnegie Institution of Washington Publication: No. 493). Repr. of 1939 ed. 39.00 (ISBN 0-404-15881-1). AMS Pr.
Tyler, Stephen A. India: An Anthropological Perspective. LC 72-76937. (Anthropology Ser.). 278p. 1973. pap. text ed. 11.95 (ISBN 0-87620-415-9); pap. text ed. 10.95 (ISBN 0-87620-414-0). Goodyear.
Vidyarthi, L. P., et al. The Sacred Complex of Kashi: A Microcosm of Indian Civilization. 1979. 20.00x (ISBN 0-8364-0335-5). South Asia Bks.
Voting, Caste, Community, Society: Explorations in Aggregate Data Analysis in India & Bangladesh. 1978. 11.00x (ISBN 0-8364-0297-9). South Asia Bks.
Walimbe, Y. S. Abhinavagupta on Indian Aesthetics. 1980. 9.50x (ISBN 0-8364-0624-9, Pub. by Ajanta). South Asia Bks.

INDIA–COMMERCE

Agarwala, P. N. India's Export Strategy. 384p. 1978. 18.00x (ISBN 0-7069-0653-5, Pub. by Croom Helm Ltd. England). Biblio Dist.
Agrawal, Chandra P. Export Methods & Services in India. 2nd ed. LC 72-902913. 336p. 1972. 7.50x (ISBN 0-8002-1411-0). Intl Pubns Serv.
Chakraborti, Haripada. Trade & Commerce of Ancient India. 354p. 1966. 10.00x (ISBN 0-87471-305-6). Rowman.
Chaudhuri, K. N. Economic Development of India Under the East India Company 1814-58. LC 78-129932. (European Understanding of India Ser). 1971. 34.95 (ISBN 0-521-07933-0). Cambridge U Pr.
Dagli, V., ed. India's Foreign Trade. (Commerce Economic Studies-9). 452p. 1974. text ed. 16.50x (ISBN 0-8426-0594-0). Verry.
Ghatak, S. Rural Money Markets in India. LC 76-905340. 1976. 12.00x (ISBN 0-8364-0463-7). South Asia Bks.
Halder, Animesh. India's Export Pattern: Analysis of Potential Diversification. LC 76-903104. 1976. 9.50x (ISBN 0-88386-503-3). South Asia Bks.
Hasan, Masood. India's Trade Relations with Rupee Payments Countries. 1972. 10.00x (ISBN 0-8426-0371-9). Verry.
Khan, A. & Arora, R. K. Public Enterprise in India. 1975. 12.00 (ISBN 0-686-20293-7). Intl Bk Dist.
Kumar, J. Indo-Chinese Trade: 1793-1833. LC 74-902720. 217p. 1974. 8.50x (ISBN 0-8364-0422-X). South Asia Bks.
Lele, Uma J. Food Grain Marketing in India: Private Performance & Public Policy. LC 75-146111. (Illus.). 1971. 32.50x (ISBN 0-8014-0618-8). Cornell U Pr.
Mathur, B. P. Public Enterprises in Perspective: Aspects of Financial Administration & Control in India. 225p. 1973. 9.50x (ISBN 0-8002-1888-4). Intl Pubns Serv.
Nayyar, D. India's Exports & Export Policies in the 1960's. LC 75-46206. (South Asian Studies). (Illus.). 378p. 1977. 39.95 (ISBN 0-521-21135-2). Cambridge U Pr.
Rangappa, K. S. & Achaya, K. T. Indian Dairy Products. 2nd ed. 1975. pap. 12.50x (ISBN 0-210-26933-2). Asia.
Reynolds, John I. Indian-American Joint Ventures: Business Policy Relationships. LC 77-18587. 1978. pap. text ed. 10.50 (ISBN 0-8191-0403-5). U Pr of Amer.
Sabade, B. R. Chambers of Commerce & Trade Associations in India. 1978. 16.00x (ISBN 0-8364-0235-9). South Asia Bks.
Sen, S. India's Bilateral Payments & Trade Agreements, 1947-8 to 1963-4. 1965. 10.00x (ISBN 0-8426-1507-5). Verry.
Sharma, T. C. & Coutinho, O. Economic & Commercial Geography of India. 2nd rev. ed. (Illus.). 400p. 1980. text ed. 22.50 (ISBN 0-7069-0546-6, Pub. by Vikas India). Advent NY.
--Economic & Commercial Geography of India. (Illus.). 1977. text ed. 13.50x (ISBN 0-7069-0546-6). Verry.
Warmington, E. H. The Commerce Between the Roman Empire & India. 448p. 1974. Repr. lib. bdg. 20.00x (ISBN 0-374-98250-3). Octagon.
Wolf, Martin. H. India's Exports. (World Bank Research Publications Ser.). (Illus.). 216p. 1981. 15.95 (ISBN 0-19-520211-2); pap. 5.95 (ISBN 0-19-520212-0). Oxford U Pr.

INDIA–CONSTITUTIONAL HISTORY

Aggarwala, R. N. National Movement & Constitutional Development of India. 8th ed. 556p. 1973. pap. 8.00x (ISBN 0-8002-1743-8). Intl Pubns Serv.
Bombwall, K. R. Foundations of Indian Federalism. 1967. 10.00x (ISBN 0-210-22721-4). Asia.
Chaube, Shibanikinkar. Constituent Assembly of India: Springboard of Revolution. LC 73-906124. 325p. 1973. 11.25x (ISBN 0-8002-0545-6). Intl Pubns Serv.
Constitution of India for the Younger Reader. 1971. pap. 1.75 (ISBN 0-88253-410-6). Ind-US Inc.
Gledhill, Alan. Republic of India, Development of Its Laws & Constitution. LC 77-98761. Repr. of 1951 ed. lib. bdg. 14.25x (ISBN 0-8371-2813-7, GLRI). Greenwood.
Gupta, D. C. Indian National Movement & Constitutional Development. 1976. 10.50 (ISBN 0-7069-0495-8). Intl Bk Dist.
Kapur, Anup C. Constitutional History of India 1765-1970. 1970. 8.75x (ISBN 0-8426-0174-0). Verry.
Menon, Vapal P. The Story of the Integration of the Indian States. LC 72-4282. (World Affairs Ser.: National & International Viewpoints). (Illus.). 542p. 1972. Repr. of 1956 ed. 25.00 (ISBN 0-405-04575-1). Arno.
Pylee, M. V. Constitutional History of India: 1600-1950. 2nd ed. vii, 163p. 1980. pap. text ed. 6.95 (ISBN 0-210-31169-X). Asia.
--India's Constitution. 3rd rev. ed. (Illus.). ix, 471p. (Orig.). 1980. pap. text ed. 11.95x (ISBN 0-210-33709-5). Asia.
Rana, M. S. Writings on Indian Constitution, 1861-1972. 496p. 1974. text ed. 22.50x (ISBN 0-8426-0710-2). Verry.
Rao, B. Shiva, ed. Framing of India's Constitution, 5 Vols. 1968. Set. 75.00x (ISBN 0-8002-1431-5). Intl Pubns Serv.
Varadachari, V. K. Governor in the Indian Constitution. 1980. 13.00x (ISBN 0-8364-0658-3, Pub. by Heritage India). South Asia Bks.

INDIA–CONSTITUTIONAL LAW

Curtis, L. G. Papers Relating to the Application of the Principle of Dyarchy to the Government of India. 667p. 1972. Repr. of 1920 ed. 45.00x (ISBN 0-7165-2117-2, Pub. by Irish Academic Pr Ireland). Biblio Dist.
Gledhill, Alan. Republic of India, Development of Its Laws & Constitution. LC 77-98761. Repr. of 1951 ed. lib. bdg. 14.25x (ISBN 0-8371-2813-7, GLRI). Greenwood.

Hidayatullah, M. Democracy in India & the Judicial Process. 1966. 5.00x (ISBN 0-210-22707-9). Asia.
Joshi, Ram. The Indian Constitution & Its Working. 1977. 6.00x (ISBN 0-8364-0068-2, Orient Longman). South Asia Bks.
Kagzi, Mangal C. The Kesavananda's Case: His Holiness Kesavananda Bharati v. State of Kerala. 345p. 1973. pap. 9.50x (ISBN 0-8002-1630-X). Intl Pubns Serv.
Khanna, H. R. Judicial Review or Confrontation. 1977. 3.75x (ISBN 0-8364-0024-0). South Asia Bks.
Mukharji, P. B. Critical Problems of the Indian Constitution. 1967. 4.00x (ISBN 0-8002-0540-5). Intl Pubns Serv.
Raman, Sunder. Fundamental Rights in the 42nd Constitutional Amendment, India. 1977. 7.50x (ISBN 0-8364-0054-2). South Asia Bks.
Revankar, Ratna G. The Indian Constitution: A Case Study of Backward Classes. LC 76-120067. 361p. 1971. 20.00 (ISBN 0-8386-7670-7). Fairleigh Dickinson.
Singhvi, L. M. Fundamental Rights & Constitutional Amendment. 740p. 1971. 25.00x (ISBN 0-8002-1438-2). Intl Pubns Serv.

INDIA–DEFENSES

Banerjee, Utpal K. Operational Analysis & Indian Defence. 1980. text ed. 40.50x (ISBN 0-391-01839-6). Humanities.
Bhatia, Shyam. India's Nuclear Bomb. 1980. text ed. 13.95x (ISBN 0-7069-0972-0, Pub. by Vikas India). Advent NY.
Jain, J. P. Nuclear India, Vols. 1-2. LC 74-904225. 1974. 32.50x (ISBN 0-88386-523-8). South Asia Bks.
Subrahmanyam, K. Perspectives in Defense Planning: Perspectives in Defense Planning. LC 72-906832. 201p. 1972. 9.50x (ISBN 0-8002-1787-X). Intl Pubns Serv.

INDIA–DESCRIPTION AND TRAVEL

Allen, Charles, ed. Plain Tales from the Raj: Images of British India in the Twentieth Century. LC 76-8693. (Illus.). 1976. 12.95 (ISBN 0-312-61390-3). St Martin.
Arrian. Anabasis of Alexander, Indica, 2 Vols. (Loeb Classical Library: No. 236, 269). 11.00x ea. Vol. 1, Bks. 1-4 (ISBN 0-674-99260-1). Vol. 2, Bks. 5-7 (ISBN 0-674-99297-0). Harvard U Pr.
Bamboat, Zenobia. Les Voyageurs francais dans l'Inde aux XVIIe et XVIIIe siecles. LC 72-83617. (Bibliothèque d'histoire coloniale). 197p. (Fr.). 1972. Repr. of 1933 ed. lib. bdg. 22.50 (ISBN 0-8337-3964-6). B Franklin.
Bendall, Cecil. A Journey in Nepal & Northern India. (Illus.). 1975. 5.95x (ISBN 0-685-89508-4). Himalaya Hse.
Blaise, Clark & Mukherjee, Bharati. Days & Nights in Calcutta. LC 75-40711. 240p. 1977. 8.95 (ISBN 0-385-02895-4). Doubleday.
Blavatsky, Helena P. The Caves & Jungles of Hindustan. De Zirkoff, Boris, ed. LC 74-26605. (Illus.). 750p. 1975. 14.50 (ISBN 0-8356-0219-2). Theos Pub Hse.
Bonsels, Waldemar. An Indian Journey. 1928. 20.00 (ISBN 0-686-17223-X). Scholars Ref Lib.
--An Indian Journey. 1977. Repr. of 1928 ed. lib. bdg. 20.00 (ISBN 0-8492-0300-7). R West.
Borooah, Anundoram. Ancient Geography of India. 120p. 1971. Repr. of 1877 ed. 7.50x (ISBN 0-8002-0435-2). Intl Pubns Serv.
Buckhory, Somduth. The Call of the Ganges: Recollections of a Magical Journey Through India. 1979. 18.00x (ISBN 0-7069-0724-8, Pub. by Vikas India). Advent NY.
Carpenter, Edward. Visit to a Gnani. 65p. 1971. Repr. of 1902 ed. 4.00 (ISBN 0-911662-44-8). Yoga.
Casimaty, Nina, ed. India & Nepal: A Travel Handbook. 1979. pap. 4.00x (ISBN 0-686-19964-2). Intl Learn Syst.
Corbett, Jim. Jim Corbett's India: Stories Selected by R. E. Hawkins. Hawkins, R. E., ed. (Illus.). 1979. 14.95 (ISBN 0-19-212968-6). Oxford U Pr.
Coryate, Thomas. T. Coryate Traveller for the English Wits: Greetings from the Court of the Great Mogul. LC 68-54628. (English Experience Ser.: No. 30). 56p. 1968. Repr. of 1616 ed. 9.50 (ISBN 90-221-0030-8). Walter J Johnson.
Coverte, Robert. A True & Almost Incredible Report of an Englishman That Travelled by Land Throw Many Kingdomes. LC 72-186. (English Experience Ser.: No. 302). 1971. Repr. of 1612 ed. 11.50 (ISBN 90-221-0302-1). Walter J Johnson.
Cunningham, Alexander. The Bhilsa Topes; or Buddhist Monuments of Central India. LC 78-72401. Repr. of 1854 ed. 47.50 (ISBN 0-404-17263-6). AMS Pr.
Della Valle, Pietro. The Travels of Pietro Della Valle to India, 2 Vols. Grey, Edward, ed. Hovers, G., tr. (Illus.). 58.00 (ISBN 0-8337-0822-8). B Franklin.
Del Vasto, Lanza. Return to the Source. Sidgwick, Jean, tr. from Fr. LC 70-169817. 319p. 1972. 6.95x (ISBN 0-8052-3441-1). Schocken.
De Rochon, Alexis M. A Voyage to Madagascar & the East Indies. Repr. of 1792 ed. 35.50 (ISBN 0-384-51590-8). Johnson Repr.
Dey, Nundo Lal. The Geographical Dictionary of Ancient & Mediaeval India. LC 42-31336. (Illus.). 272p. 1971. Repr. of 1927 ed. 19.50x (ISBN 0-8002-1453-6). Intl Pubns Serv.
Dutt, Ashok K. India in Maps. (Illus.). 1976. pap. text ed. 6.95 (ISBN 0-8403-1355-1). Kendall-Hunt.
Fa-Hsien. Travels of Fah-Hian & Sung-Yun, Buddhist Pilgrims from China to India. Beal, Samuel, tr. LC 67-66343. Repr. of 1869 ed. 12.50x (ISBN 0-678-07259-0). Kelley.
Farewell, Christopher. An East-India Colation. LC 72-171756. (No. 380). 102p. 1971. Repr. of 1633 ed. 9.50 (ISBN 90-221-0380-3). Walter J Johnson.
Farley, M. Foster. Indian Summer: An Account of a Visit to India. 211p. 1977. pap. text ed. 9.50 (ISBN 0-8191-0051-X). U Pr of Amer.
Fernandez De Figueroa, Martin. Spaniard in the Portuguese Indies: The Narrative of Martin Fernandez De Figueroa. McKenna, James B., ed. LC 67-27089. (Studies in Romance Languages: No. 31). 1967. 12.00x (ISBN 0-674-83085-7). Harvard U Pr.
Foster, W., ed. Early Travels in India, 1583-1619. 1968. Repr. 8.25x (ISBN 0-8426-1261-0). Verry.
Foster, William, compiled by. Early Travels in India: Fifteen Eighty-Three to Sixteen Nineteen. LC 70-179196. (Illus.). Repr. of 1921 ed. 26.00 (ISBN 0-404-54825-3). AMS Pr.
Hall, Basil. Travels in India, Ceylon, & Borneo. Rawlinson, H. G., ed. LC 76-174846. Repr. of 1931 ed. 15.00 (ISBN 0-405-08593-1, Blom Pubns). Arno.
Herbert, Sir Thomas. A Relation of Some Yeares Travaile Begunne Anno 1626, into Afrique & the Greater Asia. LC 76-25706. (English Experience Ser.: No. 349). 1971. Repr. of 1634 ed. 42.00 (ISBN 90-221-0349-8). Walter J Johnson.
Husaini, Khwaza K. Ma'asir-I-Jahanjiri: A Contemporary Account of Jahangir. Nizami, Azra, ed. & tr. 537p. (Persian & Eng.). 1978. lib. bdg. 35.00x (ISBN 0-210-40566-X). Asia.
Huxley, Aldous L. Jesting Pilate: An Intellectual Holiday. LC 74-11882. (Illus.). 326p. 1974. Repr. of 1926 ed. lib. bdg. 20.75x (ISBN 0-8371-7698-0, HUJP). Greenwood.
Jacquemont, Victor. Letters from India, Describing a Journey in the British Dominions of India, Tibet, Lahore & Cashmere, During the Years 1828-31, 2 vols. (Oxford in Asia Historical Reprints). (Illus.). 1976. 39.95x (ISBN 0-19-577216-4). Oxford U Pr.
Jordanus, Friar. Mirabilia Descripta: The Wonders of the East. 1967. Repr. 23.50 (ISBN 0-8337-1876-2). B Franklin.
Kaul, H. H. Travels in South Asia: A Selected & Annotated Bibliography of Guide-Books & Travel-Books on South Asia. 1979. text ed. 30.00x (ISBN 0-391-01288-6). Humanities.
Kaul, H. K. Travellers' India: An Anthology. 535p. 1980. 24.00x (ISBN 0-19-560654-X). Oxford U Pr.
Lach, Donald F. India in the Eyes of Europe: The Sixteenth Century. LC 64-19848. 1968. pap. 1.95 (ISBN 0-226-46745-7, P293, Phoen). U of Chicago Pr.
Lewis, Alun. In the Green Tree: Home Letters & Short Stories. 1949. text ed. 2.95x (ISBN 0-04-823031-6). Allen Unwin.
Locke, John C., ed. First Englishmen in India. LC 75-10575. Repr. of 1930 ed. 18.00 (ISBN 0-404-00615-9). AMS Pr.
Lopes de Castanheda, Fernam. The First Booke of the Discouerie & Conquest of the East Indias. Lichefild, N., tr. LC 72-6014. (English Experience Ser.: No. 539). 340p. 1973. Repr. of 1582 ed. 36.00 (ISBN 90-221-0539-3). Walter J Johnson.
Major, Richard H., ed. India in the Fifteenth Century. LC 79-134708. (Hakluyt Society Ser.: No. 22). 1970. lib. bdg. 26.00 (ISBN 0-8337-2189-5). B Franklin.
Mirchandani, G. G. Reporting India, 1973. annual LC 75-903643. 1975. 10.00 (ISBN 0-88386-591-2). South Asia Bks.
Moore, Fred W. Texas Short Stories & a Look at Puerto Rico. LC 78-64775. 57p. 1980. 4.95 (ISBN 0-533-04043-4). Vantage.
Muehl, John F. Interview with India. 1950. 8.50 (ISBN 0-8495-3856-4). Arden Lib.
Murphy, Dervla. On a Shoestring to Coorg. 1977. 18.50 (ISBN 0-7195-3284-1). Transatlantic.
Nagel Travel Guide to India & the Nepal. (Nagel Travel Guide Ser.). (Illus.). 816p. 1973. 55.00 (ISBN 2-8263-0023-7). Hippocrene Bks.
Natarajan, B. The City of the Cosmic Dance. LC 75-904414. 1975. 10.00x (ISBN 0-88386-611-0, Orient Longman). South Asia Bks.
Oaten, Edward F. European Travellers in India During the 15th, 16th & 17th Centuries. LC 75-137279. Repr. of 1909 ed. 21.45 (ISBN 0-404-04808-0). AMS Pr.
Rao, Shikaripur R. Lothal & the Indus Civilization. (Illus.). 215p. 1973. lib. bdg. 35.00x (ISBN 0-210-22278-6). Asia.
Reconstructing India. 1930. 12.50 (ISBN 0-685-72788-2). Norwood Edns.
Richardson, Jane. Tender Hearts of India. (Illus.). 255p. 1972. 13.00x (ISBN 0-8002-0982-6). Intl Pubns Serv.
Sharma, R. C. Settlement Geography of the Indian Desert. LC 72-906182. (Illus.). 209p. 1974. 12.50x (ISBN 0-8002-1971-6). Intl Pubns Serv.
Stein, Marc A. On Alexander's Track in the Indus: Personal Narrative of the Explorations on the North-West Frontier of India. LC 72-79947. (Illus.). Repr. of 1929 ed. 22.00 (ISBN 0-405-08995-3). Arno.
Strachey & Winterbottom. Catalogue of the Plants of Kumaon: And of the Adjacent Portions of Garhwal & Tibet. 1978. Repr. of 1918 ed. 12.50x (ISBN 0-89955-256-0, Pub. by Intl Bk Dist). Intl Schol Bk Serv.
Thapar, Raj, ed. The Invincible Traveller. (Illus.). 1980. text ed. 22.50x (ISBN 0-7069-0828-7, Pub. by Vikas India). Advent NY.
Thomson, Thomas. Western Himalayas & Tibet. 501p. 1978. Repr. of 1852 ed. 22.00 (ISBN 0-89684-155-3, Pub. by Cosmo Pubns India). Orient Bk Dist.
Tod, James. Travels in Western India. LC 4-29239. 558p. 1971. Repr. of 1839 ed. 25.00x (ISBN 0-8002-2106-0). Intl Pubns Serv.
Trevelyan, George O. The Competition Wallah. 2nd corr. ed. LC 75-41272. Repr. of 1866 ed. 25.00 (ISBN 0-404-14782-8). AMS Pr.
Valiappa, Al. Story of Our Rivers: Book II. (Nehru Library for Children). (Illus.). (gr. 1-9). 1979. pap. 1.50 (ISBN 0-89744-184-2). Auromere.
Watters, Thomas. On Yuan Chwang's Travels in India 629-645 A. D. LC 74-158213. Repr. of 1905 ed. Set. 20.00 (ISBN 0-404-06878-2). AMS Pr.
Wiles, John. The Grand Trunk Road. 1974. 9.95 (ISBN 0-236-15445-1, Pub. by Paul Elek). Merrimack Bk Serv.

INDIA–DESCRIPTION AND TRAVEL–GUIDEBOOKS

Bhardwaj, Surinder M. Hindu Places of Pilgrimage in India: A Study in Cultural Geography. LC 73-174454. (Illus.). 1973. 27.50x (ISBN 0-520-02135-5). U of Cal Pr.
Brandis, Dietrich. The Forest Flora of North-West & Central India: A Handbook of the Indigenous Trees & Shrubs of Those Countries, 2 vols. 1978. Repr. of 1874 ed. Set. 40.00x (ISBN 0-89955-276-5, Pub. by Intl Bk Dist). Intl Schol Bk Serv.
Casimaty, Nina, ed. India & Nepal: A Travel Handbook 1979-1980. (Illus.). 56p. (Orig.). 1979. pap. 6.50x (ISBN 0-8002-2430-2). Intl Pubns Serv.
Crowe, Sylvia, et al. The Gardens of Mughul India: A History & a Guide. (Illus.). 1977. 12.95 (ISBN 0-500-01078-1). Thames Hudson.
Engstrom, Barbie. India Nepal & Sri Lanka: A Guide to a Travel Experience. (Engstrom's Travel Experience Guide Ser.). (Illus.). 228p. (Orig.). 1981. pap. 14.50 (ISBN 0-916588-06-8). Kurios Pr.
Fodor's India, 1981. 1980. 14.95 (ISBN 0-679-00696-6). McKay.
Hoover, Dwight W. A Pictorial History of Indiana. LC 80-7806. 304p. 1981. 19.95x (ISBN 0-253-14693-3). Ind U Pr.
Nagel's Encyclopedia Guide: India & Nepal. (Illus.). 832p. 1980. 55.00 (ISBN 0-686-74058-0). Masson Pub.
Palmer, Paige. Travel Guide to North India. LC 79-28672. 1980. pap. 3.95 (ISBN 0-87576-088-0). Pilot Bks.
Prendergast, John. The Road to India: Guide to the Overland Routes to India. (Illus.). 1978. 18.00 (ISBN 0-7195-3396-1). Transatlantic.
Schettler, Margaret & Schettler, Rolf. Kashmir, Ladakh & Zanskar. (Travel Paperbacks Ser.). (Illus.). 192p. 1981. pap. 5.95 (ISBN 0-908086-21-0, Pub. by Lonely Planet Australia). Hippocrene Bks.

INDIA–DICTIONARIES AND ENCYCLOPEDIAS

Garrett, John. Classical Dictionary of India, 2 vols. in 1. 1973. Repr. of 1873 ed. 51.50 (ISBN 0-8337-1289-6). B Franklin.
--A Classical Dictionary of India. LC 41-40430. 806p. 1971. Repr. of 1871 ed. 22.50x (ISBN 0-8002-0294-5). Intl Pubns Serv.
Kurian, George T. Historical & Cultural Dictionary of India. LC 76-16186. (Historical & Cultural Dictionaries of Asia Ser.: No. 8). 1976. 14.50 (ISBN 0-8108-0951-6). Scarecrow.
Sharma, Jagdish S. The National Geographical Dictionary of India. LC 72-929631. 350p. 1972. 11.25x (ISBN 0-8002-0942-7). Intl Pubns Serv.
Watt, George. A Dictionary of the Economic Products of India. 6 vols. in 10. 5450p. 1972. Repr. of 1889 ed. Set. 300.00x (ISBN 0-8002-0198-1). Intl Pubns Serv.
--A Dictionary of the Economic Products of India, 6 vols. 1978. Repr. of 1889 ed. Set. 324.00 (ISBN 0-89955-259-5, Pub. by Intl Bk Dist). Intl Schol Bk Serv.

INDIA–ECONOMIC CONDITIONS

Agarwal, A. N. Indian Economy. 5th ed. LC 75-907913. 864p. 1979. 18.50x (ISBN 0-7069-0391-9). Intl Pubns Serv.
Agarwala, Ramgopal. Econometric Model of India, 1848-1961. 188p. 1970. 27.50x (ISBN 0-7146-1200-6, F Cass Co). Biblio Dist.
Ahuja, K. Idle Labour in Village India: A Study of Rajasthan. 1978. 12.50x (ISBN 0-8364-0280-4). South Asia Bks.
Ahuja, Ram. Female Offenders in India. (Illus.). 1969. 5.00x (ISBN 0-8002-0637-1). Intl Pubns Serv.
Alden, Dauril & Dean, Warren, eds. Essays Concerning the Socioeconomic History of Brazil & Portuguese India. LC 76-53761. (Illus.). 1977. 12.50 (ISBN 0-8130-0565-5). U Presses Fla.
Aquique, M. Economic History of Mithila. 1974. 9.00x (ISBN 0-88386-481-9). South Asia Bks.
Balasubramanyam, V. N. International Transfer of Technology to India. LC 73-163952. (Special Studies in International Economics & Development). 1973. 28.50x (ISBN 0-275-28245-7). Irvington.
Balfour, Edward G. Cyclopaedia of India & of Eastern & Southern Asia: Commercial, Industrial & Scientific; Products of Mineral, Vegetable & Animal Kindoms, Useful Arts & Manufactures, 3 vols. 3rd ed. LC 5-12913. 3632p. 1968. Repr. of 1885 ed. Set. 387.50x (ISBN 3-201-00028-0). Intl Pubns Serv.
Banerjea, Pramathanath. Indian Finance in the Days of the Company. (Perspectives in Asian History: No. 5). Repr. of 1928 ed. lib. bdg. 25.00x (ISBN 0-87991-820-9). Porcupine Pr.
Bansil, P. C. Agricultural Problems of India. 2nd ed. 1977. 11.00x (ISBN 0-686-26275-1). Intl Bk Dist.
Barber, William J. British Economic Thought & India Sixteen Hundred to Eighteen Fifty-Eight: A Study in the History of Development Economics. 264p. 1975. 42.00x (ISBN 0-19-828265-6). Oxford U Pr.
Bergmann, Theodore. The Development Models of India, the Soviet Union & China. (Publications of European Soc. for Rural Sociology Ser.: No. 1). (Illus.). 1977. pap. text ed. 31.25x (ISBN 90-232-1497-8). Humanities.
Bhardwaj, R. K. Urban Development in India. 1974. text ed. 21.00x (ISBN 0-8426-0654-8). Verry.
Bhatia, B. M. Poverty, Agriculture & Economic Growth. 1977. 15.00x (ISBN 0-7069-0524-5). Intl Bk Dist.
Bhatia, H. L. Centre-State Financial Relations in India. 1979. 11.00x (ISBN 0-8364-0323-1). South Asia Bks.
Bliss, C. J. & Stern, N. H. Palanpur: The Economy of an Indian Village. (Illus.). 464p. 1981. 37.50 (ISBN 0-19-828419-5). Oxford U Pr.
Bose, Atindranath N. Social & Rural Economy of Northern India, 600 B. C.-200 A.D, 2 vols. 2nd rev. ed. (Illus.). 1961. 10.00x (ISBN 0-8426-1175-4). Verry.
Brahmanda, P. R., et al, eds. Indian Economic Development & Policy: Essays in Honour of Professor V. L. D'souza. 352p. 1979. 26.00x (ISBN 0-7069-0683-7, Pub. by Croom Helm Ltd. England). Biblio Dist.
Buchanan, Daniel H. Development of Capitalistic Enterprise in India. 489p. 1966. Repr. 32.50x (ISBN 0-7146-1998-1, F Cass Co). Biblio Dist.
Butani, D. H. The Economic Story of Modern India. LC 73-903799. 182p. 1973. 5.00x (ISBN 0-8002-0589-8). Intl Pubns Serv.
Cassen, R. H. India: Population, Economy, Society. LC 77-16217. 1978. text ed. 39.50x (ISBN 0-8419-0300-X); pap. text ed. 16.95x (ISBN 0-8419-0648-3). Holmes & Meier.
Chakraborty, S. K. Managerial Development & Appraisal: Empirical Perspectives India. 1978. 15.00x (ISBN 0-8364-0135-2). South Asia Bks.
Chaudhuri, Asim. Private Economic Power in India: A Study in Genesis & Concentration. LC 76-900858. 1976. 10.00x (ISBN 0-88386-777-6). South Asia Bks.
Chaudhuri, K. N. Economic Development of India Under the East India Company 1814-58. LC 78-129932. (European Understanding of India Ser). 1971. 34.95 (ISBN 0-521-07933-0). Cambridge U Pr.
Chaudhuri, K. N. & Dewey, Clive J., eds. Economy & Society: Essays in Indian Economic & Social History. (Illus.). 1979. 16.95x (ISBN 0-19-561073-3). Oxford U Pr.
Chaudhuri, Pramit. The Indian Economy: Poverty & Development. LC 77-88457. 1979. 18.95x (ISBN 0-312-41378-5). St Martin.

Das, Binod S. Studies in the Economic History of Orissa from Ancient Times to 1833. 1978. 11.50x (ISBN 0-8364-0200-6). South Asia Bks.
Das, D. Economic History of the Deccan: From the 1st to the 6th Century A.D. 1969. 11.00x (ISBN 0-8426-1227-0). Verry.
Datt, Ruddar & Sundharam, K. P. Indian Economy (India) 10th ed. 658p. 1975. pap. text ed. 8.50x (ISBN 0-8426-0765-X). Verry.
Datta, Kalikinkar. Survey of India's Social Life & Economic Condition in the 18th Century, 1707-1813. 2nd rev. ed. 1978. 17.50x (ISBN 0-8002-0265-1). Intl Pubns Serv.
Desai, A. R. Recent Trends in Indian Nationalism. 2nd ed. LC 61-4018. 149p. 1973. 6.50x (ISBN 0-8002-1903-1). Intl Pubns Serv.
Du Mesnil-Marigny, Jules. Histoire De l'Economie Politique Des Anciens Peuples De l'Inde, De l'Egypte, De la Judee et De la Grece, 3 Vols. 3rd ed. 1967. Repr. of 1878 ed. 69.50 (ISBN 0-8337-4800-9). B Franklin.
Dutt, Romesh C. The Economic History of India. Incl. Vol. 1. The Economic History of Early British Rule; Vol. 2. India in the Victorian Age. LC 79-80224. 1902-04. Repr. Set. 46.50 (ISBN 0-8337-0981-X). B Franklin.
--Economic History of India, 2 vols. 2nd ed. LC 67-30372. Repr. of 1906 ed. 37.50x set (ISBN 0-678-06515-2). Kelley.
Eby, John W. Hindustan: As Seen by John. (Illus.). 1977. pap. 3.00 (ISBN 0-932218-05-9). Hall Pr.
Ellinwood, DeWitt, ed. India & World War One. 1978. 12.50x (ISBN 0-8364-0191-3). South Asia Bks.
Ezekiel, Hannan & Pavaskar, Madhoo. Second India Studies: Services. 1976. 4.50x (ISBN 0-333-90155-X). South Asia Bks.
Factors Which Hinder or Help Productivity Improvementt: Country Report-India. 149p. 1980. pap. 7.75 (ISBN 92-833-1468-9, APO102, APO). Unipub.
Furber, Holden. John Company at Work. LC 70-96181. 1969. Repr. lib. bdg. 24.00x (ISBN 0-374-92945-9). Octagon.
Furnivall, John S. Netherlands India: A Study of Plural Economy. LC 77-86961. Repr. of 1944 ed. 34.50 (ISBN 0-404-16712-8). AMS Pr.
Ganguli, B. N. & Gupta, D. B. Levels of Living in India: An Inter-State Profile. 1976. text ed. 13.50x (ISBN 0-8426-0920-2). Verry.
Gautam, V. Aspects of Indian Society & Economy in the Nineteenth Century. 1972. 6.00 (ISBN 0-8426-0473-1). Orient Bk Dist.
--Aspects of Indian Society & Economy in the 19th Century: A Study Based on an Evaluation of the American Consular Records. 201p. 1973. text ed. 8.25x (ISBN 0-8426-0473-1). Verry.
George, P. S. Oilseeds Economy of India. 1978. 11.00x (ISBN 0-8364-0243-X). South Asia Bks.
Gopal, Lallanji. Economic Life of Northern India: C. A.D. 700-1200. 1965. 7.00x (ISBN 0-8426-1278-5). Verry.
Gordon, A. D. Businessmen & Politics: Rising Nationalism & a Modernising Economy in Bombay, 1918-1933. 1978. 15.00 (ISBN 0-8364-0194-8). South Asia Bks.
Gujral, M. L. Economic Failures of Nehru & Indira Gandhi. 1980. text ed. 18.95x (ISBN 0-7069-0835-X, Pub. by Vikas India). Advent NY.
Gupta, Satish C. Food Prices in India. LC 77-917209. (Illus.). 1970. 8.00x (ISBN 0-8002-0631-2). Intl Pubns Serv.
Harris, Nigel. India--China: Underdevelopment & Revolution. LC 74-30894. 1974. 10.00 (ISBN 0-89089-017-X). Carolina Acad Pr.
Harriss, John. Capitalism & Peasant Farming: Agrarian Structure & Ideology in Northern Tamil Nadu. (Illus.). 330p. 1981. 24.00 (ISBN 0-19-561340-6). Oxford U Pr.
Hazari, Bharat. Structure of the Indian Economy. 1981. 12.50x (ISBN 0-8364-0675-3, Pub. by Macmillan India). South Asia Bks.
Jain, P. C. Socio-Economic Exploration of Medieval India. LC 76-904842. 1976. 17.50x (ISBN 0-88386-884-9). South Asia Bks.
Jayaraman, T. K. Economic Cooperation in the Indian Subcontinent. 1978. 7.00x (ISBN 0-8364-0174-3, Orient Longman). South Asia Bks.
Kessinger, Tom G. Vilyatpur 1848-1968: Social & Economic Change in a North Indian Village. LC 72-89788. (Illus.). 1974. 24.50x (ISBN 0-520-02340-4). U of Cal Pr.
Khan, M. Y. Indian Financial System. LC 80-904855. 464p. 1980. text ed. 27.50x (ISBN 0-7069-1101-6, Pub. by Vikas India). Advent NY.
Kher, N. N. Agrarian & Fiscal Economy in the Mauryan Age. 1973. 12.50 (ISBN 0-89684-168-5). Orient Bk Dist.
Kotwal, O. P. Indian Economy in Soviet Perspective. 158p. 1979. 10.00x (ISBN 0-8002-1005-0). Intl Pubns Serv.
Krishnaswami, K. S., et al, eds. Society & Change: Essays in Honor of Sachin Chaudhuri. (Illus.). 1978. 11.25x (ISBN 0-19-560942-5). Oxford U Pr.
Kulkarni, M. R. Industrial Development. (India; Land & People Ser.). (Illus.). 327p. 1973. 3.75x (ISBN 0-8426-0513-4). Verry.
Kumar, Dharma. India & the European Economic Community. 1967. 8.50x (ISBN 0-210-27182-5). Asia.
Kurien, C. R. Economic Changes in Tamil Nadu. 1979. 20.00x (ISBN 0-8364-0545-5). South Asia Bks.
Kuznets, Simon S., et al, eds. Economic Growth: Brazil, India, Japan. LC 55-9491. 1955. 22.50 (ISBN 0-8223-0103-2). Duke.
Lajpat Rai, Lala. Unhappy India. rev. 2nd enl. ed. LC 72-171642. Repr. of 1928 ed. 36.45 (ISBN 0-404-03803-4). AMS Pr.
Lal, Ram N. Capital Formation & Its Financing in India. 1977. 14.00x (ISBN 0-8364-0081-X). South Asia Bks.
Lamb, Helen B. Studies on India & Vietnam. Lamont, Corliss, ed. LC 76-1668. 288p. 1976. 16.50 (ISBN 0-85345-384-5, CL3845). Monthly Rev.
Lee, Terence R. Residential Water Demand & Economic Development. LC 75-429791. 1969. 6.00x (ISBN 0-8020-3245-1). U of Toronto Pr.
Lewis, John P. Quiet Crisis in India: Economic Development & American Policy. LC 73-16742. 350p. 1974. Repr. of 1962 ed. lib. bdg. 17.25x (ISBN 0-8371-7225-X, LEQC). Greenwood.
Maddison, Angus. Class Structure & Economic Growth: India & Pakistan Since the Moghuls. 1972. 7.95x (ISBN 0-393-05467-5, 05467); pap. 3.95x (ISBN 0-393-09399-9). Norton.
Maitra, Priyatosh. Underdevelopment Revisited. 1977. 7.00x (ISBN 0-8364-0075-5). South Asia Bks.
Maity, S. K. Economic Life in Northern India in the Gupta Period (Ctr. 300-500 A.D.) 2nd rev. ed. 1970. 6.50 (ISBN 0-89684-199-5). Orient Bk Dist.
Maity, Sachindra K. Economic Life in Northern India in the Gupta Period. rev. 2nd ed. 1970. 7.50x (ISBN 0-8426-0130-9). Verry.
Mal, Dilip K. Distribution of Income & Wealth in India During Five Year Plans. 1981. 9.00x (ISBN 0-8364-0735-0, Pub. by Mukhopadhyay). South Asia Bks.
Malyaro, V. The Role of the State in the Socio-Economic Structure of India. 400p. 1981. text ed. 45.00x (ISBN 0-7069-1372-8, Pub. by Vikas India). Advent NY.
Manmohan Singh, H. K. Demand Theory & Economic Calculation in a Mixed Economy. 1980. 11.50x (ISBN 0-8364-0577-3, Pub. by Macmillan India). South Asia Bks.
Mayo, Katherine. Mother India. Repr. of 1928 ed. lib. bdg. 22.50 (ISBN 0-8371-2309-7, MAMO). Greenwood.
Mehta, Balraj. Crisis of Indian Economy. 1974. text ed. 6.00x (ISBN 0-8426-0536-3). Verry.
--India & the World Oil Crisis. 1974. text ed. 7.50x (ISBN 0-8426-0691-2). Verry.
Mehta, Vadilal. Equality Through Trusteeship: India. 1977. 16.00x (ISBN 0-8364-0119-0). South Asia Bks.
Mencher, Joan P. Agriculture & Social Structure in Tamil Nadu: Past Origins, Present Transformations & Future Prospects. LC 77-80768. 1978. 15.95 (ISBN 0-89089-101-X). Carolina Acad Pr.
Moreland, William H. From Akbar to Auranqzeb: A Study in Indian Economic History. LC 77-180363. Repr. of 1923 ed. 27.50 (ISBN 0-404-56298-1). AMS Pr.
Mote, V. L., et al. Managerial Economics: Concepts & Cases-India. 1977. 8.00x (ISBN 0-8364-0431-9). South Asia Bks.
Murty, T. S. Frontiers: A Changing Concept. 1978. 18.50x (ISBN 0-8364-0175-1). South Asia Bks.
Nandy, Ashis & Owens, Raymond L. The New Vaisyas: Enterpreneurial Opportunity & Entrepreneurial Response in the Engineering Industry of an Indian City. LC 77-93390. 1978. 13.95 (ISBN 0-89089-057-9). Carolina Acad Pr.
Nanjundappa, D. M. Inter-Governmental Financial Relations in India. 132p. 1974. text ed. 9.00x (ISBN 0-8426-0725-0). Verry.
Negandhi, Anant R. Private Foreign Investment Climate in India. LC 65-64809. 1965. pap. 2.50 (ISBN 0-87744-075-1). Mich St U Busn.
Nilakanta-Sastri, K. A. Life & Culture of the Indian People: A Historical Survey. rev. 2nd ed. LC 74-903185. 284p. 1974. 9.00x (ISBN 0-85655-131-7). Intl Pubns Serv.
Pandit, Yeshwant S. India's Balance of Indebtedness: Eighteen Ninety-Eight to Nineteen Thirteen. Wilkins, Mira, ed. LC 78-3944. (International Finance Ser.). 1978. Repr. of 1937 ed. lib. bdg. 14.00x (ISBN 0-405-11244-0). Arno.
Pani, P. K. Macroeconomic Model of the Indian Economy. 1977. 13.50x (ISBN 0-8364-0088-7). South Asia Bks.
Patwardhan, Sunanda. Change Among India's Harijans: Maharashtra. (Illus.). 239p. 1973. 12.50x (ISBN 0-8002-0289-9). Intl Pubns Serv.
Pillai, S. Devadas, ed. Winners & Losers: Styles of Development & Change in an Indian Region. Baks, C. 407p. 1979. text ed. 36.00 (ISBN 0-8426-1679-9). Verry.
Prasad, D. N. External Resources in Economic Development in India. LC 72-900960. 450p. 1972. 15.00x (ISBN 0-8002-0597-9). Intl Pubns Serv.
Prasad, K. & Verma, P. Impact of Computers on Employment. 1977. 7.50x (ISBN 0-333-90176-2). South Asia Bks.
Prasad, Narmadeshwar. Change Strategy in a Developing Society: India. 1970. 9.00x (ISBN 0-8426-0168-6). Verry.
Raj, Jagdish. Economic Conflict in North India: A Study of Landlord-Tenant Relations in Oudh, 1870-1890. 1979. 14.50x (ISBN 0-8364-0339-8). South Asia Bks.
Rastogi, S. R. Wage Regulation in India. 1979. text ed. 13.50x (ISBN 0-8426-1620-9). Verry.
Ray, S. K. Economics of the Black Market. (Replica Edition Ser.). 250p. 1981. lib. bdg. 20.00x (ISBN 0-86531-149-8). Westview.
Raza, Moonis, et al, eds. Sources of Economic & Social Statistics of India. 1979. 24.00x (ISBN 0-8364-0536-6, Pub. by Eureka India). South Asia Bks.
Rothermund, D., et al, eds. Urban Growth & Rural Stagnation: Studies in the Economy of an Indian Coalfield & Its Hinterland. 1980. 36.00x (ISBN 0-8364-0662-1, Pub. by Manohar India). South Asia Bks.
Roy, Ajit. Economics & Politics of Garibi Hatao. LC 67-3054. 148p. 1973. 7.50x (ISBN 0-8002-0586-3). Intl Pubns Serv.
Saletore, R. N. Early Indian Economic History. (Illus.). 859p. 1975. 29.50x (ISBN 0-87471-599-7). Rowman.
Sasaki, Genjun H. Social & Humanistic Life in India. LC 74-924045. 291p. 1974. 11.25x (ISBN 0-8002-1984-8). Intl Pubns Serv.
Sen, Sudhir. Turning the Tide: A Strategy to Conquer Hunger & Poverty. 1978. 11.00x (ISBN 0-8364-0260-X). South Asia Bks.
Sengupta, Nirmal. Destitutes & Development. 1979. text ed. 9.00x (ISBN 0-391-01864-7). Humanities.
Sethuraman, T. V. Institutional Financing of Economic Development in India. 1970. 7.00x (ISBN 0-8426-0009-4). Verry.
Shah, C. H. India in Perspective: Development Issues, Vol. 3. 1979. text ed. 15.00x (ISBN 0-8426-1108-8). Verry.
Sharma, Arvind. The Hindu Scriptural Value System & the Economic Development of India. x, 113p. 1980. text ed. 15.00x (ISBN 0-86590-004-3). Apt Bks.
Sharma, D. P & Desai, V. V. Rural Economy of India. 1980. pap. 12.50 (ISBN 0-7069-1049-4, Pub. by Vikas India). Advent NY.
Sharma, J. N. Union & the States: A Study in Fiscal Federalism - India. 1974. text ed. 15.00x (ISBN 0-8426-0648-3). Verry.
Sharma, K. S. Institutional Structure at Capital Market in India. 307p. 1969. 9.00x (ISBN 0-8426-0456-1). Verry.
Sharma, R. K. Foreign Aid to India: An Economic Study. 1977. 11.00x (ISBN 0-8364-0064-X). South Asia Bks.
Sharma, R. S., ed. Land Revenues in India: Historical Studies. 1971. 4.00 (ISBN 0-89684-239-8). Orient Bk Dist.
Sharma, T. C. & Coutinho, O. Economic & Commercial Geography of India. 2nd rev. ed. (Illus.). 400p. 1980. text ed. 22.50 (ISBN 0-7069-0546-6, Pub. by Vikas India). Advent NY.
Shirokov, G. K. Industrialisation of India. 326p. 1975. 17.95x (ISBN 0-8464-0514-8). Beekman Pubs.
Singh, A. K. Impact of American Aid on Indian Economy. 175p. 1974. text ed. 5.50x (ISBN 0-8426-0597-5). Verry.
Singh, Tarlok. India's Development Experience. LC 74-76686. 350p. 1975. 29.95 (ISBN 0-312-41405-6). St Martin.
Singh, V. B. Social & Economic Change in India. 1967. 7.50x (ISBN 0-8188-1138-2). Paragon.
--Wage Patterns, Mobility & Savings of Workers in India. 220p. 1973. 8.50x (ISBN 0-8426-0524-X). Verry.
Sinha, P. R. Wage Determination. 362p. 1972. lib. bdg. 10.00 (ISBN 0-210-22306-5). Asia.
Sinha, R., et al. Income Distribution, Growth & Basic Needs in India. 175p. 1979. 24.00x (ISBN 0-85664-968-6, Pub. by Croom Helm Ltd England). Biblio Dist.
Spencer, Daniel L. India: Mixed Enterprise & Western Business: Experiments in Controlled Change for Growth & Profit. LC 79-1592. 1981. Repr. of 1959 ed. 21.00 (ISBN 0-88355-897-1). Hyperion Conn.
Strachey, John. India, Its Administration & Progress. LC 73-176459. Repr. of 1911 ed. 35.00 (ISBN 0-404-06295-4). AMS Pr.
Subrahmanyam, K. Defense & Development. LC 74-900257. 118p. 1973. 7.00x (ISBN 0-8002-0962-1). Intl Pubns Serv.
Survey of Research in Management, Vol. 2. 1978. 22.50x (ISBN 0-8364-0165-4). South Asia Bks.
Survey of Research in Management, India, Vol. 1. 1973. 14.00x (ISBN 0-8364-0471-8). South Asia Bks.
Swamy, Subramanian. Economic Growth in China & India, 1952-70. 1973. 8.00x (ISBN 0-226-78315-4). U of Chicago Pr.
Timberg, Thomas A. The Marwaris: From Traders to Industrialists. 1979. text ed. 15.95x (ISBN 0-7069-0528-8, Pub. by Vikas India). Advent NY.
Vaish, O. P. & Panandiker, Surekha, eds. Direct Taxes: Proposals for Reform. 117p. 1978. 10.00x (ISBN 0-7069-0681-0, Pub. by Croom Helm Ltd. England). Biblio Dist.
Vakil, C. N. Poverty & Planning. LC 73-19310. 357p. 1974. Repr. of 1963 ed. lib. bdg. 17.25x (ISBN 0-8371-7320-5, VAPP). Greenwood.
--Poverty, Planning & Inflation. 1979. 17.50x (ISBN 0-8364-0272-3). South Asia Bks.
--War Against Inflation: The Story of the Falling Rupee, 1943-1976. 1978. 14.00x (ISBN 0-8364-0163-8). South Asia Bks.
Vasudevan, A. Strategy of Planning in India. (Illus.). 1970. 9.00x (ISBN 0-8426-0114-7). Verry.
Venkatasubbiah, H. Enterprise & Economic Change, India. 1978. 11.00x (ISBN 0-8364-0169-7). South Asia Bks.
Verma, Y. P. Growth of Protectionism in India. 1974. 9.00x (ISBN 0-8426-0668-8). Verry.
Watt, George. A Dictionary of the Economic Products of India, 6 vols. in 10. 5450p. 1972. Repr. of 1889 ed. Set. 300.00x (ISBN 0-8002-0198-1). Intl Pubns Serv.
--A Dictionary of the Economic Products of India, 6 vols. 1978. Repr. of 1889 ed. Set. 324.00 (ISBN 0-89955-259-5, Pub. by Intl Bk Dist). Intl Schol Bk Serv.

INDIA–ECONOMIC CONDITIONS–1947-

Agarwal, A. N. Indian Economy. 1976. 12.00 (ISBN 0-7069-0391-9). Intl Bk Dist.
Agrawal, A. N. Indian Economy: Nature, Problems & Progress. 4th rev. & enl. ed. 848p. 1978. 15.00x (ISBN 0-7069-0391-9, Pub. by Croom Helm Ltd. England). Biblio Dist.
Ahluwalia, Isher J. Behavior of Prices & Output in India. 1979. 16.00x (ISBN 0-8364-0508-0). South Asia Bks.
Behari, Bepin. Current Economic Problems, with Special Reference to India. (Illus.). 1969. 11.00x (ISBN 0-8426-1150-9). Verry.
--Economic Growth & Technological Change in India. 1974. 12.00x (ISBN 0-686-20218-X). Intl Bk Dist.
Bhagwati, Jagdish N. & Desai, Padma. India, Planning for Industrialization: Industrialization & Trade Policies Since 1951. (Illus.). 1979. pap. 8.95x (ISBN 0-19-561154-3). Oxford U Pr.
Bhagwati, Jagdish N. & Srinivasan, T. N. Foreign Trade Regimes & Economic Development: India, Bk. 6. Bhagwati, Jagdish N. & Krueger, Anne O., eds. (Special Conference Ser.). 1975. 15.00 (ISBN 0-87014-506-1, Dist. by Columbia U Pr); pap. 5.00 (ISBN 0-686-67187-2). Natl Bur Econ Res.
Bhambri, Chander P. World Bank & India. 144p. 1980. text ed. 15.95x (ISBN 0-7069-1059-1, Pub. by Vikas India). Advent NY.
Bhatia, B. M. India's Deepening Economic Crisis. 224p. 1974. text ed. 9.00x (ISBN 0-8426-0646-7). Verry.
--India's Food Problem & Policy Since Independence. 1970. 8.25x (ISBN 0-8426-1163-0). Verry.
--Poverty, Agriculture & Economic Growth. LC 77-902903. 1977. 15.00x (ISBN 0-7069-0524-5). Intl Pubns Serv.
Birla Institute of Scientific Research, Economic Research Div. & Sinha, Bakshi D. Fiscal Policy & Economic Growth: India. 1978. text ed. 4.50x (ISBN 0-8426-1083-9). Verry.
Birla Institute of Scientific Research. Structural Transformation & Economic Development. 126p. 1980. text ed. 9.50 (ISBN 0-391-01790-X). Humanities.
Bohm, Bob. Indications: Notes on India. 220p. (Orig.). 1981. pap. 7.00 (ISBN 0-89608-125-7). South End Pr.
Bonne, Alfred. Studies in Economic Development: With Special Reference to Conditions in the Underdeveloped Areas of Western Asia and India. LC 77-27500. 1978. Repr. of 1957 ed. lib. bdg. 21.50x (ISBN 0-313-20183-8, BOED). Greenwood.
Butani, D. H. India of the Nineteen Seventies: A Panoramic View of the Evolution of India's Social Economy. 1972. 16.50x (ISBN 0-8426-0372-7). Verry.
Chakraborti, S. K. Behaviour of Prices in India, Nineteen Fifty-Two to Nineteen Seventy. 1976. 12.50x (ISBN 0-333-90148-7). South Asia Bks.

Chavan, Y. B. Winds of Change. LC 73-903437. 235p. 1973. 12.00x (ISBN 0-8002-0050-0). Intl Pubns Serv.
Dholakia, J. Unemployment & Employment Policy in India. 1977. text ed. 6.00x (ISBN 0-8426-1020-0). Verry.
Ezekiel, H. Second India Studies: Overview. 1978. 4.50x (ISBN 0-8364-0251-0). South Asia Bks.
Gadre, Kamala. Indian Way to Socialism. 1966. text ed. 9.00 (ISBN 0-8426-1698-5). Verry.
Ganguli, C. Studies in Indian Economic Problems. 1978. 11.00x (ISBN 0-8364-0242-1). South Asia Bks.
Ghatak, S. Rural Money Markets in India. LC 76-905340. 1976. 12.00x (ISBN 0-8364-0463-7). South Asia Bks.
Ghosh, A. B. Price Trends & Policies in India. 1974. 10.50x (ISBN 0-686-20291-0). Intl Bk Dist.
Ghosh, Alek. Indian Economy: Its Nature & Problems. 12th ed. LC 77-900159. (Illus.). 1970. 8.75x (ISBN 0-8002-1541-9). Intl Pubns Serv.
Gopal, Lallanji. Economic Life of Northern India. 1965. 4.50 (ISBN 0-89684-200-2). Orient Bk Dist.
Gupta, D. B. Consumption Patterns in Industry. 1974. 4.95 (ISBN 0-07-096430-0, P&RB). McGraw.
Harris, Nigel. Economic Development, Cities & Planning: The Case of Bombay. (Illus.). 1979. 8.95 (ISBN 0-19-560894-1). Oxford U Pr.
Healey, John M. Development of Social Overhead Capital in India, 1950-1960. LC 66-1142. (Illus.). 1965. 13.50x (ISBN 0-678-06272-2). Kelley.
Henderson, P. D. India: The Energy Sector. 1976. 12.95x (ISBN 0-19-560653-1). Oxford U Pr.
Jha, Prem S. India: A Political Economy of Stagnation. (Illus.). 330p. 1980. 13.95x (ISBN 0-19-561153-5). Oxford U Pr.
Johnson, B. L. C. India: Resources & Development. LC 78-15402. (Illus.). 1979. text ed. 23.50x (ISBN 0-06-493348-2). B&N.
Joshi, Y. D. Concept of Consumer Price Index & Dearness Allowance. 176p. 1974. text ed. 7.50x (ISBN 0-8426-0589-4). Verry.
Katz, S. Stanley. External Assistance & Indian Economic Growth. 5.00x (ISBN 0-210-98137-7). Asia.
Kothari's Economic & Industrial Guide of India, 1980-81. 33rd ed. LC 64-6162. 2500p. 1981. 60.00x (ISBN 0-8002-2783-2). Intl Pubns Serv.
Kulkarni, M. R. Industrial Development. (India; Land & People Ser.). (Illus.). 327p. 1973. 3.75x (ISBN 0-8426-0513-4). Verry.
Madan, G. R. India's Social Transformation: Problems of Economic Development, Vol. 1. 1979. 12.50x (ISBN 0-8364-0525-0). Southeast Acoustics.
Malgonkar, Manohar. Cue from the Inner Voice: The Choice Before Big Business. 176p. 1980. text ed. 13.95 (ISBN 0-7069-1030-3, Pub. by Vikas India). Advent NY.
Mellor, John W. The New Economics of Growth: A Strategy for India & the Developing World. LC 75-38430. (Illus.). 384p. 1976. 20.00x (ISBN 0-8014-0999-3); pap. 8.95 (ISBN 0-8014-9188-6). Cornell U Pr.
Misra, R. P. Multi-Level Planning & Integrated Rural Development in India. 1980. 15.00x (ISBN 0-8364-0576-5, Pub. by Heritage India). South Asia Bks.
Mukhopadhyay, Sudhin K. Sources of Variations in Agricultural Productivity. LC 76-902965. 1976. 9.00x (ISBN 0-333-90139-8). South Asia Bks.
Nafziger, E. Wayne. Class, Caste, & Entrepreneurship: A Study of Indian Industrialists. LC 78-16889. 1978. text ed. 12.00x (ISBN 0-8248-0575-5, Eastwest Ctr). U Pr of Hawaii.
Nair, Balakrishna N. Systemic Approaches to Indian Socio-Economic Developmentt. 1971. 18.00 (ISBN 0-686-20314-3). Intl Bk Dist.
Nair, Kusum. Blossoms in the Dust: The Human Element in Indian Development. LC 78-66080. (Midway Reprints Ser.). 1979. pap. text ed. 8.00x (ISBN 0-226-56800-8). U of Chicago Pr.
Narla, V. R. Gods, Goblins & Men. 1979. 12.00x (ISBN 0-8364-0559-5, Pub. by Minerva Associates). South Asia Bks.
Neelamegham, S., ed. Marketing Management & the Indian Economy. 1978. 20.00 (ISBN 0-7069-0667-5, Pub. by Vikas India). Advent NY.
Pachauri, R. K. Energy & Economic Development in India. LC 77-12718. (Praeger Special Studies). 1977. 23.95 (ISBN 0-03-022371-7). Praeger.
Pavaskar, M. Second India Studies: Transport. 1979. text ed. 9.00x (ISBN 0-8426-1625-X). Verry.
Pavaskar, M. & Kulkarni, R. R. Second India Studies: Communications. 1979. text ed. 9.00x (ISBN 0-8426-1626-8). Verry.
Peoples Plan II. 1977. 6.50x (ISBN 0-88386-909-8). South Asia Bks.
Prakash, S. Financing of Planned Development in India. 1968. 7.50 (ISBN 0-8426-1682-9). Verry.
Rawat, P. C. Indo-Nepal Economic Relations. LC 74-901654. 287p. 1974. 12.00x (ISBN 0-8002-0054-3). Intl Pubns Serv.
Rosen, George. Democracy & Economic Change in India. rev. ed. 1966. 25.00x (ISBN 0-520-01089-2). U of Cal Pr.
Rudra, Ashok. Indian Plan Models. 1977. Repr. 12.50x (ISBN 0-88386-993-4). South Asia Bks.
Sami, A. Intra Urban Market Geography: A Case Study of Patna. 219p. 1980. text ed. 15.75x (ISBN 0-391-02121-4). Humanities.
Sen, S. K. Studies in Economic Policy & Development of India. 1966. 5.50x (ISBN 0-8426-1508-3). Verry.
Sethi, Kiran. Executive Training in India. (Illus.). 90p. 1979. 7.50x (ISBN 0-8002-0987-7). Intl Pubns Serv.
Sharma, H. D. Research in Economics & Commerce: Methodology & Sources. 1976. 14.00 (ISBN 0-88386-750-8). South Asia Bks.
Sharma, K. L. Entrepreneurial Performance in Role Perspective. LC 75-907230. 1975. 9.50x (ISBN 0-88386-695-1). South Asia Bks.
Sharma, T. C. & Coutinho, O. Economic & Commercial Geography of India. (Illus.). 1977. text ed. 13.50x (ISBN 0-7069-0546-6). Verry.
Singh, V. B. Capitalism, Socialism & India. 1976. text ed. 9.00x (ISBN 0-8426-0922-9). Verry.
Somasekhara, N. Efficacy of Industrial Estate in India. 1975. 10.50 (ISBN 0-7069-0374-9). Intl Bk Dist.
Sreenivasan, K. Anatomy of Progress (India) 176p. 1972. 8.25x (ISBN 0-8426-0346-8). Verry.
Subrahmanian, K. K. & Pillai, P. Mohanan. Multinationals & Indian Exports. 1979. 7.50x (ISBN 0-8364-0523-4). South Asia Bks.
Subramanian, V. K. The Indian Financial System. 1979. 16.50x (ISBN 0-8364-0565-X, Pub. by Abhinav India). South Asia Bks.
Talbot, Phillips. Understanding India. LC 72-96098. (Headline Ser.: No. 214). (Illus., Orig.). 1973. pap. 2.00 (ISBN 0-87124-020-3). Foreign Policy.
Tata Economic Consultancy Services, ed. Second Maharashtra by Two Thousand & Five: A Study in Futurology. 1979. text ed. 30.00x (ISBN 0-8426-1623-3). Verry.
Tirtha, Ranjit. Society & Development in Contemporary India: Geographical Perspectives. (Illus.). 368p. 1980. 13.50 (ISBN 0-686-27540-3). R Tirtha.
Toye, F. J. Public Expenditure & Indian Development Policy, 1960-1970. LC 80-41011. 284p. Date not set. 39.50 (ISBN 0-521-23081-0). Cambridge U Pr.
Uppal, J. S. India's Economic Problems. 1975. text ed. 11.95 (ISBN 0-07-096624-9, C). McGraw.
Uppal, J. S., ed. India's Economic Problems: An Analytical Approach. LC 78-62033. 1979. 19.95x (ISBN 0-312-41409-9). St Martin.
Veit, Lawrence A. India's Second Revolution: The Dimension of Development. LC 76-853. (Illus.). 1976. 15.95 (ISBN 0-07-067395-0, P&RB). McGraw.
Venkataraman, K. Power Development in India. LC 72-10341. 178p. 1972. 14.95 (ISBN 0-470-90578-6). Halsted Pr.
Woytinsky, Wladimir S. India: The Awakening Giant. LC 57-7154. (Illus.). 1969. Repr. of 1957 ed. 12.00 (ISBN 0-527-98150-8). Kraus Repr.

INDIA–ECONOMIC POLICY

Agarwal, R. D. Economic Aspects of the Welfare State in India. LC 68-2075. (Illus.). 1967. 9.50x (ISBN 0-8002-0593-6). Intl Pubns Serv.
Agarwal, S. K. Economics of Land Consolidation in India. 1971. 7.50 (ISBN 0-8426-0367-0). Verry.
Agrawal, A. N. Economic Planning. 450p. 1980. 13.00x (ISBN 0-7069-1095-8). Intl Pubns Serv.
--Indian Economy: Nature, Problems & Progress. 4th rev. & enl. ed. 848p. 1978. 15.00x (ISBN 0-7069-0391-9, Pub. by Croom Helm Ltd. England). Biblio Dist.
Ambirajan, S. Classical Political Economy & British Policy in India. LC 76-21020. (South Asian Studies: No. 21). (Illus.). 1978. 44.50 (ISBN 0-521-21415-7). Cambridge U Pr.
Amritananda Das. Foundations of Gandhian Economics. LC 79-17126. 1979. 14.95x (ISBN 0-312-30005-0). St Martin.
Bagchi, Amiya K. Private Investment in India & Pakistan, 1900-1939. LC 79-152631. (South Asian Studies: No. 10). (Illus.). 1971. 53.50 (ISBN 0-521-07641-2). Cambridge U Pr.
Behari, Bepin. Current Economic Problems, with Special Reference to India. (Illus.). 1969. 11.00x (ISBN 0-8426-1150-9). Verry.
Bhagwati, Jagdish N. Indian Economic Policy & Performance: A Framework for a Progressive Society. (Working Papers on Development Ser.: No. 1). 1975. pap. 1.25x (ISBN 0-87725-401-X). U of Cal Intl St.
Bhatia, B. M. Poverty, Agriculture & Economic Growth. LC 77-902903. 1977. 15.00x (ISBN 0-7069-0524-5). Intl Pubns Serv.
Brahmanda, P. R., et al, eds. Indian Economic Development & Policy: Essays in Honour of Professor V. L. D'souza. 352p. 1979. 26.00x (ISBN 0-7069-0683-7, Pub. by Croom Helm Ltd. England). Biblio Dist.
Braibanti, Ralph J. & Spengler, Joseph J., eds. Administration & Economic Development in India. LC 63-9006. (Commonwealth Studies Center: No. 18). 1963. 17.75 (ISBN 0-8223-0020-6). Duke.
Chacko, George K. India: Toward an Understanding. 7.50x (ISBN 0-8084-0401-6); pap. 1.95 (ISBN 0-8084-0402-4, B14). Coll & U Pr.
Chopra, R. N. Evolution of Food Policy in India. 1981. 30.00x (ISBN 0-8364-0724-5, Pub. by Macmillan India). South Asia Bks.
Das, Nabagopal. The Indian Economy Under Planning. LC 72-907412. 140p. 1972. 7.50x (ISBN 0-8002-1542-7). Intl Pubns Serv.
Dasgupta, Ajit K. Economic Freedom, Technology & Planning for Growth. 1973. 9.00 (ISBN 0-686-20217-1). Intl Bk Dist.
Desai, P. B. Planning in India. 1980. text ed. 17.95x (ISBN 0-7069-0832-5, Pub. by Vikas India). Advent NY.
Dhesi, Autar S. Human Capital Formation & Its Utilization. (Illus.). 291p. 1979. 17.50x (ISBN 0-8002-1002-6). Intl Pubns Serv.
Divekar, V. D. Planning Process in Indian Polity. 1979. text ed. 27.00x (ISBN 0-8426-1616-0). Verry.
Dutt, Romesh C. Economic History of India, 2 vols. 817p. 1976. Set. pap. 12.50x (ISBN 0-8002-1382-3). Intl Pubns Serv.
Gadgil, D. R. Planning & Economic Policy in India. LC 73-900569. 405p. 1972. 11.25x (ISBN 0-8002-1802-7). Intl Pubns Serv.
--Planning & Economic Policy in India: Enlarged & Revised Edition. 1972. 15.00 (ISBN 0-8046-8809-5). Kennikat.
--Writings & Speeches of Professor D. R. Gadgil on Planning & Development: 1967-71. Kamat, A. R., ed. LC 75-901569. 1974. 10.00x (ISBN 0-88386-567-X). South Asia Bks.
Gandhi, Ved. Some Aspects of India's Tax Structure: An Economic Analysis. 202p. 1974. text ed. 6.00x (ISBN 0-8426-0637-8). Verry.
Ganguli, B. N. Indian Economic Thought: Nineteenth Century Perspectives. 1977. 7.50x (ISBN 0-8364-0419-X). South Asia Bks.
Gupta, Suraj B. Monetary Planning for India. 252p. 1979. text ed. 14.95x (ISBN 0-19-561145-4). Oxford U Pr.
Hasan, Masood. India's Trade Relations with Rupee Payments Countries. 1972. 10.00x (ISBN 0-8426-0371-9). Verry.
Hettne, Bjorn. The Political Economy of Indirect Rule: Mysore 1881-1947. (Scandanavian Institute of Asian Studies Monograph: No. 32). (Illus., Orig.). 1978. pap. text ed. 13.75x (ISBN 0-7007-0106-0). Humanities.
Hindustan Motors Ltd, ed. Economic Policies & Programmes in India. 1967. pap. 1.25 (ISBN 0-910824-15-0). Kallman.
Iengar, H. V. Planning in India. LC 75-903517. 1974. 5.00x (ISBN 0-8002-0302-X). Intl Pubns Serv.
Iengar, Haravu V. Business & Planned Economy. 191p. 1968. 6.75x (ISBN 0-8426-1312-9). Verry.
India's Economic Development: Aspects of Class Relations. 1981. 10.00x (ISBN 0-86131-232-5, Pub. by Macmillan India). South Asia Bks.
Khera, S. S. Government in Business. 2nd rev. ed. 1978. pap. text ed. 25.00x (ISBN 0-210-26914-6). Asia.
Kishhor, B. & Singh, B. P. Indian Economy Through the Plans. 1969. 10.00x (ISBN 0-8426-1335-8). Verry.
Kotwal, O. P. Indian Economy in Soviet Perspective. 158p. 1979. 10.00x (ISBN 0-8002-1005-0). Intl Pubns Serv.
Krishnamachari, V. T. Planning in India: Theory & Practice. rev. ed. 1977. 6.50x (ISBN 0-8364-0093-3, Orient Longman). South Asia Bks.
Lakdawal, D. T., ed. Survey of Research in Economics: Volume 1, Methods & Techniques. 1978. 14.00x (ISBN 0-8364-0224-3). South Asia Bks.
Machiraju, Hr. Fiscal Policy for Equitable Growth: An Agenda for Fiscal Reform, India. 1977. 10.00x (ISBN 0-333-90162-2). South Asia Bks.
Madan, Balkrishna. Aspects of Economic Development & Policy. 1964. 6.50x (ISBN 0-8188-1071-8). Paragon.
Mahesh-Chand. Aspects of Economic Theory, Liquidity, Growth, & Policy in India. LC 73-905813. (Illus.). 262p. 1973. 13.25x (ISBN 0-8002-0956-7). Intl Pubns Serv.
Mason, Edward S. Economic Development in India & Pakistan. LC 77-38764. (Harvard University. Center for International Affairs. Occasional Papers in International Affairs: No. 13). Repr. of 1966 ed. 11.50 (ISBN 0-404-54613-7). AMS Pr.
Mehta, Bairaj. Failures of the Indian Economy. LC 74-904219. 164p. 1974. 10.00x (ISBN 0-8002-0638-X). Intl Pubns Serv.
Mehta, Balraj. Crisis of Indian Economy. 194p. 1973. 7.00x (ISBN 0-8002-0427-1). Intl Pubns Serv.
Naik, J. A. An Alternative Polity for India. 1976. text ed. 9.00x (ISBN 0-8426-0895-8). Verry.
Nayar, Baldev R. Modernization Imperative & Indian Planning. 1972. 9.00x (ISBN 0-7069-0132-0). Intl Bk Dist.
Nayar, P. K. Leadership Bureaucracy & Planning in India. 1969. 8.25x (ISBN 0-8426-1449-4). Verry.
Patel, S. J. India We Want. 1966. 5.50x (ISBN 0-8188-1099-8). Paragon.
Pavaskar, R. M. Efficiency of Futures Training (India) 1979. text ed. 9.00x (ISBN 0-8426-1619-5). Verry.
Peoples Plan II. 1977. 6.50x (ISBN 0-88386-909-8). South Asia Bks.
Ponkshe, G. R. In Quest of a Shadow. 1966. 6.00x (ISBN 0-8188-1102-1). Paragon.
Puttaswamaiah, K. Aspects of Evaluation & Project Appraisal (India) 1979. text ed. 9.00x (ISBN 0-8426-1621-7). Verry.
Raj, A. Besant. Public Enterprise Investment Decisions in India. 1977. 13.50x (ISBN 0-8364-0456-4). South Asia Bks.
Rao, R. V. Small Industries & a Developing Economy. 1979. text ed. 11.50x (ISBN 0-391-01829-9). Humanities.
Rao, V. G. The Corporation Income Tax in India. 240p. 1980. text ed. 13.50x (ISBN 0-391-02133-8). Humanities.
Reddy, Kaipa N. The Growth of Public Expenditure in India, 1872-1968: A Secular & Time Pattern Analysis. 312p. 1972. 13.50x (ISBN 0-85655-040-X). Intl Pubns Serv.
Repetto, Robert C. Time in India's Development Programmes. LC 71-143230. (Economic Studies: No. 137). (Illus.). 1971. 10.00x (ISBN 0-674-89180-5). Harvard U Pr.
Rudra, Ashok. Indian Plan Models. 1977. Repr. 12.50x (ISBN 0-88386-993-4). South Asia Bks.
Salvi, P. G. Aid to Collaboration: A Study in Indo-U. S. Economic Relations. 1979. text ed. 12.00x (ISBN 0-8426-1618-7). Verry.
Sastry, K. S. Performance Budgeting for Planned Development. (Illus.). 235p. 1980. text ed. 12.50x (ISBN 0-391-02170-2). Humanities.
Sen, Anupam. The State, Industrialization & Class Formations in India: A Neo-Marxist Perspective on Colonialism, Underdevelopment & Development. 330p. 1982. price not set (ISBN 0-7100-0888-0). Routledge & Kegan.
Sen, S. K. Studies in Economic Policy & Development of India. 1966. 5.50x (ISBN 0-8426-1508-3). Verry.
Sengupta, Surajit. Business Law in India. 894p. (Orig.). 1979. pap. text ed. 9.95x (ISBN 0-19-560658-2). Oxford U Pr.
Seshadri, S. Parliamentary Control Over Finance. LC 75-905958. 1975. 11.00x (ISBN 0-88386-054-6). South Asia Bks.
Sethi, T. T. Price Strategy in Indian Planning. LC 72-114978. (Illus.). 565p. 1970. 15.00x (ISBN 0-8002-1833-7). Intl Pubns Serv.
Shah, Manubhai. New Role of Reserve Bank in India's Economic Development. 142p. 1974. text ed. 5.00x (ISBN 0-8426-0634-3). Verry.
Sharma, B. P. The Role of Commercial Banks in India's Developing Economy. LC 75-900036. 414p. 1974. 13.25x (ISBN 0-8002-1931-7). Intl Pubns Serv.
Singh, Charan. India's Economic Policy: Gandhian Blueprint. 1978. 8.00x (ISBN 0-8364-0166-2). South Asia Bks.
Singh, P. N. Role of Development Banks in a Planned Economy. 1974. 8.25x (ISBN 0-686-20301-1). Intl Bk Dist.
Singh, V. B. From Naoroji to Nehru: Six Essays in Indian Economic Thought. LC 75-908521. 1975. 9.50x (ISBN 0-333-90052-9). South Asia Bks.
Sreekantaradhya, B. S. Public Debt & Economic Development in India. LC 73-928092. 360p. 1972. 11.25x (ISBN 0-8002-1887-6). Intl Pubns Serv.
Suman, H. N. Direct Taxation & Economic Growth in India. 300p. 1974. text ed. 15.00x (ISBN 0-8426-0647-5). Verry.
Tyner, Wallace E. Energy Resources & Economic Development in India. 1978. lib. bdg. 19.00 (ISBN 90-277-0744-8, Pub. by Martinus Nijhoff Netherlands). Kluwer Boston.
Vakil, C. N. Poverty & Planning. LC 73-19310. 357p. 1974. Repr. of 1963 ed. lib. bdg. 17.25x (ISBN 0-8371-7320-5, VAPP). Greenwood.
Wadhva, Dharan D., ed. Some Problems of India's Economic Policy. 1978. 14.00x (ISBN 0-8364-0263-4). South Asia Bks.

Wagle, D. M. & Rao, N. V. The Power Sector in India. 1979. text ed. 12.00x (ISBN 0-8426-1624-1). Verry.
Weiner, Myron. Politics of Scarcity: Public Pressure & Political Response in India. LC 62-15047. 1962. 10.00x (ISBN 0-226-89040-6). U of Chicago Pr.
Zahir, Mohammad. Public Expenditure & Income Distribution in India. 1972. 12.00 (ISBN 0-686-20294-5). Intl Bk Dist.

INDIA–EMIGRATION AND IMMIGRATION

Dennery, Etienne. Asia's Teeming Millions. LC 70-115201. 1971. Repr. of 1931 ed. 12.50 (ISBN 0-8046-1094-0). Kennikat.
Rai, Kauleshwar. Indians & British Colonialism in East Africa, 1883-1939. 1979. 12.50x (ISBN 0-8364-0504-8). South Asia Bks.
Saran, Parmatma & Eames, Edwin, eds. New Ethnics: Asian Indians in the U. S. 410p. 1980. 29.95 (ISBN 0-03-051121-6). Praeger.
Tinker, Hugh. The Banyan Tree: Overseas Emigrants from India, Pakistan & Bangladesh. 1977. 12.95x (ISBN 0-19-215946-1). Oxford U Pr.

INDIA–FEDERAL COURT

Sharan, M. K. Court Procedure in Ancient India. 1978. 13.50x (ISBN 0-8364-0262-6). South Asia Bks.

INDIA–FOREIGN RELATIONS

Appadorai, A. Domestic Roots of India's Foreign Policy: Nineteen Forty-Seven to Nineteen Seventy-Two. 380p. 1981. 13.95 (ISBN 0-19-561144-6). Oxford U Pr.
--Essays in Indian Politics & Foreign Policy. 252p. 1971. 11.25x (ISBN 0-8002-1403-X). Intl Pubns Serv.
--Essays in Politics & International Relations. 15.00x (ISBN 0-210-98160-1). Asia.
Bhasin, Prem. Politics: National & International. 1970. 13.50 (ISBN 0-686-20285-6). Intl Bk Dist.
Bhattacharya, Sauripad. Pursuit of National Interest Through Neutralism: India's Foreign Policy in the Nehru Era. 1978. 15.00x (ISBN 0-8364-0139-5). South Asia Bks.
Burke, S. M. Mainsprings of Indian & Pakistani Foreign Policies. LC 74-78992. x, 294p. 1974. 15.00x (ISBN 0-8166-0720-6). U of Minn Pr.
Coelho, Vincent. Across the Palk Straits: India - Sri Lanka Relations. LC 76-900578. 1976. 11.00x (ISBN 0-88386-779-6). South Asia Bks.
Cohen, Stephen P. & Park, Richard L. India: Emergent Power? (Strategy Paper Ser.: No. 33). 95p. 1978. pap. 4.50 (ISBN 0-8448-1353-2). Crane-Russak Co.
Datar, Asha L. India's Economic Relations with the USSR & Eastern Europe, 1953-54 to 1969-70. LC 76-178285. (Soviet & East European Studies Ser). (Illus.). 1972. 42.50 (ISBN 0-521-08219-6). Cambridge U Pr.
Deb, Arabinda. India & Bhutan: A Study in Frontier Political Relations, 1772-1865. LC 76-905259. 1976. 7.50x (ISBN 0-88386-913-6). South Asia Bks.
Dutt, Subimal. With Nehru in the Foreign Office. 1977. 14.00x (ISBN 0-88386-905-5). South Asia Bks.
Eldridge, P. J. The Politics of Foreign Aid in India. LC 75-108903. 1970. 9.00x (ISBN 0-8052-3343-1). Schocken.
Gallo, Patrick J. India's Image of the International System. 1980. 13.00x (ISBN 0-89126-089-7). MA-AH Pub.
Gupta, Alka. UN Peacekeeping Activities in Korea: A Study of India's Role, 1947-1953. 1977. 11.00x (ISBN 0-88386-850-4). South Asia Bks.
Gupta, Karunakar. India in World Politics, a Period of Transition: Suez Crisis, 1956 - Paris Summit, 1960. 1969. 11.00x (ISBN 0-8426-1288-2). Verry.
Indian Council on World Affairs. India & the United Nations. LC 74-6708. (National Studies on International Organization-Carnegie Endowment for International Peace). 229p. 1974. Repr. of 1957 ed. lib. bdg. 15.00x (ISBN 0-8371-7544-5, INIU). Greenwood.
Kishore, Mohammad A. Jana Sangh & India's Foreign Policy. 1969. 16.50 (ISBN 0-686-20264-3). Intl Bk Dist.
Kumar, Mahendra. India & UNESCO. 296p. 1974. 13.50x (ISBN 0-8426-0724-2). Verry.
Kumar, Satish, ed. Documents on India's Foreign Policy, 1972. 1975. 25.00x (ISBN 0-88386-614-5). South Asia Bks.
--Documents on India's Foreign Policy, 1973. 1976. 27.50x (ISBN 0-8364-0397-5). South Asia Bks.
--Documents on India's Foreign Policy 1974. 1978. 27.50x (ISBN 0-8364-0133-6). South Asia Bks.
Kyger, Joanne. Japan & India Journals. 300p. 1981. pap. 10.00 (ISBN 0-939180-01-4). Tombouctou.
Lal, Nand. From Collective Security to Peacekeeping: A Study of India's Contribution to the UN Emergency Force, 1956-67. LC 76-900622. 1976. 10.00x (ISBN 0-88386-537-8). South Asia Bks.
Menon, K. P. Memories & Musings. 1979. 10.00x (ISBN 0-8364-0494-7). South Asia Bks.
Mirchandani, G. G. Reporting India, 1977-78. 1978. 14.00x (ISBN 0-8364-0271-5). South Asia Bks.
Mishra, K. P., ed. Janata's Foreign Policy. 1980. text ed. 18.95x (ISBN 0-7069-0829-5, Pub. by Vikas India). Advent NY.
Nanda, B. R., ed. Indian Foreign Policy: The Nehru Years. 1976. 12.00x (ISBN 0-8248-0486-4, Eastwest Ctr). U Pr of Hawaii.
Nandal, B. R., ed. Indian Foreign Policy: The Nehru Years. 279p. 1976. 13.50x (ISBN 0-7069-0393-5). Intl Pubns Serv.
Nath, Rakhal. New Hindu Movement, Eighteen Sixty-Six to Nineteen Eleven. 1981. 14.50x (ISBN 0-685-59382-7). South Asia Bks.
Phadnis, Urmila. Studies on Sri Lanka & India Relations. 1982. cancelled (ISBN 0-88386-893-8). South Asia Bks.
Prasad, Bimal, ed. India's Foreign Policy: Studies in Continuity & Change. 1979. text ed. 50.00x (ISBN 0-7069-0818-X, Pub. by Vikas India). Advent NY.
Rahman, M. M. Politics of Non-Alignment. 1969. 16.50 (ISBN 0-686-20286-4). Intl Bk Dist.
Raj, Aswini K. Domestic Compulsion & Foreign Policy-India. 1975. 17.50x (ISBN 0-88386-731-1). South Asia Bks.
Raj, B. V. India & Disputes in the United Nations, 1946-1954. 1959. 4.50x (ISBN 0-8426-1481-8). Verry.
Rajan, M. S. India in World Affairs 1954-56. 30.00x (ISBN 0-210-26916-2). Asia.
Rajan, M. S. & Ganguly, Shivaji, eds. India & the International System: A Selection from the Major Writings of Sisir Gupta. 400p. 1981. text ed. 40.00x (ISBN 0-7069-1072-9, Pub. by Vikas India). Advent NY.
Rao, K. S. Conflicts in Indian Polity. 1971. 5.50x (ISBN 0-8426-0366-2). Verry.
Rawlinson, H. G. Intercourse Between India & the Western World, from the Earliest Times to the Fall of Rome. LC 75-159221. 1971. Repr. of 1926 ed. lib. bdg. 14.50x (ISBN 0-374-96721-0). Octagon.
SarDesai, D. R. Indian Foreign Policy in Cambodia, Laos & Vietnam, 1947-1964. LC 68-18379. 1969. 27.50x (ISBN 0-520-01119-8). U of Cal Pr.
Sarhadi, Ajit S. India's Security in Resurgent Asia. viii, 338p. 1980. text ed. 22.50x (ISBN 0-86590-003-5). Apt Bks.
Sharma, Ram. Indian Foreign Policy: Annual Survey 1974, Vol. 4. LC 77-373140. 470p. 1980. 25.00x (ISBN 0-8002-0193-0). Intl Pubns Serv.
Sharma, Shri Ram. Indian Foreign Policy: Annual Survey. LC 77-373140. 364p. 1977. 17.50x ea. Vol. 1, 1971 (ISBN 0-8002-0190-6). Vol. 2, 1972, 366p (ISBN 0-8002-0191-4). Vol. 3, 1973, 405p (ISBN 0-8002-0192-2). Intl Pubns Serv.
Sharma, Surya P. India's Boundary & Territorial Disputes. 198p. 1971. 8.25x (ISBN 0-7069-0088-X). Intl Pubns Serv.
Singh, Baljit. Indian Foreign Policy: An Analysis. 111p. 1979. pap. 4.95 (ISBN 0-210-40570-8). Asia.
Singh, Nagendra. India & International Law. 1969. 5.00x (ISBN 0-8426-1534-2). Verry.
--India & International Law: Ancient & Mediaeval. (Illus.). 242p. 1973. 11.25x (ISBN 0-8002-1531-1). Intl Pubns Serv.
Sondhi, M. L. Non Appeasement: A New Direction for Indian Foreign Policy. 291p. 1973. text ed. 10.50x (ISBN 0-8426-0408-1). Verry.
--Non-Appeasement: A New Direction for Indian Foreign Policy. LC 72-928006. 291p. 1972. 12.00x (ISBN 0-8002-0933-8). Intl Pubns Serv.
Tharoor, Shashi. Reasons of State. 250p. 1981. text ed. 17.50x (ISBN 0-7069-1275-6, Pub by Vikas India). Advent NY.
Thomas, Raju. The Defence of India: A Budgetary Perspective of Strategy & Politics. 1978. 14.50x (ISBN 0-8364-0269-3). South Asia Bks.
Vakil, C. N. & Rao, G. R. Economic Relations Between India & Pakistan. 1968. 7.00x (ISBN 0-8426-1576-8). Verry.
Vohra, Dewan C. India's Aid Diplomacy in the Third World. 256p. 1980. text ed. 22.50 (ISBN 0-7069-1058-3, Pub. by Vikas India). Advent NY.
Warshaw, Steven, et al. India Emerges. LC 73-93983. 7.95 (ISBN 0-87297-018-3); pap. 5.95 (ISBN 0-87297-019-1, Co-Pub. by Canfield Pr). Diablo.

INDIA–FOREIGN RELATIONS–AFRICA

Ramchandani, R. H. India & Africa. 314p. 1980. text ed. 16.50x (ISBN 0-391-01796-9). Humanities.

INDIA–FOREIGN RELATIONS–CEYLON

Blackburn, Robin, ed. Explosion in the Subcontinent: India, Pakistan, Bangladesh & Ceylon. 6.50 (ISBN 0-8446-5160-5). Peter Smith.
Mason, Philip, ed. India & Ceylon: Unity & Diversity: A Symposium. 1967. pap. 5.95x (ISBN 0-19-500351-9). Oxford U Pr.

INDIA–FOREIGN RELATIONS–CHINA

Chen, K. & Uppal, J. India & China. LC 71-142355. 1971. 13.95 (ISBN 0-02-905420-6). Free Pr.
Jetly, Nancy. India-China Relations Nineteen Forty-Seven to Nineteen Seventy-Seven: A Study of Parliament's Role in the Making of Foreign Policy. 1979. text ed. 18.50x (ISBN 0-391-00986-9). Humanities.
Ram, Mohan. Politics of Sino-Indian Confrontation. 1973. 9.00 (ISBN 0-7069-0266-1). Intl Bk Dist.
Rao, G. N. India-China Border: A Reappraisal. 6.00x (ISBN 0-210-98108-3). Asia.
Trivedi, Ram Naresh. Sino-Indian Border Dispute & Its Impact on Indo-Pakistan Relations. 1977. 21.00x (ISBN 0-686-12058-2). Intl Bk Dist.

INDIA–FOREIGN RELATIONS–GREAT BRITAIN

Banerjee, K. India & Britain, 1947-1968. 1977. 14.00x (ISBN 0-88386-903-9). South Asia Bks.
Chakravorty, Birendra C. British Relations with the Hill Tribes of Assam Since Eighteen Fifty-Eight. 1981. 12.50x (ISBN 0-8364-0705-9, Pub. by Mukhopadhyay). South Asia Bks.
Hutchins, F. Illusion of Permanence: British Imperialism in India. 1967. 16.50 (ISBN 0-691-03023-5). Princeton U Pr.
Lipton, Michael. The Erosion of a Relationship: India & Britain Since 1960. (Illus.). 1976. 43.00x (ISBN 0-19-218310-9). Oxford U Pr.
Parry, Benita. Delusions & Discoveries: Studies on India in the British Imagination 1880-1930. 1972. 24.50x (ISBN 0-520-02215-7). U of Cal Pr.
Spear, Percival, ed. The Nabobs. 1980. Repr. of 1963 ed. 17.00x (ISBN 0-8364-0659-1, Pub. by Curzon Pr). South Asia Bks.
Thompson, Edward J. The Other Side of the Medal. LC 78-144848. 142p. 1974. Repr. of 1926 ed. lib. bdg. 15.00x (ISBN 0-8371-5979-2, THOS). Greenwood.

INDIA–FOREIGN RELATIONS–NEPAL

Ramakant. Indo-Nepalese Relations 1816-77. 1968. 10.00x (ISBN 0-8426-1482-6). Verry.
--Nepal-China & India. 1976. 12.00x (ISBN 0-88386-796-6). South Asia Bks.
Rawat, P. C. Indo-Nepal Economic Relations. LC 74-901654. 287p. 1974. 12.00x (ISBN 0-8002-0054-3). Intl Pubns Serv.
--Indo-Nepal Economic Relations. 1974. text ed. 13.00x (ISBN 0-8426-0656-4). Verry.
Sen, Jahar. Indo-Nepal Trade in the Nineteenth Century. 1977. 10.50x (ISBN 0-8364-0111-5). South Asia Bks.
Tyagi, Sushila. Indo Nepalese Relations: 1858-1914. LC 74-901078. 283p. 1974. 12.50x (ISBN 0-88386-511-4). South Asia Bks.

INDIA–FOREIGN RELATIONS–PAKISTAN

Blackburn, Robin, ed. Explosion in the Subcontinent: India, Pakistan, Bangladesh & Ceylon. 6.50 (ISBN 0-8446-5160-5). Peter Smith.
Gandhi, Indira. India & Bangla Desh: Selected Speeches & Statements, March-December, 1971. 200p. 1972. text ed. 4.50x (ISBN 0-391-00508-1). Humanities.
Gupta, Sisir. Kashmir: A Study of India-Pakistan Relations. 1967. 14.00x (ISBN 0-210-22625-0). Asia.
Khan, M. Asghar. The First Round: Indo-Pakistan War - 1965. 1980. text ed. 11.50x (ISBN 0-7069-0978-X, Pub. by Vikas India). Advent NY.
Singh, Lachhman. Indian Sword Strikes in East Pakistan. (Illus.). 1979. 18.00x (ISBN 0-7069-0742-6, Pub. by Vikas India). Advent NY.

INDIA–FOREIGN RELATIONS–RUSSIA

Banerjee, J. India in Soviet Global Strategy. 1977. 12.50x (ISBN 0-88386-908-X). South Asia Bks.
Chopra, Pran. Before & After the Indo-Soviet Treaty. 1972. 8.75x (ISBN 0-8426-0299-2). Verry.
Donaldson, Robert H. The Soviet-Indian Alignment: Quest for Influence 1978-1979. (Monograph in World Affairs: Vol. 16, Pt. C & D). 1979. 4.00 (ISBN 0-87940-059-5). U of Denver Intl.
--Soviet Policy Toward India: Ideology & Strategy. LC 73-89708. (Russian Research Center Studies: No. 74). 352p. 1974. text ed. 16.50x (ISBN 0-674-82776-7). Harvard U Pr.
Drieberg, T. Towards Closer Indo-Soviet Cooperation. 1974. 10.50 (ISBN 0-686-20322-4). Intl Bk Dist.
Joshi, Nirmala. Foundation of Indo-Soviet Relations. LC 75-906116. 1975. 9.00x (ISBN 0-88386-671-4). South Asia Bks.
Kaushik, Devendra. Soviet Relations with India & Pakistan. 1974. 6.60 (ISBN 0-686-20307-0). Intl Bk Dist.
Kulkarni, Maya. Indo-Soviet Political Relations Since the 1955 Bandung Conference. 1968. 4.50x (ISBN 0-8426-1342-0). Verry.
Menon, K. P. Indo-Soviet Treaty: Setting & Sequel. 1972. 6.00 (ISBN 0-686-20260-0). Intl Bk Dist.
Prasad, Bimal. Indo-Soviet Relations, Nineteen Forty-Seven - Nineteen Seventy-Two: A Documentary Study. LC 73-905180. 494p. 1973. 15.00x (ISBN 0-88386-244-1). South Asia Bks.
--Indo-Soviet Relations, 1947 to 1972: A Documentary Study. LC 73-905180. 494p. 1973. 12.50x (ISBN 0-8002-1559-1). Intl Pubns Serv.
Singh Anand, Jagjit. Indo-Soviet Relations: A More Glorious Future. 83p. 1979. 7.50x (ISBN 0-8002-1001-8). Intl Pubns Serv.
Stein, Arthur. India & the Soviet Union. LC 73-91656. 1969. 13.50x (ISBN 0-226-77172-5). U of Chicago Pr.

INDIA–FOREIGN RELATIONS–TIBET

Palakshappa, T. C. Tibetans in India: A Case Study of Mundgod Tibetans. (Illus.). 1979. text ed. 7.50x (ISBN 0-391-01191-X). Humanities.

INDIA–FOREIGN RELATIONS–UNITED STATES

Bhagat, G. Americans in India, Seventeen Eighty-Four to Eighteen-Sixty. LC 76-133012. 1970. 12.50x (ISBN 0-8147-0961-3). NYU Pr.
Desai, Tripta. Indo-American Relations Between 1940-1974. 1977. pap. text ed. 9.00 (ISBN 0-8191-0155-9). U Pr of Amer.
Hess, Gary R. America Encounters India, 1941-1947. LC 72-163196. 208p. 1972. 13.50x (ISBN 0-8018-1258-5). Johns Hopkins.
Jha, Manoranjan. Civil Disobedience & After: The American Reaction to Political Developments in India During 1930-1935. LC 73-906394. 300p. 1973. 11.25x (ISBN 0-8002-0528-6). Intl Pubns Serv.
Mokashi-Punekar, S. The Indo-Anglian Creed. (Writers Workshop Greybird Ser.). 72p. 1975. 14.00 (ISBN 0-88253-566-8); pap. text ed. 4.80 (ISBN 0-88253-565-X). Ind-US Inc.
Nayar, Baldev R. American Geopolitics & India: Study of American Foreign Policy Towards India During the 1970's. LC 76-52216. 1976. 12.00x (ISBN 0-88386-763-X). South Asia Bks.
Reynolds, John I. Indian-American Joint Ventures: Business Policy Relationships. LC 77-18587. 1978. pap. text ed. 10.50 (ISBN 0-8191-0403-5). U Pr of Amer.
Salvi, P. G. Aid to Collaboration: A Study in Indo-U. S. Economic Relations. 1979. text ed. 12.00x (ISBN 0-8426-1618-7). Verry.
Singh, A. K. Impact of American Aid on Indian Economy. 175p. 1974. text ed. 5.50x (ISBN 0-8426-0597-5). Verry.
Tewari, S. C. Indo-US Relations: 1947-1976. 1977. text ed. 12.50x (ISBN 0-391-01001-8). Humanities.

INDIA–GENEALOGY

Peirce, Ebenezer W. Indian History, Biography & Genealogy. LC 72-4336. (Select Bibliographies Reprint Ser.). 1972. Repr. of 1878 ed. 21.00 (ISBN 0-8369-6890-5). Arno.

INDIA–HISTORICAL GEOGRAPHY

Sircar, D. C. Studies in the Geography of Ancient & Medieval India. rev. 2nd ed. 401p. 1973. Repr. of 1960 ed. text ed. 13.50x (ISBN 0-8426-0519-3). Verry.

INDIA–HISTORIOGRAPHY

Devahuti. Bias in Indian Historiography. 1980. text ed. 33.75x (ISBN 0-391-02174-5). Humanities.
--Problems of Indian Historiography. 1979. text ed. 11.50x (ISBN 0-391-01862-0). Humanities.
Devahuti, ed. Problems of Indian Historiography. 1979. 13.50x (ISBN 0-8364-0352-5). South Asia Bks.
Sen, S. P. Historians & Historiography in Modern India. LC 73-905657. 463p. 1973. 25.00x (ISBN 0-8002-1495-1). Intl Pubns Serv.

INDIA–HISTORY

see also Afghan Wars

Advani, Lal K. A Prisoner's Scrap-Book. 1978. text ed. 13.50x (ISBN 0-8426-1084-7). Verry.
Agarawala, R. A. History, Art & Architecture of Jaisalmer. 1978. 42.50x (ISBN 0-8364-0319-3). South Asia Bks.
Agarwala, Ramgopal. Econometric Model of India, 1848-1961. 188p. 1970. 27.50x (ISBN 0-7146-1200-6, F Cass Co). Biblio Dist.
Antonova, K. A History of India, Book Two. 342p. 1979. 10.80 (ISBN 0-8285-1629-4, Pub. by Progress Pubs Russia). Imported Pubns.
Antonova, K., et al. A History of India, Book One. 264p. 1979. 10.80 (ISBN 0-8285-1628-6, Pub. by Progress Pubs Russia). Imported Pubns.
Ashim Kumar Roy, et al. Homage to Jaipur. LC 80-901924. (Illus.). 102p. 1979. 17.50x (ISBN 0-8002-2439-6). Intl Pubns Serv.
Banerjea, Pramathanath. Indian Finance in the Days of the Company. (Perspectives in Asian History: No. 5). Repr. of 1928 ed. lib. bdg. 25.00x (ISBN 0-87991-820-9). Porcupine Pr.

Banerjee, Gauranga N. Hellenism in Ancient India. rev. ed. 276p. 1981. text ed. 20.25x (ISBN 0-391-02417-5, Pub. by Munshiram Manoharlal India). Humanities.

Banerjee, J. India in Soviet Global Strategy. 1977. 12.50x (ISBN 0-88386-908-X). South Asia Bks.

Basham, A. L. Wonder That Was India: A Survey of the History & Culture of the Indian Sub-Continent Before the Coming of the Muslims. LC 68-10737. 1968. write for info (ISBN 0-8008-8450-7). Taplinger.

Bayley, Edward C. History of Gujarat, the Local Muhammadan Dynasties: The History of India As Told by Its Historians. 1970. Repr. of 1886 ed. 17.00x (ISBN 0-8426-0089-2). Verry.

Beveridge, Henry. Comprehensive History of India, 2 vols. 1973. 144.00 (ISBN 0-686-20205-8). Intl Bk Dist.

Bhatt, V. V. Two Decades of Development: The Indian Experiment. 6.00x (ISBN 0-8426-0635-1). Verry.

Bhattacharya, Sachchidananda. A Dictionary of Indian History. LC 77-1105. 1977. Repr. of 1972 ed. lib. bdg. 58.50x (ISBN 0-8371-9515-2, BHDI). Greenwood.

Bhattacharyya, et al, eds. The Cultural Heritage of India, 4 vols. Incl. Vol. 1. Early Phases. Radhakrishnan, S., intro. by. (ISBN 0-87481-560-6); Vol. 2. Itihasas, Puranas, Dharma & Other Shastras (ISBN 0-87481-561-4); Vol. 3. The Philosophies (ISBN 0-87481-562-2); Vol. 4. The Religions (ISBN 0-87481-563-0). (Illus.). 30.00x ea.; Set. 150.00x (ISBN 0-87481-558-4). Vedanta Pr.

Brown, W. Norman. India & Indology. Rocher, Rosane, ed. 1979. 52.00x (ISBN 0-8364-0362-2). South Asia Bks.

Chandra, Bipin. Nationalism & Colonialism in Modern India. 1979. 22.50x (ISBN 0-8364-0571-4, Pub. by Orient Longman). South Asia Bks.

Chandras, Kananur V. Four Thousand Years of Indian Education: A Short History of the Hindu, Buddhist & Moslem Periods. LC 77-81034. 1977. soft bdg. 8.00 (ISBN 0-88247-474-X). R & E Res Assoc.

Chatterjee, Sunjeeb C. Bengal Ryots. Banerjee, A. C., ed. 1977. 9.00x (ISBN 0-8364-0015-1). South Asia Bks.

Chatwin, Bruce. The Viceroy of Ouidah. LC 80-17896. 155p. 1980. 11.95 (ISBN 0-671-41253-1). Summit Bks.

Chaudhuri, K. N. & Dewey, Clive J., eds. Economy & Society: Essays in Indian Economic & Social History. (Illus.). 1979. 16.95x (ISBN 0-19-561073-3). Oxford U Pr.

Chhabra, G. S. Advanced Study in the History of Modern India: Seventeen Seven to Nineteen Forty-Seven, 3 vols. 1972. 37.50x (ISBN 0-8426-0341-7). Verry.

Chopra, Pran. India's Second Liberation. 1977. text ed. 7.95 (ISBN 0-7069-0259-9, Pub. by Vikas India). Advent NY.

Cohen, Stephen P. The Indian Army: Its Contribution to the Development of a Nation. LC 77-111421. 1971. 25.00x (ISBN 0-520-01697-1). U of Cal Pr.

Crane, Robert I. A History of South Asia. LC 73-78930. (AHA Pamphlets: No. 513). 80p. (Orig.). 1973. pap. text ed. 1.50 (ISBN 0-87229-014-X). Am Hist Assn.

D'Albuquerque, Alfonso. The Commentaries of the Great Alfonso Dalboquerque, Second Viceroy of India, 4 Vols. Birch, Walter D., ed. & tr. from Portuguese. LC 74-134712. (Hakluyt Society Ser). 1970. Repr. of 1883 ed. Set. lib. bdg. 118.00 (ISBN 0-8337-0289-0). B Franklin.

Dalton, E. T. Tribal History of Eastern India. (Illus.). 327p. 1978. Repr. of 1872 ed. 30.00 (ISBN 0-89684-123-5, Pub. by Cosmo Pubns India). Orient Bk Dist.

Dani, Ahmad Hasan. Prehistory & Prohistory of Eastern India. 1981. 28.00x (ISBN 0-8364-0734-2, Pub. by Mukhopadhyay). South Asia Bks.

Danvers, Frederick C. Portuguese in India, 2 Vols. 1966. lib. bdg. 55.00x (ISBN 0-374-92052-4). Octagon.

Dayal, John & Bose, Ajoy. The Shah Commission Begins: India Under Emergency. 1978. 13.50x (ISBN 0-8364-0179-4). South Asia Bks.

De Bary, W. T., ed. Sources of Indian Tradition, 2 vols. LC 58-4146. (Introductions to the Oriental Classics & Records of Civilization: Sources & Studies Ser.). Vol. 2, 384 Pgs. 6.00x (ISBN 0-231-08601-6). Columbia U Pr.

Del Bonta, Robert J. & Berkson, Carmel. In Praise of Hoysala Art. LC 80-901926. (Illus.). 106p. 1979. 22.50x (ISBN 0-8002-2440-X). Intl Pubns Serv.

Dewey, Clive & Hopkins, A. G. The Imperial Impact: Studies in the Economic History of Africa & India. (Commonwealth Papers Ser.: No.21). 1978. text ed. 41.75x (ISBN 0-485-17621-1, Athlone Pr). Humanities.

Dube, S. C., ed. Tribal Heritage of India: Ethnicity, Identity & Interaction, Vol. 1. 1977. 12.00x (ISBN 0-8364-0476-9). South Asia Bks.

Dunbar, George. History of India from Earliest Times to 1939, 2 vols. 1949. Set. 13.00x (ISBN 0-391-01989-9). Humanities.

Elliot, Henry M. History of India, As Told by Its Own Historians, 8 Vols. Dowson, John, ed. LC 70-166019. Repr. of 1877 ed. Set. 280.00 (ISBN 0-404-02330-4); 35.00 ea. AMS Pr.

Erskine, William. A History of India Under the Two First Sovereigns of the House of Taimur, Baber & Humayun, 2 vols. 1162p. 1972. Repr. of 1854 ed. 70.00x (ISBN 0-7165-2118-0, Pub. by Irish Academic Pr). Biblio Dist.

Firishtah, Muhammed Kasim. History of the Rise of the Mahomedan Power in India till the Year A.D. 1612, 4 Vols. Briggs, John, tr. LC 79-154112. Repr. of 1910 ed. Set. 225.00 (ISBN 0-404-56300-7). AMS Pr.

Fraser, James. The History of Nadir Shah. LC 5-1697. (Illus.). 280p. 1973. Repr. of 1742 ed. 18.75x (ISBN 0-8002-0905-2). Intl Pubns Serv.

Frazer, R. W. Literary History of India. LC 78-128001. (Studies in Asiatic Literature, No. 57). 1970. Repr. of 1898 ed. lib. bdg. 58.95 (ISBN 0-8383-1150-4). Haskell.

Ganguly, D. K. Aspects of Ancient Indian Administration. 1979. 22.50x (ISBN 0-8364-0355-X). South Asia Bks.

Ganguly, SN. Tradition, Modernity & Development. 1977. 10.00 (ISBN 0-333-90144-4). South Asia Bks.

Gerini, G. E. Researches on Ptolemy's Geography of Eastern Asia. LC 90-3098. (Illus.). 974p. 1974. 27.50x (ISBN 0-8002-0043-8). Intl Pubns Serv.

Ghosh, A. The City in Early Historical India. (Illus.). 98p. 1973. 6.50x (ISBN 0-8002-0529-4). Intl Pubns Serv.

Ghurye, G. S. Vedic India. 1979. 44.00x (ISBN 0-8364-0455-6). South Asia Bks.

Giri, V. V. My Life & Times, Vol. 1. 1976. 15.00x (ISBN 0-8002-1741-1). Intl Pubns Serv.

Golant, William. The Long Afternoon: British India 1601-1947. LC 74-15112. 282p. 1975. 17.95 (ISBN 0-312-49630-3). St Martin.

Goyal, Des Raj. Rashtriya Swayamsevak Sangh. 1979. 10.00x (ISBN 0-8364-0566-8, Pub. by Radha Krishna India). South Asia Bks.

Griffiths, Percival. Modern India. 1962. pap. 2.00 (ISBN 0-88253-203-0). Ind-US Inc.

Gupta, Hari R. Panjab on the Eve of First Sikh War. 2nd rev. ed. LC 75-903634. 1975. 12.50x (ISBN 0-88386-653-6). South Asia Bks.

Hasan, Ibn. Central Structure of the Mughal Empire. (Illus.). 1970. 11.00x (ISBN 0-8426-0197-X). Verry.

Hayashida, T. Netaji Subhas Chandra Bose: His Great Struggle & Martyrdom. 183p. 1970. 5.00x (ISBN 0-8188-1156-0). Paragon.

Hettne, Bjorn. The Political Economy of Indirect Rule: Mysore 1881-1947. (Scandanavian Institute of Asian Studies Monograph: No. 32). (Illus., Orig.). 1978. pap. text ed. 13.75x (ISBN 0-7007-0106-0). Humanities.

Hirschmann, Edwin. The White Mutiny. 1980. 24.00x (ISBN 0-8364-0639-7). South Asia Bks.

Hunter, William W. History of British India, 2 Vols. LC 73-180685. Repr. of 1900 ed. 40.00 (ISBN 0-404-03458-6). AMS Pr.

Islam, Shamsul. Chronicles of the Raj: A Study of Literary Reaction to the Imperial Idea Towards the End of the Raj. 130p. 1979. 21.50x (ISBN 0-8476-6174-1). Rowman.

Jackson, Abraham V. History of India, 9 Vols. LC 72-149391. Repr. of 1907 ed. Set. 288.00 (ISBN 0-404-09000-1); 32.00 ea. AMS Pr.

Jackson, Abraham V., ed. Historic Accounts of India by Foreign Travellers Classic, Oriental, & Occidental. LC 72-14391. (History of India: No. 9). Repr. of 1907 ed. 32.00 (ISBN 0-404-09009-5). AMS Pr.

Jadunath, Sarkar. A Short History of Aurgangzib. 1979. Repr. of 1962 ed. 10.00x (ISBN 0-8364-0568-4, Pub. by Orient Longman). South Asia Bks.

Jha, J. C. The Bhumij Revolt. (Illus.). 208p. 1967. 6.50x (ISBN 0-8426-1319-6). Verry.

Joshi, V. C., ed. Rammohun Roy & the Process of Modernization in India. 1975. 12.00 (ISBN 0-7069-0349-8). Verry.

Kapur, Jagga. What Price Perjury: Facts of the Shah Commission (India) 1978. text ed. 13.50x (ISBN 0-8426-1085-5). Verry.

Karkhanis, Sharad. Indian Politics and the Role of the Press. 226p. 1981. text ed. 17.95 (ISBN 0-7069-1278-0, Pub. by Vikas India). Asia Bk Corp.

Kher, N. N. Agrarian & Fiscal Economy in the Mauryan Age. 1973. 12.50 (ISBN 0-89684-168-5). Orient Bk Dist.

Kopf, David. The Brahmo Samaj & the Shaping of the Modern Indian Mind. LC 78-70303. 1979. text ed. 29.50 (ISBN 0-691-03125-8). Princeton U Pr.

Kopf, David & Bishop, C. James. The Indian World. LC 77-81185. (World of Asia Ser.). (Illus., Orig.). 1977. pap. text ed. 3.95x (ISBN 0-88273-503-9). Forum Pr MO.

Kublin, Hyman. India: Selected Readings. rev. ed. LC 72-7637. 230p. (gr. 9-12). 1973. pap. text ed. 6.60 (ISBN 0-395-13929-5, 2-31040). HM.

Lal, Chaman. India: Cradle of Cultures. (Illus.). 346p. 1980. text ed. 30.00x (ISBN 0-391-01872-8). Humanities.

Lane-Poole, S. Medieval India, Under Mohammedan Rule. LC 70-132442. (World History Ser., No. 48). 1970. Repr. of 1903 ed. lib. bdg. 59.95 (ISBN 0-8383-1196-2). Haskell.

Larus, Joel. Culture & Political-Military Behavior: The Hindus in Pre-Modern India. 1980. 16.50x (ISBN 0-8364-0038-0). South Asia Bks.

Lawrence, Walter R. The India We Served. 1928. Repr. 20.00 (ISBN 0-8274-2569-4). R West.

Lingat, Robert. The Classical Law of India. Derrett, J. Duncan, tr. from Fr. LC 76-81798. Orig. Title: Sources Du Droit Dans le Systeme Traditionnel De L'inde. 1973. 29.50x (ISBN 0-520-01898-2). U of Cal Pr.

Lopes de Castanheda, Fernam. The First Booke of the Discouerie & Conquest of the East Indias. Lichefild, N., tr. LC 72-6014. (English Experience Ser.: No. 539). 340p. 1973. Repr. of 1582 ed. 36.00 (ISBN 90-221-0539-3). Walter J Johnson.

Low, Anthony, ed. Congress & the Raj. 1977. 30.00x (ISBN 0-8364-0007-0). South Asia Bks.

McCrindle, J. W. The Invasion of India by Alexander the Great. 2nd ed. (Ancient India Ser). (Illus.). 432p. 1973. Repr. of 1816 ed. 18.75x (ISBN 0-8002-1591-5). Intl Pubns Serv.

Macdonell, Arthur A. India's Past: A Survey of Her Literatures, Religions, Languages & Antiquities. LC 78-20481. 1979. Repr. of 1927 ed. text ed. 26.50 (ISBN 0-88355-858-0). Hyperion Conn.

McLean, Robert, ed. India in Transition. 1982. 15.00x (ISBN 0-8364-0011-9). South Asia Bks.

Majumdar, R. C. & Chopra, P. N. Main Currents of Indian History. 1980. text ed. 12.50x (ISBN 0-391-00961-3). Humanities.

Malcolm, John. A Memoir of Central India, Including Malwa, & Adjoining Provinces: With the History, & Copious Illustrations, of the Past & Present Condition of That Country, 2 vols. 3rd ed. 1127p. 1972. Repr. of 1832 ed. 84.00x (ISBN 0-7165-2129-6, Pub. by Irish Academic Pr). Biblio Dist.

--Political History of India, 2 vols. 1970. 75.00 (ISBN 0-686-20284-8). Intl Bk Dist.

Malik, S. C., ed. Dissent, Protest & Reform in Indian Civilization. 1977. 18.50x (ISBN 0-8364-0104-2). South Asia Bks.

Masani, M. Bliss Was It in That Dawn... A Political Memoir up to Independence (India) 1978. text ed. 9.00x (ISBN 0-8426-1087-1). Verry.

Mathur, P. R. Khasi of Meghalaya. 198p. 1979. 13.50 (ISBN 0-89684-122-7, Pub. by Cosmo Pubns India). Orient Bk Dist.

Mehra, J. S. Abu to Udaipur: Celestial Simla to City of Sunrise. (Illus.). 1970. 3.95 (ISBN 0-89684-166-9). Orient Bk Dist.

Mehra, Parshotam. The North-East Frontier: A Documentary Study of the Internecine Rivalry Between India, Tibet & China, Vol. 1, 1906-14. 270p. 1979. text ed. 9.95x (ISBN 0-19-561158-6). Oxford U Pr.

Mehrotra, S. R. The Commonwealth & the Nation. 1978. 8.95 (ISBN 0-7069-0673-X, Pub. by Vikas India). Advent NY.

Menon, A. Sreedhara. Social & Cultural History of India: Kerala. 1979. text ed. 20.00 (ISBN 0-89684-079-4, Pub. by Sterling New Delhi). Orient Bk Dist.

Metcalf, Thomas R. Land, Landlords, & the British Raj: Northern India in the Nineteenth Century. LC 77-85754. (Center for South & Southeast Asia Studies, UC Berkeley). 1979. 28.50x (ISBN 0-520-03575-5). U of Cal Pr.

Minault, Gail. The Khilafat Movement: Religious Symbolism & Political Mobilization in India. 288p. Date not set. text ed. 22.50x (ISBN 0-231-05072-0). Columbia U Pr.

Mirashi, V. V. Literary & Historical Studies in Indololgy. 1976. text ed. 16.50x (ISBN 0-8426-0960-1). Verry.

Mukherjee, Prabhat. The History of Jagannath Temple. 1977. 14.50x (ISBN 0-8364-0414-9). South Asia Bks.

Mulk Raj Anand, ed. Homage to Amritsar. (Marg, a Magazine of the Arts: Vol. 30, No. 3). (Illus.). 72p. 1977. 17.50x (ISBN 0-8002-2444-2). Intl Pubns Serv.

Murthy, H. V. & Kamath, S. U. Studies in Indian Culture. (Illus.). 184p. 1973. pap. text ed. 3.75 (ISBN 0-210-22391-X). Asia.

Nanda, B. R. & Joshi, V. C., eds. Studies in Modern History, No. One. 214p. 1973. pap. text ed. 8.00x (ISBN 0-391-00624-X). Humanities.

--Studies in Modern Indian History. 1972. 15.00 (ISBN 0-8046-8819-2). Kennikat.

--Studies in Modern Indian History, No. 1. 214p. 1973. text ed. 9.00x (ISBN 0-8426-0497-9). Verry.

Noronha, R. P. A Tale Told by an Idiot. 1976. 9.00x (ISBN 0-88386-933-0). South Asia Bks.

Panikkar, K. M. An Autobiography. Krishnamurthy, K., tr. 1977. 12.50x (ISBN 0-19-560380-X). Oxford U Pr.

Patel, Satyavrata R. The Soul of India. LC 74-901610. 232p. 1974. 13.25x (ISBN 0-8002-0046-2). Intl Pubns Serv.

Patil, D. Rajaram. Cultural History from the Vayu Purana. 1973. Repr. 7.50 (ISBN 0-8426-0529-0). Orient Bk Dist.

Peirce, Ebenezer W. Indian History, Biography & Genealogy. LC 72-4336. (Select Bibliographies Reprint Ser.). 1972. Repr. of 1878 ed. 21.00 (ISBN 0-8369-6890-5). Arno.

Prinsep, H. T. History of the Political & Military Transactions in India During the Administration of the Marquis of Hastings, 1813-1823, 2 vols. (Illus.). 988p. 1972. Repr. of 1825 ed. 84.00x (ISBN 0-7165-2134-2, Pub. by Irish Academic Pr Ireland). Biblio Dist.

Puri, B. N. India in the Time of Pantanjali. 2nd ed. 1968. 6.50x (ISBN 0-8426-0031-0). Verry.

Qamber, Akhtar. The Last Musha'irah of Delhi. 1979. 18.00x (ISBN 0-8364-0537-4, Orient Longman). South Asia Bks.

Ramanappa, M. Venkata. Outlines of South Indian History. 1975. 7.75x (ISBN 0-88386-674-9). South Asia Bks.

Rao, B. S. India's Freedom Movement: Some Notable Figures. 1972. 12.95 (ISBN 0-8046-8824-9). Kennikat.

Ratnagar, Shereen. Encounters: India's Westerly Trade in the Bronze Age. 240p. 1981. 17.95 (ISBN 0-19-561253-1). Oxford U Pr.

Reid, C. Lestock. Commerce & Conquest. LC 78-115328. 1971. Repr. of 1947 ed. 12.95 (ISBN 0-8046-1119-X). Kennikat.

Rothermund, D. & Wadhwa, D. C. Zamindars, Mines & Peasants: Studies in the History of an Indian Coalfield. 1979. 16.50x (ISBN 0-8364-0331-2). South Asia Bks.

Roy, S. B. Date of Mahabharat Battle. 1977. 11.00 (ISBN 0-88386-957-8). South Asia Bks.

Rumbold, Algernon. Watershed in India 1914-1922. 1979. text ed. 47.00x (ISBN 0-485-11182-9, Athlone Pr). Humanities.

Rustomji, Nari. Bhutan: The Dragon Kingdom in Crisis. (Illus.). 1978. 8.95x (ISBN 0-19-561062-8). Oxford U Pr.

Saletore, R. N. Indian Pirates. 200p. 1980. pap. text ed. 11.25x (ISBN 0-391-02183-4, Pub. by Concept India). Humanities.

Sarkar, Jadunath. House of Shivaji: Studies & Documents on Maratha History. 1979. 11.50x (ISBN 0-8364-0343-6, Orient Longman). South Asia Bks.

Sastri, K. A. Age of Nandas & Mauryas. (Illus.). 1967. 2.50 (ISBN 0-89684-167-7). Orient Bk Dist.

Sastri, K. Nilakanta. The Pandyan Kingdom. 2nd ed. 252p. 1974. text ed. 7.50 (ISBN 0-88253-426-2). Ind-US Inc.

Sau, Ranjit. Unequal Exchange, Imperialism & Underdevelopment. (Illus.). 1978. 15.95x (ISBN 0-19-560895-X). Oxford U Pr.

Settar, S., et al. In Praise of Aihole, Badami, Mahakuta, Pattadakal. LC 80-901923. (Illus.). 134p. 1979. 32.50x (ISBN 0-8002-2442-6). Intl Pubns Serv.

Sewell, Robert T. A Forgotten Empire-Vijayanagar: A Contribution to the History of India. (Illus.). 427p. 1972. Repr. of 1900 ed. 31.00x (ISBN 0-7165-2137-7, Pub. by Irish Academic Pr). Biblio Dist.

Sharma, B. N. Social & Cultural History of Northern India c. 1000-1200 A.D. 1972. text ed. 13.75x (ISBN 0-391-00300-3). Humanities.

Sharma, Jagdish S. India Since the Advent of the British. (National Bibliography Ser No. 7). 1970. 20.00x (ISBN 0-8426-0175-9). Verry.

Sharma, R. S., ed. Land Revenues in India: Historical Studies. 1971. 4.00 (ISBN 0-89684-239-8). Orient Bk Dist.

Sharma, Sri R. Maharana Rai Singh & His Times. 1971. 3.95 (ISBN 0-89684-247-9). Orient Bk Dist.

Shastri, A. M. India As Seen in Kuttanimata of Damodargupta. 1975. 15.00 (ISBN 0-8426-0954-7). Orient Bk Dist.

--India As Seen in the Brhatsamhita of Varahamihira. (Illus.). 1969. 12.50 (ISBN 0-89684-221-5). Orient Bk Dist.

Shiva-Rao, B. India's Freedom Movement: Some Notables Figures. 336p. 1972. 12.00x (ISBN 0-8002-1553-2). Intl Pubns Serv.

Shulberg, Lucille. Historic India. LC 68-22440. (Great Ages of Man Ser.). (gr. 6 up). 1968. PLB 11.97 (ISBN 0-8094-0381-1, Pub. by Time-Life). Silver.

Singh, Hajinder. Birth of an Air Force: Memoirs of Air Vice Marshal Harjinder Singh. 1977. 15.00 (ISBN 0-8364-0107-7). South Asia Bks.

Singh, Karni. The Relations of the House of Bikaner with Central Powers, 1465-1949. LC 74-902032. xvi, 432p. 1974. 15.00x (ISBN 0-8364-0457-2). South Asia Bks.

Smith, Vincent. The Oxford History of India. Spear, Percival, ed. (Illus.). 992p. 1981. pap. 9.95 (ISBN 0-19-561297-3). Oxford U Pr.

Snelgrove, D. L. & Skorupski, T. Cultural Heritage of Ladakh. (Illus.). 1977. 55.00 (ISBN 0-7069-0474-5). Orient Bk Dist.

Spear, Percival. History of India, Vol. 2. (Illus., Orig.). 1966. pap. 3.95 (ISBN 0-14-020770-8, Pelican). Penguin.
--India: A Modern History. new, rev. & enl. ed. LC 72-81334. (History of the Modern World Ser). (Illus.). 1972. 10.00x (ISBN 0-472-07141-6). U of Mich Pr.
Srivastava, A. K. Bhagavad Gita: Economic Development & Management. 1980. 14.00x (ISBN 0-8364-0592-7, Abhinav India). South Asia Bks.
Stokes, E. T. The Peasant & the Raj. LC 77-77731. (South Asian Studies: No. 23). 1978. 37.50 (ISBN 0-521-21684-2). Cambridge U Pr.
Subrahmanian, N. History of Tamilnadu to A. D. 1336. (Illus.). 428p. 1974. text ed. 10.00 (ISBN 0-88253-434-3). Ind-US Inc.
Talwar, Bhagat R. The Talwars of Pathan Land & Subhas Chandra's Great Escape. LC 76-902650. 1976. 11.00x (ISBN 0-88386-848-2). South Asia Bks.
Tames, Richard. India & Pakistan in the Twentieth Century. (Twentieth Century World History Ser.). (Illus.). 96p. (gr. 6 up). 1981. 14.95 (ISBN 0-7134-3415-5, Pub. by Batsford England). David & Charles.
Thakur, Vijay K. Urbanization in Ancient India. 1981. 25.00x (ISBN 0-8364-0688-5, Pub. by Abhinav India). South Asia Bks.
Thapar, Romila. Ancient India. 2nd. ed. 1969. pap. 2.00 (ISBN 0-88253-275-8). Ind-US Inc.
--History of India, Vol. 1. (Orig.). 1966. pap. 4.95 (ISBN 0-14-020769-4, Pelican). Penguin.
--Medieval India. (Illus.). 1970. pap. 2.00 (ISBN 0-88253-276-6). Ind-US Inc.
Thompson, Edward. A History of India. 1927. Repr. 10.00 (ISBN 0-685-43272-6). Norwood Edns.
Vaidya, C. V. History of Medieval Hindu India, 3 vols. Incl. Vol. I. 400p. 1979. Repr. of 1921 ed (ISBN 0-89684-145-6); Vol. II. 354p. 1979. Repr. of 1924 ed (ISBN 0-89684-146-4); Vol. III. Downfall of Hindu India. 503p. 1979. Repr. of 1926 ed (ISBN 0-89684-147-2). 45.00 set (ISBN 0-686-77520-1, Pub. by Cosmo Pubns India). Orient Bk Dist.
Varadarajan, Lotika. Homage to Kalamkari. LC 80-901920. (Illus.). 134p. 1979. with boards 32.50x (ISBN 0-8002-2445-0). Intl Pubns Serv.
Venkata Ramanappa, M. N. Outlines of South Indian History. 1976. 7.50 (ISBN 0-7069-0378-1). Intl Bk Dist.
Watson, Francis. A Concise History of India. 1979. pap. 7.95 (ISBN 0-500-27164-X). Thames Hudson.
--A Concise History of India. LC 74-16890. 1975. 9.95 (ISBN 0-684-13896-4, ScribT). Scribner.
Wheeler, J. Talboy. Early Records of British India: A History of the English Settlements in India. 2nd ed. LC 73-161652. 384p. 1972. 17.50x (ISBN 0-8002-1378-5). Intl Pubns Serv.
Wilberforce, R. G. An Unrecorded Chapter of the Indian Mutiny. 1976. Repr. 12.00x (ISBN 0-8364-0477-7). South Asia Bks.
Wolpert, Stanley. A New History of India. 2nd ed. LC 81-38. (Illus.). 480p. 1982. 25.00 (ISBN 0-19-502949-6). Oxford U Pr.
--A New History of India. LC 76-42678. (Illus.). 1977. 19.95 (ISBN 0-19-502153-3); pap. 9.95x (ISBN 0-19-502154-1). Oxford U Pr.

INDIA–HISTORY–SOURCES

Correa, Gaspar. Three Voyages of Vasco Da Gama. 1964. 23.50 (ISBN 0-8337-3364-8). B Franklin.
De, S. C. Public Speeches in Ancient & Medieval India. 1977. 9.00x (ISBN 0-686-22669-0). Intl Bk Dist.
Laird, M. A., ed. Bishop Heber in Northern India: Selections from Heber's Journal. LC 70-123673. (European Understanding of India Ser). (Illus.). 1971. 32.50 (ISBN 0-521-07873-3). Cambridge U Pr.
McNeill, William H. & Sedlar, Jean W., eds. China, India & Japan: The Middle Period. 1971. pap. 4.95x (ISBN 0-19-501439-1). Oxford U Pr.

INDIA–HISTORY–EARLY TO 1000 A.D

see also Chandela Dynasty; Kushans

Agrawal, D. P. & Kusumgar, Sheela. Prehistoric Chronology & Radiocarbon Dating in India. LC 75-900640. xvi, 172p. 1974. 10.00x (ISBN 0-88386-341-3). South Asia Bks.
Agrawal, D. R. Ecology & Archaeology of Western India. 1978. 26.00x (ISBN 0-8364-0152-2). South Asia Bks.
Al-Badaoni. Muntakhabu-T-Tawarikh, 3 vols. Ranking, George, et al, eds. 1973. Repr. Vol. 1. 27.50x ea. Vol. 2 (ISBN 0-8002-1735-7). Vol. 3 (ISBN 0-8002-2387-X) (ISBN 0-8002-2388-8). Intl Pubns Serv.
Allchin, Bridget, et al, eds. The Prehistory & Palaeogeography of the Great Indian Desert. 1978. 73.00 (ISBN 0-12-050450-2). Acad Pr.
Altekar, A. S. State & Government in Ancient India. 1977. text ed. 9.00x (ISBN 0-8426-1022-7). Verry.
Altheim, Franz & Stiehl, Ruth. Geschichte Mittelasiens im Altertum. (Illus., Ger.). 1970. 164.70x (ISBN 3-11-002677-5). De Gruyter.
Asthana, Shashi P. History & Archeology of India's Contacts with Other Countries from the Earliest Times to 300 B.C. LC 76-903130. 1976. 27.00x (ISBN 0-88386-787-7). South Asia Bks.
Ayyar, R. S. Manu's Land & Trade Laws. 1976. Repr. 12.50x (ISBN 0-88386-852-0). South Asia Bks.
Basham, A. L. Aspects of Ancient Indian Culture. 1981. pap. 2.00x (ISBN 0-210-22664-1). Asia.
Bhatia, H. S., ed. International Law & Practice in Ancient India. 1977. text ed. 12.75x (ISBN 0-391-01081-6). Humanities.
Bhattacharajee. History of Ancient India. (Illus.). 1980. text ed. 25.00x (ISBN 0-391-01756-X). Humanities.
Bhattacharajee, A. History of Ancient India. 1979. text ed. 25.00x (ISBN 0-391-01758-6). Humanities.
Bhattacharyya, Narendra N. Ancient Indian Rituals & Their Social Contents. 184p. 1975. 14.50x (ISBN 0-87471-735-3). Rowman.
Biswas, Atreyi. The Political History of the Hunas in India. LC 73-907423. 1973. 11.00x (ISBN 0-88386-301-4). South Asia Bks.
Borooah, Anundoram. Ancient Geography of India. 120p. 1971. Repr. of 1877 ed. 7.50x (ISBN 0-8002-0435-2). Intl Pubns Serv.
Chakraborti, Haripada. Trade & Commerce of Ancient India. 354p. 1966. 10.00x (ISBN 0-87471-305-6). Rowman.
Chandra, Moti. Trade & Trade Routes in Ancient India. 1977. 27.50x (ISBN 0-88386-982-9). South Asia Bks.
Chapekar, Nalinee M. Ancient India & Greece. 1977. 10.00x (ISBN 0-686-22657-7). Intl Bk Dist.
Chattopadhyay, Bhaskar. Kushana State & Indian Society: A Study in Post Mauryan Polity & Society. LC 76-900378. 1975. 19.00x (ISBN 0-88386-727-3). South Asia Bks.
Chattopadhyaya, Debiprasad. Science & Society in Ancient India. (Philosophical Currents Ser.: No. 22). 1978. text ed. 34.25x (ISBN 90-6032-098-0). Humanities.
Chattopadhyaya, S. Early History of North India. 3rd rev. ed. 1976. 7.50 (ISBN 0-89684-197-9). Orient Bk Dist.
Chattopadyaya, S. Some Early Dynasties of South India. 1974. 9.00 (ISBN 0-89684-320-3). Orient Bk Dist.
Chopra, S. R., ed. Early Man in North-West India. 1979. 10.00x (ISBN 0-8364-0451-3). South Asia Bks.
Chowdhury, K. A., et al. Ancient Agriculture & Forestry in North India. (Illus.). 1978. text ed. 15.95x (ISBN 0-210-40604-6). Asia.
Das, Sukla. Crime & Punishment in Ancient India, Circa AD 300 to AD 1100. 1977. 11.00x (ISBN 0-88386-980-2). South Asia Bks.
Davids, Thomas W. Buddhist India. LC 78-38349. (Select Bibliographies Reprint Ser). Repr. of 1903 ed. 28.00 (ISBN 0-8369-6766-6). Arno.
Dey, Nundo Lal. Geographical Dictionary of Ancient & Mediaeval India. 3rd ed. (Illus.). 262p. 1971. 22.00x (ISBN 0-8426-0332-8). Verry.
Dutt, Romesh C. History of India from the Earliest Times to the Sixth Century, B.C. LC 72-14391. (History of India: No. 1). Repr. of 1906 ed. 32.00 (ISBN 0-404-09001-X). AMS Pr.
Futuhu's Salatin or Shah Namah-I Hind of Isami, Vol. 2. 1977. text ed. 15.00x (ISBN 0-210-22380-4). Asia.
Hall, Kenneth. Trade & Statecraft in the Age of the Cholas. 1980. 16.00x (ISBN 0-8364-0597-8). South Asia Bks.
Harle, J. C. Gupta Sculpture: Indian Sculpture of the Fourth to the Sixth Centuries A.D. (Illus.). 76p. 1975. 28.50x (ISBN 0-19-817322-9). Oxford U Pr.
Havell, Ernest B. The History of Aryan Rule in India. LC 72-900073. (Illus.). 613p. 1972. Repr. of 1918 ed. 22.50x (ISBN 0-8002-0911-7). Intl Pubns Serv.
Hawkridge, Emma. Indian Gods & Kings: The Story of a Living Past. facs. ed. LC 68-24853. (Essay Index Reprint Ser). 1935. 19.50 (ISBN 0-8369-0521-0). Arno.
Husain, Agha Mahdi, ed. Futuhu's Salatin or Shah Namah - I Hind of Isami, Vol. 3. 1977. text ed. 15.00 (ISBN 0-210-40578-3). Asia.
Jain, Kailash C. Ancient Cities & Towns of Rajasthan. 1967. 15.00 (ISBN 0-89684-169-3). Orient Bk Dist.
Lane-Poole, S. Medieval India Under Mohammedan Rule: A. D. 712-1764, 2 Vols. in 1. LC 52-33515. Repr. of 1951 ed. 18.00 (ISBN 0-527-54300-4). Kraus Repr.
M'Crindle, John. Invasion of India by Alexander the Great. LC 74-155621. Repr. of 1896 ed. 12.50 (ISBN 0-404-04119-1). AMS Pr.
M'Crindle, John W. Invasion of India by Alexander the Great. 1971. Repr. of 1896 ed. 11.00 (ISBN 0-403-03616-X). Scholarly.
Mahajan, V. D. History of India - from Beginning to 1526 A. D. (Illus.). 1970. 5.50x (ISBN 0-8426-0208-9). Verry.
Mahajan, Vidya D. Early History of India. 1965. 5.00x (ISBN 0-8426-1371-4). Verry.
Maity, Sachindra K. The Imperial Guptas & Their Times. LC 75-908416. 1976. 14.50x (ISBN 0-88386-811-3). South Asia Bks.
Majumdar, Asoke K. Concise History of Ancient India: Political History, No. 1. LC 78-900933. 1977. 30.00x (ISBN 0-8002-0305-4). Intl Pubns Serv.
Majumdar, R. C. Ancient India. 8th ed. (Illus.). 1977. 12.95 (ISBN 0-89684-170-7); pap. 7.50 (ISBN 0-89684-171-5). Orient Bk Dist.
Meyer, Johann J. Sexual Life in Ancient India: A Study in the Comparative History of Indian Culture, 2 vols. in one. 606p. 1971. 15.00x (ISBN 0-8002-1974-0). Intl Pubns Serv.
Mishra, Shyam M. Yasavarman of Kanauj: Study of Political History, Society & Cultural Life of Northern India. 1978. 15.00x (ISBN 0-8364-0105-0). South Asia Bks.
Mishra, Yogendra. An Early History of Vaishali. 1962. 3.95 (ISBN 0-89684-198-7). Orient Bk Dist.
Mookerji, R. K. Ancient Indian Education. 5th ed. 1974. 16.00 (ISBN 0-89684-172-3). Orient Bk Dist.
--The Gupta Empire. 5th ed. (Illus.). 1973. 4.95 (ISBN 0-686-51742-3). Orient Bk Dist.
Mukherjee, Tara B. Inter-State Relations in Ancient India. 1967. 8.25x (ISBN 0-8426-1442-7). Verry.
Nigam, Shyamsunder. Economic Organisation in Ancient India: 200 B.C. - 200 A.D. LC 75-901700. 1975. 12.50x (ISBN 0-88386-593-9). South Asia Bks.
Pargiter, F. E. Ancient Indian Historical Tradition. 2nd ed. 1972. 5.95 (ISBN 0-89684-173-1). Orient Bk Dist.
Puri, Baij N. India Under the Kushanas. (Illus.). 1965. 7.50x (ISBN 0-685-19319-5). Paragon.
Rapson, E. J. Ancient India: From the Earliest Times to the First Century A.D. (Illus.). 208p. 1974. 10.00 (ISBN 0-89005-029-5). Ares.
Saletore, B. A. Ancient Indian Political Thought & Institutions. 1971. pap. 8.25x (ISBN 0-210-33807-5). Asia.
Sankalia, H. D. Pre History of India. 1977. 12.50x (ISBN 0-8364-0101-8). South Asia Bks.
--Prehistory of India. (Illus.). 1977. text ed. 11.00x (ISBN 0-685-41706-9). Humanities.
--Prehistory of India. LC 77-906557. (Illus.). 1977. 12.50x (ISBN 0-8002-0239-2). Intl Pubns Serv.
Sarkar, K. R. Public Finance in Ancient India. 1978. 14.00x (ISBN 0-8364-0155-7). South Asia Bks.
Satyanarayana, K. A Study of the History & Culture of the Andhras: From Stone Age to Feudalism, Vol.1. LC 76-900309. 1975. 11.00x (ISBN 0-88386-025-2). South Asia Bks.
Sedlar, Jean W. India & the Greek World: A Study in the Transmission of Culture. (Illus.). 381p. 1980. 30.00x (ISBN 0-8476-6173-3). Rowman.
Sharma, R. N. Brahmins Through the Ages. 1977. 18.00x (ISBN 0-686-22659-3). Intl Bk Dist.
Shendge, Malati J. The Civilized Demons: The Harappans in the Rgveda. (Illus.). 1977. 30.00x (ISBN 0-8364-0077-1). South Asia Bks.
Sidhanta, Mirmal K. The Heroic Age of India: A Comparative Study. LC 75-928104. 1975. Repr. of 1929 ed. 12.75x (ISBN 0-8364-0409-2). South Asia Bks.
Singh, M. M. Life in North-Eastern India in Pre-Mauryan Times: With Special References to 600 B.C. to 325 B.C. 1967. 6.50 (ISBN 0-89684-243-6). Orient Bk Dist.
Smith, R. Morton. Dates & Dynasties in Earliest India. 526p. 1973. text ed. 15.00x (ISBN 0-8426-0528-2). Verry.
Smith, Vincent A. History of India from the Sixth Century B.C. to the Mohammedan Conquest, Including the Invasion of Alexander the Great. LC 72-14391. (History of India: No. 2). Repr. of 1906 ed. 32.00 (ISBN 0-404-09002-8). AMS Pr.
Stein, Burton, ed. Essays on South India. (Asian Studies at Hawaii Ser.: No. 15). 288p. (Orig.). 1975. pap. text ed. 8.50x (ISBN 0-8248-0350-7). U Pr of Hawaii.
Thakur, Upendra. Corruption in Ancient India. 1979. 13.00x (ISBN 0-8364-0514-5). South Asia Bks.
--Introduction to Homicide in India: Ancient & Early Medieval Period. 1978. 9.50x (ISBN 0-8364-0184-0). South Asia Bks.
Tripathi, R. S. History of Ancient India. 1977. 11.50 (ISBN 0-89684-216-9); pap. 6.95 (ISBN 0-686-51747-4). Orient Bk Dist.
Vidyabhusana, Satis Chandra. History of the Mediaeval School of Indian Logic. 2nd ed. LC 77-913386. 1977. 12.50x (ISBN 0-8002-0299-6). Intl Pubns Serv.
Vijnanananda, Swami, tr. from Sanskrit. The Srimad Devi Bhagawatam, Pts. I & II. LC 75-985029. 1977. 35.00x (ISBN 0-8002-0256-2). Intl Pubns Serv.

INDIA–HISTORY–1000-1526

Al-Badaoni. Muntakhabu-T-Tawarikh, 3 vols. Ranking, George, et al, eds. 1973. Repr. Vol. 1. 27.50x ea. Vol. 2 (ISBN 0-8002-1735-7). Vol. 3 (ISBN 0-8002-2387-X) (ISBN 0-8002-2388-8). Intl Pubns Serv.
Carpenter, J. Estlin. Theism in Medieval India. 1977. Repr. of 1921 ed. 20.00x (ISBN 0-8002-0231-7). Intl Pubns Serv.
Carpenter, Joseph E. Theism in Medieval India. LC 77-27152. (Hibbert Lectures: 1919). Repr. of 1921 ed. 38.50 (ISBN 0-404-60419-6). AMS Pr.
Center for Advanced Study (History) Aligarh Muslim University, et al, eds. Medieval India: A Miscellany, Vol. 4. Centre for Advanced Study (History) Aligarh Muslim University. (Illus.). 1978. text ed. 17.50x (ISBN 0-210-40597-X). Asia.
Eaton, Richard M. Sufis of Bijapur, Thirteen Hundred to Seventeen Hundred Social Roles of Sufis in Medieaval India. LC 77-71978. (Illus.). 1978. 28.50 (ISBN 0-691-03110-X). Princeton U Pr.
Elliot, Henry M. The Mohammedan Period As Described by Its Own Historians. LC 72-14391. (History of India: No. 5). Repr. of 1907 ed. 32.00 (ISBN 0-404-09005-2). AMS Pr.
Futuhu's Salatin or Shah Namah-I Hind of Isami, Vol. 2. 1977. text ed. 15.00x (ISBN 0-210-22380-4). Asia.
Husain, A. M. Tughluq Dynasty. (Illus.). 1976. Repr. of 1935 ed. 30.00x (ISBN 0-8002-0250-3). Intl Pubns Serv.
Husain, Agha Mahdi, ed. Futuhu's Salatin or Shah Namah - I Hind of Isami, Vol. 3. 1977. text ed. 15.00 (ISBN 0-210-40578-3). Asia.
Husain, Yusuf. Indo-Muslim Polity (Turko-Afghan Period) 261p. 1971. 15.00x (ISBN 0-8002-1558-3). Intl Pubns Serv.
Khani, Muhammad B. Tarikh-I-Muhammadi. 110p. 1973. pap. text ed. 5.00x (ISBN 0-210-40545-7). Asia.
Lane-Poole, Stanley. History of India from the Reign of Akbar the Great to the Fall of the Moghul Empire. LC 72-14391. (History of India: No. 4). Repr. of 1906 ed. 32.00 (ISBN 0-404-09004-4). AMS Pr.
--Mediaeval India from the Mohammedan Conquest to the Reign of Akbar the Great. LC 72-14391. (History of India: No. 3). Repr. of 1906 ed. 32.00 (ISBN 0-404-09003-6). AMS Pr.
Mahajan, V. D. History of India - from Beginning to 1526 A. D. (Illus.). 1970. 5.50x (ISBN 0-8426-0208-9). Verry.
Nizami, K. A. Medieval India: A Miscellany. Vol. 2. 15.00x (ISBN 0-210-22615-3). Asia.
Nizami, K. A., ed. Medieval India: A Miscellany, Vol. 3. 1975. lib. bdg. 15.00 (ISBN 0-210-40581-3). Asia.
Puri, Baij N. India Under the Kushanas. (Illus.). 1965. 7.50x (ISBN 0-685-19319-5). Paragon.
Sharma, L. P. Medieval History of India. 450p. 1981. text ed. 25.00x (ISBN 0-7069-1115-6, Pub. by Vikas India). Advent NY.
Sinha, B. P. Dynastic History of Magadha. 1977. 14.00x (ISBN 0-88386-821-0). South Asia Bks.
Thakur, Upendra. Introduction to Homicide in India: Ancient & Early Medieval Period. 1978. 9.50x (ISBN 0-8364-0184-0). South Asia Bks.
Vidyabhusana, Satis Chandra. History of the Mediaeval School of Indian Logic. 2nd ed. LC 77-913386. 1977. 12.50x (ISBN 0-8002-0299-6). Intl Pubns Serv.

INDIA–HISTORY–EUROPEAN SETTLEMENTS, 1500-1765

see also Mogul Empire

Correia-Afonso, John, ed. Indo-Portuguese History: Sources & Problems. 250p. 1981. 22.00 (ISBN 0-19-561261-2). Oxford U Pr.
Das, H. Norris Embassy to Aurangzib, 1699-1702. Sarkar, S. C., ed. 1959. 6.50x (ISBN 0-8426-1228-9). Verry.
Della Valle, Pietro. The Travels of Pietro Della Valle to India, 2 Vols. Grey, Edward, ed. Hovers, G., tr. (Illus.). 58.00 (ISBN 0-8337-0822-8). B Franklin.
Dodwell, Henry H. Dupleix & Clive: The Beginning of Empire. 1968. Repr. of 1920 ed. 18.50 (ISBN 0-208-00713-X, Archon). Shoe String.
Eaton, Richard M. Sufis of Bijapur, Thirteen Hundred to Seventeen Hundred Social Roles of Sufis in Medieaval India. LC 77-71978. (Illus.). 1978. 28.50 (ISBN 0-691-03110-X). Princeton U Pr.
Edwardes, Michael. Plassey: The Founding of an Empire. LC 72-109011. 1970. 6.95 (ISBN 0-8008-6315-1). Taplinger.
Edwardes, Stephen M. & Garrett, Herbert L. Mughal Rule in India. LC 75-41084. Repr. of 1930 ed. 27.50 (ISBN 0-404-14537-X). AMS Pr.
Furnivall, John S. Netherlands India: A Study of Plural Economy. LC 77-86961. Repr. of 1944 ed. 34.50 (ISBN 0-404-16712-8). AMS Pr.

Gokhale, B. G. Surat in the Seventeenth Century: A Study in Urban Hstory of Pre-Modern India. (Scandinavian Inst. of Asian Studies: No. 28). 1977. pap. text ed. 12.50x (ISBN 0-7007-0099-4). Humanities.

Gopal, Surendra. Commerce & Crafts in Gujarat, 16-17th Century. LC 76-908401. 1976. 9.00x (ISBN 0-88386-417-7). South Asia Bks.

Guha, J. P. India in the Seventeenth Century, 2 vols. 1976. 30.00 (ISBN 0-686-20251-1). Intl Bk Dist.

Habib, Irfan. An Atlas of the Mughal Empire: Political & Economic Maps with Detailed Notes, Bibliography, & Index. (Illus.). 120p. 1981. 69.00x (ISBN 0-19-560379-6). Oxford U Pr.

Hill, Samuel C. Bengal in Seventeen Fifty-Six to Seventeen Fifty-Seven: A Selection of Public & Private Papers Dealing with the Affairs of the British in Bengal During the Reign of Siraj-Udduala, 3 Vols. LC 70-180684. Repr. of 1905 ed. Set. 92.50 (ISBN 0-404-03310-5). AMS Pr.

Hunter, William W. The European Struggle for Indian Supremacy in the Seventeenth Century. LC 72-14391. (History of India: No. 7). Repr. of 1907 ed. 32.00 (ISBN 0-404-09007-9). AMS Pr.

--History of India from the First European Settlements to the Founding of the English East India Company. LC 72-14391. (History of India: No. 6). Repr. of 1906 ed. 32.00 (ISBN 0-404-09006-0). AMS Pr.

Jahangir. Memoirs. Price, D., tr. (Oriental Translation Fund Ser.: No. 2). 1969. Repr. of 1829 ed. 15.50 (ISBN 0-384-26680-0). Johnson Repr.

Khan, Asham R. Chieftains in the Mughal-Empire During the Reign of Akbar. LC 77-905394. (Illus.). 1977. 12.50x (ISBN 0-8002-0216-3). Intl Pubns Serv.

Khan, Shafaat A. Sources for the History of British India in the 17th Century. 396p. 1975. Repr. of 1926 ed. 16.00x (ISBN 0-87471-562-8). Rowman.

--Sources for the History of British India in the 17th Century. 396p. 1975. Repr. of 1926 ed. 16.00x (ISBN 0-87471-562-8). Rowman.

Kincaid, A. Charles & Parasnis, R. B. History of the Maratha People. 1968. Repr. of 1931 ed. 11.00x (ISBN 0-8426-1333-1). Verry.

Lyall, Alfred C. History of India from the Close of the Seventeenth Century to the Present Time. LC 72-14391. (History of India: No. 8). Repr. of 1907 ed. 32.00 (ISBN 0-404-09008-7). AMS Pr.

Malleson, G. B. Decisive Battles of India, 1746-1849. 1973. 16.50 (ISBN 0-686-20211-2). Intl Bk Dist.

Mill, James. The History of British India. Thomas, William, ed. LC 74-11632. (Classics of British Historical Literature Ser). 1975. lib. bdg. 20.00x (ISBN 0-226-52555-4). U of Chicago Pr.

Radwan, Ann B. The Dutch in Western India, Sixteen Hundred One-Sixteen Thirty Two. 1979. 12.50x (ISBN 0-8364-0311-8). South Asia Bks.

Richards, J. F. Mughal Administration in Golconda. (Illus.). 360p. 1975. 49.00x (ISBN 0-19-821561-4). Oxford U Pr.

Sharma, L. P. Medieval History of India. 450p. 1981. text ed. 25.00x (ISBN 0-7069-1115-6, Pub. by Vikas India). Advent NY.

Tavernier, J. B. Tavernier's Travels in India, 2 vols. Crooke, W., ed. Ball, V., tr. (Illus.). 1977. 25.00x (ISBN 0-8002-0237-6). Intl Pubns Serv.

Thompson, Edward J. & Garratt, Geoffrey T. Rise & Fulfilment of British Rule in India. LC 70-137299. Repr. of 1934 ed. 37.50 (ISBN 0-404-06395-0). AMS Pr.

Verma, D. C. History of Bijapur. LC 74-901144. iii, 306p. 1974. 12.50x (ISBN 0-88386-498-3). South Asia Bks.

Whiteway, Richard S. Rise of Portuguese Power in India 1497-1550. LC 76-407549. Repr. of 1899 ed. 17.50x (ISBN 0-678-07258-2). Kelley.

Woodford, Peggy. Rise of the Raj. (Illus.). 1978. text ed. 22.25x (ISBN 0-391-00867-6). Humanities.

INDIA-HISTORY-18TH CENTURY

Archer, Mildred. Early Views of India: The Picturesque Journeys of Thomas & William Daniell 1788-1793. (Illus.). 240p. 1980. 37.50 (ISBN 0-500-01238-5). Thames Hudson.

Banga, Indu. Agrarian System of the Sikhs Seventeen Fifty-Nine to Eighteen Forty-Nine. 1979. 18.50x (ISBN 0-88386-758-3). South Asia Bks.

Datta, Kalikinkar. Survey of India's Social Life & Economic Condition in the 18th Century. 1707-1813. 2nd rev. ed. 1978. 17.50x (ISBN 0-8002-0265-1). Intl Pubns Serv.

Desai, W. S. Bombay & the Marathas up to 1774. 1970. 8.50x (ISBN 0-8426-0019-1). Verry.

Muhammad Hadi Kamwar Khan. Tazkirat Us-Salatin Chaghta: A Mughal Chronicle of Post Aurangzeb Period 1707-1724. Alam, Muzaffar, ed. x, 452p. (Persian.). 1980. text ed. 35.00 (ISBN 0-210-40612-7). Asia.

Raghuvanshi, V. P. Indian Society in the Eighteenth Century. 1970. 21.00 (ISBN 0-686-20259-7). Intl Bk Dist.

Spear, Percival. The Oxford History of Modern India: Seventeen Forty to Nineteen Seventy-Five. 2nd ed. 1979. pap. 8.95 (ISBN 0-19-561076-8). Oxford U Pr.

Yapp, M. E. Strategies of British India: Britain, Iran, & Afghanistan, 1798-1850. (Illus.). 704p. 1980. 98.00x (ISBN 0-19-822481-8). Oxford U Pr.

INDIA-HISTORY-BRITISH OCCUPATION, 1765-1947

see also Cawnpore–Siege, 1857

Ali, Abdullah Yusuf. A Cultural History of India During the British Period. LC 75-41006. Repr. of 1940 ed. 25.50 (ISBN 0-404-14723-2). AMS Pr.

Auber, Peter. Analysis of the Constitution of the East-India Company & of the Laws Passed by the Parliament for the Government of Their Affairs, at Home & Abroad, 2 vols. (With suppl). 1966. Repr. of 1828 ed. Set. 57.50 (ISBN 0-8337-0121-5). B Franklin.

Bakshi, S. R. Simon Commission & Indian Nationalism. 1977. 11.50x (ISBN 0-88386-966-7). South Asia Bks.

Ballhatchet, Kenneth. Race, Sex & Class Under the Raj: Imperial Attitudes & Policies & Their Critics, 1793-1905. LC 79-9604. 1980. 18.50x (ISBN 0-312-66144-4). St Martin.

Barr, Pat & Desmond, Ray. Simla: A Hill Station in British India. LC 78-53492. (Illus.). 1978. encore ed. 9.95 (ISBN 0-684-16345-4, ScribT). Scribner.

Bentinck, William A. The Correspondence of Lord William Bentinck, Governor General of India 1828-1835, 2 vols. Philips, Cyril H., ed. 1977. 169.00x set (ISBN 0-19-713571-4). Oxford U Pr.

Bhanu, Dharma. History & Administration of the North-Western Provinces, Subsequently Called Agra Province, 1803-1858. 1957. 6.50x (ISBN 0-8426-1160-6). Verry.

Bhatia, H. S. Military History of British India(1607-1947) 1977. pap. text ed. 14.50x (ISBN 0-391-02010-2). Humanities.

Bhattacharjee, J. B. Cachar Under British Rule in North East India. 1977. 12.00x (ISBN 0-8364-0388-6). South Asia Bks.

--The Garos & the English. 1978. 14.00x (ISBN 0-8364-0204-9). South Asia Bks.

Bhattacharyya, Sabyasachi. Financial Foundations of the British Raj. (Indian Institute of Advanced Study, Monographs Ser.). (Illus.). 355p. 1971. 11.00x (ISBN 0-8002-0636-3). Intl Pubns Serv.

Bhutani, V. C. The Apotheosis of Imperialism: Indian Land Economy Under Curzon. 1977. text ed. 15.00x (ISBN 0-8426-0945-8). Verry.

Bhuyan, Arun. The Quit India Movement. LC 75-905098. 1975. 14.00x (ISBN 0-88386-687-0). South Asia Bks.

Bose, M. L. British Policy in the North-East Frontier Agency. 1980. text ed. 22.50x (ISBN 0-391-01833-7). Humanities.

Chakravarty, Suhash. From Khyber to Oxus: A Study in Imperial Expansion. 1977. 14.00x (ISBN 0-88386-944-6, Orient Longman). South Asia Bks.

Chakravorty, U. N. Anglo-Maratha Relations & Malcolm Seventeen Ninety-Eight to Eighteen Thirty. 1979. text ed. 15.00x (ISBN 0-210-40623-2). Asia.

Chopra, P. N. Quit India Movement. 1976. 17.50x (ISBN 0-88386-735-4). South Asia Bks.

Collins, Larry & Lapierre, Dominique. Freedom at Midnight. 1980. pap. 3.50 (ISBN 0-380-00693-6, 51003). Avon.

Compton, Herbert. A Particular Account of the European Military Adventurers of Hindustan: From 1784 to 1803. (Oxford in Asia Historical Reprints). (Illus.). 1977. 20.50x (ISBN 0-19-577227-X). Oxford U Pr.

Crane, E. A. & Roy, W. T. Birth of the Indian Nations. (A History Monograph). (Orig.). pap. text ed. 4.50 (ISBN 0-686-71772-4, 00544). Heinemann Ed.

Das, Binod S. Studies in the Economic History of Orissa from Ancient Times to 1833. 1978. 11.50x (ISBN 0-8364-0200-6). South Asia Bks.

Datta, V. N. Madan Lal Dhingra & the Revolutionary Movement. 1978. 9.50x (ISBN 0-8364-0206-5). South Asia Bks.

Dutt, Romesh C. The Economic History of India. Incl. Vol. 1. The Economic History of Early British Rule; Vol. 2. India in the Victorian Age. LC 79-80224. 1902-04. Repr. Set. 46.50 (ISBN 0-8337-0981-X). B Franklin.

Edwardes, Michael. British India, 1772-1947: A Survey of the Nature & Effects of Alien Rule. LC 68-11579. (Illus.). (YA) (gr. 10 up). 1968. 13.95 (ISBN 0-8008-1000-7). Taplinger.

Ellinwood, DeWitt, ed. India & World War One. 1978. 12.50x (ISBN 0-8364-0191-3). South Asia Bks.

Embree, Ainslie T. Charles Grant & British Rule in India. LC 77-166029. (Columbia University Studies in the Social Sciences: No. 606). 10.00 (ISBN 0-404-51606-8). AMS Pr.

Frazer, Robert W. British India. LC 70-39404. (Select Bibliographies Reprint Series). 1972. Repr. of 1896 ed. 24.25 (ISBN 0-8369-9904-5). Arno.

--British India. LC 70-39404. (Select Bibliographies Reprint Series). 1972. Repr. of 1896 ed. 24.25 (ISBN 0-8369-9904-5). Arno.

Furnivall, John S. Netherlands India: A Study of Plural Economy. LC 77-86961. Repr. of 1944 ed. 34.50 (ISBN 0-404-16712-8). AMS Pr.

Ghosh, Suresh C. Dalhousie in India: 1848-1856. LC 75-904110. 1975. 9.50x (ISBN 0-88386-577-7). South Asia Bks.

Guha, Arun C. First Spark of Revolution: The Early Phase of India's Struggle for Independence, 1900-1920. 1971. 15.00 (ISBN 0-8046-8811-7). Kennikat.

Hunter, William W. History of British India, 2 vols. 900p. 1972. Repr. of 1899 ed. Set. 22.50x (ISBN 0-8002-1500-1). Intl Pubns Serv.

Hutchins, F. Illusion of Permanence: British Imperialism in India. 1967. 16.50 (ISBN 0-691-03023-5). Princeton U Pr.

Hutchins, Francis G. India's Revolution: Gandhi & the Quit India Movement. LC 72-96630. 384p. 1973. 18.50x (ISBN 0-674-45025-6). Harvard U Pr.

India. Dominion, 2 Vols. Poplai, S. L., ed. Repr. of 1959 ed. Set. 49.00 (ISBN 0-527-44400-6). Kraus Repr.

Iqbal, Afzal. The Life & Times of Mohamed Ali: An Analysis of the Hopes, Fears, & Aspirations of Muslim India from 1778-1931. LC 75-930033. 1974. 12.50x (ISBN 0-88386-630-7). South Asia Bks.

Jeffrey, Robin. Decline of Nayar Dominance: Society & Politics in Travancore 1847-1908. LC 74-22112. 1976. 33.00x (ISBN 0-8419-0184-8). Holmes & Meier.

Josh, Sohan S. Hindustan Gadar Party: A Short History. 1977. 9.00x (ISBN 0-8364-0089-5). South Asia Bks.

Kaye, John W. Kaye's & Malleson's History of the Indian Mutiny of 1857-58, 6 Vols. Malleson, George B., ed. LC 68-31001. 1968. Repr. of 1898 ed. Set. lib. bdg. 109.50x (ISBN 0-8371-4092-7, KAIM). Greenwood.

Keene, H. G. Hindustan Under Free Lances: Seventeen Seventy to Eighteen Twenty. (Illus.). 238p. 1972. Repr. of 1907 ed. 20.00x (ISBN 0-7165-2128-8, Pub. by Irish Academic Pr). Biblio Dist.

Khan, Shafaat A. Sources for the History of British India in the Seventeenth Century. 393p. 1978. Repr. of 1925 ed. 12.50 (ISBN 0-89684-159-6, Pub. by Cosmo Pubns India). Orient Bk Dist.

Low, D. A., ed. Soundings in Modern South Asian History. LC 68-20442. (Illus.). 1968. 24.00x (ISBN 0-520-00770-0). U of Cal Pr.

Lumby, Edmond W. The Transfer of Power in India: Nineteen Forty-Five to Nineteen Forty-Seven. LC 79-1634. 1981. Repr. of 1954 ed. 22.50 (ISBN 0-88355-938-2). Hyperion Conn.

Lyall, Alfred. The Rise & Expansion of the British Dominion in India. LC 67-24585. 1968. Repr. of 1894 ed. 25.00 (ISBN 0-86527-172-0). Fertig.

--Warren Hastings. facsimile ed. LC 73-140364. (Select Bibliographies Reprint Ser). Repr. of 1889 ed. 16.00 (ISBN 0-8369-5607-9). Arno.

Lyall, Alfred C. History of India from the Close of the Seventeenth Century to the Present Time. LC 72-14391. (History of India: No. 8). Repr. of 1907 ed. 32.00 (ISBN 0-404-09008-7). AMS Pr.

Malhotra, P. L. Administration of Lord Elgin in India, Eighteen Ninety-Four to Eighteen Ninety-Nine. 1979. text ed. 15.00x (ISBN 0-7069-0747-7, Pub. by Vikas India). Advent NY.

Malleson, G. B. Decisive Battles of India, 1746-1849. 1973. 16.50 (ISBN 0-686-20211-2). Intl Bk Dist.

Mill, James. The History of British India. Thomas, William, ed. LC 74-11632. (Classics of British Historical Literature Ser). 1975. lib. bdg. 20.00x (ISBN 0-226-52555-4). U of Chicago Pr.

--History of British India, 3 vols. 1972. 135.00 (ISBN 0-686-20242-2). Intl Bk Dist.

Mishra, D. P. Living an Era: India's March to Freedom, Vol. 1. 625p. 1975. 17.00x (ISBN 0-7069-0355-2). Intl Pubns Serv.

Misra, J. P. The Administration of India Under Lord Lansdowne. LC 75-906652. 1975. 7.50x (ISBN 0-8364-0378-9). South Asia Bks.

Mookerjee. Nanda. Netaji Through German Lens. 3rd ed. 1977. pap. 8.50x (ISBN 0-8002-0329-1). Intl Pubns Serv.

Moore, R. J. Churchill, Cripps, & India, Nineteen Thirty-Nine to Nineteen Forty-Five. 1979. 33.00x (ISBN 0-19-822485-0). Oxford U Pr.

Muhammad, Shan. Khaksar Movement in India. LC 72-908754. 164p. 1973. 7.50x (ISBN 0-8002-1631-8). Intl Pubns Serv.

Murphey, Rhoads. The Outsiders: The Western Experience in India & China. LC 76-27279. (Michigan Studies on China Ser.). 1976. 19.95x (ISBN 0-472-08679-0). U of Mich Pr.

Nightingale, Pamela. Trade & Empire in Western India, 1784-1806. (South Asian Studies: No. 9). (Illus.). 1970. 24.50 (ISBN 0-521-07651-X). Cambridge U Pr.

Palmer, Julian A. Mutiny Outbreak at Meerut in 1857. (Cambridge South Asian Studies: No. 2). 1966. 19.95 (ISBN 0-521-05901-1). Cambridge U Pr.

Pandhe, Pramila. Suppression of Drama in 19th Century India. 1978. 7.50x (ISBN 0-8364-0237-5). South Asia Bks.

Pemble, John. The Raj, the Indian Mutiny, & the Kingdom of Oudh, 1801-1859. LC 76-55892. 303p. 1978. 15.00 (ISBN 0-8386-2092-2). Fairleigh Dickinson.

Perti, P. K. South Asia Frontier Policies, Administrative Problems & Lord Lansdowne. 1976. 12.50x (ISBN 0-88386-847-4). South Asia Bks.

Prabhakar, Vishnu. Story of Swarajya: Part I. (Nehru Library for Children). (Illus.). (gr. 1-10). 1979. pap. 1.50 (ISBN 0-89744-185-0). Auromere.

Prakash, Sumangal. Story of Swarajya: Part II. (Nehru Library for Children). (Illus.). (gr. 1-10). 1979. pap. 1.50 (ISBN 0-89744-186-9). Auromere.

Rawding, F. W. Gandhi & the Struggle for India's Independence. (Cambridge Topic Bks.). (Illus.). 52p. (gr. 6 up). 1981. PLB 5.95 (ISBN 0-8225-1225-4). Lerner Pubns.

Reid, Escott. Envoy to Nehru. (Illus.). 301p. 1981. 23.00x (ISBN 0-19-561258-2). Oxford U Pr.

Reynolds, Reginald. White Sahibs in India. Repr. of 1937 ed. lib. bdg. 17.25x (ISBN 0-8371-4320-9, REWS). Greenwood.

Roy, M. P. Origin, Growth, & Suppression of the Pindaris. LC 73-903242. 355p. 1973. 17.50x (ISBN 0-8002-0948-6). Intl Pubns Serv.

Russell, William H. My Indian Mutiny Diary. Edwardes, Michael, ed. Repr. of 1957 ed. 14.00 (ISBN 0-527-78120-7). Kraus Repr.

Sankhdher, B. M. India: A Nineteenth Century Study of British Imperialism in Verse. 92p. 1972. 6.00x (ISBN 0-8002-1529-X). Intl Pubns Serv.

Sareen, T. R. Indian Revolutionary Movement Abroad, 1905-1920. (Illus.). 300p. 1979. 16.50x (ISBN 0-8002-0988-5). Intl Pubns Serv.

Schact, Joseph. The Origins of Muhammadan Jurisprudence. 364p. 1979. pap. text ed. 12.50x (ISBN 0-19-825357-5). Oxford U Pr.

Selected Writings of Jawaharlal Nehru, Vol. 3. 1981. 26.00x (ISBN 0-8364-0672-9, Orient Longman). South Asia Bks.

Siddiqi, Majid H. Agrarian Unrest in North India: The United Provinces 1918-22. (Illus.). 247p. 1978. 16.00x (ISBN 0-7069-0592-X, Pub. by Croom Helm Ltd. England). Biblio Dist.

Singh, Bhim Sen. The Cripps Mission. 1979. 10.50x (ISBN 0-8364-0532-3). South Asia Bks.

Sinha, P. B. Indian National Liberation Movement & Russia: 1905-1917. 336p. 1975. text ed. 18.00x (ISBN 0-8426-0992-X). Verry.

Sita Ram. From Sepoy to Subedar: Being the Life & Adventures of Subedar Sita Ram, a Native Officer of the Bengal Army. Lunt, James, ed. (Illus.). 1970. 15.00 (ISBN 0-208-01152-8). Shoe String.

Spear, Percival. The Oxford History of Modern India: Seventeen Forty to Nineteen Seventy-Five. 2nd ed. 1979. pap. 8.95 (ISBN 0-19-561076-8). Oxford U Pr.

Spear, Percival & Spear, Margaret. India Remembered. 1981. 19.00x (ISBN 0-86131-264-3, Orient Longman). South Asia Bks.

Thompson, Edward. The Making of the Indian Princes. 1980. Repr. of 1943 ed. 14.00x (ISBN 0-7007-0124-9, Pub. by Curzon Pr). South Asia Bks.

Thompson, Edward J. & Garratt, Geoffrey T. Rise & Fulfilment of British Rule in India. LC 70-137299. Repr. of 1934 ed. 37.50 (ISBN 0-404-06395-0). AMS Pr.

Tinker, Hugh. The Ordeal of Love: C. F. Andrews & India. (Illus.). 356p. 1979. text ed. 17.95x (ISBN 0-686-70608-0). Oxford U Pr.

Venkataramani, M. S. & Shrivastava, B. K. Quit India: The American Response in the Nineteen Forty-Two Struggle. 350p. 1979. 20.00x (ISBN 0-7069-0693-4, Pub. by Croom Helm Ltd. England). Biblio Dist.

Wainwright, Mary D., ed. Brothers in India. 1979. 22.00x (ISBN 0-8364-0510-2). South Asia Bks.

Webster, John C. The Christian Community & Change in Nineteenth Century North India. LC 76-900837. 1976. 15.00x (ISBN 0-333-90123-1). South Asia Bks.

Wilkinson, Theon. Two Monsoons. (Illus.). 240p. 1976. 13.50x (ISBN 0-7156-1015-5, Pub. by Duckworth England). Biblio Dist.

Woodford, Peggy. Rise of the Raj. (Illus.). 1978. text ed. 22.25x (ISBN 0-391-00867-6). Humanities.

Worswick, Clark. The Last Empire: Photography in British India 1855-1911. LC 76-21208. (Illus.). 160p. 1976. 25.00 (ISBN 0-912334-86-X); pap. 15.00 (ISBN 0-89381-018-5). Aperture.

Yadav, K. C. The Revolt of 1857 in Haryana. 1977. 7.00x (ISBN 0-88386-978-0). South Asia Bks.

Yapp, M. E. Strategies of British India: Britain, Iran, & Afghanistan, 1798-1850. (Illus.). 704p. 1980. 98.00x (ISBN 0-19-822481-8). Oxford U Pr.

Zaidi, A. Moin, ed. The Way Out to Freedom: An Enquiry into the Quit India Movement. 1973. 13.50x (ISBN 0-88386-217-4). South Asia Bks.

INDIA–HISTORY–SEPOY REBELLION, 1857-1858

Edwardes, A. Michael. A Season in Hell. LC 72-11088. (Illus.). 326p. 1973. 12.95 (ISBN 0-8008-7015-8). Taplinger.

Pemble, John. The Raj, the Indian Mutiny, & the Kingdom of Oudh, 1801-1859. LC 76-55892. 303p. 1978. 15.00 (ISBN 0-8386-2092-2). Fairleigh Dickinson.

Rawding, F. W. The Rebellion in India, 1857. (Cambridge Introduction to the History of Mankind Ser.). (Illus.). (gr. 4-5). 1977. pap. 3.95 (ISBN 0-521-20683-9). Cambridge U Pr.

INDIA–HISTORY–1947-

see also India-Pakistan Conflict, 1965; Sino-Indian Border Dispute, 1957-

Alan. Mission with Mountbatten. 2nd ed. LC 77-4388. (Illus.). 1977. Repr. of 1972 ed. lib. bdg. 25.50x (ISBN 0-8371-9596-9, CJMM). Greenwood.

Bowles, Chester. View from New Delhi: Selected Speeches & Writings. (Illus.). 1969. 20.00x (ISBN 0-300-01233-0); pap. 1.95 (ISBN 0-300-01234-9, Y227). Yale U Pr.

Brown, W. Norman. The United States & India, Pakistan, Bangladesh. 3rd ed. LC 72-81270. (American Foreign Policy Library). Orig. Title: The United States & India & Pakistan. (Illus.). 396p. 1972. 20.00x (ISBN 0-674-92446-0); pap. 7.95x (ISBN 0-674-92447-9, HP31). Harvard U Pr.

Gopal. How India Struggled for Freedom. 1967. 8.75x (ISBN 0-8002-0642-8). Intl Pubns Serv.

Gupta, Karunakar. The Hidden History of the Sino-Indian Frontier. LC 74-903923. 200p. 1974. 9.50x (ISBN 0-88386-438-X). South Asia Bks.

History of the Freedom Movement in India, 4 vols. Incl. Vol. 1. 1750-1856. 2nd rev. ed. Majumdar, R. C. 471p. 1971. 7.50x (ISBN 0-8002-1508-7); Vol. 2. 1800-1905. 2nd rev. ed. Majumdar, R. C. 509p. 1975. 10.00x (ISBN 0-8002-1509-5); Vol. 3. 1905-1924. Chand, Tara. 527p. 1972. 7.50x (ISBN 0-8002-1510-9); Vol. 4. 1924-1947. Chand, Tara. 1972. pap. 10.00x (ISBN 0-8002-1511-7). 1973. Intl Pubns Serv.

Jain, J. P. India & Disarmament, Vol. 1: The Nehru Era, an Analytical Study. LC 74-900738. 211p. 1974. 12.00 (ISBN 0-88386-462-2). South Asia Bks.

Lyall, Alfred C. History of India from the Close of the Seventeenth Century to the Present Time. LC 72-14391. (History of India: No. 8). Repr. of 1907 ed. 32.00 (ISBN 0-404-09008-7). AMS Pr.

Mankekar, D. R. Leaves from a War Reporter's Diary. 1977. text ed. 11.95 (ISBN 0-7069-0505-9, Pub. by Vikas India). Advent NY.

Menon. Transfer of Power in India. 1980. 17.50x (ISBN 0-8364-0585-4, Pub. by Orient Longman). South Asia Bks.

Munshi, K. M. End of an Era-Hyderabad Memories. 1957. 6.75x (ISBN 0-8426-0032-9). Verry.

Nargolkar, Vasant. JP Vindicated. 1977. text ed. 9.00 (ISBN 0-8426-1044-8). Verry.

Nayar, Kuldip. India After Nehru. 1975. 9.00 (ISBN 0-686-20248-1). Intl Bk Dist.

Rawding, F. W. Gandhi & the Struggle for India's Independence. (Cambridge Topic Bks.). (Illus.). 52p. (gr. 6 up). 1981. PLB 5.95 (ISBN 0-8225-1225-4). Lerner Pubns.

Robinson, F. Separatism Among Indian Muslims. (South Asian Studies: No. 16). 400p. 1975. 39.95 (ISBN 0-521-20432-1). Cambridge U Pr.

Singh, Sukhwant. India's Wars Since Independence: Vol. 1: The Liberation of Bangladesh. 1980. text ed. 18.00x (ISBN 0-7069-1057-5, Pub. by Vikas India). Advent NY.

Spear, Percival. The Oxford History of Modern India: Seventeen Forty to Nineteen Seventy-Five. 2nd ed. 1979. pap. 8.95 (ISBN 0-19-561076-8). Oxford U Pr.

Tharyan, P. India: The Critical Decade After Nehru. 212p. 1975. text ed. 10.50x (ISBN 0-8426-0810-9). Verry.

Varkey, Ouseph. At the Crossroads: Sino- Indian Border Dispute & the Communist Party of India, 1959-1963. LC 74-903995. 300p. 1974. 12.50x (ISBN 0-88386-437-1). South Asia Bks.

Vepa, Ram K. Change & Challenge in Indian Administration. 1978. 14.00x (ISBN 0-8364-0201-4). South Asia Bks.

Wolpert, Stanley A. Tilak & Gokhale: Revolution & Reform in the Making of Modern India. (California Library Reprint Ser.). 1977. 28.50x (ISBN 0-520-03339-6). U of Cal Pr.

INDIA–HISTORY, MILITARY

Baranwal, S. P., ed. Military Year Book, 1978-1979. 13th ed. (Illus.). 1979. 25.00x (ISBN 0-8002-0984-2). Intl Pubns Serv.

Bhatia, H. S. Military History of British India. 1977. 14.00x (ISBN 0-88386-945-4). South Asia Bks.

Ghosh, Kalyan Kumar. The Indian National Army: Second Front of the Indian Independence Movement. LC 70-903119. (Illus.). 351p. 1969. 9.00x (ISBN 0-8002-1545-1). Intl Pubns Serv.

Jain, J. P. India & Disarmament, Vol. 1: The Nehru Era, an Analytical Study. LC 74-900738. 211p. 1974. 12.00 (ISBN 0-88386-462-2). South Asia Bks.

Longer, V. Red Coats to Olive Green: A History of the Indian Army 1600-1974. LC 74-903017. 543p. 1974. 13.25x (ISBN 0-8002-1907-4). Intl Pubns Serv.

Marx, Karl & Engels, Friedrich. The First Indian War of Independence Eighteen Fifty-Seven to Eighteen Fifty-Nine. 222p. 1975. 2.10 (ISBN 0-8285-0027-4, Pub. by Progress Pubs Russia). Imported Pubns.

Prasad, S. N. Survey of Work Done in the Military History of India. 1976. 6.50x (ISBN 0-88386-939-X). South Asia Bks.

Raina, Asoka. Inside R.A.W. The Story of India's Secret Service. 175p. 1981. 10.50x (ISBN 0-7069-1299-3, Pub. by Vikas India). Advent NY.

Saxena, K. M. Military System of India, 1850-1900. 1973. 15.00x (ISBN 0-8426-0621-1). Verry.

Singh, Sukhwant. India's Wars Since Independence, Vol. III. 400p. 1981. text ed. 45.00x (ISBN 0-686-73083-6, Pub. by Vikas India). Advent NY.

--India's Wars Since Independence: Defence of the Western Front, Vol. II. 350p. 1981. text ed. 35.00 (ISBN 0-7069-1277-2, Pub by Vikas India). Advent NY.

--India's Wars Since Independence: Vol. 1: The Liberation of Bangladesh. 1980. text ed. 18.00x (ISBN 0-7069-1057-5, Pub. by Vikas India). Advent NY.

INDIA–IMPRINTS

Prasher, Ram G. Indian Books, 1974 to 1975: An Annual Bibliography. 1975. 15.00 (ISBN 0-8002-1538-9). Intl Pubns Serv.

INDIA–INDUSTRIES

Anstey, Vera. The Economic Development of India. Wilkins, Mira, ed. LC 76-29760. (European Business Ser.). (Illus.). 1977. Repr. of 1952 ed. lib. bdg. 39.00x (ISBN 0-405-09775-1). Arno.

Bagchi, Amiya K. Private Investment in India & Pakistan, 1900-1939. LC 79-152631. (South Asian Studies: No. 10). (Illus.). 1971. 53.50 (ISBN 0-521-07641-2). Cambridge U Pr.

Behari, Bepin. Rural Industrialization in India. 1976. 13.50 (ISBN 0-7069-0448-6). Intl Bk Dist.

Chadda, R. S. Inventory Management in India. 2nd ed. 126p. 1971. 5.50x (ISBN 0-685-25221-3). Paragon.

Giri, V. V. Labour Problems in Indian Industry. 3rd rev. ed. 564p. 1973. pap. text ed. 12.50x (ISBN 0-210-33692-7). Asia.

Gupta, L. C. Readings in Industrial Finance, India. 1976. 14.00x (ISBN 0-333-90136-3). South Asia Bks.

Johnson, B. L. C. India: Resources & Development. LC 78-15402. (Illus.). 1979. text ed. 23.50x (ISBN 0-06-493348-2). B&N.

Klass, Morton. From Field to Factory: Community Structure & Industrialization in West Bengal. LC 78-1552. (Illus.). 1978. text ed. 18.50x (ISBN 0-915980-34-7). Inst Study Human.

Kothari's Economic & Industrial Guide of India, 1980-81. 33rd ed. LC 64-6162. 2500p. 1981. 60.00x (ISBN 0-8002-2783-2). Intl Pubns Serv.

Liedholm, Carl E. The Indian Iron & Steel Industry: An Analysis of Comparative Advantage. LC 72-619698. 1972. 8.00 (ISBN 0-87744-121-9). Mich St U Busn.

Manoharan, S. Indian Tea: Strategy for Development. LC 73-907169. 168p. 1974. 7.50x (ISBN 0-8002-0062-4). Intl Pubns Serv.

Mathur, M. M. Vanaspati Industries in India. 160p. 1981. text ed. 13.50x (ISBN 0-391-02381-0, Pub. by Concept India). Humanities.

Menezes, Francis A. Cases in Management: India. 1977. 14.00x (ISBN 0-8364-0045-3). South Asia Bks.

Nandy, Ashis & Owens, Raymond L. The New Vaisyas: Enterpreneurial Opportunity & Entrepreneurical Response in the Engineering Industry of an Indian City. LC 77-93390. 1978. 13.95 (ISBN 0-89089-057-9). Carolina Acad Pr.

Ray, Rajat K. Industrialization in India: Growth & Conflict in the Private Corporate Sector, 1914-47. 1979. text ed. 15.95x (ISBN 0-19-561064-4). Oxford U Pr.

Singh, K. R. State & Industrialization of Developing Countries. 1969. 5.50x (ISBN 0-8426-1532-6). Verry.

Sinha, Durganand. Studies in Industrial Psychology. (Illus.). 181p. 1974. 15.00x (ISBN 0-8002-2031-5). Intl Pubns Serv.

Somasekhara, N. Efficacy of Industrial Estate in India. 1975. 10.50 (ISBN 0-7069-0374-9). Intl Bk Dist.

Upadhyay, M. N. Economics of Handicrafts Industry. (Illus.). 149p. 1973. 7.50x (ISBN 0-8002-1383-1). Intl Pubns Serv.

Vepa, Ram. Joint Ventures: A New Technique for Industrial Growth, India. 1981. 17.50x (ISBN 0-8364-0695-8, Pub. by Manohar India). South Asia Bks.

Watt, Sir G. The Commercial Products of India. 1966. 17.00 (ISBN 0-934454-25-6). Lubrecht & Cramer.

INDIA–INTELLECTUAL LIFE

Aurobindo, Sri. Foundations of Indian Culture. 1979. pap. 10.00 (ISBN 0-89744-909-6). Auromere.

Jha, Akhileshwar. Intellectuals at the Crossroads: The Indian Situation. 1977. text ed. 11.00x (ISBN 0-7069-0529-6). Verry.

Kar, Bijayananda. The Theories of Error in Indian Philosophy. 1978. 11.00x (ISBN 0-8364-0304-5). South Asia Bks.

Kopf, David. The Brahmo Samaj & the Shaping of the Modern Indian Mind. LC 78-70303. 1979. text ed. 29.50 (ISBN 0-691-03125-8). Princeton U Pr.

Mookerji, Radha K. Men & Thought in Ancient India. 3rd ed. 1970. 3.50x (ISBN 0-8426-0207-0). Verry.

Oman, John C. The Mystics, Ascetics & Saints of India. lib. bdg. 75.00 (ISBN 0-8490-0698-8). Gordon Pr.

Singh, Mohinder, ed. Learned Institutions in India. 1969. 5.00x (ISBN 0-8426-0138-4). Verry.

Srivastava, H. C. Intellectuals in Contemporary India. 1979. 11.50x (ISBN 0-8364-0296-0). South Asia Bks.

INDIA–JUVENILE LITERATURE

Bothwell, Jean. First Book of India. rev. ed. LC 66-10129. (First Bks). (Illus.). (gr. 4-6). 1978. PLB 7.40 (ISBN 0-531-02229-3). Watts.

--India. 2nd rev. ed. Whipple, Jane, ed. LC 78-2511. (First Bks). (Illus.). (gr. 4-6). 1978. PLB 6.90 s&l (ISBN 0-531-02229-3). Watts.

Brown, Marcia. The Blue Jackal. LC 76-54845. (Illus.). (gr. 1-3). 1977. reinforced bdg. 6.95 (ISBN 0-684-14905-2, ScribJ). Scribner.

Dhar, Sheila. Children's History of India. 7th rev. ed. (Illus.). 178p. (gr. 5-7). pap. text ed. 1.50x (ISBN 0-88253-919-1). Ind-US Inc.

--This India. LC 75-307781. (Illus.). 208p. 1974. 5.00x (ISBN 0-8002-2083-8). Intl Pubns Serv.

Galbraith, Catherine A. & Mehta, Rama. India Now & Through Time. (gr. 6 up). 1980. 8.95 (ISBN 0-395-29207-7). HM.

Ghosh, A. Chanakya. (Illus.). (gr. 1-8). 1979. pap. 2.00 (ISBN 0-89744-152-4). Auromere.

Khanna, K. As They Saw India. (Nehru Library for Children). (Illus.). (gr. 1-9). 1979. pap. 1.50 (ISBN 0-89744-172-9). Auromere.

Learning About People & Cultures. Incl. The Mediterranean Rim (ISBN 0-88343-636-1); Southeast Asia (ISBN 0-88343-646-9); India (ISBN 0-88343-644-2). (People & Cculture Ser.). (gr. 9 up). 1974-76. 5.28 ea.; tchrs' manual 1.50 ea. McDougal-Littell.

Norris, Marianna. Young India. LC 66-14146. (Illus.). (gr. 3 up). 1966. PLB 5.95 (ISBN 0-396-06559-7). Dodd.

Singh, Mala. Kashmir. (Nehru Library for Children). (Illus.). (gr. 1-10). 1979. pap. 1.50 (ISBN 0-89744-177-X). Auromere.

Soleillant, Claude. Activities & Projects: India in Color. LC 77-79499. (Activities & Projects Ser.). (Illus.). (gr. 2 up). 1977. 9.95 (ISBN 0-8069-4550-8); PLB 9.29 (ISBN 0-8069-4551-6). Sterling.

Sterling Publishing Company Editors. India in Pictures. rev. ed. LC 68-6396. (Visual Geography Ser). (Illus.). (gr. 5 up). 1968. PLB 4.99 (ISBN 0-8069-1009-7); pap. 2.95 (ISBN 0-8069-1008-9). Sterling.

Traub, James. India: The Challenge of Change. LC 81-11106. (Illus.). 160p. (gr. 7 up). 1981. PLB 9.79 (ISBN 0-671-42834-9). Messner.

U. S. Committee For UNICEF. Hi Neighbor Book No. 4: Guinea, India, Iran, Mexico, Portugal. (Illus.). (gr. 4-6). 4.95 (ISBN 0-8038-2981-7); pap. 2.00 (ISBN 0-8038-2980-9). Hastings.

INDIA–KINGS AND RULERS

Das, Debesh. Vanishing Maharajas. 1970. 8.25x (ISBN 0-8426-0092-2). Verry.

Diver, Katherine H. Royal India. facs. ed. LC 76-142620. (Essay Index Reprint Ser). 1942. 20.00 (ISBN 0-8369-2152-6). Arno.

Godden, Rumer. Gulbadan: Portrait of a Rose Princess at the Mughal Court. LC 80-51752. (Illus.). 160p. 1981. 14.95 (ISBN 0-670-35756-1, Studio). Viking Pr.

Hawkridge, Emma. Indian Gods & Kings: The Story of a Living Past. facs. ed. LC 68-24853. (Essay Index Reprint Ser). 1935. 19.50 (ISBN 0-8369-0521-0). Arno.

Low, Sidney. The Indian States & Ruling Princes. 1929. 15.00 (ISBN 0-685-43890-2). Norwood Edns.

Malik, Zahir U. The Reign of Muhammad Shah. (Dept of History, Aligarh Muslim University Ser.). (Illus.). 1977. text ed. 25.00x (ISBN 0-210-40598-8). Asia.

Mankekar, D. R. Accession to Extinction: The Story of Indian Princes. 1974. 10.50 (ISBN 0-686-20187-6). Intl Bk Dist.

Ramusack, Barbara. The Princes of India in the Twilight of Empire: Dissolution of a Patron-Client System 1914-1939. LC 78-18161. (Illus.). 1978. 20.00x (ISBN 0-8142-0272-1). Ohio St U Pr.

Singh, R. C. Kingship in Northern India: 600-1200 A.D. 1968. 5.00x (ISBN 0-8426-1537-7). Verry.

Smith, R. Morton. Dates & Dynasties in Earliest India. 526p. 1973. text ed. 15.00x (ISBN 0-8426-0528-2). Verry.

INDIA–LANGUAGES

Bareh, Hamlet. The Language & Literature of Meghalaya. LC 78-670053. 1977. 7.50x (ISBN 0-8002-0215-5). Intl Pubns Serv.

Breton, Roland J. Atlas Geographique Des Langues et Des Ethnics De L'inde et Du Subcontinent. (Illus., Fr.). 1977. 30.00x (ISBN 2-7637-6760-5, Pub. by Laval). Intl Schol Bk Serv.

Das Gupta, Jyotirindra. Language Conflict & National Development: Group Politics & National Language Policy in India. LC 75-94992. (Center for South & Southeast Asia Studies, UC Berkeley). 1970. 19.00x (ISBN 0-520-01590-8). U of Cal Pr.

Gerow, Edwin. A Glossary of Indian Figures of Speech. (Publications in Near & Middle East Ser. A: No. 16). 436p. 1971. text ed. 60.00x (ISBN 90-2791-759-0). Mouton.

Gopal, Ram. Linguistic Affairs of India. 1967. 8.50x (ISBN 0-210-27158-2). Asia.

Gordon, Kent H. Phonology of Dhangar-Kurux. 1976. pap. 2.50x (ISBN 0-88312-853-5). Summer Inst Ling.

Mehrotra, R. R. Sociology of Secret Language. 1977. text ed. 7.50x (ISBN 0-8426-1048-0). Verry.

Prasad, N. J. The Language Issue in India. 1980. text ed. 11.25x (ISBN 0-391-01935-X). Humanities.

Reddi, G. S. Language Problem in India. 1974. text ed. 4.00x (ISBN 0-8426-0658-0). Verry.

Shukla, Shaligram. Bhojpuri Grammar. (Bhojpuri.). 1981. text ed. 10.00x (ISBN 0-87840-189-X). Georgetown U Pr.

INDIA–MAPS

Borooah, Anundoram. Ancient Geography of India. 120p. 1971. Repr. of 1877 ed. 7.50x (ISBN 0-8002-0435-2). Intl Pubns Serv.

Davies, C. Collin. Historical Atlas of the Indian Peninsula. 2nd ed. (Illus.). 1959. pap. 4.95x (ISBN 0-19-635139-1). Oxford U Pr.

Gole, Susan. Early Maps of India. (Illus.). 1976. text ed. 13.00x (ISBN 0-391-00678-9). Humanities.

Tamoskar, B. G. & Deshmukh, V. M. Geographical Interpretation of Indian Topographical Maps. 80p. 1981. 10.00x (ISBN 0-86125-401-5, Pub. by Orient Longman India). State Mutual Bk.

INDIA–NATIONAL ARMY

Mollo, Boris. The Indian Army. (Illus.). 1981. 24.95 (ISBN 0-7137-1074-8, Pub. by Blandford Pr England). Sterling.

INDIA–NATIVE RACES

Biddulph, John. Tribes of the Hindoo Koosh. (Illus.). 352p. 1971. Repr. of 1880 ed. 45.00x (ISBN 0-8002-2109-5). Intl Pubns Serv.

Dalton, Edward T. Tribal History of Eastern India. (The Native Races of India Ser). (Illus.). 420p. 1974. Repr. of 1872 ed. 37.50x (ISBN 0-8002-2108-7). Intl Pubns Serv.

Dhasmana, M. M. The Ramos of Arunachal. 1980. text ed. 16.50x (ISBN 0-391-01827-2). Humanities.

--The Ramos of Arunachal: A Socio-Cultural Study. (Illus.). 298p. 1979. 17.50x (ISBN 0-8002-2300-4). Intl Pubns Serv.

Doshi, S. L. Processes of Tribal Unification & Integration: Case Study of the Bhils. 1978. 11.00x (ISBN 0-8364-0291-X). South Asia Bks.

Engineer, Asghar Ali. The Bohras. 1980. text ed. 18.95x (ISBN 0-7069-0836-8, Pub. by Vikas India). Advent NY.

Fuchs, Stephen. The Aboriginal Tribes of India. LC 76-27186. 1977. 15.95 (ISBN 0-312-00175-4). St Martin.

Haimendorf-Von Furer, C. The Gonds of Andhra Pradesh. (Studies on Modern Asia & Africa: No. 12). 1979. text ed. 42.50x (ISBN 0-04-301090-3). Allen Unwin.

Hodson, T. C. The Meitheis. 2nd ed. Horam, M., ed. & intro. by. LC 75-903067. 1975. 10.00x (ISBN 0-88386-582-3). South Asia Bks.

Misra, Bani P. Socioeconomic Adjustments of Tribals: A Case Study of Tripura Jhumias (India) LC 76-903504. 1976. 6.50x (ISBN 0-88386-700-1). South Asia Bks.

Russell, R. V. & Lal, R. B. The Tribes & Castes of the Central Provinces of India, 4 vol. set. 1969. Repr. of 1914 ed. text ed. 105.00x (ISBN 0-391-02061-7). Humanities.

Schwartzburg, Leon. The North Indian Peasant Goes to Market. 176p. 1979. text ed. 12.00 (ISBN 0-89684-097-2, Pub. by Motilal Banarsidass India). Orient Bk Dist.

Shakespear, John. The Lushei Kuki Clans. LC 77-87057. Repr. of 1912 ed. 25.00 (ISBN 0-404-16866-3). AMS Pr.

INDIA-POLITICS AND GOVERNMENT

Ahmad, Imtiaz. Muslim Political Behaviour: A Study of the Muslim Stratagem in Indian Electoral Politics. 1982. 14.00x (ISBN 0-88386-756-7). South Asia Bks.

Aiyar, Sadashiv P. & Srinivasan, R. Studies in Indian Democracy. 1965. 10.00x (ISBN 0-8188-1005-X). Paragon.

Ali, M. Athar. Mughal Nobility Under Aurangzeb. pap. 6.00x (ISBN 0-210-31247-5). Asia.

Altekar, A. S. State & Government in Ancient India. 1977. 7.50 (ISBN 0-89684-321-1). Orient Bk Dist.

Ansari, M. A. Muslims & the Congress: Correspondence of Dr. M. A. Ansari. Hasan, M., ed. 1979. 18.50 (ISBN 0-8364-0381-9). South Asia Bks.

Appadorai, A. Essays in Indian Politics & Foreign Policy. 1971. 10.00x (ISBN 0-8426-0228-3). Verry.

Arnold, David. The Congress in Tamiland: Nationalist Politics in South India, Nineteen Nineteen to Nineteen Thirty-Seven. 1977. 12.00x (ISBN 0-88386-958-6). South Asia Bks.

Atal, Yogesh. Local Communities & National Politics: A Study in Communication Links & Political Involvement. (Illus.). 428p. 1971. 20.00x (ISBN 0-8002-0920-6). Intl Pubns Serv.

Awashti, Dhyaneshwar. Administrative History of Modern India: Sir Spencer Harcourt Butler's Administration 1918-1922. LC 73-901134. 168p. 1973. 9.50x (ISBN 0-8002-0418-2). Intl Pubns Serv.

Bahadur, Kalim. The Jama'at'i'Islami of Pakistan: Political Thought & Political Action. 1977. 12.50x (ISBN 0-8364-0058-5). South Asia Bks.

Bailey, Frederick G. Tribe, Caste & Nation. 1971. Repr. of 1960 ed. text ed. 19.50x (ISBN 0-7190-0250-8). Humanities.

Banerjea, Pramathanath. Public Administration in Ancient India. 316p. 1973. Repr. 18.75x (ISBN 0-8002-1885-X). Intl Pubns Serv.

Banerjee, J. India in Soviet Global Strategy. 1977. 12.50x (ISBN 0-88386-908-X). South Asia Bks.

Barnett, M. R. The Politics of Cultural Nationalism in South India. 1976. 28.50 (ISBN 0-691-07577-8). Princeton U Pr.

Barnett, Richard B. North India Between Empires: Awadh, the Mughals, & the British, 1720-1801. LC 78-64459. (Center for South & Southeast Asian Studies). 294p. 1980. 25.00x (ISBN 0-520-03787-1). U of Cal Pr.

Bhalla, R. P. Elections in India. LC 73-906049. 496p. 1973. 15.00x (ISBN 0-8002-0580-4). Intl Pubns Serv.

Bhambhri, C. P. The Urban Voter: Municipal Elections in Rajasthan. LC 73-907421. (Illus.). 222p. 1974. 10.00x (ISBN 0-8002-2128-1). Intl Pubns Serv.

Bhambhri, C. P. & Verma, P. S. The Urban Voter: Municipal Elections in Rajasthan, an Empirical Study. LC 73-907421. 222p. 1973. 11.50x (ISBN 0-88386-342-1). South Asia Bks.

Bhargava, B. S. Indian Local Government: A Study. 1978. 13.50 (ISBN 0-8364-0035-6). South Asia Bks.

Bhasin, Prem. Politics: National & International. 1970. 13.50 (ISBN 0-686-20285-6). Intl Bk Dist.

Bhatia, H. L. Centre-State Financial Relations in India. 1979. 11.00x (ISBN 0-8364-0323-1). South Asia Bks.

Bhatia, H. S., ed. Origin & Development of Legal & Political System in India, Vol. 1. 1976. text ed. 9.00x (ISBN 0-391-01094-8). Humanities.

--Origin & Development of Legal & Political System in India, Vol.1. 1977. text ed. 15.00 (ISBN 0-210-40590-2). Asia.

--Origin & Development of Legal & Political System in India, Vol. 2. 1978. text ed. 9.00x (ISBN 0-391-01095-6). Humanities.

--Origin & Development of Legal & Political System in India, Vol. 3. 1978. text ed. 9.00x (ISBN 0-391-01096-4). Humanities.

Bhattacharya, Bhabani. Socio-Political Currents in Bengal: Nineteenth Century Perspective. 160p. 1980. text ed. 16.50 (ISBN 0-7069-0988-7, Pub. by Vikas India). Advent NY.

Biswas, Dipti K. Political Sociology: An Introduction. 1978. 7.00x (ISBN 0-8364-0138-7). South Asia Bks.

Bjorkman, James W. Politics of Administrative Alienation in India's Rural Development Programme. 1979. 14.00x (ISBN 0-8364-0341-X). South Asia Bks.

Bose, M. L., ed. Historical & Constitutional Documents of North Eastern India. 1980. text ed. 19.50x (ISBN 0-391-01867-1). Humanities.

Bowles, R., et al. Indian: Assimilation, Integration, or Separation. 1972. pap. text ed. 3.53 (ISBN 0-13-456954-7). P-H.

Bueno De Mesquita, Bruce & Park, Richard L. India's Political System. 2nd ed. (Illus.). 1979. pap. 8.50 ref (ISBN 0-13-456921-0). P-H.

Carras, Mary C. Dynamics of Indian Political Factions: A Study of District Councils in the State of Maharashtra. LC 76-186250. (Cambridge South Asian Studies: No. 12). (Illus.). 288p. 1972. 33.95 (ISBN 0-521-08521-7). Cambridge U Pr.

Chandra, Satish. Regionalism & National Integration. 1976. 12.50x (ISBN 0-88386-870-9). South Asia Bks.

Chesney, George T. Indian Polity. rev. ed. Maheshwari, Shriram, ed. 1976. 21.00x (ISBN 0-88386-771-0). South Asia Bks.

Chintamani, Sir Shirroavoore Y. Indian Politics Since the Mutiny: Being an Account of the Development of Public Life & Political Institutions of Prominent Local Political Personalities. LC 79-4911. 1981. Repr. of 1947 ed. 19.50 (ISBN 0-88355-961-7). Hyperion Conn.

Chopra, Pran. India's Second Liberation. 1974. 16.00x (ISBN 0-262-03048-9). MIT Pr.

Cohen, Stephen P. The Indian Army: Its Contribution to the Development of a Nation. LC 77-111421. 1971. 25.00x (ISBN 0-520-01697-1). U of Cal Pr.

Cohen, Stephen P. & Park, Richard L. India: Emergent Power? (Strategy Paper Ser.: No. 33). 95p. 1978. pap. 4.50 (ISBN 0-8448-1353-2). Crane-Russak Co.

Dahanukar, Dilip S. The Lok Plan: National Planning by Life Style. 1978. 11.50x (ISBN 0-8364-0287-1, Orient Longman). South Asia Bks.

Darda, R. S. From Feudalism to Democracy. 1971. 13.50x (ISBN 0-8426-0288-7). Verry.

Das Gupta, Jyotirindra. Language Conflict & National Development: Group Politics & National Language Policy in India. LC 75-94992. (Center for South & Southeast Asia Studies, UC Berkeley). 1970. 19.00x (ISBN 0-520-01590-8). U of Cal Pr.

Dastur, A., ed. Studies in the Fourth General Election. 294p. 1972. 8.50x (ISBN 0-8188-1180-3). Paragon.

Datta, C. L. With Two Presidents: The Inside Story. (Illus.). 149p. 1970. 5.75x (ISBN 0-8002-1308-4). Intl Pubns Serv.

DeSouza, Anthony, ed. The Politics of Change & Leadership Development: New Leaders in India & Africa. 1978. 15.00x (ISBN 0-8364-0192-1). South Asia Bks.

Dhami, M. S. Minority Leaders' Image of the Indian Political System: An Exploratory Study of the Attitudes of Akali Leaders. 1975. text ed. 6.00x (ISBN 0-8426-0824-9). Verry.

Diver, Katherine H. Royal India. facs. ed. LC 76-142620. (Essay Index Reprint Ser). 1942. 20.00 (ISBN 0-8369-2152-6). Arno.

Diwan, Paras. Abrogation of the Forty-Second Amendment: Does Our Constitution Need a Second Look? (India) 1978. text ed. 12.00x (ISBN 0-8426-1069-3). Verry.

Dube, Rani. The Evil Within. 9.95 (ISBN 0-686-73465-3, Pub. by Quartet England). Charles River Bks.

Dutt, Subimal. With Nehru in the Foreign Office. 1977. 14.00x (ISBN 0-88386-905-5). South Asia Bks.

Elkins, David J. Electoral Participation in a South Indian Context. LC 74-27534. 1975. 12.95 (ISBN 0-89089-015-3). Carolina Acad Pr.

Embree, Ainslie T. India's Search for National Unity. 1981. Repr. 12.50x (ISBN 0-8364-0691-5, Pub. by Chanakya India). South Asia Bks.

Fazal-E-Rab, Syed. The JP Movement & Emergence of Janata Party: A Select Bibliography, Vol. 1: Pre-Emergency. 1977. 12.50x (ISBN 0-8364-0097-6). South Asia Bks.

Fickett, Lewis P., Jr. The Major Socialist Parties of India: A Study in Leftist Fragmentation. LC 76-20536. (Foreign & Comparative Studies-South Asian Ser.: No. 2). 1976. pap. text ed. 4.50x (ISBN 0-915984-76-8). Syracuse U Foreign Comp.

Field, John O. Consolidating Democracy: Politicalization & Partisanship in India. 1981. 22.50x (ISBN 0-8364-0707-5, Pub. by Manohar India). South Asia Bks.

Forster, E. M. Hill of Evil. LC 53-9224. (Illus.). 1971. pap. 3.95 (ISBN 0-15-640265-3, HB204, Harv). HarBraceJ.

Fox, Richard G. Kin, Clan, Raja, & Rule: State-Hinterland Relations in Preindustrial India. LC 76-129614. (Center for South & Southeast Asia Studies, UC Berkeley). 1971. 20.00x (ISBN 0-520-01807-9). U of Cal Pr.

Gangrade, Kesharichand D. Emerging Patterns of Leadership. LC 74-900834. 1974. 12.75x (ISBN 0-88386-564-5). South Asia Bks.

Ghose, S. Socialism & Communism in India. 468p. 1971. 8.25x (ISBN 0-8426-0334-4). Verry.

Ghose, S. K. Crusade & End of Indira Raj. 1978. 11.00x (ISBN 0-8364-0156-5). South Asia Bks.

Ghose, Sankar. Socialism & Communism in India. 468p. 1971. 8.50x (ISBN 0-8188-1178-1). Paragon.

--Socialism, Democracy & Nationalism in India. (Illus.). 503p. 1974. 9.00x (ISBN 0-8002-1987-2). Intl Pubns Serv.

--Socialism,Democracy & Nationalism in India. 1973. 8.50x (ISBN 0-8188-1186-2). Paragon.

Ghurye, Govind S. Whither India? LC 74-901838. 431p. 1974. 26.00x (ISBN 0-8002-0060-8). Intl Pubns Serv.

Gordon, Leonard. Bengal: The Nationalist Movement, 1876-1940. LC 73-12974. 407p. 1973. 20.00x (ISBN 0-231-03753-8). Columbia U Pr.

Goyal, Des Raj. Rashtriya Swayamsevak Sangh. 1979. 10.00x (ISBN 0-8364-0566-8, Pub. by Radha Krishna India). South Asia Bks.

Gupta, D. C. Indian Government & Politics. 1978. 20.00 (ISBN 0-7069-0521-0, Pub. by Vikas India). Advent NY.

Gupta, Giri R., ed. Cohesion & Conflict in Modern India. LC 77-86741. (Main Currents in Indian Sociology Ser.: Vol. 3). 1978. 15.95 (ISBN 0-89089-103-6). Carolina Acad Pr.

Gupta, R. C. Who Rules a Country: The Challenge of Democracy in India. 1969. 8.25x (ISBN 0-8426-1292-0). Verry.

Hanson, A. H. & Douglas, Janet. India's Democracy. (Introductions to Comparative Government Ser). 236p. 1972. 7.95x (ISBN 0-393-05469-1); pap. 4.95x (ISBN 0-393-09908-3). Norton.

Hardgrave, Robert L., Jr. India: Government & Politics in a Developing Nation. 3rd ed. 285p. 1980. pap. text ed. 9.95 (ISBN 0-15-541352-X, HC). HarBraceJ.

Harris, Nigel. India--China: Underdevelopment & Revolution. LC 74-30894. 1974. 10.00 (ISBN 0-89089-017-X). Carolina Acad Pr.

Hartmann, Horst. Political Parties in India. (Illus.). 278p. 1974. 13.00x (ISBN 0-8002-1809-4). Intl Pubns Serv.

Hettne, Bjorn. The Political Economy of Indirect Rule: Mysore 1881-1947. (Scandanavian Institute of Asian Studies Monograph: No. 32). (Illus., Orig.). 1978. pap. text ed. 13.75x (ISBN 0-7007-0106-0). Humanities.

Hiro, Dilip. Inside India Today. rev ed. LC 77-76161. 1979. pap. 5.95 (ISBN 0-85345-481-7, PB-4817). Monthly Rev.

--Inside India Today. LC 76-76161. 1977. 15.00 (ISBN 0-85345-424-8, CL4248). Monthly Rev.

Indian Institute of Public Administration. The Organisation of the Government of India. rev. 2nd ed. Mukharji, G., ed. (Illus.). 539p. 1972. 18.00x (ISBN 0-8426-0336-0). Verry.

Institute of Constitutional & Parliamentary Studies. Indian Parties & Politics. LC 72-907000. 171p. 1973. 11.25x (ISBN 0-8002-0951-6). Intl Pubns Serv.

Institute of Constitutional & Parliamentary Studies, New Delhi. Parliament & Administration in India. Singhvi, L. M., ed. LC 72-903148. 285p. 1972. 13.50x (ISBN 0-8002-0946-X). Intl Pubns Serv.

Institute Of Constitutional And Parliamentary Studies. Union State Relations in India. Kashyap, Subhash C., ed. 1969. 8.25x (ISBN 0-8426-0205-4). Verry.

Jain, R. B. Indian Parliament: Innovations, Reforms & Development. LC 76-52214. 1976. 9.00x (ISBN 0-88386-795-8). South Asia Bks.

Jayakanthan, D. Literary Man's Political Experience. 1976. 12.00 (ISBN 0-7069-0407-9). Intl Bk Dist.

Jha, Dayadhar. State Legislature in India: (Bihar) 1977. 12.50x (ISBN 0-88386-969-1). South Asia Bks.

Jha, P. Political Representation in India. 1976. 11.00x (ISBN 0-88386-774-5). South Asia Bks.

Johnson, G. Provincial Politics & Indian Nationalism. (South Asian Studies: No. 14). 300p. 1973. 29.95 (ISBN 0-521-20259-0). Cambridge U Pr.

Jones, Rodney W. Urban Politics in India: Area, Power, & Policy in a Penetrated System. LC 73-83052. 1974. 35.00x (ISBN 0-520-02545-8). U of Cal Pr.

Karkhanis, Sharad. Indian Politics and the Role of the Press. 226p. 1981. text ed. 17.95 (ISBN 0-7069-1278-0, Pub. by Vikas India). Asia Bk Corp.

Karunakaran, K. P. Democracy in India. 1978. 14.00x (ISBN 0-8364-0132-8). South Asia Bks.

Kaul, M. N. Practice & Procedure of Parliament: With Special Reference to Lok Sabha. 2nd ed. 962p. 1972. 35.00x (ISBN 0-8002-1825-6). Intl Pubns Serv.

Kaura, Uma. Muslims & Indian Nationalism, 1828-40. LC 77-74487. 1977. 11.50x (ISBN 0-88386-888-1). South Asia Bks.

Ker, James C. Political Trouble in India, 1907-1917. LC 73-907411. 472p. 1973. 14.00x (ISBN 0-8002-1814-0). Intl Pubns Serv.

Khanna, N. Miracle of Democracy in India. 124p. 1980. 4.50x (ISBN 0-89955-319-2, Pub. by Interprint India). Intl Schol Bk Serv.

Kihlberg, Mats. The Panchayati Raj of India. LC 76-903564. 9.00x (ISBN 0-88386-866-0). South Asia Bks.

Kini, N. G. The City Voter in India. LC 74-902612. 3355p. 1974. 12.75x (ISBN 0-88386-524-6). South Asia Bks.

Kohli, Suresh, ed. Corruption in India. 128p. 1975. 9.00x (ISBN 0-8002-0543-X). Intl Pubns Serv.

Kothari, Rajni, ed. State & Nation Building: A Third World Perspective. 1976. 13.00x (ISBN 0-88386-879-2). South Asia Bks.

Krishnamachari, V. T. Planning in India: Theory & Practice. rev. ed. 1977. 6.50x (ISBN 0-8364-0093-3, Orient Longman). South Asia Bks.

Kumar, Sushil & Venkataraman, K. State-Panchayati Raj Relations. 148p. 1974. lib. bdg. 7.95x (ISBN 0-210-40503-1). Asia.

Kumar, Virendra. Committees & Commissions in India 1947-73: Vols. 1-10, 1947-73. 1979. text ed. 25.00x ea. (ISBN 0-391-01934-1). Humanities.

Lal, Muni. Haryana: On High Road to Prosperity. (Illus.). 150p. 1974. 13.50x (ISBN 0-7069-0290-4). Intl Pubns Serv.

Lal, Shiv. Supreme Court on Elections. LC 75-905576. 1976. 30.00x (ISBN 0-8002-2036-6). Intl Pubns Serv.

Lall, Arthur. The Emergence of Modern India. LC 80-25028. 288p. 1981. 16.95 (ISBN 0-231-03430-X). Columbia U Pr.

McLane, John R. Indian Nationalism & the Early Congress. LC 77-72127. 1977. 32.00x (ISBN 0-691-03113-4); pap. 12.50 (ISBN 0-691-10056-X). Princeton U Pr.

Maheshwari, B. L. Centre-State Relations in the Seventies. LC 74-901888. 357p. 1973. 12.75 (ISBN 0-88386-431-2). South Asia Bks.

Maheshwari, S. R. Administrative Reforms in India. 1981. 12.00x (ISBN 0-8364-0742-3, Pub. by Macmillan India). South Asia Bks.

Malcolm, John. Political History of India, 2 vols. 1970. 75.00 (ISBN 0-686-20284-8). Intl Bk Dist.

Mallya, N. N. Indian Parliament. (India, the Land & People). (Illus.). 203p. 1972. 4.00x (ISBN 0-8426-0330-1). Verry.

Mangat Rai, E. N. Patterns of Administrative Development in Independent India. (Commonwealth Papers Ser.: No. 19). 182p. 1976. pap. text ed. 22.25x (ISBN 0-485-17619-X, Athlone). Humanities.

Mansukhani, H. L. The Jungle of Customs Law & Procedures. LC 74-900717. (Illus.). 722p. 1974. 24.00x (ISBN 0-7069-0283-1). Intl Pubns Serv.

Martin, Briton, Jr. New India, 1885: British Official Policy & the Emergence of the Indian National Congress. LC 70-98140. (Center for South & Southeast Asia Studies, UC Berkeley). 1969. 26.75x (ISBN 0-520-01580-0). U of Cal Pr.

Masani, Minoo. JP: Mission Partly Accomplished. 1977. 6.00x (ISBN 0-8364-0063-1). South Asia Bks.

Mathur, Kamala. Tripartitism in Labour Policy, the Indian Experience. 183p. 1974. 11.25x (ISBN 0-8002-2113-3). Intl Pubns Serv.

Mathur, Kuleep. Administrative Response to Emergency: A Study of Scarcity Administration in Maharashtra. LC 75-904667. 1975. 7.00x (ISBN 0-88386-642-0). South Asia Bks.

Mathur, Ramesh N. Studies in History & Politics. rev. ed. Bhandari, D. R., ed. 1958. 3.00x (ISBN 0-8426-1381-1). Verry.

Mehta, Asoka. India Today. LC 73-906812. 120p. 1973. 7.50x (ISBN 0-8002-1534-6). Intl Pubns Serv.

Mehta, Ved. The New India. 1978. 10.00 (ISBN 0-670-50735-0). Viking Pr.

Menon, K. P. Memories & Musings. 1979. 10.00x (ISBN 0-8364-0494-7). South Asia Bks.

Mersey, Clive B. Viceroys & Governors-General of India, 1757-1947. LC 70-160925. (Biography Index Reprint Ser). Repr. of 1949 ed. 18.50 (ISBN 0-8369-8088-3). Arno.

Mirchandani, G. C. Reporting India, 1976. 1977. 12.50x (ISBN 0-8364-0062-3). South Asia Bks.

Mirchandani, G. G. Reporting India, 1977-78. 1978. 14.00x (ISBN 0-8364-0271-5). South Asia Bks.

--Subverting the Constitution, India. 1977. 12.50x (ISBN 0-8364-0030-5). South Asia Bks.

--Thirty Two Million Judges: Analysis of 1977 Lok Sabha & State Elections in India. 1977. 12.00x (ISBN 0-8364-0052-6). South Asia Bks.

Misra, B. B. The Administrative History of India, 1834-1947: General Administration. 1970. 19.25x (ISBN 0-19-635267-3). Oxford U Pr.

Misra, Kashi P. Politics of Persuasion. 1967. 8.50x (ISBN 0-8188-1082-3). Paragon.

Mohan, K. T. Independence to Indira & After. 1978. text ed. 9.00 (ISBN 0-8426-1067-7). Verry.

Mookerjee, Amalendu P. Social & Political Ideas of Bipin Chandra Pal. LC 75-901635. 1974. 11.00x (ISBN 0-88386-473-8). South Asia Bks.

Mookerjee, Girija K. History of Indian National Congress (1832-1947) 276p. 1974. 15.00x (ISBN 0-8002-1504-4). Intl Pubns Serv.

Moore, R. J. The Crisis of Indian Unity, 1917-1940. 280p. 1974. 36.00x (ISBN 0-19-821560-6). Oxford U Pr.

Morris-Jones, Wyndraeth H. Parliament in India. LC 75-29074. 417p. 1975. Repr. of 1957 ed. lib. bdg. 22.75x (ISBN 0-8371-8382-0, MOPIN). Greenwood.

Mote, V. L., et al. Managerial Economics: Concepts & Cases-India. 1977. 8.00x (ISBN 0-8364-0431-9). South Asia Bks.

Munshi, K. M., ed. Indian Constitutional Papers, 2 vols. Incl. Vol. 1. Pilgrimage to Freedom (ISBN 0-8426-0029-9); Vol. 2. Munshi Papers (ISBN 0-8426-0030-2). 1967. 10.00x ea. Verry.

Nandy, Ashis. At the Edge of Psychology: Essays on Politics & Culture. 152p. 1981. 12.95 (ISBN 0-19-561205-1). Oxford U Pr.

Nayat, P. K. Leadership, Bureaucracy & Planning in India. 1969. 12.00 (ISBN 0-686-20266-X). Intl Bk Dist.

Neale, Walter C. & Adams, John. India: The Search for Unity, Democracy, & Process. 2nd ed. (New Searchlight Ser.). 1976. pap. 3.95x (ISBN 0-442-29755-6). Van Nos Reinhold.

Nehru, Jawaharlal. Independence & After. facs. ed. LC 75-134120. (Essay Index Reprint Ser). 1950. 24.00 (ISBN 0-8369-2003-1). Arno.

Pai Panandiker, V. Development Administration in India. LC 74-902560. 1974. 15.00 (ISBN 0-333-90026-X). South Asia Bks.

Pandit, H. N. P M's President: A New Concept on Trial. 1974. 6.00x (ISBN 0-8426-0762-5). Verry.

Pant, Niranjan. Politics of Panchaytirai Administration. 1979. text ed. 8.00x (ISBN 0-391-01850-7). Humanities.

Paul, Sharda. Nineteen Seventy-Seven General Elections in India. 1977. 12.00x (ISBN 0-686-12056-6). Intl Bk Dist.

Pavate, D. C. My Days As Governor. (Illus.). 1976. 10.50 (ISBN 0-7069-0315-3). Intl Bk Dist.

Pillai, Padmanabh. Perspective on Power, India & China: An Analysis of Attitudes Toward Political Power in the Two Countries Between the 7th & 2nd Centuries B.C. LC 77-74488. 1977. 11.00x (ISBN 0-88386-889-X). South Asia Bks.

Prakasa, Sri. State Governors in India. 1966. 3.50x (ISBN 0-8426-1472-9). Verry.

Prasad, G. K. Bureaucracy in India: A Sociological Study. 1974. 9.00x (ISBN 0-8426-0685-8). Verry.

Pylee, M. V. Constitutional Government in India. 3rd rev. ed. (Illus.). 1978. text ed. 27.50x (ISBN 0-210-33621-8). Asia.

Rahman, M. From Consultation to Confrontation: A Study of the Muslim League in British Indian Policies, 1906-1912. 1970. 25.00x (ISBN 0-8426-1480-X). Verry.

Rahman, M. M. Congress Crisis. 1970. 9.00 (ISBN 0-686-20206-6). Intl Bk Dist.

--Politics of Non-Alignment. 1969. 16.50 (ISBN 0-686-20286-4). Intl Bk Dist.

Ram, Mohan. Politics of Sino-Indian Confrontation. 1973. 9.00 (ISBN 0-7069-0266-1). Intl Bk Dist.

Ram Reddy, G. & Sharma, B. A., eds. State Government & Politics: Andhra Pradesh. (Illus.). 684p. 1979. 22.50x (ISBN 0-8002-0998-2). Intl Pubns Serv.

Rangaswami, Aiyangan K. Indian Cameralism. 4.00 (ISBN 0-8356-7267-0, ALS 66). Theos Pub Hse.

Rao, V. K. Indian Road to Democratic Socialism. 240p. 1976. 10.00x (ISBN 0-8002-1550-8). Intl Pubns Serv.

Rashid, S. Khalid. WAKF Administration in India: A Socio-Legal Study. 184p. 1978. 12.00x (ISBN 0-7069-0690-X, Pub. by Croom Helm Ltd. England). Biblio Dist.

Rastogi, P. N. The Nature & Dynamics of Factional Conflict. LC 75-904392. 1975. 9.00x (ISBN 0-333-90075-8). South Asia Bks.

Reddy, G. Ram. Regionalism in India: A Study of Telangana. 1979. 20.00x (ISBN 0-8364-0332-0). South Asia Bks.

Reeves, P. D. & Graham, B. D. A Handbook to Elections in Uttar Pradesh: 1920-1951. LC 75-907956. 1975. 18.00x (ISBN 0-88386-628-5). South Asia Bks.

Rosenthal, Donald B. Limited Elite: Politics & Government in Two Indian Cities. LC 70-121818. 1971. 15.00x (ISBN 0-226-72810-2). U of Chicago Pr.

Ross, Aileen. Student Unrest in India: A Comparative Approach. 1969. 13.75 (ISBN 0-7735-0041-3). McGill-Queens U Pr.

Roy, Ajit. Political Power in India: Nature & Trends. 1975. 7.50x (ISBN 0-88386-648-X). South Asia Bks.

Rudolph, Lloyd I. Modernity of Tradition: Political Development in India. 1970. pap. 4.50 (ISBN 0-226-73135-9, P350, Phoen). U of Chicago Pr.

Sankhdher, M. M. Reflections on Indian Politics. 407p. 1973. 17.50x (ISBN 0-8002-1908-2). Intl Pubns Serv.

Saraswathi, S. Minorities in Madras State: Group Interests in Modern Politics. LC 75-903357. 1974. 14.00x (ISBN 0-8364-0432-7). South Asia Bks.

Sasaki, Genjun H. Social & Humanistic Life in India. LC 74-924045. 291p. 1974. 11.25x (ISBN 0-8002-1984-8). Intl Pubns Serv.

Selected Writings of Jawaharlal Nehru, 3 vols. 1979. 16.00x ea (Orient Longman). Vol. 10. Vol. 11 (ISBN 0-8364-0345-2). Vol. 12 (ISBN 0-8364-0346-0). South Asia Bks.

Sethi, Jai D. India in Crisis. LC 75-312132. 233p. 1975. 11.00x (ISBN 0-8002-1532-X). Intl Pubns Serv.

Shakir, Moin. Politics of Minorities. 1980. 16.00x (ISBN 0-8364-0622-2, Pub. by Ajanta). South Asia Bks.

Sharma, Dasharatha. Early Chauhan Dynasties. 2nd rev. ed. 1975. 16.00 (ISBN 0-8426-0546-0). Orient Bk Dist.

Sharma, G. D. Rajput Polity: A Study of Politics & Administration of the State of Marwar, 1638-1749. 1977. 14.00x (ISBN 0-88386-887-3). South Asia Bks.

Sharma, Hari. Princes & Paramountcy. 1978. text ed. 10.50x (ISBN 0-8426-1086-3). Verry.

Sharma, L. N. The Indian Prime Minister: The Office, Its Functions & Powers. LC 76-905245. 1976. 12.50x (ISBN 0-333-90141-X). South Asia Bks.

Sharma, Miriam. The Politics of Inequality: Competition & Control in an Indian Village. LC 78-5526. (Asian Studies at Hawaii: No. 22). 1978. pap. text ed. 9.50x (ISBN 0-8248-0569-0). U Pr of Hawaii.

Sharma, R. N. Political Science in India. 1979. 28.50x (ISBN 0-8364-0328-2). South Asia Bks.

Sharma, R. S. Aspects of Political Ideas & Institutions in Ancient India. 2nd rev. ed. 1968. 4.95 (ISBN 0-89684-176-6). Orient Bk Dist.

--Indian Feudalism. rev. 2nd ed. 1981. 22.50x (ISBN 0-8364-0716-4, Pub. by Macmillan India). South Asia Bks.

Sheth, D. L., ed. Citizens & Parties: Aspects Competitive Politics in India. 1976. 9.00 (ISBN 0-88386-828-8). South Asia Bks.

Shiviah, M. New Humanism & Democratic Politics: A Study of M. N. Roy's Theory of the State. 1979. text ed. 13.50x (ISBN 0-8426-1628-4). Verry.

Shrimali, K. L. Prospects for Democracy in India. LC 78-112393. 156p. 1970. 6.95x (ISBN 0-8093-0441-4). S Ill U Pr.

Simatupang, T. B. Report from Banaran: The Story of the Experiences of a Soldier During the War of Independence. Anderson, Benedict & Graves, Elizabeth, trs. 186p. 1972. pap. 6.50 (ISBN 0-685-32890-2, A414176). Cornell Mod Indo.

Singh, Baljit & Vajpeyi, Dhirendra. Government & Politics in India. LC 81-65044. 166p. (Orig.). 1981. pap. text ed. 8.95 (ISBN 0-86590-006-X). Apt Bks.

--Government & Politics in India. 130p. 1980. cancelled (ISBN 0-86590-008-6). Apt Bks.

Singh, Bhawani. Council of States in India: A Structural & Functional Profile. (Illus.). 360p. 1973. 15.00x (ISBN 0-8002-0971-0). Intl Pubns Serv.

Singh, K. Rajendra. Politics of the Indian Ocean. 260p. 1974. text ed. 11.75x (ISBN 0-8426-0643-2). Verry.

Singh, Mohinder. The Akali Movement. 1978. 16.00x (ISBN 0-8364-0290-1). South Asia Bks.

Singhi, Narendra K. Bureaucracy: Positions & Persons - Rajasthan, India. LC 75-900687. 398p. 1974. 15.00x (ISBN 0-88386-557-2). South Asia Bks.

Sinha, Chittaranjan. Indian Civil Judiciary in Making, 1800-33. (Illus.). 209p. 1971. 8.25x (ISBN 0-8426-0296-8). Verry.

Sinha, V. B. Red Rebel in India. 1968. 8.75x (ISBN 0-8426-1543-1). Verry.

Sisson, Richard & Shrader, Lawrence L. Legislative Recruitment & Political Integration: Patterns of Political Linkage in an Indian State. (Research Monograph: No. 6). 1972. 7.00 (ISBN 0-686-23620-3, Ctr South & Southeast Asia Studies). Cellar.

Smith, Hale G. European & the Indian: European-Indian Contacts in Georgia & Florida. Repr. of 1956 ed. pap. 5.50 (ISBN 0-384-56132-2). Johnson Repr.

Smith, Morton R. Dates & Dynasties in Earliest India. 1973. 12.50 (ISBN 0-8426-0528-2). Orient Bk Dist.

Somjee, A. H. Democracy & Political Change in Village India: A Case Study. 1971. 12.50 (ISBN 0-8046-8830-3). Kennikat.

--Democratic Processes in a Developing Society. LC 79-4035. 1979. 19.95x (ISBN 0-312-19373-4). St Martin.

Thapar, Romesh. Indian Dimension: Politics of Continental Development. 1977. 12.00x (ISBN 0-7069-0538-5). Intl Bk Dist.

Thomas, Raju. The Defence of India: A Budgetary Perspective of Strategy & Politics. 1978. 14.50x (ISBN 0-8364-0269-3). South Asia Bks.

Udgaonkar, P. B. Political Institutions & Administration of Northern India, 750-1200 A.D. 1969. 6.00x (ISBN 0-8426-1574-1). Verry.

Varma, S. P. & Narain, Iqbal. Voting Behaviour in a Changing Society: A Case Study of the Fourth General Election in Rajasthan. (Illus.). 385p. 1973. text ed. 15.00x (ISBN 0-8426-0532-0). Verry.

Wadhwa, Kamlesh K. Minority Safeguards in India: Constitutional Provisions & Their Implementation. LC 75-901908. 1975. 14.00x (ISBN 0-88386-607-2). South Asia Bks.

Weiner, Myron, ed. Electoral Politics in Indian States: Three Disadvantaged Sectors. 1975. 11.00x (ISBN 0-88386-411-8). South Asia Bks.

Wilson, H. H., ed. Glossary of Judicial & Revenue Terms & of Useful Words Occuring in Official Documents Relating to the Administration of the Government of British India, Etc. 1968. Repr. of 1885 ed. 35.00x (ISBN 0-8426-1596-2). Verry.

Wirsing, Robert G. Socialist Society & Free Enterprise Politics: A Study of Voluntary Associations in Urban India. LC 76-6775. 1977. 12.95 (ISBN 0-89089-066-8). Carolina Acad Pr.

Zakaria, Rafiq. Rise of Muslims in Indian Politics: An Analysis of Developments from 1885 to 1906. 1970. 12.00x (ISBN 0-8002-1927-9). Intl Pubns Serv.

--Rise of Muslims in Indian Politics-1885-1906. 1970. 12.50x (ISBN 0-8426-0202-X). Verry.

INDIA–POLITICS AND GOVERNMENT–EARLY TO 1765

Day, U. N. Mughal Government, A. D. 1556-1707. 1971. 8.25x (ISBN 0-8426-0239-9). Verry.

Dikshit, D. P. Political History of the Chalukyas of Badami. 1980. 26.00x (ISBN 0-8364-0645-1, Pub. by Abhinav India). South Asia Bks.

Furber, Holden. John Company at Work. LC 70-96181. 1969. Repr. lib. bdg. 24.00x (ISBN 0-374-92945-9). Octagon.

Hirschmann, Edwin. The White Mutiny. 1980. 24.00x (ISBN 0-8364-0639-7). South Asia Bks.

Husain, Yusuf. Indo-Muslim Polity (Turko-Afghan Period) 261p. 1971. 15.00x (ISBN 0-8002-1558-3). Intl Pubns Serv.

Jeffrey, Robin, ed. People, Princes & Paramount Power: Society & Politics in the Indian Princely States. 1979. 15.50x (ISBN 0-19-560886-0). Oxford U Pr.

Mishra, Shyam M. Yasavarman of Kanauj: Study of Political History, Society & Cultural Life of Northern India. 1978. 15.00x (ISBN 0-8364-0105-0). South Asia Bks.

Misra, S. N. Ancient Indian Republics. LC 76-901526. 1976. 15.00x (ISBN 0-88386-799-0). South Asia Bks.

Mukerji, Shobha. Republican Trends in Ancient India. 1969. 8.25x (ISBN 0-8426-1440-0). Verry.

Mukherjee, Bharati. Kautilya's Concept of Diplomacy. 1976. 8.00 (ISBN 0-88386-504-1). South Asia Bks.

Mukherjee, Tara B. Inter-State Relations in Ancient India. 1967. 8.25x (ISBN 0-8426-1442-7). Verry.

Naqvi, Hameeda K. Urbanisation & Urban Centres Under the Great Mughals, 1556-1707. (Illus.). 210p. 1971. 11.25x (ISBN 0-8002-2129-X). Intl Pubns Serv.

Nizami, Khalig A. Some Aspects of Religion & Politics in India During the Thirteenth Century. 1973. 14.00x (ISBN 0-88386-318-9). South Asia Bks.

Rao, M. V. Studies in Kautilya. rev. ed. 1958. 5.50x (ISBN 0-8426-1486-9). Verry.

Raychaudhuri, Hemchandra. Political History of Ancient India. LC 78-174301. Repr. of 1923 ed. 27.00 (ISBN 0-404-05228-2). AMS Pr.

Roy, P. C. The Coin Age of Northern India. 1980. 27.50x (ISBN 0-8364-0641-9, Pub. by Abhinav India). South Asia Bks.

Saletore, B. A. Ancient Indian Political Thought & Institutions. 1971. pap. 8.25x (ISBN 0-210-33807-5). Asia.

Sircar, D. C. Political & Administrative Systems of Ancient & Medieval India. 1974. text ed. 15.00x (ISBN 0-8426-0670-X). Verry.

Stein, Burton. Peasant State & Society in Medieval South India. (Illus.). 550p. 1980. text ed. 31.00x (ISBN 0-19-561065-2). Oxford U Pr.

INDIA–POLITICS AND GOVERNMENT–1765-1947

Baker, C. J. & Washbrook, D. A. South India: Political Institutions & Political Change 1880-1940. 1975. text ed. 27.50x (ISBN 0-8419-5016-4). Holmes & Meier.

Bhatia, H. S., ed. Origin & Development of Legal & Political System in India, Vol.2. 1977. text ed. 15.00 (ISBN 0-210-40591-0). Asia.

Bhattacharyya, Buddhadeva. Satyagrahas in Bengal, 1921-1939. 1977. 15.00x (ISBN 0-88386-901-2). South Asia Bks.

Comming, J., ed. Political India, 1832-1932: A Cooperative Survey of a Century. 1968. Repr. of 1933 ed. 7.75x (ISBN 0-8426-1213-0). Verry.

Cross, Cecil M. Development of Self-Government in India, 1858-1914. LC 68-57597. 1968. Repr. of 1922 ed. lib. bdg. 15.00x (ISBN 0-8371-0367-3, CRSG). Greenwood.

Curtis, L. G. Papers Relating to the Application of the Principle of Dyarchy to the Government of India. 667p. 1972. Repr. of 1920 ed. 45.00x (ISBN 0-7165-2117-2, Pub. by Irish Academic Pr Ireland). Biblio Dist.

Datta, C. L. Ladakh & Western Himalayan Politics. 239p. 1973. text ed. 9.00x (ISBN 0-8426-0586-X). Verry.

Datta-Ray, B. Assam Secretariat, Eighteen Seventy-Four to Nineteen Forty-Seven: An Administrative History of North-East India. 1978. 13.50x (ISBN 0-8364-0140-9). South Asia Bks.

Eden, Emily. Up the Country. 1980. Repr. 18.00x (ISBN 0-8364-0660-5, Pub. by Curzon Pr). South Asia Bks.

Gandhi, Mohandas K. Swaraj in One Year. 2nd ed. 1921. 14.50 (ISBN 0-404-02676-1). AMS Pr.

Ghandi, Mohandas K. Nonviolence in Peace & War, 1942, 2 vols. Incl. Nonviolence in Peace & War, 1949. Ghandi, Mohandas K. LC 72-147618. (Library of War & Peace; Non-Resis. & Non-Vio.). Set. lib. bdg. 76.00 (ISBN 0-8240-0375-6); lib. bdg. 38.00 ea. Garland Pub.

Hardy, P. Muslims of British India. LC 77-184772. (South Asian Studies: No. 13). (Illus.). 300p. 1973. 39.50 (ISBN 0-521-08488-1); pap. 11.50x (ISBN 0-521-09783-5). Cambridge U Pr.

Jain, Ranbir S. Growth & Development of Governor-General's Executive Council, 1858-1919. 1962. 6.50x (ISBN 0-8426-1315-3). Verry.

Karandikar, Maheshwar A. Islam in India's Transition to Modernity. 1972. lib. bdg. 16.00 (ISBN 0-8371-2337-2, KAI/). Greenwood.

Karunakarun, K. P. Indian Politics from Dadabhai Naoroji to Gandhi. LC 76-371653. 226p. 1975. 14.00x (ISBN 0-8002-1548-6). Intl Pubns Serv.

Kaushik, P. D. Congress Ideology & Programme. 1964. 7.50x (ISBN 0-8188-1064-5). Paragon.

Lee-Warner, William. Native States of India. LC 76-144673. Repr. of 1910 ed. 27.45 (ISBN 0-404-03938-3). AMS Pr.

Lovett, H. Verney. History of the Indian Nationalist Movement. 3rd ed. LC 79-94540. Repr. of 1921 ed. lib. bdg. 18.50x (ISBN 0-678-05100-3). Kelley.

Lumby, Edmond W. The Transfer of Power in India: Nineteen Forty-Five to Nineteen Forty-Seven. LC 79-1634. 1981. Repr. of 1954 ed. 22.50 (ISBN 0-88355-938-2). Hyperion Conn.

Mehrotra, S. R. Towards India's Freedom & Partition. 1979. 20.00x (ISBN 0-7069-0712-4, Pub. by Vikas India). Advent NY.

--Towards India's Freedom & Partition. 322p. 1979. 16.00x (ISBN 0-7069-0712-4, Pub. by Croom Helm Ltd. England). Biblio Dist.

Nagar, Purushottam. Lala Lajpat Rai: The Man & His Ideas. 1978. 14.00x (ISBN 0-8364-0003-8). South Asia Bks.

Pandey, B. N., ed. Indian Nationalist Movement, Eighteen Eighty-Five to Nineteen Forty-Seven: Select Documents. LC 78-8691. 1979. 19.95x (ISBN 0-312-41385-8). St Martin.

Panikkar, K. N. British Diplomacy in North India. 1968. 12.00 (ISBN 0-686-20198-1). Intl Bk Dist.

--British Diplomacy in North India: A Study of the Delhi Residency 1803-1857. text ed. 5.50x (ISBN 0-391-00628-2). Humanities.

Rahim, Muhammad A. Lord Dalhousie's Adminstration of the Conquered & Annexed States. 1963. 7.75x (ISBN 0-8426-1479-6). Verry.

Rai, Lajpat. Life Story of Lala Lajpat Rai. Puri, R. C., ed. LC 76-903625. 1976. 9.00x (ISBN 0-88386-312-X). South Asia Bks.

Ramusack, Barbara. The Princes of India in the Twilight of Empire: Dissolution of a Patron-Client System 1914-1939. LC 78-18161. (Illus.). 1978. 20.00x (ISBN 0-8142-0272-1). Ohio St U Pr.

Rolland, Romain. Mahatma Gandhi. (Library of War & Peace; Non-Resis. & Non-Vio.). lib. bdg. 38.00 (ISBN 0-8240-0498-1). Garland Pub.

Seal, Anil. Emergence of Indian Nationalism. (Political Change in Modern Asia: No. 1). (Illus.). 1968. 39.95 (ISBN 0-521-06274-8); pap. 11.50x (ISBN 0-521-09652-9). Cambridge U Pr.

Singh, S. N. Secretary of State for India & His Council. 1962. 5.50x (ISBN 0-8426-1539-3). Verry.

Smith, William R. Nationalism & Reform in India. LC 72-85314. 496p. 1973. Repr. of 1938 ed. 18.50 (ISBN 0-8046-1716-3). Kennikat.

Spangenburg, Bradford. The British Bureaucracy in India: Status, Policy & the I.C.S. in Late Nineteenth Century. LC 76-52213. 1977. 17.50x (ISBN 0-88386-768-0). South Asia Bks.

Spear, Percival. Nabobs: A Study of the Social Life of the English in Eighteenth Century India. (Illus.). 7.50 (ISBN 0-8446-0924-2). Peter Smith.

Stokes, E. T. The Peasant & the Raj: Studies in Agrarian Society & Peasant Rebellion in Colonial India. LC 77-77731. (Cambridge South Asian Studies: No. 23). 304p. 1980. pap. 12.95x (ISBN 0-521-29770-2). Cambridge U Pr.

Strachey, John. India, Its Administration & Progress. LC 73-176459. Repr. of 1911 ed. 35.00 (ISBN 0-404-06295-4). AMS Pr.

Wolpert, Stanley A. Morley & India 1906-1910. 1967. 24.50x (ISBN 0-520-01360-3). U of Cal Pr.

Yapp, Malcolm. British Raj & Indian Nationalism. Killingray, Margaret & O'Connor, Edmund, eds. (World History Ser.). (Illus.). 32p. (gr. 10). 1980. Repr. of 1977 ed. lib. bdg. 5.95 (ISBN 0-89908-228-9); pap. text ed. 1.95 (ISBN 0-89908-203-3). Greenhaven.

INDIA–POLITICS AND GOVERNMENT–20TH CENTURY

Ambedkar, Bhimrao R. Pakistan or Partition of India. LC 77-179171. (South & Southeast Asia Studies). Repr. of 1945 ed. 32.50 (ISBN 0-404-54801-6). AMS Pr.

Aurobindo, Sri. Bande Mataram: Early Political Writings. 1979. 12.00 (ISBN 0-89744-900-2). Auromere.

Azad, Abul K. India Wins Freedom. 1978. 8.50x (ISBN 0-8364-0288-X). South Asia Bks.

Baker. Changing Political Leadership in an Indian Province: The Central Provinces & Berar 1919-1939. 1980. 11.95x (ISBN 0-19-561135-7). Oxford U Pr.

Baker, C. J. The Politics of South India, 1920-1937. LC 75-2716. (Cambridge South Asian Studies: No. 17). (Illus.). 368p. 1976. 39.95 (ISBN 0-521-20755-X). Cambridge U Pr.

Brown, Judith M. Gandhi & Civil Disobedience. LC 76-10407. (Illus.). 1977. 39.50 (ISBN 0-521-21279-0). Cambridge U Pr.

--Gandhi's Rise to Power: Indian Politics 1915-1922. LC 71-171674. (Cambridge South Asian Studies: No. 11). (Illus.). 460p. 1972. 35.00 (ISBN 0-521-08353-2); pap. 9.95x (ISBN 0-521-09873-4). Cambridge U Pr.

Chatterjee, Bimanesh. Thousand Days with Rajaji. LC 73-906982. 136p. 1974. 6.50x (ISBN 0-8002-2084-6). Intl Pubns Serv.

Choudhary, Sukhbir. Growth of Nationalism in India, 2 vols. Incl. Vol. 1. 1857-1918. 640p (ISBN 0-8002-1476-5); Vol. 2. 1919-1929. 639p (ISBN 0-8002-1477-3). 1973. 22.50x ea. Intl Pubns Serv.

Dayal, Ishwar. District Administration, India. LC 76-904844. 1976. 9.50 (ISBN 0-333-90143-6). South Asia Bks.

Desai, Morarji. The Story of My Life, 2 vols. LC 74-901103. (Illus.). vii, 651p. 1974. Set. 30.00x (ISBN 0-333-90016-2). South Asia Bks.

Gandhi, Indira. The Years of Challenge: Selected Speeches of Indira Gandhi 1966-1969. rev. ed. LC 74-168325. 498p. 1973. 7.50x (ISBN 0-8002-0980-X). Intl Pubns Serv.

Gandhi, Mohandas. Gandhi on Non-Violence: Selected Texts from Gandhi's Non-Violence in Peace & War. Merton, Thomas, ed. LC 65-15672. (Orig.). 1965. pap. 2.95 (ISBN 0-8112-0097-3, NDP197). New Directions.

Gandhi, Mohandas K. Hind Swaraj, or Indian Home Rule. 110p. (Orig.). 1981. pap. 1.50 (ISBN 0-934676-25-9). Greenlf Bks.

--Non-Violent Resistance. Kumarappa, Bharatan, ed. LC 61-16650. (YA) 1961. pap. 4.95 (ISBN 0-8052-0017-7). Schocken.

Giri, V. V. My Life & Times, Vol 1. LC 76-904158. 1976. 14.00x (ISBN 0-333-90133-9). South Asia Bks.

Gordon, A. D. Businessmen & Politics: Rising Nationalism & a Modernising Economy in Bombay, 1918-1933. 1978. 15.00 (ISBN 0-8364-0194-8). South Asia Bks.

Guham, Amalendu. Planter Raj to Swaraj: Freedom Struggle & Electoral Politics in Assam, 1926-1947. 1977. 12.00x (ISBN 0-88386-984-5). South Asia Bks.

Gupta, Bhabani. Communism in Indian Politics. LC 73-190190. (South Asian Institute Studies). 455p. 1972. 22.50x (ISBN 0-231-03568-3). Columbia U Pr.

Hartmann, Horst. Political Parties in India. 2nd rev. & ext. ed. 1977. 11.50x (ISBN 0-88386-976-4). South Asia Bks.

Hegde, K. S. Crisis in Indian Judiciary. 93p. 1973. 7.00x (ISBN 0-8002-0542-1). Intl Pubns Serv.

Jeffrey, Robin, ed. People, Princes & Paramount Power: Society & Politics in the Indian Princely States. 1979. 15.50x (ISBN 0-19-560886-0). Oxford U Pr.

Jha, Manoranjan. Civil Disobedience & After: The American Reaction to Political Developments in India During 1930-1935. LC 73-906394. 300p. 1973. 11.25x (ISBN 0-8002-0528-6). Intl Pubns Serv.

Josh, Sohan S. Hindustan Gadar Party: A Short History. 1977. 9.00x (ISBN 0-8364-0089-5). South Asia Bks.

Kashyap, Subhash. Tryst with Freedom: A Pictorial Saga. LC 73-906266. (Illus.). 89p. 1974. 17.50x (ISBN 0-8002-2115-X). Intl Pubns Serv.

Khera, S. S. Government in Business. 2nd rev. ed. 1978. pap. text ed. 25.00x (ISBN 0-210-26914-6). Asia.

Low, Anthony, ed. Congress & the Raj. 1977. 30.00x (ISBN 0-8364-0007-0). South Asia Bks.

Mahajan, V. D. Fifty Years of Modern India 1919-1969. 1970. 9.00x (ISBN 0-8426-0124-4). Verry.

Maheshwari, Shriman. President's Rule in India. 1977. 12.50x (ISBN 0-88386-985-3). South Asia Bks.

Mankekar, D. R. Accession to Extinction: The Story of Indian Princes. 1974. 10.50 (ISBN 0-686-20187-6). Intl Bk Dist.

Manor, James. Political Change in an Indian State, Mysore, 1917-1955. 1978. 12.50x (ISBN 0-8364-0069-0). South Asia Bks.

Merriam, Allen H. Gandhi & Jinnah. 1980. 16.00x (ISBN 0-8364-0039-9). South Asia Bks.

Minhas, B. S. Planning & the Poor: India. 1974. 7.50 (ISBN 0-8426-0701-3). Verry.

Misra, B. B. The Bureaucracy in India: An Historical Analysis of Development to 1947. 1977. text ed. 14.50x (ISBN 0-19-560748-1). Oxford U Pr.

Mittal, N. Freedom Movement in Punjab, 1905-1920. 12.50x (ISBN 0-88386-979-9). South Asia Bks.

Mushirut, Hasan. Nationalism & Communal Politics in India. 1979. 18.50x (ISBN 0-8364-0198-0). South Asia Bks.

Nanda, B. R., et al. Gandhi & Nehru. 76p. 1979. pap. text ed. 4.50x (ISBN 0-19-561148-9). Oxford U Pr.

Nasenko, Yuri. Jawaharlal Nehru & India's Foreign Policy. 1977. text ed. 22.50x (ISBN 0-8426-1040-5). Verry.

Neeraj, Miss Nehru & Democracy in India. LC 73-928017. 301p. 1972. 15.00x (ISBN 0-8002-1746-2). Intl Pubns Serv.

Pandley, Byanendra. The Ascendancy of the Congress in Uttar Pradesh, 1926-34: A Study in Imperfect Mobilization. (South Asian Studies). 1979. 11.95 (ISBN 0-19-560969-7). Oxford U Pr.

Panikkar, K. N., ed. National Left Movements in India. 320p. 1980. text ed. 25.00 (ISBN 0-7069-1000-1, Pub by Vikas India). Advent NY.

Pantham, Thomas. Political Parties & Democratic Concensus--India. LC 76-904867. 1976. 14.50x (ISBN 0-333-90145-2). South Asia Bks.

Raheja, Bhagwan D. Urban India & Public Policy. (Illus.). 323p. 1974. 18.75x (ISBN 0-8002-2127-3). Intl Pubns Serv.

Ramaswamy, E. A. The Worker & His Union: A Study in South India. 1977. 9.00x (ISBN 0-88386-991-8). South Asia Bks.

Saran, Parmatma. Rural Leadership in the Context of India's Modernization. 1978. 10.00x (ISBN 0-8364-0207-3). South Asia Bks.

Sen, Mohit. Revolution in India: Path & Problems. 1977. 5.50x (ISBN 0-88386-951-9, Pub. by Peoples Pub. House). South Asia Bks.

Sen Gupta, Kalyan. Pabna Disturbances & the Politics of Rent: 1873-1885. LC 74-903853. 1974. 7.75x (ISBN 0-8364-0441-6). South Asia Bks.

Sharma, S. S. Rural Elites in India. (Illus.). 267p. 1979. 15.00x (ISBN 0-8002-0999-0). Intl Pubns Serv.

Sinha, B. M. The Samba Spying Case. 200p. 1981. text ed. 15.00 (ISBN 0-7069-1392-2, Pub. by Vikas India). Advent NY.

Sinha, Sachchidanand. Emergency in Perspective: Reprieve & Challenge. 1977. 7.50x (ISBN 0-8364-0080-1). South Asia Bks.

Thakur, Janardhan. Indira Gandhi & Her Power Game. 165p. 1980. text ed. 10.50x (ISBN 0-7069-0985-2, Pub. by Vikas India). Advent NY.

Uprety, Prem R. Religion & Politics in the Punjab in the 1920's. 1981. 20.00x (ISBN 0-8364-0757-1, Pub. by Sterling). South Asia Bks.

Wadhwa, O. P. Centre-State & Inter-State Relations in India 1919-1970: A Bibliography. LC 73-904237. 148p. 1973. 11.25x (ISBN 0-8002-0279-1). Intl Pubns Serv.

Warshaw, Steven, et al. India Emerges. (Illus.). 1974. pap. text ed. 8.50 scp (ISBN 0-06-389131-X, HarpC). Har-Row.

INDIA–POLITICS AND GOVERNMENT–1947-

Appadorai, A. Towards a Just Social Order: Based on Contemporary Indian Thought. 1970. 4.50x (ISBN 0-8426-1122-3). Verry.

Banerjee, Sumanta. In the Wake of Naxalbari: A History of the Naxalite Movement in India. 436p. 1980. text ed. 22.50 (ISBN 0-8426-1656-X). Verry.

Bansal, P. L. Administrative Development in India. 196p. 1975. text ed. 9.00x (ISBN 0-8426-0835-4). Verry.

Barik, R. Politics of the JP Movement. 1977. 10.00x (ISBN 0-88386-992-6). South Asia Bks.

Berg, Lasse & Berg, Lisa. Face to Face: Fascism & Revolution in India. Kurtin, Norman, tr. from Swedish. LC 73-172283. (Illus.). 240p. 1972. 7.95 (ISBN 0-87867-014-9). Ramparts.

Bhardwaj, R. K. Municipal Administration in India: A Sociological Analysis of Rural & Urban India. 1970. 11.50x (ISBN 0-8002-1733-0). Intl Pubns Serv.

Bhargava, G. S. After Nehru. 1966. 5.50x (ISBN 0-8188-1014-9). Paragon.

Bhatia, Shyam. India's Nuclear Bomb. 1980. text ed. 13.95x (ISBN 0-7069-0972-0, Pub. by Vikas India). Advent NY.

Bhushan, Prashant. The Case That Shook India. LC 77-907825. 1978. 10.00x (ISBN 0-7069-0594-6). Intl Pubns Serv.

Bohm, Bob. Indications: Notes on India. 220p. (Orig.). 1981. pap. 7.00 (ISBN 0-89608-125-7). South End Pr.

Bose, Sajal. Underground Literature During the Emergency, India. 1978. 10.00x (ISBN 0-8364-0034-8). South Asia Bks.

Carras, Mary C. Indira Gandhi in the Crucible of Leadership. LC 78-19598. 1979. 13.95 (ISBN 0-8070-0242-9). Beacon Pr.

Chaturvedi, H. R. Bureaucracy & Local Community: Dynamics of Rural Deveolpment, India. 1977. 9.50x (ISBN 0-88386-990-X). South Asia Bks.

Chopra, Pran. Uncertain India: A Political Profile of Two Decades of Freedom. 1969. 23.00x (ISBN 0-262-03030-6). MIT Pr.

Communication Policies in India. 1977. pap. 6.75 (ISBN 92-3-101425-0, U83, UNESCO). Unipub.

Dayal, Ishwar, et al. Dynamics of Formulating Policy in Government of India. LC 76-900325. 1976. 6.00 (ISBN 0-88386-063-5). South Asia Bks.

Dean, Vera M. New Patterns of Democracy in India. 2nd ed. LC 79-78516. 1969. 14.00x (ISBN 0-674-61751-7). Harvard U Pr.

Del Vasto, Lanza. Gandhi to Vinoba: The New Pilgrimage. LC 74-6324. 1974. 7.95 (ISBN 0-8052-3554-X). Schocken.

Eldersveld, Samuel & Ahmed, Bashiruddin. Citizens & Politics: Mass Political Behavior in India. LC 77-21395. (Illus.). 1978. lib. bdg. 26.00x (ISBN 0-226-20280-1). U of Chicago Pr.

Eldridge, P. J. The Politics of Foreign Aid in India. LC 75-108903. 1970. 9.00x (ISBN 0-8052-3343-1). Schocken.

Fadia, Babulal. Pressure Groups in Indian Politics. (Illus.). 295p. 1980. text ed. 21.50x (ISBN 0-391-01795-0). Humanities.

Frankel, Francine R. India's Green Revolution: Political Costs of Economic Growth. LC 74-132237. (Center of International Studies Ser.). 1971. 17.00 (ISBN 0-691-07536-0). Princeton U Pr.

Gadre, Kamala. Indian Way to Socialism. 1966. text ed. 9.00 (ISBN 0-8426-1698-5). Verry.

Gajendragadkar, P. B. Philosophy of National Integration. LC 74-900719. 1975. 6.50x (ISBN 0-8002-1798-5). Intl Pubns Serv.

Gallo, Patrick J. India's Image of the International System. 1980. 13.00x (ISBN 0-89126-089-7). MA-AH Pub.

George, K. C. Immortal Punnapra Vayalar. LC 75-905817. 1975. 5.50x (ISBN 0-88386-693-5). South Asia Bks.

Ghose, Sankar. Changing India. 1978. 15.00x (ISBN 0-8364-0241-3). South Asia Bks.

Ghurye, G. S. India Recreates Democracy. 1979. text ed. 24.00x (ISBN 0-8426-1607-1). Verry.

Gopinath, Santha. Customer Satisfaction in the Postal Services. 105p. 1980. text ed. 10.25x (ISBN 0-391-02125-7). Humanities.

Gupta, D. C. Indian Government & Politics. 580p. 1976. 10.50x (ISBN 0-7069-0191-6). Intl Pubns Serv.

Halayya, M. Emergency: A War on Corruption. LC 75-908322. 1975. 8.00 (ISBN 0-88386-716-8). South Asia Bks.

Harrison, Selig S. India: The Most Dangerous Decades. (Illus.). 1960. 18.50x (ISBN 0-691-03025-1). Princeton U Pr.

Henderson, Michael D. Experiment with Untruth: India Under Emergency. 1978. 12.50x (ISBN 0-8364-0128-X). South Asia Bks.

Hidayatullah, M. Democracy in India & the Judicial Process. 1966. 5.00x (ISBN 0-210-22707-9). Asia.

Hull, William I. India's Political Crisis. LC 78-64277. (Johns Hopkins University. Studies in the Social Sciences. Extra Volumes-New Ser.: 7). Repr. of 1930 ed. 19.50 (ISBN 0-404-61378-0). AMS Pr.

Jagmohan. Island of Truth. 1979. 10.50 (ISBN 0-7069-0660-8, Pub. by Vikas India). Advent NY.

Jain, D. C. Parliamentary Privileges Under the Indian Constitution. 1975. text ed. 12.00x (ISBN 0-8426-0950-4). Verry.

Jha, Prem S. India: A Political Economy of Stagnation. (Illus.). 330p. 1980. 13.95x (ISBN 0-19-561153-5). Oxford U Pr.

Joshi, P. C., ed. Rammohum Roy & the Process of Modernization. 1975. 12.00 (ISBN 0-7069-0349-8). Intl Bk Dist.

Katzenstein, Mary F. Ethnicity & Equality: The Shiv Sena Party & Preferential Policies in Bombay. LC 79-4163. (Illus.). 1979. 19.50x (ISBN 0-8014-1205-6). Cornell U Pr.

Kaul, T. N. Diplomacy in Peace & War. 1979. text ed. 15.00x (ISBN 0-7069-0749-3. Pub. by Vikas India). Advent NY.

Khera, S. S. The Central Executive. (India) LC 75-905983. 1975. text ed. 9.00x (ISBN 0-8364-0483-1, Orient Longman). South Asia Bks.

Kochanek, Stanley A. Congress Party of India: The Democracy of a One-Party Diplomacy. LC 68-10393. 1968. 30.00 (ISBN 0-691-03013-8). Princeton U Pr.

Krishnan, N. No Way but Surrender: An Account of the Indo-Pakistan War in the Bay of Bengal. 80p. 1980. text ed. 10.00 (ISBN 0-7069-1018-4, Pub. by Vikas India). Advent NY.

Kumar, Virendra. Committees & Commissions in India, Vols. 4 & 5. 1978. Vol. 4. 30.00x (ISBN 0-8364-0126-3); Vol. 5. 30.00x (ISBN 0-8364-0127-1). South Asia Bks.

--Committees & Commissions in India, 1947-73, Vol. 1. LC 75-902377. 1975. 24.00x (ISBN 0-88386-935-7). South Asia Bks.

Mahajan, V. D. Fifty Years of Modern India 1919-1969. 1970. 9.00x (ISBN 0-8426-0124-4). Verry.

Mahajan, V. S. Socialistic Pattern in India. 1974. text ed. 7.50x (ISBN 0-8426-0664-5). Verry.

Maheshwari. State Governments in India. 1980. 17.00x (ISBN 0-8364-0587-0, Pub. by Macmillan India). South Asia Bks.

Mathai, M. O. My Days with Nehru. 1979. 15.00x (ISBN 0-7069-0823-6, Pub. by Vikas India). Advent NY.

Mehrotra, S. R. Towards India's Freedom & Partition. LC 79-108398. 322p. 1979. 13.50x (ISBN 0-7069-0712-4). Intl Pubns Serv.

Mehta, Ved. The New India. 1978. pap. 2.95 (ISBN 0-14-004570-8). Penguin.

Mirchandani, G. Reporting India, 1975. 1977. 11.50 (ISBN 0-88386-952-7). South Asia Bks.

Mirchandani, G. G. The People's Verdict: DCM Computer-Based Study. (Illus.). 194p. 1980. text ed. 13.50x (ISBN 0-7069-1060-5, Pub. by Vikas India). Advent NY.

Mishra, Dina N. The R. S. S. Myth & Reality. 240p. 1980. text ed. 16.50 (ISBN 0-7069-1020-6). Advent NY.

Mishra, S. N. Pattern of Emerging Leadership in Rural India. 1978. 17.00x (ISBN 0-8364-0177-8). South Asia Bks.

--Politics & Society in Rural India: A Case Study of Darauli Gram Panchayat, Siwan District, Bihar. 184p. 1980. text ed. 11.25x (ISBN 0-391-02123-0). Humanities.

Mitra, Ashok. Calcutta Diary. 206p. 1977. 25.00x (ISBN 0-7146-3082-9, F Cass Co). Biblio Dist.

--The Hoodlum Years. 1979. 7.50x (ISBN 0-8364-0530-7, Orient Longman). South Asia Bks.

Mody, Piloo. Democracy Means Bread & Freedom. 1979. 11.50x (ISBN 0-8364-0356-8). South Asia Bks.

Morris-Jones, W. H. Politics Mainly Indian. 1978. 18.00x (ISBN 0-8364-0161-1). South Asia Bks.

Mullik, B. N. My Years with Nehru, 1948-1964. 474p. 1972. 8.50x (ISBN 0-8188-1181-1). Paragon.

Narain, Iqbal. Election Studies in India. 1978. 10.00x (ISBN 0-8364-0240-5). South Asia Bks.

Narayan, Jayaprakash. Prison Diary. Shaw, A. B., ed. LC 78-5471. 156p. 1979. 9.95 (ISBN 0-295-95613-5). U of Wash Pr.

--Towards Total Revolution, 4 vols. Brahmanand, ed. LC 79-4919. 1980. Set. 50.00 (ISBN 0-295-95671-2, Pub. by Popular Prakashan India). U of Wash Pr.

Nayar, Kuldip. India After Nehru. 290p. 1975. 10.00x (ISBN 0-8002-1530-3). Intl Pubns Serv.

Pattabhiram, M., ed. General Election in India. 1962. 6.00x (ISBN 0-8188-1100-5). Paragon.
Prasad, Rai A. Socialist Thought in Modern India. LC 74-901656. 300p. 1974. 11.00x (ISBN 0-8002-0049-7). Intl Pubns Serv.
Rao, G. R. Regionalism in India. 194p. 1975. text ed. 9.00x (ISBN 0-8426-0840-0). Verry.
Reddy, G. Ram & Sharma, B. Regionalism in India: A Study of Telangana. 1980. text ed. 17.50x (ISBN 0-391-01868-X). Humanities.
Rosenthal, Donald B. The Expansive Elite: District Politics & State Policy-Making in India. 1977. 27.50x (ISBN 0-520-03160-1). U of Cal Pr.
Sabha, Lok. Political Events Annual 1975, Vol. 2. LC 77-647551. 575p. 1977. 20.00x (ISBN 0-8002-0180-9). Intl Pubns Serv.
Sarin, V. I. India's North-East in Flames. (Illus.). 200p. 1980. text ed. 13.95 (ISBN 0-7069-1068-0, Pub. by Vikas India). Advent NY.
Seminar on Leadership & Political Institutions in India. Leadership & Political Institutions in India: Proceedings. Tinker, Irene & Park, Richard L., eds. LC 69-14075. x, 486p. Repr. of 1959 ed. lib. bdg. 20.50x (ISBN 0-8371-1882-4, POII). Greenwood.
Sengupta, Surajit. Business Law in India. 894p. (Orig.). 1979. pap. text ed. 9.95x (ISBN 0-19-560658-2). Oxford U Pr.
Sethi, J. D. India's Static Power Structure. 1969. 7.75x (ISBN 0-8426-1513-X). Verry.
Shourie, Arun. Institutions in the Janata Phase. 300p. 1980. text ed. 18.00 (ISBN 0-8426-1678-0). Verry.
--Symptoms of Fascism. 322p. 1978. 16.00x (ISBN 0-7069-0696-9, Pub. by Croom Helm Ltd. England). Biblio Dist.
Shriman, Narayan. Those Ten Months: President's Rule in Gujrat. 1973. 9.00 (ISBN 0-686-20319-4). Intl Bk Dist.
Singh, Mahendra P. Split in a Predominate Party: The Indian National Congress in 1969. 1981. 24.00x (ISBN 0-8364-0721-0, Pub. by Abhinav Indian). South Asia Bks.
Singh, R. Electoral Politics in Manipur. 1981. text ed. 15.75x (ISBN 0-391-02271-7, Pub. by Concept India). Humanities.
Singh, Sampooran. India & the Nuclear Bomb. 1971. 7.50x (ISBN 0-8426-0287-9). Verry.
Srivastava, Meera. Constitutional Crisis in the States in India. 220p. 1980. text ed. 12.50x (ISBN 0-391-02135-4). Humanities.
Stern, Robert W. Process of Opposition in India: Two Case Studies of How Policy Shapes Politics. LC 78-116029. 1970. 10.00x (ISBN 0-226-77314-0). U of Chicago Pr.
Talbot, Phillips. Understanding India. LC 72-96098. (Headline Ser.: No. 214). (Illus., Orig.). 1973. pap. 2.00 (ISBN 0-87124-020-3). Foreign Policy.
Thorner, Daniel, ed. Shaping of Modern India. 1981. 28.00x (ISBN 0-8364-0678-8, Pub. by Allied India). South Asia Bks.
Veit, Lawrence A. India's Second Revolution: The Dimension of Development. LC 76-853. (Illus.). 1976. 15.95 (ISBN 0-07-067395-0, P&RB). McGraw.
Vepa, Ram K. Change & Challenge in Indian Administration. 1978. 14.00x (ISBN 0-8364-0201-4). South Asia Bks.
Vira, D. Memoirs of a Civil Servant. LC 75-904445. 1975. 10.00x (ISBN 0-88386-672-2). South Asia Bks.
Weiner, Myron. India at the Polls: The Parliamentary Elections of 1977. 1978. pap. 6.25 (ISBN 0-8447-3304-0). Am Enterprise.
--Politics of Scarcity: Public Pressure & Political Response in India. LC 62-15047. 1962. 10.00x (ISBN 0-226-89040-6). U of Chicago Pr.
Weiner, Myron, ed. Electoral Politics in the Indian States: Party Systems & Cleavages, Vol. 4. 1976. 13.00x (ISBN 0-88386-412-6). South Asia Bks.
Yunus, Mohammad. Persons, Passions & Politics. (Illus.). 333p. 1980. text ed. 15.00 (ISBN 0-7069-1017-6, Pub. by Vikas India). Advent NY.

INDIA–POPULATION

Agarwala, S. N. India's Population Problems. rev. ed. 1978. 13.00x (ISBN 0-8364-0157-3). South Asia Bks.
Bhattacharjee, P. J. & Shastri, G. N. Population in India: A Study of Inter-State Variations. 1976. 9.00 (ISBN 0-7069-0426-5). Intl Bk Dist.
Blaikie, Piers M. Family Planning in India: Diffusion & Policy. (Illus.). 168p. 1976. text ed. 24.00x (ISBN 0-8419-5800-9). Holmes & Meier.
Bose, A., et al. Population in India's Development, 1947-2000. 1974. 18.00 (ISBN 0-686-20289-9). Intl Bk Dist.
Bose, A., et al, eds. Population in India's Development, 1947-2000. 1975. text ed. 18.00x (ISBN 0-7069-0331-5). Verry.
Bose, Ashish, et al, eds. Population Statistics in India. 1977. 13.50x (ISBN 0-88386-942-X). South Asia Bks.
Cassen, R. H. India: Population, Economy, Society. LC 77-16217. 1978. text ed. 39.50x (ISBN 0-8419-0300-X); pap. text ed. 16.95x (ISBN 0-8419-0648-3). Holmes & Meier.
Chandrasekhar, S. Infant Mortality, Population Growth & Family Planning in India. LC 78-170290. (Illus.). 399p. 1972. 25.00x (ISBN 0-8078-1185-8). U of NC Pr.
Dandekar, Kumudini & Bhate, Vaijayanti. Prospects of Population Control: Evaluation of Contraception Activity. 1951-1964. 12.00 (ISBN 0-8046-8802-8). Kennikat.
Danvers, Frederik C. Portuguese in India, 2 vols. new ed. (Illus.). 1966. 85.00x set (ISBN 0-7146-2005-X, F Cass Co). Biblio Dist.
Dasgupta, Uma. Rise of an Indian Public. 1978. 16.00x (ISBN 0-8364-0292-8). South Asia Bks.
Deshpande, Madhav M. & Hook, Peter E., eds. Aryan & Non-Aryan in India. LC 78-60016. (Michigan Papers on South & Southeast Asia: No. 14). 350p. 1979. 16.50x (ISBN 0-89720-012-8); pap. 12.50x (ISBN 0-89148-014-5). Ctr S&SE Asian.
Driver, Edwin D. Differential Fertility in Central India. 1963. 13.00x (ISBN 0-691-09314-8). Princeton U Pr.
Johnson, B. L. C. India: Resources & Development. LC 78-15402. (Illus.). 1979. text ed. 23.50x (ISBN 0-06-493348-2). B&N.
Mandelbaum, David G. Human Fertility in India: Social Components & Policy Perspectives. 1974. 16.50x (ISBN 0-520-02551-2). U of Cal Pr.
Mitra, Asok. India's Population: Aspects of Quality & Control, 2 vols. 1978. 42.50x set (ISBN 0-8364-0267-7). South Asia Bks.
Poffenberger, Thomas. Fertility & Family Life in an Indian Village. LC 75-9025. (Michigan Papers on South & Southeast Asia: No. 10). (Illus.). 114p. 1975. pap. 4.50x (ISBN 0-89148-010-2). Ctr S&SE Asian.
Prabhu, John C. Social & Cultural Determinants of Fertility in India. LC 75-901184. 1974. 10.50x (ISBN 0-8002-0313-5). Intl Pubns Serv.
Seminar on Population Growth & India's Economic Development. India's Population: Some Problems in Perspective Planning-Proceedings. Agarwala, S. N., ed. LC 74-27391. 1974. Repr. of 1960 ed. lib. bdg. 16.75x (ISBN 0-8371-7905-X, AGIP). Greenwood.
Siddiqui, Nafis A. Population Geography of Muslims in India. 200p. 1976. text ed. 10.50x (ISBN 0-8426-0871-0). Verry.
Taylor, Daniel & Hamal, Hem B. Population Education for Nepal. 81p. 1974. pap. 4.00 (ISBN 0-89055-110-3). Carolina Pop Ctr.

INDIA–RACE QUESTION

Sharma, Jagdish S. India's Minorities: A Bibliographical Study. 192p. 1975. text ed. 11.75x (ISBN 0-7069-0386-2). Verry.
Weiner, M. Sons of the Soil: Migration & Ethnic Conflict in India. LC 78-51202. 1978. text ed. 28.00 (ISBN 0-691-09379-2). Princeton U Pr.

INDIA–RELATIONS (GENERAL) WITH FOREIGN COUNTRIES

Appadorai, A. & Arora, V. K. India in World Affairs, 1957-58. 1975. text ed. 18.00 (ISBN 0-8426-0823-0). Verry.
Galbraith, John K. Ambassador's Journal: A Personal Account of the Kennedy Years. LC 69-15012. 1969. 10.00 (ISBN 0-395-07708-7). HM.
Institute Of Constitutional And Parliamentary Studies. Union State Relations in India. Kashyap, Subhash C., ed. 1969. 8.25x (ISBN 0-8426-0205-4). Verry.
Kamath, Madhav V. The United States and India: Bicentennial Commemorative 1776-1976. LC 76-39929. lib. bdg. 25.00x slip case (ISBN 0-210-40588-0). Asia.
Mookerjee, Girija K. Indian Image of Nineteenth Century Europe. 1968. 3.00x (ISBN 0-210-22544-0). Asia.
Murphey, Rhoads. The Outsiders: The Western Experience in India & China. LC 76-27279. (Michigan Studies on China Ser.). 1976. 19.95x (ISBN 0-472-08679-0). U of Mich Pr.
Raghavan, M. D. India in Ceylonese History, Society & Culture. 2nd ed. 1970. 10.00x (ISBN 0-210-31211-4). Asia.
Talbot, Phillips & Poplai, S. L. India & America. LC 72-12119. 200p. 1973. Repr. of 1958 ed. lib. bdg. 15.00x (ISBN 0-8371-6713-2, TAIA). Greenwood.

INDIA–RELIGION

Abbott, John. The Keys of Power: A Study of Indian Ritual & Belief. 1974. 10.00 (ISBN 0-8216-0219-5). Univ Bks.
Ahmad, Imtiaz, ed. Religion & Rituals Among Muslims in India. 1982. 14.00x (ISBN 0-685-74912-6). South Asia Bks.
Archer, John C. Sikhs in Relation to Hindus, Moslems, Christians & Ahmadiyyas: A Study in Comparative Religion. LC 76-139895. (Illus.). 1971. Repr. of 1946 ed. 16.00 (ISBN 0-8462-1571-3). Russell.
Atkinson, Edwin F. Notes on the History of Religion in the Himalaya of the N.W.P., India. LC 78-72374. Repr. of 1883 ed. 37.50 (ISBN 0-404-17224-5). AMS Pr.
Aurobindo, Sri. Sri Aurobindo Birth Centenary Library: Complete Writings of Sri Aurobindo, 30 vols. 1979. Set. 250.00x (ISBN 0-89744-964-9); lib. bdg. 375.00x (ISBN 0-89744-965-7). Auromere.
Babb, Lawrence A. The Divine Hierarchy: Popular Hinduism in Central India. (Illus.). 266p. 1975. 17.50x (ISBN 0-231-03882-8). Columbia U Pr.
Baird, Robert D. & Bloom, Alfred. Religion & Man: Indian & Far Eastern Religious Traditions. (Religion & Man: An Introduction, Pts. 2 & 3). 1972. pap. text ed. 10.95 (ISBN 0-06-040448-5, HarpC). Har-Row.
Bhagat, M. G. Ancient Indian Asceticism. LC 76-904001. 1976. 18.50x (ISBN 0-88386-865-2). South Asia Bks.
Bhaktivedanta, Swami. The Science of Self Realization. (Illus.). 1977. 9.95 (ISBN 0-89213-101-2). Bhaktivedanta.
--Teachings of Queen Kunti. (Illus.). 1978. 9.95 (ISBN 0-89213-102-0). Bhaktivedanta.
Bhaktivedanta, Swami A. C. Beyond Birth & Death. LC 72-84844. (Illus.). 1972. pap. 1.50 (ISBN 0-912776-41-2). Bhaktivedanta.
--Nectar of Devotion. LC 78-118082. (Illus.). 1970. 9.95 (ISBN 0-912776-05-6); pap. 3.95 (ISBN 0-912776-15-3). Bhaktivedanta.
--Sri Caitanya Caritamrta: Antya-Lila, 5 vols. (Illus.). 1975. 9.95 ea. Vol. 1 (ISBN 0-912776-72-2). Vol. 2 (ISBN 0-912776-73-0). Vol. 3 (ISBN 0-912776-74-9). Vol. 4 (ISBN 0-912776-76-5). Vol. 5 (ISBN 0-912776-77-3). Bhaktivedanta.
--Sri Caitanya-Caritamrta: Madhya-Lila, 9 vols. (Illus.). 1975. 7.95 ea. Vol. 1 (ISBN 0-912776-63-3). Vol. 2 (ISBN 0-912776-64-1). Vol. 3 (ISBN 0-912776-65-X). Vol. 4 (ISBN 0-912776-66-8). Vol. 5 (ISBN 0-912776-67-6). Vol. 6 (ISBN 0-912776-68-4). Vol. 7 (ISBN 0-912776-69-2). Vol. 8, Vol. 9 (ISBN 0-912776-71-4 (ISBN 0-912776-70-6). Bhaktivedanta.
Bhaktivendanta, Swami A. C. Srimad Bhagavatam: Ninth Canto, 3 vols. LC 73-169353. (Illus., Sanskrit & Eng.). 1977. 9.95 ea. Vol. 1 (ISBN 0-912776-94-3). Vol. 2 (ISBN 0-912776-95-1). Vol. 3 (ISBN 0-912776-96-X). Bhaktivedanta.
Bhattacharyya, Narendra N. History of the Sakta Religion. LC 75-900273. 1974. 12.00x (ISBN 0-88386-566-1). South Asia Bks.
Blavatsky, Helena P. The Caves & Jungles of Hindustan. De Zirkoff, Boris, ed. LC 74-26605. (Illus.). 750p. 1975. 14.50 (ISBN 0-8356-0219-2). Theos Pub Hse.
Carpenter, J. Estlin. Theism in Medieval India. 1977. Repr. of 1921 ed. 20.00x (ISBN 0-8002-0231-7). Intl Pubns Serv.
Carpenter, Joseph E. Theism in Medieval India. LC 77-27152. (Hibbert Lectures: 1919). Repr. of 1921 ed. 38.50 (ISBN 0-404-60419-6). AMS Pr.
--Theism in Medieval India: London, 1921. LC 78-74266. (Oriental Religions Ser.: Vol. 2). 564p. 1980. lib. bdg. 60.50 (ISBN 0-8240-3901-7). Garland Pub.
Carpenter, K. Theism in Medieval India. 1977. 22.50x (ISBN 0-8364-0100-X). South Asia Bks.
Chakravarti, S. C. Bauls: The Spiritual Vikings. 1981. 10.00x (ISBN 0-8364-0671-0, Pub. by Mukhopadhyay India). South Asia Bks.
Chattopadhyaya, Sudhakar. Reflections on the Tantras. 1979. 8.25x (ISBN 0-89684-028-X). South Asia Bks.
Chinmoy, Sri. Mother India's Lighthouse: India's Spiritual Leaders. LC 74-189998. 288p. 1973. pap. 2.95 (ISBN 0-8334-1732-0). Steinerbks.
Christanand, M. The Philosophy of Indian Monotheism. 1979. 12.00x (ISBN 0-8364-0558-7, Pub. by Macmillan India). South Asia Bks.
Christanand, M. P. The Philosophy of Indian Monotheism. 132p. 1980. text ed. 12.00x (ISBN 0-333-90313-7). Humanities.
Creel, Austin. Dharma in Hindu Ethics. 1978. 11.00x (ISBN 0-88386-999-3). South Asia Bks.
Crooke, William. Religion & Folklore of Northern India. LC 72-900287. (Illus.). 471p. 1972. Repr. of 1926 ed. 21.50x (ISBN 0-8002-1915-5). Intl Pubns Serv.
Dabois, Abee J. State of Christianity in India - During the Early Nineteenth Century. 1977. 11.00x (ISBN 0-686-12059-0). Intl Bk Dist.
Dahlquist, Allan. Megasthenes & Indian Religion. 1977. 10.00 (ISBN 0-89684-277-0, Pub. by Motilal Banarsidass India). Orient Bk Dist.
--Megasthenes & Indian Religion: A Study in Motives & Types. 1977. Repr. of 1962 ed. text ed. 12.00x (ISBN 0-8426-1055-3). Verry.
Dass, Baba Hari. Sweeper to Saint: Stories of Holy India. Renu, Ma, ed. LC 80-52021. (Illus.). 200p. (Orig.). 1980. pap. 6.95 (ISBN 0-918100-03-8). Sri Rama.
Dave, H. T. Life & Philosophy of Shree Swaminarayan. new ed. Shepard, Leslie, ed. (Illus.). 274p. 1975. Repr. of 1967 ed. 8.95 (ISBN 0-04-294082-6). Weiser.
Deshpande, Madhav & Hook, Peter, eds. Aryan & Non-Aryan in India. 315p. 1979. 16.50 (ISBN 0-89720-011-X); pap. 12.50 (ISBN 0-89720-012-8). Karoma.
Deussen, Paul. The System of the Vedanta According to Badarayana's Brahma Sutras & Sankara's Commentary Thereon. Deussen, Charles, tr. 1977. text ed. 10.50x (ISBN 0-8426-1057-X). Verry.
Devaraja, N. K. Philosophy, Religion & Culture: Essays in Search of Definitions & Directions. 223p. 1974. text ed. 9.00x (ISBN 0-8426-0548-7). Verry.
Drekmeier, Charles. Kingship & Community in Early India. LC 62-9565. 1962. 19.50x (ISBN 0-8047-0114-8). Stanford U Pr.
Dutt, Nalinaksha. Buddhist Sects in India. 1978. 9.50 (ISBN 0-89684-043-3, Pub. by Motilal Banarsidas India); pap. 5.95 (ISBN 0-89684-044-1). Orient Bk Dist.
Eck, Diana L. Darsan: Seeing the Divine Image in India. 64p. 1981. pap. 3.00 (ISBN 0-89012-024-2). Anima Bks.
Eschmann, Anncharlott, et al. The Cult of Jagannath & the Regional Tradition of Orissa. 1979. 26.00 (ISBN 0-8364-0327-4). South Asia Bks.
Farquhar, J. N. Modern Religious Movements in India: New York, 1919. LC 78-74274. (Oriental Religions Ser.: Vol. 3). 497p. 1980. lib. bdg. 55.00 (ISBN 0-8240-3909-2). Garland Pub.
Feys, J. The Yogi & the Mystic. LC 76-902829. 1976. 11.00x (ISBN 0-8364-0480-7). South Asia Bks.
Feys, Jan. The Philosophy of Evolution in Sri Aurobindo & Telihard De Chardin. 276p. 1974. 13.25x (ISBN 0-8002-1797-7). Intl Pubns Serv.
Firishtah, Muhammed Kasim. History of the Rise of the Mahomedan Power in India till the Year A.D. 1612, 4 Vols. Briggs, John, tr. LC 79-154112. Repr. of 1910 ed. Set. 225.00 (ISBN 0-404-56300-7). AMS Pr.
Fuchs, Stephen. Rebellious Prophets: A Study of Messianic Movements in Indian Religions. 1965. 8.95x (ISBN 0-210-27136-1). Asia.
Gandhi, Indira. Eternal India. LC 80-51191. Orig. Title: Inde. (Illus.). 260p. 1980. 50.00 (ISBN 0-86565-003-9). Vendome.
Gargi, Balwant. Nirankari Baba. (Illus.). 172p. 1973. 9.00x (ISBN 0-8002-0934-6). Intl Pubns Serv.
Gonda, J. Visnuism & Sivaism: A Comparison. LC 71-545904. 1976. 12.50x (ISBN 0-8002-0233-3). Intl Pubns Serv.
Hopkins, Edward W. The Religions of India. LC 77-94585. 1979. Repr. of 1895 ed. lib. bdg. 65.00 (ISBN 0-89341-312-7). Longwood Pr.
Jagadiswarananda, Swami, tr. Devi-Mahatmyam (the Chandi) (Sanskrit & Eng). pap. 3.25 (ISBN 0-87481-426-X). Vedanta Pr.
Jha, Akhileshwar. The Imprisoned Mind: Guru Shisya Tradition in Indian Culture. 1980. 18.50x (ISBN 0-8364-0665-6, Pub. by Ambika India). South Asia Bks.
Kapoor, O. B. The Philosophy & Religion of Sri Caitanya: The Philosophical Background of the Hare Krishna Movement. 1977. 16.00x (ISBN 0-88386-995-0). South Asia Bks.
Kawamura, Leslie S. Bodhisattva Doctrine. 306p. 1981. pap. text ed. 7.00x (ISBN 0-919812-12-0, Pub. by Laurier U Pr). Humanities.
Keith, Arthur B. The Religion & Philosophy of the Veda & Upanishads, 2 vols. LC 71-109969. Repr. of 1925 ed. lib. bdg. 34.00x (ISBN 0-8371-4475-2, KEVU). Greenwood.
Kennedy, Melville R. The Chaitanya Movement: Calcutta & London. LC 78-74267. (Oriental Religions Ser.: Vol. 6). 283p. Date not set. lib. bdg. 33.00 (ISBN 0-8240-3904-1). Garland Pub.
Keyt, George, tr. Song of Love. Orig. Title: Gita Govinda. 123p. 1969. pap. 2.00 (ISBN 0-88253-048-8). Ind-US Inc.
Kohli, S. S. A Critical Study of Adi Granth, Being a Comprehensive & Scientific Study of Guru Granth Sahib, the Scripture of the Sikhs. 1976. Repr. of 1961 ed. text ed. 15.00x (ISBN 0-685-71570-1). Verry.
Krishna Prasad. Religious Freedom Under Indian Constitution. 1976. 9.00x (ISBN 0-88386-839-3). South Asia Bks.
Lal, R. B. Gita in the Light of Modern Science. 1971. 6.75x (ISBN 0-8426-0235-6). Verry.
Lalwani, K. C. Sramana Bhagavan Mahavira: Life & Doctrine. LC 75-904150. 1975. 10.00x (ISBN 0-88386-533-5). South Asia Bks.
Lawrence, Bruce B. Shahrastani on the Indian Religions. (Religion & Society Ser.: No. 4). 1976. text ed. 51.25x (ISBN 90-2797-681-3). Mouton.
Ling, Trevor. Karl Marx & Religion: In Europe & India. LC 79-55947. 1980. text ed. 23.00x (ISBN 0-06-494294-5). B&N.

McGavran, Donald A. Ethnic Realities & the Church: Lessons from India. LC 78-11517. (Illus.). 1979. pap. 8.95 (ISBN 0-87808-168-2). William Carey Lib.
McLean, Robert, ed. India in Transition. 1982. 15.00x (ISBN 0-8364-0011-9). South Asia Bks.
Malik, S. C., ed. Dissent, Protest & Reform in Indian Civilization. 1977. 18.50x (ISBN 0-8364-0104-2). South Asia Bks.
Martin, E. Osborn. The Gods of India: A Brief Description of Their History, Character, & Worship. LC 77-87621. 1977. Repr. of 1914 ed. lib. bdg. 40.00 (ISBN 0-89341-302-X). Longwood Pr.
Mathur, A. P. Radhasoami Faith: A Historical Study. 1974. 9.00 (ISBN 0-686-20296-1). Intl Bk Dist.
Mayeda, Sengaku, tr. A Thousand Teachings: The Upadesasahasri of Sankara. 1979. 27.50x (ISBN 0-86008-242-3, Pub. by U of Tokyo Pr). Intl Schol Bk Serv.
Mehta, Gita. Karma Cola. 1979. 9.95 (ISBN 0-671-25083-3). S&S.
Miri, Sujata. Religion & Society of North-East India. 128p. 1980. text ed. 13.95x (ISBN 0-7069-1136-9, Pub. by Vikas India). Advent NY.
Mitra, Debala. Bronzes from Achutrajpur Orissa. 1978. 50.00x (ISBN 0-8364-0136-0). South Asia Bks.
Mother India's Lighthouse: India's Spiritual Leaders & Flame-Heights of the West. LC 74-189998. 1973. 1.95 (ISBN 0-685-61448-4). Aum Pubns.
Mueller, Friedrich M. Lectures on the Origin & Growth of Religion, As Illustrated by the Religions of India. LC 73-18816. Repr. of 1882 ed. 27.50 (ISBN 0-404-11440-7). AMS Pr.
Muktanado, Swami. Lalleswhari. 1981. pap. write for info. SYDA Found.
Murphet, Howard. Sai Baba Avatar: A New Journey into Power & Glory. LC 77-83643. 1977. 8.25 (ISBN 0-9600958-2-9); pap. 3.60 (ISBN 0-9600958-3-7). Birth Day.
Mushir-Ul-Hag. Islam in Secular India. (Indian Institute of Advanced Study Monographs Ser). 110p. 1972. 8.00x (ISBN 0-8002-1594-X). Intl Pubns Serv.
Nakahura, Hajime. Religions & Philosophies of India, 3 bks. Incl. Bk. 1. 1973. 22.50 (ISBN 0-89346-084-2); Bk. 2. 1974. pap. 13.95 (ISBN 0-89346-085-0); Bk. 3. 1973. pap. 18.50 (ISBN 0-89346-086-9). Set. 63.95 (ISBN 0-89346-087-7, Pub. by Hokuseido Pr). Heian Intl.
Nandi, R. N. Religious Institutions & Cults in the Deccan. 1973. 7.50 (ISBN 0-8426-0564-9). Orient Bk Dist.
Narayan, R. K. The Ramayana of R. K. Narayan: A Shortened Modern Prose Version of the Indian Epic, Suggested by the Tamil Version of Kamban. LC 79-189514. (Illus.). 192p. 1972. 7.95 (ISBN 0-670-58950-0). Viking Pr.
Narla, V. R. Gods, Goblins & Men. 1979. 12.00x (ISBN 0-8364-0559-5, Pub. by Minerva Associates). South Asia Bks.
Newbigin, James E. The Reunion of the Church: A Defence of the South India Scheme. LC 79-4205. 1979. Repr. of 1960 ed. lib. bdg. 17.75x (ISBN 0-313-20797-6, NERU). Greenwood.
Nizami, Khalig A. Some Aspects of Religion & Politics in India During the Thirteenth Century. 1973. 14.00x (ISBN 0-88386-318-9). South Asia Bks.
Oddie, G. A. Social Protest in India: British Protestant Missionaries & Social Reforms, Eighteen Fifty to Nineteen Hundred. 1979. 17.50x (ISBN 0-8364-0195-6). South Asia Bks.
O'Flaherty, Wendy, ed. Duty in South Asia. 1978. 12.00x (ISBN 0-8364-0025-9). South Asia Bks.
O'Flaherty, Wendy D. Karma & Rebirth in Classical Indian Traditions. LC 79-64475. 400p. 1980. 29.50x (ISBN 0-520-03923-8). U of Cal Pr.
O'Malley, Lewis S. Popular Hinduism: The Religion of the Masses. LC 70-142072. 1971. Repr. of 1935 ed. 19.50 (ISBN 0-384-43305-7). Johnson Repr.
Oman, John C. The Brahmans, Theists & Muslims of India. LC 73-905235. 342p. 1973. Repr. 12.50x (ISBN 0-88386-309-X). South Asia Bks.
--Cults, Customs, & Superstitions of India: Being a Revised & Enlarged Edition of Indian Life, Religious & Social. LC 70-179232. (Illus.). Repr. of 1908 ed. 29.00 (ISBN 0-404-54859-8). AMS Pr.
--The Mystics, Ascetics & Saints of India. lib. bdg. 75.00 (ISBN 0-8490-0698-8). Gordon Pr.
Paramananda, Swami. Srimad-Bhagavad-Gita. 7th ed. Orig. Title: Bhagavad-Gita, Srimad. 1981. pap. 2.75 (ISBN 0-911564-03-9). Vedanta Ctr.
Parratt, Saroj Nalini. The Religion of Manipur. 1980. 13.00x (ISBN 0-8364-0594-3, Pub. by Mukhopadhyaya India). South Asia Bks.
Pavitranananda, Swami. A Short Life of the Holy Mother. pap. 1.25 (ISBN 0-87481-122-8). Vedanta Pr.
Prema, Nandakumar. Dante & Sri Aurobindo: A Comparative Study of "the Divine Comedy" & "Savitri". 160p. 1981. text ed. 12.50x (ISBN 0-391-02391-8, Pub. by Affiliated E-W India). Humanities.
Radhakrishnan, S. Indian Religions. 1979. 7.00x (ISBN 0-8364-0367-3). South Asia Bks.
Radhakrishnan, Sarvepalli. Religion & Culture. 176p. 1971. pap. 2.40 (ISBN 0-88253-074-7). Ind-US Inc.
Raj Gupta, Giri, ed. Religions in Modern India. (Main Currents in Indian Sociology Ser.: Vol. 5). 368p. 1981. text ed. 27.50x (ISBN 0-7069-0793-0, Pub. by Vikas India). Advent NY.
Ramacharaka, Yogi. Philosophies & Religions of India. 7.00 (ISBN 0-911662-05-7). Yoga.
Ramakrishna, Sri. Sayings of Sri Ramakrishna. 4.50 (ISBN 0-87481-431-6). Vedanta Pr.
--Words of the Master. Brahmananda, Swami, ed. pap. 1.50 (ISBN 0-87481-135-X). Vedanta Pr.
Ramakrisnananda, Swami. Life of Sri Ranauja. 1979. pap. 6.75 (ISBN 0-87481-446-4). Vedanta Pr.
Rao, K. L. The Concept of Sraddha, in the Brahmanas, Upanisads & the Gita. 1976. text ed. 6.00x (ISBN 0-8426-0894-X). Verry.
--Mahatma Gandhi & Comparative Religion. 1979. 15.00x (ISBN 0-89684-034-4). South Asia Bks.
Rao, K. L. Seshagiri. Mahatma Gandhi & Comparative Religion. 1978. 11.50 (ISBN 0-89684-034-4, Pub. by Motilal Banarsidass India). Orient Bk Dist.
Rao, P. Nagaraja. Essays in Indian Philosophy & Religion. 185p. 1972. 8.50x (ISBN 0-8426-0357-3). Verry.
Rawson, Philip. Tantra: The Indian Cult of Ecstasy. (Illus.). 1977. pap. 8.95 (ISBN 0-500-81001-X). Thames Hudson.
Rolland, Romain. Life of Ramakrishna. 4.50 (ISBN 0-87481-080-9). Vedanta Pr.
--Life of Vivekananda. 7.95 (ISBN 0-87481-090-6). Vedanta Pr.
--La Vie de Ramakrishna. 1978. 16.95 (ISBN 0-686-55279-2). French & Eur.
--La Vie de Vivekananda. 352p. 1978. 16.95 (ISBN 0-686-55280-6). French & Eur.
Schweitzer, Albert. Indian Thought & Its Development. 1962. 8.25 (ISBN 0-8446-2893-X). Peter Smith.
Sharma, Arbind. Thresholds in Hindu-Buddhist Studies. 1980. 16.50 (ISBN 0-8364-0495-5). South Asia Bks.
Sharma, J. Dream Symbolism in the Sramanic Tradition. 1981. 11.00x (ISBN 0-8364-0674-5, Pub. by Mukhopadhyay India). South Asia Bks.
Sharma, T. N. Religious Thought in India. 1980. 11.00x (ISBN 0-8364-0619-2, Pub. by Ramneek). South Asia Bks.
Sheth, Surabhi. Religion & Society in the Brahma Purana. 1979. text ed. 30.00x (ISBN 0-8426-1102-9). Verry.
Singh, Khushwant. Gurus, Godmen & Good People. LC 75-905201. 1975. 9.00x (ISBN 0-8364-0487-4, Orient Longman). South Asia Bks.
Singh, M. Mohan. Life in North-Eastern India in Pre-Mauryan Times: With Special Reference to C.600b.C.-325b.C. 1967. 7.00x (ISBN 0-8426-1533-4). Verry.
Sinha, B. C. Serpent Worship in Ancient India. 1980. 17.00x (ISBN 0-8364-0582-X, Pub. by Bks India). South Asia Bks.
--Tree Worship in Ancient India. (Illus.). 1979. 18.50x (ISBN 0-8364-0366-5). South Asia Bks.
Sinha, Raghuvir. Religion & Culture of North-Eastern India. 1977. 8.50x (ISBN 0-8364-0028-3). South Asia Bks.
Sinha, V. K., ed. Secularism in India. LC 78-901700. 1968. 6.25x (ISBN 0-8002-2420-5). Intl Pubns Serv.
Sircar, D. C. The Sakta Pithas. 1974. text ed. 4.50x (ISBN 0-8426-0590-8). Verry.
--Studies in the Religious Life of Ancient & Medieval India. 1971. 9.00 (ISBN 0-89684-326-2). Orient Bk Dist.
Spiritual Practices of India. pap. 1.25 (ISBN 0-8065-0057-3). Citadel Pr.
Srivastava, I. P. Dhrupada: A Study of Its Origin, Historical Development, Structure & Present State. (Illus.). 176p. 1980. text ed. 15.00x (ISBN 0-8426-1648-9). Verry.
Srivastava, Rama. Comparative Religion. LC 74-904268. 1974. 14.00x (ISBN 0-88386-565-3). South Asia Bks.
Subramanian, Anna A. Saints of India. (Illus.). 1978. pap. 3.25 (ISBN 0-87481-479-0). Vedanta Pr.
Suda, J. Religions in India: A Study of Their Essential Unity. 1978. text ed. 16.75x (ISBN 0-391-01085-9). Humanities.
Swarupananda, Swami, tr. Bhagavad-Gita, Srimad. (Sanskirt & Eng). 5.75 (ISBN 0-87481-064-7). Vedanta Pr.
Sykes, Marjorie. Quakers in India. (Illus.). 176p. 1980. pap. 12.95 (ISBN 0-04-275003-2). Allen Unwin.
Tapasyananda, Swami. Aratrika Hymns & Ram Nam. 1979. pap. 2.50 (ISBN 0-87481-476-6). Vedanta Pr.
Tripathi, B. D. Sadhus of India: The Sociological View. 1979. text ed. 21.00x (ISBN 0-8426-1610-1). Verry.
Troisi, J. Tribal Religion: Religious Beliefs & Practices Among the Santals. 1979. 18.00x (ISBN 0-8364-0197-2). South Asia Bks.
Tyagaraja. Spiritual Heritage of Tyagaraja. Ramanujachari, C., tr. (Sanskrit, Telegu & Eng.). 6.95 (ISBN 0-87481-440-5). Vedanta Pr.
Upanishads: The Crown of India's Soul. 1972. pap. 2.00 (ISBN 0-87847-012-3). Aum Pubns.
Uprety, Prem R. Religion & Politics in the Punjab in the 1920's. 1981. 20.00x (ISBN 0-8364-0757-1, Pub. by Sterling). South Asia Bks.
Vidyabhusan. History of the Medieval School of Indian Logic. 1977. 11.00x (ISBN 0-8364-0099-2). South Asia Bks.
Vidyarthi, R. B. Early Indian Religious Thought. LC 76-904388. 1976. 13.50x (ISBN 0-88386-874-1). South Asia Bks.
Vidyatmananda, Swami, ed. Atman Alone Abides: Conversations with Swami Atulananda. 1978. pap. 5.50 (ISBN 0-87481-480-4). Vedanta Pr.
Warder, A. K. Indian Buddhism. rev. 2nd ed. 580p. 1980. text ed. 24.00 (ISBN 0-89684-094-8, Pub. by Motilal Banarsidass India). Orient Bk Dist.
Warrier, A. G. God in Advaita. 1977. text ed. 12.00x (ISBN 0-8426-1047-2). Verry.
Watters, Thomas. On Yuan Chwang's Travels in India 629-645 A. D. LC 74-158213. Repr. of 1905 ed. Set. 20.00 (ISBN 0-404-06878-2). AMS Pr.
Webster, John, et al. Popular Religion in the Punjab Today. 1974. 7.50x (ISBN 0-88386-608-0). South Asia Bks.
Webster, John C. The Christian Community & Change in Nineteenth Century North India. LC 76-900837. 1976. 15.00x (ISBN 0-333-90123-1). South Asia Bks.
Whitehead, Henry. The Village Gods of South India: 1921. LC 78-74275. (Oriental Religions Ser.: Vol. 10). 188p. 1980. lib. bdg. 22.00 (ISBN 0-8240-3907-6). Garland Pub.

INDIA–RURAL CONDITIONS

Bhattacharya, S. N. Rural Industrialisation in India. 387p. 1981. text ed. 24.75x (ISBN 0-391-02084-6, Pub. by Concept India). Humanities.
Deogaonkar, D. Administration for Rural Development in India. 242p. 1981. text ed. 18.00x (ISBN 0-391-02275-X, Pub. by Concept India). Humanities.
Desai, A. R. Rural Sociology in India. 2nd ed. 1979. text ed. 24.00x (ISBN 0-8426-1604-7). Verry.
Franda, Marcus. India's Rural Development: An Assessment of Alternatives. LC 79-2177. (Illus.). 320p. 1980. 17.50x (ISBN 0-253-19315-X). Ind U Pr.
Guha, Sunil. Rural Manpower & Capital Formation in India. 1969. 7.75x (ISBN 0-8426-1285-8). Verry.
Heredero, J. M. Rural Development & Social Change. 1977. 10.00x (ISBN 0-88386-885-7). South Asia Bks.
Mandal, G. C. Economics of Rural Change: A Study in East India. LC 74-902863. 1974. 8.25x (ISBN 0-88386-541-6). South Asia Bks.
Mandal, R. B. Introduction to Rural Settlements. 1979. text ed. 18.50x (ISBN 0-391-01817-5). Humanities.
Mann, Harold H. Social Framework of Agriculture. LC 67-29802. 1967. 25.00x (ISBN 0-678-08007-0). Kelley.
Marriott, McKim, ed. Village India: Studies in the Little Community. (Illus.). 1955. 12.50x (ISBN 0-226-50643-6). U of Chicago Pr.
--Village India: Studies in the Little Community. LC 55-9326. 1969. pap. 3.45 (ISBN 0-226-50644-4, P328, Phoen). U of Chicago Pr.
Mellor, John W., et al. Developing Rural India: Plan & Practice. LC 68-28804. (Illus.). 1968. 24.50x (ISBN 0-8014-0296-4). Cornell U Pr.
Mohammad, Ali. Situation of Agriculture, Food & Nutrition in Rural India. 1979. 14.00x (ISBN 0-8364-0518-8). South Asia Bks.
Nair, Kusum. Blossoms in the Dust: The Human Element in Indian Development. LC 78-66080. (Midway Reprints Ser.). 1979. pap. text ed. 8.00x (ISBN 0-226-56800-8). U of Chicago Pr.
Panchanadikar, K. C. & Panchanadikar, J. Rural Modernization in India: A Study in Developmental Infra-Structure. 1979. text ed. 27.50x (ISBN 0-8426-1608-X). Verry.
Rao, R. V. Small Industries & a Developing Economy. 1979. text ed. 11.50x (ISBN 0-391-01829-9). Humanities.
Saran, Parmatma. Rural Leadership in the Context of India's Modernization. 1978. 10.00x (ISBN 0-8364-0207-3). South Asia Bks.
Saraswati, Baidyanath. Pottery-Making Cultures & Indian Civilization. 1979. 27.50x (ISBN 0-8364-0321-5). South Asia Bks.
Saxena, D. P. Rururban Migration in India. 1979. text ed. 15.00x (ISBN 0-8426-1609-8). Verry.
Shah, S. M. Rural Development in India: Planning & Problems. 1977. 10.00x (ISBN 0-8364-0032-1). South Asia Bks.
Sharma, R. N. Spatial Approach for District Planning: A Case Study of Karnal District. 138p. 1981. text ed. 13.50x (ISBN 0-391-02272-5, Pub. by Concept India). Humanities.
Srinivas, M. N. The Remembered Village. 1977. 26.75x (ISBN 0-520-02997-6); pap. 6.95 (ISBN 0-520-03948-3). U of Cal Pr.
Srivastava, U. K. Planning & Implementation of Drought-Prone Areas Programme. 1978. 12.50x (ISBN 0-8364-0299-5). South Asia Bks.
Venkatarayappa, K. N. Rural Society & Social Change. (Illus.). 264p. 1974. 13.50x (ISBN 0-8002-0059-4). Intl Pubns Serv.
Verma, H. S. Post Independence Change in Rural India: A Pilot Study of an Uttar Pradesh Village. 92p. 1981. text ed. 11.25x (ISBN 0-391-02278-4, Pub. by Concept India). Humanities.
Voting, Caste, Community, Society: Explorations in Aggregate Data Analysis in India & Bangladesh. 1978. 11.00x (ISBN 0-8364-0297-9). South Asia Bks.
Whitcombe, Elizabeth. Agrarian Conditions in Northern India, Vol. 1, The United Provinces Under British Rule, 1860-1900. LC 75-129027. (Center for South & Southeast Asia Studies, UC Berkeley). (Illus.). 1972. 27.50x (ISBN 0-520-01706-4). U of Cal Pr.

INDIA–SCHEDULED TRIBES

Deogaonkar, S. G. Problems of Development in Tribal Areas. 192p. 1980. text ed. 13.50x (ISBN 0-391-02132-X). Humanities.
Ghurye, G. S. The Scheduled Tribes of India. LC 79-66430. (Social Science Classics Ser.). 399p. 1980. text ed. 19.95 (ISBN 0-87855-308-8); pap. 7.95 (ISBN 0-87855-692-3). Transaction Bks.
Patel, M. L. Changing Land Problems of Tribal India. LC 74-900800. 160p. 1974. 9.50x (ISBN 0-8002-0531-6). Intl Pubns Serv.
Revankar, Ratna G. The Indian Constitution: A Case Study of Backward Classes. LC 76-120067. 361p. 1971. 20.00 (ISBN 0-8386-7670-7). Fairleigh Dickinson.
Vidyarthi. The Tribal Culture of India. 1980. text ed. write for info. (ISBN 0-391-01167-7). Humanities.
Vidyarthi, L. P. Tribal Culture of India. 1977. 22.50x (ISBN 0-88386-896-2). South Asia Bks.

INDIA–SOCIAL CONDITIONS

Agarwal, R. D. Economic Aspects of the Welfare State in India. LC 68-2075. (Illus.). 1967. 9.50x (ISBN 0-8002-0593-6). Intl Pubns Serv.
Ahuja, K. Idle Labour in Village India: A Study of Rajasthan. 1978. 12.50x (ISBN 0-8364-0280-4). South Asia Bks.
Alden, Dauril & Dean, Warren, eds. Essays Concerning the Socioeconomic History of Brazil & Portuguese India. LC 76-53761. (Illus.). 1977. 12.50 (ISBN 0-8130-0565-5). U Presses Fla.
All India Sociological Conference. Sociology, Social Research, & Social Problems in India. Saksena, R. N., ed. LC 77-27251. 1978. Repr. of 1961 ed. lib. bdg. 17.25x (ISBN 0-8371-7893-2, SSRP). Greenwood.
Anstey, Vera. The Economic Development of India. Wilkins, Mira, ed. LC 76-29760. (European Business Ser.). (Illus.). 1977. Repr. of 1952 ed. lib. bdg. 39.00x (ISBN 0-405-09775-1). Arno.
Approaches & Priorities in Rural Research in India. 11p. 1978. pap. 5.00 (ISBN 0-88936-113-4, IDRCTS4, IDRC). Unipub.
Atal, Yogesh. Local Communities & National Politics: A Study in Communication Links & Political Involvement. (Illus.). 428p. 1971. 20.00x (ISBN 0-8002-0920-6). Intl Pubns Serv.
Auluck, Sunita V. Intracity Residential Mobility in an Industrial City: A Case Study of Ludhiana. 180p. 1980. text ed. 10.25x (ISBN 0-391-02134-6). Humanities.
Bansal, P. L. Administrative Development in India. 196p. 1975. text ed. 9.00x (ISBN 0-8426-0835-4). Verry.
Beck, Brenda E. Perspectives on a Regional Culture: Essays About the Coimbatore Area of South India. 1979. text ed. 17.95x (ISBN 0-7069-0723-X, Pub. by Vikas India). Advent NY.
Berg, Lasse & Berg, Lisa. Face to Face: Fascism & Revolution in India. Kurtin, Norman, tr. from Swedish. LC 73-172283. (Illus.). 240p. 1972. 7.95 (ISBN 0-87867-014-9). Ramparts.
Bhardwaj, R. K. Urban Development in India. 1974. text ed. 21.00x (ISBN 0-8426-0654-8). Verry.
Bhatia, B. M. India's Food Problem & Policy Since Independence. 1970. 8.25x (ISBN 0-8426-1163-0). Verry.
Bhatnagar, C. P. The Crisis in Indian Society. LC 70-928075. 217p. 1971. 11.25x (ISBN 0-8002-0541-3). Intl Pubns Serv.

Bhatty, I. Z. Technological Change & Employment: A Study of Plantations, India. 1978. 18.50x (ISBN 0-8364-0273-1). South Asia Bks.
Bose, Ashish. Bibliography on Urbanization in India, Nineteen Forty-Seven to Seventy-Six. 1977. 12.00x (ISBN 0-8364-0385-1). South Asia Bks.
Bose, Nirmal K. The Structure of Hindu Society. Beteille, Andre, tr. 1976. 10.00x (ISBN 0-88386-781-8, Orient Longman). South Asia Bks.
Carstairs, G. M. & Kapur, R. L. The Great Universe of Kota: Stress, Change & Mental Disorder in an Indian Village. LC 75-13151. 1976. 21.50x (ISBN 0-520-03024-9). U of Cal Pr.
Cassen, R. H. India: Population, Economy, Society. LC 77-16217. 1978. text ed. 39.50x (ISBN 0-8419-0300-X); pap. text ed. 16.95x (ISBN 0-8419-0648-3). Holmes & Meier.
Chacko, George K. India: Toward an Understanding. 7.50x (ISBN 0-8084-0401-6); pap. 1.95 (ISBN 0-8084-0402-4, B14). Coll & U Pr.
Chattopadhyay, Kamaladevi. Tribalism in India. (Illus.). 1978. text ed. 16.00x (ISBN 0-7069-0652-7). Humanities.
Chaudhuri, K. N. & Dewey, Clive J., eds. Economy & Society: Essays in Indian Economic & Social History. (Illus.). 1979. 16.95x (ISBN 0-19-561073-3). Oxford U Pr.
Chekki, D. A. Sociology of Contemporary India. 1978. 12.50x (ISBN 0-8364-0245-6). South Asia Bks.
Chekki, Danesh A. The Social System & Culture of Modern India: A Research Bibliography. LC 74-19226. (Reference Library of Social Science: No. 1). 873p. 1974. lib. bdg. 85.00 (ISBN 0-8240-1056-6). Garland Pub.
Dalton, E. T. Tribal History of Eastern India. 1973. Repr. 45.00x (ISBN 0-8426-0774-9). Verry.
Darling, Malcolm L. The Punjab Peasant in Prosperity & Debt. rev. ed. Dewey, Clive, ed. 1978. 14.00x (ISBN 0-8364-0070-4). South Asia Bks.
Dasgupta, Sipra. Class Relations & Technological Change in Indian Agriculture. 1981. 16.00x (ISBN 0-8364-0676-1, Pub. by Macmillan India). South Asia Bks.
Datta, Kalikinkar. Survey of India's Social Life & Economic Condition in the 18th Century, 1707-1813. 2nd rev. ed. 1978. 17.50x (ISBN 0-8002-0265-1). Intl Pubns Serv.
De Bary, W. T., ed. Sources of Indian Tradition, 2 vols. LC 58-4146. (Introductions to the Oriental Classics & Records of Civilization: Sources & Studies Ser.). Vol. 2, 384 Pgs. 6.00x (ISBN 0-231-08601-6). Columbia U Pr.
Desai, A. R. Recent Trends in Indian Nationalism. 2nd ed. LC 61-4018. 149p. 1973. 6.50x (ISBN 0-8002-1903-1). Intl Pubns Serv.
Desai, A. R., ed. Peasant Struggles in India. 1979. 27.50x (ISBN 0-19-560803-8). Oxford U Pr.
Deshpande, C. D., et al. Impact of a Metropolitan City on the Surrounding Region. (Illus.). 167p. 1980. pap. text ed. 8.00x (ISBN 0-391-02206-7). Humanities.
Deshpande, Vasant D. Towards Social Integration. 1978. 12.00x (ISBN 0-8364-0236-7). South Asia Bks.
De Souza, Alfred, ed. Children in India: Critical Issues in Human Development. 1980. 17.50x (ISBN 0-8364-0601-X, Pub. by Manohar India). South Asia Bks.
--The Indian City: Poverty, Ecology & Urban Development. 1979. 14.50x (ISBN 0-8364-0196-4). South Asia Bks.
Dhar, D. P. Planning & Social Change: With Special Reference to India. 1976. text ed. 10.50x (ISBN 0-8426-0893-1). Verry.
Doshi, Harish. Traditional Neighborhood in a Modern City. LC 74-902204. 154p. 1974. 8.50x (ISBN 0-88386-292-1). South Asia Bks.
Dubey, S. M., et al. Family Marriage & Social Change on the Indian Fringe. 283p. 1980. 22.00 (ISBN 0-89684-259-2, Pub. by Cosmo Pubns India). Orient Bk Dist.
Dubey, S. N. Administration of Social Welfare Programmes in India. LC 73-905770. 214p. 1973. 13.25x (ISBN 0-8002-0052-7). Intl Pubns Serv.
Embree, Ainslie T. India's Search for National Unity. 1981. Repr. 12.50x (ISBN 0-8364-0691-5, Pub. by Chanakya India). South Asia Bks.
Everett, Jana M. Women & Social Change in India. 1979. 16.95 (ISBN 0-312-88731-0). St Martin.
Frykenberg, Robert. Land Tenure & Peasant in South Asia. 1979. 16.00x (ISBN 0-8364-0347-9, Orient Longman). South Asia Bks.
Gadgil, D. R. Planning & Economic Policy in India. LC 73-900569. 405p. 1972. 11.25x (ISBN 0-8002-1802-7). Intl Pubns Serv.
Gangrade, K. D. Crisis of Values: A Study in Generation Gap (India) LC 75-904390. 296p. 1975. 12.50x (ISBN 0-88386-576-9). South Asia Bks.
Ganguli, B. N. & Gupta, D. B. Levels of Living in India. 1976. 11.50x (ISBN 0-8002-1650-4). Intl Pubns Serv.
--Levels of Living in India: An Inter-State Profile. 1976. text ed. 13.50x (ISBN 0-8426-0920-2). Verry.
Gautam, V. Aspects of Indian Society & Economy in the Nineteenth Century. 1972. 6.00 (ISBN 0-8426-0473-1). Orient Bk Dist.
--Aspects of Indian Society & Economy in the 19th Century: A Study Based on an Evaluation of the American Consular Records. 201p. 1973. text ed. 8.25x (ISBN 0-8426-0473-1). Verry.
Ghose, Sankar. Changing India. 1978. 12.50x (ISBN 0-8002-0362-3). Intl Pubns Serv.
Ghosh, K. Plannning India's Future. 1978. 15.00x (ISBN 0-88386-906-3). South Asia Bks.
Gorwaney, N. Self-Image & Social Change: A Study of Female Students. 1978. text ed. 18.00x (ISBN 0-8426-1075-8). Verry.
Gough, Kathleen. Rural Society in Southeast India. (Cambridge Studies in Social Anthropology: No. 38). (Illus.). 512p. Date not set. price not set (ISBN 0-521-23889-7). Cambridge U Pr.
Gupta, Giri R., ed. Cohesion & Conflict in Modern India. LC 77-86741. (Main Currents in Indian Sociology Ser.: Vol. 3). 1978. 15.95 (ISBN 0-89089-103-6). Carolina Acad Pr.
--Contemporary India: Some Sociological Perspectives. LC 75-5479. (Main Currents in Indian Sociology Ser.: Vol. 1). 1976. 12.95 (ISBN 0-89089-052-8). Carolina Acad Pr.
--Family & Social Change in Modern India. LC 76-9126. (Main Currents in Indian Sociology Ser.: Vol. 2). 1977. 13.95 (ISBN 0-89089-060-9). Carolina Acad Pr.
Gupta, Giri Raj, ed. Main Currents in Indian Sociology: Social & Cultural Context of Medicine in India, Vol. IV: 1980. text ed. 30.00x (ISBN 0-7069-0793-0, Pub. by Vikas India). Advent NY.
Gupta, Surendra K. Citizen in the Making. LC 75-903605. 1975. 12.75x (ISBN 0-88386-581-5). South Asia Bks.
Hardgrave, Robert. Essays in the Political Sociology of South India. 1980. 15.00x (ISBN 0-8364-0605-2, Pub. by Usha). South Asia Bks.
Harris, Nigel. India--China: Underdevelopment & Revolution. LC 74-30894. 1974. 10.00 (ISBN 0-89089-017-X). Carolina Acad Pr.
Harriss, John. Capitalism & Peasant Farming: Agrarian Structure & Ideology in Northern Tamil Nadu. (Illus.). 330p. 1981. 24.00 (ISBN 0-19-561340-6). Oxford U Pr.
Heredero, J. M. Rural Development & Social Change. 1977. 10.00x (ISBN 0-88386-885-7). South Asia Bks.
Hiebert, Paul G. Konduru: Structure & Integration in a South Indian Village. LC 75-120809. (Illus.). 1971. 10.95x (ISBN 0-8166-0593-9). U of Minn Pr.
Hiro, Dilip. Inside India Today. LC 76-76161. 1977. 15.00 (ISBN 0-85345-424-8, CL4248). Monthly Rev.
Ittaman, K. P. Amini Islanders: Social Structure & Change. LC 76-901759. 1976. 13.00x (ISBN 0-88386-844-X). South Asia Bks.
Jafar, S. M. Student Unrest in India: A Select Bibliography. 1977. 12.50x (ISBN 0-8364-0095-X). South Asia Bks.
Jain, P. C. Labour in Ancient India: From the Vedic Age up to the Gupta Period. 302p. 1971. 12.50x (ISBN 0-8426-0284-4). Verry.
--Socio-Economic Exploration of Medieval India. LC 76-904842. 1976. 17.50x (ISBN 0-88386-884-9). South Asia Bks.
Jammu, P. S. Changing Social Structure in Rural Panjab. 204p. 1975. text ed. 9.00x (ISBN 0-8426-0836-2). Verry.
Jha, Akhileshwar. Modernization & the Hindu Socio-Culture. 1978. 11.00x (ISBN 0-8364-0146-8). South Asia Bks.
Jha, Shree Nagesh. Leadership & Local Politics: A Study of Meerut District District in Uttar Pradesh (India) 1923-73. 175p. 1979. text ed. 14.50 (ISBN 0-8426-1640-3). Verry.
Johnson, B. L. C. India: Resources & Development. LC 78-15402. (Illus.). 1979. text ed. 23.50x (ISBN 0-06-493348-2). B&N.
Johnson, Donald J. & Johnson, Jean E. Through Indian Eyes, Vol. 2: Forging a Nation. rev. ed. Clark, Leon E., ed. (Illus.). 156p. (gr. 9-12). 1981. pap. 5.95 (ISBN 0-938960-03-2). CITE.
Kaur, Surjit. Wastage of Children: A Family Planning Foundation (India) Book. (Illus.). 1978. text ed. 18.00x (ISBN 0-8426-1104-5). Verry.
Kessinger, Tom G. Vilyatpur 1848-1968: Social & Economic Change in a North Indian Village. LC 72-89788. (Illus.). 1974. 24.50x (ISBN 0-520-02340-4). U of Cal Pr.
Khare, B. B. India: Political Attitudes & Social Change. 1974. text ed. 15.00x (ISBN 0-8426-0641-6). Verry.
Kirpal Singh, Soodan. Aging in India. LC 75-903847. 1975. 10.00x (ISBN 0-88386-531-9). South Asia Bks.
Kohli, K. L. Mortality in India: A Statewide Study. 1978. text ed. 19.50x (ISBN 0-8426-1074-X). Verry.
Kumar, P. Economics of Water Management, India. 1977. 7.00x (ISBN 0-8364-0076-3). South Asia Bks.
Kuppuswamy, B. Social Change in India. 2nd rev. ed. 1978. text ed. 13.50 (ISBN 0-7069-0372-2). Verry.
--Social Change in India. 1975. 13.50 (ISBN 0-7069-0142-8). Intl Bk Dist.
Kuthiala, S. K. From Tradition to Modernity. (Illus.). 227p. 1973. 11.25x (ISBN 0-8002-0628-2). Intl Pubns Serv.
Lajpat Rai, Lala. Unhappy India. rev. 2nd enl. ed. LC 72-171642. Repr. of 1928 ed. 36.45 (ISBN 0-404-03803-4). AMS Pr.
Lal, Basant K. Contemporary Indian Philosophy. 1979. 14.00x (ISBN 0-89684-012-3). South Asia Bks.
Lannoy, Richard. Speaking Tree: A Study of Indian Culture & Society. 1971. 25.00 (ISBN 0-19-501469-3). Oxford U Pr.
Leach, E. R. & Mukherjee, Soumyendra N. Elites in South Asia. (Illus.). 1970. 27.50 (ISBN 0-521-07710-9). Cambridge U Pr.
Lloyd, Peter C. Slums of Hope? Shanty Towns of the Third World. LC 78-24770. 1979. 17.95x (ISBN 0-312-72963-4). St Martin.
Madan, G. R. Indian Social Problems, Vol. 2: Social Reconstruction. 2nd ed. 1974. text ed. 9.00x (ISBN 0-8426-0715-3). Verry.
--Western Sociologists on Indian Society: Marx, Spencer, Weber, Durkheim, Pareto. (International Library of Sociology). 1979. 25.50x (ISBN 0-7100-8782-9). Routledge & Kegan.
Madan, Gurmukh R. Indian Social Problems, Vol. 1. 1967. 7.00x (ISBN 0-8188-1072-6). Paragon.
Maddison, Angus. Class Structure & Economic Growth: India & Pakistan Since the Moghuls. 1972. 7.95x (ISBN 0-393-05467-5, 05467); pap. 3.95x (ISBN 0-393-09399-9). Norton.
Maitra, Priyatosh. Underdevelopment Revisited. 1977. 7.00x (ISBN 0-8364-0075-5). South Asia Bks.
Malyaro, V. The Role of the State in the Socio-Economic Structure of India. 400p. 1981. text ed. 45.00x (ISBN 0-7069-1372-8, Pub. by Vikas India). Advent NY.
Mankekar, D. R. Revolution of Rising Frustrations. (Illus.). 1975. 10.50 (ISBN 0-7069-0348-X). Intl Bk Dist.
Mayo, Katherine. Mother India. Repr. of 1928 ed. lib. bdg. 22.50 (ISBN 0-8371-2309-7, MAMO). Greenwood.
Mehta, Prayag, ed. Indian Youth: Emerging Problems & Issues. 1971. 6.75x (ISBN 0-8426-0217-8). Verry.
Mencher, Joan P. Agriculture & Social Structure in Tamil Nadu: Past Origins, Present Transformations & Future Prospects. LC 77-80768. 1978. 15.95 (ISBN 0-89089-101-X). Carolina Acad Pr.
Minhas, B. S. Planning & the Poor: India. 1974. 7.50 (ISBN 0-8426-0701-3). Verry.
Mitchell, Nora. The Indian Hill-Station: Kodaikanal. LC 72-78250. (Research Papers Ser.: No. 141). (Orig.). 1972. pap. 8.00 (ISBN 0-89065-048-9). U Chicago Dept Geog.
Mukherjee, Ramkishna. Social Indicators. 1975. 9.00x (ISBN 0-333-90090-1). South Asia Bks.
Nafziger, E. Wayne. Class, Caste, & Entrepreneurship: A Study of Indian Industrialists. LC 78-16889. 1978. text ed. 12.00x (ISBN 0-8248-0575-5, Eastwest Ctr). U Pr of Hawaii.
Nagpaul, Hans. Study of Indian Society (India) A Sociological Analysis of Social Welfare & Social Work Education. 1972. 17.50x (ISBN 0-8426-0354-9). Verry.
Naidu, Ratna. The Communal Edge to Plural Societies: India & Malaysia. 1978. text ed. 14.00x (ISBN 0-7069-0922-4). Humanities.
Nair, Balakrishna N. Systemic Approaches to Indian Socio-Economic Developmentt. 1971. 18.00 (ISBN 0-686-20314-3). Intl Bk Dist.
Nair, Kusum. Blossoms in the Dust: The Human Element in Indian Development. LC 78-66080. (Midway Reprints Ser.). 1979. pap. text ed. 8.00x (ISBN 0-226-56800-8). U of Chicago Pr.
Nanavati, Manilal B. & Vakil, Chandulal N. Group Prejudices in India: A Symposium. Repr. of 1951 ed. lib. bdg. 16.25x (ISBN 0-8371-3132-4, NAGP). Greenwood.
Nandy, Ashis. At the Edge of Psychology: Essays on Politics & Culture. 152p. 1981. 12.95 (ISBN 0-19-561205-1). Oxford U Pr.
Narayan, Shriman. India Needs(Mahatma) Gandhi. 156p. 1976. text ed. 7.50x (ISBN 0-8426-0870-2). Verry.
National Seminar on Social Statistics, India, 2 vols. 1978. Set. 47.50x (ISBN 0-685-54889-9). Vol. 1 (ISBN 0-8364-0238-3). Vol. 2 (ISBN 0-8364-0239-1). South Asia Bks.
Nayar, Baldev R. Violence & Crime in India. LC 75-908765. 1975. 9.00x (ISBN 0-333-90074-X). South Asia Bks.
Oddie, G. A. Social Protest in India: British Protestant Missionaries & Social Reforms, Eighteen Fifty to Nineteen Hundred. 1979. 17.50x (ISBN 0-8364-0195-6). South Asia Bks.
O'Malley, L. S. India's Social Heritage. 194p. 1976. 13.00x (ISBN 0-8002-1554-0). Intl Pubns Serv.
Pandey, S. N. Education & Social Changes in Bihar. 1975. 9.00 (ISBN 0-8426-0986-5). Orient Bk Dist.
--Education & Social Changes in Bihar 1900-1921: A Survey of Social History of Bihar Form Lord Curzon to Non-Cooperation Movement. 1976. text ed. 10.50x (ISBN 0-8426-0986-5). Verry.
Patwardhan, Sunanda. Change Among India's Harijans: Maharashtra. (Illus.). 239p. 1973. 12.50x (ISBN 0-8002-0289-9). Intl Pubns Serv.
--Change & Mobility Among India's Harijans. LC 73-906258. 1973. 8.00x (ISBN 0-8364-0391-6). South Asia Bks.
Pillai, S. Devadas, ed. Winners & Losers: Styles of Development & Change in an Indian Region. Baks, C. 407p. 1979. text ed. 36.00 (ISBN 0-8426-1679-9). Verry.
Punit, A. E. Social Systems in Rural India. 1979. text ed. 10.50x (ISBN 0-8426-1103-7). Verry.
Raghuvanshi, V. P. Indian Society in the Eighteenth Century. 1969. 12.50x (ISBN 0-8426-1478-8). Verry.
Rahman, Hossainur. Hindu-Muslim Relations in Bengal, 1905-1947. 1977. text ed. 12.50 (ISBN 0-210-40605-4). Asia.
Ramu, G. N. Family & Caste in Urban India: A Case Study. 224p. 1977. 14.00x (ISBN 0-7069-0530-X, Pub. by Croom Helm Ltd. England). Biblio Dist.
Rao, Hanumantha, et al. Reflections on Economic Development & Social Change. 1979. 22.50x (ISBN 0-8364-0522-6). South Asia Bks.
Rao, M., ed. Social Movements in India: Peasant & Backward Classes Movements, Vol. 1. 1980. 17.50x (ISBN 0-8364-0199-9). South Asia Bks.
Rao, M. S. Social Movements & Social Transformation: A Study of Two Backward Class Movements in India. 1979. 17.50x (ISBN 0-8364-0354-1). South Asia Bks.
Rao, S. Venugopal. Crime in Our Society. 150p. 1980. text ed. 15.00 (ISBN 0-7069-1209-8, Pub. by Vikas India). Advent NY.
Rashid, A. Society & Culture in Medieval India-1206-1556. 1969. 6.50x (ISBN 0-8426-1488-5). Verry.
Rastyannikov, V. G. Agrarian Evolution in a Multiform Structure Society: Experience of Independent India. 400p. 1981. 29.95 (ISBN 0-7100-0755-8). Routledge & Kegan.
Raza, Moonis, et al, eds. Sources of Economic & Social Statistics of India. 1979. 24.00x (ISBN 0-8364-0536-6, Pub. by Eureka India). South Asia Bks.
Reddy, V. E. & Bhat, K. S. The Out of School Youth. 1978. text ed. 18.00x (ISBN 0-8426-1076-6). Verry.
Rosen, George. Democracy & Economic Change in India. rev. ed. 1966. 25.00x (ISBN 0-520-01089-2). U of Cal Pr.
Rothermund, D. & Wadhwa, D. C. Zamindars, Mines & Peasants: Studies in the History of an Indian Coalfield. 1979. 16.50x (ISBN 0-8364-0331-2). South Asia Bks.
Rothermund, D., et al, eds. Urban Growth & Rural Stagnation: Studies in the Economy of an Indian Coalfield & Its Hinterland. 1980. 36.00x (ISBN 0-8364-0662-1, Pub. by Manohar India). South Asia Bks.
Roy, Beth. Bullock Carts & Motor Bikes: Ancient India on a New Road. LC 72-75281. (gr. 6 up). 1972. 6.95 (ISBN 0-689-30064-6). Atheneum.
Roy, Girish Chandra. Indian Culture: The Tradition of Non-Violence & Social Change in India. 1976. 11.00x (ISBN 0-88386-833-4). South Asia Bks.
Saberwal, Satish. Mobile Men: Limits to Change in Urban Punjab. 260p. 1976. 13.00x (ISBN 0-7069-0430-3). Intl Pubns Serv.
Sachchidananda & Lal. Elite & Development. 286p. 1980. text ed. 15.75x (ISBN 0-391-02129-X). Humanities.
Saintsbury, George. East India Slavery. 52p. 1972. Repr. of 1829 ed. text ed. 5.75x (ISBN 0-7165-1816-3). Humanities.
Sarikwal, R. C. Sociology of a Growing Town (Ghazibad, India) 1978. 22.50x (ISBN 0-8364-0303-7). South Asia Bks.
Sarin, V. I. India's North-East in Flames. (Illus.). 200p. 1980. text ed. 13.95 (ISBN 0-7069-1068-0, Pub. by Vikas India). Advent NY.
Saxena, D. P. Rururban Migration in India. 1979. text ed. 15.00x (ISBN 0-8426-1609-8). Verry.
Sen, Gertrude E. Voiceless India. LC 74-109975. (Illus.). 1971. Repr. of 1930 ed. lib. bdg. 20.00x (ISBN 0-8371-4481-7, SEVI). Greenwood.
Shah, C. H. India in Perspective: Development Issues, Vol. 3. 1979. text ed. 15.00x (ISBN 0-8426-1108-8). Verry.

Shankar, Pathak. Social Welfare, Health & Family Planning in India. 1979. 15.00x (ISBN 0-8364-0348-7). South Asia Bks.
Sharma, Jagdish S. India's Minorities: A Bibliographical Study. 1975. 12.50 (ISBN 0-7069-0386-2, Pub. by Vikas India). Advent NY.
Sharma, K. M. Social Assistance in India. LC 76-900836. 1976. 9.50x (ISBN 0-333-90122-3). South Asia Bks.
Sharma, S. K. & Malhotra, S. L. Integrated Rural Development in India. 1977. 6.50x (ISBN 0-8364-0078-X). South Asia Bks.
Sharma, S. S. Rural Elites in India. (Illus.). 267p. 1979. 15.00x (ISBN 0-8002-0999-0). Intl Pubns Serv.
Shekhar, C. Dynamics of Social Change. 1979. text ed. 12.00x (ISBN 0-8426-1629-2). Verry.
Shenoy, Sudha R. India: Progress or Poverty. (Institute of Economic Affairs, Research Monographs: No. 27). 1972. pap. 4.25 (ISBN 0-255-36023-1). Transatlantic.
Sheth, Surabhi. Religion & Society in the Brahma Purana. 1979. text ed. 30.00x (ISBN 0-8426-1102-9). Verry.
Singh, Andre M. & De Souza, Alfred. The Urban Poor: Slum & Pavement Dwellers in the Major Cities of India. 1981. 14.00x (ISBN 0-8364-0694-X, Pub. by Manohar India). South Asia Bks.
Singh, Andrea M. Neighbourhood & Social Networks in Urban India: South India Voluntary Associations in Dehi. LC 76-900764. 1976. 12.00x (ISBN 0-88386-783-4). South Asia Bks.
Singh, R. R., ed. Social Work Perspectives on Poverty. 1980. text ed. 12.50x (ISBN 0-391-01832-9). Humanities.
Singh, Tarlok. Poverty & Social Change: With a Reappraisal. 2nd ed. LC 74-33899. 352p. 1975. Repr. of 1969 ed. lib. bdg. 18.75x (ISBN 0-8371-8000-7, SIPO). Greenwood.
Singh, V. B. Social & Economic Change in India. 1967. 7.50x (ISBN 0-8188-1138-2). Paragon.
Sinha, M. M. The Impact of Urbanization on Land Use in the Rural-Urban Fringe: A Case Study of Patna. 258p. 1980. text ed. 18.00x (ISBN 0-391-02141-9). Humanities.
Sinha, R. Social Change in Indian Society. 1980. 11.25 (ISBN 0-391-02184-2). Humanities.
Sinha, Raghuvir. Social Change in Indian Society. rev. ed. 1978. 11.50x (ISBN 0-8364-0182-4). South Asia Bks.
Smith, William R. Nationalism & Reform in India. LC 72-85314. 496p. 1973. Repr. of 1938 ed. 18.50 (ISBN 0-8046-1716-3). Kennikat.
Somers, George E. The Dynamics of Santal Traditions in a Peasant Society. (Illus.). 256p. 1978. text ed. 11.25x (ISBN 0-87073-858-5). Schenkman.
Sopher, David E., ed. Exploration of India: Geographical Perspectives on Society & Culture. LC 79-17033. (Illus.). 1980. 22.50x (ISBN 0-8014-1258-7). Cornell U Pr.
Sovani, N. V. Urbanization & Urban India. 7.50x (ISBN 0-210-22695-1). Asia.
Sreenivasan, M. A. Labour in India - Socio-Economic Conditions of Workers in Kolar Salo Mines: A Study of Kolar Gold Field. 125p. 1980. text ed. 10.50 (ISBN 0-7069-1204-7, Pub. by Vikas India). Advent NY.
Srinivas, M. N. Social Change in Modern India. (Rabindranath Tagore Memorial Lectures). (gr. 9-12). 1966. 22.50x (ISBN 0-520-01203-8); pap. 6.95x (ISBN 0-520-01421-9, CAMPUS21). U of Cal Pr.
Srinivas, M. N., et al. Dimensions of Social Change in India. 1978. 17.50x (ISBN 0-8364-0145-X). South Asia Bks.
--The Fieldworker & the Field: Problems & Challenges in Sociological Investigation. 300p. 1979. text ed. 13.95x (ISBN 0-19-561118-7). Oxford U Pr.
Stokes, E. T. The Peasant & the Raj: Studies in Agrarian Society & Peasant Rebellion in Colonial India. LC 77-77731. (Cambridge South Asian Studies: No. 23). 304p. 1980. pap. 12.95x (ISBN 0-521-29770-2). Cambridge U Pr.
Subrahamanayam, K. Self-Reliance & National Resilience. LC 75-907181. 1975. 11.50x (ISBN 0-88386-676-5). South Asia Bks.
Thakur, Vijay K. Urbanization in Ancient India. 1981. 25.00x (ISBN 0-8364-0688-5, Pub. by Abhinav India). South Asia Bks.
Thapar, N., ed. Tribe, Caste & Religion. 1977. 8.50x (ISBN 0-88386-974-8). South Asia Bks.
Thapar, Romila. Ancient Indian Social History: Some Interpretations. 1978. 17.50x (ISBN 0-8364-0249-9, Orient Longman). South Asia Bks.
Thorner, Daniel, ed. Shaping of Modern India. 1981. 28.00x (ISBN 0-8364-0678-8, Pub. by Allied India). South Asia Bks.
Thurston, Edgar & Rangachari, K. Castes & Tribes of Southern India, 7 Vols. (Illus.). Repr. of 1909 ed. Set. 253.50 (ISBN 0-384-60438-2). Johnson Repr.
Tirtha, Ranjit. Society & Development in Contemporary India: Geographical Perspectives. (Illus.). 368p. 1980. 13.50 (ISBN 0-686-27540-3). R Tirtha.
Tripathi, B. D. Sadhus of India: The Sociological View. 1979. text ed. 21.00x (ISBN 0-8426-1610-1). Verry.
Ullrich, Helen E., ed. Competition & Modernization in South Asia. LC 75-907280. 1975. 12.00x (ISBN 0-88386-696-X). South Asia Bks.
Vaidyanathan, N. International Labour Organization Conventions & India. LC 75-904151. 1975. 9.50x (ISBN 0-88386-532-7). South Asia Bks.
Vajpeyi, Dhirendra K. Modernization & Social Change in India. 1979. 18.50x (ISBN 0-8364-0549-8). South Asia Bks.
Vatuk, Sylvia. Kinship & Urbanization: White Collar Migrants in North India. LC 75-161993. 1973. 24.75x (ISBN 0-520-02064-2). U of Cal Pr.
Venkatasubrahmanyan, T. R. Group Prejudices in India: Experiments in Learning Theory. (Illus.). 825p. 1973. 8.25x (ISBN 0-8002-1474-9). Intl Pubns Serv.
Venu, S, et al. Planning in India. 1977. 8.50x (ISBN 0-8364-0066-6, Orient Longman). South Asia Bks.
Visel, Adele. Of Brahmins & Lesser Folk. 1979. 7.95 (ISBN 0-533-04007-8). Vantage.
Von Furer-Haimendorf, Christoph. Highlanders of Arunachal Pradesh. 224p. 1981. text ed. 25.00x (ISBN 0-7069-1367-1, Pub. by Vikas India). Advent NY.
Whitcombe, Elizabeth. Agrarian Conditions in Northern India, Vol. 1, The United Provinces Under British Rule, 1860-1900. LC 75-129027. (Center for South & Southeast Asia Studies, UC Berkeley). (Illus.). 1972. 27.50x (ISBN 0-520-01706-4). U of Cal Pr.
Wiebe, Paul. Social Life in an Indian Slum. LC 75-5480. 1975. 9.25 (ISBN 0-89089-051-X). Carolina Acad Pr.
Wirsing, Robert G. Socialist Society & Free Enterprise Politics: A Study of Voluntary Associations in Urban India. LC 76-6775. 1977. 12.95 (ISBN 0-89089-066-8). Carolina Acad Pr.
Woytinsky, Wladimir S. India: The Awakening Giant. LC 57-7154. (Illus.). 1969. Repr. of 1957 ed. 12.00 (ISBN 0-527-98150-8). Kraus Repr.

INDIA–SOCIAL LIFE AND CUSTOMS

Agarwala, S. N. India's Population Problems. rev. ed. 1978. 13.00x (ISBN 0-8364-0157-3). South Asia Bks.
Ahmad, Imtiaz, ed. Family, Kinship, & Marriage Among the Muslims. LC 77-74484. 1977. 17.50x (ISBN 0-88386-757-5). South Asia Bks.
Amore, Roy C. & Shinn, Larry D. Lustful Maidens & Ascetic Kings: Buddhist & Hindu Stories of Life. (Illus.). 176p. 1981. text ed. 14.95x (ISBN 0-19-502838-4); pap. 5.95 (ISBN 0-19-502839-2). Oxford U Pr.
Anton, Rita. The Far off Hills. LC 78-60282. (Illus.). 264p. 1979. 9.95 (ISBN 0-385-14366-4). Doubleday.
Apte, M. L. Mass Culture, Language & Arts in India. 1979. text ed. 18.00x (ISBN 0-8426-1605-5). Verry.
Bailey, Frederick G. Caste & the Economic Frontier. 1957. text ed. 10.50x (ISBN 0-7190-0249-4). Humanities.
Ballhatchet, Kenneth. Race, Sex & Class Under the Raj: Imperial Attitudes & Policies & Their Critics, 1793-1905. LC 79-9604. 1980. 18.50x (ISBN 0-312-66144-4). St Martin.
Bandopadhyaya, Manik. Padma River Boatman. (Asian & Pacific Writing Ser.). 1973. 14.95x (ISBN 0-7022-0833-7); pap. 8.00x (ISBN 0-7022-0834-5). U of Queensland Pr.
Banerji, Sures C. Aspects of Ancient Indian Life from Sanskrit Sources. 179p. 1973. text ed. 11.00x (ISBN 0-8426-0406-5). Verry.
Beals, Alan R. Village Life in South India: Cultural Design & Environmental Variation. LC 74-76547. (Worlds of Man Ser). 1974. 12.75x (ISBN 0-88295-600-0); pap. 5.95x (ISBN 0-88295-601-9). Harlan Davidson.
Bhardwaj, Surinder M. Hindu Places of Pilgrimage in India: A Study in Cultural Geography. LC 73-174454. (Illus.). 1973. 27.50x (ISBN 0-520-02135-5). U of Cal Pr.
Bhattacharyya, Narendra N. Ancient Indian Rituals & Their Social Contents. 184p. 1975. 14.50x (ISBN 0-87471-735-3). Rowman.
Bose, Nirmal Kumar. Culture & Society in India. 1977. Repr. of 1967 ed. lib. bdg. 18.50x (ISBN 0-210-33830-X). Asia.
Buck, William. Ramayana. LC 78-153549. (Illus.). 1976. 16.95 (ISBN 0-520-02016-2); pap. 6.95 (ISBN 0-520-04394-4). U of Cal Pr.
Chauhan, Brij R. Towns in the Tribal Setting. (Illus.). 207p. 1972. 9.50x (ISBN 0-8002-2091-9). Intl Pubns Serv.
Chopra, Pran N. Some Aspects of Social Life During the Mughal Age, 1526-1707. 1963. 5.50x (ISBN 0-8426-1206-8). Verry.
Cormack, Margaret L. The Hindu Woman. LC 74-6750. 207p. 1974. Repr. of 1953 ed. lib. bdg. 14.00x (ISBN 0-8371-7557-7, COHW). Greenwood.
Dass, Arvind. Agrarian Relations in India. 1980. 18.50x (ISBN 0-8364-0648-6, Pub. by Manohar India). South Asia Bks.
Deshpande, C. D., et al. Impact of a Metropolitan City on the Surrounding Region. (Illus.). 167p. 1980. pap. text ed. 8.00x (ISBN 0-391-02206-7). Humanities.
Deshpande, Madhav & Hook, Peter, eds. Aryan & Non-Aryan in India. 315p. 1979. 16.50 (ISBN 0-89720-011-X); pap. 12.50 (ISBN 0-89720-012-8). Karoma.
De Viri, Anne. Indrani & I. LC 65-21134. (Orig.). 1966. 4.95 (ISBN 0-87376-004-2). Red Dust.
Douglas, Norman. Good-Bye to Western Culture: Some Footnotes on East & West. LC 70-184841. 241p. 1930. Repr. lib. bdg. 15.00x (ISBN 0-8371-6330-7, DOWC). Greenwood.
Dube, S. C., ed. Tribal Heritage of India: Ethnicity, Identity & Interaction, Vol. 1. 1977. 12.00x (ISBN 0-8364-0476-9). South Asia Bks.
Dumont, Louis. Homo Hierarchicus: The Caste System & Its Implications. rev. ed. Gulati, Basia, tr. LC 80-16480. 1981. 27.50x (ISBN 0-226-16962-6); pap. 9.95 (ISBN 0-226-16963-4, P601, Phoen). U of Chicago Pr.
Eby, John W. Hindustan: As Seen by John. (Illus.). 1977. pap. 3.00 (ISBN 0-932218-05-9). Hall Pr.
Endogenous Intellectual Creativity & Emerging New International Order. 9p. 1980. pap. 5.00 (ISBN 92-808-0116-3, TUNU 071, UNU). Unipub.
Endogenous Intellectual Creativity: The Ethos of the Composite Culture of India. 50p. 1980. pap. 5.00 (ISBN 92-808-0107-4, TUNU 075, UNU). Unipub.
Fabri, Charles. Indian Dress. 1977. Repr. of 1960 ed. 4.00x (ISBN 0-8364-0114-X). South Asia Bks.
Gandhi, Indira. Eternal India. LC 80-51191. Orig. Title: Inde. (Illus.). 260p. 1980. 50.00 (ISBN 0-86565-003-9). Vendome.
Ghoshal, Upendia N. History of Indian Public Life, Vol. 2: The Pre-Maurya & the Maurya Periods. 1966. 9.95x (ISBN 0-19-635231-2). Oxford U Pr.
Gupta, G. R. Marriage, Religion, & Society: Tradition & Change in an Indian Village. LC 73-5903. 180p. 1974. 14.95 (ISBN 0-470-33648-X). Halsted Pr.
Gupta, Giri R., ed. Family & Social Change in Modern India. LC 76-9126. (Main Currents in Indian Sociology Ser.: Vol. 2). 1977. 13.95 (ISBN 0-89089-060-9). Carolina Acad Pr.
Gupta, Shanti N. Indian Concept of Values. 1978. 11.00x (ISBN 0-8364-0071-2). South Asia Bks.
Hardiman, David. Peasant Nationalists of Gujarat: Kheda District 1917-1934. (Illus.). 300p. 1981. 16.50 (ISBN 0-19-561255-8). Oxford U Pr.
Hiro, Dilip. Inside India Today. rev ed. LC 77-76161. 1979. pap. 5.95 (ISBN 0-85345-481-7, PB-4817). Monthly Rev.
Holmes, F. Inquiry into World Cultures - India: Focus on Change. 1974. pap. text ed. 5.28 (ISBN 0-13-498980-5). P-H.
Husain, Abrar. Marriage Customs Among Muslims in India: A Sociological Study of the Shia Marriage Customs. 1976. text ed. 12.00x (ISBN 0-8426-0926-1). Verry.
Ingham, Kenneth. Reformers in India, 1793-1833: An Account of the Work of Christian Missionaries on Behalf of Social Reform. LC 73-16425. xi, 150p. 1973. Repr. of 1956 ed. lib. bdg. 13.50x (ISBN 0-374-94112-2). Octagon.
Jha, Akhileshwar. Sexual Designs in Indian Culture. 1979. text ed. 12.50x (ISBN 0-7069-0744-2). Humanities.
Kamat, Jyotsna. Social Life in Medieval Karnataka. 1980. 21.00x (ISBN 0-8364-0554-4, Pub. by Abhinav India). South Asia Bks.
Ketkar, P. R. History of Caste in India. 192p. 1979. Repr. of 1909 ed. text ed. 13.50 (ISBN 0-89684-133-2). Orient Bk Dist.
Khan, M. E. & Prasad, C. V. People's Perception About Family Planning: A Study of Andhra Pradesh & Bihar. 156p. 1980. text ed. 10.00x (ISBN 0-391-02131-1). Humanities.
Khare, Ravindra S. Hindu Hearth & Home. 300p. 1976. 16.00x (ISBN 0-8002-1493-5). Intl Pubns Serv.
Kincaid, Dennis. British Social Life in India, 1608-1937. LC 74-155238. (Illus.). 1971. Repr. of 1938 ed. 15.75 (ISBN 0-8046-1619-1). Kennikat.
--British Social Life in India 1608-1937. 2nd ed. (Illus.). 1973. 20.00 (ISBN 0-7100-7284-8). Routledge & Kegan.
Klay, John. India Discovered: The Achievement of the British Raj. (Illus.). 288p. 1981. 35.00 (ISBN 0-8317-2385-8, Rutledge Pr). Smith Pubs.
Kublin, Hyman. India. rev. ed. LC 72-3351. (Illus.). 228p. (gr. 9-12). 1973. pap. text ed. 6.60 (ISBN 0-395-13928-7, 2-31034). HM.
--India: Selected Readings. rev. ed. LC 72-7637. 230p. (gr. 9-12). 1973. pap. text ed. 6.60 (ISBN 0-395-13929-5, 2-31040). HM.
Kuppuswamy, B. Dharma & Society: A Study in Social Values, India. 1978. 12.50x (ISBN 0-8364-0120-4). South Asia Bks.
Kutty, A. R. Marriage & Kinship in an Island Society. (Illus.). 227p. 1972. 13.50x (ISBN 0-8002-1704-7). Intl Pubns Serv.
Lal, Chaman. India: Cradle of Cultures. (Illus.). 346p. 1980. text ed. 30.00x (ISBN 0-391-01872-8). Humanities.
Lal, Sheo K. The Urban Elite. LC 75-900549. 147p. 1974. 12.00x (ISBN 0-88386-561-0). South Asia Bks.
Lannoy, Richard. Speaking Tree: A Study of Indian Culture & Society. 1971. 25.00 (ISBN 0-19-501469-3). Oxford U Pr.
Lorrance, Arleen. Hello, Goodbye, I Love You. (Illus., Orig.). 1981. pap. price not set (ISBN 0-916192-18-0). L P Pubns.
Maharajah of Baroda. The Palaces of India. LC 80-51187. (Illus.). 256p. 1980. 50.00 (ISBN 0-86565-007-1). Vendome.
Mandelbaum, David G. Society in India, Volume One: Continuity & Change. 392p. 1970. pap. 9.95x (ISBN 0-520-01893-1, CAMPUS 41). U of Cal Pr.
--Society in India, Volume Two: Change & Continuity. 408p. 1970. pap. 9.95x (ISBN 0-520-01895-8, CAMPUS 42). U of Cal Pr.
Mayer, Adrian C. Caste & Kinship in Central India: A Village & Its Region. (Illus.). 1960. pap. 4.95x (ISBN 0-520-01747-1, CAMPUS 39). U of Cal Pr.
Mehta, Gita. Karma Cola. 1979. 9.95 (ISBN 0-671-25083-3). S&S.
Mehta, Prayag, ed. Indian Youth: Emerging Problems & Issues. 1971. 6.75x (ISBN 0-8426-0217-8). Verry.
Meyer, J. J. Sexual Life in Ancient India. 1971. 10.50 (ISBN 0-89684-318-1). Orient Bk Dist.
Meyer, Johann J. Sexual Life in Ancient India: A Study in the Comparative History of Indian Culture, 2 vols. in one. 606p. 1971. 15.00x (ISBN 0-8002-1974-0). Intl Pubns Serv.
Moffatt, Michael. An Untouchable Community in South India: Structure & Consensus. LC 78-51183. 1979. 25.00 (ISBN 0-691-09377-6). Princeton U Pr.
Moon, Penderel. Strangers in India. 212p. 1972. Repr. of 1944 ed. lib. bdg. 15.00 (ISBN 0-8371-5624-6, MOSI). Greenwood.
Muehl, John F. Interview with India. 1950. 8.50 (ISBN 0-8495-3856-4). Arden Lib.
Mukherjee, Bhabananda. Structure & Kinship in Tribal India. 1981. 10.00x (ISBN 0-8364-0769-5, Pub. by Minerva India). South Asia Bks.
Mukherjee, Ramkrishna. West Bengal Family Structures, 1946-1966. LC 76-904812. 1976. 12.50x (ISBN 0-8364-0478-5). South Asia Bks.
Mukhopadhyay, Sankaranande. A Profile of Sundarbans Tribes. LC 76-905288. 1976. 6.50x (ISBN 0-88386-872-5). South Asia Bks.
Nagarkar, Kiran. Seven Sixes Are Forty-Three. Slee, Shubha, tr. from Marathi. (Asian & Pacific Writing Ser.: No. 14). 213p. 1981. text ed. 15.75 (ISBN 0-7022-1503-1); pap. 8.50 (ISBN 0-7022-1502-3). U of Queensland Pr.
Nair, K. K., pseud. A Profile of Indian Culture. (The India Library Ser., Vol. 1). 202p. 1975. 8.95 (ISBN 0-88253-774-1). Ind-US Inc.
Nair, P. T. Marriage & Dowry in India. 1978. 12.50x (ISBN 0-88386-907-1). South Asia Bks.
Nilakanta-Sastri, K. A. Life & Culture of the Indian People: A Historical Survey. rev. 2nd ed. LC 74-903185. 284p. 1974. 9.00x (ISBN 0-85655-131-7). Intl Pubns Serv.
Noble, Allen G. & Dutt, Ashok K., eds. Indian Urbanization & Planning: Vehicles of Modernization. (Illus.). 366p. 1977. 16.00x (ISBN 0-8002-2305-5). Intl Pubns Serv.
Oaten, Edward F. European Travellers in India During the 15th, 16th & 17th Centuries. LC 75-137279. Repr. of 1909 ed. 21.45 (ISBN 0-404-04808-0). AMS Pr.
Oddie, G. A. Social Protest in India: British Protestant Missionaries & Social Reforms, Eighteen Fifty to Nineteen Hundred. 1979. 17.50x (ISBN 0-8364-0195-6). South Asia Bks.
O'Flaherty, Wendy, ed. Duty in South Asia. 1978. 12.00x (ISBN 0-8364-0025-9). South Asia Bks.
O'Malley, L. S. S. India's Social Heritage. LC 74-11745. 194p. 1975. Repr. of 1934 ed. lib. bdg. 13.00x (ISBN 0-374-96147-6). Octagon.
Oman, John C. Cults, Customs, & Superstitions of India: Being a Revised & Enlarged Edition of Indian Life, Religious & Social. LC 70-179232. (Illus.). Repr. of 1908 ed. 29.00 (ISBN 0-404-54859-8). AMS Pr.
--Cults, Customs & Superstitions of India. 336p. 1972. 15.00x (ISBN 0-8002-0537-5). Intl Pubns Serv.
Pandhe, Pramila. Suppression of Drama in 19th Century India. 1978. 7.50x (ISBN 0-8364-0237-5). South Asia Bks.
Prabhu, John C. Social & Cultural Determinants of Fertility in India. LC 75-901184. 1974. 10.50x (ISBN 0-8002-0313-5). Intl Pubns Serv.

Raghuvanshi, V. P. Indian Society in the Eighteenth Century. 1970. 21.00 (ISBN 0-686-20259-7). Intl Bk Dist.
Ramu, G. N. Family & Caste in Urban India. 1977. 11.00x (ISBN 0-7069-0530-X). South Asia Bks.
Rawson, Philip. Tantra: The Indian Cult of Ecstasy. (Illus.). 1977. pap. 8.95 (ISBN 0-500-81001-X). Thames Hudson.
Richardson, Jane. Tender Hearts of India. (Illus.). 255p. 1972. 13.00x (ISBN 0-8002-0982-6). Intl Pubns Serv.
Riepe, D. Indian Philosophy Since Independence. (Philosophical Currents Ser.: No. 25). 403p. 1980. text ed. 34.25x (ISBN 90-6032-113-8). Humanities.
Roy, Beth. Bullock Carts & Motor Bikes: Ancient India on a New Road. LC 72-75281. (gr. 6 up). 1972. 6.95 (ISBN 0-689-30064-6). Atheneum.
Saxena, R. K. Social Reforms: Infanticide & Sati. LC 75-906665. 1975. 8.50x (ISBN 0-88386-655-2). South Asia Bks.
Schermerhorn, R. A. Ethnic Plurality in India. LC 77-75662. 1978. text ed. 12.95x (ISBN 0-8165-0612-4); pap. text ed. 6.45x (ISBN 0-8165-0578-0). U of Ariz Pr.
Sen, Gertrude E. Voiceless India. LC 74-109975. (Illus.). 1971. Repr. of 1930 ed. lib. bdg. 20.00x (ISBN 0-8371-4481-7, SEVI). Greenwood.
Sharda, Bam D. Status Attainment in Rural India. 1977. 8.00x (ISBN 0-88386-144-5). South Asia Bks.
Sharma, B. N. Festivals of India. 1978. 30.00x (ISBN 0-8364-0283-9). South Asia Bks.
--Social Life in Northern India, A.D. 600-1000. 1966. 8.25x (ISBN 0-8426-1516-4). Verry.
Sharma, Ram N. Indian Society & Social Institutions. 280p. 1981. 22.50x (ISBN 0-8002-2812-X). Intl Pubns Serv.
--Indian Society & Social Institutions. 280p. 1981. text ed. 13.50x (ISBN 0-391-02416-7, Pub. by Munshiram Manoharlal India). Humanities.
Shaw, Ray & Zolotow, Charlotte. A Week in Lateef's World: India. (Face to Face Bks.). (gr. k-3). 1970. 7.95 (ISBN 0-02-782380-6, CCpr). Macmillan.
Shingi, P. M., et al. Rural Youth: Education, Occupation & Social Outlook. 1980. 10.00x (ISBN 0-8364-0663-X, Pub. by Abhinav India). South Asia Bks.
Singer, Milton. When a Great Tradition Modernizes: An Anthropological Approach to Indian Civilization. LC 79-26490. (Midway Reprint Ser.). 1980. pap. text ed. 17.50x (ISBN 0-226-76102-9). U of Chicago Pr.
Singh, M. Mohan. Life in North-Eastern India in Pre-Mauryan Times: With Special Reference to C.600b.C.-325b.C. 1967. 7.00x (ISBN 0-8426-1533-4). Verry.
Singh, Sarva D. Polyandry in Ancient India. 1980. text ed. 25.00x (ISBN 0-7069-0729-9, Pub. by Vikas India). Advent NY.
Singhal, D. P. Modern Indian Society & Culture. 1981. 12.50x (ISBN 0-8364-0684-2, Pub. by Meenakshi India). South Asia Bks.
Sinha, Durganand. Socialization of the Indian Child. 172p. 1981. text ed. 15.00 (ISBN 0-391-02373-X, Pub. by Concept India). Humanities.
Sinha, M. P. & Gangrade, K. D., eds. Inter-Generational Conflict in India. 1971. 12.50x (ISBN 0-8426-0270-4). Verry.
Sinha, Raghuvir. Religion & Culture of North-Eastern India. 1977. 8.50x (ISBN 0-8364-0028-3). South Asia Bks.
--Social Change in Indian Society. rev. ed. 1978. 11.50x (ISBN 0-8364-0182-4). South Asia Bks.
Soleillant, Claude. Activities & Projects: India in Color. LC 77-79499. (Activities & Projects Ser.). (Illus.). (gr. 2 up). 1977. 9.95 (ISBN 0-8069-4550-8); PLB 9.29 (ISBN 0-8069-4551-6). Sterling.
Sontheimer, Gunther-Dietz. The Joint Hindu Family: Its Evolution As a Legal Institution. 1977. 18.50x (ISBN 0-8364-0102-6). South Asia Bks.
Spear, Percival. Nabobs: A Study of the Social Life of the English in Eighteenth Century India. (Illus.). 7.50 (ISBN 0-8446-0924-2). Peter Smith.
Splendours of Tamilnadu. 1981. 28.00x (ISBN 0-8364-0762-8, Pub. by Marg India). South Asia Bks.
Sreenivasan, Kasthuri. Climbing the Coconut Tree: A Partial Autobiography. (Illus.). 178p. 1980. 13.95x (ISBN 0-19-561242-6). Oxford U Pr.
Srinivas, M. N., et al. Dimensions of Social Change in India. 1978. 17.50x (ISBN 0-8364-0145-X). South Asia Bks.
Sur, A. K. Sex & Marriage in India: An Ethnohistorical Survey. 194p. 1974. 7.50x (ISBN 0-8002-1973-2). Intl Pubns Serv.
Tandon, Prakash. Beyond Punjab: A Sequel to Punjabi Century. LC 73-123620. (Center for South & Southeast Asia Studies, Uc Berkeley). 1971. 22.75x (ISBN 0-520-01759-5). U of Cal Pr.
Thomas, T. M. Indian Educational Reforms in Cultural Perspective. 1970. 10.00x (ISBN 0-8426-0202-X). Verry.
Thurston, Edgar. Omens & Superstitions of Southern India. 1979. Repr. of 1912 ed. lib. bdg. 35.00 (ISBN 0-8414-8415-5). Folcroft.
Tirtha, Ranjit: Society & Development in Contemporary India. (Illus.). 368p. 1980. 13.50 (ISBN 0-8187-0040-8). Harlo Pr.
Varghese, Jamila. Her Gold & Her Body. 228p. 1980. text ed. 15.95 (ISBN 0-7069-0931-3, Pub. by Vikas India). Advent NY.
Vatsayayan, Kapila M. Some Aspects of Cultural Policies in India. 1970-73. pap. 3.25 (ISBN 92-3-100943-5, UNESCO). Unipub.
Vatsyayan, Kapila. Traditions of Indian Folk Dance. (Illus.). 1977. text ed. 18.00x (ISBN 0-8426-1058-8). Verry.
Vidyarthi, L. P., et al. Changing Dietary Patterns & Habits. 1979. text ed. 15.00x (ISBN 0-391-01928-7). Humanities.
Von Furer-Haimendorf, Christoph. Highlanders of Arunachal Pradesh. 224p. 1981. text ed. 25.00x (ISBN 0-7069-1367-1, Pub. by Vikas India). Advent NY.
Voting, Caste, Community, Society: Explorations in Aggregate Data Analysis in India & Bangladesh. 1978. 11.00x (ISBN 0-8364-0297-9). South Asia Bks.
Wagle, N. K., ed. Images of Maharashtra: A Regional Profile in India. 160p. 1980. pap. text ed. 10.50 (ISBN 0-7007-0144-3). Humanities.
Ward, William. View of the History, Literature, & Mythology of the Hindoos, 3 Vols. LC 71-115207. 1971. Repr. of 1882 ed. Set. 75.00x (ISBN 0-8046-1100-9). Kennikat.

INDIA-SOCIAL POLICY

Alternative Ways of Life in India: Pollution of Poverty or Bane or Affluence? 25p. 1981. pap. 5.00 (ISBN 92-808-0159-7, TUNU 113, UNU). Unipub.
Apte, M. L. Mass Culture, Language & Arts in India. 1979. text ed. 18.00x (ISBN 0-8426-1605-5). Verry.
Communication Policies in India. 1977. pap. 6.75 (ISBN 92-3-101425-0, U83, UNESCO). Unipub.
Gadgil, D. R. Planning & Economic Policy in India: Enlarged & Revised Edition. 1972. 15.00 (ISBN 0-8046-8809-5). Kennikat.
Gangrade, K. D. Social Legislation in India, 2 vols. 1978. 30.00 set (ISBN 0-8364-0232-4). South Asia Bks.
Jha, Akhileshwar. Modernization & the Hindu Socio-Culture. 1978. 11.00x (ISBN 0-8364-0146-8). South Asia Bks.
Kaufman, Harold & Singh, Avtar. Villages Upward Bound. 1975. 12.00 (ISBN 0-88386-646-3). South Asia Bks.
Mishra, Sachida N. Political Socialization in India. (Illus.). 156p. 1980. pap. text ed. 12.25x (ISBN 0-391-02207-5). Humanities.
Naik, J. A. An Alternative Polity for India. 1976. text ed. 9.00x (ISBN 0-8426-0895-8). Verry.
Nandy, Ashis. At the Edge of Psychology: Essays on Politics & Culture. 152p. 1981. 12.95 (ISBN 0-19-561205-1). Oxford U Pr.
Rao, V. & Mazumdar, H., eds. Planning for Change. 1975. 11.50x (ISBN 0-88386-675-7). South Asia Bks.
Shekhar, C. Dynamics of Social Change. 1979. text ed. 12.00x (ISBN 0-8426-1629-2). Verry.
Subba Rao, K. Social Justice & Law. LC 74-903851. 1975. 9.00x (ISBN 0-8002-1986-4). Intl Pubns Serv.
Weiner, Myron, et al. India's Preferential Policies: Migrants, the Middle Classes, & Ethnic Equality. LC 81-7523. (Chicago Originals Paperback Ser.). 176p. 1981. lib. bdg. 18.50x (ISBN 0-226-88577-1). U of Chicago Pr.

INDIA-STATISTICS

India Central Statistical Organisation. Statistical Abstract India. 21st ed. 844p. 1975. 50.00x (ISBN 0-8002-2019-6). Intl Pubns Serv.
Kulkarni, V. G. Statistical Outline of Indian Economy. 1968. 10.00x (ISBN 0-8426-1343-9). Verry.
Mukherjee, Sudhansu B. The Age Distribution of the Indian Population: A Reconstruction for the States & Territories, 1881-1961. LC 76-28367. 1977. 5.00x (ISBN 0-8248-0518-6, Eastwest Ctr.). U Pr of Hawaii.
Raza, Moonis, et al, eds. Sources of Economic & Social Statistics of India. 1979. 24.00x (ISBN 0-8364-0536-6, Pub. by Eureka India). South Asia Bks.

INDIA IN LITERATURE

Deshpande, P. G. Gandhiana - a Bibliography of Gandhian Literature. bds. 5.50x (ISBN 0-8426-1236-X). Verry.
Gupta, Brijen K. India in English Fiction, 1800-1970: An Annotated Bibliography. LC 73-4194. 1973. 10.00 (ISBN 0-8108-0612-6). Scarecrow.
Majam-Majumdar, R. C. Classical Accounts of India: Rome, Greek. Repr. of 1960 ed. 18.50x (ISBN 0-8364-0704-0, Pub. by Mukhopadhyay). South Asia Bks.
Satin, Nora. India in Modern English Fiction. 1978. Repr. of 1976 ed. lib. bdg. 25.00 (ISBN 0-8492-8045-1). R West.
Singh, Shailendra D. Novels on the Indian Mutiny. 248p. 1973. 8.50x (ISBN 0-88386-310-3). South Asia Bks.
Viswanatham, Kalive. India in English Fiction. LC 72-902912. 270p. 1971. 7.50x (ISBN 0-8002-1533-8). Intl Pubns Serv.

INDIA-PAKISTAN CONFLICT, 1965

Jai-Singh. Tanot, Loganwala & Other Battles of the Rajasthan Desert, 1965 & 1971. LC 73-904095. 193p. 1974. 7.50x (ISBN 0-8002-2055-2). Intl Pubns Serv.

INDIA-PAKISTAN CONFLICT, 1971-

Jai-Singh. Tanot, Loganwala & Other Battles of the Rajasthan Desert, 1965 & 1971. LC 73-904095. 193p. 1974. 7.50x (ISBN 0-8002-2055-2). Intl Pubns Serv.
Misra, R. P. Role of the United Nations in the Indo-Pakistan Conflict, 1971. 1973. 9.00 (ISBN 0-686-20302-X). Intl Bk Dist.

INDIA-RUBBER

see Rubber

INDIA-RUBBER INDUSTRY

see Rubber Industry and Trade

INDIAN ARTS FUND

Wilder, Mitchell A. Quiet Triumph: Forty Years with the Indian Arts Fund, Santa Fe. LC 66-13037. (Illus.). 18p. 1965. pap. 2.00 (ISBN 0-88360-010-2). Amon Carter.

INDIAN BASKETS

see Indians of North America-Industries

INDIAN BLANKETS

see Indians of North America-Textile Industry and Fabrics; Indians of South America-Textile Industry and Fabrics

INDIAN CAPTIVITIES

see Indians of North America-Captivities

INDIAN-CHINESE BORDER DISPUTE, 1957-

see Sino-Indian Border Dispute, 1957-

INDIAN CIVILIZATION

see Indians-Culture

INDIAN CLUBS

see also Callisthenics

INDIAN CORN

see Corn

INDIAN ETHICS

see Indians of North America-Ethics

INDIAN FOLK-LORE

see Folk-Lore, Indian

INDIAN LANGUAGES

see Indians-Languages; Indians of Mexico-Languages; Indians of North America-Languages

INDIAN LITERATURE

Benedict, Ruth. Tales of the Cochiti Indians. 256p. 1981. 9.95 (ISBN 0-8263-0569-5). U of NM Pr.
Brinton, Daniel G., ed. The Maya Chronicles. LC 70-83457. (Library of Aboriginal American Literature Ser.: No. 1). Repr. of 1882 ed. 22.50 (ISBN 0-404-52181-9). AMS Pr.
Carroll, Raymonde. Nukuoro Stories. (Nukuoro Texts Ser.: Vol. 1). 1980. pap. 22.00 (ISBN 0-8357-0551-X, IS-00118, Pub. by U of Mich Pr). Univ Microfilms.
Gaddis, Vincent H. American Indian Myths & Mysteries. LC 76-51215. 1977. 8.95 (ISBN 0-8019-6409-1). Chilton.
Johnson, Donald J. & Johnson, Jean E. Through Indian Eyes, Vol. 1: The Wheel of Life. rev. ed. Clark, Leon E., ed. (Illus.). 156p. (gr. 9-12). 1981. pap. text ed. 5.95 (ISBN 0-938960-02-4). CITE.
Malotki, Ekkehart, et al. Hopi Tales. Malotki, Ekkehart, tr. (Special Publications Ser.). (Illus.). 1978. pap. 8.00 (ISBN 0-89734-001-9). Mus Northern Ariz.
Marken, Jack W. American Indian: Language & Literature. LC 76-4624. (Goldentree Bibliographies in Language & Literature). 1978. pap. text ed. 12.95x (ISBN 0-88295-553-5). Harlan Davidson.
Milton, John R. American Indian Speaks: Poetry, Fiction & Art by the American Indian. LC 71-106810. (Illus.). 191p. 1969. pap. 5.00 (ISBN 0-88249-003-6). Dakota Pr.
Singh, Armitjit, et al, eds. Indian Literature: A Guide to Information Sources. LC 74-11532. (American Literature, English Literature & World Literatures in English Information Guide Ser.: Vol 36). 450p. 1981. 36.00 (ISBN 0-8103-1238-7). Gale.
Singh, Jaideva. Spanda-Karikas: The Divine Creative Impulse. Karikas & the Spanda-nirnaya Translated into English. 209p. 1981. text ed. 15.00 (ISBN 0-8426-1684-5). Verry.
Spence, Lewis. Popol Vuh: Mythic & Heroic Sagas of the Kiches of Central America. LC 75-139178. (Popular Studies in Mythology, Romance & Folklore: No. 16). Repr. of 1908 ed. 5.50 (ISBN 0-404-53516-X). AMS Pr.
Turner, Frederick W., 3rd, ed. The Portable North American Indian Reader. LC 72-12545. (Viking Portable Library: No. 77). 1977. pap. 5.95 (ISBN 0-14-015077-3). Penguin.
Vizenor, Gerald. Earthdivers: Tribal Narratives on Mixed Descent. (Illus.). 195p. 1981. 14.95 (ISBN 0-8166-1048-7). U of Minn Pr.
Wilbert, Johannes, ed. Folk Literature of the Yamana Indians: Martin Gusinde's Collection of Yamana Narratives. LC 76-20026. 1977. 24.50x (ISBN 0-520-03299-3). U of Cal Pr.

INDIAN LITERATURE (AMERICAN INDIAN)

see Indian Literature

INDIAN LITERATURE (EAST INDIAN)

see Indic Literature

INDIAN MUTINY, 1857-1858

see India-History-British Occupation, 1765-1947

INDIAN MYTHOLOGY (AMERICAN INDIAN)

see Indians-Religion and Mythology

INDIAN NATIONAL CONGRESS

Chatterjee, Basant. Congress Splits - India. 1970. 11.00x (ISBN 0-8426-0091-4). Verry.
Ghose, Sankar. Indian National Congress: Its History & Heritage. LC 76-900644. 1976. 8.00x (ISBN 0-88386-776-1). South Asia Bks.
Kaushik, P. D. Congress Ideology & Programme. 1964. 7.50x (ISBN 0-8188-1064-5). Paragon.
Kochanek, Stanley A. Congress Party of India: The Democracy of a One-Party Diplomacy. LC 68-10393. 1968. 30.00 (ISBN 0-691-03013-8). Princeton U Pr.
McLane, John R. Indian Nationalism & the Early Congress. LC 77-72127. 1977. 32.00x (ISBN 0-691-03113-4); pap. 12.50 (ISBN 0-691-10056-X). Princeton U Pr.
Martin, Briton, Jr. New India, 1885: British Official Policy & the Emergence of the Indian National Congress. LC 70-98140. (Center for South & Southeast Asia Studies, UC Berkeley). 1969. 26.75x (ISBN 0-520-01580-0). U of Cal Pr.
Rahman, M. M. Congress Crisis. 1970. 9.00 (ISBN 0-686-20206-6). Intl Bk Dist.
Sethi, J. D. India's Static Power Structure. 1969. 7.75x (ISBN 0-8426-1513-X). Verry.
Weiner, Myron. Party Building in a New Nation: The Indian National Congress. LC 67-12150. 1967. 15.00x (ISBN 0-226-89038-4). U of Chicago Pr.

INDIAN OCEAN

Colborn, J. G. The Thermal Structure of the Indian Ocean. (International Indian Ocean Expedition Oceanographic Monographs: No. 2). 144p. 1975. text ed. 15.00x (ISBN 0-8248-0349-3, Eastwest Ctr). U Pr of Hawaii.
Cole, Jean. Trimaran Against the Trades. LC 77-96854. 1970. 5.95 (ISBN 0-8286-0047-3). De Graff.
Cousteau, Jacques-Yves & Diole, Philippe. Life & Death in a Coral Sea. LC 69-13003. (The Undersea Discoveries of Jacques-Yves Cousteau). (Illus.). 1978. pap. 8.95 (ISBN 0-89104-089-7). A & W Pubs.
Gorshkov, S. G. World Ocean Atlas, Vol. 2: Atlantic & Indian Oceans. 3504p. 1979. 400.00 (ISBN 0-08-021953-5). Pergamon.
Grey, Charles. Pirates of the Eastern Seas 1618-1723: A Lurid Page of History. LC 74-115319. 1971. Repr. of 1933 ed. 15.00 (ISBN 0-8046-1110-6). Kennikat.
Howard, John K. & Starck, Walter A., 2nd. Distribution & Relative Abundance of Billfishes (Istiophoridae) of the Indian Ocean. LC 75-4747. (Studies in Tropical Oceanography Ser: No. 13). (Illus.). 1975. 10.00x (ISBN 0-87024-276-8). U Miami Marine.
Implementation of the International Indian Ocean Fishery Survey & Development Programme. (FAO Fisheries Reports: No. 180). 21p. 1977. pap. 7.50 (ISBN 0-686-67661-0, F828, FAO). Unipub.
Kaushik, Devendra. Indian Ocean: Towards a Peace Zone. 1972. 7.50 (ISBN 0-7069-0173-8). Intl Bk Dist.
Patra, Saral, ed. Indian Ocean & Great Powers. 82p. 1979. 7.50x (ISBN 0-8002-1004-2). Intl Pubns Serv.
Report of the Sixth Session of the Indian Ocean Fishery Commission. (FAO Fisheries Report: No. 234). 35p. 1981. pap. 7.50 (ISBN 92-5-100930-9, F2088, FAO). Unipub.
Schoff, Wilfred H. The Periplus of the Erythraean Sea: Travel & Trade in the Indian Ocean by a Merchant of the First Century. LC 74-929621. (Illus.). 328p. 1974. 20.00x (ISBN 0-8002-0044-6). Intl Pubns Serv.
Udintsev, G. B., ed. Geological-Geophysical Atlas of the Indian Ocean. 1976. text ed. 165.00 (ISBN 0-08-020939-4). Pergamon.

INDIAN OCEAN REGION

Adie, Ian W. Oil, Politics, & Seapower: The Indian Ocean Vortex. LC 74-29073. (Strategy Paper Ser: No. 24). 1975. 6.95x (ISBN 0-8448-0617-X); pap. 2.25x o. p. (ISBN 0-8448-0618-8). Crane-Russak Co.

Amirie, Abbas, ed. The Persian Gulf & Indian Ocean in International Politics. 1975. 15.00x (ISBN 0-8139-0846-9); pap. 7.50x (ISBN 0-685-88513-5). U Pr of Va.
Bauchar, Rene. L' Afrique Noire. et l'Ocean Indien Francophones Ahjourd'hui. (Illus.). 1973. 29.95x (ISBN 2-85258-054-3). Intl Learn Syst.
Bezboruah, Monoranjan. U. S. Strategy in the Indian Ocean: The International Response. LC 77-2786. 1977. 29.95 (ISBN 0-03-021811-X). Praeger.
Bowman, Larry W. & Clark, Ian, eds. The Indian Ocean in Global Politics. (Westview Special Studies in International Relations). 270p. 1980. lib. bdg. 25.00x (ISBN 0-86531-038-6); pap. 12.00x (ISBN 0-86531-191-9). Westview.
Colomb, John C. Slave-Catching in the Indian Ocean. LC 72-78367. (Illus.). Repr. of 1873 ed. 24.00x (ISBN 0-8371-1339-3). Greenwood.
Indian Ocean Fishery Commission. Report: Fourth Session, July 21-25, 1975, Mombasa, Kenya. (FAO Fisheries Reports: No. 166). 27p. 1976. pap. 7.50 (ISBN 0-685-65011-1, F808, FAO). Unipub.
Kerr, Alex, ed. Resources & Development in the Indian Ocean Region. 256p. 1981. lib. bdg. 29.75x (ISBN 0-86531-123-4). Westview.
Kodikara, Shelton & O'Neill, Robert. Strategic Factors in Interstate Relations in South Asia. (Canberra Papers on Strategy & Defence Ser.: No. 19). 87p. (Orig.). 1980. pap. text ed. 8.95 (ISBN 0-908160-34-8). Bks Australia.
Poulose, T. T., ed. Indian Ocean Power Rivalry. 317p. 1974. 17.00x (ISBN 0-8002-1546-X). Intl Pubns Serv.
Promotion of the Establishment of Marine Parks & Reserves in the Northern Indian Ocean Including the Red Sea & Persian Gulf. 1976. pap. 12.50x (ISBN 2-88032-032-1, IUCN39, IUCN). Unipub.
Royal Society of London. The Terrestrial Ecology of Aldabra. Stoddart, D. R. & Westoll, T. S., eds. (Illus.). 1979. lib. bdg. 61.00x (ISBN 0-85403-111-1, Pub. by Royal Soc London). Scholium Intl.
Singh, K. Rajendra. Politics of the Indian Ocean. 260p. 1974. text ed. 11.75x (ISBN 0-8426-0643-2). Verry.
Tahtinen, Dale R. Arms in the Indian Ocean. 1977. pap. 4.25 (ISBN 0-8447-3242-7). Am Enterprise.
Toussaint, Auguste. History of the Indian Ocean. Guicharnaud, June, tr. 1966. 12.50x (ISBN 0-226-80887-4). U of Chicago Pr.
Towle, Philip. Naval Power in the Indian Ocean. 121p. 1980. pap. text ed. 9.95 (ISBN 0-908160-28-3, 0479). Bks Australia.
Traveller's Guide to East Africa & the Indian Ocean. 1981. pap. 8.45 (ISBN 0-531-03966-8). Watts.

INDIAN-PAKISTAN CONFLICT, 1965
see India-Pakistan Conflict, 1965

INDIAN POETRY (AMERICAN INDIAN)
see Indian Poetry

INDIAN POETRY
Cronyn, George W., ed. American Indian Poetry: An Anthology of Songs & Chants. new ed. LC 73-133483. 1970. pap. 5.95 (ISBN 0-87140-026-X). Liveright.
Day, A. Grove. Sky Clears: Poetry of the American Indians. LC 65-38538. 1964. pap. 2.45 (ISBN 0-8032-5047-9, BB 142, Bison). U of Nebr Pr.
Eberman, Willis. Clatsop Drumbeats: Poetry. (Indian Culture Ser.). (gr. 5). 1973. 1.95 (ISBN 0-89992-040-3). MT Coun Indian.
Greasybear, Charley J. Songs. Trusky, A. Thomas & Crews, Judson, eds. LC 78-58484. (Modern & Contemporary Poets of the West). (Orig.). 1979. pap. 2.50 (ISBN 0-916272-10-9). Ahsahta Pr.
Hodge, Gene M. Four Winds, Poems from Indian Rituals. LC 77-17800. 1979. pap. 4.25 (ISBN 0-913270-07-5). Sunstone Pr.
Houston, James, ed. & illus. Songs of the Dream People: Chants & Images from the Indians & Eskimos of North America. LC 72-77130. (gr. 4 up). 1972. 5.95 (ISBN 0-689-30306-8, McElderry Bk). Atheneum.
Howard, Helen A. American Indian Poetry. (United States Authors Ser.: No. 334). 1979. lib. bdg. 13.50 (ISBN 0-8057-7271-5). Twayne.
Marriott, Alice. Maria: The Potter of San Ildefonso. rev. ed. (CAI Ser.: Vol. 27). (Illus.). 1976. Repr. of 1948 ed. 11.95 (ISBN 0-8061-0176-8). U of Okla Pr.
Neihardt, John G. Twilight of the Sioux. LC 74-134771. Orig. Title: A Cycle of the West. 1971. pap. 4.50 (ISBN 0-8032-5734-1, BB 532, Bison). U of Nebr Pr.
Norman, Howard, ed. & tr. The Wishing Bone Cycle: Narrative Poems from the Swampy Cree Indians. 192p. 1976. 9.95 (ISBN 0-88373-045-6); pap. 3.45 (ISBN 0-88373-046-4). Stonehill Pub Co.
Rothenberg, Jerome, ed. Shaking the Pumpkin: Traditional Poetry of the Indian North Americas. LC 74-171317. 1972. pap. 4.95 (ISBN 0-385-01296-9, Anch). Doubleday.
Spinden, Herbert J. Songs of the Tewa. (Illus.). 1976. 12.95 (ISBN 0-913270-55-5). Sunstone Pr.
Tedlock, Dennis, tr. Finding the Center: Narrative Poetry of the Zuni Indians. LC 78-9611. (Illus.). 1978. 19.50x (ISBN 0-8032-4401-0); pap. 4.50 (ISBN 0-8032-9400-X, BB 676, Bison). U of Nebr Pr.
Turner, Frederick W., 3rd, ed. The Portable North American Indian Reader. LC 72-12545. (Viking Portable Library: No. 77). 1977. pap. 5.95 (ISBN 0-14-015077-3). Penguin.
Wood, Nancy. Many Winters. LC 74-3554. 80p. (gr. 6 up). 1974. 7.95 (ISBN 0-385-02226-3); limited edition 25.00 (ISBN 0-385-07107-8). Doubleday.
--War Cry on a Prayer Feather: Prose & Poetry of the Ute Indians. LC 77-76272. (gr. 4 up). 1979. 7.95a (ISBN 0-385-12884-3); PLB (ISBN 0-385-12885-1). Doubleday.

INDIAN PONIES
see also Appaloosa Horse

INDIAN SHAKERS
Barnett, Homer. Indian Shakers: A Messianic Cult of the Pacific Northwest. LC 72-5482. (Arcturus Books Paperbacks). (Illus.). 383p. 1972. pap. 7.95 (ISBN 0-8093-0595-X). S Ill U Pr.
Renwick Gallery of the National Collection of Fine Arts. Shaker: Furniture & Objects from the Faith & Andrew Deming Andrews Collection. LC 73-14614. (Illus.). 88p. 1973. 14.95x (ISBN 0-87474-155-6). Smithsonian.

INDIAN STUDIES
see Indians–Study and Teaching

INDIAN TERRITORY
Abel, Annie H. The American Indian As Participant in the Civil War. LC 19-5303. (American Studies). Repr. of 1919 ed. 16.00 (ISBN 0-384-00080-0). Johnson Repr.

INDIAN TRADE FACTORIES
see Indians of North America–Commerce

INDIAN TRAILS
Beauchamp, William M. Perch Lake Mounds, with Notes on Other New York Mounds & Some Accounts of Indian Trails. LC 74-7929. Repr. of 1905 ed. 14.50 (ISBN 0-404-11815-1). AMS Pr.
Hebard, Grace R. & Brininstool, Earl A. The Bozeman Trail: Historical Accounts of the Blazing of the Overland Routes into the Northwest & the Fights with Red Cloud's Warriors, 2 vols. LC 74-7973. Repr. of 1922 ed. Set. 63.50 (ISBN 0-404-11860-7); Vol. 1. (ISBN 0-404-11861-5); Vol. 2. (ISBN 0-404-11862-3). AMS Pr.
Terrell, John U. Traders of the Western Morning: Aboriginal Commerce in Precolumbian North America. (Illus.). 1967. 8.50 (ISBN 0-686-20690-8). Southwest Mus.
Wallace, Paul A. W. Indian Paths of Pennsylvania. LC 66-4482. 1971. 9.00 (ISBN 0-685-19109-5). Pa Hist & Mus.

INDIAN WARFARE
Here are entered treatises on the indian methods of fighting. Works on Indian wars are entered under Indians of Mexico (North America, etc.)–Wars, or under names of specific Indian wars.
Bhakari, S. K. Indian Warfare. 230p. 1981. text ed. 27.00 (ISBN 0-391-02415-9, Pub. by Munshiram Manoharlal India). Humanities.
Goodwin, Grenville. Western Apache Raiding & Warfare. Basso, Keith H., ed. LC 73-142255. 1971. 10.00x (ISBN 0-8165-0345-1). U of Ariz Pr.
Henry Tall Bull & Weist, Tom. Cheyenne Warriors. (Indian Culture Ser.). (gr. 4-12). 1976. pap. 1.95 (ISBN 0-89992-015-2). MT Coun Indian.
Hofsinde, Robert. Indian Warriors & Their Weapons. (Illus.). (gr. 4-7). 1965. PLB 6.48 (ISBN 0-688-31613-1). Morrow.
Snyderman, George S. Behind the Tree of Peace: A Sociological Analysis of Iroquois Warfare. LC 76-43838. Repr. of 1948 ed. 17.00 (ISBN 0-404-15692-4). AMS Pr.

INDIANA
see also names of cities, counties, etc. in Indiana
Dorson, Richard M. Land of the Millrats. LC 81-2944. (Illus.). 336p. 1981. text ed. 22.50 (ISBN 0-674-50855-6). Harvard U Pr.
Edmonds, Thomas. Indiana Pre-License Real Estate Manual. 1977. pap. text ed. 13.00 (ISBN 0-89493-002-8). Realty Train.
Gray, Ralph D., ed. The Hoosier State: A Documentary of Indiana, 2 vols. LC 80-12496. 448p. 1981. Vol. 1. pap. 16.95 (ISBN 0-8028-1842-0); Vol. 2. pap. 18.95 (ISBN 0-8028-1843-9). Eerdmans.
Hamm, Russell L. & Bough, Max E., eds. Yearbook of Indiana Education, 1970. LC 74-12588. 1970. pap. 3.95x (ISBN 0-8134-1194-7, 1194). Interstate.
Harsey, Paula. Harris-Indiana Industrial Directory 1981. (Illus., Annual). 1981. 38.90 (ISBN 0-916512-26-6). Harris Pub.
Indiana. 28.00 (ISBN 0-89770-090-2). Curriculum Info Ctr.
Jonsson, Ingrid E. Reference Guide to Indiana. LC 77-80566. 1977. lib. bdg. 35.00 (ISBN 0-403-07220-4). Somerset Pub.
Jonsson, Ingrid Eklov. Indiana-Encylopedia of the United States. LC 76-14257. (Illus.). 1979. lib. bdg. 45.00 (ISBN 0-403-01976-1). Scholarly.
Martin, John B. Indiana: An Interpretation. LC 72-5516. (Biography Index Reprint Ser.). 1972. Repr. of 1947 ed. 27.75 (ISBN 0-8369-8136-7). Arno.

INDIANA–DESCRIPTION AND TRAVEL
Alley, Jean & Alley, Hartley. Southern Indiana. LC 65-11797. (Illus.). 128p. 1965. pap. 6.95x (ISBN 0-253-18291-3). Ind U Pr.
Combined Atlas of Randolph Co., Ind. 1865-1874-1909. 124p. 1980. 20.00 (ISBN 0-686-28103-9). Bookmark.
Dillon, Lowell I. & Lyon, Edward E. Indiana: Crossroads of America. (Regional Geography Ser.). (Illus.). 1978. pap. text ed. 9.95 (ISBN 0-8403-1893-6). Kendall-Hunt.
Federal Writers' Project. Indiana: A Guide to the Hoosier State. 564p. 1941. Repr. 49.00 (ISBN 0-403-02165-0). Somerset Pub.
McCord, Shirley S., ed. Travel Accounts of Indiana, 1679-1961: A Collection of Observations by Wayfaring Foreigners, Itinerants, & Peripatetic Hoosiers. (Illus.). 340p. 1970. 10.00x (ISBN 0-253-36040-4). Ind U Pr.
Osler, Jack. Fifty Great Mini-Trips for Indiana. (Illus.). 1978. pap. 2.95 (ISBN 0-89645-005-8). Media Ventures.
Scifres, Bill. Indiana Outdoors: A Guide to Fishing, Hunting, & Wild Crops. LC 76-11931. (Illus.). 384p. 1976. 12.50x (ISBN 0-253-14166-4); pap. 7.95x (ISBN 0-235-28335-5). Ind U Pr.
State Industrial Directories Corp. Indiana State Industrial Directory, 1981. Date not set. pap. price not set (ISBN 0-89910-046-5). State Indus D.
Thomas, David. Travels Through the Western Country in the Summer of 1816. White, George W., ed. & frwd. by. (Contributions to the History of Geology Ser.: Vol. 6). 1970. Repr. of 1819 ed. 21.75 (ISBN 0-02-853400-X). Hafner.
White, Sheryl. Beautiful Indiana. Shangle, Robert D., ed. LC 80-26310. (Illus.). 72p. 1980. 14.95 (ISBN 0-89802-160-X); pap. 7.95 (ISBN 0-89802-159-6). Beautiful Am.

INDIANA–GENEALOGY
Jackson, Ronald V. & Teeples, Gary R. Indiana Census Index 1820. LC 77-85921. (Illus.). lib. bdg. 20.00 (ISBN 0-89593-036-6). Accelerated Index.
--Indiana Census Index 1830. LC 77-85922. (Illus.). lib. bdg. 26.00 (ISBN 0-89593-037-4). Accelerated Index.
--Indiana Census Index 1840. LC 77-85925. (Illus.). lib. bdg. 57.00 (ISBN 0-89593-038-2). Accelerated Index.
--Indiana Census Index 1850. LC 77-85926. (Illus.). lib. bdg. 69.00 (ISBN 0-89593-039-0). Accelerated Index.

INDIANA–HISTORY
Baker, Ronald L. & Carmony, Marvin. Indiana Place Names. LC 74-17915. 224p. 1976. pap. 3.95x (ISBN 0-253-28340-X). Ind U Pr.
Barnhart, John D. & Riker, Dorothy L. Indiana to Eighteen Sixteen: The Colonial Period. 536p. 1971. 15.00x (ISBN 0-253-37018-3). Ind U Pr.
Black, Harry G. Trails to Hoosier Heritage. LC 80-81608. (Illus.). 114p. (Orig.). 1981. pap. 3.95 (ISBN 0-937086-00-2). HMB Pubns.
Buckley, James J. Gary Railways: Bulletin 84. (Illus.). 1975. pap. 4.00 (ISBN 0-915348-84-5). Central Electric.
Cameron, James. From the Inside Out: A Lynching in the North. LC 79-66608. 1981. 9.95 (ISBN 0-918270-05-7). That New Pub.
Cline & McHaffie. The People's Guide, 1874: Directory of Henry Co., Indiana. 398p. 1979. 20.50 (ISBN 0-686-27818-6). Bookmark.
Dillon, John B. History of Indiana from Its Earliest Exploration by Europeans to the Close of Territorial Government in 1816. LC 73-146392. (First American Frontier Ser). (Illus.). 1971. Repr. of 1859 ed. 30.00 (ISBN 0-405-02845-8). Arno.
Dreiser, Theodore. A Hoosier Holiday. LC 73-16642. (Illus.). 513p. 1974. Repr. of 1916 ed. lib. bdg. 24.75x (ISBN 0-8371-7211-X, DRHH). Greenwood.
Dunn, Jacob P. Indiana: A Redemption from Slavery. new & enl. ed. LC 72-3754. (American Commonwealths: No. 12). Repr. of 1905 ed. 32.00 (ISBN 0-404-57212-X). AMS Pr.
Esarey, Logan. The Indiana Home. LC 76-12384. (Illus.). 136p. 1976. 10.00x (ISBN 0-253-32989-2); pap. 3.95x (ISBN 0-253-28325-6). Ind U Pr.
F. A. Battey & Co. History of La Grange Co., Ind., 1882. 470p. 1979. 15.50 (ISBN 0-686-27816-X). Bookmark.
Federal Writers' Project, Indiana. The Calumet Region Historical Guide. LC 73-3619. Repr. of 1939 ed. 29.00 (ISBN 0-404-57921-3). AMS Pr.
Gray, Ralph D., ed. The Hoosier State: A Documentary of Indiana, 2 vols. LC 80-12496. 448p. 1981. Vol. 1. pap. 16.95 (ISBN 0-8028-1842-0); Vol. 2. pap. 18.95 (ISBN 0-8028-1843-9). Eerdmans.
Hall, Baynard R. The New Purchase: Or, Seven & a Half Years in the Far West. facsimile ed. LC 75-101. (Mid-American Frontier Ser.). 1975. Repr. of 1843 ed. 35.00x (ISBN 0-405-06869-7). Arno.
Lane, James B. City of the Century: A History of Gary, Indiana. LC 77-23622. (Illus.). 416p. 1978. 9.95x (ISBN 0-253-11187-0). Ind U Pr.
Lewis Publishing Co. History of Northeast Indiana, 1920: La Grange Co. 493p. 1979. 24.00 (ISBN 0-686-27815-1). Bookmark.
Lynch, Martha. Reminiscences of Adams, Jay & Randolph Cos., Ind., 1896. 363p. 1979. 17.50 (ISBN 0-686-27819-4). Bookmark.
Peckham, Howard H. Indiana, a History. (States & the Nation Ser.). (Illus.). 1978. 12.95 (ISBN 0-393-05670-8, Co-Pub by AASLH). Norton.
Philbrick, F. S., ed. The Laws of Indiana Territory: 1801-1809. (Illinois Historical Collections Ser.: Vol. 21). 1930. 7.50 (ISBN 0-912154-07-1). Ill St Hist Lib.
Phillips, Clifton J. Indiana in Transition: The Emergence of an Industrial Commonwealth, 1880-1920. (Illus.). 688p. 1968. 15.00x (ISBN 0-253-37016-7). Ind U Pr.
Smeal, Lee. Indiana Historical & Biographical Index. LC 78-53694. (Illus.). Date not set. lib. bdg. price not set (ISBN 0-89593-179-6). Accelerated Index.
Stampp, Kenneth M. Indiana Politics during the Civil War. LC 77-23629. 320p. 1978. Repr. of 1949 ed. 12.50x (ISBN 0-253-37022-1). Ind U Pr.
Strausberg, Stephen. Federal Stewardship on the Frontier. Bruchey, Stuart, ed. LC 78-56677. (Management of Public Lands in the U. S. Ser.). (Illus.). 1979. lib. bdg. 28.00x (ISBN 0-405-11354-4). Arno.
Terrell, W. H. Indiana in the War of Rebellion: Report of the Adjutant General. 616p. Repr. of 1960 ed. 15.00x (ISBN 0-253-37014-0). Ind U Pr.
The Territory of Indiana, 1800-1810. (The Territorial Papers of the United States: Vol. 7). Repr. of 1939 ed. 69.50 (ISBN 0-404-01457-7). AMS Pr.
The Territory of Indiana, 1810-1816. (The Territorial Papers of the United States: Vol. 8). Repr. of 1939 ed. 69.50 (ISBN 0-404-01458-5). AMS Pr.
Thornbrough, Emma L. Indiana in the Civil War Era 1850-1880. (Illus.). 758p. 1965. 17.50x (ISBN 0-253-37020-5). Ind U Pr.
Troyer, Byron L. Yesterday's Indiana. LC 75-14381. (Illus.). 1977. pap. 7.95 (ISBN 0-912458-84-4). E A Seemann.
Vance, Mary. Historical Society Architectural Publications: Georgia, Hawaii, Idaho, Illinois & Indiana. (Architecture Ser.: Bibliography A-157). 54p. 1980. pap. 6.00 (ISBN 0-686-26906-3). Vance Biblios.
Vexler, R. I. Indiana Chronology & Factbook, Vol. 14. 1978. 8.50 (ISBN 0-379-16139-7). Oceana.
Wilson, William E. Indiana: A History. LC 66-22445. (Illus.). 256p. 1966. pap. 6.95x (ISBN 0-253-28305-1). Ind U Pr.
Woollen, William W. Biographical & Historical Sketches of Early Indiana. facsimile ed. LC 75-131. (Mid-American Frontier Ser.). (Illus.). 1975. Repr. of 1883 ed. 32.00x (ISBN 0-405-06896-4). Arno.

INDIANA–JUVENILE LITERATURE
Bailey, Bernadine. Picture Book of Indiana. rev. ed. LC 66-705. (Illus.). (gr. 3-5). 1974. 5.50g (ISBN 0-8075-9516-0). A Whitman.
Carpenter, Allan. Indiana. LC 78-12459. (New Enchantment of America State Bks). (Illus.). (gr. 4 up). 1979. PLB 10.60 (ISBN 0-516-04114-2). Childrens.
Fradin, Dennis. Indiana: In Words & Pictures. LC 79-21383. (Young People's Stories of Our States Ser.). (Illus.). 48p. (gr. 2-5). 1980. PLB 9.25 (ISBN 0-516-03912-1). Childrens.

INDIANA–POLITICS AND GOVERNMENT
Bobbitt. Indiana Appellate Practice & Procedure, 2 vols. 1972. 59.50, with 1977 suppl (ISBN 0-672-81526-5, Bobbs-Merrill Law); 1977 suppl 10.00 (ISBN 0-672-82813-8). Michie-Bobbs.
Hyneman, Charles S., et al. Voting in Indiana: A Century of Persistence & Change. LC 78-19550. (Illus.). 314p. 1980. 18.50x (ISBN 0-253-17283-7). Ind U Pr.
Indiana Judges Association. Indiana Pattern Jury Instructions - Criminal. 250p. 1980. 50.00 (ISBN 0-87215-353-3). Michie-Bobbs.
Michie Co. & Bobbs-Merrill Staff, eds. Burns' Indiana Statutes Title Thirty Five. 1979. 2 vol. set 64.00 (ISBN 0-685-94784-X); 32.00 ea. Vol. 1 (ISBN 0-672-83711-0). Vol. 2 (ISBN 0-672-83712-9). Bobbs.

Publisher's Editorial Staff. Indiana Banking & Related Laws. 3rd ed. LC 78-15745. 1977. 50.00, with 1978 suppl (ISBN 0-672-83720-X, Bobbs-Merrill Law); 1978 suppl. 10.00 (ISBN 0-672-83721-8). Michie-Bobbs.

Rawles, William A. Centralizing Tendencies in the Administration of Indiana. (Columbia University. Studies in the Social Sciences: No. 44). 1968. Repr. of 1903 ed. 24.50 (ISBN 0-404-51044-2). AMS Pr.

Seidman, Marshall J. The Law of Evidence in Indiana. 1977. 20.50 (ISBN 0-672-82868-5, Bobbs-Merrill Law). Michie-Bobbs.

Weeden, William B. War Government, Federal & State, 1861-65. LC 75-87685. (Law, Politics & History Ser.). 1972. Repr. of 1906 ed. lib. bdg. 39.50 (ISBN 0-306-71707-7). Da Capo.

INDIANA, UNIVERSITY OF

Clark, Thomas D. Indiana University: Midwestern Pioneer, 3 vols. Incl. Vol. 1. The Early Years. (Illus.). 352p. 1970. 12.50x (ISBN 0-253-14170-2); Vol. 2. In Mid-Passage. (Illus.). 448p. 1973. 17.50x (ISBN 0-253-32995-7); Vol. 3. Years of Fulfillment. 704p. 1977. 19.95x (ISBN 0-253-32996-5). LC 74-126207. (Illus.). Set. 42.50x (ISBN 0-253-32997-3). Ind U Pr.

Lee, Dorothy S. Native North American Music & Oral Data: A Catalogue of Sound Recordings, 1893-1976. LC 78-20337. 480p. 1979. 22.50x (ISBN 0-253-18877-6). Ind U Pr.

INDIANA COMPANY

Savelle, Max. George Morgan: Colony Builder. LC 32-30652. Repr. of 1932 ed. 14.00 (ISBN 0-404-05567-2). AMS Pr.

INDIANA INFANTRY, 100TH REGIMENT, 1862-1865

Upson, Theodore F. With Sherman to the Sea: Civil War Letters, Diaries & Reminiscences. Winther, Oscar O., ed. LC 58-12211. (Indiana University Civil War Centennial Ser). (Illus.). 1968. Repr. of 1958 ed. 12.00 (ISBN 0-527-92300-1). Kraus Repr.

INDIANAPOLIS

Geib, George W. Indianapolis: Hoosiers' Circle City. Blakey, Ellen S., ed. LC 81-65677. (American Portrait Ser.). (Illus.). 224p. (gr. 11 up). 1981. 24.95 (ISBN 0-932986-19-6). Continental Herit.

INDIANAPOLIS SPEEDWAY RACE

Berger, Phil & Bortstein, Larry. The Boys of Indy. LC 76-55144. (Illus.). 1977. 8.95 (ISBN 0-89474-002-4). Corwin.

Dorson, Ron. The Indy Five Hundred. 1974. 9.95 (ISBN 0-87880-025-5). Norton.

--Stay Tuned for the Greatest Spectacle in Racing. (Illus.). 260p. 1980. lib. bdg. 9.95 (ISBN 0-915088-21-5). C Hungness.

Hungness, Carl. The Indianapolis Five-Hundred Yearbook: 1974. (Illus.). 224p. 1974. lib. bdg. 13.95 (ISBN 0-915088-03-7); pap. 9.95 (ISBN 0-915088-02-9). C Hungness.

--The Indianapolis Five-Hundred Yearbook: 1976. LC 74-84562. (Illus.). 224p. 1976. lib. bdg. 13.95 (ISBN 0-915088-09-6); pap. text ed. 9.95 (ISBN 0-915088-10-X). C Hungness.

--The Indianapolis Five-Hundred Yearbook: 1979. Mahoney, John, ed. (Illus.). 1979. 13.95 (ISBN 0-915088-20-7); pap. 9.95 (ISBN 0-915088-19-3). C Hungness.

Hungness, Carl, et al. The Indianapolis Five-Hundred Yearbook: Nineteen Seventy-Eight. (Illus.). 1978. 13.95 (ISBN 0-915088-18-5); pap. 9.95 (ISBN 0-915088-17-7). C Hungness.

--The Indianapolis Five Hundred Yearbook 1975. (Illus.). 224p. (YA) 1975. lib. bdg. 13.95 (ISBN 0-915088-06-1); pap. 9.95 (ISBN 0-915088-07-X). C Hungness.

--The Indianapolis Five Hundred Yearbook: 1977. LC 74-84562. (Illus.). 1977. lib. bdg. 13.95 (ISBN 0-915088-12-6); pap. 9.95 (ISBN 0-915088-13-4). C Hungness.

--Indianapolis Five Hundred Yearbook: 1980. (Illus.). 224p. 1980. lib. bdg. 13.95 (ISBN 0-915088-24-X); pap. 9.95 (ISBN 0-915088-23-1). C Hungness.

Libby, Bill. Champions of the Indianapolis 500. LC 76-87. (Illus.). 1976. 7.95 (ISBN 0-396-07306-9). Dodd.

Mahoney, John & Hungness, Carl, eds. The Indianapolis Five Hundred Yearbook, 1969-1972. (Illus.). 304p. lib. bdg. 24.95 (ISBN 0-915088-22-3). C Hungness.

Reed, Terry. Indy: Race & Ritual. LC 79-25342. (Illus.). 1980. pap. 8.95 (ISBN 0-89141-075-9). Presidio Pr.

Sommers, Dick. Eddie Called Me Boss. LC 79-88533. (Illus.). 256p. 1979. 12.95 (ISBN 0-686-28501-8). Warren Pub.

Yates, Brock W. Indianapolis Five Hundred. rev. ed. LC 61-10844. (Illus.). (gr. 7 up). 1961. PLB 7.89 (ISBN 0-06-026641-4, HarpJ). Harper-Row.

INDIANS

Here are entered works on the aboriginal peoples of the Western Hemisphere, including Eskimos. see also Paleo-Indians; also Indians of North America, Indians of South America, and similar headings

Brandon, William. The Last American: The Indian in American Culture. LC 73-6956. 564p. 1973. 15.00 (ISBN 0-07-007201-9, GB). McGraw.

Brandon, William, ed. American Heritage Book of the Indians. 1964. pap. 1.75 (ISBN 0-440-30113-0, LFL). Dell.

Brinton, Daniel G. The American Race: A Linguistic Classification & Ethnographic Description of the Native Tribes of North & South America. LC 4-12237. (American Studies). Repr. of 1901 ed. lib. bdg. 21.50 (ISBN 0-384-05870-1, D025). Johnson Repr.

Burlin, Natalie. The Indians Book. 59.95 (ISBN 0-8490-0401-2). Gordon Pr.

Clastres, Pierre. Society Against the State. Hurley, Robert, tr. 1977. 12.95 (ISBN 0-916354-38-5). Urizen Bks.

Coles, Robert. Eskimos, Chicanos, Indians. (Children of Crisis Ser.: Vol.4). 1978. 15.00 (ISBN 0-316-15162-9, Atlantic-Little, Brown). Little.

Collier, John. Indians of the Americas. abr. ed. (Orig.). 1952. pap. 1.95 (ISBN 0-451-61886-6, MJ1886, Ment). NAL.

Embree, Edwin R. Indians of the Americas. 1970. pap. 2.95 (ISBN 0-02-031990-8, Collier). Macmillan.

Encyclopedia of Indians of the Americas, Vols. 1-9. LC 75-170347. 1974-1981. 69.00 ea. (ISBN 0-403-03586-4). Scholarly.

Fairchild, Hoxie N. Noble Savage: A Study in Romantic Naturalism. LC 61-12130. 1961. Repr. of 1928 ed. 15.00 (ISBN 0-8462-0180-1). Russell.

Frazer, James G. & Downie, Robert A., eds. Anthologia Anthropologica: The Native Races of America. LC 73-21267. Repr. of 1939 ed. 47.50 (ISBN 0-404-11423-7). AMS Pr.

Grinnell, George B. The Story of the Indian. Repr. of 1909 ed. 35.00 (ISBN 0-8492-9965-9). R West.

International Congress Of Americanists - 29th. Indian Tribes of Aboriginal America. Tax, Sol, ed. (Illus.). 410p. 1967. Repr. of 1952 ed. 21.00x (ISBN 0-8154-0233-3). Cooper Sq.

Klar, Kathryn, et al, eds. American Indian & Indo-European Studies: Papers in Honor of Madison S. Beeler. 1980. text ed. 79.50x (ISBN 90-279-7876-X). Mouton.

Leonard, Jonathan. Ancient America. LC 67-15619. (Great Ages of Man). (Illus.). (gr. 6 up). 1967. PLB 11.97 (ISBN 0-8094-0374-9, Pub. by Time-Life). Silver.

Leonard, Jonathan N. Ancient America. (Great Ages of Man Ser). (Illus.). 1967. 12.95 (ISBN 0-8094-0352-8). Time-Life.

Lizot, Jacques. Circle of Fires: Life Among the Yanomami. Simon, Ernest, tr. from Fr. (Illus.). 224p. 1981. 22.50x (ISBN 0-8476-6968-8). Rowman.

Lowey, Warren G. Little Fox, Indian Boy. (Illus.). (gr. 3-9). 1972. 3.95 (ISBN 0-912954-02-7). Edmond Pub Co.

Mason, Otis T. Cradles of the American Aborigines. (Illus.). Repr. of 1889 ed. pap. 8.50 (ISBN 0-8466-4033-3, SJ133). Shorey.

Meyer, Roy W. History of the Santee Sioux: United States Indian Policy on Trial. LC 80-11810. xviii, 434p. 1967. pap. 7.95 (ISBN 0-8032-8109-9, BB 751, Bison). U of Nebr Pr.

Ortiz, Roxanne D., ed. American Indian Energy Resources & Development. LC 80-51952. (Development Ser.: No. 2). (Orig.). 1980. pap. 5.00 (ISBN 0-934090-02-5). U of NM Nat Am Stud.

Ortiz, Simon J. Fightback: For the Sake of the People, for the Sake of the Land. LC 80-51953. (Literature Ser.: No. 1). (Orig.). 1980. pap. 6.95 (ISBN 0-934090-03-3). U of NM Nat Am Stud.

Smole, William J. The Yanoama Indians: A Cultural Geography. (Texas Pan American Ser.). (Illus.). 286p. 1976. 17.50x (ISBN 0-292-71019-4). U of Tex Pr.

Texas University Institute Of Latin-American Studies. Some Educational & Anthropological Aspects of Latin-America. (Illus.). Repr. of 1948 ed. lib. bdg. 15.00x (ISBN 0-8371-1032-7, TLEA). Greenwood.

Thevet, Andre. The New Found Worlde, or Antarctike. Hacket, T., tr. LC 74-174794. (English Experience Ser.: No. 417). 296p. 1971. Repr. of 1568 ed. 28.00 (ISBN 90-221-0417-6). Walter J Johnson.

Verrill, A. Hyatt. The American Indian: North, South & Central America. 1977. lib. bdg. 59.95 (ISBN 0-8490-1414-X). Gordon Pr.

Viola, Herman J. The Indian Legacy of Charles Bird King. LC 76-15022. (Illus.). 162p. 1981. Repr. of 1976 ed. 25.00 (ISBN 0-87474-943-3). Ohio U Pr.

Wissler, Clark. The American Indian. 3rd ed. 8.50 (ISBN 0-8446-1482-3). Peter Smith.

INDIANS-ANTIQUITIES

see also Man, Prehistoric-America; Paleo-Indians

Aveni, Anthony F., ed. Native American Astronomy. LC 76-53569. (Illus.). 304p. 1977. text ed. 17.50x (ISBN 0-292-75511-2). U of Tex Pr.

Blakely, Robert L., ed. Biocultural Adaptation in Prehistoric America. LC 76-49155. (Southern Anthropological Society Ser: No. 11). 144p. 1977. pap. 6.50x (ISBN 0-8203-0417-4). U of Ga Pr.

Bushnell, G. H. First Americans: The Pre-Columbian Civilization. LC 68-17503. (Library of the Early Civilizations Ser). (Illus.). 1968. pap. 4.95 (ISBN 0-07-009308-3, SP). McGraw.

Curtis, Edward S. Indian Days of Long Ago. (Illus.). 1978. 8.95 (ISBN 0-913668-46-X); pap. 3.95 (ISBN 0-913668-45-1). Ten Speed Pr.

Embree, Edwin R. Indians of the Americas. 1970. pap. 2.95 (ISBN 0-02-031990-8, Collier). Macmillan.

Jenness, Diamond, ed. The American Aborigines: Their Origin & Antiquity. LC 72-94055. (Illus.). 396p. 1973. Repr. of 1933 ed. lib. bdg. 16.50x (ISBN 0-8154-0455-7). Cooper Sq.

Leone, Mark P., ed. Contemporary Archaeology: A Guide to Theory & Contributions. LC 79-156779. (Illus.). 476p. 1972. pap. 12.95x (ISBN 0-8093-0534-8). S Ill U Pr.

Patterson, Thomas C. America's Past: A New World Archaeology. 168p. 1973. pap. 5.95x (ISBN 0-673-05273-7). Scott F.

Thomas, Cyrus. Introduction to the Study of North American Archaeology. LC 72-5009. (Harvard University. Peabody Museum of Archaeology & Ethnology. Antiquities of the New World: No. 14). Repr. of 1898 ed. 34.00 (ISBN 0-404-57314-2). AMS Pr.

Willey, Gordon R. Introduction to American Archaeology, Vol. 1: North & Middle America. 1966. text ed. 26.95 (ISBN 0-13-477836-7). P-H.

--Introduction to American Archaeology, Vol. 2: South America. (Illus.). 1971. text ed. 26.95 (ISBN 0-13-477851-0). P-H.

Zubrow, Ezra B., et al, eds. New World Archaeology: Theoretical & Cultural Transformations: Readings from Scientific American. LC 74-7028. (Illus.). 1974. text ed. 20.95x (ISBN 0-7167-0503-6); pap. text ed. 10.95x (ISBN 0-7167-0502-8). W H Freeman.

INDIANS-ART

Appleton, Leroy. American Indian Design & Decoration. Orig. Title: Indian Art of the Americas. (Illus.). 1971. pap. 6.50 (ISBN 0-486-22704-9). Dover.

Bean, Lowell J. & Vane, Sylvia B. Art of the Huichol Indians. LC 78-3144. (Illus.). 212p. 1978. pap. 6.95 (ISBN 0-88401-032-5). Fine Arts Mus.

Cahill, Holger. American Sources of Modern Art. LC 78-86426. (Museum of Modern Art Publications in Reprint Ser). (Illus.). 1970. Repr. of 1933 ed. 16.00 (ISBN 0-405-01532-1). Arno.

Conn, Richard. Native American Art in the Denver Art Museum. pap. 20.00 (ISBN 0-686-75602-9). U of Wash Pr.

Cordy-Collins, Alana & Nicholson, H. B. Pre-Columbian Art from the Land Collection. Land, L. K., ed. (Illus.). 272p. (Orig.). 1979. pap. 25.00 (ISBN 0-940228-03-3). Calif Acad Sci.

Dockstader, Frederick J. Indian Art of the Americas. LC 73-89979. (Illus., Orig.). 1973. 5.00x (ISBN 0-934490-09-0). Mus Am Ind.

Dumbarton Oaks Collection. Pre-Columbian Art. Benson, Elizabeth P., ed. LC 76-8176. 1976. 22.50 (ISBN 0-226-68981-6, Chicago Visual Lib); 1 colorfiche incl. U of Chicago Pr.

Edwards, Phyllis I., et al. Indian Botanical Paintings. (Illus.). 72p. (Orig.). 1980. pap. 8.00x (ISBN 0-913196-29-0). Hunt Inst Botanical.

Frederickson, Jaye & Gibb, Sandra. The Covenant Chain: Indian Ceremonial & Trade Silver. (Illus.). 168p. 1980. 24.95 (ISBN 0-660-10347-8, 56313-8, Pub. by Natl Gallery Canada); pap. 19.95 (ISBN 0-660-10348-6, 56314-6). U of Chicago Pr.

Kubler, George. The Art and Architecture of Ancient America. 2nd ed. (Pelican History of Art Ser.: No. 21). (Illus.). 1976. 50.00 (ISBN 0-670-13377-9, Pelican). Viking Pr.

McGrew, R. Brownell. R. Brownell McGrew. LC 78-53113. (Illus.). 1978. 25.00 (ISBN 0-913504-43-2). Lowell Pr.

Orchard, William C. Beads & Beadwork of the American Indian, Vol. 11. 2nd ed. LC 75-16030. (Contributions Ser.). 1975. soft cover 5.00 (ISBN 0-934490-22-8). Mus Am Ind.

Parry, Ellwood. The Image of the Indian & the Black Man in American Art, 1590-1900. new ed. LC 73-79606. (Illus.). 180p. 1974. 12.50 (ISBN 0-8076-0706-1). Braziller.

Phelps, Steven. Art & Artefacts of the Pacific, Africa & the Americas: The James Hooper Collection. (Illus.). 487p. 1976. 52.50x (ISBN 0-8476-1368-2). Rowman.

Phillips, Philip & Brown, James A. Pre-Columbian Shell Engravings from the Craig Mound at Spiro, Oklahoma, Vol. V. LC 74-77557. (Illus.). 192p. (Orig.). 1980. Ser. ltd. ed. 60.00x (ISBN 0-686-74605-8). Peabody Harvard.

Srivastava. Mother Goddess in Indian Art, Archaeology & Literature. 1980. 32.00x (ISBN 0-686-65576-1, Pub. by Agam India). South Asia Bks.

Tiger, Peggy & Babcock, Molly. The Life & Art of Jerome Tiger: War to Peace, Death to Life. LC 80-5245. (Illus.). 300p. 1980. 45.00 (ISBN 0-8061-1656-0). U of Okla Pr.

Von Wuthenau, Alexander. Art of Terracotta Pottery in Pre-Columbian, Central, & South America. (Art of the World Library). (Illus.). 1970. 6.95 (ISBN 0-517-50855-9). Crown.

INDIANS-BIBLIOGRAPHY

Field, Thomas W. Essay Towards an Indian Bibliography. LC 67-14026. 1967. Repr. of 1873 ed. 22.00 (ISBN 0-8103-3327-9). Gale.

Newberry Library - Chicago. Dictionary Catalog of the Edward E. Ayer Collection of Americana & American Indians, 16 Vols. 1961. Set. 880.00 (ISBN 0-8161-0586-3). G K Hall.

Wolf, Carolyn E. & Folk, Karen R. Indians of North & South America: A Bibliography Based on the Collection at the Willard E. Yager Library-Museum Hartwick College, Oneonta, N.Y. LC 77-1759. 1977. 27.50 (ISBN 0-8108-1026-3). Scarecrow.

INDIANS-CIVILIZATION

see Indians-Culture

INDIANS-CULTURE

Ambler, J. Richard. The Anasazi. LC 77-76509. (Special Publications Ser.: No. 13). (Illus.). 1977. pap. 4.95 (ISBN 0-89734-005-1). Mus Northern Ariz.

Amsden, Charles A. Prehistoric Southwesterners from Basketmaker to Pueblo. 5.00 (ISBN 0-686-20683-5). Southwest Mus.

Arias-Larreta, Abraham. Literaturas Aborigenes De America. 10th ed. (Illus.). 609p. 1975. 24.90 (ISBN 0-685-56925-X); pap. 17.90 (ISBN 0-685-56926-8). Edit Indoamerica.

Copway, George. Indian Life & Indian History. LC 76-43684. Repr. of 1860 ed. 21.00 (ISBN 0-404-15517-0). AMS Pr.

Guerra, F. The Pre-Columbian Mind. LC 75-183465. 350p. 1972. 54.00 (ISBN 0-12-785286-7). Acad Pr.

Heizer, Robert F. & Whipple, M. A., eds. The California Indians: A Source Book. 2nd rev. & enl. ed. LC 72-122951. (Illus.). 1971. 20.00x (ISBN 0-520-01770-6); pap. 7.95 (ISBN 0-520-02031-6, CAL231). U of Cal Pr.

International Congress Of Americanists - 29th. Civilizations of Ancient America. Tax, Sol, ed. (Illus.). 328p. 1952. Repr. 17.50x (ISBN 0-8154-0231-7). Cooper Sq.

Koller, John M. The Indian Way. 1982. text ed. 9.95 (ISBN 0-02-365800-2). Macmillan.

Lopez, Enrique H. Conversations with Katherine Anne Porter: Refugee from Indian Creek. (Illus.). 314p. 1981. 14.95 (ISBN 0-316-53199-5). Little.

Lothrop, Samuel K. Pre-Columbian Designs from Panama: 591 Illustrations of Cocle Pottery. 6.50 (ISBN 0-8446-5508-2). Peter Smith.

Martin, Calvin. Keepers of the Game: Indian-Animal Relationship & the Fur Trade. LC 77-78381. 1978. 10.95 (ISBN 0-520-03519-4). U of Cal Pr.

Russell, Norman. Indian Thoughts: I Am Old. Date not set. 2.00 (ISBN 0-88235-026-9). San Marcos.

Saletore, R. N. Encyclopaedia of Indian Culture, Vol. 1. 425p. 1981. text ed. 45.00x (ISBN 0-391-02282-2). Humanities.

--Encyclopaedia of Indian Culture, Vol. 2. 425p. 1981. text ed. 45.00x (ISBN 0-391-02331-4). Humanities.

--Encyclopaedia of Indian Culture, Vol. 3. 425p. 1981. text ed. 45.00x (ISBN 0-391-02332-2). Humanities.

--Encyclopaedia of Indian Culture (Index & Bibliography, Vol. 4. 425p. 1981. text ed. 45.00x (ISBN 0-391-02333-0). Humanities.

Sea in the Pre-Columbian World: Conference at Dumbarton Oaks, October 26 & 27, 1974. Benson, Elizabeth P., ed. LC 76-58217. (Illus.). 188p. 1977. 18.00x (ISBN 0-88402-071-1, Ctr Pre-Columbian). Dumbarton Oaks.

Sevilla-Casas, Elias, ed. Western Expansion & Indigenous Peoples: The Heritage of Las Casas. (World Anthropology Ser.). 1977. 26.00x (ISBN 0-202-90052-5). Beresford Bk Serv.

Srivastava. Mother Goddess in Indian Art, Archaeology & Literature. 1980. 32.00x (ISBN 0-686-65576-1, Pub. by Agam India). South Asia Bks.

Stierlin, Henri. The Pre-Colombian Civilizations: The World of the Maya, Aztecs & Incas. (Illus.). Date not set. 7.98 (ISBN 0-8317-7116-X, Pub. by Mayflower Bks). Smith Pubs.

Stone, Doris. Pre-Columbian Man in Costa Rica. Flint, Emily, ed. LC 77-86538. (Peabody Museum Press Books). (Illus.). 1978. pap. 12.00 (ISBN 0-87365-792-6). Peabody Harvard.
Van Sertima, Irvan. They Came Before Columbus: The African Presence in Ancient America. 1977. 15.00 (ISBN 0-394-40245-6). Random.
Wissler, Clark. Red Man Reservations. 1971. pap. 1.95 (ISBN 0-02-038650-8, Collier). Macmillan.

INDIANS-ETHNOLOGY
see Indians; Indians of North America; also indians of South America and similar headings

INDIANS-FOLK-LORE
see Folk-Lore, Indian

INDIANS-GAMES
Blood, Charles L. American Indian Games & Crafts. (Easy-Read Activity Bks.). (Illus.). 32p. (gr. 1-3). 1981. PLB 8.90 (ISBN 0-531-04304-5). Watts.
Sutton-Smith, Brian. The Games of the Americas: A Book of Readings. LC 75-35081. (Studies in Play & Games). (Illus.). 1976. Repr. 32.00x (ISBN 0-405-07929-X). Arno.

INDIANS-GOVERNMENT RELATIONS
see also Indians, Treatment Of
Council on Interracial Books for Children, Inc. Chronicles of American Indian Protest. 2nd, rev. ed. 400p. (gr. 11-12). pap. 5.95 (ISBN 0-930040-30-9). CIBC.
Getches, David H., et al. Cases & Materials on Federal Indian Law. LC 79-3906. (American Casebook Ser.). 600p. 1979. text ed. 19.95 (ISBN 0-8299-2027-7). West Pub.
Rosen, Lawrence. American Indians & the Law. LC 77-80868. 1978. Repr. of 1976 ed. 16.95 (ISBN 0-87855-266-9). Transaction Bks.

INDIANS-HISTORY
Copway, George. Indian Life & Indian History. LC 76-43684. Repr. of 1860 ed. 21.00 (ISBN 0-404-15517-0). AMS Pr.
Grinnell, George B. The Story of the Indian. Repr. of 1909 ed. 35.00 (ISBN 0-8492-9965-9). R West.
Hunter, William W. A Brief History of the Indian People. 1978. Repr. of 1907 ed. lib. bdg. 30.00 (ISBN 0-8492-5250-4). R West.
Innis, Ben. Bloody Knife. (Illus.). 1973. 8.95 (ISBN 0-88342-029-5). Old Army.
Josephy, Alvin M., Jr. Indian Heritage of America. (Illus.). (YA) 1968. 15.95 (ISBN 0-394-43049-2). Knopf.
Lopez, Enrique H. Conversations with Katherine Anne Porter: Refugee from Indian Creek. (Illus.). 314p. 1981. 14.95 (ISBN 0-316-53199-5). Little.
Sevilla-Casas, Elias, ed. Western Expansion & Indigenous Peoples: The Heritage of Las Casas. (World Anthropology Ser.). 1977. 26.00x (ISBN 0-202-90052-5). Beresford Bk Serv.
Wise, Jennings C. & Deloria, Vine, Jr. Red Man in the New World Drama. 1971. 12.95 (ISBN 0-02-630550-X). Macmillan.

INDIANS-JUVENILE LITERATURE
Baity, Elizabeth C. Americans Before Columbus. rev. ed. (Illus.). (gr. 7 up). 1951. 7.95 (ISBN 0-670-12166-5). Viking Pr.
Furman, Abraham L., ed. Indian Stories. (Young Readers Bookshelf). (Illus.). (gr. 4-7). PLB 6.19 (ISBN 0-8313-0043-4). Lantern.
World Book-Childcraft International Inc. Staff & Garbarino, Merwyn. The Indian Book. LC 65-25105. (Childcraft Annual Ser.). (Illus.). 304p. (gr. k-6). 1980. PLB write for info. (ISBN 0-7166-0680-1). World Bk-Childcraft.

INDIANS-LANGUAGES
see also Indians of North America-Languages; Indians of South America-Languages
Brinton, Daniel G. The American Race: A Linguistic Classification & Ethnographic Description of the Native Tribes of North & South America. LC 4-12237. (American Studies). Repr. of 1901 ed. lib. bdg. 21.50 (ISBN 0-384-05870-1, D025). Johnson Repr.
Coward, Harold G., ed. Language in Indian Philosophy & Religion. 98p. 1978. pap. text ed. 5.25 (ISBN 0-919812-07-4, Pub. by Laurier U Pr Canada). Humanities.
Garcia Icazbalceta, Joaquin. Apuntes Para un Catalogo De Escritores En Lenguas Indigenas De America. LC 77-122833. (Bibliography & Reference Ser.: No. 335). 1970. Repr. of 1866 ed. lib. bdg. 25.50 (ISBN 0-8337-1787-1). B Franklin.
Matteson, Esther, et al. Comparative Studies in Amerindian Languages. (Janua Linguarum, Practica Ser: No. 127). 251p. (Orig.). 1972. pap. text ed. 57.50x (ISBN 90-2792-110-5). Mouton.

INDIANS-LEGENDS
see also Folk-Lore, Indian
Bemister, Margaret. Thirty Indian Legends of Canada. pap. 6.50 (ISBN 0-88894-025-4, Pub. by Douglas & McIntyre). Intl Schol Bk Serv.
Hansen, L. Taylor. He Walked the Americas. (Illus.). 1963. deluxe ed. 7.95 (ISBN 0-910122-19-9). Amherst Pr.
McAndrews, Anita G. & Herrera, Tomas, eds. Cuna Cosmology: Legends from Panama. LC 77-9164. (Illus., Orig.). 1978. 14.00x (ISBN 0-89410-009-2); pap. 7.00x (ISBN 0-89410-010-6). Three Continents.

INDIANS-LITERATURE
see Indian Literature

INDIANS-MEDICINE
see also Medicine-Man
Corlett, William T. The Medicine-Man of the American Indian & His Cultural Background. LC 75-23699. Repr. of 1935 ed. 33.50 (ISBN 0-404-13249-9). AMS Pr.
Krogman, William, et al. Medicine Among the American Indians: CIBA Symposia, 1939, Vol. 1, No. 1. 1981. pap. 4.95 (ISBN 0-686-69101-6). Acoma Bks.
Wah-Be-Gwo-Nese, pseud. Ojibwa Indian Legends. (Illus.). 1972. 2.95 (ISBN 0-918616-05-0). Northern Mich.

INDIANS-MYTHOLOGY
see Indians-Religion and Mythology

INDIANS-ORIGIN
Adair, James. History of the American Indians. (American Studies). Repr. of 1775 ed. 31.00 (ISBN 0-384-00305-2). Johnson Repr.
Brennan, Louis A. American Dawn: A New Model of American Prehistory. LC 71-93718. (Illus.). 1970. 14.95 (ISBN 0-02-514910-5). Macmillan.
Coffer, William E. Spirits of the Sacred Mountains: Creation Stories of the American Indian. 1978. 8.95 (ISBN 0-442-21600-9). Van Nos Reinhold.
Huddleston, Lee E. Origins of the American Indians: European Concepts, 1492-1729. (Latin American Monographs: No. 11). 189p. 1967. 10.00x (ISBN 0-292-73693-2). U of Tex Pr.
Jenness, Diamond, ed. The American Aborigines: Their Origin & Antiquity. LC 72-94055. (Illus.). 396p. 1973. Repr. of 1933 ed. lib. bdg. 16.50x (ISBN 0-8154-0455-7). Cooper Sq.
--The American Aborigines: Their Origin & Antiquity; a Collection of Papers by Ten Authors Published for Presentation at the 5th Pacific Science Congress, Canada. LC 78-180611. (Illus.). iv, 396p. 1972. Repr. of 1933 ed. 19.00 (ISBN 0-8462-1616-7). Russell.
--The American Aborigines: Their Origin & Antiquity; a Collection of Papers by Ten Authors Published for Presentation at the 5th Pacific Science Congress, Canada. LC 78-180611. (Illus.). iv, 396p. 1972. Repr. of 1933 ed. 19.00 (ISBN 0-8462-1616-7). Russell.
Kellogg, Edward P. The Roots of the American Indian. LC 79-91921. 1980. 14.95 (ISBN 0-9603914-0-1); text ed. 12.95 (ISBN 0-686-66004-8). Kellogg.
Kelly, Joyce. The Complete Visitor's Guide to Mesoamerican Ruins. (Illus.). 480p. 1981. 35.00 (ISBN 0-8061-1566-1). U of Okla Pr.
MacNeish, Richard S., intro. by. Early Man in America: Readings from Scientific American. LC 72-12251. (Illus.). 1973. text ed. 15.95x (ISBN 0-7167-0864-7); pap. text ed. 7.95x (ISBN 0-7167-0863-9). W H Freeman.
May, Julian. Before the Indians. (Illus.). 40p. (gr. k-3). 1969. reinforced bdg. 7.95 (ISBN 0-8234-0005-0). Holiday.
Menendez, Enrique C. Only the Wind. Armas, Jose, ed. Hernandez, Frances, tr. from Span. (Illus.). 182p. 1980. 9.00 (ISBN 0-918358-05-1); pap. 7.00 (ISBN 0-686-64685-1). Pajarito Pubns.
Newman, Walter S. & Salwen, Bert S., eds. Amerinds & Their Paleoenviornments in Northeastern North America, Vol. 288. 1977. 35.00 (ISBN 0-89072-034-7). NY Acad Sci.
Wauchope, Robert. Lost Tribes & Sunken Continents: Myth Method in the Study of American Indians. LC 62-18112. (Illus.). 1962. 7.50x (ISBN 0-226-87635-7, Phoen); pap. 3.95 (ISBN 0-686-76908-2, Phoen). U of Chicago Pr.
Wirth, Diane E. Discoveries of the Truth. (First Impression Ser.). (Illus.). 1978. pap. 4.95x (ISBN 0-9602096-1-1). D E Wirth.

INDIANS-PICTORIAL WORKS
Kate Cory. (Special Publications Ser). 1978. 30.00 (ISBN 0-89734-002-7). Mus Northern Ariz.

INDIANS-PICTURE WRITING
see Picture-Writing, Indian

INDIANS-RELIGION AND MYTHOLOGY
Albaum, Charlet. Ojo De Dios: Eye of God. (Illus.). 96p. (Orig.). 1972. pap. 2.50 (ISBN 0-448-01149-2). G&D.
Appleton, Leroy. American Indian Design & Decoration. Orig. Title: Indian Art of the Americas. (Illus.). 1971. pap. 6.50 (ISBN 0-486-22704-9). Dover.
Brinton, D. G. Myths of the New World: A Treatise on the Symbolism & Mythology of the Red Race of America. LC 68-24972. (American History & Americana Ser., No. 47). 1969. Repr. of 1876 ed. lib. bdg. 49.95 (ISBN 0-8383-0918-6). Haskell.
Brinton, Daniel G. The Myths of the New World. LC 71-144901. 331p. 1972. Repr. of 1876 ed. 10.00 (ISBN 0-403-00839-5). Scholarly.
--Myths of the New World: A Treatise on the Symbolism & Mythology of the Red Race of America. LC 78-31682. 1979. Repr. of 1868 ed. lib. bdg. 30.00 (ISBN 0-89341-326-7). Longwood Pr.
--Myths of the New World: A Treatise on the Symbolism & Mythology of the Red Race of America. 2nd ed. LC 69-13839. 1969. Repr. of 1876 ed. lib. bdg. 15.00x (ISBN 0-8371-2040-3, BRMN). Greenwood.
--Myths of the New World: The Symbolism & Mythology of the Indians of the Americas. LC 72-81594. (Illus.). 348p. 1976. 7.50 (ISBN 0-8334-1742-8, Steinerbooks). Multimedia.
Brinton, Daniel G., ed. Rig Veda Americanus. LC 73-83463. (Library of Aboriginal American Literature Ser.: No. 8). Repr. of 1890 ed. 14.00 (ISBN 0-404-52188-6). AMS Pr.
Brown, Vinson. Voices of Earth & Sky. LC 76-41761. (Illus.). 1976. pap. 3.95 (ISBN 0-87961-060-3). Naturegraph.
Castaneda, Carlos. Journey to Ixtlan. 1981. pap. 2.95 (ISBN 0-671-43673-2). PB.
--Separate Reality. 1981. pap. 2.95 (ISBN 0-671-43672-4). PB.
--Tales of Power. 1981. pap. 2.95 (ISBN 0-671-43674-0). PB.
--Teachings of Don Juan. 1981. pap. 2.95 (ISBN 0-671-42216-2). PB.
Coward, Harold G., ed. Language in Indian Philosophy & Religion. 98p. 1978. pap. text ed. 5.25 (ISBN 0-919812-07-4, Pub. by Laurier U Pr Canada). Humanities.
Ely, Evelyn & Hughes, Phyllis. Ojos De Dios. (Illus.). 1972. pap. 1.95 (ISBN 0-89013-056-6). Museum NM Pr.
Hansen, L. Taylor. He Walked the Americas. (Illus.). 1963. deluxe ed. 7.95 (ISBN 0-910122-19-9). Amherst Pr.
Luomala, K. Oceanic, American Indian, & African Myths of Snaring the Sun. Repr. of 1940 ed. pap. 7.00 (ISBN 0-527-02276-4). Kraus Repr.
Mackenzie, Donald. Indian Myth & Legend. LC 77-85615. 1978. Repr. of 1913 ed. lib. bdg. 50.00 (ISBN 0-89341-316-X). Longwood Pr.
MacKenzie, Donald A. Myths of Pre-Columbian America. LC 77-94602. 1978. Repr. of 1923 ed. lib. bdg. 40.00 (ISBN 0-89341-314-3). Longwood Pr.
Mooney, James. Myths of the Cherokee. LC 16-5534. (Landmarks in Anthropology Ser). Repr. of 1900 ed. 31.00 (ISBN 0-384-39920-7). Johnson Repr.
Peet, Stephen O. Myths & Symbols, or Aboriginal Religions in America. LC 76-27515. (Illus.). 1976. Repr. of 1905 ed. lib. bdg. 45.00 (ISBN 0-89341-039-X). Longwood Pr.
Poor, Laura E. Sanskrit & Its Kindred Literatures. LC 76-27525. 1976. Repr. of 1880 ed. lib. bdg. 35.00 (ISBN 0-89341-038-1). Longwood Pr.
Rajneesh, Bhagwan S. The Book of the Secrets, Vol. IV. LC 75-36733. 416p. (Orig.). 1981. pap. 5.95 (ISBN 0-06-090885-8, CN 885, CN). Har-Row.
Srivastava. Mother Goddess in Indian Art, Archaeology & Literature. 1980. 32.00x (ISBN 0-686-65576-1, Pub. by Agam India). South Asia Bks.
Walker, Deward E., Jr. Myths of Idaho Indians. rev. ed. LC 79-57484. (Gem Bk. & Anthropological Monograph). (Illus.). 188p. (Orig.). 1980. pap. 7.50 (ISBN 0-89301-066-9). U Pr of Idaho.

INDIANS-STUDY AND TEACHING
Vantine, Larry L. Teaching American Indian History: An Interdisciplinary Approach. LC 78-62223. 1978. soft cover 9.00 (ISBN 0-88247-546-0). R & E Res Assoc.

INDIANS-WRITING
see also Picture-Writing, Indian
Griffiths, Gareth. A Double Exile: African & West Indian Writing Between Two Cultures. 208p. 1980. 7.95 (ISBN 0-7145-2623-1, Pub. by M Boyars). Merrimack Bk Serv.

INDIANS, TREATMENT OF
see also Indians of North America-Government Relations
Bailey, L. R. Indian Slave Trade in the Southwest: A Study of Slave-Taking & the Traffic in Indian Captives from 1700-1935. LC 66-2888. (Illus.). 9.50 (ISBN 0-87026-028-6). Westernlore.
Bailey, M. Thomas. Reconstruction in Indian Territory. LC 77-189551. 1972. 13.50 (ISBN 0-8046-9022-7). Kennikat.
Barsh, Russel L. & Henderson, J. Youngblood. The Road: Indian Tribes & Political Liberty. 1980. 14.95x (ISBN 0-520-03629-8). U of Cal Pr.
Chamberlin, J. E. The Harrowing of Eden: White Attitudes Toward Native Americans. LC 75-9941. 1975. 8.95 (ISBN 0-8164-9251-4). Continuum.
Cook, Sherburne F. The Conflict Between the California Indian & White Civilization. LC 75-23860. 1976. 36.50x (ISBN 0-520-03142-3); pap. 6.95 (ISBN 0-520-03143-1, CAL332). U of Cal Pr.
Council on Interracial Books for Children, Inc. Chronicles of American Indian Protest. 2nd, rev. ed. 400p. (gr. 11-12). pap. 5.95 (ISBN 0-930040-30-9). CIBC.
De Las Casas, Bartolome. In Defense of the Indians. Poole, Stafford, ed. & tr. from Lat. LC 73-15094. (Illus.). 385p. 1974. 25.00 (ISBN 0-87580-042-4); boxed set of 3 vols., with hanke, friede & keen 50.00 (ISBN 0-685-38980-4, HPFK-3). N Ill U Pr.
Deloria, Vine, Jr. The Indian Affair. (Orig.). 1974. pap. 2.50 (ISBN 0-377-00022-1). Friend Pr.
Dippie, Brian W. The Vanishing American. (Illus.). 464p. 1982. 25.00x (ISBN 0-8195-5056-6). Wesleyan U Pr.
Drinnon, Richard. Facing West: The Metaphysics of Indian-Hating & Empire-Building. (Illus.). 544p. 1980. 20.00 (ISBN 0-8166-0978-0). U of Minn Pr.
Gessner, Robert. Massacre: A Survey of Today's American Indian. LC 72-38831. (Civil Liberties in American History Ser). 418p. 1972. Repr. of 1931 ed. lib. bdg. 35.00 (ISBN 0-306-70445-5). Da Capo.
Halliburton, R., Jr. Red Over Black: Black Slavery Among the Cherokee Indians. LC 76-15329. (Illus.). 1977. lib. bdg. 17.95 (ISBN 0-8371-9034-7, HAR/). Greenwood.
Hanke, Lewis. The First Social Experiments in America. 1964. 6.00 (ISBN 0-8446-1221-9). Peter Smith.
Howitt, William. Colonization & Christianity: A Popular History of the Treatment of the Natives by the Europeans in All Their Colonies. LC 70-76856. Repr. of 1838 ed. 22.75x (ISBN 0-8371-1162-5, Pub. by Negro U Pr). Greenwood.
Jacobs, Wilbur R. Dispossessing the American Indian. LC 72-37179. 1972. pap. text ed. 7.95x (ISBN 0-684-13774-7, ScribC). Scribner.
Jennings, Francis. The Invasion of America: Indians, Colonialism, and the Cant of Conquest. (Illus.). 384p. 1976. pap. 4.95 (ISBN 0-393-00830-4, Norton Lib). Norton.
Katz, Jane B., ed. Let Me Be a Free Man: A Documentary History of Indian Resistance. LC 74-11910. (Voices of the American Indian Ser.). (Illus.). 184p. (gr. 6 up). 1975. PLB 6.95 (ISBN 0-8225-0640-8). Lerner Pubns.
Lauber, Almon W. Indian Slavery in Colonial Times Within the Present Limits of the United States. LC 71-77994. (Columbia University, Studies in the Social Sciences Ser.: No. 134). Repr. of 1913 ed. 11.50 (ISBN 0-404-51134-1). AMS Pr.
Lesser, Alexander. The Pawnee Ghost Dance Hand Game: A Study of Cultural Change. LC 79-82340. (Illus.). 1978. 20.00 (ISBN 0-299-07480-3); pap. 7.95 (ISBN 0-299-07484-6). U of Wis Pr.
Mardock, Robert W. Reformers & the American Indian. LC 79-113815. (Illus.). 1971. 12.50x (ISBN 0-8262-0090-7). U of Mo Pr.
Miner, H. Craig. The Corporation & the Indian: Tribal Sovereignty & Industrial Civilization in Indian Territory. LC 75-44405. 1976. 11.00x (ISBN 0-8262-0198-9). U of Mo Pr.
Nammack, Georgiana C. Fraud, Politics & the Dispossession of the Indians: The Iroquois Land Frontier in the Colonial Period. (Civilization of the American Indian Ser.: Vol. 97). (Illus.). 128p. 1969. 9.95x (ISBN 0-8061-0854-1). U of Okla Pr.
Peithmann, Irvin M. Broken Peace Pipes: A Four-Hundred Year History of the American Indian. 320p. 1964. 11.75 (ISBN 0-398-01468-X). C C Thomas.
Priest, Loring B. Uncle Sam's Stepchildren: The Reformation of United States Indian Policy, 1865-1887. LC 79-76511. 1969. Repr. of 1942 ed. lib. bdg. 16.50x (ISBN 0-374-96574-9). Octagon.
--Uncle Sam's Stepchildren: The Reformation of United States Indian Policy, 1865-1887. LC 75-5983. x, 310p. 1975. pap. 3.95 (ISBN 0-8032-5818-6, BB 601, Bison). U of Nebr Pr.
Prucha, Francis P., ed. Cherokee Removal: The "William Penn" Essays & Other Writings by Jeremiah Evarts. LC 80-28449. 320p. 1981. 19.50x (ISBN 0-87049-313-2). U of Tenn Pr.
Roessel, Ruth. The Role of Indian Studies in American Education. (Illus.). 1974. pap. 1.25 (ISBN 0-912586-20-6). Navajo Coll Pr.
Smith, Jane F. & Kvasnicka, Robert M., eds. Indian-White Relations: A Persistent Paradox. 1981. pap. 6.95 (ISBN 0-686-73615-X, 094-9). Howard U Pr.
--Indian-White Relations: A Persistent Paradox. LC 75-22316. 354p. 1976. 15.00 (ISBN 0-88258-055-8). Howard U Pr.
Steiner, Stan. The Vanishing White Man. LC 74-15854. (Illus.). 288p. (YA) 1976. 12.95 (ISBN 0-06-014078-X, HarpT). Har-Row.
Szasz, Margaret C. Education & the American Indian: The Road to Self-Determination Since 1928. 2nd ed. LC 77-11742. (Illus.). 252p. 1979. pap. 6.95x (ISBN 0-8263-0468-0). U of NM Pr.

Whipple, Chandler. The Indian & the Whiteman in Massachusetts & Rhode Island. LC 73-93961. (First Encounter Ser). (Illus.). 156p. 1973. pap. 3.50 (ISBN 0-912944-12-9). Berkshire Traveller.

Zimmerman, Bill. Airlift to Wounded Knee. LC 76-3138. (Illus.). 348p. 1976. 14.95 (ISBN 0-8040-0691-1). Swallow.

INDIANS, TREATMENT OF–LATIN-AMERICA

see also Encomiendas (Latin-America)

Arens, Richard, ed. Genocide in Paraguay. LC 76-5726. 1977. 12.50x (ISBN 0-87722-088-3). Temple U Pr.

Helps, Arthur. Spanish Conquest in America, & Its Relation to the History of Slavery & to the Government of Colonies, 4 Vols. new ed. Oppenheim, M., ed. LC 72-15297. Repr. of 1904 ed. 85.00 (ISBN 0-404-03270-2). AMS Pr.

James, J. A. English Institutions & the American Indian. 1973. Repr. of 1894 ed. pap. 7.00 (ISBN 0-384-26743-2). Johnson Repr.

Juan, Jorge J. & De Ulloa, Antonio. Discourse & Political Reflections on the Kingdom of Peru: Their Government, Special Regimen of Their Inhabitants, & Abuses Which Have Been Introduced into One & Another, with Special Information on Why They Grew up & Some Means to Avoid Them. TePaske, John J., ed. & tr. from Span. LC 78-7135. (American Exploration & Travel Ser: No. 65). 1979. 17.50 (ISBN 0-8061-1482-7). U of Okla Pr.

Korth, Eugene H. Spanish Policy in Colonial Chile: The Struggle for Social Justice, 1535-1700. LC 68-26779. 1968. 17.50x (ISBN 0-8047-0666-2). Stanford U Pr.

Zavala, Silvio A. New Viewpoints on the Spanish Colonization of America. Coyne, Joan, tr. LC 68-10958. 1968. Repr. of 1943 ed. 6.50 (ISBN 0-8462-1115-7). Russell.

INDIANS IN ART

see subdivision Pictorial Works under Indians; Indians Of North America and similar headings

INDIANS IN LITERATURE

Barnett, Louise K. Ignoble Savage: American Literary Racism, 1790-1890. LC 75-16964. (Contributions in American Studies: No. 18). 220p. 1975. lib. bdg. 14.75x (ISBN 0-8371-8281-6, BIG/). Greenwood.

Bissell, B. The American Indian in English Literature of the 18th Century. 59.95 (ISBN 0-87968-604-9). Gordon Pr.

Dabney, Lewis M. The Indians of Yoknapatawpha: A Study in Literature & History. LC 73-77659. 136p. 1974. 12.95x (ISBN 0-8071-0058-7). La State U Pr.

Keiser, Albert. Indian in American Literature. LC 72-96160. 1970. Repr. of 1933 ed. lib. bdg. 14.50x (ISBN 0-374-94541-1). Octagon.

--The Indian in American Literature. 59.95 (ISBN 0-8490-0397-0). Gordon Pr.

Lorand Olazagasti, Adelaida. El Indio En la Narrativa Guatemalteca. pap. 4.05 (ISBN 0-8477-3138-3). U of PR Pr.

Lourie, Dick, ed. Come to Power: Writings by American Indians. LC 73-86673. 100p. 1973. 8.95 (ISBN 0-912278-45-5); pap. 3.95 (ISBN 0-912278-44-7). Crossing Pr.

Monkman, Leslie. A Native Heritage: Images of the Indian in English-Canadian Literature. 208p. 1981. 25.00x (ISBN 0-8020-5537-0). U of Toronto Pr.

Pearce, Roy Harvey & Miller, J. Hillis, eds. Savagism & Civilization: A Study of the Indian & the American Mind. LC 53-6486. 272p. 1967. pap. 3.45x (ISBN 0-8018-0525-2). Johns Hopkins.

Sayre, Robert F. Thoreau & the American Indians. LC 76-45910. 1977. text ed. 17.50 (ISBN 0-691-06330-3). Princeton U Pr.

INDIANS OF CENTRAL AMERICA

see also Mayas

American Indian Publishers, ed. Dictionary of Indian Tribes of the Americas, 4 vols. (Illus.). 1980. Set. lib. bdg. 225.00 (ISBN 0-937862-25-8). Am Indian Pubs.

The Annals of the Cakchiquels. LC 76-83461. (Library of Aboriginal American Literature: No. 6). Repr. of 1885 ed. 20.00 (ISBN 0-404-52186-X). AMS Pr.

Basso, Ellen B., ed. Carib-Speaking Indians: Culture, Society, & Language. LC 75-18138. (Anthropological Papers: No. 28). 1977. pap. 6.95x (ISBN 0-8165-0493-8). U of Ariz Pr.

Carmack, Robert M. Quichean Civilization: The Ethnohistoric, Ethnographic, & Archaelogical Sources. LC 70-149948. (Illus.). 1973. 28.50x (ISBN 0-520-01963-6). U of Cal Pr.

Colby, Benjamin N. & Van Den Berghe, Pierre L. Ixil Country: A Plural Society in Highland Guatemala. LC 68-16740. 1969. 21.50x (ISBN 0-520-01515-0). U of Cal Pr.

Gann, Thomas W. The Maya Indians of Southern Yucatan & Northern British Honduras. Repr. of 1918 ed. 19.00 (ISBN 0-403-08977-8). Scholarly.

Gonzalez, Nancie L. Black Carib Household Structure: A Study of Migration & Modernization. LC 77-93024. (Illus.). 188p. 1980. pap. text ed. 7.50 (ISBN 0-295-95733-6). U of Wash Pr.

Harrison, Peter D. & Turner, B. L., II, eds. Pre-Hispanic Maya Agriculture. LC 78-55703. (Illus.). 414p. 1978. 20.00x (ISBN 0-8263-0483-4). U of NM Pr.

Helms, Mary W. Asang: Adaptations to Culture Contact in a Miskito Community. LC 70-630257. (Illus.). 1971. 11.00 (ISBN 0-8130-0298-2). U Presses Fla.

Hinshaw, Robert E. Panajachel: A Guatemalan Town in Thirty-Year Perspective. LC 74-17838. (Pitt Latin American Ser). 1975. 16.95x (ISBN 0-8229-3296-2). U of Pittsburgh Pr.

Jenness, Aylette & Kroeber, Lisa. A Life of Their Own: An Indian Family in Latin America. LC 75-15964. (Illus., Orig.). (gr. 5 up). 1975. 8.95 (ISBN 0-690-00572-5, TYC-J). Har-Row.

Joyce, Thomas A. Central American & West Indian Archaeology. LC 77-172548. (Illus.). Repr. of 1916 ed. 19.00 (ISBN 0-405-08676-8, Blom Pubns). Arno.

Lumholtz, Carl. New Trails in Mexico: Indians of Mexico and Arizona. LC 76-176225. (Beautiful Rio Grande Classics Ser). 576p. 1971. lib. bdg. 20.00 (ISBN 0-87380-059-1). Rio Grande.

McGlynn, Eileen. Middle American Anthropology: Directory, Bibliography & Guide to the UCLA Library Collection. LC 74-620057. (UCLA Library Guide Ser. B: No. 1). (Illus., Orig.). 1975. pap. text ed. 6.00 (ISBN 0-87903-301-0). UCLA Lat Am Ctr.

Oglesby, Catharine. Modern Primitive Arts of Mexico, Guatemala & the Southwest. facs. ed. LC 75-90670. (Essay Index Reprint Ser). 1939. 16.00 (ISBN 0-8369-1215-2). Arno.

Smith, Waldemar R. Fiesta System & Economic Change. LC 77-390. 1977. 16.00x (ISBN 0-231-04180-2). Columbia U Pr.

Stone, Doris. Boruca of Costa Rica. (Harvard University Peabody Museum of Archaeology & Ethnology Papers). Repr. of 1949 ed. pap. 5.00 (ISBN 0-527-01265-3). Kraus Repr.

Tax, Sol. Penny Capitalism: A Guatemalan Indian Economy. LC 78-159254. x, 230p. 1971. Repr. of 1953 ed. lib. bdg. 16.00x (ISBN 0-374-97785-2). Octagon.

Von Hagen, Victor W. The Aztec & Maya Papermakers. LC 76-6317. (Illus.). 1978. Repr. of 1944 ed. 25.00 (ISBN 0-87817-206-8). Hacker.

Wafer, Lionel. New Voyage & Description of the Isthmus of America. Winship, George P., ed. LC 79-114820. 1970. Repr. of 1903 ed. 18.50 (ISBN 0-8337-3663-9). B Franklin.

Wagley, Charles. Economics of a Guatemalan Village. LC 41-19381. 1941. pap. 6.00 (ISBN 0-527-00557-6). Kraus Repr.

Wauchope, Robert, ed. Handbook of Middle American Indians, Vols. 1-16. Incl. Vol. 1. Natural Environment & Early Cultures. West, Robert C., ed. 578p. 1964. 40.00x (ISBN 0-292-73259-7); Vols. 2 & 3. Archaeology of Southern Mesoamerica, Pts 1 & 2. Willey, Gordon R., ed. 1965. 85.00x set (ISBN 0-292-73260-0). Vol. 2, 560p. Vol. 3, 531p; Vol. 4. Archaeological Frontiers & External Connections. Willey, Gordon R. & Ekholm, Gordon F., eds. 375p. 1966. 35.00x (ISBN 0-292-73632-0); Vol. 5. Linguistics. McQuown, Norman A., ed. 410p. 1967. 35.00x (ISBN 0-292-73665-7); Vol. 6. Social Anthropology. Nash, M., ed. 605p. 1967. 40.00x (ISBN 0-292-73666-5); Vols. 7 & 8. Ethnology, Pts. 1 & 2. Vogt, Evon Z., ed. 1969. 70.00x set (ISBN 0-292-78419-8). Vol. 7, 584p. Vol. 8, 388p; Vol. 9. Physical Anthropology. Stewart, T. Dale, ed. 304p. 1970. 45.00x (ISBN 0-292-70014-8); Vols. 10 & 11. Archaeology of Northern Mesoamerica, Pts. 1 & 2. Ekholm, Gordon F. & Bernal, Ignacio, eds. LC 64-10316. 1971. 65.00x set (ISBN 0-292-70150-0). Vol. 10, 466p. Vol. 11, 454p; Vol. 12. Guide to Ethnohistorical Sources, Pt. 1. Cline, Howard F., ed. LC 64-10316. 476p. 1972. 35.00x (ISBN 0-292-70152-7); Vol. 13. Guide to Ethnohistorical Sources, Part 2. Cline, Howard F. & Glass, John B., eds. LC 64-10316. 439p. 1973. 35.00x (ISBN 0-292-70153-5); Vols. 14 & 15. Guide to Ethnohistorical Sources (Parts 3 & 4) Cline, Howard F., et al, eds. (Illus.). 1975. 65.00x set (ISBN 0-292-70154-3). Vol. 14, 410p. Vol. 15, 425p. U of Tex Pr.

Wisdom, Charles. Chorti Indians of Guatemala. (Midway Reprint Ser). 528p. 1974. pap. 16.50x (ISBN 0-226-90283-8). U of Chicago Pr.

Wolf, Eric. Sons of the Shaking Earth. LC 59-12290. (Illus.). 1959. 15.00x (ISBN 0-226-90499-7, Phoen); pap. 4.95x (ISBN 0-226-90500-4, P90, Phoen). U of Chicago Pr.

Woods, Clyde M. & Graves, Theodore D. The Process of Medical Change in a Highland Guatemalan Town. LC 72-97396. (Latin American Studies Ser.: Vol. 21). 61p. 1973. pap. text ed. 5.00 (ISBN 0-87903-021-6). UCLA Lat Am Ctr.

INDIANS OF CENTRAL AMERICA–ANTIQUITIES

see also Guatemala–Antiquities

Gendrop, Paul & Heyden, Doris. Pre-Columbian Architecture of Mesoamerica. LC 75-8993. (History of World Architecture Ser.). (Illus.). 340p. 1976. 50.00 (ISBN 0-8109-1018-7). Abrams.

Hewett, Edgar L. Ancient Life in Mexico & Central America. LC 67-29546. (Illus.). 1968. Repr. of 1936 ed. 15.00x (ISBN 0-8196-0205-1). Biblo.

Kendall, Aubyn, ed. The Art & Archaeology of Pre-Columbian Middle America. (Reference Publications Ser.). 1977. lib. bdg. 25.00 (ISBN 0-8161-8093-8). G K Hall.

Lothrop, Samuel K. Zacualpa: A Study of Ancient Quiche Artifacts. LC 77-11508. (Carnegie Institution of Washington. Publication: No. 472). 1977. Repr. of 1936 ed. 20.00 (ISBN 0-404-16269-X). AMS Pr.

Michels, Joseph W. The Kaminaljuyu Chiefdom. LC 79-15181. (Monograph Ser. on Kaminaljuyu). (Illus.). 1979. text ed. 22.50x (ISBN 0-271-00224-7). Pa St U Pr.

Pasztory, Esther, ed. Middle Classic Mesoamerica: 400-700 A. D. (Illus.). 197p. 1978. 25.00x (ISBN 0-231-04270-1). Columbia U Pr.

Sanders, William T. & Michels, Joseph W., eds. Teotihuacan & Kaminaljuyu: A Study in Culture Contact. LC 77-21061. (Monograph Ser. on Kaminaljuyu). (Illus.). 1978. text ed. 23.50x (ISBN 0-271-00529-7). Pa St U Pr.

Spinden, Herbert J. Ancient Civilizations of Mexico & Central America. 3rd rev. ed. LC 67-29554. (Illus.). 1968. Repr. of 1928 ed. 10.50x (ISBN 0-8196-0215-9). Biblo.

INDIANS OF CENTRAL AMERICA–ART

Badner, Mino. Possible Focus of Andean Artistic Influence in Mesoamerica. Bd. with Izapan-Style Art: A Study of its Form & Meaning. Quirarte, Jacinto; Human Decapitation in Ancient Mesoamerica. Moser, Christopher L. (Studies in Pre-Columbian Art & Archaeology: Nos. 9-11). (Illus.). 1972-1973. 18.00x (ISBN 0-88402-054-1, Ctr Pre-Columbian). Dumbarton Oaks.

Bolz-Augenstein, I. & Disselhoff, H. D., eds. Praekolumbischer Kunst: Sammlung Ludwig. (Monumenta Americana Ser.: Vol. 6). (Illus.). 1971. 37.50x (ISBN 0-8150-0460-5). Wittenborn.

Keeler, Clyde E. Cuna Indian Art: The Culture & Craft of Panama's San Blas Islanders. LC 68-24875. 1969. 15.00 (ISBN 0-682-46815-0, University). Exposition.

Kendall, Aubyn, ed. The Art & Archaeology of Pre-Columbian Middle America. (Reference Publications Ser.). 1977. lib. bdg. 25.00 (ISBN 0-8161-8093-8). G K Hall.

Oglesby, Catharine. Modern Primitive Arts of Mexico, Guatemala & the Southwest. facs. ed. LC 75-90670. (Essay Index Reprint Ser). 1939. 16.00 (ISBN 0-8369-1215-2). Arno.

Osborne, Lilly D. Indian Crafts of Guatemala & El Salvador. rev. ed. (Civilization of the American Indian Ser.: No. 79). (Illus.). 1975. 24.95 (ISBN 0-8061-0673-5); pap. 9.95 (ISBN 0-8061-1288-3). U of Okla Pr.

Shao, Paul. Asiatic Influences in Pre-Columbian American Art. (Illus.). 1976. 28.50x (ISBN 0-8138-1855-9). Iowa St U Pr.

Von Winning, Hasso. Pre-Columbian Art of Mexico & Central America. LC 68-13065. (History of World Architecture Ser.). (Illus.). 1968. 45.00 (ISBN 0-8109-0423-3); ltd. ed. leather bd 125.00 (ISBN 0-8109-4751-X). Abrams.

INDIANS OF CENTRAL AMERICA–ETHNOLOGY

see Indians of Central America

INDIANS OF CENTRAL AMERICA–FOLK-LORE

see Folk-Lore, Indian

INDIANS OF CENTRAL AMERICA–LANGUAGES

see also Maya Language

Craig, Colette G. The Structure of Jacaltec. LC 76-27109. 444p. 1977. pap. text ed. 9.95x (ISBN 0-292-74002-6). U of Tex Pr.

Day, Christopher. The Jacaltec Language. (Language Science Monographs: Vol. 12). viii, 136p. (Orig.). 1973. pap. text ed. 8.00x (ISBN 0-87750-176-9). Res Ctr Lang Semiotic.

Mayers, Marvin, ed. Languages of Guatemala. (Janua Linguarum, Ser. Practica: No. 23). (Orig.). 1966. pap. text ed. 55.00x (ISBN 90-2790-642-4). Mouton.

Thomas, Cyrus. Indian Languages of Mexico & Central America & Their Geographical Distribution. Repr. of 1911 ed. 17.00 (ISBN 0-403-03612-7). Scholarly.

--Indian Languages of Mexico & Central America. Repr. of 1911 ed. pap. 17.00 (ISBN 0-8466-4042-2, SJ142). Shorey.

INDIANS OF CENTRAL AMERICA–LEGENDS

see also Folk-Lore, Indian

Baker, Betty. No Help at All. LC 76-13223. (Greenwillow Read-Alone Bks.). (Illus.). (gr. 1-4). 1978. 5.95 (ISBN 0-688-80056-4); PLB 5.71 (ISBN 0-688-84056-6). Greenwillow.

INDIANS OF CENTRAL AMERICA–ORIGIN

see Indians–Origin

INDIANS OF CENTRAL AMERICA–POTTERY

Lothrop, S. K., et al. Cocle: An Archaeological Study of Central Panama, 2 vols. Repr. of 1942 ed. Vol. 1. pap. 55.00 (ISBN 0-527-01169-X); Vol. 2. pap. 67.00 (ISBN 0-527-01170-3). Kraus Repr.

Reina, Ruben E. & Hill, Robert M., II. The Traditional Pottery of Guatemala. LC 77-17455. (Texas Pan American Ser.). (Illus.). 321p. 1978. 35.00 (ISBN 0-292-78024-9). U of Tex Pr.

INDIANS OF CENTRAL AMERICA–RELIGION AND MYTHOLOGY

Alexander, Hartley B. Latin American Mythology. LC 63-19096. (Mythology of All Races Ser.: Vol. 11). (Illus.). 1964. Repr. of 1932 ed. 25.00x (ISBN 0-8154-0006-3). Cooper Sq.

Castaneda, Carlos. Separate Reality. LC 79-139617. 1971. 11.95 (ISBN 0-671-20897-7). S&S.

Le Plongeon, Augustus. Sacred Mysteries Among the Mayas & the Quiches. LC 73-76094. (Secret Doctrine Reference Ser). (Illus.). 200p. 1973. Repr. of 1886 ed. 8.95 (ISBN 0-913510-02-5). Wizards.

Recinos, Adrian & Goetz, Delia, trs. Popol Vuh: The Sacred Book of the Ancient Quiche Maya: Spanish Version of the Original Maya. (Civilization of the American Indian Ser.: No. 29). (Eng). 1978. Repr. of 1950 ed. 10.95 (ISBN 0-8061-0205-5). U of Okla Pr.

Spence, Lewis. The Myths of Mexico & Peru. LC 76-27516. (Illus.). 1976. Repr. of 1914 ed. lib. bdg. 45.00 (ISBN 0-89341-031-4). Longwood Pr.

--Popol Vuh: Mythic & Heroic Sagas of the Kiches of Central America. LC 75-139178. (Popular Studies in Mythology, Romance & Folklore: No. 16). Repr. of 1908 ed. 5.50 (ISBN 0-404-53516-X). AMS Pr.

Warren, Kay B. The Symbolism of Subordination: Indian Identity in a Guatemalan Town. (Texas Pan American Ser.). (Illus.). 221p. 1978. text ed. 14.00x (ISBN 0-292-77546-6). U of Tex Pr.

INDIANS OF CENTRAL AMERICA–TEXTILE INDUSTRY AND FABRICS

Auld, Rhoda L. Molas: What They Are; How to Make Them; Ideas They Suggest for Creative Applique. 136p. 1980. pap. 9.95 (ISBN 0-442-20050-1). Van Nos Reinhold.

Goodman, Frances S. The Embroidery of Mexico & Guatemala. (Encore Edition). 1976. 6.95 (ISBN 0-684-15946-5, ScribT). Scribner.

INDIANS OF MEXICO

see also Aztecs; Ethnology–Mexico; Nahuas; Olmecs

Artaud, Antonin. Les Tarahumaras. 160p. 1974. 3.95 (ISBN 0-686-53838-2). French & Eur.

Aschmann, Homer. Central Desert of Baja California: Demography & Ecology. LC 66-29636. (Illus.). 1967. lib. bdg. 49.50x (ISBN 0-910950-01-6). Manessier.

Bandelier, A. F. Scientist on the Trail. Hammond, George P., ed. LC 67-24721. (Quivira Society Publications, Vol. 10). 1967. Repr. of 1949 ed. 12.00 (ISBN 0-405-00084-7). Arno.

Bandelier, A. F. & Hewett, Edgar L. On the Social Originization & Mode of Government of the Ancient Mexicans. 145p. 1975. Repr. of 1879 ed. lib. bdg. 10.00x (ISBN 0-8154-0504-9). Cooper Sq.

Beals, Ralph L. Cheran: A Sierra Tarascan Village. LC 72-95138. (Illus.). 225p. 1973. Repr. of 1946 ed. lib. bdg. 13.50x (ISBN 0-8154-0466-2). Cooper Sq.

--The Comparative Ethnology of Northern Mexico Before 1750. LC 72-95137. (Illus.). 225p. 1973. Repr. of 1932 ed. lib. bdg. 10.00x (ISBN 0-8154-0465-4). Cooper Sq.

Bennett, Wendell C. & Zingg, Robert M. The Tarahumara; an Indian Tribe of Northern Mexico. LC 75-29143. (Beautiful Rio Grande Classics Ser). (Illus.). 520p. 1975. Repr. of 1935 ed. lib. bdg. 40.00 (ISBN 0-87380-107-5). Rio Grande.

Bowen, Thomas. Trincheras Culture of Sonora, Mexico. (Anthropological Papers). Date not set. price not set (ISBN 0-8165-0424-5). U of Ariz Pr.

Burckhalter, David. The Seris. LC 75-44915. 1976. pap. 5.95 (ISBN 0-8165-0517-9). U of Ariz Pr.

Chinas, B. The Isthmus Zapotecs. LC 73-3945. (Case Studies in Cultural Anthropology). 1973. pap. text ed. 4.95 (ISBN 0-03-080301-2, HoltC). HR&W.
Clavigero, Francesco S. The History of Mexico, 2 vols. Feldman, Burton & Richardson, Robert D., eds. LC 78-60908. (Myth & Romanticism Ser.: Vol. 7). (Illus.). 1979. Set. lib. bdg. 132.00 (ISBN 0-8240-3556-9). Garland Pub.
Coolidge, Dane & Coolidge, Mary. The Last of the Seris of Mexico. LC 71-153199. (Beautiful Rio Grande Classics Ser). lib. bdg. 12.00 (ISBN 0-87380-078-8). Rio Grande.
Craine, Eugene R. & Reindorp, Reginald C., eds. Chronicles of Michoacan. LC 69-16726. (Civilization of the American Indian Ser.: No. 98). (Illus.). 1970. 14.95 (ISBN 0-8061-0887-8). U of Okla Pr.
Crumrine, N. Ross. The Mayo Indians of Sonora: A People Who Refuse to Die. LC 76-8563. 1977. 12.50x (ISBN 0-8165-0605-1); pap. text ed. 5.95x (ISBN 0-8165-0473-3). U of Ariz Pr.
De Acosta, Joseph. The Natural & Moral History of the Indies, 2 Vols. Markham, Clements R., ed. LC 75-134715. (Hakluyt Society Ser.: No. 60-61). 1970. Set. lib. bdg. 60.50 (ISBN 0-8337-0798-1). B Franklin.
De La Vega, Marguerite. Some Factors Affecting Leadership of Mexican-Americans in a High School. LC 74-76562. 1974. Repr. of 1951 ed. soft bdg. 7.00 (ISBN 0-88247-290-9). R & E Res Assoc.
De Zorita, Alonso. Life & Labor in Ancient Mexico: The Brief & Summary Relation of the Lords of New Spain. Keen, Benjamin, tr. 1964. 20.00 (ISBN 0-8135-0442-2). Rutgers U Pr.
Dobie, J. Frank. Apache Gold & Yaqui Silver. LC 76-21512. (Zia Books). (Illus.). 384p. 1976. pap. 6.95 (ISBN 0-8263-0434-6). U of NM Pr.
Dobie, J. Frank, ed. Southwestern Lore. LC 33-1134. (Texas Folklore Society Publications: No. 9). 1965. Repr. of 1931 ed. 6.95 (ISBN 0-87074-042-3). SMU Press.
--Spur-Of-The-Cock. LC 34-1434. (Texas Folklore Society Publications: No. 11). 1965. Repr. of 1933 ed. 4.95 (ISBN 0-87074-043-1). SMU Press.
Driver, Harold E. & Driver, Wilhelmine. Ethnography & Acculturation of the Chichimeca-Jonaz of Northeast Mexico. LC 63-62521. (General Publications Ser: Vol. 26). 1963. pap. text ed. 5.00x (ISBN 0-87750-116-5). Res Ctr Lang Semiotic.
Dunne, Peter M. Black Robes in Lower California. (California Library Reprint Series: No. 3). (Illus.). 1968. Repr. 26.75x (ISBN 0-520-00362-4). U of Cal Pr.
Dutton, Bertha P. Friendly People: The Zuni Indians. (Illus.). 1963. pap. 1.95 (ISBN 0-89013-002-7). Museum NM Pr.
Eddy, Frank W. Metates & Manos. (Illus.). 1964. pap. 0.95 (ISBN 0-89013-009-4). Museum NM Pr.
Friedlander, Judith N. Being Indian in Hueyapan: A Study of Forced Identity in Comtemporary Mexico. LC 74-23047. (Illus.). 224p. (Orig.). 1975. text ed. 14.95 (ISBN 0-312-07280-5); pap. text ed. 6.95 (ISBN 0-312-07315-1). St Martin.
Gann, Thomas W. The Maya Indians of Southern Yucatan & Northern British Honduras. Repr. of 1918 ed. 19.00 (ISBN 0-403-08977-8). Scholarly.
Gibson, Charles. Tlaxcala in the Sixteenth Century. (Illus.). 1952. 15.00x (ISBN 0-8047-0615-8). Stanford U Pr.
Griffen, William B. Culture Change & Shifting Populations in Central Northern Mexico. LC 69-16327. (Anthropological Papers, No. 13). 1969. pap. 5.95x (ISBN 0-8165-0140-8). U of Ariz Pr.
Historia Tolteca-Chichimeca. Mexikanische Bilderhandschrift. 1937. 13.00 (ISBN 0-384-23440-2). Johnson Repr.
Hodge, Frederick W., ed. Handbook of American Indians North of Mexico, 2 vols. Repr. of 1910 ed. 150.00 (ISBN 0-403-00355-5). Scholarly.
Holden, William C., et al. Studies of the Yaqui Indians of Sonora, Mexico. LC 76-43747. (Texas Tech. College, Bulletin: 12). Repr. of 1936 ed. 19.00 (ISBN 0-404-15586-3). AMS Pr.
Hunn, Eugene S. Tzelta Folk Zoology: The Classification of Discontinuities in Nature. LC 76-56205. (Language, Thought & Culture Ser.). 1977. 50.00 (ISBN 0-12-361750-2). Acad Pr.
Iwanska, Alicja. Purgatory & Utopia: A Mazahua Indian Village of Mexico. (Illus.). 214p. 1971. 13.25x (ISBN 0-87073-762-7); pap. text ed. 7.95x (ISBN 0-87073-763-5). Schenkman.
Kemper, Robert V. Migration & Adaptation: Tzintzuntzan Peasants in Mexico City. LC 77-2413. (Sage Library of Social Research: Vol. 43). 1977. 20.00 (ISBN 0-8039-0687-0); pap. 9.95 (ISBN 0-8039-0688-9). Sage.
Latorre, Felipe A. & Latorre, Delores L. The Mexican Kickapoo Indians. LC 75-11654. (Texas Pan American Ser). (Illus.). 421p. 1976. 22.50x (ISBN 0-292-75023-4). U of Tex Pr.
Leslie, Charles M. Now We Are Civilized: A Study of the World View of the Zapotec Indians of Mitla, Oaxaca. LC 81-14. (Illus.). xi, 108p. 1981. Repr. of 1960 ed. lib. bdg. 18.00x (ISBN 0-313-22847-7, LENW). Greenwood.
Lumholtz, Carl. Unknown Mexico: Indians of Mexico, 2 vols. LC 72-13182. (Beautiful Rio Grande Classics Ser). Set. lib. bdg. 50.00 (ISBN 0-87380-085-0). Rio Grande.
Lumholtz, Karl. Unknown Mexico: A Record of Five Years' Exploration Among the Tribes of the Western Sierra Madre, in the Tierra Caliente of Tepic & Jalisco, & Among the Tarascos of Michoacan, 2 vols. LC 72-5010. (Antiquities of the New World Ser.: Vol. 15). (Illus.). Repr. of 1902 ed. Set. 87.50 (ISBN 0-404-57315-0). Vol. 1 (ISBN 0-404-57321-5). Vol. 2. (ISBN 0-404-57322-3); Vol. 2. (ISBN 0-404-57322-3). AMS Pr.
McGee, W. J. The Seri Indians of Mexico: 1895-1896, Pt. 1. LC 78-156768. (Beautiful Rio Grande Classics Ser.: No. 17). lib. bdg. 25.00 (ISBN 0-87380-079-6). Rio Grande.
McGlynn, Eileen. Middle American Anthropology: Directory, Bibliography & Guide to the UCLA Library Collection. LC 74-620057. (UCLA Library Guide Ser. B: No. 1). (Illus., Orig.). 1975. pap. text ed. 6.00 (ISBN 0-87903-301-0). UCLA Lat Am Ctr.
Parsons, Elsie C. Mitla: Town of the Souls, & Other Zapoteco-Speaking Pueblos of Oaxaca, Mexico. LC 36-18029. (Illus.). 1936. 17.50x (ISBN 0-226-64760-9). U of Chicago Pr.
Pennington, Campbell W. The Tepehuan of Chihuahua: Their Material Culture. LC 73-99792. (Illus.). 1969. 30.00x (ISBN 0-87480-013-7); pap. 15.00x (ISBN 0-87480-147-8). U of Utah Pr.
Pozas, Ricardo. Juan the Chamula: An Ethnological Recreation of the Life of a Mexican Indian. Kemp, Lysander, tr. (Illus.). 1962. pap. 2.25 (ISBN 0-520-01027-2, CAL69). U of Cal Pr.
Romney, Kimball & Romney, Romaine. The Mixtecans of Juxtlahuaca, Mexico. LC 66-1706. 186p. 1973. pap. text ed. 6.50 (ISBN 0-88275-136-0). Krieger.
Sauer, Carl O. Aboriginal Population of Northwestern Mexico. LC 76-43815. (Ibero-Americana: 10). Repr. of 1935 ed. 11.50 (ISBN 0-404-15670-3). AMS Pr.
--The Distribution of Aboriginal Tribes & Languages in Northwestern Mexico. LC 76-43818. (Ibero-Americana: 5). Repr. of 1934 ed. 13.75 (ISBN 0-404-15671-1). AMS Pr.
Schmieder, Oscar. Settlements of the Tzapotec & Mije Indians: State of Oaxaca, Mexico. Repr. of 1930 ed. pap. 23.00 (ISBN 0-384-54130-5). Johnson Repr.
Scholes, France V., et al. Maya Chontal Indians of Acalan-Tixchel: A Contribution to the History & Ethnography of the Yucatan Peninsula. LC 68-15677. (Civilization of the American Indian Ser.: Vol. 91). (Illus.). 1968. 24.95x (ISBN 0-8061-0813-4). U of Okla Pr.
Smith, Mary E. Picture Writing from Ancient Southern Mexico: Mixtec Place Signs & Maps. LC 72-869. (Civilization of the American Indian Ser.: Vol. 124). (Illus.). 500p. 1973. 27.50x (ISBN 0-8061-1029-5). U of Okla Pr.
Starr, Frederick. In Indian Mexico: A Narrative of Travel & Labor. LC 74-9025. Repr. of 1908 ed. 49.50 (ISBN 0-404-11903-4). AMS Pr.
--The Physical Characters of the Indians of Southern Mexico. LC 74-9008. (Illus.). Repr. of 1902 ed. 19.00 (ISBN 0-404-11906-9). AMS Pr.
Steven, Hugh. Manuel. Guardarrama, Alvaro, tr. 132p. (Span.). 1981. pap. 3.25 (ISBN 0-89922-159-9). Edit Caribe.
Swanton, John R. Indian Tribes of the Lower Mississippi Valley & Adjacent Coast of the Gulf of Mexico. Repr. of 1911 ed. 29.00 (ISBN 0-403-03613-5). Scholarly.
Tannenbaum, Frank. Peace by Revolution, Mexico After 1910. LC 33-35455. (Illus.). 1933. pap. 7.50x (ISBN 0-231-08568-0). Columbia U Pr.
Taraval, Sigismundo. Indian Uprising in Lower California, 1734-1737. LC 79-137296. Repr. of 1931 ed. 24.00 (ISBN 0-404-06337-3). AMS Pr.
Thomas, Alfred B., ed. Teodora De Croix & the Northern Frontier of New Spain 1776-1783. (American Exploration & Travel Ser.: No. 5). 1968. Repr. of 1941 ed. 14.95 (ISBN 0-8061-0093-1). U of Okla Pr.
Trimborn, Hermann. Quellen Zur Kulturgeschichte Des Prakolumbischen America. Repr. of 1936 ed. pap. 15.50 (ISBN 0-384-61570-8). Johnson Repr.
Vogt, Eton L. Zinacantecos of Mexico: A Modern Maya Way of Life. LC 76-107436. (Case Studies in Cultural Anthropology). 1970. pap. text ed. 6.95 (ISBN 0-03-084016-3, HoltC). HR&W.
Wauchope, Robert, ed. Handbook of Middle American Indians, Vols. 1-16. Incl. Vol. 1. Natural Environment & Early Cultures. West, Robert C., ed. 578p. 1964. 40.00x (ISBN 0-292-73259-7); Vols. 2 & 3. Archaeology of Southern Mesoamerica, Pts 1 & 2. Willey, Gordon R., ed. 1965. 85.00x set (ISBN 0-292-73260-0). Vol. 2, 560p. Vol. 3, 531p; Vol. 4. Archaeological Frontiers & External Connections. Willey, Gordon R. & Ekholm, Gordon F., eds. 375p. 1966. 35.00x (ISBN 0-292-73632-0); Vol. 5. Linguistics. McQuown, Norman A., ed. 410p. 1967. 35.00x (ISBN 0-292-73665-7); Vol. 6. Social Anthropology. Nash, M., ed. 605p. 1967. 40.00x (ISBN 0-292-73666-5); Vols. 7 & 8. Ethnology, Pts. 1 & 2. Vogt, Evon Z., ed. 1969. 70.00x set (ISBN 0-292-78419-8). Vol. 7, 584p. Vol. 8, 388p; Vol. 9. Physical Anthropology. Stewart, T. Dale, ed. 304p. 1970. 45.00x (ISBN 0-292-70014-8); Vols. 10 & 11. Archaeology of Northern Mesoamerica, Pts. 1 & 2. Ekholm, Gordon F. & Bernal, Ignacio, eds. LC 64-10316. 1971. 65.00x set (ISBN 0-292-70150-0). Vol. 10, 466p. Vol. 11, 454p; Vol. 12. Guide to Ethnohistorical Sources, Pt. 1. Cline, Howard F., ed. LC 64-10316. 476p. 1972. 35.00x (ISBN 0-292-70152-7); Vol. 13. Guide to Ethnohistorical Sources, Part 2. Cline, Howard F. & Glass, John B., eds. LC 64-10316. 439p. 1973. 35.00x (ISBN 0-292-70153-5); Vols. 14 & 15. Guide to Ethnohistorical Sources (Parts 3 & 4) Cline, Howard F., et al, eds. (Illus.). 1975. 65.00x set (ISBN 0-292-70154-3). Vol. 14, 410p. Vol. 15, 425p. U of Tex Pr.
West, Robert C. Cultural Geography of the Modern Tarascan Area. LC 77-118761. (Illus.). 77p. 1973. Repr. of 1948 ed. lib. bdg. 22.00x (ISBN 0-8371-5078-7, SMIH). Greenwood.
Whitecotton, Joseph W. The Zapotecs: Princes, Priests & Peasants. (Civilization of the American Indian Ser: Vol. 143). (Illus.). 1977. 16.95 (ISBN 0-8061-1374-X). U of Okla Pr.
Wolf, Eric. Sons of the Shaking Earth. LC 59-12290. (Illus.). 1959. 15.00x (ISBN 0-226-90499-7, Phoen); pap. 4.95x (ISBN 0-226-90500-4, P90, Phoen). U of Chicago Pr.

INDIANS OF MEXICO-AGRICULTURE

Collier, George A. Fields of the Tzotzil: The Ecological Bases of Tradition in Highland Chiapas. LC 75-12840. (Texas Pan American Ser.). (Illus.). 270p. 1975. 15.00x (ISBN 0-292-72412-8). U of Tex Pr.
Harrison, Peter D. & Turner, B. L., II, eds. Pre-Hispanic Maya Agriculture. LC 78-55703. (Illus.). 414p. 1978. 20.00x (ISBN 0-8263-0483-4). U of NM Pr.

INDIANS OF MEXICO-ANTIQUITIES

Blanton, Richard E., ed. Monte Alban: Settlement Patterns at the Ancient Zapotec Capital. (Studies in Archaeology Ser). 1978. 25.50 (ISBN 0-12-104250-2). Acad Pr.
Bowen, Thomas. Seri Prehistory: The Archaeology of the Central Coast of Sonora, Mexico. LC 74-29360. (Anthropological Papers: No. 27). 1976. pap. 4.95x (ISBN 0-8165-0358-3). U of Ariz Pr.
Charnay, Desire. The Ancient Cities of the New World: Being Voyages & Explorations in Mexico & Central America from 1857 to 1882. Gonina, J. & Conant, Helen S., trs. from Fr. LC 72-5004. (Antiquities of the New World: Vol. 10). (Illus.). Repr. of 1887 ed. 40.00 (ISBN 0-404-57310-X). AMS Pr.
De Sahagun, Bernardino. Florentine Codex, General History of the Things of New Spain, 12 bks. Anderson, Arthur J. & Dibble, Charles E., trs. Incl. Bk. 1. Gods. 15.00x (ISBN 0-87480-000-5); Bk. 2. Ceremonies. 40.00x (ISBN 0-87480-194-X); Bk. 3. Origin of the Gods. 15.00x (ISBN 0-87480-002-1); Bks. 4 & 5. The Soothsayers, the Omens. 40.00x (ISBN 0-87480-003-X); Bk. 6. Rhetoric & Moral Philosophy. 40.00x (ISBN 0-87480-010-2); Bk. 7. Sun, Moon & Stars, & the Binding of the Years. 15.00x (ISBN 0-87480-004-8); Bk. 8. Kings & Lords. 20.00x (ISBN 0-87480-005-6); Bk. 9. Merchants. 15.00x (ISBN 0-87480-006-4); Bk. 10. People. 30.00x (ISBN 0-87480-007-2); Bk. 11. Earthly Things. 45.00x (ISBN 0-87480-008-0); Bk. 12. Conquest of Mexico. 25.00x (ISBN 0-87480-096-X). U of Utah Pr.
Field, Frederick V. Pre-Hispanic Mexican Stamp Designs. LC 73-89751. 220p. (Orig.). 1974. pap. 5.00 (ISBN 0-486-23039-2). Dover.
Hammond, Norman, ed. Mesoamerican Archaeology: New Approaches. (Illus.). 498p. 1974. 25.00x (ISBN 0-292-75008-0). U of Tex Pr.
Hewett, Edgar L. Ancient Life in Mexico & Central America. LC 67-29546. (Illus.). 1968. Repr. of 1936 ed. 15.00x (ISBN 0-8196-0205-1). Biblo.
Hunter, C. Bruce. A Guide to Ancient Mexican Ruins. (Illus.). 1977. 12.95 (ISBN 0-8061-1399-5); pap. 6.95 (ISBN 0-8061-1407-X). U of Okla Pr.
Kelly, Isabel T. Excavations at Apatzingan, Michoacan. (Illus.). 1947. pap. 15.50 (ISBN 0-384-29110-4). Johnson Repr.
Kendall, Aubyn, ed. The Art & Archaeology of Pre-Columbian Middle America. (Reference Publications Ser.). 1977. lib. bdg. 25.00 (ISBN 0-8161-8093-8). G K Hall.
Millon, Rene, ed. Urbanization at Teotihuacan, Mexico, Vol. 1, Pts. 1 & 2: The Teotihuacan Map. LC 72-7588. (Illus.). 333p. 1973. 75.00x (ISBN 0-292-78501-1). U of Tex Pr.
Paddock, John, ed. Ancient Oaxaca: Discoveries in Mexican Archeology & History. (Illus.). 1966. 25.00 (ISBN 0-8047-0170-9). Stanford U Pr.
Pasztory, Esther, ed. Middle Classic Mesoamerica: 400-700 A. D. (Illus.). 197p. 1978. 25.00x (ISBN 0-231-04270-1). Columbia U Pr.
Sanders, William T. & Price, Barbara J. Mesoamerica: The Evolution of a Civilization. (Orig.). 1968. pap. text ed. 9.95x (ISBN 0-394-30789-5, RanC). Random.
Spinden, Herbert J. Ancient Civilizations of Mexico & Central America. 3rd rev. ed. LC 67-29554. (Illus.). 1968. Repr. of 1928 ed. 10.50x (ISBN 0-8196-0215-9). Biblo.

INDIANS OF MEXICO-ARCHITECTURE

Totten, George O. Maya Architecture. LC 71-122845. (Research & Source Works Ser.: No. 513). 1971. Repr. of 1926 ed. lib. bdg. 76.50 (ISBN 0-8337-3560-8). B Franklin.

INDIANS OF MEXICO-ARMS AND ARMOR

see also Throwing Sticks

INDIANS OF MEXICO-ART

see also Aztecs-Art; Indians of Mexico-Sculpture

Benson, Elizabeth P. An Olmec Figure at Dumbarton Oaks. LC 70-184640. (Studies in Pre-Columbian Art & Archaeology: No. 8). (Illus.). 95p. 1971. pap. 4.00x (ISBN 0-88402-035-5, Ctr Pre-Columbian). Dumbarton Oaks.
Berrin, Kathleen & Seligman, Thomas K.intro. by. Art of the Huichol Indians. (Illus.). 1978. 22.50 (ISBN 0-8109-0685-6); pap. 9.25 o. p. (ISBN 0-8109-2160-X). Abrams.
Enciso, Jorge. Design Motifs of Ancient Mexico. (Illus.). 1947. pap. 3.50 (ISBN 0-486-20084-1). Dover.
--Designs from Pre-Columbian Mexico. 1971. pap. 2.25 (ISBN 0-486-22794-4). Dover.
Field, Frederick V. Pre-Hispanic Mexican Stamp Designs. LC 73-89751. 220p. (Orig.). 1974. pap. 5.00 (ISBN 0-486-23039-2). Dover.
Kendall, Aubyn, ed. The Art & Archaeology of Pre-Columbian Middle America. (Reference Publications Ser.). 1977. lib. bdg. 25.00 (ISBN 0-8161-8093-8). G K Hall.
Oglesby, Catharine. Modern Primitive Arts of Mexico, Guatemala & the Southwest. facs. ed. LC 75-90670. (Essay Index Reprint Ser). 1939. 16.00 (ISBN 0-8369-1215-2). Arno.
Ranney, Edward. Stonework of the Maya. LC 73-82769. (Illus.). 119p. 1974. pap. 9.95x (ISBN 0-8263-0277-7). U of NM Pr.
Shao, Paul. Asiatic Influences in Pre-Columbian American Art. (Illus.). 1976. 28.50x (ISBN 0-8138-1855-9). Iowa St U Pr.
Stump, Sarain. There Is My People Sleeping. (Illus.). 200p. 1970. pap. 2.95 (ISBN 0-686-74147-1). Superior Pub.
Twenty Centuries of Mexican Art. LC 79-169322. (Museum of Modern Art in Reprint Ser.). (Illus.). 200p. 1972. Repr. of 1940 ed. 23.00 (ISBN 0-405-01580-1). Arno.
Von Winning, Hasso. Pre-Columbian Art of Mexico & Central America. LC 68-13065. (History of World Architecture Ser.). (Illus.). 1968. 45.00 (ISBN 0-8109-0423-3); ltd. ed. leather bd 125.00 (ISBN 0-8109-4751-X). Abrams.

INDIANS OF MEXICO-COSTUME AND ADORNMENT

see also Indians of Mexico-Art

Cordry, Donald & Cordry, Dorothy. Mexican Indian Costumes. (Texas Pan American Ser.). (Illus.). 1968. 39.95 (ISBN 0-292-73426-3). U of Tex Pr.

INDIANS OF MEXICO-ECONOMIC CONDITIONS

Sabloff, Jeremy A. & Rathje, William L., eds. A Study of Changing Pre-Columbian Commercial Systems: Cozumel, Mexico. LC 75-20624. (Peabody Museum Monographs: No. 3). 1975. pap. 12.00 (ISBN 0-87365-902-3). Peabody Harvard.

INDIANS OF MEXICO-ETHNOLOGY

see Indians of Mexico

INDIANS OF MEXICO-FICTION

Parsons, Elsie C., ed. American Indian Life. LC 22-16158. (Illus.). 1967. 21.50x (ISBN 0-8032-3651-4); pap. 4.50 (ISBN 0-8032-5148-3, BB 364, Bison). U of Nebr Pr.

INDIANS OF MEXICO-FOLK-LORE

see Folk-Lore, Indian

INDIANS OF MEXICO–GOVERNMENT RELATIONS

see also Indians, Treatment Of

Barsh, Russel L. & Henderson, J. Youngblood. The Road: Indian Tribes & Political Liberty. 1980. 14.95x (ISBN 0-520-03629-8). U. of Cal Pr.

Iwanska, Alicja. The Truths of Others: An Essay on Nativistic Intellectuals in Mexico. LC 76-40139. (Illus.). 128p. 1978. 13.25x (ISBN 0-87073-558-6); pap. text ed. 7.95x (ISBN 0-87073-559-4). Schenkman.

INDIANS OF MEXICO–HISTORY

Beals, Ralph L. The Aboriginal Culture of the Cahita Indians. LC 76-43657. (Ibero-Americana Ser.: 19). Repr. of 1943 ed. 14.50 (ISBN 0-404-15490-5). AMS Pr.

Enock, C. Reginald. The Secret of the Pacific: Origins of the Toltecs, Aztecs, Mayas, & Incas. 1977. lib. bdg. 59.95 (ISBN 0-8490-2584-2). Gordon Pr.

Jenkins, Myra E. Tigua Indians of Ysleta Del Sur in New Mexico: History & Administration During the Spanish Colonial Period. (Library of American Indian Affairs). 65p. 1974. lib. bdg. 28.50 (ISBN 0-8287-1272-7). Clearwater Pub.

Montez, Philip. Some Differences in Factors Related to Educational Achievement of Two Mexican-American Groups: Thesis. LC 74-76669. 1974. Repr. of 1960 ed. soft bdg. 7.00 (ISBN 0-88247-277-1). R & E Res Assoc.

Motolinia, Toribio. History of the Indians of New Spain. Foster, Elizabeth A., tr. LC 73-8449. (Illus.). 294p. 1973. Repr. of 1950 ed. lib. bdg. 19.75x (ISBN 0-8371-6977-1, MONS). Greenwood.

Sabloff, Jeremy A. & Rathje, William L., eds. A Study of Changing Pre-Columbian Commercial Systems: Cozumel, Mexico. LC 75-20624. (Peabody Museum Monographs: No. 3). 1975. pap. 12.00 (ISBN 0-87365-902-3). Peabody Harvard.

Spores, Ronald. Mixtec Kings & Their People. (Civilization of the American Indian Ser.: No. 85). (Illus.). 1967. 14.95 (ISBN 0-8061-0726-X). U of Okla Pr.

INDIANS OF MEXICO–LANGUAGES

see also Aztec Language; Maya Language; Mazateco Language; Papago Language; Popoluca Language (Vera Cruz); Tarascan Language

Daly, John P. A Generative Syntax of Penoles Mixtec. (Publications in Linguistics Ser.: No. 42). 1973. pap. 4.00x (ISBN 0-88312-052-6); microfiche 1.00 (ISBN 0-88312-452-1). Summer Inst Ling.

Day, Christopher. The Jacaltec Language. (Language Science Monographs: Vol. 12). viii, 136p. (Orig.). 1973. pap. text ed. 8.00x (ISBN 0-87750-176-9). Res Ctr Lang Semiotic.

Pike, Kenneth L. Tone Languages: A Technique for Determining the Number & Type of Pitch Contrasts in a Language, with Studies in Tonemic Substitution & Fusion. 1948. pap. 6.95x (ISBN 0-472-08734-7). U of Mich Pr.

Pride, Kitty. Chatino Syntax. (Publications in Linguistics & Related Fields Ser.: No. 12). 248p. 1965. microfiche 2.00 (ISBN 0-88312-412-2). Summer Inst Ling.

Reid, et al. Diccionario Totonaco de Xicotepec de Juarez. (Vocabularios Indigenas Ser.: No. 17). 1974. pap. 12.00x (ISBN 0-88312-752-0); microfiche 3.40 (ISBN 0-88312-552-8). Summer Inst Ling.

Sauer, Carl O. The Distribution of Aboriginal Tribes & Languages in Northwestern Mexico. LC 76-43818. (Ibero-Americana: 5). Repr. of 1934 ed. 13.75 (ISBN 0-404-15671-1). AMS Pr.

Swanton, John R. Linguistic Material from the Tribes of Southern Texas & Northeastern Mexico. Repr. of 1940 ed. 25.00 (ISBN 0-403-03631-3). Scholarly.

Thomas, Cyrus. Indian Languages of Mexico & Central America & Their Geographical Distribution. Repr. of 1911 ed. 17.00 (ISBN 0-403-03612-7). Scholarly.

--Indian Languages of Mexico & Central America. Repr. of 1911 ed. pap. 17.00 (ISBN 0-8466-4042-2, SJ142). Shorey.

Turner, Paul & Turner, Shirley. Dictionary of Chontal to Spanish-English, & Spanish to Chontal. LC 78-164366. 1971. pap. 3.95x (ISBN 0-8165-0338-9). U of Ariz Pr.

INDIANS OF MEXICO–LEGENDS

see also Folk-Lore, Indian

Anaya, Rudolfo A. Heart of Aztlan. LC 76-55065. 1976. 7.50 (ISBN 0-915808-17-X); pap. 4.50 (ISBN 0-685-78786-9). Editorial Justa.

Baker, Betty. No Help at All. LC 76-13223. (Greenwillow Read-Alone Bks.). (Illus.). (gr. 1-4). 1978. 5.95 (ISBN 0-688-80056-4); PLB 5.71 (ISBN 0-688-84056-6). Greenwillow.

Beals, Carleton. Stories Told by the Aztecs: Before the Spaniards Came. LC 77-95140. (Illus.). (gr. 7 up). 1970. 8.95 (ISBN 0-200-71636-0, B79170, AbS-J). Har-Row.

Boyd, Maurice. Tarascan Myths & Legends. LC 68-59408. (History & Culture Monograph Ser. No. 4). 1969. 4.50 (ISBN 0-912646-09-8). Tex Christian.

Giddings, Ruth W. Yaqui Myths & Legends. LC 60-63129. (Illus.). 1968. pap. 3.95 (ISBN 0-8165-0467-9). U of Ariz Pr.

INDIANS OF MEXICO–MISSIONS

Aschmann, Homer. Central Desert of Baja California: Demography & Ecology. LC 66-29636. (Illus.). 1967. lib. bdg. 49.50x (ISBN 0-910950-01-6). Manessier.

Braden, Charles S. Religious Aspects of the Conquest of Mexico. LC 74-181914. Repr. of 1930 ed. 19.50 (ISBN 0-404-00925-5). AMS Pr.

Dunner, Peter M. Pioneer Jesuits in Northern Mexico. LC 78-10566. (Illus.). 1979. Repr. of 1944 ed. lib. bdg. 20.25x (ISBN 0-313-20653-8, DUPJ). Greenwood.

Shiels, William E. Gonzalo De Tapia, 1561-1594: Founder of the First Permanent Jesuit Mission in North America. LC 74-12835. (U.S. Catholic Historical Society Monograph: No. XIV). 1978. Repr. of 1934 ed. lib. bdg. 18.50x (ISBN 0-8371-7758-8, SHGT). Greenwood.

INDIANS OF MEXICO–ORIGIN

see Indians–Origin

INDIANS OF MEXICO–POTTERY

Brenner, Anita. Influence of Technique on the Decorative Style in the Domestic Pottery of Culhuacan. LC 78-82356. (Columbia Univ. Contributions to Anthropology Ser.: Vol. 13). Repr. of 1931 ed. 14.50 (ISBN 0-404-50563-5). AMS Pr.

Gilpin, Laura. Indian Arts Fund Collection. (Illus.). 1970. 3.50 (ISBN 0-89013-042-6). Museum NM Pr.

Stirling, Matthew W. Stone Monuments of Southern Mexico. Repr. of 1943 ed. 19.00 (ISBN 0-403-03697-6). Scholarly.

INDIANS OF MEXICO–RELIGION AND MYTHOLOGY

see also Mayas–Religion and Mythology

Alexander, Hartley B. Latin American Mythology. LC 63-19096. (Mythology of All Races Ser.: Vol. 11). (Illus.). 1964. Repr. of 1932 ed. 25.00x (ISBN 0-8154-0006-3). Cooper Sq.

Aveni, Anthony F. Skywatchers of Ancient Mexico. (Texas Pan American Ser.). (Illus.). 369p. 1980. text ed. 30.00x (ISBN 0-292-77557-1); pap. 6.95 cancelled (ISBN 0-292-77557-1). U of Tex Pr.

Benitez, Fernando. In the Magic Land of Peyote. Upton, John, tr. from Span. LC 74-23171. (Texas Pan American Ser). (Illus.). 226p. 1975. 11.95 (ISBN 0-292-73806-4). U of Tex Pr.

Braden, Charles S. Religious Aspects of the Conquest of Mexico. LC 74-181914. Repr. of 1930 ed. 19.50 (ISBN 0-404-00925-5). AMS Pr.

Brenner, Anita. Idols Behind Altars. LC 67-19527. (Illus.). 1929. 18.00x (ISBN 0-8196-0190-X). Biblo.

Caso, Alfonso. Aztecs, People of the Sun. Dunham, Lowell, tr. (Civilization of the American Indian Ser.: No. 50). (Illus.). 1978. Repr. of 1958 ed. 16.95 (ISBN 0-8061-0414-7). U of Okla Pr.

Castaneda, Carlos. A Separate Reality. (gr. 10-12). 1976. pap. 2.50 (ISBN 0-671-83132-1). PB.

--The Teachings of Don Juan. 1976. pap. 2.50 (ISBN 0-671-82767-7). PB.

--The Teachings of Don Juan: A Yaqui Way of Knowledge. LC 68-17303. 1968. 12.95x (ISBN 0-520-00217-2); pap. 3.95 (ISBN 0-520-02258-0, CAL253). U of Cal Pr.

Hunt, Eva. Transformation of the Hummingbird: Cultural Roots of a Zinacantecan Mythical Poem. LC 76-12909. (Symbol, Myth, & Ritual Ser.). (Illus.). 1977. 25.00x (ISBN 0-8014-1022-3). Cornell U Pr.

Nuttall, Zelia. Penitential Rite of the Ancient Mexicans. 1904. pap. 3.00 (ISBN 0-527-01189-4). Kraus Repr.

Sahagun, Fray B. A History of Ancient Mexico, 1547-1577: The Religion & the Ceremonies of the Aztec Indians. Bandelier, Fanny, tr. from Sp. LC 76-27292. (Beautiful Rio Grande Classics Ser). 1976. lib. bdg. 15.00 (ISBN 0-87380-133-4). Rio Grande.

Sandstrom, Alan. Traditional Curing & Crop Fertility Rituals Among Otomi Indians of the Sierra De Puebla, Mexico: The Lopez Manuscripts. (University Museum Occasional Papers & Monographs: No. 3). (Illus.). vi, 104p. 1981. write for info. (ISBN 0-9605982-0-0). Ind U Mus.

Spence, Lewis. Myths of Mexico & Peru. 1976. lib. bdg. 60.00 (ISBN 0-8490-0700-3). Gordon Pr.

--The Myths of Mexico & Peru. LC 76-27516. (Illus.). 1976. Repr. of 1914 ed. lib. bdg. 45.00 (ISBN 0-89341-031-4). Longwood Pr.

Vogt, Evon Z. Tortillas for the Gods: A Symbolic Analysis of Zinacanteco Rituals. 256p. 1976. 16.50x (ISBN 0-674-89554-1). Harvard U Pr.

INDIANS OF MEXICO–SCULPTURE

Aztec Stone Sculpture. (Illus.). 1976. pap. 4.00 (ISBN 0-89192-166-4, Dist. by Interbook). Ctr Inter-Am Rel.

Kampen, Michael E. The Sculptures of el Tajin, Veracruz, Mexico. LC 71-119809. (Illus.). 208p. 1972. 12.50 (ISBN 0-8130-0306-7). U Presses Fla.

INDIANS OF MEXICO–SOCIAL LIFE AND CUSTOMS

Bernal, Ignacio. The Olmec World. Heyden, Doris & Horcasitas, Fernando, trs. (Illus.). 1969. pap. 7.95 (ISBN 0-520-02891-0). U of Cal Pr.

Bricker, Victoria R. Ritual Humor in Highland Chiapas. LC 73-6501. (Texas Pan American Ser). (Illus.). 278p. 1973. 17.50x (ISBN 0-292-77004-9). U of Tex Pr.

Collier, George A. Fields of the Tzotzil: The Ecological Bases of Tradition in Highland Chiapas. LC 75-12840. (Texas Pan American Ser.). (Illus.). 270p. 1975. 15.00x (ISBN 0-292-72412-8). U of Tex Pr.

Dellenbaugh, Frederick S. The North-Americans of Yesterday: A Comparative Study of North-American Indian Life, Customs, & Products, on the Theory of the Ethnic Unity of Race. LC 74-7950. (Illus.). Repr. of 1906 ed. 44.50 (ISBN 0-404-11837-2). AMS Pr.

Haviland, John B. Gossip, Reputation, & Knowledge in Zinacantan. LC 76-8095. (Illus.). 1977. lib. bdg. 20.00x (ISBN 0-226-31955-5). U of Chicago Pr.

Morgan, Lewis H. Montezuma's Dinner. 2nd ed. 1967. pap. text ed. 0.75 (ISBN 0-935534-21-0). NY Labor News.

Salcedo, Consuelo. Mexican-American Socio-Cultural Patterns: Implications for Social Casework. LC 74-77165. 1974. Repr. of 1955 ed. soft bdg. 7.00 (ISBN 0-88247-275-5). R & E Res Assoc.

Spicer, Edward H. The Yaquis: A Cultural History. LC 79-27660. 1980. 28.50x (ISBN 0-8165-0589-6); pap. 14.50x (ISBN 0-8165-0588-8). U of Ariz Pr.

INDIANS OF NORTH AMERICA

Here are entered works on the Indians of North America in general. For works of specific tribes or groups of tribes see subdivisions–Eastern States,–Northwest, Pacific,–Southwest, New,–Southwest, Old,–The West.

see also Aleuts; Eskimos; Ethnology–North America; Mound-Builders

Abel, Annie H. The American Indian As Participant in the Civil War. LC 19-5303. (American Studies). Repr. of 1919 ed. 16.00 (ISBN 0-384-00080-0). Johnson Repr.

--History of Events Resulting in Indian Consolidation West of the Mississippi. LC 76-158219. Repr. of 1908 ed. 14.50 (ISBN 0-404-07116-3). AMS Pr.

Alexander, Hartley B. World's Rim: Great Mysteries of the North American Indians. LC 53-7703. (Illus.). xx, 259p. 1967. pap. 4.95 (ISBN 0-8032-5003-7, BB160, Bison). U of Nebr Pr.

American Indian Publishers, ed. Dictionary of Indian Tribes of the Americas, 4 vols. (Illus.). 1980. Set. lib. bdg. 225.00 (ISBN 0-937862-25-8). Am Indian Pubs.

Axtell, James, ed. The Indian Peoples of Eastern America: A Documentary History of the Sexes. (Illus.). 256p. 1981. text ed. 11.95x (ISBN 0-19-502740-X); pap. text ed. 6.95x (ISBN 0-19-502741-8). Oxford U Pr.

--The Native American People of the East. new ed. LC 72-95875. (American People Ser.). 126p. (Orig.). (gr. 9-12). 1973. PLB 7.95 (ISBN 0-88301-083-6); pap. 2.50 (ISBN 0-88301-067-4). Pendulum Pr.

Bailey, M. Thomas. Reconstruction in Indian Territory. LC 77-189551. 1972. 13.50 (ISBN 0-8046-9022-7). Kennikat.

Baker, Jim. Ways of the Warriors: Indians of the Field & Forest. 2nd ed. LC 75-14774. (Jim Baker's Historical Handbooks). (Illus.). 64p. (gr. 5-12). 1975. pap. 1.50 (ISBN 0-914482-09-2). Ohio Hist Soc.

Bancroft, Hubert H. The Native Races, 5 vols. LC 67-29422. (Works of Hubert Howe Bancroft Ser.). 1967. Repr. of 1888 ed. Set. 125.00x (ISBN 0-914888-00-5). Bancroft Pr.

Barrows, William. The Indian's Side of the Indian Question. LC 72-5517. (Select Bibliographies Reprint Ser.). 1972. Repr. of 1887 ed. 13.00 (ISBN 0-8369-6895-6). Arno.

Basso, Keith H. & Opler, Morris, eds. Apachean Culture History & Ethnology. LC 70-140453. (Anthropological Papers: No. 21). (Illus.). 172p. (Orig.). 1971. pap. 6.95x (ISBN 0-8165-0295-1). U of Ariz Pr.

--Apachean Culture History & Ethnology. LC 70-140453. (Anthropological Papers: No. 21). (Illus.). 172p. (Orig.). 1971. pap. 6.95x (ISBN 0-8165-0295-1). U of Ariz Pr.

Beals, Ralph L. The Ethnology of the Western Mixe. LC 73-75846. (Illus.). 175p. 1973. Repr. of 1945 ed. lib. bdg. 11.50x (ISBN 0-8154-0481-6). Cooper Sq.

Beckwourth, James P. & Bonner, Thomas D. The Life & Adventures of James P. Beckwourth. LC 73-88092. (Illus.). xvi, 649p. 1972. pap. 10.95 (ISBN 0-8032-0724-7) (ISBN 0-8032-6061-X, BB 773, Bison). U of Nebr Pr.

Bell, Robert E. Wichita Indians: Wichita Indian Archaeology & Ethnology: a Pilot Study. Horr, David A., ed. (Plains Indians - American Indian Ethnohistory Ser.). 1974. lib. bdg. 42.00 (ISBN 0-8240-0770-0). Garland Pub.

Berkhofer, Robert F., Jr. The White Man's Indian: Images of the American Indian from Columbus to the Present. LC 78-11047. (Illus.). 1979. pap. 4.95 (ISBN 0-394-72794-0, V-794, Vin). Random.

Beuf, Ann H. Red Children in White America. LC 76-49737. 168p. 1977. 12.00x (ISBN 0-8122-7719-8). U of Pa Pr.

Bissell, Benjamin H. American Indian in English Literature of the Eighteenth Century. (Yale Studies in English Ser.: No. 68). (Illus.). 1968. Repr. of 1925 ed. 17.50 (ISBN 0-208-00710-5, Archon). Shoe String.

Black, Nancy B. & Weidman, Bette S., eds. White on Red: Images of the American Indian. 1976. 17.50 (ISBN 0-8046-9084-7, Natl U). Kennikat.

Blu, Karen. The Lumbee Problem. LC 79-12908. (Cambridge Studies of Cultural Systems). (Illus.). 1980. 24.50 (ISBN 0-521-22525-6); pap. 6.95 (ISBN 0-521-29542-4). Cambridge U Pr.

Boas, Franz. Ethnography of Franz Boas: Letters & Diaries of Franz Boas Written on the Northwest Coast from 1886-1931. Rohner, Ronald P., ed. LC 70-77152. (Illus.). 1969. 13.00x (ISBN 0-226-06238-4). U of Chicago Pr.

Boesen, Victor & Graybill, Florence C. Edward S. Curtis: Photographer of the North American Indian. LC 76-53435. (gr. 7 up). 1977. 6.95 (ISBN 0-396-07430-8). Dodd.

Boring, Mel. Wovoka. LC 80-24003. (Story of an American Indian Ser.). (Illus.). 64p. (gr. 5 up). 1981. PLB 6.95 (ISBN 0-87518-179-1). Dillon.

Brantley, W. H., ed. Battle of Horseshoe Bend. 1955. pap. 3.50 (ISBN 0-87651-205-8). Southern U Pr.

Brookings Institution. The Problem of Indian Administration. 1971. Repr. of 1928 ed. 50.00 (ISBN 0-384-05920-1). Johnson Repr.

Brown, G. B. The Unknown Indian. 1977. lib. bdg. 59.95 (ISBN 0-8490-2789-6). Gordon Pr.

Brush, Helen N. & Dittman, Catherine P. Indian Hills: The Place, the Times, the People. Anderson, Elizabeth S., ed. LC 75-40516. (Illus.). 128p. 1976. 12.95 (ISBN 0-914628-03-8). Graphic Impress.

Capps, B. The Indians. LC 72-93991. (Old West Ser). (Illus.). (gr. 5 up). 1973. (Pub. by Time-Life). Silver.

Castile, George. North American Indians: An Introduction to the Chichimeca. (Illus.). 1978. text ed. 13.95 (ISBN 0-07-010233-3, C). McGraw.

Catlin, George. Letters & Notes on the Manners, Customs & Conditions of the North American Indians, Vol. 1. LC 64-18844. (Illus.). 264p. 1973. pap. 5.50 (ISBN 0-486-22118-0). Dover.

--Letters & Notes on the Manners, Customs & Conditions of the North American Indians, Vol. 2. LC 64-18844. (Illus.). 266p. 1973. pap. 5.50 (ISBN 0-486-22119-9). Dover.

--Life Among the Indians. 1977. Repr. 39.00 (ISBN 0-403-07273-5). Scholarly.

Champlain, Samuel. Voyages of Samuel De Champlain, 3 Vols. Slafter, Edmund F., ed. Otis, Charles P., tr. (Illus.). Set. 62.00 (ISBN 0-8337-3287-0). B Franklin.

Claiborne, Robert. The First Americans. (Emergence of Man Ser). (Illus.). 170p. 1973. 9.95 (ISBN 0-8094-1267-5); lib. bdg. avail. (ISBN 0-685-31460-X). Time-Life.

Cohn, Edgar, ed. Our Brother's Keeper: The Indian in White America. pap. 4.95 (ISBN 0-452-00557-4, F557, Mer). NAL.

Colton, Harold S. Black Sand: Prehistory in Northern Arizona. LC 73-13454. (Illus.). 132p. 1974. Repr. of 1960 ed. lib. bdg. 15.00x (ISBN 0-8371-7137-7, COBS). Greenwood.

Constitutions and Laws of the American Indian Tribes, Ser. 1, 20 vols. 1973. Repr. Set. 412.00 (ISBN 0-8420-2100-0). Scholarly Res Inc.

Constitutions and Laws of the American Indian Tribes Ser. 2, 33 vols. 1975. Repr. Set. 460.00 (ISBN 0-8420-2101-9). Scholarly Res Inc.

Corruccini, Robert S., et al, eds. Anthropological Studies Related to Health Problems of North American Indians. LC 74-5180. (American Indian Health Ser.: Vol. 4). 148p. 1974. text ed. 19.00x (ISBN 0-8422-7157-0). Irvington.

Craven, Wesley F. White, Red, & Black: The Seventeenth-Century Virginian. 1977. pap. 2.95x (ISBN 0-393-00857-6, N857, Norton Lib). Norton.

Crump, Spencer. California's Spanish Missions: An Album of Their Yesterdays and Todays. LC 73-88320. (Illus.). 96p. (Orig.). 1975. 10.00 (ISBN 0-87046-028-5). Trans-Anglo.

Curtis, Edward S. The North American Indian, Being a Series of Volumes Picturing & Describing the Indians of the U. S. & Alaska, 20 Vols., Supplement to Vol. 1-20 in 4 Vols, Vols. 4-8, 10-16, 18, 19. (Reprint, Orig, Pub, 1907-1930). 1970. Set. write for info. (ISBN 0-384-10395-2); 40.00 ea.; supplements 50.00 ea. Johnson Repr.
Curtis, William E. Children of the Sun. LC 74-7946. Repr. of 1883 ed. 15.00 (ISBN 0-404-11833-X). AMS Pr.
David, Jay, ed. The American Indian: The First Victim. 1972. pap. 3.50 (ISBN 0-688-06030-7). Morrow.
De Laguna, Frederica. The Story of a Tlingit Community: Problem in the Relationship Between Archaeological, Ethnological & Historical Methods. Repr. of 1960 ed. 21.00 (ISBN 0-403-03698-4). Scholarly.
Dellenbaugh, F. S. The North Americans of Yesterday. 1977. lib. bdg. 69.95 (ISBN 0-8490-2351-3). Gordon Pr.
Densmore, Frances. How Indians Use Wild Plants for Food, Medicine & Crafts. (Illus.). 162p. 1974. pap. 3.00 (ISBN 0-486-23019-8). Dover.
De Schweinitz, Edmund. Life & Times of David Zeisberger the Western Pioneer & Apostle of the Indians. LC 70-146391. (First American Frontier Ser). 1971. Repr. of 1870 ed. 32.00 (ISBN 0-405-02844-X). Arno.
De Smet, P. J. Life, Letters, & Travels, Eighteen Hundred One to Eighteen Seventy Three, 4 Vols. in 2. 1905. Set. 60.00 (ISBN 0-527-83900-0). Kraus Repr.
Dixon, Joseph. Vanishing Race; Little Big Horn. LC 72-13439. (Beautiful Rio Grande Classics Ser). lib. bdg. 20.00 (ISBN 0-87380-100-8). Rio Grande.
Dobie, J. Frank. Apache Gold & Yaqui Silver. LC 76-21512. (Zia Books). (Illus.). 384p. 1976. pap. 6.95 (ISBN 0-8263-0434-6). U of NM Pr.
Dodge, Richard I. Our Wild Indians, Etc. 1977. Repr. 49.00 (ISBN 0-403-08281-1). Scholarly.
Drake, Samuel G. The Book of the Indians. LC 74-7960. Repr. of 1841 ed. 49.00 (ISBN 0-404-11848-8). AMS Pr.
Drinnon, Richard. Facing West: The Metaphysics of Indian-Hating & Empire-Building. 1980. pap. 8.95 (ISBN 0-452-00541-8, F541, Mer). NAL.
Driver, Harold E. Indians of North America. 2nd rev. ed. LC 79-76207. (Illus.). 1969. 25.00x (ISBN 0-226-16466-7). U of Chicago Pr.
Driver, Harold E. & Coffin, James L. Classification & Development of North American Indian Cultures: A Statistical Analysis of the Driver-Massey Sample. LC 75-2609. (Transactions Ser: Vol. 65, Pt. 3). (Illus.). 1975. pap. 7.00 (ISBN 0-87169-653-3). Am Philos.
Driver, Harold E. & Massey, William C. Comparative Studies of North American Indians. LC 57-11239. (Transactions Ser.: Vol. 47, Pt. 2). (Illus.). 1957. pap. 8.00 (ISBN 0-87169-472-7). Am Philos.
Dukepoo, Frank. The Elder American Indian. LC 77-83494. (Elder Minority Ser). 1978. 3.50x (ISBN 0-916304-33-7). Campanile.
Dunn, Lynn P. American Indians: A Study Guide & Source Book. LC 74-31618. 1975. soft bdg. 6.00 (ISBN 0-88247-305-0). R & E Res Assoc.
Eastman, Charles A. The Indian To-Day. LC 74-7962. Repr. of 1915 ed. 17.50 (ISBN 0-404-11851-8). AMS Pr.
Edmunds, R. David, ed. American Indian Leaders: Studies in Diversity. LC 80-431. (Illus.). xiv, 257p. 1980. 19.50x (ISBN 0-8032-1800-1); pap. 5.95 (ISBN 0-8032-6705-3, BB 746, Bison). U of Nebr Pr.
Erdoes, Richard. The Sun Dance People. (Illus.). 241p. Date not set. pap. 1.95 (ISBN 0-394-70803-2, Vin). Random.
--The Sun Dance People: The Plains Indians, Their Past & Present. LC 77-155812. (Illus.). 224p. (gr. 5-8). 1972. 5.95 (ISBN 0-394-82316-8); PLB 6.99 (ISBN 0-394-92316-2). Knopf.
Essays in Anthropology Presented to A. L. Kroeber in Celebration of His Sixtieth Birthday, June 11, 1936. facs. ed. LC 68-20297. (Essay Index Reprint Ser). 1936. 21.50 (ISBN 0-8369-0422-2). Arno.
Fahey, John. The Flathead Indians. LC 73-7420. (Civilization of the American Indian Ser.: Vol. 130). (Illus.). 350p. 1974. 15.95 (ISBN 0-8061-1126-7). U of Okla Pr.
Farb, Peter. Man's Rise to Civilization: The Cultural Ascent of the Indians of North America. 2nd rev. ed. 1978. 15.00 (ISBN 0-525-15270-9). Dutton.
Fewkes, Jesse W. Preliminary Report on a Visit to the Navaho National Monument, Arizona. Repr. of 1911 ed. 19.00 (ISBN 0-403-03691-7). Scholarly.
Filson, John. Discovery, Settlement & Present State of Kentucke. 7.00 (ISBN 0-8446-2058-0). Peter Smith.
The Flood. (Indian Culture Ser.). 1976. 1.95 (ISBN 0-89992-020-9). MT Coun Indian.
Foreman, Grant. Indian Removal: The Emigration of the Five Civilized Tribes of Indians. (Civilization of the American Indian Ser.: Vol. 2). (Illus.). 434p. 1976. 16.95 (ISBN 0-8061-0019-2); pap. 8.95 (ISBN 0-8061-1172-0). U of Okla Pr.
Franklin, Paula. Indians of North America: Survey of Tribes That Inhabit the Continent. (Illus.). 1979. 9.95 (ISBN 0-679-20700-7). McKay.
Gaddis, Vincent H. American Indian Myths & Mysteries. LC 76-51215. 1977. 8.95 (ISBN 0-8019-6409-1). Chilton.
Garbarino, Merwyn S. Native American Heritage. (Illus.). 1976. 17.95 (ISBN 0-316-30120-5). Little.
Gidley, Mick, ed. The Vanishing Race: Selections from Edward S. Curtis' the North American Indian. LC 76-23476. (Illus.). 1977. 9.95 (ISBN 0-8008-7945-7). Taplinger.
Gifford, E. W. The Kamia of Imperial Valley. Repr. of 1931 ed. 19.00 (ISBN 0-403-03622-4). Scholarly.
Gilles, Albert S., Sr. Comanche Days. LC 74-77543. (Bicentennial Series in American Studies: No. 3). 1974. 6.95 (ISBN 0-87074-139-X). SMU Press.
Goodwin, Grenville. Western Apache Raiding & Warfare. Basso, Keith H., ed. LC 73-142255. 1971. 10.00x (ISBN 0-8165-0345-1). U of Ariz Pr.
Grange, Roger T., Jr. Pawnee & Lower Loup Pottery. (Publications in Anthropology: No. 3). 1968. pap. 6.00 (ISBN 0-686-20020-9). Nebraska Hist.
Graves, John. The Last Running. (Illus.). 48p. 1974. 9.50 (ISBN 0-88426-036-4). Encino Pr.
Grey Owl & Little Pigeon. Cry of the Ancients. 1974. 8.00 (ISBN 0-8309-0108-6). Herald Hse.
Grinnell, George B. The Indians of Today. LC 74-7970. (Illus.). Repr. of 1911 ed. 34.50 (ISBN 0-404-11857-7). AMS Pr.
Grisham, Noel. A Serpent for a Dove: The Suppression of the American Indian. (Illus.). 168p. 7.50 (ISBN 0-8363-0089-0). Jenkins.
Hallowell, Alfred I. Role of Conjuring in Saulteaux Society. LC 78-120622. 1970. Repr. lib. bdg. 10.50x (ISBN 0-374-93405-3). Octagon.
Hanks, Lucien M., Jr. & Hanks, Jane R. Tribe under Trust: A Study of the Blackfoot Reserve of Alberta. LC 51-4918. 206p. 1950. 15.00x (ISBN 0-8020-7016-7). U of Toronto Pr.
Hawkins, Benjamin. A Sketch of the Creek Country in the Years 1798 & 1799. Bd. with Letters of Benjamin Hawkins, 1796-1806. LC 74-2200. (Illus.). 592p. 1974. Repr. of 1848 ed. 22.50 (ISBN 0-87152-170-9). Reprint.
Heckewelder, John. History, Manners, & Customs of the Indian Nations Who Once Inhabited Pennsylvania & the Neighboring States. LC 75-146398. (First American Frontier Ser). (Illus.). 1971. Repr. of 1819 ed. 19.00 (ISBN 0-405-02853-9). Arno.
Heizer, Robert F., ed. California. (Handbook of North American Indians Ser.: Vol. 8). (Illus.). 800p. text ed. 13.50 (ISBN 0-87474-188-2). Smithsonian.
Heizer, Robert F. & Whipple, M. A., eds. The California Indians: A Source Book. 2nd rev. & enl. ed. LC 72-122951. (Illus.). 1971. 20.00x (ISBN 0-520-01770-6); pap. 7.95 (ISBN 0-520-02031-6, CAL231). U of Cal Pr.
Heline, Theodore. American Indian: Our Relations & Responsibilities. (Studies in This Changing World Ser). 1.00 (ISBN 0-87613-030-9). New Age.
Hertzberg, Hazel W. Search for an American Indian Identity: Modern Pan-Indian Movements. LC 77-140889. 1971. 16.95x (ISBN 0-8156-0076-3); pap. 10.95x (ISBN 0-8156-2245-7). Syracuse U Pr.
Higginbotham, Jay. The Mobile Indians. 1966. pap. 5.95 (ISBN 0-913208-02-7). Rockwell.
--The Pascagoula Indians. (Illus.). 1967. pap. 3.00 (ISBN 0-913208-03-5). Rockwell.
Highwater, Jamake. The Primal Mind: Vision & Reality in Indian America. LC 80-8929. 256p. 1981. 12.95 (ISBN 0-06-014866-7). Har-Row.
Hind, Henry Y. Explorations in the Interior of the Labrador Peninsula, the Country of the Montagnais & Nasquapee Indians. LC 73-12560. (Illus.). 1973. Repr. of 1863 ed. 34.00 (ISBN 0-527-40725-9). Kraus Repr.
Hodge, Frederick W., ed. Handbook of American Indians North of Mexico Nineteen Hundred & Seven to Nineteen Ten, 2 Vols. (Illus.). 1975. Repr. of 1910 ed. Set. 45.00x (ISBN 0-87471-004-9). Rowman.
--Handbook of the American Indians: North of Mexico, 2 vols. Repr. of 1912 ed. Set. lib. bdg. 90.25x (ISBN 0-8371-2509-X, HOAI). Greenwood.
Hodge, Frederick W. & Lewis, Theodore H., eds. Spanish Explorers in the Southern United States, 1528-1543. (Original Narratives). (Illus.). 1977. Repr. of 1907 ed. 18.50x (ISBN 0-06-480372-4). B&N.
Hodgson, Adam. Remarks During a Journey Through North America in the Years 1819, 1920 and 1921. LC 76-107479. Repr. of 1823 ed. 16.25x (ISBN 0-8371-3755-1). Greenwood.
Hoffman, Walter J. The Menomini Indians. (Landmarks in Anthropology Ser). (Illus.). 328p. Repr. of 1896 ed. 38.50 (ISBN 0-384-23920-X). Johnson Repr.
Hoyland, John S. Indian Crisis: The Background. facsimile ed. LC 77-140357. (Select Bibliographies Reprint Ser). Repr. of 1943 ed. 15.00 (ISBN 0-8369-5600-1). Arno.
Hudson, Charles. The Southeastern Indians. LC 75-30729. (Illus.). 1976. 25.00 (ISBN 0-87049-187-3); pap. 9.50x (ISBN 0-87049-248-9). U of Tenn Pr.
Hudson, Charles M. Catawba Nation. LC 75-119554. 136p. 1970. pap. 5.95x (ISBN 0-8203-0255-4). U of Ga Pr.
Hudson, Charles M., ed. Red, White, & Black: Symposium on Indians in the Old South. LC 70-156041. (Southern Anthropological Society Proceedings Ser: No. 5). 151p. 1971. pap. 5.25x (ISBN 0-8203-0308-9). U of Ga Pr.
Hundley, Norris, Jr., ed. The American Indian: Essays from the Pacific Historical Review. LC 74-76443. 151p. 1975. 21.75 (ISBN 0-87436-139-7); pap. text ed. 9.75 (ISBN 0-87436-140-0). ABC-Clio.
James, J. A. English Institutions & the American Indian. 1973. Repr. of 1894 ed. pap. 7.00 (ISBN 0-384-26743-2). Johnson Repr.
Johnston, Bernice. Speaking of Indians. LC 72-134776. 96p. 1970. pap. 3.95 (ISBN 0-8165-0257-9). U of Ariz Pr.
Jones, Peter. Life & Journals of Kah-Ke-Wa-Quo-Na-by. LC 76-43759. Repr. of 1860 ed. 26.00 (ISBN 0-404-15601-0). AMS Pr.
Jones, William. Ethnography of the Fox Indians. Repr. of 1939 ed. 19.00 (ISBN 0-403-03592-9). Scholarly.
Josephy, Alvin M., Jr. Indian Heritage of America. 1969. pap. 3.95 (ISBN 0-553-14978-4). Bantam.
Kehoe, Alice B. North American Indians: A Comprehensive Account. LC 80-22335. (Illus.). 564p. 1981. pap. text ed. 16.95 (ISBN 0-13-623652-9). P-H.
Kilpatrick, Jack F. & Kilpatrick, Anna G. Walk in Your Soul: Love Incantations of the Oklahoma Cherokees. LC 65-24931. 1965. 6.95 (ISBN 0-87074-085-7). SMU Press.
Kivett, Marvin F. Woodland Sites in Nebraska, Vol. 1. (Publications in Anthropology: No. 1). 1970. pap. 6.00 (ISBN 0-686-20023-3). Nebraska Hist.
Kraft, Herbert C., ed. A Delaware Indian Symposium. (Pennsylvania Historical & Museum Comm. Anthropological Ser., No. 4). (Illus.). 160p. 1974. 7.00 (ISBN 0-911124-77-2); pap. 4.00 (ISBN 0-911124-76-4). Pa Hist & Mus.
Kroeber, Alfred L. Native Tribes Map. pap. 2.25x (ISBN 0-520-00668-2). U of Cal Pr.
Kroeber, Theodora. Ishi in Two Worlds: A Biography of the Last Wild Indian in North America. LC 61-7530. (Illus.). 1961. 14.95 (ISBN 0-520-00674-7); pap. 3.95 (ISBN 0-520-00675-5, CAL94). U of Cal Pr.
Larson, Charles R. American Indian Fiction. LC 78-55698. 208p. 1978. 12.95x (ISBN 0-8263-0477-X). U of NM Pr.
Lauber, Almon W. Indian Slavery in Colonial Times Within the Present Limits of the United States. LC 71-77994. (Columbia University, Studies in the Social Sciences Ser.: No. 134). Repr. of 1913 ed. 11.50 (ISBN 0-404-51134-1). AMS Pr.
Leforge, Thomas H. Memoirs of a White Crow Indian. Marquis, Thomas B., narrated by. LC 74-6222. xxiv, 356p. 1974. 21.50x (ISBN 0-8032-0885-5); pap. 6.50 (ISBN 0-8032-5800-3, BB 584, Bison). U of Nebr Pr.
Leitch, Barbara A. A Concise Dictionary of Indian Tribes of North America. LePoer, Kendall, ed. LC 78-21347. 1980. 59.95 (ISBN 0-917256-09-3). Ref Pubns.
Lenarcic, R. J. As Long As the Grass Shall Grow. 1973. pap. text ed. 8.95x (ISBN 0-8422-0232-3). Irvington.
Leupp, Francis E. In Red Man's Land: A Study of the American Indian. LC 76-44529. (Beautiful Rio Grande Classics Ser). 1976. lib. bdg. 10.00 (ISBN 0-87380-140-7). Rio Grande.
--The Indian & His Problem. LC 10-8871. (American Studies). 1970. Repr. of 1910 ed. 18.50 (ISBN 0-384-32395-2). Johnson Repr.
Lindquist, Gustavus E. The Indian in American Life. LC 74-7977. Repr. of 1944 ed. 17.50 (ISBN 0-404-11867-4). AMS Pr.
--Red Man in the United States. LC 68-56243. (Illus.). Repr. of 1923 ed. lib. bdg. 19.50x (ISBN 0-678-00798-5). Kelley.
Long, John. Voyages & Travels of an Indian Interpreter & Trader Describing the Manners & Customs of the North American Indians. (American Studies). 1969. Repr. of 1791 ed. 14.00 (ISBN 0-384-33570-5). Johnson Repr.
McDonald, David R. & Mail, Patricia D. Tulapai to Tokay: A Bibliography of Alcohol Use & Abuse Among Native Americans of North America. LC 80-81243. (Bibliography Ser.). 1981. 25.00 (ISBN 0-87536-253-2). HRAFP.
McElwain, Thomas. Mythological Tales & the Allegany Seneca: A Study of the Socio-Religious Context of Traditional Oral Phenomena in an Iroquois Community. (Stockholm Studies in Comparative Religion Ser.: No. 17). 1978. pap. text ed. 17.75x (ISBN 91-22-00181-6). Humanities.
Mails, Thomas E. The Mystic Warriors of the Plains. LC 72-76191. 608p. 1972. 29.95 (ISBN 0-385-04741-X). Doubleday.
Marquis, Arnold. A Guide to America's Indians: Ceremonials, Reservations, & Museums. LC 74-5315. (Illus.). 400p. 1974. 15.95 (ISBN 0-8061-1133-X); pap. 8.95 (ISBN 0-8061-1148-8). U of Okla Pr.
Marx, Herbert L., Jr., ed. The American Indian: A Rising Ethnic Force. (Reference Shelf Ser: Vol. 45, No. 5). 1973. 6.25 (ISBN 0-8242-0508-1). Wilson.
Mason, Otis T. Man's Knife Among the North American Indians. 20p. Repr. of 1899 ed. pap. 3.75 (ISBN 0-8466-4051-1, SJI51). Shorey.
Maxon, James C. Indians of the Lake Mead Country. Jackson, Earl, ed. LC 73-165840. (Illus., Orig.). 1971. pap. 0.50 (ISBN 0-911408-23-1). Sw Pks Mnmts.
Mayhall, Mildred P. Kiowas. rev. ed. LC 70-163636. (Civilization of the American Indian Ser.: Vol. 63). (Illus.). 1962. 14.95 (ISBN 0-8061-0543-7). U of Okla Pr.
Meacham, Alfred B. Wi-Ne-Ma the Woman-Chief & Her People. LC 76-43773. Repr. of 1876 ed. 17.50 (ISBN 0-404-15628-2). AMS Pr.
Mead, Margaret & Bunzel, Ruth L., eds. The Golden Age of American Anthropology. LC 60-11668. (Golden Age Ser). 12.50 (ISBN 0-8076-0122-5). Braziller.
Merton, Thomas. Ishi Means Man: Essays on Native Americans. LC 75-12192. (Unicorn Keepsake Ser: Vol. 8). (Illus.). 75p. 1976. 10.00 (ISBN 0-87775-100-5); pap. 5.00 (ISBN 0-87775-074-2). Unicorn Pr.
Meyer, Kathleen A. Ishi. LC 79-25574. (Story of an American Indian Ser.). (Illus.). (gr. 5 up). 1980. PLB 6.95 (ISBN 0-87518-093-0). Dillon.
Meyer, Roy W. The Village Indians of the Upper Missouri: The Mandans, Hidatsas, & Arikaras. LC 77-4202. (Illus.). 1977. 14.95 (ISBN 0-8032-0913-4). U of Nebr Pr.
Miles, Nelson A. Personal Recollections & Observations of General Nelson A. Miles. rev. ed. LC 68-23812. (American Scene Ser). (Illus.). Repr. of 1896 ed. lib. bdg. 55.00 (ISBN 0-306-71020-X). Da Capo.
Mooney, James. Siouan Tribes of the East. LC 73-108504. (American Indian History Ser). (Illus.). 1970. Repr. of 1894 ed. 16.00 (ISBN 0-403-00348-2). Scholarly.
Moorehead, Warren K. American Indian in the United States, Period 1850-1914. facs. ed. LC 71-75512. (Select Bibliographies Reprint Ser). 1914. 35.00 (ISBN 0-8369-5014-3). Arno.
--Prehistoric Relics. facs. ed. (Illus.). Repr. pap. 16.00 (ISBN 0-8466-0157-5, SJS157). Shorey.
Morey, S. M., ed. Can the Red Man Help the White Man. LC 74-117372. 116p. 1970. pap. 3.50 (ISBN 0-685-56655-2). Waldorf Pr.
Morison, Samuel E. Samuel De Champlain: Father of New France. 1972. 10.00 (ISBN 0-316-58399-5, Pub. by Atlantic Monthly Pr). Little.
Morse, Jedidiah. Report to the Secretary of War of the United States, on Indian Affairs. LC 68-27675. (Illus.). Repr. of 1822 ed. 19.50x (ISBN 0-678-00548-6). Kelley.
--A Report to the Secretary of War of the U. S. on Indian Affairs. LC 70-108516. (Illus.). 400p. 1972. Repr. of 1822 ed. 16.00 (ISBN 0-403-00345-8). Scholarly.
National Geographic Society, ed. The World of the American Indian. LC 74-16277. (Story of Man Library). (Illus.). 400p. 1974. 9.95, avail. only from Natl. Geog. (ISBN 0-87044-151-5). Natl Geog.
Newcomb, W. W., Jr. North American Indians: An Anthropological Perspective. LC 73-88990. (Anthropology Ser.). 416p. 1974. pap. text ed. 10.95 (ISBN 0-87620-623-2). Goodyear.
North American Indians: A Dissertation Index. 1976. 28.00 (ISBN 0-8357-0134-4). Univ Microfilms.
Northsun, Nila. Small Bones, Little Eyes. Robertson, Kirk & Robertson, Kirk, eds. (Windriver Ser.). 72p. (Orig.). 1981. pap. 4.50 (ISBN 0-916918-17-3). Duck Down.
Ogden, Peter S. Traits of American Indian Life & Character. 2nd ed. Repr. of 1933 ed. 17.45 (ISBN 0-404-07149-X). AMS Pr.
Ojibwa Summer. LC 72-83228. 1972. write for info. (ISBN 0-8271-7244-3, Pub. by Barre); pap. write for info. Black Ice.
Olum, Walam. The Lenape & Their Legends. Brinton, Daniel G., tr. LC 74-108462. 262p. 1973. Repr. of 1884 ed. 7.00 (ISBN 0-403-00449-7). Scholarly.

Oswalt, Wendell H. This Land Was Theirs: A Study of North American Indians. 3rd ed. LC 77-14986. 1978. text ed. 21.95 (ISBN 0-471-02342-6). Wiley.

Owen, R. C., et al. North American Indians: A Sourcebook. 1967. text ed. 16.95 (ISBN 0-02-390030-X). Macmillan.

Palmer, Rose A. The North American Indians: An Account of the American Indians North of Mexico. LC 74-11848. (Illus.). 309p. 1975. Repr. of 1929 ed. lib. bdg. 22.50x (ISBN 0-8154-0494-8). Cooper Sq.

Parker, Arthur C. The Indian How Book. (Illus.). 6.00 (ISBN 0-8446-5234-2). Peter Smith.

Perdue, Theda. Slavery & the Evolution of Cherokee Society, 1540-1866. LC 78-16284. 1979. 12.50x (ISBN 0-87049-259-4). U of Tenn Pr.

Pickett, Albert J. History of Alabama, & Incidentally of Georgia & Mississippi, from the Earliest Period, 2 Vols. in 1. LC 76-146410. (First American Frontier Ser). (Illus.). 1971. Repr. of 1851 ed. 39.00 (ISBN 0-405-02872-5). Arno.

Porter, H. C. Inconstant Savage: England & the North American Indian, 1500-1660. 588p. 1979. 34.95 (ISBN 0-7156-0968-8, Pub. by Duckworth England). Biblio Dist.

Pouchot, M. Memoir Upon the Late War in North America, Between the French & English, 1755-60, 2 Vols. Hough, Franklin B., ed. 1866. Repr. Set. 64.00 (ISBN 0-403-03644-5). Scholarly.

Pound, Arthur & Day, Richard E. Johnson of the Mohawks. facsimile ed. LC 75-164621. (Select Bibliographies Reprint Ser). Repr. of 1930 ed. 40.00 (ISBN 0-8369-5904-3). Arno.

Poynter, Margaret. Miracle at Metlakatla. (Greatness with Faith Ser.). (Illus.). 1978. 4.95 (ISBN 0-570-07876-8, 39-1201); pap. 2.95 (ISBN 0-570-07881-4, 39-1211). Concordia.

Price, Archibald G. White Settlers & Native Peoples: An Historical Study of Racial Contacts Between English-Speaking Whites & Aboriginal Peoples in the United States, Canada, Australia, & New Zealand. LC 71-142320. (Illus.). 232p. 1972. Repr. of 1950 ed. lib. bdg. 19.75x (ISBN 0-8371-5923-7, PRWH). Greenwood.

Price, John A. Native Studies: American & Canadian Indians. 1978. pap. text ed. 8.95x (ISBN 0-07-082695-1, C). McGraw.

Prucha, Francis P. Indian Peace Medals in American History. LC 76-3772. (Illus.). 1976. 15.00 (ISBN 0-8032-0890-1). U of Nebr Pr.

Prucha, Francis P., ed. Americanizing the American Indians: Writings by the Friends of the Indian, 1880-1900. LC 72-92132. 1973. 18.50x (ISBN 0-674-02975-5). Harvard U Pr.

Radisson, Pierre E. Voyages of Peter Esprit Radisson, Being an Account of His Travels & Experiences Among the North American Indians, from 1652 to 1684. Scull, Gideon D., ed. (Illus.). 1885. 26.50 (ISBN 0-8337-3285-4). B Franklin.

Randall, Florence. American Indians. rev. ed. (Highlights Handbooks Ser.). (Illus.). (gr. 2-6). 1972. pap. 1.95 (ISBN 0-87534-111-X). Highlights.

Raphael, Ralph B. The Book of American Indians. LC 54-12972. 144p. 1973. lib. bdg. 4.95 (ISBN 0-668-00369-3). Arco.

Reference Encyclopedia of the American Indian: 1978 Edition. 3rd ed. Vol. 1, 560 Pgs. 25.00 (ISBN 0-686-62440-8); Vol. 2, 350 Pgs. 25.00 (ISBN 0-686-62441-6). B Klein Pubns.

Rich, John M. Chief Seattle's Unanswered Challenge. 1977. pap. 3.95 (ISBN 0-87770-072-9). Ye Galleon.

Rogers, Robert. A Concise Account of North America. Repr. of 1765 ed. 14.50 (ISBN 0-384-51700-5). Johnson Repr.

Sanders, Thomas E. & Peek, Walter W. Literature of the American Indian. abridged ed. 1976. pap. 7.95x (ISBN 0-02-477650-5). Macmillan.

Sandoz, Mari. These Were the Sioux. (gr. k-8). 1971. pap. 0.95 (ISBN 0-440-48792-7, YB). Dell.

Sapir, Edward. Selected Writings of Edward Sapir in Language, Culture, & Personality. Mandelbaum, David G., ed. 1949. 32.50x (ISBN 0-520-01115-5). U of Cal Pr.

Saum, Lewis O. The Fur Trader & the Indian. LC 65-23915. (Illus.). 336p. (gr. 9 up). 1965. 13.95 (ISBN 0-295-73793-X); pap. 3.95 (ISBN 0-295-74031-0). U of Wash Pr.

Savage, William W., ed. Indian Life: Transforming an American Myth. LC 77-9111. (Illus.). 1978. 12.95 (ISBN 0-8061-1434-7). U of Okla Pr.

Savishinsky, Joel S. The Trail of the Hare. new ed. (Library of Anthropology Ser.). (Illus.). 304p. 1975. 27.00x (ISBN 0-677-04140-3). Gordon.

Schell, Rolfe F. One Thousand Years on Mound Key. rev. ed. LC 68-24198. (Illus.). 1968. 3.95 (ISBN 0-87208-001-3); pap. 1.50 (ISBN 0-87208-000-5). Island Pr.

Scholder, Fritz. Indian Kitsch: The Use & Misuse of Indian Images. LC 78-65928. (Illus.). 1979. pap. 8.50 (ISBN 0-87358-190-3). Northland.

Schoolcraft, Henry R. The American Indians: Their History, Condition & Prospects from Original Notes & Manuscripts... Together with an Appendix Containing Thrilling Narratives, Daring Exploits, Etc. LC 75-7083. (Indian Captivities Ser.: Vol. 60). 1977. Repr. of 1851 ed. lib. bdg. 44.00 (ISBN 0-8240-1684-X). Garland Pub.

--Historical & Statistical Information Respecting the History, Condition & Prospects of the Indian Tribes of the United States, 7 vols. Nichols, Frances S., ed. LC 77-94466. (Illus.). Repr. of 1857 ed. Set. lib. bdg. 1500.00 (ISBN 0-404-05630-X). AMS Pr.

--Personal Memoirs of a Residence of Thirty Years with the Indian Tribes on the American Frontiers: With Brief Notices of Passing Events, Facts & Opinions, A.D. 1812 to A.D. 1842. LC 74-9021. Repr. of 1851 ed. 37.50 (ISBN 0-404-11899-2). AMS Pr.

--Personal Memoirs of a Residence of Thirty Years with the Indian Tribes on the American Frontiers: 1812-1842. facsimile ed. LC 75-119. (Mid-American Frontier Ser.). 1975. Repr. of 1851 ed. 41.00x (ISBN 0-405-06885-9). Arno.

Schultz, James W. Why Gone Those Times: Blackfoot Tales. Silliman, Eugene L., ed. (The Civilization of the American Indian Ser.: Vol. 127). (Illus.). 271p. 1980. pap. 6.95 (ISBN 0-8061-1639-0). U of Okla Pr.

Simpson, George & Yinger, J. Milton, eds. American Indians & American Life. LC 73-84761. (American Academy of Political & Social Science). vii, 226p. 1975. Repr. of 1957 ed. 15.00 (ISBN 0-8462-1739-2). Russell.

Smith, G. Hubert. Omaha Indians. Horr, David A., ed. (American Indian Ethnohistory Ser. - Plains Indians). 1974. lib. bdg. 42.00 (ISBN 0-8240-0739-5). Garland Pub.

Sorkin, Alan L. The Urban American Indian. LC 76-54459. (Illus.). 1978. 17.95 (ISBN 0-669-01296-3). Lexington Bks.

Spencer, Robert F., et al. The Native Americans: Ethnology & Backgrounds of the North American Indians. 2nd ed. (Illus.). 1977. text ed. 23.50 scp (ISBN 0-06-046371-6, HarpC). Har-Row.

Starr, Frederick. American Indians. LC 74-9024. Repr. of 1899 ed. 21.50 (ISBN 0-404-11902-6). AMS Pr.

Stein, Bennett H., ed. Tough Trip Through Paradise 1878-1879 by Andrew Garcia. (Illus.). 1967. 6.95 (ISBN 0-395-07719-2). HM.

Steiner, Stan. New Indians. 1969. pap. 2.65 (ISBN 0-440-56306-2, Delta). Dell.

Stewart, Julian H. Basin-Plateau Aboriginal Sociopolitical Groups. Repr. of 1938 ed. 22.00 (ISBN 0-403-03529-5). Scholarly.

Stirling, M. W. Historical & Ethnological Material on the Juvaro Indians. Repr. of 1938 ed. 19.00 (ISBN 0-403-03599-6). Scholarly.

Stuart, Granville. Pioneering in Montana: The Making of a State 1864-1887. Phillips, Paul C., ed. LC 77-7651. Orig. Title: Forty Years on the Frontier. (Illus.). 1977. 15.95x (ISBN 0-8032-0933-9); pap. 5.25 (ISBN 0-8032-5870-4, BB 648, Bison). U of Nebr Pr.

Swadesh, Frances L. Los Primeros Pobladores: Hispanic Americans of the Ute Frontier. LC 73-11566. 288p. 1974. text ed. 3.95x (ISBN 0-268-00505-2). U of Notre Dame Pr.

Swanton, John R. Indian Tribes of North America. 1968. Repr. of 1952 ed. 27.00 (ISBN 0-403-00051-3). Scholarly.

--The Indian Tribes of North America. LC 52-61970. (Illus.). 726p. 1979. Repr. of 1952 ed. 35.00x (ISBN 0-87474-179-3). Smithsonian.

--Indians of the Southeastern United States. LC 78-11039. (Classics of Smithsonian Anthropology Ser.: No. 1). (Illus.). 943p. 1979. pap. text ed. 17.50x (ISBN 0-87474-895-X). Smithsonian.

--The Indians' of the Southeastern United States' Repr. of 1943 ed. 69.00 (ISBN 0-403-00050-5). Scholarly.

Taylor, Colin. Warriors of the Plains. LC 73-92269. (Illus.). 1975. 15.00 (ISBN 0-668-03447-5). Arco.

Tibbles, Thomas H. The Ponca Chiefs: An Account of the Trial of Standing Bear. Graber, Kay, ed. LC 73-181595. xiv, 143p. 1972. 10.95x (ISBN 0-8032-0814-6); pap. 3.50 (ISBN 0-8032-5763-5, BB 547, Bison). U of Nebr Pr.

Tooker, Elizabeth. An Ethnography of the Huron Indians 1615-1649. Repr. of 1964 ed. 17.00 (ISBN 0-403-03593-7). Scholarly.

Turner, Frederick W., 3rd, ed. The Portable North American Indian Reader. LC 72-12545. (Viking Portable Library: No. 77). 704p. 1974. 10.00 (ISBN 0-670-11970-9). Viking Pr.

--The Portable North American Indian Reader. LC 72-12545. (Viking Portable Library: No. 77). 1977. pap. 5.95 (ISBN 0-14-015077-3). Penguin.

Turner, Geoffrey. Indians of North America. (Illus.). 1979. 12.95 (ISBN 0-7137-0843-3, Pub. by Blandford Pr England). Sterling.

U. S. Bureau of the Census. Indian Population in the U. S. & Alaska: 13th Census, 1910. LC 15-26430. 42.00 (ISBN 0-527-91780-X). Kraus Repr.

--Indian Population in the U. S. & Alaska: 15th Census, 1937. 17.00 (ISBN 0-527-91750-8). Kraus Repr.

Vandervelde, Marjorie. Could It Be Old Hiari. (Indian Culture Ser.). (gr. 5-9). 1975. 1.95 (ISBN 0-89992-040-3). MT Coun Indian.

Vanderwerth, W. C. Indian Oratory: Famous Speeches by Noted Indian Chieftains. (CAI Ser.: Vol. 110). (Illus.). 1979. pap. 6.95 (ISBN 0-8061-1575-0). U of Okla Pr.

Velie, Alan R. American Indian Literature: An Anthology. LC 78-21387. (Illus.). 1979. 16.95 (ISBN 0-8061-1530-0); pap. 7.95 (ISBN 0-8061-1523-8). U of Okla Pr.

Voegelin, Byron D. South Florida's Vanished People: Travels in the Homeland of Ancient Calusa. LC 72-94649. 1977. 5.95 (ISBN 0-87208-038-2); pap. 2.95 (ISBN 0-87208-106-0). Island Pr.

Vogel, Virgil V. Indian in American History. 1968. pap. 1.25 (ISBN 0-912008-17-2). Integrated Ed Assoc.

Volney, C. F. View of the Soil & Climate of the United States of America. Brown, C. B., tr. (Contributions to the History of Geology). (Illus.). 1968. 29.00 (ISBN 0-02-854250-9). Hafner.

Waldman, Harry, ed. Dictionary of Indians of North America, 3 vols. 1978. Set. 145.00 (ISBN 0-403-01799-8). Scholarly.

--Encyclopedia of Indians of the Americas, Vols. 1-8. LC 74-5088. 1974-81. lib. bdg. 59.00 ea. Scholarly.

Wallace, Anthony F. The Death & Rebirth of the Seneca. 416p. 1972. pap. 4.95 (ISBN 0-394-71699-X, Vin). Random.

Wallace, Paul A. Conrad Weiser, Sixteen Ninety-Six to Seventeen Sixty: Friend of Colonist & Mohawk. LC 73-102553. (Illus.). 1971. Repr. of 1945 ed. 27.50 (ISBN 0-8462-1505-5). Russell.

Walton, Joseph S. Conrad Weiser & the Indian Policy of Colonial Pennsylvania. LC 71-146425. (First American Frontier Ser). (Illus.). 1971. Repr. of 1900 ed. 20.00 (ISBN 0-405-02895-4). Arno.

Washburn, Wilcomb E. The Indian in America. LC 74-1870. (New American Nation Ser.). (Illus.). 318p. (YA) 1975. 17.50x (ISBN 0-06-014534-X, HarpT). Har-Row.

--The Indian in America. (New American Nation Ser.). (Illus.). 336p. 1975. pap. 4.95 (ISBN 0-06-131855-8, TB1855, Torch). Har-Row.

Waters, Frank. Pumpkin Seed Point: Being Within the Hopi. LC 76-75741. 175p. 1973. 9.95 (ISBN 0-8040-0255-X, SB); pap. 5.95 (ISBN 0-8040-0635-0). Swallow.

Watson, Jane W. The First Americans: Tribes of North America. (An I Am Reading Bk.). (Illus.). (gr. 1-4). 1980. 4.95 (ISBN 0-394-84194-8); PLB 5.99 (ISBN 0-394-94194-2). Pantheon.

Wax, Murray L. Indian-Americans: Unity & Diversity. LC 71-146886. (Ethnic Groups in American Life Ser). 1971. pap. 7.95 ref. ed. (ISBN 0-13-456970-9). P-H.

Wax, Rosalie H. Doing Fieldwork: Warnings & Advice. 1971. text ed. 15.00x (ISBN 0-226-86949-0, Phoen); pap. 4.95 (ISBN 0-226-86950-4, Phoen). U of Chicago Pr.

White, George. Historical Collections of Georgia. 3rd ed. Bd. with Name Index. Dutton, Alpha C. (Illus.). Repr. of 1920 ed. LC 68-9358. 1969. Repr. of 1855 ed. 30.00 (ISBN 0-8063-0376-X). Genealog Pub.

Wilson, James. The Original Americans: US Indians. (Minority Rights Group Ser.: No. 31). 28p. 1976. pap. 2.50 (ISBN 0-89192-128-1). Interbk Inc.

Wingert, Paul S. American Indian Sculpture. LC 76-43896. Repr. of 1949 ed. 27.50 (ISBN 0-404-15756-4). AMS Pr.

Wissler, Clark. Relation of Nature to Man in Aboriginal America. LC 75-160133. Repr. of 1926 ed. 22.00 (ISBN 0-404-07005-1). AMS Pr.

Wood, Mary. Life Against the Land: A Short History of the Pueblo Indians. 1978. 1.00 (ISBN 0-913488-07-0). Timberline Bks.

Wood, W. Raymond & Liberty, Margot, eds. Anthropology on the Great Plains. LC 79-28369. (Illus.). viii, 306p. 1980. 25.00x (ISBN 0-8032-4708-7). U of Nebr Pr.

Worsley, Israel. A View of the American Indians: General Character, Customs, Language, Public Festivals, Religious Rite, & Traditions. Davis, Moshe, ed. LC 77-70757. (America & the Holy Land Ser.). 1977. Repr. of 1828 ed. lib. bdg. 14.00x (ISBN 0-405-10303-4). Arno.

Worton, Stanley N. The First Americans. (American Issues in Perspective Ser.). (Illus.). 192p. (gr. 9-12). 1974. pap. text ed. 4.50x (ISBN 0-8104-6008-4). Hayden.

Yava, Aaron. Border Towns of the Navajo Nation. 2nd ed. (Illus.). 80p. 1975. pap. 4.00 (ISBN 0-914974-06-8). Holmgangers.

Zane, Polly & Zane, John. The Native Americans. LC 76-5579. (gr. 1-12). 1976. tchrs' ed 28.00 (ISBN 0-935070-01-X). Proof Pr.

INDIANS OF NORTH AMERICA-AGRICULTURE

Barrows, David P. Ethnobotany of the Coahuilla Indians of Southern California. 1977. pap. 5.95 (ISBN 0-686-22387-X). Malki Mus Pr.

Carlson, Leonard A. Indians, Bureaucrats, & Land: The Dawes Act & the Decline of Indian Farming. LC 80-1709. (Contributions in Economics & Economic History Ser.: No. 36). xii, 219p. 1981. lib. bdg. 29.95 (ISBN 0-313-22533-8, CDA/). Greenwood.

Castetter, Edward F. & Bell, Willis. Pima & Papago Indian Agriculture. LC 76-43674. Repr. of 1942 ed. 21.00 (ISBN 0-404-15510-3). AMS Pr.

Dick, Herbert W. Bat Cave. (School of American Research Monograph: No. 27). (Illus.). 114p. 1965. pap. 4.75 (ISBN 0-8263-0287-4). U of NM Pr.

Donkin, Robin. Agricultural Terracing in the Aboriginal New World. LC 77-15120. (Viking Fund Publications in Anthropology: No. 56). (Illus.). 1979. pap. 8.50x (ISBN 0-8165-0453-9). U of Ariz Pr.

Elmore, Francis H. Ethnobotany of the Navajo. LC 76-43698. (Univ. of New Mexico Bulletin: Vol. 1, No. 7). Repr. of 1944 ed. 22.50 (ISBN 0-404-15530-8). AMS Pr.

Hill, Willard W. The Agricultural & Hunting Methods of the Navaho Indians. LC 76-43742. (Yale Univ. Pubns. in Anthropology: No. 18). Repr. of 1938 ed. 19.50 (ISBN 0-404-15583-9). AMS Pr.

Smith, Harriet L. American Indian Foods & Vegetables. (A Western Americana Book). (Illus., Orig.). 1981. pap. 2.95 (ISBN 0-913626-23-6). S S S Pub Co.

Smith, Huron H. Ethnobotany of the Forest Potawatomi Indians. LC 76-43835. (Bulletin of the Public Museum of the City of Milwaukee: Vol. 7, No. 1). Repr. of 1933 ed. 29.00 (ISBN 0-404-15689-4). AMS Pr.

--Ethnobotany of the Meskwaki Indians, 2 vols. in 1. Bd. with Ethnobotany of the Menomini Indians. Repr. of 1923 ed. LC 76-43836. (Bulletin of the Public Museum of the City of Milwaukee: Vol. 4, Nos. 1 & 2). Repr. of 1928 ed. 40.50 (ISBN 0-404-15690-8). AMS Pr.

Vestal, Paul A. & Schultes, Richard E. The Economic Botany of the Kiowa Indians. LC 76-43883. (Harvard Univ., Botanical Museum). Repr. of 1939 ed. 21.50 (ISBN 0-404-15740-8). AMS Pr.

Whiting, Alfred F. Ethnobotany of the Hopi. LC 76-43890. (Museum of Northern Arizona Bulletin: No. 15). Repr. of 1939 ed. 16.00 (ISBN 0-404-15749-1). AMS Pr.

Will, George F. & Hyde, George E. Corn Among the Indians of the Upper Missouri. LC 64-63592. 323p. 1964. 18.50x (ISBN 0-8032-0892-8); pap. 3.95 (ISBN 0-8032-5846-1, BB 195, Bison). U of Nebr Pr.

Wilson, Gilbert L. Agriculture of the Hidatsa Indians: An Indian Interpretation. LC 76-43892. (Univ. of Minnesota Studies in the Social Sciences: No. 9). Repr. of 1917 ed. 24.50 (ISBN 0-404-15754-8). AMS Pr.

INDIANS OF NORTH AMERICA-AMUSEMENTS

see Indians of North America-Social Life and Customs

INDIANS OF NORTH AMERICA-ANTIQUITIES

see also Cliff-Dwellers; Cliff-Dwellings; Indians of North America-Implements; Indians of North America-Pottery; Mound-Builders; Mounds; also subdivision Antiquities under names of states, e.g. Arizona-Antiquities; also names of places, e.g. Tsura (Indian Settlement)

Alex, Lynn M. Exploring Iowa's Past: A Guide to Prehistoric Archaeology. LC 80-21391. (Illus.). 180p. 1980. pap. 7.95 (ISBN 0-87745-108-7). U of Iowa Pr.

Anderson, Duane. Western Iowa Prehistory. (Illus.). 55p. 1975. 6.95 (ISBN 0-8138-1765-X). Iowa St U Pr.

Anthropology & the American Indian: A Symposium. 122p. 1973. pap. 2.50 (ISBN 0-685-40544-3). Indian Hist Pr.

Archaelogy: Supplement to the Handbook of Middle American Indians, Vol. 1. Sabloff, Jeremy A., ed. (Illus.). 480p. 1981. text ed. 55.00x (ISBN 0-292-77556-3). U of Tex Pr.

Barnett, Franklin. Dictionary of Prehistoric Indian Artifacts of the American Southwest. LC 73-82865. (Illus.). 288p. 1973. pap. 7.95 (ISBN 0-87358-120-2). Northland.

Beauchamp, William M. Aboriginal Use of Wood in New York. LC 76-43661. (New York State Museum Bulletin: 89). Repr. of 1905 ed. 27.50 (ISBN 0-404-15493-X). AMS Pr.

--Polished Stone Articles Used by the New York Aborigines Before & During European Occupation. LC 74-7930. Repr. of 1897 ed. 17.50 (ISBN 0-404-11816-X). AMS Pr.

Bettarel, Robert L. & Smith, Hale G. The Moccasin Bluff Site & the Woodland Cultures of Southwestern Michigan. (Anthropological Papers: No. 49). 1973. pap. 6.00 (ISBN 0-932206-47-6). U Mich Mus Anthro.
Blaine, Martha R. The Ioway Indians. LC 78-21385. (Illus.). 1979. 24.95 (ISBN 0-8061-1527-0, CAI#151). U of Okla Pr.
Brose, David S. The Archaeology of Summer Island: Changing Settlement Systems in Northern Lake Michigan. (Anthropological Papers: No. 41). (Illus.). 1970. pap. 3.00x (ISBN 0-932206-39-5). U Mich Mus Anthro.
Brown, Calvin S. Archaeology of Mississippi. LC 72-5011. (Antiquities of the New World Ser.: Vol. 16). (Illus.). Repr. of 1926 ed. 49.50 (ISBN 0-404-57316-9). AMS Pr.
Chapman, Carl H. The Archaelogy of Missouri, I. LC 73-92242. 320p. 1975. 20.00x (ISBN 0-8262-0160-1). U of Mo Pr.
Chapman, Carl H. & Chapman, Eleanor F. Indians & Archaeology of Missouri. LC 64-64127. (Missouri Handbook Ser.). (Illus.). 1964. pap. 4.00x (ISBN 0-8262-0589-5). U of Mo Pr.
Crouch, Daniel J. Archaelogical Investigations of the Kiowa & Comanche Indian Agency Commissaries 34-Cm 232. (Contributions of the Museum of the Great Plains Ser.: No. 7). (Illus.). 1978. pap. 11.30 (ISBN 0-685-91362-7). Mus Great Plains.
Cushing, Frank H. Explorations of Key Dwellers' Remains on the Gulf Coast of Florida. LC 72-5007. (Antiquities of the New World Ser.: Vol. 13). (Illus.). Repr. of 1896 ed. 16.00 (ISBN 0-404-57313-4). AMS Pr.
Drucker, Philip. Indians of the Northwest Coast. 2.95 (ISBN 0-385-02443-6, B3, AMS). Natural Hist.
Dunnell, R. C. The Prehistory of Fishtrap, Kentucky. LC 72-90078. (Publications in Anthropology: No. 75). 1972. pap. 7.00 (ISBN 0-685-64463-4). Yale U Anthro.
Ferring, C. R., et al. An Archaeological Reconnaissance of Fort Sill, Oklahoma. (Contributions of the Museum of the Great Plains Ser.: No. 6). (Illus.). 1978. pap. 20.16 (ISBN 0-685-91361-9). Mus Great Plains.
Fewkes, Jessie W. & Gilman, Benjamin I. A Few Summer Ceremonials at Zuni Pueblo: Zuni Melodies, Reconnaissance of Ruins in or Near the Zuni Reservation. LC 76-21216. (A Journal of American Ethnology & Archaeology: Vol. 1). Repr. of 1891 ed. 20.00 (ISBN 0-404-58041-6). AMS Pr.
Fitting, James E. The Archaeology of Michigan: A Guide to the Prehistory of the Great Lakes Region. LC 75-14773. (Bulletin Ser.: No. 56). (Illus.). 274p. 1975. pap. text ed. 7.50x (ISBN 0-87737-033-8). Cranbrook.
Fitting, James E., ed. The Pre-History of the Burnt Bluff Area. (Anthropological Papers: No. 34). 1968. pap. 3.00x (ISBN 0-932206-32-8). U Mich Mus Anthro.
Frison, George C. The Wardell Buffalo Trap Forty Eight SU Three Hundred & One: Communal Procurement in the Upper Green River Basin, Wyoming. (Anthropological Papers: No. 48). 1973. pap. 3.00x (ISBN 0-932206-46-8). U Mich Mus Anthro.
Giammattei, Victor M. & Reichert, N. Greer. Art of a Vanished Race: The Mimbres Classic Black-on-White. LC 75-28600. (Illus.). 96p. 1975. pap. 6.95 (ISBN 0-916280-00-4). Dillon-Tyler Pubs.
Gibbon, Guy E. The Sheffield Site: An Oneota Site on the St. Croix River. LC 73-6715. (Minnesota Prehistoric Archaeology Ser., No. 10). (Illus.). 62p. 1973. pap. 4.00 (ISBN 0-87351-079-8). Minn Hist.
Gladwin, Harold, et al. Excavations at Snaketown: Material Culture. LC 65-23304. 1965. 16.50x (ISBN 0-8165-0031-2). U of Ariz Pr.
Griffin, James B. The Fort & Ancient Aspect. (Anthropological Papers: No. 28). (Illus.). 1966. pap. 6.00x (ISBN 0-932206-28-X). U Mich Mus Anthro.
Griffin, John W. & Bullen, Ripley P., eds. The Safety Harbor Site, Pinellas County, Florida. 1950. pap. 5.50 (ISBN 0-384-19990-9). Johnson Repr.
Guernsey, Samuel J. Explorations in Northeastern Arizona. 1931. pap. 15.00 (ISBN 0-527-01224-6). Kraus Repr.
Harnishfeger, Lloyd C. A Collector's Guide to American Indian Artifacts. LC 74-33525. (Bks for Adults & Young Adults). (Illus.). 96p. (gr. 5 up). 1976. PLB 6.95 (ISBN 0-8225-0759-5). Lerner Pubns.
Harrington, M. R. Sacred Bundles of the Sac & Fox Indians. (Anthropological Publications Ser.: Vol. 4-2). (Illus.). 1914. 7.00 (ISBN 0-686-24093-6). Univ Mus of U.
Harris, W. Stuart. Dead Towns of Alabama. LC 76-29655. (Illus.). 176p. 1977. 9.95 (ISBN 0-8173-5232-5). U of Ala Pr.
Haven, Samuel F. Archaeology of the United States. LC 72-4999. (Harvard University. Peabody Museum of Archaeology & Ethnology. Antiquities of the New World: No. 3). Repr. of 1856 ed. 30.00 (ISBN 0-404-57303-7). AMS Pr.
Hayden, Julian. Excavations, Nineteen Forty, at University Indian Ruin. (Illus.). 1957. pap. 4.00x (ISBN 0-911408-10-X). Sw Pks Mnmts.
Hedrick, Basil C., et al, eds. The Classic Southwest: Readings in Archaeology, Ethnohistory, & Ethnology. LC 70-184966. 206p. 1973. 10.00x (ISBN 0-8093-0547-X). S Ill U Pr.
Henry, Jeannette, ed. The American Indian Reader: Anthropology. LC 72-86873. 174p. 1972. pap. 4.00 (ISBN 0-913436-09-7). Indian Hist Pr.
Hester, T. R. & Mildner, M. P. Great Basin Atlatl Studies. Heizer, Robert F., ed. (Ballena Press Publications in Archaeology, Ethmology & History Ser.: No. 2). (Illus.). 60p. 1974. pap. 4.95 (ISBN 0-87919-036-1). Ballena Pr.
Hewett, Edgar L. Ancient Life in the American Southwest. LC 67-29548. (Illus.). 1968. Repr. of 1930 ed. 15.00x (ISBN 0-8196-0203-5). Biblo.
--General View of the Archeology of the Pueblo Region: Extracts. facs. ed. 22p. Repr. of 1904 ed. pap. 3.75 (ISBN 0-8466-0160-5, SJS160). Shorey.
Hill, James N. Broken K Pueblo: Prehistoric Social Organization in the American Southwest. LC 70-111383. (Anthropological Papers: No. 18). 149p. 1970. pap. 6.95x (ISBN 0-8165-0215-3). U of Ariz Pr.
Hinsdale, W. B. Distribution of the Aboriginal Population of Michigan. (Occasional Contributions Ser.: No. 2). (Illus.). 1968. pap. 1.00x (ISBN 0-686-53050-0). U Mich Mus Anthro.
Holmes, William H. An Ancient Quarry in Indian Territory. Repr. of 1894 ed. 19.00 (ISBN 0-403-03507-4). Scholarly.
Honea, Kenneth. Early Man Projectile Points in the Southwest. (Illus.). 1976. pap. 1.25 (ISBN 0-89013-013-2). Museum NM Pr.
Hooton, E. A. Indian Village Site & Cemetery Near Madisonville, Ohio. 1920. pap. 12.00 (ISBN 0-527-01212-2). Kraus Repr.
Hothern, Lar. North American Indian Artifacts. 2nd ed. 1980. pap. 9.95 (ISBN 0-517-54112-2). Crown.
Hrolicka, Ales. Physical Anthropology of the Lenape or Delawares, & of the Eastern Indians in General. Repr. of 1916 ed. 15.00 (ISBN 0-403-06385-X). Scholarly.
Huden, John C., ed. Archaeology in Vermont. LC 74-130409. (Illus.). 1970. pap. 3.85 (ISBN 0-8048-0929-1). C E Tuttle.
Hunt, Charles B. Death Valley: Geology, Ecology, Archaeology. LC 74-2460. 256p. 1975. 14.95 (ISBN 0-520-02460-5); CAL 315. pap. 7.95 (ISBN 0-520-03013-3). U of Cal Pr.
Irwin-Williams, Cynthia. Excavations at Magic Mountain. (Proceedings: No. 12). 1966. pap. 3.65 (ISBN 0-916278-65-4). Denver Mus Natl Hist.
Janzen, Donald E. The Naomikong Site & the Dimensions of Laurel in the Lake Superior Region. (Anthropological Papers: No. 36). (Illus.). 1968. pap. 3.00x (ISBN 0-932206-34-4). U Mich Mus Anthro.
Jenness, Diamond, ed. The American Aborigines: Their Origin & Antiquity; a Collection of Papers by Ten Authors Published for Presentation at the 5th Pacific Science Congress, Canada. LC 78-180611. (Illus.). iv, 396p. 1972. Repr. of 1933 ed. 19.00 (ISBN 0-8462-1616-7). Russell.
Jennings, Jesse D. Prehistory of North America. 2nd ed. (Illus.). 320p. 1974. text ed. 21.00 (ISBN 0-07-032454-9, C). McGraw.
Keel, Bennie C. Cherokee Archaeology: A Study of the Appalachian Summit. LC 75-41444. (Illus.). 1976. 14.50x (ISBN 0-87049-189-X). U of Tenn Pr.
Keur, Dorothy L. Big Bead Mesa: An Archaeological Study of Navaho Acculturation, 1745-1812. LC 76-43760. (Memoirs of the Society for American Archaeology: No. 1). Repr. of 1941 ed. 12.50 (ISBN 0-404-15613-4). AMS Pr.
Kidder, Alfred V. Introduction to the Study of Southwestern Archaeology. new ed. (Illus., Orig.). 1962. pap. 9.95 (ISBN 0-300-00140-1, YW-5). Yale U Pr.
Lambert, Marjorie F. & Ambler, J. R. Survey & Excavation of Caves in Hidalgo County, New Mexico. (Illus.). 1961. pap. 2.50 (ISBN 0-89013-115-5). Museum NM Pr.
Leslie, Vernon. Faces in Clay. LC 72-86083. 1973. 15.00x (ISBN 0-686-14952-1). T E Henderson.
Lewis, Thomas M. & Kneberg, Madeline. Hiwassee Island: An Archaeological Account of Four Tennessee Indian Peoples. LC 75-130688. (Illus.). 338p. 1970. 15.50 (ISBN 0-87049-123-7). U of Tenn Pr.
Lister, Florence C. & Lister, Robert H. Earl Morris & Southwestern Archaeology. LC 68-19737. (Illus.). 1977. pap. 6.95 (ISBN 0-8263-0455-9). U of NM Pr.
McBryde, Isabel. Aboriginal Prehistory in New England: An Archaeological Survey of Northeastern New South Wales. (Illus.). 400p. 1974. 45.00x (ISBN 0-424-06530-4, Pub. by Sydney U Pr). Intl Schol Bk Serv.
McGregor, John C. Southwestern Archaeology. 2nd ed. LC 65-10079. (Illus.). 1965. 20.00 (ISBN 0-252-72659-6). U of Ill Pr.
McHargue, Georgess & Roberts, Michael. A Field Guide to Conservation Archaeology in North America. LC 77-21558. (YA) 1977. 8.95 (ISBN 0-397-31724-7, JBL-J); pap. 4.95 (ISBN 0-397-31725-5). Har-Row.
McNutt, Charles. Early Puebloan Occupations Tesuque by-Pass & Upper Rio Grande Valley. (Anthropological Papers: No. 40). (Illus.). 1969. pap. 3.00x (ISBN 0-932206-38-7). U Mich Mus Anthro.
Martin, Paul S. & Willis, Elizabeth S. Anasazi Painted Pottery in the Field Museum of Natural History. LC 41-11775. (Fieldiana Anthropology Memoirs Ser: Vol. 5). 1968. Repr. of 1940 ed. 30.00 (ISBN 0-527-61900-0). Kraus Repr.
Martineau, LaVan. The Rocks Begin to Speak. DenDooven, Gweneth R., ed. LC 72-85137. (Illus.). 1973. 10.95 (ISBN 0-916122-30-1). KC Pubns.
Mason, Ronald J. Two Stratified Sites on the Door Peninsula of Wisconsin. (Anthropological Papers: No. 26). 1966. pap. 3.00x (ISBN 0-932206-27-1). U Mich Mus Anthro.
Mathews, Zena P. The Relation of Seneca False Face Masks to Seneca & Ontario Archeology. LC 77-94707. (Outstanding Dissertations in the Fine Arts Ser.). 1978. lib. bdg. 36.00x (ISBN 0-8240-3239-X). Garland Pub.
Mayer, Karl H. Mushroom Stones of Meso-America. (Illus.). 1977. pap. 4.95 (ISBN 0-916552-09-8). Acoma Bks.
Miner, Horace M. Cave Hollow, an Ozark Bluff-Dweller Site. (Anthropological Papers: No. 3). (Illus.). 1950. pap. 0.50x (ISBN 0-932206-17-4). U Mich Mus Anthro.
Morss, Noel. Ancient Culture of the Fremont River in Utah. 1931. pap. 6.00 (ISBN 0-527-01226-2). Kraus Repr.
--Archaeological Explorations on the Middle Chinlee. LC 28-11557. 1927. pap. 6.00 (ISBN 0-527-00533-9). Kraus Repr.
Olsen, Fred. On the Trail of the Arawaks. LC 73-7416. (Civilization of the American Indian Ser.: No. 129). (Illus.). 350p. 1975. 19.95 (ISBN 0-8061-1137-2); pap. 9.95 (ISBN 0-8061-1503-3). U of Okla Pr.
Pendergast, James F. & Trigger, Bruce G. Cartier's Hochelaga & the Dawson Site. LC 78-184767. (Illus.). 470p. 1972. 25.00 (ISBN 0-7735-0070-7). McGill-Queens U Pr.
Pratt, Peter P. Archaeology of the Oneida Iroguois, Vol. 1. 1976. 11.50 (ISBN 0-686-30586-8). Pierce Coll.
Price, James E. & Krakker, James J. Dalton, Occupation of the Ozark Border. Feldman, L. H., ed. LC 75-327206. (Museum Brief: No. 20). (Illus.). vii, 41p. 1975. pap. 2.30x (ISBN 0-913134-20-1). Mus Anthro Mo.
Prudden, P. M. Further Study of Prehistoric Small House-Ruins in the San Juan Watershed. LC 18-15717. 1918. pap. 5.00 (ISBN 0-527-00520-7). Kraus Repr.
Purdy, Barbara A. Florida's Prehistoric Stone Technology. LC 80-24726. (Illus.). xvi, 165p. 1981. 25.00 (ISBN 0-8130-0697-X). U Presses Fla.
Putnam, Frederic W. The Archaeological Reports of Frederic Ward Putnam. LC 78-178422. (Harvard University. Peabody Museum of Archaeology & Ethnology. Antiquities of the New World: No. 8). (Illus.). Repr. of 1973 ed. 31.50 (ISBN 0-404-57308-8). AMS Pr.
Quimby, George I. Indian Culture & European Trade Goods: The Archaeology of the Historic Period in the Western Great Lakes Region. LC 78-4996. 1978. Repr. of 1966 ed. lib. bdg. 22.50x (ISBN 0-313-20379-2, QUIC). Greenwood.
Reher, Charles A., ed. Settlement & Subsistence Along the Lower Chaco River: The CGP Survey. LC 77-71906. (Illus.). 614p. 1977. pap. 15.00x (ISBN 0-8263-0449-4). U of NM Pr.
Ritchie, William A. Archaeology of New York State. rev ed. LC 80-13378. (Illus.). 1980. Repr. of 1969 ed. write for info (ISBN 0-916346-41-2). Harbor Hill Bks.
Robbins, Louise & Neumann, George K. The Prehistoric People of the Fort Ancient Culture of the Central Ohio Valley. (Anthropological Papers: No. 47). 1972. pap. 6.00x (ISBN 0-932206-45-X). U Mich Mus Anthro.
Rogers, Spencer L. PAA KO, Part VI: The Physical Type of the Paa-Ko Population. (School of American Research Monograph: No. 19, Vol. 2). (Illus.). iii, 48p. 1954. pap. 3.00x ltd. ed. (ISBN 0-8263-0291-2). U of NM Pr.
Rohn, Arthur H. Cultural Change & Continuity on Chapin Mesa. LC 76-24089. (Illus.). 1977. 16.00x (ISBN 0-7006-0153-8). Regents Pr KS.
Seaman, N. G. Indian Relics of the Pacific Northwest. 2nd enl. ed. LC 66-28021. (Illus.). 1967. pap. 5.95 (ISBN 0-8323-0236-8). Binford.
Sears, William H. Excavations at Kolomoki: Final Report. LC 53-7144. 144p. 1956. pap. 4.50x (ISBN 0-8203-0059-4). U of Ga Pr.
Skinner, Alanson B. Notes on Iroquois Archaeology. LC 76-43827. (MAI. Indian Notes & Monographs, Miscellaneous: No. 18). 1977. Repr. of 1921 ed. 26.00 (ISBN 0-404-15679-7). AMS Pr.
Smith, Bruce D. Middle Mississippi Exploitation of Animal Populations. (Anthropological Papers: No. 57). (Illus.). 1975. pap. 4.00x (ISBN 0-932206-55-7). U Mich Mus Anthro.
Snow, Dean. The Archaeology of North America: American Indians & Their Origins. (Illus.). 272p. 1980. pap. 12.95 (ISBN 0-500-27183-6). Thames Hudson.
Snow, Dean R. Native American Prehistory: A Critical Bibliography. LC 79-2168. (Newberry Library Center for the History of the American Indian Bibliographical Ser.). 96p. 1980. pap. 3.95x (ISBN 0-253-33498-5). Ind U Pr.
South, Stanley. Method & Theory in Historical Archeology. (Studies in Archeology Ser.). 1977. 26.00 (ISBN 0-12-655750-0). Acad Pr.
Steele, William O. Talking Bones: Secrets of Indian Mound Builders. LC 76-58687. (Illus.). (gr. 2-5). 1978. 8.95 (ISBN 0-06-025768-7, HarpJ); PLB 8.79 (ISBN 0-06-025769-5). Har-Row.
Stewart, Hilary. Artifacts of the Northwest Coast Indians. 172p. text ed. 20.00x (ISBN 0-919654-01-0, Pub. by Hancock Hse); pap. 12.95 (ISBN 0-87663-641-5). Universe.
Stoltman, James B. The Laurel Culture in Minnesota. LC 73-4190. (Minnesota Prehistoric Archaeology Ser.: No. 8). (Illus.). x, 146p. 1973. pap. 5.50 (ISBN 0-87351-076-3). Minn Hist.
Streiff, Jan E., compiled by. Roster of Excavated Prehistoric Sites in Minnesota to 1972. LC 72-78032. (Minnesota Prehistoric Archaeology Ser.: No. 7). 38p. 1972. pap. 2.50 (ISBN 0-87351-071-2). Minn Hist.
Toth, Alan. Archaeology & Ceramics at the Marksville Site. (Anthropological Papers: No. 56). (Illus.). 1975. pap. 4.00x (ISBN 0-932206-54-9). U Mich Mus Anthro.
Walthall, John A. Prehistoric Indians of the Southeast: Archaeology of Alabama & the Middle South. LC 79-13722. (Illus.). 288p. 1980. 22.50x (ISBN 0-8173-0020-1). U of Ala Pr.
Wedel, Waldo R. An Introduction to Pawnee Archaeology. Repr. of 1963 ed. 17.00 (ISBN 0-403-03614-3). Scholarly.
--Prehistoric Man on the Great Plains. (Illus.). 1961. 16.95 (ISBN 0-8061-0501-1). U of Okla Pr.
White, James S. Diving for Northwest Relics. LC 79-1869. (Illus.). 1979. 8.95 (ISBN 0-8323-0329-1); pap. 6.50 (ISBN 0-8323-0330-5). Binford.
Wilford, Lloyd A. Burial Mounds of the Red River Headwaters. LC 70-113818. (Minnesota Prehistoric Archaeology Ser.: No. 5). (Illus.). 36p. 1970. pap. 2.00 (ISBN 0-87351-059-3). Minn Hist.
Wilkinson, Richard G. Prehistoric Biological Relationship in the Great Lakes Region. (Anthropological Papers: No. 43). (Illus.). 1971. pap. 3.50x (ISBN 0-932206-41-7). U Mich Mus Anthro.
Willey, Gordon R. Archeology of the Florida Gulf Coast. LC 72-5013. (Harvard University. Peabody Museum of Archaeology & Ethnology. Antiquities of the New World: No. 18). (Illus.). Repr. of 1949 ed. 57.50 (ISBN 0-404-57318-5). AMS Pr.
Williams, Stephen, ed. The Waring Papers: The Collected Works of Antonio J. Waring. LC 67-27476. (Papers of the Peabody Museum Ser.: Vol. 58). 1977. pap. 20.00 (ISBN 0-87365-169-3). Peabody Harvard.
Willoughby, Charles C. Antiquities of the New England Indians. LC 72-5012. (Harvard University. Peabody Museum of Archaeology & Ethnology. Antiquities of the New World: No. 17). (Illus.). Repr. of 1935 ed. 25.00 (ISBN 0-404-57317-7). AMS Pr.
--Indian Antiquities of the Kennebec Valley. Spiess, Arthur E., ed. (Occasional Publications in Maine Archaeology: No. 1). (Illus.). 160p. 1980. 22.00 (ISBN 0-913764-13-2). Maine St Mus.

--Indian Antiquities of the Kennebec Valley. (Illus.). 1980. 22.00 (ISBN 0-913764-13-2). Maine St Mus.
Wilmsen, Edwin N. Lithic Analysis & Cultural Inference: A Paleo-Indian Case. LC 75-89880. (Anthropological Papers: No. 16). 1970. pap. 5.95x (ISBN 0-8165-0211-0). U of Ariz Pr.
Woodbury, R. B. Prehistoric Stone Implements of Northeastern Arizona. (Illus.). 1954. 20.00 (ISBN 0-527-01286-6). Kraus Repr.
Wright, Barton. Hopi Material Culture: Artifacts Gathered by H. R. Voth in the Fred Harvey Collection. LC 78-74181. (Illus.). 1979. 14.95 (ISBN 0-87358-189-X). Northland.

INDIANS OF NORTH AMERICA–ARCHITECTURE
see also Indians of North America–Dwellings; Kivas
Volwahsen, Andreas. Living Architecture: Indian. (Illus.). 1969. 15.00 (ISBN 0-912158-36-0). Hennessey.

INDIANS OF NORTH AMERICA–ARMS AND ARMOR
see also Bow and Arrow; Throwing Sticks
Laubin, Reginald & Laubin, Gladys. American Indian Archery. LC 78-58108. (Civil. of the American Indian Ser.: Vol. 154). (Illus.). 1980. 12.50 (ISBN 0-8061-1467-3). U of Okla Pr.
Peckham, Stewart. Prehistoric Weapons in the Southwest. (Illus.). 1965. pap. 1.25 (ISBN 0-89013-017-5). Museum NM Pr.
Russell, Carl P. Guns on the Early Frontiers: A History of Firearms from Colonial Times Through the Years of the Western Fur Trade. LC 80-12570. xvi, 395p. 1980. 19.50x (ISBN 0-8032-3857-6); pap. 6.95 (ISBN 0-8032-8903-0, BB 747, Bison). U of Nebr Pr.
Wright, Barton. Pueblo Shields. LC 75-43343. (Illus.). 98p. 1976. 9.50 (ISBN 0-87358-146-6). Northland.

INDIANS OF NORTH AMERICA–ART
see also Sandpaintings
Aan-Ta-T'Loot & Pack, Raymond. Tlingit Designs & Carving Manual. LC 78-11887. (Illus.). 1978. 9.95 (ISBN 0-87564-862-2); pap. 6.95 (ISBN 0-87564-861-4). Superior Pub.
Adair, John. Navajo & Pueblo Silversmiths. (Civilization of the American Indian Ser.: No. 25). (Illus.). 1975. Repr. of 1944 ed. 10.95 (ISBN 0-8061-0133-4). U of Okla Pr.
American Indian Art: Form & Tradition. LC 72-90701. (Illus.). 1972. 8.00 (ISBN 0-912964-01-4). Minneapolis Inst Arts.
Artscanada. Stones, Bones & Skin: Ritual & Shamanic Art. (Illus.). 200p. 1981. 14.95 (ISBN 0-295-95864-2). Univ of Wash Pr.
Ashton, Robert & Stuart, Jozefa. Images of American Indian Art. LC 77-78131. 1977. 11.95 (ISBN 0-8027-0577-4); pap. 6.95 (ISBN 0-8027-7116-5). Walker & Co.
Boas, Franz. The Decorative Art of the Indians of the North Pacific Coast. LC 74-7936. (Illus.). Repr. of 1897 ed. 14.00 (ISBN 0-404-11823-2). AMS Pr.
Branson, Oscar T. Fetishes & Carvings of the Southwest. (Illus.). 1976. pap. 7.95 (ISBN 0-918080-04-5). Treasure Chest.
--Fetishes & Carvings of the Southwest. 1977. 12.95 (ISBN 0-442-21417-0). Van Nos Reinhold.
Brasser, Ted J. A Basketful of Indian Culture Change. (Illus.). 124p. 1975. pap. text ed. 3.95x (ISBN 0-660-00105-5, 56280-8, Pub. by Natl Mus Canada). U of Chicago Pr.
Broder, Patricia J. American Indian Painting & Sculpture. LC 80-66526. (Illus.). 165p. 1981. 35.00 (ISBN 0-89659-147-6). Abbeville Pr.
Coe, Ralph T. Sacred Circles: Two Thousand Years of North American Indian Art. LC 77-153583. (Illus.). 260p. 1977. pap. 15.00 (ISBN 0-295-95584-8). U of Wash Pr.
Collins, Henry B., et al. The Far North: Two Thousand Years of American Eskimo & Indian Art. LC 77-3132. (Illus.). 320p. 1977. 22.50x (ISBN 0-253-32120-4); pap. 17.50x (ISBN 0-253-28105-9). Ind U Pr.
D'Amato, Alex & D'Amato, Janet. American Indian Craft Inspirations. LC 72-83734. (Illus.). 224p. (YA) 1972. 7.95 (ISBN 0-87131-031-7). M Evans.
Davis, Starr & Davis, Richard. Tongues & Totems: Comparative Arts of the Pacific Basin. LC 74-82243. 1974. softcover 8.95 (ISBN 0-686-17270-1). Alaska Intl Art.
Dawdy, Doris O. Annotated Bibliography of American Indian Paintings. LC 66-27358. (Contributions Ser.: Vol. 21, Part 2). 1968. soft cover 2.50 (ISBN 0-934490-05-8). Mus Am Ind.
Douglas, Frederic H. & D'Harnoncourt, Rene. Indian Art of the United States. LC 74-86425. (Museum of Modern Art Publications in Reprint Ser). (Illus.). 1970. Repr. of 1941 ed. 18.00 (ISBN 0-405-01534-8). Arno.
Duff, Wilson. Arts of the Raven: Masterworks by the Northwest Coast Indian. (Illus.). 112p. 1967. pap. 11.50 (ISBN 0-295-95583-X, Pub. by Vancouver Art Canada). U of Wash Pr.
Duff, Wilson & Stewart, Hilary. Images: Stone: B.C. (Illus.). 1975. 17.95 (ISBN 0-919654-27-4, Pub. by Hancock Hse). Universe.
Erdman, Donnelley & Holstein, Philip M., eds. Enduring Visions: One Thousand Years of Southwestern Indian Art. LC 79-52784. (Illus.). 1979. pap. 12.95 (ISBN 0-934324-00-X, Pub. by Aspen Ctr Visual Arts). Pub Ctr Cult Res.
Ewers, John C. Plains Indian Painting: A Description of Aboriginal American Art. LC 76-43701. Repr. of 1939 ed. 24.50 (ISBN 0-404-15533-2). AMS Pr.
Ewers, John C., ed. Indian Art in Pipestone: George Catlin's Portfolio in the British Museum. LC 78-2974. (Illus.). 80p. 1979. 8.95x (ISBN 0-87474-420-2). Smithsonian.
Feder, Norman. American Indian Art. LC 69-12484. (Illus.). 1971. 45.00 (ISBN 0-8109-0014-9). Abrams.
--Art of the Eastern Plains Indians: The Nathan Sturges Jarvis Collection. (Illus.). 72p. (Orig.). 1964. pap. 2.50 (ISBN 0-87273-010-7). Bklyn Mus.
Feest, Christian F. Native Arts of North America. (World of Art Ser.). (Illus.). 300p. 1980. 17.95 (ISBN 0-19-520215-5); pap. 9.95 (ISBN 0-19-520216-3). Oxford U Pr.
From River Banks & Sacred Places: Ancient Indian Terracottas. pap. 2.50 (ISBN 0-87846-118-3). Mus Fine Arts Boston.
Fundaburk, Emma L. & Foreman, Mary D., eds. Sun Circles & Human Hands: The Southeastern Indians, Art & Industries. (Illus.). 10.00 (ISBN 0-910642-01-X). Fundaburk.
Garfield, Viola E. & Wingert, Paul S. Tsimshian Indians & Their Arts. LC 68-87177. (American Ethnological Society Numbered Publications Ser: No. 18). (Illus.). 108p. 1966. pap. 3.95 (ISBN 0-295-74042-6). U of Wash Pr.
Glubok, Shirley. The Art of the Northwest Coast Indians. LC 74-22384. (Illus.). 48p. (gr. 4 up). 1975. 9.95 (ISBN 0-02-736150-0). Macmillan.
--The Art of the Plains Indians. LC 75-14064. (Illus.). 48p. (gr. 4 up). 1975. 9.95 (ISBN 0-02-736360-0, 73636). Macmillan.
--The Art of the Woodland Indians. LC 76-12434. (Illus.). (gr. 4 up). 1976. 10.95 (ISBN 0-02-736440-2, 73644). Macmillan.
Grant, Campbell. Canyon De Chelly: Its People & Rock Art. LC 75-8455. 1978. 19.50x (ISBN 0-8165-0632-9); pap. 8.95 (ISBN 0-8165-0523-3). U of Ariz Pr.
--Rock Art of the American Indian. (Illus.). 192p. 1981. pap. 10.95 (ISBN 0-89646-060-6). Outbooks.
Hall, Edwin S., Jr., et al. Northwest Coast Indian Graphics: Introduction to Silk Screen Prints. LC 81-3397. (Illus.). 144p. 1981. 29.95 (ISBN 0-295-95835-9). U of Wash Pr.
Harding, Anne D. & Bolling, Patricia. Bibliography of Articles & Papers on North American Indian Art. 1980. lib. bdg. 75.00 (ISBN 0-8490-3115-X). Gordon Pr.
Harding, Anne D. & Bolling, Patricia, eds. Bibliography of Articles & Papers on North American Indian Art. 1938. 19.00 (ISBN 0-527-37800-3). Kraus Repr.
Harvey, Byron. Ritual in Pueblo Art: Hopi Life in Hopi Painting, Vol. 24. LC 67-30973. (Contributions Ser.). (Illus.). 1970. 15.00 (ISBN 0-934490-14-7); soft cover 10.00 (ISBN 0-934490-15-5). Mus Am Ind.
Hatcher, Evelyn. Visual Methaphors: A Formal Analysis of Navajo Art. LC 74-20691. (AES Ser). 1975. text ed. 20.95 (ISBN 0-8299-0026-8). West Pub.
Hawthorn, Audrey. Kwakiutl Art. LC 79-4856. (Illus.). 292p. 1979. 35.00 (ISBN 0-295-95674-7). U of Wash Pr.
Highwater, Jamake. Song from the Earth: American Indian Painting. LC 75-37201. (Illus.). 1980. pap. 12.95 (ISBN 0-8212-1091-2, 804061). NYGS.
--Song from the Earth: American Indian Painting. LC 75-37201. (Illus.). 1976. 22.50 (ISBN 0-8212-0698-2, 804053). NYGS.
--The Sweet Grass Lives on: Fifty Contemporary North American Indian Artists. LC 80-7776. (Illus.). 192p. 1980. 35.00 (ISBN 0-690-01925-4). Har-Row.
Hofsinde, Robert. Indian Arts. LC 73-137100. (Illus.). (gr. 3-7). 1971. PLB 6.48 (ISBN 0-688-31617-4). Morrow.
Holm, Bill. Crooked Beak of Heaven: Masks & Other Ceremonial Art of the Northwest Coast. LC 77-39631. (Index of Art in the Pacific Northwest Ser.: No. 3). (Illus.). 96p. 1972. pap. 7.95 (ISBN 0-295-95191-5). U of Wash Pr.
--Northwest Coast Indian Art: An Analysis of Form. LC 65-10818. (Thomas Burke Memorial Washington State Museum Monograph: No. 1). (Illus.). 133p. 1965. 12.95 (ISBN 0-295-73855-3); pap. 7.95 (ISBN 0-295-95102-8). U of Wash Pr.
Hothem, Lar. North American Indian Artifacts: A Collector's Identification & Value Guide. (Illus., Orig.). 1979. pap. 8.95 (ISBN 0-517-53956-X, Americana). Crown.
Inverarity, Robert B. Art of the Northwest Coast Indians. 2nd ed. (Illus.). 1967. pap. 10.95 (ISBN 0-520-00595-3). U of Cal Pr.
Joe, Eugene B., et al. Navajo Sandpainting Art. (Illus.). 32p. (Orig.). 1978. pap. 4.95 (ISBN 0-918080-20-7). Treasure Chest.
Kabotie, Fred & Belknap, Bill. Fred Kabotie: Hopi Indian Artist. LC 77-79071. (Illus.). 1977. 35.00 (ISBN 0-87358-164-4). Northland.
Kenny, Maurice, ed. From the Center: A Folio of Native American Art & Poetry. (Illus.). 30p. (Orig.). 1981. pap. 7.50 (ISBN 0-936574-03-8). Strawberry Pr NY.
Kew, Della & Goddard, P. E. Indian Art & Culture. 2nd ed. (Illus.). 1978. pap. 5.95 (ISBN 0-919654-13-4, Pub. by Hancock Hse). Universe.
King, Mary E. & Traylor, Idris R., Jr., eds. Art & Environment in Native America. (Special Publications: No. 7). (Illus., Orig.). 1974. pap. 8.00 (ISBN 0-89672-032-2). Tex Tech Pr.
La Farge, Oliver, et al. Introduction to American Indian Art, 2 vols. in 1. (Illus.). lib. bdg. 15.00 (ISBN 0-87380-047-8). Rio Grande.
Lee, Georgia. The Portable Cosmos: Effigies, Ornaments & Incised Stone from the Chumash Area. (Ballena Press Anthropological Papers: No. 21). (Illus.). 114p. (Orig.). 1981. pap. 6.95 (ISBN 0-87919-093-0). Ballena Pr.
Levin, et al. Art of the American Indian. Vandervelde, ed. 1973. 1.95 (ISBN 0-89992-077-2). MT Coun Indian.
McAfee, William W. Our Ancient People. 1978. 7.50 (ISBN 0-533-03370-5). Vantage.
Mallery, Garrick. Picture-Writing of the American Indians, 2 vols. (Illus.). Set. 20.00 (ISBN 0-8446-4582-6). Peter Smith.
Mathews, Zena & Jonaitis, Aldona. Native North American Art History--Selected Readings. (Illus.). 300p. (Orig.). 1981. pap. text ed. 10.95 (ISBN 0-917962-73-7). Peek Pubns.
Matthews, Washington. Navajo Weavers & Silversmiths. LC 70-97218. (Wild & Woolly West Ser., No. 7). (Illus.). 1968. 7.00 (ISBN 0-910584-81-8); pap. 1.50 (ISBN 0-910584-07-9). Filter.
Mera, H. F. Pueblo Designs: 176 Illustrations of the "Rain Bird". 1970. pap. 4.00 (ISBN 0-486-22073-7). Dover.
Mera, Harry P. Indian Silverwork of the Southwest. rev. 2nd ed. (Illus., Orig.). 1960. Repr. 7.95 (ISBN 0-912762-03-9); thin card cover 3.95 (ISBN 0-912762-02-0). King.
Milton, John R. American Indian Speaks: Poetry, Fiction & Art by the American Indian. LC 71-106810. (Illus.). 191p. 1969. pap. 5.00 (ISBN 0-88249-003-6). Dakota Pr.
Monthan, Guy & Monthan, Doris. Art & Indian Individualists. LC 74-31544. (Illus.). 168p. 1975. 35.00 (ISBN 0-87358-137-7). Northland.
--Nacimientos: Nativity Scenes by Southwest Indian Artisans. LC 79-88621. (Illus.). 1979. 16.50 (ISBN 0-87358-203-9); pap. 9.95 (ISBN 0-87358-208-X). Northland.
Morrow, Mable. Indian Rawhide: An American Folk Art. (Civilization of the American Indian Ser.: Vol. 132). (Illus.). 243p. 1980. pap. 12.50 (ISBN 0-8061-1637-4). U of Okla Pr.
Naylor, Maria, ed. Authentic Indian Designs. LC 74-17711. (Illus.). 256p. 1975. pap. 6.50 (ISBN 0-486-23170-4). Dover.
--Authentic Indian Designs: 2500 Ils. from Reports of the Bureau of American Ethnology. 10.75 (ISBN 0-8446-5228-8). Peter Smith.
Nelson, Mary C. The Legendary Artists of Taos. (Illus.). 176p. 1980. 25.00 (ISBN 0-8230-2745-7). Watson-Guptill.
New, Lloyd K., intro. by. The Institute of American Indian Arts, Alumni Exhibition. LC 73-92099. (Illus.). 72p. 1974. pap. 3.25 (ISBN 0-88360-003-X). Amon Carter.
Newcomb, Franc J. Study of Navajo Symbolism, 3 pts. in 1. Incl. Pt. 1. Navajo Symbols in Sandpaintings & Ritual Objects; Pt. 2. Navajo Picture Writing. Fishler, S. A; Pt. 3. Notes on Corresponding Symbols in Various Parts of the World. Wheelwright, Mary C. 1956. Set. pap. 13.00 (ISBN 0-527-01284-X). Kraus Repr.
Oglesby, Catharine. Modern Primitive Arts of Mexico, Guatemala & the Southwest. facs. ed. LC 75-90670. (Essay Index Reprint Ser). 1939. 16.00 (ISBN 0-8369-1215-2). Arno.
Parsons, Elsie C. Isleta Paintings. Repr. of 1962 ed. 49.00 (ISBN 0-403-03619-4). Scholarly.
Petersen, Karen D. Plains Indian Art from Fort Marion. (Civilization of the American Indian Ser.: Vol. 101). (Illus.). 1971. 19.95 (ISBN 0-8061-0888-6). U of Okla Pr.
Philbrook Art Center. Native American Art at Philbrook. LC 80-82374. (Orig.). 1980. pap. 9.95 (ISBN 0-86659-001-3). SW Art Assn.
Pohrt, Richard A. The American Indian: The American Flag. (Illus.). 152p. (Orig.). 1975. 12.50 (ISBN 0-939896-03-6); pap. 7.50 (ISBN 0-939896-02-8). Flint Inst Arts.
Reichard, Gladys A. Navajo Medicine Man Sandpaintings. (Illus.). 12.50 (ISBN 0-8446-5604-6). Peter Smith.
Rogers, Gay Ann. Tribal Designs for Needlepoint: Thirty Original Designs Adapted from Eskimo, Polynesian & Indian Art. LC 76-2814. 1977. Softbound 5.95 (ISBN 0-385-09967-3). Doubleday.
Roosevelt, Anna C. & Smith, James G., eds. The Ancestors: Native Artisans of the Americas. LC 79-89536. (Illus.). 1979. pap. 17.50 (ISBN 0-934490-00-7). Mus Am Ind.
Rose, Wendy. Lost Copper. 1980. 8.95 (ISBN 0-686-27943-3). Malki Mus Pr.
Schaafsma, Polly. Indian Rock Art of the Southwest. LC 79-9127. (Southwest Indian Arts Ser.). (Illus.). 379p. 1980. 40.00x (ISBN 0-8263-0524-5). U of NM Pr.
--Rock Art in the Cochiti Reservoir District. (Illus.). 1975. pap. 8.95 (ISBN 0-89013-063-9). Museum NM Pr.
--Rock Art in the Navajo Reservoir District. (Illus.). 1971. pap. 3.95 (ISBN 0-89013-007-8). Museum NM Pr.
--The Rock Art of Utah. Flint, Emily, ed. LC 72-173663. (Papers of the Peabody Museum Ser.: Vol.65). (Illus.). 1976. pap. 15.00 (ISBN 0-87365-186-3). Peabody Harvard.
Scholder, Fritz. Scholder - Indians. LC 79-188288. (Illus.). 1976. pap. 12.50 (ISBN 0-87358-092-3). Northland.
Sides, Dorothy. Decorative Art of the Southwestern Indians. (Illus.). 7.50 (ISBN 0-8446-2936-7). Peter Smith.
Sides, Dorothy S. Decorative Art of the Southwestern Indians. rev. ed. (Illus.). 1962. pap. 2.25 (ISBN 0-486-20139-2). Dover.
Sinclair, Lister & Pollack, Jack. The Art of Norval Morrisseau. (Illus.). 1979. 50.00 (ISBN 0-458-93820-3). Methuen Inc.
Smith, Gerald A. & Turner, Wilson G. Indian Rock Art of Southern California. LC 75-14612. (Illus.). 1975. text ed. 17.50 (ISBN 0-915158-03-5). San Bernardino.
Steltzer, Ulli. Indian Artists at Work. LC 76-49168. (Illus.). 144p. 1977. 20.00 (ISBN 0-295-95536-8); pap. 14.95 (ISBN 0-295-95598-8). U of Wash Pr.
Stewart, Hilary. Looking at Indian Art of the Northwest Coast. LC 78-73988. (Illus.). 112p. 1979. pap. 6.95 (ISBN 0-295-95645-3). U of Wash Pr.
Story, Dorothy P. Full-Color American Indian Designs for Needlepoint Rugs. LC 75-9176. (Needlepoint Ser.). 32p. (Orig.). 1975. pap. 2.00 (ISBN 0-486-23190-9). Dover.
Swinton, George. Sculpture of the Eskimo. (Illus.). 256p. 1972. 29.95 (ISBN 0-8212-0404-1, 777315). NYGS.
Tanner, Clara L. Southwest Indian Craft Arts. LC 66-24299. (Illus.). 1968. 20.00 (ISBN 0-8165-0083-5). U of Ariz Pr.
--Southwest Indian Painting: A Changing Art. rev. ed. LC 74-160812. (Illus.). 1980. 50.00 (ISBN 0-8165-0309-5). U of Ariz Pr.
Tanner, Clara L., et al. Ray Manley's Collecting Southwestern Indian Arts & Crafts. 3rd rev. ed. (Illus.). 1979. pap. 4.00 (ISBN 0-931418-03-8). R Manley.
Vaillant, George C. Indian Arts in North America. LC 72-97071. (Illus.). 63p. 1973. Repr. lib. bdg. 20.00x (ISBN 0-8154-0469-7). Cooper Sq.
Wade, Edwin L. & McChesney, Lea S. Historic Hopi Ceramics: The Thomas V. Keam Collection of the Peabody Museum of Archaeology & Ethnology, Harvard. LC 81-81627. (Peabody Museum Press Ser.). (Illus.). 602p. (Orig.). 1981. pap. text ed. write for info. (ISBN 0-87365-798-5). Peabody Harvard.
Wardwell, Allen. Objects of Bright Pride: Northwest Coast Indian Art from the American Museum of Natural History. LC 78-67113. (Illus.). 128p. 1979. pap. 19.95 (ISBN 0-295-95664-X). U of Wash Pr.
--Objects of Bright Pride: Northwest Coast Indian Art from the American Museum of Natural History. LC 78-67113. (Illus.). 1978. pap. 10.95 (ISBN 0-917418-61-1). Am Fed Arts.
Warner, John A. Heritage of Raven: Classical & Contemporary Art of the Northwest Coast Indians. Campbell, Margaret, ed. (Illus.). 1981. 24.95 (ISBN 0-87663-631-8, Pub. by Hancock Hse). Universe.
Wesche, Alice. Wild Brothers of the Indians: As Pictured by the Ancient Americans. LC 77-79064. (Illus.). (gr. 3-8). 1977. pap. 4.95 (ISBN 0-918080-21-5). Treasure Chest.
Whiteford, Andrew H. Indian Arts, North American. (Golden Guide Ser). (Illus.). (gr. 7 up). 1970. 1.95 (ISBN 0-307-24032-0, Golden Pr); PLB 10.38 (ISBN 0-307-63548-1). Western Pub.
Wilder, Mitchell A. Quiet Triumph: Forty Years with the Indian Arts Fund, Santa Fe. LC 66-13037. (Illus.). 18p. 1965. pap. 2.00 (ISBN 0-88360-010-2). Amon Carter.

Wingert, Paul S. American Indian Sculpture. LC 76-43896. Repr. of 1949 ed. 27.50 (ISBN 0-404-15756-4). AMS Pr.

Wingert, S. American Indian Sculpture: A Study of the Northwest Coast. LC 75-11063. 1976. Repr. of 1947 ed. lib. bdg. 30.00 (ISBN 0-87817-168-1). Hacker.

INDIANS OF NORTH AMERICA–BASKET MAKING

see Indians of North America–Industries

INDIANS OF NORTH AMERICA–BEADWORK

see Beadwork; Indians of North America–Costume and Adornment; Indians of North America–Textile Industry and Fabrics

INDIANS OF NORTH AMERICA–BIBLIOGRAPHY

Abler, Tom, et al, eds. Canadian Indian Bibliography Nineteen Sixty to Nineteen Seventy. LC 73-85083. 1974. 45.00x (ISBN 0-8020-2092-5). U of Toronto Pr.

Blaine, Martha R. Pawnees: A Critical Bibliography. LC 80-8034. (The Newberry Library Center for the History of the American Indian Bibliographical Ser.). (Illus.). 128p. 1981. pap. 3.95x (ISBN 0-253-31502-6). Ind U Pr.

Bramstedt, Wayne G. North American Indians in Towns & Cities: A Bibliography. (Public Administration Ser.: No. P-234). 1979. pap. 7.50 (ISBN 0-686-24900-3). Vance Biblios.

Buchanan, Jim & Burkert, Fran. A Bibliography of Current American Indian Policy. (Public Administration Ser.: P 188). 1979. pap. 7.00 (ISBN 0-686-24634-9). Vance Biblios.

Burgess, Larry E. & Hauptman, Laurence M. The Lake Mohonk Conference of Friends of the Indian: Guide to the Annual Reports. LC 74-6460. (Library of American Indian Affairs Ser.). (Illus.). 200p. 1975. lib. bdg. 15.00 (ISBN 0-88354-103-3). Clearwater Pub.

De Puy, Henry F. A Bibliography of the English Colonial Treaties with the American Indians. LC 78-108471. 1917. Repr. 19.00 (ISBN 0-403-00425-X). Scholarly.

Dobyns, Henry F. & Euler, Robert C. Indians of the Southwest: A Critical Bibliography. LC 80-8036. (The Newberry Library Center for the History of the American Indian Bibliographical Ser.). 176p. 1981. pap. 4.95x (ISBN 0-253-32658-3). Ind U Pr.

Dockstader, Fred J. The American Indian in Graduate Studies: A Bibliolgrapy of Theses & Dissertations, 2 vols, Vol. 25. 1973. Set. pap. 18.00 (ISBN 0-934490-06-6); Vol. 1. pap. 10.00 (ISBN 0-934490-07-4); Vol. 2. pap. 10.00 (ISBN 0-934490-08-2). Mus Am Ind.

Fogelson, Raymond D. The Cherokees: A Critical Bibliography. LC 78-3254. (The Newberry Library Center for the History of the American Indian Bibliographical Ser.). 112p. 1978. pap. 4.95x (ISBN 0-253-31346-5). Ind U Pr.

Green, Michael D. The Creeks: A Critical Bibliography. LC 79-2166. (Newberry Library Center for the History of the American Indian Bibliographical Ser.). 132p. (Orig.). 1980. pap. 4.95x (ISBN 0-253-31776-2). Ind U Pr.

Hargrett, Lester. Bibliography of the Constitutions & Laws of the American Indians. LC 47-31330. 19.00 (ISBN 0-527-37900-X). Kraus Repr.

Heizer, Robert & Elsasser, Albert B. California Indians: An Annotated Bibliography. (Reference Library of Social Science: Vol. 48). (LC 76-052687). 1977. lib. bdg. 27.00 (ISBN 0-8240-9866-8). Garland Pub.

Helm, June. The Indians of the Subarctic: A Critical Bibliography. LC 76-12373. (Newberry Library Center for the History of the American Indian Bibliographical Ser.). 104p. 1976. pap. 3.95x (ISBN 0-253-33004-1). Ind U Pr.

Henry, Jeannette, ed. Index to Literature on the American Indian, 1973. LC 70-141292. (Index to Literature on the American Indian Ser). 350p. 1975. 12.00 (ISBN 0-913436-30-5); pap. 10.00 (ISBN 0-913436-31-3). Indian Hist Pr.

Henry, Jeannette, et al, eds. Index to Literature on the American Indian, 1972. 1974. 12.00 (ISBN 0-913436-16-X). Indian Hist Pr.

--Index to Literature on the American Indian, 1972. LC 70-141292. 300p. 1974. pap. 10.00 (ISBN 0-913436-17-8). Indian Hist Pr.

Hill, Edward E. Office of Indian Affairs, 1824-1880: Historical Sketches. LC 73-16321. (Library of American Indian Affairs). 1974. lib. bdg. 20.00 (ISBN 0-88354-105-X). Clearwater Pub.

Hodge, William H. A Bibliography of Contemporary North American Indians: Selected & Partially Annotated with Study Guides. Prucha, Paul, intro. by. LC 75-21675. 320p. 1976. lib. bdg. 27.50 (ISBN 0-87989-102-5). Interland Pub.

Hoover, Herbert T. The Sioux: A Critical Bibliography. LC 79-2167. (Newberry Library Center for the History of the American Indian Bibliographical Ser.). 96p. (Orig.). 1979. pap. 3.95x (ISBN 0-253-34972-9). Ind U Pr.

Huntington Free Library & Reading Room. Dictionary Catalog of the American Indian Collection. 1977. lib. bdg. 350.00 (ISBN 0-8161-0065-9). G K Hall.

Index to Literature on the American Indian: 1970. LC 70-141292. 177p. 1972. pap. 12.00 (ISBN 0-913436-06-2). Indian Hist Pr.

Index to Literature on the American Indian, 1971. LC 70-141292. 230p. 1972. pap. 10.00 (ISBN 0-913436-08-9). Indian Hist Pr.

Kelso, Dianne R., compiled by. Bibliography of North American Indian Mental Health. LC 81-800. (Illus.). 404p. 1981. lib. bdg. 39.95 (ISBN 0-313-22930-9, KEB/). Greenwood.

Kidwell, Clara S. & Roberts, Charles. The Choctaws: A Critical Bibliography. LC 80-8037. (The Newberry Library Center for the History of the American Indian Bibliographical Ser.). 128p. 1981. pap. 3.95x (ISBN 0-253-34412-3). Ind U Pr.

Laird, W. David. Hopi Bibliography: Comprehensive & Annotated. LC 77-95563. 1977. pap. 7.95x (ISBN 0-8165-0566-7). U of Ariz Pr.

Lass-Woodfin, Mary J., ed. Books on American Indians & Eskimos. LC 77-17271. 1977. text ed. 20.00 (ISBN 0-8389-0241-3). ALA.

Marken, Jack W. American Indian: Language & Literature. LC 76-4624. (Goldentree Bibliographies in Language & Literature). 1978. pap. text ed. 12.95x (ISBN 0-88295-553-5). Harlan Davidson.

Marken, Jack W. & Hoover, Herbert T. Bibliography of the Sioux. LC 80-20106. (Native American Bibliography Ser.: No. 1). 388p. 1980. 17.50 (ISBN 0-8108-1356-4). Scarecrow.

Minnesota Historical Society. Chippewa & Dakota Indians: A Subject Catalog of Books, Pamphlets, Periodical Articles & Manuscripts in the Minnesota Historical Society. LC 70-102272. 131p. 1970. pap. 7.50 (ISBN 0-87351-056-9). Minn Hist.

Newberry Library - Chicago. Dictionary Catalog of the Edward E. Ayer Collection of Americana & American Indians, First Supplement, 3 vol. 1970. Set. lib. bdg. 210.00 (ISBN 0-8161-0810-2). G K Hall.

--Dictionary Catalog of the Edward E. Ayer Collection of Americana & American Indians, 16 Vols. 1961. Set. 880.00 (ISBN 0-8161-0586-3). G K Hall.

Nichols, Francis S., compiled by. Index to Schoolcraft's "Indian Tribes of the United States". Repr. of 1954 ed. 20.00 (ISBN 0-403-03611-9). Scholarly.

Perkins, David & Tanis, Norman. Native Americans of North America: A Bibliography Based on Collections in the Libraries of California State University, Northridge. (Illus.). 1975. 14.50 (ISBN 0-8108-0878-1). Scarecrow.

Ray, Roger B. The Indians of Maine & the Atlantic Provices: A Bibliographic Guide. Morris, Gerald E., ed. (Maine History Bibliographical Guide Ser.). 1977. pap. 4.00 (ISBN 0-915592-29-0). Maine Hist.

Smith, Dwight L., ed. Indians of the United States & Canada: A Bibliography. LC 73-87156. (Clio Bibliography Ser.: No. 3). 453p. 1974. text ed. 48.00 (ISBN 0-87436-124-9). ABC-Clio.

Stensland, Anna L. Literature by & About the American Indian: An Annotated Bibliography. LC 79-18073. 382p. 1979. pap. 9.25 (ISBN 0-8141-2984-6). NCTE.

Thornton, Russell & Grasmick, Mary K. Sociology of American Indians: A Critical Bibliography. LC 80-8035. (The Newberry Library Center for the History of the American Indian Bibliographical Ser.). 128p. 1981. pap. 3.95x (ISBN 0-253-35294-0). Ind U Pr.

Tooker, Elisabeth. Indians of the Northeast: A Critical Bibliography. LC 78-3252. (The Newberry Library Center for the History of the American Indian Bibliographical Ser.). 96p. 1978. pap. 4.95x (ISBN 0-253-33003-3). Ind U Pr.

Unrau, William E. The Emigrant Indians of Kansas: A Critical Bibliography. LC 79-2169. (Newberry Library Center for the History of the American Indian Bibliographical Ser.). 96p. (Orig.). 1981. pap. 3.95x (ISBN 0-253-36816-2). Ind U Pr.

Weslager, C. A. The Delawarew: A Critical Bibliography. LC 78-3250. (The Newberry Library Center for the History of the American Indian Bibliographical Ser.). 96p. 1978. pap. 4.95x (ISBN 0-253-31680-4). Ind U Pr.

INDIANS OF NORTH AMERICA–BIOGRAPHY

see also names of individual Indians, e.g. Geronimo

Alford, Thomas W. Civilization: & the Story of the Shawnees-As Told to Florence Drake. (The Civilization of the American Indian Ser.: Vol. 13). (Illus.). 203p. 1980. pap. 5.95 (ISBN 0-8061-1614-5). U of Okla Pr.

American Ethnological Society. American Indian Intellectuals: 1976 Proceedings. Liberty, Margot, ed. (Illus.). 1978. pap. text ed. 13.95 (ISBN 0-8299-0223-6). West Pub.

Axford, Roger W. Native Americans: 23 Indian Biographies. (Illus.). 128p. Date not set. pap. 4.50 (ISBN 0-935648-02-X). Halldin Pub.

Baird, W. David. Peter Pitchlynn: Chief of the Choctaws. (Civilization of the American Indian Ser: Vol. 116). (Illus.). 1977. pap. 6.95 (ISBN 0-8061-1367-7). U of Okla Pr.

Beidler, Peter G. Fig Tree John: An Indian in Fact & Fiction. LC 76-26345. 1977. 10.50x (ISBN 0-8165-0600-0); pap. 4.95x (ISBN 0-8165-0522-5). U of Ariz Pr.

Britt, Albert. Great Indian Chiefs. facs. ed. LC 76-76895. (Essay Index Reprint Ser). 1938. 19.50 (ISBN 0-8369-0006-5). Arno.

Brumble, H. David, III. An Annotated Bibliography of American Indian & Eskimo Autobiographies. LC 80-23449. xii, 170p. 1981. 10.95x (ISBN 0-8032-1175-9). U of Nebr Pr.

Buechner, Cecilia B. The Pokagons. 1976. Repr. of 1933 ed. 5.00 (ISBN 0-915056-05-4). Hardscrabble Bks.

Burt, Olive. Sacajawea. LC 78-1572. (Visual Biography Ser.). (Illus.). (gr. 6 up). 1978. PLB 6.90 s&l (ISBN 0-531-00975-0). Watts.

Campbell, C. W. Will Rogers. LC 79-4058. (Story of an American Indian Ser.). (Illus.). (gr. 5 up). 1979. PLB 6.95 (ISBN 0-87518-177-5). Dillon.

Capps, Benjamin. The Great Chiefs. LC 75-744. (The Old West). (Illus.). (gr. 5 up). 1975. kivar 12.96 (ISBN 0-8094-1494-5, Pub. by Time-Life). Silver.

Carlson, Vada & Witherspoon, Gary. Black Mountain Boy. LC 68-27160. (Illus.). 81p. 1974. 4.50 (ISBN 0-89019-008-9). Navajo Curr.

Coel, Margaret. Chief Left Hand: Southern Arapaho. LC 80-5940. (The Civilization of the American Indian Ser.: Vol. 159). (Illus.). 352p. 1981. 15.95 (ISBN 0-8061-1602-1). U of Okla Pr.

Cunningham, Maggi. Little Turtle. LC 77-16764. (Story of an American Indian Ser.). (Illus.). (gr. 5 up). 1978. PLB 6.95 (ISBN 0-87518-158-9). Dillon.

Delfeld, Paula. The Indian Priest: Philip B. Gordon, 1885-1948. 1977. 5.95 (ISBN 0-8199-0650-6). Franciscan Herald.

Dempsey, Hugh A. Crowfoot: Chief of the Blackfeet. (CAI Ser.: Vol. 122). (Illus.). 1979. pap. 6.95 (ISBN 0-8061-1596-3). U of Okla Pr.

--Red Crow, Warrior Chief. LC 80-51872. (Illus.). viii, 247p. 1980. 16.95 (ISBN 0-8032-1657-2). U of Nebr Pr.

Dennis, Henry C. The American Indian: A Chronology & Fact Book. 2nd ed. LC 76-46440. (Ethnic Chronology Ser.: No. 1). 1977. 8.50 (ISBN 0-379-00526-3). Oceana.

Deur, Lynne. Indian Chiefs. LC 75-128807. (Pull Ahead Bks). (Illus.). (gr. 6-11). 1972. PLB 4.95 (ISBN 0-8225-0461-8). Lerner Pubns.

Dockstader, Frederick J. Great North American Indians: Profiles in Life & Leadership. (Illus.). 1977. 17.95 (ISBN 0-442-02148-8). Van Nos Reinhold.

Drake, Samuel G. The Book of the Indians. LC 74-7960. Repr. of 1841 ed. 49.00 (ISBN 0-404-11848-8). AMS Pr.

Eastman, Charles A. From the Deep Woods to Civilization: Chapters in the Autobiography of an Indian. LC 77-7226. (Illus.). 1977. 14.95x (ISBN 0-8032-0936-3); pap. 3.75 (ISBN 0-8032-5873-9, BB 651, Bison). U of Nebr Pr.

--Indian Boyhood. LC 68-58282. (Illus.). (gr. 3-7). pap. 3.50 (ISBN 0-486-22037-0). Dover.

Famous American Indians. (Famous American Heroes & Leaders Ser.). 80p. (gr. 5-9). PLB 3.50 (ISBN 0-513-00597-8). Denison.

Finley, James B. Life Among the Indians: Or, Personal Reminiscences & Historical Incidents Illustrative of Indian Life & Character. facsimile ed. Clark, D. W., ed. LC 76-160972. (Select Bibliographies Reprint Ser). Repr. of 1857 ed. 28.00 (ISBN 0-8369-5840-3). Arno.

Gridley, Marion E. Contemporary Indian Leaders. LC 72-3148. (Illus.). 224p. (gr. 7 up). 1972. 4.95 (ISBN 0-396-06633-X). Dodd.

Harrell, Sara G. Tomo-Chi-Chi. LC 77-8936. (Story of an American Indian Ser.). (Illus.). (gr. 5 up). 1977. PLB 6.95 (ISBN 0-87518-146-5). Dillon.

Hartley, Lucie K. Pauline Johnson. LC 78-8040. (Story of an American Indian Ser.). (Illus.). (gr. 5 up). 1978. PLB 6.95 (ISBN 0-87518-156-2). Dillon.

Hoffman, Virginia. Navajo Biographies, Vol. 1. new ed. LC 70-113723. (Illus.). 208p. 1974. 10.00 (ISBN 0-89019-003-8). Navajo Curr.

Howard, James H., tr. & ed. The Warrior Who Killed Custer: The Personal Narrative of Chief Joseph White Bull. LC 68-25321. (Landmark Editions). (Illus.). 1968. 13.95x (ISBN 0-8032-0080-3). U of Nebr Pr.

Hyde, George E. Spotted Tail's Folk: A History of the Brule Sioux. rev. ed. LC 61-6497. (Civilization of the American Indian Ser.: Vol. 57). (Illus.). 361p. 1974. 15.95 (ISBN 0-8061-0484-8); pap. 7.95 (ISBN 0-8061-1380-4). U of Okla Pr.

Johnson, Broderick H., ed. Stories of Traditional Navajo Life & Culture. LC 77-22484. (Illus.). 1977. 9.95 (ISBN 0-912586-23-0). Navajo Coll Pr.

Johnson, R. P. Osceola. LC 72-91158. (Story of an American Indian Ser.). (Illus.). 96p. (gr. 5 up). 1973. PLB 6.95 (ISBN 0-87518-055-8). Dillon.

Johnson, William W. The Great Chiefs. (The Old West Ser.). (Illus.). 240p. 1975. 14.95 (ISBN 0-8094-1492-9). Time-Life.

Johnston, Charles H. Famous Indian Chiefs. facsimile ed. LC 76-152179. (Essay Index Reprints - Famous Leaders Ser.). Repr. of 1909 ed. 30.00 (ISBN 0-8369-2232-8). Arno.

Johnston, Johanna. The Indians & the Strangers. LC 72-1447. (Illus.). (gr. 2-5). 1972. 5.95 (ISBN 0-396-06610-0). Dodd.

Jones, J. Lee, ed. Red Raiders Retaliate: The Story of Lone Wolf, the Elder (Guipagho) Famous Kiowa Indian Chief. (Illus.). 96p. 1980. 8.95 (ISBN 0-933512-32-5). Pioneer Bk TX.

Josephy, Alvin M., Jr. Patriot Chiefs: A Chronicle of American Indian Resistance. (Illus.). 1969. pap. 3.95 (ISBN 0-14-004219-9). Penguin.

Katz, Jane. This Song Remembers: Self-Portraits of Native Americans in the Arts. (gr. 7 up). 1980. 8.95 (ISBN 0-395-29522-X). HM.

Kendall, Daythal. A Guide to Supplement to a Guide to Manuscripts Relating to the American Indian in the Library of the American Philosophical Society, Vol. 65 S. LC 81-65976. (Memoir Ser.). 1981. 15.00 (ISBN 0-87169-650-9). Am Philos.

Kostich, Dragos. George Morrison. LC 75-45210. (Story of an American Indian Ser.). (Illus.). (gr. 5 up). 1976. PLB 6.95 (ISBN 0-87518-110-4). Dillon.

Kroeber, Theodora. Ishi in Two Worlds: A Biography of the Last Wild Indian in North America. LC 75-36501. 1976. deluxe ed. 14.95 (ISBN 0-520-03152-0); pap. 8.95 (ISBN 0-520-03153-9). U of Cal Pr.

Lee, Betsy. Charles Eastman. LC 79-9193. (Story of an American Indian Ser.). (Illus.). (gr. 5 up). 1979. PLB 6.95 (ISBN 0-87518-175-9). Dillon.

McGaa, Ed. Red Cloud. 2nd ed. LC 77-12662. (Story of an American Indian Ser.). (Illus.). (gr. 5 up). 1977. PLB 6.95 (ISBN 0-87518-151-1). Dillon.

McKenney & Hall. Indian Tribes of North America with Biographical Sketches & Anecdotes of the Principal Chiefs, 3 vols. 1974. Set. 85.00 (ISBN 0-403-00355-5). Scholarly.

Mitchell, Emerson B. & Allen, T. D. Miracle Hill: The Story of a Navaho Boy. 230p. 1967. pap. 6.95x (ISBN 0-8061-1616-1). U of Okla Pr.

Moises, Rosalio, et al. A Yaqui Life: The Personal Chronicle of a Yaqui Indian. LC 76-56789. Orig. Title: The Tall Candle: the Personal Chronicle of a Yaqui Indian. (Illus.). 1977. 18.50x (ISBN 0-8032-0944-4); pap. 3.95 (ISBN 0-8032-5857-7, BB 637, Bison). U of Nebr Pr.

Molloy, Anne. Five Kidnapped Indians. (Illus.). (gr. 6-9). 1968. 7.95g (ISBN 0-8038-2245-6). Hastings.

Nee, Kay B. Powhatan. LC 73-140991. (Story of an American Indian Ser.). (Illus.). (gr. 5 up). 1971. PLB 6.95 (ISBN 0-87518-036-1). Dillon.

Nelson, Mary C. Pablita Velarde. LC 77-140992. (Story of an American Indian Ser.). (Illus.). (gr. 5 up). 1971. PLB 6.95 (ISBN 0-87518-037-X). Dillon.

Opler, Morris E. Apache Odyssey: A Journey Between Two Worlds. Spindler, George & Spindler, Louise, eds. (Case Studies in Cultural Anthropology). (Illus.). 320p. pap. text ed. 9.50x (ISBN 0-8290-0277-4). Irvington.

Powell, Peter J. The Cheyennes, Ma Heo O's People: A Critical Bibliography. LC 80-8033. (The Newberry Library Center for the History of the American Indian Bibliographical Ser.). 160p. 1981. pap. 4.95x (ISBN 0-253-30416-4). Ind U Pr.

Ross, Patrick. Tobias. 1977. pap. 1.95 (ISBN 0-8423-7250-4). Tyndale.

Schultz, J. W. My Life As an Indian. 224p. 1981. 5.95 (ISBN 0-449-90057-6). Fawcett.

Skold, Betty W. Sacagawea. LC 76-30613. (Story of an American Indian Ser.). (Illus.). (gr. 5 up). 1977. PLB 6.95 (ISBN 0-87518-095-7). Dillon.

Snow, Frances, et al. Thunder Waters: Experiences of Growing up in Different Indian Tribes. (gr. 3-8). 1975. 4.75 (ISBN 0-686-26094-5); pap. 1.95 (ISBN 0-89992-072-1). MT Coun Indian.

Spradley, James P., ed. Guests Never Leave Hungry: The Autobiography of James Sewid, a Kwakiutl Indian. (Illus.). 310p. 1972. pap. 4.95 (ISBN 0-7735-0134-7). McGill-Queens U Pr.

Standing Bear, Luther. My People the Sioux. Brininstool, E. A., ed. LC 74-77394. (Illus.). 1975. 18.50x (ISBN 0-8032-0874-X); pap. 3.95 (ISBN 0-8032-5793-7, BB 578, Bison). U of Nebr Pr.

Stout, Joseph A., Jr. Apache Lightning: The Last Great Battles of the Ajo Calientes. Orig. Title: The Victorio Campaign. 1974. 11.95 (ISBN 0-19-501842-7). Oxford U Pr.

Stump, Sarain. There Is My People Sleeping. (Illus.). 200p. 1970. pap. 2.95 (ISBN 0-686-74147-1). Superior Pub.

Supree, Burton & Ross, Ann. Bear's Heart: Scenes from the Life of a Cheyenne Artist of One Hundred Years Ago with Pictures by Himself. LC 76-48952. 1977. 8.95 (ISBN 0-397-31746-8). Lippincott.

Thatcher, B. B. Indian Biography: Or an Historical Account of Those Individuals Who Have Been Distinguished Among the North American Natives As Orators,Worriors,Statesmen & Other Remarkable Characters, 2vol. enl. ed. LC 73-14660. (Beautiful Rio Grande Classics Ser). (Illus.). lib. bdg. 20.00 (ISBN 0-87380-089-3). Rio Grande.

Urbanek, Mae. Chief Washakie. (Illus.). 150p. 5.00x (ISBN 0-940514-02-8). Urbanek.

U.S. Department of the Interior (Washington, D.C.) Biographical & Historical Index of American Indians & Persons Involved in Indian Affairs, 8 Vols. 1966. 820.00 (ISBN 0-8161-0716-5). G K Hall.

Viola, Herman J. Thomas L. McKenney, Architect of America's Early Indian Policy: 1816-1830. LC 74-18075. (Illus.). 365p. 1974. 15.00 (ISBN 0-8040-0668-7, SB). Swallow.

Wayne, Bennett, ed. Indian Patriots of the Great West. LC 73-17110. (Target Ser). (Illus.). 168p. (gr. 5-12). 1974. PLB 7.29 (ISBN 0-8116-4906-7). Garrard.

Williams, Neva. Patrick Des Jarlait: The Story of an American Indian Artist. LC 74-33523. (Voices of the American Indian). (Illus.). 56p. (gr. 5 up). 1975. PLB 5.95 (ISBN 0-8225-0642-4). Lerner Pubns.

Winter, Keith. A Shananditti: The Last of the Beothucks. pap. 7.50 (ISBN 0-88894-086-6, Pub. by Douglas & McIntyre). Intl Schol Bk Serv.

INDIANS OF NORTH AMERICA–BLANKETS

see Indians of North America–Textile Industry and Fabrics

INDIANS OF NORTH AMERICA–BOATS

Brower, Kenneth. The Starship & the Canoe. LC 77-15200. 1978. 8.95 (ISBN 0-03-039196-2). HR&W.

Doran, Edwin, Jr. Wangka: Austronesian Canoe Origins. LC 80-6108. (Illus.). 128p. 1981. 15.00x (ISBN 0-89096-107-7). Tex A&M Univ Pr.

Guy, Camil. The Weymontaching Birchbark Canoe. (Illus.). 1974. pap. 3.50 (ISBN 0-660-00085-7, 56557-2, Pub. by Natl Mus Canada). U of Chicago Pr.

McPhee, John. The Survival of the Bark Canoe. 146p. 1975. 7.95 (ISBN 0-374-27207-7). FS&G.

Sevareid, Eric. Canoeing with the Cree. LC 68-63520. (Illus.). 206p. 1980. Repr. of 1935 ed. 7.75 (ISBN 0-87351-038-0); pap. 4.50 (ISBN 0-87351-152-2). Minn Hist.

INDIANS OF NORTH AMERICA–CAPTIVITIES

Abney, A. H. Life & Adventures of L. D. Lafferty: Being a True Biography of One of the Most Remarkable Men of the Great Southwest. LC 75-7116. (Indian Captivities Ser.: Vol. 89). 1976. Repr. of 1875 ed. lib. bdg. 44.00 (ISBN 0-8240-1713-7). Garland Pub.

Baker, Charlotte A. True Stories of New England Captives Carried to Canada During the Old French & Indian Wars. LC 75-7128. (Indian Captivities Ser.: Vol. 101). 1976. Repr. of 1897 ed. lib. bdg. 44.00 (ISBN 0-8240-1725-0). Garland Pub.

Bevier, Abraham G. Indians: Or Narratives of Massacres & Depredations. LC 75-16122. 90p. 1975. pap. 2.95 (ISBN 0-912526-17-3). Lib Res.

Bleecker, Ann E. The History of Maria Kittle, Repr. Of 1797 Ed. Bd. with Miscellanies in Prose & Verse. Morris, Thomas. Repr. of 1791 ed. LC 75-7041. (Indian Captivities Ser.: Vol. 20). 1976. lib. bdg. 44.00 (ISBN 0-8240-1644-0). Garland Pub.

The Boston Gazette & the Country Journal... No. 1986; Oct. 22, 1792, Repr. Of 1792 Ed. Bd. with Affecting History of the Dreadful Distresses of Frederic Manheim's Family. Repr. of 1793 ed; Horrid Indian Cruelties. Repr. of 1799 ed; A True Narrative of the Sufferings of Mary Kinnan, Who Was Taken Prisoner by the Shawnee Nation of Indians. Repr. of 1794 ed; A Narrative of the Sufferings of James Derkinderen, Who Was Taken Prisoner by the Halifax Indians. Repr. of 1796 ed; A Journal of the Adventures of Matthew Bunn. Repr. of 1796 ed; Narrative of the Life & Adventures of Matthew Bunn. Repr. of 1827 ed. LC 75-7042. (Indian Captivities Ser.: Vol. 21). 1977. lib. bdg. 44.00 (ISBN 0-8240-1645-9). Garland Pub.

Brown, O. Z. O. Z. Brown: A True Narrative of Daniel McCollum, a Captive Among the Indians During the Revolutionary War, Repr. Of 1853. Washington, Wilcomb E., ed. Incl. James Moore Brown: The Captives of Abb's Valley, a Legend of Frontier Life. By a Son of Mary Moore. Brown, James M. Repr. of 1854 ed; Jane A. Wilson: Narrative of Sufferings...Among Comanche. in "Supplement to the Courant," XIX, No. 3, p.p. 2021, Feb. 11, 1854. Wilson, Jane A; Joseph Barney: Eighteen Years a Captive Among the Indians. A Very Interesting Narrative. In: "America's Own..."New York, 1855, VII, No. 18. Barney, Joseph. (Narratives of North American Indian Captivities Ser.: Vol. 65). 1978. lib. bdg. 44.00 (ISBN 0-8240-1689-0). Garland Pub.

Buckelew, the Indian Captive: Or the Life Story of F. M. Buckelew While a Captive Among the Lipan Indians in the Western Wilds of Frontier Texas As Related by Himself, Repr. Of 1911 Ed. Bd. with Life of M. Buckelew, the Indian Captive, As Related by Himself. Repr. of 1925 ed; In the Bosom of the Comanches: A Thrilling Tale of Savage Life, Massacre & Captivity Truthfully Told by a Surviving Captive. Babb, Theodore A. Repr. of 1912 ed. LC 75-7135. (Indian Captivities Ser.: Vol. 107). 1977. lib. bdg. 44.00 (ISBN 0-8240-1731-5). Garland Pub.

Bunn, Matthew. Journal of the Adventures of Matthew Bunn. facsimile ed. 1962. pap. 1.75 (ISBN 0-685-18889-2). Newberry.

--Narrative of Matthew Bunn. 60p. Date not set. price not set (ISBN 0-685-56551-3). Ye Galleon.

The Captivity & Sufferings of Gen. Freegift Patchin... Among the Indians... During the Border Warfare in the Time of the American Revolution, Repr. Of 1833 Ed. Bd. with U.S. Congress. House. Committee on Claims. Samuel Cozad... Report Made by Mr. E. Whittlesey from the Committee of Claims. Repr. of 1835 ed; Narrative of the Massacre by the Savages of the Wife & Children of Thomas Baldwin. (Incl. 2nd ed. of 1836). Repr. of 1835 ed; An Authentic Narrative of the Seminole War. Repr. of 1836 ed; Captivity & Sufferings of Mrs. Mason, with an Account of the Massacre of Her Youngest Child. Repr. of 1836 ed; Stories of the Revolution: With an Account of the Lost Child of the Delaware. Priest, Josiah. Repr. of 1836 ed; The Indian Captive (Charles Eaton) The Perilous Adventure (Captivity of David Morgan) in: Columbian Almanac for 1838. LC 75-7074. (Indian Captivities Ser.: Vol. 52). 1977. lib. bdg. 44.00 (ISBN 0-8240-1676-9). Garland Pub.

Captivity Tales: An Original Anthology. LC 74-15729. (Popular Culture in America Ser.). (Illus.). 1975. Repr. of 1974 ed. 15.00x (ISBN 0-405-06365-2). Arno.

Carrigan, Minnie B. Captured by the Indians: Reminiscences of Pioneer Life in Minnesota, Repr. Of 1907 Ed. Bd. with Eastern Kentucky Papers: The Founding of Harman's Station with an Account of the Indian Captivity of Mrs. Jennie Wiley. Connelley, William E. Repr. of 1910 ed. LC 75-7134. (Indian Captivities Ser.: Vol. 106). (Incl. rev. ed. of 1912). 1977. lib. bdg. 44.00 (ISBN 0-8240-1730-7). Garland Pub.

Chase, Francis. Gathered Sketches from the Early History of New Hampshire & Vermont: Containing Vivid & Interesting Account of a Great Variety of the Adventures of Our Forefathers, & of Other Incidents of Olden Time. LC 75-7092. (Indian Captivities Ser.: Vol. 68). 1976. Repr. of 1856 ed. lib. bdg. 44.00 (ISBN 0-8240-1692-0). Garland Pub.

Cook, Darius B. Six Months Among Indians. (Illus.). 101p. 1974. Repr. of 1889 ed. 4.50 (ISBN 0-915056-03-8). Hardscrabble Bks.

Crakes, Sylvester. Five Years a Captive Among the Black-feet Indians. LC 75-7099. (Indian Captivities Ser.: Vol. 74). 1976. Repr. of 1858 ed. lib. bdg. 44.00 (ISBN 0-8240-1698-X). Garland Pub.

Cutler, Jervis. Topographical Description of the State of Ohio, Indiana Territory, & Louisiana. LC 78-146388. (First American Frontier Ser). (Illus.). 1971. Repr. of 1812 ed. 12.00 (ISBN 0-405-02839-3). Arno.

--A Topographical Description of the State of Ohio, Indiana Territory, & Louisiana. Washburn, Wilcomb E., ed. LC 75-7056. (Narratives of North American Indian Captivities: Vol. 34). 1975. lib. bdg. 44.00 (ISBN 0-8240-1658-0). Garland Pub.

Dawson, Thomas F. The Ute War: A History of the White River Massacre & the Privations & Hardships of the Captive White Women Among the Hostiles on Grand River. Bd. with The Ute Massacre! Brave Miss Meeker's Captivity. Meeker, Josephine. LC 75-7119. (Indian Captivities Ser.: Vol. 93). 1976. Repr. of 1879 ed. lib. bdg. 44.00 (ISBN 0-8240-1717-X). Garland Pub.

Dickinson, Jonathan. Gods Protecting Providence Man's Surest Help & Defense...Remarkable Deliverance of Divers Person, from the Devouring Waves of the Sea...& Also...the Inhumane Canibals of Florida, Repr. Of 1699 Ed. Bd. with Good Fetch'd Out of Evil. Mather, Cotten. Repr. of 1706 ed; A Memorial of the Present Deplorable State of New England. Mather, Cotten. Repr. of 1707 ed. LC 75-7023. (Indian Captivities Ser.: Vol. 4). 1977. lib. bdg. 44.00 (ISBN 0-8240-1628-9). Garland Pub.

--Gods Protecting Providence Man's Surest Help & Defense...Remarkable Deliverance of Divers Person, from the Devouring Waves of the Sea...& Also...the Inhumane Canibals of Florida, Repr. Of 1699 Ed. Bd. with Good Fetch'd Out of Evil. Mather, Cotten. Repr. of 1706 ed; A Memorial of the Present Deplorable State of New England. Mather, Cotten. Repr. of 1707 ed. LC 75-7023. (Indian Captivities Ser.: Vol. 4). 1977. lib. bdg. 44.00 (ISBN 0-8240-1628-9). Garland Pub.

Drake, Samuel G. Indian Captivities: Being a Collection of the Most Remarkable Narratives of Persons Taken Captives by the North American Indians. LC 75-7077. (Indian Captivities Ser.: Vol. 55). 1976. Repr. of 1839 ed. lib. bdg. 44.00 (ISBN 0-8240-1679-3). Garland Pub.

--Indian Captivities: Or, Life in the Wigwam. LC 74-7961. Repr. of 1851 ed. 27.50 (ISBN 0-404-11849-6). AMS Pr.

Eastman, Ediwn. Seven & Nine Years Among the Camanches & Apaches: An Autobiography. LC 75-7115. (Indian Captivities Ser.: Vol. 88). 1977. Repr. of 1873 ed. lib. bdg. 44.00 (ISBN 0-8240-1712-9). Garland Pub.

Edgar, Matilda R. Ten Years of Upper Canada in Peace & War, 1805-1815, Being the Ridout Letters with Annotations by Matilda Edgar: Also an Appendix of the Narrative of the Captivity Among the Shawanese Indians in 1788 of Thos. Ridout. LC 75-7125. (Indian Captivities Ser.: Vol. 98). 1977. Repr. of 1890 ed. lib. bdg. 44.00 (ISBN 0-8240-1722-6). Garland Pub.

The Escape of Alexander M'Connel of Lexington, Ky. from Captivity by the Indians: In: Hunt's Family Almanac, Repr. Of 1855 Ed. Bd. with The Western Review & Miscellaneous Magazine, a Monthly Publication Devoted to Literature & Science: Vol. 177-179; Vol. 1, 353-358; A Tale of Other Times... the History of the Captivity of Jonas Groves with the Indians: In: Western Herald & Steubenville Gazette, v. 13, no. 33-34, Aug. 12, 19, 1820; The Little Osage Captive, an Authentic Narrative. Cornelius, Elias. Repr. of 1822 ed; An Interesting Narrative. Jamison, Anne. Repr. of 1824 ed; A Brief Narrative of the Sufferings of Lt. Nathan'l Segar Who Was Taken Prisoner by the Indians & Carried to Canada During the Revolutionary War. Repr. of 1825 ed; Narrative of William Biggs While He Was a Prisoner with the Kickapoo Indians. Repr. of 1825 ed. LC 75-7059. (Indian Captivities Ser.: Vol. 37). 1977. lib. bdg. 44.00 (ISBN 0-8240-1661-0). Garland Pub.

Fleming, William. A Narrative of the Sufferings, & Surprizing Deliverance of William & Elizabeth Fleming, Repr. Of 1756 Ed. Incl. John Maylem: Gallic Perfidy; a Poem. Maylem, John. Repr. of 1758 ed; A Faithful Narrative of the Many Dangers & Sufferings, As Well As Wonderful Deliverances of Robert Eastburn, During His Late Captivity Among the Indians. Repr. of 1758 ed; Die Erzehlungen Von Maria le Roy und Barbara Leininger, Welche Vierthalb Jahr Unter Den Indianern Gefangen Gewesen. Repr. of 1759 ed; A Plain Narrative of the Uncommon Sufferings, & Remarkable Deliverance of Thomas Brown, of Charlestown in New-England. Repr. of 1760 ed; A Narrative of the Uncommon Sufferings, & Surprizing Deliverance of Briton Hammon, a Negro Man,...Servant to General Winslow. Repr. of 1760 ed; A Journal of the Captivity of Jean Lowry & Her Children...in Pennsylvania. Repr. of 1760 ed; Erzehlung Eines Unter Den Indianern Gewesenger Gefangenen. Repr. of 1762 ed. (Narrative of North American Indian Captivities: Vol. 8). 1978. lib. bdg. 44.00 (ISBN 0-8240-1632-7). Garland Pub.

Fletcher, Ebenezer. Narrative of the Captivity of Ebenezer Fletcher. 28p. 1979. pap. 3.00 (ISBN 0-87770-150-4). Ye Galleon.

Frost, John. Heroic Women of the West: Comprising Thrilling Examples of Courage, Fortitude, Devotedness, & Self-Sacrifice, Among the Pioneer Mothers of the Western Country. LC 75-7090. (Indian Captivities Ser.: Vol. 66). 1976. Repr. of 1854 ed. lib. bdg. 44.00 (ISBN 0-8240-1690-4). Garland Pub.

God's Mercy Surmounting Man's Cruelty, Exemplified in the Captivity & Redemption of Elizabeth Hanson, Repr. Of 1728. Bd. with An Account of the Captivity of Elizabeth Hanson. Repr. of 1760 ed; Memoirs of Odd Adventures, Strange Deliverances, & C. in the Captivity of John Gyles. Repr. of 1736 ed; A Narrative of the Captivity of Nehemiah How, Who Was Taken by the Indians at the Great-Meadow Fort Above Fort Dummer. Repr. of 1748 ed; The Redeemed Captive. Norton, John. Repr. of 1748 ed. LC 75-7025. (Indian Captivities Ser.: Vol. 6). 1977. lib. bdg. 44.00 (ISBN 0-8240-1630-0). Garland Pub.

Gowanlock, Theresa. Two Months in the Camp of Big Bear: The Life & Adventures of Theresa Gowanlock & Theresa Delaney, Repr. Of 1885 Ed. Bd. with Cynthia Ann Parker, the Story of Her Capture at the Massacre of the Inmates of Parker's Fort: Of Her Quarter of a Century Spent Among the Comanches As the Wife of the War Chief Peta Nocona: and of Her Recapture at the Battle of Pease River by Captain L. S. Ross of the Texian Rangers. Repr. of 1886 ed. LC 75-7121. (Indian Captivities Ser.: Vol. 95). 1976. lib. bdg. 44.00 (ISBN 0-8240-1719-6). Garland Pub.

Hazelton. The Seminole Chief (Billy Bowlegs) Or the Captives of Kissimmee, Repr. Of 1865 Ed. Bd. with Old Rube, the Hunter: Or the Crow Captive. a Tale of the Great Plains. Holmes, Hamilton. Repr. of 1866 ed. LC 75-7105. (Indian Captivities Ser.: Vol. 80). 1976. lib. bdg. 44.00 (ISBN 0-8240-1704-8). Garland Pub.

Heard, J. Norman. White into Red: A Study of the Assimilation of White Persons Captured by Indians. LC 72-13133. (Illus.). 1973. 10.00 (ISBN 0-8108-0581-2). Scarecrow.

Henry, Alexander. Travels & Adventures in Canada & the Indian Territories Between the Years 1760 & 1776. LC 75-7053. (Indian Captivities Ser.: Vol. 31). 1976. Repr. of 1809 ed. lib. bdg. 44.00 (ISBN 0-8240-1655-6). Garland Pub.

Hilliard D'Auberteuil, Michel R. Mis Mac Rea, Roman Historique, Repr. Of 1784 Ed. Bd. with A True & Wonderful Narrative of the Surprising Captivity & Remarkable Deliverance of Mrs. Frances Scott. Repr. of 1786 ed; A Remarkable Narrative of the Captivity & Escape of Mrs. Frances Scott. (Incl. the Whitcomb ed. (ca 1800) & the 1811 ed.). Repr. of 1799 ed. LC 75-7037. (Indian Captivities Ser.: Vol. 16). 1976. lib. bdg. 38.00 (ISBN 0-8240-1640-8). Garland Pub.

Hobbs, James. Wild Life in the Far West...Comprising Hunting & Trapping Adventures with Kit Carson & Others: Captivity & Life Among the Comanches. LC 75-7113. (Indian Captivities Ser.: Vol. 87). 1977. Repr. of 1872 ed. 44.00 (ISBN 0-8240-1711-0). Garland Pub.

Hofland, Barbara H. The Stolen Boy: A Story Founded on Facts, Repr. Of 1828 Ed. Bd. with Seizure of the Ship Industry, by a Conspiracy, & the Consequent Sufferings of Capt. James Fox & His Companions: Their Captivity Among the Esquimaux Indians in North America; & the Miraculous Escape of the Captain. Repr. of 1830 ed; St. Maur: Or, the Captive Babes Recovered, Pub. by Emory & Waugh for the Tract Society of the Methodist Epescopal Church, New York. Repr. of 1830 ed. LC 75-7066. (Indian Captivities Ser.: Vol. 44). 1976. lib. bdg. 44.00 (ISBN 0-8240-1668-8). Garland Pub.

The Horrid Cruelty of the Indians, Exemplified in the Life of Charles Saunders, Late of Charles-Town, in South Carolina, Repr. Of 1763 Ed. Bd. with The History of the Life & Sufferings of Henry Grace...Being a Narrative of the Hardships He Underwent During Several Years Captivity Among the Savages in North America...in Which Is Introduced an Account of the Several Customs & Manners of the Different Nations of Indians. Repr. of 1764 ed; Adventure of a Young English Officer Among the Abenakee Savages. in: Bickerstaff's Boston Almanack, for the Year of Our Lord 1768. Repr. of 1767 ed; A Brief Narration of the Captivity of Isaac Hollister. Repr. of 1767 ed; Account of the Captivity of William Henry in 1755 & of His Residence Among the Senneka Indians Six Years & Seven Months till He Made His Escape from Them. Repr. of 1768 ed; A Narrative of an Extraordinary Escape Out of the Hands of the Indians, in the Gulph of St. Lawrence; Interspersed with a Description of the Coast, & Remarks on the Customs & Manners of the Savages There. Smethurst, Gamaliel. Repr. of 1774 ed. LC 75-7030. (Indian Captivities Ser.: Vol. 10). 1976. lib. bdg. 44.00 (ISBN 0-8240-1634-3). Garland Pub.

Hosmer, Margaret K. The Child Captives: A True Tale of Life Among the Indians of the West. LC 75-7109. (Indian Captivities Ser.: Vol. 83). 1976. Repr. of 1870 ed. lib. bdg. 44.00 (ISBN 0-8240-1707-2). Garland Pub.

Humphreys, David. An Essay on the Life of the Honorable Major-General Israel Putnam, Repr. Of 1788 Ed. Bd. with A Genuine & Correct Account of the Captivity, Sufferings & Deliverance of Mrs. Jemima Howe. Howe, Jemima. Repr. of 1792 ed; The Affecting History of Mrs. Howe. Repr. of 1815 ed. LC 75-7040. (Indian Captivities Ser.: Vol. 19). 1977. lib. bdg. 44.00 (ISBN 0-8240-1643-2). Garland Pub.

Hunter, John D. Manners & Customs of Several Indian Tribes Located West of the Mississippi... to Which Is Prefixed the History of the Author's Life During a Residence of Several Years Among Them. LC 75-7061. (Indian Captivities Ser.: Vol. 39). 1976. Repr. of 1823 ed. lib. bdg. 44.00 (ISBN 0-8240-1663-7). Garland Pub.

--Memoirs of a Captivity Among the Indians of North America. 2nd ed. 1981. 12.00x (ISBN 0-686-76742-X). Regent House.

--Memoirs of a Captivity Among the Indians of North America, from Childhood to the Age of Nineteen. LC 2-16705. (American Studies). Repr. of 1823 ed. 23.00 (ISBN 0-384-24925-6). Johnson Repr.

Hutchinson, K. M. Memoir of Abijah Hutchinson: A Soldier of the Revolution, Repr. Of 1843 Ed. Bd. with Narrative of the Massacre at Chicago, August 15, 1812, & of Some Preceding Events. Kinzie, Juliette A. Repr. of 1844 ed; A History of the Cooper Mines & Newgate Prison... Also, of the Captivity of Daniel Hayes... by the Indians in 1707. Phelps, Noah A. Repr. of 1845 ed; A Long Journey. the Story of Daniel Hayes. Repr. of 1876 ed; The Bible Boy Taken Captive by the Indians. Cope, Herman. Repr. of 1845 ed. LC 75-7082. (Indian Captivities Ser.: Vol. 59). 1977. lib. bdg. 44.00 (ISBN 0-8240-1683-1). Garland Pub.

Indian Atrocities: Affecting & Thrilling Anecdotes Respecting the Hardships & Sufferings of Our Brave & Venerable Forefathers, Etc, Repr. Of 1846. Bd. with The Indians: Or, Narrative of Massacres & Depredations on the Frontier in Wawasink & Its Vicinity During the American Revolution. Bevier, Abraham G. Repr. of 1846 ed; Three Years Among the Indians & Mexicans. James, Thomas. Repr. of 1846 ed. LC 75-7084. (Indian Captivities Ser.: Vol. 61). 1977. lib. bdg. 44.00 (ISBN 0-8240-1685-8). Garland Pub.

The Indian Captive: A Narrative of the Adventures & Sufferings of Matthew Brayton, in His 34 Years of Captivity Among the Indians of North-Western America, Repr. Of 1860 Ed. Bd. with The Indian Captives: In: Oquawka Spectator, Ill., V. 3, No. 16, May 17, 1860. Page, Larsena A. Repr. of 1860 ed; Short Narrative of James Kimball, 11 Years a Captive Among the Snake Indians. Repr. of 1861 ed; The Life of Joseph Persinger Who Was Taken by the Shawnee Indians When an Infant: With a Short Account of the Indian Troubles in Missouri; & a Sketch of the Adventures of the Author. Repr. of 1861 ed; In Captivity. the Experience, Privations & Dangers of Sam'l J. Brown, & Others, While Prisoners of the Hostile Sioux, During the Massacre & War of 1862. Repr. of 1862 ed; Abenteuer Unter Den Indianern: Oder, Ina's Gefangenschaft Unter Den Wilden und Ihre Wunderbare Befreiung. Repr. of 1863 ed. LC 75-7101. (Indian Captivities Ser.: Vol. 76). 1977. lib. bdg. 44.00 (ISBN 0-8240-1700-5). Garland Pub.

Indian Captivity: A True Narrative of the Capture of the Rev. O. M. Spencer by the Indians in the Neighborhood of Cincinnati. LC 75-7075. (Indian Captivities Ser.: Vol. 53). 1976. Repr. of 1835 ed. lib. bdg. 44.00 (ISBN 0-8240-1677-7). Garland Pub.

Interesting Narrative of the Sufferings of Mr. Joseph Barker & His Wife... Taken by a Scouting Party of British & Indians... in 1777, Repr. Of 1848 Ed. Bd. with An Indian Tradition. No Fiction. the Traditionary History of a Narrow & Providential Escape of Some White Men from Being Tomahawked, Scalped, & Robbed by a Party of Taw-Way Indians. Repr. of 1848 ed; The Dreadful Sufferings & Thrilling Adventures of an Overland Party of Immigrants to California, Their Terrible Conflicts with Savage Tribes of Indians!!! & Bands of Mexican Robbers!!! with Marriage, Funeral, & Other Interesting Ceremonies & Customs of Indian Life in Far West. Adam, George. Repr. of 1850 ed; History of the Revolutionary War... Brief Account of the Captivity & Cruel Sufferings of Captain Deitz & John & Robert Brice. Repr. of 1851 ed; The Life & Adventures of David C. Butterfield, a Northwestern Pioneer... Written by Himself, in His Wild Western Style. Repr. of 1851 ed. LC 75-7087. (Indian Captivities Ser.: Vol. 63). 1977. lib. bdg. 44.00 (ISBN 0-8240-1687-4). Garland Pub.

James, Edwin. Narrative of the Captivity & Adventures of John Tanner During Thirty Years Residence Among the Chippewa, Ottawa & Objibwa Tribes Etc. Loomis, Noel, ed. & intro. by. Repr. 15.00 (ISBN 0-87018-033-9). Ross.

Janney, Abel. Narrative of the Capture of Abel Janney by the Indians in 1782. from His Diary: In: Ohio State Arch. & Hist. Society Publications, Vol. 8, 465-73, Columbus. Repr. Of 1900 Ed. Bd. with The Shetek Pioneers & the Indians. Hibschman, Harry J. Repr. of 1901 ed; Captivity Among the Sioux, August 18 to September 26, 1862: In: Minnesota Historical Society Collections, Vol. 9, St. Paul, 1901, pp. 395-426. White, Mrs. N. D. (Illus.). Repr. of 1901 ed; Elizabeth Hicks, a True Romance of the American War of Independence, 1775 to 1783, Abridged from Her Own Manuscript by Her Daughter Fanny Bird, Completed & Ed. by Her Granddaughter Louisa J. Marriott. Hicks, Elizabeth. Repr. of 1902 ed; Scout Journals, 1757. Narrative of James Johnson, a Captive During French & Indian Wars. Repr. of 1902 ed. LC 75-7132. (Indian Captivities Ser.: Vol. 104). 1976. lib. bdg. 44.00 (ISBN 0-8240-1728-5). Garland Pub.

Jeffries, Ewel. A Short Biography of John Leeth, with an Account of His Life Among the Indians. Thwaites, Reuben G., ed. LC 74-180034. 12.00 (ISBN 0-405-08669-5, Pub. by Blom). Arno.

Jones, Jonathan H. A Condensed History of the Apache & Comanche Indian Tribes. LC 75-7129. (Indian Captivities Ser.: Vol. 102). 1976. Repr. of 1899 ed. lib. bdg. 44.00 (ISBN 0-8240-1726-9). Garland Pub.

A Journal Kept at Nootka Sound by John R. Jewitt, One of the Surviving Crew of the Ship Boston...Interspersed with Some Account of the Natives, Their Manners & Customs, Repr. Of 1807 Ed. Incl. A Narrative of the Adventures & Sufferings of John R. Jewitt. Alsop, Richard, ed. Repr. of 1815 ed. LC 75-7050. (Indian Captivities Ser.: Vol. 28). 1976. lib. bdg. 44.00 (ISBN 0-8240-1652-1). Garland Pub.

The Journal of Captain William Pote, Jr., During His Captivity in the French & Indian War from May 1745 to August 1747. LC 75-7127. (Indian Captivities Ser.: Vol. 100). 1976. Repr. of 1896 ed. lib. bdg. 44.00 (ISBN 0-8240-1724-2). Garland Pub.

The Journal of William Scudder, an Officer in the Late New-York Line, Who Was Taken Capture by the Indians at Fort Stanwix. LC 75-7044. (Indian Captivities Ser.: Vol. 22). 1977. Repr. of 1794 ed. lib. bdg. 44.00 (ISBN 0-8240-1646-7). Garland Pub.

Kelly, Fanny W. Narrative of My Captivity Among the Sioux Indians...with a Brief Account of General Sully's Indian Expedition in 1864, Bearing Upon Events Occurring in My Captivity. LC 75-7111. (Indian Captivities Ser.: Vol. 85). 1976. Repr. of 1871 ed. lib. bdg. 44.00 (ISBN 0-8240-1709-9). Garland Pub.

Kimber, Edward. The History of the Life & Adventures of Mr. Anderson. Washburn, Wilcomb E., ed. LC 75-7026. (Narratives of North American Indian Captivities: Vol. 7). 1975. lib. bdg. 44.00 (ISBN 0-8240-1631-9). Garland Pub.

Kinzie, Juliette. Wau-Bun, the "Early" Days in the Northwest. LC 75-7095. (Indian Captivities Ser.: Vol. 70). 1976. Repr. of 1856 ed. lib. bdg. 44.00 (ISBN 0-8240-1694-7). Garland Pub.

Knowles, Nathaniel. The Torture of Captives by the Indians of Eastern North America: In: Proceedings of the American Philosophical Society, Vol. 8I, No. 2, March 22, 1940, Repr. Of 1940 Ed. Bd. with Captivity of Jonathan Alder. Repr. of 1944 ed; Horrors of Captivity: Authentic & Thrilling Sketches of Tragedies That Occurred on the Texas Frontier During Indian Times. Hunter, John M. Repr. of 1954 ed; Indian John: Life of John W. Johnson. Repr. of 1861 ed. LC 75-7139. (Indian Captivities Ser.: Vol. 111). 1977. lib. bdg. 44.00 (ISBN 0-8240-1735-8). Garland Pub.

Lampman, Evelyn S. White Captives. LC 74-18187. 192p. (gr. 4-7). 1975. 6.95 (ISBN 0-689-50023-8, McElderry Bk). Atheneum.

Larimer, Sarah L. The Capture & Escape: Or, Life Among the Sioux. LC 75-7110. (Indian Captivities Ser.: Vol. 84). 1976. Repr. of 1870 ed. lib. bdg. 44.00 (ISBN 0-8240-1708-0). Garland Pub.

Lee, L. P. History of the Spirit Lake Massacre & of Miss Abigail Gardiners Three Month's Captivity Among the Indians. 1968. Repr. of 1857 ed. 5.50 (ISBN 0-87770-057-5). Ye Galleon.

Lee, Lorenzo P. History of the Spirit Lake Massacre! 8th March, 1857 & of Miss Abigail Gardiner's 3 Month's Captivity Among the Indians. According to Her Own Account, As Given to L. P. Lee, Repr. Of 1857 Ed. Bd. with History of the Spirit Lake Massacre & Captivity of Miss Abbie Gardner. Sharp, Abigail. Repr. of 1885 ed. LC 75-7097. (Indian Captivities Ser.: Vol. 72). 1976. lib. bdg. 44.00 (ISBN 0-8240-1696-3). Garland Pub.

Levernier, James & Cohen, Hennig, eds. The Indians & Their Captives. LC 76-57831. (Contributions in American Studies: No. 31). 1977. lib. bdg. 17.50x (ISBN 0-8371-9535-7, CIC/). Greenwood.

Life & Adventures of William Filley, Who Was Stolen from His Home by the Indians...& His Safe Return from Captivity After an Absence of 29 Years, Repr. Of 1867 Ed. Bd. with An Account of the Captivity of Hugh Gibson Among the Delaware Indians of the Big Beaver & the Muskingum from 1756 to 1759: In: Massachusetts Historical Society Collections, Vol. 6, 3rd Ser., pp. 141-153. Repr. of 1867 ed; Mary Nealy: In: Harper's New Monthly Magazine, Vol. 36, No. 213, Feb. 1868. Ellet, Elizabeth F. Repr. of 1868 ed; General Sheridan's Squaw Spy, & Mrs. Clara Blynn's Captivity Among the Wild Indians of the Prairies. Repr. of 1869 ed; Lost & Found in the Rocky Mountains: In: the Western Monthly, Vol. 2, Chicago, 1869, pp. 11-21. Hood, J. E. Repr. of 1869 ed. LC 75-7107. (Indian Captivities Ser.: Vol. 81). 1976. lib. bdg. 40.00 (ISBN 0-8240-1705-6). Garland Pub.

The Life & Travels of Josiah Mooso: A Life on the Frontier Among Indians & Spaniards, Not Seeing the Face of a White Woman for 15 Years. LC 75-7124. (Indian Captivities Ser.: Vol. 97). 1976. Repr. of 1888 ed. lib. bdg. 44.00 (ISBN 0-8240-1721-8). Garland Pub.

Life of Dr. William F. Carver of California, Champion Rifle-Shot of the World: Truthful Story of His Capture by the Indians When a Child. LC 75-7527. (Indian Captivities Ser.: Vol. 92). 1977. Repr. of 1878 ed. lib. bdg. 44.00 (ISBN 0-8240-1716-1). Garland Pub.

Loudon, Archibald. Selection of Some of the Most Interesting Narratives of Outrages Committed by the Indians in Their Wars with the White People, 2 Vols. in 1. LC 76-106124. (First American Frontier Ser). 1971. Repr. of 1808 ed. 30.00 (ISBN 0-405-02866-0). Arno.

--A Selection, of Some of the Most Interesting Narratives, of Outrages, Committed by the Indians, in Their Wars, with the White People, 2 vols. LC 75-7052. (Indian Captivities Ser.: Vols. 29 & 30). 1977. Repr. of 1811 ed. Vol. 1. lib. bdg. 44.00 (ISBN 0-8240-1653-X); Vol. 2. lib. bdg. 44.00 (ISBN 0-8240-1654-8). Garland Pub.

M'Clung, John A. Sketches of Western Adventure. LC 76-90184. (Mass Violence in America Ser). Repr. of 1832 ed. 13.00 (ISBN 0-405-01326-4). Arno.

McClung, John A. Sketches of Western Adventure: Containing an Account of the Most Interesting Incidents Connected with the Settlement of the West from 1755 to 1794. LC 75-7072. (Indian Captivities Ser.: Vol. 50). 1976. Repr. of 1832 ed. lib. bdg. 44.00 (ISBN 0-8240-1674-2). Garland Pub.

Marsh, James B. Four Years in the Rockies: Or the Adventures of Isaac P. Rose... Giving His Experience As a Hunter & Trapper. LC 75-7120. (Indian Captivities Ser.: Vol. 94). 1976. Repr. of 1884 ed. lib. bdg. 44.00 (ISBN 0-8240-1718-8). Garland Pub.

Mather, Cotten. Decennium Luctuosum. an History of...the Long War, Which New England Hath Had with the Indian Savages. LC 75-7022. (Indian Captivities Ser.: Vol. 3). 1976. Repr. of 1698 ed. lib. bdg. 44.00 (ISBN 0-8240-1627-0). Garland Pub.

Mather, Increase. An Essay for the Recording of Illustrious Providences. LC 75-7021. (Indian Captivities Ser.: Vol. 2). 1977. Repr. of 1684 ed. lib. bdg. 40.00 (ISBN 0-8240-1626-2). Garland Pub.

Meginness, John F. Biography of Frances Slocum, the Lost Sister of Wyoming: A Complete Narrative of Her Captivity & Wanderings Among the Indians. LC 74-3963. (Women in America Ser). 260p. 1974. Repr. of 1891 ed. 16.00 (ISBN 0-405-06112-9). Arno.

Memoirs of Charles Dennis Rusoe d'Eres, a Native of Canada, Who Was with the Scanyawtauragahrooote Indians Eleven Years, Repr. Of 1800 Ed. Bd. with The Life & Travels of James Tudor Owen. Repr. of 1801 ed; The Connecticut, Rhode Island, Massachusetts, New Hampshire & Vermont Farmers Almanac for 1803... Also Containing an Affecting Account of the Death of Miss Polly & Hannah Watts... Taken Prisoners & Murdered by the Indians. Repr. of 1802 ed. LC 75-7047. (Indian Captivities Ser.: Vol. 25). 1977. lib. bdg. 44.00 (ISBN 0-8240-1649-1). Garland Pub.

Meredith, Grace E. Girl Captives of the Cheyennes: A True Story of the Capture & Rescue of 4 Pioneer Girls, 1874, Repr. Of 1927 Ed. Bd. with Narrative of the Captivity of Mrs. Jane Frazier: In: Thomas' History of Allegheny County, Pennsylvania. Frazier, Jane. Repr. of 1930 ed; History of the Capture & Captivity of David Boyd from Cumberland County, Pennsylvania, in 1756. Davis, Marion M., ed. Repr. of 1931 ed; The Means Massacre, Molly Finney, the Canadian Captive. Illsley, Charles P. Repr. of 1932 ed; Narrative of Titus King of Northampton, Mass., a Prisoner of the Indians in Canada, 1755-1758. Repr. of 1938 ed. LC 75-7137. (Indian Captivities Ser.: Vol. 109). 1977. lib. bdg. 44.00 (ISBN 0-8240-1733-1). Garland Pub.

Message from the President of the United States, Transmitting a Report of the Secretary of War, Relative to Murders Committed by the Indians in the State of Tennessee. Jan. 11, 1813, Repr. Of 1812 Ed. Incl. The Travels of James Dolphin, with an Account of His Being Taken by the Indian Savages, & Redeemed by a Spanish Lady in the City of Old Mexico. Repr. of 1812 ed; A Journal: Containing an Accurate & Interesting Account of the Hardships, Sufferings, Battles, Defeat & Captivity of Those Heroic Kentucky Volunteers & Regulars, Commanded by General Winchester... Also Two Narratives by Men... Taken Captive by the Indians. Darnell, Elias. Repr. of 1813 ed; Murder of the Whole Family of Samuel Wells, Consisting of His Wife & Sister & Eleven Children, by the Indians. Repr. of 1813 ed; An Affecting Narrative of the Captivity & Sufferings of Mrs. Mary Smith, Who with Her Husband & Three Daughters Were Taken Prisoners by the Indians. Repr. of 1815 ed; An Affecting Account of the Tragical Death of Major Swan, & of the Captivity of Mrs. Swan & Infant Child, by the Savages. Swan, Eliza. Repr. of 1815 ed; Narrative of Henry Bird, Who Was Carried Away by the Indians, After the Murder of His Whole Family. Bird, Henry. Repr. of 1815 ed; A Narrative of the Life & Death of Lieut. Joseph Morgan Wilcox, Who Was Massacred by the Creek Indians on the Alabama River. Repr. of 1816 ed. LC 75-7055. (Indian Captivities Ser.: Vol. 33). 1976. lib. bdg. 44.00 (ISBN 0-8240-1657-2). Garland Pub.

Metcalf, Samuel L. A Collection of Some of the Most Interesting Narratives of Indian Warfare in the West. LC 75-7060. (Indian Captivities Ser.: Vol. 38). 1977. Repr. of 1821 ed. lib. bdg. 44.00 (ISBN 0-8240-1662-9). Garland Pub.

Methvin, John J. Andele, or the Mexican - Kiowa Captive. a Story of Real Life Among the Indians, Repr. Of 1899 Ed. Bd. with Grandfather's Captivity & Escape. Benton, Mrs. L. G. Repr; Stirring Adventures of the Joseph R. Brown Family. Their Captivity During the Indian Uprising of 1862 & Description of Their Old Home Near Sacred Heart-Destroyed by the Indians. Allanson, George G. Repr. LC 75-7131. (Indian Captivities Ser.: Vol. 103). 1976. lib. bdg. 44.00 (ISBN 0-8240-1727-7). Garland Pub.

Miller, Pierre. Captivity of Father Peter Milet: Among the Oneida Indians. His Own Narrative with Supplementary Documents, Repr. Of 1888 Ed. Bd. with Captivity Among the Oneidas in 1690-91 of Father Pierre Milet of the Society of Jesus. Repr. of 1897 ed; Lost & Found: Or 3 Months with the Wild Indians; a Brief Sketch of the Life of Ole T. Nystel, Embracing His Experience While in Captivity to the Comanches & Subsequent Liberation from Them. Repr. of 1888 ed; Wehman's Book on the Scalping Knife: Or the Log Cabin in Flames. Wehman, Henry J. Repr. of 1890 ed; Left by the Indians. Story of My Life. Fuller, Emeline L. Repr. of 1892 ed. LC 75-7123. (Indian Captivities Ser.: Vol. 96). 1976. lib. bdg. 44.00 (ISBN 0-8240-1720-X). Garland Pub.

Mrs. J. E. De Camp Sweet's Narrative of Her Captivity in the Sioux Outbreak of 1862: The Story of Nancy McClure - Captivity Among the Sioux, the Story of Mary Schwandt - the Captivity During the Sioux Outbreak, Etc, Repr. Of 1894 Ed. Bd. with Abby Byram & Her Father. the Indian Captives. with Some Account of Their Ancestors & a Register of Their Descendants. McElroy, John M. Repr. of 1898 ed; True Story of the Lost Shackle: Or Seven Years with the Indians. Dabney, Owen P. Repr. of 1897 ed. LC 75-7126. (Indian Captivities Ser.: Vol. 99). 1977. lib. bdg. 44.00 (ISBN 0-8240-1723-4). Garland Pub.

A Narrative of the Captivity & Adventures of John Tanner (U.S. Interpreter at the Saut de Ste. Marie) During 30 Years Residence Among the Indians in the Interior of North America. LC 75-7068. (Indian Captivities Ser.: Vol. 46). 1976. Repr. of 1830 ed. lib. bdg. 44.00 (ISBN 0-8240-1670-X). Garland Pub.

Narrative of the Captivity... of Mrs. Clarissa Plummer... Who with Mrs. Caroline Harris... Were... Taken Prisoners by the Camanche Tribe of Indians, Repr. Of 1838 Ed. Bd. with History of the Captivity & Providential Release Therefrom of Mrs. Caroline Harris... Who with Mrs. Clarissa Plummer... Were... with Their Unfortunate Husbands Taken Prisoner by the Comanche Tribe of Indians. Repr. of 1838 ed; A Narrative of the Captivity of Mrs. Horn, & Her 2 Children, with Mrs. Harris, by the Camanche Indians. House, E. Repr. of 1839 ed; An Authentic & Thrilling Narrative of the Captivity of Mrs. Horn. Repr. of 1851 ed; Narrative of Ransom Clark, the Only Survivor of Major Dade's Command in Florida. Repr. of 1839 ed; Historical Sketches of Roswell Franklin & Family. Hubbard, Robert. Repr. of 1839 ed. LC 75-7076. (Indian Captivities Ser.: Vol. 54). 1977. lib. bdg. 44.00 (ISBN 0-8240-1678-5). Garland Pub.

A Narrative of the Captivity of Mrs. Johnson: Containing an Account of Her Sufferings During Four Years with the Indians & French, Repr. Of 1796 Ed. Bd. with glascow ed. Repr. of 1797 ed; enl. ed. Repr. of 1814 ed. LC 75-7045. (Indian Captivities Ser.: Vol. 23). 1976. lib. bdg. 44.00 (ISBN 0-8240-1647-5). Garland Pub.

Narrative of the Capture & Providential Escape of Misses Frances & Almira Hall, 2 Respectable Young Women of the Ages of 16 & 18 Who Were Taken Prisoners by the Savages, Repr. Of 1832 Ed. Bd. with History of the War Between the United States & the Sac & Fox Nations of Indians. Wakefield, John A. Repr. of 1834 ed; Indian Massacre & Captivity of Hall Girls. Scanlan, Charles M. Repr. of 1915 ed. LC 75-7071. (Indian Captivities Ser.: Vol. 49). 1976. lib. bdg. 44.00 (ISBN 0-8240-1673-4). Garland Pub.

A Narrative of the Capture of Certain Americans, at Westmorland, by Savages, Repr. Of 1780 Ed. Bd. with 2nd ed. Repr. of 1784 ed; Sketches of the Life & Adventure of Moses Van Campen. Hubbard, John N. Repr. of 1841 ed. LC 75-7033. (Indian Captivities Ser.: Vol. 13). 1977. lib. bdg. 44.00 (ISBN 0-8240-1637-8). Garland Pub.

A Narrative of the Incidents Attending the Capture, Detention & Ransom of Charles Johnston... Who Was Made Prisoner by the Indians. LC 75-7065. (Indian Captivities Ser.: Vol. 43). 1976. Repr. of 1827 ed. lib. bdg. 44.00 (ISBN 0-8240-1667-X). Garland Pub.

A Narrative of the Sufferings of Massy Harbison from Indian Barbarity, Giving an Account of Her Captivity, the Murder of Her 2 Children, Her Escape, with an Infant at Her Breast, Repr. Of 1825 Ed. Incl. 4th, enl. ed. Repr. of 1836 ed. LC 75-7064. (Indian Captivities Ser.: Vol. 42). 1977. lib. bdg. 44.00 (ISBN 0-8240-1666-1). Garland Pub.

Narrative of the Tragical Death of Mr. Darius Barber, & His Seven Children, Who Were Inhumanly Butchered by the Indians... to Which Is Added an Account of the Captivity & Sufferings of Mrs. Barber, Repr. Of 1816 Ed. Incl. Shocking Murder by the Savage! of Mr. Darius Barber's Family in Georgia; Narrative of the Captivity & Sufferings of Mrs. Hannah Lewis, & Her 3 Children, Who Were Taken Prisoners by the Indians. Repr. of 1817 ed; Narrative of the Captivity & Providential Escape of Mrs. Lewis. Repr. of 1833 ed; Narrative of James Van Horne: On the Plains of Michigan. Repr. of 1817 ed; The Indian Captive: Or a Narrative of the Captivity & Sufferings of Zadock Steele... to Which Is Prefixed an Account of the Burning of Royalton. Repr. of 1818 ed. LC 75-7058. (Indian Captivities Ser.: Vol. 36). 1976. lib. bdg. 44.00 (ISBN 0-8240-1660-2). Garland Pub.

Newberry Library. Narratives of Captivity Among the Indians of North America, with Supplement I. LC 74-3100. 1974. Repr. of 1912 ed. 19.00 (ISBN 0-8103-3694-4). Gale.

Old Record of the Captivity of Margaret Erskine 1779, Repr. Of 1912 Ed. Bd. with Indian Horrors of the Fifties: Story & Life of the Only Known Living Captive of the Indian Horrors of Sixty Years Ago. Alexander, Jesse H. Repr. of 1916 ed. LC 75-7136. (Indian Captivities Ser.; Vol. 108). 1977. lib. bdg. 44.00 (ISBN 0-8240-1732-3). Garland Pub.

The Orphan's Experience: Or the Hunter & Trapper. Being a History of the Personal Experience of M. V. B. Morrison. LC 75-7108. (Indian Captivities Ser.: Vol. 82). 1977. Repr. of 1868 ed. lib. bdg. 44.00 (ISBN 0-8240-1706-4). Garland Pub.

The Personal Narrative of James O. Pattie of Kentucky During... Journeyings of 6 Years. LC 75-7070. (Indian Captivities Ser.: Vol. 48). 1976. Repr. of 1831 ed. lib. bdg. 44.00 (ISBN 0-8240-1672-6). Garland Pub.

Plummer, Rachael. Rachel Plummer's Narrative of 21 Months Servitude As a Prisoner Among the Commanchee Indians. Repr. of 1838 ed. 19.50 (ISBN 0-685-83962-1). Jenkins.

Pritts, Joseph. Incidents of Border Life Illustrative of the Times & Condition of the First Settlements in Parts of the Middle & Western States... Compiled from Authentic Sources. LC 75-7080. (Indian Captivities Ser.: Vol. 57). 1977. Repr. of 1839 ed. lib. bdg. 44.00 (ISBN 0-8240-1681-5). Garland Pub.

The Returned Captive: A Poem, Repr. Of 1787 Ed. Bd. with John Graham's Address to the Master & Worthy Family of His House; Shewing His Suffering Among the Indians of West Florida. Repr. of 1787 ed; New Travels to the Westward, or Unknown Parts of America. (Repr. of 1788 & 1797 eds.); The Remarkable Adventures of Jackson Johonnet, of Massachusetts...Containing an Account of His Captivity, Sufferings & Escape from Kickapoo Indians. (Repr. of 1793 & 1816 eds.). LC 75-7039. (Indian Captivities Ser.: Vol. 18). 1976. lib. bdg. 44.00 (ISBN 0-8240-1642-4). Garland Pub.

Rowlandson, Mary. A Narrative of the Captivity & Removes of Mrs. Mary Rowlandson. 122p. 1975. 9.95 (ISBN 0-87770-130-X). Ye Galleon.

Russell, James. Matilda: Or the Indian Captive. a Canadian Tale Founded on Fact. LC 75-7073. (Indian Captivities Ser.: Vol. 51). 1976. Repr. of 1833 ed. lib. bdg. 44.00 (ISBN 0-8240-1675-0). Garland Pub.

Schwandt, Mary. Captivity of Mary Schwandt. 1975. pap. 3.50 (ISBN 0-87770-153-9). Ye Galleon.

Seaver, James E. A Narrative of the Life of Mrs. Mary Jamison Who Was Taken by the Indians in the Year 1755 When Only About 12 Years of Age & Has Continued to Reside Amongst Them to the Present Time, Repr. Of 1824 Ed. Bd. with enl. ed. Morgan, Lewis H., ed. Repr. of 1856 ed. LC 75-7063. (Indian Captivities Ser.: Vol. 41). 1977. lib. bdg. 44.00 (ISBN 0-8240-1665-3). Garland Pub.

--Narrative of the Life of Mrs. Mary Jemison. 7.00 (ISBN 0-8446-2899-9). Peter Smith.

Shea, John G. Perils of the Ocean & Wilderness: Narrative of Shipwreck & Indian Captivity. (Reprints in History Ser.). Repr. of 1856 ed. lib. bdg. 21.00x (ISBN 0-697-00057-5). Irvington.

--Perils of the Ocean & Wilderness: Or, Narratives of Shipwreck & Indian Captivity, Gleaned from Early Missionary Annals. LC 75-7098. (Indian Captivities Ser.: Vol. 73). 1976. Repr. of 1857 ed. lib. bdg. 44.00 (ISBN 0-8240-1697-1). Garland Pub.

Smith, Clinton L. The Boy Captives, Being the True Story of the Experiences & Hardships of Clinton L. Smith & Jeff D. Smith, Among the Comanche & Apache Indians During the Early Days. LC 75-7138. (Indian Captivities Ser.: Vol. 110). 1976. Repr. of 1927 ed. lib. bdg. 44.00 (ISBN 0-8240-1734-X). Garland Pub.

Snelling, William J. Tales of the Northwest: On Sketches of Indian Life & Character. LC 75-7067. (Indian Captivities Ser.: Vol. 45). 1976. Repr. of 1830 ed. lib. bdg. 44.00 (ISBN 0-8240-1669-6). Garland Pub.

Stanley, Edwin J. Rambles in Wonderland: Or up the Yellowstone & Among the Geysers & Other Curiosities of the National Park. LC 75-7118. (Indian Captivities Ser.: Vol. 91). 1976. Repr. of 1878 ed. lib. bdg. 44.00 (ISBN 0-8240-1715-3). Garland Pub.

Steele, Zadock. The Indian Captive: Or, a Narrative of the Captivity & Sufferings of Zadock Steele. LC 71-173120. Repr. of 1908 ed. 14.00 (ISBN 0-405-08993-7). Arno.

The Story of Captain Jasper Parrish, Captive, Interpreter & United States Sub-Agent to the Six Nations Indians, Repr. Of 1903 Ed. Bd. with The Story of My Capture & Escape During the Minnesota Indian Massacre of 1862. with Historical Notes, Description of Pioneer Life, & Sketches & Incidents of the Great Outbreak of the Sioux or Dakota Indians As I Saw Them. Tarble, Helen M. Repr. of 1904 ed; The Story of the Rice Boys, Captured by the Indians. Parkman, Ebenezer. Repr. of 1906 ed. LC 75-7133. (Indian Captivities Ser.: Vol. 105). 1976. lib. bdg. 44.00 (ISBN 0-8240-1729-3). Garland Pub.

Stratton, Royal. Life Among the Indians: Being an Interesting Narrative of the Captivity of the Oatman Girls, Among the Apache & Mohave Indians. LC 75-7096. (Indian Captivities Ser.: Vol. 71). (Bnd. with 2nd ed., changed 1857). 1977. Repr. of 1857 ed. lib. bdg. 44.00 (ISBN 0-8240-1695-5). Garland Pub.

Stutler, Boyd B. Kinnan Massacre. 1969. soft bdg. 3.50 (ISBN 0-87012-039-5). McClain.

Summers, Thomas O. Joseph Brown: Or, the Young Tennessean Whose Life Was Saved by the Power of Prayer. an Indian Tale. Bd. with Narrative of a Captivity Among the Mohawk Indians, & a Description of New Netherland in 1642-3. Jogues, Isaac. LC 75-7091. (Indian Captivities Ser.: Vol. 67). Repr. of 1856 ed. lib. bdg. 44.00 (ISBN 0-8240-1691-2). Garland Pub.

Three Years Among the Camanches, the Narrative of Nelson Lee, the Texan Ranger, Containing a Detailed Account of His Captivity Among the Indians, His Singular Escape Through the Instrumentality of His Watch, & Fully Illustrating Indian Life As It Is on the War Path & in the Camp. LC 75-7100. (Indian CaptivitieS Ser.: Vol. 75). 1977. Repr. of 1859 ed. lib. bdg. 44.00 (ISBN 0-8240-1699-8). Garland Pub.

Todd, John. The Lost Sister of Wyoming: An Authentic Narrative, Repr. Of 1842 Ed. Bd. with Biography of Frances Slocum, the Lost Sister of Wyoming. a Complete Narrative of Her Captivity & Wanderings Among the Indians. Meginness, John F. Repr. of 1891 ed. LC 75-7081. (Indian Captivities Ser.: Vol. 58). 1976. lib. bdg. 40.00 (ISBN 0-8240-1682-3). Garland Pub.

A True History of the Captivity & Restoration of Mrs. Mary Rowlandson, Repr. Of 1682 Ed. Bd. with Humiliations Follow'd with Deliverances...with a Narrative, of a Notable Delivarance Lately Recieved by Some English Captives, from the Hands of Cruel Indians. Mather, Cotton. Repr. of 1697 ed. LC 75-7020. (Indian Captivities Ser.: Vol. 1). 1977. lib. bdg. 44.00 (ISBN 0-8240-1625-4). Garland Pub.

U. S. Congress. U. S. Congress House: Report...Washington, 1813. Washburn, Wilcomb E., ed. LC 75-7057. (Narratives of North American Captivities Ser.). 1977. lib. bdg. 44.00 (ISBN 0-8240-1659-9). Garland Pub.

VanDerBeets, Richard, ed. Held Captive by Indians: Selected Narratives, 1642-1836. LC 73-3448. (Illus.). 1973. 16.50x (ISBN 0-87049-145-8). U of Tenn Pr.

Vaughan, Alden T. & Clark, Edward W., eds. Puritans Among the Indians: Accounts of Captivity & Redemption 1676-1724. (John Harvard Library Belknap Ser.). (Illus.). 352p. 1981. text ed. 20.00x (ISBN 0-674-73901-9). Harvard U Pr.

Vide, V. V. American Tableaux, No. 1: Sketches of Aboriginal Life. LC 75-7085. (Indian Captivities Ser.: Vol. 62). 1976. Repr. of 1846 ed. lib. bdg. 44.00 (ISBN 0-8240-1686-6). Garland Pub.

Wakefield, Sarah. Six Weeks in the Sioux Tepees: A Narrative of Indian Captivity, Repr. Of 1863 Ed. Bd. with Miss Coleson's Narrative of Her Captivity Among the Sioux Indians. Coleson, Ann. Repr. of 1864 ed; Reminiscences of Col. John Ketcham, of Monroe County, Indiana, by His Pastor. Hopkins, Thomas M. Repr. of 1866 ed; Gertrude Moran: Or, Life & Adventures Among the Indians of the Far West. Repr. of 1866 ed. LC 75-7104. (Indian Captivities Ser.: Vol. 79). 1977. lib. bdg. 44.00 (ISBN 0-8240-1703-X). Garland Pub.

Wakefield, Sarah F. Six Weeks in the Sioux Tepees. Date not set. price not set (ISBN 0-87770-215-2). Ye Galleon.

Wallwille, Maria. Merkwuerdige und Interessante Lebensgeschichte der Frau Von Wallwille, Welche Vier Jahre Lang an Eien Irokesen Verheyrathet War. LC 75-7054. (Indian Captivities Ser.: Vol. 32). 1976. Repr. of 1809 ed. lib. bdg. 44.00 (ISBN 0-8240-1656-4). Garland Pub.

Walton, William. A Narrative of the Captivity & Sufferings of Benjamin Gilbert & His Family. Washburn, Wilcomb E., ed. LC 75-7036. (Narratives of North American Indian Captivities: Vol. 15). 1975. lib. bdg. 44.00 (ISBN 0-8240-1639-4). Garland Pub.

Washburn, Wilcomb E., ed. A Narrative of the Capture & Treatment of John Dodge, by the English at Detroit, Repr. Of 1779. Incl. An Entertaining Narrative of the Cruel & Barbarous Treatment & Extreme Sufferings of Mr. John Dodge During His Captivity. Repr. of 1780 ed; Narratives of a Late Expedition Against the Indians...& the Wonderful Escape of Dr. Knight & John Slover from Captivity. Brackenridge, Hugh H., ed. Repr. of 1783 ed; Indian Atrocities. Repr. of 1843 ed. (Narratives of North American Indian Captivities Ser.: Vol. 12). 1978. lib. bdg. 44.00 (ISBN 0-8240-1636-X). Garland Pub.

--A Narrative of the Lord's Wonderful Dealings with John Marrant, a Black, Repr. Of 1785. Bd. with A Very Remarkable Narrative of Luke Swetland, Who Was Taken Captive Four Times in the Space of Fifteen Months. Repr. of 1785 ed. 1875 ed. with additions incl. (ISBN 0-685-63632-1); Edward Merrifield: The Story of the Captivity & Rescue from the Indians of Luke Swetland. Merrifield, Edward. Repr. of 1915 ed; A Surprising Account of the Captivity & Escape of Philip M'Donald & Alexander M'Leod of Virginia from the Chickkemogga Indians. Repr. of 1786 ed. 1794 ed. incl. (ISBN 0-685-63633-X); A Surprising Account of the Discovery of a Lady Who Was Taken by the Indians in the Year 1777, & After Making Her Escape, She Retired to a Lonely Cave, Where She Lived Nine Years. in: Bickerstaff's Almanack for the Year...1788. Repr. of 1787 ed. 1794 ed. incl. (ISBN 0-685-63634-8). (Narratives of North American Indian Captivities Ser.). 1979. lib. bdg. 44.00 (ISBN 0-8240-1641-6). Garland Pub.

--A Short Sketch of the Life of Mr. Lent Munson: Alexander Viets Criswold. Incl. A Narrative of the Captivity & Sufferings of Mr. Ebenezer Fletcher of Newipswich. (Repr. of 1798; 2nd ed., repr. of 1813; 4th ed., enl., repr. of 1827); Surprizing Account of the Captivity of Miss Hannah Willis... to Which Is Added an Affecting History, of the Dreadful Distresses of Frederic Manheim's Family. Repr. of 1799 ed; Narrative of the Singular Adventures & Captivity of Mr. Thomas Barry, Among the Monsipi Indians, in the Unexplored Regions of North America. Repr. of 1800 ed. (Narratives of North American Indian Captivities Ser.: Vol. 24). 1980. lib. bdg. 44.00 (ISBN 0-8240-1648-3). Garland Pub.

Weiser, Reuben. Regina, the German Captive, or, True Piety Among the Lowly. LC 75-7093. (Indian Captivities Ser.: Vol. 69). 1977. Repr. of 1856 ed. lib. bdg. 44.00 (ISBN 0-8240-1693-9). Garland Pub.

Williams, J. Redeemed Captive Returning to Zion. 1908. 14.00 (ISBN 0-527-96920-6). Kraus Repr.

Williams, John. The Redeemed Captive. Clark, Edward W., ed. LC 76-8758. (Illus.). 1976. 10.00x (ISBN 0-87023-217-7). U of Mass Pr.

--The Redeemed Captive, Returning to Zion. LC 75-7024. (Indian Captivities Ser.: Vol. 5). 1976. Repr. of 1707 ed. lib. bdg. 44.00 (ISBN 0-8240-1629-7). Garland Pub.

Williams, Stephen W., ed. Redeemed Captive Returning to Zion: Or, a Faithful History of Remarkable Occurrences in the Captivity & Deliverance of Mr. John Williams. facs. ed. LC 78-109637. (Select Bibliographies Reprint Ser). 1853. 17.00 (ISBN 0-8369-5246-4). Arno.

Wilson, Jane A. A Thrilling Narrative of the Sufferings of Mrs. Jane Adeline Wilson During Her Captivity Among the Comanche Indians. 28p. 1972. 5.50 (ISBN 0-87770-122-9); pap. 3.95 (ISBN 0-685-37707-5). Ye Galleon.

Wunderbare Flucht Von Wilden (Captivity of Jakob Morgan). in: Columbian Almanac for 1839, Repr. Of 1839 Ed. Bd. with The Low Dutch Boy Prisoner: Being an Account of the Capture of Frederick Schermerhorn When a Lad of 17 Years Old by a Party of Mohawks. Priest, Josiah. Repr. of 1839 ed; A True Story of the Extraordinary Feats, Adventures & Sufferings of Matthew Calkins. Priest, Josiah. Repr. of 1840 ed; A True Narrative of the Capture of David Ogden Among the Indians in the Time of the Revolution & of the Slavery & Sufferings He Endured. Priest, Josiah. Repr. of 1840 ed; Narrative of the Extraordinary Life of John Conrad Shafford Known by Many by the Name of the Dutch Hermit. Repr. of 1840 ed; Authentic Particulars of the Death of Lieut. Thomas Boyd... in the Border War of the American Revolution Who Was Put to Death by the Indians in the Most Cruel Manner. Repr. of 1841 ed; The Fort Stanwix Captive, or New England Volunteer, Being the Extraordinary Life & Adventures of Isaac Hubbell Among the Indians of Canada & the West... & the Story of His Marriage with the Indian Princess. Priest, Josiah. Repr. of 1841 ed. LC 75-7079. (Indian Captivities Ser.: Vol. 56). 1977. lib. bdg. 44.00 (ISBN 0-8240-1680-7). Garland Pub.

INDIANS OF NORTH AMERICA-CHILDREN

Beuf, Ann H. Red Children in White America. LC 76-49737. 168p. 1977. 12.00x (ISBN 0-8122-7719-8). U of Pa Pr.

Dennis, Wayne. The Hopi Child. LC 75-169380. (Family in America Ser). (Illus.). 232p. 1972. Repr. of 1940 ed. 13.00 (ISBN 0-405-03857-7). Arno.

Eastman, Charles A. Indian Boyhood. (Illus.). 7.25 (ISBN 0-8446-0085-7). Peter Smith.

Havighurst, Robert J. & Neugarten, Bernice L. American Indian & White Children: A Sociopsychological Investigation. LC 54-11208. (Double-Page Reprint Ser). 1969. Repr. text ed. 14.50x (ISBN 0-226-31966-0). U of Chicago Pr.

Henry Tall Bull & Weist, Tom. Mista. (Indian Culture Ser.). (gr. 2-12). 1971. 1.95 (ISBN 0-89992-011-X). MT Coun Indian.

Hilger, Inez. Chippewa Child Life & Its Cultural Background. LC 76-43740. (BAE. Bulletin: 146). Repr. of 1951 ed. 17.50 (ISBN 0-404-15581-2). AMS Pr.

Leighton, Dorothea & Kluckhohn, Clyde. Children of the People. LC 77-96199. 1969. Repr. of 1947 ed. lib. bdg. 16.50x (ISBN 0-374-94902-6). Octagon.

Miller, Mary R. Children of the Salt River. LC 76-45149. (Language Science Monographs Ser.: No. 16). 1977. pap. 11.00 (ISBN 0-87750-206-4). Res Ctr Lang Semiotic.

Morey, Sylvester M. & Gilliam, Olivia L., eds. Respect for Life: The Traditional Upbringing of American Indian Children. LC 74-80759. (Illus.). 224p. (Orig.). 1974. pap. 4.95 (ISBN 0-914614-01-0). Waldorf Pr.

Opler, Morris E. Childhood & Youth in Jicarilla Apache Society. LC 76-43797. Repr. of 1946 ed. 21.00 (ISBN 0-404-15653-3). AMS Pr.

Reit, Seymour. Child of the Navajos. LC 74-162608. (Illus.). (gr. 2-5). 1971. PLB 5.95 (ISBN 0-396-06414-0). Dodd.

Simon, Rita J. & Altstein, Howard. Transracial Adoption. LC 76-44817. 1977. 21.95 (ISBN 0-471-79208-X, Pub. by Wiley-Interscience). Wiley.

Snow, Frances, et al. Thunder Waters: Experiences of Growing up in Different Indian Tribes. (gr. 3-8). 1975. 4.75 (ISBN 0-686-26094-5); pap. 1.95 (ISBN 0-89992-072-1). MT Coun Indian.

Wolcott, Harry F. Kwakiutl Village & School. LC 67-11818. (Studies in Education & Culture). (Orig.). 1967. pap. text ed. 5.95 (ISBN 0-03-061775-8, HoltC). HR&W.

INDIANS OF NORTH AMERICA-CIVILIZATION

see Indians of North America-Culture

INDIANS OF NORTH AMERICA-CLAIMS

Appraisal Associates. Kiowa, Comanche & Apache Lands in Oklahoma & Texas: Valuation Study As of 1900. 1976. lib. bdg. 250.00x (ISBN 0-8287-1093-7). Clearwater Pub.

--Omaha Tribe of Indians: Valuation Study of the Area Ceded, 1854. 1660p. 1973. lib. bdg. 450.00 (ISBN 0-8287-1156-9). Clearwater Pub.

Appraisal Associates & Davis, W. D. Minnesota Chippewa Tribe: Valuation of Ceded Lands As of 1855 & 1867. (Library of American Indian Affairs). 225p. 1973. lib. bdg. 94.00 (ISBN 0-8287-1128-3). Clearwater Pub.

Arkeson, Harry E. Appraisal of a Tract of Land in Lyman County, South Dakota. (Library of American Indian Affairs). 132p. 1973. lib. bdg. 44.00 (ISBN 0-8287-0918-1). Clearwater Pub.

Armer, Walter D. Gila River Reservation in Arizona, 1936-1961: Appraisal. (Library of American Indian Affairs). 105p. 1973. lib. bdg. 36.00 (ISBN 0-8287-1050-3). Clearwater Pub.

Aschmann, Homer. Northern Tonto Claim Area: Environment & Ecology. (Library of American Indian Affairs). 54p. 1973. lib. bdg. 21.00 (ISBN 0-8287-1151-8). Clearwater Pub.

--The Western Apache Range: Terrain & Ecological Conditions. (Library of American Indian Affairs). 54p. 1973. lib. bdg. 21.00 (ISBN 0-8287-1300-6). Clearwater Pub.

Baerreis, David A., et al. Anthropological Report on Indian Occupancy of That Portion of Royce Area 148 East of the Fox River in Illinois. (Library of American Indian Affairs). 190p. 1973. lib. bdg. 72.00 (ISBN 0-8287-0904-1). Clearwater Pub.

Barlowe, Raleigh. Spanish Land Grants in Royce's Cession 50 in Missouri. (Library of American Indian Affairs). 110p. 1973. lib. bdg. 37.50 (ISBN 0-8287-1265-4). Clearwater Pub.

Barlowe, Raleigh & Hammar, Conrad H. Sac, Fox & Iowa Tribes: Valuation of Lands in Eastern Iowa, Royce Areas 175, 226, & 244, 1833-1839. (Library of American Indian Affairs). 243p. 1973. lib. bdg. 73.50 (ISBN 0-8287-1225-5). Clearwater Pub.

--Valuation of Lands in Southcentral Iowa, 1839-1843: Royce Cession Area 262. (Library of American Indian Affairs). 195p. 1973. lib. bdg. 58.50 (ISBN 0-8287-1287-5). Clearwater Pub.

Barreis, David A., et al. The Mascoutens: An Anthropological Report. (Library of American Indian Affairs). 96p. 1973. lib. bdg. 33.00 (ISBN 0-685-32063-4). Clearwater Pub.

Barton, et al. Nez Perce Indian Reservation: Report on Possibility or Impossibility of Determining Gold Removed, to 1867. (Library of American Indian Affairs). 105p. 1973. lib. bdg. 36.00 (ISBN 0-8287-1141-0). Clearwater Pub.

Barton, Stoddard & Milhollin Co, et al. Nez Perce Indian Reservation: Report of Gold Production, 1860-1866. (Library of American Indian Affairs). 70p. 1973. lib. bdg. 25.50 (ISBN 0-8287-1140-2). Clearwater Pub.

Barton, Stoddard & Milhollin, Consulting Engineers. Cheyenne-Arapaho Indian Lands: Mineral Evaluation Covering Parts of Colorado, Kansas, Nebraska, & Wyoming. (Library of American Indian Affairs). 140p. 1973. lib. bdg. 45.00 (ISBN 0-8287-0984-X). Clearwater Pub.

Bell, Robert, et al, eds. Wichita Indian Archeology & Ethnohistory: A Pilot Study. (Library of American Indian Affairs). 340p. 1973. lib. bdg. 97.50 (ISBN 0-8287-1305-7). Clearwater Pub.

Bender, Averam B. Jicarilla Apache Indians, 1848-1887. (Library of American Indian Affairs). 185p. 1973. lib. bdg. 57.00 (ISBN 0-8287-1078-3). Clearwater Pub.

Berthrong, Donald J. Miami, Wea & Potawatomi: Historical Report on Indian Use & Occupancy of Royce Areas 132, 133, 145, 146, 180 & 181 in Northern Indiana & Southwestern Michigan. (Library of American Indian Affairs). 330p. 1973. lib. bdg. 94.50 (ISBN 0-8287-1123-2). Clearwater Pub.

Booth, Ernest G. Creek Nation Lands in Alabama: Land Appraisal As of 1832. (Library of American Indian Affairs). 1976. lib. bdg. 45.00x (ISBN 0-8287-1024-4). Clearwater Pub.

Brady, H. C. Osage Ceded Lands, 1865: Appraisal. (Library of American Indian Affairs). 120p. 1973. lib. bdg. 52.00 (ISBN 0-8287-1160-7). Clearwater Pub.

Broughton, W. A. Evaluation of the Mineral Lands in Indian Cession 175 of Eastern Iowa. (Library of American Indian Affairs). 58p. 1973. lib. bdg. 22.50 (ISBN 0-8287-1038-4). Clearwater Pub.

Brown, William C. Nez Perce Reservation Land: Appraisal. (Library of American Indian Affairs). 402p. 1973. lib. bdg. 114.00 (ISBN 0-8287-1143-7). Clearwater Pub.

Brunger, Eric, et al. Big Tree Cession: Historical Land Valuation. (Library of American Indian Affairs). 118p. 1973. lib. bdg. 39.00 (ISBN 0-8287-0954-8). Clearwater Pub.

Caddo Indian Tract Situated in Southwestern Arkansas & Northwestern Louisiana, 1835: Appraisal. (Library of American Indian Affairs). 175p. 1973. lib. bdg. 54.00 (ISBN 0-8287-0960-2). Clearwater Pub.

The Case of the Seneca Indians in the State of New York. (American Indians at Law Ser.). 1980. Repr. text ed. 32.50 (ISBN 0-930576-35-7). E M Coleman Ent.

Chalfant, Stuart A. Aboriginal Territory of the Nez Perce Indians. (Library of American Indian Affairs). 135p. 1973. lib. bdg. 43.50 (ISBN 0-8287-0891-6). Clearwater Pub.

--Columbia Salish of Central Washington: Aboriginal Land-Use & Occupancy. (Library of American Indian Affairs). 78p. 1973. lib. bdg. 29.00 (ISBN 0-8287-1009-0). Clearwater Pub.

Chapman, Carl H. Aboriginal Use & Occupancy of Lands West of the Mississippi River by the Osage Indian Tribe: Village Locations & Hunting Territories up to 1808. (Library of American Indian Affairs). 70p. 1973. lib. bdg. 26.00 (ISBN 0-8287-0892-4). Clearwater Pub.

--The Osage Indian Tribe: An Ethnographical, Historical & Archaeological Study. (Library of American Indian Affairs). 315p. 1973. lib. bdg. 91.50 (ISBN 0-8287-1161-5). Clearwater Pub.

The Cherokee Band of Indians: Anthropological Report on the Indian Occupancy of Royce Area 79, Ceded on September 14, 1816. (Library of American Indian Affairs). 246p. 1973. lib. bdg. 74.00 (ISBN 0-8287-0972-6). Clearwater Pub.

Chihsolm, Roger K. Piankeshaw Lands in Royce Area 63, Land Values As of 1805. (Library of American Indian Affairs). 110p. 1973. lib. bdg. 37.50 (ISBN 0-8287-1196-8). Clearwater Pub.

Chiricahua Apache Tribe: Appraisal of Mineral Resources in the Lands, 4 vols. (Library of American Indian Affairs). 1782p. 1973. lib. bdg. 480.00 (ISBN 0-8287-1003-1). Clearwater Pub.

Chisholm, Roger K. Chippewa, Ottawa & Potawatomie Lands in Illinois & Wisconsin: Valuation As of 1835. (Library of American Indian Affairs). 1976. lib. bdg. 67.00x (ISBN 0-8287-0996-3). Clearwater Pub.

--Kickapoo & Wea Lands in Royce Areas 73 & 74 in Illinois & Indiana, 1809, 1818: Valuation. 140p. 1973. lib. bdg. 45.00 (ISBN 0-8287-1086-4). Clearwater Pub.

--The Peoria Tribe & Kaskasia Nation: An Appraisal of Lands in Illinois, 1803 to 1820. (Library of American Indian Affairs). lib. bdg. 95.00x (ISBN 0-8287-1190-9). Clearwater Pub.

Christensen, Mervin J. & Hill, R. G. The Mohave Tribe in Arizona: An Appraisal of Land Values from 1942 to 1952 & 1940 to 1953. Ross, Norman A., ed. (Library of American Indian Affairs). 1976. lib. bdg. 50.00x (ISBN 0-8287-1131-3). Clearwater Pub.

Cline, Howard F. Provisional Historical Gazeteer with Locational Notes on Florida Colonial Communities, 1700-1823. (Library of American Indian Affairs). 240p. 1973. lib. bdg. 72.00 (ISBN 0-8287-1400-2). Clearwater Pub.

--Spanish & Mexican Land Grants in New Mexico, 1689-1848. (Library of American Indian Affairs). 325p. 1973. lib. bdg. 93.00 (ISBN 0-8287-1263-8). Clearwater Pub.

Confederated Salish & Kootenai Tribe of the Flathead Reservation: A History. (Library of American Indian Affairs). 1976. lib. bdg. 27.00x (ISBN 0-8287-1015-5). Clearwater Pub.

Coulter, John L. Potawatomi Tribe of Indians: Natural Resource, Agricultural & Economic Survey from 1795-1846 of Certain Lands Ceded by the Prairie Band. (Library of American Indian Affairs). 96p. 1973. lib. bdg. 46.00 (ISBN 0-8287-1205-0). Clearwater Pub.

--Value of Farmland & Improvements & Other Natural Resources in Iowa & Kansas, 1840-1850. (Library of American Indian Affairs). 70p. 1973. 25.50 (ISBN 0-8287-1291-3). Clearwater Pub.

Davis, W. D. Red Lake & Pembina Bands of Chippewa Indians: Valuation Study of the Red River Valley of the North Area in North Dakota & Minnesota Ceded October 3, 1863. (Library of American Indian Affairs). 410p. 1973. lib. bdg. 147.00 (ISBN 0-8287-1211-5). Clearwater Pub.

Diddock, Joseph L. Gila River Reservation Leased Land in Arizona, 1916-1937: Historical Report. (Library of American Indian Affairs). 29p. 1973. lib. bdg. 18.00 (ISBN 0-8287-1051-1). Clearwater Pub.

Doane Agricultural Service. Potawatomie Reserve Lands in Kansas, Sold by the Prairie Band, Potawatomie Indians to the Santa Fe Railroad, 1868: Appraisal. (Library of American Indian Affairs). 37p. 1973. lib. bdg. 32.00 (ISBN 0-8287-1207-7). Clearwater Pub.

Dobyns, Henry F. Yuman Complex: Prehistoric Indian Occupation Within the Eastern Area of the Yuman Complex: a Study in Applied Archaeoology, 3 vols. (Library of American Indian Affairs). 700p. 1973. lib. bdg. 130.00 (ISBN 0-8287-1322-7). Clearwater Pub.

Draper, Leroy D. Chinook Tribe & Bands Tribal Islands, Eighteen Fifty-One: Appraisal. (Library of American Indian Affairs). 180p. 1973. lib. bdg. 56.00 (ISBN 0-8287-0989-0). Clearwater Pub.

--Tillamook Band of Tillamooks & Nehalem Band of Tillamooks Tribal Lands: Appraisal. (Library of American Indian Affairs). 338p. 1973. lib. bdg. 97.50 (ISBN 0-8287-1275-1). Clearwater Pub.

Dunham, Harold H. Spanish & Mexican Land Policies & Grants in the Taos Pueblo Region, New Mexico. (Library of American Indian Affairs). 157p. 1973. lib. bdg. 50.00 (ISBN 0-8287-1264-6). Clearwater Pub.

--Taos Indians' Pueblo Land Grant: Historical Study of the Land Use Prior to 1848. (Library of American Indian Affairs). 29p. 1973. lib. bdg. 17.25 (ISBN 0-8287-1268-9). Clearwater Pub.

Edgemon, William S. Seminole Nation: Appraisal of Tracts of Land Ceded in 1823 & 1832. (Library of American Indian Affairs). 140p. 1973. lib. bdg. 45.00 (ISBN 0-8287-1239-5). Clearwater Pub.

Ellis, Florence H. Acoma-Laguna Land Claims. 318p. 1973. lib. bdg. 91.50 (ISBN 0-8287-0894-0). Clearwater Pub.

--The Hopi: Their History & Use of Lands in New Mexico & Arizona, 1200's to 1900's. (Library of American Indian Affairs). 250p. 1973. lib. bdg. 75.00 (ISBN 0-8287-1601-3). Clearwater Pub.

--Laguna Pueblo Land Claims: Anthropology. (Library of American Indian Affairs). 106p. 1973. lib. bdg. 36.00 (ISBN 0-8287-1103-8). Clearwater Pub.

--Nambe Pueblos: Anthropological Data Pertaining to Land Claims. (Library of American Indian Affairs). (Illus.). 1976. lib. bdg. 50.00x (ISBN 0-8287-1134-8). Clearwater Pub.

--The Navajo Indians: An Anthropoligical Study. (Library of American Indian Affairs). 1976. lib. bdg. 125.00x (ISBN 0-8287-1137-2). Clearwater Pub.

--The Pueblos of Zia, Santa Ana & Jemez: Anthropological Evidence in Support of Land Calims. (Library of American Indian Affairs). 1976. lib. bdg. 30.00x (ISBN 0-8287-1209-3). Clearwater Pub.

--Taos Land Claim: Anthropological Data. (Library of American Indian Affairs). 115p. 1973. lib. bdg. 39.00 (ISBN 0-8287-1269-7). Clearwater Pub.

Elmquist, Gordon E. Appraisal of the Lands of the Bay Mills Indian Community. (Library of American Indian Affairs). 90p. 1973. lib. bdg. 31.50 (ISBN 0-8287-0931-9). Clearwater Pub.

--Saginaw Chippewa: Appraisal of Lands Located in the Lower Peninsula, East Central Michigan, Royce Area No. 111, 1820. (Library of American Indian Affairs). 190p. 1973. lib. bdg. 57.00 (ISBN 0-8287-1227-1). Clearwater Pub.

--Three Affiliated Tribes of the Fort Berthold Reservation: Appraisal of Lands. (Library of American Indian Affairs). 210p. 1973. lib. bdg. 64.50 (ISBN 0-8287-1271-9). Clearwater Pub.

Englehorn, Vern A. Appraisal of Nooksack Tract, Washington, 1859. (Library of American Indian Affairs). 350p. 1973. lib. bdg. 100.00 (ISBN 0-8287-0923-8). Clearwater Pub.

--Appraisal of the Muckleshoot Tract, Washington, 1859. (Library of American Indian Affairs). 360p. 1973. lib. bdg. 102.00 (ISBN 0-8287-0939-4). Clearwater Pub.

Ewers, John C. Blackfeet & Gros Ventre Tribes of Indians, Lands in Northern Montana, 1888. (Library of American Indian Affairs). 180p. 1973. lib. bdg. 55.50 (ISBN 0-8287-0957-2). Clearwater Pub.

--Chippewa Cree Tribe of Rocky Boy, Montana, & the Little Band of Indians, 1888. (Library of American Indian Affairs). 170p. 1973. lib. bdg. 52.50 (ISBN 0-8287-0990-4). Clearwater Pub.

Fairbanks, Charles H. The Florida Indians. (Library of American Indian Affairs). 286p. 1973. lib. bdg. 84.00 (ISBN 0-8287-1041-4). Clearwater Pub.

--The Seminolee Nation: An Ethno-Historical Report of the Florida Indians As of 1823. (Library of American Indian Affairs). 1976. lib. bdg. 84.00x (ISBN 0-8287-1241-7). Clearwater Pub.

Faust, Josef & Hassler, John J. Creek Nation Lands in Oklahoma: Appraisal of Oil, Gas, Coal & Minerals. (Library of American Indian Affairs). 1976. lib. bdg. 225.00x (ISBN 0-8287-1025-2). Clearwater Pub.

Faust, Josef & Lee, Martin P. Seminole Lands: Mineral Interests in Oklahoma. (Library of American Indian Affairs). 184p. 1973. lib. bdg. 57.00 (ISBN 0-8287-1238-7). Clearwater Pub.

Fenenga, Franklin & Champe, John L. The Pawnee in Oklahoma: Anthropology Notes. (Library of American Indian Affairs). 129p. 1973. lib. bdg. 56.00 (ISBN 0-8287-1187-9). Clearwater Pub.

Fenton, Harry R. Appraisal of the Black Hills Area of South Dakota, 1877. (Library of American Indian Affairs). 190p. 1973. lib. bdg. 57.00 (ISBN 0-8287-0926-2). Clearwater Pub.

--Confederated Salish & Kootenai Tribes, Appraisal of the Lands in Montana, 1859. (Library of American Indian Affairs). 175p. 1973. lib. bdg. 54.00 (ISBN 0-8287-1013-9). Clearwater Pub.

Fenton, Harry R. & Fenton, Everett W. Kickapoo Tribal Lands in Illinois & Indiana: An Appraisal As of 1820. (Library of American Indian Affairs). 1976. lib. bdg. 225.00x (ISBN 0-8287-1091-0). Clearwater Pub.

Foley, Michael F. Yankton Tribal Lands: An Historical Analysis of the Opening & Development from 1849 to 1869. (Library of American Indian Affairs). 1976. lib. bdg. 75.00x (ISBN 0-8287-1315-4). Clearwater Pub.

Fontana, Bernard L. The Papago Tribe of Arizona: Anthropological Report. (Library of American Indian Affairs). 70p. 1973. lib. bdg. 25.50 (ISBN 0-8287-1183-6). Clearwater Pub.

Fox, Ida. Potawatomi Kansas Cession, Royce Area 266: Government Sales of Lands. (Library of American Indian Affairs). 38p. 1973. lib. bdg. 20.00 (ISBN 0-8287-1201-8). Clearwater Pub.

Full, Roy P. Appraisal of the Mineral Resources in the Lands of the Confederated Tribes of the Goshute Reservation. (Library of American Indian Affairs). 1572p. 1973. lib. bdg. 420.00 (ISBN 0-8287-0937-8). Clearwater Pub.

--Chiricahua Apache Lands: Analysis of the Mineral Production Prior to September 4, 1866. (Library of American Indian Affairs). 64p. 1973. lib. bdg. 24.00 (ISBN 0-8287-1001-5). Clearwater Pub.

--Chiricahua Apache Tract: Analysis of the Volume of Timber Cut & Consumed for Mining Operations Prior to September 4, 1886. (Library of American Indian Affairs). 41p. 1973. lib. bdg. 17.00 (ISBN 0-8287-1002-3). Clearwater Pub.

--Papago Indians: Appraisal of Mineral Resources in the Lands Acquired by U.S. in Arizona, 1916, & the Louis Maria Baca Grant, Float No. 3, 1906, 3 vols. (Library of American Indian Affairs). 1380p. 1973. lib. bdg. 337.50 (ISBN 0-8287-1179-8). Clearwater Pub.

Fuller, E. O. Appraisal of Land Included in the Agreement of Sept 26, 1872 Between the U. S. & the Eastern Shoshone Indians. (Library of American Indian Affairs). 320p. 1973. lib. bdg. 92.00 (ISBN 0-8287-0920-3). Clearwater Pub.

Garrett, H. J. & Sears, Roscoe H. Appraisal of the Creek Cession, 1856. (Library of American Indian Affairs). 110p. 1973. lib. bdg. 37.50 (ISBN 0-8287-0928-9). Clearwater Pub.

Gordon, B. L., et al. Jicarilla Apache Claim Area: Environment, Settlement, & Land Use. (Library of American Indian Affairs). 364p. 1973. lib. bdg. 103.50 (ISBN 0-8287-1075-9). Clearwater Pub.

Griffiths, Thomas M. Yankton Sioux Tribe: Appraisal of Lands in Nebraska, Iowa, Minnesota, South Dakota, & North Dakota, As of 1858. (Library of American Indian Affairs). 1976. lib. bdg. 150.00x (ISBN 0-8287-1314-6). Clearwater Pub.

Gussow, Zachary. Cheyenne & Arapahoe Aboriginal Occupation. (Library of American Indian Affairs). 64p. 1973. lib. bdg. 24.00 (ISBN 0-8287-0983-1). Clearwater Pub.

--Sauk, Fox & Iowa Indians: Ethnological Report on Their Historic Habitat. (Library of American Indian Affairs). 62p. 1973. lib. bdg. 24.00 (ISBN 0-8287-1236-0). Clearwater Pub.

Hackenberg, Robert A. Aboriginal Land Use & Occupancy of the Pima-Maricopa Indians, 2 vols. (Indian Claims Commission Ser). 634p. 1973. lib. bdg. 177.00 (ISBN 0-8287-0888-6). Clearwater Pub.

Hall, Richard B. Absentee Delaware Tribe of Oklahoma & Delaware Tribe, 1856-57: Appraisal of Land in Northeastern Kansas: a Part of Royce Area 316. (Library of American Indian Affairs). 140p. 1973. lib. bdg. 45.00 (ISBN 0-8287-0893-2). Clearwater Pub.

--Apache, Kiowa & Comanche Indian Reservation in Southwestern Oklahoma Appraisal & Valuation. (Library of American Indian Affairs). 1976. lib. bdg. 78.00x (ISBN 0-8287-0917-3). Clearwater Pub.

--Delaware Outlet in Northeastern Kansas, 1854: Appraisal. (Library of American Indian Affairs). 120p. 1973. lib. bdg. 39.00 (ISBN 0-8287-1028-7). Clearwater Pub.

--Iowa Tribe: Appraisal of Lands in Kansas & Nebraska, 1857. (Library of American Indian Affairs). 110p. 1973. lib. bdg. 38.00 (ISBN 0-8287-1073-2). Clearwater Pub.

--The Kickapoo Tribe of Kansas & the Peoria Tribe of Oklahoma, 1809: Appraisal of Lands in Western Indiana & Eastern Illinois: Royce Areas 73 & 74. (Library of American Indian Affairs). 132p. 1973. lib. bdg. 44.00 (ISBN 0-8287-1092-9). Clearwater Pub.

--Miami Indians 1805 & 1809: Appraisal of Lands in Southern Indiana: Royce Areas 56, 71, 72. (Library of American Indian Affairs). 325p. 1973. lib. bdg. 93.00 (ISBN 0-8287-1120-8). Clearwater Pub.

--Ottawa Tribe of Indians, Royce Areas 182 & 183, 1833: Appraisal of Lands in Northwestern Ohio & Southeastern Michigan. (Library of American Indian Affairs). 139p. 1973. lib. bdg. 45.00 (ISBN 0-8287-1175-5). Clearwater Pub.

--Peoria Tribe of Oklahoma, Absentee Delaware Tribe of Oklahoma and the Delaware Nation, 1804: Appraisal of Lands in Southwestern Indiana, Royce Area 49. (Library of American Indian Affairs). 190p. 1973. lib. bdg. 57.00 (ISBN 0-8287-1192-5). Clearwater Pub.

--The Peoria Tribe of Oklahoma, 1807: Appraisal of Land in Southeastern Illinois, Royce Area 63. (Library of American Indian Affairs). 246p. 1973. lib. bdg. 75.00 (ISBN 0-8287-1194-1). Clearwater Pub.

--Ponca Indians: Appraisal of Land in Northern Nebraska & Southern South Dakota, South & West of the Missouri River on Both Sides of the Niobrara River. (Library of American Indian Affairs). 182p. 1973. lib. bdg. 55.50 (ISBN 0-8287-1197-6). Clearwater Pub.

--Ponca Reservation, 1877: Appraisal of Land in Northeastern Nebraska. (Library of American Indian Affairs). 86p. 1973. lib. bdg. 31.50 (ISBN 0-8287-1199-2). Clearwater Pub.

--Senecas of Sandusky: Appraisal of Lands Royce Area 163, & the Mixed Band of Senecas & Shawnees of Lewistown, Royce Area 164, in Northwestern Ohio, 1831. (Library of American Indian Affairs). 140p. 1973. lib. bdg. 45.00 (ISBN 0-8287-1243-3). Clearwater Pub.

--United Senecas & Shawnees, 1833: Appraisal of Lands in Northeastern Oklahoma, Royce Areas 498, 499, 500, 501, 502. (Library of American Indian Affairs). 45p. 1973. lib. bdg. 18.00 (ISBN 0-8287-1282-4). Clearwater Pub.

Halpenny, Leonard. Ak Chin Reservation, Pinal County, Arizona: Decline of Ground Water Levels. (Library of American Indian Affairs). 73p. 1973. lib. bdg. 44.50 (ISBN 0-8287-0897-5). Clearwater Pub.

Harbin, Darwin. Blackfeet & Gros Ventre Tribes of Indians, Appraisal of Lands in Northern Montana, 1888. (Library of American Indian Affairs). 402p. 1973. lib. bdg. 114.00 (ISBN 0-8287-0956-4). Clearwater Pub.

--The Fort Berthold Indians: Appraisal of Land in North Dakota, 1891. (Library of American Indian Affairs). 159p. 1973. lib. bdg. 50.00 (ISBN 0-8287-1044-9). Clearwater Pub.

Hart, Gerald T. Confederated Ute Indian Lands in Southwestern Colorado, Ceded September 13, 1873: Appraisal. (Library of American Indian Affairs). 315p. 1973. lib. bdg. 91.00 (ISBN 0-8287-1016-3). Clearwater Pub.

Hickerson, Harold. Anthropological Report on the Indian Occupancy of Area 243. (Library of American Indian Affairs). 273p. 1973. lib. bdg. 81.00 (ISBN 0-8287-0907-6). Clearwater Pub.

--Anthropological Report on the Indian Use & Occupancy of Royce Area 332, Ceded by the Chippewa Indians of Lake Superior & the Mississippi Under the Treaty of September 30, 1854. (Library of American Indian Affairs). 151p. 1973. lib. bdg. 48.00 (ISBN 0-8287-0910-6). Clearwater Pub.

--The Chippewa Nation of Indians: Anthropological Report on the Indian Occupancy of Area 242, Ceded Under the Treaty of July 29, 1837. (Library of American Indian Affairs). 292p. 1973. lib. bdg. 85.00 (ISBN 0-8287-0992-0). Clearwater Pub.

Hobbs, Charles A., et al. Memorandum on Legislative History, Congressional Acts Pertaining to Indian Trust Funds: The Te-Moak Bands & Mescalero Apache. (Library of American Indian Affairs). 96p. 1973. lib. bdg. 34.50 (ISBN 0-8287-1115-1). Clearwater Pub.

Hoyt, Homer. Kootenai Tribe Lands in Northern Idaho & Montana, 1859: Appraisal. (Library of American Indian Affairs). 73p. 1973. lib. bdg. 27.00 (ISBN 0-8287-1101-1). Clearwater Pub.

--Nez Perce Tribe Lands in Northern Idaho, 1894: Appraisal. (Library of American Indian Affairs). 116p. 1973. lib. bdg. 39.00 (ISBN 0-8287-1144-5). Clearwater Pub.

--Northern Paiute Nation: Appraisal of Lands in Nevada & California, 1853-1863, 2 vols. (Library of American Indian Affairs). 540p. 1973. Set. lib. bdg. 150.00 (ISBN 0-8287-1149-6). Clearwater Pub.

--Washoe Tribe of Indians: Appraisal of Lands in Nevada, 1862, & in California, 1853. (Library of American Indian Affairs). 259p. 1973. lib. bdg. 76.50 (ISBN 0-8287-1297-2). Clearwater Pub.

Hurt, Wesley R. Anthropological Report on Indian Occupancy of Certain Territory Claimed by the Dakota Sioux Indians & by Rival Tribal Claimants. (Library of American Indian Affairs). 250p. 1973. lib. bdg. 75.00 (ISBN 0-8287-0903-3). Clearwater Pub.

Idaho Land & Appraisal Service. Appraisal of the Lands of the Goshute Tribe or Identifiable Group Represented by the Confederated Tribes of the Goshute Reservation in Utah & Nevada, 1875. (Library of American Indian Affairs). 190p. 1973. lib. bdg. 60.50 (ISBN 0-8287-0934-3). Clearwater Pub.

Idaho Land and Appraisal Service. Appraisal of the Papago Tribe of Arizona, 1916, & the Luis Maria Baca Grant, Float No. 3, 1906. 260p. 1973. lib. bdg. 101.50 (ISBN 0-8287-0940-8). Clearwater Pub.

--Appraisal of the Rental Value of the Fort Sill Apache Tribe of Oklahoma in Arizona & New Mexico: From 1848 to September 4, 1886. (Library of American Indian Affairs). 190p. 1973. lib. bdg. 57.00 (ISBN 0-8287-0941-6). Clearwater Pub.

Idaho Land & Appraisal Service. Fort Sill Apache Tribe of Oklahoma; the Chiricahua Apache Tribe; the Chiricahua & Warm Springs Tribes of Apache Indians, 1886: Appraisal. (Library of American Indian Affairs). 245p. 1973. lib. bdg. 49.00 (ISBN 0-8287-1048-1). Clearwater Pub.

--Jicarilla-Apache Reservation, 1887 & 1907: Appraisal. (Library of American Indian Affairs). 105p. 1973. lib. bdg. 36.00 (ISBN 0-8287-1079-1). Clearwater Pub.

--Jicarilla Apache Tribe, 1883: Appraisal. (Library of American Indian Affairs). 250p. 1973. lib. bdg. 75.00 (ISBN 0-8287-1081-3). Clearwater Pub.

Idaho Land and Appraisal Service. Red Lake Band of Chippewa Indians: Appraisal of Lands in Minnesota on Various Dates. 96p. 1973. lib. bdg. 34.50 (ISBN 0-8287-1213-1). Clearwater Pub.

Jablow, Joseph. Anthropological Study of Indian Tribes in Royce Areas 48, 96-A, 110, 177 & 98, Illinois & Indiana, 1640-1832, 2 vols. (Library of American Indian Affairs). 398p. 1973. lib. bdg. 160.00 (ISBN 0-8287-0913-0). Clearwater Pub.

--The Ponca Indians with Reference to Their Claim to Certain Lands. (Library of American Indian Affairs). 356p. 1973. lib. bdg. 102.00 (ISBN 0-8287-1198-4). Clearwater Pub.

James, Harry & Winter, William S. Potawatomi Lands in the Indian Territory, 1890: Appraisal. (Library of American Indian Affairs). 152p. 1973. lib. bdg. 48.00 (ISBN 0-8287-1203-4). Clearwater Pub.

Jenkins, Myra E. Laguna Pueblo Land Claims, 1598-1935. (Library of American Indian Affairs). 195p. 1973. lib. bdg. 58.50 (ISBN 0-8287-1104-6). Clearwater Pub.

Jenkins, Myra E. & Minge, Ward A. Navajo Activities Affecting the Acoma-Laguna Area, 1746-1910. (Library of American Indian Affairs). 220p. 1973. lib. bdg. 66.00 (ISBN 0-8287-1136-4). Clearwater Pub.

Johnson, Albert L. Fort Mohave Indian Reservation Lands: Planning Report & Gross Appraisel. (Library of American Indian Affairs). 157p. 1973. lib. bdg. 50.00 (ISBN 0-8287-1045-7). Clearwater Pub.

Jones, J. A. Anthropological Report on the Indian Occupancy of Royce Areas 149, 174 & 245. (Library of American Indian Affairs). 193p. 1973. lib. bdg. 58.00 (ISBN 0-8287-0908-4). Clearwater Pub.

--United Nation of Chippewa, Ottowa, & Potawatomie Indians: Anthropological Report on the Indian Occupancy of Royce Area 187 in Illinois & Wisconsin, Ceded Under the Treaty of September 26, 1833. (Library of American Indian Affairs). 80p. 1973. lib. bdg. 40.00 (ISBN 0-8287-1281-6). Clearwater Pub.

Kaltreider, D. R., et al. Kickapoo Lands in Illinois & Missouri: An Appraisal. Ross, Norman A., ed. (Library of American Indian Affairs). 1976. lib. bdg. 35.00x (ISBN 0-8287-1088-0). Clearwater Pub.

Kauth, Helen. Ottawa & Chippewa Lands in Michigan: Economic & Historical Background for a Valuation As of 1836. (Library of American Indian Affairs). 1976. lib. bdg. 67.00x (ISBN 0-8287-1171-2). Clearwater Pub.

Kelly, Isabel T. Southern Paiute Ethnography: The Eastern Bands. (Library of American Indian Affairs). 188p. 1973. lib. bdg. 57.00 (ISBN 0-8287-1262-X). Clearwater Pub.

Kent, Donald. The Niagara River & the Niagara River Strip to 1759. (Library of American Indian Affairs). 179p. 1973. lib. bdg. 55.50 (ISBN 0-8287-1146-1). Clearwater Pub.

Kent, Donald H. Six Nations, Wyandot & Delaware: Historical Report on Pennsylvania's Purchases from the Indians, 1784, 1785, & 1789: Indian Occupancy of Areas Purchased. (Library of American Indian Affairs). 270p. 1973. lib. bdg. 79.50 (ISBN 0-8287-1255-7). Clearwater Pub.

Kiepe, Werner. Uintah Valley Indian Reservation Lands in Utah, Appraisal As of 1881. (Library of American Indian Affairs). 212p. 1973. lib. bdg. 64.50 (ISBN 0-8287-1280-8). Clearwater Pub.

Kirk, Arthur S. Sac & Fox Indian Lands in Royce Area 69, Missouri 1824: Appraisal. (Library of American Indian Affairs). 160p. 1973. lib. bdg. 50.00 (ISBN 0-8287-1217-4). Clearwater Pub.

Kleinman, Frank R. & Myers, Donald D. Sioux Nation Lands Acquired by the U. S. Under the Treaty of April 29, 1968: Appraisal. (Library of American Indian Affairs). 317p. 1973. lib. bdg. 91.50 (ISBN 0-8287-1250-6). Clearwater Pub.

Kline, M., et al. The Oneida & Stockbridge Tribes: An Analysis of the Awareness of the Continental Congress & the U. S. Government of Relations & Treaties with New York State. Ross, Norman A., ed. (Library of American Indian Affairs). 1976. lib. bdg. 50.00x (ISBN 0-8287-1157-7). Clearwater Pub.

Knuth, Helen E. Chippewa Indians of Lake Superior: Economic & Historical Background of Northeastern Minnesota Lands, Sept. 30, 1854, Royce Area 332. (Library of American Indian Affairs). 100p. 1973. lib. bdg. 34.50 (ISBN 0-8287-0991-2). Clearwater Pub.

Kroeber, A. L. Mohave Tribe: Report on Aboriginal Territory & Occupancy. (Library of American Indian Affairs). 98p. 1973. lib. bdg. 34.50 (ISBN 0-8287-1133-X). Clearwater Pub.

Kuehnle, Walter R. Appraisal of Lands in Illinois & Wisconsin, Ceded by the Winnebago Indians, Royce Area 149, 1830, Royce Area 174, 1833, Royce Area 245, 1838. (Library of American Indian Affairs). 570p. 1973. lib. bdg. 158.00 (ISBN 0-8287-0921-1). Clearwater Pub.

--Appraisal of Royce Areas 147 & 148 in Illinois & Wisconsin, 1829. 84p. 1973. lib. bdg. 105.00 (ISBN 0-8287-0925-4). Clearwater Pub.

--Minnesota Chippewa Indians, 1838: Appraisal of Royce Area 242 in Wisconsin & Minnesota. (Library of American Indian Affairs). 230p. 1973. lib. bdg. 69.00 (ISBN 0-8287-1125-9). Clearwater Pub.

--Sauk & Fox Nations of Indians: Appraisal of Royce Area 50 in the States of Missouri, Illinois, & Wisconsin; 1805. (Library of American Indian Affairs). 300p. 1973. lib. bdg. 87.00 (ISBN 0-8287-1235-2). Clearwater Pub.

--Seneca Nations & Tonawanda Band of Seneca Indians, Appraisal of Lands in Wester New York State, Ceded to or Exchanged with the U. S. 1797, 1802, 1815, 1826. (Library of American Indian Affairs). 410p. 1973. lib. bdg. 115.50 (ISBN 0-8287-1242-5). Clearwater Pub.

Libby, Dorothy. Piankashaw Indians: Anthropological Report. (Library of American Indian Affairs). 280p. 1973. lib. bdg. 83.00 (ISBN 0-8287-1195-X). Clearwater Pub.

Lokken, Roscoe L. Iowa: Public Land Disposal. (Library of American Indian Affairs). 28p. 1973. lib. bdg. 17.00 (ISBN 0-8287-1071-6). Clearwater Pub.

Long, John S. Peoria Tribe: Geographical & Historical Analysis of Royce Areas 63, 73 & 74. (Library of American Indian Affairs). 30p. 1973. lib. bdg. 18.50 (ISBN 0-8287-1191-7). Clearwater Pub.

--Peoria Tribe of Oklahoma, Absentee Delaware Tribe of Oklahoma & the Delaware Nation, Analysis of the Land of Royce Area 49, in Southwestern Indiana. (Library of American Indian Affairs). 39p. 1973. lib. bdg. 20.00x (ISBN 0-8287-1193-3). Clearwater Pub.

McMullen, Allan L. Jicarilla Apache Tribal Lands Acquired by the U.S. on August 20, 1883: Valuation. (Library of American Indian Affairs). 160p. 1973. lib. bdg. 50.00 (ISBN 0-8287-1080-5). Clearwater Pub.

Manners, Robert A. Havasupai Indians: An Ethnohistorical Report. (Library of American Indian Affairs). 151p. 1973. lib. bdg. 48.00 (ISBN 0-8287-1058-9). Clearwater Pub.

--Hualapai Indians of Arizona. (Library of American Indian Affairs). 194p. 1973. lib. bdg. 58.50 (ISBN 0-8287-1060-0). Clearwater Pub.

--Southern Paiute & Chemehuevi: An Ethnohistorical Report. (Library of American Indian Affairs). 188p. 1973. lib. bdg. 57.00 (ISBN 0-8287-1261-1). Clearwater Pub.

Manypenny, George W. Potawatomic Tribe: Transcription of the Record of the Negotiation & Signing of the Treaty of February 22, 1855, at Washington, D. C. (Library of American Indian Affairs). 120p. 1973. lib. bdg. 39.00 (ISBN 0-8287-1206-9). Clearwater Pub.

Marriott, Alice. Osage Indians: Anthropological Study. (Library of American Indian Affairs). 215p. 1973. lib. bdg. 66.00 (ISBN 0-8287-1163-1). Clearwater Pub.

Martin, Howard N. Alabama & Coushatta Tribes of Texas: Ethnohistorical Analysis of Documents. (Library of American Indian Affairs). 66p. 1973. lib. bdg. 24.00 (ISBN 0-8287-0898-3). Clearwater Pub.

Mason, Bruce & Girard Co, et al. Klamath Concession: Timber Values, June 21, 1906. (Library of American Indian Affairs). 30p. 1973. lib. bdg. 21.00 (ISBN 0-8287-1096-1). Clearwater Pub.

Meltzer, Bernard C. & Schaar, Roland J. Chippewa Tract in Minnesota, April 26, 1866: Appraisal. (Library of American Indian Affairs). 345p. 1973. lib. bdg. 100.00 (ISBN 0-8287-0997-1). Clearwater Pub.

--Chippewa Tracts in Minnesota, 1848: Appraisal. (Library of American Indian Affairs). 278p. 1973. lib. bdg. 83.00 (ISBN 0-8287-0998-X). Clearwater Pub.

Miller, C. Marc. Coeur D'alene Tract, Idaho & Washington, 1873, 1887, 1891: Appraisal. (Library of American Indian Affairs). 210p. 1973. lib. bdg. 65.00 (ISBN 0-8287-1007-4). Clearwater Pub.

--Colville Tracts, State of Washington, 1872: Appraisal. (Library of American Indian Affairs). 210p. 1973. lib. bdg. 64.50 (ISBN 0-685-32086-3). Clearwater Pub.

--Duwamish, Snohomish & Suquamish Tracts: Appraisal. (Library of American Indian Affairs). 210p. 1973. lib. bdg. 65.00 (ISBN 0-8287-1029-5). Clearwater Pub.

--The Klamath Reservation, Appraisal, & Supplemental Appraisal: The Excluded Lands of the Klamath & Modoc Tribes & Yahooskin Band of Snake Indians, Oregon, 1906. (Library of American Indian Affairs). 190p. 1973. lib. bdg. 57.00 (ISBN 0-8287-1098-8). Clearwater Pub.

--Nez Perce Ceded Tract, Oregon, Washington & Idaho, 1867: Appraisal. (Library of American Indian Affairs). 217p. 1973. lib. bdg. 66.00 (ISBN 0-8287-1139-9). Clearwater Pub.

--Skagit Tract, Washington, Supplementing Appraisals of the Duwamish, Snohomish & Suquamish Tracts. (Library of American Indian Affairs). 59p. 1973. lib. bdg. 22.50 (ISBN 0-8287-1256-5). Clearwater Pub.

--S'klallam Tract: Appraisal. (Library of American Indian Affairs). 196p. 1973. lib. bdg. 60.00 (ISBN 0-8287-1258-1). Clearwater Pub.

--Skokomish Tract: Appraisal. (Library of American Indian Affairs). 188p. 1973. lib. bdg. 57.00 (ISBN 0-8287-1259-X). Clearwater Pub.

--Uintah Ute Tract: Preliminary Appraisal Report. (Library of American Indian Affairs). 50p. 1973. lib. bdg. 19.50 (ISBN 0-8287-1427-4). Clearwater Pub.

--Ute Ceded Tract, Colorado, 1873-1874. (Library of American Indian Affairs). 316p. 1973. lib. bdg. 91.50 (ISBN 0-8287-1285-9). Clearwater Pub.

--Yakima Indian Reservation: Appraisal of Patented Lands, State of Washington. (Library of American Indian Affairs). 160p. 1973. lib. bdg. 49.50 (ISBN 0-8287-1311-1). Clearwater Pub.

Miller, C. Mark. Snake-Piute Tract in Oregon, Appraisal, January 1879. (Library of American Indian Affairs). 107p. 1973. lib. bdg. 50.00 (ISBN 0-8287-1260-3). Clearwater Pub.

Minnesota Chippewa Tribe: Appraisal of Lands in Northwestern Michigan & Northern Wisconsin, 3 vols. (Library of American Indian Affairs). 557p. 1973. lib. bdg. 155.00 (ISBN 0-8287-1126-7). Clearwater Pub.

Monrad, Oscar & Sears, Roscoe H. Cherokee Outlet in the Indian Territory, State of Oklahoma: Appraisal. (Library of American Indian Affairs). 92p. 1973. lib. bdg. 33.00 (ISBN 0-8287-0976-9). Clearwater Pub.

Morrison, George A. The Gila River Indian Reservation. (Library of American Indian Affairs). 50p. 1973. lib. bdg. 23.50 (ISBN 0-8287-1049-X). Clearwater Pub.

Murray, Noble T. Washoe Tribe of Nevada & California: Appraisal of Lands. (Library of American Indian Affairs). 266p. 1973. lib. bdg. 103.00 (ISBN 0-8287-1298-0). Clearwater Pub.

Murray, William. Kickapoo Lands in Kansas 1863: Appraisal. (Library of American Indian Affairs). 89p. 1973. lib. bdg. 31.00 (ISBN 0-8287-1089-9). Clearwater Pub.

--Winnebago Lands in Iowa & Minnesota, Royce Area 267, in 1833 & 1846. 273p. 1973. lib. bdg. 81.00 (ISBN 0-8287-1307-3). Clearwater Pub.

Murray, William G. Kickapoo Tracts in Missouri & Kansas, 1835: Appraisal. (Library of American Indian Affairs). 150p. 1973. lib. bdg. 48.00 (ISBN 0-8287-1090-2). Clearwater Pub.

--Miami Tract in Kansas, 1854: Appraisal. (Library of American Indian Affairs). 107p. 1973. lib. bdg. 36.00 (ISBN 0-8287-1121-6). Clearwater Pub.

--Otoe & Missourie Tribes Iowa, Omaha, & Sac & Fox Tribes: Appraisal of Royce Area 151, in Missouri, 1836; in Iowa, 1838 & 1854. (Library of American Indian Affairs). 363p. 1973. lib. bdg. 127.20 (ISBN 0-8287-1170-4). Clearwater Pub.

--Potawatomi Tracts in Iowa & Kansas, 1846: Appraisal. (Library of American Indian Affairs). 239p. 1973. lib. bdg. 97.00 (ISBN 0-8287-1204-2). Clearwater Pub.

--Sac & Fox Cession in Iowa: Appraisal of Royce Area 152 in 1831. (Library Ofamerican Indian Affairs). 148p. 1973. lib. bdg. 48.00 (ISBN 0-8287-1215-8). Clearwater Pub.

--Sac & Fox Indian Cessions in Iowa, Royce Area 262, 1839 & 1843: Appraisal. (Library of American Indian Affairs). 380p. 1973. lib. bdg. 108.00 (ISBN 0-8287-1216-6). Clearwater Pub.

--Sac & Fox of Missouri Tract in Kansas: Appraisal, 1854. (Library of American Indian Affairs). 108p. 1973. lib. bdg. 37.50 (ISBN 0-8287-1222-0). Clearwater Pub.

--Sac, Fox, & Mississippi Tracts in Kansas 1860-67 & 1868. (Library of American Indian Affairs). 147p. 1973. lib. bdg. 48.00 (ISBN 0-8287-1226-3). Clearwater Pub.

--Shawnee Tract in Kansas, Appraisal, 1854. (Library of American Indian Affairs). 170p. 1973. lib. bdg. 52.50 (ISBN 0-8287-1244-1). Clearwater Pub.

--Sioux Cession in Iowa & Minnesota, Appraisal of Royce Area No. 153, 1831. (Library of American Indian Affairs). 165p. 1973. lib. bdg. 51.00 (ISBN 0-8287-1248-4). Clearwater Pub.

--Sioux Indian Tribe: Appraisal of Lands in North Dakota, South Dakota, Nebraska, Wyoming, & Montana in 1869. (Library of American Indian Affairs). 442p. 1973. lib. bdg. 124.50 (ISBN 0-8287-1249-2). Clearwater Pub.

Muske, H. Appraisal Report on Land Excluded from the Red Lake Reservation by Erroneous Survey. (Library of American Indian Affairs). 125p. 1973. lib. bdg. 40.50 (ISBN 0-8287-0951-3). Clearwater Pub.

Myers, Donald D. Appraisal of the Lands of the Hualapai Reservation, Arizona. (Library of American Indian Affairs). 400p. 1973. lib. bdg. 112.50 (ISBN 0-8287-0935-1). Clearwater Pub.

Myers, Donald D. & Kleinman, Frank R. Papago Tribe of Arizona: Appraisal of Lands, 1906 & 1916, 3 vols. (Library of American Indian Affairs). 930p. 1973. lib. bdg. 247.50 (ISBN 0-8287-1184-4). Clearwater Pub.

Myers, Donald D. & Kleinman, Frank R., Jr. Appraisal of the Black Hills Lands of the Sioux Nation, 1877. (Library of American Indian Affairs). 150p. 1973. lib. bdg. 48.00 (ISBN 0-8287-0927-0). Clearwater Pub.

--Appraisal of the Lands of the Fort Sill Apache Tribe of Oklahoma, 1886. (Library of American Indian Affairs). 383p. 1973. lib. bdg. 109.50 (ISBN 0-8287-0933-5). Clearwater Pub.

--Mohave Indians: Appraisal of Lands, 1853, 1865. (Library of American Indian Affairs). 175p. 1973. lib. bdg. 54.00 (ISBN 0-8287-1130-5). Clearwater Pub.

Nathan, Robert R. Paviotso-Mono Tracts of the Northern Paiute Nation, 4 vols. (Library of American Indian Affairs). 1000p. 1973. Set. lib. bdg. 247.50 (ISBN 0-8287-1186-0). Clearwater Pub.

--Valuation Report of Royce Area 242 (and 220) As of July 15, 1838, & Royce Area 268 As of April 3, 1848. (Library of American Indian Affairs). 190p. 1973. lib. bdg. 57.00 (ISBN 0-8287-1288-3). Clearwater Pub.

--Winnebago Tribe: Valuation Report on Royce Area 267, 1847. (Library of American Indian Affairs). 100p. 1973. lib. bdg. 34.50 (ISBN 0-8287-1309-X). Clearwater Pub.

Neighbours, Kenneth F. The Lipan Apache Tribe & the Mescalero Apache Tribe. (Library of American Indian Affairs). 75p. 1973. lib. bdg. 27.00 (ISBN 0-8287-1108-9). Clearwater Pub.

Nelson, H B. Samish Tribal Lands: Appraisal, 1859. (Library of American Indian Affairs). 80p. 1973. lib. bdg. 36.00 (ISBN 0-8287-1233-6). Clearwater Pub.

Neuman, Robert W. Caddoan Tribes: Data Relative to Their Historic Locations. (Library of American Indian Affairs). 150p. 1973. lib. bdg. 48.00 (ISBN 0-8287-0967-X). Clearwater Pub.

Newcombe, Dewey. Chippewa Tracts in Minnesota, 1855, 1864, 1867: Appraisal. (Library of American Indian Affairs). 314p. 1973. lib. bdg. 90.00 (ISBN 0-8287-0999-8). Clearwater Pub.

Newcombe, Dewey & Lawrence, Howard. Chippewa Tribe: Appraisal of Lands in Minnesota, Royce Area 332, 1855. (Library of American Indian Affairs). 292p. 1973. lib. bdg. 86.00 (ISBN 0-8287-1000-7). Clearwater Pub.

--Sisseton & Wahpeton Bands: Royce Area 413, 1859, Royce Area 243, 1838; Pike's Purchase Areas A&B, 1808: Appraisal of Lands in Minnesota, Wisconsin, South Dakota, & Iowa. 320p. 1973. lib. bdg. 92.00 (ISBN 0-8287-1252-2). Clearwater Pub.

Oberbillig, Ernest. Fort Sill Apache Tract: Mineral Appraisal, 1886. (Library of American Indian Affairs). 171p. 1973. lib. bdg. 52.50 (ISBN 0-8287-1046-5). Clearwater Pub.

--Fort Sill Apache Tribe of Oklahoma in Arizona & New Mexico Prior to September 4, 1886: Production & Royalty Value of the New Mexico Portion, a District by District Total. (Library of American Indian Affairs). 100p. 1973. lib. bdg. 34.50 (ISBN 0-8287-1047-3). Clearwater Pub.

--Goshute Tract in Nevada & Utah: Mineral Valuation As of 1875. (Library of American Indian Affairs). 155p. 1973. lib. bdg. 40.50 (ISBN 0-8287-1053-8). Clearwater Pub.

--Minnesota Chippewa Tribe: Mineral Appraisal of 1843. (Library of American Indian Affairs). 135p. 1973. lib. bdg. 43.50 (ISBN 0-8287-1127-5). Clearwater Pub.

--Paiute Indian Lands in California & Nevada: Mineral Valuation As of 1853-1863. (Library of American Indian Affairs). 294p. 1973. lib. bdg. 85.50 (ISBN 0-8287-1176-3). Clearwater Pub.

--San Carlos & Northern Tonto Apache Tracts in Arizona: Mineral Appraisal As of Various Dates, 1863-1960. (Library of American Indian Affairs). 78p. 1973. lib. bdg. 28.50 (ISBN 0-8287-1234-4). Clearwater Pub.

--Shoshone Lands Mineral Valuation, Nevada 1872 & California, 1853. (Library of American Indian Affairs). 208p. 1973. lib. bdg. 64.50 (ISBN 0-8287-1245-X). Clearwater Pub.

--Sioux Lands in the Black Hills, South Dakota: Mineral Value As of 1877. (Library of American Indian Affairs). 130p. 1973. lib. bdg. 42.00 (ISBN 0-8287-1419-3). Clearwater Pub.

--Washoe Indian Lands: Mineral Valuation Study. (Library of American Indian Affairs). 238p. 1973. lib. bdg. 72.00 (ISBN 0-8287-1293-X). Clearwater Pub.

--Yavapai Mineral Report. (Library of American Indian Affairs). 136p. 1973. lib. bdg. 43.50 (ISBN 0-8287-1318-9). Clearwater Pub.

Oberbilling, Ernest. Papago Tract, Arizona: Mineral Appraisal & Supplemental Report. (Library of American Indian Affairs). 433p. 1973. lib. bdg. 121.50 (ISBN 0-8287-1182-8). Clearwater Pub.

O'Boyle, Charles C. Cheyenne-Arapaho Tribes of Indians: Mineral Evaluation of Ceded Lands. (Library of American Indian Affairs). 45p. 1973. lib. bdg. 18.00 (ISBN 0-8287-0986-6). Clearwater Pub.

Opler, Morris E. The Lipan & Mescalero Apache in Texas. (Library of American Indian Affairs). 165p. 1973. lib. bdg. 51.00 (ISBN 0-8287-1107-0). Clearwater Pub.

The Ottawa, Chippewa & Potawatomie Nations of Indians: Anthropological Report on the Indian Occupancy of Royce Area 117, Ceded Under the Treaty Held at Chicago on August 29, 1821. (Library of American Indian Affairs). 217p. 1973. lib. bdg. 66.00 (ISBN 0-8287-1173-9). Clearwater Pub.

Owen, Gifford P. & Lietz, John F. Chinook Indian Lands in Washington & Oregon, 1851: Appraisal, 2 vols. (Library of American Indian Affairs). 330p. 1973. lib. bdg. 93.00 (ISBN 0-8287-0987-4). Clearwater Pub.

Palmer, Harris A. Appraisal of the Value of Lands in Royce Area 147, in Southwestern Wisconsin & Northwestern Illinois. (Library of American Indian Affairs). 206p. 1973. lib. bdg. 71.00 (ISBN 0-8287-0942-4). Clearwater Pub.

Parker, Ben H. & Vanderwilt, John W. Confederated Bands of Ute Indians: Appraisal of Mineral Resources in Lands, 5 vols. (Library of American Indian Affairs). 873p. 1973. Set. lib. bdg. 247.50 (ISBN 0-8287-1012-0). Clearwater Pub.

Plummer, Norman B. Crow Lands in Montana & Wyoming, 1868: Appraisal. (Library of American Indian Affairs). 201p. 1973. lib. bdg. 60.00 (ISBN 0-8287-1027-9). Clearwater Pub.

--Klamath & Modoc Tribes & Yahooskin Band of Snake Indians: Appraisal Report of Lands in Lakes & Klamath Counties, Oregon. (Library of American Indian Affairs). 161p. 1973. lib. bdg. 50.00 (ISBN 0-8287-1095-3). Clearwater Pub.

--Siletz Indian Reservation, Appraisal Report of Unalloted Lands Ceded Under Agreement of October 31, 1892, by the Tillamook Tribe of Indians. (Library of American Indian Affairs). 158p. 1973. lib. bdg. 50.00 (ISBN 0-8287-1247-6). Clearwater Pub.

Polland. Sac & Fox & Iowa Indian Cessions in Eastern Iowa: Appraisal of Royce Area 175 in 1833 & 1839, Royce Area 226 in 1837& 1839, Royce Area 244 in 1838 & 1839. (Library of American Indian Affairs). 328p. 1973. lib. bdg. 94.50 (ISBN 0-8287-1214-X). Clearwater Pub.

The Quileute Tribe of Indians & the Quinaielt Tribe of Indians. (Library of American Indian Affairs). 192p. 1973. lib. bdg. 73.00 (ISBN 0-8287-1210-7). Clearwater Pub.

R. H. Sears & Co. Zia, Jemez & Santa Ana Pueblo Lands, New Mexico. (Library of American Indian Affairs). 215p. 1973. lib. bdg. 66.00 (ISBN 0-8287-1323-5). Clearwater Pub.

Rambo, Edward A. Cheyenne & Arapaho Tribes in Northern & Western Oklahoma, 1891: Appraisal of Certain Lands. (Library of American Indian Affairs). 145p. 1973. lib. bdg. 46.00 (ISBN 0-8287-0982-3). Clearwater Pub.

Rands, Robert L. Acoma Land Utilization: An Ethnohistorical Report. (Library of American Indian Affairs). 189p. 1973. lib. bdg. 57.00 (ISBN 0-8287-0895-9). Clearwater Pub.

--Laguna Land Utilization: An Ethnohistorical Report. (Library of American Indian Affairs). 102p. 1973. lib. bdg. 24.00 (ISBN 0-8287-1102-X). Clearwater Pub.

Raney, Chase W. Appraisal Report of Warm Springs Ceded Tract, Oregon, 1859. (Library of American Indian Affairs). 176p. 1973. lib. bdg. 55.50 (ISBN 0-8287-0948-3). Clearwater Pub.

Ray, Verne F. Apache Indians of Texas: Ethnohistorical Analysis of Documents. (Library of American Indian Affairs). 265p. 1973. lib. bdg. 78.00 (ISBN 0-8287-0916-5). Clearwater Pub.

--The Joseph Band of Nez Perce Indians, 1805-1905. (Library of American Indian Affairs). 108p. 1973. lib. bdg. 37.50 (ISBN 0-8287-1082-1). Clearwater Pub.

Reber, Arthur W. Washoe Tribe: Fishery Evaluation. (Library of American Indian Affairs). 26p. 1973. lib. bdg. 19.50 (ISBN 0-8287-1296-4). Clearwater Pub.

Reeve, Frank D. Anthropological Report on the Navajo Indians. 99p. 1973. lib. bdg. 33.00 (ISBN 0-8287-0911-4). Clearwater Pub.

--The Navajo Indians in New Mexico, to 1870: Historical Report. (Library of American Indian Affairs). 98p. 1973. lib. bdg. 34.50 (ISBN 0-8287-1138-0). Clearwater Pub.

Riley, Carroll L. Makah Indians of Western Washington: A Study of Group Distribution, Political Organization & Concepts of Land Use. (Library of American Indian Affairs). 1976. lib. bdg. 20.00x (ISBN 0-8287-1111-9). Clearwater Pub.

--Salish & Chimakuam-Speaking Indians of the Puget Sound Basin of Washington. (Library of American Indian Affairs). 60p. 1973. lib. bdg. 22.50 (ISBN 0-8287-1231-X). Clearwater Pub.

Ross, Norman A., ed. The Klamath Tribe & Federal Management of the Tribal Forest, 3 vols. (Library of American Indian Affairs). 1976. lib. bdg. 200.00x (ISBN 0-8287-1099-6). Clearwater Pub.

Sanwick, John D. Nisqually, Steilacoom, & Squaxin Lands, State of Washington, 1855: Appraisal. (Library of American Indian Affairs). 30p. 1973. lib. bdg. 19.00 (ISBN 0-8287-1147-X). Clearwater Pub.

Saunderson, Mont H. Confederated Salish & Kootenai Tribe Lands of the Flathead Indian Reservation, 1859: Valuation. (Library of American Indian Affairs). 100p. 1973. lib. bdg. 34.50 (ISBN 0-8287-1014-7). Clearwater Pub.

--Crow Indian Lands Ceded in the Fort Laramie Treaty of 1868: Appraisal. (Library of American Indian Affairs). 80p. 1973. lib. bdg. 29.00 (ISBN 0-8287-1026-0). Clearwater Pub.

--Goshute Shoshone Indians: Appraisal of Lands, 1875. (Library of American Indian Affairs). 115p. 1973. lib. bdg. 39.00 (ISBN 0-8287-1052-X). Clearwater Pub.

--Three Affiliated Tribes of Fort Berthold Reservation, March 3, 1891: Valuation of Ceded Lands. (Library of American Indian Affairs). 74p. 1973. lib. bdg. 27.00 (ISBN 0-8287-1270-0). Clearwater Pub.

Schroeder, Albert H. Apache Indians. (Library of American Indian Affairs). 573p. 1973. lib. bdg. 159.00 (ISBN 0-8287-0914-9). Clearwater Pub.

--Yavapai History. (Library of American Indian Affairs). 310p. 1973. lib. bdg. 90.00 (ISBN 0-8287-1316-2). Clearwater Pub.

Sears, R. H. Acoma Pueblo Land, New Mexico: Appraisal Report, 1901-1936. (Library of American Indian Affairs). 246p. 1973. lib. bdg. 75.00 (ISBN 0-8287-0896-7). Clearwater Pub.

--Laguna Pueblo Land in New Mexico: Appraisal Report, 1908-1936. (Library of American Indian Affairs). 206p. 1973. lib. bdg. 63.00 (ISBN 0-8287-1105-4). Clearwater Pub.

Sears, Roscoe. Cheyenne & Arapaho Indian Reservations in the Indian Territory, State of Oklahoma, 1891: Appraisal. (Library of American Indian Affairs). 89p. 1973. lib. bdg. 31.00 (ISBN 0-8287-0979-3). Clearwater Pub.

Sears, Roscoe H. Cherokee Nation Indian Reservations in the Indian Territory, Oklahoma: Appraisal. (Library of American Indian Affairs). 73p. 1973. lib. bdg. 27.00 (ISBN 0-8287-0973-4). Clearwater Pub.

--Cheyenne & Arapaho Indian Reservation in the Indian Territory, State of Oklahoma, 1869: Appraisal. (Library of American Indian Affairs). 51p. 1973. lib. bdg. 20.00 (ISBN 0-8287-0980-7). Clearwater Pub.

Sharrock, Floyd W. & Sharrock, Susan R. Cree Indian Territorial Expansion: The Hudson Bay Area to Interior Saskatchewan & Missouri Plains. (Library of American Indian Affairs). 200p. 1973. lib. bdg. 60.00 (ISBN 0-8287-1017-1). Clearwater Pub.

Shenan, P. J. & Full, Roy P. Haulapai Indians of Arizona: Evaluation Study of Mineral Resources, 4 vols. (Library of American Indian Affairs). 1670p. 1973. lib. bdg. 450.00 (ISBN 0-8287-1057-0). Clearwater Pub.

Shennon, P. J. & Full, Roy P. Mohave Tribe of Indians of Arizona, California & Nevada & the Mohave Indians of the Colorado River Indian Tribes: Evaluation Study of Mineral Resources. (Library of American Indian Affairs). 78p. 1973. lib. bdg. 28.50 (ISBN 0-8287-1132-1). Clearwater Pub.

Shenon, P. J. & Full, R. P. Appraisal of the Mineral Resources in the Lands of the Sioux Nation Acquired Under Treaty of April 26, 1868, 4 vols. (Library of American Indian Affairs). 1860p. 1973. Set. lib. bdg. 500.00 (ISBN 0-8287-0938-6). Clearwater Pub.
Shenon, P. J. & Full, Roy P. Nez Perce Tribe of Indians: Evaluation Study of the Mineral Resources, 1867, 4 vols. (Evaluation Study of the Mineral Resources, 1867). 1100p. 1973. Set. lib. bdg. 300.00 (ISBN 0-8287-1145-3). Clearwater Pub.
--Washoe Tribe: Evaluation of Mineral Resources, 5 vols. (Library of American Indian Affairs). 1570p. 1973. lib. bdg. 420.00 (ISBN 0-8287-1295-6). Clearwater Pub.
--Western Bands of Shoshone Indians: Evaluation Study of Mineral Resources, 12 vols. (Library of American Indian Affairs). 5000p. 1973. lib. bdg. 1300.00 (ISBN 0-8287-1302-2). Clearwater Pub.
Shenon, P. J., et al. Northern Paiute Nation: Evaluation Study of Mineral Resources, 3 vols. (Library of American Indian Affairs). 1185p. 1973. Set. lib. bdg. 330.00 (ISBN 0-8287-1150-X). Clearwater Pub.
The Skagit Tribe & the Snoqualmie Tribe: Ethnological & Historical Evidence. 265p. 1973. lib. bdg. 52.00 (ISBN 0-8287-1257-3). Clearwater Pub.
Smith, Alice E. & Carstensen, Vernon. Winnebago Indians: Economic & Historical Background for Royce Areas 149, 174, 245. (Library of American Indian Affairs). 223p. 1973. lib. bdg. 67.50 (ISBN 0-8287-1306-5). Clearwater Pub.
Starkey, Harold C. & Carlson, Roy C. Lower Pen D'oreille or Kalispel Indian Lands: Northeast Washington, Northern Idaho, & Western Montana, 1903. (Library of American Indian Affairs). 197p. 1973. lib. bdg. 60.00 (ISBN 0-8287-1109-7). Clearwater Pub.
Starrett, Paul. Appraisal Report of Lands in Central Indiana: Purchased from the Miami Tribe of Indians 1818. (Library of American Indian Affairs). 170p. 1973. lib. bdg. 52.50 (ISBN 0-8287-0945-9). Clearwater Pub.
--Creek Nation: Appraisal of Ceded Lands in Southern Georgia & Southeastern Alabama. (Library of American Indian Affairs). 21p. 1973. lib. bdg. 15.00 (ISBN 0-8287-1022-8). Clearwater Pub.
--Ottawa, Chippewa & Potowatomi Nations of Indians: Appraisal of Royce Area 117, Ceded by the Treaty of August 29, 1821. (Library of American Indian Affairs). 250p. 1973. lib. bdg. 75.00 (ISBN 0-8287-1174-7). Clearwater Pub.
Steward, Julian H. Aboriginal & Historic Groups of the Ute Indians of Utah: An Analysis. (Indian Claims Commission Ser). 121p. 1973. lib. bdg. 39.00 (ISBN 0-8287-0887-8). Clearwater Pub.
Steward, Julian H. & Wheeler-Voegelin, Erminie. Northern Paiute Indians: Anthropological Report. (Library of American Indian Affairs). 313p. 1973. lib. bdg. 90.00 (ISBN 0-8287-1148-8). Clearwater Pub.
Stores, Samuel L. Creek Indian Lands in Oklahoma: Appriasal of Land Values As of 1907. (Library of American Indian Affairs). 1976. lib. bdg. 100.00x (ISBN 0-8287-1018-X). Clearwater Pub.
Stout, David B. Anthropological Reports on the Indians Occupying on Area Bounded Roughly by the Kankakee, Illinois, Mississippi, Ohio, Wabash, & Tippecanoe Rivers. (Library of American Indian Affairs). 32p. 1973. lib. bdg. 18.00 (ISBN 0-8287-0912-2). Clearwater Pub.
--Kickapoo, Illinois & Potawatomi Indians: Anthropological Reports. (Library of American Indian Affairs). 122p. 1973. lib. bdg. 40.00 (ISBN 0-8287-1087-2). Clearwater Pub.
--Saginaw Chippewa: Ethnohistorical Report on Royce Area No. 111 (Michigan), Treaty of Sept. 24, 1819. (Library of American Indian Affairs). 41p. 1973. lib. bdg. 20.50 (ISBN 0-8287-1229-8). Clearwater Pub.
Suphan, Robert J. The Umatilla, Walla Walla, & Cayuse Indians Relative to Socio-Political Organization & Land Use. (Library of American Indian Affairs). 90p. 1973. lib. bdg. 32.50 (ISBN 0-8287-1428-2). Clearwater Pub.
--The Wasco & Tenino Indians: Political Organization & Land-Use. 72p. 1973. lib. bdg. 27.00 (ISBN 0-8287-1292-1). Clearwater Pub.
Sutherland, J. Frederick. Appraisals of Land Areas in Minnesota, Treaties of February 22, 1855; March 11, 1863; May 7, 1864; March 19, 1867. (Library of American Indian Affairs). 314p. 1973. lib. bdg. 91.50 (ISBN 0-8287-0952-1). Clearwater Pub.
Tanner, Helen H. Caddo Tribe of Oklahoma, Rebuttal Statement. (Library of American Indian Affairs). 144p. 1973. lib. bdg. 46.50 (ISBN 0-8287-0963-7). Clearwater Pub.
--Chippewa of Eastern Lower Michigan: Historical Report. (Library of American Indian Affairs). 25p. 1973. lib. bdg. 16.25 (ISBN 0-8287-0993-9). Clearwater Pub.
--The Greenville Treaty, 1795. (Library of American Indian Affairs). 70p. 1973. lib. bdg. 38.00 (ISBN 0-8287-1055-4). Clearwater Pub.
--Indian Tribes in Southeastern Michigan & Northern Ohio: A History. (Library of American Indian Affairs). 55p. 1973. lib. bdg. 21.00 (ISBN 0-8287-1069-4). Clearwater Pub.
--Potawatomi Ceded Lands & an Indian History of Northeastern Illinois. (Library of American Indian Affairs). 1976. lib. bdg. 29.00x (ISBN 0-8287-1200-X). Clearwater Pub.
Tanner, Helen H., et al. Wyandot Reservations in Michigan & Ohio: An Historial Report for Appraising Land Values. Ross, Norman A., ed. (Library of American Indian Affairs). 1976. lib. bdg. 75.00x (ISBN 0-8287-1310-3). Clearwater Pub.
Taylor, H. C., Jr. Makah Indians: Anthropological Investigation Relative to Tribal Identity & Aboriginal Possession of Lands. (Library of American Indian Affairs). 61p. 1973. lib. bdg. 23.00 (ISBN 0-8287-1110-0). Clearwater Pub.
Thomas, Alfred B. The Jicarilla Apache Indians, a History, 1598-1888. (Library of American Indian Affairs). 152p. 1973. lib. bdg. 32.00 (ISBN 0-8287-1077-5). Clearwater Pub.
--The Mescalero Apache, 1653-1874. (Library of American Indian Affairs). 47p. 1973. lib. bdg. 22.50 (ISBN 0-8287-1118-6). Clearwater Pub.
Trygg, J. William. Appraisal Report: Historical & Economic Background, Land & Resource Evaluation Study of Royce Area 482, in St. Louis, Itasca & Koochiching Counties, Minnesota. (Library of American Indian Affairs). 166p. 1973. lib. bdg. 52.50 (ISBN 0-8287-0943-2). Clearwater Pub.
--Appraisal Report of Royce Areas 242, 220, & 268. 120p. 1973. lib. bdg. 39.00 (ISBN 0-8287-0946-7). Clearwater Pub.
Trygg, William J. Saginaw Chippewa Indian Tribe of Michigan: Appraisal of Royce Area No. 111, Treaty Cession Sept. 24, 1819. (Library of American Indian Affairs). 95p. 1973. lib. bdg. 33.00 (ISBN 0-8287-1230-1). Clearwater Pub.
Tucker, Elbridge A. Cherokee Outlet Lands Deeded by the Cherokee Nation to the U. S. in Trust on June 14, 1883: Appraisal. (Library of American Indian Affairs). 113p. 1973. lib. bdg. 39.00 (ISBN 0-8287-0977-7). Clearwater Pub.
Tucker, Eldridge A. Appraisal of the Lands Ceded by the Creek Nation for the Seminoles, August 7, 1856. (Library of American Indian Affairs). 115p. 1973. lib. bdg. 39.00 (ISBN 0-8287-0930-0). Clearwater Pub.
--Cherokee Outlet in Oklahoma, Appraisal, 1893. (Library of American Indian Affairs). 128p. 1973. lib. bdg. 42.00 (ISBN 0-8287-0975-0). Clearwater Pub.
U. S. Congress. Senate. Committee on Indian Affairs & U. S. Congress-House-India Affairs Committee. Indian Claims Commission Act. Bd. with Indian Claims Commission. LC 74-15122. LC 76-11750. Repr. of 1935 ed. 21.50 (ISBN 0-404-11982-4). AMS Pr.
Vaughan, John L., Jr. Shoshone Tribal Lands, California, 1853 & Nevada, 1872: Appraisal. (Library of American Indian Affairs). 91p. 1973. lib. bdg. 31.50 (ISBN 0-8287-1246-8). Clearwater Pub.
--Yavapai Tribe: Appraisal of Lands, 1873. (Library of American Indian Affairs). 114p. 1973. lib. bdg. 39.00 (ISBN 0-8287-1319-7). Clearwater Pub.
Voget, Fred W. Osage Anthropological Report. (Library of American Indian Affairs). 420p. 1973. lib. bdg. 117.00 (ISBN 0-8287-1158-5). Clearwater Pub.
Wall, Myron. Washoe Indians of California & Nevada: Timberland Valuation Study. (Library of American Indian Affairs). 93p. 1973. lib. bdg. 33.00 (ISBN 0-8287-1294-8). Clearwater Pub.
Wallace, Ernes. The Comanche, Apache & Kiowa Indians Before 1867: Habitat & Range. (Library of American Indian Affairs). 1976. lib. bdg. 99.00x (ISBN 0-8287-1600-5). Clearwater Pub.
Warner, Robert M. Saginaw Chippewa: Economic & Historical Report on Royce Area No. 111, Ceded by the Treaty of September 24, 1819. (Library of American Indian Affairs). 177p. 1973. lib. bdg. 55.50 (ISBN 0-8287-1228-X). Clearwater Pub.
Warner, Robert M. & Groesbeck, Lois J. The Sault Ste. Marie Area: Historical Report. (Library of American Indian Affairs). 21p. 1973. lib. bdg. 16.00 (ISBN 0-8287-1418-5). Clearwater Pub.
Watson, Ralph W. The Colville Tribe, San Poil & Nespelen Tribes, the Lekes, Okanogans, Methows: Appraisal of the Tribal Lands, State of Washington, 1872, 2 vols. (Library of American Indian Affairs). 291p. 1973. lib. bdg. 84.00 (ISBN 0-8287-1011-2). Clearwater Pub.
Wheeler-Voegelin, Erminie. Anthropological Report on Indian Use & Occupancy of Royce Area No. 113 (St. Martin Islands) Ceded in the Treaty of July 6, 1820 Between the U. S. & the Ottawa & Chippewa Nations of Indians; & the Area of Overlap of Royce Area 205 (Treaty of March 28, 1836) & Royce Area 111 (Treaty of Sept. 24, 1819) (Library of American Indian Affairs). 73p. 1973. lib. bdg. 27.00 (ISBN 0-8287-0906-8). Clearwater Pub.
--Ethnohistorical Report on Indian Use Occupancy of Royce Area 11, Ohio & Indiana, 2 vols. (Library of American Indian Affairs). 750p. 1973. lib. bdg. 250.00 (ISBN 0-8287-1036-8). Clearwater Pub.
Wheeler-Voegelin, Erminie & Blasingham, Emily J. United Tribes of Ottawas, Chappewas & Potawatomies: Anthropological Report on the Indian Occupancy of Royce Area 77 & Royce Area 78. (Library of American Indian Affairs). 217p. 1973. lib. bdg. 66.00 (ISBN 0-8287-1283-2). Clearwater Pub.
Wheeler-Voegelin, Erminie & Hickerson, Harold. Red Lake & Pembina Chippewa: Anthropological Report. (Library of American Indian Affairs). 200p. 1973. lib. bdg. 60.00 (ISBN 0-8287-1212-3). Clearwater Pub.
Wheeler-Voegelin, Erminie, et al. United Tribes of Sac & Fox Indians: Anthropological Report on the Indian Occupancy of Royce Area 50, Ceded Under the Treaty of November 3, 1804. (Library of American Indian Affairs). 310p. 1973. lib. bdg. 90.00 (ISBN 0-8287-1284-0). Clearwater Pub.
Williamson, M. J. The Creek Nation & Private Land Sales in Alabama, & an Appraisal of Creek Nation Lands. (Library of American Indian Affairs). 1976. lib. bdg. 99.00x (ISBN 0-8287-1021-X). Clearwater Pub.
--Osage Tribal Council, 1810: Appraisal of Lands in Missouri & Arkansas. (Library of American Indian Affairs). 250p. 1973. lib. bdg. 75.00 (ISBN 0-8287-1167-4). Clearwater Pub.
Winter, William S. Hualapai Tribal Lands in Northwestern Arizona: Appraisal. (Library of American Indian Affairs). 180p. 1973. lib. bdg. 56.00 (ISBN 0-8287-1062-7). Clearwater Pub.
Woolworth, Alan R. Yankton Sioux: Ethnohistorical Report on the Indian Occupancy of Royce Area 410. (Library of American Indian Affairs). 224p. 1973. lib. bdg. 67.50 (ISBN 0-8287-1313-8). Clearwater Pub.
Wright, Fred D. Mineral Value of Royce Area 147 in Illinois & Wisconsin, 1829. (Library of American Indian Affairs). 71p. 1973. lib. bdg. 38.00 (ISBN 0-8287-1124-0). Clearwater Pub.
Wyckoff, Don G. The Caddoan Cultural Area: An Archaeological Perspective. (Library of American Indian Affairs). 250p. 1973. lib. bdg. 75.00 (ISBN 0-8287-0966-1). Clearwater Pub.

INDIANS OF NORTH AMERICA–COMMERCE

Adams, William Y. Shonto: Study of the Role of the Trader in a Modern Navaho Community. Repr. of 1963 ed. 49.00 (ISBN 0-403-08959-X). Scholarly.
Crane, Verner. The Southern Frontier, 1670-1732. LC 76-54227. 1977. Repr. of 1956 ed. lib. bdg. 21.50x (ISBN 0-8371-9336-2, CRSF). Greenwood.
Dorchester, Guy C. Condition of the Indian Trade in North America, 1767: As Described in a Letter to Sir William Johnson. (Historical Printing Club. Publications: No. 37). 16p. 1972. Repr. of 1890 ed. pap. 11.00 (ISBN 0-8337-0474-5). B Franklin.
Hamilton, T. M. Early Indian Trade Guns: 1625-1775. LC 68-58290. (Contributions of the Museum of the Great Plains Ser.: No. 3). (Illus.). 1968. pap. 2.50 (ISBN 0-685-91360-0). Mus Great Plains.
Hanson, James A. Metal Weapons, Tools & Ornaments of the Teton Dakota Indians. LC 74-15277. (Illus.). xviii, 118p. 1975. 16.50 (ISBN 0-8032-0849-9). U of Nebr Pr.
Hunt, George T. Wars of the Iroquois: A Study in Intertribal Trade Relations. 218p. 1940. pap. 7.95x (ISBN 0-299-00164-4). U of Wis Pr.
Kersey, Harry A., Jr. Pelts, Plumes & Hides: White Traders Among the Seminole Indians, 1870-1930. LC 75-16137. (Illus.). xi, 158p. 1975. pap. 5.95 (ISBN 0-8130-0680-5). U Presses Fla.
Krech, Shepard, ed. Indians, Animals, & the Fur Trade: A Critique of Keepers of the Game. LC 81-1351. 176p. 1981. text ed. 12.00x (ISBN 0-8203-0563-4). U of Ga Pr.
McNitt, Frank. The Indian Traders. LC 62-16469. 393p. 1962. 17.95 (ISBN 0-8061-0531-3). U of Okla Pr.
Newcomb, Franc J. Navaho Neighbors. (Illus.). 1966. 12.95 (ISBN 0-8061-0704-9); pap. 5.95 (ISBN 0-8061-1040-6). U of Okla Pr.
Terrell, John U. Traders of the Western Morning: Aboriginal Commerce in Precolumbian North America. (Illus.). 1967. 8.50 (ISBN 0-686-20690-8). Southwest Mus.
Trennert, Robert A., Jr. Indian Traders on the Middle Border: The House of Ewing, 1827-54. LC 80-25018. (Illus.). xvi, 264p. 1981. 17.95x (ISBN 0-8032-4407-X). U of Nebr Pr.
Turner, Frederick J. The Character & Influence of the Indian Trade in Wisconsin. LC 78-63807. (Johns Hopkins University. Studies in the Social Sciences. Ninth Ser. 1891: 11-12). Repr. of 1891 ed. 11.50 (ISBN 0-404-61070-6). AMS Pr.
--Character & Influence of the Indian Trade in Wisconsin: A Study of the Trading Post As an Institution. 1891. 16.50 (ISBN 0-8337-3579-9). B Franklin.
--The Character & Influence of the Indian Trade in Wisconsin: A Study of the Trading Post As an Institution. Repr. of 1891 ed. pap. 8.00 (ISBN 0-384-62000-0). Johnson Repr.
--The Character & Influence of the Indian Trade in Wisconsin: A Study of the Trading Post As an Institution. Miller, David & Miller, Harry M., eds. LC 76-47331. 1977. 9.95 (ISBN 0-8061-1335-9). U of Okla Pr.
Woodward, Arthur. Indian Trade Goods. (Illus.). 1977. pap. 2.00 (ISBN 0-8323-0136-1). Binford.

INDIANS OF NORTH AMERICA–COSTUME AND ADORNMENT

see also Moccasins

Anawalt, Patricia R. Indian Clothing Before Cortes: Mesoamerican Costumes from the Codices. LC 80-5942. (The Civilization of the American Indian Ser.: Vol. 156). (Illus.). 400p. 1981. 39.95 (ISBN 0-8061-1650-1). U of Okla Pr.
Appleton, Leroy H. American Indian Design & Decoration. Orig. Title: Indian Art of the Americans. (Illus.). 10.00 (ISBN 0-8446-0007-5). Peter Smith.
Conn, Richard. Robes of White Shell & Sunrise. LC 74-16739. (Illus.). 1974. pap. 7.50 (ISBN 0-914738-04-6). Denver Art Mus.
D'Amato, Alex & D'Amato, Janet. American Indian Craft Inspirations. LC 72-83734. (Illus.). 224p. (YA) 1972. 7.95 (ISBN 0-87131-031-7). M Evans.
Haile, Berard. Head & Face Masks in Navaho Ceremonialism. LC 76-43722. Repr. of 1947 ed. 17.50 (ISBN 0-404-15565-0). AMS Pr.
Hofsinde, Robert. Indian Costumes. LC 68-11895. (Illus.). (gr. 3-7). 1968. PLB 6.48 (ISBN 0-688-31614-X). Morrow.
Koch, Ronald P. Dress Clothing of the Plains Indians. LC 76-46947. (Civilization of the American Indian Ser.: Vol. 140). (Illus.). 1977. 11.95 (ISBN 0-8061-1372-3). U of Okla Pr.
Lyford, Carrie A. Quill & Beadwork of the Western Sioux. (Illus.). 1979. pap. 5.95 (ISBN 0-933472-00-5). Johnson Bks.
Mera, H. P. Pueblo Indian Embroidery. LC 74-31607. (Illus.). 80p. 1975. lib. bdg. 15.00x (ISBN 0-88307-512-1); pap. 4.95 o. p. (ISBN 0-88307-513-X). Gannon.
Moorehead, Warren K., et al. Stone Ornaments Used by Indians in the U. S. & Canada. LC 76-43790. Repr. of 1917 ed. 55.00 (ISBN 0-404-15645-2). AMS Pr.
Orchard, William C. Beads & Beadwork of the American Indian, Vol. 11. 2nd ed. LC 75-16030. (Contributions Ser.). 1975. soft cover 5.00 (ISBN 0-934490-22-8). Mus Am Ind.
Tanner, Clara L. Ray Manley's Portraits & Turquoise of Southwest Indians. 1975. 6.00x (ISBN 0-685-99212-8). R Manley.
Walker, Louise J. Beneath the Singing Pines. (Illus.). (gr. 6-10). 1967. 7.95 (ISBN 0-910726-80-9). Hillsdale Educ.
Wildschut, William & Ewers, John C. Crow Indian Beadwork: A Descriptive & Historical Study. 2nd ed. (Contributions Ser., Vol. 16). (Illus.). 1973. pap. 5.00 (ISBN 0-934490-33-3). Mus Am Ind.
Wissler, Clark. Costumes of the Plains Indians & Structural Basis to the Decoration of Costumes Among the In Plains Indians. LC 74-9016. (Illus.). Repr. of 1915 ed. 17.00 (ISBN 0-404-11913-1). AMS Pr.

INDIANS OF NORTH AMERICA–CULTURAL ASSIMILATION

Hagan, William T. Indian Police & Judges: Experiments in Acculturation & Control. LC 79-18496. xiv, 206p. 1980. 14.95x (ISBN 0-8032-2308-0); pap. 4.95 (ISBN 0-8032-7205-7, BB722, Bison). U of Nebr Pr.
Johansen, Bruce & Maestas, Roberto. Wasi'chu: The Continuing Indian Wars. LC 79-10153. (Modern Reader Paperback Ser.). (Illus.). 268p. 1980. pap. 6.50 (ISBN 0-85345-507-4). Monthly Rev.
Kupperman, Karen O. Settling with the Indians: The Meeting of English & Indian Cultures in America, 1580-1640. 1980. 19.50x (ISBN 0-8476-6210-1). Rowman.
Mead, Margaret. Changing Culture of an Indian Tribe. LC 72-84468. (Columbia University. Contributions to Anthropology: No. 15). Repr. of 1932 ed. 25.00 (ISBN 0-404-50565-1). AMS Pr.

Pearce, Roy Harvey & Miller, J. Hillis, eds. Savagism & Civilization: A Study of the Indian & the American Mind. LC 53-6486. 271p. 1967. pap. 3.45x (ISBN 0-8018-0525-2). Johns Hopkins.

Quimby, George I. Indian Culture & European Trade Goods: The Archaeology of the Historic Period in the Western Great Lakes Region. LC 78-4996. 1978. Repr. of 1966 ed. lib. bdg. 22.50x (ISBN 0-313-20379-2, QUIC). Greenwood.

Recinos, Adrian & Goetz, Delia, trs. The Annals of the Cakchiquels. Bd. with Title of the Lords of Totonicapan. Goetz, Delia, tr. (Spanish translation by Dionisio Jose Chonay). (Civilization of the American Indian Ser: Vol. 37). 217p. 1953. pap. 5.95 (ISBN 0-8061-1152-6). U of Okla Pr.

Schultz, George A. An Indian Canaan: Isaac McCoy & the Vision of an Indian State. (Civilization of the American Indian Ser.: No. 121). (Illus.). 350p. 1972. 12.50 (ISBN 0-8061-1024-4); pap. 6.95 (ISBN 0-8061-1303-0). U of Okla Pr.

Underhill, Lonnie E. & Littlefield, Daniel F., Jr., eds. Hamlin Garland's Observations on the American Indian, 1895-1905. LC 75-19863. 9.95x (ISBN 0-8165-0485-7); pap. 5.95 (ISBN 0-8165-0505-5). U of Ariz Pr.

INDIANS OF NORTH AMERICA-CULTURE

Here is entered literature dealing with the cultural condition (i.e. arts, industries, religion and mythology, etc.) of the Indian at a given time or period.

see also Hopewell Culture

American Academy of Political & Social Science of Philadelphia, et al. American Indians & American Life. LC 57-13854. 1973. Repr. of 1957 ed. 21.00 (ISBN 0-527-02099-0). Kraus Repr.

American Society for Promoting the Civilization & General Improvement of the Indian Tribes Within the United States: The First Annual Report. LC 11-15758. Repr. of 1824 ed. 12.00 (ISBN 0-527-03244-1). Kraus Repr.

Benedict, Ruth. Patterns of Culture. 1961. 10.95 (ISBN 0-395-07405-3); pap. 4.95 (ISBN 0-395-08357-5). HM.

Boyd, Doug. Rolling Thunder. 1976. pap. 5.95 (ISBN 0-440-57435-8, Delta). Dell.

Brisbin, James S., ed. Belden, the White Chief: Or, Twelve Years Among the Wild Indians of the Plains from the Diaries & Manuscripts of George P. Belden. facsimile ed. LC 73-92900. (Illus.). xxvi, 513p. 1974. Repr. of 1870 ed. 15.00 (ISBN 0-8214-0150-5). Ohio U Pr.

Carter, E. R. Gift Is Rich. rev. ed. (Illus., Orig.). 1955. pap. 3.50 (ISBN 0-377-28071-2). Friend Pr.

Drew, Leslie & Wilson, Douglas. Argillite: Art of the Haida Native Culture. (Illus.). 300p. 1980. 40.00x (ISBN 0-87663-609-1, Pub. by Hancock Hse). Universe.

Eliot, John. John Eliot's Indian Dialogues: A Study in Cultural Interaction. Bowden, Henry W. & Ronda, James P., eds. LC 80-542. (Contributions in American History: No. 88). (Illus.). 173p. 1980. lib. bdg. 22.95 (ISBN 0-313-21031-4, RID/). Greenwood.

Ewers, John C. The Horse in Blackfoot Indian Culture with Comparative Material from Other Western Tribes. Repr. of 1955 ed. 39.00 (ISBN 0-403-03606-2). Scholarly.

Fenton, William & Gu Lick, John. Symposium on Cherokee & Iroquois Culture. Repr. of 1961 ed. 21.00 (ISBN 0-403-03703-4). Scholarly.

Fenton, William N., ed. Symposium on Local Diversity in Iroquois Culture. Repr. of 1951 ed. 21.00 (ISBN 0-403-03704-2). Scholarly.

Gower, Charlotte D. Northern & Southern Affiliations of Antillean Culture. LC 28-7691. 1927. pap. 5.00 (ISBN 0-527-00534-7). Kraus Repr.

Grey, Herman. Tales from the Mohaves. LC 69-16731. (Civilization of the American Indian Ser.: Vol. 107). 96p. 1980. pap. 3.95 (ISBN 0-8061-1655-2). U of Okla Pr.

Gunnerson, James H. The Fremont Culture: A Study in Culture Dynamics on the Northern Anasazi Frontier. LC 79-76014. (Peabody Museum Papers: Vol. 59, No. 2). 1969. pap. text ed. 15.00 (ISBN 0-87365-172-3). Peabody Harvard.

Gunther, Erna. Indian Life on the Northwest Coast of North America As Seen by the Early Explorers & Fur Traders During the Last Decade of the 18th Century. LC 72-188822. 320p. 1972. 15.00x (ISBN 0-226-31088-4). U of Chicago Pr.

Haeberlin, Herman K. The Idea of Fertilization in the Culture of the Pueblo Indians. LC 16-25723. Repr. of 1916 ed. pap. 5.00 (ISBN 0-527-00512-6). Kraus Repr.

Hamilton, Henry W. & Hamilton, Jean T. The Sioux of the Rosebud: A History in Pictures. LC 78-145506. (The Civilization of the American Indian Ser.: Vol. 111). (Illus.). 320p. 1981. pap. 12.50 (ISBN 0-8061-1622-6). U of Okla Pr.

Kew, Della & Goddard, P. E. Indian Art & Culture. 2nd ed. (Illus.). 1978. pap. 5.95 (ISBN 0-919654-13-4, Pub. by Hancock Hse). Universe.

King, Mary E. & Traylor, Idris R., Jr., eds. Art & Environment in Native America. (Special Publications: No. 7). (Illus., Orig.). 1974. pap. 8.00 (ISBN 0-89672-032-2). Tex Tech Pr.

Lang, Gottfried O. A Study in Culture Contact & Culture Change: The Whiterock Utes in Transition. (Utah Anthropological Papers: No. 15). Repr. of 1953 ed. 10.50 (ISBN 0-404-60615-6). AMS Pr.

Linton, Ralph. Acculturation in Seven Indian Tribes. 8.50 (ISBN 0-8446-1283-9). Peter Smith.

McAllester, David P. & McAllester, Susan W. Hogans: Navajo Houses & House Songs. (Illus.). 160p. 1980. 16.95 (ISBN 0-8195-5043-4, Pub. by Wesleyan U Pr). Columbia U Pr.

McLuhan & Curtiss. Touch the Earth. 1976. pap. 6.95 (ISBN 0-671-22275-9, Touchstone). S&S.

McLuhan, T. C. Touch the Earth: A Self Portrait of Indian Existence. 1976. pap. 6.95 (ISBN 0-671-22275-9, Touchstone Bks). S&S.

Marriott, Alice L. Greener Fields: Experiences Among the American Indians. Repr. of 1953 ed. lib. bdg. 15.00 (ISBN 0-8371-0562-5, MAGF). Greenwood.

Mead, Margaret. Changing Culture of an Indian Tribe. LC 72-84468. (Columbia University. Contributions to Anthropology: No. 15). Repr. of 1932 ed. 25.00 (ISBN 0-404-50565-1). AMS Pr.

Mills, George. The People of the Saints. (Illus.). 1967. 3.75 (ISBN 0-686-15926-8). Taylor Museum.

Moore. Ancestor's Footsteps. (Indian Culture Ser.). 1978. 1.95 (ISBN 0-89992-073-X). Mt Coun Indian.

Morey, Sylvester M., ed. Can the Red Man Help the White Man. LC 80-83370. (Illus.). 130p. 1970. pap. 3.50 (ISBN 0-913098-35-3). Myrin Institute.

Nequatewa, Edmund. Truth of a Hopi. LC 73-78419. (Illus.). 112p. 1973. pap. 4.95 (ISBN 0-87358-116-4). Northland.

Nichols, Claude A. Moral Education Among the North American Indians. LC 75-177112. (Columbia University. Teachers College. Contributions to Education: No. 427). Repr. of 1930 ed. 17.50 (ISBN 0-404-55427-X). AMS Pr.

Prakash, B. Aspects of Indian History & Civilization. 1965. 8.50 (ISBN 0-8426-1681-0). Verry.

Schoolcraft, Henry R. The Indian in His Wigwam: Or Characteristics of the Red Race in America. LC 74-9004. Repr. of 1848 ed. 29.00 (ISBN 0-404-11896-8). AMS Pr.

Schultz, James W. Why Gone Those Times? Silliman, Lee, ed. LC 72-9262. (Civilization of the American Indian Ser.: Vol. 127). 271p. 1974. 12.95 (ISBN 0-8061-1068-6). U of Okla Pr.

Sinclair, Lister & Pollack, Jack. The Art of Norval Morrisseau. (Illus.). 1979. 50.00 (ISBN 0-458-93820-3). Methuen Inc.

Smith, Marian W. Puyallup-Nisqually. LC 73-82360. (Columbia Univ. Contributions to Anthropology Ser.: Vol. 32). 1969. Repr. of 1940 ed. 27.00 (ISBN 0-404-50582-1). AMS Pr.

Spicer, Edward H. Cycles of Conquest: The Impact of Spain, Mexico & the United States on Indians of the Southwest, 1533-1960. LC 61-14500. (Illus.). 1962. pap. 8.95x (ISBN 0-8165-0021-5). U of Ariz Pr.

Spier, Leslie, et al, eds. Language, Culture & Personality: Essays in Memory of Edward Sapir. (Illus.). 1941. pap. 10.00x (ISBN 0-87480-011-0). U of Utah Pr.

Statement on American Indians. pap. 0.35 (ISBN 0-686-15373-1, B-124). US Catholic.

Tedlock, Dennis & Tedlock, Barbara, eds. Teachings from the American Earth: Perspectives on the Religion, Philosophy, & Spirituality of the American Indian. (Illus.). 280p. 1975. 9.95x (ISBN 0-87140-599-7). Liveright.

Teit, James A. The Lillooet Indians. LC 73-3520. (Jesup North Pacific Expedition. Publications: No. 2, Pt. 5). Repr. of 1906 ed. 20.00 (ISBN 0-404-58121-8). AMS Pr.

U. S. Bureau of Education. Indian Education & Civilization. Repr. 30.00 (ISBN 0-527-91600-5). Kraus Repr.

Vaughan, Alden T. & Richter, Daniel K. Crossing the Cultural Divide: Indians & New Englanders, 1605-1763. 76p. 1980. pap. 5.00 (ISBN 0-912296-48-8, Dist. by U Pr of Va). Am Antiquarian.

Vestal, Stanley. Happy Hunting Grounds. 219p. 1981. pap. 4.95 (ISBN 0-8061-1543-2). U of Okla Pr.

Wilson, Gilbert L. The Horse & the Dog in Hidatsa Culture. LC 76-43895. (AMNH Anthropological Papers: Vol. 15, Pt. 2). Repr. of 1924 ed. 23.00 (ISBN 0-404-15751-3). AMS Pr.

INDIANS OF NORTH AMERICA-CUSTOMS

see Indians of North America-Social Life and Customs

INDIANS OF NORTH AMERICA-DANCES

see also Ghost Dance

Boatright, Mody C. & Day, Donald, eds. From Hell to Breakfast. LC 45-1540. (Texas Folklore Society Publications: No. 19). (Illus.). 1967. Repr. of 1944 ed. 6.95 (ISBN 0-87074-012-1). SMU Press.

Burnett, Millie. Dance Down the Rain, Sing up the Corn: American Indian Chants & Games for Children. LC 75-21028. 1975. spiral bound 5.00 (ISBN 0-88247-370-0). R & E Res Assoc.

Dorsey, George A. The Cheyenne Indians: The Sun Dance, Wyoming. LC 78-177922. (Beautiful Rio Grande Classics Ser). 286p. 1972. lib. bdg. 20.00 (ISBN 0-87380-081-8). Rio Grande.

Fenton, William N. The Iroquois Eagle Dance, an Offshoot of the Calumet Dance. Repr. of 1953 ed. 25.00 (ISBN 0-403-03617-8). Scholarly.

Fergusson, Erna. Dancing Gods: Indian Ceremonials of New Mexico & Arizona. LC 31-18831. (Illus.). 286p. 1970. pap. 6.95 (ISBN 0-8263-0033-2). U of NM Pr.

Fletcher, Alice C. Indian Games & Dances with Native Songs. LC 75-136369. Repr. of 1915 ed. 11.50 (ISBN 0-404-07229-1). AMS Pr.

Frisbee, Charlotte. Music & Dance Research of the Southwestern Indians. LC 74-74663. (Detroit Studies in Music Bibliography Ser.: No. 36). 1977. 9.75 (ISBN 0-911772-86-3). Info Coord.

Haile, Berard. The Navaho Fire Dance, or Corral Dance, 3 vols. in 1. Bd. with The Navaho War Dance. Repr. of 1946 ed; Starlore Among the Navaho. Repr. of 1947 ed. LC 76-43724. 1977. Repr. of 1946 ed. 15.00 (ISBN 0-404-15568-5). AMS Pr.

Johnston, Basil H. Ojibway Heritage. (Illus.). 171p. 1976. 14.00x (ISBN 0-231-04168-3). Columbia U Pr.

Kurath, Gertrude P. Iroquois Music & Dance: Ceremonial Arts of Two Seneca Longhouses. Repr. of 1964 ed. 25.00 (ISBN 0-403-03618-6). Scholarly.

Laubin, Reginald & Laubin, Gladys. Indian Dances of North America: Their Importance to Indian Life. LC 75-40962. (The Civilization of the American Indian Ser: No.141). 1977. 29.95 (ISBN 0-8061-1319-7). U of Okla Pr.

Lesser, Alexander. Pawnee Ghost Dance Hand Game. LC 79-82340. (Columbia Univ. Contributions to Anthropology Ser.: Vol. 16). 1969. Repr. of 1933 ed. 21.00 (ISBN 0-404-50566-X). AMS Pr.

Mails, Thomas E. Sundancing at Rosebud & Pine Ridge. LC 78-55075. (Illus.). 1978. 33.00 (ISBN 0-931170-01-X). U of Nebr Pr.

Michelson, Truman. Notes on the Buffalo-Head Dance of the Bear Gens of the Fox Indians. Repr. of 1928 ed. 17.00 (ISBN 0-403-03668-2). Scholarly.

Speck, Frank G. Oklahoma Delaware Ceremonies, Feasts & Dances. LC 76-43845. (Memoirs of the American Philosophical Socisey: Vol. 7). Repr. of 1937 ed. 21.50 (ISBN 0-404-15696-7). AMS Pr.

Spier, Leslie. The Prophet Dance of the Northwest & Its Derivatives: The Source of the Ghost Dance. LC 76-43853. Repr. of 1935 ed. 18.00 (ISBN 0-404-15708-4). AMS Pr.

Walker, J. R. The Sun Dance & Other Ceremonies of the Oglala Division of the Teton Dakota. LC 76-43886. (AMNH Anthropological Papers: Vol. 16, Pt. 2). Repr. of 1917 ed. 21.50 (ISBN 0-404-15745-9). AMS Pr.

INDIANS OF NORTH AMERICA-DRAMA

Austin, Mary H. Arrow-Maker. rev. ed. LC 70-90082. (BCL Ser.: No. 2). Repr. of 1915 ed. 12.50 (ISBN 0-404-00419-9). AMS Pr.

Geiogamah, Hanay, ed. New Native American Drama: Three Plays. LC 79-4733. (Illus.). 1980. 9.95 (ISBN 0-8061-1586-6); pap. 4.95 (ISBN 0-8061-1697-8). U of Okla Pr.

Heath, Virginia S. Dramatic Elements in American Indian Ceremonials. (American History & Americana Ser., No. 47). 1970. pap. 12.95 (ISBN 0-8383-0093-6). Haskell.

Radin, Paul. Road of Life & Death. (Bollingen Ser.: Vol. 5). 1945. 22.00x (ISBN 0-691-09819-0). Princeton U Pr.

INDIANS OF NORTH AMERICA-DWELLINGS

see also Pueblos

Adams, Spencer L. The Long House of the Iroquois. LC 76-43640. (Illus.). Repr. of 1944 ed. 27.50 (ISBN 0-404-15475-1). AMS Pr.

Clutesi, George. Potlatch. 188p. 1969. pap. 2.95 (ISBN 0-686-74124-2). Superior Pub.

Indian Children of B. C. Tales from the Longhouse. 112p. 1973. pap. 2.95 (ISBN 0-686-74134-X). Superior Pub.

Laubin, Reginald & Laubin, Gladys. The Indian Tipi: Its History, Construction, & Use. 2nd ed. (Illus.). 1977. 14.95 (ISBN 0-8061-1433-9). U of Okla Pr.

Lavine, Sigmund A. The Houses the Indians Built. LC 74-25524. (Illus.). (gr. 5 up). 1975. PLB 5.95 (ISBN 0-396-07076-0). Dodd.

Morgan, Lewis H. Houses & House Life of the American Aborigines. LC 66-13881. (Illus.). 1966. 12.00x (ISBN 0-226-53699-8). U of Chicago Pr.

--Houses & House Life of the American Aborigines. LC 66-13881. 1966. pap. 2.95 (ISBN 0-226-53700-5, P211, Phoen). U of Chicago Pr.

Wilson, Gilbert L. The Hidatsa Earthlodge. Weitzner, Bella, ed. LC 76-43894. (AMNH Anthropological Papers: Vol. 33, Pt. 5). Repr. of 1934 ed. 29.00 (ISBN 0-404-15752-1). AMS Pr.

INDIANS OF NORTH AMERICA-ECONOMIC CONDITIONS

Adams, Evelyn C. American Indian Education: Government Schools & Economic Progress. LC 70-165701. (American Education Ser, No. 2). 1972. Repr. of 1946 ed. 14.00 (ISBN 0-405-03690-6). Arno.

Beaglehole, Ernest. Notes on Hopi Economic Life. LC 76-43655. (Yale University Publications in Anthropology: No. 15). Repr. of 1937 ed. 18.50 (ISBN 0-404-15489-1). AMS Pr.

Burton, Henrietta K. The Re-Establishment of the Indians in Their Pueblo Life Through the Revival of Their Traditional Crafts: A Study in Home Extension Education. LC 73-176617. (Columbia University. Teachers College. Contributions to Education: No. 673). Repr. of 1936 ed. 17.50 (ISBN 0-404-55673-6). AMS Pr.

Couro, Teo. San Diego County Indians As Farmers & Wage Earners. pap. 1.00 (ISBN 0-686-69102-4). Acoma Bks.

Gagala, Kenneth. Economics of Minorities: A Guide to Information Sources. LC 73-17573. (Economics Information Guide Ser: Vol. 2). 339p. 1976. 36.00 (ISBN 0-8103-1294-8). Gale.

Gilbreath, Larry K. Red Capitalism: An Analysis of the Navajo Economy. 150p. 1973. pap. 3.95 (ISBN 0-8061-1095-3). U of Okla Pr.

Haile, Berard. Property Concepts of the Navaho Indians. LC 76-43726. Repr. of 1954 ed. 12.50 (ISBN 0-404-15566-9). AMS Pr.

Lukaczer, Moses. The Federal Buy Indian Program: Promise Versus Performance. LC 75-32667. 126p. 1976. 8.50 (ISBN 0-87881-034-X); pap. 5.50 (ISBN 0-87881-035-8). Mojave Bks.

Mongia, J. N. Economics for Administrators. 600p. 1981. text ed. 40.00x (ISBN 0-7069-1293-4, Pub by Vikas India). Advent NY.

Mother Earth, Father Sky, & Economic Development: Navajo Resources & Their Use. (Development Ser.: No. 3). (Orig.). 1981. 12.75 (ISBN 0-686-75483-2). U of NM Nat Am Stud.

Oberg, Kalervo. The Social Economy of the Tlingit Indians. LC 73-16048. (Illus.). 144p. 1980. pap. text ed. 7.50 (ISBN 0-295-95735-2). U of Wash Pr.

Ortiz, Roxanne D., ed. Economic Development in American Indian Reservations. LC 79-64281. (Development Ser.: No. 1). (Orig.). 1979. pap. 8.95 (ISBN 0-934090-00-9). U of NM Nat Am Std.

Reno, Philip. Mother Earth, Father Sky, & Economic Development: Navajo Resources & Their Use. (Illus.). 183p. 1981. 15.95x (ISBN 0-8263-0550-4). U of NM Pr.

Sorkin, Alan L. American Indians & Federal Aid. (Studies in Social Economics). 231p. 1971. 10.95 (ISBN 0-8157-8044-3). Brookings.

Stanley, Sam, ed. American Indian Economic Development. (World Anthropology Ser.). 1978. 44.00 (ISBN 0-202-90078-9). Beresford Bk Serv.

Stites, Sara H. Economics of the Iroquois. LC 76-43861. Repr. of 1905 ed. 18.00 (ISBN 0-404-15715-7). AMS Pr.

Subcommittee On Economy In Government. American Indians: Facts - Future Toward Economic Development for Native American Communities. LC 76-128179. 1970. Repr. of 1969 ed. 10.00 (ISBN 0-405-00691-8). Arno.

Talbot, Steve. Roots of Oppression: The American Indian Question. (Orig.). 1981. 14.00 (ISBN 0-7178-0591-3); pap. 4.75 (ISBN 0-7178-0583-2). Intl Pub Co.

Weeden, William B. Indian Money As a Factor in New England Civilization. LC 78-63747. (Johns Hopkins University. Studies in the Social Sciences. Second Ser. 1884: 8-9). Repr. of 1884 ed. 11.50 (ISBN 0-404-61017-X). AMS Pr.

INDIANS OF NORTH AMERICA-EDUCATION

see also particular schools, e.g. Carlisle, Pennsylvania. United States Indian School

Adams, Evelyn C. American Indian Education: Government Schools & Economic Progress. LC 70-165701. (American Education Ser, No. 2). 1972. Repr. of 1946 ed. 14.00 (ISBN 0-405-03690-6). Arno.

Ammon, Solomon R. History & Present Development of Indian Schools in the United States. LC 75-5367. 1975. Repr. of 1935 ed. soft bdg. 8.00 (ISBN 0-88247-345-X). R & E Res Assoc.

Caldwell, Martha B. Annals of Shawnee Methodist Mission & Indian Manual Labor School. 2nd ed. LC 39-28738. (Illus.). 1977. pap. 2.95 (ISBN 0-87726-005-2). Kansas St Hist.

Coffer, William E. & Hosh, Koi. Sleeping Giants. LC 79-64248. 1979. pap. text ed. 7.50 (ISBN 0-8191-0760-3). U Pr of Amer.

Farmer, George L. Education: The Dilemma of the Indian-American. 1969. 15.00x (ISBN 0-913330-09-4). Sun Dance Bks.

Fischbacher, Theodore. A Study of the Role of the Federal Government in the Education of the American Indian. LC 74-76467. 1974. Repr. of 1967 ed. soft bdg. 10.00 (ISBN 0-88247-280-1). R & E Res Assoc.

Henry, Jeannette, ed. The American Indian Reader: Education. LC 72-86873. 300p. 1972. pap. 4.50 (ISBN 0-913436-10-0). Indian Hist Pr.

Jackson, Curtis E. Identification of Unique Features in Education at American Indian Schools. LC 74-76504. 1974. Repr. of 1965 ed. soft bdg. 8.00 (ISBN 0-88247-278-X). R & E Res Assoc.

McCallum, James D., ed. Letters of Eleazar Wheelock's Indians. LC 32-6653. (Dartmouth College Manuscript Ser.: No. 1). (Illus.). 327p. 1932. text ed. 4.00x (ISBN 0-87451-003-1). U Pr of New Eng.

Montez, Philip. Some Differences in Factors Related to Educational Achievement of Two Mexican-American Groups: Thesis. LC 74-76669. 1974. Repr. of 1960 ed. soft bdg. 7.00 (ISBN 0-88247-277-1). R & E Res Assoc.

Morey, Sylvester M. & Gilliam, Olivia L., eds. Respect for Life: The Traditional Upbringing of American Indian Children. LC 80-83371. (Illus.). 202p. 1980. pap. text ed. 4.95 (ISBN 0-913098-34-5). Myrin Institute.

Qoyawayma, Polingaysi. No Turning Back: A Hopi Indian Woman's Struggle to Live in Two Worlds. LC 64-7652. 180p. 1977. pap. 5.95 (ISBN 0-8263-0439-7). U of NM Pr.

Roessel, Robert A., Jr. Navajo Education, 1948-1978: Its Progress & Problems. (Navajo History Ser.). (Illus.). 339p. 1979. 14.95 (ISBN 0-912586-38-9). Navajo Coll Pr.

Rosier, Paul & Holm, Wayne. The Rock Point Experience: A Longitudinal Study of a Navajo School Program (Saad Naaki Bee Na'nitin) LC 80-19695. (Bilingual Education Ser.: No. 8). 95p. (Orig.). 1980. pap. text ed. 7.25x (ISBN 0-87281-119-0). Ctr Appl Ling.

Rudman, Jack. Indian Education - Elementary Teacher. (Career Examination Ser.: C-1311). (Cloth bdg. avail. on request). pap. 10.00 (ISBN 0-8373-1311-2). Natl Learning.

--Indian Education - Guidance Counselor. (Career Examination Ser.: C-1312). (Cloth bdg. avail. on request). pap. 10.00 (ISBN 0-8373-1312-0). Natl Learning.

--Indian Education - Secondary Teacher. (Career Examination Ser.: C-1313). 16.00 (ISBN 0-685-17964-8); pap. 10.00 (ISBN 0-8373-1313-9). Natl Learning.

Szasz, Margaret C. Education & the American Indian: The Road to Self-Determination Since 1928. 2nd ed. LC 77-11742. (Illus.). 252p. 1979. pap. 6.95x (ISBN 0-8263-0468-0). U of NM Pr.

Thompson, Hildegard. The Navajos Long Walk for Education. Johnson, Broderick H., ed. LC 74-29006. (Illus.). 1975. lib. bdg. 9.95 (ISBN 0-912586-21-4). Navajo Coll Pr.

U. S. Bureau of Education. Indian Education & Civilization. Repr. 30.00 (ISBN 0-527-91600-5). Kraus Repr.

U. S. Bureau of Indian Affairs. Bilingual Education for American Indians. Cordasco, Francesco, ed. LC 77-90552. (Bilingual-Bicultural Education in the U. S. Ser.). 1978. Repr. of 1971 ed. lib. bdg. 16.00x (ISBN 0-405-11091-X). Arno.

Wolcott, Harry F. Kwakiutl Village & School. LC 67-11818. (Studies in Education & Culture). (Orig.). 1967. pap. text ed. 5.95 (ISBN 0-03-061775-8, HoltC). HR&W.

INDIANS OF NORTH AMERICA-ETHICS

Lombardi, Gerald S. & Lombardi, Frances G. The Circle Without End: A Sourcebook of American Indian Ethics. (Illus.). 212p. 1981. lib. bdg. 9.95 (ISBN 0-87961-114-6); pap. 5.95 (ISBN 0-87961-117-0). Naturegraph.

Nichols, Claude A. Moral Education Among the North American Indians. LC 75-177112. (Columbia University. Teachers College. Contributions to Education: No. 427). Repr. of 1930 ed. 17.50 (ISBN 0-404-55427-X). AMS Pr.

INDIANS OF NORTH AMERICA-ETHNOLOGY

see Indians of North America

INDIANS OF NORTH AMERICA-FACTORY SYSTEM

see Indians of North America-Commerce

INDIANS OF NORTH AMERICA-FICTION

Beidler, Peter G. & Egge, Marion F. The American Indian in Short Fiction: An Annotated Bibliography. LC 79-20158. 1979. 11.00 (ISBN 0-8108-1256-8). Scarecrow.

Bleecker, Ann E. The History of Maria Kittle, Repr. Of 1797 Ed. Bd. with Miscellanies in Prose & Verse. Morris, Thomas. Repr. of 1791 ed. LC 75-7041. (Indian Captivities Ser.: Vol. 20). 1976. lib. bdg. 44.00 (ISBN 0-8240-1644-0). Garland Pub.

The Captivity & Sufferings of Gen. Freegift Patchin... Among the Indians... During the Border Warfare in the Time of the American Revolution, Repr. Of 1833 Ed. Bd. with U.S. Congress. House. Committee on Claims. Samuel Cozad... Report Made by Mr. E. Whittlesey from the Committee of Claims. Repr. of 1835 ed; Narrative of the Massacre by the Savages of the Wife & Children of Thomas Baldwin. (Incl. 2nd ed. of 1836). Repr. of 1835 ed; An Authentic Narrative of the Seminole War. Repr. of 1836 ed; Captivity & Sufferings of Mrs. Mason, with an Account of the Massacre of Her Youngest Child. Repr. of 1836 ed; Stories of the Revolution: With an Account of the Lost Child of the Delaware. Priest, Josiah. Repr. of 1836 ed; The Indian Captive (Charles Eaton) The Perilous Adventure (Captivity of David Morgan) in: Columbian Almanac for 1838. LC 75-7074. (Indian Captivities Ser.: Vol. 52). 1977. lib. bdg. 44.00 (ISBN 0-8240-1676-9). Garland Pub.

Clark, Keith & Clark, Donna, eds. Daring Donald McKay: Or Last War Trail of the Modocs. LC 74-184573. (Illus.). 1971. pap. 2.95 (ISBN 0-87595-032-9). Oreg Hist Soc.

The Contrast, or the Evils of War, & the Blessings of Christianity Exemplified in the Life & Adventures of Paul Placid, Repr. Of 1830 Ed. Bd. with A Short Biography of John Leeth, with a Brief Account of His Life Among the Indians. Repr. of 1831 ed; Or the Reward of Perseverance. Weston, William. Repr. of 1832 ed. LC 75-7069. (Indian Captivities Ser.: Vol. 47). 1977. lib. bdg. 44.00 (ISBN 0-8240-1671-8). Garland Pub.

Davis, John. The Post-Captain: Or, the Wooden Walls Well Manned; Comprehending a View of Naval Society & Manners, Repr. Of 1806 Ed. Bd. with Struggle of Capt. Thomas Keith in America, Including the Manner in Which He, His Wife & Child Were Decoyed by the Indians. Repr. of 1808 ed. LC 75-7048. (Indian Captivities Ser.: Vol. 26). 1977. lib. bdg. 44.00 (ISBN 0-8240-1650-5). Garland Pub.

Diffenderffer, Henry. The Young Merchant & the Indian Captive, a Tale Founded on Fact, Repr. Of 1851 Ed. Bd. with Revolutionary Incident, the Captivity of Capt. Jeremiah Snyder & Elias Snyder of Saugerties: In: Saugerties Telegraph, V. 5, No. 13-14, Jan. 25 & Feb. 1, 1851. De Witt, Charles G. Repr. of 1851 ed; Historical Traditions of Tennessee. the Captivity of Jane Brown & Her Family. Extract from American Whig Review, v.15, p.233-349. Repr. of 1852 ed; Scenes in Texas, Being a Recital of the Sufferings of a Lady in Her Escape from the Indians... by I. Call, Who Saw the Lady Before Her Recovery from the Affects of Her Sufferings. Call, I. Repr. of 1852 ed; The Lost Child: Or the Child Claimed by Two Mothers: a Narrative of the Loss & Discovery of Casper A. Partridge Among the Menomonee Indians, with a Concise Abstract of Court Testimony, & a Review of Commissioner Buttrick's Decision. Plimpton, Florus B. Repr. of 1852 ed; Indian Battles, Murders, Sieges & Forays in the Southwest. Containing the Narratives of Gen. Hall, Col. Brown, Capt. Carr, John Davis, John Bosley, Samuel Blair, John Rains, Dr. Shelby, Thomas Everett. Repr. of 1853 ed. LC 75-7088. (Indian Captivities Ser.: Vol. 64). 1976. lib. bdg. 44.00 (ISBN 0-8240-1688-2). Garland Pub.

Hilliard D'Auberteuil, Michel R. Mis Mac Rea, Roman Historique, Repr. Of 1784 Ed. Bd. with A True & Wonderful Narrative of the Surprising Captivity & Remarkable Deliverance of Mrs. Frances Scott. Repr. of 1786 ed; A Remarkable Narrative of the Captivity & Escape of Mrs. Frances Scott. (Incl. the Whitcomb ed. (ca 1800) & the 1811 ed.). Repr. of 1799 ed. LC 75-7037. (Indian Captivities Ser.: Vol. 16). 1976. lib. bdg. 38.00 (ISBN 0-8240-1640-8). Garland Pub.

Parsons, Elsie C., ed. American Indian Life. LC 22-16158. (Illus.). 1967. 21.50x (ISBN 0-8032-3651-4); pap. 4.50 (ISBN 0-8032-5148-3, BB 364, Bison). U of Nebr Pr.

The Returned Captive: A Poem, Repr. Of 1787 Ed. Bd. with John Graham's Address to the Master & Worthy Family of His House; Shewing His Suffering Among the Indians of West Florida. Repr. of 1787 ed; New Travels to the Westward, or Unknown Parts of America. (Repr. of 1788 & 1797 eds.); The Remarkable Adventures of Jackson Johonnet, of Massachusetts...Containing an Account of His Captivity, Sufferings & Escape from Kickapoo Indians. (Repr. of 1793 & 1816 eds.). LC 75-7039. (Indian Captivities Ser.: Vol. 18). 1976. lib. bdg. 44.00 (ISBN 0-8240-1642-4). Garland Pub.

Simms, William G. The Yemassee. Ridgely, Joseph V., ed. (Masterworks of Literature Ser). 1964. pap. 4.95x (ISBN 0-8084-0337-0, M3). Coll & U Pr.

Vestal, Stanley. Happy Hunting Grounds. LC 73-5134. (Illus.). 228p. 1975. 9.95 (ISBN 0-8061-1141-0). U of Okla Pr.

Vide, V. V. American Tableaux, No. 1: Sketches of Aboriginal Life. LC 75-7085. (Indian Captivities Ser.: Vol. 62). 1976. Repr. of 1846 ed. lib. bdg. 44.00 (ISBN 0-8240-1686-6). Garland Pub.

Waters, Frank. Man Who Killed the Deer. LC 73-149327. 266p. 1942. (SB); pap. 5.95 (ISBN 0-8040-0194-4). Swallow.

INDIANS OF NORTH AMERICA-FICTION, JUVENILE

Armer, Laura A. Waterless Mountain. (Illus.). (gr. 5-8). 1931. 8.95 (ISBN 0-679-20233-1). McKay.

Baker, Betty. Killer-Of-Death. LC 63-13676. (gr. 7 up). 1963. PLB 8.79 (ISBN 0-06-020331-5, HarpJ). Har-Row.

Baker, R. Ray. Red Brother. 1927. 2.95x (ISBN 0-685-21799-X). Wahr.

Bannon, Laura. When the Moon Is New. LC 53-7925. (Illus.). (gr. 3-5). 1953. 5.95g (ISBN 0-8075-8896-2). A Whitman.

Buff, Mary & Buff, Conrad. Hah-Nee. (gr. 4-6). 1965. reinforced bdg. 5.95 (ISBN 0-395-15081-7). HM.

Epstein, Anne M. Good Stones. (gr. 5-9). 1977. 6.95 (ISBN 0-395-25154-0). HM.

Hofland, Barbara H. The Stolen Boy: A Story Founded on Facts, Repr. Of 1828 Ed. Bd. with Seizure of the Ship Industry, by a Conspiracy, & the Consequent Sufferings of Capt. James Fox & His Companions: Their Captivity Among the Esquimaux Indians in North America; & the Miraculous Escape of the Captain. Repr. of 1830 ed; St. Maur: Or, the Captive Babes Recovered, Pub. by Emory & Waugh for the Tract Society of the Methodist Epescopal Church, New York. Repr. of 1830 ed. LC 75-7066. (Indian Captivities Ser.: Vol. 44). 1976. lib. bdg. 44.00 (ISBN 0-8240-1668-8). Garland Pub.

Moon, Grace. Chi-Wee. (gr. 4-6). 1925. 4.50 (ISBN 0-385-07259-7). Doubleday.

Roberts, Helen M. Mission Tales: Stories of the Historic California Missions, 7 Vols. LC 62-11254. (Illus.). (gr. 3-6). 1962. Set. text ed. 24.95x (ISBN 0-87015-107-X). Pacific Bks.

Sneve, Virginia D. Betrayed. LC 74-7574. 128p. (gr. 7 up). 1974. 5.95 (ISBN 0-8234-0243-6). Holiday.

Thayer, Marjorie & Emanuel, Elizabeth. Climbing Sun: The Story of a Hopi Indian Boy. LC 80-13743. (Illus.). 96p. (gr. 5 up). 1980. 6.95 (ISBN 0-396-07844-3). Dodd.

INDIANS OF NORTH AMERICA-FISHING

see Indians of North America-Hunting and Fishing

INDIANS OF NORTH AMERICA-FIVE CIVILIZED TRIBES

see Five Civilized Tribes

INDIANS OF NORTH AMERICA-FOLK-LORE

see Folk-Lore, Indian

INDIANS OF NORTH AMERICA-FOOD

Chamberlin, Ralph V. Ethno-Botany of the Gosiute Indians of Utah. LC 14-11549. 1911. pap. 7.00 (ISBN 0-527-00510-X). Kraus Repr.

Cushing, Frank H. Zuni Breadstuff. LC 74-7948. Repr. of 1920 ed. 48.50 (ISBN 0-404-11835-6). AMS Pr.

--Zuni Breadstuff, Vol. 8. LC 74-84740. (Indian Notes& Monographs). 1974. Repr. soft cover 10.00 (ISBN 0-934490-04-X). Mus Am Ind.

Grimm, William. Indian Harvests. (Illus.). 128p. (gr. 5 up). 1977. PLB 6.95 (ISBN 0-07-024840-0, GB). McGraw.

Kavasch, Barrie. Native Harvests: Recipes & Botanicals of the American Indian. LC 78-21791. 1979. 10.00 (ISBN 0-394-50411-9). Random.

--Native Harvests: Recipes & Botanicals of the American Indian. LC 78-21792. (Illus.). 1979. pap. 5.95 (ISBN 0-394-72811-4, Vin). Random.

Kavena, Juanita. Hopi Cookery. 1980. pap. 8.50 (ISBN 0-8165-0618-3). U of Ariz Pr.

Kimball, Yeffe & Anderson, Jean. Art of American Indian Cooking. LC 65-19860. 1965. 7.95 (ISBN 0-385-04260-4). Doubleday.

Southwestern Cookery: Indian & Spanish Influences. LC 72-9803. (Cookery Americana Ser). Repr. of 1973 ed. 12.00 (ISBN 0-405-05054-2). Arno.

Sweet, Muriel. Common Edible & Useful Plants of the East & Midwest. LC 75-8914. (Illus.). 64p. 1975. 6.95 (ISBN 0-87961-035-2); pap. 2.95 (ISBN 0-87961-034-4). Naturegraph.

Trapp, Juli S. Gifts of the Earth: American Indian Cookbook. (Illus.). 44p. 1981. pap. 9.95 (ISBN 0-937050-21-0). Stonehenge Books.

Weiner, Michael A. Earth Medicine - Earth Foods. 2nd ed. 1980. 15.95 (ISBN 0-02-625610-X). Macmillan.

--Earth Medicine - Earth Foods: Plant Remedies, Drugs, & Natural Foods of the North American Indian. 2nd ed. 1980. pap. 8.95 (ISBN 0-02-082490-4, Collier). Macmillan.

INDIANS OF NORTH AMERICA-FOOTWEAR

see Indians of North America-Costume and Adornment

INDIANS OF NORTH AMERICA-GAMES

Burnett, Millie. Dance Down the Rain, Sing up the Corn: American Indian Chants & Games for Children. LC 75-21028. 1975. spiral bound 5.00 (ISBN 0-88247-370-0). R & E Res Assoc.

Culin, Robert S. Games of the North American Indians. LC 73-8094. (Illus.). Repr. of 1907 ed. 85.00 (ISBN 0-404-11201-3). AMS Pr.

Culin, Stewart. Games of the North American Indians. LC 74-12653. (Illus.). 864p. 1975. Repr. of 1907 ed. 12.50 (ISBN 0-486-23125-9). Dover.

Fletcher, Alice C. Indian Games & Dances with Native Songs. LC 75-136369. Repr. of 1915 ed. 11.50 (ISBN 0-404-07229-1). AMS Pr.

Lesser, Alexander. Pawnee Ghost Dance Hand Game. LC 79-82340. (Columbia Univ. Contributions to Anthropology Ser.: Vol. 16). 1969. Repr. of 1933 ed. 21.00 (ISBN 0-404-50566-X). AMS Pr.

Whitney, Alex. Sports and Games the Indians Gave Us. (gr. 7 up). 1977. 7.95 (ISBN 0-679-20391-5). McKay.

INDIANS OF NORTH AMERICA-GIFTS

see also Potlatch

INDIANS OF NORTH AMERICA-GOVERNMENT RELATIONS

see also Indians of North America-Cultural Assimilation; Indians, Treatment Of

Abel, Annie H. History of Events Resulting in Indian Consolidation West of the Mississippi. LC 76-158219. Repr. of 1908 ed. 14.50 (ISBN 0-404-07116-3). AMS Pr.

Alden, John R. John Stuart & the Southern Colonial Frontier: A Study of Indian Relations, War, Trade, Land Problems in the Southern Wilderness, 1754-1775. LC 66-29459. (Illus.). 1966. Repr. of 1944 ed. 15.00 (ISBN 0-87752-001-1). Gordian.

Atkin, Edmond. Appalachian Indian Frontier: The Edmond Atkin Report & Plan of 1755. Jacobs, Wilbur R., ed. LC 54-12059. (Illus.). xxxviii, 108p. 1967. pap. 2.95x (ISBN 0-8032-5011-8, 374, Bison). U of Nebr Pr.

Bee, Robert. The First Americans Get to Washington: The Politics of American Indian Policy. 284p. 1981. text ed. 17.95x (ISBN 0-87073-836-4); pap. text ed. 8.95x (ISBN 0-87073-837-2). Schenkman.

Bee, Robert L. Crosscurrents Along the Colorado: The Impact of Government Policy on the Quechan Indians. 1981. 20.00x (ISBN 0-8165-0558-6); pap. 9.95x (ISBN 0-8165-0725-2). U of Ariz Pr.

Beers, Henry P. The Western Military Frontier 1815-1846. LC 75-25798. (Perspectives in American Hist. Ser.: No. 35). (Illus.). vi, 227p. Repr. of 1935 ed. lib. bdg. 15.00x (ISBN 0-87991-359-2). Porcupine Pr.

Berthrong, Donald J. The Cheyenne & Arapaho Ordeal: Reservation & Indian Life in the Indian Territory. LC 75-17795. (The Civilization of the American Indian Ser: No.136). 1976. 17.95 (ISBN 0-8061-1277-8). U of Okla Pr.

Brookings Institution. The Problem of Indian Administration. 1971. Repr. of 1928 ed. 50.00 (ISBN 0-384-05920-1). Johnson Repr.

Brown, J. Ross. Indian Affairs in Territories of Oregon & Washington: First Season, 35th Congress, January 25, 1858. (House Exec. Doc.: No. 39). 1973. 4.95 (ISBN 0-87770-091-5). Ye Galleon.

Cass, Lewis. Considerations on the Present State of the Indians, & Their Removal to the West of the Mississippi. facsimile ed. LC 75-91. (Mid-American Frontier Ser.). 1975. Repr. of 1828 ed. 9.50x (ISBN 0-405-06858-1). Arno.

Chamberlin, J. E. The Harrowing of Eden: White Attitudes Toward Native Americans. LC 75-9941. 1975. 8.95 (ISBN 0-8164-9251-4). Continuum.

Claims for Depredations by Sioux Indians. (House Exec. Doc.: No. 58). 25p. 1975. pap. 2.50 (ISBN 0-87770-141-5). Ye Galleon.

Clum, Woodworth. Apache Agent: The Story of John P. Clum. LC 77-14135. (Illus.). 1978. 13.95x (ISBN 0-8032-0967-3); pap. 4.25 (ISBN 0-8032-5886-0, BB 654, Bison). U of Nebr Pr.
Collier, Peter. When Shall They Rest? The Cherokees' Long Struggle with America. LC 73-6675. (Illus.). 192p. (gr. 7 up). 1973. reinforced bdg. 6.95 (ISBN 0-03-011176-5). HR&W.
Danziger, Edmund J., Jr. Indians & Bureaucrats: Administering the Reservation Policy During the Civil War. LC 73-85486. 250p. 1974. 14.95 (ISBN 0-252-00314-4). U of Ill Pr.
Debo, Angie. And Still the Waters Run. LC 66-20712. (Illus.). 1966. Repr. of 1940 ed. 9.50 (ISBN 0-87752-026-7). Gordian.
--Rise & Fall of the Choctaw Republic. 2nd ed. LC 69-7973. (Civilization of the American Indian Ser.: No. 6). (Illus.). 1934. pap. 6.95 (ISBN 0-8061-1247-6). U of Okla Pr.
Deloria, Vine. Behind the Trail of Broken Treaties. 256p. 1974. 8.95 (ISBN 0-440-01404-2). Delacorte.
De Puy, Henry F. A Bibliography of the English Colonial Treaties with the American Indians. LC 78-108471. 1917. Repr. 19.00 (ISBN 0-403-00425-X). Scholarly.
DeRosier, Arthur H., Jr. Removal of the Choctaw Indians. LC 70-111044. (Illus.). 1970. 12.50 (ISBN 0-87049-113-X). U of Tenn Pr.
Doster, James F. Creek Indians: Information Relative to the Claims of the Creeks Against the U. S. for Florida Lands Taken by the U. S. Under the Treaty of Moultrie Creek, 1823. Incl. Rebuttal Report on the Reliability of the Statements of Dr. John R. Swanton on the Creeks. (Library of American Indian Affairs). 376p. 1974. lib. bdg. 102.00 (ISBN 0-8287-1020-1). Clearwater Pub.
Dyer, Ruth C. The Indians' Land Title in California: A Case in Federal Equity, 1851-1942. LC 74-31772. 1975. soft bdg. 8.00 (ISBN 0-88247-338-7). R & E Res Assoc.
Ellis, Richard N. General Pope & U. S. Indian Policy. LC 72-129806. 287p. 1970. 10.00x (ISBN 0-8263-0191-6). U of NM Pr.
--General Pope & U. S. Indian Policy. LC 72-129806. 287p. 1970. 10.00x (ISBN 0-8263-0191-6). U of NM Pr.
Ellis, Richard N., ed. Western American Indian: Case Studies in Tribal History. LC 70-181597. xiv, 203p. 1972. 14.50x (ISBN 0-8032-0804-9); pap. 3.95x (ISBN 0-8032-5754-6, BB 548, Bison). U of Nebr Pr.
Executive Orders Relating to Indian Reservations: 1855-1922, 2 vols. in 1. LC 75-13936. 1975. Repr. of 1922 ed. lib. bdg. 40.00 (ISBN 0-8420-2065-9). Scholarly Res Inc.
Flexner, James T. Lord of the Mohawks: A Biography of Sir William Johnson. rev. ed. LC 77-13877. 1979. 16.95 (ISBN 0-316-28609-5). Little.
Foreman, Grant. Advancing the Frontier, 1830-1860. (Civilization of the American Indian Ser.: No. 4). (Illus.). 1968. Repr. of 1933 ed. 16.95 (ISBN 0-8061-0792-8). U of Okla Pr.
Foreman, Richard L. Indian Water Rights. 1980. pap. text ed. 8.95x (ISBN 0-8134-2160-8, 2160). Interstate.
Gates, Paul W. & Bruchey, Stuart, eds. The Rape of the Indian Lands: An Original Anthology. LC 78-56698. (Management of Public Lands in the U. S. Ser.). 1979. lib. bdg. 20.00x (ISBN 0-405-11358-7). Arno.
Gessner, Robert. Massacre: A Survey of Today's American Indian. LC 72-38831. (Civil Liberties in American History Ser). 418p. 1972. Repr. of 1931 ed. lib. bdg. 35.00 (ISBN 0-306-70445-5). Da Capo.
Getches, David H., et al. Cases & Materials on Federal Indian Law. LC 79-3906. (American Casebook Ser.). 600p. 1979. text ed. 19.95 (ISBN 0-8299-2027-7). West Pub.
Hagan, William T. United States-Comanche Relations: The Reservation Years. LC 75-43318. (Western American Ser.: No. 28). 1976. 25.00x (ISBN 0-300-01939-4). Yale U Pr.
Harmon, G. D. Sixty Years of Indian Affairs, Political, Economic & Diplomatic. 1941. 18.00 (ISBN 0-527-38100-4). Kraus Repr.
Hauptman, Laurence. The Iroquois & the New Deal. 1981. 20.00x (ISBN 0-8156-2247-3). Syracuse U Pr.
Heizer, Robert F., ed. Federal Concern About Conditions of California Indians 1853-1913: Eight Documents. (Ballena Press Publications in Archaeology, Ethnology & History Ser.: No. 13). 1979. pap. 7.95 (ISBN 0-87919-084-1). Ballena Pr.
Henry, Jeannette, ed. The American Indian Reader: Current Affairs. LC 72-86873. (The American Indian Reader Ser.). (Orig.). 1974. pap. 4.50 (ISBN 0-913436-20-8). Indian Hist Pr.
--Indian Voices: The Native American Today. LC 72-91137. (Convocations of American Indian Scholars Ser). 250p. 1974. pap. 6.00 (ISBN 0-913436-18-6). Indian Hist Pr.
Hertzberg, Hazel W. Search for an American Indian Identity: Modern Pan-Indian Movements. LC 77-140889. 1971. 16.95x (ISBN 0-8156-0076-3); pap. 10.95x (ISBN 0-8156-2245-7). Syracuse U Pr.
Hickerson, Harold. The Mississippi, Pillager & Winnibigoshish Bands of Chippewa Indians: Anthropological Report on the Indian Occupancy of Royce Area 357 in Minnesota. (Library of American Indian Affairs). 301p. 1974. lib. bdg. 84.00 (ISBN 0-8287-1129-1). Clearwater Pub.
Hill, Edward E. Office of Indian Affairs, 1824-1880: Historical Sketches. LC 73-16321. (Library of American Indian Affairs). 1974. lib. bdg. 20.00 (ISBN 0-88354-105-X). Clearwater Pub.
Hoopes, A. W. Indian Affairs & Their Administration, with Special Reference to the Far West. LC 33-5636. Repr. of 1932 ed. 16.00 (ISBN 0-527-42250-9). Kraus Repr.
Hopkins. Life Among the Paiutes: Their Wrongs & Claims. LC 71-102992. 12.95 (ISBN 0-912494-18-2); pap. 8.95 (ISBN 0-912494-06-9). Chalfant Pr.
Hough, Franklin B. Proceedings of the Commissioners of Indian Affairs. 1981. Repr. lib. bdg. 59.00 (ISBN 0-403-00389-X). Scholarly.
Howard, Milo B., Jr. & Rea, Robert R., eds. Memoire Justificatif of the Chevalier Montault De Monberaut: Indian Diplomacy in British West Florida, 1763-1765. LC 64-24955. (Southern Historical Ser: Vol. 3). 1965. 12.95x (ISBN 0-8173-5208-2). U of Ala Pr.
Jackson, Curtis E. & Galli, Marcia J. A History of the Bureau of Indian Affairs & Its Activities Among Indians. LC 76-44958. 1977. soft bdg. 12.00 (ISBN 0-88247-440-5). R & E Res Assoc.
Jackson, Helen. A Century of Dishonor: A Sketch of the United States Government's Dealing with Some of the Indian Tribes. LC 71-108499. x, 514p. 1972. Repr. of 1888 ed. 49.00 (ISBN 0-403-00382-2). Scholarly.
Jackson, Helen H. Century of Dishonor: The Early Crusade for Indian Reform. Rolle, ed. 8.00 (ISBN 0-8446-2298-2). Peter Smith.
Jacobs, Wilbur R. Dispossessing the American Indian. LC 72-37179. 1972. pap. text ed. 7.95x (ISBN 0-684-13774-7, ScribC). Scribner.
--Wilderness Politics & Indian Gifts: The Northern Colonial Frontier, 1748-1763. LC 51-2149. Orig. Title: Anglo-French Rivalry Along the Ohio & Northwest Frontier- 1748-1763. (Illus.). 1966. pap. 3.95x (ISBN 0-8032-5100-9, BB 351, Bison). U of Nebr Pr.
John, Elizabeth A. H. Storms Brewed in Other Men's Worlds: The Confrontation of Indians, Spanish, & French in the Southwest, 1540-1795. LC 75-9996. (Illus.). 840p. 1975. 21.50 (ISBN 0-89096-000-3). Tex A&M Univ Pr.
Johnson, Steven L. Guide to American Indian Documents in the Congressional Serial Set: 1817-1899. LC 75-45321. (Library of American Indian Affairs). 1977. 30.00x (ISBN 0-88354-107-6). Clearwater Pub.
Kappler, Charles J., ed. Indian Affairs; Laws & Treaties, 5 vols. LC 78-128994. Repr. of 1941 ed. Set. lib. bdg. 475.00 (ISBN 0-404-06710-7). AMS Pr.
--Indian Treaties, 1778-1883. Blue, Brantley, frwd. by. LC 72-75770. (Illus.). 1110p. 1975. Repr. of 1904 ed. 75.00x (ISBN 0-87989-025-8). Interland Pub.
Larrabee, Edward M. Recurrent Themes & Sequences in North American Indian-European Culture Contact. LC 76-24257. (Transactions Ser.: Vol. 66, Pt. 7). (Illus.). 1976. pap. 6.00 (ISBN 0-87169-667-3). Am Philos.
Lesser, Alexander. The Pawnee Ghost Dance Hand Game: A Study of Cultural Change. LC 79-82340. (Illus.). 1978. 20.00 (ISBN 0-299-07480-3); pap. 7.95 (ISBN 0-299-07484-6). U of Wis Pr.
Leupp, Francis E. Indian & His Problem. LC 72-137175. (Poverty U.S.A. Historical Records Ser). 1971. Repr. of 1910 ed. 18.00 (ISBN 0-405-03114-9). Arno.
Levitan, S. A. Big Brother's Indian Programs: With Reservations. 1971. 10.95 (ISBN 0-07-037391-4, P&RB). McGraw.
Lindquist, Gustavus E. The Indian in American Life. LC 74-7977. Repr. of 1944 ed. 17.50 (ISBN 0-404-11867-4). AMS Pr.
McNickle, D'Aracy. Native American Tribalism: Indian Survivals & Renewals. 1973. pap. 3.95 (ISBN 0-19-501724-2, 399, GB). Oxford U Pr.
McNickle, D'Arcy. Native American Tribalism. new ed. (Illus.). 120p. 1973. 9.95x (ISBN 0-19-501723-4). Oxford U Pr.
Manypenny, George Washington. Our Indian Wards. LC 68-54844. (The American Scene Ser). 1972. Repr. of 1880 ed. lib. bdg. 25.00 (ISBN 0-306-71140-0). Da Capo.
Mason, Philipp, ed. Schoolcraft's Expedition to Lake Itasca: The Discovery of the Source of the Mississippi. xxvi, 390p. 1958. 10.00 (ISBN 0-87013-040-4). Mich St U Pr.
Meyer, William. Native Americans: The New Indian Resistance. LC 71-163221. 1971. pap. 1.50 (ISBN 0-7178-0318-X). Intl Pub Co.
Miner, H. Craig & Unrau, William E. The End of Indian Kansas: A Study of Cultural Revolution, 1854-1871. LC 77-4410. (Illus.). 1977. 12.50x (ISBN 0-7006-0161-9). Regents Pr KS.
Mohr, Walter H. Federal Indian Relations, Seventeen Seventy-Four-Seventeen Eighty-Eight. LC 76-158854. Repr. of 1933 ed. 19.45 (ISBN 0-404-07147-3). AMS Pr.
Moorehead, Warren K. American Indian in the United States, Period 1850-1914. facs. ed. LC 71-75512. (Select Bibliographies Reprint Ser). 1914. 35.00 (ISBN 0-8369-5014-3). Arno.
--Prehistoric Relics. facs. ed. (Illus.). Repr. pap. 16.00 (ISBN 0-8466-0157-5, SJS157). Shorey.
Morse, Jedidiah. Report to the Secretary of War of the United States, on Indian Affairs. LC 68-27675. (Illus.). Repr. of 1822 ed. 19.50x (ISBN 0-678-00548-6). Kelley.
--A Report to the Secretary of War of the U. S. on Indian Affairs. LC 70-108516. (Illus.). 400p. 1972. Repr. of 1822 ed. 16.00 (ISBN 0-403-00345-8). Scholarly.
Nabokov, Peter, ed. Native American Testimony. LC 77-11558. 1979. pap. 4.95 (ISBN 0-06-090720-7, CN 720, CN). Har-Row.
Neils, Elaine M. Reservation to City: Indian Urbanization & Federal Relocation. LC 78-144044. (Research Papers Ser.: No. 131). 200p. 1971. pap. 8.00 (ISBN 0-89065-038-1). U Chicago Dept Geog.
Nichols, David A. Lincoln & the Indians: Civil War Policy & Politics. LC 77-12196. 1978. 16.00x (ISBN 0-8262-0231-4). U of Mo Pr.
Olson, James C. Red Cloud & the Sioux Problem. LC 65-10048. (Illus.). xii, 375p. 1965. 19.50x (ISBN 0-8032-0136-2); pap. 5.50 (ISBN 0-8032-5817-8, BB 602, Bison). U of Nebr Pr.
Painter, Charles C. The Condition of Affairs in Indian Territory & California. LC 74-15121. Repr. of 1888 ed. 14.00 (ISBN 0-404-11981-6). AMS Pr.
Peithmann, Irvin M. Broken Peace Pipes: A Four-Hundred Year History of the American Indian. 320p. 1964. 11.75 (ISBN 0-398-01468-X). C C Thomas.
Philp, Kenneth R. John Collier's Crusade for Indian Reform, 1920-1954. LC 76-4427. 1977. pap. text ed. 8.95x (ISBN 0-8165-0472-5). U of Ariz Pr.
Priest, Loring B. Uncle Sam's Stepchildren: The Reformation of United States Indian Policy, 1865-1887. LC 79-76511. 1969. Repr. of 1942 ed. lib. bdg. 16.50x (ISBN 0-374-96574-9). Octagon.
--Uncle Sam's Stepchildren: The Reformation of United States Indian Policy, 1865-1887. LC 75-5983. x, 310p. 1975. pap. 3.95 (ISBN 0-8032-5818-6, BB 601, Bison). U of Nebr Pr.
Priest, Loring B., ed. The New American State Papers: Indian Affairs Subject Set, 13 vols. LC 72-83828. (Illus.). 1973. Set. lib. bdg. 650.00 (ISBN 0-8420-1436-5). Scholarly Res Inc.
Prucha, F. P. Indian in American History. LC 74-150022. 1971. pap. text ed. 7.95 (ISBN 0-03-085193-9, HoltC). HR&W.
Prucha, Francis P. American Indian Policy in the Formative Years: The Indian Trade & Intercourse Acts, 1790-1834. LC 62-9428. 1970. pap. 3.25 (ISBN 0-8032-5706-6, BB 510, Bison). U of Nebr Pr.
--A Bibliographical Guide to the History of Indian-White Relations in the United States. LC 76-16045. 1977. lib. bdg. 27.00x (ISBN 0-226-68476-8); pap. 12.00x (ISBN 0-226-68477-6). U of Chicago Pr.
--Indian Policy in the United States: Historical Essays. LC 81-1667. (Illus.). x, 272p. 1981. 19.95x (ISBN 0-8032-3662-X). U of Nebr Pr.
Prucha, Francis P., ed. Americanizing the American Indians: Writings by the "Friends of the Indian," 1880-1900. LC 77-14102. x, 358p. 1978. pap. 4.95 (ISBN 0-8032-5881-X, BB 643, Bison). U of Nebr Pr.
--Documents of United States Indian Policy. LC 74-14081. x, 278p. 1975. 16.95x (ISBN 0-8032-0852-9); pap. 4.95x (ISBN 0-8032-5814-3, BB 599, Bison). U of Nebr Pr.
Rader, Brian F. The Political Outsiders: Blacks & Indians in a Rural Oklahoma County. LC 77-94282. 1978. pap. 12.00 perfect bdg. (ISBN 0-88247-517-7). R & E Res Assoc.
Randolph, J. Ralph. British Travelers Among the Southern Indians, 1660-1763. LC 72-858. (American Exploration & Travel Ser.: Vol. 62). 350p. 1973. 14.50 (ISBN 0-8061-1019-8). U of Okla Pr.
Rice, Jon F., Jr. To Preserve a Culture: The Twentieth Century Fight Over Indian Reorganization. (Illus.). 60p. 1981. 2.00 (ISBN 0-937352-02-0). Committee IL.
Rogin, Michael P. Fathers & Children: Andrew Jackson & the Subjugation of the American Indian. LC 76-10814. 1976. pap. 4.95 (ISBN 0-394-71881-X, Vin). Random.
Ross, Norman A., ed. Index to the Decisions of the Indian Claims Commission, 1948-1972. LC 72-13850. (Library of American Indian Affairs). 168p. 1973. lib. bdg. 18.00 (ISBN 0-88354-101-7). Clearwater Pub.
--Index to the Expert Testimony Presented Before the Indian Claims Commission. LC 72-13851. (Library of American Indian Affairs). 112p. 1973. lib. bdg. 18.00 (ISBN 0-88354-102-5). Clearwater Pub.
Royce, Charles C., ed. Indian Land Cessions in the United States. LC 78-146416. (First American Frontier Ser). (Illus.). 1971. Repr. of 1900 ed. 35.00 (ISBN 0-405-02880-6). Arno.
Ruby, Robert H. & Brown, John A. Half-Sun on the Columbia: A Biography of Chief Moses. (Civilization of the American Indian Ser.: No. 80). (Illus.). 1966. Repr. of 1965 ed. 17.95 (ISBN 0-8061-0675-1). U of Okla Pr.
Satz, Ronald N. American Indian Policy in the Jacksonian Era. LC 73-94119. (Illus.). vii, 343p. 1975. pap. 7.50x (ISBN 0-8032-5848-8, BB 628, Bison). U of Nebr Pr.
Schmeckebier, Laurence F. Office of Indian Affairs: Its History, Activities & Organizations. LC 74-175438. (Brookings Institution. Institute for Government Research. Service Monographs of the U. S. Government: No. 48). Repr. of 1927 ed. 31.50 (ISBN 0-404-07169-4). AMS Pr.
Schultz, George A. An Indian Canaan: Isaac McCoy & the Vision of an Indian State. (Civilization of the American Indian Ser.: No. 121). (Illus.). 350p. 1972. 12.50 (ISBN 0-8061-1024-4); pap. 6.95 (ISBN 0-8061-1303-0). U of Okla Pr.
Seymour, Flora W. Indian Agents of the Old Frontier. 1973. lib. bdg. 20.00x (ISBN 0-374-97290-7). Octagon.
--Indian Agents of the Old Frontier. LC 41-12500. 1975. Repr. of 1941 ed. 25.00 (ISBN 0-527-81533-0). Kraus Repr.
Sheehan, Bernard W. Seeds of Extinction: Jeffersonian Philanthropy & the American Indian. LC 72-85403. (Institute of Early American History & Culture Ser.). 344p. 1973. 19.00x (ISBN 0-8078-1203-X). U of NC Pr.
--Seeds of Extinction: Jeffersonian Philanthropy & the American Indian. 320p. 1974. pap. 5.95 (ISBN 0-393-00716-2). Norton.
Slotkin, J. S. The Peyote Religion. 195p. 1975. Repr. of 1956 ed. lib. bdg. 13.50x (ISBN 0-374-97480-2). Octagon.
Sorkin, Alan L. American Indians & Federal Aid. (Studies in Social Economics). 231p. 1971. 10.95 (ISBN 0-8157-8044-3). Brookings.
Standing Bear, Luther. Land of the Spotted Eagle. LC 77-14062. (Illus.). 1978. 16.95x (ISBN 0-8032-0964-9); pap. 4.50 (ISBN 0-8032-5890-9, BB 655, Bison). U of Nebr Pr.
Steele, William O. The Cherokee Crown of Tannassy. LC 77-19997. (YA) 1977. 7.95 (ISBN 0-910244-99-5). Blair.
Steffen, Jerome O. William Clark: Jeffersonian Man on the Frontier. LC 76-15355. (Illus.). 1978. Repr. of 1977 ed. 9.95 (ISBN 0-8061-1373-1). U of Okla Pr.
Steiner, Stan. New Indians. 1969. pap. 2.65 (ISBN 0-440-56306-2, Delta). Dell.
--New Indians. LC 67-22509. (Illus.). 1968. 12.50 (ISBN 0-06-014082-8, HarpT). Har-Row.
Stevens, Isaac I. Treaty Between the U. S. & the Dwamish, Suquamish & Other Allied & Subordinate Tribes of Indians in Washington Territory. facs. ed. 7p. Repr. of 1855 ed. pap. 3.00 (ISBN 0-8466-0108-7, SJS108). Shorey.
--Treaty Between the U. S. & the Makah Tribe. facs. ed. 8p. Repr. of 1855 ed. pap. 3.00 (ISBN 0-8466-0111-7, SJS111). Shorey.
--Treaty Between the U. S. & the Nisqually & Other Bands of Indians. facs. ed. 8p. Repr. of 1855 ed. pap. 3.00 (ISBN 0-8466-0109-5, SJS109). Shorey.
--Treaty Between the U. S. & the Yakima Nation of Indians. facs. ed. 8p. Repr. of 1855 ed. pap. 3.00 (ISBN 0-8466-0110-9, SJS110). Shorey.
Stuart, Paul. The Indian Office: Growth & Development of an American Institution, 1865-1900. Berkhofer, Robert, ed. (Studies in American History & Culture: No. 12). 1980. 29.95 (ISBN 0-8357-1079-3, Pub. by UMI Res Pr). Univ Microfilms.
Subcommittee On Economy In Government. American Indians: Facts - Future Toward Economic Development for Native American Communities. LC 76-128179. 1970. Repr. of 1969 ed. 10.00 (ISBN 0-405-00691-8). Arno.
Tatum, Lawrie. Our Red Brothers & the Peace Policy of President Ulysses S. Grant. LC 77-88093. (Illus.). 1970. 19.95x (ISBN 0-8032-0720-4). U of Nebr Pr.
Taylor, Graham D. The New Deal & American Indian Tribalism: The Administration of the Indian Reorganization Act, 1934-45. LC 79-9178. 1980. 14.50x (ISBN 0-8032-4403-7). U of Nebr Pr.
Thompson, Gerald. The Army & the Navajo: The Bosque Redondo Reservation Experiment, 1863-68. LC 75-8457. 1976. pap. 7.50 (ISBN 0-8165-0495-4). U of Ariz Pr.

Trennert, Robert A., Jr. Alternative to Extinction: Federal Indian Policy & the Beginnings of the Reservation System, 1846-51. LC 74-83203. 1975. 16.00x (ISBN 0-87722-030-1). Temple U Pr.

Uhler, Sherman P. Pennsylvania's Indian Relations to 1754. LC 76-43872. Repr. of 1951 ed. 13.00 (ISBN 0-404-15731-9). AMS Pr.

U. S. Bureau of Indian Affairs. Digest of Decisions Relating to Indian Affairs. LC 73-16017. Repr. of 1901 ed. 24.00 (ISBN 0-527-92015-0). Kraus Repr.

U. S. Congress. House. Commitee on Indian Affairs. Readjustment of Indian Affairs: Hearings. LC 74-15123. Repr. of 1934 ed. 36.00 (ISBN 0-404-11983-2). AMS Pr.

U. S. National Archives. List of Documents Concerning the Negotiation of Ratified Indian Treaties: 1801-1869. LC 49-10439. 1975. Repr. of 1949 ed. 19.00 (ISBN 0-527-03229-8). Kraus Repr.

U. S. Office Of Indian Affairs. Report of the Commissioner of Indian Affairs: Reports for the Years 1824-1899, 65 vols. Repr. of 1899 ed. Set. 2330.50 (ISBN 0-404-07550-9). AMS Pr.

U. S. Treaties, Etc. Treaties Between the United States of America & the Several Indian Tribes from 1778-1837. LC 8-20225. 1975. Repr. of 1837 ed. 30.00 (ISBN 0-527-03221-2). Kraus Repr.

U. S. 21st Congress, 1st Session, 1829-1830. Speeches on the Passage of the Bill for the Removal of the Indians. Repr. of 1830 ed. 18.00 (ISBN 0-527-91840-7). Kraus Repr.

Unrau, William E. The Emigrant Indians of Kansas: A Critical Bibliography. LC 79-2169. (Newberry Library Center for the History of the American Indian Bibliographical Ser.). 96p. (Orig.). 1981. pap. 3.95x (ISBN 0-253-36816-2). Ind U Pr.

U.S. Department of the Interior (Washington, D.C.) Biographical & Historical Index of American Indians & Persons Involved in Indian Affairs. 8 Vols. 1966. 820.00 (ISBN 0-8161-0716-5). G K Hall.

Utley, Robert M. Last Days of the Sioux Nation. (Western Americana Ser.: No. 3). (Illus.). 1963. 25.00x (ISBN 0-300-01003-6); pap. 5.95x (ISBN 0-300-00245-9, YW15). Yale U Pr.

Viola, Herman J. Diplomats in Buckskins: A History of Indian Delegations in Washington City. LC 80-607804. (Illus.). 1981. 17.50 (ISBN 0-87474-944-1). Smithsonian.

--The Indian Legacy of Charles Bird King. LC 76-15022. (Illus.). 152p. 1976. 25.00 (ISBN 0-87474-943-3). Smithsonian.

Watkins, Mel. Dene Nation: The Colony Within. LC 76-54701. 1977. 17.50x (ISBN 0-8020-2264-2); pap. 5.95 (ISBN 0-8020-6315-2). U of Toronto Pr.

Worcester, Donald, ed. Forked Tongues & Broken Treaties. LC 74-28285. (Illus.). 494p. 1975. 9.95 (ISBN 0-87004-246-7). Caxton.

Yava, Aaron. Border Towns of the Navajo Nation. 2nd ed. (Illus.). 80p. 1975. pap. 4.00 (ISBN 0-914974-06-8). Holmgangers.

Young, James R., ed. Guide to Decisions of the Interior Department on Indian Lands, 2 vols. 1980. softcover 10.00 (ISBN 0-935626-05-0). U Cal AISC.

INDIANS OF NORTH AMERICA–HANDICRAFT

see Indians of North America–Industries

INDIANS OF NORTH AMERICA–HEALTH AND HYGIENE

Barrow, Mark V., et al. Health & Diseases of American Indians North of Mexico: A Bibliography, 1800-1969. LC 70-161004. 1972. 7.00 (ISBN 0-8130-0331-8). U Presses Fla.

Devereux, George. Mohave Ethnopsychiatry & Suicide: The Psychiatric Knowledge & the Psychic Disturbances of an Indian Tribe. Repr. of 1961 ed. 42.00 (ISBN 0-403-03650-X). Scholarly.

International Symposium, 3rd, Yellowknife, NWT. Circumpolar Health: Proceedings. Shephard, Roy J. & Itoh, S., eds. LC 76-2608. (Illus.). 1976. 30.00x (ISBN 0-8020-3333-4). U of Toronto Pr.

Kelso, Dianne R., compiled by. Bibliography of North American Indian Mental Health. LC 81-800. (Illus.). 404p. 1981. lib. bdg. 39.95 (ISBN 0-313-22930-9, KEB/). Greenwood.

Lee, Melvin, et al. Diagnosis & Treatment of Prevalent Diseases of North American Indian Populations. (American Indian Health Ser.: Vol. 1). 302p. 1974. text ed. 21.50x (ISBN 0-8422-7215-1). Irvington.

Miller, Max J., et al. Diagnosis & Treatment of Prevalent Diseases of North American Indian Populations. (American Indian Health Ser.: Vol. 2). 250p. 1974. text ed. 19.50x (ISBN 0-8422-7216-X). Irvington.

Torrey, E. Fuller, et al. Community Health & Mental Health Care Delivery for North American Indians. (Health Problems of N.A. Indians Ser: Vol. 3). 1975. 19.00x (ISBN 0-8422-7218-6). Irvington.

Train, Percy, et al. Medicinal Uses of Plants by Indian Tribes of Nevada. LC 78-66077. (Adventures in Plant Medicine Ser.: Vol. 1). Date not set. Repr. of 1941 ed. lib. bdg. 15.00x (ISBN 0-88000-109-7). Quarterman.

Williams, Maud S. Growing Straight: The Fitness Secret of the American Indian. 200p. 1981. pap. 5.95 (ISBN 0-87877-057-7). Newcastle Pub.

INDIANS OF NORTH AMERICA–HISTORY

see also Indians of North America–Wars

Abel, Annie H. The American Indian Under Reconstruction. LC 25-10315. Repr. of 1925 ed. 19.50 (ISBN 0-384-00090-8). Johnson Repr.

--Slaveholding Indians, 3 vols. Incl. Vol. 1. The American Indian As Slaveholder & Secessionist. 1919. Repr. 35.00 (ISBN 0-685-26252-9); Vol. 2. The American Indian As Participant in the Civil War. 1919. Repr. 35.00 (ISBN 0-685-26253-7); Vol. 3. The American Indian Under Reconstruction. 1919. Repr. 30.00 (ISBN 0-685-26254-5). LC 70-116268. 1925. Repr. Set. 89.00 (ISBN 0-403-00471-3). Scholarly.

Alford, Thomas W. Civilization: & the Story of the Shawnees- As Told to Florence Drake. (Illus.). 1979. Repr. of 1936 ed. 12.50 (ISBN 0-8061-1590-4). U of Okla Pr.

American Ethnological Society. American Indian Intellectuals: 1976 Proceedings. Liberty, Margot, ed. (Illus.). 1978. pap. text ed. 13.95 (ISBN 0-8299-0223-6). West Pub.

Armstrong, Nancy, et al. The Heritage. (gr. 3-6). 1977. 1.95 (ISBN 0-89992-065-9). MT Coun Indian.

Armstrong, Virginia I., ed. I Have Spoken: American History Through the Voices of the Indians. LC 74-150755. xxii, 206p. 1971. (SB); pap. 6.95 (ISBN 0-8040-0530-3, Sb). Swallow.

Atkin, E. The Applalachian Indian Frontier: The Edmond Atkin Report & Plan of 1775. Jacobs, Wilbur R., ed. (Illus.). 7.50 (ISBN 0-8446-1561-7). Peter Smith.

The Autobiography of Delfina Cuero: A Diegueno Woman. 1970. pap. 4.50 (ISBN 0-686-14547-X). Malki Mus Pr.

Axtell, James. The European & the Indian: Essays in the Ethnohistory of Colonial North America. (Illus.). 256p. 1981. 19.95 (ISBN 0-19-502903-8). Oxford U Pr.

Bachman, Judith. A History of Indian Policy: Syllabus. 1978. pap. text ed. 5.75 (ISBN 0-89420-038-0, 333020); cassette recordings 146.10 (ISBN 0-89420-149-2, 333000). Natl Book.

Baird, W. David. The Quapaw Indians: A History of the Downstream People. LC 79-4731. (Civilization of the American Indian Ser.: Vol. 152). (Illus.). 1980. 19.95 (ISBN 0-8061-1542-4). U of Okla Pr.

Baker, Betty. Settlers & Strangers: Native Americans of the Desert Southwest & History As They Saw It. LC 77-4925. (Illus.). (gr. 3-6). 1977. 8.95 (ISBN 0-02-708220-2, 70822). Macmillan.

Bandelier, Adolph F. & Ten Kate, Herman F. An Outline of the Documentary History of the Zuni Tribe: Somatological Observations of Indians of the Southwest. LC 76-21219. (A Journal of American Ethnology & Archaeology: Vol. 3). Repr. of 1892 ed. 20.00 (ISBN 0-404-58043-2). AMS Pr.

Barsh, Russel L. & Henderson, J. Youngblood. The Road: Indian Tribes & Political Liberty. 1980. 14.95x (ISBN 0-520-03629-8). U of Cal Pr.

Beckham, Stephen D. Requiem for a People: The Rogue Indians & the Frontiersmen. LC 79-145497. (Civilization of the American Indian Ser.: Vol. 108). (Illus.). 1971. 9.95 (ISBN 0-8061-0942-4); pap. 5.95 (ISBN 0-8061-1036-8). U of Okla Pr.

Berkhofer, Robert F. The White Man's Indian: Images of the American Indian from Columbus to the Present. LC 77-15568. (Illus.). 1978. 15.00 (ISBN 0-394-48485-1). Knopf.

Boscana, Geronimo. Chinigchinich. LC 77-93183. 1978. 25.00 (ISBN 0-686-25511-9). Malki Mus Pr.

Britt, Albert. Great Indian Chiefs. facs. ed. LC 76-76895. (Essay Index Reprint Ser). 1938. 19.50 (ISBN 0-8369-0006-5). Arno.

Brophy, William A. & Aberle, Sophie D. The Indian: America's Unfinished Business. (Civilization of the American Indian Ser: Vol. 83). (Illus.). 1978. pap. 6.95 (ISBN 0-8061-1417-7). U of Okla Pr.

Brown, Dee. Bury My Heart at Wounded Knee: An Indian History of the American West. (Illus.). 480p. (gr. 7 up). 1972. pap. 3.50 (ISBN 0-553-13597-X, V13597-X). Bantam.

--Wounded Knee: An Indian History of the American West. 1975. pap. 1.50 (ISBN 0-440-95768-0, LFL). Dell.

Burgess, Larry E. & Hauptman, Laurence M. The Lake Mohonk Conference of Friends of the Indian: Guide to the Annual Reports. LC 74-6460. (Library of American Indian Affairs Ser.). (Illus.). 200p. 1975. lib. bdg. 15.00 (ISBN 0-88354-103-3). Clearwater Pub.

Coffer, William E. Phoenix: The Decline & Rebirth of the Indian People. 1979. 15.95 (ISBN 0-442-26131-4). Van Nos Reinhold.

Colden, Cadwallader. The History of Five Indian Nations. 6.50 (ISBN 0-8446-0064-4). Peter Smith.

--History of the Five Indian Nations. 181p. (YA) (gr. 9-12). 1958. pap. 3.95 (ISBN 0-8014-9086-3, CP86). Cornell U Pr.

--The History of the Five Indian Nations of Canada Which Are Dependent on the Province of New York, & Are a Barrier Between the English & the French. LC 72-2827. (American Explorers Ser.). Repr. of 1922 ed. 37.50 (ISBN 0-404-54908-X). AMS Pr.

Costo, Rupert, ed. Textbooks & the American Indian. LC 75-119022. 269p. 1969. pap. 5.00 (ISBN 0-913436-00-3). Indian Hist Pr.

Custer, Elizabeth B. Tenting on the Plains. 403p. 1973. Repr. of 1887 ed. 9.50 (ISBN 0-87928-042-5). Corner Hse.

Debo, Angie. History of the Indians of the United States. LC 73-108802. (Civilization of the American Indian Ser.: Vol. 106). (Orig.). 1970. 14.95 (ISBN 0-8061-0911-4). U of Okla Pr.

Dennis, Henry C. The American Indian: A Chronology & Fact Book. 2nd ed. LC 76-46440. (Ethnic Chronology Ser.: No. 1). 1977. 8.50 (ISBN 0-379-00526-3). Oceana.

De Puy, Henry F. A Bibliography of the English Colonial Treaties with the American Indians. LC 78-108471. 1917. Repr. 19.00 (ISBN 0-403-00425-X). Scholarly.

Dial, Adolph & Eliades, David K. The Only Land I Know: A History of the Lumbee Indians. LC 74-80435. (Illus.). 240p. (Orig.). 1974. 9.75 (ISBN 0-913436-28-3); pap. 6.00 (ISBN 0-913436-29-1). Indian Hist Pr.

Dictionary of Indian Tribes of the Americas, 4 vols. 2nd ed. 2000p. 1981. Set. lib. bdg. 250.00 (ISBN 0-686-30155-2). Am Indian Pubs.

Dippie, Brian W. The Vanishing American. (Illus.). 464p. 1982. 25.00x (ISBN 0-8195-5056-6). Wesleyan U Pr.

Driver, Harold E., ed. Americas on the Eve of Discovery. LC 79-15337. 1979. Repr. of 1964 ed. lib. bdg. 18.75x (ISBN 0-313-22028-X, DRAM). Greenwood.

Drury, Clifford. Nine Years with Spokane Indians: Diary of Elkanah Walker. (Illus.). 1976. 26.50 (ISBN 0-87062-117-3). A H Clark.

Drury, Clifford M. Chief Lawyer of the Nez Perce Indians, Seventeen Ninety-Six to Eighteen Seventy Six. LC 78-67267. (Northwest Historical Ser.: 14). (Illus.). 1979. 22.75 (ISBN 0-87062-127-0). A H Clark.

DuPriest, Maude W., et al. Cherokee Recollections. DuPriest, Maude W., ed. LC 76-10640. 1976. 10.00 (ISBN 0-914312-08-1). Indian Pocahontas Club.

Euler, Robert C. Havasupai Indians 1150-1890: Historical Report. (Library of American Indian Affairs). 50p. 1974. lib. bdg. 24.00 (ISBN 0-8287-1059-7). Clearwater Pub.

--Southern Paiute Ethnohistory. (Glen Canyon Ser: No. 28). Repr. of 1966 ed. 24.00 (ISBN 0-404-60678-4). AMS Pr.

Fahey, John. The Days of the Hercules. LC 78-63289. (Illus.). 1978. 10.95 (ISBN 0-89301-057-X). U Pr of Idaho.

Fenton, William N. American Indian & White Relations to 1830. LC 73-102490. 1971. Repr. of 1957 ed. 10.00 (ISBN 0-8462-1525-X). Russell.

Finerty, John F. War-Path & Bivouac: Or, the Conquest of the Sioux. (WFL Ser.). (Illus.). 1977. pap. 5.95 (ISBN 0-8061-1413-4). U of Okla Pr.

Fontana, Bernard L. Tarahumara: Where Night Is the Day of the Moon. LC 78-71375. (Illus.). 1979. 37.50 (ISBN 0-87358-183-0). Northland.

Foreman, Carolyn T. Indian Women Chiefs. LC 75-37860. 1976. Repr. of 1954 ed. 8.50 (ISBN 0-89201-019-3). Zenger Pub.

Foreman, Grant. Last Trek of the Indians. LC 73-173536. (Illus.). 1972. Repr. of 1946 ed. 26.00 (ISBN 0-8462-1197-1). Russell.

Gay, E. Jane. With the Nez Perces: Alice Fletcher in the Field, 1889-92. Hoxie, Frederick E. & Mark, Joan T., eds. LC 80-23045. (Illus.). xxxviii, 188p. 1981. 18.95 (ISBN 0-8032-3062-1). U of Nebr Pr.

Gibson, Arrell. The American Indian: Prehistory to the Present. 618p. 1981. pap. text ed. 11.95 (ISBN 0-669-04493-8). Heath.

Gidley, M. With One Sky Above Us: Life on an Indian Reservation at the Turn of the Century. LC 79-63443. 1979. 14.95 (ISBN 0-399-12420-9). Putnam.

Goodman, Jeffrey. American Genesis: The American Indian & the Origins of Modern Man. LC 80-18652. (Illus.). 288p. 1981. 11.95 (ISBN 0-671-25139-2). Summit Bks.

Goodwin, Gary C. Cherokees in Transition: A Study of Changing Culture & Environment Prior to 1775. LC 77-2709. (Research Papers). (Illus.). 1977. pap. 8.00 (ISBN 0-89065-088-8). U Chicago Dept Geog.

Gookin, Daniel. Historical Account of the Doings & Sufferings of the Christian Indians in New England in the Years 1675, 1676, 1677. LC 76-141098. (Research Library of Colonial Americana). 1972. Repr. of 1836 ed. 15.00 (ISBN 0-405-03307-9). Arno.

Hafen, Leroy R. Ute Indians & the San Juan Mining Region: Historical Summary. (Library of American Indian Affairs). 54p. 1974. lib. bdg. 25.00 (ISBN 0-8287-1286-7). Clearwater Pub.

Hagan, William T. American Indians. rev. ed. LC 78-72176. (Chicago History of American Civilization Ser.). (Illus.). 1979. lib. bdg. 15.00x (ISBN 0-226-31234-8); pap. 4.95 (ISBN 0-226-31235-6, CHAC 8). U of Chicago Pr.

--The Indian in American History. LC 71-185024. (AHA Pamphlets: No. 240). 1971. pap. text ed. 1.50 (ISBN 0-87229-001-8). Am Hist Assn.

--The Sac & Fox Indians. LC 58-6851. (The Civilization of the American Indian Ser.: Vol. 48). (Illus.). 320p. 1958. 14.95 (ISBN 0-8061-0397-3). U of Okla Pr.

Halkett, John. Historical Notes Respecting the Indians of North America. 1976. Repr. of 1825 ed. 19.00 (ISBN 0-527-37330-3). Kraus Repr.

Hamilton, Charles, ed. Cry of the Thunderbird: The American Indian's Own Story. George. LC 70-177336. (Civilization of the American Indian Ser.: Vol. 119). (Illus.). 283p. 1972. 12.95 (ISBN 0-8061-1003-1); pap. 6.95 (ISBN 0-8061-1292-1). U of Okla Pr.

Hanna, Charles A. The Wilderness Trail, 2 vols. LC 77-149659. (Illus.). Repr. of 1911 ed. 67.50 set (ISBN 0-404-03097-1). AMS Pr.

Henry, Jeannette, ed. The American Indian Reader: History. LC 72-86873. (American Indian Reader Ser.). (Orig.). 1974. pap. 4.00 (ISBN 0-913436-19-4). Indian Hist Pr.

Hickerson, Harold. The Chippewa & Their Neighbors: A Study in Ethnohistory. Spindler, George & Spindler, Louise, eds. (Studies in Anthropological Method). 144p. pap. text ed. 6.95x (ISBN 0-8290-0305-3). Irvington.

Hill, Ruth B. Hanta Yo: An American Saga. 1980. 9.95 (ISBN 0-446-96298-8); pap. 3.50 (ISBN 0-446-97857-4). Warner Bks.

Horr, David A., ed. American Indian Ethnohistory, 118 vols. (Illus.). lib. bdg. 2400.00 set (ISBN 0-685-37527-7); lib. bdg. 42.00 ea. Garland Pub.

Hyde, George E. Indians of the High Plains: From the Prehistoric Period to the Coming of Europeans. (Civilization of the American Indian Ser.: No. 54). (Illus.). 1976. 13.95 (ISBN 0-8061-0438-4); pap. 6.95 (ISBN 0-8061-1382-0). U of Okla Pr.

--Indians of the Woodlands: From Prehistoric Times to 1725. (Civilization of the American Indian Ser.: No. 64). (Illus.). 1962. pap. 7.95 (ISBN 0-8061-1058-9). U of Okla Pr.

Jacobs, Wilbur R. Wilderness Politics & Indian Gifts. (Illus.). 5.00 (ISBN 0-8446-2306-7). Peter Smith.

James, Harry C. Pages From Hopi History. LC 73-86451. 1974. pap. 6.50 (ISBN 0-8165-0500-4). U of Ariz Pr.

Jessett, Thomas E. Indian Side of the Whitman Massacre. 1972. Repr. pap. 3.00 (ISBN 0-87770-055-9). Ye Galleon.

Johansen, Bruce & Maestas, Roberto. Wasi'chu: The Continuing Indian War. LC 79-10153. 1979. 15.00 (ISBN 0-85345-484-1, CL4841). Monthly Rev.

Johnson, Elias. Legends, Traditions & Laws of the Iroquois: Or Six Nations, & History of the Tuscarora Indians. LC 76-43755. Repr. of 1881 ed. 18.75 (ISBN 0-404-15596-0). AMS Pr.

Jones, Jonathan H. A Condensed History of the Apache & Comanche Indian Tribes. LC 75-7129. (Indian Captivities Ser.: Vol. 102). 1976. Repr. of 1899 ed. lib. bdg. 44.00 (ISBN 0-8240-1726-9). Garland Pub.

Josephy, Alvin M. Red Power. pap. 3.95 (ISBN 0-07-033053-0, SP). McGraw.

Kellogg, Edward P. Roots of the American Indian. LC 79-91921. 1980. text ed. 14.95 (ISBN 0-9603914-0-1). EHUD.

King, Duane H., ed. The Cherokee Indian Nation: A Troubled History. LC 78-13222. (Illus.). 1979. 12.50 (ISBN 0-87049-227-6). U of Tenn Pr.

Kroeber, Theodora. Ishi, Last of His Tribe. (Pathfinder Ser.). (Illus.). 224p. (YA) 1973. pap. 2.25 (ISBN 0-553-13853-7, B13853-7). Bantam.

La Flesche, Francis. The Middle Five: Indian Schoolboys of the Omaha Tribe. LC 78-17409. (Illus.). xxiv, 152p. 1978. 12.50x (ISBN 0-8032-2852-X); pap. 2.95 (ISBN 0-8032-7901-9, BB 682, Bison). U of Nebr Pr.
Latta, Frank F. Handbook of Yokuts Indians. (Illus.). 1979. 24.95 (ISBN 0-686-26704-4). Bear State.
Leacock, Eleanor B. & Laurie, Nancy O., eds. North American Indians in Historical Perspective. 512p. 1971. text ed. 14.95 (ISBN 0-394-31014-4, RanC). Random.
Littlefield, Daniel F., Jr. The Cherokee Freedmen: From Emancipation to American Citizenship. LC 78-53659. (Contributions in Afro-American & African Studies: No. 40). 1978. lib. bdg. 18.95x (ISBN 0-313-20413-6, LCH/). Greenwood.
Locke, Raymond F., ed. The American Indian. (Great Adventures of History Ser.). 1976. pap. 1.75 (ISBN 0-87687-003-5, BM003). Mankind Pub.
Logan, the Last of the Race of Shikellemus, Chief of the Cayuga Nation. 1971. Repr. of 1868 ed. 8.00 (ISBN 0-87012-078-6). McClain.
Lurie, Nancy O. Kalispel: Historical Report. (Library of American Indian Affairs). 25p. 1974. lib. bdg. 16.25 (ISBN 0-8287-1084-8). Clearwater Pub.
McKenney, Thomas L. Memoirs, Official & Personal. LC 72-94789. xxvii, 340p. 1973. pap. 3.95 (ISBN 0-8032-5776-7, BB 565, Bison). U of Nebr Pr.
McNickle, D'Aracy. Native American Tribalism: Indian Survivals & Renewals. 1973. pap. 3.95 (ISBN 0-19-501724-2, 399, GB). Oxford U Pr.
McNickle, D'Arcy. Native American Tribalism. new ed. (Illus.). 120p. 1973. 9.95x (ISBN 0-19-501723-4). Oxford U Pr.
--They Came Here First: The Epic of the American Indian. 1975. lib. bdg. 17.50x (ISBN 0-374-95550-6). Octagon.
Madsen, Brigham D. The Lemhi: Sacajawea's People. LC 78-53137. (Illus., Orig.). 1980. pap. 4.95 (ISBN 0-87004-267-X). Caxton.
--The Northern Shoshoni. LC 78-53138. (Illus.). 262p. (Orig.). 1980. 17.95 (ISBN 0-87004-289-0); pap. 12.95 (ISBN 0-87004-266-1). Caxton.
Marriott, Alice & Rachlin, Carol K. American Epic: The Story of the American Indian. (Illus.). 1970. pap. 1.50 (ISBN 0-451-61503-4, MW1503, Ment). NAL.
Milanich, Jerald T. & Proctor, Samuel, eds. Tacachale: Essays on the Indians of Florida & Southeastern Georgia During the Historic Period. LC 77-20051. (Ripley T. Bullen Monographs in Anthropology & History: No. 1). (Illus.). 1978. 12.50 (ISBN 0-8130-0535-3). U Presses Fla.
Miner, H. Craig & Unrau, William E. The End of Indian Kansas: A Study of Cultural Revolution, 1854-1871. LC 77-4410. (Illus.). 1977. 12.50x (ISBN 0-7006-0161-9). Regents Pr KS.
Mohr, Walter H. Federal Indian Relations, Seventeen Seventy-Four-Seventeen Eighty-Eight. LC 76-158854. Repr. of 1933 ed. 19.45 (ISBN 0-404-07147-3). AMS Pr.
Mooney, James. Myths of the Cherokee. LC 70-108513. (American Indian History Sers). 1970. Repr. of 1900 ed. 59.00 (ISBN 0-403-00221-4). Scholarly.
Nichols, Roger L. The American Indian: Past & Present. 2nd ed. LC 80-20436. 283p. 1980. text ed. 10.95 (ISBN 0-471-06321-5). Wiley.
Novack, George. Genocide Against the Indians. pap. 0.60 (ISBN 0-87348-160-7). Path Pr NY.
Peckham, Howard & Gibson, Charles, eds. Attitudes of Colonial Powers Toward the American Indian. LC 77-99793. (University of Utah Publications in the American West: Vol. 2). 1976. 10.00 (ISBN 0-87480-116-8). U of Utah Pr.
Peithmann, Irvin M. Broken Peace Pipes: A Four-Hundred Year History of the American Indian. 320p. 1964. 11.75 (ISBN 0-398-01468-X). C C Thomas.
Penhallow, Samuel. History of the Indian Wars. 208p. 1973. Repr. of 1726 ed. 8.50 (ISBN 0-87928-044-1). Corner Hse.
Penrose, Maryly. Indian Affairs Papers: American Revolution. LC 80-24018. (Illus.). xviii, 395p. 1981. lib. bdg. 30.00 (ISBN 0-918940-07-9). Liberty Bell Assoc.
Perceval, Don. From Ice Mountain: Indian Settlement of the Americas. LC 79-53088. (Illus.). 1979. 16.00 (ISBN 0-87358-204-7). Northland.
Phillips, George H. Chiefs & Challengers. 1975. 17.95 (ISBN 0-520-02719-1). U of Cal Pr.
Phillips, George H., Jr. Indians in California History. Hundley, Norris & Schutz, John A., eds. LC 81-66060. (Golden State Ser.). (Illus.). 110p. 1981. pap. text ed. 4.95x (ISBN 0-87835-118-3). Boyd & Fraser.
Powell, Peter J. Sweet Medicine: The Continuing Role of the Sacred Arrows, The Sun Dance, & The Sacred Buffalo Hat in Northern Cheyenne History. (Illus.). 1969. 42.50 (ISBN 0-8061-0885-1). U of Okla Pr.
Powers, Bob. Indian Country of the Tubatulabal: First Residents of Kern River Valley. (Illus.). 1981. 18.00 (ISBN 0-87026-056-1). Westernlore.
Prakash, B. Aspects of Indian History & Civilization. 1965. 8.50 (ISBN 0-8426-1681-0). Verry.
Prucha, Francis P. American Indian Policy in Crisis: Christian Reformers & the Indian,1865-1900. LC 75-4957. 1976. 24.95 (ISBN 0-8061-1279-4). U of Okla Pr.
Prucha, Francis P., ed. Cherokee Removal: The "William Penn" Essays & Other Writings by Jeremiah Evarts. LC 80-28449. 320p. 1981. 19.50x (ISBN 0-87049-313-2). U of Tenn Pr.
Raphael, Ralph B. The Book of American Indians. LC 54-12972. 144p. 1973. lib. bdg. 4.95 (ISBN 0-668-00369-3). Arco.
Reid, John Phillip. A Law of Blood: The Primitive Law of the Cherokee Nation. LC 72-90901. 1970. 12.50x (ISBN 0-8147-0478-6). NYU Pr.
Riddle, Jeff. Indian History of the Modoc War. LC 73-82646. (Illus.). 295p. 1973. Repr. 10.00 (ISBN 0-912720-04-2). Pine Cone Pubs.
Roe, Melvin W., ed. Readings in the History of the American Indian. 1971. pap. 6.95 (ISBN 0-8422-0134-3). Irvington.
Roessel, Robert, Jr. Pictorial History of the Navajo from 1860-1910. (Illus.). 240p. 1980. 14.95 (ISBN 0-686-74363-6). Navajo Curr.
Rose, Wendy. Long Division: A Tribal History. 2nd, rev. ed. (Illus.). 1981. pap. 2.50 (ISBN 0-686-30235-4). Strawberry Pr NY.
Ruppel, Maxine. Vostaas: The Story of Montana's Indian Nations. (Indian Culture Ser.). (gr. 3-11). 1970. 2.00 (ISBN 0-89992-001-2). MT Coun Indian.
Russell, Howard S. Indian New England Before the Mayflower. LC 79-63082. (Illus.). 296p. 1980. 17.50 (ISBN 0-87451-162-3). U Pr of New Eng.
Sarner, Van H. The Broken Ring: The Destruction of the California Indians. LC 80-52892. (Illus.). 1981. 9.50 (ISBN 0-87026-057-X). Westernlore.
Satz, Ronald N. Tennessee's Indian Peoples: From White Contact to Removal, 1540-1840. LC 77-21634. (Tennessee Three Star Bks.). (Illus.). 1979. lib. bdg. 8.50x (ISBN 0-87049-285-3); pap. 3.50 (ISBN 0-87049-231-4). U of Tenn Pr.
Savishinsky, Joel S. & Frimmer, Susan B. The Middle Ground: Social Change in an Artic Community, 1967-1971. (Illus.). 60p. 1973. pap. text ed. 2.00x (ISBN 0-660-00061-X, 56433-9, Pub. by Natl Mus Canada). U of Chicago Pr.
Schroeder, Albert H. & Matson, Dan S. A Colony on the Move: Gaspar Castano de Sosa's Journal, 1590-1591. (School of American Research Bk). (Illus.). 1965. 8.95x (ISBN 0-8263-0295-5). U of NM Pr.
Schwatka, Frederick. Among the Apaches. (Wild & Woolly West Ser. No. 26). (Illus.). 30p. 1974. 7.00 (ISBN 0-910584-61-3); pap. 1.50 (ISBN 0-910584-35-4). Filter.
Seger, John H. Early Days Among the Cheyenne & Arapahoe Indians. Vestal, Stanley, ed. (CAI Ser.: Vol. 5). (Illus.). 1934. 8.95 (ISBN 0-8061-0344-2); pap. 4.95 (ISBN 0-8061-1533-5). U of Okla Pr.
Seymour, Flora W. Story of the Red Man. facs. ed. LC 79-124257. (Select Bibliographies Reprint Ser). 1929. 25.00 (ISBN 0-8369-5445-9). Arno.
Sheehan, Bernard. Savagism & Civility. LC 79-18189. 1980. 35.50 (ISBN 0-521-22927-8); pap. 7.50 (ISBN 0-521-29723-0). Cambridge U Pr.
Sheridan, Thomas E. & Naylor, Thomas H., eds. Raramuri: A Tarahumara Colonial Chronicle 1607-1791. LC 78-74036. 1979. pap. 7.50 (ISBN 0-87358-188-1). Northland.
Shorris, Earl. The Death of the Great Spirit. 208p. 1974. pap. 1.50 (ISBN 0-451-61355-4, MW1355, Ment). NAL.
Smith, Walker C. Everett Massacre. Repr. of 1916 ed. pap. 24.00 (ISBN 0-8466-0105-2, SJS105). Shorey.
Smith, William C. Was It Murder (Centralia Massacre) Repr. of 1922 ed. pap. 5.50 (ISBN 0-8466-0127-3, SJS127). Shorey.
Sonnichsen, C. L. The Mescalero Apaches. (The Civilization of the American Indian Ser.: Vol. 51). (Illus.). 341p. 1980. pap. 6.95 (ISBN 0-8061-1615-3). U of Okla Pr.
Spicer, Edward H. Short History of the Indians of the United States. (Orig.). 1969. pap. 6.95x (ISBN 0-442-00101-0, 101, Anv). Van Nos Reinhold.
Sprague, Marshall. Massacre: The Tragedy at White River. LC 79-18384. (Illus.). xx, 364p. 1980. 19.50x (ISBN 0-8032-4107-0); pap. 6.95 (ISBN 0-8032-9106-X, BB 702, Bison). U of Nebr Pr.
Strickland, Rennard. The Indians in Oklahoma. LC 79-6717. (Newcomers to a New Land Ser.: Vol. 9). (Illus.). 1980. 9.95 (ISBN 0-8061-1674-9); pap. 4.95 (ISBN 0-8061-1675-7). U of Okla Pr.
Sun Bear. Buffalo Hearts. 1976. pap. 4.00 (ISBN 0-686-01908-3). Bear Tribe.
Swanton, John R. Early History of the Creek Indians & Their Neighbors. LC 73-139862. Repr. of 1922 ed. 38.50 (ISBN 0-384-59000-4). Johnson Repr.
Szasz, Margaret C. Education & the American Indian: The Road to Self-Determination Since 1928. 2nd ed. LC 77-11742. (Illus.). 252p. 1979. pap. 6.95x (ISBN 0-8263-0468-0). U of NM Pr.
Thomas, Cyrus. The Cherokees in Pre-Columbian Times. LC 76-43868. Repr. of 1890 ed. 16.50 (ISBN 0-404-15727-0). AMS Pr.
Thomson, Charles. Enquiry into the Causes of the Alienation of the Delaware & Shawanees Indians from British Interests. LC 73-108549. 1970. Repr. of 1759 ed. 15.50 (ISBN 0-403-00271-0). Scholarly.
Thrapp, Dan L. General Crook & the Sierra Madre Adventure. (Illus.). 1977. pap. 5.95 (ISBN 0-8061-1370-7). U of Okla Pr.
--Victorio & the Mimbres Apaches. (The Civilization of the American Indian Ser.: Vol. 125). (Illus.). 393p. 1980. pap. 9.95 (ISBN 0-8061-1645-5). U of Okla Pr.
Tyler, Daniel, ed. Red Men & Hat-Wearers: Viewpoints in Indian History. (Illus.). 160p. 1976. pap. 5.95 (ISBN 0-87108-501-1). Pruett.
Underhill, Ruth M. Red Man's America: A History of Indians in the United States. rev. ed. LC 79-171345. 398p. 1971. pap. 7.95 (ISBN 0-226-84165-0, P437, Phoen). U of Chicago Pr.
--Red Man's America: A History of the Indians in the United States. rev. ed. LC 79-171345. (Illus.). 1971. 15.00x (ISBN 0-226-84164-2). U of Chicago Pr.
Unrau, William E. The Kansa Indians: A History of the Wind People, 1673-1873. LC 74-160508. (Civilization of the American Indian Ser: Vol. 114). (Illus.). 1971. 13.95 (ISBN 0-8061-0980-7). U of Okla Pr.
Van Every, Dale. Disinherited: The Lost Birthright of the American Indian. 1967. pap. 2.95 (ISBN 0-380-01141-7, 51326, Discus). Avon.
Vantine, Larry L. Teaching American Indian History: An Interdisciplinary Approach. LC 78-62223. 1978. soft cover 9.00 (ISBN 0-88247-546-0). R & E Res Assoc.
Vetromile, Eugene. The Abnakis & Their History. LC 76-43884. 1977. Repr. of 1866 ed. 15.00 (ISBN 0-404-15741-6). AMS Pr.
Waddell, Gene. Indians of the South Carolina Lowcountry, 1562-1751. LC 79-27308. (The South Caroliniana Ser: Bibliographical & Textual: No. 5). 484p. 1980. 30.00 (ISBN 0-87152-315-9). Reprint.
Wardell, Morris L. A Political History of the Cherokee Nation, Eighteen Thirty-Eight to Nineteen Hundred Seven. (Civilization of the American Indian Ser.: Vol. 17). (Illus.). 383p. 1980. pap. 9.95 (ISBN 0-8061-1641-2). U of Okla Pr.
Weeks, Philip & Gidney, James B. Subjugation & Dishonor: A Brief History of the Travail of the Native Americans. LC 79-28713. (Orig.). 1980. 12.50 (ISBN 0-89874-076-2); pap. 5.95 (ISBN 0-686-66018-8). Krieger.
Williams, Walter L., ed. Southeastern Indians Since the Removal Era. LC 78-10490. (Illus.). 270p. 1979. 18.50x (ISBN 0-8203-0464-6); pap. 6.00 (ISBN 0-8203-0483-2). U of Ga Pr.
Wissler, Clark. Indians of the United States: Four Centuries of Their History & Culture. LC 66-12215. 1966. 7.95 (ISBN 0-385-00757-4). Doubleday.
Wolf, Beverly H. The Ways of My Grandmothers. LC 79-91645. 224p. 1980. 9.95 (ISBN 0-688-03665-1). Morrow.
Wright, J. Leitch, Jr. Only Land They Knew: The Tragic Story of the American Indians in the Old South. (Illus.). 352p. 1981. 15.00 (ISBN 0-02-935790-X). Macmillan.

INDIANS OF NORTH AMERICA–HISTORY–SOURCES

Acts & Resolutions. LC 73-88769. (The Constitutions & Laws of the American Indian Tribes Ser. 1: Vol. 15). 1973. Repr. of 1899 ed. lib. bdg. 7.50 (ISBN 0-8420-1709-7). Scholarly Res Inc.
Acts & Resolutions of the Creek National Council of the Extra Session of April, 1894 & the Regular Session of October, 1894. LC 73-88773. (The Constitutions & Laws of the American Indian Tribes Ser. 1: Vol. 19). 1973. Repr. of 1894 ed. lib. bdg. 6.00 (ISBN 0-8420-1721-6). Scholarly Res Inc.
Acts & Resolutions of the General Council of the Choctaw Nation, Passed at Its Regular Session, 1902 & Extra Session, 1902. LC 73-88771. (The Constitutions & Laws of the American Indian Tribes Ser. 1: Vol. 17). 1973. Repr. of 1903 ed. lib. bdg. 9.00 (ISBN 0-8420-1711-9). Scholarly Res Inc.
Acts & Resolutions of the General Council of the Choctaw Nation Passed at Its Regular Session, 1903. LC 73-88770. (The Constitutions & Laws of the American Indian Tribes Ser. 1: Vol. 16). 1973. Repr. of 1904 ed. lib. bdg. 7.50 (ISBN 0-8420-1710-0). Scholarly Res Inc.
Acts & Resolutions of the General Council of the Choctaw Nation, Passed at Its Regular Session, October, 1897-& Also All the School Laws of the Choctaw Nation. LC 73-88768. (The Constitutions & Laws of the American Indian Tribes Ser. 1: Vol. 14). 1973. Repr. of 1897 ed. lib. bdg. 7.50 (ISBN 0-8420-1708-9). Scholarly Res Inc.
Acts of Council of the Choctaw Nation, Passed at the Regular Sessions of October 1895 & 1896, & the Special Session of September, 1896. LC 73-88767. (The Constitutions & Laws of the American Indian Tribes Ser. 1: Vol. 13). 1973. Repr. of 1897 ed. lib. bdg. 12.00 (ISBN 0-8420-1707-0). Scholarly Res Inc.
Atkin, Edmond. Appalachian Indian Frontier: The Edmond Atkin Report & Plan of 1755. Jacobs, Wilbur R., ed. LC 54-12059. (Illus.). xxxviii, 108p. 1967. pap. 2.95x (ISBN 0-8032-5011-8, 374, Bison). U of Nebr Pr.
Brinton, Daniel G., ed. Library of Aboriginal American Literature, 8 vols. 1977. Repr. of 1890 ed. write for info. (ISBN 0-404-52180-0). AMS Pr.
Compiled Laws of the Cherokee Nation Published by the Authority of the National Council. LC 73-88761. (The Constitutions & Laws of the American Indian Tribes Ser. 1: Vol. 9). 1973. Repr. of 1881 ed. lib. bdg. 30.00 (ISBN 0-8420-1716-X). Scholarly Res Inc.
Constitution & Laws of the Cherokee Nation. LC 73-88762. (The Constitutions & Laws of the American Indian Tribes Ser. 1: Vol. 10). 1973. Repr. of 1893 ed. lib. bdg. 40.00 (ISBN 0-8420-1717-8). Scholarly Res Inc.
Constitution & Laws of the Cherokee Nation. LC 73-88759. (The Constitutions & Laws of the American Indian Tribes Ser. 1: Vol. 7). 1973. Repr. of 1875 ed. lib. bdg. 25.00 (ISBN 0-8420-1714-3). Scholarly Res Inc.
Constitution, Laws & Treaties of the Chickasaws. LC 73-88778. (The Constitutions & Laws of the American Indian Tribes Ser. 1: Vol. 1). 1973. Repr. of 1878 ed. lib. bdg. 25.00 (ISBN 0-8420-1718-6). Scholarly Res Inc.
Eastman, Charles A. From the Deep Woods to Civilization: Chapters in the Autobiography of an Indian. LC 77-7226. (Illus.). 1977. 14.95x (ISBN 0-8032-0936-3); pap. 3.75 (ISBN 0-8032-5873-9, BB 651, Bison). U of Nebr Pr.
Eliot, John. John Eliot's Indian Dialogues: A Study in Cultural Interaction. Bowden, Henry W. & Ronda, James P., eds. LC 80-542. (Contributions in American History: No. 88). (Illus.). 173p. 1980. lib. bdg. 22.95 (ISBN 0-313-21031-4, RID/). Greenwood.
Journal of the General Council of the Indian Territory. LC 75-3700. (Constitutions & Laws of the American Indian Tribes, Ser. 2: Vol. 32). 1975. Repr. of 1871 ed. 12.00 (ISBN 0-8420-1890-5). Scholarly Res Inc.
Journal of the Sixth Annual Session of the General Council of the Indian Territory. LC 75-3701. (Constitutions & Laws of the American Indian Tribes Ser. 2: Vol. 33). 1975. Repr. of 1875 ed. 14.00 (ISBN 0-8420-1889-1). Scholarly Res Inc.
Laws & Joint Resolutions of the National Council, Passed & Adopted at the Regular Session of the National Council, of 1876, 1877 & Extra Session of 1878. LC 73-88760. (The Constitutions & Laws of the American Indian Tribes Ser.: Pt. 1, Vol. 8). 1973. Repr. of 1878 ed. lib. bdg. 12.50 (ISBN 0-8420-1715-1). Scholarly Res Inc.
Laws of the Cherokee Nation: Adopted by the Council at Various Periods - Printed for the Benefit of the Nation. LC 73-88756. (Constitutions & Laws of the American Indian Tribes Ser. 1: Vol. 5). 1973. Repr. of 1852 ed. lib. bdg. 35.00 (ISBN 0-8420-1712-7). Scholarly Res Inc.
Laws of the Cherokee Nation, Passed During the Years 1839-1867, Compiled by the Authority of the National Council. LC 73-88757. (Constitutions & Laws of the American Indian Tribes Ser. 1: Vol. 6). 1973. Repr. of 1868 ed. lib. bdg. 25.00 (ISBN 0-8420-1713-5). Scholarly Res Inc.
Laws of the Choctaw Nation Passed at the Regular Session of the General Council Convened at Tushka Humma, October 1892 & Adjourned November 4, 1892. Bd. with Laws of the Choctaw Nation Passed at the Regular Session of the General Council Convened at Tushka Humma, October 2, 1893 & Adjourned October 27, 1893; The Special Sessions Convened in February 1892 (for 1893) & Convened in June 1893. LC 75-3689. (Constitutions & Laws of the American Indian Tribes Ser. 2: Vol. 22). 1975. Repr. of 1893 ed. 12.00 (ISBN 0-8420-1880-8). Scholarly Res Inc.

Limbaugh, Ronald H. & Marquis, Thomas B., eds. Cheyenne & Sioux: The Reminiscences of Four Indians & a White Soldier. (Western American Monographs). (Illus.). 79p. 1973. 5.50 (ISBN 0-686-05515-2). Holt-Atherton.

Myers, Albert C. The Boy George Washington Aged Sixteen: His Own Account of an Iroquois Indian Dance. 1932. Repr. 15.00 (ISBN 0-685-43332-3). Norwood Edns.

Nabokov, Peter, ed. Native American Testimony. LC 77-11558. 1979. pap. 4.95 (ISBN 0-06-090720-7, CN 720, CN). Har-Row.

Patterson, J. B. The Life of Blackhawk Dictated by Himself. enlarged ed. 1975. 9.95 (ISBN 0-87770-137-7). Ye Galleon.

Reimers, Henry L. The Secret Saga of Five-Sack. 25p. 1975. pap. 3.00 (ISBN 0-87770-145-8). Ye Galleon.

Vecsey, Christopher & Venables, Robert W., eds. American Indian Environments: Ecological Issues in Native American History. LC 80-26458. (Illus.). 236p. 1980. text ed. 18.00x (ISBN 0-8156-2226-0); pap. text ed. 9.95x (ISBN 0-8156-2227-9). Syracuse U Pr.

Vogel, Virgil J. This Country Was Ours: A Documentary History of the American Indian. LC 77-156556. 512p. (YA) 1972. 13.95 (ISBN 0-06-014509-9, HarpT). Har-Row.

--This Country Was Ours: A Documentary History of the American Indian. 1972. pap. 5.95x (ISBN 0-06-131735-7, TB1735, Torch). Har-Row.

Washburn, Wilcomb E., compiled by. The American Indian & the United States: A Documentary History, 4 vols. LC 72-10259. 1973. Set. lib. bdg. 195.00 (ISBN 0-313-20137-4). Greenwood.

Wilcocke, S. H. Narrative of Occurrences in the Indian Countries of North America. 1968. Repr. of 1817 ed. 16.50x (ISBN 0-8464-0666-7). Beekman Pubs.

INDIANS OF NORTH AMERICA–HUNTING AND FISHING

Cooper, John M. Snares, Deadfalls & Other Traps of the Northern Algonquian & Northern Athapaskans. LC 76-43683. (Catholic University of America Anthropological Ser.: No. 5). Repr. of 1938 ed. 17.50 (ISBN 0-404-15516-2). AMS Pr.

Ewers, John C. The Horse in Blackfoot Indian Culture. LC 55-60591. (Classics in Smithsonian Anthropology Ser.: No. 3). (Illus.). 374p. 1980. pap. text ed. 9.95x (ISBN 0-87474-419-9). Smithsonian.

Henry Tall Bull & Weist, Tom. The Winter Hunt. (Indian Culture Ser.). (gr. 3-9). 1971. 1.95 (ISBN 0-89992-006-3). MT Coun Indian.

Hill, Willard W. The Agricultural & Hunting Methods of the Navaho Indians. LC 76-43742. (Yale Univ. Pubns. in Anthropology: No. 18). Repr. of 1938 ed. 19.50 (ISBN 0-404-15583-9). AMS Pr.

Hofsinde, Robert. Indian Hunting. (Illus.). (gr. 4-7). 1962. PLB 6.48 (ISBN 0-688-31608-5). Morrow.

Mason, Otis T. Traps of the American Indians. facs. ed. (Illus.). 17p. Repr. of 1901 ed. pap. 3.25 (ISBN 0-8466-4007-4, SJI7). Shorey.

Stanley, Samuel & Oberg, Pearl. The Hunt. (Indian Culture Ser.). 32p. (gr. 5-9). 1976. 1.95 (ISBN 0-89992-047-0). MT Coun Indian.

Stewart, Hilary. Indian Fishing: Early Methods on the Northwest Coast. LC 77-950. (Illus.). 136p. 1977. 19.95 (ISBN 0-295-95556-2); pap. 15.00 (ISBN 0-295-95803-0). U of Wash Pr.

Tanner, Adrian. Bringing Home Animals: Religious Ideology & Mode of Production of the Mistassini Cree Hunters. LC 79-11612. 1979. 25.00x (ISBN 0-312-09633-X). St Martin.

Wilson, Gilbert L. Hidatsa Eagle Trapping. LC 76-43893. (AMNH Anthropological Papers: Vol. 30, Pt. 4). Repr. of 1928 ed. 14.00 (ISBN 0-404-15753-X). AMS Pr.

INDIANS OF NORTH AMERICA–IMPLEMENTS

see also Harpoons; Throwing Sticks

Beauchamp, William M. Aboriginal Chipped Stone Implements of New York. LC 76-43659. (New York State Museum Bulletin: Vol. 4, No. 16). Repr. of 1897 ed. 14.50 (ISBN 0-404-15495-6). AMS Pr.

--Horn & Bone Implements of the New York Indians. LC 76-43662. (New York State Museum Bulletin: 50). Repr. of 1902 ed. 19.50 (ISBN 0-404-15494-8). AMS Pr.

Eddy, Frank W. Metates & Manos. (Illus.). 1964. pap. 0.95 (ISBN 0-89013-009-4). Museum NM Pr.

Hanson, James A. Metal Weapons, Tools & Ornaments of the Teton Dakota Indians. LC 74-15277. (Illus.). xviii, 118p. 1975. 16.50 (ISBN 0-8032-0849-9). U of Nebr Pr.

Jenks, Albert E. Minnesota's Browns Valley Man and Associated Burial Artifacts. LC 38-22478. 1937. pap. 5.00 (ISBN 0-527-00548-7). Kraus Repr.

Morrow, Mable. Indian Rawhide: An American Folk Art. LC 73-7427. (Civilization of the American Indian Ser.: Vol. 132). (Illus.). 200p. 1975. 24.50 (ISBN 0-8061-1136-4). U of Okla Pr.

Purdy, Barbara A. Florida's Prehistoric Stone Technology. LC 80-24726. (Illus.). xvi, 165p. 1981. 25.00 (ISBN 0-8130-0697-X). U Presses Fla.

Woodbury, R. B. Prehistoric Stone Implements of Northeastern Arizona. (Illus.). 1954. 20.00 (ISBN 0-527-01286-6). Kraus Repr.

INDIANS OF NORTH AMERICA–INDUSTRIES

see also Indians of North America–Antiquities; Indians of North America–Commerce; Indians of North America–Hunting and Fishing; Indians of North America–Pottery; Indians of North America–Textile Industry and Fabrics

Bahti, Mark. Collecting Southwestern Native American Jewelry. (Illus.). 1980. pap. 8.95 (ISBN 0-679-50960-7). McKay.

Bahti, Tom. Southwestern Indian Arts & Crafts. LC 65-499. (Illus.). 1966. 7.95 (ISBN 0-916122-25-5); pap. 2.00 (ISBN 0-916122-00-X). KC Pubns.

Baird, Genevieve. Northwest Indian Basketry. LC 76-29125. 1976. pap. 3.75 (ISBN 0-917048-01-6). Wash St Hist Soc.

Barrett, S. A. Pomo Indian Basketry. LC 76-147075. (Beautiful Rio Grande Classics Ser). lib. bdg. 12.50 (ISBN 0-87380-099-0). Rio Grande.

Beauchamp, William M. Metallic Ornaments of the New York Indians. LC 74-7928. Repr. of 1903 ed. 16.00 (ISBN 0-404-11814-3). AMS Pr.

--Wampum & Shell Articles Used by the New York Indians. LC 76-43663. (New York State Museum Bulletin: No. 41, Vol. 8). Repr. of 1901 ed. 21.50 (ISBN 0-404-15496-4). AMS Pr.

Bedford, Clay P., ed. Western North American Indian Baskets from the Collection of Clay P. Bedford. (Illus.). 68p. 1980. pap. 10.00 (ISBN 0-940228-04-1). Calif Acad Sci.

Brasser, Ted J. Bo'jou, Neejee: Profiles of Canadian Indian Art. (Illus.). 1976. pap. 16.95 (ISBN 0-660-00008-3, 56283-2, Pub. by Natl Mus Canada). U of Chicago Pr.

Cheney Cowles Memorial Museum of the Eastern Washington State Historical Society. Cornhusk Bags of the Plateau Indians. LC 76-9025. 1976. 4 color fiches 30.00 (ISBN 0-226-68987-5, Chicago Visual Lib). U of Chicago Pr.

Colton, Harold S. Hopi Kachina Dolls with a Key to Their Identification. rev ed. LC 59-5480. (Illus.). 150p. 1971. pap. 6.95 (ISBN 0-8263-0180-0). U of NM Pr.

D'Amato, Alex & D'Amato, Janet. American Indian Craft Inspirations. LC 72-83734. (Illus.). 224p. (YA) 1972. 7.95 (ISBN 0-87131-031-7). M Evans.

Densmore, Frances. Chippewa Customs. (Landmarks in Anthropology Ser). 1970. Repr. of 1929 ed. 19.50 (ISBN 0-384-11410-5). Johnson Repr.

Farrand, Livingston. Basketry Designs of the Salish Indians. LC 73-3514. (Jesup North Pacific Expedition. Publications: Vol. 1). Repr. of 1900 ed. 15.00 (ISBN 0-404-58116-1). AMS Pr.

Frank, Larry & Holbrook, Millard J. Indian Silver Jewelry of the Southwest 1868-1930. LC 78-7071. (Illus.). 1979. 29.95 (ISBN 0-8212-0740-7, 417947). NYGS.

Fundaburk, Emma L. & Foreman, Mary D., eds. Sun Circles & Human Hands: The Southeastern Indians, Art & Industries. (Illus.). 10.00 (ISBN 0-910642-01-X). Fundaburk.

Gates, Frieda. Easy to Make North American Indian Crafts. LC 80-80605. (Easy to Make Ser.). (Illus.). 48p. (gr. 3-6). 1981. PLB 5.79 (ISBN 0-8178-0007-7). Harvey.

Goetz, Helga. The Inuit Print ('Estampe Inuit) (Illus.). 1980. 24.95x (ISBN 0-660-50278-X, 56393-6, Pub. by Natl Mus Canada); pap. 17.95 (ISBN 0-660-00082-2, 56392-8, Pub. by Natl Mus Canada). U of Chicago Pr.

Guernsey, Samuel J. Explorations in Northeastern Arizona. 1931. pap. 15.00 (ISBN 0-527-01224-6). Kraus Repr.

Guernsey, Samuel J. & Kidder, A. V. Basket-Maker Caves of Northeastern Arizona. (Illus.). 1921. pap. 12.00 (ISBN 0-527-01213-0). Kraus Repr.

Hammons, Lee & Hill, Gertrude F. Turquoise & the Navajo. new ed. (Illus.). 36p. 1975. pap. 1.95 (ISBN 0-686-12041-8). Ariz Maps & Bks.

Hawkins, Elizabeth. Indian Weaving, Knitting, Basketry of the Northwest Coast. (Native Culture Ser.). (Illus.). 32p. (Orig.). 1978. pap. 3.00 (ISBN 0-88839-006-8, Pub. by Hancock Hse). Universe.

Hollister, U. S. Navajo & His Blanket. LC 72-10567. (Beautiful Rio Grande Classics Ser). lib. bdg. 15.00 (ISBN 0-87380-097-4). Rio Grande.

Hunt, B. The Complete How-to Book of Indian craft. Orig. Title: Ben Hunt's Big Indian Craft Book. 1973. pap. 4.95 (ISBN 0-02-011690-X, Collier). Macmillan.

Hunt, Ben. Indian Crafts & Lore. 1976. PLB 10.69 (ISBN 0-307-60581-7, Golden Pr); pap. 2.95 (ISBN 0-307-15989-2). Western Pub.

Ives, David J. The Crescent Hills Prehistoric Quarrying Area. LC 76-621896. (Museum Brief Ser.: No. 22). 1975. pap. 1.80x (ISBN 0-913134-22-8). Mus Anthro Mo.

Jacka, Jerry D. & Hammack, Nancy S. Indian Jewelry of the Prehistoric Southwest. LC 75-8017. (Illus.). 48p. 1975. pap. 4.95 (ISBN 0-8165-0515-2). U of Ariz Pr.

James, George W. Indian Basketry. (Illus.). 271p. 1972. pap. 4.00 (ISBN 0-486-21712-4). Dover.

--Indian Basketry. (Illus.). 8.00 (ISBN 0-8446-4563-X). Peter Smith.

--Indian Basketry, & How to Make Baskets. LC 73-119863. (Beautiful Rio Grande Classics Ser). 424p. 1971. lib. bdg. 20.00 (ISBN 0-87380-071-0). Rio Grande.

Jones, Joan M. Introducing Western Indian Basketry. (Color Guide Ser.). (Illus.). 64p. (Orig.). 1981. pap. price not set (ISBN 0-88839-122-6, Pub. by Hancock Hse). Universe.

Katzenberg, Dena S. And Eagles Sweep Across the Sky: Indian Textiles of the North American West. LC 77-83121. (Illus.). 1977. 12.00 (ISBN 0-912298-45-6). Baltimore Mus.

Mason, Bernard S. The Book of Indian Crafts & Costumes. (Illus.). 1946. 16.95 (ISBN 0-8260-5720-9). Wiley.

Matthews, Washington. Navajo Weavers & Silversmiths. LC 70-97218. (Wild & Woolly West Ser., No. 7). (Illus.). 1968. 7.00 (ISBN 0-910584-81-8); pap. 1.50 (ISBN 0-910584-07-9). Filter.

Mera, H. R. Pueblo Designs: 176 Illustrations of the Rain Bird. 8.50 (ISBN 0-8446-0206-X). Peter Smith.

Merrill, Ruth E. Plants Used in Basketry by the California Indians. (Illus.). 1980. Repr. 2.95 (ISBN 0-686-77544-9). Acoma Bks.

Minor, Marz & Minor, Nono. The American Indian Craft Book. LC 77-14075. (Illus.). 1978. 22.50x (ISBN 0-8032-0974-6); pap. 5.50 (ISBN 0-8032-5891-7, BB 661, Bison). U of Nebr Pr.

Morrow, Mable. Indian Rawhide: An American Folk Art. LC 73-7427. (Civilization of the American Indian Ser.: Vol. 132). (Illus.). 200p. 1975. 24.50 (ISBN 0-8061-1136-4). U of Okla Pr.

Navajo School Of Indian Basketry. Indian Basket Weaving. (Illus.). 1971. pap. 2.50 (ISBN 0-486-22616-6). Dover.

Newman, Sandra C. Indian Basket Weaving. LC 73-79779. (Illus.). 108p. 1974. pap. 4.95 (ISBN 0-87358-112-1). Northland.

Norbeck, Oscar E. Book of Authentic Indian Life Crafts. rev. ed. LC 74-81910. (Illus.). 260p. 1974. 9.95 (ISBN 0-87874-012-0). Galloway.

Parker, Arthur C. The Indian How Book. LC 74-18592. (Illus.). 335p. 1975. pap. 4.00 (ISBN 0-486-21767-1). Dover.

Proper, Churchill. Indian Crafts. LC 70-185672. (Handicraft Ser.: No. 4). (Illus.). 32p. (Orig.). (gr. 7-12). 1971. lib. bdg. 2.45 incl. catalog cards (ISBN 0-87157-904-9); pap. 1.25 vinyl laminated covers (ISBN 0-87157-404-7). SamHar Pr.

Rodee, Marian E. Southwestern Weaving: The Collection of the Maxwell Museum. 2nd, rev. ed. LC 76-21517. (Illus.). 318p. 1981. pap. 14.95 (ISBN 0-8263-0587-3). U of NM Pr.

Roosevelt, Anna C. & Smith, James G., eds. The Ancestors: Native Artisans of the Americas. LC 79-89536. (Illus.). 1979. pap. 17.50 (ISBN 0-934490-00-7). Mus Am Ind.

Salomon, J. H. The Book of Indian Crafts & Indian Lore. 1977. lib. bdg. 69.95 (ISBN 0-8490-1531-6). Gordon Pr.

Schneider, Richard C. Crafts of the North American Indians: A Craftsman's Manual. LC 73-13008. (Illus.). 325p. (gr. 9-12). 1981. pap. 9.95 (ISBN 0-936984-00-7). Schneider Pubs.

--Crafts of the North American Indians: A Craftsman's Manual. (Illus.). 326p. 1972. pap. 6.95 (ISBN 0-442-27442-4). Van Nos Reinhold.

Shenon, P. J., et al. Northern Paiute Nation: Evaluation Study of Mineral Resources, 3 vols. (Library of American Indian Affairs). 1185p. 1973. Set. lib. bdg. 330.00 (ISBN 0-8287-1150-X). Clearwater Pub.

Stribling, Mary Lou. Crafts from North American Indian Arts. (Arts & Crafts Ser.). (Illus.). 308p. 1975. 12.95 (ISBN 0-517-51612-8); pap. 6.95 (ISBN 0-517-51613-6). Crown.

Tanner, Clara L., et al. Ray Manley's Collecting Southwestern Indian Arts & Crafts. 3rd rev. ed. (Illus.). 1979. pap. 4.00 (ISBN 0-931418-03-8). R Manley.

Underhill, Ruth. Pueblo Crafts. (Wild & Woolly West Ser.: No. 36). (Illus.). 1979. 10.00 (ISBN 0-910584-87-7); pap. 6.00 (ISBN 0-910584-51-6). Filter.

Underhill, Ruth M. Pueblo Crafts. Beatty, Willard W., ed. LC 76-43880. (U. S. Office of Indian Affairs Indian Handcrafts: 7). Repr. of 1945 ed. 32.50 (ISBN 0-404-15737-8). AMS Pr.

--Work a Day Life of the Pueblos. Beatty, Willard W., ed. LC 76-43882. (Indian Life & Customs: No. 4). Repr. of 1946 ed. 19.50 (ISBN 0-404-15735-1). AMS Pr.

Van Voorhis, Eugene. Iroquois Watercraft. (Illus., Orig.). 1976. pap. 2.00 (ISBN 0-9603006-1-9). Freshwater Logistics.

West, George A. Copper: Its Mining & Use by the Aborigines of the Lake Superior Region. Repr. of 1929 ed. lib. bdg. 15.00 (ISBN 0-8371-4634-8, WECO). Greenwood.

Wolfe, Art, photos by. Indian Baskets of the Northwest Coast. LC 78-51216. (Illus.). 120p. (Text by Allan Lobb). 1978. 19.50 (ISBN 0-912856-37-8); ltd. ed. 30.00 (ISBN 0-912856-44-0). Graphic Arts Ctr.

Wolfson, Evelyn. American Indian Utensils: How to Make Baskets, Pottery, & Woodenware with Natural Materials. (Illus.). 1979. 8.95 (ISBN 0-679-20505-5). McKay.

Young, Stella. Navajo Native Dyes: Their Preparation & Use. LC 76-43671. Repr. of 1940 ed. 11.50 (ISBN 0-404-15504-9). AMS Pr.

INDIANS OF NORTH AMERICA–JUVENILE LITERATURE

see also Indians of North America–Fiction, Juvenile; Indians of North America–Legends–Juvenile Literature;
also Juvenile works, identified by grade key, may be found in other subdivisions

American Indian. (How & Why Wonder Books Ser.). (gr. 4-6). pap. 1.00 (ISBN 0-448-05055-2). Wonder.

Amon, Aline. Talking Hands: Indian Sign Language. LC 68-10123. (gr. 4-7). 1968. 7.95a (ISBN 0-385-08891-4); PLB (ISBN 0-385-09425-6). Doubleday.

Archer, Jules. Indian Foe, Indian Friend. LC 72-93280. (Illus.). (gr. 7-12). 1970. 6.95 (ISBN 0-02-705650-3, CCPr). Macmillan.

Armstrong, Nancy. Navajo Children. (Indian Culture Ser.). (gr. 2-6). 1975. 1.95 (ISBN 0-89992-037-3). MT Coun Indian.

Baker, Betty. Settlers & Strangers: Native Americans of the Desert Southwest & History As They Saw It. LC 77-4925. (Illus.). (gr. 3-6). 1977. 8.95 (ISBN 0-02-708220-2, 70822). Macmillan.

Baldwin, Gordon C. The Apache Indians: Raiders of the Southwest. LC 77-21439. (Illus.). 240p. (gr. 7 up). 1978. 9.95 (ISBN 0-590-07321-4, Four Winds). Schol Bk Serv.

Baylor, Byrd. They Put on Masks. LC 73-19557. (Illus.). 48p. (gr. 1-4). 1974. reinforced bdg. 7.95 (ISBN 0-684-13767-4, ScribJ). Scribner.

--When Clay Sings. LC 70-180758. (Illus.). (gr. 1-5). 1972. reinforced bdg. 8.95 (ISBN 0-684-12807-1, ScribJ). Scribner.

Bealer, Alex. Only the Names Remain: The Cherokees & the Trail of Tears. (gr. 1-3). 1972. 5.95 (ISBN 0-316-08520-0). Little.

Beals, Carleton. Incredible Incas: Yesterday & Today. LC 72-2077. (Illus.). 192p. (gr. 7 up). 1973. 8.95 (ISBN 0-200-71901-7, AbS-J). Har-Row.

Behrens, June & Brower, Pauline. Algonquian Indians: At Summer Camp. LC 76-27351. (Living Heritage Ser.). (Illus.). (gr. k-3). 1977. PLB 9.25 (ISBN 0-516-08706-1, Golden Gate). Childrens.

Bleeker, Sonia. The Apache Indians: Raiders of the Southwest. (Illus.). (gr. 4-7). 1951. PLB 6.48 (ISBN 0-688-31046-X). Morrow.

--The Cherokee: Indians of the Mountains. (Illus.). (gr. 3-6). 1952. PLB 6.67 (ISBN 0-688-31160-1). Morrow.

--The Chippewa Indians: Rice Gatherers of the Great Lakes. (Illus.). (gr. 3-6). 1955. PLB 6.67 (ISBN 0-688-31167-9). Morrow.

--The Delaware Indians: Eastern Fishermen & Farmers. (Illus.). (gr. 3-6). 1953. PLB 6.67 (ISBN 0-688-31230-6). Morrow.

--Indians of the Longhouse. (Illus.). (gr. 3-6). 1950. PLB 6.67 (ISBN 0-688-31453-8). Morrow.

--The Navajo: Herders, Weavers & Silversmiths. (Illus.). (gr. 3-6). 1958. PLB 6.67 (ISBN 0-688-31456-2). Morrow.

--The Pueblo Indians: Farmers of the Rio Grande. (Illus.). (gr. 3-6). 1955. PLB 6.67 (ISBN 0-688-31454-6). Morrow.

--The Sea Hunters: Indians of the Northwestern Coast. (Illus.). (gr. 3-6). 1951. PLB 6.67 (ISBN 0-688-31458-9). Morrow.

--The Sioux Indians: Hunters & Warriors of the Plains. (Illus.). (gr. 3-6). 1962. PLB 6.67 (ISBN 0-688-31457-0). Morrow.

Boesen, Victor & Graybill, Florence C. Edward S. Curtis: Photographer of the North American Indian. LC 76-53435. (gr. 7 up). 1977. 6.95 (ISBN 0-396-07430-8). Dodd.

Boning, Richard A. The Long Search. (The Incredible Ser). (Illus.). 48p. (gr. 5-11). 1972. PLB 5.95 (ISBN 0-87966-103-8, Pub. by Dexter & Westbrook). B Loft.

Boyd, Maurice. Kiowa Voices: Ceremonial Dance, Ritual & Song, Vol. 1. Worcester, Donald, ed. LC 81-50977. (Illus.). 165p. (gr. 3 up). 1981. pap. text ed. 25.00 (ISBN 0-912646-67-5). Tex Christian.
Chenfeld, Mimi B. & Vandervelde, Marjorie. Pow-Wow. (Indian Culture Ser.). (gr. 5-12). 1972. 1.95 (ISBN 0-89992-054-3). MT Coun Indian.
Chief Joseph's Own Story As Told by Chief Joseph in 1879. (Indian Culture Ser.). (gr. 4 up). 1972. 1.95 (ISBN 0-89992-019-5). MT Coun Indian.
Cunningham, Maggi. Little Turtle. LC 77-16764. (Story of an American Indian Ser.). (Illus.). (gr. 5 up). 1978. PLB 6.95 (ISBN 0-87518-158-9). Dillon.
D'Amato, Janet & D'Amato, Alex. Indian Crafts. (Illus.). (gr. 1-4). PLB 7.95 (ISBN 0-87460-088-X). Lion Bks.
Davis, Christopher. Plains Indians. (Illus.). (gr. 5-8). 1978. PLB 7.45 s&l (ISBN 0-531-01429-0). Watts.
Densmore, Frances. Dakota & Ojibwe People in Minnesota. LC 77-72282. (Illus.). 55p. (gr. 7-9). 1977. pap. 3.00 (ISBN 0-87351-111-5). Minn Hist.
Eastman, Charles A. Indian Boyhood. LC 68-58282. (Illus.). (gr. 3-7). pap. 3.50 (ISBN 0-486-22037-0). Dover.
Elting, Mary. The Hopi Way. LC 72-88692. (Two Worlds Bks.). (Illus.). 64p. (gr. 4 up). 1969. 3.95 (ISBN 0-87131-097-X). M Evans.
Ernst, Kathryn F. Indians: The First Americans. LC 78-13742. (Easy-Read Fact Bk.). (Illus.). (gr. 2-4). 1979. PLB 6.90 s&l (ISBN 0-531-02273-0). Watts.
Fichter, George. How the Plains Indians Lived. (gr. 6 up). 1980. 8.95 (ISBN 0-679-20683-3). McKay.
Fichter, George S. American Indian Music & Musical Instruments. (gr. 5-10). 1978. 7.95 (ISBN 0-679-20443-1). McKay.
Fowler, Carol. Daisy Hooee Nampeyo. LC 76-54809. (Story of an American Indian Ser.). (Illus.). (gr. 5 up). 1977. PLB 6.95 (ISBN 0-87518-141-4). Dillon.
Fox, George & Puffer, Lela. Okemos: Story of a Fox Indian in His Youth. (Indian Culture Ser.). (gr. 3-9). 1976. 1.95 (ISBN 0-89992-036-5). Mt Coun Indian.
Gardner, Jeanne L. Mary Jemison: Seneca Captive. LC 66-23287. (Illus.). (gr. 5-7). 1966. 5.50 (ISBN 0-15-252190-9, HJ). HarBraceJ.
Gerber, Will, et al. The Rings on Woot-Kew's Tail: Indian Legends of the Origin of the Sun, Moon & Stars. (Indian Culture Ser.). (gr. 3-9). 1973. 1.95 (ISBN 0-89992-059-4). MT Coun Indian.
Gilliland, Hap. Broken Ice. (Indian Culture Ser.). (gr. 1-8). 1972. 1.95 (ISBN 0-89992-024-1). MT Coun Indian.
--Chant of the Red Man. (Indian Culture Ser.). (Illus.). 1976. 2.95 (ISBN 0-89992-048-9). MT Coun Indian.
--Coyote's Pow-Wow. (Indian Culture Ser.). (gr. 1-6). 1972. 1.95 (ISBN 0-89992-022-5). MT Coun Indian.
--No One Like a Brother. (Indian Culture Ser.). (gr. 4-12). 1970. 1.95 (ISBN 0-89992-003-9). MT Coun Indian.
Glubok, Shirley. Art of the North American Indian. LC 64-11829. (Illus.). (gr. 2-6). 1964. PLB 8.79 (ISBN 0-06-022066-X, HarpJ). Har-Row.
--The Art of the Plains Indians. LC 75-14064. (Illus.). 48p. (gr. 4 up). 1975. 9.95 (ISBN 0-02-736360-0, 73636). Macmillan.
--The Art of the Southwest Indians. LC 78-133558. (Art of Ser). (Illus.). (gr. 4 up). 1971. 9.95 (ISBN 0-02-736120-9). Macmillan.
Gorsline, Marie & Gorsline, Douglas. North American Indians. LC 77-79843. (Picturebacks Ser.). (ps-2). 1978. PLB 4.99 (ISBN 0-394-93702-3, BYR); pap. 1.25 (ISBN 0-394-83702-9). Random.
Gridley, Marion. Indian Tribes of America. LC 76-24843. (Illus.). 1973. Repr. of 1940 ed. 4.95 (ISBN 0-528-82810-X). Rand.
Guidetti, Geri. A Seneca Garden. (Illus.). 26p. (Orig.). (gr. 2-8). 1981. pap. 3.95 (ISBN 0-938928-00-7). KMG Pubns OR.
Harrell, Sara G. Tomo-Chi-Chi. LC 77-8936. (Story of an American Indian Ser.). (Illus.). (gr. 5 up). 1977. PLB 6.95 (ISBN 0-87518-146-5). Dillon.
Hathaway, Flora. Old Man Coyote. (Indian Culture Ser.). (gr. 2-9). 1970. 1.95 (ISBN 0-89992-008-X). MT Coun Indian.
Hatheway, Flora. The Little People. (Indian Culture Ser.). (gr. 2-9). 1971. 1.95 (ISBN 0-89992-034-9). MT Coun Indian.
Heath, Monroe. Our American Indians. (Illus., Orig.). (gr. 9-12). 1961. pap. 1.95 (ISBN 0-685-52802-2). Pacific Coast.
Henry Tall Bull & Weist, Tom. Cheyenne Legends of Creation. (Indian Culture Ser.). (gr. 4-9). 1972. 1.95 (ISBN 0-89992-025-X). MT Coun Indian.
--Cheyenne Warriors. (Indian Culture Ser.). (gr. 4-12). 1976. pap. 1.95 (ISBN 0-89992-015-2). MT Coun Indian.
--Grandfather & the Popping Machine. (Indian Culture Ser.). (gr. 2-12). 1970. 1.95 (ISBN 0-89992-004-7). MT Coun Indian.
--Mista. (Indian Culture Ser.). (gr. 2-12). 1971. 1.95 (ISBN 0-89992-011-X). MT Coun Indian.
--The Spotted Horse. (Indian Culture Ser.). (gr. 2-10). 1970. 1.95 (ISBN 0-89992-002-0). MT Coun Indian.
--Veho. (Indian Culture Ser.). (gr. 2-6). 1971. 1.95 (ISBN 0-89992-007-1). MT Coun Indian.
--The Winter Hunt. (Indian Culture Ser.). (gr. 3-9). 1971. 1.95 (ISBN 0-89992-006-3). MT Coun Indian.
Hildreth, Dolly, et al. The Money God. (Indian Culture Ser.). (gr. 6). 1972. 1.95 (ISBN 0-89992-031-4). MT Coun Indian.
Hodgson, Pat. Growing up with the North American Indians. (Illus.). 72p. (gr. 6-10). 1980. 14.95 (ISBN 0-7134-2732-9, Pub. by Batsford England). David & Charles.
Hoffman, Virginia. Lucy Learns to Weave: Gathering Plants. LC 74-4894. (Illus.). 46p. (gr. 1-4). 1974. pap. 2.75 (ISBN 0-89019-009-7). Navajo Curr.
Hofsinde, Robert. The Indian & His Horse. (Illus.). (gr. 3-7). 1960. PLB 6.48 (ISBN 0-688-31421-X). Morrow.
--The Indian & the Buffalo. (Illus.). (gr. 3-7). 1961. PLB 6.67 (ISBN 0-688-31420-1). Morrow.
--Indian Beadwork. (Illus.). (gr. 5-9). 1958. PLB 6.48 (ISBN 0-688-31575-5). Morrow.
--Indian Fishing & Camping. (Illus.). (gr. 4-7). 1963. PLB 6.48 (ISBN 0-688-31797-9). Morrow.
--Indian Games & Crafts. (Illus.). (gr. 5-9). 1957. PLB 6.67 (ISBN 0-688-31607-7). Morrow.
--Indians at Home. (Illus.). (gr. 3-7). 1964. PLB 6.48 (ISBN 0-688-31611-5). Morrow.
--Indians on the Move. (Illus.). (gr. 3-7). 1970. PLB 6.48 (ISBN 0-688-31615-8). Morrow.
Hoyt, Olga. American Indians Today. LC 79-141865. (Illus.). (gr. 7 up). 1972. 8.95 (ISBN 0-200-71891-6, B02660, AbS-J). Har-Row.
Indian Canoeing. (Indian Culture Ser.). (Illus.). (gr. 6-12). 1976. 1.95 (ISBN 0-686-22273-3). MT Coun Indian.
Johnson, Gail E. Phantom Horse of Collister's Fields. (Indian Culture Ser.). (gr. 4-12). 1974. 1.95 (ISBN 0-89992-062-4). MT Coun Indian.
Jones, Jayne C. The American Indian in America, Vol. 2. LC 73-13378. (In America Bks). (Illus.). 96p. (gr. 5-11). 1973. PLB 6.95g (ISBN 0-8225-0227-5). Lerner Pubns.
--The American Indian in America, Vol.1. LC 72-3591. (In America Bks). (Illus.). 104p. (gr. 5-11). 1973. PLB 6.95g (ISBN 0-8225-0224-0). Lerner Pubns.
Katz, Jane B., ed. We Rode the Wind: Recollections of 19th-Century Tribal Life. LC 74-11909. (Voices of the American Indian Ser.). (Illus.). 112p. (gr. 7 up). 1975. PLB 6.95 (ISBN 0-8225-0639-4). Lerner Pubns.
Kirk, Ruth. David, Young Chief of the Quileutes: An American Indian Today. LC 67-10206. (Illus.). (gr. 3-5). 1967. 5.95 (ISBN 0-15-222498-X, HJ). HarBraceJ.
Kloss, Doris. Sarah Winnemucca. LC 81-390. (Story of an American Indian Ser.). (Illus.). (gr. 5 up). 1981. PLB 6.95 (ISBN 0-87518-178-3). Dillon.
Lagerquist, Syble. Philip Johnston & the Navajo Code Talkers. (Indian Culture Ser.). (gr. 4-12). 1975. 1.95 (ISBN 0-89992-038-1). MT Coun Indian.
Lavine, Sigmund A. The Ghosts the Indians Feared. LC 75-11441. (Illus.). 64p. (gr. 5 up). 1975. 5.95 (ISBN 0-396-07194-5). Dodd.
Layman, Paul E. Seal for a Pal. (Indian Culture Ser.). (gr. 4-9). 1972. 1.95 (ISBN 0-89992-029-2). MT Coun Indian.
Lyon, Nancy. Totem Poles & Tribes. LC 77-23748. (Myth, Magic & Superstition Ser.). (Illus.). (gr. 4-5). 1977. PLB 10.65 (ISBN 0-8172-1044-X). Raintree Pubs.
McDonald, W. H. Creation Tales from the Salish. (Indian Culture Ser.). (gr. 3-9). 1973. 1.95 (ISBN 0-89992-061-6). MT Coun Indian.
McGaw, Jessie B. Chief Red Horse Tells About Custer. (Illus.). 64p. (gr. 4 up). 1981. 9.25 (ISBN 0-525-66713-X, 0898-270). Elsevier-Nelson.
McGovern, Ann. If You Lived with the Sioux Indians. LC 74-7327. (Illus.). 96p. (gr. 2-4). 1974. 5.95 (ISBN 0-590-07340-0, Four Winds). Schol Bk Serv.
--If You Lived with the Sioux Indians. (gr. k-3). 1976. pap. 1.25 (ISBN 0-590-04533-4). Schol Bk Serv.
McKeown, Martha F. Come to Our Salmon Feast. LC 59-9823. (Illus.). (gr. 4-9). 1959. 5.95 (ISBN 0-8323-0157-4). Binford.
--Linda's Indian Home. LC 56-8826. (Illus.). (gr. 3-7). 1969. 5.95 (ISBN 0-8323-0151-5). Binford.
Marsh, Jessie. Chinook. (Indian Culture Ser.). 32p. (ps-9). 1976. 1.95 (ISBN 0-89992-041-1). MT Coun Indian.
Nabokov, Peter, ed. Native American Testimony: An Anthology of Indian & White Relations. First Encounter to Dispossession. LC 77-11558. (Illus.). (gr. 7 up). 1978 (ISBN 0-690-01313-2, TYC-J). PLB 8.79 (ISBN 0-690-03840-2). Har-Row.
Nearing, Penny, et al. Big Enough. (Indian Culture Ser.). (gr. 2-5). 1974. 1.95 (ISBN 0-89992-070-5). MT Coun Indian.
Parish, Peggy. Let's Be Indians. LC 62-13314. (Illus.). (gr. 1-5). 1962. PLB 8.79 (ISBN 0-06-024651-0, HarpJ). Har-Row.
Payne, Elizabeth. Meet the North American Indians. (Step-up Books Ser). (Illus.). (gr. 2-6). 1965. 3.95 (ISBN 0-394-80060-5, BYR). Random.
Pine, Tillie S. & Levine, Joseph. Indians Knew. (Illus.). (gr. 1-4). 1957. PLB 7.95 (ISBN 0-07-050031-2, GB). McGraw.
Poatgieter, Hermina. Indian Legacy: Native American Influences on World Life & Culture. (Illus.). 192p. (gr. 7 up). 1981. PLB 10.79 (ISBN 0-671-41703-7). Messner.
Pollock, Dean. Joseph, Chief of the Nez Perce. (Illus.). (gr. 5 up). 1950. 5.95 (ISBN 0-8323-0172-8). Binford.
Rachlis, Eugene & Ewers, John C. Indians of the Plains. LC 60-6402. (American Heritage Junior Library). (Illus.). 153p. (gr. 5 up). 1960. 9.95 (ISBN 0-8281-0385-2, J001-0). Am Heritage.
Ruppel, Maxine. Vostaas: The Story of Montana's Indian Nations. (Indian Culture Ser.). (gr. 3-11). 1970. 2.00 (ISBN 0-89992-001-2). MT Coun Indian.
Sandoz, Mari. These Were the Sioux. (gr. k-8). 1971. pap. 0.95 (ISBN 0-440-48792-7, YB). Dell.
Shields, Allan. Tragedy of Tenaya. (Indian Culture Ser.). (gr. 6). 1974. 2.00 (ISBN 0-89992-043-8). MT Coun Indian.
Showers, Paul. Indian Festivals. LC 70-78266. (Holiday Ser.). (Illus.). (gr. k-3). 1969. (TYC-J); PLB 7.89 (ISBN 0-690-43698-X). Har-Row.
Siegel, Beatrice. Fur Trappers & Traders: The Indians, the Pilgrims, & the Beaver. LC 80-7671. (Illus.). 64p. (gr. 3-7). 1981. 8.50 (ISBN 0-8027-6396-0); PLB 8.85 (ISBN 0-8027-6397-9). Walker & Co.
Skold, Betty W. Sacagawea. LC 76-30613. (Story of an American Indian Ser.). (Illus.). (gr. 5 up). 1977. PLB 6.95 (ISBN 0-87518-095-7). Dillon.
Skolnick, Emanuel. Alford Waters. LC 80-17192. (The Story of an American Indian Ser.). (Illus.). 64p. (gr. 5 up). 1980. PLB 6.95 (ISBN 0-87518-201-1). Dillon.
Spizzirri Publishing Co. Staff. Plains Indians: An Educational Coloring Book. Spizzirri, Linda, ed. (Illus.). 32p. (gr. 1-8). 1981. pap. 1.25 (ISBN 0-86545-025-0). Spizzirri.
Stanley, Samuel & Oberg, Pearl. The Hunt. (Indian Culture Ser.). 32p. (gr. 5-9). 1976. 1.95 (ISBN 0-89992-047-0). MT Coun Indian.
Steele, William O. Talking Bones: Secrets of Indian Mound Builders. LC 76-58687. (Illus.). (gr. 2-5). 1978. 8.95 (ISBN 0-06-025768-7, HarpJ); PLB 8.79 (ISBN 0-06-025769-5). Har-Row.
--Westward Adventure: The True Stories of Six Pioneers. LC 62-9479. (Illus.). (gr. 4-6). 1962. 5.95 (ISBN 0-15-294999-2, HJ). HarBraceJ.
Stember, Sol. Heroes of the American Indian. LC 70-100088. (Heroes of Ser). (Illus.). (gr. 8-10). 1971. 6.95 (ISBN 0-8303-0090-2). Fleet.
Summers, Thomas O. Joseph Brown: Or, the Young Tennessean Whose Life Was Saved by the Power of Prayer. an Indian Tale. Bd. with Narrative of a Captivity Among the Mohawk Indians, & a Description of New Netherland in 1642-3. Jogues, Isaac. LC 75-7091. (Indian Captivities Ser.: Vol. 67). Repr. of 1856 ed. lib. bdg. 44.00 (ISBN 0-8240-1691-2). Garland Pub.
Supree, Burton & Ross, Ann. Bear's Heart: Scenes from the Life of a Cheyenne Artist of One Hundred Years Ago with Pictures by Himself. LC 76-48952. 1977. 8.95 (ISBN 0-397-31746-8). Lippincott.
Tamarin, Alfred & Glubok, Shirley. Ancient Indians of the Southwest. LC 74-33984. 96p. (gr. 4-7). 1975. 7.95 (ISBN 0-385-09247-4); PLB (ISBN 0-385-09252-0). Doubleday.
Throssel, Richard. Blue Thunder. (Indian Culture Ser.). 32p. (gr. 6-12). 1976. 1.95 (ISBN 0-89992-046-2). MT Coun Indian.
Tunis, Edwin. Indians. rev. ed. LC 78-60175. (Illus.). (gr. 5 up). 1979. Repr. of 1959 ed. 14.95 (ISBN 0-690-03806-2, TYC-J); PLB 13.89 (ISBN 0-690-01283-7). Har-Row.
Vandervelde, Marjorie. Across the Tundra. (Indian Culture Ser.). (gr. 4-12). 1972. 1.95 (ISBN 0-89992-053-5). MT Coun Indian.
--Sam & the Golden People. (Indian Culture Ser.). (gr. 4-9). 1972. 1.95 (ISBN 0-89992-027-6). MT Coun Indian.
Voight, Virginia. Massasoit: Friend of the Pilgrims. LC 76-133552. (Indians Ser). (Illus.). (gr. 2-5). 1971. PLB 6.09 (ISBN 0-8116-6609-3). Garrard.
Warren, Elizabeth. I Can Read About Indians. LC 74-24880. (Illus.). (gr. 2-4). 1975. pap. 1.25 (ISBN 0-89375-061-1). Troll Assocs.
Wayne, Bennett, ed. Indian Patriots of the Eastern Woodlands. LC 75-20048. (Target Ser). (Illus.). 168p. (gr. 5-12). 1976. PLB 7.29 (ISBN 0-8116-4916-4). Garrard.
Whitney, Alex. Sports and Games the Indians Gave Us. (gr. 7 up). 1977. 7.95 (ISBN 0-679-20391-5). McKay.
Witt, Shirley H. The Tuscaroras. LC 75-189730. (Illus.). (gr. 5up). 1972. 6.95 (ISBN 0-02-793270-2, CCPr). Macmillan.
Wolfson. American Indian Tools & Ornaments. 1981. 8.95 (ISBN 0-679-20509-8). McKay.
Wood, J. Walter. Son of the Dine' (Indian Culture Ser.). (gr. 5-9). 1972. 1.95 (ISBN 0-89992-023-3). MT Coun Indian.
Wood, Nancy. When Buffalo Free the Mountains. LC 76-42412. (Illus.). 256p. (gr. 10-12). 1980. 14.95 (ISBN 0-385-01474-0). Doubleday.
Woolgar, Jack & Rudnicki, Barbara J. Hopi Mysteries. (Indian Culture Ser.). (gr. 5-9). 1974. 1.95 (ISBN 0-89992-060-8). MT Coun Indian.

INDIANS OF NORTH AMERICA–LAND TENURE

Appraisal Associates. Kiowa, Comanche & Apache Lands in Oklahoma & Texas: Valuation Study As of 1900. 1976. lib. bdg. 250.00x (ISBN 0-8287-1093-7). Clearwater Pub.
--Omaha Tribe of Indians: Valuation Study of the Area Ceded, 1854. 1660p. 1973. lib. bdg. 450.00 (ISBN 0-8287-1156-9). Clearwater Pub.
Appraisal Associates & Davis, W. D. Minnesota Chippewa Tribe: Valuation of Ceded Lands As of 1855 & 1867. (Library of American Indian Affairs). 225p. 1973. lib. bdg. 94.00 (ISBN 0-8287-1128-3). Clearwater Pub.
Arkeson, Harry E. Appraisal of a Tract of Land in Lyman County, South Dakota. (Library of American Indian Affairs). 132p. 1973. lib. bdg. 44.00 (ISBN 0-8287-0918-1). Clearwater Pub.
Armer, Walter D. Gila River Reservation in Arizona, 1936-1961: Appraisal. (Library of American Indian Affairs). 105p. 1973. lib. bdg. 36.00 (ISBN 0-8287-1050-3). Clearwater Pub.
Aschmann, Homer. Northern Tonto Claim Area: Environment & Ecology. (Library of American Indian Affairs). 54p. 1973. lib. bdg. 21.00 (ISBN 0-8287-1151-8). Clearwater Pub.
--The Western Apache Range: Terrain & Ecological Conditions. (Library of American Indian Affairs). 54p. 1973. lib. bdg. 21.00 (ISBN 0-8287-1300-6). Clearwater Pub.
Baerreis, David A., et al. Anthropological Report on Indian Occupancy of That Portion of Royce Area 148 East of the Fox River in Illinois. (Library of American Indian Affairs). 190p. 1973. lib. bdg. 72.00 (ISBN 0-8287-0904-1). Clearwater Pub.
Bailey, M. Thomas. Reconstruction in Indian Territory. LC 77-189551. 1972. 13.50 (ISBN 0-8046-9022-7). Kennikat.
Barlowe, Raleigh. Sac & Fox Lands: Appraisal of Portions in Royce Area 50 in Wisconsin, Illinois & Missouri, 1805. (Library of American Indian Affairs). 70p. 1974. lib. bdg. 28.50 (ISBN 0-8287-1218-2). Clearwater Pub.
--Spanish Land Grants in Royce's Cession 50 in Missouri. (Library of American Indian Affairs). 110p. 1973. lib. bdg. 37.50 (ISBN 0-8287-1265-4). Clearwater Pub.
Barlowe, Raleigh & Hammar, Conrad H. Sac, Fox & Iowa Tribes: Valuation of Lands in Eastern Iowa, Royce Areas 175, 226, & 244, 1833-1839. (Library of American Indian Affairs). 243p. 1973. lib. bdg. 73.50 (ISBN 0-8287-1225-5). Clearwater Pub.
--Valuation of Lands in Southcentral Iowa, 1839-1843: Royce Cession Area 262. (Library of American Indian Affairs). 195p. 1973. lib. bdg. 58.50 (ISBN 0-8287-1287-5). Clearwater Pub.
Barreis, David A., et al. The Mascoutens: An Anthropological Report. (Library of American Indian Affairs). 96p. 1973. lib. bdg. 33.00 (ISBN 0-685-32063-4). Clearwater Pub.
Barton, et al. Nez Perce Indian Reservation: Report on Possibility or Impossibility of Determining Gold Removed, to 1867. (Library of American Indian Affairs). 105p. 1973. lib. bdg. 36.00 (ISBN 0-8287-1141-0). Clearwater Pub.
Barton, Stoddard & Milhollin Co, et al. Nez Perce Indian Reservation: Report of Gold Production, 1860-1866. (Library of American Indian Affairs). 70p. 1973. lib. bdg. 25.50 (ISBN 0-8287-1140-2). Clearwater Pub.
Barton, Stoddard & Milhollin, Consulting Engineers. Cheyenne-Arapaho Indian Lands: Mineral Evaluation Covering Parts of Colorado, Kansas, Nebraska, & Wyoming. (Library of American Indian Affairs). 140p. 1973. lib. bdg. 45.00 (ISBN 0-8287-0984-X). Clearwater Pub.

Bell, Robert, et al, eds. Wichita Indian Archeology & Ethnohistory: A Pilot Study. (Library of American Indian Affairs). 340p. 1973. lib. bdg. 97.50 (ISBN 0-8287-1305-7). Clearwater Pub.

Bender, Averam B. Jicarilla Apache Indians, 1848-1887. (Library of American Indian Affairs). 185p. 1973. lib. bdg. 57.00 (ISBN 0-8287-1078-3). Clearwater Pub.

Bernstein, Marvin D. Indian Rights to the Subsoil Under Spanish & Mexican Law, 1387-1783. 34.00 (ISBN 0-8287-1068-6). Clearwater Pub.

Berthrong, Donald J. Miami, Wea & Potawatomi: Historical Report on Indian Use & Occupancy of Royce Areas 132, 133, 145, 146, 180 & 181 in Northern Indiana & Southwestern Michigan. (Library of American Indian Affairs). 330p. 1973. lib. bdg. 94.50 (ISBN 0-8287-1123-2). Clearwater Pub.

Bledsoe, Samuel T. Indian Land Laws. Bruchey, Stuart, ed. LC 78-53557. (Development of Public Land Law in the U. S. Ser.). 1979. Repr. of 1909 ed. lib. bdg. 41.00x (ISBN 0-405-11369-2). Arno.

Booth, Ernest G. Creek Nation Lands in Alabama: Land Appraisal As of 1832. (Library of American Indian Affairs). 1976. lib. bdg. 45.00x (ISBN 0-8287-1024-4). Clearwater Pub.

Brady, H. C. Osage Ceded Lands, 1865: Appraisal. (Library of American Indian Affairs). 120p. 1973. lib. bdg. 52.00 (ISBN 0-8287-1160-7). Clearwater Pub.

Brayer, Herbert O. Pueblo Indian Land Grants of the "Rio Abajo", New Mexico. Bruchey, Stuart, ed. LC 78-56700. (Management of Public Lands in the U. S. Ser.). 1979. Repr. of 1938 ed. lib. bdg. 10.00x (ISBN 0-405-11320-X). Arno.

Broughton, W. A. Evaluation of the Mineral Lands in Indian Cession 175 of Eastern Iowa. (Library of American Indian Affairs). 58p. 1973. lib. bdg. 22.50 (ISBN 0-8287-1038-4). Clearwater Pub.

Brown, William C. Nez Perce Reservation Land: Appraisal. (Library of American Indian Affairs). 402p. 1973. lib. bdg. 114.00 (ISBN 0-8287-1143-7). Clearwater Pub.

Brunger, Eric, et al. Big Tree Cession: Historical Land Valuation. (Library of American Indian Affairs). 118p. 1973. lib. bdg. 39.00 (ISBN 0-8287-0954-8). Clearwater Pub.

Caddo Indian Tract Situated in Southwestern Arkansas & Northwestern Louisiana, 1835: Appraisal. (Library of American Indian Affairs). 175p. 1973. lib. bdg. 54.00 (ISBN 0-8287-0960-2). Clearwater Pub.

Carlson, Leonard A. Indians, Bureaucrats, & Land: The Dawes Act & the Decline of Indian Farming. LC 80-1709. (Contributions in Economics & Economic History Ser.: No. 36). xii, 219p. 1981. lib. bdg. 29.95 (ISBN 0-313-22533-8, CDA/). Greenwood.

Chalfant, Stuart A. Aboriginal Territory of the Nez Perce Indians. (Library of American Indian Affairs). 135p. 1973. lib. bdg. 43.50 (ISBN 0-8287-0891-6). Clearwater Pub.

--Columbia Salish of Central Washington: Aboriginal Land-Use & Occupancy. (Library of American Indian Affairs). 78p. 1973. lib. bdg. 29.00 (ISBN 0-8287-1009-0). Clearwater Pub.

Chamberlin, J. E. The Harrowing of Eden: White Attitudes Toward Native Americans. LC 75-9941. 1975. 8.95 (ISBN 0-8164-9251-4). Continuum.

Chapman, Carl H. Aboriginal Use & Occupancy of Lands West of the Mississippi River by the Osage Indian Tribe: Village Locations & Hunting Territories up to 1808. (Library of American Indian Affairs). 70p. 1973. lib. bdg. 26.00 (ISBN 0-8287-0892-4). Clearwater Pub.

--The Osage Indian Tribe: An Ethnographical, Historical & Archaeological Study. (Library of American Indian Affairs). 315p. 1973. lib. bdg. 91.50 (ISBN 0-8287-1161-5). Clearwater Pub.

The Cherokee Band of Indians: Anthropological Report on the Indian Occupancy of Royce Area 79, Ceded on September 14, 1816. (Library of American Indian Affairs). 246p. 1973. lib. bdg. 74.00 (ISBN 0-8287-0972-6). Clearwater Pub.

Chihsolm, Roger K. Piankeshaw Lands in Royce Area 63, Land Values As of 1805. (Library of American Indian Affairs). 110p. 1973. lib. bdg. 37.50 (ISBN 0-8287-1196-8). Clearwater Pub.

Chiricahua Apache Tribe: Appraisal of Mineral Resources in the Lands, 4 vols. (Library of American Indian Affairs). 1782p. 1973. lib. bdg. 480.00 (ISBN 0-8287-1003-1). Clearwater Pub.

Chisholm, Roger K. Chippewa, Ottawa & Potawatomie Lands in Illinois & Wisconsin: Valuation As of 1835. (Library of American Indian Affairs). 1976. lib. bdg. 67.00x (ISBN 0-8287-0996-3). Clearwater Pub.

--Kickapoo & Wea Lands in Royce Areas 73 & 74 in Illinois & Indiana, 1809, 1818: Valuation. 140p. 1973. lib. bdg. 45.00 (ISBN 0-8287-1086-4). Clearwater Pub.

--Peoria of Oklahoma: Value of Land in Royce Area 49. (Library of American Indian Affairs). 148p. 1974. lib. bdg. 47.40 (ISBN 0-8287-1189-5). Clearwater Pub.

--The Peoria Tribe & Kaskasia Nation: An Appraisal of Lands in Illinois, 1803 to 1820. (Library of American Indian Affairs). lib. bdg. 95.00x (ISBN 0-8287-1190-9). Clearwater Pub.

Christensen, Mervin J. & Hill, R. G. The Mohave Tribe in Arizona: An Appraisal of Land Values from 1942 to 1952 & 1940 to 1953. Ross, Norman A., ed. (Library of American Indian Affairs). 1976. lib. bdg. 50.00x (ISBN 0-8287-1131-3). Clearwater Pub.

Cline, Howard F. Provisional Historical Gazeteer with Locational Notes on Florida Colonial Communities, 1700-1823. (Library of American Indian Affairs). 240p. 1973. lib. bdg. 72.00 (ISBN 0-8287-1400-2). Clearwater Pub.

--Spanish & Mexican Land Grants in New Mexico, 1689-1848. (Library of American Indian Affairs). 325p. 1973. lib. bdg. 93.00 (ISBN 0-8287-1263-8). Clearwater Pub.

Confederated Salish & Kootenai Tribe of the Flathead Reservation: A History. (Library of American Indian Affairs). 1976. lib. bdg. 27.00x (ISBN 0-8287-1015-5). Clearwater Pub.

Coulter, John L. Potawatomi Tribe of Indians: Natural Resource, Agricultural & Economic Survey from 1795-1846 of Certain Lands Ceded by the Prairie Band. (Library of American Indian Affairs). 96p. 1973. lib. bdg. 46.00 (ISBN 0-8287-1205-0). Clearwater Pub.

--Value of Farmland & Improvements & Other Natural Resources in Iowa & Kansas, 1840-1850. (Library of American Indian Affairs). 70p. 1973. 25.50 (ISBN 0-8287-1291-3). Clearwater Pub.

Cutter, Donald C. Jicarilla Apache Area of Northeastern New Mexico: Inquiry into Indian Rights in the American Southwest Under Spain, Mexico & the United States. (Library of American Indian Affairs). 35p. 1974. lib. bdg. 21.00 (ISBN 0-8287-1074-0). Clearwater Pub.

Davis, W. D. Red Lake & Pembina Bands of Chippewa Indians: Valuation Study of the Red River Valley of the North Area in North Dakota & Minnesota Ceded October 3, 1863. (Library of American Indian Affairs). 410p. 1973. lib. bdg. 147.00 (ISBN 0-8287-1211-5). Clearwater Pub.

Diddock, Joseph L. Gila River Reservation Leased Land in Arizona, 1916-1937: Historical Report. (Library of American Indian Affairs). 29p. 1973. lib. bdg. 18.00 (ISBN 0-8287-1051-1). Clearwater Pub.

Doane Agricultural Service. Potawatomie Reserve Lands in Kansas, Sold by the Prairie Band, Potawatomie Indians to the Santa Fe Railroad, 1868: Appraisal. (Library of American Indian Affairs). 37p. 1973. lib. bdg. 32.00 (ISBN 0-8287-1207-7). Clearwater Pub.

Dobyns, Henry F. Yuman Complex: Prehistoric Indian Occupation Within the Eastern Area of the Yuman Complex: a Study in Applied Archaeoology, 3 vols. (Library of American Indian Affairs). 700p. 1973. lib. bdg. 130.00 (ISBN 0-8287-1322-7). Clearwater Pub.

Doster, James F. Alabama: Historical Report on the Sale of Public Lands, 1806-1820. (Library of American Indian Affairs). 36p. 1974. lib. bdg. 21.00 (ISBN 0-8287-0900-9). Clearwater Pub.

Draper, Leroy D. Chinook Tribe & Bands Tribal Islands, Eighteen Fifty-One: Appraisal. (Library of American Indian Affairs). 180p. 1973. lib. bdg. 56.00 (ISBN 0-8287-0989-0). Clearwater Pub.

--Tillamook Band of Tillamooks & Nehalem Band of Tillamooks Tribal Lands: Appraisal. (Library of American Indian Affairs). 338p. 1973. lib. bdg. 97.50 (ISBN 0-8287-1275-1). Clearwater Pub.

Duck, Berkley W. Appraisal Report on a Tract of Ground Located in Central Indiana & Extending Eastward into Ohio. (Library of American Indian Affairs). 179p. 1974. lib. bdg. 55.00 (ISBN 0-8287-0949-1). Clearwater Pub.

Dunham, Harold H. Mexican & Pueblo Indians in New Mexico: Land Occupation & Use. 59.00 (ISBN 0-8287-1119-4). Clearwater Pub.

--Spanish & Mexican Land Policies & Grants in the Taos Pueblo Region, New Mexico. (Library of American Indian Affairs). 157p. 1973. lib. bdg. 50.00 (ISBN 0-8287-1264-6). Clearwater Pub.

--Taos Indians' Pueblo Land Grant: Historical Study of the Land Use Prior to 1848. (Library of American Indian Affairs). 29p. 1973. lib. bdg. 17.25 (ISBN 0-8287-1268-9). Clearwater Pub.

Edgemon, William S. Seminole Nation: Appraisal of Tracts of Land Ceded in 1823 & 1832. (Library of American Indian Affairs). 140p. 1973. lib. bdg. 45.00 (ISBN 0-8287-1239-5). Clearwater Pub.

Ellis, Florence H. Acoma-Laguna Land Claims. 318p. 1973. lib. bdg. 91.50 (ISBN 0-8287-0894-0). Clearwater Pub.

--The Hopi: Their History & Use of Lands in New Mexico & Arizona, 1200's to 1900's. (Library of American Indian Affairs). 250p. 1973. lib. bdg. 75.00 (ISBN 0-8287-1601-3). Clearwater Pub.

--Laguna Pueblo Land Claims: Anthropology. (Library of American Indian Affairs). 106p. 1973. lib. bdg. 36.00 (ISBN 0-8287-1103-8). Clearwater Pub.

--Nambe Pueblos: Anthropological Data Pertaining to Land Claims. (Library of American Indian Affairs). (Illus.). 1976. lib. bdg. 50.00x (ISBN 0-8287-1134-8). Clearwater Pub.

--The Navajo Indians: An Anthropoligical Study. (Library of American Indian Affairs). 1976. lib. bdg. 125.00x (ISBN 0-8287-1137-2). Clearwater Pub.

--The Pueblos of Zia, Santa Ana & Jemez: Anthropological Evidence in Support of Land Calims. (Library of American Indian Affairs). 1976. lib. bdg. 30.00x (ISBN 0-8287-1209-3). Clearwater Pub.

--Taos Land Claim: Anthropological Data. (Library of American Indian Affairs). 115p. 1973. lib. bdg. 39.00 (ISBN 0-8287-1269-7). Clearwater Pub.

Elmquist, Gordon E. Appraisal of the Lands of the Bay Mills Indian Community. (Library of American Indian Affairs). 90p. 1973. lib. bdg. 31.50 (ISBN 0-8287-0931-9). Clearwater Pub.

--Appraisal of the Lands of the Lower Sioux Community in Minnesota. (Library of American Indian Affairs). 142p. 1974. lib. bdg. 46.00 (ISBN 0-8287-0936-X). Clearwater Pub.

--Saginaw Chippewa: Appraisal of Lands Located in the Lower Peninsula, East Central Michigan, Royce Area No. 111, 1820. (Library of American Indian Affairs). 190p. 1973. lib. bdg. 57.00 (ISBN 0-8287-1227-1). Clearwater Pub.

--Three Affiliated Tribes of the Fort Berthold Reservation: Appraisal of Lands. (Library of American Indian Affairs). 210p. 1973. lib. bdg. 64.50 (ISBN 0-8287-1271-9). Clearwater Pub.

Englehorn, Vern A. Appraisal of Nooksack Tract, Washington, 1859. (Library of American Indian Affairs). 350p. 1973. lib. bdg. 100.00 (ISBN 0-8287-0923-8). Clearwater Pub.

--Appraisal of the Muckleshoot Tract, Washington, 1859. (Library of American Indian Affairs). 360p. 1973. lib. bdg. 102.00 (ISBN 0-8287-0939-4). Clearwater Pub.

--Appraisal Report on Brunot Land, Wyoming, Sold by Shoshone Tribe. (Library of American Indian Affairs). 199p. 1974. lib. bdg. 60.00 (ISBN 0-8287-0950-5). Clearwater Pub.

Ewers, John C. Blackfeet & Gros Ventre Tribes of Indians, Lands in Northern Montana, 1888. (Library of American Indian Affairs). 180p. 1973. lib. bdg. 55.50 (ISBN 0-8287-0957-2). Clearwater Pub.

--Chippewa Cree Tribe of Rocky Boy, Montana, & the Little Band of Indians, 1888. (Library of American Indian Affairs). 170p. 1973. lib. bdg. 52.50 (ISBN 0-8287-0990-4). Clearwater Pub.

Fairbanks, Charles H. The Florida Indians. (Library of American Indian Affairs). 286p. 1973. lib. bdg. 84.00 (ISBN 0-8287-1041-4). Clearwater Pub.

--The Seminolee Nation: An Ethno-Historical Report of the Florida Indians As of 1823. (Library of American Indian Affairs). 1976. lib. bdg. 84.00x (ISBN 0-8287-1241-7). Clearwater Pub.

Faust, Josef & Hassler, John J. Creek Nation Lands in Oklahoma: Appraisal of Oil, Gas, Coal & Minerals. (Library of American Indian Affairs). 1976. lib. bdg. 225.00x (ISBN 0-8287-1025-2). Clearwater Pub.

Faust, Josef & Lee, Martin P. Seminole Lands: Mineral Interests in Oklahoma. (Library of American Indian Affairs). 184p. 1973. lib. bdg. 57.00 (ISBN 0-8287-1238-7). Clearwater Pub.

Fenenga, Franklin & Champe, John L. The Pawnee in Oklahoma: Anthropology Notes. (Library of American Indian Affairs). 129p. 1973. lib. bdg. 56.00 (ISBN 0-8287-1187-9). Clearwater Pub.

Fenton, Harry R. Appraisal of the Black Hills Area of South Dakota, 1877. (Library of American Indian Affairs). 190p. 1973. lib. bdg. 57.00 (ISBN 0-8287-0926-2). Clearwater Pub.

--Confederated Salish & Kootenai Tribes, Appraisal of the Lands in Montana, 1859. (Library of American Indian Affairs). 175p. 1973. lib. bdg. 54.00 (ISBN 0-8287-1013-9). Clearwater Pub.

Fenton, Harry R. & Fenton, Everett W. Kickapoo Tribal Lands in Illinois & Indiana: An Appraisal As of 1820. (Library of American Indian Affairs). 1976. lib. bdg. 225.00x (ISBN 0-8287-1091-0). Clearwater Pub.

Foley, Michael F. Yankton Tribal Lands: An Historical Analysis of the Opening & Development from 1849 to 1869. (Library of American Indian Affairs). 1976. lib. bdg. 75.00x (ISBN 0-8287-1315-4). Clearwater Pub.

Fontana, Bernard L. The Papago Tribe of Arizona: Anthropological Report. (Library of American Indian Affairs). 70p. 1973. lib. bdg. 25.50 (ISBN 0-8287-1183-6). Clearwater Pub.

Fox, Ida. Potawatomi Kansas Cession, Royce Area 266: Government Sales of Lands. (Library of American Indian Affairs). 38p. 1973. lib. bdg. 20.00 (ISBN 0-8287-1201-8). Clearwater Pub.

Full, Roy P. Appraisal of the Mineral Resources in the Lands of the Confederated Tribes of the Goshute Reservation. (Library of American Indian Affairs). 1572p. 1973. lib. bdg. 420.00 (ISBN 0-8287-0937-8). Clearwater Pub.

--Chiricahua Apache Lands: Analysis of the Mineral Production Prior to September 4, 1866. (Library of American Indian Affairs). 64p. 1973. lib. bdg. 24.00 (ISBN 0-8287-1001-5). Clearwater Pub.

--Chiricahua Apache Tract: Analysis of the Volume of Timber Cut & Consumed for Mining Operations Prior to September 4, 1886. (Library of American Indian Affairs). 41p. 1973. lib. bdg. 17.00 (ISBN 0-8287-1002-3). Clearwater Pub.

--Papago Indians: Appraisal of Mineral Resources in the Lands Acquired by U.S. in Arizona, 1916, & the Louis Maria Baca Grant, Float No. 3, 1906, 3 vols. (Library of American Indian Affairs). 1380p. 1973. lib. bdg. 337.50 (ISBN 0-8287-1179-8). Clearwater Pub.

Full, Roy P. & Harty, Richard F. Yavapai Tribe: Evaluation Study of Mineral Resources, 1873, 3 vols. (Library of American Indian Affairs). 1340p. 1974. lib. bdg. 357.00 (ISBN 0-8287-1320-0). Clearwater Pub.

Fuller, E. O. Appraisal of Land Included in the Agreement of Sept 26, 1872 Between the U. S. & the Eastern Shoshone Indians. (Library of American Indian Affairs). 320p. 1973. lib. bdg. 92.00 (ISBN 0-8287-0920-3). Clearwater Pub.

--Tillamook: Report on 1894 Values of Lands & Resources in Washington. (Library of American Indian Affairs). 196p. 1974. lib. bdg. 60.00 (ISBN 0-8287-1278-6). Clearwater Pub.

Garrett, H. J. & Sears, Roscoe H. Appraisal of the Creek Cession, 1856. (Library of American Indian Affairs). 110p. 1973. lib. bdg. 37.50 (ISBN 0-8287-0928-9). Clearwater Pub.

Gordon, B. L., et al. Jicarilla Apache Claim Area: Environment, Settlement, & Land Use. (Library of American Indian Affairs). 364p. 1973. lib. bdg. 103.50 (ISBN 0-8287-1075-9). Clearwater Pub.

Griffiths, Thomas M. Yankton Sioux Tribe: Appraisal of Lands in Nebraska, Iowa, Minnesota, South Dakota, & North Dakota, As of 1858. (Library of American Indian Affairs). 1976. lib. bdg. 150.00x (ISBN 0-8287-1314-6). Clearwater Pub.

Gussow, Zachary. Cheyenne & Arapahoe Aboriginal Occupation. (Library of American Indian Affairs). 64p. 1973. lib. bdg. 24.00 (ISBN 0-8287-0983-1). Clearwater Pub.

--Sauk, Fox & Iowa Indians: Ethnological Report on Their Historic Habitat. (Library of American Indian Affairs). 62p. 1973. lib. bdg. 24.00 (ISBN 0-8287-1236-0). Clearwater Pub.

Hackenberg, Robert A. Aboriginal Land Use & Occupancy of the Pima-Maricopa Indians, 2 vols. (Indian Claims Commission Ser). 634p. 1973. lib. bdg. 177.00 (ISBN 0-8287-0888-6). Clearwater Pub.

Hall, Richard B. Absentee Delaware Tribe of Oklahoma & Delaware Tribe, 1856-57: Appraisal of Land in Northeastern Kansas: a Part of Royce Area 316. (Library of American Indian Affairs). 140p. 1973. lib. bdg. 45.00 (ISBN 0-8287-0893-2). Clearwater Pub.

--Apache, Kiowa & Comanche Indian Reservation in Southwestern Oklahoma Appraisal & Valuation. (Library of American Indian Affairs). 1976. lib. bdg. 78.00x (ISBN 0-8287-0917-3). Clearwater Pub.

--Appraisal of Lands in Northern Oklahoma, Cherokee Outlet, 1893. 96p. 1974. lib. bdg. 39.00 (ISBN 0-8287-0922-X). Clearwater Pub.

--Delaware Outlet in Northeastern Kansas, 1854: Appraisal. (Library of American Indian Affairs). 120p. 1973. lib. bdg. 39.00 (ISBN 0-8287-1028-7). Clearwater Pub.

--Iowa Tribe: Appraisal of Lands in Kansas & Nebraska, 1857. (Library of American Indian Affairs). 110p. 1973. lib. bdg. 38.00 (ISBN 0-8287-1073-2). Clearwater Pub.

--The Kickapoo Tribe of Kansas & the Peoria Tribe of Oklahoma, 1809: Appraisal of Lands in Western Indiana & Eastern Illinois: Royce Areas 73 & 74. (Library of American Indian Affairs). 132p. 1973. lib. bdg. 44.00 (ISBN 0-8287-1092-9). Clearwater Pub.

--Miami Indians 1805 & 1809: Appraisal of Lands in Southern Indiana: Royce Areas 56, 71, 72. (Library of American Indian Affairs). 325p. 1973. lib. bdg. 93.00 (ISBN 0-8287-1120-8). Clearwater Pub.

--Ottawa Tribe of Indians, Royce Areas 182 & 183, 1833: Appraisal of Lands in Northwestern Ohio & Southeastern Michigan. (Library of American Indian Affairs). 139p. 1973. lib. bdg. 45.00 (ISBN 0-8287-1175-5). Clearwater Pub.
--Peoria Tribe of Oklahoma, Absentee Delaware Tribe of Oklahoma and the Delaware Nation, 1804: Appraisal of Lands in Southwestern Indiana, Royce Area 49. (Library of American Indian Affairs). 190p. 1973. lib. bdg. 57.00 (ISBN 0-8287-1192-5). Clearwater Pub.
--The Peoria Tribe of Oklahoma, 1807: Appraisal of Land in Southeastern Illinois, Royce Area 63. (Library of American Indian Affairs). 246p. 1973. lib. bdg. 75.00 (ISBN 0-8287-1194-1). Clearwater Pub.
--Ponca Indians: Appraisal of Land in Northern Nebraska & Southern South Dakota, South & West of the Missouri River on Both Sides of the Niobrara River. (Library of American Indian Affairs). 182p. 1973. lib. bdg. 55.50 (ISBN 0-8287-1197-6). Clearwater Pub.
--Ponca Reservation, 1877: Appraisal of Land in Northeastern Nebraska. (Library of American Indian Affairs). 86p. 1973. lib. bdg. 31.50 (ISBN 0-8287-1199-2). Clearwater Pub.
--Senecas of Sandusky: Appraisal of Lands Royce Area 163, & the Mixed Band of Senecas & Shawnees of Lewistown, Royce Area 164, in Northwestern Ohio, 1831. (Library of American Indian Affairs). 140p. 1973. lib. bdg. 45.00 (ISBN 0-8287-1243-3). Clearwater Pub.
--United Senecas & Shawnees, 1833: Appraisal of Lands in Northeastern Oklahoma, Royce Areas 498, 499, 500, 501, 502. (Library of American Indian Affairs). 45p. 1973. lib. bdg. 18.00 (ISBN 0-8287-1282-4). Clearwater Pub.
Halpenny, Leonard. Ak Chin Reservation, Pinal County, Arizona: Decline of Ground Water Levels. (Library of American Indian Affairs). 73p. 1973. lib. bdg. 44.50 (ISBN 0-8287-0897-5). Clearwater Pub.
Harbin, Darwin. Blackfeet & Gros Ventre Tribes of Indians, Appraisal of Lands in Northern Montana, 1888. (Library of American Indian Affairs). 402p. 1973. lib. bdg. 114.00 (ISBN 0-8287-0956-4). Clearwater Pub.
--The Fort Berthold Indians: Appraisal of Land in North Dakota, 1891. (Library of American Indian Affairs). 159p. 1973. lib. bdg. 50.00 (ISBN 0-8287-1044-9). Clearwater Pub.
Hart, Gerald T. Confederated Ute Indian Lands in Southwestern Colorado, Ceded September 13, 1873: Appraisal. (Library of American Indian Affairs). 315p. 1973. lib. bdg. 91.00 (ISBN 0-8287-1016-3). Clearwater Pub.
Hatfield, James. Tillamook-Nehalem Lands. (Library of American Indian Affairs). 142p. 1974. lib. bdg. 46.00 (ISBN 0-8287-1277-8). Clearwater Pub.
Hickerson, Harold. Anthropological Report on the Indian Occupancy of Area 243. (Library of American Indian Affairs). 273p. 1973. lib. bdg. 81.00 (ISBN 0-8287-0907-6). Clearwater Pub.
--Anthropological Report on the Indian Use & Occupancy of Royce Area 332, Ceded by the Chippewa Indians of Lake Superior & the Mississippi Under the Treaty of September 30, 1854. (Library of American Indian Affairs). 151p. 1973. lib. bdg. 48.00 (ISBN 0-8287-0910-6). Clearwater Pub.
--The Chippewa Nation of Indians: Anthropological Report on the Indian Occupancy of Area 242, Ceded Under the Treaty of July 29, 1837. (Library of American Indian Affairs). 292p. 1973. lib. bdg. 85.00 (ISBN 0-8287-0992-0). Clearwater Pub.
Hobbs, Charles A., et al. Memorandum on Legislative History, Congressional Acts Pertaining to Indian Trust Funds: The Te-Moak Bands & Mescalero Apache. (Library of American Indian Affairs). 96p. 1973. lib. bdg. 34.50 (ISBN 0-8287-1115-1). Clearwater Pub.
Holbrook, M. J., et al. Appraisal Report of the Warm Springs Reservation in Oregon, 1859, 3 vols. (Library of American Indian Affairs). 682p. 1974. lib. bdg. 197.50 (ISBN 0-8287-0947-5). Clearwater Pub.
Hoyt, Homer. Kootenai Tribe Lands in Northern Idaho & Montana, 1859: Appraisal. (Library of American Indian Affairs). 73p. 1973. lib. bdg. 27.00 (ISBN 0-8287-1101-1). Clearwater Pub.
--Miami Tribe: Appraisal of Lands in North Central Indiana, Royce Areas 192-199, 251-256, & 258. (Library of American Indian Affairs). 294p. 1974. lib. bdg. 82.50 (ISBN 0-8287-1122-4). Clearwater Pub.
--Nez Perce Tribe Lands in Northern Idaho, 1894: Appraisal. (Library of American Indian Affairs). 116p. 1973. lib. bdg. 39.00 (ISBN 0-8287-1144-5). Clearwater Pub.
--Northern Paiute Nation: Appraisal of Lands in Nevada & California, 1853-1863, 2 vols. (Library of American Indian Affairs). 540p. 1973. Set. lib. bdg. 150.00 (ISBN 0-8287-1149-6). Clearwater Pub.
--Washoe Tribe of Indians: Appraisal of Lands in Nevada, 1862, & in California, 1853. (Library of American Indian Affairs). 259p. 1973. lib. bdg. 76.50 (ISBN 0-8287-1297-2). Clearwater Pub.
Hurt, Wesley R. Anthropological Report on Indian Occupancy of Certain Territory Claimed by the Dakota Sioux Indians & by Rival Tribal Claimants. (Library of American Indian Affairs). 250p. 1973. lib. bdg. 75.00 (ISBN 0-8287-0903-3). Clearwater Pub.
Idaho Land & Appraisal Service. Appraisal of the Lands of the Goshute Tribe or Identifiable Group Represented by the Confederated Tribes of the Goshute Reservation in Utah & Nevada, 1875. (Library of American Indian Affairs). 190p. 1973. lib. bdg. 60.50 (ISBN 0-8287-0934-3). Clearwater Pub.
Idaho Land and Appraisal Service. Appraisal of the Papago Tribe of Arizona, 1916, & the Luis Maria Baca Grant, Float No. 3, 1906. 260p. 1973. lib. bdg. 101.50 (ISBN 0-8287-0940-8). Clearwater Pub.
--Appraisal of the Rental Value of the Fort Sill Apache Tribe of Oklahoma in Arizona & New Mexico: From 1848 to September 4, 1886. (Library of American Indian Affairs). 190p. 1973. lib. bdg. 57.00 (ISBN 0-8287-0941-6). Clearwater Pub.
Idaho Land & Appraisal Service. Fort Sill Apache Tribe of Oklahoma; the Chiricahua Apache Tribe; the Chiricahua & Warm Springs Tribes of Apache Indians, 1886: Appraisal. (Library of American Indian Affairs). 245p. 1973. lib. bdg. 49.00 (ISBN 0-8287-1048-1). Clearwater Pub.
--Jicarilla-Apache Reservation, 1887 & 1907: Appraisal. (Library of American Indian Affairs). 105p. 1973. lib. bdg. 36.00 (ISBN 0-8287-1079-1). Clearwater Pub.
--Jicarilla Apache Tribe, 1883: Appraisal. (Library of American Indian Affairs). 250p. 1973. lib. bdg. 75.00 (ISBN 0-8287-1081-3). Clearwater Pub.
Idaho Land and Appraisal Service. Red Lake Band of Chippewa Indians: Appraisal of Lands in Minnesota on Various Dates. 96p. 1973. lib. bdg. 34.50 (ISBN 0-8287-1213-1). Clearwater Pub.
Jablow, Joseph. Anthropological Study of Indian Tribes in Royce Areas 48, 96-A, 110, 177 & 98, Illinois & Indiana, 1640-1832, 2 vols. (Library of American Indian Affairs). 398p. 1973. lib. bdg. 160.00 (ISBN 0-8287-0913-0). Clearwater Pub.
--The Ponca Indians with Reference to Their Claim to Certain Lands. (Library of American Indian Affairs). 356p. 1973. lib. bdg. 102.00 (ISBN 0-8287-1198-4). Clearwater Pub.
James, Harry & Winter, William S. Potawatomi Lands in the Indian Territory, 1890: Appraisal. (Library of American Indian Affairs). 152p. 1973. lib. bdg. 48.00 (ISBN 0-8287-1203-4). Clearwater Pub.
Jenkins, Myra E. Laguna Pueblo Land Claims, 1598-1935. (Library of American Indian Affairs). 195p. 1973. lib. bdg. 58.50 (ISBN 0-8287-1104-6). Clearwater Pub.
Jenkins, Myra E. & Minge, Ward A. Navajo Activities Affecting the Acoma-Laguna Area, 1746-1910. (Library of American Indian Affairs). 220p. 1973. lib. bdg. 66.00 (ISBN 0-8287-1136-4). Clearwater Pub.
Johnson, Albert L. Fort Mohave Indian Reservation Lands: Planning Report & Gross Appraisel. (Library of American Indian Affairs). 157p. 1973. lib. bdg. 50.00 (ISBN 0-8287-1045-7). Clearwater Pub.
Jones, J. A. Anthropological Report on the Indian Occupancy of Royce Areas 149, 174 & 245. (Library of American Indian Affairs). 193p. 1973. lib. bdg. 58.00 (ISBN 0-8287-0908-4). Clearwater Pub.
--United Nation of Chippewa, Ottowa, & Potawatomie Indians: Anthropological Report on the Indian Occupancy of Royce Area 187 in Illinois & Wisconsin, Ceded Under the Treaty of September 26, 1833. (Library of American Indian Affairs). 80p. 1973. lib. bdg. 40.00 (ISBN 0-8287-1281-6). Clearwater Pub.
Kaltreider, D. R., et al. Kickapoo Lands in Illinois & Missouri: An Appraisal. Ross, Norman A., ed. (Library of American Indian Affairs). 1976. lib. bdg. 35.00x (ISBN 0-8287-1088-0). Clearwater Pub.
Kauth, Helen. Ottawa & Chippewa Lands in Michigan: Economic & Historical Background for a Valuation As of 1836. (Library of American Indian Affairs). 1976. lib. bdg. 67.00x (ISBN 0-8287-1171-2). Clearwater Pub.
Kelly, Isabel T. Southern Paiute Ethnography: The Eastern Bands. (Library of American Indian Affairs). 188p. 1973. lib. bdg. 57.00 (ISBN 0-8287-1262-X). Clearwater Pub.
Kent, Donald. The Niagara River & the Niagara River Strip to 1759. (Library of American Indian Affairs). 179p. 1973. lib. bdg. 55.50 (ISBN 0-8287-1146-1). Clearwater Pub.
Kent, Donald H. Six Nations, Wyandot & Delaware: Historical Report on Pennsylvania's Purchases from the Indians, 1784, 1785, & 1789: Indian Occupancy of Areas Purchased. (Library of American Indian Affairs). 270p. 1973. lib. bdg. 79.50 (ISBN 0-8287-1255-7). Clearwater Pub.
Kiepe, Werner. Uintah Valley Indian Reservation Lands in Utah, Appraisal As of 1881. (Library of American Indian Affairs). 212p. 1973. lib. bdg. 64.50 (ISBN 0-8287-1280-8). Clearwater Pub.
Kinney, J. P. A Continent Lost - a Civilization Won: Indian Land Tenure in America. facsimile ed. McCurry, Dan C. & Rubenstein, Richard E., eds. LC 74-30639. (American Farmers & the Rise of Agribusiness Ser.). (Illus.). 1975. Repr. of 1937 ed. 27.00x (ISBN 0-405-06807-7). Arno.
--A Continent Lost, a Civilization Won: Indian Land Tenure in America. 336p. 1975. Repr. of 1937 ed. lib. bdg. 19.00x (ISBN 0-374-94576-4). Octagon.
Kirk, Arthur S. Sac & Fox Indian Lands in Royce Area 69, Missouri 1824: Appraisal. (Library of American Indian Affairs). 160p. 1973. lib. bdg. 50.00 (ISBN 0-8287-1217-4). Clearwater Pub.
Kleinman, Frank R. & Myers, Donald D. Sioux Nation Lands Acquired by the U. S. Under the Treaty of April 29, 1968: Appraisal. (Library of American Indian Affairs). 317p. 1973. lib. bdg. 91.50 (ISBN 0-8287-1250-6). Clearwater Pub.
Kline, M., et al. The Oneida & Stockbridge Tribes: An Analysis of the Awareness of the Continental Congress & the U. S. Government of Relations & Treaties with New York State. Ross, Norman A., ed. (Library of American Indian Affairs). 1976. lib. bdg. 50.00x (ISBN 0-8287-1157-7). Clearwater Pub.
Knuth, Helen E. Chippewa Indians of Lake Superior: Economic & Historical Background of Northeastern Minnesota Lands, Sept. 30, 1854, Royce Area 332. (Library of American Indian Affairs). 100p. 1973. lib. bdg. 34.50 (ISBN 0-8287-0991-2). Clearwater Pub.
Knuth, Helene. Ottawa & Potawatomi Lands: Economic & Historical Background for Valuation As of August 29, 1821. (Library of American Indian Affairs). 137p. 1974. lib. bdg. 45.00 (ISBN 0-8287-1172-0). Clearwater Pub.
Kroeber, A. L. Mohave Tribe: Report on Aboriginal Territory & Occupancy. (Library of American Indian Affairs). 98p. 1973. lib. bdg. 34.50 (ISBN 0-8287-1133-X). Clearwater Pub.
Kuehnle, Walter R. Appraisal of Lands in Illinois & Wisconsin, Ceded by the Winnebago Indians, Royce Area 149, 1830, Royce Area 174, 1833, Royce Area 245, 1838. (Library of American Indian Affairs). 570p. 1973. lib. bdg. 158.00 (ISBN 0-8287-0921-1). Clearwater Pub.
--Appraisal of Royce Areas 147 & 148 in Illinois & Wisconsin, 1829. 84p. 1973. lib. bdg. 105.00 (ISBN 0-8287-0925-4). Clearwater Pub.
--Minnesota Chippewa Indians, 1838: Appraisal of Royce Area 242 in Wisconsin & Minnesota. (Library of American Indian Affairs). 230p. 1973. lib. bdg. 69.00 (ISBN 0-8287-1125-9). Clearwater Pub.
--Sauk & Fox Nations of Indians: Appraisal of Royce Area 50 in the States of Missouri, Illinois, & Wisconsin; 1805. (Library of American Indian Affairs). 300p. 1973. lib. bdg. 87.00 (ISBN 0-8287-1235-2). Clearwater Pub.
--Seneca Nations & Tonawanda Band of Seneca Indians, Appraisal of Lands in Wester New York State, Ceded to or Exchanged with the U. S. 1797, 1802, 1815, 1826. (Library of American Indian Affairs). 410p. 1973. lib. bdg. 115.50 (ISBN 0-8287-1242-5). Clearwater Pub.
Le Duc, Thomas. Osage Nation: Investigation of Lands Conveyed in Trust Under Provisions of the Treaty of January 21, 1867. (Library of American Indian Affairs). 99p. 1974. lib. bdg. 45.00 (ISBN 0-8287-1165-8). Clearwater Pub.
Libby, Dorothy. Piankashaw Indians: Anthropological Report. (Library of American Indian Affairs). 280p. 1973. lib. bdg. 83.00 (ISBN 0-8287-1195-X). Clearwater Pub.
Lokken, Roscoe L. Iowa: Public Land Disposal. (Library of American Indian Affairs). 28p. 1973. lib. bdg. 17.00 (ISBN 0-8287-1071-6). Clearwater Pub.
Long, John S. Peoria Tribe: Geographical & Historical Analysis of Royce Areas 63, 73 & 74. (Library of American Indian Affairs). 30p. 1973. lib. bdg. 18.50 (ISBN 0-8287-1191-7). Clearwater Pub.
--Peoria Tribe of Oklahoma, Absentee Delaware Tribe of Oklahoma & the Delaware Nation, Analysis of the Land of Royce Area 49, in Southwestern Indiana. (Library of American Indian Affairs). 39p. 1973. lib. bdg. 20.00x (ISBN 0-8287-1193-3). Clearwater Pub.
McMullen, Allan L. Jicarilla Apache Tribal Lands Acquired by the U.S. on August 20, 1883: Valuation. (Library of American Indian Affairs). 160p. 1973. lib. bdg. 50.00 (ISBN 0-8287-1080-5). Clearwater Pub.
Manners, Robert A. Havasupai Indians: An Ethnohistorical Report. (Library of American Indian Affairs). 151p. 1973. lib. bdg. 48.00 (ISBN 0-8287-1058-9). Clearwater Pub.
--Hualapai Indians of Arizona. (Library of American Indian Affairs). 194p. 1973. lib. bdg. 58.50 (ISBN 0-8287-1060-0). Clearwater Pub.
--Southern Paiute & Chemehuevi: An Ethnohistorical Report. (Library of American Indian Affairs). 188p. 1973. lib. bdg. 57.00 (ISBN 0-8287-1261-1). Clearwater Pub.
Manypenny, George W. Potawatomic Tribe: Transcription of the Record of the Negotiation & Signing of the Treaty of February 22, 1855, at Washington, D. C. (Library of American Indian Affairs). 120p. 1973. lib. bdg. 39.00 (ISBN 0-8287-1206-9). Clearwater Pub.
Marriott, Alice. Osage Indians: Anthropological Study. (Library of American Indian Affairs). 215p. 1973. lib. bdg. 66.00 (ISBN 0-8287-1163-1). Clearwater Pub.
Martin, Howard N. Alabama & Coushatta Tribes of Texas: Ethnohistorical Analysis of Documents. (Library of American Indian Affairs). 66p. 1973. lib. bdg. 24.00 (ISBN 0-8287-0898-3). Clearwater Pub.
Mason, Bruce & Girard Co, et al. Klamath Concession: Timber Values, June 21, 1906. (Library of American Indian Affairs). 30p. 1973. lib. bdg. 21.00 (ISBN 0-8287-1096-1). Clearwater Pub.
Meltzer, Bernard C. & Schaar, Roland J. Chippewa Tract in Minnesota, April 26, 1866: Appraisal. (Library of American Indian Affairs). 345p. 1973. lib. bdg. 100.00 (ISBN 0-8287-0997-1). Clearwater Pub.
--Chippewa Tracts in Minnesota, 1848: Appraisal. (Library of American Indian Affairs). 278p. 1973. lib. bdg. 83.00 (ISBN 0-8287-0998-X). Clearwater Pub.
Miller, C. Marc. Coeur D'alene Tract, Idaho & Washington, 1873, 1887, 1891: Appraisal. (Library of American Indian Affairs). 210p. 1973. lib. bdg. 65.00 (ISBN 0-8287-1007-4). Clearwater Pub.
--Colville Tracts, State of Washington, 1872: Appraisal. (Library of American Indian Affairs). 210p. 1973. lib. bdg. 64.50 (ISBN 0-685-32086-3). Clearwater Pub.
--Duwamish, Snohomish & Soquamish Tracts: Appraisal. (Library of American Indian Affairs). 210p. 1973. lib. bdg. 65.00 (ISBN 0-8287-1029-5). Clearwater Pub.
--The Klamath Reservation, Appraisal, & Supplemental Appraisal: The Excluded Lands of the Klamath & Modoc Tribes & Yahooskin Band of Snake Indians, Oregon, 1906. (Library of American Indian Affairs). 190p. 1973. lib. bdg. 57.00 (ISBN 0-8287-1098-8). Clearwater Pub.
--Nez Perce Ceded Tract, Oregon, Washington & Idaho, 1867: Appraisal. (Library of American Indian Affairs). 217p. 1973. lib. bdg. 66.00 (ISBN 0-8287-1139-9). Clearwater Pub.
--Skagit Tract, Washington, Supplementing Appraisals of the Duwamish, Snohomish & Suquamish Tracts. (Library of American Indian Affairs). 59p. 1973. lib. bdg. 22.50 (ISBN 0-8287-1256-5). Clearwater Pub.
--S'klallam Tract: Appraisal. (Library of American Indian Affairs). 196p. 1973. lib. bdg. 60.00 (ISBN 0-8287-1258-1). Clearwater Pub.
--Skokomish Tract: Appraisal. (Library of American Indian Affairs). 188p. 1973. lib. bdg. 57.00 (ISBN 0-8287-1259-X). Clearwater Pub.
--Uintah Ute Tract: Preliminary Appraisal Report. (Library of American Indian Affairs). 50p. 1973. lib. bdg. 19.50 (ISBN 0-8287-1427-4). Clearwater Pub.
--Ute Ceded Tract, Colorado, 1873-1874. (Library of American Indian Affairs). 316p. 1973. lib. bdg. 91.50 (ISBN 0-8287-1285-9). Clearwater Pub.
--Yakima Indian Reservation: Appraisal of Patented Lands, State of Washington. (Library of American Indian Affairs). 160p. 1973. lib. bdg. 49.50 (ISBN 0-8287-1311-1). Clearwater Pub.
Miller, C. Mark. Snake-Piute Tract in Oregon, Appraisal, January 1879. (Library of American Indian Affairs). 107p. 1973. lib. bdg. 50.00 (ISBN 0-8287-1260-3). Clearwater Pub.
Miner, H. Craig & Unrau, William E. The End of Indian Kansas: A Study of Cultural Revolution, 1854-1871. LC 77-4410. (Illus.). 1977. 12.50x (ISBN 0-7006-0161-9). Regents Pr KS.
Minnesota Chippewa Tribe: Appraisal of Lands in Northwestern Michigan & Northern Wisconsin, 3 vols. (Library of American Indian Affairs). 557p. 1973. lib. bdg. 155.00 (ISBN 0-8287-1126-7). Clearwater Pub.
Monrad, Oscar & Sears, Roscoe H. Cherokee Outlet in the Indian Territory, State of Oklahoma: Appraisal. (Library of American Indian Affairs). 92p. 1973. lib. bdg. 33.00 (ISBN 0-8287-0976-9). Clearwater Pub.

Morrison, George A. The Gila River Indian Reservation. (Library of American Indian Affairs). 50p. 1973. lib. bdg. 23.50 (ISBN 0-8287-1049-X). Clearwater Pub.

Murray, Henry T. Klamath & Modoc Tribes & the Yahooskin Band of Snake Indians: Appraisal Report of Lands in Oregon. (Library of American Indian Affairs). 275p. 1974. lib. bdg. 78.00 (ISBN 0-8287-1094-5). Clearwater Pub.

--Kootenai Tribe in Idaho: Appraisal, As of March 8, 1859. (Library of American Indian Affairs). 220p. 1974. lib. bdg. 64.50 (ISBN 0-8287-1100-3). Clearwater Pub.

Murray, Noble T. Washoe Tribe of Nevada & California: Appraisal of Lands. (Library of American Indian Affairs). 266p. 1973. lib. bdg. 103.00 (ISBN 0-8287-1298-0). Clearwater Pub.

Murray, William. Kickapoo Lands in Kansas 1863: Appraisal. (Library of American Indian Affairs). 89p. 1973. lib. bdg. 31.00 (ISBN 0-8287-1089-9). Clearwater Pub.

--Winnebago Lands in Iowa & Minnesota, Royce Area 267, in 1833 & 1846. 273p. 1973. lib. bdg. 81.00 (ISBN 0-8287-1307-3). Clearwater Pub.

Murray, William G. Kickapoo Tracts in Missouri & Kansas, 1835: Appraisal. (Library of American Indian Affairs). 150p. 1973. lib. bdg. 48.00 (ISBN 0-8287-1090-2). Clearwater Pub.

--Miami Tract in Kansas, 1854: Appraisal. (Library of American Indian Affairs). 107p. 1973. lib. bdg. 36.00 (ISBN 0-8287-1121-6). Clearwater Pub.

--Omaha Tract in Nebraska, 1854: Appraisal. (Library of American Indian Affairs). 143p. 1974. lib. bdg. 46.50 (ISBN 0-8287-1155-0). Clearwater Pub.

--Osage Nation Land Cession in Missouri & Arkansas, 1810: Appraisal. (Library of American Indian Affairs). 196p. 1974. lib. bdg. 59.00 (ISBN 0-8287-1166-6). Clearwater Pub.

--Otoe & Missourie Tribes Iowa, Omaha, & Sac & Fox Tribes: Appraisal of Royce Area 151, in Missouri, 1836; in Iowa, 1838 & 1854. (Library of American Indian Affairs). 363p. 1973. lib. bdg. 127.20 (ISBN 0-8287-1170-4). Clearwater Pub.

--Pawnee Tracts in Nebraska & in Kansas: Appraisal, 2 vols. (Library of American Indian Affairs). 480p. 1974. lib. bdg. 159.00 (ISBN 0-8287-1188-7). Clearwater Pub.

--Potawatomi Tracts in Iowa & Kansas, 1846: Appraisal. (Library of American Indian Affairs). 239p. 1973. lib. bdg. 97.00 (ISBN 0-8287-1204-2). Clearwater Pub.

--Sac & Fox Cession in Iowa: Appraisal of Royce Area 152 in 1831. (Library Ofamerican Indian Affairs). 148p. 1973. lib. bdg. 48.00 (ISBN 0-8287-1215-8). Clearwater Pub.

--Sac & Fox Indian Cessions in Iowa, Royce Area 262, 1839 & 1843: Appraisal. (Library of American Indian Affairs). 380p. 1973. lib. bdg. 108.00 (ISBN 0-8287-1216-6). Clearwater Pub.

--Sac & Fox of Missouri Tract in Kansas: Appraisal, 1854. (Library of American Indian Affairs). 108p. 1973. lib. bdg. 37.50 (ISBN 0-8287-1222-0). Clearwater Pub.

--Sac, Fox, & Mississippi Tracts in Kansas 1860-67 & 1868. (Library of American Indian Affairs). 147p. 1973. lib. bdg. 48.00 (ISBN 0-8287-1226-3). Clearwater Pub.

--Seminole Lands in Florida: Appraisal. (Library of American Indian Affairs). 220p. 1974. lib. bdg. 64.50 (ISBN 0-8287-1237-9). Clearwater Pub.

--Shawnee Tract in Kansas, Appraisal, 1854. (Library of American Indian Affairs). 170p. 1973. lib. bdg. 52.50 (ISBN 0-8287-1244-1). Clearwater Pub.

--Sioux Cession in Iowa & Minnesota, Appraisal of Royce Area No. 153, 1831. (Library of American Indian Affairs). 165p. 1973. lib. bdg. 51.00 (ISBN 0-8287-1248-4). Clearwater Pub.

--Sioux Indian Tribe: Appraisal of Lands in North Dakota, South Dakota, Nebraska, Wyoming, & Montana in 1869. (Library of American Indian Affairs). 442p. 1973. lib. bdg. 124.50 (ISBN 0-8287-1249-2). Clearwater Pub.

Muske, H. Appraisal Report on Land Excluded from the Red Lake Reservation by Erroneous Survey. (Library of American Indian Affairs). 125p. 1973. lib. bdg. 40.50 (ISBN 0-8287-0951-3). Clearwater Pub.

Muske, William H. Sisseton & Wahpeton Tribes of North Dakota: Appraisal of Lands Disposed of Under the Act of April 27, 1904. (Library of American Indian Affairs). 100p. 1974. lib. bdg. 36.00 (ISBN 0-8287-1254-9). Clearwater Pub.

Myers, Donald D. Appraisal of the Lands of the Hualapai Reservation, Arizona. (Library of American Indian Affairs). 400p. 1973. lib. bdg. 112.50 (ISBN 0-8287-0935-1). Clearwater Pub.

Myers, Donald D. & Kleinman, Frank R. Papago Tribe of Arizona: Appraisal of Lands, 1906 & 1916, 3 vols. (Library of American Indian Affairs). 930p. 1973. lib. bdg. 247.50 (ISBN 0-8287-1184-4). Clearwater Pub.

Myers, Donald D. & Kleinman, Frank R., Jr. Appraisal of the Black Hills Lands of the Sioux Nation, 1877. (Library of American Indian Affairs). 150p. 1973. lib. bdg. 48.00 (ISBN 0-8287-0927-0). Clearwater Pub.

--Appraisal of the Lands of the Fort Sill Apache Tribe of Oklahoma, 1886. (Library of American Indian Affairs). 383p. 1973. lib. bdg. 109.50 (ISBN 0-8287-0933-5). Clearwater Pub.

--Mohave Indians: Appraisal of Lands, 1853, 1865. (Library of American Indian Affairs). 175p. 1973. lib. bdg. 54.00 (ISBN 0-8287-1130-5). Clearwater Pub.

--Western Bands of Shoshone: Appraisal of Lands in Nevada & California, 2 vols. (Library of American Indian Affairs). 1974. lib. bdg. 151.50 (ISBN 0-8287-1301-4). Clearwater Pub.

Myers, Donald D., et al. Appraisal of the Lands of the Fort McDowell Mohave-Apache & the Yavapai-Apache Communities in Arizona, 2 vols. (Library of American Indian Affairs). 394p. 1974. lib. bdg. 106.50 (ISBN 0-8287-0932-7). Clearwater Pub.

Nathan, Robert R. Paviotso-Mono Tracts of the Northern Paiute Nation, 4 vols. (Library of American Indian Affairs). 1000p. 1973. Set. lib. bdg. 247.50 (ISBN 0-8287-1186-0). Clearwater Pub.

--Valuation Report of Royce Area 242 (and 220) As of July 15, 1838, & Royce Area 268 As of April 3, 1848. (Library of American Indian Affairs). 190p. 1973. lib. bdg. 57.00 (ISBN 0-8287-1288-3). Clearwater Pub.

--Winnebago Tribe: Valuation Report on Royce Area 267, 1847. (Library of American Indian Affairs). 100p. 1973. lib. bdg. 34.50 (ISBN 0-8287-1309-X). Clearwater Pub.

Neighbours, Kenneth F. The Lipan Apache Tribe & the Mescalero Apache Tribe. (Library of American Indian Affairs). 75p. 1973. lib. bdg. 27.00 (ISBN 0-8287-1108-9). Clearwater Pub.

Nelson, H B. Samish Tribal Lands: Appraisal, 1859. (Library of American Indian Affairs). 80p. 1973. lib. bdg. 36.00 (ISBN 0-8287-1233-6). Clearwater Pub.

Neuman, Robert W. Caddoan Tribes: Data Relative to Their Historic Locations. (Library of American Indian Affairs). 150p. 1973. lib. bdg. 48.00 (ISBN 0-8287-0967-X). Clearwater Pub.

Newcombe, Dewey. Chippewa Tracts in Minnesota, 1855, 1864, 1867: Appraisal. (Library of American Indian Affairs). 314p. 1973. lib. bdg. 90.00 (ISBN 0-8287-0999-8). Clearwater Pub.

Newcombe, Dewey & Lawrence, Howard. Chippewa Tribe: Appraisal of Lands in Minnesota, Royce Area 332, 1855. (Library of American Indian Affairs). 292p. 1973. lib. bdg. 86.00 (ISBN 0-8287-1000-7). Clearwater Pub.

--Sisseton & Wahpeton Bands: Royce Area 413, 1859, Royce Area 243, 1838; Pike's Purchase Areas A&B, 1808: Appraisal of Lands in Minnesota, Wisconsin, South Dakota, & Iowa. 320p. 1973. lib. bdg. 92.00 (ISBN 0-8287-1252-2). Clearwater Pub.

Oberbillig, Ernest. Fort Sill Apache Tract: Mineral Appraisal, 1886. (Library of American Indian Affairs). 171p. 1973. lib. bdg. 52.50 (ISBN 0-8287-1046-5). Clearwater Pub.

--Fort Sill Apache Tribe of Oklahoma in Arizona & New Mexico Prior to September 4, 1886: Production & Royalty Value of the New Mexico Portion, a District by District Total. (Library of American Indian Affairs). 100p. 1973. lib. bdg. 34.50 (ISBN 0-8287-1047-3). Clearwater Pub.

--Goshute Tract in Nevada & Utah: Mineral Valuation As of 1875. (Library of American Indian Affairs). 155p. 1973. lib. bdg. 40.50 (ISBN 0-8287-1053-8). Clearwater Pub.

--Minnesota Chippewa Tribe: Mineral Appraisal of 1843. (Library of American Indian Affairs). 135p. 1973. lib. bdg. 43.50 (ISBN 0-8287-1127-5). Clearwater Pub.

--Paiute Indian Lands in California & Nevada: Mineral Valuation As of 1853-1863. (Library of American Indian Affairs). 294p. 1973. lib. bdg. 85.50 (ISBN 0-8287-1176-3). Clearwater Pub.

--San Carlos & Northern Tonto Apache Tracts in Arizona: Mineral Appraisal As of Various Dates, 1863-1960. (Library of American Indian Affairs). 78p. 1973. lib. bdg. 28.50 (ISBN 0-8287-1234-4). Clearwater Pub.

--Shoshone Lands Mineral Valuation, Nevada 1872 & California, 1853. (Library of American Indian Affairs). 208p. 1973. lib. bdg. 64.50 (ISBN 0-8287-1245-X). Clearwater Pub.

--Sioux Lands in the Black Hills, South Dakota: Mineral Value As of 1877. (Library of American Indian Affairs). 130p. 1973. lib. bdg. 42.00 (ISBN 0-8287-1419-3). Clearwater Pub.

--Washoe Indian Lands: Mineral Valuation Study. (Library of American Indian Affairs). 238p. 1973. lib. bdg. 72.00 (ISBN 0-8287-1293-X). Clearwater Pub.

--Yavapai Mineral Report. (Library of American Indian Affairs). 136p. 1973. lib. bdg. 43.50 (ISBN 0-8287-1318-9). Clearwater Pub.

Oberbilling, Ernest. Papago Tract, Arizona: Mineral Appraisal & Supplemental Report. (Library of American Indian Affairs). 433p. 1973. lib. bdg. 121.50 (ISBN 0-8287-1182-8). Clearwater Pub.

O'Boyle, Charles C. Cheyenne-Arapaho Tribes of Indians: Mineral Evaluation of Ceded Lands. (Library of American Indian Affairs). 45p. 1973. lib. bdg. 18.00 (ISBN 0-8287-0986-6). Clearwater Pub.

Opler, Morris E. The Lipan & Mescalero Apache in Texas. (Library of American Indian Affairs). 165p. 1973. lib. bdg. 51.00 (ISBN 0-8287-1107-0). Clearwater Pub.

Otis, D. S. The Dawes Act & the Allotment of Indian Land. (Civilization of the American Indian Ser.: Vol. 123). 215p. 1973. 9.95x (ISBN 0-8061-1039-2). U of Okla Pr.

The Ottawa, Chippewa & Potawatomie Nations of Indians: Anthropological Report on the Indian Occupancy of Royce Area 117, Ceded Under the Treaty Held at Chicago on August 29, 1821. (Library of American Indian Affairs). 217p. 1973. lib. bdg. 66.00 (ISBN 0-8287-1173-9). Clearwater Pub.

Owen, Gifford P. & Lietz, John F. Chinook Indian Lands in Washington & Oregon, 1851: Appraisal, 2 vols. (Library of American Indian Affairs). 330p. 1973. lib. bdg. 93.00 (ISBN 0-8287-0987-4). Clearwater Pub.

Palmer, Harris A. Appraisal of the Value of Lands in Royce Area 147, in Southwestern Wisconsin & Northwestern Illinois. (Library of American Indian Affairs). 206p. 1973. lib. bdg. 71.00 (ISBN 0-8287-0942-4). Clearwater Pub.

--Sac & Fox Mineral Lands in Northwestern, Illinois & Southwestern Wisconsin: Geological Study. 75p. 1974. lib. bdg. 30.00 (ISBN 0-8287-1221-2). Clearwater Pub.

Palmer, M. A. Appraisal of the Former Malheur Reservation in Eastern Oregon. (Library of American Indian Affairs). 95p. 1974. lib. bdg. 43.50 (ISBN 0-8287-0929-7). Clearwater Pub.

Parker, Ben H. & Vanderwilt, John W. Confederated Bands of Ute Indians: Appraisal of Mineral Resources in Lands, 5 vols. (Library of American Indian Affairs). 873p. 1973. Set. lib. bdg. 247.50 (ISBN 0-8287-1012-0). Clearwater Pub.

Plummer, Norman B. Appraisal Report of Chelan County, Washington. (Library of American Indian Affairs). 131p. 1974. lib. bdg. 43.50 (ISBN 0-8287-0944-0). Clearwater Pub.

--Crow Lands in Montana & Wyoming, 1868: Appraisal. (Library of American Indian Affairs). 201p. 1973. lib. bdg. 60.00 (ISBN 0-8287-1027-9). Clearwater Pub.

--Klamath & Modoc Tribes & Yahooskin Band of Snake Indians: Appraisal Report of Lands in Lakes & Klamath Counties, Oregon. (Library of American Indian Affairs). 161p. 1973. lib. bdg. 50.00 (ISBN 0-8287-1095-3). Clearwater Pub.

--Siletz Indian Reservation, Appraisal Report of Unalloted Lands Ceded Under Agreement of October 31, 1892, by the Tillamook Tribe of Indians. (Library of American Indian Affairs). 158p. 1973. lib. bdg. 50.00 (ISBN 0-8287-1247-6). Clearwater Pub.

Polland. Sac & Fox & Iowa Indian Cessions in Eastern Iowa: Appraisal of Royce Area 175 in 1833 & 1839, Royce Area 226 in 1837& 1839, Royce Area 244 in 1838 & 1839. (Library of American Indian Affairs). 328p. 1973. lib. bdg. 94.50 (ISBN 0-8287-1214-X). Clearwater Pub.

The Quileute Tribe of Indians & the Quinaielt Tribe of Indians. (Library of American Indian Affairs). 192p. 1973. lib. bdg. 73.00 (ISBN 0-8287-1210-7). Clearwater Pub.

R. H. Sears & Co. Zia, Jemez & Santa Ana Pueblo Lands, New Mexico. (Library of American Indian Affairs). 215p. 1973. lib. bdg. 66.00 (ISBN 0-8287-1323-5). Clearwater Pub.

Rambo, Edward A. Cheyenne & Arapaho Tribes in Northern & Western Oklahoma, 1891: Appraisal of Certain Lands. (Library of American Indian Affairs). 145p. 1973. lib. bdg. 46.00 (ISBN 0-8287-0982-3). Clearwater Pub.

Rands, Robert L. Acoma Land Utilization: An Ethnohistorical Report. (Library of American Indian Affairs). 189p. 1973. lib. bdg. 57.00 (ISBN 0-8287-0895-9). Clearwater Pub.

--Laguna Land Utilization: An Ethnohistorical Report. (Library of American Indian Affairs). 102p. 1973. lib. bdg. 24.00 (ISBN 0-8287-1102-X). Clearwater Pub.

Raney, Chase W. Appraisal Report of Warm Springs Ceded Tract, Oregon, 1859. (Library of American Indian Affairs). 176p. 1973. lib. bdg. 55.50 (ISBN 0-8287-0948-3). Clearwater Pub.

Raney, Frank R. & Raney, Chase W. Steilacoom, Nisqually & Squaxtin Tracts in Western Washington: Appraisal As of March 3, 1855. 176p. 1974. lib. bdg. 54.00 (ISBN 0-8287-1267-0). Clearwater Pub.

Ray, Verne F. Apache Indians of Texas: Ethnohistorical Analysis of Documents. (Library of American Indian Affairs). 265p. 1973. lib. bdg. 78.00 (ISBN 0-8287-0916-5). Clearwater Pub.

--The Joseph Band of Nez Perce Indians, 1805-1905. (Library of American Indian Affairs). 108p. 1973. lib. bdg. 37.50 (ISBN 0-8287-1082-1). Clearwater Pub.

--The Makah-Quileute Tribal Boundary. (Library of American Indian Affairs). 85p. 1974. lib. bdg. 33.00 (ISBN 0-8287-1112-7). Clearwater Pub.

Reber, Arthur W. Washoe Tribe: Fishery Evaluation. (Library of American Indian Affairs). 26p. 1973. lib. bdg. 19.50 (ISBN 0-8287-1296-4). Clearwater Pub.

Reeve, Frank D. Anthropological Report on the Navajo Indians. 99p. 1973. lib. bdg. 33.00 (ISBN 0-8287-0911-4). Clearwater Pub.

--The Navajo Indians in New Mexico, to 1870: Historical Report. (Library of American Indian Affairs). 98p. 1973. lib. bdg. 34.50 (ISBN 0-8287-1138-0). Clearwater Pub.

Riley, Carroll L. Makah Indians of Western Washington: A Study of Group Distribution, Political Organization & Concepts of Land Use. (Library of American Indian Affairs). 1976. lib. bdg. 20.00x (ISBN 0-8287-1111-9). Clearwater Pub.

--Salish & Chimakuam-Speaking Indians of the Puget Sound Basin of Washington. (Library of American Indian Affairs). 60p. 1973. lib. bdg. 22.50 (ISBN 0-8287-1231-X). Clearwater Pub.

Ross, Norman A., ed. The Klamath Tribe & Federal Management of the Tribal Forest, 3 vols. (Library of American Indian Affairs). 1976. lib. bdg. 200.00x (ISBN 0-8287-1099-6). Clearwater Pub.

Sanwick, John D. Nisqually, Steilacoom, & Squaxin Lands, State of Washington, 1855: Appraisal. (Library of American Indian Affairs). 30p. 1973. lib. bdg. 19.00 (ISBN 0-8287-1147-X). Clearwater Pub.

Saunderson, Mont H. Confederated Salish & Kootenai Tribe Lands of the Flathead Indian Reservation, 1859: Valuation. (Library of American Indian Affairs). 100p. 1973. lib. bdg. 34.50 (ISBN 0-8287-1014-7). Clearwater Pub.

--Crow Indian Lands Ceded in the Fort Laramie Treaty of 1868: Appraisal. (Library of American Indian Affairs). 80p. 1973. lib. bdg. 29.00 (ISBN 0-8287-1026-0). Clearwater Pub.

--Goshute Shoshone Indians: Appraisal of Lands, 1875. (Library of American Indian Affairs). 115p. 1973. lib. bdg. 39.00 (ISBN 0-8287-1052-X). Clearwater Pub.

--Three Affiliated Tribes of Fort Berthold Reservation, March 3, 1891: Valuation of Ceded Lands. (Library of American Indian Affairs). 74p. 1973. lib. bdg. 27.00 (ISBN 0-8287-1270-0). Clearwater Pub.

Schroeder, Albert H. Apache Indians. (Library of American Indian Affairs). 573p. 1973. lib. bdg. 159.00 (ISBN 0-8287-0914-9). Clearwater Pub.

--Yavapai History. (Library of American Indian Affairs). 310p. 1973. lib. bdg. 90.00 (ISBN 0-8287-1316-2). Clearwater Pub.

Sears, R. H. Acoma Pueblo Land, New Mexico: Appraisal Report, 1901-1936. (Library of American Indian Affairs). 246p. 1973. lib. bdg. 75.00 (ISBN 0-8287-0896-7). Clearwater Pub.

--Laguna Pueblo Land in New Mexico: Appraisal Report, 1908-1936. (Library of American Indian Affairs). 206p. 1973. lib. bdg. 63.00 (ISBN 0-8287-1105-4). Clearwater Pub.

Sears, Roscoe. Cheyenne & Arapaho Indian Reservations in the Indian Territory, State of Oklahoma, 1891: Appraisal. (Library of American Indian Affairs). 89p. 1973. lib. bdg. 31.00 (ISBN 0-8287-0979-3). Clearwater Pub.

Sears, Roscoe H. Cherokee Nation Indian Reservations in the Indian Territory, Oklahoma: Appraisal. (Library of American Indian Affairs). 73p. 1973. lib. bdg. 27.00 (ISBN 0-8287-0973-4). Clearwater Pub.

--Cheyenne & Arapaho Indian Reservation in the Indian Territory, State of Oklahoma, 1869: Appraisal. (Library of American Indian Affairs). 51p. 1973. lib. bdg. 20.00 (ISBN 0-8287-0980-7). Clearwater Pub.

Sears, Roscoe H. & Garret, H. J. Sac & Fox Tract Indian Territory: Appraisal. (Library of American Indian Affairs). 160p. 1974. lib. bdg. 50.00 (ISBN 0-8287-1223-9). Clearwater Pub.

Sharrock, Floyd W. & Sharrock, Susan R. Cree Indian Territorial Expansion: The Hudson Bay Area to Interior Saskatchewan & Missouri Plains. (Library of American Indian Affairs). 200p. 1973. lib. bdg. 60.00 (ISBN 0-8287-1017-1). Clearwater Pub.

Shenan, P. J. & Full, Roy P. Haulapai Indians of Arizona: Evaluation Study of Mineral Resources, 4 vols. (Library of American Indian Affairs). 1670p. 1973. lib. bdg. 450.00 (ISBN 0-8287-1057-0). Clearwater Pub.

Shennon, P. J. & Full, Roy P. Mohave Tribe of Indians of Arizona, California & Nevada & the Mohave Indians of the Colorado River Indian Tribes: Evaluation Study of Mineral Resources. (Library of American Indian Affairs). 78p. 1973. lib. bdg. 28.50 (ISBN 0-8287-1132-1). Clearwater Pub.
Shenon, P. J. & Full, R. P. Appraisal of the Mineral Resources in the Lands of the Sioux Nation Acquired Under Treaty of April 26, 1868, 4 vols. (Library of American Indian Affairs). 1860p. 1973. Set. lib. bdg. 500.00 (ISBN 0-8287-0938-6). Clearwater Pub.
Shenon, P. J & Full, Roy P. Nez Perce Reservation: Evaluation the Gold Mined Before April 17, 1867, 4 vols. (Library of American Indian Affairs). 1350p. 1974. lib. bdg. 372.00 (ISBN 0-8287-1142-9). Clearwater Pub.
Shenon, P. J. & Full, Roy P. Nez Perce Tribe of Indians: Evaluation Study of the Mineral Resources, 1867, 4 vols. (Evaluation Study of the Mineral Resources, 1867). 1100p. 1973. Set. lib. bdg. 300.00 (ISBN 0-8287-1145-3). Clearwater Pub.
--Washoe Tribe: Evaluation of Mineral Resources, 5 vols. (Library of American Indian Affairs). 1570p. 1973. lib. bdg. 420.00 (ISBN 0-8287-1295-6). Clearwater Pub.
--Western Bands of Shoshone Indians: Evaluation Study of Mineral Resources, 12 vols. (Library of American Indian Affairs). 5000p. 1973. lib. bdg. 1300.00 (ISBN 0-8287-1302-2). Clearwater Pub.
Shenon, P. J., et al. Northern Paiute Nation: Evaluation Study of Mineral Resources, 3 vols. (Library of American Indian Affairs). 1185p. 1973. Set. lib. bdg. 330.00 (ISBN 0-8287-1150-X). Clearwater Pub.
The Skagit Tribe & the Snoqualmie Tribe: Ethnological & Historical Evidence. 265p. 1973. lib. bdg. 52.00 (ISBN 0-8287-1257-3). Clearwater Pub.
Smith, Alice E. & Carstensen, Vernon. Winnebago Indians: Economic & Historical Background for Royce Areas 149, 174, 245. (Library of American Indian Affairs). 223p. 1973. lib. bdg. 67.50 (ISBN 0-8287-1306-5). Clearwater Pub.
Speck, Frank G. Territorial Subdivisions & Boundaries of the Wampanoag, Massachusett, & Nauset Indians. LC 76-43847. (MAI. Indian Notes & Monographs. Miscellaneous: No. 44). Repr. of 1928 ed. 15.00 (ISBN 0-404-15701-7). AMS Pr.
Starkey, Harold C. & Carlson, Roy C. Lower Pen D'oreille or Kalispel Indian Lands: Northeast Washington, Northern Idaho, & Western Montana, 1903. (Library of American Indian Affairs). 197p. 1973. lib. bdg. 60.00 (ISBN 0-8287-1109-7). Clearwater Pub.
Starrett, Paul. Appraisal Report of Lands in Central Indiana: Purchased from the Miami Tribe of Indians 1818. (Library of American Indian Affairs). 170p. 1973. lib. bdg. 52.50 (ISBN 0-8287-0945-9). Clearwater Pub.
--Creek Nation: Appraisal of Ceded Lands in Southern Georgia & Southeastern Alabama. (Library of American Indian Affairs). 21p. 1973. lib. bdg. 15.00 (ISBN 0-8287-1022-8). Clearwater Pub.
--Ottawa, Chippewa & Potowatomi Nations of Indians: Appraisal of Royce Area 117, Ceded by the Treaty of August 29, 1821. (Library of American Indian Affairs). 250p. 1973. lib. bdg. 75.00 (ISBN 0-8287-1174-7). Clearwater Pub.
Steward, Julian H. Aboriginal & Historic Groups of the Ute Indians of Utah: An Analysis. (Indian Claims Commission Ser). 121p. 1973. lib. bdg. 39.00 (ISBN 0-8287-0887-8). Clearwater Pub.
Steward, Julian H. & Wheeler-Voegelin, Erminie. Northern Paiute Indians: Anthropological Report. (Library of American Indian Affairs). 313p. 1973. lib. bdg. 90.00 (ISBN 0-8287-1148-8). Clearwater Pub.
Still & Still, Consulting Mining Engineers & Geologists. Hualapai Tribal Lands: Estimate of the Value of Minerals As of 1833, 2 vols. (Library of American Indian Affairs). 324p. 1974. lib. bdg. 68.00 (ISBN 0-8287-1061-9). Clearwater Pub.
Stores, Samuel L. Creek Indian Lands in Oklahoma: Appriasal of Land Values As of 1907. (Library of American Indian Affairs). 1976. lib. bdg. 100.00x (ISBN 0-8287-1018-X). Clearwater Pub.
Stout, David B. Anthropological Reports on the Indians Occupying on Area Bounded Roughly by the Kankakee, Illinois, Mississippi, Ohio, Wabash, & Tippecanoe Rivers. (Library of American Indian Affairs). 32p. 1973. lib. bdg. 18.00 (ISBN 0-8287-0912-2). Clearwater Pub.
--Kickapoo, Illinois & Potawatomi Indians: Anthropological Reports. (Library of American Indian Affairs). 122p. 1973. lib. bdg. 40.00 (ISBN 0-8287-1087-2). Clearwater Pub.
--Saginaw Chippewa: Ethnohistorical Report on Royce Area No. 111 (Michigan), Treaty of Sept. 24, 1819. (Library of American Indian Affairs). 41p. 1973. lib. bdg. 20.50 (ISBN 0-8287-1229-8). Clearwater Pub.
Suphan, Robert J. The Umatilla, Walla Walla, & Cayuse Indians Relative to Socio-Political Organization & Land Use. (Library of American Indian Affairs). 90p. 1973. lib. bdg. 32.50 (ISBN 0-8287-1428-2). Clearwater Pub.
--The Wasco & Tenino Indians: Political Organization & Land-Use. 72p. 1973. lib. bdg. 27.00 (ISBN 0-8287-1292-1). Clearwater Pub.
Sutherland, J. Frederick. Appraisals of Land Areas in Minnesota, Treaties of February 22, 1855; March 11, 1863; May 7, 1864; March 19, 1867. (Library of American Indian Affairs). 314p. 1973. lib. bdg. 91.50 (ISBN 0-8287-0952-1). Clearwater Pub.
Sutton, Imre. Indian Land Tenure: Bibliographical Essays & a Guide to the Literature. LC 74-30668. (The Library of American Indian Affairs). (Illus.). 1975. lib. bdg. 20.00x (ISBN 0-88354-104-1); pap. text ed. 8.95x (ISBN 0-88354-106-8). Clearwater Pub.
Tanner, Helen H. Caddo Tribe of Oklahoma, Rebuttal Statement. (Library of American Indian Affairs). 144p. 1973. lib. bdg. 46.50 (ISBN 0-8287-0963-7). Clearwater Pub.
--Chippewa of Eastern Lower Michigan: Historical Report. (Library of American Indian Affairs). 25p. 1973. lib. bdg. 16.25 (ISBN 0-8287-0993-9). Clearwater Pub.
--The Greenville Treaty, 1795. (Library of American Indian Affairs). 70p. 1973. lib. bdg. 38.00 (ISBN 0-8287-1055-4). Clearwater Pub.
--Indian Tribes in Southeastern Michigan & Northern Ohio: A History. (Library of American Indian Affairs). 55p. 1973. lib. bdg. 21.00 (ISBN 0-8287-1069-4). Clearwater Pub.
--Potawatomi Ceded Lands & an Indian History of Northeastern Illinois. (Library of American Indian Affairs). 1976. lib. bdg. 29.00x (ISBN 0-8287-1200-X). Clearwater Pub.
Tanner, Helen H., et al. Wyandot Reservations in Michigan & Ohio: An Historial Report for Appraising Land Values. Ross, Norman A., ed. (Library of American Indian Affairs). 1976. lib. bdg. 75.00x (ISBN 0-8287-1310-3). Clearwater Pub.
Taylor, H. C., Jr. Makah Indians: Anthropological Investigation Relative to Tribal Identity & Aboriginal Possession of Lands. (Library of American Indian Affairs). 61p. 1973. lib. bdg. 23.00 (ISBN 0-8287-1110-0). Clearwater Pub.
Thomas, Alfred B. The Jicarilla Apache Indians, a History, 1598-1888. (Library of American Indian Affairs). 152p. 1973. lib. bdg. 32.00 (ISBN 0-8287-1077-5). Clearwater Pub.
--The Mescalero Apache, 1653-1874. (Library of American Indian Affairs). 47p. 1973. lib. bdg. 22.50 (ISBN 0-8287-1118-6). Clearwater Pub.
Trygg, J. William. Appraisal Report: Historical & Economic Background, Land & Resource Evaluation Study of Royce Area 482, in St. Louis, Itasca & Koochiching Counties, Minnesota. (Library of American Indian Affairs). 166p. 1973. lib. bdg. 52.50 (ISBN 0-8287-0943-2). Clearwater Pub.
--Appraisal Report of Royce Areas 242, 220, & 268. 120p. 1973. lib. bdg. 39.00 (ISBN 0-8287-0946-7). Clearwater Pub.
Trygg, William J. Saginaw Chippewa Indian Tribe of Michigan: Appraisal of Royce Area No. 111, Treaty Cession Sept. 24, 1819. (Library of American Indian Affairs). 95p. 1973. lib. bdg. 33.00 (ISBN 0-8287-1230-1). Clearwater Pub.
Tucker, Elbridge A. Cherokee Outlet Lands Deeded by the Cherokee Nation to the U. S. in Trust on June 14, 1883: Appraisal. (Library of American Indian Affairs). 113p. 1973. lib. bdg. 39.00 (ISBN 0-8287-0977-7). Clearwater Pub.
Tucker, Eldridge A. Appraisal of the Lands Ceded by the Creek Nation for the Seminoles, August 7, 1856. (Library of American Indian Affairs). 115p. 1973. lib. bdg. 39.00 (ISBN 0-8287-0930-0). Clearwater Pub.
--Cherokee Outlet in Oklahoma, Appraisal, 1893. (Library of American Indian Affairs). 128p. 1973. lib. bdg. 42.00 (ISBN 0-8287-0975-0). Clearwater Pub.
Vaughan, John L., Jr. Shoshone Tribal Lands, California, 1853 & Nevada, 1872: Appraisal. (Library of American Indian Affairs). 91p. 1973. lib. bdg. 31.50 (ISBN 0-8287-1246-8). Clearwater Pub.
--Yavapai Tribe: Appraisal of Lands, 1873. (Library of American Indian Affairs). 114p. 1973. lib. bdg. 39.00 (ISBN 0-8287-1319-7). Clearwater Pub.
Voget, Fred W. Osage Anthropological Report. (Library of American Indian Affairs). 420p. 1973. lib. bdg. 117.00 (ISBN 0-8287-1158-5). Clearwater Pub.
Wall, Myron. Washoe Indians of California & Nevada: Timberland Valuation Study. (Library of American Indian Affairs). 93p. 1973. lib. bdg. 33.00 (ISBN 0-8287-1294-8). Clearwater Pub.
Wallace, Ernes. The Comanche, Apache & Kiowa Indians Before 1867: Habitat & Range. (Library of American Indian Affairs). 1976. lib. bdg. 99.00x (ISBN 0-8287-1600-5). Clearwater Pub.
Warner, Robert M. Saginaw Chippewa: Economic & Historical Report on Royce Area No. 111, Ceded by the Treaty of September 24, 1819. (Library of American Indian Affairs). 177p. 1973. lib. bdg. 55.50 (ISBN 0-8287-1228-X). Clearwater Pub.
Warner, Robert M. & Groesbeck, Lois J. The Sault Ste. Marie Area: Historical Report. (Library of American Indian Affairs). 21p. 1973. lib. bdg. 16.00 (ISBN 0-8287-1418-5). Clearwater Pub.
Watson, Ralph W. The Colville Tribe, San Poil & Nespelen Tribes, the Lekes, Okanogans, Methows: Appraisal of the Tribal Lands, State of Washington, 1872, 2 vols. (Library of American Indian Affairs). 291p. 1973. lib. bdg. 84.00 (ISBN 0-8287-1011-2). Clearwater Pub.
Wheeler-Voegelin, Erminie. Anthropological Report on Indian Use & Occupancy of Royce Area No. 113 (St. Martin Islands) Ceded in the Treaty of July 6, 1820 Between the U. S. & the Ottawa & Chippewa Nations of Indians; & the Area of Overlap of Royce Area 205 (Treaty of March 28, 1836) & Royce Area 111 (Treaty of Sept. 24, 1819) (Library of American Indian Affairs). 73p. 1973. lib. bdg. 27.00 (ISBN 0-8287-0906-8). Clearwater Pub.
--Ethnohistorical Report on Indian Use Occupancy of Royce Area 11, Ohio & Indiana, 2 vols. (Library of American Indian Affairs). 750p. 1973. lib. bdg. 250.00 (ISBN 0-8287-1036-8). Clearwater Pub.
Wheeler-Voegelin, Erminie & Blasingham, Emily J. United Tribes of Ottawas, Chappewas & Potawatomies: Anthropological Report on the Indian Occupancy of Royce Area 77 & Royce Area 78. (Library of American Indian Affairs). 217p. 1973. lib. bdg. 66.00 (ISBN 0-8287-1283-2). Clearwater Pub.
Wheeler-Voegelin, Erminie & Hickerson, Harold. Red Lake & Pembina Chippewa: Anthropological Report. (Library of American Indian Affairs). 200p. 1973. lib. bdg. 60.00 (ISBN 0-8287-1212-3). Clearwater Pub.
Wheeler-Voegelin, Erminie, et al. United Tribes of Sac & Fox Indians: Anthropological Report on the Indian Occupancy of Royce Area 50, Ceded Under the Treaty of November 3, 1804. (Library of American Indian Affairs). 310p. 1973. lib. bdg. 90.00 (ISBN 0-8287-1284-0). Clearwater Pub.
Williamson, M. J. The Creek Nation & Private Land Sales in Alabama, & an Appraisal of Creek Nation Lands. (Library of American Indian Affairs). 1976. lib. bdg. 99.00x (ISBN 0-8287-1021-X). Clearwater Pub.
--Creek Nation East of the Mississippi: Appraisal of Lands in Georgia & Alabama As of August 9, 1814. (Library of American Indian Affairs). 21p. 1974. lib. bdg. 17.00 (ISBN 0-8287-1023-6). Clearwater Pub.
--Osage Tribal Council, 1810: Appraisal of Lands in Missouri & Arkansas. (Library of American Indian Affairs). 250p. 1973. lib. bdg. 75.00 (ISBN 0-8287-1167-4). Clearwater Pub.
Winter, William S. Hualapai Tribal Lands in Northwestern Arizona: Appraisal. (Library of American Indian Affairs). 180p. 1973. lib. bdg. 56.00 (ISBN 0-8287-1062-7). Clearwater Pub.
Woolworth, Alan R. Yankton Sioux: Ethnohistorical Report on the Indian Occupancy of Royce Area 410. (Library of American Indian Affairs). 224p. 1973. lib. bdg. 67.50 (ISBN 0-8287-1313-8). Clearwater Pub.
Wright, Fred D. Mineral Value of Royce Area 147 in Illinois & Wisconsin, 1829. (Library of American Indian Affairs). 71p. 1973. lib. bdg. 38.00 (ISBN 0-8287-1124-0). Clearwater Pub.
Wyckoff, Don G. The Caddoan Cultural Area: An Archaeological Perspective. (Library of American Indian Affairs). 250p. 1973. lib. bdg. 75.00 (ISBN 0-8287-0966-1). Clearwater Pub.
Young, Mary E. Redskins, Ruffleshirts & Rednecks: Indian Allotments in Alabama & Mississippi 1830-1860. (Civilization of the American Indian Ser: No. 61). (Illus.). 1961. 11.95 (ISBN 0-8061-0510-0). U of Okla Pr.

INDIANS OF NORTH AMERICA–LAND TRANSFERS

see also Indians of North America–Government Relations; Indians of North America–Treaties

Blumenthal, Walter H. American Indians Dispossessed: Fraud in Land Cessions Forced Upon the Tribes. facsimile ed. LC 74-30620. (American Farmers & the Rise of Agribusiness Ser.). 1975. Repr. of 1955 ed. 13.00x (ISBN 0-405-06767-4). Arno.
Brashers, Charles. A Snug Little Purchase: How Richard Henderson Bought Kaintuckee from the Cherokees in 1775. LC 78-74150. (Illus.). 1979. 7.95 (ISBN 0-933362-01-3); pap. 4.95 (ISBN 0-933362-02-1). Assoc Creative Writers.
Burlingame, Merrill G. Blackfeet & Gros Ventre Tribes in Montana in the Agreement of May 1, 1888: Historical Report on Lands Ceded. (Library of American Indian Affairs). (Illus.). 80p. 1974. 31.50 (ISBN 0-8287-0955-6). Clearwater Pub.
--Flathead, Pen d'Oreille & Kutenai Indians Ceded Lands: Historical Report. (Library of American Indian Affairs). 105p. 1974. lib. bdg. 37.50 (ISBN 0-8287-1039-2). Clearwater Pub.
Cass, Lewis. Considerations on the Present State of the Indians, & Their Removal to the West of the Mississippi. facsimile ed. LC 75-91. (Mid-American Frontier Ser.). 1975. Repr. of 1828 ed. 9.50x (ISBN 0-405-06858-1). Arno.
Davis, W. H. Osage Ceded Lands: Valuation Study As of September 29, 1965. 240p. 1974. lib. bdg. 87.00 (ISBN 0-8287-1159-3). Clearwater Pub.
DeRosier, Arthur H., Jr. Removal of the Choctaw Indians. LC 70-111044. (Illus.). 1970. 12.50 (ISBN 0-87049-113-X). U of Tenn Pr.
Gates, Paul W. & Bruchey, Stuart, eds. The Rape of the Indian Lands: An Original Anthology. LC 78-56698. (Management of Public Lands in the U. S. Ser.). 1979. lib. bdg. 20.00x (ISBN 0-405-11358-7). Arno.
Goff, James H. Cherokee Nation: Land Cessions in Tennessee, Mississippi, North Carolina, Georgia, Alabama, 1785-1835. (Library of American Indian Affairs). 278p. 1974. lib. bdg. 79.50 (ISBN 0-8287-0974-2). Clearwater Pub.
Harrison, T. S. & Harrison, J. W. Appraisal of Oil & Gas Lands of the Portion of Wind River Basin, Wyoming Ceded by the Brunot Agreement of September 26, 1872. (Library of American Indian Affairs). 84p. 1974. lib. bdg. 32.00 (ISBN 0-8287-0924-6). Clearwater Pub.
Rogin, Michael P. Fathers & Children: Andrew Jackson & the Subjugation of the American Indian. LC 76-10814. 1976. pap. 4.95 (ISBN 0-394-71881-X, Vin). Random.
Royce, Charles C., ed. Indian Land Cessions in the United States. LC 78-146416. (First American Frontier Ser). (Illus.). 1971. Repr. of 1900 ed. 35.00 (ISBN 0-405-02880-6). Arno.
Saunderson, Mont H. Blackfeet Tribe Ceded Lands in Montana, Agreement of May 1, 1888: Valuation. (Library of American Indian Affairs). (Illus.). 100p. 1974. 36.00 (ISBN 0-8287-0959-9). Clearwater Pub.
Smith, James F. Cherokee Land Lottery of Georgia, 1832. LC 67-28624. (Illus.). 1969. Repr. of 1838 ed. 20.00 (ISBN 0-8063-0318-2). Genealog Pub.
Sutton, Imre. Indian Land Tenure: Bibliographical Essays & a Guide to the Literature. LC 74-30668. (The Library of American Indian Affairs). (Illus.). 1975. lib. bdg. 20.00x (ISBN 0-88354-104-1); pap. text ed. 8.95x (ISBN 0-88354-106-8). Clearwater Pub.
Trygg, William. Valuation Reports on Lands in Michigan & Indiana, Ceded by Treaty of August 29, 1921. (Library of American Indian Affairs). 88p. 1974. lib. bdg. 33.00 (ISBN 0-8287-1290-5). Clearwater Pub.

INDIANS OF NORTH AMERICA–LANGUAGES

see also Algonquian Languages; also names of languages or group of languages

Absaloka: Crow Children's Writing. (Indian Culture Ser.). 1971. 0.75 (ISBN 0-89992-009-8). MT Coun Indian.
Acts & Resolutions of the Creek National Council of the Session of May, June, October, November & December, 1895, Compiled & Translated by D.C. Watson. LC 73-88775. (Constitutions & Laws of the American Indian Tribes Ser. No. 1: Vol. 20). 1973. Repr. of 1896 ed. 6.00 (ISBN 0-8420-1722-4). Scholarly Res Inc.
Aoki, Haruo. Nez Perce Grammar. (California Library Reprint). 1974. 22.50x (ISBN 0-520-02524-5). U of Cal Pr.
Arvidson, Lucy. Alaawich. 1978. 2.00 (ISBN 0-686-25512-7). Malki Mus Pr.
Bauman, James J. Guide to Issues in Indian Language Retention. 1980. pap. text ed. 6.00x (ISBN 0-87281-132-8). Ctr Appl Ling.
Boas, Franz. Handbook of the American Indian Languages, 4 vols. Repr. Set. 225.00 (ISBN 0-403-08964-6). Scholarly.
--Introduction to Handbook of American Indian Languages. (Illus.). Repr. of 1911 ed. pap. 9.50 (ISBN 0-8466-4023-6, SJI23). Shorey.
--Introduction to Handbook of American Indian Languages. Holder, Preston, ed. Bd. with Indian Linguistic Families of America North of Mexico. Powell, J. W. LC 65-19467. xii, 221p. 1966. pap. 2.45x (ISBN 0-8032-5017-7, BB 301, Bison). U of Nebr Pr.

--Introduction to the Handbook of American Indian Languages. LC 63-21768. 70p. 1963. pap. 2.95 (ISBN 0-87840-150-4). Georgetown U Pr.

--Keresan Texts, Vols. 1 & 2. LC 73-3543. (American Ethnological Society. Publications: No. 8). Repr. of 1928 ed. Set. 44.00 (ISBN 0-404-58158-7). AMS Pr.

Boas, Franz & Swanton, John. Siouan (Teton & Santee Dialects) Dakota. Repr. of 1911 ed. pap. 10.95 (ISBN 0-8466-4029-5, SJI29). Shorey.

Bruno Natlis, Elena. Estudio Comparativo de Vocabularios Tobas y Pilagas. 107p. (Span.). 1965. pap. 49.95 (ISBN 0-686-56659-9, S-33083). French & Eur.

Bushnell, David I., Jr. Native Villages & Village Sites East of the Mississippi. Repr. of 1919 ed. 17.00 (ISBN 0-403-03660-7). Scholarly.

Campbell, Lyle & Mithun, Marianne, eds. The Languages of Native America: Historical & Comparative Assessment. 1040p. 1979. text ed. 30.00x (ISBN 0-292-74624-5). U of Tex Pr.

Chafe, Wallace, ed. American Indian Languages & American Linguistics. 1976. pap. text ed. 9.25x (ISBN 90-316-0086-5). Humanities.

Chafe, Wallace L. The Caddoan, Iroquoian, & Siouan Languages. (Trends in Linguistics, State-of-the Art Reports Ser.: No. 3). 1976. pap. text ed. 20.75x (ISBN 90-2793-443-6). Mouton.

Couro, Ted & Langdon, Margaret. Let's Talk 'Iipay Aa: An Introduction to the Mesa Grande Diegueno Language. (Illus.). 262p. (Orig.). 1975. pap. 7.50 (ISBN 0-87919-048-5). Ballena Pr.

--Let's Talk 'Iipay Aa: An Introduction to the Mesa Grande Diegueno Language. 1975. pap. 7.50 (ISBN 0-686-22652-6). Malki Mus Pr.

Crawford, James M., ed. Studies in Southeastern Indian Languages. LC 73-90840. 463p. 1975. 22.50x (ISBN 0-8203-0334-8). U of Ga Pr.

Cuoq, Jean A. Etudes Philologiques Sur Quelques Langues Sauvages De l'Amerique. 1866. 14.00 (ISBN 0-384-10370-7). Johnson Repr.

--Etudes Philologiques Sur Quelques Langues Sauvages De L'amerique (Montreal, 1866) (Canadiana Avant 1867: No. 9). 1966. 21.75x (ISBN 90-2796-328-2). Mouton.

Curtis, Edward S. The North American Indian, Being a Series of Volumes Picturing & Describing the Indians of the U. S. & Alaska, 20 Vols., Supplement to Vol. 1-20 in 4 Vols, Vols. 4-8, 10-16, 18, 19. (Reprint, Orig, Pub, 1907-1930). 1970. Set. write for info. (ISBN 0-384-10395-2); 40.00 ea.; supplements 50.00 ea. Johnson Repr.

Deloria, Ella C. Dakota Grammar. Picotte, Agnes, ed. LC 79-11241. 1979. pap. 5.95 (ISBN 0-88249-029-X). Dakota Pr.

--Speaking of Indians. Picotte, Agnes & Pavich, Paul, eds. LC 78-31797. 1979. pap. 5.95 (ISBN 0-88249-026-5). Dakota Pr.

Einaudi, Paula F. A Grammar of Biloxi. LC 75-25114. (American Indian Linguistics Ser.). 1976. lib. bdg. 42.00 (ISBN 0-8240-1965-2). Garland Pub.

Furbee-Losee, Louanna. The Correct Language, Tojolabal: A Grammar with Ethnographic Notes. LC 75-25115. (American Indian Linguistics Ser.). 1976. lib. bdg. 42.00 (ISBN 0-8240-1966-0). Garland Pub.

Galloway, Anne. Tovangar. 1978. 2.00 (ISBN 0-686-25513-5). Malki Mus Pr.

Gamble, Geoffrey. Wikchamni Grammar. LC 77-8566. (Publications in Linguistics Ser.: Vol. 89). 1978. 12.00x (ISBN 0-520-09589-8). U of Cal Pr.

Gatschet, A. S. The Karankawa Indians, the Coast People of Texas. 1891. pap. 9.00 (ISBN 0-527-01184-3). Kraus Repr.

Gibbs, George, et al. Languages of the Tribes of the Extreme Northwest, Alaska, the Aleutians & Adjacent Territories. (Illus.). Repr. of 1877 ed. pap. 8.50 (ISBN 0-8466-4019-8, SJI19). Shorey.

Goddard, P. E. Morphology of the Hupa Language. Repr. of 1905 ed. pap. 35.00 (ISBN 0-527-01359-5). Kraus Repr.

Goddard, Pliny E. Navajo Texts. LC 76-44071. (AMNH. Anthropological Papers: Vol. 34, Pt. 1). Repr. of 1933 ed. 16.00 (ISBN 0-404-15775-0). AMS Pr.

Gorbet, Larry P. A Grammar of Diegueno Nominals. LC 75-25116. (American Indian Linguistics Ser.). 1976. lib. bdg. 42.00 (ISBN 0-8240-1967-9). Garland Pub.

Green, Elton. Tuscarora Language. 1969. 4.95 (ISBN 0-930230-27-2). Johnson NC.

Haas, Mary R. Language, Culture, & History: Essays by Mary R. Haas. Dil, Anwar S., ed. LC 78-59373. (Language Science & National Development Series). 1978. 15.00x (ISBN 0-8047-0983-1). Stanford U Pr.

Haile, Berard. A Manual of Navaho Grammar. LC 73-15402. Repr. of 1926 ed. 26.00 (ISBN 0-404-11240-4). AMS Pr.

Heckewelder, John. History, Manners, & Customs of the Indian Nations Who Once Inhabited Pennsylvania & the Neighboring States. LC 75-146398. (First American Frontier Ser). (Illus.). 1971. Repr. of 1819 ed. 19.00 (ISBN 0-405-02853-9). Arno.

Hoijer, Harry. Tonkawa, an Indian Language of Texas. pap. 5.00 (ISBN 0-685-71708-9). J J Augustin.

Hoijer, Harry & Opler, Morris E. Chiricahua & Mescalero Apache Texts. LC 76-43746. (Univ. of Chicago Pubns. in Anthropology, Linguistics Ser.). Repr. of 1938 ed. 36.50 (ISBN 0-404-15783-1). AMS Pr.

Hoijer, Harry, et al. Linguistic Structures of Native America. Osgood, Cornelius, ed. Repr. of 1946 ed. pap. 19.50 (ISBN 0-685-13494-6). Johnson Repr.

Holmer, Nils M. The Ojibway on Walpole Island, Ontario: A Linguistic Study. LC 76-43748. Repr. of 1953 ed. 11.00 (ISBN 0-404-15587-1). AMS Pr.

Holmes, Ruth B. & Smith, Betty S. Beginning Cherokee. rev. ed. LC 76-16498. (Illus.). 1978. 17.50x (ISBN 0-8061-1464-9); pap. text ed. 9.95x (ISBN 0-8061-1463-0). U of Okla Pr.

Huseboe, Arthur R. & Geyer, William, eds. Where the West Begins: Essays on Middle Border & Siouxland Writing. LC 78-55073. (Illus.). 1978. pap. 3.95 (ISBN 0-931170-02-8). Ctr Western Studies.

James, Edwin, compiled by. Account of An Expedition from Pittsburgh to the Rocky Mountains, Performed in the Years 1819 & 1820, 2 Vols. LC 68-55198. 1968. Repr. of 1823 ed. Set. lib. bdg. 21.75x (ISBN 0-8371-8599-8, JAPI). Greenwood.

Jones, Louis T. Aboriginal American Oratory: The Tradition of Eloquence Among the Indian of the United States. 5.00 (ISBN 0-686-20688-6). Southwest Mus.

Jones, William. Fox Texts. LC 73-3535. (American Ethnological Society. Publications: No. 1). Repr. of 1907 ed. 28.00 (ISBN 0-404-58151-X). AMS Pr.

Jones, William, compiled by. Kickapoo Tales. Michelson, Truman, tr. LC 73-3544. (American Ethnological Society. Publications: No. 9). Repr. of 1915 ed. 16.00 (ISBN 0-404-58159-5). AMS Pr.

Jorgensen, Joseph G. Western Indians: Comparative Environments, Languages, & Cultures of One Hundred Seventy-Two Western American Indian Tribes. LC 80-12564. (Illus.). 1980. text ed. 49.95x (ISBN 0-7167-1104-4). W H Freeman.

Kaschube, Dorothea V., ed. Crow Texts. LC 78-23880. (IJAL-NATS Monograph: No. 2). 1978. pap. 11.25 (ISBN 0-226-36714-2, IS-00063, University of Chicago Press). Univ Microfilms.

Kendall, Martha B. Selected Problems in Yavapai Syntax: The Verde Valley Dialect. LC 75-25118. (American Indian Linguistics Ser.). 1976. lib. bdg. 42.00 (ISBN 0-8240-1969-5). Garland Pub.

Klar, Kathryn, et al, eds. American Indian & Indoeuropean Studies: Papers in Honor of Madison S. Beeler. Langdon, Margaret & Silver, Shirley. (Trends in Linguistics, Studies & Monographs: No. 16). 495p. 1980. 75.00 (ISBN 90-279-7876-X). Mouton.

Kuipers, Aert H. The Shuswap Language. LC 73-85775. (Janua Linguarum, Ser. Practica: No. 225). 297p. 1974. pap. text ed. 59.00x (ISBN 90-2792-672-7). Mouton.

Langdon, Margaret. Comparative Hokan-Coahuiltecan Studies. LC 72-94480. (Janua Linguarum, Ser. Critica: No. 4). (Illus.). 114p. 1974. pap. text ed. 20.75x (ISBN 90-2792-717-0). Mouton.

Lounsbury, Floyd G. Oneida Verb Morphology. LC 76-49736. (Yale University Publications in Anthropology Reprints Ser.: No. 48). 111p. 1976. pap. 6.00x (ISBN 0-87536-528-0). HRAFP.

Ludewig, H. E. Literature of American Aboriginal Languages. Trubner, Nicolas, ed. Repr. of 1858 ed. 16.00 (ISBN 0-527-58700-1). Kraus Repr.

McLean, John. Notes of a Twenty-Five Years' Service in the Hudson's Bay Territory. Wallace, W. S., ed. LC 68-28607. 1968. Repr. of 1932 ed. lib. bdg. 29.50x (ISBN 0-8371-5057-4, MCNS). Greenwood.

Maillard, Antoine S. Grammar of the Mikmaque Language of Nova Scotia. Bellenger, Joseph M., ed. LC 11-29307. (Library of American Linguistics: Vol. 9). Repr. of 1864 ed. 17.50 (ISBN 0-404-50989-4). AMS Pr.

Maring, Joel M. Speech Variation in Acoma Keresan. (PDR Publications in Speech Variation Ser.: No. 1). 1975. pap. text ed. 1.25x (ISBN 90-316-0069-5). Humanities.

Marken, Jack W. American Indian: Language & Literature. LC 76-4624. (Goldentree Bibliographies in Language & Literature). 1978. pap. text ed. 12.95x (ISBN 0-88295-553-5). Harlan Davidson.

Matthews, Washington. Grammar & Dictionary of the Language of the Hidatsa. LC 76-44080. (Shea's American Linguistics, Ser. 2: Nos.1 & 2). Repr. of 1873 ed. 27.50 (ISBN 0-404-15787-4). AMS Pr.

Moshinsky, Julius. A Grammar of Southeastern Pomo. (Publications in Linguistics Vol. 72). 1974. pap. 11.50x (ISBN 0-520-09450-6). U of Cal Pr.

Munro, Pamela E. Topics in Mojave Syntax. LC 75-25120. (American Indian Linguistics Ser.). 1976. lib. bdg. 42.00 (ISBN 0-8240-1970-9). Garland Pub.

Parker, Samuel. Journal of Exploring Tour Etc. Repr. 10.00 (ISBN 0-87018-046-0). Ross.

Parks, Douglas R. A Grammar of Pawnee. LC 75-25121. (American Indian Linguistics Ser.). 1976. lib. bdg. 42.00 (ISBN 0-8240-1971-7). Garland Pub.

Pilling, James C. Bibliographies of the Languages of the North American Indians, 9 Pts. in 3 Vols. LC 76-174200. Repr. of 1894 ed. Set. 67.50 (ISBN 0-404-07390-5). AMS Pr.

Powell, J. W. Introduction to the Study of Indian Languages with Words, Phrases & Sentences to Be Collected. 1977. lib. bdg. 69.95 (ISBN 0-8490-2074-3). Gordon Pr.

Powers, Stephen. Tribes of California. LC 75-13150. 1977. 32.50x (ISBN 0-520-03023-0); pap. 5.95 (ISBN 0-520-03172-5, CAL 327). U of Cal Pr.

Radin, P. A. Grammar of the Wappo Language. Repr. of 1929 ed. pap. 35.00 (ISBN 0-527-01383-8). Kraus Repr.

Reichard, Gladys A. Navaho Grammar. LC 73-15404. (American Ethnological Society. Publications: No. 21). Repr. of 1951 ed. 28.00 (ISBN 0-404-58171-4). AMS Pr.

Rood, David S. Wichita Grammar. LC 75-25122. (American Indian Linguistics Ser.). 1976. lib. bdg. 42.00 (ISBN 0-8240-1972-5). Garland Pub.

St. Clair, Robert N. & Leap, William L., eds. Language Renewal Among American Indian Tribes. (Orig.). 1981. pap. price not set (ISBN 0-89763-059-9). Natl Clearinghse Bilingual Ed.

Sapir, Edward, ed. Wishram Texts: Together with Wasco Tales & Myths. LC 73-3536. (American Ethnological Society. Publications: No. 2). Repr. of 1909 ed. 24.75 (ISBN 0-404-58152-8). AMS Pr.

Saubel, Katherine S. & Galloway, Anne. I'Isniyatam. 1978. 2.00 (ISBN 0-686-25514-3). Malki Mus Pr.

Sawyer, Jesse. Studies in American Indian Languages. (California Library Reprint). 1974. 24.50x (ISBN 0-520-02525-3). U of Cal Pr.

Scollon, Ronald & Scollon, Suzanne B. Linguistic Convergence: An Ethnography of Speaking at Fort Chipewyan, Alberta. (Language, Thought & Culture Ser.). 1979. 25.00 (ISBN 0-12-633380-7). Acad Pr.

Seiler, Hans J. Cahuilla Text with an Introduction. (Language Science Monographs Ser: Vol. 6). 1970. pap. text ed. 8.50x (ISBN 0-87750-148-3). Res Ctr Lang Semiotic.

Shea, John, ed. Library of American Linguistics, 13 Vols. Repr. of 1864 ed. Set. 175.00 (ISBN 0-404-50980-0). AMS Pr.

Sherzer, J. An Areal-Typological Study of American Indian Languages North of Mexico. (North-Holland Linguistics Ser.: Vol. 20). 1976. 39.00 (ISBN 0-444-11046-1, North-Holland); pap. 29.50 (ISBN 0-444-10911-0). Elsevier.

Spier, Leslie, et al, eds. Language, Culture & Personality: Essays in Memory of Edward Sapir. (Illus.). 1941. pap. 10.00x (ISBN 0-87480-011-0). U of Utah Pr.

Swanton, John R. Haida Indian Language. Repr. of 1911 ed. pap. 8.95 (ISBN 0-8466-4025-2, SJI25). Shorey.

--Linguistic Material from the Tribes of Southern Texas & Northeastern Mexico. Repr. of 1940 ed. 25.00 (ISBN 0-403-03631-3). Scholarly.

--A Structural & Lexical Comparison of the Tunica, Chitimacha & Atakapa Languages. Repr. of 1919 ed. 19.00 (ISBN 0-403-03699-2). Scholarly.

Travers, Milton A. One of the Keys: The Wampanoag Indian Contribution. LC 75-10246. (Illus.). 64p. 1975. 4.95 (ISBN 0-8158-0326-5). Chris Mass.

Uhlenbeck, Christianus C. A Concise Blackfoot Grammar. LC 76-44082. (Verhandelingen der Koninklijke Akademie Van Wetenschappen Te Amsterdam. Afdeeling Letterkunde. Nieuwe Reeks, Deel: 41). Repr. of 1938 ed. 27.50 (ISBN 0-404-15797-1). AMS Pr.

--A New Series of Blackfoot Texts. LC 76-44083. (Verhandelingen der Koninklijke Akademie Van Wetenschappen Te Amsterdam. Afdeeling Letterkunde. Nieuwe Reeks Deel: 13, No. 1). Repr. of 1912 ed. 19.50 (ISBN 0-404-15798-X). AMS Pr.

Uhlenbeck, Christianus C. & Van Gulik, R. H. A Blackfoot-English Vocabulary. LC 76-44086. (Verhardelingen der Koninklijke Akademie Van Wetenschappen Te Amsterdam. Afdeeling Letterkunde. Nieuwer Reeks: 33, No. 2). Repr. of 1934 ed. 35.50 (ISBN 0-404-15795-5). AMS Pr.

--An English-Blackfoot Vocabulary. LC 76-44087. (Verhandelingen der Koninklijke Akademie Van Wetenschappen Te Amsterdam. Afdeeling Letterkunde. Nieuwe Reeks: 29, No. 4). Repr. of 1930 ed. 26.50 (ISBN 0-404-15796-3). AMS Pr.

Voegelin, C. F. & Voegelin, F. M. Map of North American Indian Languages. rev. ed. (American Ethnological Society). 1967. 7.50 (ISBN 0-295-95274-1). U of Wash Pr.

Voorhis, Paul H. Introduction to the Kickapoo Language. (Language Science Monographs Ser: No. 13). xiv, 120p. (Orig.). 1974. pap. text ed. 7.50x (ISBN 0-87750-177-7). Res Ctr Lang Semiotic.

Weltfish, Gene. Caddoan Texts, Pawnee, South Band Dialect. LC 73-3553. (American Ethnological Society. Publications: No. 17). Repr. of 1937 ed. 21.75 (ISBN 0-404-58167-6). AMS Pr.

Williams, Marianne M. A Grammar of Tuscarora. LC 75-25124. (American Indian Linguistics Ser.). 1976. lib. bdg. 42.00 (ISBN 0-8240-1974-1). Garland Pub.

Williams, Roger. A Key into the Language of America. Teunissen, John T. & Hinz, Evelyn J., eds. LC 72-6590. 264p. 1973. 14.95x (ISBN 0-8143-1490-2). Wayne St U Pr.

--A Key into the Language of America, 2 vols. in 1. Incl. The Fourth Edition. Trumbull, J. Hammond, ed; The Narragansett Edition. Repr. of 1866 ed; The Fifth Edition. Chapin, Howard H., ed. 1936. LC 72-85014. 1973. 18.00 (ISBN 0-8462-1680-9). Russell.

Wolfart, Hans C. Plains Cree: A Grammatical Study. LC 73-79574. (Transactions Ser.: Vol. 63, Pt. 5). 1973. pap. 2.00 (ISBN 0-87169-635-5). Am Philos.

Zeisberger, David. Grammar of the Language of the Lenni Lenape, or Delaware Indians. Du Ponceau, Peter S., tr. from Ger. LC 76-43904. Repr. of 1827 ed. 29.50 (ISBN 0-404-15803-X). AMS Pr.

INDIANS OF NORTH AMERICA–LANGUAGES–DICTIONARIES

Byington, Cyrus. A Dictionary of the Choctaw Language. Repr. of 1915 ed. 39.00 (ISBN 0-403-03579-1). Scholarly.

Catschet, Albert & Swanton, John. A Dictionary of the Atakapa Language Accompanied by Text Material. Repr. of 1932 ed. 9.50 (ISBN 0-403-03577-5). Scholarly.

Dictionary of Chinook Jargon. Repr. pap. 4.95 (ISBN 0-8466-0005-6, SJS5). Shorey.

La Fleche, Francis. A Dictionary of the Osage Language. Repr. of 1932 ed. 35.00 (ISBN 0-403-03580-5). Scholarly.

Long, John. Voyages & Travels of an Indian Interpreter & Trader Describing the Manners & Customs of the North American Indians. (American Studies). 1969. Repr. of 1791 ed. 14.00 (ISBN 0-384-33570-5). Johnson Repr.

Matthews, Washington. Grammar & Dictionary of the Language of the Hidatsa. LC 76-44080. (Shea's American Linguistics, Ser. 2: Nos.1 & 2). Repr. of 1873 ed. 27.50 (ISBN 0-404-15787-4). AMS Pr.

Miller, Wick R. Newe Natekwinappeh: Shoshoni Stories & Dictionary. (Utah Anthropological Papers: No. 94). Repr. of 1972 ed. 24.00 (ISBN 0-404-60694-6). AMS Pr.

Rand, Silas T. Dictionary of the Languages of the Micmac Indians, Who Reside in Nova Scotia, New Brunswick, Prince Edward Island, Cape Breton & Newfoundland. Repr. of 1888 ed. 27.00 (ISBN 0-384-49565-6). Johnson Repr.

Zeisberger, David. Zeisberger's Indian Dictionary: English, German, Iroquois - the Onandaga & Algonquin - the Delaware. LC 76-43905. Repr. of 1887 ed. 17.50 (ISBN 0-404-15802-1). AMS Pr.

INDIANS OF NORTH AMERICA–LEGAL STATUS, LAWS, ETC.

see also Indians of North America–Claims; Indians of North America–Land Tenure; Indians of North America–Treaties

The Act of Union Between the Eastern & Western Cherokees, the Constitution & Amendments, & the Laws of the Cherokee Nation: Passed During the Session of 1868 & Subsequent Sessions. LC 75-3669. (Constitutions & Laws of the American Indian Tribes Ser. 2: Vol. 3). 1975. Repr. of 1870 ed. 12.00 (ISBN 0-8420-1836-0). Scholarly Res Inc.

Acts & Resolutions. LC 73-88769. (The Constitutions & Laws of the American Indian Tribes Ser. 1: Vol. 15). 1973. Repr. of 1899 ed. lib. bdg. 7.50 (ISBN 0-8420-1709-7). Scholarly Res Inc.

Acts & Resolutions of the General Council of the Choctaw Nation, Passed at Its Regular Session, 1902 & Extra Session, 1902. LC 73-88771. (The Constitutions & Laws of the American Indian Tribes Ser. 1: Vol. 17). 1973. Repr. of 1903 ed. lib. bdg. 9.00 (ISBN 0-8420-1711-9). Scholarly Res Inc.

Acts & Resolutions of the General Council of the Choctaw Nation Passed at Its Regular Session, 1903. LC 73-88770. (The Constitutions & Laws of the American Indian Tribes Ser. 1: Vol. 16). 1973. Repr. of 1904 ed. lib. bdg. 7.50 (ISBN 0-8420-1710-0). Scholarly Res Inc.

Acts & Resolutions of the General Council of the Choctaw Nation, Passed at Its Regular Session, October, 1897-& Also All the School Laws of the Choctaw Nation. LC 73-88768. (The Constitutions & Laws of the American Indian Tribes Ser. 1: Vol. 14). 1973. Repr. of 1897 ed. lib. bdg. 7.50 (ISBN 0-8420-1708-9). Scholarly Res Inc.

Acts & Resolutions of the General Council of the Choctaw Nation at the Called Sessions Thereof Held in April & June, 1858, the Regular Session Held in October, 1858. LC 75-3683. (Constitutions & Laws of the American Indian Tribes Ser. 2: Vol. 16). 1975. Repr. of 1859 ed. 12.00 (ISBN 0-8420-1849-2). Scholarly Res Inc.

Acts & Resolutions of the General Council of the Choctaw Nation, Passed at Its Regular Session, 1899. LC 75-3691. (Constitutions & Laws of the American Indian Tribes Ser. 2: Vol. 24). 1975. Repr. of 1900 ed. 12.00 (ISBN 0-8420-1882-4). Scholarly Res Inc.

Acts & Resolutions of the General Council of the Choctaw Nation, Passed at Its Regular Session, 1901. LC 75-3692. (Constitutions & Laws of the American Indian Tribes Ser. 2: Vol. 25). 1975. Repr. of 1902 ed. 11.00 (ISBN 0-8420-1883-2). Scholarly Res Inc.

Acts & Resolutions of the National Council of the Muskogee Nation of 1893. LC 75-3696. (Constitutions & Laws of the American Indian Tribes Ser. 2: Vol. 29). 1975. Repr. of 1894 ed. 11.00 (ISBN 0-8420-1887-5). Scholarly Res Inc.

Acts & Resolutions of the National Council of the Muskogee Nation of 1893 & 1899, Inclusive. LC 75-3697. (Constitutions & Laws of the American Indian Tribes Ser. 2: Vol. 30). 1975. Repr. of 1900 ed. 12.00 (ISBN 0-8420-1888-3). Scholarly Res Inc.

Acts of Council of the Choctaw Nation, Passed at the Regular Sessions of October 1895 & 1896, & the Special Session of September, 1896. LC 73-88767. (The Constitutions & Laws of the American Indian Tribes Ser. 1: Vol. 13). 1973. Repr. of 1897 ed. lib. bdg. 12.00 (ISBN 0-8420-1707-0). Scholarly Res Inc.

Apes, William. Indian Nullification of the Unconstitutional Laws of Massachusetts, Relative to the Marshpee Tribe: Or, the Pretended Riot Explained. (American Indians at Law Ser.). 1980. Repr. of 1835 ed. text ed. 17.50 (ISBN 0-930576-34-9). E M Coleman Ent.

Beatty, Donald R. History of the Legal Status of the American Indian with Particular Reference to California: Thesis. LC 74-76497. 1974. soft bdg. 8.00 (ISBN 0-88247-254-2). R & E Res Assoc.

Canby, William C., Jr. American Indian Law in a Nutshell. LC 81-3066. (Nutshell Ser.). 300p. 1981. pap. text ed. write for info. West Pub.

The Choctaw Laws: Passed at the Special Sessions in January, 1894, & April, 1894, & the Regular Session, October, 1894. LC 75-3690. (Constitutions & Laws of the American Indian Tribes Ser. 2: Vol. 23). 1975. Repr. of 1895 ed. 11.00 (ISBN 0-8420-1881-6). Scholarly Res Inc.

Cohen, Felix S. Legal Conscience, Selected Papers. Cohen, Lucy K., ed. 1970. Repr. of 1960 ed. 27.50 (ISBN 0-208-00813-6, Archon). Shoe String.

Compiled Laws of the Cherokee Nation Published by the Authority of the National Council. LC 73-88761. (The Constitutions & Laws of the American Indian Tribes Ser. 1: Vol. 9). 1973. Repr. of 1881 ed. lib. bdg. 30.00 (ISBN 0-8420-1716-X). Scholarly Res Inc.

Constitution & Laws of the Cherokee Nation. LC 73-88762. (The Constitutions & Laws of the American Indian Tribes Ser. 1: Vol. 10). 1973. Repr. of 1893 ed. lib. bdg. 40.00 (ISBN 0-8420-1717-8). Scholarly Res Inc.

Constitution & Laws of the Cherokee Nation. LC 73-88759. (The Constitutions & Laws of the American Indian Tribes Ser. 1: Vol. 7). 1973. Repr. of 1875 ed. lib. bdg. 25.00 (ISBN 0-8420-1714-3). Scholarly Res Inc.

The Constitution & Laws of the Cherokee Nation: Passed at Tah-le-Quah, Cherokee Nation, 1839. LC 75-3667. (Constitutions & Laws of the American Indian Tribes Ser. 2: Vol. 1). 1975. Repr. of 1840 ed. 14.00 (ISBN 0-8420-1834-4). Scholarly Res Inc.

The Constitution & Laws of the Choctaw Nation, 3 vols. LC 75-3680. (Constitutions & Laws of the American Indian Tribes Ser. 2). 1975. Repr. Vol. 13. 12.00 (ISBN 0-8420-1846-8); Vol. 14. 12.00 (ISBN 0-8420-1847-6); Vol. 15. 13.00 (ISBN 0-8420-1848-4). Scholarly Res Inc.

Constitution & Laws of the Muskogee Nation. LC 75-3694. (Constitutions & Laws of the American Indian Tribes Ser. 2: Vol. 27). 1975. Repr. of 1880 ed. 15.00 (ISBN 0-8420-1885-9). Scholarly Res Inc.

Constitution, Laws, & Treaties of the Chickasaws, by Authority. LC 75-3675. (Constitutions & Laws of the American Indian Tribes Ser. 2: Vol. 8). 1975. Repr. of 1860 ed. 17.00 (ISBN 0-8420-1841-7). Scholarly Res Inc.

Constitution, Laws, & Treaties of the Chickasaws. LC 73-88778. (The Constitutions & Laws of the American Indian Tribes Ser. 1: Vol. 1). 1973. Repr. of 1878 ed. lib. bdg. 25.00 (ISBN 0-8420-1718-6). Scholarly Res Inc.

Constitution, Laws, & Treaties of the Chickasaws. LC 75-3676. (Constitutions & Laws of the American Indian Tribes Ser. 2: Vol. 9). 1975. Repr. of 1867 ed. 17.00 (ISBN 0-8420-1842-5). Scholarly Res Inc.

Constitution, Treaties & Laws of the Chickasaw Nation. LC 75-3677. (Constitutions & Laws of the American Indian Tribes Ser. 2: Vol. 10). 1975. Repr. of 1890 ed. 22.00 (ISBN 0-8420-1843-3). Scholarly Res Inc.

Constitution, Treaties & Laws of the Choctaw Nation: Made & Enacted by the Choctaw Legislature 1887. LC 75-3686. (Constitutions & Laws of the American Indian Tribes Ser. 2: Vol. 19). 1975. Repr. of 1887 ed. 17.00 (ISBN 0-8420-1877-8). Scholarly Res Inc.

Deloria, Vine. Behind the Trail of Broken Treaties. 256p. 1974. 8.95 (ISBN 0-440-01404-2). Delacorte.

Drinnon, Richard. Facing West: The Metaphysics of Indian-Hating & Empire-Building. 1980. pap. 8.95 (ISBN 0-452-00541-8, F541, Mer). NAL.

Ericson, Jack T., ed. Indian Rights Association Papers: A Guide to the Microfilm Edition, 1864-1973. 233p. 1975. pap. 50.00 (ISBN 0-88455-947-5). Microfilming Corp.

Gasaway, Laura N., et al. American Indian Legal Materials: A Union List. (American Indians at Law Ser.). 1980. text ed. 49.50 (ISBN 0-930576-31-4). E M Coleman Ent.

General & Special Laws of the Choctaw Nation: Passed at the Regular Session of the General Council, Convened at Chahta Tamaha, October 3rd & Adjourned November 12th, 1881. LC 75-3684. (Constitutions & Laws of the American Indian Tribes Ser. 2: Vol. 17). 1975. Repr. of 1881 ed. 12.00 (ISBN 0-8420-1875-1). Scholarly Res Inc.

Getches, David H., et al. Cases & Materials on Federal Indian Law. LC 79-3906. (American Casebook Ser.). 600p. 1979. text ed. 19.95 (ISBN 0-8299-2027-7). West Pub.

Gubler, Brent H. A Constitutional Analysis of the Criminal Jurisdiction & Procedural Guarantees of the American Indian. LC 74-76508. 1974. Repr. of 1963 ed. soft bdg. 10.00 (ISBN 0-88247-281-X). R & E Res Assoc.

Hendren, Samuel R. Government & Religion of the Virginia Indians. LC 78-63845. (Johns Hopkins University. Studies in the Social Sciences. Thirteenth Ser. 1895: 11-12). Repr. of 1895 ed. 11.50 (ISBN 0-404-61102-8). AMS Pr.

Indian Territory. Annotated Statutes of the Indian Territory, 1 vol. in 2. LC 74-15117. Repr. of 1899 ed. Set. 98.50 (ISBN 0-404-12000-8). AMS Pr.

--Constitution of the State of Sequoyah, 3 vols. in 1. Bd. with A Memorial to the Congress of the United States on Behalf of the State of Sequoyah; Proposed State of Sequoyah. LC 74-15118. Repr. of 1906 ed. 18.00 (ISBN 0-404-11978-6). AMS Pr.

James, James A. English Institutions & the American Indian. LC 78-63833. (Johns Hopkins University. Studies in the Social Sciences. Twelfth Ser. 1894: 10). Repr. of 1894 ed. 11.50 (ISBN 0-404-61093-5). AMS Pr.

Johnson, Elias. Legends, Traditions & Laws of the Iroquois: Or Six Nations, & History of the Tuscarora Indians. LC 76-43755. Repr. of 1881 ed. 18.75 (ISBN 0-404-15596-0). AMS Pr.

Johnson, Steven L. Guide to American Indian Documents in the Congressional Serial Set: 1817-1899. LC 75-45321. (Library of American Indian Affairs). 1977. 30.00x (ISBN 0-88354-107-6). Clearwater Pub.

Kappler, Charles J., ed. Indian Affairs; Laws & Treaties, 5 vols. LC 78-128994. Repr. of 1941 ed. Set. lib. bdg. 475.00 (ISBN 0-404-06710-7). AMS Pr.

Laws & Joint Resolutions of the Cherokee Nation: Enacted by the National Council During the Regular & Extra Sessions of 1884-5-6. LC 75-3674. (Constitution & Laws of the American Indian Tribes Ser. 2: Vol. 7). 1975. Repr. of 1887 ed. 17.00 (ISBN 0-8420-1840-9). Scholarly Res Inc.

Laws & Joint Resolutions of the Cherokee Nation: Enacted During the Regular & Special Sessions of the Years 1881-2-3. LC 75-3673. (Constitutions & Laws of the American Indian Tribes Ser. 2: Vol. 6). 1975. Repr. of 1884 ed. 22.00 (ISBN 0-8420-1839-5). Scholarly Res Inc.

Laws & Joint Resolutions of the National Council, Passed & Adopted at the Regular Session of the National Council, of 1876, 1877 & Extra Session of 1878. LC 73-88760. (The Constitutions & Laws of the American Indian Tribes Ser.: Pt. 1, Vol. 8). 1973. Repr. of 1878 ed. lib. bdg. 12.50 (ISBN 0-8420-1715-1). Scholarly Res Inc.

Laws & Joint Resolutions of the National Council: Passed & Adopted at the Regular & Extra Sessions of 1870-2. LC 75-3670. (Constitutions & Laws of the American Indian Tribes Ser. 2: Vol. 4). 1975. Repr. of 1873 ed. 15.00 (ISBN 0-8420-1837-9). Scholarly Res Inc.

Laws & Joint Resolutions of the National Council: Passed & Adopted at the Regular Session of 1876. LC 75-3672. (Constitutions & Laws of the American Indian Tribes Ser. 2: Vol. 5). 1975. Repr. of 1877 ed. 12.00 (ISBN 0-8420-1838-7). Scholarly Res Inc.

Laws of the Cherokee Nation: Adopted by the Council at Various Periods - Printed for the Benefit of the Nation. LC 73-88756. (Constitutions & Laws of the American Indian Tribes Ser. 1: Vol. 5). 1973. Repr. of 1852 ed. lib. bdg. 35.00 (ISBN 0-8420-1712-7). Scholarly Res Inc.

Laws of the Cherokee Nation: Passed at the Annual Session of the National Council, 1845. LC 75-3668. (Constitutions & Laws of the American Indian Tribes Ser. 2: Vol. 2). 1975. Repr. of 1845 ed. 12.00 (ISBN 0-8420-1835-2). Scholarly Res Inc.

Laws of the Cherokee Nation, Passed During the Years 1839-1867, Compiled by the Authority of the National Council. LC 73-88757. (Constitutions & Laws of the American Indian Tribes Ser. 1: Vol. 6). 1973. Repr. of 1868 ed. lib. bdg. 25.00 (ISBN 0-8420-1713-5). Scholarly Res Inc.

Laws of the Chickasaw Nation, I. T. Relating to Intermarried & Adopted Citizens & Rights of Freedom. LC 75-3679. (Constitutions & Laws of the American Indian Tribes Ser. 2: Vol. 12). 1975. Repr. of 1896 ed. 11.00 (ISBN 0-8420-1845-X). Scholarly Res Inc.

Laws of the Choctaw Nation: Passed at the Regular Session of the General Council Convened at Tushka Humma, October 27th, 1889 & Adjourned November 15, 1889. LC 75-3687. (Constitutions & Laws of the American Indian Tribes Ser. 2: Vol. 20). 1975. Repr. of 1890 ed. 12.00 (ISBN 0-8420-1878-6). Scholarly Res Inc.

Laws of the Colonial & State Governments Relating to Indians & Indian Affairs, from 1633 to 1831, Inclusive. (American Indians at Law Ser.). 1980. Repr. of 1832 ed. text ed. 27.50 (ISBN 0-930576-32-2). E M Coleman Ent.

Leder, Lawrence H., ed. The Livingston Indian Records, Sixteen Sixty-Six to Seventeen Twenty-Three. (American Indians at Law Ser.). 1980. Repr. of 1956 ed. text ed. 25.00 (ISBN 0-930576-33-0). E M Coleman Ent.

Medcalf, Linda. Law & Identity: Lawyers, Native Americans & Legal Practice. LC 78-588. (Sage Library of Social Research: No. 62). 147p. 1978. 20.00x (ISBN 0-8039-0980-2); pap. 9.95x (ISBN 0-8039-0979-9). Sage.

Price, Monroe E. Law & the American Indian: Readings, Notes & Cases. (Contemporary Legal Education Ser.). 1973. 22.00 (ISBN 0-672-81770-5, Bobbs-Merrill Law). Michie-Bobbs.

Prucha, Francis P., ed. Documents of United States Indian Policy. LC 74-14081. x, 278p. 1975. 16.95x (ISBN 0-8032-0852-9); pap. 4.95x (ISBN 0-8032-5814-3, BB 599, Bison). U of Nebr Pr.

Taylor, Graham D. The New Deal & American Indian Tribalism: The Administration of the Indian Reorganization Act, 1934-45. LC 79-9178. 1980. 14.50x (ISBN 0-8032-4403-7). U of Nebr Pr.

U. S. Solicitor. Handbook of Federal Indian Law. Cohen, Felix S., ed. LC 74-38790. 1942. lib. bdg. 25.00 (ISBN 0-404-07121-X). AMS Pr.

U. S. Solicitor For The Dept. Of The Interior. Federal Indian Law. 1966. Repr. of 1958 ed. 50.00 (ISBN 0-379-00289-2). Oceana.

Viola, Herman J. Diplomats in Buckskins: A History of Indian Delegations in Washington City. LC 80-607804. (Illus.). 1981. 17.50 (ISBN 0-87474-944-1). Smithsonian.

Weil, Robert. The Legal Status of the Indian. LC 74-9015. Repr. of 1888 ed. 12.50 (ISBN 0-404-11912-3). AMS Pr.

Young, James R., ed. Guide to Decisions of the Interior Department on Indian Lands, 2 vols. 1980. softcover 10.00 (ISBN 0-935626-05-0). U Cal AISC.

INDIANS OF NORTH AMERICA–LEGENDS

see also Folk-Lore, Indian

Abbott, Katharine M. Old Paths & Legends of the New England Border: Connecticut, Deerfield, Berkshire. LC 72-75227. 1970. Repr. of 1907 ed. 22.00 (ISBN 0-8103-3562-X). Gale.

Adams, Richard C. Legends of the Delaware Indians & Picture Writings. 1976. Repr. of 1905 ed. 30.00 (ISBN 0-403-05765-5, Regency). Scholarly.

Applegate, Frank G. Indian Stories from the Pueblos. LC 78-150965. (Beautiful Rio Grande Classics Ser). (Illus.). 1977. 10.00 (ISBN 0-87380-076-1). Rio Grande.

Barnouw, Victor. Wisconsin Chippewa Myths & Tales & Their Relation to Chippewa Life. LC 76-53647. 304p. 1977. 25.00 (ISBN 0-299-07310-6); pap. 7.95 (ISBN 0-299-07314-9). U of Wis Pr.

Bartlett, Charles H. Tales of Kankakee Land. 1977. Repr. of 1907 ed. 7.50 (ISBN 0-915056-07-0). Hardscrabble Bks.

Bass, Althea. Grandfather Grey Owl Told Me. (Indian Culture Ser.). 1973. 1.95 (ISBN 0-89992-051-9). MT Coun Indian.

Beauchamp, William M. Iroquois Folk Lore. LC 74-7926. Repr. of 1922 ed. 21.00 (ISBN 0-404-11812-7). AMS Pr.

Beckwith, Martha W. Mandan-Hidatsa Myths & Ceremonies. LC 38-19412. Repr. of 1938 ed. 20.00 (ISBN 0-527-01084-7). Kraus Repr.

Benedict, Ruth. Zuni Mythology, 2 Vols. LC 75-82366. (Columbia Univ. Contributions to Anthropology Ser.: No. 21). 1969. Repr. of 1935 ed. Set. 60.00 (ISBN 0-404-50571-6); 30.00 ea. AMS Pr.

Bierhorst, John, ed. The Red Swan: Myths & Tales of the American Indians. 386p. 1981. Repr. of 1976 ed. lib. bdg. 27.50x (ISBN 0-374-90633-5). Octagon.

Bloomfield, Leonard. Plains Cree Texts. LC 73-3552. (American Ethnological Society. Publications: No. 16). Repr. of 1934 ed. 24.50 (ISBN 0-404-58166-8). AMS Pr.

--Sacred Stories of the Sweet Grass Cree. LC 74-7933. Repr. of 1930 ed. 34.50 (ISBN 0-404-11821-6). AMS Pr.

Boas & Chamberlain. Kutenai Tales. Repr. of 1918 ed. 32.00 (ISBN 0-403-03626-7). Scholarly.

Boas, Franz. Keresan Texts, Vols. 1 & 2. LC 73-3543. (American Ethnological Society. Publications: No. 8). Repr. of 1928 ed. Set. 44.00 (ISBN 0-404-58158-7). AMS Pr.

--Kwakiutl Tales. LC 70-82343. (Columbia University. Contributions to Anthropology: No. 2). Repr. of 1910 ed. 34.50 (ISBN 0-404-50552-X). AMS Pr.

--Kwakiutl Tales: New Series, 2 Vols. LC 79-82367. (Columbia Univ. Contributions to Anthropology Ser.: Vol. 26). 1969. Repr. of 1943 ed. Set. 40.00 (ISBN 0-404-50576-7); 20.00 ea. Vol. 1 (ISBN 0-404-50596-1). Vol. 2 (ISBN 0-404-50597-X). AMS Pr.

--The Mythology of the Bella Coola Indians. LC 73-3510. (Jesup North Pacific Expedition. Publications: Vol. 1, Pt. 2). Repr. of 1898 ed. 20.00 (ISBN 0-404-58113-7). AMS Pr.

Boas, Franz, ed. Folk-Tales of Salishan & Sahaptin Tribes. Tait, J. A., et al, trs. LC 18-7629. Repr. of 1917 ed. 13.00 (ISBN 0-527-01063-4). Kraus Repr.

Boatright, Mody C., ed. The Sky Is My Tipi. LC 49-1690. (Texas Folklore Society Publications: No. 22). (Illus.). 1966. Repr. of 1949 ed. 6.95 (ISBN 0-87074-010-5). SMU Press.

Boyer, L. Bryce. Childhood & Folklore: A Psychoanalytic Study of Apache Personality. (Illus.). 1979. 14.95 (ISBN 0-914434-07-1); pap. 6.95 (ISBN 0-914434-09-8). Lib Psychol Anthrop.

Bruseth, Nels. Indian Stories & Legends. 1977. pap. 3.95 (ISBN 0-87770-078-8). Ye Galleon.

Burton, Jimalee. Indian Heritage, Indian Pride: Stories That Touched My Life. LC 73-7426. (Illus.). 1981. pap. 9.95 (ISBN 0-8061-1707-9). U of Okla Pr.

Cheyenne Short Stories: A Collection of Ten Traditional Stores of the Cheyenne. (Cheyenne & Eng.). (gr. 2 up). 1977. 1.95 (ISBN 0-89992-057-8). MT Coun Indian.

Clark, Ella, ed. In the Beginning. (gr. 5 up). 1977. 1.95 (ISBN 0-89992-055-1). MT Coun Indian.

Clark, Ella E. Indian Legends from the Northern Rockies. (Civilization of the American Indian Ser.: No. 82). (Illus.). 1977. Repr. of 1966 ed. 13.95 (ISBN 0-8061-0701-4). U of Okla Pr.

--Indian Legends of the Pacific Northwest. (Illus.). (YA) (gr. 9-12). 1953. pap. 3.95 (ISBN 0-520-00243-1, CAL18). U of Cal Pr.

Clutesi, George. Son of Raven. (Illus.). 1967. pap. 2.95 (ISBN 0-686-74125-0). Superior Pub.

Coffer, William E. Where Is the Eagle? 288p. 1981. 16.95 (ISBN 0-442-26163-2). Van Nos Reinhold.

Coffin, Tristram P., ed. Indian Tales of North America: An Anthology for the Adult Reader. LC 61-11866. (American Folklore Soc. Bibliographical & Special Ser.: No. 13). 175p. 1961. pap. 5.95x (ISBN 0-292-73506-5). U of Tex Pr.

Cornplanter, Jesse J. Legends of the Longhouse. LC 63-13199. (Empire State Historical Publications Ser., No. 24). 1938. 12.50 (ISBN 0-87198-024-X). Friedman.

Cotten, Sallie S. The White Doe: The Fate of Virginia Dare, an Indian Legend. (Illus.). 94p. (gr. 8-12). 1975. Repr. of 1901 ed. 4.95 (ISBN 0-930230-30-2). Johnson NC.

Crane, Warren E. Totem Tales. Repr. of 1922 ed. pap. 10.50 (ISBN 0-8466-0119-2, SJS119). Shorey.

Curtin, Jeremiah. Myths of the Modocs: Indian Legends from the Northwest. LC 74-170711. Repr. of 1912 ed. 20.00 (ISBN 0-405-08415-3, Blom Pubns). Arno.

Cushing, Frank H. Zuni Folk Tales. LC 74-7949. Repr. of 1901 ed. 35.50 (ISBN 0-404-11836-4). AMS Pr.

De Angulo, Jaime. Indian Tales. (Illus.). 245p. 1962. pap. 3.45 (ISBN 0-8090-0049-0, AmCen). Hill & Wang.

Deloria, Ella. Dakota Texts. LC 73-3550. (American Ethnological Society. Publications: No. 14). Repr. of 1932 ed. 23.00 (ISBN 0-404-58164-1). AMS Pr.

Deloria, Ella C. Dakota Texts. Picotte, Agnes & Pavich, Paul, eds. LC 78-9556. 1978. pap. 5.95 (ISBN 0-88249-025-7). Dakota Pr.

Dorsey, George A. Traditions of the Caddo. LC 74-7956. Repr. of 1905 ed. 16.50 (ISBN 0-404-11845-3). AMS Pr.

Dutton, Bertha P. & Olin, Caroline. Myths & Legends of the Indian Southwest. (Bk 2). (Illus.). 1978. pap. 2.95 (ISBN 0-88388-062-8). Bellerophon Bks.

Earring, Monica F., et al. Prairie Legends. (Indian Culture Ser.). (gr. 6-9). 1978. 1.95 (ISBN 0-89992-069-1). Mt Coun Indian.

Faraud, Henri J. Dix-Huit Ans Chez Les Sauvages: Voyages Et Missions De Monseigneur Henry Faraud. Repr. of 1866 ed. 23.00 (ISBN 0-384-15135-3). Johnson Repr.

Farrand, Livingston. Traditions of the Quinault Indians - Extracts. facs. ed. pap. 6.50 (ISBN 0-8466-0004-8, SJS4). Shorey.

Father Powell. Ox'zem: Boxelder & His Sacred Lance. (Indian Culture Ser.). 1.95 (ISBN 0-89992-030-6). MT Coun Indian.

Father Power. Issiwin: Boxelder & His Sacred Lance. (Indian Culture Ser.). 2.00 (ISBN 0-686-22329-2). MT Coun Indian.

Federal Writers' Project, South Dakota. Legends of the Mighty Sioux. LC 73-3652. Repr. of 1941 ed. 14.00 (ISBN 0-404-57952-3). AMS Pr.

Fletcher, Alice C. Indian Story & Song from North America. LC 1432. (American Studies). 1970. Repr. of 1900 ed. 8.50 (ISBN 0-384-15990-7). Johnson Repr.

Frachtenberg, Leo J. Lower Umpqua Texts & Notes on the Kusan Dialects. LC 72-82341. (Columbia Univ. Contributions to Anthropology Ser.: Vol. 4). 1969. Repr. of 1914 ed. 16.50 (ISBN 0-404-50554-6). AMS Pr.

Gatschet, A. S. Migration Legend of the Creek Indians with a Linguistic Historical & Ethnographic Introduction, 2 Vols. in 1. LC 5-13733. Repr. of 1888 ed. 21.00 (ISBN 0-527-32700-X). Kraus Repr.

Gerber, Will, et al. The Rings on Woot-Kew's Tail: Indian Legends of the Origin of the Sun, Moon & Stars. (Indian Culture Ser.). (gr. 3-9). 1973. 1.95 (ISBN 0-89992-059-4). MT Coun Indian.

Gilmore, Melvin R. Prairie Smoke. LC 78-168148. (Illus.). Repr. of 1929 ed. 18.00 (ISBN 0-404-02776-8). AMS Pr.

Gingras, Louie & Rainboldt, Jo. Coyote & Kootenai. (gr. 2-6). 1977. 1.95 (ISBN 0-89992-067-5). MT Coun Indian.

Goddard, Pliny E. Myths & Tales from the San Carlos Apache. LC 76-43715. (AMNH. Anthropological Pap.: Vol. 29, Pt. 1). Repr. of 1918 ed. 16.50 (ISBN 0-404-15548-0). AMS Pr.

Goodwin, Grenville, ed. Myths & Tales of the White Mountain Apache. LC 39-33959. Repr. of 1939 ed. 14.00 (ISBN 0-527-01085-5). Kraus Repr.

Gringhuis, Dirk. Lore of the Great Turtle: Indian Legends of Mackinac Retold. LC 73-636148. (Illus.). 96p. (Orig.). 1970. pap. 2.50 (ISBN 0-911872-11-6). Mackinac Island.

Grinnell, George B. Blackfoot Lodge Tales. 310p. 1972. Repr. of 1892 ed. 9.00 (ISBN 0-87928-030-1). Corner Hse.

--Pawnee Hero Stories & Folktales with Notes on the Origin, Customs & Character of the Pawnee People. LC 61-10153. (Illus.). xiv, 417p. 1961. 21.50x (ISBN 0-8032-0896-0); pap. 7.50 (ISBN 0-8032-5080-0, BB 116, Bison). U of Nebr Pr.

Haile, Berard. Legend of the Ghostway Ritual. LC 76-43723. Repr. of 1950 ed. 25.00 (ISBN 0-404-15567-7). AMS Pr.

--Origin Legend of the Navaho Enemy Way. LC 76-43725. (Yale Univ. Pubns. in Anthropology: No. 17). Repr. of 1938 ed. 21.50 (ISBN 0-404-15781-5). AMS Pr.

--Origin Legend of the Navajo Flintway. LC 74-7972. Repr. of 1943 ed. 49.50 (ISBN 0-404-11859-3). AMS Pr.

Harris, Christie. Once More Upon a Totem. LC 72-86939. 208p. (gr. 4-7). 1973. 5.95 (ISBN 0-689-30088-3). Atheneum.

Hausman, Gerald. Sitting on the Blue-Eyed Bear: Navajo Myths & Legends. LC 75-23920. (Illus.). 144p. (gr. 7 up). 1976. 10.00 (ISBN 0-88208-061-X). Lawrence Hill.

Henry Tall Bull & Weist, Tom. Cheyenne Legends of Creation. (Indian Culture Ser.). (gr. 4-9). 1972. 1.95 (ISBN 0-89992-025-X). MT Coun Indian.

Hines, Donald M., ed. Tales of the Okanogans. 1976. 12.50 (ISBN 0-87770-173-3). Ye Galleon.

Hooke, Hilda M. Thunder in the Mountains: Legends of Canada. (Illus.). (gr. 5-7). 1947. 10.50x (ISBN 0-19-540043-7). Oxford U Pr.

Jacobs, Elizabeth D. & Jacobs, Melville. Nehalem Tillamook Tales. LC 60-62647. 1959. pap. 3.00 (ISBN 0-87114-006-3). U of Oreg Bks.

Jacobs, Melville. Content & Style of an Oral Literature: Clackamas Chinook Myths & Tales. LC 58-5617. 1959. 12.00x (ISBN 0-226-38973-1). U of Chicago Pr.

Jenness, Diamond. Corn Goddess & Other Tales from Indian Canada. (Illus.). viii, 112p. 1980. pap. 3.25 (ISBN 0-660-02427-6, 56308-1, Pub. by Natl Mus Canada). U of Chicago Pr.

Johnson, Broderick H., ed. Navajo Stories of the Long Walk Period. LC 73-78328. 1975. lib. bdg. 9.95 (ISBN 0-912586-16-8). Navajo Coll Pr.

Johnson, F. Roy. North Carolina Indian Legends & Myths. (Illus.). 112p. 1981. 7.50 (ISBN 0-930230-43-4). Johnson NC.

Johnston, Basil H. Ojibway Heritage. (Illus.). 171p. 1976. 14.00x (ISBN 0-231-04168-3). Columbia U Pr.

Jones, William. Fox Texts. LC 73-3535. (American Ethnological Society. Publications: No. 1). Repr. of 1907 ed. 28.00 (ISBN 0-404-58151-X). AMS Pr.

Jones, William, compiled by. Kickapoo Tales. Michelson, Truman, tr. LC 73-3544. (American Ethnological Society, Publications: No. 9). Repr. of 1915 ed. 16.00 (ISBN 0-404-58159-5). AMS Pr.

Judd, M. C. Wigwam Stories. 1977. lib. bdg. 59.95 (ISBN 0-8490-2825-6). Gordon Pr.

Kendall, Martha B. Coyote Stories, No. II. LC 81-5033. (Native American Texts Ser.: IJAL-NATS Monograph No. 6, 1980). 1981. pap. 12.00 (ISBN 0-226-36718-5, IS-00131, Pub. by Intl Journal Am Linguistics). Univ Microfilms.

Kroeber, Theodora. The Inland Whale: Nine Stories Retold from California Indian Legends. (Illus.). (YA) 1959. pap. 3.95 (ISBN 0-520-00676-3, CAL88). U of Cal Pr.

La Pointe, James. Legends of the Lakota. LC 72-91135. (Illus.). 184p. (Orig.). 1975. 11.00 (ISBN 0-913436-26-7); pap. 6.00 (ISBN 0-913436-27-5). Indian Hist Pr.

Leland, Charles G. Algonquin Legends of New England. LC 68-31217. 1968. Repr. of 1884 ed. 26.00 (ISBN 0-8103-3468-2). Gale.

Linderman, Frank B. Indian Why Stories: Sparks from War Eagle's Lodge-Fire. LC 15-19292. 1975. Repr. of 1915 ed. 18.00 (ISBN 0-527-03222-0). Kraus Repr.

Link, Margaret S., retold by. The Pollen Path: A Collection of Navajo Myths. LC 56-7272. (Illus.). 1956. 12.50x (ISBN 0-8047-0473-2). Stanford U Pr.

Lockett, Hattie G. The Unwritten Literature on the Hopi. LC 76-43767. (Arizona Univ. Social Science Bulletin: No. 2). Repr. of 1933 ed. 18.00 (ISBN 0-404-15621-5). AMS Pr.

Lummis, Charles F. The Man Who Married the Moon & Other Pueblo Indian Folk-Stories. LC 74-7989. (Illus.). Repr. of 1894 ed. 19.45 (ISBN 0-404-11877-1). AMS Pr.

Marriott, Alice. Saynday's People: The Kiowa Indians & the Stories They Told. LC 63-10928. (Illus.). 1963. pap. 2.45 (ISBN 0-8032-5125-4, BB 174, Bison). U of Nebr Pr.

--Ten Grandmothers. (Civilization of the American Indian Ser: No. 26). (Illus.). 1977. Repr. of 1945 ed. 13.95 (ISBN 0-8061-0140-7). U of Okla Pr.

--Winter Telling Stories. LC 73-78264. (Illus.). (gr. 3-7). 1969. reinforced bdg. 7.89 (ISBN 0-690-89636-0, TYC-J). Har-Row.

Marriott, Alice & Rachlin, Carol K. American Indian Mythology. LC 68-21613. (Illus.). 1968. 12.50 (ISBN 0-690-07201-5). T Y Crowell.

--American Indian Mythology. LC 68-21613. (Apollo Eds.). (Illus.). 211p. 1972. pap. 4.95 (ISBN 0-8152-0335-7, A335). T Y Crowell.

Marsh, Jessie. Indian Folk Tales from Coast to Coast. (Indian Culture Ser.). (Illus.). (gr. 3-6). 1978. 1.95 (ISBN 0-89992-068-3). Mt Coun Indian.

Masson, Marcelle. A Bag of Bones. LC 66-23398. (gr. 4 up). 1966. 8.50 (ISBN 0-911010-27-0); pap. 4.50 (ISBN 0-911010-26-2). Naturegraph.

Mathews, Cornelius, ed. Enchanted Moccasins & Other Legends of the American Indians. LC 73-119646. Repr. of 1877 ed. 24.75 (ISBN 0-404-04264-3). AMS Pr.

Matthews, Washington. Navaho Legends. LC 9-48. Repr. of 1897 ed. 16.00 (ISBN 0-527-01057-X). Kraus Repr.

Miller, Wick R. Newe Natekwinappeh: Shoshoni Stories & Dictionary. (Utah Anthropological Papers: No. 94). Repr. of 1972 ed. 24.00 (ISBN 0-404-60694-6). AMS Pr.

Mithun, Marianne & Woodbury, Hanni, eds. Northern Iroquoian Texts. LC 80-11887. (International Journal of American Linguistics-Native American Texts Ser.: Monograph No. 4). 168p. (Orig.). 1980. pap. 13.25 (ISBN 0-226-36716-9, Pub. by U of Chicago Pr). Univ Microfilms.

Momaday, N. Scott. The Way to Rainy Mountain. LC 69-19154. (Illus.). 90p. 1976. pap. 5.95 (ISBN 0-8263-0436-2). U of NM Pr.

Monckton, E. The White Canoe & Other Legends of the Ojibways. 1977. lib. bdg. 59.95 (ISBN 0-8490-2819-1). Gordon Pr.

Mooney, James. Myths of the Cherokee. LC 70-108513. (American Indian History Sers). 1970. Repr. of 1900 ed. 59.00 (ISBN 0-403-00221-4). Scholarly.

Mourning Dove. Coyote Stories. Guie, Heister D., ed. & illus. LC 76-43793. (Illus.). Repr. of 1933 ed. 17.00 (ISBN 0-404-15648-7). AMS Pr.

Newell, Gordon & Sherwood, Don. Totem Tales of Old Seattle. 1974. pap. 1.50 (ISBN 0-89174-026-0). Comstock Edns.

Olin, Caroline & Olin, D. Caroline. Myths & Legends of the Indian Southwest, Bk 1. 1st ed. (Illus.). 1978. pap. 2.95 (ISBN 0-88388-049-0). Bellerophon Bks.

Opler, Morris E. Dirty Boy: A Jicarilla Tale of Raid & War. LC 39-14218. 1938. 5.00 (ISBN 0-527-00551-7). Kraus Repr.

--Myths & Legends of the Lipan Apache Indians. LC 40-13687. Repr. of 1940 ed. 14.00 (ISBN 0-527-01088-X). Kraus Repr.

--Myths & Tales of the Chiricahua Apache Indians. LC 43-2944. Repr. of 1942 ed. 10.00 (ISBN 0-527-01089-8). Kraus Repr.

--Myths & Tales of the Jicarilla Apache Indians. LC 38-22477. (American Folklore Society Memoirs). Repr. of 1938 ed. 25.00 (ISBN 0-527-01083-9). Kraus Repr.

Palmer, William R. Why the North Star Stands Still. LC 57-11627. (Illus.). 1978. pap. 2.50 (ISBN 0-915630-12-5). Zion.

Parker, Arthur C. Seneca Myths & Folk Tales. LC 76-43803. (Buffalo Historical Society. Publication: Vol. 27). Repr. of 1923 ed. 35.00 (ISBN 0-404-15659-2). AMS Pr.

Parsons, Elsie W., ed. Kiowa Tales. LC 30-19147. Repr. of 1929 ed. 10.00 (ISBN 0-527-01074-X). Kraus Repr.

--Taos Tales. LC 41-4069. Repr. of 1940 ed. 13.00 (ISBN 0-527-01086-3). Kraus Repr.

--Tewa Tales. LC 29-6325. Repr. of 1926 ed. 16.00 (ISBN 0-527-01071-5). Kraus Repr.

Phinney, Archie. Nez Perce Texts. LC 73-82344. (Columbia Univ. Contributions to Anthropology Ser.: Vol. 25). Repr. of 1934 ed. 34.50 (ISBN 0-404-50575-9). AMS Pr.

Rachlin & Marriott. Plains Indian Mythology. (RL 7). 1977. pap. 1.75 (ISBN 0-451-61582-4, ME1582, Ment). NAL.

Radin, Paul. Literary Aspects of North American Mythology. (Folklore Ser). 10.00 (ISBN 0-685-36507-7). Norwood Edns.

Ramsey, Jarold, ed. Coyote Was Going There: Indian Literature of the Oregon Country. LC 76-49158. (Illus.). 336p. 1977. pap. 7.95 (ISBN 0-295-95731-X). U of Wash Pr.

Rand, Silas T. Legends of the Micmacs. LC 2-16471. 1971. Repr. of 1894 ed. 34.50 (ISBN 0-384-49567-2). Johnson Repr.

Reed, E. H. The Silver Arrow & Other Indian Romances of the Dune Country. 1977. lib. bdg. 59.95 (ISBN 0-8490-2605-9). Gordon Pr.

Robe, Rosebud Y. Tonweya & the Eagles & Other Lakota Indian Tales. LC 78-72470. (Illus.). (gr. 2-6). 1979. 7.95 (ISBN 0-8037-8973-4); PLB 7.45 (ISBN 0-8037-8974-2). Dial.

Saxton, Dean & Saxton, Lucille. Legends & Lore of the Papago & Pima Indians. LC 77-77801. 1973. pap. 5.95x (ISBN 0-8165-0420-2). U of Ariz Pr.

Schoolcraft, H. R. Myth of Hiawatha, & Other Oral Legends, Mythologic & Allegoric, of the North American Indians. Repr. of 1856 ed. 17.00 (ISBN 0-527-80350-2). Kraus Repr.

Schoolcraft, Henry R. Schoolcraft's Indian Legends from Algic Researches. Williams, Mentor L., ed. LC 74-12580. 322p. 1974. Repr. of 1956 ed. lib. bdg. 21.00x (ISBN 0-8371-7727-8, SCIL). Greenwood.

Shows, Harry B. & Gilliland, Hap. Legends of Chief Bald Eagle. (gr. 2-10). 1977. 1.95 (ISBN 0-89992-034-9). MT Coun Indian.

Simeon, Anne. The She-Wolf of Tsla-a-Wat: Indian Stories from British Columbia. 7.50 (ISBN 0-88894-145-5, Pub. by Douglas & McIntyre). Intl Schol Bk Serv.

Snelling, William J. Tales of the Northwest. Repr. 10.00 (ISBN 0-87018-058-4). Ross.

Speck, Frank G. Catawba Texts. LC 77-82345. (Columbia Univ. Contributions to Anthropology Ser.: Vol. 24). Repr. of 1934 ed. 14.50 (ISBN 0-404-50574-0). AMS Pr.

Spence, L. Myths & Legends of the North American Indian. LC 72-81598. (Illus.). 396p. 1975. pap. 7.50 (ISBN 0-8334-1745-2). Steinerbks.

Spier, Leslie. Yuman Tribes of the Gila River. LC 74-118641. (Illus.). 1970. Repr. of 1933 ed. lib. bdg. 17.50x (ISBN 0-8154-0333-X). Cooper Sq.

Squier, Emma-Lindsay. Children of the Twilight: Folktales of Indian Tribes. 1977. lib. bdg. 34.95 (ISBN 0-8490-1601-0). Gordon Pr.

Stands In Timber, John & Liberty, Margot. Cheyenne Memories. LC 67-24515. (Illus.). 1972. pap. 3.95 (ISBN 0-8032-5751-1, BB 544, Bison). U of Nebr Pr.

Stern, Bernhard J. Lummi Indians of Northwest Washington. LC 71-82357. (Columbia Univ. Contributions to Anthropology Ser.: Vol. 17). Repr. of 1934 ed. 15.00 (ISBN 0-404-50567-8). AMS Pr.

Swanton, John R. Haida Texts & Myths: Skidegate Dialect. LC 5-41613. (Landmarks in Anthropology Ser). Repr. of 1905 ed. pap. 28.00 (ISBN 0-384-59020-9). Johnson Repr.

Thompson, Stith, ed. Tales of the North American Indians. LC 66-22898. (Midland Bks.: No. 91). (Illus.). 416p. 1966. pap. 3.95x (ISBN 0-253-20091-1). Ind U Pr.

Thorne, J. Frederic. In the Time That Was: Being Legends of the Klingits. (Illus.). 26p. Repr. of 1909 ed. pap. 3.95 (ISBN 0-8466-4046-5, SJ146). Shorey.

Turner, Frederick W., 3rd, ed. The Portable North American Indian Reader. LC 72-12545. (Viking Portable Library: No. 77). 1977. pap. 5.95 (ISBN 0-14-015077-3). Penguin.

Waters, Frank. Masked Gods: Navaho & Pueblo Ceremonialism. LC 73-1799. 438p. 1950. 16.95 (ISBN 0-8040-0196-0, SB); pap. 8.95 (ISBN 0-8040-0641-5, SB). Swallow.

Weltfish, Gene. Caddoan Texts, Pawnee, South Band Dialect. LC 73-3553. (American Ethnological Society. Publications: No. 17). Repr. of 1937 ed. 21.75 (ISBN 0-404-58167-6). AMS Pr.

White, Leslie. Acoma Indians: Paper from the Bureau of American Ethnology Annual Report for 1929-1930. LC 72-13912. (Beautiful Rio Grande Classics Ser). lib. bdg. 17.50 (ISBN 0-87380-103-2). Rio Grande.

Wilson, Blanche N. Minnetonka Story. 6.95 (ISBN 0-87018-062-2). Ross.

Woolgar, Jack & Rudnicki, Barbara J. Hopi Mysteries. (Indian Culture Ser.). (gr. 5-9). 1974. 1.95 (ISBN 0-89992-060-8). MT Coun Indian.

Young, E. R. Stories from Indian Wigwams & Northern Campfires. 1977. lib. bdg. 59.95 (ISBN 0-8490-2671-7). Gordon Pr.

INDIANS OF NORTH AMERICA–LEGENDS–JUVENILE LITERATURE

Bass, Althea. Nightwalker & the Buffalo. (Indian Culture Ser.). (gr. 4-9). 1972. 1.95 (ISBN 0-89992-032-2). MT Coun Indian.

Baylor, Byrd. And It Is Still That Way. LC 76-42242. 128p. (gr. 1-4). 1976. reinforced bdg. 7.95 (ISBN 0-684-14676-2, ScribT). Scribner.

Beckwith, Martha W. Myths & Hunting Stories of the Mandan & Hidatsa Sioux. LC 76-43665. (Vassar College Folklore Foundation: Publication No. 10). 1977. Repr. of 1930 ed. 16.00 (ISBN 0-404-15498-0). AMS Pr.

Brown, Dee. Tepee Tales of the American Indian. LC 77-28292. (Illus.). (gr. 5 up). 1979. 7.95 (ISBN 0-03-022761-5). HR&W.

Cunningham, Maggi. The Cherokee Tale-Teller. LC 77-9580. (Illus.). (gr. 5 up). 1978. 8.95 (ISBN 0-87518-147-3). Dillon.

Dolch, Edward W. & Dolch, M. P. Lodge Stories. (Basic Vocabulary Ser). (gr. 1-6). 1957. PLB 6.57 (ISBN 0-8116-2506-0). Garrard.

--Navaho Stories. (Dolch Basic Vocabulary Ser.). (Illus.). (gr. 1-6). 1957. PLB 6.57 (ISBN 0-8116-2507-9). Garrard.

--Pueblo Stories. (Basic Vocabulary Ser.). (gr. 1-6). 1956. PLB 6.57 (ISBN 0-8116-2503-6). Garrard.

--Tepee Stories. (Dolch Basic Vocabulary Ser.). (gr. 1-6). 1956. PLB 6.57 (ISBN 0-8116-2504-4). Garrard.

--Wigwam Stories. (Dolch Basic Vocabulary Ser.). (gr. 1-6). 1956. PLB 6.57 (ISBN 0-8116-2505-2). Garrard.

Earl, Guy C. Indian Songs & Legends. LC 80-67271. 80p. 1980. 10.00 (ISBN 0-87062-135-1). A H Clark.

Fisher, Anne B. Stories California Indians Told. LC 57-8065. (Illus.). (gr. 3-7). 1957. 6.95 (ISBN 0-87466-026-2). Parnassus.

Gilliland, Hap. How the Dogs Saved the Cheyennes. (Indian Culture Ser.). (gr. 1-4). 1972. 1.95 (ISBN 0-89992-017-9). MT Coun Indian.

Gustafson, Anita & Kriney, Marilyn. Monster Rolling Skull & Other Native American Tales. LC 79-7890. (Illus.). (gr. 4-6). 1980. 7.95 (ISBN 0-690-04019-9, TYC-J); PLB 7.89 (ISBN 0-690-04020-2). Har-Row.

Harris, Christie. Sky Man on the Totem Pole. LC 74-19496. (Illus.). 176p. (gr. 4-7). 1975. PLB 7.95 (ISBN 0-689-30450-1). Atheneum.

Helm, Mike. Oregon Country Indian Legends. LC 81-51426. (Oregon Country Library: Vol. 5). 300p. (Orig.). (gr. 8 up). 1981. pap. 8.95 (ISBN 0-931742-07-2). Rainy Day Oreg.

Henry Tall Bull & Weist, Tom. The Rolling Head: Cheyenne Tales. (Indian Culture Ser.). (gr. 3-9). 1971. 1.95 (ISBN 0-89992-013-6). MT Coun Indian.

Highwater, Jamake. ANPAO: An American Indian Odyssey. LC 77-9264. (gr. 5-9). 1977. 10.95 (ISBN 0-397-31750-6, JBL-J); pap. 3.95 (ISBN 0-686-77290-3). Har-Row.

Holthaus, Mary. The Hunter & the Ravens. (Indian Culture Ser.). 32p. (gr. 1-6). 1976. 2.00 (ISBN 0-89992-049-7). MT Coun Indian.

Law, Katheryn. Salish Folk Tales. (Indian Culture Ser.). (gr. 2-8). 1972. 1.95 (ISBN 0-89992-028-4). MT Coun Indian.

Law, Kathryn. Tales from the Bitterfoot Valley. (Indian Culture Ser.). (gr. 1-4). 1971. 1.95 (ISBN 0-89992-014-4). MT Coun Indian.

Levin, Beatrice. Indian Myths from the Southeast. (Indian Culture Ser.). (gr. 4-12). 1974. 1.95 (ISBN 0-89992-071-3). MT Coun Indian.

Mayol, Lurline. Talking Totem Pole. (Illus.). (gr. 4-9). 1943. 5.95 (ISBN 0-8323-0158-2). Binford.

Roessel, Robert A., Jr. & Platero, Dillon, eds. Coyote Stories. LC 75-6717. (Illus.). 141p. (gr. 3-12). 1975. pap. 4.75 (ISBN 0-89019-039-9). Navajo Curr.

Roper, William L. Sequoyah & His Miracle. (Indian Culture Ser.). (gr. 6-12). 1972. 1.95 (ISBN 0-89992-056-X). MT Coun Indian.

Sally Old Coyote & Joy Yellow Tail Toineeta. Indian Tales of the Northern Plains. (Indian Culture Ser.). (gr. 2-5). 1972. 1.95 (ISBN 0-89992-018-7). MT Coun Indian.

Shaw, Anna M. Pima Indian Legends. LC 68-13547. (Illus.). 112p. 1968. pap. 3.95 (ISBN 0-8165-0186-6). U of Ariz Pr.

Weeks, Rupert. Pachee Goyo: History & Legends from the Shoshone. (Orig.). 1981. 12.00 (ISBN 0-686-30572-8); lib. bdg. 12.00 (ISBN 0-686-30573-6); pap. 6.00 (ISBN 0-686-30574-4). Jelm Mtn.

Wood, Jean & Armstrong, Nancy M. In Our Hogan: Adventure Stories of Navajo Children. (Indian Culture Ser.). (gr. 4-8). 1976. 1.95 (ISBN 0-89992-058-6). MT Coun Indian.

INDIANS OF NORTH AMERICA–MAGIC

Hallowell, Alfred I. Role of Conjuring in Saulteaux Society. LC 78-120622. 1970. Repr. lib. bdg. 10.50x (ISBN 0-374-93405-3). Octagon.

Harrington, Mark R. Sacred Bundles of the Sac & Fox Indians. LC 76-43732. (Univ. of Pennsylvania Museum. Anthropological Pubns: Vol. 4, No. 1). (Illus.). Repr. of 1914 ed. 30.00 (ISBN 0-404-15573-1). AMS Pr.

Kilpatrick, Jack F. & Kilpatrick, Anna G. Run Toward the Nightland: Magic of the Oklahoma Cherokees. LC 67-19814. (Illus.). 1967. pap. 6.95 (ISBN 0-87074-165-9). SMU Press.

Kluckhohn, Clyde. Navaho Witchcraft. 1962. pap. 5.95 (ISBN 0-8070-4697-3, BP243). Beacon Pr.

Whiting, Beatrice B. Paiute Sorcery. Repr. of 1950 ed. pap. 15.50 (ISBN 0-384-68180-8). Johnson Repr.

INDIANS OF NORTH AMERICA–MANUFACTURES

see Indians of North America–Industries

INDIANS OF NORTH AMERICA–MASKS

Cordry, Donald. Mexican Masks. LC 73-92100. (Illus.). 36p. 1973. pap. 2.00 (ISBN 0-88360-004-8). Amon Carter.

Dall, William. Masks, Labrets, & Certain Aboriginal Customs. facs. ed. Repr. of 1884 ed. pap. 9.95 (ISBN 0-8466-0123-0, SJS123). Shorey.

Haile, Berard. Head & Face Masks in Navaho Ceremonialism. LC 76-43722. Repr. of 1947 ed. 17.50 (ISBN 0-404-15565-0). AMS Pr.

King, Jonathan. Portrait Masks of the Northwest American Coast. (Tribal Art Ser.). (Illus.). 1979. pap. 8.95 (ISBN 0-500-06006-1). Thames Hudson.

Malin, Edward. A World of Faces. LC 77-26786. (Illus.). 1978. (Pub. by Timber Pr); pap. 10.95 (ISBN 0-917304-05-5, Pub. by Timber Pr). Intl Schol Bk Serv.

Mathews, Zena P. The Relation of Seneca False Face Masks to Seneca & Ontario Archeology. LC 77-94707. (Outstanding Dissertations in the Fine Arts Ser.). 1978. lib. bdg. 36.00x (ISBN 0-8240-3239-X). Garland Pub.

INDIANS OF NORTH AMERICA–MEDICINE

see also Medicine-Man

Bahr, Donald M., et al. Piman Shamanism & Staying Sickness: Ka: cim Mumkidag. LC 72-92103. 400p. 1974. pap. 9.95x (ISBN 0-8165-0303-6). U of Ariz Pr.

Boyd, Doug. Rolling Thunder. 1976. pap. 5.95 (ISBN 0-440-57435-8, Delta). Dell.

Corlett, William T. The Medicine-Man of the American Indian & His Cultural Background. LC 75-23699. Repr. of 1935 ed. 33.50 (ISBN 0-404-13249-9). AMS Pr.

Densmore, Frances. Menominee Music. LC 72-1882. (Music Ser.). (Illus.). 286p. 1972. Repr. of 1932 ed. lib. bdg. 19.50 (ISBN 0-306-70510-9). Da Capo.

Gilmore, Melvin. Notes on the Gynecology & Obstetrics of the Arikara Tribe of Indians, Vol. 14, No. 1. 1980. pap. 2.50 (ISBN 0-686-69103-2). Acoma Bks.

Hrdlicka, Ales. Psysiological & Medical Observations Among the Indians of Southwestern United States & Northern Mexico. Repr. of 1908 ed. 27.00 (ISBN 0-403-03693-3). Scholarly.

Jones, D. E. Sanapia: Comanchee Medicine Woman. LC 73-179548. (Case Studies in Cultural Anthropology). 1972. pap. text ed. 4.95 (ISBN 0-03-088456-X, HoltC). HR&W.

Kluckhohn, Clyde & Wyman, L. C. Introduction to Navaho Chant Practice. LC 42-2722. 1940. pap. 14.00 (ISBN 0-527-00552-5). Kraus Repr.

Kutmbiash, P. Ancient Indian Medicine. 288p. 1979. 10.00x (ISBN 0-86125-008-7, Pub. by Orient Longman India). State Mutual Bk.

Linderman, Frank B. Pretty-Shield: LC 72-3273. (Illus.). 256p. 1974. pap. 4.95 (ISBN 0-8032-5791-0, BB 580, Bison). U of Nebr Pr.

Moerman, Daniel E. American Medical Ethnobotany: A Reference Dictionary. LC 76-24771. (Reference Library of Social Science Ser.: Vol. 34). 1977. lib. bdg. 51.00 (ISBN 0-8240-9907-9). Garland Pub.

--Geraniums for the Iroquois: A Field Guide to American Indian Medicinal Plants. Irvine, Keith, ed. LC 81-52514. (Illus.). 1981. 19.95 (ISBN 0-917256-15-8); pap. 8.95 (ISBN 0-917256-17-4). Ref Pubns.

Reichard, Gladys. Navajo Medicine Man Sand Paintings. (Illus.). 1977. pap. 7.95 (ISBN 0-486-23329-4). Dover.

Stone, Eric P. Medicine Among the American Indians. LC 75-23657. (Clio Medica: 7). (Illus.). Repr. of 1932 ed. 13.00 (ISBN 0-404-58907-3). AMS Pr.

Tantaquidgeon, Gladys. Folk Medicine of the Delaware & Related Algonkian Indians. LC 73-620801. (Pennsylvania Historical & Museum Commission Anthropological Ser.: No. 3). (Illus.). 145p. 1972. 7.00 (ISBN 0-911124-70-5); pap. 4.00 (ISBN 0-911124-69-1). Pa Hist & Mus.

--A Study of Delaware Indian Medicine Practice & Folk Beliefs. LC 76-43864. (Pennsylvania Historical Commission). Repr. of 1942 ed. 18.00 (ISBN 0-404-15724-6). AMS Pr.

Taylor, Lyda A. Plants Used As Curatives by Certain Southeastern Tribes. LC 76-43866. (Botanical Museum of Harvard Univ.). Repr. of 1940 ed. 14.50 (ISBN 0-404-15725-4). AMS Pr.

Train, Percy, et al. Medicinal Uses of Plants by Indian Tribes of Nevada. LC 78-66077. (Adventures in Plant Medicine Ser.: Vol. 1). Date not set. Repr. of 1941 ed. lib. bdg. 15.00x (ISBN 0-88000-109-7). Quarterman.

Vogel, Virgil J. American Indian Medicine. LC 69-10626. (Civilization of the American Indian Ser.: Vol. 95). (Illus.). 1970. 22.50 (ISBN 0-8061-0863-0). U of Okla Pr.

Walker, James R. Lakota Belief & Ritual. DeMallie, Raymond J. & Jahner, Elaine A., eds. LC 79-19816. (Illus.). xxx, 329p. 1980. 21.50 (ISBN 0-8032-2551-2). U of Nebr Pr.

Weaver, Sally M. Medicine & Politics Among the Grand River Iroquois: A Study of the Non-Conservatives. (Illus.). 182p. 1972. pap. text ed. 6.95x (ISBN 0-660-00059-8, 56431-2, Pub. by Natl Mus Canada). U of Chicago Pr.

Weiner, Michael. Earth Medicine - Earth Foods. (Illus.). 192p. 1972. pap. 4.95 (ISBN 0-02-082480-7, Collier). Macmillan.

Wildschut, William. Crow Indian Medicine Bundles, Vol. 17. 2nd ed. Ewers, John C., ed. LC 74-33115. (Contributions Ser.). (Illus.). 1975. soft cover 10.00 (ISBN 0-934490-34-1). Mus Am Ind.

Wyman, L. C. & Kluckhohn, Clyde. Navaho Classification of Their Song Ceremonials. LC 38-23008. 1938. pap. 5.00 (ISBN 0-527-00549-5). Kraus Repr.

Wyman, Leland C. & Harris, Stuart K. Navajo Indian Medical Ethnobotany. LC 76-43902. (Univ. of New Mexico Bulletin Anthropological Ser.: Vol. 3, No. 5). Repr. of 1941 ed. 16.50 (ISBN 0-404-15761-0). AMS Pr.

INDIANS OF NORTH AMERICA–MISSIONS

see also Jesuits–Missions

Baroux, Louis. An Early Indian Mission. (Illus.). 95p. 1976. Repr. of 1913 ed. 4.50 (ISBN 0-915056-04-6). Hardscrabble Bks.

Bass, Althea. Cherokee Messenger: The Life of Samuel Austin Worcester. (Civilization of the American Indian Ser.: No. 12). (Illus.). 1968. Repr. of 1936 ed. 17.50 (ISBN 0-8061-0045-1). U of Okla Pr.

Beatty, Charles. Journal of a Two-Months Tour, with a View to Promoting Religion. LC 72-108459. 1768. 17.00 (ISBN 0-403-00456-X). Scholarly.

Berkhofer, Robert F. Salvation & the Savage: An Analysis of Protestant Missions & American Indian Response, 1787-1862. LC 77-22857. 1977. Repr. of 1965 ed. lib. bdg. 19.00x (ISBN 0-8371-9745-7, BESSA). Greenwood.

Berkhofer, Robert F., Jr. Salvation & the Savage: An Analysis of Protestant Missions & American Indian Response, 1787-1862. LC 65-11826. 1972. pap. text ed. 4.95x (ISBN 0-689-70290-6, 184). Atheneum.

Bowden, Henry W. American Indians & Christian Missions: Studies in Cultural Conflict. LC 80-27840. (Chicago History of American Religion Ser.). 1981. 14.95 (ISBN 0-226-06811-0). U of Chicago Pr.

Brainerd, David, ed. Memoirs of the Reverend David Brainerd: Missionary to the Indians on the Border of New York, New Jersey & Pennsylvania. LC 70-108477. (American Indian History Sers). 1970. Repr. of 1822 ed. 35.00 (ISBN 0-403-00233-8). Scholarly.

Brooks, Juanita, ed. Journal of the Southern Indian Mission: Diary of Thomas D. Brown. 175p. 1972. pap. 5.00 (ISBN 0-87421-047-X). Utah St U Pr.

Brown, John P. Old Frontiers: The Story of the Cherokee Indians from the Earliest Times to the Date of Their Removal to the West, 1838. LC 74-146379. (First American Frontier Ser). (Illus.). 1971. Repr. of 1938 ed. 29.00 (ISBN 0-405-02830-X). Arno.

Caldwell, Martha B. Annals of Shawnee Methodist Mission & Indian Manual Labor School. 2nd ed. LC 39-28738. (Illus.). 1977. pap. 2.95 (ISBN 0-87726-005-2). Kansas St Hist.

Claus, Tom & Kietzman, Dale, eds. Christian Leadership in Indian America. 1977. pap. 2.50 (ISBN 0-8024-1417-6). Moody.

Coleman, Sr. Bernard & LaBud, Sr. Verona. Masinaigans: The Little Book. LC 72-85332. (Illus.). 368p. 1972. 8.00 (ISBN 0-9600750-1-1). St Scholastica.

De Smet, Peter J. Western Missions & Missionaries. 562p. 1972. Repr. of 1863 ed. 37.50x (ISBN 0-87471-318-8). Rowman.

Faraud, Henri J. Dix-Huit Ans Chez Les Sauvages: Voyages Et Missions De Monseigneur Henry Faraud. Repr. of 1866 ed. 23.00 (ISBN 0-384-15135-3). Johnson Repr.

--Dix-Huit Ans Chez les Sauvages: Voyages et Missions De Mgr. Henry Faraud Paris-Bruxelles 1866. (Canadiana Avant 1867: No.12). 1966. 36.25x (ISBN 90-2796-329-0). Mouton.

Fraser, Gordon. Rain on the Desert. 160p. (Orig.). 1975. pap. 1.25 (ISBN 0-8024-7153-6). Moody.

Garrand, Victor. Augustine Laure, S.J., Missionary to the Yakimas. 1977. 7.50 (ISBN 0-87770-176-8); pap. 4.95 (ISBN 0-87770-187-3). Ye Galleon.

Gray, Elma E. & Gray, Leslie R. Wilderness Christians: The Moravian Mission to the Delaware Indians. LC 72-84988. (Illus.). xiv, 354p. 1973. Repr. of 1956 ed. 22.00 (ISBN 0-8462-1701-5). Russell.

Hare, Lloyd C. Thomas Mayhew, Patriarch to the Indians, 1593-1682. LC 76-104347. (Illus.). Repr. of 1932 ed. 20.00 (ISBN 0-404-03108-0). AMS Pr.

Harrod, Howard L. Mission Among the Blackfeet. LC 77-160494. (Civilization of the American Indian Ser.: Vol. 112). (Illus.). 1971. 10.95 (ISBN 0-8061-0966-1). U of Okla Pr.

Hayes, Alden C. The Four Churches of Pecos. LC 74-79075. (Illus.). 96p. (Orig.). 1974. pap. 3.95 (ISBN 0-8263-0330-7). U of NM Pr.

Hopkins, Samuel. Historical Memoirs, Relating to the Housatonic Indians. 1971. Repr. of 1911 ed. 14.00 (ISBN 0-384-24290-1). Johnson Repr.

Kellaway, William. The New England Company, 1649-1776. LC 74-33895. (Illus.). 303p. 1975. Repr. of 1961 ed. lib. bdg. 16.00x (ISBN 0-8371-7995-5, KENE). Greenwood.

Kino, Eusebio F. Kino's Historical Memoir of Pimeria Alta, 2 vols. in 1. LC 74-7975. Repr. of 1919 ed. 52.50 (ISBN 0-404-11863-1). AMS Pr.

Kocher, Paul. Alabado, a Story of Old California. 1978. 6.95 (ISBN 0-8199-0689-1). Franciscan Herald.

Lindquist, Gustavus E. The Indian in American Life. LC 74-7977. Repr. of 1944 ed. 17.50 (ISBN 0-404-11867-4). AMS Pr.

--Red Man in the United States. LC 68-56243. (Illus.). Repr. of 1923 ed. lib. bdg. 19.50x (ISBN 0-678-00798-5). Kelley.

Loskiel, George H. History of the Mission of the United Brethren Among the Indians in North America, 3 pts in one vol. Latrobe, Christian I., tr. 1794. 25.00 (ISBN 0-403-00358-X). Scholarly.

McCallum, James D., ed. Letters of Eleazar Wheelock's Indians. LC 32-6653. (Dartmouth College Manuscript Ser.: No. 1). (Illus.). 327p. 1932. text ed. 4.00x (ISBN 0-87451-003-1). U Pr of New Eng.

McCoy, Isaac. History of Baptist Indian Missions. LC 19-11605. 1970. Repr. of 1840 ed. 31.00 (ISBN 0-384-36590-6). Johnson Repr.

Mengarini, Gregory. Recollections of the Flathead Mission. Lothrop, Gloria, ed. LC 74-27573. (Illus.). 1977. 16.95 (ISBN 0-87062-111-4). A H Clark.

Morfi, Fray J. History of Texas 1673-1779, 2 pts. Castaneda, Carlos E., ed. LC 67-24718. (Quivira Society Publications, Vol. 6). 1967. Repr. of 1935 ed. 25.00 (ISBN 0-405-00076-6). Arno.

Olson. Bruchko. LC 73-81494. 1977. pap. 2.45 (ISBN 0-88419-133-8). Creation Hse.

Pitrone, Jean. Great Black Robe. (Illus.). 1965. 4.00 (ISBN 0-8198-0050-3); pap. 3.00 (ISBN 0-8198-0051-1). Dghtrs St Paul.

Riggs, Stephen R. Mary & I or Forty Years with the Sioux. Repr. 15.00 (ISBN 0-87018-051-7). Ross.

Ronda, James P. & Axtell, James. Indian Missions: A Critical Bibliography. LC 78-3253. (The Newberry Library Center for the History of the American Indian Bibliographical Ser.). 104p. 1978. pap. 4.95x (ISBN 0-253-32978-7). Ind U Pr.

Salsbury, Clarence G. & Hughes, Paul. The Salsbury Story: A Medical Missionary's Lifetime of Public Service. LC 72-101100. 320p. 1969. 7.50 (ISBN 0-8165-0204-8). U of Ariz Pr.

Shea, John D. History of the Catholic Missions Among the Indian Tribes of the United States, 1529-1854. LC 73-175853. Repr. of 1855 ed. 28.50 (ISBN 0-404-07176-7). AMS Pr.

Shea, John G. History of the Catholic Missions Among the Indian Tribes of the United States, 1529-1854. LC 70-83436. (Religion in America, Ser. 1). 1969. Repr. of 1857 ed. 19.50 (ISBN 0-405-00263-7). Arno.

Smith, Defost. Martyrs of the Oblong & Little Nine. 1948. 6.00 (ISBN 0-910294-11-9). Brown Bk.

Tache, Alexandre A. Vingt Annees De Missions Dans le Nord-Ouest De L'amerique. (Canadiana Before 1867 Ser). (Fr). Repr. of 1866 ed. 14.50 (ISBN 0-384-59425-5). Johnson Repr.

--Vingt Annees De Missions Dans le Nord-Ouest De L'amerique Par Mgr. Alex. Tache Eveque De Saint-Boniface (Montreal, 1866) (Canadiana Avant 1867: NO. 21). 1970. 23.50x (ISBN 90-2796-343-6). Mouton.

Teiwes, Helga. Mission San Xavier del Bac: A Photographic Essay on the Desert People & Their Church. 32p. 1973. pap. 3.50 (ISBN 0-8165-0423-7). U of Ariz Pr.

Urlsperger, Samuel. Detailed Report on the Salzburger Emigrants Who Settled in America: Vol. 2, 1734-1735. Jones, George F., ed. Lacher, Hermann J., tr. LC 67-27137. (Wormsloe Foundation Publications Ser: No. 10). 253p. 1969. 12.00x (ISBN 0-8203-0238-4). U of Ga Pr.

Washburn, Cephas. Reminiscence of the Indians. LC 7-19591. Repr. of 1869 ed. 19.50 (ISBN 0-384-65970-5). Johnson Repr.

INDIANS OF NORTH AMERICA–MIXED BLOODS

Berry, Brewton. Almost White. 1969. pap. 1.25 (ISBN 0-02-095250-3, Collier). Macmillan.

INDIANS OF NORTH AMERICA–MONEY

see also Wampum

Weeden, W. B. Indian Money As a Factor in New England Civilization. Repr. of 1884 ed. pap. 7.00 (ISBN 0-384-66385-0). Johnson Repr.

INDIANS OF NORTH AMERICA–MUSIC

Baker, Theodore. On the Music of the North American Indians (1976) bilingual ed. Harrison, Frank, ed. (Source Materials & Studies in Ethnomusicology: Vol. 9). (Illus., Eng. & Ger.). pap. 40.00 (ISBN 0-685-85950-9). Heinman.

--On the Music of the North American Indians. Buckley, Ann, tr. from Ger. (Music Reprint Ser., 1977). 1978. lib. bdg. 17.50 (ISBN 0-306-70888-4). Da Capo.

--Uber die Musik der nordamerikanischen Wilden. (Source Materials & Studies in Ethnomusicology Ser.: Vol. 9). (Dutch & Eng.). 1976. Repr. of 1882 ed. 40.00 (ISBN 90-6027-163-7, Pub. by Frits Knuf Netherlands); wrappers 27.50 (ISBN 90-6027-162-9, Pub. by Frits Knuf Netherlands). Pendragon NY.

Bierhorst, John. A Cry from the Earth: Music of the North American Indians. LC 78-21538. (Illus.). 128p. (gr. 5 up). 1979. 9.95 (ISBN 0-590-07533-0, Four Winds). Schol Bk Serv.

Boas, Franz. The Social Organization & Secret Societies of the Kwakiutl Indians. Based on Personal Observations Notes Made by Mr. George Hunt. (Landmarks in Anthropology Ser). Repr. of 1897 ed. 46.00 (ISBN 0-384-04872-2). Johnson Repr.

Burnett, Millie. Dance Down the Rain, Sing up the Corn: American Indian Chants & Games for Children. LC 75-21028. 1975. spiral bound 5.00 (ISBN 0-88247-370-0). R & E Res Assoc.

Curtis, Natalie. Indians' Book. rev. ed. (Illus.). 1968. pap. 10.00 (ISBN 0-486-21939-9). Dover.

Densmore, Frances. American Indians & Their Music. (American Studies). 1926. 11.00 (ISBN 0-384-11405-9). Johnson Repr.

--Chippewa Music, 2 vols. LC 77-164513. (Illus.). 1972. Repr. of 1913 ed. Set. lib. bdg. 45.00 (ISBN 0-306-70459-5). Da Capo.

--Chippewa Music. (2 vols. in one). Repr. 15.00 (ISBN 0-87018-067-3). Ross.

--Choctaw Music. LC 72-1883. (Music Ser.). (Illus.). 110p. 1972. Repr. of 1943 ed. lib. bdg. 14.00 (ISBN 0-306-70511-7). Da Capo.

--Mandan & Hidatsa Music. LC 72-1886. (Music Ser.). (Illus.). 236p. 1972. Repr. of 1923 ed. lib. bdg. 19.50 (ISBN 0-306-70514-1). Da Capo.

--Menominee Music. LC 72-1882. (Music Ser.). (Illus.). 286p. 1972. Repr. of 1932 ed. lib. bdg. 19.50 (ISBN 0-306-70510-9). Da Capo.

--Menominee Music. Repr. of 1932 ed. 14.00 (ISBN 0-403-03646-1). Scholarly.

--Music of Acoma, Isleta, Cochiti, & Zuni Pueblos. LC 72-1877. (Music Ser.). (Illus.). 142p. 1972. Repr. of 1957 ed. lib. bdg. 16.50 (ISBN 0-306-70505-2). Da Capo.

--Music of the Indians of British Columbia. LC 72-1879. (Music Ser.). (Illus.). 118p. 1972. Repr. of 1943 ed. lib. bdg. 14.50 (ISBN 0-306-70507-9). Da Capo.

--Music of the Maidu Indians. 1958. 7.50 (ISBN 0-686-20677-0); pap. 5.00 (ISBN 0-686-20678-9). Southwest Mus.

--The Music of the North American Indian, 14 vols. in 13. (Music Ser.). 1972. Set. 250.00 (ISBN 0-306-70517-6). Da Capo.

--Nootka & Quileute Music. LC 72-1885. (Music Ser.). (Illus.). 416p. 1972. Repr. of 1939 ed. lib. bdg. 29.50 (ISBN 0-306-70513-3). Da Capo.

--Northern Ute Music. LC 72-1887, (Music Ser.). (Illus.). 236p. 1972. Repr. of 1922 ed. lib. bdg. 19.50 (ISBN 0-306-70515-X). Da Capo.

--Papago Music. LC 72-1881. (Music Ser.). (Illus.). 276p. 1972. Repr. of 1929 ed. lib. bdg. 19.50 (ISBN 0-306-70509-5). Da Capo.

--Pawnee Music. LC 72-1880. (Music Ser.). 160p. 1972. Repr. of 1929 ed. lib. bdg. 14.50 (ISBN 0-306-70508-7). Da Capo.

--Pawnee Music. Repr. of 1929 ed. 9.00 (ISBN 0-403-03680-1). Scholarly.

--Seminole Music. LC 72-1878. (Music Ser.). (Illus.). 276p. 1972. Repr. of 1956 ed. lib. bdg. 19.50 (ISBN 0-306-70506-0). Da Capo.

--Teton Sioux Music. LC 72-1889. (Music Ser.). (Illus.). 722p. 1972. Repr. of 1918 ed. lib. bdg. 39.50 (ISBN 0-306-70516-8). Da Capo.

--Yuman & Yaqui Music. LC 72-1884. (Music Ser.). (Illus.). 272p. 1972. Repr. of 1932 ed. lib. bdg. 19.50 (ISBN 0-306-70512-5). Da Capo.

Densmore, Francis. Chippewa Music. Repr. of 1911 ed. 16.00 (ISBN 0-403-03557-0). Scholarly.

--Chippewa Music - Two. Repr. of 1913 ed. 27.00 (ISBN 0-403-03558-9). Scholarly.

--Teton Sioux Music. Repr. of 1918 ed. 38.00 (ISBN 0-403-03708-5). Scholarly.

--Yuman & Yaqui Music. Repr. of 1932 ed. 16.00 (ISBN 0-403-03737-9). Scholarly.

Fenton, William N. Sioux Music. lib. bdg. 29.00 (ISBN 0-403-08975-1). Scholarly.

Fewkes, Jessie W. & Gilman, Benjamin I. A Few Summer Ceremonials at Zuni Pueblo: Zuni Melodies, Reconnaissance of Ruins in or Near the Zuni Reservation. LC 76-21216. (A Journal of American Ethnology & Archaeology: Vol. 1). Repr. of 1891 ed. 20.00 (ISBN 0-404-58041-6). AMS Pr.

Fichter, George S. American Indian Music & Musical Instruments. (gr. 5-10). 1978. 7.95 (ISBN 0-679-20443-1). McKay.

Fletcher, Alice C. Indian Story & Song from North America. LC 76-136396. Repr. of 1900 ed. 9.50 (ISBN 0-404-07880-X). AMS Pr.

--Indian Story & Song from North America. LC 1432. (American Studies). 1970. Repr. of 1900 ed. 8.50 (ISBN 0-384-15990-7). Johnson Repr.

Fletcher, Alice C. & LaFlesche, Francis. Study of Omaha Indian Music with a Report of the Structural Peculiarities of the Music by J. C. Fillmore. 1893. pap. 8.00 (ISBN 0-527-01187-8). Kraus Repr.

Frisbee, Charlotte. Music & Dance Research of the Southwestern Indians. LC 74-74663. (Detroit Studies in Music Bibliography Ser.: No. 36). 1977. 9.75 (ISBN 0-911772-86-3). Info Coord.

Gilman, Benjamin I. Hopi Songs. LC 76-17498. (A Journal of American Ethnology & Archaeology: Vol. 5). Repr. of 1908 ed. 25.00 (ISBN 0-404-58045-9). AMS Pr.

Gosvami, O. The Story of Indian Music: Its Growth & Synthesis. LC 79-181165. 332p. 1961. Repr. 49.00 (ISBN 0-403-01567-7). Scholarly.

Hofmann, Charles. American Indians Sing. LC 67-14614. (Illus.). (gr. 3-6). 1967. 12.49 (ISBN 0-381-99608-5, A02600, JD-J). Har-Row.

--Frances Densmore & American Indian Music, Vol. 23. LC 67-30974. (Contributions Ser.). 1968. soft cover 5.00 (ISBN 0-934490-17-1). Mus Am Ind.

Hofsinde, Robert. Indian Music Makers. (Illus.). (gr. 3-7). 1967. PLB 6.48 (ISBN 0-688-31616-6). Morrow.

Hymes, Dell. In Vain I Tried to Tell You: Essays in Native American Ethnopoetics. LC 81-51138. (Conduct & Communication Ser.). 416p. (Orig.). 1981. 35.00x (ISBN 0-8122-7806-2); pap. 12.95x (ISBN 0-8122-1117-0). U of Pa Pr.

Kluckhohn, Clyde & Wyman, L. C. Introduction to Navaho Chant Practice. LC 42-2722. 1940. pap. 14.00 (ISBN 0-527-00552-5). Kraus Repr.

Kurath, Gertrude P. Dance & Song Rituals of Six Nations Reserve, Ontario. (Illus.). 205p. 1968. pap. text ed. 5.00x (ISBN 0-660-02066-1, 56320-0, Pub. by Natl Mus Canada). U of Chicago Pr.

--Iroquois Music & Dance: Ceremonial Arts of Two Seneca Longhouses. Repr. of 1964 ed. 25.00 (ISBN 0-403-03618-6). Scholarly.

--Music & Dance of the Tewa Pueblos. (Illus.). 1968. pap. 6.95 (ISBN 0-89013-035-3). Museum NM Pr.

Lee, Dorothy S. Native North American Music & Oral Data: A Catalogue of Sound Recordings, 1893-1976. LC 78-20337. 480p. 1979. 22.50x (ISBN 0-253-18877-6). Ind U Pr.

McAllester, David P. Peyote Music. pap. 15.50 (ISBN 0-384-36490-X). Johnson Repr.

Paige, Harry W. Songs of the Teton Sioux. (Great West & Indian Ser: Vol. 39). (Illus.). 1969. 8.50 (ISBN 0-87026-019-7). Westernlore.

Spinden, Herbert J., ed. & tr. Songs of the Tewa. LC 74-9023. (Eng.). Repr. of 1933 ed. 15.00 (ISBN 0-404-11901-8). AMS Pr.

Swanton, John R. & Boas, Franz. Haida Songs & Tsimshian Texts: (New Series) LC 73-3537. Repr. of 1912 ed. 23.00 (ISBN 0-404-58153-6). AMS Pr.

Underhill, Ruth M. Singing for Power: The Song Magic of the Papago Indians of Southern Arizona. (Library Reprint Ser.). 1977. 17.50x (ISBN 0-520-03310-8); pap. 2.95 (ISBN 0-520-03280-2). U of Cal Pr.

Wyman, L. C. & Kluckhohn, Clyde. Navaho Classification of Their Song Ceremonials. LC 38-23008. 1938. pap. 5.00 (ISBN 0-527-00549-5). Kraus Repr.

INDIANS OF NORTH AMERICA–MYTHOLOGY

see Folk-Lore, Indian; Indians of North America–Legends; Indians of North America–Religion and Mythology

INDIANS OF NORTH AMERICA–NAMES

Boas, Franz. Geographical Names of the Kwakiutl Indians. LC 77-82361. (Columbia Univ. Contributions to Anthropology Ser.: No. 20). 1969. Repr. of 1934 ed. 25.00 (ISBN 0-404-50570-8). AMS Pr.

Huden, John C. Indian Place Names of New England, Vol. 18. LC 62-18399. (Contributions Ser.). 1962. soft cover 7.50 (ISBN 0-934490-18-X). Mus Am Ind.

McAleer, G. A Study in the Etymology of the Indian Place Name. 1977. 59.95 (ISBN 0-8490-2709-8). Gordon Pr.

Rydjord, John. Indian Place-Names: Their Origin, Evolution, & Meanings, Collected in Kansas from the Siouan, Algonquian, Shoshonean, Caddoan, Iroquoian, & Other Tongues. LC 68-10303. (Illus.). 380p. 1981. 19.95 (ISBN 0-8061-0801-0). U of Okla Pr.

Sanchez, Nellie. Spanish & Indian Place Names of California: Their Meaning & Their Romance. Cortes, Carlos E., ed. LC 76-1573. (Chicano Heritage Ser.). (Illus.). 1976. Repr. of 1930 ed. 23.00x (ISBN 0-405-09523-6). Arno.

Trumbull, J. Hammond. Indian Names in Connecticut. xii, 93p. (Facsimile of 1881 ed.). 1974. 11.50 (ISBN 0-208-01415-2, Archon). Shoe String.

Vogel, Virgil J. Indian Place Names in Illinois. 1963. pap. 2.00 (ISBN 0-912226-01-3). Ill St Hist Soc.

INDIANS OF NORTH AMERICA–ORIGIN

see Indians–Origin

INDIANS OF NORTH AMERICA–PERIODICALS

Bush, Alfred L., ed. American Indian Periodicals in the Princeton University Library: Guide to the Collection. Date not set. 15.00x (ISBN 0-8287-0902-5). Clearwater Pub.

Harkins, Lee F., ed. American Indian, 2 Vols. LC 77-131270. 1970. Repr. slipcased 99.99 (ISBN 0-87140-523-7). Liveright.

Mason, Philipp, ed. Schoolcraft: Literary Voyager. viii, 200p. 1962. 5.00 (ISBN 0-87013-070-6). Mich St U Pr.

Murphy, James E. & Murphy, Sharon M. Let My People Know: American Indian Journalism, 1828-1978. LC 80-5941. 300p. 1981. 14.95 (ISBN 0-8061-1623-4). U of Okla Pr.

Schoolcraft, Henry R. Literary Voyager or Muzzeniegun. Mason, Philip P., ed. LC 74-12581. (Illus.). 193p. 1974. Repr. of 1962 ed. lib. bdg. 15.00x (ISBN 0-8371-7724-3, SCLV). Greenwood.

INDIANS OF NORTH AMERICA–PHILOSOPHY

Givens, Douglas R. An Analysis of Navajo Temporality. 1977. pap. text ed. 6.50 (ISBN 0-8191-0213-X). U Pr of Amer.

McNely, James K. Holy Wind in Navajo Philosophy. 1981. text ed. 14.95x (ISBN 0-8165-0710-4); pap. 6.95x (ISBN 0-8165-0724-4). U of Ariz Pr.

Singh, Jaideva. Spanda-Karikas: The Divine Creative Impulse. Karikas & the Spanda-nirnaya Translated into English. 209p. 1981. text ed. 15.00 (ISBN 0-8426-1684-5). Verry.

Walens, Stanley. Feasting with Cannibals: An Essay on Kwakiutl Cosmology. LC 81-47161. (Illus.). 236p. 1981. 15.00x (ISBN 0-691-09392-X). Princeton U Pr.

Witherspoon, Gary. The Central Concepts of Navajo World View. (PDR Press Publications on World View: No. 1). 22p. 1977. pap. text ed. 1.50x (ISBN 9-0316-0071-7). Humanities.

INDIANS OF NORTH AMERICA–PICTORIAL WORKS

Anderson, J. A. & Buechel, Eugene. Crying for a Vision: Rosebud Sioux Trilogy 1886-1976. Alinder, Jim & Doll, Don, eds. LC 76-25397. (Illus., Orig.). 1976. pap. 10.95 (ISBN 0-87100-104-7, 300). Morgan.

Andrews, R. W. Curtis' Western Indians: Life & Worksof Edw. C. Curtis. encore ed. LC 62-14491. (Illus.). 1962. encore ed. 9.95 (ISBN 0-87564-336-1). Superior Pub.

Bad Heart Bull, Amos & Blish, Helen H. Pictographic History of the Oglala Sioux. LC 66-13404. (Illus.). xxii, 530p. 1968. 23.50 (ISBN 0-8032-0002-1). U of Nebr Pr.

Catlin, George. Catlin's North American Indian Portfolio: A Reproduction. facs ed. LC 78-132585. (Reproduction). 1970. Repr. of 1844 ed. 250.00 (ISBN 0-8040-0029-8, SB). Swallow.

Cheney, Roberta C. The Big Missouri Winter Count. LC 79-15790. (Illus.). 48p. 1979. 7.00 (ISBN 0-87961-082-4); pap. text ed. 3.00 (ISBN 0-87961-081-6). Naturegraph.

Coen, Rena N. Red Man in Art. LC 72-267. (Fine Art Books for Young People). (Illus.). 72p. (gr. 5-12). 1972. PLB 4.95 (ISBN 0-8225-0171-6). Lerner Pubns.

Coleman, Michael. Michael Coleman. (Illus.). 1979. pap. 12.95 (ISBN 0-8032-6305-8, Buffalo Bill Hist. Ctr.). U of Nebr Pr.

Curtis, Edward S. Portraits from North American Indian Life. 192p. 1981. pap. 10.95 (ISBN 0-89104-003-X). A & W Pubs.

--Portraits from North American Indian Life. 192p. 1975. pap. 10.95 (ISBN 0-89104-003-X). A & W Pubs.

De Grazia, Ted. De Grazia Paints Cabeza de Vaca: The First Non-Indian in Texas, New Mexico, & Arizona, 1527-1536. 1973. 19.50 (ISBN 0-8165-0469-5). U of Ariz Pr.

DeSmet, P. J. New Indian Sketches. Repr. of 1904 ed. pap. 15.00 (ISBN 0-8466-4049-X, SJ149). Shorey.

Engel, Lorenz. Among the Plains Indians. LC 74-102895. (Nature & Man Ser.). (Illus.). (gr. 5-12). 1970. PLB 8.95g (ISBN 0-8225-0564-9). Lerner Pubns.

Fowler, Don D. In a Sacred Manner We Live: Photographs of the American Indian at the Beginning of the Twentieth Century. LC 73-185614. (Illus.). 196p. 1972. pap. 5.95 (ISBN 0-517-51735-3). Barre.

Mallery, Garrick. Picture-Writing of the American Indians, 2 vols. (Illus.). 1972. pap. 6.00 ea.; Vol. 1. pap. (ISBN 0-486-22842-8); Vol. 2. pap. (ISBN 0-486-22843-6). Dover.

Matthews, Mathew. Catlin Collection of Indian Paintings. facsimile ed. (Illus.). 17p. Repr. of 1890 ed. pap. 3.75 (ISBN 0-8466-0144-3, SJS144). Shorey.

Newcomb, William W., Jr. German Artist on the Texas Frontier: Friedrich Richard Petri. LC 77-28620. (Illus.). 258p. (Published in collaboration with the Texas Memorial Museum). 1978. 25.00 (ISBN 0-292-72717-8). U of Tex Pr.

The North American Indians: Photographs by Edward S. Curtis. LC 72-87367. (Illus.). 15.00 (ISBN 0-912334-34-7); pap. 8.95 (ISBN 0-912334-35-5). Aperture.

Nye, Wilbur S. Plains Indian Raiders: The Final Phases of Warfare from the Arkansas to the Red River. LC 67-24624. (Illus.). 1974. 22.50 (ISBN 0-8061-0803-7). U of Okla Pr.

Ohlendorf, Sheila & Wittliff, William D., eds. The Horsemen of the Americas: An Exhibition from the Hall of the Horsemen of the Americas. (Illus.). 1968. pap. 5.00 (ISBN 0-87959-028-9). U of Tex Hum Res.

O'Kane, Walter C. Hopis: Portrait of a Desert People. (Civilization of the American Indian Ser.: No. 35). (Illus.). 1973. Repr. of 1953 ed. 14.50 (ISBN 0-8061-0263-2). U of Okla Pr.

Perceval, Don & Lockett, Clay. A Navajo Sketch Book. 2nd ed. LC 62-21125. (Illus.). 1968. Repr. 14.50 (ISBN 0-87358-036-2). Northland.

Remington, Frederic. Remington's Frontier Sketches. LC 70-101992. (Research & Source Works Ser.: No. 398). (Illus.). 1970. Repr. of 1898 ed. 25.50 (ISBN 0-8337-2936-5). B Franklin.

Samuels, Peggy & Samuels, Harold. The Illustrated Biographical Encyclopedia of Artists of the American West. LC 76-2816. 1976. 30.00 (ISBN 0-385-01730-8). Doubleday.

Scherer, Joanna C. Indians: The Camera Reveals the Reality of North American Indian Life: 1847-1929. LC 73-84341. (Illus.). 1974. 12.95 (ISBN 0-517-51189-4). Crown.

Tanner, Clara L. Ray Manley's Portraits & Turquoise of Southwest Indians. 1975. 6.00x (ISBN 0-685-99212-8). R Manley.

Truettner, William H. The Natural Man Observed: A Study of Catlin's Indian Gallery. LC 78-15152. (Illus.). 323p. 1979. 40.00 (ISBN 0-87474-918-2). Smithsonian.

Viola, Herman J. The Indian Legacy of Charles Bird King. LC 76-15022. (Illus.). 152p. 1976. 25.00 (ISBN 0-87474-943-3). Smithsonian.

Warner, Rita, illus. North American Indians Coloring Album. (Illus.). 32p. (Orig.). 1978. pap. 3.50 (ISBN 0-912300-95-7, 95-7). Troubador Pr.

INDIANS OF NORTH AMERICA–PORTRAITS

see Indians of North America–Pictorial Works

INDIANS OF NORTH AMERICA–POTTERY

Baylor, Byrd. When Clay Sings. (Illus.). 32p. (gr. 1-5). pap. 2.95 (ISBN 0-689-70482-8, A-109, Aladdin). Atheneum.

Bunzel, Ruth L. Pueblo Potter: A Study of Creative Imagination in Primitive Art. LC 73-82257. (Columbia Univ. Contributions to Anthropology Ser.: Vol. 8). (Illus.). Repr. of 1929 ed. 55.00 (ISBN 0-404-50558-9). AMS Pr.

--The Pueblo Potter: A Study of Creative Imagination in Primitive Art. (Illus.). 160p. 1973. pap. 3.50 (ISBN 0-486-22875-4). Dover.

--The Pueblo Potter: A Study of Creative Imagination in Primitive Art. (Illus.). 6.50 (ISBN 0-8446-4622-9). Peter Smith.

Colton, Harold S. & Hargrave, Lyndon L. Handbook of Northern Arizona Pottery Wares. LC 76-43677. (Museum of Northern Arizona Bulletin: No. 11). Repr. of 1937 ed. 32.50 (ISBN 0-404-15511-1). AMS Pr.

Cosgrove, Harriet S. & Cosgrove, C. B. Swarts Ruin: A Typical Mimbres Site in Southwestern New Mexico. 1932. pap. 37.00 (ISBN 0-527-01234-3). Kraus Repr.

Dittert, Alfred E., Jr. & Plog, Fred. Generations in Clay: Pueblo Pottery of the American Southwest. LC 80-81831. (Illus.). 168p. 1980. 27.50 (ISBN 0-87358-271-3); pap. 14.95 (ISBN 0-87358-270-5). Northland.

Fewkes, Jesse W. Designs on Prehistoric Hopi Pottery. (Illus.). 1973. pap. 4.00 (ISBN 0-486-22959-9). Dover.

Ford, James A. Ceramic Decoration Sequence at an Old Indian Village Site Near Sicily Island, Louisiana. LC 36-19610. 1975. Repr. of 1935 ed. 10.00 (ISBN 0-527-03230-1). Kraus Repr.

Guthe, Carl E. Pueblo Pottery Making: A Study of the Village of San Ildefonso. LC 76-43718. Repr. of 1925 ed. 30.00 (ISBN 0-404-15554-5). AMS Pr.
Harlow & Young. Contemporary Pueblo Indian Pottery. (Illus.). 1974. pap. 2.25 (ISBN 0-89013-011-6). Museum NM Pr.
Harlow, Francis. Modern Pueblo Pottery. LC 76-52540. (Illus.). 1977. 25.00 (ISBN 0-87358-159-8). Northland.
Harlow, Francis H. Historic Pueblo Indian Pottery. (Illus.). 1967. pap. 2.50 (ISBN 0-89013-029-9). Museum NM Pr.
--Introduction to Hopi Pottery. (Special Publications Ser.). (Illus.). 1978. pap. 2.50 (ISBN 0-89734-022-1). Mus Northern Ariz.
Holmes, William H. Pottery of the Ancient Pueblos. (Illus.). Repr. of 1886 ed. pap. 9.95 (ISBN 0-8466-4053-8, SJI53). Shorey.
Kidder, Alfred V. Pottery of the Pajarito Plateau & of Some Adjacent Regions in New Mexico. LC 16-15195. 1915. pap. 7.00 (ISBN 0-527-00511-8). Kraus Repr.
Lambert, Marjorie F. Pueblo Indian Pottery: Materials, Tools & Tecniques. (Illus.). 1966. pap. 1.25 (ISBN 0-89013-025-6). Museum NM Pr.
Martin, Paul S. & Willis, Elizabeth S. Anasazi Painted Pottery in the Field Museum of Natural History. LC 41-11775. (Fieldiana Anthropology Memoirs Ser: Vol. 5). 1968. Repr. of 1940 ed. 30.00 (ISBN 0-527-61900-0). Kraus Repr.
Maxwell Museum of Anthropology, Univ. of New Mexico. Seven Families in Pueblo Pottery. LC 75-17376. (Illus.). 116p. 1975. pap. 5.95 (ISBN 0-8263-0388-9). U of NM Pr.
Spivey, Richard L. Maria. LC 78-71373. (Illus.). 1979. 37.50 (ISBN 0-87358-181-4). Northland.
Toulouse, Betty. Pueblo Pottery of the New Mexico Indians. LC 77-71898. (Guidebooks Ser.). (Illus.). 1977. pap. 5.95 (ISBN 0-89013-091-4). Museum NM Pr.
Tschopik, Harry. Navaho Pottery Making. (Illus.). 1941. pap. 8.00 (ISBN 0-527-01242-4). Kraus Repr.
Van Camp, Gena R. Kumeyaay Pottery: Paddle-&-Anvil Techniques of Southern California. (Anthropoligical Papers Ser.: No. 15). (Illus.). 1979. pap. 6.95 (ISBN 0-87919-086-8). Ballena Pr.
White, John K. Pottery Techniques of Native North America: An Introduction to Traditional Technology. LC 76-10710. 1976. 4 color fiches incl. 32.50 (ISBN 0-226-69815-7, Chicago Visual Lib). U of Chicago Pr.

INDIANS OF NORTH AMERICA-PSYCHOLOGY

Boyer, L. Bryce. Childhood & Folklore: A Psychoanalytic Study of Apache Personality. (Illus.). 1979. 14.95 (ISBN 0-914434-07-1); pap. 6.95 (ISBN 0-914434-09-8). Lib Psychol Anthrop.
Bryde, John F. Indian Students & Guidance. (Guidance Monograph). 1971. pap. 2.40 (ISBN 0-685-02018-5, 9-78858). HM.
--Modern Indian Psychology. LC 72-169122. 1971. pap. 8.00 (ISBN 0-88249-027-3). Dakota Pr.
Devereux, George. Reality & Dream: Psychotherapy of a Plains Indian. rev. ed & updated ed. LC 68-28676. (Illus.). 1969. 17.50x (ISBN 0-8147-0121-3). NYU Pr.
Symposium on Amerindians, Royal Society of Canada. The Patterns of Amerindian Identity: Proceedings. Tremblay, Marc-Adelard, ed. (Illus., Fr. & Eng.). 1977. pap. 20.00x (ISBN 2-7637-6784-2, Pub. by Laval). Intl Schol Bk Serv.

INDIANS OF NORTH AMERICA-RECREATION

see Indians of North America-Games

INDIANS OF NORTH AMERICA-RELIGION AND MYTHOLOGY

see also Indians of North America-Dances; Indians of North America-Magic; Katcinas; Peyotism; Totems

Alexander, Hartley B. North American Mythology. LC 63-19095. (Mythology of All Races Ser.: Vol. 10). (Illus.). 1964. Repr. of 1932 ed. 22.50x (ISBN 0-8154-0007-1). Cooper Sq.
Bailey, Paul. Ghost Dance Messiah: The Jack Wilson Story. LC 75-135152. 8.50 (ISBN 0-87026-025-1). Westernlore.
Beck, Peggy V. & Walters, Anna. The Sacred: Ways of Knowledge, Sources of Life. (Illus.). 1977. 8.00 (ISBN 0-912586-24-9). Navajo Coll Pr.
Benedict, Ruth F. Concept of the Guardian Spirit in North America. LC 24-872. 1923. pap. 7.00 (ISBN 0-527-00528-2). Kraus Repr.
Bierhorst, John, ed. The Red Swan: Myths & Tales of the American Indians. 386p. 1981. Repr. of 1976 ed. lib. bdg. 27.50x (ISBN 0-374-90633-5). Octagon.
Blanchard, Kendall. The Economics of Sainthood: Religious Change Among the Rimrock Navajos. LC 75-10141. (Illus.). 244p. 1976. 16.50 (ISBN 0-8386-1770-0). Fairleigh Dickinson.
Bloomfield, Leonard. Sacred Stories of the Sweet Grass Cree. LC 74-7933. Repr. of 1930 ed. 34.50 (ISBN 0-404-11821-6). AMS Pr.
Boas, Franz. Kwakiutl Culture As Reflected in Mythology. LC 36-6760. Repr. of 1935 ed. 13.00 (ISBN 0-527-01080-4). Kraus Repr.
--Religion of the Kwakiutl Indians, 2 Vols. LC 72-82368. (Columbia Univ. Contributions to Anthropology Ser.: No. 10). Repr. of 1930 ed. Set. 45.00 (ISBN 0-404-50560-0); 22.50 ea. AMS Pr.
Brinton, Daniel G. The Myths of the New World: A Treatise on the Symbolism & Mythology of the Red Race in America. LC 74-1038. 360p. 1974. Repr. of 1896 ed. 19.00 (ISBN 0-8103-3959-5). Gale.
--Myths of the New World Indians. LC 72-81594. (Illus.). 334p. 1976. pap. 7.50 (ISBN 0-8334-1742-8). Steinerbks.
Brown, Joseph E. Spiritual Legacy of the American Indian. LC 64-17425. (Illus., Orig.). 1964. pap. 1.25 (ISBN 0-87574-135-5). Pendle Hill.
Brown, Vinson. Voices of Earth & Sky. LC 76-41761. (Illus.). 1976. pap. 3.95 (ISBN 0-87961-060-3). Naturegraph.
Brundage, Burr C. The Phoenix of the Western World: Quetzalcoatl & the Sky Religion. LC 81-40278. (The Civilization of the American Indian Ser.: Vol. 160). (Illus.). 320p. 1981. 17.50 (ISBN 0-8061-1773-7). U of Okla Pr.
Capps, Walter H., ed. Seeing with the Native Eye: Contibutions to the Study of Native American Religion. LC 76-9980. 1976. pap. 4.95x (ISBN 0-06-061312-2, RD-177, HarpR). Har-Row.
Clark, Ella. Guardian Spirit Quest. (Indian Culture Ser.). (gr. 5-12). 1974. pap. 1.95 (ISBN 0-89992-045-4). MT Coun Indian.
Coffer, William E. Spirits of the Sacred Mountains: Creation Stories of the American Indian. 1978. 8.95 (ISBN 0-442-21600-9). Van Nos Reinhold.
Colton, Harold S. Hopi Kachina Dolls with a Key to Their Identification. rev ed. LC 59-5480. (Illus.). 150p. 1971. pap. 6.95 (ISBN 0-8263-0180-0). U of NM Pr.
Cooke, Grace. Sun Men of the Americas. 6.95 (ISBN 0-85487-035-0). De Vorss.
Cooper, John M. The Northern Algonquian Supreme Being. LC 76-43682. (Catholic University of America Anthropological Ser.: No. 2). Repr. of 1934 ed. 14.00 (ISBN 0-404-15515-4). AMS Pr.
Curtin, Jeremiah. Myths of the Modocs: Indian Legends from the Northwest. LC 74-170711. Repr. of 1912 ed. 20.00 (ISBN 0-405-08415-3, Blom Pubns). Arno.
Cushing, Frank H. Zuni Fetishes. LC 66-23329. (Illus.). 1966. 7.95 (ISBN 0-916122-28-X); pap. 3.00 (ISBN 0-916122-03-4). KC Pubns.
Dewdney, Selwyn. Sacred Scrolls of the Southern Ojibway. LC 73-90150. 1974. 17.50x (ISBN 0-8020-3321-0). U of Toronto Pr.
Dolaghan, Thomas & Scates, David R. The Navajos Are Coming to Jesus. LC 78-3609. (Illus.). 1978. pap. 4.95 (ISBN 0-87808-162-3). William Carey Lib.
Dorsey, G. A. & Voth, H. R. Oraibi Soyal Ceremony, & Oraibi Powamu Ceremony, & Mishongnovi Ceremonies of the Snake & Antelope Fraternities, & Oraibi Summer Snake Ceremony, 4 wks. in 1 vol. 1901-03. pap. 48.00 (ISBN 0-527-01863-5). Kraus Repr.
Duran, Fr. Diego. Book of the Gods & Rites & the Ancient Calendar. Horcasitas, Fernando & Heyden, Doris, trs. LC 73-88147. (Civilization of the American Indian Ser.: No. 102). (Illus.). 1971. 22.50 (ISBN 0-8061-0889-4); pap. 9.95 (ISBN 0-8061-1201-8). U of Okla Pr.
Dusenberry, Verne. The Montana Cree: A Study in Religious Persistence. (Stockholm Studies in Comparative Religion: No.3). 280p. 1962. text ed. 25.50x (ISBN 91-22-00263-4). Humanities.
Earle, Edwin & Kennard, Edward A. Hopi Kachinas. 2nd ed. LC 71-139867. (Illus.). 1971. 12.50 (ISBN 0-934490-11-2). Mus Am Ind.
Eastman, Charles A. The Soul of the Indian: An Interpretation. LC 79-26355. 1980. pap. 3.50 (ISBN 0-8032-6701-0, BB 735 BISON). U of Nebr Pr.
Emerson, Ellen. Indian Myths. 59.95 (ISBN 0-8490-0400-4). Gordon Pr.
Evers, Larry, ed. The South Corner of Time: Hopi, Navajo, Papago, & Yaqui Tribal Literature. LC 76-617570. (Sun Tracks: An American Indian Literary Magazine: Vol. 6). (Illus.). 240p. (Incl. translation from Hopi, Navajo, Papago, & Yaqui languages as well as first language texts in each). 1980. 20.00 (ISBN 0-936350-00-8); pap. 10.00 (ISBN 0-936350-01-6). Sun Tracks.
Fewkes, Jesse W. & Owens, John G. A Few Summer Ceremonials at the Tusayon Pueblos: Natal Ceremonies of the Hopi Indians,& a Report on the Present Condition of a Ruin in Arizona Called Casa Grande. LC 76-21217. (A Journal of American Ethnology & Archaeology: Vol. 2). 1977. Repr. of 1892 ed. 27.50 (ISBN 0-404-58042-4). AMS Pr.
Fewkes, Jesse W., et al. The Snake Ceremonials at Walpi. LC 76-17497. (A Journal of American Ethnology & Archaeology: Vol. 4). Repr. of 1894 ed. 17.50 (ISBN 0-404-58044-0). AMS Pr.
Fishler, Stanley A. In the Beginning: A Navaho Creation Myth. (Utah Anthropological Papers: No. 13). Repr. of 1953 ed. 26.50 (ISBN 0-404-60613-X). AMS Pr.
Gill, Sam D. Sacred Words: A Study of Navajo Religion & Prayer. LC 80-659. (Contributions in Intercultural & Comparative Studies: No. 4). (Illus.). xxvi, 257p. 1981. lib. bdg. 29.95 (ISBN 0-313-22165-0, GSW/). Greenwood.
Goddard, Pliny E. Myths & Tales from the San Carlos Apache. LC 76-43715. (AMNH. Anthropological Pap.: Vol. 29, Pt. 1). Repr. of 1918 ed. 16.50 (ISBN 0-404-15548-0). AMS Pr.
Goldman, Irving. The Mouth of Heaven: An Introduction to Kwakiutl Religious Thought. LC 80-11163. 284p. 1981. Repr. of 1975 ed. lib. bdg. 19.50 (ISBN 0-89874-136-X). Krieger.
--The Mouth of Heaven: An Introduction to Kwakiutl Religious Thought. LC 75-8742. 265p. 1975. 22.50 (ISBN 0-471-31140-5, Pub. by Wiley-Interscience). Wiley.
Haeberlin, Herman K. The Idea of Fertilization in the Culture of the Pueblo Indians. LC 16-25723. Repr. of 1916 ed. pap. 5.00 (ISBN 0-527-00512-6). Kraus Repr.
Haile, Berard. Love-Magic & Butterfly People: The Slim Curly Version of the Ajiee & Mothway Myths. LC 78-59705. (Illus.). xii, 172p. 1980. pap. 13.95x (ISBN 0-89734-026-4). Mus Northern Ariz.
--Love-Magic & Butterfly People: The Slim Curly Version of the Ajjee & Mothway Myths. LC 78-59705. (Illus.). xii, 172p. Date not set. pap. 13.95x (ISBN 0-89734-026-4, Pub by Mus Nothern Ariz). U of Nebr Pr.
--Waterway. LC 79-66605. (Illus.). vi, 153p. 1981. pap. 12.95x (ISBN 0-89734-030-2, Pub by Mus Northern Ariz). U of Nebr Pr.
Harrington, M. R. Sacred Bundles of the Sac & Fox Indians. (Anthropological Publications Ser.: Vol. 4-2). (Illus.). 1914. 7.00 (ISBN 0-686-24093-6). Univ Mus of U.
Harrington, Mark R. Religion & Ceremonies of the Lenape. LC 76-43731. (MAI Indian Notes & Monographs. Miscellaneous). Repr. of 1921 ed. 19.00 (ISBN 0-404-15572-3). AMS Pr.
Heath, Virginia S. Dramatic Elements in American Indian Ceremonials. (American History & Americana Ser., No. 47). 1970. pap. 12.95 (ISBN 0-8383-0093-6). Haskell.
Heckewelder, John. Narrative of the Mission of the United Brethren Among the Delaware & Mohegan Indians. LC 79-146399. (First American Frontier Ser). 1971. Repr. of 1820 ed. 21.00 (ISBN 0-405-02852-0). Arno.
Hendren, Samuel R. Government & Religion of the Virginia Indians. LC 78-63845. (Johns Hopkins University. Studies in the Social Sciences. Thirteenth Ser. 1895: 11-12). Repr. of 1895 ed. 11.50 (ISBN 0-404-61102-8). AMS Pr.
Hewitt, John N. Iroquoian Cosmology, 2 pts. in 1. LC 73-8095. Repr. of 1928 ed. 60.00 (ISBN 0-404-11202-1). AMS Pr.
Hildreth, Dolly, et al. The Money God. (Indian Culture Ser.). (gr. 6). 1972. 1.95 (ISBN 0-89992-031-4). MT Coun Indian.
Hultkrantz, Ake. Belief & Worship in Native North America. Vecsey, Christopher, ed. 1981. 30.00x (ISBN 0-8156-2248-1). Syracuse U Pr.
--The Religions of the American Indians. LC 73-90661. (Hermeneutics--Studies in the History of Religions: Vol. 7). 1979. 14.95 (ISBN 0-520-02653-5); pap. 5.95 (ISBN 0-520-04239-5, CAL 463). U of Cal Pr.
Hurdy, John M. American Indian Religions. 2.50 (ISBN 0-8202-0000-X). Sherbourne.
Johnson, F. Roy. North Carolina Indian Legends & Myths. (Illus.). 112p. 1981. 7.50 (ISBN 0-930230-43-4). Johnson NC.
Jorgensen, Joseph G. The Sun Dance Religion: Power for the Powerless. LC 70-182089. 1972. 25.00x (ISBN 0-226-41085-4). U of Chicago Pr.
--The Sun Dance Religion: Power for the Powerless. LC 70-182089. (Illus.). 372p. 1974. pap. 9.50x (ISBN 0-226-41086-2, P608, Phoen). U of Chicago Pr.
Kilpatrick, Jack F. & Kilpatrick, Anna G. Run Toward the Nightland: Magic of the Oklahoma Cherokees. LC 67-19814. (Illus.). 1967. pap. 6.95 (ISBN 0-87074-165-9). SMU Press.
Klah, Hasteen. Navajo Creation Myth: The Story of Emergence. LC 76-43762. (Museum of Navajo Ceremonial Art. Religion Ser.: Vol. 1). Repr. of 1942 ed. 24.50 (ISBN 0-404-15615-0). AMS Pr.
Kluckhohn, Clyde & Wyman, L. C. Introduction to Navaho Chant Practice. LC 42-2722. 1940. pap. 14.00 (ISBN 0-527-00552-5). Kraus Repr.
Kroeber, Alfred L. Yurok Myths. LC 75-3772. 460p. 1976. 25.00 (ISBN 0-520-02977-1); pap. 6.95 (ISBN 0-520-03639-5). U of Cal Pr.
LaBarre, Weston. The Peyote Cult. 4th ed. (Illus.). 296p. 1975. 15.00 (ISBN 0-208-01456-X). Shoe String.
Levi-Strauss, Claude. The Naked Man. Weightman, John & Weightman, Doreen, trs. from Fr. LC 79-3399. (Introduction to a Science of Mythology Ser.). (Illus.). 440p. 1981. 35.00 (ISBN 0-06-012584-5, HarpT). Har-Row.
Link, Margaret S., retold by. The Pollen Path: A Collection of Navajo Myths. LC 56-7272. (Illus.). 1956. 12.50x (ISBN 0-8047-0473-2). Stanford U Pr.
Lowie, Robert H. The Religion of the Crow Indians. LC 74-7986. Repr. of 1922 ed. 15.00 (ISBN 0-404-11876-3). AMS Pr.
Luckert, Karl W. A Navajo Bringing-Home Ceremony: The Claus Chee Sonny Version of Deerway Ajilee. LC 78-59701. (Illus.). xiv, 210p. 1980. pap. 14.95x (ISBN 0-89734-027-2). Mus Northern Ariz.
--Navajo Mountain & Rainbow Bridge Religion. (Illus.). vii, 157p. 1980. pap. 9.95x (ISBN 0-89734-025-6). Mus Northern Ariz.
--Navajo Mountain & Rainbow Bridge Religion. Goossen, Irvy W & Bilagody, Harry, Jr., trs. from Navajo. (American Tribal Religions Ser.: No. 1). (Illus.). 1977. pap. 6.95 (ISBN 0-89734-025-6). Mus Northern Ariz.
McClintock, Walter. The Old North Trail; or, Life, Legends & Religion of the Blackfeet Indians. LC 68-13651. (Illus.). 1968. pap. 5.95 (ISBN 0-8032-5130-0, BB 379, Bison). U of Nebr Pr.
McDonald, W. H. Creation Tales from the Salish. (Indian Culture Ser.). (gr. 3-9). 1973. 1.95 (ISBN 0-89992-061-6). MT Coun Indian.
Marriott, Alice & Rachlin, Carol. Plains Indian Mythology. LC 75-26554. (Illus.). 224p. 1975. 10.95 (ISBN 0-690-00694-2). T Y Crowell.
Marriott, Alice & Rachlin, Carol K. American Indian Mythology. (RL 7). 1972. pap. 1.95 (ISBN 0-451-61777-0, MJ1777, Ment). NAL.
Modesto, Ruby & Mount, Guy. Not for Innocent Ears: Spiritual Traditions of a Desert Cahuilla Medicine Woman. (Illus.). 128p. (Orig.). 1980. pap. 6.95 (ISBN 0-9604462-0-6). Sweetlight.
Moon, Sheila. A Magic Dwells: A Poetic & Psychological Study of the Navaho Emergence Myth. LC 72-105501. 1970. pap. 5.95 (ISBN 0-8195-6036-7, Pub. by Wesleyan U Pr). Columbia U Pr.
Mooney, James. Ghost-Dance Religion & the Sioux Outbreak of 1890. Wallace, Anthony F., ed. LC 64-24971. (Orig.). 1965. pap. 4.95 (ISBN 0-226-53517-7, P176, Phoen). U of Chicago Pr.
--Myths of the Cherokee & Sacred Formulas of the Cherokees. LC 72-188151. (Illus.). 1972. Repr. 60.00 (ISBN 0-918450-05-5). C Elder.
Myerhoff, Barbara G. Peyote Hunt: The Sacred Journey of Huichol Indians. LC 73-16923. (Symbol, Myth & Ritual Ser.). (Illus.). 288p. 1974. 24.50x (ISBN 0-8014-0817-2); pap. 6.95 1976 ed. (ISBN 0-8014-9137-1). Cornell U Pr.
O'Brien, Aileen. The Dine: Origin Myths of the Navaho Indians. Repr. of 1956 ed. 19.00 (ISBN 0-403-03581-3). Scholarly.
Opler, Morris E. Myths & Tales of the Jicarilla Apache Indians. LC 38-22477. (American Folklore Society Memoirs). Repr. of 1938 ed. 25.00 (ISBN 0-527-01083-9). Kraus Repr.
Parker, Arthur C. Seneca Myths & Folk Tales. LC 76-43803. (Buffalo Historical Society. Publication: Vol. 27). Repr. of 1923 ed. 35.00 (ISBN 0-404-15659-2). AMS Pr.
Parsons, Elsie C. Hopi & Zuni Ceremonialism. LC 34-5260. 1933. pap. 7.00 (ISBN 0-527-00538-X). Kraus Repr.
--Scalp Ceremonial of Zuni. LC 25-1663. 1924. pap. 5.00 (ISBN 0-527-00530-4). Kraus Repr.
Powers, William K. Oglala Religion. LC 76-30614. (Illus.). 1977. 14.95 (ISBN 0-8032-0910-X). U of Nebr Pr.
Rachlin & Marriott. Plains Indian Mythology. (RL 7). 1977. pap. 1.75 (ISBN 0-451-61582-4, ME1582, Ment). NAL.
Radin, Paul. Literary Aspects of North American Mythology. (Folklore Ser). 10.00 (ISBN 0-685-36507-7). Norwood Edns.
--Trickster: A Study in American Indian Mythology. Repr. of 1956 ed. lib. bdg. 15.00x (ISBN 0-8371-2112-4, RATT). Greenwood.
--The Trickster: A Study in American Indian Mythology. new ed. LC 74-88986. 223p. 1972. pap. 3.95 (ISBN 0-8052-0351-6). Schocken.
Reichard, Gladys A. Analysis of Coeur D'Alene Indian Myths. LC 48-2411. Repr. of 1947 ed. 14.00 (ISBN 0-527-01093-6). Kraus Repr.

--Navaho Religion: A Study of Symbolism. 2nd ed. LC 63-14455. (Bollingen Ser.: Vol. 18). 864p. 1963. 32.00 (ISBN 0-691-09801-8); pap. 9.95 (ISBN 0-691-01798-0). Princeton U Pr.
--Navaho Religion: A Study of Symbolism. 2nd ed. LC 63-14455. (Bollingen Ser.: Vol. 18). 864p. 1963. 32.00 (ISBN 0-691-09801-8); pap. 9.95 (ISBN 0-691-01798-0). Princeton U Pr.
Riggs, Stephen R. Tah-Koo Wah-Kan; or, the Gospel Among the Dakotas. LC 78-38460. (Religion in America, Ser. 2). 534p. 1972. Repr. of 1869 ed. 27.00 (ISBN 0-405-04081-4). Arno.
Shorris, Earl. The Death of the Great Spirit. 208p. 1974. pap. 1.50 (ISBN 0-451-61355-4, MW1355, Ment). NAL.
Smithson, Carma L. & Euler, Robert C. Havasupai Religion & Mythology. viii, 112p. Repr. of 1964 ed. 15.50 (ISBN 0-384-56210-8). Johnson Repr.
--Havasupai Religion & Mythology. (Utah Anthropological Papers: No. 68). Repr. of 1964 ed. 14.00 (ISBN 0-404-60668-7). AMS Pr.
Snyder, Gary. He Who Hunted Birds in His Father's Village: The Dimensions of a Haida Myth. LC 78-16935. 1979. 12.00 (ISBN 0-912516-37-2); pap. 5.00 (ISBN 0-912516-38-0). Grey Fox.
Spencer, Katherine. Mythology & Values: An Analysis of Navaho Chantway Myths. (American Folklore Society Memoir Ser: No. 48). 248p. 1957. pap. 5.00x (ISBN 0-292-73528-6). U of Tex Pr.
--Reflections of Social Life in the Navaho Origin Myth. LC 76-43850. (Univ. of New Mexico. Publications in Anthropology: No. 3). Repr. of 1947 ed. 13.00 (ISBN 0-404-15705-X). AMS Pr.
Swanton, John R. Myths & Tales of the Southeastern Indians. Repr. of 1929 ed. 19.00 (ISBN 0-403-03655-0). Scholarly.
--Myths & Tales of the Southeastern Indians. LC 74-9011. (Smithsonian Institution. Bureau of American Enthnology. Bulletin: 88). Repr. of 1929 ed. 20.00 (ISBN 0-404-11908-5). AMS Pr.
--Tlingit Myths & Texts. Repr. of 1909 ed. 28.00 (ISBN 0-384-59050-0). Johnson Repr.
--Tlingit Myths & Texts. Repr. of 1909 ed. 23.00 (ISBN 0-403-03710-7). Scholarly.
Tedlock, Dennis & Tedlock, Barbara, eds. Teachings from the American Earth: Indian Religion & Philosophy. (Illus.). 304p. 1976. pap. 6.95 (ISBN 0-87140-097-9). Liveright.
Terrell, John U. The Arrow & the Cross. 1979. 14.95 (ISBN 0-88496-132-X). Capra Pr.
Underhill, Ruth M. Papago Indian Religion. LC 74-82363. (Columbia Univ. Contributions to Anthropology Ser.: Vol. 33). Repr. of 1946 ed. 27.00 (ISBN 0-404-50583-X). AMS Pr.
--Red Man's Religion: Beliefs & Practices of the Indians North of Mexico. LC 65-24985. 1972. pap. 6.50 (ISBN 0-226-84167-7, P481, Phoen). U of Chicago Pr.
Underhill, Ruth M., et al. Rainhouse & Ocean: Speeches for the Papago Year. LC 79-66733. (Illus.). vi, 154p. 1980. pap. 12.95x (ISBN 0-89734-029-9). Mus Northern Ariz.
--Rainhouse & Ocean: Speeches for the Papago Year. LC 79-66733. (Illus.). vi, 154p. 1981. pap. 12.95x (ISBN 0-89734-029-9, Pub by Mus Northern Ariz). U of Nebr Pr.
Walker, James R. Lakota Belief & Ritual. DeMallie, Raymond J. & Jahner, Elaine A., eds. LC 79-19816. (Illus.). xxx, 329p. 1980. 21.50 (ISBN 0-8032-2551-2). U of Nebr Pr.
Willoya, William & Brown, Vinson. Warriors of the Rainbow: Strange & Prophetic Dreams of the Indian Peoples. (Illus.). 94p. (gr. 4 up). 1962. 8.50 (ISBN 0-911010-25-4); pap. 4.50 (ISBN 0-911010-24-6). Naturegraph.
Wissler, Clark. Social Organization & Ritualistic Ceremonies of the Blackfoot Indians, 2 parts in 1 vol. LC 74-9020. (Anthropological Papers of the American Museum of Natural History: Vol. 7). (Illus.). Repr. of 1912 ed. 24.00 (ISBN 0-404-11917-4). AMS Pr.
Wissler, Clark & Duvall, D. C. Mythology of the Blackfoot Indians. LC 74-9019. (Anthropological Papers of the American Museum of Natural History: Vol. 2, Pt. 1). (Illus.). Repr. of 1909 ed. 17.00 (ISBN 0-404-11916-6). AMS Pr.
Wood, Charles E. A Book of Tales, Being Myths of the North American Indians. 59.95 (ISBN 0-87968-770-3). Gordon Pr.
Wyman, L. C. & Kluckhohn, Clyde. Navaho Classification of Their Song Ceremonials. LC 38-23008. 1938. pap. 5.00 (ISBN 0-527-00549-5). Kraus Repr.
Wyman, Leland C. Blessingway. LC 66-28786. (Illus.). 580p. 1970. 14.50x (ISBN 0-8165-0178-5). U of Ariz Pr.
--The Sacred Mountains of the Navajo. (Special Publications Ser.: No. 4). (Illus.). 1976. pap. 1.00 (ISBN 0-89734-012-4). Mus Northern Ariz.
Zigmond, Maurice L. Kawaiisu Mythology: An Oral Tradition of South-Central California. (Anthropological Papers: No. 18). (Illus.). 252p. (Orig.). 1980. pap. 11.95 (ISBN 0-87919-089-2). Ballena Pr.

INDIANS OF NORTH AMERICA-RITES AND CEREMONIES

see also Peyotism;
also names of special ceremonies

Alexander, Hartley B. World's Rim: Great Mysteries of the North American Indians. LC 53-7703. (Illus.). xx, 259p. 1967. pap. 4.95 (ISBN 0-8032-5003-7, BB160, Bison). U of Nebr Pr.
Applegate, Richard. Atishwin: The Dream Helper in South-Central California. (Ballena Press Anthropological Papers Ser.: No. 13). 1979. pap. 5.95 (ISBN 0-87919-079-5). Ballena Pr.
Beckwith, Martha W. Mandan-Hidatsa Myths & Ceremonies. LC 38-19412. Repr. of 1938 ed. 20.00 (ISBN 0-527-01084-7). Kraus Repr.
Boyd, Doug. Rolling Thunder. 1976. pap. 5.95 (ISBN 0-440-57435-8, Delta). Dell.
Brown, Joseph E., ed. The Sacred Pipe: Black Elk's Account of the Seven Rites of Oglala Sioux. (Civilization of the American Indian Ser.: No. 36). (Illus.). 1953. 9.95 (ISBN 0-8061-0272-1). U of Okla Pr.
Chafe, Wallace L. Seneca Thanksgiving Rituals. Repr. of 1961 ed. 36.00 (ISBN 0-403-08969-7). Scholarly.
Chenfeld, Mimi B. & Vandervelde, Marjorie. Pow-Wow. (Indian Culture Ser.). (gr. 5-12). 1972. 1.95 (ISBN 0-89992-054-3). MT Coun Indian.
Clark, Ella. Guardian Spirit Quest. (Indian Culture Ser.). (gr. 5-12). 1974. pap. 1.95 (ISBN 0-89992-045-4). MT Coun Indian.
Collier, John. On the Gleaming Way: Navajos, Eastern Pueblos, Zunis, Hopis, Apaches & Their Land, & Their Meanings to the World. LC 62-12407. 163p. (Photos, Orig). 1962. pap. 5.95 (ISBN 0-8040-0232-0, SB). Swallow.
De Grazia, Ted. De Grazia Paints the Yaqui Easter. LC 68-22334. (Illus.). 1968. 19.50 (ISBN 0-8165-0023-1). U of Ariz Pr.
Eaton, Evelyn. I Send a Voice. LC 78-7273. (Illus., Orig.). 1978. 10.95 (ISBN 0-8356-0513-2, Quest); pap. 4.95 (ISBN 0-8356-0511-6, Quest). Theos Pub Hse.
Frisbie, Charlotte J., ed. Southwestern Indian Ritual Drama. LC 79-2308. (School of American Research Advanced Seminar Ser.). (Illus.). 384p. 1980. 30.00 (ISBN 0-8263-0521-0). U of NM Pr.
Gilliland, Hap. Coyote's Pow-Wow. (Indian Culture Ser.). (gr. 1-6). 1972. 1.95 (ISBN 0-89992-022-5). MT Coun Indian.
Haile, Berard. Head & Face Masks in Navaho Ceremonialism. LC 76-43722. Repr. of 1947 ed. 17.50 (ISBN 0-404-15565-0). AMS Pr.
--Love-Magic & Butterfly People: The Slim Curly Version of the Ajiee & Mothway Myths. LC 78-59705. (Illus.). xii, 172p. 1980. pap. 13.95x (ISBN 0-89734-026-4). Mus Northern Ariz.
Hale, Horatio. The Iroquois Book of Rites. (Scholarly Reprint Ser.). 1978. 27.50x (ISBN 0-8020-7101-5). U of Toronto Pr.
Harrington, Mark R. Religion & Ceremonies of the Lenape. LC 76-43731. (MAI Indian Notes & Monographs. Miscellaneous). Repr. of 1921 ed. 19.00 (ISBN 0-404-15572-3). AMS Pr.
Kemnitzer, L. S. A Grammar Discovery Procedure for the Study of a Dakota Healing Ritual. (PDR Press Publication on Nonverbal Behavior: No. 1). 1975. pap. text ed. 1.50x (ISBN 90-316-0057-1). Humanities.
LaBarre, Weston. The Peyote Cult. 4th ed. (Illus.). 296p. 1975. 15.00 (ISBN 0-208-01456-X). Shoe String.
Luckert, Karl W. Coyoteway: A Navajo Holyway Healing Ceremonial. LC 78-10358. 1979. pap. 13.95x (ISBN 0-8165-0655-8). U of Ariz Pr.
--A Navajo Bringing-Home Ceremony: The Claus Chee Sonny Version of Deerway Ajilee. LC 78-59701. (Illus.). xiv, 210p. 1980. pap. 14.95x (ISBN 0-89734-027-2). Mus Northern Ariz.
--Navajo Mountain & Rainbow Bridge Religion. (Illus.). vii, 157p. 1980. pap. 9.95x (ISBN 0-89734-025-6). Mus Northern Ariz.
McAllester, David P. & McAllester, Susan W. Hogans: Navajo Houses & House Songs. (Illus.). 160p. 1980. 16.95 (ISBN 0-8195-5043-4, Pub. by Wesleyan U Pr). Columbia U Pr.
McClintock, Walter. Four Days in a Medicine Lodge. facs. ed. 14p. Repr. of 1900 ed. pap. 3.25 (ISBN 0-8466-0097-8, SJS97). Shorey.
Matthews, Washington. The Night Chant: A Navaho Ceremony. LC 74-7991. Repr. of 1902 ed. 70.00 (ISBN 0-404-11880-1). AMS Pr.
Newcomb, Franc J. & Reichard, Gladys A. Sandpaintings of the Navajo Shooting Chant. (Illus.). 11.50 (ISBN 0-8446-5231-8). Peter Smith.
Radin, Paul. Road of Life & Death. (Bollingen Ser.: Vol. 5). 1945. 22.00x (ISBN 0-691-09819-0). Princeton U Pr.
Simmons, Marc. Witchcraft in the Southwest: Spanish & Indian Supernaturalism on the Rio Grande. LC 79-18928. (Illus.). xiv, 184p. 1980. pap. 4.75 (ISBN 0-8032-9116-7, BB 729, Bison). U of Nebr Pr.
Skinner, Alanson B. Medicine Ceremony of the Menomini, Iowa, & Wahpeton Dakota: With Notes on the Ceremony Among the Ponca, Bungi, Ojibwa & Potawatomi. LC 76-43826. (MAI. Indian Notes & Monographs: Vol. 4). Repr. of 1920 ed. 28.00 (ISBN 0-404-15678-9). AMS Pr.
Speck, Frank G. Oklahoma Delaware Ceremonies, Feasts & Dances. LC 76-43845. (Memoirs of the American Philosophical Sociey: Vol. 7). Repr. of 1937 ed. 21.50 (ISBN 0-404-15696-7). AMS Pr.
--A Study of the Delaware Indian Big House Ceremony: In Native Text Dictated by Witapanoxwe. LC 76-43846. (Publications of the Pennsylvania Historical Commission: Vol. 2). Repr. of 1931 ed. 24.00 (ISBN 0-404-15698-3). AMS Pr.
Tooker, Elisabeth. Iroquois Ceremonial of Midwinter. LC 70-119873. (New York State Studies). (Illus.). 1970. 11.95x (ISBN 0-8156-2149-3). Syracuse U Pr.
Tooker, Elisabeth, ed. Native North American Spirituality of the Eastern Woodlands: Sacred Myths, Dreams, Vision Speeches, Healing Formulas, Rituals & Ceremonials. LC 79-66573. (Classics of Western Spirituality). 320p. 1979. 11.95 (ISBN 0-8091-0304-4); pap. 7.95 (ISBN 0-8091-2256-1). Paulist Pr.
Underhill, Ruth M., et al. Rainhouse & Ocean: Speeches for the Papago Year. LC 79-66733. (Illus.). vi, 154p. 1980. pap. 12.95x (ISBN 0-89734-029-9). Mus Northern Ariz.
Voth, H. R. Oraibu Marau Ceremony-Brief Miscellaneous Hopi Papers. (Chicago Field Museum of Natural History Fieldiana Anthropology Ser). 1912. pap. 30.00 (ISBN 0-527-01871-6). Kraus Repr.
Walker, J. R. The Sun Dance & Other Ceremonies of the Oglala Division of the Teton Dakota. LC 76-43886. (AMNH Anthropological Papers: Vol. 16, Pt. 2). Repr. of 1917 ed. 21.50 (ISBN 0-404-15745-9). AMS Pr.
Waters, Frank. Masked Gods: Navaho & Pueblo Ceremonialism. LC 73-1799. 438p. 1950. 16.95 (ISBN 0-8040-0196-0, SB); pap. 8.95 (ISBN 0-8040-0641-5, SB). Swallow.
Wright, Barton. Kachinas: A Hopi Artist's Documentary. LC 73-75204. (Illus.). 272p. 1973. 40.00 (ISBN 0-87358-110-5). Northland.
Wyman, Leland C. The Mountainway of the Navajo. LC 74-83333. 328p. 1975. text ed. 14.50x (ISBN 0-8165-0412-1). U of Ariz Pr.

INDIANS OF NORTH AMERICA-SCHOOLS

see Indians of North America-Education

INDIANS OF NORTH AMERICA-SECRET SOCIETIES

Boas, Franz. The Social Organization & Secret Societies of the Kwakiutl Indians. Based on Personal Observations Notes Made by Mr. George Hunt. (Landmarks in Anthropology Ser). Repr. of 1897 ed. 46.00 (ISBN 0-384-04872-2). Johnson Repr.
Drucker, Philip. The Native Brotherhoods: Modern Inter-Tribal Organizations on the Northwest Coast. Repr. of 1958 ed. 19.00 (ISBN 0-403-03657-7). Scholarly.
Fortune, Reo F. Omaha Secret Societies. LC 70-82351. (Columbia Univ. Contributions to Anthropology Ser.: Vol. 14). Repr. of 1932 ed. 18.50 (ISBN 0-404-50564-3). AMS Pr.
Lowie, Robert H. The Tobacco Society of the Crow Indians. LC 74-7988. Repr. of 1919 ed. 13.45 (ISBN 0-404-11878-X). AMS Pr.
Wissler, Clark, ed. Societies of the Plains Indians, 13 pts. in 1 vol. LC 74-9027. (Anthropological Papers of the American Museum of Natural History: Vol. 11). (Illus.). Repr. of 1916 ed. 70.00 (ISBN 0-404-11918-2). AMS Pr.

INDIANS OF NORTH AMERICA-SIGN LANGUAGE

Amon, Aline. Talking Hands: Indian Sign Language. LC 68-10123. (gr. 4-7). 1968. 7.95a (ISBN 0-385-08891-4); PLB (ISBN 0-385-09425-6). Doubleday.
Cody, Iron Eyes. Indian Talk: Hand Signals of the North American Indians. (Illus.). (gr. 1 up). 1970. 7.95 (ISBN 0-911010-83-1); pap. 3.95 (ISBN 0-911010-82-3). Naturegraph.
Hofsinde, Robert. Indian Sign Language. (Illus.). (gr. 5 up). 1956. PLB 6.48 (ISBN 0-688-31610-7). Morrow.
Mallery, D. Garrick. Sign Language Among North American Indians Compared with That Among Other Peoples & Deaf Mutes. (with Articles by A. L. Kroeber & C. F. Vogelin) (Approaches to Semiotics Ser: No. 14). (Illus.). 552p. 1972. Repr. of 1881 ed. text ed. 64.00x (ISBN 0-686-22538-4). Mouton.
Sahi, Jyoti. The Child & the Serpent: Refelctions on Popular Indian Symbols. (Illus.). 192p. (Orig.). 1980. pap. 18.50 (ISBN 0-7100-0704-3). Routledge & Kegan.
Skelly, M., ed. Amer-Ind Gestural Code Based on Universal American Indian Hand Tlk. LC 79-19202. 528p. 1979. 34.95 (ISBN 0-444-00333-9, North Holland); pap. 18.95 (ISBN 0-686-63093-9, North Holland). Elsevier.
Tomkins, William. Indian Sign Language. Orig. Title: Universal Indian Sign Language of the Plains Indians of North America. (Illus.). 1969. pap. 2.00 (ISBN 0-486-22029-X). Dover.

INDIANS OF NORTH AMERICA-SOCIAL CONDITIONS

Alford, Thomas W. Civilization: & the Story of the Shawnees- As Told to Florence Drake. (Illus.). 1979. Repr. of 1936 ed. 12.50 (ISBN 0-8061-1590-4). U of Okla Pr.
Bahr, Howard M., et al, eds. Native Americans Today: Sociological Perspectives. (Illus.). 1971. pap. text ed. 14.95 scp (ISBN 0-06-040443-4, HarpC). Har-Row.
Burton, Henrietta K. The Re-Establishment of the Indians in Their Pueblo Life Through the Revival of Their Traditional Crafts: A Study in Home Extension Education. LC 73-176617. (Columbia University. Teachers College. Contributions to Education: No. 673). Repr. of 1936 ed. 17.50 (ISBN 0-404-55673-6). AMS Pr.
Bushnell, David L., Jr. Villages of the Algonquian, Siouan, & Caddoan Tribes West of the Mississippi. Repr. of 1922 ed. 21.00 (ISBN 0-403-03724-7). Scholarly.
Cash, J. To Be an Indian. 251p. 1971. pap. 7.50 (ISBN 0-03-086372-4, Pub. by HR&W). Krieger.
Cohen, Allan R. Tradition, Change & Conflict in Indian Family Business. (Publications of the Institute of Social Studies Paperback Ser.: No. 13). 347p. 1974. pap. text ed. 26.75x (ISBN 0-686-22579-1). Mouton.
Fergusson, Erna. Dancing Gods: Indian Ceremonials of New Mexico & Arizona. LC 31-18831. (Illus.). 286p. 1970. pap. 6.95 (ISBN 0-8263-0033-2). U of NM Pr.
Goldfrank, Esther S. Changing Configurations in the Social Organization of a Blackfoot Tribe During the Reserve Period. Bd. with Observations on Northern Blackfoot Kinship. Hanks, L. M., Jr. & Richardson, Jane. (Illus.). 37p. LC 46-1392. (American Ethnological Society Monographs: Nos. 8-9). (Illus.). 81p. 1945. 11.00 (ISBN 0-295-74067-1). U of Wash Pr.
Guillemin, Jeanne. Urban Renegades: The Cultural Strategy of American Indians. new ed. LC 74-30434. 336p. 1975. 17.50x (ISBN 0-231-03884-4). Columbia U Pr.
Johansen, Bruce & Maestas, Roberto. Wasi'chu: The Continuing Indian War. LC 79-10153. 1979. 15.00 (ISBN 0-85345-484-1, CL4841). Monthly Rev.
Knack, Martha C. Life Is with People: Household Organization of the Contemporary Paiute Indians. (Anthropological Papers Ser.: No. 19). 106p. (Orig.). 1981. pap. 6.95 (ISBN 0-87919-091-4). Ballena Pr.
Leacock, Eleanor B. & Laurie, Nancy O., eds. North American Indians in Historical Perspective. 512p. 1971. text ed. 14.95 (ISBN 0-394-31014-4, RanC). Random.
Manchip-White, John. Everyday Life of the North American Indian. 1979. 22.50 (ISBN 0-7134-0043-9, Pub. by Batsford England). David & Charles.
Scholder, Fritz. Indian Kitsch: The Use & Misuse of Indian Images. LC 78-65928. (Illus.). 1979. pap. 8.50 (ISBN 0-87358-190-3). Northland.
Smith, Maurice G. Political Organization of the Plains Indians: With Special Reference to the Council. LC 76-43837. (Nebraska Univ. Studies: Vol. 24, Nos. 1 & 2). Repr. of 1924 ed. 15.00 (ISBN 0-404-15691-6). AMS Pr.
Smithson, Carma L. The Havasupai Woman. (Utah Anthropological Papers: No. 38). Repr. of 1959 ed. 16.75 (ISBN 0-404-60638-5). AMS Pr.
Subcommittee On Economy In Government. American Indians: Facts - Future Toward Economic Development for Native American Communities. LC 76-128179. 1970. Repr. of 1969 ed. 10.00 (ISBN 0-405-00691-8). Arno.
Talbot, Steve. Roots of Oppression: The American Indian Question. (Orig.). 1981. 14.00 (ISBN 0-7178-0591-3); pap. 4.75 (ISBN 0-7178-0583-2). Intl Pub Co.
Taylor, Michael, et al. Moccasins on Pavement: The Urban Indian Experience a Denver Portrait. (Illus., Orig.). 1978. pap. 2.50 (ISBN 0-916278-19-0). Denver Mus Natl Hist.
Unger, Steven, ed. The Destruction of American Indian Families. LC 76-24533. 1977. pap. 3.50 (ISBN 0-686-24119-3). Assn Am Indian.
U. S. Bureau of Indian Affairs. Statistics of Indian Tribes, Agencies & Schools. 1976. Repr. of 1903 ed. 13.00 (ISBN 0-527-92020-7). Kraus Repr.
Van Every, Dale. Disinherited: The Lost Birthright of the American Indian. 1967. pap. 2.95 (ISBN 0-380-01141-7, 51326, Discus). Avon.

Waddell, Jack O. & Watson, O. Michael, eds. The American Indian in Urban Society. (Series in Anthropology). 414p. 1971. pap. text ed. 6.95 (ISBN 0-316-91621-8). Little.

Weeks, Philip & Gidney, James B. Subjugation & Dishonor: A Brief History of the Travail of the Native Americans. LC 79-28713. (Orig.). 1980. 12.50 (ISBN 0-89874-076-2); pap. 5.95 (ISBN 0-686-66018-8). Krieger.

INDIANS OF NORTH AMERICA-SOCIAL LIFE AND CUSTOMS

see also Indians of North America–Dances; Indians of North America–Games; Indians of North America–Hunting and Fishing; Potlatch

American Academy of Political & Social Science of Philadelphia, et al. American Indians & American Life. LC 57-13854. 1973. Repr. of 1957 ed. 21.00 (ISBN 0-527-02099-0). Kraus Repr.

American Ethnological Society. Forms of Play of Native North Americans: Proceedings. Norbeck, Edward & Ferrer, Claire R., eds. (Illus.). 1979. pap. text ed. 13.95 (ISBN 0-8299-0262-7). West Pub.

Arnold, Mary E. & Reed, Mabel. In the Land of the Grasshopper Song: Two Women in the Klamath River Indian Country in 1908-09. LC 80-12556. (Illus.). iv, 313p. 1980. 17.95x (ISBN 0-8032-1804-4); pap. 5.95 (ISBN 0-8032-6703-7, BB 740, Bison). U of Nebr Pr.

Axtell, James, ed. The Indian Peoples of Eastern America: A Documentary History of the Sexes. (Illus.). 256p. 1981. text ed. 11.95x (ISBN 0-19-502740-X); pap. text ed. 6.95x (ISBN 0-19-502741-8). Oxford U Pr.

Bahr, Don. Piman & Papago Ritual Oratory. 1975. pap. 4.50 (ISBN 0-685-64956-3). Indian Hist Pr.

Bahti, Tom. Southwestern Indian Ceremonials. LC 79-136004. (Illus.). 1970. 7.95 (ISBN 0-916122-27-1); pap. 3.00 (ISBN 0-916122-02-6). KC Pubns.

Basso, Keith H. Portraits of the Whiteman. LC 78-31535. 1979. 17.95 (ISBN 0-521-22640-6); pap. 4.95 (ISBN 0-521-29593-9). Cambridge U Pr.

Blanchard, Kendall A. Mississippi Choctaws at Play: The Serious Side of Leisure. LC 80-26527. 1981. 13.95x (ISBN 0-252-00866-9). U of Ill Pr.

Boas, Frank. Social Organization & the Secret Societies of the Kwakiutl Indians. Repr. of 1895 ed. 30.00 (ISBN 0-8466-9006-3, SJ144). Shorey.

Boas, Franz. Facial Paintings of the Indians of Northern British Columbia. LC 73-3509. (Jesup North Pacific Expedition. Publications: Vol. 1, Pt. 1). Repr. of 1898 ed. 20.00 (ISBN 0-404-58101-3). AMS Pr.

--The Social Organization & Secret Societies of the Kwakiutl Indians. Based on Personal Observations Notes Made by Mr. George Hunt. (Landmarks in Anthropology Ser). Repr. of 1897 ed. 46.00 (ISBN 0-384-04872-2). Johnson Repr.

Breton, Raymond & Akian, Gail G. Urban Institutions & People of Indian Ancestry. 52p. 1978. pap. text ed. 3.00x (ISBN 0-920380-14-X, Pub. by Inst Res Pub Canada). Renouf.

Brill, Charles. Indian & Free: A Contemporary Portrait of Life on a Chippewa Reservation. LC 73-91450. (Illus.). vi, 138p. 1974. 12.95 (ISBN 0-8166-0710-9). U of Minn Pr.

Bushnell, David I., Jr. Burials of the Algonquian, Siouan & Caddoan Tribes West of the Mississippi. Repr. of 1927 ed. 10.50 (ISBN 0-403-03545-7). Scholarly.

Collins, June M. Valley of the Spirits: The Upper Skagit Indians of Western Washington. LC 74-8719. (Illus.). 282p. 1974. text ed. 16.00 (ISBN 0-295-95327-6); pap. text ed. 8.50 (ISBN 0-295-95734-4). U of Wash Pr.

Colson, Elizabeth. The Makah Indians. LC 73-15051. (Illus.). 308p. 1974. Repr. of 1953 ed. lib. bdg. 19.00x (ISBN 0-8371-7153-9, COMI). Greenwood.

Curtis, Edward S. Portraits from North American Indian Life. 192p. 1975. pap. 10.95 (ISBN 0-89104-003-X). A & W Pubs.

Densmore, Frances. American Indians & Their Music. (American Studies). 1926. 11.00 (ISBN 0-384-11405-9). Johnson Repr.

--Chippewa Customs. (Landmarks in Anthropology Ser). 1970. Repr. of 1929 ed. 19.50 (ISBN 0-384-11410-5). Johnson Repr.

--Chippewa Customs. Repr. of 1929 ed. 29.00 (ISBN 0-403-03556-2). Scholarly.

--Chippewa Customs. LC 79-15400. (Illus.). 204p. 1979. pap. 7.50 (ISBN 0-87351-142-5). Minn Hist.

--Menominee Music. LC 72-1882. (Music Ser.). (Illus.). 286p. 1972. Repr. of 1932 ed. lib. bdg. 19.50 (ISBN 0-306-70510-9). Da Capo.

Dorsey, George A. Traditions of the Osage. LC 74-7957. Repr. of 1904 ed. 12.50 (ISBN 0-404-11846-1). AMS Pr.

Dorsey, James O. Omaha Sociology. LC 16-5488. 1971. Repr. of 1884 ed. 14.50 (ISBN 0-384-12395-3). Johnson Repr.

Durlach, Theresa M. The Relationship Systems of the Tlingit, Haida, & Tsimshian. LC 73-3547. (American Ethnological Society. Publications: No. 11). Repr. of 1928 ed. 18.00 (ISBN 0-404-58161-7). AMS Pr.

Dyen, D. & Aberle, D. F. Lexical Reconstruction. LC 73-92780. (Illus.). 484p. 1974. 59.50 (ISBN 0-521-20369-4). Cambridge U Pr.

Dyk, Walter, ed. Son of Old Man Hat: A Navaho Autobiography. LC 44-2654. 1967. pap. 4.95 (ISBN 0-8032-5054-1, BB 355, Bison). U of Nebr Pr.

Eastman, Charles A. Red Hunters & the Animal People. LC 74-7964. (Illus.). Repr. of 1904 ed. 21.00 (ISBN 0-404-11852-6). AMS Pr.

Eggan, Fred. The American Indian: Perspectives for the Study of Social Change. LC 80-67926. (Lewis Henry Morgan Lectures). 192p. 1981. 22.50 (ISBN 0-521-23752-1); pap. 6.95 (ISBN 0-521-28210-1). Cambridge U Pr.

Eggan, Fred, et al. Social Anthropology of North American Tribes. enl. ed. LC 55-5123. 574p. 1972. pap. text ed. 3.95 (ISBN 0-226-19074-9, P473, Phoen). U of Chicago Pr.

Ewers, John C. Indian Life on the Upper Missouri. (Civilization of the American Indian Ser.: No. 89). (Illus.). 1968. 12.95 (ISBN 0-8061-0777-4). U of Okla Pr.

Farrand, Livingston. Traditions of the Chilcotin Indians. LC 73-3516. (Jesup North Pacific Expedition. Publications: Vol. 2, Pt. 1). Repr. of 1900 ed. 17.50 (ISBN 0-404-58102-1). AMS Pr.

Farrand, Livingston & Kahnweiler, W. S. Traditions of the Quinault Indians. LC 73-3518. (Jesup North Pacific Expedition. Publications: Vol. 2, Pt. 3). Repr. of 1902 ed. 17.50 (ISBN 0-404-58119-6). AMS Pr.

Fewkes, Jesse W. & Owens, John G. A Few Summer Ceremonials at the Tusayon Pueblos: Natal Ceremonies of the Hopi Indians,& a Report on the Present Condition of a Ruin in Arizona Called Casa Grande. LC 76-21217. (A Journal of American Ethnology & Archaeology: Vol. 2). 1977. Repr. of 1892 ed. 27.50 (ISBN 0-404-58042-4). AMS Pr.

Fontana, Bernard L. Tarahumara: Where Night Is the Day of the Moon. LC 78-71375. (Illus.). 1979. 37.50 (ISBN 0-87358-183-0). Northland.

Fox, Robin. Keresan Bridge: A Problem in Pueblo Ethnology. (Monographs on Social Anthropology: No. 35). 1967. text ed. 20.75x (ISBN 0-485-19535-6, Athlone Pr). Humanities.

French & Indian Cruelty; Exemplified in the Life & Various Vicissitudes of Fortune, of Peter Williamson...Containing a Particular Account of the Manners, Customs, & Dress, of the Savages, Repr. Of 1757. Bd. with French & Indian Cruelty. Repr. of 1758 ed; Sufferings of... Repr. of 1796 ed; The Travels & Surprising Adventures of John Thomson, Who Was Taken, & Carried to America, & Sold for a Slave There; How He Was Taken Captive by the Savages,... & His Return to Scotland. Repr. of 1761 ed; A Full & Particular Account of the Sufferings of William Gatenby. Repr. of 1784 ed. (Narratives of North American Indian Captivities Ser.: Vol. 9). 1979. lib. bdg. 44.00 (ISBN 0-8240-1633-5). Garland Pub.

Frisbie, Charlotte J., ed. Southwestern Indian Ritual Drama. LC 79-2308. (School of American Research Advanced Seminar Ser.). (Illus.). 384p. 1980. 30.00 (ISBN 0-8263-0521-0). U of NM Pr.

Geary, Edward. Depredations & Massacre by the Snake River Indians. 16p. 1966. Repr. pap. 2.50 (ISBN 0-87770-049-4). Ye Galleon.

Gifford, Edward W & Block, Gwendoline H.compiled by. California Indian Nights Entertainment. LC 76-43713. Repr. of 1930 ed. 32.50 (ISBN 0-404-15546-4). AMS Pr.

Goldfrank, Esther S. Social & Ceremonial Organization of Cochiti. LC 28-11444. 1927. pap. 9.00 (ISBN 0-527-00532-0). Kraus Repr.

Hamilton, Charles, ed. Cry of the Thunderbird: The American Indian's Own Story. George. LC 70-177336. (Civilization of the American Indian Ser.: Vol. 119). (Illus.). 283p. 1972. 12.95 (ISBN 0-8061-1003-1); pap. 6.95 (ISBN 0-8061-1292-1). U of Okla Pr.

Heizer, Robert F. & Elsasser, Albert B. The Natural World of the California Indians. LC 79-65092. (Illus.). 1980. 14.95 (ISBN 0-520-03895-9); pap. 7.95 (ISBN 0-520-03896-7). U of Cal Pr.

Hertzberg, Hazel W. The Search for an American Indian Identity: Modern Pan-American Movements. (Illus.). 362p. 1981. pap. text ed. 10.95x (ISBN 0-8156-2245-7). Syracuse U Pr.

Highwater, Jamake. The Primal Mind. LC 80-8929. 256p. 1981. 14.95 (ISBN 0-06-014866-7, HarpT). Har-Row.

Hilger, Inez. A Social Study of One Hundred Fifty Chippewa Indian Families of the White Earth Reservation of Minnesota. LC 76-43741. Repr. of 1939 ed. 26.00 (ISBN 0-404-15582-0). AMS Pr.

Hilger, Sr. Inez. Chippewa Child Life & Its Cultural Background. Repr. of 1951 ed. 16.00 (ISBN 0-403-03555-4). Scholarly.

Hilger, Sr. M. Inez. Araphaho Child Life & Its Cultural Backgrounds. Repr. of 1952 ed. 19.00 (ISBN 0-403-03513-9). Scholarly.

Hoebel, E. A. Political Organizations and Law-Ways of the Comanche Indians. LC 42-13539. 1940. 8.00 (ISBN 0-527-00553-3). Kraus Repr.

Hofsinde, Robert. Indian Games & Crafts. (Illus.). (gr. 5-9). 1957. PLB 6.67 (ISBN 0-688-31607-7). Morrow.

Hunter, John D. Manners & Customs of Several Indian Tribes Located West of the Mississippi... to Which Is Prefixed the History of the Author's Life During a Residence of Several Years Among Them. LC 75-7061. (Indian Captivities Ser.: Vol. 39). 1976. Repr. of 1823 ed. lib. bdg. 44.00 (ISBN 0-8240-1663-7). Garland Pub.

--Memoirs of a Captivity Among the Indians of North America, from Childhood to the Age of Nineteen. LC 2-16705. (American Studies). Repr. of 1823 ed. 23.00 (ISBN 0-384-24925-6). Johnson Repr.

Interesting Narrative of the Sufferings of Mr. Joseph Barker & His Wife... Taken by a Scouting Party of British & Indians... in 1777, Repr. Of 1848 Ed. Bd. with An Indian Tradition. No Fiction. the Traditionary History of a Narrow & Providential Escape of Some White Men from Being Tomahawked, Scalped, & Robbed by a Party of Taw-Way Indians. Repr. of 1848 ed; The Dreadful Sufferings & Thrilling Adventures of an Overland Party of Immigrants to California, Their Terrible Conflicts with Savage Tribes of Indians!!! & Bands of Mexican Robbers!!! with Marriage, Funeral, & Other Interesting Ceremonies & Customs of Indian Life in Far West. Adam, George. Repr. of 1850 ed; History of the Revolutionary War... Brief Account of the Captivity & Cruel Sufferings of Captain Deitz & John & Robert Brice. Repr. of 1851 ed; The Life & Adventures of David C. Butterfield, a Northwestern Pioneer... Written by Himself, in His Wild Western Style. Repr. of 1851 ed. LC 75-7087. (Indian Captivities Ser.: Vol. 63). 1977. lib. bdg. 44.00 (ISBN 0-8240-1687-4). Garland Pub.

James, Edwin. Narrative of the Captivity & Adventures of John Tanner During Thirty Years Residence Among the Chippewa, Ottawa & Objibwa Tribes Etc. Loomis, Noel, ed. & intro. by. Repr. 15.00 (ISBN 0-87018-033-9). Ross.

Johnson, Broderick H., ed. Stories of Traditional Navajo Life & Culture. LC 77-22484. (Illus.). 1977. 9.95 (ISBN 0-912586-23-0). Navajo Coll Pr.

Jones, J. A. Traditions of the North American Indians, 3 vols. 300.00 (ISBN 0-8490-1224-4). Gordon Pr.

A Journal Kept at Nootka Sound by John R. Jewitt, One of the Surviving Crew of the Ship Boston...Interspersed with Some Account of the Natives, Their Manners & Customs, Repr. Of 1807 Ed. Incl. A Narrative of the Adventures & Sufferings of John R. Jewitt. Alsop, Richard, ed. Repr. of 1815 ed. LC 75-7050. (Indian Captivities Ser.: Vol. 28). 1976. lib. bdg. 44.00 (ISBN 0-8240-1652-1). Garland Pub.

Katz, Jane B., ed. I Am the Fire of Time: The Voices of Native American Women. 1977. pap. 6.95 (ISBN 0-525-47475-7). Dutton.

Keim, B. Randolph. Sheridans Troopers on the Borders: A Winter Campaign on the Plains. LC 77-878. (Beautiful Rio Grande Classics Ser.). 1977. lib. bdg. 15.00 (ISBN 0-87380-124-5). Rio Grande.

Knack, Martha C. Life Is with People: Household Organization of the Contemporary Paiute Indians. (Anthropological Papers Ser.: No. 19). 106p. (Orig.). 1981. pap. 6.95 (ISBN 0-87919-091-4). Ballena Pr.

Landes, Ruth. Ojibwa Woman. 1971. pap. 4.95 (ISBN 0-393-00574-7, Norton Lib.). Norton.

--Ojibwa Woman. LC 70-82362. (Columbia Univ. Contributions to Anthropology Ser.: Vol. 31). Repr. of 1938 ed. 21.00 (ISBN 0-404-50581-3). AMS Pr.

Loudon, Archibald. Selection of Some of the Most Interesting Narratives of Outrages Committed by the Indians in Their Wars with the White People, 2 Vols. in 1. LC 76-106124. (First American Frontier Ser). 1971. Repr. of 1808 ed. 30.00 (ISBN 0-405-02866-0). Arno.

Lowie, Robert H. Notes on the Social Organizations & Customs of the Mandan, Hidatsa, & Crow Indians. LC 74-7985. 1976. Repr. of 1917 ed. 13.45 (ISBN 0-404-11874-7). AMS Pr.

--Social Life of the Crow Indians. LC 74-7987. Repr. of 1912 ed. 11.50 (ISBN 0-404-11875-5). AMS Pr.

Luckert, Karl W. The Navajo Hunter Tradition. LC 75-9142. 1975. pap. 5.95x (ISBN 0-8165-0439-3). U of Ariz Pr.

McAllester, David P. & McAllester, Susan W. Hogans: Navajo Houses & House Songs. (Illus.). 160p. 1980. 16.95 (ISBN 0-8195-5043-4, Pub. by Wesleyan U Pr). Columbia U Pr.

McClintock, Walter. The Old North Trail; or, Life, Legends & Religion of the Blackfeet Indians. LC 68-13651. (Illus.). 1968. pap. 5.95 (ISBN 0-8032-5130-0, BB 379, Bison). U of Nebr Pr.

McKeown, Martha F. Come to Our Salmon Feast. LC 59-9823. (Illus.). (gr. 4-9). 1959. 5.95 (ISBN 0-8323-0157-4). Binford.

Mails, Thomas E. The Mystic Warriors of the Plains. LC 72-76191. 608p. 1972. 29.95 (ISBN 0-385-04741-X). Doubleday.

Margolin, Malcolm, ed. The Way We Lived: California Indian Reminiscences, Stories and Songs. 1981. 12.95 (ISBN 0-930588-03-7); pap. 6.95 (ISBN 0-930588-04-5). Heyday Bks.

Mathews, John J. The Osages: Children of the Middle Waters. (The Civilization of the American Indian Ser.: Vol. 60). (Illus.). 848p. 1981. pap. 14.95 (ISBN 0-8061-1770-2). U of Okla Pr.

Mead, Margaret. Changing Culture of an Indian Tribe. LC 72-84468. (Columbia University. Contributions to Anthropology: No. 15). Repr. of 1932 ed. 25.00 (ISBN 0-404-50565-1). AMS Pr.

Michelson, Truman. Notes on the Buffalo-Head Dance of the Bear Gens of the Fox Indians. Repr. of 1928 ed. 17.00 (ISBN 0-403-03668-2). Scholarly.

Minor, Marz & Minor, Nono. The American Indian Craft Book. LC 77-14075. (Illus.). 1978. 22.50x (ISBN 0-8032-0974-6); pap. 5.50 (ISBN 0-8032-5891-7, BB 661, Bison). U of Nebr Pr.

Morey, Sylvester M. & Gilliam, Olivia L., eds. Respect for Life: The Traditional Upbringing of American Indian Children. LC 80-83371. (Illus.). 202p. 1980. pap. text ed. 4.95 (ISBN 0-913098-34-5). Myrin Institute.

Morgan, Lewis H. Houses & House Life of the American Aborigines. LC 66-13881. (Illus.). 1966. 12.00x (ISBN 0-226-53699-8). U of Chicago Pr.

--Houses & House Life of the American Aborigines. LC 66-13881. 1966. pap. 2.95 (ISBN 0-226-53700-5, P211, Phoen). U of Chicago Pr.

--Montezuma's Dinner. 2nd ed. 1967. pap. text ed. 0.75 (ISBN 0-935534-21-0). NY Labor News.

Murray, Charles A. Travels in North America, Including a Summer with the Pawnees. 2nd ed. LC 68-54845. (American Scene Ser.). 878p. 1974. Repr. of 1839 ed. lib. bdg. 69.50 (ISBN 0-306-71021-8). Da Capo.

Nabokov, Peter. Indian Running. (Illus.). 208p. (Orig.). 1981. pap. 8.95 (ISBN 0-88496-162-1). Capra Pr.

--Two Leggings: The Making of a Crow Warrior. LC 67-15412. (Apollo Eds.). (Illus.). 1970. pap. 4.50 (ISBN 0-8152-0275-X, A275). T Y Crowell.

A Narrative of the Captivity & Adventures of John Tanner (U.S. Interpreter at the Saut de Ste. Marie) During 30 Years Residence Among the Indians in the Interior of North America. LC 75-7068. (Indian Captivities Ser.: Vol. 46). 1976. Repr. of 1830 ed. lib. bdg. 44.00 (ISBN 0-8240-1670-X). Garland Pub.

New Jersey State Museum, et al. The Hollywood Indian: Stereotypes of Native Americans in Films. (Illus.). 80p. (Orig.). 1981. 5.95 (ISBN 0-938766-00-7). NJ State Mus.

Niethammer, Carolyn. Daughters of the Earth. 1977. pap. 7.95 (ISBN 0-02-096150-2, 09615, Collier). Macmillan.

Nurge, Ethel, ed. The Modern Sioux: Social Systems & Reservation Culture. LC 71-88089. (Illus.). xvi, 352p. 1970. 20.00x (ISBN 0-8032-0715-8); pap. 4.50 (ISBN 0-8032-5812-7, BB 596, Bison). U of Nebr Pr.

Oberg, Kalervo. The Social Economy of the Tlingit Indians. LC 73-16048. (Illus.). 144p. 1980. pap. text ed. 7.50 (ISBN 0-295-95735-2). U of Wash Pr.

Ogden, Peter S. Traits of American Indian Life & Character. 2nd ed. Repr. of 1933 ed. 17.45 (ISBN 0-404-07149-X). AMS Pr.

Park, Willard Z. Shamanism in Western North America. LC 74-12553. 166p. 1975. Repr. of 1938 ed. lib. bdg. 16.50x (ISBN 0-8154-0497-2). Cooper Sq.

Perrot, Nicolas. Memoire Sur les Moeurs, Coustumes et Relligion Des Sauvages De L'amerique Septentrionale. 1864. 21.00 (ISBN 0-384-45770-3). Johnson Repr.

Powers, William K. Oglala Religion. LC 76-30614. (Illus.). 1977. 14.95 (ISBN 0-8032-0910-X). U of Nebr Pr.

Radin, Paul. Autobiography of a Winnebago Indian. 5.50 (ISBN 0-8446-2774-7). Peter Smith.

--Autobiography of a Winnebago Indian. 1920. pap. 1.75 (ISBN 0-486-20096-5). Dover.

Rutsch, Edward S. Smoking Technology of the Aborigines of the Iroquois Area of New York State. LC 73-92558. 252p. 1972. 20.00 (ISBN 0-8386-7568-9). Fairleigh Dickinson.

Salcedo, Consuelo. Mexican-American Socio-Cultural Patterns: Implications for Social Casework. LC 74-77165. 1974. Repr. of 1955 ed. soft bdg. 7.00 (ISBN 0-88247-275-5). R & E Res Assoc.

Seig, Louis. Tobacco, Peacepipes & Indians. LC 73-90817. (Wild & Woolly West Ser., No. 15). (Illus., Orig.). 1971. 7.00 (ISBN 0-910584-16-8); pap. 1.50 (ISBN 0-910584-91-5). Filter.

Sheridan, Thomas E. & Naylor, Thomas H., eds. Raramuri: A Tarahumara Colonial Chronicle 1607-1791. LC 78-74036. 1979. pap. 7.50 (ISBN 0-87358-188-1). Northland.

Snelling, William J. Tales of the Northwest: On Sketches of Indian Life & Character. LC 75-7067. (Indian Captivities Ser.: Vol. 45). 1976. Repr. of 1830 ed. lib. bdg. 44.00 (ISBN 0-8240-1669-6). Garland Pub.

Spencer, Katherine. Reflections of Social Life in the Navaho Origin Myth. LC 76-43850. (Univ. of New Mexico. Publications in Anthropology: No. 3). Repr. of 1947 ed. 13.00 (ISBN 0-404-15705-X). AMS Pr.

Spoehr, Alexander. Camp, Clan, & Kin, Among the Cow Creek Seminole of Florida. (Illus.). 1941-1947. pap. 12.00 (ISBN 0-527-01893-7). Kraus Repr.

Stewart, Frank H. Fundamentals of Age-Group Systems. (Studies in Anthropology Ser.). 1977. 42.00 (ISBN 0-12-670150-4). Acad Pr.

Swanton, John R. Source Material for the Social & Ceremonial Life of the Choctaw Indians. Repr. of 1931 ed. 25.00 (ISBN 0-403-03694-1). Scholarly.

Three Years Among the Camanches, the Narrative of Nelson Lee, the Texan Ranger, Containing a Detailed Account of His Captivity Among the Indians, His Singular Escape Through the Instrumentality of His Watch, & Fully Illustrating Indian Life As It Is on the War Path & in the Camp. LC 75-7100. (Indian CaptivitieS Ser.: Vol. 75). 1977. Repr. of 1859 ed. lib. bdg. 44.00 (ISBN 0-8240-1699-8). Garland Pub.

Tooker, Elisabeth, ed. Native North American Spirituality of the Eastern Woodlands: Sacred Myths, Dreams, Vision Speeches, Healing Formulas, Rituals & Ceremonials. LC 79-66573. (Classics of Western Spirituality). 320p. 1979. 11.95 (ISBN 0-8091-0304-4); pap. 7.95 (ISBN 0-8091-2256-1). Paulist Pr.

Turner, Geoffrey. Indians of North America. (Illus.). 261p. 1980. pap. 6.95 (ISBN 0-7137-1122-1, Pub. by Blandford Pr England). Sterling.

Underhill, Ruth M. Social Organization of the Papago Indians. LC 74-82347. (Columbia Univ. Contributions to Anthropology Ser.: Vol. 30). 1969. Repr. of 1939 ed. 23.00 (ISBN 0-404-50580-5). AMS Pr.

Voegelin, Erminie W. Mortuary Customs of the Shawnee & Other Eastern Tribes. LC 76-43885. (Indiana Historical Society Prehistory Research Ser.: Vol. 2, No. 4). Repr. of 1944 ed. 26.00 (ISBN 0-404-15742-4). AMS Pr.

Von Furer Haimendorf, Christoph. The Gonds of Andhra Pradesh: Tradition & Change in an Indian Tribe. (Illus.). 569p. 1981. 40.00x (ISBN 0-7069-0718-3). Advent NY.

Voth, Henry R., tr. The Traditions of the Hopi: The Stanley McCormic Hopi Expedition. LC 74-9014. Repr. of 1905 ed. 39.00 (ISBN 0-404-11911-5). AMS Pr.

Walker, Louise J. Beneath the Singing Pines. (Illus.). (gr. 6-10). 1967. 7.95 (ISBN 0-910726-80-9). Hillsdale Educ.

Washburn, Wilcomb E., ed. Savage Barbarism. Translated from the Spanish Publication of March 1790. in: "Connecticut Centinel," Vol. XXXII, Tues., Nov. 12, 1805, P. 4, Repr. Of 1805. Bd. with A Narrative of the Captivity of Joseph Bartlett Among the French & Indians. Repr. of 1807 ed; Horrid Murder. By the Indians. Extract of a Letter from a Gentleman in Augustine to His Friend in Virginia. in: "The New-Jersey & Pennsylvania Almanac for the Year 1808". Repr. of 1808 ed; A Narrative of the Captivity of Isaac Webster. Repr. of 1808 ed; A Narrative of the Life, Occurences, Vicissitudes & Present Situation of K. White. Repr. of 1809 ed. (Narratives of North American Indian Captivities Ser.). 1979. lib. bdg. 44.00 (ISBN 0-8240-1651-3). Garland Pub.

West, George A. Tobacco, Pipes & Smoking Customs of the American Indians. Repr. of 1934 ed. lib. bdg. 57.50x (ISBN 0-8371-4635-6, WETS). Greenwood.

White, Jon M. Everyday Life of the North American Indian. LC 79-84. (Illus.). 1979. text ed. 17.50x (ISBN 0-8419-0488-X). Holmes & Meier.

White, Leslie A. Pueblo of San Felipe. LC 32-30651. 1932. pap. 7.00 (ISBN 0-527-00537-1). Kraus Repr.

--Pueblo of Santo Domingo, New Mexico. LC 35-17202. 1935. pap. 14.00 (ISBN 0-527-00542-8). Kraus Repr.

Whiting, Beatrice B. Paiute Sorcery. Repr. of 1950 ed. pap. 15.50 (ISBN 0-384-68180-8). Johnson Repr.

Whitman, William. Oto. LC 78-82348. (Columbia Univ. Contributions to Anthropology Ser.: Vol. 28). Repr. of 1937 ed. 16.00 (ISBN 0-404-50578-3). AMS Pr.

Wilson, Elijah N. Among the Shoshones. facsimile ed. LC 79-162829. (Illus.). 222p. 1971. 9.00 (ISBN 0-912720-01-8). Pine Cone Pubs.

Wissler, Clark. Indians of the United States: Four Centuries of Their History & Culture. LC 66-12215. 1966. 7.95 (ISBN 0-385-00757-4). Doubleday.

--Social Organization & Ritualistic Ceremonies of the Blackfoot Indians, 2 parts in 1 vol. LC 74-9020. (Anthropological Papers of the American Museum of Natural History: Vol. 7). (Illus.). Repr. of 1912 ed. 24.00 (ISBN 0-404-11917-4). AMS Pr.

Witherspoon, Gary. Navajo Kinship & Marriage. LC 74-21340. 1975. pap. 3.95 (ISBN 0-226-90418-0, P745, Phoen). U of Chicago Pr.

Yarrow, Henry C. Introduction to the Study of Mortuary Customs of the North American Indians. Bd. with A Further Contribution to the Study of the Mortuary Customs of North American Indians. LC 74-9030. Repr. of 1881 ed. 33.00 (ISBN 0-404-11920-4). AMS Pr.

INDIANS OF NORTH AMERICA–SPORTS

see Indians of North America–Social Life and Customs

INDIANS OF NORTH AMERICA–TEXTILE INDUSTRY AND FABRICS

Amsden, Charles A. Navaho Weaving, Its Technic & History. LC 64-20401. (Beautiful Rio Grande Classics Ser). 1972. 15.00 (ISBN 0-87380-017-6). Rio Grande.

--Navaho Weaving, Its Technic & History. Repr. 15.00 (ISBN 0-686-20687-8). Southwest Mus.

Bennett, Noel. Designing with the Wool: Advanced Navajo Weaving Techniques. LC 78-51842. (Illus., Orig.). 1978. pap. 7.50 (ISBN 0-87358-171-7). Northland.

--The Weaver's Pathway: A Clarification of the Spirit Trail in Navajo Weaving. LC 73-78002. (Illus.). 104p. 1974. 8.95 (ISBN 0-87358-108-3). Northland.

Berlant, Anthony & Kahlenberg, Mary H. Walk in Beauty: The Navajo & Their Blankets. LC 75-37203. (Illus.). 1977. 27.50 (ISBN 0-8212-0691-5, 917966). NYGS.

Boyles, Margaret. American Indian Needlepoint Workbook. (Illus.). 96p. 1976. pap. 4.95 (ISBN 0-02-011160-6, Collier). Macmillan.

Bryan, Nonobah G. & Young, Stella. Navajo Native Dyes. (Wild & Woolly West Ser: No. 34). (Illus.). 1978. 7.00 (ISBN 0-910584-49-4); pap. 2.50 (ISBN 0-910584-57-5). Filter.

Dockstader, Frederick J. Weaving Arts of the North American Indian. LC 78-381. (Illus.). 1978. 25.00 (ISBN 0-690-01739-1). T Y Crowell.

Dudley, Taimi. Strip Patchwork: Quick & Easy Patchwork Using the Seminole Technique. 112p. 1980. 16.95 (ISBN 0-442-20400-0). Van Nos Reinhold.

Erickson, Jon T. & Cain, H. Thomas. Navajo Textiles from the Read Mullan Collection. (The Heard Museum Ser.). (Illus.). 80p. (Orig.). 1981. pap. 12.95 (ISBN 0-295-95858-8, Pub. by Heard Mus). U of Wash Pr.

--Navajo Textiles from the Read Mullan Collection. (Illus.). 80p. 1981. pap. 12.95 (ISBN 0-295-95858-8). U of Wash Pr.

Fox, Nancy. Pueblo Weaving & Textile Arts. (Guidebook Ser.). 1979. pap. 5.95 (ISBN 0-89013-105-8). Museum NM Pr.

Harmsen, W. D. Patterns & Sources of Navajo Weaving. rev. ed. LC 78-68721. (Illus.). 1978. write for info. Harmsen.

Hollister, U. S. Navajo & His Blanket. LC 72-10567. (Beautiful Rio Grande Classics Ser). lib. bdg. 15.00 (ISBN 0-87380-097-4). Rio Grande.

James, George W. Indian Blankets & Their Makers. LC 74-114965. (Beautiful Rio Grande Classics Ser). 352p. 1971. lib. bdg. 25.00 (ISBN 0-87380-058-3). Rio Grande.

--Indian Blankets & Their Makers. LC 73-90526. (Illus.). 320p. 1974. 10.00 (ISBN 0-486-23068-6); pap. 5.00 (ISBN 0-486-22996-3). Dover.

James, H. L. Posts & Rugs. 3rd ed. Jackson, Earl, ed. LC 75-10108. (Popular Ser: No. 15). (Illus.). 1976. 9.00 (ISBN 0-911408-33-9); pap. 7.00 (ISBN 0-911408-35-5). SW Pks Mnmts.

Kent, Kate P. Textiles of the Prehistoric Southwest. (Indian Arts Ser.). (Illus.). 416p. 1982. 45.00x (ISBN 0-8263-0591-1). U of NM Pr.

Mattera, Joanne. Navajo Techniques for Today's Weaver. (Illus.). 160p. 1975. 15.95 (ISBN 0-8230-3153-5). Watson-Guptill.

Matthews, Washington. Navajo Weavers. facs. ed. (Illus.). 16p. Repr. pap. 3.50 (ISBN 0-8466-0095-1, SJS95). Shorey.

Museum of New Mexico Press, ed. Navajo Weaving Handbook. rev. ed. LC 77-74888. (Guidebook Ser). (Illus.). 1977. pap. 5.95 (ISBN 0-89013-092-2). Museum NM Pr.

The Navajo Design Book. 1975. pap. 2.50 (ISBN 0-918858-04-6). Fun Pub.

Pendleton, Mary. Navajo & Hopi Weaving Techniques. (Illus.). 224p. 1974. 13.95 (ISBN 0-02-595500-4). Macmillan.

--Navajo & Hopi Weaving Techniques. (Illus.). 224p. 1974. pap. 5.95 (ISBN 0-02-011850-3, Collier). Macmillan.

Reichard, Gladys A. Navajo Shepherd & Weaver. 2nd ed. LC 68-25390. (Beautiful Rio Grande Classics Ser). (Illus.). 244p. 1968. Repr. of 1936 ed. lib. bdg. 10.00 (ISBN 0-87380-032-X). Rio Grande.

--Spider Woman: A Story of Navajo Weavers & Chanters. 2nd ed. LC 68-25391. (Beautiful Rio Grande Classics Ser). (Illus.). 310p. 1968. Repr. of 1934 ed. lib. bdg. 12.00 (ISBN 0-87380-033-8). Rio Grande.

--Weaving a Navajo Blanket. LC 73-86437. (Illus.). 256p. 1974. Repr. of 1936 ed. 3.00 (ISBN 0-486-22992-0). Dover.

Rodee, Marian E. Old Navajo Rugs: Their Development from 1900 to 1940. LC 80-54560. (Illus.). 96p. 1981. 25.00 (ISBN 0-8263-0566-0); pap. 15.95 (ISBN 0-8263-0567-9). U of NM Pr.

INDIANS OF NORTH AMERICA–TRAILS

see Indian Trails

INDIANS OF NORTH AMERICA–TRANSPORTATION

see also Indians of North America–Boats

Indian Canoeing. (Indian Culture Ser.). (Illus.). (gr. 6-12). 1976. 1.95 (ISBN 0-686-22273-3). MT Coun Indian.

Roe, Frank G. The Indian & the Horse. (Civilization of the American Indian Ser: Vol. 41). (Illus.). 465p. (Pap. ed 1979 repr. of 1955 ed.). 1974. 17.95 (ISBN 0-8061-0315-9); pap. 8.95 (ISBN 0-8061-1383-9, CAI41). U of Okla Pr.

INDIANS OF NORTH AMERICA–TRAPPING

see Indians of North America–Hunting and Fishing

INDIANS OF NORTH AMERICA–TREATIES

see also Indians of North America–Government Relations; Indians of North America–Land Transfers;

also names of specific treaties

Cline, Howard F. & King, Timothy. Treaties with the Creek & Seminole Indians, 1763-1815. 23.00 (ISBN 0-8287-1279-4). Clearwater Pub.

Constitution & Laws of the Muskogee Nation, As Compiled & Codified by A.P. McKellop, Under Act of October 15, 1892. LC 73-88772. (Constitutions & Laws of the American Indian Tribes, Ser 1: Vol. 18). 1973. Repr. of 1893 ed. 25.00 (ISBN 0-8420-1720-8). Scholarly Res Inc.

Constitution & Laws of the Muskogee Nation, As Compiled by L. C. Perryman, March 1st of 1890. LC 73-3695. (Constitution & Laws of the American Indian Tribes Ser. 2: Vol. 28). 1975. Repr. of 1890 ed. 20.00 (ISBN 0-8420-1886-7). Scholarly Res Inc.

Deloria, Vine, Jr. Behind the Trail of Broken Treaties. 1974. pap. 5.95 (ISBN 0-440-51403-7, Delta). Dell.

De Puy, Henry F. A Bibliography of the English Colonial Treaties with the American Indians. LC 78-164820. Repr. of 1917 ed. 11.50 (ISBN 0-404-07123-6). AMS Pr.

--A Bibliography of the English Colonial Treaties with the American Indians. LC 78-108471. 1917. Repr. 19.00 (ISBN 0-403-00425-X). Scholarly.

Kappler, Charles J., ed. Indian Affairs; Laws & Treaties, 5 vols. LC 78-128994. Repr. of 1941 ed. Set. lib. bdg. 475.00 (ISBN 0-404-06710-7). AMS Pr.

The Navajo Treaty-1868. LC 68-29989. 1968. 3.50 (ISBN 0-916122-29-8); pap. 1.00 (ISBN 0-916122-04-2). KC Pubns.

Price, Richard. The Spirit of the Alberta Indian Treaties. 202p. 1979. pap. text ed. 8.95x (ISBN 0-920380-23-9, Pub. by Inst Res Pub Canada). Renouf.

Williams, C. Herb & Neubrech, Walt. Indian Treaties: American Nightmare. LC 76-51982. (Illus.). 1977. lib. bdg. 3.95 (ISBN 0-916682-03-X); pap. 1.95 (ISBN 0-916682-04-8). Outdoor Empire.

INDIANS OF NORTH AMERICA–TRIBAL GOVERNMENT

Barsh, Russel L. & Henderson, J. Youngblood. The Road: Indian Tribes & Political Liberty. 1980. 14.95x (ISBN 0-520-03629-8). U of Cal Pr.

Buchanan, Jim & Burkert, Fran. A Bibliography of Current American Indian Policy. (Public Administration Ser.: P 188). 1979. pap. 7.00 (ISBN 0-686-24634-9). Vance Biblios.

Schusky, Ernest L., ed. Political Organization of Native North Americans. LC 79-3715. 1980. text ed. 18.25 (ISBN 0-8191-0909-6); pap. text ed. 11.25 (ISBN 0-8191-0910-X). U Pr of Amer.

INDIANS OF NORTH AMERICA–WARS

see also Indian Warfare

Andrist, Ralph K. Long Death. (Illus.). 1969. pap. 4.95 (ISBN 0-02-030290-8, Collier). Macmillan.

Armstrong, Perry A. The Sauks & the Black Hawk War. LC 76-43643. (Illus.). Repr. of 1887 ed. 47.50 (ISBN 0-404-15478-6). AMS Pr.

Bishop, Harriet E. Dakota War Whoop; or Indian Massacres & War in Minnesota. Washburn, Wilcomb E., ed. LC 75-7103. (Narratives of North American Indian Captivities Ser.: Vol. 78). 1978. Repr. of 1863 ed. lib. bdg. 44.00x (ISBN 0-8240-1702-1). Garland Pub.

Bledsoe, Anthony J. Indian Wars of the Northwest. (California Heritage Ser). 1976. lib. bdg. 18.00 (ISBN 0-685-71392-X). Sullivan Bks Intl.

Brininstool, E. A. Fighting Red Cloud's Warriors: True Tales of Indian Days When the West Was Young. LC 74-12557. (Illus.). 241p. 1974. Repr. of 1926 ed. lib. bdg. 11.50x (ISBN 0-8154-0499-9). Cooper Sq.

Brown, Dee. Bury My Heart at Wounded Knee: An Indian History of the American West. LC 70-121633. (Illus.). 1971. 10.95 (ISBN 0-03-085322-2). HR&W.

--Wounded Knee: An Indian History of the American West. Ehrlich, Amy, ed. LC 73-21821. (Illus.). 224p. (gr. 6 up). 1974. reinforced bdg. 6.95 (ISBN 0-03-091559-7). HR&W.

Bryant, Charles S. & Murch, Abel B. History of the Great Massacre by the Sioux Indians, in Minnesota, Including the Personal Narratives of Many Who Escaped. LC 73-12564. xii, 504p. 1973. Repr. of 1864 ed. 26.00 (ISBN 0-527-12950-X). Kraus Repr.

Bunnell, Lafayette H. Discovery of the Yosemite & the Indian War of 1851. facsimile ed. LC 72-146854. (Select Bibliographies Reprint Ser). Repr. of 1880 ed. 21.00 (ISBN 0-8369-5621-4). Arno.

Burns, Robert I. Jesuits & the Indian Wars of the Northwest. LC 65-22314. (Western Americana Ser.: No. 11). (Illus.). 1966. 47.00x (ISBN 0-300-00336-6). Yale U Pr.

Capps, Benjamin. The Great Chiefs. LC 75-744. (The Old West). (Illus.). (gr. 5 up). 1975. kivar 12.96 (ISBN 0-8094-1494-5, Pub. by Time-Life). Silver.

Conroy, Michael R. Mission at San y Sydro. LC 74-18207. 1975. 12.95 (ISBN 0-915626-01-2). Yellow Jacket.

Cook, Sherburne F. The Conflict Between the California Indian & White Civilization, 4 vols. in 1. LC 76-43678. (Ibero-Americana: 21-24). Repr. of 1943 ed. 27.50 (ISBN 0-404-15512-X). AMS Pr.

Corkran, David H. Carolina Indian Frontier. LC 79-120589. (Tricentennial Booklet: No. 6). 1970. pap. 2.25 (ISBN 0-87249-195-1). U of SC Pr.

Crampton, C. Gregory, ed. The Mariposa Indian War, 1850-1851: Diaries of Robert Eccleston - the California Gold Rush, Yosemite, & the High Sierra. LC 58-62761. vii, 168p. 1975. Repr. of 1957 ed. 15.00 (ISBN 0-87480-024-2). U of Utah Pr.

Dawson, Thomas & Skiff, F. J. Ute War: A History of the White River Massacre. 1980. pap. 6.95 (ISBN 0-933472-04-8). Johnson Bks.

Dillon, Richard H., ed. A Cannoneer in Navajo Country: Journal of Private Josiah M. Rice, 1851. (Illus.). 1970. limited ed. 14.50 (ISBN 0-912094-15-X). Old West.

Eggleston, George C. Red Eagle & the Wars with the Creek Indians of Alabama. LC 76-43695. Repr. of 1878 ed. 22.50 (ISBN 0-404-15528-6). AMS Pr.

Foreman, Grant. Indians & Pioneers: The Story of the American Southwest Before 1830. (Civilization of the American Indian Ser.: No. 14). (Illus.). 1967. 15.95 (ISBN 0-8061-0057-5); pap. 7.95 (ISBN 0-8061-1262-X). U of Okla Pr.

Gray, John S. Centennial Campaign: The Sioux War of 1876. LC 76-47160. (Source Custeriana Ser.: Vol. 8). (Illus.). 1977. pap. 7.95 (ISBN 0-88342-243-3). Old Army.

Hagan, William T. The Sac & Fox Indians. LC 58-6851. (The Civilization of the American Indian Ser.: Vol. 48). (Illus.). 320p. 1958. 14.95 (ISBN 0-8061-0397-3). U of Okla Pr.

Haile, Berard. Origin Legend of the Navaho Enemy Way. LC 76-43725. (Yale Univ. Pubns. in Anthropology: No. 17). Repr. of 1938 ed. 21.50 (ISBN 0-404-15781-5). AMS Pr.

Heard, Isaac V. History of the Sioux War & Massacres of 1862 & 1863. LC 2-26023. 1975. Repr. of 1864 ed. 20.00 (ISBN 0-527-03223-9). Kraus Repr.

Hecht, Robert A. Continents in Collision: The Impact of Europe on the North American Indian Societies. LC 80-1381. 337p. 1980. lib. bdg. 19.75 (ISBN 0-8191-1199-6); pap. text ed. 11.50 (ISBN 0-8191-1200-3). U Pr of Amer.

Hedren, Paul L. First Scalp for Custer: The Skirmish at Warbonnet Creek, Nebraska, July 17, 1876. LC 80-68844. (Hidden Springs of Custeriana Ser.: No. V). (Illus.). 106p. 1981. 38.00 (ISBN 0-87062-137-8). A H Clark.

Henry, Alexander. Travels & Adventures in Canada & the Indian Territories Between the Years 1760 & 1776. LC 75-7053. (Indian Captivities Ser.: Vol. 31). 1976. Repr. of 1809 ed. lib. bdg. 44.00 (ISBN 0-8240-1655-6). Garland Pub.

Hubbard, William. History of the Indian Wars in New England from the First Settlement to the Termination of the War with King Philip in 1677, 2 vols in 1. (American Classics in History & Social Science Ser: No. 202). 1971. Repr. of 1865 ed. lib. bdg. 32.50 (ISBN 0-8337-1756-1). B Franklin.

Jesup, Thomas S. Seminole Saga: The Jesup Report. Troyer, Byron L., ed. LC 73-88371. (Illus.). 28p. 1973. pap. 1.00 (ISBN 0-87208-026-9). Island Pr.

Loudon, Archibald. A Selection, of Some of the Most Interesting Narratives, of Outrages, Committed by the Indians, in Their Wars, with the White People, 2 vols. LC 75-7052. (Indian Captivities Ser.: Vols. 29 & 30). 1977. Repr. of 1811 ed. Vol. 1. lib. bdg. 44.00 (ISBN 0-8240-1653-X); Vol. 2. lib. bdg. 44.00 (ISBN 0-8240-1654-8). Garland Pub.

Manypenny, George Washington. Our Indian Wards. LC 68-54844. (The American Scene Ser). 1972. Repr. of 1880 ed. lib. bdg. 25.00 (ISBN 0-306-71140-0). Da Capo.

Marshall, S. L. Crimsoned Prairie. LC 72-4947. (Illus.). 320p. 1972. 20.00 (ISBN 0-684-13089-0, ScribT). Scribner.

Mason, John. A Brief of the Pequot War. facsimile ed. LC 71-152995. (Select Bibliographies Reprint Ser). Repr. of 1736 ed. 9.00 (ISBN 0-8369-5747-4). Arno.

Meeker, Josephine. The Ute War. LC 74-77764. 64p. 1975. 6.00 (ISBN 0-685-44126-1). Vic.

Merritt, Wesley. Three Indian Campaigns. 19p. Repr. of 1890 ed. pap. 3.95 (ISBN 0-8466-4037-6, SJ137). Shorey.

Myers, Frank. Soldiering in Dakota: Among the Indians in 1863-4-5. facsimile ed. LC 77-160983. (Select Bibliographies Reprint Ser). Repr. of 1888 ed. 24.00 (ISBN 0-8369-5851-9). Arno.

Pickett, Albert J. History of Alabama, & Incidentally of Georgia & Mississippi, from the Earliest Period, 2 Vols. in 1. LC 76-146410. (First American Frontier Ser). (Illus.). 1971. Repr. of 1851 ed. 39.00 (ISBN 0-405-02872-5). Arno.

Potomac Corral of the Westerners. Great Western Indian Fights. LC 60-15191. (Illus.). 1966. pap. 3.50 (ISBN 0-8032-5186-6, BB 339, Bison). U of Nebr Pr.

Seymour, Flora W. Story of the Red Man. facs. ed. LC 79-124257. (Select Bibliographies Reprint Ser). 1929. 25.00 (ISBN 0-8369-5445-9). Arno.

Steele, Phillip. The Last of the Cherokee Warriors. 2nd ed. (Illus.). (gr. 6-12). 1978. pap. 3.95 (ISBN 0-88289-203-7); 5.95 (ISBN 0-911116-99-0). Pelican.

Stuart, John. Memoir of Indian Wars & Other Occurrences by the Late Colonel Stuart of Greenbrier. Stuart, Charles A., ed. LC 75-140883. (Eyewitness Accounts of the American Revolution Ser., No. 3). 1970. Repr. of 1833 ed. 9.50 (ISBN 0-405-01211-X). Arno.

--Memoir of Indian Wars & Other Occurrences. 1971. Repr. of 1833 ed. 8.00 (ISBN 0-87012-079-4). McClain.

Sylvester, Herbert M. Indian Wars of New England, 3 vols. Kohn, Richard H., ed. LC 78-22399. (American Military Experience Ser.). 1979. Repr. of 1910 ed. Set. lib. bdg. 106.00x (ISBN 0-405-11875-9). Arno.

Three Years Among the Camanches, the Narrative of Nelson Lee, the Texan Ranger, Containing a Detailed Account of His Captivity Among the Indians, His Singular Escape Through the Instrumentality of His Watch, & Fully Illustrating Indian Life As It Is on the War Path & in the Camp. LC 75-7100. (Indian CaptivitieS Ser.: Vol. 75). 1977. Repr. of 1859 ed. lib. bdg. 44.00 (ISBN 0-8240-1699-8). Garland Pub.

Utley, Robert M. & Washburn, Wilcomb E. The American Heritage History of the Indian Wars. LC 77-23044. (Illus.). 352p. 1977. 12.95 (ISBN 0-8281-0202-3, Dist. by Scribner); deluxe ed. 39.95 slipcased (ISBN 0-8281-0203-1, Dist. by Scribner). Am Heritage.

Utley, Robert M., ed. Life in Custer's Cavalry: Diaries & Letters of Albert & Jennie Barnitz, 1867-1868. (Western Americana Ser.: No. 30). (Illus.). 1977. 19.50x (ISBN 0-300-02094-5). Yale U Pr.

Van Every, Dale. Ark of Empire: The American Frontier, 1784-1803. LC 76-1392. (Frontier People of America Ser.). 1976. Repr. of 1963 ed. 15.00x (ISBN 0-405-05543-9). Arno.

Walsh, Frank K. Indian Battles Along the Rogue River: One of America's Wild & Scenic Rivers. LC 72-87137. (Illus.). 32p. pap. 1.95 (ISBN 0-913508-02-0). Te-Cum-Tom.

Webb, George W. Chronological List of Engagements Between the Regular Army of the U.S. & Various Tribes of Hostile Indians...1790-1898. LC 74-15125. Repr. of 1939 ed. 16.50 (ISBN 0-404-11984-0). AMS Pr.

INDIANS OF NORTH AMERICA–WARS–FICTION

Peters, Joseph P., compiled by. Indian Battles & Skirmishes on the American Frontier 1790-1898. LC 66-29882. 256p. 1966. 27.50 (ISBN 0-405-03676-0). Arno.

INDIANS OF NORTH AMERICA–WARS–SOURCES

Carroll, John M., ed. The Papers of the Order of the Indian Wars. (Illus.). 1975. 22.50 (ISBN 0-88342-040-6). Old Army.

Smith, William H. St. Clair Papers: The Life & Public Services of Arthur St. Clair, 2 Vols. facs. ed. LC 77-117894. (Select Bibliographies Reprint Ser). 1881. Set. 56.00 (ISBN 0-8369-5347-9). Arno.

Wheelock, Edward, ed. Penhallow's Indian Wars. facsimile ed. LC 71-179534. (Select Bibliographies Reprint Ser). Repr. of 1924 ed. 18.00 (ISBN 0-8369-6663-5). Arno.

INDIANS OF NORTH AMERICA–WARS–1600-1815

see also King Philip's War, 1675-1676; Pequot War, 1636-1638; Pontiac's Conspiracy, 1763-1765; St. Clair's Campaign, 1791; Sullivan's Indian Campaign, 1779; United States–History–French and Indian War, 1755-1763; United States–History–King George's War, 1744-1748; United States–History–King William's War, 1689-1697; United States–History–Queen Anne's War, 1702-1713

Allman, C. B. Lewis Wetzel, Indian Fighter. (Illus.). 1961. 7.50 (ISBN 0-8159-6107-3). Devin.

Bevier, Abraham G. Indians: Or Narratives of Massacres & Depredations. LC 75-16122. 90p. 1975. pap. 2.95 (ISBN 0-912526-17-3). Lib Res.

The Captivity & Sufferings of Gen. Freegift Patchin... Among the Indians... During the Border Warfare in the Time of the American Revolution, Repr. Of 1833 Ed. Bd. with U.S. Congress. House. Committee on Claims. Samuel Cozad... Report Made by Mr. E. Whittlesey from the Committee of Claims. Repr. of 1835 ed; Narrative of the Massacre by the Savages of the Wife & Children of Thomas Baldwin. (Incl. 2nd ed. of 1836). Repr. of 1835 ed; An Authentic Narrative of the Seminole War. Repr. of 1836 ed; Captivity & Sufferings of Mrs. Mason, with an Account of the Massacre of Her Youngest Child. Repr. of 1836 ed; Stories of the Revolution: With an Account of the Lost Child of the Delaware. Priest, Josiah. Repr. of 1836 ed; The Indian Captive (Charles Eaton) The Perilous Adventure (Captivity of David Morgan) in: Columbian Almanac for 1838. LC 75-7074. (Indian Captivities Ser.: Vol. 52). 1977. lib. bdg. 44.00 (ISBN 0-8240-1676-9). Garland Pub.

Crane, Verner. The Southern Frontier, 1670-1732. LC 76-54227. 1977. Repr. of 1956 ed. lib. bdg. 21.50x (ISBN 0-8371-9336-2, CRSF). Greenwood.

De Hass, Wills. History of the Early Settlement & Indian Wars of Western Virginia. 1980. Repr. of 1851 ed. 15.00 (ISBN 0-87012-002-6). McClain.

Doddridge, Joseph. Notes on the Settlement & Indian Wars. 1976. Repr. of 1824 ed. 15.00 (ISBN 0-87012-001-8). McClain.

--Notes, on the Settlement & Indian Wars, of the Western Parts of Virginia & Pennsylvania, from the Year 1763 Until the Year 1783 Inclusive. LC 75-7062. (Indian Captivities Ser.: Vol. 40). 1977. Repr. of 1824 ed. lib. bdg. 44.00 (ISBN 0-8240-1664-5). Garland Pub.

Eckert, Allan W. The Frontiersmen. 1967. 17.50 (ISBN 0-316-20856-6). Little.

--Wilderness Empire. LC 69-16974. (Illus.). 1969. 17.50 (ISBN 0-316-20864-7). Little.

Filson, John. Discovery, Settlement & Present State of Kentucke. 7.00 (ISBN 0-8446-2058-0). Peter Smith.

Flexner, James T. Lord of the Mohawks: A Biography of Sir William Johnson. rev. ed. LC 77-13877. 1979. 16.95 (ISBN 0-316-28609-5). Little.

Flint, Timothy. Indian Wars of the West, Containing Biographical Sketches of Those Pioneers Who Headed the Western Settlers in Repelling the Attacks of the Savages. LC 74-146395. (First American Frontier Ser). 1971. Repr. of 1833 ed. 15.00 (ISBN 0-405-02848-2). Arno.

Glassley, Ray. Indian Wars of the Pacific Northwest. 2nd ed. LC 72-77590. (Illus.). 274p. 1972. 9.50 (ISBN 0-8323-0014-4). Binford.

Gookin, Daniel. Historical Collections of the Indians in New England, of Their Several Nations, Numbers, Customs, Manners, Religion & Government, Before the English Planted There. LC 70-141099. (Research Library of Colonial Americana). 1972. Repr. of 1792 ed. 17.00 (ISBN 0-405-03308-7). Arno.

Hecht, Robert A. Joseph Brant, Iroquois Ally of the British. new ed. Rahmas, D. Steve, ed. (Outstanding Personalities Ser.). 32p. 1975. lib. bdg. 2.95 incl. catalog cards (ISBN 0-686-11229-6); pap. 1.50 vinyl laminated covers (ISBN 0-686-11230-X). SamHar Pr.

Hubbard, W. History of the Indian Wars in New England, 2 Vols. in 1. 1865. 30.00 (ISBN 0-527-43000-5). Kraus Repr.

Hunt, George T. Wars of the Iroquois: A Study in Intertribal Trade Relations. 218p. 1940. pap. 7.95x (ISBN 0-299-00164-4). U of Wis Pr.

Lee, E. Lawrence. Indian Wars in North Carolina, 1663-1763. (Illus.). 1968. pap. 1.00 (ISBN 0-86526-084-2). NC Archives.

Littlefield, Daniel F., Jr. Africans & Creeks: From the Colonial Period to the Civil War. LC 78-75238. (Contributions in Afro-American & African Studies: No. 47). (Illus.). 1979. lib. bdg. 22.50 (ISBN 0-313-20703-8, LAF/). Greenwood.

McKnight, Charles. Our Western Border, Its Life, Combats, Adventures, Forays, Massacres, Captivities, Scouts, Red Chiefs, Pioneers, Women, One Hundred Years Ago, Carefully Written & Compiled. (Rediscovering America Ser). (Illus.). Repr. of 1876 ed. 42.50 (ISBN 0-384-34890-4, R174). Johnson Repr.

McMurtry, Richard K. John McMurtry & the American Indian: A Frontiersman in the Struggle for the Ohio Valley. LC 80-7469. (Illus., Orig.). 1980. pap. 9.95 (ISBN 0-936012-05-6). Current Issues.

Metcalf, Samuel L. A Collection of Some of the Most Interesting Narratives of Indian Warfare in the West. LC 75-7060. (Indian Captivities Ser.: Vol. 38). 1977. Repr. of 1821 ed. lib. bdg. 44.00 (ISBN 0-8240-1662-9). Garland Pub.

Moorhead, Max L. The Apache Frontier: Jacobo Ugarte & Spanish-Indian Relations in Northern New Spain, 1769-1791. LC 67-64449. (Civilization of the American Indian Ser.: No. 90). (Illus.). 1968. 15.95 (ISBN 0-8061-0787-1); pap. 7.95 (ISBN 0-8061-1312-X). U of Okla Pr.

A Narrative of the Sufferings of Massy Harbison from Indian Barbarity, Giving an Account of Her Captivity, the Murder of Her 2 Children, Her Escape, with an Infant at Her Breast, Repr. Of 1825 Ed. Incl. 4th, enl. ed. Repr. of 1836 ed. LC 75-7064. (Indian Captivities Ser.: Vol. 42). 1977. lib. bdg. 44.00 (ISBN 0-8240-1666-1). Garland Pub.

O'Donnell, James H., 3rd. Southern Indians in the American Revolution. LC 76-146662. 188p. 1973. 10.50x (ISBN 0-87049-131-8). U of Tenn Pr.

Penhallow, S. History of the Wars of New England with the Eastern Indians. 1859. 12.00 (ISBN 0-527-70500-4). Kraus Repr.

Smith, William H. Saint Clair Papers: The Life & Public Services of Arthur St. Clair, with His Correspondence & Other Papers, 2 Vols. LC 79-119058. (Illus.). 1970. Repr. of 1882 ed. lib. bdg. 95.00 (ISBN 0-686-76847-7). Da Capo.

Stone, W. L. Life of Joseph Brant, 2 Vols. 1865. Set. 46.00 (ISBN 0-527-86870-1). Kraus Repr.

Stone, William L. Life of Joseph Brant: Thayendanegea, Including the Indian Wars of the American Revolution, 2 Vols. LC 75-108544. (American Indian History Sers). 1970. Repr. of 1838 ed. Set. 33.00 (ISBN 0-403-00226-5). Scholarly.

Van Every, Dale. A Company of Heroes: The American Frontier, 1775-1783. LC 76-1391. (Frontier People of America Ser.). 1976. Repr. of 1962 ed. 15.00x (ISBN 0-405-05542-0). Arno.

--Forth to the Wilderness: The First American Frontier, 1754-1774. LC 76-1390. (Frontier People of America Ser.). 1976. Repr. of 1961 ed. 15.00x (ISBN 0-405-05541-2). Arno.

Wayne, Anthony. Anthony Wayne, a Name in Arms. Knopf, Richard C., ed. LC 74-4661. (Illus.). 566p. 1975. Repr. of 1960 ed. lib. bdg. 37.50 (ISBN 0-8371-7477-5, WAAW). Greenwood.

Wheelock, Edward, ed. Penhallow's Indian Wars. facsimile ed. LC 71-179534. (Select Bibliographies Reprint Ser). Repr. of 1924 ed. 18.00 (ISBN 0-8369-6663-5). Arno.

Withers, Alexander S. Chronicles of Border Warfare. 1980. Repr. of 1831 ed. 15.00 (ISBN 0-87012-000-X). McClain.

--Chronicles of Border Warfare; or, a History of the Settlement by the Whites of Northwestern Virginia. LC 75-146426. (First American Frontier Ser). 1971. Repr. of 1895 ed. 22.00 (ISBN 0-405-02896-2). Arno.

INDIANS OF NORTH AMERICA–WARS–1815-1895

see also Little Big Horn, Battle of the, 1876; Platte Bridge, Battle of, 1865; Sand Creek, Battle of, 1864; Washita, Battle of

Bailey, Lynn R. The Long Walk: A History of the Navajo Wars, 1846-1868. (Illus.). 300p. 9.50 (ISBN 0-87026-047-2). Westernlore.

Beal, Merrill D. I Will Fight No More Forever: Chief Joseph & the Nez Perce War. LC 62-13278. (Illus.). 384p. 1963. pap. 6.95 (ISBN 0-295-74009-4). U of Wash Pr.

Beers, Henry P. The Western Military Frontier 1815-1846. LC 75-25798. (Perspectives in American Hist. Ser.: No. 35). (Illus.). vi, 227p. Repr. of 1935 ed. lib. bdg. 15.00x (ISBN 0-87991-359-2). Porcupine Pr.

Bennett, Ben. Death, Too, for The-Heavy-Runner. (Illus.). 192p. 1981. 10.95 (ISBN 0-87842-131-9). Mountain Pr.

Bischoff, William N., intro. by. We Were Not Summer Soldiers: The Indian War Diary of Plympton J Kelly 1855-1856. LC 76-11999. Repr. 8.75 (ISBN 0-917048-00-8). Wash St Hist Soc.

Buck, Daniel. Indian Outbreaks. 1965. Repr. 8.75 (ISBN 0-87018-005-3). Ross.

Buker, George E. Swamp Sailors: Riverine Warfare in the Everglades, 1835-1842. LC 74-186326. 152p. 1975. 6.50 (ISBN 0-8130-0352-0). U Presses Fla.

Carley, Kenneth. The Sioux Uprising of 1862. rev. ed. LC 76-16499. (Illus.). 102p. 1976. 7.50 (ISBN 0-87351-102-6); pap. 4.50 (ISBN 0-87351-103-4). Minn Hist.

Cohen, Myer M. Notices of Florida & the Campaigns. Tyler, O. Z., Jr., ed. LC 64-19153. (Floridiana Facsimile & Reprint Ser). 1964. Repr. of 1836 ed. 10.75 (ISBN 0-8130-0048-3). U Presses Fla.

Custer, George A. My Life on the Plains. Quaife, Milo M., ed. LC 67-2618. (Illus.). 1966. pap. 6.95 (ISBN 0-8032-5042-8, BB 328, Bison). U of Nebr Pr.

Finerty, John F. War-Path & Bivouac: Or, the Conquest of the Sioux. (WFL Ser.). (Illus.). 1977. pap. 5.95 (ISBN 0-8061-1413-4). U of Okla Pr.

--War-Path & Bivouac: The Big Horn & Yellowstone Expedition. Quaife, Milo M., ed. LC 67-69221. (Illus.). 1966. pap. 7.50 (ISBN 0-8032-5059-2, BB 329, Bison). U of Nebr Pr.

Foreman, Grant. Advancing the Frontier, 1830-1860. (Civilization of the American Indian Ser.: No. 4). (Illus.). 1968. Repr. of 1933 ed. 16.95 (ISBN 0-8061-0792-8). U of Okla Pr.

Francke, Arthur E., Jr. Fort Mellon: Microcosm of the Second Seminole War 1837-1842. LC 77-11918. (Illus.). 1977. 8.95 (ISBN 0-916224-17-1). Banyan Bks.

Giddings, Joshua R. Exiles of Florida. Thompson, Arthur W., intro. by. LC 64-19159. (Floridiana Facsimile & Reprint Ser). (Illus.). 1964. Repr. of 1858 ed. 10.75 (ISBN 0-8130-0085-8). U Presses Fla.

--Exiles of Florida - or, the Crimes Committed by Our Government Against the Maroons Who Fled from South Carolina & Other Slave States Seeking Protection Under Spanish Laws. LC 70-82193. (Anti-Slavery Crusade in America Ser). 1969. Repr. of 1858 ed. 15.00 (ISBN 0-405-00632-2). Arno.

Grinnell, George B. Fighting Cheyennes. (Civilization of the American Indian Ser.: No. 44). (Illus.). 1977. Repr. of 1956 ed. 17.95 (ISBN 0-8061-0347-7). U of Okla Pr.

Halbert, H. S. & Ball, T. H. Creek War of 1813 & 1814. Owsley, Frank L., Jr., ed. LC 74-92656. (Southern Historical Ser: Vol. 15). 366p. 1969. Repr. of 1895 ed. 19.95x (ISBN 0-8173-5220-1). U of Ala Pr.

Horn, Tom. Life of Tom Horn, Government Scout & Interpreter, Written by Himself, Together with His Letters & Statements by His Friends: A Vindication. (Western Frontier Library: No. 26). 1964. pap. 4.95 (ISBN 0-8061-1044-9). U of Okla Pr.

Kelly, Fanny W. Narrative of My Captivity Among the Sioux Indians...with a Brief Account of General Sully's Indian Expedition in 1864, Bearing Upon Events Occurring in My Captivity. LC 75-7111. (Indian Captivities Ser.: Vol. 85). 1976. Repr. of 1871 ed. lib. bdg. 44.00 (ISBN 0-8240-1709-9). Garland Pub.

King, Charles. Campaigning with Crook. (Western Frontier Library: Vol. 25). (Illus.). 1967. Repr. of 1964 ed. 4.95 (ISBN 0-8061-0601-8). U of Okla Pr.

King, James T. War Eagle: A Life of General Eugene A. Carr. LC 63-14694. (Illus.). 1964. 19.95x (ISBN 0-8032-0092-7). U of Nebr Pr.

Laumer, Frank. Massacre! LC 68-9812. (Illus.). 1968. pap. 4.75 (ISBN 0-8130-0479-9). U Presses Fla.

Leckie, William H. The Military Conquest of the Southern Plains. (Illus.). 1963. 14.95 (ISBN 0-8061-0570-4). U of Okla Pr.

Littlefield, Daniel F., Jr. Africans & Seminoles: From Removal to Emancipation. LC 77-86. (Contributions in Afro-American & African Studies: No. 32). 1977. lib. bdg. 19.95x (ISBN 0-8371-9529-2, LAS/). Greenwood.

McConkey, H. E. Dakota War Whoop. 1864. Repr. 15.00 (ISBN 0-87018-041-X). Ross.

McNierney, Michael, ed. Taos Eighteen Forty-Seven: The Revolt in Contemporary Accounts. 1980. pap. 4.95 (ISBN 0-933472-07-2). Johnson Bks.

Mahon, John K. History of the Second Seminole War. LC 67-26604. (Illus.). 1967. 10.00 (ISBN 0-8130-0154-4). U Presses Fla.

Manring, Benjamin F. The Conquest of the Coeur D'Alenes, Spokanes & Palouses. 280p. 1975. 14.95 (ISBN 0-87770-155-5). Ye Galleon.

Marquis, Thomas B., tr. Wooden Leg: A Warrior Who Fought Custer. LC 31-10067. (Illus.). 1962. pap. 6.50 (ISBN 0-8032-5124-6, BB 126, Bison). U of Nebr Pr.

Meltzer, Milton. Hunted Like a Wolf: The Story of the Seminole War. LC 72-78464. (Illus.). 224p. (gr. 7 up). 1972. 6.95 (ISBN 0-374-33521-4). FS&G.

Miles, Nelson A. Personal Recollections & Observations of General Nelson A. Miles. rev. ed. LC 68-23812. (American Scene Ser). (Illus.). Repr. of 1896 ed. lib. bdg. 55.00 (ISBN 0-306-71020-X). Da Capo.

Mooney, James. Ghost-Dance Religion & the Sioux Outbreak of 1890. Wallace, Anthony F., ed. LC 64-24971. (Orig.). 1965. pap. 4.95 (ISBN 0-226-53517-7, P176, Phoen). U of Chicago Pr.

Motte, Jacob R. Journey into Wilderness: An Army Surgeon's Account of Life in Camp & Field During the Creek & Seminole Wars, 1836-1838. LC 75-45206. (Illus.). 1953. 9.00 (ISBN 0-8130-0166-8). U Presses Fla.

Murray, Keith A. Modocs & Their War. (Civilization of the American Indian Ser.: No. 52). (Illus.). 1976. pap. 7.95 (ISBN 0-8061-1331-6). U of Okla Pr.

Myers, Frank. Soldiering in Dakota Among the Indians in 1865. 50p. 1975. 4.95 (ISBN 0-87770-129-6). Ye Galleon.

Narrative of the Capture & Providential Escape of Misses Frances & Almira Hall, 2 Respectable Young Women of the Ages of 16 & 18 Who Were Taken Prisoners by the Savages, Repr. Of 1832 Ed. Bd. with History of the War Between the United States & the Sac & Fox Nations of Indians. Wakefield, John A. Repr. of 1834 ed; Indian Massacre & Captivity of Hall Girls. Scanlan, Charles M. Repr. of 1915 ed. LC 75-7071. (Indian Captivities Ser.: Vol. 49). 1976. lib. bdg. 44.00 (ISBN 0-8240-1673-4). Garland Pub.

Narrative of the Tragical Death of Mr. Darius Barber, & His Seven Children, Who Were Inhumanly Butchered by the Indians... to Which Is Added an Account of the Captivity & Sufferings of Mrs. Barber, Repr. Of 1816 Ed. Incl. Shocking Murder by the Savage! of Mr. Darius Barber's Family in Georgia; Narrative of the Captivity & Sufferings of Mrs. Hannah Lewis, & Her 3 Children, Who Were Taken Prisoners by the Indians. Repr. of 1817 ed; Narrative of the Captivity & Providential Escape of Mrs. Lewis. Repr. of 1833 ed; Narrative of James Van Horne: On the Plains of Michigan. Repr. of 1817 ed; The Indian Captive: Or a Narrative of the Captivity & Sufferings of Zadock Steele... to Which Is Prefixed an Account of the Burning of Royalton. Repr. of 1818 ed. LC 75-7058. (Indian Captivities Ser.: Vol. 36). 1976. lib. bdg. 44.00 (ISBN 0-8240-1660-2). Garland Pub.

Nichols, Roger L. General Henry Atkinson: A Western Military Career. (Illus.). 1965. 10.95 (ISBN 0-8061-0656-5); pap. 6.95 (ISBN 0-8061-1087-2). U of Okla Pr.

North, Luther. Man of the Plains: Recollections of Luther North, 1856-1882. Danker, Donald F., ed. LC 61-6409. (Pioneer Heritage Ser.: Vol. 4). (Illus.). 1961. 16.50 (ISBN 0-8032-0131-1). U of Nebr Pr.

Nye, Wilbur S. Plains Indian Raiders: The Final Phases of Warfare from the Arkansas to the Red River. LC 67-24624. (Illus.). 1974. 22.50 (ISBN 0-8061-0803-7). U of Okla Pr.

Peirce, Parker I. Antelope Bill. limited ed. 12.50 (ISBN 0-87018-047-9). Ross.

Peters, Joseph P., compiled by. Indian Battles & Skirmishes on the American Frontier 1790-1898. LC 66-29882. 256p. 1966. 27.50 (ISBN 0-405-03676-0). Arno.

Peters, Virginia B. The Florida Wars. (Illus.). 1979. 22.50 (ISBN 0-208-01719-4, Archon). Shoe String.

Phelps, Thomas. Reminiscences of Seattle, Washington Territory & the U.S. Sloop-Of-War Decatur During the Indian War of 1855-1856. 1971. Repr. 5.50 (ISBN 0-87770-070-2). Ye Galleon.

Pike, James. Scout & Ranger. LC 74-39282. (The American Scene Ser). (Illus.). 164p. 1972. Repr. of 1932 ed. lib. bdg. 19.50 (ISBN 0-306-70458-7). Da Capo.

Pollock, Dean. Joseph, Chief of the Nez Perce. (Illus.). (gr. 5 up). 1950. 5.95 (ISBN 0-8323-0172-8). Binford.

Remington, Frederick. Pony Tracks. (Western Frontier Library: No. 19). (Illus.). 1977. pap. 3.95 (ISBN 0-8061-1248-4). U of Okla Pr.

Rickey, Don, Jr. Forty Miles a Day on Beans & Hay: The Enlisted Soldier Fighting the Indian Wars. (Illus.). 1977. pap. 7.95 (ISBN 0-8061-1113-5). U of Okla Pr.

Riddle, Jeff C. The Indian History of the Modoc War. LC 74-78125. (Primary Source Bk.). (Illus.). 292p. 1975. 8.95 (ISBN 0-913522-03-1); pap. 5.95 (ISBN 0-913522-04-X). Urion Pr Oreg.

Schellie, Don. Vast Domain of Blood. LC 68-29143. ixx, 268p. 9.50 (ISBN 0-686-74355-5). Westernlore.

Spring, Agnes W. Caspar Collins: The Life & Exploits of an Indian Fighter of the Sixties. LC 27-11731. Repr. of 1927 ed. 16.00 (ISBN 0-404-06199-0). AMS Pr.

Thrapp, Dan L. Conquest of Apacheria. (Illus.). 1967. 17.95 (ISBN 0-8061-0751-0); pap. 7.95 (ISBN 0-8061-1286-7). U of Okla Pr.

Utley, Robert M. Frontier Regulars: The U. S. Army & the Indian, 1866-1891. LC 77-74430. (Wars of the United States Ser.). (Illus.). 476p. 1977. pap. 6.95x (ISBN 0-253-28150-4). Ind U Pr.

--Last Days of the Sioux Nation. (Western Americana Ser.: No. 3). (Illus.). 1963. 25.00x (ISBN 0-300-01003-6); pap. 5.95x (ISBN 0-300-00245-9, YW15). Yale U Pr.

Ware, Eugene F. Indian War of 1864. Walton, Clyde C., ed. LC 60-13875. (Illus.). 1963. pap. 4.95 (ISBN 0-8032-5212-9, BB 173, Bison). U of Nebr Pr.

INDIANS OF NORTH AMERICA-WARS-1866-1895

Alexander, Eveline M. Cavalry Wife: The Diary of Eveline M. Alexander, 1866-1867. Myres, Sandra L., intro. by. LC 76-30611. (Illus.). 186p. 1977. 11.50 (ISBN 0-89096-025-9). Tex A&M Univ Pr.

Bourke, John G. On the Border with Crook. LC 74-155699. 1971. pap. 8.50 (ISBN 0-8032-5741-4, BB 535, Bison). U of Nebr Pr.

Brady, Cyrus T. Indian Fights & Fighters. LC 74-156373. (Illus.). xx, 475p. 1971. 22.50x (ISBN 0-8032-1152-X); pap. 6.50 (ISBN 0-8032-5743-0, BB 538, Bison). U of Nebr Pr.

Capps, Benjamin. The Warren Wagontrain Raid. (Illus.). 1974. 8.95 (ISBN 0-8037-9810-5). Dial.

Collins, Dennis. Indians Last Fight or the Dull Knife Raid. LC 72-1004. Repr. of 1915 ed. 25.00 (ISBN 0-404-07122-8). AMS Pr.

Custer, Elizabeth B. Following the Guidon. (Western Frontier Library: Vol. 33). (Illus.). 341p. pap. 5.95 (ISBN 0-8061-1354-5). U of Okla Pr.

Custer, George A. Wild Life on the Plains & Horrors of Indian Warfare. LC 79-90403. (Mass Violence in America Ser). Repr. of 1891 ed. 20.50 (ISBN 0-405-01300-0). Arno.

Davis, Britton. The Truth About Geronimo. Quaife, M. M., ed. LC 75-37958. (Illus.). xxx, 263p. 1976. 16.95x (ISBN 0-8032-0877-4); pap. 5.25 (ISBN 0-8032-5840-2, BB 622, Bison). U of Nebr Pr.

Ellis, Richard N. General Pope & U. S. Indian Policy. LC 72-129806. 287p. 1970. 10.00x (ISBN 0-8263-0191-6). U of NM Pr.

Emmitt, Robert. The Last War Trail: The Utes & the Settlement of Colorado. (Civilization of the American Indian Ser.: Vol. 40). (Illus.). 352p. 1954. 14.95 (ISBN 0-685-25209-4); pap. 5.95 (ISBN 0-8061-1043-0). U of Okla Pr.

Keim, B. Randolph. Sheridans Troopers on the Borders: A Winter Campaign on the Plains. LC 77-878. (Beautiful Rio Grande Classics Ser.). 1977. lib. bdg. 15.00 (ISBN 0-87380-124-5). Rio Grande.

Seymour, Forest W. Sitanka: The Full Story of Wounded Knee. 1981. 9.75 (ISBN 0-8158-0399-0). Chris Mass.

Summerhayes, Martha. Vanished Arizona: Recollections of an Army Life of a New England Woman. LC 76-54922. (Beautiful Rio Grande Classics Ser.). 1976. lib. bdg. 12.00 (ISBN 0-87380-120-2). Rio Grande.

INDIANS OF NORTH AMERICA-WEAVING

see Indians of North America-Textile Industry and Fabrics

INDIANS OF NORTH AMERICA-WOMEN

Axtell, James, ed. The Indian Peoples of Eastern America: A Documentary History of the Sexes. (Illus.). 256p. 1981. text ed. 11.95x (ISBN 0-19-502740-X); pap. text ed. 6.95x (ISBN 0-19-502741-8). Oxford U Pr.

Kelley, Jane Holden. Yaqui Women: Contemporary Life Histories. LC 77-14063. (Illus.). 1978. 12.50 (ISBN 0-8032-0912-6). U of Nebr Pr.

Landes, Ruth. Ojibwa Woman. LC 70-82362. (Columbia Univ. Contributions to Anthropology Ser.: Vol. 31). Repr. of 1938 ed. 21.00 (ISBN 0-404-50581-3). AMS Pr.

Mead, Margaret. Changing Culture of an Indian Tribe. LC 72-84468. (Columbia University. Contributions to Anthropology: No. 15). Repr. of 1932 ed. 25.00 (ISBN 0-404-50565-1). AMS Pr.

Niethammer, Carolyn. Daughters of the Earth. 1977. pap. 7.95 (ISBN 0-02-096150-2, 09615, Collier). Macmillan.

Qoyawayma, Polingaysi. No Turning Back: A Hopi Indian Woman's Struggle to Live in Two Worlds. LC 64-7652. 180p. 1977. pap. 5.95 (ISBN 0-8263-0439-7). U of NM Pr.

Smithson, Carma L. The Havasupai Woman. (Illus.). viii, 170p. Repr. of 1959 ed. 18.50 (ISBN 0-384-56220-5). Johnson Repr.

Steiner, Stan, ed. Spirit Woman. LC 79-3001. (Harper Native American Publishing Program). (Illus.). 256p. 1980. 12.95 (ISBN 0-06-451975-9). Har-Row.

Stewart, Irene. A Voice in Her Tribe: A Navajo Woman's Own Story. (Ballena Prss Anthropological Papers: No. 17). (Illus.). 1980. pap. 5.95 (ISBN 0-87919-088-4). Ballena Pr.

Wilson, Gilbert L. Waheenee: An Indian Girl's Story. LC 81-2970. (Illus.). xii, 102p. 1981. 14.95x (ISBN 0-8032-4718-4); pap. 4.95 (ISBN 0-686-77458-2, BB 771, Bison). U of Nebr Pr.

Wolf, Beverly H. The Ways of My Grandmothers. 224p. 1981. pap. 5.95 (ISBN 0-688-00471-7). Morrow.

INDIANS OF NORTH AMERICA-ALASKA

Aan-Ta-T'Loot & Pack, Raymond. Tlingit Designs & Carving Manual. LC 78-11887. (Illus.). 1978. 9.95 (ISBN 0-87564-862-2); pap. 6.95 (ISBN 0-87564-861-4). Superior Pub.

Barbeau, Marius. Modern Growth of the Totem Pole on the Northwest Coast. facs. ed. 9p. Repr. pap. 3.00 (ISBN 0-8466-0098-6, SJS98). Shorey.

Cloutier, David. My Grandfather's House: Tlingit Songs of Death & Sorrow. LC 80-15499. (Illus.). 40p. (Orig.). 1980. pap. 3.00 (ISBN 0-914974-26-2). Holmgangers.

Gibbs, George, et al. Tribes of the Extreme Northwest, Alaska, the Aleutians & Adjacent Territories. (Illus.). Repr. of 1877 ed. pap. 22.50 (ISBN 0-8466-4018-X, SJ118). Shorey.

Helm, June. The Indians of the Subarctic: A Critical Bibliography. LC 76-12373. (Newberry Library Center for the History of the American Indian Bibliographical Ser.). 104p. 1976. pap. 3.95x (ISBN 0-253-33004-1). Ind U Pr.

Hippler, Arthur E. & Wood, John R. The Subarctic Athabascans: A Selected, Annotated Bibliography. LC 74-620010. 380p. 1974. pap. 15.00 (ISBN 0-88353-012-0). U Alaska Inst Res.

Michael, Henry N., ed. Lieutenant Zagoskin's Travels in Russian America, 1842-1844: The First Ethnographic & Geographic Investigations in the Yukon & Kuskokwim Valleys of Alaska. LC 67-2141. (Illus.). 1967. 22.50 (ISBN 0-8020-3164-1). U of Toronto Pr.

Morgan, Lael, ed. Alaska's Native People. LC 78-10528. (Alaska Geographic Ser.: Vol. 6, No. 3). (Illus., Orig.). 1979. pap. 19.95 album style (ISBN 0-88240-104-1). Alaska Northwest.

Niblack, Albert P. The Coast Indians of Southern Alaska & Northern British Columbia. LC 14-19260. 1971. Repr. of 1890 ed. 23.00 (ISBN 0-384-41365-X). Johnson Repr.

Oberg, Kalervo. The Social Economy of the Tlingit Indians. LC 73-16048. (Illus.). 144p. 1980. pap. text ed. 7.50 (ISBN 0-295-95735-2). U of Wash Pr.

Osgood, Cornelius. Ethnography of the Tanaina. LC 66-28293. (Yale University Publications in Anthropology Reprints Ser.: No. 16). 229p. 1966. pap. 9.00x (ISBN 0-87536-512-4). HRAFP.

--The Han Indians: A Compilation of Ethnographic & Historical Data on the Alaska-Yukon Boundary Area. LC 76-156892. (Publications in Anthropology: No. 74). 1971. pap. 7.50 (ISBN 0-685-64464-2). Yale U Anthro.

Swanton, John R. Indian Tribes of Alaska & Canada. facsimile ed. Repr. of 1952 ed. pap. 8.50 (ISBN 0-8466-0060-9, SJS60). Shorey.

--Social Conditions, Beliefs & Linguistic Relationship of the Tlingit Indians. LC 8-25731. (U. S. Bureau of American Ethnology Twenty Sixth Annual Report 1904-05). Repr. of 1908 ed. 15.50 (ISBN 0-384-59030-6). Johnson Repr.

--Tlingit Myths & Texts. Repr. of 1909 ed. 28.00 (ISBN 0-384-59050-0). Johnson Repr.

--Tlingit Myths & Texts. Repr. of 1909 ed. 23.00 (ISBN 0-403-03710-7). Scholarly.

Teichmann, Emil. Journey to Alaska in 1868. (Illus.). 1963. Repr. of 1925 ed. 17.50 (ISBN 0-87266-032-X). Argosy.

Van Stone, James W. Athapaskan Adaptations: Hunters & Fishermen of the Subarctic Forests. LC 73-89518. (Worlds of Man Ser.). 176p. 1974. text ed. 12.75x (ISBN 0-88295-610-8); pap. text ed. 5.95x (ISBN 0-88295-611-6). Harlan Davidson.

INDIANS OF NORTH AMERICA-CANADA

Bailey, Alfred G. The Conflict of European & Eastern Algonkian Cultures, 1504-1700: A Study in Canadian Civilization. 2nd ed. LC 78-434310. 1969. pap. 7.50 (ISBN 0-8020-6310-1). U of Toronto Pr.

Barbeau, Marius. Totem Poles of the Gitksan, Upper Skeena River, British Columbia. (Illus.). 1973. pap. text ed. 4.00x (ISBN 0-660-00148-9, 56520-3, Pub. by Natl Mus Canada). U of Chicago Pr.

Birket-Smith, Kaj. Contributions to Chipewyan Ethnology. LC 76-21701. (Thule Expedition Ser.: Vol. 6, No. 3). Repr. of 1930 ed. 38.50 (ISBN 0-404-58319-9). AMS Pr.

Braroe, Niels W. Indian & White: Self-Image & Interaction in a Canadian Plains Community. LC 74-25927. (Illus.). 1975. 10.00x (ISBN 0-8047-0877-0); pap. 3.95 (ISBN 0-8047-1028-7, SP-152). Stanford U Pr.

Brasser, Ted J. Bo'jou, Neejee: Profiles of Canadian Indian Art. (Illus.). 1976. pap. 16.95 (ISBN 0-660-00008-3, 56283-2, Pub. by Natl Mus Canada). U of Chicago Pr.

Campbell, Maria. People of the Buffalo. 8.50 (ISBN 0-88894-089-0, Pub. by Douglas & McIntyre). Intl Schol Bk Serv.

Clark, A. McFadyen. The Athapaskans: Strangers of the North. (Illus.). 1974. pap. 9.95 (ISBN 0-660-00034-2, 56269-7, Pub. by Natl Mus Canada). U of Chicago Pr.

Cooper, John M. The Northern Algonquian Supreme Being. LC 76-43682. (Catholic University of America Anthropological Ser.: No. 2). Repr. of 1934 ed. 14.00 (ISBN 0-404-15515-4). AMS Pr.

--Snares, Deadfalls & Other Traps of the Northern Algonquian & Northern Athapaskans. LC 76-43683. (Catholic University of America Anthropological Ser.: No. 5). Repr. of 1938 ed. 17.50 (ISBN 0-404-15516-2). AMS Pr.

Denys, Nicolas. Description - Natural History of the Coasts of North America. Ganong, William F., ed. LC 68-28597. 1968. Repr. of 1908 ed. lib. bdg. 42.25x (ISBN 0-8371-3873-6, DEDH). Greenwood.

Du Creux, Francois. History of Canada, or New France, 2 Vols. Conacher, James B., ed. Robinson, Percy J., tr. LC 69-14507. 1969. Repr. of 1951 ed. Vol. 1. lib. bdg. 26.75x (ISBN 0-8371-5070-1, DUHI); Vol. 2. lib. bdg. 25.75x (ISBN 0-8371-5071-X, DUHJ). Greenwood.

Dunning, R. W. Social & Economic Change Among the Northern Ojibwa. LC 60-50269. 1959. pap. 6.00 (ISBN 0-8020-6131-1). U of Toronto Pr.

Faraud, Henri J. Dix-Huit Ans Chez Les Sauvages: Voyages Et Missions De Monseigneur Henry Faraud. Repr. of 1866 ed. 23.00 (ISBN 0-384-15135-3). Johnson Repr.

Flannery, Regina. An Analysis of Coastal Algonquian Culture. LC 76-43705. (Catholic University of America, Anthropological Ser.: No. 7). Repr. of 1939 ed. 16.50 (ISBN 0-404-15537-5). AMS Pr.

Frideres, J. Canada's Indians: Contemporary Conflicts. 1974. text ed. 9.95 (ISBN 0-13-112763-2); pap. text ed. 7.95 (ISBN 0-13-112755-1). P-H.

Gibbs, George, et al. Tribes of the Extreme Northwest, Alaska, the Aleutians & Adjacent Territories. (Illus.). Repr. of 1877 ed. pap. 22.50 (ISBN 0-8466-4018-X, SJ118). Shorey.

Grant, W. L., ed. Voyages of Samuel De Champlain, Sixteen Four to Sixteen Eighteen. (Original Narratives). 1967. Repr. of 1907 ed. 18.50x (ISBN 0-06-480330-9). B&N.

Helm, June. The Indians of the Subarctic: A Critical Bibliography. LC 76-12373. (Newberry Library Center for the History of the American Indian Bibliographical Ser.). 104p. 1976. pap. 3.95x (ISBN 0-253-33004-1). Ind U Pr.

Henry, Alexander. Travels & Adventures in Canada & the Indian Territories Between 1760 & 1776. Bain, James, ed. (Research & Source Works Ser.: No. 342). (American Classics in History & Social Science Ser., No. 74). 1969. Repr. of 1901 ed. 18.50 (ISBN 0-8337-1665-4). B Franklin.

Hodge, F. W. Handbook of Indians of Canada: Appendix to the Tenth Report of the Geographic Board of Canada. LC 13-19843. 1913. 30.00 (ISBN 0-527-41300-3). Kraus Repr.

Holmer, Nils M. The Ojibway on Walpole Island, Ontario: A Linguistic Study. LC 76-43748. Repr. of 1953 ed. 11.00 (ISBN 0-404-15587-1). AMS Pr.

Hooke, Hilda M. Thunder in the Mountains: Legends of Canada. (Illus.). (gr. 5-7). 1947. 10.50x (ISBN 0-19-540043-7). Oxford U Pr.

Howley, James P. The Beothucks, or Red Indians, the Aboriginal Inhabitants of Newfoundland. LC 76-43749. Repr. of 1915 ed. 49.50 (ISBN 0-404-15589-8). AMS Pr.

Jaenen, Cornelius J. Friend & Foe: Aspects of French-American Cultural Contact in the Sixteenth & Seventeenth Centuries. (Illus.). 1976. 15.00x (ISBN 0-231-04088-1). Columbia U Pr.

Jenness, Diamond. The Indians of Canada. 6th ed. 1963. 17.50x (ISBN 0-8020-2286-3); pap. 9.95 (ISBN 0-8020-6326-8). U of Toronto Pr.

Lahontan, Louis A. New Voyages to North America, 2 vols. Thwaites, R. G., ed. 1967. Repr. of 1905 ed. 55.50 (ISBN 0-8337-2134-8). B Franklin.

Le Beau, Claude. Avantures Du Sr. C. le Beau, 2 Vols. Repr. of 1738 ed. Set. 38.50 (ISBN 0-384-31940-8). Johnson Repr.

Le Clercq, Chretien. New Relation of Gaspesia: With the Customs & Religion of the Gaspesian Indian. Ganong, William F., ed. LC 68-28600. 1968. Repr. of 1910 ed. lib. bdg. 33.75x (ISBN 0-8371-5044-2, LERG). Greenwood.

Lescarbot, Marc. History of New France, Vol. 1. LC 68-28596. 1968. Repr. of 1907 ed. Vol. 1. lib. bdg. 27.50x (ISBN 0-8371-5039-6, LHFA); Vol. 2. 37.75x (ISBN 0-8371-5040-X, LHFB); Vol. 3. 35.25x (ISBN 0-8371-5041-8, LHFC). Greenwood.

Mackenzie, Alexander. First Man West. Sheppe, Walter, ed. LC 76-3568. (Illus.). 366p. 1976. Repr. of 1962 ed. lib. bdg. 24.00x (ISBN 0-8371-8789-3, SHFM). Greenwood.

Manuel, George & Posluns, Michael. The Fourth World: An Indian Reality. LC 73-8040. (Illus.). 1974. text ed. 7.95 (ISBN 0-02-919990-5). Free Pr.

Marshall, Ingeborg. The Red Ochre People: How Newfoundland's Beothuck Indians Lived. 8.50 (ISBN 0-88894-157-9, Pub. by Douglas & McIntyre). Intl Schol Bk Serv.

Maurault, Joseph P. Histoire Des Abenakis: A Bibliography of Canadiana, No. 4520. (Fr). Repr. of 1866 ed. 38.50 (ISBN 0-384-35950-7). Johnson Repr.

Niblack, Albert P. The Coast Indians of Southern Alaska & Northern British Columbia. LC 14-19260. 1971. Repr. of 1890 ed. 23.00 (ISBN 0-384-41365-X). Johnson Repr.

Price, J. Indians of Canada: Cultural Dynamics. 1979. pap. 8.95 (ISBN 0-13-456962-8). P-H.

Ross, Eric. Beyond the River & the Bay: The Canadian Northwest in 1811. LC 71-486954. (Illus.). 1970. pap. 6.00 (ISBN 0-8020-6188-5). U of Toronto Pr.

Russell, Frank. Explorations in the Far North. LC 74-5873. Repr. of 1898 ed. 25.00 (ISBN 0-404-11682-5). AMS Pr.

Sagard-Theodat, Gabriel. Long Journey to the Country of the Hurons. Wrong, George M., ed. Langton, H. H., tr. LC 68-28613. 1968. Repr. of 1939 ed. lib. bdg. 29.25x (ISBN 0-8371-3861-2, SAJC). Greenwood.

Speck, Frank G. Beothuk & Micmac. LC 76-43840. (MAI. Indian Notes & Monographs. Miscellaneous: No. 22). Repr. of 1922 ed. 41.00 (ISBN 0-404-15693-2). AMS Pr.

--Naskapi: The Savage Hunters of the Labrador Peninsula. (Civilization of the American Indian Ser: Vol. 10). (Illus.). 1935. 12.50 (ISBN 0-8061-1412-6); pap. 5.95 (ISBN 0-8061-1418-5). U of Okla Pr.

Steedman, Elsie V. Ethnobotany of Thompson Indians of British Columbia. Repr. pap. 9.95 (ISBN 0-8466-4035-X, SJ135). Shorey.

Swanton, John R. Indian Tribes of Alaska & Canada. facsimile ed. Repr. of 1952 ed. pap. 8.50 (ISBN 0-8466-0060-9, SJS60). Shorey.

Teit, J. A. Tradition of the Thompson River Indians of British Columbia. Repr. of 1898 ed. 10.00 (ISBN 0-527-01058-8). Kraus Repr.

Teit, James A. Mythology of the Thompson Indians. LC 73-3529. (Jesup North Pacific Expeditions. Publications: No. 8, Pt. 2). Repr. of 1912 ed. 27.50 (ISBN 0-404-58125-0). AMS Pr.

--The Shuswap. LC 73-3522. (Jesup North Pacific Expedition. Publications: No. 2, Pt. 7). Repr. of 1909 ed. 37.50 (ISBN 0-404-58123-4). AMS Pr.

--The Thompson Indians of British Columbia. Boas, Franz, ed. LC 73-3513. (Jesup North Pacific Expedition. Publications: No. 1, Pt. 4). Repr. of 1900 ed. 32.50 (ISBN 0-404-58115-3). AMS Pr.

Van Stone, James W. Athapaskan Adaptations: Hunters & Fishermen of the Subarctic Forests. LC 73-89518. (Worlds of Man Ser.). 176p. 1974. text ed. 12.75x (ISBN 0-88295-610-8); pap. text ed. 5.95x (ISBN 0-88295-611-6). Harlan Davidson.

Vetromile, Eugene. The Abnakis & Their History. LC 76-43884. 1977. Repr. of 1866 ed. 15.00 (ISBN 0-404-15741-6). AMS Pr.

Voyage of Alexander Mackenzie. facs. ed. Repr. pap. 5.75 (ISBN 0-8466-0182-6, SJS182). Shorey.

Wallis, Wilson D. The Canadian Dakota. LC 76-43887. (AMNH Anthropological Papers: Vol. 41, Pt. 1). Repr. of 1947 ed. 32.50 (ISBN 0-404-15746-7). AMS Pr.

Watkins, Mel. Dene Nation: The Colony Within. LC 76-54701. 1977. 17.50x (ISBN 0-8020-2264-2); pap. 5.95 (ISBN 0-8020-6315-2). U of Toronto Pr.

West, John. Substance of a Journal During a Residence at the Red River Colony. 14.00 (ISBN 0-384-66930-1). Johnson Repr.

Wilson, James. Canada's Indians. (Minority Rights Group: No. 21). 1974. pap. 2.50 (ISBN 0-89192-107-9). Interbk Inc.

INDIANS OF NORTH AMERICA–EASTERN STATES

see also Five Civilized Tribes

Acts & Resolutions of the Creek National Council of the Extra Session of April, 1894 & the Regular Session of October, 1894. LC 73-88773. (The Constitutions & Laws of the American Indian Tribes Ser. 1: Vol. 19). 1973. Repr. of 1894 ed. lib. bdg. 6.00 (ISBN 0-8420-1721-6). Scholarly Res Inc.

Acts & Resolutions of the Creek National Council of the Session of May, June, October, November & December, 1895, Compiled & Translated by D.C. Watson. LC 73-88775. (Constitutions & Laws of the American Indian Tribes Ser. No. 1: Vol. 20). 1973. Repr. of 1896 ed. 6.00 (ISBN 0-8420-1722-4). Scholarly Res Inc.

Acts & Resolutions of the General Council of the Choctaw Nation at the Called Sessions Thereof Held in April & June, 1858, the Regular Session Held in October, 1858. LC 75-3683. (Constitutions & Laws of the American Indian Tribes Ser. 2: Vol. 16). 1975. Repr. of 1859 ed. 12.00 (ISBN 0-8420-1849-2). Scholarly Res Inc.

Acts & Resolutions of the General Council of the Choctaw Nation, Passed at Its Regular Session, 1899. LC 75-3691. (Constitutions & Laws of the American Indian Tribes Ser. 2: Vol. 24). 1975. Repr. of 1900 ed. 12.00 (ISBN 0-8420-1882-4). Scholarly Res Inc.

Acts & Resolutions of the General Council of the Choctaw Nation, Passed at Its Regular Session, 1901. LC 75-3692. (Constitutions & Laws of the American Indian Tribes Ser. 2: Vol. 25). 1975. Repr. of 1902 ed. 11.00 (ISBN 0-8420-1883-2). Scholarly Res Inc.

Acts & Resolutions of the General Council of the Choctaw Nation, Passed at Its Regular Session, 1904. Bd. with Acts & Resolutions of the General Council of the Choctaw Nation, Passed at Its Extraordinary & Regular Sessions, 1905. LC 75-3693. (Constitutions & Laws of the American Indian Tribes Ser. 2: Vol. 26). 1975. Repr. of 1905 ed. 14.00 (ISBN 0-8420-1884-0). Scholarly Res Inc.

Acts & Resolutions of the National Council of the Muskogee Nation of 1893. LC 75-3696. (Constitutions & Laws of the American Indian Tribes Ser. 2: Vol. 29). 1975. Repr. of 1894 ed. 11.00 (ISBN 0-8420-1887-5). Scholarly Res Inc.

Acts & Resolutions of the National Council of the Muskogee Nation of 1893 & 1899, Inclusive. LC 75-3697. (Constitutions & Laws of the American Indian Tribes Ser. 2: Vol. 30). 1975. Repr. of 1900 ed. 12.00 (ISBN 0-8420-1888-3). Scholarly Res Inc.

Adair, James. History of the American Indians. (American Studies). Repr. of 1775 ed. 31.00 (ISBN 0-384-00305-2). Johnson Repr.

Adams, Richard C. To the Delaware Indians. 1976. Repr. of 1904 ed. 19.00 (ISBN 0-403-05766-3, Regency). Scholarly.

Adams, Spencer L. The Long House of the Iroquois. LC 76-43640. (Illus.). Repr. of 1944 ed. 27.50 (ISBN 0-404-15475-1). AMS Pr.

Alabama - Coushatta (Creek) Indians. Incl. Alabama - Coushatta Indians: Ethnological Report & Statement of Testimony. Jacobson, Daniel; Ethnological Analysis of Documents Relating to the Alabama & Coushatta Tribes of the State of Texas. Martin, Howard; A History of Polk County, Texas, Indians. Marsh, Ralph H. (American Indian Ethnohistory Ser: Southern & Southeast Indians). (Illus.). lib. bdg. 42.00 (ISBN 0-8240-0758-1). Garland Pub.

Alden, John R. John Stuart & the Southern Colonial Frontier: A Study of Indian Relations, War, Trade, Land Problems in the Southern Wilderness, 1754-1775. LC 66-29459. (Illus.). 1966. Repr. of 1944 ed. 15.00 (ISBN 0-87752-001-1). Gordian.

Alford, Thomas W. Civilization: & the Story of the Shawnees-As Told to Florence Drake. (The Civilization of the American Indian Ser.: Vol. 13). (Illus.). 203p. 1980. pap. 5.95 (ISBN 0-8061-1614-5). U of Okla Pr.

Anderson, Duane C. & Semken, Holmes, eds. The Cherokee Excavations: Holocene Ecology & Human Adaptations in Northwestern Iowa. (Studies in Archaeology). 1980. 23.00 (ISBN 0-12-058260-0). Acad Pr.

Barbe-Marbois, Francois. Our Revolutionary Forefathers: The Letters of Francois, Marquis De Barbe-Marbois During His Residence in the United States As Secretary of the French Legation 1779-1785. facsimile ed. LC 71-99659. (Select Bibliographies Reprint Ser). 1929. 21.00 (ISBN 0-8369-5088-7). Arno.

Barry, Ada L. Yunini's Story of the Trail of Tears. LC 74-7924. (Illus.). Repr. of 1932 ed. 34.50 (ISBN 0-404-11810-0). AMS Pr.

Bartram, William. Travels. Van Doren, Mark, ed. (Illus.). 8.50 (ISBN 0-8446-1600-1). Peter Smith.

--Travels. 1928. pap. 4.50 (ISBN 0-486-20013-2). Dover.

Beauchamp, William M. Aboriginal Chipped Stone Implements of New York. LC 76-43659. (New York State Museum Bulletin: Vol. 4, No. 16). Repr. of 1897 ed. 14.50 (ISBN 0-404-15495-6). AMS Pr.

--Aboriginal Occupation of New York. LC 76-43660. (New York State Museum Bulletin: No. 32, Vol. 7). Repr. of 1900 ed. 22.00 (ISBN 0-404-15492-1). AMS Pr.

--Aboriginal Use of Wood in New York. LC 76-43661. (New York State Museum Bulletin: 89). Repr. of 1905 ed. 27.50 (ISBN 0-404-15493-X). AMS Pr.

--A History of the Iroquois, Now Commonly Called the Six Nations. LC 74-7925. (Illus.). Repr. of 1905 ed. 27.50 (ISBN 0-404-11811-9). AMS Pr.

--Horn & Bone Implements of the New York Indians. LC 76-43662. (New York State Museum Bulletin: 50). Repr. of 1902 ed. 19.50 (ISBN 0-404-15494-8). AMS Pr.

--Iroquois Folk Lore. LC 74-7926. Repr. of 1922 ed. 21.00 (ISBN 0-404-11812-7). AMS Pr.

--The Iroquois Trail. LC 74-7927. Repr. of 1892 ed. 15.00 (ISBN 0-404-11813-5). AMS Pr.

--Wampum & Shell Articles Used by the New York Indians. LC 76-43663. (New York State Museum Bulletin: No. 41, Vol. 8). Repr. of 1901 ed. 21.50 (ISBN 0-404-15496-4). AMS Pr.

Beaver, A. J. Sac & Fox Lands in Royce Area 50 in Illinois & Wisconsin: Soils & Soil Forming Factors. (Library of American Indian Affairs). 50p. 1974. lib. bdg. 24.00 (ISBN 0-8287-1220-4). Clearwater Pub.

Benson, Henry C. Life Among the Choctaw Indians & Sketches of the Southwest. (American Studies). Repr. of 1860 ed. 15.50 (ISBN 0-384-03928-6). Johnson Repr.

Berthrong, Donald J. Indians of Northern Indiana & Southwestern Michigan: An Historical Report on Indian Use & Occupancy of Northern Indiana & Southwestern Michigan. Horr, David A., ed. (North Central & Northeastern Indians - American Indian Ethnohistory Ser.). 1974. lib. bdg. 38.00 (ISBN 0-8240-0801-4). Garland Pub.

Beverley, Robert. The History & Present State of Virginia. Wright, Louis B., ed. (Institute of Early American History & Culture Ser.). 1960. Repr. of 1947 ed. 25.00x (ISBN 0-8078-0498-3). U of NC Pr.

--History & Present State of Virginia. Wright, Louis B., ed. LC 68-58999. (Illus.). 366p. 1968. pap. 3.95 (ISBN 0-8139-0028-X). U Pr of Va.

Blanchard, Kendall A. Mississippi Choctaws at Play: The Serious Side of Leisure. LC 80-26527. 1981. 13.95x (ISBN 0-252-00866-9). U of Ill Pr.

Bolton, Reginald P. New York City in Indian Possession, Vol. 2, No. 7. 2nd ed. (Indian Notes & Monographs). (Illus.). 1975. soft cover 6.00 (ISBN 0-934490-02-3). Mus Am Ind.

Booth, Ernest G. Creek Nation Lands in Alabama: Land Appraisal As of 1832. (Library of American Indian Affairs). 1976. lib. bdg. 45.00x (ISBN 0-8287-1024-4). Clearwater Pub.

Brickell, John. Natural History of North Carolina. (Illus.). 1968. Repr. of 1737 ed. 12.00 (ISBN 0-930230-17-5). Johnson NC.

--The Natural History of North Carolina. (American Studies). (Illus.). Repr. of 1737 ed. lib. bdg. 31.00 (ISBN 0-384-05740-3). Johnson Repr.

Brinton, Daniel G., ed. The Lenape & Their Legends. LC 77-102641. (Library of Aboriginal American Literature Ser.: No. 5). Repr. of 1884 ed. 21.50 (ISBN 0-404-52185-1). AMS Pr.

Brown, Douglas S. Catawba Indians: The People of the River. LC 65-28497. (Illus.). 1966. 14.95 (ISBN 0-87249-101-3). U of SC Pr.

Brumgardt, John R. & Bowles, Larry L. People of the Magic Waters: The Cahuilla Indians of Palm Springs. (Illus.). 1981. 9.95 (ISBN 0-88280-060-4). ETC Pubns.

Chalfant, Stuart A. Palus Indians: Ethnohistoric Report on Aboriginal Land Occupancy & Utilization. (Library of American Indian Affairs). 49p. 1974. lib. bdg. 24.00 (ISBN 0-8287-1177-1). Clearwater Pub.

Cherokee & Creek Indians. Incl. Ethnographic Report on Royce Area 79, Docket 275, Chicasaw, Cherokee, & Creek. Fairbanks, Charles H; Cherokee Treaties. Goff, John H; Findings of Fact, & Opinion. Indian Claims Commission. (American Indian Ethnohistory Ser: Southern & Southeast Indians). (Illus.). lib. bdg. 42.00 (ISBN 0-8240-0757-3). Garland Pub.

Chickasaws & Choctaws. LC 75-3678. (Constitutions & Laws of the American Indian Tribes Ser. 2: Vol. II). 1975. Repr. of 1891 ed. 12.00 (ISBN 0-8420-1844-1). Scholarly Res Inc.

The Choctaw Laws: Passed at the Special Sessions in January, 1894, & April, 1894, & the Regular Session, October, 1894. LC 75-3690. (Constitutions & Laws of the American Indian Tribes Ser. 2: Vol. 23). 1975. Repr. of 1895 ed. 11.00 (ISBN 0-8420-1881-6). Scholarly Res Inc.

Claflin, W. H. Stalling's Island Mound, Columbia County, Georgia. 1931. pap. 9.00 (ISBN 0-527-01232-7). Kraus Repr.

Clark, Jerry E. The Shawnee. LC 77-73700. (Kentucky Bicentennial Bookshelf Ser). (Illus.). 112p. 1977. 6.95 (ISBN 0-8131-0233-2). U Pr of Ky.

Cline, Howard F. Florida Indians I. Horr, David A., ed. (American Indian Ethnohistory Ser.). 1978. lib. bdg. 42.00 (ISBN 0-8240-0766-2). Garland Pub.

--Florida Indians II. Horr, David A., ed. (American Indian Ethnohistory Ser.). 1978. lib. bdg. 42.00 (ISBN 0-8240-0767-0). Garland Pub.

--Notes on Colonial Indians (Seminole) & Communities in Florida, 1700-1821. (Library of American Indian Affairs). 220p. 1974. 75.50 (ISBN 0-8287-1152-6). Clearwater Pub.

Cobb, William & Price, Andrew. History of the Mingo Indians. 1974. Repr. of 1921 ed. 3.50 (ISBN 0-87012-194-4). McClain.

Coe, Charles. Red Patriots: The Story of the Seminoles. Tebeau, Charlton W., intro. by. LC 73-5702. (Bicentennial Floridiana Facsimile & Reprint Ser.). 347p. 1974. Repr. of 1898 ed. 12.00 (ISBN 0-8130-0401-2). U Presses Fla.

Coe, Joffre L. The Formative Cultures of the Carolina Piedmont. LC 64-21423. (Transaction Ser.: Vol. 54, Pt. 5). 1980. Repr. of 1964 ed. 8.00 (ISBN 0-87169-545-6). Am Philos.

Cohen, Myer M. Notices of Florida & the Campaigns. Tyler, O. Z., Jr., ed. LC 64-19153. (Floridiana Facsimile & Reprint Ser). 1964. Repr. of 1836 ed. 10.75 (ISBN 0-8130-0048-3). U Presses Fla.

Constitution & Laws of the Chickasaw Nation Together with the Treaties of 1832, 1833, 1834, 1837, 1852, 1855, & 1866 Compiled by Davis A. Homer. LC 73-88755. (Constitution & Laws of the American Indian Tribes Ser. 1: Vol. 2). 1973. Repr. of 1899 ed. 45.00 (ISBN 0-8420-1719-4). Scholarly Res Inc.

Constitution & Laws of the Chickasaw Nation Together with the Treaties of 1832, 1833, 1834, 1837, 1852, 1855, & 1866 Compiled by Davis A. Homer. LC 73-88755. (Constitution & Laws of the American Indian Tribes Ser. 1: Vol. 2). 1973. Repr. of 1899 ed. 45.00 (ISBN 0-8420-1719-4). Scholarly Res Inc.

The Constitution & Laws of the Choctaw Nation, 3 vols. LC 75-3680. (Constitutions & Laws of the American Indian Tribes Ser. 2). 1975. Repr. Vol. 13. 12.00 (ISBN 0-8420-1846-8); Vol. 14. 12.00 (ISBN 0-8420-1847-6); Vol. 15. 13.00 (ISBN 0-8420-1848-4). Scholarly Res Inc.

Constitution & Laws of the Choctaw Nation, Together with the Treaties of 1837, 1855, 1865, 1866 Compiled by A.R. Durant, Davis Homer, & Ben Watkins. LC 73-88767. (Constitutions & Laws of the American Indian Tribes Ser 1: Vol. 12). 1973. Repr. of 1894 ed. 30.00 (ISBN 0-8420-1706-2). Scholarly Res Inc.

Constitution & Laws of the Choctaw Nation Together with the Treaties of 1855, 1865 & 1866, Compiled by Joseph P. Folsom, Commissioned for the Purpose, Chahta Tamaha, 1869. LC 73-88764. (Constitutions & Laws of the American Indian Tribes, Ser. 1: Vol. 11). 1973. Repr. of 1869 ed. 40.00 (ISBN 0-8420-1705-4). Scholarly Res Inc.

Constitution & Laws of the Choctaw Nation Together with the Treaties of 1855, 1865 & 1866, Compiled by Joseph P. Folsom, Commissioned for the Purpose, Chahta Tamaha, 1869. LC 73-88764. (Constitutions & Laws of the American Indian Tribes, Ser. 1: Vol. 11). 1973. Repr. of 1869 ed. 40.00 (ISBN 0-8420-1705-4). Scholarly Res Inc.

Constitution & Laws of the Muskogee Nation. LC 75-3694. (Constitutions & Laws of the American Indian Tribes Ser. 2: Vol. 27). 1975. Repr. of 1880 ed. 15.00 (ISBN 0-8420-1885-9). Scholarly Res Inc.

Constitution & Laws of the Muskogee Nation, As Compiled & Codified by A.P. McKellop, Under Act of October 15, 1892. LC 73-88772. (Constitutions & Laws of the American Indian Tribes, Ser 1: Vol. 18). 1973. Repr. of 1893 ed. 25.00 (ISBN 0-8420-1720-8). Scholarly Res Inc.

Constitution & Laws of the Muskogee Nation, As Compiled by L. C. Perryman, March 1st of 1890. LC 73-3695. (Constitution & Laws of the American Indian Tribes Ser. 2: Vol. 28). 1975. Repr. of 1890 ed. 20.00 (ISBN 0-8420-1886-7). Scholarly Res Inc.

Constitution & Laws of the Muskogee Nation, As Compiled by L. C. Perryman, March 1st of 1890. LC 73-3695. (Constitution & Laws of the American Indian Tribes Ser. 2: Vol. 28). 1975. Repr. of 1890 ed. 20.00 (ISBN 0-8420-1886-7). Scholarly Res Inc.

Constitution, Laws, & Treaties of the Chickasaws, by Authority. LC 75-3675. (Constitutions & Laws of the American Indian Tribes Ser. 2: Vol. 8). 1975. Repr. of 1860 ed. 17.00 (ISBN 0-8420-1841-7). Scholarly Res Inc.

Constitution, Laws, & Treaties of the Chickasaws. LC 75-3676. (Constitutions & Laws of the American Indian Tribes Ser. 2: Vol. 9). 1975. Repr. of 1867 ed. 17.00 (ISBN 0-8420-1842-5). Scholarly Res Inc.

Constitution, Treaties & Laws of the Chickasaw Nation. LC 75-3677. (Constitutions & Laws of the American Indian Tribes Ser. 2: Vol. 10). 1975. Repr. of 1890 ed. 22.00 (ISBN 0-8420-1843-3). Scholarly Res Inc.

Constitution, Treaties & Laws of the Choctaw Nation: Made & Enacted by the Choctaw Legislature 1887. LC 75-3686. (Constitutions & Laws of the American Indian Tribes Ser. 2: Vol. 19). 1975. Repr. of 1887 ed. 17.00 (ISBN 0-8420-1877-8). Scholarly Res Inc.

Corkran, David H. Carolina Indian Frontier. LC 79-120589. (Tricentennial Booklet: No. 6). 1970. pap. 2.25 (ISBN 0-87249-195-1). U of SC Pr.

Corry, John P. Indian Affairs in Georgia, 1732-1756. LC 76-43685. Repr. of 1936 ed. 21.50 (ISBN 0-404-15518-9). AMS Pr.

Coulter, John L. Potawatomi Lands in Iowa & Kansas: Value of Farmland Improvements & Other Natural Resources, 1840-1850. (Library of American Indian Affairs). 77p. 1974. lib. bdg. 38.00 (ISBN 0-8287-1202-6). Clearwater Pub.

Cushman, Horatio B. History of the Choctaw, Chickasaw & Natchez Indians. Debo, Angie, ed. LC 72-180607. 503p. (Repr. of abr. 1962 ed. of a work first published in 1899). 1972. 23.00 (ISBN 0-8462-1640-X). Russell.

Cutler, Jervis. Topographical Description of the State of Ohio, Indiana Territory, & Louisiana. LC 78-146388. (First American Frontier Ser). (Illus.). 1971. Repr. of 1812 ed. 12.00 (ISBN 0-405-02839-3). Arno.

Daves, Francis M. Cherokee Woman. 1973. 8.95 (ISBN 0-8283-1474-8). Branden.

Davis, W. H. Osage Ceded Lands: Valuation Study As of September 29, 1965. 240p. 1974. lib. bdg. 87.00 (ISBN 0-8287-1159-3). Clearwater Pub.

Debo, Angie. Rise & Fall of the Choctaw Republic. 2nd ed. LC 69-7973. (Civilization of the American Indian Ser.: No. 6). (Illus.). 1934. pap. 6.95 (ISBN 0-8061-1247-6). U of Okla Pr.

--The Road to Disappearance: A History of the Creek Indians. (CAI Ser.). (Orig.). 1979. pap. 9.95 (ISBN 0-8061-1532-7). U of Okla Pr.

Densmore, Frances. Seminole Music. LC 72-1878. (Music Ser.). (Illus.). 276p. 1972. Repr. of 1956 ed. lib. bdg. 19.50 (ISBN 0-306-70506-0). Da Capo.

DeRosier, Arthur H., Jr. Removal of the Choctaw Indians. LC 70-111044. (Illus.). 1970. 12.50 (ISBN 0-87049-113-X). U of Tenn Pr.

Dickens, Roy S., Jr. Cherokee Prehistory: The Pisgah Phase in the Appalachian Summit Region. LC 76-1972. 1976. 16.50x (ISBN 0-87049-193-8). U of Tenn Pr.

Doster, James F. Creek Indians. Horr, David A., ed. (American Indian Ethnohistory Ser.). 1978. lib. bdg. 42.00 (ISBN 0-8240-0788-3). Garland Pub.

--Creek Indians & Their Florida Lands, Seventeen Forty to Eighteen Five. (Library of American Indian Affairs). (Illus.). 268p. 1974. 76.50 (ISBN 0-8287-1019-8). Clearwater Pub.

--Creek Indians: Information Relative to the Claims of the Creeks Against the U. S. for Florida Lands Taken by the U. S. Under the Treaty of Moultrie Creek, 1823. Incl. Rebuttal Report on the Reliability of the Statements of Dr. John R. Swanton on the Creeks. (Library of American Indian Affairs). 376p. 1974. lib. bdg. 102.00 (ISBN 0-8287-1020-1). Clearwater Pub.

Downes, Randolph C. Council Fires on the Upper Ohio. LC 40-34394. (Illus.). 1940. pap. 5.95 (ISBN 0-8229-5201-7). U of Pittsburgh Pr.

Eaton, Rachel C. John Ross & the Cherokee Indians. LC 76-43694. Repr. of 1921 ed. 24.50 (ISBN 0-404-15526-X). AMS Pr.

Edmunds, R. David. The Potawatomis: Keepers of the Fire. LC 78-5628. (Civilization of the American Indian Ser: No. 145). (Illus.). 1978. 19.95 (ISBN 0-8061-1478-9). U of Okla Pr.

Eggleston, George C. Red Eagle & the Wars with the Creek Indians of Alabama. LC 76-43695. Repr. of 1878 ed. 22.50 (ISBN 0-404-15528-6). AMS Pr.

Fairbanks, Charles H. Florida Indians III. Horr, David A., ed. (American Indian Ethnohistory Ser.). 1978. lib. bdg. 42.00 (ISBN 0-8240-0759-X). Garland Pub.

--The Pascagoula, Biloxi & Mobilian Consolidated Band. (Library of American Indian Affairs Ser.). 250p. 1974. lib. bdg. 72.00 (ISBN 0-8287-1185-2). Clearwater Pub.

--The Seminole of Florida to 1823. (Library of American Indian Affairs). 292p. 1974. lib. bdg. 82.50 (ISBN 0-8287-1240-9). Clearwater Pub.

--The Seminolee Nation: An Ethno-Historical Report of the Florida Indians As of 1823. (Library of American Indian Affairs). 1976. lib. bdg. 84.00x (ISBN 0-8287-1241-7). Clearwater Pub.

Fenton, William N. The Roll Call of the Iroquois Chiefs: A Study of a Mnemonic Cane from the Six Nations Reserve. LC 76-43704. (Smithsonian Miscellaneous Collections Ser.: Vol. 3, No. 15). Repr. of 1950 ed. 20.00 (ISBN 0-404-15536-7). AMS Pr.

Filler, Louis & Guttmann, Allen, eds. The Removal of the Cherokee Nation: Manifest Destiny or National Dishonor? LC 76-53820. 128p. 1977. pap. 5.50 (ISBN 0-88275-482-3). Krieger.

Fliegel, Carl J., compiled by. Index to the Records of the Moravian Mission Among the Indians of North America, 2 vols. 1970. 375.00 (ISBN 0-89235-018-0). Res Pubns Conn.

Florida Anthropological Society. Florida Anthropological Society Publications, Nos. 1-5. Set. pap. 27.00 (ISBN 0-384-16110-3). Johnson Repr.

Fogelson, Raymond D. The Cherokees: A Critical Bibliography. LC 78-3254. (The Newberry Library Center for the History of the American Indian Bibliographical Ser.). 112p. 1978. pap. 4.95x (ISBN 0-253-31346-5). Ind U Pr.

Foreman, Grant. Five Civilized Tribes. (Civilization of the American Indian Ser.: No. 8). (Illus.). 1971. pap. 8.95 (ISBN 0-8061-0923-8). U of Okla Pr.

Foster, Laurence. Negro-Indian Relationships in the Southeast. LC 76-43708. Repr. of 1935 ed. 14.50 (ISBN 0-404-15543-X). AMS Pr.

Freedman & Registration Bills: Passed at the Special Session of the Choctaw Council Indian Territory, May, 1883. Bd. with Laws of the Choctaw Nation, Passed at the Choctaw Council at the Regular Session of 1883. LC 75-3685. (Constitutions & Laws of the American Indian Tribes Ser. 2: Vol. 18). 1975. Repr. of 1883 ed. 16.00 (ISBN 0-8420-1876-X). Scholarly Res Inc.

French, Laurence & Hornbuckle, Jim, eds. The Cherokee Perspective. 1981. 6.95 (ISBN 0-686-31803-X). Appalach Consortium.

Garbarino, M. Big Cypress: A Changing Seminole Community. LC 72-174774. (Case Studies in Cultural Anthropology). 1972. pap. text ed. 5.95 (ISBN 0-03-086672-3, HoltC). HR&W.

Gatschet, A. S. Migration Legend of the Creek Indians with a Linguistic Historical & Ethnographic Introduction, 2 Vols. in 1. LC 5-13733. Repr. of 1888 ed. 21.00 (ISBN 0-527-32700-X). Kraus Repr.

Gatschet, Albert S. Migration Legend of the Creek Indians. LC 72-83460. (Library of Aboriginal American Literature: No. 4). Repr. of 1884 ed. 19.50 (ISBN 0-404-52184-3). AMS Pr.

General & Special Laws of the Choctaw Nation: Passed at the Regular Session of the General Council, Convened at Chahta Tamaha, October 3rd & Adjourned November 12th, 1881. LC 75-3684. (Constitutions & Laws of the American Indian Tribes Ser. 2: Vol. 17). 1975. Repr. of 1881 ed. 12.00 (ISBN 0-8420-1875-1). Scholarly Res Inc.

Gilbert, William H. The Eastern Cherokees. LC 76-43714. (BAE. Anthropological Papers: No. 23). Repr. of 1943 ed. 27.50 (ISBN 0-404-15547-2). AMS Pr.

Glenn, James A. My Work Among the Florida Seminoles. (Illus.). 1981. write for info. (ISBN 0-8130-0717-8). U Presses Fla.

Glubok, Shirley. The Art of the Southeastern Indians. LC 77-20850. (Illus.). (gr. 4 up). 1978. 9.95 (ISBN 0-02-736480-1, 73648). Macmillan.

Goff, James H. Cherokee Nation: Land Cessions in Tennessee, Mississippi, North Carolina, Georgia, Alabama, 1785-1835. (Library of American Indian Affairs). 278p. 1974. lib. bdg. 79.50 (ISBN 0-8287-0974-2). Clearwater Pub.

Grassmann, Thomas. Mohawk Indians & Their Valley. LC 74-79962. (Illus.). 1969. 25.00x (ISBN 0-87343-034-4). Magi Bks.

Graymont, Barbara. Iroquois in the American Revolution. LC 73-170096. (New York State Studies). (Illus.). 1972. 14.95x (ISBN 0-8156-0083-6); pap. 6.95 (ISBN 0-8156-0116-6). Syracuse U Pr.

Graymont, Barbara, ed. Fighting Tuscarora: The Autobiography of Chief Clinton Rickard. LC 73-8208. (Illus.). 224p. 1973. 10.50 (ISBN 0-8156-0092-5). Syracuse U Pr.

Gulf Coast History & Humanities Conference. Indians of the Lower South: Past & Present: Proceedings. Mahon, John K., ed. 1974. pap. 6.95 (ISBN 0-686-11514-7). Historic Pensacola.

Gulick, John. Cherokees at the Crossroads. rev. ed. 222p. 1973. pap. text ed. 7.00 (ISBN 0-89143-062-8). U NC Inst Res Soc Sci.

Hale, Horatio E., ed. Iroquois Book of Rites. LC 74-83458. (Library of Aboriginal American Literature: No. 2). Repr. of 1883 ed. 20.00 (ISBN 0-404-52182-7). AMS Pr.

Hammar, Conrad H. Sac, Fox & Iowa Lands in South Central Iowa, 1839-1843, Royce Area 262: Valuation. 194p. 1974. lib. bdg. 58.50 (ISBN 0-8287-1224-7). Clearwater Pub.

Hamor, Ralphe. A True Discourse of the Present Estate of Virginia. LC 72-25512. (English Experience Ser.: No. 320). 70p. 1971. Repr. of 1615 ed. 13.00 (ISBN 90-221-0320-X). Walter J Johnson.

Hare, Lloyd C. Thomas Mayhew, Patriarch to the Indians, 1593-1682. LC 76-104347. (Illus.). Repr. of 1932 ed. 20.00 (ISBN 0-404-03108-0). AMS Pr.

Harrington, M. R. The Indians of New Jersey: Dickon Among the Lenapes. LC 63-15519. (Illus.). (gr. 4-6). 1963. 12.50 (ISBN 0-8135-0424-4); pap. 3.95 (ISBN 0-8135-0425-2). Rutgers U Pr.

Harrington, Mark R. Religion & Ceremonies of the Lenape. LC 76-43731. (MAI Indian Notes & Monographs. Miscellaneous). Repr. of 1921 ed. 19.00 (ISBN 0-404-15572-3). AMS Pr.

--Sacred Bundles of the Sac & Fox Indians. LC 76-43732. (Univ. of Pennsylvania Museum. Anthropological Pubns: Vol. 4, No. 1). (Illus.). Repr. of 1914 ed. 30.00 (ISBN 0-404-15573-1). AMS Pr.

Harriot, Thomas. A Briefe & True Report of the New Found Land in Virginia. LC 71-171785. (English Experience Ser.: No. 384). 48p. 1971. Repr. of 1588 ed. 7.00 (ISBN 90-221-0384-6). Walter J Johnson.

Harvey, H. History of the Shawnee Indians, from the Year 1681 to 1854, Inclusive. LC 6-10175. Repr. of 1855 ed. 16.00 (ISBN 0-527-38600-6). Kraus Repr.

Hauptman, Laurence. The Iroquois & the New Deal. 1981. 20.00x (ISBN 0-8156-2247-3). Syracuse U Pr.

Heckewelder, John. History, Manners, & Customs of the Indian Nations Who Once Inhabited Pennsylvania & the Neighboring States. LC 75-146398. (First American Frontier Ser). (Illus.). 1971. Repr. of 1819 ed. 19.00 (ISBN 0-405-02853-9). Arno.

--History, Manners, & Customs of the Indian Nations Who Once Inhabited Pennsylvania & the Neighboring States. LC 75-146398. (First American Frontier Ser). (Illus.). 1971. Repr. of 1819 ed. 19.00 (ISBN 0-405-02853-9). Arno.

--Narrative of the Mission of the United Brethren Among the Delaware & Mohegan Indians. LC 79-146399. (First American Frontier Ser). 1971. Repr. of 1820 ed. 21.00 (ISBN 0-405-02852-0). Arno.

Hendren, S. R. Government & Religion of the Virginia Indians. 1973. Repr. of 1895 ed. pap. 7.00 (ISBN 0-384-22290-0). Johnson Repr.

Hendren, Samuel R. Government & Religion of the Virginia Indians. LC 78-63845. (Johns Hopkins University. Studies in the Social Sciences. Thirteenth Ser. 1895: 11-12). Repr. of 1895 ed. 11.50 (ISBN 0-404-61102-8). AMS Pr.

Horr, David A., ed. Indians of Ohio, Indiana, Illinois, Southern Michigan & Southern Wisconsin: Findings of Fact & Opinion, 3 vols. (North Central & Northeastern Indians - American Indian Ethnohistory Ser.). 1974. Set. lib. bdg. 99.00 (ISBN 0-8240-0807-3); lib. bdg. 42.00 ea. Garland Pub.

--Piankashaw & Kaskaskia Indians. Incl. An Anthropological Report on the Piankashaw Indians. Libby, Dorothy; Report on the Piankashaw & Kaskaskia & the Treaty of Greene Ville. Stout, David B. (American Indian Ethnohistory Ser: North Central & Northeastern Indians). (Illus.). lib. bdg. 42.00 (ISBN 0-8240-0760-3). Garland Pub.

Howard, James H. Shawnee: The Ceremonialism of a Native American Tribe & Its Cultural Background. LC 80-23752. (Illus.). xvi, 454p. 1981. 26.95x (ISBN 0-8214-0417-2); pap. 14.95 (ISBN 0-8214-0614-0). Ohio U Pr.

Howard, Milo B., Jr. & Rea, Robert R., eds. Memoire Justificatif of the Chevalier Montault De Monberaut: Indian Diplomacy in British West Florida, 1763-1765. LC 64-24955. (Southern Historical Ser: Vol. 3). 1965. 12.95x (ISBN 0-8173-5208-2). U of Ala Pr.

Hubbard, W. History of the Indian Wars in New England, 2 Vols. in 1. 1865. 30.00 (ISBN 0-527-43000-5). Kraus Repr.

Hudson, Charles M., ed. Four Centuries of Southern Indians. LC 73-85028. 183p. 1975. 9.00x (ISBN 0-8203-0332-1). U of Ga Pr.

Indian Territory. Constitution of the State of Sequoyah, 3 vols. in 1. Bd. with A Memorial to the Congress of the United States on Behalf of the State of Sequoyah; Proposed State of Sequoyah. LC 74-15118. Repr. of 1906 ed. 18.00 (ISBN 0-404-11978-6). AMS Pr.

Indians of Ohio & Indiana Prior to 1795, 2 vols. Incl. The Greenville Treaty, Seventeen Ninety-Five. Tanner, Helen H; Ethnohistory of Indian Use & Occupancy in Ohio & Indiana Prior to 1795. Wheeler-Voegelin, Erminie. (American Indian Ethnohistory Ser: North Central & Northeastern Indians). (Illus.). Set. lib. bdg. 76.00 (ISBN 0-8240-0798-0); lib. bdg. 42.00 ea. Garland Pub.

Iroquois Indians, Vol. 2. Incl. Historical Report on the Niagara River to 1759. Kent, Donald H; Findings of Fact, & Opinion. Indian Claims Commission. (American Indian Ethnohistory Ser: North Central & Northeastern Indians). (Illus.). lib. bdg. 42.00 (ISBN 0-8240-0769-7). Garland Pub.

Jackson, Halliday. Civilization of the Indian Natives. 1830. 25.00 (ISBN 0-403-00383-0). Scholarly.

Janzen, Donald E. The Naomikong Site & the Dimensions of Laurel in the Lake Superior Region. (Anthropological Papers: No. 36). (Illus.). 1968. pap. 3.00x (ISBN 0-932206-34-4). U Mich Mus Anthro.

Johansen, Bruce E. The Forgotten Founders: Benjamin Franklin, the Iroquois & the Rationale for American Revolution. 200p. 1981. 10.95 (ISBN 0-87645-111-3). Gambit.

Johnson, F. Roy. The Algonquians, the Indians of That Part of the New World First Visited by the English, Vol. 2: History-Traditions. (Illus.). 240p. 1972. 8.50 (ISBN 0-930230-01-9). Johnson NC.

--The Algonquians, the Indians of the Part of the New World First Visited by the English, Vol. 1: Pre-History & Culture. (Illus.). 112p. 1972. 6.50 (ISBN 0-930230-00-0). Johnson NC.

--Tuscaroras, Vol. 1: Mythology, Medicine & Culture. (Illus.). 1968. 6.50 (ISBN 0-930230-28-0). Johnson NC.

--Tuscaroras, Vol. 2: History, Tradition & Cultural Modificatications. (Illus.). 1968. 8.50 (ISBN 0-930230-29-9). Johnson NC.

Johnson, F. Roy, ed. Stories of the Old Cherokees: A Collection. (Illus.). 112p. (gr. 4-8). 1975. 4.95 (ISBN 0-930230-23-X). Johnson NC.

Johnson, Frederick, ed. Man in Northeastern North America. LC 76-43756. (Papers of the Robert S. Peabody Foundation for Archaeology: Vol. 3). Repr. of 1946 ed. 42.50 (ISBN 0-404-15597-9). AMS Pr.

Johnston, Charles M. Valley of the Six Nations: A Collection of Documents on the Indian Lands of the Grand River. LC 65-1239. (Illus.). 1965. 17.50 (ISBN 0-8020-1339-2). U of Toronto Pr.

Jones, Charles C., Jr. Antiquities of the Southern Indians, Particularly of the Georgia Tribes. LC 70-187389. (Illus.). 548p. 1972. Repr. of 1873 ed. 21.00 (ISBN 0-87152-084-2). Reprint.

Jones, David. Journal of Two Visits Made to Some Nations of Indians on the West Side of the River Ohio in the Years 1772 & 1773 by the Rev. David Jones, Minister of Gospel at Freehold, New Jersey. LC 77-146405. (First American Frontier Ser). 1971. Repr. of 1774 ed. 9.00 (ISBN 0-405-02864-4). Arno.

Kellet, Alexander. A Pocket of Prose & Verse. Washburn, Wilcomb E., ed. LC 75-7031. (Narratives of North American Indian Captivities: Vol. 11). 1975. lib. bdg. 44.00 (ISBN 0-8240-1635-1). Garland Pub.

Kent, Donald H. Iroquois Indians, Vol. 1: History of Pennsylvania Purchases from the Indians. (American Indian Ethnohistory Ser: North Central & Northeastern Indians). (Illus.). lib. bdg. 42.00 (ISBN 0-8240-0768-9). Garland Pub.

Ketchum, William. Authentic & Comprehensive History of Buffalo, 2 Vols. 1864-65. Set. 35.00 (ISBN 0-403-00372-5). Scholarly.

Kilpatrick, Jack F. & Kilpatrick, Anna G. The Shadow of Sequoyah: Social Documents of the Cherokees, 1862-1964. LC 65-24205. (Vol. 81). 1965. 7.95 (ISBN 0-8061-0677-8); pap. 3.50 (ISBN 0-8061-1274-3). U of Okla Pr.

Kilpatrick, Jack F. & Kilpatrick, Anna G., eds. New Echota Letters: Contributions of Samuel A. Worcester to the Cherokee Phoenix. LC 68-55078. 1968. 7.95 (ISBN 0-87074-086-5). SMU Press.

Kim, Choong S. An Asian Anthropologist in the South: Field Experiences with Blacks, Indians, & Whites. LC 76-49448. 1977. 10.00x (ISBN 0-87049-201-2). U of Tenn Pr.

Kline, M., et al. The Oneida & Stockbridge Tribes: An Analysis of the Awareness of the Continental Congress & the U. S. Government of Relations & Treaties with New York State. Ross, Norman A., ed. (Library of American Indian Affairs). 1976. lib. bdg. 50.00x (ISBN 0-8287-1157-7). Clearwater Pub.

Larrabee, Edward M. Recurrent Themes & Sequences in North American Indian-European Culture Contact. LC 76-24257. (Transactions Ser.: Vol. 66, Pt. 7). (Illus.). 1976. pap. 6.00 (ISBN 0-87169-667-3). Am Philos.

Laws of the Chickasaw Nation, I. T. Relating to Intermarried & Adopted Citizens & Rights of Freedom. LC 75-3679. (Constitutions & Laws of the American Indian Tribes Ser. 2: Vol. 12). 1975. Repr. of 1896 ed. 11.00 (ISBN 0-8420-1845-X). Scholarly Res Inc.

Laws of the Choctaw Nation: Passed at the Regular Session of the General Council Convened at Tushka Humma, October 27th, 1889 & Adjourned November 15, 1889. LC 75-3687. (Constitutions & Laws of the American Indian Tribes Ser. 2: Vol. 20). 1975. Repr. of 1890 ed. 12.00 (ISBN 0-8420-1878-6). Scholarly Res Inc.

Laws of the Choctaw Nation, Passed at the Regular Session of the General Council Convened at Tushka Humma, Oct. 6, 1890, Adjourned Nov. 14, 1890. Bd. with Laws of the Choctaw Nation Made & Enacted by the General Council from 1886-1890; Laws of the Choctaw Nation Passed at the Special Session of the General Council Convened at Tushka Humma, April 6, 1891 & Adjourned April 11, 1891. LC 75-3688. (Constitutions & Laws of the American Indian Tribes Ser. 2: Vol. 21). 1975. Repr. of 1891 ed. 16.00 (ISBN 0-8420-1879-4). Scholarly Res Inc.

Laws of the Choctaw Nation Passed at the Regular Session of the General Council Convened at Tushka Humma, October 1892 & Adjourned November 4, 1892. Bd. with Laws of the Choctaw Nation Passed at the Regular Session of the General Council Convened at Tushka Humma, October 2, 1893 & Adjourned October 27, 1893; The Special Sessions Convened in February 1892 (for 1893) & Convened in June 1893. LC 75-3689. (Constitutions & Laws of the American Indian Tribes Ser. 2: Vol. 22). 1975. Repr. of 1893 ed. 12.00 (ISBN 0-8420-1880-8). Scholarly Res Inc.

Lawson, John. New Voyage to Carolina. Lefler, Hugh T., ed. 1967. 14.95 (ISBN 0-8078-1042-8); limited ed. 25.00 (ISBN 0-8078-1041-X). U of NC Pr.

Leger, Sr. Mary C. The Catholic Indian Missions in Maine (1611-1820) LC 73-3563. (Catholic University of America. Studies in American Church History: No. 8). Repr. of 1929 ed. 19.45 (ISBN 0-404-57758-X). AMS Pr.

Levin, Beatrice. Indian Myths from the Southeast. (Indian Culture Ser.). (gr. 4-12). 1974. 1.95 (ISBN 0-89992-071-3). MT Coun Indian.

Lewis, Thomas M. & Lewis, Madeline K. Eva: An Archaic Site. LC 61-18403. (Illus.). 1961. pap. 7.50x (ISBN 0-87049-035-4). U of Tenn Pr.

Littlefield, Daniel F., Jr. Africans & Seminoles: From Removal to Emancipation. LC 77-86. (Contributions in Afro-American & African Studies: No. 32). 1977. lib. bdg. 19.95x (ISBN 0-8371-9529-2, LAS/). Greenwood.

Loskiel, George H. History of the Mission of the United Brethren Among the Indians in North America, 3 pts in one vol. Latrobe, Christian I., tr. 1794. 25.00 (ISBN 0-403-00358-X). Scholarly.

Lumpkin, Wilson. Removal of the Cherokee Indians from Georgia. LC 79-90182. (Mass Violence in America Ser). Repr. of 1907 ed. 29.00 (ISBN 0-405-01325-6). Arno.

Lydekker, John W. Faithful Mohawks. LC 68-18362. (Empire State Historical Publications Ser: No. 50). (Illus.). 1968. Repr. of 1938 ed. 8.50 (ISBN 0-87198-050-9). Friedman.

Lyons, Grant. The Creek Indians. LC 77-29255. (Illus.). 96p. (gr. 4 up). 1978. PLB 7.29 (ISBN 0-671-32895-6). Messner.

McCary, Ben C. Indians in Seventhteenth Century Virginia. 93p. 1980. pap. 1.95x (ISBN 0-8139-0142-1). U Pr of Va.

M'Clung, John A. Sketches of Western Adventure. LC 76-90184. (Mass Violence in America Ser). Repr. of 1832 ed. 13.00 (ISBN 0-405-01326-4). Arno.

McDowell, William L., Jr., ed. Documents Relating to Indian Affairs, May 21, 1750-August 7, 1754. LC 70-627805. (Colonial Records of South Carolina Ser.: No. 2). 1958. 27.50x (ISBN 0-87249-911-1). U of SC Pr.

McDowell, Willian L., Jr., ed. Journals of the Commissioners of the Indian Trade, September 20, 1710 - August 29, 1718. LC 56-59120. (Colonial Records of South Carolina Ser.: No. 3). 1955. 27.50x (ISBN 0-87249-910-3). U of SC Pr.

McGinty, Garnie W. Valuation Report on Royce Area 202 in Arkansas & Louisiana. (Library of American Indian Affairs). 140p. 1974. lib. bdg. 46.00 (ISBN 0-8287-1289-1). Clearwater Pub.

McKee, Jesse O. & Schlenker, Jon A. The Choctaws: Cultural Evolution of a Native American Tribe. LC 79-17034. 1980. 17.50x (ISBN 0-87805-107-4). U Pr of Miss.

Mackenzie, Alexander. Voyages from Montreal Through the Continent of North America to the Frozen & Pacific Oceans in 1789 & 1793, with an Account of the Rise & State of the Fur Trade, 2 vols. LC 72-2721. (American Explorers Ser.). Repr. of 1922 ed. 47.50 (ISBN 0-404-54912-8). AMS Pr.

McReynolds, Edwin C. Seminoles. (Civilization of the American Indian Ser.: No. 47). (Illus.). 1957. pap. 8.95 (ISBN 0-8061-1255-7). U of Okla Pr.

Mathews, Zena P. The Relation of Seneca False Face Masks to Seneca & Ontario Archeology. LC 77-94707. (Outstanding Dissertations in the Fine Arts Ser.). 1978. lib. bdg. 36.00x (ISBN 0-8240-3239-X). Garland Pub.

Maurault, Joseph P. Histoire Des Abenakis Depuis 1605 Jusqu'a Nos Jours. (Canadiana Avant 1867: No. 17). 1970. 60.00x (ISBN 90-2796-342-8). Mouton.

Milling, Chapman J. Red Carolinians. LC 39-545. 1969. 14.95 (ISBN 0-87249-180-3). U of SC Pr.

Mithun, Marianne & Woodbury, Hanni, eds. Northern Iroquoian Texts. LC 80-11887. (International Journal of American Linguistics-Native American Texts Ser.: Monograph No. 4). 168p. (Orig.). 1980. pap. 13.25 (ISBN 0-226-36716-9, Pub. by U of Chicago Pr). Univ Microfilms.

Mooney, James. Historical Sketch of the Cherokee. LC 75-20706. (Native American Library Ser). 272p. 1975. text ed. 12.50x (ISBN 0-202-01136-4); pap. text ed. 4.95x (ISBN 0-202-01137-2). Beresford Bk Serv.

--Myths of the Cherokee. LC 16-5534. (Landmarks in Anthropology Ser). Repr. of 1900 ed. 31.00 (ISBN 0-384-39920-7). Johnson Repr.

--Myths of the Cherokee. LC 70-108513. (American Indian History Sers). 1970. Repr. of 1900 ed. 59.00 (ISBN 0-403-00221-4). Scholarly.

--The Siouan Tribes of the East. LC 2-14653. 1971. Repr. of 1895 ed. 8.00 (ISBN 0-384-39935-5). Johnson Repr.

Morgan, David P. The Mohawk That Refused to Abdicate. LC 75-12003. 1975. 25.00 (ISBN 0-89024-031-0). Kalmbach.

Morgan, L. H. League of the Iroquois. (Illus.). 11.50 (ISBN 0-8446-2612-0). Peter Smith.

Morgan, Lewis H. League of the Ho-De-No-Sau-Nee or Iroquois, 2 Vols. new ed. Lloyd, Henry M., ed. & annotations by. (Illus.). 1966. Repr. of 1904 ed. Set. 49.50 (ISBN 0-8337-2465-7). B Franklin.

--League of the Iroquois. (Illus.). 477p. 1972. pap. 4.95 (ISBN 0-8065-0293-2). Citadel Pr.

Morton, Thomas. New English Canaan or New Canaan. Containing an Abstract of New England. LC 76-25966. (English Experience Ser.: No. 140). 192p. 1969. Repr. of 1637 ed. 28.00 (ISBN 90-221-0140-1). Walter J Johnson.

Neill, Wilfred T. & Allen, E. Ross. Florida's Seminole Indians. rev. ed. LC 65-3660. (Illus.). pap. 2.95 (ISBN 0-8200-1018-9). Great Outdoors.

Nelson, Mary C. Robert Bennett. LC 75-43539. (Story of an American Indian Ser.). (Illus.). (gr. 5 up). 1976. PLB 6.95 (ISBN 0-87518-108-2). Dillon.

Newman, Walter S. & Salwen, Bert S., eds. Amerinds & Their Paleoenviornments in Northeastern North America, Vol. 288. 1977. 35.00 (ISBN 0-89072-034-7). NY Acad Sci.

Noon, John A. Law & Government of the Grand River Iroquois. 1949. pap. 15.50 (ISBN 0-384-41875-9). Johnson Repr.

Olsen, Evelyn G. Indian Blood. (Illus.). 1967. 10.00 (ISBN 0-87012-047-6). McClain.

Parker, Arthur C. Parker on the Iroquois. Fenton, William N., ed. Bd. with The Code of Handsome Lake, the Seneca Prophet. 119p; The Consitution of the Five Nations. 148p; Iroquois Uses of Maize & Other Food Plants. 158p. LC 68-31036. (Illus.). 1968. 14.95x (ISBN 0-8156-2124-8). Syracuse U Pr.

--Seneca Myths & Folk Tales. LC 76-43803. (Buffalo Historical Society. Publication: Vol. 27). Repr. of 1923 ed. 35.00 (ISBN 0-404-15659-2). AMS Pr.

Peithman, Irvin M. Unconquered Seminole Indians. LC 57-20953. (Illus., Orig.). 1956. pap. 2.95 (ISBN 0-8200-1017-0). Great Outdoors.

Peithmann, Irvin M. Indians of Southern Illinois. (Illus.). 172p. 1964. photocopy ed. spiral 11.75 (ISBN 0-398-01469-8). C C Thomas.

Penhallow, S. History of the Wars of New England with the Eastern Indians. 1859. 12.00 (ISBN 0-527-70500-4). Kraus Repr.

Perdue, Theda. Slavery & the Evolution of Cherokee Society, 1540-1866. LC 78-16284. 1979. 12.50x (ISBN 0-87049-259-4). U of Tenn Pr.

Pollard, Garland. The Pamunkey Indians of Virginia. Repr. of 1894 ed. 25.00 (ISBN 0-403-03678-X). Scholarly.

Pope, John. Tour Through the Southern & Western Territories of the United States of North America, the Spanish Dominions on the River Mississippi & the Floridas, the Countries of the Creek Nations, & Many Uninhabited Parts. LC 70-146411. (First American Frontier Ser). 1971. Repr. of 1792 ed. 9.00 (ISBN 0-405-02875-X). Arno.

Porter, Frank W. Indians in Maryland & Delaware: A Critical Bibliography. LC 79-2460. (Newberry Library Center for the History of the American Indian Bibliographical Ser.). 128p. 1979. pap. 4.95x (ISBN 0-253-30954-9). Ind U Pr.

Pratt, Peter P. Archaeology of the Oneida Iroquois, Vol. 1. 1976. 11.50 (ISBN 0-686-30586-8). Pierce Coll.

Pratt, Theodore. The Seminole. 1980. Repr. of 1954 ed. write for info. (ISBN 0-8200-1030-8). Great Outdoors.

Prince, John D. Passamaquoddy Texts. LC 73-3545. (American Ethnological Society. Publications: No. 10). Repr. of 1921 ed. 16.00 (ISBN 0-404-58160-9). AMS Pr.

Ramabhushanam, Gay. Ethnohistorical Report on Indian Use & Occupation from 1661 to 1797 of Ohio. 55p. 1974. lib. bdg. 25.50 (ISBN 0-8287-1032-5). Clearwater Pub.

Reid, John P. A Better Kind of Hatchet: Law, Trade, Diplomacy in the Cherokee Nation. LC 75-15544. 262p. 1975. 17.75x (ISBN 0-271-01197-1). Pa St U Pr.

Riecken, F. F. Sac & Fox Lands in Royce Area 262 in Iowa: Soils & Related Physical Features, 1856-1874. (Library of American Indian Affairs). 262p. 1974. lib. bdg. 75.00 (ISBN 0-8287-1219-0). Clearwater Pub.

Royce, Charles. The Cherokee Nation of Indians. Viola, Herman J., ed. LC 75-20708. (Native American Library Ser.). 288p. 1975. text ed. 12.50x (ISBN 0-202-01138-0); pap. 4.95x (ISBN 0-202-01139-9). Beresford Bk Serv.

Ruttenber, Edward M. History of the Indian Tribes of Hudson's River. (Illus.). 1872. 29.00 (ISBN 0-403-00303-2). Scholarly.

Schell, Rolfe F. One Thousand Years on Mound Key. rev. ed. LC 68-24198. (Illus.). 1968. 3.95 (ISBN 0-87208-001-3); pap. 1.50 (ISBN 0-87208-000-5). Island Pr.

Schoolcraft, Henry R. Notes on the Iroquois. LC 74-9006. Repr. of 1847 ed. 31.00 (ISBN 0-404-11898-4). AMS Pr.

--Notes on the Iroquois: Or, Contributions to the Statistics, Aboriginal History, Antiquities & General Ethnology of Western New York. LC 2-18176. 1975. Repr. of 1846 ed. 20.00 (ISBN 0-527-03226-3). Kraus Repr.

Simmons, William S. Cautantowwit's House: An Indian Burial Ground on the Island of Conanicut in Narragansett Bay. LC 77-111456. (Illus.). 198p. 1970. text ed. 12.00x (ISBN 0-87057-122-2, Pub. by Brown U Pr). U Pr of New Eng.

Sipe, C. Hale. Indian Chiefs of Pennsylvania: Or, a Story of the Part Played by the American Indian in the History of Pennsylvania, Based Primarily on the Pennsylvania Archives & Colonial Records, & Built Around the Outstanding Chiefs. LC 73-150263. 1971. Repr. of 1927 ed. 28.00 (ISBN 0-405-02905-5). Arno.

--Indian Wars of Pennsylvania: An Account of the Indian Events, in Pennsylvania, of the French & Indian War, Pontiac's War, Lord Dunmore's War, the Revolutionary War & the Indian Uprising from 1789 to 1795. LC 77-150264. (Illus.). 1971. Repr. of 1929 ed. 45.00 (ISBN 0-405-02904-7). Arno.

Skinner, Alanson B. The Indians of Manhattan Island & Vicinity. LC 76-43824. (AMNH. Guide Leaflet Ser.: No. 41). Repr. of 1915 ed. 21.00 (ISBN 0-404-15685-1). AMS Pr.

--Mascoutens of Prairie Potawatomi Indians. Repr. of 1924 ed. lib. bdg. 15.00x (ISBN 0-8371-4631-3, SKMA). Greenwood.

--Notes on Iroquois Archaeology. LC 76-43827. (MAI. Indian Notes & Monographs, Miscellaneous: No. 18). 1977. Repr. of 1921 ed. 26.00 (ISBN 0-404-15679-7). AMS Pr.

--Notes on the Eastern Cree & Northern Salteaux. LC 76-43828. (AMNH. Anthropological Papers: Vol. 9, Pt. 1). Repr. of 1911 ed. 15.50 (ISBN 0-404-15682-7). AMS Pr.

Smith, Defost. Martyrs of the Oblong & Little Nine. 1948. 6.00 (ISBN 0-910294-11-9). Brown Bk.

Smith, Huron H. Ethnobotany of the Forest Potawatomi Indians. LC 76-43835. (Bulletin of the Public Museum of the City of Milwaukee: Vol. 7, No. 1). Repr. of 1933 ed. 29.00 (ISBN 0-404-15689-4). AMS Pr.

Smith, James F. Cherokee Land Lottery of Georgia, 1832. LC 67-28624. (Illus.). 1969. Repr. of 1838 ed. 20.00 (ISBN 0-8063-0318-2). Genealog Pub.

Smith, John. A Map of Virginia: The Proceedings of the English Colonie in Virginia. LC 72-6031. (English Experience Ser.: No. 557). 164p. 1973. Repr. of 1612 ed. 18.50 (ISBN 90-221-0557-1). Walter J Johnson.

Snyderman, George S. Behind the Tree of Peace: A Sociological Analysis of Iroquois Warfare. LC 76-43838. Repr. of 1948 ed. 17.00 (ISBN 0-404-15692-4). AMS Pr.

Speck, F. G. Ethnology of the Yuchi Indians. (Illus.). 1979. Repr. of 1909 ed. text ed. 18.75x (ISBN 0-391-00956-7). Humanities.

Speck, Frank G. Chapters on the Ethnology of the Powhatan Tribes of Virginia. LC 76-43839. (MAI. Indian Notes & Monographs: Vol. 1, No. 5). Repr. of 1928 ed. 27.50 (ISBN 0-404-15694-0). AMS Pr.

--Creek Indians of Taskigi Town. LC 8-10851. (AAA Memoirs Ser.: No. 8). 1907. pap. 5.00 (ISBN 0-527-00507-X). Kraus Repr.

--Ethnology of the Yuchi Indians. LC 76-43842. (Univ. of Pennsylvania. Anthropological Publications of the Museum: Vol. 1, No. 1). Repr. of 1909 ed. 28.00 (ISBN 0-404-15704-1). AMS Pr.

--Functions of Wampum Among the Eastern Algonkian. LC 19-12781. (AAA Memoirs Ser.: No. 25). 1919. pap. 7.00 (ISBN 0-527-00524-X). Kraus Repr.

--Iroquois. 2nd ed. LC 46-2147. (Bulletin Ser.: No. 23). (Illus.). 95p. (Orig.). 1955. pap. 3.50x (ISBN 0-87737-007-9). Cranbrook.

--The Nanticoke & Conoy Indians. LC 76-43843. (Papers of the Historical Society of Delaware. New Ser.: I). Repr. of 1927 ed. 10.00 (ISBN 0-404-15703-3). AMS Pr.

--The Nanticoke Community of Delaware. LC 76-43844. (Museum of the American Indian, Heye Foundation: Vol. 2, No. 4). (Illus.). 88p. 1981. Repr. of 1915 ed. 18.00 (ISBN 0-404-15695-9). AMS Pr.

--Oklahoma Delaware Ceremonies, Feasts & Dances. LC 76-43845. (Memoirs of the American Philosophical Sociey: Vol. 7). Repr. of 1937 ed. 21.50 (ISBN 0-404-15696-7). AMS Pr.

--Penobscot Man: The Life History of a Forest Tribe in Maine. LC 72-120669. 1970. Repr. lib. bdg. 17.50x (ISBN 0-374-97533-7). Octagon.

--Penobscot Shamanism. LC 20-13167. (AAA Memoirs Ser.: No. 25). 1919. pap. 5.00 (ISBN 0-527-00527-4). Kraus Repr.

--A Study of the Delaware Indian Big House Ceremony: In Native Text Dictated by Witapanoxwe. LC 76-43846. (Publications of the Pennsylvania Historical Commission: Vol. 2). Repr. of 1931 ed. 24.00 (ISBN 0-404-15698-3). AMS Pr.

--Territorial Subdivisions & Boundaries of the Wampanoag, Massachusett, & Nauset Indians. LC 76-43847. (MAI. Indian Notes & Monographs. Miscellaneous: No. 44). Repr. of 1928 ed. 15.00 (ISBN 0-404-15701-7). AMS Pr.

Spoehr, Alexander. Camp, Clan, & Kin, Among the Cow Creek Seminole of Florida. (Illus.). 1941-1947. pap. 12.00 (ISBN 0-527-01893-7). Kraus Repr.

Starkey, Marion L. Cherokee Nation. LC 71-180620. (Illus.). 1972. Repr. of 1946 ed. 22.00 (ISBN 0-8462-1637-X). Russell.

Starr, E. History of the Cherokee Indians & Their Legends & Folklore. 1921. 30.00 (ISBN 0-527-85700-9). Kraus Repr.

Steele, William O. The Cherokee Crown of Tannassy. LC 77-19997. (YA) 1977. 7.95 (ISBN 0-910244-99-5). Blair.

Stites, Sara H. Economics of the Iroquois. LC 76-43861. Repr. of 1905 ed. 18.00 (ISBN 0-404-15715-7). AMS Pr.

The Story of Captain Jasper Parrish, Captive, Interpreter & United States Sub-Agent to the Six Nations Indians, Repr. Of 1903 Ed. Bd. with The Story of My Capture & Escape During the Minnesota Indian Massacre of 1862. with Historical Notes, Description of Pioneer Life, & Sketches & Incidents of the Great Outbreak of the Sioux or Dakota Indians As I Saw Them. Tarble, Helen M. Repr. of 1904 ed; The Story of the Rice Boys, Captured by the Indians. Parkman, Ebenezer. Repr. of 1906 ed. LC 75-7133. (Indian Captivities Ser.: Vol. 105). 1976. lib. bdg. 44.00 (ISBN 0-8240-1729-3). Garland Pub.

Suphan, Robert J. Tillamook Band: Ethnographic Report on the Identity & Localization. (Library of American Indian Affairs). 86p. 1974. lib. bdg. 27.00 (ISBN 0-8287-1274-3). Clearwater Pub.

Swanton, John R. Early Account of the Choctaw Indians. LC 67-52261. 1918. pap. 5.00 (ISBN 0-527-00521-5). Kraus Repr.

--Early History of the Creek Indians & Their Neighbors. LC 73-139862. Repr. of 1922 ed. 38.50 (ISBN 0-384-59000-4). Johnson Repr.

--Early History of the Creek Indians & Their Neighbors. Repr. of 1922 ed. 33.00 (ISBN 0-403-03582-1). Scholarly.

--Indian Tribes of the Lower Mississippi Valley & Adjacent Coast of the Gulf of Mexico. LC 11-35489. (U. S. Bureau of American Ethnology Ser: Bulletin 43). Repr. of 1911 ed. 27.00 (ISBN 0-384-59010-1). Johnson Repr.

--Indians of the Southeastern United States. Repr. of 1946 ed. lib. bdg. 53.25x (ISBN 0-8371-0978-7, SWIS). Greenwood.

--Social Organization & Social Usages of the Indians of the Creek Confederacy. LC 28-30084. (U. S. Bureau of American Ethnology. Forty Second Annual Report, 1924-25). Repr. of 1928 ed. 31.00 (ISBN 0-384-59040-3). Johnson Repr.

Sylvester, Herbert M. Indian Wars of New England, 3 vols. Kohn, Richard H., ed. LC 78-22399. (American Military Experience Ser.). 1979. Repr. of 1910 ed. Set. lib. bdg. 106.00x (ISBN 0-405-11875-9). Arno.

Tantaquidgeon, Gladys. A Study of Delaware Indian Medicine Practice & Folk Beliefs. LC 76-43864. (Pennsylvania Historical Commission). Repr. of 1942 ed. 18.00 (ISBN 0-404-15724-6). AMS Pr.

Tarbox, Increase N., ed. Sir Walter Raleigh & His Colony in America. 1966. 24.00 (ISBN 0-8337-3470-9). B Franklin.

Taylor, Lyda A. Plants Used As Curatives by Certain Southeastern Tribes. LC 76-43866. (Botanical Museum of Harvard Univ.). Repr. of 1940 ed. 14.50 (ISBN 0-404-15725-4). AMS Pr.

Thomas, Cyrus. The Cherokees in Pre-Columbian Times. LC 76-43868. Repr. of 1890 ed. 16.50 (ISBN 0-404-15727-0). AMS Pr.

Thomson, Charles. Enquiry into the Causes of the Alienation of the Delaware & Shawanees Indians from British Interests. LC 73-108549. 1970. Repr. of 1759 ed. 15.50 (ISBN 0-403-00271-0). Scholarly.

Timberlake, Henry. Memoirs of Lieut. Henry Timberlake. LC 74-146423. (First American Frontier Ser). 1971. Repr. of 1927 ed. 13.00 (ISBN 0-405-02903-9). Arno.

Todd, Helen. Tomochichi: Indian Friend of the Georgia Colony. LC 77-75268. (Illus.). 1977. 7.95 (ISBN 0-87797-040-8). Cherokee.

Tooker, Elisabeth. Iroquois Ceremonial of Midwinter. LC 70-119873. (New York State Studies). (Illus.). 1970. 11.95x (ISBN 0-8156-2149-3). Syracuse U Pr.

Trent, William. Journal of Captain William Trent from Logstown to Pickawillany, A.D. 1752. LC 79-106114. (First American Frontier Ser). 1971. Repr. of 1871 ed. 9.00 (ISBN 0-405-02894-6). Arno.

Trigger, B. G. Huron: Farmers of the North. LC 77-92315. (Case Studies in Cultural Anthropology). 1969. pap. text ed. 5.95 (ISBN 0-03-079550-8, HoltC). HR&W.

Trigger, Bruce G. The Children of Aataentsic: A History of the Huron People to 1660, 2 vols. (Illus.). 1976. lib. bdg. 45.00x set (ISBN 0-7735-0239-4). McGill-Queens U Pr.

Trigger, Bruce G., ed. Northeast. LC 77-17162. (Handbook of North American Indians Ser.: Vol. 15). (Illus.). 924p. 1979. text ed. 14.50 (ISBN 0-87474-195-5). Smithsonian.

Trowbridge, Charles C. Shawnese Traditions. Kinietz, Vernon & Voegelin, Erminie W., eds. LC 76-43871. (Michigan Univ. Museum of Anthropology. Occasional Contributions: No. 9). Repr. of 1939 ed. 17.00 (ISBN 0-404-15729-7). AMS Pr.

Trygg, William. Valuation Reports on Lands in Michigan & Indiana, Ceded by Treaty of August 29, 1921. (Library of American Indian Affairs). 88p. 1974. lib. bdg. 33.00 (ISBN 0-8287-1290-5). Clearwater Pub.

Uhler, Sherman P. Pennsylvania's Indian Relations to 1754. LC 76-43872. Repr. of 1951 ed. 13.00 (ISBN 0-404-15731-9). AMS Pr.

U. S. Department Of State. Register of the Department of State. Repr. of 1874 ed. 10.00 (ISBN 0-384-62952-0). Johnson Repr.

Van Der Donck, Adriaen. Description of the New Netherlands. O'Donnell, Thomas F., ed. LC 68-29420. (New York State Studies). 1968. 10.00x (ISBN 0-8156-2127-2). Syracuse U Pr.

Voegelin, Byron D. South Florida's Vanished People: Travels in the Homeland of Ancient Calusa. LC 72-94649. 1977. 5.95 (ISBN 0-87208-038-2); pap. 2.95 (ISBN 0-87208-106-0). Island Pr.

Voegelin, Erminie W. Mortuary Customs of the Shawnee & Other Eastern Tribes. LC 76-43885. (Indiana Historical Society Prehistory Research Ser.: Vol. 2, No. 4). Repr. of 1944 ed. 26.00 (ISBN 0-404-15742-4). AMS Pr.

Vogel, John. Indians of Ohio & Wyandot Country. 4.95 (ISBN 0-533-01630-4). Vantage.

Wagner, Gunter. Yuchi Tales. LC 73-3549. (American Ethnological Society. Publications: No. 13). Repr. of 1931 ed. 27.00 (ISBN 0-404-58163-3). AMS Pr.

Wallace, Anthony F. King of the Delawares: Teedyuscung, 1700-1763. facs. ed. LC 73-137387. (Select Bibliographies Reprint Ser). 1949. 19.00 (ISBN 0-8369-5588-9). Arno.

--The Modal Personality Structure of the Tuscarora Indians. Repr. of 1952 ed. 19.00 (ISBN 0-403-03649-6). Scholarly.

Wallace, Paul A. Indians in Pennsylvania. LC 61-63955. (Illus., Orig.). 1981. 7.00 (ISBN 0-89271-018-7); pap. 4.00 (ISBN 0-89271-017-9). Pa Hist & Mus.

Ward, Edward. A Trip to New England: With a Character of the Country & People. LC 68-57126. (Research & Source Works Ser.: No. 312). Orig. Title: Club for Colonial Reprints, Vol. (2). 1969. Repr. of 1905 ed. 19.00 (ISBN 0-8337-3686-8). B Franklin.

Wardell, Morris L. A Political History of the Cherokee Nation, Eighteen Thirty-Eight to Nineteen Hundred Seven. (Civilization of the American Indian Ser.: Vol. 17). (Illus.). 383p. 1980. pap. 9.95 (ISBN 0-8061-1641-2). U of Okla Pr.

--A Political History of the Cherokee Nation, 1838-1907. (Civilization of the American Indian Ser.: Vol. 17). (Illus.). 1938. 16.95 (ISBN 0-8061-1411-8). U of Okla Pr.

Weeden, William B. Indian Money As a Factor in New England Civilization. LC 78-63747. (Johns Hopkins University. Studies in the Social Sciences. Second Ser. 1884: 8-9). Repr. of 1884 ed. 11.50 (ISBN 0-404-61017-X). AMS Pr.

Welch, Andrew. A Narrative of the Early Days & Remembrances of Oceola Nikkanochee, Prince of Econchatti. LC 76-54519. (Bicentennial Floridiana Facsimile Ser.). 1977. Repr. of 1841 ed. 12.00 (ISBN 0-8130-0411-X). U Presses Fla.

Weslager, C. A. The Delaware Indian Westward Migration. LC 77-99286. (Illus.). 1978. 16.00 (ISBN 0-912608-06-4). Mid Atlantic.

--The Delaware Indians: A History. (Illus.). 576p. 1972. 35.00 (ISBN 0-8135-0702-2). Rutgers U Pr.

--Delaware's Buried Past: A Story of Archaeological Adventure. (Illus.). 1968. pap. 2.95 (ISBN 0-8135-0589-5). Rutgers U Pr.

Weslager, Clinton A. The Nanticoke Indians. LC 76-43888. (Pennsylvania Historical & Museum Commission). 1977. Repr. of 1948 ed. 15.00 (ISBN 0-404-15747-5). AMS Pr.

Wetmore, Ruth Y. First on the Land: The North Carolina Indians. LC 74-84151. (Illus.). 1977. 8.95 (ISBN 0-910244-80-4). Blair.

Wheeler-Voegelin, Erminie. Ethnohistorical Report on Indian Use & Occupancy from 1640 to 1806 of Royce Area 53 in Ohio & of Royce Area 54. (Library of American Indian Affairs). 260p. 1974. lib. bdg. 93.00 (ISBN 0-8287-1033-3). Clearwater Pub.

--Ethnohistorical Report on Indian Use & Occupancy from 1650 to 1819 of Royce Areas 87 & 88. (Library of American Indian Affairs). 310p. 1974. lib. bdg. 108.00 (ISBN 0-8287-1034-1). Clearwater Pub.

--Ethnohistorical Report on Indian Use & Occupancy from 1640-1808 of Royce Area 66 in Ohio & Michigan. (Library of American Indian Affairs). 460p. 1974. lib. bdg. 122.00 (ISBN 0-8287-1035-X). Clearwater Pub.

--Indians of Northwest Ohio: An Ethnohistorical Report on the Wyandot, Potawatomi, Ottawa & Chippewa of Northwest Ohio. Horr, David A., ed. (North Central & Northeastern Indians - American Indian Ethnohistory Ser.). 1974. lib. bdg. 42.00 (ISBN 0-8240-0799-9). Garland Pub.

--Miami, Wea, & El-River Indians of Southern Indian. Horr, David A., ed. (American Indian Ethnohistory Ser.). 1974. lib. bdg. 42.00 (ISBN 0-8240-0806-5). Garland Pub.

Whipple, Chandler. Indian & the Whiteman in Connecticut. LC 73-92510. (First Encounter Ser). (Illus.). 95p. (Orig.). 1972. pap. 2.95 (ISBN 0-912944-17-X). Berkshire Traveller.

--The Indian & the Whiteman in Massachusetts & Rhode Island. LC 73-93961. (First Encounter Ser). (Illus.). 156p. 1973. pap. 3.50 (ISBN 0-912944-12-9). Berkshire Traveller.

--The Indian & the Whiteman in New England. LC 73-93961. (First Encounter Ser.). (Illus., Orig.). 1976. 10.00 (ISBN 0-912944-41-2); pap. 5.95 (ISBN 0-912944-38-2). Berkshire Traveller.

Wilbur, C. Keith. The New England Indians. LC 78-61713. (Illus.). 1978. pap. 8.95 (ISBN 0-87106-004-3). Globe Pequot.

Williams, Roger. A Key into the Language of America. Teunissen, John T. & Hinz, Evelyn J., eds. LC 72-6590. 264p. 1973. 14.95x (ISBN 0-8143-1490-2). Wayne St U Pr.

--A Key into the Language of America, 2 vols. in 1. Incl. The Fourth Edition. Trumbull, J. Hammond, ed; The Narragansett Edition. Repr. of 1866 ed; The Fifth Edition. Chapin, Howard H., ed. 1936. LC 72-85014. 1973. 18.00 (ISBN 0-8462-1680-9). Russell.

Williams, Ted C. The Reservation. LC 75-46585. (Illus.). 1976. 9.95 (ISBN 0-8156-0119-0). Syracuse U Pr.

Williamson, M. J. The Creek Nation & Private Land Sales in Alabama, & an Appraisal of Creek Nation Lands. (Library of American Indian Affairs). 1976. lib. bdg. 99.00x (ISBN 0-8287-1021-X). Clearwater Pub.

Wilson, Edmund. Apologies to the Iroquois. 1966. pap. 2.95 (ISBN 0-394-70313-8, Vin). Random.

Wilson, Edmund & Mitchell, Joseph. Apologies to the Iroquois: With a Study of the Mohawks in High Street. 1978. Repr. of 1959 ed. lib. bdg. 15.50x (ISBN 0-374-98648-7). Octagon.

Wissler, Clark. The Indians of Greater New York & the Lower Hudson. LC 74-9017. (Anthropological Papers of the American Museum of Natural History: Vol. 3). Repr. of 1909 ed. 24.50 (ISBN 0-404-11914-X). AMS Pr.

Wood, William. New Englands Prospect. LC 68-54670. (English Experience Ser.: No. 68). 104p. 1968. Repr. of 1634 ed. 16.00 (ISBN 90-221-0068-5). Walter J Johnson.

--New England's Prospect. Vaughan, Alden T., ed. LC 76-45051. (Commonwealth Ser: Vol. 3). (Illus.). 1977. 12.50x (ISBN 0-87023-226-6). U of Mass Pr.

--Wood's New England Prospect. Colburn, Jeremiah, ed. 1966. 19.00 (ISBN 0-8337-3864-X). B Franklin.

Woodward, Grace S. Cherokees. (Civilization of the American Indian Ser.: No. 65). (Illus.). 1979. Repr. of 1963 ed. 15.95 (ISBN 0-8061-0554-2). U of Okla Pr.

Woodward, Thomas S. Woodward's Reminiscences of the Creek or Muscogee Indians: Alabama, Georgia & Mississippi. rev. ed. 1970. pap. 5.95 (ISBN 0-87651-010-1). Southern U Pr.

Zeisberger, David. Grammar of the Language of the Lenni Lenape, or Delaware Indians. Du Ponceau, Peter S., tr. from Ger. LC 76-43904. Repr. of 1827 ed. 29.50 (ISBN 0-404-15803-X). AMS Pr.

INDIANS OF NORTH AMERICA-NORTHWEST, OLD

Armstrong, Perry A. The Sauks & the Black Hawk War. LC 76-43643. (Illus.). Repr. of 1887 ed. 47.50 (ISBN 0-404-15478-6). AMS Pr.

Baraga, Frederick, ed. Chippewa Indians As Recorded by Rev. Frederick Baraga in Eighteen Forty-Seven. LC 77-375214. 82p. 1976. 5.00 (ISBN 0-686-28384-8). Studia Slovenica.

Barnouw, Victor. Acculturation & Personality Among the Wisconsin Chippewa. LC 76-43646. (AAA Memoir: No. 72). Repr. of 1950 ed. 19.50 (ISBN 0-404-15481-6). AMS Pr.

--Wisconsin Chippewa Myths & Tales & Their Relation to Chippewa Life. LC 76-53647. 304p. 1977. 25.00 (ISBN 0-299-07310-6); pap. 7.95 (ISBN 0-299-07314-9). U of Wis Pr.

Barrett, Samuel A. The Dream Dance of the Chippewa & Menominee Indians of Northern Wisconsin. LC 76-43647. (Bulletin of the Public Museum of the City of Milwaukee: Vol. 1). Repr. of 1911 ed. 24.50 (ISBN 0-404-15482-4). AMS Pr.

Beckwith, Hiram W. The Illinois & Indiana Indians. facsimile ed. LC 75-86. (Mid-American Frontier Ser.). 1975. Repr. of 1884 ed. 9.00x (ISBN 0-405-06854-9). Arno.

Berthrong, Donald J. Indians of Northern Indiana & Southwestern Michigan: An Historical Report on Indian Use & Occupancy of Northern Indiana & Southwestern Michigan. Horr, David A., ed. (North Central & Northeastern Indians - American Indian Ethnohistory Ser.). 1974. lib. bdg. 38.00 (ISBN 0-8240-0801-4). Garland Pub.

Blair, Emma H., ed. Indian Tribes of the Upper Mississippi Valley & Region of the Great Lakes, 2 Vols. in 1. 1911. 30.00 (ISBN 0-527-08800-5). Kraus Repr.

Bloomfield, Leonard. Menomini Texts. LC 73-3548. (American Ethnological Society. Publications: No. 12). Repr. of 1928 ed. 39.50 (ISBN 0-404-58162-5). AMS Pr.

Boller, Henry A. Among the Indians: Four Years on the Upper Missouri, 1858-1862. Quaife, Milo M., ed. LC 76-100810. (Illus.). xvi, 370p. 1972. pap. 4.50 (ISBN 0-8032-5714-7, BB 514, Bison). U of Nebr Pr.

Bray, Martha C., ed. Journals of Joseph N. Nicollet: 1836-37. Fertey, Andre, tr. 288p. 1970. 16.50 (ISBN 0-87351-062-3). Minn Hist.

Carpenter, Cecelia S. They Walked Before: The Indians of Washington State. LC 77-81590. (Illus.). 1977. pap. 5.00 (ISBN 0-917048-04-0). Wash St Hist Soc.

Chalfant, Stuart A. Coeur D'Alene Indian Aboriginal Distribution: Ethnological Field Investigation & Analysis of Historical Material. (Library of American Indian Affairs). 155p. 1974. lib. bdg. 50.00 (ISBN 0-8287-1006-6). Clearwater Pub.

Chapman, Berlin B. Otoe & Missouria Lands. (Library of American Indian Affairs). 150p. 1974. lib. bdg. 60.00 (ISBN 0-8287-1168-2). Clearwater Pub.

Chisholm, Roger K. Chippewa, Ottawa & Potawatomie Lands in Illinois & Wisconsin: Valuation As of 1835. (Library of American Indian Affairs). 1976. lib. bdg. 67.00x (ISBN 0-8287-0996-3). Clearwater Pub.

Clarkson, Ewan. Many-Forked Branch. (Illus.). 1980. 10.95 (ISBN 0-525-14358-0). Dutton.

Coleman, Sr. Bernard, et al. Old Crow Wing: History of a Village. (Illus.). 1967. pap. 2.00 (ISBN 0-9600750-2-X). St Scholastica.

Cressman, Luther S. The Sandal & the Cave: The Indians of Oregon. LC 81-915. (Oregon State Monographs--Studies in History: No. 8). (Illus.). 96p. 1981. pap. 3.95 (ISBN 0-87071-078-8). Oreg St U Pr.

Danziger, Edmund J., Jr. The Chippewas of Lake Superior. LC 78-58130. (Civilization of the American Indian Ser: No. 148). (Illus.). 1979. 16.95 (ISBN 0-8061-1487-8). U of Okla Pr.

Deland, Charles E. The Aborigines of South Dakota. LC 76-43688. (South Dakota Historical Collections: 3). 1977. Repr. of 1906 ed. 30.00 (ISBN 0-404-15521-9). AMS Pr.

Densmore, Frances. Chippewa Customs. (Landmarks in Anthropology Ser). 1970. Repr. of 1929 ed. 19.50 (ISBN 0-384-11410-5). Johnson Repr.

--Chippewa Customs. LC 79-15400. (Illus.). 204p. 1979. pap. 7.50 (ISBN 0-87351-142-5). Minn Hist.

--Chippewa Music, 2 vols. LC 77-164513. (Illus.). 1972. Repr. of 1913 ed. Set. lib. bdg. 45.00 (ISBN 0-306-70459-5). Da Capo.

Dewdney, Selwyn & Kidd, Kenneth E. Indian Rock Paintings of the Great Lakes. rev. ed. LC 67-98487. (Illus.). 1967. 15.00 (ISBN 0-8020-3172-2). U of Toronto Pr.

Ewers, John C. Chippewa Indians VI. Horr, David A., ed. (American Indian Ethnohistory Ser.). 1978. lib. bdg. 42.00 (ISBN 0-8240-0813-8). Garland Pub.

--Plains Indian Painting: A Description of Aboriginal American Art. LC 76-43701. Repr. of 1939 ed. 24.50 (ISBN 0-404-15533-2). AMS Pr.

French & Indian Cruelty; Exemplified in the Life & Various Vicissitudes of Fortune, of Peter Williamson...Containing a Particular Account of the Manners, Customs, & Dress, of the Savages, Repr. Of 1757. Bd. with French & Indian Cruelty. Repr. of 1758 ed; Sufferings of... Repr. of 1796 ed; The Travels & Surprising Adventures of John Thomson, Who Was Taken, & Carried to America, & Sold for a Slave There; How He Was Taken Captive by the Savages,... & His Return to Scotland. Repr. of 1761 ed; A Full & Particular Account of the Sufferings of William Gatenby. Repr. of 1784 ed. (Narratives of North American Indian Captivities Ser.: Vol. 9). 1979. lib. bdg. 44.00 (ISBN 0-8240-1633-5). Garland Pub.

Gussow, Zachary, et al. Sac, Fox & Iowa Indians, Vol. 1. Horr, David A., ed. (American Indian Ethnohistory Ser.). 1978. lib. bdg. 42.00 (ISBN 0-8240-0789-1). Garland Pub.

Hallowell, A. Irving. Contributions to Anthropology: Selected Papers of A. Irving Hallowell. LC 75-20890. 1976. lib. bdg. 27.00x (ISBN 0-226-31414-6). U of Chicago Pr.

Hickerson, Harold. Chippewa Indians II: Ethnohistory of Mississippi Bands, & Pillager & Winnibigoshish Bands of Chippewa. (American Indian Ethnohistory Ser: North Central & Northeastern Indians). (Illus.). lib. bdg. 42.00 (ISBN 0-8240-0809-X). Garland Pub.

--Chippewa Indians III. Horr, David A., ed. (American Indian Ethnohistory Ser.). 1978. lib. bdg. 42.00 (ISBN 0-8240-0810-3). Garland Pub.

--Chippewa Indians IV: Ethnohistory of Chippewa in Central Minnesota. (American Indian Ethnohistory Ser: North Central & Northeastern Indians). (Illus.). lib. bdg. 42.00 (ISBN 0-8240-0811-1). Garland Pub.

Hildreth, S. P. Pioneer History: Being an Account of the First Examinations of the Ohio Valley, & the Early Settlement of the Northwest Territory. LC 79-146400. (First American Frontier Ser). (Illus.). 1971. Repr. of 1848 ed. 24.00 (ISBN 0-405-02854-7). Arno.

Hilger, Inez. Chippewa Child Life & Its Cultural Background. LC 76-43740. (BAE. Bulletin: 146). Repr. of 1951 ed. 17.50 (ISBN 0-404-15581-2). AMS Pr.

--A Social Study of One Hundred Fifty Chippewa Indian Families of the White Earth Reservation of Minnesota. LC 76-43741. Repr. of 1939 ed. 26.00 (ISBN 0-404-15582-0). AMS Pr.

Hinsdale, Wilbert B. The Indians of Washtenaw County, Michigan. 1927. 1.95x (ISBN 0-685-21790-6). Wahr.
Horr, David A., ed. Indians of Ohio, Indiana, Illinois, Southern Michigan & Southern Wisconsin: Findings of Fact & Opinion, 3 vols. (North Central & Northeastern Indians - American Indian Ethnohistory Ser.). 1974. Set. lib. bdg. 99.00 (ISBN 0-8240-0807-3); lib. bdg. 42.00 ea. Garland Pub.
Hughes, Thomas. Indian Chiefs of Southern Minnesota. Repr. 8.75 (ISBN 0-87018-026-6). Ross.
Indian Claims Commission. Chippewa Indians VII: Findings of Fact, & Opinion. (American Indian Ethnohistory Ser: North Central & Northeastern Indians). (Illus.). lib. bdg. 42.00 (ISBN 0-8240-0814-6). Garland Pub.
--Sac, Fox & Iowa Indians, Vol. 3: Findings of Fact, & Opinion. (American Indian Ethnohistory Ser: North Central & Northeastern Indians). (Illus.). lib. bdg. 42.00 (ISBN 0-8240-0791-3). Garland Pub.
Indians of Northeastern Illinois. Incl. Anthropological Report on the Chippewa, Ottawa & Potawatomi Indians in Northeastern Illinois. Baerreis, David A., et al.; Identity of the Mascontens. Barraeis, David A., et al.. (American Indian Ethnohistory Ser: North Central & Northeastern Indians). (Illus.). lib. bdg. 42.00 (ISBN 0-8240-0803-0). Garland Pub.
Indians of Northern Ohio & Southeastern Michigan. Incl. An Ethnohistorical Report on the Wyandot, Ottawa, Chippewa, Munsee, Delaware, Shawnee, & Potawatomi of Ohio & Southeastern Michigan. Wheeler-Voegelin, Erminie; The Location of Indian Tribes in Southeastern Michigan & Northern Ohio, 1700-1817. Tanner, Helen H. (American Indian Ethnohistory Ser: North Central & Northeastern Indians). (Illus.). lib. bdg. 42.00 (ISBN 0-8240-0800-6). Garland Pub.
Indians of Western Illinois & Southern Wisconsin. Incl. Anthropological Report on the Chippewas, Ottawas, & Potawatomi Residing on the Illinois & Milwaukee Rivers on the Southwestern Parts of Lake Michigan. Wheeler-Voegelin, Erminie, et al.; Anthropological Report on the Chippewa, Ottawa & Potawatomi Indians of Southwest Wisconsin & Northeast Illinois. Jones, J. A. (American Indian Ethnohistory Ser: North Central & Northeastern Indians). (Illus.). lib. bdg. 42.00 (ISBN 0-8240-0802-2). Garland Pub.
Jablow, Joseph. Indians of Illinois & Indiana: Illinois, Kickapoo & Potawatomi Indians. Horr, David A., ed. (American Indian Ethnohistory Ser.: North Central & Northeastern Indians). 1974. lib. bdg. 42.00 (ISBN 0-8240-0805-7). Garland Pub.
James, Edwin. Narrative of the Captivity & Adventures of John Tanner During Thirty Years Residence Among the Chippewa, Ottawa & Objibwa Tribes Etc. Loomis, Noel, ed. & intro. by. Repr. 15.00 (ISBN 0-87018-033-9). Ross.
Jenks, Albert E. Minnesota's Browns Valley Man and Associated Burial Artifacts. LC 38-22478. 1937. pap. 5.00 (ISBN 0-527-00548-7). Kraus Repr.
Johnson, Elden, ed. Aspects of Upper Great Lakes Anthropology: Papers in Honor of Lloyd A. Wilford. LC 74-17003. (Prehistoric Archaeology Ser: No. 11). (Illus.). 190p. 1974. pap. 9.50 (ISBN 0-87351-087-9). Minn Hist.
Jones, Peter. History of the Ojibway Indians. (Select Bibliographies Reprint Ser). 1861. 22.00 (ISBN 0-8369-5290-1). Arno.
Jones, William & Michelson, Truman, eds. Ojibwa Texts, 2 vols. LC 73-3542. (American Ethnological Society. Publications: No. 7). Repr. of 1917 ed. 74.50 (ISBN 0-404-58157-9). AMS Pr.
Kauth, Helen. Ottawa & Chippewa Lands in Michigan: Economic & Historical Background for a Valuation As of 1836. (Library of American Indian Affairs). 1976. lib. bdg. 67.00x (ISBN 0-8287-1171-2). Clearwater Pub.
Keating, William H. Narrative of the Expedition to the Source of St. Peter's River. facsimile ed. (Illus.). 1825. 12.50 (ISBN 0-87018-036-3). Ross.
Keesing, Felix M. Menomini Indians of Wisconsin: A Study of Three Centuries of Cultural Contact & Changes. LC 39-15951. 1971. Repr. of 1939 ed. 20.00 (ISBN 0-384-29005-1). Johnson Repr.
Kinietz, W. Vernon. Indians of the Western Great Lakes Region. 1965. pap. 5.95 (ISBN 0-472-06107-0, 107, AA). U of Mich Pr.
--Indians of the Western Great Lakes, 1615-1760. 1965. 8.95 (ISBN 0-472-09107-7). U of Mich Pr.
Landes, Ruth. Ojibwa Sociology. LC 79-84467. (Columbia Univ. Contributions to Anthropology Ser.: Vol. 29). Repr. of 1937 ed. 16.00 (ISBN 0-404-50579-1). AMS Pr.
--Ojibwa Woman. LC 70-82362. (Columbia Univ. Contributions to Anthropology Ser.: Vol. 31). Repr. of 1938 ed. 21.00 (ISBN 0-404-50581-3). AMS Pr.
LeDuc, Thomas H. Otoe & Missouria Lands. (Library of American Indian Affairs). 183p. 1974. lib. bdg. 70.00 (ISBN 0-8287-1169-0). Clearwater Pub.
Lowie, Robert H. The Northern Shoshone. LC 74-7983. Repr. of 1909 ed. 16.00 (ISBN 0-404-11871-2). AMS Pr.
Lupold, Harry F. The Forgotten People: The Woodland Erie. 1975. 6.00 (ISBN 0-682-48390-7, University); pap. 3.00 (ISBN 0-682-48391-5). Exposition.
Lurie, Nancy O. Wisconsin Indians. LC 80-10758. (Illus.). 66p. (Orig.). 1980. pap. 2.00 (ISBN 0-87020-195-6). State Hist Soc Wis.
Lurie, Nancy O., ed. Mountain Wolf Woman, Sister of Crashing Thunder: The Autobiography of a Winnebago Indian. (Illus.). 164p. 1961. pap. 3.95 (ISBN 0-472-06109-7). U of Mich Pr.
McConkey, Lois. Sea & Cedar: How the Northwest Coast Indians Lived. (Illus.). 1973. paper-Over-boards 6.95 (ISBN 0-88894-158-7, Pub. by Douglas & McIntyre). Madrona Pubs.
McKenney, Thomas L. Sketches of a Tour to the Lakes. (Illus.). Repr. 12.50 (ISBN 0-87018-042-8). Ross.
McKnight, Charles. Our Western Border, Its Life, Combats, Adventures, Forays, Massacres, Captivities, Scouts, Red Chiefs, Pioneers, Women, One Hundred Years Ago, Carefully Written & Compiled. (Rediscovering America Ser). (Illus.). Repr. of 1876 ed. 42.50 (ISBN 0-384-34890-4, R174). Johnson Repr.
Mails, Thomas E. Fools Crow. LC 76-2803. (Illus.). 1979. 12.95 (ISBN 0-385-11332-3). Doubleday.
Mandelbaum, David G. The Plains Cree. LC 76-43772. (Vol. 37.Pt 2). Repr. of 1940 ed. 21.00 (ISBN 0-404-15626-6). AMS Pr.
Michelson, Truman. Contributions to Fox Ethnology. Repr. of 1927 ed. 19.00 (ISBN 0-403-03571-6). Scholarly.
--Fox Miscellany. Repr. of 1936 ed. 19.00 (ISBN 0-403-08986-7). Scholarly.
--Notes on the Buffalo-Head Dance of the Bear Gens of the Fox Indians. Repr. of 1928 ed. 17.00 (ISBN 0-403-03668-2). Scholarly.
Moorehead, Warren K. The Indian Tribes of Ohio: Historically Considered, a Preliminary Paper. LC 76-43783. Repr. of 1899 ed. 12.50 (ISBN 0-404-15639-8). AMS Pr.
--Primitive Man in Ohio. LC 76-43787. Repr. of 1892 ed. 19.00 (ISBN 0-404-15642-8). AMS Pr.
Newton, Stanley D. Mackinac Island & Saulte St. Marie. LC 76-4405. (Illus.). 1976. pap. 6.00 (ISBN 0-912382-19-8). Black Letter.
Ourada, Patricia K. The Menominee Indians: A History. LC 78-7942. (Civilization of the American Indian Ser: No. 146). (Illus.). 1979. 14.95 (ISBN 0-8061-1486-X). U of Okla Pr.
Paredes, J. Anthony, ed. Anishinabe: Six Studies of Modern Chippewa. LC 79-20091. (Illus.). xi, 436p. 1980. 27.50 (ISBN 0-8130-0625-2). U Presses Fla.
Quimby, George I. Indian Life on the Upper Great Lakes: 11,000 B.C. to A.D. 1800. LC 60-11799. 1971. pap. text ed. 3.95 (ISBN 0-226-70044-5, P438, Phoen). U of Chicago Pr.
Rachlin & Marriott. Plains Indian Mythology. (RL 7). 1977. pap. 1.75 (ISBN 0-451-61582-4, ME1582, Ment). NAL.
Radin, Paul. Autobiography of a Winnebago Indian. 5.50 (ISBN 0-8446-2774-7). Peter Smith.
--Autobiography of a Winnebago Indian. 1920. pap. 1.75 (ISBN 0-486-20096-5). Dover.
--Road of Life & Death. (Bollingen Ser.: Vol. 5). 1945. 22.00x (ISBN 0-691-09819-0). Princeton U Pr.
--Trickster: A Study in American Indian Mythology. Repr. of 1956 ed. lib. bdg. 15.00x (ISBN 0-8371-2112-4, RATT). Greenwood.
--The Winnebago Tribe. LC 23-14443. 1971. Repr. of 1915 ed. 42.50 (ISBN 0-384-49490-0). Johnson Repr.
--Winnebago Tribe. LC 64-63594. (Illus.). 1970. pap. 8.50 (ISBN 0-8032-5710-4, BB 512, Bison). U of Nebr Pr.
Rogers, John N. Red World & White: Memories of a Chippewa Boyhood. LC 72-9263. (Civilization of the American Indian Ser.: No. 126). 150p. 1974. 6.95 (ISBN 0-8061-1069-4). U of Okla Pr.
Rohrl, Vivian J. Change for Continuity: The People of a Thousand Lakes. LC 80-6077. 269p. 1981. lib. bdg. 19.25 (ISBN 0-8191-1538-X); pap. text ed. 10.50 (ISBN 0-8191-1539-8). U Pr of Amer.
Sagard-Theodat, Gabriel. Long Journey to the Country of the Hurons. Wrong, George M., ed. Langton, H. H., tr. LC 68-28613. 1968. Repr. of 1939 ed. lib. bdg. 29.25x (ISBN 0-8371-3861-2, SAJC). Greenwood.
Sally Old Coyote & Joy Yellow Tail Toineeta. Indian Tales of the Northern Plains. (Indian Culture Ser.). (gr. 2-5). 1972. 1.95 (ISBN 0-89992-018-7). MT Coun Indian.
Skinner, Alanson B. Medicine Ceremony of the Menomini, Iowa, & Wahpeton Dakota: With Notes on the Ceremony Among the Ponca, Bungi, Ojibwa & Potawatomi. LC 76-43826. (MAI. Indian Notes & Monographs: Vol. 4). Repr. of 1920 ed. 28.00 (ISBN 0-404-15678-9). AMS Pr.
--Observations of the Ethnology of the Sauk Indians. 1923-25. Repr. lib. bdg. 15.00 (ISBN 0-8371-4632-1, SKSI). Greenwood.
Skinner, Alanson B. & Satterlee, John V. Folklore of the Menomini Indians. LC 76-43832. (AMNH. Anthropological Papers: Vol. 13, Pt. 3). Repr. of 1915 ed. 22.00 (ISBN 0-404-15684-3). AMS Pr.
Smith, Huron H. Ethnobotany of the Menomini Indians. Repr. of 1923 ed. lib. bdg. 15.00 (ISBN 0-8371-4633-X, SMMI). Greenwood.
--Ethnobotany of the Meskwaki Indians, 2 vols. in 1. Bd. with Ethnobotany of the Menomini Indians. Repr. of 1923 ed. LC 76-43836. (Bulletin of the Public Museum of the City of Milwaukee: Vol. 4, Nos. 1 & 2). Repr. of 1928 ed. 40.50 (ISBN 0-404-15690-8). AMS Pr.
Sosin, Jack M. Whitehall & the Wilderness: The Middle West in British Colonial Policy, 1760 to 1775. LC 80-21061. (Illus.). xi, 307p. 1981. Repr. of 1961 ed. lib. bdg. 35.00x (ISBN 0-313-22678-4, SOWW). Greenwood.
Stout, David B. Anthropological Report on the Indian Occupancy of Royce Area 262 in Iowa. (Library of American Indian Affairs). 40p. 1974. lib. bdg. 23.00 (ISBN 0-8287-0909-2). Clearwater Pub.
--Sac, Fox & Iowa Indians, Vol. 2: Indians of E. Missouri, W. Illinois & S. Wisconsin, from the Proto-Historic Period to 1804. (American Indian Ethnohistory Ser: North Central & Northeastern Indians). (Illus.). lib. bdg. 42.00 (ISBN 0-8240-0790-5). Garland Pub.
Tabeau, Pierre-Antoine. Tabeau's Narrative of Loisel's Expedition to the Upper Missouri. (American Exploration & Travel Ser: No. 3). (Illus.). 1968. Repr. of 1939 ed. 14.95 (ISBN 0-8061-0080-X). U of Okla Pr.
Tanner, Helen H. Chippewa of Eastern Lower Michigan, Seventeen Eighty-Five to Eighteen Thirty-Seven. (Library of American Indian Affairs). 25p. 1974. lib. bdg. 18.00 (ISBN 0-8287-0994-7). Clearwater Pub.
--The Ojibwas: A Critical Bibliography. LC 76-12376. (Newberry Library Center for the History of the American Indian Bibliographical Ser.). 88p. 1976. pap. 3.95x (ISBN 0-253-34165-5). Ind U Pr.
--Potawatomi Ceded Lands & an Indian History of Northeastern Illinois. (Library of American Indian Affairs). 1976. lib. bdg. 29.00x (ISBN 0-8287-1200-X). Clearwater Pub.
--The Sisseton & Wahpeton Tribes in North Dakota & South Dakota & the Treaty of 1867 & the Agreement of 1872. (Library of American Indian Affairs). 134p. 1974. lib. bdg. 44.50 (ISBN 0-8287-1253-0). Clearwater Pub.
Tanner, Helen H., et al. Wyandot Reservations in Michigan & Ohio: An Historial Report for Appraising Land Values. Ross, Norman A., ed. (Library of American Indian Affairs). 1976. lib. bdg. 75.00x (ISBN 0-8287-1310-3). Clearwater Pub.
Tibbles, Thomas H. The Ponca Chiefs: An Account of the Trial of Standing Bear. Graber, Kay, ed. LC 73-181595. xiv, 143p. 1972. 10.95x (ISBN 0-8032-0814-6); pap. 3.50 (ISBN 0-8032-5763-5, BB 547, Bison). U of Nebr Pr.
Turner, Frederick J. Character & Influence of the Indian Trade in Wisconsin: A Study of the Trading Post As an Institution. 1891. 16.50 (ISBN 0-8337-3579-9). B Franklin.
--The Character & Influence of the Indian Trade in Wisconsin: A Study of the Trading Post As an Institution. Repr. of 1891 ed. pap. 8.00 (ISBN 0-384-62000-0). Johnson Repr.
--The Character & Influence of the Indian Trade in Wisconsin: A Study of the Trading Post As an Institution. Miller, David & Miller, Harry M., eds. LC 76-47331. 1977. 9.95 (ISBN 0-8061-1335-9). U of Okla Pr.
Turney-High, Harry H. The Flathead Indians of Montana. LC 38-6188. Repr. of 1937 ed. pap. 8.00 (ISBN 0-527-00547-9). Kraus Repr.
Vaudrin, Bill. Tanaina Tales from Alaska. (Civilization of the American Indians Ser.: Vol. 96). 133p. 1981. pap. 3.95 (ISBN 0-8061-1414-2). U of Okla Pr.
Wah-Be-Gwo-Nese, pseud. Ojibwa Indian Legends. (Illus.). 1972. 2.95 (ISBN 0-918616-05-0). Northern Mich.
Walker, Deward E. Indians of Idaho. LC 78-52574. (Gembook & Anthropological Monograph). 1978. 7.50 (ISBN 0-89301-053-7). U Pr of Idaho.
Wheeler-Voegelin, Erminie. Chippewa Indians I: Red Lake & Pembina Chippewa. (American Indian Ethnohistory Ser: North Central & Northeastern Indians). (Illus.). lib. bdg. 42.00 (ISBN 0-8240-0808-1). Garland Pub.
--Indians of Northwest Ohio: An Ethnohistorical Report on the Wyandot, Potawatomi, Ottawa & Chippewa of Northwest Ohio. Horr, David A., ed. (North Central & Northeastern Indians - American Indian Ethnohistory Ser.). 1974. lib. bdg. 42.00 (ISBN 0-8240-0799-9). Garland Pub.
Wheeler-Voegelin, Erminie, et al. Chippewa Indians V. Horr, David A., ed. (American Indian Ethnohistory Ser.). 1978. lib. bdg. 42.00 (ISBN 0-8240-0812-X). Garland Pub.
Wilkinson, Richard G. Prehistoric Biological Relationship in the Great Lakes Region. (Anthropological Papers: No. 43). (Illus.). 1971. pap. 3.50x (ISBN 0-932206-41-7). U Mich Mus Anthro.
Winnebago Indians. Incl. Winnebago Ethnology. Jones, J. A; Economic & Historical Background for the Winnebago Indian Claims. Smith, Alice E. & Carstensen, Vernon.; Findings of Fact, & Opinion. Indian Claims Commission. (American Indian Ethnohistory Ser: North Central & Northeastern Indians). (Illus.). lib. bdg. 42.00 (ISBN 0-8240-0761-1). Garland Pub.
Wissler, Clark. North American Indians of the Plains. LC 73-22043. 1974. Repr. of 1934 ed. lib. bdg. 23.50 (ISBN 0-8337-5204-9). B Franklin.

INDIANS OF NORTH AMERICA–NORTHWEST, PACIFIC

Adamson, T., ed. Folk-Tales of the Coast Salish. LC 36-2204. (American Folklore Society Memoirs Ser). Repr. of 1934 ed. 25.00 (ISBN 0-527-01079-0). Kraus Repr.
Artscanada. Stones, Bones & Skin: Ritual & Shamanic Art. (Illus.). 200p. 1981. 14.95 (ISBN 0-295-95864-2). Univ of Wash Pr.
Ashwell, Reg. Coast Salish: Their Art, Culture & Legends. (Native Culture Ser.). (Illus., Orig.). 1978. pap. 4.00 (ISBN 0-88839-009-2, Pub. by Hancock Hse). Universe.
--Indian Tribes of the Northwest. 74p. 1977. pap. 4.00 (ISBN 0-919654-53-3, Pub. by Hancock Hse). Universe.
Bakken, Lavolla J. Land of the North Umpquas: Peaceful Indians of the West. LC 73-84954. (Illus.). 1973. pap. 1.00 (ISBN 0-913508-03-9). Te Cum Tom.
Bancroft-Hunt, Norman & Forman, Werner. People of the Totem. LC 78-57977. (Illus.). 1979. 14.95 (ISBN 0-399-11991-4). Putnam.
Barbeau, Marius. Modern Growth of the Totem Pole on the Northwest Coast. facs. ed. 9p. Repr. pap. 3.00 (ISBN 0-8466-0098-6, SJS98). Shorey.
Barnett, Homer. Indian Shakers: A Messianic Cult of the Pacific Northwest. LC 72-5482. (Arcturus Books Paperbacks). (Illus.). 383p. 1972. pap. 7.95 (ISBN 0-8093-0595-X). S Ill U Pr.
Barnett, Homer G. The Coast Salish of British Columbia. LC 75-25251. (Univ. of Oregon Monographs, Studies in Anthropology: No. 4). (Illus.). 320p. 1975. Repr. of 1955 ed. lib. bdg. 25.00x (ISBN 0-8371-8381-2, BACSB). Greenwood.
Bataille, Gretchen M., et al, eds. The Worlds Between Two Rivers: Perspectives on American Indians in Iowa. (Illus.). 1978. 8.50 (ISBN 0-8138-1795-1). Iowa St U Pr.
Beard, Yolande S. The Wappo: A Report. 1979. pap. 5.25 (ISBN 0-686-25242-X). Malki Mus Pr.
Berreman, J. V. Tribal Distribution in Oregon. LC 37-20181. (American Anthropological Association Memoirs). Repr. of 1937 ed. pap. 5.00 (ISBN 0-527-00546-0). Kraus Repr.
Birket-Smith, Kaj & De Laguna, Frederica. The Eyak Indians of the Copper River Delta, Alaska. LC 74-7932. (Illus.). Repr. of 1938 ed. 42.50 (ISBN 0-404-11817-8). AMS Pr.
Bischoff, W. N. Kalispel Country in Washington - 1809-1903. (Library of American Indian Affairs). 80p. 1974. lib. bdg. 32.50 (ISBN 0-8287-1083-X). Clearwater Pub.
Blackfeet Indians. Incl. Ethnological Report on the Blackfeet & Gros Ventre Tribes. Ewers, John C; Findings of Fact, & Opinion. Indian Claims Commission. (American Indian Ethnohistory Ser: Plains Indians). (Illus.). lib. bdg. 42.00 (ISBN 0-8240-0755-7). Garland Pub.
Boas, Frank. Social Organization & the Secret Societies of the Kwakiutl Indians. Repr. of 1895 ed. 30.00 (ISBN 0-8466-9006-3, SJ144). Shorey.
Boas, Franz. The Decorative Art of the Indians of the North Pacific Coast. LC 74-7936. (Illus.). Repr. of 1897 ed. 14.00 (ISBN 0-404-11823-2). AMS Pr.

--Geographical Names of the Kwakiutl Indians. LC 77-82361. (Columbia Univ. Contributions to Anthropology Ser.: No. 20). 1969. Repr. of 1934 ed. 25.00 (ISBN 0-404-50570-8). AMS Pr.

--Kwakiutl Ethnography. Codere, Helen, ed. LC 66-13861. (Classics in Anthropology Ser). (Illus.). 1967. 21.00x (ISBN 0-226-06236-8). U of Chicago Pr.

--The Kwakiutl of Vancouver Island. LC 73-3526. (Jesup North Pacific Expedition. Publications: Vol. 5, Pt. 2). Repr. of 1909 ed. 58.00 (ISBN 0-404-58124-2). AMS Pr.

--The Social Organization & Secret Societies of the Kwakiutl Indians. Based on Personal Observations Notes Made by Mr. George Hunt. (Landmarks in Anthropology Ser). Repr. of 1897 ed. 46.00 (ISBN 0-384-04872-2). Johnson Repr.

--The Social Organization & the Secret Societies of the Kwakiutl Indians. 1976. Repr. of 1895 ed. 27.00 (ISBN 0-403-06712-X, Regency). Scholarly.

Boas, Franz & Hunt, George. Kwakiutl Texts. LC 73-3523. (Jesup North Pacific Expedition. Publications: No. 3). Repr. of 1905 ed. 49.50 (ISBN 0-404-58103-X). AMS Pr.

--Kwakiutl Texts--Second Series. LC 73-3662. (Jesup North Pacific Expedition. Publications: Vol. 10, Pt. 1). Repr. of 1906 ed. 30.00 (ISBN 0-404-58110-2). AMS Pr.

Brindze, Ruth. Story of the Totem Pole. (Illus.). (gr. 4-8). 1951. 6.95 (ISBN 0-8149-0277-4). Vanguard.

Brown, J. Ross. Indian Affairs in Territories of Oregon & Washington: First Season, 35th Congress, January 25, 1858. (House Exec. Doc.: No. 39). 1973. 4.95 (ISBN 0-87770-091-5). Ye Galleon.

Brown, Vinson. Peoples of the Sea Wind. 1977. pap. 7.95 (ISBN 0-02-030700-4, 03070, Collier). Macmillan.

Burns, Robert I. Jesuits & the Indian Wars of the Northwest. LC 65-22314. (Western Americana Ser.: No. 11). (Illus.). 1966. 47.00x (ISBN 0-300-00336-6). Yale U Pr.

Cary, Carl. Salish Songs & Rituals. 1969. pap. 2.00 (ISBN 0-686-14907-6); pap. 15.00 deluxe ed. (ISBN 0-686-14908-4). Goliards Pr.

Chalfant, Stuart A. The Spokan Indians in Washington: Ethnohistorical Report on Land Use & Occupancy. 41.00 (ISBN 0-8287-1266-2). Clearwater Pub.

--Wenatchi Salish of Central Washington: Report on Anthropological & Ethnographic Material Relative to Aboriginal Land Use & Occupancy. (Library of American Indian Affairs). 51p. 1974. lib. bdg. 24.00 (ISBN 0-8287-1299-9). Clearwater Pub.

Clark, Ella E. Indian Legends from the Northern Rockies. (Civilization of the American Indian Ser.: No. 82). (Illus.). 1977. Repr. of 1966 ed. 13.95 (ISBN 0-8061-0701-4). U of Okla Pr.

--Indian Legends of the Pacific Northwest. (Illus.). (YA) (gr. 9-12). 1953. pap. 3.95 (ISBN 0-520-00243-1, CAL18). U of Cal Pr.

Coast Salish & Western Washington Indians, Vol. 2. Incl. Ethnological Field Investigation & Analysis of the Puget Sound Indians. Riley, Carroll L; Influence of White Contact on Class Distinctions & Political Authority Among the Indians of Northern Puget Sound. Collins, June McC; The Quileute Indians of Puget Sound. Indian Claims Commission, et al.; Anthropological Investigation of the Medicine Creek Tribes. Taylor, Herbert C., et al.; Historical & Ethnological Study of the Snohomish Indian People. Tweddell, Colin E. (American Indian Ethnohistory Ser: Indians of the Northwest). (Illus.). lib. bdg. 42.00 (ISBN 0-8240-0784-0). Garland Pub.

Coast Salish & Western Washington Indians, Vol. 3. Incl. Anthropological Investigation of Makah Indians. Taylor, Herbert C; History of the Neah Bay Agency. Gillis, Alix J; Ethnographic Material on the Quileute Indians: Lapush & Hoh. Howeattle, Arthur, et al.; Anthropological Investigation of the Chehalis Indians. Taylor, Herbert C; John Work on the Chehalis Indians. Taylor, Herbert C; Territorial Distribution of the Aboriginal Population of Western Washington State & the Economic & Political Characteristics of Their Culture. Fried, Jacob; Handbook of Cowlitz Indians. Ray, Verne F. (American Indian Ethnohistory Ser: Indians of the Northwest). (Illus.). lib. bdg. 42.00 (ISBN 0-8240-0785-9). Garland Pub.

Coast Salish & Western Washington Indians, Vol. 4. Incl. Structure of Twana Culture. Elmendorf, William W; A Study of Religious Change Among the Skagit Indians. Collins, June M. (American Indian Ethnohistory Ser.: Indians of the Northwest). (Illus.). lib. bdg. 42.00 (ISBN 0-8240-0786-7). Garland Pub.

Cochran, George M. Indian Portraits of the Pacific Northwest. (Illus.). 1977. pap. 2.50 (ISBN 0-8323-0285-6). Binford.

Crakes, Sylvester. Five Years a Captive Among the Black-feet Indians. LC 75-7099. (Indian Captivities Ser.: Vol. 74). 1976. Repr. of 1858 ed. lib. bdg. 44.00 (ISBN 0-8240-1698-X). Garland Pub.

Crowder, David L. Tendoy, Chief of the Lemhis. LC 75-76336. (Illus., Orig.). (gr. 5-9). 1969. pap. 2.75 (ISBN 0-87004-129-0). Caxton.

Davis, Starr & Davis, Richard. Tongues & Totems: Comparative Arts of the Pacific Basin. LC 74-82243. 1974. softcover 8.95 (ISBN 0-686-17270-1). Alaska Intl Art.

Dawson, George. The Haidas. facsimile ed. 9p. Repr. of 1882 ed. pap. 3.00 (ISBN 0-8466-0096-X, SJS96). Shorey.

Dawson, George M. Notes & Observations on the Kwakiool People of the Northern Part of Vancouver Island & Adjacent Coasts, Made During the Summer of 1885: With a Vocabulary of About Seven Hundred Words. 37p. 1977. pap. 3.50 (ISBN 0-87770-118-0). Ye Galleon.

Densmore, Frances. Nootka & Quileute Music. LC 72-1885. (Music Ser.). (Illus.). 416p. 1972. Repr. of 1939 ed. lib. bdg. 29.50 (ISBN 0-306-70513-3). Da Capo.

Dillon, Richard H. Burnt-Out Fires: California's Modoc Indian War. LC 72-5846. (Illus.). 384p. 1973. 8.95 (ISBN 0-13-090993-9). P-H.

Diomedi, Alexander. Sketches of Indian Life in the Pacific Northwest. 1978. 10.95 (ISBN 0-87770-199-7). Ye Galleon.

Drucker, Philip. Cultures of the North Pacific Coast. (Culture Area Studies Ser.). (Illus., Orig.). 1965. pap. text ed. 10.95 scp (ISBN 0-8102-0087-2, HarpC). Har-Row.

--Indians of the Northwest Coast. 2.95 (ISBN 0-385-02443-6, B3, AMS). Natural Hist.

Drury, Clifford M. Chief Lawyer of the Nez Perce Indians, Seventeen Ninety-Six to Eighteen Seventy Six. LC 78-67267. (Northwest Historical Ser.: 14). (Illus.). 1979. 22.75 (ISBN 0-87062-127-0). A H Clark.

Duff, Wilson. Arts of the Raven: Masterworks by the Northwest Coast Indian. (Illus.). 112p. 1967. pap. 11:50 (ISBN 0-295-95583-X, Pub. by Vancouver Art Canada). U of Wash Pr.

Duff, Wilson & Stewart, Hilary. Images: Stone: B.C. (Illus.). 1975. 17.95 (ISBN 0-919654-27-4, Pub. by Hancock Hse). Universe.

Duncan, Janice K. Minority Without a Champion: Kanakas on the Pacific Coast, 1788-1850. LC 72-79115. (Illus.). 24p. 1972. pap. 1.00 (ISBN 0-87595-036-1). Oreg Hist Soc.

Emmons, G. T. The Tahltan Indians. (Illus.). 1979. Repr. of 1911 ed. text ed. 17.25x (ISBN 0-391-00957-5). Humanities.

Ewers, John C. Blackfeet: Raiders on the Northwestern Plains. (Civilization of the American Indian Ser.: No. 49). (Illus.). 1976. Repr. of 1958 ed. 15.95 (ISBN 0-8061-0405-8). U of Okla Pr.

Fejes, Claire. Villagers. 1981. 14.95 (ISBN 0-394-51673-7). Random.

Ford, Clellan S. Smoke from Their Fires: The Life of a Kwakiutl Chief. (Illus.). 1968. Repr. of 1941 ed. 15.00 (ISBN 0-208-00336-3, Archon). Shoe String.

Fried, Jacob. Chehalis & Chinook Territorial Distribution of Some of the Aboriginal Population of Western Washington. (Library of American Indian Affairs). 45p. 1974. 23.50 (ISBN 0-8287-0969-6). Clearwater Pub.

Fuller, E. O. Salish & Kootenai Tribes: Anthropology & Tribal History, 2 vols. 102.00 (ISBN 0-8287-1232-8). Clearwater Pub.

Garfield, Viola E. & Forrest, Linn A. Wolf & the Raven: Totem Poles of Southeastern Alaska. 2nd ed. LC 49-8492. (Illus.). 161p. 1961. pap. 6.95 (ISBN 0-295-73998-3). U of Wash Pr.

Garfield, Viola E. & Wingert, Paul S. Tsimshian Indians & Their Arts. LC 68-87177. (American Ethnological Society Numbered Publications Ser: No. 18). (Illus.). 108p. 1966. pap. 3.95 (ISBN 0-295-74042-6). U of Wash Pr.

Gatschet, Albert. An Extract from the Klamath Indians of SW Oregon. Repr. of 1890 ed. pap. 4.50 (ISBN 0-8466-0118-4, SJS118). Shorey.

Gibbs, George. Indian Tribes of Washington Territory. 56p. 1978. 6.95 (ISBN 0-87770-206-3); pap. 4.95 (ISBN 0-87770-050-8). Ye Galleon.

Gibbs, George, et al. Tribes of the Extreme Northwest, Alaska, the Aleutians & Adjacent Territories. (Illus.). Repr. of 1877 ed. pap. 22.50 (ISBN 0-8466-4018-X, SJ118). Shorey.

Goddard, Pliny E. Indians of the Northwest Coast. 2nd ed. LC 72-81191. (Handbook Ser.: No. 10). (Illus.). 175p. 1972. Repr. of 1934 ed. lib. bdg. 11.00x (ISBN 0-8154-0428-X). Cooper Sq.

Goldman, Irving. The Mouth of Heaven: An Introduction to Kwakiutl Religious Thought. LC 80-11163. 284p. 1981. Repr. of 1975 ed. lib. bdg. 19.50 (ISBN 0-89874-136-X). Krieger.

Grumet, Robert S. Native Americans of the Northwest Coast: A Critical Bibliography. LC 79-2165. (Newberry Library Center for the History of the American Indian Bibliographical Ser.). 128p. (Orig.). 1979. pap. 4.95x (ISBN 0-253-30385-0). Ind U Pr.

Gulick, Bill. Chief Joseph Country: Land of the Nez Perce. LC 79-51577. (Illus.). 450p. 1981. 29.95 (ISBN 0-87004-275-0). Caxton.

Gunther, Erna. Indian Life on the Northwest Coast of North America As Seen by the Early Explorers & Fur Traders During the Last Decades of the Eighteenth Century. LC 72-188822. (Illus.). 296p. 1975. pap. 5.95 (ISBN 0-226-31089-2, P639, Phoen). U of Chicago Pr.

Gustafson, Paula. Salish Weaving. LC 80-51075. (Illus.). 132p. 1980. 24.95 (ISBN 0-295-95755-7). U of Wash Pr.

Haeberlin, Hermann & Gunther, Erna. Indians of Puget Sound. LC 30-27636. (Publications in Anthropology Ser.: No. 4-1). (Illus.). 84p. (Orig.). 1930. pap. 3.95 (ISBN 0-295-73813-8). U of Wash Pr.

Hays, H. R. Children of the Raven: The Seven Indian Nations of the Northwest Coast. LC 75-6668. (Illus.). 352p. 1975. 12.95 (ISBN 0-07-027372-3, GB). McGraw.

Hearne, Samuel. Journey from Prince of Wale's Fort in Hudson's Bay to the Northern Ocean. LC 78-133870. (Illus.). 1971. 19.25 (ISBN 0-8048-1007-9). C E Tuttle.

--Journey from Prince of Wales's Fort in Hudson's Bay to the Northern Ocean in the Years 1769-1772. LC 68-28601. (Illus.). 1968. Repr. of 1911 ed. lib. bdg. 32.75x (ISBN 0-8371-5045-0, HEJP). Greenwood.

Hill, Beth & Hill, Ray. Indian Petroglyphs of the Pacific Northwest. LC 74-78344. (Illus.). 314p. 1975. 21.50 (ISBN 0-295-95412-4). U of Wash Pr.

Holm, Bill. Northwest Coast Indian Art: An Analysis of Form. LC 65-10818. (Thomas Burke Memorial Washington State Museum Monograph: No. 1). (Illus.). 133p. 1965. 12.95 (ISBN 0-295-73855-3); pap. 7.95 (ISBN 0-295-95102-8). U of Wash Pr.

Honigmann, John J. Kaska Indians: An Ethnographic Reconstruction. LC 64-24364. (Yale University Publications in Anthropology Reprints Ser: No. 51). 163p. 1964. pap. 6.00x (ISBN 0-87536-510-8). HRAFP.

Howe, Carrol. Ancient Modocs of California & Oregon. LC 79-1870. (Illus.). 1979. pap. 6.50 (ISBN 0-8323-0325-9). Binford.

Indian Claims Commission. Coast Salish & Western Washington Indians, Vol. 5: Findings of Fact, & Opinion. (American Indian Ethnohistory Ser: Indians of the Northwest). (Illus.). lib. bdg. 42.00 (ISBN 0-8240-0787-5). Garland Pub.

Interior Salish & Eastern Washington Indians, Vol. 1. Incl. Ethnological Field Investigation & Analysis of Historical Material Relative to Coeur D'alene Indian Aboriginal Distribution. Chalfant, Stuart A; The Coeur D'alene Country 1805-1892: an Historical Sketch. Bischoff, William N; Findings of Fact, & Opinion. Indian Claims Commission. (American Indian Ethnohistory Ser: Indians of the Northwest). (Illus.). lib. bdg. 42.00 (ISBN 0-8240-0752-2). Garland Pub.

Interior Salish & Eastern Washington Indians, Vol. 2. Incl. Aboriginal Territories of the Flathead, Pend D'oreille & Kutenai Indians of Western Montana. Chalfant, Stuart A; Economy & Land Use by the Indians of Western Montana. Malouf, Carling; Historical Report Concerning Lands Ceded to the U.S. by Flathead, Pend D'oreille & Kutenai Indians. Burlingame, Merrill G. (American Indian Ethnohistory Ser: Indians of the Northwest). (Illus.). lib. bdg. 42.00 (ISBN 0-8240-0753-0). Garland Pub.

Interior Salish & Eastern Washington Indians, Vol. 3. Incl. The Confederated Salish & Kutenai Tribes of the Flathead Reservation, Montana. Fuller, E. O; Aboriginal Territory of the Kalispel Indians. Chalfant, Stuart A; History of the Confederated Salish & Kootenai Tribes of the Flathead Reservation, Montana. Phillips, Paul C; Flathead, Kutenai & Upper Pend D'oreille Genealogies. Malouf, Carling & Phillips, Paul C.; Findings of Fact, & Opinion. Indian Claims Commission. (American Indian Ethnohistory Ser: Indians of the Northwest). (Illus.). lib. bdg. 42.00 (ISBN 0-8240-0754-9). Garland Pub.

Interior Salish & Eastern Washington Indians, Vol. 4. Incl. Ethnohistorical Report on Aboriginal Land Use & Occupancy by Spokan Indians. Chalfant, Stuart A; Ethnohistory of the Spokane Indians. Anastasio, Angelo; Ethnohistorical Report on Aboriginal Land Occupancy & Utilization by Palus Indians. Chalfant, Stuart A; Anthropological & Ethnohistorical Material Relative to Aboriginial Land Use & Occupancy by the Columbia Salish of Central Washington. Chalfant, Stuart A; Anthropological & Ethnohistorical Material Relative to Aboriginal Land Use & Occupancy by the Wenatchi Salish of Central Washington. Chalfant, Stuart A; Ethnological Notes on the Columbia, Chelan, Entiat & Wenatchee Tribes. Ray, Verne F; Findings of Fact, & Opinion. Indian Claims Commission. (American Indian Ethnohistory Ser: Indians of the Northwest). (Illus.). lib. bdg. 42.00 (ISBN 0-8240-0782-4). Garland Pub.

Inverarity, Robert B. Art of the Northwest Coast Indians. 2nd ed. (Illus.). 1967. pap. 10.95 (ISBN 0-520-00595-3). U of Cal Pr.

Iokhel'Son, V. I. The Koryak. LC 73-3661. (The Jesup North Pacific Expedition Publications: Vol. 6). Repr. of 1908 ed. 82.50 (ISBN 0-404-58106-4). AMS Pr.

--The Yukaghir & the Yukaghirized Tungus. LC 73-3531. (The Jesup North Pacific Expedition Publications: Vol. 9). Repr. of 1926 ed. 52.50 (ISBN 0-404-58109-9). AMS Pr.

Jilek, Wolfgang G. Indian Healing: Shamanic Ceremonialism in the Pacific Northwest Today. rev. ed. (Cultures in Review Ser.). Orig. Title: Salish Indian Mental Health & Culture Change. 184p. 1981. pap. text ed. 7.95 (ISBN 0-88839-120-X, Pub. by Hancock Hse). Universe.

Kaiper, Daniel & Kapier, N. Tlingit: Their Art, Culture & Legends. (Native Culture Ser.). (Illus., Orig.). 1978. pap. 4.00 (ISBN 0-88839-010-6, Pub. by Hancock Hse). Universe.

Keithan, L., ed. Monuments in Cedar. encore ed. LC 63-15216. 1963. 9.95 (ISBN 0-87564-854-1). Superior Pub.

Kip, Lawrence. Indian Council at Walla Walla, Washington. Repr. of 1897 ed. pap. 4.25 (ISBN 0-8466-0240-7, SJS240). Shorey.

Krause, Aurel. The Tlingit Indians: Results of a Trip to the Northwest Coast of America & the Bering Straits. Gunther, Erna, tr. LC 56-3408. (American Ethnological Society Monographs: No. 26). (Illus.). 320p. 1970. pap. 6.95 (ISBN 0-295-95075-7, WP58). U of Wash Pr.

Law, Katheryn. Salish Folk Tales. (Indian Culture Ser.). (gr. 2-8). 1972. 1.95 (ISBN 0-89992-028-4). MT Coun Indian.

Lewis, Albert B. Tribes of the Columbia Valley & the Coast of Washington & Oregon. LC 6-44808. 1906. pap. 5.00 (ISBN 0-527-00501-0). Kraus Repr.

Lewis, Claudia. Indian Families of the Northwest Coast: The Impact of Change. LC 70-108776. 1970. 12.00x (ISBN 0-226-47686-3). U of Chicago Pr.

Lloyd, J. P. Message of an Indian Relic: Seattle's Own Totem Pole. facs. ed. (Illus.). 21p. Repr. of 1909 ed. pap. 3.25 (ISBN 0-8466-4006-6, SJ16). Shorey.

McDonald, W. H. Creation Tales from the Salish. (Indian Culture Ser.). (gr. 3-9). 1973. 1.95 (ISBN 0-89992-061-6). MT Coun Indian.

McFeat, Tom, ed. Indians of the North Pacific Coast. LC 67-13112. 286p. (Orig.). 1967. pap. 7.95 (ISBN 0-295-74095-7). U of Wash Pr.

McWhorter, Lucullus. Tragedy of the Wahk-Shum. 1968. Repr. 4.95 (ISBN 0-87770-064-8). Ye Galleon.

Malin, Edward. A World of Faces. LC 77-26786. (Illus.). 1978. (Pub. by Timber Pr); pap. 10.95 (ISBN 0-917304-05-5, Pub. by Timber Pr). Intl Schol Bk Serv.

Manring, Benjamin F. The Conquest of the Coeur D'Alenes, Spokanes & Palouses. 280p. 1975. 14.95 (ISBN 0-87770-155-5). Ye Galleon.

Margolin, Malcolm. The Ohlone Way: Indian Life in the San Francisco & Monterey Bay Areas. LC 78-56826. (Illus., Orig.). 1978. 8.95 (ISBN 0-930588-02-9); pap. 5.95 (ISBN 0-930588-01-0). Heyday Bks.

Marsh, Jessie. Chinook. (Indian Culture Ser.). 32p. (ps-9). 1976. 1.95 (ISBN 0-89992-041-1). MT Coun Indian.

May, Allan. The Sea People of Ozette. LC 75-20421. (Illus.). 112p. (Orig.). 1975. pap. 3.95 (ISBN 0-915454-02-5). B & E Ent.

Miller, Jay & Eastman, Carol, eds. The Tsimshian & Other Peoples of the Northwest Coast. 1982. price not set. U of Wash Pr.

Murray, Alberta. These Are My Children. 1977. 9.95 (ISBN 0-87770-194-6). Ye Galleon.

Murray, Henry T. Coeur D'Alene Tribe of Northern Idaho: Appraisal of Aboriginal Lands. (Library of American Indian Affairs). 92p. 1974. lib. bdg. 36.00 (ISBN 0-8287-1008-2). Clearwater Pub.

Niblack, Albert P. The Coast Indians of Southern Alaska & Northern British Columbia. LC 14-19260. 1971. Repr. of 1890 ed. 23.00 (ISBN 0-384-41365-X). Johnson Repr.

Oregon Indians, Vol. 1. Incl. Anthropological Investigation of the Tillamook Indians. Taylor, Herbert C; Anthropological Investigation of the Chinook Indians. Taylor, Herbert C; Ethnological Report on the Identity & Localization of Certain Native Peoples of Northwestern Oregon. Suphan, Robert J; Findings of Fact, & Opinion. Indian Claims Commission. (American Indian Ethnohistory: Indians of the Northwest). (Illus.). lib. bdg. 42.00 (ISBN 0-8240-0777-8). Garland Pub.

Oregon Indians, Vol. 2. Incl. Ethnological Report on the Wasco & Tenino Indians Relative to Socio-Political Organization & Land Use. Suphan, Robert J; Ethnological Report on the Umatilla, Walla Walla & Cayuse Indians Relative to Socio-Political Organization & Land Use. Suphan, Robert J; Findings of Fact, & Opinion. Indian Claims Commission. (American Indian Ethnohistory Ser: Indians of the Northwest). (Illus.). lib. bdg. 42.00 (ISBN 0-8240-0778-6). Garland Pub.

Osgood, Cornelius. Contributions to the Ethnography of the Kutchin. LC 73-118247. (Yale University Publications in Anthropology Reprints Ser.: No. 14). 190p. 1970. pap. 7.00x (ISBN 0-87536-522-1). HRAFP.

--Ingalik Material Culture. LC 77-118248. (Yale University Publications in Anthropology Reprints Ser.: No. 22). 500p. 1970. pap. 15.00x (ISBN 0-87536-516-7). HRAFP.

Payne, Doris P. Captain Jack, Modoc Renegade. (Illus.). 1979. pap. 5.95 (ISBN 0-8323-0295-3). Binford.

Peterson, Robert M. A Case Study of a Northern California Indian Tribe: Cultural Change to 1860. LC 77-75489. 1977. 8.00 (ISBN 0-685-82440-3). R & E Res Assoc.

Powell, Jay & Jensen, Vickie. Quileute: An Introduction to the Indians of La Push. LC 75-40877. (Illus.). 80p. 1976. 11.50 (ISBN 0-295-95492-2); pap. 4.95 (ISBN 0-295-95493-0). U of Wash Pr.

Ray, Verne F. The Klamath Indians & Their Forest Resources, Oregon, 1864-1961. 44.00 (ISBN 0-8287-1097-X). Clearwater Pub.

--The Sanpoil & Nespelem: Salishan Peoples of Northeastern Washington. LC 76-43809. (Univ. of Washington Publications in Anthropology: Vol. 5). Repr. of 1933 ed. 24.50 (ISBN 0-404-15663-0). AMS Pr.

Reiss, W. & Linderman, F. B. Blackfeet Indians. 1977. lib. bdg. 75.95 (ISBN 0-8490-1513-8). Gordon Pr.

Riley, Carroll L. Ethnological Field Investigation & Analysis of Historical Material Relative to Group Distribution & Utilization of Natural Resources Among Puget Sound Indians in Washington. 59p. 1974. lib. bdg. 26.50 (ISBN 0-8287-1037-6). Clearwater Pub.

--Makah Indians of Western Washington: A Study of Group Distribution, Political Organization & Concepts of Land Use. (Library of American Indian Affairs). 1976. lib. bdg. 20.00x (ISBN 0-8287-1111-9). Clearwater Pub.

Rohner, R. P. & Rohner, E. Kwakiutl: Indians of British Columbia. LC 72-101691. (Case Studies in Cultural Anthropology). 1970. pap. text ed. 4.95 (ISBN 0-03-079070-0, HoltC). HR&W.

Ronan, Peter. Historical Sketch of the Flathead Nation. 1890. Repr. 6.95 (ISBN 0-87018-054-1). Ross.

Ruby, Robert H. & Brown, John A. The Cayuse Indians: Imperial Tribesmen of Old Oregon. LC 74-177345. (Civilization of the American Indian Ser.: Vol. 120). (Illus.). 320p. 1972. 17.95 (ISBN 0-8061-0995-5); pap. 8.95 (ISBN 0-8061-1316-2). U of Okla Pr.

--The Chinook Indians: Traders of the Lower Columbia River. LC 75-40148. (The Civilization of the American Indian Ser: Vol.138). 1976. 17.95 (ISBN 0-8061-1325-1). U of Okla Pr.

--Indians of the Pacific Northwest: A History. LC 80-5946. (Civilization of the American Indian Ser.: Vol. 158). (Illus.). 300p. 1981. 24.95 (ISBN 0-8061-1731-1). U of Okla Pr.

Ruppel, Maxine. Vostaas: The Story of Montana's Indian Nations. (Indian Culture Ser.). (gr. 3-11). 1970. 2.00 (ISBN 0-89992-001-2). MT Coun Indian.

Samuel, Cheryl. The Chilkat Dancing Blanket. 1982. price not set. U of Wash Pr.

Sapir, Edward & Swadesh, Morris. Native Accounts of Nootka Ethnography. LC 74-7999. Repr. of 1955 ed. 34.50 (ISBN 0-404-11892-5). AMS Pr.

Sapir, Edward, ed. Wishram Texts: Together with Wasco Tales & Myths. LC 73-3536. (American Ethnological Society. Publications: No. 2). Repr. of 1909 ed. 24.75 (ISBN 0-404-58152-8). AMS Pr.

Saunderson, Mont H. Blackfeet Tribe Ceded Lands in Montana, Agreement of May 1, 1888: Valuation. (Library of American Indian Affairs). (Illus.). 100p. 1974. 36.00 (ISBN 0-8287-0959-9). Clearwater Pub.

Sauter, John & Johnson, Bruce. Tillamook Indians of the Oregon Coast. LC 73-89238. (Illus.). 1974. 8.95 (ISBN 0-8323-0212-0); pap. 5.95 (ISBN 0-8323-0227-9). Binford.

Seaman, N. G. Indian Relics of the Pacific Northwest. 2nd enl. ed. LC 66-28021. (Illus.). 1967. pap. 5.95 (ISBN 0-8323-0236-8). Binford.

Sewid, James. Guests Never Leave Hungry: The Autobiography of James Sewid, a Kwakiutl Indian. Spradley, James P., ed. (Illus.). 1969. 20.00x (ISBN 0-300-01075-3). Yale U Pr.

Smith, Marian W. Indians of the Urban Northwest. LC 74-82339. (Columbia Univ. Contributions to Anthropology Ser.: Vol. 36). 1969. Repr. of 1949 ed. 29.50 (ISBN 0-404-50586-4). AMS Pr.

--Puyallup-Nisqually. LC 73-82360. (Columbia Univ. Contributions to Anthropology Ser.: Vol. 32). 1969. Repr. of 1940 ed. 27.00 (ISBN 0-404-50582-1). AMS Pr.

Spicer, Edward H., ed. Perspectives in American Indian Culture Change. LC 60-14358. (Midway Reprint Ser). 1975. pap. 17.00x (ISBN 0-226-76971-2). U of Chicago Pr.

Spier, L. Klamath Ethnography. 1930. pap. 35.00 (ISBN 0-527-01386-2). Kraus Repr.

--Klamath Ethnography. 1930. pap. 35.00 (ISBN 0-527-01386-2). Kraus Repr.

Spier, Leslie. The Prophet Dance of the Northwest & Its Derivatives: The Source of the Ghost Dance. LC 76-43853. Repr. of 1935 ed. 18.00 (ISBN 0-404-15708-4). AMS Pr.

Spinden, Herbert J. Nez Perce Indians. LC 8-34805. 1908. pap. 8.00 (ISBN 0-527-00508-8). Kraus Repr.

Spindler, George & Spindler, Louise. Native North American Cultures: Four Cases. LC 76-23178. 1977. pap. text ed. 8.95 (ISBN 0-03-018401-0, HoltC). HR&W.

Stern, Bernhard J. Lummi Indians of Northwest Washington. LC 71-82357. (Columbia Univ. Contributions to Anthropology Ser.: Vol. 17). Repr. of 1934 ed. 15.00 (ISBN 0-404-50567-8). AMS Pr.

Stewart, Hilary. Indian Artifacts of the Northwest Coast. LC 73-84986. (Illus.). 172p. 1976. 20.00 (ISBN 0-295-95419-1). U of Wash Pr.

Stock, Leon L. Seahb Siwash. (Illus.). 352p. 1981. 15.00 (ISBN 0-89962-227-5). Todd & Honeywell.

Strong, Emory. Stone Age on the Columbia River. 2nd rev. & enl. ed. LC 70-87130. (Illus.). 1967. 8.95 (ISBN 0-8323-0135-3). Binford.

Strong, Thomas N. Cathlamet on the Columbia. new ed. (Illus.). 1981. pap. 5.95 (ISBN 0-8323-0378-X). Binford.

Suttles, Wayne P. Coast Salish & Western Washington Indians, Vol. 1: The Economic Life of the Coast Salish of Haro & Rosario Straits. (American Indian Ethnohistory Ser.: Indians of the Northwest). (Illus.). lib. bdg. 42.00 (ISBN 0-8240-0783-2). Garland Pub.

Swan, James G. Haidah Indians of Queen Charlotte Islands. 17p. Repr. of 1874 ed. pap. 7.00 (ISBN 0-8466-0034-X, SJS34). Shorey.

Swanton, John R. Haida Texts & Myths: Skidegate Dialect. LC 5-41613. (Landmarks in Anthropology Ser). Repr. of 1905 ed. pap. 28.00 (ISBN 0-384-59020-9). Johnson Repr.

--Indian Tribes of Washington, Oregon & Idaho. 1979. 5.50 (ISBN 0-87770-218-7). Ye Galleon.

Taylor, Herbert C. Chinook Indians: Anthropological Identity & Aboriginal Possession of Lands. 27.00 (ISBN 0-8287-0988-2). Clearwater Pub.

--Tillamook Indians: Anthropological Identity & Aboriginal Possession of Lands. 31.00 (ISBN 0-8287-1276-X). Clearwater Pub.

Turney-High, Harry H. Ethnography of the Kutenai. LC 41-16930. 1941. pap. 14.00 (ISBN 0-527-00555-X). Kraus Repr.

Uhlenbeck, Christianus C. A Concise Blackfoot Grammar. LC 76-44082. (Verhandelingen der Koninklijke Akademie Van Wetenschappen Te Amsterdam. Afdeeling Letterkunde. Nieuwe Reeks, Deel: 41). Repr. of 1938 ed. 27.50 (ISBN 0-404-15797-1). AMS Pr.

--A New Series of Blackfoot Texts. LC 76-44083. (Verhandelingen der Koninklijke Akademie Van Wetenschappen Te Amsterdam. Afdeeling Letterkunde. Nieuwe Reeks Deel: 13, No. 1). Repr. of 1912 ed. 19.50 (ISBN 0-404-15798-X). AMS Pr.

Uhlenbeck, Christianus C. & Van Gulik, R. H. A Blackfoot-English Vocabulary. LC 76-44086. (Verhardelingen der Koninklijke Akademie Van Wetenschappen Te Amsterdam. Afdeeling Letterkunde. Nieuwe Reeks: 33, No. 2). Repr. of 1934 ed. 35.50 (ISBN 0-404-15795-5). AMS Pr.

--An English-Blackfoot Vocabulary. LC 76-44087. (Verhandelingen der Koninklijke Akademie Van Wetenschappen Te Amsterdam. Afdeeling Letterkunde. Nieuwe Reeks: 29, No. 4). Repr. of 1930 ed. 26.50 (ISBN 0-404-15796-3). AMS Pr.

Underhill, Ruth M. Indians of the Pacific Northwest. LC 76-43876. (Indian Life & Customs: No. 5). 1977. Repr. of 1945 ed. 27.50 (ISBN 0-404-15734-3). AMS Pr.

Vaughan, Thomas, ed. Paul Kane, the Columbia Wanderer: Sketches, Paintings & Comment, 1846-1847. LC 74-176250. (Illus.). 80p. 1971. pap. 3.95 (ISBN 0-87595-029-9). Oreg Hist Soc.

Walens, Stanley. Feasting with Cannibals: An Essay on Kwakiutl Cosmology. LC 81-47161. (Illus.). 236p. 1981. 15.00x (ISBN 0-691-09392-X). Princeton U Pr.

Wallas, James & Whitaker, Pamela. Kwakiutl Legends. 150p. 1981. text ed. 17.95x (ISBN 0-87663-632-6, Pub. by Hancock Hse). Universe.

Wardwell, Allen. Objects of Bright Pride: Northwest Coast Indian Art from the American Museum of Natural History. LC 78-67113. (Illus.). 1978. pap. 10.95 (ISBN 0-917418-61-1). Am Fed Arts.

Wedel, Waldo R. The Kansa Indians, Prehistoric & Historic Habitat. 20.00 (ISBN 0-8287-1085-6). Clearwater Pub.

Wessel, Thomas R. The Blackfeet Indian Reservation in Montana: Historical Report. 95.00 (ISBN 0-8287-0958-0). Clearwater Pub.

White, James S. Diving for Northwest Relics. LC 79-1869. (Illus.). 1979. 8.95 (ISBN 0-8323-0329-1); pap. 6.50 (ISBN 0-8323-0330-5). Binford.

Wingert, S. American Indian Sculpture: A Study of the Northwest Coast. LC 75-11063. 1976. Repr. of 1947 ed. lib. bdg. 30.00 (ISBN 0-87817-168-1). Hacker.

Wolcott, Harry F. Kwakiutl Village & School. LC 67-11818. (Studies in Education & Culture). (Orig.). 1967. pap. text ed. 5.95 (ISBN 0-03-061775-8, HoltC). HR&W.

Wolf, Beverly H. The Ways of My Grandmothers. 224p. 1981. pap. 5.95 (ISBN 0-688-00471-7). Morrow.

Woodcock, George. Peoples of the Coast: The Indians of the Pacific Northwest. LC 77-6964. (Illus.). 208p. 1977. 18.95x (ISBN 0-253-34344-5). Ind U Pr.

Work, John. The Snake Country Expedition of 1830-1831: John Work's Field Journal. Haines, Francis D., Jr., ed. (American Exploration & Travel Ser.: No. 59). (Illus.). 224p. 1971. 11.95 (ISBN 0-8061-0947-5). U of Okla Pr.

INDIANS OF NORTH AMERICA–SOUTHWEST, NEW

see also Pueblos

Alexander, Eveline M. Cavalry Wife: The Diary of Eveline M. Alexander, 1866-1867. Myres, Sandra L., intro. by. LC 76-30611. (Illus.). 186p. 1977. 11.50 (ISBN 0-89096-025-9). Tex A&M Univ Pr.

Allen, T. D. Navahos Have Five Fingers. LC 63-17167. (The Civilization of the American Indian Ser.: Vol. 68). (Illus.). 249p. 1981. 13.95 (ISBN 0-8061-0575-5). U of Okla Pr.

Amsden, Charles A. Navaho Weaving, Its Technic & History. Repr. 15.00 (ISBN 0-686-20687-8). Southwest Mus.

Anderson, Susanne. Song of the Earth Spirit. (Celebrating the Earth Ser). (Illus.). 128p. 1974. 14.95 (ISBN 0-913890-26-X). Friends Earth.

Apache Indians, Vol. 2. Incl. The Ascarate Grant. Bowden, Jocelyn J; An Ethnological Study of Tortugas, New Mexico. Oppenheimer, Alan J. (American Indian Ethnohistory Ser: Indians of the Southwest). (Illus.). lib. bdg. 42.00 (ISBN 0-8240-0716-6). Garland Pub.

Apache Indians, Vol. 3. Incl. Aboriginal Use & Occupation of Certain Lands by Tigua, Manso & Suma Indians. Gerald, Rex E; History & Administration of the Tigua Indians of Ysleta Del Sur During the Spanish Colonial Period. Jenkins, Myra E; Apache Ethnohistory: Government, Land & Indian Policies Relative to Lipan, Mescalero & Tigua Indians. Neighbours, Kenneth F. (American Indian Ethnohistory Ser: Indians of the Southwest). (Illus.). lib. bdg. 42.00 (ISBN 0-8240-0717-4). Garland Pub.

Armstrong, Nancy. Navajo Children. (Indian Culture Ser.). (gr. 2-6). 1975. 1.95 (ISBN 0-89992-037-3). MT Coun Indian.

Bahti, Tom. Southwestern Indian Tribes. LC 68-31188. (Illus.). 1968. 7.95 (ISBN 0-916122-26-3); pap. 3.75 (ISBN 0-916122-01-8). KC Pubns.

Bailey, F. L. Some Sex Beliefs & Practices in a Navaho Community. (Harvard University Peabody Museum of Archaeology & Ethnology Papers Ser). 1950. pap. 7.00 (ISBN 0-527-01300-5). Kraus Repr.

Bailey, Flora L. Sex Beliefs & Practices in a Navaho Community with Comparative Material from Other Navaho Areas. LC 52-8354. (Papers: Vol. 40, No. 2). 1950. pap. 10.00 (ISBN 0-87365-118-9). Peabody Harvard.

Bailey, Lynn R. Bosque Redondo: A Study of Cultural Stress at the Navajo Reservation, 1863-1868. (Illus.). 275p. 8.50 (ISBN 0-87026-043-X). Westernlore.

--If You Take My Sheep... The Evolution & Conflicts of Navajo Pastoralism, 1630-1868. (Illus.). 304p. 12.00 (ISBN 0-87026-050-2). Westernlore.

--The Long Walk. (Illus.). 1979. 9.50 (ISBN 0-87026-047-2). Westernlore.

Baird, W. David. The Quapaw Indians: A History of the Downstream People. LC 79-4731. (Civilization of the American Indian Ser.: Vol. 152). (Illus.). 1980. 19.95 (ISBN 0-8061-1542-4). U of Okla Pr.

Baker, Betty. Settlers & Strangers: Native Americans of the Desert Southwest & History As They Saw It. LC 77-4925. (Illus.). (gr. 3-6). 1977. 8.95 (ISBN 0-02-708220-2, 70822). Macmillan.

Ball, Eve. In the Days of Victorio: Recollections of a Warm Springs Apache. LC 73-101103. 1970. pap. 5.95 (ISBN 0-8165-0401-6). U of Ariz Pr.

--Indeh: An Apache Odyssey. LC 80-13186. (Illus.). 1980. 19.95 (ISBN 0-8425-1789-8). Brigham.

Bandelier, A. F. Scientist on the Trail. Hammond, George P., ed. LC 67-24721. (Quivira Society Publications, Vol. 10). 1967. Repr. of 1949 ed. 12.00 (ISBN 0-405-00084-7). Arno.

Bandelier, Adolf F. Delight Makers. LC 70-28000. 1971. pap. 7.95 (ISBN 0-15-625264-3, HB203, Harv). HarBraceJ.

--Final Report of Investigations Among the Indians of the Southwestern U.S, 2 vols. LC 74-7918. Repr. of 1892 ed. Set. 63.00 (ISBN 0-404-58054-8); index 11.50 (ISBN 0-404-58056-4). AMS Pr.

--Historical Introduction to Studies Among the Sedentary Indians of New Mexico & a Report on the Ruins of the Pueblo at Pecos. LC 76-20788. Repr. of 1881 ed. 14.00 (ISBN 0-404-58051-3). AMS Pr.

Bandelier, Adolph F. & Hewett, Edgar L. Indians of the Rio Grande Valley. LC 72-95268. (Illus.). 274p. 1973. Repr. of 1939 ed. lib. bdg. 16.50x (ISBN 0-8154-0462-X). Cooper Sq.

Bandelier, Adolph F. & Ten Kate, Herman F. An Outline of the Documentary History of the Zuni Tribe: Somatological Observations of Indians of the Southwest. LC 76-21219. (A Journal of American Ethnology & Archaeology: Vol. 3). Repr. of 1892 ed. 20.00 (ISBN 0-404-58043-2). AMS Pr.

Barnett, Franklin. Excavation of Main Pueblo at Fitzmaurice Ruin. (Special Publications Ser.: No. 10). (Illus.). 1974. pap. 7.50 (ISBN 0-89734-017-5). Mus Northern Ariz.

Barrett, Samuel A. Material Aspects of Pomo Culture, 2 pts. in 1 vol. LC 76-43649. (Bulletin of the Public Museum of the City of Milwaukee: Vol. 20). Repr. of 1952 ed. 57.50 (ISBN 0-404-15483-2). AMS Pr.

--The Washo Indians. LC 76-43651. (Bulletin of the Public Museum of the City of Milwaukee: Vol. 2, No. 1). Repr. of 1917 ed. 14.00 (ISBN 0-404-15485-9). AMS Pr.

Basehart, Harry W. Apache Indians XII. Horr, David A., ed. (American Indian Ethnohistory Ser.). 1978. lib. bdg. 42.00 (ISBN 0-8240-0713-1). Garland Pub.

--Mescalero Apache Subsistence Patterns & Socio-Political Organization, New Mexico, 1796-1875. (Library of American Indian Affairs). 166p. 1974. lib. bdg. 52.00 (ISBN 0-8287-1117-8). Clearwater Pub.

Basso, K. H. The Cibecue Apache. LC 70-100384. (Case Studies in Cultural Anthropology). 1970. pap. text ed. 5.95 (ISBN 0-03-083171-7, HoltC). HR&W.

Basso, Keith H. Portraits of the Whiteman. LC 78-31535. 1979. 17.95 (ISBN 0-521-22640-6); pap. 4.95 (ISBN 0-521-29593-9). Cambridge U Pr.

Basso, Keith H. & Opler, Morris, eds. Apachean Culture History & Ethnology. LC 70-140453. (Anthropological Papers: No. 21). (Illus.). 172p. (Orig.). 1971. pap. 6.95x (ISBN 0-8165-0295-1). U of Ariz Pr.

Baylor, Byrd. When Clay Sings. LC 70-180758. (Illus.). (gr. 1-5). 1972. reinforced bdg. 8.95 (ISBN 0-684-12807-1, ScribJ). Scribner.

Beaglehole, Ernest. Notes on Hopi Economic Life. LC 76-43655. (Yale University Publications in Anthropology: No. 15). Repr. of 1937 ed. 18.50 (ISBN 0-404-15489-1). AMS Pr.

Beaglehole, Ernest & Beaglehole, Pearl. Hopi of the Second Mesa. LC 36-5468. 1935. pap. 5.00 (ISBN 0-527-00543-6). Kraus Repr.

Beals, Alan R. & Siegel, Bernard J. Divisiveness & Social Conflict: An Anthropological Approach. 1966. 12.50x (ISBN 0-8047-0302-7). Stanford U Pr.
Bean, John Lowell & Lawton, Harry W. The Cahuilla Indians of Southern California. 1965. 1.00 (ISBN 0-686-25508-9). Malki Mus Pr.
Bean, Lowell J. Mukat's People: The Cahuilla Indians of Southern California. LC 78-145782. (Illus.). 300p. 1972. 15.95x (ISBN 0-520-01912-1); pap. 5.75x (ISBN 0-520-02627-6). U of Cal Pr.
Bender, Averam B. Apache Indians IX. Horr, David A., ed. (American Indian Ethnohistory Ser.). 1978. lib. bdg. 42.00 (ISBN 0-8240-0711-5). Garland Pub.
--Mescalero Apache Indians in New Mexico & Arizona, 1846-1880. (Library of American Indian Affairs). 238p. 1974. lib. bdg. 69.00 (ISBN 0-8287-1116-X). Clearwater Pub.
Bender, Averam B., et al. Apache Indians V. Horr, David A., ed. (American Indian Ethnohistory Ser.). 1978. lib. bdg. 42.00 (ISBN 0-8240-0720-4). Garland Pub.
Benedict, Ruth. Tales of the Cochiti Indians. 256p. 1981. 9.95 (ISBN 0-8263-0569-5). U of NM Pr.
--Tales of the Cochiti Indians. 1976. lib. bdg. 59.95 (ISBN 0-8490-2729-2). Gordon Pr.
Bennett, Kenneth A. The Indians of Point of Pines, Arizona: A Comparative Study of Their Physical Characteristics. LC 72-76616. (Anthropological Papers: No. 23). 1973. pap. 3.95x (ISBN 0-8165-0355-9). U of Ariz Pr.
Boyce, George A. When Navajos Had Too Many Sheep: The 1940's. Henry, Jeannette, ed. LC 73-93691. (Illus.). 288p. 1974. pap. 5.00 (ISBN 0-913436-13-5). Indian Hist Pr.
Branson, Oscar T. Fetishes & Carvings of the Southwest. 1977. 12.95 (ISBN 0-442-21417-0). Van Nos Reinhold.
Brant, Charles S. Jim Whitewolf: The Life of a Kiowa Apache. LC 67-25596. (Orig.). 1969. pap. 2.25 (ISBN 0-486-22015-X). Dover.
Brayer, Herbert O. Pueblo Indian Land Grants of the "Rio Abajo", New Mexico. Bruchey, Stuart, ed. LC 78-56700. (Management of Public Lands in the U. S. Ser.). 1979. Repr. of 1938 ed. lib. bdg. 10.00x (ISBN 0-405-11320-X). Arno.
Brew, J. O. Archaeology of Alkali Ridge, Southeastern Utah. 1946. pap. 49.00 (ISBN 0-685-13693-0). Kraus Repr.
Brody, J. J. Mimbres Painted Pottery. LC 76-57542. (Southwest Indian Arts Ser). (Illus.). 253p. 1977. 35.00x (ISBN 0-8263-0452-4). U of NM Pr.
Brown, Donald N. People of the Mountain Place: Picuris Pueblo, New Mexico. Date not set. price not set (ISBN 0-8165-0516-0). U of Ariz Pr.
Brown, Vinson. Pomo Indians of California & Their Neighbors. Elsasser, Albert B., ed. (American Indian Map Bk Ser.: Vol. 1). (Illus., Orig.). (gr. 4 up). 1969. 8.50 (ISBN 0-911010-31-9); pap. 4.50 (ISBN 0-911010-30-0). Naturegraph.
Browne, John R. Apache Country. (Golden West Ser.). 1978. pap. 1.50 (ISBN 0-8439-0520-4, Leisure Bks). Nordon Pubns.
Bunting, et al. Taos Adobes. 1975. pap. 7.95 (ISBN 0-89013-088-4). Museum NM Pr.
Bunzel, Ruth L. Pueblo Potter: A Study of Creative Imagination in Primitive Art. LC 73-82257. (Columbia Univ. Contributions to Anthropology Ser.: Vol. 8). (Illus.). Repr. of 1929 ed. 55.00 (ISBN 0-404-50558-9). AMS Pr.
--Zuni Texts. LC 73-3551. (American Ethnological Society. Publications: No. 15). Repr. of 1933 ed. 23.00 (ISBN 0-404-58165-X). AMS Pr.
Burton, H. K. The Re-Establishment of the Indians in Their Pueblo Life Through the Revival of Their Traditional Crafts. LC 36-35586. Repr. of 1936 ed. 11.00 (ISBN 0-527-03236-0). Kraus Repr.
Casebier, Dennis G. Camp Beale's Springs & the Hualpai Indians. LC 79-92835. (Illus.). 240p. (Orig.). 1980. 18.50 (ISBN 0-914224-08-5). Tales Mojave Rd.
Castetter, Edward F. & Bell, Willis. Pima & Papago Indian Agriculture. LC 76-43674. Repr. of 1942 ed. 21.00 (ISBN 0-404-15510-3). AMS Pr.
Castetter, Edward F. & Underhill, Ruth. The Ethnobiology of the Papago Indians. LC 76-43676. (University of New Mexico Bulletin Biological Ser.: Vol. 4). Repr. of 1935 ed. 14.00 (ISBN 0-404-15509-X). AMS Pr.
Chamberlin, Ralph V. Ethno-Botany of the Gosiute Indians of Utah. LC 14-11549. 1911. pap. 7.00 (ISBN 0-527-00510-X). Kraus Repr.
Chapin, Frederick H. The Land of the Cliff-Dwellers. LC 74-7945. Repr. of 1892 ed. 23.50 (ISBN 0-404-11832-1). AMS Pr.
Chaudhuri, Joyotpaul. Urban Indians of Arizona: Phoenix, Tucson & Flagstaff. LC 74-15604. (Institute of Government Research Ser). pap. 1.95x (ISBN 0-8165-0477-6). U of Ariz Pr.
Christensen, Mervin J. & Hill, R. G. The Mohave Tribe in Arizona: An Appraisal of Land Values from 1942 to 1952 & 1940 to 1953. Ross, Norman A., ed. (Library of American Indian Affairs). 1976. lib. bdg. 50.00x (ISBN 0-8287-1131-3). Clearwater Pub.
Clark, La Verne H. They Sang for Horses: The Impact of the Horse on Navajo & Apache Folklore. LC 66-18527. (Illus.). 1966. pap. 9.95 (ISBN 0-8165-0091-6). U of Ariz Pr.
Clemmer, Richard O. Continuities of Hopi Culture Change. 1978. pap. 9.50 (ISBN 0-916552-15-2). Acoma Bks.
Clum, W. Apache Agent: The Story of John P. Clum. 1977. lib. bdg. 59.95 (ISBN 0-8490-1441-7). Gordon Pr.
Clum, Woodworth. Apache Agent: The Story of John P. Clum. LC 77-14135. (Illus.). 1978. 13.95x (ISBN 0-8032-0967-3); pap. 4.25 (ISBN 0-8032-5886-0, BB 654, Bison). U of Nebr Pr.
Collier, John. On the Gleaming Way: Navajos, Eastern Pueblos, Zunis, Hopis, Apaches & Their Land, & Their Meanings to the World. LC 62-12407. 163p. (Photos, Orig). 1962. pap. 5.95 (ISBN 0-8040-0232-0, SB). Swallow.
Colton, Harold S. Black Sand: Prehistory in Northern Arizona. LC 73-13454. (Illus.). 132p. 1974. Repr. of 1960 ed. lib. bdg. 15.00x (ISBN 0-8371-7137-7, COBS). Greenwood.
Colton, Harold S. & Hargrave, Lyndon L. Handbook of Northern Arizona Pottery Wares. LC 76-43677. (Museum of Northern Arizona Bulletin: No. 11). Repr. of 1937 ed. 32.50 (ISBN 0-404-15511-1). AMS Pr.
Colton, Mary-Russell F. Hopi Dyes. 2nd ed. LC 78-60236. (Special Publications Ser.). (Illus.). pap. 4.95 (ISBN 0-89734-000-0). Mus Northern Ariz.
Colyer, Vincent. Peace with the Apaches of New Mexico & Arizona. facsimile ed. LC 70-165622. (Select Bibliographies Reprint Ser). Repr. of 1872 ed. 10.00 (ISBN 0-8369-5929-9). Arno.
Coolidge, Dane & Coolidge, Mary R. The Navajo Indians. LC 76-43679. Repr. of 1930 ed. 28.50 (ISBN 0-404-15513-8). AMS Pr.
Coolidge, Mary E. The Rain-Makers: Indians of Arizona & New Mexico. LC 76-43681. Repr. of 1929 ed. 27.50 (ISBN 0-404-15514-6). AMS Pr.
Cosgrove, Harriet S. & Cosgrove, C. B. Swarts Ruin: A Typical Mimbres Site in Southwestern New Mexico. 1932. pap. 37.00 (ISBN 0-527-01234-3). Kraus Repr.
Couffer, Jack & Couffer, Mike. Canyon Summer. LC 77-4323. (Illus.). (gr. 6-9). 1977. 6.95 (ISBN 0-399-20585-3). Putnam.
Couro, Ted & Langdon, Margaret. Let's Talk 'Iipay Aa: An Introduction to the Mesa Grande Diegueno Language. 1975. pap. 7.50 (ISBN 0-686-22652-6). Malki Mus Pr.
Cozzens, Samuel W. Marvelous Country. 1967. Repr. 12.50 (ISBN 0-87018-011-8). Ross.
Crampton, C. Gregory. The Zunis of Cibola. LC 77-72586. (Illus.). 1977. 20.00 (ISBN 0-87480-120-6). U of Utah Pr.
Cushing, Frank H. My Adventures in Zuni. LC 70-459. (Wild & Woolly West Ser., No. 5). (Illus.). 1967. 7.00 (ISBN 0-910584-80-X); pap. 2.50 (ISBN 0-910584-05-2). Filter.
--Zuni Breadstuff. LC 74-7948. Repr. of 1920 ed. 48.50 (ISBN 0-404-11835-6). AMS Pr.
--Zuni Fetishes. LC 66-23329. (Illus.). 1966. 7.95 (ISBN 0-916122-28-X); pap. 3.00 (ISBN 0-916122-03-4). KC Pubns.
--Zuni: Selected Writings of Frank Hamilton Cushing. Green, Jesse, ed. LC 78-14295. (Illus.). 1979. 16.95 (ISBN 0-8032-2100-2); pap. 8.50 (ISBN 0-8032-7007-0, BB 328, Bison). U of Nebr Pr.
Dale, Edward E. The Indians of the Southwest: A Century of Development Under the United States. (Civilization of the American Indian Ser: No. 28). (Illus.). 1976. pap. 8.95 (ISBN 0-8061-1314-6). U of Okla Pr.
Davis, William W. El Gringo. LC 72-9438. (The Far Western Frontier Ser.). (Illus.). 436p. 1973. Repr. of 1857 ed. 20.00 (ISBN 0-405-04968-4). Arno.
De Aberle, S. B. The Pueblo Indians of New Mexico: Their Land, Economy & Civil Organization. LC 49-2640. (American Anthropological Association Memoirs). Repr. of 1948 ed. pap. 7.00 (ISBN 0-527-00569-X). Kraus Repr.
De Grazia, Ted. De Grazia Paints the Yaqui Easter. LC 68-22334. (Illus.). 1968. 19.50 (ISBN 0-8165-0023-1). U of Ariz Pr.
De Luxan, Diego P. Expedition into New Mexico Made by Antonio De Espejo 1582-1583. Hammond, George P., ed. LC 67-24713. (Quivira Society Publications, Vol. 1). 1967. Repr. of 1929 ed. 12.00 (ISBN 0-405-00088-X). Arno.
Dennis, Wayne. The Hopi Child. LC 75-169380. (Family in America Ser). (Illus.). 232p. 1972. Repr. of 1940 ed. 13.00 (ISBN 0-405-03857-7). Arno.
Densmore, Frances. Music of Acoma, Isleta, Cochiti, & Zuni Pueblos. LC 72-1877. (Music Ser.). (Illus.). 142p. 1972. Repr. of 1957 ed. lib. bdg. 16.50 (ISBN 0-306-70505-2). Da Capo.
--Papago Music. LC 72-1881. (Music Ser.). (Illus.). 276p. 1972. Repr. of 1929 ed. lib. bdg. 19.50 (ISBN 0-306-70509-5). Da Capo.
Diamond, Rash, Leslie & Schwartz, Inc. Chronology of the Pueblo De la Yseleta Del Sur in Colorado, New Mexico & Texas, 10,000 B.C. to 1969. (Library of American Indian Affairs). 86p. 1974. lib. bdg. 33.00 (ISBN 0-8287-1004-X). Clearwater Pub.
Dillon, Richard H., ed. A Cannoneer in Navajo Country: Journal of Private Josiah M. Rice, 1851. (Illus.). 1970. limited ed. 14.50 (ISBN 0-912094-15-X). Old West.
DiPeso, Charles C. Jicarilla Apache in New Mexico & Oklahoma: Anthropological Report, 1540-1898. (Library of American Indian Affairs). 430p. 1974. lib. bdg. 115.00 (ISBN 0-8287-1076-7). Clearwater Pub.
Dobyns, Henry F. Hualapai Indians, Vol. 1: Prehistoric Indian Occupation Within the Eastern Area of the Yuman Complex: a Study in Applied Archaeology. (American Indian Ethnohistory Ser: Indians of the Southwest). (Illus.). lib. bdg. 42.00 (ISBN 0-8240-0722-0). Garland Pub.
Dobyns, Henry F. & Euler, Robert C. Indians of the Southwest: A Critical Bibliography. LC 80-8036. (The Newberry Library Center for the History of the American Indian Bibliographical Ser.). 176p. 1981. pap. 4.95x (ISBN 0-253-32658-3). Ind U Pr.
Dolaghan, Thomas & Scates, David R. The Navajos Are Coming to Jesus. LC 78-3609. (Illus.). 1978. pap. 4.95 (ISBN 0-87808-162-3). William Carey Lib.
Dorsey, G. A. & Voth, H. R. Oraibi Soyal Ceremony, & Oraibi Powamu Ceremony, & Mishongnovi Ceremonies of the Snake & Antelope Fraternities, & Oraibi Summer Snake Ceremony, 4 wks. in 1 vol. 1901-03. pap. 48.00 (ISBN 0-527-01863-5). Kraus Repr.
Dorsey, George A. Indians of the Southwest. LC 74-7952. (Illus.). Repr. of 1903 ed. 19.50 (ISBN 0-404-11841-0). AMS Pr.
Downs, James F. The Navajo. LC 70-173266. (Case Studies in Cultural Anthropology). 1972. text ed. 4.95 (ISBN 0-03-085483-0, HoltC). HR&W.
--Two Worlds of the Washo: An Indian Tribe of California & Nevada. LC 66-13592. (Case Studies in Cultural Anthropology). (Orig.). 1966. pap. text ed. 6.95 (ISBN 0-03-056610-X, HoltC). HR&W.
Dozier, Edward P. Hano: A Tewa Indian Community in Arizona. LC 65-26674. (Case Studies in Cultural Anthropology). (Orig.). 1966. pap. text ed. 4.95 (ISBN 0-03-055115-3, HoltC). HR&W.
Dumarest, Noel. Notes on Cochiti, New Mexico. LC 20-23196. 1919. pap. 7.00 (ISBN 0-527-00526-6). Kraus Repr.
Duncan, Janice K. Minority Without a Champion: Kanakas on the Pacific Coast, 1788-1850. LC 72-79115. (Illus.). 24p. 1972. pap. 1.00 (ISBN 0-87595-036-1). Oreg Hist Soc.
Dutton, B. The Rancheria, Ute & Southern Paiote Peoples. 1976. 3.95 (ISBN 0-13-752923-6, Spec). P-H.
Dyk, Walter & Dyk, Ruth B. Son of Old Man Hat II: Marriage & Adult Life. (Illus.). 624p. 1980. 27.50 (ISBN 0-231-04946-3). Columbia U Pr.
Dyk, Walter, ed. Old Mexican, Navaho Indian: A Navaho Autobiography. 1947. pap. 15.50 (ISBN 0-384-43215-8). Johnson Repr.
--Son of Old Man Hat: A Navaho Autobiography. LC 44-2654. 1967. pap. 4.95 (ISBN 0-8032-5054-1, BB 355, Bison). U of Nebr Pr.
Eddy, Frank W. Prehistory in the Navajo Reservoir District, 2 pts. (Illus.). 1966. pap. 7.95 ea. Pt. 1 (ISBN 0-89013-023-X). Pt. 2 (ISBN 0-89013-024-8). Museum NM Pr.
Eggan, Fred. Social Organization of the Western Pueblos. LC 50-9388. 1973. pap. 2.95 (ISBN 0-226-19076-5, P557, Phoen). U of Chicago Pr.
Ellis, Florence H. Nambe Pueblos: Anthropological Data Pertaining to Land Claims. (Library of American Indian Affairs). (Illus.). 1976. lib. bdg. 50.00x (ISBN 0-8287-1134-8). Clearwater Pub.
--The Navajo Indians: An Anthropoligical Study. (Library of American Indian Affairs). 1976. lib. bdg. 125.00x (ISBN 0-8287-1137-2). Clearwater Pub.
--Navajo Indians, Vol. 1: Anthropological Study of the Navajo Indians. (American Indian Ethnohistory Ser: Indians of the Southwest). (Illus.). lib. bdg. 42.00 (ISBN 0-8240-0703-4). Garland Pub.
--Pueblo Indians, Vol. Two: Archaeologic & Ethnologic Data: Acoma-Laguna Land Claims. (American Indian Ethnohistory Ser: Indians of the Southwest). (Illus.). lib. bdg. 42.00 (ISBN 0-8240-0726-3). Garland Pub.
--The Pueblos of Zia, Santa Ana & Jemez: Anthropological Evidence in Support of Land Calims. (Library of American Indian Affairs). 1976. lib. bdg. 30.00x (ISBN 0-8287-1209-3). Clearwater Pub.
Elmore, Francis H. Ethnobotany of the Navajo. LC 76-43698. (Univ. of New Mexico Bulletin: Vol. 1, No. 7). Repr. of 1944 ed. 22.50 (ISBN 0-404-15530-8). AMS Pr.
Erdoes, Richard. The Native Americans: Navajos. LC 78-57885. (Illus.). (gr. 5 up). 1978. 14.95 (ISBN 0-8069-2740-2); PLB 13.29 (ISBN 0-8069-2741-0). Sterling.
Euler, Robert C. Southern Paiute Ethnohistory. (University of Utah Anthropological Papers; No. 78, Glen Cannon Ser.: No. 28). (Illus.). 176p. 1973. pap. 15.00x (ISBN 0-87480-094-3). U of Utah Pr.
--Southern Paiute Ethnohistory. (Glen Canyon Ser: No. 28). Repr. of 1966 ed. 24.00 (ISBN 0-404-60678-4). AMS Pr.
Fewkes, Jesse W., et al. The Snake Ceremonials at Walpi. LC 76-17497. (A Journal of American Ethnology & Archaeology: Vol. 4). Repr. of 1894 ed. 17.50 (ISBN 0-404-58044-0). AMS Pr.
Fewkes, Jessie W. & Gilman, Benjamin I. A Few Summer Ceremonials at Zuni Pueblo: Zuni Melodies, Reconnaissance of Ruins in or Near the Zuni Reservation. LC 76-21216. (A Journal of American Ethnology & Archaeology: Vol. 1). Repr. of 1891 ed. 20.00 (ISBN 0-404-58041-6). AMS Pr.
Fishler, Stanley A. In the Beginning: A Navaho Creation Myth. (Utah Anthropological Papers: No. 13). Repr. of 1953 ed. 26.50 (ISBN 0-404-60613-X). AMS Pr.
Forbes, Jack D. Warriors of the Colorado: The Yumas of the Quechan Nation & Their Neighbors. (Civilization of the American Indian Ser.: No. 76). (Illus.). 1965. 19.95 (ISBN 0-8061-0649-2). U of Okla Pr.
Forrest, Earle R. The Snake Dance of the Hopi Indians. LC 61-15835. (Illus.). 8.50 (ISBN 0-87026-018-9). Westernlore.
--Snake Dance of the Hopi Indians. (Illus.). Date not set. 8.50 (ISBN 0-87026-018-9). Westernlore.
--With a Camera in Old Navaholand. LC 69-16727. (Illus.). 1970. 8.95 (ISBN 0-8061-0860-6). U of Okla Pr.
Fox, Nancy. Pueblo Weaving & Textile Arts. (Guidebook Ser.). 1979. pap. 5.95 (ISBN 0-89013-105-8). Museum NM Pr.
Fox, Robin. Keresan Bridge: A Problem in Pueblo Ethnology. (Monographs on Social Anthropology: No. 35). 1967. text ed. 20.75x (ISBN 0-485-19535-6, Athlone Pr). Humanities.
Fraser, Gordon. Rain on the Desert. 160p. (Orig.). 1975. pap. 1.25 (ISBN 0-8024-7153-6). Moody.
Frink, Maurice. Fort Defiance & the Navajos. (Illus.). 150p. (Orig.). 1981. pap. 5.95 (ISBN 0-87108-585-2). Pruett.
Frisbee, Charlotte. Music & Dance Research of the Southwestern Indians. LC 74-74663. (Detroit Studies in Music Bibliography Ser.: No. 36). 1977. 9.75 (ISBN 0-911772-86-3). Info Coord.
Frisbie, Charlotte J., ed. Southwestern Indian Ritual Drama. LC 79-2308. (School of American Research Advanced Seminar Ser.). (Illus.). 384p. 1980. 30.00 (ISBN 0-8263-0521-0). U of NM Pr.
Frisbie, Charlotte J. & McAllester, David P., eds. Navajo Blessingway Singer: The Autobiography of Frank Mitchell, 1881-1967. LC 77-75661. 1978. pap. text ed. 10.50x (ISBN 0-8165-0568-3). U of Ariz Pr.
Garcia. Desert Immigrants: The Mexican of El Paso, 1880-1920. LC 80-36862. (Western Americana Ser.: No. 32). (Illus.). 328p. 1981. text ed. 23.00x (ISBN 0-300-02520-3). Yale U Pr.
Gehm, Katherine. Sarah Winnemucca. LC 75-12600. 185p. 1975. 8.95 (ISBN 0-89019-030-5). O'Sullivan Woodside.
Gerald, Rex E. The Tigua Suma & Manso Indians of Western Texas & New Mexico: From Aboriginal Times to the 1880's. (Library of American Indian Affairs). 116p. 1974. lib. bdg. 26.50 (ISBN 0-8287-1273-5). Clearwater Pub.
Gill, Sam D. Sacred Words: A Study of Navajo Religion & Prayer. LC 80-659. (Contributions in Intercultural & Comparative Studies: No. 4). (Illus.). xxvi, 257p. 1981. lib. bdg. 29.95 (ISBN 0-313-22165-0, GSW/). Greenwood.
Gillmor, Frances & Wetherill, Louisa W. Traders to the Navajos: The Story of the Wetherills of Kayenta. LC 52-9210. 1965. pap. 6.95 (ISBN 0-8263-0040-5). U of NM Pr.

Gilman, Benjamin I. Hopi Songs. LC 76-17498. (A Journal of American Ethnology & Archaeology: Vol. 5). Repr. of 1908 ed. 25.00 (ISBN 0-404-58045-9). AMS Pr.
Gilpin, Laura. The Enduring Navaho. (Illus.). 277p. 1968. 37.50 (ISBN 0-292-78378-7). U of Tex Pr.
Givens, Douglas R. An Analysis of Navajo Temporality. 1977. pap. text ed. 6.50 (ISBN 0-8191-0213-X). U Pr of Amer.
Goddard, Pliny E. Indians of the Southwest. LC 74-20181. (Illus.). 205p. 1975. Repr. of 1931 ed. lib. bdg. 11.00x (ISBN 0-8154-0511-1). Cooper Sq.
--Myths & Tales from the San Carlos Apache. LC 76-43715. (AMNH. Anthropological Pap.: Vol. 29, Pt. 1). Repr. of 1918 ed. 16.50 (ISBN 0-404-15548-0). AMS Pr.
--Navajo Texts. LC 76-44071. (AMNH. Anthropological Papers: Vol. 34, Pt. 1). Repr. of 1933 ed. 16.00 (ISBN 0-404-15775-0). AMS Pr.
Goldfrank, Esther S. Social & Ceremonial Organization of Cochiti. LC 28-11444. 1927. pap. 9.00 (ISBN 0-527-00532-0). Kraus Repr.
Gordon, B. L., et al. Apache Indians VI. Horr, David A., ed. (American Indian Ethnohistory Ser.). 1978. lib. bdg. 42.00 (ISBN 0-8240-0708-5). Garland Pub.
Grant, Blanche C. The Taos Indians. LC 76-40917. (Beautiful Rio Grande Classics Ser). 1976. lib. bdg. 10.00 (ISBN 0-87380-137-7). Rio Grande.
Gregonis, Linda M. Hohokam Indians of the Tucson Bascu. 1979. pap. 1.95x (ISBN 0-8165-0700-7). U of Ariz Pr.
Grey, Herman. Tales from the Mohaves. LC 69-16731. (Civilization of the American Indian Ser.: Vol. 107). 96p. 1980. pap. 3.95 (ISBN 0-8061-1655-2). U of Okla Pr.
Guernsey, Samuel J. Explorations in Northeastern Arizona. 1931. pap. 15.00 (ISBN 0-527-01224-6). Kraus Repr.
Guernsey, Samuel J. & Kidder, A. V. Basket-Maker Caves of Northeastern Arizona. (Illus.). 1921. pap. 12.00 (ISBN 0-527-01213-0). Kraus Repr.
Gunn, John M. Schat-Chen: History, Traditions & Narratives of the Queres Indians of Laguna & Acoma. LC 76-43720. Repr. of 1917 ed. 22.00 (ISBN 0-404-15553-7). AMS Pr.
Gunnerson, Dolores A. The Jicarilla Apaches: A Study in Survival. LC 72-2582. (Illus.). 348p. 1973. 17.50 (ISBN 0-87580-033-5). N Ill U Pr.
--The Jicarilla Apaches: A Study in Survival. LC 72-2582. (Illus.). 348p. 1973. 17.50 (ISBN 0-87580-033-5). N Ill U Pr.
Hack, John T. Changing Physical Environment of the Hopi Indians of Arizona. (Harvard University Peabody Museum of Archaeology & Ethnology Papers). Repr. of 1942 ed. pap. 16.00 (ISBN 0-527-01288-2). Kraus Repr.
Hackenberg, Robert A. Papago Indians in Arizona: Aboriginal Land Use & Occupancy. 89.00 (ISBN 0-8287-1180-1). Clearwater Pub.
Hackett, Charles W., ed. Revolt of the Pueblo Indians of New Mexico & Otermin's Attempted Reconquest, 1680-82, 2 Vols. LC 42-22191. (Coronado Cuarto Centennial Ser.: Vols. VIII & IX). 1942. Set. 30.00x (ISBN 0-8263-0161-4). U of NM Pr.
Haeberlin, Herman K. The Idea of Fertilization in the Culture of the Pueblo Indians. LC 16-25723. Repr. of 1916 ed. pap. 5.00 (ISBN 0-527-00512-6). Kraus Repr.
Hafen, Leroy R. Ute Indians & the San Juan Mining Region: Historical Summary. (Library of American Indian Affairs). 54p. 1974. lib. bdg. 25.00 (ISBN 0-8287-1286-7). Clearwater Pub.
Haile, Berard. Head & Face Masks in Navaho Ceremonialism. LC 76-43722. Repr. of 1947 ed. 17.50 (ISBN 0-404-15565-0). AMS Pr.
--The Navaho Fire Dance, or Corral Dance, 3 vols. in 1. Bd. with The Navaho War Dance. Repr. of 1946 ed; Starlore Among the Navaho. Repr. of 1947 ed. LC 76-43724. 1977. Repr. of 1946 ed. 15.00 (ISBN 0-404-15568-5). AMS Pr.
--Origin Legend of the Navaho Enemy Way. LC 76-43725. (Yale Univ. Pubns. in Anthropology: No. 17). Repr. of 1938 ed. 21.50 (ISBN 0-404-15781-5). AMS Pr.
--Property Concepts of the Navaho Indians. LC 76-43726. Repr. of 1954 ed. 12.50 (ISBN 0-404-15566-9). AMS Pr.
Haley, James L. Apaches: A History & Culture Portrait. LC 76-42331. (Illus.). 504p. 1981. 17.95 (ISBN 0-385-12147-4). Doubleday.
Hall, Geraldine & Goossen, Irvy. Kee's Home: A Beginning Navajo-English Reader. LC 72-174991. (Illus.). (gr. 1-6). 1972. 4.95 (ISBN 0-87358-089-3). Northland.
Harlow, Francis H. Introduction to Hopi Pottery. (Special Publications Ser.). (Illus.). 1978. pap. 2.50 (ISBN 0-89734-022-1). Mus Northern Ariz.
Harvey, Byron. Ritual in Pueblo Art: Hopi Life in Hopi Painting, Vol. 24. LC 67-30973. (Contributions Ser.). (Illus.). 1970. 15.00 (ISBN 0-934490-14-7); soft cover 10.00 (ISBN 0-934490-15-5). Mus Am Ind.
Harvey, Herbert R. The Yuma Reservation: Land Use & Occupancy. 40.00 (ISBN 0-8287-1321-9). Clearwater Pub.
Hatcher, Evelyn. Visual Methaphors: A Formal Analysis of Navajo Art. LC 74-20691. (AES Ser). 1975. text ed. 20.95 (ISBN 0-8299-0026-8). West Pub.
Haury, E. W. Excavation of Los Muertos & Neighboring Ruins in the Salt River Valley, Southern Arizona. 1945. pap. 25.00 (ISBN 0-527-01260-2). Kraus Repr.
Hedrick, Basil C., et al, eds. The Classic Southwest: Readings in Archaeology, Ethnohistory, & Ethnology. LC 70-184966. 206p. 1973. 10.00x (ISBN 0-8093-0547-X). S Ill U Pr.
Hewett, Edgar L. Ancient Life in the American Southwest. LC 67-29548. (Illus.). 1968. Repr. of 1930 ed. 15.00x (ISBN 0-8196-0203-5). Biblo.
--General View of the Archeology of the Pueblo Region: Extracts. facs. ed. 22p. Repr. of 1904 ed. pap. 3.75 (ISBN 0-8466-0160-5, SJS160). Shorey.
Hewett, Edgar L. & Dutton, Bertha P. The Pueblo Indian World. Harrington, John P., ed. LC 76-43737. Repr. of 1945 ed. 18.50 (ISBN 0-404-15578-2). AMS Pr.
Hill, Willard W. The Agricultural & Hunting Methods of the Navaho Indians. LC 76-43742. (Yale Univ. Pubns. in Anthropology: No. 18). Repr. of 1938 ed. 19.50 (ISBN 0-404-15583-9). AMS Pr.
Hoffman, Virginia & Johnson, Broderick. Navajo Biographies, Vol. 2. new ed. (Illus.). 1978. 10.00 (ISBN 0-686-23792-7). Navajo Curr.
Hoijer, Harry & Opler, Morris E. Chiricahua & Mescalero Apache Texts. LC 76-43746. (Univ. of Chicago Pubns. in Anthropology, Linguistics Ser.). Repr. of 1938 ed. 36.50 (ISBN 0-404-15783-1). AMS Pr.
Hopi Indians. Incl. The Hopi: Their History & Use of Lands. Ellis, Florence H; Hopi History & Ethnobotany. Colton, Harold E; Findings of Fact, & Opinion. Indian Claims Commission. (American Indian Ethnohistory Ser: Indians of the Southwest). (Illus.). lib. bdg. 42.00 (ISBN 0-8240-0706-9). Garland Pub.
Hopkins. Life Among the Paiutes: Their Wrongs & Claims. LC 71-102992. 12.95 (ISBN 0-912494-18-2); pap. 8.95 (ISBN 0-912494-06-9). Chalfant Pr.
Hough, Walter. Hopi Indians. (Illus.). Repr. of 1915 ed. pap. 22.00 (ISBN 0-8466-4048-1, SJI48). Shorey.
Hughes, Donald J. American Indians in Colorado. (Illus.). 1977. pap. 5.00 (ISBN 0-87108-206-3). Pruett.
Indian Claims Commission. Paiute Indians, Vol. Five: Findings of Fact, & Opinion. (American Indian Ethnohistory Ser: California & Basin - Plateau Indians). (Illus.). lib. bdg. 42.00 (ISBN 0-8240-0744-1). Garland Pub.
--Puebla Indians, Vol. Five: Findings of Fact, & Opinion. (American Indian Ethnohistory Ser: Indians of the Southwest). (Illus.). lib. bdg. 42.00 (ISBN 0-8240-0729-8). Garland Pub.
Indian Tribes of Texas. (Illus.). 1971. 15.95 (ISBN 0-87244-000-1). Texian.
Iverson, Peter. The Navajo Nation. LC 80-1024. (Contributions in Ethnic Studies: No. 3). (Illus.). xxxii, 273p. 1981. lib. bdg. 25.00 (ISBN 0-313-22309-2, INN/). Greenwood.
James, George W. Lake of the Sky. 1928. 7.95 (ISBN 0-685-19482-5). Powner.
James, H. L. Posts & Rugs. 3rd ed. Jackson, Earl, ed. LC 75-10108. (Popular Ser: No. 15). (Illus.). 1976. 9.00 (ISBN 0-911408-33-9); pap. 7.00 (ISBN 0-911408-35-5). SW Pks Mnmts.
Jicarilla Apache Tribe. Apache Indians VII. Horr, David A., ed. (American Indian Ethnohistory Ser.). 1978. lib. bdg. 42.00 (ISBN 0-8240-0709-3). Garland Pub.
Joe, Eugene B., et al. Navajo Sandpainting Art. (Illus.). 32p. (Orig.). 1978. pap. 4.95 (ISBN 0-918080-20-7). Treasure Chest.
John, Elizabeth A. H. Storms Brewed in Other Men's Worlds: The Confrontation of Indians, Spanish, & French in the Southwest, 1540-1795. LC 75-9996. (Illus.). 840p. 1975. 21.50 (ISBN 0-89096-000-3). Tex A&M Univ Pr.
Johnson, Broderick & Callaway, Sydney M. Denetsosie. rev. ed. LC 73-93973. (Illus.). 51p. 1974. 4.50 (ISBN 0-89019-007-0). Navajo Curr.
Johnson, Broderick, ed. Our Friends: The Navajos. LC 76-13397. (Illus.). 1976. pap. 4.95 (ISBN 0-912586-22-2). Navajo Coll Pr.
Johnson, Broderick & Russell, Ruth, eds. Navajo Livestock Reduction: A National Disgrace. LC 74-78932. (Illus.). 1974. lib. bdg. 9.95 (ISBN 0-912586-18-4). Navajo Coll Pr.
Johnson, Broderick H., ed. Navajo Stories of the Long Walk Period. LC 73-78328. 1975. lib. bdg. 9.95 (ISBN 0-912586-16-8). Navajo Coll Pr.
--Navajos & World War II. Begay, Laura A. & Brown, Henry, trs. from Navajo. LC 77-17543. (Illus.). 1977. pap. 5.50 (ISBN 0-912586-36-2). Navajo Coll Pr.
--Stories of Traditional Navajo Life & Culture. LC 77-22484. (Illus.). 1977. 9.95 (ISBN 0-912586-23-0). Navajo Coll Pr.
Johnston, Bernice E. California's Gabrielino Indians. (Illus.). 1962. 7.50 (ISBN 0-686-20679-7); pap. 3.75 (ISBN 0-686-20680-0). Southwest Mus.
Johnston, Frank. The Serrano Indians of Southern California. 1967. 1.00 (ISBN 0-686-25509-7). Malki Mus Pr.
Jorgensen, Joseph G. & Clemmer, Richard O. Native Americans & Energy Development. LC 78-72986. (Illus.). 1978. pap. 4.50 (ISBN 0-932978-03-7). Anthropology Res.
Joseph, Alice & Spicer, Rosamond B. The Desert People. (Midway Reprint Ser). 288p. 1974. pap. 11.00x (ISBN 0-226-41197-4). U of Chicago Pr.
Joseph, Alice, et al. The Desert People: A Study of the Papago Indians. LC 73-84755. (Illus.). xvii, 287p. Date not set. Repr. of 1947 ed. cancelled (ISBN 0-8462-1736-8). Russell.
Kabotie, Fred & Belknap, Bill. Fred Kabotie: Hopi Indian Artist. LC 77-79071. (Illus.). 1977. 35.00 (ISBN 0-87358-164-4). Northland.
Kammer, Jerry. The Second Long Walk: The Navajo-Hopi Land Dispute. 1980. 14.95 (ISBN 0-8263-0549-0). U of NM Pr.
Kate Cory. (Special Publications Ser). 1978. 30.00 (ISBN 0-89734-002-7). Mus Northern Ariz.
Kavena, Juanita. Hopi Cookery. 1980. pap. 8.50 (ISBN 0-8165-0618-3). U of Ariz Pr.
Keegan, Marcia. Mother Earth, Father Sky: Pueblo & Navajo Indians of the Southwest. LC 73-7091. (Illus.). 128p. 1974. 16.95 (ISBN 0-670-49060-1, Grossman). Viking Pr.
--The Taos Indians & Their Sacred Blue Lake. LC 72-1426. (Illus.). 64p. (gr. 3-6). 1972. PLB 5.29 (ISBN 0-671-32536-1). Messner.
Kelley, Jane Holden. Yaqui Women: Contemporary Life Histories. LC 77-14063. (Illus.). 1978. 12.50 (ISBN 0-8032-0912-6). U of Nebr Pr.
Kelly, Isabel T. Southern Paiute Ethnography: The Eastern Bands. (Library of American Indian Affairs). 188p. 1973. lib. bdg. 57.00 (ISBN 0-8287-1262-X). Clearwater Pub.
--Southern Paiute Ethnology. (Glen Canyon Ser.: No. 21). Repr. of 1964 ed. 17.50 (ISBN 0-404-60669-5). AMS Pr.
Kelly, William H. Cocopa Ethnography. LC 76-18469. (Anthropological Papers Ser.: No. 29). 1977. pap. 7.95x (ISBN 0-8165-0367-2). U of Ariz Pr.
Keur, Dorothy L. Big Bead Mesa: An Archaeological Study of Navaho Acculturation, 1745-1812. LC 76-43760. (Memoirs of the Society for American Archaeology: No. 1). Repr. of 1941 ed. 12.50 (ISBN 0-404-15613-4). AMS Pr.
Kew, Della & Goddard, P. E. Indian Art & Culture. 2nd ed. (Illus.). 1978. pap. 5.95 (ISBN 0-919654-13-4, Pub. by Hancock Hse). Universe.
King, William S. Papago Population Study. 103.00 (ISBN 0-8287-1181-X). Clearwater Pub.
King, William S. & Jones, Delmos J. Papago Indians, Vol. Two: Papago Population Studies. (American Indian Ethnohistory Ser: Indians of the Southwest). (Illus.). lib. bdg. 42.00 (ISBN 0-8240-0701-8). Garland Pub.
Klah, Hasteen. Navajo Creation Myth: The Story of Emergence. LC 76-43762. (Museum of Navajo Ceremonial Art. Religion Ser.: Vol. 1). Repr. of 1942 ed. 24.50 (ISBN 0-404-15615-0). AMS Pr.
Kluckhohn, Clyde. Navaho Witchcraft. 1962. pap. 5.95 (ISBN 0-8070-4697-3, BP243). Beacon Pr.
Kluckhohn, Clyde & Leighton, Dorothea. The Navaho. rev. ed. Lucy, frwd. by. LC 62-6779. (Illus.). 365p. 1973. text ed. 16.50x (ISBN 0-674-60601-9); pap. 6.95 (ISBN 0-674-60603-5). Harvard U Pr.
Kluckhohn, Clyde & Spencer, Katharine. Bibliography of the Navaho Indians. LC 79-171546. Repr. of 1940 ed. 16.00 (ISBN 0-404-07134-1). AMS Pr.
Kluckhohn, Clyde & Wyman, L. C. Introduction to Navaho Chant Practice. LC 42-2722. 1940. pap. 14.00 (ISBN 0-527-00552-5). Kraus Repr.
Kluckhohn, Clyde, et al. Navaho Material Culture. LC 78-122217. (Illus.). 1971. 25.00x (ISBN 0-674-60620-5, Belknap Pr). Harvard U Pr.
Kluckhohn, Florence & Strodtbeck, Fred L. Variations in Value Orientations. LC 72-12497. (Illus.). 437p. 1973. Repr. of 1961 ed. lib. bdg. 31.00x (ISBN 0-8371-6740-X, KLVV); pap. 7.95 (ISBN 0-8371-8986-1, KLV:). Greenwood.
Kroeber, Alfred L. Mohave Indians. Horr, David A., ed. (American Indian Ethnohistory Ser.). 1978. lib. bdg. 42.00 (ISBN 0-8240-0738-7). Garland Pub.
--The Seri. LC 76-43764. (Southwest Museum, Papers: No. 6). Repr. of 1931 ed. 11.50 (ISBN 0-404-15619-3). AMS Pr.
--Walapai Ethnography. LC 35-6835. 1935. pap. 21.00 (ISBN 0-527-00541-X). Kraus Repr.
--Zuni Kin & Clan. LC 76-43765. (AMNH. Anthropological Papers: Vol. 18, Pt. 2). Repr. of 1917 ed. 24.50 (ISBN 0-404-15618-5). AMS Pr.
Kroeber, Theodora. The Inland Whale: Nine Stories Retold from California Indian Legends. (Illus.). (YA) 1959. pap. 3.95 (ISBN 0-520-00676-3, CAL88). U of Cal Pr.
--Ishi, Last of His Tribe. LC 64-19401. (gr. 4 up). 1964. 7.95 (ISBN 0-87466-049-1). Parnassus.
Kurath, Gertrude P. Music & Dance of the Tewa Pueblos. (Illus.). 1968. pap. 6.95 (ISBN 0-89013-035-3). Museum NM Pr.
Lagerquist, Syble. Philip Johnston & the Navajo Code Talkers. (Indian Culture Ser.). (gr. 4-12). 1975. 1.95 (ISBN 0-89992-038-1). MT Coun Indian.
Laird, Carobeth. The Chemehuevis. 1976. 15.00 (ISBN 0-686-16327-3); pap. 8.95 (ISBN 0-686-16328-1). Malki Mus Pr.
Laird, W. David. Hopi Bibliography: Comprehensive & Annotated. LC 77-95563. 1977. pap. 7.95x (ISBN 0-8165-0566-7). U of Ariz Pr.
La Lone, Mary. Gabrielino Indians of Southern California: An Annotated Ethnohistoric Bibliography. (Occasional Papers: No. 6). 72p. 1980. pap. 4.50 (ISBN 0-917956-15-X). UCLA Arch.
Lamphere, Louise. To Run After Them: Cultural & Social Bases of Cooperation in a Navajo Community. LC 77-22352. 1977. 12.50x (ISBN 0-8165-0594-2); pap. 6.50x (ISBN 0-8165-0369-9). U of Ariz Pr.
Lang, Gottfried O. A Study in Culture Contact & Culture Change: The Whiterock Utes in Transition. (Utah Anthropological Papers: No. 15). Repr. of 1953 ed. 10.50 (ISBN 0-404-60615-6). AMS Pr.
Lange, Charles H. Cochiti: New Mexico Pueblo, Past & Present. LC 58-10852. (Illus.). 642p. 1968. lib. bdg. 14.95x (ISBN 0-8093-0295-0). S Ill U Pr.
--Cochiti: New Mexico Pueblo, Past & Present. LC 58-10852. (Arcturus Books Paperbacks). (Illus.). 642p. pap. 11.95 (ISBN 0-8093-0296-9). S Ill U Pr.
Leighton, Dorothea & Kluckhohn, Clyde. Children of the People. LC 77-96199. 1969. Repr. of 1947 ed. lib. bdg. 16.50x (ISBN 0-374-94902-6). Octagon.
Leighton, Dorothea C. & Adair, John. People of the Middle Place: A Study of the Zuni Indians. LC 65-28463. (Behavior Science Monographs). xviii, 171p. 1966. pap. 8.00x (ISBN 0-87536-320-2). HRAFP.
Link, Margaret S., retold by. The Pollen Path: A Collection of Navajo Myths. LC 56-7272. (Illus.). 1956. 12.50x (ISBN 0-8047-0473-2). Stanford U Pr.
Lister, Florence C. & Lister, Robert H. Earl Morris & Southwestern Archaeology. LC 68-19737. (Illus.). 1977. pap. 6.95 (ISBN 0-8263-0455-9). U of NM Pr.
Locke, Raymond F. Book of the Navajo. rev. ed. (Illus.). 1979. pap. 3.95 (ISBN 0-87687-300-X, BM300). Mankind Pub.
Lockett, Hattie G. The Unwritten Literature on the Hopi. LC 76-43767. (Arizona Univ. Social Science Bulletin: No. 2). Repr. of 1933 ed. 18.00 (ISBN 0-404-15621-5). AMS Pr.
Longacre, William A. Archaeology As Anthropology: A Case Study. LC 79-113089. (Anthropological Papers: No. 17). 64p. 1970. pap. 3.95x (ISBN 0-8165-0219-6). U of Ariz Pr.
Longacre, William A., ed. Reconstructing Prehistoric Pueblo Societies. LC 75-107102. (School of America Research Adv. Seminar Ser.). 1972. pap. 6.95x (ISBN 0-8263-0230-0). U of NM Pr.
Luckert, Karl W. Coyoteway: A Navajo Holyway Healing Ceremonial. LC 78-10358. 1979. pap. 13.95x (ISBN 0-8165-0655-8). U of Ariz Pr.
--A Navajo Bringing-Home Ceremony: The Claus Chee Sonny Version of Deerway Ajilee. LC 78-59701. (Illus.). xiv, 210p. Date not set. pap. 14.95x (ISBN 0-89734-027-2, Pub by Mus Nothern Ariz). U of Nebr Pr.
--Navajo Mountain & Rainbow Bridge Religion. (Illus.). vii, 157p. 1981. 9.95x (ISBN 0-89734-025-6, Pub by Mus Northern Ariz). U of Nebr Pr.
--Navajo Mountain & Rainbow Bridge Religion. Goossen, Irvy W & Bilagody, Harry, Jr., trs. from Navajo. (American Tribal Religions Ser.: No. 1). (Illus.). 1977. pap. 6.95 (ISBN 0-89734-025-6). Mus Northern Ariz.
Lummis, Charles F. Land of Poco Tiempo. LC 66-22698. (Illus.). 1981. pap. 5.95 (ISBN 0-8263-0071-5). U of NM Pr.

McAfee, William W. Our Ancient People. 1978. 7.50 (ISBN 0-533-03370-5). Vantage.
McClellan, Val J. This Is Our Land. 1978. 12.50 (ISBN 0-533-02557-5). Vantage.
McGaw, William C. Savage Scene: The Life & Times of James Kirker, Frontier King. (Illus.). 288p. 1972. 10.95 (ISBN 0-8038-6712-3). Hastings.
McNely, James K. Holy Wind in Navajo Philosophy. 1981. text ed. 14.95x (ISBN 0-8165-0710-4); pap. 6.95x (ISBN 0-8165-0724-4). U of Ariz Pr.
McNierney, Michael, ed. Taos Eighteen Forty-Seven: The Revolt in Contemporary Accounts. 1980. pap. 4.95 (ISBN 0-933472-07-2). Johnson Bks.
Malotki, Ekkehart, et al. Hopi Tales. Malotki, Ekkehart, tr. (Special Publications Ser.). (Illus.). 1978. pap. 8.00 (ISBN 0-89734-001-9). Mus Northern Ariz.
Manners, Robert A. Hualapai Indians, Vol. 2: An Ethnological Report on the Hualapai (Walapai) Indians of Arizona. (American Indian Ethnohistory Ser: Indians of the Southwest). (Illus.). lib. bdg. 42.00 (ISBN 0-8240-0723-9). Garland Pub.
--Paiute Indians, Vol. One: Southern Paiute & Chemehuevi: an Ethnohistorical Report. (American Indian Ethnohistory Ser: California & Basin - Plateau Indians). (Illus.). lib. bdg. 42.00 (ISBN 0-8240-0740-9). Garland Pub.
Manners, Robert A., et al. Havasupai Indians. Horr, David A., ed. (American Indian Ethnohistory Ser.). 1974. lib. bdg. 42.00 (ISBN 0-8240-0707-7). Garland Pub.
Martin, Paul S. SU Site Excavations at a Mongollon Village, Western New Mexico, 1st, 2nd, & 3rd Seasons. (Illus.). 1940-1947. pap. 21.00 (ISBN 0-527-01892-9). Kraus Repr.
Martin, Paul S. & Willis, Elizabeth S. Anasazi Painted Pottery in the Field Museum of Natural History. LC 41-11775. (Fieldiana Anthropology Memoirs Ser: Vol. 5). 1968. Repr. of 1940 ed. 30.00 (ISBN 0-527-61900-0). Kraus Repr.
Matthews, Washington. Navajo Weavers. facs. ed. (Illus.). 16p. Repr. pap. 3.50 (ISBN 0-8466-0095-1, SJS95). Shorey.
--Navajo Weavers & Silversmiths. LC 70-97218. (Wild & Woolly West Ser., No. 7). (Illus.). 1968. 7.00 (ISBN 0-910584-81-8); pap. 1.50 (ISBN 0-910584-07-9). Filter.
Maxwell Museum of Anthropology, Univ. of New Mexico. Seven Families in Pueblo Pottery. LC 75-17376. (Illus.). 116p. 1975. pap. 5.95 (ISBN 0-8263-0388-9). U of NM Pr.
Miller, Merton L. A Preliminary Study of the Pueblo of Taos, New Mexico. LC 74-7992. Repr. of 1898 ed. 10.00 (ISBN 0-404-11879-8). AMS Pr.
Miller, Ron & Miller, Peggy Jean. The Chemehuevi Indians of Southern California. 1973. 1.00 (ISBN 0-686-25507-0). Malki Mus Pr.
Mitchell, Emerson B. & Allen, T. D. Miracle Hill: The Story of a Navaho Boy. 230p. 1967. pap. 6.95x (ISBN 0-8061-1616-1). U of Okla Pr.
Moon, Sheila. A Magic Dwells: A Poetic & Psychological Study of the Navaho Emergence Myth. LC 72-105501. 1970. pap. 5.95 (ISBN 0-8195-6036-7, Pub. by Wesleyan U Pr). Columbia U Pr.
Moriarty, James R. Chinigchinix, an Indigenous California Indian Religion. (Illus.). 1969. 7.50 (ISBN 0-686-20682-7). Southwest Mus.
Morris, Elizabeth A. Basketmaker Caves in the Prayer Rock District, Northeastern Arizona. (Anthropological Papers: No. 35). 1980. pap. 8.50x (ISBN 0-8165-0499-7). U of Ariz Pr.
Morrison, Dorothy N. Chief Sarah: Sarah Winnemucca's Fight for Indian Rights. LC 79-22545. (Illus.). 170p. 1980. 9.95 (ISBN 0-689-30752-7). Atheneum.
Morss, Noel. Ancient Culture of the Fremont River in Utah. 1931. pap. 6.00 (ISBN 0-527-01226-2). Kraus Repr.
--Archaeological Explorations on the Middle Chinlee. LC 28-11557. 1927. pap. 6.00 (ISBN 0-527-00533-9). Kraus Repr.
Museum of New Mexico Press, ed. Navajo Weaving Handbook. rev. ed. LC 77-74888. (Guidebook Ser). (Illus.). 1977. pap. 5.95 (ISBN 0-89013-092-2). Museum NM Pr.
Museum Staff. Introduction to Hopi Kachinas. (Illus.). 1977. pap. 1.50 (ISBN 0-89734-004-3). Mus Northern Ariz.
Myers, Donald D. & Kleinman, Frank R., Jr. Appraisal of the Lands of the Fort Sill Apache Tribe of Oklahoma, 1886. (Library of American Indian Affairs). 383p. 1973. lib. bdg. 109.50 (ISBN 0-8287-0933-5). Clearwater Pub.
Nabhan, Gary P. The Desert Smells Like Rain: A Naturalist in Papago Indian Country. LC 81-81505. (Illus.). 192p. 1982. 15.00 (ISBN 0-86547-049-9). N Point Pr.
Nagata, Shuichi. Modern Transformations of Moenkopi Pueblo. LC 70-76829. (Studies in Anthropology Ser: No. 6). (Illus.). 1970. pap. 10.95 (ISBN 0-252-00031-5). U of Ill Pr.
The Navajo Design Book. 1975. pap. 2.50 (ISBN 0-918858-04-6). Fun Pub.
The Navajo Indian Book. 1975. pap. 2.50 (ISBN 0-918858-03-8). Fun Pub.
Navajo Indians, Vol. 2. Incl. Navajo Activities Affecting the Acoma-Laguna Area, 1746-1910. Jenkins, Myra E; Navajo Indians. Reeve, Frank D. (American Indian Ethnohistory Ser: Indians of the Southwest). (Illus.). lib. bdg. 42.00 (ISBN 0-8240-0704-2). Garland Pub.
Navajo Indians, Vol. 3. Incl. Navajo Sacred Places. Van Valkenburgh, Richard. Kluckhohn, Clyde, ed. (Illus.); Short History of the Navajo People. Van Valkenburgh, Richard; Findings of Fact, & Opinion. Indian Claims Commission. (American Indian Ethnohistory Ser: Indians of the Southwest). (Illus.). lib. bdg. 42.00 (ISBN 0-8240-0705-0). Garland Pub.
Neithammer, Carolyn. American Indian Food & Lore. LC 73-7681. (Illus.). 256p. 1974. pap. 7.95 (ISBN 0-02-010000-0, Collier). Macmillan.
New Mexico People & Energy Collective, et al. Red Ribbons for Emma. LC 80-83883. (Illus.). 48p. (Orig.). (gr. 3 up). 1981. 5.00 (ISBN 0-938678-07-8). New Seed.
Newcomb, Franc J. Hosteen Klah: Navaho Medicine Man & Sand Painter. LC 64-20759. (Civilization of the American Indian Ser: No. 73). (Illus.). 227p. 1971. 11.95 (ISBN 0-8061-0622-0); pap. 5.95 (ISBN 0-8061-1008-2). U of Okla Pr.
--Navaho Neighbors. (Illus.). 1966. 12.95 (ISBN 0-8061-0704-9); pap. 5.95 (ISBN 0-8061-1040-6). U of Okla Pr.
--Study of Navajo Symbolism, 3 pts. in 1. Incl. Pt. 1. Navajo Symbols in Sandpaintings & Ritual Objects; Pt. 2. Navajo Picture Writing. Fishler, S. A; Pt. 3. Notes on Corresponding Symbols in Various Parts of the World. Wheelwright, Mary C. 1956. Set. pap. 13.00 (ISBN 0-527-01284-X). Kraus Repr.
Newcomb, Franc J. & Reichard, Gladys A. Sandpaintings of the Navajo Shooting Chant. 1975. pap. 7.00 (ISBN 0-486-23141-0). Dover.
Newcomb, W. W., Jr. The Indians of Texas: From Prehistoric to Modern Times. LC 60-14312. (Texas History Paperbacks: No. 4). (Illus.). 1961. 15.95x (ISBN 0-292-73271-6); pap. 7.95x (ISBN 0-292-78425-2). U of Tex Pr.
Oglesby, Catharine. Modern Primitive Arts of Mexico, Guatemala & the Southwest. facs. ed. LC 75-90670. (Essay Index Reprint Ser). 1939. 16.00 (ISBN 0-8369-1215-2). Arno.
O'Kane, Walter C. Hopis: Portrait of a Desert People. (Civilization of the American Indian Ser.: No. 35). (Illus.). 1973. Repr. of 1953 ed. 14.50 (ISBN 0-8061-0263-2). U of Okla Pr.
Opler, M. E. Childhood & Youth in Jicarilla Apache Society. (Illus.). 1946. 5.00 (ISBN 0-686-20675-4). Southwest Mus.
Opler, Morris E. Apache Life-Way. LC 65-23533. 500p. Repr. of 1941 ed. 13.50x (ISBN 0-8154-0168-X). Cooper Sq.
--Childhood & Youth in Jicarilla Apache Society. LC 76-43797. Repr. of 1946 ed. 21.00 (ISBN 0-404-15653-3). AMS Pr.
--Myths & Tales of the Jicarilla Apache Indians. LC 38-22477. (American Folklore Society Memoirs). Repr. of 1938 ed. 25.00 (ISBN 0-527-01083-9). Kraus Repr.
Ortiz, Alfonso. Tewa World: Space, Time, Being, & Becoming in a Pueblo Society. LC 72-94079. 1972. pap. 2.95 (ISBN 0-226-63307-1, P447, Phoen). U of Chicago Pr.
--Tewa World: Space, Time, Being, & Becoming in a Pueblo Society. LC 72-94079. 1969. 8.75x (ISBN 0-226-63306-3). U of Chicago Pr.
Ortiz, Alfonso, ed. Southwest. LC 77-17162. (Handbook of North American Indians Ser.: Vol. 9). (Illus.). 700p. 1980. text ed. 17.00 (ISBN 0-87474-189-0). Smithsonian.
Painter, Muriel T. Faith, Flowers, & Fiestas. (Illus.). 1962. pap. 1.95 (ISBN 0-8165-0169-6). U of Ariz Pr.
Paiute Indians, Vol. 2. Incl. Southern Paiute Ethnography. Kelly, Isabel T; Chemehuevi Notes (Notes from Informants) Van Valkenburgh, Richard F. (American Indian Ethnohistory Ser: California & Basin - Plateau Indians). (Illus.). lib. bdg. 42.00 (ISBN 0-8240-0741-7). Garland Pub.
Paiute Indians, Vol. 4. Incl. Northern Paiute Archaeology. Grosscup, Gordon L; Medicinal Uses of Plants by Indian Tribes of Nevada. Train, Percy, et al.; Notes on Snakes, Paiutes, Nez Perces at Malheur Reservation. Meacham, A. B. (American Indian Ethnohistory Ser: California & Basin - Plateau Indians). (Illus.). lib. bdg. 42.00 (ISBN 0-8240-0743-3). Garland Pub.
Palmer, William R. Why the North Star Stands Still. LC 57-11627. (Illus.). 1978. pap. 2.50 (ISBN 0-915630-12-5). Zion.
Papago Indians, Vol. 1. Incl. Papago Indians: Aboriginal Land Use & Occupancy. Hackenberg, Robert A; Acculturation at the Papago Village of Santa Rosa. Underhill, Ruth M; The Cattle Industry of the Southern Papago Districts with Some Information on the Reservation Cattle Industry As a Whole. Xavier, Gwyneth H. (American Indian Ethnohistory Ser: Indians of the Southwest). (Illus.). lib. bdg. 42.00 (ISBN 0-8240-0721-2). Garland Pub.
Papago Indians, Vol. 3. Incl. The Papago Indians of Arizona. Kelley, William H; The Papago Tribe of Arizona. Fontana, Bernard L; Findings of Fact, & Opinion. Indians Claims Commission. (American Indian Ethnohistory Ser: Indians of the Southwest). (Illus.). lib. bdg. 42.00 (ISBN 0-8240-0702-6). Garland Pub.
Parman, Donald L. The Navajos & the New Deal. LC 74-29733. (Yale Western Americana Ser.: No. 27). (Illus.). 320p. 1976. 25.00x (ISBN 0-300-01832-0). Yale U Pr.
Parsons, Elsie C. Hopi & Zuni Ceremonialism. LC 34-5260. 1933. pap. 7.00 (ISBN 0-527-00538-X). Kraus Repr.
--Notes on Zuni, 2 pts. 1917. pap. 7.00 ea. Pt. I (ISBN 0-527-00518-5). Pt. II (ISBN 0-527-00519-3). Kraus Repr.
--Pueblo Indian Journal. LC 65-104022. 1925. pap. 7.00 (ISBN 0-527-00531-2). Kraus Repr.
--Scalp Ceremonial of Zuni. LC 25-1663. 1924. pap. 5.00 (ISBN 0-527-00530-4). Kraus Repr.
--Social Organization of the Tewa of New Mexico. LC 30-5855. 1929. pap. 21.00 (ISBN 0-527-00535-5). Kraus Repr.
Parsons, Elsie W. The Pueblo of Jemez. LC 76-43805. (Phillips Academy. Papers of the Southwest Expedition: No. 3). Repr. of 1925 ed. 47.50 (ISBN 0-404-15661-4). AMS Pr.
Paul, Doris A. The Navajo Code Talkers. (Illus.). 160p. 1973. 10.00 (ISBN 0-8059-1870-1). Dorrance.
Peckham, Stewart. Prehistoric Weapons in the Southwest. (Illus.). 1965. pap. 1.25 (ISBN 0-89013-017-5). Museum NM Pr.
Pennington, Campbell W. The Tarahumar of Mexico: Their Environment & Material Culture. LC 64-1645. (Illus.). 267p. 1974. pap. 20.00x (ISBN 0-87480-093-5). U of Utah Pr.
Pennington, Campbell W., ed. The Pima Bajo (Nevome) of Central Sonora, Mexico: Vocabulario en la Lengua Nevome. 1979. 16.00x (ISBN 0-87480-125-7). U of Utah Pr.
Perceval, Don & Lockett, Clay. A Navajo Sketch Book. 2nd ed. LC 62-21125. (Illus.). 1968. Repr. 14.50 (ISBN 0-87358-036-2). Northland.
Peterson, Bonnie, ed. Dawn of the World, Stories of the Coast Miwok Indians. (Illus.). 1976. pap. 3.00 (ISBN 0-912908-04-1). Tamal Land.
Pima-Maricopa Indians, 2 vols. Incl. Aboriginal Land Use & Occupancy of the Pima-Maricopa Indians. Hackenberg, Robert; Findings of Fact, & Opinion. Indian Claims Commission. (American Indian Ethnohistory Ser: Indians of the Southwest). (Illus.). Set. lib. bdg. 84.00 (ISBN 0-8240-0730-1); lib. bdg. 42.00 ea. Garland Pub.
Plog, Fred T. A Study of Prehistoric Change. 1974. 21.00 (ISBN 0-12-785645-5). Acad Pr.
Pound, A. Johnson of the Mohawks. 1977. lib. bdg. 59.95 (ISBN 0-8490-2107-3). Gordon Pr.
Powell, John W. The Hopi Villages (the Ancient Province of Tusayan) LC 75-25049. (Wild & Woolly West Ser, No. 21). Orig. Title: Ancient Province of Tusayan. (Illus.). 48p. 1972. 7.00 (ISBN 0-910584-28-1); pap. 1.50 (ISBN 0-910584-73-7). Filter.
Pueblo Indians, Vol. 1. Incl. Anthropological Data Pertaining to the Taos Land Claim. Ellis, Florence H; Spanish & Mexican Land Policies & Grants in the Taos Pueblo Region, New Nexico. Dunham, Harold H; A Historical Study of Land Use Eastward of the Taos Indians' Pueblo Land Grant Prior to 1848. Dunham, Harold H; Findings of Fact, & Opinion. Indian Claims Commission. (American Indian Ethnohistory Ser: Indians of the Southwest). (Illus.). lib. bdg. 42.00 (ISBN 0-8240-0725-5). Garland Pub.
Pueblo Indians, Vol. 3. Incl. Anthropology of Laguna Pueblo Land Claims. Ellis, Florence H; Historical Treatise in Defense of the Pueblo of Acoma Land Claims. Minge, Ward A; Acoma Land Utilization. Rands, Robert L. (American Indian Ethnohistory Ser: Indians of the Southwest). (Illus.). lib. bdg. 42.00 (ISBN 0-8240-0727-1). Garland Pub.
Pueblo Indians, Vol. 4. Incl. History of the Laguna Pueblo Land Claims. Jenkins, Myra E; Laguna Land Utilization: an Ethnohistorical Report. Rands, Robert L. (American Indian Ethnohistory Ser: Indians of the Southwest). (Illus.). lib. bdg. 42.00 (ISBN 0-8240-0728-X). Garland Pub.
Qoyawayma, Polingaysi. No Turning Back: A Hopi Indian Woman's Struggle to Live in Two Worlds. LC 64-7652. 180p. 1977. pap. 5.95 (ISBN 0-8263-0439-7). U of NM Pr.
Quimby, Ian M. Material Culture & the Study of American Life. (A Winterthur Bk.). (Illus.). 1978. 12.95x (ISBN 0-393-05661-9); pap. 5.95x (ISBN 0-393-09037-X). Norton.
Ray, Verne F., et al. Apache Indians X. Horr, David A., ed. (American Indian Ethnohistory Ser.). 1978. lib. bdg. 42.00 (ISBN 0-8240-0718-2). Garland Pub.
Reed, Verner Z. Southern Ute Indians of Early Colorado. Jones, William R., ed. (Illus.). 1980. pap. 2.00 (ISBN 0-89646-067-3). Outbooks.
Reichard, Gladys. Navajo Medicine Man Sand Paintings. (Illus.). 1977. pap. 7.95 (ISBN 0-486-23329-4). Dover.
Reichard, Gladys A. Navaho Religion: A Study of Symbolism. 2nd ed. LC 63-14455. (Bollingen Ser.: Vol. 18). 864p. 1963. 32.00 (ISBN 0-691-09801-8); pap. 9.95 (ISBN 0-691-01798-0). Princeton U Pr.
--Navajo Shepherd & Weaver. 2nd ed. LC 68-25390. (Beautiful Rio Grande Classics Ser). (Illus.). 244p. 1968. Repr. of 1936 ed. lib. bdg. 10.00 (ISBN 0-87380-032-X). Rio Grande.
--Social Life of the Navajo Indians. LC 76-82350. (Columbia Univ. Contributions to Anthropology Ser.: Vol. 7). Repr. of 1928 ed. 27.50 (ISBN 0-404-50557-0). AMS Pr.
--Spider Woman: A Story of Navajo Weavers & Chanters. 2nd ed. LC 68-25391. (Beautiful Rio Grande Classics Ser). (Illus.). 310p. 1968. Repr. of 1934 ed. lib. bdg. 12.00 (ISBN 0-87380-033-8). Rio Grande.
Reit, Seymour. Child of the Navajos. LC 74-162608. (Illus.). (gr. 2-5). 1971. PLB 5.95 (ISBN 0-396-06414-0). Dodd.
Robbins, Wilfred W., et al. Ethnobotany of the Tewa Indians. 19.00 (ISBN 0-403-03591-0). Scholarly.
Roberts, Frank, Jr. The Village of the Great Kivas on the Zuni Reservation, New Mexico. Repr. of 1932 ed. 19.00 (ISBN 0-403-03723-9). Scholarly.
Robinson, W. W. Los Angeles from the Days of the Pueblo. Nunis, Doyce B., Jr., ed. (Orig.). 1981. pap. 6.95 (ISBN 0-87701-242-3). Chronicle Bks.
Roessel, Robert A., Jr. Navajo Education, 1948-1978: Its Progress & Problems. (Navajo History Ser.). (Illus.). 339p. 1979. 14.95 (ISBN 0-912586-38-9). Navajo Coll Pr.
Roessel, Robert, Jr. Pictorial History of the Navajo from 1860-1910. (Illus.). 240p. 1980. 14.95 (ISBN 0-686-74363-6). Navajo Curr.
Russell, Frank. The Pima Indians. new ed. Fontana, Bernard, intro. by. LC 74-78735. 496p. 1975. pap. 9.95 (ISBN 0-8165-0335-4). U of Ariz Pr.
Sando, Joe. The Pueblo Indian. 1976. pap. 6.50 (ISBN 0-685-65151-7). Indian Hist Pr.
Sapir, Edward. Southern Paiute. Bd. with Texts of the Kaibab Paiutes & Uintah Utes; Southern Paiute Dictionary. LC 76-44081. (Proceedings of the American Academy of Arts & Sciences: Vol. 65). Repr. of 1931 ed. 40.50 (ISBN 0-404-15788-2). AMS Pr.
Saunders, Charles F. Indians of the Terraced Houses: The Pueblo Indians of New Mexico & Arizona, 1902-1910. LC 73-17359. (Beautiful Rio Grande Classics Ser). lib. bdg. 15.00 (ISBN 0-87380-102-4). Rio Grande.
Saxton, Dean & Saxton, Lucille. Legends & Lore of the Papago & Pima Indians. LC 77-77801. 1973. pap. 5.95x (ISBN 0-8165-0420-2). U of Ariz Pr.
Schroeder, Albert H. Apache Indians I: A Study of the Apache Indians. (American Indian Ethnohistory Ser: Indians of the Southwest). lib. bdg. 42.00 (ISBN 0-8240-0715-8). Garland Pub.
--The Apache Indians in Texas, New Mexico & Arizona. 99.00 (ISBN 0-8287-0915-7). Clearwater Pub.
--Apache Indians IV. Horr, David A., ed. (American Indian Ethnohistory Ser.). 1978. lib. bdg. 42.00 (ISBN 0-8240-0719-0). Garland Pub.
--Santo Domingo Pueblo: History of the Aboriginal Title Area. 41.00 (ISBN 0-8287-1417-7). Clearwater Pub.
Schroeder, Albert H. & Matson, Dan S. A Colony on the Move: Gaspar Castano de Sosa's Journal, 1590-1591. (School of American Research Bk). (Illus.). 1965. 8.95x (ISBN 0-8263-0295-5). U of NM Pr.
Seiler, Hansjakob & Hioki, Kojiro. Cahuilla Dictionary. 1979. pap. 15.00 (ISBN 0-686-25243-8). Malki Mus Pr.
Seltzer, Carl C. Racial Prehistory in the Southwest & the Hawikuh Zunis. 1944. pap. 5.00 (ISBN 0-527-01256-4). Kraus Repr.
Shaw, Anna M. Pima Indian Legends. LC 68-13547. (Illus.). 112p. 1968. pap. 3.95 (ISBN 0-8165-0186-6). U of Ariz Pr.
Shaw, Anna Moore. A Pima Past. LC 73-87716. 1974. pap. 4.95 (ISBN 0-8165-0426-1). U of Ariz Pr.

Shepardson, Mary & Hammond, Blodwen. The Navajo Mountain Community: Social Organization & Kinship Terminology. LC 70-97233. 1970. 25.00x (ISBN 0-520-01570-3). U of Cal Pr.
Sides, Dorothy. Decorative Art of the Southwestern Indians. (Illus.). 7.50 (ISBN 0-8446-2936-7). Peter Smith.
Silas & the Mad-Sad People. (gr. 1-5). 1981. 3.00 (ISBN 0-938678-08-6). New Seed.
Simmons, Leo W., ed. Sun Chief: The Autobiography of a Hopi Indian. rev. ed. (Illus.). 1942. 35.00x (ISBN 0-300-00949-6); pap. 7.50x 1963 (ISBN 0-300-00227-0, YW8). Yale U Pr.
Simpson, Richard. Ooti. LC 77-79888. (Illus.). (gr. 6-12). 1977. pap. 6.95 (ISBN 0-89087-213-9). Celestial Arts.
Smith, Anne M. Ethnography of the Northern Utes. (Illus.). 1974. pap. 10.95 (ISBN 0-89013-067-1). Museum NM Pr.
Smithson, Carma L. The Havasupai Woman. (Utah Anthropological Papers: No. 38). Repr. of 1959 ed. 16.75 (ISBN 0-404-60638-5). AMS Pr.
Smithson, Carma L. & Euler, Robert C. Havasupai Religion & Mythology. (Utah Anthropological Papers: No. 68). Repr. of 1964 ed. 14.00 (ISBN 0-404-60668-7). AMS Pr.
Spencer, Katherine. Mythology & Values: An Analysis of Navaho Chantway Myths. (American Folklore Society Memoir Ser: No. 48). 248p. 1957. pap. 5.00x (ISBN 0-292-73528-6). U of Tex Pr.
--Reflections of Social Life in the Navaho Origin Myth. LC 76-43850. (Univ. of New Mexico. Publications in Anthropology: No. 3). Repr. of 1947 ed. 13.00 (ISBN 0-404-15705-X). AMS Pr.
Spicer, Edward H. Cycles of Conquest: The Impact of Spain, Mexico & the United States on Indians of the Southwest, 1533-1960. LC 61-14500. (Illus.). 1962. pap. 8.95x (ISBN 0-8165-0021-5). U of Ariz Pr.
Spier, Leslie. Havasupai Ethnography. LC 76-43852. (AMNH. Anthropological Papers: Vol. 29, Pt. 3). Repr. of 1928 ed. 57.50 (ISBN 0-404-15709-2). AMS Pr.
--Yuman Tribes of the Gila River. LC 74-118641. (Illus.). 1970. Repr. of 1933 ed. lib. bdg. 17.50x (ISBN 0-8154-0333-X). Cooper Sq.
--Yuman Tribes of the Gila River. LC 77-92480. (Illus.). 1978. pap. 6.00 (ISBN 0-486-23611-0). Dover.
Spindler, George & Spindler, Louise. Native North American Cultures: Four Cases. LC 76-23178. 1977. pap. text ed. 8.95 (ISBN 0-03-018401-0, HoltC). HR&W.
Stanford Research Institute. Jicarilla Apache Tribe of the Jicarilla Indian Reservation in New Mexico, 1849-1870: Historical & Documentary Evidence. (Library of American Indian Affairs). 108p. 1974. lib. bdg. 37.50 (ISBN 0-8287-1602-1). Clearwater Pub.
Stephen, Alexander M. Hopi Journal, 2 Vols. Parsons, Elsie C., ed. LC 77-82337. (Columbia University Contributions to Anthropology Ser.: Vol. 23). Repr. of 1936 ed. Set. 95.00 (ISBN 0-404-50573-2); 47.50 ea. Vol. 1 (ISBN 0-404-50594-5). Vol. 2 (ISBN 0-404-50595-3). AMS Pr.
Stevenson, Matilda C. The Zuni Indians: Their Mythology, Esoteric Fraternities, & Ceremonies. LC 6-35065. (U. S. Bureau of American Ethnology, 23rd Annual Report 1901-02). Repr. of 1904 ed. 69.50 (ISBN 0-384-58130-7). Johnson Repr.
Stirling, Matthew W. Origin Myth of Acoma & Other Records. Repr. of 1942 ed. 19.00 (ISBN 0-403-03676-3). Scholarly.
Stout, Joseph A., Jr. Apache Lightning: The Last Great Battles of the Ajo Calientes. Orig. Title: The Victorio Campaign. 1974. 11.95 (ISBN 0-19-501842-7). Oxford U Pr.
Strong, William D. Aboriginal Society in Southern California. Repr. of 1929 ed. pap. 35.00 (ISBN 0-527-01382-X). Kraus Repr.
Tanis, Norman E., ed. Report of Chas. A. Wetmore, Special U.S. Commissioner of Mission Indians of Southern California. (Northridge Facsimile Ser.: Pt. VII). 1977. pap. 10.00 (ISBN 0-937048-06-2). CSUN.
Tanner, Clara L. Prehistoric Southwestern Craft Arts. LC 75-19865. (Illus.). 1976. 20.00 (ISBN 0-8165-0582-9); pap. 9.95 (ISBN 0-8165-0416-4). U of Ariz Pr.
--Ray Manley's Hopi Kachina. (Illus.). 1980. 4.00 (ISBN 0-931418-06-2). R Manley.
--Ray Manley's Indian Lands. (Illus., Eng., Ger., Japanese.). 1979. 10.00x (ISBN 0-931418-04-6); pap. 6.00x (ISBN 0-931418-05-4). R Manley.
--Southwest Indian Craft Arts. LC 66-24299. (Illus.). 1968. 20.00 (ISBN 0-8165-0083-5). U of Ariz Pr.
Thomas, Alfred B., ed. Forgotten Frontiers: A Study of the Spanish Indian Policy of Don Juan Bautista De Anza, Governor of New Mexico, 1777-1787. (Civilization of the American Indian Ser.: No. 1). 1969. Repr. of 1932 ed. 19.95 (ISBN 0-8061-0014-1). U of Okla Pr.
--Teodora De Croix & the Northern Frontier of New Spain 1776-1783. (American Exploration & Travel Ser.: No. 5). 1968. Repr. of 1941 ed. 14.95 (ISBN 0-8061-0093-1). U of Okla Pr.
Thomas, Alfred B., et al. Apache Indians VIII. Horr, David A., ed. (American Indian Ethnohistory Ser.). 1978. lib. bdg. 42.00 (ISBN 0-8240-0710-7). Garland Pub.
--Apache Indians XI. Horr, David A., ed. (American Indian Ethnohistory Ser.). 1978. lib. bdg. 42.00 (ISBN 0-8240-0712-3). Garland Pub.
Thomas, D. H. The Southwestern Indian Detours. LC 77-94331. (Illus.). 1978. 8.95 (ISBN 0-918126-12-6); pap. 5.95 (ISBN 0-918126-11-8). Hunter Ariz.
Thompson, Gerald. The Army & the Navajo: The Bosque Redondo Reservation Experiment, 1863-68. LC 75-8457. 1976. pap. 7.50 (ISBN 0-8165-0495-4). U of Ariz Pr.
Thompson, Hildegard. The Navajos Long Walk for Education. Johnson, Broderick H., ed. LC 74-29006. (Illus.). 1975. lib. bdg. 9.95 (ISBN 0-912586-21-4). Navajo Coll Pr.
Thompson, Laura. Culture in Crisis: A Study of the Hopi Indians. LC 72-94984. (Illus.). x, 221p. 1973. Repr. of 1950 ed. 22.00 (ISBN 0-8462-1728-7). Russell.
Thompson, Laura & Joseph, Alice. Hopi Way. LC 65-18836. (Illus.). 1965. Repr. of 1944 ed. 14.00 (ISBN 0-8462-0612-9). Russell.
Thrapp, Dan L. Victorio & the Mimbres Apaches. (The Civilization of the American Indian Ser.: Vol. 125). (Illus.). 393p. 1980. pap. 9.95 (ISBN 0-8061-1645-5). U of Okla Pr.
Titiev, Mischa. Hopi Indians of Old Oraibi: Change & Continuity. LC 79-142590. (Illus.). 1972. 15.00x (ISBN 0-472-08900-5). U of Mich Pr.
--Old Oraibi. (Harvard Univ. PMP Ser.: Vol. 22, No. 1). (Illus.). 1944. pap. 30.00 (ISBN 0-527-01253-X). Kraus Repr.
Tschopik, Harry. Navaho Pottery Making. (Illus.). 1941. pap. 8.00 (ISBN 0-527-01242-4). Kraus Repr.
Tyler, Hamilton A. Pueblo Animals & Myths. LC 74-15902. (Civilization of American Indian Ser.: Vol. 134). 300p. 1975. 13.95 (ISBN 0-8061-1245-X). U of Okla Pr.
--Pueblo Birds & Myths. LC 78-58069. (Civilization of the American Indian Ser: No. 147). (Illus.). 1979. 13.95 (ISBN 0-8061-1483-5). U of Okla Pr.
Underhill, Ruth. First Penthouse Dwellers of America. LC 75-23849. (Illus.). 1976. lib. bdg. 15.00x (ISBN 0-88307-525-3); pap. 4.95 0. p. (ISBN 0-88307-526-1). Gannon.
--The Papago & Pima Indians of Arizona. (Wild & Woolly West Ser.: No. 37). (Illus.). 1979. 7.00 (ISBN 0-910584-85-0); pap. 2.00 (ISBN 0-910584-52-4). Filter.
Underhill, Ruth M. Autobiography of a Papago Woman. LC 37-22775. 1936. pap. 5.00 (ISBN 0-527-00545-2). Kraus Repr.
--Navajos. rev. ed. (Civilization of the American Indian Ser: No. 43). (Illus.). 1978. Repr. of 1956 ed. 12.95 (ISBN 0-8061-0341-8). U of Okla Pr.
--A Papago Calendar Record. LC 76-43878. (The Univ.of New Mexico Bulletin Anthropological Ser.: Vol. 2, No. 5). Repr. of 1938 ed. 15.00 (ISBN 0-404-15739-4). AMS Pr.
--Papago Indian Religion. LC 74-82363. (Columbia Univ. Contributions to Anthropology Ser.: Vol. 33). Repr. of 1946 ed. 27.00 (ISBN 0-404-50583-X). AMS Pr.
--The Papago Indians of Arizona & Their Relatives the Pima. LC 78-15079. (Indian Life & Customs: No. 3). 1977. Repr. of 1940 ed. 16.50 (ISBN 0-404-15736-X). AMS Pr.
--Pueblo Crafts. Beatty, Willard W., ed. LC 76-43880. (U. S. Office of Indian Affairs Indian Handcrafts: 7). Repr. of 1945 ed. 32.50 (ISBN 0-404-15737-8). AMS Pr.
--Social Organization of the Papago Indians. LC 74-82347. (Columbia Univ. Contributions to Anthropology Ser.: Vol. 30). 1969. Repr. of 1939 ed. 23.00 (ISBN 0-404-50580-5). AMS Pr.
--Work a Day Life of the Pueblos. Beatty, Willard W., ed. LC 76-43882. (Indian Life & Customs: No. 4). Repr. of 1946 ed. 19.50 (ISBN 0-404-15735-1). AMS Pr.
Ute Indians, Vol. 1. Incl. Analysis: Aboriginal Historical Groups of the Ute Indians of Utah. Steward, Julian H; Supplement: Native Components of the White River Ute Indians. Steward, Julian H. (American Indian Ethnohistory Ser: California & Basin Plateau Indians). (Illus.). lib. bdg. 42.00 (ISBN 0-8240-0736-0). Garland Pub.
Ute Indians, Vol. 2. Incl. Confederated Ute Indian Lands. Indian Claims Commission; Historical Summary of the Ute & the San Juan Mining Region. Hafen, Leroy R; Cultural Differences & Similarities Between Uintah & White River Indians. Smith, Anne M; Findings of Fact & Opinion. Indian Claims Commission. (American Indian Ethnohistory Ser: California & Basin Plateau Indians). (Illus.). lib. bdg. 42.00 (ISBN 0-8240-0737-9). Garland Pub.
Voth, H. R. Oraibu Marau Ceremony-Brief Miscellaneous Hopi Papers. (Chicago Field Museum of Natural History Fieldiana Anthropology Ser). 1912. pap. 30.00 (ISBN 0-527-01871-6). Kraus Repr.
--Traditions of the Hopi. (Chicago Field Museum of Natural History Fieldiana Anthropology Ser). 1905. pap. 22.00 (ISBN 0-527-01868-6). Kraus Repr.
Waddell, Jack O. Papago Indians at Work. LC 68-58960. (Anthropological Papers: No. 12). (Illus.). 160p. 1969. pap. 4.95x (ISBN 0-8165-0139-4). U of Ariz Pr.
Wade, Edwin L. & McChesney, Lea S. Historic Hopi Ceramics: The Thomas V. Keam Collection of the Peabody Museum of Archaeology & Ethnology, Harvard. LC 81-81627. (Peabody Museum Press Ser.). (Illus.). 602p. (Orig.). 1981. pap. text ed. write for info. (ISBN 0-87365-798-5). Peabody Harvard.
Wales, Lucy H. Navaho Territory & Its Boundaries in Arizona, Colorado & New Mexico: Biographical References. (Library of American Indian Affairs). 275p. 1974. lib. bdg. 78.00 (ISBN 0-8287-1135-6). Clearwater Pub.
Washburn, Dorothy, ed. Hopi Kachina: Spirit of Life. California Academy of Sciences. (Illus.). 160p. (Orig.). 1980. pap. 14.95 (ISBN 0-295-95751-4, Pub. by Calif Acad Sci). U of Wash Pr.
Washburn, Dorothy K., ed. Hopi Kachina: Spirit of Life. (Illus.). 158p. 1980. pap. 14.95 (ISBN 0-295-95751-4). Calif Acad Sci.
Waters, Frank. Book of the Hopi. (Illus.). 1977. pap. 3.95 (ISBN 0-14-004527-9). Penguin.
--Masked Gods: Navaho & Pueblo Ceremonialism. LC 73-1799. 438p. 1950. 16.95 (ISBN 0-8040-0196-0, SB); pap. 8.95 (ISBN 0-8040-0641-5, SB). Swallow.
--Masked Gods: Navaho & Pueblo Ceremonialism. LC 73-1799. 438p. 1950. 16.95 (ISBN 0-8040-0196-0, SB); pap. 8.95 (ISBN 0-8040-0641-5, SB). Swallow.
--Pumpkin Seed Point: Being Within the Hopi. LC 76-75741. 175p. 1973. 9.95 (ISBN 0-8040-0255-X, SB); pap. 5.95 (ISBN 0-8040-0635-0). Swallow.
Weaver, Thomas, ed. Indians of Arizona: A Contemporary Perspective. LC 73-84607. 1974. pap. 4.95x (ISBN 0-8165-0455-5). U of Ariz Pr.
Webb, George E. A Pima Remembers. LC 59-4914. (Illus.). 1959. pap. 3.95 (ISBN 0-8165-0284-6). U of Ariz Pr.
Weber, David J. The Taos Trappers: The Fur Trade in the Far Southwest, 1540-1846. 260p. 1980. pap. 6.95 (ISBN 0-8061-1702-8). U of Okla Pr.
Wheat, Margaret M. Survival Arts of the Primitive Paiutes. LC 67-30392. (Illus.). 1977. pap. 7.50 (ISBN 0-87417-048-6). U of Nev Pr.
White, Elizabeth, pseud. The Sun Girl. LC 78-67324. (Special Publications Ser.). (Illus.). 1978. Repr. of 1941 ed. 4.75 (ISBN 0-89734-046-9). Mus Northern Ariz.
White, Leslie. Acoma Indians: Paper from the Bureau of American Ethnology Annual Report for 1929-1930. LC 72-13912. (Beautiful Rio Grande Classics Ser). lib. bdg. 17.50 (ISBN 0-87380-103-2). Rio Grande.
White, Leslie A. Pueblo of San Felipe. LC 32-30651. 1932. pap. 7.00 (ISBN 0-527-00537-1). Kraus Repr.
--Pueblo of Santa Ana, New Mexico. LC 43-10004. 1942. pap. 21.00 (ISBN 0-527-00559-2). Kraus Repr.
--Pueblo of Santo Domingo, New Mexico. LC 35-17202. 1935. pap. 14.00 (ISBN 0-527-00542-8). Kraus Repr.
Whiting, Alfred F. Ethnobotany of the Hopi. LC 76-43890. (Museum of Northern Arizona Bulletin: No. 15). Repr. of 1939 ed. 16.00 (ISBN 0-404-15749-1). AMS Pr.
Whitman, William. Pueblo Indians of San Ildefonso. LC 73-82352. (Columbia Univ. Contributions to Anthropology Ser.: Vol. 34). Repr. of 1947 ed. 16.50 (ISBN 0-404-50584-8). AMS Pr.
Williams, John. The Redeemed Captive. Clark, Edward W., ed. LC 76-8758. (Illus.). 1976. 10.00x (ISBN 0-87023-217-7). U of Mass Pr.
Witherspoon, Gary. The Central Concepts of Navajo World View. (PDR Press Publications on World View: No. 1). 22p. 1977. pap. text ed. 1.50x (ISBN 9-0316-0071-7). Humanities.
--Language & Art in the Navajo Universe. (Illus.). 1977. text ed. 16.00x (ISBN 0-472-08965-X); pap. text ed. 8.95x (ISBN 0-472-08966-8). U of Mich Pr.
--Navajo Kinship & Marriage. LC 74-21340. (Illus.). xii, 138p. 1975. lib. bdg. 9.50x (ISBN 0-226-90419-9). U of Chicago Pr.
--Navajo Kinship & Marriage. LC 74-21340. 1975. pap. 3.95 (ISBN 0-226-90418-0, P745, Phoen). U of Chicago Pr.
Wood, Jean & Armstrong, Nancy M. In Our Hogan: Adventure Stories of Navajo Children. (Indian Culture Ser.). (gr. 4-8). 1976. 1.95 (ISBN 0-89992-058-6). MT Coun Indian.
Wood, Mary. Life Against the Land: A Short History of the Pueblo Indians. 1978. 1.00 (ISBN 0-913488-07-0). Timberline Bks.
Woolgar, Jack & Rudnicki, Barbara J. Hopi Mysteries. (Indian Culture Ser.). (gr. 5-9). 1974. 1.95 (ISBN 0-89992-060-8). MT Coun Indian.
Worcester, Donald E. The Apaches: Eagles of the Southwest. LC 78-21377. (Civilization of the American Indian Ser.: No. 149). (Illus.). 1979. 15.95 (ISBN 0-8061-1495-9). U of Okla Pr.
Worth, Sol & Adair, John. Through Navajo Eyes: An Exploration in Film Communication & Anthropology. LC 78-180488. (Illus.). 320p. 1973. 12.50x (ISBN 0-253-36015-3); pap. 4.50x (ISBN 0-253-36016-1). Ind U Pr.
Wright, Barton. Hopi Material Culture: Artifacts Gathered by H. R. Voth in the Fred Harvey Collection. LC 78-74181. (Illus.). 1979. 14.95 (ISBN 0-87358-189-X). Northland.
--The Unchanging Hopi. LC 74-31543. (Illus.). 128p. 1975. 12.50 (ISBN 0-87358-118-0). Northland.
Wyman, L. C. & Kluckhohn, Clyde. Navaho Classification of Their Song Ceremonials. LC 38-23008. 1938. pap. 5.00 (ISBN 0-527-00549-5). Kraus Repr.
Wyman, Leland C. Blessingway. LC 66-28786. (Illus.). 580p. 1970. 14.50x (ISBN 0-8165-0178-5). U of Ariz Pr.
--The Sacred Mountains of the Navajo. (Special Publications Ser.: No. 4). (Illus.). 1976. pap. 1.00 (ISBN 0-89734-012-4). Mus Northern Ariz.
--The Windways of the Navaho. 1962. pap. 4.00 (ISBN 0-686-15929-2). Taylor Museum.
Wyman, Leland C. & Harris, Stuart K. Navajo Indian Medical Ethnobotany. LC 76-43902. (Univ. of New Mexico Bulletin Anthropological Ser.: Vol. 3, No. 5). Repr. of 1941 ed. 16.50 (ISBN 0-404-15761-0). AMS Pr.
Yava, Aaron. Border Towns of the Navajo Nation. 2nd ed. (Illus.). 80p. 1975. pap. 4.00 (ISBN 0-914974-06-8). Holmgangers.
Yavapai Indians. Incl. A Study of Yavapai History. Schroeder, Albert H; Findings of Fact, & Opinion. Indian Claims Commission; The Yavapai Indians Sixteen Eighty-Two to Eighteen Forty-Eight. Thomas, Alfred B. (American Indian Ethnohistory Ser: Indians of the Southwest). (Illus.). lib. bdg. 33.00 (ISBN 0-8240-0714-X). Garland Pub.
Yazzie, Alfred. Navajo Police. LC 80-85450. 144p. 1980. pap. 8.95 (ISBN 0-936008-02-4). Navajo Curr.
Yazzie, Ethelou, ed. Navajo History, Vol. 1. rev. ed. LC 74-4910. (Illus.). 100p. 1974. 14.50 (ISBN 0-89019-012-7); pap. 6.95 (ISBN 0-89019-014-3). Navajo Curr.
Young, Robert W. A Political History of the Navajo Tribe. Johnson, Broderick H., ed. LC 78-5402. (Illus.). 1978. lib. bdg. 8.50 (ISBN 0-912586-37-0). Navajo Coll Pr.
Young, Stella. Navajo Native Dyes: Their Preparation & Use. LC 76-43671. Repr. of 1940 ed. 11.50 (ISBN 0-404-15504-9). AMS Pr.

INDIANS OF NORTH AMERICA-SOUTHWEST, OLD

The Old Southwest includes that southwestern section of the United States before the cessions of land from Mexico following the Mexican War: Louisiana, Texas, Arkansas, Tennessee, Kentucky and Missouri.

Bandelier, Adolf F. & Hewett, Edgar H. Indians of the Rio Grande Valley. LC 74-7920. Repr. of 1937 ed. 33.00 (ISBN 0-404-11805-4). AMS Pr.
Berlandier, Jean L. The Indians of Texas in 1830. Ewers, John C., ed. Leclercq, Patricia R., tr. LC 69-13118. (Illus.). 209p. 1969. 19.95x (ISBN 0-87474-081-9). Smithsonian.
Bushnell, David I., Jr. The Choctaw of Bayou Lacomb, St. Tammany Parish, Louisiana. Repr. of 1909 ed. 17.00 (ISBN 0-403-03559-7). Scholarly.
Chalfant, Stuart A. Aboriginal Territory of the Kalispel. (Library of American Indian Affairs). 61p. 1974. lib. bdg. 27.00 (ISBN 0-8287-0890-8). Clearwater Pub.
Chapman, Berlin B. Oto & Missouri Indians. Horr, David A., ed. (American Indian Ethnohistory Ser.). 1978. lib. bdg. 42.00 (ISBN 0-8240-0746-8). Garland Pub.
Densmore, Frances. How Indians Use Wild Plants for Food, Medicine & Crafts. Orig. Title: Use of Plants by the Chippewa Indians. (Illus.). 9.00 (ISBN 0-8446-5029-3). Peter Smith.

Dutton, Bertha P. & Olin, Caroline. Myths & Legends of the Indian Southwest. (Bk 2). (Illus.). 1978. pap. 2.95 (ISBN 0-88388-062-8). Bellerophon Bks.

Forbes, Jack D. Apache, Navaho, & Spaniard. (Civilization of the American Indian Ser.: Vol. 115). (Illus.). 304p. 1960. pap. 7.95 (ISBN 0-8061-1092-9). U of Okla Pr.

Foreman, Grant. Indians & Pioneers: The Story of the American Southwest Before 1830. (Civilization of the American Indian Ser.: No. 14). (Illus.). 1967. 15.95 (ISBN 0-8061-0057-5); pap. 7.95 (ISBN 0-8061-1262-X). U of Okla Pr.

Gatschet, A. S. The Karankawa Indians, the Coast People of Texas. 1891. pap. 9.00 (ISBN 0-527-01184-3). Kraus Repr.

Gilmore, Melvin R. Uses of Plants by the Indians of the Missouri River Region. LC 77-89833. (Illus.). 1977. 11.95x (ISBN 0-8032-0935-5); pap. 3.50 (ISBN 0-8032-5872-0, BB 644, Bison). U of Nebr Pr.

Gussow, Zachary. Anthropological Report on Indian Use & Occupancy of Royce Areas 69 & 120 in Iowa & Missouri. (Library of American Indian Affairs). 90p. 1974. lib. bdg. 34.00 (ISBN 0-8287-0905-X). Clearwater Pub.

Haile, Berard. Love-Magic & Butterfly People: The Slim Curly Version of the Ajjee & Mothway Myths. LC 78-59705. (Illus.). xii, 172p. Date not set. pap. 13.95x (ISBN 0-89734-026-4, Pub by Mus Nothern Ariz). U of Nebr Pr.

--Waterway. LC 79-66605. (Illus.). vi, 153p. 1981. pap. 12.95x (ISBN 0-89734-030-2, Pub by Mus Northern Ariz). U of Nebr Pr.

Haines, Francis. Nez Perces: Tribesmen of the Columbia Plateau. LC 55-9626. (Civilization of American Indian Ser.: No. 42). (Illus.). 1955. 14.95 (ISBN 0-8061-0325-6); pap. 6.95 (ISBN 0-8061-0982-3). U of Okla Pr.

Hebard, Grace R. Washaki: An Account of Indian Resistance of the Covered Wagon & Union Pacific Railroad Invasion of Their Territory. LC 76-43733. Repr. of 1940 ed. 29.00 (ISBN 0-404-15575-8). AMS Pr.

Hickerson, Harold. The Chippewa of the Mississippi & Lake Superior: Anthropological Report on the Indian Occupancy of Royce Area 268 & Royce Area 269 Ceded by the Pillager Band of Chippewa. (Library of American Indian Affairs). 190p. 1974. lib. bdg. 58.00 (ISBN 0-8287-0995-5). Clearwater Pub.

Hoijer, Harry. Tonkawa, an Indian Language of Texas. pap. 5.00 (ISBN 0-685-71708-9). J J Augustin.

Jelinek, Arthur. A Pre-Historic Sequence in the Middle Pecos Valley, New Mexico. (Anthropological Papers: No. 31). 1967. pap. 3.00x (ISBN 0-686-53049-7). U Mich Mus Anthro.

Kniffen, Fred. Indians of Louisiana. (Illus.). 108p. (gr. 6-12). 1976. 8.95 (ISBN 0-911116-97-4). Pelican.

Lewis, Thomas M. & Kneberg, Madeline. Tribes That Slumber: Indians of the Tennessee Region. LC 58-12085. (Illus.). 1958. pap. 7.95 (ISBN 0-87049-021-4). U of Tenn Pr.

Melody, Michael E. The Apaches: A Critical Bibliography. LC 77-6918. (Newberry Library Center for the History of the American Indian Bibliographical Ser.). 96p. 1977. pap. 3.95x (ISBN 0-253-30764-3). Ind U Pr.

Morfi, Fray J. History of Texas 1673-1779, 2 pts. Castaneda, Carlos E., ed. LC 67-24718. (Quivira Society Publications, Vol. 6). 1967. Repr. of 1935 ed. 25.00 (ISBN 0-405-00076-6). Arno.

Morrill, Sibley S. The Texas Cannibals, or, Why Father Serra Came to California. 28p. 1964. octavo wrappers 1.00 (ISBN 0-910740-04-6). Holmes.

Neighbours, Kenneth F. Indian Exodus: Texas Indian Affairs. 1972. 6.95 (ISBN 0-89015-025-7). Eakin Pubns.

Neuman, Robert W. Caddoan Indians Two. Horr, David A., ed. (American Indian Ethnohistory Ser.). 1978. lib. bdg. 42.00 (ISBN 0-8240-0764-6). Garland Pub.

Newcomb, W. W., Jr. The Indians of Texas: From Prehistoric to Modern Times. LC 60-14312. (Texas History Paperbacks: No. 4). (Illus.). 1961. 15.95x (ISBN 0-292-73271-6); pap. 7.95x (ISBN 0-292-78425-2). U of Tex Pr.

Olin, Caroline & Olin, D. Caroline. Myths & Legends of the Indian Southwest, Bk 1. 1st ed. (Illus.). 1978. pap. 2.95 (ISBN 0-88388-049-0). Bellerophon Bks.

Parsons, Elsie W. Notes on the Caddo. LC 41-19360. 1941. pap. 6.00 (ISBN 0-527-00556-8). Kraus Repr.

Randolph, J. Ralph. British Travelers Among the Southern Indians, 1660-1763. LC 72-858. (American Exploration & Travel Ser.: Vol. 62). 350p. 1973. 14.50 (ISBN 0-8061-1019-8). U of Okla Pr.

Salpointe, J. B. Soldiers of the Cross. 1977. Repr. of 1898 ed. lib. bdg. 17.95 (ISBN 0-89712-063-9). Documentary Pubns.

Shaw, Helen L. British Administration of the Southern Indians 1756-1783. LC 76-43820. Repr. of 1931 ed. 24.50 (ISBN 0-404-15675-4). AMS Pr.

Swanton, John R. Indian Tribes of the Lower Mississippi Valley & Adjacent Coast of the Gulf of Mexico. LC 11-35489. (U. S. Bureau of American Ethnology Ser: Bulletin 43). Repr. of 1911 ed. 27.00 (ISBN 0-384-59010-1). Johnson Repr.

--Source Material on the History & Ethnology of the Caddo Indians. Repr. of 1942 ed. 25.00 (ISBN 0-403-03695-X). Scholarly.

Tanner, Helen H. Caddoan Indians Four. Horr, David A., ed. (American Indian Ethnohistory Ser.). 1978. lib. bdg. 42.00 (ISBN 0-8240-0765-4). Garland Pub.

Taylor, Herbert C. The Chehalis: Anthropological Investigation Relative to Tribal Identity & Aboriginal Possession of Lands. (Library of American Indian Affairs). 34p. 1974. 20.00 (ISBN 0-8287-0970-X). Clearwater Pub.

Underhill, Ruth M., et al. Rainhouse & Ocean: Speeches for the Papago Year. LC 79-66733. (Illus.). vi, 154p. 1981. pap. 12.95x (ISBN 0-89734-029-9, Pub by Mus Northern Ariz). U of Nebr Pr.

Warren, Betsy. Indians Who Lived in Texas. LC 71-76607. (Illus.). 48p. (gr. 2 up). Date not set. Repr. of 1970 ed. 6.95 (ISBN 0-937460-02-8). Hendrick-Long.

Whipple, M. A. & Heizer, N. E. The First Californians. LC 75-165582. 1971. 5.95 (ISBN 0-917962-12-5); pap. 3.95 (ISBN 0-917962-13-3). Peek Pubns.

Williams, Stephen. Aboriginal Location of the Kadohadcho & Related Indian Tribes in Arkansas & Louisiana 1542-1954. (Indian Claims Commission Ser). 60p. 1974. lib. bdg. 27.00 (ISBN 0-8287-0889-4). Clearwater Pub.

--Caddoan Indians One. Horr, David A., ed. (American Indian Ethnohistory Ser.). 1978. lib. bdg. 42.00 (ISBN 0-8240-0763-8). Garland Pub.

Wood, Nancy. Many Winters. LC 74-3554. 80p. (gr. 6 up). 1974. 7.95 (ISBN 0-385-02226-3); limited edition 25.00 (ISBN 0-385-07107-8). Doubleday.

INDIANS OF NORTH AMERICA–THE WEST

Absaloka: Crow Children's Writing. (Indian Culture Ser.). 1971. 0.75 (ISBN 0-89992-009-8). MT Coun Indian.

Allan, Iris. White Sioux. 1969. 9.95 (ISBN 0-88826-021-0). Superior Pub.

Anderson, Eugene. The Chumash Indians of Southern California. 1973. 1.00 (ISBN 0-686-22653-4). Malki Mus Pr.

Anderson, Harry H. Sioux Occupation of Missouri Territory, 1640-1868. 24.00 (ISBN 0-8287-1251-4). Clearwater Pub.

Andrews, Lynn V. Medicine Woman. LC 80-7738. (Illus.). 288p. 1981. 12.95 (ISBN 0-06-064902-X, HarpR). Har-Row.

Andrews, Ralph W. Indians As the Westerner Saw Them. encore ed. LC 63-18495. 1963. 9.95 (ISBN 0-87564-311-6). Superior Pub.

Andrist, Ralph K. Long Death. (Illus.). 1969. pap. 4.95 (ISBN 0-02-030290-8, Collier). Macmillan.

Aoki, Haruo. Nez Perce Texts. LC 77-91776. (Publications in Linguistics: Vol. 90). 1979. 14.00x (ISBN 0-520-09593-6). U of Cal Pr.

Appraisal Associates. Kiowa, Comanche & Apache Lands in Oklahoma & Texas: Valuation Study As of 1900. 1976. lib. bdg. 250.00x (ISBN 0-8287-1093-7). Clearwater Pub.

Arapaho - Cheyenne Indians. Incl. Ethnological Report on Cheyenne & Arapaho: Aboriginal Occupation. Gussow, Zachary; Historical Development of the Arapacho-Cheyenne Land Area. Hafen, Leroy R; Cheyenne & Arapaho Indians: Historical Background, Social & Economic Conditions. Ekirch, Arthur A., Jr; Findings of Fact, & Opinion. Indian Claims Commission. (American Indian Ethnohistory Ser: Plains Indians). (Illus.). lib. bdg. 42.00 (ISBN 0-8240-0732-8). Garland Pub.

Azevedo, Warren, ed. Washo Indians of California & Nevada. (Utah Anthropological Papers: No. 67). Repr. of 1963 ed. 22.50 (ISBN 0-404-60667-9). AMS Pr.

Bad Heart Bull, Amos & Blish, Helen H. Pictographic History of the Oglala Sioux. LC 66-13404. (Illus.). xxii, 530p. 1968. 23.50 (ISBN 0-8032-0002-1). U of Nebr Pr.

Bailey, John W. Pacifying the Plains: General Alfred Terry & the Decline of the Sioux, 1866-1890. LC 78-19300. (Contributions in Military History: No. 17). 1979. lib. bdg. 18.95 (ISBN 0-313-20625-2, BAT/). Greenwood.

Barrows, David P. The Ethno-Botany of the Coahuilla Indians of Southern California. LC 76-43653. Repr. of 1900 ed. 14.00 (ISBN 0-404-15487-5). AMS Pr.

--Ethnobotany of the Coahuilla Indians of Southern California. 1977. pap. 5.95 (ISBN 0-686-22387-X). Malki Mus Pr.

Barry, Edward E. The Fort Belknap Reservation in Montana: Historical Report, 1878-1946. 89.00 (ISBN 0-8287-1043-0). Clearwater Pub.

Beals, Ralph L. California Indians Six. Horr, David A., ed. (American Indian Ethnohistory Ser.). 1978. lib. bdg. 42.00 (ISBN 0-8240-0776-X). Garland Pub.

Bean, Lowell J. & Saubel, Katherine S. Temalpakh: Cahuilla Indian Knowledge & Usage of Plants. LC 72-85815. 1972. 10.00 (ISBN 0-686-11775-1); pap. 6.50 (ISBN 0-686-28549-2). Malki Mus Pr.

Beckwith, Martha W. Mandan-Hidatsa Myths & Ceremonies. LC 38-19412. Repr. of 1938 ed. 20.00 (ISBN 0-527-01084-7). Kraus Repr.

--Myths & Hunting Stories of the Mandan & Hidatsa Sioux. LC 76-43665. (Vassar College Folklore Foundation: Publication No. 10). 1977. Repr. of 1930 ed. 16.00 (ISBN 0-404-15498-0). AMS Pr.

Beckwourth, James P. & Bonner, Thomas D. The Life & Adventures of James P. Beckwourth. LC 73-88092. (Illus.). xvi, 649p. 1972. pap. 10.95 (ISBN 0-8032-0724-7) (ISBN 0-8032-6061-X, BB 773, Bison). U of Nebr Pr.

Beemer, Eleanor. My Luiseno Neighbors. (Illus.). 91p. (Orig.). 1980. pap. 9.95 (ISBN 0-916552-20-9). Acoma Bks.

Berthrong, Donald J. The Southern Cheyennes. LC 63-8990. (Civilization of the American Indian Ser.: No. 66). (Illus.). 1975. pap. 8.95 (ISBN 0-8061-1199-2). U of Okla Pr.

Blackburn, Thomas C., ed. December's Child: A Book of Chumash Oral Narratives. LC 74-27284. 360p. 1976. 19.95 (ISBN 0-520-02930-5); pap. 5.95 (ISBN 0-520-04088-0). U of Cal Pr.

Bonner, T. D. Life & Adventures of James P. Beckwourth. 1965. Repr. 12.50 (ISBN 0-87018-003-7). Ross.

Bonner, T. D., ed. Life & Adventures of James P. Beckwourth, Mountaineer, Scout & Pioneer & Chief of the Crow Nation of Indians. LC 69-18563. (American Negro: His History & Literature Ser., No. 2). 1969. Repr. of 1856 ed. 19.00 (ISBN 0-405-01850-9). Arno.

Bowden, Charles. Killing the Hidden Waters. LC 77-5633. (Illus.). 186p. 1977. 9.95 (ISBN 0-292-76439-1). U of Tex Pr.

Bradfield, Wesley. Cameron Creek Village, a Site in the Mimbres Area in Grant County, New Mexico. LC 32-4291. (Illus.). 244p. 1973. Repr. of 1931 ed. 22.00 (ISBN 0-527-10570-8). Kraus Repr.

Brown, Dee. Bury My Heart at Wounded Knee: An Indian History of the American West. LC 70-121633. (Illus.). 1971. 10.95 (ISBN 0-03-085322-2). HR&W.

Brown, Joseph E., ed. The Sacred Pipe: Black Elk's Account of the Seven Rites of Oglala Sioux. (Civilization of the American Indian Ser.: No. 36). (Illus.). 1953. 9.95 (ISBN 0-8061-0272-1). U of Okla Pr.

--Sacred Pipe: Black Elk's Account of the Seven Rites of the Oglala Sioux. (Metaphysical Library Ser.). 1971. pap. 3.25 (ISBN 0-14-003346-7). Penguin.

Brusa, Betty W. Salinan Indians of California & Their Neighbors. LC 74-13249. (American Indian Map Bk. Ser., Vol. 2). (Illus.). 96p. 1975. 8.50 (ISBN 0-87961-023-9); pap. 4.50 (ISBN 0-87961-022-0). Naturegraph.

Burlingame, Merrill G. Blackfeet & Gros Ventre Tribes in Montana in the Agreement of May 1, 1888: Historical Report on Lands Ceded. (Library of American Indian Affairs). (Illus.). 80p. 1974. 31.50 (ISBN 0-8287-0955-6). Clearwater Pub.

--Flathead, Pen d'Oreille & Kutenai Indians Ceded Lands: Historical Report. (Library of American Indian Affairs). 105p. 1974. lib. bdg. 37.50 (ISBN 0-8287-1039-2). Clearwater Pub.

Burt, Olive. Sacajawea. LC 78-1572. (Visual Biography Ser.). (Illus.). (gr. 6 up). 1978. PLB 6.90 s&l (ISBN 0-531-00975-0). Watts.

Butler, B. Robert. When Did the Shoshoni Begin to Occupy Southern Idaho: Essays on Late Prehistoric Cultural Remains from the Upper Snake & Salmon River Countries. (Occasional Papers of the Idaho Museum of Natural History: No. 32). 95p. 1981. pap. 5.00 (ISBN 0-686-30007-6). Idaho Mus Nat Hist.

Butterworth, F. Edward. White Shadows Among the Mighty Sioux. 10.00 (ISBN 0-8309-0191-4, 17-0041-3). Independence Pr.

Campbell, Maria. People of the Buffalo. 8.50 (ISBN 0-88894-089-0, Pub. by Douglas & McIntyre). Intl Schol Bk Serv.

Capps, Ben. The Indians. (The Old West Ser.). (Illus.). 1973. 14.95 (ISBN 0-8094-1454-6). Time-Life.

Carley, Kenneth. The Sioux Uprising of 1862. rev. ed. LC 76-16499. (Illus.). 102p. 1976. 7.50 (ISBN 0-87351-102-6); pap. 4.50 (ISBN 0-87351-103-4). Minn Hist.

Catlin, George. George Catlin: Episodes from "Life Among the Indians" & "Last Rambles". Ross, Marvin C., ed. LC 59-7959. 1979. 25.00 (ISBN 0-8061-0442-2); pap. 12.50 (ISBN 0-8061-1693-5). U of Okla Pr.

--Letters & Notes on the Manners, Customs & Conditions of the North American Indians, Vol. 1. LC 64-18844. (Illus.). 264p. 1973. pap. 5.50 (ISBN 0-486-22118-0). Dover.

--Letters & Notes on the Manners, Customs & Conditions of the North American Indians, Vol. 2. LC 64-18844. (Illus.). 266p. 1973. pap. 5.50 (ISBN 0-486-22119-9). Dover.

--O-kee-pa: A Religious Ceremony & Other Customs of the Mandans. Ewers, John C., ed. LC 76-4522. (Illus.). x, 106p. 1976. pap. 7.95 (ISBN 0-8032-5845-3, BB 625, Bison). U of Nebr Pr.

Chalfant, Stuart A. The Flathead, Pend D'oreille & Kutenai Indians of Western Montana: Aboriginal Territories. 34.00 (ISBN 0-8287-1040-6). Clearwater Pub.

Chapman, Carl H. Osage Indian Village Sites & Hunting Territory in Kansas, Missouri & Oklahoma. 22.00 (ISBN 0-8287-1162-3). Clearwater Pub.

--Osage Indians, Vol. Three: The Origin of the Osage Indian Tribe: an Ethnographical, Historical & Archaeological Study. (American Indian Ethnohistory Ser.: Plains Indians). (Illus.). lib. bdg. 42.00 (ISBN 0-8240-0749-2). Garland Pub.

Chase, Don M. People of the Valley: The Concow Maidu. (Illus.). 47p. 1973. pap. 3.00 limited ed. (ISBN 0-918634-29-6). D M Chase.

Cheney, Roberta C. The Big Missouri Winter Count. LC 79-15790. (Illus.). 48p. 1979. 7.00 (ISBN 0-87961-082-4); pap. text ed. 3.00 (ISBN 0-87961-081-6). Naturegraph.

Chisholm, Roger K. The Peoria Tribe & Kaskasia Nation: An Appraisal of Lands in Illinois, 1803 to 1820. (Library of American Indian Affairs). lib. bdg. 95.00x (ISBN 0-8287-1190-9). Clearwater Pub.

Christgau, John. Spoon. LC 77-22081. (Richard Seaver Bk). 1978. 10.95 (ISBN 0-670-66455-3). Viking Pr.

Confederated Salish & Kootenai Tribe of the Flathead Reservation: A History. (Library of American Indian Affairs). 1976. lib. bdg. 27.00x (ISBN 0-8287-1015-5). Clearwater Pub.

Constitution & Laws of the Osage Nation: Passed at Pawhuska, Osage Nation, in the Years 1881 & 1882. Bd. with Constitution & Laws of the Sac & Fox Nation: Indian Territory. LC 75-3699. (Constitutions & Laws of the American Indian Tribes Ser. 2: Vol. 31). 1975. Repr. of 1888 ed. 11.00 (ISBN 0-8420-1891-3). Scholarly Res Inc.

Cook, Sherburne F. The Conflict Between the California Indian & White Civilization. LC 75-23860. 1976. 36.50x (ISBN 0-520-03142-3); pap. 6.95 (ISBN 0-520-03143-1, CAL332). U of Cal Pr.

--The Conflict Between the California Indian & White Civilization, 4 vols. in 1. LC 76-43678. (Ibero-Americana: 21-24). Repr. of 1943 ed. 27.50 (ISBN 0-404-15512-X). AMS Pr.

--The Population of the California Indians 1769-1970. LC 74-27287. 1976. 21.50x (ISBN 0-520-02923-2). U of Cal Pr.

Crow Indians. Incl. The Crow Tribe of Indians. Plummer, Norman B; Findings of Fact, & Opinion. Indian Claims Commission. (American Indian Ethnohistory Ser: Plains Indians). (Illus.). lib. bdg. 42.00 (ISBN 0-8240-0756-5). Garland Pub.

Crowder, David L. Tendoy, Chief of the Lemhis. LC 75-76336. (Illus., Orig.). (gr. 5-9). 1969. pap. 2.75 (ISBN 0-87004-129-0). Caxton.

Cutler, Jervis. Topographical Description of the State of Ohio, Indiana Territory, & Louisiana. LC 78-146388. (First American Frontier Ser). (Illus.). 1971. Repr. of 1812 ed. 12.00 (ISBN 0-405-02839-3). Arno.

Dary, David. Comanche. (Public Education Ser: No.5). (Illus.). 19p. (Orig.). 1976. pap. 1.00 (ISBN 0-89338-003-2). U of KS Mus Nat Hist.

Davis, W. N. California Indians Five: Sagebrush Corner - Opening of California's Northeast. (American Indian Ethnohistory Ser: California & Basin - Plateau Indians). (Illus.). lib. bdg. 42.00 (ISBN 0-8240-0775-1). Garland Pub.

Delano, Alonzo. Life on the Plains & Among the Diggings, Being Scenes & Adventures of an Overland Journey to California. LC 72-9440. (The Far Western Frontier Ser.). (Illus.). 396p. 1973. Repr. of 1854 ed. 18.00 (ISBN 0-405-04970-6). Arno.

Dempsey, Hugh A. Crowfoot: Chief of the Blackfeet. LC 72-865. (Civilization of the American Indian Ser.: Vol. 122). 230p. 1972. 12.95 (ISBN 0-8061-1025-2). U of Okla Pr.

Denig, Edwin T. Five Indian Tribes of the Upper Missouri: Sioux, Arickaras, Assiniboines, Crees & Crows. Ewers, John C., ed. (Civilization of the American Indian Ser.: No. 59). (Illus.). 1961. 12.95 (ISBN 0-8061-0493-7); pap. 6.95 (ISBN 0-8061-1308-1). U of Okla Pr.

--Indian Tribes of Upper Missouri. facs. ed. Repr. of 1930 ed. pap. 16.00 (ISBN 0-8466-0152-4, SJS152). Shorey.

--Of the Crow Nation. Ewers, John C., ed. LC 76-43690. (BAE. Bulletin: 151). Repr. of 1953 ed. 14.50 (ISBN 0-404-15532-4). AMS Pr.

Densmore, Frances. Mandan & Hidatsa Music. LC 72-1886. (Music Ser.). (Illus.). 236p. 1972. Repr. of 1923 ed. lib. bdg. 19.50 (ISBN 0-306-70514-1). Da Capo.

De Smet, Peter J. Western Missions & Missionaries. 562p. 1972. Repr. of 1863 ed. 37.50x (ISBN 0-87471-318-8). Rowman.

Dixon, Roland B. The Northern Maidu. LC 76-43692. (AMNH. Bulletin: No. 17). Repr. of 1905 ed. 19.50 (ISBN 0-404-15523-5). AMS Pr.

--The Shasta. LC 76-43689. (AMNH. Bulletin: No. 17). Repr. of 1907 ed. 12.50 (ISBN 0-404-15524-3). AMS Pr.

Dodge, Richard I. Our Wild Indians: Thirty Three Years' Personal Experience Among the Red Men of the Great West. (Select Bibliographies Reprint Ser). 1882. 55.00 (ISBN 0-8369-5230-8). Arno.

Dorsey, G. A. The Arapaho Sun Dance, the Ceremony of the Offerings Lodge. (Chicago Field Museum of Natural History Fieldiana Anthropology Ser). 1903. 55.00 (ISBN 0-527-01864-3). Kraus Repr.

--Cheyenne. enl. ed. (Chicago Field Museum of Natural History Fieldiana Anthropology Ser). 1905. pap. 21.00 (ISBN 0-527-01869-4). Kraus Repr.

--Traditions of the Skidi Pawnee. LC 4-28964. (American Folklore Society Memoirs). Repr. of 1904 ed. pap. 21.00 (ISBN 0-527-01060-X). Kraus Repr.

Dorsey, G. A. & Kroeber, A. L. Traditions of the Arapaho. (Chicago Field Museum of Natural History Fieldiana Anthropology Ser). 1903. pap. 30.00 (ISBN 0-527-01865-1). Kraus Repr.

Dorsey, George A. The Cheyenne. 1975. 9.95 (ISBN 0-87770-157-1). Ye Galleon.

--The Cheyenne Indians: The Sun Dance, Wyoming. LC 78-177922. (Beautiful Rio Grande Classics Ser). 286p. 1972. lib. bdg. 20.00 (ISBN 0-87380-081-8). Rio Grande.

Dorsey, James O. Omaha Sociology. LC 16-5488. 1971. Repr. of 1884 ed. 14.50 (ISBN 0-384-12395-3). Johnson Repr.

--Study of Siouan Cults. (Illus.). pap. 14.50 (ISBN 0-8466-4055-4, SJI55). Shorey.

Drake, Benjamin. Life of Tecumseh & of His Brother the Prophet: With a Historical Sketch of the Shawanoe Indians. LC 78-90173. (Mass Violence in America Ser). Repr. of 1841 ed. 12.00 (ISBN 0-405-01307-8). Arno.

Driver, Harold, et al. California Indians One: Indians Land Use & Occupancy in California, 3 vols. Beals, Ralph L., ed. (American Indian Ethnohistory Ser: California & Basin-Plateau Indians). (Illus.). lib. bdg. 42.00 (ISBN 0-8240-0771-9). Garland Pub.

Driver, Harold E., et al. California Indians Four. Horr, David A., ed. (American Indian Ethnohistory Ser.). 1978. lib. bdg. 42.00 (ISBN 0-8240-0774-3). Garland Pub.

Eastman, Charles A. Indian Boyhood. LC 68-58282. (Illus.). (gr. 3-7). pap. 3.50 (ISBN 0-486-22037-0). Dover.

--Indian Boyhood. (Illus.). 7.25 (ISBN 0-8446-0085-7). Peter Smith.

Eastman, Elaine G. Sister to the Sioux: The Memoirs of Elaine Goodale Eastman, 1885-91. Graber, Kay, ed. LC 77-25018. (Pioneer Heritage Ser: Vol. VII). (Illus.). 1978. 10.95 (ISBN 0-8032-0971-1). U of Nebr Pr.

Eastman, Mary. Dahcotah: Or, Life & Legends of the Sioux Around Fort Snelling. facsimile ed. LC 75-95. (Mid-American Frontier Ser.). (Illus.). 1975. Repr. of 1849 ed. 18.00x (ISBN 0-405-06861-1). Arno.

Ekirch, Arthur A., Jr. Cheyenne & Arapaho: Historical Background. (Library of American Indian Affairs). 45p. 1974. lib. bdg. 22.50 (ISBN 0-8287-0978-5). Clearwater Pub.

Ewers, John C. Blackfeet: Raiders on the Northwestern Plains. (Civilization of the American Indian Ser.: No. 49). (Illus.). 1976. Repr. of 1958 ed. 15.95 (ISBN 0-8061-0405-8). U of Okla Pr.

Farnham, Thomas J. Travels in the Great Western Prairies, 2 vols. in 1. LC 68-16231. (The American Scene Ser.). 612p. 1973. Repr. of 1843 ed. lib. bdg. 35.00 (ISBN 0-306-71012-9). Da Capo.

Faust, Josef & Hassler, John J. Creek Nation Lands in Oklahoma: Appraisal of Oil, Gas, Coal & Minerals. (Library of American Indian Affairs). 1976. lib. bdg. 225.00x (ISBN 0-8287-1025-2). Clearwater Pub.

Fehrenbach, T. R. Comanches. LC 73-20761. 1974. 17.50 (ISBN 0-394-48856-3). Knopf.

Fenton, Harry R. & Fenton, Everett W. Kickapoo Tribal Lands in Illinois & Indiana: An Appraisal As of 1820. (Library of American Indian Affairs). 1976. lib. bdg. 225.00x (ISBN 0-8287-1091-0). Clearwater Pub.

Flannery, Regina. Gros Ventre of Montana, 2 vols. Incl. Vol. 1. Social Life; Vol. 2. Religion & Ritual. (Illus.). 1956. Repr. 21.00 set (ISBN 0-686-10282-7). Gros Ventre Treaty.

Fletcher, Alice C. & La Flesche, Francis. The Omaha Tribe. LC 11-31959. 1971. Repr. of 1911 ed. 42.50 (ISBN 0-384-16000-X). Johnson Repr.

Fletcher, Alice C. & La Flesche, Francis. Omaha Tribe, 2 vols. Incl. Vol. 1. 312p (ISBN 0-8032-5756-2, BB 549, Bison); Vol. 2. viii, 347p (ISBN 0-8032-5757-0, BB 550, Bison). LC 72-175503. (Illus.). 1972. pap. 7.95 ea. U of Nebr Pr.

Fletcher, Alice C. & LaFlesche, Francis. Study of Omaha Indian Music with a Report of the Structural Peculiarities of the Music by J. C. Fillmore. 1893. pap. 8.00 (ISBN 0-527-01187-8). Kraus Repr.

Foley, Michael F. Yankton Tribal Lands: An Historical Analysis of the Opening & Development from 1849 to 1869. (Library of American Indian Affairs). 1976. lib. bdg. 75.00x (ISBN 0-8287-1315-4). Clearwater Pub.

Foreman, Grant. Advancing the Frontier, 1830-1860. (Civilization of the American Indian Ser.: No. 4). (Illus.). 1968. Repr. of 1933 ed. 16.95 (ISBN 0-8061-0792-8). U of Okla Pr.

--Five Civilized Tribes. (Civilization of the American Indian Ser.: No. 8). (Illus.). 1971. pap. 8.95 (ISBN 0-8061-0923-8). U of Okla Pr.

Fortune, Reo F. Omaha Secret Societies. LC 70-82351. (Columbia Univ. Contributions to Anthropology Ser.: Vol. 14). Repr. of 1932 ed. 18.50 (ISBN 0-404-50564-3). AMS Pr.

Fotine, Larry. Cowboys, Indians & Other Characters. LC 80-82354. Date not set. pap. 5.00 (ISBN 0-933830-09-2). Poly Tone.

Frison, George C. The Wardell Buffalo Trap Forty Eight SU Three Hundred & One: Communal Procurement in the Upper Green River Basin, Wyoming. (Anthropological Papers: No. 48). 1973. pap. 3.00x (ISBN 0-932206-46-8). U Mich Mus Anthro.

Gamble, Geoffrey. Wikchamni Grammar. LC 77-8566. (Publications in Linguistics Ser.: Vol. 89). 1978. 12.00x (ISBN 0-520-09589-8). U of Cal Pr.

Gates, Paul W. The Fort Belknap & Blackfeet Indian Reservation in Montana: A History of Economic Influences. 54.00 (ISBN 0-8287-1042-2). Clearwater Pub.

Gibson, Arrell M. Kickapoos: Lords of the Middle Border. (Civilization of the American Indian Ser.: No. 70). (Illus.). 1976. pap. 7.95 (ISBN 0-8061-1264-6). U of Okla Pr.

Gifford, Edward W & Block, Gwendoline H.compiled by. California Indian Nights Entertainment. LC 76-43713. Repr. of 1930 ed. 32.50 (ISBN 0-404-15546-4). AMS Pr.

Gilliland, Hap. How the Dogs Saved the Cheyennes. (Indian Culture Ser.). (gr. 1-4). 1972. 1.95 (ISBN 0-89992-017-9). MT Coun Indian.

Gilmore, Melvin R. Prairie Smoke. LC 78-168148. (Illus.). Repr. of 1929 ed. 18.00 (ISBN 0-404-02776-8). AMS Pr.

Government Surveyors' Notes & Related Data on Soils, Timber & Water in Oklahoma Territory, 1871, 1872. (Library of American Indian Affairs Ser.). 32p. 1974. lib. bdg. 19.50 (ISBN 0-8287-1054-6). Clearwater Pub.

Gray, John S. Centennial Campaign: The Sioux War of 1876. LC 76-47160. (Source Custeriana Ser.: Vol. 8). (Illus.). 1977. pap. 7.95 (ISBN 0-88342-243-3). Old Army.

Gregg, Josiah. Commerce of the Prairies. Quaife, Milo M., ed. & intro. by. 5.50 (ISBN 0-8446-2165-X). Peter Smith.

--Commerce of the Prairies. Moorhead, Max, ed. (American Exploration & Travel Ser.: No. 17). (Illus.). 1974. 19.95 (ISBN 0-8061-0299-3); pap. 7.95 (ISBN 0-8061-1059-7). U of Okla Pr.

Griffiths, Thomas M. The Pawnee: Historical & Economic Geography of the Lands. 38.00 (ISBN 0-8287-1394-4). Clearwater Pub.

--Yankton Sioux Tribe: Appraisal of Lands in Nebraska, Iowa, Minnesota, South Dakota, & North Dakota, As of 1858. (Library of American Indian Affairs). 1976. lib. bdg. 150.00x (ISBN 0-8287-1314-6). Clearwater Pub.

Grinnell, George B. Blackfoot Lodge Tales: The Story of a Prairie People. LC 62-4146. 1962. pap. 5.95 (ISBN 0-8032-5079-7, BB 129, Bison). U of Nebr Pr.

--By Cheyenne Campfires. LC 79-158083. (Illus.). 1971. pap. 6.50 (ISBN 0-8032-5746-5, BB 541, Bison). U of Nebr Pr.

--Cheyenne Indians, Their History & Ways of Life, 2 Vols. LC 62-19531. (Illus.). 1923. 30.00x (ISBN 0-8154-0090-X). Cooper Sq.

--The Cheyenne Indians: Their History & Ways of Life, 2 vols. Incl. Vol. 1. x, 358p. pap. 7.95 (ISBN 0-8032-5771-6, BB 562, Bison); Vol. 2. viii, 430p. pap. 8.95 (ISBN 0-8032-5772-4, BB 563, Bison). LC 23-17688. (Illus.). 1972. U of Nebr Pr.

--When Buffalo Ran. (Western Frontier Library: No. 31). (Illus.). 1966. 6.95 (ISBN 0-8061-0715-4); pap. 2.95 (ISBN 0-8061-1271-9). U of Okla Pr.

Grosscup, Gordon L. Paiute Archeology in Nevada & California. 24.00 (ISBN 0-8287-0067-2). Clearwater Pub.

Hafen, Leroy R. Arapaho-Cheyenne Land Area: Historical Background & Development. (Library of American Indian Affairs). 69p. 1974. lib. bdg. 28.50 (ISBN 0-8287-0953-X). Clearwater Pub.

Haines, Francis. Nez Perces: Tribesmen of the Columbia Plateau. LC 55-9626. (Civilization of American Indian Ser.: No. 42). (Illus.). 1955. 14.95 (ISBN 0-8061-0325-6); pap. 6.95 (ISBN 0-8061-0982-3). U of Okla Pr.

--Red Eagles of the Northwest: The Story of Chief Joseph & His People. LC 76-43728. (Illus.). Repr. of 1939 ed. 32.50 (ISBN 0-404-15569-3). AMS Pr.

Hall, Richard B. Apache, Kiowa & Comanche Indian Reservation in Southwestern Oklahoma Appraisal & Valuation. (Library of American Indian Affairs). 1976. lib. bdg. 78.00x (ISBN 0-8287-0917-3). Clearwater Pub.

Hamilton, Henry W. & Hamilton, Jean T. The Sioux of the Rosebud: A History in Pictures. LC 78-145506. (The Civilization of the American Indian Ser.: Vol. 111). (Illus.). 320p. 1981. pap. 12.50 (ISBN 0-8061-1622-6). U of Okla Pr.

--Sioux of the Rosebud: A History in Pictures. LC 78-145506. (Civilization of the American Indian Ser.: Vol. 111). (Illus.). 1971. 19.95 (ISBN 0-8061-0953-X). U of Okla Pr.

Hassrick, Royal B., et al. Sioux: Life & Customs of a Warrior Society. (Civilization of the American Indian Ser.: No. 72). (Illus.). 1977. Repr. of 1964 ed. 16.95 (ISBN 0-8061-0607-7). U of Okla Pr.

Hatheway, Flora. Chief Plenty Coups: Life of the Crow Indian Chief. (Indian Culture Ser.). (gr. 4). 1971. 1.95 (ISBN 0-89992-005-5). MT Coun Indian.

Heard, Isaac V. History of the Sioux War & Massacres of 1862 & 1863. LC 2-26023. 1975. Repr. of 1864 ed. 20.00 (ISBN 0-527-03223-9). Kraus Repr.

Hebard, Grace R. Washaki: An Account of Indian Resistance of the Covered Wagon & Union Pacific Railroad Invasion of Their Territory. LC 76-43733. Repr. of 1940 ed. 29.00 (ISBN 0-404-15575-8). AMS Pr.

Heizer, Robert & Elsasser, Albert B. California Indians: An Annotated Bibliography. (Reference Library of Social Science: Vol. 48). (LC 76-052687). 1977. lib. bdg. 27.00 (ISBN 0-8240-9866-8). Garland Pub.

Heizer, Robert F. California Indians Two. Horr, David A., ed. (American Indian Ethnohistory Ser.). 1978. lib. bdg. 42.00 (ISBN 0-8240-0772-7). Garland Pub.

Heizer, Robert F., ed. A Collection of Ethnographical Articles on the California Indians. (Bellena Press Pubns. in Archaeology, Ethnology & History: No. 7). (Illus.). 1976. pap. 5.95 (ISBN 0-87919-062-0). Ballena Pr.

--Federal Concern About Conditions of California Indians 1853-1913: Eight Documents. (Ballena Press Publications in Archaeology, Ethnology & History Ser.: No. 13). 1979. pap. 7.95 (ISBN 0-87919-084-1). Ballena Pr.

Henning, Dale R. The Osage Nation in Eatern Oklahoma & Northwest Arkansas, 1775-1818. 20.00 (ISBN 0-8287-1164-X). Clearwater Pub.

Henry Tall Bull & Weist, Tom. Cheyenne Legends of Creation. (Indian Culture Ser.). (gr. 4-9). 1972. 1.95 (ISBN 0-89992-025-X). MT Coun Indian.

--Cheyenne Warriors. (Indian Culture Ser.). (gr. 4-12). 1976. pap. 1.95 (ISBN 0-89992-015-2). MT Coun Indian.

--The Rolling Head: Cheyenne Tales. (Indian Culture Ser.). (gr. 3-9). 1971. 1.95 (ISBN 0-89992-013-6). MT Coun Indian.

Hickerson, Harold. Sioux Indians, Vol. One: Mdewakanton Band of Sioux Indians. (American Indian Ethnohistory Ser: Plains Indians). (Illus.). lib. bdg. 42.00 (ISBN 0-8240-0794-8). Garland Pub.

Hoebel, E. A. The Cheyennes. 2nd ed. LC 77-25471. 1978. pap. 5.95 (ISBN 0-03-022686-4, HoltC). HR&W.

--Political Organizations and Law-Ways of the Comanche Indians. LC 42-13539. 1940. 8.00 (ISBN 0-527-00553-3). Kraus Repr.

Hoig, Stan. John Simpson Smith. (Illus.). 1974. 16.00 (ISBN 0-87062-107-6). A H Clark.

--The Peace Chiefs of the Cheyennes. LC 79-4739. (Illus.). 1980. 14.95 (ISBN 0-8061-1573-4). U of Okla Pr.

Holbrook, Jeffrey. Cheyenne-Arapaho Lands in Eastern Colorado, Western Kansas, Southwestern Nebraska & Southwestern Wyoming: Appraisal. (Library of American Indian Affairs). 109p. 1974. lib. bdg. 37.00 (ISBN 0-8287-0985-8). Clearwater Pub.

Holder, Preston. The Hoe & the Horse on the Plains: A Study of Cultural Development Among North American Indians. LC 70-98474. (Illus.). xiv, 176p. 1970. 13.50x (ISBN 0-8032-0730-1); pap. 3.75x (ISBN 0-8032-5809-7, BB 594, Bison). U of Nebr Pr.

Hoover, Herbert T. The Sioux: A Critical Bibliography. LC 79-2167. (Newberry Library Center for the History of the American Indian Bibliographical Ser.). 96p. (Orig.). 1979. pap. 3.95x (ISBN 0-253-34972-9). Ind U Pr.

Horn, Tom. Life of Tom Horn, Government Scout & Interpreter, Written by Himself, Together with His Letters & Statements by His Friends: A Vindication. (Western Frontier Library: No. 26). 1964. pap. 4.95 (ISBN 0-8061-1044-9). U of Okla Pr.

Horr, David A., ed. Kiowa-Commanche Indians, 2 vols. (American Indian Ethnohistory Ser.: Plains Indians). 1974. Set. lib. bdg. 76.00 (ISBN 0-8240-0724-7); lib. bdg. 42.00 ea. Garland Pub.

Howard, Oliver O. Nez Perce Joseph. LC 70-39379. (Law, Politics, & History Ser). (Illus.). 274p. 1972. Repr. of 1881 ed. lib. bdg. 37.50 (ISBN 0-306-70461-7). Da Capo.

Hoyt, Homer. Cheyenne & Arapaho Lands in Colorado, Kansas, Wyoming, & Nebraska, 1865: Appraisal. (Library of American Indian Affairs). 358p. 1974. lib. bdg. 100.00 (ISBN 0-8287-0981-5). Clearwater Pub.

Hudson, Travis & Underhay, Ernest. Crystals in the Sky: An Intellectual Odyssey Involving Chumush Astronomy, Coamology & Rock Art. (Ballena Press Anthropolical Papers: No. 10). 1978. pap. 8.95 (ISBN 0-87919-074-4). Ballena Pr.

Hughes, Jack T. Caddoan Indians Three: Prehistory of the Caddoan - Speaking Tribes. (American Indian Ethnohistory Ser.: Plains Indians). (Illus.). lib. bdg. 42.00 (ISBN 0-8240-0815-4). Garland Pub.

Hungry Wolf, Adolf. The Blood People. (Native American Publishing Program: Vol. 9). 1977. 12.95 (ISBN 0-06-450600-2, HarpT). Har-Row.

Hurt, Wesley R. Sioux Indians, Vol. Two: Dakota Sioux Indians. (American Indian Ethnohistory Ser: Plains Indians). (Illus.). lib. bdg. 42.00 (ISBN 0-8240-0795-6). Garland Pub.

Huseboe, Arthur R. & Geyer, William, eds. Where the West Begins: Essays on Middle Border & Siouxland Writing. LC 78-55073. (Illus.). 1978. pap. 3.95 (ISBN 0-931170-02-8). Ctr Western Studies.

Hyde, George E. Indians of the High Plains: From the Prehistoric Period to the Coming of Europeans. (Civilization of the American Indian Ser.: No. 54). (Illus.). 1976. 13.95 (ISBN 0-8061-0438-4); pap. 6.95 (ISBN 0-8061-1382-0). U of Okla Pr.

--The Pawnee Indians. LC 72-9260. (Civilization of the American Indian Ser.: Vol. 128). (Illus.). 310p. 1974. 17.95 (ISBN 0-8061-1065-1). U of Okla Pr.

--Red Cloud's Folk: A History of the Oglala Sioux Indians. rev. ed. (Civilization of the American Indian Ser.: No. 15). (Illus.). 1976. Repr. of 1937 ed. 15.95 (ISBN 0-8061-0063-X). U of Okla Pr.

--A Sioux Chronicle. (Civilization of the American Indian Ser.: Vol. 45). 334p. 1956. 15.95 (ISBN 0-8061-0358-2). U of Okla Pr.

Indian Claims Commission. Osage Indians, Vol. Five: Findings of Fact, & Opinion. (American Indian Ethnohistory Ser: Plains Indians). (Illus.). lib. bdg. 42.00 (ISBN 0-8240-0751-4). Garland Pub.

--Sioux Indians, Vol. Four: Findings of Fact, & Opinion. (American Indian Ethnohistory Ser: Plains Indians). (Illus.). lib. bdg. 42.00 (ISBN 0-8240-0797-2). Garland Pub.

Indians of Illinois & Northwestern Indiana. Incl. Reports on the Kickapoo, Illinois & Potawatomi Indians. Stout, David B; Anthropological Report on the Chippewa, Ottowa, & Potawatomi Indians in Southwest Michigan. Wheeler-Voegelin, Erminie. (American Indian Ethnohistory Ser: North Central & Northeastern Indians). (Illus.). lib. bdg. 42.00 (ISBN 0-8240-0804-9). Garland Pub.

Inman, H. & Cody, W. F. Great Salt Lake Trail. (Illus.). 1897. Repr. 12.50 (ISBN 0-87018-030-4). Ross.

Irving, Washington. Tour on the Prairies. McDermott, John F., ed. (Western Frontier Library: No. 7). 1971. Repr. of 1956 ed. 6.95 (ISBN 0-8061-0351-5). U of Okla Pr.

Irwin, Charles N. The Shoshoni Indians of Inyo County, California. (Ballena Press Publications in Archaeology, Ethnology & History: No. 15). (Illus.). 114p. (Orig.). 1980. pap. 6.95 (ISBN 0-87919-090-6). Ballena Pr.

Jablow, Joseph. Indians of Illinois & Indiana: Illinois, Kickapoo & Potawatomi Indians. Horr, David A., ed. (American Indian Ethnohistory Ser.: North Central & Northeastern Indians). 1974. lib. bdg. 42.00 (ISBN 0-8240-0805-7). Garland Pub.

--Ponca Indians. Horr, David A., ed. Incl. Ethnology of the Ponca. Jablow, Joseph; Findings of Fact, & Opinion. Indian Claims Commission. (American Indian Ethnohistory Ser: Plains Indians). (Illus.). 1974. lib. bdg. 42.00 (ISBN 0-8240-0734-4). Garland Pub.

Jacobson, Daniel. Alabama-Coushatta Indians of Texas & the Coushatta Indians of Louisiana, 1540-1855. (Library of American Indian Affairs). 150p. 1974. lib. bdg. 48.00 (ISBN 0-8287-0899-1). Clearwater Pub.

James, Edwin, compiled by. Account of An Expedition from Pittsburgh to the Rocky Mountains, Performed in the Years 1819 & 1820, 2 Vols. LC 68-55198. 1968. Repr. of 1823 ed. Set. lib. bdg. 21.75x (ISBN 0-8371-8599-8, JAPI). Greenwood.

Johnson, Willis F. The Red Record of the Sioux. LC 76-43757. Repr. of 1891 ed. 44.50 (ISBN 0-404-15598-7). AMS Pr.

Jones, D. E. Sanapia: Comanchee Medicine Woman. LC 73-179548. (Case Studies in Cultural Anthropology). 1972. pap. text ed. 4.95 (ISBN 0-03-088456-X, HoltC). HR&W.

Josephy, Alvin M., Jr. The Nez Perce Indians & the Opening of the Northwest. abridged ed. LC 79-14847. (Illus.). xvi, 667p. 1979. 29.50x (ISBN 0-8032-2555-5); pap. 9.95 (ISBN 0-8032-7551-X, BB 718, Bison). U of Nebr Pr.

Kaltreider, D. R., et al. Kickapoo Lands in Illinois & Missouri: An Appraisal. Ross, Norman A., ed. (Library of American Indian Affairs). 1976. lib. bdg. 35.00x (ISBN 0-8287-1088-0). Clearwater Pub.

Kenner, Charles L. History of New Mexican-Plains Indian Relations. LC 68-31375. (Illus.). 1969. 13.95 (ISBN 0-8061-0829-0). U of Okla Pr.

Knudtson, Peter M. The Wintun Indians of California & Their Neighbors. LC 76-56357. (American Indian Map Book Ser: Vol. 3). (Illus.). 1977. 8.50 (ISBN 0-87961-063-8); pap. 4.50 (ISBN 0-87961-062-X). Naturegraph.

Kroeber, A. L. Handbook of the Indians of California. LC 75-108501. (Illus.). 1024p. 1972. Repr. of 1925 ed. 79.00 (ISBN 0-403-00369-5). Scholarly.

--Handbook of the Indians of California. LC 76-19514. (Illus.). 995p. 1976. pap. 10.00 (ISBN 0-486-23368-5). Dover.

--Handbook of the Indians of California. LC 76-19514. (Illus.). 1976. lib. bdg. 18.50x (ISBN 0-88307-585-7). Gannon.

Kroeber, A. L., et al. The Diegueno Indians. 1975. pap. 2.00 (ISBN 0-916552-02-0). Acoma Bks.

Kroeber, Alfred L. The Arapaho. 1975. 14.95 (ISBN 0-87770-158-X). Ye Galleon.

--Ethnology of the Gros Ventre. LC 76-43763. (AMNH. Anthropological Papers: Vol. 1, Pt. 4). Repr. of 1908 ed. 16.50 (ISBN 0-404-15617-7). AMS Pr.

--Yurok Myths. LC 75-3772. 460p. 1976. 25.00 (ISBN 0-520-02977-1); pap. 6.95 (ISBN 0-520-03639-5). U of Cal Pr.

Kroeker, Marvin E. Great Plains Command: William B. Hazen in the Frontier West. LC 75-17709. (Illus.). 200p. 1976. 11.95 (ISBN 0-8061-1318-9). U of Okla Pr.

Landry, Stuart O. The Caddo Indians in Louisiana & Texas. (Library of American Indian Affairs). 60p. 1974. lib. bdg. 27.00 (ISBN 0-685-39448-4). Clearwater Pub.

Lang, John D. & Taylor, Samuel, Jr. Report of a Visit to Some of the Tribes of Indians, Located West of the Mississippi River. 34p. 1973. 5.50 (ISBN 0-87770-123-7). Ye Galleon.

Lange, Charles H. Caddo Treaty of July 1, 1835: Historical & Anthropological Background. (Library of American Indian Affairs). 165p. 1974. lib. bdg. 52.00 (ISBN 0-8287-0962-9). Clearwater Pub.

Laws Relating to Osage Tribes of Indians from May 18, 1824 to March 2, 1929, Compiled by Ralph A. Barney, L.L.B. LC 73-88776. (Constitutions & Laws of the American Indian Tribes, Ser. 1: Vol. 3). 1973. Repr. of 1929 ed. 12.00 (ISBN 0-8420-1723-2). Scholarly Res Inc.

Leckie, William H. The Military Conquest of the Southern Plains. (Illus.). 1963. 14.95 (ISBN 0-8061-0570-4). U of Okla Pr.

Leforge, Thomas H. Memoirs of a White Crow Indian. Marquis, Thomas B., narrated by. LC 74-6222. xxiv, 356p. 1974. 21.50x (ISBN 0-8032-0885-5); pap. 6.50 (ISBN 0-8032-5800-3, BB 584, Bison). U of Nebr Pr.

Lesser, Alexander. Pawnee Ghost Dance Hand Game. LC 79-82340. (Columbia Univ. Contributions to Anthropology Ser.: Vol. 16). 1969. Repr. of 1933 ed. 21.00 (ISBN 0-404-50566-X). AMS Pr.

--The Pawnee Ghost Dance Hand Game: A Study of Cultural Change. LC 79-82340. (Illus.). 1978. 20.00 (ISBN 0-299-07480-3); pap. 7.95 (ISBN 0-299-07484-6). U of Wis Pr.

Lewis, Henry. Valley of the Mississippi Illustrated. Heilbron, Bertha L., ed. Poatgieter, A. H., tr. LC 67-65590. (Illus.). 423p. 1967. 39.75 (ISBN 0-87351-035-6); uncut 50.00 (ISBN 0-87351-036-4). Minn Hist.

Linderman, Frank B. Plenty-coups, Chief of the Crows. LC 30-11369. (Illus.). 1962. pap. 3.95 (ISBN 0-8032-5121-1, BB 128, Bison). U of Nebr Pr.

Llewellyn, Karl N. & Hoebel, E. Adamson. The Cheyenne Way: Conflict & Case Law in Primitive Jurisprudence. (Civilization of the American Indian Ser.: Vol. 21). (Illus.). 1978. Repr. of 1941 ed. 17.95 (ISBN 0-8061-0099-0). U of Okla Pr.

Lowie, Robert H. The Assiniboine. LC 74-7978. Repr. of 1909 ed. 22.45 (ISBN 0-404-11868-2). AMS Pr.

--The Material Culture of the Crow Indians. LC 74-7980. Repr. of 1922 ed. 11.50 (ISBN 0-404-11869-0). AMS Pr.

--Social Life of the Crow Indians. LC 74-7987. Repr. of 1912 ed. 11.50 (ISBN 0-404-11875-5). AMS Pr.

--The Sun Dance of the Crow Indians. LC 76-43771. (AMNH. Anthropological Papers: Vol. 16, Pt. 1). 1977. Repr. of 1915 ed. 12.50 (ISBN 0-404-15624-X). AMS Pr.

McClellan, Val J. This Is Our Land, Vol. 1. LC 77-151749. (Illus.). 1977. 12.50x (ISBN 0-533-02248-7). Western Pubs OH.

McFee, M. Modern Blackfeet: Montanans on a Reservation. LC 76-175713. (Case Studies in Cultural Anthropology). 1972. text ed. 4.95 (ISBN 0-03-085768-6, HoltC). HR&W.

Macgregor, Gordon, et al. Warriors Without Weapons: A Study of the Society & Personality Development of the Pine Ridge Sioux. (Midway Reprint Ser.). (Illus.). 228p. 1975. pap. text ed. 9.00x (ISBN 0-226-50034-9). U of Chicago Pr.

Madsen, Brigham D. The Lemhi: Sacajawea's People. LC 78-53137. (Illus., Orig.). 1980. pap. 4.95 (ISBN 0-87004-267-X). Caxton.

--The Northern Shoshoni. LC 78-53138. (Illus.). 262p. (Orig.). 1980. 17.95 (ISBN 0-87004-289-0); pap. 12.95 (ISBN 0-87004-266-1). Caxton.

Mails, Thomas E. Sundancing at Rosebud & Pine Ridge. LC 78-55075. (Illus.). 1978. 33.00 (ISBN 0-931170-01-X). U of Nebr Pr.

Malouf, Carling I. The Indian of Western Montana: Economy & Land Use. 28.00 (ISBN 0-8287-1067-8). Clearwater Pub.

Marquis, Thomas B. The Cheyennes of Montana. Weist, Thomas D., ed. LC 78-59715. 1978. 19.50 (ISBN 0-917256-04-2). Ref Pubns.

Marquis, Thomas B., tr. Wooden Leg: A Warrior Who Fought Custer. LC 31-10067. (Illus.). 1962. pap. 6.50 (ISBN 0-8032-5124-6, BB 126, Bison). U of Nebr Pr.

Marriott, Alice. Osage Indians, Vol. Two: Osage Research Report, & Bibliography of Basic Research References. (American Indian Ethnohistory Ser: Plains Indians). (Illus.). lib. bdg. 42.00 (ISBN 0-8240-0748-4). Garland Pub.

--Saynday's People: The Kiowa Indians & the Stories They Told. LC 63-10928. (Illus.). 1963. pap. 2.45 (ISBN 0-8032-5125-4, BB 174, Bison). U of Nebr Pr.

Martin, Viahnett S. Years with the Osage. LC 75-19578. (Illus.). 184p. (Orig.). 1975. pap. 3.00 (ISBN 0-88204-004-9). Edgemoor.

Mathews, John J. Osages: Children of the Middle Waters. (Civilization of the American Indian Ser.: No. 60). (Illus.). 1981. Repr. of 1961 ed. cancelled 24.95 (ISBN 0-8061-0498-8). U of Okla Pr.

--Wah'Kon-Tah: The Osage & the White Man's Road. (Civilization of the American Indian Ser.: Vol. 3). (Illus.). 359p. pap. 7.95 (ISBN 0-8061-1699-4). U of Okla Pr.

Matthews, Washington. Ethnography & Philology of the Hidatsa Indians: U. S. Geological & Geographical Survey of the Territories, Miscellaneous Publication, No. 7. LC 3-8072. 1971. Repr. of 1877 ed. 19.50 (ISBN 0-384-35892-6). Johnson Repr.

--Grammar & Dictionary of the Language of the Hidatsa. LC 76-44080. (Shea's American Linguistics, Ser. 2: Nos.1 & 2). Repr. of 1873 ed. 27.50 (ISBN 0-404-15787-4). AMS Pr.

Mauricio, Victoria. The Return of Chief Black Foot. (Illus.). 140p. (Orig.). 1981. pap. 5.95 (ISBN 0-89865-053-4, Unilaw). Donning Co.

Metcalf, P. Richard, ed. The Native American People of the West. new ed. LC 72-95876. (American People Ser.). 159p. (Orig.). (gr. 9-12). 1973. PLB 7.95 (ISBN 0-88301-084-4); pap. 2.50 (ISBN 0-88301-068-2). Pendulum Pr.

Meyer, Roy W. History of the Santee Sioux: United States Indian Policy on Trial. LC 80-11810. xviii, 434p. 1967. pap. 7.95 (ISBN 0-8032-8109-9, BB 751, Bison). U of Nebr Pr.

Miller, Virginia P. Ukomno'm: The Yuki Indians of Northern California. (Ballena Press Anthropological Papers: No. 14). (Illus.). 1979. pap. 6.95 (ISBN 0-87919-083-3). Ballena Pr.

Miller, Wick R. Newe Natekwinappeh: Shoshoni Stories & Dictionary. (Utah Anthropological Papers: No. 94). Repr. of 1972 ed. 24.00 (ISBN 0-404-60694-6). AMS Pr.

Milligan, Edward A. Dakota Twilight: The Standing Rock Sioux, 1874-1890. 1976. 8.50 (ISBN 0-682-48421-0, Lochinvar). Exposition.

Mooney, James. Calendar History of the Kiowa Indians. LC 78-10789. (Classics of Smithsonian Anthropology Ser.: No. 2). (Illus.). 460p. 1979. pap. text ed. 8.95x (ISBN 0-87474-655-8). Smithsonian.

--The Siouan Tribes of the East. LC 2-14653. 1971. Repr. of 1895 ed. 8.00 (ISBN 0-384-39935-5). Johnson Repr.

Mooney, James & Petter, Rodolphe C. Cheyenne Indians: Sketch of the Cheyenne Grammar. LC 8-10850. Repr. of 1907 ed. pap. 5.00 (ISBN 0-527-00505-3). Kraus Repr.

Murray, Charles A. Travels in North America, Including a Summer with the Pawnees. 2nd ed. LC 68-54845. (American Scene Ser.). 878p. 1974. Repr. of 1839 ed. lib. bdg. 69.50 (ISBN 0-306-71021-8). Da Capo.

Myers, Frank. Soldiering in Dakota: Among the Indians in 1863-4-5. facsimile ed. LC 77-160983. (Select Bibliographies Reprint Ser). Repr. of 1888 ed. 24.00 (ISBN 0-8369-5851-9). Arno.

Nabokov, Peter. Two Leggings: The Making of a Crow Warrior. LC 67-15412. (Apollo Eds.). (Illus.). 1970. pap. 4.50 (ISBN 0-8152-0275-X, A275). T Y Crowell.

Neihardt, John C. Black Elk Speaks. (gr. 10-12). pap. 2.95 (ISBN 0-671-43268-0). WSP.

Nelson, Bruce. Land of the Dacotahs. LC 65-108129. (Illus.). 1964. pap. 3.95 (ISBN 0-8032-5145-9, BB 176, Bison). U of Nebr Pr.

Nelson, John Y. Fifty Years on the Trail, a True Story of Western Life: The Adventures of John Young Nelson, As Described to Harrington O'Reilly. (Western Frontier Library: No. 22). (Illus.). 1969. Repr. of 1963 ed. 7.95 (ISBN 0-8061-0572-0). U of Okla Pr.

Newcomb, W. W. The Wichita & Affiliated Tribes: Use & Occupancy of Their Lands. 27.00 (ISBN 0-8287-1304-9). Clearwater Pub.

Nez Perce Indians. Incl. Aboriginal Territory of the Nez Perce Indians. Chalfant, Stuart A; Ethnology of the Joseph Band of the Nez Perce Indians, 1805-1905. Ray, Verne F; Findings of Fact, & Opinion. Indian Claims Commission. (American Indian Ethnohistory Ser: Indians of the Northwest). (Illus.). lib. bdg. 42.00 (ISBN 0-8240-0762-X). Garland Pub.

Nicklason, Fred & Champe, John L. Yankton & Teton Sioux, 1851: Use & Occupancy of Fort Laramie Lands. 43.00 (ISBN 0-8287-1312-X). Clearwater Pub.

Nye, Wilbur S. Bad Medicine & Good: Tales of the Kiowas. 291p. 1980. pap. 7.95 (ISBN 0-8061-1643-9). U of Okla Pr.

--Plains Indian Raiders: The Final Phases of Warfare from the Arkansas to the Red River. LC 67-24624. (Illus.). 1974. 22.50 (ISBN 0-8061-0803-7). U of Okla Pr.

Oehler, Dottlieb & Smith, David Z. Description of a Journey & Visit to the Pawnee Indians. 32p. 4.95 (ISBN 0-87770-140-7); pap. 3.00 (ISBN 0-87770-134-2). Ye Galleon.

Ortiz, Roxanne D. The Great Sioux Nation. Date not set. 8.00 (ISBN 0-686-73280-4); pap. 6.95 (ISBN 0-686-73281-2). U of NM Nat Am Std.

Osage Indians, Vol. 4. Incl. A Preliminary Survey of Missouri Archaeology. Chapman, Carl H; Osage Village Locations & Hunting Territories to 1808. Chapman, Carl H; Osage Village Sites & Hunting Territory 1808-1825. Chapman, Carl H; The Osage Nation 1775-1818. Henning, Dale R. (American Indian Ethnohistory Ser: Plains Indians). (Illus.). lib. bdg. 42.00 (ISBN 0-8240-0750-6). Garland Pub.

Paige, Harry W. Songs of the Teton Sioux. (Great West & Indian Ser: Vol. 39). (Illus.). 1969. 8.50 (ISBN 0-87026-019-7). Westernlore.

Painter, Charles C. The Condition of Affairs in Indian Territory & California. LC 74-15121. Repr. of 1888 ed. 14.00 (ISBN 0-404-11981-6). AMS Pr.

Palladino, Lawrence. The Coeur D'Alene Reservation. Bd. with Our Friends the Coeur D'Alene Indians. 1967. pap. 3.00 (ISBN 0-87770-069-9). Ye Galleon.

Parker, Samuel. Journal of Exploring Tour Etc. Repr. 10.00 (ISBN 0-87018-046-0). Ross.

Parkman, Frances. Oregon Trail. Feltskog, E. N., ed. (Illus.). 854p. 1969. 27.50 (ISBN 0-299-05070-X). U of Wis Pr.

Parkman, Francis. Oregon Trail. (Classics Ser). (gr. 6 up). 1964. pap. 1.50 (ISBN 0-8049-0037-X, CL-37). Airmont.

--Oregon Trail. (RL 8). pap. 1.75 (ISBN 0-451-51377-0, CE1377, Sig Classics). NAL.

Pawnee & Kansa (KAW) Indians. Incl. Notes on the Pawnee. Champe, John L. & Fenenga, Franklin.; Historical & Economic Geography of the Pawnee Lands. Griffiths, Thomas M; Findings of Fact, & Opinion. Indian Claims Commission; The Prehistoric & Historic Habitat of the Kansa Indians. Wedel, Waldo R. (American Indian Ethnohistory Ser: Plains Indians). (Illus.). lib. bdg. 42.00 (ISBN 0-8240-0733-6). Garland Pub.

Pepper, George H. & Wilson, Gilbert L. Hidatsa Shrine & the Beliefs Respecting It. LC 9-5503. 1908. pap. 5.00 (ISBN 0-527-00509-6). Kraus Repr.

The Plains Indian Book. 1974. pap. 2.50 (ISBN 0-918858-02-X). Fun Pub.

Pluckrose, ed. Small World of Plains Indians. (Warwick Press Ser.). (gr. k-3). 1980. PLB 6.45 (ISBN 0-531-03419-4, F28). Watts.

Potomac Corral of the Westerners. Great Western Indian Fights. LC 60-15191. (Illus.). 1966. pap. 3.50 (ISBN 0-8032-5186-6, BB 339, Bison). U of Nebr Pr.

Potts, Marie. The Northern Maidu. LC 77-10739. (Illus.). 1977. 7.00 (ISBN 0-87961-071-9); pap. 3.00 (ISBN 0-87961-070-0). Naturegraph.

Powell, Peter J. People of the Sacred Mountain: A History of the Northern Cheyenne Chiefs & Warrior Societies, 1830-1879, 2 vols. LC 76-50454. (Harper & Row Native American Publishing Program). (Illus.). 1376p. 1981. Set. 150.00 (ISBN 0-06-451550-8, HarpR); prepub. 125.00 pre-dec (ISBN 0-686-72763-0). Harrow.

--Sweet Medicine: The Continuing Role of the Sacred Arrows, The Sun Dance, & The Sacred Buffalo Hat in Northern Cheyenne History. (Illus.). 1969. 42.50 (ISBN 0-8061-0885-1). U of Okla Pr.

Powers, Stephen. Tribes of California. LC 75-13150. 1977. 32.50x (ISBN 0-520-03023-0); pap. 5.95 (ISBN 0-520-03172-5, CAL 327). U of Cal Pr.

--Tribes of California. LC 74-7994. Repr. of 1877 ed. 45.50 (ISBN 0-404-11881-X). AMS Pr.

Powers, William K. Oglala Religion. LC 76-30614. (Illus.). 1977. 14.95 (ISBN 0-8032-0910-X). U of Nebr Pr.

Rachlis, Eugene & Ewers, John C. Indians of the Plains. LC 60-6402. (American Heritage Junior Library). (Illus.). 153p. (gr. 5 up). 1960. 9.95 (ISBN 0-8281-0385-2, J001-0). Am Heritage.

Ray, Verne F. Indians of the Fort Belknap Reservation, Montana: Anthropological Considerations. 36.00 (ISBN 0-8287-1070-8). Clearwater Pub.

--The Palus Tribe: A Narrative Statement & Memorandum. 33.00 (ISBN 0-8287-1178-X). Clearwater Pub.

Read, Ethel M. Lo, the Poor Indian: A Saga of the Suisun Indians of California. LC 80-82306. 580p. (Orig.). 1980. 18.00 (ISBN 0-914330-34-9); pap. 10.00 (ISBN 0-914330-37-3). Panorama West.

Remington, Frederic. Artist Wandering Among Cheyennes. (Illus.). 11p. 1889. pap. 3.00 (ISBN 0-8466-4038-4, SJ138). Shorey.

--The Way of the Indian. LC 76-104548. Repr. of 1906 ed. lib. bdg. 17.75x (ISBN 0-8398-1755-X). Irvington.

Richardson, Rupert N. The Comanche Barrier to South Plains Settlement. LC 73-9712. 424p. 1973. Repr. of 1933 ed. 35.00 (ISBN 0-527-75230-4). Kraus Repr.

Riggs, Stephen R. Mary & I: Forty Years with the Sioux. 1971. 12.00 (ISBN 0-87928-019-0). Corner Hse.

Ritzenthaler, Robert E. Mexican Kickapoo Indians. Repr. of 1956 ed. lib. bdg. 15.00x (ISBN 0-8371-4629-1, RIMK). Greenwood.

Rodnick, David. The Fort Belknap Assiniboine of Montana: A Study in Culture Change. LC 76-43811. Repr. of 1938 ed. 24.50 (ISBN 0-404-15666-5). AMS Pr.

Roehm, Marjorie C., ed. The Letters of George Catlin & His Family: A Chronicle of the American West. 1966. 32.50x (ISBN 0-520-01078-7). U of Cal Pr.

Rogers, David B. Prehistoric Man of the Santa Barbara Coast. LC 76-43812. Repr. of 1929 ed. 38.50 (ISBN 0-404-15667-3). AMS Pr.

Rosenfelt, Willard E. The Last Buffalo: Cultural Views of the Sioux or Dakota Nation. (Illus.). (gr. 4-12). PLB 5.95 (ISBN 0-513-01253-2). Denison.

Ross, Norman A., ed. The Klamath Tribe & Federal Management of the Tribal Forest, 3 vols. (Library of American Indian Affairs). 1976. lib. bdg. 200.00x (ISBN 0-8287-1099-6). Clearwater Pub.

Sandoz, Mari. Cheyenne Autumn. 1969. pap. 2.95 (ISBN 0-380-01094-1, 52621, Discus). Avon.

--Crazy Horse, the Strange Man of the Oglalas. LC 42-50340. (Illus.). 1961. pap. 4.50 (ISBN 0-8032-5171-8, BB 110, Bison). U of Nebr Pr.

--These Were the Sioux. 1975. Repr. 7.50 (ISBN 0-8038-7060-4). Hastings.

Schusky, Ernest L. The Forgotten Sioux: An Ethnohistory of the Lower Brule Reservation. LC 75-503. (Illus.). 272p. 1975. 18.95x (ISBN 0-88229-138-6); pap. 9.95x (ISBN 0-88229-501-2). Nelson-Hall.

Seger, John H. Early Days Among the Cheyenne & Arapahoe Indians. Vestal, Stanley, ed. (CAI Ser.: Vol. 5). (Illus.). 1934. 8.95 (ISBN 0-8061-0344-2); pap. 4.95 (ISBN 0-8061-1533-5). U of Okla Pr.

Shoshone Indians. Incl. The Gosiute Indians. Malouf, Carling; The Shoshones in the Rocky Mt. Area. Hultkrantz, Ake; The Indians in Yellowstone Park. Hultkrantz, Ake; Findings of Fact, & Opinion. Indian Claims Commission. (American Indian Ethnohistory Ser: California & Basin Plateau Indians). (Illus.). lib. bdg. 42.00 (ISBN 0-8240-0735-2). Garland Pub.

Simonin, Louis L. Rocky Mountain West in 1867. Clough, Wilson O., tr. LC 66-16514. (Illus.). 1966. 11.95 (ISBN 0-8032-0175-3). U of Nebr Pr.

Sioux Indians, Vol. 3. Incl. Ethnohistorical Report on the Yankton Sioux. Woolworth, Alan R; Yankton Chronology. Champe, John L. (American Indian Ethnohistory Ser: Plains Indians). (Illus.). lib. bdg. 42.00 (ISBN 0-8240-0796-4). Garland Pub.

Smith, G. Hubert. Omaha Indians. Horr, David A., ed. (American Indian Ethnohistory Ser. - Plains Indians). 1974. lib. bdg. 42.00 (ISBN 0-8240-0739-5). Garland Pub.

Smith, Gerald A. The Mojaves: Historic Indians of San Bernardino County. (Illus.). 1977. 5.50 (ISBN 0-915158-10-8); pap. 3.50 (ISBN 0-915158-01-9). San Bernardino.

Smith, Henry. Expedition Against the Sauk & Fox Indians, 1832. 19p. 1973. Repr. of 1833 ed. pap. 2.50 (ISBN 0-87770-048-6). Ye Galleon.

Smith, Maurice G. Political Organization of the Plains Indians: With Special Reference to the Council. LC 76-43837. (Nebraska Univ. Studies: Vol. 24, Nos. 1 & 2). Repr. of 1924 ed. 15.00 (ISBN 0-404-15691-6). AMS Pr.

Spicer, Edward H., ed. Perspectives in American Indian Culture Change. LC 60-14358. (Midway Reprint Ser). 1975. pap. 17.00x (ISBN 0-226-76971-2). U of Chicago Pr.

Spindler, George & Spindler, Louise. Native North American Cultures: Four Cases. LC 76-23178. 1977. pap. text ed. 8.95 (ISBN 0-03-018401-0, HoltC). HR&W.

Spindler, Will H. Tragedy Strikes at Wounded Knee. rev. ed. LC 72-75814. (Illus.). 138p. (Orig.). 1972. pap. 1.95 (ISBN 0-88249-009-5). Dakota Pr.

Standing Bear, Luther. My People the Sioux. Brininstool, E. A., ed. LC 74-77394. (Illus.). 1975. 18.50x (ISBN 0-8032-0874-X); pap. 3.95 (ISBN 0-8032-5793-7, BB 578, Bison). U of Nebr Pr.

Steiner, Stan. The Vanishing White Man. 1977. pap. 3.95 (ISBN 0-06-090574-3, CN 574, CN). Har-Row.

Steward, Julian H. White River Ute Indians: Native Components. 50p. 1974. lib. bdg. 24.00 (ISBN 0-8287-1303-0). Clearwater Pub.

Steward, Julian H. & Wheeler-Voegelin, Erminie. Paiute Indians, Vol. Three: The Northern Paiute Indians. (American Indian Ethnohistory Ser: California & Basin - Plateau Indians). (Illus.). lib. bdg. 42.00 (ISBN 0-8240-0742-5). Garland Pub.

Stores, Samuel L. Creek Indian Lands in Oklahoma: Appriasal of Land Values As of 1907. (Library of American Indian Affairs). 1976. lib. bdg. 100.00x (ISBN 0-8287-1018-X). Clearwater Pub.

Strickland, Rennard. Fire & the Spirits: Cherokee Law from Clan to Court. LC 74-15903. (Civilization of the American Indian Ser.: Vol. 133). (Illus.). 350p. 1975. 14.95 (ISBN 0-8061-1227-1). U of Okla Pr.

Strong, William D. Aboriginal Society in Southern California. Repr. of 1929 ed. pap. 35.00 (ISBN 0-527-01382-X). Kraus Repr.

--Aboriginal Society in Southern California. 1972. 15.00 (ISBN 0-686-11774-3). Malki Mus Pr.

Tall Bull, Henry & Weist, Tom. Cheyenne Fire Fighters: Modern Indians Fighting Forest Fires. (gr. 4 up). 1973. pap. 1.95 (ISBN 0-89992-016-0). MT Coun Indian.

Tallent, Annie D. The Black Hills; or, the Last Hunting Ground of the Dakotahs. LC 74-76330. 594p. 1974. Repr. of 1899 ed. 14.95 (ISBN 0-88498-017-0); lim. leath. ed. 50.00 (ISBN 0-685-50457-3). Brevet Pr.

--The Black Hills: Or, the Last Hunting Grounds of the Dakotahs. facsimile ed. LC 75-126. (Mid-American Frontier Ser.). (Illus.). 1975. Repr. of 1899 ed. 47.00x (ISBN 0-405-06891-3). Arno.

Tanner, Helen H. Caddo Tribe of Oklahoma, Fifteen Forty-One to Eighteen Fifty Nine. (Library of American Indian Affairs). 130p. 1974. lib. bdg. 45.00 (ISBN 0-8287-0964-5). Clearwater Pub.

Taylor, Herbert C. Chehalis: Historical, Ethnographical & Archeological Report. (Library of American Indian Affairs). 35p. 1974. 21.00 (ISBN 0-8287-0971-8). Clearwater Pub.

Teit, James A. & Boas, Franz. Salishan Tribes of Western Plateaus. Repr. of 1930 ed. 40.00 (ISBN 0-8466-9000-4, SJ170). Shorey.

Tibbles, Thomas H. Buckskin & Blanket Days: Memoirs of a Friend of the Indians. LC 57-7289. 1969. pap. 3.95 (ISBN 0-8032-5199-8, BB 503, Bison). U of Nebr Pr.

Tixier, Victor. Tixier's Travels on the Osage Prairies. McDermott, John, ed. Salvan, Albert, tr. (American Exploration & Travel Ser: No. 4). (Illus.). 1968. Repr. of 1940 ed. 16.95 (ISBN 0-8061-0087-7). U of Okla Pr.

Treaties & Laws of the Osage Nation As Passed to November 26, 1890, Compiled by W. S. Fitzpatrick. LC 73-88777. (Constitutions & Laws of the American Indian Tribes Ser. 1: Vol. 4). 1973. Repr. of 1895 ed. 12.00 (ISBN 0-8420-1724-0). Scholarly Res Inc.

Trenholm, Virginia C. The Arapahoes, Our People. LC 76-108799. (Civilization of the American Indian Ser.: Vol. 105). (Illus.). 1970. 17.95 (ISBN 0-8061-0908-4). U of Okla Pr.

Trenholm, Virginia C. & Carley, Maurine. The Shoshonis: Sentinels of the Rockies. (Civilization of the American Indian Ser: No. 74). (Illus.). 1964. pap. 9.95 (ISBN 0-8061-1055-4). U of Okla Pr.

Tweddell, Colin E. Historic & Ethnographic Study of the Snohomish, Specifically Concerning Their Aboriginal & Continued Existence. (Library of American Indian Affairs). 237p. 1974. lib. bdg. 69.00 (ISBN 0-8287-1380-4). Clearwater Pub.

Underhill, Ruth M. Indians of Southern California. LC 76-43875. (Indian Life & Customs: No. 2). Repr. of 1941 ed. 14.00 (ISBN 0-404-15732-7). AMS Pr.

--The Northern Paiute Indians of California & Nevada. LC 76-43877. (Indian Life & Customs: No. 1). Repr. of 1941 ed. 14.00 (ISBN 0-404-15733-5). AMS Pr.

Vestal, Paul A. & Schultes, Richard E. The Economic Botany of the Kiowa Indians. LC 76-43883. (Harvard Univ., Botanical Museum). Repr. of 1939 ed. 21.50 (ISBN 0-404-15740-8). AMS Pr.

Voget, Fred W. Osage Indians, Vol. One: Osage Research Project. (American Indian Ethnohistory Ser: Plains Indians). (Illus.). lib. bdg. 42.00 (ISBN 0-8240-0747-6). Garland Pub.

Walker, Deward E. Conflict & Schism in Nez Perce Acculturation. (Illus.). 1968. pap. 4.00 (ISBN 0-87422-002-5). Wash St U Pr.

Walker, J. R. The Sun Dance & Other Ceremonies of the Oglala Division of the Teton Dakota. LC 76-43886. (AMNH Anthropological Papers: Vol. 16, Pt. 2). Repr. of 1917 ed. 21.50 (ISBN 0-404-15745-9). AMS Pr.

Wallace, Ernes. The Comanche, Apache & Kiowa Indians Before 1867: Habitat & Range. (Library of American Indian Affairs). 1976. lib. bdg. 99.00x (ISBN 0-8287-1600-5). Clearwater Pub.

Wallace, Ernest & Hoebel, E. Adamson. The Comanches, Lords of the South Plains. (Civilization of the American Indian Ser: No. 34). (Illus.). 15.95 (ISBN 0-8061-0249-7). U of Okla Pr.

Wallace, William J. & Wallace, Edith. Desert Foragers & Hunters: Indians of the Death Valley Region. (Illus., Orig.). 1979. pap. 3.25 (ISBN 0-916552-19-5). Acoma Bks.

Wedel, Waldo R. Prehistoric Man on the Great Plains. (Illus.). 1961. 16.95 (ISBN 0-8061-0501-1). U of Okla Pr.

Weist, Katherine, ed. Belle Highwalking: The Narrative of a Cheyenne Woman. (Indian Cult Ser.). (gr. 5 up). 1979. 5.50 (ISBN 0-686-27157-2); pap. 2.95 (ISBN 0-89992-075-6). MT Coun Indian.

Weist, Tom. A History of the Cheyenne People. (Indian Culture Ser.). (Illus.). 1977. write for info. (ISBN 0-89992-506-5); pap. write for info. (ISBN 0-89992-507-3). Mt Coun Indian.

Weltfish, Gene. The Lost Universe: Pawnee Life & Culture. LC 77-7164. (Illus.). 1977. 21.50x (ISBN 0-8032-0934-7); pap. 6.95 (ISBN 0-8032-5871-2, BB 653, Bison). U of Nebr Pr.

Wharton, Clarence R. Satanta, the Great Chief of the Kiowas & His People. LC 76-43889. Repr. of 1935 ed. 18.00 (ISBN 0-404-15748-3). AMS Pr.

Wheeler, Olin D. The Trail of Lewis & Clark: 1804-1904, 2 vols. LC 75-177829. Repr. of 1904 ed. Set. 57.50 (ISBN 0-404-06926-6). AMS Pr.

Wheeler-Voegelin, Erminie, et al. California Indians Three. Horr, David A., ed. (American Indian Ethnohistory Ser.). 1978. lib. bdg. 42.00 (ISBN 0-8240-0773-5). Garland Pub.

Wheelock, Thompson B. Expedition to the Pawnee Pict Village in 1834. 1978. pap. 3.95 (ISBN 0-87770-198-9). Ye Galleon.

Wildschut, William. Crow Indian Medicine Bundles, Vol. 17. 2nd ed. Ewers, John C., ed. LC 74-33115. (Contributions Ser.). (Illus.). 1975. soft cover 10.00 (ISBN 0-934490-34-1). Mus Am Ind.

Will, George F. & Spinden, H. J. Mandans, a Study of Their Culture, Archaeology & Language. (Illus.). 1906. pap. 9.00 (ISBN 0-527-01195-9). Kraus Repr.

Wilson, Gilbert L. Agriculture of the Hidatsa Indians: An Indian Interpretation. LC 76-43892. (Univ. of Minnesota Studies in the Social Sciences: No. 9). Repr. of 1917 ed. 24.50 (ISBN 0-404-15754-8). AMS Pr.

--Hidatsa Eagle Trapping. LC 76-43893. (AMNH Anthropological Papers: Vol. 30, Pt. 4). Repr. of 1928 ed. 14.00 (ISBN 0-404-15753-X). AMS Pr.

--The Hidatsa Earthlodge. Weitzner, Bella, ed. LC 76-43894. (AMNH Anthropological Papers: Vol. 33, Pt. 5). Repr. of 1934 ed. 29.00 (ISBN 0-404-15752-1). AMS Pr.

--The Horse & the Dog in Hidatsa Culture. LC 76-43895. (AMNH Anthropological Papers: Vol. 15, Pt. 2). Repr. of 1924 ed. 23.00 (ISBN 0-404-15751-3). AMS Pr.

Wilson, Ruby E. Frank J. North: Pawnee Scout, Commander & Pioneer. (Illus.). 1982. 18.95 (ISBN 0-8040-0767-5, SB). Swallow.

Wissler, Clark. Costumes of the Plains Indians & Structural Basis to the Decoration of Costumes Among the In Plains Indians. LC 74-9016. (Illus.). Repr. of 1915 ed. 17.00 (ISBN 0-404-11913-1). AMS Pr.

--Material Culture of the Blackfoot Indians. LC 74-9018. (Anthropological Papers of the American Museum of Natural History: Vol. 5, Pt. 1). Repr. of 1910 ed. 17.50 (ISBN 0-404-11915-8). AMS Pr.

Wright, Muriel H. A Guide to the Indian Tribes of Oklahoma. (Civilization of the American Indian Ser.: No. 33). (Illus.). 1979. Repr. of 1951 ed. 12.50 (ISBN 0-8061-0238-1). U of Okla Pr.

INDIANS OF NORTH AMERICA-UNITED STATES

see Indians of North America

INDIANS OF NORTH AMERICA, CIVILIZATION OF

see Indians of North America-Cultural Assimilation

INDIANS OF SOUTH AMERICA

see also Ethnology-South America; Incas

Alvarez De Williams, Anita. Travelers Among the Cucapa. (Baja California Travels Ser.: No. 34). 1975. 24.00 (ISBN 0-87093-234-9). Dawsons.

American Indian Publishers, ed. Dictionary of Indian Tribes of the Americas, 4 vols. (Illus.). 1980. Set. lib. bdg. 225.00 (ISBN 0-937862-25-8). Am Indian Pubs.

Arens, Richard, ed. Genocide in Paraguay. LC 76-5726. 1977. 12.50x (ISBN 0-87722-088-3). Temple U Pr.

Barrett, S. A. The Cayapa Indians of Ecuador, 2 vols. 1977. Set. lib. bdg. 250.00 (ISBN 0-8490-1588-X). Gordon Pr.

Brugger, Karl. The Chronicle of Akakor. 1977. 7.95 (ISBN 0-440-01435-2). Delacorte.

Clastres, Pierre. Chronicle of the Guayaki Indians: The Ache, Nomadic Hunters of Paraguay. Auster, P. & Davis, L., trs. 274p. 1981. 20.00 (ISBN 0-89396-031-4). Mole Pub Co.

Davis, S. H. Victims of the Miracle. (Illus.). 1977. 29.95 (ISBN 0-521-21738-5); pap. 6.95x (ISBN 0-521-29246-8). Cambridge U Pr.

A Day with Tupi. pap. 1.50 (ISBN 0-915266-01-6). Awani Pr.

De Acosta, Joseph. The Natural & Moral History of the Indies, 2 Vols. Markham, Clements R., ed. LC 75-134715. (Hakluyt Society Ser.: No. 60-61). 1970. Set. lib. bdg. 60.50 (ISBN 0-8337-0798-1). B Franklin.

De Cieza De Leon, Pedro. Travels of Pedro De Cieza De Leon 1532-50. Markham, Clements R., tr. 1964. Repr. of 1864 ed. 60.50 (ISBN 0-8337-2235-2). B Franklin.

Dobritzhoffer, Martin. An Account of the Abipones, an Equestrian People of Paraguay, 3 Vols. in 1. LC 3-21856. (Landmarks in Anthropology). 1970. Repr. of 1822 ed. 73.00 (ISBN 0-384-12055-5). Johnson Repr.

Drucker, Philip. The Northern & Central Nootkan Tribes. Repr. of 1951 ed. 39.00 (ISBN 0-403-03666-6). Scholarly.

Dumont, Jean-Paul. Under the Rainbow: Nature & Supernature Among the Panare Indians. LC 75-22049. (Texas Pan American Ser.). 192p. 1976. 12.00x (ISBN 0-292-78504-6). U of Tex Pr.

Enock, C. Reginald. The Secret of the Pacific: Origins of the Toltecs, Aztecs, Mayas, & Incas. 1977. lib. bdg. 59.95 (ISBN 0-8490-2584-2). Gordon Pr.

Falkner, Thomas. A Description of Patagonia & the Adjoining Parts of South America. LC 75-41088. Repr. of 1935 ed. 21.50 (ISBN 0-404-14747-X). AMS Pr.

Farabee, W. C. Indian Tribes of Eastern Peru. 1922. pap. 15.00 (ISBN 0-527-01216-5). Kraus Repr.

Fejos, Pal. Ethnography of the Yagua. (Illus.). 1943. pap. 15.50 (ISBN 0-384-15435-2). Johnson Repr.

Ferris, Harry B. Indians of Cuzco & the Apurimac. LC 18-6196. 1916. pap. 10.00 (ISBN 0-527-00513-4). Kraus Repr.

Fitz-Roy, Robert, et al. Narrative of the Surveying Voyages of His Majesty's Ships Adventure & Beagle, 3 Vols. in 4 Pts. Repr. of 1839 ed. Set. 170.00 (ISBN 0-404-09900-9); 43.00 ea. Vol. 1 (ISBN 0-404-09901-7). Vol. 2 Pt. 1 (ISBN 0-404-09902-5). Vol. 2 Pt. 2 (ISBN 0-404-09903-3). Vol. 3 (ISBN 0-404-09904-1). AMS Pr.

Fleming, Peter. Brazilian Adventure. 1978. Repr. of 1933 ed. lib. bdg. 25.00 (ISBN 0-8482-0822-6). Norwood Edns.

Garcilaso de la Vega. Royal Commentaries of the Incas & General History of Peru, 2 Vols. Livermore, Harold V., tr. (Texas Pan American Ser.). 1965. Set. 75.00x (ISBN 0-292-73358-5). U of Tex Pr.

Gillin, John. Barama River Caribs of British Guiana. 1936. pap. 21.00 (ISBN 0-527-01233-5). Kraus Repr.

Gordon, B. Le Roy. Human Geography & Ecology in the Sinu Country of Columbia. LC 77-4433. (Ibero-Americana: No. 39). 1977. Repr. of 1957 ed. lib. bdg. 15.00x (ISBN 0-8371-9047-9, GOHU). Greenwood.

Hemming, John. Red Gold: The Conquest of the Brazilian Indians, 1500-1760. LC 77-22863. 1978. 25.00 (ISBN 0-674-75107-8). Harvard U Pr.

Henry, Jules. Jungle People: A Kaingang Tribe of the Highlands of Brazil. (Orig.). pap. 1.95 (ISBN 0-394-70521-1, V521, Vin). Random.

Hopper, Janice H., ed. Indians of Brazil in the Twentieth Century. LC 67-14551. (Illus.). 1967. 8.95 (ISBN 0-911976-02-7); pap. 6.95 (ISBN 0-911976-03-5). ICR.

Howay, Frederick. The Atahualpa. (Illus.). 1978. 3.50 (ISBN 0-87770-197-0). Ye Galleon.

Hugh-Jones, Christine. From the Milk River. LC 76-73126. (Cambridge Studies in Social Anthropology: No. 26). (Illus.). 1980. 24.95 (ISBN 0-521-22544-2). Cambridge U Pr.

Karsten, Rafael. Toba Indians of the Bolivian Gran Chaco. 1967. text ed. 6.75x (ISBN 90-6234-023-7). Humanities.

--Totalitarian State of the Past. LC 79-86027. 1969. Repr. of 1949 ed. 15.00 (ISBN 0-8046-0617-X). Kennikat.

Kerr, John G. Naturalist in the Gran Chaco. LC 68-55200. (Illus.). 1968. Repr. of 1950 ed. lib. bdg. 16.75x (ISBN 0-8371-0511-0, KEGC). Greenwood.

Kiemen, Mathias C. The Indian Policy of Portugal in the Amazon Region, 1614-1693. 1973. lib. bdg. 14.00x (ISBN 0-374-94578-0). Octagon.

Kracke, Waud H. Force & Persuasion: Leadership in an Amazonian Society. LC 78-3179. 1979. lib. bdg. 21.00x (ISBN 0-226-45210-7). U of Chicago Pr.

La Barre, W. Aymare Indians of the Lake Titicaca Plateau, Bolivia. LC 48-5985. 1948. pap. 16.00 (ISBN 0-527-00567-3). Kraus Repr.

Lamb, F. Bruce. Wizard of the Upper Amazon: The Story of Manuel Cordova Rios. LC 73-139314. 206p. 1975. pap. 5.95 (ISBN 0-395-19918-2). HM.

Levi-Strauss, Claude. Tristes Tropiques. rev. ed. (Illus., Fr.). 1968. 21.00 (ISBN 0-685-05300-8). Adler.

--Tristes-Tropiques. Weightman, John & Weightman, Doreen, trs. from Fr. LC 79-162975. (Illus.). 1974. 12.50 (ISBN 0-689-10572-X); pap. 8.95 (ISBN 0-689-70122-5, 48). Atheneum.

Marchant, Alexander N. From Barter to Slavery: The Economic Relations of Portuguese & Indians in the Settlement of Brazil, 1500-1580. 1942. 7.50 (ISBN 0-8446-1300-2). Peter Smith.

Markham, Clements R., ed. & tr. Expeditions into the Valley of the Amazons, 1539-1540, 1639. (Hakluyt Society First Ser.: No. 24). (Illus.). 1964. Repr. of 1859 ed. 26.50 (ISBN 0-8337-2238-7). B Franklin.

Matto de Turner, Clorinda. Birds Without a Nest: A Story of Indian Life in Peru. 1977. lib. bdg. 59.95 (ISBN 0-8490-1508-1). Gordon Pr.

Maybury-Lewis, David. Akwe-Shavante Society. (Illus.). 392p. 1974. pap. 4.95x (ISBN 0-686-76959-7). Oxford U Pr.

Means, Philip A. Ancient Civilization of the Andes. LC 64-8175. 1964. Repr. of 1931 ed. 18.50 (ISBN 0-87752-072-0). Gordian.

Meggers, Betty J. Amazonia: Man & Culture in a Counterfeit Paradise. LC 74-141427. (Worlds of Man Ser). 1971. 12.75x (ISBN 0-88295-608-6); pap. 5.95x (ISBN 0-88295-609-4). Harlan Davidson.

Menezes, M. N. British Policy Towards the Amerindians in British Guiana, 1803-1973. (Illus.). 1977. 49.00x (ISBN 0-19-821567-3). Oxford U Pr.

Menezes, Mary N., ed. The Amerindians in Guyana Eighteen Hundred & Three to Eighteen Seventy Three: A Documentary History. 314p. 1979. 29.50x (ISBN 0-7146-3054-3, F Cass Co). Biblio Dist.

Metraux, Alfred. The Native Tribes' of Eastern Bolivia & Western Matto Grosso. Repr. of 1942 ed. 24.00 (ISBN 0-403-03659-3). Scholarly.

Nimuendaju, Curt. Apinaye. Lowie, Robert H., tr. (Illus.). 1967. pap. text ed. 9.50x (ISBN 9-0623-4032-6). Humanities.

Osborne, Harold. Indians of the Andes: Aymaras & Quechas. LC 72-92122. (Illus.). xiii, 266p. 1972. Repr. of 1952 ed. lib. bdg. 12.50x (ISBN 0-8154-0448-4). Cooper Sq.

--Indians of the Andes: Incas, Aymaras, & Quechuas. 1977. lib. bdg. 59.95 (ISBN 0-8490-2054-9). Gordon Pr.

Pinckard, George. Notes on the West Indies, Written During the Expedition Under the Command of the Late General Sir Ralph Abercromby, 3 Vols. LC 70-90126. Repr. of 1806 ed. Set. 64.00x (ISBN 0-8371-4984-3, Pub. by Negro U Pr). Greenwood.

Pittier De Fabrega, Henri. Ethnographic & Linguistic Notes on the Paez Indians of Tierra Adentro, Cauca, Colombia. LC 8-3129. 1907. pap. 8.00 (ISBN 0-527-00504-5). Kraus Repr.

Radin, Paul. Indians of South America. Repr. of 1942 ed. lib. bdg. 17.75x (ISBN 0-8371-1123-4, RAIS). Greenwood.

Reichel-Dolmatoff, Gerardo & De Reichel, Alicia D. People of Aritama. LC 60-14234. (Illus.). 1962. 15.00x (ISBN 0-226-70791-1). U of Chicago Pr.

Schneebaum, Tobias. Keep the River on Your Right. (Illus.). 1969. pap. 3.45 (ISBN 0-394-17175-6, B259, BC). Grove.

Smith, E. R. Araucanians or Notes of a Tour Among the Indian Tribes of Southern Chili. Repr. of 1855 ed. 17.00 (ISBN 0-527-84000-9). Kraus Repr.

Staden, Hans. Captivity of Hans Stade of Hesse, 1547-55: Among the Wild Tribes of Eastern Brazil. Burton, R. F., ed. Tootal, A., tr. 1964. 24.50 (ISBN 0-8337-0430-3). B Franklin.

Steward, Julian H., ed. Handbook of South American Indians, 7 vols. Incl. Vol. 1. The Marginal Tribes. 27.50x (ISBN 0-8154-0212-0); Vol. 2. The Andean Civilizations. 35.00x (ISBN 0-8154-0213-9); Vol. 3. The Tropical Forest Tribes. 32.50x (ISBN 0-8154-0214-7); Vol. 4. The Circum-Caribbean Tribes. 25.00x (ISBN 0-8154-0215-5); Vol. 5. The Comparative Anthropology of South American Indians. 27.50x (ISBN 0-8154-0216-3); Vol. 6. Physical Anthropology, Linguistics & Cultural Geography of South American Indians. 27.50x (ISBN 0-8154-0217-1); Vol. 7. The Index. 11.00x (ISBN 0-8154-0218-X). LC 63-17285. (Illus.). Repr. of 1957 ed. Cooper Sq.

--Handbook of the South American Indians, 7 vols. Incl. Vol.1. The Marginal Tribes. Repr. of 1946 ed; Vol.2. The Andean Civilizations. Repr. of 1946 ed; Vol.3. The Tropical Forest Tribes. Repr. of 1948 ed; Vol. 4. The Circum-Carribean Tribes. Repr. of 1948 ed; Vol.5. The Comparative Ethnology of South American Indians. Repr. of 1949 ed; Vol. 6. Physical Anthropology Linguistics & Cultural Geography of South American Indians. Repr. of 1950 ed; Vol. 7. Index. Repr. of 1959 ed. Repr. of 1946 ed. Set. 395.00 (ISBN 0-403-03595-3). Scholarly.

Trimborn, Hermann. Quellen Zur Kulturgeschichte Des Prakolumbischen America. Repr. of 1936 ed. pap. 15.50 (ISBN 0-384-61570-8). Johnson Repr.

Wagley, Charles. Welcome of Tears: The Tapirape Indians of Central Brazil. LC 76-42665. (Illus.). 1978. pap. 7.95x (ISBN 0-19-502208-4). Oxford U Pr.

Wagley, Charles & Galvao, Eduardo. Tenetehara Indians of Brazil. LC 79-82359. (Columbia Univ. Contributions to Anthropology Ser.: Vol. 35). 1969. Repr. of 1949 ed. 19.50 (ISBN 0-404-50585-6). AMS Pr.

Waldman, Harry, ed. Encyclopedia of Indians of the Americas, Vols. 1-8. LC 74-5088. 1974-81. lib. bdg. 59.00 ea. Scholarly.

Wallace, Alfred R. Narrative of Travels on Amazon & Rio Negro. LC 68-25280. (World History Ser., No. 48). 1969. Repr. of 1889 ed. lib. bdg. 37.95 (ISBN 0-8383-0251-3). Haskell.

--Narrative of Travels on the Amazon & Rio Negro, with an Account of the Native Tribes, & Observations on the Climate, Geology, & Natural History of the Amazon Valley. LC 68-55226. (Illus.). 1969. Repr. of 1889 ed. lib. bdg. 15.50x (ISBN 0-8371-1641-4, WARN). Greenwood.

Whitten, Norman E., Jr. Sacha Runa: Ethnicity & Adaptation of Ecuadorian Jungle Quichua. LC 75-28350. (Illus.). 374p. 1976. 15.00 (ISBN 0-252-00553-8); text ed. 6.95 (ISBN 0-252-00836-7). U of Ill Pr.

INDIANS OF SOUTH AMERICA–AGRICULTURE

Flores-Ochoa, Jorge A. Pastoralists of the Andes: The Alpaca Herders of Paratia. Bolton, Ralph, tr. from Spanish. LC 78-31360. (Illus.). 1979. text ed. 13.50x (ISBN 0-915980-89-4). Inst Study Human.

INDIANS OF SOUTH AMERICA–AMUSEMENTS

see Indians of South America–Social Life and Customs

INDIANS OF SOUTH AMERICA–ANTIQUITIES

see also Indians of South America–Pottery; Peru–Antiquities

Badner, Mino. Possible Focus of Andean Artistic Influence in Mesoamerica. Bd. with Izapan-Style Art: A Study of its Form & Meaning. Quirarte, Jacinto; Human Decapitation in Ancient Mesoamerica. Moser, Christopher L. (Studies in Pre-Columbian Art & Archaeology: Nos. 9-11). (Illus.). 1972-1973. 18.00x (ISBN 0-88402-054-1, Ctr Pre-Columbian). Dumbarton Oaks.

Donnan, Christopher B. & Mackey, Carol J. Ancient Burial Patterns of the Moche Valley, Peru. LC 77-10677. (Illus.). 424p. 1978. 30.00x (ISBN 0-292-70329-5). U of Tex Pr.

Engel, Frederic. Preceramic Settlement on the Central Coast of Peru: Asia, Unit I. LC 62-21774. (Transactions Ser.: Vol. 53, Pt. 3). (Illus.). 1963. pap. 2.00 (ISBN 0-87169-533-2). Am Philos.

Harrison, Margaret A., ed. Sources Cited & Artifacts Illustrated. (Handbook of Middle American Indians Ser: Vol. 16). 332p. 1976. text ed. 30.00x (ISBN 0-292-73004-7). U of Tex Pr.

Heizer, Robert F., et al, eds. Sources of Stones Used in Prehistoric Mesoamerican Sites. (Illus.). 1976. pap. 5.95 (ISBN 0-87919-060-4). Ballena Pr.

Hemming, John. Machu Picchu. Bayrd, Edwin, ed. LC 80-82066. (Illus.). 1981. 16.95 (ISBN 0-88225-302-6). Newsweek.

Hewett, Edgar L. Ancient Andean Life. LC 67-29547. (Illus.). 1968. Repr. of 1939 ed. 15.00x (ISBN 0-8196-0204-3). Biblo.

Jenness, Diamond, ed. The American Aborigines: Their Origin & Antiquity; a Collection of Papers by Ten Authors Published for Presentation at the 5th Pacific Science Congress, Canada. LC 78-180611. (Illus.). iv, 396p. 1972. Repr. of 1933 ed. 19.00 (ISBN 0-8462-1616-7). Russell.

Joyce, Thomas A. South American Archaeology. LC 70-78361. (Illus.). 1969. Repr. of 1912 ed. 25.00 (ISBN 0-87817-032-4). Hacker.

Kroeber, Alfred L. Peruvian Archeology in 1942. (Illus.). Repr. of 1944 ed. pap. 15.50 (ISBN 0-384-30465-6). Johnson Repr.

Lanning, Edward. Peru Before the Incas. LC 67-28395. 1967. pap. 3.95 (ISBN 0-13-661595-3, Spec). P-H.

Lothrop, Samuel K. Indians of the Parana Delta, Argentina. LC 76-44751. (Anthropology Ser.). (Illus.). Repr. of 1932 ed. 24.50 (ISBN 0-404-15867-6). AMS Pr.

Moseley, Michael E. Peru's Golden Treasures. Willimas, P. M., ed. LC 77-93483. (Illus.). 1978. pap. 6.00 (ISBN 0-914868-03-9). Field Mus.

Moser, Christopher L. Human Decapitation in Ancient Mesoamerica. LC 73-90952. (Studies in Pre-Columbian Art & Archaeology: No. 11). (Illus.). 72p. 1973. pap. 8.00x (ISBN 0-88402-053-3, Ctr Pre-Columbian). Dumbarton Oaks.

Sawyer, Alan R. Ancient Peruvian Ceramics: The Nathan Cummings Collection. LC 65-16883. (Illus.). 1966. 8.50 (ISBN 0-87099-037-3). Metro Mus Art.

Wilbert, Johannes. Thread of Life: Symbolism of Miniature Art from Ecuador. Bd. with Further Exploration of the Rowe Chavin Seriation & Its Implications for North Central Coast Chronology. Roe, Peter; Man & a Feline in Mochica Art. Benson, Elizabeth P. (Studies in Pre-Columbian Art & Archaeology: Nos. 12-14). (Illus.). 1974. 20.00x (ISBN 0-88402-061-4). Dumbarton Oaks.

Wilbert, Johannes & Layrisse, Miguel, eds. Demographic & Biological Studies of the Warao Indians. LC 78-620049. (Latin American Studies: Vol. 45). 1980. 29.50 (ISBN 0-87903-045-3). UCLA Lat Am Ctr.

INDIANS OF SOUTH AMERICA–ART

Badner, Mino. A Possible Focus of Andean Artistic Influence in Mesoamerica. LC 72-90528. (Studies in Pre-Columbian Art & Archaeology: No. 9). (Illus.). 56p. 1972. pap. 5.00x (ISBN 0-88402-042-8, Ctr Pre-Columbian). Dumbarton Oaks.

Bennett, Edna M. & Bennett, John F. Turquoise Jewelry of the Indians of the Southwest. (Illus.). 1973. 15.00 (ISBN 0-917834-01-1). Turquoise Bks.

Bennett, Wendell C. & D'Harnoncourt, Rene. Ancient Art of the Andes. LC 54-6135. (Museum of Modern Art - Publications in Reprint). (Illus.). Repr. of 1954 ed. 18.00 (ISBN 0-405-01521-6). Arno.

Cordy-Collins, Alana & Nicholson, H. B. Pre-Columbian Art from the Land Collection. Land, L. K., ed. (Illus.). 272p. (Orig.). 1979. pap. 25.00 (ISBN 0-940228-03-3). Calif Acad Sci.

Davis, Edward M. & Newcomb, William W., eds. Exhibicion de la Coleccion Peruana Danciger. Benavides, Magdalena, tr. from Span. (Illus.). 1960. pap. 3.00 (ISBN 0-87959-024-6). U of Tex Hum Res.

Densmore, Frances. Music of the Indians of British Columbia. LC 72-1879. (Music Ser.). (Illus.). 118p. 1972. Repr. of 1943 ed. lib. bdg. 14.50 (ISBN 0-306-70507-9). Da Capo.

Gasparini, Graziano & Margolies, Luise. Inca Architecture. Lyon, Patricia J., tr. from Sp. LC 79-3005. (Illus.). 368p. 1980. 32.50x (ISBN 0-253-30443-1). Ind U Pr.

Grieder, Terence. The Art & Archaeology of Pashash. LC 77-10677. (Illus.). 278p. 1978. 22.50x (ISBN 0-292-70328-7). U of Tex Pr.

Grove, David C. The Olmec Paintings of Oxtotitlan Cave, Guerrero, Mexico. Bd. with A Study of Olmec Iconography. Joralemon, Peter D; An Olmec Figure at Dumbarton Oaks. Benson, Elizabeth P. (Studies in Pre-Columbian Art & Archaeology: Nos. 6-8). (Illus.). 1970-71. 15.00x (ISBN 0-88402-036-3, Ctr Pre-Columbian). Dumbarton Oaks.

Handbook of the Robert Woods Bliss Collection of Pre-Columbian Art. (Illus.). 78p. 1963. pap. 5.00x (ISBN 0-88402-010-X, Ctr Pre-Columbian). Dumbarton Oaks.

Lapiner, Alan. Pre-Columbian Art of South America. LC 75-1016. (Illus.). 460p. 1976. 50.00 (ISBN 0-8109-0421-7). Abrams.

Laufer, Berthold. The Decorative Art of the Amur Tribes. LC 73-3524. (Jesup North Pacific Expedition. Publications: No. 4). Repr. of 1902 ed. 42.50 (ISBN 0-404-58104-8). AMS Pr.

Miller, Arthur G. The Mural Painting of Teotihuacan. LC 72-97208. (Illus.). 193p. 1973. 35.00x (ISBN 0-88402-049-5, Ctr Pre-Columbian). Dumbarton Oaks.

Reichel-Dolmatoff, Gerardo. Beyond the Milky Way. LC 78-620014. (Latin American Studies: Vol. 42). 1978. text ed. 25.00 (ISBN 0-87903-042-9). UCLA Lat Am Ctr.

Shaffer, Frederick W. Indian Designs from Ancient Ecuador. LC 78-65058. (Illus.). 1979. pap. 3.50 (ISBN 0-486-23764-8). Dover.

Spinden, Herbert J. Study of Maya Art: Its Subject Matter & Historical Development. (Illus.). 12.50 (ISBN 0-8446-5246-6). Peter Smith.

Supplement to the Handbook of the Robert Woods Bliss Collection of Pre-Columbian Art. (Illus.). 8p. 1969. pap. 1.00x (ISBN 0-88402-028-2, Ctr Pre-Columbian). Dumbarton Oaks.

Wilbert, Johannes. Thread of Life: Symbolism of Miniature Art from Ecuador. Bd. with Further Exploration of the Rowe Chavin Seriation & Its Implications for North Central Coast Chronology. Roe, Peter; Man & a Feline in Mochica Art. Benson, Elizabeth P. (Studies in Pre-Columbian Art & Archaeology: Nos. 12-14). (Illus.). 1974. 20.00x (ISBN 0-88402-061-4). Dumbarton Oaks.

Wood, Josephine. Indian Costumes of Guatemala. 1966. 70.00x (ISBN 3-201-00252-6). Intl Pubns Serv.

INDIANS OF SOUTH AMERICA–BIBLIOGRAPHY

Cooper, John M. Analytical & Critical Bibliography of the Tribes of Tierra Del Fuego & Adjacent Territory. (Map). 1967. pap. text ed. 13.50x (ISBN 90-6234-005-9). Humanities.

INDIANS OF SOUTH AMERICA–BLANKETS

see Indians of South America–Textile Industry and Fabrics

INDIANS OF SOUTH AMERICA–COSTUME AND ADORNMENT

see Indians of South America–Art

INDIANS OF SOUTH AMERICA–CULTURE

see also Indians of South America–Social Life and Customs

Benson, Elizabeth P., ed. The Cult of the Feline: A Conference in Pre-Columbian Iconography, October 31 & November 1, 1970. LC 72-90080. (Illus.). 166p. 1972. 15.00x (ISBN 0-88402-043-6, Ctr Pre-Columbian). Dumbarton Oaks.

Clastres, Pierre. Chronicle of the Guayaki Indians. Auster, Paul & Davis, Lydia, trs. 1981. 20.00 (ISBN 0-89396-031-4). Urizen Bks.

Goldman, Irving. The Cubeo: Indians of the Northwest Amazon. LC 79-13079. 1979. pap. 8.95 (ISBN 0-252-00770-0). U of Ill Pr.

Gower, Charlotte D. Northern & Southern Affiliations of Antillean Culture. LC 28-7691. 1927. pap. 5.00 (ISBN 0-527-00534-7). Kraus Repr.

Hugh-Jones, Stephens. Amazonian Indians. (Civilization Library). (Illus.). (gr. 5-8). 1979. PLB 7.40 s&l (ISBN 0-531-01448-7). Watts.

Pennington, Campbell W. The Pima Bajo of Central Sonora, Mexico: Vol. 1, The Material Culture. (Illus.). 372p. 1981. 30.00x (ISBN 0-87480-126-5). U of Utah Pr.

Stolpe, Hjalmar. Amazon Indian Designs from Brazilian & Guianan Wood Carvings. LC 73-92501. (Pictorial Archives Ser.). 64p. 1974. 2.50 (ISBN 0-486-23040-6). Dover.

Titiev, Mischa. Araucanian Culture in Transition. (Occasional Contributions Ser.: No. 15). (Illus.). 1951. pap. 2.50x (ISBN 0-932206-04-2). U Mich Mus Anthro.

Von Hagen, Victor W. The Jicaque (Torrupan) Indians of Honduras. LC 76-44796. (Illus.). Repr. of 1943 ed. 18.25 (ISBN 0-404-15743-2). AMS Pr.

Yde, Jens. Material Culture of the Waiwai. (Ethnographical Ser.: No. 10). (Illus.). 1965. pap. text ed. 21.25x (ISBN 0-685-92404-1). Humanities.

INDIANS OF SOUTH AMERICA–CUSTOMS

see Indians of South America–Social Life and Customs

INDIANS OF SOUTH AMERICA–ECONOMIC CONDITIONS

Bergman, Roland W. Amazon Indian Economics: The Simplicity of Shipibo Indiana Wealth. Robinson, David J., ed. LC 80-20198. (Dellplain Latin American Ser.: No. 6). 1980. 18.25 (ISBN 0-8357-0533-1, SS-00146, Pub. by Syracuse U Dept Geog). Univ Microfilms.

Brush, Stephen B. Mountain, Field, & Family: The Economy & Human Ecology of an Andean Valley. LC 77-24364. 1977. 16.00x (ISBN 0-8122-7728-7). U of Pa Pr.

Cancian, Frank. Economics & Prestige in a Maya Community: The Religious Cargo System in Zinacantan. (Illus.). 1965. 12.50x (ISBN 0-8047-0259-4); pap. 3.95 (ISBN 0-8047-0260-8, SP90). Stanford U Pr.

Murra, John V. The Economic Organization of the Inka State. Dalton, George, ed. (Research in Economic Anthropology Supplement Ser.: No. 1). 214p. 1980. 37.50 (ISBN 0-89232-118-0). Jai Pr.

Nietschmann, Bernard. Between Land & Water: The Subsistence Ecology of the Miskito Indians, Eastern Nicaraqua. LC 72-7703. 1973. 35.00 (ISBN 0-12-785562-9). Acad Pr.

INDIANS OF SOUTH AMERICA–ETHNOLOGY

see Indians of South America

INDIANS OF SOUTH AMERICA–FOLK-LORE

see Folk-Lore, Indian

INDIANS OF SOUTH AMERICA–INDUSTRIES

see also Indians of South America–Antiquities; Indians of South America–Pottery; Indians of South America–Textile Industry and Fabrics

Roth, Walter E. Additional Studies of the Arts, & Crafts, & Customs of the Guiana Indians, with Special Reference to Those of Southern British Guiana. 17.00 (ISBN 0-403-03500-7). Scholarly.

INDIANS OF SOUTH AMERICA–JUVENILE LITERATURE

Burt, Jesse & Ferguson, Robert B. Indians of the Southeast - Then & Now. LC 72-4695. (Illus.). (gr. 5 up). 1973. 8.95 (ISBN 0-687-18793-1). Abingdon.

Malaga, Rose C. Cesar Visits the Floating Island of the Uros. LC 81-90139. (Illus.). 32p. (gr. 4-6). 1981. PLB 7.95 (ISBN 0-939642-00-X). Malaga.

INDIANS OF SOUTH AMERICA–LANGUAGES

see also Guarini Language; Quechua Language; Tzoneca Language

Adams, Patsy. La Musica Culina y la Educacion Informal. (Comunidades y Culturas Peruanas). 5p. 1976. pap. 0.75 (ISBN 0-88312-789-X). Summer Inst Ling.

Brewer, Forrest & Brewer, Jean. Vocabulario Mexicano de Tetelcingo. (Vocabularios Indigenas Ser.: No. 8). 274p. 1962. pap. 4.00x (ISBN 0-88312-658-3); microfiche 2.20 (ISBN 0-88312-363-0). Summer Inst Ling.

Burns, Donald & Alcocer, Pablo H. Un Analisis Perliminar Del Discurso En Quechua. (Documentos Del Trabajo: No. 6). 1975. 2.25x (ISBN 0-88312-737-7). Summer Inst Ling.

Collard, Howard & Collard, Elizabeth. Vocabulario Mayo, Vol. 6. rev. ed. 1974. pap. 4.00x (ISBN 0-88312-657-5). Summer Inst Ling.

Day, Christopher. The Jacaltec Language. (Language Science Monographs: No. 12). 136p. 1973. pap. text ed. 18.75x (ISBN 0-686-27751-1). Mouton.

Farabee, W. C. Indian Tribes of Eastern Peru. 1922. pap. 15.00 (ISBN 0-527-01216-5). Kraus Repr.

Gerdel, Florence & Slocum, Marianna. Vocabulario Tzeltal de Bachajon. (Vocabularios Indigenas Ser.: No. 13). 215p. 1965. pap. 3.25 (ISBN 0-88312-667-2); 2.20 (ISBN 0-88312-589-7). Summer Inst Ling.

Hardman, M. J., ed. The Aymara Language in Its Social & Cultural Context: A Collection of Essays on Aspects of Aymara Language & Culture. LC 80-29666. (Social Sciences Monographs: No. 67). (Illus.). xii, 322p. pap. write for info. (ISBN 0-8130-0695-3). U Presses Fla.

Key, Harold & Key, Mary. Bolivian Indian Tribes. (Publications in Linguistics & Related Fields Ser.: No. 15). 128p. 1967. pap. 2.00x (ISBN 0-88312-015-1); microfiche 1.50x (ISBN 0-88312-415-7). Summer Inst Ling.

Levinsohn, Stephen H. The Inga Language. (Janua Linguarum Series Practica: No. 188). (Illus., Orig.). 1976. pap. text ed. 36.25x (ISBN 90-2793-381-2). Mouton.

Loos, Eugene. Estudios Panos V: Verbos Performativos. (Serie Linguistica Peruana: No. 14). 1976. pap. 3.00 (ISBN 0-685-51592-3); microfiche 2.20 (ISBN 0-88312-345-2). Summer Inst Ling.

Moore, Bruce, et al. Estudios Fonologicos De Lenguas Vernaculas Del Ecuador. 1975. pap. 3.50x (ISBN 0-88312-757-1). Summer Inst Ling.

Payne, David L. Nasalidad En Aguaruna. (Serie Linguistica Peruana: No. 15). 1976. pap. 2.75x (ISBN 0-88312-790-3). Summer Inst Ling.

Russel, Robert. Estudios Panos IV: Una Gramatica Transformacional Del Amahuaca. (Serie Linguistica Peruana: No. 13). 1975. pap. 3.15 (ISBN 0-685-51591-5); microfiche 1.60 (ISBN 0-88312-344-4). Summer Inst Ling.

Schoenhals, Alvin & Schoenhals, Louise. Vocabulario Mixe de Totontepec. (Vocabularios Indigenas Ser.: No. 14). 353p. 1965. pap. 5.00x (ISBN 0-88312-659-1). Summer Inst Ling.

Snell, Betty E. Machiguenga: Fonologia y Vocabulario Breve. (Documentos Del Trabajo (Peru): No. 5). 34p. 1975. pap. 1.35x (ISBN 0-685-51605-9). Summer Inst Ling.

Vinas L'Rquiza, M. T. Lengua Mataca, 2 vols. 1975. Set. 49.95 (ISBN 0-686-56664-5, S-33070). French & Eur.

Weber, David J. Suffix-As-Operator Analysis & the Grammar of Successive Encoding in Llacon (Huanuco) Quechua. (Documentos Del Trabajo (Peru): No. 13). 1976. pap. 2.85x (ISBN 0-88312-646-X). Summer Inst Ling.

--Los Sufijos Posesivos En el Quechua Del Huallaga (Huanuco) (Documentos Del Trabajo (Peru): No. 12). 1976. pap. 2.25 (ISBN 0-88312-647-8). Summer Inst Ling.

Weber, Diana. Presuposiciones De Preguntas En el Quechua De Huanuco. (Documentos Del Trabajo (Peru): No. 8). 14p. 1976. pap. 1.15 (ISBN 0-88312-796-2). Summer Inst Ling.

INDIANS OF SOUTH AMERICA-LEGENDS
see also Folk-Lore, Indian

Eells, Elsie S. Tales from the Amazon. LC 20-18503. (Illus.). (gr. 4-6). 1938. 4.95 (ISBN 0-396-01809-2). Dodd.

Estrella, Gregorio. Cuentos Del Hombre Cacataibo (Cashibo) II. (Comunidades y Culturas Peruanas: No. 11). 1977. 4.25x (ISBN 0-88312-745-8); microfiche 1.00 (ISBN 0-686-77053-6). Summer Inst Ling.

Fast, Gerhard. Cuentos Folkloricos De los Achual. (Comunidades y Culturas Peruanas: No. 3). 1976. 7.25x (ISBN 0-88312-746-6). Summer Inst Ling.

Hinson, Elizabeth. Cuentos Folkloricos De los Candoshi. (Comunidades y Culturas Peruanas: No. 4). 1976. 1.90x (ISBN 0-88312-747-4). Summer Inst Ling.

Levi-Strauss, Claude. From Honey to Ashes. (Science of Mythology Ser.). 1980. Repr. of 1973 ed. lib. bdg. 25.00x (ISBN 0-374-94952-2). Octagon.

Roe, Peter G. The Cosmic Zygote: Cosmology in the Amazon Basin. (Illus.). 451p. 1982. 35.00 (ISBN 0-8135-0896-7). Rutgers U Pr.

Whittaker, Arabelle & Warkentin, Viola. Chol Texts on the Supernatural. (Publications in Linguistics & Related Fields Ser.: No. 13). 171p. 1965. pap. 2.25 (ISBN 0-88312-013-5). Summer Inst Ling.

Wilbert, Johannes, ed. Folk Literature of the Yamana Indians: Martin Gusinde's Collection of Yamana Narratives. LC 76-20026. 1977. 24.50x (ISBN 0-520-03299-3). U of Cal Pr.

INDIANS OF SOUTH AMERICA-MISSIONS

Jank, Margaret. Culture Shock. 1977. pap. 3.95 (ISBN 0-8024-1679-9). Moody.

Loewen, Jacob A. Culture & Human Values: Christian Intervention in Anthropological Perspective. Smalley, William A., ed. LC 75-12653. (Applied Cultural Anthropology Ser.). 443p. (Orig.). 1975. pap. 6.95x (ISBN 0-87808-722-2). William Carey Lib.

Rippy, J. Fred & Nelson, Jean T. Crusaders of the Jungle. LC 76-123495. 1971. Repr. of 1936 ed. 15.50 (ISBN 0-8046-1382-6). Kennikat.

Rippy, James F. Crusaders of the Jungle. LC 76-136081. (Illus.). 1971. Repr. of 1936 ed. lib. bdg. 18.25x (ISBN 0-8371-5231-3, RIJU). Greenwood.

INDIANS OF SOUTH AMERICA-ORIGIN
see Indians-Origin

INDIANS OF SOUTH AMERICA-POTTERY

Isbell, William H. The Rural Foundation for Urbanism: Economic & Stylistic Interaction Between Rural & Urban Communities in Eighth-Century Peru. LC 77-1255. (Studies in Anthropology: No. 10). (Illus.). 1977. 12.50 (ISBN 0-252-00600-3). U of Ill Pr.

Kroeber, Alfred L. Peruvian Archeology in 1942. (Illus.). Repr. of 1944 ed. pap. 15.50 (ISBN 0-384-30465-6). Johnson Repr.

Menzel, D. Paraccas Pottery of Ica a Study in Style & Time. Repr. of 1964 ed. pap. 28.00 (ISBN 0-527-01406-0). Kraus Repr.

Sawyer, Alan R. Ancient Peruvian Ceramics: The Nathan Cummings Collection. LC 65-16883. (Illus.). 1966. 8.50 (ISBN 0-87099-037-3). Metro Mus Art.

INDIANS OF SOUTH AMERICA-RELIGION AND MYTHOLOGY

Alexander, Hartley B. Latin American Mythology. LC 63-19096. (Mythology of All Races Ser.: Vol. 11). (Illus.). 1964. Repr. of 1932 ed. 25.00x (ISBN 0-8154-0006-3). Cooper Sq.

Haile, Berard. Love-Magic & Butterfly People: The Slim Curly Version of the Ajilee & Mothway Myths. 1978. pap. 7.95 (ISBN 0-685-62114-6). Mus Northern Ariz.

--The Upward Moving & Emergence Way: The Gishin Biye Version. Luckert, Karl W., ed. (American Tribal Religions Ser.: Vol. 7). xvi, 239p. 1981. 17.95x (ISBN 0-8032-2320-X); pap. 11.95x (ISBN 0-8032-7212-X, BB 786). U of Nebr Pr.

--Women Versus Men: A Conflict of the Navajo Emergence - the Curly to Aheedliinii Version. Luckert, Karl W., ed. (American Tribal Religions Ser.: Vol. 6). viii, 119p. 1981. 14.95x (ISBN 0-8032-2319-6); pap. 9.95x (ISBN 0-8032-7211-1, BB 785). U of Nebr Pr.

Hugh-Jones, S. The Palm & the Pleiades. LC 78-5533. (Studies in Social Anthropology: No. 24). (Illus.). 1979. 24.95 (ISBN 0-521-21952-3). Cambridge U Pr.

Hultkrantz, Ake. The Religions of the American Indians. LC 73-90661. (Hermeneutics--Studies in the History of Religions: Vol. 7). 1979. 14.95 (ISBN 0-520-02653-5); pap. 5.95 (ISBN 0-520-04239-5, CAL 463). U of Cal Pr.

Lowie, Robert H. Myths & Traditions of the Crow Indians. LC 74-7981. Repr. of 1918 ed. 24.00 (ISBN 0-404-11872-0). AMS Pr.

Luckert, Karl W. A Navajo Bringing-Home Ceremony: The Claus Chee Sonny Version of Deerway Ajilee. 1978. pap. 8.95 (ISBN 0-89734-027-2, ATR-3). Mus Northern Ariz.

Markham, Clements R., ed. & tr. Narratives of the Rites & Laws of the Yncas. (Hakluyt Society First Ser: No. 48). (Illus.). 1964. Repr. of 1873 ed. 26.50 (ISBN 0-8337-2232-8). B Franklin.

Metraux, Alfred. Myths of the Toba & Pilaga Indians of the Gran Chaco. LC 46-4565. Repr. of 1946 ed. 10.00 (ISBN 0-527-01092-8). Kraus Repr.

Moser, Christopher L. Human Decapitation in Ancient Mesoamerica. LC 73-90952. (Studies in Pre-Columbian Art & Archaeology: No. 11). (Illus.). 72p. 1973. pap. 8.00x (ISBN 0-88402-053-3, Ctr Pre-Columbian). Dumbarton Oaks.

Reichel-Dolmatoff, Gerardo. Amazonian Cosmos: The Sexual & Religious Symbolism of the Tukano Indians. Reichel-Dolmatoff, Gerardo, tr. from Span. LC 73-133491. xxiv, 290p. 1974. pap. 7.95 (ISBN 0-226-70732-6, P574, Phoen). U of Chicago Pr.

Spence, Lewis. The Myths of Mexico & Peru. LC 76-27516. (Illus.). 1976. Repr. of 1914 ed. lib. bdg. 45.00 (ISBN 0-89341-031-4). Longwood Pr.

Teit, James A. Mythology of the Thompson Indians. LC 73-3529. (Jesup North Pacific Expeditions. Publications: No. 8, Pt. 2). Repr. of 1912 ed. 27.50 (ISBN 0-404-58125-0). AMS Pr.

Wilbert, Johannes, ed. Folk Literature of the Yamana Indians: Martin Gusinde's Collection of Yamana Narratives. LC 76-20026. 1977. 24.50x (ISBN 0-520-03299-3). U of Cal Pr.

INDIANS OF SOUTH AMERICA-SOCIAL CONDITIONS

Bastien, Joseph W. Mountain of the Condor: Metaphor & Ritual in an Andean Ayllu. (The American Ethnological Society Ser.). (Illus.). 1978. text ed. 20.95 (ISBN 0-8299-0175-2). West Pub.

Catlin, George. Letters & Notes on the Manners, Customs,& Conditions of the North American Indians. 1977. Repr. 79.00 (ISBN 0-403-07272-7). Scholarly.

Nunez Del Prado, Oscar & Whyte, William F. Kuyo Chico: Applied Anthropology in an Indian Community. LC 72-96621. 192p. 1973. 9.50x (ISBN 0-226-60886-7). U of Chicago Pr.

Redekop, Calvin. Strangers Become Neighbors. (Studies in Anabaptist & Mennonite History Ser.: No. 22). (Illus.). 312p. 1980. 19.95x (ISBN 0-8361-1228-8). Herald Pr.

Ruby, Robert H. & Brown, John A. The Spokane Indians: Children of the Sun. LC 79-108797. (The Civilization of the American Indian Ser.: Vol. 104). (Illus.). 346p. 1981. 19.95 (ISBN 0-8061-0905-X); pap. 9.95 (ISBN 0-8061-1757-5). U of Okla Pr.

Von Hagen, Victor W. The Jicaque (Torrupan) Indians of Honduras. LC 76-44796. (Illus.). Repr. of 1943 ed. 18.25 (ISBN 0-404-15743-2). AMS Pr.

Whitten, Norman E., Jr. Cultural Transformations & Ethnicity in Modern Ecuador. LC 81-4402. 850p. 1981. 33.95 (ISBN 0-252-00832-4). U of Ill Pr.

INDIANS OF SOUTH AMERICA-SOCIAL LIFE AND CUSTOMS

Baudin, Louis. Daily Life in Peru Under the Last Incas. Bradford, Winifred, tr. (Illus.). 1962. 10.95 (ISBN 0-02-507870-4). Macmillan.

Catlin, George. Letters & Notes on the Manners, Customs,& Conditions of the North American Indians. 1977. Repr. 79.00 (ISBN 0-403-07272-7). Scholarly.

Donnan, Christopher B. & Mackey, Carol J. Ancient Burial Patterns of the Moche Valley, Peru. LC 77-10677. (Illus.). 424p. 1978. 30.00x (ISBN 0-292-70329-5). U of Tex Pr.

Gillin, John P. Moche: A Peruvian Coastal Community. LC 75-11858. (Illus.). 166p. 1973. Repr. of 1947 ed. lib. bdg. 22.00x (ISBN 0-8371-5075-2, SMID). Greenwood.

Goldman, Irving. The Cubeo: Indians of the Northwest Amazon. LC 79-13079. 1979. pap. 8.95 (ISBN 0-252-00770-0). U of Ill Pr.

Gregor, Thomas. Mehinaku: The Drama of Daily Life in a Brazilian Indian Village. LC 76-54659. 1977. lib. bdg. 24.00x (ISBN 0-226-30744-1). U of Chicago Pr.

Hugh-Jones, Christine. From the Milk River. LC 76-73126. (Cambridge Studies in Social Anthropology: No. 26). (Illus.). 1980. 24.95 (ISBN 0-521-22544-2). Cambridge U Pr.

Hugh-Jones, S. The Palm & the Pleiades. LC 78-5533. (Studies in Social Anthropology: No. 24). (Illus.). 1979. 24.95 (ISBN 0-521-21952-3). Cambridge U Pr.

Karsten, Rafael. Blood Revenge, War & Victory Feasts Among the Jibaro Indians of Eastern Ecuador. Repr. of 1923 ed. 19.00 (ISBN 0-403-03543-0). Scholarly.

Murphy, Robert, et al. Women of the Forest. LC 74-9912. (Illus.). 256p. 1974. 12.50x (ISBN 0-231-03682-5); pap. 5.00x (ISBN 0-231-03881-X). Columbia U Pr.

Murphy, Robert F. Headhunter's Heritage. 1978. Repr. of 1960 ed. lib. bdg. 15.00x (ISBN 0-374-96026-7). Octagon.

Powlison, Esther & Powlison, Paul. La Fiesta Yagua, Jina: Una Rica Herencia Cultural. (Comunidades y Culturas Peruanas: No. 8). 1976. pap. 4.00 (ISBN 0-88312-761-X); microfiche 1.60 (ISBN 0-686-77054-4). Summer Inst Ling.

Reichel-Dolmatoff, G. The Shaman & the Jaguar: A Study of Narcotic Drugs Among the Indians of Colombia. LC 74-83672. 1975. 19.50x (ISBN 0-87722-038-7). Temple U Pr.

Reichel-Dolmatoff, Gerardo. Amazonian Cosmos: The Sexual & Religious Symbolism of the Tukano Indians. LC 73-133491. 1971. 17.00x (ISBN 0-226-70731-8). U of Chicago Pr.

Stein, William W. Hualcan: Life in the Highlands of Peru. LC 75-26221. (Cornell Studies in Anthropology). (Illus.). 383p. 1976. Repr. of 1961 ed. lib. bdg. 21.25x (ISBN 0-8371-8406-1, STHU). Greenwood.

Titiev, Mischa. Araucanian Culture in Transition. (Occasional Contributions Ser.: No. 15). (Illus.). 1951. pap. 2.50x (ISBN 0-932206-04-2). U Mich Mus Anthro.

Yde, Jens. Material Culture of the Waiwai. (Ethnographical Ser.: No. 10). (Illus.). 1965. pap. text ed. 21.25x (ISBN 0-685-92404-1). Humanities.

Young, Philip D. Ngawbe: Tradition & Change Among the Western Guaymi of Panama. LC 77-139804. (Studies in Anthropology Ser: No. 7). (Illus.). 1971. pap. 9.50 (ISBN 0-252-00143-5). U of Ill Pr.

INDIANS OF SOUTH AMERICA-TEXTILE INDUSTRY AND FABRICS

Lubell, Cecil. Textile Collections of the World: Vol. 1, United States & Canada. (Illus.). 320p. 1976. 30.00 (ISBN 0-442-24896-2). Van Nos Reinhold.

Tidball, Harriet. Peru: Textiles Unlimited. LC 76-24015. (Shuttle Craft Guild Monograph: No. 25). (Illus.). 36p. 1968. pap. 6.50 (ISBN 0-916658-25-2). HTH Pubs.

--Peru: Textiles Unlimited, Part II. LC 76-24015. (Shuttle Craft Guild Monograph: No. 26). (Illus.). 46p. 1969. pap. 6.50 (ISBN 0-916658-26-0). HTH Pubs.

Tsunoyama, Yokihiro. Textiles of the Andes: Catalogue of the Amano Collection. Ray, Karl, ed. Ooka, D. T., tr. from Japanese. (Illus.). 248p. 1979. Repr. of 1977 ed. 95.00 (ISBN 0-89346-017-6, Pub. by Heian/Dohosha). Heian Intl.

Wasserman, Tamara E. & Hill, Jonathan S. Bolivian Indian Textiles: Traditional Designs & Costumes. (Pictorial Archive Ser.). (Illus.). 64p. (Orig.). 1981. pap. 7.95 (ISBN 0-486-24118-1). Dover.

INDIANS OF SOUTH AMERICA-WARS

Karsten, Rafael. Blood Revenge, War & Victory Feasts Among the Jibaro Indians of Eastern Ecuador. Repr. of 1923 ed. 19.00 (ISBN 0-403-03543-0). Scholarly.

INDIANS OF SOUTH AMERICA-WEAVING
see Indians of South America-Textile Industry and Fabrics

INDIANS OF THE UNITED STATES
see Indians of North America

INDIANS OF THE WEST INDIES

Colon, Fernando. The Life of Admiral Christopher Columbus by His Son Ferdinand. Keen, Benjamin, tr. from Ital. LC 77-27400. (Illus.). 1978. Repr. of 1959 ed. lib. bdg. 28.50x (ISBN 0-313-20175-7, COAC). Greenwood.

Driver, Harold E. Indians of North America. 2nd ed. LC 79-76207. 1969. pap. 7.95 (ISBN 0-226-16467-5, P388, Phoen). U of Chicago Pr.

Fewkes, Jesse W. Aborigines of Puerto Rico & Neighboring Islands. LC 7-35402. (Landmarks in Anthropology Ser). (Illus.). 1970. Repr. of 1907 ed. 19.50 (ISBN 0-384-15550-2). Johnson Repr.

Joyce, Thomas A. Central American & West Indian Archaeology. LC 77-172548. (Illus.). Repr. of 1916 ed. 19.00 (ISBN 0-405-08676-8, Blom Pubns). Arno.

Rouse, Irving. Prehistory in Haiti: A Study in Method. LC 64-21834. (Yale University Publications in Anthropology Reprints Ser: No. 21). 202p. 1964. pap. 7.50x (ISBN 0-87536-504-3). HRAFP.

Sauer, Carl O. The Early Spanish Main. LC 66-15044. 1966. pap. 8.95x (ISBN 0-520-01415-4, CAL182). U of Cal Pr.

Simpson, Lesley B., tr. The Laws of Burgos of Fifteen Twelve to Fifteen Thirteen: Royal Ordinances for the Good Government & Treatment of the Indians. LC 78-13497. (Illus.). 1979. Repr. of 1960 ed. lib. bdg. 15.00 (ISBN 0-313-21019-5, CALB). Greenwood.

Taylor, Douglas M. Languages of the West Indies. LC 76-47382. (Studies in Atlantic History & Culture). 1977. text ed. 18.50x (ISBN 0-8018-1729-3). Johns Hopkins.

INDIANS OF THE WEST INDIES-ORIGIN
see Indians-Origin

INDIC ARCHITECTURE
see Architecture-India

INDIC ART
see Art, Indic

INDIC AUTHORS
see Authors, Indic

INDIC BALLADS AND SONGS
see also Songs, Indic

INDIC DRAMA-HISTORY AND CRITICISM

Chattopadhyay, S. Nataka Laksana Ratna Kosa: In the Perspective of Ancient Indian Drama & Dramaturgy. LC 74-902793. 1974. 13.50x (ISBN 0-8364-0438-6). South Asia Bks.

Naik, M. K. & Mokashi-Punekar, S. Perspectives on Indian Drama in English. 1977. text ed. 7.50x (ISBN 0-19-560825-9). Oxford U Pr.

INDIC FICTION
see also Short Stories, Indic

Shahane, V. A., ed. Focus on Forster's "A Passage to India". 158p. 1981. 40.00x (ISBN 0-86125-074-5, Pub. by Orient Longman India). State Mutual Bk.

Shirwadkar, Meena. Image of Woman in the Indo-Anglian Novel. 169p. 1979. 16.95 (ISBN 0-86578-063-3). Ind-US Inc.

INDIC FOLK-LORE
see Folk-Lore, Indic

INDIC INSCRIPTIONS
see Inscriptions, Indic

INDIC LANGUAGES
Here are entered works on the languages of India in general, and works not confined to the Indo-Aryan languages, or to any other special group or language.
see also Dravidian Languages; Indo-Aryan Languages; Indochinese Languages; Mon-Khmer Languages

Ballantyne, J. R., tr. & commentary by. Laghu Kaumudi of Varadaraja. 1976. Repr. 7.50 (ISBN 0-8426-0875-3). Orient Bk Dist.

Bright, William. Variation & Change in Language: Essays by William Bright. Dil, A. S., ed. LC 76-23370. (Language Science & National Development Ser.). 304p. 1976. 10.95x (ISBN 0-8047-0926-2). Stanford U Pr.

Deshpande, Madhav M. Sociolinguistic Attitudes in India: An Historical Reconstruction. (Linguistica Extranea Ser.: Studia 5). 178p. 1979. lib. bdg. 10.50 (ISBN 0-89720-007-1); pap. 7.50 (ISBN 0-89720-008-X). Karoma.
Grierson, G. A., ed. Linguistic Survey of India, 11 vols., 19 pts. 1973. Repr. 600.00 set (ISBN 0-89684-245-2). Orient Bk Dist.
Grierson, George A., ed. Linguistic Survey of India, 1903-28, 11 Vols. in 19. 1967. 600.00x set (ISBN 0-8426-1284-X). Verry.
Gumperz, John J. Language in Social Groups: Essays by John J. Gumperz. Dil, A. S., ed. LC 75-170982. (Language Science & National Development Ser). 1971. 15.00x (ISBN 0-8047-0798-7). Stanford U Pr.
Hale, Austin, ed. Patterns in Clause, Sentence & Discourse in Selected Languages in India & Nepal, 4 vols. (Publications in Linguistics Ser.: No. 41). pap. 34.00x set (ISBN 0-88312-047-X); Pt. 1. pap. 9.00x (ISBN 0-88312-048-8); Pt. 2. pap. 10.00x (ISBN 0-88312-049-6); Pt. 3. pap. 9.50x (ISBN 0-88312-050-X); Pt. 4. pap. 7.00x (ISBN 0-88312-051-8); Pt. 1. microfiche 2.50 (ISBN 0-88312-448-3); Pt. 2. microfiche 3.00 (ISBN 0-88312-449-1); Pt. 3. microfiche 2.50 (ISBN 0-88312-450-5). Summer Inst Ling.
Iyer, K. A. Vakyapadiya of Bharthari-Chapter Three. 1974. 15.00 (ISBN 0-8426-0617-3). Orient Bk Dist.
Iyer, K. A., tr. Vakyapadiya-Chapter Two. 1977. 9.50 (ISBN 0-8426-1032-4). Orient Bk Dist.
Krishnamurti, Bhadriraju. Telugu Verbal Bases. 1972. 12.50 (ISBN 0-89684-328-9). Orient Bk Dist.
Nagy, Gregory. Comparative Studies in Greek & Indic Meter. LC 73-90339. (Studies in Comparative Literature: Monograph No. 1). 360p. 1974. 16.50x (ISBN 0-674-15275-1). Harvard U Pr.
Naik, M. K., ed. Aspects of Indian Writing in English. 319p. (Orig.). 1980. pap. text ed. 5.50x (ISBN 0-333-90301-3). Humanities.
Sastry, P. V. Vaiyakarana Siddhanta Kaumudi of Bhattoji Diksita, Vol. I. 1974. 11.50 (ISBN 0-8426-0582-7). Orient Bk Dist.
Shamasastry, R. The Origin of the Devanagari Alphabets. 70p. 1973. 15.00x (ISBN 0-8002-1769-1). Intl Pubns Serv.
Sharma, P. S. The Kalasamuddesa of Bhartrhari's Vakyapadiya. 1972. 4.50 (ISBN 0-8426-0414-6). Orient Bk Dist.
Trumpp, Ernst. Grammar of the Pasto or Language of the Afghans Compared with the Iranian & North Indian Idioms. LC 7-13081. 428p. 1969. Repr. of 1873 ed. 25.00x (ISBN 3-7648-0637-0). Intl Pubns Serv.
--Grammar of the Sindhi Language Compared with the Sanskrit-Prakrit & the Cognate Indian Vernaculars. LC 11-24551. 590p. 1970. Repr. of 1872 ed. 30.00x (ISBN 0-8002-0748-3). Intl Pubns Serv.
Venkatacharya, T. Sahityakantakodhara. 96p. 1980. text ed. 10.50 (ISBN 0-8426-1650-0). Verry.
Verma, M. K. Structure of the Noun Phrase in English & Hindi. 1971. 6.95 (ISBN 0-89684-322-X). Orient Bk Dist.

INDIC LEGENDS
see Legends, Indic

INDIC LITERATURE
Here are entered works dealing with the literature of India in general, works on Indo-Aryan literature, and other works not confined to the literature of a single-language.

Alphonso-Karkala, J. B. Indo-English Literature in the Nineteenth Century. 168p. 1971. Repr. of 1970 ed. 5.00x (ISBN 0-685-25224-8). Paragon.
Amore, Roy C. & Shinn, Larry D. Lustful Maidens & Ascetic Kings: Buddhist & Hindu Stories of Life. (Illus.). 176p. 1981. text ed. 14.95x (ISBN 0-19-502838-4); pap. 5.95 (ISBN 0-19-502839-2). Oxford U Pr.
Banerji, Sures C. A Companion to Middle Indo-Aryan Literature. 1977. 14.00x (ISBN 0-88386-983-7). South Asia Bks.
Chander, Krishan. The Dreamer & Other Stories. Ratan, Jai, tr. 160p. 1970. pap. 2.50 (ISBN 0-88253-025-9). InterCulture.
Emeneau, Murray B., compiled by. Union List of Printed Indic Texts & Translations in American Libraries. 1935. pap. 25.00 (ISBN 0-527-02681-6). Kraus Repr.
Gardner, Fletcher & Waliwanag, Ildefonso. Indic Writings of the Mindoro-Palawan Axis, 3 vols. in 1. LC 77-87489. Repr. of 1940 ed. 42.50 (ISBN 0-404-16714-4). AMS Pr.
Gray, Louis H. The Narrative of Bhoja (Bhojaprabandha) by Ballala of Benares. (American Oriental Ser.: Vol. 34). 1950. pap. 5.00x (ISBN 0-940490-34-X). Am Orient Soc.
Gunnell, Bryn. The Cashew-Nut Girl & Other Stories of India. 1974. 9.95 (ISBN 0-236-17623-4, Pub. by Paul Elek). Merrimack Bk Serv.
Hopkins, Edward W. The Great Epic of India: Its Character & Origin. LC 74-901095. 480p. 1969. Repr. of 1920 ed. 17.50x (ISBN 0-8002-1470-6). Intl Pubns Serv.
Kesaven, B. S. & Mulay, Y. M., eds. The National Bibliography of Indian Literature, 1901-1953. Incl. Vol. 1. Comprising: Assamese, Bengali, English, Gujarati. 797p. 1962 (ISBN 0-8426-1447-8); Vol. 2. Comprising: Hindi, Kannada, Kashmiri, Malayalam. 632p. 1966 (ISBN 0-8426-1446-X). 25.00x ea. Verry.
Kohli, Suresh, ed. Modern Indian Short Stories. (Indian Short Stories Ser.). 164p. 1975. 5.00 (ISBN 0-88253-737-7). Ind-US Inc.
Kumar, Sharat. The Storm & Other Stories. 1976. 9.00 (ISBN 0-89253-815-5); flexible cloth 6.75 (ISBN 0-89253-816-3). Ind-US Inc.
McCutchion, David. Indian Writing in English. (Writers Workshop Greybird Ser.). 142p. 1975. 12.00 (ISBN 0-89253-596-2); pap. text ed. 8.00 (ISBN 0-88253-726-1). Ind-US Inc.
Madgulkar, Vyankatesh. The Winds of Fire. Kale, Pramod, tr. from Marathi. 113p. 1975. pap. 1.95 (ISBN 0-88253-693-1). Ind-US Inc.
Menon, R. Rabindranath. Shadows in the Sun. 1976. 8.00 (ISBN 0-89253-813-9); flexible cloth 4.80 (ISBN 0-89253-814-7). Ind-US Inc.
Moulik, Moni. Twilight. 1976. 9.00 (ISBN 0-89253-829-5); flexible cloth 6.75 (ISBN 0-89253-830-9). Ind-US Inc.
Naqvi, Rafiq A., ed. Indian Response to Literature in English (British, American, & Indo-Anglican) An Annotated Bibliography. LC 74-903521. 200p. 1974. 12.75x (ISBN 0-88386-388-X). South Asia Bks.
Obeyesekere, Ranjini & Fernando, Chitra, eds. An Anthology of Modern Writing from Sri Lanka. (Monographs of the Association for Asian Studies: No. XXXVIII). 1981. text ed. 12.95x (ISBN 0-8165-0702-3); pap. text ed. 6.50x (ISBN 0-8165-0703-1). U of Ariz Pr.
Qamber, Akhtar. Sabbatical in Japan. 1976. 8.00 (ISBN 0-89253-819-8); flexible cloth 4.00 (ISBN 0-89253-820-1). Ind-US Inc.
Satyaprakash. Kerala: A Select Bibliography. 1979. 18.50x (ISBN 0-8364-0506-4). South Asia Bks.
Shastri, P. N. & Lal, P., eds. Writers Workshop Handbook of Gujarati Literature: Vol. 1, A-F. (Writers Workshop Greybird Book). 96p. 1981. 14.00 (ISBN 0-86578-043-9); flexible bndg. 8.00 (ISBN 0-86578-042-0). Ind-US Inc.
Shimer, Dorothy B. Bhabani Bhattacharya. (World Authors Ser.: India: No. 343). 1975. lib. bdg. 12.50 (ISBN 0-8057-2151-7). Twayne.
Sivasamhita. The Siva Samhita. Srisa Chandra Vasu, tr. LC 73-3803. (Sacred Books of the Hindus: Vol. 15, Pt. 1). Repr. of 1914 ed. 14.50 (ISBN 0-404-57815-2). AMS Pr.
Srivastava, R. P. Contemporary Indian Idealism. 1973. text ed. 6.50x (ISBN 0-8426-0490-1). Verry.
Trivedi, Devika. Ikebana. (Illus.). 1976. 10.50 (ISBN 0-686-20245-7). Intl Bk Dist.
Varma, Monika. Alakananda. 1976. 8.00 (ISBN 0-89253-823-6); flexible cloth 4.80 (ISBN 0-89253-824-4). Ind-US Inc.
Winternitz, Maurice. A History of Indian Literature, 2 vols. 2nd ed. Ketkar, S. & Kohn, H., trs. Incl. Vol. 1. Introduction, Veda, National Epics, Puranas & Tantras; Vol. 2. Buddhist Literature & Jaina Literature. 1977. Repr. of 1972 ed. text ed. 37.50x (ISBN 0-391-01075-1). Humanities.

INDIC LITERATURE-HISTORY AND CRITICISM

Amur, G. S. Manohar Malgonkar. (Indian Writers Ser.). 1976. 8.50 (ISBN 0-89253-506-7). Ind-US Inc.
Artola, George T. Banners of Kamadeva, & Other Topics of Sanskrit Literature & Indian Culture. 1979. text ed. 12.00x (ISBN 0-8426-1612-8). Verry.
Bhattacharyya, N. N. History of Indian Erotic Literature. LC 76-908077. 1976. 11.00x (ISBN 0-88386-743-5). South Asia Bks.
Bhattacharyya, Suresh M. The Alamkara Section of the Agni Purana. LC 76-904737. 1976. 11.50x (ISBN 0-88386-911-X). South Asia Bks.
Chakraborti, Smarajit. The Bengali Press, 1818-1868: A Study in the Growth of Public Opinion. LC 76-905409. 1976. 9.00x (ISBN 0-88386-790-7). South Asia Bks.
Chandrasekharan, K. R. Bhabani Bhattacharya. (Indian Writers Ser.). 1976. 8.50 (ISBN 0-89253-505-9). Ind-US Inc.
Chari, S. M. Advaita & Visistadvaita: A Study Based on Vedanta Desika's Satudasani. 2nd ed. 1976. 9.00 (ISBN 0-8426-0886-9). Verry.
Clark, T. W., ed. The Novel in India: Its Birth & Development. LC 70-119719. 1970. 22.75x (ISBN 0-520-01725-0). U of Cal Pr.
Dimock, Edward C., Jr., et al. The Literatures of India: An Introduction. LC 73-87300. 1978. pap. 6.95 (ISBN 0-226-15233-2, P768, Phoen). U of Chicago Pr.
--The Literatures of India: An Introduction. LC 73-87300. xiv, 265p. 1975. 12.50x (ISBN 0-226-15232-4). U of Chicago Pr.
Jotwani, Motilal, ed. Contemporary Indian Literature & Society. 1979. 15.00x (ISBN 0-8364-0527-7). South Asia Bks.
Kaegi, Adolf. The Rigveda: The Oldest Literature of the Indians. Arrowsmith, R., tr. 198p. 1972. Repr. of 1886 ed. 13.50x (ISBN 0-8002-1924-4). Intl Pubns Serv.
Kohli, S., ed. Aspects of Indian Literature: The Changing Pattern (India) 179p. 1976. text ed. 9.00x (ISBN 0-7069-0376-5). Verry.
Kohli, Suresh, ed. Aspects of Indian Literature. 1975. 9.00 (ISBN 0-686-20194-9). Intl Bk Dist.
Krishna-Rao, A. V. The Indo-Anglian Novel & the Changing Tradition. LC 73-901609. 146p. 1972. 8.50x (ISBN 0-8002-1556-7). Intl Pubns Serv.
Krishna Rao, Angara V. The Indo-Anglian Novel & the Changing Tradition. LC 73-901609. 146p. 1972. 8.50 (ISBN 0-88386-224-7). South Asia Bks.
Lal, P. The Concept of an Indian Literature: Six Essays by P. Lal. 49p. 1973. 10.00 (ISBN 0-88253-303-7). Ind-US Inc.
Machwe, Prabhakar. Four Decades of Indian Literature. LC 76-901763. 1976. 10.00x (ISBN 0-88386-806-7). South Asia Bks.
Melwani, Murli D. Critical Essays on Indo-Anglian Themes. (Greybird Bk.). 1976. 9.00 (ISBN 0-89253-595-4); flexible bdg. 5.00 (ISBN 0-89253-128-2). Ind-US Inc.
Mohan, Ramesh. Indian Writing in English. 1979. 10.00x (ISBN 0-8364-0337-1, Orient Longman). South Asia Bks.
Mukherjee, Meenakshi, ed. Considerations: Twelve Studies in Indo-Anglian Writings. 1977. 8.00x (ISBN 0-8364-0082-8). South Asia Bks.
Murthy, H. V., ed. Vaisnavism of Samkaradeva & Ramanuja: A Comparative Study. 254p. 1973. text ed. 8.25x (ISBN 0-8426-0459-6). Verry.
Naik, M. K. Aspects of Indian Writing in English. 319p. (Orig.). 1979. pap. text ed. 4.50x (ISBN 0-333-90301-3). Humanities.
--Mulk Raj Anand. (Indian Writers Ser.). 1976. 8.50 (ISBN 0-89253-507-5). Ind-US Inc.
Parameswaran, Uma. Study of Representative Indo-English Novelists. 1976. 13.50 (ISBN 0-7069-0410-9). Intl Bk Dist.
Pargiter, F. E. The Purana Text of the Dynasties of the Kali Age. 1976. Repr. 11.00x (ISBN 0-88386-898-9). South Asia Bks.
Patil, D. R., ed. Cultural History from the Vayu Purana. 366p. 1973. text ed. 9.00x (ISBN 0-8426-0529-0). Verry.
Prasad, R. C. Early English Travellers in India. 2nd rev. ed. 391p. 1980. text ed. 27.00 (ISBN 0-8426-1649-7). Verry.
Problems of Modern Indian Literature. 1975. 12.50x (ISBN 0-88386-692-7). South Asia Bks.
Qamber, Akhtar. The Last Musha'irah of Delhi. 1979. 18.00x (ISBN 0-8364-0537-4, Orient Longman). South Asia Bks.
Raghavacharyulu, D. V. The Critical Response: Selected Essays on the American, Commonwealth,Indian & British Traditions in Literature. 1980. 13.50x (ISBN 0-8364-0632-X, Pub. by Macmillan India). South Asia Bks.
Sahai, Sachchidanand. The Ramayana in Laos-a Study in the Gvay Dvorahbi: A Shortened Modern Prose Version of the Indian Epci. 1976. Repr. of 1972 ed. 17.00x (ISBN 0-88386-869-5). South Asia Bks.
Selected Writings of Jawaharlal Nehru, Vol. 3. 1981. 26.00x (ISBN 0-8364-0672-9, Orient Longman). South Asia Bks.
Shahane, Vasant A. Ruth Prawer Jhabvala. new,enlarged ed. (Indian Writers Ser.: Vol. 11). 1981. 12.00 (ISBN 0-89253-074-X). Ind-US Inc.
Sharma, K. K. Bhabani Bhattacharya: His Vision & Themes. 1980. 10.00x (ISBN 0-8364-0584-6, Pub. by Abhinav India). South Asia Bks.
Shirwadkar, Meena. Image of Woman in the Indo-Anglian Novel. 169p. 1979. 10.00x (ISBN 0-8002-1000-X). Intl Pubns Serv.
Sidhanta, Mirmal K. The Heroic Age of India: A Comparative Study. LC 75-928104. 1975. Repr. of 1929 ed. 12.75x (ISBN 0-8364-0409-2). South Asia Bks.
Singh, R. S. Indian Novel in English: A Critical Study. 1977. text ed. 10.75x (ISBN 0-391-01079-4). Humanities.
Sivaramamurti, C. Ganga. 106p. 1981. 60.00x (ISBN 0-86125-084-2, Pub. by Orient Longman India). State Mutual Bk.
Smith, J. D. The Visaladeuarasa: A Restoration of the Text. LC 75-30441. (Cambridge Oriental Publications Ser.: No. 26). 260p. 1977. 64.00 (ISBN 0-521-20815-7). Cambridge U Pr.
Warder, A. K. Indian Kavya Literature, 3 vols. Incl. Vol. 1. Literary Criticism. 1972. 10.00 (ISBN 0-8426-0475-8); Vol. 2. Origins & Formation of the Classical Kavya. 1974. 14.50 (ISBN 0-8426-0734-X); The Early Medieval Period: Sudraka to Visakhadatta. 1977. 14.50 (ISBN 0-89684-163-4). Orient Bk Dist.
--Indian Kavya Literature: Origins & Formation on Classical Kavya, Vol.2. 1974. text ed. 19.50x (ISBN 0-8426-0734-X). Verry.
Williams, Haydn M. Studies in Modern Indian Fiction in English, 2 vols. (Greybird Book). 182p. 1975. Set. text ed. 24.00 (ISBN 0-88253-652-4); Set. pap. text ed. 15.00 (ISBN 0-88253-651-6). Ind-US Inc.
Winternitz, M. History of Indian Literature, Vol. 3, Part I. 2nd rev. ed. Jha, Subhadra, tr. 1977. 18.00 (ISBN 0-89684-217-7, Pub. by Motilal Banarsidass India). Orient Bk Dist.
Winternitz, Maurice. A History of Indian Literature, 3 vols. Ketkar, S. & Kohn, H., trs. from Ger. LC 68-12799. 1347p. 1977. Repr. of 1927 ed. Set. 57.50x (ISBN 0-8002-1503-6). Intl Pubns Serv.
Winternitz, Moriz. History of Indian Literature, Vols. 1 & 2. Ketkar, Mrs. S. & Kohn, H., trs. from Ger. LC 73-151559. (1971. Repr. of 1927, 1933 eds.). 60.00 (ISBN 0-8462-1602-7). Russell.

INDIC LITERATURE-TRANSLATIONS INTO ENGLISH

Basheer, M. Voices-The Walls. 1977. 4.00x (ISBN 0-88386-211-5). South Asia Bks.
Deshpande, Gauri. An Anthology of Indo-English Poetry. 162p. 1975. pap. text ed. 2.50 (ISBN 0-88253-455-6). Ind-US Inc.
Khan, Hazrat I. Gayan, Vadan, Nirtan. LC 80-52801. (The Collected Works of Hazrat Inayat Khan Ser.). 304p. 1980. 10.00 (ISBN 0-930872-21-5, 1006H); pap. 5.95 (ISBN 0-930872-16-9, 1006P). Sufi Order Pubns.
Lal, P. Transcreation: Two Essays. 29p. 1973. 8.00 (ISBN 0-88253-269-3). Ind-US Inc.
Masson, J. L. & Kosambi, D. D., trs. Avimaraka or Love's Enchanted World. 1970. 4.50 (ISBN 0-89684-177-4). Orient Bk Dist.
Mayeda, Sengaku, tr. A Thousand Teachings: The Upadesasahasri of Sankara. 1979. 27.50x (ISBN 0-86008-242-3, Pub. by U of Tokyo Pr). Intl Schol Bk Serv.
Raina, Trilokinath, ed. An Anthology of Modern Kashmiri Verse 1930-1960. Raina, Trithokinath, tr. from Kashmiri. 280p. 1974. lib. bdg. 12.50 (ISBN 0-88253-469-6). Ind-US Inc.
Ramakrishna, D., ed. Indian-English Prose: An Anthology. 332p. 1981. text ed. 12.50x (ISBN 0-391-02190-7, Pub. by Heinemann India). Humanities.
Sanders, Thomas E. & Peek, Walter W. Literature of the American Indian. LC 72-89050. 480p. 1973. text ed. 15.95x (ISBN 0-02-477640-8). Macmillan.
Sarma, G. P. Nationalism in Indo-Anglian Fiction. 1978. text ed. 16.75x (ISBN 0-391-01083-2). Humanities.
Van Buitenen, J. A., ed. & tr. from Sanskrit. The Mahabharata, Vol. III. Incl. Book 4: The Book of Virata; Book 5: The Book of the Effort. LC 72-97802. 1978. lib. bdg. 26.00x set (ISBN 0-226-84650-4). U of Chicago Pr.
Warder, A. K. Indian Kavya Literature: Early Medieval Period (Sudraka to Visakhadatta, Vol. 3. 1977. text ed. 19.50x (ISBN 0-8426-1053-7). Verry.
Yutang, Lin, ed. Wisdom of China & India. 1955. 5.95 (ISBN 0-394-60759-7, G59). Modern Lib.

INDIC MUSIC
see Music, Indic

INDIC MYTHOLOGY
see Mythology, Indic

INDIC PAINTING
see Painting, Indic

INDIC PAINTINGS
see Paintings, Indic

INDIC PERIODICALS

Gandhi, H. N., et al. Indian Periodicals in Print, 1973, 2 vols. LC 73-904001. 626p. 1973. Set. 37.50x (ISBN 0-8002-1547-8). Intl Pubns Serv.
Gidwani, N. N. & Navalni, K. Indian Periodicals. 1969. 16.50x (ISBN 0-8426-0125-2). Verry.
Satyaprakash. Guide to Indian Periodical Literature: 1969, Vol. 6. 1975. 45.00x (ISBN 0-88386-390-1). South Asia Bks.

INDIC PHILOSOPHY
see Philosophy, Indic

INDIC POETRY-HISTORY AND CRITICISM

Bhattacharyya, Suresh M. The Alamkara Section of the Agni Purana. LC 76-904737. 1976. 11.50x (ISBN 0-88386-911-X). South Asia Bks.
Dasgupta, Subhoranjan. Pritish Nandy. (Indian Writers Ser.: Vol. XII). 1977. 8.50 (ISBN 0-89253-450-8). Ind-US Inc.
Fraser, J. Nelson & Marathe, K. B., eds. Poems of Tukarama. Fraser, J. Nelson & Marathe, K. B., trs. 1981. Repr. of 1909 ed. 15.00x (ISBN 0-8364-0747-4, Pub. by Motilal Banarsidass). South Asia Bks.
Giri, Kalipada. Concept of Poetry: An Indian Approach. LC 75-902542. 1975. 9.00x (ISBN 0-88386-579-3). South Asia Bks.
Gokak, V. K. An Integral View of Poetry: An Indian Perspective. LC 75-908960. 1975. 11.00x (ISBN 0-88386-726-5). South Asia Bks.

Gonda, J. Vision of the Vedic Poets. (Disputationes Rheno-Trajectinae Ser.: No. 8). (Orig.). 1963. pap. text ed. 40.00x (ISBN 90-2790-034-5). Mouton.

Maini, Darshan S. Studies in Punjabi Poetry. 1979. text ed. 10.00x (ISBN 0-7069-0709-4). Humanities.

Mainkar, T. G. Rgvedic Foundations of Classical Poetics. 1977. 9.00x (ISBN 0-686-22670-4). Intl Bk Dist.

Miller, Barbara S., tr. from Sanskrit. The Hermit & the Love-Thief: Sanskrit Poems of Bhartrihari & Bilhana. LC 78-14513. 128p. 1978. 15.00 (ISBN 0-231-04644-8); pap. 6.00x (ISBN 0-231-04645-6). Columbia U Pr.

Nandy, Pritish, ed. The Vikas Book of Modern Indian Love Poetry. 1979. 10.50x (ISBN 0-7069-0748-5, Pub. by Vikas India). Advent NY.

Rahman, Anisur. Expressive Form in the Poetry of Kamala Das. 1981. 10.00x (ISBN 0-8364-0730-X, Pub. by Abhinav India). South Asia Bks.

--Form & Value in the Poetry of Nissim Ezekiel. 1981. 10.00x (ISBN 0-8364-0731-8, Pub. by Abhinav India). South Asia Bks.

Rajyalakshmi, P. V. The Lyric Spring: The Poetic Achievement of Rarojini Naidu. 1977. 11.00x (ISBN 0-8364-0056-9). South Asia Bks.

Rubin, David, tr. from Nepali. Nepali Visions, Nepali Dreams: The Poetry of Laxmiprasad Devkota. (Modern Asian Literature Ser.). 192p. 1980. 17.50x (ISBN 0-231-05014-3). Columbia U Pr.

Sachithanandan, V. Whitman & Bharati: Comparative Study. 242p. 1980. pap. text ed. 7.00x (ISBN 0-391-01740-3). Humanities.

Sen, Ramendra K. A Brief Introduction to a Comparative Study of Greek & Indian Poetics & Aesthetics. LC 76-14407. 1976. Repr. of 1954 ed. lib. bdg. 7.50 (ISBN 0-8414-7837-6). Folcroft.

Shahane, V. A., ed. Indian Poetry in English: A Critical Assessment. 1981. 14.00x (ISBN 0-8364-0685-0, Orient Longman). South Asia Bks.

Varma, Monika. Facing Four. (Greybird Book). 47p. 1975. 8.00 (ISBN 0-88253-758-X); pap. 4.80 (ISBN 0-88253-849-7). Ind-US Inc.

Warder, A. K. Indian Kavya Literature Vol. 1: Literary Criticism. 281p. 1973. text ed. 12.00x (ISBN 0-8426-0475-8). Verry.

INDIC POETRY-TRANSLATIONS INTO ENGLISH

Bowen, J. C. The Golden Pomegranate: A Selection from the Poetry of the Mogul Empire in India 1526-1858. (Illus.). 1977. Repr. of 1966 ed. 8.00x (ISBN 0-85668-073-7, Pub. by Aris & Phillips). Intl Schol Bk Serv.

Daruwalla, Keki N. Two Decades of Indian Poetry Nineteen Sixty to Nineteen Eighty. 1980. text ed. 17.50 (ISBN 0-7069-1003-6, Vikas India). Advent NY.

Dasgupta, Mary A., ed. Hers: English Verse by Indian Women. (Writers Workshop Redbirds Ser.). 106p. 1978. 10.00 (ISBN 0-86578-041-2); flexible bndg. 6.00 (ISBN 0-86578-040-4). Ind-US Inc.

Deshpande, Gauri. An Anthology of Indo-English Poetry. 162p. 1975. pap. text ed. 2.50 (ISBN 0-88253-455-6). Ind-US Inc.

Dwivedi, A. N. Indian Poetry in English: A Literary History & Anthology. 159p. 1980. text ed. 9.50x (ISBN 0-391-01789-6). Humanities.

Kurl, Shreeprakash, tr. The Devotional Poems of Mirabai. (Writers Workshop Saffronbird Ser.). 87p. 1975. 15.00 (ISBN 0-88253-722-9); pap. 6.75 (ISBN 0-89253-539-3). Ind-US Inc.

Lal, P., ed. New English Poetry by Indian Women. (Writers Workshop Redbird Ser.). 1977. flexible bdg. 8.00 (ISBN 0-89253-804-X); text ed. 14.00 (ISBN 0-89253-803-1). Ind-US Inc.

Nandy, Pritish, ed. Indian Poetry in English Today. (Indian Poetry Ser.). 140p. (Orig.). 1974. 3.95 (ISBN 0-88253-312-6). Ind-US Inc.

Parthasarathy, R., ed. Ten Twentieth Century Indian Poets. (Three Crowns New Poetry from India Ser.). 1977. pap. 5.95x (ISBN 0-19-560665-5). Oxford U Pr.

Roy, Tarapada. Where to, Tarapada-Babu? Devi, Shyamasree & Lal, P., trs. from Bengali. (Saffronbird Bk.). 51p. 1975. 10.00 (ISBN 0-88253-839-X); pap. 4.80 (ISBN 0-88253-840-3). Ind-US Inc.

Saha, P. K. Blue Magic. 80p. 1975. 14.00 (ISBN 0-88253-825-X); pap. 8.00 (ISBN 0-88253-826-8). Ind-US Inc.

Shahane, V. A., ed. Indian Poetry in English: A Critical Assessment. 1981. 14.00x (ISBN 0-8364-0685-0, Orient Longman). South Asia Bks.

INDIC SCULPTURE

see Sculpture-India

INDIC SONGS

see Songs, Indic

INDIC STUDIES

Bender, Ernest, ed. Indological Studies in Honor of W. Norman Brown. (American Oriental Ser.: Vol. 47). 1962. 10.00x (ISBN 0-940490-47-1). Am Orient Soc.

Buck, Harry M. & Yocum, Glenn A., eds. Structural Approaches to South India Studies. LC 74-77412. 1974. pap. 5.95 (ISBN 0-89012-000-5). Anima Pubns.

INDIC TALES

see Tales, Indic

INDIC WIT AND HUMOR

Mukerji, Mohan. Ham in the Sandwich. 1980. text ed. 10.50x (ISBN 0-7069-0919-4, Pub. by Vikas India). Advent NY.

INDICATING INSTRUMENTS

see Recording Instruments

INDICATOR PLANTS

see Plant Indicators

INDICATORS AND TEST-PAPERS

see also Chemical Tests and Reagents

Bishop, E. Indicators. 756p. 1973. text ed. 105.00 (ISBN 0-08-016617-2). Pergamon.

Bloomfield, Dennis A. Dye Curves: The Theory & Practice of Non-Diffusable Indicator Dilution. (Illus.). 1974. 34.50 (ISBN 0-8391-0638-6). Univ Park.

INDICES

see Indexes

INDICTMENTS

see also Grand Jury

Barth, Alan. The Price of Liberty. LC 74-176486. (Civil Liberties in American History Ser.). 1972. Repr. of 1961 ed. lib. bdg. 25.00 (ISBN 0-306-70416-1). Da Capo.

INDIFFERENTISM (RELIGION)

see also Liberalism (Religion)

Grotius, Hugo. True Religion Explained & Defended. Coventry, F., tr. LC 72-201. (English Experience Ser.: No. 318). 350p. 1971. Repr. of 1632 ed. 28.00 (ISBN 90-221-0318-8). Walter J Johnson.

INDIGNATION

see Anger

INDIGO

Gerber, Frederick H. Indigo & the Antiquity of Dyeing. LC 77-81540. 1977. pap. 4.75 (ISBN 0-685-53315-8). Arum Pr.

--Indigo & the Antiquity of Dyeing. LC 77-81540. (Illus.). 1977. pap. 4.75 (ISBN 0-9601814-1-5). Gerber Pubns.

Katzenberg, Dena S. Blue Traditions: Indigo Dyed Textiles & Related Cobalt Glazed Ceramics from the 17th Through the 19th Century. LC 73-91962. (Illus.). 1973. pap. 10.00 (ISBN 0-912298-35-9). Baltimore Mus.

Pettit, Florence H. America's Indigo Blues: Resist - Printed & Dyed Textiles of the Eighteenth Century. (Illus.). 1975. 19.95 (ISBN 0-8038-0376-1). Hastings.

Polakoff, Claire. Into Indigo: African Textiles & Dyeing Techniques. LC 77-76281. (Illus.). 1980. pap. 7.95 (ISBN 0-385-08504-4, Anch). Doubleday.

INDIRECT COSTS

see Overhead Costs

INDIRECT TAXATION

see Tariff; Taxation

INDIUM

Smith, Ivan C. & Carson, Bonnie. Indium. LC 77-88486. (Trace Metals in the Environment Ser.: Vol. 5). 1978. 29.50 (ISBN 0-250-40232-7). Ann Arbor Science.

INDIVIDUALISM

see also Collectivism; Communism; Laissez-Faire; Libertarianism; Personalism; Self-Interest; Socialism

Abrams, P. & McCulloch, A. Communes, Sociology & Society. LC 75-40985. (Themes in the Social Sciences Ser.: No. 3). 200p. 1976. 29.50 (ISBN 0-521-21188-3); pap. 7.95x (ISBN 0-521-29067-8). Cambridge U Pr.

Berman, Marshall. Politics of Authenticity: Radical Individualism & the Emergence of Modern Society. LC 77-124968. 1970. pap. 5.95x (ISBN 0-689-70288-4, 170). Atheneum.

Bettelheim, Bruno. Informed Heart. 1971. pap. 2.75 (ISBN 0-380-01302-9, 52704, Discus). Avon.

--Informed Heart: Autonomy in a Mass Age. 1960. 12.95 (ISBN 0-02-903200-8). Free Pr.

Carus, Paul. Nietzsche. LC 72-2039. (Studies in German Literature, No. 13). 1972. Repr. of 1914 ed. lib. bdg. 33.95 (ISBN 0-8383-1464-3). Haskell.

Dallmayr, Fred R. Twilight of Subjectivity: Contributions to a Post-Individualist Theory of Politics. LC 80-23433. 376p. 1981. lib. bdg. 20.00x (ISBN 0-87023-314-9); pap. text ed. 10.00x (ISBN 0-87023-315-7). U of Mass Pr.

Devane, Richard S. The Failure of Individualism: A Documented Essay. LC 75-28664. (Illus.). 1976. Repr. lib. bdg. 21.75x (ISBN 0-8371-8484-3, DEFI). Greenwood.

Donisthorpe, Wordsworth. Individualism. 59.95 (ISBN 0-8490-0403-9). Gordon Pr.

Eliot, Charles W. Conflict Between Individualism & Collectivism in a Democracy, Three Lectures. facs. ed. LC 67-22060. (Essay Index Reprint Ser). 1910. 10.00 (ISBN 0-8369-0411-7). Arno.

Fontenay, Charles L. Epistle to the Babylonians: An Essay on the Natural Inequality of Man. LC 68-9778. 1969. 12.50x (ISBN 0-87049-088-5). U of Tenn Pr.

Freud, Arthur. Of Human Sovereignty. LC 65-10993. 1965. 6.00 (ISBN 0-8022-0539-9). Philos Lib.

Hayek, Friedrich A. Individualism & Economic Order. LC 48-4149. vii, 272p. lib. bdg. 13.00 (ISBN 0-226-32089-8, Phoen). U of Chicago Pr.

Hocking, William E. The Lasting Elements of Individualism. LC 75-3186. Repr. of 1937 ed. 14.00 (ISBN 0-404-59188-4). AMS Pr.

Hoover, Clark H. American Individualism. Freidel, Frank, ed. LC 78-66528. (History of the United States 1876-1976 Ser.: Vol. 8). 1979. lib. bdg. 11.00 (ISBN 0-8240-9704-1). Garland Pub.

Hoover, Herbert. The Challenge to Liberty. LC 72-2373. (FDR & the Era of the New Deal Ser.). 212p. 1973. Repr. of 1934 ed. lib. bdg. 25.00 (ISBN 0-306-70499-4). Da Capo.

Kahn, Ludwig W. Social Ideals in German Literature. LC 75-84876. Repr. of 1938 ed. 12.95 (ISBN 0-404-03626-0). AMS Pr.

Labadie, Laurance. A Way Out: Anarchist, Mutualist & Individualist Essays. (Men & Movements in the History & Philosophy of Anarchism Ser.). 1980. lib. bdg. 59.95 (ISBN 0-686-60065-7). Revisionist Pr.

Lane, Rose W. Discovery of Freedom: Man's Struggle Against Authority. LC 73-172216. (Right Wing Individualist Tradition in America Ser). 1972. Repr. of 1943 ed. 16.00 (ISBN 0-405-00425-7). Arno.

Liao Wen-Kuei. The Individual & the Community. LC 73-14035. (International Library of Psychology, Philosophy & Scientific Method Ser). 314p. 1974. Repr. of 1933 ed. lib. bdg. 16.00x (ISBN 0-8371-7142-3, LIIN). Greenwood.

Lukes, Steven. Individualism. 172p. 1973. pap. text ed. 8.95x (ISBN 0-631-18750-2, Pub. by Basil Blackwell). Biblio Dist.

Machan, Tibor R., ed. The Libertarian Alternative: Essays in Social & Political Philosophy. LC 73-80501. 1974. 20.95x (ISBN 0-911012-72-9); pap. 11.95 (ISBN 0-88229-511-X). Nelson-Hall.

McInery, Timothy A. Private Man. 1962. 5.95 (ISBN 0-8392-1087-6). Astor-Honor.

McPherson, Thomas. Political Obligation. (Library of Political Studies). 1967. pap. text ed. 2.25x (ISBN 0-7100-3159-9). Humanities.

Moore, Charles A., ed. Status of the Individual in East & West. 20.00x (ISBN 0-87022-542-1). U Pr of Hawaii.

Moore, Harry E., Jr. Values for Freedom. LC 72-76584. 1972. 5.95 (ISBN 0-87212-026-0). Libra.

Morley, Felix, ed. Essays on Individuality. LC 76-58027. 1977. 8.00 (ISBN 0-913966-27-4, Liberty Press); pap. 3.50 (ISBN 0-913966-28-2). Liberty Fund.

Morris, Colin. The Discovery of the Individual, 1050-1200. LC 72-84235. 208p. 1973. 4.50x (ISBN 0-06-131718-7, TB1718, Torch). Har-Row.

Negrin, Su. Begin at Start: Some Thoughts on Personal Liberation & World Change. LC 72-87031. (Illus.). 176p. (Orig.). 1972. 6.95 (ISBN 0-87810-520-4); pap. 3.25 (ISBN 0-87810-020-2). Times Change.

Norton, David L. Personal Destinies-a Philosophy of Ethical Individualism. 1976. 29.00 (ISBN 0-691-07215-9); pap. 6.95 (ISBN 0-691-01975-4). Princeton U Pr.

Pole, J. R. American Individualism & the Promise of Progress: Inaugural Lecture. (Inaugural Lecture Ser.). 30p. pap. 5.95 (ISBN 0-19-951526-3). Oxford U Pr.

Redbeard, Ragnar. Might Is Right. 69.95 (ISBN 0-87700-187-1). Revisionist Pr.

Ross, James F., tr. Suarez: Disputation Six, on Formal & Universal Unity. (Medieval Philosophical Texts in Translation: No. 15). 1965. pap. 5.95 (ISBN 0-87462-215-8). Marquette.

Russell, Bertrand. Authority & the Individual. LC 68-54289. Repr. of 1949 ed. 12.50 (ISBN 0-404-05464-1). AMS Pr.

Simon, William E. A Time for Truth. LC 77-25465. 1978. 12.50 (ISBN 0-07-057378-6, GB). McGraw.

Stace, Walter T. Destiny of Western Man. Repr. of 1942 ed. lib. bdg. 14.75x (ISBN 0-8371-3375-0, STDM). Greenwood.

--The Destiny of Western Man. 1947. 17.50 (ISBN 0-384-57385-1). Johnson Repr.

Street, Charles L. Individualism & Individuality in the Philosophy of John Stuart Mill. 59.95 (ISBN 0-8490-0404-7). Gordon Pr.

Swift, Morrison I. The Horroboos. 1974. lib. bdg. 35.00 (ISBN 0-685-50722-X). Revisionist Pr.

Tucker, David. Marxism & Individualism. 1980. 22.50 (ISBN 0-312-51839-0). St Martin.

Tufts, James H. Individual - His Relation to Society As Reflected in British Ethics, 2 pts. LC 66-19697. Repr. of 1898 ed. 12.50x (ISBN 0-678-00556-7). Kelley.

University Of California Philosophical Union - 1936. Problem of the Individual: Lectures. (Publications in Philosophy Ser: Vol. 20). 1936. pap. 17.00 (ISBN 0-685-13558-6). Johnson Repr.

Wood, Ellen. Mind & Politics: An Approach to the Meaning of Liberal & Socialist Individualism. LC 74-153556. 224p. 1972. 22.75x (ISBN 0-520-02029-4). U of Cal Pr.

INDIVIDUALITY

see also Conformity; Identity; Personality; Secrecy (Psychology); Self

Bosanquet, Bernard. Principle of Individuality & Value. LC 12-14490. (Gifford Lectures). 1968. Repr. of 1912 ed. 24.00 (ISBN 0-527-10036-6). Kraus Repr.

--Value & Destiny of the Individual. LC 13-6278. (Gifford Lectures 1912). 1968. Repr. of 1913 ed. 20.00 (ISBN 0-527-10066-8). Kraus Repr.

Burridge, Kenelm. Someone, No One: An Essay on Individuality. LC 79-83979. 1979. 19.50 (ISBN 0-691-09384-9). Princeton U Pr.

Buss, A. R. & Poley, W. Individual Differences: Traits & Factors. LC 76-8909. 1976. 16.50 (ISBN 0-470-15099-8). Halsted Pr.

Claridge, Gordon S., et al. Personality Differences & Biological Variations: A Study of Twins. LC 72-10132. 1973. text ed. 28.00 (ISBN 0-08-017124-9). Pergamon.

Combs, Arthur W., et al. Perceptual Psychology: A Humanistic Approach to the Study of Persons. 492p. 1976. pap. text ed. 16.95 scp (ISBN 0-06-041346-8, HarpC). Har-Row.

Dixon, Linda K. & Johnson, Ronald C. The Roots of Individuality: A Survey of Human Behavior Genetics. LC 79-26601. 1980. pap. text ed. 10.95 (ISBN 0-8185-0376-9). Brooks-Cole.

Elias, Robert H. Entangling Alliances with None: An Essay on the Individual in the American Twenties. 256p. 1973. 8.95x (ISBN 0-393-01097-X). Norton.

Frohock, W. M. Strangers to This Ground: Cultural Diversity in Contemporary American Writing. LC 61-17183. 1961. 4.95 (ISBN 0-87074-055-5). SMU Press.

Garrison, Charles E. On Being a Person in a World of Groups. LC 81-40113. 190p. (Orig.). 1981. pap. text ed. 9.00 (ISBN 0-8191-1693-9). U Pr of Amer.

Gish, Arthur G. Beyond the Rat Race. LC 73-9336. 224p. (Orig.). 1973. pap. 1.45 (ISBN 0-87983-059-X). Keats.

Good, Paul. The Individual. (Human Behavior Ser.). 1974. 9.95 (ISBN 0-8094-1904-1); lib. bdg. avail. (ISBN 0-685-50285-6). Time-Life.

Hamburger, Jean. Discovering the Individual. 1978. 7.95 (ISBN 0-393-06433-6). Norton.

Hampshire, Stuart. Freedom of the Individual. new ed. LC 74-22929. 144p. 1975. 15.00x (ISBN 0-691-07208-6); pap. 6.95 (ISBN 0-691-01984-3). Princeton U Pr.

Hill, Brian V. Education & the Endangered Individual: A Critique of Ten Modern Thinkers. LC 73-82283. 322p. 1974. pap. text ed. 7.00x (ISBN 0-8077-2432-7). Tchrs Coll.

Jackins, Harvey. Flexible Human in the Rigid Society. 1965. pap. 0.50 (ISBN 0-911214-11-9). Rational Isl.

Kaplan, Abraham, ed. Individuality & the New Society. LC 72-103294. (Washington Paperback Ser.: No. 59). 190p. 1970. 9.50 (ISBN 0-295-95057-9); pap. 2.95 (ISBN 0-295-95140-0). U of Wash Pr.

Kinch, John W., ed. Introductory Sociology, Vol. 3: Social Development of the Individual. 1975. 3.00x (ISBN 0-86589-025-0). Individual Learn.

Lloyd, Robert. Images of Survival (NF) LC 73-1658. (Illus.). 280p. 1973. 7.95 (ISBN 0-396-06783-2). Dodd.

Morley, Felix, ed. Essays on Individuality. LC 76-58027. 1977. 8.00 (ISBN 0-913966-27-4, Liberty Press); pap. 3.50 (ISBN 0-913966-28-2). Liberty Fund.

Moustakas, Clark. Individuality & Encounter: A Brief Journey into Loneliness & Sensitivity Groups. LC 68-25353. 1968. pap. 3.45 (ISBN 0-87299-002-8). Howard Doyle.

O'Neill, John, ed. Modes of Individualism & Collectivism. LC 73-86363. 1973. 19.95 (ISBN 0-312-54320-4). St Martin.

Redman, Lenn. What Am I? (Illus.). 72p. 1980. pap. 4.95 (ISBN 0-9606258-0-1). Victor Pub Co.

Robinson, H. Alan. Meeting Individual Differences in Reading. LC 64-24978. (Supplementary Education Monograph Ser.). 1964. 6.50x (ISBN 0-226-72176-0, SEM94). U of Chicago Pr.

Roszak, Theodore. Person Planet: The Creative Disintegration of Industrial Society. LC 75-6165. 1979. pap. 5.95 (ISBN 0-385-00082-0, Anch). Doubleday.

Royce, Josiah. Conception of Immortality. 1968. Repr. of 1900 ed. lib. bdg. 15.00x (ISBN 0-8371-0207-3, ROCI). Greenwood.
--Conception of Immortality. 1900. Repr. 5.00 (ISBN 0-403-00308-3). Scholarly.
Ryden, E. Daniel. The Sovereignty of Individuality. 53p. 1977. pap. text ed. 6.50 (ISBN 0-8191-0065-X). U Pr of Amer.
Shaler, Nathaniel. The Individual: A Study of Life & Death. 59.95 (ISBN 0-87968-347-3). Gordon Pr.
Shor, Joel & Sanville, Jean. Illusion in Loving: A Psychoanalytic Approach to the Evolution of Intimacy & Autonomy. LC 77-85416. 1978. 15.00 (ISBN 0-930578-00-7). Double Helix.
Simmel, Georg. Georg Simmel, on Individuality & Social Forms. Levine, Donald N., ed. LC 78-157146. (Heritage of Sociology Ser). 1971. 20.00x (ISBN 0-226-75775-7). U of Chicago Pr.
Simon, Norma. Why Am I Different? Rubin, Caroline, ed. LC 76-41172. (Concept Books). (Illus.). 32p. 1976. 6.95g (ISBN 0-8075-9074-6). A Whitman.
Spier, Peter. People. (Illus.). 48p. (gr. 1-3). 1980. 10.00 (ISBN 0-385-13181-X); PLB (ISBN 0-385-13182-8). Doubleday.
Suran, Bernard G. Oddballs: The Social Maverick & the Dynamics of Individuality. LC 77-16660. 1978. 15.95x (ISBN 0-88229-366-4); pap. 8.95x (ISBN 0-88229-557-8). Nelson-Hall.
Thorndike, Edward L. Individuality. LC 77-16435. 1977. lib. bdg. 10.00 (ISBN 0-8414-8643-3). Folcroft.
Tyler, Fred T. Individualizing Instruction. LC 62-2192. (National Society for the Study of Education Yearbooks Ser: No. 61, Pt. 1). 1962. 6.50x (ISBN 0-226-60063-7). U of Chicago Pr.
Tyler, Leona E. Individuality: Human Possibilities & Personal Choice in the Psychological Development of Men & Women. LC 78-50897. (Social & Behavioral Science & Higher Education Ser.). 1978. text ed. 15.95x (ISBN 0-87589-365-1). Jossey-Bass.
Whyte, William H., Jr. Organization Man. 1957. 14.95 (ISBN 0-671-54330-X). S&S.

INDIVIDUALIZED INSTRUCTION

see also Open Plan Schools

Armstrong, David G. & Pinney, Robert H. Record Keeping for Individualized Instruction Programs. 64p. 1977. pap. 4.50 (ISBN 0-686-63696-1, 1601-7-06). NEA.
Association for Programmed Learning & Educational Technology. Aspects of Educational Technology X: Individualized Learning: Proceedings. 1976. 27.50x (ISBN 0-85038-461-3, Pub by Kogan Pg). Nichols Pub.
Blackburn, Jack E. & Powell, W. Conrad. One at a Time All at Once: The Creative Teacher's Guide to Individualized Instruction Without Anarchy. LC 75-21174. 1976. 12.95 (ISBN 0-87620-638-0); pap. 10.95 (ISBN 0-87620-637-2). Goodyear.
Burns, Richard W. & Klingstedt, Joe L., eds. Competency-Based Education: An Introduction. LC 73-3133. 180p. 1973. pap. 9.95 (ISBN 0-87778-061-7). Educ Tech Pubns.
Champagne, David W. & Goldman, Richard M. Handbook for Managing Individualized Learning in the Classroom. LC 75-14101. 114p. 1975. pap. 15.95 (ISBN 0-87778-081-1). Educ Tech Pubns.
Cushenbery, Donald C. Reading Improvement Through Diagnosis, Remediation & Individualized Instruction. 1977. 11.95 (ISBN 0-13-756536-4, Parker). P-H.
Dell, Helen Davis. Individualizing Instruction. LC 72-80760. (Illus.). 192p. 1972. pap. text ed. 6.95 (ISBN 0-574-18490-2, 13-1490). SRA.
Diamond, Robert M., et al. Instructional Development for Individualized Learning in Higher Education. LC 74-18398. 208p. 1975. pap. 16.95 (ISBN 0-87778-077-3). Educ Tech Pubns.
Duane, James E., ed. Individualized Instruction - Programs & Materials. LC 72-11990. 440p. 1973. 19.95 (ISBN 0-87778-043-9). Educ Tech Pubns.
Dunn, Rita & Dunn, Kenneth. Educator's Self-Teaching Guide to Individualizing Instructional Programs. 1975. 11.95 (ISBN 0-13-240663-2, Parker). P-H.
Eiss, Albert F. Individualized Learning Program. 1971. 29.95 (ISBN 0-87948-023-8). Beatty.
Flangan, John C., et al, eds. Behavioral Objectives: A Guide to Individualizing Learning, 4 vols. Incl. Social Studies (ISBN 0-88250-082-1); Language Arts (ISBN 0-88250-084-8); Mathematics (ISBN 0-88250-083-X); Science (ISBN 0-88250-081-3). 1971. Set. 60.00 set (ISBN 0-88250-075-9); pap. 33.60 (ISBN 0-686-17319-8). Cambridge Bk Co.
Galloway, David M. & Goodwin, Carole. Educating Slow-Learning & Maladjusted Children: Integration or Segregation? 1979. pap. text ed. 10.95x (ISBN 0-582-48914-8). Longman.
Gartner, Alan & Riessman, Frank. How to Individualize Learning. LC 77-89842. (Fastback Ser.: No. 100). 1977. pap. 0.75 (ISBN 0-87367-100-7). Phi Delta Kappa.
Georgiades, William, et al. New Schools for a New Age. LC 76-9909. (Illus.). 1977. pap. text ed. 9.95 (ISBN 0-87620-622-4). Goodyear.
Georgiades, William D. & Clark, Donald C. Models for Individualized Instruction. LC 73-22495. text ed. 18.95x (ISBN 0-8422-5164-2). Irvington.
Glaser, Robert. Adaptive Education: Individual Diversity & Learning. LC 76-56081. (Principles of Educational Psychology Ser.). 1977. pap. text ed. 5.95 (ISBN 0-03-015291-7, HoltC). HR&W.
Hull, Ronald E. & Mohan, Madan, eds. Individualized Instruction & Learning. LC 73-89605. 1974. 21.95x (ISBN 0-88229-113-0). Nelson-Hall.
Johnson, Rita B. & Johnson, Stuart R. Toward Individualized Learning: A Developer's Guide to Self-Instruction. LC 74-19692. 1975. text ed. 12.95 (ISBN 0-201-03420-4). A-W.
Johnson, Stuart R. & Johnson, Rita B. Developing Individualized Instructional Material. 1970. text ed. 4.44 (ISBN 0-88250-403-7). Westinghouse Learn.
Kapfer, Philip G. & Ovard, Glen F. Preparing & Using Individualized Learning Packages for Ungraded, Continuous Progress Education. LC 73-125877. 272p. 1971. pap. 17.95 (ISBN 0-87778-015-3). Educ Tech Pubns.
Kapfer, Philip G. & Kapfer, Miriam B., eds. Learning Packages in American Education. LC 72-11507. 248p. 1973. pap. 11.95 (ISBN 0-87778-047-1). Educ Tech Pubns.
Langdon, Danny G. Interactive Instructional Designs for Individualized Learning. LC 72-89577. 176p. 1973. pap. 9.95 (ISBN 0-87778-041-2). Educ Tech Pubns.
Learning Objectives for Individualized Instruction, 4 vols. Incl. Language Arts (ISBN 0-88250-772-9); Mathematics (ISBN 0-88250-773-7); Social Science (ISBN 0-88250-774-5); Science (ISBN 0-88250-775-3). 1975. 66.00 set (ISBN 0-686-26284-0); 15.00 ea. Cambridge Bk Co.
Marcus, Marie. Handbook for Individualizing Reading Instruction. (Illus.). 128p. 1974. pap. 5.95x (ISBN 0-88289-043-3). Pelican.
Messick, Samuel, et al. Individuality in Learning: Implications of Cognitive Styles & Creativity for Human Development. LC 76-11886. (Higher Education Ser.). (Illus.). 1976. 16.95x (ISBN 0-87589-281-7). Jossey-Bass.
National Conference on Personalized Instruction, 3rd & 4th, Washington, D.C. & San Francisco, 1976 & 1977. Personalized Instruction in Education Today: Proceedings. Sherman, J. Gilmour, et al, eds. LC 77-95405. (Illus.). 1978. pap. 12.00 (ISBN 0-911302-38-7). San Francisco Pr.
Neujahr, James. The Individualized Instruction Game. LC 75-22491. 1976. text ed. 8.00x (ISBN 0-8077-2485-8). Tchrs Coll.
Nussel, Edward, et al. Teacher & Individually Guided Education. LC 75-18157. (Leadership Series in Individually Guided Education). 336p. 1976. text ed. 11.95 (ISBN 0-201-19011-7); instr's guide 3.00 (ISBN 0-201-19021-4); filmstrips & cassettes 18.00 (ISBN 0-685-61963-X); filmstrips avail. (ISBN 0-201-19031-1). A-W.
Perrone, Vito. Open Education: Promise & Problems. LC 72-190068. (Fastback Ser.: No. 3). (Illus.). 1972. pap. 0.75 (ISBN 0-87367-003-5). Phi Delta Kappa.
Rapport, Virginia, ed. Learning Centers: Children on Their Own. LC 77-133244. (Illus.). 1970. pap. 2.50x (ISBN 0-87173-026-X). ACEI.
Reasoner, Charles. Portfolio of Working Materials for Individualized Instruction. 1976. 15.00 (ISBN 0-13-686337-X). P-H.
Sharan, Shlomo & Sharan, Yael. Small-Group Teaching. LC 75-42019. 256p. 1976. 18.95 (ISBN 0-87778-091-9). Educ Tech Pubns.
Sherman, Thomas M. Individually Responsive Instruction. Langdon, Danny G., ed. LC 77-25426. (Instructional Design Library Ser.). 80p. 1978. 11.95 (ISBN 0-87778-114-1). Educ Tech Pubns.
Shiman, D. A., et al. Teachers on Individualization: The Way We Do It. 1974. 9.95 (ISBN 0-07-056895-2, P&RB). McGraw.
Sorenson, Juanita S., et al. Unit Leader & Individually Guided Education. LC 75-12102. (Leadership Series in Individually Guided Education). 608p. 1976. text ed. 17.25 (ISBN 0-201-19711-1); tchr's guide 2.95 (ISBN 0-201-19721-9); cassettes & filmstrips avail. (ISBN 0-685-61033-0). A-W.
Stradley, William E. Administrator's Guide to an Individualized Performance Results Curriculum. 1973. 10.95x (ISBN 0-87628-146-3). Ctr Appl Res.
Tagatz, Glenn E. Child Development & Individually Guided Education. LC 75-12103. (Individually Guided Education-Leadership Ser.). (Illus.). 224p. 1976. pap. text ed. 7.95 (ISBN 0-201-19111-3); tchrs guide 2.95 (ISBN 0-201-19121-0). A-W.
Talmage, Harriet, ed. Systems of Individualized Education. LC 74-24478. 200p. 1975. 16.80x (ISBN 0-8211-1904-4); text ed. 15.25x (ISBN 0-685-51465-X). McCutchan.
The Teacher's Planning Pak & Guide to Individualized Instruction. (The Learning Center Set). (Illus.). 1978. pap. 7.95 (ISBN 0-913916-56-0, IP 59-0). Incentive Pubns.
Torshen, K. P. The Mastery Approach to Competency - Based Education. 1977. 21.50 (ISBN 0-12-696050-X). Acad Pr.
Turnbull. Development & Implement Individualized Education Program. 1978. 13.95 (ISBN 0-675-08318-4). Merrill.
Valletutti, P. Individualizing Educational Objectives & Programs: A Modular Approach. 1979. 16.50 (ISBN 0-8391-1265-3). Univ Park.
Weigand, J., ed. Implementing Teacher Competencies: Positive Approaches to Personalizing Education. 1977. pap. text ed. 12.95 (ISBN 0-13-451930-2). P-H.
Weisgerber, Robert A., ed. Perspectives in Individualized Learning. LC 78-138641. (Illus.). 1971. pap. text ed. 9.95 (ISBN 0-87581-077-2). Peacock Pubs.
Wiersma, William & Jurs, Stephen G. Evaluation of Instruction in Individually Guided Education. LC 75-18161. (Leadership Series in Individually Guided Education). (Illus.). 192p. 1976. text ed. 7.50 (ISBN 0-201-19211-X); instructor's guide 2.95 (ISBN 0-201-19221-7). A-W.

INDIVIDUATION

Bradford, Dennis E. The Concept of Existence: A Study of Nonexistent Particulars. LC 80-5526. 142p. 1980. lib. bdg. 16.75 (ISBN 0-8191-1124-4); pap. text ed. 7.50 (ISBN 0-8191-1127-9). U Pr of Amer.
Goldbrunner, Josef. Individuation: A Study of the Depth Psychology of Carl Gustav Jung. 1964. pap. 1.25x (ISBN 0-268-00131-6). U of Notre Dame Pr.
Jung, Carl G. Mandala Symbolism. Hull, R. F., tr. (Bollingen Ser.: Vol. 20). (Illus.). 204p. 1972. pap. 3.95 (ISBN 0-691-01781-6). Princeton U Pr.
Loux, Michael J., ed. Universals & Particulars: Readings in Ontology. LC 76-745. 359p. 1976. text ed. 16.95x (ISBN 0-268-01908-8); pap. 5.95x (ISBN 0-268-01909-6). U of Notre Dame Pr.
Meiland, Jack W. Talking About Particulars. (International Library of Philosophy & Scientific Method). 1970. text ed. 8.00x (ISBN 0-391-00056-X). Humanities.
Munitz, Milton K., ed. Identity & Individuation. LC 73-124530. (Studies in Contemporary Philosophy). 1971. o.p. 9.50x (ISBN 0-8147-5352-3); pap. 7.00x (ISBN 0-8147-5375-2). NYU Pr.
Thompson, Helen. Journey Toward Wholeness. 96p. (Orig.). 1982. pap. 3.95 (ISBN 0-8091-2422-X). Paulist Pr.
White, F. C. Plato's Theory of Particulars. Connor, W. R., ed. LC 80-2672. (Monographs in Classical Studies). 1981. lib. bdg. 45.00 (ISBN 0-405-14055-X). Arno.
Winquist, Charles E. Homecoming: Interpretation, Transformation & Individuation. LC 78-9565. 1978. pap. 7.50 (ISBN 0-89130-240-9). Scholars Pr Ca.

INDO-ARYAN LANGUAGES

see also Pali Language; Prakrit Languages; Sanskrit Language; Vedic Language

Bloch, Jules. Indo-Aryan, from the Vedas to Modern Times. rev. ed. Master, Alfred, tr. from Fr. 345p. (Orig.). 1965. pap. 30.00x (ISBN 0-8002-1557-5). Intl Pubns Serv.
Cardona, George. Studies in Indian Grammarians: One. LC 69-18745. (Transactions Ser.: Vol. 59, Pt. 1). 1969. pap. 1.00 (ISBN 0-87169-591-X). Am Philos.
Hunter, W. W. A Comparative Dictionary of the Languages of India & High Asia. 218p. 1978. Repr. of 1868 ed. 39.00 (ISBN 0-89684-144-8). Orient Bk Dist.
Pandey, Raj B. Indian Paleography, Pt. 1. 2nd ed. 1957. 8.25x (ISBN 0-8426-1458-3). Verry.
Turner, Ralph L. The Position of Romani in Indo-Aryan. 1977. lib. bdg. 59.95 (ISBN 0-8490-2460-9). Gordon Pr.
Turner, Sir Ralph. A Comparative Dictionary of the Indo-Aryan Languages. 862p. 1966. text ed. 69.00x (ISBN 0-19-713550-1). Oxford U Pr.
Wilson, H. H., ed. Glossary of Judicial & Revenue Terms & of Useful Words Occuring in Official Documents Relating to the Administration of the Government of British India, Etc. 1968. Repr. of 1885 ed. 35.00x (ISBN 0-8426-1596-2). Verry.

INDO-ARYAN LANGUAGES, MODERN

see also Bengali Language; Gujarati Language; Hindustani Language; Marathi Language; Nepali Language; Oriya Language; Pali Language; Panjabi Language

INDO-ARYAN LITERATURE

see Indic Literature

INDO-ARYAN PHILOLOGY

see also Indo-Iranian Philology; Sanskrit Philology

INDOCHINA

Here are entered works on the area comprising Laos, Cambodia and Vietnam.

Cameron, Allan W. Indochina: Prospects After "The End". 1976. pap. 3.25 (ISBN 0-8447-3210-9). Am Enterprise.
Chaumont Guitry, Guy de. Lettres d'Indochine. LC 79-179177. (South & Southeast Asia Studies). Repr. of 1951 ed. 16.00 (ISBN 0-404-54807-5). AMS Pr.
Izikowitz, Karl G. Lamet: Hill Peasants in French Indochina. LC 76-44737. 1977. Repr. of 1951 ed. 25.00 (ISBN 0-404-15938-9). AMS Pr.
Robequain, Charles. The Economic Development of French Indo-China. Ward, Isabel A., tr. LC 71-179238. (Supplement: Recent Developments in Indo-China: 1939-1943 by John, i. e. James R. Andrus & Katrine R. C. Greene). Repr. of 1944 ed. 20.50 (ISBN 0-404-54864-4). AMS Pr.
U. S. Library Of Congress - Reference Department. Indochina: A Bibliography of the Land & People. LC 68-55139. (Illus.). 1968. Repr. of 1950 ed. lib. bdg. 23.50x (ISBN 0-8371-1972-3, INBI). Greenwood.
Zasloff, Joseph J. & Brown, MacAlister. Communist Indochina & U. S. Foreign Policy: Forging New Relations. LC 77-28462. 1978. lib. bdg. 25.25x (ISBN 0-89158-150-2). Westview.

INDOCHINA-ANTIQUITIES

Groslier, Bernard P. Indochina. (Archaeologia Mundi Ser.). 1966. 29.50 (ISBN 0-88254-157-9). Hippocrene Bks.

INDOCHINA-DESCRIPTION AND TRAVEL

Brebion, Antoine. Bibliographie des voyages dans l'Indochine francaise du 9e au 19e siecle. LC 78-132542. (Bibliography & Reference Ser.: No. 395). (Geography & Discovery Ser., No. 8). 1971. Repr. of 1910 ed. lib. bdg. 24.00 (ISBN 0-8337-0359-5). B Franklin.
--Livre d'or du Cambodge de la Cochinchine et de l'Annam, 1625-1910 et bibliographie. LC 72-147145. (Research & Source Works Ser.: No. 665). 1971. Repr. of 1910 ed. lib. bdg. 14.00 (ISBN 0-8337-0360-9). B Franklin.

INDOCHINA-ECONOMIC CONDITIONS

Murray, Martin J. The Development of Capitalism in Colonial Indochina (1870-1940) LC 80-16472. 1981. 34.50x (ISBN 0-520-04000-7). U of Cal Pr.
Poole, Peter A., ed. Indochina: Perspectives for Reconciliation. LC 75-62006. (Papers in International Studies: Southeast Asia: No. 36). (Illus.). 1975. pap. 6.00x (ISBN 0-89680-022-9). Ohio U Ctr Intl.

INDOCHINA-HISTORY

Brebion, Antoine. Bibliographie des voyages dans l'Indochine francaise du 9e au 19e siecle. LC 78-132542. (Bibliography & Reference Ser.: No. 395). (Geography & Discovery Ser., No. 8). 1971. Repr. of 1910 ed. lib. bdg. 24.00 (ISBN 0-8337-0359-5). B Franklin.
Ennis, Thomas E. French Policy & Developments in Indochina. LC 72-94980. (Illus.). x, 230p. 1973. Repr. of 1936 ed. 16.00 (ISBN 0-8462-1722-8). Russell.
Lancaster, Donald. The Emancipation of French Indochina. LC 74-23161. xi, 445p. 1975. Repr. of 1961 ed. lib. bdg. 25.00x (ISBN 0-374-94719-8). Octagon.
Pinto, Roger. Aspects De L'evolution Gouvernementale De L'indochine Francaise. LC 77-179234. Repr. of 1946 ed. 16.00 (ISBN 0-404-54861-X). AMS Pr.
Thompson, Virginia M. French Indo-China. 1967. lib. bdg. 30.00x (ISBN 0-374-97866-2). Octagon.

INDOCHINA-HISTORY-1945-

Chomsky, Noam & Herman, Edward S. Political Economy of Human Rights: After the Cataclysm: Postwar Indochina & the Reconstruction of Imperial Ideology, Vol. 2. LC 79-64138. (Orig.). 1979. 15.00 (ISBN 0-89608-101-X); pap. 6.50 (ISBN 0-89608-100-1). South End Pr.
Davidson, J. A. Indo-China: Signposts in the Storm. (Illus.). 1979. text ed. 15.95x (ISBN 0-582-72603-4); pap. text ed. 10.95x (ISBN 0-582-72602-6). Longman.
Geneva - Conference - 1954. Nineteen Fifty-Four Geneva Conference Indo-China & Korea. LC 68-57791. Repr. of 1954 ed. lib. bdg. 20.50x (ISBN 0-8371-0652-4, GECO). Greenwood.
Giap, Vo Nguyen. Military Art of People's War: Selected Writings. Stetler, Russell, ed. LC 75-105317. (Illus.). 1970. pap. 5.95 (ISBN 0-85345-193-1, PB-1931). Monthly Rev.
Hammer, Ellen J. Struggle for Indochina, 1940-1955. 1955. 18.50x (ISBN 0-8047-0458-9). Stanford U Pr.

Kelly, George A. Lost Soldiers: The French Army & Empire in Crises, 1947-1962. 1965. 17.50x (ISBN 0-262-11014-8). MIT Pr.

INDOCHINA-POLITICS AND GOVERNMENT

Elliott, David W., ed. The Third Indochina Conflict. (Westview Replica Edition Ser.). 250p. 1981. lib. bdg. 18.50x (ISBN 0-89158-739-X). Westview.

Poole, Peter A., ed. Indochina: Perspectives for Reconciliation. LC 75-62006. (Papers in International Studies: Southeast Asia: No. 36). (Illus.). 1975. pap. 6.00x (ISBN 0-89680-022-9). Ohio U Ctr Intl.

INDOCHINESE ART

see Art, Indochinese

INDOCHINESE LANGUAGES

see also Austroasiatic Languages; Chinese Language; Mon-Khmer Languages; Tai Languages

Benedict, Paul K. Sino-Tibetan: A Conspectus. LC 78-154511. (Princeton-Cambridge Studies in Chinese Linguistics: No. 2). 1972. 75.00 (ISBN 0-521-08175-0). Cambridge U Pr.

Shafer, Robert. Introduction to Sino-Tibetan, 5 pts. LC 67-76846. 1966-73. Set. 250.00x (ISBN 3-447-01559-4). Intl Pubns Serv.

INDO-CHINESE MYTHOLOGY

see Mythology, Indo-Chinese

INDO-EUROPEAN ANTIQUITIES

Conference on Indo-European Studies, U. of Texas, Austin, Feb. 4-5, 1980. The Indo-Europeans in the Fourth & Third Millennia: Proceedings. Polome, Edgar C., ed. (Linguistica Extranea: Studia: No. 14). (Illus.). 245p. 1981. text ed. 21.50 (ISBN 0-89720-041-1). Karoma.

INDO-EUROPEAN LANGUAGES

see also Albanian Language; Armenian Language; Baltic Languages; Celtic Languages; Germanic Languages; Greek Language; Indo-Iranian Languages; Italic Languages and Dialects; Tokharian Language

Beekes, R. S. Development of the Proto-Indo-European Laryngeals in Greek. (Janua Linguarum, Ser. Practica: No. 42). 1969. pap. text ed. 68.25x (ISBN 90-2790-693-9). Mouton.

Benveniste, Emile. Indo-European Language & Society. Palmer, Elizabeth, tr. from Fr. LC 73-77119. (Miami Linguistics Ser: No. 12). (Illus.). 579p. 1973. 29.50x (ISBN 0-87024-250-4). U of Miami Pr.

Bradley, David. Lahu Dialects. LC 79-52679. (Faculty of Asian Studies Oriental Monograph: No. 23). (Illus., Orig.). 1980. pap. text ed. 12.95 (ISBN 0-7081-1077-0, 0309, Pub. by ANUP Australia). Bks Australia.

Brugmann, Karl. Elements of the Comparative Grammar of the Indogermanic Languages, 5 vols. Wright, Joseph, et al, trs. from Ger. 2400p. 1972. Repr. of 1888 ed. Set. 110.00x (ISBN 0-8002-1392-0). Intl Pubns Serv.

Buck, Carl D. Dictionary of Selected Synonyms in the Principal Indo-European Languages. LC 49-11769. 1949. 65.00x (ISBN 0-226-07932-5). U of Chicago Pr.

Collitz, K. H. Verbs of Motion in Their Semantic Divergence. 1931. pap. 6.00 (ISBN 0-527-00812-5). Kraus Repr.

Denison, T. S. A Mexican-Aryan Comparative Vocabulary. 1976. lib. bdg. 59.95 (ISBN 0-8490-0613-9). Gordon Pr.

Eckenstein, Lina. Spell of Words: Studies in Language Bearing on Custom. LC 68-23153. 1969. Repr. of 1932 ed. 19.00 (ISBN 0-8103-3892-0). Gale.

Eichner, Hans. Romantic & Its Cognates: The European History of a Word. LC 77-163812. 1972. 25.00x (ISBN 0-8020-5243-6). U of Toronto Pr.

Gonda, Jan. Character of the Indo-European Moods, with Special Regard to Greek & Sanskrit. LC 56-5976. 220p. 1956. 48.50x (ISBN 3-447-00344-8). Intl Pubns Serv.

Gottlieb, E. Systematic Tabulation of Indo-European Animal Names. 1931. pap. 6.00 (ISBN 0-527-00754-4). Kraus Repr.

Green, Alexander. Dative of Agency: A Chapter of Indo-European Case-Syntax. LC 14-1364. (Columbia University. Germanic Studies, Old Ser.: No. 17). Repr. of 1913 ed. 14.00 (ISBN 0-404-50417-5). AMS Pr.

Hopkins, Grace S. Indo-European Deiwos & Related Words. 1932. pap. 6.00 (ISBN 0-527-00758-7). Kraus Repr.

Kerns, J. A. & Schwartz, Benjamin. A Sketch of the Indo-European Finite Verb. (Monographs on Mediterranean Antiquity). 83p. 1972. 12.50x (ISBN 0-8147-4556-3). NYU Pr.

Krahe, Hans. Indogermanische Sprachwissenschaft, Vol. 1, Einleitung Und Lautlehre. 5th ed. (Sammlung Goeschen, Vol. 59). (Ger). 1966. 3.25x (ISBN 3-11-002730-5). De Gruyter.

Kurylowicz, J. Inflectional Categories of Indo-European. 1964. 40.80 (ISBN 3-5330-0688-3). Adler.

Lane, G. S. Words for Clothing in the Principal Indo-European Languages. 1931. pap. 6.00 (ISBN 0-527-00755-2). Kraus Repr.

Levin, Saul. Indo-European & Semitic Languages: An Exploration of Structural Similarities Related to Accent, Chiefly in Greek, Sanskrit, & Hebrew. LC 67-28937. (Illus.). 1971. 47.00 (ISBN 0-87395-055-0); microfiche 47.00 (ISBN 0-87395-155-7). State U NY Pr.

Lockwood, W. D. A Panorama of Indo-European Languages. 1972. text ed. 14.50x (ISBN 0-09-111020-3, Hutchinson U Lib); pap. text ed. 10.00x (ISBN 0-09-111021-1, Hutchinson U Lib). Humanities.

Meillet, Antoine. Indo-European Dialects. Rosenberg, S., tr. LC 67-16140. (Alabama Linguistic & Philological Ser: Vol. 15). 208p. 1968. 12.50x (ISBN 0-8173-0352-9). U of Ala Pr.

--Introduction a l'Etude Comparative Des Langues Indo-Europeennes. LC 68-11550. (Alabama Linguistic & Philological Ser: Vol. 3). 516p. 1964. pap. 11.75 (ISBN 0-8173-0301-4). U of Ala Pr.

Pokorny, Julius. Indogermanisches Etymologisches Woerterbuch, 2 vols, Vols. 1 & 2. 1648p. 1969. 240.00 set (ISBN 3-7720-0526-8, M-7478, Pub. by Francke). French & Eur.

Schwartz, Benjamin. Root & Its Modification in Primitive Indo-European. 1947. pap. 6.00 (ISBN 0-527-00786-2). Kraus Repr.

Spitzer, Leo. Essays in Historical Semantics. LC 68-10944. 1968. Repr. of 1948 ed. 10.00 (ISBN 0-8462-1112-2). Russell.

Winter, Werner, ed. Evidence for Laryngeals. (Janua Linguarum, Ser. Major: No. 11). 1965. text ed. 45.00x (ISBN 0-686-22429-9). Mouton.

Wood, Francis A. Post-Consonantal W in Indo-European. 1926. pap. 6.00 (ISBN 0-527-00807-9). Kraus Repr.

Wyatt, William F., Jr. Indo-European. LC 73-83140. (Haney Foundation Ser). 1970. 7.50x (ISBN 0-8122-7594-2). U of Pa Pr.

INDO-EUROPEAN LINGUISTICS

see Indo-European Philology

INDO-EUROPEAN MYTHOLOGY

see Mythology, Indo-European

INDO-EUROPEAN PHILOLOGY

see also names of languages and literatures belonging to the Indo-European group

Hatfield, James T., ed. Curme Volume of Linguistic Studies. 1930. pap. 12.00 (ISBN 0-527-00811-7). Kraus Repr.

Klar, Kathryn, et al, eds. American Indian & Indoeuropean Studies: Papers in Honor of Madison S. Beeler. Langdon, Margaret & Silver, Shirley. (Trends in Linguistics, Studies & Monographs: No. 16). 495p. 1980. 75.00 (ISBN 90-279-7876-X). Mouton.

Kuipers, A. H. A Dictionary of Proto-Circassian Roots. (PDR Press Publication on North Caucasian Languages: No. 1). 1975. pap. text ed. 13.75x (ISBN 90-316-0018-0). Humanities.

Lockwood, W. B. Indo-European Philology: Historical & Comparative. 1968. pap. text ed. 7.00x (ISBN 0-09-095581-1, Hutchinson U Lib). Humanities.

Ramat, Paolo, et al, eds. Linguistic Reconstruction & Indo-European Syntax: Proceedings of the Colloquium of the "Indogermanische Gesellschaft", University of Pavia, 6-7 September 1979. viii, 263p. 1980. 28.00 (ISBN 90-272-3512-0). Benjamins North Am.

Studies in Honor of Hermann Collitz. facs. ed. LC 76-84339. (Essay Index Reprint Ser). 1930. 14.50 (ISBN 0-8369-1196-2). Arno.

Taylor, Isaac. The Origin of the Aryans. 59.95 (ISBN 0-8490-0776-3). Gordon Pr.

INDO-EUROPEAN PHILOLOGY-BIBLIOGRAPHY

Meillet, Antoine. Introduction a l'Etude Comparative Des Langues Indo-Europeennes. LC 68-11550. (Alabama Linguistic & Philological Ser: Vol. 3). 516p. 1964. pap. 11.75 (ISBN 0-8173-0301-4). U of Ala Pr.

INDO-EUROPEANS

see also Armenians; Celts; Germanic Tribes; Greeks; Hittites; Illyrians; Slavs

Bongard-Levin, G. M. The Origin of Aryans. 124p. 1981. text ed. 10.25x (ISBN 0-391-02193-1, Pub. by Heinemann India). Humanities.

Cardona, George, et al, eds. Indo-European & Indo-Europeans: Papers Presented at the Third Indo-European Conference at the University of Pennsylvania. LC 68-21551. (Haney Foundation Ser.). (Illus.). 1971. text ed. 35.00x (ISBN 0-8122-7574-8). U of Pa Pr.

Cox, George W. Mythology of the Aryan Nations, 2 Vols. LC 68-8202. 1969. Repr. of 1870 ed. 35.00x (ISBN 0-8046-0091-0). Kennikat.

Hertz, Friedrich. Race & Civilization. 1970. 15.00x (ISBN 0-87068-006-4). Ktav.

Hoddinott, R. F. The Thracians. LC 80-51906. (Ancient Peoples & Places Ser.). (Illus.). 192p. 1981. 19.95 (ISBN 0-500-02099-X). Thames Hudson.

Kalyanaraman, A. Aryatarangini: The Saga of the Indo-Aryans, Vol. 2. 1970. 20.00x (ISBN 0-210-22305-7). Asia.

Keary, Charles F. Outlines of Primitive Belief Among the Indo-European Races. LC 77-85620. 1977. Repr. of 1882 ed. lib. bdg. 50.00 (ISBN 0-89341-305-4). Longwood Pr.

Klar, Kathryn, et al, eds. American Indian & Indo-European Studies: Papers in Honor of Madison S. Beeler. 1980. text ed. 79.50x (ISBN 90-279-7876-X). Mouton.

Mueller, Friedrich M. Biographies of Words & the Home of the Aryas. LC 73-18823. Repr. of 1888 ed. 15.00 (ISBN 0-404-11429-6). AMS Pr.

Poliakov, Leon. The Aryan Myth: A History of Racist & Nationalist Ideas in Europe. 1977. pap. 4.95 (ISBN 0-452-00478-0, F478, Mer). NAL.

Sergi, Giuseppe. Mediterranean Race: A Study of the Origin of European Peoples. LC 68-112231. (Illus.). 1967. pap. text ed. 11.00x (ISBN 90-6234-038-5). Humanities.

Widney, Joseph P. Race Life of the Aryan Peoples, 2 vols. Repr. of 1907 ed. lib. bdg. 65.00 set. (ISBN 0-8495-5908-1). Arden Lib.

INDO-GERMANIC LANGUAGES

see Indo-European Languages

INDO-GERMANIC PEOPLES

see Indo-Europeans

INDO-IRANIAN LANGUAGES

see also Indo-European Languages

Gorekar, N. S. Indo-Iran Relations: Cultural Aspects. 1972. 10.00x (ISBN 0-8426-0379-4). Verry.

Gray, Louis H. Indo-Iranian Phonology. LC 79-168183. (Columbia University. Indo-Iranian Ser.: No. 2). Repr. of 1902 ed. 23.00 (ISBN 0-404-50472-8). AMS Pr.

Sinha, K. P. Bishnupriya Manipuri Language. 1981. 10.00x (ISBN 0-8364-0725-3, Pub. by Mukhopadhyay). South Asia Bks.

INDO-IRANIAN PHILOLOGY

Columbia University. Columbia University Indo-Iranian Ser, 14 Vols. Repr. of 1932 ed. Set. 295.50 (ISBN 0-404-50470-1). AMS Pr.

Heesterman, J. C., et al. Pratidanam, Indian, Iranian & Indo-European Studies Presented to Franciscus Bernardus Jacobus Kuiper on His 60th Birthday. (Janua Linguarum, Ser. Major: No. 34). 1968. text ed. 140.00x (ISBN 90-2790-686-6). Mouton.

INDOLE

Erspamer, V., ed. Five-Hydroxytryptamine & Related Indolealkylamines. (Handbook of Experimental Pharmacology: Vol. 19). (Illus.). 1966. 104.00 (ISBN 0-387-03536-2). Springer-Verlag.

Houlihan, W. J. Indoles, Vol. 25, Pt. 3. 586p. 1979. 105.00 (ISBN 0-471-05132-2, Pub. by Wiley-Interscience). Wiley.

Houlihan, William, ed. Indoles, Vol. 25, Pt. 1. 587p. 1966. 77.00 (ISBN 0-471-37500-4). Krieger.

--Indoles, Vol. 25, Pt. 2. 616p. 1972. 77.00 (ISBN 0-471-37501-2). Krieger.

Phillipson, J. D. & Zenk, M. H., eds. Indole & Biogenetically Related Alkaloids. (Annual Proceedings of the Phytochemical Society of Europe: No. 17). 1981. 78.50 (ISBN 0-12-554450-2). Acad Pr.

Sundberg, Richard J. Chemistry of Indoles. (Organic Chemistry Ser.: Vol. 18). 1970. 63.50 (ISBN 0-12-676950-8). Acad Pr.

INDONESIA

Bijlmer, Hendricus J. Outlines of the Anthropology of the Timor Archipelago. LC 77-87480. (Illus.). Repr. of 1929 ed. 48.00 (ISBN 0-404-16697-0). AMS Pr.

Dalton, Bill. Indonesian Handbook. (Illus.). 1978. 8.95 (ISBN 0-9603322-0-0, Pub. by Moon Pubns). C E Tuttle.

De Wit, Augusta. Island India. 1923. 34.50x (ISBN 0-686-51407-6). Elliots Bks.

Draeger, D. F. Weapons & Fighting Arts of the Indonesian Archyselage. 12.50 (ISBN 0-685-63790-5). Wehman.

Echols, John M., ed. Preliminary Checklist of Indonesian Imprints (1945-1949) With Cornell University Holdings. 1965. pap. 3.50 (ISBN 0-685-03399-6, A806893). Cornell Mod Indo.

Fox, James J., ed. The Flow of Life: Essays on Eastern Indonesia. LC 79-9552. (Harvard Studies in Classical Anthropology: No. 2). (Illus.). 1980. 30.00x (ISBN 0-674-30675-9). Harvard U Pr.

Fryer, D. W. & Jackson, James C. Indonesia. LC 76-3707. (Nations of the Modern World Ser). 1977. 31.00x (ISBN 0-89158-028-X). Westview.

Gaudel, Andre. L' Indochine Francaise en Face du Japon. LC 73-179197. (Fr.). Repr. of 1947 ed. 19.00 (ISBN 0-404-54826-1). AMS Pr.

Indonesia. (Population Profiles Ser.: No. 14). 48p. 1980. pap. 1.50 (ISBN 0-686-61619-7, UNFPA 26, UNFPA). Unipub.

Josselin De Jong, Jan P. The Community of Erai (Wetar) LC 77-87500. (Studies in Indonesian Culture: Vol. 2). Repr. of 1947 ed. 18.00 (ISBN 0-404-16731-4). AMS Pr.

Kato, Tsuyoski. Matriliny & Migration: Evolving Minangkabau Traditions in Indonesia. LC 81-66647. (Illus.). 312p. 1982. 22.50x (ISBN 0-686-30473-X). Cornell U Pr.

Kennedy, Raymond. Ageless Indies. LC 68-56037. (Illus.). 1968. Repr. of 1942 ed. lib. bdg. 15.00x (ISBN 0-8371-0510-2, KEAI). Greenwood.

--Bibliography of Indonesian Peoples & Cultures. 2nd rev. ed. Maretzki, Thomas W. & Fischer, H. Th., eds. LC 62-20539. (Behavior Science Bibliographies Ser). xxiv, 207p. 1962. 18.00x (ISBN 0-87536-203-6). HRAFP.

Koch, Kurt E. Revival in Indonesia. LC 72-94310. 1972. pap. 3.50 (ISBN 0-8254-3007-0). Kregel.

Leifer, M. Malacca, Singapore & Indonesia. (International Straits of the World: No. 2). 288p. 1978. 35.00x (ISBN 90-286-0778-1). Sijthoff & Noordhoff.

Lundstrom-Burghoorn, Wil. Minahasa Civilization. (Gothenburg Studies in Social Anthropology Ser.: Vol. 2). 260p. 1981. pap. text ed. 22.50x (ISBN 91-7346-095-8, Pub. by Acta-Universitatis Sweden). Humanities.

Mackie, J. A., ed. The Chinese in Indonesia: Five Essays. LC 76-139. 296p. 1976. text ed. 12.00x (ISBN 0-8248-0449-X). U Pr of Hawaii.

Perry, William J. The Megalithic Culture of Indonesia. LC 77-86999. (Manchester, University. Publications. Ethnological Ser.: No. 3). Repr. of 1918 ed. 21.50 (ISBN 0-404-16773-X). AMS Pr.

Robequain, Charles. Malaya, Indonesia, Borneo, & the Philippines: A Geographical, Economic, & Political Description of Malaya, the East Indies, the Philippines. Labrde, E. D., tr. LC 75-30078. Repr. of 1954 ed. 29.50 (ISBN 0-404-59555-3). AMS Pr.

Tairas, J. N. Indonesia: A Bibliography of Bibliographies. 1975. 13.50 (ISBN 0-902675-50-8). Oleander Pr.

Tas, S. Indonesia: The Underdeveloped Freedom. LC 73-23034. 1974. pap. 8.95 (ISBN 0-672-63655-7). Pegasus.

Wilhelm, Donald. Emerging Indonesia. (Illus.). 192p. 1980. 25.00x (ISBN 0-389-20105-7). B&N.

Wolff, John U. Indonesian Conversation. 1978. 12.50 (ISBN 0-685-19866-9). Cornell SE Asia.

--Indonesian Readings. 1978. 12.50 (ISBN 0-685-19865-0). Cornell SE Asia.

INDONESIA-ANTIQUITIES

Bruner, Edward M. & Becker, Judith O., eds. Art, Ritual & Society in Indonesia. LC 79-11667. (Papers in International Studies: Southeast Asia: No. 53). (Orig.). 1979. pap. 13.00 (ISBN 0-89680-080-6). Ohio U Ctr Intl.

Forman, Bedrich. Borobudur: The Buddhist Legend in Tone. (Illus.). 1980. 16.95 (ISBN 0-686-70134-8, Mayflower Bks). Smith Pubs.

Jones, A. M. Africa & Indonesia: The Evidence of the Xylophone & Other Musical & Cultural Factors. rev. ed. (Illus.). 286p. 1971. Repr. text ed. 52.25x (ISBN 90-040-2623-1). Humanities.

Neill, Wilfred T. Twentieth-Century Indonesia. (Illus.). 413p. 1973. 25.00 (ISBN 0-231-03547-0); pap. 10.00x (ISBN 0-231-08316-5). Columbia U Pr.

Peacock, James L. Indonesia: An Anthropological Perspective. LC 72-82233. (Anthropology Ser.). 192p. 1973. text ed. 12.95 (ISBN 0-87620-417-5); pap. text ed. 10.95 (ISBN 0-87620-416-7). Goodyear.

INDONESIA-ARMY

Crouch, Harold. The Army & Politics in Indonesia. LC 77-90901. 1978. 25.00x (ISBN 0-8014-1155-6). Cornell U Pr.

INDONESIA-COMMERCE

Broek, Jan O. Economic Development of the Netherlands Indies. LC 75-143554. (Illus.). 1971. Repr. of 1942 ed. 11.00 (ISBN 0-8462-1573-X). Russell.

Mook, Hurbertus J. Van. The Netherlands Indies & Japan. LC 77-179226. Repr. of 1944 ed. 18.00 (ISBN 0-404-54853-9). AMS Pr.

Van Leur, J. C. Indonesian Trade & Society: Essays in Asian Social & Economic History. (Selected Studies on Indonesia: No. 1). 1967. 40.75x (ISBN 0-686-21859-0). Mouton.

INDONESIA-DESCRIPTION AND TRAVEL

Cool, Wouter. With the Dutch in the East: An Outline of the Military Operations in Lombock, 1894. Taylor, E. J., tr. from Dutch. LC 77-86968. (Illus.). Repr. of 1897 ed. 32.00 (ISBN 0-404-16702-0). AMS Pr.

Davis, Gloria, ed. What Is Modern Indonesian Culture? Papers in International Studies. LC 79-18979. (Southeast Asia Ser.: No. 52). 1979. pap. 18.00 (ISBN 0-89680-075-X). Ohio U Ctr Intl.

Ellis, David. Let's Look at Indonesia. 1973. pap. 1.25 (ISBN 0-85363-077-1). OMF Bks.

Forbes, Henry O. A Naturalist's Wanderings in the Eastern Archipelago: A Narrative of Travel & Exploration from 1878 to 1883. LC 77-86991. (Illus.). Repr. of 1885 ed. 41.50 (ISBN 0-404-16708-X). AMS Pr.

Greenfield, Darby. Indonesia: A Traveler's Guide. Incl. Vol. 1. Java & Sumatra (ISBN 0-902675-46-X); Vol. 2. Bali & East Indonesia. 1976. 9.95 (ISBN 0-902675-48-6). (Illus.). 1975. 9.95 (ISBN 0-686-77077-3). Oleander Pr.

Hickson, Sydney J. A Naturalist in North Celebes: A Narrative of Travels in Minahassa, the Sangir & Talaut Islands. LC 77-86952. (Illus.). Repr. of 1889 ed. 34.00 (ISBN 0-404-16726-8). AMS Pr.

Josselin De Jong, Jan P. Oirata: A Timorese Settlement on Kisar. LC 77-87501. Repr. of 1937 ed. 27.50 (ISBN 0-404-16733-0). AMS Pr.

Lanier, Alison R. Update -- Indonesia. LC 80-83915. (Counry Orientation Ser.). 1980. pap. text ed. 25.00x (ISBN 0-933662-37-8). Intercult Pr.

Middleton, Sir Henry. The Last East Indian Voyage. LC 74-25700. (English Experience Ser.: No. 307). 1971. Repr. of 1606 ed. 11.50 (ISBN 90-221-0307-2). Walter J Johnson.

Neck, Jacob Van & Walker, W. The Journall, or Daily Register, of the Voyage of Eight Shippes of Amsterdam. LC 74-80199. (English Experience Ser.: No. 680). 68p. 1974. Repr. of 1601 ed. 13.00 (ISBN 90-221-0680-2). Walter J Johnson.

Ormeling, Ferdinand J. The Timor Problem: A Geographical Interpretation of an Underdeveloped Island. LC 77-86997. Repr. of 1956 ed. 47.50 (ISBN 0-404-16769-1). AMS Pr.

Scott, Edmund. An Exact Discourse of the Subtilties, Fashishions Sic, Pollicies, Religion & Ceremonies of the East Indians,As Well Chyneses As Javans. LC 72-6030. (English Experience Ser.: No. 556). 104p. 1973. Repr. of 1606 ed. 11.50 (ISBN 90-221-0556-3). Walter J Johnson.

Williams, Maslyn. Five Journeys from Jakarta: Inside Sukarno's Indonesia. LC 74-1783. (Illus.). 383p. 1976. Repr. of 1965 ed. lib. bdg. 21.75x (ISBN 0-8371-7397-3, WIFJ). Greenwood.

INDONESIA–DESCRIPTION AND TRAVEL–VIEWS

Douwes-Dekker, Niels A. Tanah Air Kita: A Book of the Country & People of Indonesia. 2nd ed. LC 77-86970. Repr. of 1951 ed. 46.00 (ISBN 0-404-16705-5). AMS Pr.

INDONESIA–ECONOMIC CONDITIONS

Asia Pacific Centre. Markets of Asia Pacific: Indonesia. 1981. 75.00 (ISBN 0-87196-587-9); as part of set 49.95 (ISBN 0-686-72848-3). Facts on File.

Boeke, Julius H. Economics & Economic Policy of Dual Societies, As Exemplified by Indonesia. LC 75-30045. (Institute of Pacific Relations). Repr. of 1953 ed. 26.50 (ISBN 0-404-59508-1). AMS Pr.

Broek, Jan O. Economic Development of the Netherlands Indies. LC 75-143554. (Illus.). 1971. Repr. of 1942 ed. 11.00 (ISBN 0-8462-1573-X). Russell.

Collier, William L. Social & Economic Aspects of Tidal Swamp Land Development in Indonesia. (Development Studies Centre-Occasional Paper: No. 15). 71p. (Orig.). 1980. pap. 3.95 (ISBN 0-909150-90-7, 0567, Pub. by ANUP Australia). Bks Australia.

Creutzberg, P. Changing Economy in Indonesia: A Selection of Statistical Source Material from the Early 19th Century up to 1940, Volume 5 - National Income. (Illus.). 133p. 1980. pap. 21.00 (ISBN 90-247-2194-6, Pub. by Martinus Nijhoff Netherlands). Kluwer Boston.

Geertz, Clifford. Agricultural Involution: The Processes of Ecological Change in Indonesia. LC 63-20356. 1963. 16.50x (ISBN 0-520-00458-2); pap. 5.95x (ISBN 0-520-00459-0, CAMPUS11). U of Cal Pr.

--Peddlers & Princes: Social Development & Economic Change in Two Indonesian Towns. LC 62-18844. (Comparative Studies of New Nations Ser.). (Illus.). 1963. 9.00x (ISBN 0-226-28513-8). U of Chicago Pr.

--Peddlers & Princes: Social Development & Economic Change in Two Indonesian Towns. LC 62-18844. (Comparative Studies of New Nations Ser). (Illus.). 1968. pap. 3.95 (ISBN 0-226-28514-6, P318, Phoen). U of Chicago Pr.

Glassburner, Bruce, ed. Economy of Indonesia: Selected Readings. LC 77-127777. (Illus.). 448p. 1971. 32.50x (ISBN 0-8014-0600-5). Cornell U Pr.

Gupta, Syama P. A Model for Income Distribution, Employment, & Growth: A Case Study of Indonesia, Syamaprased Gupta. LC 76-53909. (World Bank Staff Occasional Paper: No. 24). (Illus.). 96p. 1977. pap. 5.50x (ISBN 0-8018-1950-4). Johns Hopkins.

Hicks, George L. & McNicoll, Geoffrey. The Indonesian Economy, Nineteen Fifty to Nineteen Sixty-Five: A Bibliography. (Bibliography Ser.: No. 9). x, 248p. 1967. 4.25 (ISBN 0-686-30909-X). Yale U SE Asia.

--The Indonesian Economy, Nineteen Fifty to Nineteen Sixty-Seven: Bibliographic Supplement. (Bibliography Ser.: No. 10). xii, 211p. 1968. 5.25 (ISBN 0-686-30908-1). Yale U SE Asia.

Indonesian Economics: The Concept of Dualism in Theory and Policy. 2nd ed. (Selected Studies on Indonesia: No. 6). 1966. 30.00x (ISBN 0-686-21238-X). Mouton.

McCawley, Peter. Industrialization in Indonesia: Developments & Prospects. (Development Studies Centre - Occasional Paper: No. 13). (Orig.). 1980. pap. text ed. 3.95 (ISBN 0-7081-1593-4, 0412, Pub. by ANUP Australia). Bks Australia.

Mansvelt. Changing Economy in Indonesia. 1977. pap. 18.50 (ISBN 90-247-1959-3, Pub. by Martinus Nijhoff Netherlands). Kluwer Boston.

Palmer, Ingrid. The Indonesian Economy Since 1965: A Case Study of Political Economy Since 1966. 1978. 27.50x (ISBN 0-7146-3088-8, F Cass Co). Biblio Dist.

Papanek, Gustav F., ed. The Indonesian Economy. LC 80-18752. 300p. 1981. 26.95 (ISBN 0-03-057429-3). Praeger.

Sethuraman, S. V. Jakarta: Urban Development & Employment. (A WEP Study). 1976. 18.55 (ISBN 92-2-101429-0); pap. 12.85 (ISBN 92-2-101428-2). Intl Labour Office.

Sievers, Allen M. The Mystical World of Indonesia: Culture & Economic Development in Conflict. LC 74-6838. (Illus.). 446p. 1975. 22.50x (ISBN 0-8018-1591-6). Johns Hopkins.

Sinha, J. N. & Sawhney, P. K. Wages & Productivity in Selected Indian Industries. 1970. 6.50x (ISBN 0-8426-0137-6). Verry.

Soemardjan, Selo. Imbalances in Development: The Indonesian Experience. LC 72-619654. (Papers in International Studies: Southeast Asia: No. 25). 1972. pap. 3.50x (ISBN 0-89680-013-X). Ohio U Ctr Intl.

Van Leur, J. C. Indonesian Trade & Society: Essays in Asian Social & Economic History. (Selected Studies on Indonesia: No. 1). 1967. 40.75x (ISBN 0-686-21859-0). Mouton.

INDONESIA–FOREIGN RELATIONS

Hatta, Mohammad. The Putera Reports: Problems in Indonesian-Japanese Wartime Co-Operation. Frederick, William H., tr. & intro. by. 114p. 1971. pap. 4.00 (ISBN 0-685-32886-4, A240084). Cornell Mod Indo.

Hyde, Douglas. Confrontation in the East. (Background Ser). 1965. 6.25 (ISBN 0-8023-1062-1). Dufour.

Lagerberg, Kees. West Irian & Jakarat Imperialism. LC 79-11232. 1979. 18.95x (ISBN 0-312-86322-5). St Martin.

Mackie, J. A. Konfrontasi: The Indonesia-Malaysia Dispute 1963-1966. (Illus.). 384p. 1974. 34.50x (ISBN 0-19-638247-5). Oxford U Pr.

Mezerik, Avrahm G., ed. Malaysia-Indonesia Conflict. 1965. pap. 15.00 (ISBN 0-685-13205-6, 86). Intl Review.

Mrazek, Rudolf. United States & the Indonesian Military, Ninety Forty-Five to Ninety Sixty-Five, 2 vols. (Dissertationes Orientales Ser.: No. 39). (Orig.). 1979. pap. text ed. 12.00x (ISBN 0-685-97142-2). Paragon.

Nishihara, Masashi. Japanese & Sukarno's Indonesia: Tokyo-Jakarta Relations, 1951-1966. LC 75-35765. (Monographs of the Center for Southeast Asian Studies, Kyoto University). (Illus.). 272p. 1976. text ed. 12.00x (ISBN 0-8248-0458-9, Eastwest Ctr); pap. text ed. 7.50x (ISBN 0-8248-0379-5, Eastwest Ctr). U Pr of Hawaii.

Pringle, Robert. Indonesia & the Philippines: American Interests in Island Southeast Asia. LC 80-13474. (Illus.). 296p. 1980. 30.00x (ISBN 0-231-05008-9); pap. 9.00x (ISBN 0-231-05009-7). Columbia U Pr.

Simon, Sheldon W. The Broken Triangle: Peking, Djakarta, & the PKI. LC 68-22279. 210p. 1969. 14.00x (ISBN 0-8018-0595-3). Johns Hopkins.

Weinstein, Franklin B. Indonesian Foreign Policy & the Dilemma of Dependence: From Sukarno to Soeharto. LC 75-36998. 1976. 28.50x (ISBN 0-8014-0939-X). Cornell U Pr.

INDONESIA–HISTORIOGRAPHY

Soedjatmoko, et al, eds. Introduction to Indonesian Historiography. LC 64-25273. (Illus.). 1965. 32.50x (ISBN 0-8014-0403-7). Cornell U Pr.

INDONESIA–HISTORY

Aveling, Harry, ed. The Development of Indonesian Society. LC 79-11452. 1979. 27.50x (ISBN 0-312-19661-X). St Martin.

Benda, Harry J. The Crescent & the Rising Sun: Indonesian Islam Under the Japanese Occupation 1942-1945. 1958. 21.25 (ISBN 0-686-20916-8). Mouton.

Benda, Harry J. & McVey, Ruth T., eds. Communist Uprisings of 1926-1927 in Indonesia: Key Documents. (Translation Ser). 1960. pap. 5.50 (ISBN 0-685-08662-3, A430989). Cornell Mod Indo.

Bunnell, Fredrick. American Reactions to Indonesia's Role in the Belgrade Conference. 86p. 1964. pap. 2.00 (ISBN 0-686-73413-0). Cornell Mod Indo.

Coast, John. Recruit to Revolution: Adventure & Politics in Indonesia. LC 76-179179. Repr. of 1952 ed. 16.00 (ISBN 0-404-54809-1). AMS Pr.

Fischer, Louis. The Story of Indonesia. LC 72-12633. (Illus.). 341p. 1973. Repr. of 1959 ed. lib. bdg. 19.75x (ISBN 0-8371-6684-5, FISI). Greenwood.

Freidus, Alberta J. Sumatran Contributions to the Development of Indonesian Literature, 1920-1942. (Asian Studies at Hawaii Ser.: No. 19). 1977. pap. text ed. 4.75x (ISBN 0-8248-0462-7). U Pr of Hawaii.

George, Margaret L. Australia & Indonesian Revolution. 236p. 1980. 27.95x (ISBN 0-522-84209-7, Pub. by Melbourne Univ Pr Australia). Intl Schol Bk Serv.

Gerbrandy, Pieter S. Indonesia. LC 70-179199. (Illus.). Repr. of 1950 ed. 20.00 (ISBN 0-404-54828-8). AMS Pr.

Hanna, Willard A. Indonesian Banda: Colonialism & Its Aftermath in the Nutmeg Islands. LC 78-15914. (Illus.). 1978. text ed. 13.50x (ISBN 0-915980-91-6). Inst Study Human.

Harsono, Ganis. Recollections of an Indonesian Diplomat in the Sukarno Era. Penders, C. L. & Hering, B. B., eds. (Sources of Modern Indonesian History & Politics Ser). (Illus.). 1977. 29.00x (ISBN 0-7022-1440-X). U of Queensland Pr.

Harvey, Barbara S. Permesta: Half a Rebellion. 1977. 5.00 (ISBN 0-686-52883-2). Cornell Mod Indo.

Hoay, Kwee Tek. Origins of the Modern Chinese Movement in Indonesia. Williams, Lea A., ed. & tr. from Indonesian. (Translation Ser). (Orig.). 1969. pap. 3.00 (ISBN 0-685-08666-6, A152835). Cornell Mod Indo.

Ingleson, John. Road to Exile: Indonesian Nationalist Movement. 1979. pap. text ed. 12.50x (ISBN 0-686-65417-X, 00130). Heinemann Ed.

James, Harold & Sheil-Small, Denis. The Undeclared War: The Story of the Indonesian Confrontation 1962-1966. (Illus.). 201p. 1971. 11.00x (ISBN 0-87471-074-X). Rowman.

Kroef. Indonesia Since Sukarno. 1978. 15.00x (ISBN 0-685-50317-8). State Mutual Bk.

Liddle, R. William, et al, eds. Political Participation in Modern Indonesia. (Monograph Ser.: No. 19). (Illus.). 206p. 1973. 7.50x (ISBN 0-686-30900-6). Yale U SE Asia.

McVey, Ruth T. Soviet View of the Indonesian Revolution. (Interim Reports Ser). 1957. pap. 2.50 (ISBN 0-685-08669-0). Cornell Mod Indo.

Moertono, Soemarsaid. State & Statecraft in Old Java: A Study of the Later Mataram Period, 16th to 19th Century. rev. ed. (Monograph Ser.: No. 43). 181p. 1981. 6.50 (ISBN 0-686-72446-1). Cornell Mod Indo.

Naerssen, F. H. & Jongh, R. C. The Economic & Administrative History of Early Indonesia. 1977. text ed. 43.50x (ISBN 90-04-04918-5). Humanities.

Neill, Wilfred T. Twentieth-Century Indonesia. (Illus.). 413p. 1973. 25.00 (ISBN 0-231-03547-0); pap. 10.00x (ISBN 0-231-08316-5). Columbia U Pr.

Penders, L. N., ed. Indonesia: Selected Documents on Colonialism & Nationalism 1830-1942. 367p. 1977. 25.00x (ISBN 0-7022-1324-1); pap. 12.95x (ISBN 0-7022-1029-3). U of Queensland Pr.

Reid, Anthony. The Blood of the People: Revolution & the End of Traditional Rule in Northern Sumatra. (Illus.). 308p. 1979. text ed. 34.50x (ISBN 0-19-580399-X). Oxford U Pr.

Ricklefs, M. C. A History of Modern Indonesia. LC 81-47063. 336p. 1981. 22.50x (ISBN 0-253-19593-4). Ind U Pr.

--Jogjakarta Under Sultan Mangkubumi 1749-1792: A History of the Division of Java. (London Oriental Ser: No. 30). 496p. 1974. text ed. 33.00x (ISBN 0-19-713578-1). Oxford U Pr.

Sastro, Ali. Milestones on My Journey. Penders, Chris L., ed. (Sources of Modern Indonesian History & Politics Ser.). (Illus.). 1979. 36.25x (ISBN 0-7022-1206-7). U of Queensland Pr.

Schrieke, B. Indonesian Sociological Studies, Vol. 1. 2nd ed. (Selected Studies on Indonesia: No. 2). 1966. 25.00x (ISBN 0-686-21789-6). Mouton.

Scott, Edmund. An Exact Discourse of the Subtilties, Fashishions Sic, Pollicies, Religion & Ceremonies of the East Indians,As Well Chyneses As Javans. LC 72-6030. (English Experience Ser.: No. 556). 104p. 1973. Repr. of 1606 ed. 11.50 (ISBN 90-221-0556-3). Walter J Johnson.

Sievers, Allen M. The Mystical World of Indonesia: Culture & Economic Development in Conflict. LC 74-6838. (Illus.). 446p. 1975. 22.50x (ISBN 0-8018-1591-6). Johns Hopkins.

Sjahrir, Sutan. Our Struggle. Anderson, Benedict R., tr. (Translation Ser). Orig. Title: Perdjuangan Kita. (Orig.). 1968. pap. 2.00 (ISBN 0-685-08667-4, 48420). Cornell Mod Indo.

Soebadio, H. & Sarvaas, C. Dynamics of Indonesian History. 1978. 58.75 (ISBN 0-444-85023-6, North-Holland). Elsevier.

Soekarno. Nationalism, Islam & Marxism. (Translation Ser). (Orig.). 1970. pap. 3.00 (ISBN 0-685-08665-8, A139054). Cornell Mod Indo.

Taylor, Alastair M. Indonesian Independence & the United Nations. LC 74-29642. (Illus.). 503p. 1975. Repr. of 1960 ed. lib. bdg. 29.50x (ISBN 0-8371-8005-8). Greenwood.

A True Relation of the Unjust Proceedings Against the English of Amboyna. LC 72-228. (English Experience Ser.: No. 306). 38p. Repr. of 1624 ed. 14.00 (ISBN 90-221-0306-4). Walter J Johnson.

Van Anrooij, Francien, et al, eds. Between People & Statistics: Essays on Modern Indonesian History, Presented to P. Creutzberg. 315p. 1980. pap. 20.00 (ISBN 90-247-2304-3, Pub. by Martinus Nijhoff Netherlands). Kluwer Boston.

Vander Veur, Paul W., compiled by. The Eurasians of Indonesia: A Political-Historical Bibliography. 105p. 1971. pap. 3.50 (ISBN 0-685-32888-0, A223745). Cornell Mod Indo.

Van Niel, Robert. Survey of Historical Source Materials in Java & Manila. LC 72-132554. (Asian Studies at Hawaii Ser.: No. 5). (Orig.). 1971. pap. text ed. 7.00x (ISBN 0-87022-841-2). U Pr of Hawaii.

Vlekke, Bernard H. The Story of the Dutch East Indies. LC 71-161775. Repr. of 1945 ed. 14.00 (ISBN 0-404-09043-5). AMS Pr.

Vlekke, Bernard H. M. Nusantara: A History of the East Indian Archipelago. Wilkins, Mira, ed. LC 76-29761. (European Business Ser.). (Illus.). 1977. Repr. of 1943 ed. lib. bdg. 29.00x (ISBN 0-405-09776-X). Arno.

Vogt, Joann. Nusantara: A History of Indonesia. 6th ed. 1965. 28.00x (ISBN 0-686-21864-7). Mouton.

Wehl, David. The Birth of Indonesia. LC 72-179249. Repr. of 1948 ed. 11.00 (ISBN 0-404-54875-X). AMS Pr.

Weinstein, Franklin B. Indonesia Abandons Confrontation. (Interim Reports Ser). 1969. pap. 3.00 (ISBN 0-685-08664-X, A80363). Cornell Mod Indo.

Wilson, Greta O., ed. Regents, Reformers, & Revolutionaries: Indonesian Voices of the Colonial Days. LC 77-20686. (Asian Studies at Hawaii: No. 21). 1978. pap. text ed. 9.00x (ISBN 0-8248-0541-0). U Pr of Hawaii.

Wolf, Charles, Jr. The Indonesian Story. LC 73-5212. 201p. 1973. Repr. of 1948 ed. lib. bdg. 14.75x (ISBN 0-8371-6866-X, WOIS). Greenwood.

INDONESIA–JUVENILE LITERATURE

Smith, Datus C., Jr. The Land & People of Indonesia. rev. ed. LC 73-37731. (Portraits of the Nations Ser.). (Illus.). (gr. 6 up). 1972. 8.95 (ISBN 0-397-31533-3). Lippincott.

INDONESIA–POLITICS AND GOVERNMENT

Akhmadi, Heri. Breaking the Chains of Oppression of the Indonesian People: Defense Statement at His Trial on Charges of Insulting the Head of State, Bandung, June 7-10, 1979. (Translation Ser.: No. 59). 201p. 1981. 8.75 (ISBN 0-686-72447-X). Cornell Mod Indo.

Anderson, Benedict R. Java in a Time of Revolution. LC 74-174891. 512p. 1972. 27.50x (ISBN 0-8014-0687-0). Cornell U Pr.

Anderson, Benedict R. & McVey, Ruth T. A Preliminary Analysis of the October 1, 1965 Coup in Indonesia: Interim Report. 162p. 1971. pap. 6.00 (ISBN 0-685-32887-2, A277720). Cornell Mod Indo.

Bernas, Joaquin G. A Historical & Juridical Study of the Philippine Bill of Rights. 1971. wrps. 10.00x (ISBN 0-686-09488-3). Cellar.

Brachman, Arnold. Communist Collapse in Indonesia. LC 70-77399. 1969. 6.95 (ISBN 0-393-05377-6). Norton.

Crouch, Harold. The Army & Politics in Indonesia. LC 77-90901. 1978. 25.00x (ISBN 0-8014-1155-6). Cornell U Pr.

Douglas, Stephen A. Political Socialization & Student Activism in Indonesia. LC 73-94394. (Studies in Social Science, Vol. 57). 1970. 13.50 (ISBN 0-252-00074-9). U of Ill Pr.

Emmerson, Donald K. Indonesia's Elite: Political Culture & Cultural Politics. LC 75-36525. 304p. 1976. 22.50x (ISBN 0-8014-0917-9). Cornell U Pr.

Feith, Herbert. Decline of Constitutional Democracy in Indonesia. (Illus.). 1962. 34.50x (ISBN 0-8014-0126-7). Cornell U Pr.

--The Indonesian Elections of 1955: Interim Report. 91p. 1957. pap. 3.50 (ISBN 0-685-32883-X). Cornell Mod Indo.

Feith, Herbert & Castles, Lance, eds. Indonesian Political Thinking, 1945-1965. LC 69-18357. 520p. 1970. 27.50x (ISBN 0-8014-0531-9). Cornell U Pr.
Gautama, Sudargo & Hornick, Robert N. An Introduction to Indonesian Law. xiii, 192p. 1974. text ed. 10.00x (ISBN 0-8377-0603-3). Rothman.
Hansen, Gary E. The Politics & Administration of Rural Development in Indonesia: The Case If Agriculture. (Research Monograph: No. 9). 1973. 9.50 (ISBN 0-686-23617-3, Ctr South & Southeast Asia Studies). Cellar.
Harsono, Ganis. Recollections of an Indonesian Diplomat in the Sukarno Era. Penders, C. L. & Hering, B. B., eds. (Sources of Modern Indonesian History & Politics Ser). (Illus.). 1977. 29.00x (ISBN 0-7022-1440-X). U of Queensland Pr.
Harvey, Barbara S. Permesta: Half a Rebellion. 1977. 5.00 (ISBN 0-686-52883-2). Cornell Mod Indo.
Hatta, Mohammad. The Putera Reports: Problems in Indonesian-Japanese Wartime Co-Operation. Frederick, William H., tr. & intro. by. 114p. 1971. pap. 4.00 (ISBN 0-685-32886-4, A240084). Cornell Mod Indo.
Hatta, Mohammed. Portrait of a Patriot: Selected Writings by Mohammad Hatta. 1972. text ed. 70.00x (ISBN 0-686-22529-5). Mouton.
Holt, Claire, et al, eds. Culture & Politics in Indonesia. LC 78-162538. 362p. 1972. 25.00x (ISBN 0-8014-0665-X). Cornell U Pr.
--Culture & Politics in Indonesia. LC 78-162538. 362p. 1972. 25.00x (ISBN 0-8014-0665-X). Cornell U Pr.
Hooker, M. B. Adat Law in Modern Indonesia. (East Asian Historical Monographs). 1979. 28.00x (ISBN 0-19-580394-9). Oxford U Pr.
Jackson, Karl D. Traditional Authority, Islam, & Rebellion: A Study of Indonesian Political Behavior. 1980. 25.00x (ISBN 0-520-03769-3). U of Cal Pr.
Jackson, Karl D. & Pye, Lucian W., eds. Political Power & Communications in Indonesia. LC 76-19976. 1978. pap. 9.95x (ISBN 0-520-04205-0). U of Cal Pr.
Kahin, George M. Nationalism & Revolution in Indonesia. (Illus.). 506p. 1970. pap. 7.95 (ISBN 0-8014-9108-8, CP108). Cornell U Pr.
Lev, Daniel S. Islamic Courts in Indonesia: A Study in the Political Bases of Legal Institutions. LC 78-182281. 304p. 1972. 25.00x (ISBN 0-520-02173-8). U of Cal Pr.
McDonald, Hamish. Suharto's Indonesia. 277p. 1981. pap. text ed. 5.95x (ISBN 0-8248-0781-2). U Pr of Hawaii.
May, Brian. The Indonesian Tragedy. (Illus.). 1978. 30.00x (ISBN 0-7100-8834-5). Routledge & Kegan.
Mortimer, Rex. Indonesian Communism Under Sukarno: Ideology & Politics, 1959-1965. LC 73-19372. 448p. 1974. 25.00x (ISBN 0-8014-0825-3). Cornell U Pr.
Nishihara, Masashi. Golkar & the Indonesian Elections of 1971. (Monograph Ser.). 70p. 1972. pap. 3.50 (ISBN 0-685-32891-0). Cornell Mod Indo.
Oey Hong Lee. Indonesian Government & Press During Guided Democracy. LC 72-192291. (Hull Monographs on South-East Asia Ser: Vol. 4). 411p. 1971. 32.50x (ISBN 0-8002-1279-7). Intl Pubns Serv.
Parente, William J. Politics in Indonesia. 1980. 23.95 (ISBN 0-03-050466-X). Praeger.
Sjahrir, Soetan. Out of Exile. Wolf, Charles, Jr., tr. Repr. of 1949 ed. lib. bdg. 15.00 (ISBN 0-8371-1045-9, SJOE). Greenwood.
Tarling, Nicholas. Sukarno & Indonesian Unity. (Studies in 20th Century History Ser.). (Orig.). 1977. pap. text ed. 4.50x (ISBN 0-686-71786-4, 00551). Heinemann Ed.
Vander Veur, Paul W., compiled by. The Eurasians of Indonesia: A Political-Historical Bibliography. 105p. 1971. pap. 3.50 (ISBN 0-685-32888-0, A223745). Cornell Mod Indo.
Van Niel, Robert. Survey of Historical Source Materials in Java & Manila. LC 72-132554. (Asian Studies at Hawaii Ser.: No. 5). (Orig.). 1971. pap. text ed. 7.00x (ISBN 0-87022-841-2). U Pr of Hawaii.
Ward, K. E. The Foundation of the Partai Muslimin Indonesia: Interim Report. 75p. 1970. pap. 3.00 (ISBN 0-685-32884-8, A216561). Cornell Mod Indo.
Wolf, Charles, Jr. The Indonesian Story. LC 73-5212. 201p. 1973. Repr. of 1948 ed. lib. bdg. 14.75x (ISBN 0-8371-6866-X, WOIS). Greenwood.

INDONESIA–RELIGION

Cooley, Frank L. Indonesia: Church & Society. (Orig.). 1968. pap. 1.95 (ISBN 0-377-18021-1). Friend Pr.
Evans, Ivor H. The Religion of the Tempusak Dusuns of North Borneo. LC 77-86972. Repr. of 1953 ed. 40.00 (ISBN 0-404-16707-1). AMS Pr.
Peacock, James L. Purifying the Faith: The Muhammadijah Movement in Indonesian Islam. LC 78-61992. 1978. 6.95 (ISBN 0-8053-7824-3). Benjamin-Cummings.
Van Akkeren, Philip. Sri & Christ: A Study of the Indigenous Church in East Java. Mackie, Annebeth, tr. from Dutch. (World Studies of Churches in Mission). 1969. pap. 4.95 (ISBN 0-377-82981-1, Pub. by Lutterworth England). Friend Pr.
Willis, Avery T., Jr. Indonesian Revival: Why Two Million Came to Christ. LC 77-12811. (Illus.). 1977. pap. 6.95 (ISBN 0-87808-428-2). William Carey Lib.

INDONESIA–SOCIAL CONDITIONS

Barnes, R. H. Kedang: A Study of the Collective Thought of an Eastern Indonesian People. (Oxford Monographs in Social Anthropology). (Illus.). 359p. 1974. 42.00x (ISBN 0-19-823185-7). Oxford U Pr.
Bruner, Edward M. & Becker, Judith O., eds. Art, Ritual & Society in Indonesia. LC 79-11667. (Papers in International Studies: Southeast Asia: No. 53). (Orig.). 1979. pap. 13.00 (ISBN 0-89680-080-6). Ohio U Ctr Intl.
Cho, Lee-Jay, et al. Population Growth of Indonesia: An Analysis of Fertility & Mortality Based on the 1971 Population Census. 1980. text ed. 14.00x (ISBN 0-8248-0691-3, Pub. by Ctr Southwest Asian Studies Kyoto Univ Japan); pap. text ed. 8.00x (ISBN 0-8248-0696-4). U Pr of Hawaii.
Cooley, Frank L. Indonesia: Church & Society. (Orig.). 1968. pap. 1.95 (ISBN 0-377-18021-1). Friend Pr.
Cultural Policy in Indonesia. (Studies & Documents on Cultural Policies). (Illus.). 46p. (Orig.). 1974. pap. 5.00 (ISBN 92-3-101128-6, U124, UNESCO). Unipub.
Environmental Changes on the Coasts of Indonesia. 52p. 1981. pap. 10.00 (ISBN 92-808-0197-X, TUNU 128, UNU). Unipub.
Geertz, Clifford. The Social History of an Indonesian Town. LC 75-29282. (Illus.). 217p. 1975. Repr. of 1965 ed. lib. bdg. 17.75x (ISBN 0-8371-8431-2, GEIT). Greenwood.
Gregerson, Marilyn & Thomas, Dorothy, eds. Notes from Indonesia: On Ethnic Minority Culture. LC 78-65445. (Museum of Anthropology: No. 6). 254p. (Orig.). 1980. pap. 9.45x (ISBN 0-88312-155-7); microfiche 2.20 (ISBN 0-88312-244-8). Summer Inst Ling.
Hansen, Gary E., ed. Agricultural & Rural Development in Indonesia. (Special Studies in Social, Political, & Economic Development). 312p. 1981. lib. bdg. 20.00x (ISBN 0-86531-124-2). Westview.
Hardjono, Joan. Transmigration in Indonesia. (Oxford in Asia Current Affairs). (Illus.). 1977. pap. 9.50x (ISBN 0-19-580344-2). Oxford U Pr.
Harvey, Barbara S. Permesta: Half a Rebellion. 1977. 5.00 (ISBN 0-686-52883-2). Cornell Mod Indo.
Holt, Claire, et al, eds. Culture & Politics in Indonesia. LC 78-162538. 362p. 1972. 25.00x (ISBN 0-8014-0665-X). Cornell U Pr.
Hooker, M. B. Adat Law in Modern Indonesia. (East Asian Historical Monographs). 1979. 28.00x (ISBN 0-19-580394-9). Oxford U Pr.
Hooykaas, C. A Balinese Temple Festival. (Bibliotheca Indonesica: No. 15). 1977. pap. 29.00 (ISBN 90-247-2002-8, Pub. by Martinus Nijhoff Netherlands). Kluwer Boston.
Kato, Tsuyoski. Matriliny & Migration: Evolving Minangkabau Traditions in Indonesia. LC 81-66647. (Illus.). 312p. 1982. 22.50x (ISBN 0-686-30473-X). Cornell U Pr.
Koentjaraningrat, R. M. Introduction to the Peoples & Cultures of Indonesia & Malaysia. LC 75-4078. 1975. pap. 6.95 (ISBN 0-8465-1670-5). Benjamin-Cummings.
Lundstrom-Burghoorn, Wil. Minahasa Civilization. (Gothenburg Studies in Social Anthropology Ser.: Vol. 2). 260p. 1981. pap. text ed. 22.50x (ISBN 91-7346-095-8, Pub. by Acta-Universitatis Sweden). Humanities.
Schrieke, B. Indonesian Sociological Studies, Vol. 1. 2nd ed. (Selected Studies on Indonesia: No. 2). 1966. 25.00x (ISBN 0-686-21789-6). Mouton.
Soemardjan, Selo. Imbalances in Development: The Indonesian Experience. LC 72-619654. (Papers in International Studies: Southeast Asia: No. 25). 1972. pap. 3.50x (ISBN 0-89680-013-X). Ohio U Ctr Intl.
Ter Haar, Barend. Adat Law in Indonesia. Hoebel, E. Adamson & Schiller, A. Arthur, eds. LC 77-86985. 1977. Repr. of 1948 ed. 26.50 (ISBN 0-404-16725-X). AMS Pr.
Van Leur, J. C. Indonesian Trade & Society: Essays in Asian Social & Economic History. (Selected Studies on Indonesia: No. 1). 1967. 40.75x (ISBN 0-686-21859-0). Mouton.
Wertheim, Willem F. Indonesian Society in Transition: A Study of Social Change. LC 80-19660. (Illus.). xiv, 394p. 1980. Repr. of 1959 ed. lib. bdg. 29.75x (ISBN 0-313-22578-8, WEIO). Greenwood.
--Indonesian Society in Transition: A Study of Social Change. LC 78-14150. 1981. Repr. of 1959 ed. 27.50 (ISBN 0-88355-823-8). Hyperion Conn.
Widjojo, Nitisastro. Population Trends in Indonesia. LC 71-106356. Orig. Title: Past & Future. 1970. 34.50x (ISBN 0-8014-0555-6). Cornell U Pr.

INDONESIAN ART

see Art, Indonesian

INDONESIAN LANGUAGE

see also Malay Language

Clark, S. J. & Siahaan, E. Structure Drill in Indonesian. LC 75-120387. 1970. pap. 2.50 (ISBN 0-8048-0915-1). C E Tuttle.
Danusugondo, Purwanto. Bahasa Indonesia for Beginners, Bk. 1. 1966. pap. 6.50x (ISBN 0-424-05280-6, Pub. by Sydney U Pr). Intl Schol Bk Serv.
--Bahasa Indonesia for Beginners, Bk. 2. 2nd ed. 1969. pap. 6.50 (ISBN 0-424-06170-8, Pub. by Sydney U Pr). Intl Schol Bk Serv.
Echols, John M. & Shadily, Hassan. An Indonesian-English Dictionary. 2nd ed. 431p. 1963. 27.50x (ISBN 0-8014-0112-7). Cornell U Pr.
Karim, A. What to Say in Bahasa Indonesia: Bahasa Indonesia Phrase Book for Travellers. 1978. pap. 3.00 (ISBN 0-8048-1282-9). C E Tuttle.
Kramer, A. L., Sr. English-Indonesian, Indonesian-English Dictionary. 19.50 (ISBN 0-87559-066-7); thumb indexed 23.00 (ISBN 0-87559-067-5). Shalom.
--Van Goor's Concise Indonesian Dictionary: English-Indonesian Indonesian-English. LC 66-23535. 1966. Repr. 8.95 (ISBN 0-8048-0611-X). C E Tuttle.
Kwee, John B. Teach Yourself Indonesian. (Teach Yourself Ser.). pap. 4.95 (ISBN 0-679-10182-9). McKay.
Macdonald, R. Ross. Indonesian Reference Grammar. rev. ed. LC 76-3734. 173p. 1976. 7.95 (ISBN 0-87840-163-6). Georgetown U Pr.
Wolff, John U. Beginning Indonesian, Pt. 1. 562p. 1978. Repr. of 1972 ed. 12.50 (ISBN 0-686-65554-0). Cornell SE Asia.
--Beginning Indonesian, Pt. 2. 2nd ed. 562p. 1980. 12.50 (ISBN 0-686-60583-7). Cornell SE Asia.
--Formal Indonesian. 460p. 1980. 12.50 (ISBN 0-686-63165-X). Cornell SE Asia.
Yohanni, Johns. Bahasa Indonesia. pap. 11.95 (ISBN 0-7081-0334-0, Pub by ANUP Australia). Bks Australia.

INDONESIAN LANGUAGES

see Austronesian Languages

INDONESIAN LITERATURE

Echols, John M. Preliminary Checklist of Indonesian Imprints During the Japanese Period: March 1962 - August 1945. 1963. pap. 1.50 (ISBN 0-686-62725-3). Cornell Mod Indo.
Hendon, Rufus S. Six Indonesian Short Stories. (Translation Ser.: No. 7). viii, 123p. 1968. 4.50 (ISBN 0-686-30906-5). Yale U SE Asia.
Johns, Anthony H. Cultural Options & the Role of Tradition: A Collection of Essays on Modern Indonesian & Malaysian Literature. LC 78-74666. 1979. pap. text ed. 9.95 (ISBN 0-7081-0341-3, Faculty of Asian Studies in Association with Australian Natn'l). Bks Australia.
Siek, Marguerite. Favourite Stories from Indonesia. bilingual ed. (The Favourite Stories Ser.). (Orig.). (gr. 5). 1981. pap. text ed. 2.50x (ISBN 0-686-74505-1, 00335). Heinemann Ed.

INDONESIAN NATIONAL CHARACTERISTICS

see National Characteristics, Indonesian

INDONESIAN POETRY–HISTORY AND CRITICISM

Aveling, Harry. Contemporary Indonesian Poetry. (Asian & Pacific Writing Ser.). 1975. 14.95x (ISBN 0-7022-0931-7); pap. 8.50x (ISBN 0-7022-0932-5). U of Queensland Pr.
--A Thematic History of Indonesian Poetry, 1920-1974. (Special Report Ser.: No. 9). wrps. 3.00x (ISBN 0-686-09460-3). Cellar.
Raffel, Burton. Development of Modern Indonesian Poetry. LC 67-63246. 1967. 21.00 (ISBN 0-87395-024-0); microfiche 21.00 (ISBN 0-87395-124-7). State U NY Pr.
Ward, Philip. Indonesian Traditional Poetry. 1975. 13.50 (ISBN 0-902675-49-4). Oleander Pr.

INDONESIAN POETRY–TRANSLATIONS INTO ENGLISH

Raffel, Burton, ed. Anthology of Modern Indonesian Poetry. 2nd ed. LC 68-19044. 1968. pap. 7.95 o. p. (ISBN 0-87395-031-3); microfiche 7.95 (ISBN 0-87395-131-X). State U NY Pr.

INDONESIAN TALES

see Tales, Indonesian

INDOOR BASEBALL

see also Softball

INDOOR GAMES

see also Amusements; Psychic Games

Ainslie, Tom. Ainslie's Complete Hoyle. LC 74-32023. 544p. 1975. 15.95 (ISBN 0-671-21967-7); pap. 7.95 (ISBN 0-671-24779-4). S&S.
Brandreth, Gyles. Home Entertainment for All the Family. LC 76-50266. (Illus.). 1977. pap. 5.95 (ISBN 0-8289-0298-4). Greene.
Cassell, Sylvia. Indoor Games & Activities. LC 60-5776. (Illus.). (gr. 2-6). 1960. 6.95 (ISBN 0-06-021150-4, HarpJ). Har-Row.
Frey, Richard L., ed. According to Hoyle. rev. ed. 1978. pap. 2.25 (ISBN 0-449-23652-8, Crest). Fawcett.
Frey, Richard L., et al. New Complete Hoyle. rev. ed. LC 55-11330. 1956. 12.95 (ISBN 0-385-00126-6). Doubleday.
Gallagher, N. Simple Pleasures: Wonderful Things to Do at Home. 1981. 11.95 (ISBN 0-201-04578-8); pap. 5.95 (ISBN 0-201-04579-6). A-W.
Hindman, D. Nine Men's Morris: Over 800 Other Indoor Games, Puzzles & Stunts. LC 77-13029. 1978. pap. 3.95 (ISBN 0-13-622530-6, Reward). P-H.
Johnson, June. Eight Hundred Thirty-eight Ways to Amuse a Child. 1962. pap. 1.95 (ISBN 0-02-080380-X, Collier). Macmillan.
Keep Busy Book for Girls. (Doubleday Activity Books). (gr. 2-4). 1.95 (ISBN 0-385-03418-0). Doubleday.
Keep Busy Book for Tots. LC 62-18086. (Doubleday Activity Bks). (Illus.). (ps-2). 1.95 (ISBN 0-385-06605-8). Doubleday.
Litsky, Frank. The Complete Book of Indoor Sports. LC 79-9634. 1981. 14.95 (ISBN 0-672-52646-8). Bobbs.
Paxman, Shirley & Paxman, Monroe. To Bed to Bed the Doctor Said. (Illus.). 40p. (gr. 3-10). 1975. pap. 2.95 (ISBN 0-914510-05-3). Evergreen.
Schwartz, Alvin. Rainy Day Book. LC 68-14288. 1968. 7.95 (ISBN 0-671-60606-9). Trident.

INDORE PROCESS

see Compost

INDRAJIT, VIVEKADIPIKA

McGregor, R. S. Language of Indrajit of Orcha. LC 68-10472. (University of Cambridge Oriental Pubns.). 1968. 49.50 (ISBN 0-521-05630-6). Cambridge U Pr.

INDUCTION (ELECTRICITY)

Kiltie, Ordean. Design Shortcuts & Procedures for Electronics Power Transformers & Inductors. LC 81-81620. (Illus.). 274p. (Orig.). 1981. 39.50 (ISBN 0-916512-27-4). Kiltie.

INDUCTION (LOGIC)

see also Induction (Mathematics)

Barker, S. F. Induction & Hypothesis: A Study of the Logic of Confirmation. (Contemporary Philosophy Ser.). 203p. 1957. 17.50x (ISBN 0-8014-0027-9). Cornell U Pr.
Blackburn, S. Reason & Prediction. LC 72-83580. (Illus.). 192p. 1973. 26.95 (ISBN 0-521-08742-2). Cambridge U Pr.
Bogdan, R. J., ed. Local Induction. LC 75-34922. (Synthese Library: No. 93). 1975. lib. bdg. 58.00 (ISBN 90-277-0649-2, Pub. by Reidel Holland). Kluwer Boston.
Burks, Arthur W. Chance, Cause, Reason: An Inquiry into the Nature of Scientific Evidence. LC 74-11617. (Illus.). 688p. 1977. lib. bdg. 27.50x (ISBN 0-226-08087-0). U of Chicago Pr.
Carnap, Rudolf & Jeffrey, Richard C., eds. Studies in Inductive Logic & Probability, Vol. 1. LC 77-136025. 1971. 25.00x (ISBN 0-520-01866-4). U of Cal Pr.
Christensen, R. Foundations of Inductive Reasoning. xii, 363p. 1964. 39.50 (ISBN 0-686-28748-7, 04-08-01). Entropy Ltd.
Cohen, L. J. & Hesse, M. B., eds. Applications of Inductive Logic: Proceedings of a Conference at the Queen's College, Oxford, August 1978. (Illus.). 410p. 1980. 65.00x (ISBN 0-19-824584-X). Oxford U Pr.
Goodman, Nelson. Fact, Fiction, & Forecast. 3rd ed. LC 73-11273. 1977. 17.50 (ISBN 0-672-51889-9); pap. text ed. 6.95x (ISBN 0-672-61347-6). Hackett Pub.
Gratry, A. Logic. Singer, Helen & Singer, Milton, trs. from Fr. xii, 628p. 1944. 25.00 (ISBN 0-87548-035-7). Open Court.
Jeffrey, Richard C., ed. Studies in Inductive Logic & Probability, Vol. II. 312p. 1980. 23.75x (ISBN 0-520-03826-6). U of Cal Pr.
Kyburg, Henry E., Jr. Induction & Probability. 1970. text ed. 12.95x (ISBN 0-02-366990-X). Macmillan.
Niiniluoto, I. & Tuomela, R. Theoretical Concepts & Hypothetico-Inductive Inference. LC 73-83567. (Synthese Library: No. 53). 1973. lib. bdg. 39.50 (ISBN 90-277-0343-4, Pub. by Reidel Holland). Kluwer Boston.
Popper, Karl R. Objective Knowledge: An Evolutionary Approach. 360p. 1972. pap. text ed. 7.95x (ISBN 0-19-875024-2). Oxford U Pr.
Rescher, Nicholas. Induction. LC 80-52598. xii, 225p. 1981. 34.95x (ISBN 0-8229-3431-0). U of Pittsburgh Pr.
Sansbury, Ralph. A Unified Theory of Probability & Inductive Inference. 1971. 10.00 (ISBN 0-686-11594-5). Abco-Malan.

Swinburne, Richard, ed. Justification of Induction. (Oxford Readings in Philosophy Ser.). 188p. 1974. pap. text ed. 5.95x (ISBN 0-19-875029-3). Oxford U Pr.
Teensma, E. Solipsism & Induction. 64p. 1974. pap. text ed. 6.50x (ISBN 90-232-1149-9). Humanities.
Venn, John. Principles of Empirical or Inductive Logic. 2nd ed. LC 77-165344. 604p. 1973. Repr. of 1907 ed. 33.50 (ISBN 0-8337-3625-6). B Franklin.
--The Principles of Inductive Logic. 2nd ed. LC 72-119162. Orig. Title: The Principles of Empirical, or Inductive Logic. 624p. 1973. 18.50 (ISBN 0-8284-0265-5). Chelsea Pub.
Von Wright, Georg H. The Logical Problem of Induction. 2nd ed. LC 78-24370. 1979. Repr. of 1957 ed. lib. bdg. 20.25x (ISBN 0-313-20830-1, WRLP). Greenwood.
Will, Frederick L. Induction & Justification: An Investigation of Cartesian Procedure in the Philosophy of Knowledge. LC 73-19079. 416p. 1974. 22.50x (ISBN 0-8014-0823-7). Cornell U Pr.

INDUCTION (MATHEMATICS)

Gelfand, S. I., et al. Sequences & Combinatorial Problems. (Pocket Mathematical Library Ser.). 1968. 18.75x (ISBN 0-677-20730-1). Gordon.
Golovina, L. & Yaglom, I. Inducton in Geometry. 133p. 1979. pap. 1.90 (ISBN 0-8285-1534-4, Pub. by Mir Pubs Russia). Imported Pubns.
Golovina, L. I. & Yaglom, I. M. Induccion En la Geometria. 126p. (Span.). 1976. pap. 1.95 (ISBN 0-8285-1687-1, Pub. by Mir Pubs Russia). Imported Pubns.
Hacking, I. The Emergence of Probability. LC 74-82224. 216p. 1975. 29.95 (ISBN 0-521-20460-7). Cambridge U Pr.
Moschovakis, Y. N. Elementary Induction on Abstract Structures. LC 73-79100. (Studies in Logic & the Foundations of Mathematics Ser.: Vol. 77). 220p. 1974. 24.50 (ISBN 0-444-10537-9, North-Holland). Elsevier.
Sominsky, I. S. The Method of Mathematical Induction. 62p. 1975. pap. 1.25 (ISBN 0-8285-1702-9, Pub. by Mir Pubs Russia). Imported Pubns.

INDUCTION MOTORS

see Electric Motors, Induction

INDULGENCES

see also Absolution; Catholic Church–Discipline; Purgatory

Enchiridion of Indulgences. new, rev. ed. maroon cloth 4.00 (ISBN 0-686-14269-1, 555/22). Catholic Bk Pub.
Lea, Henry C. History of Auricular Confession & Indulgences in the Latin Church, 3 Vols. LC 68-19287. 1968. Repr. of 1896 ed. lib. bdg. 67.25x (ISBN 0-8371-0140-9, LEHC). Greenwood.
Thurston, Herbert. The Holy Year of the Jubilee: An Account of the History & Ceremonial of the Roman Jubilee. LC 78-63481. Repr. of 1900 ed. 38.45 (ISBN 0-404-16547-8). AMS Pr.

INDUS RIVER AND VALLEY

Khan, F. A. Indus Valley & Early Iran. (Pakistan Archaeology Ser). (Illus.). 1964. 10.00x (ISBN 0-8002-1560-5). Intl Pubns Serv.
Mackay, E. J. Chanhu-Daro Excavations, 1935-1936. Repr. of 1942 ed. pap. 28.00 (ISBN 0-527-02694-8). Kraus Repr.
MacKay, Ernest J. H. The Indus Civilization. LC 77-86434. Repr. of 1935 ed. 19.00 (ISBN 0-404-16673-3). AMS Pr.
Mitchiner, John E. Studies in the Indus Valley Inscriptions. (Illus.). 1979. text ed. 12.50x (ISBN 0-391-01614-8). Humanities.
Possehl, Gregory L., ed. Ancient Cities of the Indus. LC 78-54442. (Illus.). 1979. lib. bdg. 17.50 (ISBN 0-89089-093-5). Carolina Acad Pr.
Rao, Shikaripur R. Lothal & the Indus Civilization. (Illus.). 215p. 1973. lib. bdg. 35.00x (ISBN 0-210-22278-6). Asia.
Vats, Madro S. Excavations at Harappa: Being an Account of Archaeological Excavations at Harappa Carried Out Between the Years 1920-21 & 1933-34, 2 vols. LC 77-86439. Repr. of 1940 ed. 118.00 set (ISBN 0-404-16680-6). AMS Pr.
Watson, Jane W. The Indus: South Asia's Highway of History. LC 71-95747. (Rivers of World Ser.). (Illus.). (gr. 4-7). 1970. PLB 3.68 (ISBN 0-8116-6373-6). Garrard.
Wheeler, M. Civilizations of the Indus Valley & Beyond. 1966. pap. 2.95 (ISBN 0-07-069506-7, SP). McGraw.

INDUSTRIAL ACCIDENTS

see also Disability Evaluation; Employers' Liability; Workmen'S Compensation;
also subdivision Accidents, Safety Appliances, and Safety Measures under particular industries or occupations, e.g. Railroads–Accidents

Boley, Jack. A Guide to Effective Industrial Safety. 127p. 1977. 8.95 (ISBN 0-87201-798-2). Gulf Pub.
Eastman, Crystal. Work Accidents & the Law. LC 70-89757. (American Labor, from Conspiracy to Collective Bargaining Ser., No. 1). 361p. 1969. Repr. of 1910 ed. 19.00 (ISBN 0-405-02118-6). Arno.
Ferry, Ted S. Elements of Accident Investigation. 72p. 1978. pap. 10.75 spiral (ISBN 0-398-03752-3). C C Thomas.
--Modern Accident Investigation & Analysis: An Executive Guide to Accident Investigation. 350p. 1981. 30.00 (ISBN 0-686-31806-4). Page-Ficklin.
--Modern Accident Investigation & Analysis: An Executive Guide to Accident Investigation. LC 80-21046. 273p. 1981. 27.95 (ISBN 0-471-07776-3, Pub. by Wiley-Interscience). Wiley.
Goldberg, Rosamond W. Occupational Diseases in Relation to Compensation & Health Insurance. LC 68-58581. (Columbia University. Studies in the Social Sciences: No. 345). Repr. of 1931 ed. 22.50 (ISBN 0-404-51345-X). AMS Pr.
Goldmark, Josephine & Hopkins, Mary D. Comparison of an Eight-Hour Plant & a Ten-Hour Plant: U.S. Public Health Bulletin, No. 106. Stein, Leon, ed. LC 77-70495. (Work Ser.). 1977. Repr. of 1920 ed. lib. bdg. 15.00x (ISBN 0-405-10168-6). Arno.
Klein, Earl E. Work Accidents to Miners in Illinois, Vol. 7. LC 74-1689. (Children & Youth Ser.). 275p. 1974. Repr. of 1938 ed. 17.00x (ISBN 0-405-05966-3). Arno.
Rudman, Jack. Safety Engineer. (Career Examination Ser.: C-797). (Cloth bdg. avail. on request). pap. 8.00 (ISBN 0-8373-0797-X). Natl Learning.

INDUSTRIAL ACCIDENTS–PREVENTION

see Industrial Safety

INDUSTRIAL ADMINISTRATION

see Industrial Management

INDUSTRIAL ADVERTISING

see Advertising, Industrial

INDUSTRIAL ARBITRATION

see Arbitration, Industrial

INDUSTRIAL ARCHAEOLOGY

Here are entered works on the organized study of the physical remains of industries of the 18th and 19th centuries.

Alderton, David & Booker, John. The Batsford Guide to the Industrial Archaeology of East Anglia. LC 79-56490. (Illus.). 150p. 1980. 39.00 (ISBN 0-7134-2233-5, Pub. by Batsford England). David & Charles.
Ashmore, Owen. Industrial Archaeology of Lancashire. LC 68-18643. 1969. 15.00x (ISBN 0-678-05529-7). Kelley.
Atkinson, Frank. Industrial Archaeology of North-East England, 2 vols. LC 74-81052. (Industrial Archaeology of British Isles Ser). (Illus.). 342p. 1974. Vol. 1. 5.95 (ISBN 0-7153-5911-8); Vol. 2, The Sites. 5.95 (ISBN 0-7153-6740-4). David & Charles.
Baxter, Bertram. Stone Blocks & Iron Rails. (Industrial Archeology of the British Isles Ser.). (Illus.). 4.50 (ISBN 0-7153-4004-2). David & Charles.
Booker, Frank. The Industrial Archeology of the Tamar Valley. (Industrial Archeology of the British Isles Ser.). (Illus.). 303p. 7.50 (ISBN 0-7153-5172-9). David & Charles.
Buchanan, R. A. & Cossons, Neil. Industrial Archaeology of the Bristol Region. LC 69-13758. (Illus.). 1969. 15.00x (ISBN 0-678-05511-4). Kelley.
Buchanon, C. A. & Buchanon, R. A. The Batsford Guide to the Industrial Archaeology of Central Southern England. (Illus.). 192p. 1980. 45.00 (ISBN 0-7134-1364-6, Pub. by Batsford England). David & Charles.
Butt, John. Industrial Archaeology of Scotland. LC 67-109342. (Illus.). 1967. 15.00x (ISBN 0-678-05749-4). Kelley.
Butt, John & Donnachie, Ian. Industrial Archaeology in the British Isles. LC 79-11955. (Illus.). 1979. text ed. 23.50x (ISBN 0-06-490837-2). B&N.
Cossons, Neil. The BP Book of Industrial Archaeology. LC 74-20468. (Illus.). 1975. 19.95 (ISBN 0-7153-6250-X). David & Charles.
Cossons, Neil, ed. Industrial Archaeologist's Guide, 1969-1970. 2.95 (ISBN 0-7153-4308-4). David & Charles.
Crawford, Harriet, ed. Subterranean Britain. LC 79-16858. 1979. 18.95x (ISBN 0-312-77477-X). St Martin.
English, Peter. Made in Britain: A Unique Contribution to World Industrial Archaeology, Vol. 1. Faulds, I. C., ed. 1980. text ed. 15.50x (ISBN 0-904980-28-6). Humanities.
Gribbon, H. D. History of Water Power in Ulster. LC 69-12248. (Illus.). 1969. 12.95x (ISBN 0-678-05528-9). Kelley.
Harris, Helen. Industrial Archaeology of Dartmoor. LC 68-23837. (Illus.). 1968. 11.95x (ISBN 0-678-05582-3). Kelley.
Hart, Cyril. The Industrial History of Dean: With an Introduction to Its Industrial Archaeology. (Illus.). 466p. 1971. 22.50 (ISBN 0-7153-5288-1). David & Charles.
Hudson, K. World Industrial Archaeology. LC 77-94225. (New Studies in Archaeology). 1979. 49.50 (ISBN 0-521-21991-4); pap. 14.50x (ISBN 0-521-29330-8). Cambridge U Pr.
Hudson, Kenneth. Food, Clothes & Shelter: Twentieth Century Industrial Archaeology. (Illus.). 1978. text ed. 16.25x (ISBN 0-212-97021-6). Humanities.
--Guide to the Industrial Archaeology of Europe. LC 76-160459. (Illus.). 186p. 1971. 18.00 (ISBN 0-8386-1001-3). Fairleigh Dickinson.
--Industrial Archaeology: A New Introduction. 3rd ed. (Illus.). 1976. text ed. 16.25x (ISBN 0-212-97014-3). Humanities.
--Industrial Archaeology: An Introduction. 1964. 22.50 (ISBN 0-212-35963-0). Dufour.
--A Pocket Book for Industrial Archaeologists. 1976. text ed. 5.75x (ISBN 0-212-97018-6). Humanities.
Hudson, Kenneth, ed. Industrial Archaeology, Vols. 5 & 6. LC 68-23828. 1968-69. 11.00x ea. Vol. 5 (ISBN 0-678-05501-7). Vol. 6 (ISBN 0-678-05674-9). Kelley.
Johnson, W. Branch. Industrial Archaeology of Hertfordshire. LC 71-91240. (Illus.). 1970. 10.00x (ISBN 0-678-05652-8). Kelley.
Koch, Jean E. Industrial Archeology: An Introductory Bibliography. (Architecture Ser.: No. A 32). 1979. pap. 6.50 (ISBN 0-686-24527-X). Vance Biblios.
McCollam, C. Harold. The Brick & Tile Industry in Stark County, 1809-1976. LC 76-17281. (Illus.). 200p. 1976. 12.50x (ISBN 0-87338-187-4, Pub. by Stark Cty Hist. Soc.). Kent St U Pr.
Raistrick, Arthur. Industrial Archaeology: An Historical Survey. (Illus.). 314p. 1981. pap. 6.95 (ISBN 0-586-08131-3, Pub. by Granada England). Academy Chi Ltd.
--Industrial Archaeology: An Historical Survey. (Illus.). 1972. text ed. 19.95x (ISBN 0-413-28050-0, Pub. by Eyre Methuen England). Methuen Inc.
Sande, Theodore A. Industrial Archeology. LC 75-8196. (Illus.). 200p. 1976. 19.95 (ISBN 0-8289-0290-9). Greene.
Todd, A. C. & Laws, Peter. The Industrial Archaeology of Cornwall. (Industrial Archaeology of the British Isles Ser). (Illus.). 288p. 1973. 14.95 (ISBN 0-7153-5590-2). David & Charles.
Vialls, Christine. Your Book of Industrial Archaeology. (Illus.). 80p. (gr. 4-12). 1981. 9.95 (ISBN 0-571-11633-7, Pub. by Faber & Faber). Merrimack Bk Serv.
Wilson, Aubrey. London's Industrial Heritage. LC 67-28482. (Illus.). 1967. 12.50x (ISBN 0-678-05747-8). Kelley.
Wren, Wilfrid J. Tanat Valley. LC 68-141249. (Illus.). 1968. 10.95x (ISBN 0-678-05748-6). Kelley.

INDUSTRIAL ARTS

see also Agriculture; Art Industries and Trade; Artisans; Arts and Crafts Movement; Bookbinding; Engineering; Industries, Primitive; Inventions; Machinery; Machinery in Industry; Manual Training; Manufactures; Mechanical Engineering; Mills and Mill-Work; Patents; Research, Industrial; Technical Education; Technology;
also names of specific industries, arts, trades, etc., e.g. Bookbinding; Printing; Ship-building

Ahlstrand, Eric. Datsun F Ten & Three Hundred Ten: Nineteen Seventy-Six to Seventy-Nine Shop Manual. (Illus.). pap. text ed. 10.95 (ISBN 0-89287-318-3, A202). Clymer Pubns.
AIAA Conference, 33rd Annual, 1971. Industrial Arts & Space Age Technology: Proceedings. 432p. 1971. 6.50 (ISBN 0-686-11055-2); pap. 4.50 (ISBN 0-686-11056-0). Am Indus Arts.
AIAA Conference, 34th Annual, 1972. Industrial Arts in a Changing Society: Proceedings. 570p. 1972. 6.50 (ISBN 0-686-11061-7); pap. 4.50 (ISBN 0-686-11062-5). Am Indus Arts.
AIAA Conference, 35th Annual, 1973. Industrial Arts & the Challenge of an Urban Society: Proceedings. 503p. 1973. 6.50 (ISBN 0-686-11057-9); pap. 4.50 (ISBN 0-686-11058-7). Am Indus Arts.
AIAA Conference, 36th Annual, 1074. Industrial Arts & a Humane Technology for the Future: Proceedings. 383p. 1974. 6.50 (ISBN 0-686-11080-3); pap. 4.50 (ISBN 0-686-11081-1). Am Indus Arts.
AIAA Conference, 37th Annual, 1975. Essential Development Through Industrial Arts: Proceedings. Stamm, Colleen P., ed. 1976. 7.00 (ISBN 0-686-15693-5); pap. 5.25 (ISBN 0-686-15694-3). Am Indus Arts.
Balkham, K. & Mills, R. Introductory Design Problems. (gr. 11-12). 1979. pap. text ed. 7.50x (ISBN 0-435-75860-8). Heinemann Ed.
Bauer, C. E. & Thompson, R. L. Comprehensive General Shop One. 1959. 7.00 (ISBN 0-02-810480-3). Glencoe.
Bishop, Mike. Kawasaki Snowmobiles Nineteen Seventy-Six to Nineteen Eighty: Service, Repair, Maintenance. Jorgensen, Eric, ed. (Illus.). 152p. (Orig.). 1980. pap. text ed. 8.95 (ISBN 0-89287-320-5, X995). Clymer Pubns.
Bragg, William H. Creative Knowledge. facs. ed. LC 74-134057. (Essay Index Reprint Ser). 1926. 30.00 (ISBN 0-8369-2104-6). Arno.
Clark, Edie, ed. The Forgotten Arts, Bk. 4. LC 75-10770. (Illus.). 1979. pap. 3.95 (ISBN 0-911658-95-5). Yankee Bks.
Cripps, Ann, ed. Countryman Rescuing the Past. (Countryman Ser.). (Illus.). 1975. 5.50 (ISBN 0-7153-6071-X). David & Charles.
DiPaul, H. Bert. Focusing Industrial Arts on Career Education. LC 79-53500. (Illus.). 143p. (Orig.). (gr. 9-12). 1979. pap. 3.95 (ISBN 0-9605418-0-2). DiPaul.
Feirer, John L. Industrial Arts Woodworking. (gr. 9-12). 1977. text ed. 13.96 (ISBN 0-87002-195-8); wkbk 2.88 (ISBN 0-87002-284-9); tchr's. ed. 2.52 (ISBN 0-87002-350-0). Bennett IL.
Feirer, John L. & Lindbeck. Drawing & Planning for the Industrial Arts. new ed. (Illus.). (gr. 7-12). 1975. text ed. 13.16 (ISBN 0-87002-159-1); tchr's guide, charts & worksheets 5.60 (ISBN 0-87002-162-1). Bennett IL.
The Future: A Challenge to Industrial Arts. (Monograph Ser: No. 5). 1975. pap. 2.00 (ISBN 0-686-16554-3). Am Indus Arts.
Gerbracht, Carl & Robinson, Frank E. Understanding America's Industries. (gr. 7-9). 1971. text ed. 15.72 (ISBN 0-87345-499-5). McKnight.
Groneman, Chris H. & Feirer, John L. General Industrial Education. 5th ed. LC 73-9827. Orig. Title: General Shop. (Illus.). 584p. (gr. 7-9). 1973. text ed. 14.64 (ISBN 0-07-024965-2, W); tchr's. resource guide 1.84 (ISBN 0-07-024976-8); study guide 4.60 (ISBN 0-07-024968-7). McGraw.
--General Industrial Education. 6th ed. (M-H Publications in Industrial Education). (gr. 7-9). 1979. text ed. 14.64 (ISBN 0-07-024991-1, W); study guide 4.60 (ISBN 0-07-024992-X); tchr's. guide 1.84 (ISBN 0-07-024993-8). McGraw.
Henriksen, Erik K. Jig & Fixture Design Manual. LC 73-8810. (Illus.). 308p. 1973. 35.00 (ISBN 0-8311-1098-8). Indus Pr.
Holtzappfel, John J. The Principles & Practice of Ornamental & Complex Turning. (Illus.). 656p. 1973. Repr. of 1894 ed. 15.00 (ISBN 0-486-22965-3). Dover.
Industrial Arts: A Means of Preparing Youth to Understand & Contribute to Our Industrial-Technological Society. 1976. pap. 0.55x (ISBN 0-686-16665-5). Am Indus Arts.
Industrial Arts Curriculum Project. pap. 1.00 (ISBN 0-686-18056-9). Am Indus Arts.
Industrial Crafts. LC 77-73248. 64p. (gr. 7-9). 1978. pap. text ed. 3.64 (ISBN 0-02-820450-6). Glencoe.
Jorgensen, Eric, ed. BMW Three Hundred Twenty i: Nineteen Seventy-Seven to Nineteen Eighty Shop Manual. (Illus.). 248p. (Orig.). pap. text ed. 10.95 (ISBN 0-89287-326-4, A139). Clymer Pubns.
--Chevy Malibu Chevelle MonteCarlo: 1970-1980 Shop Manual. (Illus.). pap. text ed. 10.95 (ISBN 0-89287-319-1, A246). Clymer Pubns.
--Honda Twinstar Nineteen Seventy-Eight to Nineteen Eighty: Service, Repair, Maintenance. (Illus.). pap. text ed. 9.95 (ISBN 0-89287-325-6, M324). Clymer Pubns.
--Kawasaki Nine Hundred & 1000cc Four, 1973-1979: Includes Shaft Drive Service Repair Performance. (Illus., Orig.). pap. text ed. 9.95 (ISBN 0-89287-321-3, M359). Clymer Pubns.
--Oldsmobile Cutlass: Nineteen Seventy to Nineteen Eighty Shop Manual. (Illus.). 342p. (Orig.). pap. text ed. 10.95 (ISBN 0-89287-324-8, A285). Clymer Pubns.
--Suzuki SP-DR Three Hundred Seventy & Four Hundred Singles Nineteen Seventy-Eight to Nineteen Eighty: Service, Repair, Performance. (Illus.). 224p. (Orig.). pap. text ed. 9.95 (ISBN 0-89287-327-2, M374). Clymer Pubns.
--Yamaha Snowmobiles: Nineteen Seventy-Five to Nineteen Eighty Service, Repair & Maintenance. (Illus.). 180p. (Orig.). 1980. pap. text ed. 8.95 (ISBN 0-89287-323-X, X954). Clymer Pubns.
--Yamaha YZ One Hundred to Four Hundred Sixty-Five Monoshock Nineteen Seventy-Five to Nineteen Eighty: Service, Repair, Performance. (Illus.). 293p. (Orig.). pap. text ed. 9.95 (ISBN 0-89287-329-9, M413). Clymer Pubns.
Jorqgensen, Eric, ed. Datsun Two Hundred Ten: Nineteen Seventy-Nine to Nineteen Eighty Shop Manual. (Illus.). pap. text ed. 11.95 (ISBN 0-89287-322-1, A 203). Clymer Pubns.
Lindbeck, John R. & Lathrop, Irving T. General Industry. (Illus.). (gr. 7-9). 1977. 15.96 (ISBN 0-87002-185-0). student guide 4.64 (ISBN 0-87002-196-6). answer sheet free. Bennett IL.
Miller, J. G. Comprehensive General Shop. Vol. 2. 1962. 7.00 (ISBN 0-02-821180-4). Vol. 3. 1965. Glencoe.
Olson, D. Industrial Arts for the General Shop. 4th ed. 1973. text ed. 18.00 (ISBN 0-13-459131-3). P-H.

Osborne, Harold, ed. The Oxford Companion to the Decorative Arts. (Illus.). 1200p. 1975. 49.50 (ISBN 0-19-866113-4). Oxford U Pr.
Role of Industrial Arts in Tomorrow's Schools. 1965. pap. 1.00 (ISBN 0-686-00794-8). Am Indus Arts.
Veblen, Thorstein B. Instinct of Workmanship. rev. ed. LC 63-23515. Repr. of 1918 ed. 17.50x (ISBN 0-678-00051-4). Kelley.
Wells, H. G. Work, Wealth & Happiness of Mankind, 2 Vols. LC 69-10170. (Illus.). 1968. Repr. of 1931 ed. Set. lib. bdg. 49.75x (ISBN 0-8371-0263-4, WEHM). Greenwood.
Wilber, Gordon O. & Pendered, Norman C. Industrial Arts in General Education. 4th ed. 1973. text ed. 20.95 scp (ISBN 0-7002-2425-4, HarpC). Har-Row.

INDUSTRIAL ARTS–BIBLIOGRAPHY
see also Inventors
Bolton, Henry C. Catalogue of Scientific & Technical Periodicals. 1665-1895. 2nd ed. Repr. of 1897 ed. 61.50 (ISBN 0-384-04985-0). Johnson Repr.
John Crerar Library. List of Books on the History of Industry & the Industrial Arts. LC 67-14030. 1966. Repr. of 1915 ed. 26.00 (ISBN 0-8103-3104-7). Gale.

INDUSTRIAL ARTS–BIOGRAPHY
Glenister, S. H. Stories of Great Craftsmen. facs. ed. LC 75-128247. (Essay Index Reprint Ser). 1939. 17.00 (ISBN 0-8369-1831-2). Arno.
Parton, James. Captains of Industry: Or, Men of Business Who Did Something Besides Making Money; a Book for Young Americans. LC 72-2660. (Essay Index Reprint Ser.). Repr. of 1884 ed. 25.00 (ISBN 0-8369-2853-9). Arno.

INDUSTRIAL ARTS–DICTIONARIES
Feutry, Michel, et al, eds. Dictionary of Industrial Technology: English-French-German-Portuguese-Spanish. 80.00 (ISBN 2-85608-000-6). Heinman.
Franklin, Afred L. Dictionnaire Historique Des Arts, Metiers Et Professions Exerces Dans Paris Depuis Le Treizieme Siecle. (Biblio. & Ref. Ser.: No. 198). 1968. Repr. of 1906 ed. 49.00 (ISBN 0-8337-1231-4); 40.00 (ISBN 0-685-06747-5). B Franklin.

INDUSTRIAL ARTS–EXAMINATIONS, QUESTIONS, ETC.
Arco Editorial Board. Apprentice-Mechanical Trades. 6th ed. LC 77-21217. (Orig.). 1977. pap. 6.00 (ISBN 0-668-00571-8). Arco.
Rudman, Jack. Industrial Arts - Jr. H.S. (Teachers License Examination Ser.: T-30). (Cloth bdg. avail. on request). pap. 10.00 (ISBN 0-8373-8030-8). Natl Learning.
--Industrial Arts - Sr. H.S. (Teachers License Examination Ser.: T-31). (Cloth bdg. avail on request). pap. 10.00 (ISBN 0-8373-8031-6). Natl Learning.
--Industrial Arts Education. (National Teachers Examination Ser.: NT-5). (Cloth bdg. avail. on request). pap. 9.95 (ISBN 0-8373-8415-X). Natl Learning.
--Shop Subjects. (Teachers License Examination Ser.: T-53). (Cloth bdg. avail. on request). pap. 10.00 (ISBN 0-8373-8053-7). Natl Learning.
Turner, David R. Teacher of Industrial Arts: Junior High School & High School. (Orig.). 1970. pap. 6.00 (ISBN 0-668-01307-9). Arco.

INDUSTRIAL ARTS–EXHIBITIONS
see Exhibitions

INDUSTRIAL ARTS–HISTORY
see also Industries, Primitive; Inventions
Bremner, David. Industries of Scotland. LC 69-11242. Repr. of 1869 ed. 22.50x (ISBN 0-678-05583-1). Kelley.
Brewster, Ethel H. Roman Craftsmen & Tradesmen of the Early Empire. LC 72-81956. 101p. 1972. Repr. of 1917 ed. lib. bdg. 20.00 (ISBN 0-8337-4822-X). B Franklin.
Clow, Archibald & Clow, Nan L. Chemical Revolution. facs. ed. (Essay Index Reprint Ser). 1952. 38.00 (ISBN 0-8369-1909-2). Arno.
De Baye, J. The Industrial Arts of the Anglo-Saxons. 1980. Repr. of 1893 ed. lib. bdg. 40.00 (ISBN 0-89341-380-1). Longwood Pr.
Giedion, Siegfried. Mechanization Takes Command. 1969. pap. 9.95 (ISBN 0-393-00489-9, Norton Lib.). Norton.
--Mechanization Takes Command: A Contribution to Anonymous History. (Illus.). 1948. 25.00 (ISBN 0-19-500555-4). Oxford U Pr.
Guillet, Edwin C. Pioneer Arts & Crafts. 2nd ed. LC 72-415879. (Photos). 1968. pap. 3.50 (ISBN 0-8020-6081-1). U of Toronto Pr.
Hodges, Henry. Artifacts: An Introduction to Early Materials & Technology. rev. ed. (Illus., Orig.). 1981. pap. text ed. 12.50x (ISBN 0-391-02246-6). Humanities.
Hudson, Kenneth. Industrial Archaeology of Southern England. LC 68-23822. (Illus.). 1968. 14.95x (ISBN 0-678-05606-4). Kelley.
Hughes, George B. Living Crafts. facsimile ed. LC 70-156660. (Essay Index Reprints). Repr. of 1954 ed. 25.00 (ISBN 0-8369-2509-2). Arno.
Karmarsch, Karl. Geschichte Der Technologie Seit Der Mitte Des 18. Jahrhunderts. 1872. 46.00 (ISBN 0-384-28630-5). Johnson Repr.
Miller, Walter. Daedalus & Thespis: Volume II: Sculpture, Pts. 1 & 2. Repr. of 1931 ed. 10.00x (ISBN 0-8262-0590-9). U of Mo Pr.
Mumford, Lewis. Technics & Civilization. LC 63-19641. (Illus.). 1963. pap. 6.95 (ISBN 0-15-688254-X, H030, Hbgr). HarBraceJ.
Richardson, Albert E. Georgian England: A Survey of Social Life, Trades, Industries & Art from 1700 to 1820. facs. ed. LC 67-23265. (Essay Index Reprint Ser). 1931. 28.00 (ISBN 0-8369-0823-6). Arno.
Smiles, Samuel. Industrial Biography: Iron-Workers & Tool Makers. LC 67-114712. (Illus.). Repr. of 1863 ed. 17.50x (ISBN 0-678-05727-3). Kelley.
Wolf, A. A History of Science, Technology & Philosophy in the Eighteenth Century, 2 vols. (Illus.). 20.00 (ISBN 0-8446-1484-X). Peter Smith.
--A History of Science, Technology & Philosophy in the Sixteenth & Seventeenth Centuries, 2 vols. (Illus.). 20.00 (ISBN 0-8446-1483-1). Peter Smith.

INDUSTRIAL ARTS–MUSEUMS
see Industrial Museums

INDUSTRIAL ARTS–STUDY AND TEACHING
AIAA Conference, 31st Annual, 1969. Where the Action Is: Proceedings. 1969. pap. 4.50 (ISBN 0-686-00328-4). Am Indus Arts.
American Council for Elementary School Industrial Arts. Articulation in Career Education. (Focus Ser.). 20p. 1973. pap. 1.00 (ISBN 0-686-11044-7). Am Indus Arts.
An Analysis of Graduate Work in Institutions with Programs for Industrial Arts Educational Personnel. (Monograph: No. 1). 1965. pap. 2.00 (ISBN 0-686-16553-5). Am Indus Arts.
Baird, Ronald J. Contemporary Industrial Teaching. LC 78-185957. (Illus.). 200p. 1972. text ed. 9.28 (ISBN 0-87006-130-5). Goodheart.
Bakamis, William A. Improving Instruction in Industrial Arts. 1966. 8.95 (ISBN 0-02-810270-3). Glencoe.
Baratta-Lorton, Mary B. Workjobs: Activity-Centered Learning for Early Childhood Education. 1972. text ed. 11.95 (ISBN 0-201-04311-4, Sch Div). A-W.
Barlow, Melvin L. History of Industrial Education in the United States. 1967. pap. text ed. 23.44 (ISBN 0-87002-241-5). Bennett IL.
Brown, Kenneth W. Model of a Theoretical Base for Industrial Arts Education. (William E. Warner Ser.: Monograph 1). pap. text ed. 1.25 (ISBN 0-686-21299-1). Am Indus Arts.
Brown, Walter C., et al. Modern General Shop. LC 74-23595. (Illus.). 488p. 1978. text ed. 12.96 (ISBN 0-87006-260-3). Goodheart.
Butler, F. Coit. Instructional Systems Development for Vocational & Technical Training. LC 70-168490. 384p. 1972. 19.95 (ISBN 0-87778-027-7). Educ Tech Pubns.
Career Education, Definition & Evaluation. (Focus Ser.). 24p. 1973. pap. 1.50 (ISBN 0-686-11045-5). Am Indus Arts.
Charneco Babilonia, Efrain & Llabres De Charneco, Amalia. Metodologia para la Ensenanza De las Artes Industriales y la Educacion Vocacional Industrial. LC 76-3715. 236p. (Orig.). 1976. pap. text ed. 6.25 (ISBN 0-8477-2722-X). U of PR Pr.
Curriculum Projects. (Focus Ser.). 36p. 1973. pap. 1.75 (ISBN 0-686-11049-8). Am Indus Arts.
Elementary School Career Education. (Focus Ser.). 32p. 1973. pap. 1.75 (ISBN 0-686-11048-X). Am Indus Arts.
Elementary School Industrial Arts. (Focus Ser.). 24p. 1973. pap. 1.50 (ISBN 0-686-11050-1). Am Indus Arts.
Environment. (Focus Ser.). 32p. 1973. pap. 1.75 (ISBN 0-686-11051-X). Am Indus Arts.
Federal Aid for Industrial Arts. 1966. 4.75 (ISBN 0-686-16548-9); pap. 3.75 (ISBN 0-686-16549-7). Am Indus Arts.
Gerbracht, Carl & Babcock, Robert J. Elementary School Industrial Arts. 1969. 8.95 (ISBN 0-02-816990-5). Glencoe.
Giachino, J. W. & Gallington, Ralph O. Course Construction in Industrial Arts, Vocational & Technical Education. 4th ed. 1977. text ed. 18.00 (ISBN 0-8269-4065-X). Am Technical.
Graduate Programs in Industrial Arts. (Monograph Ser.: No. 4). 90p. 1974. pap. 2.00 (ISBN 0-686-11052-8). Am Indus Arts.
Gropius, Walter. New Architecture & the Bauhaus. (Illus.). 1965. pap. 4.95 (ISBN 0-262-57006-8). MIT Pr.
Guidance in Industrial Arts Education for the 70's. 1971. pap. 1.00 (ISBN 0-686-00144-3). Am Indus Arts.
Gunther, Theresa C. Manipulative Participation in the Study of Elementary Industrial Arts. LC 70-176825. (Columbia University. Teachers College. Contributions to Education: No. 490). Repr. of 1931 ed. 17.50 (ISBN 0-404-55490-3). AMS Pr.
IA Education. 1968. pap. 1.00 (ISBN 0-686-00791-3). Am Indus Arts.
Individualized Instruction. (Focus Ser.). 32p. 1973. pap. 1.75 (ISBN 0-686-11054-4). Am Indus Arts.
Industrial Arts & the Environment. (Focus Ser.). 28p. 1973. pap. 1.50 (ISBN 0-686-11059-5). Am Indus Arts.
Industrial Arts Education: Purpose, Program, Facilities, Instruction & Supervision. 40p. 1973. pap. 1.50 (ISBN 0-686-11060-9). Am Indus Arts.
Industrial Arts in Career Education. (Focus Ser.). 28p. 1973. pap. 1.50 (ISBN 0-686-11063-3). Am Indus Arts.
Industrial Arts in the Middle School. 16p. 1971. pap. 1.50 (ISBN 0-686-11064-1). Am Indus Arts.
Industry & Career Education. (Focus Ser.). 28p. 1973. pap. 1.50 (ISBN 0-686-11065-X, A641-21370). Am Indus Arts.
Kidd, D. M. & Leighbody, G. B. Methods of Teaching Shop & Technical Subjects. LC 66-26821. 1968. pap. text ed. 6.60 (ISBN 0-8273-0360-2). Delmar.
Larson, Milton E. Teaching Related Subjects in Trade & Industrial & Technical Education. LC 72-80235. 1972. text ed. 19.95 (ISBN 0-675-09073-3). Merrill.
Middle School Industrial Arts. (Focus Ser.). 32p. 1973. pap. 1.75 (ISBN 0-686-11068-4). Am Indus Arts.
Miller, W. R. & Boyd, G. Teaching Elementary Industrial Arts. (Illus.). 224p. 1981. 9.28 (ISBN 0-87006-115-1). Goodheart.
Miller, W. R. & Boyd, T. Gardner. Teaching Elementary Industrial Arts. LC 70-117395. (Illus.). 1970. text ed. 9.28 (ISBN 0-87006-115-1). Goodheart.
Plastics. (Focus Ser.). 24p. 1973. pap. 1.75 (ISBN 0-686-11069-2). Am Indus Arts.
Potential Dropouts. (Focus Ser.). 16p. 1973. pap. 1.00 (ISBN 0-686-11070-6). Am Indus Arts.
Power Technology. (Focus Ser.). 24p. 1973. pap. 1.50 (ISBN 0-686-11071-4). Am Indus Arts.
Recommended Qualification, Duties, & Responsibilities for State & Local Supervisors. 16p. 1974. pap. 1.50 (ISBN 0-686-11079-X). Am Indus Arts.
Romano, Louis A. Manual & Industrial Education at Girard College 1831-1965: An Era in American Educational Experimentation. Cordasco, Fransecso, ed. LC 80-1075. (American Ethnic Groups Ser.). 1981. lib. bdg. 39.00x (ISBN 0-405-13450-9). Arno.
Silvius, G. Harold & Curry, Estell H. Teaching Successfully in Industrial Education. rev. ed. 1967. text ed. 16.09 (ISBN 0-87345-451-0). McKnight.
Stombaugh, Ray M. Survey of the Movements Culminating in Industrial Arts Education in Secondary Schools. LC 76-177821. (Columbia University. Teachers College. Contributions to Education: No. 670). Repr. of 1936 ed. 17.50 (ISBN 0-404-55670-1). AMS Pr.
Structure & Content Foundations for Curriculum Development. 1968. pap. 1.50 (ISBN 0-686-16551-9). Am Indus Arts.
Teacher Competencies for the Cybernated Age. (Monograph Ser.: No. 3). 30p. 1970. pap. 1.75 (ISBN 0-686-11072-2). Am Indus Arts.
Teacher Education Graduate Programs. (Focus Ser.). 20p. 1973. 1.00 (ISBN 0-686-11073-0). Am Indus Arts.
Teaching Resources. (Focus Ser.). 32p. 1973. pap. 1.75 (ISBN 0-686-11074-9). Am Indus Arts.
Technology. (Focus Ser.). 40p. 1973. pap. 2.00 (ISBN 0-686-11075-7). Am Indus Arts.
Technology in the Classroom. 32p. 1973. pap. 1.75 (ISBN 0-686-11076-5). Am Indus Arts.
Transportation. 24p. 1973. pap. 1.50 (ISBN 0-686-11077-3). Am Indus Arts.
Turner, David R. Teacher of Industrial Arts: Junior High School & High School. (Orig.). 1970. pap. 6.00 (ISBN 0-668-01307-9). Arco.
Undergraduate Teacher Education. 36p. 1973. pap. 1.75 (ISBN 0-686-11078-1). Am Indus Arts.
Willmott, John N. High School Boys Electing Industrial Arts. LC 75-177636. (Columbia University. Teachers College. Contributions to Education: No. 836). Repr. of 1941 ed. 17.50 (ISBN 0-404-55836-4). AMS Pr.
Zbar, Paul & Orne, Peter. Advanced Servicing Techniques, Vol. 1. (Illus.). 320p. (gr. 10-12). 1964. pap. 12.60x (ISBN 0-8104-0781-7); tchr's guide 2.25x (ISBN 0-8104-0365-X); wkbk. 2.25x (ISBN 0-8104-0381-1). Hayden.

INDUSTRIAL ARTS LIBRARIES
see also Technical Libraries

INDUSTRIAL ARTS SHOPS
see School Shops

INDUSTRIAL BANKING
see Loans, Personal

INDUSTRIAL BUILDINGS
see also Factories; Industrial Archaeology; Office Buildings
Bender, Richard. & Wilson, Forrest. Crack in the Rear View Mirror. 1973. 19.95x (ISBN 0-442-20686-0). Van Nos Reinhold.
Buildings for Industry. LC 72-142926. (An Architectural Record Book). (Illus.). ix, 309p. Repr. of 1957 ed. lib. bdg. 31.75x (ISBN 0-8371-5928-8, ARBI). Greenwood.
Delevoy, Robert L., et al. The Landscape of Industry. (Archives d'Architecture Moderne Ser.). Orig. Title: Le Paysage de l'Industrie Region du Nord-Wallonie-Ruhr. (Illus.). 175p. (Orig., Eng. & Fr.). 1975. pap. 25.00x (ISBN 0-8150-0926-7). Wittenborn.
Dietz, Albert G. & Cutler, Laurence S., eds. Industrialized Building Systems for Housing. 1971. 25.00x (ISBN 0-262-04034-4). MIT Pr.
Grenier, Lise & Wieser-Benedetti, Hans. Les Chateaux de l'Industrie: Lille, 1830-1930, Vol. 2. (Archives d'Architecture Moderne Ser.). (Illus.). 250p. (Fr.). 1979. pap. 27.50x (ISBN 0-8150-0920-8). Wittenborn.
Hudson, Kenneth. Industrial Archaeology of Southern England. LC 68-23822. (Illus.). 1968. 14.95x (ISBN 0-678-05606-4). Kelley.
Mills, E. Design for Industry. (Illus.). 1981. text ed. write for info (ISBN 0-408-00342-1). Butterworth.
Tandy, Clifford. The Landscape of Industry. LC 75-28033. 314p. 1975. 61.95 (ISBN 0-470-84440-X). Halsted Pr.

INDUSTRIAL BUYING
see Industrial Procurement

INDUSTRIAL CAPACITY
Increasing Industrial Productivity Through Source Data Automation. 1978. pap. 3.00 (ISBN 0-918734-20-7). Reymont.
Wein, Harold H. & Sreedharan, V. P. Optimal Staging & Phasing of Multi-Product Capacity. LC 68-64839. 1968. 14.50 (ISBN 0-87744-076-X). Mich St U Busn.

INDUSTRIAL CHEMISTRY
see Chemical Engineering; Chemistry, Technical

INDUSTRIAL COMBINATIONS
see Trusts, Industrial

INDUSTRIAL COMMUNICATION
see Communication in Management

INDUSTRIAL COSTS
see Costs, Industrial

INDUSTRIAL COUNCILS
see Works Councils

INDUSTRIAL COUNSELING
see Employee Counseling

INDUSTRIAL COURTS
see Labor Courts

INDUSTRIAL DESIGN
see Design, Industrial

INDUSTRIAL DESIGN COORDINATION
see also Letterheads; Trade-Marks
Burcaw, George E. The Saxon House. LC 79-65600. (GEM Books Ser.). (Illus.). 122p. (Orig.). 1980. pap. 7.95 (ISBN 0-89301-065-0). U Pr of Idaho.
Follis, John & Hammer, Dave. Architectural Signing & Graphics. (Illus.). 1979. 32.50 (ISBN 0-8230-7051-4, Whitney Lib). Watson-Guptill.
Lord, Kenniston W., Jr. Design of the Industrial Classroom. LC 76-46605. (Illus.). 1977. text ed. 10.95 (ISBN 0-201-04357-2). A-W.
Selame, Elinor & Selame, Joe. Developing a Corporate Identity: How to Stand Out in the Crowd. LC 74-23015. (Illus.). 224p. 1975. text ed. 19.95 (ISBN 0-912016-34-5). Lebhar Friedman.
Wolfendale, E., ed. Computer-Aided Design Techniques. (Illus.). 1971. 18.00 (ISBN 0-8088-0042-6). Davey.

INDUSTRIAL DESIGNERS
see also Design, Industrial

INDUSTRIAL DISCIPLINE
see Labor Discipline

INDUSTRIAL DISEASES
see Occupational Diseases

INDUSTRIAL DISTRICTS
Here are entered works on self-contained industrial areas within which utilities, transportation, and other general services are offered to a group of companies.
Conway, H. McKinley. Industrial Park Growth. LC 78-74931. 508p. 1978. pap. 39.00x (ISBN 0-910436-09-6). Conway Pubns.
Industrial Estates: A Tool for the Development of Backward Areas. 57p. 1973. 2.75 (ISBN 0-686-70981-0, APO32, APO). Unipub.
Japanese Industrial Estates for Small Business Development. 32p. 1973. 2.75 (ISBN 0-686-70982-9, APO37, APO). Unipub.
Wiebenson, Dora. Tony Garnier: The Cite Industrielle. LC 79-78051. (Planning & Cities Ser). (Illus.). 1969. 7.95 (ISBN 0-8076-0515-8). Braziller.

INDUSTRIAL DISTRICTS–WATER SUPPLY
see Water-Supply, Industrial

INDUSTRIAL DRAWING
see Mechanical Drawing

INDUSTRIAL EDUCATION
see Manual Training; Technical Education

INDUSTRIAL EFFICIENCY
see Efficiency, Industrial

INDUSTRIAL ELECTRONICS
see also Electronic Control

Chute, G. M. & Chute, R. D. Electronics in Industry. 4th ed. 1971. 19.95 (ISBN 0-07-010932-X, G); ans. for even-numbered problems 1.50 (ISBN 0-07-010933-8). McGraw.

Chute, George M. & Chute, Robert D. Electronics in Industry. 5th ed. (Illus.). 1979. text ed. 19.95 (ISBN 0-07-010934-6); instructor's manual 2.00 (ISBN 0-07-010935-4). McGraw.

Davis, Charles. Industrial Electronics: Design & Application. LC 72-92570. 1973. text ed. 23.95x (ISBN 0-675-09010-5); instructors manual 3.95 (ISBN 0-686-66861-8). Merrill.

Driscoll, Edward F. Industrial Electronics: Devices, Circuits & Applications. (Illus.). 420p. 1976. text ed. 21.33 (ISBN 0-8269-1625-2); tchr's. guide 2.00 (ISBN 0-685-75019-1). Am Technical.

Electronic Industries Association & Zbar, Paul B. Industrial Electronics: A Text-Lab Manual. 3rd ed. (Illus.). 320p. 1981. 12.95x (ISBN 0-07-072793-7, G). McGraw.

Haas, Alfred. Industrial Electronics: Principles & Practice. LC 78-178690. 10.95d (ISBN 0-8306-1583-0, 583). TAB Bks.

Kaganov, I. Industrial Applications of Electronics. 1966. 104.00 (ISBN 0-677-20590-2). Gordon.

Lane, Leonard C. Elementary Industrial Electronics, 2 vols. (Illus.). 1962. combined ed. 10.35 (ISBN 0-8104-0464-8); pap. text ed. 4.50 ea.; Vol. 1. pap. text ed. (ISBN 0-8104-0462-1); Vol. 2. pap. text ed. (ISBN 0-8104-0463-X). Hayden.

Miller. Industrial Electricity. (gr. 9-12). 1978. text ed. 15.92 (ISBN 0-87002-200-8); student guide 2.60 (ISBN 0-87002-244-X). Bennett IL.

Patrick, Dale R. & Fardo, Stephen W. Experimenting with Industrial Electronic Systems. LC 77-86464. 1978. 11.95 (ISBN 0-672-21472-5). Sams.

--Industrial Electronic Systems. LC 77-77402. 1978. 11.95 (ISBN 0-672-21453-9). Sams.

Rudman, Jack. Industrial Electronics. (Occupational Competency Examination Ser.: OCE-21). 14.95 (ISBN 0-8373-5771-3); pap. 9.95 (ISBN 0-8373-5721-7). Natl Learning.

Wilson, J. A. Industrial Electronics & Control. LC 78-7424. 528p. 1978. text ed. 20.95 (ISBN 0-574-21515-8, 13-4515). SRA.

--Industrial Electronics & Control. LC 78-7424. 528p. 1978. text ed. 20.95 (ISBN 0-574-21515-8, 13-4515). SRA.

INDUSTRIAL ENGINEERING

see also Automation; Costs, Industrial; Engineering Economy; Human Engineering; Industrial Relations; Industrial Statistics; Methods Engineering; Production Engineering; Psychology, Industrial; Quality Control; Standardization; Systems Engineering; Work Measurement

Ackoff, R. L. & Rivett, Patrick. Manager's Guide to Operations Research. LC 63-14115. (Managers Guide Ser.). 107p. 1963. 17.95 (ISBN 0-471-00335-2, Pub. by Wiley-Interscience). Wiley.

Adulbhan, P. & Tabucanon, M. T., eds. Decision Models for Industrial Systems Engineers & Managers. (Illus.). 467p. 1981. 70.00 (ISBN 0-08-027612-1). Pergamon.

Anthony, Robert N. Planning and Control Systems: A Framework for Analysis. LC 65-18724. 1965. 10.00x (ISBN 0-87584-047-7). Harvard Busn.

Babcock, George D. The Taylor System in Franklin Management. 2nd ed. (Management History Ser.: No. 7). (Illus.). 271p. 1972. Repr. of 1918 ed. 18.75 (ISBN 0-87960-008-X). Hive Pub.

Barnes, Ralph M. Industrial Engineering & Management Problems & Policies. (Management History Ser.: No. 62). (Illus.). 373p. 1973. Repr. of 1931 ed. 20.00 (ISBN 0-87960-066-7). Hive Pub.

Beightler, Charles S., et al. Foundations of Optimization. 2nd ed. (International Ser. in Industrial & Systems Engineering). (Illus.). 1979. text ed. 24.95 (ISBN 0-13-330332-2). P-H.

Blake, Ian F. Introduction to Applied Probability. LC 78-11360. 1979. text ed. 27.95 (ISBN 0-471-03210-7). Wiley.

Bodurtha, Frank T. Industrial Explosion Prevention & Protection. (Illus.). 1980. 21.50 (ISBN 0-07-006359-1). McGraw.

Bussey, Lynn E. The Economic Analysis of Industrial Projects. (International Ser. in Industrial & System Engineering). (Illus.). 1978. ref. 24.95 (ISBN 0-13-223388-6). P-H.

Cass, Eugene L. & Zimmer, Frederick G., eds. Man & Work in Society. 313p. (Orig.). 1975. 17.50 (ISBN 0-442-29359-3). Moffat Pub.

Cleland, David I. & Kocaoglu, Dundar F. Engineering Management. (Industrial Engineering & Management Science Ser.). (Illus.). 528p. 1981. text ed. 21.95 (ISBN 0-07-011316-5, C). McGraw.

Crawford, R. J. Plastics Engineering. (Illus.). 360p. 1981. 75.00 (ISBN 0-08-026262-7); pap. 25.00 (ISBN 0-08-026263-5). Pergamon.

Elonka, Stephen M. Standard Plant Operators Manual. 3rd ed. LC 79-22089. (Illus.). 416p. 1980. 22.95 (ISBN 0-07-019298-7). McGraw.

Enrick, Norbert L. Industrial Engineering Manual: For the Textile Industry. 2nd ed. LC 77-15461. 360p. 1978. lib. bdg. 17.50 (ISBN 0-88275-631-1). Krieger.

Ernst, R. Woerterbuch der Industriellen Technik, Vol. 1. (Ger. -Eng., Dictionary of Industrial Engineering). 1974. 80.00 (ISBN 3-87097-060-X, M-7001). French & Eur.

--Woerterbuch der Industriellen Technik, Vol. 2. (Eng. -Ger., Dictionary of Industrial Engineering). 1975. 80.00 (ISBN 3-87097-068-5, M-7000). French & Eur.

--Woerterbuch der Industriellen Technik, Vol. 3. (Ger. & Fr.). 1965. 64.00 (ISBN 3-87097-005-7, M-6999). French & Eur.

--Woerterbuch der Industriellen Technik, Vol. 4. (Fr. & Ger.). 1968. 56.00 (ISBN 3-87097-006-5, M-6998). French & Eur.

--Woerterbuch der Industriellen Technik, Vol. 5. 2nd ed. (Ger. & Span.). 1973. 56.00 (ISBN 3-87097-069-3, M-6997). French & Eur.

--Woerterbuch der Industriellen Technik, Vol. 7. (Port. & Ger.). 1963. 48.00 (ISBN 3-87097-009-X, M-6995). French & Eur.

--Woerterbuch der Industriellen Technik, Vol. 8. (Port. & Ger.). 1967. 48.00 (ISBN 3-87097-010-3, M-6994). French & Eur.

Gilbreth, Frank B. Primer of Scientific Management. 2nd ed. LC 72-9513. (Management History Ser.: No. 12). 116p. 1973. Repr. of 1914 ed. 10.00 (ISBN 0-87960-024-1). Hive Pub.

Going, Charles B. Principles of Industrial Engineering. LC 77-17900. (Management History Ser.: No. 45). 177p. Repr. of 1911 ed. 17.50 (ISBN 0-87960-049-7). Hive Pub.

Herbst, John A. & Sastry, K. V., eds. On-Stream Characterization & Control of Particulate Processes. 308p. 1981. pap. 15.00 (ISBN 0-939204-02-9, 78-19). Eng Found.

Hicks, Philip E., ed. Introduction to Industrial Engineering & Management Science. (Industrial Engineering & Management Science Ser.). 1977. text ed. 19.95 (ISBN 0-07-028767-8, C); solutions manual 4.95 (ISBN 0-07-028768-6). McGraw.

Instrumentation for the Process Industries 35th, College Station, 1980. Instrumentation Symposium for the Process Industries. 118p. 1980. pap. text ed. 15.00x (ISBN 0-87664-487-6). Instru Soc.

Instrumentation for the Process Industries, 34th, College Station, 1979. Instrumentation Symposium for the Process Industries. 118p. 1979. pap. text ed. 12.00x (ISBN 0-87664-446-9). Instru Soc.

Instrumentation Symposium for the Process Industries, College Station, TX, 1977. 1977. pap. text ed. 16.00x (ISBN 0-87664-398-5). Instru Soc.

Ireson, W. Grant & Grant, Eugene, eds. Handbook of Industrial Engineering & Management. 2nd ed. LC 71-139954. 1971. 35.00 (ISBN 0-13-378463-0). P-H.

Jensen, Paul A. & Barnes, J. Wesley. Network Flow Programming. LC 79-26939. (Industrial Engineering Ser.). 408p. 1980. text ed. 28.95 (ISBN 0-471-04471-7); sol. manual avail. (ISBN 0-471-06063-1). Wiley.

Knoeppel, C. E. Installing Efficiency Methods. LC 73-8507. (Management History Ser.: No. 49). (Illus.). 267p. 1973. Repr. of 1918 ed. 22.50 (ISBN 0-87960-052-7). Hive Pub.

Krick, Edward V. Methods Engineering. LC 62-8775. (Illus.). 530p. 1962. text ed. 31.95x (ISBN 0-471-50754-7). Wiley.

Langer, Steven, ed. Compensation of Industrial Engineering. 6th ed. 1981. 60.00 (ISBN 0-916506-63-0). Abbott Langer Assocs.

McDonough, Adrian M. & Garrett, Leonard J. Management Systems. 1965. 19.50x (ISBN 0-256-00321-1). Irwin.

McKillop, M. & McKillop, A. D. Efficiency Methods. LC 73-7983. (Management History Ser.: No. 51). (Illus.). 223p. 1973. Repr. of 1917 ed. 17.50 (ISBN 0-87960-054-3). Hive Pub.

Maynard, Harold B. Industrial Engineering Handbook. 3rd ed. 1971. 49.95 (ISBN 0-07-041084-4, P&RB). McGraw.

Morris, William T. Implementation Strategies for Industrial Engineers. LC 79-13941. (Grid Series in Industrial Engineering). 1979. pap. text ed. 16.00 (ISBN 0-88244-192-2). Grid Pub.

Mundel, Marvin E., ed. Productivity: A Series from Industrial Engineering. 1978. pap. text ed. 14.00 (ISBN 0-89806-004-4, 123). Am Inst Indus Eng.

Muther, Richard & Hales, Lee. Systematic Planning of Industrial Facilitities, 2 vols. LC 79-84256. Set. 80.00 (ISBN 0-933684-00-2). Vol 1, 1979. Vol. 2, 1980. Mgmt & Indus Res Pubns.

Rice, James O. & Rosaler, Bob. Standard Handbook for Plant Engineers. (Illus.). 1280p. 1982. 42.50 (ISBN 0-07-052160-3, P&RB). McGraw.

Rudman, Jack. Industrial Engineer. (Career Examination Ser.: C-380). (Cloth bdg. avail. on request). 10.00 (ISBN 0-8373-0380-X). Natl Learning.

--Methods Analyst. (Career Examination Ser.: C-499). (Cloth bdg. avail. on request). pap. 10.00 (ISBN 0-8373-0499-7). Natl Learning.

Ryland's Directory of the Engineering Industry 1977. 42nd ed. 1977. pap. 40.00x (ISBN 0-86108-001-7). Intl Pubns Serv.

Salvendy, Gavriel. Handbook of Industrial Engineering. 1400p. 1981. 52.95 (ISBN 0-471-05841-6, Pub. by Wiley-Interscience). Wiley.

Standards & Practices for Instrumentation Nineteen Eighty. 6th ed. 1056p. 1980. text ed. 120.00x (ISBN 0-87664-450-7). Instru Soc.

Starr, Martin K. Systems Management of Operations. (Illus.). 1971. ref. ed. 19.95 (ISBN 0-13-881524-0). P-H.

Steffy, Wilbert & Hawley, Leonard. The Industrial Engineering Plant Audit. (Illus.). 83p. 1977. 12.00 (ISBN 0-686-72875-0, AUDIT). Indus Dev Inst Sci.

Thompson, C. Bertrand. The Taylor System of Scientific Management. LC 73-6566. (Management History Ser.: No. 25). (Illus.). 183p. 1973. Repr. of 1917 ed. 22.50 (ISBN 0-87960-062-4). Hive Pub.

Thumann, Albert. Plant Engineers & Managers Guide to Energy Conservation. 1977. text ed. 22.50 (ISBN 0-442-28510-8). Van Nos Reinhold.

Trade & Technical Press, ed. Industrial Fasteners Handbook. (Illus.). 115.00x (ISBN 0-85461-062-6). Intl Ideas.

Trade & Technical Press Ltd, ed. Handbook of Instruments & Instrumentation. (Illus.). 105.00x (ISBN 0-85461-064-2). Intl Ideas.

Turner, Wayne C., et al. Introduction to Industrial & Systems Engineering. (P-H Ser. in Industrial & Systems Engineering). (Illus.). 1978. ref. ed. 19.95x (ISBN 0-13-484543-9). P-H.

ULI Industrial Council. Industrial Development Handbook. Spink, Frank H., Jr., ed. LC 75-37218. (Community Builders Handbook Ser.). (Illus.). 256p. 1975. 29.00 (ISBN 0-87420-562-X). Urban Land.

Vaughn, Richard C. Introduction to Industrial Engineering. 2nd ed. (Illus.). 1977. text ed. 21.95x (ISBN 0-8138-0832-4). Iowa St U Pr.

Vernon, Ivan R., ed. Introduction to Manufacturing Management, Vol. 1. LC 79-81737. (Manufacturing Management Ser). (Illus., Orig.). 1969. 12.50 (ISBN 0-87263-016-1). SME.

Vollmann, Thomas E. Operations Management: A Systems Model-Building Approach. LC 72-3463. 1973. text ed. 16.95 (ISBN 0-201-08177-6); instructor's manual 3.00 (ISBN 0-201-08178-4). A-W.

Zoltan, Roman, ed. Industrial Development & Industrial Policy. (Illus.). 427p. 1979. 45.00x (ISBN 963-05-2097-4). Intl Pubns Serv.

INDUSTRIAL ENGINEERING AS A PROFESSION

Kennaway, A. Engineers in Industry: A Management Guide for Engineers Who Wish to Perform Creatively in Industry. (Illus.). 130p. 1981. 24.00 (ISBN 0-08-026175-2); pap. 12.00 (ISBN 0-08-026174-4). Pergamon.

Langer, Steven. Compensation of Industrial Engineers. 5th ed. 1980. pap. 50.00 (ISBN 0-916506-50-9). Abbott Langer Assocs.

INDUSTRIAL EQUIPMENT

see also Industrial Archaeology; Industrial Equipment Leases; Office Equipment and Supplies; Replacement of Industrial Equipment

Appraisal of Machinery & Equipment. LC 73-97948. (ASA Monograph: No. 2). 1969. 5.00 (ISBN 0-937828-11-4). Am Soc Appraisers.

Corder, A. S. Maintenance Management Techniques. 1976. 22.50 (ISBN 0-07-084459-3, P&RB). McGraw.

Foster, Joseph W., 3rd, et al. Reliability, Availability & Maintainability: RAM. LC 80-81873. 272p. 1981. 39.95 (ISBN 0-930206-05-3). M-a Pr.

Franklin, Jerome D. & Jendro, David J. Equipment Management Manual, Pt. 2. (Illus.). 1977. pap. 10.00 (ISBN 0-917084-24-1). Am Public Works.

Gillies, M. T., ed. Water-Based Industrial Finishes: Recent Developments. LC 80-17520. (Chemical Technology Review: No. 167). 435p. 1980. 48.00 (ISBN 0-8155-0812-3). Noyes.

Hudson, Kenneth. Industrial Archaeology of Southern England. LC 68-23822. (Illus.). 1968. 14.95x (ISBN 0-678-05606-4). Kelley.

Industrial Furnaces - Design, Location & Equipment. (Eighty-Ninety Ser). 108p. 1974. pap. 3.75 (ISBN 0-685-44134-2, 86B). Natl Fire Prot.

Industrial Furnaces Using Special Processing Atmosphere. (Eighty-Ninety Ser). 148p. 1974. pap. 4.00 (ISBN 0-685-44135-0, 86C). Natl Fire Prot.

International Labour Office, Geneva. Audiovisual, Draughting, Office, Reproduction & Other Ancillary Equipment & Supplies: Equipment Planning Guide for Vocational & Technical Trading & Education Programmes. (No. 15). (Illus.). 279p. (Orig.). 1979. pap. 22.80 (ISBN 9-2210-2112-2). Intl Labour Office.

Kron, Joan & Slesin, Suzanne. High-Tech: The Industrial Source Book for the Home. (Illus.). 1978. 29.95 (ISBN 0-517-53262-X, Dist. by Crown). Potter.

Leff, Nathaniel H. Brazilian Capital Goods Industry, Nineteen Twenty-Nine to Nineteen Sixty Four. LC 68-21976. (Center for International Affairs Ser). 1968. 10.00x (ISBN 0-674-08090-4). Harvard U Pr.

Page, John S. Estimator's Equipment Installation Man-Hour Manual. 2nd ed. (Estimators Man-Hour Library). 280p. 1978. 25.00x (ISBN 0-87201-276-X). Gulf Pub.

Rudman, Jack. Equipment Specialist. (Career Examination Ser.: C-971). (Cloth bdg. avail. on request). pap. 8.00 (ISBN 0-8373-0971-9). Natl Learning.

Steel Wire & Products. (Industrial Equipment & Supplies Ser.). 175p. 1979. 295.00 (ISBN 0-686-31544-8). Busn Trend.

Switchgear & Switchboard Apparatus. (Industrial Equipment & Supplies). 1980. 350.00 (ISBN 0-686-31539-1). Busn Trend.

INDUSTRIAL EQUIPMENT-MAINTENANCE AND REPAIR

see Plant Maintenance

INDUSTRIAL EQUIPMENT LEASES

Anderson, Paul F. Financial Aspects of Industrial Leasing Decisions: Implications for Marketing. LC 77-75139. (MSU Business Studies Ser.). 1977. pap. 6.50 (ISBN 0-87744-145-6). Mich St U Busn.

Equipment Leasing, 1980. (Commercial Law & Practice Course Handbook Ser., 1979-80: Vol. 236). 1980. 25.00 (ISBN 0-686-50962-5, A4-3084). PLI.

Fabozzi, Frank J. Equipment Leasing: A Comprehensive Guide for Executives. 250p. 1981. 35.00 (ISBN 0-87094-264-6). Dow Jones-Irwin.

Fritch, Bruce E. & Reisman, Albert F., eds. Equipment Leasing & Leveraged Leasing. LC 80-83480. 1980. 75.00 (ISBN 0-685-85340-3, A1-1273). PLI.

Mead, H. T. & Mitchell, G. L. Plant Hire for Building & Construction. 1972. text ed. 16.95 (ISBN 0-408-00080-5). Butterworth.

Reisman, Albert F. & Fritch, Bruce E. Equipment Leasing - Leveraged Leasing. 2nd. ed. LC 80-83480. 1235p. 1980. text ed. 75.00 (ISBN 0-686-75083-7, A1-1273). PLI.

INDUSTRIAL ESPIONAGE

see Business Intelligence

INDUSTRIAL ESTATES

see Industrial Districts

INDUSTRIAL EXHIBITIONS

see Exhibitions

INDUSTRIAL FILMS

see Moving-Pictures in Industry

INDUSTRIAL GAMING

see Management Games

INDUSTRIAL HEALTH

see also Factory Laws and Legislation; Industrial Accidents; Occupational Diseases

Anton, Thomas. Occupational Safety & Health Management. 1979. text ed. 14.95 (ISBN 0-07-002106-6, C). McGraw.

Ashford, Nicholas A. Crisis in the Workplace: Occupational Disease & Injury - (a Report to the Ford Foundation) LC 75-28424. 1976. text ed. 27.50x (ISBN 0-262-01045-3). MIT Pr.

Atherley, Gordon R. Occupational Health & Safety Concepts; Chemical & Processing Hazards. (Popular Edition Ser.). (Illus.). 1978. 22.50x (ISBN 0-85334-848-0, Pub. by Applied Science). Burgess-Intl Ideas.

Bacow, Lawrence S. Bargaining for Job Safety & Health. 208p. 1980. text ed. 17.50x (ISBN 0-262-02152-8). MIT Pr.

Baetjer, Anna M. Women in Industry: Their Health & Efficiency. Stein, Leon, ed. LC 77-70480. (Work Ser.). (Illus.). 1977. Repr. of 1946 ed. lib. bdg. 25.00x (ISBN 0-405-10154-6). Arno.

Beaulieu, Harry J. & Buchan, Roy M. Quantitative Industrial Hygiene. 1981. lib. bdg. 17.50 (ISBN 0-8240-7180-8). Garland Pub.

Broadhurst, V. A. The Health & Safety at Work Act in Practice. 1978. 17.50 (ISBN 0-85501-159-9). Heyden.

Building Work. (Occupational Safety & Health Ser.: No. 42). 255p. 1981. pap. 16.00 (ISBN 92-2-101907-1, ILO 161, ILO). Unipub.

Burgess, William A. Recognition of Health Hazards in Industry: A Review of Materials & Processes. LC 81-2132. 376p. 1981. 28.00 (ISBN 0-471-06339-8, Pub. by Wiley-Interscience). Wiley.

Calabrese, E. J. Methodological Approaches to Deriving Environmental & Occupational Health Standards. 402p. 1978. 40.00 (ISBN 0-471-04544-6, Pub. by Wiley-Interscience). Wiley.

Clayton, George D. & Clayton, Florence E. Patty's Industrial Hygiene & Toxicology: General Principles, Vol. 1. 3rd rev. ed. LC 77-17515. 1978. 115.00 (ISBN 0-471-16046-6, Pub. by Wiley-Interscience). Wiley.

Corlett, E. N. & Richardson, J. Stress, Work Design & Productivity. (Wiley Ser. on Studies in Occupational Stress). 160p. 1982. 23.00 (ISBN 0-471-28044-5, Pub. by Wiley-Interscience). Wiley.

Cotlar, M. Improving the Health of Small Organizations. 1978. 13.95 (ISBN 0-87909-383-8). Reston.

Cralley, Lester & Cralley, Lewis. Patty's Industrial Hygiene & Toxicology: Theory & Rationale of Industrial Hygiene Practice, Vol. 3. LC 78-27102. 1979. 60.00 (ISBN 0-471-02698-0, Pub by Wiley-Interscience). Wiley.

Daum, Susan M. & Stellman, Jeanne M. Work Is Dangerous to Your Health: A Handbook of Health Hazards in the Workplace & What You Can Do About Them. pap. 3.95 (ISBN 0-394-71918-2, V-918, Vin). Random.

Davies, C. N. Health Conditions in the Ceramic Industry. 286p. 1970. 46.00 (ISBN 0-08-013347-9). Pergamon.

DeReamer, Russell. Modern Safety & Health Technology. LC 79-47487. 1980. 35.95 (ISBN 0-471-05729-0, Pub. by Wiley-Interscience). Wiley.

Egdahl, R. H. & Walsh, D. C., eds. Industry & HMOs: A Natural Alliance. (Springer Ser. on Industry & Health Care: Vol. 5). (Illus.). 1979. pap. 13.90 (ISBN 0-387-90366-6). Springer-Verlag.

Ffrench, G. Occupational Health. 198p. 1974. 17.50 (ISBN 0-85200-064-2). Herman Pub.

Follmann, Joseph F., Jr. The Economics of Industrial Health: History, Theory, & Practice. new ed. 1978. 27.50 (ISBN 0-8144-5444-5). Am Mgmt.

Forssman, S. & Coppee, G. H. Occupational Health Problems of Young Workers. 2nd ed. (Occupational Safety & Health Ser.: No. 26). 1975. 5.70 (ISBN 92-2-101051-1). Intl Labour Office.

Goldbeck, W. B. A Business Perspective on Industry & Health Care. LC 77-7982. (Springer Series on Industry & Health Care: Vol. 2). 1978. pap. 13.90 (ISBN 0-387-90298-8). Springer-Verlag.

--Industry's Voice in Health Policy. (Springer Ser. on Industry & Health Care: Vol. 7). 1979. pap. 12.60 (ISBN 0-387-90429-8). Springer-Verlag.

Goldsmith, Frank & Kerr, Lorin E. Occupational Safety & Health: The Control & Prevention of Work-Related Hazards. 1982. in prep. (ISBN 0-89885-092-4). Human Sci Pr.

Griscom, John H. The Sanitary Condition of the Laboring Population of New York, with Suggestions for Its Imporvement. LC 75-125742. (American Environmental Studies). Repr. of 1845 ed. 8.00 (ISBN 0-405-02667-6). Arno.

Guide to Safety & Health in Dock Work. x, 287p. 1976. 18.55 (ISBN 92-2-101081-3). Intl Labour Office.

Hart, A. W. & Hart, A. W. Industrial Hygiene. (Illus.). 400p. 1976. 19.95x (ISBN 0-13-461202-7). P-H.

Health Action: How to Improve Health & Contain Costs Strategies for Employers, Chambers of Commerce, Community Organizations, & Concerned Citizens. LC 78-65948. 1978. pap. 5.00 (ISBN 0-89834-003-9, 7025). Chamber Comm US.

Institute for Power System. Handbook of Industrial Safety & Health. 1979. 99.00x (ISBN 0-686-65621-0). State Mutual Bks.

International Labour Office, Geneva. Guide to Health & Hygiene in Agricultural Work. (Illus.). 317p. 1979. pap. 15.70 (ISBN 92-2-101974-8). Intl Labour Office.

Jacobson, Walter O. Compliance with Occupational Safety & Health Act: State Programs for State & Local Agencies in the United States. 1974. 5.00 (ISBN 0-87373-287-1, PR 741). Intl Personnel Mgmt.

Johnson. MORT Safety Assurance Systems. (Occupational Safety & Health Ser.: Vol. 4). 544p. 1980. 35.00 (ISBN 0-8247-6897-3). Dekker.

Jones, Alan, et al. Occupational Hygiene: A Practical Guide. 200p. 1981. 24.50x (ISBN 0-7099-1404-0, Pub. by Croom Helm Ltd England). Biblio Dist.

Jones, W. T. Health & Safety at Work Handbook: Basic Volume, 3 vols. 250p. 1975. 10.00x (ISBN 0-86010-014-6, Pub. by Graham & Trotman England); Supplement 1 & 2. lib. bdg. 11.00x (ISBN 0-86010-071-5); Set. pap. 21.00x (ISBN 0-686-64054-3). State Mutual Bk.

Kanh, Robert L. Work & Health. (Series in Organizational Assessment & Change). 160p. 1981. 15.95 (ISBN 0-471-05749-5, Pub. by Wiley-Interscience). Wiley.

Kearns, Joseph L. Stress in Industry. 1977. 8.50x (ISBN 0-85078-054-3); pap. 5.00x (ISBN 0-85078-055-1). Technomic.

Larson, L. A., ed. Fitness, Health, & Work Capacity. 1974. 17.95 (ISBN 0-02-359750-X). Macmillan.

Linch, A. L. Biological Monitoring for Industrial Chemical Exposure Control. LC 73-88623. (Uniscience Ser). 188p. 1974. 52.95 (ISBN 0-87819-048-1). CRC Pr.

Lusterman, Seymour. Industry Roles in Health Care. (Report Ser: No. 610). 130p. (Orig.). 1974. pap. 20.00 (ISBN 0-8237-0033-X). Conference Bd.

Lusterman, Seymour, ed. Health Care Issues for Industry. (Report Ser: No. 637). 1974. pap. 17.50 (ISBN 0-8237-0032-1). Conference Bd.

McCready, Benjamin W. On the Influence of Trades, Professions & Occupations in the United States in the Production of Disease. LC 78-180583. (Medicine & Society in America). 144p. 1972. Repr. of 1943 ed. 12.00x (ISBN 0-405-03960-3). Arno.

McLean, A., ed. Occupational Stress. (Illus.). 128p. 1974. 13.50 (ISBN 0-398-03067-7). C C Thomas.

Martin, Rollard A. Occupational Disability: Causes, Prediction, Prevention. (Illus.). 220p. 1975. 19.75 (ISBN 0-398-03224-6). C C Thomas.

Miller, Marshall L., ed. Occupational Health & Safety Regulation. LC 78-60849. 154p. 1980. pap. text ed. 22.50 (ISBN 0-86587-078-0). Gov Insts.

National Research & Appraisal Co. & Sharninghouse, Jane, eds. OSHA for Machine Tools. 1000p. 1980. 95.00 (ISBN 0-89692-101-8). Equipment Guide.

Noble, David. Facts & Observations Relative to the Influence on Manufactures Upon Health & Life. (The Development of Industrial Society Ser.). 81p. 1971. Repr. of 1843 ed. 13.00x (ISBN 0-7165-1563-6, Pub. by Irish Academic Pr). Biblio Dist.

Occupational Exposure to Airborne Substances Harmful to Health. 44p. 1981. pap. 6.50 (ISBN 92-2-102442-3, ILO 152, ILO). Unipub.

Olishifski, Julian B., ed. Fundamentals of Industrial Hygiene. LC 78-58307. 1300p. 1979. 35.00 (ISBN 0-87912-081-9, 15127); instructors guide o.p. 1.05 (ISBN 0-87912-080-0, 151-13). Natl Safety Coun.

Optimisation of the Working Environment: New Trends. (Occupational Safety & Health Ser.: No. 43). 421p. 1981. pap. 22.25 (ISBN 92-2-001905-1, ILO 162, ILO). Unipub.

Page, Robert C. Occupational Health & Mantalent Development. LC 62-9730. 722p. 1968. 10.00 (ISBN 0-87527-064-6). Green.

Peterson, Jack E. Industrial Health. (Illus.). 1977. ref. ed. 26.95 (ISBN 0-13-459552-1). P-H.

Poulton, E. C. The Environment at Work. (Illus.). 176p. 1979. 14.00 (ISBN 0-398-03848-1). C C Thomas.

Reinberg, A., et al, eds. Night & Shift Work-Biological & Social Aspects: Proceedings of the Vth International Symposium on Night and Shift Work-Scientific Committee on Shift Work of the Permanent Commission & International Association on Occupational Health (PCIAIH, Rouen, 12-16 May 1980. (Illus.). 516p. 1981. 80.00 (ISBN 0-08-025516-7). Pergamon.

Role of Medical Inspection of Labour. 1968. 4.55 (ISBN 92-2-100004-4). Intl Labour Office.

Ross, W. Donald. Practical Psychiatry for Industrial Physicians. 404p. 1956. photocopy ed. spiral 39.75 (ISBN 0-398-01613-5). C C Thomas.

Ruch, Walter E. & Held, Bruce. Respiratory Protection - OSHA & the Small Businessman. LC 75-7955. (Illus.). 1975. 15.00 (ISBN 0-250-40101-0). Ann Arbor Science.

Rudman, Jack. Industrial Hygienist. (Career Examination Ser.: C-381). (Cloth bdg. avail. on request). pap. 8.00 (ISBN 0-8373-0381-8). Natl Learning.

Safety & Health in Shipbuilding & Ship Repairing: ILO Code of Practice. 2nd ed. 1978. 15.70 (ISBN 92-2-101199-2). Intl Labour Office.

Sataloff, Joseph & Michael, Paul. Hearing Conservation. (Illus.). 376p. 1973. 21.75 (ISBN 0-398-02822-2). C C Thomas.

Schilling, R. S., ed. Occupational Health Practice. 2nd ed. LC 80-41044. (Illus.). 512p. 1981. text ed. 49.00 (ISBN 0-407-33701-6). Butterworth.

Shepard, William P. The Physician in Industry. Stein, Leon, ed. LC 77-70532. (Work Ser.). 1977. Repr. of 1961 ed. lib. bdg. 22.00x (ISBN 0-405-10200-3). Arno.

Silverman, Leslie. Particle Size Analysis in Industrial Hygiene. (Atomic Energy Commission Monographs). 315p. 1971. 40.00 (ISBN 0-12-643750-5). Acad Pr.

Slaney, Brenda, ed. Occupational Health Nursing. 177p. 1980. 22.00x (ISBN 0-85664-779-9, Pub. by Croom Helm Ltd England). Biblio Dist.

Stellman, Jeanne M. & Daum, Susan M. Work Is Dangerous to Your Health: A Handbook of Health Hazards in the Workplace & What You Can Do About Them. LC 72-12386. 1973. pap. 4.95 (ISBN 0-394-71918-2). Pantheon.

Taylor, W., ed. The Vibration Syndrome. 1974. 37.00 (ISBN 0-12-684760-6). Acad Pr.

Trade & Technical Press Editors. Handbook of Industrial Safety & Health. 1980. 108.00 (ISBN 0-85461-075-8, Pub by Trade & Tech England). Renouf.

Trevethick, R. A. Environmental & Industrial Health Hazards: A Practical Guide. 2nd ed. 1976. pap. 28.50x (ISBN 0-433-32655-7). Intl Ideas.

Walton, W. H., ed. Carbon Monoxide, Industry & Performance. 1976. pap. text ed. 27.50 (ISBN 0-08-019966-6). Pergamon.

WHO Study Group. Geneva, 1974. Early Detection of Health Impairment in Occupational Exposure to Health Hazards: Report. (Technical Report Ser.: No. 571). (Also avail. in French & Spanish). 1975. pap. 3.50 (ISBN 92-4-120571-7). World Health.

Wilder, Charles S. Selected Health Characteristics by Occupation: United States, 1975-1976. Cox, Klaudia, ed. (Ser. 10: No. 133). 1979. pap. text ed. 1.75 (ISBN 0-8406-0174-3). Natl Ctr Health Stats.

INDUSTRIAL HEALTH–GREAT BRITAIN

Collis, Edgar L. & Greenwood, Major. The Health of the Industrial Worker. Stein, Leon, ed. LC 77-70489. (Work Ser.). (Illus.). 1977. Repr. of 1921 ed. lib. bdg. 29.00x (ISBN 0-405-10161-9). Arno.

INDUSTRIAL HEALTH ENGINEERING

see Industrial Health

INDUSTRIAL HOUSEKEEPING

Educational Research Council of America. Executive Housekeeper. rev. ed. Marchak, John P., ed. (Real People at Work Ser: B). (Illus.). 1976. pap. text ed. 2.25 (ISBN 0-89247-011-9). Changing Times.

Feldman, Edwin B. Housekeeping Handbook for Institutions, Business & Industry. rev. ed. LC 75-83312. 502p. 1979. 19.95 (ISBN 0-8119-0072-X). Fell.

Sack, Thomas. Complete Guide to Building & Plant Maintenance. 2nd ed. LC 71-126828. (Illus.). 1971. 32.95 (ISBN 0-13-160101-6). P-H.

INDUSTRIAL INSURANCE

see Insurance, Industrial

INDUSTRIAL LAWS AND LEGISLATION

Here are entered works of a comprehensive character which deal with laws and legislation regulating industry. Works on the theory of state regulation of industry are entered under Industry and State; Laissez-Faire.

see also Competition, Unfair; Factory Laws and Legislation; Freedom of Movement; Labor Laws and Legislation; Occupations, Dangerous; Patent Laws and Legislation; Trade-Marks; Trade Regulation

Adams, Henry C. Two Essays: Relation of the State to Industrial Action & Economics & Jurisprudence. Dorfman, Joseph, ed. LC 75-76510. (Reprints of Economic Classics). Repr. of 1954 ed. 15.00x (ISBN 0-678-00494-3). Kelley.

Allen, Henry J. & Gompers, Samuel. Party of the Third Part: The Story of the Kansas Industrial Relations Court. LC 74-156401. (American Labor Ser., No. 2). 1971. Repr. of 1920 ed. 16.00 (ISBN 0-405-02911-X). Arno.

Bilek, Arthur J., et al. Legal Aspects of Private Security. LC 79-55202. 287p. 1981. text ed. 15.95 (ISBN 0-87084-488-1). Anderson Pub Co.

Higgins, George C. Voluntarism in Organized Labor in the United States, 1930-40. LC 76-89737. (American Labor: From Conspiracy to Collective Bargaining Ser., No. 1). 1969. Repr. of 1944 ed. 9.00 (ISBN 0-405-02126-7). Arno.

Janner, Greville. Janner's Compendium of Employment Law. 759p. 1979. text ed. 45.50x (ISBN 0-220-66363-7, Pub. by Busn Bks England). Renouf.

Keeton, G. W. & Frommel, S. N., eds. British Industry & European Law. xiv, 191p. 1974. text ed. 17.50x (ISBN 0-8377-0727-7). Rothman.

Lane, Robert. The Regulation of Businessmen: Social Conditions of Government Economic Control. LC 66-14606. 1966. Repr. of 1954 ed. 14.50 (ISBN 0-208-00515-3, Archon). Shoe String.

Leshin, Geraldine. EEO Law: Impact on Fringe Benefits. Hinman, Faye, ed. (Policy & Practice Publication). 1979. 6.00 (ISBN 0-89215-102-1). U Cal LA Indus Rel.

Macavoy, Paul W. Regulated Industries. 1979. 14.95 (ISBN 0-393-01280-8); pap. 4.95x (ISBN 0-393-95094-8). Norton.

Martin, Donald L. & Schwartz, Warren C., eds. Deregulating American Industry: Legal & Economic Problems. LC 77-5273. (Illus.). 1977. 15.95 (ISBN 0-669-01603-9). Lexington Bks.

Mitchell, Ewan. The Employer's Guide to the Law on Health, Safety & Welfare at Work. 2nd ed. 471p. 1977. text ed. 36.75x (ISBN 0-220-66341-6, Pub. by Busn Bks England). Renouf.

Pendlebury, N. Industrial Law. 1980. 11.00x (ISBN 0-905435-05-2, Pub. by DP Pubns). State Mutual Bk.

Quirk, Paul J. Industry Influence in Federal Regulatory Agencies. LC 80-8571. 264p. 1981. 19.50x (ISBN 0-691-09388-1); pap. 5.95x (ISBN 0-691-02823-0). Princeton U Pr.

Rollinson, Mark. Small Issue Industrial Development Bonds. 1978. 39.50 (ISBN 0-914470-07-8). Capital Pub Corp.

Sen, B. A Diplomat's Handbook of International Law & Practice. 2nd ed. 1979. lib. bdg. 66.00 (ISBN 9-0247-2142-3, Pub. by Martinus Nijhoff Netherlands). Kluwer Boston.

Stokes, M. Conquering Government Regulation: A Business Guide. 288p. 1981. 24.95 (ISBN 0-07-061640-X, P&RB). McGraw.

Wachter, Michael L. & Wachter, Susan M., eds. Toward a New U. S. Industrial Policy. LC 81-10312. 568p. 1982. 30.00x (ISBN 0-8122-7819-4). U of Pa Pr.

Weiss, Leonard & Strickland, Allyn. Regulation: A Case Approach. (Illus.). 1976. pap. text ed. 8.95 (ISBN 0-07-069097-9, C). McGraw.

INDUSTRIAL LAWS AND LEGISLATION–DICTIONARIES–POLYGLOT

Becker, V. Legal Dictionary for Trade & Industry. 600p. 1980. 150.00x (ISBN 0-7121-5489-2, Pub. by Macdonald & Evans). State Mutual Bk.

INDUSTRIAL LOCATION

see Industries, Location of

INDUSTRIAL MAINTENANCE

see Plant Maintenance

INDUSTRIAL MANAGEMENT

see also Assembly-Line Methods; Big Business; Business; Business Consultants; Business Intelligence; Communication in Management; Controllership; Corporate Planning; Delegation of Authority; Efficiency, Industrial; Employment Stabilization; Executives; Executives, Training of; Factory Management; Industries, Location of; Industries, Size of; Industrial Health; Industrial Organization; Industrial Procurement; Industrial Relations; Industrial Sociology; Labor Productivity; Management Audit; Management Games; Managerial Economics; Marketing; Marketing Management; Materials Management; New Business Enterprises; Office Management; Personnel Management; Production Control; Production Management; Production Standards; Sales Management; Shift Systems; Shipment of Goods; Small Business–Management; Technological Innovations; Welfare Work in Industry; Works Councils

Aaron, B. & Wedderburn, K. W., eds. Industrial Conflict. LC 72-94300. 415p. 1972. 36.50x (ISBN 0-8448-0156-9). Crane-Russak Co.

Accounting Symposium, Ohio State Univ., 1972. Behavioral Experiments in Accounting: Papers, Critiques, Discussion, & Commentary. Burns, Thomas J., ed. (Illus.). 533p. 1972. pap. 8.50x (ISBN 0-87776-307-0, AA7). Ohio St U Admin Sci.

Ackerman, Robert W. The Social Challenge to Business. 384p. 1976. 18.50x (ISBN 0-674-81190-9). Harvard U Pr.

Ackoff, R. L. Concept of Corporate Planning. LC 74-100318. 158p. 1969. 16.50 (ISBN 0-471-00290-9, Pub. by Wiley-Interscience). Wiley.

Adams, Loyce. Managerial Psychology. 1965. 9.75 (ISBN 0-8158-0034-7). Chris Mass.

Adulbhan, P. & Tabucanon, M. T., eds. Decision Models for Industrial Systems Engineers & Managers. (Illus.). 467p. 1981. 70.00 (ISBN 0-08-027612-1). Pergamon.

Alford, Leon P. The Laws of Management Applied to Manufacturing. (Management History Ser.: No. 23). 272p. 1974. Repr. of 1928 ed. 20.00 (ISBN 0-87960-035-7). Hive Pub.

American Economic Association, ed. Readings in the Social Control of Industry. LC 72-14175. (Essay Index Reprint Ser.). Repr. of 1942 ed. 25.00 (ISBN 0-518-10001-4). Arno.

American Management Association. New Products - New Profits. Marting, Elizabeth, ed. LC 64-12772. (Illus.). 1964. 12.95 (ISBN 0-8144-5088-1). Am Mgmt.

American Society for Engineering Education. Papers on Scientific Management. LC 75-6637. (Management History Ser.: No. 72). Orig. Title: American Society for the Promotion of Engineering Education Proceedings. (Illus.). 228p. 1975. Repr. of 1912 ed. 17.50 (ISBN 0-87960-110-8). Hive Pub.

Ammer, Dean S. Manufacturing Management & Control. (Illus.). 1968. pap. 8.95 (ISBN 0-13-555839-5). P-H.

Anshen, Melvin, ed. Managing the Socially Responsible Corporation. LC 73-13364. (Studies of the Modern Corporation). (Illus.). 288p. 1974. 15.95 (ISBN 0-02-900680-5). Macmillan.

Anshen, Melvin & Bach, George Leland, eds. Management & Corporations 1985. LC 75-4938. 253p. 1975. Repr. of 1960 ed. lib. bdg. 15.00 (ISBN 0-8371-8051-1, ANMC). Greenwood.

Ansoff, H. Igor. Corporate Strategy: An Analytic Approach to Business Policy for Growth & Expansion. 1965. 18.50 (ISBN 0-07-002111-2, P&RB). McGraw.

Anyon, George J. Entrepreneurial Dimensions of Management. 1973. text ed. 9.95 (ISBN 0-915180-12-X). Harrowood Bks.

Appley, Lawrence A. Management in Action. 3rd ed. 1956. 9.75 (ISBN 0-8144-5001-6). Am Mgmt.

Balfour, Campbell, ed. Participation in Industry. 217p. 1973. 15.00x (ISBN 0-87471-429-X). Rowman.

Bates, James & Parkinson, J. R. Business Economics. 2nd ed. LC 72-10187. 1969. lib. bdg. 12.50x (ISBN 0-678-06268-4). Kelley.

Batten, J. D. Developing a Tough-Minded Climate for Results. LC 65-16483. 1965. 14.95 (ISBN 0-8144-5101-2). Am Mgmt.

Batty, J., et al. Industrial Administration & Management. 4th ed. (Illus.). 592p. 1979. pap. 21.50x (ISBN 0-7121-0954-4, Pub. by Macdonald & Evans England). Intl Ideas.

Becker, Charles H. Plant Manager's Handbook. 1974. 32.95 (ISBN 0-13-680694-5). P-H.

Bedworth, David D. Industrial Systems: Planning, Analysis, Control. 510p. 1973. 28.95 (ISBN 0-8260-0867-4). Wiley.

Berriman, A. E., et al. Industrial Administration: A Series of Lectures. Chandler, Alfred D., ed. LC 79-7546. (History of Management Thought & Practice Ser.). 1980. Repr. of 1920 ed. lib. bdg. 18.00x (ISBN 0-405-12330-2). Arno.

Bethel, L., et al. Industrial Organization & Management. 5th ed. 1971. 19.50 (ISBN 0-07-005060-0, C); solutions manual 3.95 (ISBN 0-07-005061-9). McGraw.

Betts, P. W. Supervisory Studies. 1968. 9.50x (ISBN 0-7121-1929-9). Intl Pubns Serv.

Beyer, Robert & Trawicki, Donald J. Profitability Accounting: For Planning & Control. 2nd ed. (Illus.). 400p. 1972. 32.50 (ISBN 0-471-06523-4, 06961). Ronald Pr.

Bibliography on Productivity Measurement & Analysis. 75p. 1981. pap. 13.25 (ISBN 92-833-1478-6, AP0106, APO). Unipub.

Bittel, Lester R. Improving Supervisory Performance. 1976. 13.95 (ISBN 0-07-005451-7, G); course management 5.30 (ISBN 0-07-005453-3); performance portfolio 5.70 (ISBN 0-07-005452-5). McGraw.

--The Nine Master Keys of Management. (Illus.). 256p. 1972. 16.50 (ISBN 0-07-005476-2, P&RB). McGraw.

Black, Homer A., et al. Accounting in Business Decisions: Theory, Method, & Use. 3rd ed. (Illus.). 752p. 1973. 21.00x (ISBN 0-13-001545-8); accounting forms 4.95x (ISBN 0-13-001644-6); practice case 2.95x (ISBN 0-13-001230-0). P-H.

Blake, Robert R. & Mouton, Jane S. Building a Dynamic Corporation Through Grid Organization Development. Schein, Edgar, et al, eds. (Organization Development Ser). 1969. pap. text ed. 6.50 (ISBN 0-201-00612-X). A-W.

--Corporate Excellence Through Grid Organization Development. (Illus.). 392p. 1968. 11.95 (ISBN 0-87201-331-6). Gulf Pub.

--The New Managerial Grid. 342p. 1978. 12.95 (ISBN 0-87201-473-8). Gulf Pub.

Bond, Floyd A., ed. Technological Change & Economic Growth: Proceedings, C.I.C. Conference, 1964. (Michigan Business Papers: No. 41). 1965. pap. 1.00 (ISBN 0-87712-090-0). U Mich Busn Div Res.

Bower, Marvin. Will to Manage: Corporate Success Through Programmed Management. 1966. 18.50 (ISBN 0-07-006735-X, P&RB). McGraw.

Boyce, Timothy J. Fair Representation, the NLRB, & the Courts. LC 78-65072. (Labor Relations & Public Policy Ser.: No. 18). 1978. pap. 8.95 (ISBN 0-89546-007-6). Indus Res Unit-Wharton.

Brayman, Harold. Corporative Management in a World of Politics: The Public, Political & Governmental Problems of Business. 1967. 18.50 (ISBN 0-07-007350-3, P&RB). McGraw.

Bright, James R. Automation & Management. 1958. 30.00 (ISBN 0-08-022293-5). Pergamon.

Broadwell, William E., Jr. The Management of Work: A Workbook. (Business Ser). (Illus.). 1971. 8.95 (ISBN 0-201-00672-3). A-W.

Brown, Wilfred. Organization. (Illus.). 400p. 1971. 18.75x (ISBN 0-435-85103-9). Intl Pubns Serv.

Burns, Tom & Stalker, G. M. Management of Innovation. (Orig.). 1961. pap. 12.95x (ISBN 0-422-72050-X, 6, Pub. by Tavistock England). Methuen Inc.

Bursk, Edward C. & Blodgett, Timothy B., eds. Developing Executive Leaders. LC 70-160023. (Illus.). 1971. 12.50x (ISBN 0-674-19975-8). Harvard U Pr.

Bursk, Edward C. & Chapman, John F., eds. New Decision-Making Tools for Managers: Mathematical Programing As an Aid in the Solving of Business Problems. LC 63-11416. (Illus.). 1963. 20.00x (ISBN 0-674-61050-4). Harvard U Pr.

--New Decision Making Tools for Managers. 1971. pap. 1.25 (ISBN 0-451-61017-2, MY1017, Ment). NAL.

Business Management, Two. viii, 52p. 1975. pap. 3.50x (ISBN 0-900976-27-6, Pub. by Inst Marine Eng). Intl Schol Bk Serv.

Carlson, Dick. Modern Management. (Orig.). 1967. pap. text ed. 3.95 (ISBN 0-87252-006-4). Tinnon-Brown.

--Modern Management: Principles & Practices. 184p. 1962. 3.50x (ISBN 0-686-14670-0). OECD.

Chandler, Alfred D., Jr. Strategy & Structure: Chapters in the History of the American Industrial Enterprise. 1962. pap. 5.95x (ISBN 0-262-53009-0). MIT Pr.

Charnes, A. & Cooper, W. W., eds. Management Science Approaches to Manpower Planning & Organizational Design. (TIMS Studies in the Management Sciences Ser: Vol. 8). 1978. 29.50 (ISBN 0-444-85120-8, North-Holland). Elsevier.

Chemical Engineering Magazine. Skills Vital to Successful Managers. 1979. 24.50 (ISBN 0-07-010737-8, P&RB). McGraw.

Cleland, David I. & Kocaoglu, Dundar F. Engineering Management. (Industrial Engineering & Management Science Ser.). (Illus.). 528p. 1981. text ed. 21.95 (ISBN 0-07-011316-5, C). McGraw.

Cochran, Thomas C. Two Hundred Years of American Business. LC 76-9670. 1977. 15.00x (ISBN 0-465-08814-7). Basic.

Cody, John, et al, eds. Policies for Industrial Progress in Developing Countries. (World Bank Research Publications Ser.). (Illus.). 326p. 1980. text ed. 22.00 (ISBN 0-19-520176-0); pap. text ed. 7.95x (ISBN 0-19-520177-9). Oxford U Pr.

Collins, Orvis F., et al. Enterprising Man. LC 64-63821. 1964. 7.50 (ISBN 0-87744-027-1). Mich St U Busn.

Conference on Scientific Management, 1st. Addresses & Discussions at the Conference on Scientific Management: Proceedings. LC 72-90030. (Management History Ser.: No. 9). 399p. Repr. of 1912 ed. 22.50 (ISBN 0-87960-014-4). Hive Pub.

Conway, H. McKinley & Liston, Linda L. Industrial Facilities Planning. LC 76-49711. 330p. 1976. pap. 35.00x (ISBN 0-910436-05-3). Conway Pubns.

Cooke, Morris L. & Murray, Philip. Organized Labor & Production: Next Steps in Industrial Democracy. LC 73-156409. (American Labor Ser., No. 2). 1971. Repr. of 1946 ed. 16.00 (ISBN 0-405-02918-7). Arno.

Cornell, Alexander H. The Decision-Maker's Handbook. (Illus.). 1980. 13.95 (ISBN 0-13-198218-4, Spec); pap. 7.95 (ISBN 0-13-198200-1, Spec). P-H.

Cornuelle, Richard. De-Managing America: The Final Revolution. 1976. pap. 2.45 (ISBN 0-394-72099-7, 72099, Vin). Random.

Costello, Timothy & Zalkind, S. Psychology in Administration: Research Orientation Text with Integrated Readings. (Illus.). 1963. text ed. 21.00 (ISBN 0-13-732867-2). P-H.

Coventry, W. & Burstiner, I. Management: A Basic Handbook. 1977. 12.95 (ISBN 0-13-549188-6, Spec); pap. 5.95 (ISBN 0-13-549170-3, Spec). P-H.

Crozier, Michel. Bureaucratic Phenomenon. LC 63-20916. 1967. pap. 5.50 (ISBN 0-226-12166-6, P280, Phoen). U of Chicago Pr.

Dale, E. Management: Theory & Practice. (Management Ser.). (Illus.). 1978. text ed. 17.95 (ISBN 0-07-015188-1, C); instructors manual 6.95 (ISBN 0-07-015189-X). McGraw.

Dale, Ernest. Management: Theory & Practice. 3rd ed. (Management Ser.). (Illus.). 816p. 1973. text ed. 14.95 (ISBN 0-07-015165-2, C); pap. text ed. 10.95 (ISBN 0-07-015162-8); instructors manual 4.95 (ISBN 0-07-015166-0). McGraw.

--Readings in Management: Landmarks & New Frontiers. 3rd ed. (Management Ser.). (Illus.). 544p. 1975. text ed. 14.95 (ISBN 0-07-015184-9, C). McGraw.

Davis, Keith. The Challenge of Business. Kothman, Thomas H., ed. (Illus.). 544p. 1975. text ed. 15.95 (ISBN 0-07-015527-5, C); instructor's guide 2.95 (ISBN 0-07-063125-5); transparency masters 15.00 (ISBN 0-07-015529-1); student guide 5.95 (ISBN 0-07-015528-3). McGraw.

Dean, Joel. Managerial Economics. 1951. ref. ed. 19.95 (ISBN 0-13-549972-0). P-H.

Dennison, Henry S. Organization Engineering. LC 73-169665. (Management History Ser.: No. 4). 214p. 1972. Repr. of 1931 ed. 17.50 (ISBN 0-87960-001-2). Hive Pub.

Devinat, Paul. International Labour Office Studies & Reports. Chandler, Alfred D., ed. LC 79-7540. (Scientific Management in Europe: Economic Conditions No. 17,History of Management Thought & Practice Ser.: Economic Conditions, No. 17). 1980. Repr. of 1927 ed. lib. bdg. 22.00x (ISBN 0-405-12325-6). Arno.

Dively, George S. Power of Professional Management. LC 77-151052. 1971. 12.95 (ISBN 0-8144-5188-8). Am Mgmt.

Doktor, Robert H. & Moses, Michael A. Managerial Insights: Analysis, Decisions, & Implementation. (Illus.). 432p. 1973. pap. text ed. 12.95 (ISBN 0-13-550103-2). P-H.

Drucker, Peter F. Effective Executive. LC 67-11341. 1967. 10.95 (ISBN 0-06-031825-2, HarpT). Har-Row.

--Managing for Results. LC 64-12670. 1964. 11.95 (ISBN 0-06-031830-9, HarpT). Har-Row.

--Practice of Management. LC 54-8946. 1954. 11.95 (ISBN 0-06-011095-3, HarpT). Har-Row.

Dudick, Thomas S. Profile for Profitability: Using Cost Control & Profitability Analysis. LC 72-4353. (Systems & Controls for Financial Management Ser.). 253p. 1972. 33.50 (ISBN 0-471-22362-X, Pub. by Wiley-Interscience). Wiley.

Eilon, S. & King, J. R. Industrial Scheduling Abstracts: 1950-1966. 1967. 11.75 (ISBN 0-934454-50-7). Lubrecht & Cramer.

Elbourne, Edward T. Fundamentals of Industrial Administration: An Introduction to Industrial Organisation Management & Economics. Chandler, Alfred D., ed. LC 79-7544. (History of Management Thought & Practice Ser.). 1980. Repr. of 1934 ed. lib. bdg. 48.00x (ISBN 0-405-12328-0). Arno.

Evans, H. A. Cost-Keeping & Scientific Management. (Management History Ser.: No. 79). (Illus.). 252p. 1975. Repr. of 1911 ed. 18.75 (ISBN 0-87960-116-7). Hive Pub.

Ewing, David W., ed. Long-Range Planning for Management. 3rd rev. ed. LC 70-157905. (Illus.). 480p. 1972. 17.50x (ISBN 0-06-011217-4, HarpT). Har-Row.

Fenner, T. W. & Everett, J. L. Inventor's Handbook. 1968. 17.00 (ISBN 0-8206-0070-9). Chem Pub.

Firestone, Frederic N. Marginal Aspects of Management Practices. LC 59-63586. 1960. 4.50 (ISBN 0-87744-044-1). Mich St U Busn.

Florence, P. Sargant. The Logic of British & American Industry: A Realistic Analysis of Economic Structure & Government. 3rd ed. 1972. 22.75x (ISBN 0-7100-7155-8). Routledge & Kegan.

Flumiani, Carlo M. Managing the Large Corporation in a World of Conflicting & Antagonistic Forces. (Illus.). 1977. 47.15 (ISBN 0-89266-039-2). Am Classical Coll Pr.

Folts, Franklin E. Introduction to Industrial Management. LC 77-22994. 686p. 1979. Repr. of 1963 ed. 27.50 (ISBN 0-88275-566-8). Krieger.

Forrester, Jay W. Industrial Dynamics. (Illus.). 1961. pap. 19.95x (ISBN 0-262-56001-1). MIT Pr.

Franklin, B. A. The Industrial Executive. LC 73-10346. (Management History Ser.: No. 39). 153p. Repr. of 1926 ed. 12.50 (ISBN 0-87960-043-8). Hive Pub.

Friedman, Georges. Industrial Society: Emergence of the Human Problems of Automation. Stein, Leon, ed. LC 77-70497. (Work Ser.). 1977. Repr. of 1955 ed. lib. bdg. 28.00x (ISBN 0-405-10167-8). Arno.

Gantt, H. L. Industrial Leadership. LC 72-9507. (Management History Ser.: No. 42). (Illus.). 141p. 1973. Repr. of 1916 ed. 17.50 (ISBN 0-87960-044-6). Hive Pub.

--Organizing for Work. LC 72-9508. (Management History Ser.: No. 43). (Illus.). 118p. 1973. Repr. of 1919 ed. 17.50 (ISBN 0-87960-046-2). Hive Pub.

Gantt, H. L., et al. How Scientific Management Is Applied. LC 72-9521. (Management History Ser.: No. 26). (Illus.). 128p. 1973. Repr. of 1911 ed. 15.00 (ISBN 0-87960-033-0). Hive Pub.

Garrett, Leonard J. & Silver, Milton. Production Management Analysis. 2nd ed. LC 73-7831. (Harbrace Business & Economics Ser.). 1973. text ed. 21.95 (ISBN 0-15-571991-2, HC); solutions manual avail. (ISBN 0-15-571992-0, HC). HarBraceJ.

Gellerman, Saul W. Management by Motivation. LC 68-12699. (Illus.). 1968. 17.95 (ISBN 0-8144-5157-8). Am Mgmt.

--Uses of Psychology in Management. 1970. pap. 1.95 (ISBN 0-02-008220-7, Collier). Macmillan.

General Electric Company. Responsibilities of Business Leadership: Talks Presented at the Leadership Conference. (Management History Ser.: No. 75). (Illus.). 113p. 1975. Repr. of 1954 ed. 15.00 (ISBN 0-87960-112-4). Hive Pub.

George, Claude S., Jr. Management for Business & Industry. Orig. Title: Management in Industry. 1970. text ed. 20.95 (ISBN 0-13-548578-9). P-H.

George, Kenneth D. & Joll, Caroline. Industrial Organisation: Competition, Growth & Structural Change. 3rd ed. (Illus.). 336p. 1981. text ed. 35.00x (ISBN 0-04-338095-6); pap. text ed. 16.50x (ISBN 0-04-338096-4). Allen Unwin.

Gilbreth, Frank B. Primer of Scientific Management. 2nd ed. LC 72-9513. (Management History Ser.: No. 12). 116p. 1973. Repr. of 1914 ed. 10.00 (ISBN 0-87960-024-1). Hive Pub.

Gilbreth, Frank B., et al. Scientific Management Course. LC 79-92317. (Management History Ser.: No. 77). 180p. 1975. Repr. of 1912 ed. 20.00 (ISBN 0-87960-114-0). Hive Pub.

Gilbreth, Lillian M. The Psychology of Management. LC 72-9514. (Management History Ser.: No. 22). ix, 344p. 1973. Repr. of 1914 ed. 20.00 (ISBN 0-87960-026-8). Hive Pub.

Gilmer, B. V & Deci, Edward L. Industrial & Organizational Psychology. 4th ed. (M-H Series in Psychology). (Illus.). 1976. text ed. 17.95 (ISBN 0-07-023289-X, C); instructor's manual 4.95 (ISBN 0-07-023290-3). McGraw.

Gladwin, Thomas N. Environment, Planning & the Multinational Corporation. Altman, Edward I. & Walter, Ingo, eds. LC 76-10400. (Contemporary Studies in Economic & Financial Analysis: Vol. 8). 350p. 1977. lib. bdg. 30.00 (ISBN 0-89232-014-1). Jai Pr.

Glasser, Joseph. Fundamentals of Applied Industrial Management. (Illus.). 15.00 (ISBN 0-8283-1542-6). Branden.

Gould, Jay M. Technical Elite. LC 66-15566. (Illus.). 1966. 12.50x (ISBN 0-678-00131-6). Kelley.

Gouldner, Alvin W. Patterns of Industrial Bureaucracy: A Case Study of Modern Factory Administration. 1954. 12.95 (ISBN 0-02-912730-0); pap. text ed. 6.95 (ISBN 0-02-912740-8). Free Pr.

Gutsch, Roland W., et al, eds. Proceedings of the Sixth Internet Congress 1979. 1793p. 1980. pap. 165.00x (ISBN 3-18-419061-7, Pub. by VDI Verlag Germany). Renouf.

Hammeed, K. A. Enterprise: Industrial Entrepreneurship in Development. 1975. 15.00x (ISBN 0-8039-9935-6). Sage.

Haner, F. T. & Ford, James C. Contemporary Management. LC 72-95931. 1973. text ed. 17.95 (ISBN 0-675-08987-5). Merrill.

Hanika, F. New Thinking in Management. 1966. 5.25x (ISBN 0-434-90706-5). Intl Pubns Serv.

Harrell, Thomas W. Managers' Performance & Personality. 1961. pap. 3.75 (ISBN 0-538-07580-5). SW Pub.

Harrigan, Kathryn R. Strategies for Declining Businesses. LC 79-48032. 448p. 1980. 34.95x (ISBN 0-669-03641-2). Lexington Bks.

Hartness, James. The Human Factor in Works Management. LC 73-10284. (Management History Ser.: No. 46). 168p. Repr. of 1912 ed. 12.50 (ISBN 0-87960-047-0). Hive Pub.

Hastings, N. A. & Mello, J. M. Decision Networks. 196p. 1978. 43.75 (ISBN 0-471-99531-2, Pub. by Wiley-Interscience). Wiley.

Hattery, Lowell H. Executive Control & Data Processing. 1959. 3.95 (ISBN 0-685-06099-3). Anderson Kramer.

Heyel, Carl, ed. The VNR Concise Guide to Industrial Management. (Van Nostrand Reinhold Concise Management Ser.). 1979. pap. text ed. 7.95 (ISBN 0-442-23403-1). Van Nos Reinhold.

Hicks, H., et al. Modern Business Management. (Illus.). 400p. 1974. text ed. 15.95 (ISBN 0-07-028756-2, C); tchr's manual 5.95 (ISBN 0-07-028758-9); study guide 8.50 (ISBN 0-07-028757-0). McGraw.

Hicks, Herbert G., et al. Dimensions of American Business. 1975. text ed. 8.50 (ISBN 0-07-028717-1, C). McGraw.

Ho, Y. C. & Mitter, S., eds. Directions in Large-Scale Systems: Many-Person Optimization & Decentralized Control. 434p. 1976. 45.00 (ISBN 0-306-30937-8, Plenum Pr). Plenum Pub.

Hobson, John A. Rationalisation & Unemployment. Repr. of 1930 ed. lib. bdg. 12.50 (ISBN 0-8414-5088-9). Folcroft.

Holden, P. E., et al. Top Management. (Illus.). 1968. text ed. 13.95 (ISBN 0-07-029545-X, C). McGraw.

Hoxie, Robert F. Scientific Management & Labor. LC 66-21677. Repr. of 1915 ed. 15.00x (ISBN 0-678-00169-3). Kelley.

Hughes, Charles L. Goal Setting. LC 65-26864. 1965. 12.95 (ISBN 0-8144-5116-0). Am Mgmt.

Hunt, Edward E., ed. Scientific Management Since Taylor: A Collection of Authoritative Papers. LC 72-80579. (Management History Ser.: No. 2). 284p. 1972. Repr. of 1924 ed. 18.50 (ISBN 0-87960-010-1). Hive Pub.
Hussey, David. Inflation & Business Policy. LC 76-7065. (Business Strategy & Planning Ser.). (Illus.). 1976. text ed. 22.00x (ISBN 0-582-45073-X). Longman.
Industrial Relations Workshop Seminars, Inc. How to Manage with a Union, 2 vols. LC 68-13936. 1969. Set. 49.50 (ISBN 0-685-92653-2). Indus Rel Wkshp.
--Managing Without a Union: Private & Public Sectors. LC 77-88035. 1978. 39.50 (ISBN 0-685-92652-4). Indus Rel Wkshp.
International Labour Conference, 67th Session & International Labour Office. Termination of Employment at the Initiative of the Employer, Report VIII, No. 2. 147p. (Orig.). 1981. pap. 12.85 (ISBN 92-2-102412-1). Intl Labour Office.
Irwin, Manley, et al. Selected Structure & Allocation Problems in the Regulated Industries. LC 69-63030. 1969. pap. 2.00 (ISBN 0-87744-083-2). Mich St U Busn.
Jensen, Ronald & Cherrington, David J. The Business Management Laboratory: Participants' Manual. rev. ed. 1979. pap. 9.95x (ISBN 0-256-01953-3). Business Pubns.
Johnson, Richard A., et al. Management, Systems & Society: An Introduction. LC 75-13447. 576p. 1976. text ed. 18.95 (ISBN 0-87620-540-6); tchrs manual free (ISBN 0-87620-539-2). Goodyear.
--Theory & Management of Systems. 3rd ed. (Management Ser). (Illus.). 544p. 1973. text ed. 17.95 (ISBN 0-07-032634-7, C); instructor's manual 4.95 (ISBN 0-07-032635-5). McGraw.
Kappel, Frederick R. Vitality in a Business Enterprise. 1960. 12.95 (ISBN 0-07-033290-8, P&RB). McGraw.
Karpik, Lucien, ed. Organization & Environment. LC 76-22902. (Sage Studies in International Sociology: Vol. 12). 345p. 1978. 22.50 (ISBN 0-8039-9981-X); pap. 9.95x (ISBN 0-8039-9982-8). Sage.
Katz, Robert L. Management of the Total Enterprise: Cases & Concepts in Business Policy. 1970. ref. ed. 24.95 (ISBN 0-13-548933-4). P-H.
Kellogg, Marion S. Putting Management Theories to Work. LC 68-5675. 286p. 1968. 14.95 (ISBN 0-87201-463-0). Gulf Pub.
Kelly, Anthony & Harris, M. J. Management of Industrial Maintenance. (Illus.). 1978. 19.95 (ISBN 0-408-00297-2). Butterworth.
Keyes, Carl. Management Guide to Systems & Procedures. 1967. 6.95 (ISBN 0-685-20553-3). Tinnon-Brown.
King, Bert, et al, eds. Managerial Control & Organizational Democracy. LC 77-13200. (Scripta Ser. in Personality & Social Psychology). 1978. 22.95 (ISBN 0-470-99323-5). Halsted Pr.
Klatt, Lawrence A., et al. Human Resources Management: A Behavioral Systems Approach. 1978. 19.95x (ISBN 0-256-02045-0). Irwin.
Laufer, Arthur C. Operations Management. 1975. 12.50 (ISBN 0-538-07070-6). SW Pub.
Lee, John & Chandler, Alfred D., eds. Pitman's Dictionary of Industrial Administration: A Comprehensive Encyclopedia of the Organization, Administration, & Management of Modern Industry, 2 vols. LC 79-7552. (History of Management Thought & Practice Ser.). 1980. Repr. of 1928 ed. Set. lib. bdg. 125.00x (ISBN 0-405-12336-1); lib. bdg. 62.50x ea. Vol. 1 (ISBN 0-405-12337-X). Vol. 2 (ISBN 0-405-12338-8). Arno.
Lemke, Bernhard C. & Edwards, J. Don. Administrative Control & Executive Action. 2nd ed. LC 71-161870. 564p. 1971. text ed. 21.95 (ISBN 0-675-09792-4). Merrill.
Lenin, Vladimir I. El Control Obrero y la Nacionalicacion de la Industria. 254p. (Span.). 1978. 3.00 (ISBN 0-8285-1369-4, Pub. by Progress Pubs Russia). Imported Pubns.
Likert, Rensis. New Patterns of Management. 1961. 16.95 (ISBN 0-07-037850-9, C). McGraw.
Lincoln, James F. A New Approach to Industrial Economics. 1961. 4.50 (ISBN 0-8159-6301-7). Devin.
Lindsay, Franklin A. New Techniques for Management Decision Making. 1963. pap. 2.95 (ISBN 0-07-037893-2, SP). McGraw.
Long, William A. & Seo, K. K. Management in Japan & India: With Reference to the United States. LC 77-7824. (Praeger Special Studies). 1977. text ed. 34.50 (ISBN 0-03-022651-1). Praeger.
Lorsch, Jay W. & Lawrence, Paul R. Managing Group & Intergroup Relations. 1972. pap. 11.95x (ISBN 0-256-00264-9). Irwin.
Lundgren, Earl F. Organizational Management. LC 73-21940. (Illus.). 512p. 1974. text ed. 21.50 scp (ISBN 0-06-385355-8, HarpC). Har-Row.
McGregor, Douglas. Professional Manager. 1967. 14.95 (ISBN 0-07-045093-5, C). McGraw.
Mackay, R. J., ed. Business & Science. LC 75-6722. (Management History Ser.: No. 74). (Illus.). 311p. 1975. Repr. of 1932 ed. 20.00 (ISBN 0-87960-111-6). Hive Pub.
McNichols, Thomas J. Executive Policy & Strategic Planning. (Illus.). 192p. 1977. pap. 8.95 (ISBN 0-07-045683-6, C). McGraw.
Mancuso, Joseph. Managing Technology Products. LC 74-82598. 1975. Vol. 1. 8.75x (ISBN 0-89006-045-2). Artech Hse.
Martin, Jane, ed. Milestones in Development: A Cumulative Index to Industrial Development, Site Selection Handbook & Related Publications Covering a Quarter-Century of Professional Contribution. 1981. 75.00x (ISBN 0-910436-16-9). Conway Pubns.
Massie, Joseph L., et al. Management: Analysis, Concepts, Cases. 3rd ed. (Illus.). 800p. 1975. ref. ed. 21.95 (ISBN 0-13-548412-X). P-H.
Matteson, Michael T., ed. Management Classics. Ivancevich, John M. LC 76-42891. (Illus.). 1977. pap. text ed. 11.95 (ISBN 0-87620-587-2); objective tests free (ISBN 0-87620-581-3). Goodyear.
Mauser, Ferdinand F. & Schwartz, David J. American Business: An Introduction. 4th ed. (Illus.). 1978. text ed. 18.95 (ISBN 0-15-502282-2, HC); instructor's guide avail. (ISBN 0-15-502283-0); student guide 7.95 (ISBN 0-15-502284-9); manual of student assignments 7.95 (ISBN 0-15-502285-7); key to manual avail. (ISBN 0-15-502286-5); test pkgs.forms A & B avail. (ISBN 0-15-502290-3); keys to tests A & B avail. (ISBN 0-15-502291-1); instructor's tests forms A & B avail. (ISBN 0-15-502294-6); transparency masters avail. (ISBN 0-15-502287-3). HarBraceJ.
Maynard, Harold B. Handbook of Business Administration. 1967. 49.50 (ISBN 0-07-041090-9, P&RB). McGraw.
--Top Management Handbook. 1960. 49.95 (ISBN 0-07-041085-2, P&RB). McGraw.
Merkle, Judith A. Management & Ideology: The Legacy of the International Scientific Management Movement. LC 78-59447. 300p. 1980. 20.00x (ISBN 0-520-03737-5). U of Cal Pr.
Miller, David W. & Starr, Martin K. Executive Decisions & Operations Research. 2nd ed. 1969. ref. ed. 21.00 (ISBN 0-13-294538-X). P-H.
Mitchell, Don G. The Challenges Facing Management. LC 63-13488. (Moskowitz Lectures). 1963. 5.00x (ISBN 0-8147-0314-3). NYU Pr.
Mockler, Robert J. The Business Management Process. LC 73-79531. (Illus.). 700p. 1973. text ed. 12.00x (ISBN 0-88319-011-7). Austin Pr.
Moore, Carl L. Profitable Applications of the Break Even System. (Illus.). 1971. 32.95 (ISBN 0-13-726646-4, Busn). P-H.
Negandhi, Anant R. & Prasad, Benjamin S. The Frightening Angels: A Study of U. S. Multinationals in Developing Nations. rev. ed. LC 74-30491. (Illus.). 220p. 1975. 20.00x (ISBN 0-87338-169-6). Kent St U Pr.
Newman, William H. Process of Management: The Concepts, Behavior & Practice. 4th ed. 1977. pap. 21.95 (ISBN 0-13-723429-5); study guide casebook 8.95 (ISBN 0-13-723411-2). P-H.
Norman, R. G. & Bahiri, S. Productivity Measurements & Incentives. 20.00x (ISBN 0-408-70308-3). Transatlantic.
Nystrom, Harry. Creativity & Innovation. LC 78-8594. 125p. 1979. 29.75 (ISBN 0-471-99682-3, Pub. by Wiley-Interscience). Wiley.
Odiorne, George S. How Managers Make Things Happen. (Illus.). 1961. pap. 3.95 (ISBN 0-13-400531-7, Reward). P-H.
Optner, Stanford L. Systems Analysis for Business Management. 3rd ed. (Illus.). 400p. 1974. ref. ed. 18.95 (ISBN 0-13-881276-4). P-H.
Organization of Industrial Fire Loss Prevention. (Zero Ser). 1974. pap. 2.00 (ISBN 0-685-58138-1, 6). Natl Fire Prot.
Organizational Development: Theory & Practice. 1977. 10.50 (ISBN 0-8144-6513-7). Am Mgmt.
Pacifico, Carl R. & Witwer, Daniel B. Practical Industrial Management: Insights for Managers. LC 80-23190. 375p. 1981. 21.95 (ISBN 0-471-08190-6, Pub. by Wiley-Interscience). Wiley.
Parkhurst, Frederic A. Applied Methods of Scientific Management. (Management History Ser.: No. 55). 350p. Repr. of 1917 ed. 23.00 (ISBN 0-686-76979-1). Hive Pub.
Parkinson, C. Northcote, et al. Industrial Disruption. LC 73-77701. 181p. 6.95x (ISBN 0-900537-10-8). Hippocrene Bks.
Pascarella, Perry. Industry Week's Guide to Tomorrow's Executive: Humanagement in the Future Corporation. 320p. 1980. text ed. 16.95 (ISBN 0-442-23122-9). Van Nos Reinhold.
Plant, Arnold, ed. Some Modern Business Problems: A Series of Studies. facs. ed. LC 67-23260. (Essay Index Reprint Ser). 1937. 18.00 (ISBN 0-8369-0792-2). Arno.
Prasad, S. Benjamin, ed. Management in International Perspective. LC 67-10930. (Orig.). 1967. pap. text ed. 6.95x (ISBN 0-89197-289-7). Irvington.
Profitability Analysis for Managerial & Engineering Decisions. 215p. 1980. pap. 23.50x (ISBN 0-686-75486-7, AP0105, APO). Unipub.
Rice, Craig S. Power Secrets of Managing People. LC 79-21649. 249p. 1980. 18.95 (ISBN 0-13-686931-9). P-H.
Richards, Max D. & Nielander, William A. Readings in Management. 4th ed. 1974. text ed. 8.95 (ISBN 0-538-07960-6). SW Pub.
Richman, Barry M. & Copen, Melvyn R. International Management & Economic Development. LC 77-24758. 692p. 1978. Repr. of 1972 ed. lib. bdg. 24.00 (ISBN 0-88275-597-8). Krieger.
Riggs, James L., et al. Industrial Organization & Management. 6th ed. (Illus.). 1979. text ed. 21.00 (ISBN 0-07-052854-3, C); solutions manual 5.95 (ISBN 0-07-052855-1). McGraw.
Ritti, R. Richard. The Engineer & the Industrial Corporation. LC 73-133913. 1971. 17.50x (ISBN 0-231-03373-7). Columbia U Pr.
Roberts, Edward B., ed. Managerial Applications of System Dynamics. LC 77-26952. (MIT Press Wright-Allen Ser. in System Dynamics). 1978. 45.00x (ISBN 0-262-18088-X); pap. text ed. 17.50x (ISBN 0-262-68035-1). MIT Pr.
Roscoe, Edwin S., et al. Organization for Production. 5th ed. 1971. 19.95x (ISBN 0-256-00470-6). Irwin.
Rosegger, Gerhard. The Economics of Production & Innovation: An Industrial Perspective. (Illus.). 1980. 41.00 (ISBN 0-08-024047-X); pap. 17.50 (ISBN 0-08-024046-1). Pergamon.
Ross, Joel E. Managing Productivity. (Illus.). 192p. 1977. text ed. 16.95 (ISBN 0-87909-459-1). Reston.
Roy, Robert H. The Administrative Process. 248p. 1958. 15.00x (ISBN 0-8018-0566-X); pap. 2.95x (ISBN 0-8018-0567-8). Johns Hopkins.
Rubey, Harry, et al. Engineer & Professional Management. 3rd ed. (Illus.). 1971. pap. 4.50x (ISBN 0-8138-0695-X). Iowa St U Pr.
Rudge, Fred. The Key to Increased Productivity. LC 76-56968. 242p. 1977. pap. 24.50 (ISBN 0-87179-244-3). BNA.
Rudman, Jack. Director of Industrial Development. (Career Examination Ser.: C-2857). (Cloth bdg. avail. on request). 1980. pap. 14.00 (ISBN 0-8373-2857-8). Natl Learning.
--Industrial Consultant. (Career Examination Ser.: C-2771). (Cloth bdg. avail. on request). 1980. pap. 12.00 (ISBN 0-8373-2771-7). Natl Learning.
--Industrial Development Assistant. (Career Examination Ser.: C-2848). (Cloth bdg. avail. on request). 1980. pap. 12.00 (ISBN 0-8373-2848-9). Natl Learning.
--Industrial Training Supervisor. (Career Examination Ser.: C-2839). (Cloth bdg. avail. on request). 1980. pap. 12.00 (ISBN 0-8373-2839-X). Natl Learning.
Running a Professional Corporation. 7.50 (ISBN 0-914770-02-0). Littoral Develop.
Rush, Harold M. Organization Development: A Reconnaissance. (Report Ser: No. 605). 74p. (Orig.). 1973. pap. 15.00 (ISBN 0-8237-0043-7). Conference Bd.
Saaty, Thomas L. Decision Making for Leaders: The Analytical Hierarchy Process for Decisions in a Complex Work. (Industrial Management Ser.). (Illus.). 180p. 1981. text ed. 22.00 (ISBN 0-686-72072-5). Lifetime Learn.
Salvendy, Gavriel. Prediction & Developement of Industrial Work Performance. LC 73-5914. 351p. 1973. 27.75 (ISBN 0-471-75080-8, Pub. by Wiley). Krieger.
Sampson, Robert C. Managing the Managers: A Realistic Approach to Applying the Behavioral Sciences. 1965. 19.95 (ISBN 0-07-054509-X, P&RB). McGraw.
Sathe, Vijay. Controller Involvement in Management. (Illus.). 192p. 1982. text ed. 22.95 (ISBN 0-13-171660-3). P-H.
Schellenberger, Robert E. & Boseman, Glenn F. Policy Formulation & Strategy Management. LC 77-2758. (Wiley Series in Management & Administration). 1978. text ed. 23.95 (ISBN 0-471-75903-1); tchrs. manual o.p. avail. (ISBN 0-471-03725-7). Wiley.
Schlaifer, Robert. Probability & Statistics for Business Decisions. 1959. text ed. 22.95 (ISBN 0-07-055309-2, C); tchr's manual 5.95 (ISBN 0-07-055313-0); student's manual 7.95 (ISBN 0-07-055314-9). McGraw.
Schleh, Edward C. Management by Results: The Dynamics of Profitable Management. (Illus.). 1961. 18.50 (ISBN 0-07-055320-3, P&RB). McGraw.
--The Management Tactician: Executive Tactics for Getting Results. (Illus.). 288p. 1974. 13.95 (ISBN 0-07-055293-2, P&RB). McGraw.
Schoen, Sterling H. & Hilgert, Raymond L. Cases in Collective Bargaining & Industrial Relations: A Decisional Approach. 3rd ed. 1978. pap. 11.95x (ISBN 0-256-02002-7). Irwin.
Sen, Amartya K. Choice of Techniques: An Aspect of the Theory of Planned Economic Development. 3rd ed. LC 68-3220. 1968. 12.50x (ISBN 0-678-06266-8). Kelley.
Sethi, Narendra K. Management Perspectives. (Illus.). 311p. 1972. 11.00x (ISBN 0-8002-1695-4). Intl Pubns Serv.
Shepard, George H. The Application of Efficiency Principles. LC 73-10363. (Management History Ser.: No. 59). 378p. Repr. of 1917 ed. 22.50 (ISBN 0-87960-061-6). Hive Pub.
Sherman, Harvey. It All Depends: A Pragmatic Approach to Organization. LC 66-25021. 218p. 1966. pap. 6.00x (ISBN 0-8173-4833-6). U of Ala Pr.
Shubin, John A. Business Management. rev. ed. (Orig.). 1957. pap. 3.95 (ISBN 0-06-460092-0, CO 92, COS). Har-Row.
Siegel, Laurence & Lane, Irving M. Psychology in Industrial Organizations. 3rd ed. 1974. 19.95x (ISBN 0-256-01563-5). Irwin.
Silver, Gerald A. Introduction to Business. (Illus.). 1978. text ed. 15.95 (ISBN 0-07-057495-2, C); study guide 5.95 (ISBN 0-07-057497-9); transparency masters 15.00 (ISBN 0-07-057499-5); instructor's manual 4.95 (ISBN 0-07-057496-0). McGraw.
Simon, Herbert A. The New Science of Management Decision. rev. ed. LC 76-40414. 1977. ref. ed. 15.95x (ISBN 0-13-616144-8); pap. text ed. 11.95 (ISBN 0-13-616136-7). P-H.
Sittig, M. Practical Techniques for Saving Energy in the Chemical, Petroleum & Metals Industries. LC 77-71855. (Energy Technology Review No. 12; Chemical Technology Review: No. 90). (Illus.). 1977. 48.00 (ISBN 0-8155-0657-0). Noyes.
Skene Smith, N. Introductory Atlas: Economics, Commerce & Administration, a Visual Analysis, Vol. 1. 1966. 14.50 (ISBN 0-08-010966-7). Pergamon.
Slichter, Sumner H. Union Policies & Industrial Management. LC 68-23330. (Institute of Economics of the Brookings Institution Publications: No. 85). 1968. Repr. of 1941 ed. lib. bdg. 27.50x (ISBN 0-8371-0231-6, SLIM). Greenwood.
Slichter, Sumner H., et al. The Impact of Collective Bargaining on Management. 1960. 18.95 (ISBN 0-8157-7984-4). Brookings.
Sloma, Richard S. No-Nonsense Management: A General Manager's Primer. LC 77-80559. 1977. 12.95 (ISBN 0-02-929220-4). Free Pr.
Solomons, David. Divisional Performance: Measurement & Control. 1968. pap. 11.50x (ISBN 0-256-00529-X). Irwin.
Stanford, Melvin J. Management Policy. (Illus.). 1979. ref. ed. 21.95 (ISBN 0-13-548974-1). P-H.
Starr, Martin K. & Stein, Irving. The Practice of Management Science. (Illus.). 208p. 1976. 13.95 (ISBN 0-13-693630-X). P-H.
Staudt, Thomas A. & Taylor, Donald. Managerial Introduction to Marketing. 3rd ed. (Illus.). 576p. 1976. 20.95x (ISBN 0-13-550186-5). P-H.
Steffy, Wilbert, et al. Management Control Systems for Small & Medium-Sized Firms. (Illus.). 84p. 1980. 12.00 (ISBN 0-686-72878-5, MGT C). Indus Dev Inst Sci.
Stein, Leon & Taft, Philip, eds. Management of Workers: Selected Arguments, 1917-1956. LC 72-156430. (American Labor Ser., No. 2). 1971. 17.00 (ISBN 0-405-02955-1). Arno.
Steiner, George A. Top Management Planning. LC 66-20539. (Studies of the Modern Corporation Ser). (Illus.). 1969. 29.50 (ISBN 0-02-931120-9). Macmillan.
Steiner, George A. & Bryan, William G. Industrial Project Management. LC 68-12919. 243p. 1968. 7.95 (ISBN 0-913456-35-7). Interbk Inc.
Straub, Joseph T. Applied Management. 1979. 18.95 (ISBN 0-87626-014-8); student involvement guide 7.95 (ISBN 0-87626-016-4). Winthrop.
Symposium, 2nd. Genetics of Industrial Management: Proceedings. Macdonald, K. D., ed. 1976. 85.50 (ISBN 0-12-464350-7). Acad Pr.
Taylor, Frederick W. Principles of Scientific Management. 1967. pap. 4.95 (ISBN 0-393-00398-1, Norton Lib). Norton.

--Scientific Management, Comprising Shop Management, the Principles of Scientific Management, & Testimony Before the Special House Committee, 3 vols. in 1. LC 77-138133. (Illus.). Repr. of 1947 ed. lib. bdg. 33.50x (ISBN 0-8371-5706-4, TASM). Greenwood.

Taylor, Frederick W. & Gilbreth, Frank B. Principles of Scientific Management. Bd. with Primer of Scientific Management. (Hive Managemant History: No. 86). (Illus.). 250p. 1981. lib. bdg. 18.50 (ISBN 0-87960-117-5); pap. 8.95 (ISBN 0-87960-122-1). Hive Pub.

Taylor Society. Scientific Management in American Industry. Person, H. S., ed. LC 72-89989. (Management History Ser.: No. 11). (Illus.). xix, 479p. 1972. Repr. of 1929 ed. 32.50 (ISBN 0-87960-017-9). Hive Pub.

Terry, George R. Principles of Management. 7th ed. 1977. 19.95x (ISBN 0-256-00562-1). Irwin.

Thierauf, Robert J., et al. Management Principles & Practices: A Contingency & Questionnaire Approach. LC 77-23297. (Management & Administration Ser.). 819p. 1977. text ed. 26.95x (ISBN 0-471-29504-3); tchr's manual avail. (ISBN 0-471-03728-1). Wiley.

Thompson, C. Bertrand. The Theory & Practice of Scientific Management. LC 72-80596. (Management History Ser.: No. 15). vii, 319p. 1972. Repr. of 1917 ed. 22.50 (ISBN 0-87960-015-2). Hive Pub.

Todes, Jay L., et al. Management & Motivation: An Introduction to Supervision. 1977. text ed. 17.95 scp (ISBN 0-06-046636-7, HarpC); instructor's manual avail. (ISBN 0-06-366635-9). Har-Row.

Tugwell, Rexford G. The Industrial Discipline & the Governmental Arts. Stein, Leon, ed. LC 77-70541. (Work Ser.). 1977. Repr. of 1933 ed. lib. bdg. 16.00x (ISBN 0-405-10210-0). Arno.

Van Aken, J. E. On the Control of Complex Industrial Organizations. 1978. pap. 19.00 (ISBN 90-207-0791-4, Pub. by Martinus Nijhoff Netherlands). Kluwer Boston.

Vanek, Jaroslav. The Labor-Managed Economy: Essays. LC 76-16682. (Illus.). 1977. 25.00x (ISBN 0-8014-0955-1). Cornell U Pr.

Vernon, Ivan R., ed. Organization for Manufacturing, Vol. 2. LC 79-110568. (Manufacturing Management Ser). (Illus.). 1970. text ed. 11.25 (ISBN 0-87263-018-8). SME.

Vinson, Donald E. & Sciglimpaglia, Donald. The Environment of Industrial Marketing. LC 74-20124. (Marketing Ser.). 1975. pap. text ed. 14.95 (ISBN 0-88244-074-8). Grid Pub.

Vollmer, Howard M. Adaptations of Scientists & Organizations. LC 75-18091. (Science & Technology Management Ser., No. 2). Date not set. price not set (ISBN 0-685-52882-0). Pacific Bks.

Wachter, Michael L. & Wachter, Susan M., eds. Toward a New U. S. Industrial Policy. LC 81-10312. 568p. 1982. 30.00x (ISBN 0-8122-7819-4). U of Pa Pr.

Warren, E. Kirby. Long Range Planning: Executive Viewpoint. 1966. ref. ed. 15.95 (ISBN 0-13-540187-9). P-H.

Webber, Ross A. Management: Basic Elements of Managing Organizations. rev ed. 1979. write for info. (ISBN 0-256-02234-8). Irwin.

White, Harrison C. Research & Development as a Pattern in Industrial Management: A Case Study of Institutionalization & Uncertainty. Zuckerman, Harriet & Merton, Robert K., eds. LC 79-9037. (Dissertations in Sociology Ser.). 1980. lib. bdg. 24.00x (ISBN 0-405-13004-X). Arno.

Wickesberg, Albert K. Management Organization. (Illus., Orig.). 1966. pap. text ed. 6.95x (ISBN 0-89197-290-0). Irvington.

Williamson, Oliver E. Markets & Hierarchies - Analysis & Antitrust Implications: A Study in the Economics of Internal Organization. LC 74-27597. (Illus.). 1975. 17.95 (ISBN 0-02-935360-2). Free Pr.

Wilson, William. Operational Creativity. 1959. pap. 2.00 (ISBN 0-87744-050-6). Mich St U Busn.

Woodward, Joan. Industrial Organization: Theory & Practice. 2nd ed. (Illus.). 324p. 1981. 42.00 (ISBN 0-19-874123-5); pap. 20.00 (ISBN 0-19-874122-7). Oxford U Pr.

Worms, G. Modern Methods of Applied Economics. 1970. 43.00x (ISBN 0-677-01990-4). Gordon.

Wortman, Leon A. Effective Management for Engineers & Scientists. LC 80-19665. 275p. 1981. 22.95 (ISBN 0-471-05523-9, Ronald Pr). Wiley.

Zimbalist, Andrew, ed. Case Studies on the Labor Process. LC 79-3020. 314p. 1981. 16.50 (ISBN 0-85345-518-X, CL 518X); pap. 7.50 (ISBN 0-85345-519-8). Monthly Rev.

INDUSTRIAL MANAGEMENT–BIBLIOGRAPHY

Cannons, H. G. Bibliography of Industrial Efficiency & Factory Management. LC 72-9506. (Management History Ser.: No. 18). 175p. 1973. Repr. of 1920 ed. 17.50 (ISBN 0-87960-021-7). Hive Pub.

Daniells, Lorna. Business Information Sources. LC 74-30517. 1976. 16.95 (ISBN 0-520-02946-1). U of Cal Pr.

Harvard University, Graduate School of Business Administration. Subject Catalog of the Baker Library: First Supplement. 1974. 115.00 (ISBN 0-8161-1180-4). G K Hall.

INDUSTRIAL MANAGEMENT–CASE STUDIES

Bennett, Earl, et al. Business Policy: Case Problems of the General Manager. 3rd ed. (Marketing & Management Ser.). 1978. text ed. 19.95x (ISBN 0-675-08401-6); manual 3.95 (ISBN 0-686-67971-7). Merrill.

Boddewyn, J. J., ed. European Industrial Managers: West & East. LC 76-10916. 560p. 1976. 25.00 (ISBN 0-87332-085-9). M E Sharpe.

Broadwell, William E., Jr. The Management of Work: A Workbook. (Business Ser). (Illus.). 1971. 8.95 (ISBN 0-201-00672-3). A-W.

Eilon, S., et al. Exercises in Industrial Management. 1966. 10.00 (ISBN 0-312-27440-8). St Martin.

Fleenor, C. Patrick & Knudson, Harry R. Organizational Behavior: A Management Approach. (Illus.). 1978. pap. text ed. 14.95 (ISBN 0-87626-623-5). Winthrop.

Hornbruch, Frederick W., Jr. Raising Productivity: Ten Case Histories & Their Lessons. (Illus.). 384p. 1977. 17.50 (ISBN 0-07-030350-9, P&RB). McGraw.

Johnson, Rossall J. Executive Decisions. 2nd ed. 1970. text ed. 12.50 (ISBN 0-538-07370-5). SW Pub.

Katz, Robert L. Management of the Total Enterprise: Cases & Concepts in Business Policy. 1970. ref. ed. 24.95 (ISBN 0-13-548933-4). P-H.

Kaufman, Herbert. The Forest Ranger: A Study in Administrative Behavior. LC 60-6650. (Resources for the Future Ser). (Illus.). 259p. 1960. 17.50x (ISBN 0-8018-0327-6); pap. 3.95x (ISBN 0-8018-0328-4). Johns Hopkins.

Lawrence, Paul R. & Lorsch, Jay W. Organization & Environment: Managing Differentiation & Integration. LC 67-30338. 1967. 14.00x (ISBN 0-87584-064-7). Harvard Busn.

--Organization & Environment: Managing Differentiation & Integration. 1969. pap. 9.50x (ISBN 0-256-00314-9). Irwin.

Lockyer, K. G. & McEwan-Young, W. Short Cases in Industrial Management. 1972. text ed. 15.95x (ISBN 0-7002-0177-7). Intl Ideas.

Lorsch, Jay W. & Lawrence, Paul R. Managing Group & Intergroup Relations. 1972. pap. 11.95x (ISBN 0-256-00264-9). Irwin.

Massie, Joseph L., et al. Management: Analysis, Concepts, Cases. 3rd ed. (Illus.). 800p. 1975. ref. ed. 21.95 (ISBN 0-13-548412-X). P-H.

Smith, George A., Jr. & Matthews, John B., Jr. Business, Society, & the Individual. rev. ed. 1967. 20.50x (ISBN 0-256-00487-0). Irwin.

Thompson, Clarence B., ed. Scientific Management: A Collection of the More Significant Articles Describing the Taylor System of Management. LC 72-80596. (Management History Ser.: No. 1). 890p. 1972. Repr. of 1914 ed. 47.50 (ISBN 0-87960-011-X). Hive Pub.

Wasson, Chester R. Managerial Economics: Text & Cases. LC 66-11425. (Illus.). 1966. 18.50x (ISBN 0-89197-291-9); pap. text ed. 8.95x (ISBN 0-89197-834-8); instructor's manual free (ISBN 0-89197-835-6). Irvington.

Weiss, Leonard W. Case Studies in American Industry. 3rd ed. LC 78-31149. (Introduction to Economics Ser.). 1980. pap. text ed. 11.50 (ISBN 0-471-03159-3). Wiley.

Welsch, Glenn A. Cases in Profit Planning & Control. 1970. pap. text ed. 9.95 (ISBN 0-13-118471-7). P-H.

Ziegler, Raymond J., ed. Business Policies & Decision Making. LC 66-11454. 1966. pap. text ed. 6.95x (ISBN 0-89197-688-4). Irvington.

INDUSTRIAL MANAGEMENT–HANDBOOKS, MANUALS, ETC.

Bass, B. Stogdill's Handbook of Leadership. 587p. 1981. text ed. 29.95 (ISBN 0-02-901820-X). Macmillan.

Ireson, W. Grant & Grant, Eugene, eds. Handbook of Industrial Engineering & Management. 2nd ed. LC 71-139954. 1971. 35.00 (ISBN 0-13-378463-0). P-H.

Lock, Dennis, ed. Engineer's Handbook of Management Techniques. 1973. 24.00x (ISBN 0-8464-0376-5). Beekman Pubs.

Rudman, Jack. Industrial Foreman. (Career Examination Ser.: C-1956). (Cloth bdg. avail. on request). pap. 8.00 (ISBN 0-8373-1956-0). Natl Learning.

Samaras, Thomas T. Industrial Manager's Desk Handbook. (Illus.). 1980. 34.95 (ISBN 0-13-461491-7, Busn). P-H.

INDUSTRIAL MANAGEMENT–HISTORY

Cleland, David I. The Origin & Development of a Philosophy of Long-Range Planning in American Business. LC 75-41751. (Companies & Men: Business Enterprises in America). (Illus.). 1976. 24.00x (ISBN 0-405-08068-9). Arno.

Diemer, Hugo. Industrial Organization & Management. LC 73-6736. (Management History Ser.: No. 61). (Illus.). 315p. 1973. Repr. of 1915 ed. 18.50 (ISBN 0-87960-064-0). Hive Pub.

Drury, Horace B. Scientific Management. 2nd rev. ed. LC 68-56654. (Columbia University. Studies in the Social Sciences: No. 157). 1922. 21.00 (ISBN 0-404-51157-0). AMS Pr.

Farnham, Dwight T. Scientific Industrial Efficiency. LC 73-9692. (Management History Ser.: No. 36). (Illus.). 101p. 1973. Repr. of 1917 ed. 15.00 (ISBN 0-87960-039-X). Hive Pub.

Holbert, Hayward J. A History of Professional Management in American Industry. LC 75-41761. (Companies & Men: Business Enterprises in America). 1976. 21.00x (ISBN 0-405-08077-8). Arno.

Lee, Frederic S. The Human Machine & Industrial Efficiency. LC 73-9695. (Management History Ser.: No. 50). (Illus.). 126p. 1973. Repr. of 1918 ed. 15.00 (ISBN 0-87960-053-5). Hive Pub.

Wachter, Michael & Wachter, Susan M., eds. A New U. S. Industrial Power. 1981. write for info. (ISBN 0-8122-7819-4). U of Pa Pr.

INDUSTRIAL MANAGEMENT–MATHEMATICAL MODELS

see also DYNAMO (Computer Program Language)

Agee, M. & Taylor, R. Quantitative Analysis for Management Decisions. 384p. 1976. text ed. 18.95 (ISBN 0-13-746511-4). P-H.

Arrow, Kenneth J., et al, eds. Studies in Applied Probability & Management Science. 1962. 18.50x (ISBN 0-8047-0099-0). Stanford U Pr.

Buffa, Elwood S. Operations Management: Problems & Models. 3rd ed. LC 78-37167. (Management & Administration Ser). 1972. 26.95 (ISBN 0-471-11867-2). Wiley.

Coyle, R. G. Management System Dynamics. LC 76-40144. 463p. 1977. 65.25 (ISBN 0-471-99444-8, Pub. by Wiley-Interscience); pap. 29.95 (ISBN 0-471-99451-0). Wiley.

Cyert, Richard M. & March, J. G. Behavioral Theory of the Firm. 1963. ref. ed. 20.95 (ISBN 0-13-073304-0). P-H.

Dano, S. Industrial Production Models: A Theoretical Study. (Illus.). 1966. 18.20 (ISBN 0-387-80753-5). Springer-Verlag.

Enrick, Norbert L. Management Planning: A Systems Approach. 1967. 24.95 (ISBN 0-07-019524-2, P&RB). McGraw.

First Stanford Symposium. Mathematical Methods in the Social Sciences, 1959: Proceedings. Arrow, Kenneth J., et al, eds. 1960. 18.75x (ISBN 0-8047-0021-4). Stanford U Pr.

Haner, F. T. & Ford, James C. Contemporary Management. LC 72-95931. 1973. text ed. 17.95 (ISBN 0-675-08987-5). Merrill.

Hax, A. Studies in Operations Management. (Studies in Management Science & Systems Ser.: Vol. 6). 1979. 78.00 (ISBN 0-444-85161-5, North Holland). Elsevier.

Horowitz, Ira. Introduction to Quantitative Business Analysis. 2nd ed. (Illus.). 352p. 1972. text ed. 19.95 (ISBN 0-07-030398-3); solutions to problems 2.75 (ISBN 0-07-030399-1). McGraw.

Ishikawa, Akira. Corporate Planning & Control Model Systems. LC 75-13745. 166p. 1975. 15.00x (ISBN 0-8147-3751-X). NYU Pr.

Meisels, Kurt. A Primer of Linear Programming. LC 62-10307. (Illus.). 1962. 7.95x (ISBN 0-8147-0297-X). NYU Pr.

Palmer, Colin. Quantitative Aids for Management Decision Making. 1979. text ed. 21.50x (ISBN 0-566-00284-1, Pub. by Gower Pub Co England). Renouf.

Schlaifer, Robert. Introduction to Statistics for Business Decisions. 1961. text ed. 20.95 (ISBN 0-07-055308-4, C); solutions manual 4.95 (ISBN 0-07-055305-X). McGraw.

Schweyer, Herbert E. Analytic Models for Managerial & Engineering Economics. LC 64-15941. 520p. 1964. 21.00 (ISBN 0-88275-607-9). Krieger.

Vanek, Jan. The Economics of Workers' Management: A Yugoslav Case Study. 1972. text ed. 24.95x (ISBN 0-04-338053-0). Allen Unwin.

INDUSTRIAL MANAGEMENT–PROGRAMMED INSTRUCTION

Albers, Henry H. & Schoer, Lowell A. Programmed Organization & Management Principles. LC 77-3561. 128p. 1977. pap. 5.25 (ISBN 0-88275-555-2). Krieger.

INDUSTRIAL MANAGEMENT–RESEARCH

Cabell, Randolph W. & Phillips, Almarin. Problems in Basic Operations Research Methods for Management. LC 75-11958. 122p. 1975. Repr. of 1961 ed. 11.50 (ISBN 0-88275-317-7). Krieger.

Dahl, Robert A., ed. Social Science Research on Business: Product & Potential. LC 60-9783. 185p. 1959. pap. 10.00x (ISBN 0-231-02407-X). Columbia U Pr.

Graves, David, ed. Management Research: A Cross-Cultural Perspective. LC 72-83206. 350p. 1973. 14.95 (ISBN 0-444-41060-0). Elsevier.

Kaufmann, Arnold & Faure, R. Introduction to Operations Research. Sneyd, Henry C., tr. LC 67-23162. (Mathematics in Science & Engineering Ser.: Vol. 47). (Illus.). 1968. 43.50 (ISBN 0-12-402360-6). Acad Pr.

McCloskey, Joseph F., et al, eds. Operations Research for Management, Vol. 1. (Operations Research Ser). 410p. 1954. Vol. 1. 25.00x (ISBN 0-8018-0404-3). Johns Hopkins.

Technology & Employment in Industry. 389p. 1981. 28.50 (ISBN 92-2-102469-5, ILO175, ILO). Unipub.

INDUSTRIAL MANAGEMENT–STUDY AND TEACHING

Goldschmid, Harvey J., et al, eds. Industrial Concentration: The New Learning. 1974. pap. 8.95 (ISBN 0-316-31941-4). Little.

Neelamegham, S. Management Development: New Perspectives & View Points. (Illus.). 365p. 1973. 12.50x (ISBN 0-8002-1694-6). Intl Pubns Serv.

INDUSTRIAL MANAGEMENT–VOCATIONAL GUIDANCE

Place, Irene & Robertson, Leonard. Opportunities in Management Careers. 2nd ed. LC 78-60546. (gr. 8 up). 1978. PLB 6.60 (ISBN 0-685-04930-2); pap. 4.95 (ISBN 0-685-04931-0). Natl Textbk.

INDUSTRIAL MANAGEMENT–CHINA

Andors, Stephen, ed. Workers & Workplaces in Revolutionary China. Mathews, Jay, et al, trs. LC 76-53710. (The China Book Project Ser.). 1977. 25.00 (ISBN 0-87332-094-8). M E Sharpe.

Richman, Barry M. A First Hand Study of Industrial Management in Communist China. (Illus.). 1967. pap. 3.00x (ISBN 0-911798-00-5). UCLA Mgmt.

INDUSTRIAL MANAGEMENT–EUROPE

Comisso. Worker's Control Under Plan & Market. 1979. text ed. 24.50x (ISBN 0-300-02334-0). Yale U Pr.

Fishwick, Francis. Multinational Companies & Economic Concentration in Europe. 1981. 26.95 (ISBN 0-03-059124-4). Praeger.

Granick, David. Enterprise Guidance in Eastern Europe: A Comparison of Four Socialist Economies. LC 75-2992. 536p. 1975. 35.00 (ISBN 0-691-04209-8); pap. 13.50 (ISBN 0-691-10033-0). Princeton U Pr.

Jeffries, Ian, ed. The Industrial Enterprise in Eastern Europe. 176p. 1981. 21.95 (ISBN 0-03-059323-9). Praeger.

Vanek, Jan. The Economics of Workers' Management: A Yugoslav Case Study. 1972. text ed. 24.95x (ISBN 0-04-338053-0). Allen Unwin.

INDUSTRIAL MANAGEMENT–FRANCE

Savage, Dean. Founders, Heirs, & Managers: French Industrial Leadership in Transition. LC 79-13929. (Sage Library of Social Research: Vol. 91). 228p. 1979. 20.00 (ISBN 0-8039-1150-5); pap. 9.95 (ISBN 0-8039-1151-3). Sage.

INDUSTRIAL MANAGEMENT–GERMANY (FEDERAL REPUBLIC, 1949-)

Lawrence, Peter. Managers & Management in West Germany. LC 79-23970. 220p. 1980. 27.50 (ISBN 0-312-51237-6). St Martin.

Peltzer, Martin & Boer, Rolf. German Labour Management Relations Act. 384p. 1980. 66.00x (ISBN 0-7121-5515-5, Pub. by Macdonald & Evans). State Mutual Bk.

INDUSTRIAL MANAGEMENT–GREAT BRITAIN

Bakewell, K. G. Library & Information Services for Management. 1968. 13.50 (ISBN 0-208-00854-3, Linnet). Shoe String.

Dore, Ronald P. British Factory - Japanese Factory: The Origins of National Diversity in Employment Relations. LC 72-78948. 1973. 18.50x (ISBN 0-520-02268-8); pap. 7.95x (ISBN 0-520-02495-8, CAMPUS96). U of Cal Pr.

Hart, P. E. & Clarke, Roger. Concentration in British Industry 1935-1975. LC 79-41808. (Economic & Social Research Occasional Paper: No. 32). 163p. 1980. 29.50 (ISBN 0-521-23393-3). Cambridge U Pr.

Sant, Morgan & Moseley, Malcolm. Industrial Development of East Anglia. 207p. 1980. 15.70x (ISBN 0-86094-003-9, Pub. by GEO Abstracts England); pap. 10.60x (ISBN 0-686-27383-4, Pub. by GEO Abstracts England). State Mutual Bk.

Turner, H. A., et al. Management Characteristics & Labour. LC 77-76076. (DAE Papers in Industrial Relations Ser.: No. 3). (Illus.). 1977. pap. 7.95x (ISBN 0-521-29245-X). Cambridge U Pr.

INDUSTRIAL MANAGEMENT–INDIA

Davar, Rustom S. Personnel Management & Industrial Relations in India. 369p. 1976. pap. text ed. 9.00x (ISBN 0-7069-0392-7). Intl Pubns Serv.

Joshi, Arun. Lala Shri Ram: A Study in Entrepreneurship & Industrial Management. LC 75-904545. 1975. 20.00x (ISBN 0-88386-645-5). South Asia Bks.

Long, William A. & Seo, K. K. Management in Japan & India: With Reference to the United States. LC 77-7824. (Praeger Special Studies). 1977. text ed. 34.50 (ISBN 0-03-022651-1). Praeger.

Roy, S. K. & Menon, A. S., eds. Motivation & Organizational Effectiveness with Special Reference to India. 267p. 1975. text ed. 10.50x (ISBN 0-8426-0800-1). Verry.

Sethi, Narendra K. Management Perspectives. (Illus.). 311p. 1972. 11.00x (ISBN 0-8002-1695-4). Intl Pubns Serv.

INDUSTRIAL MANAGEMENT–JAPAN

Dore, Ronald P. British Factory - Japanese Factory: The Origins of National Diversity in Employment Relations. LC 72-78948. 1973. 18.50x (ISBN 0-520-02268-8); pap. 7.95x (ISBN 0-520-02495-8, CAMPUS96). U of Cal Pr.

Imai, Masaaki. Never Take Yes for an Answer: An Inside Look at Japanese Business for Foreign Businessmen. 148p. 1975. pap. 11.00x (ISBN 0-89955-243-9, Pub. by Simul). Intl Schol Bk Serv.

Japan's Community-Based Industries: A Case Study of Small Industry. 300p. 1980. pap. 25.25 (ISBN 0-686-74014-9, APO 100, APO). Unipub.

Long, William A. & Seo, K. K. Management in Japan & India: With Reference to the United States. LC 77-7824. (Praeger Special Studies). 1977. text ed. 34.50 (ISBN 0-03-022651-1). Praeger.

Sasaki, Naoto. Management & Industrial Structure in Japan. (Illus.). 160p. 1981. 24.00 (ISBN 0-08-024056-9); pap. 12.00 (ISBN 0-08-024057-7). Pergamon.

Yoshino, M. Y. Japan's Managerial System: Tradition & Innovation. 1969. pap. 6.95x (ISBN 0-262-74006-0, 192). MIT Pr.

INDUSTRIAL MANAGEMENT–LATIN AMERICA

Stinchcombe, Arthur W. Creating Efficient Industrial Management. 1974. 24.00 (ISBN 0-12-785805-9). Acad Pr.

INDUSTRIAL MANAGEMENT–PAKISTAN

White, Laurence J. Industrial Concentration & Economic Power in Pakistan. LC 73-2493. 192p. 1974. 16.50x (ISBN 0-691-04200-4). Princeton U Pr.

INDUSTRIAL MANAGEMENT–RUSSIA

Azrael, Jeremy R. Managerial Power & Soviet Politics. LC 66-21330. (Russian Research Center Studies: No. 52). 1966. 14.00x (ISBN 0-674-54750-0). Harvard U Pr.

Bergson, Abram. Planning & Productivity Under Soviet Socialism. LC 68-24703. (Benjamin Fairless Memorial Lectures). 95p. 1968. 15.00x (ISBN 0-231-03116-5). Columbia U Pr.

Conyngham, William J. Industrial Management in the Soviet Union: The Role of the CPSU in Industrial Decision-Making, 1917-1970. LC 74-170206. (Publications Ser.: No. 116). 389p. 1973. 12.95 (ISBN 0-8179-6161-5). Hoover Inst Pr.

Granick, David. Management of the Industrial Firm in the USSR. LC 74-6752. 346p. 1974. Repr. of 1954 ed. lib. bdg. 18.50x (ISBN 0-8371-7555-0, GRIF). Greenwood.

Hough, Jerry F. Soviet Prefects: The Local Party Organs in Industrial Decision-Making. LC 69-18033. (Russian Research Center Studies: No. 58). 1969. 18.50x (ISBN 0-674-82785-6). Harvard U Pr.

Liberman, E. G. Economic Methods & the Effectiveness of Production. Schultz, Arlo, tr. from Rus. LC 70-183252. (Illus.). 183p. 1971. text ed. 17.50 (ISBN 0-87332-002-6). M E Sharpe.

Ryavec, Karl W. Implementation of Soviet Economic Reforms: Political, Organizational & Social Processes. LC 75-3627. (Special Studies). (Illus.). 380p. 1975. text ed. 34.50 (ISBN 0-275-05240-0). Praeger.

INDUSTRIAL MATERIALS

see Materials

INDUSTRIAL MEDICINE

see Medicine, Industrial

INDUSTRIAL MICROBIOLOGY

see also Microbiological Synthesis

Bull, M. J. Progress in Industrial Microbiology, Vol. 14. 1978. 58.00 (ISBN 0-444-41665-X). Elsevier.

Bull, M. J., ed. Progress in Industrial Microbiology, Vol. 15. 1979. 63.00 (ISBN 0-444-41815-6, North Holland). Elsevier.

Casida, L. E. Industrial Microbiology. LC 68-22302. 1968. 40.50 (ISBN 0-471-14060-0). Wiley.

Developments in Industrial Microbiology, Vols. 16 & 17. 1975-76. Vol. 16. 25.00 (ISBN 0-934454-92-2); Vol. 17. 25.00 (ISBN 0-686-21617-2). Vol.18. 29.95 (ISBN 0-934454-83-3). Lubrecht & Cramer.

Hahn, Peter. Guide to the Literature for the Industrial Microbiologist. LC 73-19782. 206p. 1973. 25.00 (ISBN 0-306-68431-4). IFI Plenum.

Hockenhull, D. J. Progress in Industrial Microbiology, Vols. 4 & 5. Incl. Vol. 4. 214p. 44.50x (ISBN 0-677-10150-3); Vol. 5. 327p. 67.75x (ISBN 0-677-10160-0). 1969. Gordon.

Koda, Chester, ed. Developments in Industrial Microbiology, Vol. 3. LC 60-13953. 398p. 1962. 35.00 (ISBN 0-306-37033-6, Plenum Pr). Plenum Pub.

Mid-America Symposia on Spectroscopy. Developments in Applied Spectroscopy: Proceedings, 8 vols. Incl. Vol. 1. 12th Symposium. Ashby, W. D., ed. 260p. 1962. o. p. (ISBN 0-306-38301-2); Vol. 2. 13th Symposium. Ferraro, J. R. & Ziomek, J. S., eds. 438p. 1963. 42.50 (ISBN 0-306-38302-0); Vol. 3. 14th Symposium. Forrette, J. E. & Lanterman, E., eds. 419p. 1964. 42.50 (ISBN 0-306-38303-9); Vol. 4. 15th Symposium. Davis, E. N., ed. 588p. 1965. 45.00 (ISBN 0-306-38304-7); Vol. 5. 16th Symposium. Pearson, L. R. & Grove, E. L., eds. 506p. 1966. 45.00 (ISBN 0-306-38305-5); Vol. 6. 18th Symposium. Baer, W. K., et al, eds. 403p. 1968. 42.50 (ISBN 0-306-38306-3); Vol. 7, Pts. A & B. 19th Symposium. Grove, E. L. & Perkins, A. J., eds. 351p. 1969. Vol. 7, Pt. A. 37.50 (ISBN 0-306-38371-3, Plenum Pr); Pt. B. 37.50 (ISBN 0-306-38372-1). Plenum Pr). Plenum Pub.

Miller, Brimtom M. & Litsky, Warren. Industrial Microbiology. 1976. 23.95 (ISBN 0-07-042142-0, C). McGraw.

Peppler, Henry J., ed. Microbial Technology. LC 77-796. (Illus.). 464p. 1977. Repr. of 1967 ed. lib. bdg. 21.00 (ISBN 0-88275-538-2). Krieger.

Rainbow, Cyril & Rose, A. H., eds. Biochemistry of Industrial Microorganisms. 1964. 91.50 (ISBN 0-12-576050-7). Acad Pr.

Rich, Saul, ed. Developments in Industrial Microbiology, Vol. 2. LC 60-13953. 306p. 1961. 35.00 (ISBN 0-306-37032-8, Plenum Pr). Plenum Pub.

Riviere, J. Industrial Applications of Microbiology. Smith, J. & Moss, M., eds. Smith, J. & Moss, M., trs. LC 77-22815. 1978. 30.95 (ISBN 0-470-99265-4). Halsted Pr.

Schlessinger, David, ed. Microbiology 1976. LC 74-33538. (Annual Microbiology Ser.). 1976. 22.00 (ISBN 0-914826-11-5). Am Soc Microbio.

Sebek, O. K. & Laskin, A. I., eds. Genetics of Industrial Microorganisms. (Illus.). 1979. 12.00 (ISBN 0-914826-19-0). Am Soc Microbio.

Society for Industrial Microbiology. Developments in Industrial Microbiology, 11 vols. LC 60-13953. Vols. 5-15. 25.00 ea. Lubrecht & Cramer.

Thoma, R. W., ed. Industrial Microbiology. (Benchmark Papers in Microbiology: Vol. 12). 1977. 48.50 (ISBN 0-12-787540-9). Acad Pr.

INDUSTRIAL MICROSCOPY

see also Metallography

Vanek, Z., et al. Genetics of Industrial Microorganisms, 2 vols. 1973. 146.50 (ISBN 0-444-40988-2). Elsevier.

INDUSTRIAL MOBILIZATION

see also Munitions

Carroll, Berenice A. Design for Total War: Arms & Economics in the Third Reich. LC 68-15527. (Studies in European History: Vol. 17). 1968. text ed. 50.00x (ISBN 90-2790-299-2). Mouton.

Connery, Robert Howe. The Navy & the Industrial Mobilization in World War II. LC 73-166951. (FDR & the Era of the New Deal Ser). 526p. 1972. Repr. of 1951 ed. lib. bdg. 49.50 (ISBN 0-306-70322-X). Da Capo.

Fraser, Cecil E. & Teetle, Stanley F., eds. Industry Goes to War. facs. ed. LC 75-142630. (Essay Index Reprint Ser). 1941. 15.00 (ISBN 0-8369-2048-1). Arno.

INDUSTRIAL MORALE

see Employee Morale

INDUSTRIAL MUSEUMS

Biriokova, N. Applied Arts of Western Europe of XII-XVIII Centuries in the Hermitage. (Texts in French & russian). 1974. 20.00 (ISBN 0-685-86583-5, 569080991). State Mutual Bk.

Hagley Museum. Hagley Museum Guide. (Illus.). 1976. pap. 1.50 (ISBN 0-914650-14-9). Eleutherian Mills-Hagley.

Henry Ford Museum Staff. The Henry Ford Museum. (Illus.). 128p. 1972. pap. 4.95 (ISBN 0-517-50679-3). Crown.

INDUSTRIAL NOISE

Cheremisinoff, Paul N. & Cheremisinoff, Peter P. Industrial Noise Control Handbook. LC 76-46023. 1977. 37.50 (ISBN 0-250-40144-4). Ann Arbor Science.

Fader, Bruce. Industrial Noise Control. LC 81-2158. 352p. 1981. 29.95 (ISBN 0-471-06007-0, Pub. by Wiley Interscience). Wiley.

Faulkner, Lynn L., ed. Handbook of Industrial Noise Control. LC 75-41315. (Illus.). 608p. 1976. 43.00 (ISBN 0-8311-1110-0). Indus Pr.

Irwin, J. David & Graf, Edward R. Industrial Noise & Vibration Control. LC 78-7786. (Illus.). 1979. ref. 31.50 (ISBN 0-13-461574-3). P-H.

Miller, Richard K. Industrial Noise Control 1978. new ed. 1978. pap. text ed. 35.00x (ISBN 0-89671-011-4). Southeast Acoustics.

--Noise Control in Buffing & Polishing. new ed. (Illus.). 1979. pap. text ed. 35.00x (ISBN 0-89671-009-2). Southeast Acoustics.

--Noise Control Solutions for Monument Manufacturing. 1979. pap. text ed. 45.00x (ISBN 0-89671-008-4). Southeast Acoustics.

--Noise Control Solutions for the Chemical & Petroleum Industries. new ed. 1979. pap. text ed. 45.00x (ISBN 0-89671-010-6). Southeast Acoustics.

--Noise Control Solutions for the Rubber & Plastics Industry. new ed. (Illus.). 1979. pap. text ed. 45.00x (ISBN 0-89671-007-6). Southeast Acoustics.

--Noise Control Solutions for the Wire Industry. new ed. (Illus.). 1979. pap. text ed. 35.00x (ISBN 0-89671-006-8). Southeast Acoustics.

National Safety Council Staff. Industrial Noise & Hearing Conservation. Olishifski, Julian B. & Harford, Earl R., eds. LC 75-11313. (Illus.). xvi, 1120p. 1975. text ed. 34.00 (ISBN 0-87912-085-1, 151.17). Natl Safety Coun.

Webb, J. D., ed. Noise Control in Industry. 421p. 1976. text ed. 28.95x (ISBN 0-419-11220-0, Pub. by E & FN Spon England). Methuen Inc.

INDUSTRIAL NUISANCES

see Nuisances

INDUSTRIAL NURSING

see also Public Health Nursing

Educational Research Council of America. Industrial Nurse. Ferris, Theodoe N., et al, eds. (Real People at Work Ser: I). (Illus.). 1975. pap. text ed. 2.25 (ISBN 0-89247-065-8). Changing Times.

INDUSTRIAL OPHTHALMOLOGY

Fox, S. L. Industrial & Occupational Ophthalmology. (Illus.). 224p. 1973. 16.25 (ISBN 0-398-02827-3). C C Thomas.

Merte, H. J., ed. Societas Ergophthalmologica Internationalis: 5th Symposium, Bordeux 1974. 6th Symposium, Hamburg 1976. 7th Symposium, Nagoya 1978. (Problems of Industrial Medicine in Opthamology Ser.: Vol. 5-7). xvi, 750p. 1981. pap. 178.50 (ISBN 3-8055-3003-X). S Karger.

INDUSTRIAL ORGANIZATION

see also Industrial Management; Industrial Sociology; Works Councils

Argyris, Chris. Organization of a Bank: Study of the Nature of Organization & the Fusion Process. Stein, Leon, ed. LC 77-70479. (Work Ser.). 1977. Repr. of 1954 ed. lib. bdg. 20.00x (ISBN 0-405-10153-8). Arno.

Averitt, Robert T. Dual Economy. 1968. pap. 6.95x (ISBN 0-393-09781-1, NortonC). Norton.

Bethel, L., et al. Industrial Organization & Management. 5th ed. 1971. 19.50 (ISBN 0-07-005060-0, C); solutions manual 3.95 (ISBN 0-07-005061-9). McGraw.

Bramlette, Carl A., Jr. & Mescon, Michael H., eds. Individual & the Future of Organizations, Vol. 1. LC 72-619550. (Franklin Foundation Lecture Ser.). Orig. Title: Man & the Future of Organizations. 1972. pap. 3.75 (ISBN 0-88406-003-9). Ga St U Busn Pub.

Brookings, Robert S. Industrial Ownership: Its Economic & Social Significance. facsimile ed. LC 74-37872. (Select Bibliographies Reprint Ser.). Repr. of 1925 ed. 12.00 (ISBN 0-8369-6709-7). Arno.

Brown, Wilfred. Organization. (Illus.). 400p. 1971. 18.75x (ISBN 0-435-85103-9). Intl Pubns Serv.

Cadbury, Edward. Experiments in Industrial Organization. Chandler, Alfred D., ed. LC 79-7534. (History of Management Thought & Practice Ser.). 1980. Repr. of 1912 ed. lib. bdg. 25.00x (ISBN 0-405-12316-7). Arno.

Caves, Richard, et al. Competition in the Open Economy: A Model Applied to Canada. LC 79-23908. (Harvard Economic Studies: No. 150). 1980. text ed. 25.00x (ISBN 0-674-15425-8). Harvard U Pr.

Caves, Richard E. & Uekusa, Masu. Industrial Organization in Japan. 1976. 10.95 (ISBN 0-8157-1324-X); pap. 4.95 (ISBN 0-8157-1323-1). Brookings.

Champion, Dean J. The Sociology of Organizations. LC 74-12245. (Illus.). 450p. 1975. 17.50 (ISBN 0-07-010492-1, C). McGraw.

Chandler, Alfred D., Jr. Strategy & Structure: Chapters in the History of the American Industrial Enterprise. 1962. pap. 5.95x (ISBN 0-262-53009-0). MIT Pr.

Clarkson, Kenneth W. & Miller, Roger L. Industrial Organization. (Illus.). 576p. 1982. text ed. 20.95x (ISBN 0-07-042036-X, C); instructors manual 4.95x (ISBN 0-07-042037-8). McGraw.

Clegg, Stewart & Dunkerley, David. Organization, Class & Control. 1980. 40.00 (ISBN 0-7100-0421-4); pap. 20.00x (ISBN 0-7100-0435-4). Routledge & Kegan.

Corey, E. Raymond & Star, Steven H. Organization Strategy: A Marketing Approach. LC 79-132151. 1971. 22.50x (ISBN 0-87584-088-4). Harvard Busn.

Diemer, Hugo. Factory Organization & Administration, 2 vols. in 1. Chandler, Alfred D., ed. LC 79-7542. (History of Management Thought & Practice Ser.). 1980. Repr. of 1935 ed. lib. bdg. 58.00x (ISBN 0-405-12326-4). Arno.

Dunkerley, David. Foreman: Aspects of Task & Structure. (International Library of Sociology Ser.). 1975. 18.95x (ISBN 0-7100-8158-8). Routledge & Kegan.

Dutrich, John E. & Zawacki, Robert A. People & Organizations: Cases in Management & Organizational Behavior. 1981. pap. 9.95x (ISBN 0-256-02423-5). Business Pubns.

Gibb, Jack R. Trust: A New View of Personal & Organizational Development. LC 77-93139. 1978. 15.00 (ISBN 0-89615-002-X); pap. 8.95 (ISBN 0-89615-006-2). Guild of Tutors.

Greer, Douglas F. Industrial Organization & Public Policy. (Illus.). 1979. text ed. 19.95 (ISBN 0-02-347020-8). Macmillan.

Gulick, Luther H. & Urwick, Lydall, eds. Papers on the Science of Administration. LC 68-55727. (Illus.). Repr. of 1937 ed. 15.00x (ISBN 0-678-00512-5). Kelley.

Gyllenhammer, Pehr G. People at Work. LC 77-73067. (Illus.). 1977. 8.95 (ISBN 0-201-02499-3). A-W.

Hall, Robert L. Economic System in a Socialist State. LC 68-10924. 1967. Repr. of 1937 ed. 8.50 (ISBN 0-8462-1022-3). Russell.

Hicks, H., et al. Modern Business Management. (Illus.). 400p. 1974. text ed. 15.95 (ISBN 0-07-028756-2, C); tchr's manual 5.95 (ISBN 0-07-028758-9); study guide 8.50 (ISBN 0-07-028757-0). McGraw.

International Council for the Quality of Working Life. Working on the Quality of Working Life. (International Ser. on the Quality of Working Life: Vol. 8). 1979. lib. bdg. 36.75 (ISBN 0-89838-001-4, Pub. by Martinus Nijhoff Netherlands). Kluwer Boston.

Janger, Allen R. Matrix Organization of Complex Businesses, Report No. 763. LC 79-66357. (Illus., Orig.). 1979. pap. 37.50 (ISBN 0-8237-0199-9). Conference Bd.

Jelinek, Mariann, et al. Organizations by Design. 1981. pap. 13.95x (ISBN 0-256-02561-4). Business Pubns.

Jewell, Linda N. & Reitz, H. Joseph. Group Effectiveness in Organizations. (Organizational Behavior & Psychology Ser.). 1981. pap. text ed. 8.95x (ISBN 0-673-15334-7). Scott F.

Johnson, Richard A., et al. Management, Systems & Society: An Introduction. LC 75-13447. 576p. 1976. text ed. 18.95 (ISBN 0-87620-540-6); tchrs manual free (ISBN 0-87620-539-2). Goodyear.

Kanter, Rosabeth M. Men & Women of the Corporation. LC 76-43464. 1979. 15.00 (ISBN 0-465-04452-2, CN-5036); pap. 5.95x (ISBN 0-465-04453-0). Basic.

Klein, Lisl. Social Scientist in Industry. LC 75-41612. 257p. 1976. 21.95 (ISBN 0-470-15004-1). Halsted Pr.

Koch, James V. Industrial Organization & Prices. 2nd ed. (Illus.). 1980. text ed. 20.95 (ISBN 0-13-462481-5). P-H.

Konz, Stephan. Work Design. LC 78-50042. (Industrial Engineering Ser.). 1979. text ed. 24.95 (ISBN 0-88244-162-0). Grid Pub.

Lawrence, Paul R. & Lorsch, Jay W. Organization & Environment: Managing Differentiation & Integration. LC 67-30338. 1967. 14.00x (ISBN 0-87584-064-7). Harvard Busn.

--Organization & Environment: Managing Differentiation & Integration. 1969. pap. 9.50x (ISBN 0-256-00314-9). Irwin.

Lee, John. Management: A Study of Industrial Organization. Chandler, Alfred D., ed. LC 79-7550. (History of Management Thought & Practice Ser.). 1980. Repr. of 1921 ed. lib. bdg. 10.00x (ISBN 0-405-12334-5). Arno.

Library Catalogue of the Martin P. Catherwood Library of the New York State School of Industrial & Labor Relations: Fourth Supplement. (Library Catalogs & Supplements Ser.). 1980. lib. bdg. 260.00 (ISBN 0-8161-0333-X). G K Hall.

Lippitt, Gordon L., et al. Optimizing Human Resources: Readings in Individual & Organization Development. (Business Ser). (Illus.). 1971. pap. text ed. 11.95 (ISBN 0-201-04247-9). A-W.

Lorsch, Jay W. & Lawrence, Paul R. Organizational Planning: Cases & Concepts. LC 72-79316. 1972. pap. 11.95x (ISBN 0-256-00456-0). Irwin.

Low, Richard E. Modern Economic Organization. 1970. 18.50x (ISBN 0-256-00315-7). Irwin.

Marris, Robin & Wood, Adrian, eds. Corporate Economy: Growth, Competition, & Innovative Potential. (Studies in Technology & Society). 1971. 25.00x (ISBN 0-674-17252-3). Harvard U Pr.

Masson, Robert T. & Qualls, P. David, eds. Essays on Industrial Organization: In Honor of Joe S. Bain. LC 76-3610. 240p. 1976. text ed. 20.00 (ISBN 0-88410-416-8). Ballinger Pub.

Mescon, Michael H. & Bramlette, Carl A., Jr. The Individual & the Future of Organizations, Vol. 8. (Franklin Foundation Lecture Ser.). 1979. pap. 3.75 (ISBN 0-88406-129-9). Ga St U Busn Pub.

Mockler, Robert J. The Business Management Process. LC 73-79531. (Illus.). 700p. 1973. text ed. 12.00x (ISBN 0-88319-011-7). Austin Pr.

Needham, Douglas. The Economics of Industrial Structure, Conduct & Performance. LC 77-93897. 1978. 14.95x (ISBN 0-312-23665-4). St Martin.

Nicholson, T. A. Optimization in Industry, 2 vols. Incl. Vol. 1. Optimization Techniques (ISBN 0-202-37002-X); Vol. 2. Industrial Applications (ISBN 0-202-37003-8). LC 77-172860. 1972. 12.50 ea. Beresford Bk Serv.

Nystrom, P., ed. Prescriptive Models of Organizations. Starbuck, W. H. Orig. Title: TIMS Studies in the Management Sciences, Vol. 5, 1977. 1977. Repr. 24.25 (ISBN 0-7204-0573-4, North-Holland). Elsevier.

Obel, Borge. Issues of Organizational Design: A Mathematical Programming View of Organizations. (Illus.). 273p. 1981. 30.00 (ISBN 0-08-025837-9). Pergamon.

O'Shaughnessy, J. Business Organization. (Studies in Management). 1966. pap. text ed. 12.95x (ISBN 0-04-658043-3). Allen Unwin.

Phillips, Almarin, ed. Promoting Competition in Regulated Markets. (Studies in the Regulation of Economic Activity). 397p. 1975. 15.95 (ISBN 0-8157-7052-9); pap. 6.95 (ISBN 0-8157-7051-0). Brookings.

Pickering, J. F. Industrial Structure & Market Conduct. 335p. 1974. bds. 36.00x (ISBN 0-85520-040-5, Pub by Martin Robertson England); pap. 14.95x (ISBN 0-85520-039-1). Biblio Dist.

Porter, Michael E. Interbrand Choice Strategy, & Bilateral Market Power. (Economic Studies: No. 146). 1976. 13.50x (ISBN 0-674-45820-6). Harvard U Pr.

Rice, George H., Jr., ed. Industrial Organizations: Selected Readings. LC 78-59403. (Illus.). 1979. text ed. 15.00 (ISBN 0-914872-15-X). Austin Pr.

Riggs, James L., et al. Industrial Organization & Management. 6th ed. (Illus.). 1979. text ed. 21.00 (ISBN 0-07-052854-3, C); solutions manual 5.95 (ISBN 0-07-052855-1). McGraw.

Robb, Russell. Lectures on Organization. LC 73-169681. (Management History Ser.: No. 5). 78p. 1972. Repr. of 1910 ed. 10.00 (ISBN 0-87960-006-3). Hive Pub.

Rohlen, Thomas P. For Harmony & Strength: Japanese White-Collar Organization in Anthropological Perspective. LC 73-91668. 1974. 26.50x (ISBN 0-520-02674-8); pap. 7.95x (ISBN 0-520-03849-5). U of Cal Pr.

Roll, Eric. Early Experiment in Industrial Organization: History of the Firm of Boulton & Watt, 1775-1805. 320p. 1968. Repr. of 1930 ed. 30.00x (ISBN 0-686-11223-7, F Cass Co). Biblio Dist.

Rowley, Charles K. Readings in Industrial Economics, 2 vols. LC 73-76642. 1973. Vol. 1. pap. 11.50x (ISBN 0-8448-0207-7); Vol. 2. pap. 11.50x (ISBN 0-8448-0208-5). Crane-Russak Co.

Running a Professional Corporation. 7.50 (ISBN 0-914770-02-0). Littoral Develop.

Shepherd, William G. The Economics of Industrial Organization. LC 78-6285. 1979. 20.95 (ISBN 0-13-231464-9). P-H.

Sherman, Roger. The Economics of Industry. new ed. (Series in Economics). 1974. text ed. 15.95 (ISBN 0-316-78539-3). Little.

Shubik, Martin & Levitan, Richard. Market Structure & Behavior. LC 79-27108. (Illus.). 267p. 1980. text ed. 18.50x (ISBN 0-674-55026-9). Harvard U Pr.

Slichter, Sumner H. Union Policies & Industrial Management. LC 73-89763. (American Labor, from Conspiracy to Collective Bargaining Ser., No.1). 611p. 1969. Repr. of 1941 ed. 24.00 (ISBN 0-405-02148-8). Arno.

Sofer, Cyril. Organizations in Theory & Practice. LC 73-174821. 1972. text ed. 15.00x (ISBN 0-465-05324-6). Basic.

The Stability of Industrial Organisms. 57p. 1981. pap. 12.50 (ISBN 0-85198-470-3, CAB 13, CAB). Unipub.

Stout, Russell, Jr. Management or Control? The Organizational Challenge. LC 79-3302. 224p. 1980. 12.95x (ISBN 0-253-12082-9). Ind U Pr.

Studies in Canadian Industrial Organization: A Technical Report. (Royal Commission on Corporate Concentration Ser.: No. 26). 1979. pap. 9.25 (ISBN 0-660-00868-8, SSC 114, SSC). Unipub.

Thompson, James D. Organizations in Action. 1967. text ed. 15.95 (ISBN 0-07-064380-6, C). McGraw.

Tushman, Michael. Organizational Change: An Exploratory Study & Case History. LC 73-620201. (ILR Paperback Ser.: No. 15). 1974. pap. 6.75 (ISBN 0-87546-055-0); pap. 9.75 special hard bdg. o.p (ISBN 0-87546-285-5). NY Sch Indus Rel.

Udy, Stanley H., Jr. Organization of Work: A Comparative Analysis of Production Among Nonindustrial Peoples. LC 59-9547. (Comparative Studies Ser). xvi, 182p. 1967. pap. 7.50x (ISBN 0-87536-314-8). HRAFP.

Unwin, G. Industrial Organization in the Sixteenth & Seventeenth Centuries. 2nd ed. 277p. 1957. 25.00x (ISBN 0-7146-1365-7, F Cass Co). Biblio Dist.

Van Aken, J. E. On the Control of Complex Industrial Organizations. 1978. pap. 19.00 (ISBN 90-207-0791-4, Pub. by Martinus Nijhoff Netherlands). Kluwer Boston.

Vernon, Ivan R., ed. Organization for Manufacturing, Vol. 2. LC 79-110568. (Manufacturing Management Ser). (Illus.). 1970. text ed. 11.25 (ISBN 0-87263-018-8). SME.

Wallace, Donald H. Market Control in the Alumininum Industry. Wilkins, Mira, ed. LC 76-29774. (European Business Ser.). (Illus.). 1977. Repr. of 1937 ed. lib. bdg. 36.00x (ISBN 0-405-09786-7). Arno.

Warner, Malcolm. Organizational Choice & Constraint. (Illus.). 1978. 24.95 (ISBN 0-566-00180-2, 01619-5, Pub. by Saxon Hse England). Lexington Bks.

Whyte, William H., Jr. The Organization Man. 1956. pap. 6.95 (ISBN 0-671-21235-4, Touchstone Bks). S&S.

Wild, R. Work Organization: A Study of Manual Labor & Mass Production. LC 74-13085. 222p. 1975. 30.95 (ISBN 0-471-94406-8, Pub. by Wiley-Interscience). Wiley.

Wildsmith, J. R. Managerial Theories of the Firm. LC 73-82263. 200p. 1973. 12.50 (ISBN 0-8046-7073-0). Kennikat.

Williamson, Oliver E. Markets & Hierarchies - Analysis & Antitrust Implications: A Study in the Economics of Internal Organization. LC 74-27597. (Illus.). 1975. 17.95 (ISBN 0-02-935360-2). Free Pr.

Woodward, Joan. Industrial Organization: Theory & Practice. 2nd ed. (Illus.). 324p. 1981. 42.00 (ISBN 0-19-874123-5); pap. 20.00 (ISBN 0-19-874122-7). Oxford U Pr.

Worcester, Dean A. & Neese, Ronald J. Welfare Gains from Advertising: The Problem of Regulation. 1978. pap. 5.25 (ISBN 0-8447-3290-7). Am Enterprise.

INDUSTRIAL PAINTING
see Painting, Industrial

INDUSTRIAL PARKS
see Industrial Districts

INDUSTRIAL PHOTOGRAPHY
see Photography, Industrial

INDUSTRIAL PLANTS
see Factories

INDUSTRIAL POISONS
see Industrial Toxicology

INDUSTRIAL POLICE
see Police, Private

INDUSTRIAL PROCESS CONTROL
see Process Control

INDUSTRIAL PROCESSING
see Manufacturing Processes

INDUSTRIAL PROCUREMENT
see also Purchasing Agents

Ammer, Dean S. Profit-Conscious Purchasing: A Treasury of Newly-Developed Cost-Reduction Methods. 65.50 (ISBN 0-85013-086-7). Dartnell Corp.

Baron, Paul B. When You Buy or Sell a Company. LC 80-66938. 396p. Date not set. 3 ring binder 85.00 (ISBN 0-936936-51-7). Ctr Busn Info.

Corey, E. Raymond. Procurement Management: Strategy, Organization & Decision-Making. LC 78-5826. 1978. 21.50 (ISBN 0-8436-0759-9). CBI Pub.

Didactic Systems Staff. Procurement Management. (Simulation Game Ser.). 1975. pap. 24.90 (ISBN 0-89401-080-8); pap. 21.50 two or more (ISBN 0-685-78134-8). Didactic Syst.

Dowst, Somerby R. Basics for Buyers: A Practical Guide to Better Purchasing. LC 74-156479. (Illus.). 1971. 16.95 (ISBN 0-8436-1301-7). CBI Pub.

Edelberg, Guillermo S. The Procurement of Practices of the Mexican Affiliates of Selected United States Automobile Firms. Bruchey, Stuart & Bruchey, Eleanor, eds. LC 76-5005. (American Business Abroad Ser.). (Illus.). 1976. Repr. of 1976 ed. lib. bdg. 15.00x (ISBN 0-405-09274-1). Arno.

Electronics Buyer's Guide, 1980. Date not set. pap. 30.00 (ISBN 0-07-054596-0). McGraw.

Farmer, David & Taylor, Bernard, eds. Corporate Planning & Procurement. LC 74-19369. 272p. 1975. 27.50 (ISBN 0-686-74221-4). Krieger.

Hong, Alfred, ed. Marketing Economics Key Plants, 1977-78: Guide to Industrial Purchasing Power. National Edition. LC 73-642154. 1977. 90.00 (ISBN 0-914078-23-2). Marketing Econs.

National Association of Purchasing Management. Purchasing Handbook. 4th ed. Farrell, Paul V., ed. 1152p. Date not set. price not set (ISBN 0-07-045899-5, P&RB). McGraw.

Rudman, Jack. Purchase Inspector (Shop Steel) (Career Examination Ser.: C-2258). (Cloth bdg. avail. on request). 1977. pap. 8.00 (ISBN 0-8373-2258-8). Natl Learning.

Stefanelli, John M. Selection & Procurement for the Hospitality Industry. LC 80-20604. (Wiley Service Management Ser.). 502p. 1981. text ed. 19.95 (ISBN 0-471-04538-1). Wiley.

Steffy, Wilbert, et al. Industrial Purchasing Controls for the Small & Medium Sized Firm. (Illus.). 170p. 1980. 12.00 (ISBN 0-686-72865-3, IND P). Indus Dev Inst Sci.

Stevens, J. & Grant, J. The Purchasing-Marketing Interface: Text & Cases. LC 75-9965. 1976. 21.95 (ISBN 0-470-82438-7). Halsted Pr.

Stumm, David A. Advanced Industrial Selling. 426p. 1981. 17.95 (ISBN 0-8144-5665-0). Am Mgmt.

Webster, Frederick, Jr. & Wind, Yoram. Organizational Buying Behavior. LC 75-170040. (Foundations of Marketing Ser). (Illus.). 144p. 1972. pap. 7.95 ref. ed. (ISBN 0-13-640953-9). P-H.

Westing, J. H., et al. Purchasing Management: Materials in Motion. 4th ed. LC 75-38969. 624p. 1976. text ed. 26.50 (ISBN 0-471-93632-4). Wiley.

Woodside, A. G., et al, eds. Consumer & Industrial Buying Behavior. 1977. text ed. 19.95 (ISBN 0-444-00230-8, North-Holland). Elsevier.

Zarnowitz, Victor. Orders, Production & Investment: A Cyclical & Structural Analysis. (Business Cycles Ser.: No. 22). 760p. 1972. 20.00x (ISBN 0-87014-215-1, Dist. by Columbia U Pr). Natl Bur Econ Res.

Zenz, Gary L. Purchasing & the Management of Materials in Motion. 5th ed. LC 80-21649. (Marketing Ser.). 514p. 1981. text ed. 24.95 (ISBN 0-471-06091-7); tchrs.' ed. avail. (ISBN 0-471-08935-4). Wiley.

INDUSTRIAL PROCUREMENT–DATA PROCESSING

National Computing Centre Ltd., ed. Production Control Packages. LC 72-97122. (Factfinder Ser: No. 13). 100p. 1976. pap. 15.00x (ISBN 0-85012-160-4). Intl Pubns Serv.

INDUSTRIAL PROCUREMENT–MATHEMATICAL MODELS

Amihud, Yakov, ed. Bidding & Auctioning for Procurement & Allocation: Proceedings of a Conference at the Center for Applied Economics, New York University. LC 75-27104. 220p. 1976. 20.00x (ISBN 0-8147-0558-8). NYU Pr.

INDUSTRIAL PRODUCTION
see Industry; Overproduction; Supply and Demand

INDUSTRIAL PROJECT MANAGEMENT
see also Network Analysis (Planning)

Cleland, David I. & King, William R. Systems Analysis & Project Management. 2nd ed. (Management Ser.). (Illus.). 416p. 1975. text ed. 16.95 (ISBN 0-07-011310-6, C). McGraw.

CNES & Chvidchenko, Ivan. Large Space Programs Management. (Illus.). 364p. 1971. 73.25x (ISBN 0-677-50670-8). Gordon.

Davies, C., et al. Organization for Program Management. LC 78-27660. 1980. 38.50 (ISBN 0-471-27571-9, Pub. by Wiley-Interscience). Wiley.

Foxhall, William B. Professional Construction Management & Project Administration. 2nd ed. LC 76-4483. 1976. 20.50 (ISBN 0-07-021755-6, Architectural Res Bks). McGraw.

Hoare, H. R. Project Management Using Network Analysis. 1973. 19.95 (ISBN 0-07-084436-4, P&RB). McGraw.

Ludwig, Ernest E. Applied Project Management for the Process Industries. (Illus.). 374p. 1974. 29.95x (ISBN 0-87201-044-9). Gulf Pub.

Manual for Evaluation of Industrial Projects. 139p. 1980. pap. 9.00 (ISBN 0-686-72362-7, UN80/2B2, UN). Unipub.

Martin, Charles C. Project Management: How to Make It Work. LC 75-37884. (Illus.). 224p. 1976. 16.95 (ISBN 0-8144-5408-9). Am Mgmt.

Martino, R. L. Resources Management. 1970. 24.95 (ISBN 0-07-040652-9, P&RB). McGraw.

Moder, Joseph J. & Phillips, Cecil R. Project Management with CPM & PERT. 2nd ed. (Illus.). 1970. 17.95x (ISBN 0-442-15666-9). Van Nos Reinhold.

Organization for Economic Cooperation & Development. Manual of Industrial Project Analysis in Developing Countries. 454p. 1968. 12.50x (ISBN 0-686-14661-1). OECD.

Practical Appraisal of Industrial Projects-Application of Social Cost-Benefit Analysis in Pakistan. (Project Formulation & Evaluation Ser.: No. 4). 181p. 1980. pap. 13.00 (ISBN 0-686-72366-X, UN79/2B5, UN). Unipub.

Rondinelli, Dennis A. Planning Development Projects. LC 77-23072. (Community Development Ser.: Vol. 35). 1977. 33.00 (ISBN 0-87933-280-8). Hutchinson Ross.

Wooldridge, Susan. Project Management in Data Processing. (Illus.). 1976. 15.95x (ISBN 0-442-80327-3). Van Nos Reinhold.

INDUSTRIAL PROMOTION

Organization for Economic Cooperation & Development. Creation of an Industrial Promotion Service. 68p. 1973. 2.00x (ISBN 92-64-11012-7). OECD.

INDUSTRIAL PROPERTY
see also Competition, Unfair; Industrial Design Coordination; Marks of Origin; Patent Laws and Legislation; Trade-Marks

Auslander, M. Arthur. Protecting & Profiting from Your Business Ideas. LC 68-30897. (Orig.). 1969. pap. 2.95 (ISBN 0-87576-021-X). Pilot Bks.

Broughton, Robert. Measures of Property Rights. (Orig.). 1977. pap. 5.95 (ISBN 0-910286-51-5). Boxwood.

The Easement As a Conservation Technique: (EPLP 1) 1972. pap. 7.50x (ISBN 2-88032-071-2, IUCN18, IUCN). Unipub.

Grubb & Ellis Company. Successful Industrial Real Estate Brokerage. 2nd ed. 327p. (Orig.). 1980. pap. 54.95 (ISBN 0-88462-317-3). Real Estate Ed Co.

Harris, L. James & Patient, Trademark & Copyright Institute of the George Washington University, eds. Nurturing New Ideas: Legal Rights & Economic Roles. LC 76-83776. 1969. 14.50 (ISBN 0-87179-081-5). BNA.

Industrial Property Glossary. 1979. pap. 20.00 (ISBN 0-685-96910-X, WIPO58, WIPO). Unipub.

Industrial Property Laws & Treaties, 3 vols. 1976. loose leaf bdg. 140.00x ea. (WIPO). Vol. I (WIPO42). Vol. II (WIPO43). Vol. III (WIPO56). Unipub.

Industrial Property Laws & Treating. 1980. loose leaf bdg. 140.00 (ISBN 0-686-60081-9, WIPO 60, WIPO). Unipub.

Inter-American Treaties & Conventions on Industrial Property. (Treaty Ser.: No. 15). 1960. pap. 1.00 (ISBN 0-8270-0335-8). OAS.

Inventive Activity in the Asian & the Pacific Region. 152p. 1981. pap. 26.00 (ISBN 92-805-0028-7, WIPO66, WIPO). Unipub.

Jehoran, H. Cohen, ed. Protection of Geographic Denominations of Goods & Services. (Monographs in Industrial Property & Copyright Law: Vol. III). 216p. 1980. 37.50 (ISBN 90-286-0090-6). Sijthoff & Noordhoff.

Kase, Francis J., ed. Dictionary of Industrial Property, Legal & Related Terms: English, Spanish, French & German. 232p. 1980. 50.00x (ISBN 90-286-0619-X). Sijthoff & Noordhoff.

Kunstadt, Robert M. The Protection of Personal & Commercial Reputation. (IIC Studies in Industrial Property & Copyright Law: Vol. 3). 1980. pap. 36.30 (ISBN 0-89573-028-6). Verlag Chemie.

Manual of Industrial Property Conventions. 1971. Vol. I, With Suppls. 1, 2, & 3. loose leaf bdg. 30.00x (ISBN 0-686-53011-X, WIPO1, WIPO); Vol. II, Suppl. 4. loose leaf bdg. 30.00x (ISBN 0-686-53012-8, WIPO2); Vol. III Suppls. 5 & 6. loose leaf bdg. 45.00x (ISBN 0-686-53013-6, WIPO3). Unipub.

Multilateral Treaties & Conventions on Industrial Property in the Americas. (Treaty Ser.: No. 39). (Eng. , Span. , & Port.). 1973. pap. 1.00 (ISBN 0-8270-0495-8). OAS.

Paris Convention for the Protection of Industrial Property. pap. 3.00x (ISBN 0-686-53020-9, WIPO4, WIPO). Unipub.

Situation of Industrial Property in the Arab States. 1979. pap. 20.00 (ISBN 0-685-96911-8, WIPO59, WIPO). Unipub.

Umbeck, John R. A Theory of Property Rights-with Special Applications to the California Gold Rush. (Illus.). 160p. 1981. text ed. 9.50 (ISBN 0-8138-1675-0). Iowa St U Pr.

Warden, John, ed. Annual of Industrial Property Law, 1975. xvi, 512p. 1975. text ed. 36.00x (ISBN 0-85683-050-X). Rothman.

--Annual of Industrial Property Law 1977. LC 76-641044. (Illus.). 1977. 72.00x (ISBN 0-8002-0672-X). Intl Pubns Serv.

Zweigert, Konrad & Kropholler, Jan. Law of Copyright, Competition & Industrial Property. Kolle, Gert & Hallstein, Hans P., eds. (Sources of International Uniform Law Ser.: Vol. III-A First Supplement). 1340p. 1979. 175.00x (ISBN 9-0286-0099-X). Sijthoff & Noordhoff.

INDUSTRIAL PSYCHOLOGY

see Psychology, Industrial

INDUSTRIAL PUBLICITY

see also Advertising; Industrial Design Coordination; Public Relations

Barber, Harry L. How to Steal a Million Dollars in Free Publicity. 100p. (Orig.). pap. 8.97 (ISBN 0-940008-01-7). Newport Pub.

Kuswa, Webster. Sell Copy. LC 79-13996. 226p. 1979. 11.95x (ISBN 0-911654-69-0). Writers Digest.

INDUSTRIAL PURCHASING

see Industrial Procurement

INDUSTRIAL RADIOGRAPHY

see Radiography, Industrial

INDUSTRIAL RECREATION

Langer, Steven, ed. Industrial Recreation Report - 1977. 1977. pap. 60.00 (ISBN 0-916506-18-5). Abbott Langer Assocs.

Wilson, Theodore B., et al. An Introduction to Industrial Recreation: Employee Activities & Services. 1979. text ed. 14.95 (ISBN 0-8403-2031-0). Kendall-Hunt.

INDUSTRIAL RELATIONS

see also Arbitration, Industrial; Collective Bargaining; Employee Counseling; Employee-Management Relations in Government; Employees' Magazines, Handbooks, etc.; Employees' Representation in Management; Grievance Procedures; Industrial Sociology; Labor Contract; Labor Laws and Legislation; Personnel Management; Shop Stewards; Strikes and Lockouts; Trade-Unions; Unfair Labor Practices; Works Councils

also local subdivisions of countries other than United States, and names of cities, e.g. Industrial Relations–India; Industrial Relations–New York (City)

Aaron, Benjamin, ed. Reference Supplement: Labor Relations & Social Problems - A Course Book, Unit R. 5th ed. 216p. 1981. pap. text ed. 4.00 (ISBN 0-87179-345-8). BNA.

Abarbanel, Jerome. Redefining the Environment. (Key Issues Ser.: No. 9). 1972. pap. 2.00 (ISBN 0-87546-200-6). NY Sch Indus Rel.

Adler, Joseph & Doherty, Robert E., eds. Employment Security in the Public Sector: A Symposium. 1974. pap. 2.00 (ISBN 0-87546-204-9). NY Sch Indus Rel.

Allen, Henry J. & Gompers, Samuel. Party of the Third Part: The Story of the Kansas Industrial Relations Court. LC 74-156401. (American Labor Ser., No. 2). 1971. Repr. of 1920 ed. 16.00 (ISBN 0-405-02911-X). Arno.

Anderson, Howard J. Primer of Labor Relations. 21st ed. 160p. 1980. pap. 7.50 (ISBN 0-87179-343-1). BNA.

Annual Research Conference, 13th, UCLA, 1970. The Generation Gap: Implications for Labour-Management Relations: Proceedings. 2.00 (ISBN 0-89215-031-9). U Cal LA Indus Rel.

Annual Research Conference, 9th, UCLA, 1966. The City & the World of Work-a Critical Examination of Life in los Angeles & Urban America in the Mid-Sixties: Proceedings. 2.00 (ISBN 0-89215-029-7). U Cal LA Indus Rel.

Armstrong, P. J., et al. Ideology & Shopfloor Industrial Relations. 218p. 1981. 37.50x (ISBN 0-7099-0465-7, Pub. by Croom Helm Ltd England). Biblio Dist.

Auerbach, Jerold S. Labor & Liberty: The La Follette Committee & the New Deal. LC 66-28233. 1966. 18.50x (ISBN 0-672-51153-3). Irvington.

Baer, Walter E. The Operating Manager's Labor Relations Guidebook. 1978. pap. text ed. 8.95 (ISBN 0-8403-1936-3). Kendall Hunt.

--Strikes: A Study of Conflict & How to Resolve It. LC 75-26713. (Illus.). 192p. 1975. 12.95 (ISBN 0-8144-5388-0). Am Mgmt.

Bakke, E. Wight. Mutual Survival: The Goal of Unions & Management. 2nd ed. 1966. 13.50 (ISBN 0-208-00189-1, Archon). Shoe String.

Balliet, Lee. Survey of Labor Relations. 220p. 1981. text ed. 12.00 (ISBN 0-87179-347-4); pap. text ed. 8.00 (ISBN 0-87179-351-2). BNA.

Banks, Robert F. & Stieber, Jack, eds. Multinationals, Unions, & Labor Relations in Industrialized Countries. LC 77-4463. (International Report Ser.: No. 9). 208p. 1977. 10.00 (ISBN 0-87546-064-X). NY Sch Indus Rel.

Baritz, Loren. The Servants of Power. LC 73-17924. 273p. 1974. Repr. of 1960 ed. lib. bdg. 22.75 (ISBN 0-8371-7275-6, BASP). Greenwood.

Berenbeim, Ronald. Nonunion Complaint Systems: A Corporate Appraisal. LC 79-92986. (Report Ser.: No. 770). (Illus.). v, 50p. (Orig.). 1980. pap. text ed. 30.00 (ISBN 0-8237-0206-5). Conference Bd.

Berkeley, A. Eliot & Barnes, Ann, eds. Labor Relations in Hospitals & Health Care Facilities. LC 75-45236. 110p. 1976. 10.00 (ISBN 0-87179-229-X). BNA.

Berman, Edward. Labor & the Sherman Act. LC 68-27049. (Illus.). 332p. 1969. Repr. of 1930 ed. 9.00 (ISBN 0-8462-1272-2). Russell.

Bernstein, Paul. Workplace Democratization. LC 79-66569. 127p. 1980. pap. text ed. 4.95 (ISBN 0-87855-711-3). Transaction Bks.

Bhalla, A. S. & International Labour Office, eds. Technology & Employment in Industry: A Case Study Approach. 2nd rev. & enl. ed. xv, 389p. (Orig.). 1981. 25.65 (ISBN 92-2-102469-5); pap. 21.40 (ISBN 92-2-102466-0). Intl Labour Office.

Bielstein, R. M. The Practical Approach to Industrial Relations for Line Supervisors. 109p. 1965. 6.95 (ISBN 0-87201-381-2). Gulf Pub.

Blackman, John L. Presidential Seizure in Labor Disputes. LC 67-20871. (Wertheim Publications in Industrial Relations Ser). 1967. 17.50x (ISBN 0-674-70201-8). Harvard U Pr.

Blanpain, R., ed. Bulletin of Comparative Labour Relations: Workers Participation in the European Community, No. 8. 1978. pap. 24.00 (ISBN 90-312-0044-1, Pub. by Kluwer Law Netherlands). Kluwer Boston.

Blanpain, Roger. The O E C D Guidelines for Multinational Enterprises & Labour Relations: 1976-1979 Experience & Review. 366p. 1980. lib. bdg. 47.00 (ISBN 90-312-0108-1, Pub. by Kluwer Law Netherlands). Kluwer Boston.

Bloom, Gordon F. & Northrup, Herbert R. Economics of Labor Relations. 9th ed. 1981. 21.95 (ISBN 0-256-02490-1). Irwin.

Blum, Albert A., ed. International Handbook of Industrial Relations: Contemporary Developments & Research. LC 79-8586. (Illus.). xiv, 698p. 1981. 45.00 (ISBN 0-313-21303-8, BLH/). Greenwood.

Blum, Fred H. Toward a Democratic Work Process. LC 73-11840. 229p. 1974. Repr. of 1953 ed. lib. bdg. 15.00x (ISBN 0-8371-7063-X, BLDW). Greenwood.

BNA Editorial Staff. Labor Relations Yearbook - 1980. 1981. text ed. write for info. (ISBN 0-87179-358-X). BNA.

BNA Editorial Staff, ed. Labor Relations Yearbooks. Incl. 1965. 416p (ISBN 0-87179-028-9); 1966. 546p (ISBN 0-87179-029-7); 1967. 646p (ISBN 0-87179-030-0); 1969. 864p (ISBN 0-87179-032-7); 1970. 546p (ISBN 0-87179-033-5); 1971. 464p (ISBN 0-87179-034-3); 1972 O.P (ISBN 0-87179-035-1); 1973. 422p (ISBN 0-87179-036-X); 1974. 570p (ISBN 0-87179-217-6). LC 66-19726. 20.00 ea. BNA.

BNA Editorial Staff of Labor Relations Reporter. Labor Relations Yearbook--1979. 540p. 1980. 20.00 (ISBN 0-87179-334-2). BNA.

--Labor Relations Yearbook 1976. LC 66-19726. 630p. 1977. 20.00 (ISBN 0-87179-239-7). BNA.

--Labor Relations Yearbook 1977. LC 66-19726. 552p. 1978. 20.00 (ISBN 0-87179-242-7). BNA.

--Labor Relations Yearbook 1978. 556p. 1979. 20.00 (ISBN 0-87179-295-8). BNA.

Bock, Betty. Restructuring Proposals: Measuring Competition in Numerical Grids. (Report Ser: No. 619). 177p. (Orig.). 1974. pap. 12.50 (ISBN 0-8237-0050-X). Conference Bd.

Bolweg, Joep F. Job Design & Industrial Democracy. (Studies in the Quality of Working Life: No. 3). 1976. lib. bdg. 20.50 (ISBN 90-207-0634-9, Pub. by Martinus Nijhoff Netherlands). Kluwer Boston.

Boulware, Lemuel R. Truth About Boulwarism: Trying to Do Right Voluntarily. LC 77-91413. 194p. 1969. 7.50 (ISBN 0-87179-010-6); pap. 2.85 (ISBN 0-87179-108-0). BNA.

Boyce, Timothy J. Fair Representation, the NLRB, & the Courts. LC 78-65072. (Labor Relations & Public Policy Ser.: No. 18). 1978. pap. 8.95 (ISBN 0-89546-007-6). Indus Res Unit-Wharton.

Brandes, Stuart D. American Welfare Capitalism: American Welfare Capitalism: Eighteen Eighty to Nineteen-Forty. LC 75-20886. 240p. 1976. lib. bdg. 14.00x (ISBN 0-226-07121-9). U of Chicago Pr.

British Association for the Advancement of Science (Section F Economics) Economics & Technical Change. Hugh-Jones, E. M., ed. LC 71-93848. 1969. lib. bdg. 12.50x (ISBN 0-678-06265-X). Kelley.

Brookings, Robert S. Industrial Ownership: Its Economic & Social Significance. facsimile ed. LC 74-37872. (Select Bibliographies Reprint Ser.). Repr. of 1925 ed. 12.00 (ISBN 0-8369-6709-7). Arno.

Brooks, Thomas R. Toil & Trouble. rev ed. 432p. 1972. pap. 5.95 (ISBN 0-440-59016-7, Delta). Dell.

Bruce, Martin M. A Guide to Human Relations in Business & Industry. LC 73-6907. 1969. pap. 11.05 (ISBN 0-935198-00-8). M M Bruce.

Bulmer, Charles & Carmichael, John L. Employment & Labor-Relations Policy. LC 79-3145. (Policy Studies Book). 1980. 24.50 (ISBN 0-669-03388-X). Lexington Bks.

Burgoyne, Arthur G. The Homestead Strike of Eighteen Ninety-Two. LC 79-4702. (Illus.). 1979. 12.95 (ISBN 0-8229-3405-1); pap. 5.95 (ISBN 0-8229-5310-2). U of Pittsburgh Pr.

Burnett, Arthur L., et al, eds. Labor-Management Relations, Civil Service Reforms, & EEO in the Federal Service--1980. 532p. 45.00 (ISBN 0-686-64535-9). BNA.

Cabot, Stephen J. Labor Management Relations Act Manual. 1st ed. 1978. 44.00 (ISBN 0-88262-208-0, 78-60446). Warren.

Calkins, Clinch. Spy Overhead: The Story of Industrial Espionage. LC 70-156408. (American Labor Ser., No. 2). 1971. Repr. of 1937 ed. 24.00 (ISBN 0-405-02917-9). Arno.

Carter, Michael & Leahy, William, eds. New Directions in Labor Economics & Industrial Relations. 240p. 1981. text ed. 16.95 (ISBN 0-268-01458-2); pap. text ed. 6.95 (ISBN 0-268-01459-0, NDP 269). U of Notre Dame Pr.

Chamberlain, Neil W. Union Challenge to Management Control. 1967. Repr. of 1948 ed. 19.50 (ISBN 0-208-00586-2, Archon). Shoe String.

Chamberlain, Neil W. & Cullen, D. E. The Labor Sector. 2nd ed. Orig. Title: The Firm: Microeconomic Planning & Action. 1972. 17.95 (ISBN 0-07-010428-X, C). McGraw.

Chandler, Margaret K. Management Rights & Union Interests. LC 78-6226. (Illus.). 1978. Repr. of 1964 ed. lib. bdg. 27.75x (ISBN 0-313-20495-0, CHMA). Greenwood.

Clark, Paul F. The Miners' Fight for Democracy: Arnold Miller & the Reform of the United Mine Workers. (Cornell Studies in Industrial & Labor Relations: No. 21). (Illus.). 194p. 1981. 16.95 (ISBN 0-87546-086-0); pap. 9.95 (ISBN 0-87546-087-9). NY Sch Indus Rel.

Coghill, Mary A. Games & Simulatons in Industrial & Labor Relations Training. (Key Issues Ser.: No. 7). 1971. pap. 2.00 (ISBN 0-87546-207-3). NY Sch Indus Rel.

Commerce Clearing House. Guidebook to Labor Relations: 1981. 1981. 8.50 (ISBN 0-686-75935-4). Commerce.

Commons, John R. Industrial Goodwill. LC 75-89726. (American Labor, from Conspiracy to Collective Bargaining, Ser. 1). 213p. 1969. Repr. of 1919 ed. 12.00 (ISBN 0-405-02113-5). Arno.

Commons, John R., ed. Trade Unionism & Labor Problems. LC 66-21664. Repr. of 1905 ed. 22.50x (ISBN 0-678-00221-5). Kelley.

--Trade Unionism & Labor Problems, 2nd Series. LC 66-21665. Repr. of 1921 ed. 27.50x (ISBN 0-678-00287-8). Kelley.

Commons, John R., et al. Industrial Government. LC 79-89727. (American Labor, from Conspiracy to Collective Bargaining, Ser. 1). 425p. 1969. Repr. of 1921 ed. 17.00 (ISBN 0-405-02114-3). Arno.

Communicating with Subordinates. (AMACOM Reprint Collections). 1974. 7.50 (ISBN 0-8144-6937-X). Am Mgmt.

Conciliation & Arbitration of Industrial Disputes in English-Speaking Countries of Africa. (Labour-Management Relations Ser: No. 37). 208p. 1970. 2.30 (ISBN 92-2-100063-X, LMR37). Intl Labour Office.

Conciliation & Arbitration Procedures in Labour Disputes. 183p. 1980. pap. 16.00 (ISBN 92-2-102339-7, ILO 151, ILO). Unipub.

Connolly, Walter B., Jr. & Connolly, Michael J. Work Stoppages & Union Responsibility. new ed. LC 77-78310. 1977. text ed. 20.00 (ISBN 0-685-88300-0, H1-0838). PLI.

Cook, Alice H. The Working Mother: A Survey of Problems & Programs in Nine Countries. 2nd rev. ed. LC 78-620004. 1978. pap. 4.75 (ISBN 0-87546-067-4). NY Sch Indus Rel.

Cooke, Morris L. & Murray, Philip. Organized Labor & Production: Next Steps in Industrial Democracy. LC 73-156409. (American Labor Ser., No. 2). 1971. Repr. of 1946 ed. 16.00 (ISBN 0-405-02918-7). Arno.

Cooper, B. & Bartlett, A. Industrial Relations. 1976. pap. 14.95x (ISBN 0-434-90261-6). Intl Ideas.

Dahrendorf, Ralf. Class & Class Conflict in Industrial Society. 1959. 12.50x (ISBN 0-8047-0560-7); pap. 3.95 (ISBN 0-8047-0561-5, SP3). Stanford U Pr.

--Classes & Conflits De Classes Dans la Societe Industrielle. (L' Oeuvre Sociologique: No. 1). 1972. pap. 48.75x (ISBN 90-2797-014-9). Mouton.

Daniel, W. W. & McIntosh, Neil. Right to Manage: A Study of Leadership & Reform in Employee Relations. 192p. 1972. 15.95x (ISBN 0-8464-0798-1). Beekman Pubs.

De, Nitish, et al. Managing & Developing New Forms of Work Organization. (Management Development Ser.: No. 16). (Illus.). 158p. (Orig.). 1980. pap. 11.40 (ISBN 92-2-102145-9). Intl Labour Office.

De Leon, Daniel. What Means This Strike? 10th ed. 1972. pap. 0.50 (ISBN 0-935534-44-X). NY Labor News.

DeMaria. How Management Wins Union Organizing Campaigns. 1980. pap. 12.95 (ISBN 0-917386-32-9). Exec Ent.

Derber, Milton. The American Idea of Industrial Democracy, 1865-1965. LC 70-100376. 1970. 29.95 (ISBN 0-252-00085-4). U of Ill Pr.

The Development of Industrial Relations Systems: Some Implications of Japanese Experience. 1977. 4.50x (ISBN 92-64-11639-7). OECD.

Dhingra, O. P. Cases in Industrial Relations. LC 72-925737. (Illus.). 144p. 1971. 9.50x (ISBN 0-8002-0525-1). Intl Pubns Serv.

Dobson, C. R. Masters & Journeyman: A Prehistory of Industrial Relations 1717 to 1800. 212p. 1980. 24.75x (ISBN 0-8476-6768-5). Rowman.

Doeringer, Peter B., ed. Industrial Relations in International Perspective. LC 79-13690. 1981. text ed. 35.00x (ISBN 0-8419-0525-8). Holmes & Meier.

Dougherty, James L. Union-Free Labor Relations: A Step-by-Step Guide to Staying Union Free. 278p. 1980. 49.95 (ISBN 0-87201-302-2). Gulf Pub.

Douglas, Ann. Industrial Peacemaking. LC 62-14463. (Illus.). 675p. 1962. 27.50x (ISBN 0-231-02487-8). Columbia U Pr.

Douty, H. M. Wage Bargain & the Labor Management. (PSEW Ser.: No. 37). 1980. text ed. 12.00x (ISBN 0-8018-2393-5); pap. text ed. 4.95x (ISBN 0-8018-2394-3). Johns Hopkins.

--The Wage Bargain & the Labor Market. 160p. 1980. 12.00 (ISBN 0-8018-2393-5); pap. 4.95 (ISBN 0-8018-2394-3). Johns Hopkins.

Dubin, Robert. Human Relations in Administration. 4th ed. (Illus.). 640p. 1974. ref. ed. 21.00 (ISBN 0-13-446435-4). P-H.

Dubofsky, Melvyn. Industrialism & the American Worker: 1865-1920. LC 74-7326. (American History Ser.). 1975. pap. 4.95x (ISBN 0-88295-726-0). Harlan Davidson.

Dufty, N. F. Industrial Relations in the Public Sector: The Firemen. (Illus.). 1980. 25.00x (ISBN 0-7022-1408-6). U of Queensland Pr.

Dunlop, John T. Industrial Relations Systems. LC 77-24354. (Arcturus Books Paperbacks). 412p. 1977. pap. 8.95x (ISBN 0-8093-0850-9). S Ill U Pr.

Dunn, Robert W. The Americanization of Labor. LC 74-22740. (The Labor Movement in Fiction & Non-Fiction Ser.). Repr. of 1927 ed. 22.00 (ISBN 0-404-58492-6). AMS Pr.

Durand, Claude. Conscience Ouvriere & Action Syndicale. (Societe, Mouvements Sociaux & Ideologies, Etudes: No. 10). (Illus.). 1971. pap. 14.50x (ISBN 90-2796-875-6). Mouton.

Eads, George C. The Local Service Airline Experiment. (Studies in the Regulation of Economic Activity). 225p. 1972. 11.95 (ISBN 0-8157-2022-X). Brookings.

East-West Industrial Co-Operation. 122p. 1979. pap. 10.00 (ISBN 0-686-68951-8, UN79/2E25, UN). Unipub.

Edwards, Harry T., et al. Labor Relations Law in the Public Sector. 2nd ed. (Contemporary Legal Education Ser.). 1979. text ed. 23.00 (ISBN 0-672-81788-8). Bobbs.

Ellsworth, John, Jr. Factory Folkways: Study of Institutional Structure & Change. Stein, Leon, ed. LC 77-70493. (Work Ser.). 1977. Repr. of 1952 ed. lib. bdg. 20.00x (ISBN 0-405-10164-3). Arno.

Engineering Employer's Federation. Business Performance & Industrial Relations. 1972. 5.00x (ISBN 0-85038-036-7). Intl Pubns Serv.

Estey, Marten S., ed. Labor Relations Policy in an Expanding Economy: American Academy of Political & Social Science. LC 74-10648. 152p. 1974. Repr. of 1961 ed. lib. bdg. 15.00x (ISBN 0-8371-7645-X, ESLR). Greenwood.

Evatt, Herbert V. The Task of Nations. LC 79-152595. 279p. 1972. Repr. of 1949 ed. lib. bdg. 15.00x (ISBN 0-8371-6028-6, EVTN). Greenwood.

Fearn, Robert M. Labor Economics: The Emerging Synthesis. 288p. 1981. text ed. 18.95 (ISBN 0-87626-473-9). Winthrop.

Feldman, Herman. Problems in Labor Relations. LC 78-89732. (American Labor, from Conspiracy to Collective Bargaining Ser., no. 1). 353p. 1969. Repr. of 1937 ed. 14.50 (ISBN 0-405-02120-8). Arno.

Fitzgerald, Mark J. Britain Views Our Industrial Relations. 1955. 8.50x (ISBN 0-268-00025-5). U of Notre Dame Pr.

Flanders, Allan. Management & Unions. 318p. (Orig.). 1975. pap. 4.95 (ISBN 0-571-10711-7, Pub. by Faber & Faber). Merrimack Bk Serv.

Forslin, Jan, et al, eds. Automation & Industrial Workers: A Fifteen Nation Study, Vol. 1, Pt. 2. (Publications of the Vienna Centre). (Illus.). xvii, 304p. Date not set. price not set (ISBN 0-08-024310-X). Pergamon.

Fossum, John A. Labor Relations: Development Structure Process. 1979. 19.50x (ISBN 0-256-02088-4). Business Pubns.

Foulkes, F. Personnel Policies in Large Nonunion Companies. 1980. 21.95 (ISBN 0-13-660308-4). P-H.

Freedman, Audrey. Managing Labor Relations, Report No. 765. LC 79-55275. (Illus., Orig.). 1979. pap. 30.00 (ISBN 0-8237-0201-4). Conference Bd.

Friedman, Henry & Meredeen, Sander. The Dynamics of Industrial Conflict: Lessons from Ford. 386p. 1980. 32.50x (ISBN 0-85664-982-1, Pub. by Croom Helm Ltd England). Biblio Dist.

Fuji Conference, Fourth. Labor & Management: Proceedings. Nakagawa, Keiichiro, ed. 1979. 25.50x (ISBN 0-86008-243-1, Pub. by U of Tokyo Pr). Intl Schol Bk Serv.

Fulmer, William E. Problems in Labor Relations: Text & Cases. 1980. 22.95x (ISBN 0-256-02366-2). Irwin.

Gallie, D. In Search of the New Working Class. LC 77-80834. (Studies in Sociology: No. 9). (Illus.). 1978. 36.00 (ISBN 0-521-21771-7); pap. 10.95x (ISBN 0-521-29275-1). Cambridge U Pr.

Gennard, John. Job Security & Industrial Relations. 78p. 1979. 5.00x (ISBN 92-64-11835-7). OECD.

Gersuny, Carl. Work Hazards & Industrial Conflict. LC 80-51506. (Illus.). 176p. 1981. 14.00x (ISBN 0-87451-189-5). U Pr of New Eng.

Gill, Colin, et al. Industrial Relations in the Chemical Industry. 1978. text ed. 35.00x (ISBN 0-566-00215-9, Pub. by Gower Pub Co England). Renouf.

Gilmer, B. V & Deci, Edward L. Industrial & Organizational Psychology. 4th ed. (M-H Series in Psychology). (Illus.). 1976. text ed. 17.95 (ISBN 0-07-023289-X, C); instructor's manual 4.95 (ISBN 0-07-023290-3). McGraw.

Ginzberg, Eli, et al. Democratic Values & the Rights of Management. LC 63-20227. 217p. 1963. 20.00x (ISBN 0-231-02664-1). Columbia U Pr.

Gohmann, John W. Arbitration & Representation: Applications in Air & Rail Labor Relations. LC 80-84183. 228p. 1981. text ed. 24.50 (ISBN 0-8403-2335-2). Kendall-Hunt.

Gold, Charlotte. Employer-Employee Committees & Worker Participaton. (Key Issues Ser.: No. 20). 1976. pap. 3.00 (ISBN 0-87546-221-9). NY Sch Indus Rel.

Goldman, A. L. Labour Law & Industrial Relations in the U. S. A. 1979. pap. 36.00 (ISBN 90-312-0097-2, Pub. by Kluwer Law Netherlands). Kluwer Boston.

Goldman, Alvin L. The Supreme Court & Labor-Management Relations Law. LC 75-42953. 1976. 19.95 (ISBN 0-669-00496-0). Lexington Bks.

Goodman, J. F., et al. Rule-Making & Industrial Peace: Industrial Relations in the Footwear Industry. 213p. 1977. 45.00x (ISBN 0-85664-430-7, Pub. by Croom Helm Ltd England). Biblio Dist.

Goodrich, Carter L. Frontier of Control. 344p. 1980. text ed. 13.95 (ISBN 0-902818-70-8); pap. 6.95 (ISBN 0-902818-69-4). Pluto Pr.

Grant, Luke. National Erectors' Association & the International Association of Bridge & Structural Ironworkers: The United States Commission on Industrial Relations. LC 72-156414. (American Labor Ser., No. 2). 1971. Repr. of 1915 ed. 10.00 (ISBN 0-405-02922-5). Arno.

Greenberg, Paul D. & Glaser, Edward M. Some Issues in Joint Union-Management Quality of Worklife Improvement Efforts. LC 80-14044. 80p. 1980. pap. 4.00 (ISBN 0-911558-70-5). Upjohn Inst.

Greenwald, Bruce C. Adverse Selection in the Labor Market. LC 78-75052. (Outstanding Dissertations in Economics Ser.). 1979. lib. bdg. 30.00 (ISBN 0-8240-4130-5). Garland Pub.

Gregory, Charles O. & Katz, Harold A. Labor & the Law. 3rd ed. 1979. 35.00 (ISBN 0-393-01208-5); pap. text ed. 10.95x (ISBN 0-393-09995-4). Norton.

Greiner, John M., et al. Monetary Incentives & Work Standards in Five Cities: Impacts & Implications for Management & Labor. 94p. 1977. pap. 3.95 (ISBN 0-87766-187-1, 17300). Urban Inst.

A Guide to Employer-Employee Relations: A Book of Readings. LC 74-30848. 1975. pap. 5.50 (ISBN 0-87125-025-X). Cath Health.

Gunter, Hans. Transnational Industrial Relations. 1972. 27.50 (ISBN 0-312-81480-1). St Martin.

Gutman, Herbert. Work Culture & Society in Industrializing America. 1976. 12.50 (ISBN 0-394-49694-9). Knopf.

Gutman, Herbert G. Work Culture & Society in Industrializing America: Essays in America's Working Class & Social History. 1977. pap. 4.95 (ISBN 0-394-72251-5, Vin). Random.

Haber, William. Industrial Relations in the Building Industry. LC 76-156415. (American Labor Ser., No. 2). 1971. Repr. of 1930 ed. 29.00 (ISBN 0-405-02923-3). Arno.

Hagburg, Eugene C. & Levine, Marvin J. Labor Relations: An Integrated Perspective. 1978. text ed. 19.95 (ISBN 0-8299-0168-X). West Pub.

Hall, David J. Industrial Relations Problems & the Industrial Relations Act. LC 73-161725. 1972. pap. 7.50x (ISBN 0-85038-035-9). Intl Pubns Serv.

Hanslowe, Kurt L., et al. Union Security in Public Employment: Of Free Riding & Free Association. LC 78-620002. (Institute of Public Employment Monograph: No.8). 1978. pap. 3.25 (ISBN 0-87546-065-8). NY Sch Indus Rel.

Hardman, J. B., ed. American Labor Dynamics. LC 72-89736. (American Labor Ser. 1). 432p. 1969. Repr. of 1928 ed. 17.00 (ISBN 0-405-02125-9). Arno.

Hartmann, George W. & Newscomb, Theodore, eds. Industrial Conflict: Psychological Interpretation. LC 77-182. (Work Ser.). (Illus.). 1977. Repr. of 1939 ed. lib. bdg. 38.00x (ISBN 0-405-10173-2). Arno.

Harvard Business Review Editors. Harvard Business Reviews on Human Relations. LC 78-20166. (Illus.). 1979. 16.95 (ISBN 0-06-011789-3, HarpT). Har-Row.

Hegarty, Christopher & Goldberg, Philip. How to Manage Your Boss. 288p. 1981. 12.95 (ISBN 0-89256-142-4). Rawson Wade.

Heldman, Dan C., et al. Deregulating Labor Relations. LC 79-56315. 200p. (Orig.). 1981. 11.95 (ISBN 0-933028-14-8); pap. 6.95 (ISBN 0-933028-13-X). Fisher Inst.

Heron, Alexander R. Why Men Work. Stein, Leon, ed. LC 77-70502. (Work Ser.). 1977. Repr. of 1948 ed. lib. bdg. 15.00x (ISBN 0-405-10174-0). Arno.

--Why Men Work. Stein, Leon, ed. LC 77-70502. (Work Ser.). 1977. Repr. of 1948 ed. lib. bdg. 15.00x (ISBN 0-405-10174-0). Arno.

Hershfield, David C. The Multinational Union Challenges the Multinational Company. (Report Ser.: No. 658). 40p. (Orig.). 1975. pap. 20.00 (ISBN 0-8237-0077-1). Conference Bd.

Hershfield, David C., ed. Labor Relations Outlook - 1976. LC 76-3285. (Report Ser: No. 683). 57p. (Orig.). 1976. pap. 15.00 (ISBN 0-8237-0117-4). Conference Bd.

Heskes, Deborah. Supportive Services for Disadvantaged Workers & Trainees. (Key Issues Ser.: No. 12). 1973. pap. 2.00 (ISBN 0-87546-225-1). NY Sch Indus Rel.

Hieb, Elizabeth A., ed. Collection of Employer Contributions Institute, Las Vegas, Nevada, June 15 to 18, 1980: Proceedings. 77p. (Orig.). 1980. pap. 8.00 (ISBN 0-89154-138-1). Intl Found Employ.

Hildebrand, George H. & Meyers, Frederic, eds. Selected Works of Benjamin Aaron. (Monograph Ser: No. 18). 1977. 8.50 (ISBN 0-89215-076-9). U Cal LA Indus Rel.

--Selected Works of Irving Bernstein. (Monograph Ser: No. 17). 1977. 7.00 (ISBN 0-89215-075-0). U Cal LA Indus Rel.

Hoffman, Eileen B. Resolving Labor Management Disputes: A Nine-Country Comparison. (Report Ser: No. 600). (Illus.). 114p. (Orig.). 1973. pap. 17.50 (ISBN 0-8237-0049-6). Conference Bd.

Hoffner, Paul E., et al, eds. Practical Labor Relations: A Collection of Readings. LC 80-5525. 183p. 1980. pap. text ed. 8.95 (ISBN 0-8191-1119-8). U Pr of Amer.

Hofstede, G. Futures for Work. 1979. lib. bdg. 19.50 (ISBN 0-89838-015-4, Pub. by Martinus Nijhoff Netherlands). Kluwer Boston.

Holley, William H., Jr. & Jennings, Ken. The Labor Relations Process: Form & Content. 600p. 1980. text ed. 22.95 (ISBN 0-03-046556-7). Dryden Pr.

Horowitz, Morris A. New York Hotel Industry: A Labor Relations Study. LC 60-7992. (Wertheim Publications in Industrial Relations Ser): (Illus.). 1960. 14.00x (ISBN 0-674-61900-5). Harvard U Pr.

Hoxie, Robert F. Scientific Management & Labor. LC 66-21677. Repr. of 1915 ed. 15.00x (ISBN 0-678-00169-3). Kelley.

Hughes, Charles L. Making Unions Unnecessary. 1975. 7.95 (ISBN 0-917386-07-8). Exec Ent.

Hunt, Dennis D. Common Sense Industrial Relations. LC 77-89384. 1978. 14.95 (ISBN 0-7153-7453-2). David & Charles.

Hunt, James W. Employer's Guide to Labor Relations. LC 74-167769. 162p. 1979. pap. 7.50 (ISBN 0-87179-292-3). BNA.

Hyman, Richard. Industrial Relations: A Marxist Introduction. 1976. pap. 15.00 (ISBN 0-333-18667-2). Verry.

Hyman, Richard & Brough, Ian. Social Values & Industrial Relations: A Study of Fairness & Inequality. 1975. (Pub. by Basil Blackwell); pap. 14.00x (ISBN 0-631-16610-6, Pub. by Basil Blackwell). Biblio Dist.

Industrial Relations & Personnel Management in English-Speaking Africa. (Labour-Management Relations Ser: No. 40). 204p. 1972. 7.15 (ISBN 92-2-100168-7). Intl Labour Office.

Industrial Relations: Learning Guide, CEBS Course VIII. 1979. spiral bdg. 13.00 (ISBN 0-89154-105-5). Intl Found Employ.

Industrial Relations Research Association. Adjusting to Technological Change. Somers, Gerald C., et al, eds. LC 73-15246. 230p. 1974. Repr. of 1963 ed. lib. bdg. 15.00x (ISBN 0-8371-7168-7, SOTC). Greenwood.

Industrial Relations Workshop Seminars, Inc. How to Manage with a Union, 2 vols. LC 68-13936. 1969. Set. 49.50 (ISBN 0-685-92653-2). Indus Rel Wkshp.

--Managing Without a Union: Private & Public Sectors. LC 77-88035. 1978. 39.50 (ISBN 0-685-92652-4). Indus Rel Wkshp.

Institute of Industrial Relations Conference. Employment Problems in the Defense Industry: Proceedings. 1971. 2.00 (ISBN 0-89215-037-8). U Cal LA Indus Rel.

Institute of Labor & Industrial Relations. Document & Reference Text: 1971 Supplement, Vol. 2. Miller, Joe A. & Gold, Steven C., eds. 447p. 1971. pap. 15.00x (ISBN 0-87736-316-1). U of Mich Inst Labor.

International Labour Office. Asian Regional Conference, Manila, December 1980, 9th Session: Problems of Rural Workers in Asia & the Pacific, Report III. ii, 104p. (Orig.). 1980. pap. 10.00 (ISBN 92-2-102500-4). Intl Labour Office.

--Ninth Asian Regional Conference, Manila, December, 1980: Report of the Director-General Asian Development in the 1980s-Growth, Employment & Working Conditions, Report I, Pt. 1. iii, 100p. (Orig.). 1980. pap. 10.00 (ISBN 92-2-102497-0). Intl Labour Office.

--Ninth Asian Regional Conference, Manila, December 1980: Report of the Director-General Application of ILO Standards, Report I, Pt. 2. iii, 45p. (Orig.). 1980. pap. text ed. 7.15 (ISBN 92-2-102498-9). Intl Labour Office.

--Programme of Industrial Activities Advisory Committee of Salaried Employees & Professional Workers, 8th Session, Geneva, 1981: The Effects of Technological & Structural Changes on the Employment & Working Conditions of Non-Manual Workers, Report II. iv, 117p. (Orig.). 1980. pap. 8.55 (ISBN 92-2-102557-8). Intl Labour Office.

--Sixteenth Special Report of the Director-General on the Application of the Declaration Concerning the Policy of Apartheid of the Republic of South Africa. International Labour Conference, 66th Session, 1980. ILC-66-1 Special Report. 62p. (Orig.). 1980. pap. 8.55 (ISBN 92-2-102086-X). Intl Labour Office.

International Labour Office, Geneva. Technical Guide, 1980: Employment, Unemployment, Hours of Work, Wages, Vol. II. 432p. (Orig.). 1980. pap. 15.70 (ISBN 92-2-102286-2). Intl Labour Office.

International Labour Office, Iron & Steel Committee, 10th Session, Geneva, 1981. The Improvement of Working Conditions & Working Environments in the Iron & Steel Industry; Report III. v, 86p. (Orig.). 1981. pap. write for info. Intl Labour Office.

Jackson, Gordon E. How to Stay Union Free. LC 78-61773. 1978. 8.95 (ISBN 0-686-14631-X). Management Pr.

Jackson, Michael P. Industrial Relations: A Textbook. 281p. 1977. 25.00x (ISBN 0-85664-194-4, Pub. by Croom Helm Ltd England). Biblio Dist.

Jacobs, James B. & Crotty, Norma M. Guard Unions & the Future of the Prisons. LC 78-62007. (Institute of Public Employment Monograph: No. 9). 1978. pap. 3.50 (ISBN 0-87546-070-4). NY Sch Indus Rel.

Jain, Hem C., ed. Worker Participation: Success & Problems. LC 80-57. (Praeger Special Studies). 1980. 24.95 (ISBN 0-03-052451-2). Praeger.

Jennings, Kenneth M., Jr., et al. Labor Relations in a Public Service Industry: Unions, Management, & the Public Interest in Mass Transit. LC 77-13717. (Praeger Special Studies). 1978. 32.95 (ISBN 0-03-040866-0). Praeger.

Jensen, Vernon H. Heritage of Conflict: Labor Relations in the Nonferrous Metals Industry up to 1930. LC 69-10109. (Industrial & Labor Relations Ser). (Illus.). 1968. Repr. of 1950 ed. lib. bdg. 28.50x (ISBN 0-8371-0117-4, JEHC). Greenwood.

Jones, D. M. Disclosure of Financial Information to Employees. (Illus.). 268p. (Orig.). 1978. pap. 27.50x (ISBN 0-85292-169-1). Intl Pubns Serv.

Jost, Lee F. & Sutherland, C. Bruce. Guide to Professional Benefit Plan Management & Administration. 405p. (Orig.). 1980. pap. 35.00 (ISBN 0-89154-096-2). Intl Found Employ.

Juris, Hervey A. & Roomkin, Myron, eds. The Shrinking Perimeter: Unionism & Labor Relations in the Manufacturing Sector. LC 79-1864. 240p. 1980. 22.95 (ISBN 0-669-02939-4). Lexington Bks.

Justin, Jules J. Managing Without a Union. 1979. text ed. 29.95 (ISBN 0-442-23381-7). Van Nos Reinhold.

Karrass, Chester & Glasser, William. Both Win Management: A Radically New Approach to Improving Manager & Employee Performance. (Illus.). 224p. 1980. 11.95 (ISBN 0-690-01809-6). Har-Row.

Kennedy, Van Dusen. Union Policy & Incentive Wage Methods. LC 68-58598. (Columbia University Studies in the Social Sciences: No. 513). Repr. of 1945 ed. 21.00 (ISBN 0-404-51513-4). AMS Pr.

Kilgour, John G. Preventive Labor Relations. 1981. 23.95 (ISBN 0-8144-5637-5). Am Mgmt.

Kilpatrick, John A. The Changing Labor Content of American Foreign Trade: Nineteen Seventy to Nineteen Seventy-Five. Dufey, Gunter, ed. (Research for Business Decisions: Vol. 19). 93p. 1980. 21.95 (ISBN 0-8357-1103-X, Pub. by UMI Res Pr). Univ Microfilms.

King, William L. Industry & Humanity. LC 72-95460. (Social History of Canada Ser.). 1973. 17.50x (ISBN 0-8020-1947-1); pap. 7.50 (ISBN 0-8020-6174-5). U of Toronto Pr.

Knight, Robert E. Industrial Relations in the San Francisco Bay Area, 1900-1918. LC 59-15322. (Institute of Industrial Relations, UC Berkeley). 1960. 32.50x (ISBN 0-520-00658-5). U of Cal Pr.

Kochan, Thomas A. Collective Bargaining & Industrial Relations. 1980. 20.95x (ISBN 0-256-02353-0). Irwin.

Kochan, Thomas A., et al. The Effectiveness of Union-Management Safety & Health Committees. LC 77-22038. 1977. pap. 2.75 (ISBN 0-911558-02-0). Upjohn Inst.

Kornhauser, Arthur, et al, eds. Industrial Conflict. LC 77-70509. (Work Ser.). 1977. Repr. of 1954 ed. lib. bdg. 34.00x (ISBN 0-405-10179-1). Arno.

Kovach, Kenneth A. Readings & Cases in Contemporary Labor Relations 1980. LC 80-1429. 359p. 1981. pap. text ed. 12.00 (ISBN 0-8191-1362-X). U Pr of Amer.

Kujawa, D. Employment Effects of Multinational Enterprises: The Case of the United States. International Labour Office, ed. (Research on Employment Effects of Multinational Enterprises. Working Papers Ser.: No. 12). 53p. (Orig.). 1980. pap. 8.55 (ISBN 9-2210-2276-5). Intl Labour Office.

Labour Disputes, Perspective, OECD Industrial Relations Programme: Special Studies. (Document Ser.). 1979. 3.75x (ISBN 92-64-11860-8). OECD.

Langer, Steven. The Personnel-Industrial Relations Report, Pt. III: Departmental Budgets & Staffing Ratios. 1980. pap. 85.00 (ISBN 0-916506-35-5). Abbott Langer Assocs.

--The Personnel-Industrial Relations Report, Pt. II: Income by Type & Size of Employer. 1980. pap. 85.00 (ISBN 0-916506-53-3). Abbott Langer Assocs.

Levcik, Friedrich & Stankovsky, Jan. Industrial Cooperation Between East & West. LC 78-73222. 1979. 27.50 (ISBN 0-87332-126-X). M E Sharpe.

Levin, Edward & De Santis, Daniel V. Mediation: An Annotated Bibliography. LC 78-18359. (Industrial & Labor Relations Bibliography Ser.: No. 15). 1978. pap. 3.25 (ISBN 0-87546-069-0). NY Sch Indus Rel.

Levin, Noel A. Guidelines for Fiduciaries of Taft-Hartley Trusts: An ERISA Manual. 137p. 1980. 25.00 (ISBN 0-89154-135-7). Intl Found Employ.

Levine, Marvin J. & Hagburg, Eugene C. Public Sector Labor Relations. 1979. text ed. 17.95 (ISBN 0-8299-0184-1). West Pub.

Levine, Marvin J. & Hagburg, Eugene C., eds. Labor Relations in the Public Sector: Readings, Cases, & Experimental Exercises. (Orig.). 1979. pap. text ed. 10.95x (ISBN 0-89832-000-3). Brighton Pub Co.

Loftus, Joseph & Walfish, Beatrice, eds. Breakthroughs in Union-Management Cooperation. LC 77-24837. 1977. pap. text ed. 7.00 (ISBN 0-89361-002-X). Work in Amer.

McKelvey, Jean T., ed. The Duty of Fair Representation. 1977. 10.95 (ISBN 0-87546-260-X); pap. 6.95 (ISBN 0-87546-234-0). NY Sch Indus Rel.

McKenney, Ruth. Industrial Valley. Repr. of 1939 ed. lib. bdg. 17.00x (ISBN 0-8371-0585-4, MCIV). Greenwood.

Magoon, Paul M. & Richards, John B. Discipline or Disaster: Management's Only Choice. 1966. 7.50 (ISBN 0-682-44029-9, Banner). Exposition.
Managing Human Relations. pap. 10.00 (ISBN 0-686-02516-4). Preston.
Mann, Karl O., ed. Readings in Labor Relations. 110p. 1974. pap. text ed. 4.95x (ISBN 0-87128-850-8). Irvington.
Marsh, A. I. Workplace Industrial Relations in Engineering. (Illus.). 223p. 1971. 15.00x (ISBN 0-85038-013-8). Intl Pubns Serv.
Marsh, A. I., ed. Concise Encyclopedia of Industrial Relations. 1979. text ed. 46.00x (ISBN 0-566-02095-5, Pub. by Gower Pub Co England). Renouf.
Marshall, Don. R. Successful Techniques for Solving Employee Compensation Problems. LC 77-17964. 1978. 29.95 (ISBN 0-471-57297-7, Pub. by Wiley-Interscience). Wiley.
Martin, Benjamin & Kassalow, Everett M., eds. Labor Relations in Advanced Industrial Societies: Issues & Problems. LC 79-56777. 206p. 1980. text ed. 10.00 (ISBN 0-87003-015-9). Carnegie Endow.
Martin, Philip. Contemporary Labor Relations. 1979. pap. text ed. 9.95x (ISBN 0-534-00688-4). Wadsworth Pub.
Mayo, Elton. The Human Problems of an Industrial Civilization. Stein, Leon, ed. LC 77-70515. (Work Ser.). 1977. Repr. of 1933 ed. lib. bdg. 15.00x (ISBN 0-405-10184-8). Arno.
--The Social Problems of an Industrial Civilization. Stein, Leon, ed. LC 77-70516. (Work Ser.). 1977. Repr. of 1945 ed. lib. bdg. 12.00x (ISBN 0-405-10185-6). Arno.
Meltz, Noah, et al. Sharing the Work: An Analysis of the Issues in Worksharing & Jobsharing. 100p. 1981. 7.50 (ISBN 0-8020-2383-5). U of Toronto Pr.
Millis, Harry A. Organized Labor. LC 74-22752. (Labor Movement in Fiction & Non-Fiction). Repr. of 1945 ed. 57.50 (ISBN 0-404-58504-3). AMS Pr.
Mills, D. Quinn. Labor Management Relations. Davis, Keith, ed. (Management Ser.). (Illus.). 1978. text ed. 17.95 (ISBN 0-07-042367-9, C); instructor's manual 5.50 (ISBN 0-07-042368-7). McGraw.
--Labor Management Relations. Davis, Keith, ed. (Management Ser.). (Illus.). 1978. text ed. 17.95 (ISBN 0-07-042367-9, C); instructor's manual 5.50 (ISBN 0-07-042368-7). McGraw.
Mills, Daniel Q. Industrial Relations & Manpower in Construction. 1972. 20.00x (ISBN 0-262-13078-5). MIT Pr.
Montgomery, David. Workers' Control in America. LC 78-32001. (Illus.). 1979. 16.95 (ISBN 0-521-22580-9). Cambridge U Pr.
Montgomery, Royal E. Industrial Relations in the Chicago Building Trades. LC 77-156434. (American Labor Ser., No. 2). 1971. Repr. of 1927 ed. 17.00 (ISBN 0-405-02934-9). Arno.
Moore, Wilbert E. Industrial Relations & the Social Order. rev. ed. Stein, Leon, ed. LC 77-70517. (Work Ser.). (Illus.). 1977. Repr. of 1951 ed. lib. bdg. 41.00x (ISBN 0-405-10186-4). Arno.
Morris, Richard, ed. Labor & Management. LC 76-183137. (Great Contemporary Issues Ser.). (Illus.). 500p. 1973. 35.00 (ISBN 0-405-04163-2, New York Times); 30.00subscribers (ISBN 0-685-41643-7). Arno.
Morrison, Charles. An Essay on the Relations Between Labor & Capital. LC 70-38273. (The Evolution of Capitalism Ser.). 348p. 1972. Repr. of 1854 ed. 18.00 (ISBN 0-405-04128-4). Arno.
Muldoon, Joseph A. & Berdie, Mitchell. Effective Employee Assistance: A Comprehensive Guide for the Employer. 1980. 49.95 (ISBN 0-89638-048-3). CompCare.
Newhouse, Wade J. Public Sector Labor Relations Law in New York State. LC 78-50698. 1978. lib. bdg. 24.50 (ISBN 0-930342-57-7). W S Hein.
Newport, M. Gene. Labor Relations & the Supervisor. LC 68-19343. (Orig.). 1968. text ed. 8.95 (ISBN 0-201-05270-9). A-W.
Northrup, Herbert R., et al. The Objective Selection of Supervisors: A Study of Informal Industry Practice & Two Models for Improved Supervisor Selection. LC 78-61998. (Manpower & Human Resources Studies: No. 8). 1978. 25.00 (ISBN 0-89546-006-8). Indus Res Unit-Wharton.
Ottoway, Richard, ed. Humanising the Workplace: New Proposals & Perspectives. 175p. 1977. 25.00x (ISBN 0-85664-345-9, Pub. by Croom Helm Ltd England). Biblio Dist.
Owen, Trevor. Making Organisations Work. (International Ser. on the Quality of Working Life: Vol. 7). 1978. lib. bdg. 23.00 (ISBN 90-207-0778-7, Pub. by Martinus Nijhoff Netherlands); pap. 12.50 (ISBN 90-207-0779-5). Kluwer Boston.
--The Manager & Industrial Relations. 1979. 35.00 (ISBN 0-08-022471-7); pap. 12.75 (ISBN 0-08-022472-5). Pergamon.
Pardoe, Alan. A Practical Guide for Employer & Employee to the Industrial Relations Act, 1971. xx, 319p. 1972. pap. text ed. 6.50x (ISBN 0-85308-024-0). Rothman.
Peck, Cornelius J., ed. Cases & Materials on Negotiation: Unit 5, Labor Relations & Social Problems, a Course Book. 2nd ed. 280p. 1980. text ed. 9.00 (ISBN 0-87179-335-0). BNA.
Perlman, Richard. Labor Theory. LC 80-12286. 250p. 1981. Repr. of 1969 ed. lib. bdg. write for info. (ISBN 0-89874-163-7). Krieger.
Plant, Robert. Industries in Trouble. International Labour Office, ed. vi, 178p. (Orig.). 1981. 17.10 (ISBN 92-2-102678-7); pap. 11.40 (ISBN 92-2-102679-5). Intl Labour Office.
Poole, Michael. Workers' Participation in Industry. rev ed. 1978. pap. 6.50 (ISBN 0-7100-8824-8). Routledge & Kegan.
Poole, Michael & Mansfield, Roger. Managerial Roles in Industrial Relations: Towards a Definitive Survey of Research & Formulation of Models. 162p. 1980. text ed. 27.75x (ISBN 0-566-00377-5, Pub. by Gower Pub Co England). Renouf.
Productivity, Quality of Working Life & Labour-Management Relations. 23p. 1976. 2.75 (ISBN 0-686-70977-2, APO62, APO). Unipub.
Purcell, Theodore F. Blue Collar Man: Patterns of Dual Allegiance in Industry. Stein, Leon, ed. LC 77-70524. (Work Ser.). (Illus.). 1977. Repr. of 1960 ed. lib. bdg. 23.00x (ISBN 0-405-10192-9). Arno.
Radovic, Igor. How to Manage the Boss: The Radovic Rule. LC 73-80172. 1975. 5.95 (ISBN 0-87131-121-6). Brown Bk.
Radovic, Igor D. The Radovic Rule: How to Manage Your Boss. LC 73-80172. (Illus.). 160p. 1973. 5.95 (ISBN 0-87131-121-6). M Evans.
Rausch, Erwin & Wohlking, Wallace. Handling Conflict in Management: Superior-Subordinate-Group Conflict Game II. portuguese ed. 24.90 (ISBN 0-89401-039-5); pap. 21.50 two or more (ISBN 0-685-85552-X). Didactic Syst.
Reynolds, Lloyd G. Labor Economics & Labor Relations. 8th ed. (Illus.). 656p. 17.95 (ISBN 0-13-517680-8). P-H.
--Labor Economics & Labor Relations. 7th ed. (Illus.). 1978. ref. 20.95 (ISBN 0-13-517706-5). P-H.
Reynolds, Lloyd G., et al. Readings in Labor Economics & Labor Relations. 2nd ed. (Illus.). 1978. pap. text ed. 12.95 (ISBN 0-13-761569-8). P-H.
Richardson, F. L. & Walker, Charles E. Human Relations in an Expanding Company; Manufacturing Departments, Endicott Plant of the International Business Machines Corporation. Stein, Leon, ed. (Work Ser.). (Illus.). 1977. Repr. of 1948 ed. lib. bdg. 12.00x (ISBN 0-405-10196-1, 77-70528). Arno.
Rifkin, Bernard. American Labor Sourcebook. 1980. 39.95 (ISBN 0-07-052830-6, P&RB). McGraw.
Ritzman, Larry P., et al, eds. Disaggregation: Problems in Manufacturing & Service Organizations. 1979. lib. bdg. 56.00 (ISBN 0-89838-003-0, Pub. by Martinus Nijhoff Netherlands). Kluwer Boston.
Roberts, Benjamin C. Industrial Relations: Contemporary Issues. LC 68-23089. (International Institute of Labor Studies). 1969. 19.95 (ISBN 0-312-41440-4). St Martin.
Roberts, Benjamin C., ed. Towards Industrial Democracy: Europe, Japan & the United States. LC 78-71100. (Atlantic Institute for International Affairs Research Ser.: No. 2). 300p. 1979. text ed. 23.00 (ISBN 0-916672-20-4). Allanheld.
Robertson, Dennis H. Study of Industrial Fluctuation. Repr. of 1915 ed. 17.50x (ISBN 0-678-01244-X). Kelley.
Robinson, James W., et al, eds. Introduction to Labor. 1975. pap. 11.95 (ISBN 0-13-485490-X). P-H.
Ross, A. M., ed. Industrial Relations & Economic Development. (International Institute for Labor Studies). 1967. 22.50 (ISBN 0-312-41510-9). St Martin.
Rowan, Richard L. Readings in Labor Economics & Labor Relations. 4th ed. 1980. 12.95x (ISBN 0-256-02367-0). Irwin.
Rowntree, B. Seebohm. The Human Factor in Business. Chandler, Alfred D., ed. LC 79-7553. (History of Management Thought & Practice Ser.). 1980. Repr. of 1921 ed. lib. bdg. 15.00x (ISBN 0-405-12339-6). Arno.
Rudman, Jack. Administrative Labor Relations Specialist. (Career Examination Ser.: C-2027). (Cloth bdg. avail. on request). pap. 12.00 (ISBN 0-8373-2027-5). Natl Learning.
--Assistant Labor Relations Specialist. (Career Examination Ser.: C-2057). (Cloth bdg. avail on request). pap. 10.00 (ISBN 0-8373-2057-7). Natl Learning.
--Associate Labor Relations Specialist. (Career Examination Ser.: C-1946). (Cloth bdg. avail. on request). pap. 10.00 (ISBN 0-8373-1946-3). Natl Learning.
--Labor Relations Assistant. (Career Examination Ser.: C-1338). (Cloth bdg. avail. on request). pap. 10.00 (ISBN 0-8373-1338-4). Natl Learning.
--Labor Specialist. (Career Examination Ser.: C-2146). (Cloth bdg. avail. on request). 1976. pap. 10.00 (ISBN 0-8373-2146-8). Natl Learning.
--Principal Labor-Management Practices Adjustor. (Career Examination Ser.: C-613). (Dloth bdg. avail. on request). pap. 12.00 (ISBN 0-8373-0613-2). Natl Learning.
--Principal Labor Relations Analyst. (Career Examination Ser.: C-2231). (Cloth bdg. avail. on request). pap. 12.00 (ISBN 0-8373-2231-6). Natl Learning.
Sanchez, Irene, et al. The California Worker's Compensation Rehabilitation System. LC 80-70211. (Illus.). 360p. 1981. 35.00x (ISBN 0-02-927670-5). Macmillan.
Sanzotta, Donald. Manager's Guide to Interpersonal Relations. (Illus.). 1979. 12.95 (ISBN 0-8144-5508-5). Am Mgmt.
Sauermann, Heinz. Bargaining Behavior: Beitraege zur experimentellen Wirtschaftsordnung. 1978. 53.00 (ISBN 3-1634-0971-7). Adler.
Sayles, Leonard R. Behavior of Industrial Work Groups: Prediction & Control. Stein, Leon, ed. LC 77-70530. (Work Ser.). 1977. Repr. of 1958 ed. lib. bdg. 12.00x (ISBN 0-405-10198-8). Arno.
Sayre, Kenneth M., et al. Regulation, Values & the Public Interest. Stewart, James B., ed. LC 80-451. 224p. (Orig.). 1980. pap. text ed. 3.60 (ISBN 0-268-01607-0). U of Notre Dame Pr.
Schofer, Lawrence. The Formation of a Modern Labor Force: Upper Silesia 1865-1914. LC 73-90658. 1975. 24.00x (ISBN 0-520-02651-9). U of Cal Pr.
Schrank, Robert, ed. American Workers Abroad. 1979. 15.00 (ISBN 0-262-19178-4). MIT Pr.
Seashore, Stanley E. Group Cohesiveness in the Industrial Work Group. Stein, Leon, ed. LC 77-70531. (Work Ser.). 1977. Repr. of 1954 ed. lib. bdg. 12.00x (ISBN 0-405-10199-6). Arno.
Sedwick, Robert C. Interaction: Interpersonal Relationships in Organizations. (Illus.). 240p. 1974. pap. 9.95 (ISBN 0-13-469155-5). P-H.
Selekman, Benjamin M., et al. Problems in Labor Relations. 3rd ed. 1964. text ed. 18.95 (ISBN 0-07-056083-8, C); key 3.50 (ISBN 0-07-056084-6). McGraw.
Seligson, Harry & Bardwell, George. Labor-Management Relations in Colorado. LC 61-14374. 1961. 12.00 (ISBN 0-8040-0178-2). Swallow.
Shils, Edward B., et al. Industrial Peacemaker: George W. Taylor's Contributions to Collective Bargaining. LC 79-5050. (Illus.). 1979. 22.00 (ISBN 0-8122-7772-4). U of Pa Pr.
Siegel, Abraham J. & Lipsky, David B., eds. Unfinished Business: An Agenda for Labor, Management, & the Public. 1978. 9.95x (ISBN 0-262-19175-X). MIT Pr.
Slichter, Sumner H. Union Policies & Industrial Management. LC 68-23330. (Institute of Economics of the Brookings Institution Publications: No. 85). 1968. Repr. of 1941 ed. lib. bdg. 27.50x (ISBN 0-8371-0231-6, SLIM). Greenwood.
Slichter, Sumner H., et al. The Impact of Collective Bargaining on Management. 1960. 18.95 (ISBN 0-8157-7984-4). Brookings.
Smith, Russell A., et al. Labor Relations Law: Cases & Materials. 6th ed. (Contemporary Legal Education Ser.). 1979. text ed. 23.00 (ISBN 0-672-81929-5). Bobbs.
Somers, Gerald G., ed. Essays in Industrial Relations Theory. LC 70-78818. (Illus.). 1969. 8.50x (ISBN 0-8138-0838-3). Iowa St U Pr.
Spitz, John. Grievance Arbitration: Techniques & Strategies. (IPA Training Manual). 1977. 10.50 (ISBN 0-89215-083-1). U Cal LA Indus Rel.
Spivack, Julius. What You Should Know About Labor Relations. LC 66-24434. 1966. 5.95 (ISBN 0-379-11208-6). Oceana.
Steers, Richard M. & Porter, Lyman W. Motivation & Work Behavior. 2nd ed. (Management Ser.). (Illus.). 1979. text ed. 13.95 (ISBN 0-07-060941-1, C). McGraw.
Stern, Robert N. & Comstock, Philip. Employee Stock Ownership Plans (ESOPs) Benefits for Whom? LC 78-620017. (Key Issues Ser.: No. 23). 1978. pap. 3.00 (ISBN 0-87546-068-2). NY Sch Indus Rel.
Stewart, Nathaniel. Help Your Boss & Help Yourself. LC 73-87547. (Illus.). 160p. 1974. 9.95 (ISBN 0-8144-5351-1). Am Mgmt.
Stogdill, Ralph M. Managers, Employees, Organizations. 1966. 6.00x (ISBN 0-87776-125-6, R125). Ohio St U Admin Sci.
Suffern, Arthur E. Coal Miners' Struggle for Industrial Status. (Brookings Institution Reprint Ser). lib. bdg. 28.50x (ISBN 0-697-00170-9); pap. 9.95x (ISBN 0-89197-703-1). Irvington.
Swann, James P., Jr. NLRB Elections: A Guidebook for Employers. 150p. (Orig.). 1980. pap. 10.00 (ISBN 0-87179-322-9). BNA.
Taylor, Albion G. Labor Policies of the National Association of Manufacturers. LC 73-2536. (Big Business; Economic Power in a Free Society Ser.). Repr. of 1928 ed. 10.00 (ISBN 0-405-05114-X). Arno.
Taylor, Benjamin & Witney, Fred. Labor Relations Law. 3rd ed. 1979. text ed. 23.95 (ISBN 0-13-519645-0). P-H.
Ten Years Later. 72p. 1979. pap. 5.50 (ISBN 0-686-74543-4, SSC161, SSC). Unipub.
Thomason, Calvin C. & Clement, F. A. Human Relations in Action: Problems & Cases in Dealing with People. 2nd ed. Repr. of 1954 ed. lib. bdg. 15.00x (ISBN 0-8371-4040-4, THHR). Greenwood.
Torrington, Derek. Face to Face: Techniques for Handling the Personal Encounter at Work. (Illus.). 1972. 16.00x (ISBN 0-8464-0396-X). Beekman Pubs.
Training: Challenge of the 1980s. Offprint of Part 1 of the Report of the Director-General to the International Labour Conference, Geneva, 1980. 50p. (Orig.). 1980. pap. 7.15 (ISBN 92-2-102554-3). Intl Labour Office.
Tredgold, Rodger F. Human Relations in Modern Industry. 2nd rev. ed. LC 74-135212. 1963. text ed. 13.50 (ISBN 0-8236-2390-4). Intl Univs Pr.
Twentieth Century Fund. Labor Committee. Partners in Production: A Basis for Labor-Management Understanding a Report by the Labor Committee. Repr. of 1949 ed. 4.00 (ISBN 0-527-02841-X). Kraus Repr.
U. S. Commission On Industrial Relations. Efficiency Systems & Labor. LC 71-156411. (American Labor Ser., No. 2). 1971. Repr. of 1916 ed. 13.00 (ISBN 0-405-02945-4). Arno.
Vollmer, Howard M. Employee Rights & the Employment Relationship. LC 76-845. 175p. 1976. Repr. of 1960 ed. lib. bdg. 14.25x (ISBN 0-8371-8743-5, VOER). Greenwood.
Von Beyme, Klaus. Challenge to Power: Trade Unions & Industrial Relations in Capitalist Countries. LC 79-41782. (Illus.). 407p. 1980. 22.50 (ISBN 0-8039-9840-6); pap. 12.50 (ISBN 0-8039-9841-4). Sage.
Wainwright, Hilary & Elliott, Dave. The Lucas Struggle. (Allison & Busby Motive Ser.). 192p. 1981. 14.95 (ISBN 0-8052-8097-9, Pub. by Allison & Busby England); pap. 7.95 (ISBN 0-8052-8098-7). Schocken.
Walker, Charles R. Toward the Automatic Factory: A Case Study of Men & Machines. LC 76-45083. (Illus.). 1977. Repr. of 1957 ed. lib. bdg. 19.00x (ISBN 0-8371-9301-X, WATA). Greenwood.
Warne, Frank J. The Workers at War. LC 74-22762. (Labor Movement in Fiction & Non-Fiction). Repr. of 1920 ed. 20.00 (ISBN 0-404-58515-9). AMS Pr.
Warr, Peter, et al. Developing Employee Relations. 216p. 1978. text ed. 26.75x (ISBN 0-566-00209-4, Pub. by Gower Pub Co England). Renouf.
Weber, Eric. The Indispensable Employee. 1978. pap. text ed. 4.95 (ISBN 0-914094-09-2). Symphony.
--Raise Power. 1978. pap. text ed. 4.95 (ISBN 0-914094-08-4). Symphony.
Weekes, Brian, et al. Industrial Relations & the Limits of Law: The Industrial Effects of the Industrial Relations Act, 1971. (Warwick Studies in Industrial Relations). xvii, 344p. 1975. 19.50x (ISBN 0-631-16620-3). Rothman.
Werne, Benjamin. The Law & Practice of Public Employment Labor Relations, 3 vols. LC 74-79539. 1607p. 1974. 100.00 (ISBN 0-87215-168-9). Michie-Bobbs.
Wertheimer, Barbara M. & Nelson, Anne H., eds. Women As Third-Party Neutrals: Gaining Acceptability. LC 78-620003. 1978. pap. 2.75 (ISBN 0-87546-066-6). NY Sch Indus Rel.
Westin, Alan F. & Salisbury, Stephan. Individual Rights in the Corporation: A Reader on Employee Rights. LC 79-1902. 1980. 16.95 (ISBN 0-394-50715-0). Pantheon.
Whitehead, T. N. The Industrial Worker: Human Relations in a Group of Manual Workers, 2 vols. in one. Stein, Leon, ed. LC 77-70546. (Work Ser.). (Illus.). 1977. Repr. of 1938 ed. lib. bdg. 30.00x (ISBN 0-405-10214-3). Arno.
--Leadership in a Free Society: Human Relations Based on an Analysis of Present-Day Industrial Civilizations. Stein, Leon, ed. LC 77-70548. (Work Ser.). 1977. Repr. of 1936 ed. lib. bdg. 18.00x (ISBN 0-405-10215-1). Arno.
Whyte, William F., et al. Money & Motivation: An Analysis of Incentives in Industry. LC 76-49620. (Illus.). 1977. Repr. of 1955 ed. lib. bdg. 19.75 (ISBN 0-8371-9342-7, WHMOM). Greenwood.

Windmuller, John P. & Lambert, Richard D., eds. Industrial Democracy in International Perspective. LC 76-62834. (Annals Ser.: No. 431). 1977. 7.50 (ISBN 0-87761-214-5); pap. 6.00 (ISBN 0-87761-215-3). Am Acad Pol Soc Sci.

Witte, John F. Democracy, Authority, & Alienation in Work: Workers' Participation in an American Corporation. LC 80-16241. (Illus.). 1980. lib. bdg. 20.00x (ISBN 0-226-90420-2). U of Chicago Pr.

Woods, Noel S. Industrial Relations. LC 76-354394. 114p. 1975. pap. 8.50x (ISBN 0-456-01910-3). Intl Pubns Serv.

Yoder, D. Personnel Management & Industrial Relations. 6th ed. 1970. 21.00 (ISBN 0-13-659201-5). P-H.

Yoder, Dale & Heneman, Herbert G., Jr. ASPA Handbook of Personnel & Industrial Relations. 1698p. 1979. 45.00 (ISBN 0-87179-307-5). BNA.

Yoder, Dale & Heneman, Herbert G., Jr., eds. Motivation & Commitment: Wage & Salary Administration, Vol. 2. rev. ed. LC 74-24765. (ASPA Handbook of Personnel & Industrial Relations Ser.: Vol. 2). 250p. 1975. pap. 7.50 (ISBN 0-87179-201-X). BNA.

--PAIR Policy & Program Management, Vol.7. LC 74-80467. (ASPA Handbook of Personal & Industrial Relations). 182p. 1978. pap. 5.00 (ISBN 0-87179-206-0). BNA.

--Professional PAIR, Vol. VIII. (ASPA Handbook of Personnel & Industrial Relations). 268p. 1979. pap. 7.50 (ISBN 0-87179-207-9). BNA.

--Staffing Policies &Strategies: Aspa Handbook of Personnel & Industrial Relations, Vol. I. 2nd, rev. ed. (Illus.). 306p. pap. text ed. 7.50 (ISBN 0-87179-318-0). BNA.

--Training & Development, Vol.5. LC 74-80467. (ASPA Handbook of Personnel & Industrial Relations). 160p. 1977. pap. 5.00 (ISBN 0-87179-204-4). BNA.

Yoder, Dale, Jr. & Heneman, Herbert G., Jr., eds. ASPA Handbook of Personnel & Industrial Relations: Employee & Labor Relations, Vol. 3. 2nd, rev. ed. LC 79-15194. (Illus.). 232p. 1979. pap. text ed. 7.50 (ISBN 0-87179-305-9). BNA.

INDUSTRIAL RELATIONS–BIBLIOGRAPHY

Askwith, George R. Industrial Problems & Disputes. facsimile ed. LC 72-179502. (Select Bibliographies Reprint Ser). Repr. of 1920 ed. 24.00 (ISBN 0-8369-6631-7). Arno.

Cornell University. Third Supplement to the Cumulation of the Library Catalog Supplements of the New York State School of Industrial & Labor Relations. (Library Catalogs-Bib. Guides). 1979. lib. bdg. 180.00 (ISBN 0-8161-0260-0). G K Hall.

Cornell University, Martin P. Catherwood Library. Cumulation of the Library Catalog Supplements of the New York State School of Industrial and Labor Relations, First Supplement. 1977. lib. bdg. 120.00 (ISBN 0-8161-0055-1). G K Hall.

Cornell University New York State School of Industrial & Labor Relations. Cumulation of the Library Catalog Supplements of Martin P. Catherwood Library of the New York State School of Industrial & Labor Relations, 9 vols. 1976. Set. lib. bdg. 1235.00 (ISBN 0-8161-0022-5). G K Hall.

Cornell University, New York State School of Industrial & Labor Relations. Library Catalog of the Martin P. Catherwood Library of the New York State School of Industrial & Labor Relations, Seventh Supplement. 1974. lib. bdg. 120.00 (ISBN 0-8161-1079-4). G K Hall.

Kleingartner, Archie. Professional & Quasi-Union Organization & Bargaining Behavior: A Bibliography. 1972. 2.00 (ISBN 0-89215-055-6). U Cal LA Indus Rel.

Kubr, Milan, et al, eds. Management, Administration & Productivity: International Directory of Institutions & Information Sources. 2nd ed. xiii, 305p. (Orig., Eng., Fr., Span.). 1981. pap. 18.55 (ISBN 92-2-002468-3). Intl Labour Office.

Library Catalog of the Martin P. Catherwood Library of the New York State School of Industrial & Labor Relations, Fifth Supplement. (Library Catalogs & Supplements Ser.). 1981. lib. bdg. 280.00 (ISBN 0-8161-0362-3). G K Hall.

Morris, James O. & Cordova, Efren. Bibliography of Industrial Relations in Latin America. LC 67-64729. (Bibliography Ser.: No. 8). 1967. 10.00 (ISBN 0-87546-022-4). NY Sch Indus Rel.

Soltow, Martha & Sokkar, Jo A. Industrial Relations & Personnel Management: Selected Information Sources. LC 78-31795. 294p. 1979. lib. bdg. 12.00 (ISBN 0-8108-1203-7). Scarecrow.

Tudyka, Kurt P. Pressure Groups: History, Theory, Functions. 170p. 1973. 15.00x (ISBN 3-7637-0212-1). Intl Pubns Serv.

INDUSTRIAL RELATIONS–DICTIONARIES

Becker, Esther, ed. Dictionary of Personnel & Industrial Relations. 1958. 10.00 (ISBN 0-8022-0088-5). Philos Lib.

Dion, Gerald. Glossary of Terms Used in Industrial Relations. 2nd, rev. & enl. ed. 351p. (Eng. & Fr.). 1975. 19.00x (ISBN 2-7637-6733-8, Pub. by Laval). Intl Schol Bk Serv.

Doherty, Robert E. Industrial & Labor Relations Terms: A Glossary. 4th rev. ed. LC 79-18839. (ILR Bulletin: No. 44). 1979. pap. 2.50 (ISBN 0-87546-075-5). NY Sch Indus Rel.

Roberts, Harold S. Roberts' Dictionary of Industrial Relations. rev. ed. LC 78-175029. 599p. 1971. 20.00 (ISBN 0-87179-135-8). BNA.

INDUSTRIAL RELATIONS–PROGRAMMED INSTRUCTION

Hawkins, Kevin. A Handbook of Industrial Relations Pratice. (Illus.). 251p. 1979. 27.50x (ISBN 0-85038-235-1). Intl Pubns Serv.

INDUSTRIAL RELATIONS–RESEARCH

Turnbull, John G. Labor-Management Relations. LC 49-48994. (Social Science Research Council Bulletin: No. 61). 1949. pap. 2.50 (ISBN 0-527-03289-1). Kraus Repr.

INDUSTRIAL RELATIONS–STUDY AND TEACHING

Kerrison, Irvine L. & Levine, Herbert A. Labor Leadership Education: A Union-University Approach. LC 73-9255. 188p. 1973. Repr. of 1960 ed. lib. bdg. 15.00x (ISBN 0-8371-6996-8, KELE). Greenwood.

Powell, Mary Jo & Gold, Charlotte H., eds. A Manual of Style for the New York State School of Industrial & Labor Relations at Cornell University. 1973. pap. 2.00 (ISBN 0-87546-052-6). NY Sch Indus Rel.

INDUSTRIAL RELATIONS–AFRICA

Damachi, U. G., et al, eds. Industrial Relations in Africa. LC 79-12765. 32.50x (ISBN 0-312-41457-9). St Martin.

INDUSTRIAL RELATIONS–ASIA

Small Industry Bulletin for Asia & the Pacific, No.16. 189p. 1980. pap. 14.00 (ISBN 0-686-70509-2, UN80-2F4, UN). Unipub.

INDUSTRIAL RELATIONS–AUSTRALIA

Gibson, R. W. Disclosure by Australian Companies. (Illus.). 354p. 1971. 22.50x (ISBN 0-522-83996-7, Pub. by Melbourne U Pr). Intl Schol Bk Serv.

Niland, John & Dabscheck, Braham. Industrial Relations in Australia. write for info. Allen Unwin.

Walker, Kenneth F. Australian Industrial Relations Systems. rev. ed. LC 76-111488. (Wertheim Publications in Industrial Relations Ser). (Illus.). 1970. 22.50x (ISBN 0-674-05280-3). Harvard U Pr.

INDUSTRIAL RELATIONS–CANADA

Chaison, Gary N. & Rose, Joseph B., eds. Readings in Canadian Industrial Relations. LC 74-11073. 299p. 1974. text ed. 28.50x (ISBN 0-8422-5191-X); pap. text ed. 8.75x (ISBN 0-8422-0441-5). Irvington.

Congres Des Relations Industrielles. Politique Globale De la Main-D'oeuvre: Evaluation De L'experience Quebecoise. (No. 21). 1966. 6.00x (ISBN 2-7637-6326-X, Pub. by Laval). Intl Schol Bk Serv.

Dion, Gerard. La Politisation des Relations du Travail. 169p. (Fr.). 1973. pap. 6.50x (ISBN 2-7637-6700-1, Pub. by Laval). Intl Schol Bk Serv.

INDUSTRIAL RELATIONS–DENMARK

Galenson, Walter. Danish System of Labor Relations: A Study in Industrial Peace. LC 68-27059. (Illus.). 1969. Repr. of 1952 ed. 12.00 (ISBN 0-8462-1279-X). Russell.

INDUSTRIAL RELATIONS–EUROPE

Balfour, Campbell. Industrial Relations in the Common Market: France, Germany, Italy, Netherlands, Belgium, Luxembourg, Denmark, Norway, Ireland & Britain. (Illus.). 142p. 1972. 10.95x (ISBN 0-7100-7436-0); pap. 4.75 (ISBN 0-7100-7437-9). Routledge & Kegan.

Conference of the Institute of Industrial Relations. Dispute Settlement Procedures in Five Western European Countries: Proceedings. Aaron, Benjamin, ed. 1969. 2.00 (ISBN 0-89215-036-X). U Cal LA Indus Rel.

Crouch, Colin & Pizzorno, Alessandro, eds. Resurgence of Class Conflict in Western Europe Since 1968. 349p. 1981. pap. text ed. cancelled (ISBN 0-8419-0647-5). Holmes & Meier.

Facts on Europe, Economic & Labor Information for the U. S. Businessman. 1966. spiral bdg. 8.50 (ISBN 0-87330-020-3). Indus Rel.

Haraszti, Miklos. A Worker in a Worker's State. LC 77-88841. 176p. 1981. pap. 4.95 (ISBN 0-87663-561-3). Universe.

Industrial Democracy in Europe (IDE) International Research Group, ed. European Industrial Relations. (Illus.). 288p. 1981. 45.00x (ISBN 0-19-827254-5). Oxford U Pr.

Liebhaberg, Bruno. Industrial Relations & Multinational Corporations in Europe. 107p. 1981. 26.95 (ISBN 0-03-059128-7). Praeger.

McPherson, William H. Public Employee Relations in West Germany. LC 77-634396. (Comparative Studies in Public Employment Labor Relations Ser.). 1971. 10.95x (ISBN 0-87736-009-X); pap. 5.95x (ISBN 0-87736-010-3). U of Mich Inst Labor.

Multinationals in Western Europe: The Industrial Relations Experience. 2nd ed. 1976. 10.00 (ISBN 92-2-101476-2). Intl Labour Office.

Roberts, Benjamin C., ed. Towards Industrial Democracy: Europe, Japan & the United States. LC 78-71100. (Atlantic Institute for International Affairs Research Ser.: No. 2). 300p. 1979. text ed. 23.00 (ISBN 0-916672-20-4). Allanheld.

Torrington, Derek. Comparative Industrial Relations in Europe. LC 78-1359. (Contributions in Economics & Economic History: No. 21). 1978. lib. bdg. 18.95x (ISBN 0-313-20366-0, TCI/). Greenwood.

INDUSTRIAL RELATIONS–GERMANY

Chamberlin, Waldo. Industrial Relations in Germany 1914-1939. LC 75-180664. Repr. of 1942 ed. 21.50 (ISBN 0-404-56400-3). AMS Pr.

Kahn-Freund, Otto. Labour Law & Politics in the Weimar Republic. Lewis, Ron & Clark, Jon, eds. (Warwick Studies in Industrial Relations). 272p. 1981. 29.00x (ISBN 0-631-12825-5, Pub. by Basil Blackwell England). Biblio Dist.

INDUSTRIAL RELATIONS–GREAT BRITAIN

Allen, V. L. Sociology of Industrial Relations: Studies in Method. 1971. text ed. 11.00x (ISBN 0-582-44482-9). Humanities.

Askwith, George R. Industrial Problems & Disputes. facsimile ed. LC 72-179502. (Select Bibliographies Reprint Ser). Repr. of 1920 ed. 24.00 (ISBN 0-8369-6631-7). Arno.

Bagwell, P. S. Industrial Relations in Nineteenth Century Britain. 106p. 1974. 15.00x (ISBN 0-7165-2215-2, Pub. by Irish Academic Pr Ireland). Biblio Dist.

Bain, G. S. & Woolven, G. B. A Bibliography of British Industrial Relations. LC 76-53516. 1979. 115.00 (ISBN 0-521-21547-1). Cambridge U Pr.

Bowen, Peter. Social Control in Industrial Organisations. (Direct Edition Ser.). (Orig.). 1976. pap. 17.95x (ISBN 0-7100-8312-2). Routledge & Kegan.

Brown, Ernest H. The Growth of British Industrial Relations. LC 74-14024. (Illus.). 414p. 1975. Repr. of 1959 ed. lib. bdg. 26.00x (ISBN 0-8371-7781-2, BRBI). Greenwood.

Brown, William, ed. The Changing Contours of British Industrial Relations: A Survey of Manufacturing Industry. (Warwick Studies in Industrial Relations). 160p. 1981. 19.95x (ISBN 0-631-12775-5, Pub. by Basil Blackwell England); pap. 8.95x (ISBN 0-631-12826-3, Pub. by Basil Blackwell England). Biblio Dist.

Bull, George. Industrial Relations: The Boardroom Viewpoint. 208p. 1972. 8.75 (ISBN 0-370-01387-5). Transatlantic.

Burgess, Keith. The Origins of British Industrial Relations: The Nineteenth Century Experience. 331p. 1975. 21.50x (ISBN 0-87471-713-2). Rowman.

Clegg, Hugh A. The Changing System of Industrial Relations in Great Britain: A Completely Rewritten Version of "the System of Industrial Relations in Great Britain". 479p. 1979. 45.50x (ISBN 0-631-11091-7, Pub. by Basil Blackwell England); pap. 21.00x (ISBN 0-631-11101-8). Biblio Dist.

Copeman, George. Employee Share Ownership & Industrial Stability. LC 75-316794. 208p. 1975. 9.00x (ISBN 0-85292-108-X). Intl Pubns Serv.

Cronin, James E. Industrial Conflict in Modern Britain. 242p. 1979. 25.00x (ISBN 0-8476-6188-1). Rowman.

Currie, Robert. Industrial Politics. LC 78-40480. 1979. 45.00x (ISBN 0-19-827419-X). Oxford U Pr.

Dutton, H. I. & King, J. E. Ten per Cent & No Surrender: The Preston Strike, 1853-1854. (Illus.). 288p. Date not set. price not set (ISBN 0-521-23620-7). Cambridge U Pr.

Elliott, John. Conflict or Co-Operation? The Growth of Industrial Democracy. 306p. 1980. pap. 14.00x (ISBN 0-85038-106-1). Nichols Pub.

Evans, Hywell. Governmental Regulation of Industrial Relations: A Comparative Study of United States & British Experience. 1961. pap. 0.75 (ISBN 0-87546-016-X). NY Sch Indus Rel.

Fitzgerald, Mark J. Britain Views Our Industrial Relations. 1955. 8.50x (ISBN 0-268-00025-5). U of Notre Dame Pr.

Grouch, Colin. The Politics of Industrial Relations. (Political Issues of Modern Britain Ser.). 1979. text ed. 5.00x (ISBN 0-391-01163-4). Humanities.

Hawkins, Kevin. A Handbook of Industrial Relations Pratice. (Illus.). 251p. 1979. 27.50x (ISBN 0-85038-235-1). Intl Pubns Serv.

Hubbard, Gilbert E. Eastern Industrialization & Its Effect on the West. LC 77-138614. 1979. Repr. of 1935 ed. lib. bdg. 24.25x (ISBN 0-8371-5726-9, HUEI). Greenwood.

Hyman, Richard. Industrial Relations: A Marxist Introduction. 1976. pap. 15.00 (ISBN 0-333-18667-2). Verry.

Kahn-Freund, Otto. Labour Relations: Heritage & Adjustment. (British Academy Ser.). 1979. 23.00x (ISBN 0-19-725987-1). Oxford U Pr.

Levinson, Harold M. Collective Bargaining by British Local Authority Employees. LC 74-634398. (Comparative Studies in Public Employment Labor Relations Ser.). 1971. 5.00x (ISBN 0-87736-013-8); pap. 2.50x (ISBN 0-87736-014-6). U of Mich Inst Labor.

Loveridge, Raymond. Collective Bargaining by National Employees in the United Kingdom. LC 78-634399. (Comparative Studies in Public Employment Labor Relations Ser.). 1971. 10.00x (ISBN 0-87736-015-4); pap. 5.00x (ISBN 0-87736-016-2). U of Mich Inst Labor.

McIntosh, Andrew, ed. Employment Policy in the United Kingdom & the United States. LC 80-67738. 188p. (Orig.). 1981. pap. text ed. 22.50x (ISBN 0-89011-551-6). Abt Assoc.

Morrison, Charles. An Essay on the Relations Between Labor & Capital. LC 70-38273. (The Evolution of Capitalism Ser.). 348p. 1972. Repr. of 1854 ed. 18.00 (ISBN 0-405-04128-4). Arno.

Purcell, John & Smith, Robin, eds. The Control of Work. 1979. text ed. 32.00x (ISBN 0-8419-5058-X). Holmes & Meier.

Robertson, N. & Sams, K. I., eds. British Trade Unionism: Selected Documents, 2 vols. 600p. 1972. Set. 50.00x (ISBN 0-87471-098-7). Rowman.

Spero, Sterling D. Labor Relations in British Nationalized Industry. LC 55-10746. 83p. 1955. 4.50x (ISBN 0-8147-0397-6). NYU Pr.

Stephenson, Geoffrey M. & Brotherton, Christopher J. Industrial Relations: A Social Psychological Approach. LC 78-18452. 412p. 1979. 51.75 (ISBN 0-471-99701-3, Pub. by Wiley-Interscience). Wiley.

Thomson, A. W. & Engleman, S. R. Industrial Relations Act: A Review & Analysis. (Glasgow Social & Economic Research Studies: No. 2). vii, 184p. 1975. text ed. 12.50x (ISBN 0-85520-102-9). Rothman.

Thomson, A. W. J. & Beaumont, P. B. Collective Bargaining in the British Public Sector. LC 78-71279. 1979. 25.95 (ISBN 0-03-050481-3). Praeger.

Turner, H. A., et al. Management Characteristics & Labour. LC 77-76076. (DAE Papers in Industrial Relations Ser.: No. 3). (Illus.). 1977. pap. 7.95x (ISBN 0-521-29245-X). Cambridge U Pr.

Ward, J. T. & Fraser, Hamish. Workers & Employers: Documents on Trade Union & Industrial Relations in Britain Since the Early Nineteen Century. xxxii, 374p. 1981. 35.00 (ISBN 0-208-01878-6, Archon). Shoe String.

Wedderburn, K. W. & Davies, P. L. Employment Grievances & Disputes Procedures in Great Britain. LC 71-84788. 1969. 31.50x (ISBN 0-520-01408-1). U of Cal Pr.

Wigham, Eric. Strikes & the Government, 1893-1974: A History of the Peacekeeping Role of the Department of Employment & Its Predecessors (Britain) 224p. 1976. text ed. 30.00x (ISBN 0-333-15040-6). Verry.

INDUSTRIAL RELATIONS–INDIA

Agarwal, S. L. Labour Relations Law in India. 1978. 14.00x (ISBN 0-8364-0309-6). South Asia Bks.

Davar, R. S. Personnel Management & Industrial Relations in India. 1976. 12.00 (ISBN 0-7069-0392-7). Intl Bk Dist.

Goyal, R. C. Problems in Personnel & Industrial Relations in India. 439p. 1972. 16.50x (ISBN 0-8426-0314-X). Verry.

Hubbard, Gilbert E. Eastern Industrialization & Its Effect on the West. LC 77-138614. 1979. Repr. of 1935 ed. lib. bdg. 24.25x (ISBN 0-8371-5726-9, HUEI). Greenwood.

Nair, K. R. Industrial Relations in Kerala. 1974. text ed. 13.50x (ISBN 0-8426-0614-9). Verry.

INDUSTRIAL RELATIONS–JAPAN

Bennett, John W. & Ishino, Iwao. Paternalism in the Japanese Economy. LC 72-3538. 307p. 1972. Repr. of 1963 ed. lib. bdg. 16.00x (ISBN 0-8371-6424-9, BEJE). Greenwood.

Business Intercommunications, Inc. Labor-Management Relations in Foreign Capital Affiliated Enterprises in Japan. 1976. 160.00 (ISBN 0-686-19298-2). A M Newman.

Cook, Alice H., et al. Public Employee Labor Relations in Japan: Three Aspects. LC 71-634401. (Comparative Studies in Public Employment Labor Relations Ser.). 1971. 5.00x (ISBN 0-87736-019-7); pap. 3.00x (ISBN 0-87736-020-0). U of Mich Inst Labor.

Hanami, T. A. Labour Law & Industrial Relations in Japan. 1979. lib. bdg. 37.00 (ISBN 90-312-0099-9, Pub. by Kluwer Law Netherlands); pap. 20.00 (ISBN 90-312-0095-6, Pub. by Kluwer Law Netherlands). Kluwer Boston.

Hanami, Tadashi. Labor Relations in Japan Today. LC 78-71313. (Illus.). 253p. 1979. 15.00 (ISBN 0-87011-374-7). Kodansha.
Hubbard, Gilbert E. Eastern Industrialization & Its Effect on the West. LC 77-138614. 1979. Repr. of 1935 ed. lib. bdg. 24.25x (ISBN 0-8371-5726-9, HUEI). Greenwood.
Marshall, Byron K. Capitalism & Nationalism in Prewar Japan: The Ideology of the Business Elite 1868-1941. 1967. 10.00x (ISBN 0-8047-0325-6). Stanford U Pr.
Roberts, Benjamin C., ed. Towards Industrial Democracy: Europe, Japan & the United States. LC 78-71100. (Atlantic Institute for International Affairs Research Ser.: No. 2). 300p. 1979. text ed. 23.00 (ISBN 0-916672-20-4). Allanheld.
Sasaki, Naoto. Management & Industrial Structure in Japan. (Illus.). 160p. 1981. 24.00 (ISBN 0-08-024056-9); pap. 12.00 (ISBN 0-08-024057-7). Pergamon.
Taira, Koji. Economic Development & the Labor Market in Japan. LC 78-111459. (Studies of the East Asian Institute Ser). 1970. 17.50x (ISBN 0-231-03272-2). Columbia U Pr.

INDUSTRIAL RELATIONS–LATIN AMERICA

Form, William H. & Blum, Albert A., eds. Industrial Relations & Social Change in Latin America. LC 65-18667. 1965. 7.50 (ISBN 0-8130-0079-3). U Presses Fla.
Meyers, Frederic. Mexican Industrial Relations Viewed from the Perspective of the Mexican Labor Court. (Monograph: No. 24). 1979. 5.00 (ISBN 0-89215-104-8). U Cal LA Indus Rel.
Morris, James O. & Cordova, Efren. Bibliography of Industrial Relations in Latin America. LC 67-64729. (Bibliography Ser.: No. 8). 1967. 10.00 (ISBN 0-87546-022-4). NY Sch Indus Rel.
Multilateral Treaties & Conventions on Industrial Property in the Americas. (Treaty Ser.: No. 39). (Eng. , Span. , & Port.). 1973. pap. 1.00 (ISBN 0-8270-0495-8). OAS.
Story, Dale. Sectoral Clash & Industrialization in Latin America. LC 80-28553. (Foreign & Comparative Studies Latin American Ser.: No. 2). 1981. pap. text ed. 6.00x (ISBN 0-915984-93-8). Syracuse U Foreign Comp.
Wengel, Jan Ter. Allocation of Industry in the Andean Common Market. (Studies in Development & Planning: Vol. 11). 1980. lib. bdg. 19.95 (ISBN 0-89838-020-0, Pub. by Martinus Nijhoff Netherlands). Kluwer Boston.

INDUSTRIAL RELATIONS–NEW YORK (CITY)

Seidenberg, Jacob. Labor Injunction in New York City, 1935-1950. (Cornell Studies Ser.: No. 4). 1953. pap. 1.00 (ISBN 0-87546-001-1). NY Sch Indus Rel.

INDUSTRIAL RELATIONS–NIGERIA

Etukudo, Akanimo J. Waging Industrial Peace in Nigeria. 1977. 8.00 (ISBN 0-682-48850-X, University). Exposition.

INDUSTRIAL RELATIONS–NORWAY

Galenson, Walter. Labor in Norway. LC 78-102494. (Illus.). 1970. Repr. of 1949 ed. 15.00 (ISBN 0-8462-1134-3). Russell.

INDUSTRIAL RELATIONS–RUSSIA

Brown, Emily C. Soviet Trade Unions & Labor Relations. LC 66-21332. 1966. 20.00x (ISBN 0-674-82905-0). Harvard U Pr.

INDUSTRIAL RELATIONS–SOUTHERN STATES

Gilman, Glenn. Human Relations in the Industrial Southeast. LC 74-7609. (Illus.). 327p. 1974. Repr. of 1956 ed. lib. bdg. 19.50x (ISBN 0-8371-7589-5, BIHU). Greenwood.

INDUSTRIAL RELATIONS–SWEDEN

Fry, John A. Industrial Democracy & Labour Market Policy in Sweden. 1979. 35.00 (ISBN 0-08-022462-8); pap. 18.75 (ISBN 0-08-022498-9). Pergamon.
Schmidt, Folke. Law & Industrial Relations in Sweden. 255p. 1977. text ed. 21.00x (ISBN 0-8377-1107-X). Rothman.

INDUSTRIAL RELATIONS–WEST INDIES

Labour Relations in the Caribbean Region. (Labour-Management Relations Ser.: No. 43). 1974. 8.55 (ISBN 92-2-101084-8). Intl Labour Office.

INDUSTRIAL RELATIONS COUNCILS
see Works Councils

INDUSTRIAL RELATIONS RESEARCH
see Industrial Relations–Research

INDUSTRIAL RESEARCH
see Research, Industrial

INDUSTRIAL REVOLUTION
see Industry–History

INDUSTRIAL SAFETY
see also Clothing, Protective; Factory Laws and Legislation; Industrial Accidents;
also subdivisions Safety Appliances and Safety Measures under subjects, e.g. Factories–Safety Appliances

Accident Prevention: A Worker's Education Manual. 9th ed. 1978. 5.70 (ISBN 92-2-101479-7). Intl Labour Office.
American Water Works Association. Safety Practice for Water Utilities - M3. 3rd ed. (AWWA Manuals). (Illus.). 128p. pap. text ed. 8.00 (ISBN 0-89867-061-6). Am Water Wks Assn.
Annual Asse Professional Development Conference, 1968, 70, 72, 78 & 79. Proceedings. 1980. 20.00 (ISBN 0-686-21675-X). ASSE.
Anton, Thomas. Occupational Safety & Health Management. 1979. text ed. 14.95 (ISBN 0-07-002106-6, C). McGraw.
Ashford, Nicholas A. Crisis in the Workplace: Occupational Disease & Injury - (a Report to the Ford Foundation) LC 75-28424. 1976. text ed. 27.50x (ISBN 0-262-01045-3). MIT Pr.
Atherly, Gordon. Occupational Health & Safety Concepts. 1978. 20.20x (ISBN 0-85334-848-0). Intl Ideas.
Bacow, Lawrence S. Bargaining for Job Safety & Health. 208p. 1980. text ed. 17.50x (ISBN 0-262-02152-8). MIT Pr.
Bailey, Martin J. Reducing Risks to Life: Measurement of the Benefits. 1980. pap. 4.25 (ISBN 0-8447-3346-6). Am Enterprise.
Beaulieu, Harry J. & Buchan, Roy M. Quantitative Industrial Hygiene. 1981. lib. bdg. 17.50 (ISBN 0-8240-7180-8). Garland Pub.
Berman, Daniel. Death on the Job. LC 78-13914. 1979. pap. 6.50 (ISBN 0-85345-527-9, PB5279). Monthly Rev.
Binford, Charles M., et al. Loss Control in the OSHA Era. (Illus.). 288p. 1975. 19.95 (ISBN 0-07-005278-6, P&RB). McGraw.
Blake, Roland P. Industrial Safety. 3rd ed. 1963. ref. ed. 16.95 (ISBN 0-13-463133-1). P-H.
Blockley, D. I. The Nature of Structure-Design & Safety. 365p. 1980. 89.95 (ISBN 0-470-27047-0). Halsted Pr.
Bodurtha, Frank T. Industrial Explosion Prevention & Protection. (Illus.). 1980. 21.50 (ISBN 0-07-006359-1). McGraw.
Boley, Jack. A Guide to Effective Industrial Safety. 127p. 1977. 8.95 (ISBN 0-87201-798-2). Gulf Pub.
--A Guide to Effective Industrial Safety. 127p. 1977. 8.95 (ISBN 0-87201-798-2). Gulf Pub.
Bridbord, Kenneth & French, Jean, eds. Toxicological & Carcinogenic Health Hazards in the Workplace. LC 78-72073. (Illus., Orig.). 1979. text ed. 22.00x (ISBN 0-930376-05-6). Pathotox Pubs.
Broadhurst, V. A. The Health & Safety at Work Act in Practice. 1978. 17.50 (ISBN 0-85501-159-9). Heyden.
Brown, D. Systems Analysis & Design for Safety. 399p. 1976. text ed. 24.95 (ISBN 0-13-881177-6). P-H.
Browning. The Loss Rate Concept in Safety Engineering. (Occupational Safety & Health Ser.: Vol. 6). 176p. 1980. 27.50 (ISBN 0-8247-1249-8). Dekker.
Building Work. (Occupational Safety & Health Ser.: No. 42). 255p. 1981. pap. 16.00 (ISBN 92-2-101907-1, ILO 161, ILO). Unipub.
Chelius, James R. Workplace Safety & Health. 1977. pap. 4.25 (ISBN 0-8447-3274-5). Am Enterprise.
Chemical Engineering Magazine. Safe & Efficient Plant Operation & Maintenance. LC 80-14762. (Chemical Engineering Ser.). 400p. 1980. 29.50 (ISBN 0-07-010707-6); pap. 24.50 (ISBN 0-686-77571-6). McGraw.
Chicken, John C. Hazard Control Policy in Britain. LC 75-12900. 204p. 1975. text ed. 27.00 (ISBN 0-08-019739-6). Pergamon.
Chissick, S. S. & Derricott, R. Occupational Health & Safety Management. LC 79-41218. 720p. 1981. 117.00 (ISBN 0-471-27646-4, Pub. by Wiley-Interscience). Wiley.
Coe, Charles K. Cutting Costs with a Safety Program. 96p. 1977. spiral bdg. 5.00 (ISBN 0-89854-001-1). U of GA Inst Govt.
Culbertson, Charles. Origin of Safety Management & Legislative Effects. 28p. 1981. write for info. Risk & Ins.
Denton, K. Safety Management. 416p. 1982. text ed. 19.95 (ISBN 0-07-016410-X, C). McGraw.
DeReamer, Russell. Modern Safety & Health Technology. LC 79-47487. 1980. 35.95 (ISBN 0-471-05729-0, Pub. by Wiley-Interscience). Wiley.
Educational Research Council of America. Safety Engineer. rev. ed. Ferris, Theodore N. & Marchak, John P., eds. (Real People at Work Ser: F). (Illus.). 1976. pap. text ed. 2.25 (ISBN 0-89247-048-8). Changing Times.
Engineering Industry Training Board, ed. Training in Safe Working Practice for Power Press Tool Setters & Operators, 9 vols. Incl. Vol. 1. Introduction to Power Press; Vol. 3. Press Brakes; Vol. 4. Safety Tool Setting; Vol. 5. Guards; Vol. 6. Testing Press Guards; Vol. 7. Accident Prevention. 1973. Set. 21.00x (ISBN 0-89563-031-1). Intl Ideas.
Fellner, Baruch A. & Savelson, Donald W. Occupational Safety & Health: Law & Practice. 1977. 35.00 (ISBN 0-685-85381-0, A1-1238). PLI.
Gardner, James E. Safety Training for the Supervisor. 3rd ed. LC 78-52505. 1979. pap. text ed. 8.95 (ISBN 0-201-03090-X). A-W.
Gausch, John P. Balanced Involvement: Safety, Production Motivation. (Monographs: No.3). cancelled (ISBN 0-686-21671-7); cancelled (ISBN 0-686-21672-5). ASSE.
Gersuny, Carl. Work Hazards & Industrial Conflict. LC 80-51506. (Illus.). 176p. 1981. 14.00x (ISBN 0-87451-189-5). U Pr of New Eng.
Goldsmith, Frank & Kerr, Lorin E. Occupational Safety & Health: The Control & Prevention of Work-Related Hazards. 1982. in prep. (ISBN 0-89885-092-4). Human Sci Pr.
Gomez, Manuel, et al. At Work in Copper: Occupational Health & Safety in Copper Smelting, 3 vols. LC 79-63375. (Illus.). 1979. Set. pap. 70.00x (ISBN 0-918780-11-X). Inform.
Grimaldi, John V. & Simonds, Rollin H. Safety Management. 3rd ed. 1975. 20.95 (ISBN 0-256-01564-3). Irwin.
Hammar, Willie. Occupational Safety Management & Engineering. 2nd ed. (Illus.). 608p. 1981. text ed. 19.95 (ISBN 0-13-629410-3). P-H.
Hammer, Willie. Handbook of System & Product Safety. LC 72-2683. (Illus.). 368p. 1972. ref. ed. 32.95 (ISBN 0-13-382226-5). P-H.
Hazards in Construction. 1980. 60.00x (ISBN 0-686-69903-3, Pub. by Telford England). State Mutual Bk.
Hazards: Vol. 11, Proceedings. (Symposium Ser.: No. 58). 304p. 1981. 80.00x (ISBN 0-85295-120-5, Pub. by Inst Chem Eng England). State Mutual Bk.
Heinrich, Herbert W. Industrial Accident Prevention. 4th ed. 1959. text ed. 22.00 (ISBN 0-07-028058-4, C). McGraw.
Heinrich, Herbert W., et al. Industrial Accident Prevention: A Safety Management Approach. 5th rev. ed. (Illus.). 1980. text ed. 27.00 (ISBN 0-07-028061-4); instructor's manual 10.95 (ISBN 0-07-028062-2). McGraw.
Hendrick, Kingsley. Improving Employee Safety & Health Performance: A Managerial Guide. 1981. price not set (ISBN 0-8240-7269-3). Garland Pub.
Hilado, Carlos J. Handbook of Flammability Regulations. LC 75-7498. 380p. 1975. pap. 35.00x (ISBN 0-87762-159-4). Technomic.
Institute for Power System. Handbook of Industrial Fire Protection & Security. 600p. 1979. 99.00x (ISBN 0-686-65619-9). State Mutual Bks.
--Handbook of Industrial Safety & Health. 1979. 99.00x (ISBN 0-686-65621-0). State Mutual Bks.
International Labour Conference, 67th Session, 1981. Safety & Health & the Working Environment, Report VI, Pt. 2. 79p. (Orig.). 1981. pap. 8.55 (ISBN 92-2-102408-3). Intl Labour Office.
International Labour Office. Safety & Health & the Working Environment: International Labour Conference, 1981, 67th Session. 68p. (Orig.). 1980. pap. 8.55 (ISBN 92-2-102407-5). Intl Labour Office.
International Labour Office, Geneva. Building Work: A Compendium of Occupational Safety & Health. (Occupational Safety & Health Ser.: No. 42). (Illus.). 256p. (Orig.). 1980. pap. 14.25 (ISBN 92-2-101907-1). Intl Labour Office.
International Labour Office Staff. Civil Engineering Work: A Compendium of Occupational Safety Practice. (Occupational Safety & Health Ser.). viii, 153p. (Orig.). 1981. pap. 11.40 (ISBN 92-2-102577-2). Intl Labour Office.
Johnson, W., ed. Safety Assurance Systems. (Occupational Safety & Health Ser.). 1980. 35.00 (ISBN 0-8247-6897-3). Dekker.
Jones, W. T. Health & Safety at Work Handbook: Basic Volume, 3 vols. 250p. 1975. 10.00x (ISBN 0-86010-014-6, Pub. by Graham & Trotman England); Supplement 1 & 2. lib. bdg. 11.00x (ISBN 0-86010-071-5); Set. pap. 21.00x (ISBN 0-686-64054-3). State Mutual Bk.
Keller, J. J., & Assocs., Inc. Fleet Safety Compliance Manual. McDowell, George B., ed. LC 78-71720. 1979. 45.00 (ISBN 0-934674-24-8, 8M). J J Keller.
--Occupational Exposure Guide. Kleinhans, James, ed. LC 79-54214. 1979. 95.00 (ISBN 0-934674-13-2). J J Keller.
Kelman, Steven. Regulating America, Regulating Sweden: A Comparative Study of Occupational Safety & Health Policy. 280p. 1981. text ed. 19.95x (ISBN 0-262-11076-8). MIT Pr.
King, Ralph W. & Magid, John. Industrial Hazard & Safety Handbook. (Illus.). 1979. 74.95 (ISBN 0-408-00304-9). Butterworth.
Kochan, Thomas A., et al. The Effectiveness of Union-Management Safety & Health Committees. LC 77-22038. 1977. pap. 2.75 (ISBN 0-911558-02-0). Upjohn Inst.
LaDou. Occupational Health Law: A Guide for Industry. (Occupational Safety & Health Ser.: Vol. 7). 232p. 1981. 24.50 (ISBN 0-8247-1329-X). Dekker.
Lauber, R., ed. Safety of Computer Control Systems: Proceedings of the IFAC Workshop, Stuttgart, Federal Republic of Germany, 16-18 May 1979. (Illus.). 230p. 1980. 52.00 (ISBN 0-08-024453-X). Pergamon.
Leo, Anthony T. Guide to Occupational Safety Law. 1980. pap. 10.95 (ISBN 0-686-62266-9). Collegium Bk Pubs.
--Guide to Occupational Safety Law. 1980. pap. 10.95 (ISBN 0-686-62266-9). Collegium Bk Pubs.
MacAvoy, Paul W., ed. OSHA Safety Regulations: Ford Administration Papers. 1977. pap. 5.25 (ISBN 0-8447-3249-4). Am Enterprise.
McElroy, Frank E., ed. Accident Prevention Manual for Industrial Operations: Engineering & Technology Volume. LC 80-81376. 768p. 1980. 25.00 (ISBN 0-87912-026-6, 121-40). Natl Safety Coun.
Machinery & Allied Products Institute Seminar on Occupational Safety & Health, Washington, D.C., 1973. Occupational Safety & Health: A Transcript. LC 73-166354. 173p. 1973. 15.00 (ISBN 0-686-05728-7). M & A Products.
Malasky, Sol. Systems Safety: Technology & Application. 300p. 1981. lib. bdg. 32.50 (ISBN 0-8240-7280-4). Garland Pub.
Margolis, Bruce L. & Kroes, William H. The Human Side of Accident Prevention: Psychological Concepts & Principles Which Bear on Industrial Safety. (Illus.). 160p. 1975. 15.50 (ISBN 0-398-03253-X). C C Thomas.
Mendeloff, John. Regulating Safety: A Economic & Political Analysis of Occupational Safety & Health Policy. (Illus.). 1979. text ed. 20.00x (ISBN 0-262-13147-1). MIT Pr.
Miller, David E. Occupational Safety, Health, & Fire Index. (Occupational Safety and Health Ser.: Vol. 1). 1976. 38.50 (ISBN 0-8247-6462-5). Dekker.
Miller, Marshall L., ed. Occupational Health & Safety Regulation. LC 78-60849. 154p. 1980. pap. text ed. 22.50 (ISBN 0-86587-078-0). Gov Insts.
Mitchell, Ewan. The Employer's Guide to the Law on Health, Safety & Welfare at Work. 2nd ed. 471p. 1977. text ed. 36.75x (ISBN 0-220-66341-6, Pub. by Busn Bks England). Renouf.
Moran, Robert D. How to Avoid OSHA. (Illus.). 256p. 1981. 49.95 (ISBN 0-87201-652-8). Gulf Pub.
National Academy Of Engineering. Public Safety: A Growing Factor in Modern Design. (Orig.). 1970. pap. 5.50 (ISBN 0-309-01752-1). Natl Acad Pr.
National Directory of the Safety Consultants. 1980. 7.50 (ISBN 0-686-21678-4). ASSE.
National Research & Appraisal Co. & Sharninghouse, Jane, eds. OSHA for Machine Tools. 1000p. 1980. 95.00 (ISBN 0-89692-101-8). Equipment Guide.
National Safety Council. Making Safety Work. (gr. 8-9). 1976. text ed. 6.95 (ISBN 0-07-046085-X, G); teacher's manual & key 1.00 (ISBN 0-07-046086-8). McGraw.
--Meat Industry Safety Guidelines. 2nd ed. 112p. 1978. pap. 11.00 (ISBN 0-87912-043-6, 129-51). Natl Safety Coun.
National Safety Council Staff. Handbook of Occupational Safety & Health. McElroy, Frank E., ed. LC 75-11314. 272p. 1975. pap. text ed. 8.75 (ISBN 0-87912-036-3, 12903). Natl Safety Coun.
--Personnel Safety in Chemical & Allied Industries. LC 78-58303. 198p. 1979. pap. 16.00 (ISBN 0-87912-125-4, 129-96). Natl Safety Coun.
Nothstein, G. Reference Primer on the Occupational Safety & Health Act. (Illus.). 832p. 1981. text ed. 29.95 (ISBN 0-02-923110-8). Macmillan.
Occupational Exposure to Airborne Substances Harmful to Health. 44p. 1981. pap. 6.50 (ISBN 92-2-102442-3, ILO 152, ILO). Unipub.
Optimisation of the Working Environment: New Trends. (Occupational Safety & Health Ser.: No. 43). 421p. 1981. pap. 22.25 (ISBN 92-2-001905-1, ILO 162, ILO). Unipub.
OSHA Standards for General Industry. 1981. pap. 7.50 (ISBN 0-686-75925-7). Commerce.
OSHA Standards for the Construction Industry. 1981. pap. 3.50 (ISBN 0-686-75926-5). Commerce.
OSHA, Your Day in Court. (Monograph: No.4). 2.50 (ISBN 0-686-21673-3); non-members 4.00 (ISBN 0-686-21674-1). ASSE.
Page, Robert C. Occupational Health & Mantalent Development. LC 62-9730. 722p. 1968. 10.00 (ISBN 0-87527-064-6). Fireside Bks.

Peck, Theodore P., ed. Occupational Safety & Health: A Guide to Information Sources. LC 74-7199. (Management Information Guide Ser.: No. 28). 262p. 1974. 36.00 (ISBN 0-8103-0828-2). Gale.

Petersen, Dan. Analyzing Safety Performance. LC 79-19304. 344p. 1980. lib. bdg. 24.50 (ISBN 0-8240-7123-9). Garland Pub.

--The O S H A Compliance Manual. rev. ed. (Illus.). 1979. 27.50 (ISBN 0-07-049598-X, P&RB). McGraw.

--Safety Supervision. new ed. 1976. 12.95 (ISBN 0-8144-5392-9). Am Mgmt.

--Techniques of Safety Management. 2nd ed. (Illus.). 1978. 22.00 (ISBN 0-07-049596-3, P&RB). McGraw.

Petersen, Dan & Goodale, Jerry. Readings in Industrial Ancient Prevention. (Illus.). 1980. pap. text ed. 8.95 (ISBN 0-07-049591-2). McGraw.

Petersen, Daniel. Human Error Reduction & Safety Management. 272p. 1981. lib. bdg. 32.50 (ISBN 0-8240-7279-0). Garland Pub.

Poulton, E. C. The Environment at Work. (Illus.). 176p. 1979. 14.00 (ISBN 0-398-03848-1). C C Thomas.

Protecting Industrial-Business Facilities & Personnel from Terrorist Activities. 1977. pap. 5.00 (ISBN 0-918734-22-3). Reymont.

The Question of Professional Liability. (Monograph: No. 2). 2.00 (ISBN 0-686-21669-5); non-members 3.00 (ISBN 0-686-21670-9). ASSE.

Reprint of Status of the Safety Professional. cancelled (ISBN 0-686-21676-8). ASSE.

Reschenthaler, G. B. Occupational Health & Safety in Canada. 152p. 1979. pap. text ed. 5.00x (ISBN 0-920380-35-2, Pub. by Inst Res Pub Canada). Renouf.

ReVelle, Jack B. Safety Training Methods. LC 80-16601. 248p. 1980. 26.00 (ISBN 0-471-07761-5, Pub. by Wiley-Interscience). Wiley.

Rodgers, William P. Introduction to System Safety Engineering. LC 80-12545. 142p. 1980. Repr. of 1971 ed. lib. bdg. 17.50 (ISBN 0-89874-180-7). Krieger.

Rudman, Jack. Labor Safety Technician. (Career Examination Ser.: C-1595). (Cloth bdg. avail. on request). pap. 10.00 (ISBN 0-685-60438-1). Natl Learning.

Sanchez, Irene, et al. The California Worker's Compensation Rehabilitation System. LC 80-70211. (Illus.). 360p. 1981. 35.00x (ISBN 0-02-927670-5). Macmillan.

Shafai-Sahrai, Yaghoub. Determinants of Occupational Injury Experience: A Study of Matched Pairs of Companies. LC 73-620211. 120p. 1973. pap. 4.50 (ISBN 0-87744-084-0). Mich St U Busn.

Smith, Al J. Managing Hazardous Substances Accidents. (Illus.). 224p. 1981. 19.95 (ISBN 0-07-058467-2). McGraw.

Smith, Robert S. The Occupational Safety & Health Act: Its Goals & Its Achievements. LC 75-39953. 1976. pap. 3.00 (ISBN 0-8447-3193-5). Am Enterprise.

Solvent Extraction Plants. (Thirty Ser). 60p. 1974. pap. 3.00 (ISBN 0-685-44168-7, 36). Natl Fire Prot.

Tarrants, William E. The Measurement of Safety Performance. LC 79-19208. 400p. 1980. lib. bdg. 29.50 (ISBN 0-8240-7170-0). Garland Pub.

Tarrants, William E., ed. Dictionary of Terms Used in the Safety Profession. 1980. Repr. of 1971 ed. write for info. (ISBN 0-686-02409-5). ASSE.

Thurston, D. B. Design for Safety. LC 79-25241. 1980. 14.95 (ISBN 0-07-064554-X). McGraw.

Thygerson, Alton L. Safety: Concepts & Instruction. 2nd ed. (Illus.). 160p. 1976. pap. text ed. 7.95 (ISBN 0-13-785733-0). P-H.

Toxic & Hazardous Industrial Chemicals Safety Manual. 580p. Date not set. 65.00 (ISBN 0-686-76109-X, 13-101000-00). ASTM.

Trade & Technical Press Editors. Handbook of Industrial Safety & Health. 1980. 108.00 (ISBN 0-85461-075-8, Pub by Trade & Tech England). Renouf.

Trade & Technical Press Ltd, ed. Handbook of Industrial Fire Protection & Security. 105.00x (ISBN 0-85461-059-6). Intl Ideas.

Waisanen, Christine M. What to Do About OSHA. LC 78-73459. pap. 5.00 (ISBN 0-89834-002-0, 5926). Chamber Comm US.

Wells, G. L. Safety in Process Plant Design. 276p. 1981. 100.00x (ISBN 0-85295-126-4, Pub. by Inst Chem Eng England). State Mutual Bk.

--Safety in Process Plant Design. 276p. 1980. 65.95x (ISBN 0-470-26907-3). Halsted Pr.

Worker Safety Supply & Equipment Business, GB-039. 1978. 525.00 (ISBN 0-89336-088-0). BCC.

Zinngrabe, C. J. & Schumacher, F. W. Safety for Sheet Metal Workers. LC 76-49325. (gr. 9-12). 1977. pap. 3.80 (ISBN 0-8273-1614-3); tchr's guide 1.00 (ISBN 0-8273-1615-1). Delmar.

INDUSTRIAL SALVAGE

see Salvage (Waste, etc.)

INDUSTRIAL SCHOOLS

see Manual Training; Reformatories

INDUSTRIAL SECURITY MEASURES

see Industry-Security Measures

INDUSTRIAL SITES

see also Industrial Districts

Girard, Weldon. How to Make Big Money Selling Commercial & Industrial Property. 1977. 24.95 (ISBN 0-13-417956-0, Busn). P-H.

Guidelines for Assessing Industrial Environmental Impact & Environmental Criteria for the Siting of Industry. (Industry & Environment Guidelines Ser.: Vol. 1). 105p. 1981. pap. 20.00 (ISBN 92-807-1015-X, UNEP 48, UNEP). Unipub.

Martin, Jane, ed. Milestones in Development: A Cumulative Index to Industrial Development, Site Selection Handbook & Related Publications Covering a Quarter-Century of Professional Contribution. 1981. 75.00x (ISBN 0-910436-16-9). Conway Pubns.

New Project File & Site Selection Checklist. LC 79-53499. 1979. vinyl binder 35.00x (ISBN 0-910436-12-6). Conway Pubns.

Solzman, David M. Waterway Industrial Sites: A Chicago Case Study. LC 66-29231. (Research Papers Ser.: No. 107). 138p. 1967. pap. 8.00 (ISBN 0-89065-016-0). U Chicago Dept Geog.

--Waterway Industrial Sites: A Chicago Case Study. LC 66-29231. (Research Papers Ser.: No. 107). 138p. 1967. pap. 8.00 (ISBN 0-89065-016-0). U Chicago Dept Geog.

INDUSTRIAL SOCIOLOGY

Here are entered works on social relations within industry, as distinguished from labor-management relations. Works about the impact of industry on culture and societal changes, and works about the social responsibilities of businessmen are entered under Industry-Social Aspects.

see also Industrial Organization; Industry-Social Aspects

Abegglen, James C. The Japanese Factory: Aspects of Its Social Organization. Coser, Lewis A. & Powell, Walter W., eds. LC 79-6982. (Perennial Works in Sociology Ser.). (Illus.). 1979. Repr. of 1958 ed. lib. bdg. 13.00x (ISBN 0-405-12082-6). Arno.

Alderfer, Clayton P. Existence, Relatedness & Growth: Human Needs in Organizational Settings. LC 72-156839. 1972. 15.95 (ISBN 0-02-900390-3). Free Pr.

Anderson, V. V. Psychiatry in Industry. Stein, Leon, ed. LC 77-70477. (Work Ser.). 1977. Repr. of 1929 ed. lib. bdg. 25.00x (ISBN 0-405-10151-1). Arno.

Baric, L. Kinship in Industrial Society. 1971. pap. text ed. 2.45x (ISBN 0-02-972330-2). Macmillan.

Barnard, Chester I. Functions of the Executive. 30th anniversary ed. LC 68-28690. 1968. 16.50x (ISBN 0-674-32800-0); pap. 5.95x (ISBN 0-674-32803-5). Harvard U Pr.

Berg, I. Industrial Sociology. 1979. 11.95 (ISBN 0-13-463240-0); pap. 7.95 (ISBN 0-13-463232-X). P-H.

Berkman, Harold W. The Human Relations of Management. 1974. text ed. 14.95x (ISBN 0-685-70780-6). Dickenson.

Blake, Robert R. & Mouton, Jane S. Corporate Excellence Through Grid Organization Development. (Illus.). 392p. 1968. 11.95 (ISBN 0-87201-331-6). Gulf Pub.

Blake, Robert R., et al. Managing Intergroup Conflict in Industry. (Illus.). 223p. 1964. 10.95 (ISBN 0-87201-375-8). Gulf Pub.

Blauner, Robert. Alienation & Freedom: The Factory Worker & His Industry. LC 64-15820. 1964. pap. 3.45 (ISBN 0-226-05811-5, P271, Phoen). U of Chicago Pr.

Bowen, Peter. Social Control in Industrial Organisations. (Direct Edition Ser.). (Orig.). 1976. pap. 17.95x (ISBN 0-7100-8312-2). Routledge & Kegan.

Bowers, Raymond V., ed. Studies on Behavior in Organizations: A Research Symposium. LC 65-28462. 364p. 1966. 20.00x (ISBN 0-8203-0171-X). U of Ga Pr.

Bramlette, Carl A., Jr., ed. Individual & the Future of Organizations, Vol. 4. Mescon, Michael H. LC 72-619550. (Franklin Foundation Lecture Ser.). Orig. Title: Man & the Future of Organizations. 60p. 1975. pap. 3.75 (ISBN 0-88406-101-9). Ga St U Busn Pub.

Burns, Tom R., et al, eds. Work & Power: The Liberation of Work & the Control of Political Power. LC 78-63143. (Sage Studies in International Sociology: Vol. 18). (Illus.). 391p. 1979. 22.50 (ISBN 0-8039-9846-5); pap. 9.95 (ISBN 0-8039-9847-3). Sage.

Carby, Keith & Thakur, Manab. No Problems Here? Management & the Multi-Racial Workforce Including a Guide to the Race Relations Act 1976. 1977. pap. 5.00x (ISBN 0-85292-151-9). Intl Pubns Serv.

Cochrane, James L. Industrialism & Industrial Man in Retrospect: A Critical Review of the Ford Foundation's Support for the Inter-University Study of Labor. LC 79-18897. 196p. 1979. 14.75 (ISBN 0-916584-12-7, IS-00091, Pub. by Ford Found). Univ Microfilms.

Davis, Keith. Human Behavior at Work: Human Relations & Organizational Behavior. 5th ed. (Management Ser). (Illus.). 1976. text ed. 15.95 (ISBN 0-07-015489-9, C); instructor's manual 5.50 (ISBN 0-07-015518-6). McGraw.

--Organizational Behavior: A Book of Readings. 5th ed. 1977. pap. text ed. 9.95 (ISBN 0-07-015499-6, C). McGraw.

Dawley, Alan. Class & Community: The Industrial Revolution in Lynn. LC 75-29049. (Harvard Studies in Urban History Ser.). (Illus.). 1979. 17.50x (ISBN 0-674-13390-0); pap. 6.95x (ISBN 0-674-13395-1). Harvard U Pr.

DuBrin, Andrew J. Survival in the Office: How to Move Ahead or Hang On. 1977. 8.95 (ISBN 0-442-80447-4). Van Nos Reinhold.

Dufty, N. E., ed. The Sociology of the Blue Collar Worker. (International Studies in Sociology & Social Anthropology). 1969. text ed. 25.50x (ISBN 90-040-1054-8). Humanities.

Dunkerley, David. Foreman: Aspects of Task & Structure. (International Library of Sociology Ser.). 1975. 18.95x (ISBN 0-7100-8158-8). Routledge & Kegan.

Dutton, Richard. The Behavior Laboratory: A Manual. new ed. LC 74-15620. 176p. 1975. pap. text ed. 10.95 (ISBN 0-87620-112-5); instructor's guide free (ISBN 0-87620-113-3). Goodyear.

Eldridge, J. E. & Crombie, A. D. A Sociology of Organisations. (Studies in Sociology Ser.). (Illus.). 1975. pap. text ed. 7.50x (ISBN 0-04-301071-7). Allen Unwin.

Ellsworth, John, Jr. Factory Folkways: Study of Institutional Structure & Change. Stein, Leon, ed. LC 77-70493. (Work Ser.). 1977. Repr. of 1952 ed. lib. bdg. 20.00x (ISBN 0-405-10164-3). Arno.

Ewing, David W. Freedom Inside the Organization: Bringing Civil Liberties to the Workplace. 1978. pap. 3.95 (ISBN 0-07-019847-0, SP). McGraw.

Flumiani, Carlo M. The Survival of the Leadership Corporation & the Corporate State. (Illus.). 273p. 1977. 42.25 (ISBN 0-89266-042-2). Am Classical Coll Pr.

Fox, A. Sociology of Work in Industry. 1971. pap. text ed. 2.45x (ISBN 0-02-973610-2). Macmillan.

Gallie, D. In Search of the New Working Class. LC 77-80834. (Studies in Sociology: No. 9). (Illus.). 1978. 36.00 (ISBN 0-521-21771-7); pap. 10.95x (ISBN 0-521-29275-1). Cambridge U Pr.

Gardell, Bertil & Johansson, Gunn. Working Life: A Social Science Contribution to Work Reform. LC 80-40289. 347p. 1981. 45.00x (ISBN 0-471-27801-7, Pub. by Wiley-Interscience). Wiley.

Goldthorpe, John H., et al. Affluent Worker, in the Class Structure. (Studies in Sociology: No. 3). 1969. 29.95 (ISBN 0-521-07231-X); pap. 9.95x (ISBN 0-521-09533-6). Cambridge U Pr.

Hegarty, Edward J. How to Succeed in Company Politics. 2nd ed. 1976. 17.95 (ISBN 0-07-027847-4, P&RB). McGraw.

Holmstrom, M. South Indian Factory Workers. LC 75-46205. (Cambridge South Asian Studies: No. 20). 1977. 19.95 (ISBN 0-521-21134-4). Cambridge U Pr.

Hudson, Kenneth. Where We Used to Work. 1980. text ed. 20.75x (ISBN 0-212-97025-9). Humanities.

International Principles & Guidelines on Social Policy for Multinational Enterprises: Thier Usefulness & Feasibility. 1976. 7.15 (ISBN 92-2-101477-0). Intl Labour Office.

Jacquemin, A. P. & DeJong, H. W., eds. Welfare Aspects of Industrial Markets. (Nijenrode Studies in Economics: No. 2). 1977. lib. bdg. 40.00 (ISBN 90-207-0625-X, Pub. by Martinus Nijhoff Netherlands). Kluwer Boston.

Katz, Daniel & Kahn, Robert L. The Social Psychology of Organizations. 2nd ed. LC 77-18764. 838p. 1978. text ed. 26.95 (ISBN 0-471-02355-8). Wiley.

King, Charles D. & Van De Vall, Mark. Models of Industrial Democracy: Consultation, Co-Determination & Workers Management. (New Babylon Studies in the Social Sciences Ser.: No. 29). 1978. text ed. 19.75x (ISBN 0-686-26039-2). Mouton.

Kipp, E. M. People Aspects of Research & Development Management: Attracting & Retaining R & D Personnel. 1967. 29.25x (ISBN 0-677-40040-3). Gordon.

Klein, Lisl. Social Scientist in Industry. LC 75-41612. 257p. 1976. 21.95 (ISBN 0-470-15004-1). Halsted Pr.

Kumar, Krishan. Prophecy & Progress: The Sociology of Industrial & Post-Industrial Society. 1978. pap. 3.95 (ISBN 0-14-022039-9, Pelican). Penguin.

Kusterer, Ken C. Know-How on the Job: The Important Working Knowledge of "Unskilled" Workers. (Westview Replica Edition Ser.). 202p. 1980. pap. text ed. 9.50x (ISBN 0-89158-916-3). Westview.

Lederer, Emil. Die Privatangestellten in der Modernen Wirtschaftsentwicklung: White Collar Workers in Modern Economic Development. LC 74-25765. (European Sociology Ser.). 300p. 1975. Repr. 19.00x (ISBN 0-405-06519-1). Arno.

Levenstein, Adolf. Die Arbeiterfrage: The Labor Question: with Particular Consideration of the Social Psychological Side of Modern Large-Scale Industry & Its Psycho-Physical Effect on Workers. LC 74-25767. (European Sociology Ser.). 410p. 1975. Repr. 23.00x (ISBN 0-405-06521-3). Arno.

Leventman, Paula G. Professionals Out of Work. LC 80-1645. (Illus.). 1981. 19.95 (ISBN 0-02-918800-8). Free Pr.

Lorsch, Jay W. & Lawrence, Paul R. Managing Group & Intergroup Relations. 1972. pap. 11.95x (ISBN 0-256-00264-9). Irwin.

Manette, Jan. The Working Girl in a Man's World. LC 66-22896. 223p. 1966. 6.00 (ISBN 0-915988-01-1, Pub. by Hawthorne Books). Reading Gems.

Masi, Dale A. Human Services in Industry. 1981. price not set (ISBN 0-669-05104-7). Lexington Bks.

Mayo, Elton. The Human Problems of an Industrial Civilization. Stein, Leon, ed. LC 77-70515. (Work Ser.). 1977. Repr. of 1933 ed. lib. bdg. 15.00x (ISBN 0-405-10184-8). Arno.

--The Social Problems of an Industrial Civilization. Stein, Leon, ed. LC 77-70516. (Work Ser.). 1977. Repr. of 1945 ed. lib. bdg. 12.00x (ISBN 0-405-10185-6). Arno.

Meakin, David. Man & Work: Literature & Culture in Industrial Society. LC 75-45269. 215p. 1976. text ed. 18.00x (ISBN 0-8419-0259-3). Holmes & Meier.

Michelman, Irving S. The Crisis Meters: Business Response to Social Crises. LC 73-4914. 1973. lib. bdg. 15.00x (ISBN 0-678-01320-9). Kelley.

Miller, Delbert C. & Form, William H. Industrial Sociology: Work in Organizational Life. 3rd ed. (Illus.). 1979. text ed. 24.50 scp (ISBN 0-06-044471-1, HarpC). Har-Row.

Moore, Wilbert E. Industrial Relations & the Social Order. rev. ed. Stein, Leon, ed. LC 77-70517. (Work Ser.). (Illus.). 1977. Repr. of 1951 ed. lib. bdg. 41.00x (ISBN 0-405-10186-4). Arno.

Nash, Allan N. & Carroll, Stephen J. The Management of Compensation. LC 74-18922. (Behavioral Science in Industry Ser.). (Illus.). 1975. text ed. 9.95x (ISBN 0-8185-0135-9); pap. text ed. 11.95 (ISBN 0-8185-0135-9). Brooks-Cole.

Nelson, Daniel. Managers & Workers: Origins of the New Factory System in the United States, 1880-1920. 1975. 20.00x (ISBN 0-299-06900-1). U of Wis Pr.

Nichols, Theo & Beynon, Huw. Living with Capitalism: Class Relations & the Modern Factory. 1977. 18.00x (ISBN 0-7100-8594-X); pap. 10.00 (ISBN 0-7100-8595-8). Routledge & Kegan.

Offe, Claus. Industry & Inequality: The Achievement Principle in Work & Social Status. LC 76-40724. 1977. 18.95x (ISBN 0-312-41580-X). St Martin.

Parker, S. R., et al. The Sociology of Industry. 3rd ed. (Studies in Sociology Ser.). 1978. text ed. 17.95x (ISBN 0-04-301082-2); pap. text ed. 8.95x (ISBN 0-04-301083-0). Allen Unwin.

Presthus, Robert. The Organizational Society. 2nd ed. LC 77-86297. 1978. text ed. 14.95 (ISBN 0-312-58780-5); pap. text ed. 6.95x (ISBN 0-312-58781-3). St Martin.

Preston, Lee E., ed. Research in Corporate Social Performance & Policy, Vol. 3. 325p. 1981. 34.50 (ISBN 0-89232-184-9). Jai Pr.

Price, R. Masters, Unions & Men. LC 79-21229. (Illus.). 1980. 39.95 (ISBN 0-521-22882-4). Cambridge U Pr.

Quante, Wolfgang. The Exodus of Corporate Headquarters from New York City. LC 75-19809. (Special Studies). (Illus.). 234p. 1976. text ed. 27.95 (ISBN 0-275-55770-7). Praeger.

Quick, Thomas. Understanding People at Work: A Manager's Guide to the Behavioral Sciences. 1976. pap. 8.95 (ISBN 0-917386-17-5). Exec Ent.

Ritzer, George. Working: Conflict & Change. 2nd ed. (Illus.). 1977. text ed. 19.95 (ISBN 0-13-967638-4). P-H.

Rohlen, Thomas P. For Harmony & Strength: Japanese White-Collar Organization in Anthropological Perspective. LC 73-91668. 1974. 26.50x (ISBN 0-520-02674-8); pap. 7.95x (ISBN 0-520-03849-5). U of Cal Pr.

Rose, Michael. Servants of Post-Industrial Power: Sociologie Du Travail in Modern France. LC 78-65594. 1979. 22.50 (ISBN 0-87332-130-8). M E Sharpe.

Sainsaulieu, Renaud. L' Identite au Travail: Les effets culturels de l'organisation. 1977. lib. bdg. 40.00x (ISBN 2-7246-0386-9); pap. text ed. 32.50x (ISBN 2-7246-0385-0). Clearwater Pub.

Sayles, Leonard R. Behavior of Industrial Work Groups: Prediction & Control. Stein, Leon, ed. LC 77-70530. (Work Ser.). 1977. Repr. of 1958 ed. lib. bdg. 12.00x (ISBN 0-405-10198-8). Arno.

Scase, Richard, ed. Industrial Society: Class, Cleavage & Control. LC 76-47126. 1977. 17.95x (ISBN 0-312-41545-1). St Martin.

Schneider, E. V. Industrial Sociology: The Social Relations of Industry & the Community. 2nd ed. (Sociology Ser.). 1969. text ed. 16.95 (ISBN 0-07-055461-7, C). McGraw.

Shepard, Jon M. Organizational Issues in Industrial Society: A Book of Readings. (General Sociology Ser.). 496p. 1972. ref. ed. 10.95 (ISBN 0-13-641001-4). P-H.

Smith, John H. The University Teaching of Social Sciences: Industrial Sociology. 1961. pap. 2.75 (ISBN 92-3-100461-1, UNESCO). Unipub.

Staw, Barry M., ed. Psychological Foundations of Organizational Behavior. LC 76-62995. 1977. pap. text ed. 12.95 (ISBN 0-87620-736-0). Goodyear.

Stein, Leon, ed. Work or Labor: Original Anthology. LC 77-70551. (Work Ser.). (Illus.). 1977. lib. bdg. 28.00x (ISBN 0-405-10205-4). Arno.

Travers, Henry J. Organizations: Size & Intensity. LC 78-52294. 1978. pap. text ed. 6.75 (ISBN 0-8191-0483-3). U Pr of Amer.

UCLA Seminar. Humanization of the Workplace - The Swedish Experience: Proceedings. 1975. 2.00 (ISBN 0-89215-001-7). U Cal LA Indus Rel.

Van Maanen, J. Organizational Careers: Some New Perspectives. LC 76-13537. (Individuals, Groups & Organizations Ser). 1977. 23.95 (ISBN 0-471-99409-X, Pub. by Wiley-Interscience). Wiley.

Vickers, Geoffrey. Making Institutions Work. LC 73-11543. 1973. 21.95 (ISBN 0-470-90689-8). Halsted Pr.

Walker, Charles R. & Guest, Robert H. The Man on the Assembly Line. Coser, Lewis A. & Powell, Walter W., eds. LC 79-7027. (Perennial Works in Sociology Ser.). (Illus.). 1979. Repr. of 1952 ed. lib. bdg. 15.00x (ISBN 0-405-12126-1). Arno.

Wallman, Sandra. Social Anthropology of Work. LC 79-41277. (ASA Monograph Ser.: No. 19). 1980. 37.00 (ISBN 0-12-733250-2); pap. 18.50 (ISBN 0-12-733252-9). Acad Pr.

Warner, Malcolm, ed. Sociology of the Workplace. LC 73-15572. 291p. 1973. 17.95 (ISBN 0-470-92113-7). Halsted Pr.

Watson, Tony. Sociology, Work & Industry. 272p. 1980. 30.00 (ISBN 0-7100-0542-3); pap. 15.00 (ISBN 0-7100-0543-1). Routledge & Kegan.

Wheeler, David H. Our Industrial Utopia & Its Unhappy Citizens. LC 76-427888. Repr. of 1895 ed. 25.50 (ISBN 0-404-60080-8). AMS Pr.

Whitehead, T. N. The Industrial Worker: Human Relations in a Group of Manual Workers, 2 vols. in one. Stein, Leon, ed. LC 77-70546. (Work Ser.). (Illus.). 1977. Repr. of 1938 ed. lib. bdg. 30.00x (ISBN 0-405-10214-3). Arno.

Whyte, William F. Men at Work. LC 73-21104. (Illus.). 593p. 1974. Repr. of 1961 ed. lib. bdg. 38.00 (ISBN 0-8371-5976-8, WHMW). Greenwood.

Whyte, William F., ed. Industry & Society. LC 70-10019. (Illus.). vi, 211p. Repr. of 1946 ed. lib. bdg. 15.00 (ISBN 0-8371-4081-1, WHSO). Greenwood.

Wiener, A. Patterns of Control in Post-Industrial Society: Magnificent Myth. 1978. text ed. 45.00 (ISBN 0-08-021474-6); pap. text ed. 15.00 (ISBN 0-08-023100-4). Pergamon.

Witte, John F. Democracy, Authority, & Alienation in Work: Workers' Participation in an American Corporation. LC 80-16241. (Illus.). 1980. lib. bdg. 20.00x (ISBN 0-226-90420-2). U of Chicago Pr.

INDUSTRIAL STATISTICS

see also subdivision Industries under names of countries, cities, etc

Bain, Joe S. International Differences in Industrial Structure: Eight Nations in the 1950's. LC 80-14615. (Studies in Comparative Economics: No. 6). (Illus.). xiv, 209p. 1980. Repr. of 1966 ed. lib. bdg. 22.50x (ISBN 0-313-22408-0, BAID). Greenwood.

Daniel, Cuthbert. Applications of Statistics to Industrial Experimentation. LC 76-2012. (Applied Probability & Statistics Ser.). 294p. 1976. 31.00 (ISBN 0-471-19469-7, Pub. by Wiley-Interscience). Wiley.

Dietrich, C. F. Uncertainty, Calibration & Probability: The Statistics of Scientific & Industrial Measurement. LC 72-7639. 411p. 1973. 66.95 (ISBN 0-470-21440-6, Pub. by Wiley). Krieger.

Duncan, Acheson J. Quality Control & Industrial Statistics. 4th ed. 1974. 23.95x (ISBN 0-256-01558-9). Irwin.

Industrial Statistics Yearbook, 2 vols. 1979. pap. 35.00 ea. (UN). Vol. 1, General Industrial Statisics; 639 P (UN79-17-9). Vol. 2, Commodity Production Data, 67-77; 750 P (UN79-17-10). Unipub.

Lowe, C. W. Industrial Statistics, Vol. 2. 1970. 29.95x (ISBN 0-8464-0512-1). Beekman Pubs.

Oil & Gas Statistics Annual 1978 to 1979. 557p. (Orig.). 1981. pap. 32.50x (ISBN 92-64-02182-5). OECD.

Tuttle, Alva M. Use of Statistical Techniques by Ohio Manufacturers. 1963. pap. text ed. 2.00x (ISBN 0-87776-116-7, R116). Ohio St U Admin Sci.

United Nations. Yearbook of Industrial Statistics, 1976, 2 vols. Incl. Vol. 1. General Industrial Statistics, Nineteen Sixty-Seven to Nineteen Seventy-Six (ISBN 0-8002-2335-7); Vol. 2. Commodity Production Data, Nineteen Sixty-Seven to Nineteen Seventy-Six (ISBN 0-8002-2336-5). LC 76-64670. 1979. 30.00 ea. Intl Pubns Serv.

--Yearbook of Industrial Statistics, 1977, 2 vols. 11th ed. Incl. Vol. 1. General Industrial Statistics. 639p. 30.00x (ISBN 0-8002-2335-7); Vol. 2. Commodity Production Data, 1967 to 1977. 750p. 30.00x (ISBN 0-8002-2336-5). LC 76-646970. (Illus.). 1389p. 1979. write for info. Intl Pubns Serv.

--Yearbook of International Trade Statistics, 1979, 2 vols. 27th ed. Incl. Vol. 1. Trade by Country. 178p; Vol. 2. Trade by Commodity. 191p. LC 51-8987. (Illus.). 369p. (Eng. & Fr.). 1979. Set. 65.00x (ISBN 0-8002-2337-3). Intl Pubns Serv.

--Yearbook of National Accounts Statistics, 1978, 2 vols. 22nd ed. Incl. Vol. 1. Individual Country Data. 494p; Vol. 2. International Tables. 645p. LC 58-3719. (Illus.). 1979. 70.00x (ISBN 0-8002-2338-1). Intl Pubns Serv.

U. S. Bureau of Labor Statistics. Techniques of Preparing Major BLS Statistical Ser. Lipstein, Benjamin, ed. Repr. of 1954 ed. lib. bdg. 15.00 (ISBN 0-8371-2273-2, TESS). Greenwood.

Volkov, Sergei D. Statistical Strength Theory. (Russian Monographs Ser). (Illus.). 1962. 47.25x (ISBN 0-677-20350-0). Gordon.

Yearbook of Industrial Statistics, 2 vols. Vol. I. 35.00 (ISBN 0-685-33036-2, E.79.XVII.9); Vol. II. 35.00 (ISBN 0-685-33037-0, E.79.XVII.10). UN.

Yearbook of Industrial Statistics: Vol. II--Commodity Production Data 1969-1978. 747p. 1980. pap. 35.00 (ISBN 0-686-72372-4, UN80/17/10, UN). Unipub.

Yearbook of Industrial Statistics 1978: Vol. I--General Industrial Statistics. 645p. 1980. pap. 35.00 (ISBN 0-686-72371-6, UN80/17/9, UN). Unipub.

INDUSTRIAL SUPERVISORS

see Supervisors, Industrial

INDUSTRIAL SURVEYS

Here are entered works on the techniques employed. Reports, etc. of individual surveys are entered under the city or district concerned with or without subdivision Industries.

Dunham, Randall & Smith, Frank J. Organizational Surveys: An Internal Assessment of Organizational Health. 1979. pap. text ed. 8.95x (ISBN 0-673-15143-3). Scott F.

Kent, William. Investigating an Industry. LC 75-16271. (Management History Ser.: No. 65). 137p. Repr. of 1913 ed. 15.00 (ISBN 0-87960-071-3). Hive Pub.

List of Industry Analysts in the Federal Government. 1981. pap. 15.00 (ISBN 0-686-26067-8). Wash Res.

Walsh, John E., Jr. Preparing Feasibility Studies in Asia. LC 72-323074. 168p. 1971. 15.00 (ISBN 92-833-1001-2, APO55, APO). Unipub.

INDUSTRIAL TECHNICIANS

see Technicians in Industry

INDUSTRIAL TOXICOLOGY

Anderson, Kim E. & Scott, Ronald M. Fundamentals of Industrial Toxicology. (Illus.). 120p. 1981. text ed. 14.95 (ISBN 0-250-40378-1). Ann Arbor Science.

Baselt, Randall C. Biological Monitoring Methods for Industrial Chemicals. LC 79-56927. 1980. text ed. 47.00 (ISBN 0-931890-04-7). Biomed Pubns.

Clayton, George D. & Clayton, Florence E. Patty's Industrial Hygiene & Toxicology: General Principles, Vol. 1. 3rd rev. ed. LC 77-17515. 1978. 115.00 (ISBN 0-471-16046-6, Pub. by Wiley-Interscience). Wiley.

Clayton, George D. & Clayton, Florence. Patty's Industrial Hygiene & Toxicology: Toxicology, Vol. IIA. 3rd rev. ed. LC 77-17515. 1420p. 1981. 100.00 (ISBN 0-471-16042-3, Pub. by Wiley Interscience). Wiley.

Cralley, Lester & Cralley, Lewis. Patty's Industrial Hygiene & Toxicology: Theory & Rationale of Industrial Hygiene Practice, Vol. 3. LC 78-27102. 1979. 60.00 (ISBN 0-471-02698-0, Pub by Wiley-Interscience). Wiley.

Deichmann, W. B., ed. Toxicology & Occupational Medicine. (Developments in Toxicology & Environmental Science Ser.: Vol. 4). 1979. 55.00 (ISBN 0-444-00288-X, North Holland). Elsevier.

Fuller, John G. The Poison That Fell from the Sky. 1978. 6.95 (ISBN 0-394-42495-6). Random.

ILO-WHO Committee on Occupational Health. Geneva, 1968, 6th. Permissible Levels of Occupational Exposureto Airborne Toxic Substances: Report. (Technical Report Ser.: No. 415). (Also avail. in French & Spanish). 1969. pap. 1.20 (ISBN 92-4-120415-X). World Health.

Liss, Leopold, ed. Aluminum Neurotoxicity Symposium. (Neurotoxicology Ser.: Vol. 1, No. 4). (Illus.). 1980. text ed. 16.00 (ISBN 0-930376-18-8). Pathotox Pubs.

Miller, Marshall L., ed. Toxic Control: Toxic Control in the Eighties, Vol. IV. LC 80-80472. (Illus.). 224p. 1980. pap. text ed. 28.00 (ISBN 0-86587-053-5). Gov Insts.

Occupational Exposure to Airborne Substances Harmful to Health. 44p. 1981. pap. 6.50 (ISBN 92-2-102442-3, ILO 152, ILO). Unipub.

Peterson, Jack E. Industrial Health. (Illus.). 1977. ref. ed. 26.95 (ISBN 0-13-459552-1). P-H.

Plunkett, E. R. Handbook of Industrial Toxicology. 2nd ed. 1976. 40.00 (ISBN 0-8206-0201-9). Chem Pub.

Sittig, M. Toxic Metals-Pollution Control & Worker Protection. LC 76-24142. (Pollution Technology Review: No. 30). (Illus.). 1977. 39.00 (ISBN 0-8155-0636-8). Noyes.

Toxic Chemical & Explosives Facilities: Safety & Engineering Design. LC 79-9760. (Symposium Ser.: No. 96). 1979. 32.00 (ISBN 0-8412-0481-0). Am Chemical.

Tsubaki, T. & Irukayama, K., eds. Minamata Disease: Methylmercury Poisoning in Minamata & Nigata, Japan. 1977. 63.50 (ISBN 0-444-99816-0). Elsevier.

INDUSTRIAL TRAFFIC MANAGEMENT

see Shipment of Goods

INDUSTRIAL TRUSTS

see Trusts, Industrial

INDUSTRIAL UNIONS

see Trade-Unions

INDUSTRIAL VACUUM

see Vacuum Technology

INDUSTRIAL WASTES

see Factory and Trade Waste

INDUSTRIAL WATER SUPPLY

see Water-Supply, Industrial

INDUSTRIAL WELFARE WORK

see Welfare Work in Industry

INDUSTRIAL WORKERS OF THE WORLD

Brissenden, Paul F. Launching of the I. W. W. LC 78-169188. (American History & Americana Ser., No. 47). 1971. Repr. of 1913 ed. lib. bdg. 31.95 (ISBN 0-8383-1275-6). Haskell.

Brooks, John G. American Syndicalism. LC 78-86170. Repr. of 1913 ed. 10.00 (ISBN 0-404-01118-7). AMS Pr.

--American Syndicalism. LC 70-89722. (American Labor, from Conspiracy to Collective Bargaining Ser. 1). 264p. 1969. Repr. of 1913 ed. 11.00 (ISBN 0-405-02107-0). Arno.

--American Syndicalism: The I.W.W. LC 78-107407. (Civil Liberties in American History Ser). 1970. Repr. of 1913 ed. lib. bdg. 20.00 (ISBN 0-306-71887-1). Da Capo.

Chaplin, R., et al. Centralia Case: Three Views of the Armistice Day Tragedy at Centralia, Washington, November 11, 1919. LC 77-160845. (Civil Liberties in American History Ser). 1971. Repr. of 1924 ed. lib. bdg. 29.50 (ISBN 0-306-70211-8). Da Capo.

Chaplin, Ralph. Wobbly. LC 70-166089. (Civil Liberties in American History Ser). 1972. Repr. of 1948 ed. lib. bdg. 37.50 (ISBN 0-306-70212-6). Da Capo.

Conlin, Joseph R., ed. At the Point of Production: The Local History of the I.W.W. LC 80-1708. (Contributions in Labor History Ser.: No. 10). viii, 329p. 1981. lib. bdg. 29.95 (ISBN 0-313-22046-8, CPP/). Greenwood.

Flynn, Elizabeth G. Memories of the Industrial Workers of the World (IWW) (Occasional Papers: No. 24). 1977. 1.00 (ISBN 0-89977-025-8). Am Inst Marxist.

Gambs, John S. Decline of the I. W. W. LC 66-13171. 1966. Repr. of 1932 ed. 8.00 (ISBN 0-8462-0709-5). Russell.

George, Harrison. I. W. W. Trial, Story of the Greatest Trial in Labor's History by One of the Defendants. LC 70-90177. (Mass Violence in America Ser.). 9.00 (ISBN 0-405-01313-2). Arno.

Haywood, William D. Autobiography of Big Bill Haywood. LC 74-2407. 1966. pap. 2.95 (ISBN 0-7178-0011-3). Intl Pub Co.

IWW Song Book. 34th ed. 1976. pap. 0.75 (ISBN 0-917124-00-6). Indus Workers World.

Jacobs, Louis. What Does Judaism Say About... ? LC 73-77032. (The New York Times Library of Jewish Knowledge). (Illus.). 288p. 1974. 8.95 (ISBN 0-8129-0349-8). Times Bks.

Kornbluh, Joyce L., ed. Rebel Voices: An I.W.W. Anthology. LC 64-10611. (Illus.). 1968. pap. 4.95 (ISBN 0-472-06139-9, 139, AA). U of Mich Pr.

Parker, Carleton H. Casual Laborer & Other Essays. LC 67-19916. 1967. Repr. of 1920 ed. 7.50 (ISBN 0-8462-0946-2). Russell.

Radosh, R., ed. Debs. 1971. 6.95 (ISBN 0-13-197681-8). Brown Bk.

Thompson, Fred & Murfin, Patrick. The IWW: Its First Seventy Years, Nineteen Hundred & Five to Nineteen Seventy-Five. 1977. 15.00 (ISBN 0-917124-03-0); pap. 4.95 (ISBN 0-917124-04-9). Indus Workers World.

Tyler, Robert L. Rebels of the Woods: The I.W.W. in the Pacific Northwest. LC 68-1776. 1967. 7.50 (ISBN 0-87114-018-7). U of Oreg Bks.

INDUSTRIALISTS

Fraser, Colin. Tractor Pioneer: The Life of Harry Ferguson. LC 73-85451. (Illus.). vi, 294p. 1973. 15.00x (ISBN 0-8214-0134-3). Ohio U Pr.

Minnigerode, Meade. Certain Rich Men. LC 71-121489. (Essay Index Reprint Ser). 1927. 16.00 (ISBN 0-8369-1714-6). Arno.

Moore, Joseph A. Famous Leaders of Industry: Life Stories of Men Who Have Succeeded, Fifth Series. facsimile ed. LC 68-8505. (Essay Index Reprints - Famous Leaders Ser.). Repr. of 1945 ed. 23.00 (ISBN 0-8369-2326-X). Arno.

Shumway, Harry I. Famous Leaders of Industry, Fourth Series. facsimile ed. LC 76-167417. (Essay Index Reprint Ser). Repr. of 1936 ed. 26.00 (ISBN 0-8369-2441-X). Arno.

White, Trentwell M. Famous Leaders of Industry, Third Series. facsimile ed. LC 68-8505. (Essay Index Reprint Ser: Famous Leaders Ser). Repr. of 1931 ed. 23.00 (ISBN 0-8369-2259-X). Arno.

INDUSTRIALIZATION

see also Technical Assistance; Underdeveloped Areas; United Nations–Economic Assistance; United Nations–Technical Assistance

Agencies for Industrial Adaptation & Development. (Document Ser.). 1979. 3.00x (ISBN 92-64-11868-3). OECD.

Akerman, Johan. Theory of Industrialism: Causal Analysis & Economic Plans. LC 80-21155. (Illus.). Repr. of 1960 ed. lib. bdg. 19.50x (ISBN 0-87991-859-4). Porcupine Pr.

Baranson, Jack. North-South Technology Transfer: Financing & Institution Building. LC 81-80543. 159p. 1981. 15.75x (ISBN 0-912338-27-X); microfiche 12.75x (ISBN 0-912338-28-8). Lomond.

Batchelor, R. A., et al. Industrialisation & the Basis for Trade. LC 79-41582. (Economic & Social Studies: No. 32). 350p. 1980. 39.50 (ISBN 0-521-23302-X). Cambridge U Pr.

Berger, Suzanne & Piore, Michael. Dualism & Discontinuity in Industrial Societies. LC 79-25172. (Illus.). 176p. 1980. 17.95 (ISBN 0-521-23134-5). Cambridge U Pr.

Cameron, Rondo, ed. Banking & Economic Development: Some Lessons of History. 1972. text ed. 10.95x (ISBN 0-19-501428-6). Oxford U Pr.

Cameron, Rondo, et al. Banking in the Early Stages of Industrialization. 1967. 14.95x (ISBN 0-19-500843-X). Oxford U Pr.

Chenery, Hollis B. Structural Change & Development Policy. (World Bank Research Publications Ser.). (Illus.). 1980. 24.00x (ISBN 0-19-520094-2); pap. 8.95 (ISBN 0-19-520095-0). Oxford U Pr.

Chittle, Charles R. Industrialization & Manufactured Export Expansion in a Worker - Managed Economy: The Yugoslav Experience. (Kieler Studien Ser.: No. 145). 168p. 1977. 27.50x (ISBN 3-16-339672-0). Intl Pubns Serv.

Clayre, Alasdair, ed. Nature & Industrialization. (Illus.). 1977. 19.50x (ISBN 0-19-871096-8); pap. 6.95x (ISBN 0-19-871097-6). Oxford U Pr.

Daltrop, Anne. Economic Development. (Illus.). 96p. 1974. 8.50x (ISBN 0-7134-2868-6). Intl Pubns Serv.

Davis, W. Jackson. The Seventh Year: Industrial Civilization in Transition. (Illus.). 1979. 19.95 (ISBN 0-393-05693-7). Norton.

The Evolution of Industry in STPI Countries. (Science & Technology for Development: STPI Module 2). 67p. 1981. pap. 5.00 (ISBN 0-88936-257-2, IDRC TS19, IDRC). Unipub.

The Evolution of Science & Technology in STPI Countries. (Science & Technology for Development Ser.: STPI Module 3). 43p. 1981. pap. 5.00 (ISBN 0-88936-255-6, IDRC TS20, IDRC). Unipub.

Fuji Conference, Third, 1976. Marketing & Finance in the Course of Industrialization: Proceedings. Nakagawa, Keiichiro, ed. 1979. 29.50x (ISBN 0-86008-203-2, Pub. by U of Tokyo Pr). Intl Schol Bk Serv.

Hamilton, F. E., ed. Contemporary Industrialization: Spatial Analysis & Regional Analysis. (Illus.). 1978. pap. text ed. 11.95x (ISBN 0-582-48592-4). Longman.

--Industrial Change: Industrial Experience & Public Policy. (Illus.). 1978. pap. text ed. 11.95x (ISBN 0-582-48593-2). Longman.
Heard, Patricia & Butts, Miriam. Early Industrialization of America. (Jackdaw Ser: No.A32). (gr. 7 up). 1977. 6.95 (ISBN 0-670-28716-4). Viking Pr.
Hoelscher, H. E. & Hawk, M. C., eds. Industrialization & Development. LC 73-88723. (Illus.). 1969. 20.00 (ISBN 0-911302-09-3). San Francisco Pr.
Hoffmann, W. G. Growth of Industrial Economies. LC 77-81242. 1958. 15.00 (ISBN 0-379-00152-7). Oceana.
Hubbard, Gilbert E. Eastern Industrialization & Its Effect on the West. LC 77-138614. 1979. Repr. of 1935 ed. lib. bdg. 24.25x (ISBN 0-8371-5726-9, HUEI). Greenwood.
Hughes, Helen. Prospects for Partnership: Industrialization & Trade Policies in the 1970's. LC 72-12369. (International Bank for Reconstruction & Development Ser). 309p. 1974. 20.00x (ISBN 0-8018-1498-7); pap. 5.00x (ISBN 0-8018-1500-2). Johns Hopkins.
Hughes, J. R. Industrialization & Economic History: Theses & Conjectures. 1970. pap. text ed. 11.95 (ISBN 0-07-031115-3, C). McGraw.
Human Resources for Industrial Development. 2nd ed. (Studies & Reports, New Ser.: No. 71). vi, 237p. 1971. 6.85 (ISBN 92-2-100145-8). Intl Labour Office.
Inkeles, Alex & Smith, David H. Becoming Modern: Individual Change in Six Developing Countries. LC 73-92534. 416p. 1974. pap. 7.95 (ISBN 0-674-06376-7). Harvard U Pr.
Kaynor, Richard S. & Schultz, Konrad F. Industrial Development: A Practical Handbook for Planning & Implementing Development Programs. LC 72-76450. (Special Studies in International Economics & Development). 1973. 39.50x (ISBN 0-275-28683-5). Irvington.
Kemp, Tom. Historical Patterns of Industrialization. LC 77-3574. 1978. text ed. 17.00x (ISBN 0-582-48922-9); pap. text ed. 8.95x (ISBN 0-582-48923-7). Longman.
Kesselman, Steven. The Modernization of American Reform: Structures & Perceptions. Freidel, Frank, ed. LC 78-62386. (Modern American History Ser.: Vol. 10). 550p. 1980. lib. bdg. 40.00 (ISBN 0-8240-3635-2). Garland Pub.
Klass, Morton. From Field to Factory: Community Structure & Industrialization in West Bengal. LC 78-1552. (Illus.). 1978. text ed. 18.50x (ISBN 0-915980-34-7). Inst Study Human.
Kobrin, Stephen J. Foreign Direct Investment, Industrialization & Social Change. Altman, Edward I. & Walter, Ingo, eds. LC 76-10401. (Contemporary Studies in Economic & Financial Analysis: Vol. 9). 325p. 1977. lib. bdg. 30.00 (ISBN 0-89232-013-3). Jai Pr.
Kollontai, U. M., et al. Industrialisation of Developing Countries. 363p. 1975. 18.00x (ISBN 0-8464-0513-X). Beekman Pubs.
Laite, Julian. Industrial Development & Migrant Labour in Latin America. 1981. text ed. 25.00x (ISBN 0-292-73826-9). U of Tex Pr.
Leiserson, Alcira. Notes on the Process of Industrialization in Argentina, Chile, & Peru. (Politics of Modernization Ser.: No. 3). 1966. pap. 1.75x (ISBN 0-87725-203-3). U of Cal Intl St.
Lonsdale, Richard E. & Seyler, H. L., eds. Nonmetropolitan Industrialization. LC 78-20887. (Scripta Series in Geography). 1979. 15.75 (ISBN 0-470-26631-7). Halsted Pr.
Lowe, A. The Path of Economic Growth. LC 75-38186. (Illus.). 1976. 44.50 (ISBN 0-521-20888-2). Cambridge U Pr.
Maitra, Priyatosh. The Mainspring of Economic Development: The Role or Industrialization. 1980. 19.95 (ISBN 0-312-50453-5). St Martin.
Melosi, Martin V., ed. Pollution & Reform in American Cities, 1870-1930. (Illus.). 224p. 1979. text ed. 15.00x (ISBN 0-292-76459-6). U of Tex Pr.
Mokyr, Joel. Industrialization in the Low Countries, 1795-1850. LC 75-43326. (Economic in History Ser.). 1976. 25.00x (ISBN 0-300-01892-4). Yale U Pr.
Morley, James W., ed. Dilemmas of Growth in Prewar Japan. LC 79-155964. (Studies in the Modernization of Japan). 544p. 1974. 26.00x (ISBN 0-691-03074-X). Princeton U Pr.
Mott, Paul, et al. From Farm to Factory: The Development of Modern Society. LC 72-87429. 1973. pap. text ed. 6.50x (ISBN 0-675-09045-8). Merrill.
Moulder, F. V. Japan, China & the Modern World Economy. LC 76-2230. (Illus.). 1977. 24.95 (ISBN 0-521-21174-3); pap. 7.95x (ISBN 0-521-29736-2). Cambridge U Pr.
Nash, Manning. Machine Age Maya: The Industrialization of a Guatemalan Community. LC 67-20810. 1967. 8.00x (ISBN 0-226-56862-8). U of Chicago Pr.
--Machine Age Maya: The Industrialization of a Guatemalan Community. LC 67-20810. 1967. pap. 3.95x (ISBN 0-226-56863-6, P262, Phoen). U of Chicago Pr.
Noble, David. Facts & Observations Relative to the Influence on Manufactures Upon Health & Life. (The Development of Industrial Society Ser.). 81p. 1971. Repr. of 1843 ed. 13.00x (ISBN 0-7165-1563-6, Pub. by Irish Academic Pr). Biblio Dist.
North Central Regional Center for Rural Development. Rural Industrialization: Problems & Potentials. facsimile ed. 175p. 1974. pap. text ed. 8.20x (ISBN 0-8138-2465-6). Iowa St U Pr.
Park, S. S. Growth & Development: A Physical Output & Employment Strategy. LC 77-74817. 1977. text ed. 17.95 (ISBN 0-312-35128-3). St Martin.
Rabb, Theodore & Rotberg, Robert. Industrialization & Urbanization. LC 80-8675. (Studies in Interdisciplinary History). 310p. 1981. 20.00x (ISBN 0-691-05328-6); pap. 5.95x (ISBN 0-691-00785-3). Princeton U Pr.
Rostow, Walt W. Economics of Take-off into Sustained Growth. (International Economic Assn. Ser). (Illus.). 1963. 29.95 (ISBN 0-312-23555-0). St Martin.
Sutcliffe, R. B. Industry & Underdevelopment. (Economics Ser). 1971. text ed. 9.95 (ISBN 0-201-07361-7). A-W.
Tranter, N. L., ed. Population & Industrialization: The Evolution of a Concept & Its Practical Application. (Documents in Economic History Ser.). 1973. text ed. 15.75x (ISBN 0-7136-1310-6). Humanities.
Trebilcock, Clive. The Industrialization of the Continental Powers 1780-1914. (Illus.). 496p. (Orig.). 1982. text ed. price not set (ISBN 0-582-49119-3); pap. text ed. price not set (ISBN 0-582-49120-7). Longman.
Tyagunenko, V. L. Industrialization of Developing Countries. 363p. 1973. 4.75 (ISBN 0-8285-0306-0, Pub. by Progress Pubs Russia). Imported Pubns.
ULI Industrial Council. Industrial Development Handbook. Spink, Frank H., Jr., ed. LC 75-37218. (Community Builders Handbook Ser.). (Illus.). 256p. 1975. 29.00 (ISBN 0-87420-562-X). Urban Land.
Ward, Barbara. Five Ideas That Change the World. 1959. pap. 5.95x (ISBN 0-393-09438-3, NortonC). Norton.
Wilensky, Harold L. & Lebeaux, Charles N. Industrial Society & Social Welfare. 1965. pap. text ed. 5.95 (ISBN 0-02-935150-2). Free Pr.
Wils, Frits. Industrialization, Industrialists, & the Nation-State in Peru: A Comparative Sociological Analysis. LC 79-16963. (Research Ser.: No. 41). (Illus.). 1979. pap. 5.95x (ISBN 0-87725-141-X). U of Cal Intl St.
Wogart, Jan P. Industrialization in Colombia: Policies, Patterns, Perspectives. (Kieler Studien Ser.: No. 153). 176p. 1978. 35.00x (ISBN 3-16-340542-8). Intl Pubns Serv.

INDUSTRIALIZED BUILDING

Cutler, Lawrence & Cutler, Sherrie. Handbook of Housing Systems for Designers & Developers. 1974. text ed. 19.95 (ISBN 0-442-21820-6). Van Nos Reinhold.
Grubb, C. A. & Phares, M. I. Industrialization: A New Concept for Housing. LC 75-143972. (Special Studies in U.S. Economic, Social & Political Issues). 1972. 32.50x (ISBN 0-89197-794-5). Irvington.
Sullivan, Barry J. Industrialization in the Building Industry. 280p. 1980. text ed. 26.50 (ISBN 0-442-27941-8). Van Nos Reinhold.

INDUSTRIES

see Industrial Arts; Industrial Mobilization; Industry; also subdivision Industries under names of countries, etc. e.g. United States–Industries; names of particular industries

INDUSTRIES, CHEMICAL

see Chemical Industries

INDUSTRIES, ELECTRIC

see Electric Industries

INDUSTRIES, HOME

see Home Labor

INDUSTRIES, LOCATION OF

see also Factories–Location; Store Location

Accommodation of Utility Plant Within the Rights-of-Way of Urban Streets & Highways: State-of-the-Art. (Special Reports Ser: No. 44). (Illus.). 160p. 1974. 12.50 (ISBN 0-917084-06-3). Am Public Works.
Accommodation of Utility Plant Within the Rights-of-Way of Urban Streets & Highways: Manual of Improved Practice. 102p. (For use with Special Report No. 44). 1974. 12.00 (ISBN 0-917084-07-1). Am Public Works.
Bos, H. C. Spatial Dispersion of Economic Activity. 1965. 34.75x (ISBN 0-677-61510-8). Gordon.
Carlino, G. A. Economies of Scale in Manufacturing Location. (Studies in Applied Regional Science: Vol. 12). 1978. pap. 15.00 (ISBN 90-207-0721-3, Pub. by Martinus Nijhoff Netherlands). Kluwer Boston.
Carrier, Ronald E. & Schriver, William R. Plant Location Analysis: An Investigation of Plant Locations in Tennessee. (Illus.). 1969. pap. 5.00 (ISBN 0-87870-072-2). Memphis St Univ.
Chapman, James E. & Wells, William H. Factors in Industrial Location in Atlanta: 1946 to 1955. LC 58-63832. (Research Monograph: No. 8). 1958. spiral bdg. 5.00 (ISBN 0-88406-027-6). Ga St U Busn Pub.
Collins, Lyndhurst & Walker, David F., eds. Locational Dynamics of Manufacturing Activity. LC 73-21939. 412p. 1975. 58.50 (ISBN 0-471-16582-4, Pub. by Wiley-Interscience). Wiley.
Conkling, Edgar C. & Yeates, Maurice H. Man's Economic Environment. (Geography Ser.). 1976. text ed. 17.50 (ISBN 0-07-012408-6, C). McGraw.
Cross, Frank L., Jr. & Simons, John L., eds. Industrial Plant Siting. LC 75-16996. 183p. 1975. pap. 25.00x (ISBN 0-87762-163-2). Technomic.
Davidge, William F. & Hollman, Kenneth W. An Analysis of Mississippi Industrial Location Factors. 1978. 4.00 (ISBN 0-938004-02-6). U MS Bus Econ.
Delevoy, Robert L., et al. The Landscape of Industry. (Archives d'Architecture Moderne Ser.). Orig. Title: Le Paysage de l'Industrie Region du Nord-Wallonie-Ruhr. (Illus.). 175p. (Orig., Eng. & Fr.). 1975. pap. 25.00x (ISBN 0-8150-0926-7). Wittenborn.
Estall, R. C. & Buchanan, R. Olgilvie. Industrial Activity & Economic Geography: A Study of the Forces Behind the Geographical Location of Productive Activity in Manufacturing Industry. 3rd rev. ed. 1973. (Hutchinson U Lib); pap. text ed. 11.25x (ISBN 0-09-117311-6, Hutchinson U Lib). Humanities.
Gorlin, Harriet. Elements of Corporate Relocation Assistance Policies. LC 77-75943. (Report Ser.: No. 715). 1977. pap. 15.00 (ISBN 0-8237-0149-2). Conference Bd.
Greenberg, Michael, et al. A Primer on Industrial Environmental Impact. LC 78-11642. 1979. text ed. 17.95 (ISBN 0-88285-050-4). Ctr Urban Pol Res.
Grenier, Lise & Wieser-Benedetti, Hans. Les Chateaux de l'Industrie: Lille, 1830-1930, Vol. 2. (Archives d'Architecture Moderne Ser.). (Illus.). 250p. (Fr.). 1979. pap. 27.50x (ISBN 0-8150-0920-8). Wittenborn.
Gudgin, G. Industrial Location Processes & Employment Growth. 352p. 1978. text ed. 35.75x (ISBN 0-566-00144-6, Pub. by Gower Pub Co England). Renouf.
Hamilton, F. E., ed. Contemporary Industrialization: Spatial Analysis & Regional Analysis. (Illus.). 1978. pap. text ed. 11.95x (ISBN 0-582-48592-4). Longman.
--Industrial Change: Industrial Experience & Public Policy. (Illus.). 1978. pap. text ed. 11.95x (ISBN 0-582-48593-2). Longman.
--Spatial Perspectives on Industrial Organization & Decision-Making. LC 73-14379. 533p. 1974. 62.95x (ISBN 0-471-34715-9, Pub. by Wiley-Interscience). Wiley.
Hamilton, F. E. & Linge, G. J., eds. Spatial Analysis, Industry & the Industrial Environment-Progress in Research & Applications: Industrial Systems, Vol. 1. LC 78-10298. 1979. 48.95x (ISBN 0-471-99738-2, Pub. by Wiley-Interscience). Wiley.
Harper, Ann K. The Location of the United States Steel Industry, 1879-1919. Bruchey, Stuart, ed. LC 76-39829. (Nineteen Seventy-Seven Dissertations Ser.). (Illus.). 1977. lib. bdg. 18.00x (ISBN 0-405-09909-6). Arno.
Karaska, Gerald J. & Bramhall, David F., eds. Locational Analysis for Manufacturing: A Selection of Readings. (Regional Science Studies Ser.: No. 7). 1969. 23.00x (ISBN 0-262-11026-1). MIT Pr.
Kinnard, William N. & Messnen, Stephen D. Effective Business Relocation. LC 78-113590. 1970. 16.95 (ISBN 0-669-58420-7). Lexington Bks.
Latham, William R. Locational Behavior in Manufacturing Industries. (Studies in Applied Regional Science: No. 4). 1976. pap. 16.00 (ISBN 90-207-0638-1, Pub. by Martinus Nijhoff Netherlands). Kluwer Boston.
Lefeber, Louis. Location & Regional Planning, No. 7. LC 68-6272. (Training Seminar Ser). (Illus., Orig.). 1966. 7.50x (ISBN 0-8002-0844-7). Intl Pubns Serv.
Lloyd, Peter & Dicken, Peter. Location in Space. 2nd ed. 1977. text ed. 23.65 (ISBN 0-06-318058-8, IntlDept); pap. text ed. 19.80 (ISBN 0-06-318059-6). Har-Row.
Lloyd, Peter E. & Dicken, Peter. Location in Space: A Theoretical Approach to Economic Geography. 2nd ed. 1977. text ed. 22.95 scp (ISBN 0-06-044048-1, HarpC). Har-Row.
Losch, August. Economics of Location. Woglom, William H. & Stolper, Wolfgang F., trs. (Illus.). 1954. 40.00x (ISBN 0-300-00727-2). Yale U Pr.
Maunier, Rene. Origine et la Fonction Economique Des Villes: Etudes De Morphologie Sociale. LC 68-56743. (Research & Source Works Ser: No. 224). 1968. Repr. of 1910 ed. 27.50 (ISBN 0-8337-2307-3). B Franklin.
Miller, E. Willard. Manufacturing: a Study of Industrial Location. 1977. 17.95x (ISBN 0-271-01224-2, 76-1849). Pa St U Pr.
Moriarty, Barry M. Industrial Location & Community Development. LC 79-16029. 1980. 20.00x (ISBN 0-8078-1400-8); pap. 10.95x (ISBN 0-8078-4064-5). U of NC Pr.
Muther, Richard & Hales, Lee. Systematic Planning of Industrial Facilities, Vol. II. LC 79-84256. 1980. 68.00 (ISBN 0-933684-02-9). Mgmt & Indus Res Pubns.
--Systematic Planning of Industrial Facilities, Vol. 1. LC 79-84256. 1979. 18.00 (ISBN 0-933684-01-0). Mgmt & Indus Res Pubns.
New Project File & Site Selection Checklist. LC 79-53499. 1979. vinyl binder 35.00x (ISBN 0-910436-12-6). Conway Pubns.
Niemi, Albert W., Jr. State & Regional Patterns in American Manufacturing, 1860-1900. LC 73-13289. (Contributions in Economics Ser., No. 10). 209p. 1974. lib. bdg. 14.75x (ISBN 0-8371-7148-2, NAM/). Greenwood.
North Central Regional Center for Rural Development. Rural Industrialization: Problems & Potentials. facsimile ed. 175p. 1974. pap. text ed. 8.20x (ISBN 0-8138-2465-6). Iowa St U Pr.
Nourse, Hugh O. Regional Economics. LC 68-11935. (Economics Handbook). 1968. text ed. 17.95 (ISBN 0-07-047547-4, C). McGraw.
Plant Relocation: Industrial Relations Implications: a Review Based on the Glidden Decision. 1962. pap. 1.75 (ISBN 0-87330-008-4). Indus Rel.
Rees, John, et al, eds. Industrial Location & Regional Systems: Spatial Organization in the Economic Sector. (Illus.). 320p. 1981. 24.95x (ISBN 0-89789-008-6). J F Bergin.
Regional Plan Association. Office Industry: Patterns of Growth & Location. Armstrong, R. B., ed. 1972. 22.50x (ISBN 0-262-18052-9). MIT Pr.
Rowe, James E. Industrial Plant Location. (Public Administation Ser.: Bibliography P-575). 52p. 1980. pap. 5.50 (ISBN 0-686-29055-0). Vance Biblios.
Rushton, Gerard. Optimal Location of Facilities. 1979. pap. text ed. 7.95x (ISBN 0-933694-10-5). COMPress.
Schmenner, Roger W. Making Business Location Decisions. (Illus.). 352p. 1982. text ed. 29.95 (ISBN 0-13-545863-3). P-H.
Smith, David M. Industrial Location: An Economic Geographical Analysis. 2nd ed. LC 80-19231. 450p. 1981. text ed. 29.50 (ISBN 0-471-06078-X). Wiley.
Stafford, Howard A. Principles of Industrial Facility Location. LC 80-26737. (Illus.). 1980. pap. 25.00 (ISBN 0-910436-18-5). Conway Pubns.
Summers, Gene F., et al, eds. Industrial Invasion of NonMetropolitan America: A Quarter Century of Experience. LC 75-25026. (Special Studies). 1976. text ed. 26.50 (ISBN 0-275-56080-5). Praeger.
Sweet, Morris L. Industrial Location Policy for Economic Revitalization: National & International Perspectives. 200p. 1981. 23.95 (ISBN 0-03-052621-3). Praeger.
Tompkins, James A. & Moore, James M. Computer Aided Layout: A User's Guide. 1978. pap. text ed. 14.00 (ISBN 0-89806-003-6, 119). Am Inst Indus Eng.
Tong, Hsin-Min. Plant Location Decisions of Foreign Manufacturing Investors in the U.S. Dufey, Gunter, ed. (Research for Business Decisions: No. 17). 1979. 27.95 (ISBN 0-8357-1056-4). Univ Microfilms.
U. S. National Resources Planning Board. Industrial Location & National Resources. LC 43-53694. 1943. 22.00 (ISBN 0-527-92000-2). Kraus Repr.
Walker, Mabel L. Business Enterprise & the City. 1976. Repr. of 1957 ed. pap. 7.00 (ISBN 0-527-93960-9). Kraus Repr.
Warren, Kenneth. American Steel Industry Eighteen Fifty to Nineteen Seventy: A Geographical Interpretation. (Oxford Research Studies in Geography). (Illus.). 354p. 1973. 45.00x (ISBN 0-19-823214-4). Oxford U Pr.
Webber, Michael. Impact of Uncertainty on Location. 368p. 1972. 18.00x (ISBN 0-262-23054-2). MIT Pr.
Weber, Alfred. Theory of the Location of Industries. Friedrich, Carl J., tr. LC 77-102554. (Illus.). 1971. Repr. of 1929 ed. 13.50 (ISBN 0-8462-1521-7). Russell.

INDUSTRIES, LOCATION OF–AUSTRALIA

Hartley, W. A Checklist of Economic Plants in Australia. 214p. 1980. 25.00x (ISBN 0-643-02551-0, Pub. by CSIRO Australia). State Mutual Bk.

Neutze, Grahame M. Economic Policy & the Size of Cities. LC 67-89992. (Illus.). 1965. 12.50x (ISBN 0-678-05190-9). Kelley.

INDUSTRIES, LOCATION OF–CHINA

Wu, Yuan-li. Spatial Economy of Communist China: A Study on Industrial Location and Transportation. LC 67-20739. (Publications Ser.: No. 56). 1967. 16.95 (ISBN 0-8179-1561-3). Hoover Inst Pr.

INDUSTRIES, LOCATION OF–GREAT BRITAIN

Bligh & Woodgate. Pickfords Guide to Business Removals. 1977. 11.00 (ISBN 0-85941-047-1). State Mutual Bk.

Gower Publications, ed. East Anglia: A Guide to Business Locations & Expansion 1973. 1973. 25.00x (ISBN 0-8464-0347-1). Beekman Pubs.

Hays, Samuel. The Engineering Industries. 1972. pap. text ed. 5.50x (ISBN 0-435-84552-7). Heinemann Ed.

Heal, David W. The Steel Industry in Post War Britain. LC 74-80501. (Industrial Britain Ser). (Illus.). 224p. 1974. 10.00 (ISBN 0-7153-6565-7). David & Charles.

Langton, J. Geographical Change & Industrial Revolution. LC 78-67428. (Cambridge Geographical Studies: No. 11). (Illus.). 1980. 53.50 (ISBN 0-521-22490-X). Cambridge U Pr.

The London Directory of Industry & Commerce. 239p. 1981. pap. 31.00 (ISBN 0-905255-69-0, KEMP13, Kemps). Unipub.

Shafto, T. A. Guide to Modern British Industry. 1972. pap. 8.95x (ISBN 0-8464-0461-3). Beekman Pubs.

INDUSTRIES, LOCATION OF–RUSSIA

Dienes, Leslie. Locational Factors & Locational Developments in the Soviet Chemical Industry. LC 69-18023. (Research Papers Ser.: No. 119). 285p. 1969. pap. 8.00 (ISBN 0-89065-027-6). U Chicago Dept Geog.

INDUSTRIES, PRIMITIVE

see also Agriculture, Primitive; Bow and Arrow; Fishing, Primitive; Hunting, Primitive; Indians of North America–Industries; Man, Prehistoric; Nets; Pottery; Stone Implements; Weaving

Gould, Richard A., ed. Explorations in Ethnoarchaeology. LC 77-89438. (School of American Research Advanced Seminar Ser). (Illus.). 329p. 1978. 20.00x (ISBN 0-8263-0454-0); pap. 9.95x (ISBN 0-8263-0462-1). U of NM Pr.

Herskovits, Melville J. Economic Anthropology. Orig. Title: Economic Life of Primitive Peoples. 1965. pap. 7.95x (ISBN 0-393-00309-4, Norton Lib). Norton.

Hodder, Ian, ed. The Spatial Organisation of Culture. LC 78-1354. 1978. 25.95 (ISBN 0-8229-1134-5). U of Pittsburgh Pr.

Hodges, Henry. Artifacts: An Introduction to Early Materials & Technology. rev. ed. (Illus., Orig.). 1981. pap. text ed. 12.50x (ISBN 0-391-02246-6). Humanities.

Mead, Margaret. Inquiry into the Question of Cultural Stability in Polynesia. LC 70-82354. (Columbia Univ. Contributions to Anthropology Ser.: Vol. 9). Repr. of 1928 ed. 14.50 (ISBN 0-404-50559-7). AMS Pr.

Sayce, Roderick U. Primitive Arts & Crafts. (Illus.). 1963. Repr. of 1933 ed. 10.50x (ISBN 0-8196-0124-1). Biblo.

Semenov, S. A. Prehistoric Technology. Thompson, M. W., tr. (Illus.). 181p. 1976. Repr. of 1964 ed. pap. 17.50x (ISBN 0-06-496170-2). B&N.

Thurnwald, Richard. Economics in Primitive Communities. 1965. text ed. 17.00x (ISBN 90-6234-044-X). Humanities.

Udy, Stanley H., Jr. Organization of Work: A Comparative Analysis of Production Among Nonindustrial Peoples. LC 59-9547. (Comparative Studies Ser). xvi, 182p. 1967. pap. 7.50x (ISBN 0-87536-314-8). HRAFP.

INDUSTRIES, SERVICE

see Service Industries

INDUSTRIES, SIZE OF

see also Big Business; Small Business

British Association for the Advancement of Science (Section F Economics) Economics & Technical Change. Hugh-Jones, E. M., ed. LC 71-93848. 1969. lib. bdg. 12.50x (ISBN 0-678-06265-X). Kelley.

Hannah, Leslie & Kay, J. A. Concentration in Modern Industry. 1977. text ed. 17.50x (ISBN 0-333-19082-3). Humanities.

Ijiri, Y. & Simon, H. A. Skew Distributions & Sizes of Business Firms. (Studies in Mathematical & Managerial Economics: Vol. 24). 1977. 36.75 (ISBN 0-7204-0518-1, North-Holland). Elsevier.

Prais, S. J. The Evolution of Giant Firms in Britain. LC 76-18410. (NIEST Economic & Social Studies Ser.: No. 30). (Illus.). 1977. 41.50 (ISBN 0-521-21356-8). Cambridge U Pr.

INDUSTRY

see also Big Business; Business Losses; Businessmen; Costs, Industrial; Efficiency, Industrial; Employees' Representation in Management; Entrepreneur; Industrial Capacity; Industrial Equipment; Industrial Management; Industrial Organization; Industrial Promotion; Industrial Relations; Industrialization; Industries, Size of; Interindustry Economics; Machinery in Industry; Moving-Pictures in Industry; New Business Enterprises; Research, Industrial; Seasonal Variations (Economics); Small Business; Water-Supply, Industrial

Arab Directory for Commerce, Industry & Liberal Professions in the Arab Countries 1977-78. 25th ed. LC 53-32833. 1977. 125.00x (ISBN 0-8002-1213-4). Intl Pubns Serv.

Atkinson, Edward. The Industrial Progress of the Nation. LC 73-1989. (Big Business; Economic Power in a Free Society Ser.). Repr. of 1889 ed. 20.00 (ISBN 0-405-05073-9). Arno.

Banfield, Thomas C. Organization of Industry. 2nd ed. LC 68-55469. Repr. of 1848 ed. 12.50x (ISBN 0-678-00964-3). Kelley.

Brady, Robert A. Business As a System of Power. LC 76-167311. (Essay Index Reprint Ser.). Repr. of 1943 ed. 21.00 (ISBN 0-8369-2753-2). Arno.

Carey-Jones, N. S., et al. Politics, Public Enterprise & the Industrial Development Agency: Industrialisation Policies & Practices. 248p. 1975. 22.50x (ISBN 0-8419-5500-X). Holmes & Meier.

Carson, J. W. & Rickards, T. Industrial New Product Development: A Manual for the 1980's. LC 79-65781. 1979. 36.95x (ISBN 0-470-26821-2). Halsted Pr.

Chang Pei-Kang. Agriculture & Industrialization. LC 69-13854. Repr. of 1949 ed. lib. bdg. 15.00x (ISBN 0-8371-1057-2, CHAI). Greenwood.

Coker, Ed & Stuttard, Geoffrey, eds. Industrial Studies I: The Key Skills. 1975. pap. 1.95 (ISBN 0-09-911210-8, Pub. by Hutchinson). Merrimack Bk Serv.

Cole, George D. Studies in World Economics. facs. ed. LC 67-23195. (Essay Index Reprint Ser). 1934. 16.00 (ISBN 0-8369-0324-2). Arno.

Cole, Robert E. Work, Mobility, & Participation: A Comparative Study of American & Japanese Industry. LC 77-80468. 1979. 22.50x (ISBN 0-520-03542-9); pap. 7.95x (ISBN 0-520-04204-2). U of Cal Pr.

Conway, H. McKinley. New Industries of the Seventies. LC 78-62201. 1978. pap. 65.00x (ISBN 0-910436-07-X). Conway Pubns.

Davenport, Herbert J. Economics of Enterprise. LC 66-21668. Repr. of 1913 ed. 19.50x (ISBN 0-678-00424-2). Kelley.

Derrick, Paul. Men Over Industry. 1980. lib. bdg. 59.95 (ISBN 0-8490-3079-X). Gordon Pr.

Devine, P. J., et al. An Introduction to Industrial Economics. 3rd ed. (Illus., Orig.). 1979. text ed. 45.00x (ISBN 0-04-338086-7); pap. text ed. 21.00x (ISBN 0-04-338087-5). Allen Unwin.

Directory of Washington Representtatives of American Associations & Industry. 264p. 1979. 32.00 (ISBN 0-686-62452-1). B Klein Pubns.

Dunning, John H. & Pearce, Robert D. The World's Largest Industrial Enterprises. 1981. 50.00x (ISBN 0-312-89277-2). St Martin.

Edwards, Richard, ed. New York's Great Industries. LC 73-2504. (Big Business; Economic Power in a Free Society Ser.). Repr. of 1884 ed. 23.00 (ISBN 0-405-05086-0). Arno.

Ethridge, James M., ed. Directory of Directories: An Annotated Guide to Business & Industrial Directories, Professional & Scientific Rosters, & Other Lists & Guides of All Kinds. 1980. 65.00 (ISBN 0-8103-0270-5, Pub. by Information Ent); 1981 Suppl. by Directory Information Service 58.00 (ISBN 0-8103-0271-3). Gale.

Evan, William M., ed. Interorganizational Relations. LC 77-25062. 1978. pap. 9.95x (ISBN 0-8122-7745-7). U of Pa Pr.

Ferguson, C. E. Neoclassical Theory of Production & Distribution. (Illus.). 1969. 27.50x (ISBN 0-521-07453-3). Cambridge U Pr.

Frank, Charles R., Jr. Production Theory & Indivisible Commodities. LC 68-29383. (Studies in Mathematical Economics Ser.: No. 3). 1969. 17.50x (ISBN 0-691-04192-X). Princeton U Pr.

Galbraith, John K. The New Industrial State. 3rd, rev. ed. 1979. pap. 3.50 (ISBN 0-451-61764-9, ME1764, Ment). NAL.

Gephart, William F. Transportation & Industrial Development in the Middle West. 1971. lib. bdg. 14.50x (ISBN 0-374-93027-9). Octagon.

Give Us the Tools. 1979. pap. 7.00 (ISBN 0-88936-213-0, IDRC131, IDRC). Unipub.

Glover, John D. The Revolutionary Corporations: Engines of Plenty, Engines of Growth, Engines of Change. LC 80-66021. 492p. 1980. 35.00 (ISBN 0-87094-217-4). Dow Jones-Irwin.

Groneman, Chris H. & Grannis, Gary E. Exploring the Industries. LC 79-55313. 1980. pap. text ed. 14.40 (ISBN 0-8273-1757-3); instr's manual 1.55 (ISBN 0-8273-1758-1). Delmar.

Gruenberg, Michael M. & Oborne, David J. Industrial Productivity: A Psychological Perspective. LC 81-7521. 136p. 1981. 27.95 (ISBN 0-470-27194-9). Halsted Pr.

Hamlin, Scoville, ed. Menace of Overproduction. LC 76-93344. (Essay Index Reprint Ser). 1930. 16.00 (ISBN 0-8369-1295-0). Arno.

Helleiner, G. H., et al, eds. Protectionism or Industrial Adjustment. (Atlantic Papers Ser.: No. 39). 72p. 1980. write for info. (ISBN 0-916672-79-4). Allanheld.

Higham, Robert A. The Pulp, Paper & Paperboard Industry: Its Profits, Future Development & Investment Risk, 1950-2000, A Global Scenario Study. (Illus.). 225p. 1979. pap. 450.00 (ISBN 0-87930-076-0, Pub. by Eurodata Analysts England). Miller Freeman.

Hobson, John A. Incentives in the New Industrial Order. LC 79-51860. 1981. Repr. of 1922 ed. 16.00 (ISBN 0-88355-953-6). Hyperion Conn.

--Industrial System. rev. ed. LC 66-21676. Repr. of 1910 ed. 17.50x (ISBN 0-678-00537-0). Kelley.

--Work & Wealth. LC 68-30527. Repr. of 1914 ed. 17.50x (ISBN 0-678-00405-6). Kelley.

Hurley, F. Jack, ed. Industry & the Photographic Image: One Hundred & Fifty-Three Great Prints from Eighteen Fifty to the Present. 15.00 (ISBN 0-8446-5776-X). Peter Smith.

Internaional Conference on Industrial Economics, 2nd. Industrial Development & Industrial Policy: Proceedings. Roman, Zoltan, ed. 1979. 43.00 (ISBN 0-9960016-3-8, Pub. by Kiado Hungary). Heyden.

Jewkes, John, et al. Growth Through Industry: A Reconsideration of Principles Before & After the National Plan. (Institute of Economic Affairs, Readings in Political Economy Ser.: No. 2). (Orig.). 1969. pap. 4.25 (ISBN 0-255-69568-3). Transatlantic.

Johnston, Ernie. Industrial Action. 1975. pap. 1.95 (ISBN 0-09-911880-7, Pub. by Hutchinson). Merrimack Bk Serv.

Kendall, M. G., et al, eds. Mathematical Model Building in Economics & Industry. (Series One). 1968. 13.00 (ISBN 0-02-847740-5). Hafner.

--Mathematical Model Building in Economics & Industry: Series II. (Illus.). 1970. 13.00 (ISBN 0-02-847760-X). Hafner.

Kendrick, John. Understanding Productivity: An Introduction to the Dynamics of Productivity Change. LC 77-4786. (Policy Studies in Employment & Welfare: No. 31). (Illus.). 1978. text ed. 12.00x (ISBN 0-8018-1996-2); pap. text ed. 4.95x (ISBN 0-8018-1997-0). Johns Hopkins.

Killough, Hugh B. & Killough, Lucy W. Raw Materials of Industrialism. LC 79-137951. (Economic Thought, History & Challenge Ser). 1971. Repr. of 1929 ed. 17.50 (ISBN 0-8046-1453-9). Kennikat.

Kropotkin, Peter. Fields, Factories & Workshops. LC 68-56517. 1968. Repr. of 1919 ed. 20.00 (ISBN 0-405-08719-5). Arno.

Kropotkin, Petr A. Fields, Factories & Workshops or Industry Combined with Agriculture & Brain Work with Manual Work. LC 68-28589. (Illus.). 1968. Repr. of 1901 ed. lib. bdg. 15.00x (ISBN 0-8371-0135-2, KRBM). Greenwood.

Kuznets, Simon. Secular Movements in Production & Prices. LC 67-16341. Repr. of 1930 ed. 19.50x (ISBN 0-678-00318-1). Kelley.

Lewis, W. Arthur. The Theory of Economic Growth. 1955. pap. text ed. 13.50x (ISBN 0-04-330054-5). Allen Unwin.

The London Directory of Industry & Commerce. 239p. 1981. pap. 31.00 (ISBN 0-905255-69-0, KEMP13, Kemps). Unipub.

Losch, August. Economics of Location. Woglom, William H. & Stolper, Wolfgang F., trs. (Illus.). 1954. 40.00x (ISBN 0-300-00727-2). Yale U Pr.

Lustgarten, Steven. Industrial Concentration & Inflation. LC 75-18501. (Orig.). 1975. pap. 4.25 (ISBN 0-8447-3169-2). Am Enterprise.

MacGregor, David H. Enterprise, Purpose & Profit: Essays on Industry. x, 200p. 1981. Repr. of 1934 ed. lib. bdg. 16.00x (ISBN 0-87991-150-6). Porcupine Pr.

Marshall, Alfred. Industry & Trade. 4th ed. LC 72-104007. Repr. of 1923 ed. 25.00x (ISBN 0-678-00602-4). Kelley.

Miller, et al. Exploring Careers in Industry. LC 74-14422. (gr. 7-9). 1975. text ed. 15.72 (ISBN 0-87345-108-2). McKnight.

Mummery, A. F. & Hobson, John A. Physiology of Industry. LC 58-1995. Repr. of 1889 ed. 15.50x (ISBN 0-678-00673-3). Kelley.

Nourse, Edwin G. & Drury, Horace B. Industrial Price Policies & Economic Progress. (Brookings Institution Reprint Ser). (Illus.). Repr. of 1938 ed. lib. bdg. 29.50x (ISBN 0-697-00177-6). Irvington.

Nourse, Edwin G., et al. America's Capacity to Produce. (Brookings Institution Reprint Ser.). (Illus.). Repr. of 1934 ed. lib. bdg. 29.00x (ISBN 0-697-00176-8). Irvington.

Osborne, Adam. Running Wild the Next Industrial Revolution. (Orig.). 1979. pap. 3.95 (ISBN 0-931988-28-4). Osborne-McGraw.

Pigou, Arthur Cecil. Industrial Fluctuations. 2nd ed. 425p. 1968. Repr. of 1927 ed. 35.00x (ISBN 0-7146-2185-4, F Cass Co). Biblio Dist.

Prosper, Peter A., Jr. Concentration & the Rate of Change of Wages in the United States, 1950-1962. Bruchey, Stuart, ed. LC 76-4511. (Nineteen Seventy-Seven Dissertations Ser.). (Illus.). 1977. lib. bdg. 15.00x (ISBN 0-405-09922-3). Arno.

Rosenberg, Harry M. & Krasowski, Robert S. Trends in Industry Employment for North Carolina, 1940-70: The State & Multicounty Planning Regions. 1976. pap. 3.00 (ISBN 0-89055-127-8). Carolina Pop Ctr.

Rotstein, Abraham, ed. Beyond Industrial Growth. LC 76-7440. 1976. pap. 6.00 (ISBN 0-8020-6286-5). U of Toronto Pr.

Rusinoff, S. E. Mathematics for Industry. 3rd ed. (Illus.). 1968. 13.33 (ISBN 0-8269-2200-7). Am Technical.

Sallenave, Jean-Paul. Experience Analysis in Industrial Planning. LC 76-7164. (Illus.). 1976. 17.95 (ISBN 0-669-00658-0). Lexington Bks.

Schoenstadt, A. L., et al, eds. Information Linkage Between Applied Mathematics & Industry II. LC 80-17975. 1980. 20.00 (ISBN 0-12-628750-3). Acad Pr.

Shapiro, E. & White, W., eds. Capital for Productivity & Jobs. 1977. 11.95 (ISBN 0-13-113498-1, Spec); pap. 5.95 (ISBN 0-13-113480-9, Spec). P-H.

Sraffa, P. Production of Commodities by Means of Commodities. (Illus.). 99p. 1975. pap. 10.95x (ISBN 0-521-09969-2). Cambridge U Pr.

State Industrial Dirctories Corp. New Jersey State Industrial Directory, 1978. (State Industrial Directory Ser.). 1978. 87.50 (ISBN 0-916112-70-5). State Indus Dir.

State Industrial Directories Corporation. Massachusetts State Industrial Directory, 1979. (State Industrial Directory Ser.). 1979. 40.00 (ISBN 0-89910-011-2). State Indus Dir.

Stettner, N. Productivity, Bargaining & Industrial Change. 1969. 16.50 (ISBN 0-08-006756-5); pap. 7.75 (ISBN 0-08-006757-3). Pergamon.

Strong. Industrial, Labor & Community Relations. LC 68-59238. 144p. 1974. pap. 5.40 (ISBN 0-8273-0371-8); instructor's guide 1.60 (ISBN 0-8273-0372-6). Delmar.

Tawney, Richard H. Acquisitive Society. LC 28-30737. 1955. pap. 2.45 (ISBN 0-15-602846-8, HB9, Harv). HarBraceJ.

Tead, Ordway. Instincts in Industry. LC 73-89766. (American Labor, from Conspiracy to Collective Bargaining, Ser. 1). 222p. 1969. Repr. of 1918 ed. 10.00 (ISBN 0-405-02154-2). Arno.

Technology of Traditional Industry & the Role of the Craftsmen. 34p. 1980. pap. 5.00 (ISBN 92-808-0084-1, TUNU-061, UNU). Unipub.

Todd, Arthur J. Industry & Society: Sociological Appraisal of Modern Industrialism. Stein, Leon, ed. LC 77-70540. (Work Ser.). 1977. Repr. of 1933 ed. lib. bdg. 39.00x (ISBN 0-405-10209-7). Arno.

Vangermeersch, Richard. Financial Reporting Techniques in Twenty Industrial Companies Since 1861. LC 79-1238. (U of Fla. Accounting Ser.: No. 9). 1979. write for info. (ISBN 0-8130-0624-4). U Presses Fla.

Veblen, Thorstein B. Engineers & the Price System. LC 65-15955. (Illus.). Repr. of 1921 ed. 12.50x (ISBN 0-678-00058-1). Kelley.

--Vested Interests. LC 63-23513. Repr. of 1920 ed. 12.50x (ISBN 0-678-00053-0). Kelley.

Vepa, R. K. How to Set up a Small Scale Industry. 250p. 1981. text ed. 25.00 (ISBN 0-7069-1276-4, Pub by Vikas India). Advent NY.

Watts, H. D. The Large Industrial Enterprise: Some Spatial Perspectives. (Geography & Environment Ser.). (Illus.). 303p. 1980. 44.00x (ISBN 0-7099-0267-0, Pub. by Croom Helm Ltd England). Biblio Dist.

Weiss, Leonard W. Case Studies in American Industry. 3rd ed. LC 78-31149. (Introduction to Economics Ser.). 1980. pap. text ed. 11.50 (ISBN 0-471-03159-3). Wiley.

Whitehead, T. N. Leadership in a Free Society: Human Relations Based on an Analysis of Present-Day Industrial Civilizations. Stein, Leon, ed. LC 77-70548. (Work Ser.). 1977. Repr. of 1936 ed. lib. bdg. 18.00x (ISBN 0-405-10215-1). Arno.

Who's Who in Finance & Industry: 1977-78. 20th ed. LC 70-616550. 1977. 57.50 (ISBN 0-8379-0320-3). Marquis.

Winn, Daryl. Industrial Market Structure & Performance: Nineteen Sixty to Nineteen Sixty-Eight Mich. Business Studies, New Ser. (Vol. 1, No. 2). 1975. 12.00 (ISBN 0-87712-169-9). U Mich Busn Div Res.

Woodruff, A. M. & Alexander, T. G. Success & Failure in Small Manufacturing. LC 73-16632. (Illus.). 124p. 1974. Repr. of 1958 ed. lib. bdg. 15.00x (ISBN 0-8371-7203-9, WOSF). Greenwood.

INDUSTRY–BIBLIOGRAPHY

Ahn, Michael. Industrial Bibliography. LC 74-82273. (Research Report Ser.: No. 22). 1974. 6.00 (ISBN 0-87420-322-8). Urban Land.

Business Periodical Index. Annual, 01/1958-06/1959 Thru 07/1968-06/1969. 65.00 (ISBN 0-685-22242-X). Annual, 07/1969-06/1970 To Date. Wilson.

Chan, Julius. Primary Industries in Papua New Guinea After Independence. (The Australian National University Development Studies Centre Occasional Paper: No. 12). 1979. pap. 3.95 (ISBN 0-909150-64-8, 0472, Pub. by ANUP Australia). Bks Australia.

Davis, John G. & Newman, Phyllis, eds. California Manufacturers Register, 1981. 34th rev. ed. LC 48-3418. 880p. 1981. 85.00 (ISBN 0-911510-83-4). Times-M Pr.

--California Services Register, 1981. 2nd ed. 680p. 1981. 100.00 (ISBN 0-911510-84-2). Times-M Pr.

Dunning, John H. & Pearce, Robert D. The World's Largest Industrial Enterprises. 1981. 50.00x (ISBN 0-312-89277-2). St Martin.

State Industrial Directories Corp. Delaware State Industrial Directory, 1980. 1980. pap. 20.00 (ISBN 0-89910-032-5). State Indus Dir.

INDUSTRY–COSTS

see Costs, Industrial

INDUSTRY–DICTIONARIES

Freeman, Henry G. Fachenglisch Fur Technik und Industrie. 303p. (Ger. & Eng., English for Engineering and Industry). 1974. 22.50 (ISBN 3-452-17766-7, M-7376, Pub. by Carl Heymanns Verlag KG). French & Eur.

Ketchian, Sonia. Dictionnaire Petrolier des Techniques de Diagraphique, Forage et Production. 376p. (Rus., Fr., Eng. & Ger., Oil Industry Dictionary of Diagraphy, Sinking, and Production Techniques). 1965. 65.00 (ISBN 0-686-56756-0, M-6326). French & Eur.

State Industrial Directories Corp. Indiana State Industrial Directory, 1981. Date not set. pap. price not set (ISBN 0-89910-046-5). State Indus D.

--Kentucky State Industrial Directory, Nineteen Eighty-One. Date not set. pap. price not set (ISBN 0-89910-042-2). State Indus D.

--Louisiana State Industrial Directory, Nineteen Eighty-One. Date not set. pap. price not set (ISBN 0-89910-047-3). State Indus D.

--Maryland State Industrial Directory, 1978. (Maryland State Industrial Directory Ser.). 1978. 30.00 (ISBN 0-916112-65-9). State Indus Dir.

--Michigan State Industrial Directory, Nineteen Eighty-One. Date not set. pap. price not set (ISBN 0-89910-048-1). State Indus D.

--Mississippi State Industrial Directory, Nineteen Eighty-One. Date not set. pap. price not set (ISBN 0-89910-050-3). State Indus D.

--Tennessee State Industrial Directory, Nineteen Eighty-One. Date not set. pap. price not set (ISBN 0-89910-049-X). State Indus Dir.

--Vermont State Industrial Directory, Nineteen Eighty-One. Date not set. pap. price not set (ISBN 0-89910-043-0). State Indus D.

--Virginia State Industrial Directory, Nineteen Eighty-One. Date not set. pap. price not set (ISBN 0-89910-044-9). State Indus D.

Wright, Peter. Language of British Industry. 207p. 1974. text ed. 20.00x (ISBN 0-333-15359-6). Verry.

INDUSTRY–HISTORY

see also Commerce–History; Factory System; Home Labor; Machinery in Industry

Alexander, David. Retailing in England During the Industrial Revolution. 1970. text ed. 28.75x (ISBN 0-485-11116-0, Athlone Pr). Humanities.

Barker, T. C. & Harris, J. R. Merseyside Town in the Industrial Revolution: St. Helens 1750-1900. (Illus.). 508p. 1959. Repr. of 1954 ed. 27.50x (ISBN 0-7146-1268-5, F Cass Co). Biblio Dist.

Beard, Charles. The Industrial Revolution. 59.95 (ISBN 0-8490-0406-3). Gordon Pr.

Berg, Maxine. Technology & Toil: In 19th Century Britain. (Illus.). 1979. text ed. 26.00x (ISBN 0-906336-02-3); pap. text ed. 10.50x (ISBN 0-906336-03-1). Humanities.

Borrup, Roger. Plattsburgh (N.Y.) Traction Co. (Illus.). 51p. 1971. 4.50 (ISBN 0-910506-14-0). De Vito.

Bracegirdle, Brian. The Archaeology of the Industrial Revolution. LC 73-8287. (Illus.). 207p. 1973. 40.00 (ISBN 0-8386-1424-8). Fairleigh Dickinson.

Briggs, Asa. Iron Bridge to Crystal Palace: Impact & Images of the Industrial Revolution. 1979. 17.95 (ISBN 0-500-01222-9). Thames Hudson.

Brown, Joshua & Ment, David. Factories, Foundries, & Refineries: A History of Five Brooklyn Industries. LC 80-66220. (Brooklyn Rediscovery Booklet Ser.). (Illus.). 75p. 1980. pap. 3.50 (ISBN 0-933250-06-1). Bklyn Educ.

Buchanan, R. A. History & Industrial Civilization. LC 79-14550. 1979. 17.50x (ISBN 0-312-37401-1). St Martin.

Bucher, Karl. Industrial Evolution. Wickett, S. Morley, tr. from Ger. LC 68-56730. (Research & Source Works Ser.: No. 210). 1967. Repr. of 1901 ed. 20.50 (ISBN 0-8337-0408-7). B Franklin.

Buchsenschutz, B. & Blumner, Hugo. Die Hauptstatten des Gewerbfleisses im Klassischen Alterthume & die Gewerbliche Thatigkeit der Volker des Klassischen Alterthums, 2 vols. in 1. Finley, Moses, ed. LC 79-4964. (Ancient Economic History Ser.). (Ger.). 1980. Repr. of 1869 ed. lib. bdg. 20.00x (ISBN 0-405-12353-1). Arno.

Chenery, William L. Industry & Human Welfare. Stein, Leon, ed. LC 77-70487. (Work Ser.). 1977. Repr. of 1922 ed. lib. bdg. 15.00x (ISBN 0-405-10159-7). Arno.

Clarke, Penny. Growing up During the Industrial Revolution. LC 79-56472. (Growing up Ser.). (Illus.). 72p. (gr. 7 up). 1980. text ed. 14.95 (ISBN 0-7134-3370-1, Pub. by Batsford England). David & Charles.

Clawson, Dan. Bureaucracy & the Labor Process: A Study of U. S. Industry 1860-1920. LC 79-3885. 352p. 1980. 16.50 (ISBN 0-85345-542-2). Monthly Rev.

Coles, Robert. Children of Crisis, Vol. 3: The South Goes North. LC 70-162332. (Children of Crisis Ser.). (Illus.). 704p. 1972-73. 15.00 (ISBN 0-316-15172-6, Pub. by Atlantic Monthly Pr); pap. 7.95 (ISBN 0-316-15177-7). Little.

Cunningham, Hugh. Leisure in the Industrial Revolution Seventeen Eighty to Eighteen Eighty. LC 80-13354. 1980. 22.50 (ISBN 0-686-63325-3). St Martin.

Deane, Phyllis. The First Industrial Revolution. 2nd ed. LC 78-26388. 1980. 41.50 (ISBN 0-521-22667-8); pap. 9.95 (ISBN 0-521-29609-9). Cambridge U Pr.

Dodd, A. H. Industrial Revolution in North Wales. 3rd ed. (Illus.). 438p. 1971. 15.00x (ISBN 0-8426-1242-4). Verry.

Dodd, George. Days at the Factories: Manufacturing in the Nineteenth Century. (Illus.). 408p. 1975. Repr. of 1843 ed. 16.95x (ISBN 0-8464-0313-7). Beekman Pubs.

Dyer, Henry. The Evolution of Industry. LC 72-5044. (Technology & Society Ser.). 322p. 1972. Repr. of 1895 ed. 17.00 (ISBN 0-405-04696-0). Arno.

Ephraim, Asher. Relative Productivity, Factor Intensity & Technology in the Manufacturing Sectors of the U.S. & the U.K. During the Nineteenth Century. Bruchey, Stuart, ed. LC 76-39822. (Nineteen Seventy-Seven Dissertations Ser.). (Illus.). 1977. lib. bdg. 15.00x (ISBN 0-405-09902-9). Arno.

Everett, Alexander. Journal of the Proceedings of the Friends of Domestic Industry: In General Convention Met at the City of New York, October 26, 1831. Hudson, Michael, ed. Bd. with British Opinions on the Protecting System. (The Neglected American Economists Ser.). 1974. lib. bdg. 50.00 (ISBN 0-8240-1003-5). Garland Pub.

Faler, Paul G. Mechanics & Manufacturers in the Early Industrial Revolution: Lynn, Massachusetts 1780-1860. LC 80-21619. (American Social History Ser.). 310p. 1981. text ed. 34.00x (ISBN 0-87395-504-8); pap. text ed. 9.95x (ISBN 0-87395-505-6). State U NY Pr.

Fite, Gilbert C. Beyond the Fence Rows: A History of Farmland Industries Inc., 1929-1978. LC 78-62287. 1978. text ed. 15.00x (ISBN 0-8262-0258-6). U of Mo Pr.

Focal Aspects of the Industrial Revolution: 1825-42, Five Pamphlets. (The Development of Industrial Society Ser.). 198p. 1971. Repr. of 1842 ed. 25.00x (ISBN 0-7165-1562-8, Pub. by Irish Academic Pr England). Biblio Dist.

Gimpel, Jean. The Medieval Machine. 1976. 12.95 (ISBN 0-03-014636-4). HR&W.

Gras, Norman S. Industrial Evolution. LC 68-55722. Repr. of 1930 ed. 15.00x (ISBN 0-678-00462-5). Kelley.

Griffiths, Richard T. Industrial Retardation in the Netherlands: 1830-1850. (Illus.). xviii, 235p. 1980. lib. bdg. 34.00 (ISBN 90-247-2199-7, Martinus Nijhoff Pub). Kluwer Boston.

Hammond, J. L. & Hammond, B. The Town Labourer. new ed. Lovell, John, ed. LC 77-14533. (Illus.). 1978. text ed. 21.00x (ISBN 0-582-48519-3); pap. text ed. 11.50x (ISBN 0-582-48081-7). Longman.

--The Village Labourer. new ed. Mingay, Gordon E., ed. LC 77-21513. 1978. text ed. 22.00x (ISBN 0-582-48518-5); pap. text ed. 12.95x (ISBN 0-582-48082-5). Longman.

Hammond, J. L. & Hammond, Barbara. The Town Labourer, 1760-1832: The New Civilization. 342p. 1980. Repr. of 1932 ed. lib. bdg. 25.00 (ISBN 0-89984-293-3). Century Bookbindery.

Hannah, Leslie. The Rise of the Corporate Economy: The British Experience. LC 76-17228. 256p. 1976. 17.50x (ISBN 0-8018-1894-X). Johns Hopkins.

Hewings, Geoffrey J. Regional Industrial Analysis & Development. LC 77-76803. (Illus.). 1977. 14.95x (ISBN 0-312-66910-0). St Martin.

Hobshawn, Eric J. Age of Revolution: Seventeen Eighty-Nine to Eighteen Forty-Eight. (Photos). pap. 2.50 (ISBN 0-451-61740-1, ME1740, Ment). NAL.

Humphreys, Mary B., et al. The Industrial Revolution. 3rd ed. 1976. pap. text ed. 3.95x (ISBN 0-04-942151-4). Allen Unwin.

Hyde, Charles K. Detroit: An Industrial History Guide. (Illus.). 72p. 1981. pap. 5.00 (ISBN 0-8143-1696-4). Wayne St U Pr.

Jeremy, David J. Transatlantic Industrial Revolution: The Diffusion of Textile Technologies Between Britain & America, 1790-1830. (Illus.). 384p. 1981. text ed. 32.50x (ISBN 0-262-10022-3). MIT Pr.

John Crerar Library. List of Books on the History of Industry & the Industrial Arts. LC 67-14030. 1966. Repr. of 1915 ed. 26.00 (ISBN 0-8103-3104-7). Gale.

Jones, E. L. Agriculture & the Industrial Revolution. LC 74-2400. 1974. 21.95 (ISBN 0-470-44870-9). Halsted Pr.

Knight, Charles. Passages of a Working Life: During Half a Century with a Prelude of Early Reminiscences, 3 vols. (The Development of Industrial Society Ser.). 1026p. 1971. Repr. of 1865 ed. 50.00x (ISBN 0-7165-1568-7, Pub. by Irish Academic Pr). Biblio Dist.

Knox, Diana. The Industrial Revolution. Yapp, Malcolm, et al, eds. (World History Ser.). (Illus.). (gr. 10). pap. text ed. 1.95 (ISBN 0-89908-133-9); pap. text ed. 2.75 (ISBN 0-89908-108-8). Greenhaven.

Lane, Peter. The Industrial Revolution: The Birth of the Modern Age. LC 78-17537. (Illus.). 1978. text ed. 21.50x (ISBN 0-06-494034-9). B&N.

Lloyd, Humphrey. The Quaker Lloyds in the Industrial Revolution. 14.95 (ISBN 0-09-120880-7, Pub. by Hutchinson). Merrimack Bk Serv.

Lord, Eleanor L. Industrial Experiments in the British Colonies of North America. LC 78-64262. (Johns Hopkins University. Studies in the Social Sciences. Extra Volumes: 17). Repr. of 1898 ed. 13.00 (ISBN 0-404-61365-9). AMS Pr.

McGrain, John W. Pig Iron & Cotton Duck: Iron & Textile Mill Towns in Baltimore County, Maryland. (Baltimore County Heritage Publication Ser.). (Illus.). 1982. write for info. (ISBN 0-937076-01-5). Baltimore Co Pub Lib.

MacGregor, D. H. The Evolution of Industry. 1979. Repr. lib. bdg. 15.00 (ISBN 0-8495-3517-4). Arden Lib.

Mason, Otis T. The Origins of Invention: A Study of Industry Among Primitive Peoples. LC 77-38362. (Select Bibliographies Reprint Ser.). Repr. of 1895 ed. 24.00 (ISBN 0-8369-6779-8). Arno.

Mingay, G. E. Enclosure & the Small Farmer in the Age of the Industrial Revolution. (Studies in Economic & Social History). (Illus.). 1968. pap. text ed. 3.25x (ISBN 0-333-03909-2). Humanities.

Moffit, L. W. England on Eve of Industrial Revolution. 312p. 1963. 25.00x (ISBN 0-7146-1345-2, F Cass Co). Biblio Dist.

Moraze, Charles. History of Mankind: Cultural & Scientific Development: The Nineteenth Century 1775-1905: The Scientific Revolution, with the Industrial Revolution & Technical Development, Vol. 5, Pts. 1 & 2. (Illus.). 1976. text ed. 42.50x (ISBN 0-04-900026-8). Allen Unwin.

Morrison, Elting. From Know-How to Nowhere. (RL 9). pap. 1.95 (ISBN 0-451-61539-5, MJ1539, Ment). NAL.

Mulhall, Michael G. The Progress of the World: In Arts, Agriculture Commerce, Manufactures, Instruction, Railways & Public Wealth Since the Beginnng of the Nineteenth Century. (The Development of Industrial Society Ser.). 569p. 1980. Repr. 50.00x (ISBN 0-7165-1584-9, Pub. by Irish Academic Pr). Biblio Dist.

Myers, S. F., 1885- Clapp & Davies, 1886-Becken, A. C.-1897. 1974. pap. 5.50 (ISBN 0-915706-02-4). Am Reprints.

Nourse, Edwin G., et al. America's Capacity to Produce. LC 79-27946. (Institute of Economics of the Brookings Institution: No. 55). (Illus.). 608p. 1980. Repr. of 1934 ed. lib. bdg. 39.75x (ISBN 0-313-22294-0, NOAC). Greenwood.

Pike, Royston E., ed. Human Documents of the Industrial Revolution in Britain. 1966. pap. text ed. 12.50x (ISBN 0-04-942060-7). Allen Unwin.

Rodgers, Daniel T. The Work Ethic in Industrial America Eighteen Fifty to Nineteen Twenty. LC 77-81737. 1980. pap. 5.95 (ISBN 0-226-72352-6, 9-860, Phoen). U of Chicago Pr.

Rothschild, Eric, ed. The Rise of Big Business & Imperialism, Eighteen Seventy-Eight to Eighteen Ninety-Nine. (The New York Times School Microfilm Collection: Guide No. 3). 100p. (gr. 7-12). 1978. pap. 5.50 wkbk (ISBN 0-667-00552-8). Microfilming Corp.

Shephers, R. Prehistoric Mining & Allied Industries. (Studies in Archaeology Science Ser.). 1981. 38.50 (ISBN 0-12-639480-6). Acad Pr.

Speed, Peter. Social Problems of the Industrial Revolution. 160p. 1976. pap. 5.40 (ISBN 0-08-018883-4). Pergamon.

Stearns, Peter N. & Walkowitz, Daniel J., eds. Workers in the Industrial Revolution: Recent Studies of Labor in the United States & Europe. LC 73-85101. (Social History Ser). 1974. Transaction Bks.

Story, G. D. & Hayes, J. J. Industrial Revolution & Its Social Impact 1750-1850. (Research Folder Ser.: No. 4). 1973. 6.95x (ISBN 0-7022-0857-4). U of Queensland Pr.

Tames, Richard L., ed. Documents of the Industrial Revolution 1750-1850. 194p. 1971. pap. text ed. 3.25x (ISBN 0-09-106651-4). Humanities.

Tooker, Elva. Nathan Trotter: Philadelphia Merchant, 1787-1853. LC 72-5080. (Technology & Society Ser.). (Illus.). 302p. 1972. Repr. of 1955 ed. 14.00 (ISBN 0-405-04729-0). Arno.

Torres, Louis. Tuckahoe Marble: The Rise & Fall of an Industry in Eastchester, N. Y., 1822-1930. LC 76-26126. (Illus.). 1976. pap. 6.95 (ISBN 0-916346-21-8). Harbor Hill Bks.

Toynbee, Arnold. The Industrial Revolution. 7.50 (ISBN 0-8446-5832-4). Peter Smith.

Tulchinsky, Gerald J. The River Barons: Montreal Businessmen & the Growth of Industry & Transportation, 1837-53. LC 76-26019. 1976. 25.00x (ISBN 0-8020-5339-4). U of Toronto Pr.

U. S. Census Office & U. S. Treasury Dept. American Industry & Manufactures in the Nineteenth Century, 18 vols. Incl. Vol. 1. Report of the Secretary of the Treasury on the Subject of Manufactures. 16.50 (ISBN 0-08-022275-7); Vol. 2. Statement of the Arts & Manufactures of the U. S. for the Year 1810. 41.25 (ISBN 0-08-022276-5); Vol. 3. Fourth Census, 1820: Digest of Accounts of Manufacturing Establishments in the U. S. & Their Manufactures. 82.50 (ISBN 0-08-022277-3); Vol. 4. Sixth Census, 1840: Statistics of the U. S. 99.00 (ISBN 0-08-022278-1); Vol. 5. Seventh Census, 1850: Message of the President of the U. S. Communicating a Digest of the Statistics of Manufacturing. 16.50 (ISBN 0-08-022279-X); Vol. 6. Eighth Census, 1860: Manufactures in the U. S. 132.00 (ISBN 0-08-022280-3); Vol. 7. Ninth Census, 1870: Statistics of Wealth & Industry. 132.00 (ISBN 0-08-022281-1); Vol. 8. Tenth Census, 1880: Statistics of Manufactures. 165.00 (ISBN 0-08-022282-X); Vol. 9. Tenth Census, 1880: Reports on Newspaper & Periodical Press: Alaska, Seal Islands, Shipbuilding Industry, Etc. 165.00 (ISBN 0-08-022283-8); Vol. 10. Tenth Census, 1880: Report on Wages, Average Retail Prices, Trade Societies, Strikes & Lockouts, Etc., 1886. 99.00 (ISBN 0-08-022284-6); Vol. 11. Tenth Census, 1880: Reports on Power & Machines Etc. 82.50 (ISBN 0-08-022285-4); Vol. 12. Eleventh Census, 1890: Report on Manufacturing Industries: Totals for States & Industries. 132.00 (ISBN 0-08-022286-2); Vol. 13. Eleventh Census, 1890: Report on Manufacturing Industries: Statistics for Cities. 132.00 (ISBN 0-08-022287-0); Vol. 14. Eleventh Census, 1890: Report on Manufacturing Industries: Selected Industries. 99.00 (ISBN 0-08-022288-9); Vol. 15. Twelfth Census, 1900: Manufactures, U. S. by Industries. 132.00 (ISBN 0-08-022289-7); Vol. 16. Twelfth Census, 1900: Manufactures, States & Territories. 165.00 (ISBN 0-08-022290-0); Vol. 17 & 18. Twelfth Census, 1900: Manufactures, Special Reports on Selected Industries, 2 vols. Vol. 17. 165.00 (ISBN 0-08-022291-9); Vol. 18. 132.00 (ISBN 0-08-022292-7). 1971. Repr. of 1902 ed. Pergamon.

Unwin, George. Industrial Organization in the Sixteenth & Seventeenth Centuries. LC 68-58854. Repr. of 1904 ed. 24.00x (ISBN 0-678-05000-7). Kelley.
Vaizey, John. Capitalism & Socialism: A History of Industrial Growth. 294p. 1980. 31.50x (ISBN 0-297-77848-X, Pub. by Weidenfeld & Nicolson England). Biblio Dist.
Veblen, Thorstein B. Instinct of Workmanship. rev. ed. LC 63-23515. Repr. of 1918 ed. 17.50x (ISBN 0-678-00051-4). Kelley.
Vialls, Christine. The Industrial Revolution Begins. (Cambridge Topic Bks.). (Illus.). 52p. (gr. 6 up). 1981. PLB 5.95 (ISBN 0-8225-1223-8). Lerner Pubns.
Wallace, Anthony F. Rockdale. (Illus.). 1978. 17.50 (ISBN 0-394-42120-5). Knopf.
--Rockdale: The Growth of an American Village in the Early Industrial Revolution. (Illus.). 576p. 1980. pap. 6.95 (ISBN 0-393-00991-2). Norton.
Ware, Caroline F. The Early New England Cotton Manufacture: A Study in Industrial Beginnings. 13.00 (ISBN 0-384-65800-8). Johnson Repr.
Weber, Michael P. Social Change in an Industrial Town: Patterns of Progress in Warren, Pennsylvania from Civil War to World War I. LC 75-1634. 1975. 15.25x (ISBN 0-271-01201-3). Pa St U Pr.
Wyman, Mark. Hard-Rock Miners: Western Miners & the Industrial Revolution, 1860-1910. LC 78-54805. 1979. 17.95 (ISBN 0-520-03678-6). U of Cal Pr.

INDUSTRY–ORGANIZATION
see Industrial Organization

INDUSTRY–PERIODICALS–INDEXES

Bottin International: International Business Register 1981, 2 vols. 184th ed. LC 48-24844. (Illus.). 2100p. 1981. Set. 105.00x (ISBN 0-8002-2797-2). Intl Pubns Serv.
State Industrial Directories Corp. Maine State Industrial Directory 1977. (Maine State Industrial Directory Ser.). 1976. 20.00 (ISBN 0-916112-53-5). State Indus Dir.
--New Hampshire State Industrial Directory 1978-79. (New Hampshire State Industrial Directory Ser.). 1977. soft cover 20.00 (ISBN 0-916112-60-8). State Indus Dir.
--Vermont State Industrial Directory 1978-79. (Vermont State Industrial Directory Ser.). 1977. soft cover 20.00 (ISBN 0-916112-61-6). State Indus Dir.

INDUSTRY–SECURITY MEASURES

Allianz Versicherungs-AG & Muenchner Rueckversicherungs-Gesellschaft, eds. Handbook of Loss Prevention. Cahn-Speyer, P., tr. from Ger. 1978. 46.70 (ISBN 0-387-07822-3). Springer-Verlag.
Barefoot, J. Kirk. Employee Theft Investigation. LC 79-9764. 1979. 16.95 (ISBN 0-913708-33-X). Butterworth.
Berger, David L. Industrial Security. LC 79-628. 1979. 15.95 (ISBN 0-913708-32-1). Butterworth.
Bilek, Arthur J., ed. Private Security: Standards & Goals - from the Official Private Security Task Force Report. special ed. 1977. pap. text ed. 11.95 (ISBN 0-87084-716-3). Anderson Pub Co.
Burstein, Harvey. Industrial Security Management. LC 77-12762. 1977. 25.95 (ISBN 0-275-24050-9). Praeger.
Carson, Charles R. Managing Employee Honesty. LC 76-51836. (Illus.). 1977. 16.95 (ISBN 0-913708-27-5). Butterworth.
Curtis, Bob. Security Control: External Theft. LC 76-163714. (Security Control Ser.). 1971. 18.95 (ISBN 0-912016-11-6). Lebhar Friedman.
Educational Research Council of America. Plant Guard. Ferris, Theodore N. & Marchak, John P., eds. (Real People at Work: Series O). (Illus., Orig.). (gr. 5). 1976. pap. text ed. 2.25 (ISBN 0-89247-113-1). Changing Times.
Fisher, A. Security for Business & Industry. 1979. 17.95 (ISBN 0-13-798967-9). P-H.
Green, Gion & Farber, Raymond C. Introduction to Security. 2nd ed. LC 78-7318. 1978. 15.95 (ISBN 0-913708-31-3). Butterworth.
Healy, R. J. Design for Security. LC 61-21179. 1968. 32.50 (ISBN 0-471-36664-1, Pub. by Wiley-Interscience). Wiley.
Hemphill, C., Jr. Modern Security Methods. 1979. 18.95 (ISBN 0-13-597625-1). P-H.
How to Reduce Business Losses from Employee Theft & Customer Fraud. LC 78-5093. (Almar Report). 1978. 3.00 (ISBN 0-930256-03-4). Almar.
Langer, Steven, ed. The Security Report. 1978. pap. 60.00 (ISBN 0-916506-32-0). Abbott Langer Assocs.
Leininger, Sheryl, ed. Internal Theft: Investigation & Control. LC 75-17137. 256p. (Anthology). 1975. 15.95 (ISBN 0-913708-21-6). Butterworth.
Momboisse, Raymond M. Industrial Security for Strikes, Riots & Disasters. 516p. 1977. 24.75 (ISBN 0-398-01325-X). C C Thomas.
Nader, L. R. Protecting Your Business Against Employee Thefts, Shoplifters & Other Hazards. LC 72-98094. 1977. pap. 2.00 (ISBN 0-87576-032-5). Pilot Bks.
O'Block, Robert L. Security & Crime Prevention. c ed. LC 81-1353. (Illus.). 452p. 1981. pap. text ed. 14.95 (ISBN 0-8016-3738-4). Mosby.
Oliver, Eric & Wilson, John. Practical Security in Commerce & Industry. 544p. 1979. text ed. 36.00x (ISBN 0-566-02033-5, Pub by Teakfield Ltd England). Renouf.
--Practical Security in Commerce & Industry. 1979. pap. text ed. 36.00x (ISBN 0-566-02033-5, Pub. by Gower Pub Co England). Renouf.
Pike, Earl A. Protection Against Bombs & Incendiaries: For Business, Industrial & Educational Institutions. (Illus.). 92p. 1973. 9.50 (ISBN 0-398-02517-7). C C Thomas.
Post, Richard & Schachtsiek, David A. How to Develop & Operate an Effective Security Program. 1977. 65.50 (ISBN 0-85013-091-3). Dartnell Corp.
Post, Richard S. & Kingsbury, Arthur A. Security Administration: An Introduction. 3rd ed. (Illus.). 936p. 1977. 14.95 (ISBN 0-398-03572-5). C C Thomas.
Rankin, Guy R. The Professional Handbook for Patrol & Security Guards. LC 77-77264. 1977. 5.00 (ISBN 0-682-48838-0). Exposition.
Restaurant & Bar Security. 104p. 1979. pap. 8.95 (ISBN 0-913708-17-8). Butterworth.
Rudman, Jack. Safety Security Officer. (Career Examination Ser.: C-1459). (Cloth bdg. avail. on request). pap. 8.00 (ISBN 0-8373-1459-3). Natl Learning.
--Security Police Officer (U.S.P.S.) (Career Examination Ser.: C-2211). (Cloth bdg. avail. on request). pap. 8.00 (ISBN 0-8373-2211-1). Natl Learning.
Sennewald, Charles A. Effective Security Management. LC 78-6058. (Illus.). 1978. 15.95 (ISBN 0-913708-30-5). Butterworth.
Sill, Webster H., Jr. The Plant Protection Discipline: Problems & Possible Developmental Strategies. LC 78-59171. 1979. 29.95 (ISBN 0-470-26443-8). Halsted Pr.
Strauss, Sheryl, ed. Security Problems in a Modern Society. (Illus.). 314p. 1980. text ed. 9.95 (ISBN 0-409-95079-3). Butterworth.
Ursic, Henry S. & Pagano, LeRoy E. Security Management Systems. (Illus.). 384p. 1974. text ed. 29.75 photocopy ed. spiral (ISBN 0-398-02972-5). C C Thomas.
Walsh, T. J. & Healy, R. J. The Protection of Assets Manual. 1981. 212.00 (ISBN 0-930868-04-8). Merritt Co.
Walsh, Timothy J. & Healy, Richard J. Protecting Your Business Against Espionage. LC 73-84119. 1973. 16.95 (ISBN 0-8144-5311-2). Am Mgmt.

INDUSTRY–SOCIAL ASPECTS

Here are entered works about the impact of industry on culture and societal changes, and works about the social responsibilities of businessmen. Works on social relations within industry, as distinguished from labor-management relations, are entered under Industrial Sociology.
see also Industrial Sociology

Abt, Clark C. The Social Audit for Management. new ed. LC 76-30674. 1977. 19.95 (ISBN 0-8144-5384-8). Am Mgmt.
--The Social Audit: Problems & Possibilities. 1976. pap. 4.20x (ISBN 0-89011-489-7, REM-107). Abt Assoc.
Ackerman, Robert W. The Social Challenge to Business. 384p. 1976. 18.50x (ISBN 0-674-81190-9). Harvard U Pr.
Ackerman, Robert W & Bauer, Raymond A. Corporate Social Responsiveness: The Modern Dilemma. (Illus.). 472p. 1976. text ed. 24.95x (ISBN 0-87909-137-1); pap. text ed. 11.95 (ISBN 0-87909-136-3). Reston.
Allen, William R. & Bragaw, Louis K. Social Forces & the Manager: Readings & Cases. LC 81-10402. (Wiley Series in Management). 512p. 1982. text ed. 12.95 (ISBN 0-471-08611-8); price not set tchr.'s ed. (ISBN 0-471-08933-8). Wiley.
Anshen, Melvin. Corporate Strategies for Social Performance. LC 79-7888. (Studies of the Modern Corporation). 1980. 15.95 (ISBN 0-02-900730-5). Macmillan.
Anshen, Melvin, ed. Managing the Socially Responsible Corporation. LC 73-13364. (Studies of the Modern Corporation). (Illus.). 288p. 1974. 15.95 (ISBN 0-02-900680-5). Macmillan.
Barach, Jeffrey. The Individual, Business & Society. (Illus.). 1977. 16.95 (ISBN 0-13-458075-3); pap. text ed. 13.95x (ISBN 0-13-458067-2). P-H.
Bates, Albert D. Retailing & Its Environment. (Illus.). 1978. text ed. 11.95 (ISBN 0-442-80429-6). D Van Nostrand.
Bauer, Raymond A. & Fenn, Dan H., Jr. The Corporate Social Audit. LC 72-83832. (Social Science Frontiers Ser.). 1972. pap. 4.95 (ISBN 0-87154-103-3). Russell Sage.
Beesley, Michael & Evans, Tom. Corporate Social Responsibility: A Reassessment. 211p. 1978. 20.50x (ISBN 0-85664-640-7, Pub. by Croom Helm Ltd England). Biblio Dist.
Bell, Evelyn & Dunlop, Stewart. Industry & Resources. (Place & People Ser.: No. 5). (Illus.). 1977. pap. text ed. 4.95x (ISBN 0-435-34696-2). Heinemann Ed.
Benton, Lewis, ed. Private Management & Public Policy: Reciprocal Impacts. LC 79-2040. 256p. 1980. 17.95x (ISBN 0-669-03063-5). Lexington Bks.
Berry, Thomas. Management: The Managerial Ethos & the Future of Planet Earth. 1980. pap. 2.00 (ISBN 0-89012-016-1). Anima Pubns.
Bramlette, Carl A., Jr. & Mescon, Michael H., Jr., eds. The Individual & the Future of Organizations, Vol. 7. LC 72-619550. (Franklin Foundation Lecture Ser.). 1978. pap. 3.75x (ISBN 0-88406-121-3). Ga St U Busn Pub.
Bruchey, Stuart, ed. Small Business in American Life. LC 80-10994. 450p. 1980. 28.00x (ISBN 0-231-04872-6). Columbia U Pr.
Bulmer, Martin, ed. Mining & Social Change. 318p. 1978. 30.00x (ISBN 0-85664-509-5, Pub. by Croom Helm Ltd England). Biblio Dist.
Carroll, Archie B. Business & Society: Managing Corporate Social Performance. text ed. 17.95 (ISBN 0-316-13010-9); training manual free (ISBN 0-316-13011-7). Little.
Case, John, et al, eds. Workers' Control: A Reader on Labor & Social Change. pap. 3.95 (ISBN 0-394-71862-3, V-862, Vin). Random.
Cavanaugh, Gerald F. American Business Values in Transition. 224p. 1976. 11.95 (ISBN 0-13-024141-5); pap. text ed. 9.95x (ISBN 0-13-024133-4). P-H.
Chamberlain, Neil W. The Limits of Corporate Responsibility. LC 73-81035. 1973. text ed. 12.95x (ISBN 0-465-04115-9). Basic.
Chambliss, William J., ed. Problems of Industrial Society. LC 72-578. 1973. pap. text ed. 8.95 (ISBN 0-201-00958-7). A-W.
Chapman. Business in Society. 1981. text ed. write for info. (ISBN 0-408-10693-X); pap. text ed. write for info. (ISBN 0-408-10694-8). Butterworth.
Cohn, Jules. The Conscience of the Corporations: Business & Urban Affairs 1967-70. LC 77-135533. (Policy Studies in Employment & Welfare: No. 6). 144p. 1971. 10.00x (ISBN 0-8018-1231-3); pap. 4.50x (ISBN 0-8018-1230-5). Johns Hopkins.
Conference of the American Council of Learned Societies & Corning Glass Works,May 17-19,1951, Corning, New York. Creating an Industrial Civilization: Proceedings. Stein, Leon & Staley, Eugene, eds. LC 77-70536. (Work Ser.). 1977. Repr. of 1952 ed. lib. bdg. 25.00x (ISBN 0-405-10204-6). Arno.
Cook, Donald C., et al. Future of American Enterprise. (Michigan Business Papers: No. 46). 1967. pap. 1.50 (ISBN 0-87712-095-1). U Mich Busn Div Res.
Corson, John J. & Steiner, George A. Measuring Business's Social Performance: Corporate Social Audit. LC 74-19382. 1975. pap. 4.00 (ISBN 0-87186-239-5). Comm Econ Dev.
Crew, David F. Town in the Ruhr. LC 78-31526. (Social History of Bochum, 1860-1914). 352p. 1979. 20.00x (ISBN 0-231-04300-7). Columbia U Pr.
Curtiss, Ellen T. & Untersee, Philip A. Corporate Responsibilities & Opportunities to 1990. (Arthur D. Little Books). (Illus.). 1979. 25.95 (ISBN 0-669-02848-7). Lexington Bks.
Davis, Keith, et al. Business & Society: Concepts & Policy Issues. 4th ed. (Management Ser.). (Illus.). 672p. 1980. text ed. 17.95x (ISBN 0-07-015532-1, C); instr's manual 7.95 (ISBN 0-07-015533-X). McGraw.
Davis, W. Jackson. The Seventh Year: Industrial Civilization in Transition. (Illus.). 1979. pap. text ed. 6.95x (ISBN 0-393-09027-2). Norton.
Dawley, Alan. Class & Community: The Industrial Revolution in Lynn. LC 75-29049. (Harvard Studies in Urban History Ser.). (Illus.). 1979. 17.50x (ISBN 0-674-13390-0); pap. 6.95x (ISBN 0-674-13395-1). Harvard U Pr.
DeGeorge, Richard T. & Pichler, Joseph A., eds. Ethics, Free Enterprise, & Public Policy: Original Essays on Moral Issues in Business. 1978. text ed. 11.95x (ISBN 0-19-502467-2); pap. text ed. 6.95x (ISBN 0-19-502425-7). Oxford U Pr.
Dunlop, John T. Business & Public Policy. LC 80-81866. (Harvard Business School Pub. Ser.). 144p. 1981. pap. text ed. 7.95 (ISBN 0-87584-119-8). Harvard U Pr.
Epstein, Edward & Votaw, Dow. Rationality, Legitimacy, Responsibility: Search for New Directions in Business & Society. LC 78-18302. 1978. pap. 11.95 (ISBN 0-87620-807-3). Goodyear.
Estes, R. W. Corporate Social Accounting. 166p. 1976. 20.95 (ISBN 0-471-24592-5, Pub. by Wiley-Interscience). Wiley.
Ewen, Stuart. Captains of Consciousness. LC 75-34432. 1976. 10.00 (ISBN 0-07-019845-4, GB); pap. 4.95 (ISBN 0-07-019846-2). McGraw.
Farmer, Richard N. & Hogue, W. Dickerson. Corporate Social Responsibility. LC 72-96061. (Illus.). 223p. 1973. pap. text ed. 10.95 (ISBN 0-574-17930-5, 13-0930); instr's guide avail. (ISBN 0-574-17931-3, 13-0931). SRA.
Faunce, William. Problems of an Industrial Society. 2nd ed. Munson, Eric M., ed. 256p. 1981. pap. text ed. 8.95 (ISBN 0-07-020105-6, C). McGraw.
Faunce, William A. Problems of an Industrial Society. 1968. pap. 6.95 (ISBN 0-07-020103-X, C). McGraw.
Fremont-Smith, Marion R. Philanthropy & the Business Corporation. LC 72-83835. 112p. 1972. pap. 4.50 (ISBN 0-87154-279-X). Russell Sage.
Galambos, Louis P. & Spence, Barbara Barrow. The Public Image of Big Business in America, 1880-1940: A Quantitative Study in Social Change. LC 75-11347. (Illus.). 336p. 1975. 20.00x (ISBN 0-8018-1635-1). Johns Hopkins.
Gautam, Vinayshil. Enterprise & Society. 1979. text ed. 8.00x (ISBN 0-391-01861-2). Humanities.
Graham, David R. Role of Business in the Economic Redevelopment of the Rural Community. (Research Monograph: No. 36). 1973. pap. 4.00 (ISBN 0-87755-175-8). U of Tex Busn Res.
Greenwood, William T. Issues in Business & Society. 3rd ed. LC 76-12021. (Illus.). 576p. 1976. pap. text ed. 12.75 (ISBN 0-395-21410-6). HM.
Haas, John J. Corporate Social Responsibilities in a Changing Society. LC 73-78107. (Illus.). 65p. 1973. 4.00 (ISBN 0-685-32282-3). Gaus.
Heald, Morrell. The Social Responsibilities of Business: Company & Community, 1900-1960. LC 75-84490. 358p. 1970. 27.50 (ISBN 0-8295-0176-2). UPB.
Heilbroner, R. L. & London, P. Corporate Social Policy: Selections from Business & Society Review. 1975. pap. 10.95 (ISBN 0-201-04360-2). A-W.
Hewlett, Sylvia A. Cruel Dilemmas of Development: Twentieth-Century Brazil. LC 79-5198. 243p. 1980. 15.00 (ISBN 0-465-01497-6). Basic.
Hicks, Herbert G., et al. Dimensions of American Business. 1975. text ed. 8.50 (ISBN 0-07-028717-1, C). McGraw.
Hodgetts, Richard M. The Business Enterprise: Social Challenge, Social Response. LC 76-27059. (Illus.). 1977. text ed. 9.95 (ISBN 0-7216-4709-X). HR&W.
Jackson, Richard A., ed. The Multinational Corporation & Social Policy: Special Reference to General Motors in South Africa. LC 73-18872. (Special Studies). 1974. pap. 2.50 (ISBN 0-685-99394-9). Coun Rel & Intl.
Jacobs, Jane. Economy of Cities. 1970. pap. 2.95 (ISBN 0-394-70584-X, Vin). Random.
Jacoby, Neil H. Corporate Power & Social Responsibility. (Studies of the Modern Corporation Ser.). 1973. 15.00 (ISBN 0-02-915940-7). Macmillan.
Johnson, Richard A., et al. Management, Systems & Society: An Introduction. LC 75-13447. 576p. 1976. text ed. 18.95 (ISBN 0-87620-540-6); tchrs manual free (ISBN 0-87620-539-2). Goodyear.
Joint Council On Economic Education. Business & the Public Interest. 1972. 3.20 (ISBN 0-07-032721-1, G). McGraw.
Kapp, K. William. The Social Costs of Private Enterprise. LC 79-144788. (Illus.). 1971. pap. 3.95 (ISBN 0-8052-0299-4). Schocken.
Kay, Lillian W., ed. The Future Role of Business in Society. LC 77-70307. (Report Ser.: No. 710). 1977. pap. 15.00 (ISBN 0-8237-0143-3). Conference Bd.
Kelley, Florence. Modern Industry: In Relation to the Family, Health, Education, Morality. LC 75-329. (The Radical Tradition in America Ser.). 147p. 1975. Repr. of 1914 ed. 15.00 (ISBN 0-88355-233-7). Hyperion Conn.
Klein, Thomas A. Social Costs & Benefits of Business. 1977. pap. 9.95 (ISBN 0-13-815829-0). P-H.
Kobrak, Peter. Private Assumption of Public Responsibilities: The Role of American Business in Urban Manpower Programs. LC 72-83571. (Special Studies in U.S. Economic, Social & Political Issues). 1973. 29.50x (ISBN 0-275-07030-1). Irvington.
Kolasa, Blair J. Responsibility in Business: Issues & Problems. LC 72-170645. 1972. pap. text ed. 10.95 (ISBN 0-13-773739-4). P-H.
Kornhauser, Arthur. Mental Health of the Industrial Worker: A Detroit Study. LC 75-11966. 366p. 1975. Repr. of 1965 ed. 16.00 (ISBN 0-88275-295-2). Krieger.

Kugel, Yerachmiel & Gruenberg, Gladys W. Ethical Perspectives on Business & Society. LC 77-3106. 1977. 16.95 (ISBN 0-669-01482-6). Lexington Bks.

Litschert, Robert J., et al. The Corporate Role & Ethical Behavior: Concepts & Cases. (Modern Decision Analysis Ser.). 1977. 17.95x (ISBN 0-442-80402-4); instrs'. manual 2.00x (ISBN 0-442-80077-0). Van Nos Reinhold.

Loero, Guido. Boundary Conditions & Global Management. 1975. 29.50 (ISBN 0-12-455050-9). Acad Pr.

Luthans, Fred, et al. Social Issues in Business. 3rd ed. (Illus.). 1980. text ed. 19.95 (ISBN 0-02-372920-1). Macmillan.

McGrath, Phyllis S., ed. Business Credibility: The Critical Factors. LC 76-46250. (Report Ser: No. 701). (Orig.). 1976. pap. 30.00 (ISBN 0-8237-0135-2). Conference Bd.

McKie, James D., ed. Social Responsibility & the Business Predicament. (Studies in the Regulation of Economic Activity). 361p. 1975. 15.95 (ISBN 0-8157-5608-9); pap. 6.95 (ISBN 0-8157-5607-0). Brookings.

Manne, Henry G. & Wallich, Henry C. The Modern Corporation & Social Responsibility. 1972. 12.25 (ISBN 0-8447-2032-1). Am Enterprise.

Measurement of Corporate Social Performance. 1977. pap. 11.00 (ISBN 0-685-58517-4). Am Inst CPA.

Medawar, Charles. The Social Audit Consumer Handbook: A Guide to the Social Responsibilities of Business to the Consumer. (Illus.). 1978. text ed. 23.00x (ISBN 0-333-21665-2); pap. text ed. 10.25x (ISBN 0-333-21666-0). Humanities.

Molander, Earl A. Responsive Capitalism: Case Studies in Corporate Social Conduct. (Management Ser.). (Illus.). 432p. 1980. text ed. 10.00x (ISBN 0-07-042658-9, C); pap. text ed. 5.95 (ISBN 0-07-042659-7); instructor's manual 4.95 (ISBN 0-07-042659-7). McGraw.

Morrisey, T. J. Selected Readings on American Industry. 249p. 1974. text ed. 29.50x (ISBN 0-8422-5199-5); pap. text ed. 7.25x (ISBN 0-8422-0440-7). Irvington.

Morse, Dean & Warner, Aaron W., eds. Technological Innovation & Society. LC 66-18342. (Seminar on Technology & Social Change Ser.). 214p. 1966. 20.00x (ISBN 0-231-02927-6). Columbia U Pr.

Nicholson, Edward A., et al. Business Responsibility & Social Issues. new ed. 416p. 1974. text ed. 15.95 (ISBN 0-675-08826-7). Merrill.

Nicolin, Curt. Private Industry in a Public World. LC 77-73066. (Illus.). 1977. 7.95 (ISBN 0-201-05278-4). A-W.

Paluszek, John L. Will the Corporation Survive? LC 77-5730. (Illus.). 1977. pap. 7.95 (ISBN 0-87909-893-7). Reston.

Partridge, Scott H. Cases in Business & Society. (Illus.). 416p. 1982. pap. text ed. 14.95 (ISBN 0-13-117606-4). P-H.

Peterson, R. Industrial Order & Social Policy. 1973. pap. 8.95 ref. ed. (ISBN 0-13-464297-X). P-H.

Post, James. Corporate Behavior & Social Change. 300p. 1981. pap. text ed. 12.95 (ISBN 0-8359-1082-2). Reston.

Preston, Lee E. & Post, James E. Private Management & Public Policy: The Principle of Public Responsibility. (Illus.). 192p. 1975. pap. text ed. 10.95 (ISBN 0-13-710970-9). P-H.

The Quaternary Sector. 40p. 1980. pap. 5.00 (ISBN 92-808-0080-9, TUNU 030, UNU). Unipub.

Raffaele, J. A. System & Unsystem: How American Society Works. LC 74-5214. 1974. 11.95 (ISBN 0-470-70484-5); pap. 6.95x (ISBN 0-470-70483-7). Halsted Pr.

Sarason, Seymour B. Work, Aging, & Social Change: Professionals & the One Life-One Career Imperative. LC 76-27224. 1979. pap. text ed. 7.95 (ISBN 0-02-927930-5). Free Pr.

Sawyer, George. Business & Society: Managing Corporate Social Impact. LC 78-69570. (Illus.). 1978 text ed. 18.50 (ISBN 0-395-26541-X). HM

Sethi, S. Prakash. Japanese Business & Social Conflict. A Comparative Analysis of Response Patterns with American Business. LC 74-22196. 1975. text ed. 18.50 (ISBN 0-88410-274-2). Ballinger Pub.

--The Unstable Ground: Corporate Social Policy in a Dynamic Society. LC 73-18300. (Management, Accounting, & Information Systems Ser.). 576p. 1974. 19.95 (ISBN 0-471-77685-8). Wiley.

--Up Against the Corporate Wall: Modern Corporations & Social Issues of the Eighties. (Illus.). 496p. 1982. ref. ed. 18.95 (ISBN 0-686-76591-5); pap. 13.95 ref. ed. (ISBN 0-686-76592-3). P-H.

--Up Against the Corporate Wall: Modern Corporations & Social Issues of the Seventies. 3rd ed. (Illus.). 1977. pap. text ed. 14.95 (ISBN 0-13-938217-8). P-H.

Simpson, Kemper. Big Business, Efficiency & Fascism. LC 78-63717. (Studies in Fascism: Ideology & Practice). Repr. of 1941 ed. 21.50 (ISBN 0-404-16529-X). AMS Pr.

Smith, George A., Jr. & Matthews, John B., Jr. Business, Society, & the Individual. rev. ed. 1967. 20.50x (ISBN 0-256-00487-0). Irwin.

Sparer, Phineas J., ed. The Social Conscience of Business. LC 74-14909. (M. L. Seidman Town Hall Lecture Ser.). 86p. (Orig.). 1974. 5.00 (ISBN 0-87870-023-4). Memphis St Univ.

Spitzer, Carlton. Unlikely Partnership: Business Decisions & Social Policy. 1982. text ed. 22.50x (ISBN 0-582-28241-1). Longman.

Steiner, George & Steiner, John, eds. Issues in Business & Society. 2nd ed. 1977. pap. text ed. 9.95 (ISBN 0-394-31289-9). Random.

Steiner, George A. & Steiner, John F. Business, Government & Society: A Managerial Perspective. 3rd ed. 625p. 1980. text ed. 18.95 (ISBN 0-394-32445-5). Random.

Steward, Julian H., ed. Contemporary Change in Traditional Societies, 3 vols. Incl. Vol. 1. African Tribes. (Illus.). 519p. (Includes Introduction). 25.00 (ISBN 0-252-74508-6); Vol. 2. Asian Rural Societies. (Illus.). 350p. 17.50 (ISBN 0-252-74510-8); Vol. 3. Mexican & Peruvian Communities. (Illus.). 294p. 20.00 (ISBN 0-252-74511-6); pap. 5.95 (ISBN 0-252-00714-X). LC 66-25557. 1967. U of Ill Pr.

Stinchcombe, Arthur W. Creating Efficient Industrial Management. 1974. 24.00 (ISBN 0-12-785805-9). Acad Pr.

Sturdivant, Frederick & Robinson, Larry M. The Corporate Social Challenge: Cases & Commentaries. rev. ed. 1981. pap. 12.50x (ISBN 0-256-02518-5). Irwin.

Sturdivant, Frederick A. Business & Society: A Managerial Approach. rev. ed. 1981. 18.95x (ISBN 0-256-02516-9). Irwin.

Sturdivant, Frederick D. Business & Society: A Managerial Approach. rev. ed. 1981. 18.95 (ISBN 0-256-02516-9). Irwin.

The Educational Research Council. Industry: People & the Machine. (Concepts & Inquiry Ser). (gr. 4). 1975. pap. text ed. 7.24 (ISBN 0-205-04438-7, 8044384); tchrs'. guide 7.24 (ISBN 0-205-04439-5, 8044392). Allyn.

Thompson, Laurence. The Challenge of Change. LC 73-9267. 127p. 1973. Repr. of 1956 ed. lib. bdg. 15.00x (ISBN 0-8371-6998-4, THCH). Greenwood.

Townroe, Peter. The Industrial Movement: Experience in the United States & the United Kingdom. 1979. text ed. 41.00x (ISBN 0-566-00279-5, Pub. by Gower Pub Co England). Renouf.

Twiss, Brian C., ed. Social Forecasting for Company Planning. 200p. 1981. 16.50x (ISBN 0-8448-1396-6). Crane-Russak Co.

Votaw, Dow & Sethi, Prakash. The Corporate Dilemma: Traditional Values Versus Contemporary Problems. (Illus.). 288p. 1973. pap. text ed. 9.95 (ISBN 0-13-174185-3). P-H.

Wallich, Henry C., et al. New Rationale for Corporate Social Policy. LC 79-148184. 1970. pap. 2.00 (ISBN 0-87186-231-X). Comm Econ Dev.

Walton, Clarence C., ed. Business & Social Progress. LC 78-104393. 157p. 1970. 5.95 (ISBN 0-87186-323-5). Comm Econ Dev.

Wheatley, Edward W. Values in Conflict: Contemporary Issues in Business & Society. LC 76-6097. 1976. 6.95 (ISBN 0-916224-05-8). Banyan Bks.

Whiteside, Thomas. The Investigation of Ralph Nader. LC 72-79452. Orig. Title: Ralph Nader. 1972. 7.95 (ISBN 0-87795-034-2). Arbor Hse.

INDUSTRY-STATISTICS
see Industrial Statistics

INDUSTRY-SURVEYS
see Industrial Surveys

INDUSTRY (PSYCHOLOGY)
see Work

INDUSTRY, PUBLIC RELATIONS
see also Industrial Publicity

INDUSTRY AND ART
see Art and Industry

INDUSTRY AND COLLEGES
see Industry and Education

INDUSTRY AND EDUCATION
see also Education, Cooperative

Black, Gilbert J. Trends in Management & Development Education: An Economic Study. LC 79-4435. (Communications Library). 1979. 24.95x (ISBN 0-914236-24-5). Knowledge Indus.

Brickman, William & Lehrer, Stanley, eds. Automation, Education, & Human Values. (Illus.). 7.00 (ISBN 0-8446-0037-7). Peter Smith.

Burt, Samuel M. & Lessinger, Leon. Volunteer Industry Involvement in Public Education. LC 73-132557. 1970. 26.50x (ISBN 0-89197-974-3). Irvington.

Business-Higher Education Forum. Agenda for Business & Higher Education. 1980. 10.50 (ISBN 0-8268-1443-3). ACE.

Clark, Harold F. Economic Theory & Correct Occupational Distribution. Stein, Leon, ed. LC 77-70488. (Work Ser.). 1977. Repr. of 1931 ed. lib. bdg. 14.00x (ISBN 0-405-10160-0). Arno.

Dopp, Katharine E. The Place of Industries in Elementary Education. (Educational Ser.). 1908. Repr. 5.00 (ISBN 0-685-43006-5). Norwood Edns.

Harty, Sheila. Hucksters in the Classroom: A Review of Industry Propaganda in Schools. (Illus.). 190p. 1979. individuals 10.00 (ISBN 0-936758-01-5); institutions 20.00 (ISBN 0-686-28151-9). Ctr Responsive Law.

Marot, Helen. Creative Impulse in Industry: A Proposition for Educators. Stein, Leon, ed. LC 77-70514. (Work Ser.). 1977. Repr. of 1918 ed. lib. bdg. 12.00x (ISBN 0-405-10183-X). Arno.

Riendeau, Albert J. Advisory Committees for Occupational Education: A Guide to Organization & Operation. (Illus.). 1976. pap. text ed. 3.95 (ISBN 0-07-052680-X, G). McGraw.

Vanderlip, Frank A. Business & Education. LC 73-2537. (Big Business; Economic Power in a Free Society Ser.). Repr. of 1907 ed. 26.00 (ISBN 0-405-05115-8). Arno.

INDUSTRY AND STATE
Here are entered works on the relation of Industry and State in general as well as those concerned with the United States. For works on Industry and State in other countries, see local subdivisions below.
see also Agriculture and State; Commercial Policy; Economic Policy; Education, Cooperative; Foreign Trade Promotion; Forest Policy; Full Employment Policies; Government Business Enterprises; Government Competition; Government Lending; Government Ownership; Industrial Laws and Legislation; Labor Laws and Legislation; Laissez-Faire; Mercantile System; Price Regulation; Public Interest; Public Service Commissions; Railroads and State; Subsidies; Trade Regulation; Transportation and State also specific industries or commercial products

Adams, Henry C. Two Essays: Relation of the State to Industrial Action & Economics & Jurisprudence. Dorfman, Joseph, ed. LC 75-76510. (Reprints of Economic Classics). Repr. of 1954 ed. 15.00x (ISBN 0-678-00494-3). Kelley.

Agapos, A. Michael. Government-Industry & Defense: Economics & Administration. LC 74-15674. (Illus.). 226p. 1975. 15.95x (ISBN 0-8173-4604-X). U of Ala Pr.

Agencies for Industrial Adaptation & Development. (Document Ser.). 1979. 3.00x (ISBN 92-64-11868-3). OECD.

Armitage, S. M. Politics of Decontrol of Industry: Britain & the United States. (L.S.E. Research Monographs: No. 4). 1969. text ed. 9.25x (ISBN 0-297-17827-X). Humanities.

Arnold, Thurman W. The Bottlenecks of Business. LC 72-2363. (FDR & the Era of the New Deal Ser.). 352p. 1973. Repr. of 1940 ed. lib. bdg. 35.00 (ISBN 0-306-70470-6). Da Capo.

Bailey, Martin J. Reducing Risks to Life: Measurement of the Benefits. 1980. pap. 4.25 (ISBN 0-8447-3346-6). Am Enterprise.

Bartlett, Roland W. Modern Private Enterprise: Is It Successful. LC 72-93331. 1973. pap. 3.95 (ISBN 0-8134-1540-3, 1540). Interstate.

Bauer, Raymond A., et al. American Business & Public Policy: The Politics of Foreign Trade. 2nd ed. LC 63-8171. (Illus.). 1972. 34.95x (ISBN 0-202-24128-9); pap. 15.90x (ISBN 0-202-24129-7). Aldine Pub.

Beard, Charles A., ed. America Faces the Future. facsimile ed. LC 73-90608. (Essay Index Reprint Ser). 1932. 22.00 (ISBN 0-8369-1244-6). Arno.

Benton, Lewis, ed. Private Management & Public Policy: Reciprocal Impacts. LC 79-2040. 256p. 1980. 17.95x (ISBN 0-669-03063-5). Lexington Bks.

Bernstein, Marver H. Regulating Business by Independent Commission LC 77-2985. 1977. Repr. of 1955 ed. lib. bdg. 23.50x (ISBN 0-8371-9563-2, BERB). Greenwood.

Blair, John M. Economic Concentration: Structure, Behavior, & Public Policy. LC 79-187702. (Harbrace Ser. in Business & Economics). (Illus.). 832p. 1972. 16.95 (ISBN 0-15-127425-8). HarBraceJ.

Blaisdell, Thomas C., Jr. Federal Trade Commission. LC 32-26900. Repr. of 1932 ed. 10.00 (ISBN 0-404-00896-8). AMS Pr.

Blough, Roger M. The Washington Embrace of Business. LC 75-12001. (Benjamin Fairless Memorial Lectures). 161p. 1975. 12.50x (ISBN 0-915604-03-5). Columbia U Pr.

Blumberg, Paul. Industrial Democracy: The Sociology of Participation. LC 69-12382. 288p. 1974. pap. 4.95 (ISBN 0-8052-0414-8). Schocken.

Breed, Alice G. The Change in Social Welfare from Deregulation: The Case of the Natural Gas Industry. LC 78-22683. (Energy in the American Economy Ser.). (Illus.). 1979. lib. bdg. 14.00x (ISBN 0-405-11986-0). Arno.

Brown, Douglas V., et al. The Economics of the Recovery Program. LC 70-163644. (FDR & the Era of the New Deal Ser.). 1971. Repr. of 1934 ed. lib. bdg. 22.50 (ISBN 0-306-70197-9). Da Capo.

Byrom, Fletcher L. & Fraser, Douglas A. Failing Industries: The Role of Government. 90p. 1981. 10.00x (ISBN 0-915604-49-3). Columbia U Pr.

Cairncross, Alexander K. Essays in Economic Management. LC 78-37995. 219p. 1971. 17.50 (ISBN 0-87395-173-5). State U NY Pr.

Carey, Mathew. Addresses of the Philadelphia Society for the Promotion of National Industry. Hudson, Michael, ed. Bd. with Essay on Expediency & Practicability of Improving or Creating Home Markets for the Sale of Agricultural Productions & Raw Materials. Tibbits, George. (The Neglected American Economists Ser.). 1974. lib. bdg. 50.00 (ISBN 0-8240-1000-0). Garland Pub.

Caves, Richard E. & Roberts, Marc J., eds. Regulating the Product: Quality & Variety. LC 74-18123. 256p. 1975. text ed. 20.00 (ISBN 0-88410-272-6). Ballinger Pub.

Chase, Stuart. Government in Business. LC 71-136849. 296p. 1971. Repr. of 1935 ed. lib. bdg. 14.00x (ISBN 0-8371-5283-6, CHGB). Greenwood.

Clark, John M. Social Control of Business. 2nd ed. LC 68-55508. Repr. of 1939 ed. 19.50x (ISBN 0-678-00526-5). Kelley.

Cole, Roland J. & Tegeler, Philip D. Government Requirements of Small Business. LC 79-3046. (Human Affairs Research Center Ser.). 192p. 1980. 18.95 (ISBN 0-669-03307-3). Lexington Bks.

Committee for Economic Development. Redefining Government's Role in the Market System. 1979. lib. bdg. 6:50 (ISBN 0-87186-768-0); pap. 5.00 (ISBN 0-87186-068-6). Comm Econ Dev.

Cooling, B. Franklin. War, Business, & American Society: Historical Perspectives on the Military-Industrial Complex. LC 76-18163. (National University Pubns. Ser. in American Studies). 1977. 15.00 (ISBN 0-8046-9156-8). Kennikat.

Denton, Geoffrey, et al. Trade Effects of Public Subsidies to Private Enterprise. 293p. 1975. text ed. 45.00x (ISBN 0-8419-5014-8). Holmes & Meier.

Diebold, William, Jr. Industrial Policy As an International Issue. (Nineteen Eighty's Project (Council on Foreign Relations)). 1979. text ed. 9.95 (ISBN 0-07-016809-1); pap. 6.95 (ISBN 0-07-016810-5). McGraw.

Dodge, Kirsten, ed. Government & Business: Prospects for Partnership. LC 80-81347. (Symposia Ser.). (Orig.). 1980. pap. text ed. 8.50x (ISBN 0-89940-409-X). LBJ Sch Public Affairs.

Dominguez, George S. Marketing in a Regulated Environment. LC 77-22099. (Marketing Management Ser.). 1978. 29.95 (ISBN 0-471-02402-3). Ronald Pr.

Drucker, Peter F. The Future of Industrial Man: A Conservative Approach. LC 77-28895. 1978. Repr. of 1942 ed. lib. bdg. 22.75x (ISBN 0-313-20227-3, DRFI). Greenwood.

Economics of the Recovery Program. facs. ed. LC 68-29202. (Essay Index Reprint Ser). 1968. Repr. of 1934 ed. 10.25 (ISBN 0-8369-0400-1). Arno.

Edwards, Corwin D. Maintaining Competition: Requisites of a Governmental Policy. LC 71-138224. 337p. 1973. Repr. of 1949 ed. lib. bdg. 21.00x (ISBN 0-8371-5581-9, EDMC). Greenwood.

Ezekiel, Mordecai. Twenty-Five Hundred Dollars a Year. LC 72-2369. (FDR & the Era of the New Deal Ser). 348p. 1973. Repr. of 1936 ed. lib. bdg. 29.50 (ISBN 0-306-70468-4). Da Capo.

Fainsod, Merle, et al. Government & the American Economy. 3rd ed. 1959. 13.95x (ISBN 0-393-09553-3, NortonC). Norton.

Ficzere, Lajos. The Socialist State Enterprise. LC 75-502863. 160p. 1975. 11.00x (ISBN 963-05-0254-2). Intl Pubns Serv.

Fisher, Anthony. Must History Repeat Itself. 155p. 1974. 6.00 (ISBN 0-685-50126-4). Transatlantic.

Frenkel, Stephen J., ed. Industrial Action in Australia. 184p. 1981. text ed. 24.95x (ISBN 0-86861-122-0); pap. text ed. 12.50x (ISBN 0-86861-130-1). Allen Unwin.

Frese, Joseph R. & Judd, Jacob, eds. American Industrialization, Economic Expansion, & the Law. LC 81-4735. (The American Economic Enterprise Ser.: Vol. 3). 272p. 20.00 (ISBN 0-912882-50-6). Sleepy Hollow.

Fromm, Gary, ed. Studies in Public Regulation. (Regulation of Economic Activity Ser.). (Illus.). 528p. 1981. 45.00x (ISBN 0-262-06074-4). MIT Pr.
Galbraith, John K. The New Industrial State. 3rd rev. ed. 1978. 15.00 (ISBN 0-395-25712-3). HM.
Gatti, James, ed. The Limits of Government Regulation. 1981. price not set (ISBN 0-12-277620-8). Acad Pr.
George, Henry. Protection or Free Trade. LC 80-14436. 352p. 1980. 10.00x (ISBN 0-914016-70-9). Phoenix Pub.
Gerhart, Paul F. Political Activity by Public Employee Organizations at the Local Level: Threat or Promise? (Public Employee Relations Library Ser.: No. 44). pap. 6.00 (ISBN 0-87373-144-1). Intl Personnel Mgmt.
Giebelhaus, August W. Business & Government in the Oil Industry: A Case Study of Sun Oil, 1876 to 1945, Vol. 5. Porter, Glenn, ed. LC 77-7795. (Industrial Development & the Social Fabric Monographs). 425p. (Orig.). 1980. lib. bdg. 32.00 (ISBN 0-89232-089-3). Jai Pr.
Gilbert, James. Designing the Industrial State: The Intellectual Pursuit of Collectivism in America, 1880-1940. 352p. 1972. 10.00 (ISBN 0-8129-0219-X). Times Bks.
Gilbreth, Terry J. Governing Geothermal Steam: Intergovernmental Relations & Energy Policy. Bruchey, Stuart, ed. LC 78-22685. (Energy in the American Economy Ser.). 1979. lib. bdg. 22.00x (ISBN 0-405-11988-7). Arno.
Ginsburg, Douglas H. & Abernathy, William J. Government, Technology & the Future of the Automobile. (Regulation of American Business & Industry Ser.). (Illus.). 1980. 39.95 (ISBN 0-07-023291-1). McGraw.
Grant, Ronald, ed. Ethno-Nationalism, Multinational Corporations, & the Modern State. Wellhofer, E. Spencer. LC 78-74237. (Monograph Ser in World Affairs: Vol. 15, 1977-78, Pt. D). 1979. pap. 4.00 perfect bdg (ISBN 0-87940-057-9). U of Denver Intl.
Greene, James. Regulatory Problems & Regulatory Reform: The Perceptions of Business, Report No. 769. vi, 50p. (Orig.). 1980. pap. text ed. 15.00 (ISBN 0-8237-0205-7). Conference Bd.
Hamilton, F. E., ed. Industrial Change: Industrial Experience & Public Policy. (Illus.). 1978. pap. text ed. 11.95x (ISBN 0-582-48593-2). Longman.
Handlin, Oscar & Handlin, Mary F. Commonwealth: A Study of the Role of Government in the American Economy, Massachusetts, 1774-1861. rev. ed. LC 69-18032. 1969. 16.50x (ISBN 0-674-14690-5, Belknap Pr). Harvard U Pr.
Hawley, Ellis W. New Deal & the Problem of Monopoly. LC 65-24273. (Orig.). 1966. pap. 8.95 (ISBN 0-691-00564-8). Princeton U Pr.
Heath, Jim F. John F. Kennedy & the Business Community. LC 75-82114. 1969. 12.50x (ISBN 0-226-32231-9). U of Chicago Pr.
Heslop, Alan, ed. Business-Government Relations. LC 75-27052. 1976. 10.00x (ISBN 0-8147-9165-4); pap. 3.95x (ISBN 0-8147-9168-9). NYU Pr.
Holton, Richard, et al. Regulating Business: The Search for an Optimum. LC 78-50678. 1978. pap. 6.95 (ISBN 0-917616-27-8). Inst Contemporary.
Howard, Hayden R., ed. Risk & Regulated Firms. LC 72-619614. 120p. 1973. pap. 4.75 (ISBN 0-87744-119-7). Mich St U Busn.
Industrial Policy: Regional Dimensions. LC 80-8994. 1981. price not set (ISBN 0-669-04491-1). Lexington Bks.
Ingerson, Earl & Bragg, Wayne G. Science, Government & Industry for Development: The Texas Forum. LC 75-21547. (Institute of Latin American Studies-Special Publication). 470p. 1976. pap. 6.95x Span. ed. (ISBN 0-292-71035-6). U of Tex Pr.
Jacoby, Neil H. The Business-Government Relationship: A Reassessment. LC 75-15547. 192p. 1975. pap. text ed. 9.95x (ISBN 0-87620-129-X). Goodyear.
Jantscher, Gerald R. Bread Upon the Waters: Federal Aids to the Maritime Industries. (Studies in the Regulation of Economic Activity). 164p. 1975. 10.95 (ISBN 0-8157-4574-5). Brookings.
Keezer, Dexter M. & May, Stacy. The Public Control of Business: A Study of Antitrust Law Enforcement, Public Interest Regulation, & Government Participation in Business. LC 73-2515. (Big Business; Economic Power in a Free Society Ser.). Repr. of 1930 ed. 14.00 (ISBN 0-405-05095-X). Arno.
Kovaleff, Theodore P. Business & Government During the Eisenhower Administration: A Study of the Antitrust Policy of the Antitrust Division of the Justice Department. LC 79-25590. x, 313p. 1980. 17.95x (ISBN 0-8214-0416-4). Ohio U Pr.
Kugel, Yerachmiel & Cohen, Neal P. Government Regulation of Business Ethics: International Payoffs, 3 vols. LC 77-25901. 1978. looseleaf 75.00 ea. (ISBN 0-379-10258-7); Set. 225.00 (ISBN 0-686-77307-1). Oceana.
Lamb, Robert, et al, eds. Business, Media & the Law: The Troubled Confluence. LC 78-55569. 1980. 15.00x (ISBN 0-8147-0565-0). NYU Pr.
Lane, Frederic C. Profits from Power: Readings in Protection Rent & Violence-Controlling Enterprises. LC 79-13860. 1979. 24.95 (ISBN 0-87395-403-3); pap. 7.95 (ISBN 0-87395-445-9). State U NY Pr.
Lane, Robert. The Regulation of Businessmen: Social Conditions of Government Economic Control. LC 66-14606. 1966. Repr. of 1954 ed. 14.50 (ISBN 0-208-00515-3, Archon). Shoe String.
Lanzillotti, Robert F., ed. Economic Effects of Government-Mandated Costs. LC 78-14399. 1978. 18.00 (ISBN 0-8130-0626-0); pap. 9.50 (ISBN 0-8130-0614-7). U Presses Fla.
Lethbridge, David G., ed. Government & Industry Relationships: The Lubbock Memorial Lectures, 1975. 200p. 1976. text ed. 25.00 (ISBN 0-08-019733-7); pap. text ed. 17.50 (ISBN 0-08-019732-9). Pergamon.
Lodge, George C. The New American Ideology. 1975. 15.00 (ISBN 0-394-49227-7). Knopf.
Lowi, Theodore J., ed. Private Life & Public Order. (Problems of Modern Government Ser). 1968. pap. 4.95x (ISBN 0-393-09727-7, NortonC). Norton.
Lyon, Leverett S., et al. Government & Economic Life: Development & Current Issues of American Public Policy, 2 vols. LC 78-16476. (Inst. of Economics of Brookings Institution Publication: No. 79). 1978. Repr. of 1939 ed. Set. lib. bdg. 72.00x (ISBN 0-313-20601-5, LYGE). Greenwood.
Macavoy, Paul W. Regulated Industries. 1979. 14.95 (ISBN 0-393-01280-8); pap. 4.95x (ISBN 0-393-95094-8). Norton.
MacAvoy, Paul W., ed. Federal Energy Administration Regulation: Ford Administration Papers. 1977. pap. 6.25 (ISBN 0-8447-3248-6). Am Enterprise.
McCloy, John J., et al. The Great Oil Spill, the Inside Report: Gulf Oil's Bribery & Political Chicanery. LC 76-424. 340p. (Orig.). 1976. pap. 2.25 (ISBN 0-87754-044-6). Chelsea Hse.
McGrath, Phyllis S. Redefining Corporate-Federal Relations. LC 79-52413. (Report Ser.: No. 757). (Illus.). 1979. pap. 30.00 (ISBN 0-8237-0193-X). Conference Bd.
Martin, Donald L. & Schwartz, Warren C., eds. Deregulating American Industry: Legal & Economic Problems. LC 77-5273. (Illus.). 1977. 15.95 (ISBN 0-669-01603-9). Lexington Bks.
Maunder, Peter, ed. Government Intervention in the Developed Economy. LC 78-72590. 1979. 25.95 (ISBN 0-03-049501-6). Praeger.
Michalski, W., ed. The Future of Industrial Societies: Problems, Prospects, Solutions. 313p. 1979. 35.00x (ISBN 90-286-0257-7). Sijthoff & Noordhoff.
Miller, Arthur S. The Modern Corporate State: Private Governments & the American Constitution. LC 75-35350. (Contributions in American Studies: No. 23). 320p. 1976. lib. bdg. 17.95 (ISBN 0-8371-8589-0, MCS/). Greenwood.
Mitchell, Bridger M. & Kleindorfer, Paul R., eds. Regulated Industries & Public Enterprise: European & United States Perspectives. LC 79-3750. 304p. 1980. 29.95 (ISBN 0-669-03474-6). Lexington Bks.
Mitnick, Barry M. The Political Economy of Regulation: Creating, Designing, & Removing Regulatory Forms. LC 79-2612. 1980. 20.00x (ISBN 0-231-04023-7). Columbia U Pr.
Moore, Clement H. Images of Development: Egyptian Engineers in Search of Industry. 336p. 1980. text ed. 25.00x (ISBN 0-262-13161-7). MIT Pr.
Moore, W. S., ed. Regulatory Reform: Highlights of a Conference on Government Regulation. 1976. pap. 4.25 (ISBN 0-8447-3208-7). Am Enterprise.
Nader, Ralph & Green, Mark. Taming the Giant Corporation. 1976. 10.50 (ISBN 0-393-08753-0, N872, Norton Lib); pap. 3.95 (ISBN 0-393-00872-X). Norton.
Nader, Ralph, et al. Government Regulation: What Kind of Reform? 1976. pap. 3.75 (ISBN 0-8447-2070-4). Am Enterprise.
Nakagawa, Keiichiro, ed. Government & Business. 240p. 1980. 25.50x (ISBN 0-86008-265-2, Pub. by Univ Tokyo Pr Japan). Intl Schol Bk Serv.
Nordhauser, Norman. The Quest for Stability. Freidel, Frank, ed. LC 78-62510. (Modern American History Ser.: Vol. 15). 1979. lib. bdg. 24.00 (ISBN 0-8240-3638-7). Garland Pub.
Oliver, H. M., Jr. Critique of Socioeconomic Goals. (Indiana Univ. Publ. Social Science Ser.: No. 12). 1954. 13.00 (ISBN 0-527-68350-7). Kraus Repr.
Orth, Samuel P., ed. Readings on the Relation of Government to Property & Industry. LC 73-2527. (Big Business; Economic Power in a Free Society Ser.). Repr. of 1915 ed. 30.00 (ISBN 0-405-05106-9). Arno.
Owen, Bruce M. & Braeutigam, Ronald. The Regulation Game: Strategic Use of the Administration Process. LC 78-558. 1978. 20.00 (ISBN 0-88410-066-9). Ballinger Pub.
Paluszek, John L. Will the Corporation Survive? LC 77-5730. (Illus.). 1977. pap. 7.95 (ISBN 0-87909-893-7). Reston.
Partridge, Scott H. Cases in Business & Society. (Illus.). 416p. 1982. pap. text ed. 14.95 (ISBN 0-13-117606-4). P-H.
Pendergrass, Bonnie B. Public Power, Politics & Technology in the Eisenhower & Kennedy Years: The Hanford Dual-Purpose Reactor Controversy, 1956-1962. Bruchey, Stuart, ed. LC 78-22705. (Energy in the American Economy Ser.). 1979. lib. bdg. 15.00x (ISBN 0-405-12007-9). Arno.
Petersen, H. Craig. Business & Government. 478p. 1981. text ed. 19.50 scp (ISBN 0-06-045142-4, HarpC). Har-Row.
Pierce, Richard J., Jr., et al. Economical Regulation: Energy, Transportation & Utilities. (Contemporary Legal Education). 1200p. 1980. pap. text ed. 25.50 (ISBN 0-672-84200-9). Bobbs.
Pinder, John, ed. National Industrial Strategies & the World Economy. (Atlantic Institute for International Affairs Research Ser.: Vol. 6). 320p. 1981. text ed. 34.50 (ISBN 0-86598-040-3). Allanheld.
Pollack, Norman. The Populist Response to Industrial America. 1976. pap. 3.50x (ISBN 0-674-69051-6). Harvard U Pr.
President's Commission. Government & the Regulation of Corporate & Individual Decisions in the Eighties. (Illus.). 144p. 1981. 12.95 (ISBN 0-13-360834-4); pap. 4.95 (ISBN 0-13-360826-3). P-H.
Prothro, James W. Dollar Decade: Business Ideas in the 1920's. Repr. of 1954 ed. lib. bdg. 14.00x (ISBN 0-8371-2299-6, PRDD). Greenwood.
Public Economics Foundation. Attacking Regulatory Problems: An Agenda for Research in the 1980's. Ferguson, Allen R., ed. 1981. 22.50 (ISBN 0-88410-598-9). Ballinger Pub.
Raffaele, J. A. System & Unsystem: How American Society Works. LC 74-5214. 1974. 11.95 (ISBN 0-470-70484-5); pap. 6.95x (ISBN 0-470-70483-7). Halsted Pr.
Raffaele, Joseph A. System & Unsystem: How American Society Works. 388p. 1974. 13.95x (ISBN 0-87073-274-9); pap. 8.95x (ISBN 0-87073-273-0). Schenkman.
Read, Leonard E. Free Market & Its Enemy. 75p. 1965. 1.75 (ISBN 0-910614-39-3); pap. 0.50 (ISBN 0-910614-09-1). Foun Econ Ed.
Reekie, Duncan W. & Weber, Michael H. Profits, Politics & Drugs. LC 78-24496. 1979. text ed. 41.50x (ISBN 0-8419-0461-8). Holmes & Meier.
Ronen, Joshua & Saden, Simeha. Corporate Financial Information for Government Decision Making. LC 75-21495. 1975. 8.45 (ISBN 0-910586-13-6). Finan Exec.
Roos, C. F. NRA Economic Planning. LC 72-171693. (Fdr & the Era of the New Deal Ser.). 596p. 1972. Repr. of 1937 ed. lib. bdg. 55.00 (ISBN 0-306-70396-3). Da Capo.
Rosenbaum, Walter A. The Politics of Environmental Concern. 2nd ed. LC 76-41964. 1977. pap. 8.95 (ISBN 0-275-64820-6). Praeger.
Ross, A. M., ed. Industrial Relations & Economic Development. (International Institute for Labor Studies). 1967. 22.50 (ISBN 0-312-41510-9). St Martin.
Said, A. & Simmons, L. New Sovereigns: The Multinational Corporations As World Powers. 1975. pap. 3.50 (ISBN 0-13-615781-5, Spec). P-H.
Schiller, Herbert I. & Phillips, Joseph D., eds. Super-State: Readings in the Military-Industrial Complex. LC 73-104026. 1970. 20.00 (ISBN 0-252-00096-X); pap. 6.95 (ISBN 0-252-00283-0). U of Ill Pr.
Schmalensee, Richard. The Control of Natural Monopolies. LC 78-6061. 1979. 18.95 (ISBN 0-669-02322-1). Lexington Bks.
Singh, K. R. State & Industrialization of Developing Countries. 1969. 5.50x (ISBN 0-8426-1532-6). Verry.
Skuse, Allen. Government Intervention & Industrial Policy. (Studies in the British Economy Ser.). 1972. pap. text ed. 6.50x (ISBN 0-435-84556-X). Heinemann Ed.
Smith, Trevor. The Politics of the Corporate Economy. 229p. 1979. 30.50x (ISBN 0-85520-202-5, Pub by Martin Robertson England). Biblio Dist.
Sobel, Lester A., ed. Corruption in Business. new ed. LC 76-41986. 1977. lib. bdg. 17.50 (ISBN 0-87196-292-6). Facts on File.
Sokolsky, George E. Labor's Fight for Power. LC 72-137979. (American History & Culture in the Twentieth Century Ser). 1971. Repr. of 1934 ed. 13.50 (ISBN 0-8046-1434-2). Kennikat.
Stanbury, W. T. Government Regulation: Scope, Growth, Process. 267p. 1980. pap. text ed. 10.95x (ISBN 0-920380-48-4, Pub. by Inst Res Pub Canada). Renouf.
Starling, Grover. Managing the Public Sector. 1977. 18.95x (ISBN 0-256-01936-3). Dorsey.
Stein, Herbert. Economic Planning & the Improvement of Economic Policy. LC 75-27396. (Orig.). 1975. pap. 2.00 (ISBN 0-8447-3183-8). Am Enterprise.
Steiner, George & Steiner, John, eds. Issues in Business & Society. 2nd ed. 1977. pap. text ed. 9.95 (ISBN 0-394-31289-9). Random.
Steiner, George A. & Steiner, John F. Business, Government & Society: A Managerial Perspective. 3rd ed. 625p. 1980. text ed. 18.95 (ISBN 0-394-32445-5). Random.
--Business, Government & Society: Casebook. 2nd ed. 280p. 1980. pap. text ed. 7.95 (ISBN 0-394-32566-4). Random.
Stevenson, Russell B., Jr. Corporations & Information: Secrecy, Access & Disclosure. LC 79-3683. 212p. 1980. text ed. 17.95x (ISBN 0-8018-2344-7). Johns Hopkins.
Stokes, M. Conquering Government Regulation: A Business Guide. 288p. 1981. 24.95 (ISBN 0-07-061640-X, P&RB). McGraw.
Tainiter, Melvin. Scheduling Control for Industry & Government. LC 74-185676. 56p. (Orig.). pap. 3.25 (ISBN 0-87974-000-0). Timetable Pr.
Tugwell, Rexford G. Economic Basis of Public Interest. LC 68-9575. Repr. of 1922 ed. 12.50x (ISBN 0-678-00408-0). Kelley.
--The Industrial Discipline & the Governmental Arts. Stein, Leon, ed. LC 77-70541. (Work Ser.). 1977. Repr. of 1933 ed. lib. bdg. 16.00x (ISBN 0-405-10210-0). Arno.
Tuttle, Francis T. & Wall, James E. Revitalizing Communities Through Industry Service Programs. (Critical Issues Ser.: No. 2). (Illus.). 32p. (Orig.). 1979. pap. 3.00 (ISBN 0-89514-027-6, 10179). Am Voc Assn.
Twentieth Century Fund. Labor & Government: An Investigation. Bernheim, Alfred L. & Van Doren, Dorothy, eds. LC 35-9534. 1935. 22.00 (ISBN 0-527-02808-8). Kraus Repr.
Tybout, Richard A., ed. Economics of Research & Development. LC 65-18734. (Illus.). 1965. 7.50 (ISBN 0-8142-0123-7). Ohio St U Pr.
U. S. House of Representatives, Committee No. 1 of the Select Committee on Small Business. Organization & Operation of the Small Business Administration. Bruchey, Stuart & Carosso, Vincent P., eds. LC 78-19005. (Small Business Enterprise in America Ser.). (Illus.). 1979. Repr. of 1959 ed. lib. bdg. 25.00x (ISBN 0-405-11501-6). Arno.
U. S. House of Representatives, Subcommittee No. 1 of the Select Committee on Small Business. The Organization & Procedures of the Federal Regulatory Commissions & Agencies & Their Effect on Small Business, 2 vols. in 1. Bruchey, Stuart & Carosso, Vincent P., eds. LC 78-19001. (Small Business Enterprise in America Ser.). (Illus.). 1979. Repr. of 1958 ed. lib. bdg. 62.00x (ISBN 0-405-11497-4). Arno.
Urofsky, Melvin I. Big Steel & the Wilson Administration: A Study in Business-Government Relations. LC 69-12763. 1969. 8.00 (ISBN 0-8142-0006-0). Ohio St U Pr.
Vogel, David. Report of an Aspen Institute Seminar on the Corporation & Society. 4.00 (ISBN 0-686-26002-3). Aspen Inst Human.
Wachter, Michael & Wachter, Susan M., eds. A New U. S. Industrial Power. 1981. write for info. (ISBN 0-8122-7819-4). U of Pa Pr.
Warnecke, Steven, ed. International Trade & Industrial Policies: Government Intervention & an Open Global System. LC 78-611. 1978. text ed. 41.50x (ISBN 0-8419-0370-0). Holmes & Meier.
Weidenbaum, Murray L. The Future of Business Regulation: Private Action & Public Demand. 1980. pap. 5.95 (ISBN 0-8144-7533-7). Am Mgmt.
--The Future of Business Regulation: Private Action & Public Demand. LC 79-4389. (Illus.). 1979. 12.95 (ISBN 0-8144-5521-2). Am Mgmt.
Williams, Harold M. & Shapiro, Irving S. Power & Accountability. (The Benjamin F. Fairless Lectures Ser.). 64p. 1980. text ed. 10.00x (ISBN 0-915604-34-5). Carnegie-Mellon.
Winter, Ralph K. Government & the Corporation. 1978. pap. 4.25 (ISBN 0-8447-3313-X). Am Enterprise.
Wolf, Ronald H. & Mund, Vernon A. Business & Government. 434p. 1980. text ed. 19.95 (ISBN 0-89894-006-0). Advocate Pub Group.
Wormser, I. Maurice. Frankenstein, Incorporated. ix, 242p. 1981. Repr. of 1931 ed. lib. bdg. 26.00x (ISBN 0-8377-1316-1). Rothman.

Yohe, Gary W. A Comparison of Price Controls & Quantity Controls Under Uncertainty. LC 78-75060. (Outstanding Dissertations in Economics Ser.). 1979. lib. bdg. 28.00 (ISBN 0-8240-4137-2). Garland Pub.

Zimmerman, S. Mort. Business: Unsafe at Any Level. 1981. 12.50 (ISBN 0-682-49477-1). Exposition.

Zoltan, Roman, ed. Industrial Development & Industrial Policy. (Illus.). 427p. 1979. 45.00x (ISBN 963-05-2097-4). Intl Pubns Serv.

INDUSTRY AND STATE–CANADA

Safarian, A. E. Foreign Ownership of Canadian Industry. 2nd ed. LC 73-85095. 1973. pap. 8.50 (ISBN 0-8020-6216-4). U of Toronto Pr.

Studies in Canadian Industrial Organization: A Technical Report. (Royal Commission on Corporate Concentration Ser.: No. 26). 1979. pap. 9.25 (ISBN 0-660-00868-8, SSC 114, SSC). Unipub.

INDUSTRY AND STATE–CHINA

China: Rural Processing Technology. (Agricultral Services Bulletin: No. 36). 1979. pap. 6.00 (ISBN 92-5-100728-4, F1553, FAO). Unipub.

Hoffmann, Charles. Work Incentive Practices & Policies in the People's Republic of China, 1953-1965. LC 67-28936. 1967. 10.00 (ISBN 0-87395-028-3); microfiche 10.00 (ISBN 0-87395-128-X). State U NY Pr.

Jacobs, Norman. The Origin of Modern Capitalism & Eastern Asia. LC 79-1582. 1980. Repr. of 1958 ed. 19.50 (ISBN 0-88355-887-4). Hyperion Conn.

INDUSTRY AND STATE–EUROPE

Comisso. Worker's Control Under Plan & Market. 1979. text ed. 24.50x (ISBN 0-300-02334-0). Yale U Pr.

Dicksee, Lawrence R. Business Methods & the War: The Fundamentals of Manufacturing Costs: & Published Balance Sheets & Window Dressing, 3 vols. in 1. Brief, Richard P., ed. LC 80-1487. (Dimensions of Accounting Theory & Practice Ser.). 1981. Repr. of 1927 ed. lib. bdg. 18.00x (ISBN 0-686-73167-0). Arno.

Jacquemin, Alex & De Jong, Henry W. European Industrial Organization. LC 76-58378. (Problems of Economic Integration Ser.). 1977. 25.95 (ISBN 0-470-99079-1). Halsted Pr.

Kaserand, Michael & Zielinski, J. Planning in East Europe. 1971. 7.50 (ISBN 0-370-00397-7). Transatlantic.

Vernon, Raymond, ed. Big Business & the State: Changing Relations in Western Europe. LC 73-91784. 336p. 1974. text ed. 18.50x (ISBN 0-674-07275-8). Harvard U Pr.

INDUSTRY AND STATE–FRANCE

Martin, Germain. Grande Industrie Sous le Regne De Louis Quatorze. LC 70-128843. (Research & Source Works Ser.: No. 527). 1971. Repr. of 1899 ed. lib. bdg. 30.50 (ISBN 0-8337-2265-4). B Franklin.

Maunder, Peter, ed. Government Intervention in the Developed Economy. LC 78-72590. 1979. 25.95 (ISBN 0-03-049501-6). Praeger.

Nef, John U. Industry & Government in France & England, 1540-1640. 1957. pap. 3.95 (ISBN 0-8014-9053-7, CP53). Cornell U Pr.

Organization for Economic Cooperation & Development. The Industrial Policy of France. 132p. 1974. 4.00x (ISBN 92-64-11242-1). OECD.

Zysman, John. Political Strategies for Industrial Order: State, Market, & Industry in France. 1977. 24.75 (ISBN 0-520-02889-9). U of Cal Pr.

INDUSTRY AND STATE–GERMANY

Abraham, David. The Collapse of the Weimar Republic: Political Economy & Crisis. LC 80-8533. 550p. 1981. 30.00x (ISBN 0-691-05322-7); pap. 12.50x (ISBN 0-691-10118-3). Princeton U Pr.

Amman, Jost & Sachs, Hans. Book of Trades (Standebuch) Appelbaum, Stanley, tr. from Ger. LC 72-75581. (Pictorial Archive Ser.). Orig. Title: Eygentliche Beschreibung Aller Stande Auff Erden. (Illus.). 1973. Repr. of 1568 ed. 3.50 (ISBN 0-486-22886-X). Dover.

Borkin, Joseph. The Crime & Punishment of I. G. Farben. LC 78-430. 1978. 10.95 (ISBN 0-02-904630-0). Free Pr.

Jankowski, Manfred. Public Policy in Industrial Growth: The Case of the Early Ruhr Mining Region, 1766-1865. Bruchey, Stuart, ed. LC 77-77175. (Dissertations in European Economic History Ser.). (Illus.). 1977. lib. bdg. 27.00x (ISBN 0-405-10788-9). Arno.

Levy, Hermann. Industrial Germany. LC 66-31836. Repr. of 1935 ed. 25.00x (ISBN 0-678-05066-X). Kelley.

Maunder, Peter, ed. Government Intervention in the Developed Economy. LC 78-72590. 1979. 25.95 (ISBN 0-03-049501-6). Praeger.

INDUSTRY AND STATE–GREAT BRITAIN

Abraham, Neville. Big Business & Government: The New Disorder. 334p. 1975. text ed. 19.50x (ISBN 0-8419-5011-3). Holmes & Meier.

Armitage, S. M. Politics of Decontrol of Industry: Britain & the United States. (L.S.E. Research Monographs: No. 4). 1969. text ed. 9.25x (ISBN 0-297-17827-X). Humanities.

Beckett, J. V. Coal & Tobacco. (Illus.). 280p. 1981. 47.50 (ISBN 0-521-23486-7). Cambridge U Pr.

Blackaby, Frank, ed. De-Industrialisation. (Economic Policy Papers Ser.). 1979. text ed. 37.50x (ISBN 0-435-84076-2); pap. text ed. 21.50x (ISBN 0-435-84077-0). Heinemann Ed.

Broadway, Frank. State Intervention in British Industry 1964-68. LC 79-115974. 191p. 1970. 12.00 (ISBN 0-8386-7690-1). Fairleigh Dickinson.

Cole, George D. Economic Planning. LC 79-137935. (Economic Thought, History & Challenge Ser). 1971. Repr. of 1935 ed. 17.50 (ISBN 0-8046-1440-7). Kennikat.

--Self-Government in Industry. facsimile ed. LC 71-152979. (Select Bibliographies Reprint Ser). Repr. of 1918 ed. 19.00 (ISBN 0-8369-5731-8). Arno.

Davies, J. & Hughes, S. Investment in the British Economy. (Studies in the British Economy). 1979. pap. text ed. 6.00x (ISBN 0-435-84352-4). Heinemann Ed.

Fleming, John, et al. Catch Seventy-Six. (Occasional Paper: No. 47). 1977. pap. 5.95 (ISBN 0-255-36080-0). Transatlantic.

Hart, P. E. & Clarke, Roger. Concentration in British Industry 1935-1975. LC 79-41808. (Economic & Social Research Occasional Paper: No. 32). 163p. 1980. 29.50 (ISBN 0-521-23393-3). Cambridge U Pr.

Jewkes, John. Public & Private Enterprise. LC 66-12709. 1967. 4.50x (ISBN 0-226-39908-7). U of Chicago Pr.

King, M. A. Public Policy & the Corporation. (Cambridge Studies in Applied Econometrics: Vol. 3). 309p. 1977. text ed. 27.95x (ISBN 0-412-15330-0, Pub. by Chapman & Hall England). Methuen Inc.

Kirby, M. W. British Coalmining Industry, Eighteen Seventy to Nineteen Forty-Six: A Political & Economic History. LC 76-52412. 1977. 19.50 (ISBN 0-208-01656-2, Archon). Shoe String.

Knowles, Lillian C. Industrial & Commercial Revolutions in Great Britain During the Nineteenth Century. 4th ed. LC 67-27704. Repr. of 1961 ed. 17.50x (ISBN 0-678-06518-7). Kelley.

Lee, Derek. Control of the Economy. 1974. pap. text ed. 4.00x (ISBN 0-435-84542-X). Heinemann Ed.

Maunder, Peter, ed. Government Intervention in the Developed Economy. LC 78-72590. 1979. 25.95 (ISBN 0-03-049501-6). Praeger.

Nef, John U. Industry & Government in France & England, 1540-1640. 1957. pap. 3.95 (ISBN 0-8014-9053-7, CP53). Cornell U Pr.

--Industry & Government in France & England, 1540-1640. LC 68-25045. 1968. Repr. of 1940 ed. 8.00 (ISBN 0-8462-1172-6). Russell.

Redwood, John. Public Enterprise in Crisis: The Future of the Nationalised Industries. (Mainstream Ser.). 222p. 1980. 19.50x (ISBN 0-631-12582-5, Pub. by Basil Blackwell England). Biblio Dist.

Saham, Junid. British Industrial Investment in Malaysia, Nineteen Sixty-Three to Nineteen Seventy-One. (East Asian Social Science Monographs). 366p. 1981. 39.50x (ISBN 0-19-580418-X). Oxford U Pr.

Sciberras, Edmond. Multinational Electronic Companies & National Economic Policies. Altman, Edward I. & Walter, Ingo, eds. LC 76-10398. (Contemporary Studies in Economic & Financial Analysis: Vol. 6). 1977. lib. bdg. 32.50 (ISBN 0-89232-016-8). Jai Pr.

Wunderlich, Frieda. British Labor & the War. (Social Research Suppl.: No. 3). 1941. pap. 4.00 (ISBN 0-527-00863-X). Kraus Repr.

INDUSTRY AND STATE–INDIA

Iengar, Haravu V. Business & Planned Economy. 191p. 1968. 6.75x (ISBN 0-8426-1312-9). Verry.

Sen, Anupam. The State, Industrialization & Class Formations in India: A Neo-Marxist Perspective on Colonialism, Underdevelopment & Development. 330p. 1982. price not set (ISBN 0-7100-0888-0). Routledge & Kegan.

Sharma, K. L. & Singh, Harnek. Entrepreneurial Growth & Development Programmes in Northern India: A Sociological Analysis. 1980. 12.50x (ISBN 0-8364-0649-4, Pub. by Abhinav India). South Asia Bks.

Vakil, C. N., ed. Industrial Development of India: Policy & Problems. LC 73-907827. 504p. 1973. 13.50x (ISBN 0-8002-1561-3). Intl Pubns Serv.

INDUSTRY AND STATE–ITALY

Deaglio, Mario. Private Enterprise & Public Emulation. (Institute of Economic Affairs, Research Monographs: No. 5). pap. 2.50 (ISBN 0-255-69593-4). Transatlantic.

Haider, Carmen. Capital & Labor Under Fascism. LC 68-58586. (Columbia University. Studies in the Social Sciences: No. 318). Repr. of 1930 ed. 25.00 (ISBN 0-404-51318-2). AMS Pr.

Posner, M. V. & Woolf, Stuart J. Italian Public Enterprises. LC 67-4204. 1967. 10.00x (ISBN 0-674-46951-8). Harvard U Pr.

INDUSTRY AND STATE–JAPAN

Jacobs, Norman. The Origin of Modern Capitalism & Eastern Asia. LC 79-1582. 1980. Repr. of 1958 ed. 19.50 (ISBN 0-88355-887-4). Hyperion Conn.

Marshall, Byron K. Capitalism & Nationalism in Prewar Japan: The Ideology of the Business Elite 1868-1941. 1967. 10.00x (ISBN 0-8047-0325-6). Stanford U Pr.

Maunder, Peter, ed. Government Intervention in the Developed Economy. LC 78-72590. 1979. 25.95 (ISBN 0-03-049501-6). Praeger.

Murata, Kiyoji, ed. An Industrial Geography of Japan. LC 80-13404. 1980. 30.00 (ISBN 0-312-41428-5). St Martin.

INDUSTRY AND STATE–LATIN AMERICA

Jenkins, Rhys O. Dependent Industrialization in Latin America: The Automotive Industry in Argentina, Chile, & Mexico. LC 76-25352. (Illus.). 1976. text ed. 29.95 (ISBN 0-275-23220-4). Praeger.

Produccion Transferencia y Adoptacion De Technologica Industrial. (Span.). 1975. pap. 1.00 (ISBN 0-8270-6035-1). OAS.

INDUSTRY AND STATE–MALAYSIA

Saham, Junid. British Industrial Investment in Malaysia, Nineteen Sixty-Three to Nineteen Seventy-One. (East Asian Social Science Monographs). 366p. 1981. 39.50x (ISBN 0-19-580418-X). Oxford U Pr.

INDUSTRY AND STATE–PRUSSIA

Wendel, Hugo C. Evolution of Industrial Freedom in Prussia 1845-1849. facsimile ed. LC 74-109636. (Select Bibliographies Reprint Ser). 1921. 15.00 (ISBN 0-8369-5245-6). Arno.

INDUSTRY AND STATE–SWEDEN

Childs, Marquis W. Sweden: The Middle Way. LC 61-11402. (Illus.). 1961. Repr. of 1947 ed. 17.50x (ISBN 0-300-00366-8). Yale U Pr.

INDUSTRY AND WAR

see War–Economic Aspects

INDUSTRY IN ART, LITERATURE, ETC.

Arno Press & Silk, Leonard, eds. The Poetry of Industry: Two Literary Reactions to the Industrial Revolution 1755-1757. LC 70-38474. (The Evolution of Capitalism Ser.). 1972. Repr. of 1755 ed. 14.00 (ISBN 0-405-04131-4). Arno.

Burden, Charles, et al, eds. Business in Literature. LC 77-573. (English & Humanities Ser.). 1977. pap. text ed. 9.95x (ISBN 0-582-28160-1). Longman.

Doezema, Marianne. American Realism & the Industrial Age. LC 80-67347. (Themes in Art Ser.). (Illus.). 144p. 1981. pap. 9.95x (ISBN 0-910386-61-7, Pub. by Cleveland Mus Art). Ind U Pr.

Ginestier, Paul. The Poet & the Machine. Friedman, Martin B., tr. 1961. pap. 1.95 (ISBN 0-8084-0248-X, L14). Coll & U Pr.

Grant, Elliott M. French Poetry & Modern Industry, 1830-1870. 1927. pap. 13.00 (ISBN 0-527-01104-5). Kraus Repr.

Klingender, Francis D. Art & the Industrial Revolution. Elton, Arthur, ed. LC 68-17687. (Illus.). 1968. 25.00x (ISBN 0-678-07510-7). Kelley.

INDY, VINCENT D', 1851-1931

Demuth, Norman. Vincent D'Indy, 1851-1931. LC 73-6259. (Illus.). 117p. 1974. Repr. of 1951 ed. lib. bdg. 15.00x (ISBN 0-8371-6895-3, DEVD). Greenwood.

Saint-Saens, Camille. Outspoken Essays on Music. facs. ed. Rothwell, F., tr. LC 71-84335. (Essay Index Reprint Ser). 1922. 12.75 (ISBN 0-8369-1105-9). Arno.

INEBRIATES

see Alcoholics

INEBRIETY

see Alcoholism

INEFFICIENCY, INTELLECTUAL

see also Intelligence Tests; Mentally Handicapped Children

Crawshay-William, Rupert. Comforts of Unreason: A Study of the Motives Behind Irrational Thought. LC 71-98217. Repr. of 1947 ed. lib. bdg. 15.00x (ISBN 0-8371-3398-X, CRUN). Greenwood.

INEQUALITIES (MATHEMATICS)

Backenbach, E. F. & Bellman, R. An Introduction to Inequalities. LC 61-6228. (New Mathematical Library: No. 3). 1975. pap. 5.50 (ISBN 0-88385-603-4). Math Assn.

Beckenbach, E. F. & Bellman, R. Inequalities. LC 62-4593. (Ergebnisse der Mathematik und Ihrer Grenzgebiete: Vol. 30). (Illus.). 1971. 25.00 (ISBN 0-387-03283-5). Springer-Verlag.

Beckenbach, Edwin, ed. General Inequalities II. (International Ser. of Numerical Mathematics: No. 47). 505p. 1980. pap. 39.80 (ISBN 3-7643-1056-1). Birkhauser.

Carico, Charles. Systems of Linear Equations & Inequalities. 1974. 4.95x (ISBN 0-534-00330-3). Wadsworth Pub.

Duvant, G. & Lions, J. L. Inequalities in Mechanics & Physics. John, C., tr. from Fr. (Die Grundlehren der Mathematischen Wissenschaften: Vol. 219). (Illus.). 400p. 1975. 53.60 (ISBN 0-387-07327-2). Springer-Verlag.

Essen, M. R. The Cosine Pi Lambda Theorem. LC 75-17547. (Lecture Notes in Mathematics Ser.: Vol. 467). 112p. (Orig.). 1975. pap. 10.00 (ISBN 0-387-07176-8). Springer-Verlag.

Friedland, Shmuel. Nonoscillation, Disconjugacy & Integral Inequalities. LC 76-25246. 1976. 10.80 (ISBN 0-8218-2176-8, MEMO-176). Am Math.

Garsia, Adriano M. Martingale Inequalities. (Mathematics Lecture Note: Vol. 53). 1973. pap. 9.50 (ISBN 0-8053-3103-4, Adv Bk Prog). Benjamin-Cummings.

International Conference on General Inequalities, 1st, Mathematical Research Institute Oberwolfach, May 1976. Proceedings. Beckenbach, Edwin F., ed. 1978. text ed. 33.25x (ISBN 3-7643-0972-5). Renouf.

Kazarinoff, N. D. Geometric Inequalities. LC 67-6229. (New Mathematical Library: No. 4). 1975. pap. 5.50 (ISBN 0-88385-604-2). Math Assn.

Kinderlehrer, David & Stampacchia, Guido. An Introduction to Variational Inequalities & Their Applications. LC 79-52793. (Pure & Applied Mathematics Ser.). 1980. 40.00 (ISBN 0-12-407350-6). Acad Pr.

Lakshmikantham, V. & Leela, S. Differential & Integral Inequalities: Theory & Application, 2 vols. Incl. Vol. 1. Ordinary Differential Equations. 56.00 (ISBN 0-12-434101-2); Vol. 2. Functional, Partial, Abstract & Complex Differential Equations. 54.50 (ISBN 0-12-434102-0). LC 68-8425. (Mathematics in Science & Engineering Ser.: Vol. 55). 1969. Acad Pr.

Marshall, Albert & Olkin, Ingram. Inequalities: Theory of Majorization & Its Applications. LC 79-50218. (Mathematics in Science & Engineering). 1979. 60.00 (ISBN 0-12-473750-1). Acad Pr.

Mitrinovic, D. S. & Vasic, P. M. Analytic Inequalities. LC 76-116492. (Grundlehren der Mathematischen Wissenschaften: Vol. 165). (Illus.). 1970. 44.70 (ISBN 0-387-04837-5). Springer-Verlag.

Polya, G. & Szego, G. Isoperimetric Inequalities in Mathematical Physics. 1951. pap. 16.00 (ISBN 0-527-02743-X). Kraus Repr.

Schroder, Johann. Operator Inequalities. LC 79-28754. (Mathematics in Science & Engineering Ser.). 1980. 39.50 (ISBN 0-12-629750-9). Acad Pr.

Shisha, Oved, ed. Inequalities: Proceedings, 3 vols. Vol. 1, 1967. 31.50 (ISBN 0-12-640350-3); Vol. 2, 1970. 63.00 (ISBN 0-12-640302-3); Vol. 3, 1972. 54.50 (ISBN 0-12-640303-1). Acad Pr.

Solodovnikov, A. S. Systems of Linear Inequalities. 123p. 1979. pap. 2.75 (ISBN 0-8285-1515-8, Pub. by Mir Pubs Russia). Imported Pubns.

--Systems of Linear Inequalities. Glasser, Lawrence M. & Branson, Thomas P., trs. from Rus. LC 79-16106. (Popular Lectures in Mathematics Ser.). 1980. pap. text ed. 6.00x (ISBN 0-226-76786-8). U of Chicago Pr.

Szarski, J. Differential Inequalities. 1965. 15.75 (ISBN 0-02-853100-0). Hafner.

Walter, Wolfgang. Differential & Integral Inequalities. rev. ed. Rosenblatt, L. & Shampine, L., trs. from Ger. LC 72-103330. (Ergebnisse der Mathematik und Ihrer Grenzgebiete: Vol. 55). (Illus.). 1970. 42.50 (ISBN 0-387-05088-4). Springer-Verlag.

Wilf, H. S. Finite Sections of Some Classical Inequalities. LC 75-105700. (Ergebnisse der Mathematik und Ihrer Grenzgebiete: Vol. 52). (Illus.). 1970. 20.90 (ISBN 0-387-04809-X). Springer-Verlag.

INEQUALITY

see Equality

INERT ELEMENTS

see Gases, Rare

INERTIA (MECHANICS)

see also Mass (Physics)

Clotfelter, Beryl E. Reference Systems & Inertia: The Nature of Space. (Illus., Orig.). 1970. pap. 4.50x (ISBN 0-8138-1325-5). Iowa St U Pr.

INERTIAL GUIDANCE

see Inertial Navigation Systems

INERTIAL NAVIGATION (AERONAUTICS)

Farrell, James L., ed. Integrated Aircraft Navigation. 1976. 48.75 (ISBN 0-12-249750-3). Acad Pr.

INERTIAL NAVIGATION SYSTEMS

Britting, Kenneth R. Inertial Navigation Systems Analysis. LC 70-168635. 1971. 32.00 (ISBN 0-471-10485-X, Pub. by Wiley-Interscience). Wiley.

INEZ, DE CASTRO, d. 1355–DRAMA

Casona, Alejandro. Corona De Amor Y Muerte. Balseiro, Jose & Owre, J. Riis, eds. (Orig., Span). 1960. pap. 5.95x (ISBN 0-19-500844-8). Oxford U Pr.

De Montherlant, Henry. Reine Morte. 1957. 11.95 (ISBN 0-685-11525-9). French & Eur.

INFALLIBILITY OF THE CHURCH

see Catholic Church–Infallibility

INFALLIBILITY OF THE POPE

see Popes–Infallibility

INFANCY OF ANIMALS

see Animals, Infancy of

INFANT BAPTISM

see also Baptism; Predestination

Bromiley, Geoffrey W. Children of Promise: The Case for Baptizing Infants. LC 79-10346. 1979. pap. 3.95 (ISBN 0-8028-1797-1). Eerdmans.

Coleman, William V. & Coleman, Patricia R. God's Own Child: Leader's Guide. (Baptismal Program). (Illus.). 1977. pap. 4.95 (ISBN 0-89622-046-X); complete program 39.95 (ISBN 0-89622-045-1). Twenty-Third.

--God's Own Child: Parent's Book. (Baptismal Program). (Illus.). 1977. pap. 3.95 (ISBN 0-89622-047-8); complete program 39.95 (ISBN 0-685-86643-2). Twenty-Third.

Hallesby, O. Infant Baptism & Adult Conversion. 1964. pap. 3.50 (ISBN 0-8066-0400-X, 10-3346). Augsburg.

Jewett, Paul K. Infant Baptism. 1978. pap. 5.95 (ISBN 0-8028-1713-0). Eerdmans.

Newman, Albert H. History of Anti-Pedobaptism: From the Rise of Pedobaptism to A.D. 1609. LC 71-144664. Repr. of 1897 ed. 26.45 (ISBN 0-404-04686-X). AMS Pr.

INFANT EDUCATION

see Education, Preschool

INFANT MORTALITY

see Children–Mortality; Infants–Mortality

INFANT PSYCHOLOGY

Accardo, Pasquale J. Failure to Thrive in Infancy & Early Childhood: A Multidisciplinary Team Approach. 340p. text ed. 27.95 (ISBN 0-8391-1678-0). Univ Park.

Anderson, Gene C. & Raff, Beverly, eds. Newborn Behavioral Organization: Nursing Research &Implications. LC 79-2597. (Alan R. Liss Ser.: Vol. 15, No. 7). 1979. 24.00 (ISBN 0-8451-1032-2). March of Dimes.

Arlitt, Ada H. Psychology of Infancy & Early Childhood. 1979. Repr. of 1946 ed. lib. bdg. 30.00 (ISBN 0-8495-0200-4). Arden Lib.

Bailey, Rebecca A. & Burton, Elsie C. The Dynamic Self: Activities to Enhance Infant Development. (Illus.). 208p. 1981. pap. text ed. 11.95 (ISBN 0-8016-0438-9). Mosby.

Bates, Elizabeth. The Emergence of Symbols: Cognition & Communication in Infancy. LC 78-20040. (Language, Thought & Culture Ser.). 1979. 34.00 (ISBN 0-12-081540-0). Acad Pr.

Bloom, Kathleen, ed. Prospective Issues in Infancy Research. LC 80-17479. 208p. 1981. text ed. 19.95x (ISBN 0-89859-059-0). L Erlbaum Assocs.

Bower, T. G. A Primer of Infant Development. LC 76-27827. (Psychology Ser.). (Illus.). 1977. text ed. 16.95x (ISBN 0-7167-0499-4); pap. text ed. 7.95x (ISBN 0-7167-0498-6). W H Freeman.

Brazelton, T. Berry. Neonatal Behavioral Assessment Scale. (Illus.). 1974. 12.95x (ISBN 0-433-04030-0). Intl Ideas.

--Toddlers & Parents: A Declaration of Independence. 1974. 12.95 (ISBN 0-440-08750-3, Sey Lawr). Delacorte.

Bruner, Jerome S. Processes of Cognitive Growth: Infancy. LC 68-27831. (Heinz Werner Lec. Ser.: No. 3). 1968. 3.00x (ISBN 0-8271-6810-1). Clark U Pr.

Buhler, Charlotte. The First Year of Life. Greenberg, Pearl & Ripin, Rowena, trs. LC 73-16646. 281p. 1974. Repr. of 1930 ed. lib. bdg. 15.50x (ISBN 0-8371-7214-4, BUFY). Greenwood.

--The First Year of Life. Greenberg, Pearl & Ripin, Rowena, trs. LC 74-21402. (Classics in Child Development Ser). 296p. 1975. Repr. 18.00x (ISBN 0-405-06455-1). Arno.

Bullowa, Margaret, ed. Before Speech. LC 78-51671. (Illus.). 1979. 42.50 (ISBN 0-521-22031-9); pap. 11.95 (ISBN 0-521-29522-X). Cambridge U Pr.

Bzoch, Kenneth R. Assessing Language Skills in Infancy. 54p. pap. text ed. 6.75 (ISBN 0-686-72900-5). Univ Park.

Caplan, Frank, ed. The First Twelve Months of Life. 1978. pap. 3.95 (ISBN 0-553-20022-4, V13901-0). Bantam.

Church, Joseph, ed. Three Babies: Biographies of Cognitive Development. LC 78-14252. 1978. Repr. lib. bdg. 27.75x (ISBN 0-313-21029-2, CHTB). Greenwood.

Cohen, Leslie B. & Salapatek, Philip, eds. Infant Perception: From Sensation to Cognition, 2 vols. Incl. Vol. 1. Basic Visual Processes. 1975. 44.50 (ISBN 0-12-178601-3); Vol. 2. Perception of Space, Speech, & Sound. 1975. 36.00 (ISBN 0-12-178602-1). (Child Psychology Ser.). 1975. 64.50 set (ISBN 0-685-72441-7). Acad Pr.

Covin, Theron M., ed. Readings in the Psychology of Early Childhood. LC 72-85868. 488p. 1976. text ed. 18.50x (ISBN 0-8422-5238-X); pap. text ed. 14.50x (ISBN 0-8422-0491-1). Irvington.

Dunn, Judy. Distress & Comfort. (Developing Child Ser.). 1977. 6.95x (ISBN 0-674-21284-3); pap. 3.95 (ISBN 0-674-21285-1). Harvard U Pr.

Ellis, Norman R., ed. Aberrant Development in Infancy: Human & Animal Studies. LC 75-9657. 288p. 1975. 16.50 (ISBN 0-470-23859-3, Pub. by Wiley). Krieger.

Emde, Robert N., et al. Emotion Expression in Infancy: A Biobehavioral Study. LC 76-4609. (Psychological Issues Monograph: No. 37). 1976. text ed. 13.50 (ISBN 0-8236-1651-7); pap. text ed. 11.00 (ISBN 0-8236-1650-9). Intl Univs Pr.

Fitzgerald, Hiram E., et al. Developmental Psychology: The Infant & Young Child. 1977. pap. 9.95x (ISBN 0-256-01888-X). Dorsey.

Fraiberg, Selma. Every Child's Birthright. LC 77-74574. 1977. 10.95 (ISBN 0-465-02132-8). Basic.

--Insights from the Blind: Developmental Studies of Blind Children. LC 76-9676. 1977. 12.95x (ISBN 0-465-03318-0). Basic.

Gardner, Judith & Gardner, Howard. Monographs on Infancy: An Original Anthology. LC 74-21702. 316p. 1975. Repr. 19.00x (ISBN 0-405-06472-1). Arno.

Gardner, Judith K. & Gardner, Howard, eds. First Notes by Observant Parents. LC 74-21407. (Classics in Child Development Ser). 90p. 1975. Repr. 12.00x (ISBN 0-405-06459-4). Arno.

Gattegno, Caleb. The Universe of Babies: In the Beginning There Were No Words. 133p. 1973. pap. 3.85 (ISBN 0-87825-023-9). Ed Solutions.

Grrenspan, Stanley I. Psychopathology & Adaptation in Infancy & Early Childhood. 1981. pap. text ed. write for info. (ISBN 0-8236-5660-8). Intl Univs Pr.

Haith, Marshall M. Rules That Babies Look by: The Organization of Newborn Visual Activity. LC 80-10601. (Illus.). 146p. 1980. text ed. 16.50x (ISBN 0-89859-033-7). L Erlbaum Assocs.

Ibuka, Masaru. Kindergarten Is Too Late! 1980. 4.95 (ISBN 0-686-62839-X, 25363, Fireside). S&S.

Illingworth, R. S. The Development of the Infant & Young Child: Normal & Abnormal. 7th ed. (Illus.). 1980. text ed. 26.50 (ISBN 0-443-01925-8). Churchill.

Infantile Psychosis & Other Papers: Selected Papers of Margaret Mahler, Vol. 1. Incl. Vol. 2. Seperation Individuation. LC 79-51915. 1979. 40.00xset (ISBN 0-685-22268-3). Vol. 2 (ISBN 0-87668-345-6). Aronson.

Jackson, Jane F. & Jackson, Joseph H. Infant Culture. LC 78-4351. 1979. pap. 4.95 (ISBN 0-452-25221-0, Z5221, Plume). NAL.

Jersild, Arthur T., et al. Child Psychology. 7th ed. LC 74-20723. (Illus.). 640p. 1975. text ed. 19.95 (ISBN 0-13-130971-4). P-H.

Kaplan, Louise. Oneness & Separtness. 1978. 9.95 (ISBN 0-671-22854-4). S&S.

Kearsley, Richard B. & Sigel, Irving E., eds. Infants at Risk: Assessment of Cognitive Functioning. LC 78-23246. 1979. 16.50 (ISBN 0-470-26574-4). Halsted Pr.

Ligon, Ernest M., et al. Let Me Introduce My SELF. LC 76-25315. 1976. 11.95 (ISBN 0-915744-04-X); deluxe ed. 14.95 (ISBN 0-915744-05-8); pap. 7.95 (ISBN 0-915744-03-1). Character Res.

Lipsitt, Lewis P., ed. Advances in Infancy Research. 300p. 1981. 30.00 (ISBN 0-89391-045-7). Ablex Pub.

McCall, Robert B. Infants. (Illus.). 185p. 1979. 10.00 (ISBN 0-674-45265-8). Harvard U Pr.

Macfarlane, Aidan. The Psychology of Childbirth. (Developing Child Ser.). 1977. 6.95x (ISBN 0-674-72105-5); pap. 3.95 (ISBN 0-674-72106-3). Harvard U Pr.

McGraw, Myrtle B. Growth: A Study of Johnny & Jimmie. LC 74-21422. (Classics in Child Development Ser). 372p. 1975. Repr. 26.00x (ISBN 0-405-06471-3). Arno.

Marzollo, Jean. Supertot: Creative Learning Activities for Children 1-3 & Sympathetic Advice for Their Parents. LC 76-47265. (Illus.). 11.95 (ISBN 0-06-012847-X, HarpT). Har-Row.

Oates, John, ed. Early Cognitive Development. LC 78-17694. 1979. 27.95 (ISBN 0-470-26431-4). Halsted Pr.

Perez, Bernard. The First Three Years of Childhood. Christie, Alice M., ed. LC 74-21425. (Classics in Child Development Ser.). 330p. 1975. Repr. 22.00x (ISBN 0-405-06474-8). Arno.

Pulaski, Mary A. Your Baby's Mind & How It Grows: Piaget's Theory for Parents. LC 76-47263. (Illus.). 1978. 10.95 (ISBN 0-06-013461-5, HarpT). Har-Row.

Pulaski, Mary Ann. Your Baby's Mind & How It Grows. LC 76-47263. (Illus.). 224p. 1981. pap. 3.95 (ISBN 0-06-090886-6, CN 886, CN). Har-Row.

Rexford, Eveoleen N., et al, eds. Infant Psychiatry: A New Synthesis. LC 75-2774. (A Monograph of the Journal of the American Academy of Child Psychiatry Ser.). 384p. 1976. 27.50x (ISBN 0-300-01890-8). Yale U Pr.

Richards, Martin. Infancy: World of the Newborn. (Life Cycle Ser.). 1979. pap. text ed. 4.95 (ISBN 0-06-384748-5, HarpC). Har-Row.

Robeck, Mildred C. Infants & Children. (Illus.). 1978. text ed. 18.95 (ISBN 0-07-053108-0, C); instructor's manual 4.95 (ISBN 0-07-053109-9). McGraw.

Sawin, Douglas B., et al, eds. Exceptional Infant: Psychosocial Risks in Infant-Environment Transactions, Vol. 4. LC 80-14270. (Exceptional Infant Ser.). 1980. 35.00 (ISBN 0-87630-222-3). Brunner-Mazel.

Schafer, D. Sue & Moersch, Martha M., eds. Developmental Programming for Infants & Young Children, 3 vols. Incl. Vol. 1. Assessment & Application. pap. 7.00x (ISBN 0-472-08141-1); Vol. 2. Early Intervention Developmental Profile. pap. 1.25x (ISBN 0-472-08142-X); Vol. 3. Stimulation Activities. pap. 8.00x (ISBN 0-472-08143-8). LC 76-49257. 1977. Set. pap. 14.50x (ISBN 0-472-08140-3). U of Mich Pr.

Segal, Marilyn. From Birth to One Year. Bardige, Betty, ed. (Nova University Play & Learn Program). (Illus.). 67p. (gr. 9-12). pap. text ed. 5.95x (ISBN 0-935266-00-3). B L Winch.

Shaffer, David & Dunn, Judy. The First Year of Life: Psychological & Medical Implications of Early Experience. LC 78-11237. (Studies in Psychiatry). 1980. 41.75 (ISBN 0-471-99734-X, Pub. by Wiley-Interscience). Wiley.

Sherrod, Kathryn, et al. Infancy. LC 77-25205. 1978. pap. text ed. 7.95 (ISBN 0-8185-0258-4). Brooks-Cole.

Shinn, Milicent W. The Biography of a Baby. LC 74-21427. (Classics in Child Development Ser). 256p. 1975. Repr. 18.00x (ISBN 0-405-06476-4). Arno.

Spitz, Rene. Infant Psychiatry: The Selected Papers of Rene Spitz. Emde, Robert N., ed. 1981. pap. text ed. write for info. Intl Univs Pr.

Sroufe, Alan. Knowing & Enjoying Your Baby. LC 77-21703. (Illus.). 1977. 10.95 (ISBN 0-13-516690-X, Spec); pap. 3.95 (ISBN 0-13-516682-9, Spec). P-H.

Tighe, T. J. & Leaton, R. N. Habituation: Perspectives from Child Development, Animal Behavior & Neurophysiology. 1977. 19.95 (ISBN 0-470-99008-2). Halsted Pr.

Tronick, Edward. Tronick: Social Interchange in Infancy: Affect, Cognition, & Communication. (Illus.). 224p. 1982. pap. text ed. 28.95 (ISBN 0-8391-1510-5). Univ Park.

Uzgiris, Ina C. & Hunt, J. McVicker. Assessment in Infancy: Ordinal Scales of Psychological Development. LC 74-31461. 274p. 1975. 15.00 (ISBN 0-252-00465-5). U of Ill Pr.

White, Burton L. The First Three Years of Life. LC 75-22159. 1975. 10.00 (ISBN 0-13-319178-8). P-H.

Willemsen, Eleanor W. Understanding Infancy. LC 78-21181. (Psychology Ser.). (Illus.). 1979. text ed. 16.95x (ISBN 0-7167-1002-1); pap. text ed. 8.95x (ISBN 0-7167-1001-3). W H Freeman.

Ziajka, Alan. Prelinguistic Communication in Infancy. 192p. 1981. 21.95 (ISBN 0-03-058649-6). Praeger.

INFANT SALVATION

see also Children–Death and Future State; Infant Baptism; Predestination

INFANT SUDDEN DEATH

see Sudden Death in Infants

INFANT WELFARE

see Maternal and Infant Welfare

INFANTICIDE

see also Abortion

Conrad, Phil. Trial & Terror. 1978. 7.95 (ISBN 0-533-03620-8). Vantage.

Hoffer, Peter C. & Hull, N. E. Murdering Mothers: Infanticide in England & New England, 1558-1803. (NYU School of Law Ser. in Anglo-American Legal History). 208p. 1981. text ed. 22.50x (ISBN 0-8147-3412-X). NYU Pr.

Kohl, Marvin, ed. Infanticide & the Value of Life. LC 77-26376. 252p. 1978. 15.95 (ISBN 0-87975-100-2). Prometheus Bks.

Miller, Barbara D. The Endangered Sex: Neglect of Female Children in Rural North India. LC 81-3226. (Illus.). 192p. 1981. 17.50x (ISBN 0-8014-1371-0). Cornell U Pr.

Piers, Maria W. Infanticide. 1978. 7.95 (ISBN 0-393-01169-0). Norton.

Rapport a M. Le Ministre, Secretaire d'Etat de l'Interieur, Concernant les Infanticides et les Mort-Nes dans Leur Relation avec la Question des Enfant Trouves, Par M. Renacle. (Conditions of the 19th Century French Working Class Ser.). 86p. (Fr.). 1974. Repr. of 1845 ed. lib. bdg. 29.00x (ISBN 0-8287-0713-8, 1109). Clearwater Pub.

Saxena, R. K. Social Reforms: Infanticide & Sati. LC 75-906665. 1975. 8.50x (ISBN 0-88386-655-2). South Asia Bks.

Schaeffer, Francis A. & Koop, C. Everett. Whatever Happened to the Human Race? 1979. 13.95x (ISBN 0-8007-1051-7); study guide 2.95 (ISBN 0-8007-1052-5). Revell.

INFANTILE PARALYSIS

see Poliomyelitis

INFANTILISM

Stekel, Wilhelm. Patterns of Psychosexual Infantilism. 1952. 8.95x (ISBN 0-87140-840-6). Liveright.

INFANTS

see also Children; Children, First-Born; Infant Psychology

Aladjem, Silvio, et al. Clinical Perinatology. 2nd ed. LC 79-24340. (Illus.). 1979. text ed. 52.50 (ISBN 0-8016-0103-7). Mosby.

Ancona, George. It's a Baby! LC 79-10453. (Illus.). (gr. k-3). 1979. 8.95 (ISBN 0-525-32598-0). Dutton.

Aston, Athina. How to Play with Your Baby. LC 74-21748. (Illus., Orig.). 1976. pap. 5.95 (ISBN 0-916184-00-5). Fountain Pub Co NY.

Bayley, Nancy. Development of Motor Abilities During the First Three Years. 1935. pap. 4.00 (ISBN 0-527-01486-9). Kraus Repr.

Belsky, Jay. In the Beginning: Readings in Infancy. LC 81-10008. (Illus.). 328p. 1982. text ed. 25.00x (ISBN 0-231-05114-X); pap. 12.50x (ISBN 0-231-05115-8). Columbia U Pr.

Bloom, Arthur D. & James, L. S., eds. The Fetus & the Newborn. (Alan R. Less, Inc. Ser.: Vol. 17, No.1). 1981. 36.00 (ISBN 0-8451-1041-1). March of Dimes.

Bosma, James F. Third Symposium on Oral Sensation & Perception: The Mouth of the Infant. (Illus.). 484p. 1972. 58.25 (ISBN 0-398-02238-0). C C Thomas.

Brackbill, Yvonne. Infancy & Early Childhood. LC 67-15056. 1967. text ed. 12.95 (ISBN 0-02-904520-7). Free Pr.

Brazelton, T. Berry. Infants & Mothers. 1972. pap. 7.95 (ISBN 0-440-54076-3, Delta). Dell.

--Infants & Mothers: Individual Differences in Development. (Illus.). 1969. 12.95 (ISBN 0-440-04045-0, Sey Lawr). Delacorte.

Brazleton, T. B., ed. A Neonatal Behavioral Assessment Scale. (Clinics in Developmental Medicine Ser.: Vol. 50). 66p. 1973. 13.00 (ISBN 0-685-59044-5, JBL-Med-Nursing). Har-Row.

Brody, Sylvia. Patterns of Mothering: A Study of Maternal Influence During Infancy. LC 56-8839. 1970. text ed. 20.00 (ISBN 0-8236-4040-X); pap. 6.95 (ISBN 0-8236-8190-4, 024040). Intl Univs Pr.

Brody, Sylvia & Axelrad, Sidney. Anxiety & Ego Formation in Infancy. LC 74-141660. 1971. text ed. 22.50 (ISBN 0-8236-0390-3). Intl Univs Pr.

Drawbaugh, Susan M. What Pet Will I Get? LC 77-83881. 1977. 5.95 (ISBN 0-89430-017-2). Morgan-Pacific.

Dubowitz, Victor, ed. The Floppy Infant. 2nd ed. (Clinics in Developmental Medicine Ser.: No. 76). 109p. 1980. 25.00 (ISBN 0-685-24726-0, JBL-Med-Nursing). Har-Row.

Escalona, Sybelle K. & Leitch, Mary. Early Phases of Personality Development: A Non-Normative Study of Infant Behavior. 1952. pap. 5.00 (ISBN 0-527-01554-7). Kraus Repr.

Freedman, Daniel G. Human Infancy: An Evolutionary Perspective. LC 74-13497. (Child Psychology Ser.). 212p. 1974. 14.95 (ISBN 0-470-27726-2). Halsted Pr.

Gesell, Arnold. Atlas of Infant Behavior, Vol. 2. (Illus.). 1934. 125.00x (ISBN 0-685-69821-1). Elliots Bks.

Gesell, Arnold, et al. Infant & Child in the Culture of Today: The Guidance of Development in Home & Nursery School. rev. ed. LC 73-4083. (Illus.). 432p. 1974. 15.95 (ISBN 0-06-011506-8, HarpT). Har-Row.

Gesell, Arnold L. & Thompson, Helen. Infant Behavior: Its Genesis & Growth. LC 71-95101. Repr. of 1934 ed. lib. bdg. 19.50x (ISBN 0-8371-2704-1, GEIB). Greenwood.

Gibbs, Frederic A. & Gibbs, Erna L. Atlas of Electroencephalography, Vol. IV: Normal & Abnormal Infants from Birth to 11 Months of Age. 1978. 190.00 (ISBN 0-201-10055-X, Med-Nurse). A-W.

Jackson, Jane F. & Jackson, Joseph H. Infant Culture. LC 78-4351. 1979. pap. 4.95 (ISBN 0-452-25221-0, Z5221, Plume). NAL.

Johnston, Lynn. Hi Mom! Hi Dad! (Illus.). 1977. pap. 2.95 (ISBN 0-915658-06-2). Meadowbrook Pr.

Jones, Sandy. Good Things for Babies. 2nd rev. ed. (Illus.). 1980. cloth. 12.95 (ISBN 0-395-29197-6); pap. 6.95 (ISBN 0-395-29198-4). HM.

Kagan, Jerome, et al. Infancy: Its Place in Human Development. LC 77-26970. 1978. 20.00x (ISBN 0-674-45260-7); pap. 6.95 (ISBN 0-674-45261-5). Harvard U Pr.

Koch, Jarosla. Total Baby Development. 1978. pap. 3.95 (ISBN 0-671-79025-0, Wallaby). PB.

Ling, Bing-Chung. Form Discrimination As a Learning Cue in Infants. LC 41-14185. 1941. pap. 5.00 (ISBN 0-527-24852-5). Kraus Repr.

Lipsitt, Lewis P., ed. Advances in Infancy Research. 300p. 1981. 30.00 (ISBN 0-89391-045-7). Ablex Pub.

McGraw, Myrtle B. Growth: A Study of Johnny & Jimmie. LC 74-21422. (Classics in Child Development Ser). 372p. 1975. Repr. 26.00x (ISBN 0-405-06471-3). Arno.

Mahler, Margaret S., et al. The Psychological Birth of the Human Infant. LC 74-77255. 1975. text ed. 17.50x (ISBN 0-465-06659-3). Basic.

Mason, Sheila. The Baby. 48p. (gr. 9-11). 1975. pap. text ed. 3.95x (ISBN 0-521-20444-5). Cambridge U Pr.

Mayle, Peter. Great Moments in Baby History. LC 80-229. (Illus.). 1980. 9.95 (ISBN 0-02-077370-6). Macmillan.

Munger, Evelyn M. & Bowdon, Susan J. Beyond Peek-a-Boo & Pat-a-Cake: Activities for Baby's First Year. 208p. 1980. 8.95 (ISBN 0-695-81439-7). New Century.

Nagera, Humberto. Early Childhood Disturbances, the Infantile Neurosis, & the Adult Disturbances. LC 66-17526. (Psychoanalytic Study of the Child Monographs: No. 2). 1966. text ed. 10.00 (ISBN 0-8236-1520-0). Intl Univs Pr.

Provence, Sally & Lipton, Rose C. Infants in Institutions: A Comparison of Their Development During the First Year of Life with Family-Reared Infants. LC 62-21560. 1967. text ed. 15.00 (ISBN 0-8236-2648-2). Intl Univs Pr.

Rheingold, Harriet L. Modification of Social Responsiveness in Institutional Babies. 1956. pap. 4.00 (ISBN 0-527-01567-9). Kraus Repr.

Ribble, Margaretha A. The Rights of Infants: Early Psychological Needs & Their Satisfaction. 2nd ed. LC 65-24832. 1965. 15.00x (ISBN 0-231-02849-0). Columbia U Pr.

Siverman, Goldie, ed. Backpacking with Babies & Small Children. (Illus.). 1975. pap. 5.95 (ISBN 0-913140-11-2). Signpost Bk Pubns.

Smart, Mollie S. & Smart, Russell C. Development & Relationships, 4 vols. 2nd ed. Incl. Vol. 1. Infants. 370p. 8.95 (ISBN 0-02-411970-9); Vol. 2. Pre-School Children. 356p. 8.95 (ISBN 0-02-412040-5); Vol. 3. School-Age Children. 340p. 8.95 (ISBN 0-02-411990-3); Vol. 4. Adolescents. 310p. 8.95 (ISBN 0-02-412120-7). (Illus.). 1978. pap. text ed. 6.50x ea. Macmillan.

Spitz, Rene A. & Cobliner, W. Godfrey. First Year of Life: A Psychoanalytic Study of Normal & Deviant Development of Object Relations. LC 68-18382. 1966. text ed. 30.00 (ISBN 0-8236-1960-5). Intl Univs Pr.

Stack, Jack M. The Special Infant: An Interdisciplinary Approach to the Optimal Development of Infants. LC 81-4478. 1981. 24.95 (ISBN 0-89885-028-2). Human Sci Pr.

Stone, Joseph, et al. Competent Infant: Research & Commentary, 3 vols. Incl. Vol. 1. Behavior of the Newborn (ISBN 0-465-00598-5); Vol. 2. Infant's First Year (ISBN 0-465-03269-9); Vol. 3. Social Infant (ISBN 0-465-07880-X). LC 77-17673. 1974. pap. 5.95x ea.; one vol. ed. 39.50x (ISBN 0-465-01346-5). Basic.

Stone, L. Joseph, et al, eds. Behavior of the Newborn. LC 77-17627. (Competent Infant Ser.). 1978. pap. text ed. 5.95x (ISBN 0-465-00598-5). Basic.

--The Infant's First Year. LC 77-17673. (Competent Infant Ser.). 1978. pap. text ed. 5.95x (ISBN 0-465-03269-9). Basic.

--The Social Infant. LC 77-17674. (Competent Infant Ser.). 1978. pap. text ed. 5.95x (ISBN 0-465-07880-X). Basic.

Thomas, Alexander, et al. Behavioral Individuality in Early Childhood. LC 79-16817. (Illus.). 1980. Repr. of 1963 ed. lib. bdg. 17.75x (ISBN 0-313-22049-2, THBI). Greenwood.

Thomson, Ernie. It's a Baby. LC 80-925. 9.95 (ISBN 0-385-17128-5); pap. 2.99 (ISBN 0-686-74000-9). Doubleday.

Tjossem, Theodore D., ed. Intervention Strategies with High Risk Infants. (Illus.). 1976. 29.50 (ISBN 0-8391-0760-9). Univ Park.

Walcher, Dwain N. & Peters, Donald L., eds. Early Childhood: The Development of Self-Regulatory Mechanisms. 1971. 34.50 (ISBN 0-12-731750-3). Acad Pr.

Wasz-Hoeckert, O., et al. The Infant Cry: A Spectographic & Auditory Analysis. (Clinics in Developmental Medicine Ser. No. 29). 42p. 1968. 12.00 (ISBN 0-685-24737-6). Lippincott.

Wolf, Katherine M. & Auerbach, Aline B. As Your Child Grows: The First Eighteen Months. LC 55-11408. 1962. pap. 1.50 (ISBN 0-87183-045-0). Child Study.

Young, Bonnie. All About Me. 1977. 9.95 ea. Blue (ISBN 0-8024-0204-6). Pink (ISBN 0-8024-0205-4). Yellow (ISBN 0-8024-0206-2). Moody.

Youngren, Frances, ed. Our Baby, God's Gift. 1966. bds. 6.95 ea. (ISBN 0-8024-6192-1); blue bk. (ISBN 0-8024-6191-3); pink bk. (ISBN 0-685-16808-5); yellow bk. (ISBN 0-8024-6193-X). Moody.

INFANTS–CARE AND HYGIENE

see also Baby Sitters; Nurseries; Prenatal Care

Ainsworth, Mary D. Salter. Infancy in Uganda: Infant Care & the Growth of Love. LC 67-16039. (Illus.). 496p. 1967. 34.00x (ISBN 0-8018-0010-2). Johns Hopkins.

American Woman Baby & Child Care. 1981. 9.95 (ISBN 0-686-31774-2). Caroline Hse.

Anselmo, Sandra & Peterson, Jane D. A Manual for Caregivers of Infants & Toddlers. LC 77-91727. 1978. soft cover 6.00 (ISBN 0-88247-496-0). R & E Res Assoc.

Aukema, Susan & Kostick, Marilyn. The Curity Baby Book. cancelled (ISBN 0-916752-06-2). Green Hill.

--The Curity Baby Book: A Commonsense Guide to Baby Care. LC 76-48841. (Illus.). 1976. 9.95 (ISBN 0-916752-06-2). Dorison Hse.

Baumgartner, Leona, et al. The Parent's Book of Baby Care. (Good Health Books). (Illus.). 1978. pap. 2.50 (ISBN 0-448-14823-4). G&D.

Beebe, Brooke. Best Bets for Babies. (Orig.). pap. 5.95 (ISBN 0-440-50453-8, Dell Trade Pbks). Dell.

Benning, Lee Edwards. How to Bring up a Child Without Spending a Fortune. LC 75-25436. 320p. 1976. pap. 2.95 (ISBN 0-385-11513-X, Dolp). Doubleday.

Bernbeck, Rupprecht & Sinios, Alexander. Neuro-Orthopedic Screening in Infancy: Schedules, Examination & Findings. LC 78-2505. (Illus.). 120p. 1978. text ed. 16.50 (ISBN 0-8067-0231-1). Urban & S.

Better Homes & Gardens, ed. Better Homes & Gardens New Baby Book. 416p. 1980. pap. 2.95 (ISBN 0-553-20158-1). Bantam.

Better Homes & Gardens Books Editors, ed. Better Homes & Gardens New Baby Book. (Illus.). 1979. 9.95 (ISBN 0-696-00021-0). Meredith Corp.

Bibliography of Infant Foods & Nutrition 1938-1977. 322p. 1978. pap. 29.00 (ISBN 0-686-71824-0, CO 27, CSIRO). Unipub.

Bosnjak, V. Early Child Care in Yugoslavia. (International Monographs on Early Child Care). Date not set. price not set (ISBN 0-677-05460-2). Gordon.

Boston Children's Medical Center. Pregnancy, Birth & the Newborn Baby. 1972. 15.95 (ISBN 0-440-07088-0, Sey Lawr). Delacorte.

Brewer, Gail S. & Greene, Janice P. Right from the Start: Meeting the Challenges of Mothering Your Unborn & Newborn Baby. Gerras, Charlie, ed. (Illus.). 256p. (Orig.). 1981. pap. 11.95 (ISBN 0-87857-273-2). Rodale Pr Inc.

Bricklin, Alice G. Motherlove: Natural Mothering, Birth to Three Years. Williams, Betsy, ed. LC 79-9724. 1979. lib. bdg. 12.90 (ISBN 0-89471-070-2); pap. 4.95 (ISBN 0-89471-069-9). Running Pr.

Burck, Frances W. Babysense. LC 79-2476. 1979. 19.95 (ISBN 0-312-06457-8); pap. 9.95 (ISBN 0-312-06458-6). St Martin.

Caulfield, Ernest. The Infant Welfare Movement in the Eighteenth Century. (Historia Medicinae). (Illus.). Repr. of 1931 ed. lib. bdg. 15.00x (ISBN 0-87991-704-0). Porcupine Pr.

Centre for Advanced Study in the Developmental Sciences. Stimulation in Early Infancy: Proceedings. Ambrose, Anthony, ed. 1970. 42.50 (ISBN 0-12-055950-1). Acad Pr.

Cohen, Jean P. & Goirand, Roger. Your Baby: Pregnancy, Delivery, & Infant Care. (Illus.). 304p. 1981. 16.95 (ISBN 0-13-978130-7, Spec); pap. 8.95 (ISBN 0-13-978122-6). P-H.

Cohen, Monroe D., ed. Developing Programs for Infants & Toddlers. LC 76-54813. 1977. 3.25x (ISBN 0-87173-081-2). ACEI.

Cohen, Stanley A. Healthy Baby Book. 250p. Date not set. pap. 7.95 (ISBN 0-933328-11-7). Delilah Comm.

--The Healthy Baby Book. 250p. 1982. 14.95 (ISBN 0-933328-17-6). Delilah Comm.

Consumer Guide. The Complete Baby Book. 1979. 16.95 (ISBN 0-671-25197-X); pap. 7.95 (ISBN 0-671-24769-7). S&S.

Cunningham, P. J., ed. Nursery Nursing. 3rd ed. 224p. 1978. pap. 5.95 (ISBN 0-571-04940-0, Pub. by Faber & Faber). Merrimack Bk Serv.

Davis, Katherine N. A Baby Girl...Congratulations! (Illus.). 1980. pap. 2.50 (ISBN 0-8378-5034-7). Gibson.

Dewey, Evelyn. Behavior Development in Infants: A Survey of the Literature on Prenatal & Postnatal Activity 1920-1932. LC 72-343. (Body Movement Ser.: Perspectives in Research). 334p. 1972. Repr. of 1935 ed. 16.00 (ISBN 0-405-03142-4). Arno.

Feldman, Donita B., et al. Manual of Newborn Care at Grady Memorial Hospital. 255p. (Orig.). 1973. pap. 14.95 (ISBN 0-686-74197-8). Krieger.

The First Two Years; a Study of Twenty-Five Babies, Vol, II: Intellectual Development. LC 76-142316. (U of Minnesota Institute of Child Welfare, Monograph: No. VII). (Illus.). 1973. Repr. of 1933 ed. lib. bdg. 14.75x (ISBN 0-8371-5906-7, CWSH). Greenwood.

The First Two Years; a Study of Twenty-Five Babies, Vol. III: Personality Manifestations. LC 76-142316. (U of Minnesota Institute of Child Welfare Monograph: No. VIII). (Illus.). 1973. Repr. of 1931 ed. lib. bdg. 15.00x (ISBN 0-8371-5907-5, CWSI). Greenwood.

Gallagher, Eugene B. Infants, Mothers, & Doctors. LC 78-2071. 1978. 19.95 (ISBN 0-669-02269-1). Lexington Bks.

Gerber, Mrs. Dan. Bringing up Baby. (Orig.). pap. 1.95 (ISBN 0-87502-013-5). Benjamin Co.

Gerdes, M. Newell. Love of Baby. 1976. pap. 3.00 (ISBN 0-06-090536-0, CN536, CN). Har-Row.

Glickman, Beatrice M. & Springer, Nesha B. Who Cares for the Baby? Choices in Child Care. LC 77-75293. 1978. 9.95 (ISBN 0-8052-3667-8). Schocken.

Gonzalez-Mena, Janet & Eyer, Dianne W. Infancy & Caregiving. LC 79-91838. (Illus.). 163p. (Orig.). 1980. pap. text ed. 7.95 (ISBN 0-87484-515-7). Mayfield Pub.

Gordon, Ira J. Baby to Parent, Parent to Baby: A Guide to Loving & Learning in a Child's First Year. LC 76-62768. (Illus.). 1978. 8.95 (ISBN 0-312-06448-9); pap. 4.95 (ISBN 0-312-06449-7). St Martin.

Guy, May & Gilbert, Miriam. A Doctor Discusses the Care & Development of Your Baby. (Illus.). 1979. pap. 2.50 (ISBN 0-685-56949-7). Budlong.

Hagstrom, Julie. More Games Babies Play. (Illus.). 128p. 1981. pap. 4.95 (ISBN 0-89104-192-3). A & W Pubs.

Hendrick, Gladys W. My First Three Hundred Babies. LC 78-50853. 1978. 4.95 (ISBN 0-88449-030-0). Vision Hse.

Herbert-Jackson. The Infant Center. (Illus.). 1977. 17.95 (ISBN 0-8391-1157-6). Univ Park.

Honig, Alice S. & Lally, J. Ronald. Infant Caregiving: A Design for Training. (Illus.). 234p. 1981. pap. 12.95 (ISBN 0-8156-0169-7). Syracuse U Pr.

Johnson & Johnson Baby Products Company. The First Wondrous Year: You & Your Baby. (Illus.). 1979. 16.95 (ISBN 0-02-559530-X); pap. 10.95 (ISBN 0-02-077100-2). Macmillan.

Jones, Sandy. To Love a Baby. (Illus.). 192p. 1981. 15.00 (ISBN 0-395-31296-5). HM.

Kannas, Serge. La Petite Enfance. (Illus.). 1978. pap. 7.95x (ISBN 2-03-001203-3). Larousse.

Khalakdina, M. Early Child Care in India, Vol. 9. (International Monographs on Early Child Care). 1979. 24.75x (ISBN 0-677-05140-9). Gordon.

Lansky, Vicki. Feed Me, I'm Yours. 176p. 1981. pap. 2.25 (ISBN 0-553-12640-7). Bantam.

Leach, Joan & St. Louis, Patricia. Caring for Babies. LC 78-52432. (Illus.). 1978. pap. 3.50 (ISBN 0-87239-220-1, 7963). Standard Pub.

Leach, Penelope. Your Baby & Child: From Birth to Age Five. LC 77-75010. 1978. 16.95 (ISBN 0-394-40755-5). Knopf.

Leboyer, Frederick. Loving Hands: The Traditional Indian Art of Baby Massaging. 1976. 10.95 (ISBN 0-394-40469-6). Knopf.

Levine, Milton I. & Seligmann, Jean H. The Parents' Encyclopedia. (Illus.). 554p. 1973. 12.50 (ISBN 0-690-60969-8). T Y Crowell.

Levy, Janine. The Baby Exercise Book: The First Fifteen Months. Gleasure, Eira, tr. from Fr. LC 73-7030. 1974. 7.95 (ISBN 0-394-48546-7); pap. 4.95 (ISBN 0-394-73122-0). Pantheon.

McDonald, Linda. Everything You Need to Know About Babies. LC 77-21017. (Illus.). 1978. pap. 5.95 (ISBN 0-916198-04-9). Oaklawn Pr.

Mason, Sheila. The Toddler. (Illus.). 1977. 3.95x (ISBN 0-521-21391-6). Cambridge U Pr.

Moore, Mary L. Newborn & the Nurse. LC 72-180185. (Monographs in Clinical Nursing: Vol. 3). (Illus.). 1972. 12.50x (ISBN 0-7216-6490-3). Saunders.

Morrison, L. Jed & Morrison, M. K. The Onset of Parenthood: A Comprehensive, Illustrated Guide to Pregnancy, Birth & Infant Care. LC 75-17105. (Illus.). 238p. 1975. 9.95 (ISBN 0-88290-056-0). Horizon Utah.

Nash, Barbara, ed. The Complete Book of Baby Care. (Illus.). Date not set. 10.98 (ISBN 0-7064-0909-4, Mayflower Bks). Smith Pubs.

Oakley, Ann. Becoming a Mother. LC 79-22368. 1980. 18.95 (ISBN 0-8052-3735-6). Schocken.

Pillitteri, Adele. Maternal-Newborn Nursing: Care of the Growing Family. 2nd ed. 1981. text ed. write for info. (ISBN 0-316-70792-9). Little.

Pizer, Hank & Garfink, Christine. The Post Partum Book: How to Cope with & Enjoy the First Year of Parenting. LC 78-19710. 1979. 9.95 (ISBN 0-394-50524-7, GP821). Grove.

Prenatal & Infant Care Guide. (Ideals Guidelines Ser.). 96p. (Orig.). 1981. pap. 2.95 (ISBN 0-8249-4002-4). Ideals.

Princeton Center for Infancy. The Parenting Advisor. 1977. pap. 6.95 (ISBN 0-385-14330-3, Anch). Doubleday.

Princeton Center for Infancy & Early Childhood. First Twelve Months of Life. o.p. 14.95 (ISBN 0-448-02032-7); pap. 9.95 (ISBN 0-448-02149-8, Today Press). G&D.

Provence, Sally. Guide for the Care of Infants in Groups. LC 67-26025. 104p. 1967. pap. 5.75 (ISBN 0-87868-061-6, I-32). Child Welfare.

Prudden, Bonnie. How to Keep Your Child Fit from Birth to Six. LC 64-11050. (Illus.). 1964. 13.95 (ISBN 0-06-111410-3, HarpT). Har-Row.

--Your Baby Can Swim. LC 73-79534. (Illus.). 1978. pap. text ed. 6.95 (ISBN 0-9602146-0-7). Aquarian Pr.

Queenan, John T., ed. A New Life: Pregnancy, Birth, & Your Child's First Year. 1979. 19.95 (ISBN 0-442-23214-4). Van Nos Reinhold.

Resnick, Jane P. A Baby Boy...Congratulations! (Illus.). 1980. pap. 2.50 (ISBN 0-8378-5033-9). Gibson.

Ribble, Margaretha A. The Rights of Infants: Early Psychological Needs & Their Satisfaction. 2nd ed. LC 65-24832. 1965. 15.00x (ISBN 0-231-02849-0). Columbia U Pr.

Roman, Beverly. Infant Stimulation Training Skills. 1978. spiral bound 9.95 (ISBN 0-87804-316-0). Mafex.

Ross, Cathy R. & Beggs, Denise M. The Whole Baby Catalogue. LC 76-43410. (Illus.). 224p. 1977. pap. 6.95 (ISBN 0-8069-8774-X). Sterling.

Rothenberg, B. Annye, et al. Parentmaking: A Practical Handbook for Teaching Parent Classes About Babies & Toddlers. LC 81-66429. (Illus.). 460p. (Orig.). 1981. pap. 37.50 (ISBN 0-9604620-0-7). Banster Pr.

Roufberg, Ruth. Your Child from Two to Five Years: Today He Can't, Tomorrow He Can, Vol. 2. new rev ed. LC 77-169788. 144p. (Orig.). 1977. pap. 6.95 (ISBN 0-916184-02-1). Fountain Pub Co NY.

Rudman, Jack. Maternal & Child Nursing: Associate Degree. (ACT Proficiency Examination Program: PEP-37). (Cloth bdg. avail. on request). pap. 9.95 (ISBN 0-8373-5537-0). Natl Learning.

--Maternal & Child Nursing: Baccalaureate Degree. (ACT Proficiency Examination Program: PEP-38). (Cloth bdg. avail. on request). pap. 9.95 (ISBN 0-8373-5538-9). Natl Learning.

Samuels, Mike & Samuels, Nancy. The Well Baby Book. LC 78-14021. (Illus.). 1979. 19.95 (ISBN 0-671-40069-X); pap. 8.95 (ISBN 0-671-40056-8). Summit Bks.

Schreiner, Richard L., ed. Care of the Newborn. 318p. 1980. text ed. 24.00 (ISBN 0-89004-518-6). Raven.

Schwartz, Jane T. & Schwartz, Lawrence H. Vulnerable Infants: A Psychosocial Dilemma. new ed. (Illus.). 1977. pap. text ed. 10.95 (ISBN 0-07-055764-0, HP). McGraw.

Segal, Marilyn. From Birth to One Year. LC 80-13831. (The Play & Learn Ser.: Vol. 1). (Illus.). 96p. pap. 3.95 (ISBN 0-916392-50-3). Oak Tree Pubns.

Shinn, Bev & Shinn, Duane. Free & Low Cost Things for New Mothers. 1978. pap. 3.95 (ISBN 0-912732-47-4). Duane Shinn.

Shirley, Margaret M. The First Two Years; a Study of Twenty-Five Babies, Vol, I: Postural & Locomotor Development. LC 76-142316. (U of Minnesota Institute of Child Welfare, Monnograph: No. VI). (Illus.). 1973. Repr. of 1931 ed. lib. bdg. 15.00 (ISBN 0-8371-5905-9, CWSG). Greenwood.

Sills & Henry. Mother to Mother Baby Care. 1981. pap. 5.95 (ISBN 0-380-53074-0, 53074). Avon.

Smith, Lendon H. The Encyclopedia of Baby & Child Care. 1980. pap. 8.95 (ISBN 0-446-97457-9). Warner Bks.

--The Encyclopedia of Baby Child Care. rev. ed. 1981. 12.95 (ISBN 0-13-275503-3). P-H.

Stern, Leo, et al. Intensive Care in the Newborn. LC 76-22262. 296p. 1977. 37.50x (ISBN 0-89352-000-4). Masson Pub.

--Intensive Care of the Newborn II. LC 78-63400. (Illus.). 418p. 1979. 45.50x (ISBN 0-89352-022-5). Masson Pub.

Stiehm, E. Richard & Fulginiti, Vincent A. Immunologic Disorders in Infants & Children. LC 72-90730. (Illus.). 637p. 1973. pap. text ed. 27.75 (ISBN 0-7216-8602-8). Saunders.
Stoppard, Miriam. Dr. Miriam Stoppard's Book of Baby Care. LC 77-76668. (Illus.). 1977. 10.95 (ISBN 0-689-10810-9). Atheneum.
Stoutt, G. The First Month of Life. 1977. pap. 6.95 (ISBN 0-87489-067-5). Med Economics.
Stoutt, Glen R., Jr. The First Month of Life: A Parent's Guide to Care of the Newborn. 1981. pap. 1.95 (ISBN 0-451-09613-4, J9613, Sig). NAL.
Sunderman, F. William & Sunderman, F. William, Jr. The Clinical Pathology of Infancy. (Illus.). 580p. 1967. photocopy ed. spiral 57.50 (ISBN 0-398-01881-2). C C Thomas.
Volpe, Joseph J. Neonatal Neurology. (Major Problems in Clinical Pediatrics Ser.). (Illus.). 300p. 1981. text ed. write for info. (ISBN 0-7216-9077-7). Saunders.
Vosper, Jane. Good Housekeeping's Baby Book. Chapiro, Jean, ed. (Illus.). 1974. 12.50x (ISBN 0-85223-122-9). Intl Pubns Serv.
Walters, C. Etta. Mother-Infant Interaction. LC 74-12621. 1976. text ed. 24.95 (ISBN 0-87705-240-9); pap. text ed. 12.95 (ISBN 0-87705-284-0). Human Sci Pr.
Watson, Robert M. Your Second Baby First. 1968. pap. 2.45 (ISBN 0-685-42653-X). Guild Bks.
Wiener, Joan & Glick, Joyce. A Motherhood Book. 1974. 5.95 (ISBN 0-02-625350-X). Macmillan.
Williams, Herman & Barber, Lucie W. Baby's First Thirty Months. (Illus.). 1981. 5.95 (ISBN 0-89586-062-7). H P Bks.
Wudske, Vivian A., ed. American Woman Baby & Child Care. (Illus.). 1979. 9.95 (ISBN 0-918668-04-2). Paramount.
Your Infant's Care: The Practical Guide to Caring for Your New Baby. 1975. pap. 1.50 (ISBN 0-913880-03-5). Trafalgar Hse.

INFANTS–CLOTHING

Biasiny, Nan. Beautiful Baby Clothes: To Knit, Crochet & Embroider. LC 76-51753. 1977. 12.50 (ISBN 0-671-22467-0). S&S.
Martensson, Kerstin. Sew for Baby the Fun Way. (Illus.). 1974. pap. 7.95 (ISBN 0-913212-00-8). Kwik Sew.
Mensinga, Nan. Beautiful Baby Clothes. (Illus.). 1978. pap. 4.95 (ISBN 0-686-67345-X, Fireside). S&S.
Snook, Barbara. Making Baby Clothes. LC 69-11171. 1969. 4.95 (ISBN 0-8008-5075-0). Taplinger.

INFANTS–DISEASES

Altman, Arnold & Schwartz, Allen D. Malignant Diseases of Infancy, Childhood & Adolescence, Vol. 18. LC 77-79863. (Major Problems in Clinical Pediatrics). 1978. text ed. 42.00 (ISBN 0-7216-1212-1). Saunders.
Bailey, Percival, et al. Intracranial Tumors of Infancy & Childhood. (Illus.). 1939. 17.50x (ISBN 0-226-03451-8). U of Chicago Pr.
Emery, Alan E. Antenatal Diagnosis of Genetic Disease. LC 73-595585. (Illus.). 1973. 9.00x (ISBN 0-443-00986-4). Churchill.
Hanshaw, James B. & Dudgeon, John A. Viral Diseases of the Fetus & Newborn. (Major Problems in Clinical Pediatrics Ser: No. 17). 350p. 1978. 25.00 (ISBN 0-7216-4500-3). Saunders.
Infantile Psychosis & Other Papers: Selected Papers of Margaret Mahler, Vol. 1. Incl. Vol. 2. Seperation Individuation. LC 79-51915. 1979. 40.00xset (ISBN 0-685-22268-3). Vol. 2 (ISBN 0-87668-345-6). Aronson.
Milunsky, Aubrey, et al, eds. Advances in Perinatal Medicine, Vol. 1. 450p. 1981. 35.00 (ISBN 0-306-40482-6, Plenum Pr). Plenum Pub.
Mitchell, Ross F. Ellisard Mitchell's Disease in Infancy & Childhood. 7th ed. (Illus.). 436p. 1973. text ed. 24.50 (ISBN 0-443-00988-0). Churchill.
Potter, Edith L. Pathology of the Fetus & the Infant. 3rd ed. (Illus.). 1975. 77.50 (ISBN 0-8151-6760-1). Year Bk Med.
Samuels, Mike & Samuels, Nancy. The Well Baby Book. LC 78-14021. (Illus.). 1979. 19.95 (ISBN 0-671-40069-X); pap. 8.95 (ISBN 0-671-40056-8). Summit Bks.
Schreiner, Richard L. & Kisling, Jeffrey A., eds. The Newborn with Respiratory Distress: A Practical Approach to Management. 1981. text ed. 49.00 (ISBN 0-89004-559-3). Raven.
Sunderman, F. William & Sunderman, F. William, Jr. The Clinical Pathology of Infancy. (Illus.). 580p. 1967. photocopy ed. spiral 57.50 (ISBN 0-398-01881-2). C C Thomas.
Winters, Robert W. & Hasselmeyer, Eileen G. Intravenous Nutrition in the High Risk Infants. LC 74-26712. (Clinical Pediatrics, Maternal & Child Health Ser). 528p. 1975. 48.95 (ISBN 0-471-95500-0, Pub. by Wiley Medical). Wiley.
Winters, Robert W., ed. The Body Fluids in Pediatrics: Medical, Surgical, & Neonatal Disorders of Acid-Base Status, Hydration & Oxygenation. (Illus.). 1973. 32.50 (ISBN 0-316-94741-5). Little.

INFANTS–GROWTH

see Children–Growth

INFANTS–LAW

see Children–Law

INFANTS–MORTALITY

see also Sudden Death in Infants

American Association for the Study & Prevention of Infant Mortality Meeting, 1st, New Haven, 1909. Transactions. facsimile ed. LC 74-1663. (Children & Youth Ser.). 356p. 1974. Repr. of 1910 ed. 20.00x (ISBN 0-405-05944-2). Arno.
Baker, S. Josephine. Fighting for Life. facsimile ed. LC 74-1664. (Children & Youth Ser.). (Illus.). 280p. 1974. Repr. of 1939 ed. 18.00x (ISBN 0-405-05945-0). Arno.
Borg, Susan O. & Lasker, Judith. When Pregnancy Fails: Families Coping with Miscarriage, Stillbirth & Infant Death. LC 80-68167. 224p. 1981. 12.95 (ISBN 0-8070-3226-3); pap. 6.95 (ISBN 0-8070-3227-1, BP613). Beacon Pr.
Bremner, Robert H., ed. Children's Bureau Studies. LC 74-1676. (Children & Youth Ser.: Vol. 3). 386p. 1974. 23.00x (ISBN 0-405-05955-8). Arno.
Chandrasekhar, S. Infant Mortality, Population Growth & Family Planning in India. LC 78-170290. (Illus.). 399p. 1972. 25.00x (ISBN 0-8078-1185-8). U of NC Pr.
Falkner, F., ed. Fundamentals of Mortality Risks During the Perinatal Period & Infancy. (Monographs in Paediatrics: Vol. 9). (Illus.). 190p. 1977. 51.00 (ISBN 3-8055-2651-2). S Karger.
Preston, Samuel H., ed. The Effects of Infant & Child Mortality on Fertility. 1977. 27.00 (ISBN 0-12-564440-X). Acad Pr.
Rosenkrantz, Barbara G., ed. The Health of Women & Children: An Original Anthology. LC 76-43205. (Public Health in America Ser.). (Illus.). 1977. Repr. of 1977 ed. lib. bdg. 18.00x (ISBN 0-405-09876-6). Arno.
Shapiro, Sam, et al. Infant, Perinatal, Maternal, & Childhood Mortality in the United States. LC 68-29183. (Vital & Health Statistics Monographs, American Public Health Association). (Illus.). 1968. 20.00x (ISBN 0-674-45301-8). Harvard U Pr.

INFANTS–NUTRITION

see also Breast Feeding; Infants–Weaning; Milk

Applegate, Kay. The Little Book of Baby Foods. LC 78-54220. (Span. & Eng.). 1978. pap. 2.50 (ISBN 0-89016-042-2). Lightning Tree.
Bibliography of Infant Foods & Nutrition 1938-1977. 322p. 1978. pap. 29.00 (ISBN 0-686-71824-0, CO 27, CSIRO). Unipub.
Bond, Jenny T., et al, eds. Infant & Child Feeding. (Nutrition Foundation Ser.). 1981. 49.50 (ISBN 0-12-113350-8). Acad Pr.
Castle, Sue. The Complete New Guide to Preparing Baby Foods. rev. ed. LC 79-6099. (Illus.). 360p. 1981. 13.95 (ISBN 0-385-15884-X). Doubleday.
Endres, Jeannette & Rockwell, Robert E. Food, Nutrition, & the Young Child. LC 80-10848. (Illus.). 1980. pap. text ed. 11.45 (ISBN 0-8016-4139-X). Mosby.
Fischer, Josef E. Total Parenteral Nutrition. LC 75-30283. 1976. text ed. 28.50 (ISBN 0-316-28370-3). Little.
Fisk, Mary B. Baby Gourmet Cookbook. (Illus.). 1978. pap. 4.95 (ISBN 0-915696-09-6). Determined Prods.
Fomon, Samuel J. Infant Nutrition. 2nd ed. LC 74-4560. (Illus.). 575p. 1974. text ed. 27.50 (ISBN 0-7216-3809-0). Saunders.
Helmer, Barbara. Better Baby Food Cookbook. LC 80-22314. (Orig.). 1980. pap. 4.95 spiral bdg. (ISBN 0-87123-018-6, 210018). Bethany Hse.
Henderson, J. O., et al. Bibliography of Infant Foods & Nutrition: Nineteen Thirty-Eight to Nineteen Seventy-Seven. 1979. pap. 22.50x (ISBN 0-643-00316-9, Pub. by CSIRO). Intl Schol Bk Serv.
Henderson, Jane O., et al. Bibliography of Infant Foods & Nutrition: 1938-1977. 322p. 1981. 40.00x (ISBN 0-643-00316-9, Pub. by CSIRO Australia). State Mutual Bk.
Heslin, Jo-Ann & Natow, Annette B. No-Nonsense Nutrition for Your Baby's First Year. LC 78-12359. 1978. pap. 9.95 (ISBN 0-8436-2134-6). CBI Pub.
Heslin, Jo Ann, et al. No-Nonsense Nutrition for Your Baby's First Year. 288p. 1980. pap. 2.95 (ISBN 0-553-13725-5). Bantam.
Jelliffe, D. B. Infant Nutrition in the Subtropics & Tropics. 2nd ed. (Monograph Ser: No. 29). (Illus.). 335p. 1968. 17.60 (ISBN 92-4-140029-3, 788). World Health.
Lansky, Vicki. Feed Me! I'm Yours. 1974. spiral bdg 3.95 (ISBN 0-915658-01-1). Meadowbrook Pr.
Larson, Gena. Better Foods for Better Babies. 1.75 (ISBN 0-686-29782-2). Cancer Bk Hse.
Lebenthal, Emanuel, ed. Gastroenterology & Nutrition in Infancy, 2 vols. 1198p. 1981. Set. text ed. 98.00 (ISBN 0-686-77542-2). Vol. 1: Gastrointestinal Development & Perinatal Nutrition (ISBN 0-89004-526-7). Vol. 2: Gastrointestinal Disease & Nutritional Inadequancies (ISBN 0-89004-533-X). Raven.
Lorenzen, Evelyn J., ed. Dietary Guidelines. 1978. 10.95x (ISBN 0-87201-176-3). Gulf Pub.
McDonald, Linda. Baby's Recipe Book. LC 71-168374. (Illus.). 1977. pap. 3.95 (ISBN 0-498-02041-X). A S Barnes.
--Instant Baby Food. LC 75-27760. (Illus.). 113p. 1976. 5.95 (ISBN 0-916198-02-2); pap. 3.95 (ISBN 0-916198-01-4). Oaklawn Pr.
MacKeith, Ronald & Wood, Christopher. Infant Feeding & Feeding Difficulties. 5th ed. 1977. 14.95x (ISBN 0-443-01474-4). Churchill.
Merritt, D. H., ed. Infant Nutrition. (Benchmark Papers in Human Physiology: Vol. 7). 1976. 46.00 (ISBN 0-12-787070-9). Acad Pr.
O'Casey, Brenda. Natural Baby Food. 80p. 1977. 20.00 (ISBN 0-7156-0701-4, Pub. by Duckworth England); pap. 4.50 (ISBN 0-7156-0719-7, Pub. by Duckworth England). Biblio Dist.
Payne, Alma. The Baby Food Book. 1977. pap. 3.95 (ISBN 0-316-69543-2). Little.
Pearlman, Ruth. Feeding Your Baby the Safe & Healthy Way. 1971. 8.95 (ISBN 0-394-46246-7). Random.
Pipes, Peggy. Nutrition in Infancy & Childhood. LC 76-39865. (Illus.). 1977. pap. 9.95 (ISBN 0-8016-3940-9). Mosby.
Pipes, Peggy L. Nutrition in Infancy & Childhood. 2nd ed. LC 80-25068. (Illus.). 317p. 1981. pap. text ed. 11.95 (ISBN 0-8016-3941-7). Mosby.
Recommended International Code of Hygienic Practice for Food for Infants & Children. 13p. 1980. pap. 7.50 (ISBN 92-5-101014-5, F2158, FAO). Unipub.
Recommended International Standards for Foods for Infants & Children. (Codex Alimentarius Commission). 33p. 1977. pap. 4.50 (ISBN 0-685-86028-0, F612, FAO). Unipub.
Rogers, Florence K. Another Little Mouth to Feed! 1978. pap. 3.95 (ISBN 0-671-24399-3, Fireside). S&S.
Saville, Florence R. Real Food for Your Baby. LC 72-90402. 1973. 8.95 (ISBN 0-671-21475-6). S&S.
Stommel-Fugeman, Margaret, et al, eds. The Nutrition Guide to Brand Name Baby Foods. 1977. 7.95 (ISBN 0-917172-02-7). Heritage Hse-Pubs.
Thompson, Ann. The Organic Baby Food Book. 1973. 6.95 (ISBN 0-671-27107-5). Trident.
Turner, James. Making Your Own Baby Food. 128p. 1973. pap. 2.25 (ISBN 0-553-20149-2). Bantam.
Turner, Mary D. & Turner, James. Making Your Own Baby Food. rev. ed. LC 76-25808. (Illus.). 1977. 6.95 (ISBN 0-911104-89-5); pap. 3.95 (ISBN 0-911104-90-9). Workman Pub.
Visser, H. K., ed. Nutrition & Metabolism of the Fetus & Infant. (Nutricia Symposium: No. 5). 1979. lib. bdg. 56.50 (ISBN 90-247-2202-0, Pub. by Martinus Nijhoff Netherlands). Kluwer Boston.
Wilkinson, A. W., ed. The Immunology of Infant Feeding. (Ettore Majorana International Science Series - Life Sciences: Vol. 8). 144p. 1981. text ed. write for info. (ISBN 0-306-40816-3, Plenum Pr). Plenum Pub.
Williams, Phyllis S. Nourishing Your Unborn Child. 1975. pap. 1.95 (ISBN 0-380-00472-0, 42044). Avon.
Winick, Myron, ed. Nutrition & Fetal Development. LC 73-19663. 200p. 1974. 26.50 (ISBN 0-471-95435-7). Krieger.

INFANTS–PSYCHOLOGY

see Infant Psychology

INFANTS–WEANING

Forrer, Gordon R. Weaning & Human Development. LC 72-79731. 1969. 5.95 (ISBN 0-87212-020-1). Libra.
Levin, Simon S. A Philosophy of Infant Feeding. (Illus.). 188p. 1963. photocopy ed. spiral 17.95 (ISBN 0-398-01116-8). C C Thomas.

INFANTS (NEWBORN)

see also Infants (Premature); also names of special diseases of new-born infants, e.g. Erythroblastosis Fetalis

Aaronson, May & Rosenfeld, Jean. Baby & Other Teachers. (Illus.). 90p. pap. 3.75 (ISBN 0-936746-00-9, P52). Day Care Coun.
Anderson, Gene C. & Raff, Beverly, eds. Newborn Behavioral Organization: Nursing Research &Implications. LC 79-2597. (Alan R. Liss Ser.: Vol. 15, No. 7). 1979. 24.00 (ISBN 0-8451-1032-2). March of Dimes.
Beintema, David. A Neurological Study of Newborn Infants. (Clinics in Developmental Medicine Ser. No. 28). 170p. 1968. 13.00 (ISBN 0-685-24725-2, JBL-Med-Nursing). Har-Row.
Bergsma, Daniel, ed. Infant at Risk. (Symposia Ser.: Vol. 10, No. 2). 11.50 (ISBN 0-686-10021-2). March of Dimes.
Boyle, Eleanor. A New Child's Play. 1980. 9.95 (ISBN 0-500-01244-X). Thames Hudson.
Cassels, Donald E., ed. Heart & Circulation in the Newborn & Infant: A Symposium. LC 66-12966. (Illus.). 440p. 1966. 34.50 (ISBN 0-8089-0096-X). Grune.
Chasler, Charles N. The Newborn Skull: Atlas of the Normal & Abnormal Newborn & Infant Skull with Emphasis on Fetal Radiology. LC 76-9681. 228p. 1972. 25.00 (ISBN 0-87527-028-X). Green.
Ciba Foundation. Size at Birth. (Ciba Foundation Symposium: No. 27). 408p. 1975. 44.00 (ISBN 0-444-15146-X, Excerpta Medica). Elsevier.
Clausen, Joy, et al. Maternity Nursing Today. 2nd ed. (Illus.). 1976. text ed. 19.95 (ISBN 0-07-011284-3, HP). McGraw.
Congress on Perinatal Medicine, 2nd European, London, 1970. Perinatal Medicine: Proceedings. Huntingford, P. J., et al, eds. 1971. 48.00 (ISBN 3-8055-1224-4). S Karger.
Crelin, Edmund S. Functional Anatomy of the Newborn. LC 72-91292. (Illus.). 96p. 1973. 18.50x (ISBN 0-300-01632-8); pap. text ed. 7.95x (ISBN 0-300-01633-6). Yale U Pr.
Cross, K. W., et al, eds. Foetal & Neonatal Physiology: Proceedings. LC 72-93673. (Illus.). 600p. 1973. 95.00 (ISBN 0-521-20178-0). Cambridge U Pr.
Dawes, Geoffrey S. Foetal & Neonatal Physiology. 1968. 27.50 (ISBN 0-8151-2341-8). Year Bk Med.
Dubowitz, Lilly M. & Dubowitz, Victor. Gestational Age of the Newborn: A Clinical Manual. LC 76-62906. 1977. text ed. 21.95 (ISBN 0-201-01171-9, Med-Nurse). A-W.
Eisenberg, R. B. Auditory Competence in Early Life: The Roots of Communicative Behavior. (Illus.). 250p. 1975. 24.50 (ISBN 0-8391-0773-0). Univ Park.
Ewy, Donna & Ewy, Rodger. The Cycle of Life, 3 bks. in 1. Skedgell, Marian, ed. (Illus.). 384p. 1981. 17.95 (ISBN 0-525-93181-3). Dutton.
--The Cycle of Life: Guide to Parenting the Newborn. Skedgell, Marian, ed. (Illus.). 160p. 1981. pap. 7.25 (ISBN 0-525-93184-8, 0704-210). Dutton.
Feldman, Donita B., et al. Manual of Newborn Care at Grady Memorial Hospital. 255p. (Orig.). 1973. pap. 14.95 (ISBN 0-686-74197-8). Krieger.
Ferrara, Angelo & Harin, Anantham. Emergency Transfer of the High Risk Neonate: A Working Manual for Medical, Nursing & Administrative Personnel. LC 79-17689. (Illus.). 1979. pap. text ed. 25.00 (ISBN 0-8016-1565-8). Mosby.
First National Foundation-March of Dimes Perinatal Nursing Research Roundtable Conference Chicago, Ill. Newborn Behavioral Organization: Nursing Research & Implications, Proceedings. Anderson, Gene C. & Raff, Beverly, eds. LC 79-2597. (Birth Defects: Original Article Ser.: Vol. XV, No. 7). 240p. 1979. 24.00x (ISBN 0-8451-1032-2). A R Liss.
Gesell, Arnold L. The Embryology of Behavior: The Beginnings of the Human Mind. LC 72-138113. (Illus.). 289p. 1972. Repr. of 1945 ed. lib. bdg. 19.75x (ISBN 0-8371-5689-0, GEEB). Greenwood.
Goodwin, J. W., et al. Perinatal Medicine. (Illus.). 642p. 1976. 59.95 (ISBN 0-683-03649-1). Williams & Wilkins.
Hathaway, Marjie & Hathaway, Jay. Children at Birth. (Illus.). 1978. pap. 5.95 (ISBN 0-931560-00-4). Academy Pubns.
Hirata, Toshiko & Brady, June P. Newborn Intensive Care: Chemical Aspects. (Amer. Lec. Living Chemistry Ser.). (Illus.). 196p. 1977. 21.50 (ISBN 0-398-03606-3). C C Thomas.
Huntingford, Peter J., et al, eds. Perinatal Medicine. 1970. 32.00 (ISBN 0-12-362550-5). Acad Pr.
International Symposium, 2nd, Jerusalem, 1974. Bilirubin Metabolism in the Newborn. Bergsma, D., et al, eds. (International Congress Ser.: No. 380). 1976. 59.50 (ISBN 0-444-15216-4, Excerpta Medica). Elsevier.
Jenkins, G. Curtis & Newton, R. The First Year of Life. (Library of General Practice). (Illus.). 260p. 1981. pap. text ed. 21.50 (ISBN 0-443-01717-4). Churchill.
Kaltreider, D. Frank. Effects of Height & Weight on Pregnancy & the Newborn. (Illus.). 256p. 1963. photocopy ed. spiral 24.50 (ISBN 0-398-04302-7). C C Thomas.
Keay, A. J. & Morgan, D. M. Craig's Care of the Newly Born Infant. 6th ed. (Illus.). 1978. pap. text ed. 27.50 (ISBN 0-443-01756-5). Churchill.
Kelnar, G. & Harvey, D. Intensive Care of the Newborn. (Illus.). 1980. pap. text ed. 17.95 (ISBN 0-02-858020-6). Macmillan.

Klaus & Kennell. Maternal-Infant Bonding: The Impact of Early Separation or Loss on Family Development. LC 76-5397. Orig. Title: Care of the Family of the Normal or Sick Newborn. (Illus.). 224p. 1976. text ed. 14.95 (ISBN 0-8016-2631-5); pap. 11.95 (ISBN 0-8016-2630-7). Mosby.

Korones. High Risk Newborn Infants: The Basis for Intensive Nursing Care. 2nd ed. LC 75-43615. (Illus.). 288p. 1976. 13.95 (ISBN 0-8016-2736-2). Mosby.

Korones, Sheldon B. High Risk Newborn Infants: The Basis for Intensive Nursing Care. 3rd ed. LC 81-963. (Illus.). 399p. 1981. text ed. 18.50 (ISBN 0-8016-2738-9). Mosby.

Kumar, S. & Rathi, M., eds. Perinatal Medicine: Clinical & Biochemical Aspects of the Evaluation, Diagnosis & Management of the Fetus & Newborn. LC 78-40219. 1978. text ed. 45.00 (ISBN 0-08-021517-3). Pergamon.

Ligon, Ernest M., et al. Looking at Me. LC 78-72484. 1979. Repr. of 1976 ed. 12.95 (ISBN 0-8054-5633-3). Broadman.

Lubchenco, Lula O. The High Risk Infant. LC 76-1229. (Major Problems in Clinical Pediatrics: Vol. 14). (Illus.). 1976. 19.50 (ISBN 0-7216-5800-8). Saunders.

Lu Rang, Mary. Manual of Newborn Care Plans. (Spiral Manual Ser. - Nursing: Nursing). 1981. price not set spiral bdg. (ISBN 0-316-73380-6). Little.

McKilligin, Helen R. The First Day of Life: Principles of Neonatal Nursing. LC 73-98089. (Illus.). 1970. pap. text ed. 4.50 (ISBN 0-8261-1101-7). Springer Pub.

Marx, G. F. Clinical Management of Mother & Newborn. (Illus.). 1979. 31.30 (ISBN 0-387-90373-9). Springer-Verlag.

Miller, Michael E. Host Defenses in the Human Neonate. (Monographs in Neonatology). 144p. 1978. text ed. 20.25 (ISBN 0-8089-1094-9). Grune.

Neimark, Paul, et al. A Doctor Discusses Your New Baby & Your New Life. (Illus.). 1980. pap. 2.50 (ISBN 0-685-46338-9). Budlong.

Nitzan, Menachem, ed. The Influence of Maternal Hormones on the Fetus & Newborn. (Pediatric & Adolescent Endocrinology: Vol. 5). (Illus.). 1979. pap. 59.50 (ISBN 3-8055-2902-3). S Karger.

Panter, Gideon G. & Linde, Shirley M. Now That You've Had Your Baby: How to Feel Better & Happier Than Ever, After Childbirth. LC 77-8626. 1977. pap. 3.95 (ISBN 0-13-625442-X, Spec). P-H.

Roberts, David, ed. Neonatal Resuscitation: A Practical Guide, Vol. 1. (Family Practice: Review & Update Ser.). 1981. price not set (ISBN 0-12-788701-6). Acad Pr.

Roberts, Florence B. Perinatal Nursing: Care of Newborns & Their Families. (Illus.). 1976. pap. text ed. 9.95 (ISBN 0-07-053125-0, HP). McGraw.

Samson, Joan. Watching the New Baby. LC 73-84833. (Illus.). 80p. (gr. 3-6). 1974. 7.95 (ISBN 0-689-30119-7). Atheneum.

Scanlon, J. W. A System of Newborn Physical Examination. 96p. pap. text ed. 8.95 (ISBN 0-8391-1392-7). Univ Park.

Sell, Elsa J. Follow-up of the High Risk Newborn-A Practical Approach. (Illus.). 360p. 1980. text ed. 29.75 (ISBN 0-398-03913-5). C C Thomas.

Shipp, Audrey. Demographic, Socioeconomic & Health Factors Associated with Low Birth Weight, United States, 1976. (Series 21: No. 37). 1980. pap. text ed. 1.75 (ISBN 0-8406-0181-6). Natl Ctr Health Stats.

Sinclair, John C., ed. Temperature Regulation & Energy Metabolism in the Newborn. (Monographs in Neonatology Ser.). 272p. 1978. 29.25 (ISBN 0-8089-1090-6). Grune.

Smeriglio, Vincent L., ed. Newborns & Parents: Parent-Infant Contact & Newborn Sensory Stimulation. LC 80-29206. 192p. 1981. text ed. 19.95x (ISBN 0-89859-041-8). L Erlbaum Assocs.

Smith, Clement A. & Nelson, Nicholas M., eds. Physiology of the Newborn Infant. 4th ed. (Illus.). 784p. 1976. 68.50 (ISBN 0-398-03232-7). C C Thomas.

Solomon, J. B. Foetal & Neonatal Immunology. 1971. 38.00 (ISBN 0-444-10066-0, North-Holland). Elsevier.

A Star Is Born: An Album & Diary for Baby's First Year. (Biograf Publications). (Illus.). 1981. boxed 3.95x (ISBN 0-8334-4025-X). Multimedia.

Stembera, Z., et al, eds. High Risk Pregnancy & Child. Schierlova, M., tr. from Czech. (Illus.). 308p. 1976. 27.50 (ISBN 90-247-1924-0, Pub. by Nijhoff). Wright-PSG.

Stern, Leo, et al. Intensive Care in the Newborn. LC 76-22262. 296p. 1977. 37.50x (ISBN 0-89352-000-4). Masson Pub.

Swyer, P. R. & Llewellyn, Ann. The Intensive Care of the Newly Born: Physiological Principles & Practice. (Monographs in pediatrics: Vol. 6). (Illus.). 220p. 1975. 40.75 (ISBN 3-8055-2184-7). S Karger.

Tronick, Edward & Adamson, Lauren. Babies As People: New Findings on Our Social Beginnings. (Illus.). 240p. 1980. pap. 7.95 (ISBN 0-02-078070-2, Collier). Macmillan.

Turnbull, A. C. & Woodford, F. P. Prevention of Handicap Through Antenatal Care. (The Institute for Research into Mental & Multiple Handicap, Review of Research & Practice: 18). 1976. 21.50 (ISBN 0-444-15210-5, Excerpta Medica). Elsevier.

Walsh, S. Zoe, et al. The Human Fetal & Neonatal Circulation: Function & Structure. (American Lectures in Cerebral Palsy Ser.). (Illus.). 368p. 1974. 21.75 (ISBN 0-398-02662-9). C C Thomas.

Wille, Lutz & Obladen, Michael. Neonatal Intensive Care: Principles & Guidelines. (Illus.). 300p. 1981. pap. 28.40 (ISBN 0-387-10462-3). Springer-Verlag.

Willis, Anne & Ricciuti, Henry. A Good Beginning for Babies. LC 74-25867. (Illus.). 191p. 1975. pap. text ed. 4.50 (ISBN 0-912674-43-1). Natl Assn Child Ed.

Wolff, Peter H. Causes, Controls & Organization of Behavior in the Neonate. LC 66-22207. (Psychological Issues Monograph: No. 17, Vol. 5, No. 1). (Orig.). 1966. text ed. 11.00 (ISBN 0-8236-0700-3). Intl Univs Pr.

Young, Bruce K., ed. Perinatal Medicine Today: Proceedings. LC 80-17343. (Progress in Clinical & Biological Research Ser.: Vol. 44). 244p. 1980. 20.00 (ISBN 0-8451-0044-0). A R Liss.

INFANTS (NEWBORN)–BIBLIOGRAPHY

Antonov, A. N. Physiology & Pathology of the Newborn. 1945. pap. 14.00 (ISBN 0-527-01535-0). Kraus Repr.

INFANTS (NEWBORN)–DISEASES

Aladjem, Silvio & Brown, Audrey K., eds. Perinatal Intensive Care. LC 76-57754. (Illus.). 1977. 35.50 (ISBN 0-8016-0105-3). Mosby.

Avery, Mary E., et al. The Lung & Its Disorders in the Newborn Infant. 4th ed. (Major Problems in Clinical Pediatrics: Vol. 1). (Illus.). 560p. 1981. text ed. write for info. (ISBN 0-7216-1462-0). Saunders.

Bolognese, Ronald J. Perinatal Medicine: Clinical Management of the High Risk Fetus & Neonate. 332p. 1977. 33.00 (ISBN 0-683-00907-9). Williams & Wilkins.

Colen, B. D. Born at Risk. (Illus.). 240p. 1981. 9.95 (ISBN 0-312-09291-1). St Martin.

Evans, Hugh E. & Glass, Leonard. Perinatal Medicine. (Illus.). 1976. 44.00x (ISBN 0-06-140791-7, Harper Medical). Har-Row.

Friedman, William F., et al, eds. Neonatal Heart Disease. LC 73-4449. (Illus.). 386p. 1973. 49.00 (ISBN 0-8089-0802-2). Grune.

Gregory, George A. & Thibeault, Donald W. Neonatal Pulmonary Care. LC 78-7773. 1979. 34.50 (ISBN 0-201-02481-0, 02481, Med-Nurse). A-W.

Hirata, Toshiko & Brady, June P. Newborn Intensive Care: Chemical Aspects. (Amer. Lec. Living Chemistry Ser.). (Illus.). 196p. 1977. 21.50 (ISBN 0-398-03606-3). C C Thomas.

Klaus & Kennell. Maternal-Infant Bonding: The Impact of Early Separation or Loss on Family Development. LC 76-5397. Orig. Title: Care of the Family of the Normal or Sick Newborn. (Illus.). 224p. 1976. text ed. 14.95 (ISBN 0-8016-2631-5); pap. 11.95 (ISBN 0-8016-2630-7). Mosby.

Korobkin, Rowena & Guilleminault, Christian. Progress in Perinatal Neurology, Vol. 1. (Illus.). 250p. 1981. lib. bdg. 30.50 (ISBN 0-683-04751-5). Williams & Wilkins.

Larroche, Jeanne C. Developmental Pathology of the Neonate. 1977. 105.00 (ISBN 90-219-2107-3, North-Holland). Elsevier.

Lauersen, Neils H. & Hochberg, Howard. Clinical Perinatal Biochemical Monitoring. 320p. 1981. 30.00 (ISBN 0-686-77745-X, 1901-1). Williams & Wilkins.

Lough, Marvin D., et al. Newborn Respiratory Care. (Illus.). 1979. 20.95 (ISBN 0-8151-5635-9). Year Bk Med.

Lubchenco, Lula O. The High Risk Infant. LC 76-1229. (Major Problems in Clinical Pediatrics: Vol. 14). (Illus.). 1976. 19.50 (ISBN 0-7216-5800-8). Saunders.

McCracken, George H. & Nelson, John D. Antimicrobial Therapy for Newborns: Practical Application of Pharmacology to Clinical Usage. LC 77-6251. 192p. 1977. 19.50 (ISBN 0-8089-1014-0). Grune.

Magrab, Phyllis R. Early Life Conditions & Chronic Diseases. (Psychological Management of Pediatric Problems Ser.). 349p. text ed. 24.50 (ISBN 0-8391-1218-1). Univ Park.

Moore, Mary L. Newborn & the Nurse. LC 72-180185. (Monographs in Clinical Nursing: Vol. 3). (Illus.). 1972. 12.50x (ISBN 0-7216-6490-3). Saunders.

Moragas, Augusto, et al. Atlas of Neonatal Histopathology. Valdes-Dapena, Antonio & Valdes-Dapena, Marie A., trs. LC 76-45960. (Illus.). 1978. text ed. 62.50 (ISBN 0-7216-6542-X). Saunders.

O'Doherty, Neil. Atlas of the Newborn. LC 78-70614. (Illus.). 1979. text ed. 34.00 (ISBN 0-685-99716-2, JBL-Med-Nursing). Har-Row.

Rementeria, Jose L., ed. Drug Abuse in Pregnancy & Neonatal Effects. LC 77-3541. (Illus.). 1977. text ed. 23.50 (ISBN 0-8016-4108-X). Mosby.

Remington, Jack S. & Klein, Jerome O., eds. Infectious Diseases of the Fetus & Newborn Infant. LC 74-9438. (Illus.). 500p. 1976. text ed. 55.00 (ISBN 0-7216-7547-6). Saunders.

Rowe, Richard D., et al. The Neonate with Congenital Heart Disease. 2nd ed. (Illus.). 450p. 1981. text ed. 42.50 (ISBN 0-7216-7775-4). Saunders.

Schaffer, Alexander J. & Avery, Mary E. Diseases of the Newborn. 4th ed. LC 75-38155. (Illus.). 1977. text ed. 39.50 (ISBN 0-7216-7947-1). Saunders.

Stern. Intensive Care in the Newborn, Vol. III. 432p. 1981. 59.50x (ISBN 0-89352-114-0). Masson Pub.

Swischuk, Leonard E. Radiology of the Newborn & Young Infant. 2nd ed. (Illus.). 912p. 1980. 82.50 (ISBN 0-683-08053-9). Williams & Wilkins.

Symposium by the New York University Medical Center & the National Foundation-March of Dimes, New York City, Mar. 1975. Infections of the Fetus & the Newborn Infant: Proceedings. Krugman, Saul & Gershon, Anne A., eds. LC 75-13856. (Progress in Clinical & Biological Research: Vol. 3). 204p. 1975. 23.00x (ISBN 0-8451-0003-3). A R Liss.

Vulliamy, David G. The Newborn Child. 4th ed. (Illus.). 1977. pap. text ed. 12.50 (ISBN 0-443-01396-9). Churchill.

Wilson, James G. Environmental & Birth Defects. (Environmental Science: An Interdisciplinary Monograph Ser.). 1973. 44.50 (ISBN 0-12-757750-5). Acad Pr.

INFANTS (NEWBORN)–MORTALITY

see Infants–Mortality

INFANTS (NEWBORN)–SURGERY

Bennett, E. J. Fluids for Anesthesia & Surgery in the Newborn & Infant. (Illus.). 248p. 1975. 25.50 (ISBN 0-398-03279-3). C C Thomas.

Coran, Arnold G., et al. Surgery of the Neonate. Lee, Dennis C., ed. 1978. text ed. 35.00 (ISBN 0-316-08759-9, Little Med Div). Little.

Holder, Thomas M. & Ashcraft, Keith W. Pediatric Surgery. LC 78-54513. (Illus.). 1200p. 1980. text ed. write for info. (ISBN 0-7216-4737-5). Saunders.

Nixon, H. H. Pediatric Surgery. 3rd ed. Rob & Smith, eds. (Operative Surgery Ser.). 1978. 125.00 (ISBN 0-407-00634-6). Butterworth.

Redo, S. Frank. Atlas of Surgery in the First Six Months of Life. (Illus.). 1978. text ed. 31.50x (ISBN 0-06-142239-8, Harper Medical). Har-Row.

--Principles of Surgery in the First Six Months of Life. (Illus.). 195p. 1976. 26.00x (ISBN 0-06-142238-X, Harper-Medical). Har-Row.

Rickham, P. P. & Irving, Irene M. Neonatal Surgery. 2nd ed. 1978. 149.00x (ISBN 0-407-00069-0). Butterworth.

Sade, Robert M. Infant & Child Care in Heart Surgery. (Illus.). 1977. pap. 14.95 (ISBN 0-8151-7504-3). Year Bk Med.

Williams, Thomas J. Neonatal & Pediatric Cardiopulmonary Care: A Self Assessment. 1976. pap. 12.95 (ISBN 0-8151-9302-5). Year Bk Med.

Young, Daniel G. Baby Surgery: Nursing Management & Care. 167p. pap. text ed. 18.95 (ISBN 0-8391-1445-1). Univ Park.

INFANTS (PREMATURE)

Crosse, V. Mary. Crosse's Preterm Baby. rev. 8th ed. Hill, Eileen E., ed. LC 75-600. (Illus.). 304p. 1975. pap. text ed. 17.50 (ISBN 0-443-01285-7). Churchill.

Friedman, Sarah L. & Sigman, Marian, eds. Preterm Birth & Psychological Development. LC 80-980. (Developmental Psychology Ser.). 1980. 34.00 (ISBN 0-12-267880-X). Acad Pr.

Reed, Dwayne & Stanley, Fiona J., eds. Epidemiology of Prematurity. LC 77-24474. (Illus.). 384p. 1977. text ed. 22.50 (ISBN 0-8067-1611-8). Urban & S.

INFANTS, FOOD FOR

see Infants–Nutrition

INFECTION

see also Airborne Infection; Communicable Diseases; Metastasis

Allen, James C. Infection & the Compromised Host: Clinical Correlations & Therapeutic Approaches. 2nd ed. (Illus.). 285p. 1980. 29.00 (ISBN 0-686-69563-1, 0072-1). Williams & Wilkins.

Altemeier, William A, et al, eds. Manual on Control of Infection in Surgical Patients. LC 76-15400. 1976. 23.50 (ISBN 0-397-50355-5). Har-Row.

Beam, T. R., ed. Antibiotics, Hosts & Host Defences Innosocomial Infections. 20.00 (ISBN 0-915340-07-0). PJD Pubns.

Bennett, John & Brachman, Philip S. Hospital Infections. 1979. text ed. 35.00 (ISBN 0-316-08989-3). Little.

Bodey & Rodriquez. Hospital Associated Infections in the Compromised Host. (Handbook on Hospital-Associated Infection Ser.: Vol. 2). 1979. 39.75 (ISBN 0-8247-6785-3). Dekker.

Breese, Burtis B. & Hall, Caroline. Beta Hemolytic Streptococcal Diseases. (Illus.). 1978. 40.00 (ISBN 0-471-09476-5, Pub. by Wilry Med). Wiley.

Burke, John F. & Hildick-Smith, Gavin Y. The Infection-Prone Hospital Patient. 1978. text ed. 19.95 (ISBN 0-316-11680-7). Little.

Castle, M. Hospital Infection Control: Principles & Practices. LC 80-13424. 1980. 18.95 (ISBN 0-471-05395-3). Wiley.

Castle, Mary. Hospital Infection Control. LC 80-13424. 251p. 1980. 18.95 (ISBN 0-471-05395-3, Pub. by Wiley Med). Wiley.

Chandra, R. K. & Newberne, P. M. Nutrition, Immunity & Infection: Mechanisms of Interaction. (Illus.). 262p. 1977. 22.50 (ISBN 0-306-31058-9, Plenum Pr). Plenum Pub.

Controlling Infection. LC 81-6601. (Nursing Photobook Ser.). (Illus.). 160p. 1981. text ed. 12.95 (ISBN 0-916730-35-2). Intermed Comm.

Cundy, et al. Infection Control in Health Care Facilities. (Illus.). 1977. 22.50 (ISBN 0-8391-1158-4). Univ Park.

Cushing, Ralph & Krome, Ronald L. Emergency Care of Infections. (Current Concepts in Emergency Medicine: Vol. 2). Date not set. text ed. 21.50 (ISBN 0-8016-0122-3). Mosby.

Dixon, Richard E., ed. Nosocomial Infections. LC 81-50243. (Illus.). 344p. 1981. text ed. 29.50 (ISBN 0-914316-24-9); pap. text ed. 19.50 (ISBN 0-914316-29-X). Yorke Med.

Dubay, Elaine C. & Grubb, Reba D. Infection: Prevention & Control. 2nd ed. LC 77-9512. (Illus.). 1978. 11.50 (ISBN 0-8016-1463-5). Mosby.

Emond, R. T. Color Atlas of Infectious Diseases. (Year Book Color Atlas Ser). (Illus.). 384p. 1974. 35.00 (ISBN 0-8151-3118-6). Year Bk Med.

Evans, Alfred S., ed. Vital Infections of Humans: Epidemiology & Control. 2nd ed. 775p. 1981. text ed. 42.50 (ISBN 0-306-40676-4, Plenum Pr). Plenum Pub.

Friedman. Infection, Immunity & Genetics. 1978. 16.50 (ISBN 0-8391-1292-0). Univ Park.

Fuchs, Peter C. Epidemiology of Hospital Associated Infections. LC 79-17036. 1980. text ed. 25.00 (ISBN 0-89189-072-6, 45-7-011-00). Am Soc Clinical.

Fungal Infections. (Landmark Ser.). 1979. 24.50x (ISBN 0-8422-4105-1). Irvington.

Hibbard, Lester T. Infections in Obstetrics & Gynecology. LC 80-18670. (Discussions in Patient Management Ser.). 1980. pap. 8.00 (ISBN 0-87488-896-4). Med Exam.

Hodges, Robert E., ed. Human Nutrition-A Comprehensive Treatise, Vol. 4: Nutrition-Metabolic & Clinical Applications. (Illus.). 500p. 1979. 37.50 (ISBN 0-306-40203-3, Plenum Pr). Plenum Pub.

Hook, Edward W., et al, eds. Current Concepts of Infectious Diseases. LC 77-4458. 1977. 41.50 (ISBN 0-471-01598-9, Pub. by Wiley Medical). Wiley.

Imperato, P. J. Treatment & Control of Infectious Diseases in Man. (Illus.). 760p. 1974. 46.75 (ISBN 0-398-02979-2). C C Thomas.

Infection Control & Drug & Antibiotic Review. (QRB Special Edition). 1979. 25.00 (ISBN 0-86688-039-9, QRB-202). Joint Comm Hosp.

Infection Control & Drug & Antibiotic Review: QRB Special Edition. 80p. Date not set. pap. 25.00 (ISBN 0-86688-039-9). Joint Comm Hosp.

Infection Control in the Hospital. 4th ed. LC 79-9862. (Illus.). 256p. 1980. pap. 16.25 (ISBN 0-87258-262-0, 2117). Am Hospital.

McCracken, George H. & Nelson, John D. Antimicrobial Therapy for Newborns: Practical Application of Pharmacology to Clinical Usage. LC 77-6251. 192p. 1977. 19.50 (ISBN 0-8089-1014-0). Grune.

McGhee, J. R., et al, eds. Secretory Immunity & Infection. LC 78-18927. (Advances in Experimental Medicine & Biology Ser.: Vol. 107). 927p. 1978. 75.00 (ISBN 0-306-40027-8, Plenum Pr). Plenum Pub.

Mathieu, Alix & Burke, John, eds. Infection & the Perioperative Period: Pactical Considerations for Anesthesiologists & Surgeons. (Scientific Basis of Clinicla Anesthesia Ser.). 1981. write for info. (ISBN 0-8089-1325-5). Grune.

Meshelany, C. Infection Control Manual. 2nd ed. 1979. 49.95 (ISBN 0-87489-232-5). Med Economics.

Phillips, I., et al, eds. Microbiological Hazards of Infusion Therapy. LC 76-47865. (Illus.). 194p. 1976. 22.00 (ISBN 0-88416-187-0). Wright-PSG.

Pratt, William B. Chemotherapy of Infection. (Illus.). 1977. text ed. 21.95x (ISBN 0-19-502163-0); pap. text ed. 14.95x (ISBN 0-19-502162-2). Oxford U Pr.

Reeves, David S. & Geddes, A. M., eds. Recent Advances in Infection, No. 1. (Illus.). 1979. text ed. 33.00 (ISBN 0-443-01661-5). Churchill.
Rubin, Robert H. & Young, Lowell S., eds. Clinical Approach to Infection in the Compromised Host. 600p. 1981. text ed. 59.50 (ISBN 0-306-40679-9, Plenum Med Bk). Plenum Pub.
Schachter, Julius & Dawson, Chandler. Human Chlamydial Infections. LC 75-12032. (Illus.). 284p. 1978. 37.50 (ISBN 0-88416-043-2). Wright-PSG.
Thalhammer, Otto, ed. Prenatal Infections: An International Symposium. 1971. pap. 19.75 (ISBN 0-686-77267-9). Grune.
Watts, J. McK., et al. Infection in Surgery: Basic & Clinical Aspects. (Symposium Ser.). (Illus.). 488p. 1981. lib. bdg. 65.00 (ISBN 0-443-02246-1). Churchill.
Wenzel, Richard P. Handbook of Hospital Acquired Infections. 624p. 1981. 84.95 (ISBN 0-8493-0202-1). CRC Pr.
Williams. Modern Topics in Infection. Date not set. 29.50 (ISBN 0-8151-9304-1). Year Bk Med.
Williams, J. Infection in Women. Date not set. cancelled (ISBN 0-685-32593-8). Univ Park.
Willis, A. T., et al. Management of Anaerobic Infections: Prevention & Treatment. (Antimicrobial Chemotherapy Research Studies Ser.). 112p. 1981. 38.50 (ISBN 0-471-28037-2, Pub. by Res Stud Pr). Wiley.

INFECTION, AIRBORNE
see Airborne Infection

INFECTIOUS ABORTION
see Brucellosis in Cattle

INFECTIOUS DISEASES
see Communicable Diseases

INFECTIOUS HEPATITIS
see Hepatitis, Infectious

INFECTIOUS JAUNDICE
see Hepatitis, Infectious

INFERENCE (LOGIC)
see also Induction (Logic); Probabilities; Syllogism
Brown, Gillian & Currie, Karen L. Questions of Intonation. 206p. 1980. pap. text ed. 24.95 (ISBN 0-8391-1467-2). Univ Park.
Fraser, D. A. Inference & Linear Models. (Illus.). 1979. text ed. 34.50x (ISBN 0-07-021910-9, C). McGraw.
Hare, R. M. Practical Inferences. LC 70-182287. 132p. 1972. 12.95x (ISBN 0-520-02179-7). U of Cal Pr.
Harman, Gilbert H. Thought. LC 72-4044. 232p. 1973. 16.50 (ISBN 0-691-07188-8); pap. 5.95 (ISBN 0-691-01986-X). Princeton U Pr.
Hintikka, J. & Suppes, P., eds. Information & Inference. (Synthese Library Ser.). 1970. text ed. 22.00x (ISBN 90-277-0155-5). Humanities.
Raz, Joseph, ed. Practical Reasoning. LC 78-40255. (Oxford Readings in Philosophy Ser.). 1979. pap. 5.00x (ISBN 0-19-875041-2). Oxford U Pr.
Waterman, Don & Hayes-Roth, Rick, eds. Pattern-Directed Inference Systems. 1978. 47.00 (ISBN 0-12-737550-3). Acad Pr.

INFERIORITY COMPLEX
see also Attention-Seeking
Layden, Milton. Escaping the Hostility Trap: The One Sure Way to Deal with Impossible People. LC 76-54672. 1977. 7.95 (ISBN 0-13-283580-0). P-H.
Oliver Brachfeld, F. Inferiority Feelings in the Individual & the Group. Gabain, Marjorie, tr. from Fr. LC 70-169849. 301p. Repr. of 1951 ed. lib. bdg. 16.00x (ISBN 0-8371-6245-9, OLIF). Greenwood.
Ray, Marie B. The Importance of Feeling Inferior. 1971. pap. 2.95 (ISBN 0-87877-006-2, G-6). Newcastle Pub.

INFERTILITY
see Sterility

INFINITARY LANGUAGES
Barwise, J., ed. Syntax & Semantics of Infinitary Languages. LC 68-57175. (Lecture Notes in Mathematics: Vol. 72). 1968. pap. 14.70 (ISBN 0-387-04242-3). Springer-Verlag.
Dickman, M. A. Large Infinitary Languages. (Studies in Logic & the Foundations of Mathematics: Vol. 83). 1976. 49.00 (ISBN 0-444-10622-7, North-Holland). Elsevier.

INFINITE
see also Eternity; Ontology; Space and Time
Coutourat, Louis. De L'infini Mathematique. LC 68-56776. (Research & Source Works Ser.: No. 262). (Fr). 1969. Repr. of 1896 ed. 35.50 (ISBN 0-8337-0706-X). B Franklin.
Dahlstrom, Daniel O., et al, eds. Infinity: Proceedings, Vol. 55. LC 81-65757. 250p. 1982. pap. 8.00 (ISBN 0-918090-15-6). Am Cath Philo.
Leclerc, Ivor. The Nature of Physical Existence. (Muirhead Library of Philosophy). 300p. 1972. text ed. 16.50x (ISBN 0-04-100033-1). Humanities.
Lee, Charlotte A. In Touch with the Infinite. 2nd ed. 145p. 1972. 4.50 (ISBN 0-87516-169-3). De Vorss.
Levinas, Emmanuel. Totality & Infinity. Koren, Henry J., ed. Lingis, Alphonso, tr. LC 69-14432. (Philosophical Ser.). 1969. text ed. 10.00x (ISBN 0-391-01004-2). Duquesne.
Luce, Marnie & Lerner, A. B. Infinity: What Is It. LC 68-56711. (Math Concept Bks). (gr. 3-6). 1969. PLB 3.95 (ISBN 0-8225-0582-7). Lerner Pubns.
Peter, Rozsa. Playing with Infinity: Mathematical Explorations & Excursions. Dienes, Z. P., tr. (Illus.). 7.50 (ISBN 0-8446-5235-0). Peter Smith.
Singer, Dorothea W. Giordano Bruno, His Life & Thought. LC 68-23329. 1968. Repr. of 1950 ed. lib. bdg. 27.25 (ISBN 0-8371-0230-8, SIBL). Greenwood.
Sondheimer, E. & Rogerson, A. Numbers & Infinity: An Historical Account of Mathematical Concepts. LC 81-7660. 150p. Date not set. price not set (ISBN 0-521-24091-3); pap. price not set (ISBN 0-521-28433-3). Cambridge U Pr.

INFINITE PROCESSES
see Processes, Infinite

INFINITE SERIES
see Series, Infinite

INFINITESIMAL CALCULUS
see Calculus

INFINITESIMAL TRANSFORMATIONS
see Transformations, Infinitesimal

INFIRMARIES
see Hospitals

INFLAMMABLE MATERIALS
Backer, S., et al. Textile Fabric Flammability. LC 75-23061. 400p. 1976. text ed. 24.00x (ISBN 0-262-02117-X). MIT Pr.
Basic Classification of Flammable & Combustible Liquids. (Thirty Ser). 1973. pap. 2.00 (ISBN 0-685-58111-X, 321). Natl Fire Prot.
Carroll-Porczynski, C. Z. Flammability of Composite Fabrics. (Illus.). 1976. 45.00 (ISBN 0-8206-0246-9). Chem Pub.
Classification of the Flammability of Wearing Apparel. (Seven Hundred Ser). 1968. pap. 2.00 (ISBN 0-685-58211-6, 702). Natl Fire Prot.
Cleaning or Safeguarding Small Tanks & Containers. (Thirty Ser). 1970. pap. 2.00 (ISBN 0-685-58110-1, 327). Natl Fire Prot.
Code for Explosive Materials. (Forty Ser). 76p. 1973. pap. 2.00 (ISBN 0-685-44171-7, 495). Natl Fire Prot.
Code for Storage of Gaseous Oxidizing Materials. 1974. pap. 2.00 (ISBN 0-685-58202-7, 43C-T). Natl Fire Prot.
Critser, James R., Jr. Flame Retardants for Plastics, Rubber & Textiles (July 1971-June 1972) (Ser. 2-7172). 107p. 1972. 100.00 (ISBN 0-914428-11-X). Lexington Data Inc.
--Flame Retardants for Plastics, Rubber, Textiles & Paper (July 1973-June 1974) (Ser. 2-7374). 1974. 110.00 (ISBN 0-914428-22-5). Lexington Data.
Dip Tanks Containing Flammable or Combustible Liquids. (Thirty Ser). 1974. pap. 2.50 (ISBN 0-685-58108-X, 34). Natl Fire Prot.
Fire Hazard Properties of Flammable Liquids, Gases, Volatile Solids. (Thirty Ser.). 139p. 1969. pap. 3.00 (ISBN 0-685-46063-0, 325M). Natl Fire Prot.
Flammable & Combustible Liquids & Gases in Manholes & Sewers. (Thirty Ser). 1970. pap. 2.00 (ISBN 0-685-58109-8, 328). Natl Fire Prot.
Flammable & Combustible Liquids Code. (Thirty Ser). 116p. 1973. pap. 2.00 (ISBN 0-685-44165-2, NO. 30). Natl Fire Prot.
Henry, Martin, ed. The Flammable & Combustible Liquids Code Handbook. LC 79-56909. (Illus.). 256p. Date not set. 15.00 (ISBN 0-87765-174-4). Natl Fire Prot.
Hilado, Carlos J. Flammability of Cellulosic Materials, Vol. 1. LC 73-82115. (Fire & Flammability Ser.). 246p. 1973. pap. 20.00 (ISBN 0-87762-114-4). Technomic.
--Flammability of Consumer Products, Vol. 3. LC 73-82115. 140p. 1973. pap. 15.00 (ISBN 0-87762-116-0). Technomic.
--Flammability Test Method Handbook, Vol. 1. LC 73-90088. (Fire Research Ser). 120p. 1973. pap. 25.00x (ISBN 0-87762-127-6). Technomic.
--Handbook of Flammability Regulations. LC 75-7498. 380p. 1975. pap. 35.00x (ISBN 0-87762-159-4). Technomic.
--Oxygen Index of Materials, Vol. 4. LC 73-82115. (Fire & Flammability Ser.). 219p. 1973. pap. 20.00 (ISBN 0-87762-122-5). Technomic.
Hilado, Carlos J., ed. Bedding & Furniture Materials, Vol. 14. LC 73-82115. (Fire & Flammability Ser.). (Illus.). 1976. pap. 20.00x (ISBN 0-87762-174-8). Technomic.
--Flammability of Cellular Plastics, Vol. 8. LC 73-82115. (Fire & Flammability Ser.). 220p. 1974. pap. 20.00 (ISBN 0-87762-132-2). Technomic.
International Symposium on Flammability & Fire Retardants, 1977. Fire Retardants: Proceedings. Bhatnagar, Vijay M., ed. LC 77-90574. (Illus.). 1977. pap. 35.00x (ISBN 0-87762-246-9). Technomic.
Lewin, Menachem, et al, eds. Flame-Retardant Polymeric Materials, Vol. 2. LC 75-26781. (Illus.). 345p. 1978. 35.00 (ISBN 0-306-32212-9, Plenum Pr). Plenum Pub.
Meidl, James. Hazardous Materials Handbook. (Fire Science Ser). 1972. pap. text ed. 12.95x (ISBN 0-02-476370-5, 47637). Macmillan.
Meidl, James H. Flammable Hazardous Materials. 2nd ed. 1978. text ed. 18.95x (ISBN 0-02-476570-8). Macmillan.
National Academy of Sciences, ed. Fire Dynamics & Scenarios, Vol. 4. LC 77-79218. (Fire Safety Aspects of Polymeric Materials). 1978. 15.00x (ISBN 0-87762-225-6). Technomic.
Portable Shipping Tanks. (Thirty Ser). 1974. pap. 2.00 (ISBN 0-685-58105-5, 386). Natl Fire Prot.
Spray Application Using Flammable & Combustible Liquids. (Thirty Ser). 56p. 1973. pap. 2.00 (ISBN 0-685-44167-9, 33). Natl Fire Prot.
Storage of Flammable & Combustible Liquids on Farms & Isolated Construction Projects. (Thirty Ser). 1972. pap. 2.00 (ISBN 0-685-58103-9, 395). Natl Fire Prot.
Tank Vehicles for Flammable & Combustible Liquids. (Thirty Ser). 1974. pap. 2.50 (ISBN 0-685-58035-0, 385). Natl Fire Prot.
Underground Leakage of Flammable & Combustible Liquids. (Thirty Ser.). 56p. 1972. pap. 2.00 (ISBN 0-685-46064-9, 329). Natl Fire Prot.

INFLAMMATION
see also Anti-Inflammatory Agents
also particuliar inflammations, e.g. Appendicitis
Arrigoni-Martelli, Edoardo. Inflammation & Antiinflammatories. LC 77-24743. 343p. 1977. 30.00 (ISBN 0-470-99175-5). Halsted Pr.
Bonta, I. L., ed. Recent Developments in the Pharmacology of Inflammatory Mediators. (Agents & Actions Suplements: No. 2). 178p. 1977. pap. 29.00 (ISBN 3-7643-0914-8). Birkhauser.
Bonta, I. L., et al, eds. Inflammation Mechanisms & Their Impact on Therapy. (Agents & Actions Supplements: No. 3). (Illus.). 192p. 1977. pap. text ed. 60.00 (ISBN 3-7643-0913-X). Birkhauser.
Brune, K. & Baggiolini, M., eds. Arachidonic Acid Metabolism in Inflammation & Thrombosis: Proceedings of the First European Workshop on Inflammation, Basel, 1979. (Agents & Actions Supplements: No. 4). (Illus.). 300p. 1979. text ed. 38.00 (ISBN 3-7643-1095-2). Birkhauser.
Confenence on Inflammation, Princeton, 1972. Conference on Inflammation, Princeton, 1972: Mechanisms & Control. Lepow, Irwin & Ward, Peter A., eds. 43.00 (ISBN 0-12-444050-9). Acad Pr.
Gordon, J. L. & Hazleman, B. L., eds. Rheumatoid Arthritis. LC 76-51323. 1977. 41.00 (ISBN 0-7204-0621-8, North Holland). Elsevier.
Grabar, Pierre & Miescher, Peter A., eds. Mechanisms of Imflammation Induced by Immune Reactions: Fifth International Symposium of Immunopathology. (Illus.). 425p. 1968. 79.50 (ISBN 0-8089-0627-5). Grune.
Hilado, Carlos J. Surface Flame Spread, Vol. 5. LC 73-82115. (Fire & Flammability Ser.). 149p. 1973. pap. 15.00 (ISBN 0-87762-123-3). Technomic.
Metchnikoff, Elie. Lectures on the Comparative Pathology of Inflammation. LC 68-21281. 1968. lib. bdg. 9.50 (ISBN 0-88307-619-5). Gannon.
Movat, H. Z., ed. Inflammatory Reaction. (Current Topics in Pathology Ser.: Vol. 68). (Illus.). 1979. 50.80 (ISBN 0-387-09394-X). Springer-Verlag.
Movat, Henry Z., ed. Inflammation, Immunity, & Hypersensitivity: Cellular & Molecular Mechanisms. 2nd ed. 1979. text ed. 42.50 (ISBN 0-06-141804-8, Harper Medical). Har-Row.
Rainsford, K. D., et al, eds. Trace the Elements in Pathologenis & Treatment of Inflammation. Brune, K. & Whitehouse. (AAS Ser.: No. 8). 350p. 1980. softcover 79.00 (ISBN 3-7643-1201-7). Birkhauser.
Scherrer, Robert A. & Whitehouse, Michael W., eds. Antiinflamatory Agents: Chemistry & Pharmacology, Vols. 1 & 2. 1974. Vol. 1. 58.50 (ISBN 0-12-623901-0); Vol. 2. 58.50 (ISBN 0-12-623902-9); Set. 95.00 (ISBN 0-685-48715-6). Acad Pr.
Spector, W. G. & Willoughby, D. A. The Pharmacology of Inflammation. (Illus.). 118p. 1968. 19.50 (ISBN 0-8089-0615-1). Grune.
Thomas, Lewis, et al. International Symposium of Injury, Inflammation & Immunity. 422p. 1964. 19.50 (ISBN 0-685-91061-X, Pub. by W & W). Krieger.
Tripp, Alice. Basic Mechanisms of Inflammation. (Illus.). 1978. pap. text ed. 6.95 (ISBN 0-07-065222-8, HP). McGraw.
Vane, J. R. & Ferreira, S. H., eds. Anti-Inflammatory Drugs. LC 78-1606. (Handbook of Experimental Pharmacology: Vol. 50, Pt. 2). (Illus.). 1978. 203.30 (ISBN 0-387-08640-4). Springer-Verlag.
Weissmann, Gerald, ed. Advances in Inflammation Research, Vol. 2. 223p. 1981. 24.50 (ISBN 0-89004-582-8). Raven.
--Advances in Inflammation Research, Vol. 4. 1981. text ed. 21.00 (ISBN 0-89004-669-7). Raven.
--Mediators of Inflammation. LC 74-20786. 205p. 1974. 22.50 (ISBN 0-306-30815-0, Plenum Pr). Plenum Pub.
Weterman, I. T., et al, eds. Crohn's Disease Diagnosis & Treatment: Proc. Workshop. (International Congress Ser.: No. 386). 1976. pap. 58.75 (ISBN 90-219-0317-2, Excerpta Medica). Elsevier.
Willoughby, ed. Perspectives in Inflammation. (Illus.). 1977. 42.50 (ISBN 0-8391-1159-2). Univ Park.
Willoughby, D. A. & Giroud, J. P., eds. Inflamation: Mechanisms & Treatment. 1018p. 1981. pap. text ed. 64.50 (ISBN 0-8391-1650-0). Univ Park.
Zweifach, Benjamin W., et al, eds. The Inflammatory Process, Vol. 1. 2nd ed. 1974. 73.00 (ISBN 0-12-783401-X); Vol. 2. 48.75 (ISBN 0-12-783402-8); Vol. 3. 51.00 (ISBN 0-12-783403-6); Set. 133.00 (ISBN 0-685-48732-6). Acad Pr.

INFLATABLE STRUCTURES
see Air-Supported Structures

INFLATION (FINANCE)
see also Currency Question; Greenbacks; Paper Money; Price Regulation; Wage-Price Policy
Aaron, Henry J., ed. Inflation & the Income Tax. LC 76-28669. (Studies of Government Finance). 1976. 15.95 (ISBN 0-8157-0024-5); pap. 6.95 (ISBN 0-8157-0023-7). Brookings.
Ady, Ronald W. Making Money in Inflation, Deflation and Recession. 1976. 12.95 (ISBN 0-13-547794-8); pap. 3.95 (ISBN 0-13-547778-6). P-H.
Alchian, Armen A. Economic Forces at Work. LC 77-1327. 1977. 10.00 (ISBN 0-913966-30-4, Liberty Press); pap. 3.50 (ISBN 0-913966-35-5). Liberty Fund.
Aliber, Robert Z. Monetary Reform & World Inflation. LC 73-86713. (The Washington Papers: No. 12). 1973. 4.00x (ISBN 0-8039-0285-9). Sage.
Bach, G. L. The New Inflation: Causes, Effects, Cures. LC 72-2451. x, 103p. 1972. 9.00x (ISBN 0-87057-136-2, Pub. by Brown U Pr). U Pr of New Eng.
--The New Inflation: Causes, Effects, Cures. LC 72-2451. (Illus.). 113p. 1974. Repr. of 1972 ed. text ed. 9.00x (ISBN 0-87057-136-2, Pub. by Brown U Pr). U Pr of New Eng.
Bakewell, Paul, Jr. Inflation in the United States. LC 58-10622. 1958. pap. 1.00 (ISBN 0-87004-009-X). Caxton.
Barro, R. J. & Grossman, H. I. Money, Employment & Inflation. LC 75-13449. (Illus.). 304p. 1976. 24.50x (ISBN 0-521-20906-4). Cambridge U Pr.
Beigie, Carl E. Inflation Is a Social Malady. LC 78-70536. 92p. 1979. 4.00 (ISBN 0-902594-34-6). Natl Planning.
Belsley, David A., et al, eds. Inflation, Trade, & Taxes. LC 75-19099. (Illus.). 1976. 15.95 (ISBN 0-8142-0194-6). Ohio St U Pr.
Benge, Eugene J. How to Lick Inflation Before It Licks You. LC 80-29658. 176p. 1981. 9.95 (ISBN 0-8119-0342-7). Fell.
Bergstrom, A. R., et al, eds. Stability & Inflation: Essays in Memory of A. W. Phillips. LC 77-4420. 323p. 1978. 63.50 (ISBN 0-471-99522-3, Pub. by Wiley-Interscience). Wiley.
Berman, Peter I. Inflation & the Money Supply in the United States, 1956-1977. LC 78-4344. 1978. 14.95 (ISBN 0-669-02346-9). Lexington Bks.
Bethell, Tom. Television Evening News Covers Inflation: Nineteen Seventy-Eight to Seventy-Nine. Media Institute, ed. (Illus.). 52p. (Orig.). 1980. pap. 5.00 (ISBN 0-937790-00-1). Media Inst.
Bierman, Harold, Jr. Financial Management & Inflation. (Illus.). 180p. 1981. 14.95 (ISBN 0-02-903570-8). Free Pr.
Blinder, Alan S. Economic Policy & the Great Stagflation. student ed. 1981. pap. 9.50 (ISBN 0-12-106162-0). Acad Pr.
Blyth, Conrad. Inflation in New Zealand. 1978. pap. text ed. 4.95x (ISBN 0-86861-016-X). Allen Unwin.
Boeckh, J. Anthony & Coghlan, Richard T. Inflation & the Stock Market. 225p. 1981. 11.95 (ISBN 0-686-75061-6). Dow Jones-Irwin.
Borsodi, Ralph. Inflation Is Coming. 1979. lib. bdg. 59.95 (ISBN 0-685-96399-3). Revisionist Pr.
Boskin, Michael, et al. The Impact of Inflation on U.S. Productivity & International Competiveness. LC 80-83144. 69p. 1980. 7.00 (ISBN 0-89068-055-8). Natl Planning.

Bowen, Ian. Inflation & Social Justice. 35p. 1977. pap. 3.00x (ISBN 0-85564-056-1, Pub. by U of W Austral Pr). Intl Schol Bk Serv.
Bowen, William. Wage Behavior in the Postwar Period. LC 73-10582. (Princeton University Industrial Relations). (Illus.). 137p. 1973. Repr. of 1960 ed. lib. bdg. 15.00x (ISBN 0-8371-7013-3, BOWB). Greenwood.
Bowen, William G. Wage-Price Issue: A Theoretical Analysis. LC 72-90471. Repr. of 1960 ed. lib. bdg. 22.00x (ISBN 0-8371-2286-4, BOWP). Greenwood.
Bradway, Bruce M. & Pritchard, Robert E. Protecting Profits During Inflation & Recession. 130p. 1981. pap. text ed. 7.95 (ISBN 0-201-00074-1). A-W.
Brems, Hans. Inflation, Interest, & Growth: A Synthesis. LC 78-19226. 192p. 1980. 18.95 (ISBN 0-669-02466-X). Lexington Bks.
Brunner, K. & Meltzer, A. H., eds. The Problem of Inflation. (Carnegie-Rochester Conference Ser. on Public Policy: Vol. 8). 1978. 29.50 (ISBN 0-444-85147-X, North-Holland). Elsevier.
--Stabilization of the Domestic & International Economy. (Carnegie-Rochester Conference Ser.: Vol. 5). 1977. 18.50 (ISBN 0-7204-0709-5, North-Holland). Elsevier.
Brunner, Karl & Meltzer, A. H., eds. Institutions, Policies & Economic Performance. (Carnegie-Rochester Conference Series on Public Policy: Vol. 1V). 1976. pap. text ed. 19.50 (ISBN 0-7204-0564-5, North-Holland). Elsevier.
Burns, Arthur F. Reflections of an Economic Policy Maker: Speeches & Congressional Statements, 1969-1978. 1978. 17.25 (ISBN 0-8447-3319-9); pap. 9.25 (ISBN 0-8447-3333-4). Am Enterprise.
Cagan, Philip, et al. Economic Policy & Inflation in the Sixties. 1972. 8.50 (ISBN 0-8447-3078-5). Am Enterprise.
Cagan, Phillip. The Hydra-Headed Monster: The Problem of Inflation in the United States. LC 74-22830. (Orig.). 1974. pap. 4.25 (ISBN 0-8447-3143-9). Am Enterprise.
--Persistent Inflation. LC 79-1017. 280p. 1979. 20.00x (ISBN 0-231-04728-2); pap. 10.00 (ISBN 0-231-04729-0). Columbia U Pr.
Cagan, Phillip & Lipsey, Robert. The Financial Effect of Inflation. LC 78-13124. (National Bureau of Economic Research General Studies: No. 103). 96p. 1978. 15.95 (ISBN 0-88410-486-9). Ballinger Pub.
Cairncross, Alex. Inflation, Growth & International Finance. LC 75-20428. 136p. 1976. 18.00 (ISBN 0-87395-315-0). State U NY Pr.
Caplovitz, David. Making Ends Meet: How Families Cope with Inflation & Recession. LC 79-14438. (Sage Library of Social Research: No. 86). 303p. 1979. 20.00x (ISBN 0-8039-1292-7); pap. 9.95x (ISBN 0-8039-1293-5). Sage.
Case, John. Understanding Inflation. LC 80-29139. (Illus.). 224p. 1981. 9.95 (ISBN 0-688-00399-0). Morrow.
Chenoweth, Clyde G. Our Tragic Inflation Orgy & What to Do About It: An Introduction to the Fascinating Economics of Tomorrow. 1978. 8.00 (ISBN 0-682-49097-0, University). Exposition.
Chitale, V. P. Project Viability in Inflationary Conditions. 144p. 1980. text ed. 16.50x (ISBN 0-7069-1132-6, Pub. by Vikas India). Advent NY.
Cleveland, Harold Van B. & Brittain, Bruce W. The Great Inflation: A Monetarist View. LC 76-41068. 72p. 1976. 3.50 (ISBN 0-89068-003-5). Natl Planning.
Cline, William R. World Inflation & the Developing Countries. 266p. 1981. 15.95 (ISBN 0-8157-1468-8); pap. 5.95 (ISBN 0-8157-1467-X). Brookings.
Colander, David C., ed. Solutions to Inflation. 220p. 1979. pap. text ed. 7.95 (ISBN 0-15-582450-3, HC). HarBraceJ.
Committee for Economic Development. Fighting Inflation & Promoting Growth. LC 76-25444. 1976. lib. bdg. 4.00 (ISBN 0-87186-761-3); pap. 2.50 (ISBN 0-87186-061-9). Comm Econ Dev.
--Further Weapons Against Inflation. LC 70-141683. 96p. 1970. lib. bdg. 2.50 (ISBN 0-87186-740-0); pap. 1.50 (ISBN 0-87186-040-6). Comm Econ Dev.
Congressional Quarterly Staff. Taxes, Jobs, & Inflation. LC 78-13735. 1978. pap. 6.95 (ISBN 0-87187-139-4). Congr Quarterly.
Corden, W. M. Inflation, Exchange Rates, & the World Economy: Lectures on International Monetary Economics. (Business & Society Studies). 1980. pap. write for info. (ISBN 0-226-11584-4). U of Chicago Pr.
--Inflation, Exchange Rates, & the World Economy: Lectures on International Monetary Economics. LC 76-58331. (Studies in Business & Society). 1977. lib. bdg. 11.00x (ISBN 0-226-11583-6). U of Chicago Pr.
Croom, George E., Jr. & Van Der Wal, John. Now You Can Profit from Inflation. 264p. 1981. 14.95 (ISBN 0-442-25397-4). Van Nos Reinhold.
Cumes, J. W. Inflation: A Study in Stability. 202p. 1976. text ed. 16.75 (ISBN 0-08-018167-8). Pergamon.
Davidson, John. The Way to End Inflation. 1980. 7.95 (ISBN 0-533-04736-6). Vantage.
Davidson, Sidney, et al. Inflation Accounting: A Guide for the Accountant & the Financial Analyst. 1976. 21.95 (ISBN 0-07-015478-3, P&RB). McGraw.
Davis, William, ed. The Punch Book of Inflation. LC 74-31967. 1975. 4.50 (ISBN 0-7153-7014-6). David & Charles.
Davisson, Charles N. & Wilhelm, Ross. Economic Effects of the Wage-Price Guideposts. (Michigan Business Papers: No. 45). 1967. pap. 1.50 (ISBN 0-87712-094-3). U Mich Busn Div Res.
De Malynes, Gerrard. Englands View, in the Unmasking of Two Paradoxes: With a Replication Unto the Answer of Maister John Bodine. LC 79-38254. (The Evolution of Capitalism Ser.). 208p. 1972. Repr. of 1603 ed. 12.00 (ISBN 0-405-04126-8). Arno.
Dougherty, Thomas J. Controlling the New Inflation. LC 80-8962. (Illus.). 192p. 1981. 18.95x (ISBN 0-669-04512-8). Lexington Bks.
Duesenberry, James S. Can We Control Inflation? (William K. McInally Memorial Lecture Ser.: 8th). 28p. 1974. pap. 1.00 (ISBN 0-87712-164-8). U Mich Busn Div Res.
Eckstein, Otto. Core Inflation. (Illus.). 128p. 1981. 12.95 (ISBN 0-13-172643-9); pap. 7.95 (ISBN 0-13-172635-8). P-H.
Eder, G. What's Behind Inflation & How to Beat It. 1979. 9.95 (ISBN 0-13-952143-7). P-H.
Eichner, Alfred S. The Megacorp & Oligopoly. LC 79-92295. 365p. 1980. pap. 8.95 (ISBN 0-87332-168-5). M E Sharpe.
Ellis, Howard S. Notes on Stagflation. 1978. pap. 2.25 (ISBN 0-8447-3323-7). Am Enterprise.
Essays on Inflation. 6.00 (ISBN 0-686-11599-6). M & A Products.
Fallick, J. L. & Elliot, R. F., eds. Incomes Policies, Inflation & Relative Pay. (Illus.). 304p. 1981. text ed. 29.95x (ISBN 0-04-331077-X); pap. text ed. 12.50x (ISBN 0-04-331078-8). Allen Unwin.
Ferris, James J. Inflation: The Ultimate Craven Image. 192p. (Orig.). 1981. pap. 4.95 (ISBN 0-89221-087-7). New Leaf.
Fisher, David I., ed. Managing in Inflation. LC 78-63420. (Report Ser.: No. 750). 1978. pap. 15.00 (ISBN 0-8237-0186-7). Conference Bd.
Fisher, Irving. Inflation? 1979. Repr. of 1933 ed. lib. bdg. 17.50 (ISBN 0-8482-3955-5). Norwood Edns.
Flanagan, William G. How to Beat the (Financial) Squeeze: Don't Just Get Mad, Get Even. LC 79-7814. 240p. 1980. 10.95 (ISBN 0-385-14836-4). Doubleday.
Flanders, M. June & Razin, Assaf, eds. Development in an Inflationary World. (Economic Theory, Econometrics & Mathematical Economics Ser.). 1981. 55.00 (ISBN 0-12-259750-8). Acad Pr.
Fleissner, Else M. Inflation. Rahmas, D. Steve, ed. LC 72-89225. (Topics of Our Times Ser.: No. 3). 32p. (Orig.). (gr. 7-12). 1973. lib. bdg. 2.95 incl. catalog cards (ISBN 0-87157-803-4); pap. 1.50 vinyl laminated covers (ISBN 0-87157-303-2). SamHar Pr.
Flemming, John. Inflation. (Illus.). 144p. 1976. 17.95x (ISBN 0-19-877085-5); pap. 4.95x (ISBN 0-19-877086-3). Oxford U Pr.
Friedman, Irving S. Inflation: A World-Wide Disaster. 2nd ed. 320p. 1980. 14.95 (ISBN 0-395-30527-6); pap. 6.95 (ISBN 0-395-29847-4). HM.
Friedman, M. Dollars & Deficits: Inflation, Monetary Policy & the Balance of Payments. 1968. pap. 11.95 (ISBN 0-13-218289-0). P-H.
Friedman, Milton. Monetary Correction. (Institute of Economic Affairs, Occasional Papers Ser.: No. 41). 1975. 4.25 (ISBN 0-255-36058-4). Transatlantic.
--Tax Limitation, Inflation & the Role of Government. LC 78-73456. (Illus.). 110p. 1979. pap. 5.95 (ISBN 0-933028-00-8). Fisher Inst.
Friedman, Milton, et al. Essays on Inflation & Indexation. LC 74-18963. (Orig.). 1974. pap. text ed. 4.25 (ISBN 0-8447-3139-0). Am Enterprise.
--Indexing & Inflation. LC 74-19771. (Orig.). 1974. pap. 3.75 (ISBN 0-8447-2049-6). Am Enterprise.
Frisch, H., ed. Inflation in Small Countries. (Lectures Notes in Economics & Mathematical Systems: Vol. 119). 1976. pap. 16.40 (ISBN 0-387-07624-7). Springer-Verlag.
Fuller, Robert. Inflation: The Rising Cost of Living on a Small Planet. LC 79-57383. (Worldwatch Papers). 1980. pap. 2.00 (ISBN 0-916468-33-X). Worldwatch Inst.
Fusino, S. A Neo-Keynesian Theory of Inflation & Economic Growth. (Lecture Notes in Economics & Mathematical Systems Ser.: Vol. 104). v, 96p. 1974. pap. 9.90 (ISBN 0-387-06964-X). Springer-Verlag.
Gale, William A., ed. Inflation: Causes, Consequents & Control. 160p. 1981. text ed. 30.00 (ISBN 0-89946-118-2). Oelgeschlager.
Gamble, Andrew & Walton, Paul. Capitalism in Crisis: Inflation & the State. 1977. text ed. 16.50x (ISBN 0-391-00592-8); pap. text ed. 7.50x (ISBN 0-391-00593-6). Humanities.
Gapinski, James & Rockwood, Charles E. Essays in Post-Keynesian Inflation. LC 79-22879. 336p. 1979. text ed. 20.00 (ISBN 0-88410-684-5). Ballinger Pub.
Gasteyger, Curt, et al. Energy, Inflation & International Economic Relations: Atlantic Institute Studies - Two. LC 75-19764. (Special Studies). (Illus.). 256p. 1975. text ed. 24.95 (ISBN 0-275-01250-6). Praeger.
Goldschmidt, Y. & Admon, K. Profit Measurement During Inflation: Accounting, Economic & Financial Aspects. LC 77-4500. (Wiley Series in Operations Management). 1977. 32.95x (ISBN 0-471-01983-6, Pub. by Wiley-Interscience). Wiley.
Gompertz, Philip. A Child's View of Inflation. (Illus.). 40p. 1974. pap. 1.15 (ISBN 0-918248-01-9). WorDoctor.
Greaves, Percy L. Understanding the Dollar Crisis. LC 73-90023. 1973. pap. 4.95 (ISBN 0-88279-127-3). Western Islands.
Greene, James. International Experiences in Managing Inflation. (Report Ser.: No. 729). (Illus.). 1977. pap. 15.00 (ISBN 0-8237-0163-8). Conference Bd.
Griffiths, Brian. Inflation: The Price of Prosperity. LC 75-43789. 300p. 1976. text ed. 25.00x (ISBN 0-8419-0255-0). Holmes & Meier.
Hansen, H. Morris. The Wealth Transfer of Inflation: How to Compute It, Account for It, & Profit from It. LC 81-6250. 250p. 1981. 34.50 (ISBN 0-87624-014-7). Inst Busn Plan.
Harris, Seymour E. Economics of Mobilization & Inflation. LC 68-28586. (Illus.). 1968. Repr. of 1951 ed. lib. bdg. 14.50x (ISBN 0-8371-0097-6, HAEM). Greenwood.
Hayek, F. A. Choice in Currency: A Way to Stop Inflation. (Occasional Paper: No. 48). 1977. pap. 4.25 (ISBN 0-255-36078-9). Transatlantic.
Hazlitt, Henry. The Inflation Crisis, & How to Resolve It. 1978. 9.95 (ISBN 0-87000-398-4). Arlington Hse.
Heathfield, David, ed. Perspectives on Inflation: Models & Policies. (Illus.). 1979. text ed. 21.00x (ISBN 0-582-44189-7); pap. text ed. 11.95x (ISBN 0-582-44190-0). Longman.
Hinshaw, Randall, ed. Stagflation: An International Problem. (Business Economics & Finance: Vol. 10). 1977. 24.75 (ISBN 0-8247-6644-X). Dekker.
Hirsch, Fred & Goldthorpe, John H. The Political Economy of Inflation. 1978. 15.00x (ISBN 0-674-68583-0); pap. 5.95x (ISBN 0-674-68584-9). Harvard U Pr.
Hong, Byung Y. Inflation Under Pass-Along Management. 1979. 20.95 (ISBN 0-03-051331-6). Praeger.
Hussey, David. Inflation & Business Policy. LC 76-7065. (Business Strategy & Planning Ser.). (Illus.). 1976. text ed. 22.00x (ISBN 0-582-45073-X). Longman.
Inflation & Captial Markets. Sarnat, Marshall, ed. LC 77-16228. 1978. 22.50 (ISBN 0-88410-661-6). Ballinger Pub.
Inflation: The Rising Cost of Living on a Small Planet. 48p. 1980. pap. 2.95 (ISBN 0-686-61376-7, WW 34, WW). Unipub.
Iwai, Katsuhito. Disequilibrium Dynamics: A Theoretical Analysis of Inflation & Unemployment. LC 80-26445. (Cowles Foundation Monographs: No. 27). 352p. 1981. text ed. 37.50x (ISBN 0-300-02556-4). Yale U Pr.
Jackman, Richard & Klappholz, Kurt. Taming the Tiger. (Hobart Papers Special Ser.: No. 63). 1976. pap. 4.25 (ISBN 0-255-36073-8). Transatlantic.
Jefferson, Michael, et al. Inflation. 1979. 11.95 (ISBN 0-7145-3539-7); pap. 4.95 (ISBN 0-7145-3547-8). Riverrun NY.
Kemmerer, Edwin W. The ABC of Inflation. 1942. 15.00 (ISBN 0-686-17735-5). Quest Edns.
Keynes, John M. Essays in Persuasion. 1963. pap. 5.95 (ISBN 0-393-00190-3, Norton Lib). Norton.
Keyserling, Leon H. & Conference on Economic Progress Staff. Full Employment Without Inflation. (Illus.). 1975. 2.00 (ISBN 0-685-64407-3). Conf Econ Prog.
--Growth with Less Inflation or More Inflation Without Growth? (Illus.). 1970. 1.00 (ISBN 0-685-22700-6). Conf Econ Prog.
Kirkman, Patrick R. Accounting Under Inflationary Conditions. 2nd rev. ed. 1978. text ed. 29.95x (ISBN 0-04-332067-8); pap. text ed. 12.50x (ISBN 0-04-332068-6). Allen Unwin.
Klein & Wolman. Beat Inflation Strategy. 1975. 9.95 (ISBN 0-671-22063-2). S&S.
Klein, Roger & Wolman, William. The Beat Inflation Strategy. 1977. pap. 4.95 (ISBN 0-671-23080-8, Fireside). S&S.
Korliras, Panayotis G. The Economics of Disorder: A Disequilibrium Approach to the Problems of Inflation & Unemployment. (Center of Planning & Economic Research Lecture Ser.: No. 29). 1977. pap. 7.50x (ISBN 0-8002-0361-5). Intl Pubns Serv.
Krause, Lawrence B. & Salant, Walter S., eds. Worldwide Inflation: Theory & Recent Experience. LC 76-51580. 1976. 21.95 (ISBN 0-8157-5030-7); pap. 11.95 (ISBN 0-8157-5029-3). Brookings.
Kristensen, Thorkil. Inflation & Unemployment in Modern Society. 200p. 1981. 21.95 (ISBN 0-03-057003-4). Praeger.
Laege, F. K. Secular Inflation. Catty, F. B., tr. from Ger. 106p. 1961. 15.80 (ISBN 90-277-0098-2). Kluwer Boston.
Laidler, D. & Purdy, D. L. Inflation & Labour Markets. LC 74-78380. 1974. 20.00x (ISBN 0-8020-2163-8). U of Toronto Pr.
Laidler, D. E. Essays on Money & Inflation. LC 75-22170. xiv, 246p. 1979. lib. bdg. 16.00x (ISBN 0-226-46793-7); pap. 6.95 (ISBN 0-226-46792-9, P817, Phoen). U of Chicago Pr.
League of Nations, Economic, Financial & Transit Department. The Course & Control of Inflation. Wilkins, Mira, ed. LC 78-3928. (International Finance Ser.). (Illus.). 1978. Repr. of 1946 ed. lib. bdg. 11.00x (ISBN 0-405-11231-9). Arno.
Leibenstein, Harvey. Inflation, Income Distribution & X-Efficiency Theory: A Study Prepared for the International Labour Office Within the Framework of the World Employment Programme. 122p. 1980. 23.50x (ISBN 0-389-20003-4). B&N.
Lerner, Abba P. Flation: Not Inflation of Prices, Not De-Flation of Jobs. LC 72-78503. 240p. 1972. 5.95 (ISBN 0-8129-0304-8). Times Bks.
Leuthold, Steven C. The Myths of Inflation & Investing. LC 80-67811. 1980. 27.50 (ISBN 0-87251-048-4). Crain Bks.
Lincoln, Edmond E., tr. Du Pont De Nemours on the Dangers of Inflation. (Kress Library of Business & Economics: No. 7). 1949. pap. 5.00x (ISBN 0-678-09902-2, Baker Lib). Kelley.
Lindbeck, A., ed. Inflation & Employment in Open Economics: Essays by Members of the Institute for International Economic Studies, Univ. of Stockholm, Sweden. (Studies in International Economics, 1979: Vol. 5). 1979. 58.75 (ISBN 0-444-85227-1, North Holland). Elsevier.
Lindberg, Leon N. Inflation & Political Change. (Pergamon Policy Studies). 1980. 24.01 (ISBN 0-08-024625-7). Pergamon.
Looney, Robert E. The Economic Consequences of World Inflation on Semi-Dependent Countries. LC 78-65351. 1978. pap. text ed. 10.75 (ISBN 0-8191-0654-2). U Pr of Amer.
Lucas, T. S. Understanding Inflation Accounting. 1981. write for info. (ISBN 0-07-020830-1). McGraw.
Ludwig, Thomas E., et al. Inflation, Poortalk, & the Gospel. 112p. 1981. pap. 4.95 (ISBN 0-8170-0942-6). Judson.
Lustgarten, Steven. Industrial Concentration & Inflation. LC 75-18501. (Orig.). 1975. pap. 4.25 (ISBN 0-8447-3169-2). Am Enterprise.
McCulloch, J. Houston. Money & Inflation: Monetarist Approach. 121p. 1975. 7.95 (ISBN 0-12-483050-1). Acad Pr.
Market Efficiency & Inflation: Two Documents from the Cabinet Committee on Price Stability of the Johnson Administration. LC 70-83785. 1969. 6.95 (ISBN 0-405-00055-3, Pub. by Ind. Pubns.). Arno.
Mathies, F. The Ultimate Inflation Shelter. 1980. 25.00 (ISBN 0-686-58614-X). Windsor.
Mattick, Paul. Economics, Politics, & the Age of Inflation. Vale, Michel, tr. from Ger. LC 78-68044. 1979. 15.00 (ISBN 0-87332-123-5). M E Sharpe.
Maynard, Geoffrey & Van Ryckeghem, W. A World of Inflation. LC 75-26030. 272p. 1975. text ed. 21.00x (ISBN 0-06-494673-8). B&N.
Means, Gardiner. Administrative Inflation & Public Policy. 1959. 1.00 (ISBN 0-685-06096-9). Anderson Kramer.
Meany, George, et al. Government Wage-Price Guideposts in the American Economy. LC 67-25039. (Moskowitz Lectures). 82p. 1967. 5.95x (ISBN 0-8147-0295-3). NYU Pr.
Meiselman, David I. & Laffer, Arthur B., eds. The Phenomenon of Worldwide Inflation. 1975. 8.50 (ISBN 0-8447-2058-5); pap. 7.25 (ISBN 0-8447-2057-7). Am Enterprise.
Miller, Elwood. Inflation Accounting. 240p. 1980. text ed. 17.95 (ISBN 0-442-21909-1). Van Nos Reinhold.
Millet, Andrew B. The Crime of the Modern State: Inflation. (Illus.). 1979. 39.75 (ISBN 0-918968-45-3). Inst Econ Finan.

Milton. Inflation: Everyone's Problem. 4.95 (ISBN 0-8065-0320-3). Citadel Pr.
Milton, Arthur. Will Inflation Destroy America? 1977. 7.95 (ISBN 0-8065-0608-3). Citadel Pr.
Mittelbach, Frank G., ed. Taxes & Inflation & Their Effects on American Real Estate & Urban Development. (Real Estate Chair Lecture Ser.: Proceedings IV). (Illus., Orig.). 1979. pap. 5.00 (ISBN 0-911798-20-X). UCLA Mgmt.
Monetary Targets & Inflation Control. (OECD Monetary Studies). 101p. 1979. 9.50x (ISBN 92-64-11963-9). OECD.
Moore, Geoffrey. Business Cycles, Inflation & Forecasting. 1980. 42.50 (ISBN 0-88410-685-3). Ballinger Pub.
Morgan, David R. Over-Taxation by Inflation. (Hobart Papers Ser.: No. 72). 1977. pap. 6.95 (ISBN 0-255-36091-6). Transatlantic.
Morley. Inflation & Unemployment. 2nd ed. 1979. pap. 7.95 (ISBN 0-03-041016-9). Dryden Pr.
Morrison, Robert S. Inflation Can Be Stopped. LC 73-91213. (Illus.). 1973. 4.95 (ISBN 0-912400-05-6); pap. 2.00 (ISBN 0-912400-04-8). Western Res Pr.
Moulton, Harold G. Can Inflation Be Controlled. 1958. 4.95 (ISBN 0-685-06097-7). Anderson Kramer.
Muller, Fred. America's Coming Nightmare Inflation, Economic Collapse & Crime Revolution. 120p. 1980. 10.00 (ISBN 0-686-68648-9). State Ptg.
National Bureau of Economic Research Conference on Income & Wealth. Analysis of Inflation: Analysis of Inflation: Nineteen Sixty-Five to Nineteen Seventy-Four. Popkin, Joel, ed. LC 77-581. (Studies in Income & Wealth: Vol. 42). 1977. 20.00 (ISBN 0-88410-477-X). Ballinger Pub.
Neff, Cole D. Inflation: Understandable & Preventable. LC 78-73013. 90p. 1978. 4.95 (ISBN 0-8059-2600-3). Dorrance.
Niebyl, Karl H. Studies in the Classical Theories of Money. LC 70-173795. Repr. of 1946 ed. 18.75 (ISBN 0-404-04709-2). AMS Pr.
Odeh, H. S. Impact of Inflation on the Level of Economic Activity. 1970. pap. 19.25x (ISBN 0-677-61565-5). Gordon.
Okun, Arthur M. & Perry, George L., eds. Curing Chronic Inflation. 1978. 14.95 (ISBN 0-8157-6474-X); pap. 5.95 (ISBN 0-8157-6473-1). Brookings.
Parkin, Michael & Zis, George, eds. Inflation in the World Economy. (Illus.). 1976. 32.50x (ISBN 0-8020-2223-5). U of Toronto Pr.
Parsson, Jens O. Dying of Money: Lessons of the Great German & American Inflations. LC 73-92727. 372p. 1974. 11.95 (ISBN 0-914688-01-4). Wellspring Pr.
Peterson, Wallace C. Our Overloaded Economy: Inflation, Unemployment & the Crisis in American Capitalism. LC 81-51288. 288p. 1981. 12.95 (ISBN 0-87332-187-1). M E Sharpe.
Phelps, Edmund S. Inflation, Policy & Unemployment Theory. (Illus.). 1972. 15.95x (ISBN 0-393-09395-6). Norton.
Phelps, Edmund S., ed. The Microeconomic Foundations of Employment & Inflation Theory. 1973. 13.95x (ISBN 0-393-09326-3). Norton.
Pick, Franz. The U. S. Dollar: 1940-1980, an Advance Obituary. LC 81-81389. (Illus.). 76p. 1981. pap. 50.00x (ISBN 0-87551-514-2). Pick Pub.
Pierson, John H. Full Employment Without Inflation. LC 79-5446. 254p. 1980. text ed. 18.50 (ISBN 0-916672-39-5). Allanheld.
Piore, Michael J., ed. Unemployment & Inflation: Institutional & Structuralist Views. LC 79-55274. 1980. pap. 7.95 (ISBN 0-87332-165-0). M E Sharpe.
Ratcliffe, Thomas A. & Munter, Paul H. Complete Handbook of Inflation Accounting. LC 80-29378. 260p. 1981. 34.95 (ISBN 0-13-160952-1). P-H.
Riegel, E. C. Flight from Inflation: The Monetary Alternative. MacCallum, Spencer H. & Morton, George, eds. LC 76-25381. (Illus.). 1978. 10.95 (ISBN 0-9600300-9-3); pap. 6.95 (ISBN 0-686-67492-8). Heather Foun.
Robbins, et al. Inflation: Causes, Consequences, Cures. (Institute of Economic Affairs, Readings in Political Economy: No. 14). 1975. 7.50 (ISBN 0-255-36063-0). Transatlantic.
Robbins, Lord. Against Inflation. 1979. text ed. 22.50 (ISBN 0-8419-5047-4). Holmes & Meier.
Roberts, Dick & Jenness, Linda. Inflation: What Causes It, How to Fight It. 1973. pap. 0.25 (ISBN 0-87348-286-7). Path Pr NY.
Rosenn, K. S. Law & Inflation. 1978. write for info. (ISBN 0-685-81205-7, North-Holland). Elsevier.
Rosenn, Keith. Law & Inflation. LC 81-51139. 496p. 1982. 40.00x (ISBN 0-8122-7807-0). U of Pa Pr.
Sarnat, Marshall & Szego, Giorgio. Saving, Investment, & Capital Markets in an Inflationary Economy. Date not set. price not set prof. ref. (ISBN 0-88410-851-1). Ballinger Pub.
Schiff, Eric. Inflation & the Earning Power of Depreciable Assets. LC 74-24728. (Orig.). 1974. pap. 3.25 (ISBN 0-8447-3142-0). Am Enterprise.
Schmukler, Nathan & Marcus, Edward, eds. Inflation Through the Ages: Economic, Social, Psychological, & Historical Aspects. LC 81-65409. (Brooklyn College Studies on Society in Change). 840p. 1981. 42.50x (ISBN 0-930888-12-X). Brooklyn Coll Pr.
Schuettinger, Robert L. & Butler, Eamonn F. Forty Centuries of Wage & Price Control: How Not to Fight Inflation. LC 78-74609. (Policy Studies Ser.). 1979. 9.95 (ISBN 0-685-91292-2); pap. 4.95 (ISBN 0-89195-023-0). Heritage Found.
Schultz, Helen E., intro. by. Economic Calculation Under Inflation. LC 76-9439. 1976. 8.95 (ISBN 0-913966-09-6, Liberty Press). Liberty Fund.
Seed, Allen H. Inflation: Its Impact on Financial Reporting and Decision Making. LC 78-59300. 1978. 3.95 (ISBN 0-910586-24-1). Finan Exec.
Sennholz, Hans. Age of Inflation. (gr. 12). 1979. 8.95 (ISBN 0-88279-234-2); pap. 4.95 (ISBN 0-88279-129-X). Western Islands.
Shama, Avraham. Marketing in a Slow Growth Economy: The Impact of Stagflation on Consumer Psychology. LC 79-26312. (Praeger Special Studies). (Illus.). 184p. 1980. 19.95 (ISBN 0-03-052151-3). Praeger.
Shapiro, Max. The Penniless Billionaires. 1981. 15.00 (ISBN 0-8129-0923-2). Times Bks.
Sheahan, John. The Wage-Price Guideposts. (Studies in Wage-Price Policy). 1967. 11.95 (ISBN 0-8157-7842-2); pap. 4.95 (ISBN 0-8157-7841-4). Brookings.
Sherman, Howard J. Stagflation: A Radical Theory of Unemployment & Inflation. (Illus.). 1976. pap. text ed. 10.50 scp (ISBN 0-06-046106-3, HarpC). Har-Row.
Shulman, Morton. How to Invest Your Money & Profit from Inflation. 1981. pap. 2.50 (ISBN 0-345-29740-7). Ballantine.
Siven, C. H. A Study in the Theory of Inflation & Unemployment. LC 78-24271. (Studies in Monetary Economics: Vol. 4). 1979. 41.50 (ISBN 0-444-85252-2, North Holland). Elsevier.
Slawson, W. David. The New Inflation: The Collapse of Free Markets. 464p. 1981. 16.50x (ISBN 0-691-04229-2). Princeton U Pr.
Smith, Allen W. Understanding Inflation & Unemployment. 2nd ed. LC 75-29492. 176p. 1981. text ed. 15.95x (ISBN 0-88229-276-5); pap. text ed. 7.95x (ISBN 0-88229-492-X). Nelson-Hall.
Smith, Jerome F. The Coming Currency Collapse & What to Do About It! LC 80-66758. (Illus.). 250p. 1980. 13.95 (ISBN 0-916728-41-2). Bks in Focus.
Sommers, Albert T., ed. Answers to Inflation & Recession: Economic Policies for a Modern Society. LC 75-21728. (Report Ser.: No. 666). 154p. (Orig.). 1975. pap. 15.00 (ISBN 0-8237-0083-6). Conference Bd.
Sprinkel, Beryl W. & Genetski, Robert J. Winning with Money, Bk. 144. 244p. Date not set. 10.95 (ISBN 0-686-74999-5). Dow Jones-Irwin.
Staples, Fredrick. Why Inflation. 1977. pap. 2.75 (ISBN 0-915026-22-8). Counting Hse.
Stein, Ben & Stein, Herbert. Moneypower: How to Profit from Inflation. LC 79-2235. 1980. 8.95 (ISBN 0-06-014073-9, HarpT). Har-Row.
Stidger, Howe C. & Ruth, W. Inflation Management: One Hundred Practical Techniques for Business & Industry. LC 80-11271. 448p. 1980. Repr. of 1976 ed. lib. bdg. 19.95 (ISBN 0-89874-132-7). Krieger.
Tanzi, Vito. Inflation & Personal Income Tax. LC 79-52667. 1980. 27.50 (ISBN 0-521-22987-1). Cambridge U Pr.
Tax Institute & Eccles, M. S. Curbing Inflation Through Taxation. facsimile ed. LC 79-128319. (Essay Index Reprint Ser). Repr. of 1944 ed. 17.00 (ISBN 0-8369-2377-4). Arno.
Trade, Inflation & Ethics. LC 75-44723. (Critical Choices for Americans Ser.: Vol. 5). 1976. 18.95 (ISBN 0-669-00419-7). Lexington Bks.
Trevithick, J. A. & Mulvey, C. The Economics of Inflation. LC 75-256. 184p. 1975. 27.95 (ISBN 0-470-88775-3); pap. 14.95x (ISBN 0-470-26894-8). Halsted Pr.
Turner, H. A. & Zoeteweij, H. Prices, Wages & Incomes Policies in Industrialised Market Economics. 3rd ed. (Studies & Reports, New Ser.: No. 70). 1971. 5.70 (ISBN 92-2-100130-X). Intl Labour Office.
Tylecote, Andrew. The Causes of the Present Inflation: An Interdisciplinary Explanation of Inflation in Britain, Germany & the United States. LC 80-15798. 236p. 1981. text ed. 24.95x (ISBN 0-470-26953-7). Halsted Pr.
U. S. Congress - Joint Economic Committee. Employment, Growth & Price Levels, 5 Vols. 1959-1960. Repr. Set. lib. bdg. 115.00x (ISBN 0-8371-2792-0, EMGP). Greenwood.
--Relationship of Prices to Economic Stability & Growth. 1958-1959. Repr. lib. bdg. 29.50x (ISBN 0-8371-2897-8, REOP). Greenwood.
Utley, Jon B. The Inflation Survival Manual. 300p. 1981. 12.95 (ISBN 0-89803-042-0). Caroline Hse.
Wanless, P. T. & Forrester, D. A., eds. Readings in Inflation Accounting. LC 79-40741. 1979. 48.95 (ISBN 0-471-27657-X, Pub. by Wiley-Interscience). Wiley.
Ward, George K. Fires of Inflation. 1981. 6.95 (ISBN 0-533-04677-7). Vantage.
Weintraub, Sidney. Capitalism's Inflation & Unemployment Crisis. LC 77-73955. (Economics Ser.). (Illus.). 7.95 (ISBN 0-201-08502-X). A-W.
--Classical Keynesianism: Monetary Theory & the Price Level. LC 72-2573. (Illus.). 190p. 1961. Repr. lib. bdg. 18.75x (ISBN 0-8371-6421-4, WECK). Greenwood.
--Keynes, Keynesians, & Monetarists. LC 77-20307. (Illus.). 1978. pap. 9.95x (ISBN 0-8122-7741-4). U of Pa Pr.
West, Christopher J. Inflation: A Management Guide to Company Survival. 155p. 1976. 29.50 (ISBN 0-470-15087-4). Halsted Pr.
Wiegand, G. C., ed. Inflation & Monetary Crisis. 1975. pap. 4.50 (ISBN 0-8183-0138-4). Pub Aff Pr.
--The Menace of Inflation: It's Causes & Consequences. 1976. pap. 8.95 (ISBN 0-8159-6240-1). Devin.
Wiegand, G. Carl, ed. Inflation & Unemployment: Twelve American Economists Discuss the Unemployment Problem. LC 79-55282. (Orig.). 1980. pap. 8.95 (ISBN 0-8159-5825-0). Devin.
Wildman, M. S. Money Inflation in the United States: A Study in Social Pathology. 1977. lib. bdg. 69.95 (ISBN 0-8490-2276-2). Gordon Pr.
Wildman, Murray S. Money Inflation in the United States: A Study in Social Pathology. Repr. lib. bdg. 14.50x (ISBN 0-8371-1408-X, WIMI). Greenwood.
Wolfgang, Marvin E. & Lambert, Richard D., eds. Social Effects of Inflation. (The Annals of the American Academy of Political & Social Science: No. 456). 250p. 1981. 7.50 (ISBN 0-87761-264-1); pap. 6.00 (ISBN 0-87761-265-X). Am Acad Pol Soc Sci.
Woll, Artur. Inflation. 180p. 1980. 20.00x (ISBN 0-906237-09-2). Nichols Pub.
Woodward, Donald B. & Rose, Marc A. Inflation. 1979. Repr. of 1933 ed. lib. bdg. 25.00 (ISBN 0-8495-5825-5). Arden Lib.

INFLATION (FINANCE)–CHINA

Chou Shun-Hsin. The Chinese Inflation, Nineteen Thirty-Seven to Nineteen Forty-Nine. LC 62-18260. (Studies of the East Asian Institute). 1963. 18.50x (ISBN 0-231-02565-3). Columbia U Pr.
Why China Has No Inflation. 1976. pap. 1.00 (ISBN 0-8351-0429-X). China Bks.

INFLATION (FINANCE)–FRANCE

see also Assignats

The Moneymakers: A True Story of Government-Created Inflation. 1978. pap. 5.00 (ISBN 0-87651-209-0). Southern U Pr.

INFLATION (FINANCE)–GERMANY

Sennholz, Hans. Age of Inflation. (gr. 12). 1979. 8.95 (ISBN 0-88279-234-2); pap. 4.95 (ISBN 0-88279-129-X). Western Islands.

INFLATION (FINANCE)–GREAT BRITAIN

Smith, Anthony D., ed. Labour Market & Inflation. LC 68-10752. (International Institute for Labour Studies Ser.). (Illus.). 1968. 19.95 (ISBN 0-312-46305-7). St Martin.

INFLATION (FINANCE)–LATIN AMERICA

Pazos, Felipe. Chronic Inflation in Latin America. LC 71-180848. (Special Studies in International Economics & Development). 1972. 24.50x (ISBN 0-275-28282-1). Irvington.
Sherman, Howard. Estanflacion. (Span.). 1980. pap. text ed. 7.60 (ISBN 0-06-317152-X, Pub. by HarLA Mexico). Har-Row.
Wachter, Susan. Latin American Inflation. LC 75-3829. 1976. 17.95 (ISBN 0-669-99622-X). Lexington Bks.

INFLATION (FINANCE)–NEAR EAST

Lloyd, E. M. Food & Inflation in the Middle East, 1940-45. 1956. 15.00x (ISBN 0-8047-0468-6). Stanford U Pr.

INFLUENCE (PSYCHOLOGY)

see also Conformity; Imitation; Persuasion (Psychology)

Battista, O. A. People Power. LC 76-58684. Orig. Title: The Power to Influence People. pap. 8.95 (ISBN 0-915074-07-9). Research Servs Corp.
Claus, Karen E. & Bailey, June T. Power & Influence in Health Care: A New Approach to Leadership. LC 76-57769. (Illus.). 1977. pap. 10.95 (ISBN 0-8016-0417-6). Mosby.
Cohen, Arthur R. Attitude Change & Social Influence. LC 64-22400. 1964. text ed. 8.95x (ISBN 0-465-00565-9). Basic.
Gamson, William A. Power & Discontent. (Orig.). 1968. pap. text ed. 10.50x (ISBN 0-256-01101-X). Dorsey.
Hermeren, Goran. Influence in Art & Literature. LC 73-2466. (Illus.). 340p. 1975. write for info. (ISBN 0-691-07194-2). Princeton U Pr.
Higbee, Kenneth L. & Jensen, Larry C. Influence: What It Is & How to Use It. LC 77-12933. (Illus.). 1978. pap. 0.90 (ISBN 0-8425-0748-5). Brigham.
Snook, I. A. Indoctrination & Education. (Students Library of Education). 1972. 15.00x (ISBN 0-7100-7222-8). Routledge & Kegan.
--Indoctrination & Education. (Students of Library Education). 1975. pap. 7.95 (ISBN 0-7100-8163-4). Routledge & Kegan.
Sparkman, R. B. The Art of Manipulation: How to Get What You Want Out of People in Business, in Your Personal Life, & in Your Love Life. 1979. 6.95 (ISBN 0-8037-0775-4). Dial.
Tedeschi, James T., ed. Social Influence Processes. LC 79-169507. (Treatises in Social Psychology Ser.). 1972. 20.95 (ISBN 0-202-25012-1). Beresford Bk Serv.
Wheeler, Ladd, et al. Interpersonal Influence. 2nd ed. 1978. pap. text ed. 11.95 (ISBN 0-205-06061-7). Allyn.

INFLUENCE LINES

Anger, Georg & Tramm, Karl. Deflection Ordinates for Single Span & Continuous Beams. Amerongen, C. V., tr. LC 65-20500. 1965. 10.50 (ISBN 0-8044-4056-5). Ungar.
Molkenthin, A. Influence Surfaces of Two-Span Continuous Plates with Free Longitudinal Edges. dual language ed. (Illus.). 220p. (Eng, Ger.). 1971. 75.60 (ISBN 0-387-05212-7). Springer Verlag.

INFLUENZA

see also Myxoviruses

Beare, A. S., ed. Recent Influenza Research & Progress Towards Epidemiological Control. 288p. 1982. price not set (ISBN 0-8493-6250-4). CRC Pr.
Beveridge, W. I. Influenza: the Last Great Plague: An Unfinished Story of Discovery. 2nd ed. LC 77-2971. 1977. 10.95 (ISBN 0-88202-125-7). N Watson.
Choppin, P. W. & Douglas, R. G. Hospital Practice: Status Report on Influenza. LC 76-46736. (Illus.). 1977. pap. text ed. 2.50 (ISBN 0-913800-08-2). HP Pub Co.
Crosby, Alfred W., Jr. Epidemic & Peace, 1918. LC 75-23861. (Illus.). 337p. 1976. lib. bdg. 17.50x (ISBN 0-8371-8376-6, CPD/). Greenwood.
Hoyle, L. Influenza Viruses. (Virology Monographs: Vol. 4). (Illus.). 1968. 54.30 (ISBN 0-387-80892-2). Springer-Verlag.
International Association of Biological Standardization, 39th Symposium, Institute of Child Health, London November 1972. Influenza Vaccines for Men & Horses: Proceedings. Regamey, R. H. & Perkins, F. T., eds. (Immunobiological Standardization: Vol. 20). 406p. 1973. 45.00 (ISBN 3-8055-1674-6). S Karger.
International Conference on Hong Kong Influenza, Atlanta, Ga. 1969. Proceedings: Bulletin of WHO. (Vol. 41, Nos. 3-5). 414p. 1969. pap. 14.40 (ISBN 0-686-09014-4, 797). World Health.
Kilbourne, Edwin D., ed. The Influenza Viruses & Influenza. 1975. 60.50 (ISBN 0-12-407050-7). Acad Pr.
Laver, W. G. & Bachmayer, H., eds. The Influenza Virus Haemagglutinin. LC 77-17581. (Topics in Infectious Diseases: Vol 3). (Illus.). 1978. pap. 28.80 (ISBN 0-387-81459-0). Springer-Verlag.
Osborn, June, ed. Influenza in America 1918-1976: History, Science, & Politics. LC 77-14344. 1977. lib. bdg. 12.00 (ISBN 0-88202-176-1). N Watson.
Oxford. Chemotherapy & Control of Influenza. 1976. pap. 18.00 (ISBN 0-12-531750-6). Acad Pr.
Royal Society, et al. Influenza: Proceedings. (Royal Society Ser.). (Illus.). 172p. 1980. lib. bdg. 50.00x (ISBN 0-85403-138-3, Pub. by Royal Soc London). Scholium Intl.
Selby, P., ed. Influenza: Virus Vaccines & Strategy. 1976. 26.50 (ISBN 0-12-635950-4). Acad Pr.
Sell, Sarah H. & Karzon, David T., eds. Hemophilus influenzae: Proceedings of a Conference on Antigen-Antibody Systems, Epidemiology, & Immuno/Prophylaxis. LC 73-4557. (Illus.). 325p. 1973. 15.00x (ISBN 0-8265-1185-6). Vanderbilt U Pr.
Stuart-Harris, Charles H. Influenza: The Viruses & the Disease. LC 76-26808. 1976. 24.50 (ISBN 0-88416-124-2). Wright-PSG.

Symposium Organized by the International Association of Biological Standardization, 53rd, Geneva, 1977. International Symposium on Influenza Immunization: Proceedings. Perkins, F. T & Regamey, R. H., eds. (Developments in Biological Standardization: Vol. 39). (Illus.). 1977. 59.50 (ISBN 3-8055-2786-1). S Karger.

Winternitz, Milton C. Pathology of Influenza. (Illus.). 1920. 100.00x (ISBN 0-685-69886-6). Elliots Bks.

INFORMATION, FREEDOM OF
see Freedom of Information

INFORMATION, GOVERNMENT
see Government Information

INFORMATION CENTERS
see Information Services

INFORMATION DISPLAY SYSTEMS
see also Cathode Ray Tubes

Automated Education Center. Data Display Programming. LC 77-118118. 275p. 29.00 (ISBN 0-686-01994-6). Mgmt Info Serv.

Biberman, L. M., ed. Perception of Displayed Information. LC 72-97695. (Optical Physics & Engineering Ser.). (Illus.). 345p. 1973. 35.00 (ISBN 0-306-30724-3, Plenum Pr). Plenum Pub.

Blaser, A., ed. Data Base Techniques for Pictorial Applications. (Lecture Notes in Computer Sciences: Vol. 81). 599p. 1980. pap. 34.90 (ISBN 0-387-09763-5). Springer-Verlag.

Cakir, A., et al. Visual Display Terminals: A Manual Covering Ergonomics, Workplace Design, Health & Safety, Task Organization. LC 80-40070. 328p. 1980. 53.95 (ISBN 0-471-27793-2, Pub. by Wiley-Interscience). Wiley.

International Handbook of Liquid Crystal Displays 1975-1976. 2nd ed. 1976. 85.00x (ISBN 0-903969-14-9). Scholium Intl.

Jury, Eliahu I. Inners & Stability of Dynamic Systems. 320p. 1981. Repr. of 1974 ed. write for info. (ISBN 0-89874-341-9). Krieger.

Lancaster, Don. TV Typewriter Cookbook. LC 75-46215. 1976. pap. 9.95 (ISBN 0-672-21313-3). Sams.

Lee, Kaiman. Evaluation of Computer Graphic Terminals. 2nd ed. LC 74-184824. 92p. 1975. 12.00 (ISBN 0-915250-11-X). Environ Design.

Leondes, C. T., ed. Advances in Control & Dynamic Systems: Theory & Application, Vol. 17. (Serial Publication). 1981. 32.50 (ISBN 0-12-012717-2). Acad Pr.

Luenberger, David G. Introduction to Dynamic Systems: Theory, Models & Applications. LC 78-12366. 1979. 26.95 (ISBN 0-471-02594-1). Wiley.

Sherr, Solomon, ed. Fundamentals of Display System Design. LC 78-96045. 1970. 46.00 (ISBN 0-471-78570-9, Pub. by Wiley-Interscience). Wiley.

Thomas, Harry. Handbook of Information Display Devices. 1981. 24.95 (ISBN 0-8359-2743-1). Reston.

Tracton, Ken. Display Electronics. (Illus.). 1977. 11.95 (ISBN 0-8306-7861-1); pap. 6.95 (ISBN 0-8306-6861-6, 861). TAB Bks.

INFORMATION MEASUREMENT

Beauchamp, K. G. & Yuen, C. K. Digital Methods for Signal Analysis. (Illus.). 1979. text ed. 35.00x (ISBN 0-04-621027-X). Allen Unwin.

Bowen, B. A. & Brown, W. R. VLSI Systems Design for Digital Signal Processing, Vol. 1: Signal Processing & Signal Processors. (Illus.). 256p. 1982. text ed. 27.50 (ISBN 0-13-942706-6). P-H.

Feltham, Gerald A. Information Evaluation, Vol. 5. (Studies in Accounting Research). 149p. 1972. 6.00 (ISBN 0-686-31098-5). Am Accounting.

Fidelity & Security of Measurement - Data Transmission Systems. 32p. Date not set. 8.00 (ISBN 0-686-76111-1, 13-110000-12). ASTM.

Papoulis, Athanasios. Signal Analysis. 1977. text ed. 32.95 (ISBN 0-07-048460-0, C). McGraw.

INFORMATION NETWORKS, LIBRARY
see Library Information Networks

INFORMATION PROCESSING, HUMAN
see Human Information Processing

INFORMATION SCIENCE
see also Documentation; Electronic Data Processing; Information Services; Information Storage and Retrieval Systems; Library Science

Adams, Elizabeth B., ed. Management of Information Technology - Case Studies. 1975. pap. text ed. 11.95x (ISBN 0-442-80286-2). Van Nos Reinhold.

American Association for Information Science Annual Meeting 1979. Information Choices & Policies: Proceedings, Vol.16. Tally, Roy D., compiled by. LC 64-8303. 1979. 19.50 (ISBN 0-914236-47-4). Knowledge Indus.

ASIS Annual Meeting, 37th. Information Utilities: Proceedings. Zunde, Pranas, ed. LC 64-8303. (Proceedings of the ASIS Annual Meeting Ser: Vol. 11). 278p. 1974. 17.50 (ISBN 0-87715-411-2). Am Soc Info Sci.

ASIS Annual Meeting 38th. Information Revolution: Proceedings. Husbands, Charles & Tighe, Ruth, eds. LC 64-8303. (Annual Meeting Ser.: Vol. 12). 1975. 17.50 (ISBN 0-87715-412-0). Am Soc Info Sci.

ASIS Annual Meeting, 43rd, 1980. Communicating Information: Proceedings, Vol. 17. Benenfeld, Alan R., ed. LC 64-8303. (Illus.). 417p. 1980. 19.50 (ISBN 0-914236-73-3, American Society for Information Science). Knowledge Indus.

ASIS Annual Meeting,1977. Information Management in the 1980's: Proceedings, Vol. 14. LC 64-8303. 1977. pap. 17.50x (ISBN 0-914236-12-1). Knowledge Indus.

ASIS Handbook & Directory. 1975. 50.00 (ISBN 0-87715-506-2). Am Soc Info Sci.

ASIS Mid-Year Meeting, 4th. Information Roundup on Microforms & Data Processing in the Library & Information Center: Costs-Benefits-History-Trends-Proceedings. Spigai, Frances, et al, eds. LC 75-29520. 1975. 14.00 (ISBN 0-87715-112-1). Am Soc Info Sci.

ASIS Workshop on Computer Composition. Proceedings. Landau, Robert M., ed. LC 78-151299. 1971. 12.50 (ISBN 0-87715-002-8). Am Soc Info Sci.

Aspen Systems Corporation. Collective Index to the Journal of the American Society for Information Science Vol. 1-25, 1950-1974. LC 75-34696. 1975. 60.00 (ISBN 0-87715-113-X). Am Soc Info Sci.

Becker, Hal B. Functional Analysis of Information Networks: Astructured Approach to the Data Communications Environment. LC 80-15347. 296p. 1981. Repr. of 1973 ed. lib. bdg. write for info. (ISBN 0-89874-028-2). Krieger.

Blum, E. K., et al, eds. Mathematical Studies of Information Processing: Proceedings, International Conference, Kyoto, Japan, August 23-26, 1978. (Lecture Notes in Computer Science: Vol. 75). 1979. pap. 32.30 (ISBN 0-387-09541-1). Springer-Verlag.

Brenner, Everett, ed. The Information Age in Perspective: Proceedings of the ASIS Annual Meeting, 1978, Vol. 15. LC 64-8303. 1978. pap. 17.50x (ISBN 0-914236-22-9). Knowledge Indus.

Burch, J. G., et al. Information Systems: Theory & Practice. 2nd ed. 571p. 1979. 25.95 (ISBN 0-471-12322-6). Wiley.

CISM (International Center for Mechanical Sciences), Dept of Automation & Information. Quantitative-Qualitative Measure of Information. Longo, G., ed. (CISM Pubns. Ser.: No. 138). (Illus.). 51p. 1973. pap. 8.80 (ISBN 0-387-81182-6). Springer-Verlag.

Computer Science and Engineering Board. Libraries & Information Technology: A System Challenge. 96p. (Orig.). 1972. pap. text ed. 3.50 (ISBN 0-309-01938-9). Natl Acad Pr.

Courtney, James F., Jr. & Jensen, Ronald. The Systems Laboratory for Information Management. 1981. pap. 4.50x (ISBN 0-686-73764-4). Business Pubns.

Cuadra, Carlos & Luke, Ann W., eds. The Annual Review of Information Science & Technology, Vol. 5, 1970. LC 66-25096. 1970. 35.00 (ISBN 0-85229-156-6). Knowledge Indus.

Cuadra, Carlos, et al, eds. Annual Review of Information Science & Technology, Vol. 10. LC 66-25096. 1975. 27.50 (ISBN 0-87715-210-1). Am Soc Info Sci.

Cuadra, Carlos A. The Annual Review of Information Science & Technology, Vol 10, 1975. Luke, Ann W., ed. LC 66-25096. 1975. 35.00 (ISBN 0-686-67625-4). Knowledge Indus.

Cuadra, Carlos A., ed. The Annual Review of Information Science & Technology, Vol. 3, 1968. LC 66-25096. (Illus.). 1968. 35.00 (ISBN 0-685-94669-X). Knowledge Indus.

Cuadra, Carlos A. & Luke, Ann W., eds. The Annual Review of Information Science & Technology, Vol. 4, 1969. LC 66-25096. 1969. 35.00 (ISBN 0-85229-147-7). Knowledge Indus.

--The Annual Review of Information Science & Technology, Vol. 7, 1972. LC 66-25096. (Illus.). 1972. 35.00 (ISBN 0-87715-206-3). Knowledge Indus.

--The Annual Review of Information Science & Technology, Vol. 8, 1973. LC 66-25096. 1973. 35.00 (ISBN 0-87715-208-X). Knowledge Indus.

--The Annual Review of Information Science & Technology, Vol. 9, 1974. LC 66-25096. (Illus.). 1974. 35.00 (ISBN 0-87715-209-8). Knowledge Indus.

Davis, Charles H. & Rush, James E. Guide to Information Science. LC 78-75240. (Illus.). 1979. lib. bdg. 25.00 (ISBN 0-313-20982-0, DGI/). Greenwood.

Division of Science Information, National Science Foundation. Current Research on Scientific & Technical Information Transfer. LC 77-9216. (Micropapers Editions Ser). 1977. 12.95x (ISBN 0-88432-007-3). J Norton Pubs.

Donohue, Joseph C. Understanding Scientific Literatures: A Bibliometric Approach. (Illus.). 101p. 1974. 14.50x (ISBN 0-262-04039-5). MIT Pr.

Dordick, Herbert S., et al. The Emerging Network Marketplace. (Communication & Information Science Ser.). 288p. 1981. 29.50 (ISBN 0-89391-036-8). Ablex Pub.

Doyle, James M. & Grimes, George H. Reference Resources: A Systematic Approach. LC 76-7080. 1976. 12.00 (ISBN 0-8108-0928-1). Scarecrow.

Duffy, Neil & Assad, Mike. Information Management: An Executive Approach. (Illus.). 224p. 1980. 34.50x (ISBN 0-19-570190-9). Oxford U Pr.

Edelstein, Alex S., et al, eds. Information Societies: Comparing the Japanese & American Experiences. LC 78-71366. (Illus.). 1978. pap. 10.95 (ISBN 0-933236-00-X). Intl Comm Ctr.

Elias, Arthur W., ed. Key Papers in Information Science. LC 78-162999. (Key Papers Ser). 1971. 10.00 (ISBN 0-87715-101-6). Am Soc Info Sci.

Facts on File Yearbook, 1980. Date not set. 65.00 (ISBN 0-87196-039-7). Facts on File.

Garfield, Eugene. Essays of an Information Scientist, 3 vols. LC 77-602. Vols. 1 & 2 (1962-1976) 25.00 (ISBN 0-89495-001-0); Vol. 3 (1977-1978) 15.00 (ISBN 0-89495-000-2, EOIS2W). Vol. 3. ISI Pr.

--Essays of an Information Scientist, 3 vols. 1980. Set. 35.00 (ISBN 0-89495-000-2). ISI Pr.

--Essays of an Information Scientist, Vol. 3. 1980. 15.00 (ISBN 0-89495-009-6). ISI Pr.

--Essays of an Information Scientist, Vol. 4. (Illus.). 754p. 1981. price not set (ISBN 0-89495-012-6). ISI Pr.

Garvey, William D. Communication: The Essence of Science Facilitating Information Exchange Among Librarians, Scientists, Engineers, & Students. 1978. text ed. 49.00 (ISBN 0-08-022254-4); pap. text ed. 19.50 (ISBN 0-08-023344-9). Pergamon.

Griffith, Belver C., ed. Key Papers in Information Science. LC 79-24288. 439p. 1980. text ed. 25.00 (ISBN 0-914236-50-4, ASIS). Knowledge Indus.

Harris, Jessica L., ed. Cumulative Index to the Annual Review of Information Science & Technology, Vol. 1-10. LC 66-25096. 250p. 1976. lexhide 27.50 (ISBN 0-685-56510-6). Am Soc Info Sci.

Harris, Jessica L., et al, eds. Cumulative Index to the Annual Review of Information Science & Technology, Vols.1-10, 1966-1975. LC 66-25096. 1976. 35.00 (ISBN 0-87715-211-X). Knowledge Indus.

Horn, R. E. How to Write Information Mapping. 1976. 50.00 (ISBN 0-912864-05-2). Info Res Inc.

Information Transfer - ISO Standards Handbook 1. 1979. pap. 15.00 (ISBN 92-67-10017-3, UM40, UNESCO). Unipub.

International Conference on Information Sciences & Systems, 1st, Patras, Greece, Aug. 1976. Applications & Research in Information Systems & Sciences: Proceedings, 3 vols. new ed. Lainiotis, Demetrios G. & Tzannes, Nicolaos, eds. LC 77-15000. (Illus.). 1977. pap. text ed. 120.00 set (ISBN 0-89116-160-0). Hemisphere Pub.

International Research Forum on Information Science, 2nd, Royal School Librarianship, Copenhagen, Aug. 1977. Theory & Application of Information Research: Proceedings. Harbo, Ole & Kajberg, Leif, eds. 272p. 1981. text ed. 35.00 (ISBN 0-7201-1513-2, Pub. by Mansell England). Merrimack Bk. Serv.

Isis (Integrated Scientific Information System) A General Description of an Approach to Computerized Bibliographical Control. 3rd ed. 1973. 4.55 (ISBN 92-2-100113-X). Intl Labour Office.

Kent, et al. Encyclopedia of Library & Information Science, Vol. 29. 450p. 1980. 45.00 (ISBN 0-8247-2029-6). Dekker.

--Encyclopedia of Library & Information Science, Vol. 31. 512p. 1981. 45.00 (ISBN 0-8247-2031-8). Dekker.

--Encyclopedia of Library & Information Science, Vol. 32. 416p. 1981. 55.00 (ISBN 0-686-72689-8). Dekker.

--Encyclopedia of Library & Information Science, Vol. 33. 400p. 1981. price not set (ISBN 0-8247-2033-4). Dekker.

Kent, A., et al, eds. Encyclopedia of Library & Information Science, Vols. 29-31. 45.00 ea. Vol. 29 (ISBN 0-8247-2129-2). Vol. 30 (ISBN 0-8247-2130-6). Vol. 31 (ISBN 0-8247-2131-4). Dekker.

--Encyclopedia of Library & Information Science, Vol. 27. 1979. 45.00 (ISBN 0-8247-2127-6). Dekker.

Kent, Allen, et al, eds. Encyclopedia of Library & Information Science, Vol. 1. 1968. 45.00 (ISBN 0-8247-2101-2). Dekker.

--Encyclopedia of Library & Information Science, Vol. 2. 1969. 45.00 (ISBN 0-8247-2102-0). Dekker.

--Encyclopedia of Library & Information Science, Vol. 3. 1970. 45.00 (ISBN 0-8247-2103-9). Dekker.

--Encyclopedia of Library & Information Science, Vol. 4. 1970. 45.00 (ISBN 0-8247-2104-7). Dekker.

--Encyclopedia of Library & Information Science, Vol. 5. 1971. 45.00 (ISBN 0-8247-2105-5). Dekker.

--Encyclopedia of Library & Information Science, Vol. 6. 1971. 45.00 (ISBN 0-8247-2106-3). Dekker.

--Encyclopedia of Library & Information Science, Vol. 7. 1972. 45.00 (ISBN 0-8247-2107-1). Dekker.

--Encyclopedia of Library & Information Science, Vol. 8. 1972. 45.00 (ISBN 0-8247-2108-X). Dekker.

--Encyclopedia of Library & Information Science, Vol. 9. 1973. 45.00 (ISBN 0-8247-2109-8). Dekker.

--Encyclopedia of Library & Information Science, Vol. 10. 1973. 45.00 (ISBN 0-8247-2110-1). Dekker.

--Encyclopedia of Library & Information Science, Vol. 11. 1974. 45.00 (ISBN 0-8247-2111-X). Dekker.

--Encyclopedia of Library & Information Science, Vol. 12. 1974. 45.00 (ISBN 0-8247-2112-8). Dekker.

--Encyclopedia of Library & Information Science, Vol. 13. 1975. 45.00 (ISBN 0-8247-2113-6). Dekker.

--Encyclopedia of Library & Information Science, Vol. 14. 1975. 45.00 (ISBN 0-8247-2114-4). Dekker.

--Encyclopedia of Library & Information Science, Vol. 15. 1975. 45.00 (ISBN 0-8247-2115-2). Dekker.

--Encyclopedia of Library & Information Science, Vol. 16. 1975. 45.00 (ISBN 0-8247-2116-0). Dekker.

Kilgour. The Library & Information Science CumIndex, Vol. 7. LC 72-86076. 1976. 55.00 (ISBN 0-88274-006-7). R & D Pr.

King, Donald W., ed. Key Papers in the Design & Evaluation of Information Systems. LC 78-23449. (Illus.). 1978. 25.00 (ISBN 0-914236-31-8). Knowledge Indus.

Klapp, O. E. Opening & Closing. LC 77-87382. (A.S.A. Rose Monograph Ser.). (Illus.). 1978. 19.95 (ISBN 0-521-21923-X); pap. 6.95x (ISBN 0-521-29311-1). Cambridge U Pr.

Kochen, Manfred. Integrative Mechanisms in Literature Growth. LC 72-815. (Contributions in Librarianship & Information Science: No. 9). 1974. lib. bdg. 16.95 (ISBN 0-8371-6384-6, KIM/). Greenwood.

Kohonen, T. Content-Addressable Memories. (Springer Ser. in Information Sciences: Vol. 1). (Illus.). 400p. 1980. 39.00 (ISBN 0-387-09823-2). Springer-Verlag.

Kunz, Werner, et al. Methods of Analysis & Evaluation of Information Needs. 84p. 1976. text ed. 18.00 (ISBN 3-7940-3450-3, Pub. by K G Saur). Shoe String.

Lainiotis, D. G. & Tzannes, N. S., eds. A Selection of Papers from Info II, 3 vols. 1980. lib. bdg. 47.50 ea. (Pub. by Reidel Holland). Vol. 1, 530p (ISBN 90-277-1140-2). Vol. 2, 600p (ISBN 90-277-1129-1). Vol. 3, 530p (ISBN 90-277-1143-7). Kluwer Boston.

Lilley, Dorothy B. & Badough, Rose M., eds. Library & Information Sciences: A Guide to Information Sources. (Bks., Libraries, & Publishing Information Guide Ser.: Vol. 5). 200p. 1981. 36.00 (ISBN 0-8103-1501-7). Gale.

Martin, Susan K., ed. Information Politics: Proceedings of the ASIS 39th Annual Meeting. LC 64-8303. (Annual Meeting Ser.: Vol. 13). 1976. 17.50 (ISBN 0-87715-413-9). Am Soc Info Sci.

Matsuo, T. Realization Theory of Continuous-Time Dynamical Systems. (Lecture Notes in Control & Information Sciences Ser.: Vol. 32). 329p. 1981. pap. 17.40 (ISBN 0-387-10682-0). Springer-Verlag.

Miller, Mara. Where to Go for What: How to Research, Organize & Present Your Information. (Illus.). 240p. 1981. 11.95 (ISBN 0-13-957217-1, Spec); pap. 5.95 (ISBN 0-13-957209-0). P-H.

The Nationwide Provision & Use of Information. 1981. pap. 28.75 (ISBN 0-85365-563-4). Oryx Pr.

Nieman, H. Pattern Analysis. (Springer Series in Information Sciences: Vol. 4). (Illus.). 305p. 1981. 39.00 (ISBN 0-387-10792-4). Springer-Verlag.

Pugh, Eric. Third Dictionary of Acronyms & Abbreviations: More Abbreviations in Management, Technology, & Information Science. 1977. 17.50 (ISBN 0-208-01535-3, Linnet). Shoe String.

Ralston, Anthony, ed. Encyclopedia of Computer Science. 1976. 60.00 (ISBN 0-442-80321-4). Van Nos Reinhold.
Roth, Robert A. How to Conduct Surveys, Follow-up Studies, & Basic Data Collection in Evaluation Studies. (Illus.). 132p. (Orig.). 1981. pap. text ed. 8.75 (ISBN 0-8191-1650-5). U Pr of Amer.
Rowley, J. E. & Turner, C. M. The Dissemination of Information. LC 78-6138. (Grafton Library of Information Science). 1978. lib. bdg. 30.75x (ISBN 0-89158-830-2). Westview.
Rudman, Jack. Information Specialist 1. (Career Examination Ser.: C-1867). (Cloth bdg. avail. on request). pap. 8.00 (ISBN 0-8373-1867-X). Natl Learning.
--Information Specialist 2. (Career Examination Ser.: C-1868). (Cloth bdg. avail. on request). 10.00 (ISBN 0-8373-1868-8). Natl Learning.
Sager, Naomi. Natural Language Information Processing: A Computer Grammmar of English & Its Applications. 1980. text ed. 37.50 (ISBN 0-201-06769-2). A-W.
Salton, Gerard. Dynamic Information & Library Processing. (Illus.). 416p. 1975. ref. ed. 27.95 (ISBN 0-13-221325-7). P-H.
Schatz, Anne E. & Funk, Berverley M. Transcription Skills for Information Processing, Unit 2. 112p. 1981. pap. text ed. 2.92 (ISBN 0-07-055201-0, G); tchrs. manual & key 2.40 (ISBN 0-07-055212-6); cassettes 105.00 (ISBN 0-07-087832-3). McGraw.
Schatz, Anne E. & Funk, Beverley M. Transcription Skills for Information Processing, Unit 1. 96p. 1981. pap. text ed. 2.92 (ISBN 0-07-055200-2, G); cassettes 105.00 (ISBN 0-07-087831-5). McGraw.
Schutze, Gertrude. Information & Library Science Source Book: Supplement to Documentation Source Book. LC 72-1157. 1972. 16.50 (ISBN 0-8108-0466-2). Scarecrow.
Setty, K. Umapathy. Information Sources: An International Selective Guide. 1978. 12.50 (ISBN 0-7069-0628-4, Pub. by Vikas India). Advent NY.
Slamecka, V. & Borka, H., eds. Planning & Organisation of National Research Programs in Information Science. (Illus.). 83p. 1981. pap. 27.50 (ISBN 0-08-026472-7). Pergamon.
Smith, Anthony. The Geopolitics of Information: How Western Culture Dominates the World. 192p. 1981. pap. 4.95 (ISBN 0-19-520274-0, GB 655). Oxford U Pr.
--The Politics of Information: Problems of Policy of Modern Media. (Communication & Culture Ser.). 1978. text ed. 25.00x (ISBN 0-333-23610-6); pap. text ed. 10.50x (ISBN 0-333-23611-4). Humanities.
Sparck Jones, Karen & Kay, Martin. Linguistic & Information Science. (Library & Information Science Ser.). 244p. 1974. 27.50 (ISBN 0-12-656250-4). Acad Pr.
Symposium, 4th, Marianske Lazne, Sept. 1-5, 1975. Mathematical Foundations of Computer Science. Becvar, J., ed. (Lecture Notes in Computer Science: Vol. 32). x, 476p. 1975. pap. 21.40 (ISBN 0-387-07389-2). Springer-Verlag.
Systems & Policy: The Function of Information in Improving Education Systems. 1979. pap. 4.50 (ISBN 92-3-101522-2, U846, UNESCO). Unipub.
Thompson, Gordon B. Memo from Mercury: Information Technology Is Different. 62p. 1979. pap. text ed. 3.00x (ISBN 0-920380-29-8, Pub. by Inst Res Pub Canada). Renouf.
Tou, Julius T., ed. Advances in Information Systems Science. Incl. Vol. 1. 292p. 1969. 35.00 (ISBN 0-306-39401-4); Vol. 2. 479p. 1969. 35.00 (ISBN 0-306-39402-2); Vol. 3. 354p. 1970. 35.00 (ISBN 0-306-39403-0); Vol. 4. 330p. 1972. 35.00 (ISBN 0-306-39404-9); Vol. 5. 343p. 1974. 35.00 (ISBN 0-306-39405-7); Vol. 6. 209p. 1976. 35.00 (ISBN 0-306-39406-5); Vol. 7. 300p. 1978. 27.50 (ISBN 0-306-39407-3). LC 69-12544. (Illus., Plenum Pr). Plenum Pub.
--Advances in Information Systems Science, Vol. 8. 375p. 1981. text ed. price not set (ISBN 0-306-40714-0, Plenum Pr). Plenum Pub.
Trauth, E. M. & Debons, A., eds. Information Science: The Contemporary Issues. (Bks. in Lib. & Info. Sci.). 1980. cancelled (ISBN 0-8247-6853-1). Dekker.
The Use of Medical Literature. 1981. 21.00x (ISBN 0-905984-51-X, Pub. by Brit Lib England). State Mutual Bk.
User Education in Schools: A Survey of the Literature on Education for Information Use in Schools. 1981. 15.00x (ISBN 0-686-72513-1, Pub. by Brit Lib England). State Mutual Bk.
Vaillancourt, Pauline M. International Directory of Acronyms in Library, Information & Computer Sciences. 1980. 45.00 (ISBN 0-8352-1152-5). Bowker.
Vickery, B. C. Technique of Information Retrieval. 1970. 15.00 (ISBN 0-208-00983-3, Archon). Shoe String.
Vidyasagar, M. Input-Output Analysis of Large-Scale Interconnected Systems. (Lecture Notes in Control & Information Sciences Ser.: Vol. 29). 225p. 1981. pap. 16.50 (ISBN 0-387-10501-8). Springer-Verlag.
Wessel, Andrew E. The Social Use of Information: Ownership & Access. LC 76-18211. (Information Sciences Ser.). 1976. 25.50 (ISBN 0-471-93377-5, Pub. by Wiley-Interscience). Wiley.
Williams, James G & Pope, Elspeth. Simulation Activities in Library Communication & Information Science. (Communication Science & Technology Ser.: Vol. 6). 1976. 34.75 (ISBN 0-8247-6376-9). Dekker.
Williams, Martha E., ed. The Annual Review of Information Science & Technology, Vol. 11, 1976. LC 66-25096. (Illus.). 1976. 42.50 (ISBN 0-87715-212-8). Knowledge Indus.
--Annual Review of Information Science & Technology, Vol. 11. LC 66-25096. 1976. 35.00 (ISBN 0-87715-212-8). Am Soc Info Sci.
--Annual Review of Information Science & Technology, Vol. 13. LC 66-25096. 1978. 42.50 (ISBN 0-914236-21-0). Knowledge Indus.
--Annual Review of Information Science & Technology (ARIST) 1980, Vol. 15. LC 66-25096. 400p. 1980. 42.50 (ISBN 0-914236-65-2). Knowledge Indus.
--Annual Review of Information Science & Technology 1977, Vol.12. LC 66-25096. 1977. 42.50 (ISBN 0-914236-11-3). Knowledge Indus.
--Annual Review of Information Science & Techology 1979, Vol. 14. LC 66-25096. 1979. 42.50 (ISBN 0-914236-44-X). Knowledge Indus.
--Annual Review of Information Science & Technology, 1981, Vol. 16. 400p. 1981. text ed. 42.50 (ISBN 0-914236-90-3). Knowledge Indus.
--Annual Review of Information Science & Technology, 1981, Vol. 16. 400p. 1981. text ed. 42.50 (ISBN 0-914236-90-3). Knowledge Indus.
--Information Science & Technology Annual Review, 1981, Vol. 16. 400p. 1981. text ed. 42.50x (ISBN 0-914236-90-3). Knowledge Indus.
Wilson, Patrick. Public Knowledge, Private Ignorance: Toward a Library & Information Policy. LC 76-52327. (Contributions in Librarianship & Information Sciences: No. 10). 1977. lib. bdg. 15.00x (ISBN 0-8371-9485-7, WPN/). Greenwood.

INFORMATION SCIENCE–STUDY AND TEACHING

Lassia, Margaret R. Games for Information Skills. 80p. 1980. pap. text ed. 9.50x (ISBN 0-931510-06-6). Hi Willow.
The Need to Know: Teaching the Importance of Information. 1981. 18.00x (ISBN 0-905984-48-X, Pub. by Brit Lib England). State Mutual Bk.

INFORMATION SERVICES

see also Archives; Bibliographical Services; Documentation; Information Storage and Retrieval Systems; Libraries; Reference Services (Libraries); Research

American National Standards Institute. Standards Committee Z39 on Library Work, Documentation & Related Publishing Practices. American National Standard Structure for the Identification of Countries of the World for Information Interchange, Z39.27. 1976. 2.00 (ISBN 0-686-16672-8). ANSI.
Bailey, Martha J. Supervisory & Middle Managers in Libraries. LC 80-23049. 218p. 1981. 12.00 (ISBN 0-8108-1400-5). Scarecrow.
Boaz, Martha. Strategies for Meeting the Information Needs of Society in the Year 2000. LC 81-11751. 250p. 1981. lib. bdg. 22.50 (ISBN 0-87287-249-1). Libs Unl.
Boss, Richard W. & Maranjian, Lorig. Fee-Based Information Services: The Commercial Sector. 199p. 1980. 24.95 (ISBN 0-8352-1287-4). Bowker.
Carroll, John M. Confidential Information Sources: Public & Private. LC 74-20177. (Illus.). 320p. 1975. 18.95 (ISBN 0-913708-19-4). Butterworth.
Chartrand, Robert L. & Morentz, James W. Information Technology Serving Society. (Illus.). 1979. 35.00 (ISBN 0-08-021979-9). Pergamon.
Chartrand, Robert Lee & Morentz, James W., Jr., eds. Information Technology Serving Society. 1979. 25.00 (ISBN 0-08-021979-9). Chartrand.
Ching-Chih Chen & Hernon, Peter. Information Seeking: Assessing & Anticipating User Needs. 200p. 1981. 19.95x (ISBN 0-918212-50-2). Neal-Schuman.
Clinic on Library Applications of Data Processing, Proceedings, 1975. The Use of Computers in Literature Searching & Related Reference Activities in Libraries. Lancaster, F. W., ed. LC 76-1790. 1976. 8.00 (ISBN 0-87845-043-2). U of Ill Lib Info Sci.
Codlin, Ellen M., ed. ASLIB Directory: Information Sources in Science, Techonology & Commerce, Vol. 1. 4th ed. 634p. 1981. 70.00 (ISBN 0-686-72837-8, Pub by Aslib England). Gale.
--ASLIB Directory: Information Sources in the Social Sciences, Medicine & the Humanities, Vol. 2. 4th ed. 871p. 1981. 135.00 (ISBN 0-686-72838-6, Pub. by Aslib England). Gale.
Directory: Educational Documentation & Information Services. 1978. pap. 3.75 (ISBN 92-3-001565-2, U850, UNESCO). Unipub.
Divided on the Issue: A Directory of Advocacy Groups, Publications, & Information Services. 200p. 1981. pap. 14.95 (ISBN 0-918212-57-X). Neal Schuman.
Donohue, Joseph C. & Kochen, Manfred, eds. Information for the Community. LC 75-40168. 1976. text ed. 12.00 (ISBN 0-8389-0208-1). ALA.
Doyle, L. B. Information Retrieval & Processing. LC 75-1179. (Information Science Ser.). 1975. 32.95 (ISBN 0-471-22151-1, Pub. by Wiley-Interscience). Wiley.
Doyle, P. A. Guide to Basic Information Sources in English Literature. LC 75-43260. (Information ResOurces Ser). 1976. 10.95x (ISBN 0-470-15011-4, Dist. by Halsted). J Norton Pubs.
Drucker, Howard. The Organization & Management of the Resource Room: A Cookbook Approach. (Illus.). 184p. 1976. 18.75 (ISBN 0-398-03538-5). C C Thomas.
Edelstein, Alex S., et al, eds. Information Societies: Comparing the Japanese & American Experiences. LC 78-71366. (Illus.). 1978. pap. 10.95 (ISBN 0-933236-00-X). Intl Comm Ctr.
Evaluation of the Caris Pilot Project. (Illus.). 32p. 1977. pap. 2.00 (ISBN 0-88936-117-7, IDRCT55, IDRC). Unipub.
Fang, Josephine R. & Songe, Alice H. International Guide to Library, Archival, & Information Science Associations. 2nd ed. 448p. 1980. 32.50 (ISBN 0-8352-1285-8). Bowker.
Foskett, D. J., et al, eds. Library Systems & Information Services. (Illus.). 1970. pap. 13.50 (ISBN 0-208-00984-1, Archon). Shoe String.
Gale Information Guide Library. 1981. 36.00 (ISBN 0-686-75530-8). Gale.
Getting Organized: A Directory of Action Alliances, Publications, & Information Services. 200p. 1981. pap. 14.95 (ISBN 0-918212-58-8). Neal Schuman.
Giuliano, Vincent, et al. Into the Information Age: A Perspective for Federal Action on Information. 1979. pap. text ed. 8.00 (ISBN 0-8389-0283-9). ALA.
Gotsick, Pricilla S., et al. Information for Everyday Survival. LC 76-13554. 1976. pap. text ed. 10.00 (ISBN 0-8389-0211-1). ALA.
Harvey, Joan M. Specialised Information Centres. 112p. 1976. 13.50 (ISBN 0-208-01521-3, Linnet). Shoe String.
Herner, Saul & Vellucci, Matthew J., eds. Selected Federal Computer-Based Information Systems. LC 72-85016. (Illus.). ix, 215p. 1972. text ed. 15.00 (ISBN 0-87815-007-2). Info Resources.
Information Industry Market Place 1980-81. 2nd ed. 350p. 1981. pap. 32.50 (ISBN 0-8352-1291-2). Bowker.
Information Resources Management. 1979. 15.00 (ISBN 0-686-25588-7). Assn Syst Mgmt.
Josey, E. J., ed. Information Society: Issues & Answers. LC 78-17708. (Neal-Schuman Professional Bk). 1978. lib. bdg. 16.50x (ISBN 0-912700-16-5). Oryx Pr.
Katz, William A. & Tarr, Andrea. Reference & Information Services: A Reader. LC 77-20698. 1978. 15.00 (ISBN 0-8108-1091-3). Scarecrow.
Kemp, Alasdair. Current Awareness Services. (Outlines of Modern Librarianship Ser.). 181p. 1979. text ed. 12.00 (ISBN 0-85157-269-3, Pub. by Bingley England). Shoe String.
--The Nature of Knowledge: An Introduction for Librarians. 224p. 1976. 15.00 (ISBN 0-208-01528-0, Linnet). Shoe String.
Kunz, Werner & Rittel, Horst. Systems Analysis of the Logic of Research & Information Processes. 74p. 1977. text ed. 13.00 (ISBN 3-7940-3455-4, Pub. by K G Saur). Shoe String.
Library & Information Services for Special Groups. 1974. 22.50 (ISBN 0-87837-003-X). Sci Assoc Intl.
Library Association, London. The Nationwide Provision & Use of Information. 400p. 1981. pap. text ed. 28.75x (ISBN 0-85365-563-4, Pub. by Lib Assn England). Oryx Pr.
Ligon, Helen H. Successful Management Information Systems. LC 78-24565. (Research for Business Decisions Ser.: No. 9). 1978. 31.95 (ISBN 0-8357-0958-2, Pub. by UMI Res Pr). Univ Microfilms.
Marke, Julius J. & Bander, Edward J. Commercial Law Information Sources. LC 73-120909. (Management Information Guide Ser.: No. 17). 1970. 36.00 (ISBN 0-8103-0817-7). Gale.
Morse, Grant W. Guide to the Incomparable New York Times Index. LC 79-87815. (Illus.). 1980. 11.95x (ISBN 0-8303-0159-3); pap. 6.95x (ISBN 0-8303-0160-7). Fleet.
Olson, Margrethe H. Organization of Information Services: Alternative Approaches. Dufey, Gunter, ed. (Research for Business Decisions: No. 21). 306p. 1980. 31.95 (ISBN 0-8357-1105-6, Pub. by UMI Res Pr). Univ Microfilms.
Popp, F. A., et al, eds. Electromagnetic Bio-Information. (Illus.). 214p. 1979. 38.00 (ISBN 0-8067-1531-6). Urban & S.
Reference Services Review, Vol. 1, 1973. (Quarterly, Standing orders accepted). per year 30.00 (ISBN 0-685-44107-5). Pierian.
Robinson, William. Bottom Pig: A Novel of Segregation, Desegregation, & Integration. 1980. 5.75 (ISBN 0-87164-045-7). William-F.
Rowley, J. E. & Turner, C. M. The Dissemination of Information. LC 78-6138. (Grafton Library of Information Science). 1978. lib. bdg. 30.75x (ISBN 0-89158-830-2). Westview.
Rudman, Jack. Information Media Specialist. (Career Examination Ser.: C-1315). (Cloth bdg. avail. on request). pap. 8.00 (ISBN 0-8373-1315-5). Natl Learning.
--Information Specialist. (Career Examination Ser.: C-1316). (Cloth bdg. avail. on request). pap. 8.00 (ISBN 0-8373-1316-3). Natl Learning.
Schmittroth, John, Jr. & Kruzas, Anthony T., eds. Encyclopedia of Information Systems & Services. 4th ed. 1500p. 1980. 190.00 (ISBN 0-8103-0942-4). Gale.
Sherman, C. Neil, et al. Educational Information Center: An Introduction. 1969. pap. 3.50 (ISBN 0-87252-027-7). Tinnon-Brown.
Slater, Frank, ed. Cost Reduction for Special Libraries and Information Centers. LC 73-81388. 1973. 12.50 (ISBN 0-87715-104-0). Am Soc Info Sci.
Veazie, Walter & Connolly, Thomas. Marketing of Information Analysis Center Products & Services. 1971. 6.50 (ISBN 0-685-33434-1). Am Soc Info Sci.
Wall, C. Edward, ed. Public Affairs Information Service: Cumulative Author Index 1965-1969. LC 70-143248. (Cumulative Author Index Ser.: No. 3). 50.00 (ISBN 0-87650-014-9). Pierian.
Warnken, Kelly. Information Brokers. (Information Management Ser.). 224p. 1981. 24.95 (ISBN 0-8352-1347-1). Bowker.
Warnken, Kelly, ed. The Directory of Fee-Based Information Services 1980-81. LC 76-55469. 1980. pap. 6.95 (ISBN 0-936288-00-0). Info Alternative.
Weber, Ollie, ed. Information Industry Market Place, 1982: An International Directory of Information Products & Services. 250p. 1981. pap. 35.00 (ISBN 0-8352-1364-1). Bowker.
Wilson, T. D. & Stephenson, J. Dissemination of Information. 2nd ed. (Examination Guide Ser.). 1969. 10.50 (ISBN 0-208-00862-4, Archon). Shoe String.
World Guide to Technical Information & Documentation Services. 514p. 1975. pap. 22.50 (ISBN 92-3-001228-9, U726, UNESCO). Unipub.
Young, Margaret L., et al, eds. Directory of Special Libraries & Information Centers: Vol. 1-Special Libraries & Information Centers in the United States & Canada. 6th ed. LC 79-16966. 1979. 175.00 (ISBN 0-8103-0297-7). Gale.
Zamora, Gloria J. & Adamson, Martha C., eds. Conference Literature: Its Role in the Distribution of Information. (Illus.). 240p. 1981. pap. 25.00 (ISBN 0-938734-03-2). Learned Info.

INFORMATION SERVICES–GREAT BRITAIN

Ainley, Patricia. Basics of Community Information: An Action Handbook for Librarians. 1979. 15.00x (ISBN 0-902248-09-X, Pub. by AALSED England). State Mutual Bk.
Penna, et al. National Library & Information Services: A Handbook for Planners. 1977. 16.95 (ISBN 0-408-70818-2). Butterworth.

INFORMATION SERVICES, GOVERNMENT

see Government Publicity

INFORMATION STORAGE AND RETRIEVAL SYSTEMS

see also Automatic Indexing; Computers; Data Base Management; Data Tapes; Electronic Data Processing; Libraries–Automation; Microfilm Aperture Card Systems; Punched Card Systems

Artandi, Susan B. An Introduction to Computers in Information Science. 2nd ed. LC 68-12643. (Illus.). 1972. 10.00 (ISBN 0-8108-0485-9). Scarecrow.

Automated Education Center. Information System Program Planning. LC 74-88620. 20.00 (ISBN 0-686-01988-1). Mgmt Info Serv.

Bagdikian, Ben H. The Information Machines: Their Impact on Man & the Media. 10.00 (ISBN 0-8446-5845-6). Peter Smith.

Becker, Joseph & Hayes, Robert M. Information Storage & Retrieval: Tools, Elements & Theories. LC 62-12279. (Information Science Ser.). 448p. 1963. 30.95 (ISBN 0-471-06129-8, Pub. by Wiley-Interscience). Wiley.

Bennett, William R. & Davey, J. R. Data Transmission. (Inter-University Electronics Ser). (Illus.). 1964. 36.50 (ISBN 0-07-004677-8, P&RB). McGraw.

Bernstein, George B. A Fifteen-Year Forecast of Information-Processing Technology. LC 77-128581. 187p. 1969. 19.00 (ISBN 0-686-01919-9). Mgmt Info Serv.

Bing, Jon & Harvold, Trygve. Legal Decisions & Information Systems. 1977. 25.00x (ISBN 82-00-05031-9, Dist. by Columbia U Pr). Universitet.

Booth, Grayce M. Functional Analysis of Information Processing. LC 80-11247. 288p. 1981. Repr. of 1973 ed. lib. bdg. write for info. (ISBN 0-89874-135-1). Krieger.

Bracchi, G. & Lockemann, P. C., eds. Information Systems Methodology: Proceedings, 2nd Conference of the European Cooperation in Informatics, Venice, Oct. 10-12, 1978. LC 78-12358. (Lecture Notes in Computer Science: Vol. 65). 1978. pap. 31.80 (ISBN 0-387-08934-9). Springer-Verlag.

Brooke, Rosalind. Information & Advice Services. 181p. 1972. pap. text ed. 5.65x (ISBN 0-7135-1709-3, Pub. by Bedford England). Renouf.

Campbell, Bonita J. Understanding Information Systems: Foundation for Control. (Winthrop Management Ser). (Illus.). 1977. pap. text ed. 5.95 (ISBN 0-87626-889-0). Winthrop.

Casley, D. J. & Lury, D. A. Data Collection in Developing Countries. (Illus.). 1981. 45.00x (ISBN 0-19-877123-1). Oxford U Pr.

Chacko, George K. Management Information Systems. (Illus.). 454p. text ed. 27.00 (ISBN 0-89433-095-0). Petrocelli.

Chartrand, Robert Lee & Morentz, James W., Jr., eds. Information Technology Serving Society. 1979. 25.00 (ISBN 0-08-021979-9). Chartrand.

Chorafas, Dimitris. Computer Networks for Distributed Information Systems. 1980. 24.00 (ISBN 0-89433-105-1). Petrocelli.

--Data Communications for Distributed Information Systems. (Illus.). 300p. text ed. 24.00 (ISBN 0-89433-108-6). Petrocelli.

Christian, Roger W. The Electronic Library: Bibliographic Data Bases, 1978-79. 2nd ed. LC 78-18408. (Professional Librarian Ser.). 1978. pap. 24.50x (ISBN 0-914236-15-6). Knowledge Indus.

CISM (International Center for Mechanical Sciences), Dept. of Automation & Information. Information Transmission with Symbols of Different Cost. Csiszar, I., ed. (CISM Pubns. Ser.: No. 136). 36p. 1973. pap. 5.40 (ISBN 0-387-81136-2). Springer-Verlag.

Clark, Ann L. & Mandell, Steven L. A Short Course in PL-I PL-C. (Series in Data Processing & Information Systems). 1978. pap. text ed. 10.50 (ISBN 0-8299-0219-8); instrs.' manual avail. (ISBN 0-8299-0465-4). West Pub.

Clinic on Library Applications of Data Processing, Proceedings, 1975. The Use of Computers in Literature Searching & Related Reference Activities in Libraries. Lancaster, F. W., ed. LC 76-1790. 1976. 8.00 (ISBN 0-87845-043-2). U of Ill Lib Info Sci.

Cohen, Leo J. Information Resource Management. (The DA & DBA-Theory & Method Ser.). 250p. 1981. price not set (ISBN 0-939274-01-9). Mtn Hse Pub.

Couger, J. Daniel & McFadden, Fred R. Introduction to Computer-Based Information Systems. LC 74-28437. 655p. 1975. text ed. 26.95 (ISBN 0-471-17736-9). Wiley.

Cox, Nigel S. & Grose, Mitchel, eds. Organization & Handling of Bibliographic Records by Computer. LC 67-30792. 1967. 19.50 (ISBN 0-208-00237-5, Archon). Shoe String.

Dallemagne, Pierre G., ed. Oceanographic Data Reduction Manual. 296p. 1974. pap. text ed. 16.50x (ISBN 0-8422-0467-9). Irvington.

Davis, W. S. Information Processing Systems: An Introduction to Modern Computer-Based Information Systems. 2nd ed. 1981. 16.95 (ISBN 0-201-03183-3); student wkbk. 5.95 (ISBN 0-201-03185-X). A-W.

Directory of United Nations Information Systems. 215p. 1980. pap. 13.00 (ISBN 0-686-72354-6, UN80/0/2, UN). Unipub.

Directory of UN Information Systems: Information System & Data Bases 1. 465p. 1980. pap. 22.00 (ISBN 0-686-72353-8, UN80/0/1, UN). Unipub.

Dolby, J. L. Evaluation of the Utility & Cost of Computerized Library Catalogues. 1969. 18.50x (ISBN 0-262-04023-9). MIT Pr.

Dolotta, T. A., et al. Data Processing in 1980-1985: A Study of Potential Limitations to Progress. LC 76-4783. 21.00 (ISBN 0-471-21783-2); pap. 11.50 (ISBN 0-471-21786-7, Pub. by Wiley-Interscience). Wiley.

Douque, B. C. & Nijssen, G. M., eds. Data Base Description: An in-Depth Technical Evaluation of Codasyl. LC 75-11724. 382p. 1975. 37.00 (ISBN 0-444-10862-9, North-Holland). Elsevier.

Doyle, L. B. Information Retrieval & Processing. LC 75-1179. (Information Science Ser.). 1975. 32.95 (ISBN 0-471-22151-1, Pub. by Wiley-Interscience). Wiley.

Ein-Dor, Philip & Segev, Eli. Managing Management Information Systems. LC 77-10001. (Illus.). 1978. 21.00 (ISBN 0-669-01642-X). Lexington Bks.

Eldin, Hamed K. & Croft, F. Max. Information Systems: A Management Science Approach. (Illus.). 264p. 1974. 13.95x (ISBN 0-442-80050-9). Van Nos Reinhold.

Enger, Norman. Management Standards for Developing Information Systems. 1980. pap. 5.95 (ISBN 0-8144-7527-2). Am Mgmt.

Enger, Norman L. Management Standards for Developing Information Systems. new ed. LC 76-41827. (Illus.). 1977. 15.95 (ISBN 0-8144-5425-9). Am Mgmt.

Fairthorne, R. A. Towards Information Retrieval. 1968. Repr. of 1961 ed. 15.00 (ISBN 0-208-00671-0, Archon). Shoe String.

Fang, Josephine R. & Songe, Alice H. International Guide to Library, Archival, & Information Science Associations. 2nd ed. 448p. 1980. 32.50 (ISBN 0-8352-1285-8). Bowker.

Fedida, Sam & Malik, Rex. The Viewdata Revolution. LC 79-23869. 186p. 1979. 38.95x (ISBN 0-470-26879-4). Halsted Pr.

Fenichel, Carol & Hogan, Thomas. Online Searching: A Primer. 130p. 1981. text ed. 12.95x (ISBN 0-938734-01-6). Learned Info.

Fenichel, Carol, ed. Changing Patterns in Information Retrieval: Proceeding of the Tenth National Information Retrieval Colloquium. LC 66-29616. 1974. pap. 1.00 (ISBN 0-87715-106-7). Am Soc Info Sci.

Franks, L. E., ed. Data Communication: Fundamentals of Baseband Transmission. LC 74-12338. (Benchmark Papers in Electrical Engineering & Computer Science Ser: Vol. 9). 1975. 46.50 (ISBN 0-12-786480-6). Acad Pr.

Frielink, A. B., ed. Economics of Informatics. LC 74-28996. 469p. 1975. 56.00 (ISBN 0-444-10848-3, North-Holland). Elsevier.

Galatin, Malcolm, ed. Economics of Information: Annual Volume Department of Economics, Vol. 4. 1980. 21.95 (ISBN 0-915326-17-5). Cyrco Pr.

Garvin, Andrew & Bermont, Hubert. How to Win with Information or Lose Without It. (Bermont Bks.). 196p. 1980. 26.00 (ISBN 0-89696-110-9). Everest Hse.

Gessford, John E. Modern Information Systems: Designed for Decision Support. LC 78-74684. 1980. text ed. 17.95 (ISBN 0-201-03099-3). A-W.

Glasgal, Ralph. Advanced Techniques in Data Communications. LC 76-1794. (Illus.). 160p. 1976. 25.00 (ISBN 0-89006-051-7). Artech Hse.

--Basic Techniques in Data Communications. LC 77-18090. (Illus.). 1978. 25.00 (ISBN 0-89006-057-6). Artech Hse.

Goldberg, Robert & Lorin, Harold. The Economics of Information Processing: Vol. 1, Management Perspectives. 300p. 1981. 35.00 (ISBN 0-471-09206-1, Pub. by Wiley Interscience). Wiley.

--Economics of Information Processing: Vol. 2, Operation Programming & Software Models. 352p. 1981. 35.00 (ISBN 0-471-09767-5, Pub. by Wiley Interscience). Wiley.

Green, P. E. & Lucky, R. W., eds. Computer Communications. LC 74-82501. 1975. 28.95 (ISBN 0-87942-041-3). Inst Electrical.

Greenwood, William T. Decision Theory & Information Systems. LC 69-13022. 1969. text ed. 11.00 (ISBN 0-538-07050-1). SW Pub.

Grochla, Erwin & Szyperski, Norbert, eds. Information Systems & Organizational Structure. 1975. 91.75x (ISBN 3-11-004803-5). De Gruyter.

Handbook for Information Systems & Services. (Illus.). 1978. pap. 21.75 (ISBN 92-3-101457-9, U790, UNESCO). Unipub.

Hardcastle, A. R., et al. Trends in Distributed Systems. 1978. pap. 23.50x (ISBN 0-85012-201-5). Intl Pubns Serv.

Hawkins, Donald. Online Information Retrieval Bibliography 1964-1979. 175p. 1980. 25.00x (ISBN 0-938734-00-8). Learned Info.

Heaps, H. S. Information Retrieval: Computational & Theoretical Aspects. (Library & Information Science). 368p. 1978. 19.50 (ISBN 0-12-335750-0). Acad Pr.

Henley, J. P. Computer-Based Library & Information Systems. 2nd ed. (Computer Monograph Ser). 1972. text ed. 18.95 (ISBN 0-444-19584-X). Elsevier.

Herner, Saul & Vellucci, Matthew J., eds. Selected Federal Computer-Based Information Systems. LC 72-85016. (Illus.). ix, 215p. 1972. text ed. 15.00 (ISBN 0-87815-007-2). Info Resources.

Hewitt, J. OCLC: Impact & Use. 1977. pap. 10.50 (ISBN 0-88215-043-X). Ohio St U Lib.

Higgins, J. C. Information Systems for Planning & Control: Concepts & Cases. 1976. 29.95x (ISBN 0-7131-3375-9); pap. 15.95x (ISBN 0-7131-3376-7). Intl Ideas.

Hill, E., Jr. A Comparative Study of Very Large Data Bases. (Lecture Notes in Computer Sciences: Vol. 59). 1978. pap. 10.50 (ISBN 0-387-08653-6). Springer-Verlag.

Holzbauer, H. Mechanized Bibliography of Documentation & Information Services. LC 70-118116. 167p. 19.00 (ISBN 0-686-01989-X). Mgmt Info Serv.

Houghton, Bernard, ed. Computer Based Information Retrieval Systems. 1968. 12.50 (ISBN 0-208-00857-8, Archon). Shoe String.

House, William C., ed. Data Base Management. (Illus.). 470p. 1974. 21.95x (ISBN 0-442-80051-7). Van Nos Reinhold.

--Laser Beam Information Systems. 1978. text ed. 17.50 (ISBN 0-89433-049-7). Petrocelli.

IFIP Congress 77. Information Processing Seventy-Seven: Proceedings. Gilchrist, B., ed. 1977. 85.50 (ISBN 0-7204-0755-9, North-Holland). Elsevier.

IFIP Working Conference. Very Large Data Bases: Proceedings. Neuhold, E. J., ed. (IFIP Ser.). 1978. write for info. (ISBN 0-685-81210-3, North-Holland). Elsevier.

Iltam Corp for Planning & Research, International Seminar, Jerusalem, 1971. Information Storage & Retrieval: Proceedings. (Illus.). 633p. 1971. 50.00x (ISBN 0-8002-1567-2). Intl Pubns Serv.

Information Systems: Their Interconnection & Compatibility. (Illus.). 470p. 1975. pap. 42.25 (ISBN 92-0-070075-6, ISP379, IAEA). Unipub.

International Conference on Information Sciences & Systems, 1st, Patras, Greece, Aug. 1976. Applications & Research in Information Systems & Sciences: Proceedings, 3 vols. new ed. Lainiotis, Demetrios G. & Tzannes, Nicolaos, eds. LC 77-15000. (Illus.). 1977. pap. text ed. 120.00 set (ISBN 0-89116-160-0). Hemisphere Pub.

International Cooperative Information Systems. 111p. 1980. pap. 10.00 (ISBN 0-88936-252-1, IDRC156, IDRC). Unipub.

Jones, Elizabeth, ed. Declassified Documents Reference System Retrospective Collection. LC 76-39673. 1977. 2151.00 (ISBN 0-8408-0029-0). Carrollton Pr.

Katzan, Harry. Distributed Information Systems. 1979. 20.00 (ISBN 0-89433-104-3). Petrocelli.

Kent & Lancour. Encyclopedia of Library & Information Science, Vol. 28. 1980. 45.00 (ISBN 0-8247-2028-8). Dekker.

Kent, A., et al, eds. Encyclopedia of Library & Information Science, Vol. 26. 1978. 45.00 (ISBN 0-8247-2126-8). Dekker.

Kent, Allen. Information Analysis & Retrieval. LC 70-155120. (Information Science Ser). 367p. 1971. 32.95 (ISBN 0-471-46995-5). Wiley.

Kent, Allen, ed. Encyclopedia of Library & Information Science, Vol. 18. 1976. 45.00 (ISBN 0-8247-2118-7). Dekker.

--Encyclopedia of Library & Information Science, Vol. 20. 1977. 45.00 (ISBN 0-8247-2120-9). Dekker.

--Encyclopedia of Library & Information Science, Vol. 21. 1977. 45.00 (ISBN 0-8247-2121-7). Dekker.

Kent, Allen & Lancour, Harold, eds. Encyclopedia of Library & Information Science, Vol. 17. 1976. 45.00 (ISBN 0-8247-2117-9). Dekker.

--Encyclopedia of Library & Information Science, Vol. 19. 1976. 45.00 (ISBN 0-8247-2119-5). Dekker.

Kent, Allen, et al, eds. Encyclopedia of Library & Information Science, Vol. 22. 1977. 45.00 (ISBN 0-8247-2122-5). Dekker.

--Encyclopedia of Library & Information Science, Vol. 23. 1977. 45.00 (ISBN 0-8247-2123-3). Dekker.

--Encyclopedia of Library & Information Science, Vol. 24. 1978. 45.00 (ISBN 0-8247-2124-1). Dekker.

Kiewitt, Eva L. Evaluating Information Retrieval Systems: The PROBE Program. LC 78-55322. 1978. lib. bdg. 15.95 (ISBN 0-313-20521-3, KPC/). Greenwood.

King, Donald W. & Bryant, Edward C. The Evaluation of Information Services & Products. LC 76-141595. (Illus.). 306p. 1971. text ed. 23.95 (ISBN 0-87815-003-X). Info Resources.

King, Donald W., ed. Key Papers in the Design & Evaluation of Information Systems. LC 78-23449. (Illus.). 1978. 25.00 (ISBN 0-914236-31-8). Knowledge Indus.

Kleinjnen, Jack P. Computers & Profits: Quantifying Financial Benefits of Information. LC 79-14097. 1980. text ed. 15.95 (ISBN 0-201-03813-7). A-W.

Kochen, Manfred. The Growth of Knowledge: Readings on Organization & Retrieval of Knowledge. 394p. 1967. text ed. 18.00 (ISBN 0-471-49695-2, Pub. by Wiley). Krieger.

--Principles of Information Retrieval. LC 74-1204. (Information Sciences Ser). 203p. 1974. 26.50 (ISBN 0-471-49697-9, Pub. by Wiley-Interscience). Wiley.

Kowalski, R. Logic for Problem Solving. (Artificial Intelligence Ser.: Vol. 7). 295p. 1979. 18.95 (ISBN 0-444-00365-7, North Holland); pap. 9.95 (ISBN 0-444-00368-1). Elsevier.

Kraemer, Kenneth L., et al. The Management of Information Systems. 416p. 1980. 25.00x (ISBN 0-231-04886-6). Columbia U Pr.

Kuo, F. Protocols & Techniques for Data Communication Networks. 1981. 32.95 (ISBN 0-13-731729-8). P-H.

Kupfer, David J., et al. Mental Health Information Systems: Design and Implementation. (Library & Information Science Ser.: Vol. 19). 1976. 27.75 (ISBN 0-8247-6445-5). Dekker.

Lancaster, F. W. Information Retrieval Systems: Characteristics, Testing & Evaluation. 2nd ed. LC 78-11078. (Information Sciences Ser.). 381p. 1979. 26.95 (ISBN 0-471-04673-6, Pub. by Wiley-Interscience). Wiley.

--Toward Paperless Information Systems. (Library & Information Science Ser.). (192). 1978. 20.00 (ISBN 0-12-436050-5). Acad Pr.

Lancaster, F. W. & Fayen, E. G. Information Retrieval on-Line. LC 73-9697. (Information Sciences Ser.). 597p. 1973. 32.95 (ISBN 0-471-51235-4, Pub. by Wiley-Interscience). Wiley.

Lancaster, F. Wilfrid. Vocabulary Control for Information Retrieval. LC 78-186528. (Illus.). xiv, 233p. 1972. text ed. 27.50 (ISBN 0-87815-006-4). Info Resources.

Langefors, Borje. Theoretical Analysis of Information Systems. 4th ed. 400p. 1973. 21.50x (ISBN 0-442-80264-1). Van Nos Reinhold.

Langefors, Borje & Sundgren, Bo. Information Systems Architecture. 1975. 21.50x (ISBN 0-442-80300-1). Van Nos Reinhold.

Lefkovitz, David. File Structures for on-Line Systems. (Illus.). 1969. 14.85x (ISBN 0-8104-5943-4). Hayden.

Licklider, J. C. Libraries of the Future. 1965. 14.00x (ISBN 0-262-12016-X). MIT Pr.

Lomax, J. D. Data Dictionary Systems. (Illus.). 1977. pap. 45.00x (ISBN 0-85012-191-4). Intl Pubns Serv.

Lubans, John, Jr. & Chapman, Edward A., eds. Reader in Library Systems Analysis. LC 75-6253. (Reader Ser. in Library & Information Science: Vol. 16). 1975. 22.00 (ISBN 0-910972-45-1). IHS-PDS.

Lucas, Henry. The Management of Information Systems. (Management Information Systems Ser.). 1978. text ed. 19.50 (ISBN 0-07-038922-5, C); inst. manual 5.95 (ISBN 0-07-038923-3). McGraw.

Lucas, Henry C. The Analysis, Design & Implementation of Information Systems. rev. ed. (Management Information Systems Ser.). (Illus.). 416p. 1980. text ed. 23.95 (ISBN 0-07-038927-6, C); instructor's manual 9.95 (ISBN 0-07-038928-4). McGraw.

Lucas, Henry C., Jr. Implementation: The Key to Successful Information Systems. LC 80-27009. 224p. 1981. 30.00x (ISBN 0-231-04434-8). Columbia U Pr.

Lucas, Henry C., Jr. & Gibson, Cyrus F. Casebook for Management Information Systems. (Management Information Systems Ser.). 1976. pap. text ed. 10.50 (ISBN 0-07-038938-1, C). McGraw.

Lucey, T. Management Information Systems. 1980. 10.00x (ISBN 0-905435-11-7, Pub. by DP Pubns). State Mutual Bk.

Lyon, John K. Introduction to Data Base Design. LC 75-155904. (Communigraph Business Data Processing Ser). 1971. 26.95 (ISBN 0-471-55735-8, Pub. by Wiley-Interscience). Wiley.

M S D (Making Sense Out of Data) Workplan. 1974. 19.95 (ISBN 0-934752-12-5). Eckman Ctr.

Mader, Chris. Information Systems: Technology, Economics, Applications, Management. 2nd ed. LC 78-13048. 1979. text ed. 19.95 (ISBN 0-574-21150-0, 13-4150); instr's guide avail. (ISBN 0-574-21151-9, 13-4151). SRA.

Martin, E. W., Jr. & Perkins, William C. Computers & Information Systems: An Introduction. 1973. 19.95x (ISBN 0-256-01452-3). Irwin.
Martin, James & Butler, David. Viewdata & the Information Society. (Illus.). 1981. 45.00 (ISBN 0-13-941906-3). P-H.
Mathies, M. Lorraine & Watson, Peter G. Computer Based Reference Services. LC 73-9967. 270p. 1973. pap. text ed. 11.00 (ISBN 0-8389-0156-5). ALA.
Meadow, Charles T. & Cochrane. Basics of Online Searching. LC 80-23050. (Information Science Ser.). 245p. 1981. 15.95 (ISBN 0-471-05283-3, Pub. by Wiley-Interscience). Wiley.
Methlie, Laif B. Information Systems Development. 1978. 22.00x (ISBN 82-00-05216-8). Universitet.
Miller, Arthur R. Assault on Privacy: Computers, Data Banks, & Dossiers. LC 70-142588. 1971. 8.95 (ISBN 0-472-65500-0). U of Mich Pr.
Montgomery, K. Leon. Document Retrieval Systems: Factors Affecting Search Time. (Library & Information Science Ser.: Vol. 14). 160p. 1975. 19.75 (ISBN 0-8247-6195-2). Dekker.
Norback, Craig T. The Computer Invasion. LC 80-23902. 288p. 1981. text ed. 18.95 (ISBN 0-442-26121-7). Van Nos Reinhold.
Oakman, Robert L. Computer Methods for Literary Research. LC 78-31468. (Illus.). 1980. lib. bdg. 14.95x (ISBN 0-87249-381-4). U of SC Pr.
Oddy, et al. Information Retrieval Research. 1981. text ed. write for info. (ISBN 0-408-10775-8). Butterworth.
Omlor, J. Dennis. Efficiency Analysis of File Organization & Information Retrieval. Stone, Harold S., ed. LC 81-11693. (Computer Science; Distributed Database Systems Ser.: No. 10). 1981. price not set (ISBN 0-8357-1226-5, Pub. by UMI Res Pr). Univ Microfilms.
Organization for Economic Cooperation & Development. Information Technology in Local Government. (OECD Informatics Studies Ser.: No. 7). 172p. 1974. 5.00x (ISBN 92-64-11274-X). OECD.
Orientation Manual for INIS & AGRIS (OMINAS) Nineteen Seventy-Nine. 1979. pap. 11.25 (ISBN 9-2017-8279-9, IN/18/RO, IAEA). Unipub.
Orna, Elizabeth. Information Retrieval for Museums. 1980. text ed. 12.00 (ISBN 0-89664-440-5). K G Saur.
Orr, Kenneth T. Structured Requirements Definition. LC 81-80846. (Illus.). 237p. (Orig.). 1981. pap. 25.00 (ISBN 0-9605884-0-X). Orr & Assocs.
Overhage, Carl F. & Harman, R. Joyce, eds. INTREX: The Report of a Planning Conference on Information Transfer Experiments. 1965. 14.50x (ISBN 0-262-15004-2). MIT Pr.
Proceedings of Full Board Meetings, Washington, D.C., 1976. 1977. pap. 23.25 (ISBN 0-685-99120-2, ICSU5, ICSU). Unipub.
Prothro, Vivian C. Information Management Systems: A Data Base Primer. (Computer Science Ser.). 1976. 15.95x (ISBN 0-442-80336-2). Van Nos Reinhold.
Radford, K. J. Information Systems for Strategic Decisions. (Illus.). 1978. ref. ed. 14.95 (ISBN 0-87909-389-7). Reston.
Research in Industrial Education: Retrieval of Data from Information Systems. (Monograph Ser: No. 6). 1976. pap. 2.00 (ISBN 0-686-16664-7). Am Indus Arts.
Rosenfeld, J. L., ed. Information Processing, Nineteen Seventy-Four. LC 74-76063. 1107p. 1975. 97.75 (ISBN 0-444-10689-8, North-Holland). Elsevier.
Rowley, Jennifer E. Computers for Libraries. (Outlines of Modern Librarianship Ser.). Date not set. text ed. 12.00 (ISBN 0-89664-016-7). K G Saur.
Samuelson, K., et al. Information Systems & Networks: Design & Planning Guidelines of Informatics for Managers, Decision Makers & Systems Analysts. 1977. 19.50 (ISBN 0-7204-0407-X, North-Holland). Elsevier.
Sanders, James & Forsman, Carolyn. Information on Demand. (Neal-Schuman Professional Bk). 1979. lib. bdg. cancelled (ISBN 0-912700-12-2). Oryx Pr.
Schiller, Herbert I. Who Knows: Information in the Age of the Fortune 500. (Communications & Information Science Ser.). 150p. 1981. 17.50 (ISBN 0-89391-069-4). Ablex Pub.
Schmittroth, John, Jr. & Kruzas, Anthony T., eds. Encyclopedia of Information Systems & Services. 4th ed. 1500p. 1980. 190.00 (ISBN 0-8103-0942-4). Gale.
Schneider, H. J., ed. Formal Models & Practical Tools for Information Systems Design. LC 79-19860. 298p. 1980. 39.00 (ISBN 0-444-85394-4, North Holland). Elsevier.
Schneider, John, et al, eds. Survey of Commercially Available Computer-Readable Bibliographic Data Bases. LC 72-97793. cancelled (ISBN 0-87715-102-4). Am Soc Info Sci.
Schwartz, Mischa. Information Transmission, Modulation & Noise: A Unified Approach. rev. ed. (McGraw-Hill Electrical & Electronic Engineering Ser.). (Illus.). 672p. 1980. text ed. 29.50 (ISBN 0-07-055782-9); solutions manual 6.95 (ISBN 0-07-055783-7). McGraw.
Scientific American Editors. Information: A Scientific American Book. LC 66-29386. (Illus.). 1966. 14.95x (ISBN 0-7167-0967-8); pap. text ed. 7.95x (ISBN 0-7167-0966-X). W H Freeman.
Second European Congress on Information Systems & Networks. 231p. 1975. text ed. 21.50 (ISBN 3-7940-5164-5). K G Saur.
Semprevivo, Philip C. Teams in Development Information Systems. LC 80-50608. (Orig.). 1980. pap. 17.50 (ISBN 0-917072-20-0). Yourdon.
Sherrod, John, ed. Information Systems & Networks: Eleventh Annual Symposium. LC 74-11941. 200p. 1975. lib. bdg. 14.25 (ISBN 0-8371-7717-0, ISN/). Greenwood.
Sigel, Efrem, ed. Videotext: The Coming Revolution in Home-Office Information Retrieval. 1981. 14.95 (ISBN 0-517-54385-0, Harmony); pap. 8.95 (ISBN 0-517-54386-9, Harmony). Crown.
Smith, Richard M. Coordinated Indexing: Cobol Computer Programs for the Storage & Retrieval of Abstracts. 52p. 1981. spiral bd. 46.00x (ISBN 0-85365-933-8, Pub. by Lib Assn England). Oryx Pr.
Sparck-Jones, Karen. Automatic Keyword Classification for Information Retrieval. (Illus.). 1971. 17.50 (ISBN 0-208-01201-X, Archon). Shoe String.
Stern, Robert A. & Stern, Nancy. An Introduction to Computers & Information Processing. 625p. 1982. text ed. 18.95 (ISBN 0-471-08723-8) (ISBN 0-471-09941-4). Wiley.
Summary Report & Recommendations of the First Session of the IOC Panel of Experts on the Aquatic Sciences & Fisheries Information Systems (ASFIS) (Fisheries Report: No. 168). 1976. pap. 7.50 (ISBN 0-685-68959-X, FAO). Unipub.
Sundburg, M. & Goldkuhl, G. Information Systems Developement: A Systematic Approach. 1981. 24.50 (ISBN 0-13-464677-0). P-H.
Synott, William & Gruber, William H. Information Resource Management: Opportunities & Strategies for the 1980's. 352p. 1981. 21.95 (ISBN 0-471-09451-X, Pub. by Wiley-Interscience). Wiley.
Szweda, Ralph A. Information Processing Management. 2nd ed. (Illus.). 1978. 18.95x (ISBN 0-442-80509-8); instr's. manual 2.50 (ISBN 0-442-80032-0). Van Nos Reinhold.
Terminological Data Banks. (Infoterm Ser.). 1980. 45.00 (ISBN 0-686-70171-2, Dist. by Gale Research Co.). K G Saur.
Third European Congress on Information Systems & Networks "Overcoming the Language Barrier". Overcoming the Language Barrier, 2 vols. 888p. 1978. Set. pap. text ed. 72.00 (ISBN 3-7940-5184-X, Pub. by K G Saur). Gale.
Tou, Julius. Software Engineering, Vols. 1-2. 1970. Vol. 1. 44.00 (ISBN 0-12-696201-4); Vol. 2. 44.00 (ISBN 0-12-696202-2). Acad Pr.
Townley, Helen M. Systems Analysis for Information Retrieval. (The Institute of Information Scientists Monograph). 1978. lib. bdg. 18.00 (ISBN 0-233-96920-9). Westview.
Vanderbilt, Dean H. Controlled Information Sharing in a Computer Utility. LC 72-127836. 173p. 1969. 19.00 (ISBN 0-686-01943-1). Mgmt Info Serv.
Van Rijsbergen, C. J. Information Retrieval. 2nd ed. 1981. pap. text ed. 21.95 (ISBN 0-408-70951-0). Butterworth.
Van Rijsbergen, C. J., ed. Information Retrieval. 2nd ed. 1979. 35.95 (ISBN 0-408-70929-4). Butterworth.
Veim, Joanc. An Introduction to Information, Data & File Structuring. 200p. 1981. pap. 13.00x (ISBN 82-00-05322-9). Universitet.
Wessel, Andrew E. Computer-Aided Information Retrieval. 176p. 1975. 23.50 (ISBN 0-686-74202-8). Krieger.
--Implementation of Complex Information Systems. LC 79-9892. (Information Sciences Ser.). 1979. 25.50 (ISBN 0-471-02661-1, Pub. by Wiley-Interscience). Wiley.
Wiehler, G. Magnetic Peripheral Data Storage: Programmed Introduction. 28.00 (ISBN 0-85501-266-8). Heyden.
Wilson, T. D. & Stephenson, J. Dissemination of Information. 2nd ed. (Examination Guide Ser.). 1969. 10.50 (ISBN 0-208-00862-4, Archon). Shoe String.

INFORMATION STORAGE AND RETRIEVAL SYSTEMS–AGRICULTURE

Blackie, M. J. & Dent, J. B., eds. Information Systems for Agriculture. (Illus.). 1979. 24.80x (ISBN 0-85334-829-4). Intl Ideas.
Brockington, N. R. Computer Modelling in Agriculture. (Illus.). 1979. 35.00 (ISBN 0-19-854523-1). Oxford U Pr.
Cab-Cain Evaluation Project: A Comparative Study on the Performance of Two Agricultural Databases in a Computerized Current Awareness Service. 1979. pap. 8.00 (ISBN 90-220-0704-9, PDC120, PUDOC). Unipub.
Factual Data Banks in Agriculture. 1979. pap. 16.00 (ISBN 90-220-0674-3, PDC 115, PUDOC). Unipub.
Lilley. Information Sources in Agriculture & Food Science. (Butterworths Guides to Information Sources Ser.). 1981. text ed. write for info. (ISBN 0-408-10612-3). Butterworth.
Progress & Prospects in Agricultural Librarianship & Documentation. 1973. pap. 24.00 (ISBN 90-220-0460-0, PUDOC). Unipub.
Using Agris. 1981. Set. incl. audiovisual materials 140.00 (ISBN 0-686-72315-5, F2114, FAO). Unipub.

INFORMATION STORAGE AND RETRIEVAL SYSTEMS–BIOLOGY

Lewis, R., ed. Computers in the Life Sciences: Applications in Research & Education. 1979. 25.00x (ISBN 0-85664-863-9, Pub. by Croom Helm Ltd England). Biblio Dist.

INFORMATION STORAGE AND RETRIEVAL SYSTEMS–BUSINESS

Airhart, Truett E., et al. Productivity Prospectus: Securing Management's Commitment to Information Systems: Syntopican IX, Papers & Proceedings, June 29 to July 2, 1981. 1981. 3-ring polyvinyl binder 20.00 (ISBN 0-935220-06-2). IIWPA.
Benjamin, William A., ed. Harfax Directory of Industry Data Sources, 2 vol. set. 1440p. 1981. professional reference 175.00 (ISBN 0-686-73672-9). Ballinger Pub.
Brabb, George. Computers & Information Systems in Business. 2nd ed. LC 79-88716. (Illus.). 1980. text ed. 18.50 (ISBN 0-395-28671-9); inst. manual .90 (ISBN 0-395-28670-0). HM.
Brownstone, David M. & Carruth, G. Where to Find Business Information: A Worldwide Guide for Everyone Who Needs the Answers to Business Questions. 2nd ed. 650p. 1982. Set. 45.00 (ISBN 0-471-08736-X, Pub. by Wiley-Interscience). Wiley.
Business Communications, ed. New Markets for Small Business Computers, G-055. 1981. 750.00 (ISBN 0-89336-220-4, G-055). BCC.
Campbell, Malcolm. Business Information Services. 2nd ed. 192p. 1981. 20.00 (ISBN 0-208-01933-2, Linnet). Shoe String.
Cohen, Malcom S. On the Feasibility of a Labor Market Information System, 3 vols. 1974. pap. 10.95x set (ISBN 0-87736-331-5); pap. 3.95x ea. U of Mich Inst Labor.
Davis, F. T. Business Acquisitions Desk Book. 2nd ed. 415p. 1981. 39.50 (ISBN 0-87624-049-X). Inst Busn Plan.
Eliason, Alan. Business Information Processing. 496p. 1979. text ed. 18.95 (ISBN 0-574-21235-3, 13-4235); instr's guide avail. (ISBN 0-574-21236-1, 13-4236). SRA.
Ferman, Louis A. & Erfurt, John C. Overview of the Experiences of the ILIR Manpower Laboratory: The Development of a Model Approach to the Retrieval, Dissemination, & Utilization of Information on Manpower Operations. 1973. looseleaf 3.00x (ISBN 0-87736-332-3). U of Mich Inst Labor.
Hoffman, Herbert H. Alphanumeric Filing Rules for Business Documents. 118p. 1977. pap. 4.00x (ISBN 0-89537-001-8). Headway Pubns.
How to Harness Information Resources: A Systems Approach. (Management Ser.). 1976. 7.50 (ISBN 0-934356-07-6); member 5.00 (ISBN 0-686-00287-3). Assn Syst Mgmt.
Kalthoff, Robert J. & Lee, Leonard S. Productivity & Records Automation. (Illus.). 400p. 1981. text ed. 24.95 (ISBN 0-13-725234-X). P-H.
King, William R. Marketing Management Information Systems. (Priorities in Marketing Ser). 1977. text ed. 16.95x (ISBN 0-442-80395-8); pap. text ed. 9.00x (ISBN 0-442-80448-2). Van Nos Reinhold.
McCosh, Andrew, et al. Developing Managerial Information Systems. LC 80-14760. 250p. 1981. 29.95 (ISBN 0-470-26913-8). Halsted Pr.
McLeod, Raymond. Management Information Systems. LC 78-14983. 1979. text ed. 20.95 (ISBN 0-574-21245-0, 13-4245); instr's guide avail. (ISBN 0-574-21246-9, 13-4246); casebook 5.95 (ISBN 0-574-21247-7, 13-4247). SRA.
OECD. Microelectronic, Productivity & Employment. (Information Computer Communications Policy Ser.: No. 5). 290p. (Orig.). 1981. pap. 18.00x (ISBN 92-64-12162-5). OECD.
Prince, Thomas R. Information Systems for Management Planning & Control. 3rd ed. 1975. 21.95x (ISBN 0-256-01647-X). Irwin.
Saffady, William. The Automated Office: An Introduction to the Technology. Plunka, Gene A., ed. (Reference Ser.). 1981. text ed. 29.50 (ISBN 0-89258-072-0, R017). Natl Micrograph.
Shaw, Donald R. Your Small Business Computer: Evaluating, Selecting, Financing, Installing & Operating the Hardware & Software That Fits. 272p. 1980. text ed. 19.95 (ISBN 0-442-27540-4). Van Nos Reinhold.
Spigai, Frances & Sommer, Peter. A Guide to Electronic Publishing. (Publishing Technology & Management Reports). 100p. 1981. pap. 95.00 professinal (ISBN 0-914236-87-3). Knowledge Indus.
Wang, Peter C., et al, eds. Information Linkage Between Applied Mathematics & Industry. 1979. 43.50 (ISBN 0-12-734250-8). Acad Pr.
Warner-Edison Associates. Words That Mean Business: Three Thousand Terms for Access to Business Information. 175p. 1981. 49.95x (ISBN 0-918212-55-3). Neal-Schuman.
Weaver, Barbara N. & Bishop, Wiley L. The Corporate Memory: A Profitable & Practical Approach to Information Management & Retention Systems. 282p. 1981. Repr. of 1974 ed. text ed. write for info. (ISBN 0-89874-245-5). Krieger.
Wilkinson, Joseph W. Accounting Information Systems. (Wiley Series in Accounting & Information Systems). 600p. 1982. text ed. price not set (ISBN 0-471-04986-7). Wiley.
Winsbury, Rex. Viewdata in Action: A Comparative Study of Prestel. (Illus.). 288p. 1981. 39.50 (ISBN 0-07-084548-4, P&RB). McGraw.

INFORMATION STORAGE AND RETRIEVAL SYSTEMS–CHEMISTRY

Antony, Arthur. Guide to Basic Information Sources in Chemistry. LC 79-330. (Information Resources Ser.). 219p. 1979. 17.95 (ISBN 0-470-26587-6). Halsted Pr.
Arnett, Edward M. & Kent, Allen, eds. Computer Based Chemical Information. (Bks. in Library & Information Science: Vol. 4). 232p. 1973. 32.50 (ISBN 0-8247-6045-X). Dekker.
Ash, J. & Hyde, E., eds. Chemical Information Systems. LC 74-14904. 309p. 1975. 59.95 (ISBN 0-470-03444-0). Halsted Pr.
Christoffersen, Ralph E. & Olson, Edward C., eds. Computer-Assisted Drug Design. LC 79-21038. (ACS Symposium Ser.: No. 112). 1979. 40.00 (ISBN 0-8412-0521-3). Am Chemical.
Davis, Charles H. & Rush, James E. Information Retrieval & Documentation in Chemistry. LC 72-791. (Contributions in Librarianship & Information Science: No. 8). 1974. lib. bdg. 16.00 (ISBN 0-8371-6364-1, DAI/). Greenwood.
Division Of Chemistry And Chemical Technology. Chemical Structure Information Handling: A Review of the Literature, 1962-1968. LC 70-602073. (Orig.). 1969. pap. 6.95 (ISBN 0-309-01733-5). Natl Acad Pr.
Howe, W. Jeffrey, ed. Retrieval of Medicinal Chemical Information. LC 78-21611. (ACS Symposium Ser.: No. 84). 1978. 23.00 (ISBN 0-8412-0465-9). Am Chemical.
Isenhour, Thomas L. & Jurs, Peter C. Introduction to Computer Programming for Chemists: Fortran. 2nd ed. 1979. text ed. 20.95 (ISBN 0-205-05897-3). Allyn.
Lynch, M. F. Computer Handling of Chemical Structure Information. (Computer Monograph Ser). 1972. 14.95 (ISBN 0-444-19586-6). Elsevier.

INFORMATION STORAGE AND RETRIEVAL SYSTEMS–CHINESE LANGUAGE

Wang, William S-Y & Lyovin, Anatole, eds. CLIBOC: Chinese Linguistics Bibliography on Computer. LC 74-85740. (Princeton-Cambridge Studies in Chinese Linguistic Ser). 1970. 90.00 (ISBN 0-521-07455-X). Cambridge U Pr.

INFORMATION STORAGE AND RETRIEVAL SYSTEMS–CITIES AND TOWNS–PLANNING

Norris, G. & Ewart, W. Choosing & Managing Information Systems for Public Administration. 1979. text ed. 28.25x (ISBN 0-566-00244-2, Pub. by Gower Pub Co England). Renouf.
Public Works Information Systems. (Special Reports Ser: No. 36). 147p. 1970. 10.00 (ISBN 0-917084-13-6). Am Public Works.

INFORMATION STORAGE AND RETRIEVAL SYSTEMS–EDUCATION

De Land, E. C., ed. Information Technology in Health Science Education. (Computers in Biology & Medicine Ser.). 608p. 1978. 42.50 (ISBN 0-306-31113-5, Plenum Pr). Plenum Pub.
Eudised: Thesaurus Multilingue Pour le Traitement De L'information En Education. premiere francaise ed. 1974. pap. 19.50x (ISBN 0-686-21863-9). Mouton.

Mathies, Lorraine. Information Sources & Services in Education. LC 73-76472. (Fastback Ser.: No. 16). 49p. 1973. pap. 0.75 (ISBN 0-87367-016-7). Phi Delta Kappa.

User Education in Schools: A Survey of the Literature on Education for Information Use in Schools. 1981. 15.00x (ISBN 0-686-72513-1, Pub. by Brit Lib England). State Mutual Bk.

Viet, Jean, ed. Eudised: Multilingual Thesaurus for Information Processing in the Field of Education. 1st ed. 1974. pap. 19.50x (ISBN 0-686-21862-0). Mouton.

--Eudised Multilingual Thesaurus for Information Processing in the Field of Education. 391p. (Orig.). 1973. pap. text ed. 19.00x (ISBN 0-686-22571-6). Mouton.

Wood, R. & Skurnik, L. S. Item Banking. (General Ser.). (Illus.). 184p. 1969. pap. text ed. 15.00x (ISBN 0-901225-10-X, NFER). Humanities.

INFORMATION STORAGE AND RETRIEVAL SYSTEMS–ENGINEERING

Nadler, Gerald, et al. Design Concepts for Information Systems. 1975. pap. text ed. 10.00 (ISBN 0-89806-015-X, 31). Am Inst Indus Eng.

Sahney, Vinod K. & May, James L. Scheduling Computer Operations. 1972. pap. text ed. write for info. (ISBN 0-89806-017-6, 126). Am Inst Indus Eng.

Scientific & Engineering Secondary Information Transfer for Developing Countries. 1975. pap. 12.25 (ISBN 0-685-99122-9, ICSU1, ICSU). Unipub.

Shuchman, Hedvah L. Information Transfer in Engineering. (Illus.). 300p. (Orig.). 1981. pap. 45.00 (ISBN 0-9605196-0-2). Futures Group.

Smith, William A., Jr. & Wechsler, Ben L. Planning Guide for Information System Evaluation Studies. 1973. pap. text ed. 10.00 (ISBN 0-89806-016-8, 98). Am Inst Indus Eng.

INFORMATION STORAGE AND RETRIEVAL SYSTEMS–HISTORY

Murin, William J., et al, eds. Public Policy: A Guide to Information Sources. LC 80-25872. (American Government & History Information Guide Ser.: Vol. 13). 400p. 1981. 36.00 (ISBN 0-8103-1490-8). Gale.

INFORMATION STORAGE AND RETRIEVAL SYSTEMS–HUMANITIES

Doyle, P. A. Guide to Basic Information Sources in English Literature. LC 75-43260. (Information ResOurces Ser). 1976. 10.95x (ISBN 0-470-15011-4, Dist. by Halsted). J Norton Pubs.

Schoech, Dick J. Computer Use in Human Services. 288p. 1981. 24.95 (ISBN 0-87705-502-5). Human Sci Pr.

INFORMATION STORAGE AND RETRIEVAL SYSTEMS–LAW

Hafner, Carole D. An Information Retrieval System Based on a Computer Model of Legal Knowledge. Stone, Harold, ed. LC 81-7484. (Computer Science Ser.: Artificial Intelligence, No. 1). 1981. 27.95 (ISBN 0-8357-1196-X, Pub. by UMI Res Pr). Univ Microfilms.

Sprowl, James A. Manual for Computer-Assisted Legal Research. new ed. Sikes, Bette, ed. 1976. pap. 5.00 (ISBN 0-910058-76-8). Am Bar Foun.

Strong, Kline D. Retrieval Systems for Lawyers. LC 80-66349. (Illus.). 80p. (Orig.). 1980. pap. text ed. 20.00x (ISBN 0-89707-021-6, 5110057). Amer Bar Assn.

Tseng, Henry P. Complete Guide to Legal Materials in Microforms: 1978 Supplement. LC 76-15102. 1979. perfect bdg. 25.00 (ISBN 0-9602406-1-6). AMCO Intl.

Wasserman, Paul & Kaszubski, Marek, eds. Law & Legal Information Directory: A Guide to National & International Organizations, Bar Associations, Federal Court System, Federal Regulatory Agencies, Law Schools, Continuing Legal Education, Scholarships & Grants, Awards & Prizes, Special Libraries, Information Systems & Services, Research Centers, Etc. 800p. 1980. 110.00 (ISBN 0-8103-0169-5). Gale.

Weimer, David L. Improving Prosecution? The Inducement & Implementation of Innovations for Prosecution Management. LC 79-6190. (Contributions in Political Science: No. 49). (Illus.). xv, 237p. 1980. lib. bdg. 25.00 (ISBN 0-313-22247-9, WEP/). Greenwood.

Young, John H., et al, eds. Manual for the Use of Computers in Litigation. LC 79-88511. (Illus., Orig.). 1979. pap. text ed. 25.00 (ISBN 0-89707-007-0). Amer Bar Assn.

INFORMATION STORAGE AND RETRIEVAL SYSTEMS–MEDICINE

American Hospital Association. Cumulative Index of Hospital Literature. Incl. 1955-1959. 460p. 1960. casebound 31.25 (ISBN 0-87258-329-5, 1381); 1950-1954. 540p. 1955. 31.25 (ISBN 0-87258-328-7, 1380). Am Hospital.

Austin, Charles J. Information Systems for Hospital Administration. LC 79-5408. (Illus.). 1979. text ed. 25.00 (ISBN 0-914904-30-2). Health Admin Pr.

Brandejs, J. F. Health Informatics. (IFIP Medical Informatics Monograph Ser.: Vol. 2). 1976. 31.75 (ISBN 0-444-11055-0, North-Holland). Elsevier.

Current Procedural Terminology. 4th ed. 1970. pap. 12.00 (ISBN 0-89970-029-2, OP-041). AMA.

De Land, E. C., ed. Information Technology in Health Science Education. (Computers in Biology & Medicine Ser.). 608p. 1978. 42.50 (ISBN 0-306-31113-5, Plenum Pr). Plenum Pub.

Duncan, Karen, ed. Information Technology & Health Care: The Critical Issues. 200p. 1980. write for info. (ISBN 0-88283-031-7). AFIPS Pr.

First Illinois Conference on Medical Information Systems, October 1974, Urbana, IL. First Illinois Conference on Medical Information Systems: Proceedings. 1976. pap. text ed. 20.00 (ISBN 0-87664-274-1). Instru Soc.

Gouveia, W. A., et al, eds. Clinical Pharmacy & Clinical Pharmacology: Proceedings of an International Symposium Held in Sept. 1975. 1977. 66.50 (ISBN 0-7204-0596-3, North-Holland). Elsevier.

Green, Lawrence & Kansler, Connie, eds. Professional & Scientific Literature on Patient Education: A Guide to Information Sources. (Health Affairs Information Guide Ser.: Vol. 5). 330p. 1980. 36.00 (ISBN 0-8103-1422-3). Gale.

Gremy, F., et al, eds. Medical Informatics Europe 1981: Proceedings. (Lecture Notes in Medical Informatics Ser.: Vol. 11). 975p. 1981. pap. 56.20 (ISBN 0-387-10568-9). Springer-Verlag.

Howe, W. Jeffrey, ed. Retrieval of Medicinal Chemical Information. LC 78-21611. (ACS Symposium Ser.: No. 84). 1978. 23.00 (ISBN 0-8412-0465-9). Am Chemical.

Mengden, V. & Just, eds. Medical Data Transmission by Public Telephone Systems. (Illus.). 147p. 1979. pap. text ed. 24.00 (ISBN 0-8067-0961-8). Urban & S.

Schmitz, Homer. Hospital Information Systems. LC 79-15421. 188p. 1979. 26.95 (ISBN 0-89443-156-0). Aspen Systems.

Schneider, W. & Sagvall Hein, A. -L., eds. Computational Linguistics in Medicine: Proceedings of the IFIP Working Conference on Computational Linguistics in Medicine. 1978. 31.75 (ISBN 0-444-85040-6, North-Holland). Elsevier.

Schwartz, H. & Sondak, V. Computers & Medicine. LC 79-18948. 1979. pap. 35.00x (ISBN 0-89006-076-2). Artech Hse.

Shaffer, Dale E. Library Resources for Nurses: A Basic Collection for Supporting the Nursing Curriculum. 45p. 1973. pap. 3.00 (ISBN 0-915060-06-X). D E Shaffer.

TC-4 Working Conference on Hospital Information Systems, Cape Town, April 1979. Hospital Information Systems; the Art, Problems & Prospects: Proceedings. Shannon, R. H., ed. 1979. text ed. 58.75 (ISBN 0-444-85341-3, North Holland). Elsevier.

Van Egmond, J., et al, eds. Information Systems for Patient Care: Proceedings of the IFIP Working Conference on Information Systems for Patient Care Review, Analysis & Evaluation. 1976. 53.75 (ISBN 0-7204-0463-0, North-Holland). Elsevier.

INFORMATION STORAGE AND RETRIEVAL SYSTEMS–METEOROLOGY

Storage Cataloguing & Retrieval of Meteorological Information. (World Weather Watch Planning Report Ser.). 254p. 1974. pap. 32.00 (ISBN 92-63-10366-6, WMO). Unipub.

INFORMATION STORAGE AND RETRIEVAL SYSTEMS–POLITICAL SCIENCE

Englefield, Dermot. Parliament & Information. 176p. 1981. lib. bdg. 18.00x (ISBN 0-85365-570-7, Pub. by Lib Assn England); pap. text ed. 12.00x (ISBN 0-85365-993-1, Pub. by Lib Assn England). Oryx Pr.

Murin, William J., et al, eds. Public Policy: A Guide to Information Sources. LC 80-25872. (American Government & History Information Guide Ser.: Vol. 13). 400p. 1981. 36.00 (ISBN 0-8103-1490-8). Gale.

The Organization of Information Systems for Government & Public Administration. (Studies & Research: No. 8). 1979. pap. 10.00 (ISBN 92-3-101595-8, U919, UNESCO). Unipub.

INFORMATION STORAGE AND RETRIEVAL SYSTEMS–SCIENCE

Arnett, Ross H., Jr. Entomological Information Storage & Retrieval. LC 70-140434. 1970. 7.95 (ISBN 0-916846-00-8). World Natural Hist.

Baillie, A. & Gilbert, R. J., eds. Automation, Mechanisation & Data Handling in Microbiology. (Society for Applied Bacteriology Technical Ser.: No. 4). 1970. 36.50 (ISBN 0-12-073650-0). Acad Pr.

Education & Training of Users of Scientific & Technical Information. (Illus.). 1978. pap. 10.50 (ISBN 92-3-101452-8, U746, UNESCO). Unipub.

Goffman, William & Warren, Kenneth. Scientific Information Systems & the Principle of Selectivity. 20.95 (ISBN 0-03-056081-0). Praeger.

Green, Lawrence & Kansler, Connie, eds. Professional & Scientific Literature on Patient Education: A Guide to Information Sources. (Health Affairs Information Guide Ser.: Vol. 5). 330p. 1980. 36.00 (ISBN 0-8103-1422-3). Gale.

International Federation for Documentation. Directories of Science Information Sources: International Bibliography. 2nd ed. 163p. 1967. 15.00x (ISBN 0-8002-1369-6). Intl Pubns Serv.

Mount, Ellis, ed. Planning for Sci-Tech Online Searching. (Science & Technology Libraries: Vol. 1, No. 1). 1981. pap. 15.00 (ISBN 0-917724-73-9). Haworth Pr.

Networking in Sci-Tech & Information Centers. (Science & Technology Libraries Ser.: Vol. 1, No. 2). 1981. pap. 15.00 (ISBN 0-917724-72-0, B72). Haworth Pr.

Rees, Alan, ed. Contemporary Problems in Technical Library & Information Center Management: A State-of-the-Art. LC 74-14289. 1974. 18.50 (ISBN 0-87715-107-5). Am Soc Info Sci.

Science & Technology Policies Information Exchange System (SPINES) Feasibility Study. (Science Policy Studies & Documents Ser., No. 33). (Illus.). 115p. (Orig.). 1974. pap. 6.00 (ISBN 92-3-101185-5, U571, UNESCO). Unipub.

Scientific & Engineering Secondary Information Transfer for Developing Countries. 1975. pap. 12.25 (ISBN 0-685-99122-9, ICSU1, ICSU). Unipub.

UNISIST: Study Report on the Feasibility of a World Science Information System. (Illus.). 161p. (Orig.). 1971. pap. 6.75 (ISBN 92-3-100881-1, UNESCO). Unipub.

INFORMATION STORAGE AND RETRIEVAL SYSTEMS–SOCIAL SCIENCES

Cleary, Michael J. & Amsden, Robert T. A Data Analysis Handbook Using the SPSS System. (Illus., Orig.). 1979. pap. 9.50x (ISBN 0-89894-015-X). Advocate Pub Group.

DARE Information Management System: A Condensed System Description (Computer Design Version 2) (Reports and Papers in the Social Sciences: No. 31). (Illus.). 23p. 1976. pap. 2.50 (ISBN 92-3-101256-8, U148, UNESCO). Unipub.

Gillooly, William B. Literature Search: Document Retrieval in the Behavioral Sciences. (Illus., Orig.). 1969. pap. text ed. 1.25 (ISBN 0-685-16734-8). Mariner Pr.

Laska, Eugene M. & Bank, Rheta, eds. Safeguarding Psychiatric Privacy: Computer Systems & Their Uses. LC 75-15570. 452p. (Orig.). 1975. 28.00 (ISBN 0-471-51831-X). Krieger.

White, Howard D., ed. Reader in Machine-Readable Social Data. LC 77-92432. (Readers Er. in Librarianship & Information Science: Vol. 24). 1978. lib. bdg. 21.00 (ISBN 0-910972-70-2). IHS-PDS.

Wilson, Gary B., et al. A System for Record Keeping: Innovative Models for Social Services & Parent Involvement. new ed. LC 77-73770. (Illus.). 1977. pap. 5.00 (ISBN 0-89334-010-3). Humanics Ltd.

INFORMATION THEORY

see also Automatic Control; Coding Theory; Data Transmission Systems; Error-Correcting Codes (Information Theory); Information Measurement; Language and Languages; Machine Translating; Mathematical Linguistics; Modulation Theory; Punched Card Systems; Semantics; Signal Theory (Telecommunication); Speech Processing Systems; Statistical Communication Theory; Switching Theory; Telecommunication

Abramson, Norman. Information Theory & Coding. (Electronic Sciences Ser). 1963. 25.95 (ISBN 0-07-000145-6, C). McGraw.

Aczel, J. & Daroczy, Z. Measures of Information & Their Characterizations. (Mathematics in Science & Engineering Ser.). 1975. 47.00 (ISBN 0-12-043760-0). Acad Pr.

Andronov, A. A., et al. Eleven Papers on Differential Equations & Two in Information Theory. LC 51-5559. (Translations, Ser.: No. 2, Vol. 33). 1963. 29.60 (ISBN 0-8218-1733-7, TRANS 2-33). Am Math.

Ash, R. B. Information Theory. LC 65-24284. (Pure & Applied Mathematics Ser.). 339p. 1965. 36.50 (ISBN 0-470-03445-9, Pub. by Wiley-Interscience). Wiley.

Behara, M., et al, eds. Probability & Information Theory 2. LC 75-406171. (Lecture Notes in Mathematics: Vol. 296). v, 223p. 1973. pap. 10.90 (ISBN 0-387-06211-4). Springer-Verlag.

Bendat, Julius S. Principles & Applications of Random Noise Theory. rev. ed. LC 77-7225. 456p. 1978. lib. bdg. 20.50 (ISBN 0-88275-556-0). Krieger.

CISM (International Center for Mechanical Sciences), Dept. of Automation & Information, Cambridge, 1970. Information Theory & Reliable Communication. Gallager, R., ed. (CISM Pubns. Ser.: No. 30). (Illus.). 115p. 1972. pap. 12.90 (ISBN 0-387-81145-1). Springer-Verlag.

CISM (International Center for Mechanical Sciences), Dept. of Automation & Informations, 1969. Selected Topics in Information Theory. Longo, G., ed. (CISM International Center for Mechanical Sciences Ser.: No. 18). (Illus.). 111p. 1974. pap. 15.70 (ISBN 0-387-81166-4). Springer-Verlag.

Cohen, Leo J. Information Resource Management. (The DA & DBA-Theory & Method Ser.). 250p. 1981. price not set (ISBN 0-939274-01-9). Mtn Hse Pub.

Conference on Information Theory, Statistical Decision Functions, Random Processes, 4th. Transactions. Kozesnik, J., ed. 1967. 74.00 (ISBN 0-12-423858-0). Acad Pr.

Cornish, Edward, ed. The Information Society of Tomorrow. 1981. 5.95 (ISBN 0-930242-14-9). World Future.

Coyaud, Maurice. Introduction a l'Etude Des Langages Documentaires. LC 66-26623. (Alabama Linguistic & Philological Ser: Vol. 12). 1966. 11.00x (ISBN 0-8173-0105-4). U of Ala Pr.

Flavin, Matthew. Fundamental Concepts of Information Modeling. (Yourdon Press Monograph). (Illus.). 136p. (Orig.). 1981. pap. 13.00 (ISBN 0-917072-22-7). Yourdon.

Freeman, Robert R., et al, eds. Information in the Language Sciences. (Mathematical Linguistics & Automatic Language Processing: Vol. 5). 1969. 21.95 (ISBN 0-444-00036-4, North Holland). Elsevier.

Fu, K. S. & Tou, Julius T., eds. Learning Systems & Intelligent Robots. LC 74-11212. 452p. 1974. 39.50 (ISBN 0-306-30801-0, Plenum Pr). Plenum Pub.

Gallager, R. G. Information Theory & Reliable Communication. LC 68-26850. 1968. 39.95 (ISBN 0-471-29048-3). Wiley.

Gallager, Robert G. Low-Density Parity-Check Codes. (Press Research Monographs: No. 21). (Illus.). 1963. 12.00x (ISBN 0-262-07007-3). MIT Pr.

Gallaire & Minker, eds. Logic & Data Bases. 1978. 29.50 (ISBN 0-306-40060-X, Plenum Pr). Plenum Pub.

Gallaire, Herve, et al, eds. Advances in Data Base Theory, Vol. 1. 432p. 1981. 49.50 (ISBN 0-306-40629-2, Plenum Pr). Plenum Pub.

Gray, Robert M. & Davisson, Lee D., eds. Ergodic & Information Theory. (Benchmark Papers in Electrical Engineering & Computer Science: Vol. 19). 1977. 46.50 (ISBN 0-12-786590-X). Acad Pr.

Grusko, I. I., et al. Eleven Papers from the Fourth Prague Conference on Information Theory, Statistical Decision Functions, & Random Processes. LC 61-9803. (Selected Translatons in Mathematical Statistics & Probability, Ser.: Vol. 8). 1970. 26.00 (ISBN 0-8218-1458-3, STAPRO-8). Am Math.

Guiasu, Silviu. Information Theory with New Applications. (Illus.). 1977. text ed. 34.00 (ISBN 0-07-025109-6, C). McGraw.

Haber, Fred. An Introduction to Information & Communication Theory. (Advances in Modern Engineering Ser.). (Illus.). 224p. 1974. text ed. 8.95 (ISBN 0-201-02669-4). A-W.

Hamming, Richard W. Coding & Information Theory. (Illus.). 1980. text ed. 26.95 (ISBN 0-13-139139-9). P-H.

Harper, Nancy. Human Communication Theory: History of a Paraigm. 320p. 1979. pap. 9.95x (ISBN 0-8104-6091-2). Hayden.

Helmstrom, C. W. Statistical Theory of Signal Detection. 2nd ed. 1968. 26.00 (ISBN 0-08-013265-0). Pergamon.

Hyvaerinen, L. P. Information Theory for Systems Engineers. LC 79-124608. (Econometrics & Operations Research: Vol. 17). (Illus.). 1971. 29.00 (ISBN 0-387-05224-0). Springer-Verlag.

International Symposium on Probability & Information Theory, McMaster University, Canada, 1968. Proceedings. Behara, M., et al, eds. LC 76-80068. (Lecture Notes in Mathematics: Vol. 89). 1969. pap. 14.70 (ISBN 0-387-04608-9). Springer-Verlag.

Jones, D. S. Elementary Information Theory. (Oxford Applied Mathematics & Computing Science Ser.). (Illus.). 1979. 24.50x (ISBN 0-19-859636-7); pap. 9.95x (ISBN 0-19-859637-5). Oxford U Pr.

Kantor, Frederick W. Information Mechanics. LC 77-6747. 397p. 1977. 34.00 (ISBN 0-471-02968-8, Pub. by Wiley-Interscience). Wiley.

Khinchin, Alexander I. Mathematical Foundations of Information Theory. 1957. pap. text ed. 2.50 (ISBN 0-486-60434-9). Dover.

Kinneavy, James L. Theory of Discourse. 496p. 1980. pap. 8.95x (ISBN 0-393-00919-X). Norton.

Knight, Kenneth & McDaniel, Reuben. Organizations: An Information Systems Perspective. 1979. pap. 9.95x (ISBN 0-534-00583-7). Wadsworth Pub.
Kotelnikov, Vladimir A. Theory of Optimum Noise Immunity. Silverman, R. A., tr. LC 68-20594. (Illus.). 1960. pap. text ed. 3.50 (ISBN 0-486-61952-4). Dover.
Krippendorff, K. Communication & Control in Society. 1979. 55.50x (ISBN 0-677-05440-8). Gordon.
Kullbach, Solomon. Information Theory & Statistics. 10.00 (ISBN 0-8446-2412-8). Peter Smith.
Langefors, Borje & Samuelson, Kjell. Information & Data in Systems. 192p. 1976. 16.95x (ISBN 0-442-80349-4). Van Nos Reinhold.
Longo, G., ed. The Information Theory Approach to Communications. (CISM-Courses & Lectures: Vol. 229). (Illus.). 1979. pap. 49.60 (ISBN 0-387-81484-1). Springer-Verlag.
--Information Theory: New Trends & Open Problems. (International Centre for Mechanical Sciences, Courses & Lectures: No. 219). (Illus.). 1976. soft cover 30.60 (ISBN 3-211-81378-0). Springer-Verlag.
McEliece, R. J. The Theory of Information & Coding: A Mathematical Framework for Communication. (Encyclopedia of Mathematics & Its Applications: Vol. 3). 1977. text ed. 25.50 (ISBN 0-201-13502-7, Adv Bk Prog). A-W.
MacKay, Donald M. Information, Mechanism & Meaning. 1970. pap. 4.95 (ISBN 0-262-63032-X). MIT Pr.
Meetham, A. R. Encyclopedia of Linguistics, Information & Control. 1969. 115.00 (ISBN 0-08-012337-6). Pergamon.
Nauta, Doede. The Meaning of Information. LC 79-173382. (Approaches to Semiotics Ser: No. 20). (Illus.). 314p. 1972. text ed. 54.00x (ISBN 90-2791-996-8). Mouton.
Pierce, J. R. An Introduction to Information Theory: Symbols, Signals & Noise. 2nd, rev. ed. 320p. 1980. pap. 4.50 (ISBN 0-486-24061-4). Dover.
Pierce, John R. An Introduction to Information Theory: Symbols, Signals & Noise. 2nd rev. ed. Date not set. 8.75 (ISBN 0-8446-5803-0). Peter Smith.
Renyi, A. Tagebuch ueber die Informationstheorie. 160p. 1981. 14.50 (ISBN 3-7643-1006-5). Birkhauser.
Rosie, A. M. Information & Communication Theory. 2nd ed. 1973. 21.50x (ISBN 0-442-07036-5). Van Nos Reinhold.
Sakrison, D. Communication Theory: Transmission of Waveforms & Digital Information. LC 67-30084. 1968. 32.95 (ISBN 0-471-74979-6); tchrs'. manual o.p. avail. (ISBN 0-471-74978-8). Wiley.
Singh, Jagjit. Great Ideas in Information Theory, Language & Cibernetics. 7.00 (ISBN 0-8446-2946-4). Peter Smith.
Slepian, David, ed. Key Papers in the Development of Information Theory. LC 73-77997. (IEEE Press Selected Reprint Ser). 463p. 1974. 27.95 (ISBN 0-471-79852-5). Wiley.
--Key Papers in the Development of Information Theory. LC 73-77997. (Illus.). 1974. 27.95 (ISBN 0-87942-027-8). Inst Electrical.
Soroko, L. M. Holography & Coherent Optics. (Illus.). 650p. 1978. 59.50 (ISBN 0-306-40101-0, Plenum Pr). Plenum Pub.
Symposium, Brussels. Information & Prediction in Science: Proceedings. Dockx, S. & Bernays, P., eds. 1965. 46.00 (ISBN 0-12-219050-5). Acad Pr.
The Way Things Work Book of the Computer: An Illustrated Encyclopedia of Information Science, Cybernetics & Data Processing. (Illus.). 1974. 8.95 (ISBN 0-671-21900-6). S&S.
Weltner, K. The Measurement of Verbal Information in Psychology & Education. Crook, B. M., tr. from Ger. LC 73-80874. (Communications & Cybernetics Ser.: Vol. 7). (Illus.). 185p. 1974. 37.00 (ISBN 0-387-06335-8). Springer-Verlag.
Wilson, Ira G. & Wilson, Marthann E. Information, Computers & System Design. LC 74-11059. 362p. 1974. Repr. of 1965 ed. 16.00 (ISBN 0-88275-185-9). Krieger.
Wolfowitz, J. Coding Theorems of Information Theory. (Ergebnisse der Mathematik und Ihrer Grenzgebiete: Vol. 31). 1978. 31.20 (ISBN 0-387-08548-3). Springer-Verlag.
Yu, Francis T. Optics & Information Theory. LC 76-23135. 1976. 24.00 (ISBN 0-471-01682-9, Pub. by Wiley-Interscience). Wiley.

INFORMATION THEORY IN BIOLOGY

Gatlin, Lila L. Information Theory & the Living System. LC 76-187030. (Molecular Biology Ser.). (Illus.). 210p. 1972. 16.00x (ISBN 0-231-03634-5). Columbia U Pr.
Hassenstein, B. Information & Control in the Living Organism: An Elementary Introduction. 159p. 1971. pap. text ed. 9.95x (ISBN 0-412-10690-6, Pub. by Chapman & Hall England). Methuen Inc.
Neuberger, M. Florkin & Van Deenen, L. L. Comprehensive Biochemistry: Biological Information Transfer, Vol. 24. 1977. 51.75 (ISBN 0-444-41583-1). Elsevier.
Ramsey-Klee, Diane M., ed. Aids to Biological Communication: Prosthesis & Synthesis. 392p. 1970. 68.75 (ISBN 0-677-13410-X). Gordon.
Sampson, J. R. Adaptive Information Processing: An Introductory Survey. LC 76-8470. (Texts & Monographs in Computer Science Ser.). (Illus.). 1976. 17.90 (ISBN 0-387-07739-1). Springer-Verlag.
Varela, F. J. Principles of Biological Autonomy. (North Holland Ser. in General Systems Research: Vol. 2). 336p. 1979. 35.00 (ISBN 0-444-00321-5, North Holland). Elsevier.
Vassileva-Popova, J. G. & Jensen, E. V., eds. Biophysical & Biochemical Information Transfer in Recognition. LC 78-15876. 895p. 1978. 75.00 (ISBN 0-306-40036-7, Plenum Pr). Plenum Pub.
Vassileva-Popova, Julia G., ed. Physical & Chemical Bases of Biological Information Transfer. 463p. 1975. 42.50 (ISBN 0-306-30862-2, Plenum Pr). Plenum Pub.
Wrighton, R. F. Elementary Principles of Probability & Information. 1974. 20.50 (ISBN 0-12-765550-6). Acad Pr.

INFORMATION THEORY IN ECONOMICS

Galatin, Malcolm, ed. Economics of Information: Annual Volume Department of Economics, Vol. 4. 1980. 21.95 (ISBN 0-915326-17-5). Cyrco Pr.
Galatin, Malcolm & Leiter, Robert D., eds. Economics of Information. (Social Dimensions of Economics Ser.). 257p. 1981. lib. bdg. 18.00 (ISBN 0-89838-067-7). Kluwer Boston.

INFORMATION THEORY IN ESTHETICS

Moles, Abraham. Information Theory & Esthetic Perception. Cohen, Joel E., tr. LC 62-13213. (Illus.). 1966. 12.50 (ISBN 0-252-72485-2). U of Ill Pr.

INFORMATION THEORY IN PSYCHOLOGY

see also Human Information Processing

Berrien, F. Kenneth. General & Social Systems. LC 68-29552. (Illus.). 1968. 15.00x (ISBN 0-8135-0585-2). Rutgers U Pr.
Buckley, Walter, ed. Modern Systems Research for the Behavioral Scientist. LC 66-19888. (Illus.). 1968. 39.95x (ISBN 0-202-30011-0). Aldine Pub.
Hollis, Joseph W. & Hollis, Lucille U. Personalizing Information Processes. (Illus.). 1969. text ed. 17.95 (ISBN 0-02-356170-X). Macmillan.
Laszlo, Ervin. System, Structure & Experience: Toward a Scientific Theory of Mind. (Current Topics of Contemporary Thought Ser.: Vol. 1). 124p. 1969. 27.00x (ISBN 0-677-02360-X). Gordon.
Leeuwenberg, E. L. Structural Information of Visual Patterns: An Efficient Coding System in Perception. 1968. pap. text ed. 8.90x (ISBN 0-686-22463-9). Mouton.
Newbold, H. L. The Psychiatric Programming of People: Neo-Behavioral Orthomolecular Psychiatry. 170p. 1972. 17.25 (ISBN 0-08-016791-8). Pergamon.
Uttal, William R. A Taxonomy of Visual Processes. LC 80-18262. 1120p. 1981. text ed. 100.00 (ISBN 0-89859-075-2). L Erlbaum Assocs.
West, Charles K. The Social & Psychological Distortion of Information. LC 81-3941. 160p. 1981. text ed. 17.95 (ISBN 0-88229-616-7); pap. text ed. 8.95 (ISBN 0-88229-784-8). Nelson-Hall.

INFORMATIONS

see also Grand Jury; Quo Warranto

INFORMERS

Harney, Malachi L. & Cross, John C. The Informer in Law Enforcement. 2nd ed. 160p. 1968. photocopy ed. spiral 15.50 (ISBN 0-398-00782-9). C C Thomas.

INFRA-RED ASTRONOMY

Allen, David. Infrared: The New Astronomy. LC 75-16584. 228p. 1976. 17.95 (ISBN 0-470-02334-1). Halsted Pr.
Brancazio, Peter J. & Cameron, A. G., eds. Infrared Astronomy: Proceedings of a Conference Held at Goddard Space Center, 1966. LC 69-19544. (Illus.). 1968. 54.50x (ISBN 0-677-11980-1). Gordon.
Rowan-Robinson, Michael, ed. Vistas in Astronomy, Supplement: Far Infrared Astronomy. 352p. 1976. text ed. 45.00 (ISBN 0-08-020513-5). Pergamon.
Setti, Giancarlo, ed. Infrared Astronomy. (NATO Advanced Study Institutes Ser.: No. 38). 1978. lib. bdg. 42.00 (ISBN 90-277-0871-1, Pub. by Reidel Holland). Kluwer Boston.

INFRA-RED PHOTOGRAPHY

see Photography, Infra-Red

INFRA-RED RAYS

see also Infra-Red Astronomy; Infra-Red Technology

Bramson, M. A. Infrared Radiation: A Handbook for Applications. LC 66-26812. 623p. 1968. 55.00 (ISBN 0-306-30274-8, Plenum Pr). Plenum Pub.
Button, Kenneth J., ed. Infrared & Millimeter Waves: Instrumentation, Vol. II. LC 79-6949. 1979. 48.50 (ISBN 0-12-147702-9). Acad Pr.
--Infrared & Millimeter Waves: Sources of Radiation, Vol. 1. LC 79-6949. 1979. 46.50 (ISBN 0-12-147701-0). Acad Pr.
--Infrared & Millimeter Waves, Vol. 3: Submillimeter Techniques. 1980. 50.00 (ISBN 0-12-147703-7). Acad Pr.
Hadni, A. Essentials of Modern Physics Applied to the Study of the Infrared. 1967. 64.00 (ISBN 0-08-011902-6). Pergamon.
Moss, T. S. & Wolfe, W. L., eds. Infrared Physics. 1976. text ed. 47.00 (ISBN 0-08-020880-0). Pergamon.
Parker, Frank S. Applications of Infrared Spectroscopy in Biochemistry, Biology, & Medicine. LC 70-131882. 600p. 1971. 49.50 (ISBN 0-306-30502-X, Plenum Pr). Plenum Pub.
U. S. Specialty Group on Infrared Detectors. Infrared Detectors. Moss, T. S. & Wolfe, W. L., eds. 1976. text ed. 20.00 (ISBN 0-08-020548-8). Pergamon.

INFRA-RED SPECTROMETRY

Alpert, Nelson L., et al. IR-Theory & Practice of Infrared Spectroscopy. rev. 2nd ed. LC 63-17644. 380p. 1970. 29.50 (ISBN 0-306-30399-X, Plenum Pr). Plenum Pub.
--IR-Theory & Practice of Infrared Spectroscopy. LC 73-12968. 380p. 1973. pap. text ed. 7.95 (ISBN 0-306-20001-5, Rosetta). Plenum Pub.
Avram, Margareta & Mateescu, Gh. Infrared Spectroscopy: Applications in Organic Chemistry. LC 78-16322. 532p. 1979. Repr. of 1972 ed. lib. bdg. 28.50 (ISBN 0-88275-711-3). Krieger.
Becker, D. E., ed. Recommendations for the Presentation of Infrared Absorption Spectra in Data Collections-A: Condensed Phases. 1978. pap. text ed. 10.00 (ISBN 0-08-022376-1). Pergamon.
Brame, Edward & Graselli, Jeanette. Infrared & Raman Spectroscopy, Pt. A. (Practical Spectroscopy Ser.: Vol. 1). 1976. 47.50 (ISBN 0-8247-6392-0). Dekker.
Brame, Edward G. & Grasselli, Jeannette, eds. Infrared & Raman Spectroscopy, Pt. B. (Practical Spectroscopy Ser.: Vol. 1). 1977. 47.50 (ISBN 0-8247-6526-5). Dekker.
Chantry, G. W. Submillimetre Spectroscopy. 1972. 61.00 (ISBN 0-12-170550-1). Acad Pr.
Clark, R. J. & Hester, R. E., eds. Advances in Infrared and Raman Spectroscopy, 5 vols. Vol. 1. 1975 ed. 54.50 (ISBN 0-85501-181-5); Vol. 2. 1976 ed. 60.50 (ISBN 0-85501-182-3); Vol. 3. 1977 ed. 60.50 (ISBN 0-85501-183-1); Vol. 4. 1978 ed. 76.50 (ISBN 0-85501-184-X). Heyden.
--Advances in Infrared & Raman Spectroscopy, Vol. 5. 1978. casebound 83.50 (ISBN 0-85501-185-8). Heyden.
Cole, Howard, ed. Tables of Wavenumbers for the Calibration of Infrared Spectrometers, Vol. 9. 2nd ed. 1977. text ed. 37.00 (ISBN 0-08-021247-6). Pergamon.
Cook, B. W. & Jones, K. A Programmed Introduction to Infrared Spectroscopy. 1972. 24.50 (ISBN 0-85501-036-3); pap. 11.00 (ISBN 0-85501-032-0). Heyden.
Cross, A. D. & Jones, R. A. Introduction to Practical Infra-Red Spectroscopy. 3rd ed. LC 69-20393. 87p. 1969. 17.50 (ISBN 0-306-30626-3, Plenum Pr). Plenum Pub.
Dolphin, David & Wick, Alexander. Tabulation of Infrared Spectral Data. LC 76-48994. 566p. 1977. 28.50 (ISBN 0-471-21780-8). Krieger.
Espectroscopia Infarroja. (Serie Quimica: No. 12). 74p. (Span.). 1974. pap. 1.25 (ISBN 0-8270-6380-6). OAS.
Ferraro, John R. Low-Frequency Vibrations in Inorganic & Coordination Compounds. LC 74-107528. 309p. 1971. 39.50 (ISBN 0-306-30453-8, Plenum Pr). Plenum Pub.
Ferraro, John R. & Basile, Louis J., eds. Fourier Transform Infrared Spectroscopy: Applications to Chemical Systems, Vol. 2. LC 78-26956. 1979. 37.50 (ISBN 0-12-254102-2). Acad Pr.
Finch, A., et al. Chemical Applications of Far Infrared Spectroscopy. 1970. 44.00 (ISBN 0-12-256350-6). Acad Pr.
Gadsen, J. A. Infrared Spectra of Minerals & Related Inorganic Compounds. 288p. 1975. 37.95 (ISBN 0-408-70665-1). Butterworth.
Griffiths, Peter R. Chemical Infrared Fourier Transform Spectroscopy. LC 75-6505. (Chemical Analysis Ser: Vol. 43). 340p. 1975. 39.50x (ISBN 0-471-32786-7, Pub by Wiley-Interscience). Wiley.
Hair, M. L. Infrared Spectroscopy in Surface Chemistry. 336p. 1967. 45.00 (ISBN 0-8247-1285-4). Dekker.
Kendall, David N. Applied Infrared Spectroscopy. 576p. 1966. 28.50 (ISBN 0-442-15073-3, Pub. by Van Nos Reinhold). Krieger.
Lang, L., ed. Absorption Spectra in the Infrared Region, Vol. 1. 306p. 1974. 29.95 (ISBN 0-592-01257-3). Butterworth.
--Absorption Spectra in the Infrared Region, Vol. 4. 320p. 1978. lib. bdg. 28.00 (ISBN 0-88275-932-9). Krieger.
Luff, N. A. D. M. S. Working Atlas of Infrared Spectroscopy. 1972. text ed. 43.50 (ISBN 0-407-69999-6). Butterworth.
Martin, D. H., ed. Spectroscopic Techniques for Far Infra-Red Submillimeter & Millimeter Waves. 1967. 49.00 (ISBN 0-444-10244-2, North-Holland). Elsevier.
Mattson, James S., et al, eds. Infrared Correlation & Fourier Transform Spectroscopy. (Computers in Chemistry & Instrumentation: Vol. 7). 1976. 39.50 (ISBN 0-8247-6369-6). Dekker.
Miller, R. G. & Stace, B. C., eds. Laboratory Methods in Infrared Spectroscopy. 2nd ed. 1972. 52.00 (ISBN 0-85501-027-4). Heyden.
Moller, K. D. & Rothschild, W. G. Far-Infrared Spectroscopy. LC 70-118624. (Wiley Ser. in Pure & Applied Optics). 1971. 71.00 (ISBN 0-471-61313-4, Pub. by Wiley-Interscience). Wiley.
Nakanishi, Koji & Solomon, Philippa H. Infrared Absorption Spectroscopy. 2nd ed. LC 76-27393. 1977. pap. 15.95x (ISBN 0-8162-6251-9). Holden-Day.
Pinchas, S. & Laulicht, I. Infrared Spectra of Labelled Compounds. 1971. 59.50 (ISBN 0-12-556650-6). Acad Pr.
Shen, Y. R., et al, eds. Nonlinear Infrared Generation. (Topics in Applied Physics Ser.: Vol. 16). 1977. 49.40 (ISBN 0-387-07945-9). Springer-Verlag.
Socrates, G. Infrared Characteristic Group Frequencies. LC 79-1406. 153p. 1980. 72.00 (ISBN 0-471-27592-1, Pub. by Wiley-Interscience). Wiley.
Stewart, J. E. Infrared Spectroscopy: Experimental Methods & Techniques. 1970. 75.00 (ISBN 0-8247-1643-4). Dekker.
Svehla, G. Wilson & Wilson's Comprehensive Analytical Chemistry, Vol. 6: Analytical Infrared Spectroscopy. 1976. 97.75 (ISBN 0-444-41165-8). Elsevier.
Tables of Wavenumbers for the Calibration of Infra-Red Spectrometers. 169p. 1961. 14.95 (ISBN 0-306-30603-4, Consultants). Plenum Pub.
Theophanides, Theo M., ed. Infrared & Raman Spectroscopy of Biological Molecules. (NATO Advanced Study Institutes Ser.). 1979. lib. bdg. 47.50 (ISBN 90-277-0966-1, Pub. by Reidel Holland). Kluwer Boston.
Van Der Maas. Interpretation of Infrared Spectra: An Audio Visual Program. 1979. 230.00 (ISBN 0-85501-094-0). Heyden.
Van der Maas, J. H. Basic Infrared Spectroscopy. 2nd ed. 1972. 31.50 (ISBN 0-85501-031-2); pap. 17.50 (ISBN 0-85501-029-0). Heyden.
White, Robert G. Handbook of Industrial Infrared Analysis. LC 64-7506. 440p. 1964. 49.50 (ISBN 0-306-30174-1, Plenum Pr). Plenum Pub.

INFRA-RED SPECTRUM

see Spectrum, Infra-Red

INFRA-RED TECHNOLOGY

see also Photography, Infra-Red

Grunwald, Ernest, et al. Megawatt Infrared Laser Chemistry. LC 78-6721. 1978. 21.50x (ISBN 0-471-03074-0, Pub. by Wiley-Interscience). Wiley.
Hill, D. W. & Powell, T. Non-Dispersive Infrared Gas Analysis in Science, Medicine & Industry. LC 68-56425. 222p. 1968. 32.50 (ISBN 0-306-30374-4, Plenum Pr). Plenum Pub.
Hudson, Richard D., Jr. Infrared System Engineering. LC 68-8715. (Pure & Applied Optics Ser). 1969. 47.00 (ISBN 0-471-41850-1, Pub. by Wiley-Interscience). Wiley.
International Conference on Infrared Physics, 2nd, (CIRP 2), Zurich, 1979. Papers. Kneubuhl, Fritz, ed. 264p. 1980. 40.00 (ISBN 0-08-025055-6). Pergamon.
Keyes, R. J., ed. Optical & Infrared Detectors. 2nd ed. (Topics in Applied Physics Ser.: Vol. 19). (Illus.). 325p. 1981. pap. 24.80 (ISBN 0-387-10176-4). Springer-Verlag.
Kingston, R. H. Detection of Optical & Infrared Radiation. (Springer Ser. in Optical Sciences: Vol. 10). (Illus.). 1978. 23.70 (ISBN 0-387-08617-X). Springer-Verlag.
Lang, L., ed. Absorption Spectra in the Infrared Region, Vol. 3. 320p. 1977. lib. bdg. 26.50 (ISBN 0-88275-536-6). Krieger.
La Toison, M. Infrared & Its Thermal Applications. 1970. 34.75x (ISBN 0-677-61170-6). Gordon.
Wolfe, W. L. & Zissis, G. J., eds. The Infrared Handbook. LC 77-90786. (Illus.). 1978. 25.00 (ISBN 0-9603590-0-1). Environ Res Inst.

INFUSORIA

see also Ciliata

INGE, WILLIAM MOTTER

McClure, Arthur F. William Inge: A Bibliography. 1981. lib. bdg. 18.00 (ISBN 0-8240-9486-7). Garland Pub.

Shuman, R. Baird. William Inge. (Twayne's United States Authors Ser). 1965. pap. 3.45 (ISBN 0-8084-0328-1, T95, Twayne). Coll & U Pr.

INGE, WILLIAM RALPH, 1860-1954

Dark, Sidney. Five Deans: John Colet, John Donne, Jonathan Swift, Arthur Penrhyn Stanley & William Ralph Inge. LC 70-86011. (Essay & General Literature Index Reprint Ser). 1969. Repr. of 1928 ed. 11.50 (ISBN 0-8046-0555-6). Kennikat.

Helm, Robert M. Gloomy Dean: The Thought of William Ralph Inge. LC 62-14860. 1962. 7.95 (ISBN 0-910244-27-8). Blair.

INGERSOLL, CHARLES JARED, 1782-1862

Meigs, William M. Life of Charles Jared Ingersoll. LC 71-127194. (Amer. Scene Ser). 1970. Repr. of 1897 ed. lib. bdg. 35.00 (ISBN 0-306-70041-7). Da Capo.

INGERSOLL, JARED, 1722-1781

Gipson, Lawrence H. American Loyalist: Jared Ingersoll. LC 79-140529. (Historical Publications, Miscellany Ser.: No. 8). 1971. 30.00x (ISBN 0-300-01446-5); pap. 5.95x (ISBN 0-300-01424-4, Y239). Yale U Pr.

--Jared Ingersoll: A Study of American Loyalism in Relation to British Colonial Government. LC 69-14216. 1969. Repr. of 1920 ed. 12.50 (ISBN 0-8462-1309-5). Russell.

INGERSOLL, ROBERT GREEN, 1833-1899

Anderson, David D. Robert Ingersoll. (U. S. Authors Ser.: No. 204). lib. bdg. 10.95 (ISBN 0-8057-0396-9). Twayne.

Ingersoll, Robert G. & Wakefield, Eva I. Letters. LC 73-14033. (Illus.). 747p. 1974. Repr. of 1951 ed. lib. bdg. 29.00x (ISBN 0-8371-7139-3, INLE). Greenwood.

Stein, Gordon. Robert G. Ingersoll: A Checklist. LC 78-626234. (Serif Ser.: No. 9). 1969. 7.50x (ISBN 0-87338-047-9). Kent St U Pr.

INGERSOLL FAMILY

Fisher, Sidney G. Philadelphia Perspective: The Diary of Sidney George Fisher. Wainwright, Nicholas B., ed. 1967. 12.50 (ISBN 0-910732-06-X). Pa Hist Soc.

INGLIS, CHARLES, BP. OF NOVA SCOTIA, 1734-1816

Lydekker, John Wolfe. The Life & Letters of Charles Inglis: His Ministry in America & Consecration As First Colonial Bishop, from 1759-1787. LC 36-32928. (Church Historical Society Ser.: No. 20). (Illus.). 1936. text ed. 22.50x (ISBN 0-8401-5020-2). Allenson-Breckinridge.

INGOLDSBY, THOMAS, PSEUD.

see Barham, Richard Harris, 1788-1845

INGRAM'S REBELLION (VIRGINIA)

see Bacon's Rebellion, 1676

INGRATITUDE

see also Gratitude

INGRES, JEAN AUGUSTE DOMINIQUE, 1780-1867

Borden, Emanuel, ed. More Drawings of Ingres. (Master Draughtsman Ser). (Illus.). 48p. treasure trove bdg. 6.47x (ISBN 0-685-36835-1); pap. 2.95 (ISBN 0-685-36836-X). Borden.

Ingres, Jean A. Drawings of Ingres. Longstreet, Stephen, ed. (Master Draughtsman Ser). (Illus., Orig.). 1964. treasure trove bdg. 6.47x (ISBN 0-685-07265-7); pap. 2.95 (ISBN 0-685-07266-5). Borden.

Mongan, Agnes & Nace, Hans. Ingres Centennial. LC 67-18321. (Illus.). 1967. write for info. Newbury Bks Inc.

Naef, Hans. Die Bildniszeichnungen Von J.A.D. Ingres, 5 vols. only vols. 1-4 are available. (Illus.). 1980. 175.00x ea. (Pub. by Sotheby Parke Bernet England). Vol. 1 (ISBN 3-7165-0087-9). Vol. 2 (ISBN 3-7165-0249-9). Vol. 3.1979 (ISBN 3-7165-0250-2). Vol. 4 (ISBN 3-7165-0122-0). Biblio Dist.

Picon, Gaeton. Ingres. Gilbert, Stuart, tr. LC 80-51575. (Illus.). 162p. 1980. 75.00 (ISBN 0-8478-0335-X). Rizzoli Intl.

Whitely, Jon. Ingres. 1981. 27.00x (ISBN 0-905368-10-X, Pub. by Jupiter England). State Mutual Bk.

--Ingres. (Illus.). 15.95 (ISBN 0-8467-0250-9, Pub. by Two Continents); pap. text ed. 9.95 (ISBN 0-8467-0249-5). Hippocrene Bks.

INHALATION THERAPY

see also Aerosol Therapy

Assmann, David, et al. Clinical Simulations for Respiratory Care Practitioners. (Orig.). 1979. pap. 25.95 (ISBN 0-8151-0318-2). Year Bk Med.

Barnes, Thomas A. & Israel, Jacob S. Brady's Programmed Introduction to Respiratory Therapy. 2nd ed. LC 79-27753. (Illus.). 365p. 1980. pap. text ed. 14.95 (ISBN 0-87619-624-5). R J Brady.

Dekornfeld, Thomas J., ed. Selected Papers in Respiratory Therapy. 2nd ed. 1979. pap. 24.00 (ISBN 0-87488-525-6). Med Exam.

Dekornfeld, Thomas J., et al. Respiratory Therapy Examination Review Book, Vol. 2. 2nd ed. Orig. Title: Inhalation Therapy Examination Review Book, Vol. 2. 1974. ~~spiral~~ bdg. 9.50 (ISBN 0-87488-344-X). Med Exam.

Egan, Donald F. Fundamentals of Respiratory Therapy. 3rd ed. LC 76-25810. (Illus.). 1977. 26.95 (ISBN 0-8016-1503-8). Mosby.

Glover, Dennis W. & Glover, Margaret M. Respiratory Therapy: Basics for Nursing & the Allied Health Professions. LC 78-6500. (Illus.). 1978. pap. 10.50 (ISBN 0-8016-1863-0). Mosby.

Gregory, George A. & Thibeault, Donald W. Neonatal Pulmonary Care. LC 78-7773. 1979. 34.50 (ISBN 0-201-02481-0, 02481, Med-Nurse). A-W.

Heironimus, Terring W., 3rd & Bageant, Robert A. Mechanical Artificial Ventilation: A Manual for Students & Practitioners. 3rd ed. (Amer. Lec. in Anesthesiology Ser.). (Illus.). 560p. 1977. 33.50 (ISBN 0-398-03541-5). C C Thomas.

Home Use of Respiratory Therapy. (Fifty Ser). 1973. pap. 2.00 (ISBN 0-685-58083-0, 56HM). Natl Fire Prot.

Kacmarek, Robert M. & Dimas, Steven. The Essentials of Respiratory Therapy. (Illus.). 1979. 18.95 (ISBN 0-8151-4953-0). Year Bk Med.

Kracum, Vincent D. Respiratory Therapy Examination Review Book, Vol. 1. 3rd ed. 1975. spiral bdg. 9.50 (ISBN 0-87488-471-3). Med Exam.

Lough, Marvin D., et al. Newborn Respiratory Care. (Illus.). 1979. 20.95 (ISBN 0-8151-5635-9). Year Bk Med.

--Pediatric Respiratory Therapy. 2nd ed. (Illus.). 1979. 19.95 (ISBN 0-8151-5638-3). Year Bk Med.

McPherson, Steven P. Respiratory Therapy Equipment. LC 75-5602. (Illus.). 1977. text ed. 22.95 (ISBN 0-8016-3319-2). Mosby.

Mathewson, Hugh S. Pharmacology for Respiratory Therapists. LC 76-41196. (Illus.). 1977. pap. 8.95 (ISBN 0-8016-3160-2). Mosby.

Shapiro, Barry A., et al. Clinical Application of Respiratory Care. 2nd ed. (Illus.). 1979. 21.50 (ISBN 0-8151-7635-X). Year Bk Med.

Taylor, Joan P. Manual of Respiratory Therapy. 2nd ed. LC 77-22882. (Illus.). 1978. pap. text ed. 13.95 (ISBN 0-8016-0836-8). Mosby.

Tysinger, D. S., Jr. The Clinical Physics & Physiology of Chronic Lung Disease, Inhalation Therapy, & Pulmonary Function Testing. (Illus.). 264p. 1973. text ed. 17.50 (ISBN 0-398-02777-3). C C Thomas.

Wojciechowski, William V. & Neff, Paula E. Comprehensive Review of Respiratory Therapy. LC 81-1947. 400p. 1981. 19.95 (ISBN 0-471-08408-5, Pub. by Wiley Med). Wiley.

INHERITANCE (BIOLOGY)

see Heredity

INHERITANCE AND SUCCESSION

see also Decedents' Estates; Estates (Law); Executors and Administrators; Inheritance and Transfer Tax; Probate Law and Practice; Trusts and Trustees; Wills

Boucher, H. J., ed. How-to-Live-&-Die-with California Probate. (Probate Ser.). 171p. 1970. 6.95 (ISBN 0-87201-094-5). Gulf Pub.

Brittain, John A. Inheritance & the Inequality of Material Wealth. LC 77-91814. (Studies in Social Economics). 1978. 9.95 (ISBN 0-8157-1084-4); pap. 3.95 (ISBN 0-8157-1083-6). Brookings.

--The Inheritance of Economic Status. LC 76-56369. (Studies in Social Economics). 1977. 11.95 (ISBN 0-8157-1082-8); pap. 4.95 (ISBN 0-8157-1081-X). Brookings.

Comyn, J. & Johnson, R. Wills & Intestacies. LC 78-92109. 1970. 13.75 (ISBN 0-08-006691-7); pap. 6.25 (ISBN 0-08-006690-9). Pergamon.

Gavit, Bernard C. Indiana Law of Future Interest Descent & Wills. 1934. 7.00 (ISBN 0-911536-22-1). Trinity U Pr.

Goldschmidt, Walter. Kambuya's Cattle: The Legacy of an African Herdsman. LC 68-31589. 1968. 23.75x (ISBN 0-520-01472-3). U of Cal Pr.

Goody, J., et al, eds. Family & Inheritance. LC 76-10402. (Past & Present Publications Ser.). (Illus.). 1976. 45.00 (ISBN 0-521-21246-4); pap. 13.95x (ISBN 0-521-29354-5). Cambridge U Pr.

Hamnett, Ian. Chieftainship & Legitimacy. (International Library of Anthropology). 1975. 15.00x (ISBN 0-7100-8177-4). Routledge & Kegan.

Hempel, Arthur J. Claim Your Inheritance. 1975. pap. 5.00 (ISBN 0-89248-000-9). Circle Pr.

Justices & Juries in Colonial America: Two Accounts, 1680-1722. LC 77-37968. (American Law Ser.: The Formative Years). 366p. 1972. Repr. of 1972 ed. 18.00 (ISBN 0-405-03995-6). Arno.

Levin, Martin, et al. Protect Your Inheritance. 160p. 1981. pap. 6.95 (ISBN 0-8329-0102-4). New Century.

Mifsud, Frank M. Customary Land Law in Africa. (FAO Legislative Ser.: No. 7). (Orig.). 1967. pap. 4.75 (ISBN 0-685-09374-3, F 106, FAO). Unipub.

Obeyesekere, Gananath. Land Tenure in Village Ceylon. (Cambridge South Asian Studies: No. 4). 1967. 29.95 (ISBN 0-521-05854-6). Cambridge U Pr.

Reppy, Alison. Ordinance of William the Conqueror, 1072: Its Implication in the Modern Law of Succession. LC 55-5962. 1955. 15.00 (ISBN 0-379-00101-2). Oceana.

Round, Horace. Peerage & Pedigree: Studies in Peerage Law & Family History, 2 vols. (Genealogy Ser.: No. 1). 362p. 1971. Repr. of 1910 ed. Set. 65.00x (ISBN 0-7130-0020-1, Pub. by Woburn Pr England). Biblio Dist.

Round, John H. Peerage & Pedigree: Studies in Peerage Law & Family History, 2 Vols. LC 76-124476. 1970. Repr. of 1910 ed. 30.00 (ISBN 0-8063-0425-1). Genealog Pub.

Shriver, Nicholas, Jr. & Stiller, Shale E., eds. How-to-Live-&-Die-with Maryland Probate. 2nd ed. (Probate Ser.). 199p. 1975. 6.95 (ISBN 0-87201-512-2). Gulf Pub.

Sussman, Marvin B., et al. The Family & Inheritance. LC 74-104183. 1970. 13.95 (ISBN 0-87154-873-9). Russell Sage.

Swanson, Guy E. Rules of Descent: Studies in the Sociology of Parentage. (Anthropological Papers: No. 39). 1969. pap. 2.00x (ISBN 0-932206-37-9). U Mich Mus Anthro.

Wedgwood, Josiah. Economics of Inheritance. LC 74-137966. (Economic Thought, History & Challenge Ser). 1971. Repr. of 1939 ed. 14.50 (ISBN 0-8046-1467-9). Kennikat.

Wright, Minturn T., 3rd, ed. How-to-Live-&-Die-with Pennsylvania Probate. 176p. 1973. 6.95 (ISBN 0-87201-661-7). Gulf Pub.

Wypyski, Eugene M. The Law of Inheritance in All Fifty States. 3rd ed. LC 76-40542. (Legal Almanac Ser.: No. 33). 1976. lib. bdg. 5.95x (ISBN 0-379-11106-3). Oceana.

INHERITANCE AND TRANSFER TAX

see also Gifts–Taxation; Real Property and Taxation

Biskind, Elliott L., ed. Boardman's Estate Management & Accounting, 2 Vols. rev. ed. LC 64-8482. 1969. looseleaf with 1980 suppl. 85.00 (ISBN 0-87632-056-6). Boardman.

Bittker, Boris I. Federal Taxation of Income, Estates & Gifts, 4 vols. LC 80-50773. 1981. 295.00 set (ISBN 0-88262-460-1). Warren.

Clark, John A. How to Save Time & Taxes in Handling Estates. 28.50 (ISBN 0-685-02518-7). Bender.

Commerce Clearing House. Federal Estate & Gift Taxes Explained, Including Estate Planning: 1981 Edition. 1980. 9.00 (ISBN 0-686-75917-6). Commerce.

Cooper, George. A Voluntary Tax? New Perspectives on Sophisticated Estate Tax Avoidance. LC 78-20853. (Studies of Government Finance). 1979. 9.95 (ISBN 0-8157-1552-8); pap. 3.95 (ISBN 0-8157-1551-X). Brookings.

Dodge, Joseph M. Federal Taxation of Estates, Trusts & Gifts, Principles & Planning. LC 81-11602. (American Casebook Ser.). 783p. 1981. write for info. West Pub.

Engelbrecht, Ted D., et al. Federal Taxation of Estates, Gifts, & Trusts. (Illus.). 528p. 1981. 32.95 (ISBN 0-686-69612-3). P-H.

Federal Estate & Gift Taxes Code & Regulations As of April 1981. 8.50 (ISBN 0-686-75916-8). Commerce.

Federal Taxation of Estates, Gifts, & Trusts. 3rd ed. 645p. 1980. 55.00 (ISBN 0-686-28716-9, T118C). ALI-ABA.

Ferguson, M. Carr, et al. Federal Income Taxation of Estates & Beneficiaries: 1980 Supplement. LC 70-79882. 208p. 1981. pap. 7.95 (ISBN 0-316-27900-5). Little.

Harris, Homer I. & Rasch, Joseph. Handling Federal Estate & Gift Taxes, 3 vols. 2nd ed. LC 72-96007. 1972. 150.00 (ISBN 0-686-14503-8). Lawyers Co-Op.

Hartley, Thomas A. Taxation of Decedents' Estates. (Illus.). 1978. 34.95 (ISBN 0-13-886226-5, Busn). P-H.

Jantscher, Gerald R. Trusts & Estate Taxation. (Studies of Government Finance). 11.95 (ISBN 0-8157-4576-1); pap. 4.95 (ISBN 0-8157-4575-3). Brookings.

Kahn, Arnold. Filing Systems & Records Management. LC 78-31509. 1979. 15.50 (ISBN 0-07-033228-2, P&RB). McGraw.

Larsen, David C. Who Gets It When You Go? Wills, Probate, & Inheritance Taxes for the Hawaii Resident. LC 79-25776. (Illus.). 128p. 1980. pap. 4.95 (ISBN 0-8248-0695-6). U Pr of Hawaii.

Lippett, Peter E. Estate Planning: What Anyone Who Owns Anything Must Know. (Illus.). 1979. 16.95 (ISBN 0-8359-1778-9). Reston.

Looney, J. W. Estate Planning for Business Owners. King, Robert, ed. 1979. 16.95 (ISBN 0-8359-1784-3). Reston.

Morcom & Parry. Capital Transfer Tax. 2nd ed. 1977. 40.00 (ISBN 0-85941-055-2). State Mutual Bk.

Moriarty, Charles P. Adopt Your Way to Inheritance & Gift Tax Savings. LC 80-23202. 160p. 1980. 12.95 (ISBN 0-916076-31-8). Writing.

Organization for Economic Cooperation & Development, Fiscal Committee. Draft Double Taxation Convention on Estates & Inheritances: Proceedings. 128p. 1966. 2.50x (ISBN 0-686-14800-2). OECD.

Rabinowitz, Joel. Federal Estate & Gift Tax. 3rd ed. (Sum & Substance Ser.). 1979. 13.95 (ISBN 0-686-27112-2). Center Creative Ed.

Sanford, C. T. Taxing Inheritance & Capital Gains. (Institute of Economic Affairs, Hobart Papers Ser.: No. 32). 1967. pap. 2.50 (ISBN 0-685-20640-8, OW0539411). Transatlantic.

Soled, Alex J. The Essential Guide to Wills, Estates, Trusts & Death Taxes. 248p. (Orig.). 1981. pap. 12.95 (ISBN 0-940024-00-4). Chancery Pubs.

Stephens, et al. Federal Estate & Gift Taxation Study Problems. 1978. 4.95 (ISBN 0-88262-248-X). Warren.

The Taxation of Transfer of Family-Held Enterprises on Death or Inter Vivos. (Cahiers De Droit Fiscal International LXIV a). 1979. pap. 45.00 (ISBN 90-200-0562-6, Pub. by Kluwer Law Netherlands). Kluwer Boston.

Wagner, Richard E. Death & Taxes: Some Perspectives on Inheritance, Inequality, and Progressive Taxation. 1973. pap. 4.25 (ISBN 0-8447-3100-5). Am Enterprise.

--Inheritance & the State: Tax Principles for a Free & Prosperous Commonwealth. LC 77-8549. 1977. pap. 4.25 (ISBN 0-8447-3252-4). Am Enterprise.

West, Max. Inheritance Tax. 2nd rev. ed. LC 79-77988. (Columbia University. Studies in the Social Sciences: No. 11). 1971. Repr. of 1908 ed. 16.50 (ISBN 0-404-51011-6). AMS Pr.

INHERITANCE AND TRANSFER TAX–CANADA

Crumbley, D. Larry. A Practical Guide to Preparing a Federal Estate Tax Return. 7th ed. 1980. pap. 8.50 (ISBN 0-88450-057-8, 1703-B). Lawyers & Judges.

INHERITANCE AND TRANSFER TAX–GREAT BRITAIN

Berkowitz, David S. & Thorne, Samuel E., eds. British Liberties. LC 77-89201. (Classics of English Legal History in the Modern Era Ser.: Vol. 57). 486p. 1979. lib. bdg. 40.00 (ISBN 0-8240-3156-3). Garland Pub.

Harbury, C. D. & Hitchens, D. M. Inheritance & Wealth Inequality in Britain. (Illus.). 1979. text ed. 27.50x (ISBN 0-04-330296-3). Allen Unwin.

Wedgwood, Josiah. Economics of Inheritance. LC 74-137966. (Economic Thought, History & Challenge Ser). 1971. Repr. of 1939 ed. 14.50 (ISBN 0-8046-1467-9). Kennikat.

INHERITANCE AND TRANSFER TAX–INDIA

Char, T. Narasimha. Principles & Precedents of Estate Duty. 1971. lib. bdg. 20.00x (ISBN 0-210-31160-6). Asia.

INHERITANCE TAX

see Inheritance and Transfer Tax

INHIBITION

see also Habit

Boakes, R. A. & Halliday, M. S. Inhibition & Learning. 1972. 87.00 (ISBN 0-12-108050-1). Acad Pr.

Marx, Melvin H. Effects of Cumulative Training Upon Retroactive Inhibition & Transfer. (Comparitive Psychology Monographs: No. 94). Repr. of 1944 ed. pap. 5.00 (ISBN 0-527-24929-7). Kraus Repr.

Uchizono, K., ed. Excitation & Inhibition. 220p. 1975. 80.50 (ISBN 0-444-99872-1, North Holland). Elsevier.

Von Euler, U. S., et al, eds. Structure & Function of Inhibitory Neuronal Mechanisms. 1968. 79.00 (ISBN 0-08-012414-3). Pergamon.

INHIBITORS, ENZYME

see Enzyme Inhibitors

INITIAL TEACHING ALPHABET

see also Readers (I.T.A.)

Abranson, Lillian. Hanukkah ABC. (Illus.). (gr. 3-7). 1968. pap. 4.00 (ISBN 0-914080-60-1). Shulsinger Sales.

Alexenberg, Melvin. Alef Bet Zoo. (Illus.). (gr. 3-7). 1963. 5.00 (ISBN 0-914080-05-9). Shulsinger Sales.

Alexenberg, Melvin & Alexenberg, Miriam. Alef Bet Picture Dictionary. (Illus.). (gr. 3-7). 1963. 5.00 (ISBN 0-914080-06-7). Shulsinger Sales.

Azarian, Mary. A Farmer's Alphabet. LC 80-84938. (gr. 1 up). 1981. 10.95 (ISBN 0-87923-394-X); pap. 6.95 (ISBN 0-87923-397-4). Godine.

Coudron, Jill M. Alphabet Puppets. LC 78-72077. 1979. pap. 5.95 (ISBN 0-8224-0298-X). Pitman Learning.

Downing, John. The I.t.a. Symposium: Research Report on the British Experiment with i.t.a. 1967. 8.95x, cUSa (ISBN 0-8147-0130-2). NYU Pr.
Emberley, Ed. Ed Emberley's A. B. C. (Illus.). (gr. k-2). 1978. 6.95 (ISBN 0-316-23408-7). Little.
Larsen, Rayola C., ed. Alphabet Talk. (Illus., Orig.). (gr. k-3). 1980. pap. 2.50 (ISBN 0-88290-147-8). Horizon Utah.
McClenathan, Dayann. Reading with the Initial Teaching Alphabet: New Experiments & Conclusions. 1966. pap. text ed. 1.50x (ISBN 0-8134-0917-9, 917). Interstate.
Matthiesen, Thomas, photos by. ABC, an Alphabet Book. (Illus.). 64p. (gr. 3 up). 1981. 3.95 (ISBN 0-448-41054-0). G&D.
Miller, Elizabeth & Cohen, Jane. Cat & Dog Learn the ABC's. (Cat & Dog Ser.). (Illus.). 48p. (ps-3). 1981. PLB 5.90 (ISBN 0-531-04294-4). Watts.
Mitsumasa, Anno. Anno's Magical ABC: An Anamorphic Alphabet. (Illus.). 64p. 1981. 15.95 (ISBN 0-399-20788-0). Philomel.
Name Game. Hanukkah Alphabet. (Spell & Learn Ser.). (Illus.). (ps-5). 1977. pap. 1.50 (ISBN 0-914080-63-6). Shulsinger Sales.
--Alef Bet Jungle. (Spell & Learn Ser.). (Illus.). (ps-5). 1976. pap. 1.50 (ISBN 0-914080-46-6). Shulsinger Sales.
--Alef Bet Parade. (Spell & Learn Ser.). (Illus.). (ps-5). 1977. pap. 1.50 (ISBN 0-914080-48-2). Shulsinger Sales.
--Alef Bet Pet Shop. (Spell & Learn Ser.). (Illus.). (ps-5). 1976. pap. 1.50 (ISBN 0-914080-47-4). Shulsinger Sales.
--Alef Bet Toy Chest. (Spell & Learn Ser.). (Illus.). (ps-5). 1977. pap. 1.50 (ISBN 0-914080-49-0). Shulsinger Sales.
O'Halloran, George. Teach Yourself I.T.A. LC 73-85815. 1973. pap. 3.95 (ISBN 0-8224-4010-5). Pitman Learning.
Price, Marjorie. Alphadabbles: A Playful Alphabet. LC 79-18129. (Illus.). 128p. 1980. pap. 3.95 (ISBN 0-394-84303-7). Pantheon.
Scarry, Richard. Mein Allerschonstes Worterbuch: Deutsch-Englisch-Franzosisch. (Illus., Ger.). 1971. 11.95x (ISBN 3-7735-4902-4). Intl Learn Syst.
Smith, Judith M. Letter Mastery. Smith, Donald E., ed. (Michigan Tracking Program). 1976. pap. text ed. 1.75x (ISBN 0-914004-45-X). Ulrich.

INITIALISMS
see Acronyms

INITIALS
see also Alphabets; Artists' Marks; Illumination of Books and Manuscripts; Lettering; Monograms; Printing-Specimens; Type and Type-Founding
Cirker, Hayward & Cirker, Blanche. Monograms & Alphabetic Devices. (Illus., Orig.). 1970. pap. 6.00 (ISBN 0-486-22330-2). Dover.
Nesbitt, Alexander. Decorative Initials & Alphabets. (Illus.). 1959. pap. 5.00 (ISBN 0-486-20544-4). Dover.
Parks, Betsy M. The Dictionary of Initials. 1981. 12.95 (ISBN 0-8065-0750-0). Lyle Stuart.

INITIATIONS (IN RELIGION, FOLK-LORE, ETC.)
see also Baptism; Circumcision
Clymer, R. Swinburne. Philosophic Initiation. 1955. 4.95 (ISBN 0-686-05884-4). Philos Pub.
Droogers, Andre. The Dangerous Journey: Symbolic Aspects of Boys' Initiation Among the Wagenia of Kisangani, Zaire. (Change & Continuity in Africa Ser.). 1979. pap. text ed. 34.75x (ISBN 90-279-3357-X). Mouton.
Eliade, Mircea. Rites & Symbols of Initiation: The Mysteries of Birth & Rebirth. 8.50 (ISBN 0-8446-2027-0). Peter Smith.
--Rites & Symbols of Initiation: The Mysteries of Birth & Rebirth. Orig. Title: Birth & Rebirth. pap. 3.50x (ISBN 0-06-131236-3, TB1236, Torch). Har-Row.
Harley, George W. Notes on the Poro in Liberia. 1941. pap. 8.00 (ISBN 0-527-01248-3). Kraus Repr.
Henderson, Joseph L. Thresholds of Initiation. LC 67-24110. 1979. pap. 9.00x (ISBN 0-8195-6061-8, Pub. by Wesleyan U Pr). Columbia U Pr.
Jensen, Adolf E. Beschneidung und Reifezeremonien Bei Naturvoelkern. 1933. pap. 15.50 (ISBN 0-384-27160-X). Johnson Repr.
Murphy Center for Liturgical Research. Made, Not Born: New Perspectives on Christian Initiation & the Catechumenate. 192p. 1976. pap. 4.95 (ISBN 0-268-01337-3). U of Notre Dame Pr.
Zahan, Dominique. Societes D'initiation Bambara: Le N'domo, le Kore. (Lemonde D'outre-Mer Passe et Present: Etudes 8). 1960. pap. 30.00x (ISBN 90-2796-165-4). Mouton.

INITIATIONS (INTO TRADES, SOCIETIES, ETC.)
see also Greek Letter Societies; Secret Societies
Leemon, Thomas A. The Rites of Passage in a Student Culture. LC 72-81190. 1972. pap. text ed. 7.50x (ISBN 0-8077-1673-1). Tchrs Coll.
Robertson, Kirk. Origins, Initiations. 1980. 25.00 (ISBN 0-918824-19-2); pap. 4.00 (ISBN 0-918824-18-4). Turkey Pr.

INJECTIONS
see also Parenteral Therapy
Ming, Dennis & Siner, Elaine. Emergency Drug Manual. 160p. 1980. pap. 9.95 (ISBN 0-8359-1668-5). Reston.
Steinbrocker, Otto & Neustadt, David H. Aspiration & Injection Therapy in Arthritis & Musculoskeletal Disorders: A Handbook on Technique & Management. (Illus.). 1972. 12.00x (ISBN 0-06-142497-8, Harper Medical). Har-Row.

INJECTIONS, HYPODERMIC
Kurdi, William J. Hypodermoclysis. Kurdi, Kort, ed. 1980. pap. 3.95 (ISBN 0-686-28483-6). Med Educ.
Trissel, Lawrence A. Handbook on Injectable Drugs. 2nd ed. 630p. Date not set. pap. 20.00 (ISBN 0-930530-14-4). Am Soc Hosp Pharm.
--Pocket Guide to Injectable Drugs. 1981. pap. text ed. 10.00 (ISBN 0-930530-18-7). Am Soc Hosp Pharm.

INJECTIONS, HYPODERMIC–PROGRAMMED INSTRUCTION
Krueger, Elizabeth A. Hypodermic Injection: A Programed Unit. LC 66-17379. (Orig.). 1965. pap. 7.50x (ISBN 0-8077-1650-2). Tchrs Coll.

INJECTIONS, INTRAVENOUS
Aldrete. Intravenous Anesthesia. 1980. 52.95 (ISBN 0-8151-0106-6). Year Bk Med.
Dundee, John W. & Wyant, Gordon M. Intravenous Anaesthesia. LC 73-84969. 1974. text ed. 37.50 (ISBN 0-443-00977-5). Churchill.
Gahart, Betty L. Intravenous Medications: A Handbook for Nurses & Other Allied Health Personnel. 3rd ed. LC 81-4027. 258p. 1981. pap. text ed. 11.95 (ISBN 0-8016-1719-7). Mosby.

INJECTIONS, SUBCUTANEOUS
see Injections, Hypodermic

INJUNCTIONS
Kerr, William W. A Treatise on the Law & Practice of Injunctions. LC 81-81500. 743p. 1981. Repr. of 1927 ed. 75.00x (ISBN 0-912004-16-9). W W Gaunt.
Seidenberg, Jacob. Labor Injunction in New York City, 1935-1950. (Cornell Studies Ser.: No. 4). 1953. pap. 1.00 (ISBN 0-87546-001-1). NY Sch Indus Rel.
Witte, Edwin E. The Government in Labor Disputes. LC 70-89770. (American Labor, from Conspiracy to Collective Bargaining, Ser. 1). 352p. 1969. Repr. of 1932 ed. 15.00 (ISBN 0-405-02157-7). Arno.

INJURIES
see Accidents; Crash Injuries; First Aid in Illness and Injury; Sports-Accidents and Injuries; Traumatism; Wounds

INJURIES (LAW)
see Accident Law; Damages; Employers' Liability; Medical Jurisprudence; Personal Injuries; Torts

INJURIES, CRASH
see Crash Injuries

INJURIOUS INSECTS
see Insects, Injurious and Beneficial

INK
see also Printing Ink
Carvalho, David N. Forty Centuries of Ink, or a Chronological Narrative Concerning Ink & Its Backgrounds. 1971. Repr. of 1904 ed. lib. bdg. 24.50 (ISBN 0-8337-0490-7). B Franklin.

INK BRUSHWORK
see Brush Drawing

INK DRAWING
see Pen Drawing

INKBLOT TEST, RORSCHACH
see Rorschach Test

INLAND NAVIGATION
see also Canals; Inland Water Transportation; International Rivers; Intracoastal Waterways; Lakes; Rivers; Towing
Armroyd, George. Connected View of the Whole Internal Navigation of the United States. LC 77-146133. (American Classics in History & Social Science Ser.: No. 204). 1971. Repr. of 1830 ed. lib. bdg. 40.50 (ISBN 0-8337-0064-2). B Franklin.
Berna, Henri. Dictionnaire Technique et Administratif De la Navigation Interieure. 393p. (Fr.). 1977. 69.95 (ISBN 0-686-56914-8, M-6030). French & Eur.
Canal & River Cruising. 1977. pap. 2.50 (ISBN 0-8277-5219-9). British Bk Ctr.
De Salis, H. Rodolph, ed. Bradshaw's Canals & Navigable Rivers of England & Wales. LC 70-85329. Repr. of 1904 ed. 20.00x (ISBN 0-678-05551-3). Kelley.
Go South Inside: Cruising the Inland Waterway. LC 77-82090. (Illus.). 1978. 17.50 (ISBN 0-87742-070-X). Intl Marine.
Harper, Mike. Through France to the Mediterranean: Any Yachtsman's Attainable Dream. (Illus.). 216p. 1975. 15.00x (ISBN 0-85614-034-1). Intl Pubns Serv.
Jackman, William T. Development of Transportation in Modern England. LC 67-40294. Repr. of 1916 ed. 30.00x (ISBN 0-678-05178-X). Kelley.
McKnight, Hugh. The Shell Book of Inland Waterways. LC 74-20470. 1975. 19.95 (ISBN 0-7153-6884-2). David & Charles.
Phillips, John. General History of Inland Navigation, Foreign & Domestic. 5th ed. LC 76-97970. (Illus.). Repr. of 1805 ed. 25.00x (ISBN 0-678-05670-6). Kelley.
Priestley, Joseph. Priestley's Navigable Rivers & Canals, 1831. (Illus.). 702p. 1969. 7.50 (ISBN 0-7153-4395-5). David & Charles.
Willan, T. S. River Navigation in England: 1600-1750. 2nd ed. 163p. 1964. 24.00x (ISBN 0-7146-1383-5, F Cass Co). Biblio Dist.
Willan, Thomas S. River Navigation in England 1600-1750. (Illus.). Repr. of 1936 ed. 24.00x (ISBN 0-678-05204-2). Kelley.

INLAND RULES OF THE ROAD
see Inland Navigation

INLAND SHIPPING
see Inland Water Transportation

INLAND WATER TRANSPORTATION
see also Inland Navigation
American Society of Civil Engineers, compiled by. Second International Waterbone Transportation Conference. 780p. 1978. pap. text ed. 42.00 (ISBN 0-87262-099-9). Am Soc Civil Eng.
Baxter, R. E. & Phillips, C. Ports, Inland Waterways & Civil Aviation. Maunder, W. F., ed. 1979. text ed. 55.00 (ISBN 0-08-022460-1). Pergamon.
Block, Richard A., ed. Understanding T-Boat Regulations. (Illus.). 143p. 1979. pap. text ed. 12.00 (ISBN 0-934114-22-6). Marine Educ.
Ellet, Charles, Jr. Essay on the Laws of Trade. LC 65-26363. Repr. of 1839 ed. 15.00x (ISBN 0-678-00202-9). Kelley.
EMCT Staff. Competitive Position & Future of Inland Waterway Transport. (ECMT Roundtable 49). (Illus.). 95p. (Orig.). 1981. pap. text ed. 7.50 (ISBN 92-821-1065-6, 75-81-01-1). OECD.
Grains, Soybeans & User Charges: The Prospective Impact of Cost-Recovery Waterway User Charges. 2.00 (ISBN 0-686-10431-5). Natl Waterways.
Haites, Erik F., et al. Western River Transportation: The Era of Early Internal Development, 1810-1860. LC 75-12568. (Studies in Historical & Political Science: Ninety-Third Series (1975)). (Illus.). 224p. 1975. 16.00x (ISBN 0-8018-1681-5). Johns Hopkins.
Hoshi Ayao. The Ming Tribute Grain System. Elvin, Mark, tr. from Japanese. (Michigan Abstracts of Chinese & Japanese Works in Chinese History Ser.: No. 1). (Illus.). 112p. 1970. pap. 2.00 (ISBN 0-89264-901-1). U of Mich Ctr Chinese.
Howe, Charles W., et al. Inland Waterway Transportation: Studies in Public & Private Management & Investment Decisions. LC 71-85340. (Resources for the Future Ser). (Illus.). 144p. 1969. pap. 5.00x (ISBN 0-8018-1088-4). Johns Hopkins.
Hunter, Louis C. Steamboats on the Western Rivers. LC 74-96182. 1969. Repr. of 1949 ed. lib. bdg. 30.00x (ISBN 0-374-94047-9). Octagon.
Inland Waterways Guide 1974. 1974. pap. 1.95x (ISBN 0-8277-2603-1). British Bk Ctr.
Jordan, Tanis & Jordan, Martin. South America: River Trips, Vol. 2. (Illus.). 128p. 1982. pap. 9.95 (ISBN 0-933982-24-0). Bradt Ent.
McKnight, Hugh. Canal & River Craft in Pictures. LC 75-94574. (Illus.). 10.95x (ISBN 0-678-05661-7). Kelley.
Owen. Canals to Manchester. 133p. 1978. 18.00x (ISBN 0-7190-0686-4, Pub. by Manchester U Pr England). State Mutual Bk.
Preliminary Report of the Inland Waterways Commission. LC 72-2844. (Use & Abuse of America's Natural Resources Ser). 714p. 1972. Repr. of 1908 ed. 39.00 (ISBN 0-405-04529-8). Arno.
Vine, P. A. London's Lost Route to the Sea: An Historical Account of the Inland Navigations Which Linked the Thames to the English Channel. 3rd ed. (Inland Waterways Histories Ser.). 1973. 14.95 (ISBN 0-7153-6203-8). David & Charles.
Vine, Paul A. London's Lost Route to Basing-Stoke. LC 68-23819. (Illus.). 1968. 11.95x (ISBN 0-678-05641-2). Kelley.
Western Writers of America. Water Trails West. 1979. pap. 3.50 (ISBN 0-380-47688-6, 47688, Discus). Avon.
Why Congress Should Analyse the Prospect Impact of Waterway User Charges on Regions, Industries, Employment, Farming, Food Supply & Energy. 1977. 2.00 (ISBN 0-686-10434-X). Natl Waterways.

INLAND WATERWAY VESSELS–CARGO
see also Cargo Handling

INLAYING IN WOOD
see Marquetry

INNER EAR
see Labyrinth (Ear)

INNER LIGHT
Thurman, Howard. Inward Journey. LC 77-70182. 1973. pap. 2.95 (ISBN 0-913408-03-4). Friends United.
--Mysticism & the Experience of Love. LC 61-13708. (Orig.). 1961. pap. 1.10x (ISBN 0-87574-115-0). Pendle Hill.

INNESS, GEORGE, 1825-1894
Cikovsky, Nicolai, Jr. The Life & Work of George Inness. LC 76-23605. (Outstanding Dissertations in the Fine Arts - American). (Illus.). 1977. Repr. of 1965 ed. lib. bdg. 70.00 (ISBN 0-8240-2679-9). Garland Pub.
Inness, George, Jr. Life, Art, & Letters of George Inness. LC 76-87444. (Library of American Art Ser). 1969. Repr. of 1917 ed. lib. bdg. 32.50 (ISBN 0-306-71515-5). Da Capo.
McCausland, Elizabeth. George Inness. LC 76-42705. Repr. of 1946 ed. 26.00 (ISBN 0-404-15365-8). AMS Pr.
Werner, Alfred. Inness Landscapes. 88p. 1973. pap. 8.95 (ISBN 0-8230-2552-7). Watson-Guptill.

INNIS, HAROLD ADAMS, 1894-1952
Christian, William, ed. The Idea File of Harold Adam Innis. 1980. 20.00x (ISBN 0-8020-2350-9); pap. 7.50 (ISBN 0-8020-6382-9). U of Toronto Pr.
Creighton, D. G. Harold Adams Innis: Portrait of a Scholar. LC 58-854. 1978. pap. 6.00 (ISBN 0-8020-6329-2). U of Toronto Pr.
Neill, Robin. New Theory of Value: The Canadian Economics of Harold Adams Innis. LC 77-185867. 184p. 1972. pap. 3.50 (ISBN 0-8020-6152-4). U of Toronto Pr.

INNKEEPER AND GUEST
see Hotels, Taverns, etc.-Law

INNOCENTIUS 3RD, POPE, 1160 or 61-1216
Elliott-Binns, L. Innocent Third. 1968. Repr. of 1931 ed. 16.50 (ISBN 0-208-00393-2, Archon). Shoe String.
Smith, Charles E. Innocent Three, Church Defender. LC 79-88939. 1971. Repr. of 1951 ed. lib. bdg. 15.00 (ISBN 0-8371-3145-6, SMIN). Greenwood.
Tillmann, H. Pope Innocent III. (Europe in the Middle Ages Selected Studies: Vol. 13). 1979. 44.00 (ISBN 0-444-85137-2, North-Holland). Elsevier.

INNOVATIONS, AGRICULTURAL
see Agricultural Innovations

INNOVATIONS, TECHNOLOGICAL
see Technological Innovations

INNOVATIONS IN EDUCATION
see Educational Innovations

INNS
see Hotels, Taverns, etc.

INNS OF COURT, LONDON
Dillon, J. F. The Law & Jurisprudence of England & America. LC 75-99475. (American Constitutional & Legal History Ser). 1970. Repr. of 1894 ed. lib. bdg. 42.50 (ISBN 0-306-71854-5). Da Capo.
Finkelpearl, Philip J. John Marston of the Middle Temple: An Elizabethan Dramatist in His Social Setting. LC 69-12722. (Illus.). 1969. 15.00x (ISBN 0-674-47860-6). Harvard U Pr.
Wienpahl, Robert W. Music at the Inns of Court: During the Reigns of Elizabeth, James, & Charles. LC 79-14881. (Orig.). 1979. pap. 20.75 (ISBN 0-8357-0417-3, SS-00103). Univ Microfilms.

INNUIT
see Eskimos

INNUIT LANGUAGE
see Eskimo Language

INOCULATION
see also Immunity; Medicine, Preventive; Smallpox-Preventive Inoculation; Serumtherapy; Vaccination
Schaer, M. Kompendium der Schutzimpfungen. (Illus.). 1979. pap. 11.50 (ISBN 3-8055-2994-5). S Karger.

INOPERCULATES
see Discomycetes

INORGANIC CHEMISTRY
see Chemistry, Inorganic

INORGANIC FIBERS
see also Ceramic Fibers

INPUT EQUIPMENT (COMPUTERS)
see Computer Input-Output Equipment

INPUT-OUTPUT ANALYSIS
see Interindustry Economics; Linear Programming; Recursive Programming

INPUT-OUTPUT EQUIPMENT (COMPUTERS)
see Computer Input-Output Equipment

INQUESTS, CORONER'S
see Coroners

INQUIRY, COURTS OF
see Courts-Martial and Courts of Inquiry

INQUISITION
see also Persecution; Torture
Andrzejewski, Jerzy. The Inquisitors. Syrop, Konrad, tr. from Polish. LC 76-6896. 1976. Repr. of 1960 ed. lib. bdg. 15.00 (ISBN 0-8371-8868-7, ANIN). Greenwood.

Bernardus Guidonis. Manuel de l'Inquisiteur, 2 vols. in 1. Mollat, G., ed. LC 78-63183. (Heresies of the Early Christian & Medieval Era: Second Ser.). Repr. of 1927 ed. 44.50 set (ISBN 0-404-16199-5). AMS Pr.

Braunstein, Baruch. The Chuetas of Majorca. rev. ed. 1971. 20.00x (ISBN 0-87068-147-8). Ktav.

Cadoux, Cecil J. Philip of Spain & the Netherlands: An Essay on Moral Judgments in History. 1969. Repr. of 1947 ed. 17.50 (ISBN 0-208-00735-0, Archon). Shoe String.

Coulton, George G. Inquisition. LC 74-18020. 1974. Repr. of 1929 ed. lib. bdg. 10.00 (ISBN 0-8414-3647-9). Folcroft.

Davis, Georgene W. The Inquisition at Albi, 1229-1300. 322p. 1974. Repr. of 1948 ed. lib. bdg. 17.50x (ISBN 0-374-92075-3). Octagon.

Grendler, Paul F. The Roman Inquisition & the Venetian Press, 1540-1605. LC 76-45900. 1978. text ed. 28.00 (ISBN 0-691-05245-X). Princeton U Pr.

Guiraud, Jean. The Medieval Inquisition. Messenger, E. C., tr. LC 78-63181. (Hereseis 2 Ser.). 216p. 1980. Repr. of 1929 ed. 19.00 (ISBN 0-404-16222-3). AMS Pr.

--The Medieval Inquisition. Messenger, E. C., tr. LC 78-63181. (Heresies of the Early Christian & Medieval Era: Second Ser.). Repr. of 1929 ed. 21.50 (ISBN 0-404-16222-3). AMS Pr.

Hamilton, Bernard. Medieval Inquisition: Foundations of Medieval History. LC 80-27997. 110p. (Orig.). 1981. pap. text ed. 13.50x (ISBN 0-8419-0695-5). Holmes & Meier.

Haureau, Barthelemy. Bernard Delicieux et l'Inquisition Albigeoise, 1300-1320. LC 78-63180. (Heresies of the Early Christian & Medieval Era: Second Ser.). Repr. of 1877 ed. 21.50 (ISBN 0-404-16223-1). AMS Pr.

Henningsen, Gustav. The Witches' Advocate: Basque Witchcraft & the Spanish Inquisition, 1609-1614. LC 79-20340. (Basque Book Ser.). (Illus.). xxxii, 607p. 1980. 24.00 (ISBN 0-87417-056-7). U of Nev Pr.

Herculano, Alexandre. History of the Origin & Establishment of the Inquisition in Portugal. Branner, John C., tr. LC 68-54274. (Stanford University. Stanford Studies in History, Economics, & Political Science: No. 1, Pt. 2). Repr. of 1926 ed. 17.50 (ISBN 0-404-50962-2). AMS Pr.

--History of the Origin & Establishment of the Inquisition in Portugal. rev. ed. 1971. 35.00x (ISBN 0-87068-153-2). Ktav.

Kamen, Henry. Spanish Inquisition. pap. 4.95 (ISBN 0-452-00493-4, F493, Mer). NAL.

Langdon-Davies, John. The Spanish Inquisition. (Jackdaw Ser: No. 44). (Illus.). 1969. 6.95 (ISBN 0-670-66112-0, Grossman). Viking Pr.

Lea, Henry C. Chapters from the Religious History of Spain Connected with the Inquisition. LC 68-56760. (Research & Source Work Ser.: No. 245). 1967. Repr. of 1890 ed. 26.00 (ISBN 0-8337-2035-X). B Franklin.

--History of the Inquisition of Spain, 4 Vols. LC 72-181943. Repr. of 1907 ed. Set. 95.00 (ISBN 0-404-03920-0); 25.00 ea. Vol. 1 (ISBN 0-404-03921-9). Vol. 2 (ISBN 0-404-03922-7). Vol. 3 (ISBN 0-404-03923-5). Vol. 4 (ISBN 0-404-03924-3). AMS Pr.

--History of the Inquisition of the Middle Ages, 3 Vols. LC 58-9830. 1955. Repr. of 1888 ed. Set. 55.00 (ISBN 0-8462-0250-6). Russell.

--Moriscos of Spain. LC 68-56783. 1968. Repr. of 1901 ed. 20.50 (ISBN 0-8337-4218-3). B Franklin.

--Moriscos of Spain: Their Conversion & Expulsion. 1968. Repr. of 1901 ed. lib. bdg. 23.50x (ISBN 0-8371-0141-7, LEMS). Greenwood.

--Moriscos of Spain, Their Conversion & Expulsion. LC 68-26358. (Studies in Spanish Literature, No. 36). 1969. Repr. of 1901 ed. lib. bdg. 51.95 (ISBN 0-8383-0266-1). Haskell.

Liebman, Seymour B. The Inquisitors & the Jews in the New World: Summaries of Procesos 1500-1810, & Bibliographical Guide. LC 72-85110. 160p. 1973. 12.95x (ISBN 0-87024-245-8). U of Miami Pr.

--Jews in New Spain: Faith, Flame & the Inquisition. LC 70-91213. (Illus.). 1970. 19.95x (ISBN 0-87024-129-X). U of Miami Pr.

Maistre, Joseph M. De, tr. Letters on the Spanish Inquisition. LC 77-24949. 1977. Repr. of 1843 ed. 22.00 (ISBN 0-8201-1293-3). Schol Facsimiles.

Mocatta, Frederic D. The Jews of Spain & Portugal & the Inquisition. LC 72-88016. (Illus.). xxii, 106p. 1973. Repr. of 1933 ed. lib. bdg. 8.00x (ISBN 0-8154-0440-9). Cooper Sq.

Molinier, Charles. Inquisition Dans le Midi De la France Au Treizieme et Au Quatorzieme Seicle: Etude Sur les Sources De Son Histoire. 1965. Repr. of 1880 ed. 32.00 (ISBN 0-8337-2421-5). B Franklin.

Morellet, Andre. Le Manuel des Inquisiteurs a l'Usage des Inquisitions d'Espagne et du Portugal. (Holbach & His Friends Ser). 196p. (Fr.). 1974. Repr. of 1762 ed. lib. bdg. 56.50x (ISBN 0-8287-0638-7, 1525). Clearwater Pub.

Plaidy, Jean. Spanish Inquisition: Its Rise. 1966. pap. 4.95 (ISBN 0-8065-0056-5). Citadel Pr.

Roth, Cecil. A History of the Marranos. LC 74-10149. 448p. 1974. pap. 5.50 (ISBN 0-8052-0463-6). Schocken.

--Spanish Inquisition. (Orig.). 1964. pap. 4.95 (ISBN 0-393-00255-1, Norton Lib). Norton.

Turberville, A. S. Spanish Inquisition. 1968. Repr. of 1932 ed. 18.50 (ISBN 0-208-00366-5, Archon). Shoe String.

Vacandard, Elphege. The Inquisition: A Critical & Historical Study of the Coercive Power of the Church. Conway, Bertrand L., tr. from Fr. LC 76-1127. 195p. 1977. Repr. of 1926 ed. lib. bdg. 17.50 (ISBN 0-915172-09-7). Richwood Pub.

Walsh, William T. Characters of the Inquisition. LC 68-8192. (Essay & General Literature Index Reprint Ser). 1969. Repr. of 1940 ed. 12.00 (ISBN 0-8046-0486-X). Kennikat.

INQUISITIVENESS
see Curiosity

INSANE-CARE AND TREATMENT
see Mentally Ill-Care and Treatment

INSANE-LEGAL STATUS, LAWS, ETC.
see Insanity-Jurisprudence; Mental Health Laws

INSANE, CRIMINAL AND DANGEROUS
see also Criminal Liability; Forensic Psychiatry; Insanity-Jurisprudence

Biggs, John, Jr. The Guilty Mind: Psychiatry & the Law of Homicide. LC 55-10812. (Isaac Ray Award Lectures Ser). 248p. (Orig.). 1967. pap. 3.95x (ISBN 0-8018-0070-6). Johns Hopkins.

Goldstein, Abraham S. The Insanity Defense. LC 79-26323. 289p. 1980. Repr. of 1967 ed. lib. bdg. 24.00x (ISBN 0-313-22202-9, GOID). Greenwood.

Goodwin, John C. Insanity & the Criminal. 1924. 17.50 (ISBN 0-686-17699-5). Quality Lib.

Guze, Samuel B. Criminality & Psychiatric Disorders. 176p. 1976. text ed. 10.95x (ISBN 0-19-501973-3). Oxford U Pr.

Partridge, Ralph. Broadmoor: A History of Criminal Lunacy & Its Problems. LC 75-31440. (Illus.). 278p. 1976. Repr. of 1953 ed. lib. bdg. 20.25 (ISBN 0-8371-8520-3, PABRO). Greenwood.

Rabinowitz, Max. The Day They Scrambled My Brains at the Funny Factory. 1978. pap. 1.95 (ISBN 0-89083-344-3). Zebra.

Sleffel, Linda. The Law & the Dangerous Criminal. LC 77-287. (Dangerous Offender Project Ser.). 1977. 17.95 (ISBN 0-669-01481-8). Lexington Bks.

Steadman, Henry J. Beating a Rap? Defendants Found Incompetent to Stand Trial. LC 78-21110. (Studies in Crime & Justice). 1979. lib. bdg. 13.00x (ISBN 0-226-77140-7). U of Chicago Pr.

Weihofen, Henry. The Urge to Punish: New Approaches to the Problem of Mental Irresponsibility for Crime. LC 78-11363. 1979. Repr. of 1957 ed. lib. bdg. 20.75x (ISBN 0-313-21069-1, WEUP). Greenwood.

INSANE HOSPITALS
see Psychiatric Hospitals

INSANITY
Here are entered works on the legal aspects of mental disorders. Popular works and works on regional or social aspects of mental disorders are entered under Mental Illness. Systematic descriptions of mental disorders are entered under Psychology, pathological. Works on clinical aspects of mental disorders, including therapy, are entered under Psychiatry.
see also Depression, Mental; Eccentrics and Eccentricities; Genius; Hallucinations and Illusions; Hypochondria; Hysteria; Idiocy; Manic-Depressive Psychoses; Mental Illness; Neuroses; Personality, Disorders Of; Psychiatry; Psychology, Pathological; Psychoses; Schizophrenia; Stupor; Suicide

Bates, Erica. Models of Madness. 1978. 19.95x (ISBN 0-7022-1069-2); pap. 9.95x (ISBN 0-7022-1068-4). U of Queensland Pr.

Battie, William & Monro, John. A Treatise on Madness. (Illus.). 160p. 1962. Repr. of 1758 ed. 18.50x (ISBN 0-8464-0936-4). Beekman Pubs.

Briggs, Lloyd V. Two Years' Service on the Reorganized State Board of Insanity in Massachusetts, August, 1914 to August, 1916. Grob, Gerald N., ed. LC 78-22551. (Historical Issues in Mental Health Ser.). (Illus.). 1979. Repr. of 1930 ed. lib. bdg. 40.00x (ISBN 0-405-11905-4). Arno.

Brydall, John & Highmore, Anthony. Non Compos Mentis. Berkowitz, David S. & Thorne, Samuel E., eds. LC 77-86669. (Classics of English Legal History in the Modern Era Ser.: Vol. 46). 471p. 1979. lib. bdg. 40.00 (ISBN 0-8240-3095-8). Garland Pub.

Conolly, John. Indications of Insanity. 1964. Repr. 21.00x (ISBN 0-8464-0507-5). Beekman Pubs.

--On Some of the Forms of Insanity. Bd. with Inquiry Concerning the Indications of Insanity. (Contributions to the History of Psychology Ser.). 1980. Repr. of 1850 ed. 30.00 (ISBN 0-89093-315-4). U Pubns Amer.

Cotton, Henry A. The Defective Delinquent & Insane. Grob, Gerald N., ed. LC 78-22557. (Historical Issues in Mental Health Ser.). (Illus.). 1979. Repr. of 1921 ed. lib. bdg. 15.00x (ISBN 0-405-11911-9). Arno.

Esquirol, Etienne. Des Maladies Mentales: Considerees Sous les Rapports Medical Hygienique et Medico-Legal, 3 vols. in 2. LC 75-16703. (Classics in Psychiatry). (Illus., Fr.). 1976. Repr. of 1838 ed. Set. 90.00x (ISBN 0-405-07464-6); 45.00x ea. Vol. 1 (ISBN 0-405-07465-4). Vols. 2-3 (ISBN 0-405-07466-2). Arno.

Foucault, Michel. Madness & Civilization: A History of Insanity in the Age of Reason. 320p. 1973. pap. 2.95 (ISBN 0-394-71914-X, Vin). Random.

Grob, Gerald N., ed. Immigrants & Insanity: An Original Anthology. LC 78-22566. (Historical Issues in Mental Health Ser.). (Illus.). 1979. lib. bdg. 18.00x (ISBN 0-405-11920-8). Arno.

--The National Association for the Protection of the Insane & the Prevention of Insanity, 2 vols. in one. LC 78-22578. (Historical Issues in Mental Health Ser.). 1979. Repr. lib. bdg. 12.00x (ISBN 0-405-11930-5). Arno.

Jurgensen, Genevieve. The Madness of Others. Boulanger, Ghislaine, tr. 1975. 7.95 (ISBN 0-685-52102-8). Macmillan.

Kirchhoff, Theodore. Handbook of Insanity for Practitioners & Students. Repr. of 1895 ed. 25.00 (ISBN 0-89987-062-7). Darby Bks.

Neaman, Judith S. Suggestion of the Devil. 1976. Repr. of 1975 ed. lib. bdg. 13.50 (ISBN 0-374-96038-0). Octagon.

Pinel, Philippe. Treatise on Insanity. Davis, D. D., tr. from Fr. Bd. with Responsibility in Mental Disease. (Contributions to the History of Psychology Ser., Vol. III, Pt. C: Medical Psychology). 1978. Repr. of 1806 ed. 30.00 (ISBN 0-89093-167-4). U Pubns Amer.

Priest, R. G. & Steinert, J. Insanity: A Study of Major Psychiatric Disorders. 416p. 1980. 18.00x (ISBN 0-7121-0941-2, Pub. by Macdonald & Evans). State Mutual Bk.

Smith, Stephen. Who Is Insane? Grob, Gerald N., ed. LC 78-22590. (Historical Issues in Mental Health Ser.). 1979. Repr. of 1916 ed. lib. bdg. 18.00x (ISBN 0-405-11941-0). Arno.

Stearns, Henry P. Insanity: Its Causes & Prevention. Grob, Gerald N., ed. LC 78-22591. (Historical Issues in Mental Health Ser.). 1979. Repr. of 1883 ed. lib. bdg. 15.00x (ISBN 0-405-11942-9). Arno.

Thalbitzer, S. Emotion & Insanity. Repr. of 1926 ed. 12.50 (ISBN 0-89987-084-8). Darby Bks.

INSANITY-JURISPRUDENCE
Here are entered works on the legal status of persons of unsound mind. Works on the law affecting the welfare of the insane are entered under the heading Mental Health Laws. Works on psychiatry as applied in courts of law are entered under the heading Forensic Psychiatry.
see also Criminal Liability; Forensic Psychiatry; Liability (Law)

Allen, Richard C., et al, eds. Readings in Law and Psychiatry. rev. ed. LC 74-24384. (Illus.). 848p. 1975. 30.00x (ISBN 0-8018-1692-0). Johns Hopkins.

Arens, Richard. Insanity Defense. LC 72-96108. 354p. 1973. 12.50 (ISBN 0-8022-2106-8). Philos Lib.

Association Of The Bar Of The City Of New York. Mental Illness & Due Process: Report & Recommendations on Admissions to Mental Hospitals Under New York Law. (Illus.). 1962. 24.50x (ISBN 0-8014-0298-0). Cornell U Pr.

Barton, Walter E. & Sanborn, Charlotte J., eds. Law & the Mental Health Professions: Friction at the Interface. LC 77-90226. 1978. text ed. 17.50 (ISBN 0-8236-2950-3). Intl Univs Pr.

Biggs, John, Jr. The Guilty Mind: Psychiatry & the Law of Homicide. LC 55-10812. (Isaac Ray Award Lectures Ser). 248p. (Orig.). 1967. pap. 3.95x (ISBN 0-8018-0070-6). Johns Hopkins.

Brody, Baruch A. & Englehardt, H. Tristram. Mental Illness: Law & Public Policy. (Philosophy & Medicine Ser.: No. 5). 276p. 1980. lib. bdg. 29.00 (ISBN 0-686-27528-4, Pub. by Reidel Holland). Kluwer Boston.

Brooks, Alexander D. Law, Psychiatry & the Mental Health System. 1974. 26.50 (ISBN 0-316-10970-3); Suppl., 1980. pap. 8.95 (ISBN 0-316-10971-1). Little.

Fersch, Ellsworth A., Jr. Law, Psychology, & the Courts: Rethinking Treatment of the Young & the Disturbed. 184p. 1979. 17.50 (ISBN 0-398-03874-0). C C Thomas.

Fingarette, Herbert. The Meaning of Criminal Insanity. LC 70-165223. 300p. 1972. 24.50x (ISBN 0-520-02082-0); pap. 5.95x (ISBN 0-520-02631-4). U of Cal Pr.

Fingarette, Herbert & Hasse, Ann F. Mental Disabilities & Criminal Responsibilities. LC 77-91756. 1979. 24.50x (ISBN 0-520-03630-1). U of Cal Pr.

Fox, Richard W. So Far Disordered in Mind: Insanity in California, 1870-1930. LC 77-93479. 1979. 14.95x (ISBN 0-520-03653-0). U of Cal Pr.

GAP Committee on Psychiatry & Law. Psychiatry & Sex Psychopath Legislation: The 30s to the 80s, Vol. 9. LC 77-72874. (Publications: No. 98). 1977. pap. 4.00 (ISBN 0-87318-135-2, Pub. by Adv Psychiatry). Mental Health.

Glueck, Bernard. Studies in Forensic Psychiatry. LC 16-20410. (Criminal Science Monograph: No. 2). 1968. Repr. of 1915 ed. 13.00 (ISBN 0-527-34112-6). Kraus Repr.

Glueck, Sheldon. Law & Psychiatry: Cold War or Entente Cordiale. (Isaac Ray Lectures Ser). 191p. 1962. pap. 3.45x (ISBN 0-8018-0225-3). Johns Hopkins.

Jeffery, Clarence R. Criminal Responsibility & Mental Disease. 344p. 1967. 14.00 (ISBN 0-398-00922-8). C C Thomas.

Katz, Jay, et al. Psychoanalysis, Psychiatry & Law. LC 65-27757. 1967. text ed. 35.00 (ISBN 0-02-917200-4). Free Pr.

Lipsitt, Paul D. & Sales, Bruce D., eds. New Directions in Psychologal Research. 352p. 1980. text ed. 18.95 (ISBN 0-442-26267-1). Van Nos Reinhold.

Miller, Kent S. Managing Madness: The Case Against Civil Commitment. LC 76-7528. 1976. 9.95 (ISBN 0-02-921280-4). Free Pr.

Moran, Richard. Knowing Right from Wrong: The Insanity Defense of Daniel McNaughton. LC 81-65034. (Illus.). 1981. 14.95 (ISBN 0-02-921890-X). Free Pr.

Neaman, Judith S. Suggestion of the Devil. 1976. Repr. of 1975 ed. lib. bdg. 13.50 (ISBN 0-374-96038-0). Octagon.

Nissman, David M., et al. Beating the Insanity Defense: Denying the License to Kill. LC 80-8028. 1980. 18.95 (ISBN 0-669-03943-8). Lexington Bks.

Packard, Elizabeth P. Great Disclosure of Spiritual Wickedness in High Places: With Appeal to the Government to Protect the Inalienable Rights of Married Women. LC 74-3965. (Women in America Ser). (Illus.). 162p. 1974. Repr. of 1865 ed. 12.00 (ISBN 0-405-06114-5). Arno.

Pearlstein, S. Psychiatry, the Law & Mental Health. 2nd ed. LC 67-16050. (Legal Almanac Ser: No. 30). 1967. 5.95 (ISBN 0-379-11030-X). Oceana.

Polier, Justine Wise. The Rule of Law & the Role of Psychiatry (Isaac Ray Lectures) LC 68-12900. 176p. 1968. 12.00x (ISBN 0-8018-0535-X). Johns Hopkins.

Prichard, James. On the Different Forms of Insanity in Relation to Jurisprudence. Bd. with Suggestions for the Future Provision of Criminal Lunatics. Hood, W. C; Statistics of Insanity. Hood, W. C. (Contributions to the History of Psychology Ser., Vol. III, Pt. E: Insanity & Jurisprudence). 1980. Repr. of 1842 ed. 30.00 (ISBN 0-89093-328-6). U Pubns Amer.

Ray, Isaac. Contributions to Mental Pathology (1873). LC 73-9908. (Hist. of Psych. Ser.). 450p. 1973. Repr. of 1873 ed. lib. bdg. 55.00x (ISBN 0-8201-1120-1). Schol Facsimiles.

--Treatise on the Medical Jurisprudence of Insanity. Overholser, Winfred, ed. LC 62-17223. (The John Harvard Library). 1962. 18.50x (ISBN 0-674-90735-3). Harvard U Pr.

--A Treatise on the Medical Jurisprudence of Insanity. 5th ed. LC 75-16732. (Classics in Psychiatry Ser.). 1976. Repr. of 1871 ed. 37.00x (ISBN 0-405-07453-0). Arno.

Rieber, Robert W. & Vetter, Harold J., eds. The Psychological Foundations of Criminal Justice: Historical Perspectives on Forensic Psychology, Vol. 1. LC 78-18781. (Illus.). 1978. 15.00x (ISBN 0-89444-009-8). John Jay Pr.

Robinson, Daniel N. Psychology & Law: Can Justice Survive the Social Sciences? 240p. 1980. text ed. 14.95x (ISBN 0-19-502725-6); pap. text ed. 5.95x (ISBN 0-19-502726-4). Oxford U Pr.

Rosenberg, Charles E. Trial of the Assassin Guitean: Psychiatry & Law in the Gilded Age. LC 68-16713. 1976. pap. 4.95 (ISBN 0-226-72717-3, P682, Phoen). U of Chicago Pr.

--Trial of the Assassin Guiteau: Psychiatry & the Law in the Gilded Age. LC 68-16712. (Illus.). 1968. 8.00x (ISBN 0-226-72716-5). U of Chicago Pr.

Rubin, Jeffrey. Economics, Mental Health, & the Law. LC 78-19571. (Illus.). 1978. 17.95 (ISBN 0-669-02629-8). Lexington Bks.

Rubin, Sol. Psychiatry & Criminal Law. LC 64-19354. 1965. 12.50 (ISBN 0-379-00225-6). Oceana.

Shuman, Samuel I. Psychosurgery & the Medical Control of Violence: Autonomy & Deviance. LC 77-23374. 1977. 18.50x (ISBN 0-8143-1579-8). Wayne St U Pr.
Simon, Rita J. The Jury & the Defense of Insanity. 269p. 1967. 16.00 (ISBN 0-316-79149-0). Little.
Special Committee, New York City Bar Association & Fordham University School Of Law. Mental Illness, Due Process & the Criminal Defendant. LC 68-19789. 1968. 25.00 (ISBN 0-8232-0780-3). Fordham.
Steadman, Henry J. Beating a Rap? Defendants Found Incompetent to Stand Trial. LC 78-21110. (Studies in Crime & Justice). 1979. lib. bdg. 13.00x (ISBN 0-226-77140-7). U of Chicago Pr.
Szasz, Thomas. Psychiatric Slavery: The Dilemmas of Involuntary Psychiatry As Exemplified by the Case of Kenneth Donaldson. LC 76-27154. 1977. 8.95 (ISBN 0-02-931600-6). Free Pr.
Szasz, Thomas S. Law, Liberty & Psychiatry. LC 63-14187. 1968. pap. 4.95 (ISBN 0-02-074770-5, Collier). Macmillan.
--Psychiatric Justice. LC 77-18804. 1978. Repr. of 1965 ed. lib. bdg. 25.75x (ISBN 0-313-20196-X, SZPJ). Greenwood.
Weihofen, Henry. The Urge to Punish: New Approaches to the Problem of Mental Irresponsibility for Crime. LC 78-11363. 1979. Repr. of 1957 ed. lib. bdg. 20.75x (ISBN 0-313-21069-1, WEUP). Greenwood.
Wexler, David B. Mental Health Law: Major Issues. 265p. 1981. 25.00 (ISBN 0-306-40538-5, Plenum Pr). Plenum Pub.
Whitehead, Tony. Mental Illness & the Law. 192p. 1981. 19.95x (ISBN 0-631-12721-6, Pub. by Basil Blackwell England); pap. 8.95x (ISBN 0-631-12615-5, Pub. by Basil Blackwell England). Biblio Dist.

INSANITY–JURISPRUDENCE–GREAT BRITAIN

Haslam, John. Medical Jurisprudence, As It Relates to Insanity, According to the Law of England. Berkowitz, David S. & Thorne, Samuel E., eds. LC 77-86661. (Classics of English Legal History in the Modern Era Ser.: Vol. 109). 1979. lib. bdg. 55.00 (ISBN 0-8240-3096-6). Garland Pub.
Miller, Kent S. Managing Madness: The Case Against Civil Commitment. LC 76-7528. 1976. 9.95 (ISBN 0-02-921280-4). Free Pr.
Smith, Roger. Trial by Medicine: The Insanity Defense in Victorian England. 280p. 1981. 33.00x (ISBN 0-85224-407-X, Pub. by Edinburgh U Pr Scotland). Columbia U Pr.

INSANITY, DELUSIONAL

see Paranoia

INSANITY, HYSTERICAL

see Hysteria

INSANITY, PERIODIC AND TRANSITORY

see also Personality, Disorders Of

INSANITY AND ART

see Art and Mental Illness

INSANITY AND GENIUS

see Genius

INSANITY IN LITERATURE

Bucknill, John C. Mad Folk of Shakespeare. LC 74-8816. 1974. Repr. of 1867 ed. lib. bdg. 16.25 (ISBN 0-8414-3194-9). Folcroft.
De Porte, Michael V. Nightmares & Hobbyhorses: Swift, Sterne, & Augustan Ideas of Madness. LC 73-78048. (Illus.). 1974. 12.50 (ISBN 0-87328-061-X). Huntington Lib.
Doob, Penelope B. Nebuchadnezzar's Children: Conventions of Madness in Middle English Literature. 1974. 20.00x (ISBN 0-300-01675-1). Yale U Pr.
Farren, George. Essays on the Varieties in Mania, Exhibited by the Characters of Hamlet, Ophelia, Lear, & Edgar. LC 74-168009. Repr. of 1833 ed. 14.00 (ISBN 0-404-02367-3). AMS Pr.
Feder, Lillian. Madness in Literature. LC 79-3206. 1980. 17.50 (ISBN 0-691-06427-X). Princeton U Pr.
Kellogg, Abner O. Shakespeare's Delineations of Insanity, Imbecility, & Suicide. LC 77-165510. Repr. of 1866 ed. 22.45 (ISBN 0-404-03644-9). AMS Pr.
Lindsay, Jack, ed. Loving Mad Tom: Bedlamite Ballads of the 16th & 17th Century. LC 70-111205. (Illus.). Repr. of 1927 ed. lib. bdg. 12.50x (ISBN 0-678-08013-5). Kelley.
O'Brien-Moore, A. Madness in Ancient Literature. 69.95 (ISBN 0-8490-0575-2). Gordon Pr.
Peers, Edgar A. Elizabethan Drama & Its Mad Folk. LC 78-2181. 1914. lib. bdg. 20.00 (ISBN 0-8414-6825-7). Folcroft.
Shenk, Robert. The Sinner's Progress: A Study of Madness in Elizabethan Renaissance Drama. (Salzburg Elizabethan & Renaissance Studies: No. 74). 1978. pap. text ed. 25.00x (ISBN 0-391-01520-6). Humanities.
Somerville, H. Madness in Shakespearean Tragedy. 1929. lib. bdg. 20.00 (ISBN 0-8414-7850-3). Folcroft.

INSCRIPTIONS

see also Architectural Inscriptions; Brasses; Cuneiform Writing; Epitaphs; Graffiti; Historical Markers; Monograms; Petroglyphs; Runes; Seals (Numismatics)

Benson, Elizabeth P., ed. Mesoamerican Writing Systems: A Conference at Dumbarton Oaks, October 30 & 31, 1971. LC 73-93086. (Illus.). 226p. 1973. 20.00x (ISBN 0-88402-048-7, Ctr Pre-Columbian). Dumbarton Oaks.
Ehrenberg, Victor, compiled by. Documents Illustrating the Reigns of Augustus & Tiberius. 2nd ed. 1976. pap. text ed. 9.95x (ISBN 0-19-814819-4). Oxford U Pr.
Fell, Barry. America, B. C. LC 75-36269. (Illus.). 1976. 12.50 (ISBN 0-8129-0624-1, Demeter). Times Bks.
Gignoux, Phillipe. Glossaire Des Inscriptions Pehlevies et Parthes. 1972. 17.50x (ISBN 0-8002-1459-5). Intl Pubns Serv.
Graham, John A. The Hieroglyphic Inscriptions & Monumental Art of Alter De Sacrificios. LC 70-186984. (Peabody Museum Papers: Vol. 64, No. 2). 1972. pap. text ed. 15.00 (ISBN 0-87365-184-7). Peabody Harvard.
Gravestone Inscriptions & Records of Tomb Burials in the Granary Burying Ground, Boston, Massachusetts. 255p. 1918. 6.00 (ISBN 0-88389-026-7). Essex Inst.
Kaibel, G. & Lebeque, A. Inscriptiones Graecae Galliae, Hispaniae, Britanniae, Germanicae. 1977. 25.00 (ISBN 0-685-00197-0). Ares.
Kent, Roland G. Textual Criticism of Inscriptions. 1926. pap. 6.00 (ISBN 0-527-00806-0). Kraus Repr.
Masson, O. Carian Inscriptions from North Sacqara & Buhen. 120p. 1979. 75.00x (ISBN 0-686-61264-7, Pub. by Aris & Phillips). Intl Schol Bk Serv.
Matson, Esther. A Book of Inscriptions. 1977. Repr. of 1914 ed. 15.00 (ISBN 0-89984-060-4). Century Bookbindery.
Sparrow, John. Visible Words: A Study of Inscriptions in Books As Works of Art. LC 68-10027. (Illus.). 1969. 75.00 (ISBN 0-521-06534-8). Cambridge U Pr.

INSCRIPTIONS–CRETE

Hempl, George. Mediterranean Studies, 3 pts. in 1 vol. Anderson, Frederick, ed. Incl. Pt. 1, Vol. 1. The Genesis of European Alphabetic Writing; Pt. 1, Vol. 2. Minoan Seals; Pt. 2, Vol. 3. Three Papers on the History & Language of the Hittites; Pt. 3, Vol. 4. Etruscan; Pt. 3, Vol. 5. Venetic. LC 31-33039. Repr. of 1930 ed. 42.50 (ISBN 0-404-51809-5). AMS Pr.

INSCRIPTIONS–EGYPT

Edgerton, William F., ed. Medinet Habu Graffiti. LC 42-23005. (Oriental Institute Pubns. Ser: No. 36). (Illus.). 1937. 40.00x (ISBN 0-226-62133-2). U of Chicago Pr.
Leahy, M. A. The Inscriptions: Excavations at Malkata & the Birket Habu 1971-1974. (Egyptology Today: No. 2, Vol. IV). (Illus.). pap. 19.50x (ISBN 0-85668-121-0, Pub. by Aris & Phillips). Intl Schol Bk.

INSCRIPTIONS–GREAT BRITAIN

Norman, Philip. London Signs & Inscriptions. LC 68-22039. (Camden Library Ser). (Illus.). 1968. Repr. of 1893 ed. 19.00 (ISBN 0-8103-3496-8). Gale.
Okasha, Elizabeth. Hand-List of Anglo-Saxon Non-Runic Inscriptions. LC 75-129934. (Illus.). 1971. 58.00 (ISBN 0-521-07904-7). Cambridge U Pr.

INSCRIPTIONS–UNITED STATES

Read, Allen W. Classic American Graffiti: Lexical Evidence from Folk Epigraphy in Western North America; a Glossarial Study of the Low Element in the English Vocabulary. LC 76-5697. (Maledicta Press Publications Ser.: Vol. 6). 96p. 1977. pap. 6.00 (ISBN 0-916500-06-3). Maledicta.
Wright, Mildred S. Jefferson County, Texas Cemeteries, Pt. 2. LC 79-66552. (Illus.). 189p. 1981. lib. bdg. 30.00 (ISBN 0-917016-18-1); pap. 20.00 (ISBN 0-917016-19-X). M S Wright.

INSCRIPTIONS, ARAB

see Inscriptions, Hadrami

INSCRIPTIONS, ARAMAIC

Aufrecht, Walter E. & Hurd, John. A Synoptic Concordance of Aramaic Inscriptions. (International Concordance Library: Vol. I). 1975. pap. 15.00 (ISBN 0-935106-24-3). Biblical Res Assocs.
Gibson, John C. Textbook of Syrian Semitic Inscriptions: Aramaic Inscriptions, Including Inscriptions in the Dialect of Zenjirli, Vol. 2. (Illus.). 160p. 1975. 34.50x (ISBN 0-19-813186-0). Oxford U Pr.
Isbell, Charles D. Corpus of the Aramaic Incantation Bowls. LC 75-15949. (Society of Biblical Literature. Dissertation Ser.). xiv, 200p. 1975. pap. 7.50 (ISBN 0-89130-010-4, 060117). Scholars Pr Ca.

INSCRIPTIONS, ARCHITECTURAL

see Architectural Inscriptions

INSCRIPTIONS, ASSYRIAN

see Cuneiform Inscriptions

INSCRIPTIONS, BABYLONIAN

see Cuneiform Inscriptions

INSCRIPTIONS, BEHISTUN

see Cuneiform Inscriptions

INSCRIPTIONS, CHINESE

Chou, Hung-hsiang. Oracle Bone Collections in the United States. LC 74-34551. (Publications, Occasional Papers, Archaeology: Vol. 10). 1976. pap. 17.50x (ISBN 0-520-09534-0). U of Cal Pr.

INSCRIPTIONS, CUNEIFORM

see Cuneiform Inscriptions

INSCRIPTIONS, DEMOTIC

see Egyptian Language–Inscriptions

INSCRIPTIONS, EGYPTIAN

see Egyptian Language–Inscriptions

INSCRIPTIONS, GREEK

see also Inscriptions, Linear A; Inscriptions, Linear B

Academia Litterarum Borussicae, ed. Inscriptiones Graecae, 15 Vols. in 23 Pts. (Lat). 1873-1939. write for info. (ISBN 0-685-02032-0). De Gruyter.
Aranio-Ruis, V. & Olivieri, A. Inscptiones Graecae Sicilae et Infimae Italiae Ad Ius Pertinentes. 289p. 1980. 25.00 (ISBN 0-686-64210-4). Ares.
Bees, N. A. Corpus der Griechisch Christlichen Inschriften von Hellas. 1978. 25.00 (ISBN 0-89005-238-7). Ares.
Bradeen, Donald W. & McGregor, Malcolm F. Studies in Fifth-Century Attic Epigraphy. LC 72-9258. (Illus.). 150p. 1974. 9.95x (ISBN 0-8061-1064-3); pap. 4.95x (ISBN 0-8061-1364-2). U of Okla Pr.
Breccia, E., ed. Inscriptiones Graecae Aegypti, No. 2: Alexandria. 1978. 25.00 (ISBN 0-89005-242-5). Ares.
--Inscriptiones Nunc Alexandriae in Museo. 1978. 25.00 (ISBN 0-685-89477-0). Ares.
Buck, Carl D. Greek Dialects. 3rd ed. LC 55-5115. (Midway Reprint Ser). 1973. 17.00x (ISBN 0-226-07934-1). U of Chicago Pr.
Cagnat, et al. Inscriptiones Graecae: Ad Res Romanas Pertinentes, 3 vols. 1975. 75.00 (ISBN 0-89005-072-4). Ares.
Demitsas, Margarites. Sylloge Inscriptionum Graecarum et Latinarum Macedoniae, 2 vols. 1046p. 1980. 125.00 (ISBN 0-89005-324-3). Ares.
Durrbach, F., ed. Choix D'inscriptions De Delos. 1977. 25.00 (ISBN 0-89005-190-9). Ares.
Edson, C., ed. Inscriptiones Graecae. 1972. write for info. avail. (ISBN 0-685-23852-0). De Gruyter.
Gaertringen, F. Hiller v., ed. Inscriptiones Graecae: Inscriptiones Epidauri. (Illus.). 1977. Repr. of 1929 ed. 25.00 (ISBN 0-89005-207-7). Ares.
Helbing, R. Select Greek Inscriptions: Auswahl Aus Griechischen Inschriften. 1980. 10.00 (ISBN 0-89005-202-6). Ares.
Icard, Severin. Dictionary of Greek Coin Inscriptions. 1979. Repr. of 1920 ed. lib. bdg. 42.50 (ISBN 0-915262-31-2). S J Durst.
Inscriptiones Graecae: Edito Altera, 5 Vols in 7 Pts. (Lat). 1918-57. write for information (ISBN 0-685-02033-9). De Gruyter.
Jenkins, R. J. Dedalica: A Study of Dorian Plastic Art in the Seventh Century B. C. (Illus.). 1978. 10.00 (ISBN 0-89005-241-7). Ares.
Kaibel, G. & Lebeque, A., eds. Inscriptiones Graecae: Inscriptiones Galliae, Hispaniae, Britanniae, Germaniae. 1977. Repr. of 1890 ed. 25.00 (ISBN 0-89005-219-0). Ares.
Kent, John H. The Inscriptions, Nineteen Twenty-Six to Nineteen Fifty. (Corinth Ser: Vol. 8, Pt. 3). (Illus.). 1966. 30.00x (ISBN 0-87661-083-1). Am Sch Athens.
Lefebvre, G., ed. Inscriptiones Graecae Aegypti, No. 5: Christian Inscriptions. 1978. 25.00 (ISBN 0-89005-248-4). Ares.
Loewy, E. M. Inschriften Griechischer Bildhauer. 1976. 25.00 (ISBN 0-89005-112-7). Ares.
Marucchi, Orazio. Christian Epigraphy. Willis, J. Armine, tr. from It. LC 74-82057. 472p. 1975. 20.00 (ISBN 0-89005-070-8). Ares.
Meiggs, Russell & Lewis, David, eds. Selection of Greek Historical Inscriptions to the End of the 5th Century, B. C. 1969. 38.00x (ISBN 0-19-814266-8). Oxford U Pr.
Meritt, Benjamin D. Athenian Calendar in the 5th Century. facs. ed. LC 74-75510. (Select Bibliogrpahies Reprint Ser). 1928. 28.00 (ISBN 0-8369-5012-7). Arno.
--Inscriptions from the Athenian Agora. (Excavations of the Athenian Agora Picture Bks.: No. 10). (Illus.). 1966. pap. 1.50x (ISBN 0-87661-610-4). Am Sch Athens.
Meritt, Benjamin D., et al. The Athenian Tribute Lists, Vol. 3. 1968. Repr. of 1950 ed. 20.00x (ISBN 0-685-05657-0). Am Sch Athens.
Michel, C. Recueil D'inscriptions Grecques: Suppl. 1912 - 1927. 1976. 25.00 (ISBN 0-89005-110-0). Ares.
Milne, J. G. Inscriptiones Graecae Aegytpi No. 1: Cairo. 1976. 25.00 (ISBN 0-89005-111-9). Ares.
Mitford, T. B. Inscriptions of Kourion. LC 78-121295. (Memoirs Ser.: Vol. 83). (Illus.). 1971. 25.00 (ISBN 0-87169-083-7). Am Philos.
Nachmanson, Ernst. Historische Attische Inschriften. 1976. 10.00 (ISBN 0-89005-113-5). Ares.
Oikonomides, A. N. Supplementum Inscriptionum Atticarum IV. 1980. 25.00 (ISBN 0-89005-377-4). Ares.
Oikonomides, Al. N. Supplementum Inscriptionum Atticarum III. 1979. 25.00 (ISBN 0-89005-275-1). Ares.
Oikonomides, Al N., ed. Supplementum Inscriptionum Atticarum I. 1976. 25.00 (ISBN 0-89005-126-7). Ares.
Oikonomides, N., ed. Svpplementvm Inscriptionvm Atticarvm II, Vol. 2. 1978. 25.00 (ISBN 0-89005-249-2). Ares.
Pedrizet, P. & Lefebvre, G., eds. Inscriptiones Graecae Aegypti, No. 3: Abydos. 1978. 25.00 (ISBN 0-89005-243-3). Ares.
--Inscriptiones Memnonii Sive Besae Oracvli Ad Abydvm Thebaidis. 1978. 25.00 (ISBN 0-685-89476-2). Ares.
Pope, Helen. Foreigners in Attic Inscriptions. 1976. 15.00 (ISBN 0-89005-105-4). Ares.
--Non-Athenians in Attic Inscriptions. 20.00 (ISBN 0-89005-106-2). Ares.
Ramsay, William M. The Cities & Bishoprics of Phrygia. LC 75-7336. (Roman History Ser.). (Illus.). 1975. Repr. of 1895 ed. 48.00x (ISBN 0-405-07055-1). Arno.
Reilly, Linda C. Slaves in Ancient Greece. 1978. 25.00 (ISBN 0-89005-223-9). Ares.
Richardson, Bessie E. Old Age Among the Ancient Greeks. LC 74-93775. (Illus.). Repr. of 1933 ed. 21.50 (ISBN 0-404-05289-4). AMS Pr.
--Old Age Among the Ancient Greeks: The Greek Portrayal of Old Age in Literature, Art & Inscriptions. Repr. of 1933 ed. lib. bdg. 23.50x (ISBN 0-8371-0637-0, RIOA). Greenwood.
Roberts, Sally. The Attic Pyxis. 1978. 40.00 (ISBN 0-89005-210-7). Ares.
Roehl, H., ed. Inscriptiones Graecae Antiquissimae: Praeter Atticas in Attica Repertas. (Illus.). 1977. Repr. of 1882 ed. 25.00 (ISBN 0-89005-221-2). Ares.
Schwabe, Moshe & Lifshitz, Baruch. Beth She'arim, Vol. 2: The Greek Inscriptions. (Illus.). 256p. 1975. 30.00x (ISBN 0-8135-0762-6). Rutgers U Pr.
Shipp, G. Essays in Mycenaean & Homeric Greek. 1961. pap. 3.00x (ISBN 0-424-05530-9, Pub. by Sydney U Pr). Intl Schol Bk Serv.
Spiegelberg, W., ed. Inscriptiones Nominvm Graecorvm et Aegyptiacorvm Aetatis Romanae, Incisae Sivescriptae in Tabellis, (Mummy Labels) 1978. 25.00 (ISBN 0-89005-244-1). Ares.
Standerwick, H. F. Etymological Studies in the Greek Dialect Inscriptions. 1932. pap. 6.00 (ISBN 0-527-00756-0). Kraus Repr.
Strack, Max L. Inscriptiones Graecae Ptolemaicae. 1976. 15.00 (ISBN 0-89005-171-2). Ares.
Threatte, Leslie. Grammar of Attic Inscriptions: Phonology, Vol. I. 1979. 138.00x (ISBN 3-11007-344-7). De Gruyter.
Tod, M. N. The Progress of Greek Epigraphy 1937-1953. 1979. 30.00 (ISBN 0-89005-292-1). Ares.
Tracy, Stephen V. The Lettering of an Athenian Mason. (Supplement to Hesperia Ser.: No. 15). (Illus.). 1975. pap. 10.00x (ISBN 0-87661-515-9). Am Sch Athens.
Von Gaertringen, Friedrich & Kirchner, Johannes. Inscriptiones Graecae: Editio Minor, 5 vols. LC 74-77517. 2952p. 1975. Repr. 125.00 (ISBN 0-89005-013-9). Ares.
Winter, Frederick E. Greek Fortifications. LC 72-151398. (Phoenix Supplementary Volumes: No. 9). (Illus.). 1971. 22.50x (ISBN 0-8020-5225-8). U of Toronto Pr.
Woodhead, A. G. The Study of Greek Inscriptions. LC 80-41198. (Illus.). 139p. Date not set. 29.95 (ISBN 0-521-23188-4); pap. 11.95 (ISBN 0-521-29860-1). Cambridge U Pr.
Wycherley, R. E. Literary & Epigraphical Testimonia. (Athenian Agora Ser: Vol. 3). (Illus.). 1973. Repr. of 1957 ed. 15.00x (ISBN 0-87661-203-6). Am Sch Athens.

INSCRIPTIONS, HADRAMI

Bourgoin, J. Arabic Geometrical Pattern & Design. (Illus.). 6.50 (ISBN 0-8446-5104-4). Peter Smith.
Gardiner, Alan. The Kadesh Inscriptions of Remesess II. 59p. 1960. text ed. 10.50 (ISBN 0-900416-03-3, Pub. by Aris & Phillips England). Humanities.
Kouymjian, Dickran K. & Bacharach, Jere L., eds. Near Eastern Numismatics, Iconography, Epigraphy & History: Studies in Honor of George C. Miles. 1974. 55.00x (ISBN 0-8156-6041-3, Am U Beirut). Syracuse U Pr.
Mitchell, T. F. Writing Arabic: A Practical Introduction to Ruq'ah Script. 1953. pap. 8.95x (ISBN 0-19-713566-8). Oxford U Pr.

Walls, Archibald G. & Abul-Hajj, Amal. Arabic Inscriptions in Jerusalem: A Handlist. 1980. 25.00x (ISBN 0-905035-28-3, Pub. by Scorpion England). State Mutual Bk.

Winnett, F. V. & Reed, W. L. Ancient Records from North Arabia. LC 73-472676. (Illus.). 1970. 25.00x (ISBN 0-8020-5219-3). U of Toronto Pr.

INSCRIPTIONS, HIERATIC

see Egyptian Language–Inscriptions

INSCRIPTIONS, HIEROGLYPHIC

see also Egyptian Language–Inscriptions; Inscriptions, Linear A; Inscriptions, Linear B

Flammel, Nicholas. Alchemical Hieroglyphics. Orandus, Eirenaeus, tr. from Fr. 1980. Repr. of 1889 ed. 12.50 (ISBN 0-935214-04-6). Heptangle.

Graham, Ian. Corpus of Maya Hieroglyphic Inscriptions, Vol. 2, Pt. 3: Ucanal, Ixkun, Ixtutz. pap. text ed. 12.00 (ISBN 0-87365-786-1). Peabody Harvard.

--Corpus of Maya Hieroglyphic Inscriptions, Vol. 3, Pt. 2: Yaxchilan. 1979. pap. text ed. 12.00 (ISBN 0-87365-789-6). Peabody Harvard.

Graham, Ian & Von Euw, Eric. Corpus of Maya Hieroglyphic Inscriptions, Vol. 2, Pt. 1: Naranjo. LC 75-39917. 1975. pap. 12.00 (ISBN 0-87365-780-2). Peabody Harvard.

Hencken, Hugh. Mecklenburg Collection, Pt. II: The Iron Age Cemetary of Magdalenska. Condon, Lorna, ed. LC 78-52401. (American School of Prehistoric Research Bulletin Ser.: No. 32). 1978. pap. text ed. 30.00 (ISBN 0-87365-539-7). Peabody Harvard.

Von Euw, Eric. Corpus of Maya Hieroglypic Inscriptions: Xultun, Vol. 5, Pt. 1. Condon, Lorna, ed. LC 78-50627. 1978. pap. text ed. 12.00 (ISBN 0-87365-184-7). Peabody Harvard.

INSCRIPTIONS, INDIC

Sircar, D. C. Indian Epigraphical Glossary. 1966. 12.50 (ISBN 0-89684-222-3). Orient Bk Dist.

--Indian Epigraphy. (Illus.). 1965. 15.00 (ISBN 0-89684-223-1). Orient Bk Dist.

INSCRIPTIONS, ITALIC

Conway, Robert S., et al. Prae-Italic Dialects, 3 Vols. 1967. Repr. of 1933 ed. Set. 175.00 (ISBN 3-4870-1889-6). Adler.

INSCRIPTIONS, JEWISH

Chwolson, D. A. Hebrew Grave Inscriptions from the Crimea & Corpus of Hebrew in Scriptions. 1978. lib. bdg. 44.95 (ISBN 0-685-62295-9). Revisionist Pr.

Pritchard, James B. Hebrew Inscriptions & Stamps from Gibeon. (Museum Monograph). 32p. 1959. 2.00 (ISBN 0-934718-10-5). Univ Mus of U PA.

INSCRIPTIONS, KATURK

see Inscriptions, Turkish (Old)

INSCRIPTIONS, LATIN

Baldwin, Martha W. & Torelli, Mario, eds. Latin Inscriptions in the Kelsey Museum: The Dennison Collection. LC 79-19250. (Kelsey Museum of Archaeology Studies: No. 4). (Illus.). 180p. (Orig.). 1979. pap. 17.25 (ISBN 0-472-02711-5, IS-00092, Pub. by U of Mich Pr). Univ Microfilms.

Barbarino, Joseph. The Evolution of the Latin -B-U- Merger: A Quantitative & Comparative Analysis of the B-V Alteration in Latin Inscriptions. LC 78-20445. (Studies in the Romance Languages & Literatures: No. 203). 1979. 12.50x (ISBN 0-8078-9203-3). U of NC Pr.

Breccia, E., ed. Inscriptiones Nunc Alexandriae in Museo. 1978. 25.00 (ISBN 0-685-89477-0). Ares.

Burn, A. R. Romans in Britain: An Anthology of Inscriptions. 2nd ed. LC 77-75795. (Illus.). 1969. 12.95x (ISBN 0-87249-142-0). U of SC Pr.

Corpus inscriptionum Latinarum. Consilio et auctoritate Academiae Scientiarum Rei Publicae Democricae Germanicae Editum, 16 vols. in 52 parts. viii, 1487p. (Lat.). 1975. write for info. avail. (ISBN 3-11-005983-5). De Gruyter.

Demitsas, Margarites. Sylloge Inscriptionum Graecarum et Latinarum Macedoniae, 2 vols. 1046p. 1980. 125.00 (ISBN 0-89005-324-3). Ares.

Gaeng, Paul A. An Inquiry into the Local Variations in Vulgar Latin As Reflected in the Vocalism of Christian Inscriptions. (Studies in the Romance Languages & Literatures: No. 77). 1968. pap. 16.50x (ISBN 0-8078-9077-4). U of NC Pr.

--A Study of Nominal Inflection in Latin Inscriptions: A Morpho-Syntactic Analysis. (Studies in the Romance Languages & Literatures Ser: No. 182). 1977. 15.00x (ISBN 0-8078-9182-7). U of NC Pr.

Gordon, Arthur E. & Gordon, Joyce S. Album of Dated Latin Inscriptions. Incl. Pt. III. Rome & the Neighborhood, A. D. 200-525. 1965. 45.00x (ISBN 0-520-00498-1); Pt. IV. Indexes to the Album of Dated Latin Inscriptions. 1965. 40.00x (ISBN 0-520-00500-7). U of Cal Pr.

Graham, Alexander. Roman Africa. facs. ed. LC 70-157369. (Black Heritage Library Collection Ser). 1902. 24.25 (ISBN 0-8369-8807-8). Arno.

Kent, John H. The Inscriptions, Nineteen Twenty-Six to Nineteen Fifty. (Corinth Ser: Vol. 8, Pt. 3). (Illus.). 1966. 30.00x (ISBN 0-87661-083-1). Am Sch Athens.

Lindsay, W. M. Handbook of Latin Inscriptions: Illustrating the History of the Language. 134p. 1970. pap. text ed. 17.25x (ISBN 90-70265-02-8). Humanities.

Marucchi, Orazio. Christian Epigraphy. Willis, J. Armine, tr. from It. LC 74-82057. 472p. 1975. 20.00 (ISBN 0-89005-070-8). Ares.

Omeltchenko, Stephen. A Quantitative & Comparative Study of the Vocalism of the Latin Inscriptions of North American, Britain, Dalmatia, & the Balkans. (Studies in the Romance Languages & Literature Ser: No. 180). 1977. 22.00x (ISBN 0-8078-9180-0). U of NC Pr.

Rushforth, G. McN. Latin Historical Inscriptions. 1980. 10.00 (ISBN 0-89005-179-8). Ares.

--Latin Historical Inscriptions. LC 70-107831. (Select Bibliographies Reprint Ser). 1893. 17.00 (ISBN 0-8369-5196-4). Arno.

Susini, Giancarlo. The Roman Stonecutter: An Introduction to Latin Epigraphy. Badian, E., ed. Dabrowski, tr. from It. (Illus.). 84p. 1973. 12.50x (ISBN 0-87471-196-7). Rowman.

Veny, Cristobal. Inscriptions of the Balearic Isles up to the Arab Domination. 15.00 (ISBN 0-686-23376-X). Classical Folia.

INSCRIPTIONS, LINEAR A

Gordon, Cyrus H. Evidence for the Minoan Language. 1966. 12.00 (ISBN 0-911566-06-6). Ventnor.

Packard, David W. Minoan Linear A. (Illus.). 1974. 24.00x (ISBN 0-520-02580-6). U of Cal Pr.

INSCRIPTIONS, LINEAR B

see also Inscriptions–Crete

Bennett, Emmett L., Jr. Mycenae Tablets Two. Chadwick, John, ed. LC 58-7023. (Transactions Ser.: Vol. 48, Pt. 1). (Illus.). 1958. pap. 1.50 (ISBN 0-87169-481-6). Am Philos.

Chadwick, John. Decipherment of Linear B. (Illus.). 1970. 29.95 (ISBN 0-521-04599-1); pap. 7.50x (ISBN 0-521-09596-4, 596). Cambridge U Pr.

--Mycenae Tablets Three. (Transactions Ser.: Vol. 52, Pt. 7). (Illus.). 1963. pap. 1.50 (ISBN 0-87169-527-8). Am Philos.

Levin, Saul. The Linear B Decipherment Controversy Re-examined. LC 64-17579. 1964. 19.00 (ISBN 0-87395-014-3); microfiche 19.00 (ISBN 0-87395-114-X). State U NY Pr.

Ventris, M. & Chadwick, J. Documents in Mycenaean Greek. 2nd ed. (Illus.). 600p. 1973. 110.00 (ISBN 0-521-08558-6). Cambridge U Pr.

INSCRIPTIONS, MAYA

see Picture-Writing, Maya

INSCRIPTIONS, MONGOLIAN

Krueger, John R. Mongolian Epigraphical Dictionary in reverse Listing. LC 67-63757. (Uralic & Altaic Ser: Vol. 88). (Orig., Mongolian). 1967. pap. text ed. 6.00x (ISBN 0-87750-078-9). Res Ctr Lang Semiotic.

INSCRIPTIONS, NORSE

see also Inscriptions, Runic

INSCRIPTIONS, PHENICIAN

Obermann, Julian. Discoveries at Karatepe: A Phoenician Royal Inscription from Cilicia. (Supplements: 9). (Illus.). 1948. pap. 1.00 (ISBN 0-686-00045-5). Am Orient Soc.

INSCRIPTIONS, RUNIC

see also Runes

Thompson, Claiborne W. Studies in Upplandic Runography. LC 74-22284. (Illus.). 218p. 1975. 19.50x (ISBN 0-292-77511-3). U of Tex Pr.

INSCRIPTIONS, SAFAITIC

Grimme, Hubert. Texte und Untersuchungen Zur Safatenisch - Arabischen Religion. 1929. pap. 12.50 (ISBN 0-384-20070-2). Johnson Repr.

Oxtoby, Willard G. Some Inscriptions of the Safaitic Bedouin. (American Oriental Ser.: Vol. 50). (Illus.). 1968. pap. 6.00x (ISBN 0-940490-50-1). Am Orient Soc.

Winnett, F. V. & Harding, G. L. Inscriptions from Fifty Safaitic Cairns. (Near & Middle East Ser.). (Illus.). 1978. 80.00x (ISBN 0-8020-2282-0). U of Toronto Pr.

INSCRIPTIONS, SEMITIC

Gibson, John C. Textbook of Syrian Semitic Inscriptions: Volume 3, Phonecian Inscriptions, Including Inscriptions in the Mixed Dialect of Arslan Tash. (Illus.). 192p. 1981. 45.00x (ISBN 0-19-813199-2). Oxford U Pr.

Grimme, Hubert. Altsinaitische Forschungen, Epigraphisches und Historisches. 1937. pap. 12.50 (ISBN 0-384-20050-8). Johnson Repr.

Harding, G. Lankester. An Index & Concordance of Pre-Islamic Arabian Names & Inscriptions. LC 76-151372. (Near & Middle East Ser). 1971. 50.00x (ISBN 0-8020-1591-3). U of Toronto Pr.

Herr, Larry G. The Scripts of Ancient Northwest Semitic Seals. LC 78-18933. (Harvard Semitic Museum. Harvard Semitic Monographs: No. 18). (Illus.). 1978. 9.00 (ISBN 0-89130-237-9, 040018). Scholars Pr Ca.

INSCRIPTIONS, SOUTH ARABIAN

see Inscriptions, Hadrami

INSCRIPTIONS, TURKISH (OLD)

Gibson, Elsa. The Christians for Christians Inscriptions of Phrygia. LC 78-12688. (Harvard Theological Studies: No. 32). 1978. pap. 7.50 (ISBN 0-89130-262-X, 020032). Scholars Pr Ca.

INSECT BEHAVIOR

see Insects–Behavior

INSECT CONTROL

Advances in Insect Population Control by the Sterile-Male Technique. (Technical Reports Ser.: No. 44). (Illus., Orig.). 1965. pap. 9.75 (ISBN 92-0-115065-2, IDC44, IAEA). Unipub.

Aerial Control of Forest Insects in Canada. 1978. pap. 27.75 (ISBN 0-685-87289-0, SSC98, SSC). Unipub.

American Chemical Society Symposium. Chemicals Controlling Insect Behavior. Beroza, Morton, ed. 1970. 31.50 (ISBN 0-12-093050-1). Acad Pr.

Burges, H. D. & Hussey, N. W. Microbial Control of Insects & Mites. 1970. 82.00 (ISBN 0-12-143350-1). Acad Pr.

Committee on Scholarly Communication with the People's Republic of China (CSCPRC) Insect Control in the People's Republic of China: A Trip Report of the American Insect Control Delegation. LC 76-52849. (CSCPRC Report: No. 2). 1977. pap. 11.25 (ISBN 0-309-02525-7). Natl Acad Pr.

Coppel, H. C. & Mertins, J. W. Biological Insect Press Suppression. LC 76-42188. (Advanced Series in Agricultural Sciences: Vol. 4). (Illus.). 1977. 37.60 (ISBN 3-540-07931-9). Springer-Verlag.

Dethier, V. G. Man's Plague? Insects & Agriculture. LC 75-15216. (Illus.). 237p. (Orig.). 1976. 9.95 (ISBN 0-87850-026-X). Darwin Pr.

Disinfestation of Fruit by Irradiation. (Illus.). 180p. (Orig.). 1972. pap. 13.00 (ISBN 92-0-111571-7, ISP299, IAEA). Unipub.

Egerton, Frank N., ed. Ecological Studies on Insect Parasitism: An Original Anthology. LC 77-73820. (History of Ecology Ser.). 1978. lib. bdg. 18.00x (ISBN 0-405-10389-1). Arno.

Fletcher, W. W. The Pest War. LC 74-11440. 1978. pap. 13.95 (ISBN 0-470-26345-8). Halsted Pr.

Glass, E. W. Integrated Pest Management: Rationale, Potential Needs & Implementation. 1975. 5.85 (ISBN 0-686-18864-0). Entomol Soc.

Hall, Stanley A., ed. New Approaches to Pest Control & Eradication. LC 63-19396. (Advances in Chemistry Ser: No. 41). 1963. pap. 8.50 (ISBN 0-8412-0042-4). Am Chemical.

Henderson, Gary L., et al. Effects of DDT on Man & Other Mammals II. LC 73-289. 1973. 32.50x (ISBN 0-8422-7111-2). Irvington.

Hill, D. S. Agricultural Insect Pests of the Tropics. (Illus.). 584p. 1975. 60.00 (ISBN 0-521-20261-2); pap. 19.95 (ISBN 0-521-29441-X). Cambridge U Pr.

Hogner, Dorothy C. Good Bugs & Bad Bugs in Your Garden: Backyard Ecology. LC 74-6235. (Illus.). 96p. (gr. 3-7). 1974. PLB 8.79 (ISBN 0-690-00120-7, TYC-J). Har-Row.

Integrated Control of Insect Pests in the Netherlands. 304p. 1980. 52.75 (ISBN 90-220-0716-2, PDC 207, Pudoc). Unipub.

Isotopes & Radiation in Entomology. (Illus., Orig., Eng., Fr., Rus. & Span.). 1968. pap. 27.75 (ISBN 92-0-010168-2, ISP166, IAEA). Unipub.

Jukes, Thomas H., et al. Effects of DDT on Man & Other Mammals II. LC 73-289. (Illus.). 220p. 1973. text ed. 36.50x (ISBN 0-8422-7110-4). Irvington.

Lindguist, A. W., ed. Insect Population Control by the Sterile-Male Technique. (Technical Reports Ser.: No. 21). (Illus., Orig.). 1963. pap. 5.50 (ISBN 92-0-115063-6, IDC21, IAEA). Unipub.

Metcalf, Robert L. & Luckmann, William H., eds. Introduction to Insect Pest Management. LC 74-34133. (Environmental Science & Technology Ser). 587p. 1975. 32.00 (ISBN 0-471-59855-0, Pub. by Wiley-Interscience). Wiley.

Mitchell, Everett R., ed. Management of Insects Pests with Semiochemicals: Concepts & Practice. 516p. 1981. 59.50 (ISBN 0-306-40630-6, Plenum Pr). Plenum Pub.

Munro, J. W. Insects & Industry. 1929. 15.00 (ISBN 0-685-73516-8). Norwood Edns.

Philbrick, John & Philbrick, Helen. The Bug Book: Harmless Insect Controls. LC 74-75470. 128p. 1974. pap. 4.95 (ISBN 0-88266-027-6). Garden Way Pub.

Quraishi, M. Sayeed. Biochemical Insect Control: Its Impact on Economy, Environment & Natural Selection. LC 76-29701. 1977. 33.50 (ISBN 0-471-70275-7, Pub. by Wiley-Interscience). Wiley.

Rodriguez, J. G. Insect & Mite Nutrition. LC 72-96711. 717p. 1973. 68.50 (ISBN 0-444-10437-2, North-Holland). Elsevier.

Rudinsky. Forest Insect Survey & Control. 1979. 20.00 (ISBN 0-88246-100-1). Oreg St U Bkstrs.

Rudman, Jack. Foreman of Housing Exterminators. (Career Examination Ser.: C-2514). (Cloth bdg. avail. on request). pap. 10.00 (ISBN 0-686-53718-1). Natl Learning.

Shorey, H. H. & McKelvey, John J., Jr. Chemical Control of Insect Behavior: Theory & Application. LC 76-46573. (Environmental Science & Technology Ser.). 1977. 34.50 (ISBN 0-471-78840-6, Pub. by Wiley-Interscience). Wiley.

Sterility Principle for Insect Control or Eradication. (Illus.). 542p. (Orig.). 1970. pap. 56.25 (ISBN 92-0-010171-2, ISP377, IAEA). Unipub.

Symposium, Cornell University, Ithaca, New York, Oct. 1974. Insects, Science, & Society: Proceedings. Pimentel, David, ed. 1975. 30.00 (ISBN 0-12-556550-X). Acad Pr.

Symposium on the Chemistry & Action of Insect Juvenile Hormones, Washington, D. C., 1971. Insect Juvenile Hormones: Chemistry & Action. Menn, Julius J. & Beroza, Morton, eds. 1972. 42.50 (ISBN 0-12-490950-7). Acad Pr.

Watson, Theo F., et al. Practical Insect Pest Management: A Self-Instructional Manual. (Illus.). 1976. pap. text ed. 9.95x (ISBN 0-7167-0558-3). W H Freeman.

Wilson, M. Curtis, et al. Practical Insect Pest Management: Fundamentals of Applied Entomology, No. 1. LC 76-46901. (Illus.). 1977. 6.95x (ISBN 0-917974-03-4). Waveland Pr.

--Practical Insect Pest Management: Insects of Man's Household & Health, No. 5. LC 77-82251. (Illus.). 1977. 6.95x (ISBN 0-917974-07-7). Waveland Pr.

--Practical Insect Pest Management: Insects of Ornamental Plants, No. 4. LC 77-82602. (Illus.). 1977. 6.50x (ISBN 0-917974-06-9). Waveland Pr.

--Practical Insect Pest Management. 2nd. ed. LC 79-57132. (Insects of Livestock & Agronomic Crops Ser: No.2). (Illus.). 208p. 1980. pap. text ed. 8.50x (ISBN 0-917974-39-5). Waveland Pr.

Wood, David, et al, eds. Control of Insect Behavior by Natural Products: Proceedings. LC 69-13486. 1970. 38.00 (ISBN 0-12-762650-6). Acad Pr.

INSECT CONTROL–BIOLOGICAL CONTROL

Advances in Insect Population Control by the Sterile-Male Technique. (Technical Reports Ser.: No. 44). (Illus., Orig.). 1965. pap. 9.75 (ISBN 92-0-115065-2, IDC44, IAEA). Unipub.

Application of Induced Sterility for Control of Lepidopterous Populations. (Orig.). 1971. pap. 13.00 (ISBN 92-0-111271-8, ISP281, IAEA). Unipub.

Carson, Rachel. Silent Spring. (Illus.). 1962. 11.95 (ISBN 0-395-07506-8). HM.

Computer Models & Application of the Sterile-Male Technique. (Illus.). 195p. (Orig.). 1973. pap. 16.25 (ISBN 92-0-111573-3, ISP340, IAEA). Unipub.

Control of Livestock Insect Pests by the Sterile Male Technique. (Illus., Orig.). 1968. pap. 8.25 (ISBN 92-0-011368-0, IAEA). Unipub.

Controlling Fruit Flies by the Sterile-Insect Technique. (Illus.). 175p. 1976. pap. 17.25 (ISBN 92-0-111575-X, ISP392, IAEA). Unipub.

Coppel, H. C. & Mertins, J. W. Biological Insect Press Suppression. LC 76-42188. (Advanced Series in Agricultural Sciences: Vol. 4). (Illus.). 1977. 37.60 (ISBN 3-540-07931-9). Springer-Verlag.

Davidson, G. Genetic Control of Insect Pests. 1974. 26.00 (ISBN 0-12-205750-3). Acad Pr.

DeBach, P. Biological Control by Natural Enemies. LC 73-90812. (Illus.). 325p. 1974. 39.50 (ISBN 0-521-20380-5); pap. 11.95x (ISBN 0-521-09835-1). Cambridge U Pr.

Graham, Ada & Graham, Frank. Bug Hunters. LC 77-20532. (Audubon Readers: No. 2). (gr. 5 up). 1978. 6.95 (ISBN 0-440-00909-X); PLB 6.46 (ISBN 0-440-00910-3). Delacorte.

Howard, Leland O. & Fiske, William F. The Importation into the United States of the Parasites of the Gypsy Moth & the Brown-Tail Moth: Report of Progress of Previous & Concurrent Efforts of This Kind. Egerton, Frank N., 3rd, ed. LC 77-74230. (History of Ecology Ser.). (Illus.). 1978. Repr. of 1911 ed. lib. bdg. 24.00x (ISBN 0-405-10400-6). Arno.

Insect Ecology & the Sterile-Male Technique. (Illus., Orig.). 1969. pap. 8.25 (ISBN 92-0-011269-2, ISP223, IAEA). Unipub.

Laird, Marshall, ed. Blackflies: The/Future for Biological Methods in Integrated Control. LC 81-66373. 1981. price not set (ISBN 0-12-434060-1). Acad Pr.

Lindguist, A. W., ed. Insect Population Control by the Sterile-Male Technique. (Technical Reports Ser.: No. 21). (Illus., Orig.). 1963. pap. 5.50 (ISBN 92-0-115063-6, IDC21, IAEA). Unipub.

Meteorology & the Colorado Potato Beetle: Technical Note No. 137. (Illus.). 51p. 1975. pap. 15.00 (ISBN 92-63-10391-7, WMO). Unipub.

Pal, R. & Whitten, M. J., eds. The Use of Genetics in Insect Control. 1974. 58.75 (ISBN 0-444-10602-2, North-Holland). Elsevier.

Rabbinge, R. Biological Control of Fruit-Tree Red Spider Mite. (Simulation Monographs). 1976. pap. 30.00 (ISBN 90-220-0590-9, Pub. by PUDOC). Unipub.

Scruggs, C. G. The Peaceful Atom & the Deadly Fly. LC 75-28738. (Illus.). 311p. 1975. 12.95 (ISBN 0-8363-0135-8). Jenkins.

Slama, K., et al. Insect Hormones & Bioanalogues. LC 72-94418. (Illus.). 500p. 1974. pap. 66.10 (ISBN 0-387-81112-5). Springer-Verlag.

Sokoloff, A. The Biology of Tribolium: With Special Emphasis on Genetic Aspects, Vol. 3. 1978. 32.00x (ISBN 0-19-857512-2). Oxford U Pr.

The Sterile-Insect Technique & Its Field Application. (Illus.). 138p. (Orig.). 1974. pap. 11.50 (ISBN 92-0-111374-9, ISP364, IAEA). Unipub.

Sterile-Male Technique for Eradication or Control of Harmful Insects. 1969. pap. 9.75 (ISBN 92-0-111369-2, ISP224, IAEA). Unipub.

Sterility Principle for Insect Control 1974. (Illus.). 622p. 1975. pap. 56.25 (ISBN 92-0-010275-1, ISP 377, IAEA). Unipub.

Summers, Max, et al, eds. Baculoviruses for Insect Pest Control: Safety Considerations. LC 75-36871. 1975. 9.00 (ISBN 0-914826-07-7). Am Soc Microbio.

INSECT GALLS

see Galls (Botany)

INSECT METAMORPHOSIS

see Insects–Metamorphosis

INSECT POPULATIONS

Bos, H. V. & Rabbinge, R. Simulation of the Fluctuations of the Grey Larch Bud Moth Z. Diniana in the Upper Engadin. (Simulation Monographs). 1976. pap. 13.00 (ISBN 90-220-0589-5, Pub. by PUDOC). Unipub.

Insect Ecology & the Sterile-Male Technique. (Illus., Orig.). 1969. pap. 8.25 (ISBN 92-0-011269-2, ISP223, IAEA). Unipub.

Muirhead-Thompson, R. C. Ecology of Insect Vector Populations. 1968. 17.50 (ISBN 0-12-509750-6). Acad Pr.

Southwood, T. R. Ecological Methods: With Particular Reference to the Study of Insect Population. 2nd ed. LC 78-7961. 524p. 1978. 27.00x (ISBN 0-412-15760-8, Pub. by Chapman & Hall England). Methuen Inc.

Varley, G. C., et al. Insect Population Ecology: An Analytic Approach. 1974. pap. 7.95x (ISBN 0-520-02667-5). U of Cal Pr.

Weese, Asa O. Animal Ecology of an Illinois Elm-Maple Forest. pap. 6.00 (ISBN 0-384-66400-8). Johnson Repr.

INSECT SOCIETIES

see also Ants; Bees; Insect Populations; Termites; Wasps

Fabre, Jean H. Social Life in the Insect World. LC 72-164264. 1974. Repr. of 1912 ed. 28.00 (ISBN 0-8103-3967-6). Gale.

--Social Life in the Insect World. facsimile ed. Miall, Bernard, tr. LC 78-179517. (Select Bibliographies Reprint Ser). Repr. of 1912 ed. 21.00 (ISBN 0-8369-6646-5). Arno.

Goetsch, Wilhelm. Ants. (Ann Arbor Science Library Ser). (Illus.). 1957. pap. 2.95 (ISBN 0-472-05002-8, 502, AA). U of Mich Pr.

Hermann, Henry R. Social Insects, Vol. 2. 1981. 55.00 (ISBN 0-12-342202-7); subscription price 46.50 (ISBN 0-686-77701-8). Acad Pr.

Hermann, Henry R., ed. Social Insects, Vol. 1. LC 78-4871. 1979. 44.50 (ISBN 0-12-342201-9); by subscription 39.50 (ISBN 0-686-67959-8). Acad Pr.

Oster, George F. & Wilson, Edward O. Caste & Ecology in the Social Insects. LC 78-51185. (Monographs in Population Biologh: Vol. 12). (Illus.). pap. text ed. 25.00 (ISBN 0-691-08210-3); pap. 7.50 (ISBN 0-691-02361-1). Princeton U Pr.

Richard, O. W. Social Insects. (Illus.). 7.50 (ISBN 0-8446-0877-7). Peter Smith.

Simon, Hilda. Exploring the World of Social Insects. LC 74-178823. (Illus.). (gr. 6 up). 1962. 6.95 (ISBN 0-8149-0390-8). Vanguard.

Wheeler, W. M. Social Life Among the Insects: Being a Series of Lectures Delivered at the Lowell Institute in Boston in March, 1922. LC 23-12888. Repr. of 1923 ed. 23.00 (ISBN 0-384-67870-X). Johnson Repr.

Wilson, Edward O. Insect Societies. LC 74-148941. (Illus.). 1971. 25.00x (ISBN 0-674-45490-1, Belknap Pr); pap. 10.00 (ISBN 0-674-45495-2). Harvard U Pr.

INSECTICIDES

see also Insects, Injurious and Beneficial; Spraying;
also names of insecticides

Brown, A. W. & Pal, R. Insecticide Resistance in Arthropods. 2nd ed. (Monograph Ser: No. 38). (Illus.). 491p. 1971. pap. 16.40 (ISBN 92-4-140038-2, 943). World Health.

Busvine, James R. A Critical Review of the Techniques for Testing Insecticides. 2nd ed. LC 77-851432. (Illus.). 346p. 1970. 30.00x (ISBN 0-85198-030-9). Intl Pubns Serv.

Casida, John E., ed. Pyrethrum: The Natural Insecticide. 1973. 42.50 (ISBN 0-12-162950-3). Acad Pr.

Control of Pesticides: A Survey of Existing Legislation. (International Digest of Health Legislation Ser: Vol. 20, No. 4). 150p. 1969. pap. 5.60 (ISBN 92-4-169204-9, 1020). World Health.

Elliott, Michael, ed. Synthetic Pyrethroids. LC 77-1810. (ACS Symposium Ser.: No. 42). 1977. 22.50 (ISBN 0-8412-0368-7). Am Chemical.

Fest, C. & Schmidt, K. J. The Chemistry of Organophosphorus Pesticides: Reactivity-Synthesis-Mode of Action-Toxicology. LC 72-80294. (Illus.). 366p. 1973. 55.30 (ISBN 0-387-05858-3). Springer-Verlag.

Hall, Stanley A., ed. New Approaches to Pest Control & Eradication. LC 63-19396. (Advances in Chemistry Ser: No. 41). 1963. pap. 8.50 (ISBN 0-8412-0042-4). Am Chemical.

Insecticides & Application Equipment for Tsetse Control. (FAO Animal Production & Health Paper: No. 3). 1977. pap. 9.00 (ISBN 92-5-100183-9, F723, FAO). Unipub.

International Conference on Alternative Insecticides for Vector Control, Atlanta, Feb. 1971. Proceedings. (Bulletin of WHO: Vol. 44, Nos. 1-3). 470p. 1971. pap. 14.40 (ISBN 0-686-09008-X, 922). World Health.

Jacobson, Martin. Insecticides of the Future. 104p. 1975. pap. 14.75 (ISBN 0-8247-6303-3). Dekker.

Jacobson, Martin & Crosby, Donald G., eds. Naturally Occurring Insecticides. 1970. 75.00 (ISBN 0-8247-1325-7). Dekker.

Jager, K. W. Aldrin, Dieldrin, Endrin & Telodrin. 1970. 36.75 (ISBN 0-444-40898-3). Elsevier.

Kenaga, E. E. & Morgan, Robert W. Commercial & Experimental Organic Insecticides. 1978. 6.70 (ISBN 0-686-18862-4). Entomol Soc.

Killingsworth, Robert B. & Pearce, G. W., eds. Agricultural Applications of Petroleum Products. LC 54-1575. (Advances in Chemistry Ser: No. 7). 1952. pap. 8.50 (ISBN 0-8412-0008-4). Am Chemical.

Kuhr, Ronald J. & Dorough, H. Wyman. Carbamate Insecticides: Chemistry, Biochemistry & Toxicology. LC 74-25265. (Uniscience Ser.). 301p. 1976. 59.95 (ISBN 0-8493-5066-2). CRC Pr.

Matsumura, Fumio. Toxicology of Insecticides. LC 74-19258. (Illus.). 504p. 1975. 27.50 (ISBN 0-306-30787-1, Plenum Pr). Plenum Pub.

Measurements & Computations on the Behaviour of the Insecticides Azinphos-Methyl & Dimethoate in Ditches. (Agricultural Research Reports Ser.: 884). 1979. pap. 28.00 (ISBN 90-220-0695-6, PDC118, PUDOC). Unipub.

Metcalf, Robert L., Jr. & McKelvey, John J., eds. The Future for Insecticides: Needs & Prospects. LC 75-33225. 540p. 1976. 29.50 (ISBN 0-471-59860-7). Krieger.

Neal, J. W., Jr. A Manual for Determining Small Dosage Calculations of Pesticides & Conversion Tables. 1976. 6.25 (ISBN 0-686-18863-2). Entomol Soc.

O'Brien, R. D. & Yamamoto, Izuru, eds. Biochemical Toxicology of Insecticides. 1970. 32.50 (ISBN 0-12-523935-1). Acad Pr.

Osborne, ed. Consolidated List of Approved Common Names of Insecticides & Certain Other Pesticides. LC 52-44516. 1979. 3.35 (ISBN 0-686-18865-9). Entomol Soc.

Page, B. G. & Thomson, W. T. The Nineteen Eighty-One Insecticide, Herbicide, Fungicide Quick Guide. 140p. 1981. pap. 12.00 (ISBN 0-913702-11-0). Thomson Pub Ca.

Quraishi, M. Sayeed. Biochemical Insect Control: Its Impact on Economy, Environment & Natural Selection. LC 76-29701. 1977. 33.50 (ISBN 0-471-70275-7, Pub. by Wiley-Interscience). Wiley.

Ramulu, U. S. Chemistry of Insecticides & Fungicides. 342p. 1981. 25.00x (ISBN 0-686-72944-7, Pub. by Oxford & IBH India); 15.25x (ISBN 0-686-72945-5). State Mutual Bk.

Shepard, Merle, ed. Insect Pest Management. LC 73-9730. 1973. 32.50x (ISBN 0-8422-7114-7); pap. text ed. 14.50x (ISBN 0-8422-0296-X). Irvington.

Thomson, W. T. Agricultural Chemicals, Book 1: Insecticides. rev. ed. 240p. 1981. pap. 13.50 (ISBN 0-913702-13-7). Thomson Pub Ca.

Vector Control. (WHO Bulletin Supplement: Vol. 29). (Also avail. in French). 1963. pap. 4.80 (ISBN 92-4-068291-0). World Health.

Wegler, R., ed. Insecticides: Biochemical & Biological Methods, Natural Products. (Chemie der Pflanzenschutz und Schaedlingsbekaempfungsmittel). 500p. 1981. 152.30 (ISBN 0-387-10307-4). Springer-Verlag.

WHO Expert Committee on Insecticides, Geneva, 1970. Application & Dispersal of Pesticides: A Report. (Technical Report Ser: No. 465). 66p. 1971. pap. 2.00 (ISBN 92-4-120465-6, 931). World Health.

WHO Expert Committee on Insecticides, Geneva, 1968. Insecticide Resistance & Vector Control. (Technical Report Ser: No. 443). 279p. 1970. pap. 5.60 (ISBN 92-4-120443-5, 938). World Health.

Wilkinson, C. F., ed. Insecticide Biochemistry & Physiology. LC 76-10596. (Illus.). 768p. 1976. 49.50 (ISBN 0-306-30872-X, Plenum Pr). Plenum Pub.

INSECTIVOROUS PLANTS

Darwin, Charles R. Insectivorous Plants. 2nd rev. ed. LC 73-147085. Repr. of 1893 ed. 27.50 (ISBN 0-404-01928-5). AMS Pr.

Dean, Anabel. Plants That Eat Insects: A Look at Carnivorous Plants. LC 75-38480. (Science Books for Young People). (Illus.). (gr. 5-12). 1977. PLB 5.95g (ISBN 0-8225-0299-2). Lerner Pubns.

Lloyd, Francis E. The Carnivorous Plants. (Illus.). 384p. 1976. pap. 5.00 (ISBN 0-486-23321-9). Dover.

--The Carnivorous Plants. 8.75 (ISBN 0-8446-5485-X). Peter Smith.

Overbeck, Cynthia. Carnivorous Plants. (Lerner Natural Science Bks.). (Illus.). 48p. (gr. 4-10). 1981. PLB 7.95 (ISBN 0-8225-1470-2). Lerner Pubns.

Prince, J. H. Plants That Eat Animals. LC 78-14791. (Illus.). (gr. 7 up). 1979. Repr. 7.95 (ISBN 0-525-66599-4). Elsevier-Nelson.

Schnell, Donald E. Carnivorous Plants of the United States & Canada. LC 76-26883. (Illus.). 220p. 1976. 19.95 (ISBN 0-910244-90-1). Blair.

Schwartz, Randall. Carnivorous Plants. 1975. pap. 1.25 (ISBN 0-380-00518-2, 26989). Avon.

Slack, Adrian. Carnivorous Plants. (Illus.). 240p. 1980. 19.95 (ISBN 0-262-19186-5). MIT Pr.

INSECTS

see also Diptera; Entomology; Fertilization of Plants; Hemiptera; Hymenoptera; Insect Societies; Larvae–Insects; Lepidoptera; Neuroptera; Orthoptera; Scale-Insects; Wasps;
also Ants; Butterflies; Moths; Wasps; and similar headings

Amyot, Charles J. Histoire Naturelle Des Insectes, Hempteres. 751p. 1981. Repr. of 1843 ed. lib. bdg. 280.00 (ISBN 0-8287-1451-7). Clearwater Pub.

Anderson, Margaret M. Insect Friends & Enemies. (Illus.). 64p. 1981. 7.50 (ISBN 0-682-49689-8). Exposition.

Aritchie, Carson I. Insects, the Creeping Conquerors & Human History. LC 78-13420. (Illus.). (gr. 7 up). 1979. 7.95 (ISBN 0-525-66606-0). Elsevier-Nelson.

Armour, R. & Galdone, P. Insects All Around Us. 1981. 7.95 (ISBN 0-07-002266-6). McGraw.

Arnett, R. & Jacques, R., Jr. S&S Guide to Insects. 1981. 22.50 (ISBN 0-671-25013-2, Fireside); pap. 9.95 (ISBN 0-671-25014-0). S&S.

Baltazar, Clare R. & Salazar, Nelia P. Philippine Insects: An Introduction. (Illus.). 1980. text ed. 17.00x (ISBN 0-8248-0675-1, Pub. by U of Philippines Pr); pap. text ed. 12.00x (ISBN 0-8248-0676-X). U Pr of Hawaii.

Beck, Stanley D. Insect Photoperiodism. 2nd ed. LC 80-10098. 1980. 32.50 (ISBN 0-12-084380-3). Acad Pr.

Berry, R. E. Insects & Mites of Economic Importance in the Northwest. (Illus.). 1978. spiral comb bdg. 11.95 (ISBN 0-88246-002-1). Oreg St U Bkstrs.

Blackman, R. L., et al. Insect Cytogenetics. LC 80-41700. (Royal Entomological Society of London Symposium Ser.). 278p. 1981. 69.95 (ISBN 0-470-27126-4). Halsted Pr.

Bland, Roger G. & Jaques, H. E. How to Know the Insects. 3rd ed. (Pictured Key Nature Ser.). 1978. text ed. write for info. (ISBN 0-697-04753-9); wire coil avail. (ISBN 0-697-04752-0). Wm C Brown.

Borkovec, A. B. Insect Chemosterilants. (Advances in Pest Control Research Ser: Vol. 7). 144p. 1966. text ed. 9.00x (ISBN 0-470-08952-0, Pub. by Wiley). Krieger.

Borror, Donald J., et al. An Introduction to the Study of Insects. 5th ed. 26.95 (ISBN 0-03-043531-5, HoltC). HR&W.

Brady, U. Eugene, et al. Pheromones: Current Research, 2 vols, Vol. 2. 157p. 1974. text ed. 28.50x (ISBN 0-8422-7212-7). Irvington.

Brian, M. V., ed. Production Ecology of Ants & Termites. LC 76-54061. (International Biological Programme Ser.: No. 13). (Illus.). 1977. 72.50 (ISBN 0-521-21519-6). Cambridge U Pr.

Brues, Charles T. Insects, Food & Ecology. Orig. Title: Insect Dietary. (Illus.). 466p. 1972. pap. 5.00 (ISBN 0-486-21070-7). Dover.

--Insects' Food & Ecology. Orig. Title: Insect Dietary. (Illus.). 6.75 (ISBN 0-8446-4521-4). Peter Smith.

Chapman, R. F. The Insects: Structure & Function. 2nd. ed. 1976. text ed. 19.50 (ISBN 0-444-19456-8, North Holland). Elsevier.

Chapman, Royal N. Animal Ecology: Special Reference to Insects. Egerton, Frank N., 3rd, ed. LC 77-74208. (History of Ecology Ser.). 1978. Repr. of 1932 ed. lib. bdg. 27.00x (ISBN 0-405-10379-4). Arno.

Cheng, L., ed. Marine Insects. 1976. 102.50 (ISBN 0-444-11213-8, North-Holland). Elsevier.

Clausen, Lucy W. Insect Fact & Folklore. (Illus.). 1954. 4.50 (ISBN 0-02-526080-4). Macmillan.

Cogan, B. H. & Smith, K. G. Insects: Instructions for Collectors, No. 4a. 5th rev. ed. (Illus.). vi, 169p. 1974. pap. 6.00x (ISBN 0-565-05705-7, Pub. by Brit Mus Nat Hist). Sabbot-Natural Hist Bks.

Dashefsky, Howard S. & Stoffolano, John G., Jr. A Tutorial Guide to the Insect Orders. 1977. spiral bdg. 4.95x (ISBN 0-8087-0459-1). Burgess.

Davis, B. N. Insects on Nettles. (Cambridge Naturalists' Handbooks). (Illus.). 68p. Date not set. price not set (ISBN 0-521-23904-4); pap. price not set (ISBN 0-521-28300-0). Cambridge U Pr.

Denno, R. F. & Dingle, H., eds. Insect Life History Patterns: Habitat & Geographic Variation. (Proceedings in Life Sciences Ser.). (Illus.). 225p. 1981. 29.80 (ISBN 0-387-90591-X). Springer-Verlag.

Dierl, Wolfgang. Insects. LC 78-323335. (Nature Guides Ser.). (Illus.). 1979. pap. 5.95 (ISBN 0-7011-2379-6, Pub. by Chatto Bodley Jonathan). Merrimack Bk Serv.

Downer, R. G., ed. Energy Metabolism in Insects. 235p. 1981. 32.50 (ISBN 0-306-40697-7, Plenum Pr). Plenum Pub.

Dupuy, William A. Our Insect Friends & Foes. (Illus.). 5.00 (ISBN 0-8446-2013-0). Peter Smith.

Eisner, Thomas & Wilson, Edward O.intro. by. The Insects: Readings from Scientific American. LC 77-23843. (Illus.). 1977. text ed. 19.95x (ISBN 0-7167-0047-6); pap. text ed. 9.95x (ISBN 0-7167-0046-8). W H Freeman.

Emsley, Michael G. Insect Magic. (Penguin Large Format Ser.). (Illus.). 1979. pap. 9.95 (ISBN 0-14-005125-2). Penguin.

Encyclopedie Illustree Des Insects. 600p. (Fr.). 14.95 (ISBN 0-686-57156-8, M-6215). French & Eur.

Fabre, J. Henri. The Insect World of J. Henri Fabre. Teale, Edwin W., ed. LC 80-8406. (Nature Library Ser.). 352p. (Orig.). 1981. pap. 5.95 (ISBN 0-06-090806-8, CN 806, CN). Har-Row.

Fabre, Jean H. Jean Henri Fabre's Insects. Black, David, ed. (Encore Edition). (Illus.). 1979. 4.95 (ISBN 0-684-16820-0, ScribT). Scribner.

Fabricius, J. C. Systema Antialorum, Secundum Ordines, Genera, Species. 1970. Repr. of 1805 ed. 43.00 (ISBN 90-6123-060-8). Lubrecht & Cramer.

Ferris, Clifford D. & Brown, F. Martin, eds. Butterflies of the Rocky Mountain States. LC 80-22274. (Illus.). 400p. 1981. 35.00 (ISBN 0-8061-1552-1); pap. 15.95 (ISBN 0-8061-1733-8). U of Okla Pr.

Flloyd, Thomas & Swammerdam, John. The Book of Nature: The History of Insects. Sterling, Keir B., ed. LC 77-83844. (Biologists & Their World Ser.). (Illus.). 1978. Repr. of 1758 ed. lib. bdg. 38.00x (ISBN 0-405-10742-0). Arno.

Frazier, Claude A. & Brown, F. K. Insects & Allergy: And What to Do About Them. LC 79-6706. (Illus.). 350p. 1980. 14.95 (ISBN 0-8061-1518-1); pap. 8.95 (ISBN 0-8061-1706-0). U of Okla Pr.

Friedlander, C. P. The Biology of Insects. LC 76-20407. (Studies in the Biological Sciences Ser.). (Illus.). 1977. 12.50x (ISBN 0-87663-720-9). Universe.

Graham, Ada & Graham, Frank, Jr. The Milkweed & Its World of Animals. LC 74-18801. 96p. (gr. 3-5). 1976. 5.95 (ISBN 0-385-09933-9). Doubleday.

Grzimek, Bernhard, ed. Grzimek's Animal Life Encyclopedia, Vol. 2: Insects. 1975. 39.50x (ISBN 0-442-22942-9). Van Nos Reinhold.

Gupta, A. P. Insect Hemocytes. LC 78-10477. 1979. 95.00 (ISBN 0-521-22364-4). Cambridge U Pr.

Heinrich, Bernd. Bumblebee Economics. LC 78-23773. (Illus.). 1979. 17.50x (ISBN 0-674-08580-9); pap. 8.95 (ISBN 0-674-08581-7). Harvard U Pr.

Hellman, Hal. Deadly Bugs & Killer Insects. LC 78-17403. 192p. (gr. 5 up). 1978. 6.95 (ISBN 0-87131-269-7). M Evans.
Hennig, Willi. Insect Phylogeny. LC 80-40853. 514p. 1981. 78.75 (ISBN 0-471-27848-3, Pub. by Wiley-Interscience). Wiley.
Hepburn, H. R., ed. The Insect Integument. 1976. 112.50 (ISBN 0-444-41436-3). Elsevier.
Hocking, Brian. Six-Legged Science. rev. ed. 208p. 1971. 7.95x (ISBN 0-87073-860-7); pap. 4.95x (ISBN 0-87073-861-5). Schenkman.
Horn, David J. Biology of Insects. LC 76-1217. (Illus.). 1976. text ed. 14.95 (ISBN 0-7216-4780-4). HR&W.
Imms, A. D. Insect Natural History. 1973. pap. 2.95 (ISBN 0-531-06047-0, Fontana Pap). Watts.
International Symposium on Chironomidae, 7th, Dublin, August 1979. Chironomidae-Ecology Systematics Cytology & Physiology: Proceedings. Murray, D. A., ed. (Illus.). 380p. 1980. 69.00 (ISBN 0-08-025889-1). Pergamon.
Johnson, Warren T. & Lyon, H. H. Insects That Feed on Trees & Shrubs: An Illustrated Practical Guide. (Illus.). 464p. 1976. 42.50x (ISBN 0-8014-0956-X). Comstock.
Kapoor, V. C. Taxonomic Approach to Insecta. 1980. text ed. 20.00x (ISBN 0-7069-0796-5, Pub. by Vikas India). Advent NY.
Klots, Alexander B. & Klots, Elsie B. One Thousand One Questions Answered About Insects. (Illus.). 1977. pap. 4.00 (ISBN 0-486-23470-3). Dover.
Kondo, Riki H. Insects. (Instant Nature Guides). (Illus.). 1979. pap. 2.95 (ISBN 0-448-12673-7). G&D.
Lanham, Url N. The Insects. LC 64-14235. (Illus.). 1967. 17.50x (ISBN 0-231-02603-X); pap. 5.00x (ISBN 0-231-08582-6). Columbia U Pr.
Leftwich, A. W. A Dictionary of Entomology. LC 75-27143. 1976. 27.50x (ISBN 0-8448-0820-2). Crane-Russak Co.
Locke, Michael & Smith, D. S. Insect Biology in the Future: "VBW 80". 1980. 50.00 (ISBN 0-12-454340-5). Acad Pr.
Lubbock, John. On the Origin & Metamorphoses of Insects. 1978. Repr. of 1874 ed. lib. bdg. 20.00 (ISBN 0-8492-1586-2). R West.
Lutz, Frank E. Field Book of Insects of the U. S. & Canada. rev. ed. (Putnam's Nature Field Bks.). (gr. 7 up). 1948. 5.95 (ISBN 0-399-10289-2). Putnam.
McFee, Inez N. Lives of Busy Neighbors (Insects) 1924. 5.00 (ISBN 0-685-73514-1). Norwood Edns.
Marquesan Insects, Nineteen Thirty Two-Nineteen Thirty Nine, 3 vols. Repr. of 1932 ed. Vol. 1. pap. 20.00 (ISBN 0-527-02204-7); Vol. 2. pap. 31.00 (ISBN 0-527-02220-9); Vol. 3. pap. 20.00 (ISBN 0-527-02248-9). Kraus Repr.
Mazohkin-Porshnyakov, G. A. Insect Vision. LC 67-10310. 300p. 1969. 37.50 (ISBN 0-306-30268-3, Plenum Pr). Plenum Pub.
Middleton, C. H. Mister Middleton Suggests. (Illus., Orig.). pap. 4.50x (ISBN 0-392-03940-0, LTB). Sportshelf.
Milne, Lorus & Milne, Margery. Insect Worlds. (Illus.). 288p. 1980. 12.95 (ISBN 0-684-16627-5, ScribT). Scribner.
Mordue, W., et al. Insect Physiology. LC 79-27743. 1981. pap. 16.95x (ISBN 0-470-26931-6). Halsted Pr.
Nachtigall, Werner. Insects in Flight. Oldroyd, Harold & Abbott, Roger H., trs. from Ger. (Illus.). 158p. 1974. 17.95 (ISBN 0-07-045736-0, P&RB). McGraw.
Needham, James G. Elementary Lessons on Insects. (Illus.). 218p. 1929. photocopy ed. spiral 24.75 (ISBN 0-398-04376-0). C C Thomas.
Novak, J. Valdimir. Insect Hormones. 2nd ed. LC 74-26785. 600p. 1975. text ed. 52.95x (ISBN 0-412-11630-8, Pub. by Chapman & Hall England). Methuen Inc.
Perkins, John H. Insects & Experts: The Political Economy of Scientific & Technical Change. 260p. 1982. text ed. 29.50 (ISBN 0-306-40770-1, Plenum Pr). Plenum Pub.
Price, Peter W. Insect Ecology. LC 75-12720. 514p. 1975. 24.95 (ISBN 0-471-69721-4, Pub. by Wiley-Interscience). Wiley.
Raabe, Marie. Insect Neurohormones. Marshall, Nissim, tr. 300p. (Fr.). 1982. text ed. price not set (ISBN 0-306-40782-5, Plenum Pr). Plenum Pub.
Redi, F. Experiments on the Generation of Insects. Bigelow, Mab, tr. 1909. 12.00 (ISBN 0-527-74400-X). Kraus Repr.
Riley, N. D. Insects in Color. (European Ecology Ser.). (Illus.). 1963. 9.95 (ISBN 0-7137-0144-7, Pub by Blandford Pr England). Sterling.
Rosen. Species of Aphytis of the World (Hymenoptera: Aphelinidae) (Entomologica Ser.: No. 17). 1979. lib. bdg. 137.00 (ISBN 90-6193-127-4, Pub. by Junk Pubs Netherlands). Kluwer Boston.
Royal Entomological Society of London, Ninth. Diversity of Insect Faunas: Symposium. Mound, L. A. & Waloff, N., eds. 1979. 43.95 (ISBN 0-470-26544-2). Halsted Pr.
Scherer, Gerhard. Insects Etcetera: An Anthology of Arthropods, Featuring a Bounty of Beetles. Zappler, Georg, tr. from Ger. (Illus.). 108p. 1981. 50.00 (ISBN 0-933920-25-3). Hudson Hills.
Seguy, E. A. Seguy's Decorative Butterflies & Insects in Full Color. LC 77-83361. (Illus., Orig.). 1977. pap. 6.00 (ISBN 0-486-23552-1). Dover.
Sharp, Cecil J. Insects, 2 vols. (Cambridge Natural History Ser.: Vols. 5 & 6). (Illus.). Set. 17.50 (ISBN 0-8446-0907-2). Peter Smith.
Shepherd, Walter. Let's Look at Insects. 8.50x (ISBN 0-392-08023-0, SpS). Sportshelf.
Singh, Pritam. Artificial Diets for Insects, Mites, & Spiders. 606p. 1977. 75.00 (ISBN 0-306-65169-6). IFI Plenum.
Swammerdan, Jan. The Book of Nature or the History of Insects. (Illus.). 1981. Repr. of 1768 ed. lib. bdg. 120.00 (ISBN 0-8287-1469-X). Clearwater Pub.
Symposium, Cornell University, Ithaca, New York, Oct. 1974. Insects, Science, & Society: Proceedings. Pimentel, David, ed. 1975. 30.00 (ISBN 0-12-556550-X). Acad Pr.
Taylor, Ronald L. Butterflies in My Stomach: Insects in Human Nutrition. LC 75-13593. (Illus.). 224p. 1975. 8.95 (ISBN 0-912800-18-6). Woodbridge Pr.
Teale, Edwin W. Grassroot Jungles. rev. ed. LC 44-5481. (Illus.). 1937. 6.95 (ISBN 0-396-01714-2). Dodd.
Thiele, H. U. Carabid Beetles in Their Environments: A Study on Habit Selection by Adaptations in Physiology & Behaviour. LC 77-9924. (Zoophysiology & Ecology: Vol. 10). (Illus.). 1977. 56.30 (ISBN 0-387-08306-5). Springer-Verlag.
Time-Life Television. Spider & Insects. (The Wild, Wild World of Animals Ser.). (Illus.). 1977. 10.95 (ISBN 0-913948-12-8). Time-Life.
Tinbergen, Niko. Curious Naturalists. 1968. Repr. of 1959 ed. 2.95 (ISBN 0-385-02881-4, N44). Natural Hist.
Tuxen, Soren L. The Protura: A Revision of the Species of the World with Keys for Determination. 360p. 1964. 42.50x (ISBN 0-8002-1335-1). Intl Pubns Serv.
Tweedie, Michael. Atlas of Insects. LC 73-12022. (John Day Bk.). (Illus.). 128p. 1974. 10.95 (ISBN 0-381-98258-0). T Y Crowell.
--Insect Life. LC 76-53910. (Illus.). 1977. 8.95 (ISBN 0-8008-4196-4). Taplinger.
Villiard, Paul. Moths & How to Rear Them. 1975. pap. 5.00 (ISBN 0-486-23119-4). Dover.
Wallace, James, ed. Recent Advances in Phytochemistry: Vol. 10, Biochemical Interaction Between Plants & Insects. LC 67-26242. 425p. 1976. 35.00 (ISBN 0-306-34710-5, Plenum Pr). Plenum Pub.
White, M. J., ed. Genetic Mechanisms of Speciation in Insects. LC 74-80531. 196p. 1974. lib. bdg. 26.00 (ISBN 90-277-0477-5, Pub. by Reidel Holland). Kluwer Boston.
Wigglesworth, Vincent B. Insects & the Life on Man: Collected Essays on Pure Science & Applied Biology. LC 76-40479. 217p. 1976. text ed. 19.95x (ISBN 0-412-14700-9, Pub. by Chapman & Hall). Methuen Inc.
Wooton, Anthony. Insects Are Animals Too. LC 77-91775. 6.95 (ISBN 0-7153-7534-2). David & Charles.
Zahradnik, Jiri. Field Guide in Color to Insects. (Octopus Book). (Illus.). 1978. 7.95 (ISBN 0-7064-0582-X, Mayflower Bks). Smith Pubs.
Zanetti, Adriano. The World of Insects. Atthill, Catherine, tr. LC 79-1424. (Abbeville Press Encyclopedia of Natural Science). (Illus.). 1979. 13.95 (ISBN 0-89659-036-4); pap. 7.95 (ISBN 0-89659-030-5). Abbeville Pr.

INSECTS–ANATOMY
see also Nervous System–Insects
DuPorte, E. Melville. Manual of Insect Morphology. LC 76-13005. 236p. 1977. Repr. of 1959 ed. 9.50 (ISBN 0-88275-422-X). Krieger.
Frost, S. W. Insect Life & Natural History. 2nd & rev. ed. Orig. Title: General Entomology. 6.75 (ISBN 0-8446-0101-2). Peter Smith.
Hepburn, H. R., ed. The Insect Integument. 1976. 112.50 (ISBN 0-444-41436-3). Elsevier.
Horn, David J. Biology of Insects. LC 77-27756. 1978. text ed. 16.95 (ISBN 0-7216-4782-0). HR&W.
Howse, P. E. & Clement, Jean-Luc, eds. Biosystematics of Social Insects. 1981. write for info. (ISBN 0-12-357180-4). Acad Pr.
Matsuda, R. Morphology & Evolution of the Insect Abdomen. Kerkut, ed. 568p. 1976. text ed. 90.00 (ISBN 0-08-018753-6). Pergamon.
Matsuda, Ryuichi. Morphology & Evolution of the Insect Head. (Memoirs Ser: No. 4). (Illus.). 334p. 1965. 12.00 (ISBN 0-686-00423-X). Am Entom Inst.
Sharp & Muir. Comparative Anatomy of the Male Genital Tube in Coleoptera. (Illus.). 304p. 1969. 16.70 (ISBN 0-686-09300-3). Entomol Soc.
Smith, David S. Insect Cells, Their Structure & Function. text ed. 17.65 (ISBN 0-934454-51-5). Lubrecht & Cramer.
Snodgrass, Robert E. Anatomy of the Honey Bee. (Illus.). 358p. 1956. 30.00x (ISBN 0-8014-0400-2). Comstock.
--Principles of Insect Morphology. (Zoological Sciences Ser.). 1935. 29.50 (ISBN 0-07-059510-0, C). McGraw.
Tregear, R. T. & Pringle, J. W., eds. Insect Flight Muscle: Proceedings of a Symposium Held at Oxford, England, 4-6 March, 1977. 1978. 51.75 (ISBN 0-444-41612-9, Biomedical Pr). Elsevier.
Tuxen, S. L., ed. Taxonomist's Glossary of Genitalia in Insects. 1970. text ed. 27.50 (ISBN 0-934454-76-0). Lubrecht & Cramer.
Wehner, R., ed. Information Processing in the Visual Systems of Arthropods. LC 72-91887. 340p. 1973. pap. 26.40 (ISBN 0-387-06020-0). Springer-Verlag.

INSECTS–BEHAVIOR
see also Insect Societies
Atkins, Michael D. Introduction to Insect Behavior. (Illus.). 1980. pap. text ed. 9.95 (ISBN 0-686-65947-3). Macmillan.
Batra, Lekh R., ed. Insect-Fungus Symbiosis: Nutrition, Mutualism & Commensalism. LC 78-20640. (Illus.). 276p. 1979. text ed. 29.95 (ISBN 0-470-26671-6). Halsted Pr.
Callahan, Philip S. Tuning in to Nature: Solar Energy, Infrared Radiation & the Insect Communication System. (Illus.). 256p. 1976. 10.00 (ISBN 0-8159-6914-7). Devin.
Dethier, V. G. The Hungry Fly: A Physiological Study of the Behavior Associated with Feeding. (Commonwealth Fund Ser.). (Illus.). 512p. 1976. text ed. 30.00x (ISBN 0-674-42710-6). Harvard U Pr.
Dethier, Vincent G. To Know a Fly. LC 62-21838. (Illus.). 1962. pap. 4.50x (ISBN 0-8162-2240-1). Holden-Day.
Evans, Howard. Comparative Ethology & Evolution of the Sand Wasps. LC 66-18245. 1966. 27.50x (ISBN 0-674-15201-8). Harvard U Pr.
Fabre, Jean H. Social Life in the Insect World. LC 72-164264. 1974. Repr. of 1912 ed. 28.00 (ISBN 0-8103-3967-6). Gale.
Jermy, T., ed. The Host-Plant in Relation to Insect Behavior & Reproduction. LC 75-37209. 322p. 1976. 35.00 (ISBN 0-306-30909-2, Plenum Pr.). Plenum Pub.
Lee. The Hidden Events: Incredible Life & Behavior of Insects. 1982. 12.95 (ISBN 0-8120-5340-0). Barron.
Matthews, Robert W. & Matthews, Janice R. Insect Behavior. LC 78-7869. 1978. 29.50 (ISBN 0-471-57685-9, Pub. by Wiley-Interscience). Wiley.
May, Julian. Insects We Know. LC 73-4341. (Illus.). (gr. 2-4). 1973. PLB 5.95 (ISBN 0-87191-244-9). Creative Ed.
Neider, Charles, ed. Fabulous Insects. facs. ed. LC 68-16960. (Essay Index Reprint Ser). 1954. 15.50 (ISBN 0-8369-0736-1). Arno.
Rainey, R. C. Insect Flight. LC 75-22091. (Royal Entomological Society of London Symposium Ser.). 287p. 1976. 67.95 (ISBN 0-470-70550-7). Halsted Pr.
Rodriguez, J. G. Insect & Mite Nutrition. LC 72-96711. 717p. 1973. 68.50 (ISBN 0-444-10437-2, North-Holland). Elsevier.
Roeder, Kenneth D. Nerve Cells and Insect Behavior. rev. ed. LC 67-27092. (Books in Biology Ser: No. 4). 1967. 10.00x (ISBN 0-674-60800-3). Harvard U Pr.
Saunders, D. S. Insect Clocks. 292p. 1976. text ed. 37.00 (ISBN 0-08-018211-9); pap. text ed. 15.00 (ISBN 0-08-024402-5). Pergamon.
Shorey, H. H. & McKelvey, John J., Jr. Chemical Control of Insect Behavior: Theory & Application. LC 76-46573. (Environmental Science & Technology Ser.). 1977. 34.50 (ISBN 0-471-78840-6, Pub. by Wiley-Interscience). Wiley.
Stein, R. Incest & Human Love. LC 73-82641. 1973. 8.95 (ISBN 0-89388-090-6). Okpaku Communications.
Von Frisch, Karl. Dance Language & Orientation of Bees. Chadwick, Leigh E., tr. LC 67-17321. (Illus., Ger). 1967. 30.00x (ISBN 0-674-19050-5, Belknap Pr). Harvard U Pr.

INSECTS–BIBLIOGRAPHY
Bonnet, Pierre. Bibliographia Araneorum: Analyse Methodique De Toute la Litterature Araneologique Jusqu'en 1939. LC 57-58745. 832p. 1968. Repr. 40.00 (ISBN 0-686-09299-6). Entomol Soc.
Hicks, Ellis A. Check List & Bibliography on the Occurrence of Insects in Birds' Nests. 1959. incl. 1962 1971 suppl 11.50x (ISBN 0-8138-1180-5). Iowa St U Pr.

INSECTS–BIOLOGICAL CONTROL
see Insect Control–Biological Control

INSECTS–COLLECTION AND PRESERVATION
see also Zoological Specimens–Collection and Preservation
Anderson, Margaret J. Exploring the Insect World. LC 73-17412. (Illus.). 160p. (gr. 5 up). 1974. PLB 6.95 (ISBN 0-07-001625-9, GB). McGraw.
Arnett, Ross H., Jr. & Arnett, Mary E., eds. The Naturalists' Directory of Insect Collectors & Identifiers (International, Pt. I. 44th ed. (The Naturalists' Directory (International) Ser.). 96p. (Orig.). 1981. pap. 9.95 (ISBN 0-916846-15-6). Flora & Fauna.
Conklin, Gladys. The Bug Club Book: A Handbook for Young Bug Collectors. (Illus.). 96p. (gr. 4-7). 1966. 6.95 (ISBN 0-8234-0017-4). Holiday.
Peterson, Alvah. Entomological Techniques: How to Work with Insects. 10th ed. (Illus.). v, 435p. 1964. text ed. 15.00x (ISBN 0-911836-11-X). Entomological Repr.

INSECTS–CONTROL
see Insect Control

INSECTS–DEVELOPMENT
see also Insects–Metamorphosis; Larvae–Insects
Beermann, W., ed. Biochemical Differentiation in Insect Glands. LC 77-23423. (Results & Problems in Cell Differentiation: Vol. 8). (Illus.). 1977. 45.70 (ISBN 0-387-08286-7). Springer-Verlag.
Chen, P. S. Biochemical Aspects of Insect Development. (Monographs in Developmental Biology: Vol. 3). (Illus.). 1971. 43.25 (ISBN 3-8055-1265-1). S Karger.
Chu, H. F. How to Know the Immature Insects. (Pictured Key Nature Ser.). 1949. write for info. wire coil (ISBN 0-697-04807-1); wire coil 5.95x (ISBN 0-697-04806-3). Wm C Brown.
Counce, S. J. & Waddington, C. H., eds. Developmental Systems: Insects. 1973. Vol. 1. 48.50 (ISBN 0-12-193301-6); Vol. 2. 97.50 (ISBN 0-12-193302-4). Acad Pr.
Jermy, T., ed. The Host-Plant in Relation to Insect Behavior & Reproduction. LC 75-37209. 322p. 1976. 35.00 (ISBN 0-306-30909-2, Plenum Pr.). Plenum Pub.
Lawrence, P. A. Insect Development. LC 76-8196. (Royal Entomological Society of London Symposium Ser.). 1976. 34.95 (ISBN 0-470-15098-X). Halsted Pr.
Struble, D. L., et al. Pheromones: Current Research, 2 vols, Vol. 1. 176p. 1974. text ed. 28.50x (ISBN 0-8422-7211-9). Irvington.
Symposium on the Chemistry & Action of Insect Juvenile Hormones, Washington, D. C., 1971. Insect Juvenile Hormones: Chemistry & Action. Menn, Julius J. & Beroza, Morton, eds. 1972. 42.50 (ISBN 0-12-490950-7). Acad Pr.

INSECTS–DISEASES
see also Parasites–Insects
Cantwell, George, ed. Insect Diseases, Vol. 1. 326p. 1974. 39.50 (ISBN 0-8247-6117-0). Dekker.
--Insect Diseases, Vol. 2. 312p. 1974. 39.50 (ISBN 0-8247-6118-9). Dekker.
Egerton, Frank N., ed. Ecological Studies on Insect Parasitism: An Original Anthology. LC 77-73820. (History of Ecology Ser.). 1978. lib. bdg. 18.00x (ISBN 0-405-10389-1). Arno.
Maramorosch, Karl, ed. Insect & Plant Viruses: An Atlas. 1978. 59.00 (ISBN 0-12-470275-9). Acad Pr.
Panda, N. Principles of Host-Plant Resistance to Insect Pests. LC 78-59169. (Illus.). 406p. 1980. text ed. 32.50 (ISBN 0-87663-836-1). Allanheld.
Poinar, G. O. & Thomas, G. M., eds. Diagnostic Manual for the Identification of Insect Pathogens. LC 77-15977. (Illus.). 230p. 1978. 19.50 (ISBN 0-306-31097-X, Plenum Pr). Plenum Pub.
Smith, Kenneth M. Insect Virology. 1967. 38.00 (ISBN 0-12-651550-6). Acad Pr.
--Virus-Insect Relationships. (Illus.). 1977. text ed. 30.00x (ISBN 0-582-46612-1). Longman.
Snow, Keith. Insects & Diseases. LC 73-15433. (Illus.). 208p. 1974. text ed. 18.95 (ISBN 0-470-81017-3). Halsted Pr.
Steinhaus, Edward A. Disease in a Minor Chord: Being a Semihistorical & Semibiographical Account of a Period in Science When One Could Be Happily Yet Seriously Concerned with the Diseases of Lowly Animals Without Backbones, Especially the Insects. LC 75-4527. 1975. 20.00x (ISBN 0-8142-0218-7). Ohio St U Pr.
Steinhaus, Edward A., ed. Insect Pathology: An Advanced Treatise, 2 Vols. 1963. 63.00 ea. Vol. 1 (ISBN 0-12-665801-3). Vol. 2. (ISBN 0-12-665802-1). Acad Pr.
Tsetse: The Future for Biological Methods in Integrated Control. (Illus.). 1977. pap. 10.00 (ISBN 0-88936-109-6, IDRC 77, IDRC). Unipub.

INSECTS–EMBRYOLOGY
see Embryology–Insects

INSECTS–EVOLUTION
Ashburner, M., et al, eds. The Genetics of Drosphila, Vol. 3, Pt. A. Carson, H. L. 1981. price not set (ISBN 0-12-064945-4). Acad Pr.
Busvine, J. R. Insects, Hygiene & History. (Illus.). 1976. text ed. 23.75x (ISBN 0-485-11160-8, Athlone Pr). Humanities.
Callahan, Philip S. The Evolution of Insects. LC 72-80654. (Illus.). (gr. 6 up). 1972. 5.95 (ISBN 0-8234-0213-4). Holiday.
Matsuda, R. Morphology & Evolution of the Insect Abdomen. Kerkut, ed. 568p. 1976. text ed. 90.00 (ISBN 0-08-018753-6). Pergamon.
Weismann, August. Studies in the Theory of Descent, 2 vols. in 1. LC 72-1661. Repr. of 1882 ed. 57.50 (ISBN 0-404-08192-4). AMS Pr.
White, M. J., ed. Genetic Mechanisms of Speciation in Insects. LC 74-80531. 196p. 1974. lib. bdg. 26.00 (ISBN 90-277-0477-5, Pub. by Reidel Holland). Kluwer Boston.
INSECTS–EXTERMINATION
see Insect Control
INSECTS–GEOGRAPHICAL DISTRIBUTION
see also Insect Populations
Denno, R. F. & Dingle, H., eds. Insect Life History Patterns: Habitat & Geographic Variation. (Proceedings in Life Sciences Ser.). (Illus.). 225p. 1981. 29.80 (ISBN 0-387-90591-X). Springer-Verlag.
Insects of Eastern Larch, Cedar & Juniper. 99p. 1981. pap. 13.00 (ISBN 0-660-10421-0, SSC 151, SSC). Unipub.
Metzler, Eric H. Annotated Checklist & Distribution Maps of the Royal Moths & Giant Silkworm Moths (Lepidoptera: Saturniidae) in Ohio. 1980. 2.50 (ISBN 0-686-30346-6). Ohio Bio Survey.
Powell, Jerry A. & Hogue, Charles L. California Insects. LC 78-62876. (California Natural History Guide Ser.). (Illus.). 1980. 15.95 (ISBN 0-520-03806-1); pap. 7.95 (ISBN 0-520-03782-0). U of Cal Pr.
Schreiber, Harold. Disperal Centres of Sphingidae (Lepidoptera) in the Neotropical Region. (Biogeographica Ser.: No. 10). (Illus.). 1978. lib. bdg. 34.00 (ISBN 90-6193-211-4, Pub. by Junk Pubs. Netherlands). Kluwer Boston.
Wheeler, George M. & Sterling, Keir B., eds. Reports Upon Insects Collected During Geographical & Geological Explorations & Surveys West of the One Hundredth Meridan, During the Years 1872, 1873, & 1874. LC 77-81109. (Biologists & Their World Ser.). (Illus.). 1978. Repr. of 1875 ed. lib. bdg. 16.00x (ISBN 0-405-10693-9). Arno.
INSECTS–JUVENILE LITERATURE
Adler, Irving & Adler, Ruth. Insects & Plants. LC 62-19714. (Reason Why Ser). (Illus.). (gr. 3-6). 1962. PLB 8.79 (ISBN 0-381-99966-1, A38660, JD-J). Har-Row.
Allen, Gertrude E. Everyday Insects. (Illus.). (gr. k-3). 1963. reinforced bdg. 5.95 (ISBN 0-395-17891-6). HM.
Anderson, Margaret J. Exploring the Insect World. LC 73-17412. (Illus.). 160p. (gr. 5 up). 1974. PLB 6.95 (ISBN 0-07-001625-9, GB). McGraw.
Ants & Bees. (How & Why Wonder Books Ser.). (gr. 4-6). pap. 1.00 (ISBN 0-448-05030-7). Wonder.
Ants & Insects. (MacDonald Educational Ser.). (Illus., Arabic.). 3.50 (ISBN 0-86685-185-2). Intl Bk Ctr.
Bennetsen, Livonia. Under the Rainbow: Fun Book of Insects. (Illus.). 96p. (gr. 3-6). 1974. pap. 2.50 (ISBN 0-686-15407-X). Country Print.
Blassingame, Wyatt. The Little Killers: Fleas, Lice & Mosquitoes. 128p. (gr. 5 up). 1975. 5.95 (ISBN 0-399-20466-0). Putnam.
Boy Scouts Of America. Insect Life. LC 19-600. (Illus.). 64p. (gr. 6-12). 1973. pap. 0.70x (ISBN 0-8395-3353-5, 3353). BSA.
Burton, Maurice. The Life of Insects. LC 78-56576. (Easy Reading Edition of Introduction to Nature Ser.). (Illus.). 1979. lib. bdg. 7.95 (ISBN 0-686-51141-7). Silver.
Causey, Don. Killer Insects. (Illus.). (gr. 4-6). 1979. PLB 6.90 s&l (ISBN 0-531-02924-7). Watts.
Cole, Joanna. Find the Hidden Insect. LC 79-18648. (Illus.). 40p. (gr. k-3). 1979. 6.95 (ISBN 0-688-22203-X); PLB 6.67 (ISBN 0-688-32203-4). Morrow.
Conklin, Gladys. How Insects Grow. (Illus.). 128p. (gr. 3-7). 1969. 6.95 (ISBN 0-8234-0051-4). Holiday.
--When Insects Are Babies. (Illus.). (gr. k-3). 1969. reinforced bdg. 7.95 (ISBN 0-8234-0134-0). Holiday.
Crosby, Alexander L. Tarantulas. LC 80-7672. (Illus.). 64p. (gr. 3-7). 1981. 8.50 (ISBN 0-8027-6393-6); PLB 8.85 (ISBN 0-8027-6394-4). Walker & Co.
Daly, Kathleen N. A Child's Book of Insects. LC 74-14994. (gr. k-4). 1977. 6.95a (ISBN 0-385-09743-3); PLB (ISBN 0-385-09744-1). Doubleday.
Day, Jenifer W. What Is an Insect? (Child's Golden Science Bks.). (Illus.). (gr. k-4). 1976. PLB 6.92 (ISBN 0-307-61803-X, Golden Pr). Western Pub.
Devine, Bob. Mr. Baggy-Skinned Lizard. (God in Creation Ser.). (Illus.). (gr. 3-6). 1977. pap. 1.95 (ISBN 0-8024-5671-5). Moody.
Doorly, Eleanor. Insect Man. (New Windmill Ser). (Illus.). (gr. 6-8). 1936-1964. 4.25 (ISBN 0-435-12011-5). Dufour.
Dugan, William. The Bug Book. (Illus.). 24p. (ps-4). 1965. PLB 5.38 (ISBN 0-307-68903-4, Golden Pr). Western Pub.
Eighme, Lloyd. Insects You Have Seen. LC 79-24141. (Crown Ser.). (gr. 6 up). 1980. pap. 4.50 (ISBN 0-8127-0259-X). Review & Herald.
Farb, Peter. Story of Butterflies & Other Insects. LC 59-14884. (Story of Science Ser). (Illus.). (gr. 3-6). 1959. PLB 7.29 (ISBN 0-8178-3232-7). Harvey.
Fields, Alice. Insects. (gr. 2-4). 1980. PLB 6.90 (ISBN 0-531-03244-2). Watts.
Garber, Patty J., et al. Kinder-Fun Insect Series. rev. ed. Incl. Funny Little Ant; Ladybug, Ladybug; Fly, Fly; The Little Yellow Butterfly; The Little Mosquito; The Bad Little Cricket. (Illus.). 16p. (For partially-sighted & partially-hearing children). (ps-2). 1973. Set. pap. text ed. 16.00x (ISBN 0-89039-055-X). Ann Arbor Pubs.
God's Plan for Insects. 16p. (ps-3). 1980. pap. 1.50 (ISBN 0-8024-3063-5). Moody.
Griffen, Elizabeth. Dog's Book of Bugs. (Illus.). (gr. 1-4). 1967. pap. 2.95 (ISBN 0-689-70408-9, Aladdin). Atheneum.
Hopf, Alice. Bugs-Big & Little. LC 80-20705. (Illus.). 64p. (gr. 3-5). 1980. PLB 7.59 (ISBN 0-671-34014-X). Messner.
Hornblow, Leonora & Hornblow, Arthur. Insects Do the Strangest Things. LC 68-10046. (Step-up Bks). (Illus.). (gr. 2-9). 1968. 3.95 (ISBN 0-394-80072-9, BYR); PLB 4.99 (ISBN 0-394-90072-3). Random.
Hutchins, Ross E. The Bug Clan. LC 72-11254. (Illus.). 128p. (gr. 5 up). 1973. PLB 5.95 (ISBN 0-396-06771-9). Dodd.
--World of Dragonflies & Damselflies. LC 69-15910. (Illus.). (gr. 5 up). 1969. 5.95 (ISBN 0-396-07163-5). Dodd.
Insects & Spiders. LC 76-58898. (Wild, Wild World of Animals Ser.). (Illus.). 1977. lib. bdg. 11.97 (ISBN 0-686-51170-0). Silver.
Kennedy, Mary. Wings. (Illus.). 32p. 1980. pap. 1.50 (ISBN 0-590-31286-3, Schol Pap). Schol Bk Serv.
Kirkpatrick, Rena K. Look at Insects. LC 77-27130. (Look at Science Ser.). (Illus.). (gr. k-3). 1978. PLB 11.15 (ISBN 0-8393-0062-X). Raintree Child.
Little, Brown Editors, ed. Insects: East Coast Edition. (Explorer's Notebooks). (Illus.). 32p. (Orig.). (gr. 5 up). 1981. pap. 1.95 (ISBN 0-316-52771-8). Little.
--Insects: West Coast Edition. (Explorer's Notebooks). (Illus.). 32p. (Orig.). (gr. 5 up). 1980. pap. 1.95 (ISBN 0-316-52772-6). Little.
McClung, Robert M. Bees, Wasps, & Hornets. LC 73-151942. (Illus.). (gr. 3-7). PLB 6.96 (ISBN 0-688-31075-3). Morrow.
May, Julian. Insects We Know. LC 73-4341. (Illus.). (gr. 2-4). 1973. PLB 5.95 (ISBN 0-87191-244-9). Creative Ed.
Merrians, Deborah. I Can Read About Insects. new ed. LC 76-54493. (Illus.). (gr. 2-5). 1977. pap. 1.25 (ISBN 0-89375-040-9). Troll Assocs.
Morris, Dean. Insects That Live in Families. LC 77-8254. (Read About Animals Ser.). (Illus.). (gr. k-3). 1977. PLB 11.15 (ISBN 0-8393-0001-8). Raintree Child.
Naden, C. J. I Can Read About Creepy Crawly Creatures. new ed. LC 78-68469. (Illus.). (gr. 3-6). 1979. pap. 1.25 (ISBN 0-89375-207-X). Troll Assocs.
Patent, Dorothy H. How Insects Communicate. LC 75-6699. (Illus.). 128p. (gr. 4-6). 1975. 8.95 (ISBN 0-8234-0263-0). Holiday.
Petie, Haris. A Book of Big Bugs. LC 76-45379. (Illus.). (gr. 1-4). 1977. 6.95 (ISBN 0-13-079913-0). P-H.
Podendorf, Illa. Insects. (The New True Bks.). (Illus.). (gr. k-4). 1981. PLB 9.25 (ISBN 0-516-01627-X). Childrens.
Reidel, Marlene. From Egg to Butterfly. LC 81-204. (Carolrhoda Start to Finish Bks.). Orig. Title: Von der Raupe Zum Schmetterling. (Illus.). 24p. (ps-3). 1981. PLB 5.95 (ISBN 0-87614-153-X, AACR1). Carolrhoda Bks.
Rood, Ronald N. Insects. (How & Why Wonder Books Ser.). (Illus.). (gr. 4-6). pap. 1.00 (ISBN 0-448-05007-2). Wonder.
Selsam, Millicent E. & Hunt, Joyce. A First Look at Insects. LC 73-92451. (First Look at Ser). (Illus.). 32p. (gr. 2-4). 1974. PLB 5.39 (ISBN 0-8027-6182-8). Walker & Co.
Stevens, Carla. Insect Pets: Catching & Caring for Them. LC 77-9940. (Greenwillow Read-Alone Bks.). (Illus.). (gr. 1-4). 1978. 5.95 (ISBN 0-688-80121-8); PLB 5.71 (ISBN 0-688-84121-X). Greenwillow.
Swain, Ralph B. Insect Guide. LC 48-7228. 1948. 7.95 (ISBN 0-385-06826-3). Doubleday.
Thompson, Susan. Diary of a Monarch Butterfly. LC 75-1793. (Illus.). (gr. k-3). 1976. 6.50 (ISBN 0-8027-6267-0, Dist. by Walker & Co). Magic Circle Pr.
What Is a Insect? (Learning Shelf Kits Ser.). (gr. 2-4). 1977. incl. cassette & tchrs. guide 14.95 (ISBN 0-686-74391-1, 04994). Natl Geog.
World Book-Childcraft International Staff. The Bug Book. (Illus.). 304p. (gr. k-6). 1981. write for price info. (ISBN 0-7166-0681-X). World Bk-Childcraft.
Zim, Herbert S. & Cottam, Clarence A. Insects. (Golden Guide Ser.). (Illus.). (gr. 5 up). 1951. PLB 10.38 (ISBN 0-307-63504-X, Golden Pr); pap. 1.95 (ISBN 0-307-24492-X). Western Pub.
INSECTS–LARVAE
see Larvae–Insects
INSECTS–METAMORPHOSIS
Lubbock, John. On the Origin & Metamorphoses of Insects. 1978. Repr. of 1874 ed. lib. bdg. 20.00 (ISBN 0-8492-1586-2). R West.
Luscher, Martin, ed. Phase & Caste Determination in Insects - Endocrine Aspects: Proceedings of the International Congress of Entomology, 15th, Washington, D.C., 1976. text ed. 37.00 (ISBN 0-08-021256-5). Pergamon.
INSECTS–MIGRATION
Dingle, H., ed. Evolution of Insect Migration & Diapause. (Proceedings in Life Sciences). 1978. 26.30 (ISBN 0-387-90294-5). Springer-Verlag.
Johnson, C. G. Insect Migration. Head, J. J., ed. LC 76-29369. (Carolina Biology Readers Ser.). (Illus.). (gr. 11 up). 1976. pap. 1.65 (ISBN 0-89278-284-6, 45-9684). Carolina Biological.
Kaufmann, John. Insect Travelers. (Illus.). 128p. (gr. 7 up). 1972. 7.75 (ISBN 0-688-20036-2); PLB 7.44 (ISBN 0-688-30036-7). Morrow.
INSECTS–PARASITES
see Parasites–Insects
INSECTS–PHYSIOLOGY
see also Insects, Effect of Radiation On
Beament, J. W., et al, eds. Advances in Insect Physiology. Incl. Vol. 2. 1964. 57.50 (ISBN 0-12-024202-8); Vol. 3. 1966. 60.00 (ISBN 0-12-024203-6); Vol. 4. 1967. 66.00 (ISBN 0-12-024204-4); Vol. 5. 1968. 57.00 (ISBN 0-12-024205-2); Vol. 6, 1969. 46.00 (ISBN 0-12-024206-0); Vol. 7. 1970. 73.00 (ISBN 0-12-024207-9); Vol. 8. 1972. 60.50 (ISBN 0-12-024208-7); Vol. 9. Treherne, J. E. & Berridge, M. J., eds. 1972. 70.00 (ISBN 0-12-024209-5); Vol.10. 1974. 63.50 (ISBN 0-12-024210-9); Vol. 11. 1975. 68.50 (ISBN 0-12-024211-7); Vol. 12. 1977. 55.50 (ISBN 0-12-024212-5); Vol. 13. 1978. 60.00 (ISBN 0-12-024213-3). Acad Pr.
Berridge, M., et al, eds. Advances in Insect Physiology, Vol. 15. LC 63-14039. (Serial Publication). 1981. 96.00 (ISBN 0-12-024215-X). Acad Pr.
Bhaskaran, Govindan, et al, eds. Current Topics in Insect Endocrinology & Nutrition. 362p. 1981. 39.50 (ISBN 0-306-40621-7, Plenum Pr). Plenum Pub.
Bodenstein, Dietrich, ed. Milestones in Developmental Physiology of Insects: Papers in Development & Heredity. LC 70-133194. 231p. 1971. 25.00 (ISBN 0-306-50007-8, Plenum Pr). Plenum Pub.
Bursell. Introduction to Insect Physiology. 1971. 44.00 (ISBN 0-12-146650-7). Acad Pr.
Engelmann, F. The Physiology of Insect Reproduction. LC 70-114850. 1970. 59.00 (ISBN 0-08-015559-6). Pergamon.
Gilmour, D. Biochemistry of Insects. 1961. 42.00 (ISBN 0-12-284050-X). Acad Pr.
Heinrich, Bernd. Insect Thermoregulation. LC 80-19452. 328p. 1981. 35.00 (ISBN 0-471-05144-6, Pub. by Wiley-Interscience). Wiley.
Horridge, G. A., ed. The Compound Eye & Vision of Insects. (Illus.). 614p. 1975. 89.00x (ISBN 0-19-857375-8). Oxford U Pr.
Jacobson, Martin. Insect Sex Pheromones. 1972. 55.00 (ISBN 0-12-379350-5). Acad Pr.
Jones, Jack C. The Circulatory System of Insects. (Illus.). 272p. 1977. 31.00 (ISBN 0-398-03636-5). C C Thomas.
Narahashi, Toshio, ed. Neurotoxicology of Insecticides & Pheromones. LC 78-10913. 316p. 1979. 29.50 (ISBN 0-306-40067-7, Plenum Pr). Plenum Pub.
Rees, H. H. Insect Biochemistry. (Outline Studies in Biology). 64p. 1977. pap. 5.95 (ISBN 0-412-13130-7, Pub. by Chapman & Hall England). Methuen Inc.
Rockstein. Physiology of the Insecta. 2nd ed. 1974. Vol. 1, 1973. 64.50 (ISBN 0-12-591601-9); Vol. 2, 1974. 63.00 (ISBN 0-12-591602-7); Vol. 3, 1974. 63.00 (ISBN 0-12-591603-5); Vol. 4, 1974. 56.00 (ISBN 0-12-591604-3); Vol. 5, 1974. 72.00 (ISBN 0-12-591605-1); Vol. 6, 1974. 70.50 (ISBN 0-12-591606-X); 316.00 set (ISBN 0-686-67021-3). Acad Pr.
Rockstein, Morris, ed. Biochemistry of Insects. LC 77-1121. 1978. 42.50 (ISBN 0-12-591640-X). Acad Pr.
Salt, George. Cellular Defence Reactions of Insects. LC 71-118067. (Monographs in Experimental Biology: No. 16). (Illus.). 1970. 24.95 (ISBN 0-521-07936-5). Cambridge U Pr.
Saunders, D. S. Insect Clocks. 292p. 1976. text ed. 37.00 (ISBN 0-08-018211-9); pap. text ed. 15.00 (ISBN 0-08-024402-5). Pergamon.
Slama, K., et al. Insect Hormones & Bioanalogues. LC 72-94418. (Illus.). 500p. 1974. pap. 66.10 (ISBN 0-387-81112-5). Springer-Verlag.
Smith, David S. Insect Cells, Their Structure & Function. text ed. 17.65 (ISBN 0-934454-51-5). Lubrecht & Cramer.
Treherne, J. E. & Beament, J. W. Physiology of the Insect Central Nervous System. 1965. 42.50 (ISBN 0-12-698650-9). Acad Pr.
Turner, Ralph B. Analytical Biochemistry of Insects. LC 76-54362. 1977. 44.00 (ISBN 0-444-41539-4). Elsevier.
Usherwood, P. N. Insect Muscle. 1975. 97.00 (ISBN 0-12-709450-4). Acad Pr.
Wehner, R., ed. Information Processing in the Visual Systems of Arthropods. LC 72-91887. 340p. 1973. pap. 26.40 (ISBN 0-387-06020-0). Springer-Verlag.
Wigglesworth, V. B. Insect Hormones. rev. ed. Head, J. J., ed. LC 76-62977. (Carolina Biology Readers Ser.). (Illus.). (gr. 11 up). 1980. pap. 2.00 (ISBN 0-89278-270-6, 45-9670). Carolina Biological.
--Insect Hormones. (Illus.). 1970. text ed. 11.95x (ISBN 0-7167-0688-1). W H Freeman.
--Insect Physiology. 7th ed. 1974. 13.95x (ISBN 0-412-11150-0, Pub. by Chapman & Hall). Methuen Inc.
Wigglesworth, Vincent B. The Principles of Insect Physiology. 7th ed. (Illus.). 827p. 1972. 49.95x (ISBN 0-412-11400-3, Pub. by Chapman & Hall England). Methuen Inc.
INSECTS–PICTORIAL WORKS
Carr, Anna & Olkowski, William. Rodale's Color Handbook of Garden Insects. (Illus.). 1979. 14.95 (ISBN 0-87857-250-3). Rodale Pr Inc.
Milne, Lorus & Milne, Margery. The Audubon Society Field Guide to North American Insects & Spiders. LC 80-7620. (Illus.). 1008p. 1980. 11.95 (ISBN 0-394-50763-0). Knopf.
Seguy, E. A. Seguy's Decorative Butterflies & Insects in Full Color. (Illus.). 10.00 (ISBN 0-8446-5812-X). Peter Smith.
INSECTS–RESEARCH
see Entomological Research
INSECTS–AFRICA
African Trypanosomiasis. (FAO Agricultural Studies: No. 81). (Illus., Orig.). 1969. pap. 4.75 (ISBN 0-685-04901-9, F1, FAO). Unipub.
Medler, John T. Insects of Nigeria. (Memoir Ser.: No. 30). 919p. 1980. 68.00 (ISBN 0-686-27978-6). Am Entom Inst.
Penny, Norman D. & Arias, Jorge R. Insects of an Amazon Forest. LC 81-7665. (Illus.). 328p. 1982. text ed. 37.50x (ISBN 0-231-05266-9). Columbia U Pr.
Townes, Henry, et al. Catalogue & Reclassification of the Ethiopian Ichneumonidae. (Memoirs Er: No. 19). 416p. 1973. 25.00 (ISBN 0-686-08750-X). Am Entom Inst.
INSECTS–AUSTRALIA
Commonwealth Scientific & Industrial Research Institute. Scientific & Common Names of Insects & Allied Forms Occuring in Australia. 100p. (Orig.). 1980. pap. 6.00x (ISBN 0-643-00386-X, Pub. by CSIRO Australia). Intl Schol Bk Serv.
CSIRO. Insects of Australia. 1973. Repr. 50.00x (ISBN 0-522-83837-5, Pub by Melbourne U Pr). Intl Schol Bk Serv.
Healy, Anthony & Smithers, Courtenay. Australian Insects in Color. LC 75-184813. (Illus.). (gr. 9 up). 1972. 7.50 (ISBN 0-8048-1030-3). C E Tuttle.
Hughes, R. D. Living Insects. LC 74-12549. (Australian Naturalist Library). (Illus.). 304p. 1975. 14.95 (ISBN 0-8008-4929-9). Taplinger.
Insects of Australia. 1042p. 1981. 95.00x (ISBN 0-522-83837-5, Pub. by CSIRO Australia). State Mutual Bk.
Insects of Australia Supplement. 146p. 1981. 30.00x (ISBN 0-522-84070-1, Pub. by CSIRO Australia). State Mutual Bk.
The Insects of Australia: Supplement 1974. (Illus.). viii, 146p. 1975. 15.00x (ISBN 0-522-84070-1, Pub. by Melbourne U Pr). Intl Schol Bk Serv.
Mathews, E. G. Insect Ecology. (Australian Ecology Ser). (Illus.). 1977. text ed. 19.95x (ISBN 0-7022-1250-4); pap. text ed. 9.95x (ISBN 0-7022-1251-2). U of Queensland Pr.
Reid, D. G. Radar Studies of Insect Flight at Benalla Victoria, in February 1974. 1980. 10.00x (ISBN 0-643-00342-8, Pub. by CSJRO Australia). State Mutual Bk.
Scientific & Common Names of Insects & Allied Forms Occurring in Australia. 100p. 1981. 25.00x (ISBN 0-643-00386-X, Pub. by CSIRO Australia). State Mutual Bk.

Scientific & Common Names of Insects & Allied Forms Occuring in Australia. 47p. 1973. pap. 6.00 (ISBN 0-686-71843-7, CO 32, CSIRO). Unipub.
Scientific & Common Names of Insects & Allied Forms Occuring in Australia. 95p. 1980. pap. 6.00 (ISBN 0-643-00386-X, C059, CSIRO). Unipub.

INSECTS–CANADA

The Insects & Arachnids of Canada: Part 1. Collection, Preparing, & Preserving Insects. 1979. pap. 6.50 (ISBN 0-660-01650-8, SSC118, SSC). Unipub.
The Insects & Arachnids of Canada: Part 3, the Aradiadae of Canada Hemiptera: Aradidae. 1979. pap. 7.50 (ISBN 0-660-01428-9, SSC 120, SSC). Unipub.
The Insects & Arachnids of Canada, 1976: Part 2: the Bark Beetles of Canada & Alaska. (Illus.). 1977. pap. 12.95 (ISBN 0-685-79716-3, SSC52, SSC). Unipub.

INSECTS–GREAT BRITAIN

Goodden, Robert. Beningfield's Butterflies. LC 78-319587. (Illus.). 1979. 16.95 (ISBN 0-7011-2367-2, Pub. by Chatto Bodley Jonathan). Merrimack Bk Serv.
Hickin, Norman E. Caddis Larvae: Larvae of the British Trichoptera. LC 68-58408. (Illus.). 480p. 1968. 20.00 (ISBN 0-8386-6945-X). Fairleigh Dickinson.
Linssen, E. F. The Observer's Book of Insects of the British Isles. (Illus.). 1979. 3.95 (ISBN 0-684-16028-5, ScribT). Scribner.

INSECTS–HAWAII

Bryan, E. H., Jr., et al. Insects of Hawaii, Johnston Island, & Wake Island. (BMB: No. 31). Repr. of 1926 ed. pap. 8.00 (ISBN 0-527-02134-2). Kraus Repr.
Hardy, D. Elmo. Insects of Hawaii: Diptera: Cyclorrhapha IV, Vol. 14. LC 48-45482. (Illus.). 500p. (Orig.). 1981. pap. 35.00x (ISBN 0-8248-0647-6). U Pr of Hawaii.
Hardy, D. Elmo & Delfinado, Mercedes D. Insects of Hawaii, Vol. 13. LC 48-45482. (Illus.). 1980. text ed. 30.00x (ISBN 0-8248-0341-8). U Pr of Hawaii.
Zimmerman, Elwood C. & Hardy, D. Elmo. Insects of Hawaii, 13 vols. Incl. Vol. 1. Introduction; Vol. 2. Apterygota to Thysanoptera. 486p. 1948. 12.00x (ISBN 0-87022-902-8); Vol. 3. Heteroptera. 266p. 1948. 9.00x (ISBN 0-87022-903-6); Vol. 4. Homoptera: Auchenorhyncha. 278p. 1948. 9.00x (ISBN 0-87022-904-4); Vol. 5. Homoptera: Sternorhyncha. 474p. 1948. 12.00x (ISBN 0-87022-905-2); Vol. 6. Ephemeroptera-Neuroptera-Trichoptera. 218p. (Supplement to Vols. 1-5 included). 1957. 9.00x (ISBN 0-87022-906-0); Vol. 7. Macrolepidoptera. 556p. 1958. 15.00x (ISBN 0-87022-907-9); Vol. 8. Lepidoptera, Pyraloidea. 468p. 1958. 12.00x (ISBN 0-87022-908-7); Vol. 10. Diptera: Nematocera-Brachycera 1. 380p. 1960. 11.00x (ISBN 0-87022-910-9); Vol. 11. Diptera: Brachycera 2-Cyclorrhapha 1. 468p. 1964. 12.00x (ISBN 0-87022-911-7); Diptera: Dolichopodidae & Appendix (Phoridae) Tenorio, Jo Ann. 80p. (Supplement to Vol. 11). 1969. 7.00x (ISBN 0-87022-921-4); Vol. 12. Diptera: Cyclorrhapha 2. 824p. 1965. 25.00x (ISBN 0-87022-912-5); Vol. 9. Microlepidoptera, 2 parts. 1978. 60.00x set (ISBN 0-8248-0487-2). (Illus.). U Pr of Hawaii.

INSECTS–INDIA

Kalyanam, N. P. Common Insects of India. 1967. pap. 4.50x (ISBN 0-210-27166-3). Asia.

INSECTS–NEW ZEALAND

Miller, David. Common Insects in New Zealand. (Illus.). 216p. 1971. 14.95 (ISBN 0-589-00444-1, Pub. by Reed Books Australia). C E Tuttle.
Sharell, Richard. New Zealand Insects & Their Story. (Illus.). 268p. 1971. 18.40x (ISBN 0-8002-0063-2). Intl Pubns Serv.

INSECTS–NORTH AMERICA

Ashmead, W. H., et al. Insects, 2 pts. (Harriman Alaska Expedition, 1899). 1910. Pt. 1. pap. 16.00 (ISBN 0-527-38168-3); Pt. 2. pap. 16.00 (ISBN 0-527-38169-1). Kraus Repr.
Bohart, R. M. & Menke, A. S. Sphecid Wasps of the World: A Generic Revision. 1976. 68.50x (ISBN 0-520-02318-8). U of Cal Pr.
Borror, Donald J. & White, Richard E. Field Guide to the Insects of America North of Mexico. (Peterson Field Guide Ser). 1970. 11.95 (ISBN 0-395-07436-3). HM.
--A Field Guide to the Insects of America North of Mexico. LC 70-80420. (Peterson Field Guide Ser.). 1974. pap. 7.95 (ISBN 0-395-18523-8). HM.
Caldwell, John S. The Jumping Plant-Lice of Ohio (Homoptera: Chermidae) 1938. 1.00 (ISBN 0-686-30307-5). Ohio Bio Survey.
Furth, David G. The Stink Bugs of Ohio (Hemiptera: Pentatomidae) 1974. 3.00 (ISBN 0-686-30331-8). Ohio Bio Survey.
Hall, Jack C. A Review of the North & Central American Species of Paravilla Painter (Diptera--Bombyliidae) (U. C. Publications in Entomology Ser.: Vol. 92). 192p. 1981. 10.00x (ISBN 0-520-09625-8). U of Cal Pr.
Hughes, Dave & Hafele, Rick. Western Hatches. (Illus.). 240p. (Orig.). 1981. 28.95 (ISBN 0-686-73217-0); pap. 18.95 (ISBN 0-936608-12-9). F Amato Pubns.
Johnson, Dorothy M. Leafhoppers of Ohio: Subfamily Typhlocybinae. 1935. 1.50 (ISBN 0-686-30304-0). Ohio Bio Survey.
Kosztarab, Michael. The Armored Scale Insects of Ohio. 1963. 3.50 (ISBN 0-686-30321-0). Ohio Bio Survey.
Milne, Lorus & Milne, Margery. The Audubon Society Field Guide to North American Insects & Spiders. LC 80-7620. (Illus.). 1008p. 1980. 11.95 (ISBN 0-394-50763-0). Knopf.
Nelson, Dick & Nelson, Sharon. Easy Field Guide to Common Desert Insects of Arizona. (Illus.). 32p. (Orig.). (gr. 1-12). 1977. pap. 1.00 (ISBN 0-915030-13-6). Tecolote Pr.
Osborn, Herbert. The Fulgoridae of Ohio. 1938. 1.50 (ISBN 0-686-30308-3). Ohio Bio Survey.
--The Leafhoppers of Ohio. 1928. 2.00 (ISBN 0-686-30288-5). Ohio Bio Survey.
--The Membracidae of Ohio. 1940. 1.00 (ISBN 0-686-30310-5). Ohio Bio Survey.
Osborn, Herbert, et al. Recent Insect Invasions in Ohio. 1948. 1.00 (ISBN 0-686-30313-X). Ohio Bio Survey.
Richardson, John, et al. Fauna Boreali-Americana: Zoology of the Northern Parts of British America, Insecta, Pt. 4. Sterling, Keir B., ed. LC 77-81108. (Biologists & Their World Ser.). 1978. Repr. of 1837 ed. lib. bdg. 24.00x (ISBN 0-405-10692-0). Arno.
Swan, Lester A. & Papp, Charles S. The Common Insects of North America. LC 75-138765. (Illus.). 752p. 1972. (HarpT); lib. bdg. 13.27 (ISBN 0-06-014179-4). Har-Row.
Watson, S. A. The Miridae of Ohio. 1928. 1.00 (ISBN 0-686-30290-7). Ohio Bio Survey.
West, Robert M. Review of the North American Eocene & Oligocene Apatemyidae (Mammalia: Insectivora) (Special Publications: No. 3). (Illus.). 42p. 1973. pap. 2.00 (ISBN 0-89672-028-4). Tex Tech Pr.
White, Richard E. The Anobiidae of Ohio. 1962. 2.50 (ISBN 0-686-30318-0). Ohio Bio Survey.

INSECTS–PHILIPPINE ISLANDS

Baltazar, Clare R. & Salazar, Nelia P. Philippine Insects: An Introduction. (Illus.). 1980. text ed. 17.00x (ISBN 0-8248-0675-1, Pub. by U of Philippines Pr); pap. text ed. 12.00x (ISBN 0-8248-0676-X). U Pr of Hawaii.

INSECTS, AQUATIC

Jennings, Preston. Book of Trout Flies. Lyons, Nick, ed. (Illus.). 1970. 7.50 (ISBN 0-517-50204-6). Crown.
Lehmkuhl, Dennis M. How to Know the Aquatic Insects. (Pictured Key Nature Ser.). 1979. text ed. write for info. (ISBN 0-697-04766-0); wire coil avail. (ISBN 0-697-04767-9). Wm C Brown.
McCafferty, W. Patrick. Aquatic Entomology: The Fisherman's & Ecologists Illustrated Guide to Insects & Their Relatives. 496p. 1981. 50.00 (ISBN 0-686-31440-9). Sci Bks Intl.
Meck, Charles R. Meeting & Fishing the Hatches. (Illus.). 1977. 12.50 (ISBN 0-87691-232-3). Winchester Pr.
Merritt, Ricard W. & Cummins, Kenneth W. An Introduction to the Aquatic Insects of North America. (Illus.). 1978. text ed. 22.95 (ISBN 0-8403-8007-0). Kendall-Hunt.
Needham, James G. & Needham, Paul R. Guide to the Study of Freshwater Biology. 5th ed. LC 62-20742. (Illus.). 1962. pap. 5.95x (ISBN 0-8162-6310-8). Holden-Day.
Swisher, Doug & Richards, Carl. Selective Trout. (Illus.). 1971. 10.00 (ISBN 0-517-50304-2); pap. 5.95 (ISBN 0-517-52133-4). Crown.
Usinger, Robert L., ed. Aquatic Insects of California, with Keys to North American Genera & California Species. (Illus.). 1956. 26.50x (ISBN 0-520-01293-3). U of Cal Pr.

INSECTS, DESTRUCTIVE AND USEFUL

see Insects, Injurious and Beneficial

INSECTS, EFFECT OF RADIATION ON

see also Insects–Physiology; Radiation–Physiological Effect

Isotopes & Radiation in Entomology. (Illus., Orig., Eng., Fr., Rus. & Span.). 1968. pap. 27.75 (ISBN 92-0-010168-2, ISP166, IAEA). Unipub.
Isotopes & Radiation in Parasitology - 2. (Illus., Orig.). 1970. pap. 9.75 (ISBN 92-0-111170-3, ISP242, IAEA). Unipub.
Radiation & Radioisotopes Applied to Insects of Agricultural Importance. 1963. 22.75 (ISBN 92-0-010263-8, ISP74, IAEA). Unipub.

INSECTS, EFFECT OF RADIATION ON–BIBLIOGRAPHY

Marinaro, Vincent C. Modern Dry-Fly Code. (Illus.). 1970. 10.00 (ISBN 0-517-50442-1). Crown.

INSECTS, FOSSIL

Bolton, H. The Insects of the British Coal Measures, Pts. 1-2. Repr. of 1922 ed. Set. pap. 23.00 (ISBN 0-384-04980-X). Johnson Repr.
Callahan, Philip S. The Evolution of Insects. LC 72-80654. (Illus.). (gr. 6 up). 1972. 5.95 (ISBN 0-8234-0213-4). Holiday.
Kenward, H. K. The Analysis of Archaeological Insect Assemblages: A New Approach. (Archaeology of York-Principles & Methods Ser.: Vol. 19). 68p. 1978. pap. text ed. 14.95x (ISBN 0-900312-73-4, Pub. by Coun Brit Archaeology). Humanities.

INSECTS, INJURIOUS AND BENEFICIAL

see also Agricultural Pests; Galls (Botany); Garden Pests; Household Pests; Insect Control; Insecticides; Insects As Carriers of Disease; Plants–Disease and Pest Resistance;
also subdivision Diseases and Pests under names of Crops, Plants, Trees, etc. e.g. Fruit–Diseases and Pests; also specific names of insect pests

Anderson, Roger F. Forest & Shade Tree Entomology. LC 60-11714. 428p. 1960. 28.50 (ISBN 0-471-02739-1). Wiley.
Andrews, Michael. The Life That Lives on Man. LC 76-53299. (Illus.). 1978. pap. 4.95 (ISBN 0-8008-4820-9). Taplinger.
Askew, R. R. Parasitic Insects. 1971. 17.50 (ISBN 0-444-19629-3). Elsevier.
Causey, Don. Killer Insects. (Illus.). (gr. 4-6). 1979. PLB 6.90 s&l (ISBN 0-531-02924-7). Watts.
Chandler, Asa C. & Read, C. P. Introduction to Parasitology: With Special References to the Parasites of Man. 10th ed. LC 61-5670. 1961. 33.50 (ISBN 0-471-14487-8). Wiley.
Cheatum, E. P. Common Pests of the Garden, Yard, Home, & Their Control. (Illus.). 1973. pap. 1.50 (ISBN 0-934786-04-6). G Davis.
Davidson, Ralph & Lyon, William F. Insect Pests of Farm, Garden, & Orchard. 7th ed. LC 78-31366. 1979. text ed. 29.95 (ISBN 0-471-03538-6). Wiley.
Dethier, V. G. Man's Plague? Insects & Agriculture. LC 75-15216. (Illus.). 237p. (Orig.). 1976. 9.95 (ISBN 0-87850-026-X). Darwin Pr.
FAO-WHO Meeting on Insect Viruses. Geneva, 1972. Use of Viruses for the Control of Insect Pests & Disease Vectors: Report. (Technical Report Ser.: No. 531). (Also avail. in French & Spanish). 1973. pap. 1.60 (ISBN 92-4-120531-8). World Health.
Fichter, George S. Insect Pests. (Golden Guide Ser). (Illus.). (gr. 5 up). 1966. PLB 10.38 (ISBN 0-307-63534-1, Golden Pr); pap. 1.95 (ISBN 0-307-24016-9). Western Pub.
Harris, Thaddeus W. Report on the Insects of Massachusetts Injurious to Vegetation. LC 70-125746. (American Environmental Studies). 1970. Repr. of 1841 ed. 22.00 (ISBN 0-405-02671-4). Arno.
Hill, D. S. Agricultural Insect Pests of the Tropics. (Illus.). 584p. 1975. 60.00 (ISBN 0-521-20261-2); pap. 19.95 (ISBN 0-521-29441-X). Cambridge U Pr.
Hogner, Dorothy C. Good Bugs & Bad Bugs in Your Garden: Backyard Ecology. LC 74-6235. (Illus.). 96p. (gr. 3-7). 1974. PLB 8.79 (ISBN 0-690-00120-7, TYC-J). Har-Row.
Insects of Eastern Spruces, Fir & Hemlock. 1979. pap. 9.00 (ISBN 0-660-01594-3, SSC 130, SSC). Unipub.
Keegan, Hugh L. Scorpions of Medical Importance. LC 80-16419. (Illus.). 1980. 22.50x (ISBN 0-87805-124-4). U Pr of Miss.
Lamb, K. Economic Entomology in the Tropics. 1974. 25.00 (ISBN 0-12-434650-2). Acad Pr.
Leftwich, A. W. A Dictionary of Entomology. LC 75-27143. 1976. 27.50x (ISBN 0-8448-0820-2). Crane-Russak Co.
Lewis, Trevor. Thrips: Their Biology, Ecology & Economic Importance. 1973. 57.50 (ISBN 0-12-447160-9). Acad Pr.
Metcalf, Clell L., et al. Destructive & Useful Insects. 4th ed. (Agricultural Sciences Ser.). 1962. text ed. 30.95 (ISBN 0-07-041658-3, C). McGraw.
Novak, Vladimir, et al, eds. Atlas of Insects Harmful to Forest Trees, Vol. 1. (Illus.). 1977. 39.00 (ISBN 0-444-99874-8). Elsevier.
Osborn, Herbert, et al. Recent Insect Invasions in Ohio. 1948. 1.00 (ISBN 0-686-30313-X). Ohio Bio Survey.
Panda, N. Principles of Host-Plant Resistance to Insect Pests. LC 78-59169. (Illus.). 400p. 1980. text ed. 32.50 (ISBN 0-87663-836-1). Allanheld.
Pyenson, Louis L. Fundamentals of Entomology & Plant Pathology. 2nd ed. (Illus.). 1980. text ed. 22.00 (ISBN 0-87055-334-8). AVI.
Riley, Charles V. Nine Annual Reports on the Noxious, Beneficial & Other Insects of the State of Missouri, 1869-1877: With a General Index & Supplement, 10 vols. in three. Sterling, Keir B., ed. LC 77-81105. (Biologists & Their World Ser.). 1978. Repr. of 1881 ed. lib. bdg. 100.00x (ISBN 0-405-10745-5). Arno.
Simon, Hilda. Our Six-Legged Friends & Allies: Ecology in Your Back Yard. LC 74-178823. (Illus.). 96p. (gr. 6-12). 1972. 8.95 (ISBN 0-8149-0711-3). Vanguard.
Talhouk, Abdul M. Insects & Mites Injurious to Crops in Middle Eastern Countries. LC 72-422855. (Illus.). 239p. 1969. pap. 39.00x (ISBN 3-490-10618-0). Intl Pubns Serv.
The Use of Viruses for the Control on Insect Pests & Disease Vectors. (FAO Agricultural Studies: No. 91). 48p. (Orig.). 1974. pap. 4.50 (ISBN 0-685-40246-0, F490, FAO). Unipub.
Vector Control. (WHO Bulletin Supplement: Vol. 29). (Also avail. in French). 1963. pap. 4.80 (ISBN 92-4-068291-0). World Health.
Westcott, Cynthia. The Gardener's Bug Book. LC 72-89822. 720p. 1973. 15.95 (ISBN 0-385-01525-9). Doubleday.

INSECTS, INJURIOUS AND BENEFICIAL–BIOLOGICAL CONTROL

see Insect Control–Biological Control

INSECTS, INJURIOUS AND BENEFICIAL–CONTROL

see Insect Control

INSECTS, INJURIOUS AND BENEFICIAL–EXTERMINATION

see Insect Control

INSECTS, SOCIAL

see Insect Societies

INSECTS AS CARRIERS OF DISEASE

see also Flies As Carriers of Disease; Mosquitoes; Tsetse-Flies; Virus Diseases of Plants

Brewer, J. W., et al. Readings in Insect-Plant Disease Relationships. new ed. LC 72-10029. (Illus.). 1973. text ed. 29.50x (ISBN 0-8422-5071-9); pap. text ed. 13.25x (ISBN 0-8422-0264-1). Irvington.
Carter, Walter. Insects in Relation to Plant Disease. 2nd ed. LC 73-4362. 65.00 (ISBN 0-471-13849-5, Pub. by Wiley-Interscience). Wiley.
Causey, Don. Killer Insects. (Illus.). (gr. 4-6). 1979. PLB 6.90 s&l (ISBN 0-531-02924-7). Watts.
Furman, D. P. & Catts, E. P. Manual of Medical Entomology. 3rd. ed. (Illus.). 163p. 1980. pap. 8.95 (ISBN 0-521-28161-X). Cambridge U Pr.
James, M. & Harwood, Herms R. Medical Entomology. 6th ed. 1969. 19.95 (ISBN 0-02-360180-9). Macmillan.
Muirhead-Thompson, R. C. Ecology of Insect Vector Populations. 1968. 17.50 (ISBN 0-12-509750-6). Acad Pr.
Pavlovsky, Evgeny N. Natural Nidality of Transmissible Diseases: With Special Reference to the Landscape Epidemiology of Zooanthroponoses. Levine, N. D., ed. Plous, Frederick K., Jr., tr. from Rus. LC 66-11023. (Illus.). 1966. 17.50 (ISBN 0-252-72726-6). U of Ill Pr.
Snow, Keith R. Insects & Disease. LC 73-15433. 208p. 1974. 9.95 (ISBN 0-470-81017-3, Pub. by Wiley). Krieger.
Symposium Of The Entymological Society Of America - Atlantic City - 1960. Biological Transmission of Disease Agents: Proceedings. Maramorosch, K., ed. 1962. 32.50 (ISBN 0-12-470250-3). Acad Pr.
Vector Control in International Health. 144p. 1972. pap. 12.80 (ISBN 92-4-154016-8, 930). World Health.
WHO Scientific Group. Geneva, 1972. Vector Ecology: Report. (Technical Report Ser.: No. 501). (Also avail. in French & Spanish). 1972. pap. 1.60 (ISBN 92-4-120501-6). World Health.

INSECTS AS CARRIERS OF DISEASE–CONTROL

see Insect Control

INSECURITY (PSYCHOLOGY)

see Security (Psychology)

INSEMINATION, ARTIFICIAL

see Artificial Insemination

INSIDE PASSAGE

Petite, Irving. Meander to Alaska. (Illus.). 240p. 1976. pap. 3.95 (ISBN 0-915112-10-8). Seattle Bk.

INSIGNIA

see also Buttons; Campaign Insignia; Decorations of Honor; Devices; Emblems

Britton, Jack L. Uniform Insignia of the United States Military Forces. LC 80-83871. (Illus.). 1980. pap. 6.50 (ISBN 0-912958-06-5). MCN Pr.
Britton, Jack L. & Washington, George, Jr. Military Shoulder Patches of the United States Armed Forces. 3rd ed. LC 81-80699. (Illus.). 1981. 19.95 (ISBN 0-912958-13-8); pap. 12.95 (ISBN 0-912958-12-X). MCN Pr.
Clapp, Jane. Professional Ethics & Insignia. LC 74-10501. (Illus.). 1974. 32.50 (ISBN 0-8108-0735-1). Scarecrow.
Patrick, Derrick. Fetch Felix. (Illus.). 192p. 1981. 22.50 (ISBN 0-241-10371-1, Pub. by Hamish Hamilton England). David & Charles.
Rosignoli, Guido. Air Force Badges & Insignia of World War Two. LC 77-1094. (Arco Color Ser.). 1977. 7.95 (ISBN 0-668-04249-4); pap. 5.95 (ISBN 0-668-04252-4). Arco.

--Army Badges & Insignia of World War II: Great Britain, Poland, Belgium, Italy, USSR, Germany. (Illus.). 228p. 1980. 10.95 (ISBN 0-7137-0697-X, Pub. by Blandford Pr England). Sterling.

INSOLVENCY
see Bankruptcy

INSOLATION
see Solar Radiation

INSOMNIA
see also Narcotics; Sleep

Buhler, W. How to Overcome Sleeplessness. 1973. lib. bdg. 59.95 (ISBN 0-87968-493-3). Krishna Pr.

Ceres. Herbs to Help You Sleep. LC 80-50749. (Everybody's Home Herbal Ser.). (Illus.). 62p. (Orig.). 1980. pap. 1.95 (ISBN 0-394-73946-9). Shambhala Pubns.

Colligan, Douglas. Creative Insomnia. 1979. pap. 3.95 (ISBN 0-07-011797-7). McGraw.

Hartmann, Ernest. The Sleeping Pill. LC 78-6205. (Illus.). 1978. 17.50x (ISBN 0-300-02248-4). Yale U Pr.

Institute of Medicine. Sleeping Pills, Insomnia, & Medical Practice. 1979. pap. text ed. 6.00 (ISBN 0-309-02881-7). Natl Acad Pr.

James, Paul. Sleep at Last or How to Not Be an Insomniac. 192p. 1981. pap. 6.95 (ISBN 0-8317-4900-8, Rutledge Pr). Smith Pubs.

Kellerman, Henry. Sleep Disorders: Insomnia & Narcolepsy. LC 80-28517. 250p. 1981. 20.00 (ISBN 0-87630-264-9). Brunner-Mazel.

Maxman, Jerrold S. A Good Night's Sleep: A Step-by-Step Program for Overcoming Insomnia & Other Sleep Problems. (Illus.). 1981. 14.95 (ISBN 0-393-01437-1). Norton.

Regestein, Quentin R. & Rechs, James R. Sound Sleep. 1980. 10.95 (ISBN 0-671-24960-6). S&S.

Renshaw, Samuel, et al. Children's Sleep: A Series of Studies on the Influence of Motion Pictures. LC 76-124031. (Literature of Cinema Ser: Payne Fund Studies of Motion Pictures & Social Valves). Repr. of 1933 ed. 10.00 (ISBN 0-405-01631-X). Arno.

Weiman, Mark. A Bibliography of Books in English on Sleep, Dreams & Insomnia. iv, 130p. 1978. lib. bdg. 17.50 (ISBN 0-686-73174-3). Norwood Edns.

--A Bibliography of Books in English on Sleep, Dreams & Insomnia. LC 78-25842. 1978. lib. bdg. 22.50 (ISBN 0-8482-6992-6). Norwood Edns.

Weinman, Mark. A Bibliography of Books in English on Sleep, Dreams & Insomnia. 2nd ed. 130p. 1981. Repr. of 1978 ed. lib. bdg. 22.50 (ISBN 0-8495-5829-8). Arden Lib.

Williams, R. L. & Karacan, I. Sleep Disorders: Diagnosis & Treatment. LC 78-18896. 1978. 49.50 (ISBN 0-471-94682-6, Pub. by Wiley-Medical). Wiley.

INSPECTION BY SAMPLING
see Sampling

INSPECTION OF BUILDINGS
see Building Inspection

INSPECTION OF FOOD
see Food Adulteration and Inspection

INSPECTION OF MEAT
see Meat Inspection

INSPECTION OF SCHOOLS
see School Management and Organization

INSPIRATION
see also Bible–Inspiration; Creation (Literary, Artistic, etc.); Creative Ability; Enthusiasm; Revelation

Amen, Carol. Hyacinths to Feed the Soul. LC 74-33850. (Better Living Ser.). 64p. 1975. pap. text ed. 0.95 (ISBN 0-8127-0094-5). Review & Herald.

Bales, James. You Believe. Date not set. pap. 3.95 (ISBN 0-89315-425-3). Lambert Bk.

Barber, Cyril J. Vital Encounter. LC 79-89026. 1980. pap. 3.95 (ISBN 0-89840-004-X). Heres Life.

Barnard, Jerry. Something Worse Than Hell & Better Than Heaven. 1979. pap. 2.25 (ISBN 0-917726-31-6). Hunter Bks.

Baumann, Dan. Which Way to Happiness. 144p. 1981. pap. 2.50 (ISBN 0-8307-0773-5). Regal.

Bechtel, Faythelma, et al. The Creative Touch. 1974. 3.15x (ISBN 0-87813-909-5). Christian Light.

Bevan, Edwyn R. Sibyls & Seers. 1979. Repr. of 1928 ed. lib. bdg. 30.00 (ISBN 0-8495-0510-0). Arden Lib.

Birky, Lela & Conley, Lucy. The Building Christian English Ser. (gr. 3-7). 1973. send for info. (ISBN 0-686-05606-X); tchrs' ed. avail. (ISBN 0-686-05607-8). Rod & Staff.

Bowlin, William R., ed. A Book of Living Poems. LC 79-51966. (Granger Poetry Library). (Illus.). 1980. Repr. of 1934 ed. 19.00x (ISBN 0-89609-177-5). Granger Bk.

Cartland, Barbara. The Light of Love: Lines to Live by Day by Day. LC 79-20929. 1980. 9.95 (ISBN 0-525-66654-0). Elsevier-Nelson.

Cioran, E. M. The Trouble with Being Born. Howard, Richard, tr. from Fr. 208p. pap. 5.95 (ISBN 0-394-17847-5). Seaver Bks.

Coleman, Robert E., ed. One Divine Moment. (Illus., Orig.). 1970. pap. 1.95 (ISBN 0-8007-0436-3); pap. 0.95 (ISBN 0-8007-8077-9, Spire). Revell.

Collins, Camilla. In the Hollow of His Hand. 1980. pap. 3.50 (ISBN 0-8309-0262-7). Herald Hse.

Crum, Jesse K. The Art of Inner Listening. LC 74-21643. (Orig.). 1975. pap. 1.50 (ISBN 0-8356-0303-2, Quest). Theos Pub Hse.

Cubillo De Aragon, A. El Enano De las Musas. (Span.). 1971. Repr. 66.75 (ISBN 3-4870-4081-6). Adler.

Cunningham, Glenn & Sand, George. Never Quit. 144p. (gr. 6 up). 1981. PLB 7.95 (ISBN 0-912376-70-8). Chosen Bks Pub.

Custer, Stewart. Does Inspiration Demand Inerrancy. pap. 2.95 (ISBN 0-934532-07-9). Presby & Reformed.

Del Mazza, Valentino. Our Lady Among Us. 1978. 4.00 (ISBN 0-8198-0363-4); pap. 3.00 (ISBN 0-8198-0364-2). Dghtrs St Paul.

Dieterich, Robert R. The Seven Deadly Virtues. 1979. 4.75 (ISBN 0-8062-1383-3). Carlton.

Doan, Eleanor, compiled by. Your Treasury of Inspiration. rev. ed. 216p. 1980. gift ed. 9.95 (ISBN 0-310-23790-4, 9525). Zondervan.

Esses, Betty L. Se Eu Posso...Tu Podes. Date not set. 1.30 (ISBN 0-686-76437-4). Life Pubs Intl.

The Family Advent Book. LC 79-6974. (A Giniger Bk.). (Illus.). 1979. 5.95 (ISBN 0-385-15021-0). Doubleday.

Friends Anonymous. The Wise Man Stories. Smith, Harold & Smith, Alma, eds. (Orig.). 1979. pap. 2.95 (ISBN 0-87516-371-8). De Vorss.

Gerrick, David J. God Stories to Scare the Hell Out of You. (gr. 7 up). 1979. pap. text ed. 4.95 (ISBN 0-916750-24-8). Dayton Labs.

Giniger, Ken S., (compiled by. Compact Treasury of Inspiration. (Orig.). pap. 1.95 (ISBN 0-89129-229-2). Jove Pubns.

Gossett, Don. The Ministry of Angels & Believers. 1979. pap. 1.25 (ISBN 0-88368-086-6). Whitaker Hse.

--Since You Asked... (Orig.). 1979. pap. 1.75 (ISBN 0-88368-089-0). Whitaker Hse.

Grubb, Norman P. Deep Things of God. 1970. pap. 2.95 (ISBN 0-87508-209-2). Chr Lit.

Guideposts Associates. The Guideposts Treasury of Inspiration. 1980. 8.95 (ISBN 0-385-14969-7). Doubleday.

Gustafson, Janie. Celibate Passion. LC 77-20439. 1978. 8.95 (ISBN 0-06-063536-3, HarpR). Har-Row.

Hager, Wesley H. Consider the Grass: God Cares for You. (Contempo Ser.). pap. 0.95 (ISBN 0-8010-4102-3). Baker Bk.

Harding, Rosamond E. Anatomy of Inspiration. 2nd ed. 145p. 1967. 23.50x (ISBN 0-7146-2060-2, F Cass Co). Biblio Dist.

Havens, Evelyn. Five-Hundred Gems of Thought. 1978. 5.95 (ISBN 0-89543-008-8); pap. 3.95 (ISBN 0-685-87577-6). Grossmont Pr.

Herrmann, Nina. Go Out in Joy. LC 76-44972. 1977. 7.95 (ISBN 0-8042-2073-5). John Knox.

Hill, Harold & Harrell, Irene. How to Be a Winner. LC 76-12035. 1976. pap. 2.95 (ISBN 0-88270-179-7). Logos.

Hobe, Phyllis, compiled by. Fragile Moments. 1980. 14.95 (ISBN 0-8007-1176-9). Revell.

Hodgson, Joan. Why on Earth. rev. ed. 144p. 1979. pap. 4.95 (ISBN 0-85487-043-1). De Vorss.

Hunter, Charles. Follow Me! 1975. pap. 2.25 (ISBN 0-917726-35-9). Hunter Bks.

Hunter, Charles & Hunter, Frances. Angels on Assignment. 1979. pap. 3.95 (ISBN 0-917726-33-2). Hunter Bks.

--The Two Sides of a Coin. 1973. pap. 2.25 (ISBN 0-917726-36-7). Hunter Bks.

Hunter, Frances. Come Alive. 1975. pap. 3.25 (ISBN 0-917726-34-0). Hunter Bks.

--A Confession a Day Keeps the Devil Away. 1980. pap. 4.50 (ISBN 0-917726-37-5). Hunter Bks.

Hunter, Frances & Hunter, Charles. Since Jesus Passed by. 1973. pap. 2.25 (ISBN 0-917726-38-3). Hunter Bks.

Hunter, John E. & Hunter, Christine. Ten Minutes with God. LC 79-89024. 1980. 5.95 (ISBN 0-89840-006-6). Heres Life.

Hurnard, Hannah. Eagle's Wings to the Higher Places. LC 81-50721. 165p. (Orig.). 1981. pap. write for info. (ISBN 0-9603634-1-6). Rahamah Pubns.

Inrig, Gary. Quality Friendship. 192p. (Orig.). 1981. pap. 2.95 (ISBN 0-8024-2891-6). Moody.

Institute for Religious & Social Studies. Hour of Insight. facsimile ed. MacIver, R. M., ed. LC 70-167366. (Essay Index Reprint Ser). Repr. of 1954 ed. 15.00 (ISBN 0-8369-2655-2). Arno.

Jackson, Clyde O. Come Like the Benediction: A Tribute to Tuskegee Institute & Other Essays. (Illus.). 1981. 7.00 (ISBN 0-682-49723-1). Exposition.

James, Muriel & James, John. Touch a Rainbow. 1978. pap. 4.95 (ISBN 0-89087-232-5). Celestial Arts.

Johnson, Margaret. Home Before Dark. 1978. 6.95 (ISBN 0-310-26680-7). Zondervan.

Keller, W. Phillip. Still Waters. 1980. 7.95 (ISBN 0-8007-1092-4). Revell.

Kesler, Harold. Comfort One Another with These Words. Date not set. pap. 0.95 (ISBN 0-937396-11-7). Walterick Pubs.

Keyes, Ken, Jr. & Burkan, Bruce. How to Make Your Life Work. 1976. pap. 3.95 (ISBN 0-346-12226-0). Cornerstone.

Lefebvre, Dom G. God Present. 1979. pap. 3.95 (ISBN 0-03-053436-4). Winston Pr.

Lehman, James. The Old Brethren. (Orig.). 1976. pap. 2.45 (ISBN 0-89129-155-5). Jove Pubns.

Lopez, Barry. Winter Count. (Illus.). 96p. 1981. 9.95 (ISBN 0-684-16817-0, ScribT). Scribner.

McWhirter, David. Millenial Harbinger - Index. LC 81-65031. (Millenial Harbinger Ser.). 864p. 1981. 19.95 (ISBN 0-89900-228-5). College Pr Pub.

Magdalena. The Initiates. 1979. 5.75 (ISBN 0-8062-1348-5). Carlton.

The Magic Story. 1977. 2.95 (ISBN 0-442-82577-3). Peter Pauper.

Marshall, Catherine. Meeting God at Every Turn. (Illus.). 250p. 1981. 9.95 (ISBN 0-912376-61-9). Chosen Bks Pub.

Michael, Arnold. Brothers of the Grape. LC 76-142525. 1972. pap. 5.50 (ISBN 0-87516-149-9). De Vorss.

Murphey, Cecil B. Somebody Knows I'm Alive. LC 76-44967. 1978. 4.95 (ISBN 0-8042-2206-1). John Knox.

Nimeth, Albert J. Instant Inspiration. 1976. pap. 2.95 (ISBN 0-685-77506-2). Franciscan Herald.

Olsson, Norman. Inspiration from the Inner I. 182p. 1979. pap. 3.95 (ISBN 0-87707-218-3). CSA Pr.

Paulsell, William & Kelty, Matthew. Letters from a Hermit. 1978. 7.95 (ISBN 0-87243-086-3). Templegate.

Pearson, B. H. But If It Dies. pap. 1.00 (ISBN 0-87508-446-X). Chr Lit.

Phillips, Dorothy B., et al, eds. The Choice Is Always Ours. rev. ed. 480p. (Orig.). 1975. pap. 1.95 (ISBN 0-8356-0302-4, Quest). Theos Pub Hse.

Pinions. Wind on the Sand. LC 81-80879. 96p. (Orig.). 1981. pap. 3.95 (ISBN 0-8091-2390-8). Paulist Pr.

Pitcher, Arthur. Memoirs of Peter. 1981. 2.95 (ISBN 0-86544-015-8). Salvation Army.

Pollnow, Jim. My God, Why? A Mastectomy from a Husbands Point of View. LC 79-55888. 127p. 1980. pap. 3.95x (ISBN 0-9603708-0-3). J L Pollnow.

Price, Eugenia. Just As I Am. (Trumpet Bks). 1976. pap. 1.75 (ISBN 0-87981-055-6). Holman.

--Learning to Live. (Trumpet Bks). 1976. pap. 1.95 (ISBN 0-87981-062-9). Holman.

Quenon, Paul. Carved in Stone. (Illus.). 40p. 1979. pap. 2.50 (ISBN 0-87793-195-X). Ave Maria.

Ruben, William S. & Ruben, Paul. Profiles in Inspiration. 1977. pap. 1.95 (ISBN 0-532-19150-1). Woodhill.

Schaffer, Ulrich. A Growing Love: Meditations on Marriage & Commitment. rev. ed. LC 79-3758. (Illus.). 128p. 1980. pap. 3.95 (ISBN 0-06-067079-7, RD 325). Har-Row.

Sill, Sterling W. The Glory of the Sun. LC 81-80957. 380p. 1981. 10.95 (ISBN 0-88290-183-4, 1067). Horizon Utah.

Sit, Amy. Sing It! 1979. pap. 3.50 (ISBN 0-917726-39-1). Hunter Bks.

Sturholm, Larry & Roe, Jess. In the Line of Duty: The Story of Two Brave Men. LC 79-8552. 216p. 1980. 9.95 (ISBN 0-385-15396-1, Galilee). Doubleday.

Talmadge, Virginia. Dear God Little Prayers to a Big God. 1981. cloth 2.95 (ISBN 0-86544-016-6). Salvation Army.

Teresa Of Calcutta, Mother A Gift for God. LC 74-4628. (Illus.). 96p. 1974. 6.95 (ISBN 0-06-068231-0, HarpR). Har-Row.

Thielicke, Helmut. A Thielicke Trilogy. Barber, C. C. & Bromily, G. W., trs. 296p. 1980. pap. 3.95 (ISBN 0-8010-8852-6). Baker Bk.

Thomas, Cal. Public Persons & Private Lives. 1979. pap. 5.95 (ISBN 0-8499-2845-1). Word Bks.

Van Wade, David & Van Wade, Sarah. Second Chance. LC 75-20899. 1975. 5.95 (ISBN 0-88270-137-1); pap. 4.95 (ISBN 0-88270-138-X). Logos.

Waller, Charles E. The Image of God. 1979. 6.50 (ISBN 0-8062-0529-6). Carlton.

Wellington, Paul A. About to Come Forth. 1979. pap. 3.50 (ISBN 0-8309-0263-5). Herald Hse.

Whiting, Thomas A. Be Good to Yourself. LC 80-27304. 128p. 1981. 6.95 (ISBN 0-687-02800-0). Abingdon.

Wildmon, Donald E. A Gift for the Graduate. 3.95 (ISBN 0-686-12694-7). Five Star Pubs.

--Graduation Gold. 3.95 (ISBN 0-686-12695-5). Five Star Pubs.

Willer, Earl C. Treasury of Inspirational Illustrations. (Preaching Helps Ser). 1974. pap. 2.95 (ISBN 0-8010-9557-3). Baker Bk.

Williams, Steve. The Death of a Child. 1977. 3.95 (ISBN 0-686-23229-1). Firm Foun Pub.

Wright, Ralph. Ripples of Stillness. 1978. 5.95 (ISBN 0-8198-0365-0). Dghtrs St Paul.

INSTALLATION OF CARPETS
see Carpet Laying

INSTALLATION SERVICE (CHURCH OFFICERS)

Bolding, Amy. Installation Services for All Groups. LC 71-84501. 1969. 5.50 (ISBN 0-8054-3608-1). Broadman.

McCandless, Oleta R. Twenty Four Planned Services: Installations, Dedications, & Devotions. (Paperback Program Ser.). 128p. 1976. pap. 2.50 (ISBN 0-8010-6006-0). Baker Bk.

INSTALMENT CREDIT COMPANIES
see Commercial Finance Companies

INSTALMENT PLAN
see also Commercial Finance Companies; Finance Charges; Sales, Conditional

Babson, Roger W. The Folly of Instalment Buying. LC 75-39241. (Getting & Spending: the Consumer's Dilemma). 1976. Repr. of 1938 ed. 15.00x (ISBN 0-405-08006-9). Arno.

Hendricks, Gary, et al. Consumer Durables & Installment Debt: A Study of American Households. LC 72-619719. 231p. 1973. pap. 6.00 (ISBN 0-87944-117-8). Inst Soc Res.

Installment Lending Directory. 1978. 22.00 (ISBN 0-89982-088-3, 206600). Am Bankers.

Rondileau, Adrian. Education for Installment Buying. LC 77-177205. (Columbia University. Teachers College. Contributions to Education: No. 902). Repr. of 1944 ed. 17.50 (ISBN 0-404-55902-6). AMS Pr.

INSTINCT
see also Animal Intelligence; Habit; Orientation (Physiology); Orientation (Psychology); Psychology, Comparative

Ardrey, Robert. Territorial Imperative. 1968. pap. 3.25 (ISBN 0-440-58619-4, Delta). Dell.

--The Territorial Imperative: A Personal Inquiry into the Animal Origins of Property & Nations. LC 66-23572. (Illus.). 1966. 10.95 (ISBN 0-689-10015-9). Atheneum.

Bernard, L. L. Instinct: A Study in Social Psychology. 550p. 1980. Repr. of 1924 ed. lib. bdg. 40.00 (ISBN 0-89760-046-0). Telegraph Bks.

Bernard, Luther L. Instinct: A Study in Social Psychology. Coser, Lewis A. & Powell, Walter W., eds. LC 79-6984. (Perennial Works in Sociology Ser.). (Illus.). 1979. Repr. of 1924 ed. lib. bdg. 36.00x (ISBN 0-405-12084-2). Arno.

Darwin, Charles. Expression of the Emotions in Man & Animals. LC 65-17286. (Illus.). 1965. pap. 4.95 (ISBN 0-226-13656-6, P526, Phoen). U of Chicago Pr.

Darwin, Charles R. Expression of the Emotions in Man & Animals. LC 73-90703. Repr. of 1955 ed. lib. bdg. 16.75x (ISBN 0-8371-2291-0, DAEM). Greenwood.

--Expression of the Emotions in Man & Animals. Repr. of 1897 ed. 37.50 (ISBN 0-404-08410-9). AMS Pr.

Fletcher, Ronald. Instinct in Man. rev. ed. 1974. text ed. 20.00 (ISBN 0-8236-2700-4). Intl Univs Pr.

Heller, Agnes. On Instincts. Fenyo, M., tr. from Hungarian. (Dialectic & Society: No. 5). 1979. pap. text ed. 13.75x (ISBN 90-232-1705-5). Humanities.

Hinde, R. A. & Hinde, J. S. Instinct & Intelligence. rev. ed. Head, J. J., ed. LC 77-88812. (Carolina Biology Readers Ser.). 16p. 1980. pap. 1.65 (ISBN 0-89278-263-3, 45-9663). Carolina Biological.

Menninger, Karl A. Love Against Hate. LC 42-50183. 1959. pap. 3.50 (ISBN 0-15-653892-X, HB28, Harv). HarBraceJ.

Morgan, C. Lloyd. Habit & Instinct. LC 73-2978. (Classics in Psychology Ser.). Repr. of 1896 ed. 17.00 (ISBN 0-405-05150-6). Arno.

Palmeri, Rosario. Sources of Instinctive Life. LC 65-27461. 1966. 3.00 (ISBN 0-8022-1260-3). Philos Lib.

Romanes, George J. Mental Evolution in Animals: With a Posthumous Essay on Instinct by Charles Darwin. LC 71-96472. Repr. of 1884 ed. 28.00 (ISBN 0-404-05389-0). AMS Pr.

Schiller, Claire H., ed. Instinctive Behavior: The Development of a Modern Concept. LC 57-10590. (Illus.). 1964. text ed. 20.00 (ISBN 0-8236-2880-9); pap. text ed. 6.95 (ISBN 0-8236-8084-3, 022880). Intl Univs Pr.

Sivaram, M. Ananda: An Experience. 294p. 1976. 15.00x (ISBN 0-7069-0396-X). Intl Pubns Serv.

Tinbergen, Nikolaas. Study of Instinct. 1969. pap. 5.95x (ISBN 0-19-501371-9). Oxford U Pr.

--Study of Instinct. 1969. pap. 5.95x (ISBN 0-19-501371-9). Oxford U Pr.

Trotter, W. Instincts of the Herd in Peace & War. Repr. of 1916 ed. 27.50 (ISBN 0-89987-086-4). Darby Bks.

INSTITORIS, HENRICUS, d. 1508

Zilboorg, Gregory. Medical Man & the Witch During the Renaissance. LC 79-97605. 215p. Repr. of 1935 ed. 11.50x (ISBN 0-8154-0314-3). Cooper Sq.

INSTITUTE FOR DEVELOPMENTAL STUDIES

Powledge, Fred. To Change a Child: A Report on the Institute for Developmental Studies. (Illus., Orig.). 1972. 5.50 (ISBN 0-8129-6070-X). Times Bks.

INSTITUTION LIBRARIES

see also Blind, Libraries for the; Hospital Libraries

Engelbarts, Rudolf. Books in Stir: A Bibliographic Essay About Prison Libraries & About Books Written by Prisoners & Prison Employees. LC 70-180625. 1972. 10.00 (ISBN 0-8108-0450-6). Scarecrow.

INSTITUTION MANAGEMENT

see also Church Management; Office Management

Bayley, Linda, et al. Jail Library Service: A Guide for Librarians & Jail Administrators. LC 81-2023. 126p. 1981. pap. 14.00 (ISBN 0-8389-3258-4). ALA.

Powell, Ray M. Management Procedures for Institutions. LC 78-51525. (Studies in the Management of Not-for-Profit Institutions: No. 2). (Illus.). 1980. text ed. 12.95x (ISBN 0-268-01344-6). U of Notre Dame Pr.

Rudman, Jack. Senior Institution Safety Officer. (Career Examination Ser.: C-2119). (Cloth bdg. avail. on request). 1977. pap. 10.00 (ISBN 0-8373-2119-0). Natl Learning.

Vallen, J., et al. The Art & Science of Managing Hotels-Restaurants-Institutions. Orig. Title: The Art & Science of Modern Innkeeping. 1978. 14.25x (ISBN 0-8104-9470-1). Hayden.

INSTITUTIONAL CHURCH

see Church Work

INSTITUTIONAL ECONOMICS

Breit, William & Culbertson, William P., Jr., eds. Science & Ceremony: The Institutional Economics of C. E. Ayres. LC 76-8238. 228p. 1976. text ed. 14.95x (ISBN 0-292-77523-7). U of Tex Pr.

Commons, John R. Institutional Economics: It's Place in Political Economy. xii, 921p. Repr. of 1934 ed. lib. bdg. 37.50x (ISBN 0-87991-094-1). Porcupine Pr.

Copeland, Morris A. Fact & Theory in Economics. Morse, Chandler, ed. LC 73-8564. 347p. 1973. Repr. of 1958 ed. lib. bdg. 18.00x (ISBN 0-8371-6965-8, COFA). Greenwood.

Coser, Lewis A. Greedy Institutions. LC 73-10571. 1974. 12.95 (ISBN 0-02-906750-2). Free Pr.

Gruchy, Allan G. Contemporary Economic Thought. LC 79-184664. 1972. 15.00x (ISBN 0-678-00898-1). Kelley.

Powell, Ray M. Budgetary Control Procedures for Institutions. LC 78-51520. (Studies in the Managment of Not-for-Profit Institutions: No. 3). (Illus.). 1980. text ed. 12.95x (ISBN 0-268-00658-X). U of Notre Dame Pr.

Schotter, Andrew. The Economic Theory of Social Institutions. (Illus.). 240p. 1981. 29.50 (ISBN 0-521-23044-6). Cambridge U Pr.

Seckler, David. Thorstein Veblen & the Institutionalists: A Study in the Philosophy of Economics. LC 73-91642. 175p. 1975. text ed. 12.50x (ISBN 0-87081-055-3). Colo Assoc.

Steppacher, Rolf, et al, eds. Economics in Institutional Perspective: Memorial Essays in Honor of K. William Kapp. LC 76-41116. 1977. 16.95 (ISBN 0-669-00977-6). Lexington Bks.

Thompson, Carey C., ed. Institutional Adjustment: A Challenge to a Changing Economy. 194p. 1967. 12.00x (ISBN 0-292-73678-9). U of Tex Pr.

INSTITUTIONALISM (RELIGION)

Winter, Gibson. Religious Identity: The Organization of the Major Faiths. LC 68-9701. (Orig.). 1968. pap. 1.45 (ISBN 0-02-090150-X). Macmillan.

INSTITUTIONS, ASSOCIATIONS, ETC.

see Associations, Institutions, etc.

INSTITUTIONS, CHARITABLE AND PHILANTHROPIC

see Charities

INSTITUTIONS, ECCLESIASTICAL

see Religious and Ecclesiastical Institutions

INSTITUTIONS, INTERNATIONAL

see International Agencies; International Cooperation

INSTITUTIONS, PUBLIC

see Public Institutions

INSTRUCTION

see Education; Teaching; also subdivision Instruction and Study under Music and under names of musical instruments

INSTRUCTIONAL MATERIALS

see Teaching-Aids and Devices

INSTRUCTIONAL MATERIALS CENTERS

see also Instructional Materials Personnel

Allen, Kenneth W. & Allen, Loren. Organization & Administration of the Learning Resources Center in the Community College. 187p. 1973. 14.00 (ISBN 0-208-01306-7, Linnet). Shoe String.

Anderson, Jacqulyn, compiled by. How to Administer & Promote a Church Media Center: Church Media Center Development Plan, Stage 1. 1978. spiral bdg 4.95 (ISBN 0-8054-3702-9). Broadman.

--How to Classify, Catalog & Maintain Media: Church Media Center Development Plan, Stage 3. 1978. spiral bdg 4.95 (ISBN 0-8054-3704-5). Broadman.

--How to Process Media: Church Media Center Development Plan, Stage 2. 1978. pap. 4.95 (ISBN 0-8054-3703-7). Broadman.

Babin, Lawrence J. Library Media Center in the Public School. 1979. deluxe ed. 8.95 (ISBN 0-912492-12-0). Pyquag.

Beatty, LaMond F. Instructional Materials Centers. Duane, James E., ed. LC 80-21451. (The Instructional Media Library: Vol. 5). (Illus.). 104p. 1981. 13.95 (ISBN 0-87778-165-6). Educ Tech Pubns.

Blazek, Ron. Influencing Students Toward Media Center Use. LC 75-26769. (Studies in Librarianship Ser: No. 5). 238p. 1976. pap. text ed. 7.00 (ISBN 0-8389-0201-4). ALA.

Case, Robert N. & Lowrey, Anna M., eds. Curriculum Alternatives: Experiments in School Library Media Education. 254p. 1974. pap. 15.00 (ISBN 0-8389-3154-5). ALA.

Chibnall, Bernard. The Organisation of Media. 96p. 1976. 11.50 (ISBN 0-208-01525-6, Linnet). Shoe String.

Coburn, Louis. Library Media Center Problems - Case Studies. LC 73-2587. Orig. Title: Case Studies in School Library Administration. 128p. 1973. lib. bdg. 13.00 (ISBN 0-379-00019-9). Oceana.

Davidson & Steely. Using Learning Centers with Not Yet Readers: An Aid for ABC Darians. LC 77-20781. (Illus.). 1978. text ed. 12.95 (ISBN 0-87620-937-1); pap. text ed. 10.95 (ISBN 0-87620-936-3). Goodyear.

Delaney, Jack J. Media Program in the Elementory & Middle School: Its Organization & Administration. (Illus.). 222p. (Orig.). 1976. 15.00 (ISBN 0-208-01344-X, Linnet). Shoe String.

Dyer, Esther & Berger, Pam, eds. Public, School & Academic Media Centers: A Guide to Information Sources. LC 74-11554. (Books, Publishing & Libraries Information Guide Ser.: Vol. 3). 350p. 1980. 36.00 (ISBN 0-8103-1286-7). Gale.

Dyer, Esther R. Cultural Pluralism & Children's Media. (School Media Centers: Focus on Issues & Trends: No. 1). 1979. pap. 4.50 (ISBN 0-8389-3218-5). ALA.

Galvin, Thomas J., et al, eds. Excellence in School Media Programs: Essays Honoring Elizabeth T. Fast. LC 79-26944. 238p. 1980. 12.50 (ISBN 0-8389-3239-8). ALA.

Gaver, Mary V. Services of Secondary Schools Media Centers. LC 77-165675. pap. 5.00 (ISBN 0-8389-0095-X). ALA.

Gillespie, John T. Model School District Media Program. LC 77-5022. 1977. pap. text ed. 10.00 (ISBN 0-8389-3192-8). ALA.

Greff, Kasper N. & Askov, Eunice N. Learning Centers: An Ideabook for Reading & Language Arts. 1977. wire coil bdg. 5.95 (ISBN 0-8403-0931-7). Kendall Hunt.

Guide for the Conversion of School Libraries into Media Centres. (Educational Studies & Documents: No. 22). (Illus.). 1977. pap. 3.25 (ISBN 92-3-101389-0, U757, UNESCO). Unipub.

Hannigan, Jane A. & Estes, Glenn E., eds. Media Center Facilities Design. LC 78-9336. 1978. pap. 12.00 (ISBN 0-8389-3212-6). ALA.

Hart, Thomas L., ed. Instruction in School Media Center Use. LC 78-9717. 1978. pap. 9.00 (ISBN 0-8389-0255-3). ALA.

Hostrop, Richard W. Education Inside the Library Media Center. xiii, 178p. 1973. 15.00 (ISBN 0-208-01324-5, Linnet). Shoe String.

Kies, Cosette. Projecting a Positive Image Through Public Relations. (School Media Centers: Focus on Issues & Trends: No. 2). 1979. pap. 4.00 (ISBN 0-8389-3219-3). ALA.

Leopold, Carolyn C. School Libraries Worth Their Keep: A Philosophy Plus Tricks. LC 72-7497. (Illus.). 1972. 13.50 (ISBN 0-8108-0503-0). Scarecrow.

Liesener, James W. Instruments for Planning & Evaluating Library Media Programs. rev. ed. 1980. 3.00 (ISBN 0-911808-15-9). U of Md Lib Serv.

Margrabe, Mary M. Now Library-Media Center: A Stations Approach & Teaching Kit. rev. ed. LC 74-25396. (Illus.). 1975. pap. 8.95 (ISBN 0-87491-343-8). Acropolis.

Marlow, Eugene. Communications & the Corporation. LC 78-60103. (Illus.). 1978. pap. 4.95 (ISBN 0-915616-06-8). United Busn.

Martin, Betty. The Principal's Handbook on the School Library Media Center. Carson, Ben, ed. 1978. pap. 8.95 (ISBN 0-915794-22-5, 6553). Gaylord Prof Pubns.

Martin, Betty & Carson, Ben. The Principal's Handbook on the School Media Center. 212p. 1981. pap. 12.50x (ISBN 0-208-01912-X, Lib Prof Pubns). Shoe String.

Merrill, Irving R. & Drob, Harold A. Criteria for Planning the College & University Learning Resources Center. Wallington, Clint, ed. LC 77-2612. 1977. pap. 6.45 (ISBN 0-89240-003-X). Assn Ed Comm Tech.

Nickel, Mildred L. Steps to Service: A Handbook of Procedures for the School Library Media Center. LC 74-19420. 136p. 1975. pap. 5.00 (ISBN 0-8389-0161-1). ALA.

Polette, Nancy. Developing Methods of Inquiry: A Source Book for Elementary Media Personnel. LC 72-11992. 1973. 10.00 (ISBN 0-8108-0575-8). Scarecrow.

--In-Service: School Library - Media Workshops & Conferences. LC 73-12095. 1973. 11.50 (ISBN 0-8108-0658-4). Scarecrow.

Prostano, Emanuel T. & Prostano, Joyce S. The School Library Media Center. 2nd ed. LC 76-30402. (Library Science Text Ser). (Illus.). 1977. lib. bdg. 15.00x (ISBN 0-87287-137-1). Libs Unl.

Schmid, William T. Media Center Management: A Practical Guide. new ed. (Studies in Media Management). (Illus.). 1980. 16.95 (ISBN 0-8038-4730-0, Communication Arts); pap. 9.95x (ISBN 0-8038-4731-9). Hastings.

School Library Manpower Project. Occupational Definitions for School Library Media Personnel. LC 72-151111. 1970. pap. 3.00 (ISBN 0-8389-3125-1). ALA.

Shapiro, Lillian L. Teaching Yourself in Libraries. 1978. 6.00 ea. (ISBN 0-8242-0628-2); 25 or more copies 4.00 ea. Wilson.

Silverman, Eleanor. One Hundred One Media Center Ideas. LC 80-17034. 213p. 1980. pap. 13.50 (ISBN 0-8108-1329-7). Scarecrow.

Spirt, Diana L. Library-Media Manual. 1979. 6.00 (ISBN 0-8242-0615-0). Wilson.

Stroud, Janet G. Evaluative Case Studies of School Library Media Center Services: The PSES Approach. 1979. 17.00 (ISBN 0-931510-04-X). Hi Willow.

Walker, H. Thomas & Montgomery, Paula K. Teaching Media Skills: An Instructional Program for Elementary & Middle School Students. LC 76-30605. 1977. lib. bdg. 17.50x (ISBN 0-87287-135-5). Libs Unl.

Woolls, E. Blanche. Ideas for School Library Media Centers. 1978. 13.00x (ISBN 0-931510-02-3). Hi Willow.

Wynar, Christine L. Guide to Reference Books for School Media Centers. LC 73-87523. 473p. 1973. lib. bdg. 19.50- (ISBN 0-87287-069-3). Libs Unl.

INSTRUCTIONAL MATERIALS PERSONNEL

see also Audio-Visual Education

American Association of School Librarians. Certification Model for Professional School Media Personnel. 40p. 1976. pap. 2.00 (ISBN 0-8389-3179-0). ALA.

Brown, James W. & Norberg, Kenneth. Administering Educational Media: Instructional Technology & Library Services. 2nd ed. (Illus.). 384p. 1972. text ed. 17.95 (ISBN 0-07-008326-6, C). McGraw.

--Administering Educational Media: Instructional Technology & Library Services. 2nd ed. (Illus.). 384p. 1972. text ed. 17.95 (ISBN 0-07-008326-6, C). McGraw.

Erickson, Carlton W. Administering Instructional Media Programs. LC 68-12281. (Illus.). 1968. text ed. 22.95 (ISBN 0-02-333980-2, 33398). Macmillan.

Miller, James D., ed. Media Canada: Guidelines for Educators. 2nd rev. ed. 1970. 4.50 (ISBN 0-08-016508-7). Pergamon.

National Association of Secondary School Principals. The Assistant Principalship. 1970. pap. 5.50 (ISBN 0-88210-010-6). Natl Assn Principals.

Rudman, Jack. Audio-Visual Technician. (Career Examination Ser.: C-1894). (Cloth bdg. avail. on request). 1977. pap. 8.00 (ISBN 0-8373-1894-7). Natl Learning.

--Senior Audio-Visual Aid Technician. (Career Examination Ser.: C-1471). (Cloth bdg. avail. on request). pap. 8.00 (ISBN 0-8373-1471-2). Natl Learning.

Vandergrift, Kay. The Teaching Role of the School Media Specialist. (School Media Centers: Focus on Issues & Trends: No. 3). 1979. pap. 4.00 (ISBN 0-8389-3222-3). ALA.

INSTRUCTIONAL OBJECTIVES

see Education-Aims and Objectives

INSTRUCTIONAL SUPERVISION

see School Supervision

INSTRUCTIONAL SYSTEMS ANALYSIS

see Educational Statistics

INSTRUCTIONAL TECHNOLOGY

see Educational Technology

INSTRUCTIONS TO JURIES

A M J I Drafting Committee, ed. Arkansas Model Criminal Jury Instructions. 1979. 65.00 (ISBN 0-87215-229-4). Michie-Bobbs.

Aaronson, David E. Maryland Criminal Jury Instructions & Commentary. LC 75-2870. 453p. 1976. 25.00 (ISBN 0-87215-165-4). Michie-Bobbs.

Calhoun, Marcus B., et al, eds. Suggested Pattern Jury Instructions: Civil Cases, Vol. 1. LC 80-14282. 335p. 1980. ring bind 35.00 (ISBN 0-89854-060-7). U of GA Inst Govt.

Committee on Pattern Jury Instructions of the Maryland Bar Association, Inc. Maryland Pattern Jury Instructions: Civil. LC 77-72007. 1977. 47.50 (ISBN 0-686-21281-9). Lawyers Co-Op.

Dowsey, James L., Jr. Charges to the Jury in a Criminal Case for New York, 2 Vols. 1969. Set. 60.00 (ISBN 0-685-05158-7). Acme Law.

McBride, Robert L. Art of Instructing the Jury with 1978 Supplement. 545p. 1969. text ed. 45.00 (ISBN 0-686-77436-1). Anderson Pub Co.

Model Jury Instructions in Virginia: Civil, 2 vols. 1980. Set. 90.00 (ISBN 0-87215-284-7); Vol. I. (ISBN 0-87215-282-0). Vol. II. Michie-Bobbs.

Model Jury Instructions in Virginia: Criminal, 2 vols. 1979. 90.00 set (ISBN 0-87215-281-2). Vol. 1 (ISBN 0-87215-230-8). Vol. 2 (ISBN 0-87215-231-6). 1980 suppl. 20.00 (ISBN 0-87215-333-9). Michie-Bobbs.

Reid's Branson Instruction to Juries, 7 Vols. 3rd ed. Set. with 1980 suppl. 175.00 (ISBN 0-672-84048-0, Bobbs-Merrill Law); 1980 suppl. 60.00 (ISBN 0-672-84285-8). Michie-Bobbs.

Thompson, Seymour D. Charging the Jury: A Monograph. xxviii, 196p. 1980. Repr. of 1880 ed. lib. bdg. 20.00x (ISBN 0-8377-2628-X). Rothman.

INSTRUCTIVE GAMES

see Educational Games

INSTRUCTORS

see College Teachers

INSTRUMENT FLYING

Aviation Supplies & Academics. Instrument Pilot Airplane Test. 1980. pap. text ed. 9.95 (ISBN 0-686-73504-8, Pub. by ASA). Aviation.

Bohrer, Walt & Bohrer, Ann. This Is Your Captain Speaking. LC 74-31054. (Illus.). 1975. 7.95 (ISBN 0-8168-9000-5). Aero.

Culver, Henry H., Jr. IFR Pocket Simulator Procedures. LC 76-27149. (Illus.). 1976. spiral bdg. 14.95 (ISBN 0-9601062-1-9, Pub. by FIP). Aviation.

Flatau, Courtney L. & Mitchell, Jerome F. The Instrument Pilot Handbook: A Reference Manual & Exam Guide. 252p. 1980. 24.95 (ISBN 0-442-22411-7); pap. 16.95 (ISBN 0-442-22412-5). Van Nos Reinhold.

Flying Magazine Editors. Flying Wisdom. 1979. 13.95 (ISBN 0-442-22452-4). Van Nos Reinhold.

The Instrument Rating. 22nd, rev. ed. LC 77-89942. 1979. soft bdg. 17.95 (ISBN 0-87219-002-1). Pan Am Nav.

Reithmaier, L. W. Instrument Pilot's Guide. 2nd ed. LC 74-30480. (Illus.). 206p. 1974. pap. 10.95 (ISBN 0-8168-7305-4). Aero.

Taylor, Richard L. Instrument Flying. (Illus.). 288p. 1972. 8.95 (ISBN 0-02-616680-1). Macmillan.

INSTRUMENT INDUSTRY

see also Scientific Apparatus and Instruments

Advances in Instrumentation: Houston, 1976, 4 pts, Vol. 31. LC 52-29277. 1976. text ed. 30.00 ea. Pt. 1 (ISBN 0-87664-302-0). Pt. 2 (ISBN 0-87664-303-9). Pt. 3 (ISBN 0-87664-304-7). Pt. 4 (ISBN 0-87664-305-5). Set. text ed. 100.00 (ISBN 0-686-57976-3). Instru Soc.

Curtis, Tony, ed. Instruments. (Illus.). 1978. 3.95 (ISBN 0-902921-39-8). Apollo.

Instrument Maintenance Management, Vol. 11. LC 67-13017. 1976. pap. text ed. 9.00 (ISBN 0-87664-297-0). Instru Soc.

INSTRUMENT LANDING SYSTEMS

Howard, Lou T. Flying the I.L.S. Tips, Theories, Techniques. 2nd ed. (Illus.). 400p. 1979. pap. 14.50 (ISBN 0-911721-73-8, Pub. by Lgoma). Aviation.

INSTRUMENT MANUFACTURE

Horne, D. F. Dividing, Ruling & Mask-Making. LC 74-7856. (Illus.). 315p. 1974. 62.50x (ISBN 0-8448-0359-6). Crane Russak Co.

INSTRUMENTAL ANALYSIS

Bastiansen, William. Instrumental Analysis. 1979. pap. text ed. 8.50 (ISBN 0-89669-016-4). Collegium Bk Pubs.

Bauer, Henry H., et al. Instrumental Analysis. 1978. text ed. 27.95 (ISBN 0-205-05922-8). Allyn.

Ettre, Leslie & McFadden, William, eds. Ancillary Techniques of Gas Chromatography. LC 78-9476. (Chemical Analysis Ser.). 408p. 1978. Repr. of 1969 ed. lib. bdg. 24.50 (ISBN 0-88275-705-9). Krieger.

Gouw, T. H. Guide to Modern Methods of Instrumental Analysis. LC 79-171913. 510p. 1972. 38.00 (ISBN 0-471-31925-2). Krieger.

ISA Symposium, 21st, Philadelphia, May 8, 1975. Analysis Instrumentation, Vol. 13. 1975. pap. text ed. 20.00 (ISBN 0-87664-262-8). Instru Soc.

Krugers, J. & Keulemans, A. I., eds. Practical Instrumental Analysis. 1965. 29.50 (ISBN 0-444-40342-6). Elsevier.

MacLeod, A. J. Instrumental Methods of Food Analysis. LC 72-7618. (Illus.). 802p. 1973. 60.95 (ISBN 0-470-56308-7). Halsted Pr.

Mann, Charles K., et al. Instrumental Analysis. 755p. 1974. text ed. 35.50 scp (ISBN 0-06-042535-0, HarpC). Har-Row.

O'Connor, R. T., ed. Instrumental Analysis of Cotton Cellulose & Modified Cotton Cellulose. (Fiber Science Ser: Vol. 3). 504p. 1972. 59.50 (ISBN 0-8247-1500-4). Dekker.

Robinson, James W. Undergraduate Instrumental Analysis. 2nd ed. 400p. 1973. 14.75 (ISBN 0-8247-6082-4). Dekker.

Strobel, H. A. Chemical Instrumentation. 2nd ed. 1973. 26.95 (ISBN 0-201-07301-3). A-W.

Walton, Harold F. & Reyes, Jorge. Modern Chemical Analysis & Instrumentation. (Undergraduate Chemistry Ser.: Vol. 2). 368p. 1973. 23.50 (ISBN 0-8247-6033-6). Dekker.

Welcher, Frank J., ed. Standard Methods of Chemical Analysis: Instrumental Methods, Vol. IIIA. 6th ed. LC 74-23465. 996p. 1975. Repr. of 1966 ed. 43.50 (ISBN 0-88275-342-8). Kreiger.

--Standard Methods of Chemical Analysis: Instrumental Methods, Vol. IIIB. 6th ed. LC 74-23465. 1060p. 1975. Repr. of 1966 ed. 53.00 (ISBN 0-88275-253-7). Krieger.

Willard, Hobarth, et al. Instrumental Methods of Analysis. 5th ed. 850p. 1974. text ed. 18.95x (ISBN 0-442-29479-4); solutions manual 2.50x (ISBN 0-442-29483-2). D Van Nostrand.

INSTRUMENTAL BEHAVIOR

see Operant Behavior

INSTRUMENTAL MUSIC

see also Band Music; Chamber Music; Dance Music; Military Music; Orchestral Music; Percussion Music;

also Piano Music, Organ Music and similar headings

Agay, Denes. More Easy Classics to Moderns. 160p. pap. 5.95 (ISBN 0-8256-4027-X). Music Sales.

Agay, Denes, ed. Easy Classics to Moderns. 160p. pap. 5.95 (ISBN 0-8256-4017-2). Music Sales.

Applebaum, Samuel & Roth, Henry. The Way They Play: Book 5. (Illus.). 320p. 1978. 9.95 (ISBN 0-87666-449-4, Z-11). Paganiniana Pubns.

Barlow, Harold & Morgenstern, Sam, eds. Dictionary of Musical Themes. rev. ed. (Illus.). 1976. 10.95 (ISBN 0-517-52446-5). Crown.

Beck, Syndey, ed. English Instrumental Music of the Sixteenth & Seventeenth Centuries from Manuscripts in the New York Public Library, 2 vols. Incl. Vol. 1. Nine Fantasies in Four Parts. Byrd, et al.; Vol. 2. Four Suites. Locke, Mathew. write to C.F. Peters Corp. N.Y. for prices (ISBN 0-685-22863-0). NY Pub Lib.

Burnett, Millie & Cummins, Mary Ann. Texas Tales & Tunes: A Suite for Speech, Voices, & Orff Instruments. 1977. pap. 3.50 (ISBN 0-918812-00-3). Magnamusic.

Darling, J. S., ed. A Jefferson Music Book: Keyboard Pieces, Some with Violin Accompaniment. LC 76-30510. 1977. 8.95x (ISBN 0-87935-043-1, Colonial Williamsburg Foundation). U Pr of Va.

Davison, Archibald T. & Apel, Willi, eds. Historical Anthology of Music, 2 vols. Incl. Vol. 1. Oriental, Medieval, & Renaissance Music. rev. ed. (Illus.). 258p. 1949 (ISBN 0-674-39300-7); Vol. 2. Baroque, Rococo, & Pre-Classical Music. (Illus.). 303p. 1950 (ISBN 0-674-39301-5). LC 49-4339. 15.00 ea. Harvard U Pr.

Diabelli, Anton, et al. The Diabelli Variations: Variations on a Theme by Fifty Composers & Virtuosos. 1977. pap. 10.00 (ISBN 0-912028-09-2). Music Treasure.

Duckles, Vincent & Elmer, Minnie. Thematic Catalog of a Manuscript Collection of Eighteenth-Century Italian Instrumental Music in the University of California, Berkeley, Music Library. LC 63-16571. 1963. 28.75x (ISBN 0-520-00361-6). U of Cal Pr.

Foster, Stephen C. Biography, Songs, & Musical Compositions of Stephen C. Foster. LC 74-24086. Repr. of 1896 ed. 40.00 (ISBN 0-404-12915-3). AMS Pr.

Moon, John C., et al. Medleys. LC 75-19259. (Music of the Fifes & Drums Ser.: Vol. 3). 1980. pap. 2.50 (ISBN 0-87935-050-4). Williamsburg.

Oddo, Vincent. Playing & Teaching the Strings. 208p. 1979. pap. text ed. 15.95x (ISBN 0-534-00614-0). Wadsworth Pub.

Parrish, Carl. Treasury of Early Music. (Illus.). 1964. pap. 6.95x (ISBN 0-393-09444-8, NortonC). records avail. Norton.

Starr, William J. & Devine, George F., eds. Music Scores Omnibus. Incl. Pt. 2. Romantic & Impressionist Music. 1964. pap. text ed. 19.95 (ISBN 0-13-608216-5). 1964. P-H.

Verdi, Giuseppe. Falstaff. 480p. 1980. pap. 10.95 (ISBN 0-486-24017-7). Dover.

Von Wasielewski, Wilhelm J. Anthology of Instrumental Music from the End of the Sixteenth to the End of the Seventeenth Century. LC 68-14234. 50p. 1974. lib. bdg. 22.50 (ISBN 0-306-70951-1). Da Capo.

INSTRUMENTAL MUSIC-BIBLIOGRAPHY

Arling, Harry J. Trombone Chamber Music: An Annotated Bibliography. LC 78-11714. (Brass Research Ser.: No. 8). 1978. pap. text ed. 3.50 (ISBN 0-914282-23-9). Brass Pr.

Brown, Howard M. Instrumental Music Printed Before 1600: A Bibliography. LC 65-12783. (Illus.). 1965. 30.00x (ISBN 0-674-45610-6). Harvard U Pr.

Fantini, Girolamo. Modo per imparare a Sonare di Tromba. Tarr, Edward H., tr. LC 75-17501. (Brass Research Ser.: No. 7). (Illus.). 1978. Repr. of 1638 ed. 25.00 (ISBN 0-914282-10-7). Brass Pr.

Helm, Sanford M. Catalog of Chamber Music for Wind Instruments. rev. ed. LC 70-86597. (Music Reprint Ser). 1969. Repr. of 1952 ed. lib. bdg. 14.50 (ISBN 0-306-71490-6). Da Capo.

Hill, George R. A Thematic Catalog of the Instrumental Music of Florian Leopold Gassmann. (Music Indexes & Bibliographies: No. 12). 1976. 25.00 (ISBN 0-913574-12-0). Eur-Am Music.

INSTRUMENTAL MUSIC-DISCOGRAPHY

Coover, J. & Colvig, R. Medieval & Renaissance Music on Long-Playing Records. (Detroit Studies in Music Bibliography Ser.: No. 6). 1964. pap. 2.00 (ISBN 0-911772-26-X). Info Coord.

INSTRUMENTAL MUSIC-HISTORY AND CRITICISM

see also Bands (Music); Musical Instruments; Orchestra;

also various forms of instrumental music e.g. Sonata, Symphony

Barbour, J. Murray. Trumpets, Horns & Music. 1964. 10.00 (ISBN 0-87013-079-X). Mich St U Pr.

Hayes, Gerald R. Musical Instruments & Their Music: 1500-1750, 2 vols. in 1. LC 74-26053. Repr. of 1930 ed. 24.50 (ISBN 0-404-12958-7). AMS Pr.

Pearce, Wesley. Intonation Studies for Band. (Illus.). 238p. 1977. 11.00 (ISBN 0-87421-093-3). Utah St U Pr.

Von Wasielewski, Wilhelm J. Anthology of Instrumental Music from the End of the Sixteenth to the End of the Seventeenth Century. LC 68-14234. 50p. 1974. lib. bdg. 22.50 (ISBN 0-306-70951-1). Da Capo.

INSTRUMENTAL MUSIC-INSTRUCTION AND STUDY

see also names of specific musical instruments with or without the subdivision Instruction and Study

Colwell, Richard J. Teaching of Instrumental Music. (Illus.). 1969. 17.50 (ISBN 0-13-893131-3). P-H.

Green, Elizabeth A. Orchestral Bowings & Routines. 1963. pap. 4.80 (ISBN 0-87506-007-2). Campus.

John, Robert W. & Douglas, Charles N. Playing Social & Recreational Instruments. (Illus.). 144p. 1972. pap. text ed. 10.95 (ISBN 0-13-683680-1). P-H.

Kohut, Daniel L. Instrumental Music Pedagogy. (Illus.). 256p. 1973. ref. ed. 14.95 (ISBN 0-13-467944-X). P-H.

Kusel, George. The Martial Musician's Mentor: A Complete Course of Instruction for the Fife, Pt. 1. rev., 2nd ed. (Illus.). 52p. (gr. 6 up). 1979. pap. 4.95 (ISBN 0-9604476-1-X). Kusel.

Lane, William S. The Secondary School Music Laboratory: An Accelerated Program for Teaching Instrumental Skills in the General Music Classroom. (Illus.). 1977. 13.95 (ISBN 0-13-797597-X, Parker). P-H.

Pottle, Ralph R. Tuning the School Band & Orchestra. LC 72-133787. (gr. 7-12). 1980. lib. bdg. 9.00 (ISBN 0-911162-01-1); card form tuning guides for 14 different instruments 0.15 ea. Pottle.

Read, Gardner. Contemporary Instrumental Techniques. LC 75-27455. (Illus.). 1976. 17.50 (ISBN 0-02-872100-4). Schirmer Bks.

Saucier, Gene A. Woodwinds: Fundamental Performance Techniques. LC 80-5223. (Illus.). 300p. 1981. pap. text ed. 12.95 (ISBN 0-02-872300-7). Schirmer Bks.

Schneider, Max F. Beitrage Zu Einer Anleitung Clavichord und Cembalo Zu Spielen. (Keyboard Studies: Vol. 2). (Illus.). xi, 120p. 30.00 (ISBN 90-6027-339-7, Pub. by Frits Knuf Netherlands). Pendragon NY.

Turk, Daniel G. Anweisung Zum Generalbass-Spielen. Repr. of 1971 ed. wrappers 35.00 (ISBN 90-6027-137-8, Pub. by Frits Knuf Netherlands). Pendragon NY.

INSTRUMENTATION AND ORCHESTRATION

see also Arrangement (Music); Musical Instruments

Alexander, Van. First Chart. Haskell, Jimmie, ed. LC 70-182858. 112p. 1971. 9.95, incl. 2 records (ISBN 0-685-25440-2). Criterion Mus.

Berlioz, Hector. A Treatise on Modern Instrumentation & Orchestration. 1976. 49.00 (ISBN 0-403-06679-4, Regency). Scholarly.

Blatter, Alfred. Instrumentation-Orchestration. (Longman Music Ser.). 1980. pap. text ed. 18.95x (ISBN 0-582-28118-0). Longman.

Burton, Steven D. Orchestration. 500p. 1982. 19.95 (ISBN 0-13-639500-7); wkbk. 9.95 (ISBN 0-686-76603-2). P-H.

Carse, Adam. History of Orchestration. (Illus.). 7.50 (ISBN 0-8446-1816-0). Peter Smith.

--The History of Orchestration. (Illus.). 1935. pap. 5.00 (ISBN 0-486-21258-0). Dover.

Carse, Adam V. The History of Orchestration. 59.95 (ISBN 0-8490-0342-3). Gordon Pr.

Coerne, Louis A. The Evolution of Modern Orchestration. LC 74-26035. Repr. of 1908 ed. 28.50 (ISBN 0-404-12881-5). AMS Pr.

Evans, Edwin. Method of Instrumentation. Repr. lib. bdg. 25.00 (ISBN 0-403-03763-8). Scholarly.

Fiske, Roger. Score Reading, 4 vols. Incl. Vol. 1. Orchestration. 1958. 5.75 (ISBN 0-19-321301-X); Vol. 2. Musical Form. 1958. 5.75 (ISBN 0-19-321302-8); Vol. 3. Concertos. 1960. 5.75 (ISBN 0-19-321303-6); Vol. 4. Oratorios. 1955. 5.75 (ISBN 0-19-321304-4). (YA) (gr. 9up). Oxford U Pr.

Fortina, Carl. Accordion, As Written. LC 61-3658. (Illus.). 1961. pap. 3.00 (ISBN 0-910736-02-2). Holly-Pix.

Heacox, Arthur. Project Lessons in Orchestration. LC 74-28557. Repr. of 1928 ed. 18.00 (ISBN 0-404-13381-9). AMS Pr.

Jacob, Gordon. Elements of Orchestration. (Illus.). 1965. 7.95 (ISBN 0-8079-0043-5). October.

--The Elements of Orchestration. LC 76-15191. 1976. Repr. of 1962 ed. lib. bdg. 22.25x (ISBN 0-8371-8955-1, JAEO). Greenwood.

--Orchestral Technique: A Manual for Students. 2nd ed. 1940. 6.95 (ISBN 0-19-318201-7). Oxford U Pr.

Kennan, Kent. Technique of Orchestration. 2nd ed. (Music Ser). (Illus.). 1970. 19.95 (ISBN 0-13-900316-9); wkbk. 2 9.50 (ISBN 0-13-900340-1); wkbk. 6.95 (ISBN 0-13-900332-0). P-H.

Korn, Richard. Orchestral Accents. facsimile ed. LC 79-156673. (Essay Index Reprint Ser). Repr. of 1956 ed. 18.00 (ISBN 0-8369-2320-0). Arno.

Mancini, Henry. Sounds & Scores. 244p. 1973. Repr. 19.95 (ISBN 0-89524-060-2, 4001). Cherry Lane.

Mason, Daniel G. Orchestral Instruments & What They Do: A Primer for Concert-Goers. LC 75-109785. (Illus.). 1971. Repr. of 1909 ed. lib. bdg. 15.00 (ISBN 0-8371-4275-X, MAOI). Greenwood.

Oboussier, Philippe. Arranging Music for Young Players: A Handbook on Basic Orchestration. 184p. 1977. pap. 12.00 (ISBN 0-19-321495-4). Oxford U Pr.

Parrott, Ian. Method in Orchestration. (Student's Music Library Ser). 1956. 6.95 (ISBN 0-234-77310-3). Dufour.

Piston, Walter. Orchestration. (Illus.). 1955. 17.95x (ISBN 0-393-09740-4, NortonC). Norton.

Prout, E. Instrumentation. LC 68-25302. (Studies in Music, No. 42). (Illus.). 1969. Repr. of 1877 ed. lib. bdg. 45.95 (ISBN 0-8383-0314-5). Haskell.

Prout, Ebenezer. Instrumentation. LC 79-108529. 1970. Repr. of 1877 ed. 14.00 (ISBN 0-403-00324-5). Scholarly.

--The Orchestra, 2 vols. (Illus.). 577p. Repr. of 1899 ed. 49.00 (ISBN 0-403-00322-9). Scholarly.

Read, Gardner. Style & Orchestration. LC 77-15884. 1979. 19.95 (ISBN 0-02-872110-1). Schirmer Bks.

--Thesaurus of Orchestral Devices. Repr. of 1953 ed. lib. bdg. 45.00x (ISBN 0-8371-1884-0, REOD). Greenwood.

Rimsky-Korsakov, Nikolay. Principles of Orchestration. 1922. pap. text ed. 7.50 (ISBN 0-486-21266-1). Dover.

--Principles of Orchestration: With Musical Examples Drawn from His Own Works, 2 Vols. in 1. Steinberg, Maximilian, ed. 11.50 (ISBN 0-8446-2813-1). Peter Smith.

Rogers, Bernard. Art of Orchestration: Principles of Tone Color in Modern Scoring. Repr. of 1951 ed. lib. bdg. 15.00x (ISBN 0-8371-2969-9, ROAO). Greenwood.

Russo, William. Jazz Composition & Orchestration. LC 67-20580. (Illus.). 1968. 30.00x (ISBN 0-226-73212-6). U of Chicago Pr.

Sebesky, Donald. The Contemporary Arranger. LC 75-23493. 225p. 1975. spiral bdg. 20.00 (ISBN 0-88284-032-0). Alfred Pub.

Singleton, Esther. The Orchestra & Its Instruments. LC 76-22351. (Illus.). 1976. Repr. of 1917 ed. lib. bdg. 40.00 (ISBN 0-89341-004-7). Longwood Pr.

Wagner, Joseph F. Band Scoring. (Music Ser.). 1960. text ed. 15.95 (ISBN 0-07-067658-5, C). McGraw.

--Orchestration: A Practical Handbook. 1959. text ed. 15.95 (ISBN 0-07-067655-0, C); wkbk. 7.95 (ISBN 0-07-067656-9). McGraw.

INSTRUMENTS, AERONAUTICAL

see Aeronautical Instruments

INSTRUMENTS, ASTRONOMICAL

see Astronomical Instruments

INSTRUMENTS, DENTAL

see Dental Instruments and Apparatus

INSTRUMENTS, ELECTRIC

see Electric Apparatus and Appliances

INSTRUMENTS, ELECTRONIC

see Electronic Instruments

INSTRUMENTS, ENGINEERING

see Engineering Instruments

INSTRUMENTS, MATHEMATICAL

see Mathematical Instruments

INSTRUMENTS, MEASURING

see Measuring Instruments

INSTRUMENTS, MEDICAL

see Medical Instruments and Apparatus

INSTRUMENTS, METEOROLOGICAL

see Meteorological Instruments

INSTRUMENTS, MUSICAL

see Musical Instruments

INSTRUMENTS, NAUTICAL

see Nautical Instruments

INSTRUMENTS, NEGOTIABLE

see Negotiable Instruments

INSTRUMENTS, OCEANOGRAPHIC

see Oceanographic Instruments

INSTRUMENTS, OPTICAL

see Optical Instruments

INSTRUMENTS, PERCUSSION

see Percussion Instruments

INSTRUMENTS, PHYSICAL

see Physical Instruments

INSTRUMENTS, SCIENTIFIC

see Scientific Apparatus and Instruments

INSTRUMENTS, SURGICAL

see Surgical Instruments and Apparatus

INSTRUMENTS, SURVEYING

see Surveying-Instruments

INSTRUMENTS OF WAR

see Munitions

INSUBORDINATION

see also Mutiny

INSULAR FLORA AND FAUNA

see Island Flora and Fauna

INSULATING MATERIALS

see also Electric Insulators and Insulation

Business Communications Co. Substitutes for Asbestos, Gb-061: What-Who-How Much. 1981. 850.00 (ISBN 0-89336-277-8). BCC.

Hess, L. Y., ed. Insulation Guide for Buildings & Industrial Processes. LC 79-84430. (Energy Technology Review Ser.: No. 43). (Illus.). 1979. 24.00 (ISBN 0-8155-0752-6). Noyes.

National Association of Home Builders. Insulation Manual: Homes & Apartments. 2nd. ed. 149p. 1979. pap. 12.50 (ISBN 0-86718-061-7). Natl Assn Home Builders.

• Rees, G. J., ed. Semi-Insulating III-V Materials Nottingham 1980. 367p. 42.50 (ISBN 0-906812-05-4, Pub. by Shiva Pub England). Imprint Edns.

Symposium on Insulation-Materials & Processes for Aerospace & Hydrospace Applications, San Francisco, Ca. May 25-28, 1965. Proceedings. (Science of Advanced Materials & Process Engineering Ser., Vol. 8). pap. 8.00 (ISBN 0-938994-08-5). Soc Adv Material.

Thermal Insulating Measurements. 1968. pap. 3.00 (ISBN 0-685-99178-4, IIR12, IIR). Unipub.

INSULATION (ELECTRIC)

see Electric Insulators and Insulation

INSULATION (HEAT)

Burberry, Peter. Building for Energy Conservation. LC 77-17943. 1978. 16.95 (ISBN 0-470-99350-2). Halsted Pr.

Business Communications Staff. Insulation: A Resurging Business: E-035. 1981. 750.00 (ISBN 0-89336-293-X). BCC.

Close, Paul D. Sound Control & Thermal Insulation of Buildings. 1966. 24.50 (ISBN 0-442-35058-9). Van Nos Reinhold.

Comparative Tests of the Thermal Performance of an Insulated Vehicle. 1970. pap. 5.50 (ISBN 0-685-99127-X, IIR2, IIR). Unipub.

Derricott, Robert & Chissick, Seymour. Energy Conservation & Thermal Insulation: Properties of Materials - Safety & Environmental Factors. LC 80-41587. 1981. 112.50 (ISBN 0-471-27930-7, Pub. by Wiley-Interscience). Wiley.

Dillon, J. B. Thermal Insulation: Recent Developments. LC 77-15218. (Chemical Technology Review No. 99; Energy Technology Review No. 23). (Illus.). 1978. 39.00 (ISBN 0-8155-0687-2). Noyes.

Gay, Larry. The Complete Book of Insulating. LC 79-23945. (Illus.). 1980. 12.95 (ISBN 0-8289-0364-6); pap. 7.95 (ISBN 0-8289-0365-4). Greene.
Hardenbrook, Harry. Insulators Estimating Handbook. (Illus.). 128p. (Orig.). 1980. pap. 8.50 (ISBN 0-911592-50-4). F R Walker.
Heat Transmission Measurements in Thermal Insulations. 1974. 30.75 (ISBN 0-686-52110-2, 04-544000-10). ASTM.
Insulation Specification. 54p. 1981. 6.00 (ISBN 0-686-73909-4). Natl Assn Home.
Jones, R. Framing, Sheathing & Insulation. LC 73-1847. 235p. 1973. pap. 7.00 (ISBN 0-8273-0096-4); answer book 1.60 (ISBN 0-8273-0097-2). Delmar.
Kovach, E. G., ed. Thermal Energy Storage. LC 77-71233. 1977. pap. text ed. 9.50 (ISBN 0-08-021724-9). Pergamon.
Langdon, Bill. Movable Insulation. (Illus.). 1980. 14.95 (ISBN 0-87857-298-8); pap. 9.95 (ISBN 0-87857-310-0). Rodale Pr Inc.
McGrath, Ed. The Superinsulated House: A Working Guide for Owner-Builders & Architects. (Illus.). 128p. 1981. 13.95 (ISBN 0-918270-11-1); pap. 9.95 (ISBN 0-918270-12-X). That New Pub.
Marsh, Paul. Thermal Insulation & Condensation. (Illus.). 1979. text ed. 32.00x (ISBN 0-86095-814-0). Longman.
Methods of Measurement of the Insulation & Gas-Tightness of Insulated Bodies for Transport of Perishable Foodstuffs. 1970. pap. 9.00 (ISBN 0-685-99157-1, IIR4, IIR). Unipub.
NAHB Thermal Performance Guidelines: Apartments & Condominiums. 41p. 1978. pap. 7.00 (ISBN 0-86718-071-4). Natl Assn Home Builders.
National Association of Home Builders. NAHB Thermal Performance Guidelines: One & Two - Family Dwellings. rev. ed. 32p. 1978. 7.00 (ISBN 0-86718-072-2). Natl Assn Home Builders.
Nielsen, Sally E., ed. Insulating the Old House: A Handbook for the Owner. (Illus.). 1979. pap. 1.95 (ISBN 0-9600612-7-4). Greater Portland.
Probert, S. D. & Hub, D. R., eds. Thermal Insulation. (Illus.). 1968. text ed. 26.00x (ISBN 0-444-20025-8, Pub. by Applied Science). Burgess-Intl Ideas.
Sunset Editors. Insulation & Weatherstripping. LC 77-90718. (Illus.). 80p. 1978. pap. 4.95 (ISBN 0-376-01263-3, Sunset Bks). Sunset-Lane.
Thermal Insulating Covers for NPS Piping, Vessel Lagging & Dished Head Segments. 1965. pap. 6.25 (ISBN 0-686-51973-6, 12-304500-00). ASTM.
Thermal Insulating Measurements. 1968. pap. 3.00 (ISBN 0-685-99178-4, IIR12, IIR). Unipub.
Thermal Insulations in the Petrochemical Industry. (Special Technical Publications Ser.). 28p. 1975. soft cover 3.25x (ISBN 0-686-76096-4, 581, 04-581000-10). ASTM.
Thermal Transmission Measurements of Insulation. (Special Technical Publications Ser.). 458p. 1979. 39.50x (ISBN 0-686-76095-6, 660, 04-660000-10). ASTM.
Turner, William C. Thermal Insulation for Buildings: Economic Design for Comfort & Safety in Homes & Buildings. 1981. write for info. (ISBN 0-88275-985-X). Krieger.
Turner, William C. & Malloy, John F. Handbook of Thermal Insulation Design Economics for Pipes & Equipment. LC 79-13584. 376p. 1980. lib. bdg. 55.00 (ISBN 0-88275-837-3). Krieger.
--Thermal Insulation Handbook. LC 76-52962. 570p. (Orig.). 1981. Repr. of 1969 ed. 62.50 (ISBN 0-88275-510-2). Krieger.
--Thermal Insulation Handbook. 624p. 1981. 59.50 (ISBN 0-07-039805-4). McGraw.
--Thermal Insulation Handbook. 2nd ed. LC 76-52962. 570p. 1981. lib. bdg. 62.50 (ISBN 0-88275-510-2). Krieger.
United States Department of Housing & Urban Development. How to Insulate Your Home & Save Fuel. 7.50 (ISBN 0-8446-5619-4). Peter Smith.
Wolf, Ray. Rodale Plans Insulating Window Shade. (Illus.). 86p. 1980. 14.95 (ISBN 0-87857-311-9). Rodale Pr Inc.
Wood, Barry. Complete Home Insulation. (Illus.). 1979. 14.95 (ISBN 0-7153-7799-X). David & Charles.

INSULATION (SOUND)

see Soundproofing

INSULIN

see also Hypoglycemia

Altszuler, N., et al. Insulin Two. Hasselblatt, A. & Brushhausen, F. V., eds. (Handbook of Experimental Pharmacology, Vol. 32, Pt. 2). (Illus.). 880p. 1975. 158.20 (ISBN 0-387-07006-0). Springer-Verlag.
Bajaj, J. S., ed. Insulin & Metabolism. 1977. 53.75 (ISBN 90-219-2105-7, North Holland). Elsevier.
Brandenburg, D., ed. Insulin: Chemistry, Structure & Function of Insulin & Related Hormones. text ed. 112.00 (ISBN 3-11-008156-3). De Gruyter.
Brownlee, Michael. Handbook of Mellitus: Vol. 2, Islet Cell Function - Insulin Action. LC 79-26703. 250p. 1980. lib. bdg. 37.50 (ISBN 0-8240-7214-6). Garland Pub.
Federlin, K. Immunopathology of Insulin: Clinical & Experimental Studies. LC 71-154799. (Monographs on Endocrinology: Vol. 6). (Illus.). 1971. 32.70 (ISBN 0-387-05408-1). Springer-Verlag.
Frunder, H., ed. Effects & Metabolism of Insulin & Cyclic Nucleotides. (Illus.). 1978. stitched 22.00 (ISBN 0-685-87201-7). Adler.
Griffin, LaDean. Insulin Vs. Herbs & the Diabetic. 2.00 (ISBN 0-89557-015-7). Bi World Indus.
Gueriguian, J. L., et al, eds. Insulins, Growth Hormone, & Recombinant DNA Technology. 250p. 1981. 29.50 (ISBN 0-89004-544-5). Raven.
Irsigler, Karl, et al, eds. New Approaches to Diabetes Therapy. 350p. 1981. text ed. 34.50 (ISBN 0-8391-1650-0). Univ Park.
Krahl, Maurice E. Action of Insulin on Cells. (Illus.). 1961. 31.50 (ISBN 0-12-424550-1). Acad Pr.
Rieser, P. Insulin, Membranes & Metabolism. 168p. 1967. 10.95 (ISBN 0-683-07225-0, Pub by Williams & Wilkens). Krieger.
Shafrir, E., ed. Impact of Insulin on Metabolic Pathways. 1972. 43.00 (ISBN 0-12-638050-3). Acad Pr.
Symposium on Insulin Action, Toronto, 1971. Insulin Action: Proceedings. Fritz, Irving, ed. 1973. 55.50 (ISBN 0-12-268750-7). Acad Pr.

INSULL, SAMUEL, 1859-1933

McDonald, Forrest. Insull. LC 62-18110. (Illus.). 1962. 11.00x (ISBN 0-226-55718-9). U of Chicago Pr.
Ramsay, Marion L. Pyramids of Power: The Story of Roosevelt, Insull & the Utility Wars. (FDR & the Era of the New Deal Ser.). (Illus.). 342p. 1975. Repr. of 1937 ed. lib. bdg. 32.50 (ISBN 0-306-70707-1). Da Capo.

INSULTS

see Invective

INSURANCE

see also Insurance Companies; Reinsurance; Risk (Insurance); Saving and Thrift; Self-Insurance

Advice About Insurance, Credit, Budgeting. (Home Adviser Ser.). 80p. (Orig.). 1981. pap. 1.95 (ISBN 0-8326-2407-1, 7051). Delair.
Athearn, James L. Risk & Insurance. 4th ed. (Illus.). 512p. 1981. text ed. 22.50 (ISBN 0-8299-0298-8). West Pub.
--Risk & Insurance. (Illus.). 1977. text ed. 18.95 (ISBN 0-8299-0132-9). West Pub.
Barrett, Francis D., Jr. Attorney's Guide to Insurance & Risk Management. LC 77-90650. 1978. 39.50 (ISBN 0-931372-01-1). Compton & Rowe.
--Professional's Guide to Insurance & Risk Management. LC 77-90648. 1978. 39.50 (ISBN 0-931372-00-3). Compton & Rowe.
Berkeley Actuarial Research Conference, Sept. 1974. Credibility - Theory & Applications: Proceedings, Theory & Applications. Kahn, P. M., ed. 1975. 38.00 (ISBN 0-12-394650-6). Acad Pr.
Bickelhaupt, David L. General Insurance. 10th ed. 1979. text ed. 20.50x (ISBN 0-256-02150-3). Irwin.
Bickley, John S. Trends & Problems in the Distribution of Property Liability Insurance. 1956. pap. text ed. 2.00x (ISBN 0-87776-091-8, R91). Ohio St U Admin Sci.
Breault, Jerome. Insurance: Claim Your Share. 1980. 4.50 (ISBN 0-8062-1439-2). Carlton.
Breslin, Cormick L. & Troxel, Terrie E. Property-Liability Insurance Accounting & Finance. 1978. write for info. (CPCU 8). IIA.
Caputo, William V. How to Stop Being Insurance Poor. 1979. 5.95 (ISBN 0-533-03891-X). Vantage.
Changing Times Education Service Editors. Insurance. rev. ed. LC 81-7857. (Illus.). 1981. pap. text ed. 4.95 (ISBN 0-88436-813-0, CEA999051). EMC.
Construction & Erection Insurance. 48p. 1981. 36.00x (ISBN 0-686-75455-7, Pub. by Insurance Inst England). State Mutual Bk.
Crane, Frederick G. Insurance Principles & Practices. LC 79-19510. 1980. text ed. 21.95 (ISBN 0-471-01763-9). Wiley.
Cummins, J. David & Weisbart, Steven N. The Impact of Consumer Services on Independent Insurance Agency Performance. LC 76-48579. pap. 8.95 (ISBN 0-918486-01-7). IMA Ed.
Denenberg, Herbert S., et al. Risk & Insurance. 2nd ed. 1974. 19.95 (ISBN 0-13-781294-9). P-H.
Digest of Bank Insurance. 3rd ed. 1977. looseleaf 25.00 (ISBN 0-89982-041-7, 210400). Am Bankers.
Doherty, Neil. Insurance Pricing & Loss Prevention. 1976. 17.95 (ISBN 0-347-01097-0, 00308-5, Pub. by Saxon Hse). Lexington Bks.
Doman, Leon H. Supranational Regulation of Insurance. 1966. pap. 3.50 (ISBN 0-685-12055-4). Helios.
Dorfman, Mark S. Introduction to Insurance. LC 77-22029. (Illus.). 1978. ref. 19.95 (ISBN 0-13-485359-8). P-H.
Duke Law Journal. Medical Malpractice: The Duke Law Journal Symposium. LC 76-49822. 1977. 20.00 (ISBN 0-88410-701-9). Ballinger Pub.
Editors of the Fire Casualty & Surety Bulletins. Non-Resident & Surplus Line Laws: Annual Edition 1980. rev. ed. 60p. 1980. pap. 5.00 (ISBN 0-87218-306-8). Natl Underwriter.
Ford, Curtis B. How to Establish an Estate Analysis Practice. LC 78-69946. 1978. looseleaf bdg. 21.50 (ISBN 0-87218-001-8). Natl Underwriter.
Glass, Hardy F., ed. International Insurance: An Anthology of Articles, 2 Pts. LC 60-13977. 1969. pap. 3.95 (ISBN 0-87037-519-9). Helios.
Glendenning, G. William & Holtom, Robert B. Personal Lines Underwriting. 1979. write for info. (UND 62). IIA.
Greene, Mark R. Risk & Insurance. 3rd ed. LC 68-19619. 1973. text ed. 13.90 (ISBN 0-538-06320-3). SW Pub.
--Risk Aversion, Insurance, & the Future. LC 70-633854. (Sequeinnial Insurance Ser.: No. 2). 1971. 7.50 (ISBN 0-685-00048-6). Ind U Busn Res.
Guinane, George E. An Analysis of the SMP Policy: A Line-by-Line Explanation of the Special Multi-Peril Policy. 15.00 (ISBN 0-686-31022-5, 26625). Rough Notes.
Heilbroner, Robert L. & Thurow, Lester C. The Economic Problem. 1978. write for info. (CPCU 9). IIA.
Hieb, Elizabeth, ed. Institute for Fund Advisors, Lake Tahoe, June, 1977: Proceedings. 1977. spiral bdg. 10.50 (ISBN 0-89154-067-9). Intl Found Employ.
Hollingsworth, E. P., Jr. & Launie, J. J. Commercial Property & Multiple-Lines Underwriting. 1978. write for info. (UND 64). IIA.
Holtom, Robert B. Restraints on Underwriting, Risk Selection, Discrimination & the Law. LC 79-89603. 1979. text ed. 15.75 (ISBN 0-87218-303-3). Natl Underwriter.
Insurance for Nuclear Installations. (Legal Ser.: No. 6). (Illus., Orig., Eng. & Fr.). 1970. pap. 13.00 (ISBN 92-0-076070-8, ISP274, IAEA). Unipub.
Insurance Valuations, Definitions, Derivations & Appraisals. LC 72-16891. (ASA Monograph: No. 4). 1971. 5.00 (ISBN 0-937828-13-0). Am Soc Appraisers.
Jaffe, Alfred I. Insurance Producer's Handbook, Vol. 1. LC 78-58728. 1978. 29.50 (ISBN 0-87624-253-0). Inst Busn Plan.
--Insurance Producer's Handbook, Vol. 2. 1980. 39.50 (ISBN 0-87624-254-9). Inst Busn Plan.
Johnsich, John R., intro. By. Real Estate Securities & Title Insurance Terminology. (Orig.). 1980. pap. 3.95 (ISBN 0-914256-12-2). Real Estate Pub.
Koch, Harry W. Your Insurance & What You Should Know About It: California Ed. 1979. pap. 5.00 (ISBN 0-913164-81-X). Ken-Bks.
Kunreuther, Howard. Disaster Insurance Protection: Public Policy Lessons. LC 77-179. 400p. 1978. 39.95 (ISBN 0-471-03259-X, Pub. by Wiley-Interscience). Wiley.
Launie, J. J., et al. Principles of Property & Liability Underwriting. 2nd ed. 1981. write for info. (UND 61). IIA.
Lawson, Thomas. Frenzied Finance. LC 72-78767. 1905. Repr. 22.00 (ISBN 0-403-02011-5). Somerset Pub.
Lawson, Thomas W. Frenzied Finance. Vol. 1: The Crime of Amalgamated. LC 68-28640. Repr. lib. bdg. 29.50x (ISBN 0-8371-0531-5, LAFF). Greenwood.
Legg, Howard W. A Brief Outline of Insurance. 20.00 (ISBN 0-686-31023-3, 26199). Rough Notes.
Lombardi, Tarky, Jr. & Hoffman, Gerald N. Medical Malpractice Insurance: A Legislator's View. 1978. 11.95x (ISBN 0-8156-0128-X). Syracuse U Pr.
Long, John D. Ethics, Morality, & Insurance: A Long-Range Outlook. LC 71-633786. (Sesquicentennial Insurance Ser.). 1971. 8.50 (ISBN 0-685-00047-8). Ind U Busn Res.
Long, John D., ed. Issues in Insurance, 2 vols. 1978. write for info. (CPCU 10). IIA.
McEwan, Bruce. Insurance: What's It All About? 1980. 5.95 (ISBN 0-533-03805-7). Vantage.
McGill, Dan M., ed. All Lines Insurance. 1960. 7.75x (ISBN 0-256-00666-0). Irwin.
Magarick, Pat. Excessive Liability - Duties & Responsibilities of the Insurer. LC 75-44308. 1976. with 1978 suppl. 30.00 (ISBN 0-87632-157-0). Boardman.
Mehr. Plaid for Principles of Insurance. rev. ed. 1978. 5.50 (ISBN 0-256-02097-3, 03-0859-02). Learning Syst.
Mehr, Robert I. & Cammack, Emerson. Principles of Insurance. 7th ed. 1980. 19.95x (ISBN 0-256-02321-2). Irwin.
Mowbray, Albert H., et al. Insurance: Its Theory & Practice in the United States. 6th ed. LC 78-10258. 670p. 1979. Repr. of 1969 ed. lib. bdg. 29.50 (ISBN 0-88275-768-7). Krieger.
Muslehuddin. Insurance & Islamic Law. pap. 2.50 (ISBN 0-686-18372-X). Kazi Pubns.
Myers, Gerald E. Insurance Manual for Libraries. LC 77-24524. 1977. pap. 5.00 (ISBN 0-8389-0236-7). ALA.
Nelli, Humbert O. & Marshall, Robert A. The Private Insurance Business in the United States Economy. LC 76-630595. 1969. spiral bdg. 7.95 (ISBN 0-88406-012-8). Ga St U Busn Pub.
Nineteen Seventy-Eight Confidential Bank Insurance Survey Report. 1978. 7.00 (ISBN 0-89982-003-4, 212600). Am Bankers.
O'Connell, Jeffrey. Injury Industry & the Remedy of No-Fault Insurance. 272p. 1971. pap. 5.50 (ISBN 0-252-00236-9). U of Ill Pr.
Officer's Manual of Personal Finance & Insurance. rev 3rd ed. LC 79-140746. (Illus.). 320p. 1979. pap. 11.95 (ISBN 0-8117-1154-4). Stackpole.
Personal Insurance Guide. 7.50 (ISBN 0-686-31010-1, 30177). Rough Notes.
Pfeffer, Irving. Insurance & Economic Theory. 1956. 6.50x (ISBN 0-256-00408-0). Irwin.
Pfeffer, Irving & Klock, David R. Perspectives on Insurance. (Illus.). 448p. 1974. ref. ed. 19.95 (ISBN 0-13-661066-8). P-H.
Pfennigstorf, Werner. Legal Expense Insurance: The European Experience in Financing Legal Services. LC 75-996. 1975. 5.00 (ISBN 0-910058-69-5). Am Bar Foun.
Reinmuth, Dennis F. Regulation of Reciprocal Insurance Exchanges. 1967. 7.75x (ISBN 0-256-00676-8). Irwin.
Rejda, George E. Principles of Insurance. 1982. text ed. 20.95 (ISBN 0-673-15344-4). Scott F.
Riegel, R. & Miller, J. Insurance Principles & Practices: Property & Liability. 6th ed. 1976. text ed. 21.95 (ISBN 0-13-468868-6). P-H.
Rodda, William H., et al. Commercial Property Risk Management & Insurance, 2 vols. 1980. write for info. (CPCU 3). IIA.
Singh, N. Achievements of Unctad One-1964 & Unctad Two-1968, in the Field of Shipping & Indivisibles. 1969. 15.00x (ISBN 0-8426-1535-0). Verry.
Smith, Robert S., et al. Principles of Insurance Production. 1980. write for info. (PRO 81). IIA.
Special Multi-Peril Guide: A Sales Tool for Explaining the SMP Policy to Prospects. 6.00 (ISBN 0-686-31020-9, 30150). Rough Notes.
Stephenson, Gilbert T. & Wiggins, Norman A. Estates & Trusts. 5th ed. (Risk & Insurance Ser.). 480p. 1973. text ed. 19.95 (ISBN 0-13-289546-3). P-H.
Sumner, Michael. The Dollars & Sense of Hospital Malpractice Insurance. LC 78-67846. 1979. text ed. 22.50 (ISBN 0-89011-517-6). Abt Assoc.
Texas Multi-Peril Guide. 6.00 (ISBN 0-686-31021-7, 30151). Rough Notes.
Thomas, Paul I. & Reed, Prentiss B., Sr. Adjustment of Property Losses. 4th ed. (Illus.). 1977. text ed. 18.95 (ISBN 0-07-064215-X, G); instructor's manual & key 4.50 (ISBN 0-07-064216-8). McGraw.
Todd, Jerry D. Texas Insurance Fact Book, 1976. (Studies in Insurance & Actuarial Science: No. 4). 1977. pap. 3.00 (ISBN 0-87755-264-9). U of Tex Busn Res.
Vaughan, Emmett J. & Elliot, Curtis M. Fundamentals of Risk & Insurance. 2nd ed. LC 77-18769. (Wiley-Hamilton Series in Risk & Insurance). 1978. text ed. 26.50 (ISBN 0-471-90353-1); tchrs'. manual o.p. avail. (ISBN 0-471-02164-4). Wiley.
Villaronga, Luis M. The Incontestable Clause: An Historical Analysis. LC 75-26415. (S. S. Huebner Foundation Monographs: No. 5). 1976. pap. 6.95 (ISBN 0-918930-05-7). Huebner Foun Insur.
Wassell, Richard. A Textbook of Reinsurance. 224p. 1980. 27.00x (ISBN 0-85941-166-4, Pub. by Woodhead-Faulkner England). State Mutual Bk.
Waters, William R. Employer Pension Plan Membership & Household Wealth. LC 79-92473. (S. S. Huebner Foundation Monograph: No. 10). (Illus.). Date not set. pap. price not set (ISBN 0-918930-10-3). Huebner Foun Insur.
White, Jay C. Aviation Insurance Explained. 1974. pap. 7.95 (ISBN 0-911721-37-1, Pub. by Pilots). Aviation.
Williams, C. A., Jr. Risk Management & Insurance. 3rd ed. 1976. text ed. 17.95 (ISBN 0-07-070558-5, C); instr's manual 4.95 (ISBN 0-07-070559-3). McGraw.

Williams, C. Arthur, Jr. & Heins, Richard M. Risk Management & Insurance. 4th ed. (Insurance Ser.). (Illus.). 672p. 1980. text ed. 19.95 (ISBN 0-07-070564-X, C); instructor's manual 5.95 (ISBN 0-07-070565-8). McGraw.
Williams, C. Arthur, Jr., et al. Principles of Risk Management & Insurance, 2 vols. 1978. write for info. (CPCU 1). IIA.
Wood, Glenn L., et al. Personal Risk Management & Insurance, 2 vols. 2nd ed. 1980. write for info. (CPCU 2). IIA.

INSURANCE–ADJUSTMENT OF CLAIMS

Baldyga, D. G. How to Settle Your Own Insurance Claim. 1968. 4.95 (ISBN 0-02-489900-3). Macmillan.
Ehrlich, Ann. Managing Insurance Claims in the Dental Office. (Illus.). 1978. 4.95 (ISBN 0-940012-12-X). Colwell Co.
Magarick, Pat. Successful Handling of Casualty Claims. LC 73-91720. 1974. 37.50 (ISBN 0-87632-168-6). Boardman.
Rokes, Willis P. Human Relations in Handling Insurance Claims. rev. ed. 1981. 17.95x (ISBN 0-256-02504-5). Irwin.
Rudman, Jack. Insurance Fund Hearing Representative. (Career Examination Ser.: C-1546). (Cloth bdg. avail. on request). pap. 10.00 (ISBN 0-685-60432-2). Natl Learning.
Sandri-White, Alex. Insurance Claims Investigation & Adjusting. new ed. 1975. 9.50 (ISBN 0-685-56026-0). Aurea.

INSURANCE–AGENTS

see also Insurance, Life–Agents; Insurance–Vocational Guidance

Closing Talks & Techniques. 2.50 (ISBN 0-686-31041-1, 29023). Rough Notes.
Dial C for Commission. 2.50 (ISBN 0-686-31047-0, 29709). Rough Notes.
Didactic Systems Staff. Principles of Effective Insurance Agents. (Didactic Simulation Game Ser). 1973. pap. 24.90 (ISBN 0-685-77372-8); pap. 21.50 for 2 or more (ISBN 0-686-57883-X); pap. 24.90 spanish ed. (ISBN 0-89401-102-2); pap. 21.50 for 2 or more (ISBN 0-686-57884-8); pap. 0.50 leader's guide (ISBN 0-685-77375-2). Didactic Syst.
--Recruiting Effective Insurance Agents. (Didactic Simulation Game). 1973. pap. 24.90 (ISBN 0-89401-082-4); pap. 24.90 french ed. (ISBN 0-89401-083-2); pap. 21.50 for 2 or more (ISBN 0-685-77370-1); pap. 0.50 leader's guide (ISBN 0-685-77371-X). Didactic Syst.
--Selecting Effective Insurance Agents. (Simulation Game Ser.). 1973. pap. 24.90 (ISBN 0-89401-090-5); pap. 21.50 two or more (ISBN 0-685-78096-1); pap. 24.90 french ed. (ISBN 0-89401-091-3). Didactic Syst.
Donoghue, Charles. Light Your Own Fire to Bigger Sales. LC 79-88425. (Illus.). 1979. 8.75 (ISBN 0-87218-006-9). Natl Underwriter.
Earn More-Work Less. 2.50 (ISBN 0-686-31046-2, 29412). Rough Notes.
Howell, Edward B. & Howell, Richard P. Targeting in on Professional Liability. 1978. 25.00 (ISBN 0-932056-02-4). Risk Analysis.
Jaffe, Alfred I. Insurance Producer's Handbook, 2 vols. 1980. Set. 59.50 (ISBN 0-686-73129-8). Inst Busn Plan.
No Violations of Policy: An Informal History of the Independent Insurance Agents of America. 20.00 (ISBN 0-686-31038-1, 26540). Rough Notes.
One Hundred Sixty-One Direct Mail Letters. 7.50 (ISBN 0-686-31051-9, 29321). Rough Notes.
One Hundred Twenty Ideas That Have Sparked Sales. 2.50 (ISBN 0-686-31040-3, 29439). Rough Notes.
One Hundred Twenty-Two More Ideas That Have Sparked Sales. 2.50 (ISBN 0-686-31043-8, 29345). Rough Notes.
Rudman, Jack. Insurance Agent - Insurance Broker. (Career Examination Ser.: C-373). (Cloth bdg. avail. on request). pap. 8.00 (ISBN 0-685-60430-6). Natl Learning.
--Insurance Manager. (Career Examination Ser.: C-1598). (Cloth bdg. avail. on request). pap. 10.00 (ISBN 0-685-60434-9). Natl Learning.
Snouffer, Gary H. Health Insurance Agent. LC 78-26706. 1979. pap. 8.00 (ISBN 0-668-04307-5). Arco.
Top Producers' Handbook. 2.50 (ISBN 0-686-31039-X, 29441). Rough Notes.
Two Hundred & Twenty Four Answers to Objections. 2.50 (ISBN 0-686-31305-4, 29414). Rough Notes.
Vreeland, Walter M. The Care & Feeding of Agents. LC 78-53143. 1978. 8.75 (ISBN 0-87218-000-X). Natl Underwriter.
Wilmot, R., ed. Who's Who in Insurance. 303p. 1975. 26.00x (ISBN 0-86010-023-5, Pub. by Graham & Trotman England). State Mutual Bk.

INSURANCE–AGENTS–DIRECTORIES

see Insurance–Directories

INSURANCE–BIBLIOGRAPHY

Fire & Casualty Bulletin Editors. Agent's & Buyer's Guide: Annual Edition 1981. rev. ed. 550p. 1981. pap. 11.50 (ISBN 0-87218-309-2). Natl Underwriter.
Nelli, Humbert O. & Ewedemi, Soga. A Bibliography of Insurance History. 2nd ed. LC 76-6938. (Research Monograph: No. 70). 1976. spiral bd. 10.00 (ISBN 0-88406-106-X). Ga St U Busn Pub.
Thomas, Roy, ed. Insurance Information Sources. LC 75-137575. (Management Information Guide Ser.: No. 24). 1971. 36.00 (ISBN 0-8103-0824-X). Gale.

INSURANCE–DATA PROCESSING

Cissley, Charles H. Systems & Data Processing in Insurance Companies. LC 77-70940. (FLMI Insurance Education Program Ser.). (Illus.). 1977. pap. text ed. 9.50 (ISBN 0-915322-26-9); wkbk. 4.00 (ISBN 0-915322-27-7). LOMA.
Gantt, Michael D. & Gatza, James. Computers in Insurance. 1980. write for info. (CPCU 7). IIA.
Life Office Management Association, ed. Readings for the Information Systems Specialty. (FLMI Insurance Education Program Ser.). (Illus.). 186p. (Orig.). 1980. pap. text ed. 10.00 (ISBN 0-915322-39-0). Loma.

INSURANCE–DICTIONARIES

Castelo Matran, Julio. Diccionario Basico De Seguros. 312p. (Espn.). 1978. pap. 18.50 (ISBN 84-7100-049-0, S-50036). French & Eur.
Davids, Lewis E. Dictionary of Insurance. 5th ed. (Quality Paperback Ser: No. 62). (Orig.). 1979. pap. 5.95 (ISBN 0-8226-0062-5). Littlefield.
Heinze. Fachwoerterbuch des Versicherungswesen, Vol. 1. (Ger. & Eng., Dictionary of Insurance Terms). 1961. 12.50 (ISBN 3-87097-016-2, M-7392, Pub. by Brandstetter). French & Eur.
Heinze, S. Dictionary of Insurance Terms, 2 Vols. (Ger-Eng. & Eng-Ger.). 12.00 ea. Ger.-Eng (ISBN 3-8709-7016-2). Eng.-Ger (ISBN 3-8709-7017-0). Adler.
--Fachwoerterbuch des Versicherungswesen. (Ger. -Eng., Dictionary of Insurance Terms, English-German). 1961. 12.00 (ISBN 3-87097-017-0, M-7393, Pub. by Brandstetter). French & Eur.
Keim, Marianne. Insurance Language: A Running Press Glossary. LC 77-12037. 1978. lib. bdg. 12.90 (ISBN 0-89471-019-2); pap. 2.95 (ISBN 0-89471-018-4). Running Pr.
Lesobre, J. & Sommer, H. Vocabulaire Technique Des Assurances: Anglais-Francais, Francais-Anglais. 255p. (Eng.-Fr.). 1972. 27.50 (ISBN 0-686-57013-8, M-6354). French & Eur.
Levy, Michael H. A Handbook of Personal Insurance Terminology. 1968. 9.95 (ISBN 0-910580-04-9). Farnswth Pub.
Mueller-Lutz, H. L. Diccionario De Seguros. 282p. (Span., Ger., Eng. & Fr.). 1977. pap. 15.75 (ISBN 84-7100-004-0, S-50035). French & Eur.
Ruysch, W. A. Elsevier's Multilingual Dictionary of Insurance Technology. 1977. write for info. (ISBN 0-685-82355-5). Elsevier.
Strain, Robert W. Insurance Words & Their Meanings: A Dictionary of Insurance Terms. 10.00 (ISBN 0-686-31032-2, 26401). Rough Notes.

INSURANCE–DIRECTORIES

Bell, Hugh S. How to Suceed in Life Insurance Selling. 3.50 (ISBN 0-686-31052-7, 29705). Rough Notes.
--How to Succeed in Life Insurance Selling. 3.50 (ISBN 0-686-31052-7, 29705). Rough Notes.
Fire & Casualty Bulletin Editors. Agent's & Buyer's Guide: Annual Edition 1981. rev. ed. 550p. 1981. pap. 11.50 (ISBN 0-87218-309-2). Natl Underwriter.
How to Save Time & Increase Sales. 2.50 (ISBN 0-686-31042-X, 29024). Rough Notes.
Jaffe, Alfred I. & Miller, Jerome S. Business Building Letters: Ready-to-Use Letters That Build Premiums & Goodwill, 6 courses. Set. 10.00 (ISBN 0-686-31036-5, 26627). Rough Notes.
Nelli, Humbert O., ed. Index & Guide to Walford's Insurance Cyclopaedia. LC 75-38801. (Research Monograph: No. 67). 1000p. 1976. spiral bdg. 40.00 (ISBN 0-88406-099-3). Ga St U Busn Pub.
Rothschild, Bernard B. Construction Bonds & Insurance Guide. rev. ed. 1979. pap. 20.00 (ISBN 0-913962-09-0). Am Inst Arch.
Sales Ideas from the All Stars. 64p. 2.50 (ISBN 0-686-31044-6, 29413). Rough Notes.
Shields, Walter J. An Hour a Day Will Develop Your Market. 3.00 (ISBN 0-686-31053-5, 29063). Rough Notes.
Yearbook for International Insurance - Assecuranz-Compass 1980. 86th ed. 1751p. 1980. 275.00x (ISBN 0-8002-2781-6). Intl Pubns Serv.

INSURANCE–EXAMINATIONS, QUESTIONS, ETC.

Doyle, Dennis. The Complete Series 6 Study Book. (Illus.). 350p. (Orig.). 1980. pap. text ed. 23.50 (ISBN 0-914234-14-5). Human Res Dev Pr.
The Forum: Answers to Questions on Insurance Coverage. 7.50 (ISBN 0-686-31014-4, 30161). Rough Notes.
Insurance Agent & Broker. rev. ed. LC 67-12047. 1970. pap. 6.00 (ISBN 0-668-02149-7). Arco.
Rudman, Jack. Actuarial Clerk. (Career Examination Ser.: C-2417). (Cloth bdg. avail. on request). pap. 8.00 (ISBN 0-686-67755-2). Natl Learning.
--Assistant Claims Examiner. (Career Examination Ser.: C-1098). (Cloth bdg. avail. on request). pap. 8.00 (ISBN 0-8373-1098-9). Natl Learning.
--Claims Settlement Agent. (Career Examination Ser.: C-1189). (Cloth bdg. avail. on request). pap. 8.00 (ISBN 0-8373-1189-6). Natl Learning.
--Insurance Agent - Insurance Broker. (Career Examination Ser.: C-373). (Cloth bdg. avail. on request). pap. 8.00 (ISBN 0-685-60430-6). Natl Learning.
--Insurance Broker. (Career Examination Ser.: C-373). (Cloth bdg. avail. on request). pap. 8.00 (ISBN 0-8373-0373-7). Natl Learning.
--Insurance Fund Field Services Representative. (Career Examination Ser.: C-2166). (Cloth bdg. avail. on request). 1976. pap. 10.00 (ISBN 0-8373-2166-2). Natl Learning.
--Insurance Fund Hearing Representative. (Career Examination Ser.: C-1546). (Cloth bdg. avail. on request). pap. 10.00 (ISBN 0-685-60432-2). Natl Learning.
--Insurance Manager. (Career Examination Ser.: C-1598). (Cloth bdg. avail. on request). pap. 10.00 (ISBN 0-685-60434-9). Natl Learning.
--Junior Insurance Examiner. (Career Examination Ser.: C-2069). (Cloth bdg. avail. on request). 1977. pap. 8.00 (ISBN 0-685-78624-2). Natl Learning.
--Life Insurance Agent. (Career Examination Ser.: C-443). (Ckloth bdg. avail. on request). pap. 10.00 (ISBN 0-686-53361-5). Natl Learning.
--Principal Actuarial Clerk. (Career Examination Ser.: C-2424). (Cloth bdg. avail. on request). pap. 10.00 (ISBN 0-8373-2424-6). Natl Learning.
--Principal Actuary. (Career Examination Ser.: C-610). (Cloth bdg. avail. on request). pap. 12.00 (ISBN 0-8373-0610-8). Natl Learning.
--Senior Actuarial Clerk. (Career Examination Ser.: C-2418). (Cloth bdg. avail. on request). pap. 8.00 (ISBN 0-8373-2418-1). Natl Learning.
--Senior Actuary. (Career Examination Ser.: C-993). (Cloth bdg. avail. on request). pap. 10.00 (ISBN 0-8373-0993-X). Natl Learning.
--Underwriter. (Career Examination Ser.: C-2011). (Cloth bdg. avail. on request). pap. 8.00 (ISBN 0-8373-2011-9). Natl Learning.
Zelizer, Viviana. Morals & Markets. LC 78-31205. 1979. 17.50x (ISBN 0-231-04570-0). Columbia U Pr.

INSURANCE–FINANCE

see also Insurance Companies–Investments

Bachman, James E. Capitalization Requirements for Multiple Line Property Liability Insurance Companies. LC 78-57297. (S. S. Huebner Foundation Monographs: No. 6). (Illus.). 1978. pap. 10.00 (ISBN 0-918930-06-5). Huebner Foun Insur.
Skidmore, Felicity, ed. Social Security Financing. 312p. 1981. 30.00x (ISBN 0-262-19196-2). MIT Pr.
What It Costs. 1981. 12.50 (ISBN 0-686-31033-0, 30179). Rough Notes.

INSURANCE–MATHEMATICS

see also Insurance–Rates and Tables; Insurance, Life–Mathematics

Beard, E., et al. Risk Theory: The Stochastic Basis of Insurance. 2nd ed. (Monographs on Applied Probability & Statistics). 1977. 15.95x (ISBN 0-412-15100-6, Pub. by Chapman & Hall). Methuen Inc.
Borch, Karl. The Mathematical Theory of Insurance. LC 73-11670. 352p. 1974. 24.95 (ISBN 0-669-86942-2). Lexington Bks.
Rudman, Jack. Actuary. (Career Examination Ser.: C-7). (Cloth bdg. avail. on request). pap. 10.00 (ISBN 0-8373-0007-X). Natl Learning.
--Assistant Actuary. (Career Examination Ser.: C-22). (Cloth bdg. avail. on request). pap. 8.00 (ISBN 0-8373-0022-3). Natl Learning.

INSURANCE–PREMIUMS

see Insurance–Rates and Tables

INSURANCE–RATES AND TABLES

Cooper, Robert W. Investment Return & Property-Liability Insurance Ratemaking. 1974. 9.25x (ISBN 0-256-01605-4). Irwin.
Crane, Frederick G. Automobile Insurance Rate Regulation. 1962. 5.00x (ISBN 0-87776-105-1, R105). Ohio St U Admin Sci.
Freifelder, Leonard R. A Decision Theoretic Approach to Insurance Ratemaking. LC 75-26414. (S. S. Huebner Foundation Monographs: No. 4). (Illus.). 1976. pap. 9.95 (ISBN 0-918930-04-9). Huebner Foun Insur.
Hartman, Gerald R. Ratemaking for Homeowners Insurance. 1967. 8.25x (ISBN 0-256-00648-2). Irwin.
MacAvoy, Paul W., ed. Federal-State Regulation of the Pricing & Marketing of Insurance. (Ford Administration Papers on Regulatory Reforms). 1977. 5.25 (ISBN 0-8447-3253-2). Am Enterprise.
MacIntyre, Duncan M. Voluntary Health Insurance & Rate Making. LC 62-14113. 301p. 1962. 32.50x (ISBN 0-8014-0282-4). Cornell U Pr.

INSURANCE–RISK

see Risk (Insurance)

INSURANCE–SALESMANSHIP

see Insurance–Agents

INSURANCE–SELF-ASSURANCE

see Self-Insurance

INSURANCE–STATE SUPERVISION

see also Friendly Societies; Insurance Law

Broadwell, Martin M. & Simpson, William F. New Insurance Supervisor. 168p. 1981. pap. text ed. cancelled (ISBN 0-201-00568-9). A-W.
MacAvoy, Paul W., ed. Federal-State Regulation of the Pricing & Marketing of Insurance. (Ford Administration Papers on Regulatory Reforms). 1977. 5.25 (ISBN 0-8447-3253-2). Am Enterprise.
Whitford, William C. & Kimball, Spencer L. Why Process Consumer Complaints? A Case Study of the Office of the Commissioner of Insurance of Wisconsin. (Research Contribution Ser.). (Repr. from 1974 Wisconsin Law Review, No. 3). 1975. 2.00 (ISBN 0-685-56503-3). Am Bar Foun.

INSURANCE–STATISTICS

McDonald, Anne & Markowitz, Grace. Sources of Insurance Statistics. 1981. price not set. SLA.

INSURANCE–STUDY AND TEACHING

Clews, Roderick. A Textbook of Insurance Broking. 224p. 1980. 27.00x (ISBN 0-85941-121-4, Pub. by Woodhead-Faulkner England). State Mutual Bk.
Milton, Arthur. How Your Insurance Policies Rob You. LC 81-4679. 178p. 1981. 8.95 (ISBN 0-8065-0768-3). Citadel Pr.
Moore, Franklin L. Property & Casualty Insurance: Study Guide. 18.00 (ISBN 0-686-31035-7, 26629). Rough Notes.

INSURANCE–TAXATION

Lenrow, Gerald, et al. Federal Income Taxation of Insurance Companies. 3rd ed. LC 78-26091. 1979. 49.50 (ISBN 0-471-05193-4, Pub. by Ronald). Wiley.
Roberts, James E. Federal Income, Estate & Gift Taxation of Group Life Insurance. LC 76-13395. 1976. text ed. 7.95 (ISBN 0-87863-152-6). Farnswth Pub.
Stagliano, A. J. The Incidence of the Life Insurance Company Federal Income Tax. LC 79-88408. (S. S. Huebner Foundation Monograph Ser.: No. 9). 1980. pap. 12.95 (ISBN 0-918930-09-X). Huebner Foun Insur.

INSURANCE–VOCATIONAL GUIDANCE

Bloomgarden, Barry. Your Future in Insurance Careers. (Careers in Depth Ser). (gr. 7-12). 1978. PLB 5.97 (ISBN 0-8239-0455-5). Rosen Pr.
For Women: Opportunities Unlimited. 2.50 (ISBN 0-686-31048-9, 29707). Rough Notes.
Mainstream Access, Inc. The Insurance Job Finder. 256p. 1981. 16.95 (ISBN 0-13-468611-X); pap. 8.95 (ISBN 0-13-468603-9). P-H.
Sommer, Armand & Kedzie, Daniel P. Your Future in Insurance. LC 70-114117. (Career Guidance Ser). 1971. pap. 3.95 (ISBN 0-668-02249-3). Arco.
Van Gelder, Patricia. Careers in the Insurance Industry. (Career Concise Guides Ser.). (Illus.). (gr. 7 up). 1978. PLB 6.90 s&l (ISBN 0-531-01421-5). Watts.

INSURANCE–CANADA

Evans, R. G. & Williamson, M. F. Extending Canadian Health Insurance: Options for Pharmacare & Denticare. (Ontario Economic Council Research Studies). 1978. pap. 14.00 (ISBN 0-8020-3353-9). U of Toronto Pr.

INSURANCE–GREAT BRITAIN

Cannar, K. The Theory & Practice of Motor Insurance. 1978. text ed. 30.00x (ISBN 0-900886-24-2, Pub. by Witherby & Co. Ltd). State Mutual Bk.
The Insurance of UK Products Liability Risks on a World-Wide Basis. 37p. 1981. 24.00x (ISBN 0-686-75457-3, Pub. by Insurance Inst England). State Mutual Bk.

INSURANCE, ACCIDENT

see also Disability Evaluation; Industrial Accidents; Insurance, Liability; Insurance, Life–Disability Benefits; Workmen's Compensation

The Advantages & Disadvantages of the TORT System & Alternative Methods of Accident Compensation. 37p. 1981. 24.00x (ISBN 0-686-75454-9, Pub. by Insurance Inst England). State Mutual Bk.
Bickley, John S. Impact of a State Disability Act on Insurance Companies. 1954. pap. 1.00x (ISBN 0-87776-071-3, R71). Ohio St U Admin Sci.
Pickrell, Jesse F. Group Health Insurance. rev. ed. 1961. 8.00x (ISBN 0-256-00671-7). Irwin.

INSURANCE, AGRICULTURAL

A Manual on Crop Insurance for Developing Countries. (Illus.). 89p. 1976. pap. 7.50 (ISBN 0-685-66335-3, F1030, FAO). Unipub.

Ray, P. K. Agricultural Insurance: Theory & Practice & Application to Developing Countries. 2nd ed. (Illus.). 360p. 1981. 90.00 (ISBN 0-08-025787-9). Pergamon.

INSURANCE, ASSESSMENT

see also Friendly Societies

INSURANCE, AUTOMOBILE

see also Unsatisfied Judgment Funds (Traffic Accidents)

Association International du Droit d'Assurance. New Trends in Automobile Insurance in Europe. 1979. pap. 31.50 (ISBN 90-6321-014-0, Pub. by Kluwer Law Netherlands). Kluwer Boston.

Cannar, K. The Theory & Practice of Motor Insurance. 1978. text ed. 30.00x (ISBN 0-900886-24-2, Pub. by Witherby & Co. Ltd). State Mutual Bk.

Cockerell, H. A. & Dickinson, G. M. Motor Insurance & the Consumer. 192p. 1980. 30.00x (ISBN 0-85941-146-X, Pub. by Woodhead-Faulkner England). State Mutual Bk.

Council on Law Related Studies. No-Fault Auto Insurance. 1977. 24.00 (ISBN 0-379-00391-0). Oceana.

Doman, Leon H. Motor Vehicle Traffic Accident Problem: A National Solution. 1969. pap. 3.50 (ISBN 0-87037-516-4). Helios.

French, Patterson H. Automobile Compensation Plan. LC 68-58574. (Columbia University. Studies in the Social Sciences: No. 393). Repr. of 1933 ed. 21.00 (ISBN 0-404-51393-X). AMS Pr.

Gee, Harold F. Agent's Automobile Guide. 7.00 (ISBN 0-686-31026-8, 26060). Rough Notes.

Hashmi, Sajjad A. Automobile Insurance: A Long-Range Outlook. LC 72-619522. (Sesquicentennial Insurance Ser). (Illus.). 260p. 1972. 8.95 (ISBN 0-87925-000-3). Ind U Busn Res.

Keeton, Robert E., et al, eds. Crisis in Car Insurance. LC 68-20267. 1968. 19.95 (ISBN 0-252-72627-8). U of Ill Pr.

Kohl, James A. How to Save Money on Your Auto Insurance. LC 79-84203. (Illus.). 88p. 1980. pap. 10.00 (ISBN 0-935674-00-4). Jaks Pub Co.

MacPherson, Robert C. Automotive Collision Appraisal. (Illus.). 240p. 1974. pap. text ed. 10.50 (ISBN 0-07-044695-4); instructors' manual 3.50 (ISBN 0-07-044696-2); slides 70.00 (ISBN 0-07-044697-0); instructor's pkg. 77.00 (ISBN 0-07-079374-3). McGraw.

O'Connell, Jeffrey. Ending Insult to Injury: No-Fault Insurance for Products & Services. LC 74-16243. 288p. 1975. 15.00 (ISBN 0-252-00451-5). U of Ill Pr.

O'Connell, Jeffrey & Wilson, Wallace H. Car Insurance & Consumer Desires. LC 78-83554. (Illus.). 1969. 10.00 (ISBN 0-252-00033-1). U of Ill Pr.

Rosenbloom, Jerry S. Automobile Liability Claims: Insurance Company Philosophies & Practices. 1968. 7.00x (ISBN 0-256-00677-6). Irwin.

Schermer, Irwin E. Automobile Liability Insurance. LC 73-82715. 1979. looseleaf with 1978 rev. pages 125.00 (ISBN 0-87632-102-3). Boardman.

Study of the Feasibiliy of No-Fault Auto Insurance. (Policy Research Project: No. 10). 85p. 1975. 3.00 (ISBN 0-686-31366-6). LBJ Sch Public Affairs.

Webb, Bernard L. Collective Merchandising of Automobile Insurance - the Employers' View. LC 68-627179. (Research Monograph: No. 47). 1969. spiral bdg. 5.00 (ISBN 0-88406-061-6). Ga St U Busn Pub.

Widiss, Alan I, et al. No-Fault Automobile Insurance in Action: The Experience of Massachusetts, Florida, Delaware, & Michigan. LC 77-71283. 1977. 20.00x (ISBN 0-379-00391-0). Oceana.

Wiktor, Christian L. Automobile Insurance Publications. LC 73-84940. xiii, 220p. (Orig.). 1973. pap. text ed. 14.00x (ISBN 0-8377-1300-5). Rothman.

Woodroof, M. G., 3rd & Fonseca, John R. Automobile Insurance & No-Fault Law. LC 74-76324. 1974. 47.50 (ISBN 0-686-14511-9). Lawyers Co-Op.

Woodroof, M. G., 3rd & Squillante, Alphonse. Automobile Liability & the Changing Law. LC 75-39041. (Legal Almanac Ser). 128p. 1972. lib. bdg. 5.95 (ISBN 0-379-11082-2). Oceana.

INSURANCE, BUSINESS

Bardwell, Edward C. New Profits: Business Interruption Insurance. 13.50 (ISBN 0-686-31018-7, 26621). Rough Notes.

Barrett, Francis D., Jr. Accountant's Guide to Insurance & Risk Management. LC 77-90645. 39.50 (ISBN 0-931372-02-X). Compton & Rowe.

Businessowners Policy Program Guide. 5.00 (ISBN 0-686-31024-1, 30153). Rough Notes.

Catchpole, W. L. Business Guide to Insurance. 288p. 1974. 12.50x (ISBN 0-434-90220-9). Intl Pubns Serv.

Cushman, Robert F., et al. The Business Insurance Handbook. LC 80-70437. 600p. 1981. 37.50 (ISBN 0-87094-237-9). Dow Jones-Irwin.

Glendening, Frank S. Business Interruption Insurance: What Is Covered. LC 79-92558. 245p. 1980. pap. text ed. 20.00 (ISBN 0-87218-304-1). Natl Underwriter.

Hieb, Elizabeth A., ed. Corporate Benefits Management Conference, 1980: Proceedings. 102p. (Orig.). 1981. pap. 10.00 (ISBN 0-89154-136-5). Intl Found Employ.

Life Office Management Association, ed. Readings in Management Principles. (FLMI Insurance Education Program Ser.). 68p. (Orig.). 1980. pap. text ed. 5.00 (ISBN 0-915322-37-4). Loma.

MacDonald, Donald L. Corporate Risk Control. 1966. 25.95 (ISBN 0-8260-5615-6). Wiley.

Phelan, John D. Business Interruption Primer. 6.00 (ISBN 0-686-31017-9, 26260). Rough Notes.

Samuel, Millard A. How to Get Your Share of Business Insurance. 5.00 (ISBN 0-686-31050-0, 29062). Rough Notes.

Schott, Brian. RISKM: A Player's Manual. (Research Monograph: No. 66-C). 1978. 3.00 (ISBN 0-88406-122-1). Ga St U Busn Pub.

White, Edwin H. & Chasman, Herbert. Business Insurance. 4th ed. 1974. 18.00 (ISBN 0-13-100859-5, Busn). P-H.

Williams, C. A., Jr. Risk Management & Insurance. 3rd ed. 1976. text ed. 17.95 (ISBN 0-07-070558-5, C); instr's manual 4.95 (ISBN 0-07-070559-3). McGraw.

Williams, C. Arthur, Jr. & Heins, Richard M. Risk Management & Insurance. 4th ed. (Insurance Ser.). (Illus.). 672p. 1980. text ed. 19.95 (ISBN 0-07-070564-X, C); instructor's manual 5.95 (ISBN 0-07-070565-8). McGraw.

INSURANCE, BUSINESS LIFE

Glendening, Frank S. Business Interruption Insurance: What Is Covered. LC 79-92558. 245p. 1980. pap. text ed. 20.00 (ISBN 0-87218-304-1). Natl Underwriter.

Weare, Walter B. Black Business in the New South: A Social History of the North Carolina Mutual Life Insurance Company. LC 72-92690. (Blacks in the New World Ser.). (Illus.). 322p. 1973. 17.50 (ISBN 0-252-00285-7). U of Ill Pr.

INSURANCE, CASUALTY

see also Insurance, Accident; Insurance, Agricultural; Insurance, Automobile; Insurance, Liability; Insurance, Property

Arizona Property & Casualty. 1978. 13.00 (ISBN 0-930868-08-0). Merritt Co.

Arkansas Property & Casualty. 1980. 14.00 (ISBN 0-930868-09-9). Merritt Co.

Donaldson, James H. Casualty Claim Practice. 3rd ed. 1976. 23.50x (ISBN 0-256-00116-2). Irwin.

Fire & Casualty Insurance Companies. (Industry Audit Guides). 1966. pap. 6.00 (ISBN 0-685-58480-1). Am Inst CPA.

Gee, Harold F. Agent's Casualty Guide. 7.00 (ISBN 0-686-31025-X, 26100). Rough Notes.

--An Approach to Property & Casualty Insurance. 8.00 (ISBN 0-686-31028-4, 26121). Rough Notes.

Georgia Property & Casualty. 1980. 14.00 (ISBN 0-930868-36-6). Merritt Co.

Gordis, Philip. Lessons in Property & Casuality Insurance: Course 1. 58.50 (ISBN 0-686-31037-3, 26530). Rough Notes.

Gordis, Philip L. Property & Casualty Insurance: A Reservoir of Insurance Know How. 750p. lib. bdg. 25.00 (ISBN 0-686-31012-8, 26520). Rough Notes.

Illinois Property, Casualty & Health. 1978. 15.50 (ISBN 0-930868-11-0). Merritt Co.

Indiana Property & Casualty. 1978. 15.00 (ISBN 0-930868-13-7). Merritt Co.

Kulp, C. A. & Hall, J. W. Casualty Insurance. 4th ed. 1072p. 1968. 29.95 (ISBN 0-471-06568-4). Wiley.

Kulp, C. A. & Hall, John W. Casualty Insurance. 4th ed. LC 68-30893. 1968. 29.95 (ISBN 0-471-06568-4, 58871). Ronald Pr.

Louisiana Property & Casualty. 1979. 16.00 (ISBN 0-930868-15-3). Merritt Co.

Michelbacher, G. F. Multiple-Line Insurers: Their Nature & Operation. 2nd ed. (Insurance Ser.). 1970. text ed. 17.95 (ISBN 0-07-041780-6, C). McGraw.

Minnesota Property & Casualty. 1980. 15.50 (ISBN 0-930868-18-8). Merritt Co.

Mississippi Property & Casualty. 1979. 14.70 (ISBN 0-930868-20-X). Merritt Co.

Moore, Franklin L. Property & Casualty Insurance: Study Guide. 18.00 (ISBN 0-686-31035-7, 26629). Rough Notes.

N & S Dakota Property & Casualty. 1980. 15.00 (ISBN 0-930868-23-4). Merritt Co.

Rudman, Jack. Insurance Salesman. (Career Examination Ser.: C-389). (Cloth bdg. avail. on request). pap. 8.00 (ISBN 0-8373-0374-5). Natl Learning.

Siver, Edward W. An Executive Guide to Casualty & Property Insurance. LC 81-66512. 1981. 32.95 (ISBN 0-87251-049-2). Crain Bks.

Snouffer, Gary H. Property & Casualty Insurance Agent. LC 80-25678. 272p. (Orig.). 1981. pap. 12.00 (ISBN 0-668-04308-3, 4308). Arco.

South Carolina Property & Casualty. 1977. 16.60 (ISBN 0-930868-25-0). Merritt Co.

Tennessee Property & Casualty. 1980. 18.00 (ISBN 0-930868-37-4). Merritt Co.

Virginia Property & Casualty. 1980. write for info. (ISBN 0-930868-39-0). Merritt Co.

Western States Property & Causalty. 1980. 15.00 (ISBN 0-930868-31-5). Merritt Co.

Wisconsin Property & Casualty. 1977. 14.50 (ISBN 0-930868-33-1). Merritt Co.

INSURANCE, CORPORATE

see Insurance, Business

INSURANCE, DISABILITY

Arizona Life & Disability. 1980. 13.50 (ISBN 0-930868-07-2). Merritt Co.

Gordis, Philip. How to Stay Ahead Financially. 1977. 10.95 (ISBN 0-393-08794-8). Norton.

Harmelin, William. Disability Insurance: In the Business Buy-Out Agreement. 18.00 (ISBN 0-686-31054-3, 29350). Rough Notes.

Meyer, Charles W. Social Security Disability Insurance: Problems of Unexpected Growth. 1979. pap. 4.25 (ISBN 0-8447-3365-2). Am Enterprise.

O'Brien, David W. California Disability Benefits Handbook. 106p. (Orig.). 1980. pap. text ed. 7.95 (ISBN 0-9602204-6-1). Winter Brook.

Osborn, Grant M. Compulsory Temporary Disability Insurance in the United States. 1958. 7.75x (ISBN 0-256-00669-5). Irwin.

INSURANCE, EMPLOYERS' LIABILITY

see also Disability Evaluation; Industrial Accidents

Livingston, David T. Fiduciary Liability Insurance for Taft-Hartley Funds; a Comparison of Coverages. (Insurance, Liability Pensions). 68p. 1976. pap. 7.50 (ISBN 0-89154-042-3). Intl Found Employ.

INSURANCE, FIRE

see also Fireproofing

Fire & Casualty Insurance Companies. (Industry Audit Guides). 1966. pap. 6.00 (ISBN 0-685-58480-1). Am Inst CPA.

Grant, Roger H. Insurance Reform: Consumer Action in the Progressive Era. (Illus.). 1979. text ed. 14.95 (ISBN 0-8138-0935-5); pap. text ed. 9.50 (ISBN 0-8138-1210-0). Iowa St U Pr.

Huebner, S. S., et al. Property & Liability Insurance. 2nd ed. (Risk & Insurance Ser.). 1976. 20.95 (ISBN 0-13-730960-0). P-H.

Reed, P. B. & Thomas, P. I. Adjustment of Property Losses. 3rd ed. LC 69-12775. (Insurance Ser.). 1969. text ed. 19.25 (ISBN 0-07-051510-7, G). McGraw.

Rudman, Jack. Insurance Salesman. (Career Examination Ser.: C-389). (Cloth bdg. avail. on request). pap. 8.00 (ISBN 0-8373-0374-5). Natl Learning.

Salmon. Fire Insurance Principles & Practices. (Research Bulletin: No. 18). pap. 0.50 (ISBN 0-685-57190-4). Assn Sch Busn.

Smith, Harvey A. Economy in Public School Fire Insurance. LC 71-177773. (Columbia University. Teachers College. Contributions to Education: No. 428). Repr. of 1930 ed. 17.50 (ISBN 0-404-55428-8). AMS Pr.

Thomas, Paul I. & Reed, Prentiss B., Sr. Adjustment of Property Losses. 4th ed. (Illus.). 1977. text ed. 18.95 (ISBN 0-07-064215-X, G); instructor's manual & key 4.50 (ISBN 0-07-064216-8). McGraw.

INSURANCE, FIRE-RISKS

see also Electric Engineering–Insurance Requirements

INSURANCE, GROUP

Here are entered works on group insurance in general and on group life insurance. Works on group insurance in other specific fields are entered under Insurance, Casualty; Insurance, Hospitalization etc.

Batten, Robert W. & Hider, George M. Group Life & Health Insurance, Vols. 1 & 2. LC 78-71257. (FLMI Insurance Education Program Ser.). 1979. Set. pap. text ed. 19.95 (ISBN 0-915322-31-5). LOMA.

Life Office Management Association, ed. Readings for the Group Insurance Specialty. (FLMI Insurance Education Program Ser.). 45p. (Orig.). 1980. pap. 4.00 (ISBN 0-915322-40-4). Loma.

Pickrell, Jesse F. Group Health Insurance. rev. ed. 1961. 8.00x (ISBN 0-256-00671-7). Irwin.

Roberts, James E. Federal Income, Estate & Gift Taxation of Group Life Insurance. LC 76-13395. 1976. text ed. 7.95 (ISBN 0-87863-152-6). Farnswth Pub.

INSURANCE, HEALTH

see also Health Maintenance Organizations; Insurance, Life-Disability Benefits; Medical Care; Medical Care, Prepaid; Workmen's Compensation

Anderson, Odin W. The Uneasy Equilibrium: Private & Public Financing of Health Services in the United States, 1875-1965. 1968. pap. 3.95x (ISBN 0-8084-0305-2). Coll & U Pr.

Andreopoulos, Spyros, ed. National Health Insurance: Can We Learn from Canada? 296p. 1981. Repr. of 1975 ed. lib. bdg. write for info. (ISBN 0-89874-347-8). Krieger.

APA Guidelines for Psychiatric Services Covered Under Health Insurance Plans. 2nd ed. 1969. pap. 1.75 (ISBN 0-685-24844-5, P227-0). Am Psychiatric.

Austin, Charles J. The Politics of National Health Insurance: An Interdisciplinary Research Study. LC 75-14975. (Trinity Univ. Health Services Research Ser.). 1975. 7.50 (ISBN 0-911536-60-4). Trinity U Pr.

Bachman, George W. & Meriam, Lewis. The Issue of Compulsory Health Insurance. LC 75-17203. (Social Problems & Social Policy Ser.). (Illus.). 1976. Repr. of 1948 ed. 16.00x (ISBN 0-405-07475-1). Arno.

Batten, Robert W. & Hider, George M. Group Life & Health Insurance, Vols. 1 & 2. LC 78-71257. (FLMI Insurance Education Program Ser.). 1979. Set. pap. text ed. 19.95 (ISBN 0-915322-31-5). LOMA.

Bickley, John S. Impact of a State Disability Act on Insurance Companies. 1954. pap. 1.00x (ISBN 0-87776-071-3, R71). Ohio St U Admin Sci.

Blair, Roger D. & Vogel, Ronald J. The Cost of Health Insurance Administration. 128p. 1975. 21.95 (ISBN 0-669-00165-1). Lexington Bks.

Blanpain, Jan, et al. National Health Insurance & Health Resources: The European Experience. LC 77-25818. 1978. 20.00x (ISBN 0-674-26955-1). Harvard U Pr.

Bonito, Grace. Medical Insurance Billing Handbook. rev. ed. McFadden, S. Michele, ed. 1981. 16.95x (ISBN 0-89262-045-5). Career Pub.

--Medical Insurance Billing Workbook. rev. ed. McFadden, S. Michele, ed. 1981. 15.00x (ISBN 0-89262-046-3); inst. guide 12.50 (ISBN 0-89262-047-1). Career Pub.

Brown, Robert B. Guide to Health Insurance. 1981. 12.00 (ISBN 0-686-31056-X, 29122). Rough Notes.

Campbell, Rita R. & Campbell, W. Glenn. Voluntary Health Insurance in the U. S. 46p. 1960. pap. 4.25 (ISBN 0-8447-3025-4). Am Enterprise.

Carson, Clayborne. In Struggle: SNCC & the Black Awakening of the Nineteen Sixties. LC 80-16540. (Illus.). 384p. 1981. text ed. 22.00 (ISBN 0-674-44725-5). Harvard U Pr.

Catholic Health Association. National Health Insurance: Why CHA Is Taking Another Look. LC 81-67675. 52p. 1981. pap. 3.50 (ISBN 0-87125-065-9). Cath Health.

Comanor, William S. National Health Insurance in Ontario: Effects of a Policy Cost Control. 1980. pap. 4.25 (ISBN 0-8447-3379-2). Am Enterprise.

Conference on Proposed Legislation in The United States & on the British National Care Experience. National Health Insurance Schemes: Proceedings. 1972. 2.00 (ISBN 0-89215-038-6). U Cal LA Indus Rel.

Coverage & Utilization of Care for Mental Conditions Under Health Insurance: Various Studies 1973-74. 80p. 1975. 5.00 (ISBN 0-685-77440-6). Am Psychiatric.

Davidson, Stephen M., et al. The Cost of Living Longer: National Health Insurance & the Elderly. LC 79-2756. 160p. 1980. 19.95 (ISBN 0-669-03242-5). Lexington Bks.

Davis, Karen. National Health Insurance: Benefits, Costs, & Consequences. (Studies in Social Economics). 182p. 1975. 10.95 (ISBN 0-8157-1760-1); pap. 4.95 (ISBN 0-8157-1759-8). Brookings.

Egdahl, R. H. & Walsh, D. C., eds. Containing Health Benefit Costs: The Self-Insurance Option. (Springer Ser. on Industry & Health Care: Vol. 6). (Illus.). 1979. pap. 12.60 (ISBN 0-387-90385-2). Springer-Verlag.

Ehrlich, Ann. Managing Insurance Claims in the Medical Office. (Illus., Orig.). 1978. 5.95 (ISBN 0-940012-14-6). Colwell Co.

Eilers, Robert D. Regulation of Blue Cross & Blue Shield Plans. 1963. 9.00x (ISBN 0-256-00644-X). Irwin.

Eilers, Robert D. & Moyerman, Sue S. National Health Insurance. 362p. 1971. 10.75x (ISBN 0-256-00612-1). Irwin.

Elling, Ray H., ed. National Health Care: Issues & Problems in Socialized Medicine. (Controversy Ser). 287p. 1971. 9.95x (ISBN 0-88311-204-3); pap. 3.95x (ISBN 0-88311-205-1). Lieber-Atherton.

Evans, R. G. & Williamson, M. F. Extending Canadian Health Insurance: Options for Pharmacare & Denticare. (Ontario Economic Council Research Studies). 1978. pap. 14.00 (ISBN 0-8020-3353-9). U of Toronto Pr.

Fain, Tyrus G., et al, eds. National Health Insurance. LC 77-22947. (Public Documents Ser.). 1977. 38.50 (ISBN 0-8352-0960-1). Bowker.
Feder, et al. Insuring the Nation's Health: Market Competition, Catastrophic & Comprehensive Approaches. 227p. 1981. pap. 9.95 (ISBN 0-87766-298-3, 32400). Urban Inst.
Feder, J., et al, eds. National Health Insurance: Conflicting Goals & Policy Choices. LC 80-80045. 721p. 1980. text ed. 25.00x (ISBN 0-686-70298-0); pap. 12.50 (ISBN 0-87766-271-1). Urban Inst.
Feder, Judith. Medicare: The Politics of Federal Hospital Insurance. LC 77-4611. (Illus.). 1977. 19.95- (ISBN 0-669-01447-8). Lexington Bks.
Fisher, Peter. Prescription for National Health Insurance. LC 72-77266. (Illus.). 158p. 1972. 7.00 (ISBN 0-88427-007-6). North River.
Fordney, Marilyn T. Insurance Handbook for the Medical Office. 2nd ed. (Illus.). 475p. 1981. pap. text ed. write for info. (ISBN 0-7216-3814-7). Saunders.
--Insurance Handbook for the Medical Office. LC 76-22293. (Illus.). 1977. soft cover 16.95 (ISBN 0-7216-3812-0); text ed. 19.95 (ISBN 0-7216-3811-2). Saunders.
Frech, H. E. & Ginsburg, Paul B. Public Insurance in Private Medical Markets: Some Problems of National Health Insurance. 1978. pap. 4.25 (ISBN 0-8447-3303-2). Am Enterprise.
Friedman, Kenneth M. & Rakoff, Stuart H. Toward a National Health Policy: Public Policy & the Control of Health Care Costs. 1977. 20.50 (ISBN 0-669-00563-0). Lexington Bks.
Gaines, Price, ed. Time Saver for Health Insurance. LC 76-6783. 141p. 1981. pap. 13.25 (ISBN 0-87218-017-4). Natl Underwriter.
--Who Writes What: Nineteen Eighty-One Edition. LC 76-6787. 498p. 1980. pap. 10.50 (ISBN 0-87218-013-1). Natl Underwriter.
Glaser, William A. Health Insurance Bargaining: Foreign Lessons for Americans. 1978. 18.95 (ISBN 0-470-99398-7). Halsted Pr.
Gordis, Philip. How to Stay Ahead Financially. 1977. 10.95 (ISBN 0-393-08794-8). Norton.
Greenfield, Margaret. Meeting the Costs of Health Care: The Bay Area Experience & the National Issues. LC 72-5657. 182p. 1972. pap. 4.50x (ISBN 0-87772-086-X). Inst Gov Stud Berk.
Greider, Janice E. & Beadles, William T. Principles of Life Insurance, Vol. 1. rev. ed. 1973. pap. 9.00 (ISBN 0-256-01396-9). Irwin.
H. F. M. A. Staff. Review Procedures for the Medicare Hospital Statement of Reimbursable Cost. 2nd ed. 249p. 1977. pap. 2.00x (ISBN 0-930228-04-9). Hospital Finan.
Hirshfield, Daniel S. Lost Reform: The Campaign for Compulsory Health Insurance in the United States from 1932 to 1943. LC 71-115187. (Commonwealth Fund Publications Ser). 1970. 12.50x (ISBN 0-674-53917-6). Harvard U Pr.
Hyman, Herbert H. Health Planning: A Systematic Approach. LC 75-37405. 460p. 1976. text ed. 27.50 (ISBN 0-912862-17-3). Aspen Systems.
Illinois Life & Health. 1978. 14.00 (ISBN 0-930868-10-2). Merritt Co.
Illinois Property, Casualty & Health. 1978. 15.50 (ISBN 0-930868-11-0). Merritt Co.
Indiana Life & Health. 1977. 15.00 (ISBN 0-930868-12-9). Merritt Co.
Kiesler, Charles A., et al. Psychology & National Health Insurance: A Source Book. (Orig.). 1979. lib. bdg. 19.50x (ISBN 0-912704-13-6); pap. 15.00x (ISBN 0-912704-11-X). Am Psychol.
Laird, Melvin R., et al. Health Insurance: What Should Be the Federal Role? LC 75-15058. (Orig.). 1975. pap. 3.75 (ISBN 0-8447-2065-8). Am Enterprise.
Lee, A. James. Employment, Unemployment & Health Insurance: Behavioral & Descriptive Analysis of Health Insurance Loss Due to Unemployment. LC 78-66689. 1979. text ed. 19.50 (ISBN 0-89011-516-8). Abt Assoc.
Lieberman, Marvin, ed. The Impact of National Health Insurance on New York. 1977. pap. 8.95 (ISBN 0-88202-120-6). N Watson.
Louisiana Life & Health. 1980. 16.00 (ISBN 0-930868-14-5). Merritt Co.
Lusterman, Seymour. Industry Roles in Health Care. (Report Ser: No. 610). 130p. (Orig.). 1974. pap. 20.00 (ISBN 0-8237-0033-X). Conference Bd.
--Top Executives View Health Care Issues. LC 72-188149. (Report Ser: No. 552). 43p. 1972. pap. 5.00 (ISBN 0-8237-0055-0). Conference Bd.
McGuire, Thomas. Financing Psychotherapy: Costs Effects & Public Policy. 1981. 25.00 (ISBN 0-88410-711-6). Ballinger Pub.
Marmor, Theodore R. The Politics of Medicare. LC 76-169517. 160p. 1973. 18.95x (ISBN 0-202-24036-3); pap. 6.95 (ISBN 0-202-24037-1). Aldine Pub.
Marshall, Robert A. & Zubay, Eli A. The Debit System of Marketing Life & Health Insurance. LC 74-23820. 1975. 15.95 (ISBN 0-13-197384-3). Ga St U Busn Pub.
Mauksch, Ingeborg G., ed. National Health Insurance. LC 79-88380. (Nursing Dimensions Ser.: Vol. VII, No. 3). 1979. pap. text ed. 6.95 (ISBN 0-913654-57-4). Nursing Res.
Medicare Audit Guide. (Industry Audit Guides). 1969. pap. 4.50 (ISBN 0-685-58490-9). Am Inst CPA.
Meyer, Mitchell. Dental Insurance Plans. LC 75-42840. (Report Ser.: No. 680). (Illus.). 1976. pap. 15.00 (ISBN 0-8237-0114-X). Conference Bd.
Meyer, William F. Life & Health: Insurance Law. LC 72-76891. (Insurance Law Library). 1972. 47.50 (ISBN 0-686-14516-X). Lawyers Co-Op.
Minnesota Life & Health. 1979. 15.50 (ISBN 0-930868-17-X). Merritt Co.
Mississippi Life & Health. 1980. 14.00 (ISBN 0-930868-19-6). Merritt Co.
Morreale, Joseph C., ed. The U. S. Medical Care Industry: The Economist's Point of View. (Michigan Business Papers: No. 60). 131p. 1974. pap. 5.50 (ISBN 0-87712-166-4). U Mich Busn Div Res.
Munts, Raymond. Bargaining for Health: Labor Unions, Health Insurance, & Medical Care. 1967. 25.00 (ISBN 0-299-04320-7). U of Wis Pr.
Myers, Robert J. Medicare. 1970. 12.00x (ISBN 0-256-00373-4). Irwin.
N & S Dakota Life & Health. 1980. 15.00 (ISBN 0-930868-22-6). Merritt Co.
National Health Insurance Proposals. (Legislative Analysis Ser). (Orig.). 1974. pap. 3.75 (ISBN 0-8447-0166-1). Am Enterprise.
Numbers, Ronald L. Almost Persuaded: American Physicians & Compulsory Health Insurance, 1912-1920. LC 77-17254. (The Henry E. Sigerist Supplements to the Bulletin of the History of Medicine, New Ser.: No. 1). (Illus.). 1978. text ed. 11.50x (ISBN 0-8018-2052-9). Johns Hopkins.
Oddo, Ronald M. The Complete Guide to Ohio Health Insurance Claims Processing. 365p. 1981. Repr. 95.00 (ISBN 0-938936-03-4). Daring Pr.
Pauly, Mark V., ed. National Health Insurance: What Now, What Later, What Never? 1980. 16.95 (ISBN 0-8447-2184-0); pap. 8.25 (ISBN 0-8447-2185-9). Am Enterprise.
Pickrell, Jesse F. Group Health Insurance. rev. ed. 1961. 8.00x (ISBN 0-256-00671-7). Irwin.
Poen, Monte M. Harry S. Truman versus the Medical Lobby: The Genesis of Medicare. LC 78-59724. 1979. text ed. 20.00x (ISBN 0-8262-0257-8). U of Mo Pr.
Prudential Insurance Company of America. Health Insurance Fundamentals. LC 76-17650. (Self-Teaching Guides Ser.). 1976. pap. text ed. 4.95 (ISBN 0-471-01937-2). Wiley.
Prussin, Jeffrey A. Employee Health Benefits: HMOs & Mandatory Dual Choice. LC 76-24131. 230p. 1976. 49.50 (ISBN 0-912862-27-0). Aspen Systems.
Reed, Louis S., et al. Health Insurance & Psychiatric Care: Utilization & Cost. 412p. 1972. 8.00 (ISBN 0-685-31187-2, 217). Am Psychiatric.
Rosett, Richard N., ed. The Role of Health Insurance in the Health Services Sector. LC 76-8856. (Universities-National Bureau Conference Ser.: No. 27). 1976. 20.00 (ISBN 0-87014-272-0). N Watson.
Roth, Russell & Furstenberg, Frank F. National Health Insurance. 11.25 (ISBN 0-8447-2026-7). Am Enterprise.
Scheidemandel, Patricia, et al. Health Insurance for Mental Illness. 89p. 1968. pap. 3.00 (ISBN 0-685-24845-3, P195-0). Am Psychiatric.
Silverman, Milton, et al. Pills & the Public Purse. LC 80-6058. 300p. 1981. 15.95 (ISBN 0-520-04381-2). U of Cal Pr.
Skidmore, Max J. Medicare & the American Rhetoric of Reconciliation. LC 67-16144. 206p. 1970. 12.95x (ISBN 0-8173-4718-6). U of Ala Pr.
Snouffer, Gary H. Health Insurance Agent. LC 78-26706. 1979. pap. 8.00 (ISBN 0-668-04307-5). Arco.
Social Security Benefits Including Medicare, June 1981. 1981. pap. 1.50 (ISBN 0-686-75929-X). Commerce.
Somers, Herman M. & Somers, Anne R. Doctors, Patients, & Health Insurance: The Organization & Financing of Medical Care. 1961. 15.95 (ISBN 0-8157-8036-2). Brookings.
South Carolina Life & Health. 1976. 15.08 (ISBN 0-930868-24-2). Merritt Co.
Spiegel, Allen D. The Medicaid Experience. LC 78-27669. (Illus.). 418p. 1979. text ed. 35.75 (ISBN 0-89443-088-2). Aspen Systems.
Spiegelman, Mortimer. Ensuring Medical Care for the Aged. 1960. 8.75x (ISBN 0-256-00681-4). Irwin.
Steskal, T. J. Understanding Medicare. 93p. (Orig.). 1980. pap. 9.95 (ISBN 0-937978-00-0, MC-1). Info Prods.
Stoeber, Edward A. How to Use Life & Health Insurance in Business & Estate Planning. 3rd ed. LC 80-82132. 183p. 1980. pap. 15.00 (ISBN 0-87218-405-6). Natl Underwriter.
Taylor, Malcolm. Health Insurance & Canadian Public Policy: The Seven Decisions That Created the Canadian Health Insurance System. (Canadian Public Administration Ser.). 1978. 21.95x (ISBN 0-7735-0307-2); pap. 10.95 (ISBN 0-7735-0308-0). McGill-Queens U Pr.
Tennessee Life & Health. 1980. 18.00 (ISBN 0-930868-38-2). Merritt Co.
Virginia Life & Health. 1979. 15.00 (ISBN 0-930868-26-9). Merritt Co.
Webber, Irving L., ed. Medical Care Under Social Security: Potentials & Problems. LC 53-12339. (Center for Gerontological Studies & Programs Ser.: Vol. 15). 1966. pap. 3.75 (ISBN 0-8130-0237-0). U Presses Fla.
Weeks, David A. National Health Insurance & Corporate Benefit Plans: An Interim Report. (Report Ser: No. 633). 1974. pap. 15.00 (ISBN 0-8237-0040-2). Conference Bd.
West Virginia Life & Health-Property & Liability. 1977. 15.50 (ISBN 0-930868-29-3). Merritt Co.
Western States Life & Health. 1979. 15.00 (ISBN 0-930868-30-7). Merritt Co.
Williams, Pierce. The Purchase of Medical Care Through Fixed Periodic Payment. LC 75-17251. (National Bureau of Economic Research Ser.). 1975. Repr. 21.00x (ISBN 0-405-07525-1). Arno.
Wisconsin Life & Health. 1978. 14.50 (ISBN 0-930868-32-3). Merritt Co.
Wolfson, A. D. & Tuohy, Carolyn J. Opting Out of Medicare: Private Medical Markets in Ontario. 256p. 1980. pap. 12.50 (ISBN 0-8020-3373-3). U of Toronto Pr.
Ziegler, A. Insurance & Third-Party-Payable Claims. (Illus.). 1979. pap. 12.00 (ISBN 0-87489-152-3). Med Economics.

INSURANCE, HOSPITALIZATION

see also Hospital Care; Medical Care, Prepaid

Feder, Judith. Medicare: The Politics of Federal Hospital Insurance. LC 77-4611. (Illus.). 1977. 19.95- (ISBN 0-669-01447-8). Lexington Bks.
Graham, Nancy. Quality Assurance in Hospitals: Strategies for Assessment & Implementation. 400p. 1981. text ed. price not set (ISBN 0-89443-391-1). Aspen Systems.
Sloan, Frank A. & Steinwald, Bruce. Insurance, Regulation, & Hospital Costs. LC 79-3752. (Illus.). 288p. 1980. 25.95x (ISBN 0-669-03472-X). Lexington Bks.
Wilder, C. S. Hospital & Surgical Insurance Coverage United States 1974. Stevenson, Taloria, ed. (Ser.10, No. 117). 1977. pap. text ed. 1.50 (ISBN 0-8406-0109-3). Natl Ctr Health Stats.

INSURANCE, INDEMNITY

see Insurance, Liability

INSURANCE, INDUSTRIAL

Marshall, Robert A. & Zubay, Eli A. The Debit System of Marketing Life & Health Insurance. LC 74-23820. 1975. 15.95 (ISBN 0-13-197384-3). Ga St U Busn Pub.

INSURANCE, LIABILITY

see also Insurance, Accident; Insurance, Automobile; Insurance, Employers' Liability

Bagwell, W. Ray. Property & Liability Insurance Management Model. 1972. 10.95 (ISBN 0-88406-118-3). Ga St U Busn Pub.
Bishop, Joseph W., Jr. The Law of Corporate Officers & Directors: Indemnification & Insurance. LC 80-52859. 1981. 65.00 (ISBN 0-88262-504-7). Warren.
Guide to Liability Insurance. 7.50 (ISBN 0-686-31016-0, 30164). Rough Notes.
Huebner, S. S., et al. Property & Liability Insurance. 2nd ed. (Risk & Insurance Ser.). 1976. 20.95 (ISBN 0-13-730960-0). P-H.
--Property & Liability Insurance. 3rd ed. (Illus.). 608p. 1982. ref. ed. 24.95 (ISBN 0-13-730978-3). P-H.
O'Connell, Jeffrey. Ending Insult to Injury: No-Fault Insurance for Products & Services. LC 74-16243. 288p. 1975. 15.00 (ISBN 0-252-00451-5). U of Ill Pr.
Pierce, John E. Development of Comprehensive Insurance for the Household. 1958. 8.95x (ISBN 0-256-00673-3). Irwin.
Rosenbloom, Jerry S. Automobile Liability Claims: Insurance Company Philosophies & Practices. 1968. 7.00x (ISBN 0-256-00677-6). Irwin.
Schaeftler, Michael A. The Liabilities of Office: Indemnification & Insurance of Corporate Officers & Directors. 1976. 22.50 (ISBN 0-316-77276-3). Little.
Strain, Robert W. IASA Property-Liability Insurance Accounting. 1974. 21.50 (ISBN 0-930868-05-6). Merritt Co.
Sullivan, Gene. Products Liability: Who Needs It? LC 78-70485. 1979. text ed. 12.75 (ISBN 0-87218-003-4). Natl Underwriter.
West Virginia Life & Health-Property & Liability. 1977. 15.50 (ISBN 0-930868-29-3). Merritt Co.

INSURANCE, LIFE

see also Annuities; Insurance, Business Life; Insurance, Group; Insurance, Industrial; Insurance, Savings-Bank Life; Life Insurance Stocks; Probabilities

Arizona Life & Disability. 1980. 13.50 (ISBN 0-930868-07-2). Merritt Co.
Belth, Joseph M. Life Insurance: A Consumer's Handbook. LC 72-76943. 272p. 1973. 12.50x (ISBN 0-253-14800-6). Ind U Pr.
--Participating Life Insurance Sold by Stock Companies. 1965. 8.25x (ISBN 0-256-00639-3). Irwin.
Black, Kenneth, Jr. & Huebner, S. S. Life Insurance. x10th ed. (Illus.). 784p. 1982. 26.00 (ISBN 0-13-535799-3). P-H.
Brennan, Michael J. & Schwartz, Eduardo S. Pricing & Investment Strategies for Guaranteed Equity-Linked Life Insurance. LC 78-62409. (S. S. Huebner Foundation Monograph Ser.: No.7). (Illus.). 1979. pap. 12.00 (ISBN 0-918930-07-3). Huebner Foun Insur.
Brown, Robert B. Guide to Life Insurance. 1981. 12.00 (ISBN 0-686-31055-1, 29121). Rough Notes.
Buley, R. Carlyle. American Life Convention 1906-1952: A Study in the History of Life Insurance, 2 Vols. 1953. Set. 89.00x (ISBN 0-89197-012-6). Irvington.
Cissley, Charles H. Management Science in Life Companies. LC 75-32898. 1975. pap. 4.50 (ISBN 0-915322-15-3). LOMA.
Clough, Shepard B. Century of American Life Insurance: A History of the Mutual Life Insurance Company of New York, 1843-1943. LC 78-100150. Repr. of 1946 ed. lib. bdg. 17.25x (ISBN 0-8371-3713-6, CLAL). Greenwood.
Consumer Reports Editors. The Consumers Union Report on Life Insurance: A Guide to Planning & Buying the Protection You Need. 384p. 1981. 14.95 (ISBN 0-03-059109-0); pap. 7.95 (ISBN 0-03-059108-2). HR&W.
Cummins. An Econometric Model of the Life Insurance Sector of the U. S. Economy. LC 73-11654. 1975. 24.95 (ISBN 0-669-89490-7). Lexington Bks.
Cummins, J. David. Development of Life Insurance Surrender Values in the United States. LC 73-87483. (S. S. Huebner Foundation Monographs: No. 2). 1973. pap. 6.95 (ISBN 0-918930-02-2). Huebner Foun Insur.
Czuber, Eman. Wahrscheinlichkeitsrechnung & 'ihre Anwendung Auf Fehlerausgleichung, Statistik & Lebensversicherung, 2 Vols. (Bibliotheca Mathematica Teubneriana Ser.: Nos. 23 & 24). (Ger). 1969. Repr. of 1938 ed. Set. 42.50 (ISBN 0-384-10585-8). Johnson Repr.
Dacey. What's Wrong with Your Life Insurance. 1966. pap. 2.95 (ISBN 0-02-079490-8, Collier). Macmillan.
Dacey, Norman F. What's Wrong with Your Life Insurance. 1966. pap. 6.95 (ISBN 0-02-529340-0, CCPr). Macmillan.
Fogiel, Max. How to Pay Lots Less for Life Insurance. LC 76-22597. 1971. 11.95 (ISBN 0-87891-502-8). Res & Educ.
--How to Pay Lots Less for Life Insurance. LC 76-22597. 1971. 11.95 (ISBN 0-87891-502-8). Res & Educ.
Gaines, Price, ed. Interest-Adjusted Index: Nineteen Eighty-One Edition. LC 76-6788. 410p. 1980. pap. 18.00 (ISBN 0-87218-012-3). Natl Underwriter.
--Life Rates & Data, 1981. LC 76-7124. 768p. 1981. pap. 12.25 (ISBN 0-87218-015-8). Natl Underwriter.
--Who Writes What: Nineteen Eighty-One Edition. LC 76-6787. 498p. 1980. pap. 10.50 (ISBN 0-87218-013-1). Natl Underwriter.
Gordis, Philip. How to Stay Ahead Financially. 1977. 10.95 (ISBN 0-393-08794-8). Norton.
Grant, Roger H. Insurance Reform: Consumer Action in the Progressive Era. (Illus.). 1979. text ed. 14.95 (ISBN 0-8138-0935-5); pap. text ed. 9.50 (ISBN 0-8138-1210-0). Iowa St U Pr.
Gregg, Davis W. & Lucas, Vane B., eds. Life & Health Insurance Handbook. 3rd ed. 1973. 17.50x (ISBN 0-256-00169-3). Irwin.
Greider, Janice E. & Beadles, William T. Law & the Life Insurance Contract. 4th ed. 1979. 17.95x (ISBN 0-256-02158-9). Irwin.
--Principles of Life Insurance, Vol. 1. rev. ed. 1973. pap. 9.00 (ISBN 0-256-01396-9). Irwin.
Grossman, Eli A. Life Reinsurance. 79p. (Orig.). 1980. pap. text ed. 4.50 (ISBN 0-915322-38-2). Loma.
Huebner, S. S. & Black, K. Life Insurance. 9th ed. (Illus.). 608p. 1976. 21.95 (ISBN 0-13-535781-0). P-H.
Huebner, Solomon S. Economics of Life Insurance. 3rd ed. LC 59-10395. 1959. 28.00x (ISBN 0-89197-131-9). Irvington.
Illinois Life & Health. 1978. 14.00 (ISBN 0-930868-10-2). Merritt Co.
Indiana Life & Health. 1977. 15.00 (ISBN 0-930868-12-9). Merritt Co.

Jones-Lee, M. W. The Value of Life. LC 76-7395. 1976. 13.00x (ISBN 0-226-40794-2). U of Chicago Pr.
Josephson, Halsey D. The Tired Tirade. rev. ed. LC 68-54555. 1976. text ed. 6.95 (ISBN 0-87863-132-1). Farnswth Pub.
King, George. Student Guide for Law & the Life Insurance Contract. rev. ed. (FLMI Insurance Education Program Ser.). 1976. pap. 4.50 (ISBN 0-915322-19-6). LOMA.
Lance, William L. Life Insurance, Spend It & Keep It: How to Make a Tax-Free Exchange of Your Life Insurance & Earn Tax-Deferred Interest. (Illus.). 52p. 1980. pap. 8.00 (ISBN 0-686-27280-3). Truth Pub MN.
Life Assurance & Pensions in the European Community. 37p. 1981. 18.00x (ISBN 0-686-75458-1, Pub. by Insurance Inst England). State Mutual Bk.
Life Office Management Association, ed. Student Guide for Management Principles. 1981. 4.50 (ISBN 0-915322-30-7). LOMA.
Louisiana Life & Health. 1980. 16.00 (ISBN 0-930868-14-5). Merritt Co.
McCahan, David, ed. Life Insurance Trends at Mid-Century. 1950. 4.50x (ISBN 0-256-00658-X). Irwin.
McGill, Dan M. Life Insurance. rev. ed. 1967. 15.50x (ISBN 0-256-00331-9). Irwin.
McGill, Dan M., ed. Beneficiary in Life Insurance. rev. ed. 1956. 7.75x (ISBN 0-256-00662-8). Irwin.
McIntosh, Frank S., ed. How I Got My Piece of the Rock & Vital Life Insurance Information. 1979. pap. 19.95 (ISBN 0-686-26460-6). Ins Res Svc.
Marshall, Robert A. Life Insurance Company Mergers & Consolidations. 1972. 10.00x (ISBN 0-256-00653-9). Irwin.
Mehr. Plaid for Life Insurance. 1979. pap. 5.50 (ISBN 0-256-02101-5, 03-1293-01). Learning Syst.
Mehr, Robert I. Life Insurance: Theory & Practice. rev. ed. 1977. 19.95x (ISBN 0-256-01938-X). Business Pubns.
Milton. Life Insurance Stocks: The Modern Gold Rush. 2.95 (ISBN 0-8065-0322-X). Citadel Pr.
Minnesota Life & Health. 1979. 15.50 (ISBN 0-930868-17-X). Merritt Co.
Mississippi Life & Health. 1980. 14.00 (ISBN 0-930868-19-6). Merritt Co.
Munch. Life Insurance in Estate Planning. 1981. text ed. write for info. (ISBN 0-316-58930-6). Little.
Murrah, Charles R. Don't Talk to Me About Death. LC 77-75935. 1978. text ed. 3.95 (ISBN 0-87863-147-X). Farnswth Pub.
N & S Dakota Life & Health. 1980. 15.00 (ISBN 0-930868-22-6). Merritt Co.
Nontax & Tax Aspects of Life Insurance. 53p. 1980. pap. 10.00 (ISBN 0-686-29225-1, T182). ALI-ABA.
O'Halloran, T. P. You Sign the Little Cheque & We Sign the Big One. 1978. pap. text ed. 10.00 (ISBN 0-900886-28-5, Pub. by Witherby & Co. Ltd). State Mutual Bk.
Organization for Economic Cooperation & Development. Financial Guarantees Required from Life Assurance Concerns. 96p. 1971. 3.00x (ISBN 0-686-14799-5). OECD.
Orren, Karen. Corporate Power & Social Change: The Politics of the Life Insurance Industry. LC 73-8118. (Illus.). 216p. 1974. 14.00x (ISBN 0-8018-1507-X); pap. 4.45x (ISBN 0-8018-1828-1). Johns Hopkins.
Pearson, John S. Student Guide for Principles of Life Insurance, Pt. 1. (FLMI Insurance Education Program Ser.). 1972. pap. 4.00 (ISBN 0-915322-01-3). LOMA.
--Teaching Part 1: Principles of Life Insurance. 1972. pap. 8.00 (ISBN 0-915322-02-1). LOMA.
Pexa, Robert J. The Life Insurance War. LC 80-80013. (Illus.). 170p. (Orig.). 1980. pap. 6.95 (ISBN 0-9604170-0-1). Myleen Pr.
Pritchett, Bruce M. A Study of Capital Mobilization: The Life Insurance Industry of the 19th Century. Bruchey, Stuart, ed. LC 76-45109. (Nineteen Seventy-Seven Dissertations Ser.). (Illus.). 1977. lib. bdg. 28.00x (ISBN 0-405-09921-5). Arno.
Prudential Insurance Company of America. Life Insurance Fundamentals. LC 76-17652. (Self-Teaching Guides). 1976. pap. text ed. 8.95 (ISBN 0-471-01938-0). Wiley.
Readings for the Life Insurance Investments Specialty, II. (FLMI Insurance Education Program Ser.). 204p. 1980. pap. text ed. 9.00 (ISBN 0-915322-35-8). LOMA.
Rosler, Lee. Opportunities in Life Insurance Sales. LC 74-83737. 128p. (gr. 8-12). 1974. PLB 6.60 (ISBN 0-8442-6451-2); pap. 4.95 (ISBN 0-8442-6450-4). Natl Textbk.
--Opportunities in Life Insurance Sales. LC 65-19433. 1965. pap. 4.95 (ISBN 0-910580-54-5). Farnswth Pub.
Russell, George H. & Black, Kenneth. Human Behavior & Life Insurance. 1963. ref. ed. 10.95 (ISBN 0-13-444687-9). P-H.
Rykunyk, Mike. An Informed Approach to Life Insurance. 176p. 1982. 6.95 (ISBN 0-8059-2807-3). Dorrance.
Schwarzschild, Stuart. Rights of Creditors in Life Insurance Policies. 1963. 8.95x (ISBN 0-256-00680-6). Irwin.
Shy, DeWitt M. Live Smart-Die Smarter. LC 78-53620. 1978. 7.95 (ISBN 0-87397-136-1). Strode.
Sorensen, Marlene. Teaching Legal Aspects of Life Insurance, Pt. 3. (FLMI Insurance Education Program Ser.). 1978. instrs.' manual 8.00x (ISBN 0-915322-29-3). LOMA.
South Carolina Life & Health. 1976. 15.08 (ISBN 0-930868-24-2). Merritt Co.
Spielman, Peter & Zelman, Aaron. The Life Insurance Conspiracy: Made Elementary by Holmes & Watson. 1979. pap. 4.95 (ISBN 0-671-24377-2, Fireside). S&S.
Sprague, Thomas B. A Treatise on Life Insurance Accounts: Forming Pt. II on "Life Insurance in 1872", 2 vols. in one. Brief, Richard P., ed. LC 80-1526. (Dimensions of Accounting Theory & Practice Ser.). 1981. Repr. of 1911 ed. lib. bdg. 24.00x (ISBN 0-405-13547-5). Arno.
Stagliano, A. J. The Incidence of the Life Insurance Company Federal Income Tax. LC 79-88408. (S. S. Huebner Foundation Monograph Ser.: No. 9). 1980. pap. 12.95 (ISBN 0-918930-09-X). Huebner Foun Insur.
Stalson, J. Owen. Marketing Life Insurance. 1969. Repr. of 1949 ed. 11.95x (ISBN 0-256-00538-9). Irwin.
Stoeber, Edward A. How to Use Life & Health Insurance in Business & Estate Planning. 3rd ed. LC 80-82132. 183p. 1980. pap. 15.00 (ISBN 0-87218-405-6). Natl Underwriter.
Tennessee Life & Health. 1980. 18.00 (ISBN 0-930868-38-2). Merritt Co.
VanCaspel, Venita. Life Insurance: The Great National Consumer Dilemma. 1980. pap. 1.50 (ISBN 0-8359-4022-5). Reston.
Virginia Life & Health. 1979. 15.00 (ISBN 0-930868-26-9). Merritt Co.
Weisbart, Steven N. Extraterritorial Regulation of Life Insurance. 1975. 10.95x (ISBN 0-256-01753-0). Irwin.
West Virginia Life & Health-Property & Liability. 1977. 15.50 (ISBN 0-930868-29-3). Merritt Co.
Western States Life & Health. 1979. 15.00 (ISBN 0-930868-30-7). Merritt Co.
Will, Charles A. Life Company Underwriting. LC 74-78029. (FLMI Insurance Education Program Ser.). 1974. pap. 11.00 (ISBN 0-915322-07-2). LOMA.
Williamson, Harold F. & Smalley, Orange A. Northwestern Mutual Life: A Century of Trusteeship. LC 75-41787. (Companies & Men: Business Enterprises in America). (Illus.). 1976. Repr. of 1957 ed. 26.00x (ISBN 0-405-08102-2). Arno.
Wisconsin Life & Health. 1978. 14.50 (ISBN 0-930868-32-3). Merritt Co.
Wynn, Stephen. World Trends in Life Insurance. 119p. 1975. 15.95 (ISBN 0-85227-041-0, Pub. by Wiley). Krieger.
Zelizer, Viviana. Morals & Markets. LC 78-31205. 1979. 17.50x (ISBN 0-231-04570-0). Columbia U Pr.

INSURANCE, LIFE–ACCOUNTING

Life Office Management Association, ed. Student Guide to Accounting: for Life Insurance Companies. (FLMI Insurance Education Program Ser.). 97p. (Orig.). 1980. wkbk. 4.00 (ISBN 0-915322-42-0). Loma.
The Life Underwriter's Accounting System. (Orig.). (gr. 3 up). 12.00 (ISBN 0-686-31058-6); parents & teacher's guide for children 5.25 (ISBN 0-9606258-1-X, 27485); a 2-book pocket envelope 10.20 (ISBN 0-686-31059-4, 27486). Rough Notes.
Readings for the Managerial Accounting Speciality. (FLMI Insurance Education Program Ser.). 1981. pap. write for info (ISBN 0-915322-45-5). LOMA.
Strain, Robert W., ed. Life Insurance Accounting: Insurance Accounting & Statistical Association. 1977. text ed. 21.50 (ISBN 0-930868-00-5). Merritt Co.
Van House, Charles & Hammond, Rogers. Accounting for Life Insurance Companies. 1969. 11.50x (ISBN 0-256-00570-2). Irwin.
Yahr, Robert B. Are There Any GA (A P) S in Financial Reporting for the Life Insurance Industry? Dufey, Gunter, ed. LC 80-39883. (Research for Business Decisions: No. 29). 182p. 1981. 29.95 (ISBN 0-8357-1146-3, Pub. by UMI Res Pr). Univ Microfilms.

INSURANCE, LIFE–AGENTS

Life Sales Leadership Techniques. 1981. 7.50 (ISBN 0-686-31057-8, 29201). Daily Journal Books, 2. Financial Statement Book. Instruction Manual (27487). Rough Notes.
Rosler, Lee. Opportunities in Life Insurance Sales. LC 74-83737. 128p. (gr. 8-12). 1974. PLB 6.60 (ISBN 0-8442-6451-2); pap. 4.95 (ISBN 0-8442-6450-4). Natl Textbk.
Snouffer, Gary H. Life Insurance Agent. LC 77-14575. 1979. pap. text ed. 8.00 (ISBN 0-668-04306-7, 4306). Arco.
Stone, Mildred F. Extraordinary Ellen: The First Lady of Life Insurance. LC 79-90520. 1979. pap. 4.95 (ISBN 0-87863-195-X). Farnswth Pub.
Thompson, Hamilton B. Life Insurance As It's Really Sold! From Approach to Close. 4.00 (ISBN 0-686-31049-7, 29706). Rough Notes.

INSURANCE, LIFE–DISABILITY BENEFITS

Cooper, Robert W. An Historical Analysis of the Tontine Principle. LC 72-92061. (S. S. Huebner Foundation Monographs: No. 1). 1972. pap. 6.95 (ISBN 0-918930-01-4). Huebner Foun Insur.

INSURANCE, LIFE–EXAMINATIONS, QUESTIONS, ETC.

see Insurance–Examinations, Questions, etc.

INSURANCE, LIFE–MATHEMATICS

see also Probabilities

Harper, Floyd S. & Workman, Lewis C. Fundamental Mathematics of Life Insurance. 1970. 10.75x (ISBN 0-256-00231-2). Irwin.
Menge, Walter O. & Fischer, Carl H. The Mathematics of Life Insurance. 2nd ed. LC 65-12855. 1965. text ed. 8.95x (ISBN 0-914004-00-X). Ulrich.
Workman, Lewis C. Teaching Part 6: Fundamental Mathematics of Life Insurance. 1975. 8.00 (ISBN 0-915322-08-0). LOMA.
--Workbook for Fundamental Mathematics of Life Insurance. 1970. pap. 6.50 (ISBN 0-915322-00-5). LOMA.

INSURANCE, LIFE–MEDICAL EXAMINATIONS

International Congress of Life Insurance, 13th, Madrid 1979. Annals of Life Insurance Medicine: Proceedings, Vol. 6. Tanner, E. & Hefti, M. L., eds. (Illus.). 270p. 1980. 37.80 (ISBN 0-387-10050-4). Springer-Verlag.
Singer, Richard B. & Levinson, Louis, eds. Medical Risks: Patterns of Mortality & Survival. LC 74-31609. 1976. 37.95 (ISBN 0-669-98228-8). Lexington Bks.

INSURANCE, LIFE–CANADA

Pedoe, Arthur. Life Insurance, Annuities, & Pensions: A Canadian Text. 3rd ed. 1978. 25.00x (ISBN 0-8020-2316-9). U of Toronto Pr.

INSURANCE, LIFE–GREAT BRITAIN

Babbage, Charles. Comparative View of the Various Institutions for the Assurance of Lives. LC 67-18568. Repr. of 1826 ed. 12.50x (ISBN 0-678-00335-1). Kelley.
Dodds, J. C. The Investment Behaviour of British Life Insurance Companies. 193p. 1979. 50.00x (ISBN 0-7099-0058-9, Pub. by Croom Helm Ltd England). Biblio Dist.
Franklin, Peter J. & Woodhead, Caroline. The U. K. Life Assurance Industry: A Study in Applied Economics. (Illus.). 390p. 1980. 80.00x (ISBN 0-85664-654-7, Pub. by Croom Helm Ltd England). Biblio Dist.
Rosin, Albert. Lebensversicherung und Ihre Geistesgeschichtlichen Grundlagen. Repr. of 1932 ed. pap. 7.00 (ISBN 0-384-52050-2). Johnson Repr.

INSURANCE, LIGHTNING

see also Insurance, Fire

INSURANCE, MARINE

see also Salvage

Bes, J. Chartering & Shipping Terms: Time-Sheet Supplements, Vols. 2 & 3. Set. 70.00 (ISBN 0-685-11999-8). Heinman.
Duer, John. The Law & Practice of Marine Insurance, Deduced from a Critical Examination of the Adjudged Cases, the Nature & Analogies of the Subject, & the General Usage of Commercial Nations, 2 vols. LC 72-37972. (American Law Ser.: The Formative Years). 1650p. 1972. Repr. of 1846 ed. Set. 70.00 (ISBN 0-405-04010-5); 35.00 ea. Vol. 1. Vol. 2. Arno.
Huebner, S. S., et al. Property & Liability Insurance. 2nd ed. (Risk & Insurance Ser.). 1976. 20.95 (ISBN 0-13-730960-0). P-H.
International Union Of Marine Insurance & International Chamber Of Commerce. Tables of Practical Equivalents of the Principal Terms, Clauses & Conditions of Cover Used in Various Countries for the Insurance of Cargo Against the Risks of International Transport, 2 vols. 3rd rev. ed. 1969. pap. 8.50 (ISBN 0-87037-518-0). Helios.
International Union Of Marine Insurance Cargo Loss Prevention Committee. Time-Bar on Cargo Claims. 2nd ed. rev. ed. 1969. pap. 4.50 (ISBN 0-87037-520-2). Helios.
Lambeth, R. J. Templeman on Marine Insurance: Its Principles & Practice. 5th ed. 574p. 1981. 48.00x (ISBN 0-7121-1395-9). Sheridan.
Mankabady, S. Collision at Sea: A Guide to the Legal Consequences. 1978. 36.75 (ISBN 0-444-85155-0, North-Holland). Elsevier.
Martin, Frederick. History of Lloyd's & of Marine Insurance in Great Britain. LC 76-156387. (Research & Source Works Ser.: No. 737). 1971. Repr. of 1876 ed. lib. bdg. 25.50 (ISBN 0-8337-2268-9). B Franklin.
Mullins, Hugh A. & Buglass, Leslie J. Marine Insurance Digest. 2nd ed. LC 59-15426. 1959. 7.00x (ISBN 0-87033-046-2). Cornell Maritime.
Pinkernelle, E., tr. from Ger. German General Rules of Marine Insurance. 1977. 11.25x (ISBN 3-11-006879-6). De Gruyter.
Winter, William D. Marine Insurance. 3rd ed. (Insurance Ser.). (Illus.). 1952. text ed. 19.50 (ISBN 0-07-071119-4, C). McGraw.

INSURANCE, MULTIPLE LINE

Bickelhaupt, David L. Transition to Multiple-Line Insurance Companies. 1961. 8.25x (ISBN 0-256-00640-7). Irwin.
Swift, Walter D. Multiple Line Adjusting: A Guide to Professional Claim Practices. pap. text ed. 12.00 (ISBN 0-686-31015-2, 26021). Rough Notes.

INSURANCE, MUTUAL

see Insurance

INSURANCE, PARTNERSHIP

see Insurance, Business Life

INSURANCE, PHYSICIANS'

see Physicians–Insurance Requirements

INSURANCE, POSTAL LIFE

see Insurance, Life

INSURANCE, PROPERTY

see also Insurance, Casualty; Insurance, Fire; Insurance, Marine

Arizona Property & Casualty. 1978. 13.00 (ISBN 0-930868-08-0). Merritt Co.
Arkansas Property & Casualty. 1980. 14.00 (ISBN 0-930868-09-9). Merritt Co.
Bachman, James E. Capitalization Requirements for Multiple Line Property Liability Insurance Companies. LC 78-57297. (S. S. Huebner Foundation Monographs: No. 6). (Illus.). 1978. pap. 10.00 (ISBN 0-918930-06-5). Huebner Foun Insur.
Bagwell, W. Ray. Property & Liability Insurance Management Model. 1972. 10.95 (ISBN 0-88406-118-3). Ga St U Busn Pub.
Gee, Harold F. An Approach to Property & Casualty Insurance. 8.00 (ISBN 0-686-31028-4, 26121). Rough Notes.
Georgia Property & Casualty. 1980. 14.00 (ISBN 0-930868-36-6). Merritt Co.
Gordis, Philip. Lessons in Property & Casuality Insurance: Course 1. 58.50 (ISBN 0-686-31037-3, 26530). Rough Notes.
Gordis, Philip L. Property & Casualty Insurance: A Reservoir of Insurance Know How. 750p. lib. bdg. 25.00 (ISBN 0-686-31012-8, 26520). Rough Notes.
Homeowners Seventy Six Policy Program Guide. 60p. 6.00 (ISBN 0-686-31011-X, 30180). Rough Notes.
Huebner, S. S., et al. Property & Liability Insurance. 2nd ed. (Risk & Insurance Ser.). 1976. 20.95 (ISBN 0-13-730960-0). P-H.
--Property & Liability Insurance. 3rd ed. (Illus.). 608p. 1982. ref. ed. 24.95 (ISBN 0-13-730978-3). P-H.
Illinois Property, Casualty & Health. 1978. 15.50 (ISBN 0-930868-11-0). Merritt Co.
Indiana Property & Casualty. 1978. 15.00 (ISBN 0-930868-13-7). Merritt Co.
The Insuring of Condominiums & Cooperatives. 8.00 (ISBN 0-686-31019-5, 26628). Rough Notes.
Louisiana Property & Casualty. 1979. 16.00 (ISBN 0-930868-15-3). Merritt Co.
Melchior, William T. Insuring Public School Property. LC 75-177068. (Columbia University. Teachers College. Contributions to Education: No. 168). Repr. of 1925 ed. 17.50 (ISBN 0-404-55168-8). AMS Pr.
Minnesota Property & Casualty. 1980. 15.50 (ISBN 0-930868-18-8). Merritt Co.
Mississippi Property & Casualty. 1979. 14.70 (ISBN 0-930868-20-X). Merritt Co.
Moore, Franklin L. Property & Casualty Insurance: Study Guide. 18.00 (ISBN 0-686-31035-7, 26629). Rough Notes.
N & S Dakota Property & Casualty. 1980. 15.00 (ISBN 0-930868-23-4). Merritt Co.
Nye, David J. A Simulation Analysis of Capital Structure in a Property Insurance Firm. LC 75-3908. (S. S. Huebner Foundation Monographs: No. 3). (Illus.). 1975. pap. 8.95 (ISBN 0-918930-03-0). Huebner Foun Insur.
Pierce, John E. Development of Comprehensive Insurance for the Household. 1958. 8.95x (ISBN 0-256-00673-3). Irwin.
Siver, Edward W. An Executive Guide to Casualty & Property Insurance. LC 81-66512. 1981. 32.95 (ISBN 0-87251-049-2). Crain Bks.
Snouffer, Gary H. Property & Casualty Insurance Agent. LC 80-25678. 272p. (Orig.). 1981. pap. 12.00 (ISBN 0-668-04308-3, 4308). Arco.
South Carolina Property & Casualty. 1977. 16.60 (ISBN 0-930868-25-0). Merritt Co.
Strain, Robert W. IASA Property-Liability Insurance Accounting. 1974. 21.50 (ISBN 0-930868-05-6). Merritt Co.
Tennessee Property & Casualty. 1980. 18.00 (ISBN 0-930868-37-4). Merritt Co.
Virginia Property & Casualty. 1980. write for info. (ISBN 0-930868-39-0). Merritt Co.

West Virginia Life & Health-Property & Liability. 1977. 15.50 (ISBN 0-930868-29-3). Merritt Co.
Western States Property & Causalty. 1980. 15.00 (ISBN 0-930868-31-5). Merritt Co.
Wisconsin Property & Casualty. 1977. 14.50 (ISBN 0-930868-33-1). Merritt Co.

INSURANCE, SAVINGS-BANK LIFE

Johnson, Donald R. Savings Bank Life Insurance. 1963. pap. 8.50x (ISBN 0-256-00647-4). Irwin.

INSURANCE, SELF

see Self-Insurance

INSURANCE, SICKNESS

see Insurance, Health

INSURANCE, SOCIAL

see Social Security

INSURANCE, STATE AND COMPULSORY

see Social Security

INSURANCE, STRIKE

see also Insurance, Unemployment

INSURANCE, TRANSPORTATION

see Insurance, Marine

INSURANCE, UNEMPLOYMENT

see also Supplemental Unemployment Benefits

Altman, Ralph. Availability for Work, a Study in Unemployment Compensation. LC 68-8935. (Illus.). 1968. Repr. of 1950 ed. lib. bdg. 17.25x (ISBN 0-8371-0004-6, ALAW). Greenwood.
Atkinson, R. C. The Federal Role in Unemployment Compensation Administration: A Report Prepared for the Committee on Social Security. LC 77-74927. (American Federalism-the Urban Dimension). 1978. Repr. of 1941 ed. lib. bdg. 12.00x (ISBN 0-405-10476-6). Arno.
Avrutis, Raymond. How to Collect Unemployment Benefits. LC 75-859. 1975. pap. 1.25 (ISBN 0-8052-0490-3). Schocken.
Becker, Joseph. Experience Rating in Unemployment Insurance: An Experiment in Competitive Socialism. LC 72-4026. (Illus.). 419p. 1972. 25.00x (ISBN 0-8018-1429-4). Johns Hopkins.
Becker, Joseph M. Shared Government in Employment Security. LC 74-6703. 501p. 1975. Repr. of 1959 ed. lib. bdg. 23.50x (ISBN 0-8371-7547-X, BESG). Greenwood.
--Unemployment Benefits: Should There Be a Compulsory Federal Standard? 1980. pap. 4.25 (ISBN 0-8447-3389-X). Am Enterprise.
Blaustein, Saul J. & Craig, Isabel. An International Review of Unemployment Insurance Schemes. (Studies in Unemployment Insurance). 1977. pap. 4.00 (ISBN 0-911558-22-5). Upjohn Inst.
Blaustein, Saul J. & Kozlowski, Paul J. Interstate Differences in Unemployment Insurance Benefit Cost: A Cross Section Study. 1978. pap. 1.50 (ISBN 0-911558-00-4). Upjohn Inst.
Bowers, Edison L., et al. Financing Unemployment Compensation: Ohio's Experience. 1957. 4.00x (ISBN 0-87776-089-6, R89). Ohio St U Admin Sci.
Douglas, Paul H. Social Security in the United States: An Analysis & Appraisal of the Federal Social Security Act. LC 71-137164. (Poverty U.S.A. Historical Record Ser). 1971. Repr. of 1936 ed. 16.00 (ISBN 0-405-03102-5). Arno.
Employment Security Clerk. 5th ed. LC 75-26006. (Orig.). 1975. pap. 6.00 (ISBN 0-668-00700-1). Arco.
Hamermesh, Daniel S. Jobless Pay & the Economy. LC 76-47369. (Policy Studies in Employmennt & Welfare: No. 29). (Illus.). 128p. 1977. 8.50x (ISBN 0-8018-1927-X); pap. 3.95x (ISBN 0-8018-1928-8). Johns Hopkins.
How to Collect Unemployment Insurance: Even If You're Not Eligible. 1981. pap. 4.95 (ISBN 0-686-30632-5). Loompanics.
Keeling, B. Lewis. Payroll Records & Accounting. 1975. text ed. 6.84 (ISBN 0-538-01460-1). SW Pub.
Mackin, Paul J. Benefit Financing in Unemployment Insurance: A Problem of Balancing Responsibilities. LC 78-23336. (Studies in Unemployment Insurance), 1978. pap. 3.00 (ISBN 0-911558-61-6). Upjohn Inst.
Nelson, Daniel. Unemployment Insurance: The American Experience, 1915-1935. (Illus.). 320p. 1969. 25.00x (ISBN 0-299-05200-1). U of Wis Pr.
Rudman, Jack. Senior Unemployment Insurance Claims Examiner. (Career Examination Ser.: C-2285). (Cloth bdg. avail. on request). 1977. pap. 10.00 (ISBN 0-8373-2285-5). Natl Learning.
--Unemployment Insurance Claims Clerk. (Career Examination Ser.: C-850). (Cloth bdg. avail. on request). pap. 8.00 (ISBN 0-8373-0850-X). Natl Learning.
--Unemployment Insurance Claims Examiner. (Career Examination Ser.: C-851). (Cloth bdg. avail. on request). pap. 8.00 (ISBN 0-8373-0851-8). Natl Learning.
--Unemployment Insurance Investigator. (Career Examination Ser.: C-2364). (Cloth bdg. avail. on request). pap. 8.00 (ISBN 0-8373-2364-9). Natl Learning.
Unemployment Compensation Amendments. (Legislative Analyses). 1976. pap. 3.75 (ISBN 0-8447-0176-9). Am Enterprise.

INSURANCE, WORKING-MEN'S

see Social Security

INSURANCE ADJUSTING

see Insurance–Adjustment of Claims

INSURANCE AGENTS

see Insurance–Agents

INSURANCE COMPANIES

Baum, Daniel J. The Investment Function of Canadian Financial Institutions. LC 72-86435. (Special Studies in International Economics & Development). 1973. 38.50x (ISBN 0-275-28684-3). Irvington.
Bawcutt, Paul. Captive Insurance Companies. 160p. 1980. 54.00x (ISBN 0-85941-077-3, Pub. by Woodhead-Faulkner England). State Mutual Bk.
Blair, Roger D. & Vogel, Ronald J. The Cost of Health Insurance Administration. 128p. 1975. 21.95 (ISBN 0-669-00165-1). Lexington Bks.
Brown, Antony. Lloyd's of London. LC 73-91848. (Illus.). 216p. 1974. 25.00x (ISBN 0-8128-1671-4). Stein & Day.
Cissley, Charles H. Management Science in Life Companies. LC 75-32898. 1975. pap. 4.50 (ISBN 0-915322-15-3). LOMA.
Didactic Systems Staff. Management by Objectives for Insurance Companies. (Simulation Game Ser.). 1972. pap. 24.90 (ISBN 0-89401-054-9); pap. 21.50 two or more (ISBN 0-685-78128-3). Didactic Syst.
Gloster, Jesse E. North Carolina Mutual Life Insurance Company: Its Historical Development & Current Operations. LC 75-41758. (Companies & Men: Business Enterprises in America). (Illus.). 1976. 25.00x (ISBN 0-405-08074-3). Arno.
Jaffee, Cabot L. & Burroughs, Wayne A. Problems in Insurance Company Management: An In-Basket Training Exercise. LC 77-153065. (Business Ser). (Illus.). 1971. pap. text ed. 9.95 (ISBN 0-201-03291-0). A-W.
James, Marquis. The Metropolitan Life: A Study in Business Growth. LC 75-41765. (Companies & Men: Business Enterprises in America). (Illus.). 1976. Repr. of 1947 ed. 32.00x (ISBN 0-405-08080-8). Arno.
Keller, Morton. Life Insurance Enterprise, 1885-1910: A Study in the Limits of Corporate Power. LC 63-10868. (Center for the Study of the History of Liberty in America Ser). (Illus.). 1963. 16.50x (ISBN 0-674-53150-7, Belknap Pr). Harvard U Pr.
Life Office Management Association. Life Company Operations. LC 74-83846. 1974. 10.00 (ISBN 0-915322-10-2); student guide 4.50 (ISBN 0-915322-11-0); Teaching Part 2, 1975. 8.00 (ISBN 0-915322-09-9). LOMA.
Life Office Management Association, ed. Student Guide for Management Principles. 1981. 4.50 (ISBN 0-915322-30-7). LOMA.
Lilly, Claude C., III, et al. Oracle I. LC 81-80590. 351p. 1981. text ed. 50.00 (ISBN 0-87218-310-6). Natl Underwriter.
McGuire, Patrick E. Customer Relations in Financial Institutions. (Report No. 761). (Illus., Orig.). 1979. pap. 15.00 (ISBN 0-8237-0197-2). Conference Bd.
Marshall, Robert A. Life Insurance Company Mergers & Consolidations in the Southeast. LC 71-10036. (Research Monograph: No. 52). 1970. spiral bdg. 3.00 (ISBN 0-88406-064-0). Ga St U Busn Pub.
Mass Life & Health. 1977. 12.00 (ISBN 0-930868-16-1). Merritt Co.
Missouri Life & Health Property & Casualty. 1980. 17.50 (ISBN 0-930868-21-8). Merritt Co.
Mueller-Lutz, Heinz L. Basic Principles of Insurance Management. Weissman, Fred, tr. LC 66-22891. (Illus.). 1966. 6.95 (ISBN 0-87037-514-8). Helios.
Post, James E. Risk & Response. (Illus.). 1976. 21.50 (ISBN 0-669-00645-9). Lexington Bks.
Puth, Robert C. Supreme Life: The History of a Negro Life Insurance Company. LC 75-41780. (Companies & Men: Business Enterprises in America). 1976. 20.00x (ISBN 0-405-08095-6). Arno.
Sommer, Armand & Kedzie, Daniel P. Your Future in Insurance. LC 70-114117. (Career Guidance Ser). 1971. pap. 3.95 (ISBN 0-668-02249-3). Arco.
Survey of Current Management Techniques in the Insurance Industry. 37p. 1981. 24.00x (ISBN 0-686-75459-X, Pub. by Insurance Inst England). State Mutual Bk.
Tobias, Andrew. The Invisible Bankers: Everything the Insurance Industry Never Wanted You to Know. 1982. 14.95 (ISBN 0-686-76564-8, Linden). S&S.
Webb, Bernard L., et al. Insurance Company Operations. 1978. write for info. (CPCU 5). IIA.
Weisbart, Steven N. & Skipper, Harold D., eds. Privacy & the Insurance Industry. LC 79-21197. (Research Monograph: No. 83). 1979. pap. 14.95 (ISBN 0-88406-123-X). Ga St U Busn Pub.

INSURANCE COMPANIES–DIRECTORIES

see Insurance–Directories

INSURANCE COMPANIES–EMPLOYEES

see also Insurance–Agents

Augustus, Betty. Local Agency Office Handbook for Beginners. 6.00 (ISBN 0-686-31034-9, 26420). Rough Notes.
Roush, John H., Jr. Management Audits of Branch Claims Offices of National Insurance Companies. LC 74-31546. 197p. 1975. 17.00 (ISBN 0-9600830-1-4). J H Roush.

INSURANCE COMPANIES–INVESTMENTS

Burgh, Edward M. Mortgage Investing by Life Insurance Companies. LC 80-80943. (FLMI Insurance Education Program Ser.). (Illus.). 202p. (Orig.). 1980. pap. text ed. 12.00 (ISBN 0-915322-36-6). Loma.
Cummins, J. David. Investment Activities of Life Insurance Companies. 1977. 16.00x (ISBN 0-256-01974-6). Irwin.
Hooley, Richard W. Financing the Natural Gas Industry. LC 68-59256. (Columbia University. Studies in the Social Sciences: No. 602). Repr. of 1961 ed. 18.50 (ISBN 0-404-51602-5). AMS Pr.
Pritchett, Bruce M. A Study of Capital Mobilization: The Life Insurance Industry of the 19th Century. Bruchey, Stuart, ed. LC 76-45109. (Nineteen Seventy-Seven Dissertations Ser.). (Illus.). 1977. lib. bdg. 28.00x (ISBN 0-405-09921-5). Arno.
Schultz, Robert E. Life Insurance Housing Projects. 1956. 6.50x (ISBN 0-256-00678-4). Irwin.
Snider, H. Wayne. Life Insurance Investment in Commercial Real Estate. 1956. 6.50x (ISBN 0-256-00679-2). Irwin.

INSURANCE COMPANIES–TAXATION

see Insurance–Taxation

INSURANCE COMPANY OF NORTH AMERICA

James, Marquis. Biography of a Business, 1792-1942: Insurance Company of North America. LC 75-43409. (Companies & Men: Business Enterprises in America). (Illus.). 1976. Repr. of 1942 ed. 31.00x (ISBN 0-405-08079-4). Arno.

INSURANCE ENGINEERING

see also Fire Extinction; Fire Prevention

INSURANCE LAW

Anderson, Ronald A. Couch on Insurance, 24 vols. 2nd ed. LC 59-1915. 1971. 876.00 set (ISBN 0-686-14510-0). Lawyers Co-Op.
Anderson, Ronald T. Agent's Legal Responsibility. LC 80-83690. 168p. 1980. text ed. 12.75 (ISBN 0-87218-307-6). Natl Underwriter.
Angell, Joseph K. A Treatise on the Law of Fire & Life Insurance. LC 76-37965. (American Law Ser.: The Formative Years). 600p. 1972. Repr. of 1854 ed. 26.00 (ISBN 0-405-03992-1). Arno.
Castelo, Julio. The Insurance Market in Latin America, Portugal, & Spain. LC 73-90846. 220p. 1977. text ed. 15.00x (ISBN 0-8203-0377-1). U of Ga Pr.
Court Decisions: Coverage Interpretations That Help You Understnad & Sell Insurance. 7.50 (ISBN 0-686-31013-6, 30035). Rough Notes.
District of Columbia Insurance: Annotated Code. pap. 3.50 (ISBN 0-685-14181-0). Lerner Law.
Dobbyn, John F. Insurance Law in a Nutshell. LC 81-7468. (Nutshell Ser.). 315p. 1981. pap. text ed. 6.95 (ISBN 0-686-72639-1). West Pub.
Duer, John. The Law & Practice of Marine Insurance, Deduced from a Critical Examination of the Adjudged Cases, the Nature & Analogies of the Subject, & the General Usage of Commercial Nations, 2 vols. LC 72-37972. (American Law Ser.: The Formative Years). 1650p. 1972. Repr. of 1846 ed. Set. 70.00 (ISBN 0-405-04010-5); 35.00 ea. Vol. 1. Vol. 2. Arno.
Garon, Philip A., ed. Insurance Law Anthology, Vol. 1. (National Law Anthology Ser.). 1981. text ed. 59.95 (ISBN 0-914250-21-3). Intl Lib.
Gould Editorial Staff. Insurance Laws of the United States. (Supplemented annually). looseleaf 7.50 (ISBN 0-87526-179-5). Gould.
Horn, Ronald C. Subrogation in Insurance Theory & Practice. 1964. 9.25x (ISBN 0-256-00651-2). Irwin.
Howell, Edward B. & Howell, Richard P. Targeting in on Professional Liability. 1978. 25.00 (ISBN 0-932056-02-4). Risk Analysis.
Indiana Insurance Laws. 4th ed. 1979. 35.00 (ISBN 0-672-82765-4, Bobbs-Merrill Law). Michie-Bobbs.
Insurance Agent & Broker. rev. ed. LC 67-12047. 1970. pap. 6.00 (ISBN 0-668-02149-7). Arco.
Insurance Law (N. Y.) 1974 ed. 238p. 5.50 (ISBN 0-87526-077-2). Gould.
Insurer's Tort Law. 1971. 14.30 (ISBN 0-914770-01-2). Littoral Develop.
Kimball, Spencer. Insurance & Public Policy: A Study in the Legal Implementation of Social & Economic Public Policy, Based on Wisconsin Records, 1835-1959. 1960. 7.50x (ISBN 0-299-02140-8); enl. ed. 17.00x (ISBN 0-299-02149-1). U of Wis Pr.
Lorrimer, James, et al. The Legal Environment of Insurance, 2 vols. 1978. write for info. (CPCU 6). IIA.
MacAvoy, Paul W., ed. Federal-State Regulation of the Pricing & Marketing of Insurance. (Ford Administration Papers on Regulatory Reforms). 1977. 5.25 (ISBN 0-8447-3253-2). Am Enterprise.
Patterson, Edwin W. The Insurance Commissioner in the United States. Repr. of 1927 ed. 31.00 (ISBN 0-384-45145-4). Johnson Repr.
Pfennigstorf, Werner. German Insurance Laws: Statutes & Regulations Concerning Insurance Supervision & Insurance Contracts. LC 75-18609. 1975. 27.00 (ISBN 0-910058-73-3). Am Bar Foun.
Pfennigstorf, Werner, tr. from Ger. German Insurance Laws: Statutes & Regulations Concerning Insurance Supervision & Contracts, 1977 Supplement. 1977. pap. 3.00 (ISBN 0-910058-85-7). Am Bar Foun.
Prudential Insurance Company of America. New York State Insurance Law. LC 76-28412. (Self-Teaching Guides). 1977. 3.95 (ISBN 0-471-02108-3). Wiley.
The Regulation of Insurance Companies in the United States & the European Communities: A Comprehensive Study. Date not set. price not set (ISBN 0-89834-040-3). Chamber Comm US.
Sorensen, Marlene. Teaching Legal Aspects of Life Insurance, Pt. 3. (FLMI Insurance Education Program Ser.). 1978. instrs.' manual 8.00x (ISBN 0-915322-29-3). LOMA.
Taylor, Irwin M. Law of Insurance. 2nd ed. LC 68-16508. (Illus.). 1968. 5.95 (ISBN 0-379-11037-7). Oceana.
Texas Local Recording Agent's Licensing Course. 1980. correspondence course 63.00 (ISBN 0-930868-34-X). Merritt Co.
Weese, Samuel H. Non-Admitted Insurance in the United States. (S. S. Huebner Foundation for Insurance). 1971. 8.25x (ISBN 0-256-00683-0). Irwin.

INSURANCE LAW, INTERNATIONAL

Doman, Leon H. Supranational Regulation of Insurance. 1966. pap. 3.50 (ISBN 0-685-12055-4). Helios.

INSURANCE STATISTICS

see Insurance–Rates and Tables

INSURANCE STOCKS

see also Life Insurance Stocks

INSURGENCY

see also Government, Resistance to; Guerrilla Warfare; Internal Security; Peasant Uprisings; Subversive Activities; Terrorism

Ash, William. Morals & Politics: The Ethics of Revolution. (Direct Editions Ser.). 1977. pap. 9.00 (ISBN 0-7100-8558-3). Routledge & Kegan.
British Government. Handbook on Anti-Mau Mau Operations. 170p. 1977. pap. 8.00 (ISBN 0-87364-099-3). Paladin Ent.
Dellheim, S. D. Intelligence Requirements for Domestic Urban Insurgency. new ed. 1978. pap. 5.95 (ISBN 0-930788-00-1, SPR-5591). Scott Protective.
International Countermeasures Handbook 1979-80. 1980. 50.00 (ISBN 0-531-03918-8). Watts.
Khairallah, David. Insurrection Under International Law. 1973. 20.00 (ISBN 0-86685-176-3). Intl Bk Ctr.
Mao Tse-Tung. Mao Tse-Tung on Revolution & War. Rejai, M., ed. 10.00 (ISBN 0-8446-5275-X). Peter Smith.
Nachalo, Sophia & Vochek, Yarostan. Letters of Insurgents. 1976. 6.75 (ISBN 0-934868-13-1). Black & Red.
O'Neill, Bard, et al, eds. Political Violence & Insurgency: A Comparative Approach. LC 74-25006. 1974. write for info. (ISBN 0-915222-01-9). Phoenix Assocs.
O'Neill, Brad E., et al, eds. Insurgency in the Modern World. (Westview Special Study Ser.). (Illus.). 320p. 1980. lib. bdg. 27.75x (ISBN 0-89158-598-2). Westview.
Szatmary, David P. Shays' Rebellion: The Making of an Agrarian Insurrection. LC 79-22522. 1980. lib. bdg. 14.00x (ISBN 0-87023-295-9). U of Mass Pr.
U.S. Army. Civil Disturbances Handbook for Small Unit Leaders. (Illus.). 1977. pap. 4.00 (ISBN 0-87364-090-X). Paladin Ent.

INSURRECTIONS

see Revolutions; Slavery in the United States–Insurrections, etc.

INTAGLIO PRINTS

see Engravings

INTAGLIOS

see also Gems; Seals (Numismatics)

Neverov, O., compiled by. Antique Intaglios. Date not set. 10.95 (ISBN 0-89893-005-7). CDP.

INTANGIBLE PROPERTY
see Copyright; Intellectual Property; Licenses; Patents; Trade-Marks
INTANGIBLE PROPERTY-TAXATION
see also Friendly Societies; Insurance-Agents; Insurance, Fire; Insurance Law; Taxation of Bonds, Securities, etc.
INTARSIA
see Marquetry
INTEGER PROGRAMMING
see also Programming (Electronic Computers)

Balinski, M. L., ed. Approaches to Integer Programming. LC 74-83270. (Mathematical Programming Study: Vol. 2). 197p. 1975. pap. 23.50 (ISBN 0-7204-0359-6, North-Holland). Elsevier.

Garfinkel, Robert & Nemhauser, George L. Integer Programming. LC 72-3881. (Decision & Control Ser.). 528p. 1972. 35.50x (ISBN 0-471-29195-1, Pub. by Wiley-Interscience). Wiley.

Glover, Fred. A Fresh Look at Heuristic Principles for Integer Progamming. 1977. 2.50 (ISBN 0-686-64187-6). U CO Busn Res Div.

Greenberg, Harold. Integer Programming. (Mathematics in Science & Engineering Ser., Vol. 76). 1971. 32.50 (ISBN 0-12-299450-7). Acad Pr.

Hausmann, D., ed. Integer Programming & Related Areas: A Classified Bibliography 1976 - 1978. Compiled at the Institute Fuer Oekonometrie und Operations Research, Univ of Bonn. LC 78-18918. (Lecture Notes in Economics & Mathematical Systems: Vol. 160). 1978. pap. 18.50 (ISBN 0-387-08939-X). Springer-Verlag.

Institute of Operations Research, Sponsored by IBM, University of Bonn, Germany, Sept. 8-12, 1975. Studies in Integer Programming: Proceedings of a Workshop Held in Bonn. Hammer, P. L., ed. (Annals of Discrete Mathematics). 1977. 58.75 (ISBN 0-7204-0765-6, North-Holland). Elsevier.

Kastning, C., ed. Integer Programming & Related Areas. (Lecture Notes in Economics & Mathematical Systems: Vol. 128). 1976. soft cover 20.30 (ISBN 0-387-07788-X). Springer-Verlag.

NATO Advanced Study Institute, Versailles, France, September 2-13, 1974. Combinatorial Programming: Methods & Application, Proceedings. Roy, B., ed. (NATO Advanced Study Institutes: No. C19). 386p. 1975. 47.50 (ISBN 9-0277-0506-2, Pub. by Reidel Holland). Kluwer Boston.

Salkin, Harvey M. Integer Programming. (Illus.). 450p. 1975. text ed. 21.95 (ISBN 0-201-06841-9). A-W.

Taha, Hamdy A. Integer Programming Theory. 1975. 36.50 (ISBN 0-12-682150-X). Acad Pr.

Zionts, Stanley. Linear & Integer Programming. (Illus.). 528p. 1974. text ed. 22.95 (ISBN 0-13-536763-8). P-H.

INTEGRAL CALCULUS
see Calculus, Integral
INTEGRAL EQUATIONS
see also Calculus, Operational; Functional Analysis; Integral Transforms

Ahiezer, N. I., et al. Fifteen Papers on Real & Complex Functions, Series, Differential & Integral Equations. LC 51-5559. (Translations Ser.: No. 2, Vol. 86). 1970. 29.20 (ISBN 0-8218-1786-8, TRANS 2-86). Am Math.

Albrecht, Julius & Collatz, Lothar, eds. Numerical Treatment of Integral Equations. (International Ser. of Numerical Mathematics Ser.: No. 53). 283p. 1981. pap. 33.00 (ISBN 3-7643-1105-3). Birkhauser.

Anderson, R. S. & De Hoog, F. R., eds. Application & Numberical Solution of Intergral Equations. (Mechanics Analysis Ser.: No. 6). 265p. 1980. 27.50x (ISBN 90-286-0450-2). Sijthoff & Noordhoff.

Atkinson, Kendall E. A Survey of Numerical Methods for the Solution of Fredholm Integral Equations of the Second Kind. LC 75-28900. (Illus., Orig.). 1976. pap. text ed. 20.50 (ISBN 0-686-24262-9). Soc Indus-Appl Math.

Baker, Christopher. The Numerical Treatment of Integral Equations. (Monographs on Numerical Analysis). (Illus.). 1048p. 1977. text ed. 69.00x (ISBN 0-19-853406-X). Oxford U Pr.

Bart, H., et al. Minimal Factorization of Matrix & Operator Functions. (Operator Theory: Advances & Applications Ser.: No. 1). 236p. 1979. pap. 17.50 (ISBN 3-7643-1139-8). Birkhauser.

Bocher, M. An Introduction to the Study of Integral Equations. 2nd ed. (Cambridge Tracts in Mathematics & Mathematical Physics Ser.: No. 10). 1971. Repr. of 1926 ed. 8.25 (ISBN 0-02-841570-1). Hafner.

Cochran, J. A. Analysis of Linear Integral Equations. 1972. 24.95 (ISBN 0-07-011527-3, C). McGraw.

Conference on Qualitative Theory of Nonlinear Differential & Integral Equations, Wisconsin. Studies in Applied Mathematics Five: Advances in Differential & Integral Equations. Proceedings. Nohel, John S., ed. (Illus.). 1969. text ed. 12.50 (ISBN 0-686-24260-2). Soc Indus-Appl Math.

Corduneanu, Constantin. Principles of Differential & Integral Equations. 2nd ed. LC 77-2962. 1977. text ed. 10.95 (ISBN 0-8284-0295-7). Chelsea Pub.

Delves, L. M. & Walsh, J., eds. Numerical Solution of Integral Equations. (Illus.). 352p. 1974. 39.50x (ISBN 0-19-853342-X). Oxford U Pr.

Gohberg, I. C. & Fel'dman, I. A. Convolution Equations & Projection Methods for Their Solution. LC 73-22275. (Translations of Mathematical Monographs: Vol. 41). 262p. 1974. 48.40 (ISBN 0-8218-1591-1, MMONO-41). Am Math.

Goldberg, ed. Solution Methods for Integral Equations: With Applications. (Mathematical Concepts & Methods in Science & Engineering: Vol. 18). 1979. 35.00 (ISBN 0-306-40254-8, Plenum Pr). Plenum Pub.

Graef, John R. Stability of Dynamical Systems: Theory & Application. (Lecture Notes in Pure& Applied Mathematics: Vol. 28). 1977. 24.75 (ISBN 0-8247-6410-2). Dekker.

Hilbert, David. Integralgleichungen. (Ger). 14.95 (ISBN 0-8284-0091-1). Chelsea Pub.

Hochstadt, Harry. Integral Equations. LC 73-4230. (Pure & Applied Mathematics Ser.). 304p. 1973. 33.95 (ISBN 0-471-40165-X, Pub. by Wiley-Interscience). Wiley.

Hoheisel, Guido. Integral Equations. Tropper, A. Mary, tr. LC 68-15581. 1968. 8.50 (ISBN 0-8044-4405-6). Ungar.

Honig, C. S. Volterra Stieltjes-Integral Equations. (Mathematics Studies Ser: Vol. 16). 157p. 1975. pap. 24.50 (ISBN 0-444-10850-5, North-Holland). Elsevier.

Jaswon, M. A. & Symm, G. T. Integral Equation Methods in Potential Theory & Elastostatics. 1978. 45.50 (ISBN 0-12-381050-7). Acad Pr.

Kagiwada, H. & Kalaba, R. Integral Equations via Imbedding Methods. LC 74-13228. (Applied Mathematics & Computation Ser.: No. 6). 1974. text ed. 22.50 (ISBN 0-201-04106-5, Adv Bk Prog); pap. text ed. 12.50 (ISBN 0-201-04107-3, Adv Bk Prog). A-W.

Kanwal, Ram P. Linear Integral Equations: Theory & Techniques. 1971. 46.50 (ISBN 0-12-396550-0). Acad Pr.

Lakshmikantham, V. & Leela, S. Differential & Integral Inequalities: Theory & Application, 2 vols. Incl. Vol. 1. Ordinary Differential Equations. 56.00 (ISBN 0-12-434101-2); Vol. 2. Functional, Partial, Abstract & Complex Differential Equations. 54.50 (ISBN 0-12-434102-0). LC 68-8425. (Mathematics in Science & Engineering Ser.: Vol. 55). 1969. Acad Pr.

LaSalle, J. P. The Stability of Dynamical Systems. (CBMS Regional Conference Ser.: Vol. 25). (Orig.). 1976. pap. text ed. 9.50 (ISBN 0-89871-022-7). Soc Indus-Appl Math.

Levinson, Norman. Gap & Density Theorems. LC 41-6147. (Colloquium, Pbns. Ser.: Vol. 26). 1963. Repr. of 1940 ed. 19.60 (ISBN 0-8218-1026-X, COLL-26). Am Math.

Londen, S. O. & Staffan, O. J., eds. Volterra Equations: Proceedings, Helsinki Symposium, Finland, August 11-14, 1978. (Lecture Notes in Mathematics: Vol. 737). 1979. pap. 16.80 (ISBN 0-387-09534-9). Springer-Verlag.

Mikhlin, S. G. Linear Integral Equations. (Russian Monographs & Texts on the Physical Sciences Ser). 1961. 35.75x (ISBN 0-677-20320-9). Gordon.

Miller, Richard K. & Sell, George R. Volterra Integral Equations & Topological Dynamics. LC 52-42839. (Memoirs: No. 102). 1979. pap. 9.60 (ISBN 0-8218-1802-3, MEMO-102). Am Math.

Moiseiwitsch, Benjamin L. Integral Equations. LC 76-10282. (Longman Mathematical Texts). (Illus.). 1977. pap. text ed. 11.95x (ISBN 0-582-44288-5). Longman.

Paley, Raymond E. & Wiener, Norbert. Fourier Transforms in the Complex Domain. LC 35-3273. (Colloquium, Pbns. Ser.: Vol. 19). 1978. Repr. of 1934 ed. 27.60 (ISBN 0-8218-1019-7, COLL-19). Am Math.

Petrovskii, Ivan G. Lectures on the Theory of Integral Equations. LC 57-3179. (Illus.). 1957. 9.00x (ISBN 0-910670-09-9). Graylock.

Ramm, A. Theory & Applications of Some New Classes of Integral Equations. 344p. 1981. pap. 19.80 (ISBN 0-387-90540-5). Springer-Verlag.

Schwabik, Stefan, et al. Differential & Integral Equations: Boundry Value Problems & Adjoints. 1979. 39.50 (ISBN 90-277-0802-9, Pub. by Reidel Holland). Kluwer Boston.

Srivastava, H. M. & Buschman, R. G. Convolution Integral Equations with Special Function Kernels. LC 76-52979. 1977. 14.95 (ISBN 0-470-99050-3). Halsted Pr.

Steklov Institute of Mathematics, Academy of Sciences, U S S R, No. 97 & Maslennikov, M. Y. Milne Problem with Anisotropic Scattering: Proceedings. 1969. 37.20 (ISBN 0-8218-1897-X, STEKLO-97). Am Math.

Symposium in Pure Mathematics - Chicago - 1966. Singular Integrals: Proceedings, Vol. 10. Calderon, A. P., ed. LC 67-16553. 1967. 30.00 (ISBN 0-8218-1410-9, PSPUM-10). Am Math.

Symposium on the Numerical Treatment of O.D.E. Integral & Integro-Differential Equations. Rome 1960. 680p. 1961. 31.50 (ISBN 3-7643-0378-6). Birkhauser.

Tsokos, Chris P. & Padgett, W. J. Random Integral Equations with Applications to Life Sciences & Engineering. 1974. 46.00 (ISBN 0-12-702150-7). Acad Pr.

Vekua, N. P. Systems of Singular Integral Equations. 1967. 45.25x (ISBN 0-677-61340-7). Gordon.

Walter, Wolfgang. Differential & Integral Inequalities. rev. ed. Rosenblatt, L. & Shampine, L., trs. from Ger. LC 72-103330. (Ergebnisse der Mathematik und Ihrer Grenzgebiete: Vol. 55). (Illus.). 1970. 42.50 (ISBN 0-387-05088-4). Springer-Verlag.

INTEGRAL FUNCTIONS
see Functions, Entire
INTEGRAL TRANSFORMS

Davies, B. Integral Transforms & Their Applications. LC 77-27330. (Applied Mathematical Sciences Ser.: Vol. 25). (Illus.). 1978. pap. 16.30 (ISBN 0-387-90313-5). Springer-Verlag.

Erdelyi, Arthur, ed. Tables of Integral Transforms, Vol. 1. (Illus.). 1954. text ed. 32.50 (ISBN 0-07-019549-8, P&RB). McGraw.

Giffin, Walter C. Transform Techniques for Probability Modeling. (Operation Research Industrial Engineering Ser.). 1975. 46.50 (ISBN 0-12-282750-3). Acad Pr.

Katz, M. B. Questions of Uniqueness & Resolution in Reconstruction of 2-D & 3-D Objects from Their Projections. (Lecture Notes in Biomathematics: Vol. 26). 1979. pap. 11.30 (ISBN 0-387-09087-8). Springer-Verlag.

Oberhettinger, F. Tables of Bessel Transforms. LC 72-88727. 289p. 1972. pap. 13.00 (ISBN 0-387-05997-0). Springer-Verlag.

Sneddon, Ian N. The Use of Integral Transforms. (Illus.). 560p. 1972. text ed. 28.50 (ISBN 0-07-059436-8, C). McGraw.

Wolf, K. B. Integral Transforms in Science & Engineering. (Mathematical Concepts & Methods in Science & Engineering Ser.: Vol. 11). 475p. 1978. 32.50 (ISBN 0-306-39251-8, Plenum Pr). Plenum Pub.

INTEGRALS

Alfsen, E. M. Compact Convex Sets & Boundary Integrals. LC 72-136352. (Ergebnisse der Mathematik und Ihrer Grenzgebiete: Vol. 57). (Illus.). 1971. 29.00 (ISBN 0-387-05090-6). Springer-Verlag.

Babenko, K. I., et al. Twelve Papers on Approximations & Integrals. LC 51-5559. (Translations Ser.: No. 2, Vol. 44). 1966. Repr. of 1965 ed. 21.20 (ISBN 0-8218-1744-2, TRANS 2-44). Am Math.

Bleistein, Norman & Handlesman, Richard. Asymptotic Expansions of Integrals. LC 74-3376. 1975. text ed. 18.50x (ISBN 0-03-083596-8). Irvington.

Bochner, Salomon. Fouriersche Integrale. LC 49-22695. (Ger). 8.95 (ISBN 0-8284-0042-3). Chelsea Pub.

Boudreaux, Edward A., et al. Numerical Tables of Two-Center Overlap Integrals. 1970. text ed. 28.00 (ISBN 0-8053-1064-9, Adv Bk Prog). Benjamin-Cummings.

Brucker, A. M. Differentiation of Integrals: Supplement to American Mathematical Monthly, November 1971. (Slaught Memorial Paper: No. 12). 51p. pap. 2.00 (ISBN 0-88385-415-5). Math Assn.

Butzer, P. L. & Berens, H. Semi-Groups of Operators & Approximation. LC 68-11980. (Grundlehren der Mathematischen Wissenschaften: Vol. 145). 1967. 33.90 (ISBN 0-387-03832-9). Springer-Verlag.

Chakravarti, P. C. Integrals & Sums. 1970. text ed. 23.50x (ISBN 0-485-11114-4, Athlone Pr). Humanities.

Copson, Edward T. Asymptotic Expansions. (Cambridge Tracts in Mathematics & Mathematical Physics). 1965. 21.50 (ISBN 0-521-04721-8). Cambridge U Pr.

Dwight, Herbert B. Tables of Integrals & Other Mathematical Data. 4th ed. 1961. 16.95 (ISBN 0-02-331170-3, 33117). Macmillan.

Ferguson, LeBaren O. Approximation by Polynomials with Integral Coefficients. LC 79-20331. (Mathematical Surveys: Vol. 17). 1980. 28.80 (ISBN 0-8218-1517-2). Am Math.

Gohberg, Israel, et al. Einfuhrung in Die Theorie der Eindimensionalen Singularen Integraloperatoren. (Mathematische Reihe: No. 63). (Illus.). 379p. (Ger.). 1979. 59.50 (ISBN 3-7643-1020-0). Birkhauser.

Gradshteyn, I. S., et al. Tables of Integrals, Series & Products. 1980. 19.50 (ISBN 0-12-294760-6). Acad Pr.

Hudson, Ralph G. Table of Integrals. 1917. text ed. 13.50 (ISBN 0-471-41877-3, Pub. by Wiley-Interscience). Wiley.

Jacobs, Konrad. Measure & Integral. (Probability & Mathematical Statistics). 1978. 55.00 (ISBN 0-12-378550-2). Acad Pr.

Konrod, Aleksandr S. Nodes & Weights of Quadrature Formulas. LC 65-15002. 143p. 1965. 47.50 (ISBN 0-306-65111-4). IFI Plenum.

Kral, J. Integral Operators in Potential Theory. (Lecture Notes in Mathematics Ser.: Vol. 823). 171p. 1981. pap. 11.80 (ISBN 0-387-10227-2). Springer-Verlag.

McShane, Edward J. Integration. (Mathematical Ser.: Vol. 7). 1961. 28.00 (ISBN 0-691-07982-X). Princeton U Pr.

Nielsen. Direct Integrel Theory. (Lecture Notes in Pure & Applied Mathematics Ser.: Vol. 61). 184p. 1980. 23.50 (ISBN 0-8247-6971-6). Dekker.

Osher, S. J. Two Papers on Similarity of Certain Volterra Integral Operators. LC 52-42839. (Memoirs: No. 73). 1967. pap. 7.20 (ISBN 0-8218-1273-4, MEMO-73). Am Math.

Petit Bois, G. Tables of Indefinite Integrals. 1906. pap. text ed. 5.00 (ISBN 0-486-60225-7). Dover.

Sadowsky, Cora. Interpolation of Operators & Singular Integrals. (Pure & Applied Math Ser.: Vol. 53). 1979. 35.00 (ISBN 0-8247-6883-3). Dekker.

Schochetman, Irwin E. Integral Operators in the Theory of Induced Banach Representations. LC 78-15819. (Memoirs: No. 207). 1978. 9.60 (ISBN 0-8218-2207-1). Am Math.

Segal, I. E. & Kunze, R. A. Integrals & Operators. 2nd rev ed. LC 77-16682. (Grundlehren der Mathematischen Wissenschaften: Vol. 228). 1978. Repr. 37.80 (ISBN 0-387-08323-5). Springer-Verlag.

Shilov, G. E. & Gurevich, B. L. Integral, Measure & Derivative: A Unified Approach. Silverman, Richard, tr. 1977. pap. text ed. 4.50 (ISBN 0-486-63519-8). Dover.

Sobel, M., et al. Dirichlet Distribution: Type 1. LC 74-6283. (Selected Tables in Mathematical Statistics: Vol. 4). 1977. 26.00 (ISBN 0-8218-1904-6, TABLES-4). Am Math.

Spiegel, Murray R. Real Variables. 1969. pap. 6.95 (ISBN 0-07-060221-2, SP). McGraw.

Symposium in Pure Mathematics - Chicago - 1966. Singular Integrals: Proceedings, Vol. 10. Calderon, A. P., ed. LC 67-16553. 1967. 30.00 (ISBN 0-8218-1410-9, PSPUM-10). Am Math.

Wheeden, Richard & Zygmund, Antoni. Measure & Integral. (Monographs & Textbooks in Pure & Applied Mathamatics). 1977. 19.75 (ISBN 0-8247-6499-4). Dekker.

INTEGRALS, DEFINITE
see also Numerical Integration

Carslaw, Horatio S. Introduction to the Theory of Fourier's Series & Integrals. 3rd ed. (Illus.). 1952. pap. 6.00 (ISBN 0-486-60048-3). Dover.

Fichtenholz, G. M. The Definite Integral. Silverman, R. A., tr. from Rus. LC 78-149513. (Pocket Mathematical Library Ser.). (Illus.). 97p. 1973. 23.25x (ISBN 0-677-21090-6). Gordon.

--The Indefinite Integral. Schwartz, Jacob D., ed. Silverman, Richard A., tr. from Rus. LC 76-135120. (Pocket Mathematical Library Ser.). (Illus.). 148p. 1971. 34.75x (ISBN 0-677-21030-2). Gordon.

INTEGRALS, DOUBLE
see Integrals, Multiple
INTEGRALS, ELLIPTIC
see Functions, Elliptic
INTEGRALS, GENERALIZED
see also Integrals, Haar; Measure Theory

Bartle, Robert G. Elements of Integration. LC 75-15979. 129p. 1966. 20.95 (ISBN 0-471-05457-7). Wiley.

Berberian, Sterling K. Measure & Integration. LC 74-128871. 1970. Repr. of 1965 ed. text ed. 11.95 (ISBN 0-8284-0241-8). Chelsea Pub.

Bichteler, K. Integration Theory: With Special Attention to Vector Measures. LC 72-97636. (Lecture Notes in Mathematics: Vol. 315). 357p. 1973. pap. 14.30 (ISBN 0-387-06158-4). Springer-Verlag.

Bishop, Errett & Cheng, Henry. Constructive Measure Theory. LC 52-42839. (Memoirs: No. 116). 1972. pap. 6.40 (ISBN 0-8218-1816-3, MEMO-116). Am Math.

Burkill, John C. Lebesgue Integral. (Cambridge Tracts in Mathematics & Mathematical Physics). 1951. 14.50 (ISBN 0-521-04382-4). Cambridge U Pr.

Gunther, N. Integrales De Stieltjes. LC 50-1366. (Fr). 19.95 (ISBN 0-8284-0063-6). Chelsea Pub.

Guzman, M. De. Differentiation of Integrals in R to the nth Power. (Lecture Notes in Mathematics: Vol. 481). xii, 226p. 1975. pap. 12.20 (ISBN 0-387-07399-X). Springer-Verlag.

Hawkins, Thomas. Lebesgue's Theory of Integration: Its Origins & Development. 3rd ed. LC 74-8402. xv, 227p. 1975. text ed. 11.95 (ISBN 0-8284-0282-5). Chelsea Pub.

Kingman, John F. & Taylor, S. J. Introduction to Measure & Probability. 1966. 44.50 (ISBN 0-521-05888-0). Cambridge U Pr.

Klambauer, G. Real Analysis. LC 72-93078. 416p. 1973. 22.95 (ISBN 0-444-00133-6, North Holland). Elsevier.

McBride, Adam C. Fractional Calculus & Integral Transforms of Generalized Functions. (Research in Mathematics Ser.: No. 31). 179p. (Orig.). 1979. pap. text ed. 17.95 (ISBN 0-273-08415-1). Pitman Pub MA.

Nielsen, Niels. Die Gammafunktion, 2 vols. in 1. Incl. Integrallogarithmus. LC 64-13785. (Ger.). 1965. 16.50 (ISBN 0-8284-0188-8). Chelsea Pub.

Pesin, Ivan N. Classical & Modern Integration Theories. (Probability & Mathematical Statistics Ser.: Vol. 8). (Rus). 1970. 32.50 (ISBN 0-12-552550-8). Acad Pr.

Pfeffer, Washek F. Integrals & Measures. (Monographs in Pure & Applied Mathematics: Vol. 42). 1977. 24.50 (ISBN 0-8247-6530-3). Dekker.

Weir, A. J. General Integration & Measure. LC 73-91620. (Illus.). 344p. 1974. 35.50 (ISBN 0-521-20407-0); pap. 13.95 (ISBN 0-521-29715-X). Cambridge U Pr.

Whitney, Hassler. Geometric Integration Theory. (Mathematical Ser.: Vol. 21). 1957. 28.00x (ISBN 0-691-07972-2). Princeton U Pr.

INTEGRALS, HAAR

Nachbin, Leopoldo. The Haar Integral. LC 75-42042. 168p. 1976. Repr. of 1965 ed. 9.75 (ISBN 0-88275-374-6). Krieger.

INTEGRALS, HYPERELLIPTIC

see also Functions, Elliptic

INTEGRALS, IMPROPER

Neri, U. Singular Integrals. LC 76-166077. (Lecture Notes in Mathematics: Vol. 200). 1971. pap. text ed. 11.20 (ISBN 0-387-05502-9). Springer-Verlag.

INTEGRALS, MULTIPLE

Ledermann, Walter. Multiple Integrals. (Library of Mathematics Ser.). (Illus.). 1966. pap. 5.00 (ISBN 0-7100-4358-9). Routledge & Kegan.

Major, P. Multiple Wiener-Ito Integrals. (Lecture Notes in Mathematics Ser.: Vol. 849). 127p. 1981. pap. 9.80 (ISBN 0-387-10575-1). Springer-Verlag.

Morrey, Charles B. Multiple Integrals in the Calculus of Variations. (Grundlehren der Mathematischen Wissenschaften: Vol. 130). 1966. 42.20 (ISBN 0-387-03524-9). Springer-Verlag.

Stroud, A. Approximate Calculation of Multiple Integrals. LC 77-159121. (Automatic Computation Ser). (Illus.). 1972. ref. ed. 29.50 (ISBN 0-13-043893-6). P-H.

--Approximate Calculation of Multiple Integrals. LC 77-159121. (Automatic Computation Ser). (Illus.). 1972. ref. ed. 29.50 (ISBN 0-13-043893-6). P-H.

INTEGRALS, STOCHASTIC

Bharucha-Reid, A. T. Random Integral Equations. (Mathematics in Science & Engineering Ser.: Vol. 96). 1972. 46.00 (ISBN 0-12-095750-7). Acad Pr.

Ito, Kiyosi, ed. Proceedings of the International Symposium on Stochastic Differential Equations, Kyoto, 1976. LC 78-19655. 1978. 50.00 (ISBN 0-471-05375-9, Pub. by Wiley-Interscience). Wiley.

McKean, H. P., Jr. Stochastic Integrals. (Probability & Mathematical Statistics Ser.: Vol. 5). 1969. 28.00 (ISBN 0-12-483450-7). Acad Pr.

Meyer, P. A. Martingales & Stochastic Integrals I. LC 72-88111. (Lecture Notes in Mathematics: Vol. 284). vi, 89p. 1972. pap. 6.30 (ISBN 0-387-05983-0). Springer-Verlag.

Tsokos, C. P. & Padgett, W. J. Random Integral Equations with Applications to Stochastic Systems. (Lecture Notes in Mathematics: Vol. 233). 174p. 1971. pap. 7.00 (ISBN 0-387-05660-2). Springer-Verlag.

INTEGRATED CIRCUITS

Barber, A. Practical Guide to Digital Integrated Circuits. 1976. 14.95 (ISBN 0-13-690743-1). P-H.

Barna, A. A. VHSIC (Very High Speed Integrated Circuits) Technologies & Tradeoffs. LC 81-4356. 175p. 1981. 15.00 (ISBN 0-471-09463-3, Pub. by Wiley-Interscience). Wiley.

Barna, Arpad & Porat, Dan I. Integrated Circuits in Digital Electronics. LC 73-6709. 483p. 1973. 40.00 (ISBN 0-471-05050-4, Pub. by Wiley-Interscience). Wiley.

Becher, William D. Logical Design Using Integrated Circuits. 1977. text ed. 21.50x (ISBN 0-8104-5859-4). Hayden.

Buchsbaum, Walter H. Encyclopedia of Integrated Circuits: A Handbook of Essential Reference Data. LC 80-21596. 420p. 1981. 19.95 (ISBN 0-13-275875-X). P-H.

Camenzind, Hans R. Electronic Integrated Systems Design. LC 78-12195. (Illus.). 342p. 1980. Repr. of 1972 ed. lib. bdg. 18.50 (ISBN 0-88275-763-6). Krieger.

Carr, William N. & Mize, Jack P. MOS-LSI Design & Application. LC 72-7407. (Texas Instruments Electronics Ser.). (Illus.). 320p. 1972. 35.00 (ISBN 0-07-010081-0, P&RB). McGraw.

Cirovic, Michael M. Integrated Circuits: A User's Handbook. (Illus.). 1977. text ed. 22.95 (ISBN 0-87909-356-0); students manual avail. Reston.

Cockin, J. A. High Speed Pulse Technique. Hammond, P., ed. 263p. 1975. text ed. 27.00 (ISBN 0-08-018774-9); pap. text ed. 14.50 (ISBN 0-08-018773-0). Pergamon.

Comer, David J. Electronic Design with Integrated Circuits. LC 80-23365. (Electrical Engineering Ser.). (Illus.). 416p. 1981. text ed. 24.95 (ISBN 0-201-03931-1). A-W.

Connelly, J. A. Analog Integrated Circuits: Devices, Circuits, Systems & Applications. LC 74-20947. 401p. 1975. 38.00 (ISBN 0-471-16854-8, Pub. by Wiley-Interscience). Wiley.

Coughlin, Robert F. & Driscoll, Frederick F., Jr. Operational Amplifiers & Linear Integrated Circuits. 2nd ed. (Illus.). 400p. 1982. 19.95 (ISBN 0-13-637785-8). P-H.

Deboo, Gordon J. & Burrous, Clifford N. Integrated Circuits & Semiconductor Devices: Theory & Application. 2nd ed. (Illus.). 1977. text ed. 19.95 (ISBN 0-07-016246-8, G); instructor's manual 3.00 (ISBN 0-07-016247-6). McGraw.

DeForest, W. S. Photoresist: Materials & Processes. 1975. 26.95 (ISBN 0-07-016230-1, P&RB). McGraw.

Dempsey, John A. Basic Digital Electronics with MSI Applications. LC 75-9009. 320p. 1976. text ed. 20.95 (ISBN 0-201-01478-5). A-W.

Dooley, D. J., ed. Data Conversion Integrated Circuits. LC 80-10541. 1980. 26.95 (ISBN 0-87942-131-2). Inst Electrical.

Dooley, Daniel J. Data-Conversion Integrated Circuits. (IEEE Press Selected Reprint Ser.). 298p. 1980. 26.95 (ISBN 0-471-08154-X, Pub. by Wiley-Interscience); pap. 17.50 (ISBN 0-471-08155-8). Wiley.

Eimbinder, Jerry, ed. Application Considerations for Linear Integrated Circuits. LC 71-111352. 337p. 1970. 26.75 (ISBN 0-471-23440-0). Krieger.

--Designing with Linear Integrated Circuits. LC 68-56161. 301p. 1969. 19.75 (ISBN 0-471-23455-9, Pub. by Wiley). Krieger.

Elliott, D. J. Integrated Circuit Fabrication Technology. 1982. price not set (ISBN 0-07-019238-3). McGraw.

Elmasry, M. I. Digital MOS Integrated Circuits. 450p. 1981. 36.00 (ISBN 0-471-86202-9, Pub. by Wiley Interscience); pap. 23.50 (ISBN 0-471-86203-7). Wiley.

Engineering Staff of Texas Instruments Inc., Semiconductor Group. The Interface Circuits Data Book for Design Engineers. LC 81-51166. 1981. pap. 10.95 (ISBN 0-89512-109-3, LCC5921). Tex Instr Inc.

Fitchen, Franklin C. Electronic Integrated Circuits & Systems. LC 79-23338. 432p. 1980. lib. bdg. 21.50 (ISBN 0-89874-027-4). Krieger.

--Electronic Integrated Circuits & Systems. 1970. 16.95 (ISBN 0-442-22406-0). Van Nos Reinhold.

Flynn, George. MOS Digital ICS. LC 75-28961. (Illus.). 1975. pap. 6.50 (ISBN 0-672-21299-4). Sams.

Fredericksen, Thomas M. Intuitive IC Electronics: A Sophisticated Primer for Engineers & Technicians. (Illus.). 208p. 1981. 18.50 (ISBN 0-07-021923-0, P&RB). McGraw.

Friedman, Herbert. Practical Low-Cost IC Projects. 2nd ed. LC 79-62996. 1979. pap. 4.50 (ISBN 0-672-21599-3). Sams.

Glaser, Arthur & Subak-Sharpe, Gerald E. Integrated Circuit Engineering: Fabrication, Design, Application. LC 77-73945. 1977. text ed. 28.95 (ISBN 0-201-07427-3, 0-201-07428). A-W.

Gray, P. R., et al, eds. Analog MOS Integrated Circuits. LC 80-22116. 1980. 30.95 (ISBN 0-87942-141-X). Inst Electrical.

Gray, Paul. Analog MOS Integrated Circuits. LC 80-22116. 405p. 1980. 30.95 (ISBN 0-471-08966-4, Pub. by Wiley-Interscience); pap. 20.00 (ISBN 0-471-08964-8). Wiley.

Gray, Paul R. & Meyer, Robert G. Analysis & Design of Analog Integrated Circuits. LC 77-7211. 1977. text ed. 27.95 (ISBN 0-471-01367-6); solutions manual avail. (ISBN 0-471-03047-3). Wiley.

Grebene, A. B. Analog Integrated Circuits. (IEEE Reprint Ser.). 439p. 1978. 31.95x (ISBN 0-471-05210-8, Pub. by Wiley-Interscience); pap. 20.95x (ISBN 0-686-67364-6). Wiley.

Grebene, A. B., ed. Analog Integrated Circuits. LC 78-59636. 1978. 31.95 (ISBN 0-87942-113-4). Inst Electrical.

Grebene, Alan B. Analog Integrated Circuit Design. LC 78-15389. 416p. 1978. Repr. of 1972 ed. lib. bdg. 21.50 (ISBN 0-88275-710-5). Krieger.

Green, Wayne. IC Projects for the Amateur & Experimenter. LC 70-170666. 1971. pap. 5.95 (ISBN 0-8306-0568-1, 568). TAB Bks.

Grinich, Victor. Introduction to Integrated Circuits. (Illus.). 672p. 1975. text ed. 24.50 (ISBN 0-07-024875-3, C); instructors' manual 4.50 (ISBN 0-07-024876-1). McGraw.

Hall, Jerry & Watts, Charles. Learning to Work with Integrated Circuits. LC 77-77774. 49p. pap. 2.00 (ISBN 0-87259-331-2). Am Radio.

Hallmark, Clayton L. The Master IC Cookbook. (Illus.). 476p. (Orig.). 1980. 16.95 (ISBN 0-8306-9964-3); pap. 10.95 (ISBN 0-8306-1199-1, 1199). TAB Bks.

Hamilton, Douglas & Howard, William. Basic Integrated Circuits. (Illus.). 608p. 1975. text ed. 27.50 (ISBN 0-07-025763-9, C); solutions manual 5.50 (ISBN 0-07-025764-7). McGraw.

Healy, James. Automatic Testing & Evaluation of Digital Integrated Circuits. (Illus.). 256p. 1980. text ed. 21.95 (ISBN 0-8359-0256-0). Reston.

Heinlein, W. E. & Holmes, W. H. Active Filters for Integrated Circuits. 65.50 (ISBN 0-387-91070-0). Springer Verlag.

Heiserman, D. Handbook of Digital IC Applications. 1980. 22.95 (ISBN 0-13-372698-3). P-H.

Heiserman, David L. Beginner's Handbook of IC Projects. (Illus.). 272p. 1981. 18.95 (ISBN 0-13-074229-5); pap. 12.95 (ISBN 0-13-074286-4). P-H.

Herpy, Miklos. Analog Integrated Circuits: Operational Amplifiers & Analog Multipliers. LC 77-21008. 479p. 1980. 64.95 (ISBN 0-471-99604-1, Pub. by Wiley-Interscience). Wiley.

Hibberd, R. G. Basic Principles of Integrated Circuits. LC 74-187918. (Illus.). 267p. 1972. 15.00 (ISBN 0-8022-2082-7). Philos Lib.

--Integrated Circuit Pocket Book. (Illus.). 1972. pap. 10.95 (ISBN 0-408-00076-7, NB 11, Pub. by Newnes-Butterworth). Hayden.

--Questions & Answers on Integrated Circuits. 1978. 3.25 (ISBN 0-408-00115-1, NB 71, Pub. by Newnes-Butterworth). Hayden.

Hibberd, Robert G. Integrated Circuits: A Basic Course for Engineers & Technicians. (Texas Instruments Electronics Ser.). 1969. 22.50 (ISBN 0-07-028651-5, P&RB). McGraw.

Hnatek, E. R. User's Guidebook to Digital CMOS Integrated Circuits. 1981. 24.50 (ISBN 0-07-029067-9). McGraw.

Hope, Gordon S. Integrated Devices in Digital Circuit Design. LC 80-17172. 368p. 1981. 29.95 (ISBN 0-471-07920-0, Pub. by Wiley-Interscience). Wiley.

Jung, Walter. IC Timer Cookbook. LC 77-72622. (Illus.). 1977. pap. 9.95 (ISBN 0-672-21416-4). Sams.

Kahng, D., ed. Advances in Applied Solid State Science, Supplement, 2A: Silicon Integrated Circuits. (Serial Publication). 1981. 51.00 (ISBN 0-12-002954-5); lib. ed. 66.50 (ISBN 0-12-002955-3); microfiche ed. 36.00 (ISBN 0-12-002956-1). Acad Pr.

Kahng, Dawon, ed. Advances in Solid State Science, Supplement 2B: Silicon Integrated Circuits. (Serial Publication). 1981. 39.00 (ISBN 0-12-002957-X); lib. ed. 51.00 (ISBN 0-12-002958-8); microfiche ed. 27.50 (ISBN 0-12-002959-6). Acad Pr.

Khambata, A. J. Introduction to Large Scale Integration. LC 69-16126. 216p. 1973. Repr. of 1969 ed. 11.25 (ISBN 0-88275-099-2). Krieger.

Kiver, Milton S. Transistor & Integrated Electronics. 4th ed. 1972. 17.95 (ISBN 0-07-034942-8, G). McGraw.

Lancaster, Don. User's Guide to TTL: Wall Chart. 1974. 2.95 (ISBN 0-672-21080-0). Sams.

Lancaster, Donald E. TTL Cookbook. LC 73-90295. (Illus., Orig.). 1974. pap. 9.50 (ISBN 0-672-21035-5). Sams.

Lenk, J. Manual for Integrated Circuit Users. LC 72-96757. 1973. 21.95 (ISBN 0-87909-482-6). Reston.

Lenk, John D. Handbook of Integrated Circuits: For Engineers & Technicians. (Illus.). 1978. ref. 19.95 (ISBN 0-8359-2744-X). Reston.

Levine, M. Digital Theory & Experimentation Using Integrated Circuits. LC 73-12863. 1974. pap. 14.95 ref. ed. (ISBN 0-13-212258-8). P-H.

Marston, R. M. One Hundred & Ten Integrated Circuit Projects for the Home Constructor. 2nd ed. (Illus.). 1978. pap. 8.50 (ISBN 0-592-00058-3, NB 9, Pub. by Butterworth). Hayden.

Mazda, F. F. Integrated Circuits. LC 77-71418. (Illus.). 1978. 35.50 (ISBN 0-521-21658-3). Cambridge U Pr.

Melen, Roger & Garland, Harry. Understanding CMOS Integrated Circuits. 2nd ed. LC 79-62990. 1979. pap. 5.50 (ISBN 0-672-21598-5). Sams.

Mendelson, R. M. Interrelated Intergrated Electronics Circuits for the Radio Amateur, Technicians, Hobbyist & CB'er. 128p. 1979. pap. 7.70 (ISBN 0-8104-0760-4). Hayden.

Meyer, Robert G., ed. Integrated Circuit Operational Amplifiers. LC 78-59635. 1978. 25.95 (ISBN 0-87942-115-0). Inst Electrical.

Millman, Jacob. Microelectronics: Digital & Analog Circuits & Systems. (Illus.). 1979. text ed. 26.95 (ISBN 0-07-042327-X, C); solution manual 6.95 (ISBN 0-07-042328-8); transparency masters 9.95 (ISBN 0-07-042329-6); transparency masters for solution manual avail. (ISBN 0-07-042339-3). McGraw.

Millman, Jacob & Halkias, Christos. Electronic Fundamentals & Applications for Engineers & Scientists. 1975. text ed. 24.95 (ISBN 0-07-042310-5, C); solutions manual 2.95 (ISBN 0-07-042311-3). McGraw.

--Integrated Electronics: Analog Digital Circuits & Systems. Terman, F. E., ed. (Electrical & Electronic Engineering Ser.). (Illus.). 900p. 1972. text ed. 24.50 (ISBN 0-07-042315-6, C); ans. bk. 4.95 (ISBN 0-07-042317-2); soln. manual 4.95 (ISBN 0-07-042316-4). McGraw.

Milnes, A. G. Semiconductor Devices & Integrated Electronics. 1008p. 1980. text ed. 26.50 (ISBN 0-442-23660-3). Van Nos Reinhold.

Moschytz, George S. Linear Integrated Networks: Fundamentals. (Bell Laboratory Ser). 674p. 1974. text ed. 18.50x (ISBN 0-442-25581-0). Van Nos Reinhold.

Muller, Richard S. & Kamins, Theodore I. Device Electronics for Integrated Circuits. LC 77-1332. 1977. 29.95 (ISBN 0-471-62364-4). Wiley.

Noll, Edward M. Linear Principles, Experiments, & Projects. 2nd ed. LC 78-63123. 1978. pap. 9.95 (ISBN 0-672-21568-3). Sams.

Oberman, R. M. Digital Circuits for Binary Arithmetic. 340p. 1979. 43.95x (ISBN 0-470-26373-3). Halsted Pr.

Passahow, Edward. Digital Integrated Circuits for Electronics Technicians. (Illus.). 1978. text ed. 12.95 (ISBN 0-07-048710-3, G); instructor's manual 2.50 (ISBN 0-07-048711-1). McGraw.

Patrick, Dale R. & Patrick, Stephen. Instrumentation Training Course, 2 vols. 2nd ed. Incl. Vol. 1, Pneumatic Instruments. pap. 13.95 (ISBN 0-672-21579-9, 21579); Vol. 2, Electronic Instruments. pap. 11.95 (ISBN 0-672-21580-2, 21580). LC 79-63866. 1979. Set. pap. 24.95 (ISBN 0-672-21581-0). Sams.

Penny, William M. & Lau, Lillian, eds. Mos Integrated Circuits: Theory, Fabrication, Design & Systems Applications of MOS LSI. LC 79-1039. (American Micro Systems Inc. Bks.). 454p. 1979. Repr. of 1972 ed. 21.50 (ISBN 0-88275-897-7). Krieger.

Planer, G. & Phillips, L. Thick Film Circuits: Applications & Technology. LC 72-87040. 159p. 1973. 16.50x (ISBN 0-8448-0112-7). Crane-Russak Co.

Pletsch, Bill. Integrated Circuits: Making the Miracle Chip. 80p. 1978. pap. 6.00 (ISBN 0-686-27006-1). Palmer-Pletsch.

Prensky, Sol & Seidman, Arthur. Linear Integrated Circuits. 2nd ed. (Illus.). 1981. text ed. 21.95 (ISBN 0-8359-4241-4). Reston.

Prensky, Sol D. Manual of Linear Integrated Circuits. LC 73-15979. (Illus.). 240p. 1974. 21.95 (ISBN 0-87909-466-4). Reston.

Rakes, Charles. Integrated Circuit Projects. 2nd ed. LC 79-63867. (Illus.). 1979. pap. 5.50 (ISBN 0-672-21616-7). Sams.

Rosenthal, Murray P. Understanding Integrated Circuits. (Illus.). 128p. 1975. pap. text ed. 6.50 (ISBN 0-8104-5526-9). Hayden.

Rutkowski, George B. Handbook of Integrated-Circuit Operational Amplifiers. (Illus.). 304p. 1975. ref. ed. 18.95 (ISBN 0-13-378703-6). P-H.

Segallis, William. Guide to Electronic Components. LC 75-2065. 1975. 39.95 (ISBN 0-8436-0208-2). CBI Pub.

Sessions, Kenneth W. & Tuite, Donald. New IC FET Principles & Projects. LC 72-86692. (Illus.). 160p. 1972. pap. 4.95 (ISBN 0-8306-1613-6, 613). TAB Bks.

Shacklette, L. & Ashworth, H. Using Digital & Analog Intergrated Circuits. (Illus.). 1978. pap. text ed. 15.95 (ISBN 0-13-939488-5). P-H.

Smith, J. E., ed. Integrated Injection Logic. LC 80-18841. 1980. 34.95 (ISBN 0-87942-137-1). Inst Electrical.

Sonde, B. S. Introduction to System Design Using Integrated Circuits. LC 80-26988. 261p. 1981. 24.95 (ISBN 0-470-27110-8). Halsted Pr.

Spencer, John D. & Pippenger, Dale E. The Voltage Regulator Handbook for Design Engineers. LC 77-87869. 1977. pap. 4.40 (ISBN 0-89512-101-8, LCC4350). Tex Instr Inc.

Stout, David F. & Kaufman, Milton. Handbook of Microcircuit Design & Application. (Illus.). 1979. 32.50 (ISBN 0-07-061796-1, P&RB). McGraw.

Tab Editorial Staff. Master Transistor - IC Substitution Handbook. LC 76-45065. 1976. pap. 8.95 (ISBN 0-8306-5970-6, 970). TAB Bks.

Taub, Herbert & Schilling, Donald. Digital Integrated Electronics. (E & EE). (Illus.). 1976. text ed. 25.95 (ISBN 0-07-062921-8, C); solutions manual 5.00 (ISBN 0-07-062922-6); ans. bk. 1.95 (ISBN 0-07-062929-3). McGraw.

Texas Instruments Inc. Digital-Integrated-Circuit, Operational-Amplifier & Optoelectronic Circuit Design. (Illus.). 1976. 21.50 (ISBN 0-07-063753-9, P&RB). McGraw.

--M O S, Special-Purpose Bipolar Integrated-Circuits & R-F Power Transistor Circuit Design. (Illus.). 1976. 21.50 (ISBN 0-07-063751-2, P&RB). McGraw.

Texas Instruments, Inc. Power-Transistor & TTL Integrated-Circuit Applications. (Texas Instruments Ser.). (Illus.). 1977. 21.50 (ISBN 0-07-063754-7, P&RB). McGraw.

Till, William C. & Luxon, James T. Integrated Circuits: Materials, Devices & Fabrication. (Illus.). 512p. 1982. 32.95 (ISBN 0-13-469031-1). P-H.

Tischler, Morris. Tischler: Experiments in Amplifiers, Filters, Oscillators. Haas, Mark, ed. (Linear Integrated Circuit Applications). (Illus.). 176p. Date not set. pap. text ed. 6.95 lab manual (ISBN 0-07-064780-1). McGraw.

Topfer, Morton L. Thick Film Microelectronics. 1971. 17.95x (ISBN 0-442-28564-7). Van Nos Reinhold.

Tracton, Ken. IC Function Locator. 1978. leatherette 8.95 (ISBN 0-8306-8960-5); pap. 5.95 (ISBN 0-8306-7960-X, 960). TAB Bks.

--Integrated Circuits Guidebook. LC 75-13015. (Illus.). 196p. 1975. 8.95 (ISBN 0-8306-5771-1); pap. 5.95 (ISBN 0-8306-4771-6, 771). TAB Bks.

Turner, Rufus P. ABC's of Integrated Circuits. 2nd ed. LC 77-83682. 1977. pap. 3.95 (ISBN 0-672-21462-8). Sams.

--Getting Acquainted with the IC. LC 78-65668. 1978. pap. 4.95 (ISBN 0-672-21520-9). Sams.

--Simple IC Test Instruments You Can Build. LC 79-90832. 1979. pap. 4.95 (ISBN 0-672-21683-3). Sams.

United Tech. Pubs. Modern Applications of Linear IC's. LC 73-90737. 1974. pap. 9.95 (ISBN 0-8306-3708-7, 708). TAB Bks.

Veronis, Andrew. Integrated Circuit Fabrication Technology. (Illus.). 1978. text ed. 19.95 (ISBN 0-8359-3092-0); students manual avail. Reston.

Wakerly, John. Logic Design Projects Using Standard Integrated Circuits. LC 76-5471. 250p. 1976. text ed. 12.95 (ISBN 0-471-91705-2). Wiley.

Weber, Samuel. Large & Medium Scale Integration: Devices & Application. (Illus.). 320p. 1974. 26.50 (ISBN 0-07-068815-X, P&RB). McGraw.

Wojslaw, Charles F. Integrated Circuits: Theory & Applications. (Illus.). 1978. text ed. 18.95 (ISBN 0-87909-379-X); students manual avail. Reston.

Young, Thomas. Linear Integrated Circuits. LC 80-22791. (Electronic Technology Ser.). 495p. 1981. text ed. 21.95 (ISBN 0-471-97941-4). Wiley.

INTEGRATED DATA PROCESSING
see Electronic Data Processing

INTEGRATION, NUMERICAL
see Numerical Integration

INTEGRATION, RACIAL
see Race Relations

INTEGRATION IN EDUCATION
see Articulation (Education); School Integration

INTEGRATORS
see also Planimeter

INTEGRITY
see Self-Respect

INTEGUMENT (SKIN)
see Skin

INTELLECT
see also Age and Intelligence; Creation (Literary, Artistic, etc.); Imagination; Inefficiency, Intellectual; Intelligence Tests; Knowledge, Theory of; Logic; Maze Tests; Memory; Perception; Reason; Reasoning (Psychology); Self-Organizing Systems; Senses and Sensation; Thought and Thinking; Wisdom

Allen, Myron S. Psycho-Dynamic Synthesis. LC 66-17160. 248p. 1979. Repr. of 1966 ed. soft cover 11.95 (ISBN 0-918936-07-1). Astara.

Arendt, Hannah. The Life of the Mind. LC 80-25403. 1981. pap. 9.95 (ISBN 0-15-651992-5). Harbracej.

Armstrong, D. M. Materialist Theory of the Mind. (International Library of Philosophy & Scientific Method). 1968. text ed. 24.50x (ISBN 0-7100-3634-5). Humanities.

Bailes, Frederick. Basic Principles of the Science of Mind. 3rd ed. Bailes, Mrs. Frederick, ed. 182p. 1980. pap. 7.95 (ISBN 0-87516-404-8). De Vorss.

Bain, Alexander. Senses & the Intellect. (Contributions to the History of Psychology Ser.: No. 4, Pt. A Orientations). 1978. Repr. of 1855 ed. 30.00 (ISBN 0-89093-153-4). U Pubns Amer.

Barzun, Jacques. The House of Intellect. (Midway Reprint Ser.). viii, 274p. 1975. pap. text ed. 6.95x (ISBN 0-226-03855-6). U of Chicago Pr.

Bateson, Gregory. Mind & Nature. (New Age Ser.). 1979. pap. 3.50 (ISBN 0-553-13724-7). Bantam.

Bindra, Dalbir. A Theory of Intelligent Behavior. LC 75-46519. 447p. 1976. 30.50 (ISBN 0-471-07320-2, Pub. by Wiley-Interscience). Wiley.

Blanchard, O. K. Insanely Sane. 1981. 5.75 (ISBN 0-8062-1731-6). Carlton.

Blum, Jeffrey. Pseudoscience & Mental Ability: The Origins & Fallacies of the IQ Controversy. LC 77-81371. 1979. pap. 5.95 (ISBN 0-85345-496-5, PB4965). Monthly Rev.

Bode, Boyd H. How We Learn. LC 77-138204. 308p. 1972. Repr. of 1940 ed. lib. bdg. 20.00x (ISBN 0-8371-5562-2, BOWL). Greenwood.

Bohman, Svante. What Is Intelligence? 148p. 1981. pap. text ed. 26.75x (ISBN 0-686-72182-9, Pub. by Almqvist & Wiksell Sweden). Humanities.

Bosanquet, Bernard. Three Chapters on the Nature of Mind. Bosanquet, Helen, ed. LC 23-2356. 1968. Repr. of 1923 ed. 11.00 (ISBN 0-527-10054-4). Kraus Repr.

Brainerd, Charles J. Piaget's Theory of Intelligence. (Illus.). 1978. 18.95 (ISBN 0-13-675108-3). P-H.

Brearley, Molly & Hitchfield, Elizabeth. Guide to Reading Piaget. LC 67-25234. 1969. 8.00x (ISBN 0-8052-3092-0); pap. 3.45 (ISBN 0-8052-0222-6). Schocken.

Brim, Orville G., Jr., et al. American Beliefs & Attitudes About Intelligence. LC 75-76746. 1969. 9.95 (ISBN 0-87154-152-1). Russell Sage.

Broad, C. D. The Mind & Its Place in Nature. (International Library of Philosophy, Psychology & Scientific Method). 1976. Repr. of 1925 ed. 55.00x (ISBN 0-7100-3034-7). Humanities.

Brody, Erness B. & Brody, Nathan, eds. Intelligence: Nature, Determinants, & Consequences. 1976. 24.00 (ISBN 0-12-134250-6). Acad Pr.

Butcher, H. J. & Lomax, D. E., eds. Readings in Human Intelligence. 1972. 13.95x (ISBN 0-416-60260-6); pap. 12.95x (ISBN 0-416-60260-6). Methuen Inc.

Cancro, Robert, ed. Intelligence: Genetic & Environmental Influences. LC 79-153576. 300p. 1971. 34.50 (ISBN 0-8089-0689-5). Grune.

--Intelligence: Genetic & Environmental Influences. LC 79-153576. 300p. 1971. 34.50 (ISBN 0-8089-0689-5). Grune.

Carlisle, Thomas. A Ride on the Wave of the Future: An Essay on Human Potential. LC 78-55736. (Illus.). 1978. saddlestich 2.00 (ISBN 0-914580-08-6). Angst World.

Carlson, Eric T., et al, eds. Benjamin Rush's Lectures on the Mind. LC 80-70300. (Memoir Ser.: Vol. 144). 1981. 15.00 (ISBN 0-87169-144-2). Am Philos.

Chomsky, Noam. Rules & Representations. LC 79-26145. (Woodbridge Lectures Ser.: No. 11). 1980. 7.50x (ISBN 0-231-04826-2). Columbia U Pr.

Claremont, C. A. Intelligence & Mental Growth. 1928. 12.50 (ISBN 0-932062-30-X). Sharon Hill.

Cohen, Daniel. Intelligence: What Is It? LC 73-80178. (Illus.). 160p. (gr. 5 up). 1974. 5.95 (ISBN 0-87131-127-5). M Evans.

Cooper, Clara. The Relation Between Morality & Intellect: A Compendium of Evidence Contributed by Psychology, Criminology, & Sociology. LC 71-176638. (Columbia University. Teachers College. Contributions to Education: No. 607). Repr. of 1935 ed. 17.50 (ISBN 0-404-55607-8). AMS Pr.

Crosson, Frederick J., ed. Human & Artificial Intelligence. LC 78-131431. (Orig.). 1970. pap. text ed. 6.95x (ISBN 0-89197-220-X). Irvington.

Cunningham, Michael. Intelligence: Its Organization & Development. 1972. 26.00 (ISBN 0-12-199150-4). Acad Pr.

Custance, Arthur C. The Mysterious Matter of the Mind. (Christian Free University Curriculum Ser.). 1979. pap. 3.95 (ISBN 0-310-38011-1). Zondervan.

Cutten, George B. Mind: Its Origin & Goal. 1925. 15.00x (ISBN 0-685-89766-4). Elliots Bks.

Dale, Arbie M. & Snow, Leida. Twenty Minutes a Day to a More Powerful Intelligence. 1979. pap. 2.25 (ISBN 0-87216-646-5). Playboy Pbks.

Decarie, Therese G. Intelligence & Affectivity in Early Childhood: An Experimental Study of Jean Piaget's Object Concept & Object Relations. LC 65-28439. 1966. text ed. 17.00 (ISBN 0-8236-2720-9). Intl Univs Pr.

Doman, Glenn & Armentrout, J. Michael. The Universal Multiplication of Intelligence. LC 80-66236. (The Gentle Revolution Ser.). 223p. 1980. 12.50 (ISBN 0-936676-02-7). Better Baby.

Drake, D. Mind & Its Place in Nature. LC 26-1041. Repr. of 1925 ed. 13.00 (ISBN 0-527-25120-8). Kraus Repr.

Eckberg, Douglas L. Intelligence & Race: The Origins & Dimensions of the IQ Controversy. LC 79-19795. (Illus.). 298p. 1979. 27.95 (ISBN 0-03-052556-X). Praeger.

Ehrlich, Paul R. & Feldman, Shirley. The Race Bomb: Skin Color, Prejudice, & Intelligence. LC 76-52821. (Illus.). 1977. 9.95 (ISBN 0-8129-0681-0). Times Bks.

The Exercise of Intelligence: The Biosocial Preconditions for the Operation of Intelligence. Smith, Malcom T. LC 79-13723. 140p. 1980. lib. bdg. 17.50 (ISBN 0-8240-7165-4). Garland Pub.

Eysenck, H. Intelligence Controversy: H. J. Eysenck vs Leon Kamin. LC 80-28571. 192p. 1981. 12.95 (ISBN 0-471-08884-6, Pub. by Wiley-Interscience). Wiley.

Eysenck, H. J. Check Your Own IQ. (Illus., Orig.). 1962. pap. 2.50 (ISBN 0-14-020656-6, Pelican). Penguin.

--Know Yourself. (Gift Pack Ser.). 1976. pap. 5.95 (ISBN 0-14-095499-6). Penguin.

Eysenck, H. J. & Fulker, D. W. The Structure & Measurement of Intelligence. (Illus.). 1979. 20.80 (ISBN 0-387-09028-2). Springer-Verlag.

Ferraworth, James R. The Major Problems of Our Contemporary Society in the Critical Views of Our Intelligentsia: The Results of a Survey. (Illus.). 129p. 1981. 53.45 (ISBN 0-89266-313-8). Am Classical Coll Pr.

Flavell, John H. Development Psychology of Jean Piaget. 1973. pap. 13.95x (ISBN 0-442-22416-8). Van Nos Reinhold.

Flores, Zella K. The Relation of Language Difficulty to Intelligence & School Retardation in a Group of Spanish-Speaking Children. LC 74-833371. 1975. Repr. of 1926 ed. soft bdg. 8.00 (ISBN 0-88247-355-7). R & E Res Assoc.

Formanek, Ruth & Gurian, Anita. Charting Intellectual Development: A Practical Guide to Piagetian Tasks. 2nd ed. (Illus.). 144p. 1981. 14.75 (ISBN 0-398-04476-7). C C Thomas.

Fowler, L. N. How to Measure the Quality & Intensity of Your Mental Powers from the Physical Structure of Your Cranial Capacity. (Illus.). 1980. Repr. of 1842 ed. deluxe ed. 37.45 (ISBN 0-89901-000-8). Found Class Reprints.

Friedman, Morton P., et al, eds. Intelligence & Learning. (NATO Conference Series III-Human Factors: Vol. 14). 605p. 1981. 42.50 (ISBN 0-306-40643-8, Plenum Pr). Plenum Pub.

Furst, Charles. Origins of the Mind: Mind-Brain Connections. 1979. 11.95 (ISBN 0-13-642777-4, Spec); pap. 5.95 (ISBN 0-13-642769-3, Spec). P-H.

Galton, Francis. Hereditary Genius. (Classics in Psychology Ser.). 1979. Repr. of 1869 ed. 27.50x (ISBN 0-312-36989-1). St Martin.

Gardner, Judith K. & Gardner, Howard, eds. Factors Determining Intellectual Attainment: An Original Anthology. LC 74-21406. (Classics in Child Development Ser). 204p. 1975. Repr. 14.00x (ISBN 0-405-06458-6). Arno.

Garforth, Francis W., ed. John Locke's of the Conduct of the Understanding. LC 66-20498. 1966. text ed. 8.75 (ISBN 0-8077-1401-1); pap. text ed. 4.00x (ISBN 0-8077-1398-8). Tchrs Coll.

Gesell, Arnold, et al. Biographies of Child Development: The Mental Growth Careers of Eight-Four Infants & Children. LC 74-21409. (Classsics in Child Development Ser). (Illus.). 350p. 1975. Repr. 23.00x (ISBN 0-405-06461-6). Arno.

Giammatteo, Michael C. Rings Around Your Mind: How to Program Your Mind to Control Stress, Fear, & Self-Destructive Behavior Patterns. (Illus.). 1976. pap. text ed. 10.00 (ISBN 0-918428-08-4). Sylvan Inst.

Glover, J. C. B., ed. The Philosophy of Mind. (Oxford Readings in Philosophy). 1977. pap. text ed. 8.95x (ISBN 0-19-875038-2). Oxford U Pr.

Glover, John A. A Parent's Guide to Intelligence Testing. LC 78-25991. 1979. 17.95x (ISBN 0-88229-423-7); pap. 8.95 (ISBN 0-88229-670-1). Nelson-Hall.

Grover, Sonja C. The Cognitive Basis of the Intellect: A Response to Jensen's "Bias in Mental Testing". LC 81-40303. 148p. (Orig.). 1981. lib. bdg. 17.75 (ISBN 0-8191-1741-2); pap. text ed. 8.50 (ISBN 0-8191-1742-0). U Pr of Amer.

Guilford, J. P. Way Beyond the IQ: Guide to Improving Intelligence & Creativity. LC 77-80536. 1977. pap. 7.95 (ISBN 0-930222-01-6). Creat Educ Found.

Guilford, Joy P. & Hoepfner, R. Analysis of Intelligence. (Psychology Ser.). 1971. 32.00 (ISBN 0-07-025137-1, C). McGraw.

Haslam, John. Sound Mind: Or Contributions to the Natural History & Physiology of the Human Intellect. LC 78-72797. Repr. of 1819 ed. 21.50 (ISBN 0-404-60860-4). AMS Pr.

Hegel, Georg W. The Life of the Mind in Representational Charts. Gary, Charles E., ed. (Illus.). 1979. 37.75 (ISBN 0-89266-202-6). Am Classical Coll Pr.

Herrnstein, R. J. I. Q. in the Meritocracy. 1973. 7.95 (ISBN 0-316-35864-9, Pub by Atlantic Monthly Pr). Little.

Hobhouse, Leonard T. Mind in Evolution. LC 73-2968. (Classics in Psychology Ser.). Repr. of 1915 ed. 22.00 (ISBN 0-405-05140-9). Arno.

Hoorweg, J. C. Protein-Energy Malnutrition & Intellectual Abilities: A Study of Teenage Ugandan Children. (Communications, Ser.: No. 5). 1976. pap. text ed. 12.25x (ISBN 90-2797-752-6). Mouton.

Howard, Vernon. Esoteric Mind Power. 196p. 1980. pap. 5.50 (ISBN 0-87516-401-3). De Vorss.

Hughes, Thomas L. The Fate of Facts in a World of Men: Foreign Policy & Intelligence Making. (Headline Ser.: 233). 1976. pap. 2.00 (ISBN 0-87124-038-6, 76-45580). Foreign Policy.

Humphrey, George. The Story of Man's Mind. 1978. Repr. of 1923 ed. lib. bdg. 25.00 (ISBN 0-8482-4398-6). Norwood Edns.

Hunt, J. M. Intelligence & Experience. (Illus.). 1961. 19.95 (ISBN 0-471-06907-8). Wiley.

Ingalese, Richard. The History & Power of Mind. (Newcastle Arcana). 332p. 1976. pap. 4.95 (ISBN 0-87877-037-2, P-37). Newcastle Pub.

Jensen, Arthur R., et al. Environment, Heredity, & Intelligence. (Reprint Ser.: No. 2). 5.95 (ISBN 0-916690-02-4). Harvard Educ Rev.

Johnson, Samuel. Elementa Philosophica. LC 31-9265. 1968. Repr. of 1752 ed. 12.00 (ISBN 0-527-46440-6). Kraus Repr.

Jordan, Elijah. The Life of Mind. LC 75-3205. Repr. of 1925 ed. 22.00 (ISBN 0-404-59203-1). AMS Pr.

Joseph, Andre. Intelligence, IQ & Race: When, How & Why They Became Associated. LC 77-81023. 1977. soft bdg. 8.00 (ISBN 0-88247-479-0). R & E Res Assoc.

Keating, Daniel, ed. Intellectual Talent, Research & Development: Proceedings. LC 75-30554. 366p. 1976. 24.50x (ISBN 0-8018-1743-9); pap. 5.95x (ISBN 0-8018-1744-7). Johns Hopkins.

Koplowitz, Wilfred D. Teaching Intelligence, a Survey of College & University Courses on the Subject of Intelligence. 90p. (Orig.). 1980. pap. 3.75 (ISBN 0-938450-00-X). NISC.

Kreskin. Kreskin's Mind Power Book. LC 77-24545. (Illus.). 1977. 8.95 (ISBN 0-07-035480-4, GB). McGraw.

Krishnamurti, J. The Awakening of Intelligence. 1976. pap. 3.95 (ISBN 0-380-00462-3, 55327, Discus). Avon.

Kuo, You-Yuh. Teaching Strategies for Developing Intellectual Abilities. 1976. pap. 5.00 (ISBN 0-9601274-1-0). East West Cult.

Landau, Abraham. Intelligence Anxiety & Pleasure. LC 60-13652. 1962. 6.00 (ISBN 0-8022-0912-2). Philos Lib.

Langer, Susanne K. Mind: An Essay on Human Feeling, Vol. 2. LC 72-4011. 1973. 19.50x (ISBN 0-8018-1428-6); pap. 6.95x (ISBN 0-8018-1607-6). Johns Hopkins.

--Mind: An Essay on Human Feeling Vol. 1. LC 66-25745. (Illus.). 1967. 22.50x (ISBN 0-8018-0360-8); pap. 4.95x (ISBN 0-8018-1150-3, JH70). Johns Hopkins.

Lebrun, Yvan & Hoops, Richard. Intelligence & Aphasia. (Neurolinguistics Ser.: Vol. 2). 140p. 1974. pap. text ed. 15.75 (ISBN 90-265-0182-X, Pub. by Swets Pub Serv Holland). Swets North Am.

Leland, Charles G. The Mystic Will. 1976. Repr. of 1907 ed. 6.00 (ISBN 0-911662-58-8). Yoga.

Lewis, M. Origins of Intelligence. LC 75-31530. (Illus.). 413p. 1976. 19.50 (ISBN 0-306-30867-3, Plenum Pr). Plenum Pub.

Lowenfeld, Viktor & Brittain, W. Lambert. Creative & Mental Growth. 7th ed. 1982. text ed. 17.95 (ISBN 0-686-75023-3). Macmillan.

Machado, Luis A. The Right to Be Intelligent. 85p. 1980. 12.75 (ISBN 0-08-025781-X). Pergamon.

Mann, Mildred. Mind & Consciousness. 2nd ed. Connaway, Leonebel & Reed, Faith, eds. 1978. 4.00 (ISBN 0-89369-099-6). Soc Pragmatic.

Manning, William R. Early Diplomatic Relations Between the United States & Mexico. LC 68-55101. 1968. Repr. of 1916 ed. lib. bdg. 19.00x (ISBN 0-8371-0558-7, MAUM). Greenwood.

Matarazzo, Joseph D. & Wechsler, David. Wechsler's Measurement & Appraisal of Adult Intelligence. 5th ed. (Illus.). 1972. 21.95x (ISBN 0-19-502296-3). Oxford U Pr.

Maxwell, James. Sixteen Years On: A Follow-up of the Nineteen Forty-Seven Scottish Mental Survey. (Scottish Council for Research in Education Ser.: No. 58). 1969. 8.75x (ISBN 0-8426-1382-X); pap. 6.75x (ISBN 0-8426-1602-0). Verry.

Mead, Cyrus D. The Relations of General Intelligence to Certain Mental & Physical Traits. LC 77-177063. (Columbia University. Teachers College. Contributions to Education). Repr. of 1916 ed. 17.50 (ISBN 0-404-55076-2). AMS Pr.

Meeker, Mary. Structure of Intellect: Its Interpretation & Uses. LC 69-17296. 1969. text ed. 17.95 (ISBN 0-675-09516-6). Merrill.

Mitchell, William. The Place of Minds in the World. LC 77-27201. (Gifford Lectures: 1924-26). Repr. of 1933 ed. 27.50 (ISBN 0-404-60477-3). AMS Pr.

Molow, L. Paul & Molow, Doree. Your Fantastic Mind. 3.95 (ISBN 0-533-01679-7). Vantage.

Montagu, Ashley. On Being Intelligent. LC 72-11742. 236p. 1973. Repr. of 1951 ed. lib. bdg. 15.00 (ISBN 0-8371-6704-3, MOOB). Greenwood.

--Race & IQ. 320p. 1975. 15.95 (ISBN 0-19-501884-2). Oxford U Pr.

--Race & IQ. 336p. 1975. pap. 5.95 (ISBN 0-19-501885-0, GB425, GB). Oxford U Pr.

Mooney, Tom. The Early History of a Purpose Machine. 1976. 5.95 (ISBN 0-9601240-1-2); pap. 2.95 (ISBN 0-9601240-2-0). Mooney.

Moore, T. W., et al. Conditioning & Instrumental Learning. 2nd ed. (Illus.). 1977. pap. text ed. 6.95 (ISBN 0-07-042902-2, C). McGraw.

Morris, Charles W. Six Theories of Mind. 1932. 10.50x (ISBN 0-226-54004-9). U of Chicago Pr.

Muller, F. Max. The Science of Thought, 2 vols. 325p. 1981. Repr. of 1887 ed. Set. lib. bdg. 100.00 (ISBN 0-89760-576-4). Telegraph Bks.

Noble, Daniel. The Human Mind in Its Relations with the Brain & Nervous System. LC 78-72817. (Brainedness, Handedness, & Mental Abilities Ser.). Repr. of 1858 ed. 22.50 (ISBN 0-404-60886-8). AMS Pr.

Oliverio, A., ed. Genetics, Environment & Intelligence. 1977. 91.25 (ISBN 0-7204-0644-7, North-Holland). Elsevier.

Paterson, Donald G. Physique & Intellect. Repr. of 1930 ed. lib. bdg. 14.25x (ISBN 0-8371-2886-2, PAPI). Greenwood.

Phillips, John L., Jr. The Origins of Intellect: Piaget's Theory. 2nd ed. LC 75-5703. (Illus.). 1975. text ed. 14.95x (ISBN 0-7167-0579-6); pap. text ed. 7.95x (ISBN 0-7167-0580-X). W H Freeman.

Piaget, Jean. Adaptation & Intelligence: Organic Selection & Phenocopy. Eames, Steward, tr. LC 79-25592. 130p. 1980. 11.00 (ISBN 0-226-66777-4). U of Chicago Pr.

--Origins of Intelligence in Children. Cook, Margaret, tr. 1966. text ed. 22.50 (ISBN 0-8236-3900-2); pap. text ed. 6.95 (ISBN 0-8236-8207-2, 023900). Intl Univs Pr.

--The Psychology of Intelligence. 1971. Repr. of 1950 ed. 16.95 (ISBN 0-7100-3136-X). Routledge & Kegan.

--Psychology of Intelligence. (Quality Paperback: No. 222). 1976. Repr. of 1966 ed. pap. 3.95 (ISBN 0-8226-0222-9). Littlefield.

Porter, Noah. The Human Intellect. 4th ed. LC 75-3319. Repr. of 1870 ed. 48.00 (ISBN 0-404-59299-6). AMS Pr.

Poujol, F. A. Dictionnaire des Facultes Intellectuelles et Affectives de l'ame ou l'on Traite des Passions, des Vertus, des Vices, Des Defauts. Migne, J. P., ed. (Encyclopedie Theologique Ser.: Vol. 39). 560p. (Fr.). Date not set. Repr. of 1849 ed. lib. bdg. 72.00x (ISBN 0-89241-245-3). Caratzas Bros.

Pyle, David W. Intelligence: An Introduction. (Illus.). 1979. 16.00x (ISBN 0-7100-0306-4); pap. 7.95 (ISBN 0-7100-0307-2). Routledge & Kegan.

Raaheim, Kjell. Problem Solving & Intelligence. 1974. pap. 9.00x (ISBN 8-200-08976-2, Dist. by Columbia U Pr). Universitet.

Rappard, Hans V. Psychology As Self Knowledge: The Development of the Concept of the Mind in German Rationalistic Psychology & Its Relevance Today. Ligne, Faili, tr. 1978. pap. text ed. 18.50x (ISBN 90-232-1629-6). Humanities.

Ratzenhoffer, G. Die Kritik des Intellects: Positive Erkenntnisheorie. (Ger.). 1902. text ed. 17.00x (ISBN 90-6090-091-X). Humanities.

Reimold, Orlando S. One Mind's Eye-View of the Mind. 1979. 9.50 (ISBN 0-8022-2231-5). Philos Lib.

Resnick, Lauren B., ed. The Nature of Intelligence. LC 75-37871. 364p. 1976. 17.95 (ISBN 0-470-01384-2). Halsted Pr.

Rhine, J. B. New World of the Mind. 1962. pap. 5.00 (ISBN 0-688-06015-3). Morrow.

--The Reach of the Mind. (Illus.). pap. 4.95 (ISBN 0-688-31014-1). Morrow.

Richardson, Frederick, ed. & intro. by. Brain & Intelligence: The Ecology of Child Development. LC 72-88238. (Illus.). 400p. 1973. text ed. 16.00x (ISBN 0-87971-008-X). Natl Educ Pr.

Riegel, K. F., ed. Intelligence: Alternative Views of a Paradigm. (Human Development: Vol. 16, No. 1-2). 132p. 1974. pap. 9.75 (ISBN 3-8055-1710-6). S Karger.

Robb, George P., et al. Assessment of Individual Mental Ability. LC 73-177298. 354p. 1972. text ed. 17.50 scp (ISBN 0-7002-2357-6, HarpC). Har-Row.

Rosenzweig, Mark R., ed. Intelligence & Affectivity: Their Relationship During Child Development. Brown, T. A. & Kaegi, C. E., trs. (Illus.). 1981. 8.00 (ISBN 0-8243-2901-5). Annual Reviews.

Roslansky, J. Human Mind. LC 67-30304. (Nobel Conference Lectures Ser.). 9.50x (ISBN 0-8303-0095-3, Acad Edns). Fleet.

Rueppell, H. & Rueppell, Marlies. Intelligenzfoerderung - Moeglichkeiten und Grenzen. Schmitz-Scherzer, R., ed. (Psychologische Praxis: Band 49). (Illus.). 105p. 1976. 13.25 (ISBN 3-8055-2303-3). S Karger.

Russell, Bertrand. Sceptical Essays. (Unwin Paperback Ser.). 1960. pap. 4.50 (ISBN 0-04-104003-1). Allen Unwin.

Sagan, Carl, ed. Communication with Extraterrestrial Intelligence. 1973. pap. 6.95 (ISBN 0-262-69037-3). MIT Pr.

Sears, Pauline S., ed. Intellectual Development. new ed. LC 73-146672. (Readings in Educational Research Ser.). 1971. 10 or more copies 25.00 23.65 (ISBN 0-471-76975-4); text ed. 26.25 (ISBN 0-686-67150-3). McCutchan.

Sexton, Thomas & Poling, Donald. Can Intelligence Be Taught? (Fastback Ser.: No. 29). (Illus., Orig.). 1973. pap. 0.75 (ISBN 0-87367-029-9). Phi Delta Kappa.

Shouksmith, George. Intelligence, Creativity & Cognitive Style. 1970. 32.00 (ISBN 0-7134-0980-0, Pub. by Batsford England). David & Charles.

Simon, Brian. Intelligence, Psychology & Education: A Marxist Critique. 280p. 1971. 16.00x (ISBN 0-8464-0520-2). Beekman Pubs.

Smee, Alfred. The Mind of Man: Being a Natural System of Mental Philosophy. LC 78-72825. (Brainedness, Handedness, & Mental Abilities Ser.). (Illus.). Repr. of 1875 ed. 21.50 (ISBN 0-404-60893-0). AMS Pr.

Spearman, Charles. The Nature of "Intelligence" & the Principles of Cognition. LC 73-2990. (Classics in Psychology Ser). Repr. of 1923 ed. 18.00 (ISBN 0-405-05163-8). Arno.

Spencer, Herbert. Education-Intellectual, Moral & Physical. (Educational Ser.). 1896. Repr. 20.00 (ISBN 0-685-43181-9). Norwood Edns.

Sprott, Richard L., ed. Age, Learning Ability & Intelligence. 176p. 1980. text ed. 15.00 (ISBN 0-442-27895-0). Van Nos Reinhold.

Sternberg, Robert J. Intelligence, Information Processing, & Analogical Reasoning: The Componential Analysis of Human Abilities. LC 77-4178. (Experimental Psychology Ser.). 1977. 19.95 (ISBN 0-470-99137-2). Halsted Pr.

Sternberg, Robert J. & Detterman, Douglas K., eds. Human Intelligence: Perspectives on Its Theory & Measurement. LC 79-17994. 1979. 16.50 (ISBN 0-89391-030-9). Ablex Pub.

Stewart, Rosemarie, ed. East Meets West: The Transpersonal Approach. LC 80-53952. 202p. 1981. pap. 5.25 (ISBN 0-8356-0544-2, Quest). Theos Pub Hse.

Taine, H. A. On Intelligence. 1871. Repr. 50.00 (ISBN 0-8274-3065-5). R West.

Taine, Hippolyte A. On Intelligence. (Contributions to the History of Psychology Ser.). 1978. 30.00 (ISBN 0-89093-152-6). U Pubns Amer.

Terman, Lewis M. Genius & Stupidity: A Study. LC 74-21430. (Classics in Child Development Ser). 70p. 1975. 9.00x (ISBN 0-405-06479-9). Arno.

Thurstone, Louis L. The Nature of Intelligence. LC 72-13862. (Illus.). 167p. 1973. Repr. of 1924 ed. lib. bdg. 15.00x (ISBN 0-8371-6761-2, THNI). Greenwood.

Turner, Charles H. Maps of the Mind. 1981. 14.95 (ISBN 0-02-547740-4). Macmillan.

University Of California Philosophical Union - 1935. Nature of Mind: Lectures. (Publications in Philosophy Ser: Vol. 19). 1936. pap. 17.00 (ISBN 0-685-13526-8). Johnson Repr.

Van Der Post, Laurens. Intuition, Intellect & the Racial Question. 40p. 1976. Repr. of 1964 ed. pap. 1.50 (ISBN 0-913098-13-2). Myrin Institute.

Vernon, Philip E. Intelligence & Cultural Environment. (Illus.). 275p. 1972. pap. 7.95x (ISBN 0-416-65800-8). Methuen Inc.

--Intelligence: Heredity & Environment. LC 78-11975. (Psychology Ser.). (Illus.). 1979. pap. text ed. 10.95x (ISBN 0-7167-0737-3). W H Freeman.

Walters, Frederick C. A Statistical Study of Certain Aspects of the Time Factor in Intelligence. LC 77-177666. (Columbia University. Teachers College. Contributions to Education). Repr. of 1927 ed. 17.50 (ISBN 0-404-55248-X). AMS Pr.

Waters, T. A. Psychologistics. 1977. pap. 2.95 (ISBN 0-346-12290-2). Cornerstone.

Wechsler, David. The Selected Papers of David Wechsler. 1974. 28.50 (ISBN 0-12-741250-6). Acad Pr.

Welford, A. T. Skilled Performance: Perceptual & Motor Skills. 1976. pap. 5.95x (ISBN 0-673-07709-8). Scott F.

Welsh, George S. Creativity & Intelligence: A Personality Approach. LC 75-16305. 1975. pap. text ed. 8.00 (ISBN 0-89143-060-1). U NC Inst Res Soc Sci.

Wentworth, M. M. Individual Differences in the Intelligence of School Children. pap. 15.50 (ISBN 0-384-66750-3). Johnson Repr.

Whimbey, Arthur. Intelligence Can Be Taught. 1980. pap. 5.95 (ISBN 0-525-93128-7). Dutton.

Wintercross, Paul W. The Absolutely Definite Philosophy for the Intelligence of Contemporary Man. (Illus.). 1980. deluxe ed. 39.75 (ISBN 0-89266-221-2). Am Classical Coll Pr.

Zedler, Beatrice H., ed. Saint Thomas Aquinas: On the Unity of the Intellect Against the Averroists. (Medieval Philosophical Texts in Translation: No. 19). 1968. pap. 5.95 (ISBN 0-87462-219-0). Marquette.

INTELLECT–NUTRITIONAL ASPECTS

see also Psychology, Physiological

Cott, Allan. The Orthomolecular Approach to Learning Disabilities. LC 77-22609. 1977. pap. text ed. 3.50x (ISBN 0-87879-174-4). Acad Therapy.

Lloyd-Still, J. D. Malnutrition and Intellectual Development. LC 76-17432. (Illus.). 202p. 1976. 19.50 (ISBN 0-88416-181-1). Wright-PSG.

Malnutrition & Mental Development in Man, 2 vols. Incl. Vol. 1. Hermann, Harold W., et al, eds. 164p (ISBN 0-8422-7259-3); Vol. 2. Kallen, David J., et al, eds. 169p. 1976. text ed. 21.50x ea. Irvington.

Serban, George, ed. Nutrition & Mental Functions. LC 74-28371. (Advances in Behavioral Biology Ser.: Vol. 14). (Illus.). 278p. 1975. 27.50 (ISBN 0-306-37914-7, Plenum Pr). Plenum Pub.

Sunderlin, Sylvia, ed. Nutrition & Intellectual Growth in Children. (Illus.). 1973. pap. 2.00x (ISBN 0-87173-035-9). ACEI.

Watson, George. Personality Strength & Psychochemical Energy. LC 79-1690. 1979. 9.95 (ISBN 0-06-014587-0, HarpT). Har-Row.

INTELLECT AND AGE

see Age and Intelligence

INTELLECTRONICS

see Artificial Intelligence; Bionics

INTELLECTUAL COOPERATION

see also Congresses and Conventions; Cultural Relations; Educational Exchanges; Endowment of Research; Exchange of Persons Programs; Exchanges, Literary and Scientific; International Education; International Years of the Quiet Sun, 1964-1965; Internationalism; Library Cooperation; University Cooperation

also subdivision Relations (General) Under names of countries, e.g. United States–Relations (General) with Latin America

Cudworth, Ralph. True Intellectual System of the Universe. Repr. of 1678 ed. 211.00 (ISBN 3-7728-0103-X). Adler.

Duggan, Stephen P. A Professor at Large. LC 72-4507. (Essay Index Reprint Ser.). Repr. of 1943 ed. 25.00 (ISBN 0-8369-2942-X). Arno.

Klineberg, Otto. International Exchanges in Education, Science & Culture: Suggestions for Research. (Publications of the International Social Science Council: No. 18). (Orig.). 1966. pap. text ed. 5.60x (ISBN 0-686-22437-X). Mouton.

Merritt, Richard L., ed. Communication in International Politics. LC 72-165042. 480p. 1972. 25.00 (ISBN 0-252-00210-5). U of Ill Pr.

Sanford, Daniel S. Inter-Institutional Agreements in Higher Education. LC 75-177226. (Columbia University. Teachers College. Contributions to Education: No. 627). Repr. of 1934 ed. 17.50 (ISBN 0-404-55627-2). AMS Pr.

Scanlon, David G., ed. International Education: A Documentary History. LC 64-12575. (Orig.). 1960. text ed. 8.75 (ISBN 0-8077-2098-4); pap. 4.00x (ISBN 0-8077-2095-X). Tchrs Coll.

University Of Chicago - Graduate Library School Conference - 23rd. Iron Curtains & Scholarship. Winger, Howard W., ed. (Studies in Library Science). 1958. 6.75x (ISBN 0-226-90199-8). U of Chicago Pr.

Wells, Herbert G. World Brain. facs. ed. LC 78-128332. (Essay Index Reprint Ser). 1938. 17.00 (ISBN 0-8369-2033-3). Arno.

INTELLECTUAL FREEDOM

see Censorship; Freedom of Information; Liberty of Speech; Teaching, Freedom of

INTELLECTUAL INEFFICIENCY

see Inefficiency, Intellectual

INTELLECTUAL LIFE

see also Intellectuals; Learning and Scholarship; Popular Culture;

also subdivision Intellectual Life under names of countries, cities, etc., e.g. France–Intellectual Life

Ben-David, Joseph & Clark, Terry N. Culture & Its Creators. LC 76-610. 1977. 17.00x (ISBN 0-226-04222-7). U of Chicago Pr.

Benge, Ronald. Libraries & Cultural Change. 1970. 17.50 (ISBN 0-208-00882-9, Linnet). Shoe String.

Berman, Ronald S. Intellect & Education in a Revolutionary Society. (Bicentennial Lectures Ser). 19p. 1974. 1.00 (ISBN 0-8447-1311-2). Am Enterprise.

Cage, John, et al. The Poets' Encyclopedia. Andre, Michael & Rothenberg, Erika, eds. (Illus.). 1979. 14.95 (ISBN 0-934450-02-1). Unmuzzled Ox.

Cox, C. B. & Dyson, A. E., eds. The Twentieth-Century Mind: History, Ideas, & Literature in Britain, Vol. I: Nineteen Hundred to Nineteen Eighteen. 540p. 1972. pap. text ed. 6.95x (ISBN 0-19-281118-5). Oxford U Pr.

--The Twentieth-Century Mind: History, Ideas, & Literature in Britain, Vol. II: Nineteen Eighteen to Nineteen Forty-Five. 526p. 1972. pap. text ed. 16.75x (ISBN 0-19-212192-8). Oxford U Pr.

--The Twentieth Century Mind: History, Ideas, & Literature in Britain, Vol. III: Nineteen Forty-Five to Nineteen Sixty-Five. 522p. 1972. pap. text ed. 16.75x (ISBN 0-19-212193-6). Oxford U Pr.

Curtis, James M. Culture As Polyphony: An Essay on the Nature of Paradigms. LC 77-25242. 1978. text ed. 15.00 (ISBN 0-8262-0251-9). U of Mo Pr.

Gella, Aleksander, ed. The Intelligentsia & the Intellectuals: Theory, Method & Case Study. LC 75-38421. (Sage Studies in International Sociology: Vol. 5). (Illus.). 235p. 1976. 22.50x (ISBN 0-8039-9958-5); pap. 9.95 (ISBN 0-8039-9972-0). Sage.

Guevara, Carlos I. & Sesman, Myrna. La Madre y el Aprendizaje Del Nino: La Experiencia Urbana Puertorriquena. LC 77-9261. 1978. pap. 5.50 (ISBN 0-8477-2739-4). U of PR Pr.

Hamerton, Philip G. The Intellectual Life. 1979. Repr. of 1904 ed. lib. bdg. 30.00 (ISBN 0-8492-5325-X). R West.

--Intellectual Life. LC 72-3346. (Essay Index Reprint Ser.). Repr. of 1873 ed. 22.00 (ISBN 0-8369-2905-5). Arno.

--The Intellectual Life. LC 77-2568. 1977. Repr. of 1904 ed. lib. bdg. 25.00 (ISBN 0-8414-4761-6). Folcroft.

Hirschman, Albert O. The Passions & the Interests: Political Arguments for Capitalism Before Its Triumph. 1977. 12.50 (ISBN 0-691-04214-4); pap. 4.95 (ISBN 0-691-00357-2). Princeton U Pr.

Institute for Religious & Social Studies. New Horizons in Creative Thinking. MacIver, R. M., ed. LC 75-26660. (Religion & Civilization Series). 159p. 1975. Repr. of 1954 ed. lib. bdg. 15.00x (ISBN 0-8371-8371-5, MANHC). Greenwood.

Kampf, Louis. On Modernism: The Prospects for Literature & Freedom. 1967. 15.00x (ISBN 0-262-11020-2). MIT Pr.

Mandel, Siegfried. Group Forty Seven: The Reflected Intellect. LC 73-8698. (Crosscurrents-Modern Critiques Ser.). 245p. 1973. 8.95 (ISBN 0-8093-0641-7). S Ill U Pr.

Millas, Jorge. The Intellectual & Moral Challenge of Mass Society. Parent, David J., tr. from Span. LC 77-71315. (Illinois Language & Culture Ser: Vol. 3). 1977. 16.50 (ISBN 0-8357-0199-9, IS-00021, Pub. by Applied Literature Press). Univ Microfilms.

Miller, Perry. The Responsibility of Mind in a Civilization of Machines: Essays by Perry Miller. Crowell, John & Searl, Stanford J., Jr., eds. LC 79-4699. (New England Writers Ser.). 1979. lib. bdg. 14.50x (ISBN 0-87023-281-9). U of Mass Pr.

Mullin, Arthur, ed. The Questing Mind: Readings for Background & Comprehension. LC 68-22410. (Orig.). 1968. pap. 7.50 (ISBN 0-672-63095-8). Odyssey Pr.

Odegaard, Charles E., et al. Man & Learning in Modern Society. LC 59-15076. (Illus.). 203p. 1959. 10.50 (ISBN 0-295-73835-9). U of Wash Pr.

Rohwer, W., et al. Understanding Intellectual Development. LC 73-22554. 1974. pap. text ed. 10.95 (ISBN 0-03-089543-X, HoltC). HR&W.

Social Aspects of Endogenous Intellectual Creativity: The Problem of Obstacles Guidelines for Research. 9p. 1980. pap. 5.00 (ISBN 92-808-0113-9, TUNU 073, UNU). Unipub.

Vysny, P. Neo-Slavism & the Czechs, 1898-1914. LC 76-4239. (Soviet & East European Studies). (Illus.). 1977. 41.00 (ISBN 0-521-21230-8). Cambridge U Pr.

Wender, Herbert. Growth of Modern Thought & Culture. 1959. 3.75 (ISBN 0-8022-1850-4). Philos Lib.

INTELLECTUAL PROPERTY

see also Copyright; Industrial Property

Convention Establishing the World Intellectual Property Organization: (1967) 24p. 1970. pap. 3.00x (ISBN 0-686-53002-0, WIPO10, WIPO). Unipub.

Records of the Intellectual Property Conference of Stockholm, 1967, Vols. I & II. 1971. Set. 180.00x (ISBN 0-686-53023-3, WIPO30, WIPO). Unipub.

Sperber, Philip. Intellectual Property Management - Law - Business - Strategy. LC 74-21479. 1974. with 1978 rev. pages 67.50 (ISBN 0-87632-150-3). Boardman.

INTELLECTUALS

see also Professions;

also subdivision Intellectual Life under names of countries, cities, etc., e.g. France–Intellectual Life

Benda, Julien. Treason of the Intellectuals. Aldington, Richard, tr. 1969. pap. 5.95 (ISBN 0-393-00470-8, Norton Lib). Norton.

Bronowski, Jacob. On Being an Intellectual. LC 70-570. 1968. pap. 1.25 (ISBN 0-87391-013-3). Smith Coll.

Bruce-Briggs, B., ed. The New Class? LC 78-62999. (McGraw-Hill Paperbacks Ser.). 252p. 1981. pap. 5.95 (ISBN 0-07-008573-0). McGraw.

Brym, Robert J. Intellectuals & Politics. (Controversies in Sociology Ser.: No. 9). (Orig.). 1980. text ed. 14.95x (ISBN 0-04-322005-3); pap. text ed. 6.95x (ISBN 0-04-322006-1). Allen Unwin.

Cadwallader, Barrie. Crisis of the European Mind: A Study of Andre Malraus & Drieu la Rochelle. 267p. 1981. text ed. 67.00x (ISBN 0-7083-0759-0). Verry.

Chomsky, Noam. American Power & the New Mandarins. LC 69-11864. 1969. 10.00 (ISBN 0-394-41498-5). Pantheon.

Coser, Lewis A. Men of Ideas. LC 65-10957. 1965. 7.95 (ISBN 0-02-906790-1); pap. 3.45 (ISBN 0-02-906770-7). Free Pr.

Curti, Merle. American Paradox: The Conflict of Thought & Action. LC 72-11304. 116p. 1973. Repr. of 1956 ed. lib. bdg. 15.00x (ISBN 0-8371-6647-0, CUAP). Greenwood.

Earnest, Ernest. The Single Vision: The Alienation of American Intellectuals. LC 78-116132. 1970. 10.00x (ISBN 0-8147-0459-X); pap. 9.00x (ISBN 0-8147-0460-3). NYU Pr.

Fermi, Laura. Illustrious Immigrants: The Intellectual Migration from Europe, 1930-41. 2nd ed. LC 76-154689. 1971. pap. 18.00x (ISBN 0-226-24376-1). U of Chicago Pr.

Fredrickson, George M. Inner Civil War: Northern Intellectuals & the Crisis of the Union. 1968. pap. 4.95x (ISBN 0-06-131358-0, TB1358, Torch). Har-Row.

Fyvel, T. R. Intellectuals Today: Problems in a Changing Society. LC 68-16655. 1968. 6.95x (ISBN 0-8052-3115-3). Schocken.

Geiger, Theodor. Aufgaben und Stellung der Intelligenz in der Gesellschaft: The Task & Position of Intellectuals in Society. LC 74-25749. (European Sociology Ser.). 174p. 1975. Repr. 13.00x (ISBN 0-405-06504-3). Arno.

Grunfeld, Frederic V. Prophets Without Honor, a Background to Freud, Kafka, Einstein & Their World. LC 78-31645. (Illus.). 368p. 1979. 15.00 (ISBN 0-03-017871-1). HR&W.

Hofstadter, Richard. Anti-Intellectualism in American Life. 1963. 13.95 (ISBN 0-394-41535-3). Knopf.

--Anti-Intellectualism in American Life. 1966. pap. 3.95 (ISBN 0-394-70317-0, Vin). Random.

Holbrook, David. Education, Nihilism & Survival. 1978. pap. 7.50 (ISBN 0-232-51384-8). Attic Pr.

Hollander, Paul. Political Pilgrims: Travels of Western Intellectuals to the Soviet Union, China, & Cuba 1928-1978. LC 80-29417. 320p. 1981. 25.00 (ISBN 0-19-502937-2). Oxford U Pr.

Howe, Irving. Steady Work: Essays in the Politics of Democratic Radicalism 1953-1966. LC 66-22275. 1967. pap. 2.45 (ISBN 0-15-684930-5, HB126, Harv). HarBraceJ.

Macdonald, H. Malcolm, ed. The Intellectual in Politics. LC 66-29160. (Quarterly Ser). 1966. 10.00 (ISBN 0-87959-074-2). U of Tex Hum Res.

Marcaccio, Michael D. The Hapgoods: Three Earnest Brothers. LC 77-5102. 1977. 15.00x (ISBN 0-8139-0693-8). U Pr of Va.

Nichols, Ray. Treason, Tradition, & the Intellectual: Julien Benda & Political Discourse. LC 78-7785. 1979. 16.00x (ISBN 0-7006-0175-9). Regents Pr KS.

O'Brien, Conor Cruise & Vanech, William Dean, eds. Power & Consciousness. LC 69-19260. (Schweitzer Lecture Ser). 1969. 12.00x (ISBN 0-8147-0327-5). NYU Pr.

Rand, Ayn. For the New Intellectual. 1961. 10.95 (ISBN 0-394-42526-X). Random.

Sartre, Jean-Paul. Plaidoyer pour les Intellectuels. 1972. 3.95 (ISBN 0-686-54990-2). French & Eur.

Shortt, S. E. The Search for an Ideal: Six Canadian Intellectuals & Their Convictions in an Age of Transition, 1890-1930. 1976. 17.50x (ISBN 0-8020-5350-5); pap. 7.50 (ISBN 0-8020-6285-7). U of Toronto Pr.

Spooner, John D. Smart People: A User's Guide to the Experts. 1979. 9.95 (ISBN 0-316-80740-0). Little.

Steinberg, Stephen. Academic Melting Pot. LC 73-9656. (Illus.). 1977. pap. text ed. 4.95 (ISBN 0-87855-635-4). Transaction Bks.

Stuart, Roger W. Thought Brigade. 1963. 7.50 (ISBN 0-8392-1118-X). Astor-Honor.

Wilson, Daniel J. Arthur O. Lovejoy & the Quest for Intelligibility. LC 79-25902. xvii, 248p. 1980. 18.00x (ISBN 0-8078-1431-8). U of NC Pr.

Young, Michael. The Rise of the Meritocracy. 1962. pap. 2.95 (ISBN 0-14-020485-7, Pelican). Penguin.

INTELLECTUALS–GREAT BRITAIN

Chamberlain, John. The Letters of John Chamberlain, 2 vols. McClure, Norman E., ed. LC 78-23784. 1979. Repr. of 1939 ed. Set. lib. bdg. 72.50x (ISBN 0-313-20710-0, CHLE). Greenwood.

Foot, Michael. Debts of Honour. 240p. 1981. 13.95 (ISBN 0-06-039001-8). Har-Row.

INTELLECTUALS–RUSSIA

Acton, E. Alexander Herzen & the Role of the Intellectual Revolutionary. LC 78-56747. 1979. 22.95 (ISBN 0-521-22166-8). Cambridge U Pr.

Berlin, Isaiah. Russian Thinkers. (Pelican Ser.). 1979. pap. 3.95 (ISBN 0-14-022260-X). Penguin.

Churchward, L. G. The Soviet Intelligentsia: An Essay on the Social Structure & Roles of the Soviet Intellectuals During the 1960's. (Illus.). 218p. 1973. 18.00 (ISBN 0-7100-7475-1). Routledge & Kegan.

Pomper, Philip. Russian Revolutionary Intelligentsia. LC 75-107303. (AHM Europe Since 1500 Ser.). 1970. pap. 5.95x (ISBN 0-88295-749-X). Harlan Davidson.

INTELLIGENCE

see Intellect

INTELLIGENCE, ARTIFICIAL

see Artificial Intelligence

INTELLIGENCE, BUSINESS

see Business Intelligence

INTELLIGENCE LEVELS

see also Intelligence Tests

Bridge, R. Gary, et al. The Determinants of Educational Outcomes: Impact of Families, Peers, Teachers & Schools. LC 78-26467. 1979. 19.50 (ISBN 0-88410-182-7). Ballinger Pub.

Brigham, C. C. Study of American Intelligence. LC 23-6849. Repr. of 1923 ed. 16.00 (ISBN 0-527-10891-X). Kraus Repr.

Bronner, Augusta F. A Comparative Study of the Intelligence of Delinquent Girls. LC 72-176594. (Columbia University. Teachers College. Contributions to Education: No. 68). Repr. of 1914 ed. 17.50 (ISBN 0-404-55068-1). AMS Pr.

Calhoun, Daniel H. The Intelligence of a People. (Illus.). 392p. 1973. 28.00 (ISBN 0-691-04619-0, 400); pap. 9.95 (ISBN 0-691-00587-7). Princeton U Pr.

Denko, Joanne D. Through the Keyhole at Gifted Men & Women: A Study of 159 Adults of High IQ. LC 77-80608. 1977. pap. 24.25 (ISBN 0-8357-0260-X, SS-00032). Univ Microfilms.

Dobzhansky, Theodosius. Genetic Diversity & Human Equality. LC 73-76262. 1973. pap. 3.95x (ISBN 0-465-09710-3, CN-5010). Basic.

Genua, Albert J. How to Increase Your I.Q. in Thirty Days. 1980. 7.50 (ISBN 0-682-49361-9). Exposition.

Hunt, J. McVicker, ed. Human Intelligence. LC 78-164977. 293p. 1972. pap. 4.95 (ISBN 0-87855-502-1). Transaction Bks.

Klineberg, Otto. Negro Intelligence & Selective Migration. LC 74-12884. 66p. 1975. Repr. of 1935 ed. lib. bdg. 15.00x (ISBN 0-8371-7771-5, KLNI). Greenwood.

McKane, Keith. A Comparison of the Intelligence of Deaf & Hearing Children: A Study of the Reactions of Comparable Groups of Deaf & Hearing Children to Three Performance Scales & a Non-Language Test. LC 74-177030. (Columbia University. Teachers College. Contributions to Education: No. 585). Repr. of 1933 ed. 17.50 (ISBN 0-404-55585-3). AMS Pr.

Portenier, Lillian G. Pupils of Low Mentality in High School. LC 76-177158. (Columbia University. Teachers College. Contributions to Education: No. 568). Repr. of 1933 ed. 17.50 (ISBN 0-404-55568-3). AMS Pr.

Senna, Carl, ed. The Fallacy of I. Q. LC 72-93380. 180p. 1973. 8.95 (ISBN 0-685-28733-5, 89388-X). Okpaku Communications.

Serebriakoff, Victor. How Intelligent Are You? 128p. 1974. pap. 1.50 (ISBN 0-451-09295-3, E9295, Sig). NAL.

Shuey, Audrey M. Testing of Negro Intelligence. 2nd rev. & enl. ed. 1966. 16.50x (ISBN 0-911396-00-4). Soc Sci Pr.

Sperry, Len. Learning Performance & Individual Differences: Essays & Readings. 326p. 1972. pap. 4.95x (ISBN 0-673-07799-3). Scott F.

Steacy, Frederick W. Interrelations of Mental Abilities. LC 76-177742. (Columbia University. Teachers College. Contributions to Education: No. 95). Repr. of 1919 ed. 17.50 (ISBN 0-404-55095-9). AMS Pr.

Tanser, Harry A. Settlement of Negroes in Kent County Ontario, and a Study of the Mental Capacity of Their Descendents. LC 76-107487. Repr. of 1939 ed. 11.75x (ISBN 0-8371-3789-6). Greenwood.

Teagarden, Florence M. A Study of the Upper Limits of the Development of Intelligence. LC 75-177723. (Columbia University. Teachers College. Contributions to Education: No. 156). Repr. of 1924 ed. 17.50 (ISBN 0-404-55156-4). AMS Pr.

Viaud, Gaston. Intelligence, Its Evolution & Forms. Pomerans, A. J., tr. LC 72-10983. (Illus.). 127p. 1973. Repr. of 1960 ed. lib. bdg. 15.00 (ISBN 0-8371-6640-3, VIIN). Greenwood.

INTELLIGENCE LEVELS–TESTING

see Intelligence Tests

INTELLIGENCE OF ANIMALS

see Animal Intelligence; Instinct; Psychology, Comparative

INTELLIGENCE SERVICE

see also Espionage; Military Intelligence; Secret Service

Blackstock, Paul W. & Schaf, Frank, Jr. Intelligence, Espionage, Counterespionage & Covert Operations: A Guide to Information Sources. LC 74-11567. (International Relations Information Guide Ser.: Vol. 2). 1978. 36.00 (ISBN 0-8103-1323-5). Gale.

Blum, Richard H., ed. Surveillance & Espionage in a Free Society. LC 72-85979. (Special Studies in U.S. Economic, Social & Political Issues). 1972. 28.00x (ISBN 0-275-28643-6); pap. text ed. 8.50x (ISBN 0-89197-957-3). Irvington.

Donner, Frank J. The Age of Surveillance: The Aims & Methods of America's Political Intelligence System. LC 79-3479. 1980. 17.95 (ISBN 0-394-40298-7). Knopf.

Fitzgibbon, Constantine. Secret Intelligence in the Twentieth Century. LC 76-9110. 1976. 25.00 (ISBN 0-8128-1937-3). Stein & Day.

Harger, Richard. The Scourge of Secrecy: A Personal Testimony & Testimony & Appeal. LC 80-50239. 218p. 1980. pap. 6.80 (ISBN 0-936472-00-6). Gordy Pr.

Haswell, Jock. Spies & Spymasters: A Concise History of Intelligence. (Illus.). 1977. 10.95 (ISBN 0-500-01178-8). Thames Hudson.

Hilsman, Roger. Strategic Intelligence & National Decisions. LC 80-29549. 187p. 1981. Repr. of 1956 ed. lib. bdg. 18.50x (ISBN 0-313-22717-9, HILI). Greenwood.

Jeffreys-Jones, Rhodri. American Espionage: From Secret Service to C.I.A. LC 77-74854. (Illus.). 1977. 14.95 (ISBN 0-02-916360-9). Free Pr.

Kirkpatrick, Lyman B., Jr. U. S. Intelligence Community: Foreign Policy & Domestic Activities. 212p. 1973. 7.95 (ISBN 0-8090-9501-7, AmCen). Hill & Wang.

Macy, Christy & Kaplan, Susan. Documents. (Illus., Orig.). 1980. pap. 8.95 (ISBN 0-14-004993-2). Penguin.

Meyer, Cord. Facing Reality: From World Federalism to the CIA. LC 79-1677. (Illus.). 416p. 1980. 15.95 (ISBN 0-06-013032-6, HarpT). Har-Row.

Pfaltzgraff, Robert L., et al. Intelligence Poligy & National Security. 1981. 32.50 (ISBN 0-208-01918-9, Archon). Shoe String.

Platt, Washington. National Character in Action: Intelligence Factors in Foreign Relations. 1961. 17.50x (ISBN 0-8135-0382-5). Rutgers U Pr.

Ransom, Harry H. Intelligence Establishment. LC 70-115480. 1970. 15.00x (ISBN 0-674-45816-8). Harvard U Pr.

Schultz, D. O. & Norton, L. A. Police Operational Intelligence. rev. ed. 244p. 1973. 15.50 (ISBN 0-398-02832-X). C C Thomas.

Smith, Myron J., Jr. The Secret Wars: A Guide to Sources in English: Vol. 2, Intelligence, Propaganda & Psychological Warfare, Covert Operations, 1945-1980. Burns, Richard D., ed. (War-Peace Bibliography Ser.: No. 13). 375p. 1981. 67.50 (ISBN 0-87436-303-9). ABC Clio.

Thorpe, Elliott R. East Wind, Rain: The Intimate Account of an Intelligence Officer in the Pacific 1939-49. LC 69-12586. 1969. 7.95 (ISBN 0-87645-020-6). Gambit.

Wilcox, Laird M., compiled by. Bibliography on Espionage & Intelligence Operations. (Orig.). 1981. pap. text ed. 9.95 (ISBN 0-933592-23-X). Edit Res Serv.

Wilensky, Harold L. Organizational Intelligence: Knowledge & Policy in Government & Industry. LC 67-17388. 1969. 11.50x (ISBN 0-465-05317-3); pap. text ed. 5.95x (ISBN 0-465-05318-1). Basic.

Wise, David. The American Police State: The Government Against the People. 1976. 12.95 (ISBN 0-394-49677-9). Random.

--The American Police State: The Government Against the People. 1978. pap. 4.95 (ISBN 0-394-72498-4, Vin). Random.

Wise, David & Ross, Thomas B. Invisible Government. 1964. 10.00 (ISBN 0-394-43077-8). Random.

Wittman, George. The Role of American Intelligence Organizations. (Reference Shelf Ser.). 1976. 6.25 (ISBN 0-8242-0599-5). Wilson.

Wohlstetter, Roberta. Pearl Harbor: Warning & Decision. 1962. 18.50x (ISBN 0-8047-0597-6); pap. 5.95 (ISBN 0-8047-0598-4, SP14). Stanford U Pr.

INTELLIGENCE SERVICE–GREAT BRITAIN

Lesberg, Sandy. The Q Factor: The True Story of Charles Fraser-Smith, World War II British Intelligence Escape, Deception & Survival Expert, the "Q" of the James Bond Novels. LC 79-83768. (Illus.). Date not set. 12.95 (ISBN 0-85690-081-8). Peebles Pr.

INTELLIGENCE SERVICE–RUSSIA

Blackstock, Paul W. The Secret Road to World War Two. LC 69-2054. 1972. 9.50 (ISBN 0-8129-0083-9). Times Bks.

Lewis, David. Sexpionage: The Exploitation of Sex by Soviet Intelligence. LC 76-2534. (Illus.). 192p. 1976. 8.95 (ISBN 0-15-181380-9). HarBraceJ.

Shragin, Boris & Todd, Albert, eds. Landmarks: A Collection of Essays on the Russian Intelligentsia. Schwartz, Marian, tr. LC 77-880. 1977. text ed. 19.95x (ISBN 0-918294-00-2). Karz Pub.

INTELLIGENCE TESTING

see Intelligence Tests

INTELLIGENCE TESTS

see also Stanford-Binet Test; Wechsler Intelligence Scale for Children

Abelson, Harold H. The Improvement of Intelligence Testing. LC 76-176502. (Columbia University Teachers College Contributions to Education: No. 273). Repr. of 1927 ed. 17.50 (ISBN 0-404-55273-0). AMS Pr.

Allen, Clinton M. Some Effects Produced in an Individual by Knowledge of His Own Intellectual Level. LC 73-176511. (Columbia University. Teachers College. Contributions to Education: No. 401). Repr. of 1930 ed. 17.50 (ISBN 0-404-55401-6). AMS Pr.

Allen, William S. A Study in Latin Prognosis. LC 70-176513. (Columbia University. Teachers College. Contributions to Education: No. 135). Repr. of 1923 ed. 17.50 (ISBN 0-404-55135-1). AMS Pr.

Andrulis, Richard S. Adult Assessment: A Source Book of Tests & Measures of Human Behavior. 340p. 1977. ed. spiral bdg. 16.00photocopy (ISBN 0-398-03603-9). C C Thomas.

Arco Editiorial Board. Practice for Air Force Placement Tests. 4th ed. LC 77-2201. 1977. lib. bdg. 9.00 (ISBN 0-668-04262-1); pap. 6.00 (ISBN 0-668-04270-2). Arco.

Arco Editorial Board. Junior Administrator Development Examination: JADE. LC 67-19565. (Illus., Orig.). 1967. lib. bdg. 7.50 (ISBN 0-668-01791-0); pap. 5.00 o. p. (ISBN 0-668-01643-4). Arco.

Atkins, Ruth E. The Measurement of the Intelligence of Young Children by an Object-Fitting Test. LC 75-12673. (Univ. of Minnesota Institute of Child Welfare Monograph: No. 5). (Illus.). 89p. 1975. Repr. of 1931 ed. lib. bdg. 15.00 (ISBN 0-8371-8083-X, CWAI). Greenwood.

Bailor, Edwin M. Content & Form in Tests of Intelligence. LC 70-176529. (Columbia University. Teachers College. Contributions to Education: No. 162). Repr. of 1924 ed. 17.50 (ISBN 0-404-55162-9). AMS Pr.

Barclay, James R. Controversial Issues in Testing. (Guidance Monograph). 1968. pap. 2.40 (ISBN 0-395-09932-3, 9-78832). HM.

Barrett, Albert M. When Thinking Begins: Lessons Learned from Helping Preaverage Intelligence Individuals. (Illus.). 84p. 1973. text ed. 8.75 (ISBN 0-398-02770-6). C C Thomas.

Barthelmess, Harriet M. The Validity of Intelligence Test Elements. LC 70-176537. (Columbia University. Teachers College. Contributions to Education: No. 505). Repr. of 1931 ed. 17.50 (ISBN 0-404-55505-5). AMS Pr.

Bauernfeind, Robert H. School Testing Programs. (Guidance Monograph). 1968. pap. 2.40 (ISBN 0-395-09927-7, 9-78826). HM.

Bere, May. A Comparative Study of the Mental Capacity of Children of Foreign Parentage. (Columbia University. Teachers College. Contributions to Education: No. 154). Repr. of 1924 ed. 17.50 (ISBN 0-404-55154-8). AMS Pr.

Bernard, William & Leopold, Jules. Test Yourself. 4th ed. LC 64-9047. (Illus.). 1962. pap. 3.50 (ISBN 0-8019-1378-0). Chilton.

Block, N. J. & Dworkin, Gerald, eds. The IQ Controversy. LC 75-38113. 1976. pap. 7.95 (ISBN 0-394-73087-9). Pantheon.

Bond, Elden A. Tenth-Grade Abilities & Achievements. LC 79-176577. (Columbia University. Teachers College. Contributions to Education: No. 813). Repr. of 1940 ed. 17.50 (ISBN 0-404-55813-5). AMS Pr.

Boody, Bertha M. Psychological Study of Immigrant Children at Ellis Island. LC 79-129391. (American Immigration Collection, Ser. 2). 1970. Repr. of 1926 ed. 9.00 (ISBN 0-405-00546-6). Arno.

Bridges, Sydney. I. Q. - One Hundred & Fifty. 1973. 8.50x (ISBN 0-85078-060-8); pap. 5.00x (ISBN 0-85078-061-6). Technomic.

Brody, Erness B. & Brody, Nathan, eds. Intelligence: Nature, Determinants, & Consequences. 1976. 24.00 (ISBN 0-12-134250-6). Acad Pr.

Buhler, Charlotte. The First Year of Life. Greenberg, Pearl & Ripin, Rowena, trs. LC 73-16646. 281p. 1974. Repr. of 1930 ed. lib. bdg. 15.50x (ISBN 0-8371-7214-4, BUFY). Greenwood.

Buros, Oscar K., ed. Intelligence Tests & Reviews. LC 75-8112. 1975. 70.00x (ISBN 0-8032-1163-5). U of Nebr Pr.

--Mental Measurements Yearbook. Incl. 1st. LC 39-3422. 1938. 20.00x (ISBN 0-910674-12-4); 2nd. 1941. 30.00x (ISBN 0-910674-13-2); 3rd. 1949. 35.00x (ISBN 0-910674-03-5); 4th. 1953. 40.00x (ISBN 0-910674-04-3); 5th. 1959. 60.00x (ISBN 0-8032-1164-3); 6th. 1965. 45.00x (ISBN 0-910674-06-X); 7th, 2 vols. 1972. Set. 95.00x (ISBN 0-8032-1160-0); 8th, 2 vols. LC 39-3422. 1978. Set. 120.00x (ISBN 0-910674-24-8). LC 39-3422. U of Nebr Pr.

--Personality Tests & Reviews-One. 1970. 50.00x (ISBN 0-910674-10-8). U of Nebr Pr.

Cattell, Psyche. Measurement of Intelligence of Infants & Young Children. (Illus.). 1960. 15.50 (ISBN 0-384-07925-3). Johnson Repr.

Chapman, James C. Individual Differences in Ability & Improvement & Their Correlations. LC 74-176636. (Columbia University. Teachers College. Contributions to Education: No. 63). Repr. of 1914 ed. 17.50 (ISBN 0-404-55063-0). AMS Pr.

Chen, Hsuan-Shan. The Comparative Coachability of Certain Types of Intelligence Tests. (Columbia University. Teachers College. Contributions to Education: No. 338). Repr. of 1928 ed. 17.50 (ISBN 0-404-55338-9). AMS Pr.

Clem, Orlie M. Detailed Factors in Latin Prognosis. LC 78-176653. (Columbia University. Teachers College. Contributions to Education: No. 144). Repr. of 1924 ed. 17.50 (ISBN 0-404-55144-0). AMS Pr.

Crabbs, Lelah M. Measuring Efficiency in Supervision & Teaching. LC 73-176676. (Columbia University. Teachers College. Contributions to Education: No. 175). Repr. of 1925 ed. 17.50 (ISBN 0-404-55175-0). AMS Pr.

Cunningham, Bess V. The Prognostic Value of a Primary Group Test: A Study of Intelligence & Relative Achievement in the First Grade. LC 70-176683. (Columbia University. Teachers College. Contributions to Education: No. 139). Repr. of 1923 ed. 17.50 (ISBN 0-404-55139-4). AMS Pr.

Cunningham, Kenneth S. The Measurement of Early Levels of Intelligence. LC 72-176701. (Columbia University. Teachers College. Contributions to Education: No. 259). Repr. of 1927 ed. 17.50 (ISBN 0-404-55259-5). AMS Pr.

Dodge, Arthur F. Occupational Ability Patterns. LC 78-176724. (Columbia University. Teachers College. Contributions to Education: No. 658). Repr. of 1935 ed. 17.50 (ISBN 0-404-55658-2). AMS Pr.

Dupuy, Harold J. The Construction & Utility of Three Indexes of Intellectual Achievement. Stevenson, Taloria, ed. Incl. An Index of Intellectual Development (ID; A Socio-Intellectual-Status (SIS) Index; A Differential-Intellectual-Development (DID) Index (U.S. Children & Youth 6-17 Years. (Ser. 2: No. 74). 1977. pap. text ed. 1.85 (ISBN 0-8406-0106-9). Natl Ctr Health Stats.

Educational & Other Aspects of the Nineteen Forty-Seven Scottish Mental Survey. (Scottish Council for Research in Education Ser.: No. 41). 1958. 3.50x (ISBN 0-8426-1248-3). Verry.

Ehrlich, Paul R. & Feldman, Shirley. The Race Bomb: Skin Color, Prejudice, & Intelligence. LC 76-52821. (Illus.). 1977. 9.95 (ISBN 0-8129-0681-0). Times Bks.

Eisner, Harry. Classroom Teachers' Estimation of Intelligence & Industry of High School Students. LC 79-176743. (Columbia University. Teachers College. Contributions to Education: No. 726). Repr. of 1937 ed. 17.50 (ISBN 0-404-55726-0). AMS Pr.

Evans, B. H. & Waites, B. A. IQ & Mental Testing. 1980. text ed. 30.00x (ISBN 0-391-01911-2); pap. text ed. 13.00x (ISBN 0-391-01912-0). Humanities.

Eysenck, H. J. Check Your Own I. Q. lib. bdg. 8.50x (ISBN 0-88307-341-2). Gannon.

--The Measurement of Intelligence. 488p. 1973. 24.00 (ISBN 0-683-02803-0, Pub. by W & W). Krieger.

Eysenck, H. J. & Fulker, D. W. The Structure & Measurement of Intelligence. (Illus.). 1979. 20.80 (ISBN 0-387-09028-2). Springer-Verlag.

Eysenck, Hans J. Know Your Own I.Q. (Orig.). 1962. pap. 2.95 (ISBN 0-14-020516-0, Pelican). Penguin.

Fixx, James F. Games for the Super-Intelligent. 128p. 1974. pap. 2.50 (ISBN 0-445-08518-5). Popular Lib.

--More Games for the Superintelligent. LC 76-7695. 1976. 6.95 (ISBN 0-385-11039-1). Doubleday.

Flemming, Cecile W. Detailed Analysis of Achievement in the High School: Comparative Significance of Certain Mental, Physical & Character Traits for Success. LC 79-176778. (Columbia University. Teachers College. Contributions to Education: No. 196). Repr. of 1925 ed. 17.50 (ISBN 0-404-55196-3). AMS Pr.

Flynn, James R. Race, IQ, & Jensen. 320p. 1980. 27.50 (ISBN 0-7100-0651-9). Routledge & Kegan.

Fortna, Richard O. & Boston, Bruce O. Testing the Gifted Child: An Interpretation in Lay Language. LC 76-46730. 1976. pap. text ed. 3.75 (ISBN 0-86586-085-8). Coun Exc Child.

Freeman, Frank N. & Flory, C. D. Growth in Intellectual Ability As Measured by Repeated Tests. 1937. pap. 7.00 (ISBN 0-527-01495-8). Kraus Repr.

Friedman, Bertha B. Foundations of the Measurement of Values: The Methodology of Location & Quantification. LC 76-176788. (Columbia University. Teachers College. Contributions to Education: No. 914). Repr. of 1946 ed. 17.50 (ISBN 0-404-55914-X). AMS Pr.

Glover, John A. A Parent's Guide to Intelligence Testing. LC 78-25991. 1979. 17.95x (ISBN 0-88229-423-7); pap. 8.95 (ISBN 0-88229-670-1). Nelson-Hall.

Goldfarb, William. An Investigation of Reaction Time in Older Adults & Its Relationship to Certain Observed Mental Test Patterns. LC 78-176811. (Columbia University. Teachers College. Contributions to Education: No. 831). Repr. of 1941 ed. 17.50 (ISBN 0-404-55831-3). AMS Pr.

Goodenough, Florence & Maurer, Katharine. The Mental Growth of Children from Two to Fourteen Years: Study of the Predictive Value of the Minnesota Pre-School Scales. LC 70-141548. (Univ. of Minnesota Institute of Child Welfare Monographs: No. 20). (Illus.). 130p. 1975. Repr. of 1942 ed. lib. bdg. 15.75x (ISBN 0-8371-5895-8, CWGM). Greenwood.

Goodenough, Florence L. The Kuhlman-Binet Test for Children of Pre-School Age. LC 73-9226. 146p. 1973. Repr. of 1928 ed. lib. bdg. 15.00x (ISBN 0-8371-6990-9, CWGT). Greenwood.

--Measurement of Intelligence by Drawings. LC 74-21410. (Classics in Child Development Ser). 196p. 1975. Repr. 16.00x (ISBN 0-405-06462-4). Arno.

--Mental Testing: Its History, Principles & Applications. Repr. of 1949 ed. 23.00 (ISBN 0-384-19230-0). Johnson Repr.

Goodman, Jerome D. & Sours, John A. Child Mental Status Exam. LC 67-18208. 1967. text ed. 12.50x (ISBN 0-465-01010-5). Basic.

Gould, Stephen J. The Mismeasure of Man. (Illus.). 1981. 14.95 (ISBN 0-393-01489-4). Norton.

Graves, Katharine B. The Influence of Specialized Training on Tests of General Intelligence. LC 73-176818. (Columbia University. Teachers College. Contributions to Education: No. 143). Repr. of 1924 ed. 17.50 (ISBN 0-404-55143-2). AMS Pr.

Guidelines for Testing Minority Group Children. 18p. 0.35 (ISBN 0-686-74911-1). ADL.

Guilford, Joy P. & Hoepfner, R. Analysis of Intelligence. (Psychology Ser.). 1971. 32.00 (ISBN 0-07-025137-1, C). McGraw.

Harris, Dale B. & Pinder, Glenn D. Goodenough-Harris Test Examination of Intellectual Maturity of Youths 12-17 Years: Demographic & Socioeconomic Factors. (Ser. 11: No. 159). 70p. 1976. pap. text ed. 1.50 (ISBN 0-8406-0068-2). Natl Ctr Health Stats.

Herrnstein, R. J. I. Q. in the Meritocracy. 1973. 7.95 (ISBN 0-316-35864-9, Pub by Atlantic Monthly Pr). Little.

Hildreth, G. H. Resemblance of Siblings in Intelligence & Achievement. LC 78-176862. (Columbia University. Teachers College. Contributions to Education: No. 186). Repr. of 1925 ed. 17.50 (ISBN 0-404-55186-6). AMS Pr.

Hill, Evelyn F. The Holtzman Inkblot Technique: A Handbook for Clinical Application. LC 74-184959. (Social & Behavioral Science Ser.). 1972. 25.95x (ISBN 0-87589-121-7). Jossey-Bass.

Houts, Paul L., ed. The Myth of Measurability. 320p. (Orig.). 1977. pap. 6.95 (ISBN 0-89104-240-7). A & W Pubs.

Hunsicker, L. M. Study of the Relationship Between Rate & Ability. LC 74-176888. (Columbia University. Teachers College. Contributions to Education: No. 185). Repr. of 1925 ed. 17.50 (ISBN 0-404-55185-8). AMS Pr.

Ingalls, Robert P. Mental Retardation: The Changing Outlook. LC 77-23359. 1978. text ed. 22.95x (ISBN 0-471-42716-0). Wiley.

Irion, Theophile W. Comprehension Difficulties of Ninth Grade Students in the Study of Literature. (Columbia University. Teachers College. Contributions to Education: No. 189). Repr. of 1925 ed. 17.50 (ISBN 0-404-55189-0). AMS Pr.

Jennings, H. S., et al. Scientific Aspects of the Race Problem. LC 73-127591. (Essay Index Reprint Ser). 1941. 19.00 (ISBN 0-8369-1774-X). Arno.

Jensen, Arthur R. Bias in Mental Testing. LC 79-7583. (Illus.). 1980. 29.95 (ISBN 0-02-916430-3). Free Pr.

--Straight Talk About Mental Testing. 320p. 1981. 12.95 (ISBN 0-02-916440-0). Macmillan.

Jones, Vernon A. Effect of Age & Experience on Tests of Intelligence. LC 75-176919. (Columbia University. Teachers College. Contributions to Education: No. 203). Repr. of 1926 ed. 17.50 (ISBN 0-404-55203-X). AMS Pr.

Kaufman, Alan S. Intelligent Testing with the WISC-R. LC 78-31174. (Personality Processes Ser.). 268p. 1979. 27.50 (ISBN 0-471-04971-9, Pub. by Wiley-Interscience). Wiley.

Keliher, Alice V. A Critical Study of Homogeneous Grouping with a Critique of Measurement As the Basis for Classification. LC 77-176930. (Columbia University. Teachers College. Contributions to Education: No. 452). Repr. of 1931 ed. 17.50 (ISBN 0-404-55452-0). AMS Pr.

Kelley, T. L. Essential Traits of Mental Life. (Harvard Studies in Education: Vol. 26). 1935. pap. 15.50 (ISBN 0-384-29090-6). Johnson Repr.

Kennon, L. H. Tests of Literary Vocabulary for Teachers of English. LC 70-176966. (Columbia University. Teachers College. Contributions to Education: No. 223). Repr. of 1926 ed. 17.50 (ISBN 0-404-55223-4). AMS Pr.

King, Leo H. Mental & Interest Tests, Their Evaluation & Comparative Effectiveness As Factors of Prognosis in Secondary Education. LC 77-176957. (Columbia University. Teachers College. Contributions to Education: No. 444). Repr. of 1931 ed. 17.50 (ISBN 0-404-55444-X). AMS Pr.

Kirkpatrick, Clifford. Intelligence & Immigration. LC 76-129405. (American Immigration Collection, Ser. 2). 1970. Repr. of 1926 ed. 8.00 (ISBN 0-405-00558-X). Arno.

Klein, Stanley D. Psychological Testing of Children: A Consumer's Guide with Special Emphasis on the Psychology Assessment of Children with Disabilities. 1978. pap. 4.95 (ISBN 0-930958-01-2). Exceptional Parent.

Lawler, James. IQ, Heritability & Racism. 1978. pap. 3.95 (ISBN 0-7178-0554-9). Intl Pub Co.

Linden, James D. & Linden, Kathryn W. Tests on Trial. (Guidance Monograph). 1968. pap. 2.60 (ISBN 0-395-09930-7, 9-78830). HM.

Linden, Kathryn W. & Linden, James D. Modern Mental Measurement: A Historical Perspective. (Guidance Monograph). 1968. pap. 2.60 (ISBN 0-395-09924-2, 9-78823). HM.

Liu, Herman C. Non-Verbal Intelligence Tests for Use in China. LC 76-177001. (Columbia University. Teachers College. Contributions to Education: No. 126). Repr. of 1922 ed. 17.50 (ISBN 0-404-55126-2). AMS Pr.

Liungman, Karl. What Is I.Q.? 1975. pap. 5.95 (ISBN 0-86033-040-0). Gordon-Cremonesi.

Lord, Frederic M. & Novick, Melvin R. Statistical Theories of Mental Test Scores. 1968. text ed. 26.95 (ISBN 0-201-04310-6). A-W.

Lutterjohann, Martin. IQ Tests for Children. LC 77-1520. 192p. 8.95 (ISBN 0-8128-2272-2); pap. 4.95 (ISBN 0-8128-2271-4). Stein & Day.

--IQ Tests for School Children: How to Test Your Child's Intelligence. (Illus.). 1980. 10.95 (ISBN 0-8128-2587-X); pap. 5.95 (ISBN 0-8128-6026-8). Stein & Day.

Lyman, Howard B. Intelligence, Aptitude & Achievement Testing. (Guidance Monograph). 1968. pap. 2.40 (ISBN 0-395-09928-5, 9-78827). HM.

McCall, William A. Correlation of Some Psychological & Educational Measurements with Special Attention to the Measurement of Mental Ability. LC 75-177017. (Columbia University. Teachers College. Contributions to Education: No. 79). Repr. of 1916 ed. 17.50 (ISBN 0-404-55079-7). AMS Pr.

Matarazzo, Joseph D. & Wechsler, David. Wechsler's Measurement & Appraisal of Adult Intelligence. 5th ed. (Illus.). 1972. 21.95x (ISBN 0-19-502296-3). Oxford U Pr.

Megargee, Edwin I. The California Psychological Inventory Handbook. LC 76-186581. (Social & Behavioral Science Ser.). 1972. 26.95x (ISBN 0-87589-122-5). Jossey-Bass.

Mercer, Jane R. Labeling the Mentally Retarded. 1973. pap. 7.95x (ISBN 0-520-02428-1). U of Cal Pr.

Meyering, Ralph A. Uses of Test Data in Counseling. (Guidance Monograph). 1968. pap. 2.40 (ISBN 0-395-09920-X, 9-78819). HM.

Meyers, C. E., et al. Primary Abilities at Mental Age Six. 1962. pap. 4.00 (ISBN 0-527-01592-X). Kraus Repr.

Moriarty, Alice E. Constancy & IQ Change: A Clinical View of Relationships Between Tested Intelligence & Personality. (Illus.). 130p. 1966. photocopy ed. spiral 19.75 (ISBN 0-398-01347-0). C C Thomas.

Mosher, Raymond M. A Study of the Group Method of Measurement of Sight-Singing. LC 75-177092. (Columbia University. Teachers College. Contributions to Education: No. 194). Repr. of 1925 ed. 17.50 (ISBN 0-404-55194-7). AMS Pr.

Mullan, E. H. Mentality of the Arriving Immigrant. LC 77-129408. (American Immigration Collection, Ser. 2). (Illus.). 1970. Repr. of 1917 ed. 7.50 (ISBN 0-405-00562-8). Arno.

Munzert, Alfred W. Self-Scoring I.Q. Test. Elskamp, Karen K., ed. Date not set. pap. 1.50 (ISBN 0-917292-00-6). Hemisphere NY.

--Test Your I.Q. (Test Yourself Ser.). 1980. pap. 3.95 (ISBN 0-671-34035-2). Monarch Pr.

Myklebust, Helmer R. The Pupil Rating Scale: Screening for Learning Disabilities. 1971. pap. 19.50 (ISBN 0-8089-0684-4); record forms, pkg. of 50 13.00 (ISBN 0-8089-0794-8); specimen set manual, 1 record form 13.00 (ISBN 0-8089-0752-2); computer scoring from, 50 scoring forms, 2 class header sheets, school report form 31.25 (ISBN 0-8089-0989-4). Grune.

Newman, Isadore, et al. An Introduction to the Basic Concepts & Techniques of Measurement & Evaluation. 4th ed. 210p. 1976. pap. text ed. 5.00 (ISBN 0-917180-05-4). I Newman.

Oetting, Eugene R. & Thornton, George C., 3rd. Exercises in Psychological Testing. (Holzman Ser). (Illus., Orig.). 1968. pap. text ed. 11.50 scp (ISBN 0-06-044908-X, HarpC); instructor's manual avail. (ISBN 0-06-364894-6). Har-Row.

Peterson, Joseph. Early Conceptions & Tests of Intelligence. Repr. of 1925 ed. lib. bdg. 15.00x (ISBN 0-8371-2836-6, PETI). Greenwood.

Pinneau, S. R. Changes in Intelligence Quotient: Infancy to Maturity. 1961. text ed. 7.88 (ISBN 0-395-09455-0). HM.

Popham, W. James, ed. Criterion-Referenced Measurement: An Introduction. LC 75-146292. 128p. 1971. 14.95 (ISBN 0-87778-006-4). Educ Tech Pubns.

Rasch, G. Probalistic Models for Some Intelligence & Attainment Tests. LC 80-16546. 208p. 1980. lib. bdg. 21.00x (ISBN 0-226-70553-6); pap. 9.00x (ISBN 0-226-70554-4). U of Chicago Pr.

Rinsland, Henry D. Analysis of Completion Sentences & Arithmetical Problems As Items for Intelligence Tests. LC 73-177192. (Columbia University. Teachers College. Contributions to Education: No. 666). Repr. of 1935 ed. 17.50 (ISBN 0-404-55666-3). AMS Pr.

Robb, George P., et al. Assessment of Individual Mental Ability. LC 73-177298. 354p. 1972. text ed. 17.50 scp (ISBN 0-7002-2357-6, HarpC). Har-Row.

Sattler, Jerome M. Assessement of Children's Intelligence & Special Abilities. 2nd ed. 850p. 1981. text ed. 24.95 (ISBN 0-205-07362-X, 7973624); tchrs ed. free (ISBN 0-205-07379-4, 7973799); write for info. study guide. Allyn.

--Assessment of Children's Intelligence. LC 74-95832. (Books in Psychology). (Illus.). 1975. text ed. 17.00 (ISBN 0-7216-7944-7). HR&W.

Scarr, Sandra W. Race, Social Class & Individual Differences in I. Q. Race, Social Class & Individual Differences. 560p. 1981. text ed. 29.95 (ISBN 0-89859-055-8). L Erlbaum Assocs.

Senna, Carl, ed. The Fallacy of I. Q. LC 72-93380. 180p. 1973. 8.95 (ISBN 0-685-28733-5, 89388-X). Okpaku Communications.

Simpson, Benjamin R. Correlations of Mental Abilities. (Columbia University. Teachers College. Contributions to Education: No. 53). Repr. of 1912 ed. 17.50 (ISBN 0-404-55053-3). AMS Pr.

Smith, Max. Relationship Between Item Validity & Test Validity. LC 79-177767. (Columbia University. Teachers College. Contributions to Education: No. 621). Repr. of 1934 ed. 17.50 (ISBN 0-404-55621-3). AMS Pr.

Snedden, Donald S. Study in Disguised Intelligence Tests: Interview Form. LC 71-177765. (Columbia University. Teachers College. Contributions to Education: No. 291). Repr. of 1927 ed. 17.50 (ISBN 0-404-55291-9). AMS Pr.

Steacy, Frederick W. Interrelations of Mental Abilities. LC 76-177742. (Columbia University. Teachers College. Contributions to Education: No. 95). Repr. of 1919 ed. 17.50 (ISBN 0-404-55095-9). AMS Pr.

Stern, William L. Psychological Methods of Testing Intelligence. Whipple, G. M., tr. from Ger. Bd. with Selected Essays. Binet, Alfred, et al.. (Contributions to the History of Psychology Ser., Vol. IV, Pt. B: Psychometrics & Educational Psychology). 1978. Repr. of 1914 ed. 30.00 (ISBN 0-89093-164-X). U Pubns Amer.

Taylor, Grace A. Inventory of the Minds of Individuals of Six & Seven Years Mental Age. LC 76-177726. (Columbia University. Teachers College. Contributions to Education: No. 134). Repr. of 1923 ed. 17.50 (ISBN 0-404-55134-3). AMS Pr.

Taylor, Howard F. The I.Q. Game: A Methodological Inquiry into the Heredity-Environment Controversy. 300p. 1980. 19.50 (ISBN 0-8135-0902-5). Rutgers U Pr.

Terman, Lewis M. The Measurement of Intelligence. LC 74-21431. (Classics in Child Development Ser). 376p. 1975. Repr. 28.00x (ISBN 0-405-06480-2). Arno.

Thorndike, Edward L., et al. The Measurement of Intelligence. LC 73-2993. (Classics in Psychology Ser). Repr. of 1927 ed. 29.00 (ISBN 0-405-05165-4). Arno.

Tilton, John W. Relation Between Association & the Higher Mental Processes. LC 71-177706. (Columbia University. Teachers College. Contributions to Education: No. 218). Repr. of 1926 ed. 17.50 (ISBN 0-404-55218-8). AMS Pr.

Tinkelman, Sherman. Difficulty Prediction of Test Items. LC 70-177703. (Columbia University. Teachers College. Contributions to Education: No. 941). Repr. of 1947 ed. 17.50 (ISBN 0-404-55941-7). AMS Pr.

Tuckman, Jacob. Influence of Varying Amounts of Punishment on Mental Connections. LC 74-177692. (Columbia University. Teachers College. Contributions to Education: No. 590). Repr. of 1933 ed. 17.50 (ISBN 0-404-55590-X). AMS Pr.

Vincent, Elizabeth L. A Study of Intelligence Test Elements. (Columbia University. Teachers College. Contributions to Education: No. 152). Repr. of 1924 ed. 17.50 (ISBN 0-404-55152-1). AMS Pr.

Wagner, Eva. Reading & Ninth Grade Achievement. LC 71-176792. (Columbia University. Teachers College. Contributions to Education: No. 756). Repr. of 1938 ed. 17.50 (ISBN 0-404-55756-2). AMS Pr.

Walters, Frederick C. A Statistical Study of Certain Aspects of the Time Factor in Intelligence. LC 77-177666. (Columbia University. Teachers College. Contributions to Education). Repr. of 1927 ed. 17.50 (ISBN 0-404-55248-X). AMS Pr.

Wechsler, David. The Selected Papers of David Wechsler. 1974. 28.50 (ISBN 0-12-741250-6). Acad Pr.

Wesman, Alexander G. A Study of Transfer of Training from High School Subjects to Intelligence. LC 78-177650. (Columbia University. Teachers College. Contributions to Education: No. 909). Repr. of 1945 ed. 17.50 (ISBN 0-404-55909-3). AMS Pr.

Whipple, Guy M. Manual of Mental & Physical Tests, Part One: Simpler Processes. (Educational Ser.). 1914. Repr. 20.00 (ISBN 0-685-43653-5). Norwood Edns.

--Manual of Mental & Physical Tests, Part Two: Complex Processes. (Educational Ser.). 1915. Repr. 20.00 (ISBN 0-685-43654-3). Norwood Edns.

Wylie, Andrew T. The Opposites Test. LC 74-177617. (Columbia University. Teachers College. Contributions to Education: No. 170). Repr. of 1925 ed. 17.50 (ISBN 0-404-55170-X). AMS Pr.

INTELLIGENT MACHINES

see Artificial Intelligence; Conscious Automata; Logic Machines

INTEMPERANCE

see Alcoholism; Liquor Problem; Temperance

INTENDANTS

Baxter, Douglas C. Servants of the Sword: French Intendants of the Army, 1630-70. LC 75-40115. 288p. 1976. 17.50 (ISBN 0-252-00291-1). U of Ill Pr.

Becquart-Leclerq, Jeanne, ed. Paradoxes du Pouvoir Local. (Travaux et Recherches Ser: No. 38). 1977. lib. bdg. 28.75x (ISBN 2-7246-0346-X, Pub. by Presses De la Foundation Nationale Sciences Politiques); pap. text ed. 20.00x (ISBN 2-7246-0339-7). Clearwater Pub.

Fisher, Lillian E. Intendant System in Spanish America. LC 77-91350. 1970. Repr. of 1929 ed. text ed. 12.50 (ISBN 0-87752-033-X). Gordian.

Gruder, Vivian R. Royal Provincial Intendants: A Governing Elite in Eighteenth Century France. 1968. 22.50x (ISBN 0-8014-0164-X). Cornell U Pr.

INTENSION (PHILOSOPHY)

see Semantics (Philosophy)

INTENSIVE CARE UNITS

see also Coronary Care Units; Recovery Room (Surgery)

Baldwin, Linda & Pierce, Ruth. Mobile Intensive Care: A Problem Oriented Approach. LC 78-18240. (Illus.). 1978. pap. 12.95 (ISBN 0-8016-0428-1). Mosby.

Beal, John M. & Eckenhoff, James E. Intensive & Recovery Room Care. 1969. text ed. 15.95 (ISBN 0-02-307400-0). Macmillan.

Berk, J. L., et al, eds. Handbuch der Intensivmedizin. 1979. pap. 58.75 (ISBN 3-8055-2941-4). S Karger.

Burrell, Zeb, Jr. & Burrell, Lennette O. Critical Care. 3rd ed. LC 76-53564. (Illus.). 1977. lib. bdg. 15.95 (ISBN 0-8016-0914-3). Mosby.

Burrell, Zeb L., Jr. & Burrell, Lenette O. Critical Care. 4th ed. LC 81-9544. (Illus.). 544p. 1981. text ed. 19.95 (ISBN 0-8016-0906-2). Mosby.

Clarke, D. B. & Barnes, A. D., eds. Intensive Care for Nurses. 2nd ed. (Illus.). 208p. 1975. 7.50 (ISBN 0-632-00696-X, Blackwell). Mosby.

Colen, B. D. Born at Risk. (Illus.). 240p. 1981. 9.95 (ISBN 0-312-09291-1). St Martin.

Daly, Barbara J. Intensive Care Nursing. LC 78-78019. (Current Clinical Nursing Ser.). 1979. pap. 13.50 (ISBN 0-87488-575-2). Med Exam.

Davis, Joan E. & Mason, Celestine B. Neurologic Critical Care. 1979. text ed. 16.95 (ISBN 0-442-22004-9). Van Nos Reinhold.

Emery, E. R., et al. Principles of Intensive Care. LC 73-93515. (Medibooks Ser.). 1973. pap. 6.00 (ISBN 0-668-03461-0). Arco.

Finn, R. & Drury, P. A Guide to the Intensive Therapy Unit. 1974. 6.95 (ISBN 0-407-72755-8). Butterworth.

Frey, R., et al, eds. Mobile Intensive Care Units: Advanced Emergency Care Delivery Systems. (Anaesthesiology & Resuscitation: Vol. 95). 1976. pap. 27.00 (ISBN 0-387-07561-5). Springer-Verlag.

Goldin, Marshall D. Intensive Care of the Surgical Patient. 1981. 45.00 (ISBN 0-8151-3732-X). Year Bk Med.

--Yearbook of Intensive Care of the Surgical Patient. 1981. 45.00 (ISBN 0-8151-3732-X). Year Bk Med.

Hanson, Gillian C. & Wright, P. L. Medical Management of the Critically Ill. 1070p. 1979. text ed. 127.00 (ISBN 0-8089-1066-3). Grune.

Hayne, Arlene & Hayne, Bailey. Organization & Management of Critical Care. 350p. 1982. text ed. price not set (ISBN 0-89443-397-0). Aspen Systems.

Hazzard, Mary E. Critical Care Nursing. (Nursing Outline Ser.). 1978. spiral bdg. 9.50 (ISBN 0-87488-384-9). Med Exam.

Hill, D. W. & Dolan, A. H. Instrumentation for Intensive Care. 320p. 1976. 44.00 (ISBN 0-8089-0886-3). Grune.

Hospital Instrumentation Care & Servicing for Critical Care Units. LC 77-1393. 192p. 1977. 10.00 (ISBN 0-87664-324-1); study guide 4.00 (ISBN 0-87664-357-8). Instru Soc.

Jones, E. Sherwood. Essential Intensive Care. (Illus.). 1978. text ed. 15.00 (ISBN 0-397-58236-6, JBL-Med-Nursing). Har-Row.

Ledingham, I., ed. Recent Advances in Intensive Therapy, No. 1. (Recent Advances in Intensive Therapy Ser.). (Illus.). 1978. 35.00 (ISBN 0-443-01432-9). Churchill.

Marini, John J. Respiratory, Medicine & Intensive Care for the House Officer. (House Officer Ser.). 150p. 1981. pap. 9.95 (ISBN 0-683-05551-8). Williams & Wilkins.

Meltzer, L. E., et al. Concepts & Practices of Intensive Care for Nurse Specialists. 2nd ed. LC 75-27692. 1976. 24.95 (ISBN 0-913486-48-5). Charles.

Millar, Sally, et al, eds. Methods in Critical Care. LC 79-67786. (American Association of Critical Care Nurses Ser.). (Illus.). 484p. 1980. pap. 17.95 (ISBN 0-7216-1006-4). Saunders.

Missen, Janet. Principles of Intensive Care for Nurses. (Illus.). 1975. pap. text ed. 14.95x (ISBN 0-433-22080-5). Intl Ideas.

O'Connor, Andrea B., ed. Nursing: Critically Ill Patients. LC 78-140953. (Contemporary Nursing Ser.). 249p. 1978. pap. text ed. 7.95 (ISBN 0-937126-20-9). Am Journal Nurse.

Oh & Teik. Intensive Care Manual. (Illus.). 200p. 1980. text ed. 29.95 (ISBN 0-409-31380-7). Butterworth.

Roberts, Keith D. & Edwards, Jennifer M. Paediatric Intensive Care: A Manuel for Resident Medical Officers & Senior Nurses. 2nd ed. (Illus.). 1976. 28.25 (ISBN 0-632-08020-5, Blackwell). Mosby.

Rogers, Robert M. Respiratory Intensive Care. (American Lectures in Circulation Ser.). (Illus.). 448p. 1977. 37.50 (ISBN 0-398-03601-2). C C Thomas.

Secor, Jane. Patient Care in Respiratory Problems. LC 70-81827. (Monographs in Clinical Nursing: Vol. 1). (Illus.). 1969. 9.95x (ISBN 0-7216-8045-3). Saunders.

Skillman, John J., ed. Intensive Care. (Illus.). 560p. 1975. 28.50 (ISBN 0-316-79660-3). Little.

Stern. Intensive Care in the Newborn, Vol. III. 432p. 1981. 59.50x (ISBN 0-89352-114-0). Masson Pub.

Sweetwood, Hannelore. Nursing in the Intensive Respiratory Care Unit. 2nd ed. LC 78-10617. 1979. text ed. 26.50 (ISBN 0-8261-1202-1). Springer Pub.

Thornton, Andrew J. & Levy, Cyril J. Topics in Anaesthesia & Intensive Care. (Medical Bks.). 1979. lib. bdg. 14.95 (ISBN 0-8161-2195-8, Hall Medical). G K Hall.

Tinker, Jack & Porter, Susan W. A Course in Intensive Therapy Nursing. 294p. 1980. 30.00x (ISBN 0-7131-4347-9, Pub. by Arnold Pubs England). State Mutual Bk.

Turner, Phyllis S. Self-Assessment of Current Knowledge in Intensive Care Nursing. 1980. pap. 9.75 (ISBN 0-87488-227-3). Med Exam.

Vestal, Katherine W. Pediatric Critical Care Nursing. LC 80-22913. 450p. 1981. 19.95 (ISBN 0-471-05674-X, Pub. by Wiley Med). Wiley.

Weil, M. H. & DaLuz, P. L., eds. Manual of Critical Care Medicine. LC 77-24959. (Illus.). 1978. 30.60 (ISBN 0-387-90270-8). Springer-Verlag.

Weil, Max Harry & Henning, Robert S., eds. Handbook of Critical Care Medicine. (Illus.). 1978. 39.95 (ISBN 0-8151-9191-X, Pub. by Symposia Special). Year Bk Med.

Zschoche, Donna A. Mosby's Comprehensive Review of Critical Care. 2nd ed. LC 80-16790. (Illus.). 959p. 1980. text ed. 27.95 (ISBN 0-8016-5697-4). Mosby.

INTENT, CRIMINAL

see Criminal Intent

INTENTION (LOGIC)

Anscombe, G. E. Intention. 2nd ed. 93p. (Orig.). 1963. pap. text ed. 6.50x (ISBN 0-8014-9803-1). Cornell U Pr.

Aquila, Richard E. Intentionality: A Study of Mental Acts. LC 76-15160. 1977. 15.00x (ISBN 0-271-01228-5). Pa St U Pr.

Diamond, Cora & Teichman, Jenny, eds. Intention & Intentionality: Essays in Honour of G. E. M. Anscombe. LC 79-2478. (Illus.). 1980. 35.00x (ISBN 0-8014-1275-7). Cornell U Pr.

INTERACTION, SOCIAL

see Social Interaction

INTERACTION ANALYSIS IN EDUCATION

Amidon, Edmund J. & Hough, John B. Interaction Analysis: Theory, Research & Application. LC 67-23976. (Education Ser). (Illus., Orig.). 1967. pap. 9.95 (ISBN 0-201-00234-5). A-W.

Bassett, Ronald E. & Smythe, Mary-Jeanette. Communication & Instruction. LC 78-23390. 1979. text ed. 13.50 scp (ISBN 0-06-040526-0, HarpC); inst. manual free (ISBN 0-06-360544-9). Har-Row.

Berman, Louise M. & Roderick, Jessie A., eds. Feeling, Valuing & the Art of Growing: Insights into the Affective. LC 76-54454. (ASCD Yearbook, 1977). 1977. 9.75 (ISBN 0-87120-082-1, 610-77104). Assn Supervision.

Daniel, Charlie & Daniel, Becky. Warm Smiles, Happy Faces. (gr. k-4). 1978. 4.95 (ISBN 0-916456-24-2, GA79). Good Apple.

Dickson, Mimi & Robitscher, Jean. Learning Joy: A Book for Parents & Teachers Who Want to Help Children Find Themselves--& Joy. LC 77-76833. (Illus.). 1977. 4.95 (ISBN 0-87426-045-0). Whitmore.

Downey, Meriel. Interpersonal Judgments in Education. 1977. text ed. 15.70 (ISBN 0-06-318051-0, IntlDept); pap. text ed. 7.80 (ISBN 0-06-318052-9, IntlDept). Har-Row.

Flanders, Ned A. Analyzing Teaching Behavior. (Education Ser). 1970. 19.95 (ISBN 0-201-02052-1). A-W.

Gammage, Philip. Teacher & Pupil: Some Socio-Psychological Aspects. (Students Library of Education). 1971. 10.00x (ISBN 0-7100-7135-3); pap. 4.50 (ISBN 0-7100-7136-1). Routledge & Kegan.

Ginott, Haim G. Teacher & Child. Markel, Robert, ed. LC 70-182448. 228p. 1972. 9.95 (ISBN 0-02-543340-7). Macmillan.

Heller, Robert W. & Rosenthal, Alice M., eds. Child & the Articulated Curriculum. LC 68-59060. 1968. pap. 2.50x (ISBN 0-8134-1071-1, 1071). Interstate.

Hennings, Dorothy G. Mastering Classroom Communication: What Interaction Analysis Tells the Teacher. LC 74-3722. 208p. 1975. pap. text ed. 7.95 (ISBN 0-87620-551-1). Goodyear.

Jones, Richard M. Fantasy & Feeling in Education. LC 68-29430. 1968. 15.00x (ISBN 0-8147-0220-1). NYU Pr.

King, Ronald. All Things Bright & Beautiful? A Sociological Study of Infants' Classrooms. LC 78-4518. 155p. 1978. 27.75 (ISBN 0-471-99653-X, Pub. by Wiley-Interscience). Wiley.

Laramy, John E. Organizational Behavior in Schools Differing in Architectural Openness. LC 76-17454. 1976. saddlestitched 1.95x (ISBN 0-8134-1833-X, 1833). Interstate.

Medway, Peter. Finding a Language: Autonomy & Learning in School. (Chameleon Education Ser.). 148p. (Orig.). 1981. pap. 4.95 (ISBN 0-686-30978-2). Writers & Readers.

Westbury, Ian & Bellack, Arno A., eds. Research into Classroom Processes: Recent Developments & Next Steps. LC 70-170131. 280p. 1971. text ed. 14.25x (ISBN 0-8077-2327-4). Tchrs Coll.

INTERACTION OF ATMOSPHERE AND OCEAN

see Ocean-Atmosphere Interaction

INTERACTIONS, HYPERFINE

see Hyperfine Interactions

INTERALLIED MILITARY MISSION TO HUNGARY, 1919-1920

Bandholtz, Harry H. Undiplomatic Diary. LC 77-160009. Repr. of 1933 ed. 27.50 (ISBN 0-404-00494-6). AMS Pr.

INTER-AMERICAN CONFERENCES

see also Pan-Americanism

Gregg, Robert W., ed. International Organization in the Western Hemisphere. LC 68-15908. 1968. 12.95x (ISBN 0-8156-2117-5). Syracuse U Pr.

Inman, Samuel G. Inter-American Conferences: 1826-1954. Davis, Harold E., ed. (Facsimile of 1969 ed.). 1976. student ed. 5.00 (ISBN 0-87419-035-5); lib. bdg. 7.00 (ISBN 0-87419-014-2). U Pr of Wash.

Inter-American Institute Of International Legal Studies. Inter-American System: Its Development & Strengthening. Garcia-Amador, F. V., ed. LC 66-17245. 1966. 20.00 (ISBN 0-379-00261-2). Oceana.

INTER-AMERICAN CONVENTIONS

see Pan-American Treaties and Conventions

INTER-AMERICAN COOPERATION

see Pan-Americanism

INTER-AMERICAN RELATIONS

see Pan-Americanism

INTER-AMERICAN TREATIES

see Pan-American Treaties and Conventions

INTERCEPTION OF COMMUNICATIONS, UNAUTHORIZED

see Eavesdropping

INTERCHANGE OF LIBRARIANS

see Librarians, Interchange of

INTERCHANGE OF PERSONS

see Exchange of Persons Programs

INTERCHANGE OF POPULATION

see Population Transfers

INTERCHANGE OF STUDENTS

see Students, Interchange Of

INTERCHANGE OF TEACHERS

see Teachers, Interchange Of

INTERCHURCH COOPERATION

see Interdenominational Cooperation

INTERCOASTAL SHIPPING

see also Coastwise Shipping

INTER-COLLEGE COOPERATION

see University Cooperation

INTERCOMMUNICATION SYSTEMS
see also Closed-Circuit Television; Loud-Speakers; Police Communication Systems; Public Address Systems

INTERCOMMUNION
see also Church Membership

Raphael, Bishop. Anglican-Orthodox Intercommunion. pap. 0.25 (ISBN 0-686-05405-9). Eastern Orthodox.

Ware, K. Communion & Intercommunion. 1980. pap. 1.95 (ISBN 0-937032-20-4). Light&Life Pub Co MN.

INTERCONNECTED ELECTRIC UTILITY SYSTEMS
see Electric Utilities

INTERCONTINENTAL BALLISTIC MISSILE BASES

Ball, Desmond J. Politics & Force Levels: The Strategic Missile Program of the Kennedy Administration. LC 78-57302. 400p. 1981. 27.50x (ISBN 0-520-03698-0). U of Cal Pr.

Beard, Edmund. Developing the ICBM: A Study in Bureaucratic Politics. (Institute of War & Peace Studies). 273p. 1976. 17.50x (ISBN 0-231-04012-1). Columbia U Pr.

INTERCULTURAL COMMUNICATION

Asante, Molefi K., et al, eds. Handbook of Intercultural Communication. LC 78-2468. 1979. 29.95x (ISBN 0-8039-0954-3). Sage.

Bowie, Theodore, ed. East-West In Art. LC 66-12723. (Illus.). 192p. (Orig.). 1966. pap. 6.50x (ISBN 0-253-11901-4). Ind U Pr.

Brislin, Richard W. & Pedersen, Paul. Cross-Cultural Orientation Programs. LC 75-41358. 224p. 1976. 14.50 (ISBN 0-470-14993-0). Halsted Pr.

Brislin, Richard W., ed. Culture Learning: Concepts, Applications, & Research. 1977. pap. text ed. 10.00x (ISBN 0-8248-0544-5, Eastwest Ctr). U Pr of Hawaii.

Condon, John C. & Yousef, Fathi S. An Introduction to Intercultural Communication. LC 74-14633. (No. 19). 326p. 1975. pap. 7.50 (ISBN 0-672-61328-X, SC19). Bobbs.

Conference On Science - Philosophy And Religion - 6th Symposium. Approaches to Group Understanding. Bryson, L., et al, eds. 858p. 1964. Repr. of 1947 ed. 35.00x (ISBN 0-8154-0036-5). Cooper Sq.

Curriculum Guidelines for Multiethnic Education. 49p. 1.00 (ISBN 0-686-74900-6). ADL.

Davey, William G., ed. Intercultural Theory & Practice: A Case Method Approach. (Illus.). 190p. (Orig.). 1981. text ed. 15.00 (ISBN 0-933934-08-4). Soc Intercult Ed Train & Res.

Dawson, J. L. & Blowers, G. H., eds. Perspectives in Asian Cross-Cultural Psychology: Selected Papers of the First Asian Regional Conference of the IACCP, March 19-23, 1979. 1981. pap. write for info. (ISBN 90-265-0359-8). Swets North Am.

Dodd, Carley H. Dynamics of Intercultural Communication. 300p. 1981. pap. text ed. price not set (ISBN 0-697-04174-3). Wm C Brown.

Dufrenoy, Marie-Louise. L' Orient Romanesque En France, 1704-1789: Tome III, L'idee De Progres L'orient. 509p. (Fr.). 1975. pap. text ed. 40.00x (ISBN 90-6203-108-0). Humanities.

Fischer, Heinz-Dietrich & Merrill, John C., eds. International & Intercultural Communication. (Humanistic Studies in the Communication Arts). 1976. 24.95 (ISBN 0-8038-3402-0); pap. text ed. 12.50x (ISBN 0-8038-3403-9). Hastings.

Gerbner, George, ed. Mass Media Policies in Changing Cultures. LC 77-2399. 1977. 29.50x (ISBN 0-471-01514-8, Pub. by Wiley-Interscience). Wiley.

Grant, Carl A., ed. Multicultural Education: Commitments, Issues & Applications. 1977. 7.00 (ISBN 0-87120-084-8). Assn Supervision.

Hall, Edward T. Beyond Culture. LC 74-3550. 1977. pap. 4.50 (ISBN 0-385-12474-0, Anch). Doubleday.

--The Silent Language. LC 72-97265. 240p. 1973. pap. 3.95 (ISBN 0-385-05549-8, Anch). Doubleday.

Heller, L. G. Communicational Analysis & Methodology for Historians. LC 72-75003. 1972. 15.00x (ISBN 0-8147-3362-X). NYU Pr.

Jain, Nemi C., ed. International & Intercultural Communication Annual, Vol. V. 140p. (Orig.). 1979. pap. text ed. 7.50 (ISBN 0-686-30716-X). Intercult Pr.

Kochman, Thomas. Black & White Styles in Conflict. LC 81-3405. 1981. price not set (ISBN 0-226-44954-8). U of Chicago Pr.

Levine, Deena & Adelman, Mara B. Beyond Language: Intercultural Communication for ESL. (Illus.). 200p. 1982. pap. 8.95 (ISBN 0-13-076000-5). P-H.

Nordenstreng, Kaarle & Schiller, Herbert I., eds. National Sovereignty & International Communication: A Reader. LC 78-16046. (Communication & Information Science Ser.). 1979. 32.00 (ISBN 0-89391-008-2). Ablex Pub.

Oliver, Robert T. Culture & Communication: The Problem of Penetrating National & Cultural Boundries. (American Lecture Communication). 184p. 1962. photocopy ed. spiral 14.75 (ISBN 0-398-01422-1). C C Thomas.

Prosser, Michael H. The Cultural Dialogue: An Introduction to Intercultural Communication. LC 77-89049. (Illus.). 1978. text ed. 13.95 (ISBN 0-395-24448-X). HM.

Read, William H. America's Mass Media Merchants. LC 76-17231. (Illus.). 224p. 1977. 14.00x (ISBN 0-8018-1851-6). Johns Hopkins.

Rich, Andrea L. Interracial Communication. (Auer Ser.). 212p. 1974. pap. text ed. 11.50 scp (ISBN 0-06-045391-5, HarpC). Har-Row.

Ross, E. Lamar, ed. Interethnic Communication. LC 77-27456. 157p. 1978. 11.50x (ISBN 0-8203-0441-7); pap. 5.95 (ISBN 0-8203-0442-5). U of Ga Pr.

Samovar, Larry A. & Porter, Richard E. Intercultural Communication: A Reader. 2nd ed. 1976. pap. 10.95x (ISBN 0-534-00448-2). Wadsworth Pub.

Samovar, Larry A., et al. Understanding Intercultural Communication. 240p. 1980. pap. text ed. 9.95x (ISBN 0-534-00862-3). Wadsworth Pub.

Sitaram, K. S. & Cogdell, Roy T. Foundations of Intercultural Communication. new ed. 1976. text ed. 13.95x (ISBN 0-675-08626-4). Merrill.

Symposium on Humane Responsibility in Intercultural Communication. Communicating Across Cultures for What? Saito, Mitsuko & Condon, John C., eds. 1977. pap. 10.50x (ISBN 0-89955-242-0, Pub. by Simul). Intl Schol Bk Serv.

Van Nieuwenhuijze, C. A. Cross Cultural Studies. (Publications of the Institute of Social Studies Ser.: No. 5). 1963. 26.25x (ISBN 90-2790-103-1). Mouton.

Wilber, Ken. No Boundary: Eastern & Western Approaches to Personal Growth. LC 81-40489. (Illus.). 174p. 1981. pap. 5.95 (ISBN 0-394-74881-6). Shambhala Pubns.

INTERCULTURAL EDUCATION
see also Race Awareness

Ball, Geraldine. Innerchange Language Arts Resource Ser for Junior High. 1977. 95.00 (ISBN 0-86584-031-8). Human Dev Train.

--Innerchange Language Arts Resource Set for Senior High. 1977. 95.00 (ISBN 0-86584-026-1). Human Dev Train.

Brickman, William W. Bibliographical Essays on Comparative & International Education. LC 76-28420. 1976. Repr. of 1975 ed. lib. bdg. 17.50 (ISBN 0-8414-1783-0). Folcroft.

Brislin, Richard W. & Pedersen, Paul. Cross-Cultural Orientation Programs. 223p. 1976. 14.50 (ISBN 0-470-14993-0, Pub. by Wiley). Krieger.

Brislin, Richard W., ed. Culture Learning: Concepts, Applications, & Research. 1977. pap. text ed. 10.00x (ISBN 0-8248-0544-5, Eastwest Ctr). U Pr of Hawaii.

Carr, Albert. Black Is a Word. 30p. (gr. k up). 1972. lib. bdg. 1.70 (ISBN 0-686-02466-4); pap. 1.50 (ISBN 0-686-02467-2); coated stock 1.50 (ISBN 0-686-02468-0). Pacific Ed Pubns.

Cheyney, Arnold B. Teaching Children of Different Cultures in the Classroom: A Language Approach. (Elementary Education Ser.). 1976. pap. text ed. 10.50 (ISBN 0-675-08622-1). Merrill.

Cole, Ann, et al. Children Are Children Are Children: An Activity Approach to Exploring Brazil, France, Iran, Japan, Nigeria, & the U.S.S.R. (Illus.). 1978. 11.95 (ISBN 0-316-15114-9); pap. 7.95 (ISBN 0-316-15113-0). Little.

Conference On Educational Problems Of Special Cultural Groups - Teachers College - Columbia University - 1949. Cultural Groups & Human Relations. facs. ed. Allport, G. W., et al, eds. LC 77-117772. (Essay Index Reprint Ser). 1951. 16.00 (ISBN 0-8369-1792-8). Arno.

Cook, Lloyd A. Intergroup Education. LC 71-100151. Repr. of 1954 ed. lib. bdg. 18.50x (ISBN 0-8371-3397-1, COIE). Greenwood.

Cook, Lloyd A., ed. Toward Better Human Relations. facsimile ed. LC 70-90626. (Essay Index Reprint Ser). 1952. 15.00 (ISBN 0-8369-1284-5). Arno.

Garcia, Ricardo. Fostering a Pluralistic Society Through Multi-Ethnic Education. LC 78-50372. (Fastback Ser.: No. 107). 49p. 1978. pap. 0.75 (ISBN 0-87367-107-4). Phi Delta Kappa.

Hamnett, Michael P., ed. Research in Culture Learning: Language & Conceptual Studies. Brislin, Richard W. LC 80-21761. 195p. 1980. pap. 10.00x (ISBN 0-8248-0738-3). U Pr of Hawaii.

Henderson, J. L. Education for World Understanding. 1969. 12.25 (ISBN 0-08-013217-0); pap. 5.75 (ISBN 0-08-013216-2). Pergamon.

Herman, Judith, ed. The Schools & Group Identity: Educating for a New Pluralism. (Illus.). 1974. pap. 1.75 (ISBN 0-87495-010-4). Am Jewish Comm.

Hoopes, David S. Intercultural Education. LC 79-93119. (Fastback Ser.: No. 142). (Orig.). 1980. pap. 0.75 (ISBN 0-87367-142-2). Phi Delta Kappa.

International - Intercultural Education in the Four-Year College. (Occasional Publication Ser.: No. 22). 88p. 1976. pap. 3.00 (ISBN 0-89192-198-2). Interbk Inc.

Kohls, L. Robert. Developing Intercultural Awareness. (Illus.). 100p. 1981. pap. text ed. 10.00 (ISBN 0-933934-07-6). Soc Intercult Ed Train & Res.

Pasternak, Michael G. Helping Kids Learn Multi-Cultural Concepts: A Handbook of Strategies. LC 79-63052. (Illus.). 1979. pap. text ed. 9.95 (ISBN 0-87822-194-8). Res Press.

Pusch, Margaret D., et al. Multicultural Education: A Cross-Cultural Training Approach. LC 79-92379. (Illus., Orig.). 1980. pap. text ed. 11.95 (ISBN 0-933662-06-8). Intercult Pr.

Ramirez, Manuel, 3rd & Castandea, Alfredo. Cultural Democracy, Biocognitive Development & Education. 1974. 17.50 (ISBN 0-12-577250-5). Acad Pr.

Renwick, George W. Evaluation Handbook for Cross-Cultural Training & Multicultural Education: Practical Guidelines. LC 79-92378. (Intercultural Handbks.). (Illus.). 1980. pap. text ed. 4.50 (ISBN 0-933662-08-4). Intercult Pr.

Simerville, Clara L. Home Visits Abroad. LC 62-74039. (Illus.). 1961. pap. 5.95 (ISBN 0-87071-306-X). Oreg St U Pr.

Sims, William E. & De Martinez, Bernice B. Perspectives in Multicultural Education. LC 81-40171. (Illus.). 230p. (Orig.). 1981. lib. bdg. 18.50 (ISBN 0-8191-1687-4); pap. text ed. 9.75 (ISBN 0-8191-1688-2). U Pr of Amer.

Tiedt, Pamela & Tiedt, Iris M. Multicultural Teaching: A Handbook of Activities, Information, & Resources. new ed. 1979. text ed. 19.95 (ISBN 0-205-06445-0); pap. text ed. 12.95 (ISBN 0-205-06522-8, 2365227). Allyn.

Trueba, Henry T. & Barnett-Mizrahi, Carol, eds. Bilingual Multicultural Education & the Professional: From Theory to Practice. 1979. pap. text ed. 15.95 (ISBN 0-88377-138-1). Newbury Hse.

US: A Cultural Mosaic. 380p. (gr. 6-8). 12.50 (ISBN 0-686-74871-9). ADL.

Verma & Bagley, eds. Self-Concept, Achievement & Multicultural Education. 150p. 1981. text ed. 42.50x (ISBN 0-333-30944-8, Pub. by Macmillan England). Humanities.

Walsh, John E. Intercultural Education in the Community of Man. LC 72-93149. 236p. 1973. 12.00x (ISBN 0-8248-0260-8, Eastwest Ctr). U Pr of Hawaii.

Weeks, William W., et al, eds. A Manual of Structured Experiences for Cross-Cultural Learning. LC 79-100422. 1977. pap. text ed. 5.95 (ISBN 0-933934-05-X). Intercult Pr.

Weiss, Bernard J., ed. American Education & the European Immigrant: 1840-1940. LC 81-1773. 225p. 1982. 16.95 (ISBN 0-252-00879-0). U of Ill Pr.

Willie, Charles V. The Ivory & Ebony Towers: Race Relations & Higher Education. LC 80-8946. 192p. 1981. 19.95x (ISBN 0-669-04479-2). Lexington Bks.

Wilson, Thomasyne L. Toward Equitable Education: A Handbook for Multicultural Consciousness for Early Childhood. LC 76-53958. 1976. 9.50 (ISBN 0-686-23417-0). Ujamaa Dev Educ.

INTERCULTURAL RELATIONS
see Cultural Relations

INTERDENOMINATIONAL COOPERATION

Ernst, Eldon. Moment of Truth for Protestant America: Interchurch Campaigns Following World War I. LC 74-16567. (American Academy of Religion. Dissertation Ser.). 1974. pap. 7.50 (ISBN 0-88420-120-1, 010103). Scholars Pr Ca.

Rosseau, Richard W., ed. Interreligious Dialogue: Facing the Next Frontier, Vol. 1. LC 81-52035. (Modern Theological Themes Ser.: Selections from the Literature). 133p. (Orig.). 1981. pap. 13.50x (ISBN 0-940866-00-5). Ridge Row.

INTERDICT (CANON LAW)

Krehbiel, Edward B. The Interdict: Its History & Operation, with Special Attention to the Time of Innocent the Third, 1198-1216. 184p. 1977. Repr. of 1909 ed. lib. bdg. 17.50x (ISBN 0-915172-21-6). Richwood Pub.

INTERDICTION (CIVIL LAW)
see also Guardian and Ward

INTEREST (LAW)
see also Damages

INTEREST (PSYCHOLOGY)
see also Attention; Attention-Seeking; Curiosity

Dewey, John. Interest & Effort in Education. LC 74-18471. (Arcturus Books Paperbacks). 120p. 1975. pap. 6.95 (ISBN 0-8093-0716-2). S Ill U Pr.

Freeman, Larry G. & Freeman, Ruth. Child & His Picture Book. rev. ed. LC 66-29514. (Head Start Program Ser.). 1967. 7.00 (ISBN 0-87282-062-9). Century Hse.

O'Shea, Harriet E. A Study of the Effect of the Interest of a Passage of Learning Vocabulary. LC 71-177138. Repr. of 1930 ed. 17.50 (ISBN 0-404-55351-6). AMS Pr.

Sarhan, El-Demerdash A. Interests & Culture: A Comparative Study of Interests, Concerns, Wishes, Likes, Dislikes, & Happiest Days of Egyptian & American Children. LC 72-177228. (Columbia University. Teachers College. Contributions to Education: No. 959). Repr. of 1950 ed. 17.50 (ISBN 0-404-55959-X). AMS Pr.

Sterner, Alice P. Radio, Motion Picture & Reading Interests: A Study of High School Pupils. LC 77-177824. (Columbia University. Teachers College. Contributions to Education: No. 932). Repr. of 1947 ed. 17.50 (ISBN 0-404-55932-8). AMS Pr.

Strong, Edward K., Jr. Vocational Interests of Men & Women. 1943. 27.50x (ISBN 0-8047-0375-2). Stanford U Pr.

Thorndike, Edward L. The Psychology of Wants, Interests & Attitudes. LC 35-1773. (Psychology Ser). Repr. of 1935 ed. 18.50 (ISBN 0-384-60370-X). Johnson Repr.

INTEREST AND USURY
see also Discount

Anthony, Robert N. Accounting for the Cost of Interest. LC 75-12484. 128p. 1975. 15.95 (ISBN 0-669-00027-2). Lexington Bks.

Arno Press & Silk, Leonard, eds. Religious Attitudes Toward Usury: Two Early Polemics. LC 79-38471. (The Evolution of Capitalism Ser.). 1972. 19.00 (ISBN 0-405-04135-7). Arno.

Baily, Francis. The Doctrine of Interest & Annuities: Analytically Investigated & Explained; Together with Several Useful Tables Connected with the Subject. Brief, Richard P., ed. LC 80-1470. (Dimensions of Accounting Theory & Practice Ser.). 1981. Repr. of 1908 ed. lib. bdg. 15.00x (ISBN 0-405-13500-9). Arno.

Bohm-Bawerk, Eugen V. The Positive Theory of Capital. facsimile ed. Smart, William, tr. LC 70-175689. (Select Bibliographies Reprint Ser). Repr. of 1891 ed. 24.00 (ISBN 0-8369-6604-X). Arno.

Bohm-Bawerk, Eugen Von. Capital & Interest, 3 vols. Incl. Vol. 1. History & Critique of Interest Theories. 512p (ISBN 0-910884-09-9); Vol. 2. Positive Theory of Capital. 480p (ISBN 0-910884-10-2); Vol. 3. Further Essays on Capital & Interest. 256p (ISBN 0-910884-11-0). LC 58-5555. 1959. 3 vols. 47.50 (ISBN 0-910884-07-2). Libertarian.

Bohm Von-Bawerk, Eugene. Capital & Interest. Smart, William, tr. LC 68-54734. Repr. of 1890 ed. lib. bdg. 19.50x (ISBN 0-678-00610-5). Kelley.

Bonello, Frank J. The Formulation of Expected Interest Rates. LC 71-627748. 1969. 8.00 (ISBN 0-87744-092-1). Mich St U Busn.

Campbell, David P. & Strong, Edward K., Jr. Strong-Campbell Interest Inventory. prices on request (ISBN 0-8047-1068-6). Stanford U. Pr.

Cassel, Gustav. Nature & Necessity of Interest. LC 77-147898. Repr. of 1903 ed. 13.50x (ISBN 0-678-00848-5). Kelley.

Chalmers, Eric B. International Interest Rate War. LC 74-185905. 1972. 19.95 (ISBN 0-312-42280-6). St. Martin.

Conard, Joseph W. Behavior of Interest Rates: A Progress Report. (General Ser.: No. 81). 1966. 8.00x (ISBN 0-87014-081-7, Dist. by Columbia U Pr). Natl Bur Econ Res.

Culpeper, Thomas. A Tract Against Usurie. LC 74-80170. (English Experience Ser.: No. 649). 22p. 1974. Repr. of 1621 ed. 3.50 (ISBN 90-221-0649-7). Walter J Johnson.

Darst, David M. The Complete Bond Book: A Guide to All Types of Fixed-Income Securities. (Illus.). 352p. (Orig.). 1975. 22.50 (ISBN 0-07-017390-7, P&RB). McGraw.

Dempsey, Bernard W. The Frontier Wage. LC 60-9601. 1960. 4.95 (ISBN 0-8294-0022-2). Loyola.

Divine, Thomas F. Interest, an Historical & Analytical Study in Economics & Modern Ethics. 1959. 10.95 (ISBN 0-87462-405-3). Marquette.

The Exploitation Theory of Socialism - Communism. 3rd rev. ed. LC 74-83838. (Capital & Interest Ser.). 176p. 1975. pap. 5.00 (ISBN 0-910884-03-X). Libertarian.

Fenton, Roger. A Treatise of Usurie. LC 74-28855. (English Experience Ser.: No. 736). 1975. Repr. of 1611 ed. 13.00 (ISBN 9-0221-0736-1). Walter J Johnson.

Fetter, Frank A. Capital, Interest & Rent: Essays in the Theory of Distribution. Rothbard, Murray N., ed. LC 76-25587. (Studies in Economic Theory). 400p. 1976. 12.00 (ISBN 0-8362-0684-3); pap. 5.00x (ISBN 0-8362-0685-1). NYU Pr.
Financial Publishing Co. Coupon Interest Calendar - 360-Day Basis No. 360. 20.00 (ISBN 0-685-02539-X). Finan Pub.
--Coupon Interest Calendar - 365-Day Basis No. 365. 25.00 (ISBN 0-685-02538-1). Finan Pub.
--Monthly Payment Direct Reduction Loan Amortization Schedules No.185. 13th ed. 40.00 (ISBN 0-685-02550-0). Finan Pub.
Fisher, Irving. Theory of Interest. LC 56-4884. Repr. of 1930 ed. 25.00x (ISBN 0-678-00003-4). Kelley.
--The Theory of Interest: As Determined by Impatience to Spend Income & Opportunity to Invest It. LC 77-22591. (Illus.). Repr. of 1930 ed. lib. bdg. 8.95x (ISBN 0-87991-864-0). Porcupine Pr.
Ford, James L. & Stark, T. Long & Short-Term Interest Rates. LC 67-9408. (Illus.). 1967. 6.00x (ISBN 0-678-06255-2). Kelley.
Gray, Jean M. The Term Structure of Interest Rates in the United States, 1884-1914. LC 77-14785. (Dissertations in American Economic History Ser.). 1978. 21.00 (ISBN 0-405-11037-5). Arno.
Havighurst, Clark C., ed. Consumer Credit Reform. LC 79-111218. (Law & Contemporary Problems Ser.). 1970. 10.00 (ISBN 0-379-11513-1). Oceana.
Hawawini, Gabriel A. & Vora, Ashok. The History of Interest Approximations. original anthology ed. Brief, Richard P., ed. LC 80-1459. (Dimensions of Accounting Theory & Practice Ser.). 1981. lib. bdg. 25.00x (ISBN 0-405-13480-0). Arno.
Hawtrey, Ralph G. Century of Bank Rate. Repr. of 1939 ed. 22.50x (ISBN 0-678-05175-5). Kelley.
Hirshleifer, Jack. Investment, Interest, & Capital. (Finance Ser). 1970. text ed. 16.95x (ISBN 0-13-502955-4). P-H.
Hoffman, Charles H. The True Nature of Discounts & Interest Charges. 1980. pap. 4.29 (ISBN 0-934914-31-1). NACM.
Homer, Sidney. A History of Interest Rates. 2nd ed. 1977. 45.00 (ISBN 0-8135-0840-1). Rutgers U Pr.
Homer, Sidney & Johannesen, Richard I. The Price of Money, 1946-1969: An Analytical Study of U. S. & Foreign Interest Rates. 1969. 10.50 (ISBN 0-8135-0607-7). Rutgers U Pr.
International Economic Association. Theory of Interest Rates: Proceedings. Hahn, F. H. & Brechling, F. P., eds. 1965. 25.00 (ISBN 0-312-79835-0). St Martin.
Karr, Frederic H. Interest on Third Party Accounts: A Desk Top Primer. 160p. 1980. 19.95 (ISBN 0-03-058024-2). Praeger.
Kellison, Stephen G. Theory of Interest. 1971. Repr. of 1970 ed. 14.50x (ISBN 0-256-00283-5). Irwin.
Kellogg, Edward. New Monetary System: The Only Means of Securing the Respective Rights of Labor & of Protecting the Public from Financial Revulsions. rev. ed. Putnam, Mary K., ed. 1967. Repr. of 1861 ed. 23.00 (ISBN 0-8337-1907-6). B Franklin.
Kemmerer, Edwin W. Seasonal Variations in the Relative Demand for Money & Capital in the United States. Bruchey, Stuart, ed. LC 80-1154. (The Rise of Commercial Banking Ser.). (Illus.). 1981. Repr. of 1910 ed. lib. bdg. 45.00x (ISBN 0-405-13660-9). Arno.
Keynes, John M. General Theory of Employment, Interest & Money. LC 36-27176. 1965. pap. 4.95 (ISBN 0-15-634711-3, H044, Hbgr). HarBraceJ.
Keyserling, Leon H. Tight Money & Rising Interest Rates. (Illus.). 1960. 0.50 (ISBN 0-685-41563-5). Conf Econ Prog.
Keyserling, Leon H. & Conference on Economic Progress Staff. The Toll of Rising Interest Rates. (Illus.). 1964. 0.50 (ISBN 0-685-41560-0). Conf Econ Prog.
King, Leo H. Mental & Interest Tests, Their Evaluation & Comparative Effectiveness As Factors of Prognosis in Secondary Education. LC 77-176957. (Columbia University. Teachers College. Contributions to Education: No. 444). Repr. of 1931 ed. 17.50 (ISBN 0-404-55444-X). AMS Pr.
Lelievre, Charles. Le Travail et l'Usure Dans l'Antiquite. LC 72-179395. (Research & Source Works Ser.: No. 894). 36p. (Fr.). 1972. Repr. of 1866 ed. 16.00 (ISBN 0-8337-2065-1). B Franklin.
Lindahl, Erik R. Studies in the Theory of Money & Capital. LC 70-117915. (Illus.). Repr. of 1939 ed. 17.50x (ISBN 0-678-00655-5). Kelley.
Locke, John. Several Papers Relating to Money, Interest & Trade, Etc. LC 67-29701. Repr. of 1696 ed. 19.50x (ISBN 0-678-00334-3). Kelley.
Loosigian, Allan M. Interest Rate Futures. LC 79-21762. 1980. 24.95 (ISBN 0-87128-579-7, Pub. by Dow Jones). Dow Jones-Irwin.
Lugg, George W. The Interest Game. LC 80-50470. 104p. (Orig.). 1980. pap. 3.95x (ISBN 0-935834-02-8). Rainbow-Betty.
Lutz, F. A. The Theory of Interest. Witlich, Claus, tr. from Ger. 336p. 1967. lib. bdg. 37.00 (ISBN 90-277-0099-0, Pub. by Reidel Holland). Kluwer Boston.
Malkiel, B. G. Term Structure of Interest Rates: Expectations & Behavior Patterns. 1966. 21.00 (ISBN 0-691-04181-4). Princeton U Pr.
Mark, Jeffrey. An Analysis of Usury. 1980. lib. bdg. 59.95 (ISBN 0-8490-3085-4). Gordon Pr.
--The Modern Idolatry: Being an Analysis of Usury & the Pathology of Debt. 1980. lib. bdg. 69.95 (ISBN 0-8490-3078-1). Gordon Pr.
Massaro, Vincent G. A Guide to Forecasting Interest Rates. (Report Ser: No. 601). 32p. (Orig.). 1973. pap. 5.00 (ISBN 0-8237-0031-3). Conference Bd.
Massie, Joseph. An Essay on the Governing Causes of the Natural Rate of Interest: Wherein the Sentiments of Sir William Petty & Mr. Locke, on That Head, Are Considered. (History of English Economic Thought Ser). pap. 15.50 (ISBN 0-384-35820-9). Johnson Repr.
Nelson, Benjamin. Idea of Usury: From Tribal Brotherhood to Universal Brotherhood. 2nd ed. LC 71-76205. 1969. pap. 2.95 (ISBN 0-226-57161-0, P342, Phoen). U of Chicago Pr.
Paish, Frank W. Long-Term & Short-Term Interest Rates in the United Kingdom. LC 67-4633. 1967. 5.00x (ISBN 0-678-06764-3). Kelley.
Palgrave, Robert H. Bank Rate & the Money Market in England, France, Germany, Holland, & Belgium 1844-1900. Repr. of 1903 ed. lib. bdg. 16.00x (ISBN 0-8371-0604-4, PABR). Greenwood.
Patinkin, Don. Money, Interest, & Prices: An Integration of Monetary & Value Theory. 2nd ed. 1965. text ed. 35.50 scp (ISBN 0-06-045030-4, HarpC). Har-Row.
Pring, Martin J. How to Forecast Interest Rates: A Guide to Profits for Consumers, Managers & Investors. 192p. 1981. 14.95 (ISBN 0-07-050865-8, P&RB). McGraw.
Qureshi, A. I. Islam & the Theory of Interest. 4.95 (ISBN 0-686-18373-8). Kazi Pubns.
Robinson, Joan. The Rate of Interest & Other Essays. LC 79-51867. 1981. Repr. of 1952 ed. 17.00 (ISBN 0-88355-959-5). Hyperion Conn.
Rosen, Lawrence R. The Dow Jones-Irwin Guide to Interest. rev. ed. 1981. 14.95 (ISBN 0-87094-260-3). Dow Jones-Irwin.
Ryan, F. W. Usury & Usury Laws. 1977. lib. bdg. 69.95 (ISBN 0-8490-2791-8). Gordon Pr.
Scovell, Clinton H. Interest As a Cost. LC 75-18483. (History of Accounting Ser.). (Illus.). 1976. Repr. 18.00x (ISBN 0-405-07565-0). Arno.
Sherman, Michael. Compound Interest Tables. 1979. pap. 2.95 (ISBN 0-930306-17-1). Delphi Info.
Todhunter, Ralph. Institute of Acturies' Text Book of the Principles of Interest, Life Annuities & Assurances, & Their Practical Application. Brief, Richard P., ed. LC 80-1529. (Dimensions of Accounting Theory & Practice Ser.). 1981. Repr. of 1901 ed. lib. bdg. 19.00x (ISBN 0-405-13550-5). Arno.
Usury Laws & Modern Business Transactions 1980 Course Handbook. (Commercial Law & Practice Course Handbook Ser. 1979-80: Vol. 227). 321p. 1978. pap. 25.00 (ISBN 0-685-07688-1, A4-3076). PLI.
Van Horne, James C. Financial Market Rates & Flows. (Illus.). 1978. pap. text ed. 10.95 (ISBN 0-13-316190-0). P-H.
--Function & Analysis of Capital Market Rates. LC 73-99453. 1970. pap. 10.95 ref. ed. (ISBN 0-13-331934-2). P-H.
WFI Publishing Company. Directory of Banks & Savings Institutions Which Pay the Highest Interest in the World. 1979. pap. 4.95 (ISBN 0-933560-04-4). WFI Pub Co.
Wicksell, Knut. Interest & Prices. LC 65-16993. Repr. of 1936 ed. 13.50x (ISBN 0-678-00086-7). Kelley.
--Value, Capital & Rent. LC 68-58668. (Illus.). Repr. of 1954 ed. 13.50x (ISBN 0-678-00652-0). Kelley.
Wilson, Thomas. Discourse Upon Usury. new ed. 392p. 1962. 30.00x (ISBN 0-7146-1260-X, F Cass Co). Biblio Dist.
World Interest Rates. (World Ser: No. 6). 20p. 1971. 10.50x (ISBN 0-8002-0663-0). Intl Pubns Serv.

INTEREST AND USURY–MATHEMATICAL MODELS

Ford, James L. & Stark, T. Long & Short-Term Interest Rates. LC 67-9408. (Illus.). 1967. 6.00x (ISBN 0-678-06255-2). Kelley.
Slovin, M. B. & Sushka, M. E. Interest Rates on Savings Deposits: Theory, Estimation, & Policy. LC 74-16931. (Illus.). 192p. 1975. 18.95 (ISBN 0-669-96453-0). Lexington Bks.

INTEREST AND USURY–PROBLEMS, EXERCISES, ETC.

Filmer, Sir Robert. A Disclosure Whether It May Be Lawful to Take Use for Money. Berkowitz, David S. & Thorne, Samuel E., eds. LC 77-89250. (Classics of English Legal History in the Modern Era Ser.: Vol. 79). 166p. 1979. lib. bdg. 40.00 (ISBN 0-8240-3179-2). Garland Pub.
Sheppard, N. E. & Baillie, D. C. Compound Interest. LC 61-65433. 1960. pap. 12.50x (ISBN 0-8020-2027-5). U of Toronto Pr.

INTEREST AND USURY–TABLES, ETC.

see also Investments–Tables, etc.

Combined Payments & Constant Percent Tables: Quarterly Loan Schedules No. 188. 40.00 (ISBN 0-685-26871-3). Finan Pub.
Estes, Jack C. Compound Interest & Annuity Tables. 240p. (Orig.). 1976. pap. 3.95 (ISBN 0-07-019683-4, SP). McGraw.
--Handbook of Interest & Annuity Tables. 1976. 24.50 (ISBN 0-07-019681-8, P&RB). McGraw.
--Interest Amortization Tables. (McGraw-Hill Paperbacks). 224p. (Orig.). 1976. pap. 4.95 (ISBN 0-07-019680-X, SP). McGraw.
Financial Three Hundred Sixty-Five Day Simple Interest Tables, No. 64: Five Percent to Ten Percent by One Quarter. 35.00 (ISBN 0-685-32726-4). Finan Pub.
Glover, James W. & Carver, Henry C. Tables of Compound Interest Functions & Logarithms of Compound Interest Functions. 1921. 3.00x (ISBN 0-685-21808-2). Wahr.
Interest Rates, 1960-1974: A Recalculation on a Homogeneous Basis of the Interest Rates in 15 Countries Published in OECD Financial Statistics. 1976. 15.00x (ISBN 92-64-01503-5). OECD.
Kent, Frederick C. & Kent, Maude E. Compound Interest & Annuity Tables. 1963. pap. 3.50 (ISBN 0-07-034121-4, SP). McGraw.
Lake, A. V., et al. Lake's Monthly Installment Interest & Discount Book. 6th ed. LC 26-8678. 28.00 (ISBN 0-910860-01-7). Lake.
Sherman, Michael. Delphi Mortgage Yield Tables. 1973. 25.00 (ISBN 0-930306-00-7). Delphi Info.
--Payment Table for Monthly Mortgage Loans Publication, No. 475. 1975. pap. 2.50 (ISBN 0-930306-04-X). Delphi Info.
--Payment Tables for Monthly Mortgage Loans Publications, No. 674. 1974. pap. 3.00 (ISBN 0-930306-05-8). Delphi Info.
--Simple Interest Installment Loan Payment Tables. 1977. pap. 7.50 (ISBN 0-930306-02-3). Delphi Info.

INTEREST AND USURY–GREAT BRITAIN

Blaxton, John. The English Usurer: Or, Usury Condemned. LC 73-6102. (English Experience Ser.: No. 578). 80p. 1973. Repr. of 1634 ed. 9.50 (ISBN 90-221-0578-4). Walter J Johnson.
Chapman, R. A. Decision Making: A Case Study of the Decision to Raise the Bank Rate in September 1957. (Library of Political Studies). 1969. text ed. 5.75x (ISBN 0-7100-6302-4). Humanities.
Some Thoughts on the Interest of Money in General, & Particularly in the Publick Funds. Repr. of 1738 ed. 18.50 (ISBN 0-384-56610-3). Johnson Repr.

INTERFACES, CHEMISTRY OF

see Surface Chemistry

INTERFERENCE (LIGHT)

see also Electric Waves; Holography

Francon, Maurice. Optical Interferometry. 1966. 50.50 (ISBN 0-12-266350-0). Acad Pr.
Steel, William H. Interferometry. (Cambridge Monographs on Physics). 1967. 35.50 (ISBN 0-521-06547-X). Cambridge U Pr.

INTERFERENCE MICROSCOPE

Ross, K. F. Phase Contrast & Interference Microscopy. 1967. 21.50 (ISBN 0-312-60410-6). St Martin.
Tolansky, S. Interference Microscopy for the Biologist. (American Lecture Living Chemistry). (Illus.). 180p. 1968. pap. 19.75 (ISBN 0-398-01930-4). C C Thomas.
--Multiple Beam Interference Microscopy of Metals. 1970. 25.50 (ISBN 0-12-692650-6). Acad Pr.

INTERFEROMETER

Brown, R. H. Intensity Interferometer: Its Applications to Astronomy. 084p. 29.95 (ISBN 0-686-30861-1). Halsted Pr.
Brown, R. Hanbury. The Intensity Interferometer: Its Application to Astronomy. LC 74-14878. 184p. 1974. 26.95 (ISBN 0-470-10797-9). Halsted Pr.
Schuman, W. & Dubas, M. Holographic Interferometry: From the Scope of Deformation Analysis of Opaque Bodies. (Springer Ser. in Optical Sciences: Vol. 16). (Illus.). 1979. 34.00 (ISBN 0-387-09371-0). Springer-Verlag.
Tolansky, S. Multiple-Beam Interferometry of Surfaces & Films. (Illus.). 1971. pap. text ed. 3.00 (ISBN 0-486-62215-0). Dover.
--Multiple-Beam Interferometry of Surfaces & Films. (Illus.). 6.00 (ISBN 0-8446-0275-2). Peter Smith.

INTERFERONS

Colowick, Sidney & Pestka, Sidney, eds. Methods in Enzymology: Vol. 78, Interferons, Pt. A. 1981. price not set. Acad Pr.
Edelhart, Michael & Lindenmann, Jean. Interferon: The New Hope for Cancer. 224p. 1981. 11.95 (ISBN 0-201-03943-5). A-W.
Friedman, Robert M. Interferons: A Primer. LC 81-2887. 1981. 17.50 (ISBN 0-12-268280-7). Acad Pr.
Gresser, I., ed. Interferons, 1980, Vol. 2. LC 79-41412. (Interferon Ser.). 1981. 16.50 (ISBN 0-686-72573-5). Acad Pr.
Interferons, 2 vols. Incl. Vol. 1. Dubovi, Edward, et al. (ISBN 0-8422-7247-X); Vol. 2. Morahan, Page S., et al. (ISBN 0-8422-7248-8). 1977. text ed. 32.50x ea. Irvington.
Khan, Amanullah, et al, eds. Interferon: Properties & Clinical Uses. (Illus.). 750p. 1980. 15.00 (ISBN 0-935994-00-9). Wadley Inst Molecular Med.
Meeting Held at the Gulbenkian Institute of Science, Oeiras, Portugal, Sept. 1973. Effects of Interferon on Cells, Viruses & the Immune System: Proceedings. Geraldes, A., ed. 1975. 93.00 (ISBN 0-12-280650-6). Acad Pr.
Rita, G., ed. The Interferons. LC 68-23504. 1968. 43.00 (ISBN 0-12-589050-8). Acad Pr.
Solov'ev, V. D. & Bektemirov, T. A. Interferon: Theory & Applications. LC 73-79428. (Illus.). 300p. 1973. 35.00 (ISBN 0-306-30725-1, Plenum Pr). Plenum Pub.
Stewart, W. E. The Interferon System. 2nd, enl. ed. (Illus.). 493p. 1981. 46.70 (ISBN 0-387-81634-8). Springer-Verlag.
--The Interferon System. LC 79-10970. (Illus.). 1979. 51.50 (ISBN 0-387-81505-8). Springer-Verlag.
Stewart, William E., et al. Interferons & Their Actions. 224p. 1977. 64.95 (ISBN 0-8493-5159-6). CRC Pr.
Stinebring, W. & Chapple, P. J., eds. Human Interferon: Production & Clinical Use. LC 78-13393. (Advances in Experimental Medicine & Biology Ser.: Vol. 110). 229p. 1978. 29.50 (ISBN 0-306-40053-7, Plenum Pr). Plenum Pub.
Stringfellow, ed. Interferon & Interfaron Inducers: Clinical Applications. (Modern Pharmacology-Toxicology Ser.: Vol. 17). 336p. 1980. 39.50 (ISBN 0-8247-6931-7). Dekker.
Vilcek, J. Interferon. (Virology Monographs: Vol. 6). 1969. 20.90 (ISBN 0-387-80933-3). Springer-Verlag.
Vilcek, Jan, et al, eds. Regulatory Functions of Interferons, Vol. 350. LC 80-25207. (Annals of the New York Academy of Sciences). 641p. 1980. 124.00x (ISBN 0-89766-089-7); pap. 124.00x (ISBN 0-89766-090-0). NY Acad Sci.

INTERGOVERNMENTAL FISCAL RELATIONS

see also Grants-In-Aid; Intergovernmental Tax Relations

Advisory Committee to the Dept of Housing & Urban Development. Revenue Sharing & the Planning Process: Shifting the Locus of Responsibility for Domestic Problem Solving. LC 74-6418. 108p. 1974. pap. 6.25 (ISBN 0-309-02214-2). Natl Acad Pr.
Bahl, Roy W. & Vogt, Walter. Fiscal Centralization & Tax Burdens: State and Regional Finance of City Services. LC 75-31649. 192p. 1976. text ed. 19.50 (ISBN 0-88410-423-0). Ballinger Pub.
Bird, Richard M. Central-Local Fiscal Relations & the Provision of Urban Public Services. LC 79-55416. (Centre for Research on Federal Financial Relations - Research Monograph: No. 30). 57p. (Orig.). 1980. pap. text ed. 12.95 (ISBN 0-908160-47-X, 0580). Bks Australia.
Break, George F. Intergovernmental Fiscal Relations in the United States. (Studies of Government Finance). 1967. 14.95 (ISBN 0-8157-1074-7); pap. 5.95 (ISBN 0-8157-1073-9). Brookings.
Caputo, David A. & Cole, Richard L. Revenue Sharing: Methodological Approaches & Problems. LC 75-45862. 1976. 19.95 (ISBN 0-669-00238-0). Lexington Bks.
Dommel, Paul R. The Politics of Revenue Sharing. LC 74-376. (Illus.). 224p. 1974. 10.00x (ISBN 0-253-34551-0). Ind U Pr.
Fogelson, Robert M., et al, eds. Federal Aid to the Cities: An Original Anthology. LC 77-74925. (American Federalism-the Urban Dimension). (Illus.). 1978. lib. bdg. 34.00x (ISBN 0-405-10481-2). Arno.
Harris, Lowell. Federal - State - Local Fiscal Relationships. 1976. Repr. of 1967 ed. 25.00 (ISBN 0-527-89013-8). Kraus Repr.
Heller, Walter. New Dimensions of Political Economy. 1967. pap. 3.95x (ISBN 0-393-09755-2). Norton.
Heller, Walter, et al. Revenue Sharing & the City. Perloff, Harvey S. & Nathan, Richard P., eds. LC 77-86396. (Resources for the Future, Inc Publications). Repr. of 1968 ed. 14.50 (ISBN 0-404-60333-5). AMS Pr.

Heller, Walter W. New Dimensions of Political Economy. LC 66-23467. (Godkin Lectures Ser.: 1966). 1966. 10.00x (ISBN 0-674-61100-4). Harvard U Pr.

Heller, Walter W., et al. Revenue Sharing & the City. LC 68-16164. (Resources for the Future Ser). 124p. (Orig.). 1968. pap. 2.50x (ISBN 0-8018-0266-0). Johns Hopkins.

Hirsch, Werner Z., ed. Elements of Regional Accounts. (Resources for the Future Ser). 240p. 1964. 16.00x (ISBN 0-8018-0275-X). Johns Hopkins.

Hirsch, Werner Z., et al. Fiscal Pressures on the Central City: The Impact of Commuters, Nonwhites & Overlapping Governments. LC 70-170272. (Special Studies in U.S. Economic, Social & Political Issues). 1971. 28.00x (ISBN 0-89197-759-7). Irvington.

Juster, F. Thomas, ed. The Economic & Political Impact of General Revenue Sharing. LC 76-620084. 308p. 1977. 13.00 (ISBN 0-87944-217-4). Inst Soc Res.

Larkey, Patrick D. Evaluating Public Programs: The Impact of General Revenue-Sharing on Municipal Fiscal Behavior. LC 78-51176. 1979. 20.00 (ISBN 0-691-07601-4). Princeton U Pr.

Li Chuan-Shih. Central & Local Finance in China. LC 68-57573. (Columbia University. Studies in the Social Sciences: No. 226). Repr. of 1922 ed. 17.50 (ISBN 0-404-51226-7). AMS Pr.

Marlin, John T. Revenue Sharing Renewal, No. 15. (COMP Papers Ser.). 52p. pap. 7.50 (ISBN 0-916450-36-8). Coun on Municipal.

Martin, R. C. The Cities & the Federal System. LC 77-74949. (American Federalism-the Urban Dimension). 1978. Repr. of 1965 ed. lib. bdg. 15.00x (ISBN 0-405-10495-2). Arno.

Mathews, Russell. Revenue Sharing in Federal Systems. LC 79-55746. (Centre for Research on Federal Financial Relations - Research Monograph: No. 31). 89p. (Orig.). 1980. pap. text ed. 12.95 (ISBN 0-908160-25-9, 0587). Bks Australia.

Maxwell, James A. Commonwealth-State Financial Relations in Australia. LC 67-30708. 1967. 12.50x (ISBN 0-522-83829-4, Pub. by Melbourne U Pr). Intl Schol Bk Serv.

Maxwell, James A. & Aronson, J. Richard. Financing State & Local Governments. 3rd ed. LC 76-54871. (Studies of Government Finance). 1977. 14.95 (ISBN 0-8157-5512-0); pap. 5.95 (ISBN 0-8157-5511-2). Brookings.

Minge, David & Blevins, Audie, Jr. Effect of Law on County & Municipal Expenditures, As Illustrated by the Wyoming Experience. new ed. LC 75-19122. (Illus.). 217p. 1975. pap. 4.50 (ISBN 0-915876-02-7). Wyoming Law Inst.

Musgrave, Richard A., ed. Essays in Fiscal Federalism. LC 76-49481. (Brookings Institution, Studies of Government Finance Ser.). (Illus.). 1977. Repr. of 1965 ed. lib. bdg. 22.25x (ISBN 0-8371-9366-4, MUEFF). Greenwood.

Nathan, Richard P., et al. Monitoring Revenue Sharing. 394p. 1975. 14.95 (ISBN 0-8157-5984-3); pap. 5.95 (ISBN 0-8157-5983-5). Brookings.

--Revenue Sharing: The Second Round. LC 76-51884. 1977. 11.95 (ISBN 0-8157-5986-X); pap. 4.95 (ISBN 0-8157-5985-1). Brookings.

Reagan, Michael D. & Sanzone, John G. The New Federalism. 2nd ed. 208p. 1981. pap. text ed. 3.95x (ISBN 0-19-502772-8). Oxford U Pr.

Scheffer, Walter F. General Revenue Sharing & Decentralization. LC 75-40955. 250p. 1976. 12.50 (ISBN 0-8061-1332-4); pap. 5.95x (ISBN 0-8061-1343-X). U of Okla Pr.

Tax Policy League. Tax Relations Among Governmental Units. LC 77-74959. (American Federalism-the Urban Dimension). 1978. Repr. of 1938 ed. lib. bdg. 14.00x (ISBN 0-405-10502-9). Arno.

Terrell, Paul & Weisner, Stan. The Social Impact of Revenue Sharing: Planning, Participation, & the Purchase of Service. LC 76-12882. (Illus.). 1976. 22.95 (ISBN 0-275-23470-3). Praeger.

U.S Advisory Commission on Intergovernmental Relations. The Role of Equalization in Federal Grants. LC 77-74926. (American Federalism-the Urban Dimension). (Illus.). 1978. Repr. of 1964 ed. lib. bdg. 15.00x (ISBN 0-405-10475-8). Arno.

U.S. House Committee on Government Operations. Federal-State-Local Relations: Federal Grants-in Aid State & Local Officials, 2 vols. in 1. LC 77-74935. (American Federalism-the Urban Dimension). 1978. lib. bdg. 32.00 (ISBN 0-405-10482-0). Arno.

U.S. Treasury Department, the Committee on Intergovernmental Fiscal Relations. Federal, State & Local Government Fiscal Relations. LC 77-74967. (American Federalism-the Urban Dimension). (Illus.). 1978. Repr. of 1943 ed. lib. bdg. 36.00x (ISBN 0-405-10510-X). Arno.

Veeraraghavachar, S. M. Union-State Financial Relations in India. 1969. 9.00x (ISBN 0-8426-1577-6). Verry.

Waldhorn, Steven & Sneed, Joseph, eds. Restructuring the Federal System. LC 74-80584. 261p. 1975. 19.50x (ISBN 0-8448-0373-1). Crane-Russak Co.

Walker, Larry. State Legislative Control of Federal Aid Funds: The Case of Oklahoma. (Legislative Research Ser.: No. 13). 1978. 4.00 (ISBN 0-686-04911-X). Univ OK Gov Res.

Wright, Deil S., et al. Assessing the Impacts of General Revenue Sharing in the Fifty States: A Survey of State Administrators. LC 75-29490. (Illus.). 1975. pap. text ed. 5.00 (ISBN 0-89143-063-6). U NC Inst Res Soc Sci.

INTERGOVERNMENTAL TAX RELATIONS

see also Taxation, Double

Diamond, Walter & Diamond, Dorothy. International Tax Treaties of All Nations, 6 vols, Series B. LC 77-16742. 1978. lib. bdg. 50.00 (ISBN 0-379-00725-8). Oceana.

Diamond, Walter H. & Diamond, Dorothy B. International Tax Treaties of All Nations, 11 vols. LC 75-33646. 1000p. 1976. text ed. 50.00x ea. Oceana.

Hutchinson, Ruth G. State-Administered Locally-Shared Taxes. LC 68-58593. (Columbia University. Studies in the Social Sciences: No. 355). Repr. of 1931 ed. 16.50 (ISBN 0-404-51355-7). AMS Pr.

Johnson, Harry L., ed. State & Local Tax Problems. LC 69-10113. 1969. 12.50x (ISBN 0-87049-089-3). U of Tenn Pr.

Musgrave, Richard A., ed. Essays in Fiscal Federalism. LC 76-49481. (Brookings Institution, Studies of Government Finance Ser.). (Illus.). 1977. Repr. of 1965 ed. lib. bdg. 22.25x (ISBN 0-8371-9366-4, MUEFF). Greenwood.

Newcomer, Mabel. Separation of State & Local Revenues in the United States. LC 68-56675. (Columbia University. Studies in the Social Sciences: No. 180). Repr. of 1917 ed. 17.50 (ISBN 0-404-51180-5). AMS Pr.

OECD Staff. Model Convention for Mutual Administrative Assistance in the Recovery of Tax Claims. (Oecd Committee for Fiscal Affairs Ser.). 64p. (Orig.). 1981. pap. 7.50x (ISBN 92-64-12191-9). OECD.

Owens, Elisabeth A. Bibliography on Taxation of Foreign Operations & Foreigners. LC 68-23792. 112p. (Orig.). 1968. pap. 5.00x (ISBN 0-915506-09-2). Harvard Law Intl Tax.

Tax Policy League. Tax Relations Among Governmental Units. LC 77-74959. (American Federalism-the Urban Dimension). 1978. Repr. of 1938 ed. lib. bdg. 14.00x (ISBN 0-405-10502-9). Arno.

INTERINDUSTRY ECONOMICS

see also Diversification in Industry

Almon, Clopper, et al. Nineteen Eighty Five Interindustry Forecasts of the American Economy. LC 73-21608. (Illus.). 224p. 1974. 19.95 (ISBN 0-669-92494-6). Lexington Bks.

Bacharach, M. Biproportional Matrices & Input Output Change. LC 77-75823. (Department of Applied Economics Monographs: No. 16). (Illus.). 1970. 29.50 (ISBN 0-521-07594-7). Cambridge U Pr.

Carter, Anne P. Structural Change in the American Economy. LC 73-95516. (Studies in Technology & Society). 1970. 16.50x (ISBN 0-674-84370-3). Harvard U Pr.

Conference on Research in Income & Wealth. Input-Output Analysis: An Appraisal. LC 75-19705. (National Bureau of Economic Research Ser.). (Illus.). 1975. Repr. of 1955 ed. 21.00x (ISBN 0-405-07585-5). Arno.

Correa, Hector. Integrated Economic Accounting: Theory & Applications to National, Real, & Financial Economic Planning. LC 76-17445. 1976. 26.95 (ISBN 0-669-00779-X). Lexington Bks.

Csepinszky. Input-Output Techniques. 1976. 29.00 (ISBN 0-9960004-7-X, Pub. by Kaido Hungary). Heyden.

Dorfman, R., et al. Linear Programming & Economic Analysis. 1958. text ed. 21.95 (ISBN 0-07-017621-3, P&RB). McGraw.

Giarrantani, Frank. Regional & Interregional Input-Output Analysis: An Annotated Bibliography. LC 75-45868. 1976. 6.00 (ISBN 0-89092-008-7). West Va U Pr.

Isard, Walter & Langford, Thomas. Regional Input-Output Study: Recollections, Reflections & Diverse Notes on the Philadelphia Experience. (Regional Science Studies Ser: No. 10). 1971. 17.50x (ISBN 0-262-09013-9). MIT Pr.

Koehler, G. J., et al, eds. Optimization Over Leontief Substitution Systems. LC 74-28992. 1975. 29.50 (ISBN 0-444-10956-0, North-Holland). Elsevier.

Lee, Tong H., et al. Regional & Interregional Intersectoral Flow Analysis: The Method & an Application to the Tennessee Economy. LC 72-187360. 168p. 1973. 10.50x (ISBN 0-87049-139-3). U of Tenn Pr.

Leontief, Wassily W. Input-Output Economics. 1966. 19.95x (ISBN 0-19-500616-X). Oxford U Pr.

Macrakis, Michael S., ed. Energy: Demand, Conservation, & Institutional Problems. LC 74-2257. 450p. 1974. 35.00x (ISBN 0-262-13091-2). MIT Pr.

Miernyk, William H. Impact of the Space Program on a Local Economy. LC 67-24344. 167p. 1967. 6.50 (ISBN 0-937058-04-1). West Va U Pr.

Miernyk, William H., et al. Impact of the Space Program on a Local Economy. (Illus.). 6.00 (ISBN 0-685-30821-9). McClain.

Miyazawa, K. Input-Output Analysis & the Structure of Income Distribution. (Lecture Notes in Economics & Math Systems: Vol. 116). 150p. 1976. pap. 9.90 (ISBN 0-387-07613-1). Springer-Verlag.

Morishima, Michio. Equilibrium, Stability, & Growth: A Multi-Sectoral Analysis. 1964. 29.95x (ISBN 0-19-828145-5). Oxford U Pr.

O'Connor, Robert & Henry, Edmund W. Input-Output Analysis & Its Applications. LC 75-24778. 1975. 16.25 (ISBN 0-02-849850-X). Hafner.

Polenske, Karen R. State Estimates of the Gross National Product 1947, 1958, 1963. LC 79-145900. (Multiregional Input Output Study: Vol. 1). 320p. 1972. 29.95 (ISBN 0-669-62539-6). Lexington Bks.

Rodgers, John M. State Estimates of Commodity Trade Flows, 1963. LC 73-8811. (Multiregional Input-Output Study: Vol. 5). (Illus.). 272p. 1973. 25.50 (ISBN 0-669-89227-0). Lexington Bks.

Strout, Alan M. Technological Change & United States Energy Consumption, 1939-1954. Bruchey, Stuart, ed. LC 78-22753. (Energy in the American Economy Ser.). (Illus.). 1979. lib. bdg. 22.00x (ISBN 0-405-12017-6). Arno.

Theil, H. System-Wide Explorations in International Economics, Input-Output Analysis, & Marketing Research. (Lectures in Economics Ser.: Vol. 2). 139p. 1980. 29.50 (ISBN 0-444-85377-4). Elsevier.

Tilanus, C. B. Input-Output Experiments. 1964. 19.25x (ISBN 0-677-61165-X). Gordon.

Todaro, Michael P. Development Planning: Models & Methods. (Illus.). 111p. 1971. pap. 5.95x (ISBN 0-19-519647-3). Oxford U Pr.

Treml, Vladimir G., ed. Studies in Soviet Input-Output Analysis. LC 77-2739. (Praeger Special Studies). 1977. text ed. 44.50 (ISBN 0-275-56550-5). Praeger.

Tsukui, J. & Murakami, Y. Turnpike Optimality in Input-Output Systems: Theory & Application for Planning. (Contributions to Economic Analysis Ser.: Vol. 122). 1979. 51.25 (ISBN 0-444-85221-2, North Holland). Elsevier.

Wu, Nesa & Coppins, Richard. Linear Programming & Extensions. (Industrial Engineering & Management Science Ser.). (Illus.). 480p. 1981. 27.95 (ISBN 0-07-072117-3, C); solutions manual 8.95 (ISBN 0-07-072118-1). McGraw.

INTERINDUSTRY ECONOMICS–BIBLIOGRAPHY

Harmston, Floyd K. & Lund, Richard E. Application of an Input-Output Framework to a Community Economic System. LC 67-63043. 1967. 10.00x (ISBN 0-8262-0577-1). U of Mo Pr.

Riley, Vera & Allen, Robert L. Interindustry Economic Studies. (Operations Research Ser). 288p. 1955. pap. 14.00x (ISBN 0-8018-0558-9). Johns Hopkins.

INTERIOR DECORATION

see also Church Decoration and Ornament; Color in Architecture; Coverlets; Drapery; Floor Coverings; Furniture; House Furnishings; Interior Decorators; Lighting; Lighting, Architectural and Decorative; Mural Painting and Decoration; Paper-Hanging; Screens; Staircases; Stove-Plates; Tapestry; Texture Painting; Upholstery; Wall-Paper

Alexander, Mary Jean. Decorating Made Simple. LC 64-13823. 1964. pap. 3.50 (ISBN 0-385-01695-6, Made). Doubleday.

Allen, Phyllis S. Decorate for Living. LC 79-1228. (Illus.). 1979. pap. 9.95 (ISBN 0-8425-1627-1). Brigham.

--The Young Decorator. LC 74-23449. (Illus.). 220p. (gr. 10-12). 1975. pap. text ed. 12.95x (ISBN 0-8425-0062-6). Brigham.

Alpern, Andrew. Apartments for the Affluent: A Historical Survey of Buildings in New York. (Illus.). 1975. 34.50 (ISBN 0-07-001372-1, P&RB). McGraw.

Antiques Magazine & Winchester, Alice, eds. Living with Antiques: A Treasury of Private Homes in America. 1963. 15.00 (ISBN 0-525-14793-4). Dutton.

Apartment Life Editors. The Apartment Book. (Illus.). 1979. 27.50 (ISBN 0-517-53699-4, Harmony). Crown.

Architectural Record Editors. Interior Spaces Designed by Architects. 1974. 32.50 (ISBN 0-07-002220-8, P&RB). McGraw.

Artistic Houses: American Victorian Homes. LC 69-18531. (Illus.). 1969. 38.50 (ISBN 0-405-08215-0, Pub. by Blom). Arno.

Artley, Alexandra, ed. Artist, Architect & Patron. (Illus.). 96p. 1980. 22.50 (ISBN 0-85139-075-7). Eastview.

Baillie, Sheila & Skjelver, Mabel R. Graphics for Interior Space. LC 79-64692. (Illus.). 1979. pap. 9.50x (ISBN 0-8032-6054-7). U of Nebr Pr.

Baker, Bill. House of Ideas. LC 73-11734. (Illus.). 288p. 1974. 19.95 (ISBN 0-02-506280-8, 50628). Macmillan.

Banov, Abel & Lytle, Marie-Jeanne. Successful Wallcoverings & Decoration. 2nd ed. Case, Virginia A., ed. (Successful Ser.). (Illus.). 136p. Date not set. cancelled (ISBN 0-89999-021-5); pap. 7.95 (ISBN 0-89999-022-3). Structures Pub.

Billcliffe, Roger. Charles Rennie Mackintosh: The Complete Furniture, Furniture Drawings, & Interior Designs. LC 78-72303. (Illus.). 1979. 60.00 (ISBN 0-8008-1773-7). Taplinger.

Bjerregaard, Kirsten, ed. Design from Scandinavia: Scandinavian Interiors, No. 6. (Illus.). 1978. pap. 12.95 (ISBN 0-917304-51-9, Pub. by World Pictures). Intl Schol Bk Serv.

--Design from Scandinavia: Scandinavian Interiors, No. 7. (Illus.). 1978. pap. 12.95 (ISBN 87-87541-04-1, Pub. by World Pictures). Intl Schol Bk Serv.

--Design from Scandinavia: Scandinavian Interiors, No. 8. (Illus.). 1978. pap. 12.95 (ISBN 87-87541-08-4, Pub. by World Pictures). Intl Schol Bk Serv.

Bradford, Barbara T. Designs for Casual Living. (Illus.). 1977. 16.95 (ISBN 0-671-21969-3). S&S.

--Luxury Designs for Apartment Living. LC 77-16899. (Illus.). 352p. 1981. 29.95 (ISBN 0-385-12769-3). Doubleday.

Brown, Erica. Interior Views: Design at Its Best. LC 80-5356. 176p. 1980. 25.00 (ISBN 0-670-39978-7, Studio). Viking Pr.

Burden, Ernest. Entourage: A Tracing File for Architecture & Interior Design Drawing. (Illus.). 256p. 1981. 15.95 (ISBN 0-07-008930-2). McGraw.

Butler, Margaret & Greves, Beryl. Fabric Furnishings. 1972. 27.00 (ISBN 0-7134-2754-X, Pub. by Batsford). David & Charles.

Chamberlain, Narcissa. Old Rooms for New Living. (Illus.). 1977. 13.95 (ISBN 0-8038-5346-7). Hastings.

Chamberlain, Samuel. Salem Interiors. (Illus.). 1966. 12.50 (ISBN 0-8038-6642-9). Hastings.

Chamberlain, Samuel & Chamberlain, Narcissa G. The Chamberlain Selection of New England Rooms, 1639-1863. 1973. 20.00 (ISBN 0-8038-1176-4). Hastings.

The Complete Family Interior Decorating Book. (Illus.). 520p. 1981. 8.95 (ISBN 0-686-31187-6, 2542). Playmore & Prestige.

Conran, Terence. The Kitchen Book. (Illus.). 1977. 35.00 (ISBN 0-517-53131-3). Crown.

Cook, Clarence. The House Beautiful: Essays on Beds & Tables, Stools & Candlesticks. 1980. Repr. of 1878 ed. 30.00 (ISBN 0-88427-029-7). Caroline Hse.

Crane, Catherine. What Do You Say to a Naked Room? (Illus.). 1979. 19.95 (ISBN 0-8037-9745-1); pap. 12.95 (ISBN 0-8037-9641-2). Dial.

Crane, Catherine C., ed. Residential Interiors Today. (Illus.). 1977. (Whitney Lib); pap. 9.95 (ISBN 0-8230-7444-7). Watson-Guptill.

D'Arcy, Barbara. Bloomingdale's Book of Home Decorating. LC 73-4064. (Illus.). 264p. 1973. 15.95 (ISBN 0-06-010948-3, HarpT). Harper-Row.

Davis, Melinda. Storage: A House & Garden Book. LC 77-88766. 1979. pap. 6.95 (ISBN 0-394-73464-5). Pantheon.

Day, Lewis F. Everyday Art. LC 76-17763. (Aesthetic Movement Ser.: Vol. 19). 1977. Repr. of 1882 ed. lib. bdg. 44.00 (ISBN 0-8240-2468-0). Garland Pub.

Designers Guild. Soft Furnishings: Ideas & Fabrics by Designers. 1980. pap. text ed. 14.95 (ISBN 0-374-51614-6). FS&G.

Donovan, Carrie. Living Well: The New York Times Book of Interior Design & Decoration. Filley, Patrick, ed. LC 81-50088. (Illus.). 256p. 1981. 35.00 (ISBN 0-8129-0993-3); prepub. 30.00 pre-Dec. (ISBN 0-686-74666-X). Times Bks.

Draycon, R. N. Home Decorating. (Invest in Living Ser.). (Illus.). 1977. pap. 6.25x (ISBN 0-7158-0462-6). Intl Pubns Serv.

Dresser, Christopher. Art of Decorative Design. (Library of Victorian Culture). (Illus.). 1977. pap. text ed. 10.00 (ISBN 0-89257-030-X). Am Life Foun.

Duprey, Kenneth. Old Houses on Nantucket. 15.00 (ISBN 0-8038-0193-9). Architectural.

Eames, Alexandra. Windows & Walls: Designs-Patterns-Projects. LC 80-80753. 160p. 1980. 17.95 (ISBN 0-8487-0507-6). Oxmoor Hse.

Eastlake, Charles L. Hints on Household Taste in Furniture, Upholstery & Other Details. LC 73-177519. (Illus.). Repr. of 1872 ed. 18.00 (ISBN 0-405-08480-3). Arno.

Edis, Robert W. Decoration of Town Houses. 2nd ed. (Illus.). 1976. Repr. 17.50x (ISBN 0-85409-909-3). Charles River Bks.
Editors of Architectural Digest. Celebrity Homes. Rense, Paige, ed. (Large Format Ser.). (Illus.). 1979. pap. 14.95 (ISBN 0-14-005229-1). Penguin.
Editors of Better Homes & Gardens Books. Better Homes & Gardens: New Decorating Book. (Illus.). 432p. 1981. 29.92 (ISBN 0-696-00092-X). Meredith Corp.
Estes, Hiawatha T. Distinctive Homes. (Illus.). 1981. 2.00 (ISBN 0-911008-18-7). H Estes.
--Hallmark Homes. (Illus.). 1981. 2.00 (ISBN 0-911008-20-9). H Estes.
--Homes by Hiawatha. (Illus.). 1981. 2.00 (ISBN 0-911008-21-7). H Estes.
--Prize Homes. (Illus.). 1981. 2.00 (ISBN 0-911008-22-5). H Estes.
--Ranch & Modern Homes. (Illus.). 1981. 3.00 (ISBN 0-911008-19-5). H Estes.
--Town & Country Homes. (Illus.). 1981. 2.00 (ISBN 0-911008-23-3). H Estes.
Faulkner, Ray & Faulkner, Sarah. Inside Today's Home. 4th ed. LC 74-11832. (Illus.). 1975. text ed. 19.95 (ISBN 0-03-089480-8, HoltC). HR&W.
Faulkner, Sarah. Planning a Home: A Practical Guide to Interior Design. LC 78-22021. 1979. pap. text ed. 18.95 (ISBN 0-03-045471-9, HoltC); projects manual 8.95 (ISBN 0-03-045476-X). HR&W.
Frankel, Virginia. What Your House Tells About You. 1972. 5.95 (ISBN 0-671-27089-3). Trident.
Frankl, Paul T. Form & Reform: Practical Handbook of Modern Interiors. LC 72-143347. (Illus.). 1972. Repr. of 1930 ed. 15.00 (ISBN 0-87817-067-7). Hacker.
--New Dimensions: The Decorative Arts of Today in Words and Pictures. LC 75-15851. (Architecture and Decorative Arts Ser.). (Illus.). 122p. 1975. Repr. of 1928 ed. lib. bdg. 37.50 (ISBN 0-306-70741-1). Da Capo.
Frazier, David. Around the House. (Illus.). 1979. pap. 6.95 (ISBN 0-8256-3143-2, Quick Fox). Music Sales.
Frey, Iris I. Staple It. 1979. 12.95 (ISBN 0-517-53254-9); pap. 8.95 (ISBN 0-517-53255-7). Crown.
Friedman, Julius & Beckman, John. Special Rooms: Louisville, Kentucky. LC 80-83167. (Illus.). 88p. (Orig.). 1981. pap. 12.95 (ISBN 0-937246-01-8). Chicago Review.
Friedmann, Arnold. Interior Design. 2nd ed. LC 75-26331. 448p. 1976. text ed. 19.95 (ISBN 0-444-00178-6, North Holland). Elsevier.
Garee, Betty, ed. Ideas for Making Your Home Accessible. LC 79-51595. (Illus.). 1979. 6.50 (ISBN 0-915708-08-6). Cheever Pub.
Geck, Francis J. Interior Design & Decoration - an Outline. 4th ed. 259p. 1971. write for info. wire coil (ISBN 0-697-08308-X). Wm C Brown.
Gilbert, Rose B. & McMillan, Patricia H. The You-Do-It Book of Early American Decorating. LC 77-15150. (Illus.). 1979. 17.95 (ISBN 0-385-12711-1). Doubleday.
Goldstein, Harriet I. & Goldstein, Vetta. Art in Everyday Life. 4th ed. (Illus.). 1954. text ed. 18.95 (ISBN 0-02-344480-0, 34448). Macmillan.
Graff, Arden. The Best Building on the Block. (Orig.). 1981. pap. 4.95 (ISBN 0-934892-01-6). Interiors.
Guild, Robin. Homeworks: The Complete Guide to Displaying Your Possessions. 1979. 29.95 (ISBN 0-442-24576-9). Van Nos Reinhold.
Halse, Albert O. The Use of Color in Interiors. 2nd ed. (Illus.). 1978. 27.50 (ISBN 0-07-025624-1, P&RB). McGraw.
Hatje, Gerd & Kaspar, Peter, eds. Decorating for Modern Living. (Illus.). 1977. pap. 8.95 (ISBN 0-8109-2059-X). Abrams.
Haven, Sharon O. Room to Grow: Making Your Child's Bedroom a Special Place. Cohen, Liza, ed. (Illus.). 1979. write for info. (ISBN 0-931018-02-1). Two Step Bks.
Haweis, Mrs. E. The Art of Decoration. LC 76-17761. (Aesthetic Movement Ser.: Vol. 17). 1977. Repr. of 1889 ed. lib. bdg. 44.00x (ISBN 0-8240-2466-4). Garland Pub.
Hedden, Jay W. Successful Living Rooms. LC 77-26025. (Illus.). 1978. 13.95 (ISBN 0-912336-60-9); pap. 6.95 (ISBN 0-912336-61-7). Structures Pub.
Helsel, Marjorie B. The Home Decorator's Color Book. 1972. pap. 2.95 (ISBN 0-686-66668-2, Fireside). S&S.
--The Interior Designer's Bedspread & Canopy Sketchfile. (Illus.). 192p. 1975. 15.95 (ISBN 0-8230-7290-8, Whitney Lib). Watson-Guptill.
--Interior Designer's Drapery Sketchfile. (Illus.). 1969. 15.95 (ISBN 0-8230-7289-4, Whitney Lib). Watson-Guptill.
Henton, Richard W. Quick-Sketch: A New Technique in Interior Design Graphics. 144p. 1980. pap. text ed. 8.95 (ISBN 0-8403-2233-X). Kendall-Hunt.
Hicks, David. Living with Design. LC 79-1980. (Illus.). 1979. 29.95 (ISBN 0-688-03501-9). Morrow.
Hines, Millie, ed. Crafty Ideas for the Home. (Illus.). 96p. (Orig.). 1980. pap. 2.00 (ISBN 0-918178-20-7). Simplicity.
--Easy Ways to Decorate Your Kitchen. (Illus.). 96p. (Orig.). 1981. pap. 2.00 (ISBN 0-918178-24-X). Simplicity.
Hope, Thomas. Household Furniture & Interior Decoration: Classic Style Book of the Regency Period. (Illus.). 1971. pap. 5.00 (ISBN 0-486-21710-8). Dover.
--Household Furniture & Interior Decoration: Executed from Designs by Thomas Hope. (Illus.). 1970. Repr. of 1807 ed. 16.50 (ISBN 0-685-04855-1). Transatlantic.
House & Garden, ed. Twentieth Century Decorating Architecture & Gardens. LC 80-12593. (Illus.). 320p. 1980. 34.95 (ISBN 0-03-047581-3); pre-Jan. 29.95 (ISBN 0-686-77496-5). HR&W.
Housing Press. The House & Home for Interior Design. LC 77-10867. (Illus.). 1979. 16.95 (ISBN 0-07-030473-4, P&RB). McGraw.
Hunt, Isabel. Leisuretime: House Beautiful: Clever New Ideas for Homemakers. LC 74-19758. (Leisuretime Ser.). (Illus.). 96p. 1975. bds. 5.95 (ISBN 0-668-03697-4). Arco.
Hurst, A. E. & Goodier, J. M. Painting & Decorating. 620p. 1980. 75.00x (ISBN 0-85264-243-1, Pub. by Griffin England). State Mutual Bk.
The Interiors Book of Shops & Restaurants. (Illus.). 144p. 1981. 25.00 (ISBN 0-8230-7284-3, Whitney Lib). Watson-Guptill.
Jarry, M. Carpets of the Manufacture De la Savonnerie. 33.50 (ISBN 0-87245-156-9). Textile Bk.
Katz, Marjorie P. Instant-Effect Decorating. LC 76-168690. (Illus.). 320p. 1972. 8.95 (ISBN 0-87131-066-X). M Evans.
Kettell, R. H., ed. Early American Rooms. (Illus.). 15.00 (ISBN 0-8446-2367-9). Peter Smith.
Kettell, Russell H., ed. Early American Rooms Sixteen Fifty-Sixteen Fifty-Eight. (Illus.). 1966. pap. 6.95 (ISBN 0-486-21633-0). Dover.
Kleeman, Walter. The Challenge of Interior Design. 304p. 1981. 19.95 (ISBN 0-8436-0133-7). CBI Pub.
Knackstedt, Mary V. Interior Design for Profit. Haney, Laura J., ed. 1980. 17.00 (ISBN 0-9604676-0-2). Kobro Pubns.
Larsen, Jack L. & Weeks, Jeanne. Fabrics for Interiors. 1975. 16.95 (ISBN 0-442-24683-8); pap. 8.95 (ISBN 0-442-24684-6). Van Nos Reinhold.
Lefebvre, Adrian. The New Frontiers of Interior Decoration. (Illus.). 1980. deluxe ed. 41.75 (ISBN 0-930582-60-8). Gloucester Art.
Lindahl, Judy. Decorating with Fabric: An Idea Book. rev. ed. 128p. 1980. pap. 4.95 (ISBN 0-9603032-1-9). Lindahl.
--Energy Saving Decorating. new ed. LC 81-90134. (Illus.). 128p. (Orig.). 1981. pap. 4.95 (ISBN 0-9603032-3-5). Lindahl.
--The Shade Book. rev. ed. (Illus.). 128p. pap. 4.95 (ISBN 0-9603032-2-7). Lindahl.
Loftie, W. J., et al. A Plea for Art in the House & House Decoration & Dress & Music in the House. Stansky, Peter & Shewan, Rodney, eds. LC 76-18320. (Aesthetic Movement & the Arts & Crafts Movement Ser.). 1978. Repr. lib. bdg. 44.00x (ISBN 0-8240-2460-5). Garland Pub.
Lowe, David. Chicago Interiors. (Illus.). 1980. pap. 10.95 (ISBN 0-8092-5992-3). Contemp Bks.
Lyon, Jean. Decorating with Antiques & Collectibles. (Illus.). 1980. pap. 7.95 (ISBN 0-89145-110-2). Collector Bks.
McClellan, Brenda. Successful Home Decorating. Case, Virginia A., ed. (Successful Ser.). (Illus.). 136p. Date not set. cancelled (ISBN 0-89999-021-5); pap. 7.95 (ISBN 0-89999-022-3). Structures Pub.
Magnani, Franco. One Room Interiors. (Illus.). 1979. 22.50 (ISBN 0-8230-7379-3). Watson-Guptill.
Magnani, Franco, ed. Living Spaces: 150 Design Ideas from Around the World. (Illus.). 1978. 22.50 (ISBN 0-8230-7356-4, Whitney Lib). Watson-Guptill.
Maier, Manfred. Basic Principles of Design. 392p. 1981. pap. 35.00 (ISBN 0-442-21206-2). Van Nos Reinhold.
Milady Editors. Total Look in Interior Design. 1969. 5.25 (ISBN 0-87350-252-3). Milady.
Morrison, Alex. Photofinish. 144p. 1981. 16.95 (ISBN 0-442-21262-3). Van Nos Reinhold.
Murphy, Dennis G. The Materials of Interior Design. Murphy, Gladys N., ed. (Interior Furnishings & Products Ser.). (Illus.). 208p. (Orig.). 1978. 10.50 (ISBN 0-938614-00-2, 211-196). Stratford Hse.
Naar, Jon & Siple, Molly. Living in One Room: Ingenius Ideas to Transform a Single Room into All You Ever Wanted in a Full Apartment - A Place to Work, Indulge Your Hobbies, & Entertain As Well As Eat & Sleep. 1976. 10.95 (ISBN 0-394-40846-2). Random.
Obst, Frances M. Art & Design for Home Living. 1963. text ed. 12.95x (ISBN 0-685-14648-0). Macmillan.
O'Connell, C. B. Home Furnishing Self Help. LC 68-12618. 1968. 10.00 (ISBN 0-8108-0180-9). Scarecrow.
Orr, Monica, ed. Special Rooms: Louisville, Kentucky. LC 80-83167. 72p. (Orig.). 1980. pap. 12.95 (ISBN 0-937246-01-8). Hawley Cooke Orr.
Paint & Wallpaper. (Home Repair & Improvement Ser.). (Illus.). 1976. 10.95 (ISBN 0-8094-2354-5). Time-Life.
Panero, Julius & Zelnik, Martin. Human Dimensions & Interior Space. (Illus.). 1979. 32.50 (ISBN 0-8230-7271-1). Watson-Guptill.
Pautz, Phyllis. Decorating with Plant Crafts & Natural Material. LC 70-150912. 1971. 9.95 (ISBN 0-385-08327-0). Doubleday.
Porter, Donald. Making Loose Covers. 1975. 17.95 (ISBN 0-7134-2911-9, Pub. by Batsford England). David & Charles.
Pressman, Andy & Pressman, Peter. Integrated Space Systems: Vocabulary for Room Language. 128p. 1980. 16.95 (ISBN 0-442-23162-8); pap. 9.95 (ISBN 0-442-23167-9). Van Nos Reinhold.
Rense, Paige. Decorating for Celebrities: Interviews with Twenty of the World's Best Interior Designers. LC 78-22644. (Illus.). 240p. 1980. 22.95 (ISBN 0-385-14810-0). Doubleday.
Rense, Paige, ed. Architectural Digest California Interiors. LC 79-84685. (The Worlds of Architectural Digest Ser.). (Illus.). 1979. 14.95 (ISBN 0-89535-032-7). Knapp Pr.
--Architectural Digest, Celebrity Homes. LC 77-84047. (Illus.). 1977. 35.00x (ISBN 0-89535-001-7). Knapp Pr.
--Architectural Digest International Interiors. LC 77-17004. (Illus.). 1979. 35.00 (ISBN 0-89535-003-3). Knapp Pr.
--Architectural Digest New York Interiors. LC 79-84686. (The Worlds of Architectural Digest Ser.). (Illus.). 1979. 14.95 (ISBN 0-89535-031-9). Knapp Pr.
--Architectural Digest Traditional Interiors. LC 79-84682. (The Worlds of Architectural Digest Ser.). (Illus.). 1979. 14.95 (ISBN 0-89535-034-3). Knapp Pr.
--Celebrity Homes II. LC 81-3786. 256p. 1981. 40.00 (ISBN 0-89535-048-3). Knapp Pr.
Rodgers, Dorothy. My Favorite Things. LC 64-22105. (Illus.). 1977. pap. 8.95 (ISBN 0-689-70548-4). Atheneum.
Rogers, Meyric R. American Interior Design: The Traditions & Development of Domestic Design from Colonial Times to the Present. LC 75-22838. (America in Two Centuries Ser). (Illus.). 1976. Repr. of 1947 ed. 23.00x (ISBN 0-405-07709-2). Arno.
Ruggiero, Joseph. Found Objects: A Guide to Decorating with Natural & Man-Made Materials. (Illus.). 224p. 1981. 29.95 (ISBN 0-517-54147-5). Potter.
St. Marie, Satenig S. Homes Are for People. LC 72-10244. (Illus.). 412p. 1973. text ed. 18.95 (ISBN 0-471-82635-9). Wiley.
Schneider, R. Interior Design Careers. 1976. 6.36 (ISBN 0-13-392795-4); pap. text ed. 5.12 (ISBN 0-13-392787-3). P-H.
Schofield, Maria, ed. Decorative Art & Modern Interiors: Environments for People. LC 80-81603. (Decorative Art & Modern Interiors, Theme Changes Annually). (Illus.). 192p. 1980. 29.95 (ISBN 0-688-03480-2). Morrow.
--Decorative Art & Modern Interiors: Themes in Nature. LC 78-71658. (Illus.). 1979. 29.95 (ISBN 0-688-03480-2). Morrow.
--Decorative Art & Modern Interiors 1977. 1977. 27.50 (ISBN 0-442-27423-8). Van Nos Reinhold.
--Decorative Art & Modern Interiors 1978. 1978. 29.95 (ISBN 0-442-27421-1). Van Nos Reinhold.
Scrivens, Steven. Interior Planting in Large Buildings: A Handbook for Architects Interior Designers & Horticulturists. LC 80-23565. 129p. 1981. 44.95 (ISBN 0-470-27067-5). Halsted Pr.
Seale, William. Recreating the Historic House Interior. LC 78-14361. (Illus.). 1979. text ed. 22.00 (ISBN 0-910050-32-5). AASLH.
--A Tasteful Interlude: American Interiors Through the Camera's Eye, 1860 to 1917. (Illus.). 288p. 1981. pap. 12.95 (ISBN 0-910050-49-X). AASLH.
Shipway, Verna C. & Shipway, Warren. Decorative Design in Mexican Homes. (Illus.). 1966. 18.95 (ISBN 0-8038-0058-4). Architectural.
Siegel, Herbert. A Guide to Business Principles & Practices for Interior Designers. (Illus.). 1963. 19.50 (ISBN 0-8230-7251-7, Whitney Lib). Watson-Guptill.
Skurka, Norma. The New York Times Book of Interior Design & Decoration. LC 76-9690. (Illus.). 1976. 25.00 (ISBN 0-8129-0653-5). Times Bks.
Skurka, Norma & Gili, Oberto. Underground Interiors: Adventures in Decorating & Design. LC 72-85241. (Illus.). 124p. 1973. 14.95 (ISBN 0-8129-0293-9); pap. 6.95 (ISBN 0-8129-6227-3). Times Bks.
Staff of Previews. The New Previews Book of Dream Houses. 1979. (Dist. by Crown); pap. 8.95 (ISBN 0-517-53712-5). Crown.
Stramesi, Annette. Creative Home Decorating. 1981. 7.95 (ISBN 0-916752-14-3). Caroline Hse.
--The Inside Story: Creative Home Decorating. LC 77-71482. 144p. 1977. 7.95 (ISBN 0-916752-14-3). Dorison Hse.
Sulahria, Julie J. Inside Design: Creating Your Environment. 1977. text ed. 20.50 scp (ISBN 0-06-453508-8, HarpC). Har-Row.
Sunset Editors. Picture Framing & Wall Display. LC 79-88158. (Illus.). 104p. 1979. pap. 3.95 (ISBN 0-376-01421-0, Sunset Bks). Sunset-Lane.
--Pillows: How to Make. LC 80-80859. (Illus.). 80p. (Orig.). 1980. pap. 3.95 (ISBN 0-376-01431-8, Sunset Bks). Sunset-Lane.
Sylvia's Home Help Series. Artistic Homes; or, How to Furnish with Taste. Stansky, Peter & Shewan, Rodney, eds. LC 76-17759. (Aesthetic Movement & the Arts & Crafts Movement Ser.). 1978. Repr. of 1881 ed. lib. bdg. 44.00x (ISBN 0-8240-2464-8). Garland Pub.
Todd, Dorothy & Mortimer, Raymond. The New Interior Decoration. LC 77-4444. (Architecture & Decorative Art Ser.). (Illus.). 1977. Repr. of 1929 ed. lib. bdg. 45.00 (ISBN 0-306-70899-X). Da Capo.
Trupp, Beverly. Color It Home: A Builder's Guide to Interior Design & Merchandising. (Illus.). 240p. 1981. 34.95 (ISBN 0-8436-0136-1). CBI Pub.
Varney, Carleton. There's No Place Like Home: Confessions of an Interior Designer. LC 80-1020. 228p. 1980. 12.95 (ISBN 0-672-51872-4). Bobbs.
Wade, Carlson. Floor Decorating. LC 76-10883. (Illus.). 1979. 15.00 (ISBN 0-498-01810-5). A S Barnes.
--Wall Decorating. LC 75-20608. (Illus.). 1977. 15.00 (ISBN 0-498-01754-0). A S Barnes.
Weiss. Working Places. 1980. 17.95 (ISBN 0-312-88646-2); pap. 8.95 (ISBN 0-312-88985-2). St Martin.
Weiss, Jeffery. Great Kitchens. 96p. 1981. pap. 9.95 (ISBN 0-312-34605-0). St Martin.
Weiss, Jeffrey. Great Bathrooms. 96p. 1981. pap. 9.95 (ISBN 0-312-34486-4). St Martin.
--Great Kids' Rooms. (Illus.). 96p. 1981. pap. 9.95 (ISBN 0-312-34601-8). St Martin.
Wharton, Edith & Codman, Ogden. The Decoration of Houses. (Illus.). 1978. 14.95 (ISBN 0-393-04468-8, Norton Lib); pap. 3.95 (ISBN 0-393-00840-1). Norton.
Wharton, Edith & Codman, Ogden, Jr. The Decoration of Houses. facsimile ed. LC 75-932. (Leisure Class in America Ser.). (Illus.). 1975. Repr. of 1914 ed. 21.00x (ISBN 0-405-06938-3). Arno.
Whiton, Sherrill. Interior Design & Decoration. 4th ed. (Illus.). 1974. scp 37.95 (ISBN 0-397-47315-X, HarpC); pap. 30.50 scp (ISBN 0-397-47302-8, HarpC). Har-Row.
Wilk, Christopher. Marcel Breuer: Furniture & Interior Design. LC 81-81191. (Illus.). 192p. 1981. 22.50 (ISBN 0-87070-264-5); pap. 12.50 (ISBN 0-87070-263-7). Museum Mod Art.
Wilkins, W. Home Decorating. pap. 6.95 (ISBN 0-408-00243-3, NB 61, Pub. by Newnes-Technical). Hayden.
Wilkinson, Jule, ed. Special Atmosphere Themes for Foodservice. LC 78-184740. 1972. 12.95 (ISBN 0-8436-0536-7). CBI Pub.
Wilson, Jose & Leaman, Arthur. The Second Complete Home Decorating Catalogue. rev. ed. LC 80-26201. (Illus.). 224p. 1981. 18.95 (ISBN 0-03-055941-3); pap. 10.95 (ISBN 0-03-055936-7). HR&W.
Wise, Herbert H. Rooms with a View. (Illus.). 1978. pap. 6.95 (ISBN 0-8256-3128-9, Quick Fox). Music Sales.
Wise, Herbert H. & Friedman-Weiss, Jeffrey. Living Places. LC 76-8071. 1976. pap. 6.95 (ISBN 0-8256-3067-3, Quick Fox). Music Sales.
Zakas, Spiros & Miner, Margaret. Lifespace: Designs for Today's Home. LC 77-24208. (Illus.). 1977. 5.98 (ISBN 0-02-633410-0). Macmillan.

INTERIOR DECORATION-BIBLIOGRAPHY

American Institute of Decorators. Interior Design & Decoration: A Bibliography. LC 61-7059. 86p. 1961. 5.00 (ISBN 0-87104-254-1). NY Pub Lib.

Vance, Mary. Interior Design & Decoration: A Bibliography of Books. (Architecture Ser.: Bibliography A-257). 75p. 1980. pap. 8.00 (ISBN 0-686-29056-9). Vance Biblios.

INTERIOR DECORATION–ENCYCLOPEDIAS, YEARBOOKS

Aronson, Joseph. Encyclopedia of Furniture. rev. ed. (Illus.). (YA) (gr. 9 up). 1965. 11.95 (ISBN 0-517-03735-1). Crown.

Goodier, J. H. Dictionary of Painting & Decorating. 308p. 1974. 39.50x (ISBN 0-85264-224-5, Pub. by Griffin England). State Mutual Bk.

INTERIOR DECORATION–HANDBOOKS, MANUALS, ETC.

Allen, Phyllis S. Beginnings of Interior Environment. 4th ed. LC 76-12563. (Illus.). 1977. 17.95x (ISBN 0-8425-1444-9); pap. 12.95x (ISBN 0-8425-1448-1). Brigham.

Apartment Life Editors. The Apartment Book. (Illus.). 1979. 27.50 (ISBN 0-517-53699-4, Harmony). Crown.

Avery, James R. & Null, Roberta L. Environmental Design Laboratory Guide. 3rd ed. (Illus.). 1978. pap. text ed. 6.95 (ISBN 0-8403-1077-3). Kendall-Hunt.

Banov, Abel & Lytle, Marie-Jeanne. Book of Successful Painting. LC 74-21836. (Illus.). 114p. 1975. 12.00 (ISBN 0-912336-11-0); pap. 4.95 (ISBN 0-912336-12-9). Structures Pub.

Barkin, Carol & James, Elizabeth. Slapdash Decorating. LC 78-32134. (Illus.). (gr. 7 up). 1979. pap. 3.95 (ISBN 0-671-33027-6). Wanderer Bks.

Cary, Jane R. How to Create Interiors for the Disabled: A Guidebook for Family & Friends. LC 77-88781. 1978. 15.00 (ISBN 0-394-41376-8); pap. 5.95 (ISBN 0-394-73595-1). Pantheon.

Cornell, Jane. Successful Custom Interiors. Horowitz, Shirley M., ed. LC 79-15910. (Successful Ser.). (Illus.). 1979. 13.95 (ISBN 0-912336-87-0); pap. 6.95 (ISBN 0-912336-88-9). Structures Pub.

Dalsgaard, Per & Erichson, Elisabeth. Bright Ideas for Your Home. LC 78-4730. (Illus.). 1978. 14.95 (ISBN 0-06-010972-6, HarpT). Har-Row.

Faulkner, Sarah. Planning a Home: A Practical Guide to Interior Design. LC 78-22021. (Illus.). 384p. 1979. 22.50 (ISBN 0-03-053631-6). HR&W.

Frazier, Alton E. Good Taste Begins with You. Ide, Arthur F., ed. LC 79-9441. (Illus., Orig.). 1980. Ide Hse.

Goodier, J. H. Painting & Decorating: A Guide for Houseowner & Decorator. (Illus.). 1977. 17.95x (ISBN 0-7114-4612-1). Intl Ideas.

Graff, Arden. Arden Graff's Interior Design Kit. (Illus., Orig.). 1979. wkbk. 9.95 (ISBN 0-934892-00-8). Interiors.

Grow, Lawrence. The Old House Book of Bedrooms. (The Old House Book Ser.). (Illus.). 96p. 1980. 15.00 (ISBN 0-446-51216-8); pap. 7.95 (ISBN 0-446-97553-2). Warner Bks.

--The Old House Book of Living Rooms & Parlors. (The Old House Book Ser.). (Illus.). 150p. 1980. 15.00 (ISBN 0-446-51215-X); pap. 7.95 (ISBN 0-446-97552-4). Warner Bks.

Grow, Lawrence, ed. The Brand New Old House Catalogue. (Illus.). 224p. 1980. 17.95 (ISBN 0-446-51214-1); pap. 9.95 (ISBN 0-446-97557-5). Warner Bks.

Hatje, Gerd & Kaspar, Peter. Sixteen Hundred & One Decorating Ideas for Modern Living: A Practical Guide to Home Furnishing & Interior Design. LC 73-19988. (Illus.). 320p. 1974. 25.00 (ISBN 0-8109-0129-3). Abrams.

James, Elizabeth & Barkin, Carol. A Place of Your Own. (Illus.). 96p. (gr. 3). 1981. 10.25 (ISBN 0-525-37100-1, Skinny Book); pap. cancelled (ISBN 0-525-37099-4, Skinny Book). Dutton.

Kinney, Cle & Roberts, Barry. Don't Move--Improve! Hundreds of Ways to Make a Good House Better. LC 78-3305. (Funk & W Bk.). (Illus.). 1979. 14.95 (ISBN 0-308-10314-9). T Y Crowell.

Levenson, Helene. Creating an Interior: A Complete Guide to Interior Design. (Illus.). 1980. 22.95 (ISBN 0-13-189019-0, Spec); pap. 12.95 (ISBN 0-13-189001-8). P-H.

Miller, Charlotte S. Interior Decorating Made Easy: The Do-It-Yourself Guide to Basics. LC 81-90244. (Illus.). 258p. 1981. 9.95 (ISBN 0-9606646-8-8). Miller Assocs.

Morton, Ruth. Interior Design: The Home-Its Furnishing & Equipment. Zinkus, Dan & Newman, Carol, eds. (Illus.). 184p. (Orig.). (gr. 9-12). 1979. pap. 3.99 (ISBN 0-07-043426-3, W). McGraw.

Murphy, Dennis G. The Business of Interior Design. Murphy, Gladys N., ed. LC 60-2339. (Professional Practices & Reference Guidelines Ser.). (Illus.). 136p. 1975. pap. 9.50 (ISBN 0-938614-01-0). Stratford Hse.

Naar, Jon & Moore, Mary E. Your Space. LC 79-16355. 1979. 12.95 (ISBN 0-312-89826-6); pap. 6.95 (ISBN 0-312-89827-4). St Martin.

Nichole, Louis. Designer Accessories to Make for Your Home. Speiser, W., ed. LC 77-20530. (Illus.). 1978. pap. 7.95 (ISBN 0-8329-0181-4). New Century.

Parker, Dorothy. Ms. Pinchpenny's Book of Interior Design. 1979. 12.95 (ISBN 0-442-26558-1). Van Nos Reinhold.

Richards, Delphene & Bishop, Carolyn, eds. Home Decorating Guide. LC 73-11786. (Family Circle Books). (Illus.). 128p. 1976. 7.98x (ISBN 0-405-09843-X). Arno.

Roda, Janet. Fabric Decorating for the Home: One Hundred and Thirty Room-by-Room Projects. LC 76-14112. (Illus.). 1976. 19.95 (ISBN 0-8487-0422-3). Oxmoor Hse.

Roy, Doreen. Champagne Decorating on a Beer Budget. LC 76-55704. (Illus.). 1977. 10.95 (ISBN 0-8128-2202-1); pap. 6.95 (ISBN 0-8128-2203-X). Stein & Day.

Schram, Joseph. Successful Children's Rooms. Horowitz, Shirley, ed. LC 79-11967. (Successful Ser.). (Illus.). 1979. 13.95 (ISBN 0-912336-89-7); pap. 6.95 (ISBN 0-912336-90-0). Structures Pub.

Schreiber, Joanne. Sewing to Decorate Your Home. LC 77-16946. 1979. pap. 6.95 (ISBN 0-385-12560-7, Dolp). Doubleday.

Sunset Editors. Curtains, Draperies & Shades. LC 78-70270. (Illus.). 104p. 1979. pap. 4.95 (ISBN 0-376-01733-3, Sunset Bks). Sunset-Lane.

--Hot Tubs, Spas & Home Saunas. LC 78-70274. (Illus.). 80p. 1979. pap. 3.95 (ISBN 0-376-01242-0, Sunset Bks). Sunset-Lane.

--Indoor Plants: Decorating with. LC 79-90333. (Illus.). 80p. 1980. pap. 3.95 (ISBN 0-376-03341-X, Sunset Bks). Sunset-Lane.

Turner, William. How to Work with an Interior Designer. (Illus.). 160p. 1981. 19.95 (ISBN 0-8230-7260-6); pap. 12.95 (ISBN 0-8230-7262-2). Watson-Guptill.

Varney, Carleton. Be Your Own Decorator. LC 78-10242. 1979. pap. 9.95 (ISBN 0-87223-549-1, Dist. by Har-Row). Wideview Bks.

--Be Your Own Decorator. LC 78-10242. (Illus.). 1978. 17.95 (ISBN 0-87223-514-9, Dist. by Har-Row). Playboy.

Von Furstenberg, Egon & Fisher, Karen. The Power Look at Home: Decorating for Men. LC 79-26436. (Illus.). 1980. 25.00 (ISBN 0-688-03599-X). Morrow.

Williams, Adele. Thrift Shop Decorating. LC 75-31071. 1976. 9.95 (ISBN 0-87795-127-6); pap. 3.95 (ISBN 0-87795-132-2). Arbor Hse.

INTERIOR DECORATION–HISTORY

Ball, V. K. Architecture & Interior Design: Europe & America from the Colonial Era to Today, 2 vol. set. LC 79-24851. 890p. 1980. Set. 80.00 (ISBN 0-471-08721-1, Pub. by Wiley-Interscience); Set. pap. 50.00 (ISBN 0-471-08720-3); write for info. (ISBN 0-471-05161-6). Wiley.

Ball, Victoria K. Architecture & Interior Design: Europe & America from the Colonial Era to Today. LC 79-24851. 442p. 1980. 45.00 (ISBN 0-471-05161-6, Pub. by Wiley-Interscience); pap. 27.50 (ISBN 0-471-08722-X). Wiley.

Cook, Clarence. The House Beautiful: Essays on Beds & Tables, Stools & Candlesticks. LC 78-14326. (Illus.). 336p. 1980. Repr. of 1878 ed. 30.00 (ISBN 0-88427-029-7, Dist. by Caroline House). North River.

Editors of Better Homes & Gardens Books. New Decorating Book. (Illus.). 432p. (YA) 1981. 29.95 (ISBN 0-696-00092-X). BH&G.

Fry, Charles R. Art Deco Interiors in Color. LC 77-75887. (Illus.). 1977. pap. 5.00 (ISBN 0-486-23527-0). Dover.

Garrett, Elisabeth D. Antiques Book of American Interiors: The Colonial & Federal Styles. (Illus.). 160p. 1980. 17.95 (ISBN 0-517-54563-2). Crown.

Jarry, Madeleine. Chinoiserie: Chinese Influence on European Decorative Art: Seventeenth & Eighteenth Centuries. (Illus.). 256p. 1981. casebound 95.00 (ISBN 0-686-73660-5). Vendome.

Larrabee, Eric & Vignelli, Massimo. Knoll Design. (Illus.). 300p. 1981. 65.00 (ISBN 0-8109-0907-3). Abrams.

Mayhew, Edgar D. & Myer, Minor, Jr. Documentary History of American Interiors: From Colonial Era to Nineteen Fifteen. (Illus.). 304p. 1980. 45.00 (ISBN 0-684-16293-8). Scribner.

Rense, Paige, ed. Architectural Digest Historic Interiors. LC 77-84683. (The Worlds of Architectural Digest Ser.). (Illus.). 1979. 14.95 (ISBN 0-89535-033-5). Knapp Pr.

Schwartz, Marvin D. American Interiors 1675-1885: A Guide to the American Period Rooms in the Brooklyn Museum. LC 68-57682. (Illus.). 124p. (Orig.). 1968. pap. 4.95 (ISBN 0-87273-016-6). Bklyn Mus.

Sweeney, John A. The Treasure House of Early American Rooms. (Illus.). 1978. Repr. 5.98 (ISBN 0-517-24947-2). Crown.

Thornton, Peter. Seventeenth Century Interior Decoration in England, France & Holland. LC 77-91067. (Illus.). 439p. 1981. pap. 19.95x (ISBN 0-300-02776-1). Yale U Pr.

INTERIOR DECORATION–VOCATIONAL GUIDANCE

Ball, Victoria K. Opportunities in Interior Design. LC 76-51706. (Illus.). (YA) (gr. 8 up). 1977. PLB 6.60 (ISBN 0-8442-6524-1); pap. 4.95 (ISBN 0-8442-6523-3). Natl Textbk.

Greer, Michael. Your Future in Interior Design. (Careers in Depth Ser.). 1980. lib. bdg. 5.97 (ISBN 0-8239-0524-1). Rosen Pr.

INTERIOR DECORATION–EUROPE

Jarry, Madeleine. Chinoiserie: Chinese Influence on European Decorative Art: Seventeenth & Eighteenth Centuries. (Illus.). 256p. 1981. casebound 95.00 (ISBN 0-686-73660-5). Vendome.

Thornton, Peter. Seventeenth Century Interior Decoration in England, France & Holland. LC 77-91067. (Studies in British Art Ser.). (Illus.). 1978. 55.00x (ISBN 0-300-02193-3). Yale U Pr.

INTERIOR DECORATION–FRANCE

Fregnac, Claude & Andrews, Wayne. The Great Houses of Paris. (Illus.). 1979. 50.00 (ISBN 0-670-34972-0, The Vendome Pr.). Viking Pr.

Fry, Charles R. Art Deco Interiors in Color. LC 77-75887. (Illus.). 1977. pap. 5.00 (ISBN 0-486-23527-0). Dover.

Parker, James & Le Corbeiller, Clare. A Guide to the Wrightsman Galleries at The Metropolitan Museum of Art. LC 78-21154. 1979. pap. 3.95 (ISBN 0-87099-186-8). Metro Mus Art.

Thornton, Peter. Seventeenth Century Interior Decoration in England, France & Holland. LC 77-91067. (Studies in British Art Ser.). (Illus.). 1978. 55.00x (ISBN 0-300-02193-3). Yale U Pr.

INTERIOR DECORATION–GREAT BRITAIN

Ayres, James. The Shell Book of the Home in Britain: Decoration, Design & Construction of Vernacula Interiors, 1500-1850. (Shell Book Ser.). (Illus.). 240p. 1981. 25.00 (ISBN 0-571-11625-6, Pub. by Faber & Faber). Merrimack Bk Serv.

Beard, Geoffrey. Craftsmen & Interior Decoration in England Sixteen-Sixty to Eighteen-Twenty. LC 81-2648. (Illus.). 320p. 1981. 85.50x (ISBN 0-8419-0703-X). Holmes & Meier.

Garrett, Elisabeth D. Antiques Book of Victorian Interiors. (Illus.). 160p. 1981. 19.95 (ISBN 0-686-74645-7). Crown.

Hope, Thomas. Household Furniture & Interior Decoration: Classic Style Book of the Regency Period. (Illus.). 8.00 (ISBN 0-8446-0146-2). Peter Smith.

Johnson, David. Home Decorating. LC 78-74079. (Penny Pinchers Ser.). 1979. 2.95 (ISBN 0-7153-7751-5). David & Charles.

Loftie, M. J., et al. The Dining Room & the Drawing Room & the Bedroom & the Boudoir. Stansky, Peter & Shewan, Rodney, eds. LC 76-18321. (Aesthetic Movement & the Arts & Crafts Movement Ser.). 1978. lib. bdg. 44.00x (ISBN 0-8240-2461-3). Garland Pub.

Sullivan, Caroline. Making Soft Furnishings. LC 78-74080. (Penny Pincher Ser.). 1979. 2.95 (ISBN 0-7153-7752-3). David & Charles.

Thornton, Peter. Seventeenth Century Interior Decoration in England, France & Holland. LC 77-91067. (Studies in British Art Ser.). (Illus.). 1978. 55.00x (ISBN 0-300-02193-3). Yale U Pr.

INTERIOR DECORATION–JAPAN

Morse, Edward S. Japanese Homes & Their Surroundings. LC 76-157262. (Illus.). 1971. pap. 5.50 (ISBN 0-8048-0998-4). C E Tuttle.

--Japanese Homes & Their Surroundings. (Illus.). 8.50 (ISBN 0-8446-2620-1). Peter Smith.

--Japanese Homes & Their Surroundings. (Illus.). 1961. pap. 5.00 (ISBN 0-486-20746-3). Dover.

INTERIOR DECORATION–MEXICO

Shipway, Verna C. & Shipway, Warren. Mexican Interiors. 1979. 18.95 (ISBN 0-8038-0159-9). Hastings.

INTERIOR DECORATORS

Fisher, Richard B. Syrie Maugham. (Illus.). 104p. 1979. 22.00 (ISBN 0-7156-1307-3, Pub. by Duckworth England). Biblio Dist.

INTER-LIBRARY LOANS

see also Exchanges, Literary and Scientific

Palmour, Vernon E., et alcompiled by. A Study of the Characteristics, Costs, & Magnitude of Interlibrary Loans in Academic Libraries. LC 70-39344. 1972. lib. bdg. 15.00 (ISBN 0-8371-6340-4, PIL/). Greenwood.

Thomson, Sarah K. Interlibrary Loan Involving Academic Libraries, Acrl. LC 70-124575. (A.C.R.L. Monograph Ser.: No. 32). 1970. pap. text ed. 5.00 (ISBN 0-8389-3010-7). ALA.

--Interlibrary Loan Policies Directory. LC 74-32182. 496p. 1975. 9.00 (ISBN 0-8389-0197-2). ALA.

--Interlibrary Loan Procedure Manual. LC 71-125942. (Orig.). 1970. lib. bdg. 5.00 (ISBN 0-8389-3113-8). ALA.

INTERLINGUA (INTERNATIONAL AUXILIARY LANGUAGE ASSOCIATION)

see also English Language–Dictionaries–Interlingua

INTERLUDES, ENGLISH

Bernard, Jules E., Jr. Prosody of the Tudor Interlude. LC 69-15677. (Yale Studies in English Ser.: No. 90). 1969. Repr. of 1939 ed. 18.50 (ISBN 0-208-00782-2, Archon). Shoe String.

Hopper, Vincent F. & Lahey, Gerald B., eds. Medieval Mysteries, Moralities & Interludes. LC 61-18362. (gr. 10 up). 1962. pap. text ed. 3.95 (ISBN 0-8120-0135-4). Barron.

Loomis, Roger S. & Wells, Henry W., eds. Representative Medieval & Tudor Plays. LC 77-111109. (Play Anthology Reprint Ser). 1942. 20.50 (ISBN 0-8369-8202-9). Arno.

New Custom. LC 78-133716. (Tudor Facsimile Texts. Old English Plays: No. 46). Repr. of 1908 ed. 31.50 (ISBN 0-404-53346-9). AMS Pr.

Trial of Treasure. LC 70-133749. (Tudor Facsimile Texts. Old English Plays: No. 38). Repr. of 1908 ed. 31.50 (ISBN 0-404-53338-8). AMS Pr.

INTERMARRIAGE (RACIAL)

see Interracial Marriage

INTERMEDIATE SCHOOL DISTRICTS

see School Districts

INTERMEDIATE SCHOOLS

see Middle Schools

INTERMEDIATE STATE

see also Death; Eschatology; Future Life; Heaven; Hell; Purgatory; Soul

INTERMENT

see Burial

INTERMETALLIC COMPOUNDS

Kornilov, Ivan I. Chemistry of Metallides. LC 65-23386. 156p. 1966. 34.50 (ISBN 0-306-10758-9, Consultants). Plenum Pub.

Kripyakevich, I. P. Systematic Classification of Types of Intermetallic Structures. LC 64-24934. 35p. 1964. 20.00 (ISBN 0-306-10683-3, Consultants). Plenum Pub.

Wallace, W. E. Rare Earth Intermetallics. (Materials Science Ser.). 1973. 48.00 (ISBN 0-12-732850-5). Acad Pr.

Westbrook, J. H., ed. Intermetallic Compounds. LC 76-30325. 1977. Repr. of 1967 ed. lib. bdg. 34.50 (ISBN 0-88275-494-7). Krieger.

INTERMITTENT FEVER

see Malaria

INTERMUNICIPAL LAW

see Conflict of Laws

INTERNAL COMBUSTION ENGINES

see Gas and Oil Engines

INTERNAL CONVERSION (NUCLEAR PHYSICS)

see also Auger Effect; Beta Rays; Electrons–Emission; X-Rays

Hamilton, Joseph H., ed. Internal Conversion Processes. 1966. 55.50 (ISBN 0-12-321850-0). Acad Pr.

INTERNAL EAR

see Labyrinth (Ear)

INTERNAL FRICTION

Nowick, A. S. & Berry, B. S. Anelastic Relaxation in Crystalline Solids. (Materials Science Ser.). 1972. 45.00 (ISBN 0-12-522650-0). Acad Pr.

Postnikov, V. S., et al. Internal Friction in Metals & Alloys. LC 67-25402. 266p. 1967. 35.00 (ISBN 0-306-10795-3, Consultants). Plenum Pub.

INTERNAL FRICTION (LIQUIDS)

see Viscosity

INTERNAL MEDICINE

see also Cardiology; Endocrinology; Gastroenterology; Hematology; Nephrology

Advances in Internal Medicine & Pediatrics, Vol. 44. (Illus.). 190p. 1980. 52.00 (ISBN 0-387-09869-0). Springer-Verlag.

Blackshear, P. J. Key References in Internal Medicine. 1981. pap. text ed. write for info. (ISBN 0-443-08079-8). Churchill.

Bollet, Alfred J., ed. Harrison's Principles of Internal Medicine Patient Management Cases PreTest Self-Assessment & Review. (Illus.). 248p. (Orig.). 1980. 27.50 (ISBN 0-07-051647-2). McGraw Pretest.

Botez, M. I. & Reynolds, E. H., eds. Folic Acid in Neurology, Psychiatry, & Internal Medicine. LC 78-57243. 550p. 1979. text ed. 49.50 (ISBN 0-89004-338-8). Raven.

Bucher, Rue & Stelling, Joan G. Becoming Professional. LC 77-6257. (Sage Library of Social Research: Vol. 46). (Illus.). 296p. 1977. 20.00 (ISBN 0-8039-0607-2); pap. 9.95 (ISBN 0-8039-0608-0). Sage.

Burton, J. L. Aids to Postgraduate Medicine. 3rd ed. (Aids to...Ser.). (Illus.). 1978. pap. text ed. 7.00 (ISBN 0-443-01812-X). Churchill.

Callen, Jeffery P. Cutaneous Aspects of Internal Disease. 1980. 79.95 (ISBN 0-8151-1411-7). Year Bk Med.

Cluysenaer, O. J. & VanTongeren, J. H. Malabsorption in Coeliac Sprue. 1977. lib. bdg. 47.50 (ISBN 90-247-2000-1, Pub. by Martinus Nijhoff Netherlands). Kluwer Boston.

Cohen, Lawrence. A Synopsis of Medicine in Dentistry. 2nd ed. LC 77-24482. (Illus.). 254p. 1977. text ed. 10.50 (ISBN 0-8121-0608-3). Lea & Febiger.

Collins, R. Douglas. Illustrated Diagnosis of Localized Diseases. LC 74-6001. (Illus.). 224p. 1974. text ed. 45.00 (ISBN 0-397-50332-6, JBL-Med-Nursing). Har-Row.

Coodley, Eugene, et al, eds. Internal Medicine Update, Nineteen Seventy-Nine Nineteen Eighty. (Hahnemann Symposia). 416p. 1979. 45.50 (ISBN 0-8089-1172-4). Grune.

Faber, Knud H. Nosography. 2nd rev ed. LC 75-23706. (Illus.). 1976. Repr. of 1930 ed. 22.00 (ISBN 0-404-13258-8). AMS Pr.

Fishman, Mark C., et al. Medicine. Thaler, Malcolm S., ed. (Illus.). 500p. 1981. pap. text ed. 19.75 (ISBN 0-397-50436-5, JBL-Med-Nursing). Har-Row.

Fream, William C. Notes on Medical Nursing. 2nd ed. LC 77-1480. (Illus.). 1977. pap. text ed. 8.25 (ISBN 0-443-01612-7). Churchill.

Freinkel, Norbert, ed. Contemporary Metabolism: Analytical Reviews of Basic & Clinical Progress, Vol. 1. (Illus.). 497p. 1979. 29.50 (ISBN 0-306-40127-4, Plenum Pr). Plenum Pub.

Friedman, Eli, ed. Internal Medicine: Review & Assessment. Stillman, Richard M. 448p. 1981. 15.00 (ISBN 0-8385-4040-6). ACC.

Friedmann, Lawrence W. & Edagawa, Naoyushi. Treatment of Disordered Function from Pain to Sexual Complaints: An Introduction to the Edagawa Method. (Illus.). 192p. 1981. 20.00x (ISBN 0-682-49665-0, University). Exposition.

Greene, Bruce M. & Robertson, David, eds. Problems in Internal Medicine. (Orig.). 1980. pap. text ed. write for info. (ISBN 0-8391-1594-6). Univ Park.

Hemker, H. C. Prothrombin & Related Coagulation Factors. 1975. lib. bdg. 47.50 (ISBN 90-6021-236-3, Pub. by Leiden Univ Holland). Kluwer Boston.

Holsinger, James W., ed. Self-Assessment of Current Knowledge in Internal Medicine. 4th ed. LC 79-91971. 1980. pap. 16.50 (ISBN 0-87488-257-5). Med Exam.

Hurst, J. Willis & Hurst, John W., Jr. Hurst, the Heart Self-Assessment & Review with CME. (Illus.). 270p. (Orig.). 1980. 65.00 (ISBN 0-07-079066-3, HP). McGraw.

Ingelfinger, Franz J., et al, eds. Controversy in Internal Medicine II. LC 73-76267. (Illus.). 829p. 1974. 21.50 (ISBN 0-7216-5026-0). Saunders.

International Congress of Internal Medicine, 12th, Tel Aviv, 1974. Frontiers of Internal Medicine 1974: Proceedings. Blondheim, S. H., ed. xxii, 450p. 1976. 115.00 (ISBN 3-8055-2205-3). S Karger.

International Congress on Internal Medicine, 13th, Helsinki, August 1976. Internal Medicine: 1976 Topics: Proceedings. Louhija, A. & Valtonen, V., eds. (Illus.). 1977. 131.75 (ISBN 3-8055-2641-5). S Karger.

Isselbacher, K. J., et al. Harrison's Principles of Internal Medicine PreTest Self-Assessment & Review with CME. (Illus.). 290p. (Orig.). 1980. 70.00 (ISBN 0-07-079160-0). McGraw Pretest.

Isselbacher, Kurt J., et al. Update One: Harrison's Principles of Internal Medicine. 9th ed. (Illus.). 304p. 1981. text ed. 30.00 (ISBN 0-07-032131-0). McGraw.

Isselbacher, Kurt J., et al, eds. Harrison's Principles of Internal Medicine. 9th ed. (Illus.). 1980. text ed. 45.00 1 vol. ed. (ISBN 0-07-032068-3); text ed. 55.00 2 vol. ed. (ISBN 0-07-032069-1); medical review bk. 25.00 (ISBN 0-07-051657-X). McGraw Pretest.

Kleid, Jack J., et al. Textbook Study Guide of Internal Medicine. 3rd ed. (Medical Examination Review Book: Vol. 2A). 1976. pap. 8.50 spiral bdg. (ISBN 0-87488-123-4). Med Exam.

Krishnankutty, P. K. Textbook of Internal Medicine. 512p. 1979. 20.00x (ISBN 0-86125-282-9, Pub. by Orient Longman India). State Mutual Bk.

Lubin. Consultative Internal Medicine. 1981. 21.95 (ISBN 0-409-95011-4). Butterworth.

McCombs, Robert P. Fundamentals of Internal Medicine. 4th ed. (Illus.). 1971. 25.00 (ISBN 0-8151-5808-4). Year Bk Med.

MacLeod, John, ed. Davidson's Principles & Practice of Medicine. 12th ed. LC 77-30073. (Illus.). 1978. pap. text ed. 21.75 (ISBN 0-443-01566-X). Churchill.

Major, David, ed. Internal Medicine Update, 1980 to 1981. (Hahnemann Symposia Ser.). 1981. price not set (ISBN 0-8089-1388-3, 792658). Grune.

Mitchell, S. Weir. Doctor & Patient. LC 71-180584. (Medicine & Society in America Ser). 182p. 1972. Repr. of 1888 ed. 13.00 (ISBN 0-405-03961-1). Arno.

Patient Care Flow Chart Nineteen Eighty. 566p. 1980. 52.00 (ISBN 0-471-08162-0, Pub. by Wiley Med). Wiley.

Pieroni, Robert E. Internal Medicine Review. LC 75-21781. (Arco Medical Review Ser.). pap. text ed. 11.00 (ISBN 0-668-03881-0, 3881). Arco.

--Speciality Board Review: Internal Medicine. (Illus.). 160p. (Orig.). 1981. text ed. 14.00 (ISBN 0-668-04818-2, 4818). Arco.

Reller, L. Barth, et al. Clinical Internal Medicine. 1979. 16.95 (ISBN 0-316-73970-7). Little.

Rolleston, Humphrey D. Internal Medicine. LC 75-23653. (Clio Medica: No. 4). Repr. of 1930 ed. write for info. (ISBN 0-404-58904-9). AMS Pr.

Rose, Burton D. Clinical Physiology of Acid Base & Electrolyte Disorders. 1st ed. (Illus.). 1977. pap. text ed. 13.95 (ISBN 0-07-053621-X, HP). McGraw.

Sellink, J. L. Radiological Atlas of Common Diseases of the Small Bowel. 1976. lib. bdg. 95.00 (ISBN 90-207-0476-1, Pub. by Martinus Nijhoff Netherlands). Kluwer Boston.

Smith, Lloyd H., Jr. & Wyngaarden, James B., eds. Review of General Internal Medicine: A Self-Assessment Manual. LC 79-3922. (Illus.). 330p. 1980. pap. text ed. 14.95 (ISBN 0-7216-8419-X). Saunders.

Spivak, Jerry L. & Barnes, H. Verdain. Manual of Clinical Problems in Internal Medicine: Annotated with Key References. 2nd ed. LC 74-4944. 1978. text ed. 12.95 spiral bound (ISBN 0-316-80714-1). Little.

Stern, Neuton S. Rare Diseases in Internal Medicine. 592p. 1966. photocopy ed. spiral 58.75 (ISBN 0-398-01858-8). C C Thomas.

Stollerman, Gene H., ed. Advances in Internal Medicine, Vol. 27. Date not set. price not set (ISBN 0-8151-8297-X). Year Bk Med.

Stollerman, Gene H., et al, eds. Advances in Internal Medicine, Vol. 24. (Illus.). 1979. 38.00 (ISBN 0-8151-8294-5). Year Bk Med.

--Advances in Internal Medicine, Vol. 25. 1980. 38.50 (ISBN 0-8151-8295-3). Year Bk Med.

Thorn, et al, eds. Harrison's Principles of Internal Medicine. 8th ed. (Illus.). 1976. text ed. 45.00 1 vol. ed. (ISBN 0-07-064518-3, 64518-3, HP); text ed. 55.00 2 vol. ed. (ISBN 0-07-064519-1, 64519-1). McGraw.

Veith, Ilza, tr. The Yellow Emperor's Classic of Internal Medicine. 1966. 22.50x (ISBN 0-520-01296-8); pap. 6.95 (ISBN 0-520-02158-4, CAL238). U of Cal Pr.

Villaverde, Manuel M. Internal Medicine: Medical Examination Manual. 1979. pap. text ed. 14.95 (ISBN 0-442-25094-0). Van Nos Reinhold.

Wisch, Nathaniel, et al, eds. Internal Medicine Specialty Board Review. 6th ed. 1978. spiral bdg. 16.50 (ISBN 0-87488-303-2). Med Exam.

INTERNAL MIGRATION

see Migration, Internal

INTERNAL REVENUE

see also Income Tax; Inheritance and Transfer Tax; Licenses

Larson, Martin A. The I. R. S. Versus the Middle Class or How the Average Citizen Can Protect Himself Against the Fedral Tax Collector. LC 79-67271. (Orig.). 1980. 12.95 (ISBN 0-8159-5824-2); pap. 5.95 (ISBN 0-8159-5827-7). Devin.

Meier, E. J. Taxpayers, Politics, & the IRS! LC 79-66929. 1980. 7.95 (ISBN 0-533-04428-6). Vantage.

Rudman, Jack. Senior Excise Tax Investigator. (Career Examination Ser.: C-2419). (Cloth bdg. avail. on request). pap. 8.00 (ISBN 0-8373-2419-X). Natl Learning.

INTERNAL REVENUE LAW

Commerce Clearing House. U.S. Excise Tax Guide: 1981. 232p. 1981. 6.00 (ISBN 0-686-75939-7). Commerce.

Ferleger, Herbert R. David A. Wells & the American Revenue System 1865-1870. LC 77-7106. (Perspectives in American History Ser.: No. 32). Repr. of 1942 ed. lib. bdg. 19.50x (ISBN 0-87991-356-8). Porcupine Pr.

Kahn, Douglas A. & Waggoner, Laurence W. Provisions of the Internal Revenue Code & Treasury Regulations: 1981 Supplement. 1981. write for info. (ISBN 0-316-48205-6). Little.

Reams, Bernard D., Jr., ed. Internal Revenue Acts of the United States: 1909-1950, 144 vols. in 146 bks. LC 78-71405. 176000p. 1979. Repr. Set. lib. bdg. 5975.00 (ISBN 0-930342-69-0). W S Hein.

Rudman, Jack. Excise Tax Investigator. (Career Examination Ser.: C-972). (Cloth bdg. avail. on request). pap. 6.00 (ISBN 0-8373-0972-7). Natl Learning.

U.S. General Accounting Office. How the Internal Revenue Service Selects Individual Income Tax Returns for Audit. 1980. pap. 5.00 (ISBN 0-89499-007-1). Bks Business.

Wilson, J. Eugene. How to Fight the IRS & Win! Wilson, Caroline L., ed. LC 79-90658. (Illus.). 368p. 24.95 (ISBN 0-9601416-4-2); pap. 19.95 (ISBN 0-9601416-3-4). J C Print.

INTERNAL ROTATION (MOLECULAR)

see Molecular Rotation

INTERNAL SECURITY

see also Loyalty Oaths; Loyalty-Security Program, 1947-; Subversive Activities

Blum, Richard H., ed. Surveillance & Espionage in a Free Society. LC 72-85979. (Special Studies in U.S. Economic, Social & Political Issues). 1972. 28.00x (ISBN 0-275-28643-6); pap. text ed. 8.50x (ISBN 0-89197-957-3). Irvington.

Bowden, Tom. The Breakdown of Public Security: The Case of Ireland 1916-1921 & Palestine 1936-1939. LC 76-56682. (Sage Studies in Twentieth Century History: Vol. 8). (Illus.). 342p. 1977. 20.00 (ISBN 0-8039-9865-1); pap. 9.95 (ISBN 0-8039-9866-X). Sage.

Brown, Lester R. Redefining National Security. LC 77-86155. (Worldwatch Papers). 1977. pap. 2.00 (ISBN 0-916468-13-5). Worldwatch Inst.

Buzby, Walter J. & Paine, David. Hotel & Motel Security Management. LC 76-12555. 256p. 1976. 17.95 (ISBN 0-913708-24-0). Butterworth.

Caughey, John. In Clear & Present Danger: The Crucial State of Our Freedom. 1980. Repr. of 1958 ed. lib. bdg. 14.50x (ISBN 0-374-91339-0). Octagon.

Caughey, John W. In Clear & Present Danger. (Midway Reprint Ser). 224p. 1975. pap. 7.95x (ISBN 0-226-09799-4). U of Chicago Pr.

Clubb, O. Edmund. The Witness & I. LC 74-11385. 314p. 1975. 16.00x (ISBN 0-231-03859-3). Columbia U Pr.

Enloe, Cynthia. Ethnic Soldiers: State Security in a Divided Society. LC 79-5418. 270p. 1980. 19.00x (ISBN 0-8203-0507-3). U of Ga Pr.

Fernandez, Eduardo B., et al. Database Security & Integrity. LC 80-15153. (IBM Systems Programming Ser.). (Illus.). 288p. 1981. text ed. 18.95 (ISBN 0-201-14467-0). A-W.

Fisher, A. Security for Business & Industry. 1979. 17.95 (ISBN 0-13-798967-9). P-H.

Fund for the Republic, Inc. Digest of the Public Record of Communism in the United States. Grob, Gerald, ed. LC 76-46078. (Anti-Movements in America). 1977. lib. bdg. 43.00x (ISBN 0-405-09951-7). Arno.

Krapels, Edward N. Oil Crisis Management: Strategic Stockpiling for International Security. LC 80-13358. 192p. 1980. text ed. 15.00 (ISBN 0-8018-2374-9). Johns Hopkins.

Nader, L. R. Protecting Your Business Against Employee Thefts, Shoplifters & Other Hazards. LC 72-98094. 1977. pap. 2.00 (ISBN 0-87576-032-5). Pilot Bks.

Pfaltzgraff, Robert, Jr. & Lambert, Richard D., eds. National Security Policy for the 1980's. (The Annals of the American Academy of Political & Social Science: No. 457). 250p. 1981. 7.50 (ISBN 0-87761-266-8); pap. 6.00x (ISBN 0-87761-267-6). Am Acad Pol Soc Sci.

Reeves, Thomas C., ed. McCarthyism. LC 78-2879. (American Problem Studies). (Illus.). 144p. 1978. pap. text ed. 5.50 (ISBN 0-88275-674-5). Krieger.

Rorty, James. McCarthy & the Communists. LC 78-138179. 163p. 1972. Repr. of 1954 ed. lib. bdg. 15.00x (ISBN 0-8371-5636-X, ROCO). Greenwood.

Rudman, Jack. Supervising Security Officer. (Career Examination Ser.: C-2205). (Cloth bdg. avail. on request). pap. 10.00 (ISBN 0-8373-2205-7). Natl Learning.

Security Through Science & Engineering, Nineteen Eighty International Conference, September 23-26, 1980. Proceedings. 1980. 33.50 (ISBN 0-89779-042-1). U of Ky OES Pubns.

Theoharis, Athan. Seeds of Repression: Harry S. Truman & the Origins of McCarthyism. LC 71-116089. 256p. 1971. 6.95 (ISBN 0-8129-0169-X); pap. 2.95 (ISBN 0-8129-6283-4). Times Bks.

Wagner, Thomas J., et al. Basic Security Training Manual. 136p. 1979. text ed. 10.75 (ISBN 0-398-03949-6). C C Thomas.

Wilkins, Barry. The Internal Auditor's Information Security Handbook. 1979. pap. text ed. 12.00 (ISBN 0-89413-080-3). Inst Inter Aud.

INTERNALIZATION

see also Identification (Psychology)

INTERNATIONAL

Braunthal, Julius. History of the International: World Socialism Nineteen Forty-Three to Nineteen Sixty-Eight. LC 67-17667. 656p. 1980. lib. bdg. 40.75x (ISBN 0-89158-369-6). Westview.

Drachkovitch, Milorad M., ed. The Revolutionary Internationals, 1864-1943. 1966. 15.00x (ISBN 0-8047-0293-4). Stanford U Pr.

Foster, William Z. History of the Three Internationals: The World Socialist & Communist Movements from 1848 to the Present. LC 68-30822. (Illus.). 1968. Repr. of 1955 ed. lib. bdg. 34.25x (ISBN 0-8371-0076-3, FOTI). Greenwood.

Lademacher, Horst. Die Zimmerwalder Bewegung: Protokolle und Korrespondenz, 2 bande. 1967. 263.00x (ISBN 0-686-21244-4). Mouton.

Marx, Karl. The Civil War in France. 144p. 1934. 5.00 (ISBN 0-88286-035-6). C H Kerr.

Stekloff, G. M. History of the First International. 3rd ed. Paul, Eden & Paul, Cedar, trs. LC 68-10945. 1968. Repr. of 1928 ed. 12.50 (ISBN 0-8462-1040-1). Russell.

INTERNATIONAL ADMINISTRATION

see International Agencies; International Organization

INTERNATIONAL AFFAIRS AND CHRISTIANITY

see Christianity and International Affairs

INTERNATIONAL AFRICAN INSTITUTE

International African Institute. Cumulative Bibliography of African Studies, International African Institute,London Author Catalog, 2 vols. 1973. Set. lib. bdg. 170.00 (ISBN 0-8161-1045-X). G K Hall.

--Cumulative Bibliography of African Studies, International African Institute, London Classified Catalog, 3 vols. 1973. Set. lib. bdg. 255.00 (ISBN 0-8161-1076-X). G K Hall.

INTERNATIONAL AGENCIES

Here are entered works on public international organizations and agencies of international government. Particular organizations are entered under their respective names.

see also International Officials and Employees; International Organization; United Nations–Economic Assistance; United Nations–Technical Assistance

Abels, Harriette S. Future Government. Schroeder, Howard, ed. LC 80-14940. (Our Future World Ser.). (Illus.). 48p. (gr. 4 up). PLB 6.95 (ISBN 0-89686-082-5); pap. 3.25 (ISBN 0-89686-091-4). Crestwood Hse.

Agreements & Working Arrangements with Other International Organizations. (WMO Ser: No. 60). (Illus.). 1978. pap. 12.00 (ISBN 0-685-89406-1, W-374, WMO). Unipub.

Alexandrowicz, Charles H. Law Making Functions of the Specialized Agencies of the United Nations. 181p. 1973. text ed. 9.75x (ISBN 0-207-12740-9). Rothman.

Broad Terms for United Nations Programmes & Activities, 1979. 186p. 1980. pap. 13.00 (ISBN 0-686-68945-3, UN79/0/1, UN). Unipub.

California University - Committee On International Relations. Problems of War & Peace in the Society of Nations. facs. ed. LC 67-23188. (Essay Index Reprint Ser). 1937. 15.00 (ISBN 0-8369-0270-X). Arno.

Corbett, Percy E. Growth of World Law. LC 70-132236. 1971. 16.00 (ISBN 0-691-09223-0). Princeton U Pr.

Gruhn, Isebill V. Regionalism Reconsidered: The Economic Commission for Africa. LC 79-5060. (Special Studies on Africa). 1979. lib. bdg. 18.00x (ISBN 0-89158-576-1). Westview.

International Institute for the Unification of Private Law. Digest of Legal Activities of International Organizations & Other Institutions. 4th ed. LC 74-19327. 1980. 85.00 (ISBN 0-379-00525-5); suppplement 1977 15.00 (ISBN 0-379-00525-5). Oceana.

Jacobson, Harold K. Networks of Interdependence: International Organizations & the Global Political System. 1979. text ed. 19.95 (ISBN 0-394-32153-7). Knopf.

Jordan, Robert S., ed. International Administration: Its Evolution & Contemporary Applications. 1971. pap. 6.95x (ISBN 0-19-501462-6). Oxford U Pr.

Jutte, Rudiger. The Future of International Organization. 1981. 22.50 (ISBN 0-312-31476-0). St Martin.

Kay, David A. & Skolnikoff, Eugene B., eds. World Eco-Crisis: International Organizations in Response. LC 79-178153. 332p. 1972. 20.00 (ISBN 0-299-06151-5, 615); pap. 5.95x (ISBN 0-299-06154-X). U of Wis Pr.

Kirgis, Frederic L. Supplement to International Organizations in Their Legal Setting, Documents, Comments & Questions: 1981 Supplement. (American Casebook Ser.). 218p. 1981. pap. text ed. 7.95 (ISBN 0-686-74739-9). West Pub.

Koo, Wellington, Jr. Voting Procedure in International Political Organizations. LC 79-137253. Repr. of 1947 ed. 26.45 (ISBN 0-404-03774-7). AMS Pr.

Lawson, Ruth C., ed. International Regional Organizations: Constitutional Foundations. LC 74-10016. 387p. 1975. Repr. of 1962 ed. lib. bdg. 26.00x (ISBN 0-8371-7655-7, LARO). Greenwood.

Loveday, Alexander. Reflections on International Administration. LC 74-9168. 334p. 1974. Repr. of 1956 ed. lib. bdg. 17.25x (ISBN 0-8371-7618-2, LOIA). Greenwood.

Luard, Evan. International Agencies: The Emerging Framework of Interdependence. LC 76-2128. 1977. lib. bdg. 40.00 (ISBN 0-379-00686-3). Oceana.

Meerhaeghe, M. A. International Economic Institutions. 2nd ed. LC 75-179701. 1972. 22.50x (ISBN 0-312-42070-6). St. Martin.
Merillat, Herbert C., ed. Legal Advisors & International Organizations. LC 66-22029. 1966. 8.50 (ISBN 0-379-00294-9). Oceana.
The Organization Context of Development: Illuminating Paths for Wider Participation. 35p. 1980. pap. 5.00 (ISBN 92-808-0079-5, TUNU 043, UNU). Unipub.
Orr, David W. & Soroos, Marvin S., eds. The Global Predicament: Ecological Perspectives on World Order. LC 78-10207. 1979. 19.00 (ISBN 0-8078-1346-X); pap. 9.00x (ISBN 0-8078-1349-4). U of NC Pr.
Peaslee, Amos J. International Governmental Organizations: Constitutional Documents, Pts. 3 & 4. 3rd rev. ed. Xydis, Dorothy P., compiled by. 1979. lib. bdg. 146.00 (ISBN 90-247-2087-7, Pub. by Martinus Nijhoff Netherlands). Kluwer Boston.
Pelton, Joseph N. Global Communications Satellite Policy: INTELSAT, Politics & Functionalism. LC 74-77978. 183p. 1974. 14.50 (ISBN 0-912338-32-6); microfiche 11.50 (ISBN 0-912338-33-4). Lomond.
Rapaport, Jacques, et al. Small States & Territories: Status & Problems. LC 72-140128. (UNITAR Studies). 1971. 11.00 (ISBN 0-405-02237-9). Arno.
Report of the Eighteenth Conference on International Organizations for the Joint Study of Programmes. 28p. 1976. pap. 7.50 (ISBN 92-5-100037-9, F2063, FAO). Unipub.
Rubinstein, Alvin Z. Soviets in International Organizations: Changing Policy Toward Developing Countries, 1953-1963. 1964. 24.00 (ISBN 0-691-08717-2). Princeton U Pr.
Schwebel, Stephen M., ed. Effectiveness of International Decisions. LC 76-140512. 1971. 28.00 (ISBN 0-379-00462-3). Oceana.
Singh, Lalita P. Politics of Economic Cooperation in Asia: A Study of Asian International Organizations. LC 66-17956. 1966. 7.00x (ISBN 0-8262-0054-0). U of Mo Pr.
Stevens, Robert D. & Stevens, Helen C., eds. Reader in Documents of International Organizations. LC 73-93966. (Reader Ser. in Library & Information Science: Vol. 13). 1974. 21.00 (ISBN 0-910972-40-0). IHS-PDS.
Taylor, Paul. International Co-Operation Today: The European & the Universal Pattern. 1971. 19.95 (ISBN 0-236-17644-7, Pub. by Paul Elek). Merrimack Bk Serv.
Tharp, Paul A., Jr., ed. Regional International Organizations: Structures & Functions. LC 74-141782. 1971. text ed. 8.95 (ISBN 0-312-66920-8). St Martin.
Wallace, Don, Jr. & Escobar, Helga, eds. The Future of International Economic Organizations. LC 75-44942. (Special Studies). 1977. text ed. 23.95 (ISBN 0-275-22990-4). Praeger.
Weiss, Thomas G. International Bureaucracy: An Analysis of the Operation of Functional Global International Secretariats. LC 75-2. 160p. 1975. 19.95x (ISBN 0-669-99341-7). Lexington Bks.
White, Lyman C. International Non-Governmental Organizations: Their Purposes, Methods, & Accomplishments. LC 68-8340. (Illus.). 1968. Repr. of 1951 ed. lib. bdg. 16.25x (ISBN 0-8371-0266-9, WHIN). Greenwood.
Yearbook of International Organizations 1978-1979. 17th ed. 1123p. 125.00 (ISBN 0-686-74472-1). Gale.

INTERNATIONAL AGENCIES-DIRECTORIES
Angel, Juvenal L. Directory of International Agencies. 1970. 25.00 (ISBN 0-671-17027-9). Monarch Pr.
Annual International Congress Calendar, 1980. 20th ed. LC 60-1648. (Illus., Orig., Eng. & Fr.). 1980. pap. 47.50x (ISBN 0-8002-2393-4). Intl Pubns Serv.
Haas, Michael. Basic Documents of Asian Regional Organizations, 8 vols. LC 74-2248. 1979. 47.50 ea. (ISBN 0-379-00177-2). Oceana.
Peaslee, Amos J. International Governmental Organizations: Constitutional Documents, Pts. 3 & 4. 3rd rev. ed. Xydis, Dorothy P., compiled by. 1979. lib. bdg. 146.00 (ISBN 90-247-2087-7, Pub. by Martinus Nijhoff Netherlands). Kluwer Boston.
Yearbook of International Organizations: Latest Edition. 1979. 119.00 (ISBN 92-834-1241-9). Adler.

INTERNATIONAL AGREEMENTS
see International Obligations; Treaties

INTERNATIONAL AGRICULTURAL COOPERATION
Blau, G. International Commodity Arrangements & Policies. 1964. pap. 4.50 (ISBN 0-685-36304-X, F241, FAO). Unipub.
D'A. Shaw, Robert. Jobs & Agricultural Development. LC 79-145446. (Monographs: No. 3). 84p. 1970. 1.00 (ISBN 0-686-28692-8). Overseas Dev Council.
FAO General Commemorative Conference, 16 November 1970. Report. 1970. pap. 4.50 (ISBN 0-685-36328-7, F193, FAO). Unipub.
Goldberg, Ray A. International Agribusiness Coordination. (Concepts in Agribusiness Management Ser). 184p. 1980. 17.50 (ISBN 0-88410-284-X). Ballinger Pub.
Jaggi, E. Agricultural Co-Operatives & Associations in Switzerland. Morley, J. A., tr. 71p. 1974. 20.00x (ISBN 0-85042-008-3, Pub. by Plunkett Found England). State Mutual Bk.
Mosher, Arthur T. Technical Co-Operation in Latin-American Agriculture. LC 75-26310. (World Food Supply Ser). (Illus.). 1976. Repr. of 1957 ed. 27.00x (ISBN 0-405-07788-2). Arno.
Pearse, Andrew. Seeds of Plenty, Seeds of Want: A Critical Analysis of the Green Revolution. 280p. 1980. 22.50x (ISBN 0-19-877150-9). Oxford U Pr.
Plunkett Foundation for Co-Operatives Studies, ed. Year Book of Agricultural Co-Operation 1979. 219p. 1979. 40.00x (ISBN 0-85042-028-8, Pub. by Plunkett Found England). State Mutual Bk.
Royal Institute Of International Affairs. World Agriculture: An International Survey. Repr. of 1932 ed. 25.50 (ISBN 0-384-52303-X). Johnson Repr.

INTERNATIONAL ALPHABET
see Phonetic Alphabet; Transliteration

INTERNATIONAL AMERICAN CONFERENCES
see Inter-American Conferences

INTERNATIONAL AND MUNICIPAL LAW
Falk, R. A. Aftermath of Sabbatino. LC 65-19486. (Hammarskjold Forum Ser.: No. 7). 1965. 12.50 (ISBN 0-379-11807-6). Oceana.
Hendry, James M. Treaties & Federal Constitutions. LC 75-1361. 186p. 1975. Repr. of 1955 ed. lib. bdg. 15.00 (ISBN 0-8371-8010-4, HETF). Greenwood.
Masters, Ruth D. International Law in National Courts. LC 71-76631. (Columbia University. Studies in the Social Sciences: No. 370). Repr. of 1932 ed. 20.00 (ISBN 0-404-51370-0). AMS Pr.
Schachter, Oscar, et al. Toward Wider Acceptance of U N Treaties. LC 79-140127. (UNITAR Studies). 1971. 10.00 (ISBN 0-405-02236-0). Arno.
Schwebel, Stephen M., ed. Effectiveness of International Decisions. LC 76-140512. 1971. 28.00 (ISBN 0-379-00462-3). Oceana.
Triska, Jan F. & Slusser, Robert M. The Theory, Law & Policy of Soviet Treaties. 1962. 25.00x (ISBN 0-8047-0122-9). Stanford U Pr.
Vallat, F. A. International Law & the Practitioner. 1966. 13.50 (ISBN 0-379-11906-4). Oceana.

INTERNATIONAL ARBITRATION
see Arbitration, International

INTERNATIONAL ASSOCIATION OF BRIDGE AND STRUCTURAL IRON WORKERS
Burns, William J. Masked War: The Story of a Peril That Threatened the United States. LC 76-90168. (Mass Violence in America Ser). Repr. of 1913 ed. 11.50 (ISBN 0-405-01303-5). Arno.

INTERNATIONAL ASSOCIATION OF MACHINISTS
Perlman, Mark. Machinists: A New Study in American Trade Unionism. LC 61-16695. (Wertheim Publications in Industrial Relations Ser). (Illus.). 1961. 16.50x (ISBN 0-674-54050-6). Harvard U Pr.

INTERNATIONAL ATOMIC ENERGY AGENCY
IAEA Laboratory Activities: 5th Report. (Technical Reports Ser.: No. 90). (Illus., Orig.). 1968. pap. 5.50 (ISBN 92-0-175168-0, IDC90, IAEA). Unipub.
IAEA Research Contracts: 14th Annual Report. (Technical Reports Series, No. 154). 184p. (Orig.). 1974. pap. 17.25 (ISBN 92-0-175074-9, IDC154, IAEA). Unipub.
Regulations for Safe Transport or Radioactive Materials: Advisory Material. (Safety Ser.: No. 37). 190p. (Orig.). 1974. pap. 14.50 (ISBN 92-0-123273-X, ISP324, IAEA). Unipub.
Safeguards Techniques, 2 Vols. (Illus., Orig.). 1970. Vol. 1. pap. 44.00 (ISBN 92-0-070270-8, ISP260-1, IAEA); Vol. 2. pap. 35.75 (ISBN 92-0-070370-4, ISP260-2). Unipub.

INTERNATIONAL BANK FOR RECONSTRUCTION AND DEVELOPMENT
Cheng, Hang-Sheng. International Bond Issues of the Less-Developed Countries: Diagnosis & Prescription. 1969. 7.50x (ISBN 0-8138-0218-0). Iowa St U Pr.
Hurni, Bettina S. The Lending Policy of the World Bank in the Nineteen Seventies: Analysis & Evaluation. LC 79-16529. (Westview Special Studies in International Economies & Business). (Illus.). 170p. 1980. lib. bdg. 20.00x (ISBN 0-89158-681-4). Westview.
Mason, Edward S. & Asher, Robert E. The World Bank Since Bretton Woods. LC 73-1089. 1973. 21.95 (ISBN 0-8157-5492-2). Brookings.
Reid, Escott. Strengthening the World Bank. LC 73-87437. (Illus.). xx, 290p. 1973. 7.50x (ISBN 0-226-70934-5). U of Chicago Pr.

INTERNATIONAL BANKING
see Banks and Banking, International

INTERNATIONAL BIBLIOGRAPHY
see Bibliography, International

INTERNATIONAL BIMETALLISM
see Bimetallism

INTERNATIONAL BIOLOGICAL PROGRAM
Cooper, J. P., ed. Photosynthesis & Productivity in Different Environments. (International Biological Programme Ser.: No. 3). (Illus.). 550p. 1975. 99.00 (ISBN 0-521-20573-5). Cambridge U Pr.
Frankel, O. H. & Hawkes, J. G., eds. Crop Genetic Resources for Today & Tomorrow. LC 74-82586. (International Biological Programme Ser.: Vol. 2). (Illus.). 544p. 1975. 75.00 (ISBN 0-521-20575-1). Cambridge U Pr.
Golley, F. B., et al, eds. Small Mammals. LC 74-25658. (International Biological Programme Ser.: No. 5). (Illus.). 448p. 1975. 65.00 (ISBN 0-521-20601-4). Cambridge U Pr.
International Biological Program, National Research Council. Productivity of World Ecosystems. 1975. pap. 16.00 (ISBN 0-309-02317-3). Natl Acad Pr.
Japan International Biological Program Synthesis Series, Vols. 1-13. 3112p. 1975. Set. 270.00 (ISBN 0-86008-146-X, Pub. by U of Tokyo). Intl Schol Bk Serv.
Peterken, G. F. Guide to the Check Sheet of International Biological Programme Areas. (International Biological Program Handbook No. 4). (Illus.). 1968. pap. 3.50 (ISBN 0-632-04670-8, Blackwell). Mosby.
Pirie, N. W., ed. Food Protein Sources. LC 74-12962. (International Biological Programme Ser.: No. 4). (Illus.). 288p. 1975. 47.50 (ISBN 0-521-20588-3). Cambridge U Pr.
Van Dyne, G. M. Grasslands, Systems Analysis & Man. Breymeyer, A. I., ed. LC 77-28249. (International Biological Programme Ser.: No. 19). 1980. 140.00 (ISBN 0-521-21872-1). Cambridge U Pr.
Worthington, E. B., ed. The Evolution of IBP, Vol. 1. LC 75-2722. (International Biological Programme Ser.). (Illus.). 276p. 1975. 49.50 (ISBN 0-521-20736-3). Cambridge U Pr.

INTERNATIONAL BOUNDARIES
see Boundaries

INTERNATIONAL BOUNDARY AND WATER COMMISSION (U. S. AND MEXICO)
Hundley, Norris, Jr. Dividing the Waters: A Century of Controversy Between the United States & Mexico. LC 66-18468. 1966. 21.50x (ISBN 0-520-00586-4). U of Cal Pr.

INTERNATIONAL BROTHERHOOD OF TEAMSTERS, CHAUFFEURS, WAREHOUSEMEN AND HELPERS OF AMERICA
Brill, Steven. The Teamsters. 1979. pap. 2.75 (ISBN 0-671-82905-X). PB.
--The Teamsters. 1978. 11.95 (ISBN 0-671-22771-8). S&S.
Dobbs, Farrell. Teamster Bureaucracy. LC 76-52771. (Illus.). 1977. 17.00 (ISBN 0-913460-52-4); pap. 4.95 (ISBN 0-913460-53-2). Monad Pr.
--Teamster Politics. LC 75-17324. (Illus.). 256p. 1975. 17.00 (ISBN 0-913460-38-9); pap. 4.95 (ISBN 0-913460-39-7). Monad Pr.
--Teamster Power. LC 73-78115. 256p. 1973. 17.00 (ISBN 0-913460-20-6, Dist. by Path Pr NY); pap. 4.95 (ISBN 0-913460-21-4). Monad Pr.
Moldea, Dan E. The Hoffa Wars. 1979. pap. 2.75 (ISBN 0-441-34010-5, Charter Bks). Ace Bks.
A Profile of the Teamsters Union. 47p. 1961. pap. 4.50 (ISBN 0-87330-007-6). Indus Rel.

INTERNATIONAL BUSINESS ENTERPRISES
see also Corporations, Foreign; Foreign Licensing Agreements; Investments, Foreign
Adams, J. D. & Whalley, J. The International Taxation of Multinational Enterprise in Developed Countries. LC 77-13. 1977. lib. bdg. 19.95x (ISBN 0-8371-9530-6, ADI/). Greenwood.
Aggarwal, Raj Kumar. The Management of Foreign Exchange: Optimal Policies for a Multinational Company. rev. ed. Bruchey, Stuart, ed. LC 80-563. (Multinational Corporations Ser.). 1980. lib. bdg. 19.00x (ISBN 0-405-13359-6). Arno.
Aitken, Thomas. The Multinational Man: The Role of the Manager Abroad. LC 73-10602. 176p. 1973. 16.95 (ISBN 0-470-01793-7). Halsted Pr.
Ajami, Riad A. Arab Response to Multinationals. 1979. 20.95 (ISBN 0-03-048436-7). Praeger.
Alexandrides, C. G., ed. International Business Systems Perspectives. LC 72-619616. (Illus., Orig.). 1973. pap. 10.95 (ISBN 0-88406-000-4). Ga St U Busn Pub.
American Arbitration Association. New Strategies for Peaceful Resolution of International Business Disputes. LC 78-158817. 1972. 11.50 (ISBN 0-379-00066-0). Oceana.
Anderson, Dole A., et al, eds. International Business, Nineteen Seventy-Nine: A Selection of Current Readings. LC 76-635130. (Sixth in a Biennial Ser.). (Orig.). 1979. pap. 7.25 (ISBN 0-87744-160-X). Mich St U Busn.
Apter, David E. & Goodman, Louis W., eds. Multinational Corporation & Social Change. LC 75-1989. 225p. 1976. text ed. 21.95 (ISBN 0-275-23020-1); pap. 10.95 (ISBN 0-275-64580-0). Praeger.
Arpan, Jeffrey & Radebaugh, Lee. International Accounting & Multinational Enterprises. 400p. 1981. text ed. 21.50 (ISBN 0-88262-539-X). Warren.
Ayarslan, Solmaz D. A Dynamic Stochastic Model for Current Asset & Liability Management of a Multinational Corporation. Bruchley, Stuart, ed. LC 80-565. (Multinational Corporations Ser.). (Illus.). 1980. lib. bdg. 25.00x (ISBN 0-405-13362-6). Arno.
Banks, Robert F. & Stieber, Jack, eds. Multinationals, Unions, & Labor Relations in Industrialized Countries. LC 77-4463. (International Report Ser.: No. 9). 208p. 1977. 10.00 (ISBN 0-87546-064-X). NY Sch Indus Rel.
Barnet & Muller. Global Reach. 1976. 7.95 (ISBN 0-671-22104-3, Touchstone Bks). S&S.
Barnet, Richard J. & Muller, Ronald E. Global Reach: The Power of the Multinational Corporations. LC 74-2794. 1975. 15.95 (ISBN 0-671-21835-2); pap. 7.95 (ISBN 0-671-22104-3). S&S.
Basche, James R., Jr. U. S. Business Support for International Public Service Activities, Pt. 2: Support from Foreign Affiliates-Brazil. (Report Ser: No. 616). 25p. (Orig.). 1974. pap. 10.00 (ISBN 0-8237-0057-7). Conference Bd.
--U. S. Business Support for International Public Service Activities Part 2: Support from Foreign Affiliates-the Philippines. (Report Ser.: No. 657). 24p. (Orig.). 1975. pap. 20.00 (ISBN 0-8237-0076-3). Conference Bd.
--U. S. Support for International Public Service Activities, Pt. 2: Support from Foreign Affiliates-Mexico. (Report Ser: No. 617). 26p. (Orig.). 1974. pap. 10.00 (ISBN 0-8237-0059-3). Conference Bd.
Bassiry, Reza. Power Vs. Profit: Multinational Corporation-Nation State Interaction. Bruchey, Stuart, ed. LC 80-566. (Multinational Corporations Ser.). 1980. lib. bdg. 25.00x (ISBN 0-405-13363-4). Arno.
Beeth, Gunnar. International Management Practice: An Insider's View. LC 73-75669. 1973. 17.95 (ISBN 0-8144-5321-X). Am Mgmt.
Behrman, Jack N. Conflicting Constraints on the Multinational Enterprise: Potential for Resolution. LC 74-80755. 301p. 1974. pap. 5.50 (ISBN 0-685-56606-4, FMME 27, FMME). Unipub.
Behrman, Jack N. & Fischer, William A. Overseas R & D Activities of Transnational Companies. LC 79-25296. 336p. 1980. text ed. 30.00 (ISBN 0-89946-016-X). Oelgeschlager.
Bergsten, C. Fred, et al. American Multinationals & American Interests. LC 77-91786. 1978. 21.95 (ISBN 0-8157-0920-X); pap. 13.95 (ISBN 0-8157-0919-6). Brookings.
Biersteker, Thomas J. Distortion or Development? Contending Perspectives on the Multinational Corporation. 1979. text ed. 20.00x (ISBN 0-262-02133-1). MIT Pr.
Black, Robert & Blank, Stephen. Multinationals in Contention: Responses at Governmental & International Levels. LC 78-66971. (Report Ser.: No. 749). (Illus.). 1978. pap. 30.00 (ISBN 0-8237-0185-9). Conference Bd.
Blake, David H. & Lambert, Richard D., eds. The Multinational Corporation. new ed. LC 72-85688. (The Annals of the American Academy of Political & Social Science: No. 403). 300p. 1972. 7.50 (ISBN 0-87761-154-8); pap. 6.00 (ISBN 0-87761-153-X). Am Acad Pol Soc Sci.
Blank, Stephen, et al. Assessing the Political Environment: An Emerging Function in International Companies. (Report Ser.: No. 794). (Illus.). viii, 72p. (Orig.). 1980. pap. text ed. 45.00 (ISBN 0-8237-0230-8). Conference Bd.
Blin, Jean, et al. The Impact of Flexible Exchange Rates on International Business. 1981. write for info. (ISBN 0-89068-058-2). Natl Planning.
Boarman, Patrick M. & Schollhammer, Hans, eds. Multinational Corporations & Governments: Business-Government Relations in an International Context. LC 75-8402. (Illus.). 256p. 1975. text ed. 24.95 (ISBN 0-275-00900-9). Praeger.
Brooke, Michael Z. & Remers, H. Lee. The Strategy of Multinational Enterprise. 277p. 1979. text ed. 21.95 (ISBN 0-686-31211-2). Pitman Pub MA.

Brooke, Michael Z. & Remmers, H. Lee. International Management & Business Policy. LC 78-69612. (Illus.). 1978. Repr. of 1977 ed. text ed. 20.95 (ISBN 0-395-26505-3). HM.
Brooke, Michael Z. & Remmers, H. Lee, eds. The Multinational Company in Europe: Some Key Problems. LC 73-93992. (Illus.). 224p. 1974. Repr. of 1972 ed. text ed. 10.00x (ISBN 0-472-08182-9). U of Mich Pr.
Brooks, Michale Z. & Van Beusedom, Mark. International Corporate Planning. 323p. text ed. 24.95 (ISBN 0-273-01130-8). Pitman Pub MA.
Brookstone, Jeffrey M. The Multinational Businessman & Foreign Policy: Entrepreneurial Politics in East-West Trade & Investment. LC 76-12845. (Illus.). 1976. text ed. 22.95 (ISBN 0-275-23360-X). Praeger.
Browndorf, Eric & Reimer, Scott. Bibliography of Multinational Corporations & Foreign & Direct Investment. Simmonds, Kenneth R., ed. LC 78-24051. (Multinational Corporations Law). 1979. 75.00 (ISBN 0-379-20374-X). Oceana.
Bruchey, Stuart, ed. Multinational Corporations Series, 35 bks. 1980. Set. lib. bdg. 912.00x (ISBN 0-405-13350-2). Arno.
Buckley, Peter J. & Casson, Mark. The Future of the Multinational Enterprise. LC 76-6058. 120p. 1976. text ed. 21.00x (ISBN 0-8419-0272-0). Holmes & Meier.
Business International Corporation. International Business Report, 1980-81: Key Developments & Corporate Strategies. 352p. 1981. 39.50 (ISBN 0-03-059187-2). Praeger.
Carter, E. Eugene & Rodriguez, Rita M. International Financial Management. 2nd ed. (Illus.). 1979. text ed. 22.95 (ISBN 0-13-472977-3). P-H.
Cateora, Philip R. & Hess, John M. International Marketing, Bk. 270. 4th ed. 749p. Date not set. 20.50 (ISBN 0-686-74987-1). Dow Jones-Irwin.
Chandler, Alfred D., Jr. & Bruchley, Stuart, eds. Giant Enterprise: Ford, General Motors, & the Automobile Industry. LC 80-18483. (Multinational Corporations Ser.). 1980. Repr. of 1964 ed. lib. bdg. 25.00x (ISBN 0-405-13349-9). Arno.
Channon, Derek F. & Jalland, Michael. Multinational Strategic Planning. 1979. 35.00 (ISBN 0-8144-5575-1). Am Mgmt.
Clapham, Michael. Multinational Enterprises & Nation States. (The Stamp Memorial Lectures). 1975. pap. text ed. 2.75x (ISBN 0-485-16429-9, Athlone Pr). Humanities.
Clerin, Rose M. Taxation Planning for Middle East Operations. 1978. pap. 19.00 (ISBN 90-200-0515-4, Pub. by Kluwer Law Netherlands). Kluwer Boston.
Cleveland, Harlan, et al. The Overseas Americans. Bruchey, Stuart, ed. LC 80-558. (Multinational Corporations Ser.). 1980. Repr. of 1960 ed. lib. bdg. 29.00x (ISBN 0-405-13354-5). Arno.
Cohen, Benjamin I. Multinational Firms & Asian Exports. LC 74-17551. (Illus.). 192p. 1975. 15.00x (ISBN 0-300-01812-6). Yale U Pr.
Committee of Experts on Restrictive Business Practices. Mergers & Competition Policy: Proceedings. 71p. 1975. 5.00x (ISBN 92-64-11257-X). OECD.
Connor, John M. Market Power of Multinationals: A Quantitative Analysis of U. S. Corporations in Brazil & Mexico. LC 77-14302. (Praeger Special Studies). 1977. 28.95 (ISBN 0-03-023036-5). Praeger.
Coolidge, Philip, et al, eds. The OECD Guidelines for Multinational Enterprises: A Business Appraisal. LC 77-90874. (Orig.). 1977. pap. text ed. 10.00 (ISBN 0-935328-02-5). Intl Law Inst.
Cooperation in Documentation & Communication. Bibliographical Notes for Understanding the Transnational Corporations & the Third World. Strharsky, Harry & Riesch, Mary, eds. LC 75-8120. 1975. pap. 3.95 (ISBN 0-914958-03-8). CoDoC.
Corporate Investment & Acquisitions by Foreign Companies in the U. S. A. Proceedings of the 1978 Graham & Trotman Conference. 186p. 1978. 110.00x (ISBN 0-86010-156-8, Pub. by Graham & Trotman England). State Mutual Bk.
Creamer, Daniel, et al. Overseas Research & Development by United States Multinationals, 1966-1975: Estimates of Expenditures & a Statistical Profile. LC 76-8343. (Report Ser.: No. 685). (Illus.). 1976. pap. 15.00 (ISBN 0-8237-0119-0). Conference Bd.
Cronje, Suzanne, et al. The Lonrho Connections: A Multinational & Its Politics in Africa. LC 76-51608. (Illus.). 1977. 15.00 (ISBN 0-89475-000-3). Bellwether CA.
Crosswell, C. Legal Aspects of International Business. 1980. 40.00 (ISBN 0-379-20683-8). Oceana.
Cunningham, Gary M. An Accounting Research Framework for Multinational Enterprises. Dufey, Gunter, ed. LC 78-24444. (Research for Business Decisions Ser.: No. 5). 1978. 31.95 (ISBN 0-8357-0968-X, Pub. by UMI Res Pr). Univ Microfilms.
Daniels, John D., et al. International Business: Environments & Operations. 2nd ed. LC 78-67456. 1979. text ed. 19.95 (ISBN 0-201-01395-9); instr's manual avail. (ISBN 0-201-01396-7). A-W.
Davis, Stanley M., ed. Managing & Organizing Multinational Corporations. LC 77-1760. 1978. text ed. 55.00 (ISBN 0-08-021267-0); pap. text ed. 14.00 (ISBN 0-08-021266-2). Pergamon.
De Bodinat, Henri. Influence in the Multinational Corporation: The Case of Manufacturing. Bruchey, Stuart, ed. LC 80-567. (Multinational Corporations Ser.). 1980. lib. bdg. 29.00x (ISBN 0-405-13364-2). Arno.
Desatnick, Robert L. & Bennett, Margo L. Human Resource Management in the Multinational Company. LC 77-15803. 1978. 20.00x (ISBN 0-89397-031-X). Nichols Pub.
Devanna, Mary A. & Tichy, Noel M., eds. Organization Design for Multinational Corporations. (Praeger Special Studies Ser.). (Illus.). 1980. 20.95 (ISBN 0-03-051101-1). Praeger.
Directory of International Business Travel & Relocation. 1st ed. (Illus.). 900p. 1980. 125.00 (ISBN 0-8103-0997-1). Gale.
Doing Business in Saudi Arabia & the Arab Gulf States: 1978-79. 1979. 65.00 (ISBN 0-916400-06-9). Inter-Crescent.
Doz, Yves L. Government Control & Multinational Strategic Management: Power Systems & Telecommunication Equipment. LC 79-11793. (Praeger Special Studies Ser.). 298p. 1979. 24.95 (ISBN 0-03-049476-1). Praeger.
Dubin, Michael. Foreign Acquisitions & the Spread of the Multinational Firm. Bruchey, Stuart, ed. LC 80-572. (Multinational Corporations Ser.). (Illus.). 1980. lib. bdg. 19.00x (ISBN 0-405-13366-9). Arno.
Duerr, Michael & Roach, John M. Organization & Control of International Operations. (Report Ser.: No. 597). 1973. text ed. 15.00 (ISBN 0-8237-0182-4). Conference Bd.
Duerr, Michael G. & Greene, James. Foreign Nationals in International Management. (Managing International Business Ser.: No. 2). 1968. pap. 5.00 (ISBN 0-8237-0027-5). Conference Bd.
Dunning, John & Stepford, John. World Directory of Multinational Enterprises, 2 vols. 1500p. 1980. 195.00 set (ISBN 0-686-65762-4); Vol. 1. (ISBN 0-87196-440-6); Vol. 2. (ISBN 0-87196-441-4). Facts on File.
Dunning, John H. International Production & the Multinational Enterprise. (Illus.). 416p. 1981. text ed. 40.00x (ISBN 0-04-330319-6); pap. text ed. 18.50x (ISBN 0-04-330320-X). Allen Unwin.
Dunning, John H., ed. Economic Analysis & the Multinational Enterprise. 405p. 1981. Repr. of 1976 ed. text ed. 37.50x (ISBN 0-04-330246-7). Allen Unwin.
--The Multinational Enterprise. 1971. text ed. 36.00x (ISBN 0-04-330189-4). Allen Unwin.
Dymsza, W. Multinational Business Strategy. 1971. pap. text ed. 8.95 (ISBN 0-07-018570-0, C). McGraw.
Edge, Alfred G., et al. The Multinational Management Game. 1980. pap. 7.95x (ISBN 0-256-02362-X). Business Pubns.
Edwards, C. International Restrictive Business Practices. 1960. text ed. 12.25 (ISBN 0-02-908970-0). Free Pr.
Eells, Richard. Global Corporations: The Emerging System of World Economic Power. rev. ed. LC 75-18008. 1976. pap. text ed. 5.95 (ISBN 0-02-909270-1). Free Pr.
Eells, Richard, ed. International Business Philanthropy. LC 79-7338. (Studies of the Modern Corporation Ser.). (Illus.). 1979. 12.95 (ISBN 0-02-909260-4). Free Pr.
Eiteman, David K. & Stonehill, Arthur I. Multinational Business Finance. 2nd ed. LC 78-55818. 1979. text ed. 19.95 (ISBN 0-201-01744-X). A-W.
England, George W., et al. Organizational Functioning in Cross-Cultural Perspective. LC 78-31169. 1979. 17.50x (ISBN 0-87338-225-0). Kent St U Pr.
Fallon, N. Winning Business in Saudi Arabia. 61p. 1976. 65.00x (ISBN 0-86010-043-X, Pub. by Graham & Trotman England). State Mutual Bk.
Fatemi, Nasrollah S., et al. Multinational Corporations. 2nd rev. ed. LC 75-29728. 300p. 1976. 12.00 (ISBN 0-498-01879-2); pap. 4.95 (ISBN 0-498-04097-6). A S Barnes.
Fayerweather, John. Executive Overseas: Administrative Attitudes & Relationships in a Foreign Culture. LC 59-11259. 1959. 11.95x (ISBN 0-8156-2026-8). Syracuse U Pr.
--International Business Strategy & Administration. LC 78-5675. 1978. 22.50 (ISBN 0-88410-669-1). Ballinger Pub.
Fayerweather, John & Kapoor, Ashok. Strategy & Negotiation for the International Corporation: Guidelines & Cases. LC 76-10537. 1976. 17.50 (ISBN 0-88410-299-8). Ballinger Pub.
Federal Regulation of International Business, 2 vols. Date not set. 175.00 (ISBN 0-89834-028-4, 6325); optional 3rd vol. 50.00 (ISBN 0-686-75090-X). Chamber Comm US.
Feinschreiber, Robert, ed. Subpart F: Foreign Subsidiaries & Their Tax Consequences. LC 79-88374. 260p. 1979. 35.00 (ISBN 0-916592-28-6). Panel Pubs.
Feld, Werner J. Multinational Enterprises & U. N. Politics: The Quest for Codes of Conduct. (Pergamon Policy Studies). (Illus.). 1980. 28.00 (ISBN 0-08-022488-1). Pergamon.
Fieldhouse, David K. Unilever Overseas: The Anatomy of a Multinational. LC 78-20358. (Publications Ser.: No. 205). 1979. pap. 25.00 (ISBN 0-8179-7051-7). Hoover Inst Pr.
Finnie, David H. Desert Enterprise: The Middle East Oil Industry in Its Local Environment. Bruchey, Stuart, ed. LC 80-559. (Multinational Corporations Ser.). (Illus.). 1980. Repr. of 1958 ed. lib. bdg. 24.00x (ISBN 0-405-13356-1). Arno.
Fishwick, Francis. Multinational Companies & Economic Concentration in Europe. 1981. 26.95 (ISBN 0-03-059124-4). Praeger.
Franko, Lawrence. European Multinationals. 1976. text ed. 15.80 (ISBN 0-06-318049-9, IntlDept). Har-Row.
Franko, Lawrence G. The European Multinationals: A Renewed Challenge to American & British Big Business. LC 76-1155. 1976. 16.95 (ISBN 0-89223-032-0). Greylock Pubs.
Freeman, Orville. The Multinational Company: Instrument for World Growth. 144p. 1981. 18.95 (ISBN 0-03-059052-3). Praeger.
Friedman, Wolfgang & Kalmanoff, George, eds. Joint International Business Ventures. LC 61-7173. 1961. 25.00x (ISBN 0-231-02465-7). Columbia U Pr.
Friedmann, Wolfgang & Mates, Leo, eds. Joint Business Ventures of Yugoslav Enterprises & Foreign Firms. 192p. (Orig.). 1968. pap. 10.00x (ISBN 0-8377-0526-6). Rothman.
Frith Overseas Research Ltd. Winning Business in Egypt. 98p. 1978. 99.00x (ISBN 0-86010-121-5, Pub. by Graham & Trotman England). State Mutual Bk.
Frommel, S. N. Taxation of Branches & Subsidiaries in Western Europe, Canada & the USA. 1978. pap. 34.00 (ISBN 90-200-0508-1, Pub. by Kluwer Law Netherlands). Kluwer Boston.
Functioning of the Multinational Corporation: A Global Comparative Study. (Policy Studies). Date not set. 20.01 (ISBN 0-08-025087-4). Pergamon.
George, Abraham M. Foreign Exchange Management & the Multinational Corporation: A Manager's Guide. LC 78-19738. 1978. 28.95 (ISBN 0-03-046641-5). Praeger.
Germidis, Dimitri, ed. International Subcontracting: A New Form of Investment. (Illus.). 227p. (Orig.). 1981. pap. text ed. 13.50x (ISBN 92-64-12129-3, 41-80-08-1). OECD.
Ghertman, M. & Leontiades, J. European Research in International Business. 1978. 46.50 (ISBN 0-444-85089-9, North-Holland). Elsevier.
--European Research in International Business. 1978. 46.50 (ISBN 0-444-85089-9, North-Holland). Elsevier.
Gilpin, Robert G., Jr. U. S. Power & the Multinational Corporation: The Political Economy of Direct Foreign Investment. LC 75-7265. 1975. 10.95x (ISBN 0-465-08951-8). Basic.
Gladwin, Thomas N. Environment, Planning & the Multinational Corporation. Altman, Edward I. & Walter, Ingo, eds. LC 76-10400. (Contemporary Studies in Economic & Financial Analysis: Vol. 8). 350p. 1977. lib. bdg. 30.00 (ISBN 0-89232-014-1). Jai Pr.
Gladwin, Thomas N. & Walter, Ingo. Multinationals Under Fire: Lessons in the Management of Conflict. LC 79-21741. 689p. 1980. 38.50x (ISBN 0-471-01969-0, Pub. by Wiley-Interscience). Wiley.
Goehle, Donna G. Decision Making in Multinational Corporations. Dufey, Gunter, ed. (Research for Business Decisions: No. 18). 237p. 1980. 31.95 (ISBN 0-8357-1102-1, Pub. by UMI Res Pr). Univ Microfilms.
Gonzalez, Richard F. & Negandhi, Anant R. United States Overseas Executive: His Orientations & Career Patterns. LC 66-64923. 1967. pap. 2.00 (ISBN 0-87744-078-6). Mich St U Busn.
Grewlich, Klaus W. Transnational Enterprises in a New International System. 240p. 1981. 42.50 (ISBN 90-286-0650-5). Sijthoff & Noordhoff.
Grieves, Forest L., ed. Transnationalism in World Politics & Business. LC 79-1397. (Pergamon Policy Studies). 240p. 1979. 33.00 (ISBN 0-08-023892-0). Pergamon.
Grunberg, Leon. Failed Multinational Ventures. LC 80-8364. (Illus.). 1981. write for info. (ISBN 0-669-04032-0). Lexington Bks.
Gunnemann, Jon P., ed. The Nation-State & Transnational Corporations in Conflict. LC 75-3623. (Special Studies). 1975. pap. 3.50 (ISBN 0-685-99395-7). Coun Rel & Intl.
Gunter, Hans. Transnational Industrial Relations. 1972. 27.50 (ISBN 0-312-81480-1). St Martin.
Handbook of International Trade & Development Statistics: Supplement 1980. 33.00 (ISBN 0-686-75223-6, E/F.80.I I.D. 10). UN.
Haner, F. T. Global Business Strategy for the Nineteen Eighties. LC 80-12524. 244p. 1980. 24.95 (ISBN 0-03-047196-6). Praeger.
Harrington, Fred H. God, Mammon, & the Japanese: Dr. Horace N. Allen & Korean-American Relations, 1884 to 1905. Bruchey, Stuart, ed. LC 80-560. (Multinational Corporations Ser.). (Illus.). 1980. Repr. of 1944 ed. lib. bdg. 35.00x (ISBN 0-405-13357-X). Arno.
Hawkins, Robert G., ed. Research in International Business & Finance, Vol. 1. 330p. 1979. 37.50 (ISBN 0-89232-031-1). Jai Pr.
Hazari, Bharat R. The Pure Theory of International Trade & Distortions. LC 78-9092. 1978. 30.95 (ISBN 0-470-26430-6). Halsted Pr.
Hedlund, Gunnar & Otterbeck, Lars. The Multinational Corporation, the Nation State & the Trade Unions: An European Perspective. LC 76-42447. (Illus.). 1977. 17.50x (ISBN 0-87338-198-X, Pub. by Comparative Adm. Research Institute). Kent St U Pr.
Heenan, David A. & Perlmutter, Howard V. Multinational Organization Development. 1978. pap. text ed. 6.50 (ISBN 0-201-02953-7). A-W.
Heller, Kenneth H. The Impact of U. S. Income Taxation on the Financing & Earnings Remittance Decisions of U. S.-Based Multinational Firms with Controlled Foreign Corporations. Bruchey, Stuart, ed. LC 80-575. (Multinational Corporations Ser.). (Illus.). 1980. lib. bdg. 35.00x (ISBN 0-405-13368-5). Arno.
Hellinger, Stephen H. & Hellinger, Douglas A. Unemployment & the Multinationals: A Strategy for Technological Change in Latin America. 1976. 13.95 (ISBN 0-8046-9126-6, National University Pub). Kennikat.
Hellman, Rainer. Transnational Control of Multinational Corporations. LC 77-7342. (Praeger Special Studies). 1977. text ed. 21.95 (ISBN 0-03-021941-8). Praeger.
Henley, Donald S., compiled by. International Business-1975: A Selection of Current Readings. LC 76-635130. x, 423p. 1975. pap. 6.00 (ISBN 0-87744-130-8). Mich St U Busn.
Henning, Charles N., et al. International Financial Management. (Illus.). 1978. text ed. 20.50x (ISBN 0-07-028175-0, C); instructor's manual 4.95 (ISBN 0-07-028176-9). McGraw.
Hernes, Helga, ed. The Multinational Corporation: A Guide to Information Sources. LC 73-17509. (International Relations Information Guide Series: Vol. 4). 1977. 36.00 (ISBN 0-8103-1327-8). Gale.
Hershfield, David C. The Multinational Union Challenges the Multinational Company. (Report Ser.: No. 658). 40p. (Orig.). 1975. pap. 20.00 (ISBN 0-8237-0077-1). Conference Bd.
Hildebrandt, Herbert W., ed. International Business Communication: Theory, Practice, Teaching Throughout the World. (Michigan International Business Studies: No. 17). (Illus.). 170p. (Orig.). 1981. pap. price not set (ISBN 0-87712-213-X). U Mich Busn Div Res.
Hood, Neil & Young, Stephen. The Economics of Multinational Enterprise. (Illus.). 1979. pap. text ed. 19.95x (ISBN 0-582-44388-1). Longman.
Horst, Thomas. Income Taxation & Competitiveness in the United States, West Germany, France, the United Kingdom & Japan. LC 77-90041. (Committee on Changing International Realities Ser.). 48p. (Orig.). 1977. pap. 3.00 (ISBN 0-89068-042-6). Natl Planning.
Hulbert, James M. & Brandt, William K. Managing the Multinational Subsidiary. LC 80-23924. 1980. 22.95 (ISBN 0-03-057436-6). HR&W.
Hymer, S. The Multinational Corporation. Cohen, R. B., et al, eds. LC 79-52327. (Illus.). 1979. 39.50 (ISBN 0-521-22695-3). Cambridge U Pr.
Ibrahim A. Al-Moneef. Transfer of Management Technology to Developing Nations: The Role of Multinational Oil Firms in Saudi Arabia. Brouchey, Stuart, ed. LC 80-564. (Multinational Corporations Ser.). 1980. lib. bdg. 45.00x (ISBN 0-405-13361-8). Arno.
Ijalaye, David A. The Extension of Corporate Personality in International Law. 1978. 27.50 (ISBN 0-379-20328-6). Oceana.

International Business Unit, Dept. of Management Science, U. of Manchester Institute of Science & Technology. International Business Bibliography. LC 76-27166. (Reference Library of Social Science Ser.: Vol. 36). 1977. lib. bdg. 47.00 (ISBN 0-8240-9899-4). Garland Pub.

International Fiscal Association. Work in Intergovernmental Organizations on Transnational Companies. (Congress Seminar Series of the Inter-National Fiscal Association: No. 1). 1979. pap. 16.00 (ISBN 90-200-0491-3, Pub. by Kluwer Law Netherlands). Kluwer Boston.

International Labour Office. Employment Effects of Multinational Enterprises in Industrialised Countries. ix, 100p. (Orig.). 1981. pap. 4.40 (ISBN 92-2-102741-4). Intl Labour Office.

International Principles & Guidelines on Social Policy for Multinational Enterprises: Thier Usefulness & Feasibility. 1976. 7.15 (ISBN 92-2-101477-0). Intl Labour Office.

Irish, Donald P., ed. Multinational Corporations in Latin America: Private Rights & Public Responsibilities. LC 77-620055. (Papers in International Studies: Latin America: No. 2). (Illus.). 1977. pap. 9.00x (ISBN 0-89680-067-9). Ohio U Ctr Intl.

Jacoby, Neil H., et al. Bribery & Extortion in World Business. LC 77-6942. (Studies of the Modern Corporation). 1977. 12.95 (ISBN 0-02-916000-6). Free Pr.

Jadwani, Hassanand T. Some Aspects of the Multinational Corporation's Exposure to the Exchange Rate Risk. Bruchey, Stuart, ed. LC 80-576. (Multinational Corporations Ser.). (Illus.). 1980. lib. bdg. 18.00x (ISBN 0-405-13369-3). Arno.

Jeannet, Jean-Pierre. Transfer of Technology within Multinational Corporations: An Exploratory Analysis. Bruchey, Stuart, ed. LC 80-577. (Multinational Corporations Ser.). 1980. lib. bdg. 20.00x (ISBN 0-405-13370-7). Arno.

Jilling, Michael. Foreign Exchange Risk Management in U. S. Multinational Corporations. LC 78-24052. (Research for Business Decisions Ser.: No. 6). 1978. 27.95 (ISBN 0-8357-0952-3). Univ Microfilms.

Joyner's Guide to Official Washington for Doing Business Overseas. 364p. 1981. cancelled (ISBN 0-08-025108-0, JOY 3, Joyner's). Unipub.

Kapoor, A. International Business Negotiations: A Study in India. LC 70-114622. 361p. 1973. 12.00 (ISBN 0-87850-016-2); pap. 6.00x (ISBN 0-87850-017-0). Darwin Pr.

Kapoor, A., ed. Asian Business & Environment in Transition: Selected Readings & Essays. LC 73-20719. 667p. 1976. 9.95x (ISBN 0-87850-020-0). Darwin Pr.

Kapoor, Ashok, ed. International Business in the Middle East: Case Studies. (Special Studies in International Economics & Business). 1979. lib. bdg. 20.00x (ISBN 0-89158-257-6). Westview.

Katzan, Harry, Jr. Multinational Computer Systems: An Introduction to Transnational Data Flow & Data Regulation. (Van Nostrand Reinhold International Series on Data Communications & Networks). 224p. 1980. text ed. 16.95 (ISBN 0-442-21573-8). Van Nos Reinhold.

Keagan, Warren J. Mulitnational Marketing Management. 2nd ed. (Illus.). 1980. text ed. 22.00 (ISBN 0-13-605055-7). P-H.

Kelly, Marie W. Foreign Investment Evaluation Practices of U. S. Multinational Corporations. Dufey, Gunter, ed. LC 81-4714. (Research for Business Decisions: No. 40). 240p. 1981. 31.95 (ISBN 0-8357-1183-8, Pub. by UMI Res Pr). Univ Microfilms.

Kindleberger, Charles P., ed. International Corporation: A Symposium. 1970. pap. 7.95x (ISBN 0-262-61014-0). MIT Pr.

Kolde, E. International Business Enterprise. 2nd ed. LC 78-37518. (Illus.). 672p. 1973. ref. ed. 22.95 (ISBN 0-13-472381-3). P-H.

Kolde, Endel. The Pacific Quest: The Concept & Scope of an Oceanic Community. LC 76-41117. (Pacific Rim Research Series: No. 1). 1976. 17.95 (ISBN 0-669-00978-4). Lexington Bks.

Konz, Leo E. The International Transfer of Commercial Technology: The Role of the Multinational Corporation. Bruchey, Stuart, ed. LC 80-580. (Multinational Corporations Ser.). (Illus.). 1980. lib. bdg. 20.00x (ISBN 0-405-13372-3). Arno.

Kugel, Yerachmiel & Gruenberg, Gladys. International Payoffs: A Dilemma for Business. LC 76-48404. 1977. 18.95 (ISBN 0-669-01150-9). Lexington Bks.

--Selected Readings on International Payoffs. LC 76-48404. 1977. 19.95 (ISBN 0-669-01458-3). Lexington Bks.

Kujawa, D. Employment Effects of Multinational Enterprises: The Case of the United States. International Labour Office, ed. (Research on Employment Effects of Multinational Enterprises. Working Papers Ser.: No. 12). 53p. (Orig.). 1980. pap. 8.55 (ISBN 9-2210-2276-5). Intl Labour Office.

Kujawa, Duane, ed. American Labor & the Multinational Corporation. LC 72-85977. (Special Studies in International Economics & Development). 1973. 39.50x (ISBN 0-275-28717-3). Irvington.

Kumar, Krishna, ed. Transnational Enterprises: Their Impact on Third World Secieties & Cultures. (Westview Special Studies in International Business & Economics). (Illus.). 400p. 1980. lib. bdg. 27.75x (ISBN 0-89158-852-3). Westview.

Kumar, Krishna & McLeod, Maxwell G., eds. Multinationals from Developing Countries. LC 80-8531. 1981. 22.95 (ISBN 0-669-04113-0). Lexington Bks.

Kuusi, Juha. Host State & the Transnational Corporation. 1980. text ed. 31.50 (ISBN 0-566-00249-3, Pub. by Gower Pub Co England). Renouf.

Lall, Sanjaya. The Multinational Corporation. 224p. 1980. 32.50 (ISBN 0-8419-5083-0). Holmes & Meier.

LaPalombara, Joseph & Blank, Stephen. Multinational Corporations & Developing Countries. LC 79-92481. (Report Ser.: No. 767). (Illus.). xiv, 215p. (Orig.). 1980. pap. text ed. 30.00 (ISBN 0-8237-0203-0). Conference Bd.

--Multinational Corporations in Comparative Perspective. LC 77-83253. (Report Ser.: No. 725). (Illus.). 1977. pap. 15.00 (ISBN 0-8237-0159-X). Conference Bd.

Lea, Sperry & Webley, Simon. Multinational Corporations in Developed Countries: A Review of Recent Research & Policy Thinking. LC 73-77813. 88p. 1973. 2.00 (ISBN 0-902594-07-9). Natl Planning.

Ledogar, Robert J. Hungry for Profits: U. S. Food & Drug Multinationals in Latin America. LC 75-39985. (International Documentation Ser: No. 70). 1976. 7.95 (ISBN 0-89021-034-9); pap. 5.95 (ISBN 0-89021-038-1). IDOC.

Lees, F. A. International Banking & Finance. LC 73-11884. 419p. 1974. text ed. 36.95 (ISBN 0-470-52273-9). Halsted Pr.

Levinson, Charles. International Trade Unionism. (Ruskin House Series in Trade Union Studies). 1972. text ed. 15.95x (ISBN 0-04-331049-4). Allen Unwin.

Liebhaberg, Bruno. Industrial Relations & Multinational Corporations in Europe. 107p. 1981. 26.95 (ISBN 0-03-059128-7). Praeger.

Lietaer, Bernard A. The Role of European Multinationals in Latin America: The Positive Sum Game. LC 79-91943. (Praeger Special Studies Ser.). 298p. 1980. 24.95 (ISBN 0-03-046251-7). Praeger.

Logar, Cyril M. Location of Responsibility for Product Policy Decisions of United States-Based Multinational Firms Manufacturing Consumer Goods. Bruchey, Stuart, ed. LC 80-581. (Multinational Corporations Ser.). (Illus.). 1980. lib. bdg. 20.00x (ISBN 0-405-13373-1). Arno.

Long, Frank. Restrictive Business Practices, Transnational Corporations & Development. (Dimensions of International Business Ser.). 192p. 1981. lib. bdg. 19.00 (ISBN 0-89838-057-X, Pub. by Martinus Nijhoff). Kluwer Boston.

Macaluso, Donald G. The Financial Advantage of Multinational Firm During Tight Credit Periods in Host Countries. Bruchey, Stuart, ed. LC 80-582. (Multinational Corporations Ser.). 1980. lib. bdg. 15.00x (ISBN 0-405-13374-X). Arno.

Madden, Carl H., ed. The Case for the Multinational Corporation. LC 76-12863. (Special Studies). 1976. text ed. 25.95 (ISBN 0-275-23980-2). Praeger.

Madsen, Axel. Private Power: Multinational Corporations for the Survival of Our Planet. LC 80-19372. 256p. 1980. 12.95 (ISBN 0-688-03735-6). Morrow.

Martyn, Howe. Multinational Business Management. LC 75-116682. 1970. 32.50x (ISBN 0-669-58818-0). Irvington.

Mascarenhas, Oswald A. Towards Measuring the Technological Impact of Multinational Corporations in the Less Developed Countries. Bruchey, Stuart, ed. LC 80-583. (Multinational Corporations Ser.). 1980. lib. bdg. 35.00x (ISBN 0-405-13375-8). Arno.

Masini, Jean, et al. Multinationals in Africa: A Case Study of the Ivory Coast. LC 78-19462. (Praeger Special Studies). 1978. 23.95 (ISBN 0-03-046256-8). Praeger.

Mason, R. H., et al. The Economics of International Business. 464p. 1981. Repr. of 1975 ed. text ed. 23.50 (ISBN 0-89874-248-X). Krieger.

Mason, R. Hal, ed. International Business in the Pacific Basin. LC 78-346. 1978. 19.95 (ISBN 0-669-02189-X). Lexington Bks.

Mason, R. Hal, et al. International Business. 2nd ed. LC 80-23483. (Management & Administration Ser.). 428p. 1981. text ed. 22.95 (ISBN 0-471-06217-0). Wiley.

Mathewson, G. F. & Quirin, G. D. Fiscal Transfer Pricing in Multinational Corporations. (Ontario Economic Council Research Studies). (Orig.). 1979. pap. 10.00 (ISBN 0-8020-3360-1). U of Toronto Pr.

Matthews, Harry G. Multinational Corporations & Black Power. 136p. 1976. text ed. 11.25 (ISBN 0-87073-776-7). Schenkman.

May, Herbert K. The Multinational Corporations in Latin America. 1977. pap. 8.25 (ISBN 0-685-79717-1, CoA). Unipub.

Mekeirle, Joseph O. Multinational Corporations: The ECISM Guide to Information Sources. 71.95 (ISBN 0-03-046261-4). Praeger.

Molineu, Harold. Multinational Corporations & International Investment in Latin America: A Selected Bibliography. LC 77-620052. (Papers in International Studies: Latin America: No. 3). 1977. pap. 9.00x (ISBN 0-89680-068-7). Ohio U Ctr Intl.

Moore, Russell M. Multinational Corporations & the Regionalization of the Latin American Automotive Industry. Bruchey, Stuart, ed. LC 80-584. (Multinational Corporations Ser.). 1980. lib. bdg. 29.00x (ISBN 0-405-13376-6). Arno.

Moran, Theodore H. Multinational Corporations & the Politics of Dependence: Copper in Chile. LC 74-2973. (Harvard University Center for International Affairs, Ser.). 320p. 1975. 21.00 (ISBN 0-691-04204-7); pap. 6.95 (ISBN 0-691-00359-9). Princeton U Pr.

Mueller, Gerhard G. & Choi, Frederick D. Introduction to Multinational Accounting. (Illus.). 1978. ref. 21.95 (ISBN 0-13-489302-6). P-H.

Multinationals from Small Countries. 1977. 20.00x (ISBN 0-262-01050-X). MIT Pr.

Multinationals in Western Europe: The Industrial Relations Experience. 2nd ed. 1976. 10.00 (ISBN 92-2-101476-2). Intl Labour Office.

Murray, Robin. Multinationals Beyond the Market. 344p. 1981. 34.95 (ISBN 0-470-27240-6). Halsted Pr.

Myers, Desaix, III, et al. U. S. Business in South Africa: The Economic, Political & Moral Issues. LC 79-3638. 392p. 1980. 17.50x (ISBN 0-253-11486-1). Ind U Pr.

Nair, Basskaran. Mass Media & the Transnational Corporation: A Study of Media-Corporate Relationship & Its Consequencees on the Third World. 180p. 1981. 18.00 (ISBN 9971-69-005-5, Pub. by Singapore U Pr); pap. 9.50 (ISBN 9971-69-022-5, Pub. by Singapore U Pr). Ohio U Pr.

Negandhi, Anant R. Quest for Survival & Growth: A Comparative Study of American, European, & Japanese Multinationals. LC 78-71603. 1979. 29.95 (ISBN 0-03-046416-1). Praeger.

Newbould, Gerald D., et al. Going International: The Experience of Smaller Companies Overseas. LC 78-15729. 1978. 30.95 (ISBN 0-470-26493-4). Halsted Pr.

Newfarmer, Richard. Transnational Conglomerates & the Economics of Dependent Development. Altman, Edward I. & Walter, Ingo, eds. LC 78-13842. (Contemporary Studies in Economic & Financial Analysis). (Orig.). 1980. lib. bdg. 35.00 (ISBN 0-89232-110-5). Jai Pr.

Nieckels, Lars. Transfer Pricing in Multinational Firms: A Heuristic Programming Approach & Case Studies. LC 76-6174. 1976. 24.95 (ISBN 0-470-15084-X). Halsted Pr.

Noer, David M. Multinational People Management: A Guide for Organizations & Employees. LC 75-13802. 164p. 1975. 10.00 (ISBN 0-87179-220-6). BNA.

Northrup, Herbert R. & Rowan, Richard L. Multinational Collective Bargaining Attempts: The Record, the Cases, & the Prospects. (Multinational Industrial Relations Ser.: No. 6). 580p. 1979. 27.50 (ISBN 0-89546-016-5). Indus Res Unit-Wharton.

O'Connor, Walter F. An Inquiry into the Foreign Tax Burdens If U. S. Based Multinational Corporations. Bruchey, Stuart, ed. LC 80-586. (Multinational Corporations Ser.). 1980. lib. bdg. 39.00x (ISBN 0-405-13377-4). Arno.

Ogram, Ernest W., Jr. The Emerging Pattern of the Multinational Corporation. LC 65-64947. (Research Monograph: No. 31). 1965. spiral bdg. 5.00 (ISBN 0-88406-047-0). Ga St U Busn Pub.

Ozawa, Terutomo. Multinationalism, Japanese Style: The Political Economy of Outward Dependency. LC 79-84007. 1979. 20.00x (ISBN 0-691-04221-7). Princeton U Pr.

Parker, John E. The Economics of Innovation: The National & Multinational Enterprise in Technological Change. 2nd ed. (Illus.). 1978. text ed. 38.00x (ISBN 0-582-44612-0). Longman.

Peninou, Georges, et al. Multinational Corporations & European Public Opinion. LC 78-58894. (Praeger Special Studies). 1978. 23.95 (ISBN 0-03-046191-X). Praeger.

Penrose, Edith T. The Large International Firm in Developing Countries. LC 76-7581. (Illus.). 1976. Repr. of 1968 ed. lib. bdg. 20.50x (ISBN 0-8371-8850-4, PELI). Greenwood.

Persaud, Thakoor. Conflicts Between Multinational Corporations & Less Developed Countries: The Case of Bauxite Mining in the Caribbean with Special Reference to Guyana. Bruchey, Stuart, ed. LC 80-587. (Multinational Corporations Ser.). 1980. lib. bdg. 25.00x (ISBN 0-405-13378-2). Arno.

Plasschaert, Sylvain R. Transfer Pricing & Multinational Corporation: An Overview of Concepts, Mechanisms & Regulations. LC 79-84708. (Praeger Special Studies Ser.). 126p. 1979. 21.95 (ISBN 0-03-052396-6). Praeger.

Policy Instructions to Build up an Infrastructure for the Generation of Technology. (Science & Technology for Development Ser.: STPI Module 5). 57p. 1981. pap. 5.00 (ISBN 0-88936-263-7, IDRC TS26, IDRC). Unipub.

Pomper, Claude L. International Investment Planning: An Integrated Approach. (Studies in Mathematical & Managerial Economics: Vol. 22). 1976. 34.25 (ISBN 0-7204-0380-4, North-Holland). Elsevier.

Practical & Legal Considerations in the International Licensing of Technology, Part III, Folio 8. pap. write for info. ALI-ABA.

Prasad, S. Benjamin & Shetty, Y. Krishna. An Introduction to Multinational Management. (Illus.). 256p. 1976. 12.95 (ISBN 0-13-489203-8). P-H.

Pratten, C. F. Labour Productivity Differentials Within International Companies. LC 76-8294. (Department of Applied Economics. Occasional Papers: No. 50). (Illus.). 1976. pap. 15.95x (ISBN 0-521-29102-X). Cambridge U Pr.

Przeworski, Joanne F. The Decline of the Copper Industry in Chile & the Entrance of North American Capital, 1870 to 1916. Bruchey, Stuart, ed. LC 80-609. (Multinational Corporations Ser.). 1980. lib. bdg. 29.00x (ISBN 0-405-13379-0). Arno.

Raveed, Sion. Joint Ventures Between U. S. Multinational Firms & Host Governments in Selected Developing Countries. Bruchey, Stuart, ed. LC 80-590. (Multinational Corporations Ser.). (Illus.). 1980. lib. bdg. 25.00x (ISBN 0-405-13381-2). Arno.

Reimann, Guenter. Patents for Hitler. LC 78-63708. (Studies in Fascism: Ideology & Practice). Repr. of 1945 ed. 18.00 (ISBN 0-404-16978-3). AMS Pr.

Renforth, William & Raveed, Sion. A Comparative Study of Multinational Corporation Joint International Business Ventures with Family Firm or Non-Family Firm Partners. Bruchey, Stuart, ed. LC 80-782. (Multinational Corporations Ser.). 1980. lib. bdg. 18.00x (ISBN 0-405-13395-2). Arno.

Review of Multinational Corporations in Brazil & Mexico: Structural Sources of Economic & Noneconomic Power. 26p. 1977. pap. 5.00 (ISBN 0-685-80146-2, CoA). Unipub.

Richman, Barry M. & Copen, Melvyn R. International Management & Economic Development. LC 77-24758. 692p. 1978. Repr. of 1972 ed. lib. bdg. 24.00 (ISBN 0-88275-597-8). Krieger.

Robinson, Richard D. National Control of Foreign Business: A Survey of Fifteen Countries. LC 75-44938. (Special Studies). (Illus.). 1976. text ed. 45.00 (ISBN 0-275-56500-9). Praeger.

Robock, Stefan H., et al. International Business & Multinational Enterprises. rev ed. 1977. 21.95x (ISBN 0-256-01974-6). Irwin.

Rodriguez, Rita M. Foreign-Exchange Management in U.S. Multinationals. LC 78-54703. 144p. 1980. 17.95x (ISBN 0-669-02330-2). Lexington Bks.

Rueschhoff, Norlin G. International Accounting & Financial Reporting. LC 76-12871. (Special Studies). 1976. 24.95 (ISBN 0-275-23110-0). Praeger.

Rugman, Alan. Inside the Multinationals: The Economics of Internal Markets. 220p. 1981. text ed. 27.50x (ISBN 0-231-05384-3). Columbia U Pr.

Rugman, Alan M. Multinationals in Canada: Theory, Performance, Economic Impact. 1980. lib. bdg. 18.95 (ISBN 0-89838-036-7, Pub. by Martinus Nijhoff Netherlands). Kluwer Boston.

Rutenberg, Daniel P. Multinational Management. 450p. 1982. 19.95 (ISBN 0-686-76613-X). Winthrop.

Sagafi-nejad, Tagi & Belfield, Robert. Transnational Corporations, Technology Transfer & Development: A Bibliographic Sourcebook. LC 80-36887. (Pergamon Policy Studies on International Development). 150p. 1981. 25.00 (ISBN 0-08-026299-6). Pergamon.

Said, A. & Simmons, L. New Sovereigns: The Multinational Corporations As World Powers. 1975. pap. 3.50 (ISBN 0-13-615781-5, Spec). P-H.

Schachter, Oscar & Hellawell, Robert. Competition in International Business. LC 81-3856. 448p. 1981. 30.00x (ISBN 0-231-05220-0). Columbia U Pr.

Schaupp, Dietrich L. A Cross-Cultural Study of a Multinational Company: Attitudinal Responses to Participative Management. LC 78-8453. (Praeger Special Studies). 1978. 21.95 (ISBN 0-03-022871-9). Praeger.

Schnitzer, Martin. Role of U. S. Multinationals in East-West Trade. LC 78-19794. 168p. 1980. 21.50 (ISBN 0-03-043026-7). Praeger.

Schooler, Robert D. An Introduction to International Business: The Dominant Aspect of International Relations. LC 78-71778. 1979. pap. text ed. 5.00x (ISBN 0-87543-146-1). Lucas.

Sciberras, Edmond. Multinational Electronic Companies & National Economic Policies. Altman, Edward I. & Walter, Ingo, eds. LC 76-10398. (Contemporary Studies in Economic & Financial Analysis: Vol. 6). 1977. lib. bdg. 32.50 (ISBN 0-89232-016-8). Jai Pr.

Sethi, S. Prakash & Holton, Richard H., eds. Management of the Multinationals: Policies, Operations, & Research. LC 73-17644. (Illus.). 1974. 19.95 (ISBN 0-02-928410-4). Free Pr.

Shea, Donald R., et al, eds. Reference Manual on Doing Business in Latin America. LC 79-22412. 1979. 30.00 (ISBN 0-930450-12-4); pap. 20.00 (ISBN 0-930450-13-2). Univ of Wis Latin Am.

Sichel, Werner, ed. The Economic Effects of Multinational Corporations. (Michigan Business Papers: No. 61). 1975. pap. 4.50 (ISBN 0-87712-171-0). U Mich Busn Div Res.

Siddiqi, Shahid. Planning & Control of Multinational Marketing Strategy: The Issue of Integration. Bruchey, Stuart, ed. LC 80-592. (Multinational Corporations Ser.). 1980. lib. bdg. 25.00x (ISBN 0-405-13384-7). Arno.

Simmonds, K. Multinational Corporations Law, Vols. 1-2. 1979. Set. 75.00 (ISBN 0-379-20373-1). Oceana.

--Multinational Corporations Law, Release 3. 1980. 50.00 (ISBN 0-379-20373-1). Oceana.

Singh, V. B. Multinational Corporations & India. (Illus.). 161p. 1979. 10.00x (ISBN 0-8002-0992-3). Intl Pubns Serv.

Sklar, Holly, ed. Trilateralism: The Trilateral Commission & Elite Planning for World Management. LC 80-51040. (Orig.). 1980. 20.00 (ISBN 0-89608-104-4); pap. 9.00 (ISBN 0-89608-103-6). South End Pr.

Sklar, Richard L. Corporate Power in an African State: The Political Impact of Multinational Mining Companies in Zambia. LC 74-81440. 1975. 30.00x (ISBN 0-520-02814-7). U of Cal Pr.

Skully, Michael T., ed. A Multinational Look at the Transnational Corporation. 1978. 24.95x (ISBN 0-909162-04-2). Australiana.

The Social & Economic Impacts of Transnational Corporations: Case Studies of the U. S. Paper Industry in Brazil. 1977. pap. 6.25 (ISBN 0-915814-14-5, FMME7, FMME). Unipub.

Social & Labour Practices of Some European-Based Multinationals in the Metal Trades. 1976. 14.25 (ISBN 92-2-101474-6). Intl Labour Office.

Solomon, Lewis D. Multinational Corporations & the Emerging World Order. (National University Publications). 1978. 16.50 (ISBN 0-8046-9196-7). Kennikat.

Sorey, Gordon K. The Foreign Policy of a Multinational Enterprise: An Analysis of the Policy Interactions of Dow Chemical Company & the U. S. Bruchey, Stuart, ed. LC 80-593. (Multinational Corporations Ser.). 1980. lib. bdg. 15.00x (ISBN 0-405-13385-5). Arno.

Spaght, Monroe E. The Multinational Corporation. LC 78-58383. 1978. 6.00x (ISBN 0-915604-16-7). Columbia U Pr.

--The Multinational Corporation. (Benjamin F. Fairless Lectures). 1978. text ed. 6.00x (ISBN 0-915604-16-7). Carnegie-Mellon.

Stanford Research Institute. Foreign Investment: Five Studies from the International Development Center, An Original Anthology. Bruchey, Stuart, ed. LC 80-605. (Multinational Corporations Ser.). (Illus.). 1980. lib. bdg. 45.00x (ISBN 0-405-13351-0). Arno.

Steiner, George A. & Cannon, Warren M., eds. Multinational Corporate Planning. LC 66-20539. 348p. 1966. 8.50 (ISBN 0-913456-26-8). Interbk Inc.

Stobaugh, Robert B. & Robbins, Sidney M. Money in the Multinational Enterprise. 1973. text ed. 13.50x (ISBN 0-465-04715-7). Basic.

Stoever, William A. Renegotiations in International Business Transactions: The Process of Dispute-Resolution Between Multinational Investors & Host Societies. LC 79-4727. 1981. 27.95 (ISBN 0-669-03057-0). Lexington Bks.

Stopford. Directory of Multinational Enterprise. Date not set. price not set. Sijthoff & Noordhoff.

Stopford, John M. Growth & Organizational Change in the Multinational Firm. Bruchey, Stuart, ed. LC 80-594. (Multinational Corporations Ser.). (Illus.). 1980. lib. bdg. 18.00x (ISBN 0-405-13386-3). Arno.

Streng, William P. International Business Transactions Tax & Legal Handbook. (Illus.). 1977. 39.95 (ISBN 0-13-467662-9, Busn). P-H.

Surrey, Walter S. & Wallace, Don, Jr., eds. A Lawyer's Guide to International Business Transactions, Pt. IV. 471p. 1980. 55.00 (ISBN 0-686-28717-7, B96B4). ALI-ABA.

Swent, Christine W. & Unterman, Lee D. The Future of the United States Multinational Corporation. LC 74-34223. x, 161p. 1975. 12.50x (ISBN 0-8139-0631-8). U Pr of Va.

Szuprowicz, Bohdan O. & Szuprowicz, Maria R. Doing Business with People's Republic of China: Industries & Markets. 449p. 1978. 29.95 (ISBN 0-471-03389-8, Pub. by Wiley-Interscience). Wiley.

Teece, David J. Multinational Corporation & the Resource Cost of International Technology Transfer. LC 76-26053. 1976. professional ref. 19.00 (ISBN 0-88410-053-7). Ballinger Pub.

Telesio, Piero. Foreign Licensing Policy in Multinational Enterprises. (Praeger Special Studies). 21.95 (ISBN 0-03-047476-0). Praeger.

Thorelli, Hans B. & Graves, R. L. International Operations Simulation. LC 64-16969. 1964. 17.00 (ISBN 0-02-932540-4). Free Pr.

Thwaite, et al. Pamphlets on American Business Abroad: An Original Anthology. Bruchey, Stuart & Bruchey, Eleanor, eds. LC 76-5053. (American Business Abroad Ser.). (Illus.). 1976. Repr. of 1976 ed. 23.00x (ISBN 0-405-09294-6). Arno.

Tindall, Robert Emmett. Multinational Enterprises: Legal & Management Structures & Interrelationship with Ownership, Control, Antitrust, Labor Taxation & Disclosure. LC 75-14173. 430p. 1975. text ed. 28.00x (ISBN 0-379-00310-4). Oceana.

Torneden, Roger L. Foreign Disinvestment by U. S. Multinational Corporations: With Eight Case Studies. LC 75-1136. (Special Studies). (Illus.). 174p. 1975. text ed. 24.95 (ISBN 0-275-05830-1). Praeger.

Toyne, Brian. Host Country Managers of Multinational Firms: An Evaluation of Variables Affecting Their Managerial Thinking Patterns. Bruchey, Stuart, ed. LC 80-599. (Multinational Corporations Ser.). (Illus.). 1980. lib. bdg. 29.00x (ISBN 0-405-13389-8). Arno.

Transfer Pricing & Multi-National Enterprises. 1979. 9.00x (ISBN 92-64-11947-7). OECD.

Tsurumi, Yoshi. The Japanese Are Coming: A Multinational Interaction of Firms & Politics. LC 76-23262. 1976. 19.50 (ISBN 0-88410-651-9). Ballinger Pub.

Ture, Norman B., et al. U. S. Taxation of American Business Abroad. LC 75-27224. (AEI - Hoover Policy Studies Ser.). (Orig.). 1975. pap. 5.25 (ISBN 0-8447-3177-3). Am Enterprise.

Turner, Louis. Invisible Empires: Multinational Companies & the Modern World. LC 79-134582. 1971. 6.95 (ISBN 0-15-145301-2). HarBraceJ.

--Multinational Companies & the Third World. 294p. 1973. 8.95 (ISBN 0-8090-7159-2); pap. 3.45 (ISBN 0-8090-1379-7). Hill & Wang.

U. S. Department of Commerce. Statistics on American Business Abroad, 1950-1975: An Original Anthology. Bruchey, Stuart & Bruchey, Eleanor, eds. LC 76-5035. (American Business Abroad Ser.). (Illus.). 1976. 23.00x (ISBN 0-405-09301-2). Arno.

Vaitsos, Constantine V. Intercountry Income Distribution & Transnational Enterprises. 192p. 1974. 33.00x (ISBN 0-19-828195-1). Oxford U Pr.

Van Zandt, Harold. International Business Prospects: Nineteen Seventy-Seven to Nineteen Ninety-Nine. LC 78-15745. (Key Issues Lecture Ser). 1978. 8.50 (ISBN 0-672-97221-2); pap. 5.50 (ISBN 0-672-97220-4). Bobbs.

Vernon, Raymond. The Economic & Political Consequences of Multinational Enterprise: An Anthology. LC 72-79081. 150p. (Orig.). 1972. pap. 3.00x (ISBN 0-87584-098-1). Harvard Busn.

--Sovereignty at Bay: The Multinational Spread of U. S. Enterprises. LC 73-167766. (Illus.). 1971. text ed. 12.95x (ISBN 0-465-08096-0). Basic.

--Storm Over the Multinationals: The Real Issues. 1977. 15.00x (ISBN 0-674-83875-0). Harvard U Pr.

Vinh Quang Tran. Foreign Exchange Management in Multinational Firms. Dufey, Gunter, ed. (Research for Business Decisions: No. 26). 246p. 1980. 31.95 (ISBN 0-8357-1133-1, Pub. by UMI Res Pr). Univ Microfilms.

Wages & Working Conditions in Multinational Enterprises. 2nd ed. 1978. 8.55 (ISBN 92-2-101475-4). Intl Labour Office.

Walmsley, John. Joint Ventures in Saudi Arabia. 1979. 55.00x (ISBN 0-86010-166-5, Pub. by Graham & Trotman England). State Mutual Bk.

Wattenberg, Ben J. & Whalen, Richard J. The Wealth Weapon: U.S. Foreign Policy & Multinational Corporations. LC 79-66448. 127p. 1980. 16.95 (ISBN 0-87855-340-1); pap. 6.95 (ISBN 0-87855-820-9). Transaction Bks.

Weston, J. Fred & Sorge, Bart W. Guide to International Financial Management. 1977. 15.95 (ISBN 0-07-069488-5, C); text ed. 9.95 (ISBN 0-07-069487-7). McGraw.

--International Managerial Finance. 1972. 19.95x (ISBN 0-256-01390-X). Irwin.

Wiechmann, Ulrich E. Marketing Management in Multinational Firms: The Consumer Packaged Goods Industry. LC 75-19831. (Special Studies). 1976. text ed. 22.95 (ISBN 0-275-55850-9). Praeger.

Wilkins, Mira. Emergence of Multinational Enterprise: American Business Abroad from the Colonial Era to 1914. LC 71-122218. 1970. 17.50x (ISBN 0-674-24830-9). Harvard U Pr.

--The Maturing of Multinational Enterprise: American Business Abroad from 1914 to 1970. LC 73-88499. (Studies in Business History: No. 27). 1974. text ed. 25.00x (ISBN 0-674-55475-2). Harvard U Pr.

Williamson, Harold F., ed. Evolution of International Management Structures. LC 74-83671. 254p. 16.50x (ISBN 0-87413-109-X). U Delaware Pr.

Wilpert, Bernhard, et al, eds. Workers' Participation in an Internationalized Economy. LC 78-1388. 1978. 17.50x (ISBN 0-87338-214-5). Kent St U Pr.

Wilson, Brent D. Disinvestment of Foreign Subsidiaries. Dufey, Gunter, ed. (Research for Business Decisions). 112p. 1980. 23.95 (ISBN 0-8357-1132-3, Pub. by UMI Res Pr). Univ Microfilms.

Wilson, Donald T. International Business Transactions in a Nutshell. LC 80-39793. (Nutshell Ser.). 400p. 1981. pap. text ed. 7.95 (ISBN 0-8299-2119-2). West Pub.

Wilson, J. S., ed. Multinational Enterprises. 1974. 40.00 (ISBN 9-0286-0124-4). Heinman.

Winchester, Mark B. International Essays for Business Decision Makers, Vol. 3. LC 77-89595. 1979. 17.95 (ISBN 0-8144-5516-6). Am Mgmt.

Winning Business in Arab Markets: Proceedings of the 1975 Graham & Trotman Conference. 162p. 1975. 77.00x (ISBN 0-86010-044-8, Pub. by Graham & Trotman England). State Mutual Bk.

Winning Business in the USSR. 94p. 1978. 33.00x (ISBN 0-86010-122-3, Pub. by Graham & Trotman England). State Mutual Bk.

Wood, Douglas & Byrne, James. International Business Finance. LC 80-23951. 400p. 1981. text ed. 47.50x (ISBN 0-8419-0663-7). Holmes & Meier.

World Symposium on the Importance of the Patent System to Developing Countries. 1978. pap. 25.00 (ISBN 0-685-65239-4, WIPO 52, WIPO). Unipub.

Yoshino, M. Y. Japan's Multinational Enterprises. 1976. 14.00x (ISBN 0-674-47259-4). Harvard U Pr.

Young, Oran R. Compliance & Public Authority: A Theory with International Applications. LC 79-2193. (Resources for the Future Ser.). 1979. 12.95x (ISBN 0-8018-2279-3). Johns Hopkins.

Zenoff, D. B. International Business Management: Text & Cases. 1971. 13.50 (ISBN 0-02-431470-6). Macmillan.

INTERNATIONAL BUSINESS ENTERPRISES–ACCOUNTING

Alhashim, Dhia D. & Robertson, James W. Accounting for Multinational Enterprises. LC 77-13732. (Key Issues Lecture Ser). 1978. 13.95 (ISBN 0-672-97209-3); pap. 7.95 (ISBN 0-672-97183-6). Bobbs.

Giannotti, John B. & Smith, Richard W. Treasury Management Practioners' Handbook: A Practical Approach to Treasury Management in the Multinatioanl Corporation. LC 8-1523. 536p. 1981. 39.50 (ISBN 0-471-08062-4, Pub. by Wiley Interscience). Wiley.

Miller, Elwood L. Accounting Problems of Multinational Enterprises. LC 78-20273. (Illus.). 1979. 21.00 (ISBN 0-669-02712-X). Lexington Bks.

OECD. Accounting Practices in OECD Member Countris. (International Investment & Multinational Enterprises). (Illus.). 250p. (Orig.). 1980. pap. text ed. 13.50x (ISBN 92-64-12076-9). OECD.

Watt, George C., et al. Accounting for the Multinational Corporation. LC 78-60558. 1978. 25.00 (ISBN 0-87094-171-2). Dow Jones-Irwin.

INTERNATIONAL BUSINESS MACHINES CORPORATION

Engelbourg, Saul. International Business Machines: A Business History. LC 75-41753. (Companies & Men: Business Enterprises in America). (Illus.). 1976. 29.00x (ISBN 0-405-08070-0). Arno.

IBM: Small Systems. 1979. text ed. 46.25x (ISBN 0-903796-47-3, Pub. by Online Conferences England). Renouf.

MacTalley, Truman & MacTalley, Truman, eds. IBM: Colossus in Transition. LC 81-50092. (Illus.). 352p. 1981. 16.95 (ISBN 0-8129-1000-1). Times Bks.

Richardson, F. L. & Walker, Charles E. Human Relations in an Expanding Company: Manufacturing Departments, Endicott Plant of the International Business Machines Corporation. Stein, Leon, ed. (Work Ser.). (Illus.). 1977. Repr. of 1948 ed. lib. bdg. 12.00x (ISBN 0-405-10196-1, 77-70528). Arno.

INTERNATIONAL CIVIL AVIATION ORGANIZATION

Buergenthal, Thomas. Law-Making in the International Civil Aviation Organization, Vol. 7. 1969. 10.00x (ISBN 0-8156-2139-6). U Pr of Va.

INTERNATIONAL CIVIL SERVICE

see International Officials and Employees

INTERNATIONAL CLAIMS

see Claims; Government Liability (International Law)

INTERNATIONAL COMPETITION

see Competition, International

INTERNATIONAL CONFERENCE ON MARITIME LAW, BRUSSELS, 1922

Yiannopoulos, Athanassios N. Negligence Clauses in Ocean Bills of Lading: Conflict of Laws & the Brussels Convention of 1924, a Comparative Study. LC 62-10479. 1962. 15.00x (ISBN 0-8071-0840-5). La State U Pr.

INTERNATIONAL CONFERENCES, CONGRESSES AND CONVENTIONS

see Congresses and Conventions

INTERNATIONAL CONGRESS OF THE P. E. N. CLUBS, 17TH, LONDON, 1941

Ould, Hermon, ed. Writers in Freedom. LC 73-105819. 1970. Repr. of 1941 ed. 12.00 (ISBN 0-8046-0969-1). Kennikat.

INTERNATIONAL COOKERY

see Cookery, International

INTERNATIONAL COOPERATION

Here are entered general works on international cooperative activities with or without the participation of governments.

see also Agriculture, Cooperative; Arbitration, International; Congresses and Conventions; Economic Assistance; European Cooperation; Intellectual Cooperation; International Agencies; International Education; International Organization; Internationalism; League of Nations; Pan-Americanism; Reconstruction (1939-1951); Technical Assistance; United Nations–Economic Assistance; United Nations–Technical Assistance

Anshen, Ruth N., ed. Beyond Victory. facsimile ed. LC 75-156605. (Essay Index Reprint Ser). Repr. of 1943 ed. 18.00 (ISBN 0-8369-2303-0). Arno.

Boardman, Robert. International Organization & the Conservation of Nature. LC 80-8638. 232p. 1981. 22.50x (ISBN 0-253-16474-5). Ind U Pr.

Brown, Lester R. The Interdependence of Nations. LC 72-90074. (Headline Ser.: No. 212). (Illus., Orig.). 1972. pap. 2.00 (ISBN 0-87124-018-1). Foreign Policy.

Brown, Seyom. New Forces in World Politics. LC 74-912. 200p. 1974. 11.95 (ISBN 0-8157-1118-2); pap. 4.95 (ISBN 0-8157-1117-4). Brookings.

Butler, Nicholas M. Why War. (Essay & General Literature Index Reprint Ser). 1969. Repr. of 1941 ed. 12.50 (ISBN 0-8046-0058-9). Kennikat.

Carr, Edward H. Nationalism & After. 1945. 9.95 (ISBN 0-312-56000-1). St Martin.

Cherry, Colin. World Communications: Threat or Promise - A Socio-Technical Approach. rev. ed. LC 78-3761. 1978. 38.50 (ISBN 0-471-99616-5); pap. 15.95 (ISBN 0-471-99660-2, Pub. by Wiley-Interscience). Wiley.

Committee for International Environmental Programs. Institutional Arrangements for International Environmental Cooperation. LC 72-188498. 80p. 1972. pap. 3.75 (ISBN 0-309-01946-X). Natl Acad Pr.

Coomer, James C., ed. Quest for a Sustainable Society. LC 80-24158. (Pergamon Policy Studies on International Development). 230p. 1981. 26.50 (ISBN 0-08-027168-5). Pergamon.

Cuff, R. D. & Granatstein, J. L. American Dollars-Canadian Prosperity. 1978. 15.95 (ISBN 0-89522-015-6). Samuel Stevens.

Davis, Harriet E., ed. Pioneers in World Order. facs. ed. LC 70-128232. (Essay Index Reprint Ser). 1944. 17.00 (ISBN 0-8369-1913-0). Arno.

De Huszar, George B., ed. Persistent International Issues. LC 79-142645. (Essay Index Reprint Ser.). Repr. of 1947 ed. 18.00 (ISBN 0-8369-2772-9). Arno.

Dolman, Anthony J. Resources, Regimes, World Order. (Pergamon Policy Studies on International Development Ser.). 425p. 1981. 39.51 (ISBN 0-08-028080-3); pap. 10.91 (ISBN 0-08-028079-X). Pergamon.

Employment, Trade & North-South Co-Operation. 263p. 1981. pap. 17.50 (ISBN 92-2-102531-4, ILO178, ILO). Unipub.

Fayerweather, John, ed. International Business-Government Affairs: Toward an Era of Accommodation. LC 73-12445. 164p. 1973. 15.00 (ISBN 0-88410-256-4). Ballinger Pub.

Finger, Seymour M. & Harbert, Joseph R., eds. U.S. Policy in International Institutions: Defining Reasonable Options in an Unreasonable World. LC 78-4335. (Special Studies in International Relations & U.S. Foreign Policy Ser.). (Illus.). 1978. lib. bdg. 32.50 (ISBN 0-89158-077-8); pap. text ed. 13.50 (ISBN 0-89158-078-6). Westview.

Fischer. A Collection of International Concessions & Related Instruments, Vols. 9-10. 1980. 45.00 ea. Vol. 9 (ISBN 0-379-10084-3). Vol. 10 (ISBN 0-379-10085-1). Oceana.

Foell, Wesley K. Management of Energy-Environment Systems: Methods & Case Studies. LC 78-13617. (Wiley Iiasa International Institute Series on Applied Systems Analysis). 1979. 52.50 (ISBN 0-471-99721-8, Pub by Wiley-Interscience). Wiley.

Foreman, Clark. The New Internationalism. facsimile ed. LC 71-37342. (Select Bibliographies Reprint Ser). Repr. of 1934 ed. 13.00 (ISBN 0-8369-6689-9). Arno.

Haas, Ernst B. The Obsolescence of Regional Integration Theory. LC 75-620124. (Research Ser: No. 25). 136p. 1976. pap. 2.95x (ISBN 0-87725-125-8). U of Cal Intl St.

Hoole, Francis W., et al, eds. Making Ocean Policy: The Politics of Government Organization. (Westview Special Studies in Natural Resources & Energy Management). 300p. 1981. lib. bdg. 23.75x (ISBN 0-89158-966-X). Westview.

Hoover, Herbert C. & Gibson, H. Problems of Lasting Peace. LC 42-16570. 1969. Repr. of 1942 ed. 12.00 (ISBN 0-527-42420-X). Kraus Repr.

Huntley, James R. Uniting the Democracies: Institutions of the Emerging Atlantic-Pacific System. LC 78-20565. 1980. 29.50x (ISBN 0-8147-3396-4). NYU Pr.

International Cooperation in Terminology. (Infoterm Ser.: Vol. 3). 333p. 1975. pap. text ed. 35.00 (ISBN 3-7940-5503-9, Pub. by K G Saur). Gale.

International Symposium on the Judicial Settlement of International Disputes. Proceedings. Bernhardt, R. & Mosler, H., eds. LC 74-5923. (Beitrage Zum Auslandischen Oeffentlichen Rechtund Voelkerecht: Vol. 62). 550p. 1974. 46.10 (ISBN 0-387-06756-6). Springer-Verlag.

Kling, Blair B. & Pearson, M. N., eds. The Age of Partnership: Europeans in Asia Before Dominion. LC 78-31650. 1979. text ed. 12.50x (ISBN 0-8248-0495-3). U Pr of Hawaii.

Ladd, William. An Essay on a Congress of Nations for the Adjustment of International Disputes Without Resort to Arms. LC 72-137550. (Peace Movement in America Ser). 1162p. 1972. Repr. of 1916 ed. lib. bdg. 11.95x (ISBN 0-89198-078-4). Ozer.

Laseron, Charles F. & Brunnschweiller, Rudolph O. American Institutions & Organizations Interested in Asia. rev. ed. LC 61-11435. 1961. text ed. 10.00x (ISBN 0-8008-0176-8). Taplinger.

Marvin, Francis S., ed. Unity of Western Civilization. LC 77-128277. (Essay Index Reprint Ser). 1929. 17.00 (ISBN 0-8369-1889-4). Arno.

Merritt, Richard L. & Russett, Bruce M., eds. From National Development to Global Community: Essays in Honor of Karl W. Deutsch. (Illus.). 416p. 1981. text ed. 37.50x (ISBN 0-04-327060-3); pap. text ed. 16.95x (ISBN 0-04-327061-1). Allen Unwin.

Mowat, Robert B. International Relations. facs. ed. LC 67-22105. (Essay Index Reprint Ser). 1931. 12.25 (ISBN 0-8369-0725-6). Arno.

National Association for Women Deans, Administrators, & Counselors. Global Communication & Understanding. 1978. pap. 3.00 (ISBN 0-686-12124-4). Natl Assn Women.

NATO: The Next Thirty Years. (Significant Issues Ser.: Vol. I, No. 6). 25p. 1979. pap. 5.00 (ISBN 0-89206-012-3, CSIS007, CSIS). Unipub.

Page, Kirby. American Peace Policy. LC 73-147610. (Library of War & Peace; Kellogg Pact & the Outlawry of War). lib. bdg. 38.00 (ISBN 0-8240-0369-1). Garland Pub.

Pastubov, V. D. A Guide to the Practice of International Conferences. (Studies in the Administration of International Law & Organization). 1945. Repr. of 1945 ed. pap. 15.00 (ISBN 0-527-00882-6). Kraus Repr.

Richardson, John H. Economic Disarmament: A Study of International Cooperation. LC 75-41228. Repr. of 1931 ed. 18.50 (ISBN 0-404-14591-4). AMS Pr.

--Economic Disarmament: A Study on International Cooperation. LC 77-5720. 1977. Repr. of 1931 ed. lib. bdg. 16.75x (ISBN 0-8371-9640-X, RIED). Greenwood.

Robbins, Lionel C. Economic Planning & International Order. LC 72-4294. (World Affairs Ser.: National & International Viewpoints). 348p. 1972. Repr. of 1937 ed. 16.00 (ISBN 0-405-04586-7). Arno.

Sandler, Todd, et al. The Political Economy of Public Goods & International Cooperation. LC 78-55185. (Monograph Ser in World Affairs: Vol. 15, 1977-78 Ser., Pt. C). 1978. pap. 4.00 perfect bdg. (ISBN 0-87940-056-0). U of Denver Intl.

Shaffer, Stephen M. & Shaffer, Lisa R. The Politics of International Cooperation: A Comparison of U. S. Experience in Space & in Security. (Monograph Series in World Affairs). 73p. Date not set. pap. 4.00 (ISBN 0-87940-063-3). U of Denver Intl.

Shotwell, James T. On the Rim of the Abyss. LC 73-147590. (Library of War & Peace; Int'l. Organization, Arbitration & Law). lib. bdg. 38.00 (ISBN 0-8240-0351-9). Garland Pub.

Simmons, James R. Quest for Ethics. LC 62-15036. 1962. 2.75 (ISBN 0-8022-1573-4). Philos Lib.

Smith, Elise C., ed. Toward Internationalism: Readings in Cross-Cultural Communication. LC 78-17153. 1979. pap. text ed. 9.95 (ISBN 0-88377-123-3). Newbury Hse.

Steel, Ronald, ed. World Affairs: National & International Viewpoints, 41 bks. 1972. Repr. 900.00 (ISBN 0-405-04560-3). Arno.

Stewart, Maxwell S. Building for Peace at Home & Abroad. facsimile ed. LC 71-134138. (Essay Index Reprint Ser). Repr. of 1943 ed. 16.00 (ISBN 0-8369-2372-3). Arno.

Sullivan, David S. & Sattler, Martin J., eds. Change & the Future International System. 1972. 20.00x (ISBN 0-231-03565-9); pap. 5.00x (ISBN 0-231-08304-1). Columbia U Pr.

Tomasic, Roman & Feeley, Malcolm, eds. Neighborhood Justice: An Assessment of an Emerging Idea. (Professional Ser.). (Illus.). 320p. 1981. text ed. 27.50x (ISBN 0-582-28253-5). Longman.

Torpats, John. Economic Basis for World Peace. LC 73-137963. (Economic Thought, History & Challenge Ser). 1971. Repr. of 1941 ed. 12.50 (ISBN 0-8046-1464-4). Kennikat.

Trilateral Commission. Trilateral Commission Task Force Reports: 1-7: A Compilation of Reports from the First Two Years of the Trilateral Commission. LC 77-2476. 209p. 1977. 12.00x (ISBN 0-8147-8159-4) (ISBN 0-8147-8160-8). NYU Pr.

Walsh, A. E. & Paxton, John. Competition Policy: European & International Trends & Practices. LC 74-33134. 200p. 1975. 25.00 (ISBN 0-312-15540-9). St Martin.

Ward, Barbara. Spaceship Earth. LC 66-18062. (George B Pegram Ser). 1966. 15.00x (ISBN 0-231-02951-9); pap. 5.00x (ISBN 0-231-08586-9). Columbia U Pr.

Warner, Amos G. Three Phases of Cooperation in the West. (Johns Hopkins University Studies in Historical & Political Science, Ser. 6: Nos. 7, 8). 79p. Repr. of 1888 ed. pap. 7.00 (ISBN 0-384-66803-8). Johnson Repr.

Zimmern, Alfred E. America & Europe & Other Essays. facs. ed. LC 78-84350. (Essay Index Reprint Ser). 1929. 14.50 (ISBN 0-8369-1117-2). Arno.

--Prospects of Democracy & Other Essays. facs. ed. LC 68-8506. (Essay Index Reprint Ser). 1929. 17.00 (ISBN 0-8369-1017-6). Arno.

INTERNATIONAL COOPERATION IN ATOMIC ENERGY RESEARCH

see Atomic Energy Research

INTERNATIONAL COOPERATION IN EDUCATION

see Educational Exchanges

INTERNATIONAL COOPERATION IN SCIENCE

see Science–International Cooperation

INTERNATIONAL COPYRIGHT

see Copyright, International

INTERNATIONAL COURT OF JUSTICE

see Hague–International Court of Justice

INTERNATIONAL COURTS

see also Jurisdiction (International Law)
also names of individual courts, e.g. Hague–Permanent Court of International Justice

Dawson, Frank G. & Head, Ivan L. International Law, National Tribunals, & Rights of Aliens, Vol. 10. 1971. 10.00x (ISBN 0-8156-2152-3). U Pr of Va.

Grieves, Forest L. Supranationalism & International Adjudication. LC 69-17362. (Illus.). 1969. 19.95 (ISBN 0-252-00012-9). U of Ill Pr.

Hudson, M. O. International Tribunals: Past & Future. (Studies in the Administration of International Law Organization). 1944. Repr. of 1944 ed. pap. 16.00 (ISBN 0-527-00880-X). Kraus Repr.

Jessup, Philip C. United States & the World Court. Incl. What's Wrong with International Law? Friedman, Wolfgang; Foreign Policy of a Free Democracy. Jessup, Philip C; Fallacy of a "Preventive" War. Jessup, Philip C; Legal Process & International Order. Kelsen, Hans. LC 70-147750. (Library of War & Peace; International Law). lib. bdg. 38.00 (ISBN 0-8240-0490-6). Garland Pub.

Kelsen, Hans. Peace Through Law. LC 76-147757. (Library of War & Peace; International Law). lib. bdg. 38.00 (ISBN 0-8240-0492-2). Garland Pub.

Ralston, Jackson H. Law & Procedure of International Tribunals. LC 75-147738. (Library of War & Peace; International Law). lib. bdg. 38.00 (ISBN 0-8240-0496-5). Garland Pub.

Sandifer, D. V. Evidence Before International Tribunals. Repr. of 1939 ed. 23.00 (ISBN 0-527-78700-0). Kraus Repr.

Sandifer, Durward V. Evidence Before International Tribunals. rev. ed. LC 75-1242. (Procedural Aspects of International Law Inst.: Vol. 13). (Illus.). 500p. 1975. 27.50x (ISBN 0-8139-0616-4). U Pr of Va.

Seidl-Hohenveldern, Ignaz. The Austrian-German Arbitral Tribunal, Vol. 11. 1972. 10.00x (ISBN 0-8156-2159-0). U Pr of Va.

Tomasic, Roman & Feeley, Malcolm, eds. Neighborhood Justice: An Assessment of an Emerging Idea. (Professional Ser.). (Illus.). 320p. 1981. text ed. 27.50x (ISBN 0-582-28253-5). Longman.

White, Gillian. The Use of Experts by International Tribunals, Vol. 4. 1965. 10.00x (ISBN 0-8139-0837-X). U Pr of Va.

INTERNATIONAL CRIMINAL COURT (PROPOSED)

Ferencz, Benjamin. An International Criminal Court: A Step Toward World Peace, 2 vols. LC 80-10688. 1212p. 1980. Vol. 1. lib. bdg. 37.50 ea. (ISBN 0-379-20389-8). Vol. 2 (ISBN 0-379-20390-1). Oceana.

INTERNATIONAL CRIMINAL LAW

see International Offenses

INTERNATIONAL DEBTS

see Debts, External

INTERNATIONAL DEVELOPMENT ASSOCIATION

Dupuy, R. J. The Right to Development at the International Level. 458p. 1981. 40.00 (ISBN 90-286-0990-3). Sijthoff & Noordhoff.

Honadle, George & Klaus, Rudi, eds. International Development Administration: Implementation Analysis for Development Projects. LC 79-65182. (Praeger Special Studies). 236p. 1979. 23.95 (ISBN 0-03-051041-4). Praeger.

INTERNATIONAL ECONOMIC INTEGRATION

see also Customs Unions;
also names of international organizations established to integrate the economies of various countries, e.g. European Economic Community

Adams, F. Gerard & Glickman, Norman. Modeling the Multiregional Economic System: Perspectives for the Eighties. LC 79-48005. (Wharton Econometric Ser.). 1980. 24.95x (ISBN 0-669-03627-7). Lexington Bks.

Amacher, Ryan C., et al, eds. Challenge to a Liberal International Economic Order. 1979. 17.25 (ISBN 0-8447-2151-4); pap. 9.25 (ISBN 0-8447-2152-2). Am Enterprise.

Bracewell-Milnes, Barry. Eastern & Western European Economic Integration. LC 76-6671. (Illus.). 300p. 1976. text ed. 22.50 (ISBN 0-312-22470-2). St Martin.

Collins, Doreen. Social Policy of the European Economic Community. LC 75-22282. 286p. 1975. 30.95 (ISBN 0-470-16583-9). Halsted Pr.

Congress of the International Economic Association, 4th, Budapest, Hungary. Economic Integration: Worldwide, Regional, Sectoral: Proceedings. Machlup, Fritz, ed. LC 76-10281. 1977. 43.95 (ISBN 0-470-01381-8). Halsted Pr.

Corea, Gamani. Need for Change: Towards the New International Economic Order. LC 80-40800. 350p. 1980. 27.50 (ISBN 0-08-026095-0). Pergamon.

Einzig, Paul & Quinn, Brian S. The Euro-Dollar System: Practice & Theory of International Interest Rates. 6th ed. LC 77-78988. 1977. 17.95x (ISBN 0-312-26741-X). St Martin.

Inter-American Institute of International Legal Studies, ed. Instruments of Economic Integration in Latin America & in the Caribbean, 2 vols. rev ed. LC 75-30735. 800p. 1975. text ed. 45.00 ea. (ISBN 0-379-00331-7). Oceana.

Krauss, Melvyn B., ed. The Economics of Integration: A Book of Readings. 1973. pap. text ed. 14.95x (ISBN 0-04-330222-X). Allen Unwin.

Latham, A. J. The International Economy & the Undeveloped World, 1865-1914. (Illus.). 217p. 1978. 21.50x (ISBN 0-8476-6088-5). Rowman.

Llewellyn, David T. International Financial Integration: The Limits of Sovereignty. LC 80-11699. (Problems of Economic Integration Ser.). 215p. 1981. 32.95x (ISBN 0-470-26960-X). Halsted Pr.

Lortie, Pierre. Economic Integration & the Law of Gatt. LC 75-3626. (Special Studies). (Illus.). 202p. 1975. text ed. 25.95 (ISBN 0-275-05230-3). Praeger.

Machlup, Fritz. A History of Thought on Economic Integration. LC 76-54770. 323p. 1977. 22.50x (ISBN 0-231-04298-1). Columbia U Pr.

Meerhaeghe, M. A. International Economic Institutions. 2nd ed. LC 75-179701. 1972. 22.50x (ISBN 0-312-42070-6). St. Martin.

The New International Economic Order. (Dag Hammerskjold Library Bibliographic Ser.: No. 30). 128p. 1980. pap. 11.00 (ISBN 0-686-72364-3, UN80/1/15, UN). Unipub.

Ropeka, W. International Order & Economic Integration. Trinks, G. E., et al, trs. from Ger. 276p. 1960. lib. bdg. 26.00 (ISBN 90-277-0100-8, Pub. by Reidel Holland). Kluwer Boston.

Rosenne, Shabtai. The World Court: What It Is, How It Works. 3rd rev. ed. LC 62-9743. 290p. 1974. lib. bdg. 22.50 (ISBN 0-379-00206-X). Oceana.

Senin, Mikhail. Socialist Integration: The Theoretical & Practical Considerations Governing the Economic Relations Among Socialist Countries. 284p. 1975. 16.00x (ISBN 0-8464-0860-0). Beekman Pubs.

Shoup, Carl S., ed. Fiscal Harmonization in Common Markets, 2 Vols. Vol. 1. Theory, Vol. 2. Practice. LC 66-14789. 1966. Set. 50.00x (ISBN 0-231-08964-3). Columbia U Pr.

Simai, M. & Garam, Katalin, eds. Economic Intergration. 1977. 30.00 (ISBN 0-9960004-6-1, Pub. by Kiado Hungary). Heyden.

Simai, Mihaly & Garam, Katalin, eds. Economic Integration: Concepts, Theories & Problems. LC 78-308400. 423p. 1977. 32.50x (ISBN 963-05-1188-6). Intl Pubns Serv.

Singer, Hans W. & Ansari, Javed A. Rich & Poor Countries. LC 76-49137. 1977. text ed. 16.50x (ISBN 0-8018-1933-4). Johns Hopkins.

Sutton, Anthony C. & Wood, Patrick M. Trilaterals Over Washington, 2 vols. 390p. 1981. Set. pap. 11.90 (ISBN 0-933482-03-5); pap. 5.95 ea. Vol. 1 (ISBN 0-933482-01-9). Vol. 2 (ISBN 0-933482-02-7). August Corp.

Tinbergen, Jan. International Economic Integration. 2nd rev. ed. 1965. 14.75 (ISBN 0-444-40573-9). Elsevier.

Vanek, Jaroslav. General Equilibrium of International Discrimination: The Case of Customs Unions. LC 65-11593. (Economic Studies: No. 123). 1965. 10.00x (ISBN 0-674-34400-6). Harvard U Pr.

INTERNATIONAL ECONOMIC RELATIONS

see also Balance of Payments; Commercial Policy; Economic Assistance; International Business Enterprises; International Economic Integration; International Finance; Investments, Foreign; Technical Assistance;
also subdivision Foreign Economic Relations under names of countries, e.g. United States–Foreign Economic Relations

Abbott, George C. International Indebtedness & the Developing Countries. LC 79-5070. 1979. 25.00 (ISBN 0-87332-149-9). M E Sharpe.

Abegglen, James C., et al. U.S.-Japan Economic Relations: A Symposium on Critical Issues. LC 80-620017. (Research Papers & Policy Studies: No. 1). 68p. 1980. pap. 5.00x (ISBN 0-912966-25-4). IEAS Ctr Chinese Stud.

Abolfathi, Farid, et al. The OPEC Market to Nineteen Eighty-Five. LC 76-44612. (Illus.). 1977. 24.95 (ISBN 0-669-01102-9). Lexington Bks.

Adams, F. Gerard & Glickman, Norman. Modeling the Multiregional Economic System: Perspectives for the Eighties. LC 79-48005. (Wharton Econometric Ser.). 1980. 24.95x (ISBN 0-669-03627-7). Lexington Bks.

Adams, Tim. Third World Out! Hardy, A. L., ed. LC 78-74429. 1978. pap. 4.00 (ISBN 0-686-23919-9). Central FL Voters.

Ajami, Riad A. Arab Response to Multinationals. 1979. 20.95 (ISBN 0-03-048436-7). Praeger.

Allen, Polly R. & Kenen, Peter B. Asset Markets, Exchange Rates, & Economic Integration. LC 79-16874. (Illus.). 1980. 55.00 (ISBN 0-521-22982-0). Cambridge U Pr.

Alvarez, Francisco C. New Horizons for the Third World. 1976. 6.00 (ISBN 0-8183-0246-1). Pub Aff Pr.

Amstutz, Mark R. Economics & Foreign Policy: A Guide to Information Sources. LC 74-11566. (Vol. 7). 1977. 36.00 (ISBN 0-8103-1321-9). Gale.

Anell, Lars. Recession, the Western Economies & the Changing World Order. 1981. price not set (ISBN 0-312-66576-8). St Martin.

Anell, Lars & Nygren, Birgitta. The Developing Countries & the World Economic Order. 208p. 1980. pap. 8.95 (ISBN 0-416-74630-6, 2002). Methuen Inc.

Arad, Uzi B., et al. Sharing Global Resources. LC 78-13233. (Council on Foreign Relations 1980's Project). (Illus.). 1979. text ed. 9.95 (ISBN 0-07-002150-3, P&RB); pap. 6.95 (ISBN 0-07-002151-1). McGraw.

Ashworth, William. A Short History of the International Economy Since 1850. 3rd ed. 1976. text ed. 23.00x (ISBN 0-582-44060-2); pap. text ed. 12.50x (ISBN 0-582-44061-0). Longman.

Atimono, Emiko. Law & Diplomacy in Commodity Economics. 200p. 1982. text ed. 57.95x (ISBN 0-8419-5080-6). Holmes & Meier.

Avery, William & Rapkin, David P., eds. America in a Changing Global Economy. 1982. text ed. 20.00x (ISBN 0-582-28269-1); pap. text ed. 9.95x (ISBN 0-582-28270-5). Longman.

Azzam, Salem, frwd. by. The Muslim World & the Future Economic Order. 383p. 1980. 29.95x (ISBN 0-906041-10-4, Pub. by Islamic Council of Europe England); pap. 14.95x (ISBN 0-906041-09-0). Intl Schol Bk Serv.

Backman, Jules & Bloch, Ernest, eds. Multinational Corporations, Trade & the Dollar in the Seventies. LC 74-77713. (Key Issues Lecture Ser.). 108p. 1974. 7.95x (ISBN 0-8147-0977-X); pap. 3.95x (ISBN 0-8147-0978-8). NYU Pr.

Baer, George W. International Organizations, Nineteen Eighteen to Nineteen Forty-Five: A Guide to Research & Research Materials. Kimmich, Christoph M., ed. LC 80-53893. 261p. 1981. lib. bdg. 17.50 (ISBN 0-8420-2179-5). Scholarly Res.

Balances of Payments of OECD Countries 1960-1977. 1979. 13.00x (ISBN 92-64-01877-8). OECD.

Balassa, Bela. The Newly Industrialized Countries in the World Economy. LC 80-20787. 450p. 1981. 45.00 (ISBN 0-08-026336-4); pap. 18.50 (ISBN 0-08-026335-6). Pergamon.

Baldwin, Robert E. International Trade & Finance: Readings. Richardson, J. David, ed. (Orig.). 1974. pap. text ed. 9.95 (ISBN 0-316-07921-9). Little.

Ball, R. J., ed. The International Linkage Economic Modes. LC 72-88287. (Contributions to Economic Analysis Ser.: Vol. 78). 435p. 1973. 49.00 (ISBN 0-444-10464-X, North-Holland). Elsevier.

Balogh, Thomas. Fact & Fancy in International Economic Relations: An Essay on International Monetary Reform. LC 73-7993. 132p. 1973. text ed. 19.50 (ISBN 0-08-017740-9). Pergamon.

Banks, Ferdinand E. The International Economy: A Modern Approach. LC 77-26560. (Illus.). 1979. 17.95 (ISBN 0-669-01504-0). Lexington Bks.

Batchelder, Alan & Haitani, Kanji. International Economics: Theory & Practice. LC 70-21770. (Economics Ser.). 471p. 1981. text ed. 22.00 (ISBN 0-88244-231-7). Grid Pub.

Batra, R. N. The Pure Theory of International Trade Under Uncertainty. LC 74-4820. 1975. text ed. 27.95 (ISBN 0-470-05687-8). Halsted Pr.

Bauer, Robert A., ed. The Interaction of Economics & Foreign Policy. LC 75-2243. (A Kenyon Public Affairs Forum Publication Ser). 1975. 10.00x (ISBN 0-8139-0639-3); pap. 2.95x (ISBN 0-8139-0640-7). U Pr of Va.

Bedjaoui, Mohammed. Towards a New International Economic Order. LC 79-22943. Orig. Title: Pour un Nouvel Ordre Economique International. 1979. text ed. 29.50x (ISBN 0-8419-0585-1); pap. text ed. 17.95 (ISBN 0-8419-0588-6). Holmes & Meier.

Behrman, Jere R. Development, the International Economic Order, & Commodity Agreements. LC 78-52500. (Perspectives in Economics). (Illus.). 1978. pap. text ed. 6.95 (ISBN 0-201-08367-1). A-W.

Beigie, Carl E. & Hero, Alfred O., Jr., eds. Natural Resources in U. S. - Canadian Relations: Perspectives, Prospects, & Policy Options, Vol. 3. 240p. 1981. lib. bdg. 18.50x (ISBN 0-89158-556-7); pap. text ed. 8.50x (ISBN 0-89158-879-5). Westview.

Bergsten, A. Fred & Krause, Lawrence B., eds. World Politics & International Economics. 1975. 18.95 (ISBN 0-8157-0916-1); pap. 6.95 (ISBN 0-8157-0915-3). Brookings.

Bergsten, C. F. The International Economic Policy of the United States: Selected Papers of C. Fred Bergsten, 1977-1979. LC 79-3040. 416p. 1980. 28.95x (ISBN 0-669-03314-6). Lexington Bks.

Bergsten, C. Fred. Managing International Economic Interdependence: Selected Papers of C. Fred Bergsten. LC 77-2517. 1977. 23.95 (ISBN 0-669-01516-4). Lexington Bks.

Bergsten, Fred C. Toward a New International Economic Order. LC 74-16635. 1975. 23.95 (ISBN 0-669-96677-0). Lexington Bks.

Bhagwati, Jagdish N. Amount & Sharing of Aid. LC 73-123777. (Monographs: No. 2). 208p. 1970. 1.50 (ISBN 0-686-28693-6). Overseas Dev Council.

Bhagwati, Jagdish N., ed. The New International Economic Order: The North South Debate. 1977. pap. 11.00x (ISBN 0-262-52042-7). MIT Pr.

Biersteker, Thomas J. Distortion or Development? Contending Perspectives on the Multinational Corporation. (Illus.). 216p. 1981. pap. 7.95x (ISBN 0-262-52065-6). MIT Pr.

Blake, O. & Walters, R. Politics of Global Economic Relations. (Illus.). 272p. 1976. pap. 10.95 (ISBN 0-13-684712-9). P-H.

Block, Fred L. The Origins of International Economic Disorder: A Study of United States International Monetary Policy from World War Two to the Present. LC 75-7190. 1977. pap. 6.95x (ISBN 0-520-03729-4). U of Cal Pr.

Bognar, J. New Forces & Currents in the International Economy. (Studies in Developing Countries Ser.: No. 83). 30p. 1975. pap. 6.00x (ISBN 0-8002-2188-5). Intl Pubns Serv.

Bos, H. C., ed. Towards Balanced International Growth. 1969. 31.75 (ISBN 0-444-10153-5, North-Holland). Elsevier.

Brada, Josef C., intro. by. Quantitative & Analytic Studies in East-West Economic Relations. LC 76-10986. (Studies in East European & Soviet Planning Development & Trade: No. 24). (Illus.). 1976. pap. text ed. 6.00 (ISBN 0-89249-015-2). Intl Development.

Brandt, Willy & Sampson, Anthony, eds. North-South: A Program for Survival (The Brandt Report) 320p. (Orig.). 1980. pap. text ed. 4.95 (ISBN 0-262-52059-1). MIT Pr.

Brown, Lester R. The Interdependence of Nations. (Development Papers: No. 10). 70p. 1972. pap. 1.00 (ISBN 0-686-28679-0). Overseas Dev Council.

Brubacker, Earl R. Individual Values & Global Sharing. 192p. 1980. 18.50x (ISBN 0-8147-1031-X). NYU Pr.

Brunner, Karl, ed. The First World & the Third World: Essays on the New International Economic Order. LC 78-62660. 1978. 9.95 (ISBN 0-932468-00-4); pap. 3.95 (ISBN 0-932468-01-2). U Rochester Policy.

Buckley, Peter J. & Roberts, Brian R. European Direct Investment in the U.S.A. Before World War I. 1981. 25.00 (ISBN 0-312-26940-4). St Martin.

Butwell, Richard, ed. Foreign Policy & the Developing Nation. LC 68-55041. 244p. 1969. 15.00x (ISBN 0-8131-1185-4). U Pr of Ky.

Cabrera, Gilberto R. Fundamentos Del Comercio Internacional. 7.50 (ISBN 0-8477-2602-9). U of PR Pr.

Calleo, David P. & Rowland, Benjamin M. America & the World Political Economy: Atlantic Dreams & National Realities. LC 72-88911. (Midland Bks.: No. 160). 384p. 1973. pap. 3.95x (ISBN 0-253-20160-8). Ind U Pr.

Camps, M. & Gwin, C. Collective Management: The Reform of Global Economic Organizations. (Council on Foreign Relations Ser.). 1981. write for info (ISBN 0-07-009708-9, P&RB); pap. write for info. (ISBN 0-07-009709-7). McGraw.

Carbaugh, Robert J. International Economics. (Illus.). 1980. text ed. 17.95 (ISBN 0-87626-381-3). Winthrop.

Carlson, Jack & Graham, Hugh. The Economic Importance of Exports to the United States, Vol. II. LC 80-66694. (Significant Issues Ser.: No. 6). 128p. 1980. 5.95 (ISBN 0-686-77783-2). CSI Studies.

Chachiliades, Miltiades. International Trade Theory & Policy. 2nd ed. (Economic Handbk Ser). (Illus.). 1977. text ed. 21.95 (ISBN 0-07-010344-5, C). McGraw.

Clark, Ian. Reform & Resistance in the International Order. LC 79-54017. 1980. 29.50 (ISBN 0-521-22998-7); pap. 8.95 (ISBN 0-521-29763-X). Cambridge U Pr.

Cline, William. Policy Alternatives for a New International Economic Order. LC 79-87553. 1979. 26.95 (ISBN 0-03-049471-0); pap. 9.95 (ISBN 0-03-049466-4). Praeger.

Cline, William R., ed. Policy Alternatives for a New International Economic Order: An Economic Analysis. LC 79-87553. 410p. 1979. pap. 7.95 (ISBN 0-03-049466-4). Overseas Dev Council.

Coburn, Gordon C. The Emerging Conflict Between the United States & Europe for the New Leadership of the World. (Illus.). 1979. deluxe ed. 47.45 (ISBN 0-930008-30-8). Inst Econ Pol.

Coffey, Peter. World Monetary Crisis. LC 74-14711. 128p. 1974. 18.95 (ISBN 0-312-89180-6). St Martin.

Committee for Economic Development. International Economic Consequences of High-Priced Energy. LC 75-22468. 116p. 1975. lib. bdg. 4.00 (ISBN 0-87186-759-1); pap. 2.50 (ISBN 0-87186-059-7). Comm Econ Dev.

--Toward a New International Economic System: A Joint Japanese-American View. LC 74-79477. 64p. 1974. pap. 2.00 (ISBN 0-87186-054-6). Comm Econ Dev.

Connolly, M. B. & Swoboda, A. K. International Trade & Money. 1973. pap. text ed. 9.95x (ISBN 0-04-330220-3). Allen Unwin.

Cooper, Richard N. The Economics of Interdependence. (Council on Foreign Relations Ser.). 316p. 1980. 20.00x (ISBN 0-231-05070-4); pap. 6.50x (ISBN 0-231-05071-2). Columbia U Pr.

Corden, W. M. Inflation, Exchange Rates, & the World Economy: Lectures on Int'l Monetary Economics. rev. ed. 160p. 1981. 15.00 (ISBN 0-226-11585-2). U of Chicago Pr.

Cuddy, J. D. International Price Indexation. (Illus.). 1977. 17.95 (ISBN 0-347-01140-3, 00684-X, Pub. by Saxon Hse England). Lexington Bks.

Daly, D. J., ed. International Comparisons of Prices & Output. (Studies in Income & Wealth: No. 37). 340p. 1972. text ed. 15.00x (ISBN 0-87014-244-5, Dist. by Columbia U Pr). Natl Bur Econ Res.

Dammann, Erik. The Future in Our Hands. (Illus.). 1979. 25.00 (ISBN 0-08-024284-7); pap. 11.50 (ISBN 0-08-024283-9). Pergamon.

Deland, Isidore. The United States, Europe, Israel & the Approaching Collapse of the World Order. (Illus.). 1978. deluxe ed. 69.50 (ISBN 0-930008-00-6). Inst Econ Pol.

Denoon, David B., ed. The New International Economic Order: A U. S. Response. LC 79-1997. (A UNA-USA Bk.). 1979. 25.00x (ISBN 0-8147-1769-1); pap. 11.50x (ISBN 0-8147-1770-5). NYU Pr.

De Rivero, Oswaldo. New Economic Order & International Development Law. LC 79-41222. 132p. 1980. 18.50 (ISBN 0-08-024706-7). Pergamon.

De Saint Phalle, Thibaut. U. S. Productivity & Competitiveness in International Trade, Vol. II. LC 80-68434. (Significant Issues Ser.: No. 12). 115p. 1980. 5.95 (ISBN 0-89206-028-X). CSI Studies.

Despres, Emile. International Economic Reform: Collected Papers of Emile Despres. Meier, Gerald M., ed. 311p. 1973. text ed. 9.95x (ISBN 0-19-501610-6). Oxford U Pr.

Deutsch, Karl W. & Fritsch, Bruno, eds. Problems of World Modeling: Political & Social Implications. LC 77-953. 1977. 25.00 (ISBN 0-88410-656-X). Ballinger Pub.

Development Co-Operation, 1978 Review. 1978. 17.00x (ISBN 92-64-11866-7). OECD.

Development Co-Operation, 1979 Review. 292p. 1979. 19.00x (ISBN 92-64-12019-X). OECD.

Dhonte, Pierre. Clockwork Debt: Trade & the External Debt of Developing Countries. LC 79-1753. 144p. 1979. 16.95 (ISBN 0-669-02925-4). Lexington Bks.

Diamond, Solomon. Roots of Psychology: Psychology Recollected. LC 72-76919. (Illus.). 800p. 1973. text ed. 25.95x (ISBN 0-465-07137-6). Basic.

Dolman, Anthony J., ed. Global Planning & Resource Management: Toward International Decision Making in a Divided World. (Pergamon Policy Studies on International Development). 272p. 1980. 20.00 (ISBN 0-08-026309-7); pap. 7.95 (ISBN 0-08-026320-8). Pergamon.

Dornbusch, Rudiger & Frenkel, Jacob A., eds. International Economic Policy: Theory & Evidence. 1979. pap. 7.95 (ISBN 0-8018-2133-9). Johns Hopkins.

Douglass, Gordon K. The New Interdependence: The European Community & the United States. LC 79-5121. 160p. 1979. 17.95 (ISBN 0-669-03203-4). Lexington Bks.

Drucker, Peter. Age of Discontinuity. 1978. pap. 4.95 (ISBN 0-06-090591-3, CN591, CN). Har-Row.

Dumont, Rene. Utopia or Else... LC 74-32587. 188p. 1975. 10.00x (ISBN 0-87663-218-5). Universe.

Dunn, Robert M., Jr. The Canada-U.S. Captial Market. LC 78-71657. 148p. 1978. 6.00 (ISBN 0-88806-046-7). Natl Planning.

Editors of the Overseas Assignment Directory. Business with China. LC 79-11413. 1979. pap. 19.95 (ISBN 0-914236-39-3). Knowledge Indus.

Ellsworth, Paul T. & Leith, J. Clark. The International Economy. 5th ed. (Illus.). 608p. 1975. text ed. 17.50x (ISBN 0-02-332760-X, 33276). Macmillan.

Employment, Trade & North-South Co-Operation. 263p. 1981. pap. 17.50 (ISBN 92-2-102531-4, ILO178, ILO). Unipub.

Erb, Guy F. Negotiations on Two Fronts: Manufactures & Commodities. LC 78-57199. (Development Papers: No. 25). 80p. 1978. pap. 1.50 (ISBN 0-686-28674-X). Overseas Dev Council.

Erlanger, George C. The International Monetary Chaos & a Positive Plan for the Monetary Reconstruction of the World. (Illus.). 147p. 1981. 67.85 (ISBN 0-918968-90-9). Inst Econ Finan.

Evans, John W. Kennedy Round in American Trade Policy: The Twilight of the GATT? LC 77-139725. (Center for International Affairs Ser). 1971. 18.50x (ISBN 0-674-50275-2). Harvard U Pr.

Faaland, Just, ed. Aid & Influence: The Case of Bangladesh. LC 80-13481. 1980. 25.00 (ISBN 0-312-01492-9). St Martin.

Fallenbuchl, Zbigniew M. & McMillan, Charles H., eds. Partners in East-West Economic Relations: The Determinants of Choice. (Pergamon Policy Studies). (Illus.). 1980. 47.00 (ISBN 0-08-022497-0). Pergamon.

Fawcett, James. International Economic Conflicts: Their Prevention & Resolution. LC 77-374401. 1977. 15.00x (ISBN 0-905118-06-5). Intl Pubns Serv.

Finger, Seymour M. & Harbert, Joseph R., eds. U. S. Policy in International Institutions: Defining Reasonable Options in an Unreasonable World. rev. & updated ed. (Special Studies in International Relations). 200p. (Orig.). 1981. lib. bdg. 20.00x (ISBN 0-86531-105-6); pap. 8.50x (ISBN 0-86531-106-4). Westview.

Finnin, William M., Jr. & Smith, Gerald A., eds. The Morality of Scarcity: Limited Resources & Social Policy. LC 78-21514. 1979. 10.95x (ISBN 0-8071-0485-X). La State U Pr.

Fitt, Yann, et al. The World Economic Crisis: American Imperialism at Bay. 224p. (Orig.). 1980. 16.95 (ISBN 0-905762-53-3, Pub. by Zed Pr); pap. 6.95 (ISBN 0-905762-54-1). Lawrence Hill.

Flammang, Robert. U. S Programs That Impede U. S. Export Competitveness: The Regulatory Environment, Vol. II. LC 80-80933. (Significant Issues Ser.: No. 3). 45p. 1980. 5.95 (ISBN 0-89206-017-4). CSI Studies.

Fleming, Harold M. States, Contracts & Progress. LC 60-10207. (Orig.). 1960. 7.50 (ISBN 0-379-00053-9). Oceana.

Fleming, J. Marcus. Essays in International Economics. 1971. 16.50x (ISBN 0-674-26435-5). Harvard U Pr.

Fordwor, Kwame D. The African Development Bank: Problems of International Cooperation. LC 80-24607. (Pergamon Policy Studies on International Development). 300p. 1981. 30.00 (ISBN 0-08-026339-9). Pergamon.

Foreign Policy Association Editors. Trade & the Dollar: Coping with Interdependence. (Headline Ser.: No. 242). (Illus.). 1978. pap. 2.00 (ISBN 0-87124-052-1). Foreign Policy.

Frank, Andre G. Reflections on the World Economic Crisis. LC 80-8088. 192p. 1981. 13.50 (ISBN 0-85345-563-5); pap. 5.50 (ISBN 0-85345-564-3, PB5643). Monthly Rev.

Freeman, Donald B. International Trade, Migration & Capital Flows: A Quantitative Analysis of Spatial Economic Interaction. LC 73-75154. (Research Papers Ser.: No. 146). (Illus.). 201p. 1973. pap. 8.00 (ISBN 0-89065-053-5). U Chicago Dept Geog.

Friedrich, Klaus. International Economics. (Illus.). 375p. 1974. text ed. 16.95 (ISBN 0-07-022435-8, C). McGraw.

Gardner, Richard N. Sterling-Dollar Diplomacy in Current Perspective: The Origins & the Prospects of Our International Economic Order. LC 79-26572. 1980. 25.00x (ISBN 0-231-04944-7); pap. 7.50x (ISBN 0-231-04945-5). Columbia U Pr.

Gasteyger, Curt, et al. Energy, Inflation & International Economic Relations: Atlantic Institute Studies - Two. LC 75-19764. (Special Studies). (Illus.). 256p. 1975. text ed. 24.95 (ISBN 0-275-01250-6). Praeger.

GATT Activities in 1976. 1977. pap. 5.00 (ISBN 0-685-86539-8, GATT). Unipub.

GATT Activities in 1978 & Results of the Tokyo Round Multilateral Trade Negotiations. 1979. pap. 7.00 (ISBN 0-686-59422-3, G125, Gatt). Unipub.

Geiger, Theodore & Geiger, Frances M. Welfare & Efficiency: Their Interactions in Western Europe & Implications for International Economic Relations. LC 78-63434. 160p. 1978. 7.00 (ISBN 0-89068-045-0). Natl Planning.
Geisst, Charles R. Raising International Capital: International Markets & the European Institutions. 176p. 1979. 20.95x (ISBN 0-566-00282-5, 03296-4, Pub. by Saxon Hse England). Lexington Bks.
Ghatak, Subrata. Monetary Economics in Developing Countries. Date not set. 25.00 (ISBN 0-312-54418-9). St Martin.
Gilpin, Robert G., Jr. U. S. Power & the Multinational Corporation: The Political Economy of Direct Foreign Investment. LC 75-7265. 1975. 10.95x (ISBN 0-465-08951-8). Basic.
Glejser, H. Quantitative Studies of International Economic Relations. 1976. 46.50 (ISBN 0-444-10902-1, North-Holland). Elsevier.
Global Economic Challenge: Trade Policy, Energy & Jobs, & Technology Transfer, Vol. II. 1980. pap. 3.00 (ISBN 0-934654-23-9). UNA-USA.
Gold, Bela. Productivity, Technology, & Capital Economic Analysis, Managerial Strategies, & Government Policies. LC 79-4749. 1979. 26.95 (ISBN 0-669-02957-2). Lexington Bks.
Golt, Sidney. The GATT Negotiations, 1973-79: The Closing Stage. LC 78-54114. 70p. 1978. 3.00 (ISBN 0-902594-32-X). Natl Planning.
Gomes, Leonard. International Economic Problems. 1979. 17.95x (ISBN 0-312-42158-3). St Martin.
Gordon, Richard L. Coal & Canada-U.S. Energy Relations. LC 76-20420. 76p. 1976. 3.00 (ISBN 0-88806-017-3). Natl Planning.
Gordon, Robert & Pelkmans, Jacques. Challenges to Interdependent Economies. (Illus.). 1979. text ed. 9.95 (ISBN 0-07-023810-3, P&RB); pap. 6.95 (ISBN 0-07-023811-1). McGraw.
Gould, Lawrence V. & Targ, Harry R. Global Dominance & Dependence: Readings in Theory & Research. 1980. pap. cancelled. Kings Court.
Goulet, Denis & Kallab, Valeriana, eds. Development from Tradition: Views from Several Cultures. 322p. 1981. write for info. Overseas Dev Council.
Grassman, Sven & Lundberg, Erik, eds. World Economic Order: Past & Prospects. LC 79-18803. 1980. 37.50x (ISBN 0-312-89046-X). St Martin.
Grieves, Forest L., ed. Transnationalism in World Politics & Business. LC 79-1397. (Pergamon Policy Studies). 240p. 1979. 33.00 (ISBN 0-08-023892-0). Pergamon.
Grotewold, Andreas. The Regional Theory of World Trade. LC 79-83769. (Illus.). 1979. 8.45x (ISBN 0-933550-00-6). Ptolemy Pr.
Grubel, Herbert F. International Economics. rev. ed. 1981. 20.95 (ISBN 0-256-02493-6). Irwin.
Grundy, Kenneth W., et al, eds. Evaluating Transnational Programs in Government & Business. 1980. 29.50 (ISBN 0-08-025101-3). Pergamon.
Haberler, Gottfried. The World Economy, Money, & the Great Depression. LC 75-42762. 1976. pap. 3.25 (ISBN 0-8447-3198-6). Am Enterprise.
Hamilton, Barry E. The New Emerging Afro-Arab & European Combine. (Illus.). 167p. 1980. deluxe ed. 59.75 (ISBN 0-930008-61-8). Inst Econ Pol.
Hanabusa, Masamichi. Trade Problems Between Japan & Western Europe. LC 79-88567. (Illus.). 138p. 1979. 24.95 (ISBN 0-03-053361-9). Praeger.
Hanright, Roger K. The Approaching Third World Conflagration: The Oil Crisis & the Division of the World into Two Maximal Empires As a Solution to Avoid the Universal Catastrophe. (Illus.). 143p. 1980. deluxe ed. 61.75 (ISBN 0-930008-60-X). Inst Econ Pol.
Hansen, Roger D. Beyond the North-South Stalemate. LC 78-10607. 348p. 1979. pap. 5.95 (ISBN 0-07-026049-4). Overseas Dev Council.
Hansen, Roger D. & Overseas Development Council Staff. The U. S. & World Development: Agenda for Action, 1976. LC 76-4936. (Agenda Ser.). 240p. 1976. pap. 4.95 (ISBN 0-275-85670-4). Overseas Dev Council.
Haq, Khadija. A New Strategy for North-South Negotiations. (Policy Studies). 1980. 25.00 (ISBN 0-686-77706-9). Pergamon.
Haq, Khadija, ed. Dialogue for a New Order. LC 80-12972. (Pergamon Policy Studies on International Development). 328p. 1980. 32.50 (ISBN 0-08-025105-6). Pergamon.
--Equality of Opportunity Within & Among Nations. LC 77-14405. (Praeger Special Studies). 1977. 27.95 (ISBN 0-03-040856-3). Praeger.
Harrod, Roy. International Economics. (Cambridge Economic Handbook Ser). 1957. pap. 10.95x (ISBN 0-521-08780-5). Cambridge U Pr.
Harrod, Roy F. & Hague, Douglas C., eds. International Trade Theory in a Developing World: Proceedings. (International Economic Assn. Ser). 1969. 29.95 (ISBN 0-312-42385-3). St Martin.
Hartland-Thunberg, Penelope. Trading Blocs, U.S. Exports, & World Trade. (Westview Special Studies in International Economics & Business). 197p. 1980. lib. bdg. 23.25xx (ISBN 0-89158-967-8). Westview.
Heaton, Frederick L. The Choice for Humanity: World Catastrophe or the Political Division of the Earth. (Illus.). 159p. 1980. deluxe ed. 55.25 (ISBN 0-930008-62-6). Inst Econ Pol.
Heilperin, Michael A. International Monetary Economics. LC 78-21878. (Studies in International Economics: No. 2). (Illus.). xiv, 281p. Repr. of 1939 ed. lib. bdg. 17.50x (ISBN 0-87991-851-9). Porcupine Pr.
Helleiner, G. K. Protectionism or Industrial Adjustment, No. 39. (The Atlantic Papers). 72p. 1980. pap. 4.75 (ISBN 0-916672-79-4, Pub. by Atlantic Inst France). Allanheld.
Hilton, Stanley E. Brazil & the Great Powers, 1930-1939: The Politics of Trade Rivalry. (Latin American Monographs Ser.: No. 38). 326p. 1975. 15.00x (ISBN 0-292-70713-4). U of Tex Pr.
Hinshaw, Randall, ed. Key Issues in International Monetary Reform. (Business Economics & Finance Ser.: Vol. 4). 170p. 1975. 22.75 (ISBN 0-8247-6324-6). Dekker.
Hirsch, Fred, et al. Alternatives to Monetary Disorder. (Nineteen Eighties Project (Council on Foreign Relations)). 1977. pap. 3.95 (ISBN 0-07-029047-4, P&RB). McGraw.
Hogan & Hartson. Legal Considerations Relating to U. S.-Brazilian Ventures. LC 79-55257. 1979. pap. 10.00 (ISBN 0-89834-013-6, 6023). Chamber Comm US.
Hood, Neil & Young, Stephen. The Economics of Multinational Enterprise. (Illus.). 1979. pap. text ed. 19.95x (ISBN 0-582-44388-1). Longman.
Hossain, Kamal, ed. Legal Aspects of the New International Economic Order. 300p. 1980. 32.50x (ISBN 0-89397-088-3). Nichols Pub.
Howe, James W. & Overseas Development Council Staff. The U. S. & the Developing World: Agenda for Action, 1974. LC 74-4234. (Agenda Ser.). 228p. 1974. pap. 3.95 (ISBN 0-686-28670-7). Overseas Dev Council.
--The U. S. & World Development: Agenda for Action, 1975. LC 75-11641. (Agenda Ser.). 288p. 1975. pap. 4.95 (ISBN 0-275-89310-3). Overseas Dev Council.
Hunter, Robert E. & Overseas Development Council Staff. The United States & the Developing World: Agenda for Action, 1973. LC 73-76292. (Agenda Ser.). 172p. 1973. pap. 2.50 (ISBN 0-686-28671-5). Overseas Dev Council.
ILO International Labour Office, ed. Employment, Growth & Basic Needs: A One-World Problem. LC 77-70278. 256p. 1977. pap. 3.95 (ISBN 0-686-28705-3). Overseas Dev Council.
Interdependence & Development. 1979. 8.00x (ISBN 92-64-21989-7). OECD.
International Fiscal Association. Work in Intergovernmental Organizations on Transnational Companies. (Congress Seminar Series of the Inter-National Fiscal Association: No. 1). 1979. pap. 16.00 (ISBN 90-200-0491-3, Pub. by Kluwer Law Netherlands). Kluwer Boston.
International Investment & Multinational Enterprises - Review of the 1976 Declarations & Decisions. 67p. 1979. 6.00x (ISBN 92-64-11970-1). OECD.
Investing in Developing Countries. 4th rev. ed. 1979. 12.00x (ISBN 92-64-11880-2). OECD.
Jensen, F. B. & Walter, I., eds. Readings in International Economic Relations. 1966. 14.50x (ISBN 0-471-06636-2). Wiley.
Johnson, Harry G. World Economy at the Crossroads: A Survey of Current Problems of Money, Trade & Economic Development. 1965. pap. 3.95x (ISBN 0-19-500336-5). Oxford U Pr.
Kamrany, Nake, ed. The New Economics of the Less Developed Countries: Changing Perceptions in the North-South Dialogue. LC 77-14602. (Westview Special Studies in Social Political, & Economic Development Ser.). 1978. lib. bdg. 29.25x (ISBN 0-89158-449-8). Westview.
Katz, Samuel I., ed. U. S.-European Monetary Relations. 1979. 15.25 (ISBN 0-8447-2150-6); pap. 7.25 (ISBN 0-8447-2149-2). Am Enterprise.
Katzenstein, Peter J., ed. Between Power & Plenty: Foreign Economic Policies of Advanced Industrial States. LC 77-91053. 352p. 1978. 25.00 (ISBN 0-299-07560-5); pap. 8.95 (ISBN 0-299-07564-8). U of Wis Pr.
Kegley, Charles W., Jr. & McGowan, Patrick, eds. The Political Economy of Foreign Policy Behavior. LC 80-252248. (Sage International Yearbook of Foreign Policy Studies: Vol. 6). 312p. 1981. 22.50 (ISBN 0-8039-1160-2); pap. 9.95 (ISBN 0-8039-1161-0). Sage.
Kenen, Peter & Lubitz, Raymond. International Economics. 3rd ed. LC 71-135021. (Foundations of Modern Economics Ser). (Illus.). 1971. pap. 9.95 ref. ed. (ISBN 0-13-472613-8). P-H.
Kenwood, A. G. & Lougheed, A. L. The Growth of the International Economy, 1820-1960. LC 70-171174. 328p. 1971. 23.00 (ISBN 0-87395-137-9). State U NY Pr.
Keynes, John M. The Collected Writings of John Maynard Keynes, Vol. 25, Activities 1940-44: Shaping the Postwar World: The Clearing Union. Moggridge, D., ed. LC 76-13349. 360p. 1980. 42.50 (ISBN 0-521-22018-1). Cambridge U Pr.
--The Collected Writings of John Maynard Keynes, Vol. 27, Activities 1940-46: Shaping the Postwar World: Employment & Commodities. Moggridge, D., ed. LC 76-13349. 424p. 1980. 42.50 (ISBN 0-521-23074-8). Cambridge U Pr.
--The Collected Writings of John Maynard Keynes, Vol. 26, Activities 1943-46: Shaping the Postwar World: Bretton Woods & Reparations. Moggridge, D., ed. LC 76-13349. 1980. 42.50 (ISBN 0-521-22939-1). Cambridge U Pr.
Kindleberger, Charles P. International Money: A Collection of Essays. 336p. 1981. text ed. 37.50x (ISBN 0-04-332077-5); pap. text ed. 14.50x (ISBN 0-04-332078-3). Allen Unwin.
--Power & Money: The Politics of International Economics & the Economics of International Politics. LC 70-116852. 1970. 5.95x (ISBN 0-465-06134-6). Basic.
Kindleberger, Charles P. & Lindert, Peter. International Economics. 6th ed. 1978. 19.25x (ISBN 0-256-02028-0). Irwin.
Klass, Michael W., et al. International Mineral Cartels & Embargoes: Policy Implications for the United States. LC 80-11123. 350p. 1980. 31.95 (ISBN 0-03-044366-0). Praeger.
Kohl, Wilfred L., ed. Economic Foreign Policies of Industrial States. LC 76-43584. 1977. 21.50 (ISBN 0-669-00958-X). Lexington Bks.
Kolko, Joyce. America & the Crisis of World Capitalism. LC 74-253. 216p. 1976. pap. 4.95x (ISBN 0-8070-4791-0, BP533). Beacon Pr.
Kostyukhin, D. The World Market Today. 320p. 1979. pap. 3.40 (ISBN 0-8285-0390-7, Pub. by Progress Pubs Russia). Imported Pubns.
Kreinin, Mordechai E. International Economics: A Policy Approach. 3rd ed. 464p. 1979. text ed. 20.95 (ISBN 0-15-541540-9, HC). HarBraceJ.
Krueger, Anne O. Liberalization Attempts & Consequences. (Studies in International Econimic Relations; Special Conference Ser. on Foreign Trade Regimes & Economic Development: No. 9; No. 10). 1978. 18.50 (ISBN 0-88410-483-4). Ballinger Pub.
Laffer & Miles. International Economics: In an Integrated World. 416p. 1981. 19.95 (ISBN 0-8302-4028-4). Goodyear.
Laszlo, Ervin, ed. The Implementation of the New International Economic Order. (Pergamon Policy Studies). Date not set. text ed. price not set (ISBN 0-08-025111-0). Pergamon.
--World Leadership & the New International Economic Order. (Pergamon Policy Studies). Date not set. text ed. price not set (ISBN 0-08-025112-9). Pergamon.
Laszlo, Ervin & Kurtzman, Joel, eds. Political & Institutional Issues of the New International Economic Order. (Pergamon Policy Studies on the New International Economic Order). 208p. 1981. text ed. 20.00 (ISBN 0-08-025122-6). Pergamon.
--The Structure of the World Economy & Prospects for a New International Economic Order. LC 79-23350. (Pergamon Policy Studies on the New International Economic Order Ser.). 120p. 1980. 16.50 (ISBN 0-08-025119-6). Pergamon.
--The United States, Canada & the New International Economic Order. (Policy Studies). 1979. 20.00 (ISBN 0-08-025113-7). Pergamon.
--Western Europe & the New International Economic Order: Representative Samples of European Perspectives. LC 80-16620. (Pergamon Policy Studies). 120p. 1980. 16.50 (ISBN 0-08-025114-5). Pergamon.
Laszlo, Ervin, et al. The Objectives of the New International Economic Order. LC 78-14766. (Pergamon Policy Studies). 288p. 1978. 20.00 (ISBN 0-08-023697-9). Pergamon.
--R C D C (Regional Cooperation Among Developing Countries) The New Imperative of Development in the 1980's. 75p. 1981. pap. 10.00 (ISBN 0-686-71860-7). Pergamon.
--The Obstacles to the New International Economic Order. LC 79-28723. (Pergamon Policy Studies on the New International Economic Order). 170p. 1980. 20.00 (ISBN 0-08-025110-2); pap. 7.95 (ISBN 0-08-025970-7). Pergamon.
Laudicina, Paul A. World Poverty & Development: A Survey of American Opinion. LC 73-89873. (Monographs: No. 8). 126p. 1973. 2.50 (ISBN 0-686-28687-1). Overseas Dev Council.
Laule, Gerhard, tr. The Effects of Losses in One Country on the Income Tax Treatment in Other Countries of an Associated Companies Engaged in International Activities. (Cahiers De Droit Fiscal International LXIV B). 1979. pap. 45.00 (ISBN 90-200-0563-4, Pub. by Kluwer Law Netherlands). Kluwer Boston.
Leamer, Edward E. & Stern, Robert M., eds. Quantitative International Economics. LC 79-118034. 209p. 1970. 19.95x (ISBN 0-202-06066-7). Aldine Pub.
Leeds, Roger S. Co-Financing for Development: Why Not More? LC 80-80117. (Development Papers: No. 29). 64p. 1980. pap. 3.00 (ISBN 0-686-28119-5). Overseas Dev Council.
Levcik, Friedrich & Stankovsky, Jan. Industrial Cooperation Between East & West. LC 78-73222. 1979. 27.50 (ISBN 0-87332-126-X). M E Sharpe.
Lewis, W. Arthur. The Evolution of the International Economic Order. LC 77-15374. 1973. 11.00 (ISBN 0-691-04219-5); pap. 4.95 (ISBN 0-691-00360-2). Princeton U Pr.
Long, Frank, ed. The Political Economy of EEC Relations with African, Caribbean & Pacific States: Contributions to the Understanding of the Lome Convention on North-South Relations. 192p. 1980. 26.00 (ISBN 0-08-024077-1). Pergamon.
Losman, Donald L. International Economic Sanctions: The Cases of Cuba, Israel, & Rhodesia. LC 78-21429. 1979. 12.95x (ISBN 0-8263-0500-8). U of NM Pr.
Lozoya, Jorge & Estevez, Jaime, eds. Latin America & the New International Economic Order. LC 79-27384. (Pergamon Policy Studies in the New International Economic Order). 112p. 1980. 16.50 (ISBN 0-08-025118-8). Pergamon.
Lozoya, Jorge A. & Bhattacharya, A. K. The Financial Issues of the New International Economic Order. LC 79-29709. (Pergamon Policy Studies on International Development). 256p. 1980. 20.00 (ISBN 0-08-025121-8). Pergamon.
Lozoya, Jorge A., ed. International Trade, Industrialization & the New International Economic Order. (Pergamon Policy Studies). Date not set. text ed. price not set (ISBN 0-08-025120-X). Pergamon.
--The Social & Cultural Issues of the New International Economic Order. (Pergamon Policy Studies). Date not set. text ed. price not set (ISBN 0-08-025123-4). Pergamon.
MacBean, A. I. & Snowden, N. International Institutions in Trade & Finance. (Studies in Economics: No. 18). (Illus.). 272p. 1981. text ed. 29.95x (ISBN 0-04-382032-8); pap. text ed. 11.95x (ISBN 0-04-382033-6). Allen Unwin.
MacBean, Alasdair. A Positive Approach to the International Economic Order, Pt. 1: Trade & Structural Adjustment. LC 78-70406. 82p. 1978. 3.00 (ISBN 0-902594-33-8). Natl Planning.
MacBean, Alasdair & Balasubramanyam, V. N. A Positive Approach to the International Economic Order, Pt. II: Nontrade Issues. 1980. 5.00 (ISBN 0-902594-37-0). Natl Planning.
McCulloch, Rachel. Research & Development As a Determinant of U.S. International Competitiveness. LC 78-63432. 60p. 1978. 3.00 (ISBN 0-89068-044-2). Natl Planning.
McGinnis, James B. Bread & Justice: Toward a New International Economic Order. LC 79-90224. 372p. 1979. pap. text ed. 4.95 (ISBN 0-8091-9537-2); tchrs. ed. 7.95 (ISBN 0-8091-9536-4). Paulist Pr.
McLaughlin, Martin M. & Overseas Development Council Staff. The United States & World Development: Agenda 1979. LC 78-71589. (Agenda Ser.). 280p. 1979. pap. 5.95 (ISBN 0-686-28666-9). Overseas Dev Council.
Macrothesaurus for Information Processing in the Field of Economic & Social Development: New English Edition. 1979. 30.00 (ISBN 92-64-11882-9). OECD.
Magdoff, Harry & Sweezy, Paul M. The Deepening Crisis of U.S. Capitalism: Essays by Harry Magdoff & Paul M. Sweezy. LC 80-8935. 256p. 1981. 16.00 (ISBN 0-85345-573-2); pap. 6.50 (ISBN 0-85345-574-0). Monthly Rev.
Magee, Stephen P. International Trade. LC 78-74686. (Perspectives on Economics Ser.). (Illus.). 1980. pap. text ed. 6.95 (ISBN 0-201-08365-5). A-W.

Mahbub ul Haq. The Third World & the International Economic Order. (Development Papers: No. 22). 54p. 1976. pap. 1.50 (ISBN 0-686-28676-6). Overseas Dev Council.

Malmgren, Harald B. International Economic Peacekeeping in Phase II. LC 77-190727. 1972. 8.95 (ISBN 0-8129-0389-7); pap. 3.95 (ISBN 0-8129-6204-4). Times Bks.

--Trade for Development. LC 76-152712. (Monographs: No. 4). 88p. 1971. 1.00 (ISBN 0-686-28691-X). Overseas Dev Council.

Marcuzzi, G. European Ecosystems. (Biogeographica: Vol. 15). 1979. lib. bdg. 158.00 (ISBN 90-6193-216-5, Pub. by Junk Pubs. Netherlands). Kluwer Boston.

Mason, C. M., ed. Effective Management of Resources: The International Politics of the North Sea. 1979. 22.50x (ISBN 0-89397-043-3). Nichols Pub.

Mason, R. H., et al. The Economics of International Business. 464p. 1981. Repr. of 1975 ed. text ed. 23.50 (ISBN 0-89874-248-X). Krieger.

Mason, R. Hal, et al. International Business. 2nd ed. LC 80-23483. (Management & Administration Ser.). 428p. 1981. text ed. 22.95 (ISBN 0-471-06217-0). Wiley.

Mathieson, John A. The Advanced Developing Countries: Emerging Actors in the World Economy. LC 79-91996. (Development Papers: No. 28). 72p. 1979. pap. 3.00 (ISBN 0-686-28672-3). Overseas Dev Council.

Meade, J. E. The Theory of International Economic Policy: The Balance of Payments, Vol. 1. (RIIA Ser.). 448p. 1951. 29.50x (ISBN 0-19-214553-3). Oxford U Pr.

Meagher, Robert F. An International Redistribution of Wealth & Power: A Study of the Charter of Economic Rights & Duties of States. (Pergamon Policy Studies). 1979. text ed. 34.50 (ISBN 0-08-022478-4). Pergamon.

Meerhaeghe, M. A. International Economic Institutions. 2nd ed. LC 75-179701. 1972. 22.50x (ISBN 0-312-42070-6). St. Martin.

Megrelis, Christian. Keys to the Future: From Free Trade to Fair Trade. LC 80-5075. 1980. 19.95 (ISBN 0-669-03705-2). Lexington Bks.

Meier, Gerald M. International Economics: The Theory of Policy. (Illus.). 1980. text ed. 16.95x (ISBN 0-19-502636-5). Oxford U Pr.

--International Trade & Development. LC 73-13405. 208p. 1975. Repr. of 1963 ed. lib. bdg. 19.50x (ISBN 0-8371-7061-3, MEIT). Greenwood.

Menon, Bhashkar P. Global Dialogue: The New International Economic Order. 1977. text ed. 21.00 (ISBN 0-08-021498-3); pap. text ed. 8.50 (ISBN 0-08-021499-1). Pergamon.

Mersky, Roy M., ed. Conference on Transnational Economic Boycotts & Coercion, 2 vols. LC 78-7049. 1978. 85.00 set (ISBN 0-379-20335-9). Oceana.

Metzger, Stanley D. Law & Policymaking for Trade Among Have & Have-Not Nations. Carey, John, ed. LC 68-22787. (Hammarskjold Forum Ser.: No. 11). 1968. 10.00 (ISBN 0-379-11811-4). Oceana.

Mezerik, Avrahm G., ed. Trade, Aid & Economic Development. 1964. pap. 15.00 (ISBN 0-685-13210-2, 81). Intl Review.

The Middle East & the Attempt at World Economic Hegemony. 1976. 44.75 (ISBN 0-685-85009-9). Inst Econ Finan.

Mikdashi, Zuhayr, ed. Arab-European Business Cooperation. 1979. pap. 26.00 (ISBN 90-200-0554-5, Pub. by Kluwer Law Netherlands). Kluwer Boston.

Mikesell, Raymond F. & Farah, Mark G. U. S. Export Competitiveness in Manufactures in Third World Countries, Vol. II. LC 80-67711. (Significant Issues Ser.: No. 9). 144p. 1980. 5.95 (ISBN 0-89206-026-3). CSI Studies.

Mikesell, Raymond F. & Furth, J. Herbert. Foreign Dollar Balances & the International Role of the Dollar. (Studies in International Economic Relations: No. 8). 1974. 10.00x (ISBN 0-87014-262-3, Dist. by Columbia U Pr). Natl Bur Econ Res.

Milner, Chris & Greenaway, David. An Introduction to International Economics. (Illus.). 1979. pap. text ed. 13.95x (ISBN 0-582-45576-6). Longman.

Mirow, Kurt R. & Maurer, Harry. Webs of Power: International Cartels & the World Economy. 525p. 1982. 15.95 (ISBN 0-395-30536-5). HM.

Moving Toward Change: Some Thoughts on the International Economic Order. 137p. 1976. pap. 6.00 (ISBN 92-3-101365-3, U394, UNESCO). Unipub.

Muller, Ronald E. Revitalizing America. 1980. 13.95 (ISBN 0-671-24889-8). S&S.

--Revitalizing America: Politics for Prosperity. 1982. pap. 6.95 (ISBN 0-671-43831-X, Touchstone Bks). S&S.

Mundell, Robert A. & Swoboda, Alexander K., eds. Monetary Problems of the International Economy. pap. write for info. (ISBN 0-226-55066-4). U of Chicago Pr.

Munoz, Heraldo, ed. From Dependency to Development: Strategies to Overcome Underdevelopment & Inequality. (Westview Special Studies in Social, Political, & Economic Development). 300p. 1981. lib. bdg. 28.50x (ISBN 0-89158-902-3); pap. text ed. 12.50 (ISBN 0-86531-079-3). Westview.

Myrdal, Gunnar. An International Economy: Problems & Perspectives. LC 77-25683. 1978. Repr. of 1956 ed. lib. bdg. 29.75x (ISBN 0-313-20078-5, MYIC). Greenwood.

Mytelka. Regional Development in a Global Economy. LC 79-10192. 1979. text ed. 19.50 (ISBN 0-300-02342-1). Yale U Pr.

Nairn, Ronald C. Wealth of Nations in Crisis. LC 79-90284. 289p. 1979. 12.95 (ISBN 0-934018-00-6). Bayland Pub.

National Accounts of OECD Countries, Nineteen Sixty to Nineteen Seventy-Seven, Vol. II, Detailed Tables. 264p. 1979. 17.50x (ISBN 92-64-01958-8). OECD.

Nawaz, Tawfique, compiled by. The New International Economic Order: A Bibliography. LC 79-28077. 200p. 1980. lib. bdg. 27.50 (ISBN 0-313-22111-1, NAI/). Greenwood.

Neale, Alan D. The Flow of Resources from Rich to Poor. LC 72-38760. (Harvard University. Center for International Affairs. Occasional Papers in International Affairs: No. 2). Repr. of 1961 ed. 11.50 (ISBN 0-404-54602-1). AMS Pr.

Neuberger, Egon & Lara, Juan. The Foreign Trade Practices of Centrally Planned Economies & Their Effects on U.S. International Competitiveness. LC 77-90040. 56p. 1977. 3.00 (ISBN 0-89068-043-4). Natl Planning.

Neuberger, Egon & Tyson, Laura D., eds. The Impact of International Economic Disturbances on the Soviet Union & Eastern Europe. (Pergamon Policy Studies). 60.00 (ISBN 0-08-025102-1). Pergamon.

Nicol, Davidson & Echeverria, Luis, eds. Regionalism & the New International Economic Order: Studies Presented to the UNITAR-CEESTEM Club of Rome Conference at the United Nations. (Pergamon Policy Studies on International Development). 448p. 1981. 45.00 (ISBN 0-08-026318-6); pap. 19.50 (ISBN 0-08-026331-3). Pergamon.

Njoku, John E. Analyzing Nigerian-Americans Under a New Economic Order. LC 80-5916. 128p. (Orig.). 1981. pap. text ed. 7.50 (ISBN 0-8191-1448-0). U Pr of Amer.

Nolde, Boris E. Russia in the Economic War (Economic & Social History of the World War) 1928. 42.50x (ISBN 0-686-51304-5). Elliots Bks.

Noreng, Oystein. Oil Politics in the Nineteen-Eighties: Patterns of International Cooperation. (Illus.). 1978. text ed. 9.95x (ISBN 0-07-047185-1, P&RB); pap. 5.95x (ISBN 0-07-047186-X). McGraw.

Nurkse, Ragnar. Equilibrium & Growth in the World Economy: Economic Essays. Haberler, Gottfried & Stern, Robert M., eds. LC 61-11007. (Economic Studies: No. 118). (Illus.). 1961. 17.50x (ISBN 0-674-26000-7). Harvard U Pr.

OAS General Secretariat Department of Publications, ed. Boletin Estadistico De la OEA. (Periodical-Quarterly Ser.). 207p. 4.00 (ISBN 0-686-68291-2). OAS.

OECD. Collective Bargaining & Government Policies in Ten OECD Countries: Austria, Canada, France, Germany, Italy, Japan, N. Zealand, Sweden, UK & US. (Illus.). 151p. (Orig.). 1980. pap. 9.00x (ISBN 92-64-12011-4). OECD.

--National Accounts of OECD Countries, Nineteen Sixty-One to Nineteen Seventy-Eight, Vol. II. (Illus.). 284p. 1980. pap. 18.00x (ISBN 92-64-02094-2, 30-80-03-3). OECD.

--Policy Implications of Data Network Developments in the OECD Area. (Information Computer Communications Policy: No. 3). (Illus.). 206p. (Orig., Fr.). 1980. pap. 12.50x (ISBN 92-64-12005-X, 93-79-02-1). OECD.

Ohlin, Bertil, et al, eds. The International Allocation of Economic Activity. LC 77-11048. 1978. text ed. 54.50x (ISBN 0-8419-0342-5). Holmes & Meier.

Oliver, Robert W. International Economic Co-Operation & the World Bank. 421p. 1975. text ed. 35.00x (ISBN 0-8419-5013-X). Holmes & Meier.

Olson, Robert K. U. S. Foreign Policy & the New International Economic Order. (Special Studies in International Relations). 184p. 1981. lib. bdg. 20.00x (ISBN 0-86531-125-0). Westview.

Oppenheimer, Peter, ed. Issues in International Economics. (Oxford International Symposia). 300p. 1980. 40.00 (ISBN 0-85362-186-1, Oriel). Routledge & Kegan.

Organization for Economic Cooperation & Development. International Direct Investment: Policies, Procedures & Practices in OECD Member Countries, 1979. 72p. (Orig.). 1980. pap. text ed. 4.25x (ISBN 92-64-12026-2, 21 80 02 1). OECD.

Pearce, I. F. International Trade. 1970. text ed. 17.95x (ISBN 0-393-09948-2, NortonC). Norton.

Pincus, John. Economic Aid & International Cost Sharing. (Illus.). 240p. 1965. 16.00x (ISBN 0-8018-0533-3). Johns Hopkins.

Poniachek, Harvey A. Monetary Independence Under Flexible Exchange Rates. (Illus.). 1979. 18.95 (ISBN 0-669-02728-6). Lexington Bks.

Poulson, Barry W., et al, eds. U. S.-Mexico Economic Relations. (Special Studies in International Economics & Business). 1979. lib. bdg. 36.75x (ISBN 0-89158-469-2). Westview.

Pugel, Thomas A. International Market Linkages & U.S. Manufacturing: Prices, Profits, & Patterns. LC 78-24108. 1979. reference 15.00 (ISBN 0-88410-490-7). Ballinger Pub.

Raichur, S. & Liske, C. T., eds. The Politics of Aid, Trade & Investment. LC 75-31886. (Comparative Political Economics & Public Policy Ser.). 218p. 1976. 25.95 (ISBN 0-470-54117-2). Halsted Pr.

Ramesh, Jairam & Weiss, Charles, Jr., eds. Mobilizing Technology for World Development. LC 79-5349. 240p. 1979. pap. 6.95 (ISBN 0-03-055451-9). Overseas Dev Council.

Rangarajan, L. N. Commodity Conflict: The Political Economy of International Commodity Negotiations. LC 77-22674. (Illus.). 1978. 32.50x (ISBN 0-8014-1154-8). Cornell U Pr.

Ranis, Gustav. The United States & the Developing Economies. rev. ed. 1973. 8.95x (ISBN 0-393-05461-6, NortonC); pap. 5.95x (ISBN 0-393-09999-7). Norton.

Reubens, Edwin P., ed. The Challenge of the New International Economic Order. (Westview Special Studies in International Economics & Business). 220p. 1981. lib. bdg. 26.50 (ISBN 0-89158-762-4); pap. text ed. 12.00x (ISBN 0-86531-078-5). Westview.

Revenue Statistics of OECD Members Countries, Nineteen Sixty-Five to Nineteen Seventy-Eight. 235p. 1979. 17.00x (ISBN 92-64-01959-6). OECD.

Richardson, John H. Economic Disarmament: A Study of International Cooperation. LC 75-41228. Repr. of 1931 ed. 18.50 (ISBN 0-404-14591-4). AMS Pr.

Richardson, Neil R. Foreign Policy & Economic Dependence. LC 78-6451. 226p. 1978. text ed. 12.95x (ISBN 0-292-72425-X). U of Tex Pr.

Ringquist, Wilfred D. The Approaching Trade War Between the United States & the Rest of the World. (Illus.). 136p. 1980. deluxe ed. 43.55 (ISBN 0-918968-69-0). Inst Econ Finan.

Robertson, Jerome B. Jerusalem, Germany, Soviet Russia & the Approaching Danger of a New World Conflagration. (The Most Meaningful Contemporary Historical Trends Library). (Illus.). 161p. 1981. 63.85 (ISBN 0-930008-85-5). Inst Econ Pol.

Ropke, Wilhelm. International Economic Disintegration. LC 78-11239. (Studies in International Economics: No. 4). xii, 283p. Repr. of 1942 ed. lib. bdg. 17.50x (ISBN 0-87991-853-5). Porcupine Pr.

Ross, Arthur. Politics & Economics in an Interdependent World. LC 78-24281. 1979. 15.00 (ISBN 0-8122-7762-7). U of Pa Pr.

Rothstein, Robert L. Global Bargaining: UNCTAD & the Quest for a New International Economic Order. LC 78-70316. 1979. 21.00x (ISBN 0-691-07610-3); pap. 6.95 (ISBN 0-691-02190-2). Princeton U Pr.

--The Weak in the World of the Strong: The Third World in the International System. LC 77-7889. (Institute of War & Peace Studies). 1977. 18.00x (ISBN 0-231-04338-4). Columbia U Pr.

Royal Institute of International Affairs, ed. The Chatham House Annual Review: International Economic & Monetary Issues, Vol. 1. (PPS on International Politics). (Illus.). 200p. 1981. 20.01 (ISBN 0-08-027532-X). Pergamon.

Royle, Edward F. The Metaphysics of the Oils, the New Power Structure of the World & the Nature of the Postpetroleum Era. (Illus.). 142p. 1980. deluxe ed. 59.75 (ISBN 0-930008-58-8). Inst Econ Pol.

Rugman, Alan M. International Diversification & the Multinational Enterprise. (Illus.). 160p. 1979. 16.95 (ISBN 0-669-02772-3). Lexington Bks.

Sachs, Ignacy. Studies in Political Economy of Development. LC 79-40488. 1980. 45.00 (ISBN 0-685-97187-2) (ISBN 0-685-97188-0). Pergamon.

Samuelson, Paul, ed. International Economic Relations. (International Economics Association Ser). 1969. lib. bdg. 19.95 (ISBN 0-312-42175-3). St Martin.

Sandler, Todd, ed. The Theory & Structures of International Political Economy. (Westview Special Studies in International Economics & Business). 280p. 1980. lib. bdg. 26.25x (ISBN 0-89158-765-9). Westview.

Saunders, C. T. East & West in the Energy Squeeze. 1980. 32.50 (ISBN 0-312-22473-7). St Martin.

Saunders, C. T., ed. Money & Finance in East & West. (East-West European Economic Interaction Ser.: Vol. 4). 1979. pap. 34.10 (ISBN 0-387-81507-4). Springer-Verlag.

Sawyer, J. A., ed. Modelling the International Transmission Mechanism. (Contributions to Economic Analysis Ser.: Vol. 121). 1979. 73.25 (ISBN 0-444-85223-9, North Holland). Elsevier.

Scammell, W. M. The International Economy Since Nineteen Forty-Five. LC 79-27416. 1980. 25.00 (ISBN 0-312-42191-5). St Martin.

--International Monetary Policy. LC 74-26769. 1976. pap. 16.95 (ISBN 0-470-15197-8). Halsted Pr.

Scheuer, Sidney H. The Ethics of International Economics: An Innovative Approach to World Affairs. 192p. 1980. 8.50 (ISBN 0-682-49653-7). Exposition.

Schiavo-Campo, Salvatore. International Economics. 1978. text ed. 16.95 (ISBN 0-87626-386-4). Winthrop.

Schmitz, W., ed. Convertibility, Multilateralism & Freedom: World Economic Policy in the Seventies. Essays in Honour of Reinhard Kamitz. LC 76-186940. 400p. 1972. 37.80 (ISBN 0-387-81056-0). Springer-Verlag.

Schnitzer, Martin. Role of U. S. Multinationals in East-West Trade. LC 78-19794. 168p. 1980. 21.50 (ISBN 0-03-043026-7). Praeger.

Schooler, Robert D. An Introduction to International Business: The Dominant Aspect of International Relations. LC 78-71778. 1979. pap. text ed. 5.00x (ISBN 0-87543-146-1). Lucas.

Schwarzenberger, Georg. Economic World Order: A Basic Problem of International Economic Law. LC 70-132276. 1971. 11.00 (ISBN 0-379-11911-0). Oceana.

Sengupta, Arjun, ed. Commodities, Finance & Trade: Issues in the North-South Negotiations. LC 79-17881. (Contributions in Economics & Economic History: No. 30). (Illus.). 1980. lib. bdg. 28.50 (ISBN 0-313-21469-7, SEC/). Greenwood.

Servan-Schreiber, Jean-J. The American Challenge. Steel, Ronald, tr. from Fr. LC 68-19793. 1979. pap. 5.95 (ISBN 0-689-70586-7, 249). Atheneum.

Sewell, John & Overseas Development Council Staff. The United States & World Development: Agenda 1977. LC 76-30725. (Agenda Ser.). 272p. 1977. pap. 4.95 (ISBN 0-275-65000-6). Overseas Dev Council.

Sewell, John W. The United States & World Development: Agenda 1980. 256p. 1980. 23.95 (ISBN 0-03-058993-2); pap. 6.95 (ISBN 0-03-058992-4). Praeger.

Sewell, John W. & Overseas Development Council Staff. The United States & World Development: Agenda 1980. LC 80-82415. 242p. 1980. pap. 6.95 (ISBN 0-03-058992-4). Overseas Dev Council.

Shonfield, Andrew. International Economic Relations: The Western System in the 1960s & 1970s. LC 76-54540. (The Washington Papers: No. 42). 88p. 1977. 4.00 (ISBN 0-8039-0790-7). Sage.

Shonfield, Andrew, et al. International Economic Relations of the Western World 1959-1971, Vol. 1. Shonfield, Andrew, ed. (Royal Institute of International Affairs Ser). 448p. 1976. 45.00x (ISBN 0-19-218314-1). Oxford U Pr.

Shuster, M. R. The Public International Law of Money. (Illus.). 359p. 1973. 32.00x (ISBN 0-19-825308-7). Oxford U Pr.

Silver, Morris. Affluence, Altruism, & Atrophy: The Decline of the Welfare State. LC 79-3528. 200p. 1980. 18.50x (ISBN 0-8147-7810-0). NYU Pr.

Singh, Jyoti S. A New International Economic Order: Toward a Fair Redistribution of the World's Resources. LC 76-54508. (Special Studies). 1977. text ed. 20.95 (ISBN 0-275-24170-X). Praeger.

Sjostedt, Gunnar. The External Role of the European Community. 1977. 24.95 (ISBN 0-566-00172-1, 01455-9, Pub. by Saxon Hse England). Lexington Bks.

Smith, Gordon W. The External Public Debt Prospects of the Non-Oil-Exporting Developing Countries. LC 77-90866. (Monographs: No. 10). 64p. 1977. 4.00 (ISBN 0-686-28685-5). Overseas Dev Council.

Snider, Delbert A. Introduction to International Economics. 7th ed. 1979. 19.95x (ISBN 0-256-02176-7). Irwin.

Sodersten, Bo. International Economics. 2nd ed. LC 79-15789. 1980. 16.00x (ISBN 0-312-42110-9). St Martin.

Spero, Joan E. The Politics of International Economic Relations. 2nd ed. 350p. 1981. text ed. 14.95x (ISBN 0-312-62704-1); pap. text ed. 8.95x (ISBN 0-686-71652-3). St Martin.
--The Politics of International Economic Relations. 2nd ed. 350p. 1981. text ed. 14.95x (ISBN 0-312-62704-1); pap. text ed. 8.95x (ISBN 0-686-71652-3). St Martin.
--The Politics of International Economic Relations. LC 76-41546. 1977. 14.95x (ISBN 0-312-62702-5); pap. text ed. 6.95x (ISBN 0-312-62703-3). St Martin.
Strange, Susan. International Economic Relations of the Western World, 1959-71, Vol. 2: International Monetary Relations. Shonfield, Andrew, ed. 1976. 45.00x (ISBN 0-19-218317-6). Oxford U Pr.
Sumner, William G. Earth-Hunger & Other Essays. 404p. 1980. text ed. 19.95 (ISBN 0-87855-323-1); pap. text ed. 6.95 (ISBN 0-87855-705-9). Transaction Bks.
Tasca, Diane, et al, eds. United States-Japanese Economic Relations: Cooperation, Competition & Confrontation. (Policy Studies). 1980. 18.25 (ISBN 0-08-025129-3). Pergamon.
Thinking & Doing. 96p. 1981. pap. 7.50 (ISBN 92-3-101841-8, U1075, UNESCO). Unipub.
Trade Monopolies in Eastern Europe, Nineteen Seventy-Nine to Nineteen Eighty. 4th ed. 163p. (Orig.). 1979. pap. 35.00x (ISBN 90-6156-520-0). Intl Pubns Serv.
Twitchett, Carol C. A Framework for Development: The EEC & the ACP. 160p. 1981. text ed. 28.50x (ISBN 0-04-338094-8). Allen Unwin.
Tyler, William G. Issues & Prospects for New International Economic Order. LC 77-78367. (Illus.). 1977. 19.95 (ISBN 0-669-01445-1). Lexington Bks.
United Nations. World Economic Survey, 1979-80. LC 48-1401. 116p. (Orig.). 1980. pap. 10.00x (ISBN 0-8002-1108-1). Intl Pubns Serv.
--Yearbook of Industrial Statistics, 1977, 2 vols. 11th ed. Incl. Vol. 1. General Industrial Statistics. 639p. 30.00x (ISBN 0-8002-2335-7); Vol. 2. Commodity Production Data, 1967 to 1977. 750p. 30.00x (ISBN 0-8002-2336-5). LC 76-646970. (Illus.). 1389p. 1979. write for info. Intl Pubns Serv.
--Yearbook of International Trade Statistics, 1979, 2 vols. 27th ed. Incl. Vol. 1. Trade by Country. 178p; Vol. 2. Trade by Commodity. 191p. LC 51-8987. (Illus.). 369p. (Eng. & Fr.). 1979. Set. 65.00x (ISBN 0-8002-2337-3). Intl Pubns Serv.
--Yearbook of National Accounts Statistics, 1978, 2 vols. 22nd ed. Incl. Vol. 1. Individual Country Data. 494p; Vol. 2. International Tables. 645p. LC 58-3719. (Illus.). 1979. 70.00x (ISBN 0-8002-2338-1). Intl Pubns Serv.
U. S. Department Of State. Sino-Soviet Economic Offensive in the Less Developed Countries. (Illus.). Repr. of 1958 ed. lib. bdg. 15.00 (ISBN 0-8371-2270-8, SISE). Greenwood.
Vajda, Imre & Simai, M., eds. Foreign Trade in a Planned Economy. LC 74-149433. 1971. 38.50 (ISBN 0-521-08153-X). Cambridge U Pr.
Van Bochove, C. A., et al, eds. Modeling for Government & Business. 1977. lib. bdg. 40.00 (ISBN 90-207-0732-9, Martinus Nijhoff Pubs). Kluwer Boston.
Van Lith, Jan A., ed. Change & the New International Economic Order. (Tilburg Studies in Economics: Vol. 20). 1980. lib. bdg. 14.95 (ISBN 0-89838-028-6, Pub. by Martinus Nijhoff Netherlands). Kluwer Boston.
Van Meerhaeghe, Marcel A. A Handbook of International Economic Institutions. 472p. 1980. lib. bdg. 76.50 (ISBN 90-247-2357-4, Pub. by Martinus Nijhoff Netherlands). Kluwer Boston.
Vienna Institute for Comparative Economic Studies. Comecon Data Nineteen Seventy-Nine. LC 80-17577. 436p. 1980. text ed. 45.50x (ISBN 0-8419-0607-6). Holmes & Meier.
Villamil, Jose, ed. Transnational Capitalism & National Development: New Perspectives on Dependence. LC 78-26672. (Harvester Studies in Development). 1979. text ed. 37.50x (ISBN 0-391-00963-X). Humanities.
Wadsworth, J. E. & De Juvigny, F. Leonard. New Approaches in Monetary Policy, No. 4. (Financial & Monetary Policy Issues Ser.). 406p. 1979. 40.00x (ISBN 90-286-0848-6). Sijthoff & Noordhoff.
Wallace, Don, Jr. International Regulation of Multinational Corporations. LC 75-8411. (Special Studies). (Illus.). 1976. text ed. 24.95 (ISBN 0-275-05880-8). Praeger.
Wallace, Don, Jr. & Escobar, Helga, eds. The Future of International Economic Organizations. LC 75-44942. (Special Studies). 1977. text ed. 23.95 (ISBN 0-275-22990-4). Praeger.
Walsh, A. E. & Paxton, John. Trade & Industrial Resources of the Common Market & EFTA Countries: A Comparative Statistical Analysis. 176p. 1970. text ed. 40.00x (ISBN 0-8377-1302-1). Rothman.
Walter, Ingo. International Economics. 3rd ed. LC 80-21541. 510p. 1981. text ed. 21.95 (ISBN 0-471-04957-3). Wiley.
Waring, F. A. Foreign Economic Policy. 1966. pap. 3.00x (ISBN 0-85564-036-7, Pub by U of W Austral Pr). Intl Schol Bk Serv.
Watts, Nita, ed. Economic Relations Between East & West. (International Economics Association Publications). 1979. 34.50x (ISBN 0-312-23508-9). St Martin.
Weiller, Jean & Coussy, Jean, eds. Economie Internationale 1: Automatismes et Structures (Faits, Theorie et Politiques) (Textes De Sciences Sociales: No.13). 340p. 1975. pap. text ed. 25.50x (ISBN 90-2797-666-X). Mouton.
Weiss, Leonard. Trade Liberalization & the National Interest, Vol. II. LC 80-80932. (Significant Issues Ser.: No. 2). 60p. 1980. 5.95 (ISBN 0-89206-016-6). CSI Studies.
Wells, Louis T. & Vernon, Raymond. Manager in the International Economy. 4th ed. (Illus.). 1981. text ed. 21.00 (ISBN 0-13-549550-4). P-H.
Wells, Louis T., Jr. & Vernon, Raymond. Economic Environment of International Business. 3rd ed. (Illus.). 272p. 1981. text ed. 14.95 (ISBN 0-13-224329-6). P-H.
Westshore, Inc. Doing Business with the Russians. (Praeger Special Studies). 1979. 20.95 (ISBN 0-03-048456-1). Praeger.
Whale, Philip B. International Trade. LC 67-16354. Repr. of 1932 ed. 20.00x (ISBN 0-678-05093-7). Kelley.
Whiting, D. P. International Trade & Payments. (Illus.). 160p. 1978. pap. 13.95x (ISBN 0-7121-0952-8). Intl Ideas.
Who Owns Whom: Australasia & Far East 1979-1980. 9th ed. LC 72-62467. 1190p. 1979. 175.00x (ISBN 0-8002-2415-9). Intl Pubns Serv.
Williamson, Robert B., et al. Latin American-U. S. Economic Interactions: Conflict, Accommodation & Policies for the Future. 380p. 1975. 16.25 (ISBN 0-8447-2051-8); pap. 8.25 (ISBN 0-8447-2050-X). Am Enterprise.
Woodrow Wilson Foundation. Political Economy of American Foreign Policy: Its Concepts, Strategy, & Limits. LC 68-56044. (Illus.). 1968. Repr. of 1955 ed. lib. bdg. 17.00x (ISBN 0-8371-0759-8, WFAF). Greenwood.
World Development Report, 1979: The World Bank. (Illus.). 1979. 9.95 (ISBN 0-19-502637-3); pap. 3.50 (ISBN 0-19-502638-1). Oxford U Pr.
World Economic Survey 1978 - Current Trends in the World Economy. 125p. 1980. pap. 10.00 (ISBN 0-686-68980-1, UN80/2C1, UN). Unipub.
World Trade Annual Supplement, 1978, 5 vols. 110.00 ea.; Set. 550.00 (ISBN 0-8027-5978-5). Vol. 1 (ISBN 0-8027-5969-6). Vol. 2 (ISBN 0-8027-5971-8). Vol. 3 (ISBN 0-8027-5972-6). Vol. 4 (ISBN 0-8027-5973-4). Vol. 5 (ISBN 0-8027-5974-2). Walker & Co.
World Trade Annual, 1978, 5 vols. 50.00 ea.; Set. 250.00 (ISBN 0-8027-5977-7). Vol. 1 (ISBN 0-8027-5963-7). Vol. 2 (ISBN 0-8027-5964-5). Vol. 3 (ISBN 0-8027-5965-3). Vol. 4 (ISBN 0-8027-5966-1). Vol. 5 (ISBN 0-8027-5968-8). Walker & Co.
Yeager, Leland B. International Monetary Relations: Theory, History & Policy. 2nd ed. 667p. 1976. text ed. 33.50 scp (ISBN 0-06-047323-1, HarpC). Har-Row.
Zurawicki, L. Multinational Enterprises in the West & East. 218p. 1979. 27.50x (ISBN 90-286-0419-7). Sijthoff & Noordhoff.
Zwass, Adam. Money, Banking, & Credit in the Soviet Union & Eastern Europe. LC 78-64910. 1979. 18.50 (ISBN 0-87332-124-3). M E Sharpe.

INTERNATIONAL EDUCATION

Here are entered works on education for international understanding, world citizenship etc.
see also Intellectual Cooperation; Internationalism; Students, Interchange Of; Teachers, Interchange Of

Arndt, Christian O. & Everett, Samuel, eds. Education for a World Society: 11th Yearbook of John Dewey Society. LC 72-142603. (Essay Index Reprint Ser.). Repr. of 1951 ed. 18.00 (ISBN 0-8369-2383-9). Arno.
ASCD 1973 Yearbook Committee. Education for Peace: Focus on Mankind. Henderson, George, ed. LC 44-6213. (Yearbook Ser. 1973). (Illus., Orig.). 1973. 7.50 (ISBN 0-87120-017-1, 17946). Assn Supervision.
Bailey, Stephen K., ed. Higher Education in the World Community. 1976. 15.00 (ISBN 0-8268-1321-6). ACE.
Brown, Walter T., ed. CISP International Studies Funding Book. 2nd ed. 1979. Repr. looseleaf 50.00 (ISBN 0-939288-00-1). CISP.
Butts, Robert F. American Education in International Development. facs. ed. LC 73-117763. (Essay Index Reprint Ser). 1963. 15.00 (ISBN 0-8369-1786-3). Arno.
Cherrington, Ben M. Methods of Education in International Attitudes. LC 77-176642. (Columbia University. Teachers College. Contributions to Education: No. 595). Repr. of 1934 ed. 17.50 (ISBN 0-404-55595-0). AMS Pr.
Council on International Educational Exchange. The Whole World Handbook: A Guide to Study, Travel, & Work Abroad. 352p. 1981. pap. 7.95 (ISBN 0-525-93171-6, 0558-017). Dutton.
Deutsch, Steven E. International Education & Exchange: A Sociological Analysis. LC 77-84488. 1970. 10.00 (ISBN 0-8295-0175-4). UPB.
Education for International Understanding. (Orig.). 1964. pap. 2.25 (ISBN 92-3-100437-9, UNESCO). Unipub.
Gray, George W. Education on an International Scale: A History of the International Education Board, 1923-1938. LC 78-800. (Illus.). 1978. Repr. of 1941 ed. lib. bdg. 15.25x (ISBN 0-313-20268-0, GREI). Greenwood.
Halls, W. D. International Equivalences in Access to Higher Education. (Studies on International Equivalences of Degrees). 137p. 1972. pap. 7.00 (ISBN 92-3-100909-5, U327, UNESCO). Unipub.
Henderson, J. L. Education for World Understanding. 1969. 12.25 (ISBN 0-08-013217-0); pap. 5.75 (ISBN 0-08-013216-2). Pergamon.
Howard, John R., ed. An Overview of International Studies. LC 72-86185. 232p. 1972. 29.50x (ISBN 0-8422-5030-1). Irvington.
The International Bureau of Education in the Service of Educational Development. 152p. 1980. pap. 7.50 (ISBN 0-686-60077-0, U949, UNESCO). Unipub.
Leach, R. J. International Schools & Their Role in the Field of International Education. 1969. 22.00 (ISBN 0-08-013037-2); pap. 10.75 (ISBN 0-08-013036-4). Pergamon.
Methods of Establishing Equivalences Between Degrees & Diplomas. (Studies on International Equivalences of Degrees). 143p. 1970. pap. 7.50 (ISBN 92-3-100824-2, U380, UNESCO). Unipub.
Morrissett, Irving & Williams, Ann M., eds. International Perspectives on Social-Political Education. LC 81-5739. 1980. pap. 14.95 (ISBN 0-89994-253-9). Soc Sci Ed.
Open Doors: Report on Internatkional Education Exchange, 1978-1979. 157p. 1980. pap. 15.00 (ISBN 0-87206-098-5, IIE-22, IIE). Unipub.
Overly, Norman V. & Kimpston, Richard D., eds. Global Studies: Problems & Promises for Elementary Teachers. LC 76-40696. 1976. pap. text ed. 4.50 (ISBN 0-87120-095-3, 611-76086). Assn Supervision.
Paulsen, F. Robert, ed. Changing Dimensions in International Education. LC 73-76783. 220p. 1969. 2.00 (ISBN 0-8165-0179-3). U of Ariz Pr.
Pierce, Lucia & Pierce, Lucia. International Training. 1981. pap. cancelled (ISBN 0-915432-81-1). NE Conf Teach Foreign.
Scanlon, David G. & Shields, James J., eds. Problems & Prospects in International Education. LC 68-23008. 1968. text ed. 16.50x (ISBN 0-8077-2101-8). Tchrs Coll.
Shane, Harold G., ed. United States & International Education. (National Society for the Study of Education Yearbooks Ser: No. 68, Pt. 1). 1969. 7.50x (ISBN 0-226-60094-7). U of Chicago Pr.
Study Abroad: 22nd Edition, 1979-1980, 1980-1981. 1979. pap. 9.95 (ISBN 92-3-001592-X, U879, UNESCO). Unipub.
Sutton, Francis, et al. Internationalizing Higher Education: A United States Approach. (No. 13). 48p. 1974. pap. 1.00 (ISBN 0-89192-151-6). Interbk Inc.
Tysse, Agnes M., ed. International Education: The American Experience, A Bibliography, 2 pts, Vol. 2, Periodical Articles. rev. ed. Incl. Part 1. General; Part 2. Area Studies, & Indexes. LC 73-16429. 1977. 45.00 (ISBN 0-8108-1009-3). Scarecrow.
Tysse, Agnes N. International Education: the American Experience a Bibliography: Vol. 1: Dissertations & Theses. 1974. 10.00 (ISBN 0-8108-0686-X). Scarecrow.
Zweig, Michael. Idea of a World University. Taylor, Harold, ed. LC 66-17970. 224p. 1967. 8.95x (ISBN 0-8093-0233-0). S Ill U Pr.

INTERNATIONAL EDUCATIONAL EXCHANGES

see Educational Exchanges

INTERNATIONAL EXCHANGE

see Foreign Exchange

INTERNATIONAL EXCHANGE OF PERSONS PROGRAMS

see Exchange of Persons Programs

INTERNATIONAL EXCHANGE OF STUDENTS

see Students, Interchange of

INTERNATIONAL EXCHANGES, LITERARY AND SCIENTIFIC

see Exchanges, Literary and Scientific

INTERNATIONAL EXHIBITIONS

see Exhibitions

INTERNATIONAL FEDERATION

see International Organization

INTERNATIONAL FINANCE

see also Balance of Payments; Banks and Banking, International; Debts, External; Foreign Exchange; International Liquidity; Loans, Foreign

Aliber, Robert Z. Exchange Risk & Corporate International Finance. LC 78-4645. 1978. 24.95 (ISBN 0-470-26307-5). Halsted Pr.
--The International Money Game. 3rd, expanded ed. LC 78-73770. 1979. 12.95 (ISBN 0-465-03375-X); pap. 6.95x (ISBN 0-465-03376-8). Basic.
--National Monetary Policies & the International Financial System. LC 74-75610. (Studies in Business & Society Ser). viii, 332p. 1974. text ed. 19.00x (ISBN 0-226-01390-1). U of Chicago Pr.
Argy, Victor. The Post War International Money Crisis: An Analysis. 472p. (Orig.). 1981. text ed. 37.50x (ISBN 0-04-332075-9); pap. text ed. 15.95x (ISBN 0-04-332076-7). Allen Unwin.
Backman, Jules & Bloch, Ernest, eds. Multinational Corporations, Trade & the Dollar in the Seventies. LC 74-77713. (Key Issues Lecture Ser.). 108p. 1974. 7.95x (ISBN 0-8147-0977-X); pap. 3.95x (ISBN 0-8147-0978-8). NYU Pr.
Baldwin & Richardson. International Trade & Finance. 2nd ed. 1981. pap. text ed. 11.95 (ISBN 0-316-07922-7). Little.
Balogh, Thomas. Fact & Fancy in International Economic Relations: An Essay on International Monetary Reform. LC 73-7993. 132p. 1973. text ed. 19.50 (ISBN 0-08-017740-9). Pergamon.
Basagni, Fabio & Uri, Pierre, eds. Monetary Relations & World Development. LC 77-15650. 1977. 19.85 (ISBN 0-03-041591-8). Praeger.
Beter, Peter D. Conspiracy Against the Dollar: The Politics of the New Imperialism. LC 73-79850. 96p. 1973. 5.95 (ISBN 0-8076-0709-6); pap. 2.95 (ISBN 0-8076-0710-X). Braziller.
Bird, Graham. The International Monetary System & the Less Developed Countries. LC 78-65139. (Praeger Special Studies Ser.). 1979. 28.95 (ISBN 0-03-051211-5). Praeger.
Block, Fred L. The Origins of International Economic Disorder: A Study of United States International Monetary Policy from World War Two to the Present. LC 75-7190. 1977. pap. 6.95x (ISBN 0-520-03729-4). U of Cal Pr.
Burns, Joseph M. Accounting Standards & International Finance: With Special Reference to Multinationals. LC 76-40618. 1976. pap. 4.25 (ISBN 0-8447-3225-7). Am Enterprise.
Cairncross, Alex. Inflation, Growth & International Finance. LC 75-20428. 136p. 1976. 18.00 (ISBN 0-87395-315-0). State U NY Pr.
Cantelon, Willard. The Day the Dollar Dies: Biblical Prophecy of a New World System in the End Times. LC 72-94186. 190p. 1973. pap. 2.50 (ISBN 0-88270-170-3). Logos.
Carlson, Robert S., et al. International Finance: Cases & Simulation. LC 80-81213. 400p. 1980. pap. text ed. 6.95 (ISBN 0-201-00903-X). A-W.
Carter, E. Eugene & Rodriguez, Rita M. International Financial Management. 2nd ed. (Illus.). 1979. text ed. 22.95 (ISBN 0-13-472977-3). P-H.
Casey, Douglas. The International Man. 14.95 (ISBN 0-932496-01-6). Green Hill.
Casey, Douglas R. International Investing. 150p. 1981. pap. 9.95 (ISBN 0-89696-130-3). Everest Hse.
Chacholiades, Miltiades. International Monetary Theory & Policy. (Illus.). 1977. 24.00 (ISBN 0-07-010340-2, C). McGraw.
Chalmers, Eric B. International Interest Rate War. LC 74-185905. 1972. 19.95 (ISBN 0-312-42280-6). St. Martin.
Channon, Derek F. British Banking Strategy & the International Challenge. 1977. text ed. 35.00x (ISBN 0-333-19808-5). Verry.
Cheng, Hang-Sheng. International Bond Issues of the Less-Developed Countries: Diagnosis & Prescription. 1969. 7.50x (ISBN 0-8138-0218-0). Iowa St U Pr.
Committee for Economic Development. Strengthening the World Monetary System. LC 73-84800. 87p. 1973. pap. 1.50 (ISBN 0-87186-051-1). Comm Econ Dev.
Connolly, M. B. & Swoboda, A. K. International Trade & Money. 1973. pap. text ed. 9.95x (ISBN 0-04-330220-3). Allen Unwin.
Coombs, C. A. The Arena of International Finance. 243p. 1976. 25.50 (ISBN 0-471-01513-X, Pub. by Wiley-Interscience). Wiley.
--The Arena of International Finance. 1976. 25.50 (ISBN 0-471-01513-X, Pub. by Wiley-Interscience). Wiley.

Corden, W. M. Inflation, Exchange Rates, & the World Economy: Lectures on International Monetary Economics. LC 76-58331. (Studies in Business & Society). 1977. lib. bdg. 11.00x (ISBN 0-226-11583-6). U of Chicago Pr.

Coty, Francois. Tearing Away the Veils of International Finance. 1979. lib. bdg. 69.95 (ISBN 0-8490-3011-0). Gordon Pr.

Dalgaard, Bruce R. South Africa's Impact on Britain's Return to Gold, 1925. Bruchey, Stuart, ed. LC 80-2801. (Dissertations in European Economic History II). (Illus.). 1981. lib. bdg. 18.00x (ISBN 0-405-13985-3). Arno.

Davidson, Paul. International Money & the Real World. 450p. 1981. 34.95 (ISBN 0-470-27256-2). Halsted Pr.

Davidson, William H. Experience Effects in International Investment & Technology Transfer. Dufey, Gunter, ed. LC 80-39884. (Research for Business Decisions Ser.: No. 34). 160p. 1981. 29.95 (ISBN 0-8357-1148-X, Pub. by UMI Res Pr). Univ Microfilms.

Dreyer, Jacob S. Composite Reserve Assets in the International Monetary System, Vol. 2. Altman, Edward I. & Walter, Ingo, eds. LC 76-5757. (Contemporary Studies in Economic and Financial Analysis). 325p. 1977. lib. bdg. 30.00 (ISBN 0-89232-003-6). Jai Pr.

Dufey, Gunter & Giddy, Ian H. International Money Market. LC 78-1298. (Foundations of Finance Ser.). (Illus.). 1978. ref. ed. o.p. 13.95 (ISBN 0-13-470914-4); pap. 10.95 (ISBN 0-13-470914-4). P-H.

Eckes, Alfred E., Jr. A Search for Solvency: Bretton Woods & the International Monetary System, 1941-1971. LC 75-14433. 369p. 1975. 17.50x (ISBN 0-292-70712-6). U of Tex Pr.

Economides, Chris. Earned International Reserve Units: The Catalyst of Two Complementary World Problems - Monetary & Development. 24p. 1976. pap. text ed. 8.50 (ISBN 0-08-021178-X). Pergamon.

Einzig, Paul. Behind the Scenes of International Finance. Wilkins, Mira, ed. LC 78-3912. (International Finance Ser.). 1978. Repr. of 1931 ed. lib. bdg. 12.00x (ISBN 0-405-11216-5). Arno.

--World Finance, Nineteen Fourteen to Nineteen Thirty-Five. Wilkins, Mira, ed. LC 78-3911. (International Finance Ser.). 1978. Repr. of 1935 ed. lib. bdg. 25.00x (ISBN 0-405-11215-7). Arno.

Elton, E. & Gruber, M. International Capital Markets. LC 75-17829. (Studies in Financial Economics: Vol. 1). 387p. 1976. 49.00 (ISBN 0-444-10867-X, North-Holland). Elsevier.

Fallon, Nicholas. Middle East Oil Money & Its Future Expenditure. 1975. 25.00x (ISBN 0-86010-024-3). Intl Pubns Serv.

Feiger, George & Jacquillat, Bertrand. International Finance: Text & Cases. new ed. 496p. 1980. text ed. 21.95 (ISBN 0-205-07137-6, 1071378); tchr's ed. avail. (ISBN 0-205-07138-4). Allyn.

Feinschreiber, Robert, ed. Earnings & Profits: The International Aspects. LC 79-52908. 192p. 1979. 35.00 (ISBN 0-916592-30-8). Panel Pubs.

Feis, Herbert. Europe the World's Banker, Eighteen Seventy to Nineteen Fourteen. LC 74-7665. Repr. of 1930 ed. 19.50x (ISBN 0-678-00044-1). Kelley.

Fleming, J. Marcus. Essays on Economic Policy. LC 77-15991. 1978. 25.00x (ISBN 0-231-04366-X). Columbia U Pr.

Friedmann, Wolfgang G., et al. International Financial Aid. LC 66-20494. 1966. 25.00x (ISBN 0-231-02953-5). Columbia U Pr.

Gibson, Norman R. The Case for International Money. Wilkins, Mira, ed. LC 78-3913. (International Finance Ser.). 1978. lib. bdg. 18.00x (ISBN 0-405-11217-3). Arno.

Gold, Joseph. Legal & Institutional Aspects of the International Monetary System. Evensen, Jane B. & Oh, Jai K., eds. 1979. 17.50 (ISBN 0-686-23762-5). Intl Monetary Fund.

Halm, George N. A Guide to International Monetary Reform. LC 74-28969. 1975. 15.95 (ISBN 0-669-98061-7). Lexington Bks.

Hawkins, Robert G., ed. Research in International Business & Finance, Vol. 2. 350p. 1981. 37.50 (ISBN 0-89232-140-7). Jai Pr.

--Research in International Business & Finance, Vol. 3. 300p. 1981. 37.50 (ISBN 0-89232-245-4). Jai Pr.

Heller, H. Robert. International Monetary Economics. (Illus.). 256p. 1974. ref. ed. 18.95 (ISBN 0-13-473140-9). P-H.

Henning, Charles N., et al. International Financial Management. (Illus.). 1978. text ed. 20.50x (ISBN 0-07-028175-0, C); instructor's manual 4.95 (ISBN 0-07-028176-9). McGraw.

Herring, R. J. & Marston, R. C. National Monetary Policies & International Financial Markets. (Contributions to Economic Analysis: Vol. 104). 1977. 39.00 (ISBN 0-7204-0519-X, North-Holland). Elsevier.

Hirsch, Fred, et al. Alternatives to Monetary Disorder. (Nineteen Eighties Project (Council on Foreign Relations)). 1977. pap. 3.95 (ISBN 0-07-029047-4, P&RB). McGraw.

International Center for Settlement of Investment Disputes. Investment Laws of the World, Binder 10. 1979. 75.00 (ISBN 0-379-00650-2); Set. 800.00 (ISBN 0-686-77393-4). Oceana.

International Centre For Settlement Of Investment Disputes. Convention on the Settlement of Investment Disputes Between States & Nationals of Other States, 4 vols. in 5. 17.50 ea. Oceana.

Jacobsson, Erin E. A Life for Sound Money: Per Jacobsson-His Biography. LC 78-41135. (Illus.). 1979. 49.00x (ISBN 0-19-828411-X). Oxford U Pr.

Kenen, P. B., ed. International Trade & Finance. LC 75-2717. (Illus.). 580p. 1976. 32.50 (ISBN 0-521-20719-3). Cambridge U Pr.

Kenen, Peter & Lubitz, Raymond. International Economics. 3rd ed. LC 71-135021. (Foundations of Modern Economics Ser). (Illus.). 1971. pap. 9.95 ref. ed. (ISBN 0-13-472613-8). P-H.

Kettell, Brian. The Finance of International Business. 264p. 1979. 33.00x (ISBN 0-86010-151-7, Pub. by Graham & Trotman England). State Mutual Bk.

Kim, Suk H. An Introduction to International Financial Management. LC 80-5203. 302p. 1980. pap. text ed. 10.75 (ISBN 0-8191-1054-X). U Pr of Amer.

Kindleberger, Charles P. Europe & the Dollar. 1966. pap. 6.95x (ISBN 0-262-61005-1). MIT Pr.

--International Money: A Collection of Essays. 336p. 1981. text ed. 37.50x (ISBN 0-04-332077-5); pap. text ed. 14.50x (ISBN 0-04-332078-3). Allen Unwin.

Kinney, William P. The Monetary Maze: Gold, the International Monetary System, & the Emerging World Economy. LC 76-52187. 1977. pap. text ed. 4.95 (ISBN 0-8403-1700-X). Kendall-Hunt.

Kolde, E. International Business Enterprise. 2nd ed. LC 78-37518. (Illus.). 672p. 1973. ref. ed. 22.95 (ISBN 0-13-472381-3). P-H.

League of Nations, Secretariat, Economic, Financial & Transit Department. International Currency Experience, Lessons of the Inter-War Period. Wilkins, Mira, ed. LC 78-3932. (International Finance Ser.). 1978. Repr. of 1944 ed. lib. bdg. 16.00x (ISBN 0-405-11235-1). Arno.

Lees, Francis A. & Eng, Maximo. International Financial Markets: Development of the Present System & Future Prospects. LC 73-13345. (Special Studies). (Illus.). 576p. 1975. pap. text ed. 12.95 (ISBN 0-275-89180-1). Praeger.

Lessard, Donald, ed. International Financial Management Theory & Application. LC 79-501. 626p. 1979. pap. text ed. 13.95 (ISBN 0-88262-344-3). Warren.

Llewellyn, David T. International Financial Integration: The Limits of Sovereignty. LC 80-11699. (Problems of Economic Integration Ser.). 215p. 1981. 32.95x (ISBN 0-470-26960-X). Halsted Pr.

Lomax, D. F. & Gutmann, P. T. The Euromarkets & International Financial Policies. 259p. 1981. 34.95x (ISBN 0-470-26923-5). Halsted Pr.

Macaluso, Donald G. The Financial Advantage of Multinational Firm During Tight Credit Periods in Host Countries. Bruchey, Stuart, ed. LC 80-582. (Multinational Corporations Ser.). 1980. lib. bdg. 15.00x (ISBN 0-405-13374-X). Arno.

McDaniels, John F., ed. International Financing & Investment. LC 62-20225. 1964. 40.00 (ISBN 0-379-12852-7). Oceana.

Machlup, Fritz. International Payments, Debts & Gold: Collected Essays. 2nd ed. LC 76-20371. 1976. pap. 12.50x (ISBN 0-8147-5412-0). NYU Pr.

Machlup, Fritz, et al, eds. International Mobility & Movement of Capital. (Universities-National Bureau Conference Ser.: No. 24). 680p. 1972. text ed. 20.00x (ISBN 0-87014-249-6, Dist. by Columbia U Pr). Natl Bur Econ Res.

McKinnon, Ronald I. Money in International Exchange: The Convertible Currency System. 1979. text ed. 13.95x (ISBN 0-19-502408-7); pap. text ed. 9.95x (ISBN 0-19-502409-5). Oxford U Pr.

Madden, John T. & Nadler, Marcus. International Money Markets. LC 68-23311. Repr. of 1935 ed. lib. bdg. 37.50 (ISBN 0-8371-0552-8, MAIM). Greenwood.

Mandel, Ernest. Decline of the Dollar: A Marxist View of the Monetary Crisis. LC 72-85799. 128p. 1973. 10.00 (ISBN 0-913460-04-4, Dist. by Path Pr Inc Ny). Monad Pr.

Massaro, Vincent G. Transnational Money Management. LC 78-72556. (Report Ser.: No. 743). (Illus.). 1978. pap. 30.00 (ISBN 0-8237-0176-X). Conference Bd.

Mendelsohn, M. Stefan. Money on the Move: The Modern International Capital Market. (Illus.). 1979. 16.50 (ISBN 0-07-041474-2). McGraw.

Metzler, Lloyd A. & Haberler, Gottfried. International Monetary Policies. Wilkins, Mira, ed. LC 78-3938. (International Finance Ser.). 1978. Repr. of 1947 ed. lib. bdg. 10.00x (ISBN 0-405-11239-4). Arno.

Meyer, Richard H. Bankers' Diplomacy: Monetary Stabilization in the Twenties. LC 79-111120. (Columbia Studies in Economics Ser.: No. 4). 170p. 1970. 20.00x (ISBN 0-231-03325-7). Columbia U Pr.

Murphy, J. Carter. International Monetary System: Beyond the First Stage of Reform. 1979. pap. 7.25 (ISBN 0-8447-3362-8). Am Enterprise.

Mutti, John. Taxes, Subsidies & Competitiveness Internationally. (Committee on Changing International Realities Ser.). 1981. pap. price not set (ISBN 0-89068-059-0). Natl Planning.

Nordyke, James W. International Finance & New York. Bruchey, Stuart & Bruchey, Eleanor, eds. LC 76-5024. (American Business Abroad Ser.). 1976. 19.00x (ISBN 0-405-09291-1). Arno.

OECD Staff. Experience with Controls on International Portfolio Operations in Shares & Bonds. (Illus.). 63p. (Orig.). 1981. pap. text ed. 7.00x (ISBN 92-64-12138-2, 21-80-07-1). OECD.

--National Accounts of OECD Countries 1950-1979, Vol. 1. 89p. (Orig.). 1981. pap. text ed. 7.50x (ISBN 92-64-02117-5, 30-81-01-3). OECD.

Oh, John. International Financial Management: Problems, Issues & Experiences, Vol. 34. Altman, Edward I. & Walter, Ingo, eds. LC 81-81655. (Contemporary Studies in Economic & Financial Analysis). 300p. 1981. 32.50 (ISBN 0-89232-228-4). Jai Pr.

Oliver, Robert W. International Economic Co-Operation & the World Bank. 421p. 1975. text ed. 35.00x (ISBN 0-8419-5013-X). Holmes & Meier.

Oppenheim, Peter. The Language of International Finance in English: Money & Banking. (English for Careers Ser.). (Illus.). (gr. 10 up). 1976. pap. text ed. 3.50 (ISBN 0-88345-272-3). Regents Pub.

Organization for Economic Cooperation & Development. Monetary Policy in France. (Monetary Studies Ser.: No. 5). 106p. 1975. 5.25 (ISBN 0-686-14847-9). OECD.

--Monetary Policy in the U. S. (Monetary Studies Ser.: No. 4). 216p. 1974. 9.50 (ISBN 0-686-14846-0). OECD.

Quinn, Brian S. The New Euromarkets: A Theoretical & Practical Study of International Financing in the Eurobond & Eurocurrency Markets. LC 75-4755. 1975. 27.95 (ISBN 0-470-70266-4). Halsted Pr.

Reed, Howard C. The Preeminence of International Financial Centers. 160p. 1981. 19.95 (ISBN 0-03-059317-4). Praeger.

Riehl, Heinz & Rodriquez, Rita M. Foreign Exchange Markets. (Illus.). 1977. 24.50 (ISBN 0-07-052670-2, P&RB). McGraw.

Riley, James C. International Government Finance & the Amsterdam Capital Market: 1740-1815. LC 79-152. (Illus.). 1980. 37.50 (ISBN 0-521-22677-5). Cambridge U Pr.

Roderick, Robert. The Greek Position. 1981. 14.95 (ISBN 0-671-61015-5, Wyndham). S&S.

Royal Institute Of International Affairs. Problem of International Investment. LC 67-55858. Repr. of 1937 ed. 30.00x (ISBN 0-678-05195-X). Kelley.

Sargent, J. R. Europe & the Dollar in World-Wide Disequilibrium. (Financial & Monetary Policy Issues Ser.: No. 5). 360p. 1981. 69.25 (ISBN 90-286-0700-5). Sijthoff & Noordhoff.

Sarnat, Marshall S. & Szego, Giorgio P., eds. International Finance & Trade, Vol. I. LC 79-11158. 1979. 27.50 (ISBN 0-88410-673-X). Ballinger Pub.

--International Finance & Trade, Vol. II. LC 79-1158. (Illus.). 1979. 27.50 (ISBN 0-88410-679-9); Vol. I & II. 40.00 (ISBN 0-88410-680-2). Ballinger Pub.

Savage, Donald T. Money & Banking. LC 76-56134. 1977. text ed. 26.50x (ISBN 0-471-75519-2); tchrs. manual avail. (ISBN 0-471-02578-X). Wiley.

Scammell, W. M. International Trade & Payments: A Theoretical Approach. LC 73-87879. 640p. 1974. text ed. 16.95 (ISBN 0-312-42350-0). St Martin.

Schiavo-Campo, Salvatore. International Economics. 1978. text ed. 16.95 (ISBN 0-87626-386-4). Winthrop.

Schrecker, Ellen. The Hired Money. Wilkins, Mira, ed. LC 78-3947. (International Finance Ser.). (Illus.). 1978. lib. bdg. 26.00x (ISBN 0-405-11247-5). Arno.

Sherbiny, Nalem A. & Sirageldin, Ismail, eds. Manpower Planning in the Oil Countries. (Research in Human Capital & Development: Supplement No. 1). 350p. 1981. 37.50 (ISBN 0-89232-129-6). Jai Pr.

Siebel, Ulf R. German Restrictions on Capital Transactions with Foreigners. 176p. 1980. 36.00x (ISBN 0-7121-5512-0, Pub. by Macdonald & Evans). State Mutual Bk.

Sirc, L. Outline of International Finance: Exchange Rates & Payments Between Countries. LC 74-3259. 1974. 16.95 (ISBN 0-470-79325-2). Halsted Pr.

Solomon, Robert. The International Monetary System: 1945-1976: an Insiders View. LC 76-10094. 1977. 17.50 (ISBN 0-06-013898-X, HarpT). Har-Row.

Southard, Frank, Jr. The Finances of European Liberation: With Special Reference to Italy. Wilkins, Mira, ed. LC 78-3950. (International Finance Ser.). 1978. Repr. of 1946 ed. lib. bdg. 14.00x (ISBN 0-405-11251-3). Arno.

Steinberg, Eleanor B. & Yager, Joseph A. New Means of Financing International Needs. LC 77-21275. 1978. 14.95 (ISBN 0-8157-8116-4); pap. 5.95 (ISBN 0-8157-8115-6). Brookings.

Stem, Carl H., et al, eds. Eurocurrencies & the International Monetary System. LC 76-29115. (Conference Proceedings). 1976. 17.25 (ISBN 0-8447-2091-7); pap. 9.25 (ISBN 0-8447-2090-9). Am Enterprise.

Sukijasovic, Miodrag. Foreign Investment in Yugoslavia. 1971. 12.00 (ISBN 0-379-00476-3). Oceana.

Swoboda, A. K., ed. Europe & the Evolution of the International Monetary System. 1973. 25.00 (ISBN 9-0286-0173-2). Heinman.

Tew, Brian. The Evolution of the International Monetary System 1945-1977. 1979. pap. 12.95 (ISBN 0-470-26705-4). Halsted Pr.

Third Paris-Dauphine Conference on Money & International Monetary Problems, March 28-30, 1974. Recent Issues in International Monetary Economics: Proceedings. Claasen, E. M. & Salin, P., eds. LC 75-44183. 1976. 85.50 (ISBN 0-444-11023-2, North-Holland). Elsevier.

Triffin, Robert. Our International Monetary System. 1968. pap. text ed. 4.50x (ISBN 0-394-30714-3). Phila Bk Co.

United Nations, Department of Economic Affairs. International Capital Movements During the Inter-War Period. Wilkins, Mira, ed. LC 78-23883. (International Finance Ser.). (Illus.). 1978. Repr. of 1949 ed. lib. bdg. 10.00x (ISBN 0-405-11252-1). Arno.

U. S. Senate, Executive Document. International Monetary Conference. Wilkins, Mira, ed. LC 78-3952. (International Finance Ser.: No. 58). (Illus.). 1978. Repr. of 1879 ed. lib. bdg. 54.00x (ISBN 0-405-11253-X). Arno.

Van Dormael, Armand. Bretton Woods: Birth of a Monetary System. LC 77-10651. 1978. text ed. 32.50x (ISBN 0-8419-0326-3). Holmes & Meier.

Versluysen, Eugene. The Political Economy of International Finance. 350p. 1981. 25.00x (ISBN 0-312-62235-X). St Martin.

--The Political Economy of International Finance. 350p. 1981. 25.00x (ISBN 0-312-62235-X). St Martin.

Weston, J. Fred & Sorge, Bart W. Guide to International Financial Management. 1977. 15.95 (ISBN 0-07-069488-5, C); text ed. 9.95 (ISBN 0-07-069487-7). McGraw.

--International Managerial Finance. 1972. 19.95x (ISBN 0-256-01390-X). Irwin.

Whitman, Marina. Government Risk-Sharing in Foreign Investment. 1965. 25.00x (ISBN 0-691-04134-2). Princeton U Pr.

Wilkins, Mira, ed. British Parliamentary Reports on International Finance, 2 vols. in one. LC 78-3907. (International Finance Ser.). 1978. Repr. of 1931 ed. lib. bdg. 24.00x (ISBN 0-405-11212-2). Arno.

--International Finance Series, Fifty-Three Bks, 53 bks. (Illus.). 1978. lib. bdg. 1096.00x set (ISBN 0-405-11200-9). Arno.

Willett, Thomas D. Floating Exchange Rates & International Monetary Reform. LC 77-13327. 1977. pap. 5.25 (ISBN 0-8447-3271-0). Am Enterprise.

--International Liquidity Issues. 1980. pap. 5.25 (ISBN 0-8447-3388-1). Am Enterprise.

Wionczek, Miguel S. International Indebtedness & World Economic Stagnation. 135p. 1981. 17.50 (ISBN 0-08-024702-4). Pergamon.

Wiseley, William. A Tool of Power: The Political History of Money. LC 76-57701. 300p. 1977. 29.95 (ISBN 0-471-02235-7, Pub. by Wiley-Interscience). Wiley.

Wood, Douglas & Byrne, James. International Business Finance. LC 80-23951. 400p. 1981. text ed. 47.50x (ISBN 0-8419-0663-7). Holmes & Meier.

World Bank. World Bank Operations: Sectoral Programs & Policies. LC 72-4032. 526p. 1973. 25.00x (ISBN 0-8018-1448-0); pap. 6.50x (ISBN 0-8018-1449-9). Johns Hopkins.

INTERNATIONAL FISCAL RELATIONS
see Intergovernmental Fiscal Relations
INTERNATIONAL GEOPHYSICAL YEAR, 1957-1958
see also Project Vanguard
INTERNATIONAL GRANTS-IN-AID
see Economic Assistance; International Relief
INTERNATIONAL INSTITUTIONS
see International Cooperation
INTERNATIONAL INSTITUTE OF AGRICULTURE
Hobson, Asher. International Institute of Agriculture. 1931. 26.00 (ISBN 0-384-23740-1); pap. 21.50 (ISBN 0-384-23730-4). Johnson Repr.
INTERNATIONAL INSURANCE LAW
see Insurance Law, International
INTERNATIONAL JOINT COMMISSION (U. S. AND CANADA) 1909-
Chacko, Chirakaikaran J. International Joint Commission Between the United States of America & the Dominion of Canada. LC 68-58554. (Columbia University. Studies in the Social Sciences: No. 358). Repr. of 1932 ed. 30.00 (ISBN 0-404-51358-1). AMS Pr.
INTERNATIONAL JURISDICTION
see Jurisdiction (International Law)
INTERNATIONAL LABOR ACTIVITIES
see also names of individual labor organizations, e.g. International Labor Organization
Flanagan, Robert J. & Weber, Arnold R. Bargaining Without Boundaries: The Multinational Corporation & International Labor Relations. LC 74-5724. (Studies in Business & Society Ser). xviii, 258p. 1974. text ed. 14.50x (ISBN 0-226-25312-0). U of Chicago Pr.
International Labour Conference, 53rd Session, 1969. World Employment Programme: Report of the Director-General. 2nd ed. 1970. 3.00 (ISBN 92-2-100136-9). Intl Labour Office.
International Labour Office. Report of the Director-General: International Labour Conference, 67th Session, 1981. xiii, 111p. (Orig.). 1981. pap. 11.40 (ISBN 92-2-102393-1). Intl Labour Office.
Lenin, V. I. On Proletarian Internationalism. 382p. 1976. 2.50 (ISBN 0-8285-1633-2, Pub. by Progress Pubs Russia). Imported Pubns.
Lenin, Vladimir I. On the International Working Class & Communist Movement. 414p. 1978. 3.60 (ISBN 0-8285-0151-3, Pub. by Progress Pubs Russia). Imported Pubns.
Logue, John. Toward a Theory of Trade Union Internationalism. (University of Gothenberg (Sweden), Research Section Post-War History Publications Ser.: No. 7). 66p. (Orig.). 1980. pap. 2.95 (ISBN 0-933522-02-9). Kent Popular.
Lorwin, Lewis. International Labor Movement: History, Policies, Outlooks. LC 73-13404. 366p. 1973. Repr. of 1953 ed. lib. bdg. 21.50 (ISBN 0-8371-7060-5, LOLM). Greenwood.
Ponomarev, B. N., et al. The International Working Class Movement. 1980. 11.50 (ISBN 0-8285-1889-0, Pub. by Progress Pubs Russia). Imported Pubns.
Rowan, Richard L. & O'Brien, Rae A. Multinational Union Organizations in the Public Service & White-Collar Industries. 1980. pap. 15.00 (ISBN 0-89546-022-X). Indus Res Unit-Wharton.
Rowan, Richard L., et al. Multinational Union Organizations in the Manufacturing & Processing Industries. LC 80-53989. (Multinational Industrial Relations Ser.). 213p. (Orig.). 1980. pap. 15.00 (ISBN 0-89546-021-1). Indus Res Unit-Wharton.
Vaidyanathan, N. International Labour Organization Conventions & India. LC 75-904151. 1975. 9.50x (ISBN 0-88386-532-7). South Asia Bks.
INTERNATIONAL LABOR LAWS AND LEGISLATION
see Labor Laws and Legislation, International
INTERNATIONAL LABOR OFFICE
Galenson, Walter. The International Labor Organization: An American View. LC 80-52295. 352p. 1981. 21.50x (ISBN 0-299-08540-6); pap. 7.75 (ISBN 0-299-08544-9). U of Wis Pr.
International Labour Conference, 66th Session & International Labour Office. International Labour Conference Sixty-Six Session. Report of the Committee of Experts on the Application of Conventions & Recommendations (Articles 19, 22 & 35 of the Constitution) Vol. A: General Report & Observations Concerning Particular Countries Report III, Part 4a. xv, 242p. (Orig.). 1980. pap. 17.10 (ISBN 92-2-102092-4). Intl Labour Office.
International Labour Office. Financial Report & Audited Financial Statements for the Fifty-Sixth Financial Period (1978-79) & Reports of the External Auditor. ii, 53p. (Orig.). 1980. pap. 12.85 (ISBN 92-2-102088-6). Intl Labour Office.
--ILO Medium-Term Plan, 1982-1987. Report on Programme Implementation 1978-1979. Supplement of the Report of the Director-General: Documents of the 212th (Feb.-March Session of the Governing Body) 297p. (Orig.). 1980. pap. 15.70 (ISBN 92-2-102085-1). Intl Labour Office.
--Information & Proposals Concerning the Programme & Budget for the 1980-81 & Other Financial & Administrative Questions. Report II. International Labour Conference, 66th Session, 1980. iii, 112p. (Orig.). 1980. pap. 14.25 (ISBN 92-2-102087-8). Intl Labour Office.
INTERNATIONAL LABOR ORGANIZATION
Alcock, Antony. History of the International Labor Organization. 1971. Repr. lib. bdg. 20.00x (ISBN 0-374-90127-9). Octagon.
Ayusawa, Iwao. A History of Labor in Modern Japan. LC 76-20683. 406p. 1976. Repr. of 1966 ed. lib. bdg. 25.00x (ISBN 0-8371-8991-8, AYHL). Greenwood.
Bloss, Esther. Labor Legislation in Czechoslovakia. LC 79-76641. (Columbia University Studies in the Social Sciences: No. 446). Repr. of 1938 ed. 18.50 (ISBN 0-404-51446-4). AMS Pr.
Geneva Institute Of International Relations. Problems of Peace, First Ser. LC 73-105015. (Essay Index Reprint Ser). 1927. 22.00 (ISBN 0-8369-1468-6). Arno.
Haas, Ernst B. Beyond the Nation-State: Functionalism & International Organization. LC 64-21999. 1964. 22.50x (ISBN 0-8047-0186-5); pap. 6.95 (ISBN 0-8047-0187-3, SP83). Stanford U Pr.
International Labour Office. Constitution of the International Labour Organisation & Standing Orders of the International Labour Conference, 1980 Edition. 84p. (Eng., Fr., Sp.). 1980. pap. 5.70 (ISBN 92-2-002471-3). Intl Labour Office.
--General Survey of the Reports Relating to Convention No. 138 & Recommendation No. 146 Concerning Minimum Age: International Labour Conference, 67th Session, 1981. ix, 209p. (Orig.). 1981. pap. 15.70 (ISBN 9-221-02402-4). Intl Labour Office.
--Report of the Committee of Experts on the Application of Conventions & Recommendations: International Labour Conference 67th Session, 1981, Report III (pt. 4a) xv, 244p. (Orig.). 1981. pap. 17.10 (ISBN 9-22102-401-6). Intl Labour Office.
--Report of the Director-General: International Labour Conference, 67th Session, 1981. iii, 49p. (Orig.). 1981. pap. 8.55 (ISBN 9-22102-394-X). Intl Labour Office.
International Labour Office, Central Library, Geneva. International Labour Documentation: Cumulative Edition 1970-71, 2 vols. 1972. Set. lib. bdg. 210.00 (ISBN 0-685-24887-9). G K Hall.
Johnston, George A. International Labour Organisation: Its Work for Social & Economic Progress. LC 74-112270. (Europa's International Relations Ser). 1970. 8.95x (ISBN 0-900362-23-5). Intl Pubns Serv.
Kruglak, Gregory T. The Politics of United States Decision-Making in United Nations Specialized Agencies: The Case of the International Labor Organization. LC 80-5318. 300p. 1980. lib. bdg. 18.50 (ISBN 0-8191-1075-2); pap. text ed. 10.75 (ISBN 0-8191-1076-0). U Pr of Amer.
Landy, E. A. Effectiveness of International Supervision: Three Decades of I. L. O. Experience. LC 66-11877. 1966. 20.00 (ISBN 0-379-00283-3). Oceana.
Morse, David A. The Origin & Evolution of the I. L. O. & Its Role in the World Community. LC 68-66942. (Pierce Ser.: No. 2). 136p. 1969. 3.50 (ISBN 0-87546-025-9). NY Sch Indus Rel.
Pease, M. Consolidated Index to the ILO Legislative Series: 1919-1970. LC 75-802. 280p. 1975. 35.00 (ISBN 0-89111-000-3). UNIFO Pubs.
Stewart, Bryce M. Canadian Labor Laws & the Treaty. LC 77-76689. (Columbia University. Studies in Social Sciences: No. 278). 1969. Repr. of 1926 ed. 32.50 (ISBN 0-404-51278-X). AMS Pr.
INTERNATIONAL LAW
see also Aggression (International Law); Alien Property; Aliens; Allegiance; Arbitration, International; Asylum, Right of; Atomic Weapons (International Law); Autonomy; Boundaries; Civil Rights (International Law); Civil War; Claims; Colonies (International Law); Consular Law; Consuls; Diplomatic and Consular Service; Diplomatic Protection; Diplomats; Eminent Domain (International Law); Equality of States; Exterritoriality; Extradition; Fishery Law and Legislation; Foreign Offices; Freedom of the Seas; Government Liability (International Law); Insurance Law, International; International and Municipal Law; International Cooperation; International Courts; International Offenses; International Organization; Intervention (International Law); Investments, Foreign (International Law); Labor Laws and Legislation, International; Maritime Law; Military Law; Natural Law; Naturalization; Neutrality; Occupancy (International Law); Persons (International Law); Pirates; Political Crimes and Offenses; Recognition (International Law); Refugees, Political; Repatriation; Salvage; Sanctions (International Law); Self-Defense (International Law); Slave-Trade; Sovereignty; Space Law; State Succession; Territorial Waters; Territory, National; Treaties; War (International Law); War, Maritime (International Law); Water-Rights (International Law)
also subdivisions Laws and Legislation and Laws and Regulations under topics of international concern
Academie De Droit International Recueil Des Cours, Collected Courses of the Hague Academy of International Law, 1980, Vol. I, Tome 166. 448p. 1981. 37.50x (ISBN 90-286-2731-6). Sijthoff & Noordhoff.
Akehurst, Michael. A Modern Introduction to International Law. 3rd ed. (Minerva Ser. of Students' Handbooks). 1977. text ed. 29.95x (ISBN 0-04-341013-8); pap. text ed. 13.75x (ISBN 0-04-341014-6). Allen Unwin.
Amacher, Ryan C. & Sweeney, Richard J., eds. The Law of the Sea: U.S. Interests & Alternatives. LC 76-1303. (Conference Proceedings Ser.). 1976. 14.25 (ISBN 0-8447-2073-9); pap. 6.25 (ISBN 0-8447-2072-0). Am Enterprise.
American Catholic Philosophical Association. Natural Law & International Relations, Vol. 24. 1950. pap. 12.00 (ISBN 0-384-40940-7). Johnson Repr.
American Society Of International Law. International Law in the Twentieth Century. Gross, Leo, ed. LC 69-16894. (Orig.). 1969. pap. text ed. 18.95x (ISBN 0-89197-234-X). Irvington.
Anand, R. P. New States & International Law. 1972. 6.50x (ISBN 0-686-20280-5). Intl Bk Dist.
Arangio-Ruiz, G. U. N. Declaration on Friendly Relations & the System of Sources of International Law. 354p. 1979. 27.50x (ISBN 90-286-0149-X). Sijthoff & Noordhoff.
Asian States & the Development of Universal International Law. 1974. 9.50x (ISBN 0-7069-0086-3). Intl Bk Dist.
Association of Student International Law Societies & American Society of International Law. Philip C. Jessup International Law Moot Court Competition, 10 vols. LC 80-85091. 1981. Set. lib. bdg. 450.00 (ISBN 0-89941-094-4). W S Hein.
Audretsch, H. Supervision in European Community Law: Observance by the Member States of Their Treaty Obligations - a Treatise on International & Supranational Supervision. 1978. 63.50 (ISBN 0-444-85037-6, North-Holland). Elsevier.
Australian Yearbook of International Law 1970-1973, Vol. 1. 1975. 30.00 (ISBN 0-379-00482-8). Oceana.
Baade, H. W., ed. Soviet Impact on International Law. LC 65-22170. 1965. 10.00 (ISBN 0-379-11505-0). Oceana.
Bara, Louis. Science de la Paix. LC 78-147448. (Library of War & Peace; Problems of the Organized Peace Movement: Selected Documents). lib. bdg. 38.00 (ISBN 0-8240-0238-5). Garland Pub.
Beaufre, Andre. Strategy for Tomorrow. LC 73-94041. 91p. 1975. pap. 10.50x (ISBN 0-8448-1096-7). Crane-Russak Co.
Benton, E. J. International Law & the Diplomacy of the Spanish-American War. 1977. lib. bdg. 59.95 (ISBN 0-8490-2062-X). Gordon Pr.
Bergmann, Lothar. Der Begehungsort Im Internationalen Strafrecht Deutschlands, Englands und der Vereinigten Staaten Von Amerika. (Neue Koelner Rechtswissenschaftliche Abhandlungen Ser.: Vol. 48). (Ger). 1966. pap. 17.75x (ISBN 3-11-001077-1). De Gruyter.
Berne Convention for the Protection of Literary & Artistic Works (Texts) Nineteen Sixty-Eight Supplement (Stockholm Act, 1967) 1968. loose leaf bdg. 5.00x (ISBN 0-686-53124-8, WIPO6, WIPO). Unipub.
Bernier, Ivan. International Legal Aspects of Federalism. xiv, 296p. (Orig.). 1973. 19.50 (ISBN 0-208-01384-9, Archon). Shoe String.
Bischel, Jon E., ed. Income Tax Treaties. LC 78-58373. 1978. text ed. 30.00 (ISBN 0-685-65701-9, J3-1412). PLI.
Black, C. E. & Falk, Richard A., eds. Future of International Legal Order, 4 vols. Incl. Vol. 1. Trends & Patterns. 1969. 32.50 (ISBN 0-691-09215-X); Vol. 2. Wealth & Resources. 1970. 25.00 (ISBN 0-691-09217-6); Vol. 3. Conflict Management. 416p. 1971. 27.50 (ISBN 0-691-09220-6); Vol. 4. The Structure of the International Environment. 600p. 1972. 27.50 (ISBN 0-691-09221-4). (Center of International Studies, Princeton Univ.). Princeton U Pr.
Boehme, Eckart, ed. From the Law of the Sea Towards an Ocean Space Regime: Practical & Legal Implications of the Marine Revolution. 174p. 1972. pap. 25.00x (ISBN 3-7875-2119-4). Intl Pubns Serv.
Boguslavsky, M. M. Copyright in International Relations: International Protection of Literary & Scientific Works. Catterns, David, ed. Poulet, N., tr. from Rus. 224p. 1979. 30.00x (ISBN 0-9595513-0-1, Pub. by Australian Copyright Council Australia). Rothman.
Bokor, Hanna. New States & International Law. LC 74-24762. 1970. 8.75x (ISBN 0-8002-0863-3). Intl Pubns Serv.
Bowett, D. The Legal Regime of Islands in International Law. 337p. 1979. 30.00x (ISBN 90-286-0968-7). Sijthoff & Noordhoff.
Bowett, Derek. The Legal Regime of Islands in International Law. 1978. lib. bdg. 32.50 (ISBN 0-379-20346-4). Oceana.
Bowie, Robert R. Suez Nineteen Fifty-Six. (International Crisis & the Role of Law Ser). 164p. 1974. 9.95x (ISBN 0-19-519805-0); pap. 4.95x (ISBN 0-19-519804-2). Oxford U Pr.
Bridgman, Raymond. First Book of World Law. LC 79-147597. (Library of War & Peace; International Law). lib. bdg. 38.00 (ISBN 0-8240-0358-6). Garland Pub.
Brierly, James L. Law of Nations: An Introduction to the International Law of Peace. new ed. Waldock, Humphrey, ed. 1978. 9.95x (ISBN 0-19-825105-X). Oxford U Pr.
British Year of International Law, 1930, Vol. 11. (Royal Institute of International Affairs Ser.). 1930. text ed. 15.95x (ISBN 0-19-214633-5). Oxford U Pr.
Brownlie, Ian. Principles of Public International Law. 3rd ed. 1980. 46.00x (ISBN 0-19-876066-3); pap. 27.50x (ISBN 0-19-876067-1). Oxford U Pr.
Bryant, Robert D. A World Rule of Law, a Way to Peace. LC 76-24727. 1977. soft bdg. 12.00 (ISBN 0-88247-412-X). R & E Res Assoc.
Burlamaqui, Jean J. The Principles of Natural & Politic Law. 5th ed. Nugent, Thomas, tr. LC 70-38249. (The Evolution of Capitalism Ser.). 500p. 1972. Repr. of 1807 ed. 29.00 (ISBN 0-405-04114-4). Arno.
Butler, W. E. International Law in Comparative Perspective. 324p. 1980. 42.50x (ISBN 90-286-0089-2). Sijthoff & Noordhoff.
Butler, W. E., ed. A Sourcebook on Socialist International Organizations. 1168p. 1980. 125.00x (ISBN 90-286-0798-6). Sijthoff & Noordhoff.
Cairnes, John E. Political Essays. LC 66-22615. Repr. of 1873 ed. 17.50x (ISBN 0-678-00206-1). Kelley.
Carlston, Kenneth S. Law & Organization in World Society. LC 62-13211. 1962. 17.95 (ISBN 0-252-72512-3). U of Ill Pr.
Carnegie Endowment for International Peace, Washington. Division of International Law. Monograph Series. 1937-45. Repr. Set. 150.00 (ISBN 0-384-07699-8). Johnson Repr.
Cassese, A., ed. U. N. Law-Fundamental Rights: Two Topics in International Law. 268p. 1979. 38.00x (ISBN 90-286-0828-1). Sijthoff & Noordhoff.
Chatterjee, S. K. Legal Aspects of International Drug Control. 612p. 1981. 117.00 (ISBN 90-286-2091-5). Sijthoff & Noordhoff.
Convention Establishing the World Intellectual Property Organization: (1967) 24p. 1970. pap. 3.00x (ISBN 0-686-53002-0, WIPO10, WIPO). Unipub.
Convention for the Protection of Producers of Phonograms Against Unauthorized Duplication of Their Phonograms. 1974. pap. 3.00x (ISBN 0-686-53125-6, WIPO 27, WIPO). Unipub.
Convention Relating to the Distribution of Programme-Carrying Signals Transmitted by Satellite. 1974. pap. 3.00x (ISBN 0-686-53126-4, WIPO 28, WIPO). Unipub.
Convention to Prevent & Punish the Acts of Terrorism Taking the Form of Crimes Against Persons & Related Extortion That Are of International Significance. (Treaty Ser.: No. 37). 18p. (Eng., Span., Port. & Fr.). 1971. pap. 1.00 (ISBN 0-8270-0480-X). OAS.
Corbett, Percy E. Growth of World Law. LC 70-132236. 1971. 16.00 (ISBN 0-691-09223-0). Princeton U Pr.

--Law in Diplomacy. 9.50 (ISBN 0-8446-1125-5). Peter Smith.
--Study of International Law. (Orig.). 1955. pap. text ed. 2.35 (ISBN 0-685-19772-7). Phila Bk Co.
Crane, Robert T. The State in Constitutional & International Law. LC 78-63921. (Johns Hopkins University. Studies in the Social Sciences. Twenty-Fifth Ser. 1907: 6-7). Repr. of 1907 ed. 13.50 (ISBN 0-404-61172-9). AMS Pr.
Csabafi, Inre A. Concept of State Jurisdiction in International Space Law: A Study in the Progressive Development of Space Law in the United Nations. 197p. (Orig.). 1971. pap. 27.50x (ISBN 90-247-5015-6). Intl Pubns Serv.
David Davies Memorial Institute of International Studies, ed. The International Disputes: The Legal Aspects. 344p. 1972. 12.00x (ISBN 0-900362-39-1). Intl Pubns Serv.
Dawson, Frank G. & Head, Ivan L. International Law, National Tribunals, & Rights of Aliens, Vol. 10. 1971. 10.00x (ISBN 0-8156-2152-3). U Pr of Va.
Deak, Francis & Jessup, Philip, eds. A Collection of Neutrality Laws, Regulations & Treaties of Various Countries, 2 vols. LC 70-138607. 1970. Repr. of 1939 ed. lib. bdg. 53.00x (ISBN 0-8371-5715-3, DENL). Greenwood.
Delupis, Ingrid. International Law & the Independent State. LC 73-94048. 236p. 1974. 32.50x (ISBN 0-8448-0317-0). Crane-Russak Co.
De Rivero, Oswaldo. New Economic Order & International Development Law. LC 79-41222. 132p. 1980. 18.50 (ISBN 0-08-024706-7). Pergamon.
De Visscher, Charles. Theory & Reality in Public International Law. rev. ed. Corbett, P. E., tr. LC 67-21020. (Center of International Studies Ser). 1968. 32.50x (ISBN 0-691-09210-9). Princeton U Pr.
De Vries, H. P. & Rodriguez-Novas, J. The Law of the Americas. LC 66-27792. 1965. 20.00 (ISBN 0-379-00268-X). Oceana.
Dhokalia, R. P. The Codification of Public International Law. LC 66-11927. 1971. 22.50 (ISBN 0-379-00264-7). Oceana.
Di Marzo, Luigi. Component Units of Federal States & International Agreement. LC 80-83265. 272p. 1981. 45.00x (ISBN 90-286-0330-1). Sijthoff & Noordhoff.
Douglas, William O. Towards a Global Federalism. LC 68-31494. (James Stokes Lectureship on Politics). 177p. 1968. 10.00x (ISBN 0-8147-0129-9). NYU Pr.
Drobnig, Ulrich. American-German Private International Law. LC 79-132281. (Parker School Studies in Private International Law Ser). 1972. lib. bdg. 20.00 (ISBN 0-379-11418-6). Oceana.
Eagleton, C. Responsibility of States in International Law. Repr. of 1928 ed. 19.00 (ISBN 0-527-26050-9). Kraus Repr.
Edwards, Charles S. Hugo Grotius, the Miracle of Holland: A Study of Political & Legal Thought. LC 81-4592. 288p. 1981. text ed. 19.95x (ISBN 0-88229-624-8). Nelson-Hall.
Egyptian Review of International Law 1945-1974, Vols. 1-36. 1974. Set. 540.00 (ISBN 0-686-57565-2); 22.50 ea. Oceana.
Elias, T. O. New Horizons in International Law. 1979. lib. bdg. 36.00 (ISBN 0-379-20499-1). Oceana.
Elliot, Jonathan. The American Diplomatic Code, Embracing a Collection of Treaties & Conventions Between U.S. & Foreign Powers from 1778 to 1834, 2 Vols. LC 74-129032. (Research & Source Works Ser.: No. 605). 1971. Repr. lib. bdg. 63.00 (ISBN 0-8337-1036-2). B Franklin.
Erickson, Richard J. International Law & the Revolutionary State: A Case Study of the Soviet Union & Customary International Law. LC 72-8649. 320p. 1972. lib. bdg. 20.00 (ISBN 0-379-00169-1). Oceana.
Falk, Richard A. The Role of Domestic Courts in International Legal Order, Vol. 3. 1964. 10.00x (ISBN 0-8139-0836-1). U Pr of Va.
Feilchenfeld, Ernst H. The International Economic Law of Belligerent Occupation. xii, 181p. Repr. of 1942 ed. 23.00 (ISBN 0-384-15413-1). Johnson Repr.
Feinberg, Nathan. Studies in International Law. 640p. 1979. text ed. 34.50x (ISBN 965-223-324-2, Pub. by Magnes Israel). Humanities.
Fenwick, C. Foreign Policy & International Law. LC 68-57015. 1968. 8.50 (ISBN 0-379-00366-X). Oceana.
Finch, George A. The Sources of Modern International Law. ix, 124p. Repr. of 1937 ed. 15.50 (ISBN 0-384-15685-1). Johnson Repr.
Finnegan, Richard B., et al. Law & Politics in the International System: Case Studies in Conflict Resolution. LC 79-66153. (Illus.). 1979. pap. text ed. 9.00 (ISBN 0-8191-0793-X). U Pr of Amer.
Fisher, Herbert A. Common Weal. facs. ed. LC 68-22911. (Essay Index Reprint Ser). 1924. 16.00 (ISBN 0-8369-0440-0). Arno.
Fisher, Roger. Improving Compliance with International Law. LC 80-14616. (Procedural Aspects of International Law Ser.: Vol. 14). 1981. 20.00x (ISBN 0-8139-0859-0). U Pr of Va.
--Points of Choice. LC 78-40067. (International Crises & the Role of Law Ser.). 1978. pap. 4.95 (ISBN 0-19-825324-9). Oxford U Pr.
Franck, Thomas M. Control of Sea Resources by Semi-Autonomous States. LC 78-69499. 1978. pap. 1.75 (ISBN 0-87003-032-9). Carnegie Endow.
Frank, Ruddy, ed. American International Law Cases, 1783-1968, 20 vols. LC 78-140621. (American International Law Cases Ser). 1977. lib. bdg. 45.00 ea. Oceana.
Freeman, A. V. International Responsibility of States for Denial of Justice. LC 39-17013. Repr. of 1938 ed. 30.00 (ISBN 0-527-31400-5). Kraus Repr.
Friedmann, Wolfgang, ed. Public & Private Enterprise in Mixed Economies. LC 73-12406. 410p. 1974. 25.00x (ISBN 0-231-03776-7). Columbia U Pr.
Friedmann, Wolfgang G., et al, eds. Transnational Law in a Changing Society: Essays in Honor of Philip C. Jessup. LC 71-187029. 324p. 1972. 20.00x (ISBN 0-231-03619-1). Columbia U Pr.
Fulbecke, William. The Pandectes of the Law of Nations. LC 79-84109. (English Experience Ser.: No.928). 192p. 1979. Repr. of 1602 ed. lib. bdg. 18.00 (ISBN 90-221-0928-3). Walter J Johnson.
Gifford, William C., Jr. International Tax Planning. 2nd ed. 746p. 1979. 45.00 (ISBN 0-87179-271-0). BNA.
Glassner, Martin I. Bibliography on Land-Locked States. LC 80-51737. 60p. 1980. 20.00x (ISBN 90-286-0290-9). Sijthoff & Noordhodf.
Gorove, Stephen, ed. Legal Aspects of International Investment. (L. Q. C. Lamar Society of International Law, University of Mississippi Law Center, Monograph: No. 1). viii, 79p. (Orig.). 1977. pap. text ed. 10.00x (ISBN 0-8377-0607-6). Rothman.
Green, Leslie C. International Law Through the Cases. 4th ed. (Illus.). 1978. lib. bdg. 50.00 (ISBN 0-379-20404-5); pap. text ed. 29.50 (ISBN 0-379-20405-3). Oceana.
Grenville, J. A. Major International Treaties, 1914-1973. LC 75-163352. 1975. pap. 8.95 (ISBN 0-8128-1848-2). Stein & Day.
Grieves, Forest L. International Law, Organization, & the Environment: A Bibliography & Research Guide. LC 74-77640. (Institute of Government Research Ser). 1974. pap. 3.50x (ISBN 0-8165-0463-6). U of Ariz Pr.
Grotius Society. Grotius Society Transactions, 45 vols. incl. index. LC 16-15222. 1915-59. Set. 550.00 (ISBN 0-379-20500-9); 20.00 ea. Oceana.
Guide to the Application of the Paris Convention for the Protection of Industrial Property. 1968. 35.00x (ISBN 0-686-53003-9, WIPO44, WIPO). Unipub.
Guide to the International Registration of Marks. 1977. pap. 12.00x (ISBN 0-686-53005-5, WIPO39, WIPO). Unipub.
Hackworth, Green H. Digest of International Law from 1906 to 1944, 8 vols. LC 70-147741. (Library of War & Peace; International Law). Set. lib. bdg. 400.00 (ISBN 0-8240-0489-2). Garland Pub.
The Hague Agreement Concerning the International Deposit of Industrial Designs. 1975. pap. 4.00x (ISBN 0-686-53004-7, WIPO13, WIPO). Unipub.
Haraszti, G., ed. Questions of International Law. 255p. 1977. 28.50x (ISBN 90-286-0386-7). Sijthoff & Noordhoff.
Harcourt, George G. Letters by Historicus on Some Questions of International Law. Repr. of 1863 ed. 16.00 (ISBN 0-527-37750-3). Kraus Repr.
Henkin, Louis. How Nations Behave. 2nd ed. LC 79-1015. 1979. 25.00x (ISBN 0-231-04756-8); pap. 10.00x (ISBN 0-231-04757-6). Columbia U Pr.
Herczegh, Geza. General Principles of Law & the International Legal Order. LC 75-7993. 129p. 1969. 11.25x (ISBN 0-8002-1451-X). Intl Pubns Serv.
Hingorani, R. C., ed. Modern International Law. lib. bdg. 17.50 (ISBN 0-379-20439-8). Oceana.
Hoyt, Edwin C. National Policy & International Law: Case Studies from American Canal Policy. (Monograph Ser. in World Affairs, Vol. 4: 1966-67 Ser., Pt. A). 4.00 (ISBN 0-87940-011-0). U of Denver Intl.
Hudson, Manley. International Legislation, 9 Vols. Set. 540.00 (ISBN 0-379-20110-0); 60.00 ea. Oceana.
Hull, W. I. Two Hague Conferences & Their Contributions to International Law. LC 8-28855. Repr. of 1908 ed. 24.00 (ISBN 0-527-43200-8). Kraus Repr.
Ijalaye, David A. The Extension of Corporate Personality in International Law. 1978. 27.50 (ISBN 0-379-20328-6). Oceana.
International Law & the Middle East Crisis: A Symposium, Vol. 4. 1957. 5.00 (ISBN 0-930598-03-2). Tulane Stud Pol.
The International Law of the Future: Postulates, Principles & Proposals. (Studies in the Administration of International Law & Organization). 1944. Repr. of 1944 ed. pap. 7.00 (ISBN 0-527-00879-6). Kraus Repr.
International Law Quarterly: Nineteen Forty Seven - Nineteen Fifty One, 4 vols. 1968. 50.00 ea. (ISBN 0-379-20550-5). Oceana.
Italian Society For International Organization. Italian Practice in International Law, 1861-1942, 10 Vols. Ago, Robert, ed. LC 79-147818. 40.00 ea. (ISBN 0-379-10000-2). Oceana.
Jackson, David C. The "Conflicts" Process: Jurisdiction & Choice in Private International Law. LC 75-33647. 400p. 1975. text ed. 28.00 (ISBN 0-379-00382-1). Oceana.
Jacobini, H. B. A Study of the Philosophy of International Law As Seen in Works of Latin American Writers. LC 78-20471. 1980. Repr. of 1954 ed. 16.50 (ISBN 0-88355-849-1). Hyperion Conn.
Jaffe, Louis L. Judicial Aspects of Foreign Relations. 1933. 15.50 (ISBN 0-384-26660-6). Johnson Repr.
Jennings, R. Y. & Brownlie, Ian, eds. The British Year Book of International Law: 1976-1977, Vol. XLVIII. 1978. 89.00x (ISBN 0-19-818172-8). Oxford U Pr.
Jessup, P. C. The Use of International Law. LC 79-173670. 164p. 1972. Repr. of 1959 ed. lib. bdg. 22.50 (ISBN 0-306-70407-2). Da Capo.
Jessup, Philip C. The Prince of International Justice. LC 76-158460. (Jacob Blaustein Lectures in International Affairs Ser.: No. 2). 82p. 1971. 10.00x (ISBN 0-231-03545-4). Columbia U Pr.
--Transnational Law. 1956. 24.50x (ISBN 0-685-89792-3). Elliots Bks.
Joyner, Nancy D. Aerial Hijacking As an International Crime. LC 74-8380. 352p. 1974. lib. bdg. 21.00 (ISBN 0-379-00004-0). Oceana.
Kelsen, Hans. General Theory of Law & State. Wedberg, Anders, tr. LC 61-12122. 1961. Repr. of 1945 ed. 25.00 (ISBN 0-8462-0215-8). Russell.
Khadduri, Majid. Major Middle Eastern Problems in International Law. 1972. pap. 5.25 (ISBN 0-8447-3080-7). Am Enterprise.
Kirkemo, Ronald B. An Introduction to International Law. LC 73-81677. 1974. 17.95x (ISBN 0-88229-118-1). Nelson-Hall.
--An Introduction to International Law. (Quality Paperback: No. 312). 235p. 1975. pap. 3.95 (ISBN 0-8226-0312-8). Littlefield.
Knechtle, A. A. Basic Problems in International Fiscal Law. Weisflog, W. E., tr. 1979. pap. 27.00 (ISBN 90-200-0550-2, Pub. by Kluwer Law Netherlands). Kluwer Boston.
Ko Swan Sik, et al, eds. Netherlands Yearbook of International Law, Vol. XI: 1980. 400p. 1981. 40.00 (ISBN 90-286-2711-1). Sijthoff & Noordhoff.
Kronmiller, Theodore G., ed. The Lawfullness of Deep Seabed Mining, Vols. 1 & 2. LC 79-23232. 1980. Set. lib. bdg. 80.00 (ISBN 0-379-20461-4). Vol. 1, 521p (ISBN 0-379-20461-4). Vol. 2, 460p (ISBN 0-379-20462-2). Oceana.
Kuhn, Arthur K. Comparative Commentaries on Private International Law or Conflict of Laws. xi, 381p. 1981. Repr. of 1937 ed. lib. bdg. 32.50x (ISBN 0-8377-0737-4). Rothman.
--Pathways in International Law, a Personal Narrative. Repr. of 1953 ed. lib. bdg. 15.00x (ISBN 0-8371-2211-2, KUPI). Greenwood.
Lamenek, K., ed. Agreements of International Organizations & the Vienna Convention on the Law of Treaties: Oesterreich, Zeitschrift fuer Oeffentiliches Recht Suppl. 1. 1971. pap. 33.90 (ISBN 0-387-81010-2). Springer-Verlag.
Larson, Arthur. When Nations Disagree: A Handbook on Peace Through Law. LC 61-15490. (Edward Douglass White Lectures). 1961. 17.50x (ISBN 0-8071-0605-4). La State U Pr.
Lautepacht, Hersch. International Law: The Law of Peace, 4 vols. Lauterpacht, E., ed. Incl. Vol. 1. 500p. 1970 (ISBN 0-521-07643-9); Vol. 2. 624p. 1975 (ISBN 0-521-20480-1); Vol. 3, Pts. 2-6. 1977 (ISBN 0-521-21207-3); Vol. 4, Pts. 7-8. 1978 (ISBN 0-521-21524-2). LC 70-92250. 97.50 ea. Cambridge U Pr.
Lauterpacht, Hersch. Function of Law in the International Community. LC 79-147755. (Library of War & Peace; International Law). lib. bdg. 38.00 (ISBN 0-8240-0493-0). Garland Pub.
Lauterpacht, Hersh. Function of Law in the International Community. 1966. Repr. of 1933 ed. 25.00 (ISBN 0-208-00434-3, Archon). Shoe String.
--Private Law Sources & Analogies of International Law, with Special Reference to International Arbitration. 1970. Repr. of 1927 ed. 22.50 (ISBN 0-208-00814-4, Archon). Shoe String.
Legal Problems Associated with Ocean Data Acquisition Systems (ODAS) (Intergovernmental Oceanographic Commission Technical Ser. No. 5). 1970. pap. 2.25 (ISBN 92-3-100762-9, U350, UNESCO). Unipub.
Levi, Werner. Contemporary International Law: A Concise Introduction. 1978. lib. bdg. 29.75x (ISBN 0-89158-184-7); pap. text ed. 11.00x (ISBN 0-89158-187-1). Westview.
--Law & Politics in the International Society. LC 76-22580. (Sage Library of Social Research: Vol. 32). 224p. 1976. 20.00 (ISBN 0-8039-0617-X); pap. 9.95 (ISBN 0-8039-0618-8). Sage.
Lillich, Richard B., ed. The Valuation of Nationalized Property in International Law, Vol. 2. LC 70-177376. (Virginia Legal Studies). 200p. 1973. 15.00x (ISBN 0-8139-0465-X). U Pr of Va.
--The Valuation of Nationalized Property in International Law, Vol. 3. (Virginia Legal Studies). 1975. 15.00x (ISBN 0-8139-0613-X). U Pr of Va.
Lipstein, Kurt. Principles of the Conflict of Laws: National & International. 160p. 1981. 21.50 (ISBN 90-286-0750-1). Sijthoff & Noordhoff.
Lisbon Agreement for the Protection of Appellations of Origin & Their International Registration & Regulations of October 5, 1976. 24p. 1976. pap. 3.00x (ISBN 0-686-53009-8, WIPO15, WIPO). Unipub.
Livermore, Sarah, et al, eds. The American Bar - The Canadian Bar - The International Bar: 1981. 63rd ed. LC 18-21110. 3062p. 1981. 130.00 (ISBN 0-931398-06-1). R B Forster.
Locarno Agreement Establishing an International Classification for Industrial Designs. 24p. 1977. pap. 3.00x (ISBN 0-686-53010-1, WIPO19, WIPO). Unipub.
Loebenstein, E. International Mutual Assistance in Administrative Matters. LC 72-96054. (Osterreichische Zeitschrift Fuer Offentliches Recht: Suppl. 2). 93p. 1972. pap. 24.80 (ISBN 0-387-81120-6). Springer-Verlag.
MacDonald, R. The International Law & Policy of Human Welfare. 708p. 1978. 92.50x (ISBN 90-286-0808-7). Sijthoff & Noordhoff.
McDougal, Myres S. & Reisman, W. Michael. International Law in Contemporary Perspective: The Public Order of the World Community. (University Casebook Ser.). 1500p. 1981. text ed. write for info. (ISBN 0-88277-035-7). Foundation Pr.
McMahon, M. M. Conquest & Modern International Law. LC 41-1044. Repr. of 1940 ed. 21.00 (ISBN 0-527-03235-2). Kraus Repr.
McNair, Arnold Duncan. The Development of International Justice: Two Lectures Delivered at the Law Center of New York University in December 1953. LC 54-9041. 1954. 4.50x (ISBN 0-8147-0275-9). NYU Pr.
McWhinney, E. The International Law of Detente. 260p. 1978. 37.50x (ISBN 90-286-0338-7). Sijthoff & Noordhoff.
--The World Court & the Contemporary International Law-Making Process. 227p. 1979. 35.00x (ISBN 90-286-0908-3). Sijthoff & Noordhoff.
McWhinney, Edward. Conflict & Compromise: International Law & World Order in a Revolutionary Age. LC 80-29045. 152p. 1981. text ed. 17.50x (ISBN 0-8419-0694-7); pap. text ed. 8.50x (ISBN 0-8419-0696-3). Holmes & Meier.
McWhinney, Edward, ed. International Law of Communications. LC 73-140557. 1971. 17.50 (ISBN 0-379-00138-1). Oceana.
Madrid Agreement Concerning the International Registration of Marks & Regulations of June 21, 1974. 1975. pap. 4.00x (ISBN 0-686-53014-4, WIPO11, WIPO). Unipub.
Madrid Agreement for the Repression of False or Deceptive Indications of Source on Goods. 1975. pap. 3.00x (ISBN 0-686-53127-2, WIPO 12, WIPO). Unipub.
Maine, Sir Henry J. International Law. LC 79-1612. 1980. Repr. of 1894 ed. 18.50 (ISBN 0-88355-915-3). Hyperion Conn.
Malawar, Stuart S. Imposed Treaties & International Law. LC 77-82277. 1977. lib. bdg. 17.50 (ISBN 0-930342-07-0). W S Hein.
Malawer, Stuart S. Studies in International Law. 2nd ed. LC 77-71708. 1977. lib. bdg. 27.50 (ISBN 0-9601384-1-2). W S Hein.
Margalith, Aaron M. The International Mandates. LC 78-64278. (Johns Hopkins University. Studies in the Social Sciences. Extra Volumes-New Ser.: 8). Repr. of 1930 ed. 23.00 (ISBN 0-404-61379-9). AMS Pr.
Martens, Georg F. Von, ed. Nouveau Recueil General De Traites & Autres Actes Relatifs Aux Rapports De Droit International, 35 vols. 28645p. 2450.00 (ISBN 0-384-35551-X); pap. 2250.00 (ISBN 0-384-35550-1). Johnson Repr.

Marvin, Francis S., ed. Evolution of World-Peace: Essays. Unity Ser. 4. facs. ed. LC 68-20318. (Essay Index Reprint Ser). 1921. 12.25 (ISBN 0-8369-0682-9). Arno.
--Western Races & the World. Unity Ser. 5. facs. ed. LC 68-22929. (Essay Index Reprint Ser). 1968. Repr. of 1922 ed. 15.00 (ISBN 0-8369-0684-5). Arno.
Mason, C. M., ed. Effective Management of Resources: The International Politics of the North Sea. 1979. 22.50x (ISBN 0-89397-043-3). Nichols Pub.
Merryman, John H. International Law, Development & the Transit Trade of Landlocked States: The Case of Bolivia. 1969. 13.50x (ISBN 3-7875-2114-3). Intl Pubns Serv.
Mill, James. Essays on Jurisprudence Government, Liberty of the Press, Law of Nations, Education, Colony & Prison Discipline. LC 66-21685. Repr. of 1825 ed. 17.50x (ISBN 0-678-00297-5). Kelley.
Miller, William G. Lectures on the Philosophy of Law, Designed Mainly As an Introduction to the Study of International Law. xv, 432p. 1979. Repr. of 1884 ed. lib. bdg. 35.00x (ISBN 0-8377-0834-6). Rothman.
Model Law Concerning the Protection of Performers, Producers of Phonograms & Broadcasting Organizations with a Commentary on It. 1974. pap. 3.00x (ISBN 0-686-53019-5, WIPO50, WIPO). Unipub.
Model Law for Developing Countries on Appellations of Origin & Indications of Source. 1975. pap. 12.00x (ISBN 0-686-53015-2, WIPO49, WIPO). Unipub.
Model Law for Developing Countries on Marks, Trade Names, & Acts of Unfair Competition. 1967. pap. 12.00x (ISBN 0-686-53018-7, WIPO47, WIPO). Unipub.
Moore, John B. Digest of International Law, 8 Vols. LC 77-101908. Repr. of 1906 ed. Set. 250.00 (ISBN 0-404-04420-4); 32.50 ea. AMS Pr.
Morse, C. G. Torts in Private International Law. LC 78-5881. (Problems in Private International Law Ser.: Vol. 2). 1979. 53.75 (ISBN 0-444-85168-2, North Holland). Elsevier.
Multilateral Agreements. (Legal Ser.: No. 1). 1959. pap. 9.75 (ISBN 92-0-176059-0, IAEA). Unipub.
Nanyenya-Takirambudde, Peter. Technology Transfer & International Law. LC 79-23571. 190p. 1980. 22.95 (ISBN 0-03-047531-7). Praeger.
Nice Agreement Concerning the International Classification of Goods & Services for the Purposes of Registration of Marks. 1970. pap. 3.00x (ISBN 0-686-53128-0, WIPO 14, WIPO). Unipub.
OAS General Secretariat, Dept. of Publications. Sexto Curso de Derecho Internationsl Organizado Por el Comite Juridico Interamericano: Julio-Agosto de 1979, Conferencias e Informes. 630p. (Span.). 1979. pap. text ed. 25.00 (ISBN 0-8270-1144-X). OAS.
OAS General Secretariat Office of Development & Codification of International Law. Actas Y Documentos Segunda Conferencia Especializada Interamerica Sobre Derecho Internacional Privado, Vol. 1. (International Law). 455p. 1980. lib. bdg. 25.00 (ISBN 0-8270-1113-X). OAS.
OAS General Secretariat Office of Development & Codification of Inernational Law. Actas Y Documentos Segunda Conferencia Especializada Interamericana Sobre Derecho Internacional Privado, Vol. 3. (International Law Ser.). 469p. 1980. text ed. 25.00 (ISBN 0-8270-1115-6). OAS.
OAS General Secretatiat Office of Development & Codification of International Law. Actas Y Documentos Segunda Conferencia Especializada Interamericana Sobre Derecho Internacional Privado, Vol. 2. (International Law Ser.). 450p. 1980. text ed. 25.00 (ISBN 0-8270-1114-8). OAS.
Offner, Eric D. International Trademark Service, 3 vols. LC 79-89849. 1970. 96.00 (ISBN 0-912166-04-5). Fieldston.
--International Trademark Service: Supplement, 1971, 1972, 1973. 1973. 35.00 (ISBN 0-685-22596-8). Fieldston.
Okolie, Charles. International Law & the Developing Countries. LC 74-81841. 1978. 22.00 (ISBN 0-685-59259-6). NOK Pubs.
Onuf, Nicholas G, ed. Law Making in the Global Community. 600p. 1980. lib. bdg. write for info. (ISBN 0-89089-169-9). Carolina Acad Pr.
Ostrower, Alexander. Language, Law, & Diplomacy, 2 Vols. LC 63-15015. 1965. 20.00x (ISBN 0-8122-7408-3). U of Pa Pr.
Panhuys. Yearbook of the A. A. A. 1974. (Association of Attenders & Alumni of the Hague Academy of International Law Ser: No. 44). 1977. pap. 47.00 (ISBN 90-247-1945-3, Pub. by Martinus Nijhoff Netherlands). Kluwer Boston.
Paris Convention for the Protection of Industrial Property. pap. 3.00x (ISBN 0-686-53020-9, WIPO4, WIPO). Unipub.
Patel, Satyavrata R. World Constitutional Law & Practice - Major Constitutions & Governments. 1970. 11.00x (ISBN 0-8426-0161-9). Verry.
Patent Cooperation Treaty (PCT) 1970. pap. 6.00x (ISBN 0-686-53021-7, WIPO21, WIPO). Unipub.
Peaslee. Agriculture - Commodities - Fisheries - Food - Plants, Pt. 2. (International Governmental Organizations Constitutional Documents). 1975. lib. bdg. 89.00 (ISBN 90-247-1687-X, Pub. by Martinus Nijhoff Netherlands). Kluwer Boston.
--Communications, Transport, Travel. (International Governmental Organizations Constitutional Documents: Pt. 5). 1976. lib. bdg. 131.50 (ISBN 90-247-1826-0, Pub. by Martinus Nijhoff Netherlands). Kluwer Boston.
--General & Regional - Political - Economic - Social - Legal - Defense, 2 vols. (International Government Organizations Constitutional Documents: Pt. 1). 1974. lib. bdg. 191.00 (ISBN 90-247-1601-2, Pub. by Martinus Nijhoff Netherlands). Kluwer Boston.
Perkins, John A. The Prudent Peace: Law As Foreign Policy. LC 80-1200. 1981. lib. bdg. 28.00x (ISBN 0-226-65873-2). U of Chicago Pr.
Phillimore, Walter G. Three Centuries of Peace Treaties & Their Teachings, 1582-1913. LC 73-147602. (Library of War & Peace; International Law). lib. bdg. 38.00 (ISBN 0-8240-0363-2). Garland Pub.
Ralston, Jackson H. Law & Procedure of International Tribunals. LC 75-147738. (Library of War & Peace; International Law). lib. bdg. 38.00 (ISBN 0-8240-0496-5). Garland Pub.
Ramcharan. The International Law Commission. 1977. pap. 34.00 (ISBN 90-247-1984-4, Pub. by Martinus Nijhoff Netherlands). Kluwer Boston.
Ramundo, Bernard A. Peaceful Coexistence: International Law in the Building of Communism. LC 67-12421. 262p. 1967. 18.00x (ISBN 0-8018-0542-2). Johns Hopkins.
Ranshofen-Wertheimer, E. F. The International Secretariat: A Great Experiment in International Administration. (Studies in the Administration of International Law & Organization). Repr. of 1945 ed. pap. 28.00 (ISBN 0-527-00881-8). Kraus Repr.
Records of the Diplomatic Conference on the International Protection of Performers, Producers of Phonograms & Broadcasting Organizations. 1968. pap. 30.00x (ISBN 0-686-53022-5, WIPO37, WIPO). Unipub.
Records of the Intellectual Property Conference of Stockholm, 1967, Vols. I & II. 1971. Set. 180.00x (ISBN 0-686-53023-3, WIPO30, WIPO). Unipub.
Reeves, John. History of the English Law, 4 Vols. 2nd ed. LC 68-57387. Repr. of 1787 ed. Set. 75.00x (ISBN 0-678-04529-1). Kelley.
Regala, Roberto. Law & Diplomacy in a Changing World. 1967. 12.50 (ISBN 0-379-00342-2). Oceana.
Root, Elihu. Addresses on International Subjects. facs. ed. LC 74-86780. (Essay Index Reprint Ser). 1916. 22.00 (ISBN 0-8369-1191-1). Arno.
Rosenne, Shabtai, ed. League of Nations Committee of Experts for the Progressive Codification of International Law. LC 77-165998. 1972. Set. lib. bdg. 75.00 (ISBN 0-379-00147-0). Oceana.
--League of Nations Conference for the Codification of International Law (1930, 4 vols. 1630p. 1975. Set. lib. bdg. 200.00 (ISBN 0-379-10100-9); lib. bdg. 50.00 ea.; Vol. 1. lib. bdg. (ISBN 0-379-10101-7); Vol. 2. lib. bdg. (ISBN 0-379-10102-5); Vol. 3. lib. bdg. (ISBN 0-379-10103-3); Vol. 4. lib. bdg. (ISBN 0-379-10104-1). Oceana.
Royal Institute of International Affairs. British Yearbook of Internaional Law. Incl. Vol. 3. 1965. 15.95x (ISBN 0-19-214625-4); Vol. 7. 1965. 15.95x (ISBN 0-19-214629-7); Vol. 39, 1963. Waldock, H. & Jennings, R. Y., eds. 1965. 24.95x (ISBN 0-19-214622-X); Vol. 40, 1964. Waldock, H. & Jennings, R. Y., eds. 1966. 24.95x (ISBN 0-19-214623-8); Vol. 41, 1965-66. Waldock, H. & Jennings, R. Y., eds. 1968. 24.95x (ISBN 0-19-214657-2); Waldock, H. & Jennings, R. Y., eds. 1969. 24.95x (ISBN 0-19-214658-0); Vol. 44. Waldcock, H. & Jennings, R. Y., eds. 1970. 24.95x (ISBN 0-19-214660-2); Vol. 45. Waldock, H. & Jennings, R. Y., eds. 1973. 59.50x (ISBN 0-19-214661-0). (Royal Institute of International Affairs Ser.). Oxford U Pr.
Sahovic, Milan, ed. Principles of International Law Concerning Friendly Relations & Cooperation. LC 73-8985. 1973. lib. bdg. 17.50 (ISBN 0-379-00020-2). Oceana.
Schermers, Harry G. International Institutional Law, 2 vols. in 1, Vols. I & II. rev. ed. 1088p. 1981. 175.00 (ISBN 90-286-0320-4). Sijthoff & Noordhoff.
Schwartzenberger, Georg & Keeton, George W. Making International Law Work. LC 70-147758. (Library of War & Peace; International Law). lib. bdg. 38.00 (ISBN 0-8240-0491-4). Garland Pub.
Schwarzenberger, Georg. The Dynamics of International Law. xii, 139p. 1976. text ed. 15.00x (ISBN 0-903486-19-9). Rothman.
--The Inductive Approach to International Law. LC 65-17479. 1965. 12.50 (ISBN 0-379-00260-4). Oceana.
Schwarzenberger, Georg & Brown, E. D. A Manual of International Law. 6th ed. lix, 612p. 1976. text ed. 27.50x (ISBN 0-903486-26-1). Rothman.
Scott, James B. Law, the State & the International Community. Repr. of 1939 ed. lib. bdg. 38.00x (ISBN 0-8371-2809-9, SCLI). Greenwood.
Session D'Athenes Nineteen Seventy-Nine: Travaux Preparatoires. (Institut De Droit International. Annuaire: Vol. 58, Tome I). 1979. 178.50 (ISBN 3-8055-2987-2). S Karger.
Sheikh, Ahmed. International Law & National Behavior: A Behavioral Interpretation of Contemporary International Law & Politics. LC 73-19922. 352p. 1974. pap. text ed. 14.50x (ISBN 0-471-78230-0). Wiley.
Shih-Tsai Chen, Samuel. Basic Documents of International Organization. rev. ed. 1979. pap. text ed. 9.95 (ISBN 0-8403-1947-9, 40194701). Kendall-Hunt.
Simmonds, K. Multinational Corporations Law, Vols. 1-2. 1979. Set. 75.00 (ISBN 0-379-20373-1). Oceana.
--Multinational Corporations Law, Release 3. 1980. 50.00 (ISBN 0-379-20373-1). Oceana.
Sinclair, Ian M. The Vienna Convention on the Law of Treaties. LC 72-13210. (Melland Schill Ser.: N. 13). 96p. 1973. lib. bdg. 11.00 (ISBN 0-379-11913-7). Oceana.
Singh, N. Human Rights & International Co-Operation. LC 70-904156. 1969. 12.50x (ISBN 0-8002-0907-9). Intl Pubns Serv.
Stewart, V. Lorne, intro. by. Justice & Troubled Children Around the World, Vol. 1. LC 79-3154. 1981. 17.50x (ISBN 0-8147-7809-7). NYU Pr.
Stone, Julius. Israel & Palestine: Assault on the Law of Nations. LC 80-8875. 208p. 1981. text ed. 17.50x (ISBN 0-8018-2535-0). Johns Hopkins.
Storme, M. Towards a Justice with a Human Face. 1978. lib. bdg. 79.00 (ISBN 90-268-0974-3, Pub. by Kluwer Law Netherlands). Kluwer Boston.
Sukijasovic, Miodrag. Foreign Investment in Yugoslavia. 1971. 12.00 (ISBN 0-379-00476-3). Oceana.
Summers, Lionel M. The International Law of Peace. LC 72-4367. 272p. 1972. lib. bdg. 13.50 (ISBN 0-379-00133-0). Oceana.
Sweeney, Joseph M., et al. Cases & Materials on the International Legal System. 2nd ed. LC 81-3093. (University Casebook Ser.). 1356p. 1981. text ed. write for info. (ISBN 0-88277-032-2). Foundation Pr.
Tabory, Mala. Multilingualism in International Law & Institutions. LC 80-51742. 304p. 1980. 32.50x (ISBN 90-286-0210-0). Sijthoff & Noordhoff.
Taracouzio, T. A. The Soviet Union & International Law: A Study Based on the Legislation, Treaties & Foreign Relations of the Union of Socialist Soviet Republics. Repr. of 1935 ed. 26.00 (ISBN 0-527-88900-8). Kraus Repr.
Third United Nations Conference on the Law of the Sea: Official Records, Vol. IX. 191p. 1979. pap. 14.00 (ISBN 0-686-68976-3, UN79/5/3, UN). Unipub.
Thomas, Ann V. & Thomas, A. J., Jr. A World Rule of Law: Prospects & Problems. LC 74-13554. 1975. 6.95 (ISBN 0-87074-144-6). SMU Press.
Tobin, Harold J. Termination of Multipartite Treaties. LC 33-34572. (Columbia University. Studies in the Social Sciences: No. 388). Repr. of 1933 ed. 24.50 (ISBN 0-404-51388-3). AMS Pr.
Tunkin, G. I. Theory of International Law. Butler, William E., tr. from Russian. LC 73-92258. 480p. 1974. text ed. 22.50x (ISBN 0-674-88001-3). Harvard U Pr.
Umozurike, U. O. International Law & Colonialism in Africa. LC 74-81843. Date not set. cancelled (ISBN 0-88357-032-7). NOK Pubs.
University of Cambridge, Squire Law Library. Catalogue of International Law, 4 vols. LC 71-147816. 400p. 1972. 200.00 set (ISBN 0-379-20030-9); 50.00 ea. Oceana.
Vattel, Emmerich De. The Law of Nations. LC 75-31104. Repr. of 1863 ed. 57.50 (ISBN 0-404-13519-6). AMS Pr.
Verwey, Wil D. Economic Development, Peace, & International Law. 1972. text ed. 36.50x (ISBN 90-232-0992-3). Humanities.
Von Glahn, Gerhard. Law Among Nations: An Introduction to Public International Law. 3rd ed. (Illus.). 1976. text ed. 18.95 (ISBN 0-02-423150-9). Macmillan.
Weis, P. Nationality & Statelessness in International Law. rev. ed. 400p. 1979. 62.50x (ISBN 90-286-0329-8). Sijthoff & Noordhoff.
Weis, Paul. Nationality & Statelessness in International Law. LC 78-14149. 1979. Repr. of 1956 ed. 26.50 (ISBN 0-88355-822-X). Hyperion Conn.
Weston, Burns H., et al. International Law & World Order: An Introductory Problem-Oriented Coursebook. LC 80-15873. (American Casebook Ser.). 1195p. 1980. text ed. 23.95 (ISBN 0-8299-2097-8). West Pub.
Wheaton, Henry. Elements of International Law. LC 78-157426. (American Constitutional & Legal History Ser). 360p. 1972. Repr. of 1836 ed. lib. bdg. 39.50 (ISBN 0-306-70206-1). Da Capo.
Whiteman, Marjorie M. Damages in International Law, 2 vols. 1976. Repr. of 1937 ed. Set. 71.00 (ISBN 0-527-95970-7). Kraus Repr.
Williams, Bruce S. State Security & the League of Nations. LC 75-177845. Repr. of 1927 ed. 26.00 (ISBN 0-404-06959-2). AMS Pr.
Wilson, Robert R. International Law & Contemporary Commonwealth Issues. LC 79-142294. (Commonwealth Studies Center: No. 38). (Illus.). 1971. 12.75 (ISBN 0-8223-0246-2). Duke.
Woolsey, Theodore D. Introduction to the Study of International Law Designed As an Aid in Teaching, & in Historical Studies. 4th ed. 487p. 1981. Repr. of 1874 ed. lib. bdg. 37.50x (ISBN 0-8377-1313-7). Rothman.
World Peace Through Law Centre. The Geneva World Conference, 1967: Proceedings. 747p. 1969. 12.50x (ISBN 0-8002-1452-8). Intl Pubns Serv.
Wright, Quincy. Contemporary International Law: A Balance Sheet. rev. ed. (Orig.). 1961. pap. text ed. 2.45x (ISBN 0-685-19716-6). Phila Bk Co.
--The Enforcement of International Law Through Municipal Law in the United States. Repr. of 1916 ed. 15.50 (ISBN 0-384-69485-3). Johnson Repr.
--International Law & the United Nations. LC 74-27430. 1976. Repr. of 1960 ed. lib. bdg. 16.00x (ISBN 0-8371-7900-9, WRIL). Greenwood.
Zagayko, Florence F. International Law: A Classification for Libraries. LC 65-17043. 1965. 15.00 (ISBN 0-379-00256-6). Oceana.

INTERNATIONAL LAW–ADDRESSES, ESSAYS, LECTURES

Ansay, T., et al. Recueil Des Cours De L'academie De Droit International De la Haye: Collected Courses of the Hague Academy of Int'l Law, Vol. 156 (1977-III) 482p. 1980. 40.00x (ISBN 90-286-0600-9). Sijthoff & Noordhoff.
Bassiouni, M. Cherif. International Criminal Law: A Draft International Criminal Code. LC 80-50452. 286p. 1980. 50.00x (ISBN 90-286-0130-9). Sijthoff & Noordhoff.
Columbia Law Review. Essays on International Law. 1965. 20.00 (ISBN 0-379-00330-9); pap. 8.50 (ISBN 0-685-18989-9). Oceana.
Durante, F., et al. Recueil Des Cours De La'academie De Droit International De la Haye: Collected Courses of the Hague Academy of International Law, Vol. 152 (1976-iv) 478p. 1980. 40.00x (ISBN 90-286-0590-8). Sijthoff & Noordhoff.
Elias, T. O., ed. Nigerian Annual of International Law. 1979. pap. 49.50 (ISBN 0-19-575455-7). Oxford U Pr.
Engel, Salo & Metall, R. A., eds. Law, State & International Legal Order: Essays in Honor of Hans Kelsen. LC 64-16881. 1964. 19.50x (ISBN 0-87049-052-4). U of Tenn Pr.
Falk, Richard A. & Mendlovitz, Saul H., eds. The Strategy of World Order, 4 vols. Incl. Vol. 1. Toward a Theory of War Prevention. Lasswell, Harold D., frwd. by. pap. 3.50 (ISBN 0-911646-01-9); Vol. 2. International Law. Friedmann, Wolfgang, frwd. by. pap. 3.50 (ISBN 0-911646-02-7); Vol. 3. The United Nations. Schacter, Oscar, frwd. by. pap. 4.50 (ISBN 0-911646-03-5); Vol. 4. Disarmament & Economic Development. Singer, David, frwd. by. pap. 4.50 (ISBN 0-911646-04-3). 1966. pap. 14.00 set (ISBN 0-911646-00-0). Inst World Order.
Garner, James W. Studies in Government & International Law. Fairlie, John A., ed. 574p. 1972. Repr. of 1943 ed. lib. bdg. 23.00x (ISBN 0-8371-5966-0, GASG). Greenwood.
Head, I. L., ed. This Fire-Proof House. LC 66-29647. 1967. 9.00 (ISBN 0-379-00282-5). Oceana.
Jessup, P. C. The Use of International Law. LC 79-173670. 164p. 1972. Repr. of 1959 ed. lib. bdg. 22.50 (ISBN 0-306-70407-2). Da Capo.

Kalshoven, Frits, et al, eds. Essays on the Development of the International Legal Order: In Memory of Haro F. van Panhuys. 240p. 1980. 50.00x (ISBN 90-286-0360-3). Sijthoff & Noordhoff.

Lepawsky, Albert, et al, eds. Search for World Order: Studies by Students & Colleagues of Quincy Wright. LC 75-147119. (Orig.). 1971. 38.50x (ISBN 0-89197-479-2). Irvington.

Lerner, Natan. U. N. Convention on the Elimination of Al Forms of Racial Discrimination. LC 80-51738. 278p. 1980. 37.50x (ISBN 90-286-0160-0). Sijthoff & Noordhoff.

Metzger, Stanley D. International Law, Trade & Finance: Realities & Prospects. LC 62-20101. 1963. 14.00 (ISBN 0-379-11603-0). Oceana.

Moskowitz, Moses. The Roots & Reaches of United Nations Actions & Decisions. LC 80-51741. 220p. 1980. 28.50x (ISBN 90-286-0140-6). Sijthoff & Noordhoff.

Mosler, Hermann. The International Society As a Legal Community. LC 80-50454. (Collected Courses, the Hague Academy of International Law: Vol. 140, 1974-IV). 327p. 1980. pap. 27.50x (ISBN 90-286-0080-9). Sijthoff & Noordhoff.

OAS General Secretariat. Recomendaciones E Informes Del Comite Jurico Interamericano Documetos Oficiales: Vol. 2, 1974-1977. 675p. 1981. 50.00 (ISBN 0-8270-1284-5). OAS.

Root, Elihu. Men & Policies: Addresses. facs. ed. Bacon, Robert & Scott, J. B., eds. LC 68-22942. (Essay Index Reprint Ser). 1968. Repr. of 1924 ed. 19.50 (ISBN 0-8369-0832-5). Arno.

Schwarzenberger, Georg, ed. Law, Justice & Equity. LC 67-20413. 1967. 14.00 (ISBN 0-379-00344-9). Oceana.

Sinha, S. Prakash. Asylum & International Law. (Orig.). 1971. pap. 50.00x (ISBN 90-247-5063-6). Intl Pubns Serv.

Sumanpouw, Mathilde. Les Nouvelles Conventions De la Haye: Leur Application Par les Juges Nationaux, Vol. II. 260p. (Fr.). 1981. 45.00x (ISBN 90-286-0870-2). Sijthoff & Noordhoff.

Van Dijk, P. Judicial Review of Governmental Action & the Requirement of an Interest to Sue. LC 80-51740. 618p. 1980. 100.00x (ISBN 90-286-0120-1). Sijthoff & Noordhoff.

Vitta, E. & Brownlie, I. Recueil Des Cours L'academie De Droit International De la Haye: Collected Courses of the Hague Academy of Int'l Law, Vol. 162 (1979-i) 1980. 40.00x (ISBN 90-286-0530-4). Sijthoff & Noordhoff.

Wilson, H. H. The Rig-Veda Sanhita, 7 vols. Incl. Vol. I. 348p. Repr. of 1850 ed (ISBN 0-89684-125-1); Vol. II. 346p. Repr. of 1854 ed (ISBN 0-89684-126-X); Vol. III. 249p. Repr. of 1857 ed (ISBN 0-89684-127-8); Vol. IV. 179p. Repr. of 1857 ed (ISBN 0-89684-128-6); Vol. V. 314p. Repr. of 1866 ed (ISBN 0-89684-129-4); Vol VI. 443p. Repr. of 1888 ed (ISBN 0-89684-130-8); Vol. VII. 436p. Repr. of 1888 ed (ISBN 0-89684-131-6). 1977. 120.00 set (ISBN 0-686-77518-X, Pub. by Cosmo Pubns India). Orient Bk Dist.

Wilson, Robert R. International Law Standard & Commonwealth Developments. LC 66-22940. (Commonwealth Studies Center: No. 27). 1966. 14.75 (ISBN 0-8223-0191-1). Duke.

INTERNATIONAL LAW–BIBLIOGRAPHY

Brownlie, William H., ed. Basic Documents in International Law. 2nd ed. 1972. 22.00x (ISBN 0-19-876023-X); pap. 14.50x (ISBN 0-19-876024-8). Oxford U Pr.

Hathaway, Barbara D. Julius Stone: A Bio-Bibliography. (Legal Bibliography Ser.: No. 20). 51p. (Orig.). 1980. pap. 15.00 (ISBN 0-935630-02-3). U of Tex Tarlton Law Lib.

Myers, Denys P. Manual of Collections of Treaties & of Collections Relating to Treaties. 1922. 43.00 (ISBN 0-8337-2499-1). B Franklin.

Strollreither, Konrad. Internationale Bibliographie der Juristischen Nachschlagewerke. LC 55-10789. 611p. 1955. 85.00x (ISBN 3-465-00388-8). Intl Pubns Serv.

University of Cambridge, Squire Law Library. Catalogue of International Law, 4 vols. LC 71-147816. 400p. 1972. 200.00 set (ISBN 0-379-20030-9); 50.00 ea. Oceana.

INTERNATIONAL LAW–CASES

Bishop, William W., Jr. International Law: Cases & Materials. 3rd ed. 1122p. 1971. 26.00 (ISBN 0-316-09664-4). Little.

Cohen, Jerome A., ed. China's Practice of International Law: Some Case Studies. LC 72-80656. (Studies in East Asian Law: No. 6). (Illus.). 420p. 1973. 20.00x (ISBN 0-674-11975-4). Harvard U Pr.

Deak, Francis. American International Law Cases: 1971-1978, Vols. 1-20. 45.00 ea. (ISBN 0-379-20075-9). Oceana.

Donelan, M. D. & Grieve, M. J. International Disputes: Case Histories, 1945-1970. LC 73-78089. 280p. 1973. 19.95 (ISBN 0-312-42000-5). St Martin.

DuBoff, Leonard D., ed. Art Law, Domestic & International. LC 75-7668. (Illus.). x, 627p. 1975. text ed. 27.50x (ISBN 0-8377-0503-7). Rothman.

Feinberg, Nathan. Studies in International Law. 640p. 1981. text ed. 46.00 (ISBN 0-86598-051-9, Pub. by Magnes Israel). Allanheld.

Frank, Ruddy, ed. American International Law Cases, 1783-1968, 20 vols. LC 78-140621. (American International Law Cases Ser). 1977. lib. bdg. 45.00 ea. Oceana.

Great Britain: The Case of Great Britain As Laid Before the Tribunal of Arbitration, 3 vols. 1976. Repr. of 1872 ed. Set. 132.00 (ISBN 0-527-35710-3). Kraus Repr.

Henkin, Louis, et al. Cases & Materials on International Law. 2nd ed. LC 80-17731. (American Casebook Ser.). 1210p. 1980. text ed. 22.95 (ISBN 0-8299-2099-4). West Pub.

International Institute for the Unification of Private Law. Digest of Legal Activities of International & Other Institutions, Release 1. 4th ed. 1980. 85.00 (ISBN 0-379-00545-X). Oceana.

Jennings, R. Y. & Brownlie, Ian, eds. The British Year Book of International Law 1978, Vol. XLIX. (British Year Book of International Law). (Illus.). 1980. 89.00x (ISBN 0-19-818178-7). Oxford U Pr.

Milner, Alan, ed. Modern African Contract Cases. LC 72-165489. 1972. lib. bdg. 22.50 (ISBN 0-379-00044-X). Oceana.

Orfield, Lester B. & Re, E. D. Cases & Materials on International Law. 2nd ed. 1965. 20.00 (ISBN 0-672-80979-6, Bobbs-Merrill Law). Michie-Bobbs.

Parry, C., ed. British International Law Cases, 9 vols. Incl. Vol. 1. 1964. 42.50 (ISBN 0-379-14021-7); Vol. 2. 1965. 42.50 (ISBN 0-379-14022-5); Vol. 3. 1966. 42.50 (ISBN 0-379-14023-3); Vol. 4. 1966. 42.50 (ISBN 0-379-14024-1); Vol. 5. 1966. 42.50 (ISBN 0-379-14025-X); Vol. 6. 1967. 42.50 (ISBN 0-379-14026-8); Vol. 7. 1969. 42.50 (ISBN 0-379-14027-6); Vol. 8. 1971. 42.50 (ISBN 0-379-14028-4); Vol. 9. 1973. 60.00 (ISBN 0-379-14029-2). LC 63-22348. Oceana.

Parry, Clive, ed. Commonwealth International Law Cases, 10 vols. LC 73-20151. 1977. lib. bdg. 45.00 ea (ISBN 0-379-00950-1). Oceana.

Ruddy, F. American International Law Cases, Vols. 21-22. 1980. 45.00 ea. (ISBN 0-379-20400-2). Vol. 21. Vol. 22 (ISBN 0-379-20401-0). Oceana.

Stephen, Robert M. Developing an Understanding of World Problems. LC 69-15389. 1969. text ed. 7.00 (ISBN 0-379-00362-7). Oceana.

Tobin, Harold J. Termination of Multipartite Treaties. LC 33-34572. (Columbia University. Studies in the Social Sciences: No. 388). Repr. of 1933 ed. 24.50 (ISBN 0-404-51388-3). AMS Pr.

World Court Reports, 1922-1942, 4 Vols. 1969. Repr. of 1922 ed. Set. lib. bdg. 200.00 (ISBN 0-379-00428-3); lib. bdg. 50.00 ea. Vol. 1 (ISBN 0-379-00429-1). Vol. 2 (ISBN 0-379-00430-5). Vol. 3 (ISBN 0-379-00431-3). Vol. 4 (ISBN 0-379-00432-1). Oceana.

Zivier, Ernst R. The Legal Status of the Land Berlin: A Survey After the Quadripartite Agreement. Ulrich, Paul S., tr. from Ger. (International Law & Politics Ser.: Vol. 8a). 1979. pap. text ed. 27.50x (ISBN 3-87061-150-2). Intl Pubns Serv.

INTERNATIONAL LAW–HISTORY

Bhatia, H. S., ed. International Law & Practice in Ancient India. 1977. text ed. 12.75x (ISBN 0-391-01081-6). Humanities.

Cohen, Jerome A. & Chiu, Hungdah. People's China & International Law, 2 vols. LC 73-2475. (Studies in East Asian Law). 1974. Set. 100.00 (ISBN 0-691-09229-X); pap. 32.50 (ISBN 0-691-09231-1). Princeton U Pr.

Fernandez, Alejandro M. International Law in Philippine Relations: 1898-1946. 1971. 7.00x (ISBN 0-8248-0439-2). U Pr of Hawaii.

Goebel, Julius. Equality of States: A Study in the History of Law. LC 73-109921. Repr. of 1923 ed. 12.50 (ISBN 0-404-02849-7). AMS Pr.

Grotius, Hugo. The Rights of War & Peace, Including the Law of Nature & of Nations. LC 78-20466. 1980. Repr. of 1901 ed. text ed. 31.50 (ISBN 0-88355-845-9). Hyperion Conn.

Lange, Christian L. Histoire De la Doctrine Pacifique. LC 79-147755. (Library of War & Peace; International Law). lib. bdg. 38.00 (ISBN 0-8240-0361-6). Garland Pub.

Lautepacht, Hersch. International Law: The Law of Peace, 4 vols. Lauterpacht, E., ed. Incl. Vol. 1. 500p. 1970 (ISBN 0-521-07643-9); Vol. 2. 624p. 1975 (ISBN 0-521-20480-1); Vol. 3, Pts. 2-6. 1977 (ISBN 0-521-21207-3); Vol. 4, Pts. 7-8. 1978 (ISBN 0-521-21524-2). LC 70-92250. 97.50 ea. Cambridge U Pr.

Lorton, David. The Juridical Terminology of International Relations in Egyptian Texts Through Dynasty XVIII. LC 73-8114. (Near Eastern Studies). 208p. 1974. 14.50x (ISBN 0-8018-1535-5). Johns Hopkins.

Ralston, Jackson H. International Arbitration from Athens to Locarno. LC 75-147737. (Library of War & Peace; Int'l. Organization, Arbitration & Law). 38.00 (ISBN 0-8240-0472-8). Garland Pub.

Rosenne, Shabtai, ed. League of Nations Conference for the Codification of International Law (1930, 4 vols. 1630p. 1975. Set. lib. bdg. 200.00 (ISBN 0-379-10100-9); lib. bdg. 50.00 ea.; Vol. 1. lib. bdg. (ISBN 0-379-10101-7); Vol. 2. lib. bdg. (ISBN 0-379-10102-5); Vol. 3. lib. bdg. (ISBN 0-379-10103-3); Vol. 4. lib. bdg. (ISBN 0-379-10104-1). Oceana.

Ruddy, Francis S. International Law in the Enlightenment: The Background of Emmerich De Vattel's "Le Droit Des Gens". LC 75-4423. 400p. 1975. 40.00 (ISBN 0-379-00292-2). Oceana.

Scott, James B. Law, the State & the International Community. Repr. of 1939 ed. lib. bdg. 38.00x (ISBN 0-8371-2809-9, SCLI). Greenwood.

Singh, Nagendra. India & International Law. 1969. 5.00x (ISBN 0-8426-1534-2). Verry.

Ward, Robert P. Enquiry into the Foundation & History of the Law of Nations in Europe, from the Time of the Greeks & Romans to the Age of Grotius, 2 vols. LC 77-147603. (Library of War & Peace; International Law). Set. lib. bdg. 66.00 (ISBN 0-8240-0364-0); lib. bdg. 38.00 ea. Garland Pub.

INTERNATIONAL LAW–OUTLINES, SYLLABI, ETC.

Hackworth, Green H. Digest of International Law: Washington, D.C., 1940-1944, 8 vols. LC 73-5440. Repr. of 1944 ed. Set. 395.00 (ISBN 0-404-11140-8); Vol. 1. (ISBN 0-404-11141-6); Vol. 2. (ISBN 0-404-11142-4); Vol. 3. (ISBN 0-404-11143-2); Vol. 4. (ISBN 0-404-11144-0); Vol. 5. (ISBN 0-404-11145-9); Vol. 6. (ISBN 0-404-11146-7); Vol. 7. (ISBN 0-404-11147-5); Vol. 8. (ISBN 0-404-11148-3). AMS Pr.

INTERNATIONAL LAW–SOURCES

see also Treaties

Brownlie, William H., ed. Basic Documents in International Law. 2nd ed. 1972. 22.00x (ISBN 0-19-876023-X); pap. 14.50x (ISBN 0-19-876024-8). Oxford U Pr.

Collins, Edward, Jr. International Law in a Changing World. 1970. text ed. 21.95 (ISBN 0-394-30098-X, RanC). Random.

International Centre For Settlement Of Investment Disputes. Convention on the Settlement of Investment Disputes Between States & Nationals of Other States, 4 vols. in 5. 17.50 ea. Oceana.

Oda, Shigeru. The International Law of the Ocean Development: Basic Documents. LC 72-76418. 510p. Vol. 1 (1972) 55.00x (ISBN 90-286-0122-8); Vol. 2 (1974) 70.00x (ISBN 90-286-0224-0). Intl Pubns Serv.

INTERNATIONAL LAW–STUDY AND TEACHING

Collins, Edward, Jr. International Law in a Changing World. 1970. text ed. 21.95 (ISBN 0-394-30098-X, RanC). Random.

Dupuy, Rene J. & Tunkin, Gregory. Comparability of Degrees & Diplomas in International Law. (International Equivalences of Degrees Studies). 75p. (Orig.). 1973. pap. 4.00 (ISBN 92-3-101057-3, U94, UNESCO). Unipub.

Studies in the Administration of International Law & Organization, Vols. 1-9. 1944-48. pap. 142.00 (ISBN 0-527-00878-8). Kraus Repr.

INTERNATIONAL LAW–YEARBOOKS

Annuaire Francais De Droit International 1978, Vol. 24. LC 57-28515. (Fr.). 1979. 125.00 (ISBN 2-222-02320-3). Intl Pubns Serv.

Bouchez, L. J., et al, eds. Netherlands Yearbook of International Law: State Immunity from Attachment & Execution, Vol. X. 650p. 1980. 40.00x (ISBN 90-286-0710-2). Sijthoff & Noordhoff.

Centre National De la Recherche Scientifique, ed. Annuaire Francais De Droit International, Vol. 25. LC 57-28515. 1288p. 1979. 125.00x (ISBN 2-222-02737-3). Intl Pubns Serv.

The Italian Yearbook of International Law 1975, Vol. 1. LC 76-8042. 1977. lib. bdg. 35.00 (ISBN 0-379-00828-9). Oceana.

Jennings, R. Y. & Brownlie, Ian. The British Year Book of International Law 1979, Vol. 50. 464p. 1981. 98.00x (ISBN 0-19-825360-5). Oxford U Pr.

Jennings, R. Y. & Brownlie, Ian, eds. The British Year Book of International Law 1978, Vol. XLIX. (British Year Book of International Law). (Illus.). 1980. 89.00x (ISBN 0-19-818178-7). Oxford U Pr.

Matthews, James M., ed. Kime's International Law Directory for 1980. 88th ed. 809p. 1981. 52.50x (ISBN 0-900503-12-2). Intl Pubns Serv.

Waldock, Humphrey, ed. The British Year Book of International Law, 1972-1973, Vol. 46. 600p. 1975. 85.00x (ISBN 0-19-214662-9). Oxford U Pr.

The Work of the International Law Commission. 325p. 1980. pap. 16.00 (ISBN 0-686-70510-6, UN80-5-11, UN). Unipub.

Yearbook of the International Law Commission Nineteen Seventy-Eight: Part One of Documents of the Thirtieth Session, Vol. 2. 289p. 1979. pap. 18.00 (ISBN 0-686-70513-0, UN79-5-6(PT.1), UN). Unipub.

Yearbook of the International Law Commission: Nineteen Seventy-Nine, Vol.1. 247p. 1980. pap. 17.00 (ISBN 0-686-70512-2, UN80-5-4, UN). Unipub.

INTERNATIONAL LAW (ISLAMIC LAW)

Hamidullah, M. The Muslim Conduct of State. pap. 7.95 (ISBN 0-686-18542-0). Kazi Pubns.

Khadduri, Majid, intro. by. & tr. The Islamic Law of Nations: Shaybani's Siyar. 366p. 1966. 23.50x (ISBN 0-8018-0334-9). Johns Hopkins.

INTERNATIONAL LAW, PRIVATE

see Conflict of Laws

INTERNATIONAL LIQUIDITY

see also Balance of Payments; Gold; Special Drawing Rights

Dreyer, Jacob S. Composite Reserve Assets in the International Monetary System, Vol. 2. Altman, Edward I. & Walter, Ingo, eds. LC 76-5757. (Contemporary Studies in Economic and Financial Analysis). 325p. 1977. lib. bdg. 30.00 (ISBN 0-89232-003-6). Jai Pr.

INTERNATIONAL LOANS

see Loans, Foreign

INTERNATIONAL MARRIAGES

see Marriages, International

INTERNATIONAL MILITARY TRIBUNAL

International Conference on Military Trials, London, 1945. Report of Robert H. Jackson, U.S. Representative to the International Conference on Military Trials, London, 1945. LC 72-178907. Repr. of 1949 ed. 31.00 (ISBN 0-404-10023-6). AMS Pr.

INTERNATIONAL MOLDERS' UNION OF NORTH AMERICA

Stockton, Frank T. The International Molders Union of North America. LC 74-22759. Repr. of 1921 ed. 14.00 (ISBN 0-404-58512-4). AMS Pr.

INTERNATIONAL MONETARY FUND

Dam, Kenneth W. The Role of Rules in the International Monetary System. LC 76-47303. 1976. pap. 1.50 (ISBN 0-916770-03-6). Law & Econ U Miami.

De Beaufort-Wijnholds, J. A. & Debeaufort. The Need for International Reserves & Credit Facilities. (Publications of the Netherlands Institute of Bankers & Stock Brokers Ser: No. 31). 1977. pap. 23.00 (ISBN 90-207-0713-2, Pub. by Martinus Nijhoff Netherlands). Kluwer Boston.

De Vries, Margaret G. The International Monetary Fund, 1966-1971: The System Under Stress, 2 vols. Incl. Vol. 1. Narrative. 11.00 (ISBN 0-686-20503-0); Vol. 2. Documents. 6.00 (ISBN 0-686-20504-9). 1977. Set. 15.00 (ISBN 0-686-20502-2). Intl Monetary.

Diebold, William, Jr. Dollars, Jobs, Trade & Aid. LC 72-93265. (Headline Ser.: No. 213). (Illus., Orig.). 1972. pap. 2.00 (ISBN 0-87124-019-X). Foreign Policy.

Erlanger, George C. The International Monetary Chaos & a Positive Plan for the Monetary Reconstruction of the World. (Illus.). 147p. 1981. 67.85 (ISBN 0-918968-90-9). Inst Econ Finan.

Field, A. N. The Bretton Woods Plot: The Twin Evils of the International Monetary Fund & the World Bank for Reconstruction & Development. 1979. lib. bdg. 69.95 (ISBN 0-8490-2879-5). Gordon Pr.

Gilbert, Milton. Quest for World Monetary System: Gold-Dollar System & It's Aftermath. LC 80-17865. 255p. 1980. 21.95 (ISBN 0-471-07998-7, Pub. by Wiley-Interscience). Wiley.

Gold, Joseph. Fund Agreement in the Courts. 1962. 3.50 (ISBN 0-686-00618-6). Intl Monetary.

--Membership & Nonmembership in the International Monetary Fund: A Study in International Law & Organization. 1974. 10.00 (ISBN 0-686-05842-9). Intl Monetary.

--The Stand-By Arrangements of the International Monetary Fund: A Commentary on Their Formal, Legal & Financial Aspects. 295p. 1970. 4.00 (ISBN 0-686-01023-X). Intl Monetary.

International Monetary Fund, Bureau of Language Services. IMF Glossary: English-French-Spanish. 1979. pap. 5.00 (ISBN 0-686-25172-5). Intl Monetary.

International Monetary Fund Seminar, 1970. International Reserves: Needs & Availability: Proceedings. 552p. 1970. 6.00 (ISBN 0-686-01024-8). Intl Monetary.

The International Monetary Fund, 1945-1965: Twenty Years of International Monetary Cooperation, 3 vols. Incl. Vol. 1. Chronicle. Horsefield, J. Keith. 663p. 5.00 (ISBN 0-686-01029-9); Vol. 2. Analysis. De Vries, Margaret G., et al. 621p. 5.00 (ISBN 0-686-01030-2); Vol. 3. Documents. Horsefield, J. Keith, ed. 549p. 5.00 (ISBN 0-686-01031-0). 1969. 12.50 set (ISBN 0-686-01028-0). Intl Monetary.

Machlup, Fritz. Remaking the International Monetary System: The Rio Agreement & Beyond. LC 68-31419. (Committee for Economic Development Ser). 161p. 1968. 10.00x (ISBN 0-8018-0416-7); pap. 3.45x (ISBN 0-8018-0417-5). Johns Hopkins.
Officer, Lawrence H. & Willett, Thomas D. International Monetary System. 4.50x (ISBN 0-87543-096-1). Lucas.
Payer, Cheryl. The Debt Trap: The IMF & the Third World. LC 74-24794. 256p. 1975. pap. 5.95 (ISBN 0-85345-376-4, PB3764). Monthly Rev.
Poniachek, Harvey A. Monetary Independence Under Flexible Exchange Rates. (Illus.). 1979. 18.95 (ISBN 0-669-02728-6). Lexington Bks.
Stem, Carl H., et al, eds. Eurocurrencies & the International Monetary System. LC 76-29115. (Conference Proceedings). 1976. 17.25 (ISBN 0-8447-2091-7); pap. 9.25 (ISBN 0-8447-2090-9). Am Enterprise.
Williamson, John. The Failure of World Monetary Reform, 1971-74. LC 77-71278. 221p. 1977. 18.50x (ISBN 0-8147-9173-5); pap. 8.50x (ISBN 0-8147-9174-3). NYU Pr.

INTERNATIONAL NEWS
see Foreign News

INTERNATIONAL OBLIGATIONS
see also Treaties
Bilder, Richard B. Managing the Risks of International Agreement. LC 80-52288. 320p. 1981. 22.50x (ISBN 0-299-08360-8). U of Wis Pr.

INTERNATIONAL OFFENSES
see also Aggression (International Law); Crimes against Humanity; Genocide; Terrorism; War Crimes
Bassiouni, M. Cherif. International Criminal Law: A Draft International Criminal Code. LC 80-50452. 286p. 1980. 50.00x (ISBN 90-286-0130-9). Sijthoff & Noordhoff.
Bassiouni, M. Cherif & Nanda, Ved P. A Treatise on International Criminal Law, Vol.2: Jurisdiction & Cooperation. 448p. 1973. 59.50 (ISBN 0-398-02573-8); pap. 49.50 (ISBN 0-398-02628-9). C C Thomas.
Bassiouni, M. Cherif & Nanda, Ved P., eds. A Treatise on International Criminal Law, Vol. 1: Crimes & Punishment. 778p. 1973. pap. text ed. 54.75 (ISBN 0-398-02557-6). C C Thomas.
United Nations. United Nations Crime Conference: Sixth U.N. Congress on the Prevention of Crime & the Treatment of Offenders, Caracas, 1980, Keynote Documents Edition. MacNamara, Donald E., ed. 550p. 1981. 47.50 (ISBN 0-686-31384-4). UNIFO Pubs.

INTERNATIONAL OFFICIALS AND EMPLOYEES
Crosswell, Carol M. Protection of International Personnel Abroad. LC 52-10152. 1952. 12.50 (ISBN 0-379-00036-9). Oceana.
Graham, Norman A. & Jordan, Robert S., eds. The Changing Role & Concepts of the International Civil Service. (Pergamon Policy Studies). 1980. 27.00 (ISBN 0-08-024643-5). Pergamon.
--The International Civil Service: Changing Role & Concepts. LC 79-19471. (Pergamon Policy Studies). 200p. 1980. 27.00 (ISBN 0-08-024643-5). Pergamon.
Langrod, Georges. International Civil Service. LC 63-22349. 1964. 25.00 (ISBN 0-379-00216-7). Oceana.
Loveday, Alexander. Reflections on International Administration. LC 74-9168. 334p. 1974. Repr. of 1956 ed. lib. bdg. 17.25x (ISBN 0-8371-7618-2, LOIA). Greenwood.
McLaren, Robert I. Civil Servants & Public Policy: A Comparative Study of International Secretaries. 144p. 1980. text ed. 9.25 (ISBN 0-88920-088-2, Pub. by Laurier U Pr Canada). Humanities.
Plantley. The International Civil Service: Law & Management. LC 80-82069. 472p. 1981. 59.50x (ISBN 0-89352-103-5). Masson Pub.
Weiss, Thomas G. International Bureaucracy: An Analysis of the Operation of Functional Global International Secretariats. LC 75-2. 160p. 1975. 19.95x (ISBN 0-669-99341-7). Lexington Bks.

INTERNATIONAL ORGANIZATION
Here are entered works on theories and efforts leading toward worldwide or regional political organization of nations.
see also Church and International Organization; Concert of Europe; European Federation; International Agencies; International Cooperation; International Law; International Officials and Employees; International Trusteeships; Mandates; Reconstruction (1914-1939); Reconstruction (1939-1951); Regionalism (International Organization); Security, International; World Politics; also names of specific organizations, e.g. United Nations, Pan American Union
Atherton, Alexine L., ed. International Organizations: A Guide to Information Sources. LC 73-17502. (International Relations Guide Ser.: Vol. 1). 1976. 36.00 (ISBN 0-8103-1324-3). Gale.
Bennett, A. International Organization: Principles & Issues. 2nd ed. (Illus.). 1980. text ed. 14.95 (ISBN 0-13-473447-5). P-H.
Beres, Louis R. & Targ, Harry R. Constructing Alternative World Futures: Reordering the Planet. LC 76-54678. 264p. 1977. text ed. 15.50x (ISBN 0-87073-566-7); pap. text ed. 7.95x (ISBN 0-87073-567-5). Schenkman.
Bibo, Istvan. The Paralysis of International Institutions & the Remedies: A Study of Self-Determination, Concord Among the Major Powers & Political Arbitration. LC 75-17182. 152p. 1976. 27.95 (ISBN 0-470-07208-3). Halsted Pr.
Bridgman, Raymond. World Organization. LC 77-147575. (Library of War & Peace; Int'l. Organization, Arbitration & Law). 38.00 (ISBN 0-8240-0341-1). Garland Pub.
Brinton, Clarence C. From Many, One: The Process of Political Integration. LC 70-143309. 1971. Repr. of 1948 ed. lib. bdg. 15.00x (ISBN 0-8371-5964-4, BRFO). Greenwood.
Brunner, K. & Meltzer, A. International Organization, National Policies & Economic Development. (Carnegie-Rochester Conference Ser. on Public Policy: Vol. 6). 1977. 19.50 (ISBN 0-7204-0744-3, North-Holland). Elsevier.
Bull, Hedley. The Anarchical Society: A Study of Order in World Politics. LC 76-21786. 335p. 1977. 22.50x (ISBN 0-231-04132-2); pap. 8.00x (ISBN 0-231-04133-0). Columbia U Pr.
Carlston, Kenneth S. Law & Organization in World Society. LC 62-13211. 1962. 17.95 (ISBN 0-252-72512-3). U of Ill Pr.
Chen, Samuel S. The Theory & Practice of International Organization. 2nd ed. 133p. 1974. text ed. 29.75x (ISBN 0-8422-5139-1). Irvington.
Claude, Inis L., Jr. Power & International Relations. 1962. text ed. 15.95 (ISBN 0-394-30133-1). Random.
--Swords into Plowshares: The Problems & Progress of International Organization. 4th ed. 1971. text ed. 18.95 (ISBN 0-394-31003-9). Random.
The Concept of International Organization. 245p. 1981. pap. 15.75 (ISBN 92-3-101742-X, U1094, UNESCO). Unipub.
Corwin, Edward S. Constitution & World Organization. facs. ed. LC 73-117869. (Select Bibliographies Reprint Ser). 1944. 11.00 (ISBN 0-8369-5322-3). Arno.
Deutsch, Karl W., et al. Political Community & the North Atlantic Area: International Organization in the Light of Historical Experience. LC 69-13882. Repr. of 1957 ed. lib. bdg. 15.00x (ISBN 0-8371-1054-8, DEPO). Greenwood.
Eaton, Howard O., et al. Federation: The Coming Structure of World Government. 1944. 12.50x (ISBN 0-8061-0129-6). U of Okla Pr.
Falk, Richard A. A Global Approach to National Policy. LC 75-2817. 384p. 1975. text ed. 18.50x (ISBN 0-674-35445-1). Harvard U Pr.
--A Study of Future Worlds. LC 74-10139. (Preferred Worlds for the 1990's Ser.). (Illus.). 1975. pap. text ed. 10.95 (ISBN 0-02-910080-1). Free Pr.
Feinschreiber, Robert, ed. International Reorganizations: The New Rules. LC 79-88375. 164p. 1979. 35.00 (ISBN 0-916592-29-4). Panel Pubs.
Friedrich, Carl J. Inevitable Peace. Repr. of 1948 ed. lib. bdg. 15.00x (ISBN 0-8371-2397-6, FRIN). Greenwood.
Geneva Institute Of International Relations. Problems of Peace, Fifth Series. facs. ed. LC 71-121470. (Essay Index Reprint Ser). 1930. 19.00 (ISBN 0-8369-1808-8). Arno.
Goodman, Elliot R. The Soviet Design for a World State. LC 60-7625. (Studies of the Russian Institute). 512p. 1960. 25.00x (ISBN 0-231-02339-1). Columbia U Pr.
Goodrich, Leland M. & Kay, David A., eds. International Organization: Politics & Process. 1973. 25.00 (ISBN 0-299-06250-3); pap. 9.95x (ISBN 0-299-06254-6). U of Wis Pr.
Haas, Michael. International Organization: An Interdisciplinary Bibliography. LC 68-28099. (Bibliographical Ser.: No. 41). 944p. 1971. 35.00 (ISBN 0-8179-2411-6). Hoover Inst Pr.
Hammer, Conrad H. Toward a Simpler World: The Community Idea. 1978. 10.00 (ISBN 0-533-03331-4). Vantage.
Hansen, A. H., et al. United States After War. facs. ed. LC 69-18571. (Essay Index Reprint Ser). 1945. 14.50 (ISBN 0-8369-1069-9). Arno.
Hobson, John A. Towards International Government. LC 70-147581. (Library of War & Peace; Int'l. Organization, Arbitration & Law). lib. bdg. 38.00 (ISBN 0-8240-0345-4). Garland Pub.
Holcombe, Arthur N. Strategy of Peace in a Changing World. LC 67-27085. 1967. 16.50x (ISBN 0-674-84075-5). Harvard U Pr.
Hudson, Manley O. Progress in International Organization. ix, 162p. 1981. Repr. of 1932 ed. lib. bdg. 20.00x (ISBN 0-8377-0637-8). Rothman.
Hutchins, Robert M. Saint Thomas & the World State. (Aquinas Lecture). 1949. 6.95 (ISBN 0-87462-114-3). Marquette.
Jessup, Philip C., et al. International Regulation of Economic & Social Questions: International Organization by Joseph L. Chamberlain. LC 77-18933. (Illus.). 1978. Repr. of 1955 ed. lib. bdg. 16.75x (ISBN 0-313-20206-0, JEIR). Greenwood.
Jordan, Robert S., ed. International Administration: Its Evolution & Contemporary Applications. 1971. pap. 6.95x (ISBN 0-19-501462-6). Oxford U Pr.
--International Administration: Its Evolution & Contemporary Applications. 1971. pap. 6.95x (ISBN 0-19-501462-6). Oxford U Pr.
Kelsen, Hans. Peace Through Law. LC 76-147757. (Library of War & Peace; International Law). lib. bdg. 38.00 (ISBN 0-8240-0492-2). Garland Pub.
Keys, Donald. Earth at Omega: Passage to Planetization. (gr. 11-12). Date not set. text ed. 12.95 (ISBN 0-8283-1743-7); pap. text ed. 9.95 (ISBN 0-8283-1745-3). Branden.
Kothari, Rajni. Footsteps into the Future. LC 74-31357. (Preferred Worlds for the 1990's Ser.). 1975. 8.95 (ISBN 0-02-917570-4); pap. text ed. 7.95 (ISBN 0-02-917580-1). Free Pr.
Kuehl, Warren F. Seeking World Order: The United States & International Organization to 1920. LC 69-19952. 1969. 10.00 (ISBN 0-8265-1137-6). Vanderbilt U Pr.
Lagos, Gustavo & Godoy, Horacio H. Revolution of Being: A Latin American View of the Future. LC 77-3848. (Preferred Worlds for the 1990's). 1977. 14.95 (ISBN 0-02-917840-1). Free Pr.
Lemp, Helena B. Manual for the Organization of Scientific Congresses. 1978. pap. 19.75 (ISBN 3-8055-2962-7). S Karger.
Lindberg, Leon N. & Scheingold, Stuart A., eds. Regional Integration: Theory & Research. LC 77-139717. (Illus.). 1970. 22.50x (ISBN 0-674-75326-7); pap. 6.95x (ISBN 0-674-75327-5). Harvard U Pr.
Mangone, Gerard J. The Idea & Practice of World Government. LC 74-3620. 278p. 1974. Repr. of 1951 ed. lib. bdg. 15.00x (ISBN 0-8371-7453-8, MAPW). Greenwood.
--A Short History of International Organization. LC 74-10653. 326p. 1975. Repr. of 1954 ed. lib. bdg. 16.50x (ISBN 0-8371-7652-2, MAIO). Greenwood.
Millard, Everett L. Freedom in a Federal World. 5th ed. LC 60-16492. 1970. 7.50 (ISBN 0-379-00450-X). Oceana.
Northedge, F. S. International Political System. 336p. 1976. pap. 9.95 (ISBN 0-571-11009-6, Pub. by Faber & Faber). Merrimack Bk Serv.
Organization to Build a World Community, San Francisco, July 20-25, 1975. World Citizens Assembly: Report of Proceedings. 1976. 5.30 (ISBN 0-686-17524-7). World Citizens.
Ramos, Alberto G. The New Science of Organizations: A Reconceptualization of the Wealth of Nations. 224p. 1981. 25.00 (ISBN 0-8020-5527-3). U of Toronto Pr.
Riches, Cromwell A. Majority Rule in International Organization: A Study of the Trend from Unanimity to Majority Decision. LC 78-64297. (Johns Hopkins University. Studies in the Social Sciences. Extra Volumes.: 28). Repr. of 1940 ed. 27.00 (ISBN 0-404-61397-7). AMS Pr.
Riggs, Robert E. & Mykletun, I. Jostein. Beyond Functionalism: Attitudes Toward International Organization in Norway & the United States. LC 79-11306. (Illus.). 1979. 19.50x (ISBN 0-8166-0898-9). U of Minn Pr.
Schiffer, Walter. The Legal Community of Mankind. LC 74-152603. 367p. 1972. Repr. of 1954 ed. lib. bdg. 21.00x (ISBN 0-8371-6038-3, SCLC). Greenwood.
Schuman, Frederick L. The Commonwealth of Man: An Inquiry into Power Politics & World Government. LC 76-30305. 1977. Repr. of 1972 ed. lib. bdg. 31.25x (ISBN 0-8371-9372-9, SCCO). Greenwood.
Shih-Tsai Chen, Samuel. Basic Documents of International Organization. rev. ed. 1979. pap. text ed. 9.95 (ISBN 0-8403-1947-9, 40194701). Kendall-Hunt.
Shimm, Melvin G. European Regional Communities: A New Era on the Old Continent. LC 62-20226. (Orig.). 1962. 10.00 (ISBN 0-379-11502-6). Oceana.
Social Science Research Council Reviews. Incl. No. 1. Research in Political Science. 64p. 1968; No. 2. Research on International Organizations. Goodwin, G. L. & Strange, Susan. 57p. 1968; No. 4. Social Research on Automation. Sadler, Philip. 66p. 1968; No. 6. Comparability in Social Research. Stacey, Margaret, ed. 134p. 1969; No. 7. The Population Census. Benjamin, Bernard. 170p. 1970; No. 8. Longitudinal Studies & the Social Sciences. Wall, W. D. & Williams, H. L. 245p. 1970; No. 9. Research in Economic & Social History. 128p. 1971. 5.00x ea. Intl Pubns Serv.
Society for International Development, 1973. Political & Social Realities of Development: Recognition & Response. LC 64-8541. 1973. 12.50 (ISBN 0-379-12008-9). Oceana.
Thomas, Harold. The World Power Foundation: Its Goals & Platform. 1980. pap. 6.95 (ISBN 0-686-29511-0). Loompanics.
Tinkler, Hugh. Race, Conflict & the International Order: From Empire to United Nations. LC 77-79017. (The Making of the 20th Century Ser.). (Illus.). 1977. 17.95x (ISBN 0-312-66130-4). St Martin.
Tyagi, A. R. International Administration-Indian Perspective. 1969. 9.00x (ISBN 0-8426-1573-3). Verry.
Wehr, Paul & Washburn, Michael. Peace & World Order Systems: Teaching & Research. LC 75-23614. (Sage Library of Social Research: Vol. 25). 255p. 1976. 20.00 (ISBN 0-8039-0552-1); pap. 9.95 (ISBN 0-8039-0553-X). Sage.
Williams, Walter, Jr. Intergovernmental Military Forces & World Public Order. LC 75-167280. 718p. 1972. lib. bdg. 32.50x (ISBN 0-379-00063-6). Oceana.
Wood, Robert S., ed. The Process of International Organization. 1971. pap. text ed. 7.50 (ISBN 0-685-55645-X, 31301). Phila Bk Co.
Woolf, Leonard. International Government: Two Reports. LC 79-149532. (Library of War & Peace; Int'l. Organization, Arbitration & Law). lib. bdg. 38.00 (ISBN 0-8240-0481-7). Garland Pub.

INTERNATIONAL ORGANIZATIONS
see International Agencies

INTERNATIONAL PAYMENTS, BALANCE OF
see Balance of Payments

INTERNATIONAL PEASANTS' UNION
Jackson, George D., Jr. Comintern & Peasant in East Europe, 1919-1930. LC 66-15489. 1966. 20.00x (ISBN 0-231-02912-8). Columbia U Pr.

INTERNATIONAL POLICE
see also United Nations-Armed Forces
Garrison, Omar V. The Secret World of Interpol. LC 76-24523. 1976. 8.95 (ISBN 0-931116-00-7). Ralston-Pilot.
Wainhouse, David W., et al. International Peacekeeping at the Crossroads: National Support--Experience & Prospects. LC 73-7887. (Illus.). 640p. 1974. 32.50x (ISBN 0-8018-1478-2). Johns Hopkins.
Zacher, Mark W. International Conflicts & Collective Security: 1946-1977. LC 78-19775. (Praeger Special Studies). 1979. 25.95 (ISBN 0-03-044261-3). Praeger.

INTERNATIONAL POLITICS
see World Politics

INTERNATIONAL PRIVATE LAW
see Conflict of Laws

INTERNATIONAL PROPAGANDA
see Propaganda, International

INTERNATIONAL RELATIONS
Here are entered works dealing with the theory of international intercourse. Historical accounts are entered under the headings World Politics; United States-Politics and Government; etc. Works dealing with foreign relations from the point of view of an individual state are entered under the name of the state with subdivision Foreign Relations.
see also Alliances; Ambassadors; Arbitration, International; Balance of Power; Boundaries; Catholic Church-Relations (Diplomatic); Christianity and International Affairs; Competition, International; Congresses and Conventions; Consuls; Cultural Relations; Detente; Diplomacy; Diplomatic and Consular Service; Diplomatic Negotiations in International Disputes; Diplomatic Protection; Diplomats; Disarmament; Foreign News; Foreign Offices; Geography, Political; Geopolitics; Intergovernmental Fiscal Relations; International Cooperation; International Courts; International Economic Relations; International Law; International Organization; Monroe Doctrine; Munitions; Nationalism; Pan-Pacific Relations; Peace; Propaganda, International; Reconstruction (1914-1939); Reconstruction (1939-1951); Refugees, Political; Security, International; Treaties; World Politics

also subdivision Foreign Relations under names of countries, e.g. France–Foreign Relations; also names of international alliances, congresses, treaties, etc. e.g. Holy Alliance; Versailles, Treaty of, 1918

Akindele, R. A. The Organization & Promotion of World Peace: A Study of Universal-Regional Relationships. LC 74-79987. 240p. 1975. 20.00x (ISBN 0-8020-5314-9). U of Toronto Pr.

Aliano, Richard A. The Crime of World Power: Politics Without Government in the International System. LC 77-25866. 1978. 15.00 (ISBN 0-399-12027-0). Putnam.

Allison, Graham & Szanton, Peter. Remaking Foreign Policy: The Organizational Connection. LC 76-9334. 1976. 12.00x (ISBN 0-465-06908-8). Basic.

Anand, R. P. Cultural Factors in International Relations. 1981. 20.00x (ISBN 0-8364-0727-X, Pub. by Abhinav India). South Asia Bks.

Andren, Nils & Birnbaum, Karl E. Belgrade & Beyond: The CSCE Process in Perspective. (East West Perspectives: No. 5). 27.50x (ISBN 90-286-0250-X). Sijthoff & Noordhoff.

Andrews, William G. Politics of International Crisis. (New Perspectives in Political Science Ser: No. 28). 1970. pap. 4.95x (ISBN 0-442-00339-0, NP28). Van Nos Reinhold.

Anne. To the Whole World: An Open Letter. 1978. pap. 2.50 (ISBN 0-914350-33-1). Vulcan Bks.

Arbatov, G. The War of Ideas in Contemporary International Relations. 313p. 1973. 4.20 (ISBN 0-8285-0325-7, Pub. by Progress Pubs Russia). Imported Pubns.

Arnold-Foster, Mark. World at War. (RL 8). 1974. pap. 1.95 (ISBN 0-451-05775-9, J5775, Sig). NAL.

Ashley, Richard K. Political Economy of War & Peace. 320p. 1980. 30.00 (ISBN 0-89397-087-5). Nichols Pub.

Axline, Andrew W. & Stegenga, James A. The Global Community: A Brief Introduction to International Relations. 2nd ed. 200p. 1981. price not set (HarpC). Har-Row.

Ayoob, Mohadded. Conflict & Intervention in the Third World. 1980. 27.50x (ISBN 0-312-16228-6). St Martin.

Bakeless, John, ed. Report of the Round Tables & General Conferences at the Twelfth Session (Institute of Politics, Williams College) 1932. 32.50x (ISBN 0-686-51301-0). Elliots Bks.

Baldwin, Christopher. The Major Problems of the World at the End of the 20th Century & Possible Solutions to Avoid an Epochal Catastrophe. (Illus.). 149p. 1980. 49.75 (ISBN 0-930008-65-0). Inst Econ Pol.

Bara, Louis. Science de la Paix. LC 78-147448. (Library of War & Peace; Peace Movement: Selected Documents). lib. bdg. 38.00 (ISBN 0-8240-0238-5). Garland Pub.

Barnds, William J., ed. Japan & the United States: Challenges & Opportunities. LC 79-1551. 1979. 19.00x (ISBN 0-8147-1020-4); pap. 8.00x (ISBN 0-8147-1021-2). NYU Pr.

Barnet, Richard. Roots of War. 1973. pap. 5.95 (ISBN 0-14-021698-7, Pelican). Penguin.

Barrat, John & Louw, Michael, eds. International Aspects of Overpopulation. LC 71-179498. 1972. text ed. 19.95 (ISBN 0-312-41965-1). St. Martin.

Basiuk, Victor. Technology, World Politics, & American Policy. LC 76-51841. (Institute of War & Peace Studies). 409p. 1977. 22.50x (ISBN 0-685-74998-3). Columbia U Pr.

Bauer, Robert A., ed. The Interaction of Economics & Foreign Policy. LC 75-2243. (A Kenyon Public Affairs Forum Publication Ser). 1975. 10.00x (ISBN 0-8139-0639-3); pap. 2.95x (ISBN 0-8139-0640-7). U Pr of Va.

Beer, Francis A. Peace Against War: The Ecology of International Violence. LC 80-27214. (International Relations Ser.). (Illus.). 1981. text ed. 19.95x (ISBN 0-7167-1250-4); pap. text ed. 9.95x (ISBN 0-7167-1251-2). W H Freeman.

Beitz, Charles R. Political Theory & International Relations. LC 79-83976. 1979. 16.50x (ISBN 0-691-07614-6); pap. 5.95 (ISBN 0-691-02192-9). Princeton U Pr.

Beloff, Max. Foreign Policy & the Democratic Process. LC 76-57665. (The Albert Shaw Lectures on Diplomatic History, 1954). 1977. Repr. of 1955 ed. lib. bdg. 15.00 (ISBN 0-8371-9463-6, BEFO). Greenwood.

Benson, Vladimir. The Failure of the American Dream & the Moral Responsibility of the United States for the Crisis in the Middle East & for the Collapse of the World Order. (Illus.). 1978. deluxe ed. 49.50 (ISBN 0-930008-13-8). Inst Econ Pol.

Beres, Louis R. The Management of World Power: A Theoretical Analysis. (Monograph Ser. in World Affairs, Vol. 10: 1972-73 Ser., Pt. C). 4.00 (ISBN 0-87940-035-8). U of Denver Intl.

--People, States, & World Order. LC 80-83099. 237p. 1981. pap. text ed. 7.95 (ISBN 0-87581-267-8). Peacock Pubs.

--Transforming World Politics: The National Roots of World Peace. (Monograph Ser. in World Affairs, Vol. 12: 1974-75 Ser., Pt. D). 4.00 (ISBN 0-87940-044-7). U of Denver Intl.

Berman, Maureen R. & Johnson, Joseph E., eds. Unofficial Diplomats. LC 77-9376. 1977. 16.00x (ISBN 0-231-04396-1); pap. 6.00 (ISBN 0-231-04397-X). Columbia U Pr.

Best, Geoffrey. Humanity in Warfare. 400p. 1980. 25.00x (ISBN 0-231-05158-1). Columbia U Pr.

Bilgrami, S. J. International Organization. (Illus.). 1979. text ed. 17.50x (ISBN 0-7069-0548-2, Pub. by Vikas India). Advent NY.

Bishop, Vaughn F. & Meszaros, J. William. Comparing Nations: The Developed & the Developing Worlds. 1979. text ed. 15.95 (ISBN 0-669-01142-8). Heath.

Black, C. E. & Falk, Richard A., eds. Future of International Legal Order, 4 vols. Incl. Vol. 1. Trends & Patterns. 1969. 32.50 (ISBN 0-691-09215-X); Vol. 2. Wealth & Resources. 1970. 25.00 (ISBN 0-691-09217-6); Vol. 3. Conflict Management. 416p. 1971. 27.50 (ISBN 0-691-09220-6); Vol. 4. The Structure of the International Environment. 600p. 1972. 27.50 (ISBN 0-691-09221-4). (Center of International Studies, Princeton Univ.). Princeton U Pr.

Black, J. E. & Thompson, K. W., eds. Foreign Policies in a World of Change. (New Reprints in Essay & General Literature Index Ser.). 1975. Repr. of 1963 ed. 53.00 (ISBN 0-518-10196-7, 10196). Arno.

Blaney, Harry C. Global Challenges. 1979. 12.95 (ISBN 0-531-05408-X); pap. 6.95 (ISBN 0-531-05619-8). Watts.

Bloomfield, Lincoln P. The Foreign Policy Process: A Modern Primer. (Illus.). 256p. 1982. pap. 9.95 reference (ISBN 0-13-326504-8). P-H.

Blount, George. Peace Through World Government. 1974. pap. 5.00 (ISBN 0-87716-055-4, Pub. by Moore Pub Co). F Apple.

Boasson, Charles & Nurock, Max, eds. The Changing International Community: Some Problems of Its Laws, Structures, & Peace Research & the Middle East Conflict. (New Babylon Studies in Social Sciences: No. 18). 1973. text ed. 37.75x (ISBN 90-2797-292-3). Mouton.

Bonkovsky, Frederick O., ed. International Norms & National Behavior. LC 79-21206. (Orig.). 1980. pap. 8.95 (ISBN 0-8028-1803-X). Eerdmans.

Botkin, James W., et al. No Limits to Learning: Bridging the Human Gap: the Club of Rome Report. LC 79-40911. 1979. 17.00 (ISBN 0-08-024705-9); pap. 7.75 (ISBN 0-08-024704-0). Pergamon.

Boyce, P. J. Foreign Affairs for New States: Some Questions of Credentials. LC 77-87169. 1978. 21.50x (ISBN 0-312-29837-4). St Martin.

Bozeman, Adda B. Future of Law in a Multicultural World. LC 78-131127. 1971. 17.50 (ISBN 0-691-05643-9); pap. 6.95 (ISBN 0-691-01060-9). Princeton U Pr.

Bremer, Stuart A. Simulated Worlds: A Computer Model of National Decision-Making. LC 76-3244. 1976. text ed. 25.00 (ISBN 0-691-05661-7). Princeton U Pr.

Brezhnev, Leonid I. Selected Speeches & Writings on Foreign Affairs. LC 78-40614. 1978. text ed. 45.00 (ISBN 0-08-023569-7). Pergamon.

Brockreide, Wayne & Scott, Robert L. Moments in the Rhetoric of the Cold War. (Orig.). 1970. pap. text ed. 3.50 (ISBN 0-685-04767-9). Phila Bk Co.

Brodie, Bernard. War & Politics. 514p. 1973. 11.95 (ISBN 0-02-315020-3); pap. 7.75 (ISBN 0-685-28575-8). Macmillan.

Brown, Lester R. Our Daily Bread. LC 75-851. (Headline Ser.: No. 225). (Illus.). 1975. pap. 2.00 (ISBN 0-87124-030-0). Foreign Policy.

Brown, Robert W., et al. Africa & International Crises. LC 77-17820. (Foreign & Comparative Studies-Eastern Africa Ser.: No. 22). 106p. 1976. pap. text ed. 4.50x (ISBN 0-915984-19-9). Syracuse U Foreign Comp.

Bryce, James. International Relations. LC 66-21391. Repr. of 1922 ed. 8.50 (ISBN 0-8046-0053-8). Kennikat.

Buchan, Alastair. Change Without War: The Shifting Structure of World Power. LC 74-19962. 112p. 1975. 17.95 (ISBN 0-312-12880-0). St Martin.

Buchanan, William. How Nations See Each Other: A Study in Public Opinion. LC 70-138210. (Illus.). 220p. 1972. Repr. of 1953 ed. lib. bdg. 20.50x (ISBN 0-8371-5565-7, BUNS). Greenwood.

Buck, Philip W. & Travis, Martin B., Jr., eds. Control of Foreign Relations in Modern Nations. 1957. 13.95x (ISBN 0-393-09528-2, NortonC). Norton.

Bull, Hedley. The Anarchical Society: A Study of Order in World Politics. LC 76-21786. 335p. 1977. 22.50x (ISBN 0-231-04132-2); pap. 8.00x (ISBN 0-231-04133-0). Columbia U Pr.

Burgess, Philip M., et al. International & Comparative Politics: A Handbook. 1978. pap. text ed. 14.95 (ISBN 0-205-06009-9). Allyn.

Burton, John W. Systems, States, Diplomacy & Rules. 256p. 1968. 28.95 (ISBN 0-521-07316-2). Cambridge U Pr.

Butow, R. J. C. The John Doe Associates: Backdoor Diplomacy for Peace, 1941. LC 73-89857. (Illus.). xii, 468p. 1974. 18.50x (ISBN 0-8047-0852-5). Stanford U Pr.

Butterfield, Herbert. International Conflict in the Twentieth Century. LC 74-6777. 123p. 1974. Repr. of 1960 ed. lib. bdg. 15.00 (ISBN 0-8371-7569-0, BUIC). Greenwood.

Butterworth, Robert L. Moderation from Management: International Organizations & Peace. LC 77-26248. 1978. pap. text ed. 4.95 (ISBN 0-916002-32-2, Pub. by U Ctr Intl St). U of Pittsburgh Pr.

Buzan, B. G. & Jones, R. J., eds. Change & the Study on International Relations. 1981. 25.00x (ISBN 0-312-12858-4). St Martin.

Callahan, Patrick, et al, eds. Describing Foreign Policy Behavior. (Illus.). 416p. 1981. 32.50 (ISBN 0-8039-1708-2). Sage.

Carlson, Ellsworth C. Kaiping Mines, 1877-1912. rev. 2nd ed. LC 71-148943. (East Asian Monographs Ser: No. 3). 1971. pap. 9.00x (ISBN 0-674-49700-7). Harvard U Pr.

Carr, Edward H. International Relations Between the Two World Wars: 1919-1939. (Illus.). 1947. 15.95 (ISBN 0-312-42315-2). St Martin.

--Twenty Years' Crisis, Nineteen Nineteen to Nineteen Thirty-Nine: An Introduction to the Study of International Relations. 2nd ed. 1946. 18.95 (ISBN 0-312-82425-4). St Martin.

--Twenty Years' Crisis, 1919-1939: An Introduction to the Study of International Relations. pap. 3.95x (ISBN 0-06-131122-7, TB1122, Torch). Har-Row.

Carr, William G. Pawns in the Game. 1978. pap 4.00x (ISBN 0-911038-29-9). Noontide.

Catudal, Honore M., Jr. The Exclave Problem of Western Europe. LC 78-24487. (Illus.). 1979. 12.50x (ISBN 0-8173-4729-1). U of Ala Pr.

Centre for the Analysis of Conflict, London. International Relations Theory: A Critical Bibliography. Groom, A. J., ed. 1978. 22.50 (ISBN 0-89397-026-3); pap. 12.50 (ISBN 0-903804-17-4). Nichols Pub.

Charlesworth, James C. America's Changing Role As a World Leader. Lambert, Richard D., ed. LC 76-85466. (Annals Ser.: 384). 1969. 7.50 (ISBN 0-87761-118-1); pap. 6.00 (ISBN 0-87761-117-3). Am Acad Pol Soc Sci.

Chittick, William O. The Analysis of Foreign Policy Outputs. Wahlke, John C., ed. (Political Science Ser). 272p. 1975. text ed. 13.50x (ISBN 0-675-08703-1). Merrill.

Choucri, Nazli & Robinson, Thomas W., eds. Forecasting in International Relations: Theory, Methods, Problems, Prospects. LC 78-19169. (Illus.). 1978. text ed. 36.95x (ISBN 0-7167-0059-X). W H Freeman.

Christiansen, Bjorn. Attitudes Towards Foreign Affairs As a Function of Personality. LC 72-14085. (Illus.). 283p. 1974. Repr. of 1959 ed. lib. bdg. 15.00x (ISBN 0-8371-6754-X, CHFA). Greenwood.

Cioffi-Revilla, Claudio A. Mathematical Models in International Relations: A Bibliography. LC 79-25527. (Technical Papers Ser.: No. 4). (Orig.). 1979. pap. text ed. 7.00 (ISBN 0-89143-088-1). U NC Inst Res Soc Sci.

Clapham, Christopher. Foreign Policy Making in Developing States. LC 77-71401. (Praeger Special Studies). 1979. 23.95 (ISBN 0-03-046691-1). Praeger.

Clark, Ian. Reform & Resistance in the International Order. LC 79-54017. 1980. 29.50 (ISBN 0-521-22998-7); pap. 8.95 (ISBN 0-521-29763-X). Cambridge U Pr.

Clark, Ronald W. The Greatest Power on Earth: The International Race for Supremacy. LC 80-7899. (Illus.). 352p. 1981. 13.95 (ISBN 0-06-014846-2, HarpT). Har-Row.

Claude, Inis L., Jr. Power & International Relations. 1962. text ed. 15.95 (ISBN 0-394-30133-1). Random.

Cleveland, Harlan. The Third Try at World Order. 3.95 (ISBN 0-686-25998-X). Aspen Inst Human.

Cohen, Bernard C. Political Process & Foreign Policy: The Making of the Japanese Peace Settlement. LC 80-19832. x, 293p. 1980. Repr. of 1957 ed. lib. bdg. 37.50x (ISBN 0-313-22715-2, COPF). Greenwood.

Connelly, Philip & Perlman, Robert. The Politics of Scarcity: Resource Conflicts in International Relations. (Royal Institute of International Affairs Ser). 192p. 1975. 12.50 (ISBN 0-19-218308-7). Oxford U Pr.

Consensus & Peace. 231p. 1981. pap. 20.75 (ISBN 92-3-101851-5, U1055, UNESCO). Unipub.

Consolidated Index to the Survey of International Affairs 1920-1938 & Documents on International Affairs 1928-1938. 272p. 1967. pap. 25.00 (ISBN 0-384-09760-X). Johnson Repr.

Corbett, Percy E. Law in Diplomacy. 9.50 (ISBN 0-8446-1125-5). Peter Smith.

Cot, J. International Conciliation. (Europa's International Relations Ser). 368p. 1972. 13.95x (ISBN 0-900362-40-5). Intl Pubns Serv.

Couloumbis, Ted & Wolfe, James. Introduction to International Relations: Power & Justice. 2nd ed. 448p. 1982. 18.95 (ISBN 0-13-485292-3). P-H.

Cox, K. R., et al, eds. Locational Approaches to Power & Conflict. LC 76-127983. 352p. 1974. 19.95 (ISBN 0-470-18122-2). Halsted Pr.

Crozier, Brian, ed. Annual of Power & Conflict, 1979-80: A Survey of Political Violence & International Influence. 9th ed. LC 77-370326. 510p. 1980. 65.00x (ISBN 0-8002-2671-2). Intl Pubns Serv.

Dadie, Bernard B. Hommes de Tous les Continents. pap. 6.95 (ISBN 0-685-35631-0). French & Eur.

Davies, John P., Jr. Foreign & Other Affairs. 7.50 (ISBN 0-8446-0576-X). Peter Smith.

Davison, W. Phillips & Gordenker, Leon, eds. Resolving Nationality Conflicts: The Role of Public Opinion Research. LC 80-15128. 245p. 1980. 25.50 (ISBN 0-03-056229-5). Praeger.

Davison, W. Phillips, et al. News from Abroad & the Foreign Policy Public. LC 80-68024. (Headline Ser.: No. 250). (Illus.). 64p. (Orig.). 1980. pap. 2.00 (ISBN 0-87124-063-7). Foreign Policy.

De Beaufort-Wijnholds, J. A. & Debeaufort. The Need for International Reserves & Credit Facilities. (Publications of the Netherlands Institute of Bankers & Stock Brokers Ser: No. 31). 1977. pap. 23.00 (ISBN 90-207-0713-2, Pub. by Martinus Nijhoff Netherlands). Kluwer Boston.

De Leon, Daniel. Reform or Revolution. 1977. pap. 0.50 (ISBN 0-935534-37-7). NY Labor News.

De Molinari, Gustave. Society of Tomorrow: A Forecast of Its Political & Economic Organization. LC 71-147501. (Library of War & Peace; the Political Economy of War). lib. bdg. 38.00 (ISBN 0-8240-0295-4). Garland Pub.

Deutsch, K. Analysis of International Relations. 2nd ed. (Foundations of Modern Political Science Ser.). 1978. pap. 9.95 (ISBN 0-13-033217-8). P-H.

Deutsch, Karl W. Tides Among Nations. LC 78-57053. 1979. 19.95 (ISBN 0-02-907300-6). Free Pr.

Deutsch, Karl W. & Fritsch, Bruno, eds. Problems of World Modeling: Political & Social Implications. LC 77-953. 1977. 25.00 (ISBN 0-88410-656-X). Ballinger Pub.

Dobrosielski, Marian, ed. Peaceful Coexistence: Essays in Honor of the Thirtieth Anniversary of the Polish Institute of International Affairs. (UCIS Ser. in Russian & East European Studies). 160p. 1980. pap. text ed. 7.95 (ISBN 0-916002-42-X, Pub. by U Ctr Intl St). U of Pittsburgh Pr.

Doctor, Adi H. International Relations: An Introductory Study. 1969. 6.50x (ISBN 0-8426-1241-6). Verry.

Donelan, Michael. The Reason of States. 1979. pap. text ed. 9.95x (ISBN 0-04-320132-6). Allen Unwin.

Doran, Charles F. The Politics of Assimilation: Hegemony & Its Aftermath. LC 77-148241. (Illus.). 256p. 1971. 16.50x (ISBN 0-8018-1218-6). Johns Hopkins.

Douglas, Roy. Advent of War, Nineteen Thirty-Nine to Nineteen Forty. LC 78-12266. 1979. 21.95 (ISBN 0-312-00650-0). St Martin.

Douglas, William O. International Dissent. 1971. 4.95 (ISBN 0-394-43072-7). Random.

--International Dissent: Six Steps Towards World Peace. LC 74-119448. 1971. pap. 1.95 (ISBN 0-394-70871-7, V645, Vin). Random.

Dunn, Frederick S. Practice & Procedure of International Conferences. LC 70-158959. Repr. of 1929 ed. 14.50 (ISBN 0-404-02221-9). AMS Pr.

--War & the Minds of Men. LC 79-131371. 1971. Repr. of 1950 ed. 12.00 (ISBN 0-208-00945-0, Archon). Shoe String.

East, Maurice A., et al, eds. Why Nations Act: Theoretical Perspectives for Comparative Foreign Policy Studies. Salmore, Stephen A. & Hermann, Charles F. LC 77-22119. (Sage Focus Editions: Vol. 2). 234p. 1978. 22.50 (ISBN 0-8039-0718-4); pap. 9.95 (ISBN 0-8039-0719-2). Sage.

Eayrs, James. Diplomacy & Its Discontents. LC 73-163811. 198p. 1971. pap. 5.00 (ISBN 0-8020-6121-4). U of Toronto Pr.

Eckhard, Frederic & Linden, Ronald H., eds. Issues Before the Thirty-Third General Assembly of the United Nations. LC 76-640166. 1978. 10.00x (ISBN 0-8147-2155-9); pap. 7.50x (ISBN 0-8147-2156-7). NYU Pr.

Economic Relations Between East & West: Prospects & Problems. 1978. pap. 2.00 (ISBN 0-8157-2091-2). Brookings.
Eden, A. Foreign Affairs. LC 39-17206. Repr. of 1939 ed. 19.00 (ISBN 0-527-26310-9). Kraus Repr.
Educational Research Council of America. Nations in Action: International Tensions. (Challenges of Our Time Ser.). (gr. 7). 1972. pap. text ed. 9.32 (ISBN 0-205-05033-6, 8050333); tchrs'. guide 6.60 (ISBN 0-205-05034-4, 8050341). Allyn.
Ellul, Jaques. Betrayal of the West. O'Connell, Matthew J., tr. from Fr. LC 77-26796. 1978. 9.95 (ISBN 0-8164-9338-3). Continuum.
El Mallakh, Ragai & Atta, Jacob K. The Absorptive Capacity of Kuwait: Domestic & International Perspectives. LC 81-47026. (Illus.). 1981. 21.95 (ISBN 0-669-04541-1). Lexington Bks.
Evan, William M. Knowledge & Power in a Global Society. LC 81-8728. (Sage Focus Editions Ser.). (Illus.). 320p. 1981. pap. 9.95 (ISBN 0-8039-1660-4). Sage.
--Knowledge & Power in a Global Society. LC 81-8728. (Sage Focus Editions Ser.). (Illus.). 320p. 20.00 (ISBN 0-8039-1659-0). Sage.
Falk, Richard A. A Global Approach to National Policy. LC 75-2817. 384p. 1975. text ed. 18.50x (ISBN 0-674-35445-1). Harvard U Pr.
--A Study of Future Worlds. LC 74-10139. (Preferred Worlds for the 1990's Ser.). (Illus.). 1975. pap. text ed. 10.95 (ISBN 0-02-910080-1). Free Pr.
Farges, Albert M. By the End of the Century, Who Will Be Number One? (Illus.). 1980. deluxe ed. 55.15 (ISBN 0-930008-55-3). Inst Econ Pol.
Farrell, John C. & Smith, Asa P., eds. Theory & Reality in International Relations. LC 68-18993. 108p. 1967. pap. 5.00x (ISBN 0-231-08587-7). Columbia U Pr.
Farvar, Taghi. International Development & the Human Environment. new ed. 1973. pap. 14.95 (ISBN 0-02-468980-7). Macmillan Info.
Fedder, Edwin H., ed. Defense Politics of the Atlantic Alliance. 180p. 1980. 23.50 (ISBN 0-03-058018-8). Praeger.
Feld, Werner. International Relations: A Transnational Policy Approach. LC 77-25959. (Illus.). 433p. 1979. text ed. 14.50x (ISBN 0-88284-058-4). Alfred Pub.
Ferraris, Luigi V., ed. Report on a Negotiation: Helsinki-Geneva-Helsinki Nineteen Seventy-Two to Nineteen Seventy-Five. Barber, Marie-Claire, tr. from Italian. (Collections De Relations Internationales Ser.). 439p. 1980. 46.00x (ISBN 9-0286-0779-X). Sijthoff & Noordhoff.
Finlay, David J. & Hovet, Thomas, Jr. Seven Thousand Three Hundred & Four: International Relations on the Planet Earth. 352p. 1975. text ed. 20.50 scp (ISBN 0-06-042067-7, HarpC); instructor's manual avail. (ISBN 0-06-362082-0). Har-Row.
Finnegan, Richard B., et al. Law & Politics in the International System: Case Studies in Conflict Resolution. LC 79-66153. (Illus.). 1979. pap. text ed. 9.00 (ISBN 0-8191-0793-X). U Pr of Amer.
Fischer, Louis. This Is Our World. LC 74-1514. (Illus.). 522p. 1974. Repr. of 1956 ed. lib. bdg. 25.00x (ISBN 0-8371-7389-2, FIOW). Greenwood.
Fisher, Glen. American Communication in a Global Society. LC 79-9331. (Communication & Information Science Ser.). 1979. 17.50 (ISBN 0-89391-025-2). Ablex Pub.
Fisher, Roger. International Conflict for Beginners. 8.00 (ISBN 0-8446-5851-0). Peter Smith.
--International Conflicts for Beginners. (Illus.). 1970. pap. 4.95x (ISBN 0-06-131911-2, TB1911, Torch). Har-Row.
Fliess, Peter J. International Relations in the Bipolar World. 5.50 (ISBN 0-8446-2069-6). Peter Smith.
Foreign Policy Association. Great Decisions 1976. (gr. 10-12). 1976. pap. text ed. 5.20 (ISBN 0-205-05383-1, 7653832); tchrs' guide 2.20 (ISBN 0-205-06115-X). Allyn.
Fox, William T., ed. Theoretical Aspects of International Relations. (International Studies Ser). 1959. 4.95x (ISBN 0-268-00273-8). U of Notre Dame Pr.
Franck, Thomas M. & Weisband, Edward. Word Politics: Verbal Strategy Among the Superpowers. 1971. 12.95 (ISBN 0-19-501460-X); pap. 5.95x (ISBN 0-19-501459-6). Oxford U Pr.
Franck, Thomas M. & Weisband, Edward, eds. Secrecy & Foreign Policy. 480p. 1974. 19.50 (ISBN 0-19-501746-3). Oxford U Pr.
Frankel, Charles. Morality & U. S. Foreign Policy. (Headline Ser.: No. 224). (Orig.). 1975. pap. 2.00 (ISBN 0-87124-029-7). Foreign Policy.
Frankel, Joseph. International Relations in a Changing World. rev. ed. 1980. 14.50x (ISBN 0-19-219147-0); pap. text ed. 5.95x (ISBN 0-19-289128-6). Oxford U Pr.
Frei, Daniel. International Crisis & Crisis Management. LC 78-58474. 1978. 24.95 (ISBN 0-03-046346-7). Praeger.
Gareau, Frederick H. The Cold War, 1947-67: A Quantitative Study. (Monograph Ser. in World Affairs, Vol. 6: 1968-69 Ser., Pt. A). 4.00 (ISBN 0-87940-018-8). U of Denver Intl.
Garnett, John C., ed. Theories of Peace & Security: A Reader in Contemporary Strategic Thought. 1970. 15.95 (ISBN 0-312-79695-1); pap. 6.95 (ISBN 0-312-79660-9). St Martin.
Gessert, Robert & Hehir, J. Bryan. The New Nuclear Debate. LC 76-3357. (Special Studies). (Orig.). 1976. pap. 2.00t (ISBN 0-87641-215-0). Coun Rel & Intl.
Gijlstra, D. J., et al, eds. Legal Issues of European Integration. 120p. 1980. pap. 18.50 (ISBN 90-268-1079-2, Pub. by Kluwer Law Netherlands). Kluwer Boston.
Glassner, Martin I. Access to the Sea for Developing Land-Locked States. LC 71-598487. (Illus.). 1970. 35.00x (ISBN 9-0247-5022-9). Intl Pubns Serv.
Glipin, Robert. War & Change in World Politics. LC 81-2885. (Illus.). 192p. Date not set. price not set (ISBN 0-521-24018-2). Cambridge U Pr.
Global Analysis & Its Applications, 3 vols. (Illus.). 699p. (Orig.). 1975. Vol. 1. pap. 18.00 (ISBN 0-685-52332-2, ISP355-1, IAEA); Vol.2. pap. 28.50 (ISBN 0-685-52333-0, ISP355-2); Vol. 3. pap. 24.50 (ISBN 0-685-52334-9, ISP355-3). Unipub.
Global Militarization & Its Remedy. 27p. 1980. pap. 5.00 (ISBN 92-808-0063-9, TUNU 044, UNU). Unipub.
Global Processes & the World in the Nineteen Eighties: Prolegomenon 1 for a GIPD World Model. 42p. 1981. pap. 5.00 (ISBN 92-808-0317-4, TUNU142, UNU). Unipub.
Goldmann, Kjell & Sjostedt, Gunnar, eds. Power, Capabilities, Interdependence: Problems in the Study of International Influence. LC 77-84076. (Sage Modern Politics Ser.: Vol. 3). (Illus.). 300p. 1979. 22.50 (ISBN 0-8039-9884-8); pap. 9.95 (ISBN 0-8039-9885-6). Sage.
Goldstein, Martin E. Nuclear Proliferation: International Politics in a Multinuclear World. LC 80-1367. 79p. 1980. pap. text ed. 6.00 (ISBN 0-8191-1243-7). U Pr of Amer.
Gompert, David C., et al. Nuclear Weapons & World Politics. LC 77-8695. (Nineteen Eighties Project-Council on Foreign Relations). 1977. text ed. 11.95 (ISBN 0-07-023713-1, P&RB); pap. 6.95 (ISBN 0-07-023714-X). McGraw.
Gordon, Lincoln. Growth Policies & the International Order. (Council on Foreign Relations 1980's Project). (Illus.). 1979. text ed. 9.95 (ISBN 0-07-023812-X, P&RB). McGraw.
Gould, Lawrence V. & Targ, Harry R. Global Dominance & Dependence: Readings in Theory & Research. 1980. pap. cancelled. Kings Court.
Graduate Institute Of International Studies - Geneva. World Crisis by the Professors of the Institute. facs. ed. LC 73-86753. (Essay Index Reprint Ser). 1938. 17.00 (ISBN 0-8369-1133-4). Arno.
Graham, Daniel O. A New Strategy for the West: NATO After Detente. LC 77-89607. 1977. 3.00 (ISBN 0-89195-020-6). Heritage Found.
Graham, Malbone W. American Diplomacy in the International Community. facs. ed. LC 70-76900. (Essay Index Reprint Ser). 1948. 15.75 (ISBN 0-8369-1037-0). Arno.
Granger, John V. Technology & International Relations. LC 78-15363. (Illus.). 1979. text ed. 19.95x (ISBN 0-7167-1004-8); pap. text ed. 9.95x (ISBN 0-7167-1003-X). W H Freeman.
Green, Carol N., ed. Unravel the World: A Resources Bibliography for Global Understanding. 1975. pap. text ed. 0.50 (ISBN 0-88441-417-5, 26-702). GS.
Grieves, Forest L. Conflict & Order: An Introduction to International Relations. LC 76-10901. (Illus.). 1976. pap. text ed. 15.95 (ISBN 0-395-24332-7); inst. manual 1.50 (ISBN 0-395-24335-1). HM.
Gromyko, A. A. Only for Peace. (Illus.). 1979. text ed. 46.00 (ISBN 0-08-023582-4); pap. text ed. 19.00 (ISBN 0-08-024513-7). Pergamon.
Groom, A. J. & Mitchell, C. International Relations Theory: A Critical Bibliography. 222p. 1980. pap. 12.50x (ISBN 0-686-77490-6). Nichols Pub.
Groom, A. J. & Taylor, Paul, eds. Functionalism: Theory & Practice in International Relations. LC 73-93664. 354p. 1975. 34.50x (ISBN 0-8448-0305-7). Crane-Russak Co.
--International Organization: A Conceptual Approach. 1978. 25.00 (ISBN 0-89397-025-5). Nichols Pub.
Grundy, Kenneth W., et al, eds. Evaluating Transnational Programs in Government & Business. 1980. 29.50 (ISBN 0-08-025101-3). Pergamon.
Guetzkow, Harold & Valadez, Joseph J., eds. Simulated International Processes: Theories & Research in Global Modeling. LC 80-29047. (Illus.). 400p. 1981. 29.95 (ISBN 0-8039-1574-8). Sage.
Gwatkin, Davidson R. A Population Strategy for the Nineteen Eighties: Health, Mortality, & Development. 224p. 1981. write for info. Overseas Dev Council.
Haas, Ernest B. & Whiting, Allen S. Dynamics of International Relations. LC 74-25993. 557p. 1975. Repr. of 1956 ed. lib. bdg. 36.25x (ISBN 0-8371-7879-7, HAIR). Greenwood.
Haas, Ernst. Collective Security & the Future International System. (Monograph Ser. in World Affairs, Vol. 5: 1967-68 Ser., Pt. A). 4.00 (ISBN 0-87940-015-3). U of Denver Intl.
Halle, Louis J. The Society of Man. LC 78-31208. 1979. Repr. of 1965 ed. lib. bdg. 16.75x (ISBN 0-313-20942-1, HASM). Greenwood.
Halle, Louis J. & Thompson, Kenneth W., eds. Foreign Policy & the Democratic Process: The Geneva Papers. LC 78-64523. 1978. pap. text ed. 6.00 (ISBN 0-8191-0633-X). U Pr of Amer.
Hamon, Augustin F., ed. Enquete sur la Guerre et le Mititarisme. LC 70-147470. (Library of War & Peace; the Character & Causes of War). lib. bdg. 38.00 (ISBN 0-8240-0262-8). Garland Pub.
Handel, Michael. Weak States in the International System. (Illus.). 318p. 1981. 27.50x (ISBN 0-7146-3117-5, F Cass Co). Biblio Dist.
Handlin, Oscar. The Distortion of America. 1981. 9.95 (ISBN 0-316-34316-1). Little.
Hansen, Roger D. Beyond the North-South Stalemate. (Council on Foreign Relations, 1980's Project). (Illus.). 1979. 12.95 (ISBN 0-07-026048-6, P&RB). McGraw.
Haq, Khadija. A New Strategy for North-South Negotiations. (Policy Studies). 1980. 25.00 (ISBN 0-686-77706-9). Pergamon.
Hare, A. Paul & Blumberg, Herbert H. A Search for Peace & Justice: Reflections of Michael Scott. (Illus.). 255p. 1980. 19.50x (ISBN 0-8476-3612-7). Rowman.
Harris, Errol E. Annihilation & Utopia: The Principles of International Politics. 1966. text ed. 10.50x (ISBN 0-04-327010-7). Humanities.
Harrison, Michael M. The Reluctant Ally: France & Atlantic Security. LC 80-8865. 320p. 1981. text ed. 24.00x (ISBN 0-8018-2474-5). Johns Hopkins.
Hartmann, Frederick H. Relations of Nations. 5th ed. Carroll, James, ed. (Illus.). 700p. 1978. text ed. 21.95 (ISBN 0-02-351270-9, 35127). Macmillan.
Hawrylyshyn, Bohdan. Condemned to Co-Exist: Road Maps to the Future. (Illus.). 200p. 1980. 31.00 (ISBN 0-08-026115-9); pap. 11.00 (ISBN 0-08-026114-0). Pergamon.
Heisler, Martin O. & Lambert, Richard D., eds. Ethnic Conflict in the World Today. LC 77-81968. (Annals of the American Academy of Political & Social Science: No. 433). 1977. pap. 6.00 (ISBN 0-87761-219-6). Am Acad Pol Soc Sci.
Henderson, Gregory, et al. Public Diplomacy & Political Change: Four Case Studies: Okinawa, Peru, Czechoslovakia, Guinea. LC 72-14204. (Special Studies in International Politics & Government). 1973. 24.50x (ISBN 0-275-28710-6). Irvington.
Henkin, Louis. How Nations Behave. 2nd ed. LC 79-1015. 1979. 25.00x (ISBN 0-231-04756-8); pap. 10.00x (ISBN 0-231-04757-6). Columbia U Pr.
Henry, Clement M. Politics & International Relations in the Middle East: An Annotated Bibliography. 107p. (Orig.). 1980. pap. 4.00 (ISBN 0-932098-18-5). Ctr for NE & North Aafrican Stud.
Herz, John H. The Nation-State & the Crisis of World Politics: Essays on International Politics in the Twentieth Century. LC 76-7507. 1976. pap. text ed. 9.95x (ISBN 0-679-30308-1). Longman.
Hess, J. Daniel. From the Other's Point of View. LC 79-22405. 1980. pap. 7.95 (ISBN 0-8361-1912-6). Herald Pr.
Hindmarsh, Albert E. Force in Peace: Force Short of War in International Relations. LC 72-89264. 264p. 1973. Repr. of 1933 ed. 15.00 (ISBN 0-8046-1757-0). Kennikat.
Hinshaw. Domestic Goals & Financial Interdependence: The Frankfurt Dialogue. (Business Economics & Finance Ser.: Vol. 12). 1980. 25.00 (ISBN 0-8247-6999-6). Dekker.
Hinsley, Francis H. Power & the Pursuit of Peace. (Orig.). 1968. pap. 13.95x (ISBN 0-521-09448-8). Cambridge U Pr.
Holbraad, Carsten. Superpowers & International Conflict. LC 79-9942. 1979. 25.00x (ISBN 0-312-77674-8). St Martin.
Holsti, Kalvei J. International Politics: A Framework for Analysis. 3rd ed. (Illus.). 1977. 17.95 (ISBN 0-13-473371-1). P-H.
Holsti, O. R., et al. Unity & Disintegration in International Alliances. 293p. 1973. 19.50 (ISBN 0-471-40835-2, Pub. by Wiley). Krieger.
Hopkins, Terence K. & Wallerstein, Immanuel, eds. Processes of the World-System. LC 79-27385. (Political Economy of the World-System Annuals: Vol. 3). (Illus.). 320p. 1980. pap. 22.50 (ISBN 0-8039-1378-8); pap. 9.95 (ISBN 0-8039-1379-6). Sage.
Hoskins, Halford. Atlantic Pact. 5.00 (ISBN 0-8183-0229-1). Pub Aff Pr.
Howard, Nigel. Paradoxes of Rationality: Games, Metagames & Political Behavior. 1971. 23.00x (ISBN 0-262-08046-X). MIT Pr.
Howe, Russell W. Weapons: The International Game of Arms, Money & Diplomacy. LC 79-7494. 1980. 19.95 (ISBN 0-385-12809-6). Doubleday.
Hoxha, Enver. Imperialism & the Revolution. new ed. LC 79-84364. 1979. pap. 5.95 (ISBN 0-933774-00-1). World View Pubns.
Hugo, Grant. Appearance & Reality in International Relations. LC 72-137420. 207p. 1970. 15.00x (ISBN 0-231-03468-7). Columbia U Pr.
IFAC - IFORS Symposium, 1st, Algiers, Algeria, May 1973. Systems Approaches to Developing Countries: Proceedings. Cuenod, M. A. & Kahne, S., eds. LC 73-77508. 470p. 1973. 35.00 (ISBN 0-87664-211-3). Instru Soc.
Institute for the Study of Conflict, ed. Annual of Power & Conflict Nineteen Seventy-Nine to Nineteen Eighty. 465p. 1980. 50.00x (ISBN 0-8448-1386-9). Crane-Russak Co.
International Affairs Nineteen Thirty-Nine to Nineteen Seventy-Nine. LC 80-22312. 1981. text ed. 24.75 (ISBN 0-8419-0677-7); pap. 12.00 (ISBN 0-8419-0678-5). Holmes & Meier.
Interrelations: Resources, Environment, Population & Development. 106p. 1980. pap. 6.00 (ISBN 0-686-72361-9, UN80/2A8, UN). Unipub.
Jacobson, Harold K. Networks of Interdependence: International Organizations & the Global Political System. 1979. text ed. 19.95 (ISBN 0-394-32153-7). Knopf.
Jacobson, Harold K., ed. The Shaping of Foreign Policy. (Controversy Ser). 214p. 1969. 9.95x (ISBN 0-202-24071-1); pap. 3.95x (ISBN 0-202-24072-X). Lieber-Atherton.
Jervis, Robert. Logic of Images in International Relations. LC 79-90951. 1970. 14.00x (ISBN 0-691-07532-8). Princeton U Pr.
--Perception & Misperception in International Politics. (Center for International Affairs at Harvard Ser.). 1976. text ed. 32.00 (ISBN 0-691-05656-0); pap. 13.50 (ISBN 0-691-10049-7). Princeton U Pr.
Jessup, Phillip C. Birth of Nations. LC 73-15515. (Illus.). 361p. 1974. 17.50x (ISBN 0-231-03721-X). Columbia U Pr.
Jones, Roy E. Principles of Foreign Policy: The Civil State in Its World Setting. LC 79-9835. 1979. 25.00x (ISBN 0-312-64561-9). St Martin.
Jones, Walter & Rosen, Steven J. The Logic of International Relations. 4th ed. (Illus.). 560p. (Orig.): 1981. pap. text ed. 12.95 (ISBN 0-87626-510-7, W5107-5); tchr's manual free (ISBN 0-87626-511-5, W5115-8). Winthrop.
Joyce, James A. Red Cross International & the Strategy of Peace. LC 59-10744. (Illus.). 1959. 12.50 (ISBN 0-379-00062-8). Oceana.
Joynt, Carey B. & Corbett, Percy E. Theory & Reality in World Politics. LC 77-14693. 1978. 10.95 (ISBN 0-8229-1132-9). U of Pittsburgh Pr.
Kalijarvi, Thorsten V., et al. Modern World Politics. 2nd ed. (Essay Index Reprint Ser.). Repr. of 1945 ed. 43.00 (ISBN 0-518-10148-7). Arno.
Kaplan, Morton A. The Life and Death of the Cold War: Selected Studies in Postwar Statecraft. LC 76-20539. 1976. 20.95x (ISBN 0-88229-335-4); pap. 10.95 (ISBN 0-88229-500-4). Nelson-Hall.
--Systems & Process in International Politics. LC 74-13081. 324p. 1975. pap. 6.95 (ISBN 0-88275-212-X). Krieger.
--Towards Professionalism in International Theory: Macrosystems Analysis. LC 78-65223. 1979. 17.95 (ISBN 0-02-916750-7). Free Pr.
Kaplan, Morton A., ed. Great Issues of International Politics. 2nd ed. LC 73-84931. 576p. 1974. text ed. 34.95x (ISBN 0-202-24139-4); pap. text ed. 14.95x (ISBN 0-202-24140-8). Aldine Pub.
--Isolation or Interdependence? LC 74-32547. 1975. 15.95 (ISBN 0-02-916940-2). Free Pr.
Katzenstein, Peter J., ed. Between Power & Plenty: Foreign Economic Policies of Advanced Industrial States. LC 77-91053. 352p. 1978. 25.00 (ISBN 0-299-07560-5); pap. 8.95 (ISBN 0-299-07564-8). U of Wis Pr.

Kaufman, Edy. The Super Powers & Their Spheres of Influence. LC 76-24651. 1977. 18.95x (ISBN 0-312-77630-6). St Martin.
Kaul, Triloki N. The Kissinger Years. 112p. 1980. Repr. 7.50 (ISBN 0-86578-001-3). Ind-US Inc.
Keeton, George W. & Schwarzenberger, Georg, eds. The Year Book of World Affairs, 1980. LC 47-29156. 300p. 1980. 38.75 (ISBN 0-89158-876-0). Westview.
Kegley, Charles W., Jr., et al, eds. International Events & the Comparative Analysis of Foreign Policy. LC 74-23206. (Illus.). 350p. 1975. 14.95x (ISBN 0-87249-326-1); pap. 7.95x (ISBN 0-87249-333-4). U of SC Pr.
Kendle, John. Round Table Movement & Imperial Union. LC 73-81758. 1974. 22.50x (ISBN 0-8020-5292-4). U of Toronto Pr.
Kennan, George, et al. Encounters with Kennan: The Great Debate. 218p. 1979. 23.50x (ISBN 0-7146-3132-9, F Cass Co). Biblio Dist.
Kent, Randolph C. & Nielsson, G. P., eds. Study & Teaching of International Relations: A Perspective on Mid-Career Education. 1980. 26.50x (ISBN 0-89397-057-3). Nichols Pub.
Kersten, Lawrence & Kersten, Karen K. The Love Exchange. LC 81-65745. 384p. 1981. 15.95 (ISBN 0-8119-0426-1). Fell.
King, Alexander. The State of the Planet: A Report Prepared by the International Federation of Institutes for Advanced Study, Stockholm. (Illus.). 1980. 27.00 (ISBN 0-08-024717-2); pap. 12.00 (ISBN 0-08-024716-4). Pergamon.
Klepacki, Z. M. The Origins of International Organizations. 149p. 1978. 21.00x (ISBN 90-286-0228-3). Sijthoff & Noordhoff.
Knorr, Klaus. The Power of Nations. LC 74-25920. 1975. 16.95x (ISBN 0-465-06142-7); pap. 6.95x (ISBN 0-465-06143-5). Basic.
Krippendorff, Ekkehart. International Relations As a Social Science. 225p. 1981. text ed. 17.00x (ISBN 0-391-02356-X, Pub. by Radiant Pubs India). Humanities.
Kubalkova, V. & Cruickshank, A. A. Marxism-Leninism & the Theory of International Relations. 1980. 40.00x (ISBN 0-7100-0361-7). Routledge & Kegan.
Kumar, Mahendra. Violence & Nonviolence in International Relations. 256p. 1976. text ed. 11.25x (ISBN 0-391-00622-3). Humanities.
Lall, Arthur. Modern International Negotiation. LC 66-17587. 404p. 1966. 22.50x (ISBN 0-231-02935-7). Columbia U Pr.
Landheer, B. World Society: How Is an Effective & Desireable World Order Possible? LC 73-879471. 211p. 1971. 27.50x (ISBN 9-0247-5088-1). Intl Pubns Serv.
Langguth, A. J. Hidden Terrors. LC 77-88769. 1979. pap. 3.95 (ISBN 0-394-73802-0). Pantheon.
LaRouche, Lyndon H., Jr. Why Revival of "SALT" Won't Stop War. 116p. (Orig.). 1980. pap. 3.95 (ISBN 0-933488-08-4). New Benjamin.
Laszlo, Ervin. A Strategy for the Future: The Systems Approach to World Order. LC 73-92679. 224p. 1974. 8.95 (ISBN 0-8076-0743-6); pap. 4.95 (ISBN 0-8076-0744-4). Braziller.
Lebedev, N. I. A New Stage in International Relations. LC 77-30488. 1978. text ed. 30.00 (ISBN 0-08-022246-3). Pergamon.
Lebow, Richard N. Between War & Peace: The Nature of International Crisis. LC 80-21982. 410p. 1981. text ed. 24.50 (ISBN 0-8018-2311-0). Johns Hopkins.
Lesher, Grif, ed. Organizing for Community Education on International Issues. LC 74-34805. 1975. pap. text ed. 2.00 (ISBN 0-87003-003-5). Carnegie Endow.
Levi, Werner. Law & Politics in the International Society. LC 76-22580. (Sage Library of Social Research: Vol. 32). 224p. 1976. 20.00 (ISBN 0-8039-0617-X); pap. 9.95 (ISBN 0-8039-0618-8). Sage.
Lindsay, Michael. Is Peaceful Co-Existence Possible. xvi, 252p. 1960. 5.00 (ISBN 0-87013-052-8). Mich St U Pr.
Linnemann, H., et al, eds. Model of International Relations in Agriculture. (Contributions to Economic Analysis Ser.: Vol. 124). 1979. 39.00 (ISBN 0-444-85169-0, North Holland). Elsevier.
Liska, George. Alliances & the Third World. LC 68-17254. (Studies in International Affairs, No. 5: No. 5). 70p. (Orig.). 1968. pap. 2.95x (ISBN 0-8018-0377-2). Johns Hopkins.
Luard, E. Human Rights & Foreign Policy. LC 80-41774. 32p. pap. 6.75 (ISBN 0-08-027405-6). Pergamon.
Luard, Evan. Types of International Society. LC 75-43173. 1976. 19.95 (ISBN 0-02-919450-4). Free Pr.
Luttwak, Edward N. Strategy & Politics. LC 79-65224. 1980. text ed. 16.95 (ISBN 0-87855-346-0). Transaction Bks.
McCormick, Donald. Approaching Nineteen-Eighty-Four. LC 80-67578. 192p. 1980. 19.95 (ISBN 0-7153-7654-3). David & Charles.
McGinn, Charles. Victory Without War. (Illus.). 153p. (Orig.). 1980. pap. 3.95 (ISBN 0-89260-193-0). Hwong Pub.
McGowan, Patrick J., ed. Sage International Yearbook of Foreign Policy Studies, Vol. 3. LC 72-98039. 320p. 1975. 22.50 (ISBN 0-8039-0323-5); pap. 9.95x (ISBN 0-8039-0324-3). Sage.
McHenry, Donald F. Ethics & Foreign Policy. LC 80-68410. (Distinguished Cria Lecture on Morality & Foreign Policy Ser.). 1980. pap. 4.00 (ISBN 0-87641-220-7). Coun Rel & Intl.
Machlup, Fritz. Remaking the International Monetary System - the Rio Agreement & Beyond. LC 68-31419. 176p. 1968. pap. 3.00 (ISBN 0-87186-224-7). Comm Econ Dev.
McLaughlin, Martin M. & Overseas Development Council. The United States & World Development: Agenda 1979. 1979. 23.95 (ISBN 0-03-049146-0); pap. 4.95 student ed (ISBN 0-03-049151-7). Praeger.
McMurry, Ruth E. & Lee, Muna. Cultural Approach. LC 72-159057. 1971. Repr. of 1947 ed. 15.00 (ISBN 0-8046-1680-9). Kennikat.
Macridis, Roy C., ed. Foreign Policy in World Politics. 5th ed. 1976. 11.95 (ISBN 0-13-326488-2). P-H.
Macrothesaurus for Information Processing in the Field of Economic & Social Development: New English Edition. 1979. 30.00 (ISBN 92-64-11882-9). OECD.
Mandel, Robert. Perception, Decision Making & Conflict. LC 78-65350. 1978. pap. text ed. 8.50 (ISBN 0-8191-0652-6). U Pr of Amer.
Manley, Robert H., ed. Building Positive Peace: Actors & Factors. LC 81-43025. 242p. 1981. lib. bdg. 19.00 (ISBN 0-8191-1516-9); pap. text ed. 9.75 (ISBN 0-8191-1517-7). U Pr of Amer.
Manning, C. A. The Nature of International Society. LC 75-23427. 220p. 1962. 31.95 (ISBN 0-470-56760-0). Halsted Pr.
Mansbach, Richard W. & Vasquez, John A. In Search of Theory: A New Paradigm for Global Politics. LC 80-19365. 544p. 1981. 25.00x (ISBN 0-231-05060-7). Columbia U Pr.
Markel, Lester, et al. Public Opinion & Foreign Policy. LC 78-167404. (Essay Index Reprint Ser). 1972. Repr. of 1949 ed. 17.00 (ISBN 0-8369-7242-2). Arno.
Martell, John. Twentieth Century World. 3rd ed. (Illus.). 1981. pap. 13.95x (ISBN 0-245-53578-0). Intl Ideas.
Martin, John. Dictators & Democracies Today. facs. ed. LC 68-16953. (Essay Index Reprint Ser). 1935. 14.75 (ISBN 0-8369-0680-2). Arno.
Matsumoto, Nancy, ed. The United States & the Global Environment: A Guide to American Organizations Concerned with International Environment Issues. LC 79-53313. (Who's Doing What Ser.: No. 9). 100p. (Orig.). 1981. pap. 20.00x (ISBN 0-912102-45-4). Cal Inst Public.
Mayr, Kaspar. Der Andere Weg: Dokumente und Materialen. LC 73-147444. (Library of War & Peace: Histories of the Organized Peace Movement). lib. bdg. 38.00 (ISBN 0-8240-0234-2). Garland Pub.
Meadows, Dennis L. & Meadows, Donella, eds. Toward Global Equilibrium: Collected Papers. LC 72-81804. (Illus.). 400p. 1973. 27.50x (ISBN 0-262-13143-9). MIT Pr.
Merrell, V. Dallas. Huddling: The Informal Way to Management Success. LC 78-31941. 1979. 11.95 (ISBN 0-8144-5506-9). Am Mgmt.
Merritt, Richard, ed. Foreign Policy. 1974. pap. 5.00 (ISBN 0-918592-09-7). Policy Studies.
Merritt, Richard L., ed. Foreign Policy Analysis. LC 75-27808. (Policy Studies Organization Study). 176p. 1975. 17.95 (ISBN 0-669-00251-8). Lexington Bks.
Mezerik, A. G., ed. International Debate, 1969. 15.00 (ISBN 0-685-58891-2). Intl Review.
Michelmann, Hans J. Organisational Effectiveness in a Multinational Bureaucracy. LC 78-60532. 1979. 26.95 (ISBN 0-03-047211-3). Praeger.
Millis, Walter & Real, James. Abolition of War. 1963. pap. 1.95 (ISBN 0-685-14563-8). Macmillan.
Misra, K. P. & Beal, Richard S., eds. International Relations Theory: Western & Non-Western Perspectives. 272p. 1980. text ed. 20.00 (ISBN 0-7069-1087-7, Pub. by Vikas India). Advent NY.
Misra, Kashi P. Politics of Persuasion. 1967. 8.50x (ISBN 0-8188-1082-3). Paragon.
Mitchell, C. R. The Structure of International Conflict. LC 79-25423. 400p. 1981. 35.00 (ISBN 0-312-76763-3). St Martin.
Mitchell, Jeremy, ed. Research in International Organization. pap. text ed. 4.00x (ISBN 0-435-82841-X). Heinemann Ed.
Mitrany, David. The Progress of International Government. 1933. 19.50x (ISBN 0-686-51293-6). Elliots Bks.
Modelski, George. Principles of World Politics. LC 70-163237. 1972. 16.95 (ISBN 0-02-921440-8). Free Pr.
Morgan, Patrick M. Theories & Approaches to International Politics. 3rd ed. LC 79-66439. 302p. 1981. 24.95 (ISBN 0-87855-350-9); text ed. 24.95 (ISBN 0-686-68062-6); pap. 9.95 (ISBN 0-87855-791-1); pap. text ed. 9.95 (ISBN 0-686-68063-4). Transaction Bks.
Morgenthau, Hans J. Politics Among Nations: The Struggle for Power & Peace. 5th, rev. ed. 1978. 27.95 (ISBN 0-394-50085-7); text ed. 18.95 (ISBN 0-394-32193-6). Knopf.
Morse, Edward L. Modernization & the Transformation of International Relations. LC 75-32367. (Perspectives on Modernization Ser.). 1976. 14.95 (ISBN 0-02-922200-1). Free Pr.
Mowat, Robert B. International Relations. facs. ed. LC 67-22105. (Essay Index Reprint Ser). 1931. 12.25 (ISBN 0-8369-0725-6). Arno.
Multilateral Treaties in Respect of Which the Secretary General Performs Depository Functions. 677p. 1980. pap. 34.00 (ISBN 0-686-68960-7, UN80/5/10, UN). Unipub.
Narayanan, K. R. & Misra, K. P., eds. Nonalignment in Contemporary International Relations. 275p. 1981. text ed. 27.50x (ISBN 0-7069-1286-1, Pub by Vikas India). Advent NY.
National Association for Women Deans, Administrators, & Counselors. Global Communication & Understanding. 1978. pap. 3.00 (ISBN 0-686-12124-4). Natl Assn Women.
Negishi, T. General Equilibrium Theory & International Trade. (Studies in Mathematical & Managerial Economics: Vol. 13). 1972. 36.75 (ISBN 0-444-10340-6, North-Holland). Elsevier.
Nelson, Jack A. Hunger for Justice: The Politics of Food & Faith. LC 79-21072. 1980. pap. 4.95 (ISBN 0-88344-196-9). Orbis Bks.
Neumann, George B. A Study of International Attitudes of High School Students with Special Reference to Those Nearing Completion of Their High School Courses. LC 77-177118. (Columbia University. Teachers College. Contributions to Education: No. 239). Repr. of 1926 ed. 17.50 (ISBN 0-404-55239-0). AMS Pr.
Nixon, Richard. The Real War. 1980. 12.50 (ISBN 0-686-72844-0). Warner Bks.
Northedge, F. S. & Donelan, M. D. International Disputes: The Political Aspects. LC 70-149885. 1971. 19.95 (ISBN 0-312-42035-8). St. Martin.
--International Disputes: The Political Aspects. 1971. 15.00x (ISBN 0-900362-36-7). State Mutual Bk.
Northedge, F. S., ed. The Foreign Policies of the Powers. LC 75-3762. 1975. 17.95 (ISBN 0-02-923170-1); pap. text ed. 8.95 (ISBN 0-02-923180-9). Free Pr.
--The Use of Force in International Relations. LC 74-10140. 1974. 17.95 (ISBN 0-02-923210-4). Free Pr.
Northrop, F. S. The Meeting of East & West. LC 79-89839. (Illus.). 1979. 27.00 (ISBN 0-918024-10-2); pap. text ed. 17.00 (ISBN 0-918024-11-0). Ox Bow.
Northrop, Kenneth. A Violent World Ahead. (Illus.). 1979. deluxe ed. 46.75 (ISBN 0-930008-19-7). Inst Econ Pol.
Nove, Alec. East-West Trade: Problems, Prospects, Issues. LC 78-52025. (The Washington Papers: No. 53). 1978. pap. 4.00 (ISBN 0-8039-1039-8). Sage.
O'Faolain, Sean. Foreign Affairs. 192p. 1978. pap. 3.50 (ISBN 0-14-004552-X, Pub. by Penguin England). Irish Bk Ctr.
Ofoegbu, Ray. A Foundation Course in International Relations for African Students. 224p. (Orig.). 1980. pap. text ed. 10.50x (ISBN 0-04-327058-1). Allen Unwin.
Organski, A. F. & Kugler, Jacek. The War Ledger. LC 79-23366. (Illus.). xii, 292p. 1981. pap. 6.50 (ISBN 0-226-63280-6). U of Chicago Pr.
Osgood, Charles E. An Alternative to War or Surrender. LC 62-19089. (Illus.). 1962. pap. 4.95 (ISBN 0-252-72312-0). U of Ill Pr.
Osgood, Robert E. Containment, Soviet Behavior, & Grand Strategy. LC 81-82418. (Policy Papers in International Affairs Ser.: No. 16). x, 75p. 1981. pap. 5.50x (ISBN 0-87725-516-4). U of Cal Intl St.
Ossenbeck, Frederick J. & Kroeck, Patricia C., eds. Open Space & Peace. LC 64-18827. (Publications Ser.: No. 35). 1964. 10.95 (ISBN 0-8179-1351-3). Hoover Inst Pr.
Ostrower, Alexander. Language, Law, & Diplomacy, 2 Vols. LC 63-15015. 1965. 20.00x (ISBN 0-8122-7408-3). U of Pa Pr.
The Outlawry of War: A Constructive Policy for World Peace. 1978. Repr. of 1927 ed. 20.00 (ISBN 0-8492-6745-5). R West.
Owen, Harold. Aftermath. (Illus.). 1970. 10.25x (ISBN 0-19-211195-7). Oxford U Pr.
Oye, Kenneth A., et al, eds. Eagle Entangled: U. S. Foreign Policy in a Complex World. (Illus.). 1979. text ed. 19.95x (ISBN 0-582-29003-1); pap. text ed. 11.95x (ISBN 0-582-29002-3). Longman.
Page, Kirby. Dollars & World Peace. LC 79-147503. (Library of War & Peace; the Political Economy of War). lib. bdg. 38.00 (ISBN 0-8240-0297-0). Garland Pub.
Palley, Marion & Hale, George. The Politics of Intergovernmental Relations. (Politics & Public Policy Ser.). 225p. (Orig.). 1980. pap. text ed. 7.50 (ISBN 0-87187-161-0). Congr Quarterly.
Parkinson, F. The Philosophy of International Relations: A Study in the History of Thought. LC 77-11197. (Sage Library of Social Research: Vol. 52). 245p. 1977. 20.00x (ISBN 0-8039-0689-7); pap. 9.95 (ISBN 0-8039-0690-0). Sage.
Patra, Saral, ed. Indian Ocean & Great Powers. 82p. 1979. 7.50x (ISBN 0-8002-1004-2). Intl Pubns Serv.
Paxton, John. World Legislatures. LC 74-24740. 192p. 1975. 18.95 (ISBN 0-312-89145-8). St Martin.
Pearson, Lester B. Democracy in World Politics. 1955. 13.00x (ISBN 0-691-05609-9). Princeton U Pr.
Penrose, Edith Tilton, et al, eds. New Orientations: Essays in International Relations. 136p. 1970. 24.00x (ISBN 0-7146-2593-0, F Cass Co). Biblio Dist.
Penrose, Ernest Francis. Revolution in International Relations. 290p. 1965. 25.00x (ISBN 0-7146-1570-6, F Cass Co). Biblio Dist.
Pettman, Ralph. Biopolitics & International Values: Investigating Liberal Norms. LC 80-22926. (PPS on International Politics). 196p. 1981. 20.00 (ISBN 0-08-026329-1); pap. 9.95 (ISBN 0-08-026328-3). Pergamon.
--State & Class: A Sociology of International Affairs. 1979. write for info. (ISBN 0-312-75602-X). St Martin.
Phelps, Christina. The Anglo-American Peace Movement in the Mid-Nineteenth Century. facsimile ed. LC 76-37906. (Select Bibliographies Reprint Ser). Repr. of 1930 ed. 15.00 (ISBN 0-8369-6744-5). Arno.
Pieper, F. C., ed. SISCIS: Subject Index to Sources of Comparative International Statistics. LC 78-323066. 745p. 1978. 200.00x (ISBN 0-900246-23-5). Intl Pubns Serv.
Plischke, Elmer. Foreign Relations Decision-Making: Options Analysis. LC 73-85566. 52p. 1973. pap. 4.00 (ISBN 0-934484-04-X). Inst Mid East & North Africa.
--Microstates in World Affairs. 1977. pap. 6.25 (ISBN 0-8447-3241-9). Am Enterprise.
Pollock, John C. The Politics of Crisis Reporting: American Journalism & Foreign Affairs. LC 78-19772. (Praeger Special Studies). 1979. 16.95 (ISBN 0-03-044336-9). Praeger.
Posses, F. The Art of International Negotiation. 195p. 1978. text ed. 23.50x (ISBN 0-220-66315-7, Pub. by Busn Bks England). Renouf.
Prescott, D. A. Education & International Relations. (Harvard Studies in Education: Vol. 14). 1930. pap. 15.50 (ISBN 0-384-47730-5). Johnson Repr.
President's Commission. The United States & the World Community in the Eighties. (Illus.). 128p. 1981. 12.95 (ISBN 0-13-937904-5); pap. 4.95 (ISBN 0-13-937896-0). P-H.
Puchala, Donald J. International Politics Today. (Illus., Orig.). 1971. pap. text ed. 11.95 scp (ISBN 0-06-045295-1, HarpC). Har-Row.
Rajan, M. S. & Ganguly, Shivaji, eds. Great Power Relations: World Order & the Third World. 400p. 1980. text ed. 40.00 (ISBN 0-7069-1073-7, Pub. by Vikas India). Advent NY.
Ramcharan, R. G., ed. Human Rights: Thirty Years After the Universal Declaration. 1978. lib. bdg. 50.00 (ISBN 9-0247-2145-8, Pub. by Martinus Nijhoff Netherlands). Kluwer Boston.
Records of the Paris Conference, Nineteen Seventy-One. 1974. 50.00x (ISBN 0-686-53026-8, WIPO34, WIPO). Unipub.
Records of the Strasbourg Diplomatic Conference on the International Patent Classification, 1971. 1973. 50.00x (ISBN 0-686-53027-6, WIPO33, WIPO). Unipub.
Records of the Vienna Diplomatic Conference on the Trademark Registration Treaty, 1973. 1975. 100.00x (ISBN 0-686-53028-4, WIPO35, WIPO). Unipub.
Records of the Washington Diplomatic Conference on the Patent Cooperation Treaty, 1970. 1972. 120.00x (ISBN 0-686-53029-2, WIPO32, WIPO). Unipub.
Records on the International Conference of States on the Protection of Phonograms, 1971. 1975. pap. 60.00x (ISBN 0-686-53024-1, WIPO36, WIPO). Unipub.

Reinsch, Paul S. World Politics at the End of the Nineteenth Century, As Influenced by the Oriental Situation. LC 72-79835. (China Library Ser.). (Illus.). 1972. Repr. of 1900 ed. lib. bdg. 23.00 (ISBN 0-8420-1362-8). Scholarly Res Inc.
Reports on the Work of the Five Main Committees on the Intellectual Property Conference of Stockholm, 1967. 1967. pap. 5.00x (ISBN 0-686-53030-6, WIPO29, WIPO). Unipub.
Revesz, Geza. The Origins & Prehistory of Language. Butler, J., tr. from Ger. LC 78-138128. 240p. Repr. of 1956 ed. lib. bdg. 15.00x (ISBN 0-8371-4167-2, RELA). Greenwood.
Reychler, Luc. Patterns of Diplomatic Thinking: A Cross National Study of Structural & Social-Psychological Determinants. LC 78-19774. (Praeger Special Studies). 1979. 24.95 (ISBN 0-03-046636-9). Praeger.
Reynolds, P. A. An Introduction to International Relations. 2nd ed. 352p. 1980. pap. text ed. 12.95x (ISBN 0-582-29502-5). Longman.
Rodkey, Frederick S. Turco-Egyptian Question in the Relations of England, France, & Russia, 1832-1841. LC 76-180616. 1972. Repr. of 1924 ed. 13.00 (ISBN 0-8462-1624-8). Russell.
Roffman, Howard. Understanding the Cold War. LC 75-5251. 198p. 1976. 11.50 (ISBN 0-8386-1740-9). Fairleigh Dickinson.
Rohrer, Daniel M. Freedom of Speech & Human Rights: An International Perspective. 1979. pap. text ed. 9.95 (ISBN 0-8403-1987-8, 40198701). Kendall-Hunt.
The Role of Patent Information in Research & Development: WIPO Moscow Symposium, 1974. 1975. pap. 50.00x (ISBN 0-686-53031-4, WIPO45, WIPO). Unipub.
Rome Convention for the Protection of Performers, Producers of Phonograms & Broadcasting Organizations. 15p. 1976. pap. 3.00x (ISBN 0-686-53032-2, WIPO38, WIPO). Unipub.
Rosecrance, Richard. International Relations: Peace or War. (Illus.). 288p. (Orig.). 1972. pap. text ed. 9.95 (ISBN 0-07-053698-8, C). McGraw.
Rosecrance, Richard N. Action & Reaction in World Politics: International Systems in Perspective. LC 77-2329. 1977. Repr. of 1963 ed. lib. bdg. 32.00x (ISBN 0-8371-9548-9, ROAR). Greenwood.
Rosen, Stephen & Jones, Walter. The Logic of International Relations. 3rd ed. (Illus.). 1980. pap. 12.95 (ISBN 0-87626-420-8). Winthrop.
Rosenau, J. N. National Leadership & Foreign Policy: A Case Study in the Mobilization of Public Support. (Center of International Studies Ser.). 1963. 24.00 (ISBN 0-691-09321-0). Princeton U Pr.
Rosenau, James N. International Politics & Foreign Policy. 2nd ed. LC 61-14106. 1969. text ed. 19.95 (ISBN 0-02-926980-6). Free Pr.
--Scientific Study of Foreign Policy. 2nd ed. (Essays on the Analysis of World Politics). 1980. 27.50x (ISBN 0-89397-074-3); pap. 15.00x (ISBN 0-89397-075-1). Nichols Pub.
--Study of Global Interdependence: Essays on the Transnationalization of World Affairs. (Essays on the Analysis of World Politics). 1980. 27.50x (ISBN 0-89397-078-6); pap. 15.00x (ISBN 0-89397-079-4). Nichols Pub.
--Study of Political Adaptation. (Essays on the Analysis of World Politics). 1980. 25.00x (ISBN 0-89397-076-X); pap. 15.00x (ISBN 0-89397-077-8). Nichols Pub.
Rosenau, James N., ed. Comparing Foreign Policies: Theories, Findings, & Methods. LC 72-98047. 442p. 1974. 21.50 (ISBN 0-470-73613-5). Halsted Pr.
Rosenau, James N., et al. World Politics. LC 75-22766. (Illus.). 1976. text ed. 17.95 (ISBN 0-02-927040-5). Free Pr.
Rostow, Eugene V. Law, Power, & the Pursuit of Peace. LC 67-10669. (Roscoe Pound Lecture Ser.). 1968. 10.95x (ISBN 0-8032-0156-7). U of Nebr Pr.
Rout, Leslie B., Jr. Politics of the Chaco Peace Conference, 1935-1939. (Latin American Monographs: No. 19). (Illus.). 286p. 1970. 12.50x (ISBN 0-292-70049-0). U of Tex Pr.
Royal Institute of International Affairs. Reports on Nationalism by a Study Group of Members of the Royal Institute of International Affairs: Proceedings. 360p. 1963. 28.50x (ISBN 0-7146-1571-4, F Cass Co). Biblio Dist.
--South-Eastern Europe. 2nd rev. ed. Repr. of 1939 ed. 18.50 (ISBN 0-384-56750-9). Johnson Repr.
Rummel, Rudolph J. & Tanter, Raymond. Dimensions of Conflict Behavior Within & Between Nations, 1955-1960. 1974. codebk. 8.00 (ISBN 0-89138-072-8). ICPSR.
Rundle, R. N. International Affairs, Eighteen Ninety to Nineteen Thirty Nine. LC 79-12170. (Illus.). 1980. text ed. 29.50x (ISBN 0-8419-0516-9); pap. text ed. 12.95x (ISBN 0-8419-0601-7). Holmes & Meier.
Russell, Frank M. Theories of International Relations. LC 72-4297. (World Affairs Ser.: National & International Viewpoints). 658p. 1972. Repr. of 1936 ed. 30.00 (ISBN 0-405-04588-3). Arno.
Said, Abdul A. & Lerche, Charles Q. Concepts of International Politics: A Global Perspective. 3rd ed. 1979. text ed. 17.95 (ISBN 0-13-166033-0). P-H.
Santiago, Miriam D. International Relations. 1975. wrps. 5.50x (ISBN 0-686-18684-2). Cellar.
Schamis, Gerardo J. War & Terrorism in International Affairs. Salti, Danielle, tr. from Span. LC 79-91346. 100p. (Orig.). 1980. pap. 3.95 (ISBN 0-87855-808-X). Transaction Bks.
Schleicher, Charles P. International Behavior: Analysis & Operations. LC 72-91179. 1973. pap. text ed. 4.95x (ISBN 0-675-09022-9). Merrill.
Schuman, Frederick L. The Commonwealth of Man: An Inquiry into Power Politics & World Government. LC 76-30305. 1977. Repr. of 1972 ed. lib. bdg. 31.25x (ISBN 0-8371-9372-9, SCCO). Greenwood.
Schwab, George, ed. Ideology & Foreign Policy. 1978. 12.95 (ISBN 0-915326-07-8). Cyrco Pr.
--Ideology & Foreign Policy: A Global Perspective. 226p. 1981. Repr. of 1978 ed. pap. text ed. 10.95x (ISBN 0-8290-0393-2). Irvington.
Schwartz, Pushpa N., ed. Confrontation of Co-Operation? Twelfth World Conference of the Society for International Development Proceedings. 1976. pap. text ed. 17.50 (ISBN 0-08-020491-0). Pergamon.
Scott, James B. Law, the State, & the International Community, 2 Vols. LC 70-153354. Repr. of 1939 ed. Set. 32.00 (ISBN 0-404-05638-5). AMS Pr.
Serfaty, Simon. The United States, Western Europe, & the Third World: Allies & Adversaries, Vol. II. LC 80-50588. (Significant Issues Ser.: No. 4). 53p. 1980. 5.95 (ISBN 0-89206-018-2). CSI Studies.
Shaping Accelerated Development & International Changes. 45p. 1980. pap. 3.00 (ISBN 0-686-68971-2, UN80/2A4, UN). Unipub.
Sheikh, Ahmed. International Law & National Behavior: A Behavioral Interpretation of Contemporary International Law & Politics. LC 73-19922. 352p. 1974. pap. text ed. 14.50x (ISBN 0-471-78230-0). Wiley.
Shiels, Frederick L. The New American Foreign Policy: A Primer for the 1980's. 1979. pap. text ed. 9.95 (ISBN 0-686-62267-7). Collegium Bk Pubs.
Shih-Tsai Chen, Samuel. The Theory & Practice of International Organization. rev. ed. 1979. text ed. 14.95 (ISBN 0-8403-1946-0, 40194601). Kendall-Hunt.
Simpson, Smith. The Crisis in American Diplomacy. 300p. 1980. 10.95 (ISBN 0-8158-0388-5). Chris Mass.
Simpson, William G. Which Way Western Man? LC 79-91738. 758p. 1980. pap. 7.00 (ISBN 0-937944-01-7). Natl Alliance.
Singer, Marshall. Weak States in a World of Power: The Dynamics of International Relationships. LC 70-158070. 1972. 16.95 (ISBN 0-02-928900-9). Free Pr.
Singh, K. Rajendra. The Indian Ocean: Big Power Presence & Local Response. 1978. 16.00x (ISBN 0-88386-885-7). South Asia Bks.
Singham, A. W., ed. The Nonaligned Movement in World Politics. LC 78-51457. 324p. 1978. pap. 7.95 (ISBN 0-88208-086-5). Lawrence Hill.
Snyder, Glenn H. & Diesing, Paul. Conflict Among Nations: Bargaining, Decision Making & System Structure in International Crisis. LC 77-72135. 1978. 38.50 (ISBN 0-691-05664-1); pap. 13.50 (ISBN 0-691-10057-8). Princeton U Pr.
Society for International Development. International Development, 1965. LC 64-8541. 1966. 12.50 (ISBN 0-379-12002-X). Oceana.
--International Development, 1971: Development Targets for the 70's - Jobs & Justice. LC 64-8541. 1972. 12.50 (ISBN 0-379-12007-0). Oceana.
Sondermann, Fred, et al. The Theory & Practice of International Relationships. 5th ed. (Illus.). 1979. pap. text ed. 11.50 (ISBN 0-13-914507-9). P-H.
Sorel, Albert. Europe Under the Old Regime. 5.00 (ISBN 0-8446-2974-X). Peter Smith.
Sorey, Gordon K. The Foreign Policy of a Multinational Enterprise: An Analysis of the Policy Interactions of Dow Chemical Company & the U. S. Bruchey, Stuart, ed. LC 80-593. (Multinational Corporations Ser.). 1980. lib. bdg. 15.00x (ISBN 0-405-13385-5). Arno.
Spanier, J. Games Nations Play. 3rd ed. LC 77-89738. 1978. pap. 11.95 (ISBN 0-03-022206-0, HoltC). HR&W.
Spiegel, Steven L. Dominance & Diversity: The International Hierarchy. LC 80-8295. 317p. 1980. lib. bdg. 19.00 (ISBN 0-8191-1331-X); pap. text ed. 10.50 (ISBN 0-8191-1332-8). U Pr of Amer.
Sternheimer, Stephen. East-West Technology Transfers: Japan & the Communist Bloc. LC 80-50901. (The Washington Papers: No. 76). (Illus.). 88p. 1980. pap. 4.00 (ISBN 0-8039-1485-7). Sage.
Stillman, Edmund O. & Pfaff, William. The Politics of Hysteria: The Sources of Twentieth-Century Conflict. LC 81-4630. x, 273p. 1981. Repr. of 1964 ed. lib. bdg. 25.00x (ISBN 0-313-22973-2, STPOH). Greenwood.
Stoessinger, John G. The Might of Nations. 6th ed. 1979. pap. text ed. 10.95x (ISBN 0-394-32261-4). Random.
Stoke, Harold W. The Foreign Relations of the Federal State. LC 78-64284. (Johns Hopkins University. Studies in the Social Sciences. Extra Volumes.: 14). Repr. of 1931 ed. 23.00 (ISBN 0-404-61384-5). AMS Pr.
Stokes, Bruce. Local Responses to Global Problems: A Key to Meeting Basic Human Needs. LC 77-94930. (Worldwatch Papers). 1978. pap. 2.00 (ISBN 0-916468-16-X). Worldwatch Inst.
Stone, Julius. Israel & Palestine: Assault on the Law of Nations. LC 80-8875. 208p. 1981. text ed. 17.50x (ISBN 0-8018-2535-0). Johns Hopkins.
Strasbourg Agreement Concerning the International Patent Classification. 19p. 1971. pap. 3.00x (ISBN 0-686-53033-0, WIPO22, WIPO). Unipub.
Strasbourg Conference on the International Patent Classification. 1971. pap. 4.00x (ISBN 0-686-53034-9, WIPO23, WIPO). Unipub.
Streeten, Paul. Recent Issues in World Development: A Collection of Survey Articles. (Illus.). 450p. 1981. 152.00 (ISBN 0-08-026812-9). Pergamon.
Stuart, Douglas T. & Tow, William T., eds. China, the Soviet Union & the West: Strategic & Political Dimensions for the Nineteen Eighties. (Special Studies in International Relations). 320p. (Orig.). 1981. lib. bdg. 28.75x (ISBN 0-86531-091-2); pap. text ed. 12.50x (ISBN 0-86531-168-4). Westview.
Sturzo, Luigi. The International Community & the Right of War. LC 68-9649. 1971. Repr. of 1929 ed. 21.50 (ISBN 0-86527-104-6). Fertig.
Suhrke, Astri & Noble, Lela G. Ethnic Conflict in International Relations. LC 77-83444. (Praeger Special Studies). 1978. 24.95 (ISBN 0-03-040681-1). Praeger.
Sullivan, David S. & Sattler, Martin J., eds. Change & the Future International System. 1972. 20.00x (ISBN 0-231-03565-9); pap. 5.00x (ISBN 0-231-08304-1). Columbia U Pr.
Sullivan, Michael P. International Relations: Theories & Evidence. (Illus.). 400p. 1976. 18.95 (ISBN 0-13-473470-X). P-H.
Suyin, Han. Asia Today: Two Outlooks. (Beatty Memorial Lectures Ser.). 1969. 5.25x (ISBN 0-7735-0061-8); pap. 2.75 (ISBN 0-7735-0062-6). McGill-Queens U Pr.
Szent-Miklosy, Istvan. Atlantic Union Movement: Significance in World Politics. (Illus.). 264p. 7.95 (ISBN 0-685-41740-9). Fountainhead.
Taft, William H. & Bryan, William J. World Peace: A Written Debate. Repr. of 1917 ed. 12.00 (ISBN 0-527-88632-7). Kraus Repr.
Takagi, Yasaka. Toward International Understanding. enl. ed. 450p. 1971. 8.00x (ISBN 0-86008-112-5, Pub by U of Tokyo Pr). Intl Schol Bk Serv.
Tarrow, Sidney, et al. Territorial Politics in Industrial Nations. LC 77-83439. (Praeger Special Studies). 1978. 32.50 (ISBN 0-03-040961-6). Praeger.
Taylor, Trevor, ed. Approaches & Theory in International Relations. LC 77-8093. (Illus.). 1978. pap. text ed. 11.50x (ISBN 0-582-48540-1). Longman.
Thanassecos, Luc. Chronologie Des Relations Internationales, 1914-1971: Exposes Thematiques. 1972. pap. 25.50x (ISBN 90-2796-970-1). Mouton.
Thompson, Kenneth. Ethics, Functionalism, & Power in International Politics: The Crisis in Values. LC 78-24061. 1979. 12.50x (ISBN 0-8071-0492-2). La State U Pr.
Thompson, Kenneth W. Understanding World Politics. LC 74-12569. 234p. 1975. text ed. 11.95x (ISBN 0-268-00564-8). U of Notre Dame Pr.
Tomashevsky, D. Lenin's Ideas & Modern International Relations. 288p. 1974. 3.85 (ISBN 0-8285-0307-9, Pub. by Progress Pubs Russia). Imported Pubns.
Tompkins, E. Berkeley, ed. Peaceful Change in Modern Society. LC 74-152429. (Publications Ser.: No. 101). 158p. 1971. 8.95 (ISBN 0-8179-6011-2); pap. 5.95 (ISBN 0-8179-6012-0). Hoover Inst Pr.
Toynbee, Arnold J. & Ashton-Gwatkin, Frank T., eds. The World in March Nineteen Thirty Nine. Repr. of 1946 ed. 50.00 (ISBN 0-384-61134-6); pap. 45.00 (ISBN 0-685-13639-6). Johnson Repr.
Trademark Registration Treaty (TRT) 1973. pap. 6.00x (ISBN 0-686-53035-7, WIPO16, WIPO). Unipub.
Transborder Data Flows & the Protection of Privacy. (Document Ser.). 1979. 20.00x (ISBN 92-64-01926-X). OECD.
Trevelyan, Humphrey. Diplomatic Channels. LC 73-81316. 160p. 1973. 7.95 (ISBN 0-87645-080-X). Gambit.
Trilateral Commission. Trilateral Commission Task Force Reports 15-19. 472p. 1981. text ed. 30.00x (ISBN 0-8147-8166-7) (ISBN 0-8147-8167-5). NYU Pr.
Tripathi, K. S. Evolution of Nuclear Strategy. 1970. 7.00 (ISBN 0-686-20226-0). Intl Bk Dist.
Tucker, Robert W. The Inequality of Nations. LC 76-9673. 1979. pap. 4.95 (ISBN 0-465-03246-X, CN5046). Basic.
Tunis Model Law on Copyright for Developing Countries. 26p. 1976. pap. 6.00x (ISBN 0-686-53036-5, WIPO51, WIPO). Unipub.
Unilateral Force in International Relations. Incl. Some Neglected Aspects of War. Mahan, Alfred T; Power That Makes for Peace. Pritchett, Henry S; Capture of Private Property at Sea. Corbett, Julian S; Ewige Friede. Von Stengel, Karl. (Library of War & Peace; Int'l. Organization, Arbitration & Law). lib. bdg. 38.00 (ISBN 0-8240-0348-9). Garland Pub.
University Of California. Publications in International Relations, 5 Vols. 1923-57. 115.50 (ISBN 0-685-13624-8); pap. 98.50 (ISBN 0-685-13625-6). Johnson Repr.
Valenta, Jiri. Soviet Intervention in Czechoslovakia, 1968: Anatomy of a Decision. LC 78-20522. 224p. 1981. pap. 5.95 (ISBN 0-8018-2540-7). Johns Hopkins.
Van Dyke, Vernon. International Politics. 3rd ed. 1972. text ed. 16.95 (ISBN 0-13-472928-5). P-H.
Vienna Agreement Establishing an International Classification of the Figurative Elements of Marks. 20p. 1973. pap. 3.00x (ISBN 0-686-53037-3, WIPO17, WIPO). Unipub.
Vienna Agreement for the Protection of Type Faces & Their International Deposit. pap. 5.00x (ISBN 0-686-53038-1, WIPO18, WIPO). Unipub.
Vincent, Jack E. Handbook of International Relations. LC 68-8679. 1969. pap. 4.50 (ISBN 0-8120-0368-3). Barron.
--Project Theory: Interpretations & Policy Relevance. LC 78-59172. 1978. pap. text ed. 11.25 (ISBN 0-8191-0551-1). U Pr of Amer.
--Understanding International Relations. 1978. pap. text ed. 14.75 (ISBN 0-8191-0538-4). U Pr of Amer.
Vital, David. The Inequality of States: A Study of the Small Power in International Relations. LC 80-11343. (Illus.). 198p. 1980. Repr. of 1967 ed. lib. bdg. 19.75x (ISBN 0-313-22357-2, VIIS). Greenwood.
Von Weizsacker, Carl F. The Politics of Peril: Economics, Society & the Prevention of War. LC 78-4991. 1978. 12.95 (ISBN 0-8164-9345-6). Continuum.
Walsh, Edmund A., ed. History & Nature of International Relations. facs. ed. LC 74-88036. (Essay Index Reprint Ser). 1922. 24.00 (ISBN 0-8369-1161-X). Arno.
Waltz, Kenneth N. Man, the State & War: A Theoretical Analysis. LC 59-11482. (Institute of War & Peace Studies Ser). 1959. 17.50x (ISBN 0-231-02292-1); pap. 6.00x (ISBN 0-231-08564-8). Columbia U Pr.
--Theory of International Politics. LC 78-62549. (Political Science Ser.). (Illus.). 1979. pap. text ed. 8.50 (ISBN 0-201-08349-3). A-W.
Ward, Barbara. Spaceship Earth. LC 66-18062. (George B Pegram Ser). 1966. 15.00x (ISBN 0-231-02951-9); pap. 5.00x (ISBN 0-231-08586-9). Columbia U Pr.
Watson, Adam. Toleration in Religion & Politics. LC 80-65746. (Second Annual Distinguished Cria Lecture on Morality & Foreign Policy Ser.). 1980. pap. 4.00 (ISBN 0-87641-218-5). Coun Rel & Intl.
Watt, D. C. Survey of International Affairs, 1962. (Royal Institute of International Affairs Ser). 1970. 26.00x (ISBN 0-19-214732-3). Oxford U Pr.
Watt, D. C., ed. Greenwich Forum V: Europe & the Sea: the Cause for & Against a New International Regime for the North Sea and Its Approaches. 1981. text ed. 49.95 (ISBN 0-86103-039-7). Butterworth.
Weigert, Hans W. Generals & Geographers: The Twilight of Geopolitics. LC 70-167434. (Essay Index Reprint Ser.). Repr. of 1942 ed. 18.00 (ISBN 0-8369-2728-1). Arno.
Weldon, John. Nineteen Eighties, Decade of Shock. LC 80-81458. 1980. pap. 3.95 (ISBN 0-89051-063-6). CLP Pubs.

Wendzel, Robert L. International Relations: A Policymaker Focus. 2nd ed. LC 79-1215. 1979. text ed. 9.95x (ISBN 0-471-05261-2). Wiley.
West, Robert H. The Invisible World. 275p. 1980. Repr. of 1939 ed. lib. bdg. 30.00 (ISBN 0-8482-7063-0). Norwood Edns.
Wight, Martin. Power Politics. Bull, Hedley, ed. LC 77-11020. 1978. text ed. 29.50x (ISBN 0-8419-0344-1). Holmes & Meier.
Wilcox, Wayne. Protagonist Powers & the Third World. Lambert, Richard D., ed. LC 76-102760. (The Annals of the American Academy of Political & Social Science: Vol. 386). 1969. 7.50 (ISBN 0-87761-122-X); pap. 6.00 (ISBN 0-87761-121-1). Am Acad Pol Soc Sci.
Wilhelm, Donald. Creative Alternatives to Communism: Guidelines for the Future. 188p. 1980. 12.95x (ISBN 0-8290-0298-7); pap. 6.95x (ISBN 0-8290-0299-5). Irvington.
Winslow, Earle M. The Pattern of Imperialism: A Study in the Theories of Power. LC 78-159238. xii, 278p. 1971. Repr. lib. bdg. 15.00x (ISBN 0-374-98685-1). Octagon.
Woito, Robert. To End War: A New Approach to International Conflict. 6th ed. 512p. 1981. 16.95 (ISBN 0-8298-0464-1); pap. 9.95 (ISBN 0-8298-0476-5). Pilgrim NY.
Wolfe, James H. & Couloumbis, Theo. A. Introduction to International Relations: Power & Justice. (Illus.). 1978. text ed. 17.95 (ISBN 0-13-485300-8). P-H.
Wolfers, Arnold & Martin, Laurence W., eds. The Anglo-American Tradition in Foreign Affairs: Readings from Thomas More to Woodrow Wilson. 1956. text ed. 17.50x (ISBN 0-686-51345-2). Elliots Bks.
Woolf, Leonard. War for Peace. LC 75-148376. (Library of War & Peace; the Character & Causes of War). lib. bdg. 38.00 (ISBN 0-8240-0465-5). Garland Pub.
Wright. Understanding Intergovernmental Relations. LC 77-26967. 1978. pap. text ed. 6.95 (ISBN 0-87872-152-5). Duxbury Pr.
Wright, Quincy. On Predicting International Relations: The Year 2000. (Monograph Ser. in World Affairs, Vol. 7: 1969-70 Ser, Pt. A). 4.00 (ISBN 0-87940-022-6). U of Denver Intl.
Ziegler. War, Peace & International Relations. 2nd ed. 1981. pap. text ed. 8.95 (ISBN 0-316-98493-0). Little.
Ziegler, David W. War, Peace & International Politics. 1977. pap. text ed. 9.95 (ISBN 0-316-98770-0); instr. manual free (ISBN 0-316-98771-9). Little.
Zimmerman, William. Soviet Perspectives on International Relations, 1956-1967. LC 68-56326. (Studies of the Russian Inst. Columbia Univ). 1969. 23.00x (ISBN 0-691-07525-5); pap. 7.95 (ISBN 0-691-02168-6). Princeton U Pr.
Zinnes, Dina A. & Gillespie, John V., eds. Mathematical Models in International Relations. LC 75-25000. (Special Studies). (Illus.). 1976. text ed. 45.00 (ISBN 0-275-55870-3). Praeger.

INTERNATIONAL RELATIONS–ADDRESSES, ESSAYS, LECTURES

Art, Robert J. & Jervis, Robert, eds. International Politics: Anarchy, Force, Imperialism. 1973. pap. text ed. 11.95 (ISBN 0-316-05244-2). Little.
Barker, Charles A., ed. Power & Law: American Dilemma in World Affairs. LC 76-135660. (Illus.). 224p. 1971. 15.50x (ISBN 0-8018-1254-2). Johns Hopkins.
Burton, J. W. Nonalignment. 1967. 4.50 (ISBN 0-685-11966-1). Heineman.
California University Committee on International Relations. Problems of Hemispheric Defense. LC 77-167322. (Essay Index Reprint Ser.). Repr. of 1942 ed. 12.50 (ISBN 0-8369-2759-1). Arno.
Cohen, Raymond. Threat Perception in International Crisis. LC 79-3964. 214p. 1979. 17.50 (ISBN 0-299-08000-5). U of Wis Pr.
Cordier, Andrew W., ed. Columbia Essays in International Affairs: The Dean's Papers, Vol. 2, 1966. LC 66-14078. 324p. 1967. 25.00x (ISBN 0-231-03047-9). Columbia U Pr.
--Columbia Essays in International Affairs: The Dean's Papers, Vol. 3, 1967. LC 66-14078. 441p. 1968. 25.00x (ISBN 0-231-03156-4). Columbia U Pr.
--Columbia Essays in International Affairs: The Dean's Papers, Vol. 4, 1968. LC 66-14078. 295p. 1969. 25.00x (ISBN 0-231-03270-6). Columbia U Pr.
--Columbia Essays in International Affairs: The Dean's Papers, Vol. 5, 1969. LC 66-14078. 328p. 1970. 25.00x (ISBN 0-231-03487-3). Columbia U Pr.
Falk, Richard A. & Mendlovitz, Saul H., eds. The Strategy of World Order, 4 vols. Incl. Vol. 1. Toward a Theory of War Prevention. Lasswell, Harold D., frwd. by. pap. 3.50 (ISBN 0-911646-01-9); Vol. 2. International Law. Friedmann, Wolfgang, frwd. by. pap. 3.50 (ISBN 0-911646-02-7); Vol. 3. The United Nations. Schacter, Oscar, frwd. by. pap. 4.50 (ISBN 0-911646-03-5); Vol. 4. Disarmament & Economic Development. Singer, David, frwd. by. pap. 4.50 (ISBN 0-911646-04-3). 1966. pap. 14.00 set (ISBN 0-911646-00-0). Inst World Order.
Gati, Charles. Caging the Bear: Containment & the Cold War. LC 73-19522. 1974. pap. text ed. 5.95 (ISBN 0-672-61351-4). Bobbs.
Goldwin, Robert A., ed. Beyond the Cold War. LC 72-10851. (Essay Index Reprint Ser.). 1973. Repr. of 1965 ed. 19.00 (ISBN 0-8369-7218-X). Arno.
Grieves, Forest L., ed. Transnationalism in World Politics & Business. LC 79-1397. (Pergamon Policy Studies). 240p. 1979. 33.00 (ISBN 0-08-023892-0). Pergamon.
Hartmann, Frederick H. World in Crisis. 4th ed. Carroll, James J., ed. 519p. 1973. pap. text ed. 10.95 (ISBN 0-02-351380-2). Macmillan.
Harvard University, Center for International Affairs. Occasional Papers in International Affairs, 30 vols. Repr. of 1973 ed. Set. write for info (ISBN 0-404-54600-5). AMS Pr.
Hilsman, Roger & Good, Robert C., eds. Foreign Policy in the Sixties: The Issues & the Instruments. 311p. 1965. pap. 4.95x (ISBN 0-8018-0273-3). Johns Hopkins.
James, Alan, ed. The Bases of International Order: Essays in Honour of C. A. W. Manning. 17.95x (ISBN 0-19-215801-5). Oxford U Pr.
Kertesz, Stephen D. & Fitzsimons, M. A. Diplomacy in a Changing World. LC 74-2587. (International Studies of the Committee on International Relations, U. of Notre Dame). 407p. 1974. Repr. of 1959 ed. lib. bdg. 19.25x (ISBN 0-8371-7408-2, KEDI). Greenwood.
Lepawsky, Albert, et al, eds. Search for World Order: Studies by Students & Colleagues of Quincy Wright. LC 75-147119. (Orig.). 1971. 38.50x (ISBN 0-89197-479-2). Irvington.
Liggio, Leonard P. & Martin, James J., eds. Watershed of Empire: Essays on New Deal Foreign Policy. LC 76-4291. 1976. pap. 3.95 (ISBN 0-87926-020-3). R Myles.
Merritt, Richard L., ed. Communication in International Politics. LC 72-165042. 480p. 1972. 25.00 (ISBN 0-252-00210-5). U of Ill Pr.
Pettman, Ralph, ed. Moral Claims in World Affairs. LC 78-11431. 1979. 18.95 (ISBN 0-312-54755-2). St Martin.
Porter, Brian, ed. The Aberystwyth Papers: International Politics 1919-1969. 400p. 1972. 17.75x (ISBN 0-19-215193-2). Oxford U Pr.
Rakove, Milton L., ed. Arms & Foreign Policy in the Nuclear Age. 1972. pap. text ed. 6.95x (ISBN 0-19-501470-7). Oxford U Pr.
Rosenau, James, et al. The Analysis of International Politics. LC 70-184005. 1972. 17.95 (ISBN 0-02-927030-8). Free Pr.
Rosenau, James N. In Search of Global Patterns. LC 75-20950. (Illus.). 1976. 19.95 (ISBN 0-02-927050-2). Free Pr.
Stack, John F., Jr., ed. Ethnic Identities in a Transnational World. LC 80-1199. (Contributions in Political Science Ser.: No. 52). 264p. 1981. lib. bdg. 27.50 (ISBN 0-313-21088-8, SEI/). Greenwood.
Streeten, Paul. The Frontiers of Development Studies. 498p. 1979. Repr. of 1972 ed. text ed. 7.50x (ISBN 0-333-13195-9, Pub. by Macmillan England). Humanities.
Wright, Quincy. Problems of Stability & Progress in International Relations. LC 76-3755. 378p. 1976. Repr. of 1954 ed. lib. bdg. 26.25x (ISBN 0-8371-8788-5, WRPS). Greenwood.

INTERNATIONAL RELATIONS–BIBLIOGRAPHY

Amstutz, Mark R. Economics & Foreign Policy: A Guide to Information Sources. LC 74-11566. (Vol. 7). 1977. 36.00 (ISBN 0-8103-1321-9). Gale.
Boulding, Elise, et al. Bibliography on World Conflict & Peace. (Special Studies in Peace, Conflict & Conflict Resolution). 1979. lib. bdg. 19.50x (ISBN 0-89158-374-2). Westview.
Conover, Helen F. A Guide to Bibliographic Tools for Research in Foreign Affairs, 2 vols. lib. bdg. 250.00 (ISBN 0-8490-1917-6). Gordon Pr.
Council on Foreign Relations, Inc. (New York) Catalog of the Foreign Relations Library, First Supplement. 1979. lib. bdg. 325.00 (ISBN 0-8161-0306-2). G K Hall.
Dimitrov, Th. World Bibliography on International Documentation, 2 vols. LC 80-5653. 846p. 1981. 95.00 (ISBN 0-89111-010-0). UNIFO Pubs.
Kreslins, Janis A., ed. Foreign Affairs Bibliography: 1962-1972. LC 75-29085. 921p. 1976. 49.50 (ISBN 0-8352-0784-6). Bowker.
Langer, William L. & Armstrong, Hamilton F., eds. Foreign Affairs Bibliography, 1919-1932. LC 60-11311. 1960. Repr. of 1933 ed. 20.00 (ISBN 0-8462-0223-9). Russell.
Palmer, Robert J. Foreign Affairs Fifty-Year Index 1922-1972. LC 24-9921. 1282p. 1973. 46.75 (ISBN 0-8352-0584-3). Bowker.
Pfaltzgraff, Robert, Jr., ed. Study of International Relations: A Guide to Information Sources. LC 73-17511. (International Relations Information Guide Ser.: Vol. 5). 220p. 1977. 36.00 (ISBN 0-8103-1331-6). Gale.
Roberts, Henry L., ed. Foreign Affairs Bibliography 1942-1952. LC 54-12196. 1969. Repr. 29.50 (ISBN 0-8352-0212-7). Bowker.
--Foreign Affairs Bibliography, 1952-62. LC 33-7094. 752p. 1964. 29.50 (ISBN 0-8352-0046-9). Bowker.
Stanford University, Hoover Institution on War, Revolution & Peace. Catalog of the Arabic Collection. 1969. 80.00 (ISBN 0-8161-0170-1). G K Hall.
--Catalog of the Chinese Collection, 13 Vols. 1969. Set. 980.00 (ISBN 0-8161-0168-X). G K Hall.
Stanford University, Hoover Institution on War, Revolution, & Peace. The Catalog of the Chinese Collection: Second Supplement, 2 vols. 1977. Set. lib. bdg. 260.00 (ISBN 0-8161-0039-X). G K Hall.
Stanford University, Hoover Institution on War, Revolution & Peace. Catalog of the Japanese Collection, 7 Vols. 1969. Set. 600.00 (ISBN 0-8161-0169-8). G K Hall.
Stanford University, Hoover Institution on War, Revolution, & Peace. Catalog of the Japanese Collection: Second Supplement. 1977. lib. bdg. 130.00 (ISBN 0-8161-0040-3). G K Hall.
Stanford University, Hoover Institution on War, Revolution & Peace. Catalog of the Turkish & Persian Collections. 1969. 75.00 (ISBN 0-8161-0171-X). G K Hall.
Stanford University, Hoover Institution on War, Peace & Revolution. Catalog of the Western Language Collection, 63 Vols. 1969. Set. 5200.00 (ISBN 0-8161-0859-5). G K Hall.
Stanford University, Hoover Institution on War, Revolution & Peace. The Catalog of the Western Language Collections: Second Supplement, 6 vols. 1977. Set. lib. bdg. 840.00 (ISBN 0-8161-0037-3). G K Hall.
--Catalogs of the Western Language Serials & Newspaper Collection, 3 Vols. 1969. 230.00 (ISBN 0-8161-0167-1). G K Hall.
Survey of International Affairs, Indexes, 1920-1930. Repr. of 1932 ed. pap. 42.00, incl. suppl. vols (ISBN 0-384-58817-4). Johnson Repr.
U. S. Library Of Congress - General Reference And Bibliography Division. Guide to Bibliographic Tools for Research in Foreign Affairs. 2nd ed. LC 68-55129. (Illus.). 1968. Repr. of 1958 ed. lib. bdg. 15.00 with suppl (ISBN 0-8371-3171-5, GUBT). Greenwood.
Wright, Moorhead, et al. Essay Collections in International Relations: A Classified Bibliography. (Reference Library of Social Science: Vol. 45). (LC 76-052692). 1977. lib. bdg. 24.00 (ISBN 0-8240-9868-4). Garland Pub.

INTERNATIONAL RELATIONS–COLLECTIONS

Goldwin, Robert A. & Pearce, Tony, eds. Readings in World Politics. 2nd ed. (Orig.). 1970. pap. text ed. 6.95x (ISBN 0-19-501339-5). Oxford U Pr.
Hoffman, Stanley, ed. Contemporary Theory in International Relations. LC 77-24275. (Illus.). 1977. Repr. of 1960 ed. lib. bdg. 23.50 (ISBN 0-8371-9750-3, HOCT). Greenwood.
Vambery, Joseph T. & Vambery, Rose V. Cumulative List & Index of Treaties & International Agreements Registered with the United Nations, December 1969 Thru December 1974, 2 vols. LC 77-82663. 1977. 55.00 ea. (ISBN 0-379-00740-1). Oceana.

INTERNATIONAL RELATIONS–DICTIONARIES

Haensch, Guenther. Woerterbuch der Internationalen Beziehungen und der Politik. 2nd ed. (Ger., Eng., Fr. & Span., Dictionary of International Relations & Politics). pap. 40.00 (ISBN 3-19-006211-0, M-6993). French & Eur.

INTERNATIONAL RELATIONS–MORAL AND RELIGIOUS ASPECTS

Bawa Muhaivaddeen, M. R. The Truth & Unity of Man: Letters in Response to a Crisis. LC 80-18050. 144p. 1980. 10.00 (ISBN 0-914390-15-5); pap. 3.95 (ISBN 0-914390-14-7). Fellowship Pr PA.
Bennett, John C. Moral Tensions in International Affairs. LC 64-8199. (Ethics & Foreign Policy Ser). 1964. pap. 0.50 (ISBN 0-87641-108-1). Coun Rel & Intl.
Bennett, John C. & Seifert, Harvey. U. S. Foreign Policy & Christian Ethics. 1977. soft cover 7.95 (ISBN 0-664-24756-3). Westminster.
Kirkemo, Ronald. Between the Eagle & the Dove: The Christian & American Foreign Policy. LC 76-12300. (Illus.). 1976. pap. 4.95 (ISBN 0-87784-775-4). Inter-Varsity.
Lindsell, Harold. The Gathering Storm. 1980. pap. 5.95 (ISBN 0-8423-0986-1). Tyndale.
--The Gathering Storm. 1980. pap. 5.95 (ISBN 0-8423-0986-1). Tyndale.
Nitze, Paul H. Recovery of Ethics. (Ethics & Foreign Policy Ser). 1960. pap. 0.50 (ISBN 0-87641-104-9). Coun Rel & Intl.
Pettman, Ralph, ed. Moral Claims in World Affairs. LC 78-11431. 1979. 18.95 (ISBN 0-312-54755-2). St Martin.
Rosenau, James N. Race in International Politics: A Dialogue in Five Parts. (Monograph Ser. in World Affairs, Vol. 7: 1969-70 Ser, Pt. B). 4.00 (ISBN 0-87940-023-4). U of Denver Intl.
Thompson, Kenneth W. Christian Ethics & the Dilemmas of Foreign Policy. LC 59-15344. 1959. 12.75 (ISBN 0-8223-0175-X). Duke.
--Moral Issue in Statecraft: Twentieth-Century Approaches & Problems. LC 66-21758. (Rockwell Lectures). 1966. 8.95x (ISBN 0-8071-0812-X). La State U Pr.
--Morality & Foreign Policy. LC 79-23211. 250p. 1980. 16.95x (ISBN 0-8071-0656-9). La State U Pr.

INTERNATIONAL RELATIONS–OUTLINES, SYLLABI, ETC.

Dougherty, James E. & Pfaltzgraff, Robert L. Contending Theories of International Relations: A Comprehensive Survey. 2nd ed. 592p. 1980. pap. text ed. 18.50 scp (ISBN 0-06-045215-3, HarpC). Har-Row.

INTERNATIONAL RELATIONS–PSYCHOLOGICAL ASPECTS

Dillon, Wilton. Gifts & Nations: The Obligation to Give, Receive & Repay. (New Babylon Studies in the Social Sciences: No. 5). (Illus., Orig.). 1968. pap. text ed. 8.90x (ISBN 0-686-22435-3). Mouton.
Farrell, John C. & Smith, Asa P., eds. Image & Reality in World Politics. LC 68-18994. 140p. (Orig.). 1968. pap. 5.00x (ISBN 0-231-08588-5). Columbia U Pr.
Holsti, Ole R. Crisis Escalation War. 290p. 1972. 12.00 (ISBN 0-7735-0117-7). McGill-Queens U Pr.
Janis, Irving. Victims of Groupthink: A Psychological Study of Foreign-Policy Decisions & Fiascoes. 1973. pap. text ed. 9.25 (ISBN 0-395-14044-7). HM.
Kisker, George W., ed. World Tension: The Psychopathology of International Relations. LC 69-10114. 1969. Repr. of 1951 ed. lib. bdg. 15.75x (ISBN 0-8371-0516-1, KIIR). Greenwood.
North, Robert C., et al. Content Analysis: A Handbook with Applications for the Study of International Crisis. (Handbooks for Research in Political Behavior). 1963. pap. 6.95x (ISBN 0-8101-0176-9). Northwestern U Pr.

INTERNATIONAL RELATIONS–RESEARCH

Bertelsen, Judy S., ed. Non-State Nations in International Politics: Comparative System Analyses. LC 75-36404. 1978. text ed. 29.95 (ISBN 0-275-56320-0). Praeger.
Bobrow, Davis B. International Relations: New Approaches. LC 72-77282. 1972. pap. text ed. 3.95 (ISBN 0-02-904370-0). Free Pr.
Burton, John W. World Society. LC 71-176252. (Illus.). 250p. 1972. 26.50 (ISBN 0-521-08425-3); pap. 7.95x (ISBN 0-521-09694-4). Cambridge U Pr.
Choucri, Nazli & North, Robert. Nations in Conflict: National Growth & International Violence. LC 74-23453. (Illus.). 1975. text ed. 24.95x (ISBN 0-7167-0773-X). W H Freeman.
Cottam, Richard W. Foreign Policy Motivation: A General Theory & a Case Study. LC 76-6659. 1977. 16.95 (ISBN 0-8229-3323-3). U of Pittsburgh Pr.
Falkowski, Lawrence. Presidents, Secretaries of State & Crisis Management in U.S. Foreign Relations: A Model & Predictive Analysis. LC 77-27049. (Westview Special Studies in International Relations & U.S. Foreign Policy Ser.). (Illus.). 1978. lib. bdg. 23.75x (ISBN 0-89158-072-7); pap. text ed. 9.50x (ISBN 0-89158-073-5). Westview.
Frankel, Joseph. Contemporary International Theory & the Behavior of States. (Illus.). 144p. 1973. pap. text ed. 4.95x (ISBN 0-19-888083-9). Oxford U Pr.
Galtung, J. Essays in Peace Research: Peace & Social Structure, Vol. 3. 1978. pap. text ed. 33.00x (ISBN 87-7241-370-0). Humanities.
Gillispie, John V. & Zinnes, Dina A., eds. Mathematical Systems in International Relations Research. LC 75-23964. 1977. text ed. 45.95 (ISBN 0-275-55620-4). Praeger.
Gross, Feliks. World Politics & Tension Areas. LC 65-19520. (Illus.). 1966. 12.50x (ISBN 0-8147-0173-6). NYU Pr.
Herman, Charles F., ed. International Crises. LC 74-165102. 1973. 19.95 (ISBN 0-02-914560-0). Free Pr.

Jensen, Lloyd. Explaining Foreign Policy. 272p. (Orig.). 1982. pap. 9.95 reference (ISBN 0-13-295600-4). P-H.

Lentner, Howard H. Foreign Policy Analysis: A Comparative & Conceptual Analysis. LC 73-85554. 1974. text ed. 11.95x (ISBN 0-675-08884-4). Merrill.

Lieber, Robert J. Theory & World Politics. 176p. 1972. ref. ed. 7.95 (ISBN 0-87626-872-6); pap. text ed. 7.95 (ISBN 0-87626-871-8). Winthrop.

McGowan, Patrick J., ed. Sage International Yearbook of Foreign Policy Studies, Vol. 3. LC 72-98039. 320p. 1975. 22.50 (ISBN 0-8039-0323-5); pap. 9.95x (ISBN 0-8039-0324-3). Sage.

Riggs, Robert E. & Mykletun, I. Jostein. Beyond Functionalism: Attitudes Toward International Organization in Norway & the United States. LC 79-11306. (Illus.). 1979. 19.50x (ISBN 0-8166-0898-9). U of Minn Pr.

Rummel, R. J. The Dimensions of Nations, Vol. 1. LC 72-84054. 416p. 1972. 25.00x (ISBN 0-8039-0170-4). Sage.

Russett, Bruce M., ed. Peace, War & Numbers. LC 72-77769. 352p. 1972. 25.00x (ISBN 0-8039-0164-X). Sage.

Sullivan, Michael P., et al. Cumulation Papers in International Research, Pt. C, 1980-1981. Hopmann, P. Terrence & Zinnes, Dina A., eds. (Monograph Series in World Affairs: Vol. 18). (Orig.). 1981. pap. 5.00 (ISBN 0-87940-066-8). U of Denver Intl.

Vincent, Jack E. Factor Analysis in International Relations: Interpretation, Problem Areas, & an Application. LC 71-137854. (U of Fla. Social Sciences Monographs: No. 43). 1971. pap. 3.50 (ISBN 0-8130-0315-6). U Presses Fla.

--Factor Analysis in International Relations: Interpretation, Problem Areas, & an Application. LC 71-137854. (U of Fla. Social Sciences Monographs: No. 43). 1971. pap. 3.50 (ISBN 0-8130-0315-6). U Presses Fla.

Wilkenfeld, Jonathan, et al. Foreign Policy Behavior: The Interstate Behavior Analysis Model. LC 80-13161. (Illus.). 288p. 1980. 22.50 (ISBN 0-8039-1476-8). Sage.

World Directory of Peace Research Institutions. (Reports & Papers in the Social Sciences Ser.: No. 49). 213p. 1981. pap. 10.00 (ISBN 92-3-101902-3, U1090, UNESCO). Unipub.

Young, Oran R. Intermediaries: Third Parties in International Crises. (Center of International Studies). 1967. 28.00x (ISBN 0-691-05621-8). Princeton U Pr.

Zinnes, Dina A. Contemporary Research in International Relations: A Perspective & a Critical Assessment. LC 75-11290. (Illus.). 1976. 25.00 (ISBN 0-02-935730-6). Free Pr.

INTERNATIONAL RELATIONS–SOURCES

Dumont, Jean, et al, eds. Corps Universel Diplomatique Du Droit Des Gens, 8 Vols. LC 72-164796. Repr. of 1731 ed. Set. lib. bdg. 600.00 (ISBN 0-404-01810-6); lib. bdg. 75.00 ea. AMS Pr.

--Corps Universel Diplomatique: Supplement, 5 Vols. LC 72-953. Repr. of 1739 ed. Set. lib. bdg. 375.00 (ISBN 0-404-01820-3); lib. bdg. 75.00 ea. AMS Pr.

Hrabak, Diane E., ed. Worldwide Government Directory. LC 81-80273. 800p. 1981. 125.00 (ISBN 0-939304-00-7). Lambert Pubns.

Kenworthy, Leonard S. Free & Inexpensive Materials on World Affairs. LC 68-56447. 1969. pap. text ed. 3.50x (ISBN 0-8077-1608-1). Tchrs Coll.

Snyder, Louis L., ed. Fifty Major Documents of the Twentieth Century. (Orig.). 1955. pap. 5.95x (ISBN 0-442-00005-7, 5, Anv). Van Nos Reinhold.

INTERNATIONAL RELATIONS–STUDY AND TEACHING

Belfiglio, Valentine J. American Foreign Policy. LC 78-66047. (Illus.). 1979. pap. text ed. 8.00 (ISBN 0-8191-0681-X). U Pr of Amer.

Fenton, Thomas, ed. Education for Justice (Resource Manual) LC 74-83519. 464p. 1975. pap. 7.95x (ISBN 0-88344-119-5). Orbis Bks.

Foreign Policy Association. Great Decisions. (gr. 9-12). 1974. pap. text ed. 3.52 (ISBN 0-03-011846-8); tchr's guide 1.32 (ISBN 0-03-012301-1). HR&W.

--Great Decisions '77. LC 58-59828. (Great Decisions Ser.). (Illus.). 1977. pap. 5.00 (ISBN 0-87124-040-8). Foreign Policy.

--Great Decisions '79. LC 58-59828. (Illus.). 1979. pap. 5.00 (ISBN 0-87124-049-1). Foreign Policy.

Foreign Policy Association Editors. Great Decisions Nineteen Eighty. LC 58-59828. (Illus.). 1980. pap. 5.00 (ISBN 0-87124-056-4). Foreign Policy.

Fox, William T. American Study of International Relations. LC 67-65726. (Studies in International Affairs: No. 6). 1967. 5.95x (ISBN 0-87249-111-0); pap. 2.25x (ISBN 0-87249-008-4). U of SC Pr.

Herz, Martin F. How the Cold War Is Taught: Six American History Textbooks Examined. LC 78-11053. 82p. 1978. pap. 3.00 (ISBN 0-89633-009-5). Ethics & Public Policy.

International Studies in Six European Countries: United Kingdom, France, Federal Republic of Germany, Netherlands, Sweden, Italy. LC 76-54268. 1976. pap. 7.00 (ISBN 0-916584-03-8). Ford Found.

Knorr, Klaus & Rosenau, James N., eds. Contending Approaches to International Politics. LC 68-27404. (Center of International Studies Ser.). 1969. 21.00 (ISBN 0-691-05638-2); pap. 6.95 (ISBN 0-691-02164-3). Princeton U Pr.

McGowan, Patrick J. & Shapiro, Howard B. The Comparative Study of Foreign Policy: A Survey of Scientific Findings. LC 72-98040. (Sage Library of Social Research: Vol. 4). 1973. 18.00x (ISBN 0-8039-0258-1); pap. 8.95x (ISBN 0-8039-0207-7). Sage.

Mathisen, Trygve. Methodology in the Study of International Relations. LC 74-3753. 265p. 1974. Repr. of 1959 ed. lib. bdg. 15.50x (ISBN 0-8371-7472-4, MASI). Greenwood.

Morgan, Patrick M. Theories & Approaches to International Politics. LC 79-66439. 310p. 1975. text ed. 12.95 (ISBN 0-87855-127-1). Transaction Bks.

Pettman, Ralph. Human Behavior & World Politics: An Introduction to International Relations. LC 75-10759. 352p. text ed. 15.95 (ISBN 0-312-39760-7); pap. text ed. 7.95 (ISBN 0-312-39795-X). St Martin.

Wright, Quincy. The Study of International Relations. LC 55-5046. 1980. 34.50x (ISBN 0-89197-558-6); pap. text ed. 18.50x (ISBN 0-89197-956-5). Irvington.

INTERNATIONAL RELATIONS–YEARBOOKS

ACP States Yearbook, 1980 to 1981. 670p. 1981. pap. 257.25 (ISBN 2-8029-0014-5, ED13, Edns Delta). Unipub.

Defense Foreign Affairs Handbook 1980. Date not set. 70.00x (ISBN 0-531-03917-X). Key Bk Serv.

International Yearbook & Statesmen's Who's Who: 1974. 22nd ed. text ed. 35.00x (ISBN 0-8277-0485-2). British Bk Ctr.

Jones, Peter, ed. The International Yearbook of Foreign Policy Analysis, Vol. 2. LC 75-21728. 266p. 1976. 17.50x (ISBN 0-8448-0762-1). Crane-Russak Co.

McGowan, Pat & Kegley, Charles W., Jr., eds. Threats, Weapons, & Foreign Policy. LC 79-26659. (Sage International Yearbook of Foreign Policy Studies: Vol. 5). 324p. 1980. 22.50x (ISBN 0-8039-1154-8); pap. 9.95 (ISBN 0-8039-1155-6). Sage.

McGowan, Patrick J., ed. Sage International Yearbook of Foreign Policy Studies, Vol. 1. LC 72-98039. 320p. 1973. 22.50 (ISBN 0-8039-0202-6). Sage.

--Sage International Yearbook of Foreign Policy Studies, Vol. 2. LC 72-98039. 351p. 1974. 20.00x (ISBN 0-8039-0471-1); pap. 9.95 (ISBN 0-8039-0496-7). Sage.

Watt, D. C. Survey of International Affairs 1963. (Royal Institute of International Affairs). 1977. 55.00x (ISBN 0-19-214733-1). Oxford U Pr.

Yearbook of World Problems & Human Potential, 1976. 1000p. 1975. 65.00x (ISBN 92-834-1232-X). Intl Pubns Serv.

INTERNATIONAL RELIEF

see also Disaster Relief; Refugees, Political; also subdivisions Civilian Relief or Hospitals, Charities, etc. under names of wars

Callahan, Daniel & Clark, Phillip G., eds. Ethical Issues of Population Aid: Culture, Economics & International Assistance. 1981. text ed. 24.50x (ISBN 0-8290-0364-9). Irvington.

The Europa Yearbook 1981: A World Survey, 1981, 2 vols. 22nd ed. LC 59-2942. iii, 3600p. 1981. Set. 180.00x (ISBN 0-686-65097-2). Vol. 1 (ISBN 0-905118-59-6). Vol. 2 (ISBN 0-905118-60-X). Intl Pubns Serv.

Mooneyham, W. Stanley. Sea of Heartbreak. (Illus.). 1980. pap. 2.95 (ISBN 0-88270-414-1). Logos.

Myrdal, Alva, et al. America's Role in International Social Welfare. 7.00 (ISBN 0-8446-1320-7). Peter Smith.

Roddy, Lee. On Wings of Love. 128p. 1981. pap. 3.95 (ISBN 0-8407-5758-1). Nelson.

Yarrow, C. H. Quaker Experiences in International Conciliation. LC 78-7415. 1978. 15.00x (ISBN 0-300-02260-3). Yale U Pr.

INTERNATIONAL RIVERS

Garretson, Albert H., et al. The Law of International Drainage Basins. LC 67-25904. 1968. 45.00 (ISBN 0-379-00320-1). Oceana.

Rios y Lagos Internacionales-Utilizacion Para Fines Agricolas E Industriales: Documento De Antecedentes. 4th rev. ed. (Serie De Derecho y Relaciones Internacionales). (Span.). 1971. 3.00 (ISBN 0-8270-5210-3). OAS.

INTERNATIONAL SALES

see Export Sales

INTERNATIONAL SECURITY

see Security, International

INTERNATIONAL SOCIALIST CONGRESS

Bernstein, Samuel. First International in America. LC 62-52478. 1962. 15.00x (ISBN 0-678-00102-2). Kelley.

Drachkovitch, Milorad M., ed. The Revolutionary Internationals, 1864-1943. 1966. 15.00x (ISBN 0-8047-0293-4). Stanford U Pr.

Fainsod, Merle. International Socialism & the World War. 1966. lib. bdg. 15.50x (ISBN 0-374-92679-4). Octagon.

Foster, William Z. History of the Three Internationals: The World Socialist & Communist Movements from 1848 to the Present. LC 68-30822. (Illus.). 1968. Repr. of 1955 ed. lib. bdg. 34.25x (ISBN 0-8371-0076-3, FOTI). Greenwood.

Guillaume, James. Internationale: Documents & Souvenirs Eighteen Sixty-Four to Seventy-Eight, 4 Vols. in 2. (Fr). 1969. 91.00 (ISBN 0-8337-1487-2). B Franklin.

Haupt, Georges. Socialism & the Great War: The Collapse of the Second International. 280p. 1972. 24.95x (ISBN 0-19-827184-0). Oxford U Pr.

Joll, James. The Second International 1889-1914. 2nd ed. 1975. 21.50x (ISBN 0-7100-7966-4). Routledge & Kean.

Selections from the Writings of European Socialists on World War I: The Crisis in German Socialism. Incl. Krise und Die Aufgaben der Internationalem Sozialdemokratie. Axelrod, Paul; Internationale der Arbeiter Klass und der Europaische Krieg. Bernstein, Eduard; Vor und Nach Dem 4 August 1914. Borchardt, Julian; Klassenkampf Gegen Den Krieg. Liebknecht, Karl; Militarimus, Krieg und Arbeiterklasse. Luxemburg, Rosa. LC 77-147524. (Library of War & Peace; Labor, Socialism & War). lib. bdg. 38.00 (ISBN 0-8240-0312-8). Garland Pub.

INTERNATIONAL SPACE COOPERATION

see Astronautics–International Cooperation

INTERNATIONAL SYSTEM OF UNITS

see Metric System

INTERNATIONAL TELEPHONE AND TELEGRAPH CORPORATION

Sampson, Anthony. The Sovereign State of ITT. LC 79-96745. 335p. 1980. pap. 7.95 (ISBN 0-8128-6060-8). Stein & Day.

INTERNATIONAL TRADE

see Commerce

INTERNATIONAL TRADE REGULATION

see Foreign Trade Regulation

INTERNATIONAL TRAVEL REGULATIONS

see also Aliens; Emigration and Immigration Law; Foreign Exchange–Law

Gear, H. S. & Deutschman, Z. Disease Control & International Travel: A Review of the International Sanitary Regulations, Vol. 10, Nos. 9-10. (Illus., Eng, Fr, Span.). pap. 1.20 (ISBN 92-4-158001-1). World Health.

INTERNATIONAL TRIBUNALS

see International Courts

INTERNATIONAL TRUSTEESHIPS

see also Mandates; State Succession

Hall, H. D. Mandates, Dependencies, & Trusteeship. (Studies in the Administration of International Law & Organization). 1948. pap. 25.00 (ISBN 0-527-00887-7). Kraus Repr.

Sady, Emil J. The United Nations & Dependent Peoples. LC 74-4730. 205p. 1974. Repr. of 1956 ed. lib. bdg. 15.00x (ISBN 0-8371-7483-X, SAUN). Greenwood.

Toussaint, Charmian E. The Trusteeship System of the United Nations. LC 75-27689. 1976. Repr. of 1956 ed. lib. bdg. 18.25x (ISBN 0-8371-8460-6, TOTS). Greenwood.

INTERNATIONAL UNION, UNITED AUTOMOBILE, AEROSPACE, AND AGRICULTURAL IMPLEMENT WORKERS OF AMERICA

El-Messidi, Kathy G. The Bargain: The Story Behind the Thirty Year Honeymoon of GM & UAW. LC 78-26325. 1979. 10.00 (ISBN 0-8424-0120-2). Nellen Pub.

Friedlander, Peter. The Emergence of a UAW Local, 1936-1939: A Study in Class & Culture. LC 74-26020. 1975. 9.95 (ISBN 0-8229-3295-4). U of Pittsburgh Pr.

Howe, I. & Widick, B. J. The UAW & Walter Reuther. LC 72-2375. (FDR & the Era of the New Deal Ser.). 324p. 1973. Repr. of 1949 ed. lib. bdg. 29.50 (ISBN 0-306-70485-4). Da Capo.

Kornhauser, Arthur & Sheppard, Harold. When Labor Votes. LC 76-2533. (Illus.). 352p. 1976. Repr. of 1956 ed. lib. bdg. 23.75x (ISBN 0-8371-8787-7, KOWL). Greenwood.

Kruchko, John G. Birth of a Union Local: The History of UAW Local 674, Norwood, Ohio, 1933-1940. LC 72-619603. 1972. pap. 1.75 (ISBN 0-87546-046-1). NY Sch Indus Rel.

Marquart, Frank. An Auto Worker's Journal: The UAW from Crusade to One-Party Union. LC 75-11993. 200p. 1975. 10.95 (ISBN 0-271-01196-3). Pa St U Pr.

Meier, August & Rudwick, Elliott. Black Detroit & the Rise of the UAW. (Illus.). 1979. 17.95 (ISBN 0-19-502561-X). Oxford U Pr.

Reuther, Victor G. The Brothers Reuther & the Story of the U.A.W. A Memoir. 1979. pap. 8.95 (ISBN 0-395-27515-6). HM.

Snyder, Carl D. White-Collar Workers & the UAW. LC 72-88954. 224p. 1973. 12.50 (ISBN 0-252-00286-5). U of Ill Pr.

INTERNATIONAL UNION OF MINE, MILL AND SMELTER WORKERS

Suggs, George G., Jr. Colorado's War on Militant Unionism: James H. Peabody & the Western Federation of Miners. LC 70-39624. 242p. 1972. 14.50x (ISBN 0-8143-1471-6). Wayne St U Pr.

INTERNATIONAL UNION OF OPERATING ENGINEERS

Mangum, Garth L. Operating Engineers: The Economic History of a Trade Union. LC 63-19144. (Wertheim Publications in Industrial Relations Ser). (Illus.). 1964. 18.50x (ISBN 0-674-64050-0). Harvard U Pr.

INTERNATIONAL VISITORS

see Visitors, Foreign

INTERNATIONAL WORKINGMEN'S ASSOCIATION

Lawrence & Wishart Ltd., ed. Documents of the First Council of the International Working Men's Association: 1864-1872, 5 vols. 705p. 1974. 60.00x (ISBN 0-8464-0340-4). Beekman Pubs.

Mattern, Carolyn J., ed. Papers of the International Workingmen's Association: Guide to a Microfilm Edition. (Guides to Historical Resources Ser.). 1972. pap. 1.00 (ISBN 0-87020-151-4). State Hist Soc Wis.

INTERNATIONAL YEARS OF THE QUIET SUN, 1964-1965

Annals of the International Year of the Quiet Sun. Incl. Vol. 1. Geophysical Measurements: Techniques, Observational Schedules & Treatment of Data. 1968. 25.00x (ISBN 0-262-09005-8); Vol. 2. Solar & Geophysical Events 1960-1965 (Calendar Record) 1968. 20.00x (ISBN 0-262-09006-6); Vol. 3. The Proton Flare Project. 1969. 25.00x (ISBN 0-262-09007-4); Vol. 4. Solar-Terrestrial Physics: Solar Aspects. 1969. 25.00x (ISBN 0-262-09008-2); Vol. 5. Solar-Terrestrial Physics: Terrestrial Aspects. 1969. 25.00x (ISBN 0-262-09009-0); Vol. 6. Survey of IQSY Observations & Bibliography. 1970. 30.00x (ISBN 0-262-09010-4); Vol. 7. Sources & Availability of IQSY Data. 1970. 25.00x (ISBN 0-262-09011-2). MIT Pr.

Dolgin, I. M. & Gavrilova, L. A. Meteorological Conditions in the Arctic During the International Year of the Quiet Sun. 122p. 1971. 11.50 (ISBN 0-7065-1126-3, Pub. by IPST). Intl Schol Bk Serv.

INTERNATIONALER BUND FREIER EVANGELISCHER GEMEINDEN

Olson, Arnold T. Believers Only. LC 64-22145. 6.95 (ISBN 0-911802-00-2). Free Church Pubns.

INTERNATIONALISM

see also Nationalism; also headings beginning with the word International, e.g. International Cooperation; International Organization

Boy Scouts of America. Citizenship in the World. LC 19-600. (Illus.). 64p. (gr. 6-12). 1972. pap. 0.70x (ISBN 0-8395-3254-7, 3254). BSA.

Cooper, Sandi, ed. Internationalism in Nineteenth Century Europe. LC 74-147743. (Library of War & Peace; Documentary Anthologies). lib. bdg. 38.00 (ISBN 0-8240-0505-8). Garland Pub.

Davis, Jerome. Citizens of One World. (Orig.). 1961. pap. 1.95 (ISBN 0-8065-0185-5, X-68). Citadel Pr.

Earle, Edward M., ed. Nationalism & Internationalism: Essays Inscribed to Carlton J. H. Hayes. LC 74-4429. xvii, 508p. 1974. Repr. of 1951 ed. lib. bdg. 25.00x (ISBN 0-374-92447-3). Octagon.

Foreman, Clark. The New Internationalism. facsimile ed. LC 71-37342. (Select Bibliographies Reprint Ser). Repr. of 1934 ed. 13.00 (ISBN 0-8369-6689-9). Arno.

Goodman, Elliot R. The Soviet Design for a World State. LC 60-7625. (Studies of the Russian Institute). 512p. 1960. 25.00x (ISBN 0-231-02339-1). Columbia U Pr.

Josephson, Harold. James T. Shotwell & the Rise of Internationalism in America. LC 74-2874. (Illus.). 330p. 1975. 16.50 (ISBN 0-8386-1524-4). Fairleigh Dickinson.

Leone, Bruno, ed. Internationalism: Opposing Viewpoints. (ISMS Ser.). (Illus.). (gr. 9-12). 1978. 8.95 (ISBN 0-912616-59-8); pap. 3.95 (ISBN 0-912616-58-X). Greenhaven.

Meinecke, Friedrich. Cosmopolitanism & the National State: Welburgertum Und Nationalstaat. Kimber, Robert B., tr. LC 65-17150. 1970. 25.00 (ISBN 0-691-05177-1). Princeton U Pr.

Mische, Gerald & Mische, Patricia. Toward a Human World Order: Beyond the National Security Straitjacket. LC 76-41440. 412p. 1977. 9.95 (ISBN 0-8091-0216-1); pap. 2.95 (ISBN 0-8091-1977-3). Paulist Pr.

Pentland, Charles. International Theory & European Integration. LC 73-10832. 1973. 17.95 (ISBN 0-02-925210-5). Free Pr.

Semyonov, V. Nations & Internationalism. 303p. 1979. 6.30 (ISBN 0-8285-1503-4, Pub. by Progress Pubs Russia). Imported Pubns.

Shafer, Boyd C. Nationalism & Internationalism: Belonging in Human Experience. 1981. pap. 4.95 (ISBN 0-89874-260-9). Krieger.

Smith, Elise C., ed. Toward Internationalism: Readings in Cross-Cultural Communication. LC 78-17153. 1979. pap. text ed. 9.95 (ISBN 0-88377-123-3). Newbury Hse.

Ward, Barbara. Five Ideas That Change the World. 1959. pap. 5.95x (ISBN 0-393-09438-3, NortonC). Norton.

INTERNATIONALIZED TERRITORIES
see also International Trusteeships; Mandates

INTERNMENT CAMPS
see Concentration Camps

INTERNS (CLINICAL PSYCHOLOGY)

Finn, Michael H. & Brown, Fred, eds. Training for Clinical Psychology: Proceedings of the Springfield Mt. Sinai Conferences on Intern Training in Clinical Psychology. LC 59-13114. 1960. text ed. 15.00 (ISBN 0-8236-6620-4). Intl Univs Pr.

INTERNS (EDUCATION)
see also Student Teaching

Meyers, Edward C. & Cannon, Wendell E. The Recruitment & Training of Teacher Interns. 150p. 1960. 3.95 (ISBN 0-88474-008-0). U of S Cal Pr.

National Society for Internships & Experiential Education. The Experienced Hand: A Student's Handbook on Getting an Internship & Making the Most of It. Date not set. price not set. Carroll Pr.

INTERNS (MEDICINE)

Gottlieb, Arlan J., et al. The Whole Internist Catalog: A Compendium of Clues to Diagnosis & Management. LC 79-66034. (Illus.). 509p. 1980. pap. text ed. 19.50 (ISBN 0-7216-4179-2). Saunders.

Moser, Robert H. House Officer Training: A Casual Perspective. (American Lecture Medical Writing & Communication). 128p. 1970. photocopy ed. spiral 12.75 (ISBN 0-398-01357-8). C C Thomas.

Pullen, Roscoe. The Internship. (American Lecture Internal Medicine). 1952. photocopy ed. spiral 4.95 (ISBN 0-398-04397-3). C C Thomas.

Sobol, Harriet. The Interns. (Illus.). (gr. 6 up). Date not set. 8.95 (ISBN 0-686-76709-8). Coward.

INTEROCEANIC CANALS
see Canals

INTEROCEPTION

Kezdi, P., ed. Baroreceptors & Hypertension. 1967. 67.00 (ISBN 0-08-012488-7). Pergamon.

INTERPERSONAL COMMUNICATION

Adler, Ron, et al. Interplay: The Process of Interpersonal Communication. LC 80-11169. 306p. (Orig.). 1980. pap. text ed. 12.95 (ISBN 0-03-049586-5, HoltC); tchrs. manual avail. (ISBN 0-03-054161-1); skills manual avail. HR&W.

Argyle, Michael & Trower, Peter. Person to Person: Ways of Communicating. (Life Cycle Ser.). 1979. pap. text ed. 4.95 scp (ISBN 0-06-384746-9, HarpC). Har-Row.

Arnold, William E. & Hirsch, Robert O. Communicating Through Behavior. (Illus.). 300p. 1977. pap. text ed. 10.95 (ISBN 0-8299-0133-7). West Pub.

Bach, George R. & Wyden, Peter. The Intimate Enemy: How to Fight Fair in Love & Marriage. 384p. 1981. pap. 2.95 (ISBN 0-380-00392-9, 54452). Avon.

Barker, Larry L., et al. Groups in Process: An Introduction to Small Group Communication. LC 78-17202. 1979. 15.95 (ISBN 0-13-365361-7). P-H.

Barnhart, Sarah A. Introduction to Interpersonal Communication. 1976. pap. text ed. 6.95 scp (ISBN 0-690-00855-4, HarpC). Har-Row.

Bennett, A. E., ed. Communications Between Doctors & Patients. (Nuffield Publications Ser.). 1976. pap. 7.00x (ISBN 0-19-721392-8). Oxford U Pr.

Blakeman, John, et al. IPC: Interpersonal Communication Skills for Correctional Management. 118p. (Orig.). 1977. pap. text ed. 8.95x (ISBN 0-914234-69-2); Trainer Guide. pap. text ed. 12.95x (ISBN 0-914234-70-6). Human Res Dev Pr.

Brooks, W. D. & Vogel, R. A., eds. Interpersonal Communication. LC 76-44141. (Ser. in Speech Communication). 1977. pap. text ed. 5.95 (ISBN 0-8465-7603-1); instr's. guide 3.95 (ISBN 0-8465-7607-4). Benjamin-Cummings.

Brooks, William D. & Emmert, Philip. Interpersonal Communication. 2nd ed. 368p. 1980. pap. write for info. (ISBN 0-697-04172-7); instrs.' manual avail. (ISBN 0-697-04180-8). Wm C Brown.

Bullowa, Margaret, ed. Before Speech. LC 78-51671. (Illus.). 1979. 42.50 (ISBN 0-521-22031-9); pap. 11.95 (ISBN 0-521-29522-X). Cambridge U Pr.

Carr, Jacquelyn B. Communicating & Relating. LC 78-58969. 1979. pap. text ed. 12.95 (ISBN 0-8053-1820-8); instr's guide 3.95 (ISBN 0-8053-1821-6). Benjamin-Cummings.

Devito, Joseph A. The Interpersonal Communication Book. 2nd ed. (Illus.). 1980. pap. text ed. 13.50 scp (ISBN 0-06-041654-8, HarpC); instructional strategies avail. (ISBN 0-06-361635-1). Har-Row.

Eadie & Kline. Orientations to Interpersonal Communication. Applbaum, Ronald & Hart, Roderick, eds. (MODCOM Modules in Speech Communication Ser.). 1976. pap. text ed. 2.50 (ISBN 0-574-22512-9, 13-5512). SRA.

Egan, Gerard. You & Me: The Skills of Communicating & Relating to Others. LC 77-6475. (Illus.). 1977. pap. text ed. 10.95 (ISBN 0-8185-0238-X); instructor's manual free (ISBN 0-685-79911-5). Brooks-Cole.

Eglash, Albert. Humanistic Communication in Love, Sex, & Intimacy. LC 79-54710. (Beyond Assertion Training: Humanistic Communication Skills Ser.: No. 2). (Illus.). 1980. pap. 20.00 (ISBN 0-935320-10-5). Quest Pr.

--Humanistic Communication Skills for Nurses: Sharing, Caring, Trusting. LC 79-54709. (Beyond Assertion Training: Humanistic Communication Skills Ser.: No. 4). (Illus., Orig.). 1980. 30.00 (ISBN 0-935320-09-1). Quest Pr.

Fairfield, James G. T. When You Don't Agree. LC 77-3133. 1977. pap. text ed. 3.95 (ISBN 0-8361-1819-7). Herald Pr.

Faules, Don F. & Alexander, Dennis C. Communication & Social Behavior: A Symbolic Interaction Perspective. LC 76-46610. (Speech Communication Ser.). (Illus.). 1978. pap. text ed. 9.95 (ISBN 0-201-01982-5); instr's manual 3.00 (ISBN 0-201-01979-5). A-W.

Forrest, Mary & Olson, Margot. Exploring Speech Communication: An Introduction. 433p. 1981. pap. text ed. 13.50 (ISBN 0-8299-0381-X). West Pub.

Freidman, Paul G. Interpersonal Communication: Innovations in Instruction. 160p. 1978. pap. 7.50 (ISBN 0-686-63720-8, 1497-9-06). NEA.

Gaw. It Depends: Appropriate Interpersonal Communication. LC 81-416. 393p. 1981. 9.95 (ISBN 0-88284-124-6). Alfred Pub.

Gearhart, Sally & Rennie, Susan. A Feminist Tarot. 4th ed. (Illus.). 1981. pap. 5.00 (ISBN 0-930436-01-6). Persephone.

Giffin, Kim & Barnes, Richard. Trust of Self & Others. (Interpersonal Communication Ser.). (Illus.). 96p. 1976. pap. text ed. 5.95 (ISBN 0-675-08647-7). Merrill.

Giffin, Kim & Patton, Bobby R. Basic Readings in Interpersonal Communication: Theory & Application. 2nd ed. (Auer Ser.). 272p. 1976. pap. text ed. 11.50 scp (ISBN 0-06-042329-3, HarpC). Har-Row.

--Fundamentals of Interpersonal Communication. 2nd ed. (Auer Ser.). 263p. 1976. text ed. 15.50 scp (ISBN 0-06-042315-3, HarpC); instructor's manual free (ISBN 0-06-362351-X). Har-Row.

Gilmore, Susan K. & Fraleigh, Patrick W. Communication at Work. LC 80-69467. (Illus.). 150p. (Orig.). 1980. 6.95 (ISBN 0-938070-00-2). Friendly Pr.

Goldman, Alan. Unveiling the Self: Frontiers in Human Communication. 1979. pap. text ed. 15.95 (ISBN 0-8403-2072-8). Kendall-Hunt.

Gottman, John, et al. A Couple's Guide to Communication. LC 76-23968. 1976. pap. text ed. 9.95 (ISBN 0-87822-127-1). Res Press.

Gulley, Halbert & Leathers, Dale G. Communication & Group Process. 3rd ed. LC 76-44532. 1977. text ed. 15.95 (ISBN 0-03-089406-9, HoltC). HR&W.

Gumpert, Gary & Cathcart, Robert, eds. Inter-Media: Interpersonal Communication in a Media World. LC 78-12227. 1979. 9.95x (ISBN 0-19-502505-9). Oxford U Pr.

Hargie, Owen, et al. Social Skills in Interpersonal Communication. 198p. 1981. 28.00x (ISBN 0-7099-0279-4, Pub. by Croom Helm LTD England). Biblio Dist.

Hess, Herbert J. & Tucker, Charles O. Talking About Relationships. 2nd ed. 80p. 1980. pap. text ed. 3.50x (ISBN 0-917974-47-6). Waveland Pr.

Hinz, Robert B. Intimacy: A Game of Discovery. LC 80-50527. (Illus.). 68p. (Orig.). 1980. pap. 4.95 (ISBN 0-9604470-0-8). Pisces Eye.

Howard, J. Grant. Trauma of Transparency: A Biblical Approach to Inter-Personal Communication. 2nd ed. (Critical Concern Bks.). 235p. (Orig.). 1981. pap. 5.95 (ISBN 0-930014-73-1); study guide 2.95 (ISBN 0-930014-74-X). Multnomah.

Huseman, Richard C., et al. Readings in Interpersonal & Organizational Communication. 3rd ed. 1977. text ed. 15.95 (ISBN 0-205-05900-7, 485777-1). Allyn.

Jandt, Fred E. The Process of Interpersonal Communication. 1976. pap. text ed. 9.50 scp (ISBN 0-06-384253-X, HarpC); tchr's ed. free (ISBN 0-06-373300-5). Har-Row.

Johnson, David W. Reaching Out: Interpersonal Effectiveness & Self-Actualization. 2nd ed. (Illus.). 320p. 1981. text ed. 15.95 (ISBN 0-13-753327-6); pap. text ed. 11.95 (ISBN 0-13-753319-5). P-H.

Kelley, Kay. Bette Banana Sings the Blues, Banana Style. Mersereau, R. E., ed. LC 78-63575. (Illus.). 1979. pap. 6.95x (ISBN 0-917466-04-7). Spec Features Wkshp.

Kelly, Eugene W., Jr. Effective Interpersonal Communication: A Manual for Skill Development. 1977. pap. text ed. 7.50x (ISBN 0-8191-0125-7). U Pr of Amer.

Keltner, John W. Elements of Interpersonal Communication. 1973. pap. 9.95x (ISBN 0-534-00290-0). Wadsworth Pub.

Koile, Earl. Listening As a Way of Becoming. LC 76-48520. 1977. 5.95 (ISBN 0-87680-510-1, 61001). Word Bks.

Larson, Roland & Larson, Doris. I Need to Have You Know Me. (Orig.). 1980. pap. 7.95 (ISBN 0-03-053431-3). Winston Pr.

Lucero, Maryetta. Why Don't You Love Yourself: Some Information on Dealing with Yourself & Others. LC 75-46072. 1976. pap. 3.50 (ISBN 0-89016-021-X). Lightning Tree.

McCroskey, James C., et al. Introduction to Interpersonal Communication. LC 71-126966. 1971. text ed. 14.95x (ISBN 0-13-485425-X). P-H.

MacRae, Donald L., et al. You & Others: An Introduction to Interpersonal Communication. (Illus.). 1976. pap. text ed. 9.95 (ISBN 0-07-082256-5, C). McGraw.

Miller, Gerald R. & Steinberg, Mark. Between People: A New Analysis of Interpersonal Communication. LC 74-18926. (Illus.). 352p. 1975. text ed. 14.95 (ISBN 0-574-17501-6, 13-5500); study activity guide 3.25 (ISBN 0-574-17502-4, 13-5502). SRA.

Miller, Sherod, et al. Straight Talk: How to Improve Your Relationships Through Better Communication. LC 80-51251. 1980. 13.95 (ISBN 0-89256-143-2). Rawson Wade.

Morse, Ben W. & Phelps, Lynn A. Interpersonal Communication: A Relational Perspective. 1980. 15.95x (ISBN 0-8087-3963-8). Burgess.

Moulton, Eugene R. & Held, McDonald W. Communication: A Creative Process. LC 76-1043. 1976. pap. text ed. 10.95x (ISBN 0-8087-1378-7). Burgess.

Pace, R. Wayne & Boren, Robert. R. The Human Transaction: Facets, Functions, & Forms of Interpersonal Communication. 300p. 1973. text ed. 10.95x (ISBN 0-673-05840-9). Scott F.

Patton, Bobby R. & Giffin, Kim. Interpersonal Communication in Action: Basic Text & Readings. 3rd ed. (Illus.). 499p. 1980. pap. text ed. 13.50 scp (ISBN 0-06-045062-2, HarpC); avail. (ISBN 0-06-364975-6). Har-Row.

Patton, Bobby R. & Patton, Bonnie R. Female-Male: Living Together. (Interpersonal Communication Ser.). (Illus.). 1976. pap. text ed. 5.95 (ISBN 0-675-08643-4); instructor's manual 3.95 (ISBN 0-686-67248-8). Merrill.

Peitchinis, Jacquelyn. Staff-Patient Communication in the Health Services. LC 76-15415. 1976. text ed. 11.50 (ISBN 0-8261-2040-7); pap. text ed. 6.95 (ISBN 0-8261-2041-5). Springer Pub.

Pine, John C., ed. Interpersonal Communication. 2nd ed. LC 80-54. 88p. 1980. pap. 7.50x (ISBN 0-89854-057-7). U of GA Inst Govt.

Reid, Paul E. A Model of Interpersonal Speech Communication. LC 79-64197. 1979. pap. text ed. 6.25 (ISBN 0-8191-0755-7). U Pr of Amer.

Riley, Donald P., et al. Parent-Child Communication. LC 77-13652. (Workshop Models for Family Life Education Ser.). 1977. plastic 8.95 (ISBN 0-87304-157-7). Family Serv.

Roloff, Michael E. Interpersonal Communication: The Social Exchange Approach. LC 81-4451. (The Sage CommText Ser.: Vol. 6). (Illus.). 149p. 1981. 14.00 (ISBN 0-8039-1604-3); pap. 6.95 (ISBN 0-8039-1605-1). Sage.

Rossiter, Charles M. & Pearce, W. B., Jr. Communicating Personally: A Theory of Interpersonal Communication and Human Relationships. LC 74-23546. (SC Ser: No. 21). 286p. 1975. pap. 6.50 (ISBN 0-672-61352-2). Bobbs.

Ruben, Brent D. Interact 2. 1977. wkbk. 7.95x (ISBN 0-89529-025-1). Avery Pub.

Rush, John A. Communication Effectiveness (Advanced) Training Manual. (Illus.). 1978. pap. text ed. 11.00x (ISBN 0-920124-05-4). Humanity Pubns.

Russell, Charles, et al. Interpersonal Communication for Pharmacists: An Interactionist Approach. 176p. 1981. 11.95 (ISBN 0-8385-4306-5). ACC.

Sathre-Eldon, et al. Let's Talk: An Introduction to Interpersonal Communication. 3rd ed. 1980. pap. text ed. 7.95x (ISBN 0-673-15376-2). Scott F.

Savary, Louis & Paolini, Mary. Interpersonal Communication. LC 75-1432. (Communication Eduction Ser.). (gr. 9-12). 1975. pap. text ed. 4.00 (ISBN 0-8294-0245-4); tchrs. guide 1.50 (ISBN 0-685-58315-5). Loyola.

Schwartz, Gary, et al. Love & Commitment. LC 79-25460. (Sociological Observations: Vol. 9). (Illus.). 271p. 1980. 20.00 (ISBN 0-8039-1419-9); pap. 9.95 (ISBN 0-8039-1420-2). Sage.

Shuter, Robert. Understanding Misunderstandings: Exploring Interpersonal Communication. 1978. pap. text ed. 10.50 scp (ISBN 0-06-046132-2, HarpC). Har-Row.

Smith, R. Dennis & Williamson, L. Keith. Interpersonal Communication: Roles, Rules, Strategies & Games. 2nd ed. 370p. 1981. pap. text ed. write for info. (ISBN 0-697-04182-4); instr.' manual avail. (ISBN 0-697-04188-3). Wm C Brown.

Solomon, Arthur, et al. Interpersonal Communication: A Cross-Disciplinary Approach. 120p. 1970. 12.75 (ISBN 0-398-01810-3). C C Thomas.

Stewart, John. Bridges Not Walls. 2nd ed. LC 76-46606. (Speech Communication Ser.). 1977. pap. 8.95 (ISBN 0-201-07227-0). A-W.

Stewart, John & D'Angelo, Gary. Together-Communicating Interpersonally. 2nd ed. LC 79-26426. (Speech Communication Ser.). (Illus.). 1980. pap. 11.50 (ISBN 0-201-07506-7). A-W.

Strayhorn, Joseph M., Jr. Talking It Out: A Guide to Effective Communication & Problem Solving. LC 77-81298. 1977. pap. text ed. 5.95 (ISBN 0-87822-140-9). Res Press.

Tubbs, Stewart L. & Moss, Sylvia. Interpersonal Communication. 2nd ed. 299p. 1981. pap. text ed. 10.95 (ISBN 0-394-32684-9). Random.

Verderber, Rudolph F. & Verderber, Kathleen S. Inter-Act: Using Interpersonal Communication Skills. 2nd ed. 368p. 1980. pap. text ed. 10.95x (ISBN 0-534-00785-6). Wadsworth Pub.

Weaver, Richard L., II. Understanding Interpersonal Communication. 2nd ed. 1981. pap. text ed. 10.95x (ISBN 0-673-15436-X). Scott F.

Webb, Ralph, Jr. Interpersonal Speech Communication: Principles & Practices. (Illus.). 320p. 1975. pap. text ed. 14.95 (ISBN 0-13-475103-5). P-H.

Weinhold, Barry & Elliott, Lynn C. Transpersonal Communication. LC 79-10871. (Illus.). 1979. text ed. 9.95 (ISBN 0-13-930396-0, Spec); pap. 4.95 (ISBN 0-13-930388-X). P-H.

Wells, Theodora. Keeping Your Cool Under Fire: Communicating Non-Defensively. Manley, Robert G., ed. (Illus.). 1979. 11.95 (ISBN 0-07-069250-5). McGraw.

Yudkovitz, Elaine, et al. Communication Therapy in Childhood Schizophrenia: An Auditory Monitoring Approach. LC 76-46358. 224p. 1976. 19.25 (ISBN 0-8089-0993-2). Grune.

Ziajka, Alan. Prelinguistic Communication in Infancy. 192p. 1981. 21.95 (ISBN 0-03-058649-6). Praeger.

INTERPERSONAL PERCEPTION
see Social Perception

INTERPERSONAL RELATIONS
see also Conflict of Generations; Dependency (Psychology); Group Relations Training; Interpersonal Communication; Intimacy (Psychology); Personal Space; Machiavellianism (Psychology); Social Participation; Teacher-Student Relationships

Adam, B. A. The Survival of Domination: Inferiorization & Everyday Life. 1978. 15.00 (ISBN 0-444-99047-X, Pub. by Elsevier). Greenwood.

Ainsworth, Mary D., et al. Patterns of Attachment: A Psychological Study of the Strange Situation. LC 78-13303. 391p. 1979. 24.95 (ISBN 0-470-26534-5). Halsted Pr.

Allen, Bud & Bosta, Diana. Library of Lesson Plans: Vol. 2, No. 4, Human Relations. 55p. 1981. vinyl 29.95x (ISBN 0-939438-12-7). Rae John.

Allen, Graham A. Sociology of Friendship & Kinship. (Studies in Sociology Ser.). (Orig.). 1979. text ed. 22.50x (ISBN 0-04-301104-7); pap. text ed. 8.95x (ISBN 0-04-301105-5). Allen Unwin.

Alloway, Thomas, ed. Communication & Affect - a Comparative Approach. 1972. 23.00 (ISBN 0-12-053050-3). Acad Pr.

Andelin, Helen. Fascinating Womanhood. 320p. 1980. pap. 2.75 (ISBN 0-553-13988-6). Bantam.

Arnold, William V., et al. Divorce: Prevention or Survival. LC 77-22066. 1977. pap. 4.95 (ISBN 0-664-24142-5). Westminster.

Athos, A. & Gabarro, J. Interpersonal Behavior. 1978. 23.95 (ISBN 0-13-475004-7). P-H.

Austin, William G. & Worchel, Stephen. The Social Psychology of Intergroup Relations. LC 78-13197. (Psychology Ser.). 1979. text ed. 18.95 (ISBN 0-8185-0278-9). Brooks-Cole.

Bach, George R. & Deutsch, Ronald M. Pairing. 1971. pap. 2.95 (ISBN 0-380-00394-5, 55350). Avon.

Bales, R. F. Personality & Interpersonal Behavior. LC 71-84682. 1970. text ed. 15.95 (ISBN 0-03-080450-7, HoltC). HR&W.

Ball, Donald W. Microecology: Social Situations & Intimate Space. LC 72-10541. (Studies in Sociology Ser). 40p. 1973. pap. text ed. 2.50 (ISBN 0-672-61209-7). Bobbs.

Balswick, Jack. Why I Can't Say I Love You. LC 77-92472. 1978. 6.95 (ISBN 0-8499-0079-4, 0079-4). Word Bks.

Bannister, Kathleen & Pincus, Lily. Shared Phantasy in Marital Problems: Therapy in a Four Person Relationship. 80p. 1971. 3.50x (ISBN 0-686-77025-0, CBO-903-C). Natl Assn Soc Wkrs.

Barbara, Dominick A. How to Make People Listen to You. 188p. 1971. pap. 9.75 photocopy ed. spiral (ISBN 0-398-02223-2). C C Thomas.

Barnlund, Dean C. Public & Private Self in Japan & the United States. (Illus.). 201p. 1975. pap. 13.50x (ISBN 0-89955-244-7, Pub. by Simul). Intl Schol Bk Serv.

Beardsley, Lou. Mothers-in-Law Can Be Fun. LC 80-84763. 1981. pap. 4.95 (ISBN 0-89081-281-0). Harvest Hse.

Becvar, Raphael J. Skills for Effective Communication: A Guide to Building Relationships. LC 73-19914. (Wiley Self-Teaching Guides). 218p. 1974. pap. text ed. 7.95x (ISBN 0-471-06143-3). Wiley.

Bell, Gary & Seay, Davin R. Lost but Not Forever. LC 80-81472. 1981. pap. 4.95 (ISBN 0-89081-253-5). Harvest Hse.

Bell, Robert. Having It Your Way: The Strategy of Settling Everyday Conflicts. (Illus.). 1977. 8.95 (ISBN 0-393-01164-X). Norton.

Bennis, Warren, et al. Essays in Interpersonal Dynamics. 1979. pap. text ed. 8.95x (ISBN 0-256-02231-3). Dorsey.

Berenson, F. M. Understanding Persons: Personal & Impersonal Relations. 19.95 (ISBN 0-312-83154-4). St Martin.

Bernhard, Yetta. Self-Care. LC 75-9448. 1975. 11.95 (ISBN 0-89087-110-8); pap. 7.95 (ISBN 0-89087-111-6). Celestial Arts.

Berscheid, Ellen & Walster, Elaine H. Interpersonal Attraction. 2nd ed. LC 77-77726. (Topics in Social Psychology). (Illus.). 1978. pap. text ed. 8.95 (ISBN 0-201-00569-7). A-W.

Billig, M. Social Psychology & Intergroup Relations. (European Monographs in Social Psychology). 1976. 57.50 (ISBN 0-12-097950-0). Acad Pr.

Bishop, Beata & McNeill, Pat. The Eggshell Ego: An Irreverent Look at Today's Male. LC 77-8249. 1978. pap. 3.95 (ISBN 0-89490-021-8). Enslow Pubs.

Blau, Peter M. Exchange & Power in Social Life. LC 64-23827. 1964. 25.95 (ISBN 0-471-08030-6). Wiley.

Bonino, Jose M. Room to Be People: An Interpretation of the Message of the Bible for Today's World. Leach, Vickie, tr. from Span. LC 78-14662. 80p. 1979. pap. 3.95 (ISBN 0-8006-1349-X, 1-1349). Fortress.

Borman, Ernest, et al. Interpersonal Communication in the Modern Organization. 2nd ed. (Illus.). 304p. 1982. text ed. 18.95 (ISBN 0-13-475061-6). P-H.

Bossevain, Jeremy. Friends of Friends: Networks, Manipulators, & Coalitions. LC 74-83521. 288p. 1975. 19.95 (ISBN 0-312-30590-7). St Martin.

Bowers, Warner F. Interpersonal Relationships in the Hospital. 136p. 1960. ed. spiral bdg. 14.75photocopy (ISBN 0-398-00203-7). C C Thomas.

Bowlby, John. The Making & Breaking of Affectional Bonds. 1979. 14.95x (ISBN 0-422-76850-2, Pub. by Tavistock England); pap. 6.95x (ISBN 0-422-76860-X). Methuen Inc.

Bramson, Robert M. Coping with Difficult People. 240p. 1981. 11.95 (ISBN 0-385-17362-8, Anchor Pr). Doubleday.

Brancaleone, Jim. Man with a Broken Heart. (Orig., LC 77-072049). 1977. pap. 3.50 (ISBN 0-9601186-1-6). Heartbeat.

Brenton, Myron. Friendship. LC 74-78533. 1974. 6.95 (ISBN 0-8128-1727-3). Stein & Day.

Brilliant, Ashleigh. Appreciate Me Now & Avoid the Rush. 160p. (Orig.). 1981. 9.95 (ISBN 0-912800-97-6); pap. 4.95 (ISBN 0-912800-94-1). Woodbridge Pr.

Broderick, Carlfred. Couples. 1981. pap. 5.95 (ISBN 0-671-43827-1, Touchstone Bks). S&S.

Brothers, Joyce. What Every Woman Should Know About Men. 1982. 13.95 (ISBN 0-671-25020-5). S&S.

Brown, Charles T. & Keller, Paul T. Monologue to Dialogue: An Exploration of Interpersonal Commuication. 2nd ed. LC 78-16541. (Special Communication Ser.). 1979. pap. 11.95 (ISBN 0-13-600825-9). P-H.

Brown, John T. Fundamental Perspectives on Interpersonal Communication. (The Social Science of Human Communication Ser.). (Illus.). 200p. (Orig.). 1981. pap. 5.00 (ISBN 0-938742-00-0). Victoria Isl.

Bruce, Martin M. A Guide to Human Relations in Business & Industry. LC 73-6907. 1969. pap. 11.05 (ISBN 0-935198-00-8). M M Bruce.

Burgess, Robert L. & Huston, Ted L., eds. Social Exchange in Developing Relationships. LC 79-6934. 1979. 30.00 (ISBN 0-12-143550-4). Acad Pr.

Burkett, David & Narcisco, John. Declare Yourself: Discovering the Me in Relationships. LC 75-11802. (Illus.). 1975. 9.95 (ISBN 0-13-197582-X, Spec); pap. 3.95 (ISBN 0-13-197574-9, Spec). P-H.

Burns, Sherman. From the Heart. 64p. (Orig.). 1981. pap. 3.95 (ISBN 0-686-30386-5). Vistula Pr.

Burton, Genevieve. Interpersonal Relations - a Guide for Nurses. 4th ed. LC 77-2948. 1977. pap. text ed. 7.95 (ISBN 0-8261-0294-8). Springer Pub.

Byrne, Donn E. The Attraction Paradigm. (Personality & Psychopathology Ser.: Vol. 11). 1971. 50.50 (ISBN 0-12-148650-8). Acad Pr.

Calden, George. I Count - You Count. LC 76-7235. 1975. pap. 3.95 (ISBN 0-913592-64-1). Argus Comm.

Caplan, Gerald & Killilea, Marie, eds. Support Systems & Mutual Help. LC 76-7473. (Illus.). 336p. 1976. 39.00 (ISBN 0-8089-0927-4). Grune.

Carkhuff, Robert R. Helping & Human Relations: A Primer for Lay & Professional Helpers, 2 Vols. LC 73-82021. 1969. text ed. 12.95 ea. (HoltC); Vol. 1. (ISBN 0-03-081214-3); Vol. 2. (ISBN 0-03-081215-1). HR&W.

Carlson, Dwight L. Overcoming Hurts & Anger. LC 80-83852. 1981. pap. 4.95 (ISBN 0-89081-277-2). Harvest Hse.

Carr, Jacquelyn B. Communicating & Relating. LC 78-58969. 1979. pap. text ed. 12.95 (ISBN 0-8053-1820-8); instr's guide 3.95 (ISBN 0-8053-1821-6). Benjamin-Cummings.

Carson, Robert C. Interaction Concepts of Personality. LC 73-15045. (Perspectives in Personality Ser.). 1969. 13.50 (ISBN 0-202-25035-0); pap. 5.95 (ISBN 0-202-25047-4). Beresford Bk Serv.

Centre for Advanced Study in the Developmental Sciences Study Group. The Origins of Human Social Relations: Proceedings. Schaffer, H. R., ed. 1971. 44.00 (ISBN 0-12-622550-8). Acad Pr.

Channels, Vera G. Experiences in Interpersonal Relationships. 335p. 1975. pap. text ed. 4.95 (ISBN 0-8134-1703-1, 1703); teacher's manual 0.50 (ISBN 0-8134-1708-2, 1708). Interstate.

Charon, J. Symbolic Interactionism: An Introduction, an Interpretation, an Integration. 1979. pap. 10.95 (ISBN 0-13-870105-9). P-H.

Chelune, Gordon J., et al. Self-Disclosure: Origins, Patterns, & Implications of Openness in Interpersonal Relationships. LC 79-88766. (Social & Behavioral Science Ser.). 1979. text ed. 18.95x (ISBN 0-87589-433-X). Jossey-Bass.

Claremont De Castillejo, Irene. Knowing Woman: A Feminine Psychology. LC 72-80470. 1973. 8.00 (ISBN 0-913430-01-3). C G Jung Foun.

--Knowing Woman: Feminine Psychology. 192p. 1974. pap. 3.50 (ISBN 0-06-090349-X, CN349, CN). Har-Row.

Coffey, Alan, et al. Human Relations: Law Enforcement in a Changing Community. (Illus.). 304p. 1982. reference 18.95 (ISBN 0-13-445700-5). P-H.

Cohen, Sara K. Whoever Said Life Is Fair? 1980. 7.95 (ISBN 0-684-16449-3). Scribner.

Cohen, Steven M. Interethnic Marriage & Friendship. Zuckerman, Harriet & Merton, Robert K., eds. LC 79-8985. (Dissertations on Sociology Ser.). 1980. lib. bdg. 25.00x (ISBN 0-405-12958-0). Arno.

Colangelo, Nicholas, et al. Multicultural Nonsexist Education: A Human Relations Approach. 1979. pap. text ed. 14.95 (ISBN 0-8403-2052-3). Kendall-Hunt.

Cole, Jim. The Holder-a View of Our Relationship. 1975. pap. 3.75 (ISBN 0-9601200-4-1). J Cole.

--Holder: A View of Our Relationships. (Illus.). pap. 3.75 (ISBN 0-88310-006-1). Publishers Consult.

Coleman, Emily & Edwards, Betty. Brief Encounters. 1980. pap. 4.95 (ISBN 0-385-15579-4, Anch). Doubleday.

Combs, James E. & Mansfield, Michael. Drama in Life: The Uses of Communication in Society. (Humanistic Studies in the Communication Arts). 1976. 19.95 (ISBN 0-8038-1555-7); pap. 10.50x (ISBN 0-8038-1556-5). Hastings.

Comfort, Alex. I & That. 1979. 6.95 (ISBN 0-517-53749-4). Crown.

Cook, Mark & Wilson, Glenn, eds. Love & Attraction: An International Conference. LC 78-40286. 1979. text ed. 72.00 (ISBN 0-08-022234-X). Pergamon.

Cooper, Cary L. & Alderfer, Clayton. Advances in Experiential Social Processes. LC 77-22060. (Advances in Experimental Social Processes Ser.: Vol. 1). 1978. 36.25 (ISBN 0-471-99546-0, Pub. by Wiley-Interscience). Wiley.

Costello, Andrew. How to Deal with Diffficult People. 112p. (Orig.). 1980. pap. 2.95 (ISBN 0-89243-128-8). Liguori Pubns.

Coulson, William R. A Sense of Community: That Education Might Be Personal. LC 73-76604. 1973. pap. text ed. 5.95x (ISBN 0-675-08929-8). Merrill.

Crenshaw, Theresa & Crenshaw, Roger. Expressing Your Feelings: The Key to an Intimate Relationship. 240p. (Orig.). (gr. 11-12). 1981. pap. text ed. 9.95x (ISBN 0-8290-0252-9). Irvington.

Cromwell, Otis & Roark, Stanford. A Course in Human Relations, 3 modules. 1975. leader's guides 6.16 ea.; pupil's wkbks. 2.20 ea.; tchrs' kits 74.80 ea. Har-Row.

David, Jay. The Meeting Book: Never Be Lonely Again. 1979. pap. 2.95 (ISBN 0-346-12391-7). Cornerstone.

Davis, Bruce & Wright, Genny. Hugs & Kisses. LC 77-5283. (Illus.). 1978. 2.95 (ISBN 0-89480-008-6). Workman Pub.

Davis, Murray S. Intimate Relations. LC 73-1859. (Illus.). 1973. 12.95 (ISBN 0-02-907020-1); pap. 3.95 (ISBN 0-02-907200-X). Free Pr.

Derenski, Arlene & Landsburg, Sally B. The Age Taboo: Older Women-Younger Men Relationships. 254p. 1981. 12.95 (ISBN 0-316-51366-0). Little.

De Ville, Jard. Nice Guys Finish First: How to Get People to Do What You Want...& Love You for It. LC 79-637. 1979. 7.95 (ISBN 0-688-03471-3). Morrow.

Dickenson, Rosalind E. Communication Nil! 1979. 5.00 (ISBN 0-682-49346-5). Exposition.

Diedrich, Richard C. Guidance Personnel & Other Professionals. (Guidance Monograph). 1968. pap. 2.40 (ISBN 0-395-09908-0). HM.

Dobson, James. What Wives Wish Their Husbands Knew About Women. 1975. 5.95 (ISBN 0-8423-7890-1). Tyndale.

Doise, W. & Douglas, G. Groups & Individuals. LC 77-84800. (Illus.). 1978. 29.95 (ISBN 0-521-21953-1); pap. 8.95x (ISBN 0-521-29320-0). Cambridge U Pr.

DuBrin, Andrew. Human Relations: A Job-Oriented Approach. 2nd ed. 300p. 1981. text ed. 17.95 (ISBN 0-8359-3002-5); instr's. manual free (ISBN 0-8359-3003-3). Reston.

DuBrin, Andrew J. Human Relations: A Job Oriented Approach. (Illus.). 1978. text ed. 17.95 (ISBN 0-87909-371-4); instrs'. manual avail. Reston.

Duck, S. & Gilmour, R., eds. Personal Relationship, Vol. 1: Studying Personal Relationships. LC 80-41360. 1981. 24.00 (ISBN 0-12-222801-4). Acad Pr.

--Personal Relationships, Vol. 2: Developing Personal Relatlionships. LC 80-41360. 1981. 24.00 (ISBN 0-12-222802-2). Acad Pr.

Duck, Steve, ed. Theory & Practice in Interpersonal Attraction. 1977. 64.50 (ISBN 0-12-222850-2). Acad Pr.

Duck, Steven. The Study of Acquaintance. 1977. 24.95 (ISBN 0-566-00160-8, 01085-5, Pub. by Saxon Hse England). Lexington Bks.

Dyer, William G. Creating Closer Families: Principles of Positive Family Interaction. LC 75-20169. (Illus.). 144p. 1975. pap. 6.95 (ISBN 0-8425-0726-4). Brigham.

Egan, Gerard. Interpersonal Living: A Skills - Contract Approach to Human Relations Training in Groups. LC 76-6651. 1976. pap. text ed. 10.95 (ISBN 0-8185-0189-8). Brooks-Cole.

--You & Me: The Skills of Communicating & Relating to Others. LC 77-6475. (Illus.). 1977. pap. text ed. 10.95 (ISBN 0-8185-0238-X); instructor's manual free (ISBN 0-685-79911-5). Brooks-Cole.

Eggleston, S. John. Social Context of the School. (Student's Lib. of Ed.). 1967. text ed. 3.75x (ISBN 0-7100-4217-5); pap. text ed. 2.75x (ISBN 0-7100-4210-8). Humanities.

Eisler, Richard M. & Frederiksen, Lee W. Perfecting Social Skills: A Guide to Interpersonal Behavior Development. (Applied Clinical Psycholgy Ser.). 225p. 1981. 18.95 (ISBN 0-306-40592-X, Plenum Pr). Plenum Pub.

Ellenson, Ann. Human Relations. (Illus.). 304p. 1973. ref. ed. 16.95 (ISBN 0-13-445643-2). P-H.

Emery, Stewart. Actualizations: You Don't Have to Rehearse to Be Yourself. Rogin, Neal, ed. 222p. 1980. Repr. of 1978 ed. 14.95 (ISBN 0-8290-0222-7). Irvington.

Englebardt, Leland S. Living Together: What's the Law? 1981. 10.95 (ISBN 0-517-54072-X, Michelman Books). Crown.

Eshleman, J. Ross & Clarke, Juanne N. Intimacy, Commitments & Marriage: Development of Relationships. 1978. pap. text ed. 15.95 (ISBN 0-205-05932-5); instr's manual (ISBN 0-205-05934-1). Allyn.

Evans, K. M. Sociometry & Education. 1962. text ed. 6.75x (ISBN 0-7100-3487-3). Humanities.

Fast, Julius. Incompatability of Men & Women & How to Overcome It. LC 70-164549. 192p. 1971. 5.95 (ISBN 0-87131-065-1). M Evans.

Fasteau, Marc. The Male Machine. 1976. pap. 4.95 (ISBN 0-440-55356-3, Delta). Dell.

Fasteau, Marc F. The Male Machine. LC 74-9858. (Illus.). 240p. 1974. 8.95 (ISBN 0-07-019985-X, GB). McGraw.

Filley, Alan C. Interpersonal Conflict Resolution. 180p. 1975. pap. 8.95x (ISBN 0-673-07589-3). Scott F.

Filsinger, Erik E. & Lewis, Robert A. Marital Observation & Behavioral Assessment. (Sage Focus Editions: Vol. 34). 320p. 1981. 20.00 (ISBN 0-8039-1570-5); pap. 9.95 (ISBN 0-8039-1571-3). Sage.

Fischer, Claude S., et al. Networks & Places: Social Relations in the Urban Setting. LC 76-55101. (Illus.). 1977. 19.95 (ISBN 0-02-910240-5). Free Pr.

Fischer, Joel, ed. Interpersonal Helping: Emerging Approaches for Social Work Practice. (Illus.). 704p. 1973. pap. 13.75 (ISBN 0-398-02565-7). C C Thomas.

Fisher, Bruce. Rebuilding: When Your Relationship Ends. LC 79-24440. 1981. pap. 5.95 (ISBN 0-915166-30-5). Impact Pubs Cal.

Flanders, James P. Practical Psychology. 352p. 1976. text ed. 17.50 (ISBN 0-06-042084-7, HarpC); instructor's manual avail. (ISBN 0-06-362088-X). Har-Row.

Flax, Carol & Ubell, Earl. Mother, Father, You: The Adults Guide to Getting Along Great with Parents & in-Laws. LC 80-5189. 224p. 1980. 12.95 (ISBN 0-87223-614-5, Dist. by Har-Row). Wyden.

Fletcher, Kenneth, et al. Extend: Youth Reaching Youth. LC 74-77684. 112p. (Orig.). 1974. pap. 3.95 (ISBN 0-8066-1435-8, 10-2150). Augsburg.

Foa, Uriel G. & Foa, Edna B. Societal Structures of the Mind. (Illus.). 468p. 1974. pap. 37.50 (ISBN 0-398-02932-6). C C Thomas.

Foote, Nelson N. & Cottrell, Leonard S., Jr. Identity & Interpersonal Competence: A New Direction in Family Research. LC 56-11957. 1955. pap. 14.00x (ISBN 0-226-25685-5). U of Chicago Pr.

Freedman, Hy. Sex Link: The Three-Billion-Year-Old Urge & What the Animals Do About It. LC 77-8546. 224p. 1977. 8.95 (ISBN 0-87131-242-5). M Evans.

Fruehling, Rosemary T. Working at Human Relations. Herr, Edwin L., ed. (Cooperative Work Experience Education for Careers Program). (Illus.). (gr. 11-12). 1976. pap. text ed. 5.04 (ISBN 0-07-028331-1, G); tchr's manual & key 2.75 (ISBN 0-07-028332-X); program guide 5.95 (ISBN 0-07-028339-7). McGraw.

Fulmer, Robert M. Practical Human Relations. 1977. 17.95x (ISBN 0-256-01908-8). Irwin.

Gahagan, Judy. Interpersonal & Group Behaviour. (Essential Psychology Ser.). 1977. pap. 4.50x (ISBN 0-416-82750-0). Methuen Inc.

Gallen, Richard, et al. The Unmarried Couple's Legal Handbook: The Questions You Should Ask, The Answers You Should Know. (Orig.). pap. 6.95 (ISBN 0-440-59219-4, Delta). Dell.

Gathorne-Hardy, Jonathan. Marriage, Love, Sex & Divorce: What Brings Us Together, What Drives Us Apart. 384p. 1981. 13.95 (ISBN 0-671-40103-3). Summit Bks.

Gazda, George M., et al. Human Relations Development: A Manual for Educators. 2nd ed. 1977. text ed. 10.95x (ISBN 0-205-05566-4); pap. text ed. 9.95x (ISBN 0-685-71782-8). Allyn.

Gelles, Richard J. The Violent Home: A Study of Physical Aggression Between Husbands & Wives. LC 73-94288. (Sage Library of Social Research: Vol. 13). 232p. 1974. 20.00x (ISBN 0-8039-0381-2); pap. 9.95x (ISBN 0-8039-0449-5). Sage.

Gellis, Audrey. How to Meet Men Now That You're Liberated. 1978. pap. 1.95 (ISBN 0-445-04288-5). Popular Lib.

Genne, Elizabeth S. & Genne, William H. First of All Persons: A New Look at Men-Women Relationships. (Orig.). 1973. pap. 1.95 (ISBN 0-377-03041-4). Friend Pr.

Gerhardt, Sidney & McKay, Elizabeth. There Is a Better Way of Living! A Sensible Approach to Personal & Family Growth. LC 75-14443. 128p. 1975. 5.95 (ISBN 0-8164-9268-9). Continuum.

Gerl, George & Lane, George. Two Called Together. 1978. pap. text ed. 4.00 (ISBN 0-8294-0274-8); tchr's ed. 4.00 (ISBN 0-8294-0277-2). Loyola.

Getz, Gene A. Building up One Another. 1976. pap. 3.95 (ISBN 0-88207-744-9). Victor Bks.
Giammatteo, Michael C. Myths Away, or Myths Are a Way. (Illus., Orig.). 1973. pap. 5.00 (ISBN 0-918428-04-1). Sylvan Inst.
Glad, Donald D. & Glad, Virginia B. Interpersonality Synopsis. 1963. 4.95 (ISBN 0-87212-006-6). Libra.
Glidewell, John C. Choice Points: Essays on the Emotional Problems of Living with People. 1970. 11.00x (ISBN 0-262-07038-3); pap. 3.95x (ISBN 0-262-57026-2). MIT Pr.
Goffman, Erving. Behavior in Public Places: Notes on the Social Organization of Gatherings. LC 62-11850. 1963. 15.95 (ISBN 0-02-911930-8); pap. 4.50 (ISBN 0-02-911940-5). Free Pr.
Goldberg, Jan, et al. The Statue of Liberty Is Cracking up: A Guide to Loving, Leaving, & Living Again. 1979. 8.95 (ISBN 0-15-184916-1). HarBraceJ.
Goldstein, Arnold P. & Sorcher, Melvin. Changing Supervisor Behavior. LC 73-10059. 1974. text ed. 12.75 (ISBN 0-08-017742-5); pap. text ed. 6.75 (ISBN 0-08-017769-7). Pergamon.
Goldstine, Daniel. The Dance-Away Lover. 1978. pap. 2.50 (ISBN 0-345-29763-6). Ballantine.
Goodlad, John I., et al. Toward a Mankind School: An Adventure in Humanistic Education. 256p. 1974. 8.95 (ISBN 0-07-023624-0, P&RB). McGraw.
Gordon, Leonard V. Measurement of Interpersonal Values. LC 74-22623. 122p. (Orig.). 1975. text ed. 12.00 (ISBN 0-574-72770-1); pap. text ed. 8.20 (ISBN 0-574-72764-7). SRA.
Greenburger, Francis & Kiernan, Thomas. How to Ask for More, & Get It: The Art of Creative Negotiation. LC 77-80889. 1978. 7.95 (ISBN 0-385-12495-3). Doubleday.
Grossack, Martin M. Love & Reason. 1976. pap. 3.00 (ISBN 0-685-78289-1). Inst. Rat Liv.
Grove, Theodore S. Experiences in Interpersonal Communication. (Illus.). 224p. 1976. pap. 11.95 (ISBN 0-13-294975-X). P-H.
Halacy, D. S., Jr. Social Man: The Relationships of Humankind. (Nature of Man Ser.: Bk. 4). 176p. (gr. 7up). 1973. 6.25 (ISBN 0-8255-4041-0). Macrae.
Hall, Francine S. & Hall, Douglas T. Two-Career Couple. (Illus.). 1979. 10.95 (ISBN 0-201-02733-X); pap. 5.95 (ISBN 0-201-02734-8). A-W.
Hall, Manly P. Incompatibility: A Crisis in Modern Living. pap. 1.75 (ISBN 0-89314-320-0). Philos Res.
Hall, Marie B. Common Sense & the Battle of the Sexes. 68p. 1973. pap. 2.50 (ISBN 0-89314-977-2). Veritat Found.
Hallinan, P. K. Where's Michael? LC 77-15952. (Illus.). (ps-3). 1978. PLB 8.65 (ISBN 0-516-03668-8). Childrens.
Halliwell, L. M., ed. People Working Together. 1969. pap. 8.50x (ISBN 0-7022-0632-6). U of Queensland Pr.
Halpern, Howard. Cutting Loose: An Adult Guide to Terms with Your Parents. 1978. pap. 2.75 (ISBN 0-553-14940-7). Bantam.
Hamersma, Richard J. & Mark, Robert A. The Seven-Pillared Relationship. LC 79-20450. 192p. 1981. 13.95 (ISBN 0-88229-443-1). Nelson-Hall.
Haney, William V. Communication & International Relations. 4th ed. 1979. text ed. 20.50x (ISBN 0-256-02244-5). Irwin.
Harcum, E. Rae. Psychology for Daily Living: Simple Guidance in Human Relations for Parents, Teachers, & Others. LC 79-1048. 1979. 15.95x (ISBN 0-88229-384-2); pap. 8.95 (ISBN 0-88229-696-5). Nelson-Hall.
Hargreaves, David H. Interpersonal Relations & Education. (International Library of Sociology). 1972. 25.00x (ISBN 0-7100-7245-7). Routledge & Kegan.
--Interpersonal Relations & Education. rev. ed. (International Library of Sociology). 1975. pap. 8.95 (ISBN 0-7100-8081-6). Routledge & Kegan.
Harris, Philip R. & Moran, Robert T. Managing Cultural Differences. 432p. 1979. 19.95 (ISBN 0-87201-160-7). Gulf Pub.
Hauck, Paul A. Overcoming Jealousy & Possessiveness. LC 81-3040. 1981. pap. 5.95 (ISBN -0664-24374-6). Westminster.
Hawthorn, Jeremy. Identity & Relationship. LC 77-26780. 1973. 17.50 (ISBN 0-8414-4857-4). Folcroft.
Headington, Bonnie J. Communication in the Counseling Relationship. LC 78-9026. 1979. 15.50 (ISBN 0-910328-24-2); pap. 10.00 (ISBN 0-910328-24-2). Carroll Pr.
Heartbreak, U. S. A. by One Hundred Girls. 240p. 1981. write for info. (ISBN 0-936066-03-2). Suffolk Hse.
Held, Ronald G. Learning Together. 1976. pap. 1.25 (ISBN 0-88243-571-X, 02-0571). Gospel Pub.
Henderson, George. Human Relations: From Theory to Practice. LC 73-19387. (Illus.). 450p. 1981. pap. 9.95x (ISBN 0-8061-1709-5). U of Okla Pr.
--Human Relations: From Theory to Practice. LC 73-19387. (Illus.). 500p. 1974. 19.50x (ISBN 0-8061-1184-4). U of Okla Pr.
Henley, Nancy & Thorne, Barrie. She Said - He Said. 1976. perfect bdg. 3.00 (ISBN 0-912786-36-1). Know Inc.
Henry, Jules. Pathways to Madness. 512p. 1973. pap. 4.95 (ISBN 0-394-71882-8, Vin). Random.
Henry, Mark & Henry, Mary F. A Patchwork Family. Lyman, intro. by. LC 77-82403. (Illus.). 1978. pap. 4.95 (ISBN 0-8054-5586-8). Broadman.
Hodgetts, Richard M. Modern Human Relations. 512p. 1980. text ed. 21.95 (ISBN 0-03-054276-6). Dryden Pr.
Hof, Larry & Miller, William. Marriage Enrichment: Philosophy Process & Program. (Illus.). 192p. 1980. text ed. 14.95 (ISBN 0-87619-717-9). R J Brady.
Hopson, Barrie & Hopson, Charlotte. Intimate Feedback: Lover's Guide to Getting in Touch with Each Other. 1976. pap. 1.50 (ISBN 0-451-06894-7, W6894, Sig). NAL.
Horner, Althea. Being & Loving. LC 77-73972. 1978. 9.95 (ISBN 0-8052-3681-3). Schocken.
Huseman, Richard C., et al. Interpersonal Communication in Organizations. 1975. text ed. 17.95 (ISBN 0-205-04897-8, 484897-7). Allyn.
Huston, Theodore, ed. Foundations of Interpersonal Attraction. 1974. 32.00 (ISBN 0-12-362950-0). Acad Pr.
Hyatt, Ralph I. Before You Love Again. (Paperbacks Ser.). 192p. 1980. pap. 3.95 (ISBN 0-07-031555-8, GB). McGraw.
If You've Ever Loved a Married Man: By One Who Did. 1978. pap. 1.95 (ISBN 0-914938-03-7). Dune Pubs.
Ihara, Toni & Warner, Ralph. The Living Together Kit. 1979. pap. 2.50 (ISBN 0-449-24172-6, Crest). Fawcett.
Irish, Richard K. How to Live Separately Together: A Guide for Working Couples. LC 78-22637. 264p. 1981. 11.95 (ISBN 0-385-14650-7, Anchor Pr). Doubleday.
Isaacs, Susan. Social Development in Young Children: A Study of Beginning. 1965. text ed. 7.50x (ISBN 0-391-02051-X). Humanities.
James, Muriel & Savary, Louis. The Heart of Friendship. LC 74-25702. 1978. pap. 4.95 (ISBN 0-06-064113-4, RD 254, HarpR). Har-Row.
Jellison, Jerald M. I'm Sorry - I Didn't Mean to - & Other Lies We Love to Tell. LC 77-10125. 1977. 7.95 (ISBN 0-89456-005-0). Chatham Sq.
Jewett, Paul K. El Hombre como Varon y Hembra. Vilela, Ernesto S., tr. from Eng. 205p. (Orig., Span.). 1979. pap. 4.95 (ISBN 0-89922-132-7). Edit Caribe.
Johnson, David W. Human Relations & Your Career: A Guide to Interpersonal Skills. (Illus.). 1978. 13.95 (ISBN 0-13-445601-7). P-H.
Jones, John E. & Pfeiffer, J. William, eds. The Annual Handbook for Group Facilitators 1981. LC 73-92841. (Ser. in Human Relations Training). 296p. (Orig.). 1981. pap. 20.00 (ISBN 0-88390-004-1); looseleaf ntbk. 44.50 (ISBN 0-88390-003-3). Univ Assocs.
--Annual Handbook for Group Facilitators, 1973. LC 73-92841. (Series in Human Relations Training). 290p. 1973. pap. 20.00 (ISBN 0-88390-081-5); looseleaf ntbk. 44.50 (ISBN 0-88390-073-4). Univ Assocs.
--The Annual Handbook for Group Facilitators, 1979. LC 73-92841. (Ser. in Human Relations Training). 296p. 1979. pap. 20.00 (ISBN 0-88390-095-5); looseleaf notebook 44.50 (ISBN 0-88390-093-9). Univ Assocs.
Kardos, Lajos, ed. Attitudes, Interaction & Personality. Dajka, B., et al, trs. (Illus.). 149p. 1980. 10.50x (ISBN 963-05-2088-5). Intl Pubns Serv.
Kassorla, Irene. Putting It All Together. 224p. 1976. pap. 2.50 (ISBN 0-446-91802-4). Warner Bks.
Katz, Mort. Living Together: A Daily Workbook for Strengthening Relationships. (Illus.). 1981. pap. 5.95 (ISBN 0-87863-002-3). Farnswth Pub.
Kelley, Harold H. Personal Relationships: Their Structures & Processes. LC 79-11609. 1979. 16.50x (ISBN 0-470-26730-5). Halsted Pr.
Kelley, Harold H. & Thibaut, John W. Interpersonal Relations: A Theory of Interdependence. LC 78-164. 341p. 1978. 30.95 (ISBN 0-471-03473-8, Pub. by Wiley-Interscience). Wiley.
Kelley, Jan D. & Winship, Barbara J. I Am Worth It. LC 78-26111. 1979. 13.95 (ISBN 0-88229-291-9). Nelson-Hall.
Kelling, George W. Blind Mazes: A Study of Love. LC 78-24254. 218p. 1979. text ed. 17.95x (ISBN 0-88229-242-0). Nelson-Hall.
Keyes, Ken, Jr. A Conscious Person's Guide to Relationships. LC 78-71456. 1979. pap. 3.95 (ISBN 0-915972-00-X). Living Love.
Kiesler, Sara B. Interpersonal Processes in Groups & Organizations. Mackenzie, Kenneth D., ed. LC 77-86018. (Organizational Behavior Ser.). 1978. pap. text ed. 9.95x (ISBN 0-88295-451-2). Harlan Davidson.
King-Farlow, John. Self-Knowledge & Social Relations. 1978. 15.00 (ISBN 0-88202-182-6). N Watson.
Klein, Mavis. How to Choose a Mate. 160p. 1981. 12.00 (ISBN 0-7145-2727-0, Pub. by M. Boyars). Merrimack Bk Serv.
Klimek, David. Beneath Mate Selection & Marriage: The Unconscious Motives in Human Pairing. 1979. 14.95 (ISBN 0-442-23074-5). Van Nos Reinhold.
Klinzing, Dennis & Klinzing, Dene. The Hospitalized Child: Communication Techniques for Health Personnel. (Illus.). 1977. pap. text ed. 10.95 (ISBN 0-13-394817-X). P-H.
Knapp, Mark L. Social Intercourse: From Greeting to Goodbye. 1978. pap. text ed. 13.95 (ISBN 0-205-05961-9, 4859618); instr's man. o.p. avail. (ISBN 0-205-05962-7). Allyn.
Kornhaber, Bruce & Stanicek, Frank. Making It Happen: The Art of Relating Humanly. 1978. pap. text ed. 8.95x (ISBN 0-917974-26-3). Waveland Pr.
Kreis, Bernadine. To Love Again: An Answer to Loneliness. LC 75-2070. 200p. 1975. 6.95 (ISBN 0-8164-9261-1). Continuum.
Kristy, Norton F. Staying in Love: Reinventing Marriage & Other Realationships. (Orig.). pap. 2.75 (ISBN 0-515-05089-X). Jove Pubns.
Kvols-Riedler, Bill & Kvols-Riedler, Kathy. Understanding Yourself & Others. (Illus.). 222p. (Orig.). 1981. pap. 6.95 (ISBN 0-933450-01-X). RDIC Pubns.
Laing, R. D. Self & Others. 1972. pap. 2.50 (ISBN 0-14-021376-7, Pelican). Penguin.
Laing, Ronald D., et al. Interpersonal Perception. LC 66-17767. (Illus.). 1966. text ed. 6.95 (ISBN 0-8261-0851-2). Springer Pub.
Landorf, Joyce. Tough & Tender. rev. ed. 1981. 7.95 (ISBN 0-8007-1283-8). Revell.
Langer, Ellen J. & Dweck, Carol S. Personal Politics: The Psychology of Making It. (Illus.). 192p. 1973. pap. text ed. 9.95x (ISBN 0-13-657247-2). P-H.
Langone, John. Like, Love, Lust: A View of Sex & Sexuality. 144p. 1981. pap. 2.25 (ISBN 0-380-54189-0, 54189). Avon.
Larsen, Earnest. Love Is a Hunger. LC 79-53701. (Illus., Orig.). 1979. pap. 5.95 (ISBN 0-89638-037-8). CompCare.
Lecker, Sidney. How to Get the One You Love to Say Yes. Larsen, Madelyn, ed. LC 79-22931. (Illus.). 224p. 1980. 8.95 (ISBN 0-346-12461-1). Cornerstone.
Lee, Albert & Lee, Carol A. The Total Couple. 1977. 7.95 (ISBN 0-89328-010-0). Lorenz Pr.
Leedy, G. Frank. Check List for Marriage. LC 72-181367. 1971. 5.00 (ISBN 0-87212-023-6). Libra.
Leviton, Charles D. & Hill, Stephanie. A Fresh Start--- for a New Age Relationship. LC 79-66745. 1979. 10.95 (ISBN 0-934962-00-6). Synergy Hse.
Levy, Ronald. Self-Revelation Through Relationships. LC 73-167896. 1972. 9.95 (ISBN 0-13-803569-5). P-H.
Linder, Darwyn E., ed. Psychological Dimensions of Social Interaction: Readings & Perspectives. LC 72-4707. 1973. pap. text ed. 9.95 (ISBN 0-201-04246-0). A-W.
Lissfelt, J. Fred. Kaffeeklatsch. (Orig.). 1955. pap. 2.50 (ISBN 0-910286-23-X). Boxwood.
Littauer, Florence. Pursuit of Happiness. LC 80-85333. 1981. pap. 4.95 (ISBN 0-89081-284-5). Harvest Hse.
Losoncy. Turning People on: How to Be an Encouraging Person. LC 77-4686. 1977. 11.95 (ISBN 0-13-933242-1, Spec); pap. 5.95 (ISBN 0-13-933234-0). P-H.
McCall, George J., et al. Social Relationships. LC 78-115939. (Observations Ser.). 1970. text ed. 7.95x (ISBN 0-202-30062-5). Beresford Bk Serv.
Mace, David & Mace, Vera. How to Have a Happy Marriage. LC 77-7575. 1977. 6.95 (ISBN 0-687-17830-4). Abingdon.
--We Can Have Better Marriages If We Really Want Them. LC 73-17468. (Illus.). 176p. 1974. 7.95 (ISBN 0-687-44282-6). Abingdon.
McGuire, James & Priestley, Philip. Life After School: A Social Skills Curriculum. (Illus.). 230p. 1981. 24.00 (ISBN 0-08-025192-7); pap. 12.00 (ISBN 0-08-025193-5). Pergamon.
Mack, Wayne. Homework Manual for Biblical Counseling: Personal & Interpersonal Problems, Vol. 1. 1979. pap. 5.50 (ISBN 0-87552-356-0). Presby & Reformed.
McWilliams, Peter A. It's Nice to Know Someone Like You. (Illus.). 64p. (Orig.). 1981. pap. 4.95 (ISBN 0-88396-151-2). Blue Mtn Pr CO.
Maier, Norman R. Problem-Solving Discussions & Conferences: Leadership Methods & Skills. 1963. text ed. 15.95 (ISBN 0-07-039715-5, C). McGraw.
Malone, John. Straight Women-Gay Men: A Special Relationship. 1980. 8.95 (ISBN 0-8037-8174-1). Dial.
--Straight Women-Gay Men: A Special Relationship. 1980. 8.95 (ISBN 0-8037-8174-1). Dial.
Marwell, G. & Schmidt, D. R. Cooperation: An Experimental Analysis. 1975. 30.50 (ISBN 0-12-476350-2). Acad Pr.
Mayeroff, Milton. On Caring. 1972. pap. 1.95 (ISBN 0-06-080242-1, P242, PL). Har-Row.
Mihaly, Mary E. Getting Your Own Way: A Guide to Growing up Assertively. LC 78-27050. 180p. (gr. 7 up). 1979. 6.95 (ISBN 0-87131-285-9). M Evans.
Millar, Dan & Millar, Frank. Messages & Myths: Understanding Interpersonal Communication. LC 75-33811. 250p. 1976. pap. text ed. 7.95x (ISBN 0-88284-022-3). Alfred Pub.
Miller, Gerald R., ed. Explorations in Interpersonal Communication. LC 76-6315. (Sage Annual Reviews of Communication Research: Vol. 5). 278p. 1976. 22.50 (ISBN 0-8039-0665-X); pap. 9.95 (ISBN 0-8039-0666-8). Sage.
Miller, Sherod, et al. Couple Communication I: Talking Together. (Couple Communication Ser.). 1979. pap. 8.95 (ISBN 0-917340-09-4). Interpersonal Comm.
Mitchelson, Marvin. Living Together. 1981. 10.95 (ISBN 0-671-24981-9). S&S.
Molton, Warren L. Friends, Partners, & Lovers. 1979. pap. 5.95 (ISBN 0-8170-0815-2). Judson.
Montagu, Ashley. Education & Human Relations. LC 72-11333. 191p. 1973. Repr. of 1958 ed. lib. bdg. 15.00 (ISBN 0-8371-6659-4, MOEH). Greenwood.
Montefiore, Alan, ed. Philosophy & Personal Relations: An Anglo-French Study. 208p. 1973. 9.00 (ISBN 0-7735-0179-7). McGill-Queens U Pr.
Murstein, Bernard I. Exploring Intimate Life Styles. LC 77-27272. 1978. text ed. 18.95 (ISBN 0-8261-2380-5); pap. text ed. 11.95 (ISBN 0-8261-2381-3). Springer Pub.
Namboodiri, Krishnan, ed. Survey Sampling & Measurement. (Quantitative Studies in Social Relations Ser.). 1978. 33.50 (ISBN 0-12-513350-2). Acad Pr.
Newcomb, Theodore M. The Acquaintance Process. LC 61-9361. 1961. 28.50x (ISBN 0-03-010520-X). Irvington.
Newcomb, Theodore M. & Wilson, Everett K., eds. College Peer Groups: Problems & Prospects for Research. LC 65-29033. (NORC Monographs in Social Research Ser.: No. 8). 1966. 10.95x (ISBN 0-202-09002-7). NORC.
Nouwen, Henri J. M. Intimacy. LC 80-8906. 160p. 1981. pap. 3.95 (ISBN 0-06-066323-5, RD359, HarpR). Har-Row.
O'Banion, Terry & O'Connell, April. Shared Journey: An Introduction to Encounter. 1970. pap. text ed. 11.95 (ISBN 0-13-807834-3). P-H.
Ofshe, Richard. Interpersonal Behavior in Small Groups. (Illus.). 816p. 1973. text ed. 24.95x (ISBN 0-13-475020-9). P-H.
Ogilvie, Lloyd J. The Beauty of Caring. LC 80-80464. 1981. pap. 4.95 (ISBN 0-89081-244-6). Harvest Hse.
--The Beauty of Sharing. LC 80-8880. (Orig.). 1981. pap. 4.95 (ISBN 0-89081-246-2). Harvest Hse.
Olsen, Paul. The Future of Being Human. LC 74-31004. 192p. 1975. 6.95 (ISBN 0-87131-173-9). M Evans.
An Overview of Communication & Interpersonal Relationships. (MODCOM Modules in Speech Communication Ser.). 1976. pap. text ed. 2.50 (ISBN 0-574-22520-X, 13-5520). SRA.
Ovesen, Ellis. Lives Touch. LC 73-81822. (Illus.). 96p. (Orig.). 1973. pap. 3.25 (ISBN 0-88489-053-8). St Marys.
Pace, R., et al. Communicating Interpersonally: A Reader. LC 72-92574. 1973. pap. text ed. 8.95x (ISBN 0-675-09002-4). Merrill.
Panzarella, Andrew. Microcosm: A Radical Experiment in Re-Education for Becoming a Person. 1972. pap. 4.95 (ISBN 0-88489-013-9). St Marys.
Pearce, Jane & Newton, Saul. Conditions of Human Growth. 1969. 6.95 (ISBN 0-685-08130-3); pap. 4.95 (ISBN 0-8065-0177-4). Citadel Pr.
Peele, Stanton & Brodsky, Archie. Love & Addiction. 1976. pap. 2.25 (ISBN 0-451-06985-4, E6985, Sig). NAL.
Pfeiffer, J. William & Jones, John E. Reference Guide to Handbooks & Annuals. rev. ed. LC 75-14661. 166p. 1981. pap. 9.50 (ISBN 0-88390-069-6). Univ Assocs.

Pfeiffer, J. William & Jones, John E., eds. Annual Handbook for Group Facilitators, 1972. LC 73-92841. (Series in Human Relations Training). 272p. 1972. pap. 20.00 (ISBN 0-88390-085-8); looseleaf ntbk. 44.50 (ISBN 0-88390-072-6). Univ Assocs.
--A Handbook of Structured Experiences for Human Relations Training, Vol. VIII. LC 73-92840. (Ser. in Human Relations Training). 142p. (Orig.). 1981. pap. 9.50 (ISBN 0-88390-048-3). Univ Assocs.
--A Handbook of Structured Experiences for Human Relations Training, 8 vols. LC 73-92840. (Series in Human Relations Training). 1973-81. pap. 9.50 ea.; Vol. 1. Rev. Ed. (ISBN 0-88390-041-6); Vol. 2. Rev. Ed. (ISBN 0-88390-042-4); Vol. 3. Rev. Ed. (ISBN 0-88390-043-2); Vol. 4. (ISBN 0-88390-044-0). Vol. 5 (ISBN 0-88390-045-9). Vol. 6 (ISBN 0-88390-046-7). Vol. 7 (ISBN 0-88390-047-5). Vol.8 (ISBN 0-88390-048-3). Univ Assocs.
Phillips, Gerald M. & Erickson, Eugene C. Interpersonal Dynamics in the Small Group. 1970. text ed. 7.95 (ISBN 0-394-30704-6, RanC). Random.
Pietsch, William V. Human Be-Ing: How to Have a Creative Relationship Instead of a Power Struggle. 1975. pap. 1.95 (ISBN 0-451-08784-4, J8784, Sig). NAL.
Purnell, Dick. Why Couples Break up. (Dynamic Relationship Ser.). 1982. pap. 1.95 (ISBN 0-86605-022-1). Campus Crusade.
Rajouane, Maggie. Loving the Single Man. 1977. Repr. text ed. 9.95 (ISBN 0-914094-05-X). Symphony.
Rathjen, Diana P. & Foreyt, John P., eds. Social Competence: Interventions for Children & Adults. LC 80-118. (Pergamon General Psychology Ser.: No. 91). (Illus.). 300p. 1980. 26.50 (ISBN 0-08-025965-0). Pergamon.
Raush, Harold L., et al. Communication, Conflict & Marriage: Explorations in the Theory & Study of Intimate Relationships. LC 73-18506. (Social & Behavioral Science Ser.). 1974. 15.95x (ISBN 0-87589-210-8). Jossey-Bass.
Raven, Bertran & Rubin, Jeffrey. Social Psychology: People in Groups. LC 75-32693. 592p. 1976. 24.95 (ISBN 0-471-70970-0). Wiley.
Reeves, Elton. How to Get Along with (Almost) Everybody. 200p. 1975. pap. 3.95 (ISBN 0-8065-0479-X). Citadel Pr.
Reflections on Relationships. (gr. 11-12). 1978. wkbk. 6.00 (ISBN 0-13-770081-4). P-H.
Roberts, Shelley & Hilliard, Fred. What to Do with a Liberated Woman. new ed. (Illus.). 1978. pap. 3.95 (ISBN 0-918484-02-2). Smugglers.
Rosenfels, Paul. Love & Power: The Psychology of Interpersonal Creativity. LC 66-25081. 1966. 4.95 (ISBN 0-87212-009-0). Libra.
Ruben, Brent. Human Communication Handbook: Simulations & Games, Vol. 2. 1978. pap. text ed. 11.75 (ISBN 0-8104-5765-2). Hayden.
Ruben, Brent D. & Budd, Richard W. Human Communication Handbook: Simulations & Games, Vol. 1. (Illus.). 1975. pap. text ed. 11.75 (ISBN 0-8104-5524-2). Hayden.
Rubin, Zick, ed. Doing Unto Others: Joining, Molding, Conforming, Helping, Loving. (Patterns of Social Behavior Ser). 160p. 1975. pap. 3.45 (ISBN 0-13-217596-7, Spec, Spec). P-H.
Rudman, Jack. Director of Community Relations. (Career Examination Ser.: C-1856). (Cloth bdg. avail. on request). pap. 10.00 (ISBN 0-8373-1856-4). Natl Learning.
--Human Relations Aide. (Career Examination Ser.: C-1307). (Cloth bdg. avail. on request). pap. 8.00 (ISBN 0-8373-1307-4). Natl Learning.
--Human Relations Representative. (Career Examination Ser.: C-1308). (Cloth bdg. avail. on request). pap. 8.00 (ISBN 0-8373-1308-2). Natl Learning.
--Human Relations Training Officer. (Career Examination Ser.: C-1309). (Cloth bdg. avail. on request). pap. 8.00 (ISBN 0-8373-1309-0). Natl Learning.
--Senior Human Relations Representative. (Career Examination Ser.: C-2584). (Cloth bdg. avail. on request). pap. 10.00 (ISBN 0-8373-2584-6). Natl Learning.
Ruesch, Jurgen. Semiotic Approaches to Human Relations. 1972. 115.00x (ISBN 90-2792-299-3). Mouton.
Russell, Letty M. The Future of Partnership. LC 78-20805. 1979. pap. 6.95 (ISBN 0-664-24240-5). Westminster.
Russo, Anthony. Filling Gaps: An Interpersonal Skills Approach. 1978. pap. 6.95 (ISBN 0-89529-044-8). Avery Pub.
Safilios-Rothschild, Constantina. Love, Sex & Sex Roles. LC 76-44439. 1977. 9.95 (ISBN 0-13-540948-9, Spec); pap. 5.95 (ISBN 0-13-540930-6). P-H.
--Relationships. (Special Issue of Psychology of Women Quarterly: Vol. 5, No. 3). 1981. pap. 9.95 (ISBN 0-89885-085-1). Human Sci Pr.
Sager, Clifford J. & Hunt, Bernice. Intimate Partners: Hidden Patterns in Love Relationships. (McGraw-Hill Paperbacks Ser.). 204p. 1981. pap. 4.95 (ISBN 0-07-054428-X). McGraw.
--Intimate Partners: Hidden Patterns in Love Relationships. 1979. 8.95 (ISBN 0-07-054427-1, GB). McGraw.
Sammon, Sean D., et al. Fidelity: Issues of Emotional Living in an Age of Stress for Clergy & Religious. Hart, Joseph L., ed. LC 81-533. 148p. (Orig.). 1981. pap. 5.00 (ISBN 0-89571-011-0). Affirmation.
Sampson, Elois S. The Tall Stance. 1979. 5.50 (ISBN 0-682-49434-8). Exposition.
Sanderson, Gregg. What Ever Happened to "Happily Ever After"? A Step-by-Step Guide to Happier Relationships. 180p. (Orig.). (YA) 1980. pap. 5.95 (ISBN 0-9605868-0-6). Adventures in Living.
Sarraute, Nathalie. Between Life & Death. Jolas, Maria, tr. from Fr. 1980. pap. 11.95 (ISBN 0-7145-0122-0); pap. 4.95 (ISBN 0-7145-0123-9). Riverrun NY.
Schachter, Stanley. Psychology of Affiliation: Experimental Studies of the Sources of Gregariousness. 1959. 5.95x (ISBN 0-8047-0566-6). Stanford U Pr.
Scheidel, Thomas M. Speech Communication & Human Interaction. 2nd ed. 1976. text ed. 10.95x (ISBN 0-673-15005-4). Scott F.
Schickel, Richard. Singled Out: A Civilized Guide to Sex & Sensibility for the Suddenly Single Man-or Women. LC 80-54080. 128p. 1981. 8.95 (ISBN 0-670-64710-1). Viking Pr.
Schmidt, Martin F. & Bernthal, Wilmar F. Explorations in Human Relations. 208p. 1959. 3.50 (ISBN 0-686-64180-9). U CO Busn Res Div.
Schmidt, Paul F. Coping with Difficult People. LC 79-27486. (Christian Care Books). 1980. pap. 5.95 (ISBN 0-664-24299-5). Westminster.
Schulman, Ken. Connecting. 1979. text ed. 10.95 (ISBN 0-914094-13-0). Symphony.
Schur, Edwin M. Labeling Deviant Behavior: Its Sociological Implications. (Demearath Ser). 1971. pap. text ed. 10.95 scp (ISBN 0-06-045812-7, HarpC). Har-Row.
Schutz, William C. The Interpersonal Underworld. LC 66-28683. Orig. Title: Firo: A Three-Dimensional Theory of Interpersonal Behavior. 1966. pap. 5.95x (ISBN 0-8314-0011-0). Sci & Behavior.
Schwan, Kas, et al. The Living Together Book. LC 79-67611. (Illus.). 64p. (Orig.). 1980. pap. 4.95 (ISBN 0-87223-601-3, Dist. by Har-Row). Wideview Bks.
Schwartz, Roslyn & Schwartz, Leonard. Becoming a Couple: Making the Most Out of Every Stage in Your Relationship. 1980. text ed. 9.95 (ISBN 0-13-072173-5, Spec); (Spec). P-H.
Scott, Michael D. & Powers, William G. Interpersonal Communication: A Question of Needs. LC 77-76342. (Illus.). 1978. text ed. 12.95 (ISBN 0-395-25055-2); inst. manual 0.60 (ISBN 0-395-25056-0). HM.
Sedwick, Robert C. Interaction: Interpersonal Relationships in Organizations. (Illus.). 240p. 1974. pap. 9.95 (ISBN 0-13-469155-5). P-H.
Selman, Robert L. The Growth of Interpersonal Understanding: Developmental & Clinical Analysis. (Developmental Psychology Ser.). 1980. 25.00 (ISBN 0-12-636450-8). Acad Pr.
Shain, Merle. Some Men Are More Perfect Than Others. 144p. 1980. pap. 4.98 (ISBN 0-686-65666-0). Bantam.
--When Lovers Are Friends. 112p. 1980. pap. 2.50 (ISBN 0-553-20506-4). Bantam.
Shave, David W. The Therapeutic Listener. 320p. 1974. 15.00 (ISBN 0-88275-116-6). Krieger.
Shedd, Charlie W. Talk to Me. 1976. pap. 1.50 (ISBN 0-89129-112-1). Jove Pubns.
Shor, Joel & Sanville, Jean. Illusion in Loving. LC 77-85416. 1978. text ed. 15.00 (ISBN 0-930578-00-7). Intl Univs Pr.
Simons, Joseph & Reidy, Jeanne. Risk of Loving. LC 68-54376. 1973. pap. 4.95 (ISBN 0-8164-9141-0). Continuum.
Smart, Laura S & Smart, Mollie S. Families: Developing Realtionships. 2nd ed. (Illus.). 1980. text ed. 18.95 (ISBN 0-02-411930-X). Macmillan.
Smith, Gerald W. Hidden Meanings. LC 76-56897. 1977. pap. 4.95 (ISBN 0-89087-149-3). Celestial Arts.
Smith, O. C., Jr. The First Collected Insights of the Prophet O. C. 1978. 4.00 (ISBN 0-682-48784-8). Exposition.
Smith, Riley K & Tessina, Tina B. How to Be a Couple & Still Be Free. LC 80-8669. 1980. lib. bdg. 11.95x (ISBN 0-89370-651-5). Borgo Pr.
Somerville, Rose M., ed. Intimate Relationships: Marriage, Family & Lifestyles Through Literature. (Family & Consumer Science Ser.). (Illus.). 480p. 1975. ref. ed. o.p. 16.95 (ISBN 0-13-476861-2); pap. 11.95 (ISBN 0-13-476879-5). P-H.
Soules, Jim. How to Single Out Your Mate: A Guide for Twogetherness in the 80's. 140p. 1980. pap. 4.95 (ISBN 0-936890-05-3). Comm Creat.
Spangler, David. Relationships & Identity. 104p. 1981. pap. 4.95 (ISBN 0-905249-31-3, Pub. by Findhorn-Thule Scotland). Hydra Bk.
Sparkman, R. B. The Art of Manipulation: How to Get What You Want Out of People in Business, in Your Personal Life, & in Your Love Life. 1979. 6.95 (ISBN 0-8037-0775-4). Dial.
Stein, Joseph. Making Life Meaningful. LC 78-15347. 1979. 13.95 (ISBN 0-88229-375-3); pap. 6.95 (ISBN 0-88229-651-5). Nelson-Hall.
Steinmetz, Lawrence L. Human Relations: People & Work. (Illus.). 1979. text ed. 18.50 scp (ISBN 0-06-046422-4, HarpC); inst. manual avail. (ISBN 0-06-366430-5). Har-Row.
Steinmetz, Suzanne K. Cycle of Violence: Assertive, Aggressive, & Abusive Family Interation. LC 77-24411. (Praeger Special Studies). 1977. text ed. 21.95 (ISBN 0-03-022876-X); pap. 9.95 (ISBN 0-03-046806-X). Praeger.
Stephens, Ken. Discipleship Evangelism: Study Guide. 1981. pap. 2.50 (ISBN 0-89081-286-1). Harvest Hse.
Stevenson, James. Monty. (Illus.). 32p. 1980. Repr. pap. 1.95 (ISBN 0-590-30268-X, Schol Pap). Schol Bk Serv.
Sugarman, Daniel A. Priceless Gifts: A Psychologist Guide to Loving & Caring. 1978. 9.95 (ISBN 0-02-615270-3). Macmillan.
Sullivan, Harry S. Interpersonal Theory of Psychiatry. Perry, Helen S. & Gawel, Mary L., eds. 1968. pap. 3.25 (ISBN 0-393-00138-5, Norton Lib). Norton.
Sunila, Joyce. The New Lovers: Younger Men-Older Women. (Orig.). 1980. pap. 2.25 (ISBN 0-449-14332-5, GM). Fawcett.
Swensen, Clifford H., Jr. Introduction to Interpersonal Relations. 1973. text ed. 11.95x (ISBN 0-673-07597-4). Scott F.
Tagiuri, Renato & Petrullo, Luigi, eds. Person Perception & Interpersonal Behavior. 1958. 17.50x (ISBN 0-8047-0542-9). Stanford U Pr.
Tannenbaum, Arnold S. Social Psychology of the Work Organization. LC 66-16965. (Behavior Science in Industry Ser). (Orig.). 1966. pap. text ed. 6.95 (ISBN 0-8185-0317-3). Brooks-Cole.
Taylor, Anita & Taylor, Robert. Couples: The Art of Staying Together. rev. ed. 1980. 8.95 (ISBN 0-87491-219-9); pap. 5.95 (ISBN 0-87491-403-5). Acropolis.
Tedeschi, James, et al. Conflict, Power & Games: The Experimental Study of Interpersonal Relations. (Treatises in Social Psychology). 280p. 1973. 15.95x (ISBN 0-202-25018-0). Beresford Bk Serv.
Tedeschi, James T., ed. Social Influence Processes. LC 79-169507. (Treatises in Social Psychology Ser.). 1972. 20.95 (ISBN 0-202-25012-1). Beresford Bk Serv.
Thibaut, John W. & Kelley, Harold H. Social Psychology of Groups. LC 59-11813. (Illus.). 313p. 1959. 23.50 (ISBN 0-471-85866-8). Wiley.
Timmons, Tim. Loneliness Is Not a Disease. LC 80-83845. 1981. pap. 4.95 (ISBN 0-89081-264-0). Harvest Hse.
Torrington, Derek. Face to Face: Techniques for Handling the Personal Encounter at Work. (Illus.). 1972. 16.00x (ISBN 0-8464-0396-X). Beekman Pubs.
Toward Intimacy. 1978. pap. 3.95 (ISBN 0-87705-337-5). Human Sci Pr.
Town Hall Inc. People in Your Life. facs. ed. Hughes, Margaret M., ed. LC 71-142706. (Essay Index Reprint Ser). 1951. 16.00 (ISBN 0-8369-2204-2). Arno.
Training in Human Relations. (Leadership Pamphlet Ser.: No.16). 1959. 1.40 (ISBN 0-88379-027-0). Adult Ed.
Triandis, Harry C. Interpersonal Behavior. LC 76-14005. 1977. pap. text ed. 15.95 (ISBN 0-8185-0188-X). Brooks-Cole.
Turpin, John C. & Turpin, Barbara H. A Positive Approach to Personal Growth. (Illus.). 130p. (Orig.). 1981. pap. text ed. write for info. (ISBN 0-939506-00-9). Turpin & Assocs.
Tway, Eileen, ed. Reading Ladders for Human Relations. 6th ed. 1980. 9.95 (ISBN 0-8268-1414-X). ACE.
Understanding How Groups Work. (Leadership Pamphlet Ser.: No. 4). 1955. 1.40 (ISBN 0-88379-017-3). Adult Ed.
Viscott, David. How to Live with Another Person. LC 74-80711. 148p. 1974. 6.95 (ISBN 0-87795-092-X). Arbor Hse.
--How to Live with Another Person. 1976. pap. 2.25 (ISBN 0-671-83566-1, 80272). PB.
Viscott, David S. How to Live with Another Person. LC 74-80711. (Priam Ser.). 1979. pap. 4.50 (ISBN 0-87795-241-8). Arbor Hse.
Wallace, Walter L. Student Culture: Social Structure & Continuity in a Liberal Arts College. LC 66-15212. (NORC Monographs in Social Research Ser.: No. 9). 1966. 9.50x (ISBN 0-202-09006-X). NORC.
Walton, Richard E. Interpersonal Peacemaking: Confrontations & Third Party Consultation. (Organization Development Ser). (Orig.). 1969. pap. text ed. 6.50 (ISBN 0-201-08435-X). A-W.
Wanderer, Dr. Zev & Fabian, Erika. Making Love Work: New Techniques in the Art of Staying Together. 1979. 10.95 (ISBN 0-399-12427-6). Putnam.
Warschaw, Tessa A. Winning by Negotiation. LC 80-14535. 264p. 1980. 10.95 (ISBN 0-07-000780-2, GB). McGraw.
Weber, Eric. Getting Together. 1977. Repr. text ed. 7.95 (ISBN 0-914094-04-1). Symphony.
--How to Pick up Girls. 1981. cancelled (ISBN 0-914094-00-9). Green Hill.
Webster, Murray, Jr. & Sobieszek, Barbara. Sources of Self Evaluation: A Formal Theory of Significant Others & Social Influence. LC 74-5066. 189p. 1974. 26.95 (ISBN 0-471-92440-7, Pub. by Wiley-Interscience). Wiley.
Wheeler, Ladd, et al. Interpersonal Influence. 2nd ed. 1978. pap. text ed. 11.95 (ISBN 0-205-06061-7). Allyn.
White, Ellen G. How to Get Along with Others. (Uplook Ser.). 1964. pap. 0.75 (ISBN 0-8163-0072-0, 08835-1). Pacific Pr Pub Assn.
Wilding, Michael. Living Together. 1974. 14.95x (ISBN 0-7022-0895-7); pap. 7.95x (ISBN 0-7022-0896-5). U of Queensland Pr.
Witenberg, Earl G., ed. Interpersonal Explorations in Psychoanalysis: New Directions in Theory & Practice. LC 75-174819. 1973. text ed. 13.95x (ISBN 0-465-03391-1). Basic.
Worchel, S. & Goethals, G. Adjustment & Human Relations. 592p. 1981. text ed. 16.95 (ISBN 0-394-32226-6); wkbk. 5.95 (ISBN 0-394-32737-3). Knopf.
Wright, Donald K. & Field, David D. A Human Relations Guide. LC 72-8998. 92p. 1972. pap. text ed. 5.95x (ISBN 0-8422-0272-2). Irvington.
Wright, H. Norman. Communication: Key to Your Marriage. rev. ed. LC 73-88317. 208p. 1979. pap. 4.95 (ISBN 0-8307-0726-3, 5415004). Regal.
Wright, Milton. Getting Along with People: A Guide to Personal Success. 1977. lib. bdg. 15.00 (ISBN 0-8414-9598-X). Folcroft.
Zaleznik, Abraham & Moment, D. Dynamics of Interpersonal Behavior. LC 64-23867. 1964. 25.95 (ISBN 0-471-98120-6, Pub. by Wiley-Hamilton). Wiley.
Zeller, William. Understanding & Accepting Ourselves & Others. pap. 0.65 (ISBN 0-8199-0397-3, L38912). Franciscan Herald.
Zerof, Herbert G. Finding Intimacy: The Art of Happiness in Living Together. 224p. (Orig.). 1981. pap. 6.95 (ISBN 0-86683-618-7). Winston Pr.
Znaniecki, Florian. Social Relations & Social Roles. (Reprints in Sociology Ser). lib. bdg. 28.50x (ISBN 0-697-00219-5); pap. 8.95x (ISBN 0-89197-940-9). Irvington.
Zola, Marion. All the Good Ones Are Married. Kane, Susan N., ed. LC 80-5776. 256p. 1981. 12.95 (ISBN 0-8129-0967-4). Times Bks.

INTERPLANETARY COMMUNICATION
see Interstellar Communication

INTERPLANETARY PROPULSION
see Space Vehicles-Propulsion Systems

INTERPLANETARY VOYAGES
Here are entered early, imaginary and descriptive accounts of travel beyond the earth.
see also Space Flight to Mars

Bergier, Jacques. Extraterrestrial Visitations from Prehistoric Times to the Present. 1974. pap. 1.50 (ISBN 0-451-05942-5, W5942, Sig). NAL.
Berrill, N. J. Worlds Without End. 1964. 5.95 (ISBN 0-02-510340-7). Macmillan.
Chatelain, Maurice. Our Ancestors Came from Outer Space. 1979. pap. 2.25 (ISBN 0-440-16654-3). Dell.
Clarke, Arthur C. Challenge of the Spaceship. 1980. pap. 2.50 (ISBN 0-671-82139-3). PB.
--Report on Planet Three & Other Speculations. LC 74-156515. 1972. 9.95 (ISBN 0-06-010793-6, HarpT). Har-Row.
Cohen, Daniel. The Ancient Visitors. LC 75-21220. 224p. (gr. 4-7). 1976. 7.95 (ISBN 0-385-09786-7). Doubleday.
Colby, C. B. Beyond the Moon: Future Explorations in Interplanetary Space. (Illus.). (gr. 4-7). 1971. PLB 5.29 (ISBN 0-698-30023-8). Coward.
Countryman, Jack. Atlantis & the Seven Stars. LC 77-9182. 1979. 7.95 (ISBN 0-312-05946-9). St Martin.
Drake, W. Raymond. Gods & Spacemen of Greece & Rome. (Orig.). (RL 9). 1977. pap. 1.50 (ISBN 0-451-07620-6, W7620, Sig). NAL.

--Gods & Spacemen of the Ancient Past. 1974. pap. 1.50 (ISBN 0-451-06140-3, W6140, Sig). NAL.

Fowler, Raymond E. The Andreasson Affair. LC 78-11659. 1979. 9.95 (ISBN 0-13-036608-0). P-H.

Goran, Morris. The Modern Myth: Ancient Astronauts & UFOs. LC 76-50190. (Illus.). 1978. 8.95 (ISBN 0-498-02008-8). A S Barnes.

Heppenheimer, T. A. Toward Distant Suns. (Illus.). 256p. 1979. 19.95 (ISBN 0-8117-1578-7). Stackpole.

Macvey, John W. Interstellar Travel: Past, Present & Future. 1978. pap. 2.25 (ISBN 0-380-41368-X, 41368). Avon.

--Interstellar Travel: Past, Present & Future. LC 77-8766. (Illus.). 1977. 25.00x (ISBN 0-8128-2278-1). Stein & Day.

Mooney, Richard E. Colony: Earth. LC 73-90698. 304p. 1974. 25.00x (ISBN 0-8128-1658-7). Stein & Day.

--Gods of Air & Darkness. LC 75-8926. 192p. 1975. 25.00 (ISBN 0-8128-1815-6). Stein & Day.

Murchie, Guy. Music of the Spheres: The Material Universe from Atom to Quasar, Simply Explained, 2 Vols. rev. ed. (Illus.). (YA) (gr. 7-12). Vol. 1. pap. 5.00 (ISBN 0-486-21809-0); Vol. 2. pap. 5.00 (ISBN 0-486-21810-4). Dover.

--Music of the Spheres: The Material Universe from Atom to Quasar, Simply Explained, 2 vols. (Illus.). 20.00 set (ISBN 0-8446-0815-7). Peter Smith.

Navia, Luis E. A Bridge to the Stars: Our Ancient Cosmic Legacy. 1977. 10.95 (ISBN 0-89529-004-9). Avery Pub.

Nicolson, Iain. Road to the Stars. (Illus.). 1978. 14.95 (ISBN 0-688-03336-9). Morrow.

Shaw, Bob. Galactic Tours. (Illus.). 96p. 1981. 15.95 (ISBN 0-86276-005-4). Proteus Pub NY.

Sitchin, Zecharia. The Twelfth Planet. 1978. pap. 2.95 (ISBN 0-380-39362-X, 50351). Avon.

--The Twelfth Planet. LC 75-37857. 356p. 1976. 25.00 (ISBN 0-8128-1939-X). Stein & Day.

Sixteenth Annual Meeting, Anaheim, California, 1970. Space Shuttles & Interplanetary Missions: Proceeding. (Advances in the Astronautical Sciences Ser.: Vol. 28). 1970. 35.00 (ISBN 0-87703-055-3). AM Astronaut.

Steiger, Brad. Worlds Before Our Own. LC 78-18232. 1978. 8.95 (ISBN 0-399-12215-X, Pub. by Berkley). Putnam.

Story, Ronald. The Space Gods Revealed: A Close Look at the Theories of Erich Von Daniken. LC 75-30347. (Illus.). 192p. (YA) 1976. 10.95 (ISBN 0-06-014141-7, HarpT). Har-Row.

Thorne, Ian. Ancient Astronauts. Schroeder, Howard, ed. LC 78-7973. (Search for the Unknown Ser.). (Illus.). (gr. 4). 1978. PLB 6.95 (ISBN 0-913940-86-0); pap. 2.95 (ISBN 0-89686-007-8). Crestwood Hse.

Vance, Adrian. UFO's, the Eye & the Camera. LC 76-48205. (Illus.). 1977. 8.95 (ISBN 0-87929-046-3). Barlenmir.

Von Daniken, Erich. Chariots of the Gods: Unsolved Mysteries of the Past. (Illus.). 1970. 8.95 (ISBN 0-399-10128-4). Putnam.

Von Daniken, Frich. Chariots of the Gods? 1980. pap. 2.50 (ISBN 0-425-04381-9). Berkley Pub.

INTERPLEADER

see Actions and Defenses

INTERPOLATION

see also Approximation Theory; Numerical Integration; Spline Theory

Bergh, J. & Lofstrom, J. Interpolation Spaces: An Introduction. 1976. 32.80 (ISBN 0-387-07875-4). Springer-Verlag.

Davis, Philip J. Interpolation & Approximation. LC 75-2568. (Illus.). 416p. 1975. pap. text ed. 5.50 (ISBN 0-486-62495-1). Dover.

Jordan, Charles. Calculus of Finite Differences. 3rd ed. LC 65-29977. 22.50 (ISBN 0-8284-0033-4). Chelsea Pub.

Steffensen, John F. Interpolation. 2nd ed. LC 50-12797. 14.95 (ISBN 0-8284-0071-7). Chelsea Pub.

Triebel, H. Interpolation Theory: Function Spaces, Differential Operators. (North-Holland Mathematical Library: Vol. 18). 1978. 73.25 (ISBN 0-7204-0710-9, North-Holland). Elsevier.

Walsh, J. L. Interpolation & Approximation by Rational Functions in the Complex Domain. rev. ed. LC 60-3978. (Colloquium Pbns. Ser.: Vol. 20). 1966. 39.60 (ISBN 0-8218-1020-0, COLL-20). Am Math.

INTERPRETATION

see Hermeneutics

INTERPRETATION, BIBLICAL

see Bible-Criticism, Interpretation, etc.

INTERPRETATION, MUSICAL

see Music-Interpretation (Phrasing, Dynamics, etc.)

INTERPRETATION, PHOTOGRAPHIC

see Photographic Interpretation

INTERPRETATION AND CONSTRUCTION (LAW)

see Law-Interpretation and Construction

INTERPRETATIVE SPEECH

see Oral Interpretation

INTERPRETERS

see Translators

INTERPRETING AND TRANSLATING

see Translating and Interpreting

INTERPRETIVE DANCING

see Modern Dance

INTERRACIAL ADOPTION

Blank, Joseph P. Nineteen Steps up the Mountain. 1977. pap. 1.95 (ISBN 0-515-04442-3). Jove Pubns.

Duling, Gretchen A. Adopting Joe: A Black Vietnamese Child. LC 76-20946. (Illus.). 1977. pap. 2.95 (ISBN 0-8048-1203-9). C E Tuttle.

Grow, Lucille J. & Shapiro, Deborah. Black Children-White Parents: A Study of Transracial Adoption. LC 74-29169. (Orig.). 1975. pap. 7.95 (ISBN 0-87868-152-3). Child Welfare.

--Transracial Adoption Today: Views of Adoptive Parents & Social Workers. LC 75-7553. 1975. pap. 4.75 (ISBN 0-87868-153-1). Child Welfare.

Ladner, Joyce. Mixed Families. pap. 3.95 (ISBN 0-686-31407-7). NACAC.

--Mixed Families: Adopting Across Racial Boundaries. 1978. pap. 3.95 (ISBN 0-385-12793-6, Anch). Doubleday.

Shornack, Lawrence L. Adoptive Parent Study: A Report of Survey of Parents Raising Adopted Minority, Older, & Handicapped Children. 1976. 1.25 (ISBN 0-918416-01-9). Open Door Soc.

Simon & Altstein. Transracial Adoption. 18.95 (ISBN 0-686-31406-9). NACAC.

Simon, Rita J. & Altstein, Howard. Transracial Adoption. LC 76-44817. 1977. 21.95 (ISBN 0-471-79208-X, Pub. by Wiley-Interscience). Wiley.

--Transracial Adoption: A Follow-Up. LC 80-8770. 1981. write for info. (ISBN 0-669-04357-5). Lexington Bks.

Zastrow, Charles H. Outcome of Black Children White Parents Transracial Adoptions. LC 76-56070. 1977. soft bdg. 10.00 (ISBN 0-88247-456-1). R & E Res Assoc.

INTERRACIAL MARRIAGE

Cohen, Steven M. Interethnic Marriage & Friendship. Zuckerman, Harriet & Merton, Robert K., eds. LC 79-8985. (Dissertations on Sociology Ser.). 1980. lib. bdg. 25.00x (ISBN 0-405-12958-0). Arno.

Connor, John W. A Study of the Marital Stability of Japanese War Brides. LC 75-36569. 1976. perfect bdg. softcover 9.00 (ISBN 0-88247-376-X). R & E Res Assoc.

Devos, George A. Personality Patterns & Problems of Adjustment in American-Japanese Intercultural Marriages, No. 49. (Asian Folklore & Social Life Monograph). 300p. 1973. 7.30 (ISBN 0-89986-046-X). E Langstaff.

Dunlap, James. Intermarriage Prevents Disease. 1978. pap. 2.50 (ISBN 0-686-22704-2). World Intl.

Gordon, Albert I. Intermarriage: Interfaith, Interracial, Interethnic. LC 80-19279. (Illus.). xiii, 420p. 1980. Repr. of 1966 ed. lib. bdg. 29.75x (ISBN 0-313-22711-X, GOIN). Greenwood.

Kahane, Meir. Why Be Jewish? Intermarriage, Assimilation, & Alienation. LC 77-8774. 264p. 1981. pap. 6.95 (ISBN 0-8128-6129-9). Stein & Day.

Kannan, C. T. Inter-Racial Marriages in London: A Comparative Study. 1972. 10.00 (ISBN 0-685-79107-6). Heinman.

Martinez-Alier, Verena. Marriage, Class & Colour in Nineteenth Century Cuba. LC 73-82463. 224p. 1974. pap. 10.95x (ISBN 0-521-09846-7). Cambridge U Pr.

Mayer, Egon & Sheingold, Carl. Intermarriage & the Jewish Future. LC 79-63378. 46p. 1980. pap. 1.50 (ISBN 0-87495-031-7). Am Jewish Comm.

Porterfield, Ernest. Black & White Mixed Marriages. LC 77-87996. 206p. 1978. 17.95x (ISBN 0-88229-131-9); pap. 8.95x (ISBN 0-88229-484-9). Nelson-Hall.

INTERROGATION

see Questioning

INTERROGATORIES (CRIMINAL PROCEDURE)

see Preliminary Examinations (Criminal Procedure)

INTERSCHOLASTIC ATHLETICS

see School Sports

INTERSEXUALITY

see Hermaphroditism

INTERSTATE AGREEMENTS

Leach, Richard H. & Sugg, Redding S. Administration of Interstate Compacts. Repr. of 1959 ed. lib. bdg. 15.00x (ISBN 0-8371-2154-X, LEIC). Greenwood.

INTERSTATE COMMERCE

see also Bills of Lading; Railroad Law; Restraint of Trade; Trade Regulation

Baxter, Maurice G. Steamboat Monopoly: Gibbons Vs Ogden, 1824. 1972. pap. text ed. 3.10x (ISBN 0-394-31491-3). Phila Bk Co.

Corwin, Edward S. Commerce Power Versus States Rrights. 1959. 8.00 (ISBN 0-8446-1130-1). Peter Smith.

Fellmeth, Robert. Interstate Commerce Omission: The Report on the Interstate Commerce Commission & Transportation. LC 70-112514. (Ralph Nader Study Group Reports). 1970. 8.95 (ISBN 0-670-40019-X, Grossman). Viking Pr.

Frankfurter, Felix. Commerce Clause Under Marshall, Taney & Waite. 6.00 (ISBN 0-8446-2086-6). Peter Smith.

Gavit, Bernard C. Commerce Clause of the United States Constitution. LC 77-121284. Repr. of 1932 ed. 36.00 (ISBN 0-404-02688-5). AMS Pr.

Judson, Frederick N. The Law of Interstate Commerce & Its Federal Regulation. xix, 509p. 1981. Repr. of 1905 ed. lib. bdg. 38.50x (ISBN 0-8377-0735-8). Rothman.

Kallenbach, Joseph E. Federal Cooperation with the States Under the Commerce Clause. LC 69-10112. 1969. Repr. of 1942 ed. lib. bdg. 22.25x (ISBN 0-8371-0507-2, KACC). Greenwood.

Keller, John J. Interstate Motor Carrier Forms Manual: Private, Contract, Exempt. rev. ed. Nelson, Harold C., et al, eds. LC 76-7194. 1979. 69.00 (ISBN 0-686-16913-1). J J Keller.

Kitch, Edmund W. Regulation, Federalism & Interstate Commerce. Tarlock, A. Dan, ed. LC 80-23166. 176p. 1981. lib. bdg. 22.50 (ISBN 0-89946-065-8). Oelgeschlager.

Macveagh, Rogers. The Transportation Act 1920. Bruchey, Stuart, ed. LC 80-1330. (Railroads Ser.). 1981. Repr. of 1923 ed. lib. bdg. 85.00x (ISBN 0-405-13804-0). Arno.

Newcomb, H. T. The Work of the Interstate Commerce Commission. Bruchey, Stuart, ed. LC 80-1334. (Railroads Ser.). (Illus.). 1981. Repr. of 1905 ed. lib. bdg. 12.00x (ISBN 0-405-13808-3). Arno.

Posner, Richard. Robinson-Patman Act. 1977. pap. 4.25 (ISBN 0-8447-3228-1). Am Enterprise.

Reynolds, George G. Distribution of Power to Regulate Interstate Carriers Between the Nation & the States. LC 68-57578. (Columbia University. Studies in the Social Sciences: No. 295). Repr. of 1928 ed. 28.50 (ISBN 0-404-51295-X). AMS Pr.

Rutledge, Wiley. Declaration of Legal Faith. LC 74-114563. (American Constitutional & Legal History Ser). 1970. Repr. of 1947 ed. lib. bdg. 14.95 (ISBN 0-306-71921-5). Da Capo.

Ryden, Elihu D. Federal Fertility in the Stream of Commerce. LC 72-86198. 56p. 1972. pap. text ed. 3.50x (ISBN 0-8422-0220-X). Irvington.

INTERSTATE COMPACTS

see Interstate Agreements

INTERSTATE CONTROVERSIES

Rice, William G. Tale of Two Courts: Judicial Settlement of Controversies Between the States of the Swiss & American Federations. 150p. 1967. 15.00x (ISBN 0-299-04390-8). U of Wis Pr.

INTERSTATE COOPERATION

see Interstate Agreements

INTERSTATE DISPUTES

see Interstate Controversies

INTERSTATE RELATIONS

see also Interstate Agreements; Interstate Controversies

Litwak, Robert, ed. Sources of Inter-State Conflict. LC 80-28448. (Security in the Persian Gulf Ser.: Vol. 2). 100p. 1981. pap. text ed. 10.00 (ISBN 0-86598-045-4). Allanheld.

INTERSTELLAR COMMUNICATION

see also Astronautics-Communication Systems; Radio Astronomy

Cameron, A. G. W., ed. Interstellar Communication: The Search for Extraterrestrial Life. (Illus.). 1963. pap. 9.50 (ISBN 0-8053-1751-1, Adv Bk Prog). Benjamin-Cummings.

Mathes, J. H. & Huett, Lenora. The Amnesia Factor. LC 75-9446. 1975. pap. 4.95 (ISBN 0-89087-023-3). Celestial Arts.

Ponnamperuma, Cyril & Cameron, A. G. W., eds. Interstellar Communication: Scientific Perspectives. (Illus.). 272p. 1974. pap. text ed. 11.50 (ISBN 0-395-17809-6). HM.

Sagan, Carl & Shklovskii, I. S. Intelligent Life in the Universe. LC 64-18404. 1978. pap. text ed. 12.50x (ISBN 0-8162-7913-6). Holden-Day.

Sagan, Carl & Shklovsky, I. S. Intelligent Life in the Universe. 1968. pap. 3.95 (ISBN 0-440-54056-9, Delta). Dell.

Truck, Fred. The Development of Signs in Space: A Futurist Communication from Bolon Dzacab. 5.00 (ISBN 0-938236-03-2). Cookie Pr.

UNA-USA National Policy Panel. Space Communications: Increasing UN Responsiveness to the Problems of Mankind. LC 78-163097. (Illus.). 64p. 1971. pap. text ed. 1.00x (ISBN 0-934654-07-7). UNA-USA.

INTERSTELLAR MATTER

see also Nebulae; Planetary Nebulae

Balian, R., et al, eds. Atomic & Molecular Physics & the Interstellar Matter, 2 vols. LC 75-23253. 1975. Set. 78.00 (ISBN 0-444-10856-4, North-Holland). Elsevier.

Boschke, F., ed. Cosmochemistry. LC 51-5479. (Topics in Current Chemistry: Vol. 44). (Illus.). 200p. 1973. 27.10 (ISBN 0-387-06457-5). Springer-Verlag.

Cadle, Richard D. Particles in the Atmosphere & Space. 236p. 1966. 13.50 (ISBN 0-442-15170-5, Pub. by Van Nos Reinhold). Krieger.

Carson, T. R. & Roberts, M. J., eds. Atoms & Molecules in Astrophysics. (A NATO Advanced Study Institute Volume). 1973. 58.00 (ISBN 0-12-161050-0). Acad Pr.

Chiu Hone-Yeel & Muriel, Amador. Galactic Astronomy, Vols. 1 & 2. 1970. Vol. 1. 73.25x (ISBN 0-677-13750-8); Vol. 2. 63.75x (ISBN 0-677-13760-5); Set. 123.25 (ISBN 0-677-13770-2). Gordon.

Dyson, J. E. & Williams, D. A. The Physics of the Interstellar Medium. 176p. 1981. 45.00x (ISBN 0-686-73065-8, Pub. by Manchester U Pr England). State Mutual Bk.

Elsaesser, H. & Fechtig, H., eds. Interplanetary Dust & Zodiacal Light. LC 78-2597. 1976. pap. 21.20 (ISBN 0-387-07615-8). Springer-Verlag.

Gordon, Mark A. & Snyder, Lewise. Molecules in the Galactic Environment. LC 73-6555. 475p. 1973. 28.25 (ISBN 0-471-31608-3, Pub. by Wiley). Krieger.

Kaplan, S. A. & Pikelner, S. B. Interstellar Medium. LC 70-85076. (Illus.). 1970. 22.50x (ISBN 0-674-46075-8). Harvard U Pr.

Lynds, Beverly T., ed. Dark Nebulae, Globules, & Protostars. LC 73-152040. (Illus.). 158p. 1971. 7.50x (ISBN 0-8165-0300-1). U of Ariz Pr.

Martin, P. G. Cosmic Dust. (Studies in Physics). (Illus.). 1979. 45.00x (ISBN 0-19-851458-1). Oxford U Pr.

NATO Advanced Study Institute, Schliersee, Germany, April, 1973. Interstellar Medium: Proceedings. Pinkau, K., ed. LC 73-91208. (NATO Advanced Study Institutes: No. C-6). 1973. lib. bdg. 37.00 (ISBN 90-277-0417-1, Pub. by Reidel Holland). Kluwer Boston.

Randall, Charles A., ed. Extra-Terrestrial Matter. LC 69-15447. (Illus.). 331p. 1969. 15.00 (ISBN 0-87580-009-2). N Ill U Pr.

Schatzman, Evry & Biermann, Ludwig. Cosmic Gas Dynamics. LC 73-16025. 291p. 1974. 23.00 (ISBN 0-471-75720-9, Pub. by Wiley). Krieger.

Skobel'tsyn, D. V., ed. Methods in Stellar Atmosphere & Interplanetary Plasma Research. (P. N. Lebedev Physics Institute Ser.: Vol. 62). (Illus.). 202p. 1974. 39.50 (ISBN 0-306-10905-0, Consultants). Plenum Pub.

Solomon, P. M. & Edmunds, M. G. Giant Molecular Clouds in the Galaxy. (Illus.). 348p. 1980. 48.00 (ISBN 0-08-023068-7). Pergamon.

Spitzer, Lyman, Jr. Diffuse Matter in Space. (Tracts on Physics & Astronomy, Vol. 28). 1968. 27.00 (ISBN 0-470-81710-0, Pub. by Wiley-Interscience). Wiley.

--Physical Processes in the Interstellar Medium. LC 77-14273. 1978. 23.00 (ISBN 0-471-02232-2, Pub. by Wiley-Interscience). Wiley.

Symposium on Cosmical Gas Dynamics,6th, et al. Interstellar Gas Dynamics: Proceedings. Habing, H. J., ed. LC 78-124849. (IAU Symposia: No.39). 388p. 1970. lib. bdg. 42.00 (ISBN 90-277-0172-5, Pub. by Reidel Holland). Kluwer Boston.

Symposium Organized by the International Astronomical Union, 52nd, the State Univ. of N.Y. at Albany, May-June, 1972. Interstellar Dust & Related Topics: Proceedings. Greenberg, J. M. & Van de Hulst, H. C., eds. LC 73-88590. 500p. 1973. lib. bdg. 84.00 (ISBN 90-277-0396-5, Pub. by Reidel Holland); pap. text ed. 50.00 (ISBN 90-277-0397-3, Pub. by Reidel Holland). Kluwer Boston.

Van Woerden, H., ed. Topics in Interstellar Matter. (Astrophysics & Space Science Library: No. 70). 1977. lib. bdg. 39.50 (ISBN 90-277-0835-5, Pub. by Reidel Holland). Kluwer Boston.

INTERSTELLAR VOYAGES

see Interplanetary Voyages

INTERURBAN RAILROADS

see Street-Railroads

INTERVALS (MUSIC)

see Musical Intervals and Scales

INTERVENTION (INTERNATIONAL LAW)

see also Jurisdiction (International Law); Monroe Doctrine; Neutrality

Chakrabarti, R. Intervention & the Problem of Its Control in the Twentieth Century. 240p. 1974. text ed. 12.00x (ISBN 0-8426-0686-6). Verry.

Halpern, Manfred. Morality & Politics of Intervention. LC 63-12832. (Ethics & Foreign Policy Ser). 1963. pap. 0.50 (ISBN 0-87641-105-7). Coun Rel & Intl.

Kane, William Everett. Civil Strife in Latin America: A Legal History of U.S. Involvement. LC 76-184954. (American Society of International Law Ser). (Illus.). 240p. 1972. 16.00x (ISBN 0-8018-1368-9). Johns Hopkins.

Lillich, Richard B. Humanitarian Intervention & the United Nations. LC 73-78927. (Procedural Aspects of International Law Institute, & Virginia Law Studies). 250p. 1973. 12.50x (ISBN 0-8139-0505-2). U Pr of Va.

Little, Richard. Intervention: External Involvement in Civil Wars. 236p. 1975. 19.50x (ISBN 0-87471-755-8). Rowman.

Mack, Andrew, et al, eds. Imperialism, Intervention & Development. 393p. 1979. 32.00x (ISBN 0-686-28574-3, Pub. by Croom Helm Ltd England). Biblio Dist.

Martin, Charles E. Policy of the United States As Regards Intervention. LC 21-3655. (Columbia University. Studies in the Social Sciences: No. 211). Repr. of 1921 ed. 16.50 (ISBN 0-404-51211-9). AMS Pr.

Ministers of Foreign Affairs of the American Republics-6th-San Jose-Costa Rica-1960. Final Act: Meeting of Consultation. (Sp.). pap. 1.00 (ISBN 0-8270-1675-1). OAS.

Moore, John N. Law & the Indo-China War. LC 73-166383. 704p. 1972. 42.50 (ISBN 0-691-03089-8); pap. 15.50 (ISBN 0-691-10004-7). Princeton U Pr.

Perkins, Whitney T. Constraint of Empire: The United States & Caribbean Interventions. LC 80-27269. (Contributions in Comparative Colonial Studies: No. 8). 320p. 1981. lib. bdg. 35.00 (ISBN 0-313-22266-5, PCE/). Greenwood.

Stern, Ellen P., ed. The Limits of Military Intervention. LC 77-5588. (Sage Series on Armed Forces & Society: Vol. 12). 1977 (ISBN 0-8039-0810-5). pap. 12.50 (ISBN 0-8039-0811-3). Sage.

Thomas, Aaron J. & Thomas, Ann. Dominican Republic Crisis, 1967. Carey, John, ed. LC 67-14395. (Hammarskjold Fourm Ser.: No. 9). 1967. 10.00 (ISBN 0-379-11809-2). Oceana.

Vincent, R. J. Nonintervention & International Order. LC 72-6526. (Center of International Studies, Princeton Univ.). 464p. 1974. 30.00x (ISBN 0-691-05652-8). Princeton U Pr.

Von Mises, Ludwig. A Critique of Interventionism. 1977. 8.95 (ISBN 0-87000-382-8). Arlington Hse.

Young, Oran R. Intermediaries: Third Parties in International Crises. (Center of International Studies). 1967. 28.00x (ISBN 0-691-05621-8). Princeton U Pr.

INTERVENTION (PSYCHOLOGY)

see Operant Behavior

INTERVERTEBRAL DISK

Kramer. Intervertebral Disc Diseases. Date not set. price not set (ISBN 0-8151-5153-5). Year Bk Med.

INTERVIEWING

see also Employment Interviewing; Interviewing in Psychiatry; Interviews; Questioning; Social Case Work

Allen, Bud & Bosta, Diana. Library of Lesson Plans: Vol. 2, No. 3, Corrective Interviewing for Supervisors. 55p. 1981. vinyl 29.95x (ISBN 0-939438-11-9). Rae John.

Benjamin, Alfred D. The Helping Interview. 3rd ed. LC 80-81650. 208p. 1981. pap. text ed. 7.95 (ISBN 0-395-29648-X). HM.

Bessell, Robert. Interviewing & Counselling. 1976. 22.50 (ISBN 0-7134-0965-7, Pub. by Batsford England). David & Charles.

Black, J. M. How to Get Results from Interviewing: A Practical Guide for Operating Management. 1970. 19.95 (ISBN 0-07-005510-6, P&RB). McGraw.

Cannell, Charles F., et al. A Technique for Evaluating Interviewer Performance. LC 74-620203. 138p. 1975. pap. 6.50 (ISBN 0-87944-174-7). Inst Soc Res.

Cross, Crispin P., ed. Interviewing & Communication in Social Work. (Library of Social Work). 192p. 1974. 16.00 (ISBN 0-7100-7879-X); pap. 6.00 (ISBN 0-7100-7880-3). Routledge & Kegan.

Downs, Cal W., et al. The Organizational Communicator. (Illus.). 1977. text ed. 16.95 scp (ISBN 0-06-041734-X, HarpC); instructor's manual avail. (ISBN 0-06-361742-0). Har-Row.

--Professional Interviewing. (Illus.). 432p. 1980. text ed. 15.50 (ISBN 0-06-041739-0, HarpC); pap. text ed. 10.50 scp (ISBN 0-06-041736-6). Har-Row.

Fear, Richard A. McGraw-Hill Course in Effective Interviewing. 1973. 42.50 (ISBN 0-07-079484-7, P&RB). McGraw.

Fletcher, John. Interview at Work. 1973. 14.95x (ISBN 0-7156-0727-8). Intl Ideas.

Garrett, Annette. Interviewing: Its Principles & Methods. 2nd ed. LC 72-78003. 1972. 8.00 (ISBN 0-87304-098-8); pap. 5.00 (ISBN 0-87304-097-X). Family Serv.

Gorden, Raymond L. Interviewing: Strategy, Techniques & Tactics. 3rd ed. 1980. 19.25x (ISBN 0-256-02370-0). Dorsey.

Groves, Robert M. & Kahn, Robert L. Surveys by Telephone: A National Comparison with Personal Interviews. LC 79-51703. (Quantitative Studies in Social Relations Ser.). 1979. 25.00 (ISBN 0-12-304650-5). Acad Pr.

How to Conduct an Appraisal Interview. (Fr. & Span. eds. avail.). 1975. pap. 11.00 (ISBN 0-686-10556-7). Preston.

Hyman, Herbert H. Interviewing in Social Research. LC 54-11209. (Illus.). 1954. 17.50x (ISBN 0-226-36539-5); pap. 5.95 (ISBN 0-226-36538-7, P627, Phoen). U of Chicago Pr.

Interviewing & Counseling. 163p. 1981. pap. text ed. 15.00 (ISBN 0-686-30445-4, B214). ALI-ABA.

Ives, Edward D. The Tape-Recorded Interview: A Manual for Field Workers in Folklore & Oral History. LC 79-20527. 1980. lib. bdg. 9.75x (ISBN 0-87049-257-8); pap. text ed. 5.50x (ISBN 0-87049-291-8). U of Tenn Pr.

Ivey, Allen E. & Authier, Jerry. Microcounseling: Innovations in Interviewing, Counseling, Psychotherapy & Psychoeducation. 2nd ed. (Illus.). 624p. 1978. 29.75 (ISBN 0-398-03712-4). C C Thomas.

Kadushin, Alfred. The Social Work Interview. LC 70-190192. 337p. 1972. 13.50x (ISBN 0-231-03290-0). Columbia U Pr.

Kahn, R. L. & Cannell, C. F. Dynamics of Interviewing: Theory, Technique & Cases. 368p. 1957. 27.95 (ISBN 0-471-45441-9). Wiley.

Maier, Norman R. F. The Appraisal Interview: Three Basic Approaches. LC 75-40984. 228p. 1976. pap. 15.00 (ISBN 0-88390-111-0). Univ Assocs.

Morgan, Henry H. The Interviewer's Manual. 55p. 1973. pap. text ed. 8.70 (ISBN 0-15-816860-7, Psych Corp). HarBraceJ.

O'Leary, Lawrence R. Interviewing for the Decisionmaker. LC 75-44322. 144p. 1976. 14.95x (ISBN 0-88229-215-3); pap. 8.95 (ISBN 0-88229-512-8). Nelson-Hall.

Olson, Richard F. Managing the Interview. LC 80-17112. (Self-Teaching Guide Ser.). 183p. 1980. 7.95 (ISBN 0-471-04859-3, Pub. by Wiley-Interscience). Wiley.

Peven, Dorothy, et al. Interviewing: A Syllabus. (Orig.). 1979. pap. 2.00x (ISBN 0-918560-24-1). A Adler Inst.

Polansky, Norman A. Ego Psychology & Communication: Theory for the Interview. LC 74-116533. 1971. 19.95x (ISBN 0-202-26052-6). Aldine Pub.

Richetto & Zima. Fundamentals of Interviewing. new ed. Applbaum, Ronald & Hart, Roderick, eds. (MODCOM Modules in Speech Communication Ser.). 1976. pap. text ed. 2.50 (ISBN 0-574-22523-4, 13-5523). SRA.

Riker, William H. Study of Local Politics. (Orig.). 1959. pap. text ed. 2.35 (ISBN 0-685-19773-5). Phila Bk Co.

Royal, Robert F. & Schutt, Steven R. The Gentle Art of Interviewing & Interrogation: A Professional Manual & Guide. 1976. 12.95 (ISBN 0-13-351247-9, Busn). P-H.

Slavens, Thomas P. Informational Interviews & Questions. LC 77-18502. 1978. 10.00 (ISBN 0-8108-1102-2). Scarecrow.

Staff of the Survey Research Center. Interviewer's Manual. rev. ed. LC 76-630039. 145p. 1976. 12.00 (ISBN 0-87944-195-X); pap. 8.00 (ISBN 0-87944-194-1). Inst Soc Res.

Steinmetz, Lawrence L. Interviewing Skills for Supervisory Personnel. (Business Ser). (Illus.). 1971. pap. text ed. 8.95 (ISBN 0-201-07280-7). A-W.

Stewart, Charles J. Interviewing Principles & Practices: A Project Text. 112p. 1980. 6.95 (ISBN 0-8403-2210-0). Kendall-Hunt.

Stewart, Charles J. & Cash, William B., Jr. Interviewing: Principles & Practices. 3rd ed. 288p. 1981. pap. text ed. write for info. (ISBN 0-697-04193-X). Wm C Brown.

--Interviewing: Principles & Practices. 2nd ed. 320p. 1978. pap. text ed. write for info. (ISBN 0-697-04149-2); instrs.' manual avail. (ISBN 0-686-67922-9). Wm C Brown.

Turner, David R. Employment Interviewer. 6th ed. LC 68-20391. (Orig.). 1968. lib. bdg. 12.00 (ISBN 0-668-01922-0); pap. 8.00 (ISBN 0-668-00008-2). Arco.

Uris, Auren. Executive Interviewer's Deskbook. 222p. 1978. 49.95 (ISBN 0-87201-395-2). Gulf Pub.

Weinberg, Eve. Community Surveys with Local Talent: A Handbook. (Report Ser: No. 123). 1971. 5.00 (ISBN 0-932132-15-4). NORC.

Wicks, Robert J. & Josephs, Ernest H., Jr. Techniques in Interviewing for Law Enforcement & Corrections Personnel: A Programmed Text. 152p. 1977. pap. 10.75 (ISBN 0-398-03677-2). C C Thomas.

INTERVIEWING–PROGRAMMED INSTRUCTION

Effective Interviewing for the Supervisor. (PRIME VII Ser.). 1965. 25.00 (ISBN 0-8144-1038-3). Am Mgmt.

Ilyin, Donna. Ilyin Oral Interview Test. (Illus.). 1976. tchrs.' manual 15.95 (ISBN 0-88377-057-1); 50 scoring sheets 4.50 (ISBN 0-685-57363-X). Newbury Hse.

Schollick, Nigel & Bloxsom, Peter. Staff Appraisal-Self Appraisal: A Programmed Guide to Interviews. (Illus.). 1972. 18.95x (ISBN 0-7114-4919-8). Intl Ideas.

INTERVIEWING (JOURNALISM)

Brady, John. The Craft of Interviewing. 244p. 1975. 9.95 (ISBN 0-911654-44-5). Writers Digest.

--The Craft of Interviewing. LC 77-76543. 1977. pap. 3.95 (ISBN 0-394-72469-0, Vin). Random.

Broughton, Irv. The Art of Interviewing for Television, Radio & Film. (Illus.). 1981. 14.95 (ISBN 0-8306-9743-8, 1125). TAB Bks.

Hilton, Jack & Knoblauch, Mary. On Television: A Survival Guide for Media Interviews. (Illus.). 176p. 1980. 11.95 (ISBN 0-8144-5627-8). Am Mgmt.

Metzler, K. Creative Interviewing: The Writer's Guide to Gathering Information by Asking Questions. 1977. 12.95 (ISBN 0-13-189720-9); pap. 8.95 (ISBN 0-13-189712-8). P-H.

Presson, Hazel. Student Journalist & Interviewing. LC 67-10292. (Student Journalist Ser). (gr. 7 up). 1979. PLB 7.97 (ISBN 0-8239-0488-1). Rosen Pr.

INTERVIEWING, MEDICAL

see Medical History Taking

INTERVIEWING IN PSYCHIATRY

Argelander, Hermann. The Initial Interview in Psychotherapy. Bernays, Hella F., tr. from Ger. LC 75-17113. 146p. 1976. text ed. 19.95 (ISBN 0-87705-248-4). Human Sci Pr.

Bird, Brian. Talking with Patients. 2nd ed. LC 73-2804. 365p. 1973. 15.50 (ISBN 0-397-50313-X, JBL-Med-Nursing). Har-Row.

Cormier, William H. & Cormier, L. Sherilyn. Interviewing Strategies for Helpers: A Guide to Assessment, Treatment & Evaluation. LC 78-12849. (Psychology Ser.). (Illus.). 1979. text ed. 21.95 (ISBN 0-8185-0282-7). Brooks-Cole.

Davis, John D. The Interview As Arena: Strategies in Standardized Interviews & Psychotherapy. LC 73-107647. 1971. 10.00x (ISBN 0-8047-0729-4). Stanford U Pr.

Easson, William M. Psychiatry: Patient Management Review. LC 76-41171. 1977. pap. 8.00 (ISBN 0-668-04058-0). Arco.

Evans, D. R., et al. Essential Interviewing: A Programmed Approach to Effective Communication. LC 79-13719. 1979. pap. text ed. 9.95 (ISBN 0-8185-0342-4). Brooks-Cole.

Hartman, Henry L. Basic Psychiatry for Corrections Workers. 488p. 1978. 23.75 (ISBN 0-398-03663-2). C C Thomas.

Looff, David H. Getting to Know the Troubled Child. LC 75-43691. 1976. pap. 6.95x (ISBN 0-87049-190-3). U of Tenn Pr.

MacKinnon, Roger A. & Michels, Robert. Psychiatric Interview in Clinical Practice. LC 70-151680. 1971. 16.00 (ISBN 0-7216-5973-X). Saunders.

Polansky, Norman A. Ego Psychology & Communication: Theory for the Interview. LC 74-116533. 1971. 19.95x (ISBN 0-202-26052-6). Aldine Pub.

Reinsch, Lamar & Stano, Michael. Communications in Interviews. 256p. 1982. pap. 11.95 (ISBN 0-13-153502-1). P-H.

Siegman, Aron Wolfe & Pope, Benjamin. Studies in Dyadic Communication: Proceedings of a Research Conference on the Interview. 356p. 1972. text ed. 21.00 (ISBN 0-08-015867-6). Pergamon.

Sullivan, Harry S. Psychiatric Interview. 1970. pap. 2.95 (ISBN 0-393-00506-2, Norton Lib). Norton.

INTERVIEWS

see also Interviewing

Clark, Lawrence P. Introduction to Surveys & Interviews. (Learning Packages in the Policy Sciences: No. 12). (Illus.). 56p. 1978. pap. text ed. 2.50 (ISBN 0-936826-01-0). Pol Stud Assocs.

Coleman, Terry. The Scented Brawl: Selected Articles & Interviews. 1979. 19.95 (ISBN 0-241-10042-9, Pub. by Hamish Hamilton England). David & Charles.

Dorn, Edward. Interviews. Allen, Donald, ed. LC 78-6100. (Writing: 38). 126p. 1980. pap. 5.00 (ISBN 0-87704-038-9). Four Seasons Foun.

Drake, J. D. Interviewing for Managers. LC 73-162471. 1972. 14.50 (ISBN 0-8144-5269-8). AM Mgmt.

Frum, Barbara. As It Happened. 1977. 10.00 (ISBN 0-7710-3195-5). McClelland.

Golson, G. Barry, ed. The Playboy Interview. 722p. 1981. 19.95 (ISBN 0-686-73588-9); pap. 9.95 (ISBN 0-686-73589-7). Playboy.

Gray, Barry. Barry Gray: My Night People. LC 75-14039. 192p. 1975. 7.95 (ISBN 0-671-22090-X). S&S.

Greico, William. O-My-God an Interview. 1978. perfect bdg. 3.50 (ISBN 0-88252-082-2). Paladin Hse.

Grice, Charles R., Jr. Fifteen Tips on Handling Job Interviews. McFadden, S. Michele, ed. 1981. pap. text ed. 29.50 30 copy pack 1.00 ea. (ISBN 0-89262-043-9). Career Pub.

Herst. Selling Yourself. 10.95 (ISBN 0-686-31285-6). New Century.

Higginbotham, James B. & Cox, Keith K. Focus Group Interviews: A Reader. LC 79-15536. 124p. 1979. pap. 14.00 (ISBN 0-87757-123-6). Am Mktg.

Komar, John J. The Interview Game: Winning Strategies for the Job Seeker. 1979. pap. 4.95 (ISBN 0-695-81302-1). New Century.

Lebherz, Richard. Conversations with Practically Everybody. 1977. 8.95 (ISBN 0-8062-0813-9). Carlton.

Maleady, Antoinette. Record & Tape Reviews Index, 1971. LC 72-3355. 1972. 10.00 (ISBN 0-8108-0522-7). Scarecrow.

Martin, Dick. The Executive's Guide to Handling a Press Interview. LC 77-593. 1977. 3.95 (ISBN 0-87576-058-9). Pilot Bks.

Medley, Anthony H. Sweaty Palms: The Neglected Art of Being Interviewed. LC 78-1258. 1978. pap. 4.95 (ISBN 0-534-97999-8, Lifetime Learning Pubns.). CBI Pub.

Schollick, Nigel & Bloxsom, Peter. Staff Appraisal-Self Appraisal: A Programmed Guide to Interviews. (Illus.). 1972. 18.95x (ISBN 0-7114-4919-8). Intl Ideas.

Sevareid, Eric. Conversations with Eric Sevareid. 1977. 6.00 (ISBN 0-8183-0248-8). Pub Aff Pr.

Shouksmith, George. Assessment Through Interviewing. 2nd ed. 1978. text ed. 18.00 (ISBN 0-08-021152-6); pap. text ed. 8.50 (ISBN 0-08-021151-8). Pergamon.

INTESTACY

see Inheritance and Succession

INTESTINAL AND PARASITIC WORMS

see Worms, Intestinal and Parasitic

INTESTINAL INFECTIONS

see Intestines–Bacteriology

INTESTINAL OBSTRUCTIONS

see Intestines–Obstructions

INTESTINAL WORMS

see Worms, Intestinal and Parasitic

INTESTINES

see also Colon (Anatomy); Duodenum; Rectum

Bottone, Edward J., ed. Yersinia Enterocolitica. 240p. 1981. 69.95 (ISBN 0-8493-5545-1). CRC Pr.

Clearfield, Harris R. & Dinoso, Vicente P., eds. Gastrointestinal Emergencies: Thirty-Fourth Hahnemann Symposium. LC 75-37629. (34th). (Illus.). 400p. 1976. 48.00 (ISBN 0-8089-0713-1). Grune.

Csaky, T. Z., ed. Intestinal Absorption & Malabsorption. LC 74-80532. 318p. 1975. 27.00 (ISBN 0-89004-020-6). Raven.

Forth, W. & Rummel, W., eds. Pharmacology of Intestinal Absorption: Gastrointestinal Absorption of Drugs. 1976. text ed. 140.00 (ISBN 0-08-016210-X). Pergamon.

Friedman, M. H., ed. Functions of the Stomach & Intestine. (Illus.). 450p. 1976. 29.50 (ISBN 0-8391-0715-3). Univ Park.

Kenny, Alexander D., ed. Intestinal Calcium Absorption & Its Regulation. 176p. 1981. 49.95 (ISBN 0-8493-5701-2). CRC Pr.

Latimer, Paul R. Behavioral Medicine & Irritable Bowel Syndrome. (General Psychology Ser.). Date not set. price not set (ISBN 0-08-025085-8). Pergamon.

McColl, Ian & Sladen, G. E., eds. Intestinal Absorption in Man. 1975. 56.50 (ISBN 0-12-482150-2). Acad Pr.

Mechanisms of Intestinal Secretion. LC 79-2066. (Kroc Foundation Ser.: Vol. 12). 319p. 1979. 28.00x (ISBN 0-8451-0302-4). A R Liss.

Morton. Guts. 2nd ed. (Studies in Biology: No. 7). 1979. 5.95 (ISBN 0-8391-0154-6). Univ Park.

Robinson, J. W. Intestinal Ion Transport. (Illus.). 1976. 39.50 (ISBN 0-8391-0876-1). Univ Park.

Todd, Ian P., ed. Intestinal Stomas. 1979. 28.50x (ISBN 0-433-32501-1). Intl Ideas.

Voino. Pathogenesis of Intestinal Infections. 1977. 30.00 (ISBN 0-9960006-9-0, Pub. by Kaido Hungary). Heyden.

Wrong, O. M., et al. Large Intestine: Its Role in Mammalian Nutrition & Homeostasis. LC 81-4915. 230p. 1981. 24.95 (ISBN 0-470-27167-1). Halsted Pr.

INTESTINES–BACTERIOLOGY

Drasar, D. R. & Hill, M. J. Human Intestinal Flora. 1974. 45.00 (ISBN 0-12-221750-0). Acad Pr.

Olitzki, A. Enteric Fevers. Causing Organisms & Host's Reactions. Grumbach, A., ed. (Bibliotheca Microbiologica: Vol. 10). 1972. pap. 87.00 (ISBN 3-8055-1237-6). S Karger.

INTESTINES–DISEASES
see Constipation; Diarrhea; Digestive Organs–Diseases; Dysentery; Enteritis; Intestines–Radiography
INTESTINES–INTUSSUSEPTION
see Intussuseption in Children
INTESTINES–OBSTRUCTIONS
Morson, B. C. Histological Typing of Intestinal Tumours. LC 70-101520. (International Histological Classification of Tumours (World Health Organization) Ser.). (Illus.). 69p. 1976. text ed. 53.00 (ISBN 92-4-176015-X); text & slides 142.00 (ISBN 0-89189-114-5). Am Soc Clinical.
INTESTINES–RADIOGRAPHY
Marshak, Richard H. & Lindner, Arthur E. Radiology of the Small Intestine. 2nd ed. LC 75-5053. (Illus.). 705p. 1976. text ed. 42.50 (ISBN 0-7216-6127-0). Saunders.
Nelson, R. S. Radioactive Phosphorus in the Diagnosis of Gastrointestinal Cancer. (Recent Results in Cancer Research: Vol. 10). (Illus.). 1967. 11.30 (ISBN 0-387-03958-9). Springer-Verlag.
INTESTINES–SURGERY
see also Hernia; Intestines–Obstructions
Drobni. Surgery of the Intestines. 1975. 35.00 (ISBN 0-9960008-1-X, Pub. by Kaido Hungary). Heyden.
Drobni, S. Surgery of the Intestines. 1977. 35.00x (ISBN 963-05-0632-7). Intl Pubns Serv.
Ellis, Leslie E. & Ellis, C. Arthur. Lose Weight Without Dieting: Facts & Fictions About Intestinal Bypass Surgery. LC 73-3522. (Illus.). 112p. 1976. 9.95 (ISBN 0-917172-00-0). Heritage Hse Pubs.
Greenlee, Herbert B. Surgery of the Small & Large Intestine. (Illus.). 1973. 27.50 (ISBN 0-8151-3972-1). Year Bk Med.
Hill, Graham L. Ileostomy: Surgery, Physiology & Management. LC 75-44116. (Illus.). 208p. 1976. 29.50 (ISBN 0-8089-0928-2). Grune.
Mahoney, Joanne M. Guide to Ostomy Nursing Care. (Illus.). 1976. 8.95 (ISBN 0-316-54388-8). Little.
INTIMACY (PSYCHOLOGY)
Bernhard, Yetta. Self-Care. LC 75-9448. 1975. 11.95 (ISBN 0-89087-110-8); pap. 7.95 (ISBN 0-89087-111-6). Celestial Arts.
Brancaleone, Jim. Man with a Broken Heart. (Orig., LC 77-072049). 1977. pap. 3.50 (ISBN 0-9601186-1-6). Heartbeat.
Chaikin, Alan L. & Derlega, Valerian J. Sharing Intimacy: What We Reveal to Others & Why. 1975. 10.95 (ISBN 0-13-807867-X, Spec); pap. 3.45 (ISBN 0-13-807859-9). P-H.
Crenshaw, Theresa & Crenshaw, Roger. Expressing Your Feelings: The Key to an Intimate Relationship. 240p. (Orig.). (gr. 11-12). 1981. pap. text ed. 9.95x (ISBN 0-8290-0252-9). Irvington.
Dauw, Dean C. Stranger in Your Bed: A Guide to Emotional Intimacy. LC 78-23444. 1979. 13.95 (ISBN 0-88229-472-5). Nelson-Hall.
Davis, Murray S. Intimate Relations. LC 73-1859. (Illus.). 1973. 12.95 (ISBN 0-02-907020-1); pap. 3.95 (ISBN 0-02-907200-X). Free Pr.
Flanders, James P. Practical Psychology. 352p. 1976. text ed. 17.50 (ISBN 0-06-042084-7, HarpC); instructor's manual avail. (ISBN 0-06-362088-X). Har-Row.
Greenwald, Jerry. Creative Intimacy. 1977. pap. 2.75 (ISBN 0-515-05971-4). Jove Pubns.
Hogenboom, N. G. Incongruity & Incompatibility in Intimate Partner Relationships. 16p. 1974. pap. 4.00 (ISBN 90-220-0473-2, Pub. by PUDOC). Unipub.
Hopson, Barrie & Hopson, Charlotte. Intimate Feedback: Lover's Guide to Getting in Touch with Each Other. 1976. pap. 1.50 (ISBN 0-451-06894-7, W6894, Sig). NAL.
Hunter, J. F. Sexual Morality & Personal Intimacy. LC 79-27352. 1980. 14.95 (ISBN 0-312-71346-0). St Martin.
Jones, Sandy. To Love a Baby. (Illus.). 192p. 1981. 15.00 (ISBN 0-395-31296-5). HM.
Kilpatrick, William K. Identity & Intimacy. 272p. 1975. pap. 4.95 (ISBN 0-440-54576-5, Delta). Dell.
Levinger, George & Raush, Harold L., eds. Close Relationships: Perspectives on the Meaning of Intimacy. LC 77-900. (Illus.). 1977. 12.00x (ISBN 0-87023-238-X). U of Mass Pr.
Luthman, Shirley G. Intimacy: The Essence of Male & Female. LC 72-81832. 1977. pap. 6.95 (ISBN 0-936094-01-X). Mehetabel & Co.
Myers, Lonny & Leggitt, Hunter. Adultery & Other Private Matters: Your Right to Personal Freedom in Marriage. LC 75-4701. (Illus.). 221p. 1975. 15.95 (ISBN 0-911012-51-6). Nelson-Hall.
Olthuis, James. I Pledge You My Troth: Marriage, Family, Friendship. LC 74-25695. 160p. 1975. 4.95 (ISBN 0-06-066394-4, RD-155, HarpR). Har-Row.
Sager, Clifford J. & Hunt, Bernice. Intimate Partners: Hidden Patterns in Love Relationships. 1979. 8.95 (ISBN 0-07-054427-1, GB). McGraw.
Shor, Joel & Sanville, Jean. Illusion in Loving: A Psychoanalytic Approach to the Evolution of Intimacy & Autonomy. 1979. pap. 2.95 (ISBN 0-14-005119-8). Penguin.
--Illusion in Loving: A Psychoanalytic Approach to the Evolution of Intimacy & Autonomy. LC 77-85416. 1978. 15.00 (ISBN 0-930578-00-7). Double Helix.
Soules, Jim. How to Single Out Your Mate: A Guide for Twogetherness in the 80's. 140p. 1980. pap. 4.95 (ISBN 0-936890-05-3). Comm Creat.
Stark, Edward. Intimacy. 1978. pap. 1.95 (ISBN 0-8439-0524-7, Leisure Bks). Nordon Pubns.
INTOLERANCE
see Fanaticism; Liberty of Conscience; Religious Liberty; Toleration
INTOXICANTS
see Alcohol; Alcoholic Beverages; Liquors; Stimulants
INTOXICATION
see Alcoholism; Drunkenness (Criminal Law); Liquor Problem; Narcotic Habit; Temperance
INTRACOASTAL NAVIGATION
see Intracoastal Waterways
INTRACOASTAL WATERWAYS
see also Canals; Inland Navigation
Fagan, Brian. California Coastal Passages. Young, Noel, ed. (Illus.). (Orig.). 1981. pap. 16.95 (ISBN 0-88496-161-3, Co-Pub by ChartGuide). Capra Pr.
Hadfield, Charles & Norris, John. Waterways to Stratford. 2nd ed. (Canal of the British Isles Ser.). (Illus.). 1962. 4.95 (ISBN 0-7153-4231-2). David & Charles.
Inland & Maritime Waterways & Ports: Proceedings of the XXV Congress of the Permanent International Association of Navigation Congresses, (PIANC) Edinburgh, Scotland, 11 vols. (Illus.). 2750p. 1981. 400.00 (ISBN 0-08-026750-5). Pergamon.
Intracostal Waterway. 1939. 39.00 (ISBN 0-403-02213-4). Somerset Pub.
Legget, Robert F. Ottawa Waterway: Gateway to a Continent. LC 75-6780. (Illus.). 320p. 1975. 20.00 (ISBN 0-8020-2189-1); pap. 7.50 (ISBN 0-8020-6300-4). U of Toronto Pr.
The Ocean Highway. LC 72-10937. 1939. 39.00 (ISBN 0-403-02183-9). Somerset Pub.
Paget-Tomlinson, E. Britain's Canal & River Craft. 1981. 30.00x (ISBN 0-686-77415-9, Pub. by Moorland). State Mutual Bk.
Priestley, Joseph. Priestley's Navigable Rivers & Canals, 1831. (Illus.). 702p. 1969. 7.50 (ISBN 0-7153-4395-5). David & Charles.
Theberge, Clifford & Theberge, Elaine. The Trent-Severn Waterway: A Traveler's Companion. new ed. (Illus.). 1978. 13.95 (ISBN 0-89522-009-1); pap. 8.95 (ISBN 0-89522-010-5). Samuel Stevens.
Ware, M. E. Narrow Boats at Work. 144p. 1981. 40.00x (ISBN 0-686-73695-8, Pub. by Moorland). State Mutual Bk.
INTRACORPOREAL ARTIFICIAL HEART
see Heart, Artificial
INTRACRANIAL ANEURYSMS
Dandy, Walter E. Intracranial Arterial Aneurysms. (Illus.). 1969. Repr. of 1944 ed. 18.50 (ISBN 0-02-843550-8). Hafner.
Hopkins, Leo N. & Long, Donlin M., eds. Neurosurgery of Aneurysms. (Seminars in Neurological Surgery Ser.). 1981. text ed. 35.50 (ISBN 0-89004-481-3). Raven.
INTRACRANIAL TUMORS
see also Brain–Diseases
Bailey, Percival. Intracranial Tumors. 2nd ed. (Illus.). 524p. 1948. ed. spiral bdg. 49.50photocopy (ISBN 0-398-04197-0). C C Thomas.
Bailey, Percival, et al. Intracranial Tumors of Infancy & Childhood. (Illus.). 1939. 17.50x (ISBN 0-226-03451-8). U of Chicago Pr.
Cuneo, Henry M. & Rand, Carl W. Brain Tumors of Childhood. (American Lecture Neurology). (Illus.). 236p. 1952. 25.50 (ISBN 0-398-04235-7). C C Thomas.
Cushing, Harvey. Intracranial Tumors: Notes Upon a Series of Two Thousand Verified Cases with Surgical-Mortality Percentages Pertaining Thereto. (Illus.). 154p. 1932. ed. spiral bdg. 18.75photocopy (ISBN 0-398-04236-5). C C Thomas.
Cushing, Harvey & Bailey, Percival. Tumors Arising from the Blood Vessels of the Brain: Angiomatous Malformations & Hemangioblastomas. (Illus.). 232p. 1928. ed. spiral bdg. 24.50photocopy (ISBN 0-398-04238-1). C C Thomas.
Dandy, Walter E. Benign Tumors in the Third Ventricle of the Brain: Diagnosis & Treatment. (Illus.). 1933. ed. spiral bdg. 18.50photocopy (ISBN 0-398-04241-1). C C Thomas.
--Selected Writings of Walter E. Dandy. (Illus.). 800p. 1957. ed. spiral bdg. 69.50photocopy (ISBN 0-398-04242-X). C C Thomas.
Davidoff, L. M., et al. Neuroradiology Workshop. Incl. Vol. 1. Scalp, Skull & Meninges. (Illus.). 264p. 1961. 68.00 (ISBN 0-8089-0112-5); Vol. 2. Intracranial Tumors Other Than Meningiomas. (Illus.). 410p. 1963. 83.75 (ISBN 0-8089-0113-3); Vol. 3. Non-Neoplastic Intracranial Lesions. (Illus.). 584p. 1968. 104.00 (ISBN 0-8089-0114-1). LC 60-16433. Grune.
Paoletti, P., et al, eds. Multidisciplinary Aspects of Brain Tumor Therapy. (Neurooncology Ser.: Vol. 1). 404p. 1979. write for info. (Noth Holland). Elsevier.
Vinkin, P. J. & Bruyn, G. W. Handbook of Clinical Neurology, Vol. 16: Tumors of the Brain & Skull, Pt. 1. (Illus.). 700p. 1975. 146.50 (ISBN 0-444-10495-X, North-Holland). Elsevier.
INTRAMURAL SPORTS
American Alliance for Health, Physical Education & Recreation. Intramural Portfolio. 1978. pap. 4.50 (ISBN 0-685-29042-5, 245-26220). AAHPERD.
Beeman, Harris F., et al. Intramural Sports: A Text & Study Guide. 3rd, rev. ed. LC 79-92382. 128p. 1980. pap. text ed. 7.95x (ISBN 0-916622-16-9). Princeton Bk Co.
Colgate, John A. Administration of Intramural & Recreational Activities: Everyone Can Participate. LC 77-9265. 1978. text ed. 21.95 (ISBN 0-471-01728-0). Wiley.
Hendy, C. Martin & McGregor, Ian. Intramurals: A Teacher's Guide. (Illus.). 1979. pap. text ed. 4.95 (ISBN 0-918438-45-4). Leisure Pr.
Hyatt, Ronald W. Intramural Sports: Organization & Administration. LC 76-29694. (Illus.). 1977. pap. text ed. 10.95 (ISBN 0-8016-2320-0). Mosby.
Kleindienst, V. K. & Weston, A. Recreational Sports Program: Schools...Colleges...Communities. LC 77-16808. 1978. 17.95 (ISBN 0-13-767905-X). P-H.
McGuire, Raymond & Mueller, Pat, eds. Bibliography of References for Intramural & Recreational Sports. LC 79-127170. 1975. pap. text ed. 5.25 (ISBN 0-918438-07-1). Leisure Pr.
Manjone, Joseph A. & Bowen, Robert T. Co-Rec Intramural Sports Handbook. 1978. pap. text ed. 4.95 (ISBN 0-918438-10-1). Leisure Pr.
Means, L. Intramurals: Their Organization & Administration. 2nd ed. 1973. ref. ed. 16.95 (ISBN 0-13-477216-4). P-H.
Mueller, Pat & Reznik, John W. Intramural-Recreational Sports: Programming & Administration. 5th ed. LC 78-10122. 1979. text ed. 19.95 (ISBN 0-471-04911-5). Wiley.
Nordly, Carl L. The Administration of Intramural Athletics for Men in Colleges & Universities. LC 70-177108. (Columbia University. Teachers College. Contributions to Education: No. 716). Repr. of 1937 ed. 17.50 (ISBN 0-404-55716-3). AMS Pr.
Peterson, James A. Intramural Administration: Theory & Practice. 384p. 1976. 15.95 (ISBN 0-13-477232-6). P-H.
Peterson, James A. & Preo, Lawrence S., eds. Intramural Director's Handbook. 1978. pap. text ed. 8.95 (ISBN 0-918438-08-X). Leisure Pr.
Rokosz, Francis M. Structured Intramurals. LC 74-12918. (Illus.). 306p. 1975. text ed. 10.50 (ISBN 0-7216-7635-9). HR&W.
Sattler, Thomas P., et al, eds. Theoretical & Operational Aspects of Intramural Sports. 1978. pap. text ed. 8.95 (ISBN 0-918438-44-6). Leisure Pr.
Tyler, Coulbourn. Intramural Director's Guide to Program Evaluation. 104p. (Orig.). 1981. pap. text ed. 7.95 (ISBN 0-918438-67-5). Leisure Pr.
INTRAOCULAR PRESSURE, HIGH
see Glaucoma
INTRATRACHEAL ANESTHESIA
Gillespie, Noel A. Endotracheal Anesthesia. rev. ed. Bamforth, Betty J. & Siebecker, Karl L., eds. (Illus.). 256p. 1963. 17.50x (ISBN 0-299-00280-2). U of Wis Pr.
INTRAUTERINE CONTRACEPTIVES
see also Birth Control; Contraception
Edelman, David A., et al. Intrauterine Devices & Their Complications. (Medical Bks.). 1979. lib. bdg. 20.00 (ISBN 0-8161-2134-6, Hall Medical). G K Hall.
Elstein, Max & Sparks, Richard. Intrauterine Contraception, Vol. 1. Briggs, Michael, ed. (Annual Research Reviews Ser.). 1978. 12.00 (ISBN 0-88831-021-8). Eden Med Res.
Hafez, E. S. & Van Os, W. A., eds. Medicated Intrauterine Devices: Physiological & Clinical Aspects. (Developments in Obstetrics & Gynecology: No. 5). (Illus.). 245p. 1980. lib. bdg. 55.00 (ISBN 90-247-2371-X, Pub. by Martinus Nijhoff Netherlands). Kluwer Boston.
International Conference on Intrauterine Contraception, 3rd, Cairo, 1974. Analysis of Intrauterine Contraception: Proceedings. Hefnawi, F. & Segal, S. J., eds. 1976. 51.25 (ISBN 0-444-11043-7, North-Holland). Elsevier.
Kolbe, Helen K. Intrauterine Devices Abstracts: A Guide to the Literature, 1976-1979. (Population Information Library Ser.: Vol. 1). 575p. 1980. 75.00 (ISBN 0-306-65191-2, IFI). Plenum Pub.
Moghissi, Kamran S., ed. Controversies in Contraception. LC 78-15812. 250p. 1979. 15.00 (ISBN 0-686-74095-5). Krieger.
Newton, John R. Managing Patients with Intrauterine Devices. 1979. pap. 6.95 (ISBN 0-917634-07-1). Creative Infomatics.
Snowden, Robert. The IUD. 117p. text ed. 9.95 (ISBN 0-85664-439-0). Univ Park.
Wheeler, Robert G., et al, eds. Intrauterine Devices: Development, Evaluation, & Program Implementation. 1974. 35.00 (ISBN 0-12-745550-7). Acad Pr.
Wishik, Samuel M. & Hulka, Jaroslav F. Casebook for the Intrauterine Contraception Device. 2nd ed. 1974. pap. 2.30 (ISBN 0-89055-122-7). Carolina Pop Ctr.
INTRAVENOUS FEEDING
see Artificial Feeding
INTRAVENOUS INJECTIONS
see Injections, Intravenous
INTRAVENOUS THERAPY
Coco, Charlene D. Intravenous Therapy: A Handbook for Practice. LC 79-19930. 1980. pap. text ed. 10.50 (ISBN 0-8016-0995-X). Mosby.
Gahart, Betty L. Intravenous Medications: A Handbook for Nurses & Other Allied Health Personnel. 2nd ed. LC 76-30576. (Illus.). 1977. pap. text ed. 10.95 (ISBN 0-8016-1718-9). Mosby.
Kurdi, William J. I. V. Equipment Safety Manual. Kurdi, Kevin J., ed. 1980. pap. 4.95 (ISBN 0-686-28482-8). Med Educ.
--Modern Intravenous Therapy Procedures. Kurdi, James K., ed. 1980. pap. text ed. 24.95 (ISBN 0-686-28481-X). Med Educ.
Managing I. V. Therapy. LC 79-28050. (Nursing Photobook Ser.). (Illus.). 1979. text ed. 12.95 (ISBN 0-916730-18-2). InterMed Comm.
Phillips, I., et al, eds. Microbiological Hazards of Infusion Therapy. LC 76-47865. (Illus.). 194p. 1976. 22.00 (ISBN 0-88416-187-0). Wright-PSG.
Plumer, Ada L. Principles & Practices of Intravenous Therapy. 2nd ed. 1975. pap. 9.95 (ISBN 0-316-71133-0). Little.
Scranton, Pierce E. Practical Techniques in Venipuncture. (Illus.). 180p. 1977. pap. 5.00 (ISBN 0-683-07551-9). Williams & Wilkins.
Towse, G., ed. The Role of Intravenous Miconazole in the Treatment of Systemic Mycoses. (Royal Society of Medicine International Congress & Symposium Ser.: No. 45). 1981. write for info. (ISBN 0-8089-1399-9). Grune.
INTRENCHMENTS
see also Attack and Defense (Military Science); Mines, Military
Ashworth, Tony. Trench Warfare. LC 80-13696. 258p. 1980. text ed. 43.50x (ISBN 0-8419-0615-7). Holmes & Meier.
INTRODUCTION OF ANIMALS
see Animal Introduction
INTRODUCTION OF PLANTS
see Plant Introduction
INTRODUCTION OF SPEAKERS
see Public Speaking–Introductions, Anecdotes, Etc.
INTROSPECTION
Constas, Robert. Death Does Not Exist - Psychology of Becoming Oneself. 1979. pap. 2.00 (ISBN 0-911794-48-4). Aqua Educ.
Dorsey, John M., ed. The Growth of Self-Insight. LC 61-18939. (Leo M. Franklin Memorial Lectures in Human Relations Ser: Vol. 10). 1962. 6.95x (ISBN 0-8143-1186-5). Wayne St U Pr.
Frisch, Ann & Frisch, Paul. Discovering Your Hidden Self. (RL 10). 1976. pap. 1.75 (ISBN 0-451-06994-3, E6994, Sig). NAL.
Hong, Edna. The Downward Ascent. LC 78-66942. 1979. pap. 3.50 (ISBN 0-8066-1679-2, 10-1955). Augsburg.
Leban, Adrienne. Inner Energy. Stiskin, Nahum, ed. LC 78-73472. (Illus.). 1979. pap. 5.95 (ISBN 0-394-73777-6). Autumn Pr.
Lefebvre, Vladimir A. The Structure of Awareness: Toward a Symbolic Language of Human Reflexion. LC 76-51843. (Library of Social Research: Vol. 41). 200p. 1977. 20.00 (ISBN 0-8039-0720-6); pap. 9.95 (ISBN 0-8039-0721-4). Sage.
Schuurman, C. J. Intrance: Fundamental Psychological Problems of the Inner & Outer World. Boer-Hoff, Louise E., tr. from Dutch. LC 78-70618. (Illus.). 1981. pap. 6.95 (ISBN 0-89793-023-1). Hunter Hse.

INTROSPECTION (THEORY OF KNOWLEDGE)
see Self-Knowledge, Theory of
INTROVERSION
see also Autism
Lloyd, Craig. Aggressive Introvert: Herbert Hoover & Public Relations Management, 1912-1932. LC 72-12608. 220p. 1973. 10.75 (ISBN 0-8142-0181-4). Ohio St U Pr.
Schwegler, Raymond A. A Study of Introvert-Extravert Responses to Certain Test Situations. LC 76-177805. (Columbia University. Teachers College. Contributions to Education: No. 361). Repr. of 1929 ed. 17.50 (ISBN 0-404-55361-3). AMS Pr.
Shapiro, Kenneth & Alexander, Irving E. The Experience of Introversion: An Integration of Phenomenological Empirical & Jungian Approaches. LC 74-83142. 1975. 12.50 (ISBN 0-8223-0328-0). Duke.
INTRUSIONS (GEOLOGY)
see also Sills (Geology)
Gilbert, Grove K. Report of the Geology of the Henry Mountains: U.S. Geographical & Geological Survey of the Rocky Mounntain Region. Albritton, Claude C., Jr., ed. LC 77-6519. (History of Geology Ser.). (Illus.). 1978. Repr. of 1877 ed. lib. bdg. 15.00x (ISBN 0-405-10441-3). Arno.
INTUITION
see also Knowledge, Theory Of; Perception; Reality
Allen, Myron S. Psycho-Dynamic Synthesis. LC 66-17160. 248p. 1979. Repr. of 1966 ed. soft cover 11.95 (ISBN 0-918936-07-1). Astara.
Brandt, Richard B. Philosophy of Schleiermacher: The Development of His Theory of Scientific & Religious Knowledge. LC 68-19265. 1968. Repr. of 1941 ed. lib. bdg. 16.75x (ISBN 0-8371-0027-5, BRPS). Greenwood.
Bunge, Mario. Intuition & Science. LC 75-11792. 142p. 1975. Repr. of 1962 ed. lib. bdg. 15.00x (ISBN 0-8371-8066-X, BUIS). Greenwood.
Fisher, Milton. Intuition: How to Use It for Success & Happiness. 192p. 1981. 11.50 (ISBN 0-525-93111-2, 01214-360). Dutton.
Hudson, W. D. Ethical Intuition. (Orig.). 1967. pap. 4.50 (ISBN 0-312-26495-X, E63500). St Martin.
Levinas, Emmanuel. The Theory of Intuition in Husserl's Phenomenology. Orianne, Andre, tr. from Fr. (Studies in Phenomenology & Existential Philosophy). 165p. 1973. 11.95x (ISBN 0-8101-0413-X). Northwestern U Pr.
Troelstra, A. S. Principles of Intuitionism. LC 74-88182. (Lecture Notes in Mathematics: Vol. 95). 1969. pap. 10.70 (ISBN 0-387-04614-3). Springer-Verlag.
Van Der Post, Laurens. Intuition, Intellect & the Racial Question. 40p. 1976. Repr. of 1964 ed. pap. 1.50 (ISBN 0-913098-13-2). Myrin Institute.
Vaughan, Frances E. Awakening Intuition. LC 77-27685. 1979. pap. 3.95 (ISBN 0-385-13371-5, Anch). Doubleday.
INTUITION (PSYCHOLOGY)
see also Perception
Bastick, T. Intuition: How We Think & Act. 1981. price not set (ISBN 0-471-27992-7, Pub. by Wiley Interscience). Wiley.
Berne, Eric. Intuition & Ego States: The Origins of Transactional Analysis. McCormick, Paul, ed. LC 76-57549. (Illus.). 1977. pap. 4.95 (ISBN 0-89489-001-8). TA Press.
Burden, Virginia. The Process of Intuition. rev. ed. LC 75-4170. 100p. 1975. pap. 2.50 (ISBN 0-8356-0466-7, Quest). Theos Pub Hse.
Fischbein, E., ed. The Intuitive Sources of Probabilistic Thinking in Children. LC 75-22376. (Synthese Library: No.85). xiii, 201p. 1975. lib. bdg. 39.50 (ISBN 90-277-0626-3, Pub. by Reidel Holland). Kluwer Boston.
INTUITION OF DURATION
see Time Perception
INTUITIONISTIC MATHEMATICS
Dummett, Michael & Minio, Robert. Elements of Intuitionism. (Oxford Logic Guides Ser.). 1977. text ed. 45.00x (ISBN 0-19-853158-3). Oxford U Pr.
Luckhardt, H. Extensional Goedel Functional Interpretation: A Consistency Proof of Classical Analysis. LC 72-96046. (Lecture Notes in Mathematics: Vol. 306). 161p. 1973. pap. 8.50 (ISBN 0-387-06119-3). Springer-Verlag.
Troelstra, A. S. Choice Sequences: A Chapter of Intuitionistic Mathematics. (Oxford Logic Guides Ser.). 1977. 22.50x (ISBN 0-19-853163-X). Oxford U Pr.
--Metamathematical Investigations of Intuitionistic Arithmetic & Analysis. (Lecture Notes in Mathematics: Vol. 344). pap. 19.20 (ISBN 0-387-06491-5). Springer-Verlag.
INTUSSUSEPTION IN CHILDREN
Ravitch, Mark M. Intussusception in Infants & Children. (Illus.). 156p. 1981. 28.50 (ISBN 0-87527-169-3). Green.
INVALID COOKERY
see Cookery for the Sick
INVALIDS
see also Convalescence; Handicapped; Occupational Therapy
INVALIDS–RECREATION
see Handicapped–Recreation
INVARIANT IMBEDDING
Angel, Edward & Bellman, Richard. Dynamic Programming & Partial Differential Equations. (Mathematics in Science & Engineering Ser: Vol. 88). 1972. 36.50 (ISBN 0-12-057950-2). Acad Pr.
Lee, E. Stanley. Quasilinearization & Invariant Imbedding. (Mathematics in Science & Engineering Ser.,: Vol. 41). 1968. 48.00 (ISBN 0-12-440250-X). Acad Pr.
Meyer, Gunther H. Initial Value Methods for Boundary Value Problems: Theory & Applications of Invariant Imbedding. (Mathematics in Science & Engineering Ser.). 1973. 38.00 (ISBN 0-12-492950-8). Acad Pr.
Shimizu, Akinao & Aoki, Katsutada. Application of Invariant Imbedding to Reactor Physics. (Nuclear Science & Technology Ser). 1972. 34.50 (ISBN 0-12-640150-0). Acad Pr.
INVARIANTS
see also Invariant Imbedding
Conley, C. Isolated Invariant Sets & the Morse Index. LC 78-1577. (Conference Board of the Mathematical Sciences Ser.: No. 38). 1978. 12.80 (ISBN 0-8218-1688-8, CBMS 38). Am Math.
Dieudonne, J. A. & Carrell, James B. Invariant Theory: Old & New. 1971. 17.00 (ISBN 0-12-215540-8). Acad Pr.
Fogarty, John. Invariant Theory. (Math Lecture Notes Ser.: No. 29). 1969. 17.50 (ISBN 0-8053-2570-0, Adv Bk Prog); pap. 8.50 (ISBN 0-8053-2571-9, Adv Bk Prog). Benjamin-Cummings.
Grace, John A. & Young, Alfred. The Algebra of Invariants. LC 65-11860. 1965. 13.95 (ISBN 0-686-70735-4). Chelsea Pub.
Hauptman, H. Crystal Structure Determination: The Role of Cosine Semivariants. LC 72-80574. 407p. 1972. 45.00 (ISBN 0-306-30703-0, Plenum Pr). Plenum Pub.
Hilbert, D., et al. Hilbert's Papers on Invariant Theory. LC 78-17596. (LIE Groups: History Frontiers & Applications Ser.: No. 8). 1978. 35.00 (ISBN 0-915692-26-0). Math Sci Pr.
Karras, U., et al. Cutting and Pasting of Manifolds: SK-Groups. LC 73-76374. (Mathematics Lecture Ser: No. 1). 70p. 1973. pap. 3.00 (ISBN 0-914098-10-1). Publish or Perish.
Logan, John D., ed. Invariant Variational Principles. 1977. 30.00 (ISBN 0-12-454750-8). Acad Pr.
Olum, Paul. Invariants for Effective Homotopy Classification & Extension of Mappings. LC 52-42839. (Memoirs: No. 37). 1978. pap. 12.00 (ISBN 0-8218-1237-8, MEMO-37). Am Math.
Sakurai, J. J. Invariance Principles & Elementary Particles. (Investigations in Physics Ser.: Vol. 10). 1964. 20.00x (ISBN 0-691-07987-0). Princeton U Pr.
Sanders, Gerald A. Invariant Ordering. (Janua Linguarum Series Minor: No. 198). 156p. (Orig.). 1975. pap. text ed. 27.50x (ISBN 0-686-22607-0). Mouton.
Springer, T. A. Invariant Theory. LC 77-5890. (Lecture Notes in Mathematics: Vol. 585). 1977. pap. 9.80 (ISBN 0-387-08242-5). Springer-Verlag.
INVARIANTS, DIFFERENTIAL
see Differential Invariants
INVASION OF PRIVACY
see Privacy, Right of
INVASIONS OF ROME, BARBARIAN
see Barbarian Invasions of Rome
INVECTIVE
see also Satire
Flynn, Charles P. Insult & Society: Patterns of Comparative Interaction. 1976. 11.50 (ISBN 0-8046-9152-5, National University Pub). Kennikat.
The Insult Dictionary: How to Get What You Want in Five Nasty Languages. 1981. pap. 4.95 (ISBN 0-686-29649-4). Natl Textbk.
McPhee, Nancy. Book of Insults: Ancient & Modern. 1980. pap. 2.95 (ISBN 0-14-005365-4). Penguin.
--The Book of Insults Ancient & Modern. LC 78-19201. (Illus.). 1978. 6.95 (ISBN 0-312-08929-5). St Martin.
Markert, Ludwig. Struktur und Bezeichnung des Scheltworts. (Beiheft 40 zur fur die Alttesta-Mentliche Wissenschaft). 1977. text ed. 69.50x (ISBN 3-11-005813-8). De Gruyter.
Roback, A. A. A Dictionary of International Slurs. LC 76-5696. (Maledicta Press Publications Ser.: Vol. 5). 1979. pap. 15.00 (ISBN 0-916500-05-5). Maledicta.
Roylance, William H. Complete Book of Insults, Boasts & Riddles. 1970. 10.95 (ISBN 0-13-157453-1, Reward); pap. 3.95 (ISBN 0-13-157479-5). P-H.
Safian, Louis H. Two Thousand More Insults. 224p. 1976. pap. 3.95 (ISBN 0-8065-0521-4). Citadel Pr.
INVENTIONS
see also Creation (Literary, Artistic, etc.); Inventors; Patents; Research, Industrial; Technological Innovations; Technology Transfer
Arnold, Tom & Vaden, Frank S. Invention Protection for Practicing Engineers. (Professional Engineering Career Development). 1971. 14.95x (ISBN 0-8464-0528-8). Beekman Pubs.
Baker, Henry E. Colored Inventor: A Record of Fifty Years. LC 71-75851. (American Negro: His History & Literature, Ser. No. 2). 1969. pap. 1.00 (ISBN 0-405-01943-2). Arno.
Baker, R. New & Improved. 168p. 1981. 30.00x (ISBN 0-686-73697-4, Pub. by Brit Lib England). State Mutual Bk.
Beard, Charles A., ed. Century of Progress. facs. ed. LC 79-128205. (Essay Index Reprint Ser). 1932. 25.00 (ISBN 0-8369-1903-3). Arno.
Berle, Alf K. Inventions, Patents & Their Management. 602p. 1959. 23.50 (ISBN 0-442-00712-4, Pub. by Van Nos Reinhold). Krieger.
Black, William C. Hooked on Flies: Confessions of a Pattern Inventor. 160p. 1980. 13.50 (ISBN 0-87691-312-5). Winchester Pr.
Brown, Mike. The New Nineteen Eighty Suppressed Inventions & How They Work. 2nd ed. 106p. 1974. pap. 11.95 (ISBN 0-686-70916-0). Madison Co.
Burlingame, Roger. Engines of Democracy: Inventions & Society in Mature America. LC 75-22804. (America in Two Centuries Ser). (Illus.). 1976. Repr. of 1940 ed. 37.00x (ISBN 0-405-07676-2). Arno.
--March of the Iron Men: A Social History of Union Through Invention. LC 75-22805. (America in Two Centuries Ser). (Illus.). 1976. Repr. of 1938 ed. 31.00x (ISBN 0-405-07677-0). Arno.
Calvert, Robert, ed. The Encyclopedia of Patent Practice & Invention Management. LC 74-1028. 880p. 1974. Repr. of 1964 ed. 41.50 (ISBN 0-88275-181-6), Krieger.
Carter, E. F. Dictionary of Inventions & Discoveries. rev. 2nd ed. LC 75-37058. 208p. 1976. 14.50x (ISBN 0-8448-0867-9). Crane-Russak Co.
Clarke, Arthur C. Profiles of the Future. 1977. pap. 2.25 (ISBN 0-445-04061-0). Popular Lib.
Clarke, Donald. Enciclopedia De los Inventos. 2nd ed. 128p. (Espn.). 1978. 25.50 (ISBN 84-7091-134-1, S-50483). French & Eur.
Cohen, Randy & Anderson, Alexandra. Why Didn't I Think of That. (Illus.). 1980. pap. 5.95 (ISBN 0-449-90037-1, Columbine). Fawcett.
Conference of the Universities. The Rate & Direction of Inventive Activity: Economic & Social Factors: Proceedings. LC 75-19703. (National Bureau of Economic Research Ser.). (Illus.). 1975. Repr. 36.00x (ISBN 0-405-07583-9). Arno.
Cook, Charles L. Inventor's Guide in a Series of Four Parts: How to Protect, Search, Compile Facts & Sell Your Invention. (Illus.). 1979. 11.95 (ISBN 0-9604670-0-9). C L Cook.
Cook, Chester L. Inventor's Guide in a Series of Four Parts: How to Protect, Search, Compile Facts & Sell Your Invention. rev. ed. (Illus.). 52p. 1981. Repr. of 1979 ed. saddle stitch 11.95 (ISBN 0-9604670-1-7). C L Cook.
Cooper, Grace R. The Sewing Machine: Its Invention & Development. LC 75-619415. (Illus.). 238p. 1977. 20.00x (ISBN 0-87474-330-3). Smithsonian.
Dionne, Narcisse E. Inventaire chronologique des livres, 5 pts. in 1 vol. LC 70-164837. Repr. of 1912 ed. 45.00 (ISBN 0-404-02138-7). AMS Pr.
Fenner, T. W. & Everett, J. L. Inventor's Handbook. 1968. 17.00 (ISBN 0-8206-0070-9). Chem Pub.
Flumiani, C. M. The Theory of Inventiveness. LC 68-23100. (Illus.). 32p. 1972. 39.45 (ISBN 0-913314-15-3). Am Classical Coll Pr.
Gilfillan, S. C. Sociology of Invention. 1970. pap. 3.95 (ISBN 0-262-57020-3). MIT Pr.
--Supplement to the Sociology of Invention. LC 75-97497. (Illus.). 1971. 10.00 (ISBN 0-911302-16-6). San Francisco Pr.
Goff, Harry. Inventions Wanted. 1981. cancelled (ISBN 0-914960-24-5). Green Hill.
--Inventions Wanted! LC 79-56695. (Illus.). 160p. (Orig.). 1980. text ed. 8.95 (ISBN 0-914960-27-X, Dist. by Caroline Hse); pap. 5.95 (ISBN 0-914960-24-5). Academy Bks.
Greene, Orville & Durr, Frank. The Practical Inventor's Handbook. LC 78-26666. (Illus.). 1979. 19.95 (ISBN 0-07-024320-4, P&RB). McGraw.
Gregory, James, ed. The Patent Book. LC 78-68388. (Illus.). 1979. 12.95 (ISBN 0-89479-037-4). A & W Pubs.
Hadamard, Jacques. Psychology of Invention in the Mathematical Field. 1945. pap. text ed. 3.00 (ISBN 0-486-20107-4). Dover.
Hallock, Robert L. Inventing for Fun & Profit. 1978. 6.95 (ISBN 0-517-53311-1). Crown.
His Maiesties Gracious Grant & Privilege to William Braithwaite, for the Sole Printing & Publishing Musicke, His Way. LC 73-6105. (English Experience Ser.: No. 573). 1973. Repr. of 1636 ed. 3.50 (ISBN 90-221-0573-3). Walter J Johnson.
Illustrated Science & Invention Encyclopedia: How It Works, 21 vols. 1976. 146.58 (ISBN 0-87475-800-9). Stuttman.
Inventions, 2 vols. (British Parliamentary Papers Ser.). 1971. Set. 171.00x (ISBN 0-7165-1450-8, Pub. by Irish Academic Pr Ireland). Biblio Dist.
Jerrome, Edward G. Tales of Invention. (Pacemaker True Adventures Ser.). (Illus., Orig.). 1973. pap. text ed. 2.64 (ISBN 0-8224-9186-9); tchrs' manual free. Pitman Learning.
Jewkes, John, et al. Sources of Invention. 2nd ed. LC 79-90986. 1971. pap. 6.95x (ISBN 0-393-00502-X, Norton Lib). Norton.
Jouffroy, A. Dictionnaire des Inventions et Decouvertes Anciennes et Modernes, 2 vols. Migne, J. P., ed. (Nouvelle Encyclopedie Theologique Ser.: Vols. 35-36). 1424p. (Fr.). Date not set. Repr. of 1860 ed. lib. bdg. 181.00x (ISBN 0-89241-277-1). Caratzas Bros.
Kivenson, Gilbert. The Art & Science of Inventing. 1977. 13.95 (ISBN 0-442-24442-8). Van Nos Reinhold.
Meinhardt, Peter. Inventions, Patents, & Trademarks in Great Britain. 420p. 1971. 25.00x (ISBN 0-8464-0529-6). Beekman Pubs.
Model Law for Developing Countries on Inventions. 1965. pap. 12.00x (ISBN 0-686-53017-9, WIPO46, WIPO). Unipub.
Morison, Elting E. Men, Machines, & Modern Times. 1966. 8.00x (ISBN 0-262-13025-4); pap. 3.45 (ISBN 0-262-63018-4). MIT Pr.
National Academy Of Engineering. Process of Technological Innovation. LC 72-601240. (Illus., Orig.). 1969. pap. 4.75 (ISBN 0-309-01726-2). Natl Acad Pr.
National Geographic Society. Those Inventive Americans. LC 75-125340. (Special Publications Ser.). (Illus.). 1971. avail. only from natl. geog. 6.95 (ISBN 0-87044-089-6). Natl Geog.
New & Improved . . . Inventors & Inventions That Have Changed the Modern World. 1981. 15.00x (ISBN 0-686-77432-9, Pub. by Brit Lib England). State Mutual Bk.
Norman, Bruce. The Inventing of America. LC 76-11686. (Illus.). 1976. 18.50 (ISBN 0-8008-4220-0). Taplinger.
Pearsall, Ronald. Collecting Mechanical Antiques. LC 73-76415. (Illus.). 197p. 1973. 7.95 (ISBN 0-668-02967-6). Arco.
Pressman, David R. Patent It Yourself! How to Protect, Patent & Market Your Inventions. LC 78-10232. 1979. 15.95 (ISBN 0-07-050780-5, P&RB). McGraw.
Reefman, William E. How to Sell Your Own Invention. (Illus.). 1977. pap. 10.00 (ISBN 0-912256-11-7). Halls of Ivy.
Schmookler, Jacob. Invention & Economic Growth. LC 66-14453. 1966. 16.50x (ISBN 0-674-46400-1). Harvard U Pr.
--Patents, Inventions & Economic Change: Data & Selected Essays. Griliches, Zvi & Hurwicz, Leonid, eds. LC 74-188355. (Illus.). 320p. 1972. 15.00x (ISBN 0-674-65770-5). Harvard U Pr.
Schwenck, James E. & McNair, Eric P. How to Become a Successful Inventor: Design a Gadget in Your Spare Time & Strike It Rich! 1974. 7.95 (ISBN 0-8038-3031-9). Hastings.
Shuldner, Herbert. The Popular Science Book of Gadgets: Ingenious Devices for the Home. Michaelman, Herbert, ed. 1980. 16.95 (ISBN 0-517-54280-3, Michelman Books); pap. 9.95 (ISBN 0-517-54443-1, Michelman Books). Crown.
Tesla, Nilola & Valic, B. Nikola Tesla: My Inventions. (Illus.). 1977. 30.00x (ISBN 0-89918-777-3, Y-777). Vanous.
Thring, M. W. & Laithwaite, E. R. How to Invent. (Illus.). 1977. 17.00 (ISBN 0-8206-0251-5). Chem Pub.
Ullrich, Hanns. Standards of Patentability for European Inventions. (IIC Studies: Vol. 1). 1977. pap. 34.20 (ISBN 3-527-25695-4). Verlag Chemie.
Whitehurst, Bert W. Financing Your Inventions. (Illus.). lib. bdg. 13.75 (ISBN 0-686-51721-0); pap. text ed. 8.50 (ISBN 0-918602-00-9). Galleon-Whitehurst.
--How to Sell Inventions. 2nd ed. (Illus.). 58p. (Orig.). 1981. lib. bdg. 12.95 (ISBN 0-686-72209-4); pap. text ed. 9.50 (ISBN 0-686-72210-8). Galleon-Whitehurst.
--How to Sell Inventions. rev., enl. ed. (Illus.). 1979. lib. bdg. 14.00x (ISBN 0-918602-21-1); pap. text ed. 9.00 (ISBN 0-918602-01-7). Galleon-Whitehurst.
Yerkes, Robert M., ed. New World of Science. facs. ed. LC 68-58818. (Essay Index Reprint Ser). 1920. 25.00 (ISBN 0-8369-1166-0). Arno.

INVENTIONS–BIBLIOGRAPHY

Forbes, Eric G. & Pacela, Allan F. A Source Book of Government-Owned Biomedical Inventions. LC 77-88370. (Illus.). 1978. looseleaf 82.50x (ISBN 0-930844-02-5). Quest Pub.

INVENTIONS–HISTORY

Beckman, Johann. A History of Inventions & Discoveries. 1976. Repr. of 1817 ed. 295.00 (ISBN 0-403-06509-7, Regency). Scholarly.

Byrn, Edward W. Progress of Invention in the Nineteenth Century. LC 78-81454. (Illus.). 1970. Repr. of 1900 ed. 18.00 (ISBN 0-8462-1357-5). Russell.

Darmstaedter, Ludwig, et al. Handbuch Zur Geschichte der Naturwissenschaften und der Technik. 2nd rev. enl. ed. LC 9-606. 1908. 46.00 (ISBN 0-527-21500-7). Kraus Repr.

Daumas, Maurice, ed. The History of Technology & Invention, Vol. 3. (Illus.). 1978. 30.00 (ISBN 0-517-52037-0). Crown.

--A History of Technology & Invention Progress Through the Ages, Vol. 1: The Origins of Technological Civilization to 1450. 520p. 1980. 40.00x (ISBN 0-7195-3730-4, Pub. by Murray Pubs England). State Mutual Bk.

--History of Technology & Invention Process Through the Ages, Vol. 2: The First Stages of Mechanization 1450-1725. 694p. 1980. 40.00x (ISBN 0-7195-3731-2, Pub. by Murray Pubs England). State Mutual Bk.

--A History of Technology & Invention Progress Through the Ages, Vol. 3: The Expansion of Mechanization 1725-1860. 700p. 1980. 40.00x (ISBN 0-7195-3732-0, Pub. by Murray Pubs England). State Mutual Bk.

--History of Technology & Invention: Progress Through the Ages, 2 vols. Incl. Vol. 1. The Origins of Technological Civilization (ISBN 0-517-50727-7); Vol. 2. The First Stages of Mechanization (ISBN 0-517-50728-5). (Illus.). 1969. 25.00 ea. Crown.

De Bono, Edward. Eureka. LC 73-21084. (Illus.). 1979. pap. 10.00 (ISBN 0-03-049826-0). HR&W.

Dickman, Lloyd H. Would Dad Be Surprised. 1980. 6.95 (ISBN 0-533-04233-X). Vantage.

Giedion, Siegfried. Mechanization Takes Command. 1969. pap. 9.95 (ISBN 0-393-00489-9, Norton Lib.). Norton.

--Mechanization Takes Command: A Contribution to Anonymous History. (Illus.). 1948. 25.00 (ISBN 0-19-500555-4). Oxford U Pr.

Graham-Cameron, Mike. Home Sweet Home. (Illus.). 32p. 1980. pap. 1.60 ea. (Pub. by Dinosaur Pubns); pap. in 5 pk. avail. (ISBN 0-85122-174-2). Merrimack Bk Serv.

Hall. Pneumatics of Hero of Alexandria. 141p. 1971. text ed. 12.00 (ISBN 0-685-56997-7). N Watson.

Hatfield, Stafford H. The Conquest of Thought by Invention in the Mechanical State of the Future. 1979. Repr. of 1929 ed. lib. bdg. 15.00 (ISBN 0-8495-2289-7). Arden Lib.

Hathaway, Esse V. Partners in Progress. facs. ed. LC 68-29213. (Essay Index Reprint Ser.). 1968. Repr. of 1935 ed. 16.00 (ISBN 0-8369-0518-0). Arno.

Heher, J. M., ed. Great Scientific Adventures: Program Guide. 100p. (gr. 9-12). 1980. pap. text ed. 7.95 (ISBN 0-667-00594-3). Microfilming Corp.

Kaempffert, Waldemar B., ed. A Popular History of American Invention, 2 vols. LC 74-9385. (Illus.). Repr. of 1924 ed. Set. 125.00 (ISBN 0-404-11921-2); Vol. 1. (ISBN 0-404-11922-0); Vol. 2. (ISBN 0-404-11923-9). AMS Pr.

Proctor, Thomas. Gorgeous Gallery of Gallant Inventions, 1578. Rollins, Hyder E., ed. LC 72-102534. 1971. Repr. of 1926 ed. 12.00 (ISBN 0-8462-1517-9). Russell.

Rickards, Maurice, ed. New Inventions. 1969. 3.50 (ISBN 0-8038-5012-3). Hastings.

Ries, Estelle H. The Ingenuity of Man. LC 75-8726. (Illus.). 333p. 1975. Repr. of 1962 ed. lib. bdg. 17.25x (ISBN 0-8371-8041-4, RIIM). Greenwood.

Saltz, Elizabeth. Growth of American Culture & Inventions. 64p. 1981. pap. 6.95 (ISBN 0-89962-228-3). Todd & Honeywell.

The Smithsonian Book of Invention. LC 78-62960. (Illus.). 256p. 1978. 19.95 (ISBN 0-89599-002-4). Smithsonian Expo.

Vanderbilt, Byron M. Inventing: How the Masters Did It. LC 74-14959. 1974. 12.95 (ISBN 0-87716-054-6, Pub. by Moore Pub Co). F Apple.

INVENTIONS–JUVENILE LITERATURE

Baldwin, Gordon C. Inventors & Inventions of the Ancient World. LC 73-76461. (Illus.). 256p. (gr. 7-11). 1973. 7.95 (ISBN 0-590-07164-5, Four Winds). Schol Bk Serv.

Benjamin, Alan. One Thousand Inventions. LC 80-80659. (Illus.). 10p. (ps up). 1980. spiral bdg. 4.95 (ISBN 0-590-07749-X, Four Winds). Schol Bk Serv.

Caney, Steven. Inventions & Contraptions. LC 78-73723. (Illus.). 256p. (Orig.). (gr. 4-6). Date not set. 12.50 (ISBN 0-89480-077-9); pap. 5.95 (ISBN 0-89480-076-0). Workman Pub.

Garrison, Webb. Why Didn't I Think of That: From Alarm Clocks to Zippers. LC 77-5806. (Illus.). (gr. 3-7). 1977. PLB 6.95 (ISBN 0-13-958603-2). P-H.

Klein, Aaron E. & Klein, Cynthia L. The Better Mousetrap: A Miscellany of Gadgets, Labor-Saving Devices, & Inventions That Intrigue. LC 81-3796. (Illus.). 192p. (gr. 6 up). 1981. 10.95 (ISBN 0-8253-0030-4). Beaufort Bks NY.

Leslie, Sarah. Who Invented It & What Makes It Work. LC 75-39568. (Illus.). 72p. (gr. 2-6). 1976. 4.95 (ISBN 0-448-47612-6). Platt.

Marzell, Ernst S. Great Inventions. LC 77-171532. (Real Life Bks). (Illus.). 32p. (gr. 5-9). 1973. PLB 4.95 (ISBN 0-8225-0705-6). Lerner Pubns.

Murphy, Jim. Weird & Wacky Inventions. LC 77-15859. (Illus.). (gr. 3-5). 1978. 7.95 (ISBN 0-517-53318-9). Crown.

Weiss, Harvey. How to Be an Inventor. LC 79-7823. (Illus.). 96p. (gr. 5 up). 1980. 8.95 (ISBN 0-690-04052-0, TYC-J); PLB 8.79 (ISBN 0-690-04053-9). Har-Row.

Wulffson, Don L. The Invention of Ordinary Things. LC 80-17498. (Illus.). 96p. (gr. 3 up). 1981. 6.95 (ISBN 0-688-41978-X); PLB 6.67 (ISBN 0-688-51978-4). Lothrop.

INVENTORIES

see also Commercial Finance Companies; Inventory Control; Inventory Shortages

Cotter, Arundel. Fool's Profits. Brief, Richard P., ed. LC 80-1481. (Dimensions of Accounting Theory & Practice Ser.). 1981. Repr. of 1940 ed. lib. bdg. 16.00x (ISBN 0-405-13511-4). Arno.

Devine, Carl T. Inventory Valuation & Periodic Income. Brief, Richard P., ed. LC 80-1486. (Dimensions of Accounting Theory & Practice Ser.). 1981. Repr. of 1942 ed. lib. bdg. 19.00x (ISBN 0-405-13516-5). Arno.

Staples, Frederick. The Inventories. LC 74-20116. 104p. 1975. text ed. 6.45 (ISBN 0-915026-19-8). Counting Hse.

U. S. Congress - Joint Economic Committee. Inventory Fluctuations & Economic Stabilization. LC 70-94622. (Illus.). 1971. Repr. of 1961 ed. lib. bdg. 26.25x (ISBN 0-8371-3046-8, INFL). Greenwood.

Whitin, Thomson M. Theory of Inventory Management. Repr. of 1957 ed. lib. bdg. 15.00x (ISBN 0-8371-3406-4, WHIM). Greenwood.

INVENTORIES–MATHEMATICAL MODELS

Arrow, Kenneth J., et al. Studies in the Mathematical Theory of Inventory & Production. 1958. 18.50x (ISBN 0-8047-0541-0). Stanford U Pr.

Arrow, Kenneth J., et al, eds. Studies in Applied Probability & Management Science. 1962. 18.50x (ISBN 0-8047-0099-0). Stanford U Pr.

Hadley, George & Whitin, T. M. Analysis of Inventory Systems. (Illus.). 1963. ref. ed. 21.95 (ISBN 0-13-032953-3). P-H.

Scarf, Herbert E., et al, eds. Multistage Inventory Models & Techniques. 1963. 15.00x (ISBN 0-8047-0188-1). Stanford U Pr.

INVENTORS

see also Engineers

Baker, Henry E. Colored Inventor: A Record of Fifty Years. LC 71-75851. (American Negro: His History & Literature, Ser. No. 2). 1969. pap. 1.00 (ISBN 0-405-01943-2). Arno.

Baker, R. New & Improved. 168p. 1981. 30.00x (ISBN 0-686-73697-4, Pub. by Brit Lib England). State Mutual Bk.

Burt, McKinley, Jr. Black Inventors of America. 1969. pap. 6.85 (ISBN 0-89420-095-X, 296959). Natl Book.

Cohen, Scott. Meet the Makers. LC 78-21354. 1979. 8.95 (ISBN 0-312-52835-3). St Martin.

Edison, Thomas A. Diary of Thomas A. Edison. LC 71-107081. (Illus.). 1971. pap. 3.95 (ISBN 0-85699-018-3). Chatham Pr.

Faussig, F. W. Psychology of Inventors & Money-Makers. (Illus.). 103p. 1981. 43.25 (ISBN 0-89920-020-6). Am Inst Psych.

Feldman, Anthony & Ford, Peter. Scientists & Inventors. (Horizons of Knowledge Ser.). (Illus.). 1979. 19.95 (ISBN 0-87196-410-4). Facts on File.

Hathaway, Esse V. Partners in Progress. facs. ed. LC 68-29213. (Essay Index Reprint Ser.). 1968. Repr. of 1935 ed. 16.00 (ISBN 0-8369-0518-0). Arno.

Iles, George. Leading American Inventors. facs. ed. LC 68-8472. (Essay Index Reprint Ser). 1968. Repr. of 1912 ed. 24.00 (ISBN 0-8369-0557-1). Arno.

The Indefatigable Mr. Woodcroft' The Legacy of Invention. 1981. pap. 6.00x (ISBN 0-902914-53-7, Pub. by Brit Lib England). State Mutual Bk.

Johnson, F. Roy & Stephenson, Frank, Jr. The Gatling Gun & Flying Machine of Richard & Henry Gatling. (Illus.). 1979. 9.50 (ISBN 0-930230-37-X). Johnson NC.

Kirby, Richard S., ed. Inventors & Engineers of Old New Haven. facs. ed. LC 78-86765. (Essay Index Reprint Ser). 1939. 13.00 (ISBN 0-8369-1144-X). Arno.

Kurylo, Friedrich & Susskind, Charles. Ferdinand Braun: A Life of the Nobel Prize Winner & Inventor of the Cathode-Ray Oscilloscope. (Illus.). 304p. 1981. 27.50 (ISBN 0-262-11077-6). MIT Pr.

Lehrburger, Egon. Inventors. LC 68-2276. (Pegasus Books: No. 5). (Illus.). 1965. 10.50x (ISBN 0-234-77841-5). Intl Pubns Serv.

Lord, Athena V. Pilot for Spaceship Earth: R. Buckminster Fuller, Architect, Inventor & Poet. LC 77-12629. (Illus.). (gr. 5 up). 1978. 8.95 (ISBN 0-02-761420-4, 76142). Macmillan.

National Geographic Society. Those Inventive Americans. LC 75-125340. (Special Publications Ser.). (Illus.). 1971. avail. only from natl. geog. 6.95 (ISBN 0-87044-089-6). Natl Geog.

Neumeyer, Fredrik & Stedman, John C. Employed Inventor in the United States. 1971. 30.00x (ISBN 0-262-14006-3). MIT Pr.

New & Improved . . . Inventors & Inventions That Have Changed the Modern World. 1981. 15.00x (ISBN 0-686-77432-9, Pub. by Brit Lib England). State Mutual Bk.

Oppenheimer, Francis J. Ezekiel to Einstein: Israel's Gifts to Science & Invention. facsimile ed. LC 70-167398. (Essay Index Reprint Ser). Repr. of 1940 ed. 9.75 (ISBN 0-8369-2438-X). Arno.

Prager, Frank D., ed. The Autobiography of John Fitch. LC 76-8596. (Memoirs Ser.: Vol. 113). (Illus.). 1976. pap. 7.00 (ISBN 0-87169-113-2). Am Philos.

Strickland, Mary. Memoir of the Life, Writings & Mechanical Inventions of Edmund Cartwright. LC 70-149329. (Documents of Social History). Repr. of 1843 ed. lib. bdg. 17.50x (ISBN 0-678-07769-X). Kelley.

Susskind, Charles. Twenty-Five Engineers & Inventors. LC 76-40764. (Illus.). 1977. 7.50 (ISBN 0-911302-29-8). San Francisco Pr.

Tesla, Nikola. Inventions, Researchs, & Writings. Repr. of 1894 ed. 12.00 (ISBN 0-913022-23-3). Angriff Pr.

Tesla, Nilola & Valic, B. Nikola Tesla: My Inventions. (Illus.). 1977. 30.00x (ISBN 0-89918-777-3, Y-777). Vanous.

Train, John. The Money Masters: Nine Great Investors, Their Winning Strategies & How You Can Apply Them. LC 78-20192. 1980. 11.95 (ISBN 0-06-014373-8, HarpT). Har-Row.

Wile, Frederic W. Emile Berliner: Maker of the Microphone. LC 74-4699. (Telecommunications Ser). (Illus.). 380p. 1974. Repr. of 1926 ed. 21.00x (ISBN 0-405-06062-9). Arno.

Williams, James C. At Last Recognition in America, Vol. 1. LC 78-3007. (Illus.). 1978. 18.50 (ISBN 0-931564-00-X). BCA Pub.

INVENTORS–JUVENILE LITERATURE

Manchester, Harland. New Trail Blazers of Technology. LC 76-16760. (Illus.). 192p. (gr. 6 up). 1976. 7.95 (ISBN 0-684-14718-1, ScribT). Scribner.

O'Sullivan, Tom, illus. The World's Greatest Inventors. LC 78-66934. (Pandabacks). (Illus.). (gr. 1-5). pap. 0.95 (ISBN 0-448-49614-3). Platt.

Ott, Virginia & Swanson, Gloria. Man with a Million Ideas: Fred Jones, Genius Inventor. LC 76-22444. (Adult & Young Adult Bks). (Illus.). (gr. 6 up). 1976. PLB 6.95 (ISBN 0-8225-0761-7). Lerner Pubns.

Pizer, Vernon. Shortchanged by History: America's Neglected Innovators. LC 78-24141. (Illus.). (gr. 6-8). 1979. 8.95 (ISBN 0-399-20665-5). Putnam.

Sweet, Dovie D. Red Light, Green Light: The Life of Garrett Morgan & the Invention of the Stoplight. (gr. k-4). 1978. 5.00 (ISBN 0-682-49088-1). Exposition.

INVENTORY

see also Warehouses

INVENTORY CONTROL

see also Inventories; Materials Management; Stores or Stock-Room Keeping

Appel, Gerald. Winning Stock Selection Systems. 1979. 50.00 (ISBN 0-686-51195-6). Boardroom.

Atkinson, Chuck. Inventory Management for Small Computers. LC 80-68566. 140p. 1981. pap. 12.95 (ISBN 0-918398-48-7). Dilithium Pr.

Banks, Jerry & Hohenstein, Charles L., Jr. Procurement & Inventory Ordering Tables. LC 77-8663. 1978. pap. text ed. 14.50 (ISBN 0-08-021945-4). Pergamon.

Battersby, Albert. Guide to Stock Control. 2nd ed. 1971. 12.95x (ISBN 0-8464-0463-X). Beekman Pubs.

Buffa, Elwood S. & Miller, Jeffrey G. Production-Inventory Systems: Planning & Control. 3rd ed. 1979. 21.95x (ISBN 0-256-02041-8). Irwin.

Dudick, T. S. & Cornell, R. Inventory Control for the Financial Executive. 251p. 1979. 31.95 (ISBN 0-471-01503-2, Pub. by Wiley-Interscience). Wiley.

Eilon, S. & Lampkin, W. Inventory Control Abstracts: 1953-1965. 1968. 14.70 (ISBN 0-934454-53-1). Lubrecht & Cramer.

Ghattas, Emile. Inventory Management in Lebanon. 1977. 15.00x (ISBN 0-8156-6047-2, Am U Beirut). Syracuse U Pr.

Graham, Gordon. Automated Inventory Management for the Distributor. LC 80-17655. 350p. 1980. 21.50 (ISBN 0-8436-0794-7). CBI Pub.

Greene, J. H. Production & Inventory Control Handbook. 1970. 49.95 (ISBN 0-07-024332-8, P&RB). McGraw.

Greene, James H. Production & Inventory Control: Systems & Decisions. rev. ed. 1974. text ed. 20.95x (ISBN 0-256-01431-0). Irwin.

Jannis, C. Paul, et al. Managing & Accounting for Inventories: Control, Income Recognition, & Tax Strategy. 3rd ed. 1979. 37.95 (ISBN 0-471-05016-4, Pub by Ronald Pr). Wiley.

Jones, E. R. Simplified Inventory System: For Collectors Investors & Dealers. LC 75-25315. (Illus.). 128p. 1975. 7.50 (ISBN 0-9600934-2-7). E R Jones.

Kobert, Norman. Inventory Strategies. 1979. 50.00 (ISBN 0-932648-03-7). Boardroom.

Kuehne, Robert S. & Baker, R. Jerry. Inventory Management Factomatic--a Portfolio of Successful Forms, Reports, Records & Procedures. (Illus.). 1978. 39.95 (ISBN 0-13-502369-6, Busn). P-H.

Larson, S. Inventory Systems & Controls Handbook. 1976. 27.95 (ISBN 0-13-502351-3); pap. 9.95 (ISBN 0-13-502963-5). P-H.

McCarthy, Thomas & Morison, Thomas L. Controlling & Accounting for Supplies. 4.95 (ISBN 0-686-11620-8, 7576). Natl Assn Accts.

Magee, John R. & Boodman, D. M. Production Planning & Inventory Control. 2nd ed. 1967. pap. text ed. 19.50 (ISBN 0-07-039488-1, C). McGraw.

Montgomery, Douglas C. & Berry, William L., eds. Production Planning, Scheduling & Inventory Control: Concepts, Techniques, & Systems. 1974. pap. text ed. 14.00 (ISBN 0-89806-022-2, 199). Am Inst Indus Eng.

Nador, Eliezer. Inventory Systems. 356p. 1981. Repr. of 1966 ed. lib. bdg. price not set (ISBN 0-89874-367-2). Krieger.

Peterson, Rein & Silver, Edward A. Decision Systems for Inventory Management & Production Planning. LC 78-4980. (Ser. in Management Administration). 1979. text ed. 29.95 (ISBN 0-471-68327-2). Wiley.

Plossl, G. & Wright, O. Production & Inventory Control: Principles & Techniques. 1967. ref. ed. 21.95 (ISBN 0-13-725127-0). P-H.

Plossl, George W. & Welch, W. Evert. The Role of Top Management in the Control of Inventory. (Illus.). 1978. 16.95 (ISBN 0-8359-6697-6). Reston.

Reinfeld, Nyles V. Production & Inventory Control. 1981. text ed. 19.95 (ISBN 0-8359-5629-6). Reston.

Sandilya, M. S. & Gopalakrishnan, P. Inventory Management: Text & Cases. 1981. 12.00x (ISBN 0-8364-0714-8, Pub. by Macmillan India). South Asia Bks.

Srbich, Alex L., ed. Bibliography. 6th ed. LC 79-90368. 1979. pap. 7.50 (ISBN 0-935406-01-8). Am Prod & Inventory.

Steffy, Wilbert, et al. Inventory Controls for the Small & Medium Sized Firm: Computer-Aided Inventory Control & Manual Inventory Control Methods. (Illus.). 85p. 1980. 12.00 (ISBN 0-686-72877-7, INV C). Indus Dev Inst Sci.

Super, Donald E. Work Values Inventory: MRC Machine-Scorable Test Booklets. 41.24 (ISBN 0-395-09529-8); directions manual 2.51 (ISBN 0-395-09530-1); specimen set. pap. 2.16 (ISBN 0-395-09531-X). HM.

Techniques in Inventory Management. 5.95 (ISBN 0-686-09792-0, 6436). Natl Assn Accts.

Thomas, Adin B. Stock Control in Manufacturing Industries. 2nd ed. 240p. 1980. text ed. 29.50 (ISBN 0-566-02140-4, Pub. by Gower Pub Co England). Renouf.

Wallace, Tom. Dictionary. 4th ed. LC 79-90362. 1980. pap. 7.50 ref. (ISBN 0-935406-00-X). Am Prod & Inventory.

INVENTORY CONTROL–MATHEMATICAL MODELS

Johnson, Lynwood A. & Montgomery, Douglas C. Operations Research in Production Planning, Scheduling, & Inventory Control. LC 73-17331. 525p. 1974. text ed. 30.95 (ISBN 0-471-44618-1). Wiley.

Levine, Kenneth C. & Thomas, William R. Optimization of Continuous Expected Value Models. LC 71-626077. (Research Monograph: No. 45). 1968. spiral bdg. 5.00 (ISBN 0-88406-059-4). Ga St U Busn Pub.

Love, Stephen. Inventory Control. (Industrial Engineering & Management Science Ser.). (Illus.). 1979. text ed. 16.50 (ISBN 0-07-038782-6, C); solutions manual 8.50 (ISBN 0-07-038783-4). McGraw.
Prekopa, A., ed. Inventory Control & Water Storage. (Colloquia Mathematica: Vol. 7). 1974. 39.00 (ISBN 0-444-10606-5, North-Holland). Elsevier.
Reisman, A., et al. Industrial Inventory Control. (Studies in Operations Research Ser.). 192p. 1972. 37.50x (ISBN 0-677-04180-2). Gordon.
Schneeweiss, C. A. Inventory-Production Theory: A Linear Policy Approach. LC 77-13254. (Lecture Notes in Economics & Mathematical Systems: Vol. 151). 1977. pap. text ed. 10.70 (ISBN 0-387-08443-6). Springer-Verlag.

INVENTORY MANAGEMENT
see Inventory Control

INVENTORY SHORTAGES
see also Shoplifting
Curtis, Bob. Security Control: Internal Theft. LC 72-90623. (Security Control Ser.). 1973. 18.95 (ISBN 0-912016-14-0). Lebhar Friedman.

INVERSE FUNCTIONS
see Functions, Inverse

INVERSIONS (GEOMETRY)
see also Involutes (Mathematics)
Bakelman, I. Ya. Inversions. Teller, Joan W. & Williams, Susan, trs. from Rus. LC 74-5727. (Popular Lectures in Mathematics Ser). 82p. 1975. pap. text ed. 4.50x (ISBN 0-226-03499-2). U of Chicago Pr.
Twomey, S. Introduction to the Mathematics of Inversion in Remote Sensing & Indirect Measurements. (Developments in Geomathematics Ser.: Vol. 3). 1977. 80.50 (ISBN 0-444-41547-5, North Holland). Elsevier.

INVERTEBRATES
see also Arachnida; Arthropoda; Brachiopoda; Coelenterata; Crustacea; Echinodermata; Insects; Mollusks; Myriapoda; Nervous System-Invertebrates; Polyzoa; Protozoa; Sponges; Worms
Acton, Ronald T., et al. Invertebrate Immune Defense Mechanisms. 1973. 23.50x (ISBN 0-8422-7054-X). Irvington.
Alexander, R. McNeill. The Invertebrates. LC 78-6275. (Illus.). 1979. 65.50 (ISBN 0-521-22120-X); pap. 17.95x (ISBN 0-521-29361-8). Cambridge U Pr.
Allen, Richard K. Common Intertidal Invertebrates of Southern California. 1976. pap. text ed. 8.95 (ISBN 0-917962-10-9). Peek Pubns.
Autrum, H., ed. Comparative Physiology & Evolution of Vision in Invertebrates: Invertebrate Visual Centers & Behavior II. (Handbook of Sensory Physiology Ser.: Vol. VII, 6c). (Illus.). 660p. 1981. 159.30 (ISBN 0-387-10422-4). Springer-Verlag.
--Comparative Physiology & Evolution of Vision in Invertebrates B: Invertebrate Visual Centers & Behavior I. (Handbook of Sensory Physiology: Vol. VII, Pt. 6B). (Illus.). 650p. 1980. 159.00 (ISBN 0-387-08703-6). Springer-Verlag.
--Comparative Physiology & Evolution of Vision in Invertebrates: A: Invertebrate Photoreceptors. LC 78-21470. (Handbook of Sensory Physiology: Vol. 7, Pt. 6A). (Illus.). 1979. 184.80 (ISBN 0-387-08837-7). Springer-Verlag.
--Comparitive Physiology & Evolution of Vision in Invertebrates C: Invertebrate Visual Centers & Behavior II. (Handbook of Sensory Physiology Ser.: Vol. VII-6c). (Illus.). 660p. 1981. 159.30 (ISBN 0-387-10422-4). Springer-Verlag.
Barrington, E. J. Intervertebrate Structure & Function. 2nd ed. 1979. pap. 20.95x (ISBN 0-470-26503-5). Halsted Pr.
Barth, Robert H. The Invertebrate World. 1981. text ed. 24.95 (ISBN 0-03-013276-2, HoltC). HR&W.
Beck, D Elden & Braithwaite, Lee F. Invertebrate Zoology Laboratory Workbook. 3rd ed. (Illus.). 1968. spiral bdg. 10.95x (ISBN 0-8087-0211-4). Burgess.
Beklemishev, V. N. Principles of Comparative Anatomy of Invertebrates, 2 Vols. Kabata, Z., ed. McLennan, J. M., tr. LC 70-97749. 1970. Set. pap. 45.00x (ISBN 0-226-04175-1). U of Chicago Pr.
Blackman, Rodger. Aphids. (Invertebrate Types Ser.). (Illus.). 176p. 1981. pap. 12.00 (ISBN 0-08-025943-X). Pergamon.
Borradaile, L. A. & Potts, F. A. Invertebrata. 4th ed. 1961. text ed. 29.95x (ISBN 0-521-04285-2). Cambridge U Pr.
Brown, Frank A. Selected Invertebrate Types. 1950. 27.50 (ISBN 0-471-10857-X). Wiley.
Brusca, Gary J. General Patterns of Invertebrate Development. (Illus.). 134p. 1975. pap. 7.15x (ISBN 0-916422-03-8). Mad River.
Brusca, Richard C. Common Intertidal Invertebrates of the Gulf of California. rev. ed. (Illus.). 513p. 1980. pap. 26.95x (ISBN 0-8165-0682-5). U of Ariz Pr.
Buchsbaum, Ralph. Animals Without Backbones. rev., 2nd ed. LC 48-9508. (Illus.). 405p. 1975. pap. 9.50 (ISBN 0-226-07870-1). U of Chicago Pr.
--Animals Without Backbones: An Introduction to the Invertebrates. rev. ed. LC 48-9508. (Illus.). (gr. 9 up). 1948. text ed. 16.00x (ISBN 0-226-07869-8). U of Chicago Pr.
Bullough, William S. Practical Invertebrate Anatomy. 2nd ed. 1958. 17.95 (ISBN 0-312-63490-0). St Martin.
Calow, P. Invertebrate Biology: A Functional Approach. 224p. 1981. pap. 21.95 (ISBN 0-470-27238-4). Halsted Pr.
Chatton, E. Les Peridiniens Parasites. 1975. Repr. lib. bdg. 90.00x (ISBN 3-87429-100-6). Lubrecht & Cramer.
Clark, Robert B. Dynamics in Metazoan Evolution: The Origin of the Coelom & Segments. 1964. 45.00x (ISBN 0-19-854353-0). Oxford U Pr.
Clarkson, E. N. Invertebrate Palaeontology & Evolution. (Illus.). 1979. text ed. 40.00x (ISBN 0-04-560007-4); pap. text ed. 19.95x (ISBN 0-04-560008-2). Allen Unwin.
Clyne, Densey. The Garden Jungle. 184p. 1980. 27.95x (ISBN 0-00-216411-6, Pub. by W Collins Australia). Intl Schol Bk Serv.
Cooper, Edwin L., ed. Contemporary Topics in Immunobiology: Vol. 4, Invertebrate Immunology. LC 78-165398. (Illus.). 299p. 1974. 25.00 (ISBN 0-306-37804-3, Plenum Pr). Plenum Pub.
Corning, W. C., et al. Invertebrate Learning. Incl. Vol. 1, Protozoans Through Annelids. 296p. 1973. 34.50 (ISBN 0-306-37671-7); Vol. 2, Arthropods & Gastropod Mollusks. 284p. 1973. 34.50 (ISBN 0-306-37672-5); Vol. 3, Cephalopods & Echinoderms. 220p. 1975. 32.50 (ISBN 0-306-37673-3). LC 72-90335. (Illus., Plenum Pr). Plenum Pub.
Dales, R. P. Dales Practical Invertebrate Zoology. 2nd ed. LC 81-6570. 363p. 1981. 32.95 (ISBN 0-470-27226-0). Halsted Pr.
Dales, R. Phillips, ed. Practical Invertebrate Zoology. LC 75-93029. (Biology Ser). (Illus.). 368p. 1970. 9.95 (ISBN 0-295-95012-9). U of Wash Pr.
Davidson, Elizabeth W., ed. Pathogenesis of Invertebrate Microbial Diseases. 500p. 1981. text ed. 40.00 (ISBN 0-86598-014-4). Allanheld.
Edmondson, W. T. Marine Biology: Ecology of Invertebrates, Vol. 3. 1966. 52.25x (ISBN 0-677-65100-7). Gordon.
Elliott, J. M. Some Methods for the Statistical Analysis of Samples of Benthic Invertebrates. 2nd ed. 1977. 11.00x (ISBN 0-900386-29-0, Pub. by Freshwater Bio). State Mutual Bk.
Engemann, Joseph G. & Hegner, Robert W. Invertebrate Zoology. 3rd ed. 1981. text ed. 20.95 (ISBN 0-686-72536-0). Macmillan.
Freeman, W. H. & Bracegirdle, Brian. An Atlas of Invertebrate Structure. (Heinemann Biology Atlases Ser.). 1971. text ed. 15.50x (ISBN 0-435-60315-9). Heinemann Ed.
Fretter, V. & Graham, A. A Functional Anatomy of Invertebrates: Excluding Land Anthropods. 1976. 64.50 (ISBN 0-12-267550-9). Acad Pr.
Fretter, Vera & Peake, J., eds. Pulmonates: Vol. 2A, Systematics, Evolution & Ecology. 1979. 72.00 (ISBN 0-12-267502-9). Acad Pr.
--Pulmonates: Vol. 2b, Economic Malacology with Particular Reference to Achatina Fulica. 1979. 35.50 (ISBN 0-12-267541-X). Acad Pr.
George, J. David & George, Jennifer. Marine Life: An Illustrated Encyclopedia of Invertebrates in the Sea. LC 79-10976. 1979. 49.00x (ISBN 0-471-05675-8, Pub. by Wiley-Interscience). Wiley.
Gosner, K. L. Guide to Identification of Marine & Estuarine Invertebates: From Cape Hatteras to the Bay of Fundy. 693p. 1971. pap. 26.50 (ISBN 0-471-31901-5). Wiley.
Greenberg, Idaz. Field Guide to Marine Invertebrates. (Illus.). 1980. plastic card 3.95 (ISBN 0-913008-11-7). Seahawk Pr.
Hart, C. W. & Fuller, Samuel L. H., eds. Pollution Ecology of Estuarine Invertebrates. LC 79-18151. (Water Pollution Ser.). 1979. 36.00 (ISBN 0-12-328440-6). Acad Pr.
Hegner, Robert W. & Engemann, Joseph G. Invertebrate Zoology. 2nd ed. (Illus.). 1968. text ed. 15.95 (ISBN 0-02-353120-7). Macmillan.
Hickman, Cleveland P. Biology of the Invertebrates. 2nd ed. LC 72-83970. (Illus.). 720p. 1973. text ed. 18.95 (ISBN 0-8016-2170-4). Mosby.
Highnam, Kenneth C. & Hill, Leonard. The Comparative Endocrinology of the Invertebrates. LC 77-15979. (Contemporary Biology Ser). 1978. 29.50 (ISBN 0-8391-1193-2). Univ Park.
Ho, Ju-Shey. Laboratory Manual for Invertebrate Zoology. LC 77-94106. (Illus.). 1978. 7.95x (ISBN 0-89260-120-5). Hwong Pub.
House, M. R. The Origin of Major Invertebrate Groups. (Systematics Association Ser.: No. 12). 1979. 95.00 (ISBN 0-12-357450-1). Acad Pr.
Hoyle, Graham. Identified Neurons & Behavior of Arthropods. (Illus.). 608p. 1977. 39.50 (ISBN 0-306-31001-5, Plenum Pr). Plenum Pub.
Hunt, S. Polysaccharide-Protein Complexes in Invertebrates. 1970. 50.50 (ISBN 0-12-362050-3). Acad Pr.
Ivleva, I. V. Mass Cultivation of Invertebrates-Biology & Methods. Mercado, A., tr. from Rus. (Israel Program for Scientific Translations Ser). (Illus.). vi, 150p. 1974. 17.50x (ISBN 0-7065-1280-4, Pub. by IPST). Intl Schol Bk Serv.
Kaestner, A. Invertebrate Zoology: Vol. 1, Porifera, Cnidaria, Platyhelminthes, Aschelminthes, Mollusca, Annelida & Related Phyla. 597p. 1980. Repr. of 1967 ed. 29.95 (ISBN 0-470-45415-6). Krieger.
Kaestner, Alfred. Invertebrate Zoology: Arthropod Relatives, Chelicerata, Myriapoda, Vol. 2. Levi, Herbert W., tr. 482p. 1979. Repr. of 1968 ed. lib. bdg. 25.00 (ISBN 0-88275-692-3). Krieger.
--Invertebrate Zoology: Vol. 2, Arthropod Relatives, Chelicerata, Chelicerata, Myrlapoda. LC 78-9320. 538p. 1980. Repr. of 1970 ed. lib. bdg. 26.50 (ISBN 0-88275-818-7). Krieger.
Kaiser, Hans E. Species-Specific Potential of Invertebrates for Toxicological Research. 224p. text ed. 29.95 (ISBN 0-8391-1502-4). Univ Park.
Kummel, Bernhard & Gould, Stephen J., eds. Status of Invertebrate Paleontology, 1953, Vol. 112, No. 3. LC 79-8351. (The History of Paleontology Ser.). (Illus.). 1980. Repr. of 1954 ed. lib. bdg. 16.00x (ISBN 0-405-12715-4). Arno.
Kurstak, Edouard & Marqmorosch, Karl, eds. Invertebrate Tissue Culture: Applications in Medicine, Biology & Agriculture. 1976. 38.00 (ISBN 0-12-429740-4). Acad Pr.
Lamy. Invertebrate Oxygen-Binding Proteins. 864p. 1981. write for info. Dekker.
Laverack, M. S. & Dando, J., eds. Essential Invertebrate Zoology. 2nd ed. LC 78-25963. 1979. pap. text ed. 16.95 (ISBN 0-470-26605-8). Halsted Pr.
Lewis, S. M. & Coster, J., eds. Quality Control in Haematology. 1976. 36.00 (ISBN 0-12-446850-0). Acad Pr.
Light, William J. Spionidae: Invertebrates of the San Francisco Bay Estuary System, Vol. 1. Lee, Welton L., ed. (Illus.). 1978. text ed. 10.00x (ISBN 0-910286-58-2). Boxwood.
Lincoln, R. J. & Sheals, J. G. Collecting Invertebrate Animals. LC 79-14530. (Illus.). 1980. 22.50 (ISBN 0-521-22851-4); pap. 6.95 (ISBN 0-521-29677-3). Cambridge U Pr.
Lindberg, David R. Acmaeidae: Invertebrates of the San Francisco Bay Estuary System, Vol. 2. Lee, Welton, ed. (Illus.). 1980. text ed. 12.50x (ISBN 0-910286-72-8). Boxwood.
Ludwig, William B. & Roach, Lee S. Studies on the Animal Ecology of the Hocking River Basin: The Bottom Invertebrates of the Hocking River & The Plankton of the Hocking River. 1932. 2.00 (ISBN 0-686-30299-0). Ohio Bio Survey.
Lutz, H., ed. Invertebrate Organ Cultures. (Documents in Biology Ser.: Vol. 2). 1970. 54.50x (ISBN 0-677-30100-6). Gordon.
Maramorosch, Karl, ed. Invertebrate Immunity: Mechanisms of Invertebrate Vector-Parasite Relations. 1975. 34.00 (ISBN 0-12-470265-1). Acad Pr.
Meglitsch, Paul A. Invertebrate Zoology. 2nd ed. (Illus.). 1972. text ed. 21.95x (ISBN 0-19-501522-3). Oxford U Pr.
Mellanby, Helen. Animal Life in Fresh Water. 6th ed. LC 75-17181. 308p. 1963. pap. text ed. 10.95x (ISBN 0-412-21360-5, Pub. by Chapman & Hall England). Methuen Inc.
Morris, Robert H., et al. Intertidal Invertebrates of California. LC 77-92946. (Illus.). 904p. 1980. 45.00x (ISBN 0-8047-1045-7). Stanford U Pr.
Nichols, David & Cooke, John. Oxford Book of Invertebrates. 1971. 29.95 (ISBN 0-19-910008-X). Oxford U Pr.
Olive, John H. & Smith, Kenneth R. Benthic Macroinvertebrates As Indexes of Water Quality in the Scioto River Basin, Ohio. 1975. 8.00 (ISBN 0-686-30332-6). Ohio Bio Survey.
Pimentel, Richard A. Invertebrate Identification Manual. (Illus.). 1967. pap. text ed. 8.95x (ISBN 0-442-17578-7). Van Nos Reinhold.
Prasad, S. N. Life of Invertebrates. 800p. 1980. text ed. 50.00 (ISBN 0-7069-1042-7, Pub. by Vikas India). Advent NY.
Ramsay, James A. Physiological Approach to the Lower Animals. 2nd ed. LC 68-21398. (Illus.). 1968. text ed. 29.50 (ISBN 0-521-07185-2); pap. 8.50x (ISBN 0-521-09537-9). Cambridge U Pr.
Ratcliffe, N. A. & Rowley, A. F., eds. Invertebrate Blood Cells: General Aspects, Animals Without True Circulatory Systems to Cephalopods, Vol. 1. LC 80-41248. 1981. 79.50 (ISBN 0-12-582101-8). Acad Pr.
Ricketts, Edward F. & Calvin, Jack. Between Pacific Tides. 4th rev. ed. LC 68-17140. (Illus.). 1968. 12.50 (ISBN 0-8047-0641-7); text ed. 9.50x (ISBN 0-8047-0642-5). Stanford U Pr.
Rozsa, K. S., ed. Neurotransmitters in Invertebrates: Proceedings of a Satellite Symposium of the 28th International Congress of Physiological Sciences, Veszprem, Hungary, 1980. LC 80-42251. (Advances in Physiological Sciences: Vol. 22). (Illus.). 400p. 1981. 50.00 (ISBN 0-08-027343-2). Pergamon.
Russell-Hunter, W. D. Biology of Higher Invertebrates. (Orig.). 1969. pap. text ed. 7.95 (ISBN 0-02-404600-0). Macmillan.
--Biology of Lower Invertebrates. (Illus.). 1968. pap. text ed. 5.95x (ISBN 0-02-359010-6). Macmillan.
--A Life of Invertebrates. 1979. text ed. 22.95 (ISBN 0-02-404620-5). Macmillan.
Salanki. Neurobiology of Invertebrates: Gastropoda Brain. 1976. 47.00 (ISBN 0-9960001-3-5, Pub. by Kaido Hungary). Heyden.
Salanki, J., ed. Neurobiology Invertebrates: Proceedings of a Satellite Symposium of the 28th International Congress of Physiological Sciences, Tihany, Hungary, 1980. LC 80-42252. (Illus.). 400p. 1981. 50.00 (ISBN 0-08-027344-0). Pergamon.
--Neurobiology of Invertebrates Gastropoda Brain. 1976. 45.00x (ISBN 963-05-1080-4). Intl Pubns Serv.
Selsam, Millicent & Hunt, Joyce. A First Look at Animals Without Backbones. LC 76-12056. (A First Look at Ser.). (gr. 2-4). 1976. PLB 6.85 (ISBN 0-8027-6269-7). Walker & Co.
Sherman, Irwin W. & Sherman, Vilia G. The Invertebrates: Function & Form: A Laboratory Guide. 2nd ed. (Illus.). 352p. 1976. pap. text ed. 11.95 (ISBN 0-02-409840-X). Macmillan.
Smith, R. I., et al. Keys to Marine Invertebrates of the Woods Hole Region. (Illus.). 1964. 5.00 (ISBN 0-912544-01-5). Marine Bio.
Smith, Ralph I. & Carlton, James T., eds. Light's Manual: Intertidal Invertebrates of the Central California Coast. 3rd ed. 1975. 26.50x (ISBN 0-520-02113-4). U of Cal Pr.
Sparks, Albert K. Invertebrate Pathology: Noncommunicable Diseases. 1972. 55.50 (ISBN 0-12-656450-7). Acad Pr.
Stancyk, Stephen E., ed. Reproductive Ecology of Marine Invertebrates. (Belle W. Baruch Library in Marine Science Ser.). 1979. lib. bdg. 27.50 (ISBN 0-87249-379-2). U of SC Pr.
Tombes, A. S. Introduction to Invertebrate Endocrinology. 1970. 31.50 (ISBN 0-12-693050-3). Acad Pr.
Vago, C. Invertebrate Tissue Culture. 1971-72. Vol. 1. 56.50 (ISBN 0-12-709901-8); Vol. 2. 56.50 (ISBN 0-12-709902-6); 84.00 set (ISBN 0-686-76836-1). Acad Pr.
Wagstaffe, Reginald & Fidler, J. Havelock. Preservation of Natural History Specimens. Incl. Vol. 1. Invertebrates. (Illus.). 220p. (ISBN 0-8464-0749-3); Vol. 2. Vertebrates, Geology, & Botany. (Illus.). 420p. (ISBN 0-8464-0750-7). 1971. 49.00x set (ISBN 0-8464-0751-5). Beekman Pubs.
Walls, Jerry G. Starting with Marine Invertebrates. (Illus.). 160p. (Orig.). 1974. 7.95 (ISBN 0-87666-767-1, PS-729). TFH Pubns.
Wells, Martin. Lower Animals. LC 68-13140. 1968. pap. 2.95 (ISBN 0-07-069255-6, SP). McGraw.
Wesenberg-Lund, C. Biologie der Suesswassertiere: Wirbellose Tiere. (Illus.). 1967. 80.00 (ISBN 3-7682-0426-X). Lubrecht & Cramer.
Wessells, Norman K., intro. by. Vertebrate Structures & Functions: Readings from Scientific American. LC 73-17004. (Illus.). 1974. text ed. 19.95x (ISBN 0-7167-0890-6); pap. text ed. 9.95x (ISBN 0-7167-0889-2). W H Freeman.
Wolken, Jerome J. Invertebrate Photoreceptors: A Comparative Analysis. 1971. 30.00 (ISBN 0-12-762350-7). Acad Pr.
Zaika, V. E. Specific Production of Aquatic Invertebrates. Gollek, B., ed. Mercado, A., tr. from Rus. LC 73-12320. 154p. 1973. 43.95 (ISBN 0-470-98111-3). Halsted Pr.
Zeiller, Warren. Tropical Marine Invertebrates of Southern Florida & the Bahama Islands. LC 74-2467. (Illus.). 144p. 1974. 34.50x (ISBN 0-471-98153-2, Pub. by Wiley-Interscience). Wiley.
Zoological Society Of London - 23rd Symposium. Invertebrate Receptors. Newall, ed. 1968. 54.00 (ISBN 0-12-613323-9). Acad Pr.

INVERTEBRATES, FOSSIL

see also names of individual fossil phyla, classes, orders, etc. e.g. Mollusks, Fossil

Dacque, Edgar. Vergleichende Biologische Formenkunde der Fossilen Niederen Tiere: Biological Comparative Morphology of Lower Fossil Animals. Gould, Stephen J., ed. LC 79-8329. (The History of Paleontology Ser.). (Illus., Ger.). 1980. Repr. of 1921 ed. lib. bdg. 65.00x (ISBN 0-405-12710-3). Arno.

Hartzschel, Walter. Treatise on Invertebrate Paleontology, Pt. W. Suppl.1 Miscellanea, Trace Fossils & Problematica. 2nd. rev. & enl. ed. LC 53-12913. (Illus.). 1975. 20.00x (ISBN 0-8137-3027-9). Geol Soc.

McAlester, A. Lee. Type Species of Paleozoic Nuculoid Bivalve Genera. LC 68-23891. (Memoir: No. 105). (Illus.). 1968. 9.50x (ISBN 0-8137-1105-3). Geol Soc.

Moore, Raymond C. Treatise on Invertebrate Paleontology, Pt. U: Echinodermata 3, 2 vols. LC 53-12913. (Illus.). 1966. 27.50x (ISBN 0-8137-3022-8). Geol Soc.

Moore, Raymond C., ed. Treatise on Invertebrate Paleontology, Pt. C: Protista 2 (Foraminifera, et., 2 vols. LC 53-12913. 1964. 37.00x (ISBN 0-8137-3003-1). Geol Soc.

--Treatise on Invertebrate Paleontology, Pt. D: Protista 3 (Radiolarians, Tintinnines) LC 53-12913. (Illus.). 1954. 12.50x (ISBN 0-8137-3004-X). Geol Soc.

--Treatise on Invertebrate Paleontology, Pt. F: Coelenterata. LC 53-12913. (Illus.). 1956. 23.50x (ISBN 0-8137-3006-6). Geol Soc.

--Treatise on Invertebrate Paleontology: Part G - Bryozoa. LC 53-12913. 1953. 16.00x (ISBN 0-8137-3007-4). Geol Soc.

--Treatise on Invertebrate Paleontology, Pt. H: Brachiopoda, 2 vols. LC 53-12913. (Illus.). 1965. 37.50x (ISBN 0-8137-3008-2). Geol Soc.

--Treatise on Invertebrate Paleontology, Pt. I: Mollusca 1. LC 53-12913. (Illus.). 1960. 19.75x (ISBN 0-8137-3009-0). Geol Soc.

--Treatise on Invertebrate Paleontology, Pt. K: Mollusca 3. LC 53-12913. (Illus.). 1964. 23.75x (ISBN 0-8137-3011-2). Geol Soc.

--Treatise on Invertebrate Paleontology: Part L - Mollusca 4 (Ammmonoidea) LC 53-12913. 1957. 22.50x (ISBN 0-8137-3012-0). Geol Soc.

--Treatise on Invertebrate Paleontology, Pt. N: Mollusca 6 (Bivalvia, Vols. 1-2. LC 53-12913. (Illus.). 1969. 38.25x (ISBN 0-8137-3014-7). Geol Soc.

--Treatise on Invertebrate Paleontology, Pt. O: Arthropoda 1. LC 53-12913. (Illus.). 1959. 23.50x (ISBN 0-8137-3015-5). Geol Soc.

--Treatise on Invertebrate Paleontology, Pt. P: Arthropoda 2. LC 53-12913. (Illus.). 1955. 14.00x (ISBN 0-8137-3016-3). Geol Soc.

--Treatise on Invertebrate Paleontology, Pt. Q: Arthropoda 3. LC 53-12913. (Illus.). 1961. 22.75x (ISBN 0-8137-3017-1). Geol Soc.

--Treatise on Invertebrate Paleontology, Pt. R. Arthropoda 4, Vols. 1-2. LC 53-12913. (Illus.). 1969. 26.00x (ISBN 0-8137-3018-X). Geol Soc.

--Treatise on Invertebrate Paleontology, Pt. S: Echinodermata 1, 2 vols. LC 53-12913. (Illus.). 1968. 26.00x (ISBN 0-8137-3020-1). Geol Soc.

--Treatise on Invertebrate Paleontology, Pt. W: Miscellanea. LC 53-12913. (Illus.). 1962. 14.00x (ISBN 0-8137-3024-4). Geol Soc.

Moore, Raymond C. & Teichert, Curt, eds. Treatise on Invertebrate Paleontology: Part T: Echinodermata 2 (Crinoidea, 3 vols. LC 53-12913. (Treatise on Invertebrate Paleontology). (Illus.). 1978. Set. 55.00x (ISBN 0-8137-3021-X); Vol. 1. 27.00x (ISBN 0-686-52382-2); Vol. 2. 26.00x (ISBN 0-686-52383-0); Vol. 3. 13.00x (ISBN 0-686-52384-9). Geol Soc.

Moore, Raymond C., et al. Invertebrate Fossils. 1952. text ed. 26.00 (ISBN 0-07-043020-9, C). McGraw.

Robison, Richard A. & Tiechert, Curt, eds. Treatise on Invertebrate Paleontology: Introduction (Fossilization, Biogeography & Biostratigraphy, Pt. A. LC 53-12913. 1979. 25.00x (ISBN 0-8137-3001-5). Geol Soc.

Shimer, Harvey W. & Shrock, Robert R. Index Fossils of North America. (Illus.). 1944. 55.00x (ISBN 0-262-19001-X). MIT Pr.

Shrock, Robert R. & Twenhofel, William H. Principles of Invertebrate Paleontology. 2nd ed. (International Ser. in the Earth & Planetary Sciences: Geography Ser.). 1953. text ed. 26.00 (ISBN 0-07-057165-1, C). McGraw.

Tasch, Paul. Paleobiology of the Invertebrates: Data Retrieval from the Fossil Record. 2nd ed. LC 79-14929. 975p. 1980. text ed. 36.95 (ISBN 0-471-05272-8). Wiley.

INVESTIGATIONS

see also Criminal Investigation; Fire Investigation; Governmental Investigations

Akin, Richard H. The Private Investigator's Basic Manual. 208p. 1979. 16.25 (ISBN 0-398-03520-2). C C Thomas.

Arco Editorial Board. Investigator-Inspector. 4th ed. LC 78-24190. 1979. pap. 10.00 (ISBN 0-668-01670-1, 1670-1). Arco.

Barefoot, J. Kirk. Undercover Investigation. (Illus.). 100p. 1975. 13.50 (ISBN 0-398-03345-5). C C Thomas.

Dellheim, S. D. Forensic Handbook. new ed. (Illus.). 1978. pap. 3.95 (ISBN 0-930788-01-X, SPR-5592). Scott Protective.

DiDomenico, Joseph M. Investigative Technique for the Retail Security Investigator. LC 79-12097. 1979. 14.95 (ISBN 0-912016-82-5). Lebhar Friedman.

Golec, Anthony M. Techniques of Legal Investigation. (Illus.). 280p. 1976. 19.75 (ISBN 0-398-03522-9). C C Thomas.

Grau, Joseph J. Criminal & Civil Investigation Handbook. (Illus.). 1088p. 1982. 39.50 (ISBN 0-07-024130-9). McGraw.

Kaplan, Abraham. The Conduct of Inquiry. 1964. pap. text ed. 12.95 scp (ISBN 0-8102-0144-5, HarpC). Har-Row.

Levin, Jack. Estadistica en Investigacion. (Span.). 1979. pap. text ed. 7.80 (ISBN 0-06-315012-3, Pub. by HarLA Mexico). Har-Row.

Mouzakis. Investigative Guidelines & Procedures, No. 1. 1981. text ed. 43.95 (ISBN 0-409-95016-5). Butterworth.

Plutchik, Robert. Fundamentos De Investigacion Experimental. rev. ed. 1975. pap. text ed. 9.00 (ISBN 0-06-316991-6, IntlDept). Har-Row.

Rhodes, Gerald. Committees of Inquiry. 232p. 1975. 21.50x (ISBN 0-8448-0757-5). Crane-Russak Co.

Rudman, Jack. Chief Special Investigator. (Career Examination Ser.: C-1591). (Cloth bdg. avail. on request). pap. 12.00 (ISBN 0-8373-1591-3). Natl Learning.

--Complaint Investigator. (Career Examination Ser.: C-1863). (Cloth bdg. avail. on request). pap. 8.00 (ISBN 0-8373-0950-6). Natl Learning.

--Hospital Case Investigator. (Career Examination Ser.: C-1889). (Cloth bdg. avail. on request). pap. 8.00 (ISBN 0-8373-1889-0). Natl Learning.

--Investigator. (Career Examination Ser.: C-377). (Cloth bdg. avail. on request). pap. 8.00 (ISBN 0-8373-0377-X). Natl Learning.

--Principal Investigator. (Career Examination Ser.: C-1791). (Cloth bdg. avail. on request). pap. 10.00 (ISBN 0-8373-1791-6). Natl Learning.

--Principal Special Investigator. (Career Examination Ser.: C-1590). (Cloth bdg. avail. on request). pap. 10.00 (ISBN 0-8373-1590-5). Natl Learning.

--Private Investigator. (Career Examination Ser.: C-2462). (Cloth bdg. avail. on request). pap. 10.00 (ISBN 0-8373-2462-9). Natl Learning.

--Senior Special Investigator. (Career Examination Ser.: C-1589). (Cloth bdg. avail. on request). pap. 10.00 (ISBN 0-8373-1589-1). Natl Learning.

--Special Investigator. (Career Examination Ser.: C-1588). (Cloth bdg. avail. on request). pap. 8.00 (ISBN 0-8373-1588-3). Natl Learning.

--Supervising Investigator. (Career Examination Ser.: C-2106). (Cloth bdg. avail. on request). 1977. pap. 10.00 (ISBN 0-8373-2106-9). Natl Learning.

Scott, James D. Investigative Methods. (Illus.). 1978. ref. ed. 14.95 (ISBN 0-87909-392-7); instrs'. manual avail. Reston.

INVESTIGATIONS, GOVERNMENTAL

see Governmental Investigations

INVESTIGATOR (SHIP)

McClure, Robert J. The Discovery of the North-West Passage by H.M.S. Investigator: 1850-54. Osborn, Sherard, ed. LC 74-5853. Repr. of 1856 ed. 26.50 (ISBN 0-404-11660-4). AMS Pr.

INVESTITURE

see also Bishops; Church and State

Cantor, Norman F. Church, Kingship & Lay Investiture in England, 1089-1135. 1969. lib. bdg. 18.50x (ISBN 0-374-91273-4). Octagon.

Morrison, Karl E., ed. The Investiture Controversy: Issues, Ideals & Results. LC 77-15654. (European Problem Studies). 144p. 1976. pap. text ed. 5.50 (ISBN 0-88275-634-6). Krieger.

Robinson, Ian S. Authority & Resistance in the Investiture Contest. LC 78-9110. 1978. text ed. 39.50x (ISBN 0-8419-0407-3). Holmes & Meier.

Tellenbach, Gerd. Church, State & Christian Society at the Time of the Investiture Contest. 1979. text ed. 15.00x (ISBN 0-391-00153-1). Humanities.

INVESTMENT ADVISERS

Counseling the Investment Adviser 1977. (Corporate Law & Practice Course Handbook Ser., 1976-77: Vol. 231). 1977. pap. 20.00 (ISBN 0-685-85295-4, B4-5511). PLI.

Rudman, Jack. Investment Analyst. (Career Examination Ser.: C-2333). (Cloth bdg. avail. on request). pap. 10.00 (ISBN 0-685-60436-5). Natl Learning.

INVESTMENT AND SAVING

see Saving and Investment

INVESTMENT BANKING

see also Development Banks; Syndicates (Finance)

Anthony, Vivian. Banks & Markets. (Studies in the British Economy). 1974. pap. text ed. 6.95x (ISBN 0-435-84558-6). Heinemann Ed.

Carosso, Vincent P. Investment Banking in America: A History. Sears, Martin V. & Katz, Irving, eds. LC 70-99515. (Studies in Business History: No. 25). 1970. 25.00x (ISBN 0-674-46574-1). Harvard U Pr.

--More Than a Century of Investment Banking: The Didder, Peabody & Co. Story. (Illus.). 1979. 10.95 (ISBN 0-07-010136-1, P&RB). McGraw.

Carosso, Vincent P., ed. Two Private Banking Partnerships: An Original Anthology. LC 75-2676. (Wall Street & the Security Market Ser.). (Illus.). 1975. 34.00x (ISBN 0-405-07238-4). Arno.

Davey, Patrick J. Investment Banking Arrangements. LC 76-313. (Report Ser.: No. 681). 1976. pap. 30.00 (ISBN 0-8237-0115-8). Conference Bd.

Galston, Arthur. Security Syndicate Operations: Organization, Management & Accounting. enl. & rev. ed. LC 75-2634. (Wall Street & the Security Market Ser.). 1975. Repr. of 1928 ed. 16.00x (ISBN 0-405-06959-6). Arno.

Goldsmith, Raymond W. Financial Intermediaries in the American Economy Since 1900. LC 75-19713. (National Bureau of Economic Research Ser.). (Illus.). 1975. Repr. 25.00x (ISBN 0-405-07593-6). Arno.

Medina, Harold R. Corrected Opinion of Harold R. Medina, United States Circuit Judge in United States of America, Plaintiff, V. Henry S. Morgan, Harold Stanley et. Al.... facsimile ed. LC 75-2647. (Wall Street & the Security Market Ser.). 1975. Repr. of 1954 ed. 25.00x (ISBN 0-405-06972-3). Arno.

Security Dealers of North America, 2 vols. 1981. 192.00 set (ISBN 0-686-10240-1). Standard Poors.

Warburg, Paul M. The Federal Reserve System: Its Origin & Growth-Reflections & Recollections, 2 vols. facsimile ed. LC 75-2680. (Wall Street & the Security Markets Ser.). 1975. Repr. of 1930 ed. Set. 100.00x (ISBN 0-405-07242-2). Arno.

Willis, Henry P. & Bogen, Jules I. Investment Banking. rev. ed. LC 75-2686. (Wall Street & the Security Market Ser.). 1975. Repr. of 1936 ed. 40.00x (ISBN 0-405-07247-3). Arno.

INVESTMENT CASTING

see Precision Casting

INVESTMENT CLUBS

see also Investment Trusts

Sederberg, Arelo. The Stock Market Investment Club Handbook. 288p. 1971. 7.50 (ISBN 0-8202-0089-1). Sherbourne.

INVESTMENT COMPANIES

see Investment Trusts

INVESTMENT IN REAL ESTATE

see Real Estate Investment

INVESTMENT TRUSTS

see also Investment Clubs

Baum, Daniel J. The Investment Function of Canadian Financial Institutions. LC 72-86435. (Special Studies in International Economics & Development). 1973. 38.50x (ISBN 0-275-28684-3). Irvington.

Brown, Thomas E. A Layman's Guide to Oil & Gas Investments. 136p. 1981. 9.95 (ISBN 0-87201-344-8). Gulf Pub.

Bullock, Hugh. The Story of Investment Companies. LC 59-13778. (Illus.). 305p. 1959. 22.50x (ISBN 0-231-02378-2). Columbia U Pr.

Cam, Gilbert A. Survey of the Literature on Investment Companies, 1864-1957. 1964. pap. 3.00 (ISBN 0-87104-173-1). NY Pub Lib.

Commerce Clearing House, Inc. Small Business Investment Companies. Bruchey, Stuart & Carosso, Vincent P., eds. LC 78-18958. (Small Business Enterprise in America Ser.). 1979. Repr. of 1959 ed. lib. bdg. 12.00x (ISBN 0-405-11462-1). Arno.

Flynn, John T. Investment Trusts Gone Wrong! facsimile ed. LC 75-2629. (Wall Street & Security Market Ser.). 1975. Repr. of 1930 ed. 17.00x (ISBN 0-405-06955-3). Arno.

Fowler, John F., Jr. American Investment Trusts. facsimile ed. LC 75-2633. (Wall Street & the Security Market Ser.). 1975. Repr. of 1928 ed. 26.00x (ISBN 0-405-06958-8). Arno.

Friend, I., et al. Mutual Funds & Other Institutional Investors: A New Perspective. 1970. 19.95 (ISBN 0-07-022456-0, P&RB). McGraw.

Grayson, Theodore J. Investment Trusts: Their Origin, Development, & Operation. facsimile ed. LC 75-2636. (Wall Street & the Security Market Ser.). 1975. Repr. of 1928 ed. 27.00x (ISBN 0-405-06961-8). Arno.

Heflebower, R. B. Cooperatives & Mutuals in the Market System. LC 79-5407. 1980. 22.50 (ISBN 0-299-07850-7). U of Wis Pr.

Kaufman, Stanley. Practical & Legal Manual for the Investor. LC 56-5060. (Legal Almanac Ser: No. 42). (Orig.). 1956. 4.95 (ISBN 0-379-11042-3). Oceana.

Mead, Stuart B. Mutual Fund & Investment Company Performance in the Fifties. LC 61-64380. 1961. pap. 2.50 (ISBN 0-87744-049-2). Mich St U Busn.

Meidner, Rudolf. Employee Investment Funds: An Approach to Collective Capital Formation. (Illus.). 1978. text ed. 18.95x (ISBN 0-04-331072-9). Allen Unwin.

Metzger, Bert L. Highlights of Largest Profit Sharing Trusts in U. S. 16p. 1975. pap. 1.00 (ISBN 0-911192-20-4). Profit Sharing.

Steiner, William H. Investment Trusts: American Experience. facsimile ed. LC 75-2671. (Wall Street & the Security Market Ser.). 1975. Repr. of 1929 ed. 20.00x (ISBN 0-405-07234-1). Arno.

INVESTMENTS

see also Annuities; Bank Investments; Bonds; Brokers; Building and Loan Associations; Capital Investments; Insurance Companies–Investments; Investment Advisers; Investment Banking; Investment Trusts; Jewelry As an Investment; Loans; Mortgages; Porcelain As an Investment; Real Estate Investment; Saving and Thrift; Securities; Speculation; Stock-Exchange; Stocks

Abramovitz, Moses, et al. The Allocation of Economic Resources. LC 59-7420. 1959. pap. 4.85x (ISBN 0-8047-0569-0). Stanford U Pr.

Abrams, Don. The Profit-Taker: The Proven Rapid Money-Maker in Good & Bad Markets. LC 79-22695. 124p. 1980. 9.95 (ISBN 0-471-06228-6, Pub. by Wiley-Interscience). Wiley.

Aby, Carroll D. & Vaughn, Donald E., Jr., eds. Investment Classics. LC 78-27774. 1979. pap. text ed. 14.95 (ISBN 0-87620-444-2). Goodyear.

Ahlers, David M. A New Look at Portfolio Management. Altman, Edward I. & Walter, Ingo, eds. LC 76-10448. (Contemporary Studies in Economic & Financial Analysis: Vol. 5). 1977. lib. bdg. 30.00 (ISBN 0-89232-012-5). Jai Pr.

Altman, Edward I. Financial Handbook. 5th ed. 1736p. 1981. 42.50 (ISBN 0-471-07727-5, Pub. by Ronald Pr). Wiley.

Amling, Frederick. Investments: An Introduction to Analysis & Management. 4th ed. (Illus.). 1978. ref. 21.00 (ISBN 0-13-504308-5). P-H.

Andersen, Ian. Making Money. LC 77-93232. 1978. 10.00 (ISBN 0-8149-0797-0). Vanguard.

Anderson, Frank R. Quality Controlled Investing: Or How to Avoid the Pick & Pray Method. LC 78-7607. 160p. 1978. 21.95 (ISBN 0-471-04382-6, Pub. by Wiley-Interscience). Wiley.

Angell, James W. Investment & Business Cycles. 363p. Repr. of 1941 ed. lib. bdg. 19.50x (ISBN 0-678-00973-2). Kelley.

Aplin, Richard D., et al. Capital Investment Analysis: Using Discounted Cash Flows. 2nd ed. LC 78-50041. (Agricultural Economics Ser.). 1977. pap. text ed. 12.95 (ISBN 0-88244-153-1). Grid Pub.

Appel, Gerald. Ninety-Nine Ways to Make Money in a Depression. rev. ed. (Illus.). 256p. Date not set. 14.95 (ISBN 0-87000-501-4). Arlington Hse.

Appel, Gerald & Hitschler, Fred. Stock Market Trading Systems: A Guide to Investment Strategy. LC 79-55228. 218p. 1980. 30.00 (ISBN 0-87094-195-X). Dow Jones-Irwin.

Appleman, Jean. The Midas Touch: Dynamics of Market Investment. LC 75-18229. 260p. 1975. pap. 9.95 (ISBN 0-916036-00-6). Am Pub.

Appleman, M. Understanding Your Customer: Psychological Aspects of Investing. 1973. 5.00 (ISBN 0-13-936252-5). P-H.

Armfield, W. A., Jr. The Energy Investment Game: How to Play It & Win with Oil & Gas. LC 80-19221. (Illus.). 222p. 1980. 24.95 (ISBN 0-87624-128-3); pap. 6.95 (ISBN 0-87624-127-5). Inst Busn Plan.

Ashford, Mark. Psychic Adventure on Wall Street: Or You Can Win the Wall Street Game! 1979. 6.00 (ISBN 0-682-49400-3). Exposition.

Atkinson, Thomas R. Pattern of Financial Asset Ownership: Wisconsin Individuals, 1949. (Financial Research Program Ser.). 1956. 9.00 (ISBN 0-691-04155-5, Dist. by Princeton U Pr). Natl Bur Econ Res.

Auster, Rolf. Tax Tested Strategies in Securities & Options Investments. LC 80-24880. 226p. 1980. 24.95 (ISBN 0-87624-582-3). Inst Busn Plan.

Barnes, Leo & Feldman, Stephen. Handbook of Wealth Management. (Illus.). 1977. 42.50 (ISBN 0-07-003765-5, P&RB). McGraw.

Batliwalla, Minoo R. Investment Decision: Capital Budgeting with the Aid of the Discounted Cash Flow Technique. (Illus.). 1978. text ed. 30.00 (ISBN 0-210-22356-1). Asia.

Baudisch, A. V. Investments That Beat Inflation to the Punch. LC 71-103721. (Orig.). 1970. pap. 2.00 (ISBN 0-87576-025-2). Pilot Bks.

Bauman, W. Scott & Klein, Thomas A. Investment Profit Correlation: A Regression Model of Profits from Common Stock Investments. (Michigan Business Reports: No. 55). 1968. pap. 3.00 (ISBN 0-87712-073-0). U Mich Busn Div Res.

Bawa, V. S., et al. Estimation Risk & Optimal Portfolio Choice. (Studies in Bayesian Econometrics: Vol. 3). 1979. 29.50 (ISBN 0-444-85344-8, North Holland). Elsevier.

Beadle, Patricia. Investing in the Eighties: What to Buy & When. (Illus.). 208p. 1981. 10.95 (ISBN 0-686-72890-4). HarBraceJ.

Beckhardt, Israel. The Small Investor's Guide to Gold. 1979. pap. 2.95 (ISBN 0-532-23232-1). Woodhill.

Beckner, Steven K. The Hard Money Book: An Insider's Guide to Successful Investment in Currency, Gold, Silver & Precious Stones. LC 79-84366. (Orig.). 1979. pap. 19.00 (ISBN 0-933722-00-1). Capitalist Reporter.

Becky, Steven K. The Hard Money Book: An Insider's Guide to Successful Investment in Currency, Gold, Silver, & Precious Stones. (Illus.). 160p. 1980. 14.95 (ISBN 0-8015-3281-7, Hawthorn); pap. 7.95 (ISBN 0-8015-3282-5, Hawthorn). Dutton.

Bellemore, Douglas H. & Ritchie, John C., Jr. Principles, Practices & Analysis: Principles & Analysis. 4th ed. 1974. text ed. 14.95 (ISBN 0-538-06420-X). SW Pub.

Bennett, John B. & Doelling, Norman. Investing in Japanese Securities: Profit & Protection for the Intelligent Investor. LC 72-83672. 112p. 1972. pap. 3.00 (ISBN 0-8048-1063-X). C E Tuttle.

Bereny, Justin A. The Emerging Solar Technologies: An Investment Overview. 100p. 1982. 125.00 (ISBN 0-89934-146-2). Solar Energy Info.

Bernstein, Jacob. The Investor's Quotient: The Psychology of Successful Investing in Commodities & Stock. LC 80-17127. 275p. 1980. 16.95 (ISBN 0-471-07849-2). Wiley.

Bicksler, James L., ed. Capital Market Equilibrium & Efficiency: Implications for Accounting, Finance, & Portfolio Decision Making. 1977. 38.50 (ISBN 0-669-86660-1). Lexington Bks.

Bicksler, James L. & Samuelson, Paul A., eds. Investment Portfolio Decision-Making. LC 73-1561. 1974. 19.95 (ISBN 0-669-86215-0). Lexington Bks.

Bierman, Harold, Jr. & Smidt, Seymour. The Capital Budgeting Decision: Economic Analysis of Investment Projects. 5th ed. (Illus.). 1980. text ed. 23.95 (ISBN 0-02-309480-X). Macmillan.

Bines, Harvey E. Law of Investment Management. 1978. 56.00 (ISBN 0-88262-150-5, 77-10130). Warren.

Blackman, Richard. Follow the Leaders. 1979. 3.95 (ISBN 0-346-12382-8). Cornerstone.

Blanchard, James U., III, ed. The Expert's "Alternative Investment" Handbook. 238p. 1980. 19.95 (ISBN 0-686-73976-0). Alexandria Hse.

Blotnick, Srully. Winning: The Psychology of Successful Investing. 1978. 15.95 (ISBN 0-07-006119-X, P&RB). McGraw.

Bookbinder, Albert I. A. Investment Decision Making. LC 67-29760. (Illus.). 145p. 1968. 4.95x (ISBN 0-916106-00-4). Prog Pr.

Bracewell-Milnes, J. B. & Huiskamp, J. C. Investment Incentives. (International Series of the Fiscal-Economic Institute, Erasmus Univ., Rotterdam). 1977. pap. 25.00 (ISBN 90-200-0499-9, Pub. by Kluwer Law Netherlands). Kluwer Boston.

Branch, Ben. Fundamentals of Investing. LC 75-26703. 1976. 24.50 (ISBN 0-471-09650-4). Wiley.

Brennan, Mary E. & Hieb, Elizabeth A., eds. Investment Institute Hollywood, Florida, April 27 to 30, 1980: Proceedings. 137p. 1980. pap. 10.00 (ISBN 0-89154-134-9). Intl Found Employ.

Bridwell, Rodger W. The Battle for Financial Security: How to Invest in the Runaway 80's. 288p. 1980. 12.95 (ISBN 0-8129-0898-8). Times Bks.

Browne, Harry & Coxon, Terry. Inflation-Proofing Your Investments: A Permanent Program That Will Help You Protect Your Savings Against Inflation or Depression. LC 80-26086. (Illus.). 1980. 14.95 (ISBN 0-688-03576-0). Morrow.

Brownstone, David M. & Franck, Irene M. The VNR Investor's Dictionary. 320p. 1980. 16.95 (ISBN 0-442-21578-9). Van Nos Reinhold.

Business Investment Management: A MAPI Study & Manual. non-members 20.00 (ISBN 0-686-11603-8); members 12.00 (ISBN 0-686-11604-6). M & A Products.

Bussey, Lynn E. The Economic Analysis of Industrial Projects. (International Ser. in Industrial & System Engineering). (Illus.). 1978. ref. 24.95 (ISBN 0-13-223388-6). P-H.

Cairncoss, Alexander K. Home & Foreign Investment, 1870-1913. LC 74-17410. 251p. Repr. of 1953 ed. lib. bdg. 15.00x (ISBN 0-678-01023-4). Kelley.

Cantelon, Willard. New Money or None. 1979. pap. 2.95 pocketsize (ISBN 0-88270-388-9). Logos.

Casey, Douglas R. Crisis Investing. 1981. pap. 3.50 (ISBN 0-671-42678-8). PB.

--International Investing. 150p. 1981. pap. 9.95 (ISBN 0-89696-130-3). Everest Hse.

Cavelti, Peter. How to Invest in Gold. 192p. (Orig.). 1980. pap. 5.95 (ISBN 0-695-81423-0). New Century.

Changing Times Education Service Editors. Saving & Investing. rev. ed. LC 81-7860. (Illus.). 1981. pap. text ed. 4.45 (ISBN 0-88436-807-6, CEA994051). EMC.

Chase, Samuel, Jr. Asset Prices in Economic Analysis. LC 63-13588. (California Library Reprint Series: No. 22). 1971. 21.50x (ISBN 0-520-01928-8). U of Cal Pr.

Choksi, Armeane, et al. The Planning of Investment Programs in the Fertilizer Industry. LC 78-8436. (World Bank Ser: No. 2). 1978. text ed. 19.50x (ISBN 0-8018-2138-X); pap. text ed. 8.95x (ISBN 0-8018-2153-3). Johns Hopkins.

Christy, G. A. & Clendenin, J. C. Introduction to Investments. 8th ed. (Finance Ser.). 784p. 1982. 20.95 (ISBN 0-07-010833-1, C). McGraw.

--Introduction to Investments. 5th ed. (Illus.). 704p. 1973. text ed. 16.00 (ISBN 0-07-010825-0, C); instructors' manual 4.95 (ISBN 0-07-010826-9). McGraw.

Christy, G. A., et al. Introduction to Investments. 7th ed. (Finance Ser.). (Illus.). 1977. text ed. 17.95 (ISBN 0-07-010827-7, C); instructors' manual 4.95 (ISBN 0-07-010828-5). McGraw.

Church, Albert M. The Sophisticated Investor: How to Target Prime Investment Opportunities. (Illus.). 224p. 1981. 15.95 (ISBN 0-13-822767-5); pap. 7.95 (ISBN 0-686-73241-3). P-H.

Coates, Robert. Investment Strategy. (Illus.). 1978. text ed. 17.95 (ISBN 0-07-011471-4); instructor's manual 5.95 (ISBN 0-07-011472-2); study guide 6.50 (ISBN 0-07-011473-0). McGraw.

Cobleigh, Ira & Dorfman, Bruce. The Dowbeaters: How to Buy Stocks That Go up. (Illus.). 1979. 10.95 (ISBN 0-02-526500-8). Macmillan.

Cohen, Bernard. Compendium of Finance. LC 68-55511. Repr. of 1822 ed. 25.00x (ISBN 0-678-01042-0). Kelley.

Cohen, Jerome B., et al. Guide to Intelligent Investing. LC 77-83590. 1978. 12.50 (ISBN 0-87094-152-6). Dow Jones-Irwin.

Coleman, David. For the Long Term. LC 78-59906. 1979. 12.95 (ISBN 0-930726-05-7); pap. 8.95 (ISBN 0-930726-04-9). Concept Pub.

Cowing, Cedric B. Populist, Plungers, & Progressives: A Social History of Stock & Commodity Speculation, 1890-1936. LC 65-12988. (Orig.). 1969. 20.00 (ISBN 0-691-04555-0); pap. 8.95 (ISBN 0-691-00563-X). Princeton U Pr.

Craig, Gary H. Unscrewing the Small Investor. 156p. 1976. 7.95 (ISBN 0-442-80141-6). Van Nos Reinhold.

Crane, Burton. The Sophisticated Investor. rev. ed. 1964. pap. 2.95 (ISBN 0-671-68072-2, Fireside). S&S.

Croom, George E., Jr. & Van Der Wal, John. Now You Can Profit from Inflation. 264p. 1981. 14.95 (ISBN 0-442-25397-4). Van Nos Reinhold.

Crowell, Richard A. Stock Market Strategy. (Illus.). 1977. 21.95 (ISBN 0-07-014720-5, P&RB). McGraw.

Crumbley, Larry & Crumbley, Tony L. The Financial Management of Your Coin-Stamp Estate. LC 77-13026. 1978. 16.50 (ISBN 0-668-04444-6). Arco.

Curley, Anthony J. & Bear, Robert M. Investment Analysis & Management. 1979. text ed. 24.50 scp (ISBN 0-06-041452-9, HarpC); inst. manual free (ISBN 0-06-361451-0); scp data deck 29.50 (ISBN 0-06-041454-5). Har-Row.

Cuse, Arthur. How to Make it in Gold & Not Get @#$! (Orig.). 1974. pap. 9.95 (ISBN 0-917474-02-3). Guideline Pub.

Dahl, Cornwall. Consistent Profits in Short Selling Speculation. (Illus.). 267p. 1976. 41.50 (ISBN 0-89266-011-2). Am Classical Coll Pr.

D'Ambrosio, Charles. Guide to Successful Investing. 1969. pap. text ed. 11.95x (ISBN 0-13-370817-9). P-H.

D'Ambrosio, Charles A. Principles of Modern Investments. LC 75-34094. (Illus.). 512p. 1976. text ed. 21.95 (ISBN 0-574-19210-7, 13-2210); instr's guide avail. (ISBN 0-574-19211-5, 13-2211). SRA.

Dames, Ralph T. The Winning Option. LC 79-23369. 128p. 1980. 14.95 (ISBN 0-88229-527-6). Nelson-Hall.

D'Arcy, G. Minot. Investment Counsel. 1964. 5.95 (ISBN 0-8392-1052-3). Astor-Honor.

Davidson, William H. Experience Effects in International Investment & Technology Transfer. Dufey, Gunter, ed. LC 80-39884. (Research for Business Decisions Ser.: No. 34). 160p. 1981. 29.95 (ISBN 0-8357-1148-X, Pub. by UMI Res Pr). Univ Microfilms.

Deutch, Howard E. High Profits Without Risk. (Illus.). 1977. 15.95x (ISBN 0-917244-01-X). Jefren Pub.

Dirks, Ray. Heads You Win, Tails You Win. LC 78-27174. 1979. 10.95 (ISBN 0-8128-2581-0). Stein & Day.

--Heads You Win, Tales You Win. 192p. 1980. pap. 3.50 (ISBN 0-553-14073-6). Bantam.

Dobson, Edward D. The Trading Rule That Can Make You Rich: Precision Bid Commodity Trading. LC 79-64620. (Illus.). 1979. pap. 25.00 (ISBN 0-934380-03-1). Traders Pr.

Dore, M. H. Dynamic Investment Planning. 1978. text ed. 29.50x (ISBN 0-8419-5511-5). Holmes & Meier.

Dougall, Herbert & Corrigan, Francis J. Investments. 10th ed. LC 78-453. (Illus.). 1978. ref. ed. 21.95 (ISBN 0-13-504597-5). P-H.

Dreman, David. Contrarian Investment Strategy: The Psychology of Stock-Market Success. LC 78-21820. (Illus.). 1980. 12.95 (ISBN 0-394-42390-9). Random.

Dreman, David N. Psychology & the Stock Market. new ed. LC 76-49986. 1977. 13.95 (ISBN 0-8144-5429-1). Am Mgmt.

Drollinger, William C. Tax Shelters & Tax-Free Income for Everyone, Vol. 1. 4th ed. LC 72-94179. 1979. 19.95 (ISBN 0-914244-04-3). Epic Pubns.

Dunst, Klaus H. Portfolio Management. 1979. 46.00x (ISBN 3-11007-748-5). De Gruyter.

Duthy, Robin V. Alternative Investment: A Guide to Opportunity in the Collectibles Market. 272p. 1980. 22.50 (ISBN 0-8129-0865-1). Times Bks.

Dyckman, T. R. Investment Analysis & General Price-Level Adjustments, Vol. 1. (Studies in Accounting Research). 76p. 1969. 6.00 (ISBN 0-686-31093-4). Am Accounting.

Dyke, Bill & Jones, Bill. The Horse Business: An Investor's Guide. (Illus.). 1974. 10.00 (ISBN 0-912830-22-0). Printed Horse.

Eisner, Robert. Factors in Business Investment. LC 78-7548. (National Bureau of Economic Research Ser.: No. 102). 1978. 22.50 (ISBN 0-88410-484-2). Ballinger Pub.

Eiteman, Wilford J. Personal Finance & Investment. 1952. 3.25 (ISBN 0-685-79083-5). Masterco Pr.

Elliott, R. N. Nature's Law & the Secret of the Universe. (Illus.). 1980. Repr. 99.75 (ISBN 0-89901-008-3). Found Class Reprints.

Elton, Edwin J. & Gruber, Martin J. Modern Portfolio Theory & Investment Analysis. LC 80-19517. (Illus.). 553p. 1981. 22.95 (ISBN 0-471-04690-6). Wiley.

Engel, Louis & Wyckoff, Peter. How to Buy Stocks. 6th rev. ed. 1976. 11.95 (ISBN 0-316-23906-2). Little.

--How to Buy Stocks. 6th rev. ed. 1977. pap. 3.50 (ISBN 0-553-20455-6). Bantam.

Fabozzi, Frank J. & Zarb, Frank G. The Handbook of Financial Markets: Securities, Options and Futures. LC 80-70448. 825p. 1981. 37.50 (ISBN 0-87094-216-6). Dow Jones-Irwin.

Fama, Eugene F. Foundations of Finance: Portfolio Decisions & Securities Prices. LC 75-36771. (Illus.). 1976. text ed. 17.50x (ISBN 0-465-02499-8). Basic.

Farrell, Maurice, ed. Dow Jones Investors Handbook, 1980. LC 66-17650. (Illus.). 160p. (Orig.). 1980. pap. 5.95 (ISBN 0-87128-590-8, Pub. by Dow Jones). Dow Jones-Irwin.

Felsen, Jerry. Cybernetic Approach to Stock Market Analysis: Versus Efficient Market Theory. LC 74-34512. 1975. 15.00 (ISBN 0-682-48224-2, University). Exposition.

--Cybernetic Approach to Stock Market Analysis vs Efficient Market Theory. LC 74-34512. 1975. 20.00 (ISBN 0-916376-01-X). CDS Pub.

--Low-Cost, Personal-Computer-Based Investment Decision Systems. LC 77-83508. 1977. pap. 20.00 (ISBN 0-916376-03-6). CDS Pub.

Feng, P. Y. The ASE-OTC Dividend Reinvestment Handbook. 100p. (Orig.). Date not set. pap. 7.95 (ISBN 0-934036-06-3). PMF Research.

--The Dividend Reinvestment Catalog. 330p. 1981. pap. 8.50 (ISBN 0-934036-05-5). PMF Research.

--The Dividend Reinvestment Directory. LC 79-87718. 1979. pap. 4.95 (ISBN 0-934036-01-2). PMF Research.

--The Dividend Reinvestment Guide. LC 79-87719. 1979. pap. 3.95 (ISBN 0-934036-02-0). PMF Research.

--The Dividend Reinvestment Handbook. 2nd ed. LC 80-84630. 701p. 1981. pap. 25.00 (ISBN 0-934036-04-7). PMF Research.

--The Dividend Reinvestment Handbook. LC 79-84219. 1979. pap. 18.50 (ISBN 0-934036-00-4). PMF Research.

Ferris, Paul. The City. (Jackdaw Ser: No. 134). (gr. 7 up). 1974. 6.95 (ISBN 0-670-22445-6). Viking Pr.

Findlay, M. Chapman & Williams, Edward E. Investment Analysis. (Illus.). 480p. 1974. ref. ed. 21.00 (ISBN 0-13-502633-4). P-H.

Fischer, Donald E. & Jordan, Ronald J. Security Analysis & Portfolio Management. 2nd ed. 1979. 19.95 (ISBN 0-13-798850-8). P-H.

Fitzgerald, T. H. Money Market Directory 1981: Institutional Investors & Their Portfolio Managers. 1980. 265.00 (ISBN 0-939712-00-8). Money Mkt.

Flumiani, C. M. How to Protect Your Money from the Destructive Powers of Inflation, Business Depressions, Political Turmoil, Wars, Revolutions & How to Double Your Patrimony Safely Every Five Years. (Illus.). 114p. 1974. 60.00 (ISBN 0-913314-37-4). Am Classical Coll Pr.

--The Wall Street Manual for Teenagers. (Illus.). 80p. (gr. 7-12). 1973. 19.75 (ISBN 0-913314-24-2). Am Classical Coll Pr.

Flumiani, C. M., ed. The Wall Street Library, 3 vols. (The New Stock Market Library Book). (Illus.). deluxe ed. 137.45 (ISBN 0-918968-26-7). Inst Econ Finan.

Ford, Norman D. Investing to Beat Inflation. 169p. 1979. 4.95 (ISBN 0-686-63829-8). Harian.

Fosback, Norman G. Stock Market Logic: A Sophisticated Approach to Profits on Wall Street. LC 76-28826. (Illus.). 1976. 30.00 (ISBN 0-917604-48-2); pap. 20.00 (ISBN 0-917604-49-0). Inst Econmetric.

Francis, Clark & Archer, Stephen H. Portfolio Analysis. 2nd ed. (Foundations of Finance Ser.). (Illus.). 1979. text ed. 21.00 (ISBN 0-13-686675-1). P-H.

Francis, Jack C. Investments: Analysis & Management. 2nd ed. 1976. 18.95 (ISBN 0-07-021787-4, C); solutions manual 4.95 (ISBN 0-07-021788-2). McGraw.

Fraser, James. Investment Sources. 1979. 5.00 (ISBN 0-87034-057-3). Fraser Pub Co.

Fraser, James L. Ten Rules for Investing. Repr. of 1964 ed. 1.50 (ISBN 0-87034-030-1). Fraser Pub Co.

Frost, A. John & Prechter, Robert R., Jr. Elliott Wave Principle: Key to Stock Market Profits. LC 78-70643. 1978. 21.00 (ISBN 0-932750-00-1). New Classics Lib.

Fund Advisors Institute, July 1975, Denver, Colorado: Proceedings. (Pensions). 221p. 1976. pap. 6.50 (ISBN 0-89154-039-3). Intl Found Employ.

Gale, Jack L. Commercial Investment Brokerage: An Introduction with Case Studies. 296p. 1979. pap. 18.00 (ISBN 0-913652-19-9). Realtors Natl.

Geczi, Mike. Futures: The Anti-Inflation Investment. 1980. pap. 2.95 (ISBN 0-380-75713-3, 75713, Discus). Avon.

Gitman, Lawrence J. & Joehnk, Michael D. Fundamentals of Investing. 736p. 1981. text ed. 21.50 scp (ISBN 0-06-042338-2, HarpC). Har-Row.

Glubetich, Dave. How to Grow a Moneytree. Wigginton, Dave, ed. 1977. pap. 6.95 (ISBN 0-9601530-0-4). Impact Pub.

Goff, T. G. Theory & Practice of Investment. (Illus.). 220p. 1971. 12.50x (ISBN 0-434-90665-4). Intl Pubns Serv.

Goldberg, Richard H. Planting Your Money Tree: A Guide for the Small Investor. LC 77-23814. 1977. 7.95 (ISBN 0-89456-004-2). Chatham Sq.

Golden, James R. Investment Behavior by United States Railroads: 1870-1914. LC 75-2582. (Dissertations in American Economic History). (Illus.). 1975. 23.00x (ISBN 0-405-07202-3). Arno.

Goldsmith, Raymond W., ed. Institutional Investors & Corporate Stock: A Background Study. (Studies in Capital Formation & Financing Ser.: No. 13). 400p. 1973. text ed. 15.00x (ISBN 0-87014-237-2, Dist. by Columbia U Pr). Natl Bur Econ Res.

Gorove, Stephen, ed. Legal Aspects of International Investment. (L. Q. C. Lamar Society of International Law, University of Mississippi Law Center, Monograph: No. 1). viii, 79p. (Orig.). 1977. pap. text ed. 10.00x (ISBN 0-8377-0607-6). Rothman.

Graham, Benjamin. The Intelligent Investor: A Book of Practical Counsel. 4th rev. ed. LC 78-156524. (Illus.). 1973. 12.95 (ISBN 0-06-011591-2, HarpT). Har-Row.

Graham, Benjamin, et al. Security Analysis. 4th ed. 1962. text ed. 22.50 (ISBN 0-07-023957-6, C). McGraw.

Grant, Mary M. & Cote, Norma, eds. Directory of Business & Financial Services. 7th ed. LC 75-34228. 1976. 18.80 (ISBN 0-87111-212-4). SLA.

Griffith, B. Barret. Investing Is Adventure. 1965. Repr. of 1949 ed. flexible cover 4.00 (ISBN 0-87034-012-3). Fraser Pub Co.
Grosvenor, William M. American Securities: The Causes Influencing Investment & Speculation & the Fluctuations in Values, 1872 to 1885. Repr. of 1885 ed. lib. bdg. 18.75x (ISBN 0-8371-1100-5, GRAS). Greenwood.
Grushcow, Jack & Smith, Courtney. Profits Through Seasonal Trading. 184p. 1980. 37.95 (ISBN 0-471-06158-1, Ronald). Ronald Pr.
Haag, Leonard H. Cash Management & Short Term Investments for Colleges & Universities. Wainwright, Abbott, ed. LC 77-21132. 1977. 15.00 (ISBN 0-915164-05-1). Natl Assn Coll.
Hagin, Robert. The Dow Jones-Irwin Guide to Modern Portfolio Theory. LC 79-51785. 1980. 14.50 (ISBN 0-87094-181-X). Dow Jones-Irwin.
--Modern Portfolio Theory. 1980. pap. 11.95x (ISBN 0-256-02379-4). Irwin.
Hahn, L. Albert. Economics of Illusion. Repr. of 1949 ed. flexible cover 8.00 (ISBN 0-87034-040-9). Fraser Pub Co.
Hancock, William A. Saving Money Through Ten-Year Trusts. (Illus.). 1979. 15.95 (ISBN 0-07-025983-6, P&RB). McGraw.
Hanford, Lloyd, Sr. Analysis & Management of Investment Property. 3rd ed. 1970. pap. text ed. 12.50 (ISBN 0-912104-06-6). Inst Real Estate.
Hardy, C. Colburn. Dun & Bradstreet's Guide to Your Investments: 1982. LC 73-18050. (Illus.). 224p. 1982. 16.75 (ISBN 0-06-014935-3, HarpT); pap. 9.95 (ISBN 0-06-090928-5, CN 928). Har-Row.
Hatch, Janice H., ed. Investments Institute, Hollywood, Fla., April 27-30, 1975: Proceedings. (Pensions, Investments). 182p. 1975. spiral binding 10.50 (ISBN 0-89154-036-9). Intl Found Employ.
Hayden, Vern. Money: Use It or Lose It. (Illus.). 128p. 1980. 10.95 (ISBN 0-937602-00-0). Hayden Hse.
Hayes, Douglas A. & Bauman, W. Scott. Investments: Analysis & Management. 3rd ed. (Illus.). 1976. text ed. 19.95 (ISBN 0-02-352710-2). Macmillan.
Hefferlin, Jonathan. Making Inflation Pay: How Limited Funds in Gold, Silver, Coins, Stamps, Real Estate at the Right Time Can Win Big. 224p. 1981. 10.95 (ISBN 0-936602-09-0). Harbor Pub CA.
Hefferling, Jonathan. Making Inflation Pay. (Illus.). 224p. 1980. 9.95 (ISBN 0-937554-00-6). Regency Pubs CA.
Herrick, Tracy G. Bank Analysts Handbook. LC 78-987. 1978. 39.95 (ISBN 0-471-02025-7, Pub. by Wiley-Interscience). Wiley.
Herzfeld, Thomas J. The Investor's Guide to Closed-End Funds: The Herzfeld Hedge. (Illus.). 1979. 19.50 (ISBN 0-07-028417-2). McGraw.
Hicks, Tyler G. How to Build a Second Income Fortune in Your Spare Time. 1965. pap. 3.95 (ISBN 0-13-402941-0, Reward). P-H.
--Sixty Day Fully Financed Fortune. 2nd ed. 150p. 1981. pap. 29.50 (ISBN 0-914306-54-5). Intl Wealth.
Hieb, Elizabeth, ed. Institute for Fund Advisors, Denver, May 10-12,1978: Proceedings. 1978. pap. 10.50 (ISBN 0-89154-083-0). Intl Found Employ.
Hieb, Elizabeth A., ed. Investments Institute, Lake Tahoe, Nevada, May 6-9, 1979: Proceedings. 1979. pap. text ed. 10.00 (ISBN 0-89154-110-1). Intl Found Employ.
--Investments Institute, Miami, April 1978: Proceedings. 1978. pap. 7.50 (ISBN 0-89154-079-2). Intl Found Employ.
Hirshleifer, Jack. Investment, Interest, & Capital. (Finance Ser). 1970. text ed. 16.95x (ISBN 0-13-502955-4). P-H.
Huang, S. Investment Analysis & Management. (Illus.). 500p. 1981. 19.95 (ISBN 0-87626-453-4). Winthrop.
Huff, Charles & Marinacci, Barbara. Commodity Speculation for Beginners: A Guide to the Futures Market. (Illus.). 224p. 1980. 11.95 (ISBN 0-02-555450-6). Macmillan.
Institutional Investor Study Report, 6 vols. 1971. Repr. 50.00 set (ISBN 0-405-03259-5). Arno.
Insull, Isidore K. Most Followed Investing Formulas for Assured Success in Wall Street. (Illus.). 129p. 1980. 49.45 (ISBN 0-918968-73-9). Inst Econ Finan.
International Centre for Settlement of Investment Disputes. Investment Laws of the World: The Developing Nations, 9 vols. LC 77-72048. 1973-79. looseleaf 75.00 ea. (ISBN 0-379-00650-2); index 75.00 (ISBN 0-379-00650-2). Oceana.
Investment Companies. (Industry Audit Guides). 1973. pap. 7.00 (ISBN 0-685-58483-6). Am Inst CPA.
Investment Fundamentals. rev. ed. 1975. 5.00 (ISBN 0-89982-175-8, 270800). Am Bankers.
Jessup, Paul F. Competing for Stock Market Profits. LC 73-15961. 276p. 1974. text ed. 13.50 (ISBN 0-471-44263-1). Wiley.
Johnsich, John R., intro. by. Title Insurance & Real Estate Securities Terminology. (Orig.). 1980. pap. 3.95 (ISBN 0-914256-11-4). Real Estate Pub.
Johnson, Philip M. How to Maximize Your Advertising Investment. LC 80-10997. 224p. 1980. 21.50 (ISBN 0-8436-0769-6). CBI Pub.
Johnson, Timothy E. Investment Principles. LC 77-13345. (Illus.). 1978. ref. 19.95 (ISBN 0-13-504506-1). P-H.
Jones, Charles P., et al. Essentials of Modern Investments. LC 77-71239. 450p. 1977. 23.50 (ISBN 0-8260-4812-9). Wiley.
Jorgenson, W. L. & Jorgenson, B. J. Corporate Profiles for Executives & Investors. 1977. pap. 9.95 (ISBN 0-685-76961-5). J Lloyd Corp.
Kantor, Herman I. Doctors Must Invest! a Primer on Where! LC 72-94163. (Illus.). 144p. 1974. 10.00 (ISBN 0-87527-110-3). Green.
Katz, Howard S. Honest Money Now! LC 78-75028. 1979. pap. 4.95 (ISBN 0-916728-22-6). Bks in Focus.
Kaufman, S. L. Investors Legal Guide. 2nd ed. 1979. 5.95 (ISBN 0-379-11126-8). Oceana.
Kellett, Richard. Ordinary Shares for Ordinary Savers. (Institute of Economic Affairs, Hobart Papers Ser.: No. 16). pap. 2.50 (ISBN 0-685-27187-0). Transatlantic.
Kendrick, David A. & Stoutjesdijk, Ardy J. The Planning of Industrial Investment Programs: A Methodology. LC 78-8428. (World Bank Ser: No. 1). 1979. text ed. 14.00x (ISBN 0-8018-2139-8); pap. text ed. 5.95x (ISBN 0-8018-2152-5). Johns Hopkins.
Klein, Howard J. Fad Money: How to Make Money from Fads, Crazes, & Trends. 1979. 8.95 (ISBN 0-531-09912-1). Watts.
Kogelschatz, Deane. Everyman's Guide to Financial Survival. (Illus.). 188p. 1981. 13.95 (ISBN 0-87364-216-3). Paladin Ent.
Kuklin, R. M. Learn to Invest & Trade on Wall Street. LC 79-64472. (Illus.). 1979. 12.95 (ISBN 0-933962-00-2); pap. 6.95 (ISBN 0-933962-01-0). Mercantine Pr.
Kuyvenhoven, Arie. Planning with the Semi Input-Output Method. (Studies in Development & Planning: Vol. 10). 266p. 1978. lib. bdg. 26.00 (ISBN 90-207-0798-1, Pub. by Martinus Nijhoff Netherlands). Kluwer Boston.
Latane, Henry A., et al. Security Analysis & Portfolio Management. 2nd ed. 1975. 27.95 (ISBN 0-8260-5256-8). Wiley.
Lattanzi, A. Functions of the Purchase & Sales Department. 1974. text ed. 14.95 (ISBN 0-13-332221-1). P-H.
Laurence, Michael. Playboy's Investment Guide. LC 77-167610. 288p. 1975. pap. 2.50 (ISBN 0-87216-643-0). Playboy Pbks.
Laves, Walter Herman. German Governmental Influence on Foreign Investment, 1871-1914. Wilkins, Mira, ed. LC 76-29742. (European Business Ser.). 1977. Repr. of 1977 ed. lib. bdg. 14.00x (ISBN 0-405-09759-X). Arno.
LeBaron, Dean. The Ins and Outs of Institutional Investing. LC 76-40961. 176p. 1976. 16.95x (ISBN 0-88229-343-5). Nelson-Hall.
Lees, Francis A. Foreign Banking & Investment in the United States: Issues & Alternatives. LC 76-4782. 1976. 25.95 (ISBN 0-470-15212-5). Halsted Pr.
Leuthold, Steven C. The Myths of Inflation & Investing. LC 80-67811. 1980. 27.50 (ISBN 0-87251-048-4). Crain Bks.
Levine, Sumner N. The Dow Jones-Irwin Business & Investment Almanac, Nineteen Eighty-Two. 720p. 1981. 19.95 (ISBN 0-87094-273-5). Dow Jones-Irwin.
Levine, Sumner N., ed. Investment Manager's Handbook. LC 79-53965. 1037p. 1980. 37.50 (ISBN 0-87094-207-7). Dow Jones-Irwin.
Levitt, Arthur, Jr. How to Make Your Money Make Money. LC 80-70617. 220p. 1981. 11.95 (ISBN 0-87094-236-0). Dow Jones-Irwin.
Lichello, Robert. Superpower Investing. LC 74-78729. 1974. 8.95 (ISBN 0-87863-042-2). Farnswth Pub.
Lin Tso. Complete Guide to Listed Options. 1981. 19.95 (ISBN 0-13-161216-6); pap. 11.95 (ISBN 0-13-161208-5). P-H.
Little, Royal. How to Lose One Hundred Million Dollars & Other Valuable Advice. LC 79-11628. (Illus.). 1979. 12.50 (ISBN 0-316-52786-6). Little.
Loeb, Gerald M. The Battle for Investment Survival. rev. ed. 9.95 (ISBN 0-671-21303-2). S&S.
--Battle for Investment Survival. rev. ed. 1965. pap. 2.45 (ISBN 0-671-21304-0, Fireside). S&S.
Loftus, John A. Investment Management: An Analysis of the Experience of American Management Investment Trusts. LC 78-64181. (Johns Hopkins University. Studies in the Social Sciences. Fifty-Ninth Ser. 1941: 1). Repr. of 1941 ed. 16.00 (ISBN 0-404-61289-X). AMS Pr.
Lorie & Brealy. Modern Development in Invest. Mngt. 2nd ed. 1978. pap. 15.95 (ISBN 0-03-040716-8). Dryden Pr.
Lovejoy, Frederick A. Divestment for Profit. LC 75-161689. 1971. 18.55 (ISBN 0-910586-02-0). Finan Exec.
Lutkin, Anthony. The Thirteen Deceits of the Wall Street Intellectuals. (Illus.). 1978. 39.75 (ISBN 0-89266-142-9). Am Classical Coll.
McGuire, C. B. Rational Investment Behavior in the Face of Floods. LC 79-135090. 151p. 1969. 34.50 (ISBN 0-686-01920-2). Mgmt Info Serv.
McLendon, Gordon. Get Really Rich in the Coming Super Metals Boom. 1981. 12.95 (ISBN 0-671-43225-7). S&S.
--Get Really Rich in the Coming Super Metals Boom. 1981. pap. 4.95 (ISBN 0-671-43202-8). PB.
McMillan, Lawrence G. Options As a Strategic Investment. (Illus.). 1980. text ed. 19.95 (ISBN 0-13-638387-4). P-H.
Malkiel, Burton. A Random Walk Down Wall Street. rev. ed. (Illus.). 1973. 13.95 (ISBN 0-393-05500-0); pap. 5.95x (ISBN 0-393-09246-1). Norton.
Malkiel, Burton G. The Inflation Beater's Investment Guide: Winning Strategies for the 1980's. 1980. 8.95 (ISBN 0-393-01355-3). Norton.
Manners, George E., Jr. & Louderback, Joseph G. Managing Return on Investment: Implications for Pricing, Volume, & Funds Flow. LC 80-8817. 192p. 1981. 22.95x (ISBN 0-669-04383-4). Lexington Bks.
Margolius, Sidney. The Innocent Investor. Bd. with The Shaky Ground Floor. 1971. 6.95 (ISBN 0-671-27075-3). Trident.
Market Value Methods for Intercorporate Investments in Stock. (Accounting Research Monograph: No. 2). 1976. pap. 6.50 (ISBN 0-685-58516-6). Am Inst CPA.
Markowitz, Harry M. Portfolio Selection: Efficient Diversification of Investments. (Cowles Foundation Monograph: No. 16). 1971. pap. 7.95x (ISBN 0-300-01372-8, Y232). Yale U Pr.
Markstein, David. How to Make Your Money Do More. 1971. 6.95 (ISBN 0-671-27064-8). Trident.
Markstein, David L. The Get Rich Book: Markstein's Guide to Much Bigger Investment Income. LC 76-8332. 1976. 7.95 (ISBN 0-916852-01-6). Pay Day Pr.
Martin, Gary. Twenty-Five per Cent More Guaranteed. 28p. 1976. pap. 9.95 (ISBN 0-686-19037-8). La Belle.
Mayo, Herbert B. Basic Investments. 544p. 1980. text ed. 21.95 (ISBN 0-03-054691-5). Dryden Pr.
Meeker, James E. The Work of the Stock Exchange (Revised Edition) facsimile ed. LC 75-2649. (Wall Street & the Security Market Ser.). (Illus.). 1975. Repr. of 1930 ed. 44.00x (ISBN 0-405-06974-X). Arno.
Meltzer, Yale. Putting Money to Work: An Investment Primer. LC 75-43923. (Illus.). 256p. 1976. pap. 5.95 (ISBN 0-13-744524-5, Spec, Spec). P-H.
Mendelson, Morris & Robbins, Sidney. Investment Analysis & Securities Markets. LC 75-36776. 1976. text ed. 17.50x (ISBN 0-465-03594-9). Basic.
Miller, James. A Key to Financial Survival: The Secret Investment Diary of a Portfolio Manager. LC 77-1071. 1977. pap. 2.95 (ISBN 0-87576-060-0). Pilot Bks.
Moody, John. Profitable Investing: Fundamentals of the Science of Investing. facsimile ed. LC 75-2651. (Wall Street & the Security Market Ser.). 1975. Repr. of 1925 ed. 19.00x (ISBN 0-405-06976-6). Arno.
Morgan, James W. Proposal Format for Successful Private Sector Investments. (Designed to accompany "Successful Fund-Raising"). 1976. 4.00 (ISBN 0-686-16390-7); Set. 22.95 (ISBN 0-686-16391-5). Grantsman Ent.
Nagan, Peter. Fail Safe Investing: How to Make Money with Less Than Ten Thousand Dollars...Without Losing Sleep. 192p. 1981. 9.95 (ISBN 0-399-12616-3). Putnam.
Narbeth, Colin & Lyon, David. Successful Investing in Stamps & Banknotes. 145p. 1975. 9.00x (ISBN 0-86010-007-3, Pub. by Graham & Trotman). State Mutual Bk.
Nauheim, Fred. Move Your Assets to Beat Inflation. (Illus.). 288p. 1980. 11.95 (ISBN 0-13-604611-8). P-H.
Neitzel, James J., ed. Investments Institute, April 1976, Palm Springs, California: Proceedings. 1976. spiral bdg. 10.50 (ISBN 0-89154-051-2). Intl Found Employ.
--Investments Institute, New Orleans, May, 1977: Proceedings. 1977. spiral bdg. 12.50 (ISBN 0-89154-066-0). Intl Found Employ.
Nelson, Paula. The Joy of Money. 1977. pap. 2.95 (ISBN 0-553-20451-3). Bantam.
--The Joy of Money: A Contemporary Woman's Guide to Financial Freedom. LC 75-9847. 248p. 1975. 7.95 (ISBN 0-8128-1816-4). Stein & Day.
Nelson, Wayne F. How to Buy Money: Investing Wisely for Maximum Return. LC 81-3751. 10.95 (ISBN 0-686-75370-4). McGraw.
Nemet, Roslyn. Investment Tips for Today's Woman. (Orig.). 1981. pap. 2.25 (ISBN 0-8439-8038-9, Tiara Bks). Nordon Pubns.
Nicholas, Ted. Income Portfolio. new, rev. ed. 1981. 9.95 (ISBN 0-913864-25-0). Enterprise Del.
Nickell, S. J. The Investment Decision of Firms. LC 78-73957. (Economic Handbooks Ser.). 1975. 42.50 (ISBN 0-521-22465-9); pap. 13.95x (ISBN 0-521-29511-4). Cambridge U Pr.
Noddings, Thomas C. Advanced Investment Strategies. LC 78-62631. 1978. 17.50 (ISBN 0-87094-170-4). Dow Jones-Irwin.
Nomura Research Institute. Investing in Japan. (Illus.). 208p. 1980. 25.00x (ISBN 0-85941-067-6). Herman Pub.
Osborn, Roger. Mathematics of Investment. (Illus.). 9.50 (ISBN 0-8363-0066-1). Jenkins.
Patterson, E. M. & Wilkins, Mira, eds. America's Changing Investment Market. LC 76-29983. (European Business Ser.). (Illus.). 1977. Repr. of 1916 ed. lib. bdg. 21.00x (ISBN 0-405-09748-4). Arno.
Pogue, Gerald & Modigliani, Franco. A Study of Investment Performance Fees. LC 74-315. Date not set. price not set (ISBN 0-669-91884-9). Lexington Bks.
Porter, Sylvia. Sylvia Porter's New Money Book for the 80's. 1328p. 1980. pap. 9.95 (ISBN 0-380-51060-X, 51060). Avon.
Pratt, Shannon. Valuing a Business: The Analysis & Appraisal of Closely Held Companies. LC 80-85475. 424p. 1981. 42.50 (ISBN 0-87094-205-0). Dow Jones-Irwin.
Preston, Robert L. Building Your Fortune with Silver. 112p. 1973. pap. 2.00 (ISBN 0-89036-024-3). Hawkes Pub Inc.
--How to Prepare for the Coming Crash. 128p. 1971. pap. 2.95 (ISBN 0-89036-025-1). Hawkes Pub Inc.
Rachlin, Robert. Return on Investment: Strategies for Profit. LC 75-44668. 1976. 14.95 (ISBN 0-938712-00-4). Marr Pubns.
Randle, Paul A. & Swensen, Philip R. Managing Your Money: An Investment Guide for Professionals & Entrepreneurs. 224p. 1979. 19.95 (ISBN 0-534-97996-3); pap. 12.95 (ISBN 0-534-97994-7). CBI Pub.
--Managing Your Money: An Investment Guide for Professionals & Entrepreneurs. LC 79-12669. 1979. 19.95 (ISBN 0-534-97996-3); pap. 12.95 (ISBN 0-534-97994-7). Lifetime Learn.
Reily, F. Investment Analysis & Portfolio Management. LC 78-56196. 1979. 22.95 (ISBN 0-03-013576-1). Dryden Pr.
Reis, Bernard J. False Security: The Betrayal of the American Investor. facsimile ed. LC 75-2663. (Wall Street & the Security Markets Ser.). 1975. 22.00 (ISBN 0-405-06987-1). Arno.
Renwick, F. B. Introduction to Investments & Finance: Theory and Analysis. 1971. text ed. 19.95x (ISBN 0-02-399560-2). Macmillan.
Rice, Samuel O., ed. Fundamentals of Investment. facsimile ed. LC 75-2664. (Wall Street & the Security Market Ser.). 1975. Repr. of 1925 ed. 23.00x (ISBN 0-405-06988-X). Arno.
Rider, Paul R. & Fischer, Carl H. Mathematics of Investment. 1962. Repr. of 1951 ed. text ed. 8.95x (ISBN 0-914004-02-6). Ulrich.
Roalman, A. R. Investor Relations That Work. 320p. 1981. 34.95 (ISBN 0-8144-5620-0). Am Mgmt.
Roalman, Arthur R., ed. Investor Relations Handbook. LC 73-85192. 240p. 1974. 17.95 (ISBN 0-8144-5349-X). Am Mgmt.
Roderick, Clayton A. The Stock Market Power of Inflation Survival & New Guide to Prosperity in Times of Crises & Depressions. (Illus.). 1980. deluxe ed. 49.75 (ISBN 0-918968-47-X). Inst Econ Finan.
Rogers, Mary & Joyce, Nancy. Women & Money. (Illus.). 1978. 8.95 (ISBN 0-07-053495-0, GB). McGraw.
Romero, George. The Great Dollar Deception: Losing When You Think You're Winning. LC 80-66757. 176p. 1980. 14.95 (ISBN 0-916728-43-9). Bks in Focus.
Rosenberg, Claude N., Jr. The Common Sense Way to Stock Market Profits. rev. ed. 1978. pap. 1.95 (ISBN 0-451-08397-0, J8397, Sig). NAL.
Ross, Charles M. A Guide for the Perplexed Investor. 1981. 5.95 (ISBN 0-8062-1832-0). Carlton.
Rowley, J. C. & Trivedi, P. K. Econometrics of Investment. LC 74-32176. (Monographs on Applied Econometrics). 1975. 36.85 (ISBN 0-471-74361-5, Pub. by Wiley-Interscience). Wiley.

Rubinstein, David H. Invest for Retirement: A Conservative Investor's Guide. LC 81-65507. 320p. 1981. 12.95 (ISBN 0-02-927530-X). Free Pr.
Rudd, Andrew & Clasing, Henry K., Jr. Modern Portfolio Strategy. 1981. 21.50 (ISBN 0-87094-191-7). Dow Jones-Irwin.
Ruff, Howard J. How to Prosper During the Coming Bad Years. LC 78-13919. 1979. 8.95 (ISBN 0-8129-0804-X). Times Bks.
Rukeyser, Louis. How to Make Money in Wall Street. LC 73-14055. 288p. 1974. 7.95 (ISBN 0-385-07505-7). Doubleday.
Rush, Richard H. Automobiles As an Investment. (Illus.). 224p. 1982. 14.95 (ISBN 0-686-76674-1). Macmillan.
Ruthberg, Sidney. Playboy's Investment & Financial Planning Guide for Singles. LC 81-80402. 288p. 1981. 12.95 (ISBN 0-87223-701-X). Seaview Bks.
Sakolski, Aaron M. Principles of Investment. facsimile ed. LC 75-2665. (Wall Street & the Security Market Ser.). 1975. Repr. of 1925 ed. 29.00x (ISBN 0-405-06989-8). Arno.
Sauvain, Harry C. Investment Management. 4th ed. 592p. 1973. ref. ed. 21.00 (ISBN 0-13-503094-3). P-H.
Schneider, Bernard. Your Money - Going or Growing? (Illus.). (gr. 7 up). 1978. wkbk 2.25 (ISBN 0-912486-33-3). Finney Co.
Schulman, Martin Bud. The Professional's Investment Guide: How to Multiply the Profits from Your Practice. rev. ed. LC 76-8269. 1976. 28.50 (ISBN 0-87491-024-2). Acropolis.
Schultz, Harry. Bear Market Investment Strategies. LC 80-70618. 232p. 1981. 14.95 (ISBN 0-87094-224-7). Dow Jones-Irwin.
Schwartz, Daniel. The National Directory of Income Opportunities. LC 77-95320. 1978. 15.00 (ISBN 0-87863-153-4). Farnswth Pub.
Schwed, Fred, Jr. Where Are the Customers Yachts? (Illus.). 4.50 (ISBN 0-910944-33-4). Magee.
Schwilling, Werner. Lexikon der Geldenlage. (Ger.). 1974. 35.00 (ISBN 3-478-51560-2, M-7258). French & Eur.
Schwimmer, Martin J. & Malca, Edward. Pension & Institutional Portfolio Management. LC 76-6473. (Special Studies). (Illus.). 120p. 1976. text ed. 22.95 (ISBN 0-275-56730-3). Praeger.
Scoville, Ogden D. The Small Investor's Handbook for Long-Term Security or Quick Profit. 1971. pap. 4.50 (ISBN 0-06-463324-1, EH 324, EH). Har-Row.
Shapiro, E. & White, W., eds. Capital for Productivity & Jobs. 1977. 11.95 (ISBN 0-13-113498-1, Spec); pap. 5.95 (ISBN 0-13-113480-9, Spec). P-H.
Sharpe, W. Investments. 2nd ed. 1981. 21.00 (ISBN 0-13-504613-0). P-H.
Sharpe, W. F. Portfolio Theory & Capital Markets. (Foundations of American Government & Political Science). 1970. 17.95 (ISBN 0-07-056487-6, C). McGraw.
Sherwood, Hugh C. How Corporate & Municipal Debt Is Rated: An Inside Look at Standard & Poor's Rating System. LC 63-12099. 180p. 1976. 29.95 (ISBN 0-471-78585-7). Krieger.
--How to Invest in Bonds. LC 74-81543. 176p. 1976. pap. 3.95 (ISBN 0-07-056685-2, SP). McGraw.
Shulman, Morton. How to Invest Your Money & Profit from Inflation. (Illus.). 160p. 1980. 10.95 (ISBN 0-394-51064-X). Random.
Silver, A. David. The Radical New Road to Wealth. rev. ed. 1981. pap. 15.00 (ISBN 0-914306-53-7). Intl Wealth.
Smith, Adam. The Money Game. 1976. pap. 2.45 (ISBN 0-394-72103-9, Vin). Random.
Smith, Albert C., Jr. The Little Guy's Stock Market Survival Guide. Smith, Albert, III, ed. LC 78-73336. (Illus., Orig.). 1979. pap. 5.95 (ISBN 0-933086-01-6). Cromwell-Smith.
Smith, Keith V. & Eiteman, David K. Essentials of Investing. 1974. 19.95x (ISBN 0-256-01554-6). Irwin.
Smith, Milton. Money Today, More Tomorrow. 320p. 1981. 14.95 (ISBN 0-87626-593-X); pap. text ed. 9.95 (ISBN 0-87626-592-1). Winthrop.
Smith, Thurman L. Investors Can Beat Inflation. rev. ed. LC 79-52816. 150p. 1981. pap. 4.95 (ISBN 0-89709-018-7). Liberty Pub.
Smitley, Robert L. Popular Financial Delusions. Repr. of 1963 ed. flexible cover 9.00 (ISBN 0-87034-004-2). Fraser Pub Co.
Soble, Ron. Smart Money in Hard Times: A Guide to Inflationproof Investments. Orig. Title: Smart Money. 1975. pap. 1.75 (ISBN 0-451-06447-X, E6447, Sig). NAL.
Spencer, Robert L. The Performance of the Best Investment Advisory Services. LC 77-85330. 1977. 25.00 (ISBN 0-9601412-1-9). Odd John.
Sprecher, C. Ronald. Essentials of Investments. LC 77-74380. (Illus.). 1977. text ed. 19.25 (ISBN 0-395-25454-X); inst. manual 0.70 (ISBN 0-395-25455-8). HM.
Sprecher, R. Ronald. Introduction to Investment Management. 1975. text ed. 20.50 (ISBN 0-395-18706-0); instructor's manual pap. 1.50 (ISBN 0-395-18784-2). HM.
Staley, Eugene. War & the Private Investor. 1967. Repr. 23.00 (ISBN 0-86527-206-9). Fertig.
Stallworthy, E. A. Control of Investment in New Manufacturing Facilities. 1973. 19.95x (ISBN 0-8464-0284-X). Beekman Pubs.
Standard & Poor's Research Dept. Standard & Poor's Rating Guide. Incl. Corporate Bonds; Commercial Paper; Municipal Bonds; International Securities. (Illus.). 1979. 19.95 (ISBN 0-07-051883-1). McGraw.
Stein, Ben & Stein, Herbert. Moneypower: How to Make Inflation Make You Rich. 224p. 1981. pap. 2.95 (ISBN 0-380-54809-7, 54809). Avon.
--Moneypower: How to Profit from Inflation. LC 79-2235. 1980. 8.95 (ISBN 0-06-014073-9, HarpT). Har-Row.
Steinmetz, Lawrence L. Managing the Marginal & Unsatisfactory Performer. LC 78-83467. (Business Ser). (Illus.). 1969. pap. 7.95 (ISBN 0-201-07276-9); instr's guide 1.50 (ISBN 0-201-07277-7). A-W.
Stermole, Franklin J. Economic Evaluation & Investment Decision Methods. 3rd ed. 1980. text ed. 24.50 (ISBN 0-9603282-3-8); solutions manual 6.50 (ISBN 0-9603282-3-8). Invest Eval.
Sterne, George & Von Hoelscher, Russ. Investment Opportunities of the 1980's. 260p. 1981. 19.95 (ISBN 0-940398-01-X). Profit Ideas.
Stevens, Mark. Leveraged Finance: How to Raise & Invest Cash. LC 79-23897. 228p. 1980. 17.95 (ISBN 0-13-535104-9, Busn). P-H.
Stevenson, Richard A. & Jennings, Edward H. Fundamentals of Investments. 2nd ed. (Illus.). 608p. 1980. text ed. 20.50 (ISBN 0-8299-0299-6). West Pub.
--Fundamentals of Investments. LC 75-42350. (Illus.). 580p. 1976. text ed. 16.95 (ISBN 0-8299-0077-2); instrs.' manual avail. (ISBN 0-8299-0575-8). West Pub.
Stevenson, Richard A. & Phillips, Susan M. Investment Environment, Analysis & Alternatives: A Book of Readings. (Illus.). 1977. pap. text ed. 13.50 (ISBN 0-8299-0117-5). West Pub.
Stigum, Marcia. The Money Market: Myth, Reality & Practice. LC 78-59224. 1978. 27.50 (ISBN 0-87094-167-4). Dow Jones-Irwin.
Stock Market Profits with Convertibles. LC 74-17847. 9.95 (ISBN 0-89058-602-0). R H M Pr.
Stoken, Dick. What They Are, What They Mean, How to Profit by Them. (Illus.). 1978. 19.50 (ISBN 0-07-061632-9, P&RB). McGraw.
Sturgis, Henry S. Investment: A New Profession. facsimile ed. LC 75-2672. (Wall Street & the Security Market Ser.). 1975. Repr. of 1924 ed. 17.00x (ISBN 0-405-07235-X). Arno.
Sturm, James L. Investing in the United States, 1798-1893: Upper Wealth-Holders in a Market Economy. Bruchey, Stuart, ed. (Nineteen Seventy-Seven Dissertations Ser.). (Illus.). 1977. lib. bdg. 15.00x (ISBN 0-405-09929-0). Arno.
Sutton, J. Doctor's Simple, Scientific Approach to Stock Market Success. 1971. 34.95 (ISBN 0-13-216911-8). P-H.
Sutton, Robert M. What You Should Know to Make Money from Your Investments. 1979. 10.00 (ISBN 0-682-49206-X, Banner). Exposition.
Sylvester, Richard R. Investment Strategy. Date not set. 29.95 (ISBN 0-932010-22-9). Phd Pub.
Thole, B. L. & Gilissen, Theodor. Dictionary of Stock Market Terms in Four Languages. (Eng., Fr., Ger. & Dutch.). 18.50 (ISBN 0-87559-068-3). Shalom.
Tobia, Andrew. The Only Investment Guide You'll Ever Need. 200p. 1981. pap. 2.75 (ISBN 0-553-14481-2). Bantam.
Tobias, Andrew. The Only Investment Guide You'll Ever Need. LC 77-84395. 1978. 5.95 (ISBN 0-15-169941-0). HarBraceJ.
Trainer, M. Ann. A Beginner's Workbook to Safe & Profitable Investing. 1977. 6.00 (ISBN 0-682-48876-3). Exposition.
Trester, Kenneth R. The Compleat Option Player. (Illus.). 316p. 1977. 20.00 (ISBN 0-9604914-0-6). Investrek.
Tso, Lin. Complete Investor's Guide to Listed Options: Calls & Puts. 240p. 1980. 19.95 (ISBN 0-13-161216-6, Spec); pap. 11.95 (ISBN 0-13-161208-5). P-H.
Tuccille, Jerome. Dynamic Investing: The System for Automatic Profits -- No Matter Which Way the Market Goes. 1981. pap. 9.95 (ISBN 0-453-00398-2, H398). NAL.
--Everything the Beginner Needs to Know to Invest Shrewdly. 1978. 8.95 (ISBN 0-87000-408-5). Arlington Hse.
--Everything the Beginner Needs to Know to Invest Shrewdly: A Step-by-Step Guide to the Basics of Financial Growth. 192p. 1979. pap. 4.50 (ISBN 0-06-463476-0, EH 476, EH). Har-Row.
--Mind Over Money: Why Most People Lose Money in the Stock Market & How You Can Become a Winner. LC 79-22813. 1980. 8.95 (ISBN 0-688-03595-7). Morrow.
Tucker, Gilbert M. Your Money & What to Do With It. 1960. 4.50 (ISBN 0-8159-7401-9). Devin.
United Business Services, ed. Successful Investing. 1979. 14.95 (ISBN 0-671-24604-6). S&S.
Unterman, Dr. Israel. Understanding the Balance Sheet & Profit & Loss Statement. rev. ed. LC 73-77431. 1976. 7.95 (ISBN 0-910580-14-6). Farnswth Pub.
VanCaspel, Venita. Energizing Your Investments. 1980. pap. 1.50 (ISBN 0-8359-1678-2). Reston.
Vignola, Leonard, Jr. Strategic Divestment. LC 73-85193. 160p. 1974. 12.95 (ISBN 0-8144-5347-3). Am Mgmt.
Waldmann, Raymond J. Direct Investment & Development in the U.S. A Guide to Incentive Programs, Laws & Restrictions, 1981-82. rev. ed. LC 80-51673. 453p. 1981. pap. text ed. 75.00 (ISBN 0-933678-01-0). Transnatl Invest.
Waldmann, Raymond J., ed. Investment Incentive Programs of the Pacific Basin. (Illus.). 390p. 1980. 150.00 (ISBN 0-939322-00-5). Intl Busn Educ.
Watson, Walter A. Master Plan for Financial Security. 1966. pap. 3.95 deluxe ed. (ISBN 0-685-21860-0). Watson Pub.
Weber, John. Growth Opportunity Analysis. (Illus.). 304p. 1976. pap. text ed. 8.95x (ISBN 0-87909-307-2); instrs'. manual avail. Reston.
Welch, William B. Strategies for Put & Call Option Trading. (Illus.). 224p. (Orig.). 1981. pap. text ed. 12.95 (ISBN 0-87626-826-2, W8262-5). Winthrop.
When to Sell: Inside Strategies for Stock Market Profits. 272p. 1977. 9.95 (ISBN 0-374-28906-9). FS&G.
Whitehouse, Brian. Investing Your Money. Date not set. 4.50x (ISBN 0-392-09270-0, SpS). Sportshelf.
Whitman, Martin & Shubik, Martin. The Aggressive Conservative Investor. LC 78-21593. 1979. 15.95 (ISBN 0-394-50457-7). Random.
Widicus, Wilber W. & Stitzel, Thomas E. Personal Investing, Bk. 227. 3rd ed. 525p. Date not set. 18.95 (ISBN 0-686-74998-7). Dow Jones-Irwin.
Widicus, Wilbur W. & Stitzel, Thomas E. Personal Investing. 3rd ed. 1980. 18.95x (ISBN 0-256-02341-7). Irwin.
Williams, Arthur. Managing Your Investment Manager: The Complete Guide to Selection, Measurement, & Control. LC 79-56084. 210p. 1980. 27.50 (ISBN 0-87094-187-9). Dow Jones-Irwin.
Williams, John B. Theory of Investment Value. LC 38-12316. Repr. of 1938 ed. 19.50x (ISBN 0-678-08050-X). Kelley.
Woodrow, Raymond J. Management for Research in U. S. Universities. LC 77-27085. 1978. 15.00 (ISBN 0-915164-05-1). Natl Assn Coll.
Woy, James B., ed. Investment Information: A Detailed Guide to Selected Sources. LC 79-118791. (Management Information Guides Ser.: No. 19). 1970. 36.00 (ISBN 0-8103-0819-3). Gale.
Wuliger, Betty S. Dollars & Sense: Protecting Your Money & Making It Grow-a Unique Primer for the Individual Investor. 1976. 11.95 (ISBN 0-394-40221-9). Random.
Wyckoff, Richard D. The Fundamental Rules of Successful Investing. (Illus.). 121p. 1981. 57.85 (ISBN 0-918968-85-2). Inst Econ Finan.
--New Techniques for Stock Market Profits. 1979. deluxe ed. 67.75 (ISBN 0-918968-24-0). Inst Econ Finan.
Youngquist, Walter. Investing in Natural Resources. 2nd ed. LC 80-67667. 281p. 1980. 14.95 (ISBN 0-87094-221-2). Dow Jones-Irwin.
Zahorchak, Michael G. The Art of Low Risk Investing. 2nd ed. 1977. pap. 7.95 (ISBN 0-442-29577-4). Van Nos Reinhold.

INVESTMENTS–BIBLIOGRAPHY

Carpenter, Edward. Iolaus: An Anthology of Friendship. 3rd ed. LC 76-174018. 1971. Repr. of 1920 ed. 19.00 (ISBN 0-8103-3790-8). Gale.

INVESTMENTS–CASE STUDIES

Atkinson, T. R. Pattern of Financial Asset Ownership: Wisconsin Individuals, 1949, Vol. 7. (National Bureau of Economic Research). 1956. 13.50 (ISBN 0-691-04155-5). Princeton U Pr.
Atkinson, Thomas R. Pattern of Financial Asset Ownership: Wisconsin Individuals, 1949. (Financial Research Program Ser.). 1956. 9.00 (ISBN 0-691-04155-5, Dist. by Princeton U Pr). Natl Bur Econ Res.
Carrington, John C. & Edwards, George T. Financing Industrial Investment. LC 78-65708. 1979. 29.95 (ISBN 0-03-049761-2). Praeger.
Train, John. The Money Masters. 320p. 1981. pap. 4.95 (ISBN 0-14-005944-X). Penguin.
Twark, Alan J., et al. Security Analysis & Portfolio Management: A Casebook. LC 72-83245. 200p. 1973. pap. 12.95x (ISBN 0-8162-8946-8); instructors manual 2.50x (ISBN 0-8162-8956-5). Holden-Day.

INVESTMENTS–MATHEMATICAL MODELS

Brown, J. P. The Economic Effects of Floods. LC 72-86100. (Lecture Notes in Economics & Mathematical Systems: Vol. 70). v, 87p. 1972. pap. 6.30 (ISBN 0-387-05925-3). Springer-Verlag.
Hart, William L. Mathematics of Investment. 5th ed. 448p. 1975. text ed. 17.95x (ISBN 0-669-93690-1); instr's manual 1.95 (ISBN 0-669-93708-8). Heath.
Jacoby, Henry D. Analysis of Investment in Electric Power. Bruchey, Stuart, ed. LC 78-22688. (Energy in the American Economy Ser.). (Illus.). 1979. lib. bdg. 20.00x (ISBN 0-405-11991-7). Arno.
Solnik, B. H. European Capital Markets: Towards a General Theory. LC 73-6594. (Illus.). 128p. 1973. 14.95 (ISBN 0-669-87064-1). Lexington Bks.

INVESTMENTS–TABLES, ETC.

Financial Publishing Co. Continuous Compounding Savings Factor Tables No. 534. 15.00 (ISBN 0-685-02537-3). Finan Pub.
--Expanded Bond Values Tables. No. 63. pocket ed. 27.50 (ISBN 0-685-02541-1). Finan Pub.
--Expanded Bond Values Tables. No. 63. pocket ed. 27.50 (ISBN 0-685-02541-1). Finan Pub.
Johnson, Ramon E. & Pratt, Richard T. Tables for Investment Decision Making. 272p. 1981. pap. text ed. 9.95 (ISBN 0-8403-2382-4). Kendall-Hunt.
Residual Lease Tables. 5.00 (ISBN 0-685-59989-2). Finan Pub.

INVESTMENTS–AFRICA

Frankel, S. Herbert. Capital Investment in Africa: Its Course & Effects. LC 68-9593. (Illus.). 1970. Repr. 28.50 (ISBN 0-86527-021-X). Fertig.

INVESTMENTS–AUSTRALIA

Carr, David W. Foreign Investment & Development in the Southwest Pacific: With Special Reference to Austrailia & Indonesia. LC 78-8598. (Praeger Special Studies). 1978. 24.50 (ISBN 0-03-042271-X). Praeger.

INVESTMENTS–EUROPE

Bernard, Jean-Pierre. The Swiss Investment Catalog. 55p. 1981. 5.95 (ISBN 0-686-73718-0). Alexandria Hse.
Fleetwood, Jucker & Elver, Erin. Sweden's Capital Imports & Exports. Wilkins, Mira, ed. LC 76-29743. (European Business Ser.). (Illus.). 1977. Repr. of 1947 ed. lib. bdg. 28.00x (ISBN 0-405-09760-3). Arno.

INVESTMENTS–GREAT BRITAIN

Dodds, J. C. The Investment Behaviour of British Life Insurance Companies. 193p. 1979. 50.00x (ISBN 0-7099-0058-9, Pub. by Croom Helm Ltd England). Biblio Dist.
Firth, Michael A. Investment Analysis: The Techniques of Appraising the British Stock Market. 1975. 23.65 (ISBN 0-06-318028-6, IntlDept). Har-Row.
Hughes, S. & Davies, J. R. Investment in the British Economy. (Studies in the British Economy Ser.). (Orig.). 1981. pap. text ed. 6.00x (ISBN 0-686-77443-4). Heinemann Ed.
Rayner, Anthony C. & Little, I. M. Higgledy Piggledy Growth Again. LC 66-73566. (Illus.). 1966. 11.50x (ISBN 0-678-06261-7). Kelley.
Shaw, E. R. London Money Market. 2nd ed. 1978. pap. text ed. 14.95x (ISBN 0-434-91832-6). Intl Ideas.
Shone, Robert. Price & Investment Relationships. 1975. 39.95 (ISBN 0-236-17600-5, Pub. by Paul Elek). Merrimack Bk Serv.

INVESTMENTS–INDIA

Bagchi, Amiya K. Private Investment in India & Pakistan, 1900-1939. LC 79-152631. (South Asian Studies: No. 10). (Illus.). 1971. 53.50 (ISBN 0-521-07641-2). Cambridge U Pr.
Challa, Krishna. Investment & Returns in Exploration & the Impact on the Supply of Oil & Natural Gas Reserves. Bruchey, Stuart, ed. LC 78-22667. (Energy in the American Economy Ser.). (Illus.). 1979. lib. bdg. 14.00x (ISBN 0-405-11971-2). Arno.
Markensten, Klas. Foreign Investment & Development in India, No. 8. (Scandinavian Inst. of Asian Studies). 295p. 1975. pap. text ed. 19.00x (ISBN 0-7007-0057-9). Humanities.
Mote, V. L. Capital Investment Decisions. 1979. 10.00x (ISBN 0-8364-0376-2). South Asia Bks.
Paul, Samuel & Rangarajan, C. Short-Term Investment Forecasting: An Exploratory Study. LC 75-903519. 1974. 12.00 (ISBN 0-8364-0466-1). South Asia Bks.

INVESTMENTS, AMERICAN

Angell, James W. Financial Foreign Policy of the United States. LC 65-18785. 1965. Repr. of 1933 ed. 7.50 (ISBN 0-8462-0625-0). Russell.

Arnold, Dean A. American Economic Enterprises in Korea, 1895-1939. Bruchey, Stuart & Bruchey, Eleanor, eds. (American Business Abroad Ser.). (Illus.). 1976. 32.00x (ISBN 0-405-09264-4). Arno.

Barlow, E. R. & Wender, Ira T. Foreign Investment & Taxation. LC 55-9771. (Illus.). 508p. 1955. 4.00x (ISBN 0-915506-01-7). Harvard Law Intl Tax.

Beard, Charles A. Devil Theory of War: An Inquiry into the Nature of History & the Possibility of Keeping Out of War. LC 68-54771. (Illus.). 1968. Repr. of 1936 ed. lib. bdg. 15.00 (ISBN 0-8371-0300-2, BEDT). Greenwood.

Bruchey, Stuart & Bruchey, Eleanor, eds. American Business Abroad Ser, 50 vols. 1976. Repr. 1070.00x (ISBN 0-405-09261-X). Arno.

--Estimates of United States Direct Foreign Investment, 1929-1943 & 1947: An Original Anthology. LC 76-5008. (American Business Abroad Ser.). (Illus.). 1976. Repr. of 1976 ed. 22.00x (ISBN 0-405-09277-6). Arno.

Carret, Philip L. The Art of Speculation (Revised Edition) facsimile ed. LC 75-2625. (Wall Street & the Security Markets Ser.). 1975. Repr. of 1930 ed. 23.00x (ISBN 0-405-06951-0). Arno.

Dunn, Robert W. American Foreign Investments. Richt, Adrian, ed. LC 76-5003. (American Business Abroad Ser.). 1976. Repr. of 1926 ed. 26.00x (ISBN 0-405-09272-5). Arno.

Dunning, John H. American Investment in British Manufacturing Industry. Bruchey, Stuart & Bruchey, Eleanor, eds. LC 76-5004. (American Business Abroad Ser.). (Illus.). 1976. 22.00x (ISBN 0-405-09273-3). Arno.

Esslen, Rainer. The Complete Book of International Investing: How to Buy Foreign Securities & Who's on the Internationalinvestment Scene. 1977. 24.95 (ISBN 0-07-019665-6, P&RB). McGraw.

Fleisig, Heywood. Long Term Capital Flows & the Great Depression: The Role of the United States, 1927-1933. facsimile ed. LC 75-2580. (Dissertations in American Economic History). 1975. 26.00x (ISBN 0-405-07200-7). Arno.

Hufbauer, G. & Adler, F. W. Overseas Manufacturing Investment & the Balance of Payments. Bruchey, Stuart & Bruchey, Eleanor, eds. LC 76-5047. (American Business Abroad Ser.). 1976. Repr. of 1968 ed. 12.00x (ISBN 0-405-09311-X). Arno.

Hunt, Pearson. Portfolio Policies of Commercial Banks in the United States 1920-1939. Bruchey, Stuart, ed. LC 80-1187. (The Rise of Commercial Banking Ser.). 1981. Repr. of 1940 ed. lib. bdg. 12.00x (ISBN 0-405-13657-9). Arno.

Johnson, Arno H., et al. The American Market of the Future. LC 66-22222. 1966. 6.95x (ISBN 0-8147-0219-8). NYU Pr.

Jones, Chester L. Caribbean Interests of the United States. LC 73-111719. (American Imperialism: Viewpoints of United States Foreign Policy, 1898-1941). 1970. Repr. of 1919 ed. 17.00 (ISBN 0-405-02029-5). Arno.

Kujawa, Duane, ed. American Labor & the Multinational Corporation. LC 72-85977. (Special Studies in International Economics & Development). 1973. 39.50x (ISBN 0-275-28717-3). Irvington.

Lary, Hal B., et al. The United States in the World Economy. LC 75-26859. (Economic Series: No. 23). 216p. 1975. Repr. of 1943 ed. lib. bdg. 16.25x (ISBN 0-8371-8257-3, LAUS). Greenwood.

Lewis, Cleona & Schlotterbeck, Karl T. America's Stake in International Investments. Bruchey, Stuart & Bruchey, Eleanor, eds. LC 76-5015. (American Business Abroad Ser.). 1976. Repr. of 1938 ed. 42.00x (ISBN 0-405-09283-0). Arno.

McKenzie, Fred A. The American Invaders. Bruchey, Stuart & Bruchey, Eleanor, eds. LC 76-5016. (American Business Abroad Ser.). 1976. Repr. of 1902 ed. 16.00x (ISBN 0-405-09284-9). Arno.

Magdoff, Harry. Age of Imperialism. LC 69-19788. 1969. 6.00 (ISBN 0-85345-082-X, CL082X); pap. 3.95 (ISBN 0-85345-101-X, PB101X). Monthly Rev.

Marer, Paul. U. S. Financing of East-West Trade: Studies in East European & Soviet Planning, Development, & Trade. (No. 22). 1975. pap. text ed. 8.00 (ISBN 0-89249-030-6). Intl Development.

Musgrave, Peggy B. United States Taxation of Foreign Investment Income: Issues & Arguments. LC 68-58098. (Illus.). 186p. (Orig.). 1969. pap. 6.00 (ISBN 0-915506-10-6). Harvard Law Intl Tax.

Stern, Siegfried. The United States in International Banking. Bruchey, Stuart & Bruchey, Eleanor, eds. LC 76-5036. (American Business Abroad Ser.). 1976. Repr. of 1952 ed. 28.00x (ISBN 0-405-09302-0). Arno.

Stobaugh, Robert B. Nine Investments Abroad & Their Impact at Home. 1976. text ed. 12.00x (ISBN 0-87584-113-9). Harvard U Pr.

Thwaite, et al. Pamphlets on American Business Abroad: An Original Anthology. Bruchey, Stuart & Bruchey, Eleanor, eds. LC 76-5053. (American Business Abroad Ser.). (Illus.). 1976. Repr. of 1976 ed. 23.00x (ISBN 0-405-09294-6). Arno.

U. S. Congress, House of Representatives. The Overseas Private Investment Corporation: A Critical Analysis. Bruchey, Stuart & Bruchey, Eleanor, eds. LC 76-5055. (American Business Abroad Ser.). (Illus.). 1976. Repr. of 1973 ed. 12.00x (ISBN 0-405-09313-6). Arno.

U. S. Congress, Senate. American Petroleum Interests in Foreign Countries. Bruchey, Stuart & Bruchey, Eleanor, eds. LC 76-5037. (American Business Abroad Ser.). (Illus.). 1976. Repr. of 1946 ed. 30.00x (ISBN 0-405-09303-9). Arno.

U. S. Department of Commerce. U. S. Business Investments in Foreign Countries: A Supplement to the Survey of Current Business. Bruchey, Stuart & Bruchey, Eleanor, eds. LC 76-5038. (American Business Abroad Ser.). (Illus.). 1976. Repr. of 1960 ed. 12.00x (ISBN 0-405-09304-7). Arno.

Waldmann, Raymond J. & Theurer, Martin. Investitionsrecht und Wirtschaftsfoerderung in USA. German American Chamber of Commerce, ed. (Ger.). 1981. 80.00 (ISBN 0-86640-001-X). German Am Chamber.

INVESTMENTS, AMERICAN–AFRICA

Myers, Desaix, III, et al. U. S. Business in South Africa: The Economic, Political & Moral Issues. LC 79-3638. 392p. 1980. 17.50x (ISBN 0-253-11486-1). Ind U Pr.

Rogers, Barbara. White Wealth & Black Poverty: American Investments in Southern Africa. LC 75-35353. (Studies in Human Rights: No. 2). 288p. 1976. lib. bdg. 17.50 (ISBN 0-8371-8277-8, RWW/). Greenwood.

U. S. Bureau of Foreign Commerce & Blankenheimer, Bernard. Investment in Union of South Africa: Conditions & Outlook for United States Investors. Repr. of 1954 ed. lib. bdg. 16.00x (ISBN 0-8371-2222-8, INSA). Greenwood.

INVESTMENTS, AMERICAN–AUSTRALIA

Brash, Donald T. American Investment in Australian Industry. LC 66-31366. 1966. 17.50x (ISBN 0-674-02500-8). Harvard U Pr.

INVESTMENTS, AMERICAN–BOLIVIA

Marsh, Margaret C. Bankers in Bolivia: A Study in American Foreign Investment. LC 76-99250. Repr. of 1928 ed. 19.75 (ISBN 0-404-04190-6). AMS Pr.

INVESTMENTS, AMERICAN–CANADA

Cuff, R. D. & Granatstein, J. L. American Dollars-Canadian Prosperity. 1978. 15.95 (ISBN 0-89522-015-6). Samuel Stevens.

Globerman, Steven. U.S. Ownership of Firms in Canada: Issues & Policy Approaches. LC 79-51649. 104p. 1979. 5.00 (ISBN 0-88806-052-1). Natl Planning.

INVESTMENTS, AMERICAN–CHINA

Vevier, Charles. United States & China, Nineteen Six-Nineteen Thirteen: A Study of Finance & Diplomacy. LC 68-9547. (Illus.). 1968. Repr. of 1955 ed. lib. bdg. 15.00 (ISBN 0-8371-0258-8, VEUS). Greenwood.

INVESTMENTS, AMERICAN–COLOMBIA

Rippy, Fred J. The Capitalists & Columbia. Bruchey, Stuart & Bruchey, Eleanor, eds. LC 76-5031. (American Business Broad Ser.). (Illus.). 1976. Repr. of 1931 ed. 18.00x (ISBN 0-405-09298-9). Arno.

INVESTMENTS, AMERICAN–EUROPE

Hu, Y. S. Impact of U. S. Investment in Europe: A Case Study of the Automotive & Computer Industries. LC 73-5163. (Special Studies in International Economics & Development). 1973. 37.50x (ISBN 0-275-28746-7); pap. text ed. 18.50x (ISBN 0-89197-792-9). Irvington.

Mikesell. Nonfuel Minerals: U.S. Investment Policies Abroad. LC 75-8169. (The Washington Papers: No. 23). 104p. 1975. 4.00 (ISBN 0-8039-0550-5). Sage.

Southard, Frank A., Jr. American Industry in Europe. Bruchey, Stuart & Bruchey, Eleanor, eds. LC 76-5032. (American Business Abroad Ser.). (Illus.). 1976. Repr. of 1931 ed. 18.00x (ISBN 0-405-09299-7). Arno.

INVESTMENTS, AMERICAN–GERMANY

Sutton, Antony C. Wall Street & the Rise of Hitler. LC 76-14011. (Orig.). 1976. 8.95 (ISBN 0-89245-004-5). Seventy Six.

INVESTMENTS, AMERICAN–INDIA

Kapoor, A. International Business Negotiations: A Study in India. LC 70-114622. 361p. 1973. 12.00 (ISBN 0-87850-016-2); pap. 6.00x (ISBN 0-87850-017-0). Darwin Pr.

INVESTMENTS, AMERICAN–LATIN AMERICA

Behrman, Jack N. Decision Criteria for Foreign Direct Investment in Latin America. LC 74-75185. 89p. 1974. pap. 5.00 (ISBN 0-685-56603-X, CoA). Unipub.

Gregersen, Hans M. & Contreras, Arnoldo. U. S. Investment in the Forest-Based Sector in Latin America: Problems & Potentials. LC 74-21754. (Resources for the Future). (Illus.). 128p. (Orig.). 1975. pap. 4.50x (ISBN 0-8018-1704-8). Johns Hopkins.

Ray, Phillip A. South Wind Red. LC 62-17968. 1962. pap. 2.00 (ISBN 0-911956-12-3). Constructive Action.

Shea, Donald R., et al, eds. Reference Manual on Doing Business in Latin America. LC 79-22412. 1979. 30.00 (ISBN 0-930450-12-4); pap. 20.00 (ISBN 0-930450-13-2). Univ of Wis Latin Am.

Tratado Interamericano De Asistencia Reciproca, 2 vols. Incl. Vol. 1. Aplicaciones, 1948-1959. 5.00 (ISBN 0-8270-0670-5); Vol. 2. Aplicaciones, 1960-1972. 5.00 (ISBN 0-8270-0675-6); Vol. 3. Aplicaciones, 1973-1976. (Eng. & Span.). 2.00 ea.. (Serie De Tratados Multilaterales, Convenciones y Acuerdos). (Span.). 5.00 ea. OAS.

U. S. Department of Commerce. U. S. Investments in the Latin American Economy. Bruchey, Stuart & Bruchey, Eleanor, eds. LC 76-5039. (American Business Abroad Ser.). (Illus.). 1976. Repr. of 1957 ed. 15.00 (ISBN 0-405-09305-5). Arno.

Winkler, Max. Investments of United States Capital in Latin America. LC 73-123497. 1971. Repr. of 1929 ed. 13.50 (ISBN 0-8046-1384-2). Kennikat.

INVESTMENTS, AMERICAN–SOUTH AMERICA

Novaes, Rubem. Brazilian Investment Policy: Priorities & Perspectives. LC 79-52098. 1979. pap. 4.00 (ISBN 0-89834-010-1, 6022). Chamber Comm US.

Opinion Leaders & Private Investment: An Attitude Survey in Chile & Venezuela. 1977. pap. 5.50 (ISBN 0-915814-13-7, COA4, COA). Unipub.

Phelps, Dudley M. Migration of Industry to South America. Repr. of 1936 ed. lib. bdg. 15.00x (ISBN 0-8371-2826-9, PHIS). Greenwood.

INVESTMENTS, BRITISH

Adler, Dorothy R. British Investment in American Railways 1834-1898. Hidy, Muriel E., ed. LC 79-122437. 1970. 11.50x (ISBN 0-8139-0311-4). U Pr of Va.

Atkin, John Michael. British Overseas Investment: 1918-1931. Bruchey, Stuart, ed. LC 77-81821. (Dissertations in European Economic History Ser.). (Illus.). 1977. lib. bdg. 28.00x (ISBN 0-405-10774-9). Arno.

Clarke, W. M. Private Enterprise in Developing Countries. 1969. pap. 4.20 (ISBN 0-08-012142-X). Pergamon.

Paterson, Donald G. British Direct Investment in Canada, 1890-1914. LC 76-22429. 1976. 17.50x (ISBN 0-8020-5354-8). U of Toronto Pr.

Payne, Peter L., ed. Studies in Scottish Business History. LC 67-20815. (Illus.). 1967. 30.00x (ISBN 0-678-05076-7). Kelley.

Rippy, J. Fred. British Investment in Latin America: 1822-1949. Wilkins, Mira, ed. LC 76-29755. (European Business Ser.). 1977. Repr. of 1959 ed. lib. bdg. 15.00x (ISBN 0-405-09771-9). Arno.

Sun, E-Tu Zen. Chinese Railways & British Interests, Eighteen Ninety-Eight to Nineteen Eleven. LC 74-152540. (Illus.). 1971. Repr. of 1954 ed. 12.00 (ISBN 0-8462-1613-2). Russell.

Thorner, Daniel. Investment in Empire: British Railway & Steam Shipping Enterprise in India, 1825-1849. Wilkins, Mira, ed. LC 76-29991. (European Business Ser.). 1977. Repr. of 1950 ed. lib. bdg. 13.00x (ISBN 0-405-09723-9). Arno.

Wilkins, Mira. British Overseas Investments, 1907-1948: An Original Anthology. LC 76-29782. (European Business Ser.). 1977. Repr. of 1977 ed. lib. bdg. 25.00x (ISBN 0-405-09783-2). Arno.

Wilkins, Mira, ed. Issues & Insights on International Investment: An Original Anthology. LC 76-29781. (European Business Ser.). 1977. Repr. of 1977 ed. lib. bdg. 10.00x (ISBN 0-405-09792-1). Arno.

INVESTMENTS, FOREIGN

see also Corporations, Foreign; Debts, External; Foreign Licensing Agreements; Loans, Foreign; Technical Assistance

Bayliss, B. T. & Philip, A. Butt. Capital Markets & Industrial Investment in Germany & France: Lessons for the U. K. 1979. text ed. 29.50x (ISBN 0-566-00335-X, Pub. by Gower Pub Co England). Renouf.

Behrman, Jack N. Decision Criteria for Foreign Direct Investment in Latin America. LC 74-75185. 89p. 1974. pap. 5.00 (ISBN 0-685-56603-X, CoA). Unipub.

Bloomfield, Arthur I. Capital Imports & the American Balance of Payments, 1934-39. LC 66-23017. (Illus.). Repr. of 1950 ed. 17.50x (ISBN 0-678-00165-0). Kelley.

Bos, H. C., et al. Private Foreign Investment in Developing Countries: A Quantitative Study on the Evaluation of Its Macro-Economic Impact. LC 73-91763. (International Studies in Economics & Econometrics: No. 7). 300p. 1974. lib. bdg. 53.00 (ISBN 90-277-0410-4, Pub. by Reidel Holland); pap. text ed. 28.00 (ISBN 90-277-0439-2, Pub. by Reidel Holland). Kluwer Boston.

Callis, Helmut G. Foreign Capital in Southeast Asia. Bruchey, Stuart & Bruchey, Eleanor, eds. LC 76-4998. (American Business Abroad Ser.). (Illus.). 1976. Repr. of 1942 ed. 12.00x (ISBN 0-405-09267-9). Arno.

Carr, David W. Foreign Investment & Development in the Southwest Pacific: With Special Reference to Austrailia & Indonesia. LC 78-8598. (Praeger Special Studies). 1978. 24.50 (ISBN 0-03-042271-X). Praeger.

Casey, Douglas. The International Man. 14.95 (ISBN 0-932496-01-6). Green Hill.

Cassel, Gustav. Foreign Investments. Wilkins, Mira, ed. LC 78-3902. (International Finance Ser.). 1978. Repr. of 1928 ed. lib. bdg. 15.00x (ISBN 0-405-11207-6). Arno.

Crouchley, Arthur Edwin. Investment of Foreign Capital in Egyptian Companies & Public Debt. Wilkins, Mira, ed. LC 76-29989. (European Business Ser.). 1977. Repr. of 1936 ed. lib. bdg. 13.00x (ISBN 0-405-09721-2). Arno.

Crowe, Kenneth C. America for Sale. LC 79-90694. 1980. pap. 5.95 (ISBN 0-385-15616-2, Anch). Doubleday.

Daniel, James & Bruchley, Stuart, eds. Private Investment: The Key to International Industrial Development: a Report of the San Francisco Conference. LC 80-606. (Multinational Corporations Ser.). 1980. Repr. of 1958 ed. lib. bdg. 26.00x (ISBN 0-405-13355-3). Arno.

Davies, A. Emil. Investments Abroad. Wilkins, Mira, ed. LC 76-29984. (European Business Ser.). 1977. Repr. of 1927 ed. lib. bdg. 13.00x (ISBN 0-405-09749-2). Arno.

Day, Adrian. Investing Without Borders. 1981. 19.95 (ISBN 0-932496-10-5). Alexandria Hse.

Delupis, Ingrid. Finance & Protection of Investments in Developing Countries. 183p. 1973. 21.95 (ISBN 0-7161-0173-4, Pub. by Wiley). Krieger.

Eastman, H. C. & Stykolt, S. Tariff & Competition in Canada. (Illus.). 1968. 19.95 (ISBN 0-312-78540-2). St Martin.

Elton, E. & Gruber, M. International Capital Markets. LC 75-17829. (Studies in Financial Economics: Vol. 1). 387p. 1976. 49.00 (ISBN 0-444-10867-X, North-Holland). Elsevier.

Esslen, Rainer. The Complete Book of International Investing: How to Buy Foreign Securities & Who's on the Internationalinvestment Scene. 1977. 24.95 (ISBN 0-07-019665-6, P&RB). McGraw.

FitzGerald, E. V. Public Sector Investment Planning for Developing Countries. 1978. text ed. 28.50x (ISBN 0-8419-5027-X). Holmes & Meier.

Foreign Investment in Egypt. 1979. pap. 6.25 (ISBN 0-915814-19-6, COA29, CoA). Unipub.

Frank, Isaiah. Foreign Enterprise in Developing Countries. 1980. 15.00 (ISBN 0-8018-2343-9); pap. 5.95 (ISBN 0-8018-2378-1). Johns Hopkins.

Frank, Robert H. & Freeman, Richard T. Distributional Consequences of Direct Foreign Investment. (Economic Theory, Econometrics & Mathematical Economic Ser.). 1978. 22.00 (ISBN 0-12-265050-6). Acad Pr.

Fry, Earl H. Financial Invasion of the U. S. A. A Threat to American Society? (Illus.). 1979. 9.95 (ISBN 0-07-022591-5). McGraw.

Gilman, Martin G. The Financing of Foreign Direct Investment. 200p. 1981. write for info. (ISBN 0-312-28982-0). St Martin.

Green, Robert T. Political Instability As a Determinant of U. S. Foreign Investment. (Studies in Marketing: No. 17). (Illus.). 1972. pap. 4.00 (ISBN 0-87755-172-3). U of Tex Busn Res.

Greene, James & Bauer, David. Foreign Investment & Employment: An Examination of Foreign Investments to Make 58 Products Overseas. (Report Ser.: No. 656). 47p. (Orig.). 1975. pap. 20.00 (ISBN 0-8237-0075-5). Conference Bd.

Grieves, Forest L., ed. Transnationalism in World Politics & Business. LC 79-1397. (Pergamon Policy Studies). 240p. 1979. 33.00 (ISBN 0-08-023892-0). Pergamon.

Grosse, Robert E. Foreign Investment Codes & Location of Direct Investment. LC 80-15194. 174p. 1980. 21.95 (ISBN 0-03-057024-7). Praeger.

Guisinger, Stephen E., ed. Trade & Investment Policies in the Americas. LC 73-84723. 1973. 5.95 (ISBN 0-87074-136-5). SMU Press.

Haendel, Dan. Foreign Investment: The Management of Political Risk. (Westview Special Studies in International Economics). 1978. lib. bdg. 24.75x (ISBN 0-89158-253-3). Westview.

Hymer, Stephen H. The International Operations of National Firms: A Study of Direct Foreign Investment. LC 75-33365. (Economic Monograph Ser.). 208p. 1976. text ed. 14.50x (ISBN 0-262-08085-0). MIT Pr.
International Investment & Multinational Enterprises. rev. ed. 32p. 1980. 3.00x (ISBN 9-264-12023-8). OECD.
Investing in Developing Countries. 4th rev. ed. 1979. 12.00x (ISBN 92-64-11880-2). OECD.
Isaiah. Foreign Enterprise in Developing Countries. 224p. 1980. pap. 5.95 (ISBN 0-8018-2378-1). Comm Econ Dev.
Iversen, Carl. Aspects of the Theory of International Capital Movements. 2nd ed. LC 67-27678. Repr. of 1936 ed. 19.50x (ISBN 0-678-00327-0). Kelley.
Jilling, Michael. Foreign Exchange Risk Management in U. S. Multinational Corporations. LC 78-24052. (Research for Business Decisions Ser.: No. 6). 1978. 27.95 (ISBN 0-8357-0952-3). Univ Microfilms.
Joyner's Guide: Doing Business Abroad. 1980. pap. 95.00 (ISBN 0-686-61572-7, JOY 2, Joyner's). Unipub.
Kapoor, A. International Business Negotiations: A Study in India. LC 70-114622. 361p. 1973. 12.00 (ISBN 0-87850-016-2); pap. 6.00x (ISBN 0-87850-017-0). Darwin Pr.
Kapoor, A., ed. Asian Business & Environment in Transition: Selected Readings & Essays. LC 73-20719. 667p. 1976. 9.95x (ISBN 0-87850-020-0). Darwin Pr.
Knudsen, Harald. Expropriation of Foreign Investments in Latin America. 356p. 1975. pap. 19.50x (ISBN 8-200-01385-5, Dist. by Columbia U Pr). Universitet.
Kobrin, Stephen J. Foreign Direct Investment, Industrialization & Social Change. Altman, Edward I. & Walter, Ingo, eds. LC 76-10401. (Contemporary Studies in Economic & Financial Analysis: Vol. 9). 325p. 1977. lib. bdg. 30.00 (ISBN 0-89232-013-3). Jai Pr.
Kojima, Kiyoshi. Direct Foreign Investment: A Japanese Model of Multinational Business Operations. LC 78-61337. (Praeger Special Studies). 1979. 27.95 (ISBN 0-03-047471-X). Praeger.
Krasner, Stephen D. Defending the National Interest: Raw Material Investments & U. S. Foreign Policy. LC 78-51175. (Center for International Affairs at Harvard Ser.). 1978. 22.50 (ISBN 0-691-07600-6); pap. 5.95 (ISBN 0-691-02182-1). Princeton U Pr.
Lal, D. Appraising Foreign Investment in Developing Countries. 1975. 18.50x (ISBN 0-8419-5300-7). Holmes & Meier.
Lamont, Douglas F. Foreign State Enterprises: A Threat to American Business. LC 78-19818. 1979. 12.95 (ISBN 0-465-02482-3). Basic.
Lewis, Cleona & Schlotterbeck, Karl T. America's Stake in International Investments. Bruchey, Stuart & Bruchey, Eleanor, eds. LC 76-5015. (American Business Abroad Ser.). 1976. Repr. of 1938 ed. 42.00x (ISBN 0-405-09283-0). Arno.
Lillich, Richard B. The Protection of Foreign Investment: Six Procedural Studies, Vol. 5. 1965. 10.00x (ISBN 0-8139-0838-8). U Pr of Va.
McCracken, Paul W. & Benoit, Emile. Balance of Payments & Domestic Prosperity. (Michigan International Business Studies: No. 1). 1963. pap. 1.25 (ISBN 0-87712-115-X). U Mich Busn Div Res.
Machlup, Fritz, et al, eds. International Mobility & Movement of Capital. (Universities-National Bureau Conference Ser.: No. 24). 680p. 1972. text ed. 20.00x (ISBN 0-87014-249-6, Dist. by Columbia U Pr). Natl Bur Econ Res.
McKay, John P. Pioneers for Profit: Foreign Entrepreneurship & Russian Industrialization, 1885-1913. LC 79-103932. 1970. 14.00x (ISBN 0-226-55990-4). U of Chicago Pr.
Marcus, Edward & Marcus, Mildred R. Investment & Development Possibilities in Tropical Africa. Wilkins, Mira, ed. LC 76-29767. (European Business Ser.). 1977. Repr. of 1960 ed. lib. bdg. 17.00x (ISBN 0-405-09781-6). Arno.
May, Herbert K. The Role of Foreign Investment in Latin America: Some Considerations & Definitions. LC 74-14344. 101p. 1974. pap. 4.00 (ISBN 0-685-56610-2, FMME 6, FMME). Unipub.
Meier, Gerald M. Problems of Cooperation for Development. 272p. 1974. pap. text ed. 5.95x (ISBN 0-19-501867-2). Oxford U Pr.
Mikesell, Raymond F. Foreign Investment in Copper Mining: Case Studies of Mines in Peru & Papua New Guinea. LC 75-11356. (Resources for the Future Ser). (Illus.). 166p. 1975. 12.00x (ISBN 0-8018-1750-1). Johns Hopkins.
Mintz, Ilse. Deterioration in the Quality of Foreign Bonds Issued in the United States, 1920-1930. Wilkins, Mira, ed. LC 78-3939. (International Finance Ser.). (Illus.). 1978. Repr. of 1951 ed. lib. bdg. 10.00x (ISBN 0-405-11240-8). Arno.
Molineu, Harold. Multinational Corporations & International Investment in Latin America: A Selected Bibliography. LC 77-620052. (Papers in International Studies: Latin America: No. 3). 1977. pap. 9.00x (ISBN 0-89680-068-7). Ohio U Ctr Intl.
Montavon, Remy, et al. The Role of Multinational Companies in Latin America: A Case Study in Mexico. 124p. 1980. 27.50 (ISBN 0-03-057973-2). Praeger.
Moore, John R. The Impact of Foreign Direct Investment on an Underdeveloped Economy: The Venezuelan Case. Bruchey, Stuart & Bruchey, Eleanor, eds. LC 76-5018. (American Business Abroad Ser.). 1976. lib. bdg. 21.00x (ISBN 0-405-09285-7). Arno.
Nkrumah, Kwame. Neo-Colonialism: The Last Stage of Imperialism. LC 66-18026. (Illus., Orig.). 1965. pap. 3.25 (ISBN 0-7178-0140-3). Intl Pub Co.
Organization for Economic Cooperation & Development. Foreign Investment in Yugoslavia (1974) 58p. 1974. 2.50x (ISBN 92-64-11207-3). OECD.
Osborne, Harrison. The Foreign Economic Invasion of the United States & the Drastically Changed Character of the International Economic Structure. (Illus.). 1978. 47.85 (ISBN 0-930008-12-X). Inst Econ Pol.
Oyaide, William J. The Role of Direct Private Foreign Investment in Economic Development. 1977. pap. text ed. 9.00 (ISBN 0-8191-0329-2). U Pr of Amer.
Parry, Thomas G. The Multinational Enterprise. Altman, Edward I. & Walter, Ingo, eds. LC 77-24394. (Contemporary Studies in Economic & Financial Analysis Ser.). 1980. lib. bdg. 29.50 (ISBN 0-89232-092-3). Jai Pr.
Patterson, E. M. & Wilkins, Mira, eds. America's Changing Investment Market. LC 76-29983. (European Business Ser.). (Illus.). 1977. Repr. of 1916 ed. lib. bdg. 21.00x (ISBN 0-405-09748-4). Arno.
Platt, D. C., ed. Business Imperialism, Eighteen Forty to Nineteen Thirty: An Inquiry Based on British Experience in Latin America. (Illus.). 1978. 54.00x (ISBN 0-19-828271-0). Oxford U Pr.
Pring, Martin J. International Investing Made Easy. new ed. 224p. 1980. 15.95 (ISBN 0-07-050872-0, P&RB). McGraw.
Remer, Charles F. Foreign Investments in China. LC 67-24594. 1968. 29.50 (ISBN 0-86527-067-8). Fertig.
Robinson, Richard D. National Control of Foreign Business: A Survey of Fifteen Countries. LC 75-44938. (Special Studies). (Illus.). 1976. text ed. 45.00 (ISBN 0-275-56500-9). Praeger.
Robinson, Richard D., et al. Foreign Investment in the Third World: A Comparative Study of Selected Developing Country Investment Promotion Programs. 1980. 10.00 (ISBN 0-89834-012-8, 6005). Chamber Comm US.
Royal Institute Of International Affairs. Problem of International Investment. LC 67-55858. Repr. of 1937 ed. 30.00x (ISBN 0-678-05195-X). Kelley.
Royal Institute of International Affars: Problem of International Investment. 371p. 1965. 32.50x (ISBN 0-7146-1247-2, F Cass Co). Biblio Dist.
Seminar Summary on "The Role of Japan in Latin America". 19p. 1980. pap. 4.50 (ISBN 0-686-61370-8, COA 40, COA). Unipub.
Shawcross, et al. Overseas Investment or Economic Nationalism? (Institute of Economic Affairs, Occasional Papers Ser.: No. 15). pap. 2.50 (ISBN 0-255-69544-6). Transatlantic.
Shea, Donald R. & Swacker, Frank W., eds. Business & Legal Aspects of Latin American Trade & Investment. LC 76-44061. 1977. pap. 15.00 (ISBN 0-930450-11-6). Univ of Wis Latin Am.
Singer, Stuart R. & Weiss, Stanley. Foreign Investment in the United States: 1980 Course Handbook. LC 79-92658. 617p. 1980. pap. text ed. 25.00 (ISBN 0-686-68824-4, B4-6531). PLI.
Solnik, B. H. European Capital Markets: Towards a General Theory. LC 73-6594. (Illus.). 128p. 1973. 14.95 (ISBN 0-669-87064-1). Lexington Bks.
Southern California Research Council, Foreign Investment in Southern California: An Economic Profile, No. 23. 1976. pap. 4.00 (ISBN 0-686-17279-5). Econ Res Ctr.
Stanford Research Institute. Foreign Investment: Five Studies from the International Development Center, An Original Anthology. Bruchey, Stuart, ed. LC 80-605. (Multinational Corporations Ser.). (Illus.). 1980. lib. bdg. 45.00x (ISBN 0-405-13351-0). Arno.
Stobaugh, Robert B., et al. Nine Investments Abroad & Their Impact at Home: Case Studies on Multinational Enterprises & the U.S. Economy. LC 74-20368. 250p. 1976. 12.00x (ISBN 0-87584-113-9). Harvard Busn.
Stoever, William A. Renegotiations in International Business Transactions: The Process of Dispute-Resolution Between Multinational Investors & Host Societies. LC 79-4727. 1981. 27.95 (ISBN 0-669-03057-0). Lexington Bks.
Sullivan, Jeremiah J. & Heggelund, Per O. Foreign Investment in the U. S. Fishing Industry. LC 79-2074. (Pacific Rim Research Ser.: No. 3). 208p. 1979. 21.95 (ISBN 0-669-03066-X). Lexington Bks.
Suzman, Cedric L., et al. Foreign Direct Investment in the Southeast: West Germany, the United Kingdom, & Japan. Suzman, Cedric L. & Gentry, Celestea, eds. LC 79-66996. (Papers on International Issues: No. 1). (Orig.). 1979. pap. 4.00 (ISBN 0-935082-00-X). Southern Ctr Intl Stud.
Thoman, G. Richard. Foreign Investment & Regional Development: The Theory & Practice of Investment Incentives, with a Case Study of Belgium. LC 72-85978. (Special Studies in International Economics & Development). 1973. 32.50x (ISBN 0-275-28681-9). Irvington.
Truitt, J. Frederick. Expropriation of Private Foreign Investment. LC 74-633855. (International Business Research Institute Ser: No. 3). 160p. 1974. 8.00 (ISBN 0-685-38968-5). Ind U Busn Res.
United Nations Economic Commission for Europe. Factors of Growth & Investment Policies: An International Approach. 1978. pap. 23.00 (ISBN 0-08-021992-6). Pergamon.
U. S. Federal Trade Commission. Report of the Federal Trade Commission on Foreign Ownership in the Petroleum Industry. Wilkins, Mira, ed. LC 76-29746. (European Business Ser.). (Illus.). 1977. Repr. of 1923 ed. lib. bdg. 14.00x (ISBN 0-405-09763-8). Arno.
U.S. Dept. of Commerce, Bureau of Foreign & Domestic Commerce. Investments in Latin America & the British West Indies. Wilkins, Mira, ed. LC 76-29754. (European Business Ser.: Special Agent Ser. 169). (Illus.). 1977. Repr. of 1918 ed. lib. bdg. 33.00x (ISBN 0-405-09770-0). Arno.
Vasey, Lloyd R., ed. ASEAN & a Positive Strategy for Foreign Investment. 1978. pap. text ed. 8.00x (ISBN 0-8248-0621-2). U Pr of Hawaii.
Webley, Simon. Foreign Direct Investment in the United States: Opportunities & Impediments. LC 74-14056. 50p. 1974. 2.00 (ISBN 0-902594-25-7). Natl Planning.
Westshore, Inc. Doing Business with the Russians. (Praeger Special Studies). 1979. 20.95 (ISBN 0-03-048456-1). Praeger.
Whitman, Marina. Government Risk-Sharing in Foreign Investment. 1965. 25.00x (ISBN 0-691-04134-2). Princeton U Pr.
Wilkins, Mira. Foreign Enterprise in Florida: The Impact of Non-U. S. Direct Investments. LC 79-844. 1979. 15.00 (ISBN 0-8130-0623-6). U Presses Fla.
--Foreign Investments in the United States: Department of Commerce & Department of Treasury Estimates. LC 76-29783. (European Business Ser.). 1977. Repr. of 1977 ed. lib. bdg. 29.00x (ISBN 0-405-09788-3). Arno.
Wilkins, Mira, ed. European Foreign Investments, As Seen by the U.S. Department of Commerce. An Original Anthology. LC 76-29779. (European Business Ser.). 1977. lib. bdg. 21.00x (ISBN 0-405-09791-3). Arno.
--Issues & Insights on International Investment: An Original Anthology. LC 76-29781. (European Business Ser.). 1977. Repr. of 1977 ed. lib. bdg. 10.00x (ISBN 0-405-09792-1). Arno.
Wood, Gordon. Borrowing & Business in Australia: A Study of the Correlation Between Imports of Capital & Changes in National Prosperity. Wilkins, Mira, ed. LC 76-29986. (European Business Ser.). (Illus.). 1977. Repr. of 1930 ed. lib. bdg. 17.00x (ISBN 0-405-09718-2). Arno.
Wu, Chun-hsi. Dollars, Dependents, & Dogma: Overseas Chinese Remittances to Communist China. LC 67-24368. (Publications Ser.: No. 55). 1967. 13.95 (ISBN 0-8179-1551-6). Hoover Inst Pr.
Zagaris, Bruce. Foreign Investment in the United States. LC 79-20638. (Praeger Special Studies Ser.). (Illus.). 334p. 1980. 26.95 (ISBN 0-03-052401-6). Praeger.
Zupnick, Elliot. Foreign Investment in the U. S. Costs & Benefits. LC 80-66684. (Headline Ser.: No. 249). (Illus.). 80p. (Orig.). 1980. pap. 2.00 (ISBN 0-87124-061-0). Foreign Policy.

INVESTMENTS, FOREIGN-LAW AND LEGISLATION

Ball, George, et al. Conference on Foreign Direct Investment in the United States: Proceedings. (Orig.). pap. text ed. 10.00 (ISBN 0-935328-00-9). Intl Law Inst.
Browndorf, Eric & Reimer, Scott. Bibliography of Multinational Corporations & Foreign & Direct Investment. Simmonds, Kenneth R., ed. LC 78-24051. (Multinational Corporations Law). 1979. 75.00 (ISBN 0-379-20374-X). Oceana.
Brucher, Horst & Pulch, Dieter. The German Law of Foreign Investment Shares. 124p. 1980. 18.00x (ISBN 0-7121-5503-1, Pub. by Macdonald & Evans). State Mutual Bk.
Campbell, Dennis, ed. Legal Aspects of Alien Acquisitions of Real Property. 218p. 1980. lib. bdg. 42.00 (ISBN 90-2681-169-1, Pub. by Kluwer Law Netherlands). Kluwer Boston.
The Changing Legal Investment Environment in Venezuela: Management Implications. 15p. 1980. pap. 4.00 (ISBN 0-686-61369-4, COA 39, COA). Unipub.
Dickie, Robert B. Foreign Investment: France, a Case Study. LC 72-97988. 1970. 12.50 (ISBN 0-379-00390-2). Oceana.
Estudio Comparativo De las Legislaciones Latino Americanas Sobre Regulacion y Control de la Inversin Privada-Extranqera. (Span.). 1975. 10.00 (ISBN 0-8270-5235-9). OAS.
Friedmann, Wolfgang & Mates, Leo, eds. Joint Business Ventures of Yugoslav Enterprises & Foreign Firms. 192p. (Orig.). 1968. pap. 10.00x (ISBN 0-8377-0526-6). Rothman.
Gorove, Stephen. Legal Aspects of International Investment. (L.Q.C. Lamar Society of International Law, University of Mississippi Law Center Monograph: No. 1). 1977. pap. text ed. 15.00x (ISBN 0-8377-0607-6). U MS Law Ctr.
Henderson, J. Foreign Investment Laws & Agriculture. (FAO Legislative Ser.: No. 9). (Orig.). 1970. pap. 14.25 (ISBN 0-685-02924-7, F194, FAO). Unipub.
LaFave, Wayne R. & Hay, Peter, eds. International Trade, Investment, & Organization. LC 66-25556. 1967. 25.00 (ISBN 0-252-74504-3). U of Ill Pr.
Mueller, Rudolf & Schneider, Hannes. The German Law Against Restraints of Competition. 208p. 1980. 39.00x (ISBN 0-7121-5511-2, Pub. by Macdonald & Evans). State Mutual Bk.
Organization for Economic Cooperation & Development. Foreign Investment in Yugoslavia (1974) 58p. 1974. 2.50x (ISBN 92-64-11207-3). OECD.
Rosendahl, Roger, et al, eds. Legal Environment for Foreign Direct Investment in the United States. (Orig.). 1972. pap. text ed. 12.00 (ISBN 0-935328-01-7). Intl Law Inst.
Shea, Donald R. & Swacker, Frank W., eds. Business & Legal Aspects of Latin American Trade & Investment. LC 76-44061. 1977. pap. 15.00 (ISBN 0-930450-11-6). Univ of Wis Latin Am.
Temple Lang, John. Common Market & Common Law: Legal Aspects of Foreign Investment & Economic Integration in the European Community, with Ireland As a Prototype. LC 66-26774. 1966. 12.50x (ISBN 0-226-79213-7). U of Chicago Pr.

INVESTMENTS, FOREIGN (INTERNATIONAL LAW)

Delupis, Ingrid. Finance & Protection of Investments in Developing Countries. LC 73-12149. 183p. 1973. 30.95 (ISBN 0-470-20637-3). Halsted Pr.
Meron, Theodor. Investment Insurance in International Law. LC 76-2451. 700p. 1976. lib. bdg. 70.00 (ISBN 0-379-00246-9). Oceana.
Metzger, Stanley D. International Law, Trade & Finance: Realities & Prospects. LC 62-20101. 1963. 14.00 (ISBN 0-379-11603-0). Oceana.
Organization for Economic Cooperation & Development. International Direct Investment: Policies, Procedures & Practices in OECD Member Countries, 1979. 72p. (Orig.). 1980. pap. text ed. 4.25x (ISBN 92-64-12026-2, 21 80 02 1). OECD.
Rubin, Seymour J. Private Foreign Investment. 118p. 1956. 8.50x (ISBN 0-8018-0570-8). Johns Hopkins.
Shaw, Crawford, ed. Legal Problems in International Trade & Investment. LC 62-3307. 1962. 17.50 (ISBN 0-379-12851-9). Oceana.

INVESTMENTS, JAPANESE

Sekiguchi, Sueo. Japanese Direct Foreign Investment. LC 78-59177. (Atlantic Institute for International Affairs Research Studies: Vol. 1). 171p. 1979. text ed. 20.00 (ISBN 0-916672-17-4). Allanheld.

INVESTORS

see Capitalists and Financiers

INVISIBLE WORLD

see Spirits

INVOCATION OF SAINTS

see Saints-Cultus

INVOLUTES (MATHEMATICS)

Boltianski, V. G. La Envolvente. 88p. (Span.). 1977. pap. 1.30 (ISBN 0-8285-1452-6, Pub. by Mir Pubs Russia). Imported Pubns.

Khiralla, T. W. On the Geometry of External Involute Spur Gears. LC 76-49243. (Illus.). 1976. 25.00 (ISBN 0-9601752-1-0). T W Khiralla.

Tuplin, William A. Involute Gear Geometry. 10.50 (ISBN 0-8044-4939-2). Ungar.

INYO COUNTY, CALIFORNIA

Mitchell, Roger. Inyo-Mono Jeep Trails. (Illus.). 1969. wrappers 1.25 (ISBN 0-910856-33-8). La Siesta.

IODIDES

Biological Separations in Iodinated Density-Gradient Media. 205p. 12.00 (ISBN 0-904147-02-9). Info Retrieval.

IODINE

Control of Iodine in the Nuclear Industry. (Technical Reports Ser.: No. 148). (Illus.). 101p. (Orig.). 1973. pap. 10.25 (ISBN 92-0-025073-4, IDC148, IAEA). Unipub.

ION BOMBARDMENT

see also Ion Implantation

Applications of Ion Beams to Materials: 1975. (Institute of Physics Conference Ser.: No. 28). 1975. 62.50 (ISBN 0-9960030-7-X, Pub. by Inst Physics England). Heyden.

Centre National de la Recherche Scientifique. Ionic Bombardment: Theory & Applications. (Illus.). 1964. 73.25x (ISBN 0-677-10040-X). Gordon.

Low-Energy Ion Beams Nineteen Seventy-Seven: Salford. (Institute of Physics Conference Ser.: No. 38). 1978. 75.00 (ISBN 0-9960031-8-5, Pub. by Inst Physics England). Heyden.

Mayer, J. W., et al. Ion Implantation. 1970. 43.00 (ISBN 0-12-480850-6). Acad Pr.

Meyer, Otto & Kappeler, Franz, eds. Ion Beam Surface Layer Analysis, 2 vols. Incl. Vol. 1. 494p (ISBN 0-306-35045-9); Vol. 2. 491p (ISBN 0-306-35046-7). LC 76-2606. 1976. Ea. 45.00 (ISBN 0-686-63987-1, Plenum Pr); Set. 45.00 (ISBN 0-686-63988-X). Plenum Pub.

Saris, F. W. & Van Der Weg, W. F. Atomic Collisions in Solids. 1976. 158.75 (ISBN 0-444-11073-9, North-Holland). Elsevier.

Wilson, I. H., ed. Low-Energy Ion Beams Nineteen Eighty. (Institute of Physics Conference Ser.: No. 54). 1981. 85.00 (ISBN 0-9960033-4-7, Pub. by Inst Physics England). Heyden.

Wolicki, E. A., et al, eds. Ion Beam Analysis: Proceedings of the Third International Conference, Washington, D.C., June 1977. 1978. 134.25 (ISBN 0-444-85121-6, North-Holland). Elsevier.

Ziegler, James F., ed. New Uses of Ion Acceleration. LC 75-16315. 482p. 1975. 35.00 (ISBN 0-306-30853-3, Plenum Pr.). Plenum Pub.

ION EXCHANGE

Anderson, W. P., ed. Ion Transport in Plants. 1973. 103.00 (ISBN 0-12-058250-3). Acad Pr.

Brice, David K. Ion Implantation Range & Energy Deposition Distributions, Vol. 1: High Incident Ion Energies. LC 74-34119. 590p. 1975. 79.50 (ISBN 0-306-67401-7). IFI Plenum.

Calmon, C. & Gold, H. Ion Exchange for Pollution Control, 2 vols. 1979. Vol. 1, 272p. 69.95 (ISBN 0-8493-5153-7); Vol. 2, 288p. 74.95 (ISBN 0-8493-5154-5). CRC Pr.

Clarkson, D. Ion Transport & Cell Structure in Plants. LC 74-7132. 1974. text ed. 36.95 (ISBN 0-470-15985-5). Halsted Pr.

Critser, James R., Jr. Ion Exchange-Chromatography: Processes & Equipment, 1973. (Ser. 7-1973). 1974. 100.00 (ISBN 0-914428-23-3). Lexington Data.

Emelity, L. A. Operation & Control of Ion-Exchange Processes for Treatment of Radioactive Wastes. 1967. pap. 10.25 (ISBN 92-0-125067-3, IAEA). Unipub.

Kozhevnikov, A. V. Electron-Ion Exchangers: A New Group of Redoxites. Pick, A., ed. Kondor, R., tr. from Rus. LC 74-32247. 129p. 1975. 30.95 (ISBN 0-470-50626-1). Halsted Pr.

Kunin, Robert. Elements of Ion Exchange. LC 60-8970. 194p. 1971. Repr. of 1960 ed. 10.50 (ISBN 0-88275-036-4). Krieger.

Marcus, Y. & Howery, D. G. Ion Exchange Equilibrium Constants. 1976. pap. 10.00 (ISBN 0-08-020992-0). Pergamon.

Marinsky & Marcus. Ion Exchange & Solvent Extraction. (Ion Exchange & Solvent Extraction Ser.: Vol. 8). 464p. 1981. price not set (ISBN 0-8247-1333-8). Dekker.

Marinsky, J. A. & Marcus, Y., eds. Ion Exchange & Solvent Extraction, Vol. 1. 1966. 49.50 (ISBN 0-8247-1451-2). Dekker.

--Ion Exchange & Solvent Extraction, Vol. 3. 168p. 1973. 32.75 (ISBN 0-8247-1453-9). Dekker.

--Ion Exchange & Solvent Extraction, Vol. 4. 288p. 1973. 39.75 (ISBN 0-8247-6014-X). Dekker.

--Ion Exchange & Solvent Extraction, Vol. 5. 294p. 1973. 39.75 (ISBN 0-8247-6061-1). Dekker.

Marinsky, Jacob A. & Marcus, Yizhok, eds. Ion Exchange & Solvent Extraction, Vol. 7. 1977. 47.75 (ISBN 0-8247-6571-0). Dekker.

Paterson, R. An Introduction to Ion Exchange. 1970. 17.50 (ISBN 0-85501-011-8). Heyden.

PTC 31-1973. 1974: Ion Exchange Equipment. 1979. pap. text ed. 6.00 (ISBN 0-685-41933-9, C00016). ASME.

Research in Ion Exchange Chromatography. 183p. 1958. 39.50 (ISBN 0-306-10546-2, Consultants). Plenum Pub.

Rieman, W. & Walton, H. Ion Exchange in Analytical Chemistry. LC 74-105870. 1970. 36.00 (ISBN 0-08-015511-1). Pergamon.

Shatenshtein, A. I. Isotopic Exchange & the Replacement of Hydrogen in Organic Compounds. LC 62-12859. 308p. 1962. 35.00 (ISBN 0-306-10547-0, Consultants). Plenum Pub.

Sykova, Eva, et al, eds. Ion-Selective Microelectrodes & Their Use in Excitable Tissues. 360p. 1981. 39.50 (ISBN 0-306-40723-X, Plenum Pr). Plenum Pub.

Walton, H. F., ed. Ion-Exchange Chromatography. LC 75-31610. (Benchmark Papers in Analytical Chemistry Ser: Vol. 1). 400p. 1976. 51.00 (ISBN 0-12-787725-8). Acad Pr.

ION EXCHANGE RESINS

see also Gums and Resins

Kunin, Robert. Ion Exchange Resins. LC 58-6078. 518p. 1972. Repr. of 1958 ed. 23.50 (ISBN 0-88275-065-8). Krieger.

ION FLOW DYNAMICS

see also Magnetohydrodynamics; Plasma (Ionized Gases)

AGARD-NATO. Instrumentation for High Speed Plasma Flow. (Agardographs Ser.: No. 96). 1966. 54.00x (ISBN 0-677-11020-0). Gordon.

Petrucci, S., ed. Ionic Interactions: From Dilute Solutions to Fused Salts. (Physical Chemistry Ser.: Vol. 22). 1971. Vol. 1. 56.50 (ISBN 0-12-553001-3); Vol. 2. 50.00 (ISBN 0-12-553002-1). Acad Pr.

Samaras, Demetrios G. Theory of Ion Flow Dynamics. LC 78-153896. 1971. pap. text ed. 7.50 (ISBN 0-486-60309-1). Dover.

Schultz, Stanley, ed. Ion Transport by Epithelia. (Society of General Physiologists Ser.: Vol. 36). 279p. 1981. text ed. 32.00 (ISBN 0-89004-610-7). Raven.

ION IMPLANTATION

Chernow, Fred, et al, eds. Ion Implantation in Semiconductors, 1976. LC 77-2980. 754p. 1977. 59.50 (ISBN 0-306-36256-2, Plenum Pr). Plenum Pub.

Crowder, Billy L., ed. Ion Implantation in Semiconductors & Other Material. LC 73-14789. (IBM Research Symposia Ser.). 654p. 1973. 49.50 (ISBN 0-306-30756-1, Plenum Pr). Plenum Pub.

Dearnaly, G., et al. Ion Implantation. LC 72-93492. (Defects in Crystalline Solids Ser.: Vol. 8). 800p. 1974. 117.00 (ISBN 0-444-10488-7, North-Holland). Elsevier.

Eisen, Fred H. & Chadderton, Lewis T., eds. Ion Implantation. LC 71-153515. (Illus.). 480p. 1971. 104.00x (ISBN 0-677-15000-8). Gordon.

Herman, H., ed. Treatise on Materials Science & Technology: Vol. 18 Ion Implantation. 1980. 55.00 (ISBN 0-12-341818-6). Acad Pr.

Namba, Susumu, ed. Ion Implantation in Semiconductors: Science & Technology. LC 75-8985. 742p. 1975. 55.00 (ISBN 0-306-30841-X, Plenum Pr). Plenum Pub.

Scully, J. C., ed. Ion Implantation & Ion Beam Analysis Techniques in Corrosion Studies. 1977. pap. text ed. 16.00 (ISBN 0-08-021420-7). Pergamon.

Vashishta, P., et al, eds. Fast Ion Transport in Solids. LC 79-18065. 800p. 1979. 65.00 (ISBN 0-444-00353-3, North Holland). Elsevier.

Wilson, Robert. G. & Brewer, George R. Ion Beams: With Applications to Ion Implantation. 512p. 1979. Repr. of 1973 ed. lib. bdg. 27.50 (ISBN 0-88275-899-3). Krieger.

Winterbon, K. Bruce. Ion Implantation Range & Energy Deposition Distributions, Vol. 2: Low Incident Ion Energies. LC 74-34119. 341p. 1975. 65.00 (ISBN 0-306-67402-5). IFI Plenum.

ION MICROSCOPE

see Field-Ion Microscope

ION ROCKETS

AGARD-NATO. Physics & Technology of Ion Motors. (Agardographs Ser.: No. 88). (Illus.). 1966. 93.00x (ISBN 0-677-10570-3). Gordon.

Brewer, G. R. Ion Propulsion, Technology & Applications. 1970. 114.50 (ISBN 0-677-02600-5). Gordon.

Langmuir, David B., ed. Electrostatic Propulsion. (Progress in Astronautics & Aeronautics: Vol. 5). 1961. 19.00 (ISBN 0-12-535105-4). Acad Pr.

IONESCO, EUGENE, 1912-

Coe, Richard N. Eugene Ionesco. 6.00 (ISBN 0-8446-5711-5). Peter Smith.

--Eugene Ionesco. 1968. pap. 1.50 (ISBN 0-394-17161-6, B 235, BC). Grove.

Grossvogel, David I. The Blasphemers: The Theatre of Brecht, Ionesco, Beckett, Genet. 1965. pap. 3.95 (ISBN 0-8014-9006-5, CP6). Cornell U Pr.

Hayman, Ronald. Eugene Ionesco. LC 75-10103. (World Dramatists Ser.). (Illus.). 150p. 1976. 10.95 (ISBN 0-8044-2388-1). Ungar.

Hughes, Griffith & Bury, Ruth. Eugene Ionesco: A Bibliography. 127p. 1975. pap. text ed. 5.00x (ISBN 0-7083-0565-2). Verry.

Ionesco, Eugene. Fragments of a Journal. Pace, Jean, tr. 1968. pap. 12.00 (ISBN 0-686-66239-3, ST00035). Grove.

--Journal en Miettes. 224p. 1973. 3.95 (ISBN 0-686-54195-2). French & Eur.

--Rhinoceros: Deuxieme Edition. Ellison, Reuben Y., et al, eds. LC 75-14361. 1976. pap. text ed. 9.95 (ISBN 0-03-013731-4, HoltC). HR&W.

Lamont, Rosette C. & Friedman, Melvin J., eds. The Two Faces of Ionesco. LC 76-51038. 1978. 15.00x (ISBN 0-87875-110-6). Whitston Pub.

Lewis, Allan. Ionesco. (World Authors Ser.: France: No. 239). lib. bdg. 10.95 (ISBN 0-8057-2452-4). Twayne.

Pronko, Leonard C. Eugene Ionesco. LC 65-16380. (Columbia Essays on Modern Writers Ser.: No. 7). (Orig.). 1965. pap. 2.00 (ISBN 0-231-02681-1). Columbia U Pr.

Vernois. La Dynamique Theatrale d'Eugene Ionesco. 32.50 (ISBN 0-685-34259-X). French & Eur.

Wulbern, Julian H. Brecht & Ionesco: Commitment in Context. LC 71-129767. (Illus.). 1971. 15.00 (ISBN 0-252-00129-X). U of Ill Pr.

IONIA, ASIA MINOR

Hogarth, David G. Ionia & the East. LC 68-25242. (World History Ser., No. 48). 1969. Repr. of 1909 ed. lib. bdg. 47.95 (ISBN 0-8383-0956-9). Haskell.

IONIAN ISLANDS

Davies, Derek A. C. Greek Islands. LC 73-158639. (This Beautiful World Ser.: Vol. 27). (Illus.). 130p. (Orig.). 1971. pap. 4.95 (ISBN 0-87011-154-X). Kodansha.

Denham, H. M. The Ionian Islands to Rhodes: A Sea-Guide. (Illus.). 1976. 19.95 (ISBN 0-393-03195-0). Norton.

Foss, Arthur. Ionian Islands. 1970. 12.00 (ISBN 0-571-08944-5). Transatlantic.

--The Ionian Islands: Zakynthos to Corfu. (Illus.). 274p. 1969. 7.95 (ISBN 0-571-08944-5, Pub. by Faber & Faber). Merrimack Bk Serv.

Young, Martin. Corfu & the Other Ionian Islands. LC 70-862207. (Illus.). 344p. 1971. 10.00x (ISBN 0-224-01307-6). Intl Pubns Serv.

--The Travellers' Guide to Corfu & the Other Ionian Islands. LC 77-363313. (Travellers' Guide Ser.). (Illus.). 358p. 1979. 9.95 (ISBN 0-224-01307-6, Pub. by Chatto Bodley Jonathan). Merrimack Bk Serv.

IONIANS

Huxley, G. L. Early Ionians. 1966. pap. text ed. 8.50x (ISBN 0-7165-2065-6). Humanities.

--The Early Ionians. (Illus.). 220p. 1972. Repr. of 1966 ed. 17.00x (ISBN 0-7165-2065-6, Pub. by Irish Academic Pr Ireland). Biblio Dist.

IONIC BOMBARDMENT

see Ion Bombardment

IONIC CRYSTALS

see also Polarons

Devreese, J. T., ed. Polarons in Ionic Crystals & Polar Semiconductors: Proceedings of the 1971 Antwerp Advanced Study Institute. 1972. 88.00 (ISBN 0-444-10409-7, North-Holland). Elsevier.

Farge, Y. & Fontana, M. P. Electronic & Vibrational Properties of Point Defects in Ionic Crystals. (Defects in Crystalline Solids Ser.: Vol. 11). 271p. 1979. 48.75 (ISBN 0-444-85272-7, North Holland). Elsevier.

Skolbel'tsyn, D. V., ed. Surface Properties of Semiconductors & Dynamics of Ionic Crystals. LC 77-136983. (P. N. Lebedev Physics Institute Ser.: Vol. 48). 148p. 1971. 27.50 (ISBN 0-306-10854-2, Consultants). Plenum Pub.

Sprackling, M. T. The Plastic Deformation of Simple Ionic Crystals. 1977. 39.00 (ISBN 0-12-657850-8). Acad Pr.

IONIC EQUILIBRIUM

Butler, James N. Ionic Equilibrium. (Illus.). 1964. 20.95 (ISBN 0-201-00730-4). A-W.

--Solubility & pH Calculations. LC 64-15563. (Chemistry Ser). (Orig.). (gr. 9 up). 1964. pap. 5.95 (ISBN 0-201-00733-9). A-W.

Margolis, Emil J. Chemical Principles in Calculations of Ionic Equilibria. (Orig.). 1966. pap. text ed. 5.95x (ISBN 0-02-376060-5). Macmillan.

Massey, H. S., et al. Electronic & Ionic Impact Phenomena: Slow Collisions of Heavy Particles, Vol. 3. 872p. 1971. 95.00x (ISBN 0-19-851252-X). Oxford U Pr.

Prue, J. E. Ionic Equilibria. 1966. 15.00 (ISBN 0-08-011344-3). Pergamon.

Robbins, Omer, Jr. Ionic Reactions & Equilibria. 1967. pap. text ed. 4.95x (ISBN 0-02-402010-9). Macmillan.

Russotti, H. The Study of Ionic Equilibria: An Introduction. (Illus.). 1978. pap. text ed. 15.50x (ISBN 0-582-44175-7). Longman.

IONIC FLOWS

see Ion Flow Dynamics

IONIC PROPULSION

see Ion Rockets

IONIC SOLUTIONS

Moeller, T. & O'Connor, R. Ions in Aqueous Systems. 1971. text ed. 11.95 (ISBN 0-07-042647-3). McGraw.

Smedley, Stuart I. The Interpretation of Ionic Conductivity in Liquids. 180p. 1980. 25.00 (ISBN 0-306-40529-6, Plenum Pr). Plenum Pub.

IONIZATION

see also Auger Effect; Chemical Equilibrium; Collisions (Nuclear Physics); Hydrogen-Ion Concentration; Ion Exchange; Ionic Equilibrium; Scintillation Counters

Bock, R., ed. Heavy Ion Collisions: Heavy Ion Reactors & Microscopic Properties of Nuclear States, Vol. 1. 1979. 97.75 (ISBN 0-7204-0738-9, North Holland). Elsevier.

Duncan, A. B. Rydberg Series in Atoms & Molecules. (Physical Chemistry Ser, Vol. 23). 1971. 26.50 (ISBN 0-12-223950-4). Acad Pr.

Jones, J. R. The Ionisation of Carbon Acids. 1974. 36.50 (ISBN 0-12-389750-5). Acad Pr.

Reams, Carey A. Choose! Life or Death: Reams Biological Theory of Ionization. 1978. pap. 3.95 (ISBN 0-89221-046-X). New Leaf.

Reed, Rowland I. Ion Production by Electron Impact. 1962. 37.00 (ISBN 0-12-585250-9). Acad Pr.

Serjeant, E. P. & Dempsey, B., eds. Ionisation Constants of Organic Acids in Aqueous Solution. (Chemical Data Ser.: Vol. 23). (Illus.). 1979. text ed. 190.00 (ISBN 0-08-022339-7). Pergamon.

Sulman, Felix G. The Effect of Air Ionization, Electric Fields, Atmospherics & Other Electric Phenomena on Man & Animal. (Environmental Studies Ser.). (Illus.). 424p. 1980. text ed. 24.75 (ISBN 0-398-03929-1); pap. text ed. 18.75 (ISBN 0-398-03930-5). C C Thomas.

IONIZATION CHAMBERS

see also Bubble Chamber; Cloud Chamber; Nuclear Counters; Spark Chambers

IONIZATION OF GASES

see also Air, Ionized; Photoionization of Gases

Cherrington, B. E. Gaseous Electronics & Gas Lasers. 1979. text ed. 48.00 (ISBN 0-08-020622-0). Pergamon.

Danilov, A. D. Chemistry of the Ionosphere. LC 68-31236. (Monographs in Geoscience Ser.). 296p. 1970. 32.50 (ISBN 0-306-30357-4, Plenum Pr). Plenum Pub.

International Conference on Phenomena in Ionized Gases, 12th, the Netherlands, 1975. Phenomena in Ionized Gases, Pt. 2, Invited Papers: Proceedings. Holscher, J. G. & Schram, D. C., eds. 1976. 41.50 (ISBN 0-444-11074-7, North-Holland). Elsevier.

International Conference on Phenomena in Ionized Gases, 12th. Proceedings: Part I - Contributed Papers. Holscher, J. G. & Schram, D. C., eds. 408p. 1975. 58.75 (ISBN 0-444-10945-5, North-Holland); Pt. 2: Invited Paper. 38.00 (ISBN 0-444-11074-7). Elsevier.

Lighthill, M. J., et al, eds. Dynamics of Ionized Gases. Imai, Isao & Sato, Hiroshi. 1978. 38.00x (ISBN 0-86008-079-X, Pub. by U of Tokyo Pr). Intl Schol Bk Serv.

McDaniel, Earl W. & Mason, Edward A. The Mobility & Diffusion of Ions in Gases. LC 72-13414. 372p. 1973. 35.50 (ISBN 0-471-58387-1, Pub. by Wiley). Krieger.

Nasser, Essam. Fundamentals of Gaseous Ionization & Plasma Electronics. LC 77-125275. (Plasma Physics Ser). 1971. 46.00 (ISBN 0-471-63056-X, Pub. by Wiley-Interscience). Wiley.

Pfotzer, G., et al. Time Pattern of Ionizing Radiation in Balloon Altitudes in High Latitudes, 2 Pts in 1. 1962. pap. 8.90 (ISBN 0-387-02880-3). Springer-Verlag.

Shuler, Kurt E., ed. Ionization in High Temperature Gases. (Progress in Astronautics & Aeronautics: Vol. 12). 1963. 14.00 (ISBN 0-12-535112-7). Acad Pr.

Spitzer, L. Physics of Fully Ionized Gases. 2nd ed. 1962. 17.00 (ISBN 0-470-81723-2). Wiley.

A Survey of Phenomena in Ionized Gases: Invited Papers. (Eng., Fr., Rus. & Ger.). 1968. pap. 44.00 (ISBN 92-0-030068-5, ISP178, IAEA). Unipub.

Thomson, Joseph J. & Thomson, George P. Conduction of Electricity Through Gases, 2 Vols. LC 68-8881. (Illus.). 1969. pap. text ed. 4.50 ea.; Vol. 1. pap. text ed. (ISBN 0-486-62007-7); Vol. 2. pap. text ed. (ISBN 0-486-62008-5). Dover.

IONIZED AIR

see Air, Ionized

IONIZING RADIATION
see also Beta Rays; Cosmic Rays; Gamma Rays; Ultra-Violet Rays; X-Rays
Mladjenovic, M. Radioisotope & Radiation Physics: An Introduction. 1973. 38.50 (ISBN 0-12-502350-2). Acad Pr.
Soyka, Fred. The Ion Effect. 2.50 (ISBN 0-686-29966-3). Cancer Bk Hse.
Tait, W. H. Radiation Detection. LC 80-40240. 1980. text ed. 54.95 (ISBN 0-408-10645-X). Butterworth.
IONOSPHERE
Al'pert, Y. L. Radio Wave Propagation & the Ionosphere, Vol. 1: The Ionosphere. 2nd ed. LC 75-167674. (Illus.). 430p. 1973. 45.00 (ISBN 0-306-17141-4, Consultants). Plenum Pub.
Anastassiades, M. A., ed. Solar Eclipses & the Ionosphere. LC 71-119056. 309p. 1970. 34.50 (ISBN 0-306-30480-5, Plenum Pr). Plenum Pub.
Becker, Walter. Tables of Ordinary & Extraordinary Refractive Indices, Group Refractive Indices & - H-Sub-Ox - F Curves for Standard Ionospheric Layer Models. 1960. 7.10 (ISBN 0-387-02580-4). Springer-Verlag.
Brown, G. M. Ionosphere. (Progress in Radio Science Ser.: Vol. 3). 1965. 19.50 (ISBN 0-444-40087-7). Elsevier.
Danilov, A. D. Chemistry of the Ionosphere. LC 68-31236. (Monographs in Geoscience Ser.). 296p. 1970. 32.50 (ISBN 0-306-30357-4, Plenum Pr). Plenum Pub.
Giraud, A. & Petit, M. Ionospheric Techniques & Phenomena. (Geophysics & Astrophysics Monographs: No. 13). 1978. 45.00 (ISBN 90-277-0499-6, Pub. by Reidel Holland); pap. write for info. (ISBN 90-277-0500-3, Pub. by Reidel Holland). Kluwer Boston.
Harrison, John A. Story of the Ionosphere. (Illus.). 1963. 5.25 (ISBN 0-7175-0112-4). Dufour.
Ivanov-Kholodnyi, G. S. & Nikol' skii, G. M. The Sun & the Ionosphere: Short-Wave Solar Radiation & Its Effect on the Ionosphere. 400p. 1971. 42.50x (ISBN 0-7065-1180-8, Pub. by IPST). Intl Schol Bk Serv.
Manning, Laurence A. Bibliography of the Ionosphere: An Annotated Survey Through 1960. 1962. 20.00x (ISBN 0-8047-0125-3). Stanford U Pr.
Ratcliffe, J. A. An Introduction to the Ionosphere & Magnetosphere. LC 74-171680. (Illus.). 200p. 1972. 35.50 (ISBN 0-521-08341-9). Cambridge U Pr.
Rawer, Karl. Ionosphere: Its Significance for Geophysics & Radio Communication. Katz, Ludwig, tr. LC 57-6113. 1957. 11.50 (ISBN 0-8044-4788-8). Ungar.
Risbeth, Henry & Garriott, O. K. Introduction to Ionospheric Physics. (International Geophysics Ser.: Vol. 14). 1969. 50.50 (ISBN 0-12-588940-2). Acad Pr.
Skovli, G., ed. Polar Ionosphere & Magnetospheric Processes. 1970. 73.25x (ISBN 0-677-13930-6). Gordon.
Symposium On Ionospheric Physics - Alpbach - 1964. High Latitude Particles & the Ionosphere: Proceedings. Maehlum, B., ed. 1965. 50.50 (ISBN 0-12-465550-5). Acad Pr.
IONOSPHERIC RADIO WAVE PROPAGATION
see also Magneto-Ionic Theory
Al'pert, Y. L. Radio Wave Propagation & the Ionosphere. LC 61-17727. 214p. 1963. 37.50 (ISBN 0-306-10590-X, Consultants). Plenum Pub.
--Radio Wave Propagation & the Ionosphere, Vol. 1: The Ionosphere. 2nd ed. LC 75-167674. (Illus.). 430p. 1973. 45.00 (ISBN 0-306-17141-4, Consultants). Plenum Pub.
Al'pert, Y. L. & Fligel', D. S. Propagation of ELF & VLF Waves Near the Earth. LC 75-167674. (Illus.). 280p. 1974. 42.50 (ISBN 0-306-17142-2, Consultants). Plenum Pub.
Alpert, Yakov L., ed. Radio Wave Propagation & the Ionosphere: Propagation of Electromagnetic Waves Near the Earth, Vol. 2. 2nd ed. LC 75-167674. 268p. 1974. 42.50 (ISBN 0-306-17142-2, Plenum Pr). Plenum Pub.
ESRIN-ESLAB Symposium,2nd Frascati,Itay23-27,September,1968. Low-Frequency Waves & Irregularities in the Ionosphere: Proceedings. D'Angelo, N., ed. (Astrophysics & Space Science Library: No.14). 218p. 1969. lib. bdg. 37.00 (ISBN 90-277-0114-8, Pub. by Reidel Holland). Kluwer Boston.
Folkestad, K., ed. Ionospheric Radio Communications. LC 68-20271. 468p. 1968. 42.50 (ISBN 0-306-30336-1, Plenum Pr). Plenum Pub.
Gurevich, A. Nonlinear Phenomena in the Ionosphere. (Physics & Chemistry in Space Ser.: Vol. 10). (Illus.). 1978. 52.00 (ISBN 0-387-08605-6). Springer-Verlag.
Kasha, Michael A. Ionosphere & Its Interaction with Satellites. (Illus.). 1969. 45.25x (ISBN 0-677-02090-2). Gordon.
Saveskie, Peter N. Radio Propagation Handbook. (Illus., Orig.). 1980. 17.95 (ISBN 0-8306-9949-X); pap. 10.95 (ISBN 0-8306-1146-0, 1146). TAB Bks.
Whale, H. A. Effects of Ionospheric Scattering on Very-Long Distance Radio Communication. LC 76-84765. 179p. 1969. 29.50 (ISBN 0-306-30420-1, Plenum Pr). Plenum Pub.
Yeh, K. C. & Liv, C. H. Theory of Ionospheric Waves. (International Geophysics Ser., Vol. 17). 1972. 60.00 (ISBN 0-12-770450-7). Acad Pr.
IONOSPHERIC RESEARCH
Grandal, Bjorn & Holtet, Jan A., eds. Dynamical & Chemical Coupling of the Neutral & Ionized Atmosphere. (Nato Advanced Study Institute Ser. C: No. 35). 1977. lib. bdg. 47.50 (ISBN 90-277-0840-1, Pub. by Reidel Holland). Kluwer Boston.
IONS
see also Anions; Cations; Cloud Chamber; Complex Ions; Electric Discharges through Gases; Electrolysis; Electrons; Ion Bombardment; Ion Rockets; Ionic Solutions; Metal Ions; Particle Accelerators; Plasma (Ionized Gases); Thermionic Emission
Allsop, R. T. & Healey, J. A. Chemical Analysis, Chromatography, & Ion Exchange. 1974. pap. text ed. 5.50x (ISBN 0-435-65954-5); tchr's guide 3.25x (ISBN 0-435-65955-3). Heinemann Ed.
Andersen, Hans H., ed. Bibliography & Index of Experimental Range & Stopping Power Data. LC 77-22415. 1978. text ed. 48.00 (ISBN 0-08-021604-8). Pergamon.
Ausloos, ed. Kinetics of Ion-Molecule Reactions. (NATO Advanced Studies Institute Ser.: Series B: Physics, Vol. 40). 1979. 49.50 (ISBN 0-306-40153-3, Plenum Pr). Plenum Pub.
Ausloos, Pierre, ed. Interactions Between Ions & Molecules. LC 74-31389. (NATO Advanced Study Institutes Ser. B-Physics: Vol. 6). 690p. 1975. 59.50 (ISBN 0-306-35706-2, Plenum Pr). Plenum Pub.
Ausloos, Pierre J., ed. Ion-Molecule Reactions in the Gas Phase. LC 66-28609. (Advances in Chemistry Ser: No. 58). 1966. 26.00 (ISBN 0-8412-0059-9). Am Chemical.
Bartlett, Paul D. Nonclassical Ions: Reprints & Commentary. 1965. pap. 9.50 (ISBN 0-8053-0571-8, Adv Bk Prog). Benjamin-Cummings.
Bartolo, Baldassare Di, ed. Optical Properties of Ions in Solids. LC 75-1190. (NATO Advanced Study Institutes Ser. Ser. B: Physics: Vol. 8). 490p. 1975. 45.00 (ISBN 0-306-35708-9, Plenum Pr). Plenum Pub.
Brown, H. C., ed. The Nonclassical Ion Problem. (Illus.). 301p. 1977. 24.95 (ISBN 0-306-30950-5, Plenum Pr). Plenum Pub.
Brown, Herbert C. Explorations in the Nonclassical Ion Area. 1976. pap. text ed. 12.75 (ISBN 0-08-020488-0). Pergamon.
Copeland, J. L. Transport Properties of Ionic Liquids. 1974. 24.50x (ISBN 0-677-02830-X). Gordon.
Dobler, Max. Ionophores & Their Structure. LC 81-4373. 350p. 1981. 35.00 (ISBN 0-471-05270-1, Pub. by Wiley-Interscience). Wiley.
Eisenberg, Adi, ed. Ions in Polymers. LC 80-19321. (Advances in Chemistry Ser.: No. 187). 1980. 43.50 (ISBN 0-8412-0482-9). Am Chemical.
Engleman, R., ed. Nonradiative Decay of Ions & Molecules in Solids. 1979. 58.75 (ISBN 0-444-85244-1, North Holland). Elsevier.
Everett. Ions in Macromolecular & Biological Systems. 1978. 39.50 (ISBN 0-8391-1290-4). Univ Park.
Franklin, J. L., ed. Ion-Molecule Reactions, 2 vols. LC 77-179758. 1972. Vol. 1, 362p. 42.50 (ISBN 0-306-30551-8, Plenum Pr); Vol. 2. 42.50 (ISBN 0-306-30552-6). Plenum Pub.
Ions & Ion Pairs & Their Role in Chemical Reactions: International Symposium on Ions & Ion Pairs & Their Role in Chemical Reactions, Syracuse, New York, 1978. 30.00 (ISBN 0-08-022355-9). Pergamon.
Ions Can Do Strange Things. cancelled (ISBN 0-686-13627-6). OMango.
Knewstubb, P. F. Mass Spectrometry & Ion-Molecule Reactions. LC 69-16282. (Cambridge Chemistry Textbooks Ser). (Illus.). 1969. 27.50 (ISBN 0-521-07489-4); pap. 11.50x (ISBN 0-521-09563-8). Cambridge U Pr.
Leffert, H. L., ed. Growth Regulation by Ion Fluxes. LC 80-13986. (Annals of the New York Academy of Sciences: Vol. 339). 335p. 60.00x (ISBN 0-89766-049-8). NY Acad Sci.
Limiting Steps in Ion Uptake by Plants from Soil. (Technical Reports Ser: No. 65). 1966. pap. 11.25 (ISBN 92-0-115566-2, IDC65, IAEA). Unipub.
Littmark, U. & Ziegler, J. F. Handbook of Range Distributions for Energetic Ions in All Elements. LC 79-27825. (The Stopping & Ranges of Ions in Matter Ser.: Vol. 6). 490p. 72.00 (ISBN 0-08-023879-3). Pergamon.
Low-Energy Ion Beams Nineteen Seventy-Seven: Salford. (Institute of Physics Conference Ser.: No. 38). 1978. 75.00 (ISBN 0-9960031-8-5, Pub. by Inst Physics England). Heyden.
Luebbers, D. W., et al. eds. Progress in Enzyme & Ion-Selective Electrodes. (Illus.). 240p. 1981. pap. 27.20 (ISBN 0-387-10499-2). Springer-Verlag.
McDaniel, Earl W., et al. Ion-Molecule Reactions. LC 70-91647. 374p. 1970. 33.95 (ISBN 0-471-58386-3, Pub. by Wiley). Krieger.
McLafferty, F. W., ed. Mass Spectrometry of Organic Ions. 1963. 71.50 (ISBN 0-12-483650-X). Acad Pr.
Mc Manus, Samuel P., ed. Organic Reactive Intermediates. (Organic Chemistry Ser.). 1973. 65.00 (ISBN 0-12-485450-8). Acad Pr.
Marinsky, J. A. & Marcus, Y., eds. Ion Exchange & Solvent Extraction, Vol. 6. 312p. 1974. 47.75 (ISBN 0-8247-6047-6). Dekker.
Massey, H. S. Electronic & Ionic Impact Phenomena, 2 vols. Incl. Vol. 1. Collision of Electrons with Atoms. Massey, H. S. & Burhop, E. H. 49.95x (ISBN 0-19-851247-3); Vol. 2. Electron Collisions with Molecules & Photoionization. Massey, H. S. 41.00x (ISBN 0-19-851249-X). 1969. Oxford U Pr.
Massey, Harrie. Negative Ions. 3rd ed. LC 74-31792. (Cambridge Monographs on Physics). (Illus.). 600p. 1976. 126.00 (ISBN 0-521-20775-4). Cambridge U Pr.
Mott, N. F. & Massey, H. S. Theory of Atomic Collisions. 3rd ed. (International Series of Monographs on Physics). (Illus.). 1965. 65.00x (ISBN 0-19-851242-2). Oxford U Pr.
Mullins, L. J. Ion Transport in Heart. 144p. 1981. 16.50 (ISBN 0-89004-645-X). Raven.
NATO Sponsored Advanced Study Institute on Fast Ion Transport in Solids, Solid State Batteries & Devices, Belgirate, Italy, Sept. 1972. Fast Ion Transport in Solids: Proceedings. Van Gool, W., ed. LC 72-96146. 420p. 1973. 58.75 (ISBN 0-444-10432-1, North-Holland). Elsevier.
Neel, L., ed. Nonlinear Behaviour of Molecules, Atoms & Ions in Electric, Magnetic or Electromagnetic Fields. 1979. 88.00 (ISBN 0-444-41790-7). Elsevier.
Olah, George A. & Schleyer, Paul, eds. Miscellaneous Ions, Theory & Structure. LC 67-13956. (Reactive Intermediates in Organic Chemistry: Carbonium Ions). 531p. (Orig.). 1976. 50.50 (ISBN 0-471-65342-X). Krieger.
Papovych, Orest. Tetraphenylborates. (IUPAC Solubility Data Ser.). 260p. 1981. 100.00 (ISBN 0-08-023928-5). Pergamon.
Picraux, S. T., et al, eds. Applications of Ion Beams to Metals. LC 74-4395. 706p. 1974. 49.50 (ISBN 0-306-30781-2, Plenum Pr). Plenum Pub.
Scully, J. C., ed. Ion Implementation & Ion Beam Analysis Techniques in Corrosion: Selected Papers Presented at the Conference at the Corrosion & Protection Centre, UMIST, Manchester, 28-30 June 1978. 148p. 1981. 16.00 (ISBN 0-08-026135-3). Pergamon.
Sellin, A., ed. Structure & Collisions of Ions & Atoms. (Topics in Current Physics: Vol 5). (Illus.). 1978. 41.60 (ISBN 0-387-08576-9). Springer-Verlag.
Szwarc, Michael, ed. Ions & Ion Pairs in Organic Reactions, Vol. 1. 411p. 1972. 26.50 (ISBN 0-471-84307-5). Krieger.
--Ions & Ion Pairs in Organic Reactions: Role of Ions & Ion Pairs in Chemical Reactions, Vol. 2. 582p. 1974. 40.50 (ISBN 0-471-84308-3). Krieger.
Taylor, R. H. Magnetic Ions in Metals: A Review of Thier Study by Electron Spin Resonance. LC 76-53798. 1977. 21.95 (ISBN 0-470-99024-4). Halsted Pr.
Thomas, J. P. & Cachard, A., eds. Material Characterization Using Ion Beams. LC 77-13269. (NATO Advanced Study Institutes Ser. B: Physics, Vol. 28). 535p. 1977. 49.50 (ISBN 0-686-64758-0, Plenum Pr). Plenum Pub.
Valyi, L. Atom & Ion Sources. LC 76-44880. 1978. 85.50 (ISBN 0-471-99463-4, Pub. by Wiley-Interscience). Wiley.
Vesely, J., et al. Analysis with Ion-Selective Electrodes. 1978. 74.95 (ISBN 0-470-26296-6). Halsted Pr.
Wilson, I. H., ed. Low-Energy Ion Beams Nineteen Eighty. (Institute of Physics Conference Ser.: No. 54). 1981. 85.00 (ISBN 0-9960033-4-7, Pub. by Inst Physics England). Heyden.
IONS–SPECTRA
Abragam, A. & Bleaney, B. Electron Paramagnetic Resonance of Transition Ions. (International Series of Monographs on Physics). 1970. 9.00x (ISBN 0-19-851250-3). Oxford U Pr.
Cooks, R. G., et al. Metastable Ions. LC 72-97419. 312p. 1973. 49.00 (ISBN 0-444-41119-4). Elsevier.
Fiermans, L. & Vennik, J., eds. Electron & Ion Spectroscopy of Solids. LC 78-6171. (NATO Advanced Study Institutes Ser.: Series B, Physics, Vol. 32). 487p. 1978. 47.50 (ISBN 0-306-35732-1, Plenum Pr). Plenum Pub.
Hartmann, H. & Wanczek, K. P. Ion Cyclotron Resonance Spectrometry. (Lecture Notes in Chemistry: Vol. 7). (Illus.). 1978. pap. 15.60 (ISBN 0-387-08760-5). Springer-Verlag.
Herzberg, Gerhard. Spectra & Structures of Simple Free Radicals: An Introduction to Molecular Spectroscopy. LC 70-124722. (Baker Non-Resident Lectureships in Chemistry Ser.). 240p. 1971. 25.00x (ISBN 0-8014-0584-X). Cornell U Pr.
Wilson, Robert G. Ion Nass Spectra. 442p. (Orig.). 1974. 29.75 (ISBN 0-471-94965-5). Krieger.
IORGA, NICOLAE, 1871-1940
Oldson, William O. The Historical & Nationalistic Thought of Nicolae Iorga. (East European Monographs: No. 5). 1973. 14.00x (ISBN 0-231-03747-3). East Eur Quarterly.
IOWA
see also names of cities, counties, towns, etc. in Iowa
Anderson, Wayne I. Geology of Iowa. (Illus.). 1982. write for info. (ISBN 0-8138-1505-3). Iowa St U Pr.
Andrews, Clarence A., ed. Clarence Andrews' Christmas in Iowa. LC 79-89445. (Illus.). 128p. 1979. 7.95 (ISBN 0-934582-00-9). Midwest Heritage.
--Growing up in Iowa. (Illus.). 1978. 8.95 (ISBN 0-8138-1940-7). Iowa St U Pr.
Bauer, Douglas. Prairie City, Iowa. LC 79-10314. 1979. 10.95 (ISBN 0-399-12359-8). Putnam.
Beacon Presse Staff, ed. Who's Who in Iowa. 64p. (Orig.). 1980. pap. 4.95 (ISBN 0-935954-03-1). Beacon Presse IA.
Dahl, Orin L. Des Moines: Capital City. LC 78-68066. (American Portrait Ser.). 1978. 19.95 (ISBN 0-932986-02-1). Continent Herit.
Federal Writers' Project. Iowa: A Guide to the Hawkeye State. 583p. 1938. Repr. 48.00 (ISBN 0-403-02166-9). Somerset Pub.
Frankland, Phillip & Airola, Stephen. Atlas of Selected Iowa Services. LC 78-16807. 1978. pap. text ed. 6.95x (ISBN 0-87745-085-4). U of Iowa Pr.
Garland, Hamlin. Iowa, O Iowa. 1979. Repr. of 1935 ed. lib. bdg. 30.00 (ISBN 0-8482-4185-1). Norwood Edns.
How Iowa Cooks. 1964. 4.25 (ISBN 0-686-15945-4); supplement incl. Tipton Woman.
Iowa. 28.00 (ISBN 0-89770-091-0). Curriculum Info Ctr.
Lokken, Roscoe L. Iowa: Public Land Disposal. LC 72-2854. (Use & Abuse of America's Natural Resources Ser). 320p. 1972. Repr. of 1942 ed. 17.00 (ISBN 0-405-04518-2). Arno.
Stanford, John. Tornado! Accounts of Tornadoes in Iowa. (Illus.). 1977. pap. 4.95 (ISBN 0-8138-0365-9). Iowa St U Pr.
Wall, Joseph F. Iowa. (States & the Nation Ser.). (Illus.). 1978. 12.95 (ISBN 0-393-05671-6, Co-Pub by AASLH). Norton.
Zielinski, John. Unknown Iowa. pap. 7.95 (ISBN 0-686-52156-0). Wallace-Homestead.
IOWA–ANTIQUITIES
Alex, Lynn M. Exploring Iowa's Past: A Guide to Prehistoric Archaeology. LC 80-21391. (Illus.). 180p. 1980. pap. 7.95 (ISBN 0-87745-108-7). U of Iowa Pr.
Anderson, Duane. Eastern Iowa Prehistory. 108p. 1981. 10.95 (ISBN 0-8138-1865-6). Iowa St U Pr.
--Western Iowa Prehistory. (Illus.). 55p. 1975. 6.95 (ISBN 0-8138-1765-X). Iowa St U Pr.
IOWA–BIBLIOGRAPHY
Vexler, R. I. Iowa Chronology & Factbook, Vol. 15. 1978. 8.50 (ISBN 0-379-16140-0). Oceana.
IOWA–DESCRIPTION AND TRAVEL
Berger, Brian. Beautiful Iowa. Shangle, Robert D., ed. LC 79-28596. (Illus.). 72p. 1980. 14.95 (ISBN 0-89802-107-3); pap. 7.95 (ISBN 0-89802-106-5). Beautiful Am.
Bowles, John B. Distribution & Biogeography of Mammals of Iowa. (Special Publications: No. 9). (Illus., Orig.). 1975. pap. 8.00 (ISBN 0-89672-034-9). Tex Tech Pr.
Federal Writers' Project. Iowa: A Guide to the Hawkeye State. 583p. 1938. Repr. 48.00 (ISBN 0-403-02166-9). Somerset Pub.
Nelson, H. L. A Geography of Iowa. 1976. 3.95 (ISBN 0-87069-172-4). Wallace-Homestead.
Pelzer, Louis. Marches of the Dragoons in the Mississippi Valley: 1833-1850. facsimile ed. LC 75-116. (Mid-American Frontier Ser.). 1975. Repr. of 1917 ed. 18.00x (ISBN 0-405-06882-4). Arno.
Stanek, Edward & Stanek, Jacqueline. Iowa's Magnificent County Courthouse. 1976. softbound 7.95 (ISBN 0-87069-164-3). Wallace-Homestead.
IOWA–HISTORY
Carlson, Norman, ed. Iowa Trolleys: Bulletin-114. LC 73-90937. (Illus.). 1975. 25.00 (ISBN 0-915348-14-4). Central Electric.

Houlette, William. Iowa, the Pioneer Heritage. 5.95 (ISBN 0-87069-069-8). Wallace-Homestead.

Iowa State Historical Society. Documentary Material Relating to the History of Iowa, 3 vols. Shambaugh, Benjamin F., ed. LC 74-19610. Repr. of 1901 ed. Set. 67.50 (ISBN 0-404-12339-2). AMS Pr.

Jackson, Ronald V. & Teeples, Gary R. Iowa Census Index 1840. LC 77-87433. (Illus.). lib. bdg. 26.00 (ISBN 0-89593-041-2). Accelerated Index.

--Iowa Census Index 1850. LC 77-85928. (Illus.). lib. bdg. 30.00 (ISBN 0-89593-042-0). Accelerated Index.

--Iowa Territorial Census Index 1836. LC 77-85927. (Illus.). lib. bdg. 14.00 (ISBN 0-89593-040-4). Accelerated Index.

James, J. A. Constitution & Admission of Iowa into the Union. 1973. Repr. of 1900 ed. pap. 7.00 (ISBN 0-384-26742-4). Johnson Repr.

James, James A. Constitution & Admission of Iowa into the Union. LC 78-63875. (Johns Hopkins University. Studies in the Social Sciences. Eighteenth Ser. 1900: 7). Repr. of 1900 ed. 11.50 (ISBN 0-404-61131-1). AMS Pr.

Kirkpatrick, Inez E. A Postal History of Sioux City. (Illus.). 1977. lib. bdg. 13.50x (ISBN 0-916170-07-1); pap. 10.00x (ISBN 0-916170-12-8). J-B Pubs.

Kwasky, Albert. The Old Lady in Dubuque. 1979. 7.95 (ISBN 0-533-03615-1). Vantage.

Lee, Deemer. Esther's Town. 190p. 1980. 12.95 (ISBN 0-8138-0460-4). Iowa St U Pr.

Macy, Jesse. Institutional Beginnings in a Western State (Iowa) LC 78-63746. (Johns Hopkins University. Studies in the Social Sciences. Second Ser. 1884: 7). Repr. of 1884 ed. 11.50 (ISBN 0-404-61016-1). AMS Pr.

Mattice, Beatrice H. They Walked These Hills Before Me: An Early History of the Town of Conesville. 1980. pap. 8.95 (ISBN 0-686-64343-7). Hope Farm.

Mills, George S. Rogues & Heroes from Iowa's Amazing Past. facsimile ed. LC 77-153160. (Illus.). 260p. 1972. pap. 9.95x (ISBN 0-8138-2415-X). Iowa St U Pr.

Pellegreno, Ann H. Iowa Takes to the Air: 1845-1918, Vol. 1. LC 79-55458. (Illus.). (YA) 1981. 14.95 (ISBN 0-935092-01-3). Aerodrome Pr.

Sage, Leland L. A History of Iowa. 368p. 1974. 13.95 (ISBN 0-8138-0840-5). Iowa St U Pr.

Schwieder, Dorothy, ed. Patterns & Perspectives in Iowa History. 450p. 1973. 8.50x (ISBN 0-8138-1215-1). Iowa St U Pr.

Shambaugh, Benjamin F. Constitution & Records of the Claim Association of Johnson County, Iowa. Bruchey, Stuart, ed. LC 78-53565. (Development of Public Lands Law in the U. S. Ser.). 1979. Repr. of 1894 ed. lib. bdg. 15.00x (ISBN 0-405-11384-6). Arno.

Smeal, Lee. Iowa Historical & Biographical Index. LC 78-53695. (Illus.). Date not set. lib. bdg. price not set (ISBN 0-89593-180-X). Accelerated Index.

Sopp, LaVerne. Personal Name Index to the Eighteen Fifty-Six City Directories of Iowa. (Genealogy & Local History Ser.: Vol. 13). 400p. 1980. 36.00 (ISBN 0-8103-1486-X). Gale.

Vexler, R. I. Iowa Chronology & Factbook, Vol. 15. 1978. 8.50 (ISBN 0-379-16140-0). Oceana.

IOWA–IMPRINTS

Historical Records Survey: Check List of Iowa Imprints, 1838-1860. 1940. pap. 6.00 (ISBN 0-527-01912-7). Kraus Repr.

IOWA–JUVENILE LITERATURE

Brown, Don. Tell a Tale of Iowa. (Illus.). 1968. 4.95 (ISBN 0-87069-068-X); pap. 1.50 (ISBN 0-87069-067-1). Wallace-Homestead.

Carpenter, Allen. Iowa. LC 79-11802. (New Enchantment of America State Bks.). (Illus.). (gr. 4 up). 1979. PLB 10.60 (ISBN 0-516-04115-0). Childrens.

Fradin, Dennis. Iowa: In Words & Pictures. LC 79-19399. (Young People's Stories of Our States Ser.). (Illus.). 48p. (gr. 2-5). 1980. PLB 9.25 (ISBN 0-516-03915-6). Childrens.

Posten, Margaret L. This Is the Place - Iowa. 3rd ed. (Illus.). (gr. 7-10). 1970. 7.95x (ISBN 0-8138-1702-1). Iowa St U Pr.

IOWA–POLITICS AND GOVERNMENT

Allen, Edward S. Freedom in Iowa: The Role of the Iowa Civil Liberties Union. 1977. 7.50x (ISBN 0-8138-0700-X). Iowa St U Pr.

Bowman, Harold M. Administration of Iowa: A Study in Centralization. LC 70-82248. (Columbia University, Studies in the Social Sciences Ser.: No. 46). Repr. of 1903 ed. 18.50 (ISBN 0-404-51046-9). AMS Pr.

Hahn, Harlan. Urban-Rural Conflict: The Politics of Change. LC 73-127985. 288p. 1971. 18.00x (ISBN 0-8039-0080-5). Sage.

James, J. A. Constitution & Admission of Iowa into the Union. 1973. Repr. of 1900 ed. pap. 7.00 (ISBN 0-384-26742-4). Johnson Repr.

Larew, James C. A Party Reborn: The Democrats of Iowa, 1950-1974. LC 80-51855. (Illus.). 216p. 1980. 12.00x (ISBN 0-89033-002-6); pap. 6.00 (ISBN 0-686-69969-6). State Hist Iowa.

Macy, J. Institutional Beginnings in a Western State: Iowa. pap. 7.00 (ISBN 0-384-34942-0). Johnson Repr.

Rosenburg, Morton M. Iowa on the Eve of the Civil War: A Decade of Frontier Politics. LC 77-177343. (Illus.). 288p. 1972. 14.50x (ISBN 0-8061-0989-0); pap. 6.95 (ISBN 0-8061-1242-5). U of Okla Pr.

Shambaugh, Benjamin F., compiled by. The Messages & Proclamations of the Governors of Iowa, 7 vols. LC 74-19616. Repr. of 1905 ed. Set. 245.00 (ISBN 0-404-12431-3). AMS Pr.

IOWA, UNIVERSITY OF–CHILD WELFARE RESEARCH STATION

Iowa Child Welfare Research Station, State University of Iowa. Fortieth Anniversary of the Iowa Child Welfare Research Station, 1917-1957. 1959. pap. 5.00 (ISBN 0-527-01581-4). Kraus Repr.

IOWA CAVALARY–SEVENTH REGIMENT, 1862-1866

Ware, Eugene F. Indian War of 1864. Walton, Clyde C., ed. LC 60-13875. (Illus.). 1963. pap. 4.95 (ISBN 0-8032-5212-9, BB 173, Bison). U of Nebr Pr.

IOWA INFANTRY–MORMON BATTALION, 1846-1847

Cooke, Philip St. George. Exploring Southwestern Trails Eighteen Forty-Six to Eighteen Fifty-Four: The Journal of Philip St. George Cooke, the Journal of William Henry Chase Whiting & the Diaries of Francois Xavier Aubry. Bieber, Ralph P. & Bender, Averam B., eds. LC 74-7196. (Southwest Historical Ser.: Vol. 7). (Illus.). 383p. Repr. of 1938 ed. lib. bdg. 20.00x (ISBN 0-87991-302-9). Porcupine Pr.

Gudde, Erwin G. Bigler's Chronicle of the West: The Conquest of California, Discovery of Gold, & Mormon Settlement As Reflected in Henry William Bigler's Diaries. LC 62-17519. (Illus.). 1962. 15.00 (ISBN 0-520-00528-7). U of Cal Pr.

IQBAL, MUHAMMAD, SIR, 1877-1938

Brohi, A. K. Iqbal & the Concept of Islamic Socialism. pap. 0.75 (ISBN 0-686-18447-5). Kazi Pubns.

Nadvi, A. H. A. Glory of Iqbal. 6.50 (ISBN 0-686-18323-1). Kazi Pubns.

Naim, C. M., ed. Iqbal, Jinnah, & Pakistan: The Vision & the Reality. LC 79-25477. (Foreign & Comparative Studies-South Asian Ser: No. 5). 216p. (Orig.). 1979. pap. text ed. 6.50x (ISBN 0-915984-81-4). Syracuse U Foreign Comp.

IQSY

see International Years of the Quiet Sun, 1964-1965

IRA, VERMONT

Peck, Simon L. History of the Town of Ira, Vermont. LC 71-83074. (21 Photos). 1970. Repr. of 1926 ed. 15.00 (ISBN 0-8048-0875-9). C E Tuttle.

IRAN

Arasteh, A. R. Faces of Persian Youth: A Sociological Study. 1970. 30.00 (ISBN 0-685-00395-7). Heinman.

--Man & Society in Iran. 1970. 35.00 (ISBN 0-685-12031-7). Heinman.

Bartol'd, Vasilii V. Mussulman Culture. Suhrawardy, Shahid, tr. from Rus. LC 77-10749. (Studies in Islamic History: No. 3). xxviii, 146p. Repr. lib. bdg. 13.50x (ISBN 0-87991-452-1). Porcupine Pr.

Curzon, George N. Persia & the Persian Question, 2 vols. new ed. 1966. 75.00x set (ISBN 0-7146-1969-8, F Cass Co). Biblio Dist.

--Persia & the Persian Question, 2 vols. 1976. lib. bdg. 200.00 (ISBN 0-8490-2422-6). Gordon Pr.

Elwell-Sutton, L. P. Modern Iran. 1976. lib. bdg. 59.95 (ISBN 0-8490-2267-3). Gordon Pr.

Field, Henry. Contributions to the Anthropology of Iran. (Illus.). 1939. pap. 35.00 (ISBN 0-527-01889-9). Kraus Repr.

Forbis, William H. Fall of the Peacock Throne: The Story of Iran. LC 78-2125. (Illus.). 1980. 15.95 (ISBN 0-06-011301-4, HarpT). Har-Row.

Graham, Robert. Iran: The Illusion of Power. LC 78-65258. (Illus.). 272p. 1980. 17.95x (ISBN 0-312-43587-8); pap. 6.95 (ISBN 0-312-43589-4). St Martin.

Haas, William S. Iran. LC 79-181934. Repr. of 1946 ed. 21.50 (ISBN 0-404-03019-X). AMS Pr.

Harnack, Curtis. Persian Lions, Persian Lambs. (Illus.). 280p. 1981. pap. 12.00 (ISBN 0-8138-1336-0). Iowa St U Pr.

Hillman, Michael C. Hedayat's "The Blind Owl". Forty Years After. (Middle East Monograph: No. 4). 223p. 1978. pap. 6.95x (ISBN 0-292-73006-3). U of Tex Pr.

Hureau, Jean. Iran Today. 256p. 1979. 14.95 (ISBN 2-8525-8020-9, Pub. by J A Editions France). Hippocrene Bks.

Iran: Concepts of Biotic Community Conservation. (Illus.). 1976. pap. 7.50x (ISBN 2-88032-048-8, IUCN56, IUCN). Unipub.

Knanishu, Joseph. About Persia & Its People. LC 77-87649. Repr. of 1899 ed. 24.00 (ISBN 0-404-16418-8). AMS Pr.

Millett, Kate. Going to Iran. (Illus.). 1981. 13.95 (ISBN 0-698-11095-1). Coward.

Millspaugh, A. C. The American Task in Persia. LC 73-6293. (The Middle East Ser.). Repr. of 1925 ed. 19.00 (ISBN 0-405-05350-9). Arno.

Namikawa, Banri. Iran. LC 73-79762. (This Beautiful World Ser.: Vol. 45). (Illus.). 130p. (Orig.). 1973. pap. 4.95 (ISBN 0-87011-213-9). Kodansha.

O'Donnell, Terence. Garden of the Brave in War: Recollections of Iran. 1980. 10.95 (ISBN 0-89919-016-2). HM.

Rudkin, Anthony & Butcher, Irene, eds. Book World Directory of Arab Counties, Turkey & Iran. 1981. text ed. 78.00 (ISBN 0-7201-0830-6, Pub. by Mansell England). Merrimack Bk Serv.

--Book World Directory of the Arab Countries, Turkey & Iran. 1981. 85.00 (ISBN 0-8103-1185-2, Pub. by Mansell England). Gale.

Shabaz, A. D. Land of the Lion & the Sun: Persia. 1977. lib. bdg. 59.95 (ISBN 0-8490-2125-1). Gordon Pr.

Waring, Edward S. A Tour to Sheeraz by the Route of Kazroon & Feerozabad. LC 73-6309. (The Middle East Ser.). Repr. of 1807 ed. 19.00 (ISBN 0-405-05370-3). Arno.

Wilson, Arnold T. Persia. 1976. lib. bdg. 69.95 (ISBN 0-8490-2421-8). Gordon Pr.

IRAN–ANTIQUITIES

Bokonyi, S. The Animal Remains from Four Sites in the Kermanshah Valley, Iran: Asiab, Sarab, Dehsavar & Sighbid. 1977. 10.00x (ISBN 0-904531-88-0, Pub. by BAR). State Mutual Bk.

Fukai, Shinji. Ceramics of Ancient Persia. (Illus.). 222p. 1981. 95.00 (ISBN 0-8348-1523-0). Weatherhill.

--Persian Glass. LC 77-23736. (Illus.). 1977. 50.00 (ISBN 0-8348-1515-X). Weatherhill.

Herzfeld, E. E. Archaeological History of Iran. 1976. lib. bdg. 59.95 (ISBN 0-8490-1446-8). Gordon Pr.

Hicks, Jim. The Persians. (Emergence of Man Ser.). (Illus.). 1975. 9.95 (ISBN 0-8094-1297-7). Time-Life.

Hume, Gary W. The Ladizian: An Industry of the Asian Chopper-Chopping Tool Complex in Iranian Baluchistan. (Illus.). 355p. 1976. 12.00 (ISBN 0-8059-2091-9). Dorrance.

Jackson, Abraham V. Persia Past & Present. LC 76-149392. (Illus.). Repr. of 1906 ed. 57.50 (ISBN 0-404-09014-1). AMS Pr.

Johnson, Gregory A. Local Exchange & Early State Development in Southwestern Iran. (Anthropological Papers: No. 51). (Illus.). 1973. pap. 4.00x (ISBN 0-932206-49-2). U Mich Mus Anthro.

Lamberg-Karlovsky, C. C. Excavations at Tepe Yahya, Iran, 1967-1969: Progress Report No. 1. LC 74-143902. (ASPR Bulletin: No. 27). 1970. pap. text ed. 12.00 (ISBN 0-87365-528-1). Peabody Harvard.

Matheson, Sylvia A. Persia: An Archaeological Guide. new ed. (Illus.). 360p. 1976. pap. 13.95 (ISBN 0-571-04888-9, Pub. by Faber & Faber). Merrimack Bk Serv.

Moorey, P. R. Ancient Persian Bronzes in the Adam Collection. 208p. 1974. 36.00 (ISBN 0-571-10216-6, Pub. by Faber & Faber). Merrimack Bk Serv.

--Kish Excavations 1923-1933: With a Microfiche Catalogue of the Objects of the Ashmolean Museum. (Illus.). 1978. 49.50x (ISBN 0-19-813191-7). Oxford U Pr.

Oriental Institute. Persepolis & Ancient Iran. LC 76-7942. 1976. 1 color & 11 black & white fiches incl. 50.00 (ISBN 0-226-69493-3, Chicago Visual Lib); 1 color & 11 black-&-white fiches incl. U of Chicago Pr.

Schmidt, Erich F. Excavations at Tepe Hissar, Damghan. (Illus.). 478p. 1936. 30.00 (ISBN 0-686-11911-8). Univ Mus of U PA.

Stein, Mark A. Old Routes of Western Iran: Narrative of an Archaeological Journey. (Illus.). Repr. of 1940 ed. lib. bdg. 29.50x (ISBN 0-8371-2256-2, STOR). Greenwood.

Stronach, David. Pasargadae: A Report on the Excavations Conducted by the British Institute of Persian Studies from 1961 to 1963. (Illus.). 1978. 79.00x (ISBN 0-19-813190-9). Oxford U Pr.

Vidyarthi, L. P. The Sacred Complex of Kashi. 1979. text ed. 17.50x (ISBN 0-391-01856-6). Humanities.

Watson, Patty Jo. Archaeological Ethnography in Western Iran. LC 78-5853. (Viking Fund Publications in Anthropology Ser.: No. 57). 1979. pap. 9.95x (ISBN 0-8165-0577-2). U of Ariz Pr.

Wright, Henry T. Archaeological Investigations in Northeastern Xuzestan, 1976. (Technical Reports Ser.: No. 10). (Illus., Orig., Contributions 5 in research reports in archaeology). 1979. pap. 6.00x (ISBN 0-932206-80-8). U Mich Mus Anthro.

IRAN–BIBLIOGRAPHY

Harvard University Library. Harvard University Library Catalogue of Arabic, Persian & Ottoman Turkish Bks, 5 Vols. LC 68-29108. 1968. Set. text ed. 195.00x (ISBN 0-674-10050-6). Harvard U Pr.

Pearson, James D., ed. A Bibliography of Pre-Islamic Persia. LC 75-306315. 328p. 1975. 42.00 (ISBN 0-7201-0365-7, Pub. by Mansell England). Merrimack Bk Serv.

Schwab, M. Bibliographie de la Perse. (Fr.). 1876. pap. text ed. 9.50x (ISBN 90-6041-062-9). Humanities.

U. S. Library Of Congress - General Reference And Bibliography Division. Iran: A Selected & Annotated Bibliography. LC 68-55131. (Illus.). 1968. Repr. of 1951 ed. lib. bdg. 14.00x (ISBN 0-8371-0718-0, IRSB). Greenwood.

Wilson, Arnold T. Bibliography of Persia. 1976. lib. bdg. 59.95 (ISBN 0-8490-1500-6). Gordon Pr.

IRAN–BIOGRAPHY

Arasteh, A. R. Rumi the Persian. 1965. pap. 7.50 (ISBN 0-686-51193-X). Heinman.

Davis, F. Hadland, ed. Jami, Persian Mystic & Poet. 103p. 1981. pap. 3.25 (ISBN 0-88004-003-3). Sunwise Turn.

DeFelice, Gerald T. Death in Egypt. 400p. (Orig.). 1981. pap. 29.95 (ISBN 0-686-30237-0). Une Pub.

Hedayat, Sadeq. Haji Agha: Portrait of an Iranian Confidence Man. Wickens, G. M., tr. from Persian. (Middle East Monograph: No. 6). 130p. (Orig.). 1979. pap. text ed. 4.95x (ISBN 0-292-73010-1, Pub by Ctr Mid East Stud). U of Tex Pr.

O'Donnell, Terence. Garden of the Brave in War. LC 80-14656. 1980. 10.95 (ISBN 0-89919-016-2). Ticknor & Fields.

IRAN–COMMERCE

Major Companies of Iran 1979-80. 1979. 55.00x (ISBN 0-685-94072-1). Nichols Pub.

IRAN–DESCRIPTION AND TRAVEL

Barbaro, Josafa & Contarini, Amrogio. Travels to Tana & Persia. Thomas, William, tr. (Hakluyt Soc. First Ser.: No. 49). 1963. 23.50 (ISBN 0-8337-0162-2). B Franklin.

Beny, Roloff. Iran: Elements of Destiny. LC 78-53014. (Illus.). 1978. 50.00 (ISBN 0-89696-000-5). Everest Hse.

Chardin, John. Sir John Chardin's Travels in Persia. LC 76-181928. (BCL Ser.: No. I). Repr. of 1927 ed. 24.50 (ISBN 0-404-01449-6). AMS Pr.

Ferrier, J. P. Caravan Journeys & Wanderings in Persia, Afghanistan, Turkistan & Beloochistan. (Oxford in Asia Historical Reprints Ser.). (Illus.). 1977. 26.00x (ISBN 0-19-577214-8). Oxford U Pr.

Forbes-Leith, F. A. Checkmate: Fighting Tradition in Central Persia. LC 73-6279. (The Middle East Ser.). Repr. of 1927 ed. 15.00 (ISBN 0-405-05335-5). Arno.

Fraser, James B. A Winter's Journey (Tatar) from Constantinople to Tehran, 2 vols. in 1. LC 73-6281. (The Middle East Ser.). Repr. of 1838 ed. 48.00 (ISBN 0-405-05339-8). Arno.

Hedin, Sven A. Overland to India, 2 Vols. 1910. Set. lib. bdg. 68.50x (ISBN 0-8371-3894-9, HEOI). Greenwood.

Helms, Cynthia. An Ambassador's Wife in Iran. LC 80-25090. (Illus.). 284p. 1981. 12.95 (ISBN 0-396-07881-8). Dodd.

Herbert, Sir Thomas. A Relation of Some Yeares Travaile Begunne Anno 1626, into Afrique & the Greater Asia. LC 76-25706. (English Experience Ser.: No. 349). 1971. Repr. of 1634 ed. 42.00 (ISBN 90-221-0349-8). Walter J Johnson.

Hobson, Sarah. Masquerade: An Adventure in Iran. Orig. Title: Through Persia in Disguise. (Illus.). 1979. 10.00 (ISBN 0-89733-013-7). Academy Chi Ltd.

Iran Pocket Guide. (Illus.). 1974. pap. 1.25x (ISBN 0-686-19965-0). Intl Learn Syst.

Issari, Mohammed Ali & Paul, Doris A. A Picture of Persia. LC 76-678. 1977. 15.00 (ISBN 0-682-48410-5, University). Exposition.

Jackson, Abraham V. Persia Past & Present. LC 76-149392. (Illus.). Repr. of 1906 ed. 57.50 (ISBN 0-404-09014-1). AMS Pr.

Kinneir, John M. A Geographical Memoir of the Persian Empire. LC 73-6283. (The Middle East Ser.). Repr. of 1813 ed. 31.00 (ISBN 0-405-05341-X). Arno.

Maitra, K. M., tr. Persian Embassy to China. 1970. Repr. of 1934 ed. 9.50 (ISBN 0-8188-0102-6). Paragon.

Mirza, Youel B. When I Was a Boy in Persia. LC 77-87650. (Illus.). Repr. of 1920 ed. 20.00 (ISBN 0-404-16419-6). AMS Pr.

The Nagel Travel Guide to Iran. (Nagel Travel Guide Ser.). (Illus.). 392p. 1974. 38.00 (ISBN 2-8263-0454-2). Hippocrene Bks.

Sheil, Mary. Glimpses of Life & Manners in Persia. LC 73-6299. (The Middle East Ser.). Repr. of 1856 ed. 25.00 (ISBN 0-405-05356-8). Arno.

Sherley, Anthony. Sir A. Sherley His Relation of Travels into Persia. LC 74-80232. (English Experience Ser.: No. 695). 140p. 1974. Repr. of 1613 ed. 15.00 (ISBN 90-221-0695-0). Walter J Johnson.

Stark, Freya. The Valley of the Assassins: & Other Persian Travels. 1978. Repr. of 1934 ed. lib. bdg. 20.00 (ISBN 0-8482-6381-2). Norwood Edns.

Stein, Mark A. Old Routes of Western Iran: Narrative of an Archaeological Journey. (Illus.). Repr. of 1940 ed. lib. bdg. 29.50x (ISBN 0-8371-2256-2, STOR). Greenwood.

Sykes, P. M., ed. The Glory of the Shia World. LC 73-6302. (The Middle East Ser.). Repr. of 1910 ed. 18.00 (ISBN 0-405-05362-2). Arno.

Vambery, Arminius. Arminius Vambery: His Life & Adventures. LC 73-6307. (The Middle East Ser.). Repr. of 1883 ed. 21.00 (ISBN 0-405-05369-X). Arno.

IRAN–ECONOMIC CONDITIONS

Amuzegar, Jahangir. Iran: An Economic Profile. LC 77-5286. 1977. 12.95 (ISBN 0-916808-12-2). Mid East Inst.

Amuzegar, Jahangir & Fekrat, M. Ali. Iran: Economic Development Under Dualistic Conditions. LC 79-153044. (Publications of the Center for Middle Eastern Studies Ser.: No. 7). 1971. 9.50x (ISBN 0-226-01754-0). U of Chicago Pr.

Arab World Business Guides. Nineteen Eighty Businessman's Guide to the Arab World & Iran: 1980. 1980. pap. 30.00 (ISBN 0-931000-13-0). Guides Multinatl Busn.

Baldwin, George B. Planning & Development in Iran. LC 67-18377. 224p. 1967. 14.50x (ISBN 0-8018-0052-8). Johns Hopkins.

Bricault, G. C. Major Companies of Iran 1978-1979. 260p. 1978. pap. 40.00x (ISBN 0-86010-109-6). Intl Pubns Serv.

Economic Development & the Village in Iran: Prospects for an Alternative Approach. 26p. 1981. pap. 5.00 (ISBN 92-808-0149-X, TUNU 118, UNU). Unipub.

Employment & Income Policies for Iran. vi, 100p. 1973. 6.85 (ISBN 92-2-100192-X). Intl Labour Office.

Fesharaki, Fereidun. Development of the Iranian Oil Industry: International & Domestic Aspects. LC 75-19782. (Special Studies). (Illus.). 300p. 1976. text ed. 31.95 (ISBN 0-275-55600-X). Praeger.

Hallak, J., et al. The Financial Aspects of First-Level Education in Iran. LC 72-93794. (Financing Educational Systems Ser.). (Illus.). 59p. (Orig.). 1973. pap. 4.50 (ISBN 92-803-1051-8, U272, UNESCO). Unipub.

Issawi, Charles. Economic History of Iran, 1800-1914. Polk, William R., ed. LC 70-153883. (Publications of the Center for Middle Eastern Studies Ser: No. 8). 1971. 17.50x (ISBN 0-226-38606-6). U of Chicago Pr.

Johnson, Gail C. High Level Manpower in Iran: From Hidden Conflict to Crisis. LC 79-21419. (Praeger Special Studies Ser.). 136p. 1980. 24.50 (ISBN 0-03-053366-X). Praeger.

Katouzian, Homa. The Political Economy of Modern Iran: Despotism & Pseudo-Modernism, 1926-1979. 448p. 1981. 40.00x (ISBN 0-8147-4577-6); pap. 19.50x (ISBN 0-8147-4578-4). NYU Pr.

Kedourie, Elie & Haim, Sylvia G., eds. Towards a Modern Iran: Studies in Thought, Politics & Society. 1980. 29.50x (ISBN 0-7146-3145-0, F Cass Co). Biblio Dist.

Looney. Economic Origins of the Iranian Revolution. (Pergamon Policy Studies). 225p. Date not set. text ed. price not set (ISBN 0-08-025950-2). Pergamon.

Mahdi, Ali-Akbar. A Selected Bibliography on Political Economy of Iran. (Public Administration Ser.: Bibliography P-598). 104p. 1980. pap. 15.25 (ISBN 0-686-29067-4). Vance Biblios.

Major Companies of Iran. 1977. softcover 26.00 (ISBN 0-531-03273-6). Watts.

Millspaugh, A. C. The American Task in Persia. LC 73-6293. (The Middle East Ser.). Repr. of 1925 ed. 19.00 (ISBN 0-405-05350-9). Arno.

Millspaugh, Arthur. Americans in Persia. LC 76-9837. (Politics & Strategy of World War II Ser.). 1976. Repr. of 1946 ed. lib. bdg. 27.50 (ISBN 0-306-70764-0). Da Capo.

Mossavar-Rahmane, Bijan. Energy Policy in Iran: Domestic Choices & International Implications. LC 80-27995. (PPS on Science & Technnology Ser.). (Illus.). 160p. 1981. 15.00 (ISBN 0-08-026293-7). Pergamon.

Motamen, Homa. Expenditure of Oil Revenue: An Optimal Control Approach with Application to the Iranian Economy. LC 29-20567. 1979. 27.50x (ISBN 0-312-27605-2). St Martin.

IRAN–FOREIGN RELATIONS

Cottrell, Alvin J. & Dougherty, James E. Iran's Quest for Security: U. S. Arms Transfers & the Nuclear Option. LC 77-80298. (Foreign Policy Reports Ser.). 1977. 5.00 (ISBN 0-89549-004-8). Inst Foreign Policy Anal.

Elwell-Sutton, Laurence P. Persian Oil: A Study in Power Politics. LC 75-6469. (History & Politics of Oil Ser). 343p. 1976. Repr. of 1955 ed. 19.50 (ISBN 0-88355-288-4). Hyperion Conn.

Entner, Marvin L. Russo-Persian Commercial Relations, 1828-1914. LC 65-64001. (U of Fla. Social Science Monographs: No. 28). (Illus.). 1965. pap. 3.00 (ISBN 0-8130-0073-4). U Presses Fla.

Grayson, Benson L. United States-Iranian Relations. LC 81-40305. 194p. (Orig.). 1981. lib. bdg. 19.50 (ISBN 0-8191-1797-8); pap. text ed. 9.50 (ISBN 0-8191-1796-X). U Pr of Amer.

Lenczowski, George. Russia & the West in Iran, 1918-1948: A Study in Big Power Rivalry. LC 68-23307. (Illus.). 1968. Repr. of 1949 ed. lib. bdg. 26.50x (ISBN 0-8371-0144-1, LERW). Greenwood.

McManus, Doyle. Free at Last! The Complete Story of the Hostages' 444- Day Ordeal & the Secret Negotiations to Set Them Free. (Illus., Orig.). 1981. pap. 3.50 (ISBN 0-451-11054-4, AE1054, Sig). NAL.

Millspaugh, Arthur. Americans in Persia. LC 76-9837. (Politics & Strategy of World War II Ser.). 1976. Repr. of 1946 ed. lib. bdg. 27.50 (ISBN 0-306-70764-0). Da Capo.

Moody, Sid. Four Hundred Forty-Four Days: The American Hostage Story. Date not set. 8.95 (ISBN 0-8317-4570-3, Mayflower Bks). Smith Pubs.

Pelletier, Jean & Adams, Claude. The Canadian Caper. LC 81-38365. (Illus.). 264p. 1981. Repr. 12.95 (ISBN 0-688-00756-2). Morrow.

Ramazani, Rouhollah K. Foreign Policy of Iran, 1500-1941: A Developing Nation in World Affairs. LC 66-12469. 1966. 12.95x (ISBN 0-8139-0200-2). U Pr of Va.

--Iran's Foreign Policy, 1941-1973: A Study of Foreign Policy in Modernizing Nations. LC 74-16467. 1975. 20.00x (ISBN 0-8139-0594-X). U Pr of Va.

Rezun, Miron. The Soviet Union & Iran, No. 8. (Collection De Relations Internationales Ser.). 425p. 1981. 39.50x (ISBN 90-286-2621-2). Sijthoff & Noordhoff.

Rubin, Barry. Paved with Good Intentions: The American Experience & Iran. 426p. 1981. pap. 5.95 (ISBN 0-14-005964-4). Penguin.

Stempel, John D. Inside the Iranian Revolution. LC 81-47564. 352p. 1981. 17.50x (ISBN 0-253-14200-8). Ind U Pr.

Wead, R. Douglas. The Iran Crisis. (Orig.). 1980. pap. 2.95 (ISBN 0-88270-433-8). Logos.

IRAN–HISTORICAL GEOGRAPHY

Herbert, Thomas. Travels in Persia, Sixteen Twenty-Seven to Sixteen Twenty-Nine. Foster, William, ed. LC 78-39468. (Select Bibliographies Reprint Series). 1972. Repr. of 1929 ed. 19.75 (ISBN 0-8369-9912-6). Arno.

Hole, Frank, et al. Prehistory & Human Ecology of the Deh Luran Plain: An Early Village Sequence from Khuzistan, Iran. new ed. (Memoirs Ser.: No. 1). (Illus.). 1969. pap. 8.00x (ISBN 0-932206-63-8). U Mich Mus Anthro.

IRAN–HISTORY

Ahsan, M. M. Social Life Under the Abbasids. (Arab Background Ser.). (Illus.). 1979. text ed. 33.00x (ISBN 0-582-78079-9). Longman.

Algar, Hamid. Religion & State in Iran, Seventeen Eighty-Five to Nineteen Six: The Role of the 'Ulama in the Qajar Period. LC 72-79959. (Near Eastern Center, UCLA). 1969. 22.00x (ISBN 0-520-04100-3). U of Cal Pr.

Amirsadeghi, Hossein, ed. Twentieth Century Iran. LC 77-9569. (Illus.). 1977. text ed. 35.50x (ISBN 0-8419-0325-5). Holmes & Meier.

Atkin, Muriel. Russia & Iran, Seventeen Eighty to Eighteen Twenty-Eight. LC 80-10391. (Illus.). 1980. 20.00x (ISBN 0-8166-0924-1). U of Minn Pr.

Banani, Amin. The Modernization of Iran, 1921-1941. (Illus.). 1961. 10.50x (ISBN 0-8047-0050-8). Stanford U Pr.

Bausani, Alessandro. The Persians. 1971. 9.95 (ISBN 0-236-17760-5, Pub. by Paul Elek). Merrimack Bk Serv.

Benjamin, S. G. The Story of Persia. 1977. lib. bdg. 59.95 (ISBN 0-8490-2685-7). Gordon Pr.

Benjamin, Samuel G. Persia. LC 70-39191. (Select Bibliographies Reprint Ser.). 1887. 22.00 (ISBN 0-8369-6793-3). Arno.

Bosworth, C. E. The Medieval History of Iran, Afghanistan & Central Asia. 374p. 1980. 75.00x (ISBN 0-86078-000-7, Pub. by Variorum England). State Mutual Bk.

Boyle, J. A., ed. Persia: History & Heritage. (Illus.). 1978. text ed. 21.00x (ISBN 0-04-950017-1); pap. 13.50 (ISBN 0-04-950018-X). Allen Unwin.

Browne, Edward G. Persian Revolution of 1905-09. 1966. Repr. 30.00x (ISBN 0-7146-1968-X, F Cass Co). Biblio Dist.

Brydges, Harford J. The Dynasty of the Kajars. LC 73-6272. (The Middle East Ser.). Repr. of 1833 ed. 35.00 (ISBN 0-405-05327-4). Arno.

Budge, Ernest A. The Histories of Rabban Hormizd the Persian & Rabban Bar-'Idta, 3 pts. in 2 vols. LC 73-18847. (Luzac's Semitic Text & Translation Ser.: Nos. 9, 10, 11). Repr. of 1902 ed. 46.00 set (ISBN 0-404-11336-2). AMS Pr.

Busse, Heribert, tr. History of Persia Under Qajar Rule. LC 74-183229. 494p. 1972. 27.50x (ISBN 0-231-03197-1). Columbia U Pr.

Cambridge History of Iran. Incl. Vol. 1. The Land of Iran. Fisher, W. B., ed. 1968. 62.00 (ISBN 0-521-06935-1); Vol. 4. Frye, R. N., ed. 1975. 62.00 (ISBN 0-521-20093-8); Vol. 5. The Saljug & Mongol Periods. Boyle, J. A., ed. LC 67-12845. 1968. 62.00 (ISBN 0-521-06936-X). LC 67-12845. (Illus.). Cambridge U Pr.

Cameron, George G. History of Early Iran. (Midway Reprint Ser.). 1976. pap. 12.00x (ISBN 0-226-09226-7). U of Chicago Pr.

Church, Alfred J. The Story of the Persian War: From Herodotus. LC 77-6999. 1977. Repr. of 1888 ed. lib. bdg. 35.00 (ISBN 0-89341-250-3). Longwood Pr.

Frye, Richard N. Islamic Iran & Central Asia (7th-12th Centuries) 380p. 1980. 75.00x (ISBN 0-86078-044-9, Pub. by Variorum England). State Mutual Bk.

Gail, Marzieh. Persia & the Victorians. 1977. lib. bdg. 59.95 (ISBN 0-8490-2423-4). Gordon Pr.

Geiger, Wilhelm & Kuhn, Ernst, eds. Grundriss der iranischen Philologie, 2 vols. 1769p. 1974. Repr. of 1904 ed. 279.95x (ISBN 3-11-002491-8). De Gruyter.

Ghirshman, R. Iran. (Illus.). 1978. pap. 3.95 (ISBN 0-14-020239-0, Pelican). Penguin.

Irving, Clive. Crossroads of Civilization: Three Thousand Years of Persian History. (Illus.). 1979. text ed. 21.50x (ISBN 0-06-493238-9). B&N.

Keddie, Nikki R. & Yann, Richard. Roots of Revolution: An Interpretive History of Modern Iran. LC 81-40438. (Illus.). 316p. 1981. text ed. 25.00 (ISBN 0-300-02606-4); pap. 5.95 (ISBN 0-300-02611-0, YF-24). Yale U Pr.

Khan, M. S. Studies in Miskawayh's Contemporary History (340-369 A. H.) LC 79-26702. 300p. (Orig.). 1980. 22.75 (ISBN 0-8357-0499-8, SS-00111). Univ Microfilms.

Krusinski, J. History of the Late Revolution in Persia, 2 vols. in 1. LC 73-6285. (The Middle East Ser.). Repr. of 1740 ed. 34.00 (ISBN 0-405-05342-8). Arno.

Lambton, A. K. Theory & Practice in Medieval Persian Government. 332p. 1980. 75.00x (ISBN 0-86078-067-8, Pub. by Variorum England). State Mutual Bk.

Lenczowski, George. Russia & the West in Iran, 1918-1948: A Study in Big Power Rivalry. LC 68-23307. (Illus.). 1968. Repr. of 1949 ed. lib. bdg. 26.50x (ISBN 0-8371-0144-1, LERW). Greenwood.

Lenczowski, George C., ed. Iran Under the Pahlavis. LC 76-26773. (Publication Ser.: No. 164). (Illus.). 1978. 19.95 (ISBN 0-8179-6641-2). Hoover Inst Pr.

Le Strange, Guy. The Lands of the Eastern Caliphate. LC 77-180355. (Cambridge Geographical Ser.). Repr. of 1905 ed. 41.50 (ISBN 0-404-56287-6). AMS Pr.

--Mesopotamia & Persia Under the Mongols in the Fourteenth Century A.D. (Studies in Islamic History: No. 18). 104p. Repr. of 1903 ed. lib. bdg. 13.50x (ISBN 0-87991-108-5). Porcupine Pr.

Lockhart, Laurence. Nadir Shah: A Critical Study Based Mainly Upon Contemporary Sources. LC 78-180358. Repr. of 1938 ed. 28.45 (ISBN 0-404-56290-6). AMS Pr.

Mather, Maurice W. & Hewitt, Joseph. Xenophon's Anabasis, Bks. 1-4. (Illus.). (YA) 1976. pap. 10.95x (ISBN 0-8061-1347-2). U of Okla Pr.

Minorsky, Vladimir. The Turks, Iran & the Caucasus in the Middle Ages. 368p. 1980. 69.00x (ISBN 0-86078-028-7, Pub. by Variorum England). State Mutual Bk.

Moore, Diane M. Iran: In a Persian Market. LC 79-93424. 118p. (Orig.). 1980. pap. 7.95 (ISBN 0-686-61402-X). D M Moore.

Nixon, Anthony. The Three English Brothers Sir T. Sherley His Travels, Sir A. Sherley His Ambassage to the Christian Princes, Master R. Sherley His Wars Against the Turkes. LC 72-26473. (English Experience Ser.: No. 270). 80p. 1970. Repr. of 1607 ed. 11.50 (ISBN 90-221-0270-X). Walter J Johnson.

Noeldeke, Theodor. The Iranian National Epic. Bogadov, Leonid T., tr. LC 79-13091. 161p. Repr. of 1930 ed. lib. bdg. 15.00x (ISBN 0-87991-460-2). Porcupine Pr.

Perry, John R. Karim Khan Zand: A History of Iran, 1747-1779. LC 78-26553. (Publications of the Center for Middle Eastern Studies: No. 12). (Illus.). 1979. lib. bdg. 12.50x (ISBN 0-226-66098-2). U of Chicago Pr.

Porada, Edith & Dyson, R. H. Ancient Iran. (Art of the World Library). 6.95 (ISBN 0-517-50828-1). Crown.

Rogers, Robert W. A History of Ancient Persia. (Illus.). 393p. 1980. Repr. of 1929 ed. lib. bdg. 75.00 (ISBN 0-89984-428-6). Century Bookbindery.

Ross, E. Denison. The Persians. 1978. Repr. of 1931 ed. lib. bdg. 45.00 (ISBN 0-8492-2374-1). R West.

Ross, E. Denison, Jr. The Persians. 142p. 1980. Repr. lib. bdg. 30.00 (ISBN 0-89987-713-3). Darby Bks.

Savory, Roger M. Iran Under the Safavids. LC 78-73817. (Illus.). 300p. 1980. 34.50 (ISBN 0-521-22483-7). Cambridge U Pr.

Shaban, M. A. The Abbasid Revolution. 1979. 32.00 (ISBN 0-521-07849-0); pap. 11.95 (ISBN 0-521-29534-3). Cambridge U Pr.

Shuster, William M. Strangling of Persia: Story of the European Diplomacy & Oriental Intrigue That Resulted in the Denationalization of Twelve Million Mohammedans, a Personal Narrative. LC 69-10154. 1969. Repr. of 1912 ed. lib. bdg. 24.50x (ISBN 0-8371-0224-3, SHSP). Greenwood.

Smith, John M., Jr. History of the Sarbadar Dynasty, 1336-1381, A. D., & Its Sources. LC 68-54393. (Near & Middle East Monographs). (Illus.). 1970. text ed. 74.00x (ISBN 90-2791-714-0). Mouton.

Sterling, Martie & Sterling, Robin. Last Flight from Iran. 272p. (Orig.). 1981. pap. 2.50 (ISBN 0-553-20005-4). Bantam.

Stevens, Roger. The Land of the Great Sophy. LC 78-73476. (Illus.). 1979. 11.95 (ISBN 0-8008-4540-4). Taplinger.

Sykes, Perry. A History of Persia. 1976. lib. bdg. 69.95 (ISBN 0-8490-1982-6). Gordon Pr.

Tynianov, Iurri N. Death & Diplomacy in Persia. Brown, A., tr. from Rus. LC 74-10092. (Illus.). 357p. 1974. Repr. of 1938 ed. 22.50 (ISBN 0-88355-178-0). Hyperion Conn.

Upton, Joseph M. History of Modern Iran: An Interpretation. LC 60-7207. (Middle Eastern Monographs Ser: No. 2). 1960. pap. 4.50x (ISBN 0-674-39900-5). Harvard U Pr.

Vlin, Robert. Iran: A People in Revolution. (Illus.). Date not set. price not set (ISBN 0-916650-14-6); pap. price not set (ISBN 0-916650-15-4). Banner Pr IL.

Waldman, Marilyn R. Toward a Theory of Historical Narrative: A Case Study in Perso-Islamicate Historiography. LC 79-886. 1980. 15.00x (ISBN 0-8142-0297-7). Ohio St U Pr.

Wilber, Donald N. Iran-Past & Present. 8th ed. 1976. 23.00x (ISBN 0-691-03108-8); pap. 6.95 (ISBN 0-691-00021-2). Princeton U Pr.

--Riza Shah Pahlavi: The Resurrection & Reconstruction of Iran 1878-1944. LC 74-34518. 1975. 15.00 (ISBN 0-682-48206-4, University). Exposition.

IRAN–HISTORY–TO 640

Alexander, William. The Tragedie of Darius. LC 72-6936. (English Experience Ser.: No. 293). 80p. Repr. of 1603 ed. 11.50 (ISBN 90-221-0293-9). Walter J Johnson.

Altheim, Franz & Stiehl, Ruth. Geschichte Mittelasiens im Altertum. (Illus., Ger.). 1970. 164.70x (ISBN 3-11-002677-5). De Gruyter.

Arrian. Anabasis of Alexander, Indica, 2 Vols. (Loeb Classical Library: No. 236, 269). 11.00x ea. Vol. 1, Bks. 1-4 (ISBN 0-674-99260-1). Vol. 2, Bks. 5-7 (ISBN 0-674-99297-0). Harvard U Pr.

Cambridge History of Iran. Incl. Vol. 1. The Land of Iran. Fisher, W. B., ed. 1968. 62.00 (ISBN 0-521-06935-1); Vol. 4. Frye, R. N., ed. 1975. 62.00 (ISBN 0-521-20093-8); Vol. 5. The Saljug & Mongol Periods. Boyle, J. A., ed. LC 67-12845. 1968. 62.00 (ISBN 0-521-06936-X). LC 67-12845. (Illus.). Cambridge U Pr.

Cameron, George C. History of Early Iran. 1976. lib. bdg. 69.95 (ISBN 0-8490-1972-9). Gordon Pr.

Cameron, George G. History of Early Iran. LC 68-57592. (Illus.). 1968. Repr. of 1936 ed. lib. bdg. 19.50x (ISBN 0-8371-0338-X, CAEI). Greenwood.

Cao Xueqin. The Persian Expedition. rev. ed. Warner, Rex, tr. (Classics Ser.). 1950. pap. 3.50 (ISBN 0-14-044007-0). Penguin.

Cassin-Scott, Jack. The Greek & Persian Armies. (Men-at-Arms Ser.). (Illus.). 48p. 1978. pap. 7.95 (ISBN 0-85045-271-6). Hippocrene Bks.

Church, Alfred J. The Story of the Persian War: From Herodotus. 1979. Repr. of 1881 ed. lib. bdg. 20.00 (ISBN 0-8482-7577-2). Norwood Edns.

Dicks, Brian. The Ancient Persians: How They Lived & Worked. 1979. 14.95 (ISBN 0-7153-7711-6). David & Charles.

Frye, Richard N., ed. Sasanian Remains from Qasr-i Abu Nasr: Seals, Sealings, & Coins. LC 72-80657. (Iranian Ser: No. 1). (Illus.). 224p. 1973. 12.50x (ISBN 0-674-78960-1). Harvard U Pr.

Hicks, Jim. The Persians. (Emergence of Man Ser.). (Illus.). 1975. 9.95 (ISBN 0-8094-1297-7). Time-Life.

O'Kane, John, tr. from Persian. The Ship of Sulaiman. LC 70-186605. 250p. 1972. 17.50x (ISBN 0-231-03654-X). Columbia U Pr.

Olmstead, Arthur T. History of the Persian Empire. LC 48-7317. (Illus.). 1959. pap. 7.95 (ISBN 0-226-62777-2, P36, Phoen). U of Chicago Pr.

Rogers, Robert W. A History of Ancient Persia. facsimile ed. LC 70-168502. (Select Bibliographies Reprint Ser). Repr. of 1929 ed. 35.00 (ISBN 0-8369-5942-6). Arno.

Xenohpon. The Historie of Xenophon. Bingham, J., tr. LC 74-80234. (English Experience Ser.: No. 704). 142p. 1974. Repr. of 1623 ed. 25.00 (ISBN 90-221-0704-3). Walter J Johnson.

Xenophon. March up Country: A Modern Translation of the Anabasis. Rouse, W. H., tr. 1958. pap. 2.45 (ISBN 0-472-06095-3, 95, AA). U of Mich Pr.

IRAN–INTELLECTUAL LIFE

Chelkowski, Peter J., ed. Ta'ziyeh: Ritual & Drama in Iran. LC 78-20543. 1979. 28.50x (ISBN 0-8147-1375-0). NYU Pr.

IRAN–JUVENILE LITERATURE

Fox, Paula. Portrait of Ivan. LC 74-93085. (Illus.). (gr. 5-7). 1969. 7.95 (ISBN 0-87888-015-1). Bradbury Pr.

Hinckley, Helen. The Land & People of Iran. rev. ed. LC 70-37733. (Portraits of the Nations Series). (Illus.). 1973. 8.79 (ISBN 0-397-31202-4, JBL-J). Har-Row.

Miller, William M. Tales of Persia: A Book for Children. LC 79-51273. (Illus.). 145p. (gr. 2-8). 1979. 5.00 (ISBN 0-8059-2635-6). Dorrance.

U. S. Committee For UNICEF. Hi Neighbor Book No. 4: Guinea, India, Iran, Mexico, Portugal. (Illus.). (gr. 4-6). 4.95 (ISBN 0-8038-2981-7); pap. 2.00 (ISBN 0-8038-2980-9). Hastings.

Wiedel, Janine. Looking at Iran. LC 78-6038. (Looking at Other Countries Ser.). (Illus.). (gr. 4-7). 1979. 7.95 (ISBN 0-397-31797-2). Lippincott.

IRAN–POLITICS AND GOVERNMENT

Akhavi, Shahrough. Religion & Politics in Contemporary Iran: Clergy-State Relations in the Pahlavi Period. LC 79-22084. 1980. lib. bdg. 29.00 (ISBN 0-87395-408-4); pap. 9.95 (ISBN 0-87395-456-4). State U NY Pr.

Albert, David H. Tell the American People: Perspectives on the Iranian Revolution. rev. ed. LC 80-83577. 1980. 14.95 (ISBN 0-86571-001-5); pap. 4.95 (ISBN 0-86571-003-1). New Soc Pubs.

Algar, Hamid, tr. from Persian. Constitution of the Islamic Republic of Iran. 94p. 1980. 7.95 (ISBN 0-933782-07-1); pap. 2.95 (ISBN 0-933782-02-0). Mizan Pr.

Amirsadeghi, Hossein, ed. Twentieth Century Iran. LC 77-9569. (Illus.). 1977. text ed. 35.50x (ISBN 0-8419-0325-5). Holmes & Meier.

Aspects of the Iranian Revolution. 35p. 1980. pap. 5.00 (ISBN 92-808-0038-8, TUNU 064, UNU). Unipub.

Baraheni, Reza. The Crowned Cannibals: Writings on Repression in Iran. 1977. pap. 3.95 (ISBN 0-394-72357-0, V-357, Vin). Random.

Batra, Ravi. Muslim Civilization & the Crisis in Iran. LC 80-53736. 218p. (Orig.). 1981. 15.00 (ISBN 0-939352-00-1); pap. 8.00 (ISBN 0-939352-00-1). Venus Bks.

Bayne, E. A. Four Ways of Politics: State & Nation in Italy, Somalia, Israel, Iran. LC 65-14723. 1965. 7.50 (ISBN 0-910116-60-1). Am U Field.

--Persian Kingship in Transition. LC 68-30502. 1968. 7.50 (ISBN 0-910116-65-2). Am U Field.

Benham, Djamchid. Cultural Policy in Iran. LC 72-96471. (Studies & Documents on Cultural Policies). (Illus.). 46p. (Orig.). 1973. pap. 5.00 (ISBN 92-3-101002-6, U125, UNESCO). Unipub.

Bill, James A. The Politics of Iran: Groups, Classes & Modernization. LC 73-187714. 176p. 1972. pap. text ed. 8.95 (ISBN 0-675-09102-0). Merrill.

Bonine, Michael E. & Keddie, Nikki R., eds. Continuity & Change in Modern Iran. LC 80-19468. 225p. 1981. pap. text ed. 7.95x (ISBN 0-87395-466-1, BOCC-P). State U NY Pr.

--Modern Iran: The Dialectics of Continuity & Change. LC 80-19463. 400p. 1981. text ed. 34.00x (ISBN 0-686-72180-2, BOMI). State U NY Pr.

Carroll, Maurice, et al. No Hiding Place: The New York Times Inside Report on America Held Hostage. Jellinek, Roger, ed. 320p. 1981. 14.95 (ISBN 0-8129-0980-1). Times Bks.

Cottam, Richard W. Nationalism in Iran: Updated Through 1978. LC 78-12302. 1979. 15.95 (ISBN 0-8229-3396-9); pap. 6.95 (ISBN 0-8229-5299-8). U of Pittsburgh Pr.

Dehquani-Tafti, H. B. The Hard Awakening. 1981. 10.95 (ISBN 0-8164-0496-8). Seabury.

Economic Development & the Village in Iran: Prospects for an Alternative Approach. 26p. 1981. pap. 5.00 (ISBN 92-808-0149-X, TUNU 118, UNU). Unipub.

Engelmeyer, Shelon D. & Wagman, Robert J. Hostage. 128p. pap. 5.95 (ISBN 0-89803-084-6). Caroline Hse.

Forbis, William H. Fall of the Peacock Throne: The Story of Iran. (McGraw-Hill Paperbacks Ser.). (Illus.). 320p. 1981. pap. 6.95 (ISBN 0-07-021486-7). McGraw.

Graham, Robert. Iran. LC 79-2512. 1979. pap. 5.95 (ISBN 0-312-43588-6). St Martin.

Halliday, Fred. Iran: Dictatorship & Development. (Illus.). 1979. pap. 3.95 (ISBN 0-14-022010-0, Pelican). Penguin.

Hoveyda, Fereydour. The Last Days of the Shah. 1980. 9.95 (ISBN 0-686-61454-2, Wyndam Bks). S&S.

Inlow, E. Burke. Shahanshah: A Study of Monarchy of Iran. 1979. 13.95 (ISBN 0-89684-051-4, Pub. by Motilal Banarsidass, India). Orient Bk Dist.

Jabbari, Ahmad & Olson, Robert, eds. Iran: Essays on a Revolution in the Making. (Illus.). 214p. (Orig.). 1981. pap. 4.95 (ISBN 0-939214-00-8). Mazda Pubs.

Jazani, Bizhan. Capitalism & Revolution in Iran: Selected Writings. 1981. 17.00 (ISBN 0-905762-82-7, Pub. by Zed Pr); pap. 7.95 (ISBN 0-905762-57-6). Lawrence Hill.

Johnson, Gail C. High Level Manpower in Iran: From Hidden Conflict to Crisis. LC 79-21419. (Praeger Special Studies Ser.). 136p. 1980. 24.50 (ISBN 0-03-053366-X). Praeger.

Johnson, Gregory A. Local Exchange & Early State Development in Southwestern Iran. (Anthropological Papers: No. 51). (Illus.). 1973. pap. 4.00x (ISBN 0-932206-49-2). U Mich Mus Anthro.

Katouzian, Homa. The Political Economy of Modern Iran: Despotism & Pseudo-Modernism, 1926-1979. 448p. 1981. 40.00x (ISBN 0-8147-4577-6); pap. 19.50x (ISBN 0-8147-4578-4). NYU Pr.

Keddie, Nikki R. Iran: Religion, Politics & Society--Collected Essays. 243p. 1980. pap. 9.95x (ISBN 0-7146-4031-X, F Cass Co); 29.50x (ISBN 0-686-31761-0). Biblio Dist.

--Religion & Rebellion in Iran: The Iranian Tobacco Protest of 1891-1892. 163p. 1966. 25.00x (ISBN 0-7146-1971-X, F Cass Co). Biblio Dist.

Keddie, Nikki R. & Yann, Richard. Roots of Revolution: An Interpretive History of Modern Iran. LC 81-40438. (Illus.). 316p. 1981. text ed. 25.00 (ISBN 0-300-02606-4); pap. 5.95 (ISBN 0-300-02611-0, YF-24). Yale U Pr.

Kedourie, Elie & Haim, Sylvia G., eds. Towards a Modern Iran: Studies in Thought, Politics & Society. 1980. 29.50x (ISBN 0-7146-3145-0, F Cass Co). Biblio Dist.

Kuniholm, Bruce R. The Origins of the Cold War in the Near East: Great Power Conflict and Diplomacy in Iran, Turkey, and Greece. LC 79-83999. (Illus.). 1979. 27.50x (ISBN 0-691-04665-4); pap. 10.50 (ISBN 0-691-10083-7). Princeton U Pr.

Lambton, A. K. Theory & Practice in Medieval Persian Government. 332p. 1980. 75.00x (ISBN 0-86078-067-8, Pub. by Variorum England). State Mutual Bk.

Looney. Economic Origins of the Iranian Revolution. (Pergamon Policy Studies). 225p. Date not set. text ed. price not set (ISBN 0-08-025950-2). Pergamon.

McDaniel, Robert A. The Shuster Mission & the Persian Constitutional Revolution. LC 72-96696. (Studies in Middle Eastern History: No. 1). 1974. 25.00x (ISBN 0-88297-004-6). Bibliotheca.

Mahdi, Ali-Akbar. A Selected Bibliography on Political Economy of Iran. (Public Administration Ser.: Bibliography P-598). 104p. 1980. pap. 15.25 (ISBN 0-686-29067-4). Vance Biblios.

Millspaugh, Arthur. Americans in Persia. LC 76-9837. (Politics & Strategy of World War II Ser.). 1976. Repr. of 1946 ed. lib. bdg. 27.50 (ISBN 0-306-70764-0). Da Capo.

Pahlavi, Ashraf. Faces in a Mirror: Memoirs from Exile. LC 80-13509. 1980. 12.95 (ISBN 0-13-299131-4). P-H.

Queen, Richard & Hass, Patricia. Inside & Out: Hostage to Iran, Hostage to Myself. (Illus.). 1981. 12.95 (ISBN 0-399-12645-7). Putnam.

Roosevelt, K. Countercoup: The Struggle for the Control of Iran. (McGraw-Hill Paperback Ser.). 1981. pap. price not set (ISBN 0-07-053593-0, SP). McGraw.

Roosevelt, Kermit. Countercoup: The Struggle for the Control of Iran. (Illus.). 1979. 12.95 (ISBN 0-07-053590-6, GB). McGraw.

Salinger, Pierre. America Held Hostage: The Secret Negotiations. LC 81-43127. (Illus.). 350p. 1981. 16.95 (ISBN 0-385-17750-X). Doubleday.

Shuster, William M. Strangling of Persia: Story of the European Diplomacy & Oriental Intrigue That Resulted in the Denationalization of Twelve Million Mohammedans, a Personal Narrative. LC 69-10154. 1969. Repr. of 1912 ed. lib. bdg. 24.50x (ISBN 0-8371-0224-3, SHSP). Greenwood.

Siddiqi, Amir H. Caliphate & Kingship in Mediaeval Persia. LC 77-10621. (Studies in Islamic History: No. 14). 112p. Repr. of 1937 ed. lib. bdg. 12.50x (ISBN 0-87991-463-7). Porcupine Pr.

Singh, K. R. Iran: Quest for Security. 421p. 1980. text ed. 37.50x (ISBN 0-7069-1259-4, Pub. by Vikas India). Advent NY.

Stempel, John D. Inside the Iranian Revolution. LC 81-47564. 352p. 1981. 17.50x (ISBN 0-253-14200-8). Ind U Pr.

Wead, R. Douglas. The Iran Crisis. (Orig.). 1980. pap. 2.95 (ISBN 0-88270-433-8). Logos.

Zabih, Sepehr. The Mossadegh Era: Roots of the Iranian Revolution. LC 81-80670. 180p. 1981. 9.95 (ISBN 0-930720-68-7); pap. 5.95 (ISBN 0-930720-69-5). Liberator Pr.

Ziring, Lawrence. Iran, Turkey, & Afghanistan: A Political Chronology. 240p. 1981. 23.95 (ISBN 0-03-058651-8). Praeger.

Zonis, Marvin. Political Elite of Iran. LC 74-90966. (Princeton Studies on the Near East). 1971. 26.00 (ISBN 0-691-03083-9); pap. 6.95 (ISBN 0-691-00019-0). Princeton U Pr.

IRAN–RELIGION

Akhavi, Shahrough. Religion & Politics in Contemporary Iran: Clergy-State Relations in the Pahlavi Period. LC 79-22084. 1980. lib. bdg. 29.00 (ISBN 0-87395-408-4); pap. 9.95 (ISBN 0-87395-456-4). State U NY Pr.

Bowman, Raymond A. Aramaic Ritual Texts from Persepolis. LC 65-55148. (Oriental Institute Pubns. Ser: No. 91). 1970. 35.00x (ISBN 0-226-62194-4). U of Chicago Pr.

Keddie, Nikki R. Religion & Rebellion in Iran: The Iranian Tobacco Protest of 1891-1892. 163p. 1966. 25.00x (ISBN 0-7146-1971-X, F Cass Co). Biblio Dist.

Kedourie, Elie & Haim, Sylvia G., eds. Towards a Modern Iran: Studies in Thought, Politics & Society. 1980. 29.50x (ISBN 0-7146-3145-0, F Cass Co). Biblio Dist.

Mills, Lawrence H. Our Own Religion in Ancient Persia. LC 74-21262. Repr. of 1913 ed. 45.00 (ISBN 0-404-12811-4). AMS Pr.

Mulla Firuz Bin Kaus, tr. from Mahabhadian. The Desatir. LC 73-84045. (Secret Doctrine Reference Ser.). 208p. 1980. pap. 6.95 (ISBN 0-913510-33-5). Wizards.

Ray, Ajit K. The Religious Ideas of Rammohun Roy: A Survey of His Writings on Religion Particularly in Persian, Sanskrit, & Bengali. 1976. 7.50x (ISBN 0-88386-925-X). South Asia Bks.

Wead, R. Douglas. The Iran Crisis. (Orig.). 1980. pap. 2.95 (ISBN 0-88270-433-8). Logos.

Widengren, Geo. Iran & Islam. (Jordon Lectures in Comparative Religion Ser: No. 10). 160p. 1979. cancelled (ISBN 0-485-17410-3, Athlone Pr). Humanities.

Wilson, Samuel G. Persian Life & Customs. 3rd ed. LC 76-178305. Repr. of 1900 ed. 24.50 (ISBN 0-404-06996-7). AMS Pr.

IRAN–SOCIAL CONDITIONS

Bill, James A. The Politics of Iran: Groups, Classes & Modernization. LC 73-187714. 176p. 1972. pap. text ed. 8.95 (ISBN 0-675-09102-0). Merrill.

Bonine, Michael E. & Keddie, Nikki R., eds. Continuity & Change in Modern Iran. LC 80-19468. 225p. 1981. pap. text ed. 7.95x (ISBN 0-87395-466-1, BOCC-P). State U NY Pr.

--Modern Iran: The Dialectics of Continuity & Change. LC 80-19463. 400p. 1981. text ed. 34.00x (ISBN 0-686-72180-2, BOMI). State U NY Pr.

Braswell, George W., Jr. To Ride a Magic Carpet. LC 77-78472. 1977. 3.95 (ISBN 0-8054-6308-9). Broadman.

Fraser, James B. Narrative of the Residence of the Persian Princes in London in 1835 & 1836, 2 vols. in 1. LC 73-6280. (The Middle East Ser.). Repr. of 1838 ed. 34.00 (ISBN 0-405-05336-3). Arno.

Issawi, Charles. Economic History of Iran, 1800-1914. Polk, William R., ed. LC 70-153883. (Publications of the Center for Middle Eastern Studies Ser: No. 8). 1971. 17.50x (ISBN 0-226-38606-6). U of Chicago Pr.

Kazemi, Farhad. Poverty & Revolution in Iran: The Migrant Poor, Urban Marginality & Politics. 180p. 1981. text ed. 17.50x (ISBN 0-8147-4576-8). NYU Pr.

Paydarfar, Ali A. Social Change in a Southern Province of Iran. LC 75-15427. (Comparative Urban Studies Monograph Ser: No. 1). (Illus.). 190p. 1974. pap. text ed. 5.50 (ISBN 0-89143-044-X). U NC Inst Res Soc Sci.

Prigmore, Charles S. Social Work in Iran Since the White Revolution. LC 75-9807. 208p. 1976. 13.95x (ISBN 0-8173-4500-0). U of Ala Pr.

IRAN–SOCIAL LIFE AND CUSTOMS

Abbot, John. The Iranians: How They Live & Work. 168p. 1978. text ed. 8.95 (ISBN 0-03-042496-8, HoltC). HR&W.

Donaldson, Bess A. The Wild Rue. LC 73-6277. (The Middle East Ser.). Repr. of 1938 ed. 12.00 (ISBN 0-405-05332-0). Arno.

Edwards, Arthur C. Persian Caravan. facsimile ed. LC 70-110224. (Short Story Index Reprint Ser.). 1928. 15.00 (ISBN 0-8369-3311-7). Arno.

Fischer, Michael M. Iran: From Religious Dispute to Revolution. LC 79-24330. (Harvard Studies in Cultural Anthropology: No. 3). (Illus.). 328p. 1980. text ed. 17.50x (ISBN 0-674-46615-2). Harvard U Pr.

Forbes-Leith, F. A. Checkmate: Fighting Tradition in Central Persia. LC 73-6279. (The Middle East Ser.). Repr. of 1927 ed. 15.00 (ISBN 0-405-05335-5). Arno.

Kulsan, Nah'Nah. Customs & Manners of the Women of Persia. Atkinson, James, tr. LC 72-164039. (Research & Source Works Ser.: No. 528). 1971. Repr. of 1832 ed. lib. bdg. 20.50 (ISBN 0-8337-0110-X). B Franklin.

Moore, Diane M. Iran: In a Persian Market. LC 79-93424. 118p. (Orig.). 1980. pap. 7.95 (ISBN 0-686-61402-X). D M Moore.

Sarkissian, Henry A. Tales of One Thousand & One Iranian Days. 1981. 8.95 (ISBN 0-533-04476-6). Vantage.

Sheil, Mary. Glimpses of Life & Manners in Persia. LC 73-6299. (The Middle East Ser.). Repr. of 1856 ed. 25.00 (ISBN 0-405-05356-8). Arno.

Sykes, P. M., ed. The Glory of the Shia World. LC 73-6302. (The Middle East Ser.). Repr. of 1910 ed. 18.00 (ISBN 0-405-05362-2). Arno.

Wilson, Samuel G. Persian Life & Customs. 3rd ed. LC 76-178305. Repr. of 1900 ed. 24.50 (ISBN 0-404-06996-7). AMS Pr.

IRANIAN ARCHITECTURE

see Architecture–Iran

IRANIAN CIVILIZATION

see Civilization, Iranian

IRANIAN LANGUAGES

see Avesta Language; Kurdish Language; Persian Language

IRANIAN LITERATURE

see also Indic Literature; Indo-Iranian Philology

Ishaque, M. Four Eminent Poetesses of Iran. 1976. lib. bdg. 59.95 (ISBN 0-8490-1860-9). Gordon Pr.

Rypka, J., et al. History of Iranian Literature. enl. & rev. ed. Jahn, Karl, ed. Van Popta-Hope, P., tr. from Ger. 928p. 1968. 79.00 (ISBN 90-277-0143-1, Pub. by Reidel Holland). Kluwer Boston.

Sharma, Nasira, ed. Echoes of Iranian Revolution: Poems of Revolt & Liberation. 1979. text ed. 11.95 (ISBN 0-7069-0925-9, Pub. by Vikas India). Advent NY.

Southgate, Minoo, ed. Modern Persian Short Stories. LC 79-89930. 228p. (Orig.). 1980. 14.00x (ISBN 0-89410-032-7, 033-5); pap. 7.00x (ISBN 0-89410-033-5). Three Continents.

IRANIAN POTTERY

see Pottery, Iranian

IRAQ

Adams, Doris G. Iraq's People & Resources. LC 80-19079. (University of California Publications in Economics Ser.: Vol. XVIII). (Illus.). viii, 160p. 1980. Repr. of 1958 ed. lib. bdg. 18.75x (ISBN 0-313-22759-4, ADIP). Greenwood.

Baali, Fuad. Relation of the People to the Land in Southern Iraq. LC 66-64914. (U of Fla. Social Sciences Monograph: No. 31). 1966. 3.00 (ISBN 0-8130-0010-6). U Presses Fla.

Drower, Ethel S. Folk-Tales of Iraq. LC 78-63226. (Illus.). 30.50 (ISBN 0-404-16165-0). AMS Pr.

Emanuel, W. V. Wild Asses: A Journey Through Persia. LC 76-180336. Repr. of 1939 ed. 27.50 (ISBN 0-404-56248-5). AMS Pr.

Fichter, George. Iraq. (First Bks). (Illus.). (gr. 4-6). 1978. PLB 7.40 s&l (ISBN 0-531-02236-6). Watts.

Field, Henry. Anthropology of Iraq Pt. 1, Pt. 1. (Illus.). 1940. pap. 28.00 (ISBN 0-527-01890-2). Kraus Repr.

Hamilton, Archibald M. Road Through Kurdistan. LC 70-180345. Repr. of 1937 ed. 26.00 (ISBN 0-404-56275-2). AMS Pr.

Harris, George L., et al. Iraq. LC 58-14179. (Survey of World Cultures Ser). xvi, 350p. (YA) (gr. 10 up). 1958. 15.00x (ISBN 0-87536-905-7). HRAFP.

Jacobsen, Thorkild. Toward the Image of Tammuz & Other Essays on Mesopotamian History & Culture. Moran, William L., ed. LC 76-95925. (Semitic Ser: No. 21). 1970. 25.00x (ISBN 0-674-89810-9). Harvard U Pr.

--The Treasures of Darkness: A History of Mesoptamian Religon. LC 75-27576. (Illus.). 1976. 20.00x (ISBN 0-300-01844-4); pap. 6.95x (ISBN 0-300-02291-3). Yale U Pr.
Kramer, Samuel N. Cradle of Civilization. LC 67-29528. (Great Ages of Man). (Illus.). (gr. 6 up). 1967. PLB 11.97 (ISBN 0-8094-0378-1, Pub. by Time-Life). Silver.
--Cradle of Civilization. (Great Ages of Man Ser). (Illus.). 1967. 12.95 (ISBN 0-8094-0356-0); lib. bdg. avail. (ISBN 0-685-20547-9). Time-Life.
Ministry of Planning Central Statistical Organization. Annual Abstract of Statistics, Iraq, 1976. LC 72-622806. 1977. pap. 17.50x (ISBN 0-8002-0258-9). Intl Pubns Serv.
Rossi, Pierre. Iraq, the Land of the New River. (Illus.). 1981. 60.00 (ISBN 0-88254-603-1, Pub. by J. A. Editions France). Hippocrene Bks.

IRAQ-ANTIQUITIES

Adams, Robert M. Heartland of Cities: Surveys of Ancient Settlement & Land Use on the Central Floodplain of the Euphrates. LC 80-13995. (Illus.). 384p. 1981. lib. bdg. 35.00x (ISBN 0-226-00544-5). U of Chicago Pr.
Adams, Robert M. & Nissen, Hans J. The Uruk Countryside: The Natural Setting of Urban Societies. LC 78-179489. 1972. 20.00x (ISBN 0-226-00500-3). U of Chicago Pr.
Budge, Ernest A. By Nile & Tigris. LC 75-28120. (Illus.). Repr. of 1920 ed. Set. 75.00 (ISBN 0-404-11312-5). AMS Pr.
Cassin, Elena. La Splendeur Divine: Introduction a L'etude De la Mentalite Mesopotamienne. (Civilisations et Societes: No. 8). pap. 28.75x (ISBN 90-2796-077-1). Mouton.
Chiera, Edward. They Wrote on Clay: The Babylonian Tablets Speak Today. Cameron, George G., ed. LC 38-27631. (Illus.). 1938. 9.50x (ISBN 0-226-10424-9). U of Chicago Pr.
--They Wrote on Clay: The Babylonian Tablets Speak Today. Cameron, George G., ed. LC 38-27631. (Illus.). 1956. pap. 3.50 (ISBN 0-226-10425-7, P2, Phoen). U of Chicago Pr.
Ellis, Richard S. A Bibliography of Mesopotamian Archeological Sites. 175p. 1972. 47.50x (ISBN 3-447-01434-2). Intl Pubns Serv.
--Foundation Deposits in Ancient Mesopotamia. LC 78-63541. (Yale Near Eastern Researches: No. 2). Repr. of 1968 ed. 27.50 (ISBN 0-404-60262-2). AMS Pr.
Fagan, Brian M. Return to Babylon: Travelers, Archaeologists & Monuments in Mesopotamia. LC 79-18194. (Illus.). 1979. 14.95 (ISBN 0-316-27306-6). Little.
Hancock, Percy S. Mesopotamian Archaeology. (Illus.). Repr. of 1912 ed. lib. bdg. 45.00 (ISBN 0-87821-031-8). Milford Hse.
Hancock, Percy S. P. Mesopotamian Archaeology. LC 77-6996. 1977. Repr. of 1912 ed. lib. bdg. 45.00 (ISBN 0-89341-218-X). Longwood Pr.
Handcock, P. S. Mesopotamian Archaeology. Repr. of 1912 ed. 24.00 (ISBN 0-527-37500-4). Kraus Repr.
Heyerdahl, Thor. The Tigris Expedition: In Search of Our Beginnings. LC 80-1862. 360p. 1981. 17.95 (ISBN 0-385-17357-1). Doubleday.
Leacroft, Helen & Leacroft, Richard. The Buildings of Ancient Mesopotamia. LC 73-22559. (Illus.). 40p. (gr. 6 up). 1975. PLB 7.95 (ISBN 0-201-09447-9, 9447, A-W Childrens). A-W.
Levine, Louis D. & Young, T. Cuyler, Jr., eds. Mountains & Lowlands: Essays in the Archaeology of Greater Mesopotamia. LC 77-75777. (Bibliotheca Mesopotamica: Vol. 7). (Illus.). 405p. 1977. text ed. 21.00 (ISBN 0-89003-053-7); pap. 16.50 (ISBN 0-89003-052-9). Undena Pubns.
Lloyd, Seton. The Archaeology of Mesopotamia: From the Old Stone Age to the Persian Conquest. 1980. pap. 8.95 (ISBN 0-500-79007-8). Thames Hudson.
--The Archaeology of Mesopotamia: From the Old Stone Age to the Persian Conquest. (Illus.). 1978. 17.95 (ISBN 0-500-78007-2). Thames Hudson.
--Foundations in the Dust: The Story of Mesopotamian Exploration. rev. enl. ed. (Illus.). 216p. 1981. 19.95 (ISBN 0-500-05038-4). Thames Hudson.
McCown, Donald E., et al. Nippur II: The North Temple & Sounding E: Excavations of the Joint Expedition to Nippur of the American Schools of Oriental Research & the Oriental Institute of the University of Chicago. LC 77-74719. (Oriental Institute Publications: No. 97). (Illus.). lib. bdg. 50.00x (ISBN 0-918986-04-4). Oriental Inst.
Oppenheim, A. Leo. Letters from Mesopotamia: Official, Business, & Private Letters on Clay Tablets from Two Millennia. LC 67-20576. 1967. 10.50x (ISBN 0-226-63190-7). U of Chicago Pr.
Pallis, Svend A. The Antiquity of Iraq. LC 78-72755. (Ancient Mesopotamian Texts & Studies). Repr. of 1956 ed. 37.50 (ISBN 0-404-18199-6). AMS Pr.
Perkins, Ann L. The Comparative Archeology of Early Mesopotamia. LC 49-10748. (Studies in Ancient Oriental Civilization: No. 25). (Illus.). xx, 201p. (Orig.). 1977. pap. text ed. 14.00x (ISBN 0-226-62396-3). Oriental Inst.
--The Comparative Archeology of Early Mesopotamia. LC 49-10748. (Studies in Ancient Oriental Civilization: No. 25). (Illus.). 1977. pap. 14.00x (ISBN 0-226-62396-3). U of Chicago Pr.
Reiner, Erica & Pingree, David. The Venus Tablet of Ammisaduqa. LC 75-26241. (Bibliotheca Mesopotamica Ser: Vol. 2, Pt. 1). 60p. 1975. pap. 6.75 (ISBN 0-89003-010-3). Undena Pubns.
Wright, Henry T. The Administration of Rural Production in an Early Mesopotamian Town. new ed. (Anthropological Papers: No. 38). 1969. pap. 3.00x (ISBN 0-932206-36-0). U Mich Mus Anthro.

IRAQ-ECONOMIC CONDITIONS

Al-Eyd, Kadhim A. Oil Revenues & Accelerated Growth: Absorptive Capacity in Iraq. LC 79-18596. 206p. 1979. 22.95 (ISBN 0-03-053306-6). Praeger.
Gabbay, Rony. Communism & Agrarian Reform in Iraq. 240p. 1978. 32.00x (ISBN 0-85664-567-2, Pub. by Croom Helm Ltd England). Biblio Dist.
Jalal, F. Role of Government in the Industrialization of Iraq. 160p. 1972. 26.00x (ISBN 0-7146-2586-8, F Cass Co). Biblio Dist.
Kelidar, Abbas, ed. Integration of Modern Iraq. 1979. 19.95x (ISBN 0-312-41891-4). St Martin.
Langley, Kathleen M. Industrialization of Iraq. LC 61-7179. (Middle Eastern Monographs Ser: No. 5). (Illus.). 1961. pap. 4.50x (ISBN 0-674-45251-8). Harvard U Pr.
Penrose, Edith & Penrose, E. F. Iraq: Economics, Oil & Politics. LC 77-16007. (Nations of the Modern World Ser.). 1978. lib. bdg. 39.75x (ISBN 0-89158-804-3). Westview.
Samarraie, Husam. Agriculture in Iraq During the Third Century. (Arab Background Ser.). 1972. 15.00x (ISBN 0-86685-026-0). Intl Bk Ctr.

IRAQ-FOREIGN RELATIONS

Al-Marayati, Abid A. Diplomatic History of Modern Iraq. 1961. 6.00 (ISBN 0-8315-0108-1). Speller.
Hussein, Saddam. Social & Foreign Affairs in Iraq. Kishtainy, Khalid W., tr. 123p. 1979. 25.00x (ISBN 0-7099-0070-8, Pub. by Croom Helm Ltd England). Biblio Dist.
McLaurin, R. D., et al. Foreign Policy Making in the Middle East: Domestic Influences on Policy in Egypt, Iraq, Israel, & Syria. LC 76-24360. (Special Studies). 1977. text ed. 29.95 (ISBN 0-275-23870-9); pap. 10.95 (ISBN 0-275-65010-3). Praeger.
Mezerik, Avrahm G., ed. Kuwait-Iraq Dispute. 1961. pap. 15.00 (ISBN 0-685-13204-8, 66). Intl Review.

IRAQ-HISTORY

Al-Arif, Ismail. Iraq Reborn: A Firsthand Account of the 1958 Revolution & After. 1982. 9.50 (ISBN 0-533-05009-X). Vantage.
Algar, Hamid. Mirza Malkum Khan: A Biographical Essay in 19th Century Iranian Modernism. LC 78-187750. 1973. 28.50x (ISBN 0-520-02217-3). U of Cal Pr.
Atiyyah, Ghassan R. Iraq, Nineteen Hundred Eight to Nineteen Twenty-One: A Socio-Political Study. 407p. 1975. 15.00x (ISBN 0-89955-250-1, Pub. by Arab Inst Res). Intl Schol Bk Serv.
Batatu, John. The Old Social Classes & the Revolutionary Movements of Iraq: A Study of Iraq's Old Landed & Commercial Classes & of Its Communists. LC 78-51157. (Princeton Studies on the Near East). (Illus.). 1979. 85.00 (ISBN 0-691-05241-7). Princeton U Pr.
Fariq, Khurshid A. Tarikh Al-Ridda: Gleaned from al-Iktifa of al-Balansi with Notes & an Introduction. 183p. (Arabic.). 1981. text ed. write for info. (ISBN 0-7069-1334-5, Pub. by Vikas India). Advent NY.
Guyot, Charles. The Legend of the City of Ys. Cavanagh, Deirdre, tr. from Fr. LC 78-10235. Orig. Title: La Legende de la Ville D'ys: D'apres les Anciens Textes. (Illus.). 1979. lib. bdg. 12.00x (ISBN 0-87023-264-9). U of Mass Pr.
Le Strange, Guy. The Lands of the Eastern Caliphate. LC 77-180355. (Cambridge Geographical Ser.). Repr. of 1905 ed. 41.50 (ISBN 0-404-56287-6). AMS Pr.
--Mesopotamia & Persia Under the Mongols in the Fourteenth Century A.D. (Studies in Islamic History: No. 18). 104p. Repr. of 1903 ed. lib. bdg. 13.50x (ISBN 0-87991-108-5). Porcupine Pr.
Lloyd, S. The Ruined Cities of Iraq. (Illus.). 72p. 1980. 10.00 (ISBN 0-89005-375-8). Ares.
Lloyd, Seton. Foundations in the Dust: A Story of Mesopotamian Exploration. LC 76-46179. Repr. of 1947 ed. 21.50 (ISBN 0-404-15364-X). AMS Pr.
Longrigg, Stephen. Four Centuries of Modern Iraq. (Arab Background Ser.). 18.00x (ISBN 0-86685-019-8). Intl Bk Ctr.
--Iraq Nineteen Hundred to Nineteen Fifty. (Arab Background Ser.). 1968. 16.00x (ISBN 0-86685-020-1). Intl Bk Ctr.
Oppenheim, A. Leo. Ancient Mesopotamia: Portrait of a Dead Civilization. 2nd rev. ed. LC 64-19847. (Illus.). 1977. lib. bdg. 22.00x (ISBN 0-226-63186-9); pap. 6.95 (ISBN 0-226-63187-7). U of Chicago Pr.
Penrose, Edith & Penrose, E. F. Iraq: Economics, Oil & Politics. LC 77-16007. (Nations of the Modern World Ser.). 1978. lib. bdg. 39.75x (ISBN 0-89158-804-3). Westview.
Roux, Georges. Ancient Iraq. rev. ed. 480p. 1980. pap. 5.95 (ISBN 0-14-020828-3, Pelican). Penguin.
Wakehurst, John D. The Truth About Mesopotamia, Palestine & Syria. LC 79-2887. 221p. 1981. Repr. of 1923 ed. 19.50 (ISBN 0-8305-0054-5). Hyperion Conn.
Weisberg, David B. Guild Structure & Political Allegiance in Early Achaemenid Mesopotamia. LC 78-63540. (Yale Near Eastern Researches: No. 1). Repr. of 1967 ed. 22.50 (ISBN 0-404-60261-4). AMS Pr.

IRAQ-POLITICS AND GOVERNMENT

Al-Arif, Ismail. Iraq Reborn: A Firsthand Account of the 1958 Revolution & After. 1982. 9.50 (ISBN 0-533-05009-X). Vantage.
Edmonds, Cecil J. Kurds, Turks, & Arabs: Politics, Travel, & Research in North-Eastern Iraq, 1919-1925. LC 80-1930. Repr. of 1957 ed. 49.50 (ISBN 0-404-18960-1). AMS Pr.
Ellis, Maria deJ. Agriculture & the State in Ancient Mesopotamia: An Introduction to Problems of Land Tenure. (Occasional Publications of the Babylonian Fund: Vol. 1). 1976. 20.00 (ISBN 0-934718-28-8). Univ Mus of U PA.
Foster, Henry A. The Making of Modern Iraq: A Product of World Forces. LC 77-173537. (Illus.). ix, 319p. 1972. Repr. of 1935 ed. 15.00 (ISBN 0-8462-1664-7). Russell.
Gabbay, Rony. Communism & Agrarian Reform in Iraq. 240p. 1978. 32.00x (ISBN 0-85664-567-2, Pub. by Croom Helm Ltd England). Biblio Dist.
Gallman, Waldemar J. Iraq under General Nuri: My Recollections of Nuri al-Said 1954-1958. (Illus.). 255p. 1964. 16.50x (ISBN 0-8018-0210-5). Johns Hopkins.
Ghareeb, Edmund. The Kurdish Question in Iraq. LC 81-8897. (Contemporary Issues in the Middle East Ser.). (Illus.). 336p. 1981. 22.00 (ISBN 0-8156-0164-6). Syracuse U Pr.
Ireland, Philip W. Iraq: A Study in Political Development. LC 75-83852. (Illus.). 1970. Repr. of 1937 ed. 15.00 (ISBN 0-8462-1412-1). Russell.
Jalal, F. Role of Government in the Industrialization of Iraq. 160p. 1972. 26.00x (ISBN 0-7146-2586-8, F Cass Co). Biblio Dist.
Kelidar, Abbas, ed. Integration of Modern Iraq. 1979. 19.95x (ISBN 0-312-41891-4). St Martin.
Khadduri, Majid. Independent Iraq, Nineteen Thirty-Two to Nineteen Fifty-Eight: A Study in Iraqi Politics. 2nd ed. LC 80-1919. Repr. of 1960 ed. 41.50 (ISBN 0-404-18972-5). AMS Pr.
--Republican Iraq: A Study in Iraqi Politics Since the Revolution of 1958. LC 80-1923. Repr. of 1969 ed. 37.00 (ISBN 0-404-18973-3). AMS Pr.
--Socialist Iraq: A Study in Iraqi Politics Since 1968. LC 78-51916. 1978. 12.95 (ISBN 0-916808-16-5). Mid East Inst.
Kimball, Lorenzo K. The Changing Pattern of Political Power in Iraq, 1958-1971. 7.95 (ISBN 0-8315-0120-0). Speller.
O'Ballance, Edgar. Kurdish Revolt, Nineteen Sixty-One to Nineteen Seventy. 189p. 1973. 15.00 (ISBN 0-208-01395-4, Archon). Shoe String.

IRAQ-SOCIAL LIFE AND CUSTOMS

Aspects of Iraqi Cultural Policy. (Studies & Documents on Cultural Policies). 39p. 1980. pap. 4.00 (ISBN 92-3-101745-4, U-995, UNESCO). Unipub.
Batatu, John. The Old Social Classes & the Revolutionary Movements of Iraq: A Study of Iraq's Old Landed & Commercial Classes & of Its Communists. LC 78-51157. (Princeton Studies on the Near East). (Illus.). 1979. 85.00 (ISBN 0-691-05241-7). Princeton U Pr.
Fernea, Elizabeth Warnock. Guests of the Sheik: An Ethnology of an Iraqi Village. LC 65-13098. 1969. pap. 3.95 (ISBN 0-385-01485-6, A693, Anch). Doubleday.
Hussein, Saddam. Social & Foreign Affairs in Iraq. Kishtainy, Khalid W., tr. 123p. 1979. 25.00x (ISBN 0-7099-0070-8, Pub. by Croom Helm Ltd England). Biblio Dist.

IREBY, ENGLAND (LANCASHIRE)

Chippindall, W. H. History of the Township of Ireby. 1935. 13.00 (ISBN 0-384-08885-6). Johnson Repr.

IRELAND, WILLIAM HENRY, 1777-1835

Bodde, D. Shakespeare & the Ireland Forgeries. LC 75-22073. (Studies in Shakespeare, No. 24). 1975. lib. bdg. 40.95 (ISBN 0-8383-2084-8). Haskell.
Chalmers, George. Apology for the Believers in the Shakespeare Papers. LC 77-96373. (Eighteenth Century Shakespeare). Repr. of 1797 ed. lib. bdg. 35.00x (ISBN 0-678-05140-2). Kelley.
--Supplemental Apology for the Believers in the Shakespeare-Papers. LC 70-96374. (Eighteenth Century Shakespeare). Repr. of 1799 ed. lib. bdg. 30.00x (ISBN 0-678-05141-0). Kelley.
Mair, John. Fourth Forger. LC 71-153227. 1971. Repr. of 1938 ed. 13.00 (ISBN 0-8046-1537-3). Kennikat.
Malone, Edmond. Inquiry into the Authenticity of Certain Miscellaneous Papers & Legal Instruments. LC 73-96356. (Eighteenth Century Shakespeare). Repr. of 1796 ed. lib. bdg. 25.00x (ISBN 0-678-05123-2). Kelley.

IRELAND

see also Northern Ireland;
also names of cities, towns and counties in Ireland, e.g. Dublin; Kerry

Aalen, F. H. Man & the Landscape in Ireland. 1978. 29.50 (ISBN 0-12-041350-7). Acad Pr.
Adams, Michael. Censorship: The Irish Experience. 265p. 1968. 15.00x (ISBN 0-686-28344-9, Pub. by Irish Academic Pr). Biblio Dist.
Bryan, Walter. Improbable Irish. LC 77-86659. 1969. 4.95 (ISBN 0-8008-4170-0). Taplinger.
Dobrin, Arnold. Ireland: The Edge of Europe. LC 70-117146. (World Neighbors Ser). (Illus.). (gr. 6 up). 1971. 7.95 (ISBN 0-525-67030-0); PLB 6.80 (ISBN 0-525-67031-9). Elsevier-Nelson.
Evans, E. E. The Personality of Ireland. LC 72-83667. (Wiles Lectures, 1971). (Illus.). 176p. 1973. 18.95 (ISBN 0-521-08684-1). Cambridge U Pr.
Ireland. (Panorama Bks.). (Illus., Fr.). 4.95 (ISBN 0-685-11258-6). French & Eur.
Ireland: A Directory 1981. 15th ed. 390p. 1981. 55.00x (ISBN 0-312-43590-8). St Martin.
Landreth, H. Dear Dark Head, an Intimate Story of Ireland. Repr. of 1936 ed. 20.00 (ISBN 0-527-54200-8). Kraus Repr.
Laurence, Dan, ed. Bernard Shaw: The Matter with Ireland. 1979. 12.95x (ISBN 0-8464-0087-1). Beekman Pubs.
Lewis, Samuel. Topographical Dictionary of Ireland, 3 Vols. LC 75-102611. (Irish Culture & History Ser). 1970. Repr. of 1837 ed. Set. 150.00x (ISBN 0-8046-0788-5). Kennikat.
Millman, Lawrence. Our Like Will Not Be There Again: Notes from the West of Ireland. 1977. 7.95 (ISBN 0-316-57386-8). Little.
Newman, Jeremiah. The State of Ireland. 128p. 1977. 6.00x (ISBN 0-906127-00-9, Pub. by Irish Academic Pr Ireland). Biblio Dist.
O'Brien, Elinor. The Land & People of Ireland. rev. ed. LC 76-38335. (Portraits of the Nations Ser.). (Illus.). (gr. 6 up). 1972. 8.79 (ISBN 0-397-31299-7, JBL-J). Har-Row.
O'Clery, Helen. Ireland. (Pegasus Books: No. 10). (Illus.). 1967. 10.50x (ISBN 0-234-77995-0). Intl Pubns Serv.
Phillimore, William P. & Thrift, Gertrude. Indexes to Irish Wills, 5 Vols. in 1. LC 72-112827. (Illus.). 1970. Repr. of 1909 ed. 30.00 (ISBN 0-8063-0440-5). Genealog Pub.
Regional Problems & Policies in OECD Countries: Vol. 1, France, Italy, Ireland, Denmark, Sweden, Japan. 1976. 7.00x (ISBN 92-64-11486-6). OECD.
White, Carolyn. History of Irish Fairies. 1976. pap. 3.95 (ISBN 0-85342-455-1). Irish Bk Ctr.
Who Owns Whom: United Kingdom & the Republic of Ireland 1980-81, 2 vols. 23rd ed. LC 59-52911. 2200p. 1980. 190.00x (ISBN 0-8002-2418-3). Intl Pubns Serv.

IRELAND-ANTIQUITIES

Barrow, George L. The Round Towers of Ireland. (Illus.). 230p. 1979. 35.00 (ISBN 0-906187-04-4, Pub. by Acad Pr Ireland). Devin.
Burl, Aubrey. Rings of Stone: The Prehistoric Stone Circles of Britain & Ireland. LC 79-17741. (Illus.). 280p. 1980. 19.95 (ISBN 0-89919-000-6). Ticknor & Fields.
Dix, Ernest R. Catalogue of Early Dublin Printed Books, 1601-1700, 4 vols in 2. LC 71-132673. 1971. Repr. of 1898 ed. Set. lib. bdg. 47.00 (ISBN 0-8337-0873-2). B Franklin.
Dublin University. Catalogue of Fifteenth Century Books in the Library of Trinity College, Dublin, & in Marsh's Library, Dublin, with a Few from Other Collections. Abbott, T. K., ed. LC 70-128846. (Bibliography & Reference Ser.: No. 360). 1970. Repr. of 1905 ed. lib. bdg. 21.00 (ISBN 0-8337-0001-4). B Franklin.
Eager, Alan R. A Guide to Irish Bibliographical Material: A Bibliography of Irish Bibliographies and Sources of Information. LC 80-12368. xv, 502p. 1980. lib. bdg. 65.00 (ISBN 0-313-22343-2, EIB/). Greenwood.
Forde-Johnston, J. Prehistoric Britain & Ireland. 1976. 11.50 (ISBN 0-393-05605-8). Norton.

Harding, D., ed. Hillforts: Later Prehistoric Earthworks in Britain & Ireland. 1976. 94.50 (ISBN 0-12-324750-0). Acad Pr.

Hooton, E. A. & Dupertius, C. Wesley. Physical Anthropology of Ireland, 2 vols. (Harvard University Peabody Museum of Archaeology & Ethnology Papers Ser). 1955. Set. pap. 64.00 (ISBN 0-527-01275-0). Kraus Repr.

Joyce, Patrick W. Social History of Ancient Ireland, 2 Vols. LC 68-56473. (Illus.). 1968. Repr. of 1913 ed. Set. 40.00 (ISBN 0-405-08677-6, Blom Pubns); 20.00 ea. Vol. 1 (ISBN 0-405-08678-4). Vol. 2 (ISBN 0-405-08679-2). Arno.

Macalister, R. A. The Archaeology of Ireland. LC 78-87056. (Illus.). 1973. Repr. lib. bdg. 35.00 (ISBN 0-87821-027-X). Milford Hse.

Macalister, Robert A. Ancient Ireland: A Study in the Lessons of Archeology & History. LC 72-83747. (Illus.). Repr. of 1935 ed. 18.00 (ISBN 0-405-08757-8, Pub. by Blom). Arno.

--The Archaeology of Ireland. rev. ed. LC 70-172160. (Illus.). Repr. of 1949 ed. 25.00 (ISBN 0-405-08758-6, Pub. by Blom). Arno.

--Ireland in Pre-Celtic Times. LC 68-56469. (Illus.). 1969. Repr. of 1921 ed. 22.00 (ISBN 0-405-08759-4, Pub. by Blom). Arno.

McLaren, Duncan. In Ruins: The Once Great Houses of Ireland. LC 80-7662. (Illus.). 96p. 1980. 22.50 (ISBN 0-394-51095-X). Knopf.

Movius, Hallam L. Irish Stone Age, Its Chronology, Development & Relationships. Repr. of 1942 ed. lib. bdg. 28.75x (ISBN 0-8371-1152-8, MOIS). Greenwood.

Norman, E. R. & St Joseph, J. K. Early Development of Irish Society: The Evidence of Aerial Photography. LC 71-85734. (Air Surveys Ser.: No. 3). (Illus.). 1969. 32.50 (ISBN 0-521-07471-1). Cambridge U Pr.

O'Meadhra, Vaininn. Early Christian, Viking & Romanesque Art: Motif Pieces from Ireland. (Illus.). 260p. (Orig.). 1979. pap. text ed. 33.75x (ISBN 91-22-00270-7). Humanities.

O'Riordain, Sean P. Antiquities of the Irish Countryside. 5th ed. (Illus.). 1979. 23.00x (ISBN 0-416-85630-6); pap. 9.95 (ISBN 0-416-85610-1). Methuen Inc.

Wilde, Jane F. Ancient Cures, Charms & Usages of Ireland. LC 74-137347. 1970. Repr. of 1890 ed. 24.00 (ISBN 0-8103-3599-9). Gale.

Willoughby, Bob, ed. Voices from Ancient Ireland. (Illus.). 64p. (Orig.). 1981. pap. 7.95 (ISBN 0-330-26274-2, Pub. by Pan Bks England). Irish Bk Ctr.

Wood-Martin, W. G. Traces of the Elder Faiths of Ireland, 2 Vols. LC 70-102631. (Irish Culture & History Ser). Repr. of 1902 ed. Set. 40.00x (ISBN 0-8046-0807-5). Kennikat.

IRELAND-BIBLIOGRAPHY

Brown, Stephen J., ed. Ireland in Fiction: A Guide to Irish Novels, Tales, Romances, & Folk-Lore. LC 76-113998. (Bibliography & Reference Ser.: No. 311). 1970. Repr. of 1919 ed. text ed. 18.50 (ISBN 0-8337-0388-9). B Franklin.

Dix, Ernest R. Catalogue of Early Dublin Printed Books, 1601-1700, 4 vols in 2. LC 71-132673. 1971. Repr. of 1898 ed. Set. lib. bdg. 47.00 (ISBN 0-8337-0873-2). B Franklin.

Elton, G., ed. Annual Bibliography of British & Irish History, 1978. 1979. text ed. 26.75x (ISBN 0-391-01054-9). Humanities.

Hanson, Lawrence W. Contemporary Printed Sources for British & Irish Economic History, 1701-1750. 1964. 165.00 (ISBN 0-521-05196-7). Cambridge U Pr.

Henderson, G. P. & Henderson, S. P., eds. Directory of British Associations & Associations in Ireland. 6th ed. xiv, 486p. 1980. 125.00 (ISBN 0-686-74473-X). Gale.

Kenney, James F. Sources for the Early History of Ireland: Ecclesiastical. 1967. lib. bdg. 50.00x (ISBN 0-374-94560-8). Octagon.

Maltby, Arthur & McKenna, Brian. Irish Official Publications: A Guide to Republic of Ireland Papers, with a Breviate of Reports 1922-1972. (Guides to Official Publications Ser.: Vol. 7). 388p. 1980. 54.00 (ISBN 0-08-023703-7). Pergamon.

National Library Of Ireland - Dublin. Manuscript Sources for the History of Irish Civilisation, 11 Vols. 1965. Set. lib. bdg. 960.00 (ISBN 0-8161-0662-2). G K Hall.

Wagner, Henry R., ed. Irish Economics Seventeen Hundred to Seventeen Eighty-Three. LC 79-95162. Repr. of 1907 ed. 11.50x (ISBN 0-678-00559-1). Kelley.

IRELAND-BIOGRAPHY

Barrington, George. The Life, Times, & Adventures of George Barrington, the Celebrated Thief & Pickpocket. Bd. with The Memoirs of George Barrington, Containing Every Emarkable Circumstance, from His Birth to the Present Time. LC 80-2470. 1981. 29.50 (ISBN 0-404-19102-9). AMS Pr.

Blue Book Nineteen Seventy-Six: Leaders of the English-Speaking World, 2 vols. LC 73-13918. 1979. Set. 85.00 (ISBN 0-8103-0216-0). Gale.

Boylan, Henry. A Dictionary of Irish Biography. LC 78-67791. 1978. text ed. 25.00x (ISBN 0-06-490620-5). B&N.

Buckland, Patrick. James Craig. (Gill's Irish Lives Ser.). 143p. 1980. 20.00 (ISBN 0-7171-1078-8, Pub. by Gill & Macmillan Ireland); pap. 6.50 (ISBN 0-7171-0984-4). Irish Bk Ctr.

Byrne, Miles. Memoirs of Miles Byrne, 3 vols. in one. Repr. of 1863 ed. 36.00x (ISBN 0-686-28340-6, Pub. by Irish Academic Pr). Biblio Dist.

Coughlan, Rupert. Napper Tandy. (Illus.). 1976. 18.50 (ISBN 0-900068-34-5). Irish Bk Ctr.

Cox, Tom. Damned Englishman: A Study of Erskine Childers (1870-1922) LC 73-86542. 1975. 10.00 (ISBN 0-682-47821-0, University). Exposition.

Edwards, Ruth D. Patrick Pearse. 384p. 1980. pap. 7.95 (ISBN 0-571-11351-6, Pub. by Faber & Faber). Merrimack Bk Serv.

Falkiner, Litton C. Essays Relating to Ireland. LC 74-102600. (Irish Culture and History Ser). 1970. Repr. of 1909 ed. 12.50 (ISBN 0-8046-0777-X). Kennikat.

Griffin, Gerald. Wild Geese, Pen Portraits of Famous Irish Exiles. LC 77-2922. 1938. lib. bdg. 17.50 (ISBN 0-8414-4405-6). Folcroft.

Inglis, Brian. Roger Casement. LC 73-15422. 1974. 8.95 (ISBN 0-15-178327-6). HarBraceJ.

Moss, Laurence S. Mountifort Longfield: Ireland's First Professor of Political Economy. LC 75-34003. 240p. 1976. 14.95x (ISBN 0-916054-02-0, Caroline Hse Inc). Green Hill.

Moynihan, James H. The Life of Archbishop John Ireland. LC 76-6358. (Irish Americans Ser). (Illus.). 1976. Repr. of 1953 ed. 27.00 (ISBN 0-405-09351-9). Arno.

Murphy, Dervla. Wheels Within Wheels: Unraveling an Irish Past. 1980. 10.95 (ISBN 0-89919-006-5, Ticknor & Fields). HM.

O'Flanagan, J. Roderick. Lives of the Lord Chancellors & Keepers of the Great Seal of Ireland, 2 Vols. LC 71-112406. Repr. of 1870 ed. 50.00x (ISBN 0-678-04540-2). Kelley.

--Lives of the Lord Chancellors & Keepers of the Great Seal of Ireland, 2 Vols. 1971. Repr. of 1870 ed. 50.00x (ISBN 0-8377-2500-3). Rothman.

Tierney, Michael. Eoin Macneill: Scholar & Man of Action, 1867 - 1945. Martin, F. X., ed. (Illus.). 492p. 1981. 67.50x (ISBN 0-19-822440-0). Oxford U Pr.

White, Terence De Vere. The Anglo-Irish. (Illus.). 293p. 1975. text ed. 15.00x (ISBN 0-575-00764-8). Verry.

IRELAND-CHURCH HISTORY

see also Celtic Church

Bell, Philip. Disestablishment in Ireland & Wales. (Church Historical Society Ser.: No. 90). 1969. 21.50x (ISBN 0-8401-5090-3). Allenson-Breckinridge.

Bolster, Evelyn. A History of the Diocese of Cork from Earliest Times to the Reformation. (Illus.). 548p. 1972. 27.00x (ISBN 0-686-28339-2, Pub. by Irish Academic Pr). Biblio Dist.

De Paor, Maire & De Paor, Liam. Early Christian Ireland. (Illus.). 1978. pap. 7.95 (ISBN 0-500-27110-0). Thames Hudson.

Hanly, John, ed. The Letters of Saint Oliver Plunkett, Sixteen Twenty-Five to Sixteen Eighty-One: Archbishop of Armagh & Primate of All Ireland. 1979. text ed. 75.00x (ISBN 0-391-01120-0, Dolmen Pr). Humanities.

Harney, Martin P. Medieval Ties Between Italy & Ireland. 1963. 1.50 (ISBN 0-8198-0101-1). Dghtrs St Paul.

Hughes, Kathleen. Church in Early Irish Society. (Methuen Library Reprints Ser.). 1980. 39.95x (ISBN 0-416-74390-0). Methuen Inc.

--Early Christian Ireland. Elton, G. R., ed. LC 72-1498. (Sources of History Ser). 320p. 1973. 22.50x (ISBN 0-8014-0721-4); pap. 7.95 (ISBN 0-8014-9135-5, CP135). Cornell U Pr.

McDowell, R. B. Church of Ireland. (Studies in Irish History). 1975. 12.95x (ISBN 0-7100-8072-7). Routledge & Kegan.

Plummer, Charles. Vitae Sanctorum Hiberniae, 2 Vols. 1910. 48.00x set (ISBN 0-19-821390-5). Oxford U Pr.

Watt, John. The Church in Medieval Ireland, Vol. 5. (Gill History of Ireland Ser.). 1973. pap. 3.25 (ISBN 0-7171-0562-8). Irish Bk Ctr.

Whyte, J. H. Church & State in Modern Ireland: 1923 to 1979. 2nd ed. 491p. 1980. 32.50x (ISBN 0-389-20010-7). B&N.

Winnett, Arthur R. Peter Browne: Provost, Bishop, Metaphysician. (Church Historical Society Ser.: No. 95). 1974. text ed. 17.50x (ISBN 0-8401-5095-4). Allenson-Breckinridge.

IRELAND-CIVILIZATION

Akenson, Donald H. The United States & Ireland. LC 73-82348. (American Foreign Policy Library). 210p. 1973. 12.50x (ISBN 0-674-92460-6). Harvard U Pr.

De Breffny, Brian, ed. The Irish World. LC 77-6659. (Illus.). 1977. 40.00 (ISBN 0-8109-1120-5). Abrams.

Drudy, P. J., ed. Anglo-Irish Studies Three. 1977. text ed. 12.50x (ISBN 0-391-00820-X). Humanities.

--Anglo-Irish Studies Two. 1976. text ed. 10.00x (ISBN 0-391-01218-5). Humanities.

Farag, Fahmy. The Opposing Virtues: Two Essays. (New Yeats Papers: No. 15). 1978. pap. text ed. 9.25x (ISBN 0-85105-323-8, Dolmen Pr). Humanities.

Green, Alice S. The Making of Ireland & Its Undoing 1200-1600. facsimile ed. LC 75-37883. (Select Bibliographies Reprint Ser). Repr. of 1908 ed. 25.00 (ISBN 0-8369-6720-8). Arno.

Gregory, Lady Coole. 64p. 1971. Repr. of 1913 ed. 11.00x (ISBN 0-7165-1372-2, Pub. by Cuala Press Ireland). Biblio Dist.

Hull, Eleanor. History of Ireland & Her People, Vol. 1: From Earlier Times to the Tudor Period. LC 72-7296. (Select Bibliographies Reprint Ser.). 1972. Repr. of 1926 ed. 33.00 (ISBN 0-8369-6956-1). Arno.

--History of Ireland & Her People, Vol. 2: From the Stuart Period to Modern Times. LC 72-7296. (Select Bibliographies Reprint Ser.). 1972. Repr. of 1926 ed. 32.00 (ISBN 0-8369-6960-X). Arno.

Joyce, Patrick W. Social History of Ancient Ireland, 2 Vols. LC 68-56473. (Illus.). 1968. Repr. of 1913 ed. Set. 40.00 (ISBN 0-405-08677-6, Blom Pubns); 20.00 ea. Vol. 1 (ISBN 0-405-08678-4). Vol. 2 (ISBN 0-405-08679-2). Arno.

Macalister, Robert A. Ancient Ireland: A Study in the Lessons of Archeology & History. LC 72-83747. (Illus.). Repr. of 1935 ed. 18.00 (ISBN 0-405-08757-8, Pub. by Blom). Arno.

National Library of Ireland. Manuscript Sources for the History of Irish Civilisation: First Supplement, 3 vols. MacLochlainn, Alf, ed. 1979. Set. lib. bdg. 375.00 (ISBN 0-8161-0248-1). G K Hall.

National Library of Ireland - Dublin. Sources for the History of Irish Civilisation: Articles in Irish Periodicals, 9 vols. 1970. Set. 950.00 (ISBN 0-8161-0858-7). G K Hall.

O'Faolain, Sean. Irish: A Character Study. 1979. pap. 5.95 (ISBN 0-8159-5812-9). Devin.

Porter, Arthur K. Crosses & Culture of Ireland. LC 68-56480. (Illus.). 1969. Repr. of 1931 ed. 25.00 (ISBN 0-405-08860-4, Pub. by Blom). Arno.

Scherman, Katharine. The Flowering of Ireland: Saints, Scholars & Kings. (Illus.). 320p. 1981. 15.95 (ISBN 0-316-77284-4). Little.

Sheehy, Jeanne. The Rediscovery of Ireland's Past: The Celtic Revival 1830-1930. (Illus.). 1980. 19.95 (ISBN 0-500-01221-0). Thames Hudson.

Walsh, J. J. The World's Debt to the Irish. 75.00 (ISBN 0-87968-360-0). Gordon Pr.

IRELAND-COMMERCE

Chambers Commercial Guide to Ireland, 1975. 1975. lib. bdg. 8.50x (ISBN 0-8277-2848-4). British Bk Ctr.

Thom's Commercial Directory of Ireland 1979-1980. 129th ed. LC 7-24316. (Illus.). 976p. 1979. 55.00x (ISBN 0-8002-2450-7). Intl Pubns Serv.

IRELAND-DESCRIPTION AND TRAVEL

Atlas of Ireland. (Illus.). 112p. 1980. lib. bdg. 99.50 (ISBN 0-686-70053-8). St Martin.

Barrington, Jonah. Ireland of Sir Jonah Barrington: Selections from His Personal Sketches. Staples, Hugh B., ed. LC 67-21201. (Illus.). 352p. 1967. 14.50 (ISBN 0-295-95127-3). U of Wash Pr.

Barry, Terence B. The Medeival Moated Sites of South-Eastern Ireland. 1977. 25.00x (ISBN 0-904531-69-4, Pub. by BAR). State Mutual Bk.

Begley, Monie. Rambles in Ireland. LC 77-78830. (Illus.). 1977. 15.00 (ISBN 0-8159-5214-7). Devin.

Birnbaum, Stephen. Great Britain & Ireland Nineteen Eighty-Two. (The Get 'em & Go Travel Guide Ser.). 704p. 1981. pap. 10.95 (ISBN 0-395-31535-2). HM.

Boll, Heinrich. Irish Journal. Vennewitz, Leila, tr. from Ger. 1967. pap. 3.95 (ISBN 0-07-006415-6, GB). McGraw.

Bulfin, William. Rambles in the West of Ireland. abr. ed. 90p. 1979. pap. 3.75 (ISBN 0-85342-585-X). Irish Bk Ctr.

Carr, John. The Stranger in Ireland: Or, a Tour in the Southern & Western Part of That Country in the Year 1805. (Illus.). 532p. 1970. Repr. of 1806 ed. 47.50x (ISBN 0-87471-303-X). Rowman.

Clark, Wallace. Sailing Round Ireland. 1976. 22.50 (ISBN 0-7134-3133-4, Pub. by Batsford England). David & Charles.

Compton, Paul A. Northern Ireland: A Census Atlas. 1978. text ed. 39.00x (ISBN 0-7171-0891-0). Humanities.

Corkery, Daniel. The Hidden Ireland. 1967. pap. 5.95 (ISBN 0-7171-0079-0). Irish Bk Ctr.

Country Inns: Ireland. 1981. 5.95 (ISBN 0-89102-208-2). B Franklin.

Davies, Derek A. C. Ireland. LC 72-77797. (This Beautiful World Ser: Vol. 37). (Illus.). 118p. (Orig.). 1972. pap. 4.95 (ISBN 0-87011-180-9). Kodansha.

De Breffny, Brian. Castles of Ireland. (Illus.). 1977. 19.95 (ISBN 0-500-24100-7). Thames Hudson.

--Land of Ireland. LC 79-11461. (Illus.). 1979. 35.00 (ISBN 0-8109-1250-3). Abrams.

De Breffny, Brian & Mott, George. The Churches & Abbeys of Ireland. (Illus.). 1976. 14.95 (ISBN 0-393-04441-6). Norton.

Eagle, Dorothy & Carnell, Hilary. The Oxford Literary Guide to the British Iles. (Illus.). 464p. 1980. pap. 8.95 (ISBN 0-19-285098-9, GB 617). Oxford U Pr.

Evans, E. E. Irish Heritage. (Illus.). 1950. 15.00 (ISBN 0-85221-009-4). Dufour.

Feehan, John M. The Magic of the Kerry Coast. 122p. 1979. pap. 4.75 (ISBN 0-85342-584-1). Irish Bk Ctr.

FitzGibbon, Theodora. Taste of Ireland. LC 78-80422. (Illus.). 1969. 5.95 (ISBN 0-395-07681-1). HM.

Giraldus. Cambrensis Historical Works. Wright, Thomas, ed. LC 68-55551. (Bohn's Antiquarian Library Ser). Repr. of 1863 ed. 35.00 (ISBN 0-404-50015-3). AMS Pr.

Gorham, M. Ireland from Old Photographs. 1979. pap. 11.95 (ISBN 0-7134-2195-9, Pub. by Batsford England). David & Charles.

Gwynn, Stephen. The Charm of Ireland: Her Places of Beauty, Entertainment, Sport, & Historic Association. Repr. of 1927 ed. 17.50 (ISBN 0-685-64783-8). Norwood Edns.

Hickin, Norman. Irish Nature. (Illus.). 240p. 1980. 29.50x (ISBN 0-8476-6291-8). Rowman.

Jennett, Sean. The West of Ireland. (Illus.). 1980. 14.95 (ISBN 0-393-01338-3). Norton.

Lavelle, Des. Skellig: Island Outpost of Europe. 1976. 10.95 (ISBN 0-7735-0276-9). McGill-Queens U Pr.

McNally, Kenneth. The Batsford Colour Book of Ireland. (Illus.). 64p. 1981. Repr. of 1975 ed. 11.00 (ISBN 0-7134-2904-6, Pub. by Batsford England). David & Charles.

--Batsford Colour Book of Ireland. 1975. 11.95 (ISBN 0-7134-2904-6, Pub. by Batsford England). David & Charles.

--The Islands of Ireland. (Illus.). 1979. 17.95 (ISBN 0-393-04509-9). Norton.

Maxwell, Constantia. The Stranger in Ireland. facs. ed. (Sackville Library). 340p. 1979. Repr. of 1954 ed. 25.00 (ISBN 0-7171-0966-6). Irish Bk Ctr.

Morton, H. V. The Magic of Ireland. (Illus.). 1978. 12.95 (ISBN 0-396-07605-X). Dodd.

Mould, Daphne D. Irish Pilgrimage. 1957. 20.00 (ISBN 0-686-17250-7). Scholars Ref Lib.

N. Ireland Backed by S. Ireland. pap. 2.50 (ISBN 0-8277-2408-X). British Bk Ctr.

O'Brien, Henry. Atlantis in Ireland: Round Towers of Ireland. LC 73-94419. (Illus.). 544p. 1976. pap. 9.95 (ISBN 0-8334-1758-4, Steinerbooks). Multimedia.

Payne, Robert. A Briefe Description of Ireland Made in 1589. LC 72-6023. (English Experience Ser.: No. 548). 16p. 1973. Repr. of 1589 ed. 5.00 (ISBN 90-221-0548-2). Walter J Johnson.

Pochin Mould, D. D. The Mountains of Ireland. rev. ed. (Illus.). 1976. 14.95 (ISBN 0-7171-0815-5). Irish Bk Ctr.

Reilly, Cyril & Reilly, Renee. I Am of Ireland. (Illus.). 60p. (Orig.). 1981. pap. 6.95 (ISBN 0-03-059058-2). Winston Pr.

Reilly, Cyril A. & Reilly, Renee T. An Irish Blessing. (Illus.). 1977. pap. 6.95 (ISBN 0-03-021271-5). Winston Pr.

Sheehy, Terence. Ireland. (Illus.). 1979. 15.95 (ISBN 0-8317-4992-X, Mayflower Bks). Smith Pubs.

--Ireland in Colour. (Illus.). 79p. 1975. 14.95 (ISBN 0-393-04409-2). Norton.

Smith-Gordon, Lionel. Rural Reconstruction in Ireland. 1919. 32.50x (ISBN 0-685-69866-1). Elliots Bks.

Synge, John M. John M. Synge in West Kerry. Orig. Title: In West Kerry. 88p. 1979. pap. 3.50 (ISBN 0-85342-582-5). Irish Bk Ctr.

Teg, William. Vikings & Vagabonds. 1955. 3.00 (ISBN 0-8158-0197-1). Chris Mass.

Uris, Jill & Uris, Leon. Ireland: A Terrible Beauty. (Illus.). 1978. pap. 8.95 (ISBN 0-553-01208-8). Bantam.

Uris, Leon & Uris, Jill. Ireland: a Terrible Beauty. LC 73-9182. 304p. 1975. 24.95 (ISBN 0-385-07563-4). Doubleday.

Vaughn-Thomas, Wynford. The Countryside of Great Britain & Ireland. LC 79-12671. (Illus.). 1979. 14.95 (ISBN 0-8317-1794-7, Mayflower Bks). Smith Pubs.

Veber, May. Ireland Observed. Joss, Jean, tr. (Observed Ser.). (Illus.). 1980. 24.95 (ISBN 0-19-520201-5). Oxford U Pr.

Walker, Brian M., et al. Faces of Ireland: 1875-1925. 1981. 50.00x (ISBN 0-904651-47-9, Pub. by Appletree Ireland). State Mutual Bk.

Ward, Philip. Come with Me to Ireland. (Illus.). 6.50 (ISBN 0-902675-36-2). Oleander Pr.

Whelpton, Barbara. Unknown Ireland. LC 65-9275. (Unknown Guide Ser.). (Illus.). 1964. 12.50x (ISBN 0-85307-039-3). Intl Pubns Serv.
Woods, Cedric S. Freshwater Life in Ireland. 1974. 7.00x (ISBN 0-7165-2280-2, Pub. by Irish Academic Pr Ireland); pap. 2.50x o. p. (ISBN 0-7165-2281-0). Biblio Dist.
Young, Arthur. A Tour in Ireland: 1776-1779, 2 vols. 4th ed. Hutton, A. W., ed. 1970. Repr. of 1892 ed. Set. 27.00x (ISBN 0-686-28472-0, Pub. by Irish Academic Pr). Biblio Dist.

IRELAND–DESCRIPTION AND TRAVEL–GUIDEBOOKS

Abse, Joan. The Art Galleries of Britain & Ireland: A Guide to Their Collections. LC 75-24944. (Illus.). 248p. 1975. 15.00 (ISBN 0-8386-1850-2). Fairleigh Dickinson.
Arthur Frommer's Guide to Dublin & Ireland, 1981-82. 215p. Date not set. pap. 2.95 (ISBN 0-671-41431-3). Frommer-Pasmantier.
Arthur Frommer's Guide to Dublin, Ireland: 1981-82. pap. 2.95 (ISBN 0-671-41431-3). Frommer-Pasmantier.
Automobile Association. AA Ireland: Where to Go, What to Do. (Illus.). 204p. 1981. pap. 7.95 (ISBN 0-86145-035-3, Pub. by Auto Assn-British Tourist Authority England). Merrimack Bk Serv.
Automobile Association of England, ed. Treasures of Britain. 3rd ed. (Illus.). 1976. 24.95 (ISBN 0-393-08743-3). Norton.
Bartholomew, John. Observer's Tourist Atlas of Great Britain & Ireland. (Observer Bks.). (Illus.). 1977. 2.95 (ISBN 0-684-15210-X, ScribT). Scribner.
Begley, Monie. Rambles in Ireland. rev. ed. LC 79-27302. (Illus.). 1979. 9.95 (ISBN 0-416-00651-5). Methuen Inc.
Blue Guide - Ireland. 1979. 27.95 (ISBN 0-528-84633-7); pap. 19.95 (ISBN 0-528-84632-9). Rand.
British Tourist Authority. AA Touring Guide to Ireland. (Illus.). 1979. 22.95 (ISBN 0-09-127020-0, Pub. by B T A). Merrimack Bk Serv.
Courtenay, Ashley. Nineteen Eighty Let's Halt Awhile in Ireland. 1980. pap. 5.95 (ISBN 0-8038-4330-5). Hastings.
Cox, Thornton. Ireland. (Thornton Cox's Travellers' Guides Ser.). Date not set. pap. 5.95 (ISBN 0-8038-7159-7). Hastings.
Eagle, Dorothy & Carnell, Hilary, eds. The Oxford Illustrated Literary Guide to Great Britain & Ireland. (Illus.). 352p. 1981. 29.95 (ISBN 0-19-869125-4). Oxford U Pr.
Egon Ronay's Guide 1977: Hotels, Restaurants & Inns in Great Britain & Ireland. 1977. pap. 8.95 (ISBN 0-8277-4928-7). British Bk Ctr.
Fodor's Ireland, 1981. 1980. 12.95 (ISBN 0-679-00697-4); pap. 9.95 (ISBN 0-679-00698-2). McKay.
Guide to Great Britain & Ireland. (Foreign Guides). 1981. pap. 7.95 (ISBN 0-528-84535-7). Rand.
Guide to Hotels & Restaurants, 1978: Great Britain & Ireland. (A.A. Guides Ser.). (Illus.). 1978. pap. 8.95x (ISBN 0-09-132001-1). Standing Orders.
Harrison, John & Harrison, Shirley. Ireland. (Pocket Guides). pap. 3.95 (ISBN 0-528-84312-5). Rand.
Harvard Student Agencies. Let's Go, Britain & Ireland: The Budget Guide 1980 to 1981 Edition. (Illus.). 1980. pap. 5.50 (ISBN 0-525-93090-6). Dutton.
Ireland on Fifteen Dollars a Day, 1979-80. 320p. pap. 4.95 (ISBN 0-671-41421-6). Frommer-Pasmantier.
Jones, J. Sydney. Bike & Hike: Sixty Tours Around Great Britain & Ireland. (Illus., Orig.). 1978. pap. 3.95 (ISBN 0-8467-0439-0, Pub. by Two Continents). Hippocrene Bks.
Kehoe, William & Kehoe, Constance. Enjoying Ireland. rev. ed. 288p. 1981. pap. 6.95 (ISBN 0-8159-5406-9). Devin.
Michelin Guides & Maps. Michelin Red Guide to Great Britain & Ireland. (Red Guide Ser.). 1981. 12.95 (ISBN 2-06-006501-1). Michelin.
Murphy, Marese. Thornton Cox Travellers Guide to Ireland. (Illus.). 1977. pap. 5.95 (ISBN 0-8038-7159-7). Hastings.
Nagel Editorial Staff. Nagel's Guide to Ireland. (Encyclopedia Guides Ser.). 1980. 38.00 (ISBN 2-8263-0736-3). Hippocrene Bks.
The Nagel Travel Guide to Great Britain & Ireland. (Nagel Travel Guide Ser.). (Illus.). 750p. 1974. 45.00 (ISBN 2-8263-0405-4). Hippocrene Bks.
Nagel's Encyclopedia Guide: Ireland. (Illus.). 352p. 1979. 38.00 (ISBN 2-8263-0736-3). Masson Pub.
Ransom, P. J. Holiday Cruising in Ireland: A Guide to Irish Inland Waterways. (Illus.). 152p. 1971. 4.50 (ISBN 0-7153-5003-X). David & Charles.
Ronay, Egon. Egon Ronay's Lucasa Guide 1981: To Hotels, Resturants, Inns in Great Britain & Ireland & Guide to 740 Furnished Apartments in London. rev. ed. LC 74-644899. (Illus.). 830p. 1981. pap. 12.95 (ISBN 0-03-058958-4). HR&W.
Rose, H. Your Guide to Ireland. 1965. 5.25x (ISBN 0-8002-0780-7). Intl Pubns Serv.
Simpson, Norman T. Country Inns & Back Roads: Britain & Ireland. (Illus., Orig.). 1980. pap. 6.95 (ISBN 0-912944-58-7). Berkshire Traveller.
Southwest Ireland, Yorr Guide. pap. 2.95 (ISBN 0-8277-2433-0). British Bk Ctr.
Suilleabhain, Sean O. Irish Walk Guides: No. 1, Southwest. Lynam, Joss, ed. (Irish Walk Guide Ser.). 1978. pap. 2.95 (ISBN 0-7171-0907-0). Irish Bk Ctr.
Verstappen, Peter, ed. Rand McNally Guide to Great Britain & Ireland. LC 78-70556. (Illus.). 1981. pap. 7.95 (ISBN 0-528-84535-7). Rand.
Whilde, Tony. Irish Walk Guides: West, Clare, Galway, Mayo. Lynam, Joss, ed. (Irish Walk Guide Ser.: No. 2). (Illus.). 1978. pap. 2.95 (ISBN 0-7171-0908-9). Irish Bk Ctr.

IRELAND–ECONOMIC CONDITIONS

Balfour, Arthur J., et al. Against Home Rule. Rosenbaum, S., ed. LC 75-102591. (Irish Culture & History Ser). (Illus.). 1970. Repr. of 1912 ed. 14.50 (ISBN 0-8046-0768-0). Kennikat.
Cairnes, John E. Political Essays. LC 66-22615. Repr. of 1873 ed. 17.50x (ISBN 0-678-00206-1). Kelley.
Crumpe, Samuel. Essay on the Best Means of Providing Employment for the People. 2nd. ed. LC 67-29499. Repr. of 1795 ed. 19.50x (ISBN 0-678-00410-2). Kelley.
Cullen, L. M. Anglo-Irish Trade Sixteen Hundred Sixty to Eighteen Hundred. LC 68-56548. 1968. 15.00x (ISBN 0-678-06757-0). Kelley.
--Economic History of Ireland Since 1660. pap. 14.95 (ISBN 0-7134-1382-4, Pub. by Batsford England). David & Charles.
Donnelly, James S. Land & People of Nineteenth-Century Cork. 1975. 42.50 (ISBN 0-7100-7986-9). Routledge & Kegan.
Godkin, James. Land-War in Ireland. LC 72-102605. (Irish Culture & History Ser). 1970. Repr. of 1870 ed. 22.50 (ISBN 0-8046-0782-6). Kennikat.
Green, Alice S. The Making of Ireland & Its Undoing 1200-1600. facsimile ed. LC 75-37883. (Select Bibliographies Reprint Ser). Repr. of 1908 ed. 25.00 (ISBN 0-8369-6720-8). Arno.
Kiernan, Thomas J. History of the Financial Administration of Ireland to Eighteen Seventeen. (Perspectives in European History: No. 29). Repr. of 1930 ed. lib. bdg. 20.00x (ISBN 0-87991-822-5). Porcupine Pr.
Lane, Padraig. Ireland. (Illus.). 96p. 1974. 17.50x (ISBN 0-7134-2845-7). Intl Pubns Serv.
Malthus, Thomas R. The Occasional Papers on Population & Political Economy from Contemporary Journals. Semmel, Bernard, ed. 1963. 23.50 (ISBN 0-8337-2197-6). B Franklin.
Marx, Karl & Engels, Frederick. Ireland & the Irish Question. Dixon, Richard, ed. Ryazanskaya, S., et al, trs. from Fr., Ger. & It. LC 73-188754. 518p. 1972. pap. 3.25 (ISBN 0-7178-0342-2). Intl Pub Co.
Morris, Lloyd R. Celtic Dawn: A Survey of the Renascence in Ireland, 1889-1916. LC 78-132944. 1971. Repr. of 1917 ed. 11.00x (ISBN 0-8154-0359-3). Cooper Sq.
Nicholls, Kenneth. Gaelic & Gaelicised Ireland in the Middle Ages. (Gill History of Ireland: Vol. 4). (Illus.). 212p. 1972. pap. 5.75 (ISBN 0-7171-0561-X). Irish Bk Ctr.
O'Brien, George A. Economic History of Ireland from the Union to the Famine. LC 68-56554. Repr. of 1921 ed. lib. bdg. 19.50x (ISBN 0-678-00816-7). Kelley.
--Economic History of Ireland from the Union to the Famine. LC 68-56554. Repr. of 1921 ed. lib. bdg. 19.50x (ISBN 0-678-00816-7). Kelley.
--The Economic History of Ireland in the Eighteenth Century. LC 77-24245. (Perspectives in European History Ser.: No. 15). (Illus.). 437p. Repr. of 1918 ed. lib. bdg. 20.00x (ISBN 0-87991-622-2). Porcupine Pr.
--Economic History of Ireland in the Seventeenth Century. LC 68-56555. Repr. of 1919 ed. lib. bdg. 15.00x (ISBN 0-678-00817-5). Kelley.
--Economic History of Ireland in the Seventeenth Century. LC 68-56555. Repr. of 1919 ed. lib. bdg. 15.00x (ISBN 0-678-00817-5). Kelley.
O'Tuathaigh, Gearoid. Ireland Before the Famine. (Gill History of Ireland: Vol. 9). 248p. 1972. pap. 5.75 (ISBN 0-7171-0566-0). Irish Bk Ctr.
Petty, William. History of the Survey of Ireland, Commonly Called the Down Survey. Larcom, Thomas A., ed. LC 67-20090. Repr. of 1851 ed. 19.50x (ISBN 0-678-00341-6). Kelley.
Plunkett, Horace. Ireland in the New Century. LC 77-102625. (Irish Culture & History Ser). 1970. Repr. of 1904 ed. 14.50 (ISBN 0-8046-0801-6). Kennikat.
Postlethwayt, Malachy. Britain's Commercial Interest Explained & Improved, 2 Vols. LC 68-22376. Repr. of 1757 ed. Set. 45.00x (ISBN 0-678-00392-0). Kelley.
Potter, George. To the Golden Door. LC 73-3928. (Illus.). 631p. 1974. Repr. of 1960 ed. lib. bdg. 35.00x (ISBN 0-8371-6862-7, POGD). Greenwood.
Smith, Elizabeth. The Irish Journals of Elizabeth Smith Eighteen Forty to Eighteen Fifty. Thomson, David & McGusty, Moyra, eds. (Illus.). 352p. 1980. 39.95x (ISBN 0-19-822471-0). Oxford U Pr.
Solow, Barbara L. Land Question & the Irish Economy, 1870-1903. LC 78-158431. (Economic Studies: No. 139). (Illus.). 1971. 10.00x (ISBN 0-674-50875-0). Harvard U Pr.
--Land Question & the Irish Economy, 1870-1903. LC 78-158431. (Economic Studies: No. 139). (Illus.). 1971. 10.00x (ISBN 0-674-50875-0). Harvard U Pr.
Thornton, William T. Plea for Peasant Proprietors. LC 68-58028. Repr. of 1848 ed. 15.00x (ISBN 0-678-00569-9). Kelley.

IRELAND–EMIGRATION AND IMMIGRATION

Adams, William F. Ireland & Irish Emigration to the New World from Eighteen Fifteen to the Famine. LC 79-90753. 444p. 1980. Repr. of 1932 ed. 20.00 (ISBN 0-8063-0868-0). Genealog Pub.
Byrne, Stephen. Irish Immigration to the United States: What It Has Been and What It Is. LC 69-18763. (American Immigration Collection Ser., No. 1). (Illus.). 1969. Repr. of 1873 ed. 9.50 (ISBN 0-405-00511-3). Arno.
Clark, Dennis. The Irish Relations: Trials of an Immigrant Tradition. LC 81-65293. 224p. 1981. 19.00 (ISBN 0-8386-3083-9). Fairleigh Dickinson.
Davin, N. F. The Irishman in Canada. 718p. Repr. of 1877 ed. 30.00x (ISBN 0-7165-0060-4, Pub. by Irish Academic Pr Ireland). Biblio Dist.
Hale, Edward E. Letters on Irish Emigration. LC 70-39376. (Select Bibliographies Reprint Series). 1972. Repr. of 1852 ed. 10.00 (ISBN 0-8369-9910-X). Arno.
Kennedy, Robert E., Jr. The Irish: Emigration, Marriage, & Fertility. LC 70-187740. 304p. 1973. 23.75x (ISBN 0-520-01987-3); pap. 5.95x (ISBN 0-520-02896-1). U of Cal Pr.
Lockhart, Audrey. Some Aspects of Irish Emmigration from Ireland to the North American Colonies Between 1660-1775. LC 76-6351. (Irish Americans Ser.). 1976. 15.00 (ISBN 0-405-09345-4). Arno.
Maguire, Edward J., ed. Reverend John O'Hanlon's The Irish Emmigrant's Guide to the United States. LC 76-6352. (Irish Americans Ser). 1976. 17.00 (ISBN 0-405-09346-2). Arno.
Marshall, William F. Ulster Sails West. LC 76-56641. 1979. pap. 5.00 (ISBN 0-8063-0754-4). Genealog Pub.
Potter, George. To the Golden Door. LC 73-3928. (Illus.). 631p. 1974. Repr. of 1960 ed. lib. bdg. 35.00x (ISBN 0-8371-6862-7, POGD). Greenwood.
Schrier, Arnold. Ireland & the American Emigration, 1850-1900. LC 70-83864. (Illus.). 1970. Repr. of 1958 ed. 9.50 (ISBN 0-8462-1416-4). Russell.
Woodham-Smith, Cecil B. Great Hunger. LC 62-11223. (Illus.). 1963. 16.95 (ISBN 0-06-014740-7, HarpT). Har-Row.

IRELAND–FOREIGN RELATIONS

Dangerfield, George. The Damnable Question: A Study in Anglo-Irish Relations. pap. 5.95 (ISBN 0-316-17201-4, Atlantic-Little, Brown). Little.
--The Damnable Question: A Study of Anglo-Irish Relations. 1976. 14.95 (ISBN 0-316-17200-6, Pub. by Atlantic Monthly Pr). Little.
De Vere, Aubrey. English Misrule & Irish Misdeeds. LC 77-102597. (Irish Culture & History Ser). 1970. Repr. of 1848 ed. 12.75 (ISBN 0-8046-0775-3). Kennikat.
Fuller, R. Buckminster. Critical Path. 448p. 1981. 15.95 (ISBN 0-312-17488-8). St Martin.
Murray, Alice E. History of the Commercial & Financial Relations Between England & Ireland from the Period of the Restoration. LC 75-122235. (Research & Source Works Ser: No. 482). 1970. Repr. of 1903 ed. lib. bdg. 29.00 (ISBN 0-8337-2491-6). B Franklin.
Townshend, Charles. The British Campaign in Ireland, Nineteen Nineteen to Nineteen Twenty-One. (Oxford Historical Monographs). (Illus.). 256p. 1978. pap. 12.95x (ISBN 0-19-821874-5). Oxford U Pr.
Whitlock, Dorothy, et al, eds. Ireland in Early Medieval Europe. LC 80-40325. (Studies in Memory of Kathleen Hughes). (Illus.). 400p. Date not set. 95.00 (ISBN 0-521-23547-2). Cambridge U Pr.

IRELAND–GENEALOGY

Burke, John. A Genealogical & Heraldic History of the Commoners of Great Britain & Ireland. LC 76-44267. 1977. 85.00 (ISBN 0-8063-0742-0). Genealog Pub.
Burke, John B. The General Armory of England, Scotland, Ireland, & Wales. LC 66-28797. (Illus.). 1976. 50.00 (ISBN 0-8063-0064-7). Genealog Pub.
Cochran, Alice L. The Saga of an Irish Immigrant Family: The Descendants of John Mullanphy. LC 76-6328. (Irish Americans Ser.). 1976. 17.00 (ISBN 0-405-09325-X). Arno.
Crisp, Frederick A. & Howard, Joseph J. Visitation of Ireland, 6 vols. in 1. LC 72-10820. (Illus.). 1973. Repr. of 1918 ed. 30.00 (ISBN 0-8063-0543-6). Genealog Pub.
Egan, Joseph J. & Egan, Mary J. History of Clan Egan: The Birds of the Forest of Wisdom. LC 79-25089. (Illus.). 332p. (Orig.). 1979. pap. 26.50 (ISBN 0-8357-0492-0, SS-00124). Univ Microfilms.
Falley, Margaret D. Irish & Scotch-Irish Ancestral Research, 2 vols. 1962. 35.85 (ISBN 0-686-15423-1). M D Falley.
Farrar, Henry. Irish Marriages: Being an Index to the Marriages in Walker's Hibernian Magazine, 1771-1812, 2 vols. in 1. LC 72-5685. 1972. Repr. of 1897 ed. 20.00 (ISBN 0-8063-0517-7). Genealog Pub.
Jones, George A. Crown & Sword: The Milesian-Celtic Heritage of Ireland & Britain. LC 76-44145. 1977. pap. 3.95 (ISBN 0-917610-00-8). Rookfield.
Lodge, John. Peerage of Ireland, or a Genealogical History of the Present Nobility of That Kingdom, 7 Vols. Archdall, Mervyn, ed. LC 77-172749. Repr. of 1789 ed. Set. 150.00 (ISBN 0-404-07970-9); 22.50 ea. AMS Pr.
MacLysaght, Edward. The Families of Ireland. 450p. Date not set. 40.00x (ISBN 0-686-26446-0, Pub. by Irish Academic Pr). Biblio Dist.
Matheson, Robert E. Special Report on Surnames in Ireland: Varieties & Synonymes of Surnames & Christian Names in Ireland. LC 68-54684. 1975. Repr. of 1901 ed. 12.50 (ISBN 0-8063-0187-2). Genealog Pub.
Moore, Thomas. Memoirs of Captain Rock (pseud.) the Celebrated Irish Chieftain: With Some Account of His Ancestors. LC 75-28831. Repr. of 1824 ed. 26.00 (ISBN 0-404-13821-7). AMS Pr.
O'Hart, J. The Irish & Anglo-Irish Landed Gentry When Cromwell Came to Ireland. 804p. 1969. Repr. of 1884 ed. 30.00x (ISBN 0-7165-0038-8, Pub. by Irish Academic Pr Ireland). Biblio Dist.
O'Hart, John. Irish Pedigrees: Or, the Origin & Stem of the Irish Nation, 2 vols. 5th ed. LC 76-12097. 1976. Repr. of 1892 ed. Set. 60.00 (ISBN 0-8063-0737-4). Genealog Pub.
O'Laughlin, Michael C. The Complete Book for Tracing Your Irish Ancestors. (Irish Genealogy Ser.). (Illus.). 224p. 1981. lib. bdg. write for info. (ISBN 0-940134-01-2). Irish Genealog.
--The O'Donaghue Book: Irish Family Histories Ser. 50p. 1981. 9.95 (ISBN 0-940134-16-0). Irish Genealog.
--The O'Laughlin Book. (Irish Family Histories Ser.). 50p. 1981. 9.95 (ISBN 0-940134-17-9). Irish Genealog.
--Three Hundred Great Families of Ireland. (Irish Genealogical Ser.). 300p. 1981. text ed. 24.95 (ISBN 0-940134-11-X). Irish Genealog.

IRELAND–HISTORIC HOUSES, ETC.

Barrow, George L. The Round Towers of Ireland. (Illus.). 230p. 1979. 35.00 (ISBN 0-906187-04-4, Pub. by Acad Pr Ireland). Devin.
Barry, Terence B. The Medeival Moated Sites of South-Eastern Ireland. 1977. 25.00x (ISBN 0-904531-69-4, Pub. by BAR). State Mutual Bk.
De Breffny, Brian & Mott, George. The Churches & Abbeys of Ireland. (Illus.). 1976. 14.95 (ISBN 0-393-04441-6). Norton.
Historic Houses, Castles & Gardens in Great Britain & Ireland 1980. LC 57-35834. (Illus.). 167p. (Orig.). 1980. pap. 4.50x (ISBN 0-900486-26-0). Intl Pubns Serv.

IRELAND–HISTORY

see also Fenians

Akenson, Donald H. Between Two Revolutons: Islandmagee County Antrim, Seventeen Ninety-Eight to Nineteen Twenty. (Illus.). 221p. 1979. 17.50 (ISBN 0-208-01827-1, Archon). Shoe String.
Bailey, Anthony. Acts of Union: Reports on Ireland, 1973-79. 1980. 8.95 (ISBN 0-394-51073-9). Random.
Ball, F. Elrington. A History of the County of Dublin, 6 vols. (Sackville Library). 1168p. 1979. Repr. of 1902 ed. 100.00 (ISBN 0-7171-0971-2). Irish Bk Ctr.
Barnard, T. C. Cromwellian Ireland: English Government & Reform in Ireland 1649-1660. (Oxford Historical Monographs). 352p. 1975. text ed. 45.00x (ISBN 0-19-821858-3). Oxford U Pr.

Barrow, George L. The Round Towers of Ireland. (Illus.). 230p. 1979. 35.00 (ISBN 0-906187-04-4, Pub. by Acad Pr Ireland). Devin.
Beckett, J. C. Confrontations: Studies in Irish History. 175p. 1972. 13.50x (ISBN 0-87471-147-9). Rowman.
Beckett, James C. Short History of Ireland. 6th ed. 1975. 17.50x (ISBN 0-391-02079-X, Hutchinson U Lib); pap. text ed. 10.25x (ISBN 0-391-02080-3). Humanities.
Beckett, James G. Making of Modern Ireland, 1603-1923. 1966. 13.95 (ISBN 0-394-43473-0). Knopf.
Bell, J. Bowyer. The Secret Army: The Ira, 1916-1979. rev. ed. (Illus.). 508p. 1980. text ed. 30.00x (ISBN 0-262-02145-5). MIT Pr.
Berardis, Vincenzo. Italy & Ireland in the Middle Ages. 1977. lib. bdg. 59.95 (ISBN 0-8490-2089-1). Gordon Pr.
Berleth, Richard. The Twilight Lords: An Irish Chronicle. LC 77-15125. 1978. 12.95 (ISBN 0-394-49667-1). Knopf.
Bew, Paul. Land & the National Question in Ireland Eighteen Fifty-Eight to Eighty-Two. (Illus.). 1979. text ed. 15.50x (ISBN 0-391-00960-5). Humanities.
Bhreathnach, Eibhlin. Life & People of the Middle Ages: Ireland, England & Europe C. 500- C. 1250. (Illus.). pap. text ed. cancelled (ISBN 0-7171-0787-6). Irish Bk Ctr.
Blunt, Wilfrid S. The Land War in Ireland. LC 75-28808. Repr. of 1912 ed. 41.50 (ISBN 0-404-13801-2). AMS Pr.
Bowden, Tom. The Breakdown of Public Security: The Case of Ireland 1916-1921 & Palestine 1936-1939. LC 76-56682. (Sage Studies in Twentieth Century History: Vol. 8). (Illus.). 342p. 1977. 20.00 (ISBN 0-8039-9865-1); pap. 9.95 (ISBN 0-8039-9866-X). Sage.
Bowen, Desmond. The Protestant Crusade in Ireland, 1800-70: A Study of Protestant-Catholic Relations Between the Act of Union & Disestablishment. 1978. 23.95x (ISBN 0-7735-0295-5). McGill-Queens U Pr.
Bowen, Elizabeth. Bowen's Court. LC 64-19368. (Neglected Books of the Twentieth Century). (Illus.). (gr. 10-12). 1979. pap. 6.95 (ISBN 0-912946-67-9). Ecco Pr.
Boylan, Henry. A Dictionary of Irish Biography. LC 78-67791. 1978. text ed. 25.00x (ISBN 0-06-490620-5). B&N.
Bradshaw, Brendan. The Irish Constitutional Revolution in the Sixteenth Century. LC 78-58785. 1979. 41.50 (ISBN 0-521-22206-0). Cambridge U Pr.
Brendan-Bradley, Patrick. Bantry Bay: Ireland in the Days of Napoleon & Wolfe Tone. LC 31-24620. Repr. of 1931 ed. 14.50 (ISBN 0-384-05660-1). Johnson Repr.
Brown, Malcolm. The Politics of Irish Literature: From Thomas Davis to W. B. Yeats. LC 72-152328. (Washington Paperback Ser.: No. 67). 443p. 1972. 12.00 (ISBN 0-295-95170-2); pap. 3.95 (ISBN 0-295-95280-6). U of Wash Pr.
Brynn, Edward. Crown & Castle: British Rule in Ireland 1800-1830. (Illus.). 1978. text ed. 32.00x (ISBN 0-7705-1496-0). Humanities.
Bufwack, Mary S. Village Without Violence: An Examination of a Northern Irish Community. 256p. 1981. text ed. 16.50x (ISBN 0-87073-849-6); pap. text ed. 7.95x (ISBN 0-87073-875-5). Schenkman.
Burke, William P. The Irish Priests in Penal Times. 508p. 1968. Repr. of 1914 ed. 19.00x (ISBN 0-7165-0034-5, Pub. by Irish Academic Pr Ireland). Biblio Dist.
Butler, William F. Confiscation in Irish History. LC 76-102594. (Irish Culture & History Ser). 1970. Repr. of 1917 ed. 12.50 (ISBN 0-8046-0771-0). Kennikat.
Calder, Grace J., ed. Carlyle's Dubliners. 1980. 22.50x (ISBN 0-85105-268-1, Dolmen Pr). Humanities.
Campion, Edmund. A Historie of Ireland. LC 41-6539. 1977. Repr. of 1633 ed. 30.00x (ISBN 0-8201-1191-0). Schol Facsimiles.
Carroll, Francis M. American Opinion & the Irish Question: 1910-1923. LC 78-58897. 1978. 25.00x (ISBN 0-312-02890-3). St Martin.
Carroll, Joseph. Ireland in the War Years: 1939-1945. LC 74-16547. 1975. 14.50x (ISBN 0-8448-0607-2). Crane-Russak Co.
Carter, Carolle J. The Shamrock & the Swastika: German Espionage in Ireland in World War II. LC 76-14103. (Illus.). 1977. 12.95 (ISBN 0-87015-221-1). Pacific Bks.
Caulfield, Malachy. The Easter Rebellion. LC 74-5550. 375p. 1975. Repr. of 1963 ed. lib. bdg. 21.00x (ISBN 0-8371-7507-0, CAER). Greenwood.
Chauvire, Roger. A Short History of Ireland. 4.95 (ISBN 0-8159-6811-6). Devin.
Clark, Samuel. Social Origins of the Irish Land War. LC 79-83980. 1979. 28.50 (ISBN 0-691-05272-7); pap. 8.95 (ISBN 0-691-10068-3). Princeton U Pr.
Cobden, Richard. England, Ireland, & America. LC 77-28350. 1980. text ed. 15.95x (ISBN 0-915980-44-4). Inst Study Human.
Collins, M. E. Conquest & Colonisation. (History of Ireland Ser.: Vol. 2). (Illus.). 240p. 1969. pap. text ed. 8.50 (ISBN 0-7171-0256-4). Irish Bk Ctr.
--Ireland, Eighteen Hundred to Nineteen Seventy. (Illus.). 1976. pap. text ed. 6.95x (ISBN 0-582-22140-4). Longman.
Comerford, Anthony. Easter Rising: Dublin 1916. (Jackdaw Ser: No. 61). (Illus.). 1969. 6.95 (ISBN 0-670-28732-6, Grossman). Viking Pr.
Coogan, Timothy P. Ireland Since the Rising. LC 75-35333. (Illus.). 355p. 1976. Repr. of 1966 ed. lib. bdg. 27.50x (ISBN 0-8371-8560-2, COIR). Greenwood.
Costello, Peter. The Heart Grown Brutal: The Irish Revolution in Literature, from Parnell to the Death of Yeats, 1891-1939. (Illus.). 330p. 1977. 24.50x (ISBN 0-8476-6007-9). Rowman.
Costigan, Giovanni. A History of Modern Ireland: With a Sketch of Earlier Times. LC 69-15699. (Illus.). 1970. pap. 7.50 (ISBN 0-672-63547-X). Pegasus.
Coughlan, Rupert. Napper Tandy. (Illus.). 1976. 18.50 (ISBN 0-900068-34-5). Irish Bk Ctr.
Coupland, Reginald. American Revolution & the British Empire. LC 65-18801. 1965. Repr. of 1930 ed. 7.50 (ISBN 0-8462-0601-3). Russell.
Croker, Thomas C., ed. Narratives Illustrative of the Contests in Ireland in 1641 & 1690. (Camden Society, London. Publications. First Ser.: No. 14). Repr. of 1841 ed. 17.50 (ISBN 0-404-50114-1). AMS Pr.
--Narratives Illustrative of the Contests in Ireland in 1641 & 1690. 1841. 19.50 (ISBN 0-384-10190-9). Johnson Repr.
Cronin, Sean. Irish Nationalism: A History of Its Roots & Ideology. (Illus.). 394p. 1981. 17.50 (ISBN 0-8264-0062-0). Continuum.
Cronne, H. A., et al, eds. Essays in British & Irish History in Honour of James Eadie Todd. 1977. Repr. of 1949 ed. lib. bdg. 25.00 (ISBN 0-8495-0711-1). Arden Lib.
--Essays in British & Irish History in Honour of James Eadie Todd. Quinn, D. B. 1977. Repr. of 1949 ed. lib. bdg. 30.00 (ISBN 0-8482-3478-2). Norwood Edns.
Crowley, Flor. In West Cork Long Ago. 127p. (Orig.). pap. 4.50 (ISBN 0-85342-600-7). Irish Bk Ctr.
Cullen, L. M. Economic History of Ireland Since 1660. pap. 14.95 (ISBN 0-7134-1382-4, Pub. by Batsford England). David & Charles.
Curran, Joseph M. The Birth of the Irish Free State, 1921-1923. LC 79-4088. 1980. 22.75x (ISBN 0-8173-0013-9). U of Ala Pr.
Curtis, Edmund. History of Ireland. 6th ed. 1961. pap. 15.95x (ISBN 0-416-67730-4). Methuen Inc.
--A History of Medieval Ireland from 1086 to 1513. 1976. lib. bdg. 59.95 (ISBN 0-8490-1977-X). Gordon Pr.
Davies, G. L. & Stephens, Nicholas. Ireland. (Illus.). 1978. 20.95x (ISBN 0-416-84640-8). Methuen Inc.
Davies, Rowland. Journal of the Very Rev. Rowland Davies, from March 8, 1688-9, to September 29, 1690. Caulfield, Richard, ed. LC 71-163674. (Camden Society, London. Publications, First Ser.: No. 68). Repr. of 1857 ed. 21.00 (ISBN 0-404-50168-0). AMS Pr.
--Journal of the Very Rev. Rowland Davies, Ll.D. Dean of Ross from March 8, 1688-9 to September 29, 1690. 1857. 23.00 (ISBN 0-384-10995-0). Johnson Repr.
De Breffny, Brian. Land of Ireland. LC 79-11461. (Illus.). 1979. 35.00 (ISBN 0-8109-1250-3). Abrams.
Delaney, E. J. & Feehan, J. M. Comic History of Ireland. 125p. 1951. pap. 4.50 (ISBN 0-85342-058-0). Irish Bk Ctr.
Denieffe, Joseph. A Personal Narrative of the Irish Revolutionary Brotherhood. (Illus.). 293p. 1969. Repr. of 1906 ed. 17.00x (ISBN 0-686-28341-4, Pub. by Irish Academic Pr). Biblio Dist.
De Tocqueville, Alexis. Journeys to England & Ireland. Mayer, J. P., ed. LC 78-67392. (European Political Thought Ser.). 1979. Repr. of 1958 ed. lib. bdg. 15.00x (ISBN 0-405-11745-0). Arno.
Devoy, J. Recollections of an Irish Rebel. 508p. 1969. Repr. of 1929 ed. 25.00x (ISBN 0-7165-0045-0, Pub. by Irish Academic Pr Ireland). Biblio Dist.
Dolley, Michael. Anglo-Norman Ireland, Vol. 3. (Gill History of Ireland). (Illus.). 210p. 1973. pap. 3.25 (ISBN 0-7171-0560-1). Irish Bk Ctr.
Donnelly, James S. Land & People of Nineteenth-Century Cork. 1975. 42.50 (ISBN 0-7100-7986-9). Routledge & Kegan.
Drudy, P. J., ed. Anglo Irish Studies, No. 4. 1979. text ed. 14.75x (ISBN 0-391-01178-2). Humanities.
--Irish Studies, Vol. 1. LC 80-40084. 192p. 1981. 29.50 (ISBN 0-521-23336-4). Cambridge U Pr.
Duffy, Charles G. My Life in Two Hemispheres, 2 vols. 1969. Repr. of 1898 ed. Set. write for info. (ISBN 0-7165-0603-3, Pub. by Irish Academic Pr Ireland); Vol. 1, 335pgs. 20.00x (ISBN 0-686-30762-3); Vol. 2, 395pgs. 20.00x (ISBN 0-7165-0561-4). Biblio Dist.
--Young Ireland. LC 71-127257. (Europe 1815-1945 Ser.). 796p. 1973. Repr. of 1881 ed. lib. bdg. 59.50 (ISBN 0-306-71119-2). Da Capo.
Dunleavy, Gareth W. & Dunleavy, Janet E. The O'Conor Papers: A Descriptive Catalog & Surname Register of the Materials at Clonalis House. LC 76-53652. 1977. 50.00 (ISBN 0-299-07240-1, IS-00016, Pub. by Univ. of Wisconsin Pr). Univ Microfilms.
Dwyer, P. Siege of Londonderry. 1971. Repr. of 1689 ed. 17.00x (ISBN 0-8464-0847-3). Beekman Pubs.
The Easter Proclamation of the Irish Republic, 1916. 1975. pap. text ed. 2.25x (ISBN 0-85105-289-4, Dolmen Pr). Humanities.
Edwards, R. Dudley & Williams, T. Desmond, eds. The Great Famine: Studies in Irish History, 1845-1852. LC 76-173534. (Illus.). xx, 517p. (With a new preface & biblio. by E. R. R. Green). 1976. Repr. of 1957 ed. 30.00 (ISBN 0-8462-1793-7). Russell.
Edwards, Ruth D. An Atlas of Irish History. 2nd ed. (Illus.). 180p. 1981. 19.95x (ISBN 0-416-08110-X); pap. 8.95x (ISBN 0-416-08120-7). Methuen Inc.
Egan, Joseph J. & Egan, Mary J. History of Clan Egan: The Birds of the Forest of Wisdom. LC 79-25089. (Illus.). 332p. (Orig.). 1979. pap. 26.50 (ISBN 0-8357-0492-0, SS-00124). Univ Microfilms.
Ellis, Peter B. The Boyne Water: The Battle of the Boyne, 1690. LC 76-6753. 175p. 1976. text ed. 18.95x (ISBN 0-312-09415-9). St Martin.
--Hell or Connaught: The Cromwellian Colonization of Ireland. LC 74-24650. 288p. 1975. 17.95 (ISBN 0-312-36715-5). St Martin.
Elton, G., ed. Annual Bibliography of British & Irish History: Publications of 1977. 1978. text ed. 26.75x (ISBN 0-391-00881-1). Humanities.
--Annual Bibliography of British & Irish History: Publications of 1979, Vol. 5. 1981. text ed. 30.00x (ISBN 0-391-01774-8). Humanities.
--Annual Bibliography of British & Irish History, 1978. 1979. text ed. 26.75x (ISBN 0-391-01054-9). Humanities.
--Annual Bibliography of British & Irish History 1976. 1977. text ed. 28.50x (ISBN 0-391-00753-X). Humanities.
Erasmus, Desiderius. One Dialogue or Colloquy Entitled Diversoria. LC 71-26509. (English Experience Ser.: No. 244). 20p. 1970. Repr. of 1566 ed. 7.00 (ISBN 90-221-0244-0). Walter J Johnson.
--Utile Dulce: Or, Trueths Libertie; Seven Wittie-Wise "Dialogues". Burton, William, tr. LC 73-7084. (English Experience Ser.: No. 591). 160p. 1973. Repr. of 1606 ed. 16.00 (ISBN 90-221-0591-1). Walter J Johnson.
Falkiner, Litton C. Essays Relating to Ireland. LC 74-102600. (Irish Culture and History Ser). 1970. Repr. of 1909 ed. 12.50 (ISBN 0-8046-0777-X). Kennikat.
Finnegan, T. A. Sligo: Sinbad's Yellow Shore. 1979. pap. text ed. 5.25x (ISBN 0-85105-332-7, Dolmen Pr). Humanities.
Fitzgerald, Brian. The Anglo-Irish: Three Representative Types, Cork, Ormonde, Swift, 1602-1745. LC 76-22190. 1976. Repr. of 1952 ed. lib. bdg. 25.00 (ISBN 0-8414-4211-8). Folcroft.
Fitzpatrick, J. B. Ireland & the Making of Britain. 59.95 (ISBN 0-8490-0422-5). Gordon Pr.
Fitzpatrick, Thomas. Bloody Bridge. LC 71-102602. (Irish Culture & History Ser). 1970. Repr. of 1903 ed. 14.50 (ISBN 0-8046-0779-6). Kennikat.
Flackes, W. D. Northern Ireland: A Political Directory 1968-79. 1980. 25.00 (ISBN 0-686-60013-4). St Martin.
Foley, Gerry. Ireland in Rebellion. (Interviews with Cathal Goulding & Tomas MacGiolla). pap. 0.60 (ISBN 0-87348-254-9). Path Pr NY.
Forbes, Crosby & Lee, Henry. Massachusetts Help to Ireland During the Great Famine. LC 67-24085. (Illus.). 1967. 6.00x (ISBN 0-937650-00-5). Mus Am China.
Froude, James A. English in Ireland in the Eighteenth Century, 3 Vols. LC 70-99246. Repr. of 1881 ed. Set. 75.00 (ISBN 0-404-02640-0). AMS Pr.
Gallagher, Frank. Days of Fear: Diary of a Hunger Strike. 117p. pap. 1.00 (ISBN 0-85342-069-6). Irish Bk Ctr.
Gallagher, Frank & Hogan, David. The Four Glorious Years. 1971. Repr. of 1953 ed. 27.00 (ISBN 0-384-17583-X). Johnson Repr.
--The Four Glorious Years. 1971. Repr. of 1953 ed. 27.00 (ISBN 0-384-17583-X). Johnson Repr.
Gilbert, John T., ed. History of the Irish Confederation & the War in Ireland, 1641-1649, Containing a Narrative of Affairs of Ireland, 7 vols. LC 72-144616. Repr. of 1891 ed. Set. 210.00 (ISBN 0-404-02840-3). AMS Pr.
Gipson, Lawrence H. The British Empire Before the American Revolution, 15 vols. Incl. Vol. 1. The British Isles & the American Colonies: Great Britain & Ireland, 1748-1754. rev. ed. 1958 (ISBN 0-394-41784-4); Vol. 2. The British Isles & the American Colonies: The Southern Plantations, 1748-1754. rev. ed. 1960 (ISBN 0-394-41782-8); Vol. 3. The British Isles & the American Colonies: The Northern Plantations, 1748-1754. rev. ed. 1960 (ISBN 0-394-41783-6); Vol. 4. Zones of International Friction: North America, South of the Great Lakes Region, 1748-1754 (ISBN 0-394-45340-9); Vol. 4. Zones of International Friction: The Great Lakes Frontier, Canada, the West Indies, India, 1748-1754014vol. 5 (ISBN 0-394-45341-7); Vol. 6. The Great War for the Empire: The Years of Defeat, 1754-1757 (ISBN 0-394-42718-1); Vol. 7. The Great War for the Empire: The Victorious Years, 1758-1760 (ISBN 0-394-45057-4); Vol. 8. The Great War for the Empire: The Culmination, 1760-1763 (ISBN 0-394-42719-X); Vol. 9. The Triumphant Empire: The Triumphant Empire. 1956 (ISBN 0-394-44963-0); Vol. 10. The Triumphant Empire: Thunder-Clouds Gather in the West, 1763-1766. 1961 (ISBN 0-394-41785-2); Vol. 11. The Triumphant Empire: The Rumbling of the Coming Storm, 1766-1770. 1965 (ISBN 0-394-41791-7); Vol. 12. The Triumphant Empire: Britain Sails into the Storm, 1770-1776. 1965 (ISBN 0-394-41795-X); Vol. 13. The Triumphant Empire: The Empire Beyond the Storm, 1770-1776. 1967 (ISBN 0-394-41797-6); Vol. 14. A Bibliographical Guide to the History of the British Empire, 1748-1776. 1968 (ISBN 0-394-41686-4); Vol. 15. A Guide to Manuscripts Relating to the History of the British Empire, 1748-1776. 1970 (ISBN 0-394-41786-0). Vols. 2-7, 9, 11-15. 15.00 ea. Knopf.
Giraldus. Cambrensis Historical Works. Wright, Thomas, ed. LC 68-55551. (Bohn's Antiquarian Library Ser). Repr. of 1863 ed. 35.00 (ISBN 0-404-50015-3). AMS Pr.
--The English Conquest of Ireland. Furnivall, F. J., ed. (EETS, OS Ser.: No. 107). Repr. of 1896 ed. 10.00 (ISBN 0-527-00111-2). Kraus Repr.
--English Conquest of Ireland, A.D. 1166-1185. LC 68-25237. (British History Ser., No. 30). 1969. Repr. of 1896 ed. lib. bdg. 49.95 (ISBN 0-8383-0947-X). Haskell.
Greaves, C. Desmond. Liam Mellows & the Irish Revolution. 400p. 1970. 18.00x (ISBN 0-8464-0565-2). Beekman Pubs.
Gregory. Gods & Fighting Men: The Story of the Tuatha De Danaan & of the Fianna of Ireland. 2nd ed. 1976. pap. text ed. 7.50x (ISBN 0-7705-1413-8). Humanities.
Gregory, Isabella A. A Book of Saints & Wonders: Put Down Here by Lady Gregory According to the Old Writings & Memory of the People of Ireland. (CECWLG Ser.). (Illus.). 116p. 1971. 13.95x (ISBN 0-19-519685-6). Oxford U Pr.
Griffin, William D. Ireland: A Chronology & Fact Book. LC 73-12694. (World Chronology Ser.). 160p. 1973. lib. bdg. 8.50x (ISBN 0-379-16302-0). Oceana.
Hackett, Francis. The Story of the Irish Nation. 1930. Repr. 25.00 (ISBN 0-8274-3522-3). R West.
Harkness, D. W. The Restless Dominion. LC 73-114761. 1970. 18.50x (ISBN 0-8147-0463-8). NYU Pr.
Hay, Edward. History of the Irish Insurrection. 1973. lib. bdg. 69.95 (ISBN 0-685-37597-8). Revisionist Pr.
Hayes-McCoy, G. A. A History of Irish Flags from Earliest Times. (Reference Bks.). 1980. lib. bdg. 45.00 (ISBN 0-8161-8400-3). G K Hall.
Henley, Pauline. Spenser in Ireland. LC 70-131741. 1970. Repr. of 1928 ed. 7.00 (ISBN 0-403-00628-7). Scholarly.
--Spenser in Ireland. LC 76-81491. (Illus.). 1969. Repr. of 1928 ed. 9.00 (ISBN 0-8462-1404-0). Russell.
Henry, Robert M. Evolution of Sinn Fein. LC 73-102608. (Irish Culture & History Ser). 1970. Repr. of 1920 ed. 15.00 (ISBN 0-8046-0785-0). Kennikat.
Herity, Michael & Eogan, George. Ireland in Prehistory. (Illus.). 1976. 30.00 (ISBN 0-7100-8413-7). Routledge & Kegan.
Hickey, D. J. & Doherty, J. E. Dictionary of Irish History Since 1800. 615p. 1980. 38.50x (ISBN 0-389-20160-X). B&N.
Hinton, Edward M. Ireland Through Tudor Eyes. 111p. 1980. Repr. of 1935 ed. lib. bdg. 22.50 (ISBN 0-89987-362-6). Darby Bks.

--Ireland Through Tudor Eyes. 1979. Repr. of 1935 ed. lib. bdg. 22.50 (ISBN 0-8495-2279-X). Arden Lib.
Holinshed. Irish Chronicle Fifteen Seventy-Seven: The Historie of Ireland from the First Inhabitation Thereof, Unto the Years 1509. LC 78-12424. (Dolemen Edition: No. XXVIII). 1979. Repr. of 1577 ed. text ed. 96.75x (ISBN 0-391-00562-6, Dolmen Pr). Humanities.
Hughes, Kathleen. Early Christian Ireland. Elton, G. R., ed. LC 72-1498. (Sources of History Ser). 320p. 1973. 22.50x (ISBN 0-8014-0721-4); pap. 7.95 (ISBN 0-8014-9135-5, CP135). Cornell U Pr.
Hull, Eleanor. History of Ireland & Her People, Vol. 1: From Earlier Times to the Tudor Period. LC 72-7296. (Select Bibliographies Reprint Ser.). 1972. Repr. of 1926 ed. 33.00 (ISBN 0-8369-6956-1). Arno.
--History of Ireland & Her People, Vol. 2: From the Stuart Period to Modern Times. LC 72-7296. (Select Bibliographies Reprint Ser.). 1972. Repr. of 1926 ed. 32.00 (ISBN 0-8369-6960-X). Arno.
Irish Conference of Historians - 4th. Irish Historical Studies: No. 3. 5.95 (ISBN 0-685-32720-5). Dufour.
Jackson, T. A. Ireland Her Own: An Outline History of the Irish Struggle for National Freedom and Independence. 516p. 1970. pap. 1.95 (ISBN 0-7178-0285-X). Intl Pub Co.
James, Francis G. Ireland in the Empire, 1688-1770: A History of Ireland from the Williamite Wars to the Eve of the American Revolution. LC 72-87772. (Historical Monographs Ser: No. 68). (Illus.). 1973. 17.50x (ISBN 0-674-46626-8). Harvard U Pr.
Johnston, Edith M. Ireland in the Eighteenth Century. (Gill History of Ireland: Vol. 8). 224p. 1974. pap. 6.95 (ISBN 0-7171-0565-2). Irish Bk Ctr.
Kaufman, Daniel. Ireland: Presences. (Illus.). 112p. 1980. 19.95 (ISBN 0-312-43591-6). St Martin.
Kiernan, Thomas J. History of the Financial Administration of Ireland to Eighteen Seventeen. (Perspectives in European History: No. 29). Repr. of 1930 ed. lib. bdg. 20.00x (ISBN 0-87991-822-5). Porcupine Pr.
Kinahan, Coralie. You Can't Shoot the English. 1980. 10.00 (ISBN 0-533-04570-3). Vantage.
Landon, Michael L. Erin & Britannia: The Historical Backround to a Modern Tragedy. LC 79-27005. (Illus.). 288p. 1981. text ed. 18.95x (ISBN 0-88229-643-4); pap. text ed. 8.95 (ISBN 0-88229-766-X). Nelson-Hall.
Lecky, W. E. History of Ireland in the Eighteenth Century. abr. ed. Curtis, L. P., Jr., ed. LC 78-184286. (Classics of British Historical Literature Ser). 1972. pap. 3.95 (ISBN 0-226-46995-6, P464, Phoen). U of Chicago Pr.
--A History of Ireland in the 18th Century, 5 vols. 500.00 (ISBN 0-8490-0331-8). Gordon Pr.
Lecky, William E. History of Ireland in the Eighteenth Century, 5 Vols. new ed. LC 70-77896. Repr. of 1893 ed. Set. 57.50 (ISBN 0-404-03940-5); 15.00 ea. Vol. 1 (ISBN 0-404-03941-3). Vol. 2 (ISBN 0-404-03942-1). Vol. 3 (ISBN 0-404-03943-X). Vol. 4 (ISBN 0-404-03944-8). Vol. 5 (ISBN 0-404-03945-6). AMS Pr.
--A History of Ireland in the 18th Century, 5 vols. 1972. Repr. of 1892 ed. Set. 49.00 (ISBN 0-403-03601-1). Scholarly.
Lee, J. J., ed. Ireland Nineteen Forty-Five to Nineteen Seventy. (Thomas Davis Ser.). 1979. text ed. 23.50x (ISBN 0-06-494129-9). B&N.
Lee, Joseph. The Modernisation of Irish Society 1848-1914. (Gill History of Ireland: Vol. 10). 192p. 1973. pap. 5.50 (ISBN 0-7171-0567-9). Irish Bk Ctr.
Le Fanu, William R. Seventy Years of Irish Life: Being Anecdotes & Reminiscences. LC 75-28821. Repr. of 1893 ed. 27.00 (ISBN 0-404-13813-6). AMS Pr.
Lethbridge, T. C. Herdsmen & Hermits: Celtic Seafarers in the Northern Seas. 1977. lib. bdg. 59.95 (ISBN 0-8490-1941-9). Gordon Pr.
Lethbridge, Thomas C. Herdsmen & Hermits. 1950. text ed. 4.25x (ISBN 0-391-01986-4). Humanities.
Lille Symposium June-July 1978. Ireland at the Crossroads: Proceedings. Rafroidi, Patrick & Joannon, Pierre, eds. 1979. pap. text ed. 8.00x (ISBN 2-85939-111-8). Humanities.
Lydon, James. Ireland in the Later Middle Ages. (Gill History of Ireland: Vol. 6). 300p. 1973. pap. 6.50 (ISBN 0-7171-0563-6). Irish Bk Ctr.
Lydon, James & Maccurtin, Margaret, eds. Gill History of Ireland, 11 vols. Set. pap. 60.00 (ISBN 0-686-16761-9). Irish Bk Ctr.
Lyle, M. K. Out of the Past: Ulster Voices Speak. 1981. 11.50 (ISBN 0-533-04292-5). Vantage.
Lynch, Ann. Man & Environment in South-West Ireland, 4000 B.C. - A.D. 800: A Study of Man's Impact on the Development of Soil & Vegetation. 175p. 1981. 42.00x (ISBN 0-86054-112-6, Pub. by BAR). State Mutual Bk.
Lyons, F. S. Culture & Anarchy in Ireland Eighteen Nineteen to Nineteen Thirty-Nine: The Ford Lectures 1978. 1979. 17.50x (ISBN 0-19-822493-1). Oxford U Pr.
Lyons, F. S. & Hawkins, R. A., eds. Ireland Under the Union: Varieties of Tension. (Illus.). 348p. 1980. 42.00x (ISBN 0-19-822469-9). Oxford U Pr.
McAliskey, Bernadette D. The Irish Struggle: Nineteen Seventy to Nineteen Eighty. 1982. lib. bdg. 25.00 (ISBN 0-913460-80-X); pap. 6.95 (ISBN 0-913460-79-6). Monad Pr.
McCaffrey, Lawrence J. Ireland: From Colony to Nation State. 1979. 14.95 (ISBN 0-13-506196-2); pap. 11.95 (ISBN 0-13-506188-1). P-H.
Maccall, Seamus. A Little History of Ireland. LC 80-21515. 59p. (Orig.). 1980. pap. 3.50 (ISBN 0-937702-00-5). Irish Bks Media.
McCormack, W. J. Sheridan le Fanu & Victorian Ireland. (Illus.). 334p. 1980. text ed. 42.00x (ISBN 0-19-812629-8). Oxford U Pr.
Maccurtain, Margaret. Tudor & Stuart Ireland. (Gill History of Ireland: Vol. 7). (Illus.). 224p. 1972. pap. 5.75 (ISBN 0-7171-0564-4). Irish Bk Ctr.
MacDonagh, Oliver. Ireland: The Union & Its Aftermath. 1977. text ed. 25.00x (ISBN 0-04-941004-0); pap. text ed. 8.95x (ISBN 0-04-941005-9). Allen Unwin.
McDowell, R. B., ed. Social Life in Ireland 1800-1845. (Irish Life & Culture Ser.). (Illus.). 1976. pap. 3.95 (ISBN 0-85342-295-8). Irish Bk Ctr.
McDowell, Robert B. Ireland in the Age of Imperialism & Revolution, Seventeen Sixty to Eighteen Hundred One. 748p. text ed. 84.00x (ISBN 0-19-822480-X). Oxford U Pr.
Macgearailt, Gearoid. Celts & Normans. (History of Ireland Ser.: Vol. 1). (Illus.). 288p. 1969. pap. text ed. 6.95 (ISBN 0-7171-0255-6). Irish Bk Ctr.
MacHale, John. A Ballad-History of Ireland. 1981. pap. 5.95 (ISBN 0-934906-01-7). R J Liederbach.
MacLysaght, Edward. Changing Times: Ireland Since Eighteen Ninety-Eight. 1978. text ed. 18.25x (ISBN 0-901072-88-5). Humanities.
--Irish Life in the Seventeenth Century. 324p. 1979. 15.00x (ISBN 0-7165-2343-4, Pub. by Irish Academic Pr); pap. 7.50x (ISBN 0-7165-2342-6, Pub. by Irish Academic Pr). Biblio Dist.
MacManus, Seumas. The Story of the Irish Race. rev. ed. 12.50 (ISBN 0-8159-6827-2). Devin.
--The Story of the Irish Race: A Popular History of Ireland. 1979. Repr. of 1922 ed. lib. bdg. 50.00 (ISBN 0-89987-550-5). Darby Bks.
MacNeill, Eoin. Phases of Irish History. LC 76-102614. (Irish Culture & History Ser). 1970. Repr. of 1919 ed. 17.50 (ISBN 0-8046-0791-5). Kennikat.
McNeill, Mary. Vere Foster. LC 73-180713. (Illus.). 256p. 1972. 17.50x (ISBN 0-8173-4450-0). U of Ala Pr.
McNeill, T. E. Anglo-Norman Ulster: The History & Archaeology of an Irish Barony 1177-1400. (Illus.). 166p. 1980. text ed. 32.50x (ISBN 0-85976-057-X). Humanities.
MacNiochaill, Gearoid. Ireland Before the Vikings. (Gill History of Ireland: Vol. 1). (Illus.). 184p. 1972. pap. 6.95 (ISBN 0-7171-0558-X). Irish Bk Ctr.
Macthomais, Eamonn. Gur Cake & Coal Blocks. (Illus.). 1976. pap. 5.95 (ISBN 0-905140-07-9). Irish Bk Ctr.
Magnusson, Magnus. Landlord or Tenant? A View of Irish History. LC 79-305778. (Illus.). 1979. 10.50 (ISBN 0-370-30130-7, Pub. by Chatto Bodley Jonathan). Merrimack Bk Serv.
Maltby, Arthur & Maltby, Jean. Ireland in the Nineteenth Century: A Breviate of Official Publications. (Guides to Official Publications Ser.: Vol. 4). (Illus.). 1979. 55.00 (ISBN 0-08-023688-X). Pergamon.
Mansergh, Nicholas. The Irish Question, 1840-1921. 1976. pap. 8.50 (ISBN 0-8020-6321-7). U of Toronto Pr.
Martin, F. X & Byrne. The Scholar Revolutionary: Eoin Macneil 1867-1945, & the Making of the New Ireland. (Illus.). 320p. 1973. 20.00x (ISBN 0-7165-0577-0, Pub. by Irish Academic Pr Ireland). Biblio Dist.
Martin, Francis X., ed. Leaders & Men of the Easter Rising: Dublin 1916. LC 67-13383. 276p. 1967. 20.00x (ISBN 0-8014-0290-5). Cornell U Pr.
Mill, John S. John Stuart Mill on Ireland. LC 78-13054. 1979. text ed. 14.95x (ISBN 0-915980-46-0). Inst Study Human.
Moody, T. W. Davitt & Irish Revolution: Eighteen Forty-Six to Eighteen Eighty-Two. (Illus.). 628p. 1981. 74.00 (ISBN 0-19-822382-X). Oxford U Pr.
--The Ulster Question, 1603-1973. (Illus.). 1974. pap. 4.95 (ISBN 0-85342-399-7). Irish Bk Ctr.
Moody, T. W., ed. Early Modern Ireland, 1534-1691. (New History of Ireland Ser.). (Illus.). 1976. 29.95x (ISBN 0-19-821739-0). Oxford U Pr.
Moore, Thomas. Memoirs of Captain Rock (pseud.) the Celebrated Irish Chieftain: With Some Account of His Ancestors. LC 75-28831. Repr. of 1824 ed. 26.00 (ISBN 0-404-13821-7). AMS Pr.
Morgan & Purdie, eds. Ireland: Divided Nation, Divided Class. 1980. lib. bdg. 17.50 (ISBN 0-906133-20-3, Pub. by Ink Links); pap. 6.95 (ISBN 0-906133-21-1). Path Pr NY.
Morrison, Alex. Early Man in Britain & Ireland. 1980. write for info. (ISBN 0-312-22463-X). St Martin.
Moryson, Fynes. An Itinerary. LC 70-38150. (English Experience Ser.: No. 387). 1971. Repr. of 1617 ed. 104.00 (ISBN 90-221-0387-0). Walter J Johnson.
Neill, Kenneth. An Illustrtated History of the Irish People. (Illus.). 256p. 1980. 19.95 (ISBN 0-8317-5004-9, Mayflower Bks). Smith Pubs.
Neill, Kenneth, ed. Modern Historical Documents. 1977. pap. text ed. 1.50 (ISBN 0-7171-0842-2). Irish Bk Ctr.
Nicholls, Kenneth. Gaelic & Gaelicised Ireland in the Middle Ages. (Gill History of Ireland: Vol. 4). (Illus.). 212p. 1972. pap. 5.75 (ISBN 0-7171-0561-X). Irish Bk Ctr.
O'Ballance, Edgar. Terror in Ireland: The Heritage of Hate. (Illus.). 280p. 1981. 14.95 (ISBN 0-89141-100-3). Presidio Pr.
O'Brien, George. The Economic History of Ireland in the 17th Century. 69.95 (ISBN 0-8490-0082-3). Gordon Pr.
O'Brien, George A. Economic History of Ireland from the Union to the Famine. LC 68-56554. Repr. of 1921 ed. lib. bdg. 19.50x (ISBN 0-678-00816-7). Kelley.
--Economic History of Ireland from the Union to the Famine. LC 68-56554. Repr. of 1921 ed. lib. bdg. 19.50x (ISBN 0-678-00816-7). Kelley.
--The Economic History of Ireland in the Eighteenth Century. LC 77-24245. (Perspectives in European History Ser.: No. 15). (Illus.). 437p. Repr. of 1918 ed. lib. bdg. 20.00x (ISBN 0-87991-622-2). Porcupine Pr.
--Economic History of Ireland in the Seventeenth Century. LC 68-56555. Repr. of 1919 ed. lib. bdg. 15.00x (ISBN 0-678-00817-5). Kelley.
--Economic History of Ireland in the Seventeenth Century. LC 68-56555. Repr. of 1919 ed. lib. bdg. 15.00x (ISBN 0-678-00817-5). Kelley.
O'Broin, Leon. Dublin Castle & the 1916 Rising. LC 78-138554. 1971. 14.50x (ISBN 0-8147-6150-X). NYU Pr.
O'Casey, Sean. The Story of the Irish Citizen Army. 72p. 1981. pap. 4.50 (ISBN 0-904526-50-X, Pub. by the Journeyman Press, England). Lawrence Hill.
O'Connor, Frank. Big Fellow. 1965. 6.95 (ISBN 0-87243-020-0). Templegate.
O'Connor, James. History of Ireland, 1798-1924, 2 vol. 710p. Repr. of 1926 ed. 58.00 (ISBN 0-384-42893-2). Johnson Repr.
O'Corrain, Donncha. Ireland Before the Normans. (Gill History of Ireland: Vol. 2). (Illus.). 222p. 1972. pap. 6.95 (ISBN 0-7171-0559-8). Irish Bk Ctr.
O'Curry, Eugene. Lectures in the Manuscript Materials of Ancient Irish History, 2 vols in 1. Repr. of 1861 ed. 46.50 (ISBN 0-685-06758-0). B Franklin.
O'Donovan, John, ed. Annals of the Four Masters, 7 Vols. LC 70-158820. Repr. of 1854 ed. Set. 402.50 (ISBN 0-404-04820-X); 57.50 ea. AMS Pr.
O'Faolain, Sean. Irish: A Character Study. 1979. pap. 5.95 (ISBN 0-8159-5812-9). Devin.
O'Farrell, P. J. England & Ireland Since 1800. 189p. 1975. pap. text ed. 3.95x (ISBN 0-19-289045-X). Oxford U Pr.
O'Hegarty, Patrick S. A History of Ireland Under the Union 1801-1922. LC 52-10517. 1969. Repr. of 1952 ed. 36.00 (ISBN 0-527-68240-3). Kraus Repr.
O'Kearney, Nicholas, ed. The Battle of Gabhra. 176p. Repr. of 1854 ed. 16.50 (ISBN 0-384-42995-5). Johnson Repr.
Orel, Harold, ed. Irish History & Culture: Aspects of a People's Heritage. LC 75-35532. (Illus.). 320p. 1976. pap. 8.95x (ISBN 0-7006-0137-6). Regents Pr Ks.
O'Sullivan, Humphrey. The Diary of Humphrey O'Sullivan 1827-1835. De Bhaldraithe, Tomas, tr. from Irish. Orig. Title: Cin Lae Amhlaoibh. (Illus.). 139p. 1979. pap. 4.50 (ISBN 0-85342-588-4). Irish Bk Ctr.
O'Sullivan Bear, Philip. Ireland Under Elizabeth. LC 70-102595. (Irish Culture & History Ser). 1970. Repr. of 1903 ed. 16.50 (ISBN 0-8046-0772-9). Kennikat.
Otway-Ruthven, A. J. A History of Medieval Ireland. 2nd ed. LC 79-18849. (Illus.). 1979. 22.50x (ISBN 0-312-38139-5). St Martin.
Petty, W. The Political Anatomy of Ireland. 260p. 1970. Repr. of 1691 ed. 30.00x (ISBN 0-7165-0093-0, Pub. by Irish Academic Pr Ireland). Biblio Dist.
Power, Patrick. Sex & Marriage in Ancient Ireland. (Irish Life & Culture Ser.). 1977. pap. 3.75 (ISBN 0-85342-475-6). Irish Bk Ctr.
Ranelagh, John. Ireland: An/Illustrated History. (Illus.). 268p. 1981. 25.00 (ISBN 0-19-520261-9). Oxford U Pr.
Reeve, Carl & Barton, Ann. James Connolly & the United States: The Road to the 1916 Irish Rebellion. (AIMS Historical Ser.: No. 10). 1978. text ed. 16.00x (ISBN 0-391-00879-X). Humanities.
Reid, John P. In a Defiant Stance: The Conditions of Law in Massachusetts Bay, the Irish Comparison, & the Coming of the American Revolution. LC 76-42453. 1977. 16.75x (ISBN 0-271-01240-4). Pa St U Pr.
Robbins, Frank. Under the Starry Plough: Recollections of the Irish Citizen Army. (Illus.). 251p. (Orig.). 1977. pap. text ed. 5.95x (ISBN 0-906187-00-1, Pub. by Acad Pr Ireland). Facsimile Bk.
Ryan, Desmond. The Sword of Light, from the Four Masters to Douglas Hyde, 1636-1938. LC 74-9698. 1939. 22.50 (ISBN 0-8414-7307-2). Folcroft.
--The Sword of Light: From the Four Masters to Douglas Hyde, 1636-1938. LC 78-5092. 1979. Repr. of 1939 ed. lib. bdg. 30.00 (ISBN 0-8495-4607-9). Arden Lib.
Saul, George B. Traditional Irish Literature: A Brief Introduction. rev. ed. LC 71-120997. 115p. 1970. 10.00 (ISBN 0-8387-7686-8). Bucknell U Pr.
Schelling, Felix E. English Chronicle Play. LC 65-15877. (Studies in Drama, No. 39). 1969. Repr. of 1902 ed. lib. bdg. 37.95 (ISBN 0-8383-0618-7). Haskell.
Share, Bernard. The Emergency - Neutral Ireland 1939-45. (Illus.). 1978. 18.50 (ISBN 0-7171-0916-X). Irish Bk Ctr.
Sheehy, C. When the Normans Came to Ireland. 1975. pap. 2.75 (ISBN 0-85342-393-8). Irish Bk Ctr.
Sheehy, Jeanne. The Rediscovery of Ireland's Past: The Celtic Revival 1830-1930. (Illus.). 1980. 19.95 (ISBN 0-500-01221-0). Thames Hudson.
Silke, John J. Kinsale: The Spanish Intervention in Ireland at the End of the Elizabethan Wars. LC 77-96148. (Illus.). 1970. 25.00 (ISBN 0-8232-0865-6). Fordham.
Smith, Howard. Ireland. LC 74-176702. (Illus.). 136p. 1974. 8.75x (ISBN 0-563-10785-5). Intl Pubns Serv.
Stanford, William B. Ireland & the Classical Tradition. 261p. 1976. 17.50x (ISBN 0-87471-924-0). Rowman.
Stephens, James. The Insurrection in Dublin. 1979. text ed. 12.50x (ISBN 0-391-00942-7); pap. text ed. 4.50x (ISBN 0-391-00943-5). Humanities.
Strauss, Eric. Irish Nationalism & British Democracy. LC 75-8727. 307p. 1975. Repr. of 1951 ed. lib. bdg. 16.50x (ISBN 0-8371-8046-5, STINA). Greenwood.
Swords, Liam, ed. Irish-French Connection Fifteen Seventy-Eight to Nineteen Seventy-Eight. (Orig.). 1979. pap. text ed. 6.25x (ISBN 0-391-01706-3). Humanities.
Taylor, J. F. Owen Roe O'Neill. 1981. Repr. 7.50 (ISBN 0-916620-27-1). Portals Pr.
Thebaud, A. J. The Irish Race in the Past & Present. 1977. lib. bdg. 59.95 (ISBN 0-8490-2077-8). Gordon Pr.
Tierney, Mark. The Birth of Modern Ireland. (Illus.). 256p. 1969. pap. 8.50 glossary index (ISBN 0-7171-0257-2). Irish Bk Ctr.
--Modern Ireland Since Eighteen Fifty. 2nd rev. ed. 1978. pap. 4.95 (ISBN 0-7171-0886-4). Irish Bk Ctr.
Townshend, Charles. The British Campaign in Ireland, Nineteen Nineteen to Nineteen Twenty-One. (Oxford Historical Monographs). (Illus.). 256p. 1978. pap. 12.95x (ISBN 0-19-821874-5). Oxford U Pr.
True Report of the Success Which God Gave Unto Our English Soldiers in Ireland, 1580. LC 72-6016. (English Experience Ser.: No. 541). 1973. Repr. of 1581 ed. 5.00 (ISBN 90-221-0541-5). Walter J Johnson.
Ua Clerigh, Arthur. History of Ireland to the Coming of Henry Second. LC 73-102596. (Irish Culture & History Ser). 1970. Repr. of 1910 ed. 22.00 (ISBN 0-8046-0773-7). Kennikat.
Unwin, J. C. The Hungry Forties: Life Under the Bread Tax. 288p. Date not set. Repr. of 1904 ed. 24.00x (ISBN 0-686-28338-4, Pub. by Irish Academic Pr). Biblio Dist.
Ward, Alan J. The Easter Rising: Revolution & Irish Nationalism. LC 79-55729. (AHM Europe Since 1500 Ser.). (Illus., Orig.). 1980. pap. text ed. 5.95x (ISBN 0-88295-803-8). Harlan Davidson.
Ware, James. Ancient Irish Histories, 4 vols. in 2. LC 71-102590. (Irish Culture & History Ser). 1970. Repr. of 1809 ed. Set. 55.00x (ISBN 0-8046-0767-2). Kennikat.
--Two Histories of Ireland. LC 71-171796. (English Experience Ser.: No. 421). 500p. 1971. Repr. of 1633 ed. 80.00 (ISBN 90-221-0421-4). Walter J Johnson.

White, Terence De Vere. The Anglo-Irish. (Illus.). 293p. 1975. text ed. 15.00x (ISBN 0-575-00764-8). Verry.

Whitlock, Dorothy, et al, eds. Ireland in Early Medieval Europe. LC 80-40325. (Studies in Memory of Kathleen Hughes). (Illus.). 400p. Date not set. 95.00 (ISBN 0-521-23547-2). Cambridge U Pr.

Wilkinson, Burke. The Zeal of the Convert. LC 76-3922. 1976. 9.95 (ISBN 0-88331-086-4). Luce.

Woodham-Smith, Cecil. Great Hunger. 1980. pap. 8.95 (ISBN 0-525-47643-1). Dutton.

Woodward, Otway. Divided Island. (Studies in 20th Century History Ser.). 48p. 1977. pap. text ed. 4.50x (ISBN 0-435-31761-X). Heinemann Ed.

Wyse Jackson, Robert. Story of Limerick. 1974. pap. 1.75 (ISBN 0-85342-376-8). Irish Bk Ctr.

IRELAND–HISTORY–FICTION

Macken, Walter. Silent People. 1962. Repr. 10.95 (ISBN 0-02-578000-X). Macmillan.

Saul, George B. Wild Queen. LC 67-30726. (Illus.). 1967. 4.95 (ISBN 0-910244-45-6). Blair.

IRELAND–HISTORY–SOURCES

Cecil, Robert. Letters from Sir Robert Cecil to Sir George Carew. 1864. 15.50 (ISBN 0-384-53140-7). Johnson Repr.

Curtis, Edmund & McDowell, R. B., eds. Irish Historical Documents. 1977. 38.00x (ISBN 0-416-85930-5). Methuen Inc.

Essex, Arthur C. Essex Papers. Airy, O., ed. Repr. of 1890 ed. 22.50 (ISBN 0-384-14670-8). Johnson Repr.

Griffin, William D. Ireland: A Chronology & Fact Book. LC 73-12694. (World Chronology Ser.). 160p. 1973. lib. bdg. 8.50x (ISBN 0-379-16302-0). Oceana.

Meyer, Kuno, ed. Life of Colman Son of Luachan. LC 78-72616. (Royal Irish Academy. Todd Lecture Ser.: Vol. 17). Repr. of 1911 ed. 18.50 (ISBN 0-404-60577-X). AMS Pr.

O'Donovan, John, ed. Annals of the Four Masters, 7 Vols. LC 70-15820. Repr. of 1854 ed. Set. 402.50 (ISBN 0-404-04820-X); 57.50 ea. AMS Pr.

Salisbury, Robert C. Letters from Sir Robert Cecil to Sir George Carew. Maclean, John, ed. LC 17-1256. (Camden Society, London. Publications, First Series: No. 88). Repr. of 1864 ed. 14.00 (ISBN 0-404-50188-5). AMS Pr.

IRELAND–INDUSTRIES

Kane, Robert J. The Industrial Resources of Ireland. 456p. Date not set. Repr. of 1845 ed. 31.00x (ISBN 0-686-28342-2, Pub. by Irish Academic Pr). Biblio Dist.

Thom's Commercial Directory of Ireland, 1978. 128th ed. LC 72-4316. (Illus.). 1978. 42.50x (ISBN 0-8002-0336-4). Intl Pubns Serv.

IRELAND–INTELLECTUAL LIFE

Costello, Peter. The Heart Grown Brutal: The Irish Revolution in Literature, from Parnell to the Death of Yeats, 1891-1939. (Illus.). 330p. 1977. 24.50x (ISBN 0-8476-6007-9). Rowman.

Davis, Thomas. Essays Literary & Historical. O'Donoghue, D. J., ed. 456p. 1973. Repr. of 1914 ed. 19.50 (ISBN 0-685-26065-8). Lemma.

Gregory, Isabella A. Ideals in Ireland. LC 75-28815. Repr. of 1901 ed. 11.00 (ISBN 0-404-13808-X). AMS Pr.

IRELAND–JUVENILE LITERATURE

Dobrin, Arnold. Ireland: The Edge of Europe. LC 70-117146. (World Neighbors Ser). (Illus.). (gr. 6 up). 1971. 7.95 (ISBN 0-525-67030-0); PLB 6.80 (ISBN 0-525-67031-9). Elsevier-Nelson.

MacMahon, Bryan. Brendan of Ireland. (Children Everywhere Ser). (Illus.). (gr. 2-4). 1967. PLB 4.95 (ISBN 0-8038-0705-8); PLB 3.33 i.t.a. ed. (ISBN 0-8038-0706-6). Hastings.

Sasek, Miroslav. This Is Ireland. (Illus.). (gr. 3 up). 1965. 6.95g (ISBN 0-02-778350-2). Macmillan.

Stein, Wendy. A Book of Ancient Ireland. (Illus.). 1978. pap. text ed. 2.50 (ISBN 0-88388-060-1). Bellerophon Bks.

Stevens, Patricia B. God Save Ireland! The Irish Conflict in the Twentieth Century. LC 73-19067. 224p. (gr. 7 up). 1974. 10.95 (ISBN 0-02-788180-6). Macmillan.

IRELAND–MAPS

Andrews, J. H. A Paper Landscape: The Ordnance Survey in Nineteenth-Century Ireland. (Illus.). 366p. 1975. 75.00x (ISBN 0-19-823209-8). Oxford U Pr.

Edwards, Ruth D. An Atlas of Irish History. 2nd ed. (Illus.). 180p. 1981. 19.95x (ISBN 0-416-08110-X); pap. 8.95x (ISBN 0-416-08120-7). Methuen Inc.

Fullard, Harold, ed. Esso Road Atlas Great Britain & Ireland. 6th ed. LC 73-160942. (Illus.). 235p. 1979. 13.50x (ISBN 0-540-05326-0). Intl Pubns Serv.

IRELAND–POLITICS AND GOVERNMENT

Ayearst, Morley. The Republic of Ireland: Its Government & Politics. LC 79-90900. 1970. 10.95x (ISBN 0-8147-0019-5). NYU Pr.

Bax, Mart. Harpstrings & Confessions: Machine-Style Politics in the Irish Republic. 1977. pap. text ed. 23.25x (ISBN 90-232-1481-1). Humanities.

Beyond Orange & Green: The Political Eonomy of the Northern Ireland Crisis. 176p. 1978. 12.95 (ISBN 0-905762-16-9, Pub. by Zed Pr); pap. 5.95 (ISBN 0-905762-17-7). Lawrence Hill.

Blanshard, Paul. The Irish & Catholic Power: An American Interpretation. LC 70-112321. 375p. 1972. Repr. of 1953 ed. lib. bdg. 16.75x (ISBN 0-8371-4708-5, BLIC). Greenwood.

Boyle, Andrew. The Riddle of Erskine Childers. 1978. 15.95 (ISBN 0-09-128490-2, Pub. by Hutchinson). Merrimack Bk Serv.

Boyle, Kevin, et al. Law & State: The Case of Northern Ireland. LC 75-10914. 206p. 1975. 10.00x (ISBN 0-87023-197-9). U of Mass Pr.

Bradshaw, Brendan. The Irish Constitutional Revolution in the Sixteenth Century. LC 78-58785. 1979. 41.50 (ISBN 0-521-22206-0). Cambridge U Pr.

Bromage, Mary C. Churchill & Ireland. 1964. 7.95x (ISBN 0-268-00049-2). U of Notre Dame Pr.

Budge, Ian & O'Leary, Cornelius. Belfast: Approach to Crisis. LC 72-85194. 1973. 18.95 (ISBN 0-312-07420-4). St Martin.

Burke, Edmund. Letters, Speeches & Tracts on Irish Affairs. Arnold, Mathew, ed. LC 75-28809. Repr. of 1881 ed. 36.00 (ISBN 0-404-13802-0). AMS Pr.

Cahill, Kevin M. Irish Essays. LC 80-80550. 140p. 1980. 9.00 (ISBN 0-89444-028-4). John Jay Pr.

Carty, R. K. Party & Parish Pump: Electoral Politics in Ireland. 207p. 1981. text ed. 11.00x (ISBN 0-88920-105-6, Pub. by Laurier U Pr). Humanities.

Childers, Erskine. Military Rule in Ireland. 59.95 (ISBN 0-8490-0637-6). Gordon Pr.

Chubb, Basil. The Government & Politics of Ireland. LC 77-93493. 1970. 10.00x (ISBN 0-8047-0708-1). Stanford U Pr.

Clarke, Maude V. Fourteenth Century Studies. facs. ed. Sutherland, L. G. & McKisack, M., eds. LC 67-30181. (Essay Index Reprint Ser). 1937. 18.50 (ISBN 0-8369-0310-2). Arno.

Clarkson, J. Dunsmore. Labour & Nationalism in Ireland. LC 78-12024. (Columbia University Studies in the Social Sciences: No. 266). Repr. of 1925 ed. 31.50 (ISBN 0-404-51266-6). AMS Pr.

Coogan, Tim P. On the Blanket: The H-Block Story. 6.95 (ISBN 0-907085-01-6). Turtle Isl Foun.

Davis, E. E. & Sinnott, R. Attitudes in the Republic of Ireland Relevant to the Northern Ireland Problem: Vol. 1: Descriptive Analysis & Some Comparisons with Attitudes in Northern Ireland & Great Britain. 1981. 25.00x (ISBN 0-686-75525-1, Pub. by ESRI Ireland). State Mutual Bk.

Dolley, Michael. Anglo-Norman Ireland, Vol. 3. (Gill History of Ireland). (Illus.). 210p. 1973. pap. 3.25 (ISBN 0-7171-0560-1). Irish Bk Ctr.

Donaldson, Alfred G. Some Comparative Aspects of Irish Law. LC 57-8815. (Commonwealth Studies Center: No. 3). 1957. 14.75 (ISBN 0-8223-0047-8). Duke.

Duffy, Charles G. My Life in Two Hemispheres, 2 vols. 1969. Repr. of 1898 ed. Set. write for info. (ISBN 0-7165-0603-3, Pub. by Irish Academic Pr Ireland); Vol. 1, 335pgs. 20.00x (ISBN 0-686-30762-3); Vol. 2, 395pgs. 20.00x (ISBN 0-7165-0561-4). Biblio Dist.

Ellis, P. Berresford, ed. James Connolly: Selected Writings. LC 73-90071. (Modern Reader Paperbacks Ser.). 320p. 1976. 11.95 (ISBN 0-85345-326-8, PB-3527); pap. 5.95 (ISBN 0-85345-348-9). Monthly Rev.

Evelegh, Robin. Peace Keeping in a Democratic Society: The Lessons of Northern Ireland. 1978. 17.95x (ISBN 0-7735-0502-4). McGill-Queens U Pr.

Eversley, George J. Gladstone & Ireland: The Irish Policy of Parliament from 1850-1894. LC 74-114520. 1971. Repr. of 1912 ed. lib. bdg. 14.25x (ISBN 0-8371-4795-6, EVGI). Greenwood.

Farrell, Brian. Chairman or Chief? (Studies in Irish Political Culture). (Illus.). 124p. 1971. pap. 3.75 (ISBN 0-7171-0535-0). Irish Bk Ctr.

Flackes, W. D. Northern Ireland: A Political Directory 1968-79. 1980. 25.00 (ISBN 0-686-60013-4). St Martin.

Ford, P. & Ford, G. A Select List of Reports of Inquiries of the Irish Dail & Senate: Fifty Years of Policy Making, 1922-72. 64p. 1974. 15.00x (ISBN 0-7165-2254-3, Pub. by Irish Academic Pr Ireland). Biblio Dist.

Fuller, R. Buckminster. Critical Path. 448p. 1981. 15.95 (ISBN 0-312-17488-8). St Martin.

Gallagher, Frank. The Indivisible Island: The Story of the Partition of Ireland. LC 74-5772. (Illus.). 316p. 1974. Repr. of 1957 ed. lib. bdg. 18.00x (ISBN 0-8371-7515-1, GAII). Greenwood.

Garvin, Tom. The Evolution of Irish Nationalist Politics. 250p. 1981. text ed. 27.00x (ISBN 0-8419-0741-2). Holmes & Meier.

Gibbon, Peter. The Origins of Ulster Unionism: The Formation of Popular Protestant Politics & Ideology in Nineteenth-Century Ireland. (Illus.). 163p. 1975. 16.50x (ISBN 0-87471-761-2). Rowman.

Good, James W. Irish Unionism. LC 70-102607. Repr. of 1920 ed. 12.50 (ISBN 0-8046-0784-2). Kennikat.

Gwynn, Denis. The Life of John Redmond. facsimile ed. LC 77-169761. (Select Bibliographies Reprint Ser). Repr. of 1932 ed. 45.00 (ISBN 0-8369-5981-7). Arno.

Gwynn, Stephen. Henry Grattan & His Times. facsimile ed. LC 78-175699. (Select Bibliographies Reprint Ser). Repr. of 1939 ed. 24.00 (ISBN 0-8369-6614-7). Arno.

Gwynn, Stephen L. Henry Grattan & His Times. LC 76-114534. (Illus.). 1971. Repr. of 1939 ed. lib. bdg. 17.25x (ISBN 0-8371-4828-6, GWHG). Greenwood.

Hechter, Michael. Internal Colonialism: The Celtic Fringe in British National Development. LC 73-84392. 1975. 25.00x (ISBN 0-520-02559-8); pap. 7.50x (ISBN 0-520-03512-7). U of Cal Pr.

Henry, Robert M. Evolution of Sinn Fein. facsimile ed. LC 77-146858. (Select Bibliographies Reprint Ser). Repr. of 1920 ed. 18.00 (ISBN 0-8369-5625-7). Arno.

Heslinga, M. R. The Irish Border As a Cultural Divide: A Contribution of the Study of Regionalism in the British Isles. 1980. pap. text ed. 18.75x (ISBN 90-232-0864-1). Humanities.

Hinton, Edward M. Ireland Through Tudor Eyes. LC 73-15942. 1935. Repr. lib. bdg. 17.50 (ISBN 0-8414-4793-4). Folcroft.

Johnston, Edith M. Great Britain & Ireland Seventeen Sixty-Eighteen Hundred: A Study in Political Administration. LC 78-2887. (St. Andrews University Publications Ser.: No. 55). 1978. Repr. of 1963 ed. lib. bdg. 34.50x (ISBN 0-313-20341-5, JOGB). Greenwood.

King, Richard A. Swift in Ireland. LC 79-171231. (English Literature Ser., No. 33). 1972. Repr. of 1895 ed. lib. bdg. 33.95 (ISBN 0-8383-1338-8). Haskell.

Lane, Dermot A., ed. Ireland, Liberation & Theology. LC 77-79989. 1978. pap. 4.95x (ISBN 0-88344-217-5). Orbis Bks.

Larkin, Emmet. The Roman Catholic Church & the Creation of the Modern Irish State, 1878-1886. LC 75-7169. (Memoirs Ser: Vol. 108). (Illus.). 1975. pap. 7.50 (ISBN 0-87169-108-6). Am Philos.

--The Roman Catholic Church in Ireland & the Fall of Parnell, 1888-1891. LC 78-22056. 1979. 19.00x (ISBN 0-8078-1352-4). U of NC Pr.

Lecky, Wm. Edward. Leaders of Public Opinion in Ireland, 2 vols. LC 76-159800. (Europe 1815-1945 Ser). 720p. 1973. Repr. of 1903 ed. Set. lib. bdg. 59.50 (ISBN 0-306-70574-5). Da Capo.

Lynch, Kathleen M. Roger Boyle: First Earl of Orrery. LC 65-17438. (Illus.). 1965. 15.00x (ISBN 0-87049-060-5). U of Tenn Pr.

Lyons, F. S. & Hawkins, R. A., eds. Ireland Under the Union: Varieties of Tension. (Illus.). 348p. 1980. 42.00x (ISBN 0-19-822469-9). Oxford U Pr.

Lyons, Francis S. The Irish Parliamentary Party, 1890-1910. LC 74-12646. 284p. 1975. Repr. of 1951 ed. lib. bdg. 15.50x (ISBN 0-8371-7734-0, LYIP). Greenwood.

McAliskey, Bernadette D. The Irish Struggle: Nineteen Seventy to Nineteen Eighty. 1982. lib. bdg. 25.00 (ISBN 0-913460-80-X); pap. 6.95 (ISBN 0-913460-79-6). Monad Pr.

McAllister, Ian. The Northern Ireland Social Democratic & Labour Party: Political Opposition in a Divided Society. 1978. text ed. 31.50x (ISBN 0-8419-5035-0). Holmes & Meier.

MacAmhlaigh, Donall. An Irish Navvy: The Diary of an Exile. Iremonger, Valentin, tr. 1964. pap. 5.95 (ISBN 0-7100-2854-7). Routledge & Kegan.

MacArdle, Dorothy. The Irish Republic. 1965. 10.00 (ISBN 0-374-17728-7). FS&G.

McCaffrey, Lawrence J. Daniel O'Connell & the Repeal Year. LC 65-27011. 272p. 1966. 10.00x (ISBN 0-8131-1115-3). U Pr of Ky.

--Irish Federalism in the 1870's: A Study in Conservative Nationalism. LC 62-21773. (Transactions Ser.: Vol. 52, Pt. 6). 1962. pap. 1.00 (ISBN 0-87169-526-X). Am Philos.

McCaffrey, Lawrence J., ed. Irish Nationalism & the American Contribution. LC 76-6354. (Irish Americans Ser). 1976. 15.00 (ISBN 0-405-09347-0). Arno.

McCann, Eamonn. War & an Irish Town. rev. 2nd ed. 176p. 1981. pap. 5.95 (ISBN 0-86104-302-2). Pluto Pr.

McCraken, J. L. Representative Government in Ireland: A Study of Dail Eireann, 1919-48. LC 75-31470. (Illus.). 1976. Repr. of 1958 ed. lib. bdg. 16.00x (ISBN 0-8371-8534-3, MCRG). Greenwood.

McDowell, R. B. Public Opinion & Government Policy in Ireland, 1801-1846. LC 74-31010. 303p. 1975. Repr. of 1952 ed. lib. bdg. 17.00x (ISBN 0-8371-7915-7, MCPO). Greenwood.

McDowell, Robert B. Ireland in the Age of Imperialism & Revolution, Seventeen Sixty to Eighteen Hundred One. 748p. text ed. 84.00x (ISBN 0-19-822480-X). Oxford U Pr.

--The Irish Administration, 1801-1914. LC 75-35336. 328p. 1976. Repr. of 1964 ed. lib. bdg. 24.75 (ISBN 0-8371-8561-0, MCIA). Greenwood.

--Irish Public Opinion, 1750-1800. LC 70-114543. 306p. 1975. Repr. of 1944 ed. lib. bdg. 14.75x (ISBN 0-8371-4742-5, MCIP). Greenwood.

MacGreil, Michael. Prejudice & Tolerance in Ireland. LC 79-49275. 600p. 1980. 31.95 (ISBN 0-03-056718-1). Praeger.

Malcomson, A. P. John Foster: The Politics of the Anglo-Irish Ascendancy. 1978. 55.00x (ISBN 0-19-920087-4). Oxford U Pr.

Manning, Maurice. Irish Political Parties. 2nd ed. (Studies in Irish Political Culture Ser.). (Illus.). 1972. pap. 3.75 (ISBN 0-7171-0536-9). Irish Bk Ctr.

Mansergh, A. The Government of Northern Ireland: A Study in Devolution. 59.95 (ISBN 0-8490-0255-9). Gordon Pr.

Marx, Karl & Engels, Frederick. Ireland & the Irish Question. Dixon, Richard, ed. Ryazanskaya, S., et al, trs. from Fr., Ger. & It. LC 73-188754. 518p. 1972. pap. 3.25 (ISBN 0-7178-0342-2). Intl Pub Co.

Marx, Karl & Engels, Friedrich. Ireland & the Irish Question. 518p. 1971. 3.25 (ISBN 0-8285-0030-4, Pub. by Progress Pubs Russia). Imported Pubns.

Mitchel, John. An Apology for the British Government in Ireland. LC 75-28830. Repr. of 1905 ed. 13.25 (ISBN 0-404-13820-9). AMS Pr.

Mitchell, Arthur. Labour in Irish Politics: Eighteen Ninty to Nineteen Thirty: the Irish Labor Movement in an Age of Revolution. (Illus.). 317p. 1974. 20.00x (ISBN 0-686-28343-0, Pub. by Irish Academic Pr). Biblio Dist.

Molony, Chartres J. Riddle of the Irish. LC 74-102619. (Irish Culture & History Ser). 1970. Repr. of 1927 ed. 12.00 (ISBN 0-8046-0796-6). Kennikat.

Morgan & Purdie, eds. Ireland: Divided Nation, Divided Class. 1980. lib. bdg. 17.50 (ISBN 0-906133-20-3, Pub. by Ink Links); pap. 6.95 (ISBN 0-906133-21-1). Path Pr NY.

Morgan, J. H., ed. New Irish Constitution. LC 70-118490. 1971. Repr. of 1912 ed. 22.50 (ISBN 0-8046-1367-2). Kennikat.

Moss, Warner. Political Parties in the Irish Free State. LC 68-58610. (Columbia University. Studies in the Social Sciences: No. 382). Repr. of 1933 ed. 20.00 (ISBN 0-404-51382-4). AMS Pr.

Murphy, John. Ireland in the Twentieth Century. (Gill History of Ireland: Vol. 11). 192p. 1975. pap. 5.50 (ISBN 0-7171-0568-7). Irish Bk Ctr.

Norman, Edward. History of Modern Ireland. LC 78-160166. 1971. 9.95x (ISBN 0-87024-205-9). U of Miami Pr.

Nowlan, Kevin B. The Politics of Repeal. LC 75-35339. 248p. 1976. Repr. of 1965 ed. lib. bdg. 15.25x (ISBN 0-8371-8562-9, NOPR). Greenwood.

O'Ballance, Edgar. Terror in Ireland: The Heritage of Hate. (Illus.). 280p. 1981. 14.95 (ISBN 0-89141-100-3). Presidio Pr.

O'Brien, Joseph V. William O'Brien & the Course of Irish Politics, 1881-1918. LC 74-22970. 350p. 1976. 26.50x (ISBN 0-520-02886-4). U of Cal Pr.

O'Brien, William. Irish Ideas. LC 79-102620. (Irish Culture & History Ser). 1970. Repr. of 1893 ed. 12.00 (ISBN 0-8046-0797-4). Kennikat.

O'Broin, Leon. Dublin Castle & the 1916 Rising. LC 78-138554. 1971. 14.50x (ISBN 0-8147-6150-X). NYU Pr.

O'Connell, Maurice R. Irish Politics & Social Conflict in the Age of the American Revolution. LC 76-2388. (Illus.). 444p. 1976. Repr. of 1965 ed. lib. bdg. 30.00 (ISBN 0-8371-8758-3, OCIP). Greenwood.

O'Donnell, F. Hugh. History of the Irish Parliamentary Party, 2 Vols. LC 70-102623. (Irish Culture & History Ser). 1970. Repr. of 1910 ed. Set. 45.00x (ISBN 0-8046-0800-8). Kennikat.

O'Faolain, Sean. King of the Beggars. LC 75-7242. (Illus.). 338p. 1975. Repr. of 1938 ed. lib. bdg. 16.25x (ISBN 0-8371-8104-6, OFKB). Greenwood.

O'Farrell, Patrick. Ireland's English Question: Anglo-Irish Relations, 1534-1970. LC 75-159481. (Fabric of British History Ser). 1972. 11.50x (ISBN 0-8052-3424-1); pap. 4.95 (ISBN 0-8052-0348-6). Schocken.
O'Leary, Cornelius. Irish Elections, 1918 - 1977: Parties, Voters & Proportional Representation. 1979. 19.95x (ISBN 0-312-43597-5). St Martin.
O'Sullivan, Donal. The Irish Free State & Its Senate: A Study in Contemporary Politics. LC 72-4286. (World Affairs Ser.: National & International Viewpoints). 696p. 1972. Repr. of 1940 ed. 30.00 (ISBN 0-405-04579-4). Arno.
O'Tuathaigh, Gearoid. Ireland Before the Famine. (Gill History of Ireland: Vol. 9). 248p. 1972. pap. 5.75 (ISBN 0-7171-0566-0). Irish Bk Ctr.
Pearse, P. H. The Letters of P. H. Pearse. O'Buachalla, Seamas, ed. 528p. 1980. text ed. 31.25x (ISBN 0-391-01678-4). Humanities.
Penniman, Howard R., ed. Ireland at the Polls: The Dial Elections of 1977. 1978. pap. 6.25 (ISBN 0-8447-3300-8). Am Enterprise.
Plunkett Foundation for Co-Operative Studies, ed. Irish Co-Operative Movement: Its History & Development by Patrick Bolger. (Institute of Public Administration Ser.). 434p. 1977. 50.00x (ISBN 0-902173-75-8, Pub. by Plunkett Found England). State Mutual Bk.
Plunkett, Horace. Ireland in the New Century. LC 77-102625. (Irish Culture & History Ser). 1970. Repr. of 1904 ed. 14.50 (ISBN 0-8046-0801-6). Kennikat.
Sacks, Paul M. The Donegal Mafia: An Irish Political Machine. LC 75-43332. (Illus.). 1976. 20.00x (ISBN 0-300-02020-1). Yale U Pr.
Sharp, Granville. Declaration of the People's Natural Right to a Share in the Legislature. LC 74-119046. (Era of the American Revolution Ser). 1971. Repr. of 1774 ed. lib. bdg. 27.50 (ISBN 0-306-71955-X). Da Capo.
Sheridan, Thomas. Some Revelations on Irish History. Bannister, Saxe, ed. LC 73-102592. (Irish Culture & History Ser). Repr. of 1870 ed. 14.50 (ISBN 0-8046-0769-9). Kennikat.
Smith, Elizabeth. The Irish Journals of Elizabeth Smith Eighteen Forty to Eighteen Fifty. Thomson, David & McGusty, Moyra, eds. (Illus.). 352p. 1980. 39.95x (ISBN 0-19-822471-0). Oxford U Pr.
Stewart, A. T. The Ulster Crisis. (Illus.). 288p. (Orig.). 1969. pap. 6.50 (ISBN 0-571-08066-9, Pub. by Faber & Faber). Merrimack Bk Serv.
Summerfield, Henry, ed. A. E. S. Contributions to the Irish Statesman. (Collected Edition of the Writings of G. W. Russell II). 1979. text ed. 52.00x (ISBN 0-391-01121-9). Humanities.
Tarpey, Marie V. The Role of Joseph McGarrity in the Struggle for Irish Independence. LC 76-6368. (Irish Americans Ser). 1976. 22.00 (ISBN 0-405-09360-8). Arno.
Whyte, J. H. Church & State in Modern Ireland: 1923 to 1979. 2nd ed. 491p. 1980. 32.50x (ISBN 0-389-20010-7). B&N.
Younger, Carlton. Ireland's Civil War. LC 70-79855. 1969. 10.00 (ISBN 0-8008-4240-5). Taplinger.

IRELAND-SOCIAL CONDITIONS

Budge, Ian & O'Leary, Cornelius. Belfast: Approach to Crisis. LC 72-85194. 1973. 18.95 (ISBN 0-312-07420-4). St Martin.
Connell, Kenneth H. The Population of Ireland, 1750-1845. LC 74-9165. 293p. 1975. Repr. of 1950 ed. lib. bdg. 18.75x (ISBN 0-8371-7620-4, COPI). Greenwood.
Cosgrave, D. North Dublin: City & County. 138p. 1977. Repr. of 1909 ed. 6.00x (ISBN 0-906127-02-5, Pub. by Irish Academic Pr Ireland). Biblio Dist.
Costello, Peter. The Heart Grown Brutal: The Irish Revolution in Literature, from Parnell to the Death of Yeats, 1891-1939. (Illus.). 330p. 1977. 24.50x (ISBN 0-8476-6007-9). Rowman.
Cullen, Louis M. The Emergence of Modern Ireland, Sixteen Hundred to Nineteen Hundred. LC 81-6548. 200p. 1981. text ed. 30.00x (ISBN 0-8419-0727-7). Holmes & Meier.
Fuller, R. Buckminster. Critical Path. 448p. 1981. 15.95 (ISBN 0-312-17488-8). St Martin.
Hannan, D. F. Displacement & Development: Class, Kinship & Social Change in Irish Rural Communities. 1981. 25.00x (ISBN 0-686-75524-3, Pub. by ESRI Ireland). State Mutual Bk.
Heslinga, M. R. The Irish Border As a Cultural Divide: A Contribution of the Study of Regionalism in the British Isles. 1980. pap. text ed. 18.75x (ISBN 90-232-0864-1). Humanities.
Kaim-Caudle, Peter, ed. Social Policy in the Irish Republic. 1967. text ed. 3.75x (ISBN 0-7100-4023-7). Humanities.
Lane, Padraig. Ireland. (Illus.). 96p. 1974. 17.50x (ISBN 0-7134-2845-7). Intl Pubns Serv.
McDowell, Robert B. Irish Public Opinion, 1750-1800. LC 70-114543. 306p. 1975. Repr. of 1944 ed. lib. bdg. 14.75x (ISBN 0-8371-4742-5, MCIP). Greenwood.
MacGreil, Michael. Prejudice & Tolerance in Ireland. LC 79-49275. 600p. 1980. 31.95 (ISBN 0-03-056718-1). Praeger.
MacKinnon, Kenneth. Language, Education & Social Processes in a Gaelic Communtiy. (Direct Editions Ser.). (Orig.). 1977. pap. 10.95 (ISBN 0-7100-8466-8). Routledge & Kegan.
MacLysaght, Edward. Irish Life in the Seventeenth Century. 324p. 1979. 15.00x (ISBN 0-7165-2343-4, Pub. by Irish Academic Pr); pap. 7.50x (ISBN 0-7165-2342-6, Pub. by Irish Academic Pr). Biblio Dist.
MacNeill, Eoin. Celtic Ireland. 59.95 (ISBN 0-87968-824-6). Gordon Pr.
Mogey, John M. Rural Life in Northern Ireland: Five Regional Studies Made for the Northern Ireland Council of Social Service, Inc. LC 77-87692. Repr. of 1947 ed. 38.00 (ISBN 0-404-16488-9). AMS Pr.
Morgan, Austen & Purdie, Bob, eds. Ireland, Divided Nation, Divided Class. 225p. 1980. text ed. 20.00x (ISBN 0-906133-20-3, Pub. by Ink Links England); pap. text ed. 8.75x (ISBN 0-906133-21-1). Humanities.
Nicholls, Kenneth. Gaelic & Gaelicised Ireland in the Middle Ages. (Gill History of Ireland: Vol. 4). (Illus.). 212p. 1972. pap. 5.75 (ISBN 0-7171-0561-X). Irish Bk Ctr.
O'Brien, George A. Economic History of Ireland from the Union to the Famine. LC 68-56554. Repr. of 1921 ed. lib. bdg. 19.50x (ISBN 0-678-00816-7). Kelley.
O'Connell, Maurice R. Irish Politics & Social Conflict in the Age of the American Revolution. LC 76-2388. (Illus.). 444p. 1976. Repr. of 1965 ed. lib. bdg. 30.00 (ISBN 0-8371-8758-3, OCIP). Greenwood.
Potter, George. To the Golden Door. LC 73-3928. (Illus.). 631p. 1974. Repr. of 1960 ed. lib. bdg. 35.00x (ISBN 0-8371-6862-7, POGD). Greenwood.
Power, Patrick. Sex & Marriage in Ancient Ireland. (Irish Life & Culture Ser.). 1977. pap. 3.75 (ISBN 0-85342-475-6). Irish Bk Ctr.
Schrier, Arnold. Ireland & the American Emigration, 1850-1900. LC 70-83864. (Illus.). 1970. Repr. of 1958 ed. 9.50 (ISBN 0-8462-1416-4). Russell.
Sheehy, Michael. Is Ireland Dying? Culture & the Church in Modern Ireland. LC 69-16059. 1969. 5.95 (ISBN 0-8008-4250-2). Taplinger.
Unwin, J. C. The Hungry Forties: Life Under the Bread Tax. 288p. Date not set. Repr. of 1904 ed. 24.00x (ISBN 0-686-28338-4, Pub. by Irish Academic Pr). Biblio Dist.

IRELAND-SOCIAL LIFE AND CUSTOMS

Allingham, William. Laurence Bloomfield in Ireland: A Modern Poem. LC 71-148742. Repr. of 1864 ed. 22.00 (ISBN 0-404-00346-X). AMS Pr.
Arensberg, Conrad M. Irish Countryman. LC 68-13630. 1968. Repr. of 1937 ed. 2.50 (ISBN 0-385-09075-7, B18, AMS). Natural Hist.
--The Irish Countryman: An Anthropological Study. 7.50 (ISBN 0-8446-1031-3). Peter Smith.
Cahill, Kevin M. Irish Essays. LC 80-80550. 140p. 1980. 9.00 (ISBN 0-89444-028-4). John Jay Pr.
Cullen, L. M. Life in Ireland. 1979. pap. 14.95 (ISBN 0-7134-1449-9, Pub. by Batsford England). David & Charles.
Daunt, W. J. A Life Spent for Ireland. 440p. 1972. Repr. of 1896 ed. 17.00x (ISBN 0-7165-0025-6, Pub. by Irish Academic Pr Ireland). Biblio Dist.
Delaney, Mary M. Of Irish Ways. (BN 4000 Ser.). 368p. 1980. pap. 4.95 (ISBN 0-06-464035-3). Har-Row.
--Of Irish Ways. LC 73-11876. (Heritage Bks). (Illus.). 1973. 8.95 (ISBN 0-87518-061-2). Dillon.
Evans, E. E. Irish Heritage. (Illus.). 1950. 15.00 (ISBN 0-85221-009-4). Dufour.
Evans, E. Estyn. Irish Folkways. (Illus.). 1966. 20.00 (ISBN 0-7100-1344-2); pap. 11.95 (ISBN 0-7100-2888-1). Routledge & Kegan.
Fox, R. The Tory Islanders. LC 77-83992. (Illus.). 1978. 27.95 (ISBN 0-521-21870-5); pap. 7.95x (ISBN 0-521-29298-0). Cambridge U Pr.
Garvey, Michael. State O'Chassis. 1980. 8.95 (ISBN 0-88347-107-8). Thomas More.
Gwynn, Stephen L. Irish Books & Irish People. facs. ed. LC 74-86756. (Essay Index Reprint Ser.). 1920. 12.00 (ISBN 0-8369-1136-9). Arno.
Healy, Maurice. The Old Munster Circuit. 272p. 1979. pap. 6.25 (ISBN 0-85342-597-3). Irish Bk Ctr.
Joyce, Patrick W. Social History of Ancient Ireland, 2 Vols. LC 68-56473. (Illus.). 1968. Repr. of 1913 ed. Set. 40.00 (ISBN 0-405-08677-6, Blom Pubns); 20.00 ea. Vol. 1 (ISBN 0-405-08678-4). Vol. 2 (ISBN 0-405-08679-2). Arno.
Krans, Horatio S. Irish Life in Irish Fiction. LC 3-22087. Repr. of 1903 ed. 22.50 (ISBN 0-404-03778-X). AMS Pr.
Molony, Chartres J. Riddle of the Irish. LC 74-102619. (Irish Culture & History Ser). 1970. Repr. of 1927 ed. 12.00 (ISBN 0-8046-0796-6). Kennikat.
Murphy, Michael J. Mountain Year: Life on the Slopes of Slieve Gullion. 1964. 6.25 (ISBN 0-8023-1079-6). Dufour.
O'Kearney, Nicholas, ed. Feis Tighe Chonuin Chinn-Shleibhe. 215p. Repr. of 1855 ed. 16.50 (ISBN 0-384-43005-8). Johnson Repr.
O'Neill, Timothy P. Life & Tradition in Rural Ireland. (Life & Tradition Ser). (Illus.). 160p. 1977. 19.50x (ISBN 0-460-04227-0, J M Dent England). Biblio Dist.
Reilly, Cyril & Reilly, Renee. I Am of Ireland. (Illus.). 60p. (Orig.). 1981. pap. 6.95 (ISBN 0-03-059058-2). Winston Pr.
Summerfield, Henry, ed. Selections from the Contributions to the Irish Homestead by G. W. Russell-A.E, 2 vols. (Collected Edition of the Writings of G. W. Russell: Vol. I). 1978. 50.00x ea. Vol. 1 (ISBN 0-391-00848-X). Vol. 2 (ISBN 0-391-00858-7). Humanities.
Sutherland, Halliday. Irish Journey. 5.95 (ISBN 0-8159-5815-3). Devin.
Synge, J. M. In Wicklow, West Kerry & Connemara. (Illus.). 166p. 1980. 19.50x (ISBN 0-8476-6260-8). Rowman.
Synge, John M. John M. Synge in Connemara. Orig. Title: In Connemara. 92p. 1979. pap. 3.95 (ISBN 0-85342-583-3). Irish Bk Ctr.
Wallace, Martin. The Irish: How They Live & Work. (How They Live & Work Ser.). (Illus.). 1974. 11.95 (ISBN 0-7153-5492-2). David & Charles.

IRELAND IN LITERATURE

Brown, Stephen. Ireland in Fiction. 382p. Repr. of 1919 ed. 13.00x (ISBN 0-686-28347-3, Pub. by Irish Academic Pr). Biblio Dist.
Frenzel, Herbert. John Millington Synge's Work As a Contribution to Irish Folk-Lore & to the Psychology of Primitive Tribes. LC 72-191249. 1932. lib. bdg. 10.00 (ISBN 0-8414-4284-3). Folcroft.
O'Donoghue, David J. Poets of Ireland: A Biographical & Bibliographical Dictionary of Irish Writers of English Verse. (Library of Literature, Drama & Criticism). 1970. Repr. of 1912 ed. 34.50 (ISBN 0-384-42975-0). Johnson Repr.

IRENAEUS, SAINT, 130-200

Burghardt, W. J. & Lawler, T. C., eds. St. Irenaeus: Proof of the Apostolic Preaching. LC 78-62503. (ACW Ser.: No. 16). 242p. 1952. 10.95 (ISBN 0-8091-0264-1). Paulist Pr.

IRENICS

see Christian Union

IRIAN

see New Guinea

IRIAN BARAT, INDONESIA

Lijphart, Arend. Trauma of Decolonization: The Dutch & West New Guinea. (Studies in Political Science: No. 17). 1966. 25.00x (ISBN 0-300-00720-5). Yale U Pr.

IRIARTE Y OROPESA, TOMAS DE, 1750-1791

Cox, R. Merritt. Tomas de Iriarte. (World Authors Ser.: Spain: No. 228). lib. bdg. 10.95 (ISBN 0-8057-2456-7). Twayne.

IRIGOYEN, HIPOLITO, PRES. ARGENTINE REPUBLIC, 1852-1933

Potash, Robert A. The Army & Politics in Argentina, 1928-1945: Yrigoyen to Peron. LC 69-13182. (Illus.). 1969. 15.00x (ISBN 0-8047-0683-2). Stanford U Pr.

IRIS (PLANT)

Dykes, William R. The Genus Iris. 1975. Repr. of 1913 ed. 25.00 (ISBN 0-486-23037-6). Dover.
--A Handbook of Garden Irises. LC 75-42381. (Illus.). 1976. Repr. of 1924 ed. write for info (ISBN 0-685-78307-3). Theophrastus.
Mathen, Brian. The Iris. LC 81-40493. (Illus.). 176p. 1981. 40.00x (ISBN 0-87663-372-6). Universe.
Price, Molly. The Iris Book. (Illus.). 224p. 1973. Repr. of 1966 ed. pap. 4.00 (ISBN 0-486-21522-9). Dover.
Randall, Harry. Irises. LC 78-80737. 1969. 8.95 (ISBN 0-8008-4245-6). Taplinger.
Warburton, Bee, ed. The World of Irises. LC 77-73698. (Illus.). 1978. 15.00 (ISBN 0-9601242-1-7). Am Iris.

IRISH AMERICANS

Akenson, Donald H. The United States & Ireland. LC 73-82348. (American Foreign Policy Library). 210p. 1973. 12.50x (ISBN 0-674-92460-6). Harvard U Pr.
Bagenal, Philip H. The American Irish & Their Influence on Irish Politics. LC 74-145469. (The American Immigration Library). viii, 252p. 1971. Repr. of 1882 ed. lib. bdg. 12.75 (ISBN 0-89198-001-6). Ozer.
Bayor, Ronald H. Neighbors in Conflict: The Irish, Germans, Jews & Italians of New York City, 1929-1941. 2nd ed. LC 77-14260. 256p. 1980. pap. 5.95 (ISBN 0-8018-2370-6). Johns Hopkins.
--Neighbors in Conflict: The Irish, Germans, Jews, & Italians of New York City, 1929-1941. LC 77-14260. (Studies in Historical & Political Science, 96th Ser: No. 2). 1978. text ed. 16.00x o. p. (ISBN 0-8018-2024-3); pap. 5.95 (ISBN 0-8018-2370-6). Johns Hopkins.
Birmingham, Stephen. Real Lace: America's Irish Rich. LC 73-4061. (Illus.). 336p. 1973. 12.95 (ISBN 0-06-010336-1, HarpT). Har-Row.
Blessing, Patrick. The British & Irish in Oklahoma. LC 79-6722. (Newcomers to a New Land Ser.: Vol. 3). (Illus.). 96p. (Orig.). 1980. pap. 2.95 (ISBN 0-8061-1672-2). U of Okla Pr.
Brown, Thomas N. Irish-American Nationalism, Eighteen Seventy to Eighteen Ninety. LC 80-11094. (Critical Periods of History). xvii, 206p. 1980. Repr. of 1966 ed. lib. bdg. 19.00x (ISBN 0-313-22204-5, BRIA). Greenwood.
Buckley, John P. The New York Irish: Their View of American Foreign Policy, 1914-1921. LC 76-6327. (Irish Americans Ser). 1976. 23.00 (ISBN 0-405-09324-1). Arno.
Byrne, Stephen. Irish Immigration to the United States: What It Has Been and What It Is. LC 69-18763. (American Immigration Collection Ser., No. 1). (Illus.). 1969. Repr. of 1873 ed. 9.50 (ISBN 0-405-00511-3). Arno.
Clark, Dennis. The Irish in Philadelphia: Ten Generations of Urban Experience. LC 72-95884. 275p. 1974. 12.50x (ISBN 0-87722-057-3). Temple U Pr.
Clark, Dennis J. Irish Blood: Northern Ireland and the American Conscience. LC 76-21808. (National University Publications Ser. in American Studies). 1977. 11.00 (ISBN 0-8046-9163-0). Kennikat.
Condon, Edward O. The Irish Race in America: Bicentennial Edition. new ed. LC 75-35480. 352p. pap. 4.95 (ISBN 0-916590-01-1). Ogham Hse.
Conzen, Kathleen N. Immigrant Milwaukee, 1836-1860. (Studies in Urban History). 1976. text ed. 16.50x (ISBN 0-674-44436-1). Harvard U Pr.
Cuddy, Joseph E. Irish-America & National Isolationism: 1914-1920. LC 76-6332. (Irish Americans Ser). 1976. 16.00 (ISBN 0-405-09328-4). Arno.
D'Arcy, William. Fenian Movement in the U. S. 1858-1886. LC 70-151542. 1971. Repr. of 1947 ed. 18.00 (ISBN 0-8462-1534-9). Russell.
Doyle, David N. Irish-Americans, Native Rights & National Empires: The Structure, Divisions, & Attitudes of the Catholic Minority in the Decade of Expansion, 1890-1901. LC 76-6336. (Irish Americans Ser). 1976. 20.00 (ISBN 0-405-09332-2). Arno.
Fallows, Marjorie R. Irish Americans: Identity & Assimilation. (Ethnic Groups in American Life Ser.). 1979. ref. ed. 11.95 (ISBN 0-13-506261-6); pap. text ed. 8.95 (ISBN 0-13-506253-5). P-H.
Flannery, John B. The Irish Texans. (The Texians & Texans Ser.). (Illus.). 174p. 1980. 8.95 (ISBN 0-933164-33-5); pap. 6.95 (ISBN 0-933164-58-0). U of Tex Inst Tex Culture.
Gabriel, Richard A. The Irish & Italians: Ethnics in City & Suburb. Cordasco, Francesco, ed. LC 80-857. (American Ethnic Groups Ser.). 1981. lib. bdg. 29.00x (ISBN 0-405-13420-7). Arno.
Glasco, Laurence A. Ethnicity & Social Structure: Irish, Germans & Native-Born of Buffalo, N.Y., 1850-1860. Cordasco, Francesco, ed. LC 80-859. (American Ethnic Groups Ser.). 1981. lib. bdg. 35.00x (ISBN 0-405-13422-3). Arno.
Greeley, Andrew M. The Irish Americans. LC 81-47353. 256p. 1981. 12.95 (ISBN 0-06-038001-2, HarpT). Har-Row.
--That Most Distressful Nation: The Taming of the American Irish. LC 74-182501. 288p. 1973. 8.95 (ISBN 0-8129-0246-7); pap. 2.95 (ISBN 0-8129-6219-2). Times Bks.
Griffin, William D. The Irish in America: Chronology & Factbook. LC 73-3405. (Ethnic Chronology Ser.). 160p. 1973. 8.50 (ISBN 0-379-00501-8). Oceana.
--A Portrait of the Irish in America. (Illus.). 320p. 1981. 30.00 (ISBN 0-684-16800-6, ScribT). Scribner.
Gudelunas, William A., Jr. & Shade, William G. Before the Molly Maguires: The Emergence of the Ethno-Religious Factor in the Politics of the Lower Anthracite Region, 1844-1872. LC 76-6344. (Irish Americans Ser). 1976. 12.00 (ISBN 0-405-09339-X). Arno.
Handlin, Oscar. Boston's Immigrants: A Study of Acculturation. rev. & enl. ed. LC 59-7653. (Illus.). 1959. 20.00x (ISBN 0-674-07980-9, Belknap Pr); pap. 6.95x (ISBN 0-674-07985-X). Harvard U Pr.
Johnson, James E. Irish in America. LC 66-10148. (In America Bks.). (Illus.). (gr. 5 up). 1966. PLB 6.95g (ISBN 0-8225-0203-8). Lerner Pubns.
Joyce, William L. Editors & Ethnicity: A History of the Irish-American Press, 1848-1883. LC 76-6349. (Irish Americans Ser). 1976. 15.00 (ISBN 0-405-09343-8). Arno.

Lannie, Vincent P. The Irish Community in America: An Annotated & Classified Bibliographical Guide. 1976. PLB 14.50 (ISBN 0-89102-060-8). B Franklin.
McCaffrey, Lawrence J., ed. Irish Americas Series, 42 bks. 1976. Set. 874.00 (ISBN 0-405-09317-9). Arno.
McGee, Thomas D. A History of the Irish Settlers in North America, from the Earliest Period to the Census of 1850. LC 78-145486. (The American Immigration Library). 240p. 1971. Repr. of 1852 ed. lib. bdg. 11.95x (ISBN 0-89198-018-0). Ozer.
--A History of the Irish Settlers in North America: From the Earliest Period to the Census of 1850. LC 74-2606. 240p. 1974. Repr. of 1852 ed. 12.50 (ISBN 0-8063-0618-1). Genealog Pub.
Maguire, John F. Irish in America. LC 69-18784. (American Immigration Collection Ser., No. 1). 1969. Repr. of 1868 ed. 18.50 (ISBN 0-405-00532-6). Arno.
O'Brien, Michael J. A Hidden Phase of American History: Ireland's Part in America's Struggle for Liberty. facsimile ed. LC 76-165648. (Select Bibliographies Reprint Ser). Repr. of 1919 ed. 35.00 (ISBN 0-8369-5957-4). Arno.
--A Hidden Phase of American History: Ireland's Part in America's Struggle for Liberty. LC 72-10442. (Illus.). 1973. Repr. of 1919 ed. 18.50 (ISBN 0-8063-0528-2). Genealog Pub.
--Irish at Bunker Hill. 1969. 10.00 (ISBN 0-8159-5813-7). Devin.
O'Grady, Joseph P. How the Irish Became Americans. (The Immigrant Heritage of America Ser). lib. bdg. 11.95 (ISBN 0-8057-3229-2). Twayne.
--Irish-Americans & Anglo-American Relations, 1880-1888. LC 76-6360. (Irish Americans Ser). 1976. 20.00 (ISBN 0-405-09353-5). Arno.
Potter, George. To the Golden Door. LC 73-3928. (Illus.). 631p. 1974. Repr. of 1960 ed. lib. bdg. 35.00x (ISBN 0-8371-6862-7, POGD). Greenwood.
Roberts, Edward F. Ireland in America. LC 74-22756. (Labor Movement in Fiction & Non-Fiction). 1976. Repr. of 1931 ed. 18.00 (ISBN 0-404-58509-4). AMS Pr.
Roney, Frank. Irish Rebel & California Labor Leader: An Autobiography. Cross, Ira B., ed. LC 76-6363. (Irish Americans Ser.). (Illus.). 1976. Repr. of 1931 ed. 37.00 (ISBN 0-405-09355-1). Arno.
Schrier, Arnold. Ireland & the American Emigration, 1850-1900. LC 70-83864. (Illus.). 1970. Repr. of 1958 ed. 9.50 (ISBN 0-8462-1416-4). Russell.
Shannon, William V. The American Irish: A Political & Social Portrait. new expanded ed. (Illus.). 484p. 1974. pap. 4.95 (ISBN 0-02-036850-X, Collier). Macmillan.
Vinyard, JoEllen M. The Irish on the Urban Frontier: Detroit, 1850-1880. LC 76-6369. (Irish Americans Ser). 1976. 25.00 (ISBN 0-405-09361-6). Arno.
Walsh, James P., ed. The Irish: America's Political Class. LC 76-6370. (Irish Americans Ser). (Illus.). 1976. 31.00 (ISBN 0-405-09362-4). Arno.
Wittke, Carl. Irish in America. LC 75-102559. 1970. Repr. of 1956 ed. 16.00 (ISBN 0-8462-1462-8). Russell.
--Irish in America. LC 68-9259. 1968. pap. 2.95 (ISBN 0-8077-2345-2). Tchrs Coll.

IRISH ARCHITECTURE
see Architecture–Ireland

IRISH ART
see Art, Irish

IRISH AUTHORS
see Authors, Irish

IRISH BALLADS AND SONGS
see also Ballads, Irish; Folk-Songs, Irish; Songs, Irish
Greaves, C. Desmond. The Easter Rising in Song & Ballad. 88p. 1980. 10.00 (ISBN 0-900707-51-8, Pub. by Stanmore Pr England); pap. 4.95 (ISBN 0-900707-51-8). Facsimile Bk.
Harvey, William. Irish Life & Humour in Anecdote & Story. 1975. Repr. of 1904 ed. 35.00 (ISBN 0-8274-4070-7). R West.
Healy, James. Irish Ballads & Songs of the Sea. 144p. 1967. pap. 4.50 (ISBN 0-85342-074-2). Irish Bk Ctr.
Healy, James N. Irish Ballads: Second Book of. 3rd ed. 1968. pap. 4.50 (ISBN 0-85342-081-5). Irish Bk Ctr.
O'Keeffe, Daniel. Irish Ballads: First Book of. 1968. pap. 4.50 (ISBN 0-85342-080-7). Irish Bk Ctr.

IRISH BULLS
see Irish Wit and Humor

IRISH CONFEDERATION, 1642-1648
Gilbert, John T., ed. History of the Irish Confederation & the War in Ireland, 1641-1649, Containing a Narrative of Affairs of Ireland, 7 vols. LC 72-144616. Repr. of 1891 ed. Set. 210.00 (ISBN 0-404-02840-3). AMS Pr.

IRISH DRAMA (ENGLISH)
Bickley, Francis. J. M. Synge & the Irish Dramatic Movement. LC 68-25027. (Illus.). 1968. Repr. of 1912 ed. 6.50 (ISBN 0-8462-1140-8). Russell.
Clarke, Austin. Liberty Lane: A Ballad Play of Dublin in Two Acts with a Prologue by Austin Clarke. (Dolmen Editions: No. XXVII). 1978. text ed. 22.25x (ISBN 0-85105-324-6, Dolmen Pr). Humanities.
Corrigan, Robert W., ed. Masterpieces of Modern Irish Theater. Incl. Countess Cathleen. Yeats, William B; Riders to the Sea. Synge, John M; Playboy of the Western World. Synge, John M; Silver Tassie. O'Casey, Sean; Cock-a-Doodle-Dandy. O'Casey, Sean. 1967. pap. 1.95 (ISBN 0-02-012190-3, 01219, Collier). Macmillan.
Feeney, William, ed. Lost Plays of the Irish Renaissance, Vol. 2. 10.00 (ISBN 0-912262-70-2). Proscenium.
Ferrar, Harold. Denis Johnston's Irish Theatre. (The Irish Theatre Ser.: No.5). 144p. (Orig.). 1973. pap. text ed. 5.25x (ISBN 0-85105-208-8, Dolmen Pr). Humanities.
Hogan, Robert & Kilroy, James. The Modern Irish Drama 1: The Irish Literary Theater 1899-1901. (The Irish Theatre Ser.: No. 6). 160p. (Orig.). 1975. text ed. 12.00x (ISBN 0-391-00377-1, Dolmen Pr); pap. text ed. 7.50x (ISBN 0-391-00378-X). Humanities.
Marriott, James W., ed. One-Act Plays of Today. LC 79-50028. (One-Act Plays in Reprint Ser.: No. 2). 1980. Repr. of 1925 ed. 21.75x (ISBN 0-8486-2051-8). Core Collection.
O'Brien, Seumas. Duty & Other Irish Comedies. LC 77-89724. (One-Act Plays in Reprint Ser.). 1977. Repr. of 1916 ed. 14.50x (ISBN 0-8486-2029-1). Core Collection.
Robinson, Lennox. Irish Theatre. LC 79-92980. (Studies in Drama, No. 39). 1969. Repr. of 1939 ed. lib. bdg. 33.95 (ISBN 0-8383-1201-2). Haskell.
Weygandt, Cornelius. Irish Plays & Playwrights. LC 79-17616. (Illus.). 1979. Repr. of 1913 ed. lib. bdg. 22.50x (ISBN 0-313-22040-9, WEIP). Greenwood.

IRISH DRAMA (ENGLISH)–BIBLIOGRAPHY
French, Frances-Jane. Abbey Theatre Series of Plays: A Bibliography. 1970. 7.25 (ISBN 0-85105-149-9). Dufour.
King, Kimball. Ten Modern Irish Playwrights: A Comprehensive Annotated Bibliography. LC 78-68289. (Reference Library of Humanities). 1979. lib. bdg. 18.00 (ISBN 0-8240-9789-0). Garland Pub.
Mikhail, E. H. Bibliography of Modern Irish Drama, 1899-1970. LC 72-1373. 63p. 1972. 10.50 (ISBN 0-295-95229-6). U of Wash Pr.

IRISH DRAMA (ENGLISH)–HISTORY AND CRITICISM
Bickley, F. L. J. M. Synge & the Irish Dramatic Movement. 59.95 (ISBN 0-8490-0430-6). Gordon Pr.
Bird, Alan. The Plays of Oscar Wilde. (Critical Studies Ser.). 220p. 1977. 18.50x (ISBN 0-06-490415-6). B&N.
Canfield, Curtis, ed. Plays of the Irish Renaissance, 1880-1930. LC 73-4881. (Play Anthology Reprint Ser.). Repr. of 1929 ed. 28.00 (ISBN 0-8369-8248-7). Arno.
Duggan, George C. Stage Irishman. LC 70-91899. (Illus.). 1937. 18.00 (ISBN 0-405-08468-4, Blom Pubns). Arno.
Ellis-Fermor, Una. The Irish Dramatic Movement. 241p. 1977. Repr. of 1939 ed. 23.75x (ISBN 0-8476-6015-X). Rowman.
Familiar Epistles to Frederick J(ones), Esq., on the Present State of the Irish Stage, Repr. Of 1804. Bd. with The Amazoniad; or, Figure & Fashion: An Heroic Poem. Repr. of 1806 ed; Histrionic Epistles. Repr. of 1807 ed; The Battles of Talavera. a Poem. 2nd ed. Repr. of 1809 ed. 1979. lib. bdg. 42.00 (ISBN 0-8240-2139-8). Garland Pub.
Hogan, Robert & Burnham, R. The Art of the Amateur Nineteen Sixteen to Nineteen Twenty: The Modern Irish Drama V. (Irish Theatre Ser.: No. 11). 400p. 1980. text ed. 49.50x (ISBN 0-391-02153-2). Humanities.
Hogan, Robert & Kilroy, James. The Modern Irish Drama, No. 3: The Abbey Theatre, the Years of Synge 1905-1909. (Irish Theatre Ser.: No. 8). 1978. text ed. 30.00x (ISBN 0-391-00754-8, Dolmen Pr). Humanities.
--Modern Irish Drama, Vol. 2: Laying the Foundations, 1902-1904. (Irish Theatre Ser: No. 7). 164p. 1976. text ed. 21.00x (ISBN 0-391-00609-6, Dolmen Pr). Humanities.
Hogan, Robert, et al. Modern Irish Drama IV: The Rise of the Realists. 1979. text ed. 45.00x (ISBN 0-391-01118-9, Dolmen Pr). Humanities.
Hughes, Samuel C. Pre-Victorian Drama in Dublin. LC 73-122840. (Research & Source Works Ser.: No. 708). 1970. Repr. of 1904 ed. lib. bdg. 15.00 (ISBN 0-8337-1760-X). B Franklin.
Malone, Andrew E. Irish Drama. LC 65-16243. 1929. 18.00 (ISBN 0-405-08777-2, Pub. by Blom). Arno.
Mikhail, E. H. Bibliography of Modern Irish Drama, 1899-1970. LC 72-1373. 63p. 1972. 10.50 (ISBN 0-295-95229-6). U of Wash Pr.
Setterquist, Jan. Ibsen & the Beginnings of Anglo-Irish Drama. Liljegren, S. B., ed. Incl. John Millington Synge. (Irish Language & Literature Institute). 92p. Repr. of 1952 ed (ISBN 0-88211-045-4); Edward Martyn. (Upsala Irish Studies). 116p. Repr. of 1960 ed (ISBN 0-88211-048-9). LC 73-80308. 1973. Repr. 7.50 ea. S A Russell.

IRISH FICTION
see also Short Stories, Irish
Greene, David. Writing in Irish Today. (Irish Life & Culture Ser.). pap. 1.95 (ISBN 0-85342-282-6). Irish Bk Ctr.
Island Stories: Tales & Legends from the West. O'Sullivan, Paul, ed. (A World of Stone Ser.: Bk. 3). (Illus.). 1977. pap. 4.95 (ISBN 0-905140-22-2). Irish Bk Ctr.

IRISH FICTION (ENGLISH)–BIBLIOGRAPHY
Brown, Stephen J., ed. Ireland in Fiction: A Guide to Irish Novels, Tales, Romances, & Folk-Lore. LC 76-113998. (Bibliography & Reference Ser.: No. 311). 1970. Repr. of 1919 ed. text ed. 18.50 (ISBN 0-8337-0388-9). B Franklin.

IRISH FICTION (ENGLISH)–HISTORY AND CRITICISM
Chesnutt, Margaret. Studies in Short Stories of William Carleton. (Gothenborg Studies in English: No. 34). 1976. pap. text ed. 13.50x (ISBN 91-7346-027-3). Humanities.
Flanagan, Thomas J. The Irish Novelists, 1800-1850. LC 76-21874. 362p. 1976. Repr. of 1959 ed. lib. bdg. 25.00x (ISBN 0-8371-9004-5, FLIN). Greenwood.
Raleigh, John H. The Chronicle of Leopold & Molly Bloom: "Ulysses" As Narrative. LC 76-20025. 1978. 20.00x (ISBN 0-520-03301-9). U of Cal Pr.
Wolff, Robert L. William Carleton, Irish Peasant Novelist: A Preface to His Fiction. LC 79-4399. 200p. 1980. lib. bdg. 18.00 (ISBN 0-8240-3527-5). Garland Pub.

IRISH FOLK-LORE
see Folk-Lore, Irish

IRISH FOLK SONGS
see Folk-Songs, Irish

IRISH HARP
see Harp

IRISH IN FOREIGN COUNTRIES
Burchell, R. A. The San Francisco Irish, Eighteen Forty-Eight to Eighteen Eighty. 1980. 16.95 (ISBN 0-520-04003-1). U of Cal Pr.
Davin, N. F. The Irishman in Canada. 718p. Repr. of 1877 ed. 30.00x (ISBN 0-7165-0060-4, Pub. by Irish Academic Pr Ireland). Biblio Dist.
Davis, Richard P. Irish Issues in New Zealand Politics, 1868-1922. LC 75-332097. 248p. 1974. 19.25x (ISBN 0-8002-0466-2). Intl Pubns Serv.
Denvir, John. The Life Story of an Old Rebel. 306p. 1972. Repr. of 1910 ed. 15.00x (ISBN 0-7165-0012-4, Pub. by Irish Academic Pr Ireland). Biblio Dist.
Dolan, Jay P. The Immigrant Church: New York's Irish & German Catholics, 1815-1865. LC 75-12552. 1975. text ed. 16.00x (ISBN 0-8018-1708-0); pap. 3.95x (ISBN 0-8018-2018-9). Johns Hopkins.
Ellis, Eilish. Emigrants from Ireland, 1847-1852: State-Aided Emigration Schemes from Crown Estates in Ireland. LC 76-39654. 1978. Repr. of 1960 ed. 5.00 (ISBN 0-8063-0748-X). Genealog Pub.
Greeley, Andrew M. The Irish Americans: The Rise to Money & Power. LC 81-47353. 215p. 1981. 12.95 (ISBN 0-06-038001-2). Har-Row.
Hennessy, Maurice N. The Wild Geese: The Irish Soldier in Exile. LC 74-13747. (Illus.). 228p. 1975. 9.95 (ISBN 0-8159-7215-6). Devin.
Lees, Lynn H. Exiles of Erin: Irish Migrants in Victorian London. LC 78-11046. 1979. 20.00x (ISBN 0-8014-1176-9). Cornell U Pr.
McCaffrey, Lawrence J. The Irish Diaspora in America. LC 75-23894. (Midland Bks.: No. 215). 224p. 1978. pap. 3.95x (ISBN 0-253-20215-9). Ind U Pr.
Mannion, John J. Irish Settlements in Eastern Canada: A Study of Cultural Transfer & Adaptation. LC 73-84354. (Illus.). 1974. pap. 8.50 (ISBN 0-8020-6371-3). U of Toronto Pr.
O'Brien, Michael J. Irish Settlers in America: A Consolidation of Articles from the Journal of the American Irish Historical Society, 2 vols. LC 78-78381. 1979. Repr. of 1941 ed. Set. 50.00 (ISBN 0-8063-0837-0). Genealog Pub.

IRISH IN LITERATURE
Duggan, George C. Stage Irishman. LC 70-91899. (Illus.). 1937. 18.00 (ISBN 0-405-08468-4, Blom Pubns). Arno.
Kelley, Mary E. Irishman in the English Novel of the Nineteenth Century. LC 78-121149. (English Literature Ser., No. 33). 1970. Repr. of 1939 ed. lib. bdg. 33.95 (ISBN 0-8383-1096-6). Haskell.

IRISH LAND QUESTION
see Land Tenure–Ireland

IRISH LANGUAGE
see also Celtic Languages; Gaelic Language
Best, R. I. Bibliography of Irish Philology & of Printed Irish Literature. LC 14-3208. (Library of Literature, Drama & Criticism). 1970. Repr. of 1913 ed. 19.50 (ISBN 0-384-13160-3). Johnson Repr.
Dillon, Myles & Croinin, D. O. Teach Yourself Irish. (Teach Yourself Ser.). pap. 3.95 (ISBN 0-679-10183-7). McKay.
Dinneen. Irish-English Dictionary. 30.00x (ISBN 0-686-12048-5). Colton Bk.
Dinneen, Patrick S., rev. by. Irish-English Dictionary. 15.00 (ISBN 0-87559-070-5); thumb indexed 18.50 (ISBN 0-685-32982-8, 071-3). Shalom.
Joyce, P. W. English As They Speak It in Ireland. 59.95 (ISBN 0-8490-0107-2). Gordon Pr.
Kiberd, Declan. Synge & the Irish Language. 294p. 1979. 25.00x (ISBN 0-8476-6159-8). Rowman.
Learn Irish for English Speakers. pap. 8.50 (ISBN 0-685-90820-8, 046-1). Saphrograph.
Lehmann, R. P. & Lehmann, W. P. An Introduction to Old Irish. (Introductions to the Older Languages of Europe Ser.: No. 1). 201p. 1975. 18.50x (ISBN 0-87352-289-3). Modern Lang.
MacAlister, R. Stewart. The Secret Languages of Ireland. LC 74-1322. Repr. of 1937 ed. lib. bdg. 35.00 (ISBN 0-8414-6115-5). Folcroft.
MacAlister, Robert A. The Secret Languages of Ireland. 284p. 1980. Repr. of 1937 ed. lib. bdg. 35.00 (ISBN 0-8495-3529-8). Arden Lib.
O'Rahilly. Irish Dialects: Past & Present. 1972. 12.50x (ISBN 0-686-09295-3). Colton Bk.
Pokorny, Julius. A Concise Old Irish Grammar & Reader, 2 vols. LC 78-72643. (Celtic Language & Literature: Goidelic & Brythonic). Repr. of 1923 ed. Set. 30.00 (ISBN 0-404-17576-7). AMS Pr.
Stokes, Whitley, ed. The Old Irish Glosses at Wurzburg & Carlsruhe. LC 78-72645. (Celtic Language & Literature: Goidelic & Brythonic). Repr. of 1887 ed. 29.00 (ISBN 0-404-17587-2). AMS Pr.
--Three Irish Glossaries. LC 78-72647. (Celtic Language & Literature: Goidelic & Brythonic). Repr. of 1862 ed. 27.50 (ISBN 0-404-17597-X). AMS Pr.
Windisch, Ernst W. A Concise Irish Grammar with Pieces for Reading. Moore, N., tr. from Ger. LC 78-72659. Repr. of 1882 ed. 16.50 (ISBN 0-404-17615-1). AMS Pr.

IRISH LANGUAGE–TO 1100
MacAlister, Robert A. The Secret Languages of Ireland. LC 78-72637. (Celtic Language & Literature: Goidelic & Brythonic). Repr. of 1937 ed. 24.50 (ISBN 0-404-17566-X). AMS Pr.
Meyer, Kuno. Miscellanea Hibernica. pap. 5.50 (ISBN 0-384-38450-1). Johnson Repr.
Thurneysen, R. Grammar of Old Irish. 1961. 30.00x (ISBN 0-686-00866-9). Colton Bk.
--Old Irish Reader. 1949. 7.50x (ISBN 0-686-00879-0). Colton Bk.

IRISH LANGUAGE–TEXTS
Meyer, Kuno. A Primer of Irish Metrics. LC 78-72640. (Celtic Language & Literature: Goidelic & Brythonic). Repr. of 1909 ed. 14.50 (ISBN 0-404-17569-4). AMS Pr.
O'hogain, Daithi. Breacadh. 1973. pap. 3.95 (ISBN 0-85342-316-4). Irish Bk Ctr.

IRISH LEGENDS
see Legends, Irish

IRISH LITERATURE (COLLECTIONS)
Comprises literature in the Irish language and literature written by Irish authors in English or other languages.
Atkinson, Robert. The Book of Leinster. LC 78-72619. (Celtic Language & Literature: Goidelic & Brythonic). Repr. of 1880 ed. 135.00 (ISBN 0-404-17536-8). AMS Pr.
Atkinson, Robert, ed. The Book of Ballymote. LC 78-72618. (Celtic Language & Literature: Goidelic & Brythonic). Repr. of 1887 ed. 130.00 (ISBN 0-404-17535-X). AMS Pr.
Bax, Clifford, ed. Florence Farr, Bernard Shaw & W. B. Yeats. 104p. 1971. Repr. of 1941 ed. 10.00x (ISBN 0-7165-1394-3, Pub. by Cuala Press Ireland). Biblio Dist.
Brown, Peter. The Book of Kells. abr. ed. (Illus.). 1981. 22.50 (ISBN 0-500-23326-8). Thames Hudson.
Campbell, J. F. Leabhar Na Feinne. 272p. 1972. Repr. of 1872 ed. 36.00x (ISBN 0-7165-2060-5, Pub. by Irish Academic Pr Ireland). Biblio Dist.
Carpenter, Andrew & Fallon, Peter, eds. The Writers: A Sense of Ireland. 1980. 20.00 (ISBN 0-905140-76-1). Braziller.

Casey, Juanita, et al. Paddy No More - Modern Irish Short Stories. LC 77-85604. 1978. 9.95 (ISBN 0-917712-03-X). Longship Pr.
Chadwick, Norah K. An Early Irish Reader. LC 78-72634. (Celtic Language & Literature: Goidelic & Brythonic). Repr. of 1927 ed. 14.50 (ISBN 0-404-17559-7). AMS Pr.
Cross, Tom P. & Slover, Clark H., eds. Ancient Irish Tales. (Illus.). 1969. Repr. of 1936 ed. 18.50x (ISBN 0-06-480177-2). B&N.
Forkner, Ben, ed. Modern Irish Short Stories. 512p. 1980. 15.95 (ISBN 0-670-48324-9). Viking Pr.
Golden, Sean & Fallon, Peter, eds. Soft Day: A Miscellany of Contemporary Irish Writing. LC 78-63298. 1979. text ed. 16.95 (ISBN 0-268-01694-1); pap. text ed. 5.95x (ISBN 0-268-01695-X). U of Notre Dame Pr.
Gregory, Augusta I. Poets & Dreamers: Studies & Translations from the Irish. LC 67-27603. 1967. Repr. of 1903 ed. 12.50 (ISBN 0-8046-0184-4). Kennikat.
--Poets & Dreamers: Studies & Translations from the Irish by Lady Gregory, Including Nine Plays by Douglas Hyde. 5th ed. (The Coole Edition of the Collected Works of Lady Gregory Ser.). 290p. 1974. text ed. 21.00x (ISBN 0-19-519790-9). Oxford U Pr.
Island Stories: Tales & Legends from the West. O'Sullivan, Paul, ed. (A World of Stone Ser.: Bk. 3). (Illus.). 1977. pap. 4.95 (ISBN 0-905140-22-2). Irish Bk Ctr.
Kenny, Herbert A. Literary Dublin: A History. LC 72-6626. (Illus.). 1974. 12.00 (ISBN 0-8008-4921-3). Taplinger.
Leabhar Breac. LC 78-72638. (Celtic Language & Literature: Goidelic & Brythonic). Repr. of 1876 ed. 145.00 (ISBN 0-404-17565-1). AMS Pr.
Lover, Samuel. Legends & Stories of Ireland. 280p. 1980. Repr. of 1902 ed. lib. bdg. 25.00 (ISBN 0-8482-1620-2). Norwood Edns.
McCarthy, Justin, et al, eds. Irish Literature, 10 Vols in 5. (Library of Literature, Drama & Criticism). 1970. Repr. of 1904 ed. Set. 269.50 (ISBN 0-384-36570-1). Johnson Repr.
McMahon, Sean, ed. The Best from "The Bell". Great Irish Writing. 187p. 1978. 16.75x (ISBN 0-8476-6152-0). Rowman.
Marcus, David, ed. New Irish Writing. 3.95 (ISBN 0-686-73470-X, Pub. by Quartet England). Charles River Bks.
Meyer, Kuno, ed. The Triads of Ireland. LC 78-72688. (Royal Irish Academy. Todd Lecture Ser.: Vol. 13). Repr. of 1906 ed. 14.50 (ISBN 0-404-60573-7). AMS Pr.
O'Brien, Edna, ed. Some Irish Loving: A Selection. LC 78-20180. 1979. 12.50 (ISBN 0-06-013192-6, HarpT). Har-Row.
O'Faolain, Sean. Selected Stories of Sean O'Faolain. LC 78-5780. 1978. 9.95 (ISBN 0-316-63285-6, Atlantic-Little, Brown). Little.
Rafroidi, Patrick. Irish Literature in English: The Romantic Period (1789-1850, Vol. I, Pts. 1, 2 & 3. (Illus.). 1980. text ed. 67.50x (ISBN 0-391-01032-8). Humanities.
--Irish Literature in English: The Romantic Period, (1789-1850, Vol. II, Pt. IV, Bibliography. 1980. text ed. 67.50x (ISBN 0-391-01033-6). Humanities.
Read, Charles A. The Cabinet of Irish Literature, 4 vols. 150.00 (ISBN 0-686-19842-5). Ridgeway Bks.
Rhys, Grace. A Celtic Anthology. LC 74-34570. 1972. Repr. of 1927 ed. lib. bdg. 25.00 (ISBN 0-8414-7324-2). Folcroft.
Royal Irish Academy. Todd Lecture Series, Vols. 1-17. Repr. of 1935 ed. Set. 388.00 (ISBN 0-404-60560-5). AMS Pr.
--Todd Lecture Series, Vols. 1-17. Repr. of 1935 ed. Set. 388.00 (ISBN 0-404-60560-5). AMS Pr.
Yeats, William B. & Higgins, F. R., eds. Broadsides: A Collection of Old & New Songs. (Illus.). 62p. 1971. Repr. of 1935 ed. 13.00x (ISBN 0-7165-1381-1, Pub. by Cuala Press Ireland). Biblio Dist.

IRISH LITERATURE-BIBLIOGRAPHY

Best, R. I. Bibliography of Irish Philology & of Printed Irish Literature. LC 14-3208. (Library of Literature, Drama & Criticism). 1970. Repr. of 1913 ed. 19.50 (ISBN 0-384-13160-3). Johnson Repr.
Dix, Ernest R. Catalogue of Early Dublin Printed Books, 1601-1700, 4 vols in 2. LC 71-132673. 1971. Repr. of 1898 ed. Set. lib. bdg. 47.00 (ISBN 0-8337-0873-2). B Franklin.
Harmon, Maurice. Select Bibliography for the Study of Anglo-Irish Literature & Its Background. (An Irish Studies Handbook). (Illus.). 1977. text ed. 19.50x (ISBN 0-88835-000-7). Humanities.
Hogan, Robert, ed. Dictionary of Irish Literature. LC 78-20021. 1979. lib. bdg. 39.95 (ISBN 0-313-20718-6, HDI/). Greenwood.
Kersnowski, Frank L., et al. A Bibliography of Modern Irish & Anglo-Irish Literature. (Checklists in the Humanities & Education Ser.). 1976. 9.00 (ISBN 0-911536-63-9). Trinity U Pr.
McKenna, Brian, ed. Irish Literature, Eighteen Hundred-Eighteen Seventy-Five: A Guide to Information Sources. LC 74-11540. (American Literature, English Literature & World Literatures in English Information Guide Ser.: Vol. 13). 1978. 36.00 (ISBN 0-8103-1250-6). Gale.
Miller, Liam, compiled by. The Dolmen Press XXV Years: Illustrated Bibliography of the Dolmen Press 1951-1976. (Dolmen Editions Ser.: No. XxV). 1976. text ed. 39.00x (ISBN 0-85105-309-2, Dolmen Pr). Humanities.
Sellery, J'nan M. & Harris, William O. Elizabeth Bowen: A Descriptive Bibliography. (Tower Bibliographical Ser.: No. 16). 1980. 25.00 (ISBN 0-87959-080-7). U of Tex Hum Res.

IRISH LITERATURE-HISTORY AND CRITICISM

Bhatnagar, K. C. The Symbolic Tendency in Irish Renaissance. 1973. Repr. of 1962 ed. 5.00 (ISBN 0-8274-1798-5). R West.
Bhatnager, K. C. The Symbolic Tendency in the Irish Renaissance. LC 74-7226. lib. bdg. 5.00 (ISBN 0-8414-3182-5). Folcroft.
Bowen, Zack, ed. Irish Renaissance Annual I. (Irish Renaissance Annual Ser.). 192p. 1980. 8.00 (ISBN 0-87413-168-5). U Delaware Pr.
Boyd, Ernest A. Appreciations & Depreciations: Irish Literary Studies. facs. ed. LC 68-16913. (Essay Index Reprint Ser). 1918. 13.00 (ISBN 0-8369-0235-1). Arno.
Brown, Malcolm. The Politics of Irish Literature: From Thomas Davis to W. B. Yeats. LC 72-152328. (Washington Paperback Ser.: No. 67). 443p. 1972. 12.00 (ISBN 0-295-95170-2); pap. 3.95 (ISBN 0-295-95280-6). U of Wash Pr.
Brown, Stephen J. Ireland in Fiction: A Guide to Irish Novels, Tales, Romances & Folklore. 362p. Repr. of 1919 ed. 22.00 (ISBN 0-403-04119-8). Somerset Pub.
Carpenter, Andrew, ed. Place, Personality & the Irish Writer. (Irish Literary Studies Ser.: No. 1). 1977. text ed. 23.50x (ISBN 0-06-490727-9). B&N.
Connellan, Owen, ed. Imtheacht Ne Tromdhaimhe; or, the Proceedings of the Great Bardic Institution. 340p. Repr. of 1860 ed. 16.50 (ISBN 0-384-09757-X). Johnson Repr.
Costello, Peter. The Heart Grown Brutal: The Irish Revolution in Literature, from Parnell to the Death of Yeats, 1891-1939. (Illus.). 330p. 1977. 24.50x (ISBN 0-8476-6007-9). Rowman.
Cronin, John. The Anglo-Irish Novel: Vol. 1--The Nineteenth Century. 157p. 1980. 20.00x (ISBN 0-389-20014-X). B&N.
Cross, Tom P. Harper & Bard. 1978. Repr. of 1931 ed. lib. bdg. 15.00 (ISBN 0-8492-3951-6). R West.
--Harper & the Bard: The Beauties of Irish Literature. 59.95 (ISBN 0-8490-0282-6). Gordon Pr.
Dunn, Douglas. Two Decades of Irish Writing: A Critical Survey. 1975. 18.95 (ISBN 0-8023-1253-5). Dufour.
Dunn, Douglas, ed. Two Decades of Irish Writing: A Critical Survey. (Essays, Prose, & Scottish Literature). 1979. 10.95 (ISBN 0-85635-070-2, Pub. by Carcanet New Pr England). Persea Bks.
Eglinton, John. Argle-Irish Essays. 1918. 10.00 (ISBN 0-8274-1346-7). R West.
Flower, Robin. Irish Tradition. 1947. pap. 4.95x (ISBN 0-19-815216-7). Oxford U Pr.
Gregory, Augusta I. Poets & Dreamers: Studies & Translations from the Irish by Lady Gregory, Including Nine Plays by Douglas Hyde. 5th ed. (The Coole Edition of the Collected Works of Lady Gregory Ser.). 290p. 1974. text ed. 21.00x (ISBN 0-19-519790-9). Oxford U Pr.
Gwynn, Stephen. To-Day & to-Morrow in Ireland. 1973. Repr. of 1903 ed. 25.00 (ISBN 0-8274-0212-0). R West.
Gwynn, Stephen L. Irish Books & Irish People. facs. ed. LC 74-86756. (Essay Index Reprint Ser.). 1920. 12.00 (ISBN 0-8369-1136-9). Arno.
Hall, Wayne E. Shadowy Heroes: Irish Literature of the 1890's. LC 80-21383. (Irish Studies). (Illus.). 1980. 20.00x (ISBN 0-8156-2231-7). Syracuse U Pr.
Harper. Critical Edition of Yeats' A Vision. 1980. text ed. 42.50x (ISBN 0-333-21299-1). Humanities.
Hayman, David & Anderson, Elliott, eds. In the Wake of the "Wake". 216p. 1978. 18.50 (ISBN 0-299-07600-8). U of Wis Pr.
Hoare, Dorothy M. The Works of Morris & of Yeats in Relation to Early Saga Literature. LC 72-139476. 1971. Repr. of 1937 ed. 11.00 (ISBN 0-8462-1382-6). Russell.
--Works of Morris & Yeats in Relation to Early Saga Literature. LC 72-193501. 1973. lib. bdg. 10.95 (ISBN 0-8414-5087-0). Folcroft.
Hogan, Robert. Mervyn Wall. 75p. 1972. 4.50 (ISBN 0-8387-1065-4). Bucknell U Pr.
Hull, Eleanor. Text Book of Irish Literature, 2 Vols. LC 70-153595. Repr. of 1908 ed. Set. 43.50 (ISBN 0-404-09244-6). AMS Pr.
Hull, Eleanor, ed. Cuchullin Saga in Irish Literature. (Grimm Library: No. 8). Repr. of 1898 ed. 22.50 (ISBN 0-404-53553-4). AMS Pr.
Hyde, Douglas. A Literary History of Ireland. 1980. 28.50x (ISBN 0-312-48741-X). St Martin.
--A Literary History of Ireland from Earliest Times to the Present Day. LC 77-94590. 1979. Repr. of 1910 ed. lib. bdg. 65.00 (ISBN 0-89341-183-3). Longwood Pr.
--The Story of Early Gaelic Literature. LC 72-13812. 1972. Repr. lib. bdg. 20.00 (ISBN 0-8414-1296-0). Folcroft.
Imran Brain. Voyage of Bran, Son of Febal, to the Land of the Living, 2 Vols. Meyer, Kuno, tr. LC 70-144520. (Grimm Library: Nos. 4, 6). Repr. of 1897 ed. Set. 54.50 (ISBN 0-404-53580-1). AMS Pr.
Jochum, K. P. W. B. Yeats: A Classified Bibliography of Criticism. 1978. 42.50 (ISBN 0-252-00577-5). U of Ill Pr.
Kain, Richard M. Dublin in the Age of William Butler Yeats & James Joyce. (Centers of Civilization Ser: No. 7). (Illus.). 1967. Repr. of 1962 ed. 6.95 (ISBN 0-8061-0535-6). U of Okla Pr.
Kenner, Hugh. Joyce's Voices. LC 76-38887. (Quantum Book Ser.). 1978. 10.00x (ISBN 0-520-03206-3, CAL 426); pap. 2.95 (ISBN 0-520-03935-1). U of Cal Pr.
Krans, Horatio S. Irish Life in Irish Fiction. LC 3-22087. Repr. of 1903 ed. 22.50 (ISBN 0-404-03778-X). AMS Pr.
Lady Gregory. Poets & Dreamers: Studies & Translations from the Irish. LC 73-17133. (Studies in Irish Literature, No. 16). 1974. lib. bdg. 51.95 (ISBN 0-8383-1725-1). Haskell.
Law, Hugh A. Anglo-Irish Literature. LC 74-8122. 1972. Repr. of 1926 ed. lib. bdg. 20.00 (ISBN 0-8414-5725-5). Folcroft.
Luke, Peter, ed. Enter Certain Players: Edwards, Mac Liammoir & the Gate 1928-1978. (Illus.). 1978. text ed. 26.00x (ISBN 0-85105-346-7, Dolmen Pr); pap. text ed. 9.25x (ISBN 0-85105-345-9). Humanities.
McCarthy, Justin, et al, eds. Irish Literature, 10 Vols in 5. (Library of Literature, Drama & Criticism). 1970. Repr. of 1904 ed. Set. 269.50 (ISBN 0-384-36570-1). Johnson Repr.
MacDonagh, Thomas. Literature in Ireland. 1973. Repr. of 1916 ed. 25.00 (ISBN 0-8274-1347-5). R West.
Magee, William K. Irish Literary Portraits. facs. ed. LC 67-23243. (Essay Index Reprint Ser). 1935. 12.25 (ISBN 0-8369-0665-9). Arno.
Mercier, Vivian. Irish Comic Tradition. 1969. pap. 4.95 (ISBN 0-19-500297-0, 284, GB). Oxford U Pr.
Moore, George. Hail & Farewell. Cave, Richard, ed. (Illus.). 774p. 1980. text ed. 35.00x (ISBN 0-7705-1467-7). Humanities.
Nennius Abbot Of Bangor. The Irish Nennius from Leabhar Na H-Uidre & Homilies & Legends from Leabhar Breac. Hogan, Edmund, ed. LC 78-72685. (Royal Irish Academy. Todd Lecture Ser.: Vol. 6). Repr. of 1895 ed. 16.50 (ISBN 0-404-60566-4). AMS Pr.
Nutt, Alfred T. Critical Study of Gaelic Literature Indispensable for the History of the Gaelic Race. LC 78-102861. (Research & Source Works Ser.: No. 204). 1971. Repr. of 1904 ed. 11.00 (ISBN 0-8337-2593-9). B Franklin.
O'Curry, Eugene. Lectures in the Manuscript Materials of Ancient Irish History, 2 vols in 1. Repr. of 1861 ed. 46.50 (ISBN 0-685-06758-0). B Franklin.
Rafroidi, Patrick & Brown, Terence. The Irish Short Story. 1979. text ed. 29.25x (ISBN 0-391-01703-9). Humanities.
Ronsley, Joseph, ed. Myth & Reality in Irish Literature. 329p. 1977. text ed. 14.50 (ISBN 0-88920-039-4, Pub. by Laurier U Pr Canada). Humanities.
Saul, George B. Traditional Irish Literature: A Brief Introduction. rev. ed. LC 71-120997. 115p. 1970. 10.00 (ISBN 0-8387-7686-8). Bucknell U Pr.
Schleifer, Ronald, ed. The Genres of the Irish Literary Revival. 190p. 1980. 16.95 (ISBN 0-937664-53-7). Pilgrim Bks OK.
Shloss, Carol. Flannery O'Connor's Dark Comedies: The Limits of Inference. Rubin, Louis D., Jr., ed. LC 80-10609. (Southern Literary Studies). 184p. 1980. 14.95x (ISBN 0-8071-0674-7). La State U Pr.
Smith, B. L. O'Casey's Satiric Vision. LC 78-10583. 1979. 12.50x (ISBN 0-87338-218-8). Kent St U Pr.
Stanford, William B. Ireland & the Classical Tradition. 261p. 1976. 17.50x (ISBN 0-87471-924-0). Rowman.
Thornton, Weldon. J. M. Synge & the Western Mind. (Irish Literary Studies: No. 4). 1979. text ed. 20.75x (ISBN 0-901072-89-3). Humanities.
Yeats, W. B. The Death of Cuchulain: Manuscript Materials, Including the Author's Final Text. Marcus, Phillip L., ed. LC 80-25851. (The Cornell Yeats Ser.). (Illus.). 208p. 1981. 35.00x (ISBN 0-8014-1379-6). Cornell U Pr.
Yeats, W. B. & Kinsella, Thomas. Davis, Mangan, Ferguson. (Anglo-Irish Studies 2, Tower Ser). 1971. 7.95 (ISBN 0-85105-166-9). Dufour.
Yeats, William B. Discoveries. 56p. 1971. Repr. of 1907 ed. 13.00x (ISBN 0-7165-1337-4, Pub. by Cuala Press Ireland). Biblio Dist.
--Essays, Nineteen Thirty-One to Nineteen Thirty-Six. 114p. 1971. Repr. of 1937 ed. 13.00x (ISBN 0-7165-1383-8, Pub. by Cuala Press Ireland). Biblio Dist.
Yeats, William B. & Kinsella, T. Davis, Mangan, Ferguson: Tradition & the Irish Writer. (Tower Ser. of Anglo Irish Studies). 1970. pap. text ed. 1.75 (ISBN 0-85105-166-9, Dolmen Pr). Humanities.

IRISH LITERATURE-TO 1100

Meyer, Kuno. Miscellanea Hibernica. pap. 5.50 (ISBN 0-384-38450-1). Johnson Repr.
Saul, George B. Traditional Irish Literature: A Brief Introduction. rev. ed. LC 71-120997. 115p. 1970. 10.00 (ISBN 0-8387-7686-8). Bucknell U Pr.
Windisch, Ernest W. & Stokes, Whitley, eds. Irische Texte: Mit Uebersetzung und Woerterbuch, 5 vols. Incl. Vol. 1. 70.00 (ISBN 0-404-18231-3); Vol. 2. The Destruction of Troy. 20.00 (ISBN 0-404-18232-1); Vol. 3. Mittelirische Verslehren. 48.00 (ISBN 0-404-18233-X); Vol. 4. Acallamh na Senorach; Bd. with In Catch Cathardam, 2 pts. in 1. 95.00 (ISBN 0-404-18234-8); Vol. 5. Die Altirische Heldensage Tain bo Cualnge. 117.00 (ISBN 0-404-18235-6). LC 78-72655. (Celtic Language & Literature: Goidelic & Brythonic). Repr. of 1909 ed. Set. 350.00 (ISBN 0-404-18230-5). AMS Pr.

IRISH LITERATURE (ENGLISH)

Browne, Ray B., et al, eds. Celtic Cross. facs. ed. LC 78-121453. (Essay Index Reprint Ser). 1964. 19.00 (ISBN 0-8369-1744-8). Arno.
Hogan, Robert, ed. Dictionary of Irish Literature. LC 78-20021. 1979. lib. bdg. 39.95 (ISBN 0-313-20718-6, HDI/). Greenwood.
Lyons, F. S. & Hawkins, R. A., eds. Ireland Under the Union: Varieties of Tension. (Illus.). 348p. 1980. 42.00x (ISBN 0-19-822469-9). Oxford U Pr.
O'Buachalla, Seamas, ed. The Literary Writings of Patrick Pearse. 254p. 1979. pap. 6.25 (ISBN 0-85342-599-X). Irish Bk Ctr.

IRISH LITERATURE (ENGLISH)-BIBLIOGRAPHY

Finneran, Richard J., ed. Anglo-Irish Literature: A Review of Research. LC 74-31959. (Reviews of Research). 1976. 24.00x (ISBN 0-87352-252-4); pap. 12.00x (ISBN 0-87352-253-2). Modern Lang.
Hogan, Robert, ed. Dictionary of Irish Literature. LC 78-20021. 1979. lib. bdg. 39.95 (ISBN 0-313-20718-6, HDI/). Greenwood.
Maguire, William J. Irish Literary Figures (Swift, St Sterne, Goldsmith, Wilde, Yeats, Joyce) 1973. lib. bdg. 22.50 (ISBN 0-685-38007-6). Folcroft.

IRISH LITERATURE (ENGLISH)-HISTORY AND CRITICISM

Beckett, J. C. The Anglo-Irish Tradition. LC 76-528. 1977. 16.50x (ISBN 0-8014-1056-8). Cornell U Pr.
Bolt, Sydney. Preface to James Joyce. (Preface Bks.). (Illus.). 1981. text ed. 14.95x (ISBN 0-582-35194-4); pap. text ed. 8.95x (ISBN 0-582-35195-2). Longman.
De Almeida, Hermione. Byron & Joyce Through Homer: Don Juan & Ulysses. 256p. 1981. 20.00x (ISBN 0-231-05092-5). Columbia U Pr.
Finneran, Richard J., ed. Anglo-Irish Literature: A Review of Research. LC 74-31959. (Reviews of Research). 1976. 24.00x (ISBN 0-87352-252-4); pap. 12.00x (ISBN 0-87352-253-2). Modern Lang.
Harmon, Maurice, ed. Image & Illusion: Anglo-Irish Literature & Its Contexts. 174p. 1979. text ed. 26.00x (ISBN 0-905473-42-6). Humanities.
Kearney, Colbert. The Writings of Brendan Behan. LC 77-24780. 1977. 16.95x (ISBN 0-312-89442-2). St Martin.
McCarthy, Patrick A. The Riddles of Finnegans Wake. LC 79-24075. 184p. 1980. 16.50 (ISBN 0-8386-3005-7). Fairleigh Dickinson.
MacDonagh, Thomas. Literature in Ireland. LC 79-102612. (Irish Culture & History Ser). 1970. Repr. of 1916 ed. 13.00 (ISBN 0-8046-0789-3). Kennikat.
Metress, Seamus P. The Irish-American Experience: A Guide to the Literature. LC 80-69050. 226p. (Orig.). 1981. lib. bdg. 19.75 (ISBN 0-8191-1694-7); pap. text ed. 10.25 (ISBN 0-8191-1695-5). U Pr of Amer.
Norris, Margot. The Decentered Universe of Finnegan's Wake: A Structuralist Analysis. LC 76-25507. 1978. pap. text ed. 3.95 (ISBN 0-8018-2148-7). Johns Hopkins.

O'Rourke, Brian. The Conscience of the Race: Sex & Religion in Irish & French Novels 1941-1973. 72p. 1980. 10.00x (ISBN 0-906127-22-X, Pub. by Irish Academic Pr Ireland). Biblio Dist.

Seymour, John. Anglo-Irish Literature from Twelve Hundred to Fifteen Eighty-Two. LC 72-191857. 1929. lib. bdg. 8.00 (ISBN 0-8414-8117-2). Folcroft.

Taylor, Estella R. Modern Irish Writers: Cross Currents of Criticism. LC 69-14108. 1969. Repr. of 1954 ed. lib. bdg. 15.00x (ISBN 0-8371-0678-8, TAIW). Greenwood.

IRISH MISSIONARIES

see Missionaries, Irish

IRISH MUSIC

see Music, Irish

IRISH MYTHOLOGY

see Mythology, Irish

IRISH NATIONAL CHARACTERISTICS

see National Characteristics, Irish

IRISH NEWSPAPERS

Joyce, William L. Editors & Ethnicity: A History of the Irish-American Press, 1848-1883. LC 76-6349. (Irish Americans Ser). 1976. 15.00 (ISBN 0-405-09343-8). Arno.

Munter, R. L. History of the Irish Newspaper, Sixteen Eighty-Five - Seventeen Sixty. 49.50 (ISBN 0-521-05786-8). Cambridge U Pr.

IRISH PERIODICALS

Madden, Richard R. History of Irish Periodical Literature from the End of the Seventeenth to the Middle of the Nineteenth Century, 2 Vols. Repr. of 1867 ed. 46.00 (ISBN 0-384-34980-3). Johnson Repr.

IRISH POETRY (COLLECTIONS)

Comprises poetry in Irish language and poetry written by Irish authors in English or other languages.

Bradley, Anthony, ed. Contemporary Irish Poetry: An Anthology. LC 76-50244. 1980. 17.95 (ISBN 0-520-03389-2). U of Cal Pr.

Brooke, Charlotte, ed. Reliques of Irish Poetry, 1789. Bd. with A Memoir of Miss Brooke, 1816. Seymour, A. C. LC 76-133327. 544p. 1970. 54.00x (ISBN 0-8201-1082-5). Schol Facsimiles.

Brooke, Stopford & Rolleston, T. W., eds. A Treasury of Irish Poetry. LC 78-74812. (Granger Poetry Library). 1979. Repr. of 1900 ed. 34.50x (ISBN 0-89609-130-9). Granger Bk.

Colum, Padraic. Irish Elegies. 4th ed. 1976. text ed. 11.75x (ISBN 0-85105-315-7, Dolmen Pr). Humanities.

Cooke, John. The Dublin Book of Irish Verse 1728-1909. 1909. lib. bdg. 20.00 (ISBN 0-8414-2386-5). Folcroft.

Garrity, Devin A., ed. New Irish Poets, Anthology. (Illus.). 6.50 (ISBN 0-8159-6302-5). Devin.

Gregory, Padric. Modern Anglo-Irish Verse. Repr. of 1914 ed. 20.00 (ISBN 0-686-18770-9). Scholars Ref Lib.

--Modern Anglo-Irish Verse. 1977. Repr. of 1914 ed. 20.00 (ISBN 0-89984-189-9). Century Bookbindery.

Gregory, Padric, ed. Modern Anglo-Irish Verse: An Anthology Selected from the Work of Living Irish Poets. LC 75-28816. Repr. of 1914 ed. 32.50 (ISBN 0-404-13809-8). AMS Pr.

Keefe, Joan, ed. & tr. Irish Poems, from Cromwell to the Famine: A Miscellany. LC 76-755. 100p. 1976. 12.00 (ISBN 0-8387-1887-6). Bucknell U Pr.

Mangan, James C., tr. Poets & Poetry of Munster: A Selection of Irish Songs by the Poets of the Last Century. 5th ed. LC 75-28824. Repr. of 1909 ed. 34.50 (ISBN 0-404-13816-0). AMS Pr.

Meyer, Kuno, tr. Selections from Ancient Irish Poetry. LC 75-28829. Repr. of 1911 ed. 10.50 (ISBN 0-404-13819-5). AMS Pr.

Montague, John, ed. Book of Irish Verse. 400p. 1977. 14.95 (ISBN 0-02-585630-8, 58563). Macmillan.

Moult, Thomas, ed. Best Poems of 1924. LC 79-50845. (Granger Poetry Library). (Illus.). 1979. Repr. of 1925 ed. 15.00x (ISBN 0-89609-163-5). Granger Bk.

--Best Poems of 1925. LC 79-51986. (Granger Poetry Library). (Illus.). 1981. Repr. of 1926 ed. 15.00x (ISBN 0-89609-180-5). Granger Bk.

--Best Poems of 1926. LC 79-50846. (Granger Poetry Library). (Illus.). 1979. Repr. of 1927 ed. 15.00x (ISBN 0-89609-164-3). Granger Bk.

--Best Poems of 1927. LC 79-51986. (Granger Poetry Library). 1981. Repr. of 1928 ed. 15.00x (ISBN 0-89609-185-6). Granger Bk.

--Best Poems of 1928. LC 79-51986. (Granger Poetry Library). (Illus.). 1981. Repr. of 1929 ed. 15.00x (ISBN 0-89609-192-9). Granger Bk.

--Best Poems of 1929. LC 79-51986. (Granger Poetry Library). (Illus.). 1981. Repr. of 1929 ed. 15.00x (ISBN 0-89609-194-5). Granger Bk.

--Best Poems of 1933. LC 79-51986. (Granger Poetry Library). (Illus.). 1981. Repr. of 1933 ed. 15.00x (ISBN 0-89609-187-2). Granger Bk.

--Best Poems of 1934. LC 79-51986. (Granger Poetry Library). (Illus.). 1981. Repr. of 1934 ed. 15.00x (ISBN 0-89609-188-0). Granger Bk.

--Best Poems of 1935. LC 79-51986. (Granger Poetry Library). (Illus.). 1981. Repr. of 1935 ed. 15.00x (ISBN 0-89609-189-9). Granger Bk.

--Best Poems of 1936. LC 79-51986. (Granger Poetry Library). (Illus.). 1981. Repr. of 1936 ed. 15.00x (ISBN 0-89609-190-2). Granger Bk.

--Best Poems of 1937. LC 79-51986. (Granger Poetry Library). (Illus.). 1981. Repr. of 1937 ed. 15.00x (ISBN 0-89609-191-0). Granger Bk.

Murphy, Gerard, ed. Early Irish Lyrics: Eighth to Twelfth Century. 1956. 24.00x (ISBN 0-19-815207-8). Oxford U Pr.

O'Daly, John, ed. Laoithe Fiannuigheachta, 2 vols. 592p. 1859-61. Repr. 16.50 (ISBN 0-384-42965-3). Johnson Repr.

O'Rahilly, Thomas F., compiled by. Danta Gradha: An Anthology of Irish Love Poetry (A.D. 1350-1750) 2nd rev. ed. LC 75-28836. Repr. of 1926 ed. 11.50 (ISBN 0-404-13825-X). AMS Pr.

O Tuama, Sean. An Duanaire - an Irish Anthology: Poems of the Dispossessed, 1600-1900. Kinsella, Thomas, tr. LC 81-51145. (Illus.). 380p. (Orig., Gaelic & Eng.). 1981. 25.00x (ISBN 0-8122-7813-5); pap. 12.95 (ISBN 0-686-76604-0). U of Pa Pr.

O'Tuama, Sean & Kinsella, Thomas. An Dunaire, Sixteen Hundred to Nineteen Hundred: Poems of the Dispossessed. (Illus.). 432p. 1980. text ed. 31.25x (ISBN 0-85105-363-7, Dolmen Pr); pap. text ed. 11.75x (ISBN 0-85105-364-5, Dolmen Pr). Humanities.

Paul, W. J. Modern Irish Poetry, 2 vols. 1977. Repr. of 1894 ed. 50.00 (ISBN 0-89984-087-6). Century Bookbindery.

--Modern Irish Poets, 2 vols. 1979. Repr. of 1894 ed. Set. lib. bdg. 100.00 (ISBN 0-8495-4336-3). Arden Lib.

Robinson, Lennox, compiled by. A Little Anthology of Modern Irish Verse. 52p. 1971. Repr. of 1928 ed. 10.00x (ISBN 0-7165-1368-4, Pub. by Cuala Press Ireland). Biblio Dist.

Ryan, Desmond, ed. The Nineteen Sixteen Poets. LC 79-18768. 224p. 1980. Repr. of 1963 ed. lib. bdg. 17.50x (ISBN 0-313-22100-6, RYNI). Greenwood.

Wolfe, Humbert. Poems from the Irish. LC 74-7474. lib. bdg. 8.50 (ISBN 0-8414-9515-7). Folcroft.

IRISH POETRY–BIBLIOGRAPHY

O'Donoghue, David J. Poets of Ireland. LC 68-30622. 1968. Repr. of 1912 ed. 32.00 (ISBN 0-8103-3152-7). Gale.

--Poets of Ireland: A Biographical & Bibliographical Dictionary of Irish Writers of English Verse. (Library of Literature, Drama & Criticism). 1970. Repr. of 1912 ed. 34.50 (ISBN 0-384-42975-0). Johnson Repr.

IRISH POETRY–HISTORY AND CRITICISM

Clarke, Austin. Poetry in Modern Ireland. LC 74-12114. 1973. lib. bdg. 8.50 (ISBN 0-8414-3363-1). Folcroft.

--Poetry in Modern Ireland. 1978. Repr. of 1951 ed. lib. bdg. 10.00 (ISBN 0-8495-0904-1). Arden Lib.

De Vere, Aubrey. Irish Odes & Other Poems. 59.95 (ISBN 0-8490-0426-8). Gordon Pr.

Dillon, Myles. Early Irish Literature. LC 48-6027. 1948. 13.00x (ISBN 0-226-14918-8). U of Chicago Pr.

Dunn, Douglas, ed. Two Decades of Irish Writing: A Critical Survey. (Essays, Prose, & Scottish Literature). 1979. 10.95 (ISBN 0-85635-070-2, Pub. by Carcanet New Pr England). Persea Bks.

Graves, Alfred P. Irish Literary & Musical Studies. facs. ed. LC 67-23224. (Essay Index Reprint Ser). 1914. 16.00 (ISBN 0-8369-0494-X). Arno.

Harmon, Maurice, ed. Irish Poetry After Yeats: Seven Poets. 231p. 1981. 13.95 (ISBN 0-316-34688-8); pap. 8.95 (ISBN 0-316-34688-8). Little.

--Richard Murphy: Poet of Two Traditions. (Interdisciplinary Studies). (Illus.). 1978. text ed. 13.75x (ISBN 0-905473-17-5). Humanities.

Kershowski, Frank. Outsiders: Poets of Contemporary Ireland. LC 74-21131. (History & Culture Monograph Ser.: No. 12). 1975. pap. 5.00 (ISBN 0-912646-03-9). Tex Christian.

Meyer, Kuno. Ueber die Aelteste Irische Dichtung. LC 78-72641. (Celtic Language & Literature: Goidelic & Brythonic). Repr. of 1914 ed. 57.50 (ISBN 0-404-17574-0). AMS Pr.

Quiggin, E. C. Prolegomena to the Study of the Later Irish Bards, 1200-1500. (Studies in Irish Literature, No. 16). 1970. pap. 12.95 (ISBN 0-8383-0064-2). Haskell.

Robinson, Lennox. A Little Anthology of Modern Irish Verse. LC 75-12772. 1972. Repr. of 1928 ed. lib. bdg. 20.00 (ISBN 0-8414-7381-1). Folcroft.

Welch, Robert. Irish Poetry from Moore to Yeats. 248p. 1980. text ed. 23.25x (ISBN 0-901072-93-1). Humanities.

--Irish Poetry from Moore to Yeats. LC 79-54105. (Irish Literary Studies: No. 5). 1980. text ed. 23.50x (ISBN 0-389-20000-X). B&N.

Yeats, William B. & Johnson, Lionel. Poetry & Ireland. 64p. 1971. Repr. of 1908 ed. 13.00x (ISBN 0-7165-1338-2, Pub. by Cuala Press Ireland). Biblio Dist.

Young, Dudley. Out of Ireland: A Reading of Yeat's Poetry. (Essays, Prose, & Scottish Literature). 1979. 10.95 (ISBN 0-85635-119-9, Pub. by Carcanet New Pr England). Persea Bks.

IRISH POETRY–TRANSLATIONS INTO ENGLISH

Carney, James. Medieval Irish Lyrics. 1967. 16.50x (ISBN 0-520-00210-5). U of Cal Pr.

Gwynn, Edward, ed. Poems from the Dindshenchas. LC 78-72686. (Royal Irish Academy. Todd Lecture Ser.: Vol. 7). Repr. of 1900 ed. 16.50 (ISBN 0-404-60567-2). AMS Pr.

Hardiman, J. Irish Minstrelsy: Or Bordic Remains of Ireland, 2 vols. 908p. 1971. Repr. of 1831 ed. 30.00x (ISBN 0-7165-0333-6, Pub. by Irish Academic Pr Ireland). Biblio Dist.

Hyde, Douglas. Poems from the Irish. Gibbon, Monk, ed. 1963. 4.25 (ISBN 0-685-09194-5). Dufour.

Lucy, Sean, ed. Love Poems of the Irish. 182p. 1967. pap. 5.95 (ISBN 0-85342-103-X). Irish Bk Ctr.

MacCumaill, Finn. Fianaigecht. LC 78-72614. (Royal Irish Academy. Todd Lecture Ser.: Vol. 16). Repr. of 1910 ed. 17.00 (ISBN 0-404-60576-1). AMS Pr.

MacDonagh, Thomas. Literature in Ireland. LC 79-102612. (Irish Culture & History Ser). 1970. Repr. of 1916 ed. 13.00 (ISBN 0-8046-0789-3). Kennikat.

Merriman, Brian. The Midnight Court & the Adventures of a Luckless Fellow. 79p. 1980. Repr. of 1926 ed. lib. bdg. 10.00 (ISBN 0-8495-5408-X). Arden Lib.

Murphy, Gerard, ed. Early Irish Lyrics: Eighth to Twelfth Century. 1956. 24.00x (ISBN 0-19-815207-8). Oxford U Pr.

O'Connell, Richard, tr. More Irish Poems. 1976. pap. 4.00 (ISBN 0-685-63923-1). Atlantis Edns.

O'Connor, Frank, ed. Kings, Lords & Commons. facs. ed. LC 72-75716. (Granger Index Reprint Ser). 1959. 15.00 (ISBN 0-8369-6034-3). Arno.

O'Faolain, Sean, compiled by. Silver Branch. facsimile ed. LC 68-58822. (Granger Index Reprint Ser). 1938. 12.00 (ISBN 0-8369-6035-1). Arno.

IRISH POETRY (ENGLISH) (COLLECTIONS)

Alspach, Russell K. Irish Poetry, from the English Invasion to 1798. 2nd rev. ed. LC 75-28807. Repr. of 1960 ed. 16.50 (ISBN 0-404-13800-4). AMS Pr.

Gamble, W. Two Irish Poets. LC 73-12449. (Goldsmith & Moore). 1948. lib. bdg. 10.00 (ISBN 0-8414-4400-5). Folcroft.

Gregory, Padric, ed. Modern Anglo-Irish Verse: An Anthology Selected from the Work of Living Irish Poets. LC 75-28816. Repr. of 1914 ed. 32.50 (ISBN 0-404-13809-8). AMS Pr.

Hoagland, Kathleen, ed. One Thousand Years of Irish Poetry. 832p. 1981. 12.95 (ISBN 0-517-34295-2). Devin.

Macdonagh, Donagh & Robinson, Lennox, eds. Oxford Book of Irish Verse Seventeenth to Twentieth Century. 1958. 24.95 (ISBN 0-19-812115-6). Oxford U Pr.

IRISH POETRY (ENGLISH)–HISTORY AND CRITICISM

Clarke, Austin. Poetry in Modern Ireland. 2nd ed. 77p. pap. 1.25 (ISBN 0-85342-040-8). Irish Bk Ctr.

Harmon, Maurice, ed. Irish Poetry After Yeats: Seven Poets. 1981. 13.95 (ISBN 0-316-34686-1); pap. 8.95 (ISBN 0-316-34688-8). Little.

Lucy, Sean, ed. Irish Poets in English. 224p. 1973. pap. 5.25 (ISBN 0-85342-301-6). Irish Bk Ctr.

IRISH QUESTION

see also Home Rule (Ireland); Land Tenure–Ireland

Brynn, Edward. Crown & Castle: British Rule in Ireland 1800-1830. (Illus.). 1978. text ed. 32.00x (ISBN 0-7705-1496-0). Humanities.

Clarkson, J. Dunsmore. Labour & Nationalism in Ireland. LC 78-12024. (Columbia University Studies in the Social Sciences: No. 266). Repr. of 1925 ed. 31.50 (ISBN 0-404-51266-6). AMS Pr.

Eversley, G. Shaw-Lefevre. Peel & O'connell. LC 71-102610. (Irish Culture & History Ser). 1970. Repr. of 1887 ed. 15.50 (ISBN 0-8046-0787-7). Kennikat.

Fields, Rona M. Northern Ireland: Society Under Siege. LC 80-80316. 267p. 1981. pap. 5.95 (ISBN 0-87855-806-3). Transaction Bks.

Gallagher, Frank. The Indivisible Island: The Story of the Partition of Ireland. LC 74-5772. (Illus.). 316p. 1974. Repr. of 1957 ed. lib. bdg. 18.00x (ISBN 0-8371-7515-1, GAII). Greenwood.

Gwynn, Stephen. Henry Grattan & His Times. facsimile ed. LC 78-175699. (Select Bibliographies Reprint Ser). Repr. of 1939 ed. 24.00 (ISBN 0-8369-6614-7). Arno.

Gwynn, Stephen L. Henry Grattan & His Times. LC 76-114534. (Illus.). 1971. Repr. of 1939 ed. lib. bdg. 17.25x (ISBN 0-8371-4828-6, GWHG). Greenwood.

Harkness, D. W. The Restless Dominion. LC 73-114761. 1970. 18.50x (ISBN 0-8147-0463-8). NYU Pr.

Heyck, Thomas W. The Dimensions of British Radicalism: The Case of Ireland, 1874-95. LC 74-11247. 300p. 1974. 19.95 (ISBN 0-252-00423-X). U of Ill Pr.

Jones, Harry S. Spenser's Defense of Lord Grey. 1919. pap. 5.50 (ISBN 0-384-27770-5). Johnson Repr.

Larkin, Emmet. The Roman Catholic Church in Ireland & the Fall of Parnell, 1888-1891. LC 78-22056. 1979. 19.00x (ISBN 0-8078-1352-4). U of NC Pr.

McCaffrey, Lawrence J. Irish Federalism in the 1870's: A Study in Conservative Nationalism. LC 62-21773. (Transactions Ser.: Vol. 52, Pt. 6). 1962. pap. 1.00 (ISBN 0-87169-526-X). Am Philos.

--The Irish Question, Eighteen Hundred to Nineteen Twenty-Two. LC 68-12962. 212p. 1968. 14.00 (ISBN 0-8131-1152-8); pap. 4.00x (ISBN 0-8131-0117-4). U Pr of Ky.

Marx, Karl & Engels, Frederick. Ireland & the Irish Question. Dixon, Richard, ed. Ryazanskaya, S., et al, trs. from Fr., Ger. & It. LC 73-188754. 518p. 1972. pap. 3.25 (ISBN 0-7178-0342-2). Intl Pub Co.

Molony, Chartres J. Riddle of the Irish. LC 74-102619. (Irish Culture & History Ser). 1970. Repr. of 1927 ed. 12.00 (ISBN 0-8046-0796-6). Kennikat.

O'Brien, Conor C. Parnell & His Party: 1880-90. 1957. 36.00x (ISBN 0-19-821237-2). Oxford U Pr.

O'Farrell, Patrick. Ireland's English Question: Anglo-Irish Relations, 1534-1970. LC 75-159481. (Fabric of British History Ser). 1972. 11.50x (ISBN 0-8052-3424-1); pap. 4.95 (ISBN 0-8052-0348-6). Schocken.

Plunkett, Horace. Ireland in the New Century. LC 77-102625. (Irish Culture & History Ser). 1970. Repr. of 1904 ed. 14.50 (ISBN 0-8046-0801-6). Kennikat.

Schools Councils History 13-16 Project. The Irish Question. (Modern World Problems Ser.). (Illus.). 1979. lib. bdg. 9.95 (ISBN 0-912616-72-5); pap. text ed. 4.45 (ISBN 0-912616-71-7). Greenhaven.

Tansill, Charles C. America & the Fight for Irish Freedom. 1957. 12.95 (ISBN 0-8159-5002-0). Devin.

IRISH REPUBLICAN ARMY

Bell, J. Bowyer. The Secret Army: The Ira, 1916-1979. rev. ed. (Illus.). 508p. 1980. text ed. 30.00x (ISBN 0-262-02145-5). MIT Pr.

Burton, Frank. The Politics of Legitimacy: Struggles in a Belfast Community. (International Library of Sociology). 1978. 21.00 (ISBN 0-7100-8966-X). Routledge & Kegan.

Carter, Carolle J. The Shamrock & the Swastika: German Espionage in Ireland in World War II. LC 76-14103. (Illus.). 1977. 12.95 (ISBN 0-87015-221-1). Pacific Bks.

General Headquarters; Ireland. Handbook for Volunteers of the Irish Republican Army. Repr. of 1956 ed. pap. 3.00 (ISBN 0-87364-074-8). Paladin Ent.

IRISH SETTERS

see Dogs–Breeds–Irish Setters

IRISH SONGS

see Songs, Irish

IRISH TALES

see Tales, Irish

IRISH TERRIER

see Dogs–Breeds–Irish Terrier

IRISH WIT AND HUMOR

Dunne, Finley P. Mr. Dooley's Philosophy. (Illus.). 1978. Repr. of 1900 ed. lib. bdg. 20.00 (ISBN 0-8495-1027-9). Arden Lib.

Greeley, Andrew M. That Most Distressful Nation: The Taming of the American Irish. LC 74-182501. 288p. 1973. 8.95 (ISBN 0-8129-0246-7); pap. 2.95 (ISBN 0-8129-6219-2). Times Bks.

Gwynn, Stephen L. Irish Books & Irish People. facs. ed, LC 74-86756. (Essay Index Reprint Ser.). 1920. 12.00 (ISBN 0-8369-1136-9). Arno.

Harvey, William. Irish Life & Humour in Anecdote & Story. 1975. Repr. of 1904 ed. 35.00 (ISBN 0-8274-4070-7). R West.

Irish Wit & Humor: Anecdote Biography of Swift, Curran, O'Leary & O'Connell. Repr. of 1878 ed. 30.00 (ISBN 0-8274-4162-2). R West.

Irish Wit & Wisdom. 1976. 2.95 (ISBN 0-442-82567-6). Peter Pauper.
Keene, Charles, et al. Mr. Punch's Irish Humour in Picture & Story. 25.00 (ISBN 0-8274-4164-9). R West.
McCann, Sean. The Wit of the Irish. LC 77-129885. 1970. 2.95 (ISBN 0-87695-115-9). Sherbourne.
O'Donoghue, D. J., ed. The Humour of Ireland. 20.00 (ISBN 0-8274-4172-X). R West.
O'Donoghue, David J. The Humour of Ireland, Selected. LC 75-28833. (Illus.). Repr. of 1894 ed. 38.50 (ISBN 0-404-13823-3). AMS Pr.

IRISH WIT AND HUMOR–HISTORY AND CRITICISM

Mercier, Vivian. Irish Comic Tradition. 1969. pap. 4.95 (ISBN 0-19-500297-0, 284, GB). Oxford U Pr.

IRISH WOLF HOUND

see Dogs–Breeds–Irish Wolf Hounds

IRON

see also Building, Iron and Steel; Cast Iron; Iron Ores; Steel; Taconite; Wrought-Iron

American Welding Society. Iron & Steel Gas-Welding Rods: A5.2-69. 3.50 (ISBN 0-685-65964-X). Am Welding.
Berglund, Abraham & Wright, Phillip G. Tariff on Iron & Steel. (Brookings Institution Reprint Ser). Repr. of 1929 ed. lib. bdg. 24.50x (ISBN 0-697-00151-2). Irvington.
Cesaire, Aime. Ferrements. pap. 8.95 (ISBN 0-685-33975-0). French & Eur.
CNRS. New Physical, Mechanical & Chemical Properties of Very High Purity Iron. 93.00 (ISBN 0-677-30730-6). Gordon.
Cordero, Raymond & Serjeantson, Richard, eds. Iron & Steel Works of the World 1978. 7th ed. LC 75-314459. 1978. 100.00x (ISBN 0-900542-21-7). Intl Pubns Serv.
Deutscher Normenausschuss-DNA, ed. Steel & Iron: Standards on Quality. 2nd ed. (DIN Pocketbook Ser.: No. 4). 394p. 1973. pap. text ed. 67.50x (ISBN 3-410-10896-3). Intl Pubns Serv.
Din Steel & Iron: Standards on Quality. 104.00 (ISBN 0-686-28162-4, 10827-2/04). Heyden.
Din Steel & Iron: Standards on Weights & Measures. 108.00 (ISBN 0-01-112512-8). Heyden.
Herbert, Peter & Schiffer, Nancy. Antique Iron, American & European: 15th Century Through 1850. LC 79-88255. (Illus.). 1979. 35.00 (ISBN 0-916838-26-9). Schiffer.
Iron & Steel Committee,Tenth Session, Geneva, 1981. General Report, Report I. International Labour Office, ed. vi, 166p. (Orig.). 1981. pap. 11.40 (ISBN 92-2-102686-8). Intl Labour Office.
Lepp, Henry, ed. Geochemistry of Iron. LC 74-23287. (Benchmark Papers in Geology Ser). 439p. 1975. 54.50 (ISBN 0-12-786939-5). Acad Pr.
Lovenberg, Walter, ed. Iron-Sulfur Proteins, 3 vols. Incl. Biological Properties. Vol. 1, 1973. 60.50 (ISBN 0-12-456001-6); Molecular Properties. Vol. 2, 1974. 56.00 (ISBN 0-12-456002-4); Vol. 3. 1977. 63.00 (ISBN 0-12-456003-2). 1973. 147.00 set (ISBN 0-685-40605-9). Acad Pr.
Proceedings of the Third International Iron & Steel Congress. 1979. 40.00 (ISBN 0-87170-074-3). ASM.
Saville, J. P. Iron and Steel. (World Resources Ser.). 1977. 9.95x (ISBN 0-8448-1208-0). Crane-Russak Co.
Source Book on Ductile Iron. (TN 719.5.s68). 1977. 38.00 (ISBN 0-87170-035-2). ASM.
Subcommittee on Iron. Iron. (Medical & Biologic Effects of Environmental Pollutants Ser.). 248p. pap. text ed. 22.95 (ISBN 0-8391-0126-0). Univ Park.
Tatsch, J. H. Iron Deposits: Origin, Evolution, & Present Characteristics. LC 76-28095. (Illus.). 600p. Date not set. text ed. 180.00 (ISBN 0-912890-12-6). Tatsch.
Von Gustorf, Ernest A., ed. The Organic Chemistry of Iron, Vol. 2. (Organometallic Chemistry Ser.). Date not set. price not set (ISBN 0-12-417102-8). Acad Pr.
White, D. How to Find Out About Iron & Steel. 1970. 16.00 (ISBN 0-08-015790-4); pap. 9.50 (ISBN 0-08-015789-0). Pergamon.

IRON–DICTIONARIES

Freeman, H. Taschenwoerterbuch Eisen und Stahl. 600p. (Ger. & Eng., Dictionary of Iron and Steel). 1966. 12.50 (ISBN 3-19-006215-3, M-7634, Pub. by M. Hueber). French & Eur.
Freeman, Henry G. Pocket Dictionary Iron & Steel. LC 76-354255. 11.25x ea.; Vol. 1. German-English. (ISBN 3-19-006214-5); Vol. 2. English-German. (ISBN 3-19-006215-3). Intl Pubns Serv.

IRON–METALLURGY

see also Sintering

Davis, Edward W. Pioneering with Taconite. LC 64-64494. (Illus.). 246p. 1964. 5.00 (ISBN 0-87351-023-2). Minn Hist.
Kumar, Rajendra. Physical Metallurgy of Iron & Steel. 1968. 20.00x (ISBN 0-210-22658-7). Asia.
Rozdzienski, Walenty. Officina Ferraria: A Polish Poem of 1612 Describing the Noble Craft of Ironwork. Rozanski, Waclow & Smith, Cyril S., eds. Pluszczewski, Stefan, tr. LC 76-26592. (SHOT Monograph Ser.: No. 9). 1977. text ed. 14.00x (ISBN 0-262-18079-0). MIT Pr.
Strassburger, J. H., ed. Blast Furnace: Theory & Practice, 2 Vols. 1969. Set. 200.75x (ISBN 0-677-10420-0). Gordon.
Van Der Merwe, Nikolaas J. Carbon - Fourteen Dating of Iron. LC 75-76206. 1969. 8.50x (ISBN 0-226-84974-0). U of Chicago Pr.

IRON–STRUCTURAL

see also Building, Iron and Steel; Plates, Iron and Steel; Ships, Iron and Steel; Steel, Structural

IRON, WROUGHT

see Wrought-Iron

IRON AGE

see also Archaeology; Bronze Age

Boardman, John, et al, eds. The European Community in Later Prehistory: Studies in Honour of C. F. C. Hawkes. (Illus.). 294p. 1971. 22.50x (ISBN 0-87471-033-2). Rowman.
Cunliffe, Barry. Iron Age Communities in Britain. 2nd ed. (Archaeology of Britain Ser). (Illus.). 1978. 42.00 (ISBN 0-7100-8725-X). Routledge & Kegan.
Forde-Johnston, J. Hillforts of the Iron Age in England & Wales: A Survey of the Surface Evidence. (Illus.). 331p. 1976. 55.00x (ISBN 0-87471-802-3). Rowman.
Glob, P. V. The Bog People: Iron-Age Man Preserved. Bruce-Mitford, R. L., tr. LC 69-20391. (Illus.). 200p. 1969. 19.95 (ISBN 0-8014-0492-4). Cornell U Pr.
Harding, D., ed. Hillforts: Later Prehistoric Earthworks in Britain & Ireland. 1976. 94.50 (ISBN 0-12-324750-0). Acad Pr.
Harding, D. W. The Iron Age in Lowland Britain. 1974. 31.00x (ISBN 0-7100-7677-0). Routledge & Kegan.
Mallery, Arlington & Harrison, Mary R. The Rediscovery of Lost America: The Story of the Pre-Columbian Iron Age in America. 1979. pap. 8.95 (ISBN 0-525-47545-1). Dutton.
Oliver, R. A. & Fagan, B. M. Africa in the Iron Age. LC 74-25639. (Illus.). 300p. 1975. 29.95 (ISBN 0-521-20598-0); pap. 7.95x (ISBN 0-521-09900-5). Cambridge U Pr.
Randall-MacIver, David. The Iron Age in Italy. LC 74-9221. (Illus.). 243p. 1974. Repr. of 1927 ed. lib. bdg. 27.00x (ISBN 0-8371-7633-6, RAIA). Greenwood.
Reynolds, Peter J. Life in the Iron Age. LC 78-56800. (Cambridge Topic Bks). (Illus.). (gr. 5-10). 1978. PLB 5.95 (ISBN 0-8225-1214-9). Lerner Pubns.
Small, A. Monte Irsi, Southern Italy: The Canadian Excavations in the Iron Age & Roman Sites 1971-1972. 1977. 25.00x (ISBN 0-904531-66-X, Pub. by BAR). State Mutual Bk.
Smith, Christopher. Fisherwick: Reconstruction of an Iron Age Landscape. 1979. 24.00x (ISBN 0-86054-047-2, Pub. by BAR). State Mutual Bk.
Vasic, Rastko. The Chronology of the Early Iron Age in Serbia. 1977. 25.00x (ISBN 0-904531-86-4, Pub. by BAR). State Mutual Bk.
Waldbauum, Jane C. From Bronze to Iron: The Transition from the Bronze Age to the Iron Age in the Eastern Mediterranean. (Studies in Mediterranean Archaeology Ser.: No. LIV). (Illus.). 1978. pap. text ed. 42.00x (ISBN 91-85058-79-3). Humanities.
Wells, Peter S. Meckelenburg Collection, Pt. II: The Emergence of an Iron Age Economy. Condon, Lorna, ed. LC 81-81958. (American School of Prehistoric Research Bulletin Ser.: No. 33). (Illus.). 243p. (Orig.). 1981. pap. text ed. write for info. (ISBN 0-87365-536-2). Peabody Harvard.
Wertime, Theodore A. & Muhly, James D., eds. The Coming of the Age of Iron. LC 79-26420. (Illus.). 580p. 1980. 29.50x (ISBN 0-300-02425-8). Yale U Pr.

IRON ALLOYS

Touloukian, Y. S. & Ho, C. Y. Properties of Selected Ferrous Alloying Elements, Vol. III. (M-H-CINDAS Data Series on Material Properties). 288p. 1981. text ed. 33.50 (ISBN 0-07-065034-9). McGraw.

IRON AND STEEL BUILDING

see Building, Iron and Steel

IRON AND STEEL SHIPS

see Ships, Iron and Steel

IRON AND STEEL WORKERS

see also Strikes and Lockouts–Steel Industry

Abel, I. W. Collective Bargaining: Labor Relations in Steel, Then & Now. LC 76-14369. (Benjamin Fairless Memorial Lectures). 84p. 1976. 8.50x (ISBN 0-915604-05-1). Columbia U Pr.
Bodnar, John. Immigration & Industrialization: Ethnicity in an American Mill Town, 1870-1940. LC 77-74549. 1977. 11.95 (ISBN 0-8229-3348-9). U of Pittsburgh Pr.
Bowen, Peter. Social Control in Industrial Organisations. (Direct Edition Ser.). (Orig.). 1976. pap. 17.95x (ISBN 0-7100-8312-2). Routledge & Kegan.
Brody, David. Steelworkers in America: The Nonunion Era. 1970. pap. 5.95x (ISBN 0-06-131485-4, TB1485, Torch). Har-Row.
--Steelworkers in America: The Nonunion Era. LC 76-83855. (Illus.). 1970. Repr. of 1960 ed. 13.00 (ISBN 0-8462-1406-7). Russell.
Brooks, Robert R. As Steel Goes: Unionism in a Basic Industry. LC 40-27479. (History of American Economy Ser). 1970. Repr. of 1940 ed. 14.00 (ISBN 0-384-05935-X). Johnson Repr.
Cherry, Mike. On High Steel: The Education of an Ironworker. LC 74-77935. 320p. 1974. 7.95 (ISBN 0-8129-0470-2). Times Bks.
--Steel Beams & Iron Men. LC 80-66246. (Illus.). 96p. (gr. 5 up). 1980. 9.95 (ISBN 0-590-07591-8, Four Winds). Schol Bk Serv.
Davis, Rebecca H. & Olsen, Tillie. Life in the Iron Mills. 176p. 1972. pap. 4.50 (ISBN 0-912670-05-3). Feminist Pr.
Educational Research Council of America. Ironworker. Ferris, Theodore N. & Marchak, John P., eds. (Real People at Work: Series O). (Illus., Orig.). (gr. 5). 1976. pap. text ed. 2.25 (ISBN 0-89247-092-5). Changing Times.
--Steelworker. Ferris, Theodore N. & Marchak, John P., eds. (Real People at Work: Series M). (Illus., Orig.). (gr. 5). 1976. pap. text ed. 2.25 (ISBN 0-89247-108-5). Changing Times.
Fitch, John A. The Steel Worker. LC 70-89757. (American Labor, from Conspiracy to Collective Bargaining Ser., No. 1). 393p. 1969. Repr. of 1910 ed. 17.00 (ISBN 0-405-02121-6). Arno.
Livernash, Edward, et al. Collective Bargaining in the Basic Steel Industry. LC 76-9742. 1976. Repr. of 1961 ed. lib. bdg. 22.00x (ISBN 0-8371-8913-6, LICB). Greenwood.
Rudman, Jack. Gang Foreman (Structures - Group C) (Iron Works) (Career Examination Ser.: C-292). (Cloth bdg. avail. on request). pap. 8.00 (ISBN 0-8373-0292-7). Natl Learning.
Stieber, Jack. Steel Industry Wage Structure: A Study of the Joint Union-Management Job Evaluation Program in the Basic Steel Industry. LC 59-12977. (Wertheim Publications in Industrial Relations Ser). (Illus.). 1959. 15.00x (ISBN 0-686-76876-0). Harvard U Pr.
Walker, Charles R. Steel: Diary of a Furnace Worker. Stein, Leon, ed. LC 77-70544. (Work Ser.). 1977. Repr. of 1922 ed. lib. bdg. 12.00x (ISBN 0-405-10213-5). Arno.

IRON CURTAIN LANDS

see Communist Countries

IRON DEFICIENCY ANEMIA

Andrews, J. & Williams, E. Woodford, eds. Iron, Anaemia, & Old Age. (Gerontologia Clinica: Vol. 13, No. 1-2). 1971. pap. 13.25 (ISBN 3-8055-0889-1). S Karger.
Fairbanks, Virgil F., et al. Clinical Disorders of Iron Metabolism. 2nd ed. LC 75-139797. (Illus.). 486p. 1971. 68.50 (ISBN 0-8089-0677-1). Grune.
IAEA-USAID-WHO Joint Meeting. Geneva, 1974. Control of Nutritional Anaemia with Special Reference to Iron Deficiency: Report. (Technical Report Ser.: No. 580). (Also avail. in French & Spanish). 1975. pap. 2.80 (ISBN 92-4-120580-6). World Health.
Pollitt, Ernesto & Leibel, Rudolph, eds. Iron Deficiency, Brain Biochemistry & Behavior. 1982. text ed. price not set (ISBN 0-89004-690-5). Raven.
Vannotti, A., et al, eds. Iron Deficiency: Pathgenesis, Clinical Aspects, Therapy. 1971. 98.50 (ISBN 0-12-714750-0). Acad Pr.

IRON-FOUNDING

see also Cast Iron; Founding; Pattern-Making

IRON IN THE BODY

see also Iron Metabolism

Cook, James D. Iron. (Methods in Hematology Ser.: Vol. 1). (Illus.). 224p. 1980. 32.00 (ISBN 0-443-08118-2). Churchill.
Jacobs, A. & Worwood, M., eds. Iron in Biochemistry & Medicine. 1974. 103.50 (ISBN 0-12-379150-2). Acad Pr.
Schlessinger, David, ed. Microbiology 1974. LC 74-33538. (Annual Microbiology Ser.). 1975. 22.00 (ISBN 0-914826-02-6). Am Soc Microbio.
Zaino, Edward C. & Roberts, Richard H., eds. Chelation Therapy in Chronic Iron Overload. (Illus.). 1978. 23.50 (ISBN 0-8151-9853-1, Pub. by Symposia Special). Year Bk Med.

IRON INDUSTRY AND TRADE

see also Cast Iron; Enameled Ware; Hardware; Iron and Steel Workers; Steel Industry and Trade; Wrought-Iron

Andonyev, S. & Filipyev, O. Dust & Fume Generation in the Iron & Steel Industry. 223p. 1977. 5.40 (ISBN 0-8285-0677-9, Pub. by Mir Pubs Russia). Imported Pubns.
Bining, Arthur C. British Regulation of the Colonial Iron Industry. LC 68-55481. Repr. of 1933 ed. 12.50x (ISBN 0-678-00924-4). Kelley.
--Pennsylvania Iron Manufacture in the Eighteenth Century. LC 72-120547. Repr. of 1938 ed. lib. bdg. 12.50x (ISBN 0-678-00678-4). Kelley.
--Pennsylvania Iron Manufacture in the Eighteenth Century. rev. ed. (Illus.). 214p. 1973. 8.50 (ISBN 0-911124-72-1); pap. 4.50 (ISBN 0-911124-71-3). Pa Hist & Mus.
Bruce, Kathleen. Virginia Iron Manufacture in the Slave Era. LC 67-30856. Repr. of 1930 ed. 19.50x (ISBN 0-678-00414-5). Kelley.
Bugayev, K., et al. Iron & Steel Production. Savin, Ivan V., tr. from Rus. (Illus.). 246p. 1971. 12.00x (ISBN 0-8464-0533-4). Beekman Pubs.
Burrows, Fredrika A. Cannonball & Cranberries. LC 76-3143. (Illus.). 1976. 4.95 (ISBN 0-88492-011-9); pap. 2.50 (ISBN 0-88492-012-7). W S Sullwold.
Chapman, H. H., et al. The Iron & Steel Industries of the South. 1953. pap. 13.70x (ISBN 0-8173-5203-1). U of Ala Pr.
The Establishment of Iron & Steel Industries in Developing Countries & Its Impact on Training & the Development of Skills: Report II. ii, 48p. (Orig.). 1981. pap. write for info. (ISBN 92-2-102687-6). Intl Labour Office.
French, Benjamin F. History of the Rise & Progress of the Iron Trade of the United States, 1621-1857. LC 68-55712. Repr. of 1858 ed. 13.50x (ISBN 0-678-00963-5). Kelley.
Harrison, T. S. Handbook of Analytical Control of Iron & Steel Production. LC 78-41222. (Series in Analytical Chemistry). 1979. 114.95 (ISBN 0-470-26538-8). Halsted Pr.
Hartley, Edward N. Ironworks on the Saugus: The Lynn & Braintree Ventures of the Company of Undertakers of the Ironworks in New England. (Illus.). 1971. 14.95x (ISBN 0-8061-0366-3); pap. 6.95x (ISBN 0-8061-0957-2). U of Okla Pr.
Hogan, William T. An Economic History of the Iron & Steel Industry in the United States, 5 vols. LC 75-158965. 1971. Set. 100.00x (ISBN 0-669-59964-6); Vol. I. 20.00 (ISBN 0-669-81760-0); Vol. II. 22.50 (ISBN 0-669-81778-3); Vol. III. 30.00 (ISBN 0-669-81786-4); Vol. IV. 27.50 (ISBN 0-669-81794-5); Vol. V. 27.50 (ISBN 0-669-81802-X). Lexington Bks.
Ingham, John N. The Iron Barons: A Social Analysis of an American Urban Elite, 1874-1965. LC 77-84761. (Illus.). 1978. lib. bdg. 19.95x (ISBN 0-8371-9891-7, IIB/). Greenwood.
International Labour Office, Iron & Steel Committee, 10th Session, Geneva, 1981. The Improvement of Working Conditions & Working Environments in the Iron & Steel Industry: Report III. v, 86p. (Orig.). 1981. pap. write for info. Intl Labour Office.
The Iron & Steel Industry in 1978. 49p. 1980. pap. 4.50x (ISBN 92-64-02058-6). OECD.
Iron & Steel Institute. Iron & Steel Dictionary: German-English & English-German. 2nd ed. 1962. 22.50x (ISBN 3-514-00197-9). Intl Pubns Serv.
--Iron & Steel Dictionary: German-French & French-German. 1962. 22.50x (ISBN 3-514-00209-6). Intl Pubns Serv.
--Iron & Steel Dictionary: German-Italian & Italian-German. 1969. 22.50x (ISBN 3-514-00012-3). Intl Pubns Serv.
--Iron & Steel Dictionary: German-Spanish & Spanish-German. 2nd ed. 1966. 22.50x (ISBN 3-514-00011-5). Intl Pubns Serv.
LaFayette, Kenneth D. Flaming Brands: Fifty Years of Iron Making in the Upper Peninsula of Michigan, 1848-1898. LC 77-72800. (Illus.). 1977. 4.75 (ISBN 0-918616-01-8). Northern Mich.
Lewis, W. David. Iron & Steel in America. (Industry in America Ser.). (Illus.). 1976. pap. 2.50 (ISBN 0-914650-10-6). Eleutherian Mills-Hagley.
Manners, Gerald. The Changing World Market for Iron Ore, 1950-1980: An Economic Geography. LC 70-146734. (Resources for the Future Ser). (Illus.). 416p. 1971. 27.50x (ISBN 0-8018-1308-5). Johns Hopkins.
Pearse, John B. A Concise History of the Iron Manufacture of the American Colonies up to the Revolution & of Pennsylvania Until the Present Time. (Illus.). 1876. 22.50 (ISBN 0-8337-2698-6). B Franklin.
Peters, A. T. Ferrous Production Metallurgy. 496p. 1981. 35.00 (ISBN 0-471-08597-9, Pub. by Wiley-Interscience). Wiley.
Pierce, Arthur D. Iron in the Pines: The Story of New Jersey's Ghost Towns & Bog Iron. (Illus.). 1966. pap. 3.95 (ISBN 0-8135-0514-3). Rutgers U Pr.
Pounds, Norman J. Geography of Iron & Steel. 4th rev. ed. (Orig.). 1968. pap. text ed. 6.00x (ISBN 0-09-106261-6, Hutchinson U Lib). Humanities.

Scrivenor, Harry. History of the Iron Trade: From the Earliest Records to the Present Period. 327p. 1967. Repr. of 1854 ed. 30.00x (ISBN 0-7146-1150-6, F Cass Co). Biblio Dist.
Smiles, Samuel. Industrial Biography: Iron-Workers & Tool Makers. LC 67-114712. (Illus.). Repr. of 1863 ed. 17.50x (ISBN 0-678-05727-3). Kelley.
Swank, James H. History of the Manufacture of Iron in All Ages. 2nd ed. 1965. Repr. of 1892 ed. 22.50 (ISBN 0-8337-3463-6). B Franklin.
Walsh, William D. The Diffusion of Technological Change in the Pennsylvania Pig Iron Industry: 1850-1870. LC 75-2601. (Dissertations in American Economic History). (Illus.). 1975. 20.00x (ISBN 0-405-07222-8). Arno.
Wertime, Theodore A. Coming of the Age of Steel. LC 60-14362. (Illus.). 1962. 12.50x (ISBN 0-226-89389-8). U of Chicago Pr.

IRON INDUSTRY AND TRADE–VOCATIONAL GUIDANCE

Sullivan, John W. Aim for a Job in the Iron & Steel Industry. LC 67-12977. (Aim High Vocational Guidance Ser.). (gr. 7-12). 1969. PLB 5.97 (ISBN 0-8239-0097-5). Rosen Pr.

IRON INDUSTRY AND TRADE–EUROPE

Cunliffe, Barry & Rowley, Trevor. Lowland Iron Age Communities in Europe. 1978. 20.00x (ISBN 0-86054-028-6, Pub. by BAR). State Mutual Bk.
Greer, Guy. Ruhr-Lorraine Industrial Problem. (Brookings Institution Reprint Ser). Repr. of 1925 ed. lib. bdg. 27.00x (ISBN 0-697-00156-3). Irvington.
Handbook of the European Iron & Steel Works. 6th ed. LC 63-32146. 1978. 115.00x (ISBN 0-8002-2370-5). Intl Pubns Serv.
Vial, Jean. L' Industrialisation De la Siderurgie Francaise 1814-1864, 2 vols. (Industrie et Artisanat: No. 3). (Illus.). 1967. pap. 64.00x (ISBN 90-2796-134-4). Mouton.

IRON INDUSTRY AND TRADE–GREAT BRITAIN

Ashton, Thomas S. Iron & Steel in the Industrial Revolution. LC 74-555. Repr. of 1924 ed. 17.50x (ISBN 0-678-06751-1). Kelley.
Bell, Florence E. At the Works: A Study of a Manufacturing Town. LC 69-10847. 1907. 15.00x (ISBN 0-678-05510-6). Kelley.
Bining, Arthur C. British Regulation of the Colonial Iron Industry. LC 68-55481. Repr. of 1933 ed. 12.50x (ISBN 0-678-00924-4). Kelley.
Birch, Alan. Economic History of the British Iron & Steel Industry, 1784-1879. LC 67-29908. 1967. 25.00x (ISBN 0-678-05026-0). Kelley.
--Economic History of the British Iron & Steel Industry: 1784-1879. (Illus.). 398p. 1967. 28.50x (ISBN 0-7146-1272-3, F Cass Co). Biblio Dist.
Fell, Alfred. Early Iron Foundary of Furness & Districts. LC 68-121907. (Illus.). Repr. of 1908 ed. 25.00x (ISBN 0-678-05168-2). Kelley.
Gale, W. K. & Nicholls, C. R. The Lilleshall Company Limited: A History 1764-1964. 144p. 1981. 30.00x (ISBN 0-86190-000-6, Pub. by Moorland). State Mutual Bk.
Hyde, Charles K. Technological Change & the British Iron Industry, 1700-1870. LC 76-45901. 1977. text ed. 22.00 (ISBN 0-691-05246-8). Princeton U Pr.
McCloskey, Donald N. Economic Maturity & Entrepreneurial Decline: British Iron & Steel, 1870-1913. LC 72-92131. (Economic Studies: No. 142). 192p. 1973. text ed. 11.00 (ISBN 0-674-22875-8). Harvard U Pr.
Roepke, Howard G. Movememts of the British Iron & Steel Industry, 1720 to 1951. LC 80-23128. (Illinois Studies in the Social Sciences: Vol. 36). (Illus.). vii, 198p. 1981. Repr. of 1956 ed. lib. bdg. 25.00x (ISBN 0-8371-9096-7, ROMB). Greenwood.
Scrivenor, Harry. History of the Iron Trade of Great Britain from the Earliest Records to the Present Period. 2nd ed. LC 68-20033. Repr. of 1854 ed. 25.00x (ISBN 0-678-05142-9). Kelley.
Straker, Ernst. Wealden Iron. LC 69-17028. Repr. of 1931 ed. 19.50x (ISBN 0-678-05518-1). Kelley.
Vialls, Christine. Coalbrookdale & the Iron Revolution: Introduction to the History of Mankind. LC 77-94224. (Illus.). 3.95 (ISBN 0-521-21672-9). Cambridge U Pr.

IRON INDUSTRY AND TRADE–JAPAN

Kawata, Sukiyuki, ed. Japan's Iron & Steel Industry 1979. 28th ed. LC 55-33803. (Illus.). 1979. pap. 27.50x (ISBN 0-8002-2382-9). Intl Pubns Serv.

IRON METABOLISM

Bergsma, Daniel, ed. Iron Metabolism & Thalassemia. LC 76-25835. (Alan R. Liss, Inc. Ser: Vol 12, No. 8). 1976. 22.00 (ISBN 0-686-18085-2). March of Dimes.
Bernat, I., ed. Iron Metabolism. 500p. 1978. 39.50 (ISBN 0-306-30829-0, Plenum Pr). Plenum Pub.
Bezkorovainy, Anatoly. Biochemistry of Nonheme Iron. (Biochemistry of the Elments Ser.: Vol. 1). 430p. 1981. 45.00 (ISBN 0-306-40501-6, Plenum Pr). Plenum Pub.
Ciba Foundation. CIBA Foundation Symposium 51: Iron Metabolism. 1977. 38.75 (ISBN 0-444-15273-3, Excerpta Medica). Elsevier.
Conference Sponsored by National Foundation-March of Dimes, Key Biscayne, Florida, Nov. 1975. Iron Metabolism & Thalassemia: Proceedings. Bergsma, Daniel, et al, eds. LC 76-25835. (Birth Defects Original Article Ser.: Vol. 12, No. 8). 212p. 1976. 26.00x (ISBN 0-8451-1006-3). A R Liss.
Cook, James D. Iron. (Methods in Hematology Ser.: Vol. 1). (Illus.). 224p. 1980. 32.00 (ISBN 0-443-08118-2). Churchill.
Fairbanks, Virgil F., et al. Clinical Disorders of Iron Metabolism. 2nd ed. LC 75-139797. (Illus.). 486p. 1971. 68.50 (ISBN 0-8089-0677-1). Grune.
Jacobs, A. & Worwood, M., eds. Iron in Biochemistry & Medicine, II. 1981. 98.50 (ISBN 0-12-378980-X). Acad Pr.
Kief, H., et al. Iron Metabolism & Its Disorders. (International Congress Ser.: No. 366). 1976. 49.75 (ISBN 0-444-15189-3, Excerpta Medica). Elsevier.
Muller-Eberhard, Ursula, ed. Iron Excess: Aberrations of Iron & Porphyrin Metabolism. LC 77-8101. (Seminars in Hematology Reprint Ser.). 272p. 1977. 40.25 (ISBN 0-8089-1040-X). Grune.
Neilands, J. B. Microbial Iron Metabolism: A Comprehensive Treatise. 1974. 68.50 (ISBN 0-12-515250-7). Acad Pr.
--Microbial Iron Metabolism: A Comprehensive Treatise. 1974. 68.50 (ISBN 0-12-515250-7). Acad Pr.

IRON MINES AND MINING

Boyum, Burton H. Saga of Iron Mining in Michigan's Upper Peninsula. 1977. pap. 3.75 (ISBN 0-938746-03-0). Marquette Cnty Hist.
Harvey, Katherine A. The Lonaconing Journals: The Founding of a Coal & Iron Community,1837-1840. LC 76-50177. (Transactions Ser.: Vol.67,Pt.2). (Illus.). 1977. pap. 7.50 (ISBN 0-87169-672-X). Am Philos.
Hochschild, Harold K. Macintyre Mine: From Failure to Fortune. (Illus.). 27p. 1962. pap. 3.95 (ISBN 0-8156-8024-4, Pub. by Adirondack Museum). Syracuse U Pr.
Landis, Paul H. Three Iron Mining Towns: A Study in Cultural Change. LC 72-112555. (Rise of Urban America). 1970. Repr. of 1938 ed. 9.00 (ISBN 0-405-02462-2). Arno.
Mussey, Henry R. Combination in the Mining Industry: A Study in Concentration in Lake Superior Iron Ore Production. LC 68-56674. (Columbia University, Studies in the Social Sciences Ser.: No. 60). Repr. of 1905 ed. 16.50 (ISBN 0-404-51060-4). AMS Pr.
Wirth, Fremont P. The Discovery & Exploitation of the Minnesota Iron Lands. Bruchey, Stuart, ed. LC 78-53544. (Development of Public Lands in the U. S. Ser.). 1979. Repr. of 1937 ed. lib. bdg. 16.00x (ISBN 0-405-11393-5). Arno.

IRON ORES

Brown, T. E., et al. Field Excursions, East Texas: Clay, Glauconite, Ironstone Deposits. (Illus.). 48p. 1969. 1.00 (ISBN 0-686-29317-7, GB 9). Bur Econ Geology.
Earney, Fillmore C. Researcher's Guide to Iron Ore: An Annotated Bibliography on the Economic Geography of Iron Ore. LC 74-76986. 1974. lib. bdg. 50.00 (ISBN 0-87287-095-2). Libs Unl.
Grout, Frank F. & Wolff, J. Fred. Geology of the Cuyuna District, Minnesota: A Progress Report. LC 55-9000. (Bulletin: No. 36). (Illus.). 1955. 3.00x (ISBN 0-8166-0106-2). Minn Geol Survey.

IRON ORGANIC COMPOUNDS

see Organoiron Compounds

IRON WORKERS

see Iron and Steel Workers

IRON-WORKS

Clarke, Mary S. Pioneer Iron Works. LC 68-21134. (Illus.). (gr. 7 up). 1968. pap. 2.95 (ISBN 0-9603346-2-9). Hilltop Pr.
Gardner, J. Starkie. English Ironwork of the Seventeenth & Eighteenth Centuries. LC 69-16319. (Illus.). Repr. of 1911 ed. 30.00 (ISBN 0-405-08551-6, Blom Pubns.). Arno.

IRONING

see Laundry and Laundry Industry

IRONSIDE, EDMUND, SIR, 1880-1959

Ironside, Edmund. Time Unguarded. Macleod, Roderick & Kelly, Denis, eds. LC 74-64. (Illus.). 434p. 1974. Repr. of 1963 ed. lib. bdg. 23.50x (ISBN 0-8371-7369-8, IRTG). Greenwood.
Soutar, Andrew. With Ironside in North Russia. LC 77-115585. (Russia Observed, Series I). 1970. Repr. of 1940 ed. 12.00 (ISBN 0-405-03062-2). Arno.

IRONWORK

see Architectural Ironwork; Blacksmithing; Forging; Welding; Wrought-Iron

IRONY

Dyson, Anthony E. The Crazy Fabric: Essays in Irony. LC 72-10871. (Essay Index Reprint Ser.). 1973. Repr. of 1965 ed. 16.00 (ISBN 0-8369-7214-7). Arno.
Kierkegaard, Soren. The Concept of Irony: With Constant Reference to Socrates. Capel, Lee M., tr. LC 66-10227. (Midland Bks.: No. 111). 1968. pap. 4.95x (ISBN 0-253-20111-X). Ind U Pr.
McDowell, Frederick P. Ellen Glasgow & the Ironic Art of Fiction. 304p. 1960. pap. 5.95 (ISBN 0-299-02114-9). U of Wis Pr.
Muecke, Douglas C. Irony. (Critical Idiom Ser.: Vol. 13). 1970. pap. 5.50x (ISBN 0-416-65420-7). Methuen Inc.
Reinitz, Richard. Irony & Consciousness: American Historiography & Reinhold Niebuhr's Vision. LC 77-92574. 232p. Date not set. 19.50 (ISBN 0-8387-2062-5). Bucknell U Pr.
States, Bert O. Irony & Drama: A Poetics. LC 73-148023. 264p. 1971. 17.50x (ISBN 0-8014-0629-3). Cornell U Pr.
Vellacott, P. Ironic Drama. LC 74-19522. 276p. 1975. 36.00 (ISBN 0-521-20590-5); pap. 10.50 (ISBN 0-521-09896-3). Cambridge U Pr.
Wessell, Leonard P. Karl Marx, Romantic Irony & the Proletariat: Studies in the Mythopoetic Origins of Marxism. LC 79-12386. 1979. text ed. 25.00x (ISBN 0-8071-0587-2). La State U Pr.

IRONY IN LITERATURE

Booth, Wayne C. A Rhetoric of Irony. LC 73-87298. xviii, 292p. 1975. 16.00x (ISBN 0-226-06552-9); pap. 5.95 (ISBN 0-226-06553-7, P641). U of Chicago Pr.
Dempster, Germaine. Dramatic Irony in Chaucer. 1959. text ed. 8.50x (ISBN 0-391-00492-1). Humanities.
Good, Edwin M. Irony in the Old Testament. (Bible & Literature Ser.: No. 3). (Orig.). 1981. pap. text ed. 9.95x (ISBN 0-907459-05-6, Pub. by Almond Pr England). Eisenbrauns.
Green, D. H. Irony in the Medieval Romance. LC 78-14930. 1979. 69.00 (ISBN 0-521-22458-6). Cambridge U Pr.
Levy, Diane W. Ironic Techniques in Anatole France: Essay on Les Sept Femmes de la Barbe-Bleue. LC 78-18827. (Studies in the Romance Languages & Literatures: No. 201). 1978. pap. 12.00x (ISBN 0-8078-9201-7). U of NC Pr.
Moglen, Helene. The Philosophical Irony of Laurence Sterne. LC 75-4574. 1975. 8.25 (ISBN 0-8130-0363-6). U Presses Fla.
Muecke, Douglas C. Irony. (Critical Idiom Ser.: Vol. 13). 1970. pap. 5.50x (ISBN 0-416-65420-7). Methuen Inc.
Murillo, Louis A. Cyclical Night: Irony in James Joyce & Jorge Luis Borges. LC 68-54022. (Illus.). 289p. 1968. 16.00x (ISBN 0-674-18040-2). Harvard U Pr.
O'Hara, Daniel T. Tragic Knowledge: Yeat's Autobiography & Hermeneutics. LC 80-26825. 224p. 1981. 22.50x (ISBN 0-231-05204-9). Columbia U Pr.
Tener, Robert L. The Phoenix Riddle: A Study of Irony in Comedy. (SSEL Poetic Drama Ser.: No. 44). (Orig.). 1979. pap. text ed. 25.00x (ISBN 0-391-01612-1). Humanities.
Thompson, Alan R. The Dry Mock, a Study of Irony in Drama. LC 80-20927. (Studies in Comparative Literature: No. 4). Repr. of 1948 ed. lib. bdg. 17.50x (ISBN 0-87991-507-2). Porcupine Pr.
Wilde, Alan. Horizons of Assent: Modernism, Postmodernism, & the Ironic Imagination. LC 80-22576. 224p. 1981. text ed. 15.00x (ISBN 0-8018-2449-4). Johns Hopkins.

IROQUOIAN LANGUAGES

Mithun, Marianne & Woodbury, Hanni, eds. Northern Iroquoian Texts. LC 80-11887. (International Journal of American Linguistics-Native American Texts Ser.: Monograph No. 4). 168p. (Orig.). 1980. pap. 13.25 (ISBN 0-226-36716-9, Pub. by U of Chicago Pr). Univ Microfilms.
Morgan, L. H. League of the Iroquois. (Illus.). 11.50 (ISBN 0-8446-2612-0). Peter Smith.
Morgan, Lewis H. League of the Ho-De-No-Sau-Nee or Iroquois, 2 Vols. new ed. Lloyd, Henry M., ed. & annotations by. (Illus.). 1966. Repr. of 1904 ed. Set. 49.50 (ISBN 0-8337-2465-7). B Franklin.

IROQUOIS INDIANS

see Indians of North America–Eastern States; Seneca Language

IRRADIATION

see also Radioactivation Analysis

Berdjis, Charles C. Pathology of Irradiation. LC 71-110278. 722p. 1970. 52.50 (ISBN 0-683-00601-0, Pub. by Williams & Wilkins). Krieger.
Biological Effects of Neutron & Proton Irradiation, 2 vols. (Illus., Orig.). 1964. 22.00 ea. (IAEA). Vol. 1 (ISBN 92-0-010064-3, ISP80-1). Vol. 2 (ISBN 92-0-010164-X, ISP80-2). Unipub.
Improvement of Food Quality by Irradiation. (Illus.). 188p. (Orig.). 1974. pap. 14.75 (ISBN 92-0-011174-2, ISP370, IAEA). Unipub.
Irradiation Facilities for Research Reactors. (Illus.). 478p. (Orig., Eng. & Fr.). 1973. pap. 37.50 (ISBN 92-0-050073-0, ISP316, IAEA). Unipub.
Kreuzer, Rudolf, ed. Freezing & Irradiation of Fish. (Illus.). 548p. 56.25 (ISBN 0-85238-008-9, FN 50, FNB). Unipub.
Leteurtre, J. & Quere, Y. Irradiation Effects in Fissile Materials. (Defects in Crystalline Solids Ser.: Vol. 6). 1972. 24.50 (ISBN 0-444-10382-1, North-Holland). Elsevier.
Manual of Food Irradiation Dosimetry. (Illus.). 1978. pap. 19.50 (ISBN 92-0-115277-9, IDC 178, IAEA). Unipub.
Neutron Irradiaton of Seeds, Three. (Technical Reports Ser.: No. 141). (Illus.). 132p. (Orig.). 1973. pap. 13.50 (ISBN 92-0-115272-8, IDC141, IAEA). Unipub.
Odum, Howard T. & Pigeon, Robert F., eds. A Tropical Rain Forest: A Study of Irradiation & Ecology at El Verde, Puerto Rico, 3vols. LC 70-606844. 652p. 1970. pap. 10.00 (ISBN 0-686-75819-6). DOE.
Panel, Vienna, March 18-22, 1974. Requirements for the Irradiaton of Food on a Commercial Scale: Proceedings. (Illus.). 216p. 1975. pap. 20.50 (ISBN 92-0-111275-0, ISP394, IAEA). Unipub.
The Technical Basic for Legislation on Irradiated Food. (FAO Atomic Energy Ser.: No. 6). (Orig.). 1966. pap. 4.50 (ISBN 0-685-09411-1, F458, FAO). Unipub.
Wholesomeness of Irradiated Food. (Food & Nutrition Ser: No. 6). 44p. 1978. pap. 6.25 (ISBN 92-5-100282-7, F495, FAO). Unipub.

IRRATIONAL NUMBERS

see Numbers, Irrational

IRRELIGION

see also Agnosticism; Atheism; Free Thought; Rationalism; Secularism

IRREVERSIBLE COMA

see Brain Death

IRREVERSIBLE PROCESSES

Day, W. A. The Thermodynamics of Simple Materials with Fading Memory. LC 77-183992. (Springer Tracts in Natural Philosophy: Vol. 22). (Illus.). 152p. 1972. 19.60 (ISBN 0-387-05704-8). Springer-Verlag.
Garrido, L. M., et al, eds. Irreversibility in the Many-Body Problem. LC 72-87519. 470p. 1972. 45.00 (ISBN 0-306-30711-1, Plenum Pr). Plenum Pub.
Haase, Rolf. Thermodynamics of Irreversible Processes. (Chemical Engineering Ser). (Illus.). 1969. text ed. 25.95 (ISBN 0-201-02651-1). A-W.
Knof, Hans. Thermodynamics of Irreversible Processes in Liquid Metals. 1966. 6.75x (ISBN 0-408-00131-3). Transatlantic.
Lavenda, B. H. Thermodynamics of Irreversible Processes. LC 76-22604. 1978. 43.95x (ISBN 0-470-98898-3). Halsted Pr.
Prigogine, I. Introduction to Thermodynamics of Irreversible Processes. 3rd ed. LC 67-29540. 1968. 19.50 (ISBN 0-470-69928-0, Pub. by Wiley-Interscience). Wiley.
Prigogine, Ilya. From Being to Becoming: Time & Complexity in the Physical Sciences. LC 79-26774. (Illus.). 1980. pap. text ed. 12.95x (ISBN 0-7167-1108-7). W H Freeman.
Ullmaier, H. Irreversible Properties of Type Two Superconductors. (Springer Tracts in Modern Physics Ser.: Vol. 76). (Illus.). 180p. 1975. 30.20 (ISBN 0-387-07424-4). Springer-Verlag.

IRRIGATION

see also Arid Regions; Dams; Irrigation Farming; Reservoirs; Saline Irrigation; Windmills

Alston, Richard M. Commercial Irrigation Enterprise: The Fear of Water Monopoly & the Genesis of Market Distortion in the Nineteenth Century American West. LC 77-14752. (Dissertations in American Economic History Ser.). 1978. 25.00 (ISBN 0-405-11025-1). Arno.
Amerian Society of Civil Engineers, compiled by. Legal, Institutional, & Social Aspects of Irrigation & Drainage & Water Resources Planning & Management. 912p. 1979. pap. text ed. 49.50 (ISBN 0-87262-140-5). Am Soc Civil Eng.
American Society of Civil Engineers, compiled By. Agricultural & Urban Considerations in Irrigation & Drainage. 808p. 1974. pap. text ed. 32.50 (ISBN 0-87262-067-0). Am Soc Civil Eng.
--Consumptive Use of Water. 232p. 1974. pap. text ed. 10.75 (ISBN 0-87262-068-9). Am Soc Civil Eng.
--Contribution of Irrigation & Drainage to World Food Supply. 432p. 1975. pap. text ed. 22.00 (ISBN 0-87262-114-6). Am Soc Civil Eng.
--Irrigation & Drainage in an Age of Competition for Resources. 560p. 1975. pap. text ed. 19.00 (ISBN 0-87262-123-5). Am Soc Civil Eng.
--Irrigation & Drainage in the Nineteen Eighties. 448p. 1979. pap. text ed. 27.00 (ISBN 0-87262-181-2). Am Soc Civil Eng.

--Operation & Maintenance of Irrigation & Drainage Systems. LC 79-55951. (Manuel & Report on Engineering Practice Ser: No. 57). 280p. 1980. pap. text ed. 28.00 (ISBN 0-87262-231-2). Am Soc Civil Eng.
--Water Management for Irrigation & Drainage. 640p. 1977. pap. text ed. 46.00 (ISBN 0-87262-097-2). Am Soc Civil Eng.
ASCE Conference, Irrigation & Drainage Division, 1980. Irrigation & Drainage: Today's Challenges. Eggleston, Jerry, ed. LC 80-66950. 512p. 1980. pap. text ed. 38.50 (ISBN 0-87262-251-7). Am Soc Civil Eng.
ASCE Irrigation & Drainage Division, July 1976. Environmental Aspects of Irrigation & Drainage: Proceedings. American Society of Civil Engineers, compiled By. 752p. 1976. pap. text ed. 37.50 (ISBN 0-87262-171-5). Am Soc Civil Eng.
Bergmann, Hellmuth. Guide to the Economic Evaluation of Irrigation Projects. 134p. 1976. 18.00x (ISBN 9-2641-1021-6). OECD.
Booher, L. J. Surface Irrigation. (FAO Agricultural Development Papers: No. 95). (Illus.). 160p. (Orig.). 1974. pap. 7.50 (ISBN 92-5-100081-6, F455, FAO). Unipub.
Bowden, Leonard W. Diffusion of the Decision to Irrigate: Simulation of the Spread of a New Resource Management Practice in the Colorado Northern High Plains. LC 65-22712. (Research Papers Ser.: No. 97). 146p. 1965. pap. 8.00 (ISBN 0-89065-010-1). U Chicago Dept Geog.
Brough, Charles H. Irrigation in Utah. LC 78-64265. (Johns Hopkins University. Studies in the Social Sciences. Extra Volumes: 19). Repr. of 1898 ed. 21.50 (ISBN 0-404-61367-5). AMS Pr.
Carruthers, Ian, ed. Social & Economic Perspectives on Irrigation. 100p. 1981. pap. 22.00 (ISBN 0-08-026780-7). Pergamon.
The Contribution of Varietal Tolerance for Problem Soils to Yield Stability in Rice. (IRRI Research Paper Ser.: No. 43). 15p. 1979. pap. 5.00 (ISBN 0-686-70538-6, R083, IRRI). Unipub.
Coward, E. Walter, ed. Irrigation & Agricultural Development in Asia: Perspectives from the Social Sciences. LC 79-24319. (Illus., Orig.). 1980. 27.50x (ISBN 0-8014-1132-7); pap. 9.95x (ISBN 0-8014-9871-6). Cornell U Pr.
Davison, Stanley S. Leadership of the Reclamation Movement, 1875-1902. Bruchey, Stuart, ed. LC 78-53545. (Development of Public Land Law in the U. S. Ser.). (Illus.). 1979. lib. bdg. 21.00x (ISBN 0-405-11365-X). Arno.
Denitrification Loss of Fertilizer Nitrogen in Paddy Soils - Its Recognition & Impact. (IRRI Research Paper Ser.: No. 37). 10p. 1979. pap. 5.00 (ISBN 0-686-70539-4, R077, IRRI). Unipub.
Downing, Theodore E. & Gibson, McGuire, eds. Irrigation's Impact on Society. LC 74-15602. (Anthropological Papers: No. 25). 140p. 1974. pap. text ed. 5.95x (ISBN 0-8165-0419-9). U of Ariz Pr.
Finkel, Herman J., ed. CRC Handbook of Irrigation Technology, Vol. I. 368p. 1981. 59.95 (ISBN 0-8493-3231-1). CRC Pr.
Fukuda, Hitoshi. Irrigation in the World - Comparative Developments. (Illus.). 1977. 42.50x (ISBN 0-86008-174-5, Pub. by U of Tokyo Pr). Intl Schol Bk Serv.
Green, Donald E. Land of the Underground Rain: Irrigation on the Texas High Plains, 1910-1970. LC 72-7589. (Illus.). 313p. 1973. pap. 8.95x (ISBN 0-292-74629-6). U of Tex Pr.
Gupta, I. C. Use of Saline Water in Agriculture. 210p. 1981. 50.00x (ISBN 0-686-76671-7, Pub. by Oxford & IBH India). State Mutual Bk.
Hagen, R. M., et al, eds. Irrigation of Agricultural Lands. (Illus.). 1967. 22.50 (ISBN 0-89118-012-5). Am Soc Agron.
Hall, A. Drought & Irrigation in North-East Brazil. LC 77-82497. (Latin American Studies: No. 29). (Illus.). 1978. 23.95 (ISBN 0-521-21811-X). Cambridge U Pr.
Hanks, R. J. & Hill, R. W. Modeling Crop Responses to Irrigation in Relation to Soils, Climate & Salinity. (IIIC Publication: No. 4). 71p. 1981. 17.25 (ISBN 0-08-025513-2). Pergamon.
Helfman, Elizabeth S. Wheels, Scoops, & Buckets: How People Lift Water for Their Fields. LC 68-27709. (Illus.). (gr. 4-6). 1968. 6.75 (ISBN 0-688-41154-1). Lothrop.
Hexem, Roger W. & Heady, Earl O. Water Production Functions for Irrigated Agriculture. 1978. text ed. 10.50x (ISBN 0-8138-1785-4). Iowa St U Pr.
International Irrigation Information Center, Bet Dagan, Israel, ed. Irrigation Equipment Manufacturers Directory. 2nd ed. LC 79-42940. (IIIC Publications: No. 5). 312p. 1980. 58.00 (ISBN 0-08-025512-4). Pergamon.
International Irrigation Information Center Bet Dagan, Israel, ed. Irrigation: International Guide to Organizations & Institutions. LC 80-49935. 165p. 1980. 46.00 (ISBN 0-08-026363-1). Pergamon.
Irrigation. (Terminology Bulletin: No. 34). 1979. pap. 7.50 (ISBN 92-5-000668-3, F1544, FAO). Unipub.
Irrigation Canal Lining. (FAO Land & Water Development Ser.: No. 1). 1978. pap. 14.25 (ISBN 92-5-100165-0, F1332, FAO). Unipub.
Irrigation Policy & Management in Southeast Asia. 198p. 1978. pap. 16.00 (ISBN 0-686-70578-5, R009, IRRI). Unipub.
Isotope & Radiation Techniques in Soil Physics & Irrigation Studies. (Illus., Orig., Eng. , Fr. , Rus. & Span.). 1967. pap. 27.75 (ISBN 92-0-010467-3, ISP158, IAEA). Unipub.
Israelsen, Orson W. & Hansen, Vaughn E. Irrigation Principles & Practices. 3rd ed. LC 62-15179. 1962. 28.95 (ISBN 0-471-42999-6). Wiley.
Lampen, Dorothy. Economic & Social Aspects of Federal Reclamation. Bruchey, Stuart, ed. LC 78-56686. (Management of Public Lands in the U. S. Ser.). (Illus.). 1979. Repr. of 1930 ed. lib. bdg. 10.00x (ISBN 0-405-11338-2). Arno.
Leliavsky, S. Irrigation & Hydraulic Design, Vol. 3. 765p. 1960. text ed. 49.95x (ISBN 0-412-05120-6, Pub. by Chapman & Hall England). Methuen Inc.
Localized Irrigation. (Irrigation & Drainage: No. 36). 198p. 1980. pap. 14.25 (ISBN 92-5-100986-4, F2130, FAO). Unipub.
Maass, Arthur & Anderson, Raymond L. And the Desert Shall Rejoice: Conflict, Growth, & Justice in Arid Environments. LC 77-17866. 1978. 25.00x (ISBN 0-262-13134-X). MIT Pr.
Mead, Elwood. Irrigation Institutions: A Discussion of the Economic & Legal Questions Created by the Growth of Irrigated Agriculture in the West. LC 72-2856. (Use & Abuse of America's Natural Resources Ser.). 406p. 1972. Repr. of 1903 ed. 19.00 (ISBN 0-405-04520-4). Arno.
--Irrigation Institutions: A Discussion of the Economic & Legal Questions Created by the Growth of Irrigated Agriculture in the West. Repr. of 1903 ed. 23.00 (ISBN 0-384-37880-3). Johnson Repr.
Pair, Claude, ed. Sprinkler Irrigation. 4th ed. LC 75-24934. (Illus.). 16.00 (ISBN 0-935030-00-X). Irrigation.
Report of the Sixth Session of the European Commission of Agriculture, Working Party of Water Resources & Irrigation. 25p. 1978. pap. 7.50 (ISBN 92-5-100345-9, F1231, FAO). Unipub.
Research Issues in Irrigation Systems in Developing Countries: Proceedings. 1978. pap. 4.00 (ISBN 0-686-23890-7). Lincoln Inst Land.
Ruttan, Vernon W. The Economic Demand for Irrigated Acreage: New Methodology & Some Preliminary Projections 1954-1980. (Resources for the Future Ser). (Illus.). 162p. 1965. 12.00x (ISBN 0-8018-0571-6). Johns Hopkins.
Sally, H. L. Lining of Earthen Irrigation Channels. 6.50x (ISBN 0-210-22631-5). Asia.
Smythe, William E. Conquest of Arid America. LC 76-8950. (Americana Library Ser.: No. 14). (Illus.). 1969. 10.50 (ISBN 0-295-95029-3); pap. 3.95 (ISBN 0-295-95100-1, ALP14). U of Wash Pr.
Soil-Moisture & Irrigation Studies. 1966. pap. 6.50 (ISBN 92-0-011067-3, ISP133, IAEA). Unipub.
Soil-Moisture & Irrigation Studies - 2. 189p. 1973. pap. 14.75 (ISBN 92-0-011073-8, ISP327, IAEA). Unipub.
Sole, William C. History of Irrigation in Adams County. 1969. pap. 1.95 (ISBN 0-934858-07-1). Adams County.
Stern, Peter H. Small Scale Irrigation: A Manual of Low-Cost Technology. (Illus.), 152p. (Orig.). 1979. pap. 10.75 (ISBN 0-903031-64-7, Pub. by Intermediate Tech England). Intermediate Tech.
Townley, John M. Turn This Water into Gold: The Story of the Newlands Project. LC 77-82449. (Illus.). 1977. 12.50 (ISBN 0-686-23018-3). Nevada Hist Soc.
Value to Agriculture of High-Quality Water from Nuclear Desalination. 1969. pap. 12.00 (ISBN 92-0-041069-3, IAEA). Unipub.
Walters, Stanley D. Water for Larsa: An Old Babylonian Archive Dealing with Irrigation. LC 76-99845. (Near Eastern Researches Ser.: No. 4). (Illus.). 1970. 17.50x (ISBN 0-300-01228-4). Yale U Pr.
Wilkinson, J. C. Water & Tribal Settlements in South-East Arabia: A Study of Aflaj of Oman. (Oxford Research Studies in Geography). (Illus.). 1977. 45.00x (ISBN 0-19-823217-9). Oxford U Pr.
Withers, Bruce & Vipond, Stanley. Irrigation: Design & Practice. (Illus.). 304p. 1974. 24.00 (ISBN 0-7134-2817-1, Pub. by Batsford England). David & Charles.
--Irrigation: Design & Practice. 2nd ed. LC 80-66673. (Illus.). 300p. 1980. soft cover 13.95x (ISBN 0-8014-9874-0). Cornell U Pr.
Worthington, E. Barton, ed. Arid Land Irrigation in Developing Countries: Environmental Problems & Effects. 1977. text ed. 105.00 (ISBN 0-08-021588-2). Pergamon.
Yaron, B., et al, eds. Arid Zone Irrigation. LC 73-76816. (Ecological Studies Ser.: Vol. 5). (Illus.). 500p. 1973. 52.00 (ISBN 0-387-06206-8). Springer-Verlag.
Yates, Herbert. Pioneer Project. 1968. pap. 3.95 (ISBN 0-8323-0201-5). Binford.
Young, Virgil E. Sprinkler Irrigation System. rev. 3rd ed. (Illus.). 200p. (Orig.). 1976. pap. text ed. 4.98 (ISBN 0-916970-01-9). Mist'er Rain.
Zimmerman, Josef. Irrigation. 516p. 1966. 31.50 (ISBN 0-471-98379-9, Pub. by Wiley). Krieger.

IRRIGATION–ASIA

Wade, Robert. Irrigation & Agricultural Politics in South Korea. (Special Studies in Social, Political, & Economic Development Ser.). 160p. 1981. lib. bdg. 22.50 (ISBN 0-86531-264-8). Westview.

IRRIGATION–CHINA

Chi Ch'ao-Ting. Key Economic Areas in Chinese History. LC 70-104612. (Illus.). Repr. of 1936 ed. 12.50x (ISBN 0-678-00594-X). Kelley.
Workshop on Efficient Use & Maintenance of Irrigation Systems at the Farm Level in China. Proceedings. (Water Resource Ser.: No. 51). 108p. 1980. pap. 9.00 (ISBN 0-686-72367-8, UN79/2F16, UN). Unipub.

IRRIGATION–EGYPT

Butzer, Karl & Freeman, Leslie G., eds. Early Hydraulic Civilization in Egypt. LC 75-36398. (Prehistoric Archaeology & Ecology Ser). (Illus.). 1976. 9.00x (ISBN 0-226-08634-8); pap. 3.25x (ISBN 0-226-08635-6). U of Chicago Pr.
Peel, Sidney C. Binding of the Nile & the New Soudan. LC 74-94484. Repr. of 1904 ed. 14.50x (ISBN 0-8371-2369-0, Pub. by Negro U Pr). Greenwood.

IRRIGATION–GREAT BRITAIN

Vaughan, Rowland. Most Approved & Long Experienced Water-Workes. LC 77-7437. (English Experience Ser.: No. 898). 1977. Repr. of 1610 ed. lib. bdg. 14.00 (ISBN 90-221-0898-8). Walter J Johnson.

IRRIGATION–INDIA

Michael, A. M. Irrigation: Theory & Practice. 1978. text ed. 30.00 (ISBN 0-7069-0613-6, Pub. by Vikas India). Advent NY.
Pandey, M. P. The Impact of Irriation on Rural Development. 1980. text ed. 9.00x (ISBN 0-391-01846-9). Humanities.
Paustian, Paul W. Canal Irrigation in the Punjab. LC 68-58614. (Columbia University. Studies in the Social Sciences: No. 322). Repr. of 1930 ed. 17.50 (ISBN 0-404-51322-0). AMS Pr.

IRRIGATION–MEXICO

Cummings, Ronald G. Water Resource Management in Northern Mexico. LC 72-4030. (Resources for the Future Ser). (Illus.). 80p. 1972. pap. 3.50x (ISBN 0-8018-1426-X). Johns Hopkins.
O'Brien, Michael J., et al. A Late Formative Irrigation Settlement Below Monte Alban: Survey & Excavation on the Xoxocotlan Piedmont, Oaxaca, Mexico. (Institute of Latin American Studies Special Publications). (Illus.). 266p. 1981. pap. 16.95x (ISBN 0-292-74628-8). U of Tex Pr.

IRRIGATION–PALESTINE

Lowdermilk, Walter C. Palestine: Land of Promise. rev. ed. LC 68-23308. (Illus.). 1968. Repr. of 1944 ed. lib. bdg. 14.00x (ISBN 0-8371-2616-9, LOPL). Greenwood.

IRRIGATION FARMING

Israelsen, Orson W. & Hansen, Vaughn E. Irrigation Principles & Practices. 3rd ed. LC 62-15179. 1962. 28.95 (ISBN 0-471-42999-6). Wiley.
Mechanization of Irrigated Crop Production. (FAO Agricultural Services Bulletin: No. 28). (Illus.). 1977. pap. 24.75 (ISBN 92-5-100254-1, F717, FAO). Unipub.
Shalhevet, J., et al, eds. Irrigation of Field & Orchard Crops Under Semi-Arid Conditions. (Illus.). 110p. 1980. pap. 10.50 (ISBN 0-08-025511-6). Pergamon.
Wang, Jaw-Kai & Hagan, Ross E. Irrigated Rice Production Systems. (Tropical Agriculture Ser.). 1980. lib. bdg. 36.25x (ISBN 0-89158-486-2). Westview.

IRRITABILITY

see also Excitation (Physiology); Plants–Irritability and Movements

IRVINE RANCH, CALIFORNIA

Cleland, Robert G. The Irvine Ranch. 3rd ed. LC 78-133487. (Illus.). 1978. pap. 5.00 (ISBN 0-87328-015-6). Huntington Lib.

IRVING, HENRY, SIR, 1838-1905

Archer, William. Henry Irving, Actor & Manager. LC 70-107156. 1970. Repr. of 1883 ed. 17.00 (ISBN 0-403-00468-3). Scholarly.
Bingham, Madeleine. Henry Irving: The Greatest Victorian Actor. LC 76-41231. (Illus.). 1978. 12.95 (ISBN 0-8128-2160-2). Stein & Day.
Brereton, Austin. Henry Irving. 75p. 1981. Repr. of 1905 ed. lib. bdg. 30.00 (ISBN 0-89984-065-5). Century Bookbindery.
--Life of Henry Irving, 2 Vols. in 1. LC 74-88604. (Illus.). 1908. 25.00 (ISBN 0-405-00835-X, Blom Pubns). Arno.
Craig, Edward G. Henry Irving. LC 79-91486. (Illus.). 1930. 15.00 (ISBN 0-405-08380-7, Blom Pubns). Arno.
Hughes, Allan. Henry Irving, Shakespearean. LC 79-54019. (Illus.). 304p. 1981. 44.50 (ISBN 0-521-22192-7). Cambridge U Pr.
Jones, Henry A. Shadow of Henry Irving. LC 77-91527. 1931. 10.00 (ISBN 0-405-08674-1, Blom Pubns). Arno.
Menpes, Mortimer. Henry Irving. 52p. 1981. Repr. of 1906 ed. lib. bdg. 25.00 (ISBN 0-89984-345-X). Century Bookbindery.
Saintsbury, Harry A. & Palmer, Cecil, eds. We Saw Him Act: A Symposium on the Art of Sir Henry Irving. LC 78-113453. (Illus.). 1939. 22.00 (ISBN 0-405-08909-0). Arno.
Stoker, Bram. Personal Reminiscences of Henry Irving, 2 Vols. Repr. of 1906 ed. Set. lib. bdg. 32.25x (ISBN 0-8371-2845-5, STHI). Greenwood.
Winter, William. Wreath of Laurel, Being Speeches on Dramatic & Kindred Occasions. LC 73-130098. (Drama Ser). 1970. Repr. of 1898 ed. lib. bdg. 15.00 (ISBN 0-8337-3828-3). B Franklin.

IRVING, WASHINGTON, 1783-1859

Adams, Charles. Memoir of Washington Irving. LC 70-148869. (Select Bibliographies Reprint Ser.). 1972. Repr. of 1870 ed. 17.00 (ISBN 0-8369-5641-9). Arno.
--Memoir of Washington Irving. LC 70-148869. (Select Bibliographies Reprint Ser.). 1972. Repr. of 1870 ed. 17.00 (ISBN 0-8369-5641-9). Arno.
Aderman, Ralph M., et al, eds. Complete Works of W. Irving: 1802-1823, Vol. 1. (Critical Editions Program: The Complete Works of Washington Irving). 1978. 30.00 (ISBN 0-8057-8522-1). Twayne.
--The Complete Works of Washington Irving: Letters, Eighteen Hundred Two to Eighteen Twenty-Three. (Twayne's Critical Editions Program: Vol. 1). 1978. lib. bdg. 30.00 (ISBN 0-8057-8522-1). G K Hall.
Bowden, Mary W. Washington Irving. (United States Authors Ser.: No. 379). 1981. lib. bdg. 9.95 (ISBN 0-8057-7314-2). Twayne.
Bruce, Wallace. Along the Hudson with Washington Irving. LC 77-776. 1913. lib. bdg. 20.00 (ISBN 0-8414-9880-6). Folcroft.
Butler, Joseph T. Washington Irving's Sunnyside. LC 74-6757. (Sleepy Hollow Restorations Guidebook). (Illus.). 80p. 1974. 3.95 (ISBN 0-912882-13-1); pap. 1.95 (ISBN 0-912882-12-3). Sleepy Hollow.
Curtis, George W. Washington Irving: A Sketch. LC 76-28379. 1976. Repr. of 1901 ed. lib. bdg. 20.00 (ISBN 0-8414-3489-1). Folcroft.
Hedges, William L. Washington Irving: An American Study, 1802-1832. LC 80-23564. (The Goucher College Ser.). xiv, 274p. 1980. Repr. of 1965 ed. lib. bdg. 27.50x (ISBN 0-313-21159-0, HEWI). Greenwood.
Hellman, George S. Letters of Washington Irving to Henry Brevoort. 1979. Repr. of 1918 ed. lib. bdg. 100.00 (ISBN 0-8495-2275-7). Arden Lib.
Hellman, George S., ed. Letters of Henry Brevoort to Washington Irving: Together with Other Unpublished Brevoort Papers. 1979. Repr. of 1918 ed. lib. bdg. 75.00 (ISBN 0-8495-2288-9). Arden Lib.
Hitchcock, Thomas. Unhappy Loves of Men of Genius: Gibbon, Johnson, Goethe, Mozart & Irving. 1979. Repr. of 1892 ed. lib. bdg. 25.00 (ISBN 0-8492-5322-5). R West.
Ingraham, Charles A. Washington Irving & Other Essays. 1978. Repr. of 1922 ed. lib. bdg. 30.00 (ISBN 0-8495-2601-9). Arden Lib.
Irving, Pierre M. The Life & Letters of Washington Irving, 4 vols. LC 67-23893. 1967. Repr. of 1863 ed. 55.00 set (ISBN 0-8103-3044-X). Gale.
Irving, Washington. The Complete Works of Washington Irving -- the Sketch Book of Geoffrey Crayon, Gentleman. Springer, Haskell S., ed. (Critical Editions Ser.). 1978. lib. bdg. 25.00 (ISBN 0-8057-8510-8). Twayne.
--Complete Works of Washington Irving: Journals & Notebooks, Vol. 2, 1807-1822. Schlissel, Lillian & Reinhart, Walter A., eds. 1981. 32.00 (ISBN 0-8057-8501-9). Twayne.
--Letters from Sunnyside & Spain. Williams, S. T., ed. 1928. 13.50x (ISBN 0-685-89761-3). Elliots Bks.
--The Poems of Washington Irving. 19p. 1980. Repr. of 1931 ed. lib. bdg. 10.00 (ISBN 0-8492-1631-1). R West.
--Washington Irving: Representative Selections. Pochmann, Henry A., ed. 1971. 24.00 (ISBN 0-403-01039-X). Scholarly.

Johnston, Johanna. The Heart That Would Not Hold: A Biography of Washington Irving. LC 72-122821. 376p. 1971. 7.95 (ISBN 0-87131-057-0). M Evans.
Kime, Wayne R. Pierre M. Irving & Washington Irving: A Collaboration of Life & Letters. 362p. 1977. text ed. 11.00 (ISBN 0-88920-056-4, Pub. by Laurier U Pr Canada); pap. text ed. 8.25 (ISBN 0-88920-055-6). Humanities.
Kime, Wayne R., ed. Washington Irving Miscellaneous Writings, 1803-1859: The Complete Works of W. Irving, 2 vols. (Critical Editions Program). 1981. lib. bdg. 75.00 (ISBN 0-8057-8520-5). Twayne.
Langfeld, William R. Washington Irving. 90p. 1980. Repr. of 1933 ed. lib. bdg. 20.00 (ISBN 0-8495-3253-1). Arden Lib.
--Washington Irving, a Bibliography. LC 72-194090. 1933. lib. bdg. 7.25 (ISBN 0-8414-5711-5). Folcroft.
Myers, Andrew, ed. The Knickerbocker Tradition: Washington Irving's New York. LC 74-678. 160p. 1974. buckram bound 8.00 (ISBN 0-912882-08-5). Sleepy Hollow.
Myers, Andrew B. Worlds of Washington Irving. LC 74-76746. (Illus.). 1974. 8.95 (ISBN 0-87104-249-5, Co-Pub by Sleepy Hollow Rest.); pap. 5.50 (ISBN 0-87104-252-5). NY Pub Lib.
Myers, Andrew B., ed. Century of Commentary on the Works of Washington Irving, 1860-1974. LC 74-7843. (Illus.). 1976. 20.00 (ISBN 0-912882-28-X). Sleepy Hollow.
--Washington Irving: A Tribute. LC 77-189961. (Illus.). 86p. 1972. 3.95 (ISBN 0-912882-04-2); pap. 2.95 (ISBN 0-912882-05-0). Sleepy Hollow.
Payne, William M. Leading American Essayists: Biographies of Leading Americans. facs. ed. LC 68-26466. (Essay Index Reprint Ser). 1968. Repr. of 1910 ed. 23.00 (ISBN 0-8369-0778-7). Arno.
Putnam, George H. Washington Irving: His Life & Work. LC 78-10597. 1978. Repr. of 1903 ed. lib. bdg. 10.00 (ISBN 0-8414-6819-2). Folcroft.
Reichart, Walter A. Washington Irving & Germany. LC 72-6208. 212p. 1972. Repr. of 1957 ed. lib. bdg. 15.00x (ISBN 0-8371-6459-1, REWI). Greenwood.
Reichart, Walter A. & Schlissel, Lillian, eds. Washington Irving Journals & Notebooks, The Complete Works of W. Irving, 1807-122, Vol. 2. (Critical Editions Program Ser.). 1981. lib. bdg. 32.00 (ISBN 0-8057-8501-9). Twayne.
Roth, Martin. Comedy & America: The Lost World of Washington Irving. (Literary Criticism Ser.). 1976. 15.00 (ISBN 0-8046-9132-0, Natl U). Kennikat.
Springer, Haskell S., compiled by. Washington Irving: A Reference Guide. (Ser. Seventy). 1976. lib. bdg. 20.00 (ISBN 0-8161-1101-4). G K Hall.
Stoddard, Richard H. The Life of Washington Irving. LC 74-17482. 1974. lib. bdg. 12.50 (ISBN 0-8414-7816-3). Folcroft.
--The Works of Washington Irving, 3 vols. 1885. Repr. 85.00 set (ISBN 0-8274-3767-6). R West.
Terrell, Dahlia, ed. The Crayon Miscellany. (Critical Editions Program: The Complete Works of Washington Irving). 1979. 27.50 (ISBN 0-8057-8518-3). Twayne.
Van Doren, Carl. Tales by Washington Irving. 452p. 1980. Repr. of 1918 ed. lib. bdg. 25.00 (ISBN 0-89984-476-6). Century Bookbindery.
Warner, Charles D. Washington Irving. LC 80-23548. (American Men & Women of Letters Ser.). 310p. 1981. pap. 4.95 (ISBN 0-87754-153-1). Chelsea Hse.
--The Work of Washington Irving. LC 76-23148. 1893. lib. bdg. 10.00 (ISBN 0-8414-9427-4). Folcroft.
--The Work of Washington Irving. 1973. Repr. of 1893 ed. 10.00 (ISBN 0-8274-0692-4). R West.
Warner, Charles D., et al. Studies of Irving. LC 73-9634. 1974. Repr. of 1880 ed. lib. bdg. 25.00 (ISBN 0-8414-2848-4). Folcroft.
Widdemer, Mabel C. Washington Irving: Boy of Old New York. LC 62-16619. (Childhood of Famous Americans Ser.). (Illus.). (gr. 3-7). 1946. 3.95 (ISBN 0-672-50183-X). Bobbs.
Williams, S. T. Bibliography of Washington Irving. 1979. 36.50 (ISBN 0-685-94325-9). Porter.
Williams, Stanley T. Bibliography of the Writings of Washington Irving. LC 79-123513. (Bibliography & Reference Ser.: No. 344). 1970. Repr. of 1936 ed. lib. bdg. 22.50 (ISBN 0-8337-3802-X). B Franklin.
--A Bibliography of the Writings of Washington Irving. LC 72-194069. 1936. lib. bdg. 25.00 (ISBN 0-8414-9739-7). Folcroft.
--Life of Washington Irving, 2 Vols. LC 73-154672. 1971. Repr. of 1935 ed. lib. bdg. 60.00x (ISBN 0-374-98630-4). Octagon.

IRWIN, JAMES BENSON
Irwin, James B. & Emerson, William A., Jr. To Rule the Night: The Discovery Voyage of Astronaut Jim Irwin. (Illus.). 1973. 6.95 (ISBN 0-87981-024-6). Holman.
Irwin, James B., Jr. & Emerson, W. A. Un Astronauta y la Lumbrera De la Noche. Date not set. Repr. of 1978 ed. 3.95 (ISBN 0-311-01066-0). Casa Bautista.

ISAAC, THE PATRIARCH
Lindsay, Gordon. Isaac & Rebekah. (Old Testament Ser.). 1.25 (ISBN 0-89985-127-4). Christ Nations.
Nee, Watchman. Changed into His Likeness. 1969. 3.00 (ISBN 0-87508-411-7); pap. 2.50 (ISBN 0-87508-410-9). Chr Lit.
--Changed into His Likeness. 1978. pap. 1.95 (ISBN 0-8423-0228-X). Tyndale.
Speigel, Shalom. The Last Trial: On the Legend & Lore of the Command to Abraham to Offer Isaac As a Sacrifice - the Akedah. LC 79-12664. (The Jewish Legacy Ser.). 1979. pap. 5.95x (ISBN 0-87441-290-0). Behrman.
Stern, Chaim. Isaac: The Link in the Chain. 1977. text ed. 7.95 (ISBN 0-8315-0077-8). Speller.

ISABEL 1ST, LA CATOLICA, QUEEN OF SPAIN, 1451-1504
Fernandez-Armesto, Felipe. Ferdinand & Isabella. LC 73-14366. (Illus.). 232p. 1975. 15.00 (ISBN 0-8008-2621-3). Taplinger.
Isabel la Catolica. (Span.). 7.50 (ISBN 84-241-5417-7). E Torres & Sons.
Plunket, Ierne A. Isabel of Castille. LC 73-14464. (Illus.). Repr. of 1919 ed. 30.00 (ISBN 0-404-58282-6). AMS Pr.

ISABEL DE BRAGANCA, PRINCESS, 1846-1921
Comfort, Mildred H. Princess Isabel of Brazil. LC 68-57047. (American Background Bks). (Illus.). (gr. 5-9). 1969. 4.95 (ISBN 0-02-832120-0, 83212). Kenedy.

ISABELLA D'ESTE, CONSORT OF FRANCIS 2ND, MARQUIS DE MANTUA, 1474-1539
Ady, Julia M. Isabella D'Este, Marchioness of Mantua, 1474-1539, 2 Vols. LC 79-154139. Repr. of 1907 ed. Set. 49.50 (ISBN 0-404-09214-4). AMS Pr.
Cartwright, Julia. Isabella D'Este Marchioness of Mantua, 1474-1539, 2 vols. 1977. Repr. of 1903 ed. 50.00 set (ISBN 0-8274-4296-3). R West.
Verheyen, Egon. The Paintings in the "Studiolo" of Isabella d'Este at Mantua. LC 76-164021. (College Art Association Monographs: Vol. 23). (Illus.). 1971. 17.50x (ISBN 0-8147-8751-7). NYU Pr.

ISABELLA STEWART GARDNER MUSEUM, BOSTON
Hadley, Rollin V. The Isabella Stewart Gardner Museum. LC 81-50895. (Museums Discovered Ser.). (Illus.). 208p. 1981. 22.50 (ISBN 0-686-75685-1, Woodbine Bks); deluxe ed. 27.50 leather (ISBN 0-686-75686-X). Shorewood Fine Art.

ISAEUS, fl. 4TH CENTURY
Isaeus. The Speeches of Isaeus. Connor, W. R., ed. LC 78-18614. (Greek Texts & Commentaries Ser.). (Illus.). 1979. Repr. of 1904 ed. lib. bdg. 50.00x (ISBN 0-405-11453-2). Arno.
Wevers, Richard F. Isaeus: Chronology, Prosopography, & Social History. LC 68-57403. (Studies in Classical Literature). (Orig.). 1969. pap. text ed. 15.50x (ISBN 0-686-22438-8). Mouton.

ISAIAH, THE PROPHET
Alexander, Joseph A. Commentaries on the Prophecies of Isaiah. 10th ed. 1980. 19.95 (ISBN 0-310-20000-8, 6526). Zondervan.
Allis, Oswald T. The Unity of Isaiah: A Study in Prophecy. 1974. pap. 2.75 (ISBN 0-8010-0111-0). Baker Bk.
Driver, S. R. Isaiah: His Life & Times. 228p. 1981. Repr. lib. bdg. 20.00 (ISBN 0-89984-158-9). Century Bookbindery.
Heifner, Fred. Isaiah: Messenger of God. (gr. 1-6). 1978. 5.50 (ISBN 0-8054-4243-X). Broadman.
Isaiah: A New Translation. LC 78-188581. (Illus.). 192p. 1973. 12.50 (ISBN 0-686-73768-7); pap. 4.50 (ISBN 0-8276-0005-4, 151). Jewish Pubn.
Lindsay, Gordon. Isaiah & Jeremiah. (Old Testament Ser.). 1.25 (ISBN 0-89985-155-X). Christ Nations.
Siegel, Jonathan P. The Severus Scroll & 1Q1SA. LC 75-28372. (Society of Biblical Literature, Masoretic Studies). 1975. pap. 7.50 (ISBN 0-89130-028-7, 060502). Scholars Pr Ca.
Tassell, Paul. Contemporary Outlines from Isaiah. (Pocket Pulpit Library). 1979. pap. 1.65 (ISBN 0-8010-8805-4). Baker Bk.
Willis, John T. Isaiah. Jones, David G., ed. (Living Word Commentary - Old Testament Ser.). 465p. 1980. 14.95 (ISBN 0-8344-0115-0). Sweet.

ISAMURANG LANGUAGE
see Batan Language

ISCHEMIA, CEREBRAL
see Cerebral Ischemia

ISCHEMIC HEART DISEASE
see Coronary Heart Disease

ISENHEIM, GERMANY (ANTONITE MONASTERY)
Nochlin, Linda. Mathis at Colmar: A Visual Confrontation. LC 63-2298. (Illus., Orig.). 1963. 5.25 (ISBN 0-87376-002-6). Red Dust.

ISHERWOOD, BENJAMIN FRANKLIN, 1822-1915
Sloan, Edward W., III. Benjamin Franklin Isherwood, Naval Engineer. LC 79-6123. (Navies & Men Ser.). (Illus.). 1980. Repr. of 1965 ed. lib. bdg. 25.00x (ISBN 0-405-13077-5). Arno.

ISHERWOOD, CHRISTOPHER BRADSHAW-ISHERWOOD, 1904-
Finney, Brian. Christopher Isherwood: A Critical Biography. (Illus.). 1979. 14.95 (ISBN 0-19-520134-5). Oxford U Pr.
Funk, Robert W. Christopher Isherwood: A Reference Guide. (Reference Bks.). 1979. lib. bdg. 24.00 (ISBN 0-8161-8072-5). G K Hall.
Heilbrun, Carolyn. Christopher Isherwood. LC 73-126543. (Columbia Essays on Modern Writers). 48p. (Orig.). 1970. pap. 2.00 (ISBN 0-231-03257-9). Columbia U Pr.
Isherwood, Christopher. Christopher & His Kind. 1977. pap. 2.75 (ISBN 0-380-01795-4, 35394, Discus). Avon.
--My Guru & His Disciple. 352p. 1981. pap. 4.95 (ISBN 0-14-005837-0). Penguin.
Piazza, Paul. Christopher Isherwood: Myth & Anti-Myth. LC 77-14271. 1978. 15.00x (ISBN 0-231-04118-7). Columbia U Pr.
Spender, Stephen. Letters to Christopher: Stephen Spender's Letters to Christopher Isherwood 1929-1939, with "the Line of the Branch" - Two Thirties Journal. Bartlett, Lee, ed. (Illus.). 230p. (Orig.). 1980. 14.00 (ISBN 0-87685-470-6); pap. 7.50 (ISBN 0-87685-469-2). Black Sparrow.
Summers, Claude J. Christopher Isherwood. LC 80-5335. (Modern Literature Ser.). 192p. 1981. pap. 4.95 (ISBN 0-8044-6885-0). Ungar.
--Christopher Isherwood. LC 80-5335. (Modern Literature Ser.). 192p. 1980. 10.95 (ISBN 0-8044-2846-8). Ungar.

ISHI, d. 1916
Heizer, Robert F. & Kroeber, Theodora, eds. Ishi the Last Yahi: A Documentary History. LC 76-19966. (Illus.). 1979. 17.50 (ISBN 0-520-03296-9); pap. 6.95 (ISBN 0-520-04366-9). U of Cal Pr.
Kroeber, Theodora. Ishi in Two Worlds: A Biography of the Last Wild Indian in North America. LC 61-7530. (Illus.). 1961. 14.95 (ISBN 0-520-00674-7); pap. 3.95 (ISBN 0-520-00675-5, CAL94). U of Cal Pr.
--Ishi in Two Worlds: A Biography of the Last Wild Indian in North America. LC 75-36501. 1976. deluxe ed. 14.95 (ISBN 0-520-03152-0); pap. 8.95 (ISBN 0-520-03153-9). U of Cal Pr.
--Ishi, Last of His Tribe. LC 64-19401. (gr. 4 up). 1964. 7.95 (ISBN 0-87466-049-1). Parnassus.

ISHIHARA, KANJI, 1889-1949
Peattie, Mark. Ishiwara Kanji & Japan's Confrontation with the West. 420p. 1975. 30.00x (ISBN 0-691-03099-5). Princeton U Pr.

ISI-XOSA
see Xosa Language

ISIDORIUS, SAINT, BP. OF SEVILLE, d. 636
Brehaut, Ernest. Encyclopedist of the Dark Ages, Isidore of Seville. (Columbia University. Studies in History, Economics, & Public Law: Vol. 48, No. 1). 1967. Repr. of 1912 ed. 21.50 (ISBN 0-8337-0361-7). B Franklin.
Tilton, Rafeal. Isidore Finds Time to Care: A Story About Isidore. (Stories About Christian Heroes Ser.). (Illus.). 32p. (Orig.). (gr. 6-9). 1980. pap. 1.95 (ISBN 0-03-056877-3). Winston Pr.

ISIS
Brady, Thomas A. Sarapis & Isis: Collected Essays. Mitchel, Fordyce, ed. 1978. 25.00 (ISBN 0-89005-253-0). Ares.
Patricia. Osiris & Isis. (Illus.). 267p. (Orig.). 1980. pap. 7.95 (ISBN 0-935146-19-9). Morningland.
Solmsen, Friedrich. Isis Among the Greeks & Romans. LC 79-1149. (Martin Classical Lectures Ser). 1979. 12.50x (ISBN 0-674-46775-2). Harvard U Pr.
Witt, R. E. Isis in the Graeco-Roman World. LC 72-146278. (Aspects of Greek & Roman Life Ser). (Illus.). 1971. 27.50x (ISBN 0-8014-0633-1). Cornell U Pr.

ISLAM
see also Caliphate; Civilization, Islamic; Dervishes; Koran; Muslims;
also special headings with Islam added in parentheses; subdivision Islam under special topics, e.g. Marriage–Islam; headings beginning with the words Islamic and Muslim
Abdalati, Hammudah. The Family Structure in Islam. LC 77-79635. 1976. 10.95 (ISBN 0-89259-004-1). Am Trust Pubns.
--Islam in Focus. 2nd ed. LC 75-4382. (Illus.). 202p. 1975. pap. 5.00 (ISBN 0-89259-000-9). Am Trust Pubns.
Adams, Charles C. Islam & Modernism in Egypt: A Study of the Modern Reform Movement Inaugurated by Muhammed 'Abduh. LC 68-25061. 1968. Repr. of 1933 ed. 18.00 (ISBN 0-8462-1218-8). Russell.
Affifi, A. E. Mystical Philosophy of Muhyid Din Ibn-Ul-Arabi. 1964. 11.00x (ISBN 0-87902-035-0). Orientalia.
Ahmad, K. Islam & the West. pap. 2.00 (ISBN 0-686-18572-2). Kazi Pubns.
Ahmad, Khurshid, ed. Islam: Its Meaning & Message. 279p. 1980. 17.50 (ISBN 0-86037-002-X, Pub. by Islamic Council of Europe England); pap. 8.95x (ISBN 0-86037-000-3). Intl Schol Bk Serv.
Ahmed, K. Fanaticism, Intolerance & Islam. pap. 1.00 (ISBN 0-686-18491-2). Kazi Pubns.
--The Religion of Islam. pap. 0.95 (ISBN 0-686-18481-5). Kazi Pubns.
Ajijola, A. D. Essence of Faith in Islam. pap. 7.95 (ISBN 0-686-63898-0). Kazi Pubns.
AlFarugi, Isma'Il R. Islam. (Illus.). 1978. pap. 3.95 (ISBN 0-89505-022-6). Argus Comm.
Al-Ghazzali. The Book of Knowledge. 1970. 14.00x (ISBN 0-87902-106-3). Orientalia.
--Worship in Islam. Calverley, Edwin E., ed. LC 79-2860. 242p. 1981. Repr. of 1925 ed. 21.50 (ISBN 0-8305-0032-4). Hyperion Conn.
Al-Husaini, Ishak M. The Moslem Brethren: The Greatest of the Modern Islamic Movements. LC 79-2866. 186p. 1981. Repr. of 1956 ed. 18.00 (ISBN 0-8305-0039-1). Hyperion Conn.
Ali, Z. Glimpses of Islam. pap. 1.50 (ISBN 0-686-18475-0). Kazi Pubns.
Ali, Zaki. Islam in the World. LC 74-180314. (Mid-East Studies). Repr. of 1947 ed. 31.00 (ISBN 0-404-56209-4). AMS Pr.
Allama Sir Abdullah al-Mamun alsuhrawardy. The Sayings of Muhammad. LC 79-52559. (Islam Ser.). 1980. Repr. of 1941 ed. lib. bdg. 12.00x (ISBN 0-8369-9266-0). Arno.
Ansari, F. R. Islam & the Western Civilization. pap. 1.00 (ISBN 0-686-18533-1). Kazi Pubns.
--Philosophy of Worship in Islam. pap. 0.75 (ISBN 0-686-18603-6). Kazi Pubns.
--Through Science & Philosophy to Islam. pap. 0.95 (ISBN 0-686-18536-6). Kazi Pubns.
--What Is Islam? pap. 0.95 (ISBN 0-686-18478-5). Kazi Pubns.
Ansari, Z. I. Bilal: The First Muezzin of Islam. pap. 0.70 (ISBN 0-686-18326-6). Kazi Pubns.
Arberry, Arthur J. Revelation and Reason in Islam. LC 80-1936. Repr. of 1957 ed. 20.00 (ISBN 0-404-18952-0). AMS Pr.
Arnold, E. Pearls of the Faith: Islam's Rosary. pap. 3.25x (ISBN 0-87902-044-X). Orientalia.
Arnold, T. Preaching of Islam. 1968. 10.75x (ISBN 0-87902-045-8). Orientalia.
Arnold, T. W. Preaching of Islam. 7.95 (ISBN 0-686-18455-6). Kazi Pubns.
Arnold, T. W. & Guillaume, A. The Legacy of Islam. 1976. lib. bdg. 75.00 (ISBN 0-8490-2141-3). Gordon Pr.
Ashraf. Lessons in Islams, 5. 3.95 (ISBN 0-686-18391-6). Kazi Pubns.
Audah, A. Q. Islam Between Ignorant Followers & Incapable Scholars. pap. 2.25 (ISBN 0-686-18505-6). Kazi Pubns.
Avicenna. Avicenna on Theology. Arberry, Arthur J., tr. LC 78-59000. 1979. Repr. of 1951 ed. 11.00 (ISBN 0-88355-676-6). Hyperion Conn.
Ayoub, Mahmoud. Redemptive Suffering in Islam. (Religion & Society Ser.: No. 10). 1978. 35.75 (ISBN 90-279-7948-0). Mouton.
Badri, M. B. Islam & Alcoholism. LC 76-42173. 1976. 1.95 (ISBN 0-89259-005-X). Am Trust Pubns.
Baillie, N. B. Digest of Moohammudan Law, 2 Vols. 1965. 27.00x (ISBN 0-87902-048-2). Orientalia.
Bawa Muhaiyaddeen, M. R. The Asma'ul-Husna: The 99 Beautiful Names of Allah. (Illus.). 211p. 1979. pap. 4.95 (ISBN 0-914390-13-9). Fellowship Pr PA.
Bell, Joseph N. Love Theory in Later Hanbalite Islam. LC 78-5904. 1979. PLB 39.00 (ISBN 0-87395-244-8). State U NY Pr.
Blunt, W. S. The Future of Islam. 4.95 (ISBN 0-686-18484-X). Kazi Pubns.
Blyden, Edward. Christianity, Islam, & the Negro. Fyfe, C., ed. 1967. 24.50x (ISBN 0-85224-085-6, Pub. by Edinburgh U Pr Scotland). Columbia U Pr.
Broomhall, Marshall. Islam in China: A Neglected Problem. 1980. lib. bdg. 75.00 (ISBN 0-8490-3137-0). Gordon Pr.
Brown, Marguerite. Magnificent Muslims. 1981. 6.00 (ISBN 0-911026-10-X). New World Press NY.
Bukhsh, S. K. Islamic Studies. 5.95 (ISBN 0-686-18357-6). Kazi Pubns.
Carra de Vaux, Bernard. Les Penseurs de l'Islam, 5 vols. LC 80-2197. Repr. of 1926 ed. Set. 200.00 (ISBN 0-404-18990-3). AMS Pr.
Chattopadhya, A. Why Have I Accepted Islam? pap. 1.75 (ISBN 0-686-18476-9). Kazi Pubns.

Christopher, John B. The Islamic Tradition. (Major Traditions in World Civilization Ser.). 1972. pap. text ed. 8.50 scp (ISBN 0-06-041283-6, HarpC). Har-Row.
Corlett, William & Moore, John. Questions of Human Existence As Answered by Major World Religions: The Islamic Space. LC 79-15204. 1980. 8.95 (ISBN 0-87888-154-9). Bradbury Pr.
Cragg. House of Islam. 2nd ed. LC 74-83949. 1975. pap. 4.95 (ISBN 0-686-66335-7). Duxbury Pr.
Cragg, Kenneth. Councils in Contemporary Islam. 1965. 15.00x (ISBN 0-85224-087-2, Pub. by Edinburgh U Pr Scotland). Columbia U Pr.
--The House of Islam. 2nd ed. (Religious Life of Man Ser). 1975. pap. text ed. 8.95x (ISBN 0-8221-0139-4). Dickenson.
Cragg, Kenneth & Speight, R. Marston. Islam from Within: Anthology of a Religion. LC 78-24004. (The Religious Life of Man Ser.). (Illus.). 1980. pap. 6.95 (ISBN 0-87872-212-2). Duxbury Pr.
Dale, Stephen F. Islamic Society on the South Asian Frontier: The Mappilas of Malabar, 1498 - 1922. (Illus.). 352p. 1981. 49.00x (ISBN 0-19-821571-1). Oxford U Pr.
Diamond, Michael J. & Gowing, Peter G. Islam & Muslims: Some Basic Information. 100p. 1981. pap. write for info. (ISBN 0-686-30367-9, Pub. by New Day Philippines). Cellar.
Doi, A. R. Introducing Islam. pap. 4.95 (ISBN 0-686-63902-2). Kazi Pubns.
Donaldson, Dwight M. The Shi'ite Religion: A History of Islam in Persia & Irak. LC 80-1933. 45.00 (ISBN 0-404-18959-8). AMS Pr.
Doray, S. J. Gateway to Islam, 4. pap. 4.95 (ISBN 0-686-18395-9). Kazi Pubns.
Dorman, Harry G. Toward Understanding Islam: Contemporary Apologetic of Islam & Missionary Policy. LC 79-176727. (Columbia University. Teachers College. Contributions to Education: No. 940). Repr. of 1948 ed. 17.50 (ISBN 0-404-55940-9). AMS Pr.
Edmonds, I. G. Islam. LC 77-2664. (First Bks.). (gr. 5-8). 1977. PLB 7.40 s&l (ISBN 0-531-01288-3). Watts.
Eickelman, Dale F. Moroccan Islam: Tradition & Society in a Pilgrimage Center. (Modern Middle East Ser.: No. 1). 322p. 1981. pap. text ed. 8.95x (ISBN 0-292-75062-5). U of Tex Pr.
Eliot, Charles. Turkey in Europe. 459p. 1965. 30.00x (ISBN 0-7146-1970-1, F Cass Co). Biblio Dist.
Esin, Emel. Mecca the Blessed, Madinah the Radiant. 1963. 21.95 (ISBN 0-236-31090-9, Pub. by Paul Elek). Merrimack Bk Serv.
Ewert, Christian. Islamische Funde in Balaguer und die Aljaferia in Zaragoza. (Madrider Forschungen, Vol. 7). (Illus.). 281p. 1971. 150.00x (ISBN 3-11-003613-4). De Gruyter.
Farah, Caesar E. Islam--Beliefs & Observances. 3rd ed. 306p. (gr. 11-12). 1982. pap. text ed. 3.95 (ISBN 0-8120-2358-7). Barron.
--Islam: Beliefs & Observances. rev. ed. LC 72-135505. (Orig.). (YA) 1970. text ed. op (ISBN 0-8120-6022-9); pap. 3.95 (ISBN 0-8120-0277-6). Barron.
Farid, A. H. Prayers of Muhammad. 1969. 10.25x (ISBN 0-87902-050-4). Orientalia.
Ferber, Stanley, ed. Islam & the Medieval West. (Illus.). 1975. pap. 22.00 (ISBN 0-87395-802-0). State U NY Pr.
Fry, George C. & King, James R. Islam: A Survey of the Muslim Faith. (Illus.). 204p. (Orig.). 1980. pap. 5.95 (ISBN 0-8010-3497-3). Baker Bk.
Gauhar, Altaf, ed. The Challenge of Islam. 393p. 1980. 35.00x (ISBN 0-906041-02-3, Pub. by Islamic Council of Europe England); pap. 14.95x (ISBN 0-906041-03-1). Intl Schol Bk Serv.
Ghazzali, Al. Mysteries of Worship in Islam: The Book of the Ihya' on Worship Translated with Commentary & Introduction. Calverley, E. E., tr. pap. 10.00 (ISBN 0-87902-200-0). Orientalia.
Gibb, H. A. Modern Trends in Islam. LC 76-159188. xiii, 141p. 1971. Repr. of 1947 ed. lib. bdg. 16.00x (ISBN 0-374-93046-5). Octagon.
Gibb, H. A. & Kramers, J. H., eds. Shorter Encyclopedia of Islam. (Illus.). 1957. 65.00x (ISBN 0-8014-0150-X). Cornell U Pr.
Gibb, Hamilton A., ed. Whither Islam? A Survey of Modern Movements in the Moslem World. LC 73-180338. Repr. of 1932 ed. 27.00 (ISBN 0-404-56263-9). AMS Pr.
Grunebaum, Gustave E., ed. Mediaeval Islam: A Study in Cultural Orientation. 2nd ed. 1961. pap. 5.95 (ISBN 0-226-31025-6, p69, Phoen). U of Chicago Pr.
Guillaume, Alfred. Islam. 1954. pap. 3.50 (ISBN 0-14-020311-7, Pelican). Penguin.
Hakim, K. A. Islam & Communism. pap. 5.50 (ISBN 0-686-18576-5). Kazi Pubns.
--Islamic Ideology. 6.95 (ISBN 0-686-18571-4). Kazi Pubns.
Hameed, Hakeem A., ed. Islam at a Glance. 125p. 1981. text ed. 15.00x (ISBN 0-7069-1313-2, Pub. by Vikas India). Advent NY.
Hameedullah. Introduction to Islam. pap. 4.95 (ISBN 0-686-18488-2). Kazi Pubns.
Hameedullah, M. Islam, a General Picture. pap. 4.00 (ISBN 0-686-63903-0). Kazi Pubns.
Hameedullah, Muhammad. Introduction to Islam. 276p. (Orig.). 1977. pap. 5.00x (ISBN 0-939830-13-2, Pub. by IIFSO Kuwait). New Era Pubns MI.
Hashim, A. S. Eleven Surahs Explained. (Islamics Books for Children: Bk. 3). pap. 3.50 (ISBN 0-686-18412-2); pap. 30.00 entire ser. (ISBN 0-686-18413-0). Kazi Pubns.
--Ibadat. (Islamic Books for Children: Bk. 2). pap. 3.95 (ISBN 0-686-18414-9); pap. 30.00 entire ser. (ISBN 0-686-18415-7). Kazi Pubns.
Hashim, S. S. Iman, Basic Beliefs. (Islamic Books for Children: Bk. 1). pap. 3.50 (ISBN 0-686-18416-5); pap. 30.00 entire ser. (ISBN 0-686-18417-3). Kazi Pubns.
Heikal, Mohamed. The Road to Ramadan: The Inside Story of How the Arabs Prepared for & Almost Won the October 1973 War. LC 75-8287. (Illus.). 288p. 1975. 8.95 (ISBN 0-8129-0567-9). Times Bks.
Hitti, Philip K. Islam: A Way of Life. LC 78-104054. 1971. pap. 4.45 (ISBN 0-89526-992-9). Regnery-Gateway.
Hourani, George F., ed. Essays on Islamic Philosophy & Science. LC 74-13493. 1974. 35.00 (ISBN 0-87395-224-3). State U Ny Pr.
Hughes, Thomas P. Dictionary of Islam. (Illus.). 750p. 1977. Repr. of 1885 ed. 39.00 (ISBN 0-89684-103-0, Pub. by Cosmo Pubns India). Orient Bk Dist.
--A Dictionary of Islam, 2 vols. 1980. Set. lib. bdg. 199.95 (ISBN 0-8490-3121-4). Gordon Pr.
--Dictionary of Islam. LC 71-14622. (Illus.). 1976. Repr. of 1885 ed. 30.00x (ISBN 0-8002-0207-4). Intl Pubns Serv.
--A Dictionary of Islam. 1976. Repr. 35.00x (ISBN 0-8364-0395-9). South Asia Bks.
--A Dictionary of Islam: A Cyclopedia of the Muhammadan Religion. (Reprints in History). (Illus.). lib. bdg. 35.00x (ISBN 0-697-00053-2); pap. 12.50x (ISBN 0-89197-728-7). Irvington.
--Dictionary of Islam: Being a Cyclopaedia of the Doctrines, Rites, Ceremonies, & Customs, Together with the Technical & Theological Terms, of the Muhannadan Religion. (Illus.). 1977. Repr. of 1885 ed. text ed. 25.00x (ISBN 0-391-01066-2). Humanities.
--Notes on Muhammadanism: Being Outlines of the Religious System of Islam. LC 74-83164. (Islam & MidEast Ser). 1976. Repr. of 1877 ed. 25.00 (ISBN 0-8420-1756-9). Scholarly Res Inc.
Humayun, Kabir. Science, Democracy, and Islam: And Other Essays. LC 80-2195. Repr. of 1955 ed. 20.00 (ISBN 0-404-18967-9). AMS Pr.
Hurgronje, Christian S. Mohammedanism: Lectures in Its Origin, Its Religious & Political Growth, & Its Present State. LC 79-2865. 184p. 1980. Repr. of 1916 ed. 16.00 (ISBN 0-8305-0038-3). Hyperion Conn.
Iqbal, A. Diplomacy in Islam. 5.50 (ISBN 0-686-18588-9). Kazi Pubns.
Iqbal, Afzal. The Prophet's Diplomacy: The Art of Negotiation As Conceived & Developed by the Prophet of Islam. rev. ed. LC 74-20174. (God Ser.: No. 801). 164p. 1975. 8.00 (ISBN 0-89007-006-7). C Stark.
Iqbal, M. The Reconstruction of Religious Thoughts in Islam. 4.95 (ISBN 0-686-18482-3). Kazi Pubns.
Islam Series. 1980. Set. lib. bdg. 229.00x (ISBN 0-8369-9259-8). Arno.
Izutsu, Toshihiko. The Concept of Belief in Islamic Theology. LC 79-52553. (Islam Ser.). 1980. Repr. of 1965 ed. lib. bdg. 20.00x (ISBN 0-8369-9261-X). Arno.
Jameelah, M. Islam & Modernism. pap. 5.50 (ISBN 0-686-18574-9). Kazi Pubns.
--Islam & Orientalism. pap. 1.50 (ISBN 0-686-18573-0). Kazi Pubns.
--Islam in Theory & Practice. pap. 6.50 (ISBN 0-686-18501-3). Kazi Pubns.
--Islam vs Ahl-al-Kitab, Past & Present. pap. 6.95 (ISBN 0-686-18570-6). Kazi Pubns.
--Islam vs the West. pap. 1.50 (ISBN 0-686-18568-4). Kazi Pubns.
Jang, A. Notes on Islam. pap. 1.25 (ISBN 0-686-18487-4). Kazi Pubns.
Jansen, Godfrey. Militant Islam. LC 79-2623. 1980. 8.95 (ISBN 0-06-012202-1, HarpT). Har-Row.
--Militant Islam. LC 79-2623. 1980. pap. 3.95 (ISBN 0-06-090759-2, CN 759, CN). Har-Row.
Jeffery, Arthur, ed. A Reader on Islam. LC 79-52557. (Islam Ser.). 1980. Repr. of 1962 ed. lib. bdg. 50.00x (ISBN 0-8369-9264-4). Arno.
Jeffrey, Arthur, ed. Islam: Muhammad & His Religion. LC 58-9958. 1958. pap. 5.75 (ISBN 0-672-60348-9, LLA137). Bobbs.
Kamal, A. A. Everyday Fiqh, 2 vols. Set. pap. 12.50 (ISBN 0-686-63899-9). Kazi Pubns.
Keddie, Nikki R., ed. Scholars, Saints & Sufis: Muslim Religious Institutions Since 1500. LC 77-153546. (Near Eastern Center, UCLA). 350p. 1972. pap. 8.95x (ISBN 0-520-03644-1). U of Cal Pr.
Kedourie, Elie. Afghani & Abduh: Essay on Religious Unbelief & Political Activism in Modern Islam. 97p. 1966. 24.00x (ISBN 0-7146-1989-2, F Cass Co). Biblio Dist.
--Islam in the Modern World. 336p. 1981. 16.95 (ISBN 0-686-69288-8). HR&W.
Khan, M. Y. God, Soul & Universe in Science & Islam. 1969. 3.25 (ISBN 0-87902-170-5). Orientalia.
Kritzeck, James, ed. The World of Islam. LC 79-52558. (Islam Ser.). (Illus.). 1980. Repr. of 1959 ed. lib. bdg. 32.00x (ISBN 0-8369-9265-2). Arno.
Kyani, A. S. Islam & Muslims in Red Regimes. pap. 3.50 (ISBN 0-686-18575-7). Kazi Pubns.
Lalljee, Yousuf N. Know Your Islam. LC 81-51707. 256p. 1981. pap. 2.50 (ISBN 0-940368-02-1). Tahrike Tarsile Quran.
Lammens, H. Islam Beliefs & Institutions. Ross, Ed, tr. 1969. Repr. of 1929 ed. 26.50x (ISBN 0-7146-1991-4, F Cass Co). Biblio Dist.
Lammens, Henri. Islam: Beliefs & Institutions. 1976. lib. bdg. 59.95 (ISBN 0-8490-2080-8). Gordon Pr.
Le Tourneau, Roger. L' Islam Contemporain. LC 80-1922. Repr. of 1950 ed. write for info. (ISBN 0-404-18975-X). AMS Pr.
Lewis, B., et al, eds. Encyclopedia of Islam, 5 vols. Incl. Vol. 1. A-B: Fasc. 1-22. Gibb, H. A., et al, eds. 1960. text ed. 185.25x (ISBN 90-040-0530-7); Vol. 2. C-G: Fasc. 23-40. Lewis, B., et al, eds. 1965. 178.75x (ISBN 90-040-0531-5); Vol. 3. H-Iram: Fasc. 41-60. 1969. text ed. 225.75x (ISBN 90-040-3275-4); Vols. 4 & 5. I-Ram &K-Ha: Fasc. 61-78. 1978. text ed. 275.00 (ISBN 0-685-23323-5). Humanities.
Lewis, Bernard. Race & Color in Islam. 1980. Repr. lib. bdg. 11.00x (ISBN 0-374-94974-3). Octagon.
Lichenstadter, Ilse. Islam & the Modern Age. 10.95 (ISBN 0-685-60132-3, Pub by Twayne). Cyrco Pr.
Lichtenstadter, Ilse. Islam & the Modern Age. 228p. 1958. text ed. 24.00x (ISBN 0-8290-0179-4). Irvington.
Macdonald, Duncan B. Aspects of Islam. facsimile ed. LC 77-179530. (Select Bibliographies Reprint Ser). Repr. of 1911 ed. 23.00 (ISBN 0-8369-6659-7). Arno.
--Development of Muslim Theology, Jurisprudence, & Constitutional Theory. LC 65-18818. 1965. Repr. of 1903 ed. 9.00 (ISBN 0-8462-0647-1). Russell.
--Religious Attitude & Life in Islam. LC 70-121277. Repr. of 1909 ed. 20.50 (ISBN 0-404-04125-6). AMS Pr.
MacDonald Presentation Volume: A Tribute to Duncan Black Macdonald, Consisting of Articles by Former Students, Presented to Him on His Seventieth Birthday, April 9, 1933. facs. ed. LC 68-22109. (Essay Index Reprint Ser). 1933. 18.75 (ISBN 0-8369-0645-4). Arno.
McNeill, William H. & Waldman, Marilyn, eds. The Islamic World. (Readings in World History Ser). 1973. pap. 6.95x (ISBN 0-19-501571-1). Oxford U Pr.
Margoliouth, David S. Mohammed & the Rise of Islam. LC 73-14455. Repr. of 1905 ed. 30.00 (ISBN 0-404-58273-7). AMS Pr.
Martin, Richard C. Islam: A Cultural Perspective. (Illus.). 192p. 1982. pap. text ed. 7.95 (ISBN 0-13-506345-0). P-H.
Massey, Kundan. Tide of the Supernatural: A Call to Love for the Muslim World. Baker, Barbara, ed. 184p. (Orig.). 1980. pap. 4.95 (ISBN 0-918956-70-6). Campus Crusade.
Ma Sung-T'ing. Islam: A Special Issue of "Yu Kung". (National Peking University & Chinese Assn. for Folklore, Folklore & Folkliterature Ser.: No. 104). (Chinese.). 6.00 (ISBN 0-89986-182-2). E Langstaff.
Maududi, A. A. Fundamentals of Islam. 4.95 (ISBN 0-686-18489-0). Kazi Pubns.
--Political Theory of Islam. pap. 1.00 (ISBN 0-686-18547-1). Kazi Pubns.
--The Religion of Truth. pap. 0.95 (ISBN 0-686-18537-4). Kazi Pubns.
--Towards Understanding Islam. pap. 3.00 (ISBN 0-686-18479-3). Kazi Pubns.
Maududi, S. A. Towards Understanding Islam. 3.85x (ISBN 0-87902-065-2). Orientalia.
Maulana-Muhammad-Ali. Religion of Islam. 1978. 37.50x (ISBN 0-8002-1916-3). Intl Pubns Serv.
Mawdudi, Sayyid A. Towards Understanding Islam. Ahmad, Khurshid, tr. from Urdu. 179p. (Orig.). 1980. pap. 3.50x (ISBN 0-939830-22-1, Pub. by IIFSO Kuwait). New Era Pubns MI.
Mez, Adam. The Renaissance of Islam. Bukhsl, Salahuddin K & Margoliovth, D. S., trs. LC 70-180361. Repr. of 1937 ed. 27.00 (ISBN 0-404-56293-0). AMS Pr.
Minai, Naila. Women in Islam. LC 80-52405. 320p. 1981. 11.95 (ISBN 0-87223-666-8). Seaview Bks.
Moses Ben Maimon. Epistle to Yemen. 1952. 12.00 (ISBN 0-527-65400-0). Kraus Repr.
Muhajir, A. M. Islam in Practical Life. 1968. 6.50x (ISBN 0-87902-067-9). Orientalia.
--Tenets of Islam. 1969. 6.50x (ISBN 0-87902-107-1). Orientalia.
Muhajir, M. R. Islam in Practical Life. 5.50 (ISBN 0-686-18502-1). Kazi Pubns.
Muradpuri, M. A. Conflict Between Socialism & Islam. pap. 3.00 (ISBN 0-686-18579-X). Kazi Pubns.
Nadui, A. H. A. Islam: The Perfect Religion & a Way of Life. pap. 1.00 (ISBN 0-686-18498-X). Kazi Pubns.
Nadvi. An Easy History of the Prophet of Islam. pap. 3.00 (ISBN 0-686-18309-6). Kazi Pubns.
--Saviors of Islamic Spirit: Vol. I, II. 16.95 (ISBN 0-686-18312-6). Kazi Pubns.
Nadvi, A. Islam: The Only Way. pap. 0.75 (ISBN 0-686-18499-8). Kazi Pubns.
Nadvi, A. H. Four Pillars of Islam. 7.50 (ISBN 0-686-18597-8). Kazi Pubns.
--Islam & the World. 5.95 (ISBN 0-686-18625-7). Kazi Pubns.
--Religion & Civilization. 2.95 (ISBN 0-686-18566-8). Kazi Pubns.
Nasr, Seyyed H. Ideals & Realities of Islam. 192p. 1972. pap. 4.95x (ISBN 0-8070-1131-2, BP439). Beacon Pr.
--Islam & the Plight of Modern Man. LC 75-29014. (World of Islam Ser.). 1976. text ed. 24.00x (ISBN 0-582-78053-5). Longman.
Naumani, M. Islamic Faith & Practice. 6.75 (ISBN 0-686-18497-1). Kazi Pubns.
--What Islam Is? 3.95 (ISBN 0-686-18477-7). Kazi Pubns.
Obermann, Julian, ed. Nissim ben Jacob ben Nissim Ibn Shahin (Studies in Islam & Judaism) The Arabic Original of Ibn Shabin's Book of Comfort. LC 78-63561. (Yale Oriental Ser. Researches: No. 17). Repr. of 1933 ed. 72.50 (ISBN 0-404-60287-8). AMS Pr.
O'Dea, Thomas F., et al. Religion & Man: Judiasm, Christianity & Islam. 1972. pap. text ed. 10.95 scp (ISBN 0-06-044893-8, HarpC). Har-Row.
O'Leary, De Lacy. Islam at the Cross Roads: A Brief Survey of the Present Position and Problems of the World of Islam. LC 80-1916. 1981. Repr. of 1923 ed. 26.50 (ISBN 0-404-18983-0). AMS Pr.
Oster, Kenneth. Islam Reconsidered: A Brief Historical Background to the Religion & Thought of the Moslem World. 1979. 7.50 (ISBN 0-682-49189-6, University). Exposition.
Palacios, Miguel A. Islam & the Divine Comedy. 295p. 1968. Repr. of 1926 ed. 28.50x (ISBN 0-7146-1995-7, F Cass Co). Biblio Dist.
Parshall, Phil. New Paths in Muslim Evangelism: Evangelical Approaches to Contextualization. 200p. (Orig.). 1980. pap. 6.95 (ISBN 0-8010-7056-2). Baker Bk.
Peacock, James L. Muslim Puritans: Reformist Psychology in Southeast Asian Islam. LC 76-55571. 1978. 24.00x (ISBN 0-520-03403-1). U of Cal Pr.
Peters, Rudilph. Islam & Colonialism. (Religion & Society Ser.). 1980. text ed. 37.50x (ISBN 90-279-3347-2). Mouton.
Planhol, Xavier De. World of Islam. 142p. 1959. pap. 6.95x (ISBN 0-8014-9830-9). Cornell U Pr.
Qaderi, M. Taleem-Ul-Islam, 4. pap. 3.50 (ISBN 0-686-18387-8). Kazi Pubns.
Qazi, M. A. Bilal: The First Muadhdhin of the Prophet of Islam. pap. 3.00 (ISBN 0-686-18325-8). Kazi Pubns.
Quasem, M. A. Al-Ghazali on Islamic Guidance. 124p. 1980. 9.95x (ISBN 0-89955-208-0, Pub. by M A Quasem Malaysia); pap. 6.95x (ISBN 0-89955-209-9). Intl Schol Bk Serv.
Qutb, M. Islam: The Misunderstood Religion. pap. 3.95 (ISBN 0-686-18500-5). Kazi Pubns.
Qutb, S. This Religion of Islam. pap. 1.50 (ISBN 0-686-18480-7). Kazi Pubns.
Qutb, Sayyed. Islam & Universal Peace. LC 77-89635. 1977. 2.75 (ISBN 0-89259-007-6). Am Trust Pubns.
Qutb, Sayyid. Al-Mustaqbal li-hadha ad-Din. 118p. (Orig., Arabic.). 1978. pap. 2.35x (ISBN 0-939830-16-7, Pub. by IIFSO Kuwait). New Era Pubns MI.
--Hadha ad-Din. 96p. (Orig., Arabic.). 1978. pap. 1.75x (ISBN 0-939830-18-3, Pub. by IIFSO Kuwait). New Era Pubns MI.
--Islam, the Religion of the Future. 127p. (Orig.). 1978. pap. 2.55x (ISBN 0-939830-06-X, Pub. by IIFSO Kuwait). New Era Pubns MI.
--Ma alim fi at-Tariq. 186p. (Orig., Arabic.). 1978. pap. 3.75x (ISBN 0-939830-17-5, Pub. by IIFSO Kuwait). New Era Pubns MI.
--Milestones. 303p. (Orig.). 1978. pap. 5.95x (ISBN 0-939830-07-8, Pub. by IIFSO Kuwait). New Era Pubns MI.
--This Religion of Islam. 104p. (Orig.). 1977. pap. 2.25x (ISBN 0-939830-08-6, Pub. by IIFSO Kuwait). New Era Pubns MI.

Rahman, A. Essentials of Islam. pap. 4.95 (ISBN 0-686-67786-2). Kazi Pubns.

Ramadhan, S. Islam & Nationalism. pap. 1.00 (ISBN 0-686-18586-2). Kazi Pubns.

Rauf, Abdul. Bilal Ibn Rabah. LC 76-49691. 1977. pap. 2.75 (ISBN 0-89259-008-4). Am Trust Pubns.

Rauf, M. A. Islamic Religious Knowledge, 3 vols. 7.50 (ISBN 0-686-18392-4). Kazi Pubns.

Rizwani, S. Islamic Manifesto. pap. 1.25 (ISBN 0-686-18495-5). Kazi Pubns.

Robson, J., tr. Mishkat Al-Masabih, 2 vols. Set. 52.00x (ISBN 0-87902-068-7); Vol. 1. 28.00x (ISBN 0-87902-297-3); Vol. 2. 26.00x (ISBN 0-87902-298-1). Orientalia.

Rosenthal, Erwin I. Studia Semitica, 2 vols. Incl. Vol. 1. Jewish Themes. 57.00 (ISBN 0-521-07958-6); Vol. 2. Islamic Themes. 45.00 (ISBN 0-521-07959-4). (Oriental Publications Ser.: Nos. 16 & 17). Cambridge U Pr.

Sachedina, Abdulaziz A. Islamic Messianism: The Idea of Mahdi in Twelver Shi'ism. LC 80-16767. 1980. text ed. 34.00x (ISBN 0-87395-442-4); pap. text ed. 14.95x (ISBN 0-686-63007-6). State U NY Pr.

Said, Edward W. Covering Islam: How the Media & the Experts Determine How We See the Rest of the World. 192p. 1981. 8.95 (ISBN 0-394-50923-4); pap. 3.95 (ISBN 0-394-74808-5). Pantheon.

Sanderson, Richard N. The Islamic Movement & the Threat to Western Civilization. (Illus.). 141p. 1980. deluxe ed. 57.45 (ISBN 0-930008-59-6). Inst Econ Pol.

Sayili, Aydin. The Observatory in Islam. Cohen, I. Bernard, ed. LC 80-2144. (Development of Science Ser.). (Illus.). 1981. lib. bdg. 45.00x (ISBN 0-405-13951-9). Arno.

Schacht, Joseph & Bosworth, C. E., eds. The Legacy of Islam. 2nd ed. (Legacy Ser). (Illus.). 583p. 1974. text ed. 33.00x (ISBN 0-19-821913-X). Oxford U Pr.

Schaefer, Udo. The Light Shineth in Darkness: Five Studies in Revelation After Christ. Neri, Helene M. & Coburn, Oliver, trs. LC 78-320332. 1977. pap. 4.95 (ISBN 0-85398-072-1, 332-028-10, Pub. by G Ronald England). Baha'i.

Schimmel, Annemarie. Islamic Calligraphy. (Illus.). 1970. 30.00 (ISBN 0-685-00757-X). Adler.

Schuon, Frithjot. Understanding Islam. Matheson, D. M., tr. (Unwin Paperback Ser.). 1976. pap. 5.25 (ISBN 0-04-297035-0). Allen Unwin.

Sell, Charles E. The Faith of Islam. LC 74-83171. (Islam & Mideast Ser.). 1976. Repr. of 1920 ed. 26.00 (ISBN 0-8420-1763-1). Scholarly Res Inc.

Servier, Andre. Islam & the Psychology of the Musulman. 1977. lib. bdg. 59.95 (ISBN 0-8490-2079-4). Gordon Pr.

Shad, A. R. Primer of Islam, Vol. 1. 2.00 (ISBN 0-686-63909-X). Kazi Pubns.

Shari'ati, Ali. On the Sociology of Islam. 3rd ed. Algar, Hamid, tr. from Persian. LC 79-83552. 1980. 9.45 (ISBN 0-933782-01-2); pap. 4.95 (ISBN 0-933782-00-4). Mizan Pr.

Siddiqui, A. A. Elementary Teachings of Islam. pap. 1.50 (ISBN 0-686-18397-5). Kazi Pubns.

Siddiqui, A. H. Islam & the Remaking of Humanity. pap. 9.95 (ISBN 0-686-63904-9). Kazi Pubns.

--What Islam Gave to Humanity? pap. 1.50 (ISBN 0-686-63918-9). Kazi Pubns.

Siddiqui, M. A. A. Principle of Islam. pap. 0.75 (ISBN 0-686-18486-6). Kazi Pubns.

Siddiqui, M. M. Women in Islam. 1969. 4.25x (ISBN 0-87902-069-5). Orientalia.

Siddiqui, M. S. Call to Islam. pap. 1.75 (ISBN 0-686-63897-2). Kazi Pubns.

Smith, Wilfred C. Islam in Modern History. 1957. 22.50x (ISBN 0-691-03030-8); pap. 6.95 (ISBN 0-691-01991-6). Princeton U Pr.

Subhan, S. A. Islam: Its Belief & Practices. 1938. 4.75x (ISBN 0-87902-190-X). Orientalia.

Swartz, Merlin L., et al. Studies on Islam. 298p. 1981. 17.50x (ISBN 0-19-502716-7); pap. 7.95x (ISBN 0-19-502717-5). Oxford U Pr.

Tabbarah, A. The Spirit of Islam. 20.00x (ISBN 0-86685-029-5). Intl Bk Ctr.

Taylor, John B. The World of Islam. (Orig.). 1979. pap. 3.95 (ISBN 0-377-00086-8). Friend Pr.

Tenets of Islam. 4.95 (ISBN 0-686-18485-8). Kazi Pubns.

Trimingham, J. Spencer. Sufi Orders in Islam. 1971. 36.00x (ISBN 0-19-826524-7). Oxford U Pr.

--The Sufi Orders in Islam. 344p. 1973. pap. 4.95 (ISBN 0-19-501662-9, GB). Oxford U Pr.

Tritton, Arthur S. Islam. LC 79-52566. (Islam Ser.). 1980. Repr. of 1951 ed. lib. bdg. 16.00x (ISBN 0-8369-9269-5). Arno.

--Islam: Belief & Practices. LC 79-2883. 200p. 1981. Repr. of 1954 ed. 18.00 (ISBN 0-8305-0051-0). Hyperion Conn.

Von Grunebaum, G. E. Muhammaden Festivals: Typical Elements of Islamic Ritual, Prayer & Pilgrimage. new ed. (Illus.). 1976. text ed. 7.50x (ISBN 0-7007-0087-0). Humanities.

Waddy, Charis. The Muslim Mind. LC 76-6522. (Illus.). 216p. 1976. text ed. 20.00x (ISBN 0-582-78061-6). Longman.

Wahab, A. Shadowless Prophet of Islam. 4.95 (ISBN 0-686-18427-0). Kazi Pubns.

Watt, W. M. The Formative Period of Islamic Thought. 1973. 18.00x (ISBN 0-85224-245-X, Pub. by Edinburgh U Pr Scotland). Columbia U Pr.

Watt, W. Montgomery. What Is Islam? 2nd ed. (Arab Background Ser.). 1979. text ed. 25.00x (ISBN 0-582-78302-X). Longman.

Welch, Alford T. & Cachia, Pierre J., eds. Islam: Past Influence & Present Challenge. LC 79-14225. 1979. 35.00 (ISBN 0-87395-391-6). State U NY Pr.

Wendell, Hasan & Al-Banna, Hasan. Five Tracts of Hasan Al-Banna: A Selection from the Majmu'at Rasa'il Al-'imam Al-Shahid Hasan Al-Banna. LC 77-83119. (Publications in Near Eastern Studies: Vol. 20). 1978. pap. 13.000 (ISBN 0-520-09584-7). U of Cal Pr.

Widengren, Geo. Iran & Islam. (Jordon Lectures in Comparative Religion Ser: No. 10). 160p. 1979. cancelled (ISBN 0-485-17410-3, Athlone Pr). Humanities.

Williams, John A., ed. Islam. LC 61-15500. (Great Religions of Modern Man Ser). 1961. 8.95 (ISBN 0-8076-0165-9). Braziller.

Zakariya, M. The Virtues of Salat. 1970. 3.25x (ISBN 0-87902-193-4). Orientalia.

Zuhur-U'D, A. M. M. An Examination of the Mystical Tendencies in Islam. 224p. 1973. 7.50x (ISBN 0-87902-252-3). Orientalia.

ISLAM–BIBLIOGRAPHY

Grimwood-Jones, Diana, ed. Middle East & Islam: A Bibliographical Introduction. 2nd rev. & enl. ed. LC 72-85349. 429p. 1979. 50.00x (ISBN 3-85750-032-8). Intl Pubns Serv.

Grimwood-Jones, Diana, et al, eds. Arab-Islamic Bibliography: Based on Giuseppe Gabrieli's Manvale Di Bibliografia Muselmana. 1977. text ed. 52.00x (ISBN 0-391-00691-6). Humanities.

Lewis & Schacht, eds. Encyclopedia of Islam Index, 3 vols. 1980. pap. text ed. 33.00x (ISBN 90-04-06002-2). Humanities.

Pearson, J. D., ed. Index Islamicus: First Supplement 1956-1960. 1962. 42.00 (ISBN 0-7201-0381-9, Pub. by Mansell England). Merrimack Bk Serv.

--Index Islamicus: Primary Sequence 1906-1955. 1958. 59.00 (ISBN 0-7201-0380-0, Pub. by Mansell England). Merrimack Bk Serv.

--Index Islamicus: Second Supplement, 1961-1965. 372p. 1975. Repr. of 1967 ed. 42.00 (ISBN 0-7201-0382-7, Pub. by Mansell England). Merrimack Bk Serv.

--Index Islamicus: Third Supplement 1966-1970. 1972. 42.00 (ISBN 0-7201-0282-0, Pub. by Mansell England). Merrimack Bk Serv.

Sardar, Ziauddin. Islam: Outline of a Classification Scheme. 1979. 17.50 (ISBN 0-85157-285-5, Pub. by Bingley England). Shoe String.

ISLAM–EDUCATION

Ahmed, K. Principles of Islamic Education. 1.00 (ISBN 0-686-18355-X). Kazi Pubns.

Dodge, Bayard. Muslim Education in Medieval Times. LC 63-144. 1962. 3.75 (ISBN 0-916808-02-5). Mid East Inst.

Sharif, M. M. Islamic & Educational Studies. 4.50 (ISBN 0-686-18356-8). Kazi Pubns.

ISLAM–HISTORIOGRAPHY

Rasul, M. G. Origin & Development of Muslim Historiography. 1970. 4.25x (ISBN 0-87902-183-7). Orientalia.

Rosenthal, Franz. History of Muslim Historiography. 1968. text ed. 93.50x (ISBN 90-04019-06-5). Humanities.

Thanvi, A. A. Bahishti Zewar (Heavenly Ornaments) 14.95 (ISBN 0-686-63896-4). Kazi Pubns.

Waardenburg, Jean-Jacques. L'islam Dans le Miroir De L'Occident: Comment Quelques Orientalistes Occidentaux Se Sont Penches Sur L'islam et Se Sont Forme une Image De Cette Religion. 3 ed. (Recherches Mediterraneennes: Etudes 3). 1970. 35.50x (ISBN 90-2796-304-5). Mouton.

ISLAM–HISTORY

Ali, Syed A. The Spirit of Islam: A History of the Evolution & Ideals of Islam with a Life of the Prophet. rev ed. 515p. 1974. Repr. of 1922 ed. text ed. 17.00x (ISBN 0-391-00341-0). Humanities.

Ali ibn Isma'il, A. H., et al. Al ibanah 'an usul addiyanah. Klein, W. C., tr. (American Oriental Ser.: Vol. 19). 1940. pap. 12.00 (ISBN 0-527-02693-X). Kraus Repr.

Al-Sayyid-Marsot, A. L., ed. Society & the Sexes in Medieval Islam. LC 79-63268. (Giorgio Levi Della Vida Biennial Conference Ser.: Vol. 6). 149p. 1979. pap. 18.50 (ISBN 0-89003-033-2). Undena Pubns.

Arnold, Thomas W. The Preaching of Islam: A History of Propagation of the Muslim Faith. LC 72-180319. (Mid-East Studies). Repr. of 1913 ed. 24.00 (ISBN 0-404-56214-0). AMS Pr.

Asghar Ali. The Origin & Development of Islam. 1980. 17.00x (ISBN 0-8364-0590-0, Orient Longman). South Asia Bks.

Becker, Carl H. Beitrage zur Geschicte Agyptens unter Dem Islam, 2 vols. in 1. LC 77-10579. (Studies in Islamic History: No. 5). Repr. of 1903 ed. lib. bdg. 17.50x (ISBN 0-87991-454-8). Porcupine Pr.

Bell, Richard. Origin of Islam in Its Christian Environment. 224p. 1968. Repr. of 1926 ed. 25.00x (ISBN 0-7146-1977-9, F Cass Co). Biblio Dist.

Bosworth, C. E. The Islamic Dynasties. 245p. 1980. pap. 9.00x (ISBN 0-85224-402-9, Pub. by Edinburgh U Pr Scotland). Columbia U Pr.

--The Islamic Dynasties. 1967. (Pub. by Edinburgh U Pr Scotland). Columbia U Pr.

Bosworth, C. E., ed. Iran & Islam. 1972. 32.50x (ISBN 0-85224-085-6, Pub. by Edinburgh U Pr Scotland). Columbia U Pr.

Bulliet, Richard W. Conversion to Islam in the Medieval Period: An Essay in Quantitative History. (Illus.). 158p. 1979. text ed. 15.00x (ISBN 0-686-74083-1). Harvard U Pr.

Crone, Patricia & Cook, M. Hagarism: The Making of the Islamic World. LC 75-41714. 268p. 1977. 29.95 (ISBN 0-521-21133-6). Cambridge U Pr.

Daniel, Norman. Islam, Europe, & Empire. 1967. 35.00x (ISBN 0-85224-108-9, Pub. by Edinburgh U Pr Scotland). Columbia U Pr.

Donaldson, Dwight M. The Shi, Its Religion: A History of Islam in Persia & Iraq. 1976. lib. bdg. 59.95 (ISBN 0-8490-2598-2). Gordon Pr.

Donner, Fred M. The Early Islamic Conquests. LC 80-8544. (Princeton Studies on the Near East). (Illus.). 328p. 1981. 20.00x (ISBN 0-691-05327-8). Princeton U Pr.

Duckworth, John, et al. Muhammad & the Arab Empire. Yapp, Malcolm & Killingray, Margaret, eds. (World History Ser.). (Illus.). (gr. 10). 1980. lib. bdg. 5.95 (ISBN 0-89908-036-7); pap. text ed. 1.95 (ISBN 0-89908-011-1). Greenhaven.

El Badri, Nassan, et al. Ramadan War. 1978. 14.75 (ISBN 0-88254-460-8); pap. 6.95 (ISBN 0-686-77347-0). Hippocrene Bks.

El Droubie, Riadh. Islam. (Living Religions Ser.). (Illus.). 1976. pap. 3.50x (ISBN 0-7062-3595-9). Intl Pubns Serv.

Esposito, John L., ed. Islam & Development: Religion & Sociopolitical Change. LC 80-25119. (Contemporary Issues in the Middle East Ser.). 292p. 1980. text ed. 22.00x (ISBN 0-8156-2229-5); pap. text ed. 9.95x (ISBN 0-8156-2230-9). Syracuse U Pr.

Fahmy, Aly M. Muslim Naval Organization in the Eastern Mediterranean from 7th to 10th Century A. D. 1948. 13.75x (ISBN 0-8426-1256-4). Verry.

Faizi, A. Q. The Prince of Martyrs: A Brief Account of Imam Husayn. 1977. pap. 2.25 (ISBN 0-85398-073-X, 339-003-10, Pub. by G Ronald England). Baha'i.

Faqih, I. Glimpses of Islamic History. 10.95 (ISBN 0-686-63900-6). Kazi Pubns.

Frye, Richard N. Islamic Iran & Central Asia (7th-12th Centuries) 380p. 1980. 75.00x (ISBN 0-86078-044-9, Pub. by Variorum England). State Mutual Bk.

Gibb, Hamilton A. Mohammedanism: An Historical Survey. 2nd ed. 1953. pap. 3.95x (ISBN 0-19-500245-8, 90). Oxford U Pr.

Graham, William A. Divine Word & Prophetic Word in Early Islam: A Reconsideration of the Sources, with Special Reference to the Divine Saying or Hadith Qudsi. (Religion & Society Ser.). 1977. text ed. 37.75x (ISBN 90-279-7612-0). Mouton.

Hanee, S. What Everyone Should Know About Islam & Muslims. pap. 7.95 (ISBN 0-686-63919-7). Kazi Pubns.

Hodgson, Marshall G. Venture of Islam: Conscience & History in World Civilization, 3 vols. LC 73-87243. 1975. 30.00x ea.; Vol. 1. (ISBN 0-226-34678-1); Vol. 2. (ISBN 0-226-34680-3); Vol. 3. (ISBN 0-226-34681-1). U of Chicago Pr.

Holt, P. M., et al, eds. The Cambridge History of Islam: Islamic Society & Civilisation, Vol. 2B. LC 73-77291. (Illus.). 1978. 59.00 (ISBN 0-521-21949-3); pap. 21.95 (ISBN 0-521-29138-0). Cambridge U Pr.

--Cambridge History of Islam. Incl. Vol. 1A. Central Islamic Lands from Pre-Islamic Times to the First World War. 59.00 (ISBN 0-521-21946-9); pap. 19.95 (ISBN 0-521-29135-6); Vol. 1B. Central Islamic Lands Since 1918. 42.00 (ISBN 0-521-21947-7); pap. 14.95 (ISBN 0-521-29136-4); Vol. 2A. The Indian Subcontinent, Southeast Asia, Africa & the Muslim West. 48.00 (ISBN 0-521-21948-5); pap. 18.50 (ISBN 0-521-29137-2); Vol. 2B. Islamic Society & Civilization. 59.00 (ISBN 0-521-21949-3); pap. 21.95 (ISBN 0-521-29138-0). 1977-78. Set. 178.00 (ISBN 0-521-22310-5); Set. pap. 62.00 (ISBN 0-521-08755-4). Cambridge U Pr.

Johnson, Paul. Civilizations of the Holy Land. LC 78-73358. (Illus.). 1979. 14.95 (ISBN 0-689-10973-3). Atheneum.

Karim, F. Heroes of Islam. Incl. Bk. 1. Muhammad; Bk. 2. Abu Bakr; Bk. 3. Umar; Bk. 4. Othman; Bk. 5. Ali; Bk. 6. Khalid Bin Walid; Bk. 7. Mohammad Bin Qasim; Bk. 8. Mahmood of Ghazni; Bk. 9. Mohyuddin; Bk. 10. Sultan Tipu; Bk. 11. Aisha the Truthful; Bk. 12. Hussain the Martyr; Bk. 13. Some Companions of the Prophet - I; Bk. 14. Some Companions of the Prophet - II; Bk. 15. Some Companions of the Prophet - III. pap. 15.00 complete set (ISBN 0-686-18393-2); pap. 1.50 ea bk. Kazi Pubns.

Kister, M. J. Studies in Jahiliyya & Early Islam. 360p. 1980. 75.00x (ISBN 0-86078-068-6, Pub. by Variorum England). State Mutual Bk.

Laffin, John. The Dagger of Islam. 224p. 1981. pap. 2.95 (ISBN 0-553-14287-9). Bantam.

Levtzion, Nehemia, ed. Conversion to Islam. LC 77-26771. 1979. text ed. 32.50x (ISBN 0-8419-0343-3). Holmes & Meier.

Levy, Reuben. A Baghdad Chronicle. LC 77-10580. (Studies in Islamic History Ser.: No. 17). (Illus.). Repr. of 1929 ed. lib. bdg. 17.50x (ISBN 0-87991-466-1). Porcupine Pr.

Lewis, Bernard. Islam in History. LC 72-6284. 300p. 1972. 17.50 (ISBN 0-912050-35-7, Library Pr). Open Court.

--Studies in Classical & Ottoman Islam (7th-16th Centuries) 414p. 1980. 68.00x (ISBN 0-902089-97-8, Pub. by Variorum England). State Mutual Bk.

Lewis, Bernard, ed. Islam, from the Prophet Muhammad to the Capture of Constantinople Vol. 1: Politics & War. (Documentary History of Western Civilization Ser.). 1973. pap. 6.95x (ISBN 0-06-131749-7, TB1749, Torch). Har-Row.

--Islam, from the Prophet Muhammad to the Capture of Constantinople, Vol. 2: Religion & Society. 1973. pap. 5.95x (ISBN 0-06-131750-0, TB1750, Torch). Har-Row.

Lokkegaard, Frede. Islamic Taxation in the Classic Period. LC 78-2387. (Studies in Islamic History: No. 10). 286p. Repr. of 1950 ed. lib. bdg. 17.50x (ISBN 0-87991-459-9). Porcupine Pr.

Makdisi, George. Islam & the Medieval West: Aspects of Intercultural Relations. Semaan, Khalil I., ed. LC 79-18678. 1979. lib. bdg. 34.00 (ISBN 0-87395-409-2); pap. 12.95 (ISBN 0-87395-455-6). State U NY Pr.

Margolliouth, David S. The Early Development of Mohammedanism. LC 77-27156. (Hibbert Lectures: 1913). Repr. of 1914 ed. 18.00 (ISBN 0-404-60415-3). AMS Pr.

Martin, B. G. Muslim Brotherhoods in 19th Century Africa. LC 75-35451. (African Studies Ser.: No. 18). 1977. 31.95 (ISBN 0-521-21062-3). Cambridge U Pr.

Memon, Muhammed U. Ibn Taimaya's Struggle Against Popular Religion with an Annotated Translation of His Kitab Iqtida Assirat Al Mustaquin Mukhalafat Ashab Al-Jahim. (Religion & Society: No. 1). 1976. text ed. 70.00x (ISBN 90-2797-591-4). Mouton.

Moore, George F. History of Religions: Judaism, Christianity, Mohammedanism, Vol. II. (International Theological Library). 568p. 1965. Repr. of 1920 ed. text ed. 13.95x (ISBN 0-567-07203-7). Attic Pr.

Nadawi, Abul H. Islam & the World. Kidwai, Mohammad A., tr. from Arabic. 218p. (Orig.). 1977. pap. 4.50x (ISBN 0-939830-04-3, Pub. by IIFSO Kuwait). New Era Pubns MI.

Nadvi. Saviors of Islamic Spirit: Vol. 1, II. 16.95 (ISBN 0-686-18312-6). Kazi Pubns.

Naff, Thomas & Owen, Roger, eds. Studies in Eighteenth-Century Islamic History. LC 77-22012. 462p. 1977. 24.95x (ISBN 0-8093-0819-3). S Ill U Pr.

Peretz, Don, et al. Islam: Legacy of the Past, Challenge of the Future. LC 80-27443. 160p. 1981. 9.95 (ISBN 0-88427-048-3, Dist. by Caroline Hse). North River.

Sabini, John. Armies in the Sand: The Struggle for Mecca & Medina. (Illus.). 224p. 1981. 16.95 (ISBN 0-500-01246-6). Thames Hudson.

Saunders, J. J. A History of Medieval Islam. 1966. Repr. of 1965 ed. 20.00x (ISBN 0-7100-2077-5). Routledge & Kegan.

--A History of Medieval Islam. (Illus.). 1978. pap. 8.95 (ISBN 0-7100-0050-2). Routledge & Kegan.

Schacht, Joseph & Bosworth, C. E., eds. The Legacy of Islam. 2nd ed. (Illus.). 1979. pap. 7.95 (ISBN 0-19-285081-4, GB579, GB). Oxford U Pr.

Scott, S. P. History of the Moorish Empire in Europe, 3 vols. 1977. Set. lib. bdg. 300.00 (ISBN 0-8490-2004-2). Gordon Pr.

Shaban, M. A. Islamic History: A.D. 750 to 1055, (A.H. 132 to 448) New Interpretation II, Vol. 2. LC 75-39390. (Illus.). 190p. 1976. 37.50 (ISBN 0-521-21198-0); pap. 11.95 (ISBN 0-521-29453-3). Cambridge U Pr.

Smith-Savage, E. & Smith, M. B. Islamic Geomancy & a Thirteenth-Century Divinatory Device. LC 79-65001. (Studies in Near Eastern Culture & Society: Vol. 2). 91p. 1979. pap. 15.25 (ISBN 0-89003-038-3). Undena Pubns.

Tibawi, A. L. Arabic & Islamic Themes: Historical, Education & Literary Studies. 1976. text ed. 27.00x (ISBN 0-7189-0164-9). Verry.

Tisdall, W. The Sources of Islam. Muir, William, tr. 102p. 1974. 7.50x (ISBN 0-8002-1993-7). Intl pubns Serv.

Ullman, M. Islamic Medicine. 1978. 10.00x (ISBN 0-85224-325-1, Pub. by Edinburgh U Pr Scotland). Columbia U Pr.

Watt, W. M. The Influence of Islam Upon Medieval Europe. 1973. 7.50x (ISBN 0-85224-218-2, Pub. by Edinburgh U Pr Scotland). Columbia U Pr.

Wellhausen, Julius. The Religio-Political Factions in Early Islam. Ostle, R. C. & Walzer, S. M., trs. 1975. 24.50 (ISBN 0-444-10872-6, North Holland). Elsevier.

Wensinck, A. J. A Handbook of Early Muhammadan Tradition. (Studies in Islamic History: No. 21). 268p. Repr. of 1927 ed. lib. bdg. 17.50x (ISBN 0-87991-075-5). Porcupine Pr.

Wismar, Adolph L. Study in Tolerance As Practiced by Muhammed & His Immediate Successors. LC 27-24455. (Columbia University. Contributions to Oriental History & Philology: No. 13). Repr. of 1927 ed. 14.00 (ISBN 0-404-50543-0). AMS Pr.

Yasin, Mohammad. A Social History of Islamic India. rev. ed. LC 74-902126. 206p. 1974. 12.00x (ISBN 0-88386-459-2). South Asia Bks.

Zaydan, Jirji. Umayyads & Abbasids. Margoliuth, D. S., tr. from Arabic. LC 79-2889. 325p. 1981. Repr. of 1907 ed. 26.50 (ISBN 0-8305-0056-1). Hyperion Conn.

--Umayyads & Abbasids: Being the Fourth Part of the Author's History of Islamic Civilization. (Studies in Islamic History: No. 22). xiv, 325p. Repr. of 1907 ed. lib. bdg. 20.00x (ISBN 0-87991-060-7). Porcupine Pr.

ISLAM–RELATIONS

Arnold, Thomas W. The Preaching of Islam: A History of Propagation of the Muslim Faith. LC 72-180319. (Mid-East Studies). Repr. of 1913 ed. 24.00 (ISBN 0-404-56214-0). AMS Pr.

Bury, George W. Pan-Islam. LC 80-1938. Repr. of 1919 ed. 30.00 (ISBN 0-404-18956-3). AMS Pr.

Hassan, Farooq. The Concept of State & Law in Islam. LC 80-69038. 321p. (Orig.). 1981. lib. bdg. 20.75 (ISBN 0-8191-1426-X); pap. text ed. 11.75 (ISBN 0-8191-1427-8). U Pr of Amer.

Kamil, A. Abd-Al-Qadir. Islam & the Race Question. (Race Question & Modern Thought). (Orig.). 1970. pap. 2.50 (ISBN 92-3-100833-1, U342, UNESCO). Unipub.

Lichtenstadter, Ilse. Islam & the Modern Age. 228p. 1958. text ed. 24.00x (ISBN 0-8290-0179-4). Irvington.

Procler, Jesse H., ed. Islam & International Relations. LC 80-1914. 1981. Repr. of 1965 ed. 27.50 (ISBN 0-404-18969-5). AMS Pr.

ISLAM–RELATIONS–CHRISTIANITY

see also Jesus Christ–Islamic Interpretations; Missions to Muslims

Ansari, F. R. Islam & Christianity in the Modern World. pap. 4.95 (ISBN 0-686-18577-3). Kazi Pubns.

Basetti-Sami, Giulio. Koran in the Light of Christ. 1977. 8.50 (ISBN 0-8199-0713-8). Franciscan Herald.

Becker, C. H. Christianity & Islam. Chaytor, H. J., tr. LC 74-608. 120p. 1974. Repr. of 1909 ed. lib. bdg. 18.50 (ISBN 0-8337-4816-5). B Franklin.

Browne, Lawrence E. The Eclipse of Christianity in Asia. 1967. Repr. 19.50 (ISBN 0-86527-049-X). Fertig.

Kritzeck, James. Peter the Venerable & Islam. (Princeton Studies on the Near East Ser). 1964. 25.00 (ISBN 0-691-03043-X). Princeton U Pr.

Smith, Henry P. The Bible & Islam. LC 73-2227. (The Jewish People; History, Religion, Literature Ser.). Repr. of 1897 ed. 24.00 (ISBN 0-405-05288-X). Arno.

Southern, R. W. Western Views of Islam in the Middle Ages. LC 62-13270. 1978. 12.50x (ISBN 0-674-95055-0); pap. 3.95x (ISBN 0-674-95065-8). Harvard U Pr.

Wismer, Don. The Islamic Jesus: An Annotated Bibliography of Sources in English & French. LC 76-24737. (Reference Library of the Humanities Ser.: Vol. 58). 1977. lib. bdg. 33.00 (ISBN 0-8240-9940-0). Garland Pub.

ISLAM–RELATIONS–JUDAISM

Geiger, Abraham. Judaism & Islam. rev. ed. (Library of Jewish Classics). 1970. 15.00x (ISBN 0-87068-058-7). Ktav.

Torrey, Charles C. Jewish Foundation of Islam. rev. ed. LC 67-18817. 1968. 15.00x (ISBN 0-87068-117-6). Ktav.

ISLAM–AFRICA

Atterbury, Anson P. Islam in Africa. LC 73-91254. Repr. of 1899 ed. 15.50x (ISBN 0-8371-2064-0, Pub. by Negro U Pr). Greenwood.

Berger, Morroe. Islam in Egypt Today: Social & Political Aspects of Popular Religion. LC 70-113597. 1970. 23.95 (ISBN 0-521-07834-2). Cambridge U Pr.

Brett, Michael, ed. Northern Africa: Islam & Modernization. 156p. 1973. 25.00 (ISBN 0-7146-2972-3, F Cass Co). Biblio Dist.

Bunger, Robert L. Islamization Among the Upper Pokomo. 2nd ed. LC 80-242. (Foreign & Comparative Studies-African Ser.: No. 33). 128p. (Orig.). 1979. pap. 8.00 (ISBN 0-915984-55-5). Syracuse U Foreign Comp.

Hurreiz, Sayyid H. Ja'Aliyyin Folktales: An in Interplay of African Arabian & Islamic Elements. LC 76-24190. (Africa Ser.: No. 8). 1977. pap. text ed. 20.00x (ISBN 0-87750-185-8). Res Ctr Lang Semiotic.

Lewis, I. M., ed. Islam in Tropical Africa. 2nd ed. LC 79-3292. 324p. 1980. 25.00x (ISBN 0-253-14956-8); pap. 10.95x (ISBN 0-253-28514-3). Ind U Pr.

Mason, John P. Island of the Blest: Islam in a Libyan Oasis Community. LC 77-620016. (Papers in International Studies: Africa: No. 31). (Illus.). 1977. pap. 10.00x (ISBN 0-89680-063-6). Ohio U Ctr Int.

Oded, Arye. Islam in Uganda. 382p. 1974. casebound 19.95 (ISBN 0-87855-171-9). Transaction Bks.

Ryan, Patrick J. Imale: Yoruba Participation in the Muslim Tradition. LC 76-57774. 1978. pap. 9.00 (ISBN 0-89130-132-1). Scholars Pr Ca.

Sheppard, Roscoe B. Islamic Africa. LC 77-155410. Repr. of 1914 ed. 9.50x (ISBN 0-8371-6105-3, Pub. by Negro U Pr). Greenwood.

Trimingham, J. Spencer. History of Islam in West Africa. (Oxford Paperbacks Ser). 1970. pap. 5.95x (ISBN 0-19-285038-5). Oxford U Pr.

--The Influence of Islam Upon Africa. 2nd ed. (Arab Background Ser.). (Illus.). 1980. text ed. 25.00x (ISBN 0-582-78499-9). Longman.

--Islam in Ethiopia. (Illus.). 299p. 1965. Repr. 27.50x (ISBN 0-7146-1731-8, F Cass Co). Biblio Dist.

Trimingham, John S. Islam in East Africa. LC 79-52567. (Islam Ser.). 1980. Repr. of 1964 ed. lib. bdg. 18.00x (ISBN 0-8369-9270-9). Arno.

--Islam in West Africa. 1959. 29.95x (ISBN 0-19-826511-5). Oxford U Pr.

Willis, John Ralph, ed. Studies in West African Islamic History: The Cultivators of Islam, Vol. 1. (Illus.). 325p. 1979. 37.50x (ISBN 0-7146-1737-7, F Cass Co). Biblio Dist.

Works, John A., Jr. Pilgrims in a Strange Land: Hausa Communities in Chad. LC 76-23138. 1976. 17.50x (ISBN 0-231-03976-X). Columbia U Pr.

ISLAM–EGYPT

Berger, Morroe. Islam in Egypt Today: Social & Political Aspects of Popular Religion. LC 70-113597. 1970. 23.95 (ISBN 0-521-07834-2). Cambridge U Pr.

Harris, Christina. Nationalism & Revolution in Egypt: The Role O the Muslim Brotherhood. LC 79-2861. 276p. 1981. Repr. of 1964 ed. 22.50 (ISBN 0-8305-0034-0). Hyperion Conn.

ISLAM–INDIA

Ahmad, Aziz. An Intellectual History of Islamic India. 1970. 13.00x (ISBN 0-85224-057-0, Pub. by Edinburgh U Pr Scotland). Columbia U Pr.

Husain, Abrar. Marriage Customs Among Muslims in India: A Sociological Study of the Shia Marriage Customs. 1976. text ed. 12.00x (ISBN 0-8426-0926-1). Verry.

Mahmood, Tahir. Muslim Personal Law. 1977. text ed. 12.50x (ISBN 0-7069-0532-6). Humanities.

Mahood, Tahir. Family Planning: The Muslim Viewpoint. 143p. 1977. 10.00x (ISBN 0-7069-0545-8, Pub. by Croom Helm Ltd. England). Biblio Dist.

Nanji, Azim. The Nizari Ismaili Tradition in the Indo-Pakistan Subcontinent. LC 78-12990. (Monographs in Islamic Religion & Theology). 1979. 25.00x (ISBN 0-88206-020-1). Caravan Bks.

Robinson, F. Separatism Among Indian Muslims. (South Asian Studies: No. 16). 400p. 1975. 39.95 (ISBN 0-521-20432-1). Cambridge U Pr.

Sharif, Ja'Far. Islam in India. Crooke, William, ed. Herklots, G. A., tr. from Hindustani. (Illus.). 414p. 1972. Repr. of 1921 ed. text ed. 15.00x (ISBN 0-7007-0015-3). Humanities.

Smith, Wilfred C. Modern Islam in India: A Social Analysis. rev. ed. LC 78-188163. (Illus., With bibliography from the 1943 ed.). 1972. Repr. of 1946 ed. 20.00 (ISBN 0-8462-1652-3). Russell.

--Modern Islam in India: A Social Analysis. LC 70-179243. Repr. of 1946 ed. 17.00 (ISBN 0-404-54869-5). AMS Pr.

ISLAM–INDONESIA

Archer, Raymond L. Muhammadan Mysticism in Sumatra. LC 77-87487. (Royal Asiatic Society, Malayan Branch. Journal: Vol. 15). Repr. of 1937 ed. 16.50 (ISBN 0-404-16695-4). AMS Pr.

Benda, Harry J. The Crescent & the Rising Sun: Indonesian Islam Under the Japanese Occupation 1942-1945. 1958. 21.25 (ISBN 0-686-20916-8). Mouton.

Federspiel, Howard. Persatuan Islam: Islamic Reform in Twentieth Century Indonesia. (Monograph Ser). (Orig.). 1970. pap. 7.50 (ISBN 0-685-08668-2, A145586). Cornell Mod Indo.

Noer, Deliar. Administration of Islam in Indonesia. (Monograph Ser.). 1978. pap. 4.50 (ISBN 0-686-65348-3). Cornell Mod Indo.

Peacock, James L. Purifying the Faith: The Muhammadijah Movement in Indonesian Islam. LC 78-61992. 1978. 6.95 (ISBN 0-8053-7824-3). Benjamin-Cummings.

Siegel, James T. The Rope of God. LC 69-15942. (Library Reprint Ser.: Vol. 96). 1978. 23.75x (ISBN 0-520-03714-6). U of Cal Pr.

Van Nieuwenhuijze, C. A. Aspects of Islam in Post Colonial Indonesia: Five Essays. 1958. 23.75x (ISBN 0-686-21860-4). Mouton.

ISLAM–MALAYA

Kessler, Clive S. Islam & Politics in a Malay State: Kelantan, 1838-1969. LC 77-14682. (Illus.). 1978. 20.00x (ISBN 0-8014-1103-3). Cornell U Pr.

Yegar, Moshe. Isalm & Islamic Istitutions in British Malaya: Policies & Implementation. 302p. 1979. text ed. 23.00x (ISBN 965-223-310-2, Pub. by Magnes Israel). Humanities.

ISLAM–MAURITANIA

Stewart, C. C. & Stewart, E. K. Islam & Social Order in Mauritania: A Case Study from the Nineteenth Century. (Oxford Studies in African Affairs Ser.). 1973. 24.00x (ISBN 0-19-821688-2). Oxford U Pr.

ISLAM–PAKISTAN

Abbott, Freeland. Islam & Pakistan. (Illus.). 1968. 22.50x (ISBN 0-8014-0003-1). Cornell U Pr.

Nanji, Azim. The Nizari Ismaili Tradition in the Indo-Pakistan Subcontinent. LC 78-12990. (Monographs in Islamic Religion & Theology). 1979. 25.00x (ISBN 0-88206-020-1). Caravan Bks.

ISLAM–RUSSIA

Bennigsen, Alexandre & Lemercier-Quelquejay, Chantal. Les Mouvements Nationaux Chez les Musulmans De Russie, 2 tomes. Incl. Tome I. Le "Sultangalievisme" Au Tatarstan. (No. 3). 1960. pap. 27.05x (ISBN 0-686-22176-1); Tome II. La Presse et le Mouvement National Chez les Musulmans De Russie Avant 1920. (No. 4). (Illus.). 1964. pap. 46.50x (ISBN 90-2796-244-8). (Mouvements Sociaux et Ideologies, Documents et Temoignages). Mouton.

ISLAM–TURKEY

Hasluck, F. W. Christianity & Islam Under the Sultans, 2 vols. LC 72-13668. 1973. Repr. of 1929 ed. Set. lib. bdg. 55.00x (ISBN 0-374-93747-8). Octagon.

Leder, Arnold. Catalysts of Change: Marxist versus Muslim in a Turkish Community. LC 76-29323. (Middle East Monograph: No. 1). 70p. 1976. pap. text ed. 3.95x (ISBN 0-292-71042-9). U of Tex Pr.

Lewis, Bernard. Studies in Classical & Ottoman Islam (7th-16th Centuries) 414p. 1980. 68.00x (ISBN 0-902089-97-8, Pub. by Variorum England). State Mutual Bk.

ISLAM AND CHRISTIANITY

see Christianity and Other Religions–Islam

ISLAM AND ECONOMICS

Afzal-Ur-Rehman. Economic Doctrines of Islam, 3. 13.50 (ISBN 0-686-18354-1). Kazi Pubns.

Ahmed, M. Economics of Islam. 4.50 (ISBN 0-686-18350-9). Kazi Pubns.

Mannan, M. M. Islamic Economics in Theory & Practice. 6.95 (ISBN 0-686-18374-6). Kazi Pubns.

Maududi, A. A. Economic Problems of Man & Its Islamic Solution. pap. 1.25 (ISBN 0-686-18349-5). Kazi Pubns.

Muslim Students' Association. Contemporary Aspects of Economic Thinking in Islam. 1976. pap. 2.50 (ISBN 0-89259-003-3). Am Trust Pubns.

Rodinson, Maxime. Islam & Capitalism. Pearce, Brian, tr. from Fr. 335p. 1978. pap. 8.95x (ISBN 0-292-73816-1). U of Tex Pr.

Siddiqui, M. N. The Economic Enterprise in Islam. pap. 1.95 (ISBN 0-686-18376-2). Kazi Pubns.

--Some Aspects of the Islamic Economy. pap. 1.95 (ISBN 0-686-18378-9). Kazi Pubns.

Yusaf, S. M. Economic Justice in Islam. 3.95 (ISBN 0-686-18351-7). Kazi Pubns.

Zaman, S. M. H. Trade in Islam. pap. 1.00 (ISBN 0-686-18377-0). Kazi Pubns.

ISLAM AND STATE

Hasluck, F. W. Christianity & Islam Under the Sultans, 2 vols. LC 72-13668. 1973. Repr. of 1929 ed. Set. lib. bdg. 55.00x (ISBN 0-374-93747-8). Octagon.

Lambton, Ann K. State & Government in Medieval Islam: An Introduction to the Study of Islamic Political Theory; the Jurists. (London Oriental Ser.: Vol. 36). 368p. 1981. 55.00 (ISBN 0-19-713600-1). Oxford U Pr.

Maududi, A. A. First Principles of Islamic State. pap. 1.00 (ISBN 0-686-18587-0). Kazi Pubns.

Rosenthal, Erwin I. Islam in the Modern National State. 1966. 34.50 (ISBN 0-521-06134-2). Cambridge U Pr.

Shariati, Ali. Marxism & Other Western Fallacies: An Islamic Critique. Algar, Hamid, ed. Campbell, R., tr. from Persian. LC 79-29729. (Orig.). 1980. 9.45 (ISBN 0-933782-05-5); pap. 4.45 (ISBN 0-933782-06-3). Mizan Pr.

Sherwani, Haroon K. Studies in Muslim Political Thought & Administration. 4th ed. LC 77-25472. (Studies in Islamic History Ser.). Repr. of 1963 ed. lib. bdg. 17.50x (ISBN 0-87991-468-8). Porcupine Pr.

ISLAMIC ARCHITECTURE

see Architecture, Islamic

ISLAMIC ART

see Art, Islamic

ISLAMIC CALENDAR

see Calendar, Islamic

ISLAMIC CITIES AND TOWNS

see Cities and Towns, Islamic

ISLAMIC CIVILIZATION

see Civilization, Islamic

ISLAMIC COINS

see Coins, Islamic

ISLAMIC CONVERTS TO CHRISTIANITY

see Converts From Islam

ISLAMIC COUNTRIES

see also Arab Countries

Geertz, Clifford. Islam Observed: Religious Development in Morocco & Indonesia. 1971. pap. 3.95 (ISBN 0-226-28511-1, P439, Phoen). U of Chicago Pr.

Lewis, B., et al, eds. Encyclopedia of Islam, 5 vols. Incl. Vol. 1. A-B: Fasc. 1-22. Gibb, H. A., et al, eds. 1960. text ed. 185.25x (ISBN 90-040-0530-7); Vol. 2. C-G: Fasc. 23-40. Lewis, B., et al, eds. 1965. 178.75x (ISBN 90-040-0531-5); Vol. 3. H-Iram: Fasc. 41-60. 1969. text ed. 225.75x (ISBN 90-040-3275-4); Vols. 4 & 5. I-Ram &K-Ha: Fasc. 61-78. 1978. text ed. 275.00 (ISBN 0-685-23323-5). Humanities.

Linant De Bellefonds, Y. Traite De Droit Musulman Compare: Filiation - Incapacites - Liberalites Entre Vifs, Tome 3. (Recherches Mediterraneennes: No. 9). 1973. pap. 47.75x (ISBN 90-2797-199-4). Mouton.

Toynbee, Arnold J. The Islamic World Since the Peace Settlement. Repr. of 1927 ed. pap. 42.00 (ISBN 0-384-61120-6). Johnson Repr.

Udovitch, A. L., ed. Islamic Middle East 700-1900: Studies in Economic & Social History. LC 79-52703. (Illus.). 832p. 1981. 24.95x (ISBN 0-87850-030-8). Darwin Pr.

Weekes, Richard V., ed. Muslim Peoples: A World Ethnographic Survey. LC 77-84759. (Illus.). 1978. lib. bdg. 37.50 (ISBN 0-8371-9880-1, WMW/). Greenwood.

ISLAMIC COUNTRIES–HISTORY

Brockelmann, C. History of the Islamic Peoples. 1980. 15.00 (ISBN 0-7100-1118-0); pap. cancelled (ISBN 0-7100-0521-0). Routledge & Kegan.

Bulliet, Richard W. The Patricians of Nishapur: A Study in Medieval Islamic Social History. LC 70-173413. (Middle Eastern Studies: No. 16). (Illus.). 280p. 1972. 16.50x (ISBN 0-674-65792-6). Harvard U Pr.

Darke, Hubert, tr. from Persian. The Book of Government or Rules for Kings: The Siyar Al-Muluk or Siyasat-nama of Nizam Al-Mulk. rev ed. (Persian Heritage Ser.). 1978. 20.00x (ISBN 0-7100-8619-9). Routledge & Kegan.

Holt, P. M. & Lambton, Ann, eds. Cambridge History of Islam: Central Islamic Lands Since 1918, Vol. 1B. 1977. 42.00 (ISBN 0-521-21947-7); pap. 14.95 (ISBN 0-521-29136-4). Cambridge U Pr.

Holt, P. M., et al, eds. Cambridge History of Islam. Incl. Vol. 1A. Central Islamic Lands from Pre-Islamic Times to the First World War. 59.00 (ISBN 0-521-21946-9); pap. 19.95 (ISBN 0-521-29135-6); Vol. 1B. Central Islamic Lands Since 1918. 42.00 (ISBN 0-521-21947-7); pap. 14.95 (ISBN 0-521-29136-4); Vol. 2A. The Indian Subcontinent, Southeast Asia, Africa & the Muslim West. 48.00 (ISBN 0-521-21948-5); pap. 18.50 (ISBN 0-521-29137-2); Vol. 2B. Islamic Society & Civilization. 59.00 (ISBN 0-521-21949-3); pap. 21.95 (ISBN 0-521-29138-0). 1977-78. Set. 178.00 (ISBN 0-521-22310-5); Set. pap. 62.00 (ISBN 0-521-08755-4). Cambridge U Pr.

Jafri, Syed H. Origins & Early Development in Shi'a Islam. (Arab Background Ser). 1979. text ed. 30.00x (ISBN 0-582-78080-2). Longman.

Le Strange, Guy. Lands of the Eastern Caliphate, Mesopotamia, Persia & Central Asia from the Moslem Conquest to the Time of Timur. 536p. 1966. Repr. 32.50x (ISBN 0-7146-1972-8, F Cass Co). Biblio Dist.

Mottahedeh, Roy P. Loyalty & Leadership in an Early Islamic Society. LC 79-3224. (Princeton Studies in the Near East Ser.). 1980. 16.50x (ISBN 0-691-05296-4). Princeton U Pr.

Pantke, Mechthild. Der Arabische Bahram-Roman: Untersuchungen zur Quellen - und Stoffgeschichte. (Studien zur Sprache, Geschichte und Kultur des Islamischen Orients N. F., Vol. 6). 230p. 1973. 57.25x (ISBN 3-11-003990-7). De Gruyter.

Ross, Edward D. Islam. LC 79-2880. 127p. 1981. Repr. of 1931 ed. 14.50 (ISBN 0-8305-0048-0). Hyperion Conn.

Shaban, M. A. Islamic History A. D. Six Hundred to Seven Fifty: New Interpretation I. LC 79-145604. 1971. 37.50 (ISBN 0-521-08137-8); pap. 11.95 (ISBN 0-521-29131-3). Cambridge U Pr.

ISLAMIC COUNTRIES–POLITICS

Al Tunisi, Khayr. Surest Path: The Political Treatise of a Nineteenth-Century Muslim Statesman. Brown, Leon C., tr. LC 67-25399. (Middle Eastern Monographs Ser: No. 16). pap. 4.50x (ISBN 0-674-85695-3). Harvard U Pr.

Ayoob, Mohammed. The Politics of Islamic Reassertion. 1981. price not set (ISBN 0-312-62707-6). St Martin.

Krosney, Herbert & Weissman, Steve. The Islamic Bomb. Chase, Edward T., ed. 1981. 14.95 (ISBN 0-8129-0978-X). Times Bks.

Maududi, A. A. Rights of Non-Muslims in Islamic State. pap. 1.00 (ISBN 0-686-18545-5). Kazi Pubns.

Rosenthal, Erwin I. Islam in the Modern National State. 1966. 34.50 (ISBN 0-521-06134-2). Cambridge U Pr.

Ruhullah Al-Mausavi Al-Khumayni. Islam & Revolution. Algar, Hamid, tr. from Persian. LC 80-24032. (Orig.). 1981. 19.95 (ISBN 0-933782-04-7). Mizan Pr.

Sherwani, H. K. Studies in Muslim Political Thought & Administration. 4.95 (ISBN 0-686-18544-7). Kazi Pubns.

Spector, Ivar. The Soviet Union & the Muslim World, 1917-1958. LC 56-44083. (Illus.). 340p. 1959. 10.50 (ISBN 0-295-73937-1). U of Wash Pr.

Watt, W. M. Islamic Political Thought. 186p. 1980. pap. 6.50x (ISBN 0-85224-403-7, Pub. by Edinburgh U Pr Scotland). Columbia U Pr.

ISLAMIC COUNTRIES–RELATIONS (GENERAL) WITH GREAT BRITAIN

Chew, Samuel C. Crescent & the Rose: Islam & England During the Renaissance. 1965. lib. bdg. 27.50x (ISBN 0-374-91501-6). Octagon.

--The Crescent & the Rose: Islam & England During the Renaissance. 59.95 (ISBN 0-87968-962-5). Gordon Pr.

ISLAMIC DECORATION AND ORNAMENT

see Decoration and Ornament, Islamic

ISLAMIC EMPIRE

Here are entered works dealing with the Near East alone, or the Near East, North Africa and Islamic Spain as a whole during the period 622-1517, i.e., from the rise and expansion of Islam to the creation of the Ottoman Empire.

see also Mamelukes

Ahmad Ibn Yahya, Al-Baladuri. Origins of the Islamic State, 2 vols. Incl. Vol. 1. Hitti, Philip K., tr. Repr. of 1916 ed (ISBN 0-404-51694-7); Vol. 2. Murgotten, Francis C., tr. Repr. of 1924 ed (ISBN 0-404-51695-5). LC 76-82247. (Columbia University Studies in the Social Sciences: No. 163 & No. 163a). Set. 49.50 (ISBN 0-404-51163-5). AMS Pr.

Atiya, Aziz S. Crusade in the Later Middle Ages. LC 67-28472. (Illus.). 1965. 22.00 (ISBN 0-527-03700-1). Kraus Repr.

Dols, M. W. The Black Death in the Middle East. 1976. 28.00 (ISBN 0-691-03107-X). Princeton U Pr.

Farah, Caesar E. The Dhayl in Medieval Arabic Historiography. (American Oriental Society Essays: 6). 1967. pap. 3.00 (ISBN 0-940490-96-X). Am Orient Soc.

Gibb, Hamilton A. Arab Conquests in Central Asia. LC 75-11477. (BCL Ser.: I). Repr. of 1923 ed. 16.00 (ISBN 0-404-02718-0). AMS Pr.

Goitein, S. D. A Mediterranean Society: The Jewish Communities of the Arab World As Portrayed in the Documents of the Cairo Geniza. Incl. Vol. I. Economic Foundations. 1968. 30.00x (ISBN 0-520-00484-1); Vol. 2. The Community. 1971. 32.50x (ISBN 0-520-01867-2); Vol. 3. The Family. 1978. 32.50x (ISBN 0-520-03265-9). LC 67-22430. (Near Eastern Center, UCLA). U of Cal Pr.

Kennedy, Hugh. The Early Abbasid Caliphate: A Political History. 238p. 1981. 27.50x (ISBN 0-389-20018-2). B&N.

Khan, M. S. Studies in Miskawayh's Contemporary History (340-369 A. H.) LC 79-26702. 300p. (Orig.). 1980. 22.75 (ISBN 0-8357-0499-8, SS-00111). Univ Microfilms.

Kissling, H. J., et al. Muslim World: A Historical Survey Part Three: The Last Great Muslim Empires. 1969. text ed. 44.50x (ISBN 90-040-2104-3). Humanities.

Lombard, Maurice. Espaces et Reseaux Du Haut Moyen Age. (Le Savoir Historique: No. 2). 1973. pap. 15.50 (ISBN 0-686-21810-8). Mouton.

Muhammad Ibn Ahmad. Travels of Ibn Jubayr. 2nd ed. Wright, William, ed. LC 77-173005. Repr. of 1907 ed. 24.50 (ISBN 0-404-03480-2). AMS Pr.

Pirenne, Henri. Mohammed & Charlemagne. (B & N Paperback Ser.). (Orig.). 1968. pap. 5.95x (ISBN 0-06-480687-1, 444). B&N.

ISLAMIC EMPIRE–HISTORY

Al-Sabi, Hilal. Rusum Dar Al-Khila Fah (Rules & Regulations of Abbasid Court) Salem, Elie A., ed. 1977. 19.95x (ISBN 0-8156-6046-4, Am U Beirut). Syracuse U Pr.

Bacharach, Jere L. A Near East Studies Handbook. rev. ed. LC 76-56610. (Illus.). 166p. 1977. 15.00 (ISBN 0-295-95549-X); pap. 5.95 (ISBN 0-295-95551-1). U of Wash Pr.

Balyuzi, H. M. Muhammad & the Course of Islam. (Illus.). 1976. 18.50 (ISBN 0-85398-060-8, 339-001-10, Pub. by G Ronald England). Baha'i.

Bowen, Harold. The Life & Times of Ali ibn Isa: The Good Vizier. LC 77-180320. (Mid-East Studies Ser.). Repr. of 1928 ed. 37.50 (ISBN 0-404-56215-9). AMS Pr.

Bulliet, Richard W. Conversion to Islam in the Medieval Period: An Essay in Quantitative History. (Illus.). 158p. 1979. text ed. 15.00x (ISBN 0-686-74083-1). Harvard U Pr.

Goldston, Robert. The Sword of the Prophet: A History of the Arab World from the Time of Mohammed to the Present Day. (Illus.). 1979. 8.95 (ISBN 0-8037-8372-8). Dial.

Ibn Al-Titaka. Al-Fakhri: On the Systems of Government and the Moslem Dynasties. Whitting, C. E., tr. LC 80-2201. Repr. of 1947 ed. 35.00 (ISBN 0-404-18968-7). AMS Pr.

Lambton, Ann K. State & Government in Medieval Islam: An Introduction to the Study of Islamic Political Theory; the Jurists. (London Oriental Ser.: Vol. 36). 368p. 1981. 55.00 (ISBN 0-19-713600-1). Oxford U Pr.

Mason, Herbert. Two Statesmen of Medieval Islam: Vizir Ibn Hubayra (499-560 A. H., 1105-1165 A. D.) & Califh an-Nasir Li Din Allah (553-622 A. H., 1158-1225 A. D.) 146p. 1972. text ed. 26.25x (ISBN 90-2796-979-5). Mouton.

Muir, William. The Caliphate: Its Rise, Decline, & Fall. LC 74-180365. Repr. of 1924 ed. 52.50 (ISBN 0-404-56305-8). AMS Pr.

Scott, Samuel P. History of the Moorish Empire in Europe, 3 Vols. LC 74-153600. Repr. of 1904 ed. Set. 135.00 (ISBN 0-404-09670-0). AMS Pr.

Spuler, Bertold. The Muslim World: A Historical Survey, 2 vols. Incl. Vol. 1. Age of the Caliphs. text ed. 20.00x (ISBN 0-685-23328-6); Vol. 2. The Mongol Period. text ed. 10.00x (ISBN 0-685-23329-4). 1960. Humanities.

Stern, S. M. Documents from Islamic Chanceries. LC 74-93306. (Oriental Studies: No. 3). (Illus.). 1970. 19.50x (ISBN 0-87249-178-1). U of SC Pr.

Stewart, Desmond. Early Islam. LC 67-27863. (Great Ages of Man Ser.). (gr. 6 up). 1967. PLB 11.97 (ISBN 0-8094-0377-3, Pub. by Time-Life). Silver.

Van Vloten, Gerlof. De Opkomst der Abbasiden in Chorasan. LC 77-10454. (Studies in Islamic History: No. 16). 154p. 1977. Repr. of 1891 ed. lib. bdg. 15.00x (ISBN 0-87991-465-3). Porcupine Pr.

ISLAMIC EMPIRE–POLITICS

Banisadr, Abolhassan. The Fundamental Principles & Precepts of Islamic Government. Ghanoonparvar, Mohammed R., tr. from Persian. 144p. (Orig.). 1981. pap. 5.95 (ISBN 0-939214-01-6). Mazda Pubs.

Husaini, S. A. Q. The Constitution of the Arab Empire. 4.95 (ISBN 0-686-18334-7). Kazi Pubns.

Ibn Al-Tiqtaqa. Al-Fakhri: On the Systems of Government & the Moslem Dynasties. Whitting, C. E., tr. LC 79-2869. 326p. 1981. Repr. of 1947 ed. 26.50 (ISBN 0-8305-0041-3). Hyperion Conn.

Ibn Al-Titaka. Al-Fakhri: On the Systems of Government and the Moslem Dynasties. Whitting, C. E., tr. LC 80-2201. Repr. of 1947 ed. 35.00 (ISBN 0-404-18968-7). AMS Pr.

Siddiqi, Amir H. Caliphate & Kingship in Mediaeval Persia. LC 77-10621. (Studies in Islamic History: No. 14). 112p. Repr. of 1937 ed. lib. bdg. 12.50x (ISBN 0-87991-463-7). Porcupine Pr.

ISLAMIC ETHICS

Adb al-Wahhab ibn Ali, Taj. Kitab Mu'id an-Ni'am Wa-Mubid an-Niqam: The Restorer of Favours & the Restrainer of Chastisements. LC 78-53829. (Luzac's Semitic Text & Translation Ser.: Vol. 18). 1978. Repr. of 1908 ed. 32.50 (ISBN 0-404-11291-9). AMS Pr.

Al-Jahiz, Abu. The Epistle on Singing-Girls by Jahiz. Beeston, A. F., ed. (Approaches to Arabic Literature Ser.). 134p. 30.00x (ISBN 0-89410-299-0, Pub. by Aris & Phillips England); pap. 16.00x (ISBN 0-89410-300-8). Three Continents.

Al-Qaradawi, Yusuf. The Permissible & the Prohibited in Islam. Siddiqui, Mohammed M., tr. from Arabic. LC 80-81562. Orig. Title: Al-Halal Wal-Haram Fil Islam. 509p. (Orig., Eng.). 1981. 16.00 (ISBN 0-89259-016-5); pap. 12.50 (ISBN 0-89259-022-X). Am Trust Pubns.

Dar, B. A. Qur'anic Ethics. 1970. 4.50x (ISBN 0-87902-160-8). Orientalia.

--Quranic Ethics. pap. 2.50 (ISBN 0-686-18602-8). Kazi Pubns.

Hashim, A. S. Islamic Ethics. (Islamic Books for Children: Bk. 7). pap. 3.50 (ISBN 0-686-18404-1); pap. 30.00 entire ser. (ISBN 0-686-18405-X). Kazi Pubns.

McDonough, Sheila. The Authority of the Past. LC 76-141690. (American Academy of Religion. Studies in Religion). 46p. 1970. pap. 4.50 (ISBN 0-89130-153-4, 010001). Scholars Pr Ca.

Makari, Victor E. Ibn Taymiyyah's Ethics: The Social Factor. Little, H. Ganse, Jr., ed. LC 81-1019. (American Academy of Religion Dissertation Ser.). 1981. pap. write for info. (ISBN 0-89130-477-0). Scholars Pr CA.

Maududi, A. A. Ethical Viewpoint of Islam. pap. 1.00 (ISBN 0-686-18492-0). Kazi Pubns.

Morewedge, Parviz, ed. Islamic Philosophy & Mysticism. LC 80-14364. (Studies in Islamic Philosophy & Science). 1981. write for info. (ISBN 0-88206-302-2). Caravan Bks.

Quasem, Mohammad A. The Ethics of Al-Ghazali. LC 78-15259. (Monographs in Islamic Religion & Theology). 1978. 25.00x (ISBN 0-88206-021-X). Caravan Bks.

Quasem, Muhammad A. The Ethics of al-Ghazali: A Composite Ethics in Islam. 1975. 17.85 (ISBN 0-686-18952-3); pap. 9.00 (ISBN 0-686-18953-1). Quasem.

Shad, A. R. Muslim Etiquettes. 1981. 14.95 (ISBN 0-686-77429-9). Kazi Pubns.

ISLAMIC INTERNATIONAL LAW

see International Law (Islamic Law)

ISLAMIC LAW

Aghnides, Nicolas P. Mohammedan Theories of Finance, with an Introduction to Mohammedan Law & a Bibliography. LC 72-82246. (Columbia University Studies in the Social Sciences: No. 166). Repr. of 1916 ed. 39.50 (ISBN 0-404-51166-X). AMS Pr.

Algar, Hamid, tr. from Persian. Constitution of the Islamic Republic of Iran. 94p. 1980. 7.95 (ISBN 0-933782-07-1); pap. 2.95 (ISBN 0-933782-02-0). Mizan Pr.

Al-Qaradawi, Yusuf. The Permissible & the Prohibited in Islam. Siddiqui, Mohammed M., tr. from Arabic. LC 80-81562. Orig. Title: Al-Halal Wal-Haram Fil Islam. 509p. (Orig., Eng.). 1981. 16.00 (ISBN 0-89259-016-5); pap. 12.50 (ISBN 0-89259-022-X). Am Trust Pubns.

Anderson, James N. Islamic Law in the Modern World. LC 75-31816. 106p. 1976. Repr. of 1959 ed. lib. bdg. 15.00 (ISBN 0-8371-8451-7, ANIL). Greenwood.

Anderson, Norman. Law Reform in the Muslim World. (Univ. of London Logical Ser.: No. 11). 1976. text ed. 27.25x (ISBN 0-485-13411-X, Athlone Pr). Humanities.

Audah, Abdul Q. Al-Islam bain Jahl 'Abna'ihi wa Ajz Ulama'ihi. 79p. (Orig., Arabic.). 1980. pap. 1.55x (ISBN 0-939830-12-4, Pub. by IIFSO Kuwait). New Era Pubns MI.

Audah, Adbul Q. Islam Between Ignorant Followers & Incapable Scholars. 115p. (Orig.). pap. 2.50x (ISBN 0-939830-01-9, Pub. by IIFSO Kuwait). New Era Pubns MI.

Baillie, N. A Digest of Muhammadan Law, 2 vols. 30.00 set (ISBN 0-686-18561-7). Kazi Pubns.

Burton, J. The Collection of the Qur'an. LC 76-27899. 1977. 38.50 (ISBN 0-521-21439-4); pap. 12.95 (ISBN 0-521-29652-8). Cambridge U Pr.

Chaudhri, A. R. Substance of Muhammahan Law. 1970. 3.85x (ISBN 0-87902-157-8). Orientalia.

Chejne, Anwar. Succession to the Rule in Muslim. 154p. (Orig.). 1981. pap. 4.85 (ISBN 0-88004-001-7). Sunwise Turn.

Coulson, Noel. A History of Islamic Law. 1964. 8.00x (ISBN 0-85224-354-5, Pub. by Edinburgh U Pr Scotland). Columbia U Pr.

Coulson, Noel J. Conflicts & Tensions in Islamic Jurisprudence. Polk, William R., ed. LC 79-80433. (Publications of the Center for Middle Eastern Studies Ser: No. 5). 1969. 5.50x (ISBN 0-226-11610-7). U of Chicago Pr.

El-Awa, Mohammed. Punishment in Islamic Law. LC 80-65482. 150p. (Orig.). 1981. 12.25 (ISBN 0-89259-015-7); pap. 8.50 (ISBN 0-89259-020-3). Am Trust Pubns.

Foda, Ezzeldin. The Projected Arab Court of Justice: A Study in Regional Jurisdiction with Specific Reference to the Muslim Law of Nations. LC 79-2858. 258p. 1981. Repr. of 1957 ed. 22.50 (ISBN 0-8305-0031-6). Hyperion Conn.

Fyzee, Asaf A. Outlines of Muhammadan Law. 4th ed. (Illus.). 1976. 11.00x (ISBN 0-19-560375-3). Oxford U Pr.

Giorgio Levi Della Vida Conference-2nd-los Angeles-1969. Proceedings: Theology & Law in Islam. Von Grunebaum, G. E., ed. 113p. 1971. 47.50x (ISBN 3-447-01273-0). Intl Pubns Serv.

Goldziher, Ignaz. Introduction to Islamic Theology & Law. Lewis, Bernard, ed. Hamori, Andras & Hamori, Ruth, trs. from Ger. LC 80-7523. (Modern Classics in Near Eastern Studies). 325p. 1981. 25.00 (ISBN 0-691-07257-4); pap. 9.95 (ISBN 0-691-10099-3). Princeton U Pr.

Hamilton, C. The Hedaya: A Commentary on the Musulman Laws. 1963. 32.00x (ISBN 0-87902-163-2). Orientalia.

Ibn Fudi, Uthman. Bayan Wujub Al-Hijra Ala L-Ibad. El Masri, F. H., ed. & tr. from Arabic. (Fontes Historical Africannae - Arabic Ser.). 358p. 1978. text ed. 49.50x (ISBN 0-19-822703-5). Oxford U Pr.

Khadduri, Majid. Law of War & Peace in Islam: A Study of Moslem International Law. LC 76-147599. (Library of War & Peace; International Law). lib. bdg. 38.00 (ISBN 0-8240-0360-8). Garland Pub.

--War & Peace in the Law of Islam. LC 77-2418. Repr. of 1955 ed. 24.50 (ISBN 0-404-10925-X). AMS Pr.

Khadduri, Majid, intro. by. & tr. Islamic Jurisprudence: Shafi'i's Risala. 374p. 1961. 24.00x (ISBN 0-8018-0333-0). Johns Hopkins.

Khali, Ibn I. Maliki Law. Ruxton, F. H., tr. from Fr. LC 79-1611. 1980. Repr. of 1916 ed. 31.50 (ISBN 0-88355-914-5). Hyperion Conn.

MacDonald, D. B. Development of Muslim Jurisprudence & Constitutional Theory. 1964. 7.60x (ISBN 0-87902-173-X). Orientalia.

Macnauhten, William H. Principles of Muhammadan Law. 140p. (Orig.). 1981. pap. 5.50 (ISBN 0-88004-010-6). Sunwise Turn.

Markby, William. An Introduction to Hindu & Mohammedan Law. LC 78-58189. 1978. Repr. of 1906 ed. lib. bdg. 25.00 (ISBN 0-89341-509-X). Longwood Pr.

Maududi, A. Islamic Law & Constitution. 1969. pap. 5.75 (ISBN 0-87902-176-4). Orientalia.

Maududi, A. A. Islamic Law & Constitution. 5.50 (ISBN 0-686-18557-9). Kazi Pubns.

--Questions of Dress. pap. 1.50 (ISBN 0-686-63910-3). Kazi Pubns.

Merchant, M. N. Quranic Laws. pap. 3.95 (ISBN 0-686-18550-1). Kazi Pubns.

Merchant, M. V. Qur'anic Laws. 1971. 5.50x (ISBN 0-87902-177-2). Orientalia.

Muslehuddin. Insurance & Islamic Law. pap. 2.50 (ISBN 0-686-18372-X). Kazi Pubns.

Pearl, David. A Textbook of Muslim Law. 317p. 1979. 35.00x (ISBN 0-85664-959-7, Pub. by Croom Helm Ltd England). Biblio Dist.

Qadri, A. A. Islamic Jurisprudence in the Modern World. 535p. 1973. 15.00x (ISBN 0-87902-232-9). Orientalia.

--Justice in Historical Islam. 3.95 (ISBN 0-686-18555-2). Kazi Pubns.

--Muslim Personal Law. pap. 4.00 (ISBN 0-686-18553-6). Kazi Pubns.

Rahim, Abdur. The Principles of Muhammadan Jurisprudence According to the Hanali, Maliki, Shafi'i & Hanbali Schools. LC 79-2879. 443p. 1981. Repr. of 1911 ed. 33.50 (ISBN 0-8305-0047-2). Hyperion Conn.

Schacht, Joseph. Introduction to Islamic Law. 1964. 24.95x (ISBN 0-19-825161-0). Oxford U Pr.

Siddiqui, A. H. Jehad in Islam. pap. 1.95 (ISBN 0-686-63906-5). Kazi Pubns.

Siddiqui, M. I. Penal Law of Islam. 1980. 9.95 (ISBN 0-686-64662-2). Kazi Pubns.

Siddiqui, M. S. Islamic Sharia & the Muslims. pap. 2.50 (ISBN 0-686-63905-7). Kazi Pubns.

Valiuddin, Mir. The Quranic Sufism. 221p. 1981. pap. 11.50 (ISBN 0-88004-007-6). Sunwise Turn.

Wakin, Jeanette A., ed. The Function of Documents in Islamic Law: The Chapters on Sale from Tahawi's Kitab Al Shurut Al-Kibar. LC 75-171178. 1972. 33.00 (ISBN 0-87395-100-X); microfiche 33.00 (ISBN 0-87395-104-2). State U NY Pr.

ISLAMIC LAW–AFRICA

Anderson, Norman. Islamic Law in Africa. new ed. 396p. 1970. 32.00x (ISBN 0-7146-1905-1, F Cass Co). Biblio Dist.

ISLAMIC LAW–ASIA

Mahmood, Tahir. Muslim Personal Law. 1977. text ed. 12.50x (ISBN 0-7069-0532-6). Humanities.

ISLAMIC LEARNING AND SCHOLARSHIP

Ahmad, Nafis. Muslim Contributions to Geography. (Illus.). 178p. (Orig.). 1981. pap. 7.50 (ISBN 0-88004-014-9). Sunwise Turn.

Mason, Herbert W., et al, eds. Humaniora Islamica: An Annual Publication of Islamic Studies & the Humanities, Vol. 1. 1973. pap. text ed. 40.00x (ISBN 0-686-31749-1). Mouton.

--Humaniora Islamica: An Annual Publication of Islamic Studies & the Humanities, Vol. 2. 310p. 1974. pap. text ed. 50.00x (ISBN 0-686-27750-3). Mouton.

Myers, Eugene A. Arabic Thought & the Western World in the Golden Age of Islam. LC 64-15696. pap. 4.95 (ISBN 0-8044-6562-2). Ungar.

Rosenthal, Franz. The Classical Heritage in Islam. Marmorstein, Emile, tr. LC 69-12476. 1975. 30.00 (ISBN 0-520-01997-0). U of Cal Pr.

ISLAMIC LEGENDS

see Legends, Islamic

ISLAMIC LITERATURE

see also Koran

Arberry, Arthur J. Aspects of Islamic Civilization As Depicted in the Original Texts. LC 77-673. 1977. Repr. of 1964 ed. lib. bdg. 29.25 (ISBN 0-8371-9494-6, ARAI). Greenwood.

Hashim, A. S. Al-Khulafe al-Rashidoon. (Islamic Books for Children: Bk. 6). pap. 3.00 (ISBN 0-686-18406-8); pap. 30.00 entire ser. (ISBN 0-686-18407-6). Kazi Pubns.

Jeffery, Arthur, ed. A Reader on Islam. LC 79-52557. (Islam Ser.). 1980. Repr. of 1962 ed. lib. bdg. 50.00x (ISBN 0-8369-9264-4). Arno.

Khumayni, Ruh A. Islam & Revolution: Writings & Declarations of Imam Khomeini. Algar, Hamid, tr. LC 80-24032. 480p. 1981. 19.95 (ISBN 0-933782-04-7). Mizan Pr.

Kritzeck, James, ed. Anthology of Islamic Literature: From the Rise of Islam to Modern Times. 1975. pap. 5.95 (ISBN 0-452-00498-5, F498, Mer). NAL.

Muhammad & Ali, Hazrat. Excellent Sayings of Muhammad & Ali. Campbell, Charles I., tr. from Arabic. 1978. pap. 5.00 (ISBN 0-917220-02-1). Khaneghah & Maktab.

Shah, Idries. Pleasantries of Mulla Nasrudin. 1971. pap. 5.75 (ISBN 0-525-47306-8). Dutton.

Utas, Bo. Tariq Ut-Tahqiq. (Scandinavian Institute of Asian Studies Monograph: No. 13). 300p. (Orig.). 1975. pap. text ed. 12.50x (ISBN 0-7007-0062-5). Humanities.

ISLAMIC LITERATURE–HISTORY AND CRITICISM

Arberry, Arthur J. Aspects of Islamic Civilization: As Depicted in the Original Texts. 1967. pap. 4.95 (ISBN 0-472-06130-5, 130, AA). U of Mich Pr.

DeLamotte, Roy C. Jalaluddin Rumi: Songbird of Sufism. LC 80-5884. 187p. 1980. lib. bdg. 16.75 (ISBN 0-8191-1286-0); pap. text ed. 8.75 (ISBN 0-8191-1287-9). U Pr of Amer.

Hamalian, Leo & Yohannan, John. New Writing from the Middle East. (Orig.). 1978. pap. 2.95 (ISBN 0-451-61639-1, ME1639, Ment). NAL.

Lyons, M. C., ed. An Arabic Translation of Themistius Commentary on Aristoteles De Anima. LC 73-1153. (Oriental Studies: No. 2). 1973. 27.50x (ISBN 0-87249-287-7). U of SC Pr.

Pfannmueller, Gustav. Handbuch der Islam-Literatur. viii, 436p. (Ger.). 1974. Repr. of 1923 ed. 86.00x (ISBN 3-11-002488-8). De Gruyter.

Schimmel, Annemarie. As Through a Veil: Mystical Poetry in Islam. (Lectures on the History of Religion Ser.: No. 12). (Illus.). 328p. 1982. text ed. 22.50x (ISBN 0-231-05246-4). Columbia U Pr.

--Islamic Religious Poetry. 1982. 22.50x (ISBN 0-231-05246-4). Columbia U Pr.

Wansbrough, J. Quranic Studies: Sources & Methods of Scriptural Interpretations, Vol. 31. (London Oriential Ser). 1977. 55.00x (ISBN 0-19-713588-9). Oxford U Pr.

ISLAMIC MUSIC

see Music, Islamic

ISLAMIC MYSTICISM

see Mysticism–Islam

ISLAMIC PAINTING

see Painting, Islamic

ISLAMIC PHILOSOPHY

see Philosophy, Islamic

ISLAMIC POTTERY

see Pottery, Islamic

ISLAMIC SECTS

see also Assassins (Ismailites); Bektashi; Motazilites; Shiites; Wahhabiyah

Abd-Al-Kahir Ibn-Tahir Ibn Muhammad, Abu M. Moslem Schisms & Sects: Being the History of the Various Philosophic Systems Developed in Islam. Seelye, Kate C., tr. LC 75-158216. (Columbia University Oriental Studies: No. 15). 1920. 20.00 (ISBN 0-404-50505-8). AMS Pr.

Wansbrough, John. The Sectarian Milieu: Content & Composition of Islamic Salvation History. (London Oriental Ser.: No. 34). 1979. 39.00x (ISBN 0-19-713596-X). Oxford U Pr.

ISLAMIC SECTS–MISSIONS

see also Ahmadiyya

ISLAMIC SOCIOLOGY

see Sociology, Islamic

ISLAMIC TEXTILE FABRICS

see Textile Fabrics, Islamic

ISLAMIC THEOLOGY

see also God (Islam); Mysticism–Islam

Al-Qibrisi, Shaykh N. Mercy Oceans: Teachings of Maulana Abdullah al-Faiza ad-Daghestani. 190p. (Orig.). 1980. pap. 4.75x (ISBN 0-939830-11-6, Pub. by Leon). New Era Pubns MI.

Al-Wahhab, Muhammad I. Essay on the Unicity of Allah. Al-Faruqi, Isma'il R., tr. from Arabic. 191p. (Orig.). 1979. pap. 4.65x (ISBN 0-939830-21-3, Pub. by IIFSO Kuwait). New Era Pubns MI.

--Kitab Al Tawhid. 120p. (Orig., Arabic.). 1978. pap. 2.35x (ISBN 0-939830-20-5, Pub. by IIFSO Kuwait). New Era Pubns MI.

Boewering, Gerhard. The Mystical Vision of Existence in Islam Classical. (Studien zur Sprache, Geschichte und Kultur desislamischen Orients, Beihefte zur "der Islam"). 296p. 1979. text ed. 79.00x (ISBN 3-11-007546-6). De Gruyter.

Cook, M. Early Muslim Dogma. 256p. Date not set. 49.50 (ISBN 0-521-23379-8). Cambridge U Pr.

Craig, William L. The Kalam Cosmological Argument. LC 77-17232. (Library of Philosophy & Religion Ser). 1979. text ed. 23.50x (ISBN 0-06-491308-2). B&N.

Deedat, A. Quran, the Ultimate Miracle. pap. 2.95 (ISBN 0-686-63913-8). Kazi Pubns.

Doj, A. R. Quran, an Introduction. pap. 4.95 (ISBN 0-686-63911-1). Kazi Pubns.

Farook, Omar & Rauf, A. Quran for Children. pap. 4.95 (ISBN 0-686-63912-X). Kazi Pubns.

Frank, Richard M. Beings & Their Attributes. LC 78-6957. 1978. 33.00 (ISBN 0-87395-378-9). State U NY Pr.

Giorgio Levi Della Vida Conference-2nd-los Angeles-1969. Proceedings: Theology & Law in Islam. Von Grunebaum, G. E., ed. 113p. 1971. 47.50x (ISBN 3-447-01273-0). Intl Pubns Serv.

Goldziher, Ignaz. Introduction to Islamic Theology & Law. Lewis, Bernard, ed. Hamori, Andras & Hamori, Ruth, trs. from Ger. LC 80-7523. (Modern Classics in Near Eastern Studies). 325p. 1981. 25.00 (ISBN 0-691-07257-4); pap. 9.95 (ISBN 0-691-10099-3). Princeton U Pr.

Hakim, Khalifa A. The Metaphysics of Rumi. 157p. 1981. pap. 4.25 (ISBN 0-88004-004-1). Sunwise Turn.

Hazrath Ali-Ibne-Abu Talib. Nahjul Balagha. Syed Mohammed Askari Jafery, tr. from Arabic. 416p. 1981. 5.00 (ISBN 0-686-30244-3); pap. 3.00 (ISBN 0-686-30245-1). Tahrike Tarsile Quran.

Husain, Ashfaque. The Spirit of Islam. 95p. 1981. text ed. 10.00x (ISBN 0-391-02192-3, Pub. by Heinemann India). Humanities.

Hussain, Ahmed. The Philosophy of Faqirs. 126p. (Orig.). 1981. pap. 4.50 (ISBN 0-88004-006-8). Sunwise Turn.

Klein, F. A. Religion of Islam. 241p. 1978. Repr. of 1906 ed. 16.50 (ISBN 0-89684-153-7). Orient Bk Dist.

Lammens, H. Islam Beliefs & Institutions. Ross, Ed, tr. 1969. Repr. of 1929 ed. 26.50x (ISBN 0-7146-1991-4, F Cass Co). Biblio Dist.

Malik, Charles, ed. God & Man in Contemporary Islamic Thought. 1972. 16.95x (ISBN 0-8156-6035-9, Am U Beirut). Syracuse U Pr.

Mas'Ud Ibn Umar Al-Taftazani. A Commentary on the Creed of Islam. LC 79-52565. (Islam Ser.). 1980. Repr. of 1950 ed. lib. bdg. 18.00x (ISBN 0-8369-9268-7). Arno.

Morewedge, Parviz, ed. Islamic Philosophical Theology. LC 79-14405. 1979. 35.00 (ISBN 0-87395-242-1). State U NY Pr.

Muhammad'Abduh. The Theology of Unity. LC 79-52560. (Islam Ser.). 1980. Repr. of 1966 ed. lib. bdg. 15.00x (ISBN 0-8369-9267-9). Arno.

Qayyum, A. On Striving to Be a Muslim. pap. 5.50 (ISBN 0-686-63908-1). Kazi Pubns.

Saporetti, C. Assur 114446: La Famiglia "A". Bucellati, G., ed. (Cybernetica Mesopotamia Ser.: Vol. 1). 139p. 1979. pap. 9.50 soft only (ISBN 0-89003-036-7). Undena Pubns.

Sharif, Ja'Far. Islam in India, or the Qanun-I-Islam: The Customs of the Musalmans of India. rev. ed. Herklots, G. A., tr. from Urdu. (Illus.). 374p. 1972. Repr. of 1921 ed. 10.50x (ISBN 0-8426-0375-1). Verry.

Siddigri, A. H. The Islamic Concept of Religion & Its Revival. 1981. 14.95 (ISBN 0-686-77428-0). Kazi Pubns.

Siddiqui, A. H. Selections from Quran & Hadith. pap. 9.95 (ISBN 0-686-63914-6). Kazi Pubns.

Sweetman, James W. Islam & Christian Theology: A Study of the Interpretations of Theological Ideas in the Two Religions, 3 vols. 1980. Set. lib. bdg. 229.95 (ISBN 0-8490-3136-2). Gordon Pr.

Tritton, Arthur S. Muslim Theology. LC 79-2885. 218p. 1980. Repr. of 1947 ed. 18.00 (ISBN 0-8305-0052-9). Hyperion Conn.

Troll, Christian. Sayyid Ahmad Khan: A Reinterpretation of Muslim Theology. 1978. text ed. 16.00x (ISBN 0-7069-0626-8). Humanities.

Wansbrough, J. Quranic Studies: Sources & Methods of Scriptural Interpretations, Vol. 31. (London Oriential Ser). 1977. 55.00x (ISBN 0-19-713588-9). Oxford U Pr.

Wensinck, A. J. Muslim Creed: Its Genesis & Historical Development. 304p. 1965. 29.50x (ISBN 0-7146-1997-3, F Cass Co). Biblio Dist.

Wolfson, Harry A. The Philosophy of the Kalam. LC 74-78718. 864p. 1976. 30.00x (ISBN 0-674-66580-5). Harvard U Pr.

ISLAMIC WOMEN

see Women, Muslim

ISLAND ARCS

Mattson, Peter H., ed. West Indies Island Arcs. (Benchmark Papers in Geology Ser.: Vol. 33). 1977. 51.50 (ISBN 0-12-787060-1). Acad Pr.

Sugimura, A. & Uyeda, S. Island Arcs. LC 77-180008. (Developments in Geotectonics: Vol. 3). (Illus.). 240p. 1973. 53.75 (ISBN 0-444-40970-X). Elsevier.

ISLAND FLORA AND FAUNA

Adams, C. D. Flowering Plants of Jamaica. 848p. 16.00 (ISBN 0-685-25504-2). Horticultural.

Amos, William H. Wildlife of the Islands. (Wildlife Habitat Ser.). (Illus.). 1980. 18.95 (ISBN 0-8109-1763-7). Abrams.

Berrill, N. J. Life of Sea Islands. (Our Living World of Nature Ser). (Illus.). 1969. 9.95 (ISBN 0-07-005026-0, P&RB); by subscription 3.95 (ISBN 0-07-046011-6). McGraw.

Bramwell, D. Plants & Islands. LC 79-50299. 1980. 63.50 (ISBN 0-12-125460-7). Acad Pr.

Carlquist, Sherwin. Island Biology. LC 73-4643. (Illus.). 660p. 1974. 32.50x (ISBN 0-231-03562-4); pap. 15.00x (ISBN 0-231-08364-5). Columbia U Pr.

Hatt, Robert, et al. Island Life: A Study of Land Vertebrates of the Islands of Eastern Lake Michigan. LC 48-7777. (Bulletin Ser.: No. 27). (Illus.). 179p. 1948. text ed. 7.00x (ISBN 0-87737-009-5). Cranbrook.

Island Life. LC 77-95115. (Wild, Wild World of Animals Ser.). (Illus.). 1978. lib. bdg. 11.97 (ISBN 0-686-51171-9). Silver.

Lack, David. Island Biology. LC 75-7194. (Studies in Ecology: Vol. 3). 1976. 46.50x (ISBN 0-520-03007-9). U of Cal Pr.

Time-Life Books, ed. Island Life. (Wild, Wild World of Animals). (Illus.). 1978. 10.95 (ISBN 0-913948-19-5). Time-Life.

Wallace, Alfred R. Island Life. 3rd, rev. ed. LC 72-1667. Repr. of 1911 ed. 34.50 (ISBN 0-404-08183-5). AMS Pr.

Weller, Milton W. The Island Waterfowl. new ed. (Illus.). 144p. 1980. text ed. 11.95 (ISBN 0-8138-1310-7). Iowa St U Pr.

Williamson, Mark. Island Populations. (Illus.). 200p. 1981. 49.50 (ISBN 0-19-854134-1). Oxford U Pr.

ISLANDS

see also Coral Reefs and Islands; Island Arcs; Island Flora and Fauna; United States–Territories and Possessions

Anderson, D. The Evergreen Islands. (Illus.). 240p. 1980. pap. 7.95 (ISBN 0-686-74118-8). Superior Pub.

Babcock, W. H. The Legendary Islands of the Atlantic. 1973. lib. bdg. 14.00x (ISBN 0-374-90320-4). Octagon.

Berrill, N. J. Life of Sea Islands. (Our Living World of Nature Ser). (Illus.). 1969. 9.95 (ISBN 0-07-005026-0, P&RB); by subscription 3.95 (ISBN 0-07-046011-6). McGraw.

Brothwell, Don & Dimbley, Geoffrey, eds. Environmental Aspects of Coasts & Islands. 206p. 1981. 48.00x (ISBN 0-86054-110-X, Pub. by BAR). State Mutual Bk.

Coxon, Philip. The World of an Island. 1978. 7.95 (ISBN 0-571-10999-3, Pub. by Faber & Faber). Merrimack Bk Serv.

Coysh, Victor. Alderney. (Island Ser.). (Illus.). 160p. 1974. 15.95 (ISBN 0-7153-6386-7). David & Charles.

Dommen, Edward, ed. Islands. (Illus.). 135p. 1981. 18.00 (ISBN 0-08-026799-8). Pergamon.

Ecological Guidelines for Island Development. (Illus.). 1974. pap. 7.50x (ISBN 2-88032-001-1, IUCN20, IUCN). Unipub.

Fowles, John. Islands. 1978. 10.95 (ISBN 0-316-28960-4). Little.

Gleasner, Bill & Gleasner, Diana. Sea Islands of the South. LC 79-24730. (Illus.). 176p. 1980. pap. 8.95 (ISBN 0-914788-21-3). East Woods.

Irving, Celia. Adriatic Islands & Corfu. 1971. 7.50x (ISBN 0-460-03922-9). Intl Pubns Serv.

Kennedy, Jo M. Dauphin Island. 1980. 5.95 (ISBN 0-87397-168-X). Strode.

Kolar, Vladimir. Islands of the Adriatic. (Illus.). 1978. 19.95 (ISBN 0-8467-0465-X, Pub. by Two Continents). Hippocrene Bks.

Kwon, H. J. Barrier Islands of the Northern Gulf of Mexico Coast: Sediment Sources & Development. (Coastal Studies, Vol. 25). (Illus.). viii, 52p. 1970. pap. 4.00x (ISBN 0-8071-0034-X). La State U Pr.

Laycock, George. Islands & Their Mysteries. LC 77-6265. (Illus.). 112p. (gr. 5-9). 1977. 7.95g (ISBN 0-590-07455-5, Four Winds). Schol Bk Serv.

Leatherman, Stephen, ed. Barrier Islands: From the Gulf of St. Lawrence to the Gulf of Mexico. LC 79-15954. 1979. 22.50 (ISBN 0-12-440260-7). Acad Pr.

Macdonald, Donald. Lewis: A History of the Island. 256p. 1981. 50.00x (ISBN 0-903065-23-1, Pub. by Wright Pub Scotland). State Mutual Bk.

--Lewis: A History of the Island. (Illus.). 1978. 19.95x (ISBN 0-8464-0564-4). Beekman Pubs.

Meinicke, C. E. Die Inseln des Stillen Oceans, 2 vols. (Ger.). 1875. text ed. 56.50x (ISBN 90-6041-043-2). Humanities.

Mitchell-Thome, Raoul C. Geology of the Middle Atlantic Islands. (Beitraege zur regionalen Geologie der Erde: Vol. 12). (Illus.). 1976. lib. bdg. 116.80x (ISBN 3-443-11012-6). Lubrecht & Cramer.

Obee, B. The Gulf Islands. (Illus.). 1981. pap. 5.95 (ISBN 0-686-74140-4). Superior Pub.

Raspe, Rudolf E. Introduction to the Natural History of the Terrestrial Sphere. facsimile ed. 1970. 26.50 (ISBN 0-02-850840-8). Hafner.

Russell, Franklin. Secret Islands. (Illus.). 1966. 5.95 (ISBN 0-393-07381-5). Norton.

Russell, Robert. The Island. LC 72-83352. 368p. 1972. 9.95 (ISBN 0-8149-0721-0). Vanguard.

Sachet, Marie-Helene & Fosberg, F. Raymond. Island Bibliographies Supplement. LC 55-60007. 448p. 1971. text ed. 11.00 (ISBN 0-309-01932-X). Natl Acad Pr.

Schwartz, Maurice L., ed. Barrier Islands. LC 73-12838. (Benchmark Papers in Geology Ser.). 464p. 1973. text ed. 50.00 (ISBN 0-12-787447-X). Acad Pr.

Thomas, Bill. The Island: A Native History of America's Coastal Islands. (Illus.). 1980. 29.95 (ISBN 0-393-01373-1). Norton.

Westbrook, Perry D. Biography of an Island. LC 57-12360. 1970. 8.95 (ISBN 0-498-07005-0). A S Barnes.

ISLANDS, IMAGINARY

see Geographical Myths

ISLANDS OF LANGERHANS

see Pancreas

ISLANDS OF THE AEGEAN

Bodnar, Edward W. & Mitchell, Charles. Cyriacus of Ancona's Journeys in the Propontis & the Northern Aegean: 1444-1445. LC 75-35466. (Memoirs Ser.: Vol. 112). 1976. pap. 6.00 (ISBN 0-87169-112-4). Am Philos.

Craik, Elizabeth M. The Dorian Aegean. (States & Cities of Ancient Greece Ser.). 1979. 22.50 (ISBN 0-7100-0378-1). Routledge & Kegan.

Davies, Derek A. C. Greek Islands. LC 73-158639. (This Beautiful World Ser.: Vol. 27). (Illus.). 130p. (Orig.). 1971. pap. 4.95 (ISBN 0-87011-154-X). Kodansha.

Davis, Ellen N. The Vapheio Cups & Aegean Gold & Silver Ware. LC 76-23609. (Outstanding Dissertations in the Fine Arts). (Illus.). 1977. Repr. of 1973 ed. lib. bdg. 63.00 (ISBN 0-8240-2681-0). Garland Pub.

DeBosset, C. P. Proceedings in Parga & the Ionian Islands. (Illus.). 1976. 15.00 (ISBN 0-916710-27-0). Obol Intl.

Denham, H. M. The Aegean: A Sea-Guide to Its Coasts & Islands. rev., 3rd ed. (Illus.). 1976. 19.95 (ISBN 0-393-03197-7). Norton.

--The Ionian Islands to Rhodes: A Sea-Guide. (Illus.). 1976. 19.95 (ISBN 0-393-03195-0). Norton.

Doumas, C., ed. Thera & the Aegean World, Vol. I. 822p. 1978. text ed. 85.00x (ISBN 0-9506133-0-4, Pub. by Aris & Phillips England). Humanities.

Hood, Sinclair. The Home of the Heroes: The Aegean Before the Greeks. (Illus.). 144p. 1975. pap. 7.50 (ISBN 0-500-29009-1). Transatlantic.

Kasperson, Roger E. The Dodecanese: Diversity & Unity in Island Politics. LC 66-29232. (Research Papers Ser.: No. 108). 184p. 1967. pap. 8.00 (ISBN 0-89065-017-9). U Chicago Dept Geog.

Tozer, H. F. The Islands of the Aegen. (Illus.). 1976. 20.00 (ISBN 0-916710-26-2). Obol Intl.

ISLANDS OF THE INDIAN OCEAN

Moor, J. H. Notices of the Indian Archipelago & Adjacent Countries. 398p. 1968. Repr. of 1837 ed. 85.00x (ISBN 0-7146-2020-3, F Cass Co). Biblio Dist.

Ommanney, Francis D. The Shoals of Capricorn. LC 74-15555. (Illus.). 322p. 1975. Repr. of 1952 ed. lib. bdg. 19.50x (ISBN 0-8371-7823-1, OMSC). Greenwood.

Scott, Sir Robert. Limuria: The Lesser Dependencies of Maritius. LC 75-3741. (Illus.). 1976. Repr. of 1961 ed. lib. bdg. 19.25x (ISBN 0-8371-8058-9, SCLIM). Greenwood.

Shand, R. T., ed. The Island Stats of the Pacific & Indian Oceans: Anatomy of Development. (Development Studies Centre-Monographs: No. 23). 512p. 1981. pap. text ed. 13.95 (ISBN 0-909150-15-X, 0088, Pub. by ANUP Australia). Bks Australia.

ISLANDS OF THE PACIFIC

see also Micronesia

Adam, T. R. Western Interests in the Pacific Realm. 6.50 (ISBN 0-8446-1507-2). Peter Smith.

Corkran, Herbert. Mini-Nations & Macro-Cooperation: The Caribbean & the South Pacific. 1977. 10.00 (ISBN 0-88265-011-4). North Am Intl.

Coxe, William. Account of the Russian Discoveries Between Asia & America. 3rd ed. LC 78-107912. (Illus.). Repr. of 1787 ed. 25.00x (ISBN 0-678-00626-1). Kelley.

De Smith, Stanley A. Microstates & Micronesia: The Problems of America's Pacific Islands & Other Minute Territories. LC 74-92526. (Studies in Peaceful Change: Vol. 4). (Illus.). 1970. 10.00x (ISBN 0-8147-0118-3). NYU Pr.

Giles, William E. A Cruise in a Queensland Labour Vessel to the South Seas. Scarr, Deryck, ed. (Pacific History Ser.: No. 1). (Illus.). 1968. 7.50x (ISBN 0-87022-295-3). U Pr of Hawaii.

Grimshaw, Beatrice. In the Strange South Seas. facs. ed. LC 72-152920. (Black Heritage Library Collection Ser). 1908. 30.50 (ISBN 0-8369-8764-0). Arno.

Harris, N. V. Tropical Pacific. LC 66-69488. (Illus.). 1966. 5.00x (ISBN 0-340-08069-8). Intl Pubns Serv.

Haun, Connie M. Faraway Places. 1977. 6.95 (ISBN 0-533-02689-X). Vantage.

Hempenstall, Peter J. Pacific Islanders Under German Rule: A Study in the Meaning of Colonial Resistance. LC 78-58251. (Illus.). 1979. text ed. 24.95 (ISBN 0-7081-1350-8, 0531, Pub. by ANUP Australia). Bks Australia.

Hinz, Earl R. Landfalls of Paradise: The Guide to Pacific Islands. LC 79-17600. (Illus.). 384p. 1980. 29.95 (ISBN 0-930030-13-3). Western Marine Ent.

Institute of Pacific Relations. An Economic Survey of the Pacific Area, 3 pts. Field, Frederick V., ed. Incl. Pt. 1. Population & Land Utilization. Pelzer, Karl J. 1971. Repr. of 1941 ed. 13.00 (ISBN 0-8462-1607-8); Pt. 2. Transportation by Katrine R. Greene & Foreign Trade in the Pacific Area by Joseph D. Phillips. 1971. Repr. of 1942 ed. 12.00 (ISBN 0-8462-1605-1); Pt. 3. Industrialization of the Western Pacific. Mitchell, Kate L. 1971. Repr. of 1942 ed. 15.00 (ISBN 0-685-22982-3). LC 75-151554. (Illus.). Russell.

Livingston, William S. & Louis, W. Roger, eds. Australia, New Zealand, & the Pacific Islands Since the First World War. 261p. 1979. text ed. 17.95x (ISBN 0-292-70344-9). U of Tex Pr.

Louis, William R. National Security & International Trusteeship in the Pacific. LC 78-149493. 1972. 13.00 (ISBN 0-87021-400-4). Naval Inst Pr.

Maude, H. E. Of Islands & Men: Studies in Pacific History. 1968. 23.50x (ISBN 0-19-550177-2). Oxford U Pr.

Munz, P. Feel of Truth. 1969. 15.00x (ISBN 0-589-04070-7). Intl Pubns Serv.

Oliver, Douglas. The Pacific Islands. rev. ed. LC 73-77010. (Illus.). 480p. 1975. pap. text ed. 5.95x (ISBN 0-8248-0397-3). U Pr of Hawaii.

Pacific Islands Year Book 1979. 13th ed. LC 79-522889. (Illus.). 1977. 30.00x (ISBN 0-8002-1774-8). Intl Pubns Serv.

Planck, Charles & Planck, Carolyn. Pacific Paradise on a Low Budget. LC 72-3809. (Illus.). 200p. 1973. pap. 3.50 (ISBN 0-87491-332-2). Acropolis.

Ralston, Caroline. Grass Huts & Warehouses: A Study of Five Pacific Beach Communities of the Nineteenth Century. LC 77-92406. 1978. text ed. 14.00x (ISBN 0-8248-0597-6). U Pr of Hawaii.

Robarts, Edward. The Marquesan Journal of Edward Robarts: 1797-1824. Dening, Greg, ed. (Pacific History Ser.: No. 6). 350p. 1974. text ed. 15.00x (ISBN 0-8248-0297-7). U Pr of Hawaii.

Roberts, Stephen H. Population Problems of the Pacific. LC 71-99884. Repr. of 1927 ed. 29.50 (ISBN 0-404-00599-3). AMS Pr.

Seabrook, W. B. The Magic Island. 1977. Repr. of 1929 ed. lib. bdg. 20.00 (ISBN 0-8414-7934-8). Folcroft.

Seabury, Paul. America's Stake in the Pacific. LC 81-2137. 91p. (Orig.). 1981. pap. 4.00 (ISBN 0-89633-045-1). Ethics & Public Policy.

Shand, R. T., ed. The Island Stats of the Pacific & Indian Oceans: Anatomy of Development. (Development Studies Centre-Monographs: No. 23). 512p. 1981. pap. text ed. 13.95 (ISBN 0-909150-15-X, 0088, Pub. by ANUP Australia). Bks Australia.

Siers, James. Rarotonga. LC 78-670044. (Illus.). 1977. 10.00x (ISBN 0-8002-0218-X). Intl Pubns Serv.

Sunset Editiors. Islands of the South Pacific: Travel Guide. 3rd ed. LC 79-88018. (Illus.). 128p. 1979. pap. 5.95 (ISBN 0-376-06385-8, Sunset Bks). Sunset-Lane.

Syme, Ronald. Isles of the Frigate Bird. 240p. 1975. 12.95 (ISBN 0-7181-1378-0, Pub. by Michael Joseph). Merrimack Bk Serv.

Thompson, L. The Native Culture of the Marianas Islands. Repr. of 1945 ed. 7.00 (ISBN 0-527-02293-4). Kraus Repr.

Tyler, Charles M. The Island World of the Pacific Ocean. 1977. lib. bdg. 75.00 (ISBN 0-8490-2081-6). Gordon Pr.

Waldo, Myra. Myra Waldo's Travel Guide to the South Pacific, 1981. (Illus.). 360p. 1981. pap. 8.95 (ISBN 0-02-098920-2, Collier). Macmillan.

Wells, Marjorie. Micronesian Handicraft Books of the Trust Territory of the Pacific Islands. 1981. 6.50 (ISBN 0-8062-1781-2). Carlton.

Young Nations Conference, Sydney, 1976. Paradise Postponed: Essays on Research & Development in the South Pacific: Proceedings. Mamak, Alexander & McCall, Grant, eds. 1979. text ed. 29.00 (ISBN 0-08-023005-9); pap. text ed. 13.25 (ISBN 0-08-023004-0). Pergamon.

ISLANDS OF THE PACIFIC–BIBLIOGRAPHY

Leeson, Ida. A Bibliography of Bibliographies of the South Pacific. (South Pacific Commission Ser.). 72p. 1954. text ed. 1.95x (ISBN 0-19-550151-9). Oxford U Pr.

Richstad, Jim & McMillan, Michael, eds. Mass Communication & Journalism in the Pacific Islands: A Bibliography. LC 77-20795. 1978. text ed. 15.00x (ISBN 0-8248-0497-X, Eastwest Ctr). U Pr of Hawaii.

ISLE OF MAN

Corran, H. S. Isle of Man. (Islands Ser.). 1977. 13.50 (ISBN 0-7153-7417-6). David & Charles.

Cubbon, A. M. Prehistoric Sites in the Isle of Man. pap. 2.95 (ISBN 0-686-10856-6). British Am Bks.

Davey, Peter. Man & Environment in the Isle of Man. 1978. 60.00x (ISBN 0-86054-034-0, Pub. by BAR). State Mutual Bk.

Hendry, R. Preston. Isle of Man Railway Album. LC 75-28. (Illus.). 96p. 1976. 13.50 (ISBN 0-7153-6828-1). David & Charles.

Killip, Christopher. The Isle of Man: A Book About the Manx. (Illus.). 96p. 1980. 25.00 (ISBN 0-7287-0187-1); pap. 12.95 (ISBN 0-7287-0186-3). Eastview.

Kinvig, R. H. The Isle of Man: A Social, Cultural and Political History. LC 75-15412. (Illus.). 1975. Repr. 14.95 (ISBN 0-8048-1165-2). C E Tuttle.

Manx Ancient & Historic Monuments. pap. 2.95 (ISBN 0-686-10851-5). British Am Bks.

Moore, A. W. A History of the Isle of Man, 2 vol. set. 34.50 (ISBN 0-686-10847-7). British Am Bks.

Morris, Ronald W. The Prehistoric Rock Art of Galloway & the Isle of Man. (Illus.). 1979. 25.00 (ISBN 0-7137-0974-X, Pub by Blandford Pr England). Sterling.

Quarmby, F. Banknotes & Banking in the Isle of Man. 1971. 7.50 (ISBN 0-685-51509-5, Pub by Spink & Son England). S J Durst.

Shearwater Press, ed. The Isle of Man & the English Counties. 100p. 100.00x (ISBN 0-686-75610-X, Pub. by Shearwater England). State Mutual Bk.

--Maps of the Isle of Man, Twelve Eighty to Seventeen Sixty. 90.00x (ISBN 0-904980-00-6, Pub. by Shearwater England). State Mutual Bk.

Stenning, E. H. Portrait of the Isle of Man. 3rd ed. LC 66-4371. (Portrait Bks.). (Illus.). 192p. 1975. 12.50x (ISBN 0-7091-5190-X). Intl Pubns Serv.

Tynwald: Symbol of an Ancient Kingdom. pap. 1.95 (ISBN 0-686-10860-4). British Am Bks.

ISLE OF WIGHT

Dicks, Brian. The Isle of Wight. LC 78-74082. 1979. 14.95 (ISBN 0-7153-7657-8). David & Charles.

Hughes, Pennethorne. The Isle of Wight: A Shell Guide. (Shell Guide Ser.). (Illus.). 278p. 1967. 7.95 (ISBN 0-571-08318-8, Pub. by Faber & Faber). Merrimack Bk Serv.

Kitchenside, G. M. Isle of Wight Album. 15.95x (ISBN 0-392-07969-0, SpS). Sportshelf.

Long, William H. A Dictionary of the Isle of Wight Dialect, & of Provincialisms Used in the Island, with Illustrative Anecdotes & Tales. LC 76-9101. 1976. Repr. of 1886 ed. lib. bdg. 20.00 (ISBN 0-8414-5740-9). Folcroft.

Patterson, A. Temple. Hampshire & the Isle of Wight. 1976. 17.95 (ISBN 0-7134-3221-7, Pub. by Batsford England). David & Charles.

Sanders, Penny. Portraits of the Isle of Wight. (Illus.). 9.95 (ISBN 0-906230-01-2, Pub. by Kingsmead Pr England). State Mutual Bk.

Wilson, Lawrence P. Portrait of the Isle of Wight. LC 65-29951. (Portrait Books Ser). (Illus.). 1965. 10.50x (ISBN 0-7091-3319-7). Intl Pubns Serv.

ISLE OF WIGHT COUNTY, VIRGINIA–HISTORY

Boddie, John B. Seventeenth Century Isle of Wight County, Virginia: Including Abstracts of County Records. LC 73-2146. 1980. Repr. of 1938 ed. 25.00 (ISBN 0-686-66834-0). Genealog Pub.

Chapman, Blanche A. Wills & Administrations of Isle of Wight County, Virginia, 1647-1800. LC 74-18117. 1975. Repr. of 1938 ed. 17.50 (ISBN 0-8063-0647-5). Genealog Pub.

ISMAILITES

see also Assassins (Ismailites); Fatimites

Lewis, Bernard. The Origins of Isma'ilism: A Study of the Historical Background of the Fatimid Caliphate. LC 74-180357. Repr. of 1940 ed. 14.50 (ISBN 0-404-56289-2). AMS Pr.

Makarem, Sami N. Doctrine of Ismailis. 1972. 6.00x (ISBN 0-89955-249-8, Pub. by Arab Inst Res). Intl Schol Bk Serv.

Poonawala, Ismail K. Bibliography of Ismaili Literature. LC 77-15698. (Studies in Near Eastern Culture & Society: Vol. 1). 1977. text ed. 40.00 (ISBN 0-685-42507-X). Undena Pubns.

ISMAY, HASTINGS LIONEL ISMAY, BARON, 1887-1965

Ismay, Lord. The Memoirs of General Lord Ismay. LC 73-22504. (Illus.). 488p. 1974. Repr. of 1960 ed. lib. bdg. 21.75x (ISBN 0-8371-6280-7, ISMF). Greenwood.

ISOBARIC SPIN

Anderson, J. D., et al, eds. Nuclear Isospin. 1969. 60.00 (ISBN 0-12-058150-7). Acad Pr.

Wilkinson, D. H., ed. Isospin in Nuclear Physics. 1970. 88.00 (ISBN 0-444-10309-0, North-Holland). Elsevier.

ISOBARS

see Atmospheric Pressure

ISOCRATES

Burk, August. Die Padagogik Des Isokrates Als Grundelgung Des Humanistichen Bildungsideals. 1923. pap. 15.50 (ISBN 0-384-06535-X). Johnson Repr.

Hubbell, Harry M. The Influence of Isocrates on Cicero, Dionysius & Aristides. 1913. 32.50x (ISBN 0-686-50045-8). Elliots Bks.

Isocrates. Ad Demonicum et Panegyricus. Connor, W. R. & Sandys, J. E., eds. LC 78-18604. (Greek Texts & Commentaries Ser.). (Illus., Gr. & Eng.). 1979. Repr. of 1872 ed. lib. bdg. 15.00x (ISBN 0-405-11444-3). Arno.

--Cyprian Orations. Connor, R. W. & Forster, Edward S., eds. LC 78-18574. (Greek Texts & Commentaries Ser). 1979. lib. bdg. 15.00x (ISBN 0-405-11418-4). Arno.

ISOCYANIDES

Ugi, Ivar. Isonitrile Chemistry. (Organic Chemistry Ser.: Vol. 20). 1971. 49.50 (ISBN 0-12-706150-9). Acad Pr.

ISOENZYMES

Brewer, G. J. Introduction to Isozyme Techniques. 1970. 35.50 (ISBN 0-12-133250-0). Acad Pr.

Clark, Peggy, et al. Isozymes: Biochemical & Genetic Studies. LC 73-10223. 242p. 1973. text ed. 27.50x (ISBN 0-8422-7126-0). Irvington.

Lang, H., ed. Creatine Kinase Isoenzyme: Patophysiology & Clinical Applications. (Illus.). 350p. 1981. 39.50 (ISBN 0-387-10714-2). Springer-Verlag.

Latner, A. L., ed. Isoenzymes in Biology & Medicine. 1968. 46.00 (ISBN 0-12-437550-2). Acad Pr.

Markert, Clement L., ed. Isozymes, 4 vols. Incl. Vol. 1. Molecular Structure. 56.50 (ISBN 0-12-472701-8); Vol. 2. Physiological Function. 56.50 (ISBN 0-12-472702-6); Vol. 3. Developmental Biology. 63.00 (ISBN 0-12-472703-4); Vol. 4. Genetics & Evolution. 58.50 (ISBN 0-12-472704-2). 1975. 191.00 set (ISBN 0-686-77086-2). Acad Pr.

Rattazzi, Mario C., et al, eds. Isozymes: Current Topics in Biological & Medical Research, Vol. 3. LC 77-12288. 212p. 1979. 22.00x (ISBN 0-8451-0252-4). A R Liss.

--Isozymes: Current Topics in Biological & Medical Research, Vol. 4. LC 77-12288. 218p. 1980. 26.00 (ISBN 0-8451-0253-2). A R Liss.

--Isozymes: Current Topics in Biological & Medical Research, Vol. 1. LC 77-12288. 202p. 1977. 19.00 (ISBN 0-8451-0250-8). A R Liss.

--Isozymes: Current Topics in Biological & Medical Research, Vol.2. LC 77-12288. 176p. 1977. 16.00 (ISBN 0-8451-0251-6). A R Liss.

Shugar, D. & Shugar, D., eds. Enzymes & Isoenzymes: Structure, Properties & Function. 1970. 57.50 (ISBN 0-12-640860-2). Acad Pr.

Weinhouse, S. Isozymes & Enzyme Regulation in Cancer. (Illus.). 1976. 49.50 (ISBN 0-8391-0735-8). Univ Park.

Wolf, P., ed. Tumor Associated Markers: The Importance of Identification in Clinical Medicine. LC 79-87540. (Illus.). 208p. 1979. 25.50x (ISBN 0-89352-065-9). Masson Pub.

ISOGONIC LINES

see Magnetism, Terrestrial

ISOLATION, SOCIAL

see Social Isolation

ISOLATION ORGAN PERFUSION (PHYSIOLOGY)

see Isolation Perfusion (Physiology)

ISOLATION PERFUSION (PHYSIOLOGY)

Berger, Edward G. The Physiology of Adequate Perfusion. LC 78-15591. (Illus.). 1979. 22.95 (ISBN 0-8016-0618-7). Mosby.

Ritchie, H. D. & Hardcastle, J. D. Isolated Organ Perfusion. (Illus.). 1973. 17.95x (ISBN 0-8464-0534-2). Beekman Pubs.

Ritchie, H. D. & Hardcastle, J. D., eds. Isolated Organ Perfusion. (Illus.). 1973. 39.50 (ISBN 0-8391-0707-2). Univ Park.

ISOMERISM

see also Stereochemistry

Bamford, C. H. & Tipper, C. F., eds. Comprehensive Chemical Kinetics, Vols. 1-7, 9, 10, 12 & 13. Incl. Vol. 1. Practice of Kinetics. 1969. 73.25 (ISBN 0-444-40673-5); Vol. 2. Theory of Kinetics. 1969. 73.25 (ISBN 0-444-40674-3); Vol. 3. Formation & Decay of Excited Species. 1970. 68.50 (ISBN 0-444-40802-9); Vol. 4. Decomposition of Inorganic & Organometallic Compounds. 1972. 63.50 (ISBN 0-444-40936-X); Vol. 5. Decomposition & Isomerization of Organic Compounds. 1972. 107.50 (ISBN 0-444-40861-4); Vol. 6. Reactions of Non-Metallic Inorganic Compounds. 1972. 92.75 (ISBN 0-444-40944-0); Vol. 7. Reactions of Metallic Salts & Complexes & Organometallic Compounds. 1972. 97.75 (ISBN 0-444-40913-0); Vol. 9. Addition & Elimination Reactions of Aliphatic Compounds. LC 72-83195. 1973. 92.75 (ISBN 0-444-41051-1); Vol. 10. Ester Formation & Hydrolysis & Related Reactions. 1972. 63.50 (ISBN 0-444-40957-2); Vol. 12. Electrophilic Substitution at a Saturated Carbon Atom. 1973. 63.50 (ISBN 0-444-41052-X); Vol. 13. Reactions of Aromatic Compounds. 1972. 92.75 (ISBN 0-444-40937-8). write for info. for subscription prices (ISBN 0-685-56648-X). Elsevier.

Gajewski, Joseph J. Hydrocarbon Thermal Isomerizations. LC 80-70594. 1981. price not set (ISBN 0-12-273350-9). Acad Pr.

ISOMETRIC EXERCISE

O'Relly, Edward. Sexercises: Isometric & Isotunic. 1967. 4.95 (ISBN 0-685-92126-3, 083205). Crown.

Petrofsky, Jerrold S. Isometric Exercise & Its Clinical Implications. (Illus.). 184p. 1981. 16.75 (ISBN 0-398-04520-8). C C Thomas.

Rossman, Isadore & Obeck, Victor. Isometrics: The Static Way to Physical Fitness. LC 66-24095. (Illus.). 1966. 7.95 (ISBN 0-87396-017-3); pap. 3.95 (ISBN 0-87396-018-1). Stravon.

Wallis, Earl L. & Logan, Gene A. Isometric Exercises for Figure Improvement & Body Conditioning. (Illus.). 1964. pap. 1.95 (ISBN 0-13-506469-4). P-H.

Wiederanders, Rex E. & Addeo, Edmond G. Biotonics: Stamina Through Six-Second Exercises That Really Work. LC 77-8208. (Funk & W Bk.). (Illus.). 1977. 7.95 (ISBN 0-308-10332-7). T Y Crowell.

ISOPERIMETRICAL PROBLEMS

see Calculus of Variations

ISOPODA

Naylor, E. British Marine Isopods. (Synopses of the British Fauna Ser.). 1972. 4.50 (ISBN 0-12-515150-0). Acad Pr.

ISOPTERA

see Termites

ISOQUINOLINE

Grethe, G. Isoquinolines, Vol. 38. (Pt. 1). 561p. 1981. 125.00 (ISBN 0-471-37481-4, Pub. by Wiley-Interscience). Wiley.

Shamma, Maurice. The Isoquinoline Alkaloids: Chemistry & Pharmacology. 1972. 43.50 (ISBN 0-12-638250-6). Acad Pr.

Shamma, Maurice & Moniot, Jerome L., eds. Isoquinoline Alkaloids Research: 1972-1977. LC 77-26929. (Illus.). 443p. 1978. 39.50 (ISBN 0-306-31059-7, Plenum Pr). Plenum Pub.

ISOSTASY

Cathles, Lawrence M. The Viscosity of the Earth's Mantle. LC 74-16162. (Illus.). 400p. 1975. 35.00 (ISBN 0-691-08140-9). Princeton U Pr.

Daly, Reginald A. Strength & Structure of the Earth. 1969. Repr. of 1940 ed. 21.75 (ISBN 0-02-843520-6). Hafner.

Popper, P. Isostatic Pressing. 1976. 17.50 (ISBN 0-85501-176-9). Heyden.

ISOTHERMS

see Atmospheric Temperature

ISOTOPE SEPARATION

see also Calutron; Nuclear Fuels

International Conference on Electromagnetic Isotope Separators & Related ION Accelerators. Electromagnetic Isotope Separators & Related Ion Accelerators: Proceedings. Amiel, S., et al, eds. 1977. 115.00 (ISBN 0-685-82368-7, North-Holland). Elsevier.

Spindel, William, ed. Isotope Effects in Chemical Processes. LC 71-84867. (Advances in Chemistry Ser.: No. 89). 1969. 24.00 (ISBN 0-8412-0090-4). Am Chemical.

Villani, Stelio. Isotope Separation. rev. 2nd ed. LC 76-13786. (Nuclear Science Technology Ser.). (Illus.). 1976. text ed. 29.80 (ISBN 0-89448-009-X). Am Nuclear Soc.

ISOTOPES

see also Calutron; Isotope Separation; Radioactive Tracers; Radioisotopes; Tracers (Chemistry); also subdivision Isotopes under names of elements, e.g. Carbon–Isotopes

Advisory Group Meeting, Vienna, Jan. 27-31, 1975. Interpretation of Environmental Isotope and Hydrochemcal Data in Groundwater Hydrology: Proceedings. (Panel Proceedings Ser.). (Illus., Orig.). 1976. pap. 22.79 (ISBN 92-0-141076-X, ISP429, IAEA). Unipub.

Audouze, Jean, ed. CNO Isotopes in Astrophysics. (Astrophysics & Space Science Lib. Ser.: No. 67). 1977. lib. bdg. 29.00 (ISBN 90-277-0807-X, Pub. by Reidel Holland). Kluwer Boston.

Baillie, T. Stable Isotopes. 1978. 44.50 (ISBN 0-8391-1234-3). Univ Park.

Barbier, E., ed. The Application of Nuclear Techniques to Geothermal Studies: Proceedings. 1978. pap. text ed. 77.00 (ISBN 0-08-021670-6). Pergamon.

Buncel, E. Carbanions: Mechanistic & Isotopic Aspects. (Reaction Mechanisms in Organic Chemistry Ser.: Vol. 9). 1974. 44.00 (ISBN 0-444-41190-9). Elsevier.

Buncel, E. & Lee, C. C., eds. Isotopes in Hydrogen Transfer Processes, Vol. 2: Isotopes in Organic Chemistry. 1976. 73.25 (ISBN 0-444-41352-9). Elsevier.

--Isotopes in Molecular Rearrangements,Vol. 1: Isotopes in Organic Chemistry. 320p. 1975. 63.50 (ISBN 0-444-41223-9). Elsevier.

Chapman, J. M. & Ayrey, G. The Use of Radioactive Isotopes in the Life Sciences. (Illus.). 176p. 1981. text ed. 28.50x (ISBN 0-04-570011-7); pap. text ed. 12.50x (ISBN 0-04-570012-5). Allen Unwin.

Cleland, W., et al, eds. Isotope Effects of Enzyme Catalyzed Reactions. (Illus.). 1977. 49.50 (ISBN 0-8391-0851-6). Univ Park.

Collins, Clair J. & Bowman, Newell S., eds. Isotope Effects in Chemical Reactions. LC 75-143546. (ACS Monograph: No. 167). 1971. 34.75 (ISBN 0-8412-0289-3). Am Chemical.

Environmental Isotope Data No. 1: World Survey of Isotope Concentration in Precipitation (1953-1963) (Technical Reports Ser.: No. 96). (Orig.). 1969. pap. 23.25 (ISBN 92-0-145069-9, IDC96, IAEA). Unipub.

Environmental Isotope Data No. 5: World Survey of Isotope Concentration in Precipitation (1970-1971) (Technical Report Ser: No. 165). 309p. 1975. pap. 22.50 (ISBN 92-0-145075-3, IDC165, IAEA). Unipub.

Environmental Isotope Data No. 6: World Survey of Isotope Concentration in Precipitation (1972-1975) (Technical Reports Ser.: No. 192). 1979. pap. 21.25 (ISBN 92-0-145179-2, IDC192, IAEA). Unipub.

Faure, Gunter. Principles of Isotope Geology. LC 77-4479. (Intermediate Geology Ser.). 1977. text ed. 35.50 (ISBN 0-471-25665-X). Wiley.

International Union of Pure & Applied Chemistry. Isotope Mass Effects in Chemistry & Biology: Proceedings of a Symposium, Vienna, 1963. 346p. 1976. 28.00 (ISBN 0-08-020778-2). Pergamon.

Isotope Hydrology, 1978, 2 vols. 1979. Vol. 1. pap. 54.50 (ISBN 92-0-040079-5, ISP 493-1, IAEA); Vol. 2. pap. 66.75 (ISBN 92-0-040179-1, ISP 493-2, IAEA). Unipub.

Isotope Studies on Wheat Fertilization. (Illus.). 99p. (Orig.). 1975. pap. 10.25 (ISBN 92-0-115074-1, IDC157, IAEA). Unipub.

Isotope Techniques for Hydrology. (Technical Reports Ser.: No. 23). (Orig.). 1964. pap. 5.50 (ISBN 92-0-145064-8, IDC23, IAEA). Unipub.

Isotope Techniques in Groundwater Hydrology, 1974, 2 vols. (Illus.). 1003p. (Orig.). 1975. Set. pap. 78.00 (ISBN 0-685-52196-6, ISP373, IAEA); 39.00 ea. Vol. 1 (ISP373-1). Vol. 2 (ISP373-2). Unipub.

Isotopes & Radiation in Soil Organic-Matter Studies. (Illus., Orig., Eng. , Fr. , Rus. & Span.). 1968. pap. 36.75 (ISBN 92-0-010368-5, ISP190, IAEA). Unipub.

Isotopes in Lake Studies. 290p. 1980. pap. 37.50 (ISBN 92-0-141179-0, ISP511, IAEA). Unipub.

Jaeger, E. Lectures in Isotope Geology. Hunziker, J. C., ed. (Illus.). 1979. 28.40 (ISBN 0-387-09158-0). Springer-Verlag.

Klein, E. Roseland & Klein, Peter D., eds. Stable Isotopes: Proceedings of the Third International Conference. 1979. 48.50 (ISBN 0-12-413650-8). Acad Pr.

Lawrence, John H. & Hamilton, J. G., eds. Advances in Biological & Medical Physics, 17 vols. Incl. Vol. 1. 1948 (ISBN 0-12-005201-6); Vol. 2. 1951 (ISBN 0-12-005202-4); Vol. 3. Lawrence, John H. & Tobias, Cornelius, eds. 1953 (ISBN 0-12-005203-2); Vol. 4. 1956 (ISBN 0-12-005204-0); Vol. 5. 1957 (ISBN 0-12-005205-9); Vol. 6. Tobias, Cornelius A. & Lawrence, John H., eds. 1958 (ISBN 0-12-005206-7); Vol. 7. 1960 (ISBN 0-12-005207-5); Vol. 8. 1962 (ISBN 0-12-005208-3); Vol. 9. Lawrence, John H. & Gofman, John W., eds. (ISBN 0-12-005209-1); Vol. 10. 1965 (ISBN 0-12-005210-5); Vol. 11. 1967. o.s.i (ISBN 0-12-005211-3); Vol. 12. 1968 (ISBN 0-12-005212-1); Vol. 13. 1971 (ISBN 0-12-005213-X); Vol. 14. 1973 (ISBN 0-12-005214-8); Vol. 15. 1974 (ISBN 0-12-005215-6); Vol. 16. 1978. 48.50 (ISBN 0-12-005216-4); lib. bdg. 59.50 (ISBN 0-12-005274-1); microfiche 35.00 (ISBN 0-12-005275-X); Vol. 17. 1980. 55.00 (ISBN 0-12-005217-2); lib. bdg. 71.50 (ISBN 0-12-005276-8); microfiche 38.50 (ISBN 0-12-005277-6). 49.00 ea. Acad Pr.

Lederer, C. Michael & Shirley, V. S. Table of Isotopes. 7th ed. LC 78-14938. 1978. 57.00 (ISBN 0-471-04179-3); pap. 37.00 (ISBN 0-471-04180-7, Pub. by Wiley-Interscience). Wiley.

McLean, F. C. & Budy, A. M. Radiation, Isotopes, & Bone. (Atomic Energy Commission Monographs). 1964. 13.50 (ISBN 0-12-484950-4). Acad Pr.

Melander, Lars & Saunders, William H., Jr. Reaction Rates of Isotopic Molecules. LC 79-12368. 1980. 34.50 (ISBN 0-471-04396-6, Pub. by Wiley-Interscience). Wiley.

Rabinovich, I. B. Influence of Isotopy on the Physicochemical Properties of Liquids. LC 69-17695. 304p. 1970. 42.50 (ISBN 0-306-10835-6, Consultants). Plenum Pub.

Rock, Peter A., ed. Isotopes & Chemical Principles. LC 75-2370. (ACS Symposium Ser.: 11). 1975. 18.25 (ISBN 0-8412-0225-7). Am Chemical.

Romer, Alfred, ed. Radiochemistry & the Discovery of Isotopes. LC 74-91273. 1970. lib. bdg. 10.50 (ISBN 0-88307-628-4). Gannon.

--Radiochemistry & the Discovery of Isotopes. LC 74-91273. (Classics of Science Ser). (Orig., Fr. & Ger.). 1970. pap. text ed. 3.50 (ISBN 0-486-62507-9). Dover.

Stable Isotopes in the Life Sciences. 1978. pap. 48.75 (ISBN 92-0-011077-0, ISP 442, IAEA). Unipub.

Statistical Treatment of Environmental Isotope Data in Precipitation. 255p. 1981. pap. 34.25 (ISBN 92-0-145081-8, IDC206, IAEA). Unipub.

Tolgyessy, J., et al. Isotope Dilution Analysis. 196p. 1972. 27.00 (ISBN 0-08-015856-0). Pergamon.

ISOTOPES–THERAPEUTIC USE

Isotope Techniques for Studying Animal Protein Production from Non-Protein Nitrogen. (Technical Reports Ser.: No. 111). (Orig.). 1970. pap. 7.00 (ISBN 92-0-115470-4, IDC111, IAEA). Unipub.

ISOTOPIC CESIUM

see Cesium–Isotopes

ISOTOPIC INDICATORS

see Radioactive Tracers

ISOZYMES

see Isoenzymes

ISRAEL

see also Palestine

Arian, Asher, ed. Israel: A Developing Society. 456p. 1980. pap. text ed. 14.25x (ISBN 90-232-1710-1). Humanities.

Baal-Teshuva, Jacob. Mission of Israel. 1963. 6.95 (ISBN 0-8315-0046-8). Speller.

Bazak Guide to Israel 1981-1982. LC 66-1422. (Illus.). 500p. (Orig.). 1981. pap. 7.95 (ISBN 0-06-090847-5, CN 847, CN). Har-Row.

Beaucamp, Evode. Prophetes d'Israel ou le Dramed'une Alliance. 1968. pap. 4.00x (ISBN 2-7637-6406-1, Pub. by Laval). Intl Schol Bk Serv.

--Les Sages d'Isreal ou le Fruit d'une Fidelite. 1968. pap. 3.80x (ISBN 2-7637-6407-X, Pub. by Laval). Intl Schol Bk Serv.

Ben-Arieh, Yehoshua. The Rediscovery of the Holy Land in the Nineteenth Century. (Illus.). 266p. 1980. 18.95 (ISBN 0-8143-1654-9, Co-Pub by Magnes Press, Hebrew University, & Israel Exploration Society). Wayne St U Pr.

Ben-Meir, Alon. Israel: The Challenge of the Fourth Decade. 224p. 1978. text ed. 12.95x (ISBN 0-8290-0392-4). Irvington.

--Israel: The Challenge of the Fourth Decade. 1978. 12.95 (ISBN 0-915326-19-1). Cyrco Pr.

Berger, L., ed. Israel Year Book 1980. 35th ed. LC 51-36641. 1980. 35.00x (ISBN 0-8002-2718-2). Intl Pubns Serv.

Blaiklock, E. M. Eight Days in Israel. 128p. 25.00x (ISBN 0-686-75529-4, Pub. by Ark Pub England). State Mutual Bk.

Bloice, Carl. Israel: Image & Reality: a Journalist's First-Hand Report. 48p. 1973. pap. 0.65 (ISBN 0-87898-103-9). New Outlook.

Brooks, Pat. Hear O Israel. LC 81-82259. (Orig.). 1981. pap. 5.00 (ISBN 0-932050-12-3). New Puritan.

Buber, Martin & Magnes, J. L., eds. Towards Union in Palestine: Essays on Zionism & Jewish-Arab Cooperation. LC 76-97272. (Judaica Ser.). 124p. 1972. Repr. of 1947 ed. lib. bdg. 15.00x (ISBN 0-8371-2564-2, BUUP). Greenwood.

Ceperley, Gordon. A Promised Land for a Chosen People. LC 79-65616. (Illus., Orig.). 1979. pap. 2.50 (ISBN 0-915540-25-8). Friends Israel-Spearhead Pr.

Coder, S. Maxwell. Israel's Destiny. 1978. pap. 2.25 (ISBN 0-8024-4182-3). Moody.

Cohen, Gary & Kirban, Salem. Israel, Land of Promise, Land of Peace. LC 74-77252. (Illus.). 1974. pap. 3.95 (ISBN 0-912582-16-2). Kirban.

Cohen, Israel, ed. The Rebirth of Israel. LC 75-6427. (The Rise of Jewish Nationalism & the Middle East Ser.). 338p. 1975. Repr. of 1952 ed. 23.50 (ISBN 0-88355-314-7). Hyperion Conn.

--Zionist Work in Palestine. LC 75-6428. (The Rise of Jewish Nationalism & the Middle East Ser.). (Illus.). 208p. 1975. Repr. of 1911 ed. 22.50 (ISBN 0-88355-315-5). Hyperion Conn.

Davis, Moshe, ed. World Jewry & the State of Israel. LC 77-72730. (Indivual Publications Ser.). 1977. lib. bdg. 12.00x (ISBN 0-405-10305-0). Arno.

De Almeida, Abrago. Israel, Gog y el Anticristo. (Span.). Date not set. 2.25 (ISBN 0-686-76298-3). Life Pubs Intl.

DeCaro, Louis. Israel Today: Fulfillment of Prophecy? 1975. pap. 4.50 (ISBN 0-87552-249-1). Presby & Reformed.

De Ridder, Richard R. My Hearts Desire for Israel. (World Focus Books). pap. 1.95 (ISBN 0-87552-254-8). Presby & Reformed.

The Directory of Israel 1980. 25th ed. 439p. 1980. 70.00x (ISBN 0-8002-2460-4). Intl Pubns Serv.

Duhamel, Georges. Israel, Clef de l'Orient. 112p. 1957. 7.95 (ISBN 0-686-55176-1). French & Eur.

Ellis, Harry B. The Dilemma of Israel. 1970. pap. 5.25 (ISBN 0-8447-1041-5). Am Enterprise.

Epp, Frank H. The Israelis. 208p. 1979. 13.95 (ISBN 0-8361-1924-X). Herald Pr.

Essrig, Harry & Segal, Abraham. Israel Today. rev. ed. LC 77-7536. (Illus.). (YA) (gr. 8-10). 1977. text ed. 8.50 (ISBN 0-8074-0007-6, 142601); tchrs'. guide 5.00 (ISBN 0-8074-0050-5, 202601). UAHC.

Fabian, Larry L. & Schiff, Ze'ev, eds. Israelis Speak: About Themselves & the Palestinians. LC 75-51150. 1977. text ed. 10.00 (ISBN 0-87003-007-8); pap. text ed. 5.00 (ISBN 0-87003-008-6). Carnegie Endow.

Frankel, William. Israel Observed. 288p. 1981. 14.95 (ISBN 0-500-01247-4). Thames Hudson.

Friedlander, Dov & Goldscheider, Calvin. The Population of Israel: Growth, Policy & Implications. LC 78-13139. 264p. 1979. 20.00x (ISBN 0-231-04572-7). Columbia U Pr.

Friendly, Alfred. Israel's Oriental Immigrants & Druzes. (Minority Rights Group: No. 12). 1972. pap. 2.50 (ISBN 0-89192-101-X). Interbk Inc.

Gamsey, Robert. Ingathering. 1961. 4.50 (ISBN 0-87315-020-1); pap. 1.50 (ISBN 0-87315-021-X). Golden Bell.

Gervasi, Frank. Case for Israel. 1967. 5.50 (ISBN 0-670-20579-6). Viking Pr.

Hauff, Louis H. Israel in Bible Prophecy. 1961. pap. 1.00 (ISBN 0-88243-532-9, 02-0532). Gospel Pub.

Hendriksen, William. Israel in Prophecy. 1968. pap. 1.95 (ISBN 0-8010-4048-5). Baker Bk.

Hertz, Joseph H., ed. A Book of Jewish Thoughts. 1976. Repr. 6.95 (ISBN 0-8197-0252-8). Bloch.

Heschel, Abraham J. Israel: An Echo of Eternity. (Illus.). 230p. 1969. pap. 3.95 (ISBN 0-374-50740-6, N358). FS&G.

Horowitz, Irving L. Israeli Ecstacies - Jewish Agonies. 240p. 1974. 12.95 (ISBN 0-19-501747-1). Oxford U Pr.

Impe, Jack Van & Campbell, Roger F. Israel's Final Holocaust. 1980. pap. 4.95 (ISBN 0-8407-9400-2). Nelson.

Israel. (Panorama Bks.). (Illus., Fr.). 4.95 (ISBN 0-685-11260-8). French & Eur.

Israel Directory, 1977: The Register of Commerce & Industry in Israel. 42nd ed. 1975. 20.00x (ISBN 0-8002-1595-8). Intl Pubns Serv.

Israeli Govt. Atlas of Israel. 1970. 239.00 (ISBN 0-444-40740-5). Elsevier.

Kirban, Salem. The Day Israel Dies! (Illus.). 1975. pap. 2.95 (ISBN 0-912582-21-9). Kirban.

Kittel, Rudolf. Great Men & Movements in Israel. rev. ed. LC 66-29121. (Library of Biblical Studies). 1968. 20.00x (ISBN 0-87068-071-4). Ktav.

Leroy-Beaulieu, Anatole. Israel Among the Nations: A Study of the Jews & Antisemitism. facsimile ed. Hellman, Frances, tr. from Fr. LC 74-27996. (Modern Jewish Experience Ser.). (Eng.). 1975. Repr. of 1904 ed. 24.00x (ISBN 0-405-06723-2). Arno.

Lewittes, M. Religious Foundations of the Jewish State: The Concept & Practice of Jewish Statehood from Biblical Times to the Modern State of Israel. 20.00x (ISBN 0-87068-433-7). Ktav.

Lindsay, Gordon. The Miracle of Israel. 1.00 (ISBN 0-89985-188-6). Christ Nations.

Lumer, Hyman. Israel Today: War or Peace? 1970. pap. 0.45 (ISBN 0-87898-061-X). New Outlook.

--Which Way Israel? 1966. pap. 0.20 (ISBN 0-87898-010-5). New Outlook.

McEleney, Neil J. Melody of Israel. (Bible Ser.). pap. 1.00 (ISBN 0-8091-5089-1). Paulist Pr.

Malgo, Wim. On the Border of Two Worlds. 0.95 (ISBN 0-686-12833-8). Midnight Call.

Mark, Emanuel, ed. A Composite Portrait of Israel. LC 80-40889. 1981. 31.00 (ISBN 0-12-476450-9). Acad Pr.

Mauro, Philip. Hope of Israel. pap. 4.95 (ISBN 0-685-19833-2). Reiner.

Mehdi, M. T., ed. Palestine & the Bible. LC 71-114557. 1971. pap. 3.00 (ISBN 0-911026-06-1). New World Press NY.

Meyer, F. B. Israel. 1972. pap. 1.75 (ISBN 0-87508-347-1). Chr Lit.

Meyer, Nathan M. The Land of Miracles. (Illus.). pap. 1.50 (ISBN 0-88469-021-0). BMH Bks.

Miller, Irving. Israel: The Eternal Idea. 1955. 17.50x (ISBN 0-686-50046-6). Elliots Bks.

Naamani, Israel T. The State of Israel. LC 79-12757. (Illus.). 1980. pap. 6.95x (ISBN 0-87441-278-1). Behrman.

Orlinsky, H. M. Israel Exploration Journal Reader, 2 vols. (The Library of Biblical Studies). Set. 99.50x (ISBN 0-87068-267-9). Ktav.

Patai, Raphael. Israel Between East & West: A Study in Human Relations. rev. ed. LC 70-98711. 1970. lib. bdg. 15.50 (ISBN 0-8371-3719-5, PAI/). Greenwood.

Polish, David. Israel - Nation & People. 15.00x (ISBN 0-87068-290-3). Ktav.

Rapaport, et al. Early Child Care in Israel. (International Monograph on Early Childcare). 1976. 23.25x (ISBN 0-677-05270-7). Gordon.

Rodinson, Maxime. Israel: A Colonial-Settler State? Thorstad, David, tr. from Fr. LC 73-78187. 96p. (Orig.). 1973. 12.00 (ISBN 0-913460-22-2, Dist. by Path Pr NY); pap. 3.45 (ISBN 0-913460-23-0). Monad Pr.

Rubin, Gail. Psalmist with a Camera. LC 79-5086. (Illus.). 116p. 1979. 16.95 (ISBN 0-89659-076-3); pap. 10.95 (ISBN 0-89659-071-2). Abbeville Pr.

Ruderman, Jerome L. Israel: A Resource Guide for Teachers of Social Studies. 31p. 0.75 (ISBN 0-686-74971-5). ADL.

Sher, Hanan, ed. Facts About Israel. 2nd ed. LC 55-19995. (Illus.). 232p. (Orig.). 1978. pap. 5.00x (ISBN 0-8002-2247-4). Intl Pubns Serv.

Sirof, Harriet. The Junior Encyclopedia of Israel. (Illus.). 1980. 16.95 (ISBN 0-8246-0228-5). Jonathan David.

Sterling Publishing Company Editors. Israel in Pictures. rev. ed. LC 62-12601. (Visual Geography Ser). (Illus.). 64p. (gr. 5 up). 1974. PLB 4.99 (ISBN 0-8069-1027-5); pap. 2.95 (ISBN 0-8069-1026-7). Sterling.

Stone, Julius. Israel & Palestine: Assault on the Law of Nations. 208p. 1981. 17.50 (ISBN 0-8018-2535-0). Johns Hopkins.

Tcholakian, Arthur. Israel, Land of Promise. LC 73-79133. (Illus.). 1973. 4.95 (ISBN 0-8128-1601-3). Stein & Day.

Walvoord, John F. Israel in Prophecy. 1978. pap. 4.95 (ISBN 0-310-34081-0). Zondervan.

Wcela, Emil A. The Story of Israel. (God's Word Today: Vol. 4). 1977. pap. 2.95 (ISBN 0-916134-25-3). Pueblo Pub Co.

Yerby, Robert. The Once & Future Israel. 1978. pap. 3.95 (ISBN 0-685-88389-2). Reiner.

Zweig, Ferdynand. Israel: The Sword & the Harp. LC 74-86291. 326p. 1970. 15.00 (ISBN 0-8386-7534-4). Fairleigh Dickinson.

ISRAEL–ANTIQUITIES

Aharoni, Yohanan. The Archeology of the Land of Israel. Aharoni, Miriam, ed. Rainey, Anson F., tr. Date not set. price not set (ISBN 0-664-21384-7). Westminster.

Avigad, Nahman. Beth She'Arim, Vol. 3: The Excavations, 1953-58. 312p. 1976. 30.00x (ISBN 0-8135-0763-4). Rutgers U Pr.

James, Frances W. The Iron Age at Beth-Shan: A Study of Levels VI-IV. (Museum Monographs). (Illus.). 369p. 1966. soft bound 8.00 (ISBN 0-934718-20-2). Univ Mus of U PA.

Marks, Anthony E., ed. Prehistory & Paleoenvironments in the Central Negev, Israel: The Avdat-Aqev Area, Part I. LC 75-40116. (Illus.). 1976. pap. 20.00 (ISBN 0-87074-153-5). SMU Press.

Meyers, Eric M., et al. Ancient Synagogue Excavations at Khirbet Shema' Upper Galilee, Israel, 1970-1972. LC 76-40864. (Illus.). 1977. 29.75 (ISBN 0-8223-0377-9). Duke.

Orlinsky, Harry M. Ancient Israel. 2nd ed. Fox, Edward W., ed. (Development of Western Civilization). (Illus.). 164p. 1960. pap. 2.95 (ISBN 0-8014-9849-X). Cornell U Pr.

Rambaud, Alfred N. De Byzantino Hippodromo et Circensibus Factionibus. 1870. 20.50 (ISBN 0-8337-2896-2). B Franklin.

Wilson, Clifford. Ebla Tablets: Secrets of a Forgotten City. rev. & enlarged ed. LC 79-50907. (Illus.). 1979. pap. 3.50 (ISBN 0-685-95015-8, Master Bks). CLP Pubs.

Yadin, Yigael. Hazor: The Rediscovery of a Great Citadel of the Bible. (Illus.). 1975. 20.00 (ISBN 0-394-49454-7). Random.

ISRAEL–ARMED FORCES

Bell, J. Bowyer. Terror Out of Zion: The Irgun, Lehl, Stern & the Palestine Underground, 1929-1949. LC 75-26172. (Illus.). 1977. 13.95 (ISBN 0-312-79205-0). St Martin.

Bowden, Tom. Army in the Service of the State. LC 78-313930. 1979. 14.00x (ISBN 965-20-0023-X, Pub. by Turtledove Pub Ltd Israel). Intl Schol Bk Serv.

Dayan, Moshe. Diary of the Sinai Campaign. LC 78-27859. (Illus.). 1979. Repr. of 1966 ed. lib. bdg. 20.75x (ISBN 0-313-20928-6, DADO). Greenwood.

Jacobs, Monty. Birth of the Israel Air Force. (Illus.). 1954. 3.00 (ISBN 0-914080-43-1). Shulsinger Sales.

Larteguy, Jean. The Walls of Israel. De Kay, Ormond, tr. from Fr. LC 78-88700. 240p. 1969. 5.95 (ISBN 0-87131-017-1). M Evans.

Perlmutter, Amos. Military & Politics in Israel: Nation Building & Role Expansion. 2nd rev. ed. (Illus.). 161p. 1977. 23.50x (ISBN 0-7146-3100-0, F Cass Co). Biblio Dist.

Rothenberg, Gunther E. Anatomy of the Israeli Army. LC 79-88523. (Illus.). 1979. 17.95 (ISBN 0-88254-491-8). Hippocrene Bks.

Weizman, Ezer. On Eagles' Wings. (Illus.). 1979. pap. 2.50 (ISBN 0-425-04022-4). Berkley Pub.

ISRAEL–BIOGRAPHY

Blaikie, William G. Heroes of Israel. 1982. lib. bdg. 19.50 (ISBN 0-86524-082-5). Klock & Klock.

Dayan, Moshe. Diary of the Sinai Campaign. LC 78-27859. (Illus.). 1979. Repr. of 1966 ed. lib. bdg. 20.75x (ISBN 0-313-20928-6, DADO). Greenwood.

Eckman, Lester & Hirschler, Gertrude. Menahem Begin. LC 78-54565. 1979. 11.95 (ISBN 0-88400-051-6). Shengold.

Golan, Aviezer & Pinkas, Danny. Shula: Code Name the Pearl. 1980. 10.95 (ISBN 0-440-01516-2). Delacorte.

Gruber, Ruth. Raquela: A Woman of Israel. LC 78-107. (Illus.). 1978. 11.95 (ISBN 0-698-10895-7). Coward.

Kendrick, L. Garland. The Journey to the Promised Land. 1978. 7.95 (ISBN 0-533-03527-9). Vantage.

Netanyahu, Benjamin & Netanyahu, Iddo, eds. Portrait of a Hero: The Letters of Yoni (1963-1976) LC 80-5414. (Illus.). 1981. 12.95 (ISBN 0-394-51376-2). Random.

Rosenblum, Morris. Heroes of Israel. LC 77-100087. (Heroes of Ser). (Illus.). (gr. 8-10). 1972. 6.95 (ISBN 0-8303-0086-4). Fleet.

Sevela, Ephraim. Farewell, Israel! Browne, Edmund, tr. from Russian. 1977. 12.95 (ISBN 0-89526-699-7). Regnery-Gateway.

Slater, Robert. Rabin of Israel: A Biography. (Illus.). 304p. 1977. 17.50x (ISBN 0-8476-3127-3). Rowman.

Who's Who in Israel & in the Work for Israel Abroad, 1981-82. 19th ed. LC 46-6380. 616p. 1981. 75.00x (ISBN 0-8002-2808-1). Intl Pubns Serv.

Winer, Gershon. Founding Fathers of Israel. 1971. 7.95 (ISBN 0-8197-0264-1). Bloch.

ISRAEL–DESCRIPTION AND TRAVEL

Agnon, S. Y. In the Heart of the Seas: A Story of a Journey to the Land of Israel. Lask, I. M., tr. from Hebrew. LC 66-30349. (Illus.). 128p. 1980. pap. 4.95 (ISBN 0-8052-0647-7). Schocken.

Alexander, Morris. Israel & Me. (Illus.). 278p. 1977. 12.50x (ISBN 0-87073-204-8). Schenkman.

--Israel & Me. LC 76-40091. 1977. 10.00 (ISBN 0-8467-0265-7, Pub. by Two Continents). Hippocrene Bks.

Bellow, Saul. To Jerusalem & Back. 1977. pap. 1.95 (ISBN 0-380-01676-1, 33472). Avon.

--To Jerusalem & Back: A Personal Account. 1977. Repr. lib. bdg. 10.95 (ISBN 0-8161-6480-0, Large Print Bks). G K Hall.

DeCaro, Louis. Israel Today. pap. 4.50 (ISBN 0-8010-2852-3). Baker Bk.

Dehan, Emmanuel. Our Visit to Israel. rev. ed. (Illus.). 1978. pap. 7.95 (ISBN 0-8197-0031-2). Bloch.

Edelman, Lily. Modern Israel. pap. 2.00 (ISBN 0-87980-101-8). Wilshire.

Harris, Bill. Israel. (Illus.). 1980. 24.95 (ISBN 0-686-68761-2, Mayflower Bks). Smith Pubs.

Harvard Student Agencies. Let's Go, Greece, Israel & Europe: The Budget Guide 1981 to 1982 Edition. (Illus.). 352p. 1981. pap. 5.95 (ISBN 0-525-93146-5). Dutton.

Hazelton, Lesley. Where Mountains Roar: A Personal Report from the Sinai & Negev Desert. LC 79-22009. (Illus.). 240p. 1980. 12.95 (ISBN 0-03-045321-6). HR&W.

Holmes, Reed. Israel, Land of Zion. LC 78-16153. 1978. 15.00 (ISBN 0-8309-0222-8). Herald Hse.

Jacoby, Hilla & Jacoby, Max, photos by. The Land of Israel. (Illus.). 1978. 40.00 (ISBN 0-500-24101-5). Thames Hudson.

Koch, Kurt E. The Coming One. LC 72-85597. 1972. pap. 2.50 (ISBN 0-8254-3011-9). Kregel.

Larsen, Elaine. Israel. (Batsford Countries Ser.). Date not set. 10.95 (ISBN 0-8038-3400-4). Hastings.

Louvish, Misha, ed. Facts About Israel. pap. 2.95 (ISBN 0-685-32919-4). Assoc Bk.

Maidat, Rita. The Twins Visit Israel. (Shayna & Keppi Ser.). (Illus.). (gr. 3-10). 1978. pap. 2.00 (ISBN 0-914080-72-5). Shulsinger Sales.

Malka, Victor. Israel Observed. Spatz, Erwin, ed. Joss, Jean, tr. (Observed Ser.). (Illus.). 1980. 24.95 (ISBN 0-19-520170-1). Oxford U Pr.

Rudoff, Carol. Images of Israel. LC 77-81181. (Illus.). 1978. pap. 4.95 (ISBN 0-930048-03-2). Prologue.

Serruya, Colette. Lake Kinneret: Lake of Tiberias, Sea of Galilee. (Monographiae Biologicae: No.32). 1978. lib. bdg. 68.50 (ISBN 90-619-3085-5, Pub. by Junk Pubs Netherlands). Kluwer Boston.

ISRAEL–DESCRIPTION AND TRAVEL–GUIDEBOOKS

Breakstone, David & Jochnowitz, Cindy. The Israel Experience Book. new ed. LC 76-56985. 1977. pap. 4.95 (ISBN 0-8197-0021-5). Bloch.

Finegan, Jack. Discovering Israel: A Popular Guide to the Holy Land. LC 80-26952. (Illus.). 176p. 1981. pap. 6.95 (ISBN 0-8028-1869-2). Eerdmans.

Fodor's Israel, 1981. 1981. 12.95 (ISBN 0-679-00699-0); pap. 9.95 (ISBN 0-679-00700-8). McKay.

Gack, Christopher & Wobcke, Manfred. Israel & the Occupied Territories. (Travel Paperbacks Ser.). (Illus.). 192p. 1981. pap. 5.95 (ISBN 0-908086-22-9, Pub. by Lonely Planet Australia). Hippocrene Bks.

Gavron, Daniel. Walking Through Israel. 448p. 1980. 12.95 (ISBN 0-395-27777-9). HM.

Israel on Twenty Dollars a Day: 1980-81 Edition. 344p. 1981. pap. 4.95 (ISBN 0-671-25490-1). Frommer-Pasmantier.

Lewensohn, Avraham. Israel Tourguide. (Illus.). 600p. (Orig.). 1980. pap. 9.95 (ISBN 0-89961-005-6). SBS Pub.

Nagel Travel Guide to Israel. (Nagel Travel Guide Ser.). (Illus.). 432p. 1971. 30.00 (ISBN 0-685-31332-8). Hippocrene Bks.

Nagel's Encyclopedia Guide: Israel. (Illus.). 432p. 1978. 30.00 (ISBN 2-8263-0049-0). Masson Pub.

Nir, Dov. The New Comprehensive Guide to Israel. 4.95 (ISBN 0-87677-143-6). Hartmore.

Vilnay, Zev. The Guide to Israel 1980. 21st ed. LC 66-33490. (Illus.). 662p. 1979. 10.00x (ISBN 0-8002-2713-1). Intl Pubns Serv.

Willcox, Kathleen M. Your Guide to Israel. LC 66-70968. (Your Guide Ser.). 1966. 5.25x (ISBN 0-8002-0781-5). Intl Pubns Serv.

ISRAEL–ECONOMIC CONDITIONS

Akzin, Benjamin & Dror, Yehezkel. Israel: High-Pressure Planning. (National Planning Ser.: No. 5). (Orig.). 1966. pap. 3.95x (ISBN 0-8156-2091-8). Syracuse U Pr.

Curtis, Michael & Chertoff, Mordecai S., eds. Israel: Social Structure & Change. LC 73-78696. (Third World Ser). 460p. 1973. pap. 5.95 (ISBN 0-87855-575-7). Transaction Bks.

Davis, Uri. Israel: Utopia Incorporated. 182p. 1977. 10.00 (ISBN 0-905762-12-6, Pub. by Zed Pr); pap. 6.00 (ISBN 0-905762-13-4). Lawrence Hill.

Flink, Salomon J. Israel: Chaos & Challenge: Politics vs. Economics. 265p. 1980. 18.00x (ISBN 965-20-0027-2, Pub. by Turtledove Pr Israel). Intl Schol Bk Serv.

Globerson, Arye. Higher Education & Employment: A Case Study of Israel. LC 78-60131. (Praeger Special Studies). 1979. 22.95 (ISBN 0-03-046226-6). Praeger.

Greenwald, Carol S. Recession As a Policy Instrument: Israel, 1965-1969. LC 73-2895. 154p. 1973. 12.00 (ISBN 0-8386-1396-9). Fairleigh Dickinson.

Horowitz, David. The Enigma of Economic Growth: A Case Study of Israel. LC 77-184338. (Special Studies in International Economics & Development). 1972. 27.50x (ISBN 0-275-28272-4). Irvington.

Laufer, L. Israel & the Developing Countries: New Approaches to Cooperation. 1967. Repr. of 1967 ed. 7.00 (ISBN 0-527-02824-X); pap. 4.00 (ISBN 0-527-02851-7). Kraus Repr.

Lerner, Abba P. & Ben-Shahar, Haim. The Economics of Efficiency & Growth: Lessons from Israel & the West Bank. LC 74-32140. 192p. 1975. 19.50 (ISBN 0-88410-276-9). Ballinger Pub.

Mandell, Lewis F. The Demand for Money in Israel. (Business Economics & Finance Ser.: Vol. 3). 136p. 1975. 19.75 (ISBN 0-8247-6290-8). Dekker.

Michaely, Michael. Foreign Trade Regimes & Economic Development: Israel, Bk. 3. Bhagwati, Jagdish N. & Krueger, Anne O., eds. (Special Conference Ser). 1975. 12.50 (ISBN 0-87014-503-7, Dist. by Columbia U Pr). Natl Bur Econ Res.

Neeman, Yaakov, ed. Conference on the Tax Consequences of American Investments in Israel: Proceedings. Nov. 12-14, 1972. x, 337p. (Orig.). 1974. 20.00x (ISBN 0-8377-0902-4). Rothman.

Pack, Howard. Structural Change & Economic Policy in Israel. LC 75-140536. (Economic Growth Center Ser.). 1971. 20.00x (ISBN 0-300-01415-5). Yale U Pr.

Prausnitz, Moshe W. From Hunter to Farmer & Trader: Studies in the Lithic Industries of Israel & Adjacent Countries (from the Mesolithic to the Chalcolithic Age). 1970. 37.50x (ISBN 3-7749-1128-2). Intl Pubns Serv.

Rosenblatt, Bernard A. The American Bridge to the Israel Commonwealth. LC 75-392. 128p. 1975. Repr. of 1959 ed. lib. bdg. 15.00x (ISBN 0-8371-8020-1, ROAB). Greenwood.

Rubner, Alex. Economy of Israel. 307p. 1959. 23.50x (ISBN 0-7146-1249-9, F Cass Co). Biblio Dist.

Uri, Pierre, ed. Israel & the Common Market. (Illus.). 702p. 1971. 35.00x (ISBN 0-8002-0898-6). Intl Pubns Serv.

Van Arkadie, Brian. Benefits & Burdens: A Report on the West Bank & Gaza Strip Economies Since 1967. LC 76-57443. 1977. pap. text ed. 3.75 (ISBN 0-87003-006-X). Carnegie Endow.

ISRAEL–EMIGRATION AND IMMIGRATION

Deshen, Shlomo & Shokeid, Moshe. The Predicament of Homecoming: Cultural & Social Life of North African Immigrants in Israel. Turner, Victor, ed. (Symbol, Myth, & Ritual Ser). (Illus.). 251p. 1974. 25.00x (ISBN 0-8014-0885-7). Cornell U Pr.

Gerber, Israel J. The Heritage Seekers--Black Jews in Search of Identity. LC 77-2907. 1977. 9.95 (ISBN 0-8246-0214-5). Jonathan David.

--The Heritage Seekers: Black Jews in Search of Identity. David, Jonathan, ed. LC 77-2907. 1977. 9.95 (ISBN 0-8246-0214-5). Inst Jewish Stud.

Kraines, Oscar. The Impossible Dilemma: Who Is a Jew in the State of Israel? 1976. 6.95 (ISBN 0-8197-0392-3). Bloch.

Kushner, Gilbert. Immigrants From India in Israel: Planned Change in an Administered Community. LC 72-82945. 1973. pap. 2.00 (ISBN 0-8165-0210-2). U of Ariz Pr.

Morris, Yaakov. Pioneers from the West. LC 76-97299. (Judaica Ser). (Illus.). 160p. 1972. Repr. of 1953 ed. lib. bdg. 15.00 (ISBN 0-8371-2624-X, MOPW). Greenwood.

Ritterband, P. Education, Employment & Migration. LC 76-62584. (ASA Rose Monographs). (Illus.). 1978. 19.95 (ISBN 0-521-21586-2); pap. 6.95x (ISBN 0-521-29192-5). Cambridge U Pr.

Willner, Dorothy. Nation-Building & Community in Israel. LC 68-20884. (Illus.). 1969. 25.00x (ISBN 0-691-03070-7). Princeton U Pr.

Zvi. LC 78-56149. 1978. pap. 2.95 (ISBN 0-915540-23-1). Friends Israel-Spearhead Pr.

ISRAEL–FOREIGN RELATIONS

Amos, John W. Arab-Israeli Military Political Relations: Arab Perceptions & the Politics of Escalation. 1979. text ed. 39.50 (ISBN 0-08-023865-3). Pergamon.

Bhutani, Surendra. Israeli-Soviet Cold War. LC 75-903197. 216p. 1975. 15.00x (ISBN 0-8002-1598-2). Intl Pubns Serv.

Brecher, Michael. Decisions in Israel's Foreign Policy. LC 73-77143. 675p. 1975. 40.00x (ISBN 0-300-01660-3). Yale U Pr.

--The Foreign Policy System of Israel: Setting, Images, Process. LC 73-179469. (Illus.). 692p. 1972. 40.00x (ISBN 0-300-01549-6). Yale U Pr.

Cohen, Aharon. Israel & the Arab World. abr. ed. 448p. 1976. pap. 5.95 (ISBN 0-8070-0245-3, BP527). Beacon Pr.

Crosbie, Sylvia K. A Tacit Alliance: France & Israel from the Suez to the Six Day War. (Studies of the Middle East Institute, Columbia University). 304p. 1974. 21.00 (ISBN 0-691-07557-3). Princeton U Pr.

Curtis, Michael & Gitelson, Susan A., eds. Israel in the Third World. LC 75-44817. 520p. (Orig.). 1976. 19.95 (ISBN 0-87855-130-1); pap. text ed. 6.95x (ISBN 0-87855-603-6). Transaction Bks.

Drinan, Robert F. Honor the Promise: America's Commitment to Israel. LC 73-9022. 1977. 7.95 (ISBN 0-385-08699-7). Doubleday.

Eckman, Lester. Soviet Policy Towards Jews & Israel. LC 73-93237. 1974. 6.95 (ISBN 0-88400-005-2). Shengold.

Fishman, Hertzel. American Protestantism & a Jewish State. LC 72-3746. (Schaver Publication Fund for Jewish Studies Ser). 254p. 1973. 12.95x (ISBN 0-8143-1481-3). Wayne St U Pr.

Flapan, Simha, ed. When Enemies Dare to Talk: An Israeli-Palestinian Debate (5-6 September 1978) Organised by "New Outlook". 129p. 1979. 25.00x (ISBN 0-7099-0174-7, Pub. by Croom Helm Ltd England). Biblio Dist.

Harkabi, Yehoshafat. Arab Attitudes to Israel. 1974. casebound 19.95x (ISBN 0-87855-168-9). Transaction Bks.

--Arab Strategies & Israel's Response. LC 77-70273. 1977. 12.95 (ISBN 0-02-913760-8); pap. 4.95 (ISBN 0-02-913780-2). Free Pr.

Harkavy, Robert E. Spectre of a Middle Eastern Holocaust: The Strategic & Diplomatic Implications of the Israeli Nuclear Weapons Program, Pt. D, 1976-77 Ser. (Monograph Ser. in World Affairs: Vol. 14). pap. 4.00 perfect bdg. (ISBN 0-87940-053-6). U of Denver Intl.

Herzog, Chaim. Who Stands Accused? Israel Answers Its Critics. 1978. 10.00 (ISBN 0-394-50132-2). Random.

Israel & South Africa: The Progression of a Relationship. LC 76-47719. 1978. pap. 6.00 (ISBN 0-911026-03-7). New World Press NY.

Kaufman, Edy, ed. Israeli-Latin American Relations. Shapira, Yoram & Barromi, Joel. LC 77-80861. 256p. 1979. 19.95 (ISBN 0-87855-210-3). Transaction Bks.

Kenen, I. L. Israel's Defense Line: Her Friends & Foes in Washington. LC 81-81866. 400p. 1981. 19.95 (ISBN 0-87975-159-2); pap. 9.95 (ISBN 0-87975-145-2). Prometheus Bks.

Lustick, Ian. Israel & Jordan: The Implications of an Adversarial Partnership. LC 78-620041. (Policy Papers in International Affairs Ser.: No. 6). (Illus.). 1978. pap. 2.00x (ISBN 0-87725-506-7). U of Cal Intl St.

McLaurin, R. D., et al. Foreign Policy Making in the Middle East: Domestic Influences on Policy in Egypt, Iraq, Israel, & Syria. LC 76-24360. (Special Studies). 1977. text ed. 29.95 (ISBN 0-275-23870-9); pap. 10.95 (ISBN 0-275-65010-3). Praeger.

Malgo, Wim. Begin with Sadat. 1.95 (ISBN 0-686-27717-1). Midnight Call.

Rafael, Gideon. Destination Peace: Three Decades of Israeli Foreign Policy: a Personal Memoir. (Illus.). 400p. 1981. 16.95 (ISBN 0-8128-2812-7). Stein & Day.

Reich, Bernard. The Quest for Peace: U. S. - Israeli Relations & the Arab-Israeli Conflict. LC 76-45940. 495p. 1977. text ed. 24.95 (ISBN 0-87855-226-X). Transaction Bks.

Roberts, Samuel J. Survival or Hegemony? The Foundations of Israeli Foreign Policy. LC 73-8134. (Studies in International Affairs: No. 20). 174p. 1974. 12.95x (ISBN 0-8018-1541-X); pap. 3.95x (ISBN 0-8018-1543-6). Johns Hopkins.

Ro'i, Yaacov. Soviet Decision Making in Practice: The USSR & Israel, 1947-54. LC 79-64857. 540p. 1980. 22.95 (ISBN 0-87855-267-7). Transaction Bks.

Safran, Nadav. Israel: The Embattled Ally. LC 77-22357. 1978. 25.00x (ISBN 0-674-46881-3, Belknap Pr); pap. 9.95 (ISBN 0-674-46882-1). Harvard U Pr.

Smith, Wilbur M. Egypt & Israel: Coming Together? 1978. pap. 3.95 (ISBN 0-8423-0683-8). Tyndale.

Stevens, Richard P. Weizmann & Smuts: A Study in Zionist-South African Cooperation. (No. 43). 1976. 6.00 (ISBN 0-686-15605-6); pap. 4.00 (ISBN 0-686-15606-4). Inst Palestine.

Stevens, Richard P. & Elmessiri, Abdelwahab M. Israel & South Africa: The Progression of a Relationship. LC 77-83663. pap. 6.95x (ISBN 0-930244-00-1). North American Inc.

Tomeh, George J. Israel & South Africa: The/Unholy Alliance. LC 72-93084. 76p. (Orig.). 1973. pap. text ed. 3.00 (ISBN 0-911026-02-9). New World Press NY.

Vogel, Rolf, ed. German Path to Israel. LC 70-88600. 1970. 14.95 (ISBN 0-8023-1229-2). Dufour.

Watterson, John S. The Egypt-Israel Treaty & the Peace-War Prospects for the World. (Illus.). 1979. deluxe ed. 59.75 (ISBN 0-930008-40-5). Inst Econ Pol.

Weizman, Ezer. The Battle for Peace. LC 80-71057. (Illus.). 408p. 1981. 15.95 (ISBN 0-553-05002-8). Bantam.

ISRAEL–HISTORY

Anderson, Roy A. & Hoffman, Jay M. All Eyes on Israel. rev. ed. (Illus.). 1978. pap. 2.25 (ISBN 0-930718-15-1). Harvest Pr Texas.

Bain, Kenneth R. The March to Zion: United States Policy & the Founding of Israel. LC 79-7413. 256p. 1980. 15.95 (ISBN 0-89096-076-3). Tex A&M Univ Pr.

Balabkins, Nicholas. West German Reparations to Israel. LC 70-152724. 1971. 25.00 (ISBN 0-8135-0691-3). Rutgers U Pr.

Ben-Gurion, David. Rebirth & Destiny of Israel. (Return to Zion Ser.). 539p. Repr. of 1954 ed. lib. bdg. 35.00x (ISBN 0-87991-139-5). Porcupine Pr.

Blenkinsopp, J. Gibeon & Israel: The Role of Gibeon & the Gibeonites in the Political and Religious History of Early Israel. LC 74-171672. (Society for Old Testament Studies Monographs). 1972. 29.50 (ISBN 0-521-08368-0). Cambridge U Pr.

Bright, John. A History of Israel. 3rd ed. LC 80-22774. 1981. 18.95 (ISBN 0-664-21381-2). Westminster.

Cameron, James. The Making of Israel. LC 77-76041. (Illus.). 1977. 7.95 (ISBN 0-8008-5084-X). Taplinger.

Charles, Robert H. A Critical History of the Doctrine of a Future Life, in Israel, in Judaism, & in Christianity. LC 79-8600. Repr. of 1899 ed. 38.50 (ISBN 0-404-18455-3). AMS Pr.

Cohen, Yona. Jerusalem Under Siege. Shefer, Dorothea, tr. from Hebrew. (Illus.). 326p. 1981. text ed. 12.00 (ISBN 0-86628-017-0). Ridgefield Pub.

Davis, John J. & Whitcomb, John C. A History of Israel. (Old Testament Studies). 1980. 14.95 (ISBN 0-8010-2888-4). Baker Bk.

--History of Israel. 14.95 (ISBN 0-88469-061-X). BMH Bks.

Dayan, Moshe. Moshe Dayan: Story of My Life. (Illus.). 1977. pap. 2.95 (ISBN 0-446-83425-4). Warner Bks.

Deacon, Richard. The Israeli Secret Service. LC 78-56985. (Illus.). 1978. 9.95 (ISBN 0-8008-4266-9). Taplinger.

De Mirabaud, Jean-Baptiste. Opinion des Anciens sur les Juifs. (Holbach & His Friends Ser). 129p. (Fr.). 1974. Repr. of 1769 ed. lib. bdg. 41.50x (ISBN 0-8287-0623-9, 1530). Clearwater Pub.

Derogy, Jacques & Carmel, Hesi. Untold History of Israel. LC 78-74552. Orig. Title: L' Histoire Secrete d'Israel. (Illus.). 396p. (Orig.). 1980. pap. 7.95 (ISBN 0-394-17651-0, E756, Ever). Grove.

--Untold History of Israel. LC 78-74552. Orig. Title: Histoire Secrete D'Israel. (Illus.). 1980. 12.50 (ISBN 0-394-50622-7, GP827). Grove.

De Vaux, Roland. The Early History of Israel. 1978. 30.00 (ISBN 0-664-20762-6). Westminster.

Eban, Abba. My Country. LC 72-2725. 1972. 15.00 (ISBN 0-394-46314-5). Random.

Edelman, Lily. Israel. 1958. 20.00 (ISBN 0-686-17232-9). Scholars Ref Lib.

Ellis, Harry B. Israel: One Land, Two Peoples. LC 73-175104. (Illus.). 210p. 1972. 10.95 (ISBN 0-690-45028-1). T y Crowell.

Ellison, H. J. The Mystery of Israel: Has God Cast Away His People? 3rd ed. 1976. pap. 4.95 (ISBN 0-85364-169-2). Attic Pr.

Elon, Amos. Understanding Israel: A Social Studies Approach. new ed. Sugarman, Morris J., ed. LC 76-18282. (Illus.). 256p. (gr. 9 up). 1976. pap. text ed. 5.95x (ISBN 0-87441-234-X). Behrman.

Eytan, Walter. The First Ten Years: A Diplomatic History of Israel. (Return to Zion Ser.). (Illus.). x, 239p. Repr. of 1958 ed. lib. bdg. 17.50x (ISBN 0-87991-140-9). Porcupine Pr.

Feinberg, Charles L. Israel: At the Center of History & Revelation. rev. ed. LC 80-12894. 1980. Repr. of 1974 ed. text ed. 10.95 (ISBN 0-930014-38-3). Multnomah.

Fohrer, Georg. Geschichte der Israelitischen Religion. xvi, 367p. (Ger.). 1969. 24.00x (ISBN 3-11-002652-X). De Gruyter.

Forster, Arnold. Report from Israel. 72p. pap. 1.25 (ISBN 0-686-74976-6). ADL.

Garcia-Granados, Jorge. The Birth of Israel: The Drama As I Saw It. (Return to Zion Ser.). viii, 291p. Repr. of 1948 ed. lib. bdg. 20.00x (ISBN 0-87991-141-7). Porcupine Pr.

Grand, Tamar & Grand, Samuel. Children of Israel. (gr. 3-4). 1972. text ed. 5.50 (ISBN 0-8074-0131-5, 121320); tchr's guide 2.25 (ISBN 0-8074-0132-3, 201320); fun & act bk. 3.00 (ISBN 0-8074-0133-1, 121322). UAHC.

Hausner, Gideon. Justice in Jerusalem. 1978. 12.95 (ISBN 0-930832-55-8). Herzl Pr.

Heaton, E. W. Everyday Life in Old Testament Times. LC 76-29288. (Illus.). 1977. lib. rep. ed. 17.50x (ISBN 0-684-14836-6). Scribner.

Hirschmann, Ira A. Life Line to a Promised Land. (Return to Zion Ser.). (Illus.). xvi, 214p. Repr. of 1946 ed. lib. bdg. 15.00x (ISBN 0-87991-120-4). Porcupine Pr.

Hong, Christopher C. Israel in Ancient Near Eastern Setting. LC 80-11683. 312p. (Orig.). 1980. pap. 20.25 (ISBN 0-8357-0507-2, SS-00131). Univ Microfilms.

Horowitz, Aharon. The Quarternary of Israel. LC 78-8855. 1979. 50.00 (ISBN 0-12-356170-1). Acad Pr.

Horowitz, Dan & Lissak, Moshe. Origins of the Israeli Polity: Palestine Under the Mandate. Hoffman, Charles, tr. LC 78-3175. 1979. lib. bdg. 19.00x (ISBN 0-226-35366-4). U of Chicago Pr.

Howard, Harry N. The King-Crane Commission. (Return to Zion Ser.). (Illus.). xiv, 369p. Repr. of 1963 ed. lib. bdg. 25.00x (ISBN 0-87991-121-2). Porcupine Pr.

Ishida, Tomoo. The Royal Dynasties in Ancient Israel. 1977. 51.25x (ISBN 3-1100-6519-3). De Gruyter.

Jaffe, Eliezer D. Pleaders & Protesters: The Future of Citizens' Organizations in Israel. LC 80-68431. 40p. 1980. pap. 2.50 (ISBN 0-87495-028-7). Am Jewish Comm.

Kampelman, Max M. Jewish Power: Myth or Reality. 21p. 1.50 (ISBN 0-686-74974-X). ADL.

Kedourie, Elie & Haim, Sylvia G., eds. Palestine & Israel in the Nineteenth & Twentieth Centuries. 250p. 1981. 29.50x (ISBN 0-7146-3121-3, F Cass Co). Biblio Dist.

Knox, D. E. The Making of a New Eastern Question: British Palestine Policy & the Origins of Israel, 1917-1925. 1981. 19.95 (ISBN 0-8132-0555-7). Cath U Pr.

Knox, Edward D. The Making of a New Eastern Question: British Palestine Policy & the Origins of Israel, 1917-1925. 1981. write for info. (ISBN 0-8132-0544-1). Cath U Pr.

Kuntz, J. Kenneth. The People of Ancient Israel: An Introduction to the Old Testament Literature, History & Thought. (Illus.). 1974. pap. text ed. 15.50 scp (ISBN 0-06-043822-3, HarpC). Har-Row.

Larteguy, Jean. The Walls of Israel. De Kay, Ormond, tr. from Fr. LC 78-88700. 240p. 1969. 5.95 (ISBN 0-87131-017-1). M Evans.

Lewisohn, Ludwig. Israel. LC 76-138122. 1971. Repr. of 1925 ed. lib. bdg. 15.00x (ISBN 0-8371-5698-X, LEIS). Greenwood.

Lieblich, Amia. Tin Soldiers on Jerusalem Beach. LC 78-51810. 1978. 10.95 (ISBN 0-394-42738-6). Pantheon.

Litvinoff, Barnet. Israel: A Chronology & Fact Book. LC 73-12571. (World Chronology Ser.). 160p. 1974. lib. bdg. 8.50 (ISBN 0-379-16310-1). Oceana.

Metzger, Lauro V. The Political Theory of the State of Israel. (Illus.). 1978. 47.50 (ISBN 0-89266-131-3). Am Classical Coll Pr.

Meyer, Nathan M. The Land of Miracles. (Illus.). pap. 1.50 (ISBN 0-88469-021-0). BMH Bks.

Nashif, Taysir N. The Palestine Arab & Jewish Leaderships: A Comparative Study. (Illus.). 1979. text ed. 10.50x (ISBN 0-210-40596-1). Asia.

Neilson, Francis. From UR to Nazareth: An Economic Inquiry into the Religious & Political History of Israel. 75.00 (ISBN 0-87700-010-7). Revisionist Pr.

Nicholson, Ernest W. Exodus & Sinai in History & Tradition. pap. 4.95 (ISBN 0-8042-0200-1). John Knox.

Oliphant, Laurence. Life in the Holy Land. (Illus.). 475p. 1980. 13.95x (ISBN 0-686-64377-1). Behrman.

O'Neill, Bard. Revolutionary Warfare in the Middle East: The Israelis vs. the Fedayeen. new ed. LC 74-79038. (Illus.). 1974. 6.00 (ISBN 0-87364-000-4). Paladin Ent.

Parmelee, Alice. A History of the People of Israel, Bk. 4. LC 80-81097. (All About the Bible). 148p. (Orig.). 1980. pap. 4.95 (ISBN 0-8192-1273-3). Morehouse.

Payne, David. The Kingdoms of the Lord. 304p. (Orig.). 1981. pap. 9.95 (ISBN 0-8028-1856-0). Eerdmans.

Peres, Shimon. From These Men: Seven Founders of the State of Israel. Simpson, Philip, tr. 1980. 10.95 (ISBN 0-671-61016-3). S&S.

Petrie, Flinders. Ancient Egypt & Ancient Israel. 150p. 1980. 12.50 (ISBN 0-89005-337-5). Ares.

Ramsey, George W. Quest for the Historical Israel. LC 80-82188. 208p. (Orig.). 1981. pap. 12.50 (ISBN 0-8042-0187-0). John Knox.

Rebirth of Israel. Date not set. 7.95 (ISBN 0-686-76250-9). Feldheim.

Ritchie, John. From Egypt to Canaan. 102p. 1981. pap. 3.50 (ISBN 0-8254-3614-1). Kregel.

Robinson, H. Wheeler. History of Israel. rev. ed. Brockington, L. H., ed. (Studies in Theology: No. 42). 1964. pap. 8.95x (ISBN 0-8401-6042-9). Allenson-Breckinridge.

--History of Israel: Its Facts & Factors. 2nd rev. ed. (Studies in Theology). 206p. 1967. pap. 13.50x (ISBN 0-7156-0163-6, Pub. by Duckworth England). Biblio Dist.

Sachar, Howard M. Egypt & Israel. 1981. 19.95 (ISBN 0-399-90124-8). Marek.

--A History of Israel: From the Rise of Zionism to Our Time. LC 76-13710. (Illus.). 1979. 9.95 (ISBN 0-394-73679-6). Knopf.

Samuel, Herbert. Grooves of Change: A Book of Memoirs. (Return to Zion Ser.). (Illus.). 378p. Repr. of 1946 ed. lib. bdg. 25.00x (ISBN 0-87991-137-9). Porcupine Pr.

Samuel, Rinna. Israel: Promised Land to Modern State. (Illus.). 175p. 1971. Repr. of 1969 ed. 16.00x (ISBN 0-85303-135-5, Pub. by Vallentine Mitchell England). Biblio Dist.

Segre, V. D. Israel: A Society in Transition. 1971. 10.95x (ISBN 0-19-215172-X). Oxford U Pr.

Smith, James E. Divided We Fall. LC 79-67439. 96p. (Orig.). 1980. pap. 1.95 (ISBN 0-87239-381-X, 40086). Standard Pub.

Swift, Fletcher H. Education in Ancient Israel, from Earliest Times to 70 A.D. LC 73-86728. xii, 134p. Date not set. Repr. of 1919 ed. cancelled (ISBN 0-8462-1759-7). Russell.

Torrey, Charles C., ed. The Chronicler's History of Israel: Chronicles-Ezra-Nehemiah Restored to Its Original Form. LC 72-85281. 240p. 1973. Repr. of 1954 ed. 12.50 (ISBN 0-8046-1709-0). Kennikat.

Viteles, Harry. A History of the Co-Operative Movement in Israel, 7 vols. Incl. Bk. 1. The Evolution of the Co-Operative Movement. 6.50x (ISBN 0-686-02378-1); Bk. 2. The Evolution of the Kibbutz Movement. 16.25x (ISBN 0-686-02379-X); Bk. 3. Analysis of the Four Sectors of the Kibbutz Movement. 16.25x (ISBN 0-686-02380-3); Bk. 4. Co-Operative Smallholders Settlements. 9.75x (ISBN 0-686-02381-1); Bk. 5. Workers, Producers, Transportation & Service Co-Operatives. 9.75x (ISBN 0-686-02382-X); Bk. 6. Central Agricultural Co-Operatives. 15.00x (ISBN 0-686-02383-8); Bk. 7. Consumers Co-Operatives. 13.20x (ISBN 0-686-02384-6). 81.00x set (ISBN 0-686-02377-3). Hartmore.

Whitelam, Keith W. The Just King: Monarchical Judicial Authority in Ancient Israel. (Journal for the Study of the Old Testament Supplement Ser.: No. 12). 1979. text ed. 19.95 (ISBN 0-905774-18-3, Pub. by JSOT Pr England). Eisenbrauns.

Wood, James E. Nationhood & the Kingdom. LC 76-48576. 1977. bds. 3.25 (ISBN 0-8054-8805-7). Broadman.

ISRAEL–HISTORY–FICTION

Uris, Leon. Exodus. LC 62-16691. 1958. 14.95 (ISBN 0-385-05082-8). Doubleday.

ISRAEL–INTELLECTUAL LIFE

Cultural Policy in Israel. (Studies & Documents on Cultural Policies). (Illus.). 79p. (Orig.). 1974. pap. 5.00 (ISBN 92-3-101066-2, U126, UNESCO). Unipub.

Eakin, Frank E. Religion & Culture of Israel: Selected Issues. 1977. pap. 10.50 (ISBN 0-8191-0208-3). U Pr of Amer.

Kimpel, Ben F. Philosophies of Life of Ancient Greeks & Israelites. LC 80-81697. 1981. 17.50 (ISBN 0-8022-2371-0). Philos Lib.

ISRAEL–JUVENILE LITERATURE

Fine, Helen. Behold, the Land: Ayin Letzion. rev. ed. LC 67-21069. (gr. 5-8). 1977. text ed. 6.50 (ISBN 0-8074-0129-3, 127270). UAHC.

Frankel, Max & Hoffman, Judy. I Live in Israel. Fishman, Priscilla, ed. LC 79-12833. (Illus.). (gr. 3-4). 1979. pap. text ed. 3.95x (ISBN 0-87441-317-6). Behrman.

Gidal, Sonia & Gidal, Tim. My Village in Israel. (Illus.). (gr. 5-6). 1959. PLB 5.69 (ISBN 0-394-91912-2). Pantheon.

Goldman, Louis & Reit, Seymour. Week in Hagar's World: Israel. LC 69-16487. (Face to Face Bks.). (Illus.). (gr. k-3). 1969. 4.50g (ISBN 0-02-736210-8, CCPr); text ed. 1.36 (ISBN 0-02-736200-0, CCPr). Macmillan.

Hoffman, Gail. The Land & People of Israel. rev. ed. LC 77-37286. (Portraits of the Nations Ser.). (Illus.). (gr. 6 up). 1972. 8.95 (ISBN 0-397-31258-X, JBL-J). Har-Row.

Kubie, Nora B. First Book of Israel. rev. ed. LC 74-31166. (First Bks). (Illus.). (gr. 4-6). 1978. PLB 7.40 (ISBN 0-531-02239-0). Watts.

--Israel. 2nd rev. ed. (First Bks). (Illus.). (gr. 4-6). 1978. PLB 7.40 s&l (ISBN 0-531-02239-0). Watts.

--Jews of Israel: History & Sources. Silberman, Mark, ed. LC 75-18510. (Illus.). 128p. (Orig.). (gr. 5-6). 1975. pap. text ed. 3.95x (ISBN 0-87441-246-3). Behrman.

Lehman, Emil. Israel: Idea & Reality. (Illus.). (gr. 8 up). 3.95x (ISBN 0-8381-0205-0, 10-205). United Syn Bk.

Rachleff, Owen S. Young Israel: A History of the Modern Nation the First 20 Years. (Illus.). (gr. 7 up). 1981. PLB 7.95 (ISBN 0-87460-115-0). Lion Bks.

Rutland, Jonathan. Take a Trip to Israel. (Take a Trip to Ser.). (Illus.). 32p. (gr. 1-3). 1981. lib. bdg. 6.90 (ISBN 0-531-04318-5). Watts.

Zohar, Danah. Israel. LC 77-88352. (Countries Ser.). (Illus.). 1978. lib. bdg. 7.95 (ISBN 0-686-51152-2). Silver.

ISRAEL–MAPS

Carta. Israel Motor Atlas. rev. ed. (Illus.). 1978. pap. 6.35 (ISBN 0-930038-06-1). Arbit.

--Israel Road Guide. rev. ed. (Illus.). 1978. pap. 10.95 (ISBN 0-930038-07-X). Arbit.

ISRAEL–POLITICS AND GOVERNMENT

Arian, Alan. The Choosing People: Voting Behavior in Israel. LC 72-7828. (Illus.). 276p. 1973. 17.50 (ISBN 0-8295-0249-1). UPB.

Aronoff, M. J. Power & Ritual in the Israel Labor Party: A Study in Political Anthropology. (Illus., Orig.). 1977. pap. text ed. 23.25x (ISBN 90-232-1453-6). Humanities.

Avi-hai, Avraham. Ben Gurion: State Builder. 365p. 1974. casebound 12.95 (ISBN 0-87855-156-5). Transaction Bks.

Badi, Joseph, ed. Fundamental Laws of the State of Israel. LC 61-8605. 451p. 1961. text ed. 38.00x (ISBN 0-8290-0174-3). Irvington.

Bayne, E. A. Four Ways of Politics: State & Nation in Italy, Somalia, Israel, Iran. LC 65-14723. 1965. 7.50 (ISBN 0-910116-60-1). Am U Field.

Bee, Noah. In Spite of Everything: History of the State of Israel. LC 73-77304. (Illus.). 200p. 1973. 7.95 (ISBN 0-8197-0297-8). Bloch.

Bernstein, Marver H. Politics of Israel: The First Decade of Statehood. LC 69-13825. Repr. of 1957 ed. lib. bdg. 17.50x (ISBN 0-8371-2036-5, BEPI). Greenwood.

Birnbaum, Ervin. Politics of Compromise: State & Religion in Israel. LC 70-92557. 348p. 1970. 18.00 (ISBN 0-8386-7567-0). Fairleigh Dickinson.

Blenkinsopp, J. Gibeon & Israel: The Role of Gibeon & the Gibeonites in the Political and Religious History of Early Israel. LC 74-171672. (Society for Old Testament Studies Monographs). 1972. 29.50 (ISBN 0-521-08368-0). Cambridge U Pr.

Caso, Adolph. They Too Made America Great. 175p. 1978. 12.50 (ISBN 0-8283-1699-6). Dante U Am.

Cohen, Joseph E. Anarchism & Libertarian Socialism in Israel: A Study of Anti-Statist Movements. 1979. lib. bdg. 42.95 (ISBN 0-686-24784-1). M Buber Pr.

Cultural Policy in Israel. (Studies & Documents on Cultural Policies). (Illus.). 79p. (Orig.). 1974. pap. 5.00 (ISBN 92-3-101066-2, U126, UNESCO). Unipub.

Czudnowski, Moshe M. & Landau, Jacob M. The Israeli Communist Party. LC 65-19765. (Studies Ser.: No. 9). 1965. pap. 5.95 (ISBN 0-8179-3092-2). Hoover Inst Pr.

Dacey, Norman F. Democracy in Israel. 1981. lib. bdg. 59.95 (ISBN 0-686-73182-4). Revisionist Pr.

--Democracy in Israel. 74p. Date not set. pap. 3.00 (ISBN 0-911038-68-X). Inst Hist Rev.

--Democracy in Israel. 73p. (Orig.). 1976. pap. 2.50 (ISBN 0-911038-68-X, Inst Hist Rev). Noontide.

Deacon, Richard. The Israeli Secret Service. LC 78-56985. (Illus.). 318p. 1980. pap. 4.95 (ISBN 0-8008-4267-7). Taplinger.

Debates of the Israeli Knesset, 1967-1968. 1977. 25.00 (ISBN 0-686-18945-0). Inst Palestine.

Edelman, Lily. Modern Israel. pap. 2.00 (ISBN 0-87980-101-8). Wilshire.

Eisenberg, Dennis, et al. The Mossad: Israel's Secret Intelligence Service--Inside Stories. (Illus.). 1979. pap. 2.75 (ISBN 0-451-08883-2, E8883, Sig). NAL.

--The Mossad: Israel's Secret Intelligence Service-the Inside Stories. LC 78-18824. (Illus.). 1978. 9.95 (ISBN 0-448-22201-9). Paddington.

Elazar, Daniel J. Self Rule-Shared Rule. LC 79-120721. 1979. 18.00x (ISBN 965-20-0010-8, Pub. by Turtledove Pub Ltd Israel). Intl Schol Bk Serv.

Elazar, Daniel J. & Aviad, Janet. Religion & Politics in Israel: The Interplay of Judaism & Zionism. 32p. 1981. pap. 2.50 (ISBN 0-87495-033-3). Am Jewish Comm.

Etzioni-Halevy, Eva & Shapira, Rina. Political Culture in Israel: Cleavage & Integration Among Israeli Jews. LC 76-24350. (Special Studies). 1977. text ed. 26.95 (ISBN 0-275-23790-7). Praeger.

Freudenheim, Y. Government in Israel. LC 66-17246. 1967. 15.00 (ISBN 0-379-00248-5). Oceana.

George, Donald E. Israeli Occupation: International Law & Political Realities. 1980. 12.50 (ISBN 0-682-49439-9). Exposition.

Harkabi, Yehoshafat. Palestinians & Israel. 285p. 1974. casebound 14.95 (ISBN 0-87855-172-7). Transaction Bks.

Hen-Tov, Jacob. Communism & Zionism in Palestine: The Comintein & the Political Unrest in the 1920's. 200p. 1974. 16.25 (ISBN 0-87073-326-5). Schenkman.

Isaac, Rael J. Israel Divided: Ideological Politics in the Jewish State. LC 75-36944. (Illus.). 1977. 16.50x (ISBN 0-8018-1737-4); pap. 3.95x (ISBN 0-8018-2015-4). Johns Hopkins.

--Party & Politics in Israel: Three Visions of a Jewish State. (Professional Ser.). (Illus.). 256p. 1980. text ed. 22.50x (ISBN 0-582-28196-2). Longman.

Israel Yearbook on Human Rights, Vols. IV & V. Vol. IV, 1974, 439p. 10.00 (ISBN 0-686-74972-3); Vol. V, 1975, 412p. 10.00 (ISBN 0-686-74973-1). ADL.

Katz, Alfred. Government & Politics in Contemporary Israel, 1948 to Present. LC 79-5508. 1980. pap. text ed. 10.50 (ISBN 0-8191-0908-8). U Pr of Amer.

Lagerwist, Frank A. Israel & the Politics of Terrorism in the Middle East. (Illus.). 143p. 1981. 69.85 (ISBN 0-930008-93-6). Inst Econ Pol.

Landau, Asher F. Selected Judgments of the Supreme Court of Israel: Special Volume. 191p. 1971. 14.95 (ISBN 0-87855-175-1). Transaction Bks.

Liebman, Charles S. Pressure Without Sanctions: The Influence of World Jewry on Israeli Policy. LC 75-18242. 304p. 1976. 18.00 (ISBN 0-8386-1791-3). Fairleigh Dickinson.

Mahler, Gregory S. The Knesset: Parliament in the Israeli Political System. LC 80-67633. 256p. 1981. 22.00 (ISBN 0-8386-3071-5). Fairleigh Dickinson.

Medding, P. Y. Mapai in Israel: Political Organisation & Government in a New Society. LC 75-184900. 352p. 37.50 (ISBN 0-521-08492-X). Cambridge U Pr.

Menuhin, Moshe. The Decadence of Judaism in Our Time. 585p. 1969. 13.00x (ISBN 0-911038-88-4, Inst Hist Rev). Noontide.

Merhav, Peretz. The Israeli Left: History, Problems, Documents. LC 77-84578. 1980. 15.00 (ISBN 0-498-02184-X). A S Barnes.

Metzger, Jan, et al. This Land Is Our Land. 272p. 1981. 35.00 (ISBN 0-86232-086-0, Pub. by Zed Pr). Lawrence Hill.

Metzger, Lauro V. The Political Theory of the State of Israel. (Illus.). 1978. 47.50 (ISBN 0-89266-131-3). Am Classical Coll Pr.

Misrahi, R. La Philosophie Politique et L'etat D'israel. (Archives Positivistes: No. 7). 391p. 1976. pap. text ed. 29.00x (ISBN 90-2797-942-1). Mouton.

Naamani, Israel T., et al, eds. Israel: Its Politics & Philosophy. rev. ed. LC 73-15645. 447p. 1973. pap. 4.95x (ISBN 0-87441-249-8). Behrman.

Nachmias, David & Rosenbloom, David H. Bureaucratic Culture: Citizens & Administrators in Israel. LC 78-17638. 1978. 17.95x (ISBN 0-312-10808-7). St Martin.

Nashif, Taysir N. The Palestine Arab & Jewish Leaderships: A Comparative Study. (Illus.). 1979. text ed. 10.50x (ISBN 0-210-40596-1). Asia.

Nisan, Mordechai. Israel & the Territories. LC 79-111044. 1979. 15.00x (ISBN 965-20-0005-1, Pub. by Turtledove Pub Ltd Israel). Intl Schol Bk Serv.

Penniman, Howard R., ed. Israel at the Polls: The Knesset Elections of 1977. 1979. pap. 8.25 (ISBN 0-8447-3305-9). Am Enterprise.

Peretz, Don. The Government & Politics of Israel. 1979. lib. bdg. 24.75x (ISBN 0-89158-086-7); pap. text ed. 10.00x (ISBN 0-89158-087-5). Westview.

Perlmutter, Amos. Military & Politics in Israel: Nation Building & Role Expansion. 2nd rev. ed. (Illus.). 161p. 1977. 23.50x (ISBN 0-7146-3100-0, F Cass Co). Biblio Dist.

--Military & Politics in Israel 1948-1967. rev ed. 176p. 1981. 23.50x (ISBN 0-7146-2392-X, F Cass Co). Biblio Dist.

--Politics & the Military in Israel, 1967-1977. 222p. 1978. 23.50x (ISBN 0-7146-3079-9, F Cass Co). Biblio Dist.

Poliak, A. N. Geopolitics of Israel & the Middle East. 1978. lib. bdg. 49.95 (ISBN 0-685-62294-0). Revisionist Pr.

Rabin, Yitzhak. The Rabin Memoirs. LC 79-9273. (Illus.). 1979. 12.95 (ISBN 0-316-73002-5). Little.

Rosenblatt, Bernard A. The American Bridge to the Israel Commonwealth. LC 75-392. 128p. 1975. Repr. of 1959 ed. lib. bdg. 15.00x (ISBN 0-8371-8020-1, ROAB). Greenwood.

Schiff, Gary S. Tradition & Politics: The Religious Parties of Israel. LC 77-5723. 1977. 14.95x (ISBN 0-8143-1580-1). Wayne St U Pr.

Schnall, David. Radical Dissent in Contemporary Israeli Politics: Cracks in the Wall. (Praeger Special Studies). 1978. 24.95 (ISBN 0-03-047096-X). Praeger.

Segre, Dan V. A Crisis of Identity: Israel & Zionism. 1980. 14.95 (ISBN 0-19-215862-7). Oxford U Pr.

Shapiro, Yonathan. The Formative Years of the Israeli Labour Party: The Organization of Power, 1919-1930. LC 74-22992. (Sage Studies in Twentieth Century History: Vol. 4). 278p. 1976. 20.00x (ISBN 0-8039-9936-4). Sage.

Sharkansky, Ira. Wither the State? Politics & Public Enterprise in Three Countries. LC 79-18780. 1979. 15.00 (ISBN 0-934540-01-2); pap. text ed. 8.95x (ISBN 0-934540-00-4). Chatham Hse Pubs.

Shem-Ur, Ora. The Challenges of Israel. LC 80-52915. 80p. 1980. 4.95 (ISBN 0-88400-071-0). Shengold.

Stein, Sarah K., ed. Leaders in Israel: Thumb-Nail Sketches of the Officers of the First Provisional Government. LC 71-179743. (Biography Index Reprint Ser). Repr. of 1948 ed. 10.00 (ISBN 0-8369-8111-1). Arno.

Tamarin, G. R. The Israeli Dilemma: Essays on a Warfare State. (Publications of Polemological Centre of the Free University of Brussels: Vol. 2). 202p. 1973. pap. text ed. 16.00 (ISBN 90-237-6220-7, Pub. by Swets Serv Holland). Swets North Am.

Weiner, Herbert. Wild Goats of Ein Gedi. LC 61-12601. (Temple Bks). 1970. pap. 2.95 (ISBN 0-689-70235-3, T-16). Atheneum.

Weizman, Ezer. The Battle for Peace. LC 80-71057. (Illus.). 408p. 1981. 15.95 (ISBN 0-553-05002-8). Bantam.

Wistrich, Robert, ed. The Left Against Zion: Communism, Israel & the Middle East. 309p. 1979. 24.00x (ISBN 0-85303-193-2, Pub by Vallentine Mitchell England); pap. 9.95x (ISBN 0-85303-199-1). Biblio Dist.

Yehoshua, A. B. Between Right & Right. LC 80-721. 224p. 1981. 11.95 (ISBN 0-385-17035-1). Doubleday.

Yogev, Gedalia, ed. The Political & Diplomatic Documents of the State of Israel, December, 1947-May, 1948, 2 vols. (Documents on the Foreign Policy of Israel Ser.). 1980. Set. 69.95 (ISBN 0-87855-396-7). Transaction Bks.

Zucker, Norman L. The Coming Crisis in Israel: Private Faith & Public Policy. 1973. 15.00x (ISBN 0-262-24018-1); pap. 4.95 (ISBN 0-262-74012-5). MIT Pr.

ISRAEL–RELATIONS (GENERAL) WITH THE UNITED STATES

Davis, Moshe, ed. Israel: Its Role in Civilization. LC 77-70673. (America & the Holy Land Ser.). 1977. Repr. of 1956 ed. lib. bdg. 23.00 (ISBN 0-405-10241-0). Arno.

Ennes, James M., Jr. Assault on the Liberty: The True Story of the Israeli Attack on an American Intelligence Ship. LC 79-4793. 1980. 13.95 (ISBN 0-394-50512-3). Random.

ISRAEL–RELIGION

Abramov, S. Zalman. Perpetual Dilemma: Jewish Religion in the Jewish State. 1979. pap. 7.50 (ISBN 0-8074-0088-2, 382500, WUPJ). UAHC.

Blenkinsopp, J. Gibeon & Israel: The Role of Gibeon & the Gibeonites in the Political and Religious History of Early Israel. LC 74-171672. (Society for Old Testament Studies Monographs). 1972. 29.50 (ISBN 0-521-08368-0). Cambridge U Pr.

Cohn, Haim H. Jewish Law in Ancient & Modern Israel. 1971. 20.00x (ISBN 0-87068-137-0). Ktav.

Cross, Frank M. Canaanite Myth & Hebrew Epic: Essays in the History of the Religion of Israel. LC 72-76564. 1973. 18.50x (ISBN 0-674-09175-2). Harvard U Pr.

Eakin, Frank E. Religion & Culture of Israel: Selected Issues. 1977. pap. 10.50 (ISBN 0-8191-0208-3). U Pr of Amer.

Elazar, Daniel J. & Aviad, Janet. Religion & Politics in Israel: The Interplay of Judaism & Zionism. 32p. 1981. pap. 2.50 (ISBN 0-87495-033-3). Am Jewish Comm.

Fohrer, Georg. Geschichte der Israelitischen Religion. xvi, 367p. (Ger.). 1969. 24.00x (ISBN 3-11-002652-X). De Gruyter.

Harrelson, Walter J. From Fertility Cult to Worship. LC 66-14929. (Scholars Press Reprint Ser.: No. 4). pap. 9.00x (ISBN 0-89130-379-0, 00 07 04). Scholars Pr CA.

Kaufmann, Yehezkel. The Religion of Israel: From Its Beginnings to the Babylonian Exile. Greenberg, Moshe, tr. LC 60-5466. 498p. 1972. pap. 8.95 (ISBN 0-8052-0364-8). Schocken.

Mayes, Andrew D. Israel in the Period of the Judges. (Studies in Biblical Theology, Second Ser.: No. 29). 1974. text ed. 9.95x o. p. (ISBN 0-8401-4079-7); pap. text ed. 7.45x (ISBN 0-8401-3079-1). Allenson-Breckinridge.

Menuhin, Moshe. The Decadence of Judaism in Our Time. 585p. 1969. 13.00x (ISBN 0-911038-88-4, Inst Hist Rev). Noontide.

Raven, John H. History of the Religion of Israel in Old Testament Theology. (Twin Brooks Ser.). pap. 9.95 (ISBN 0-8010-7691-9). Baker Bk.

Saggs, H. W. The Encounter with the Divine in Mesopotamia & Israel. (Jordan Lectures in Comparative Religion, 12th Ser). 1978. text ed. 31.25x (ISBN 0-485-17412-X, Athlone Pr). Humanities.

Sanchez, Benjamin M. Israel & the Prophecies. pap. 3.10 (ISBN 0-913558-06-0). Educator Pubns.

Thomson, J. The Samaritans: Their Testimony to the Religion of Israel. 1976. lib. bdg. 59.95 (ISBN 0-8490-2564-8). Gordon Pr.

Zucker, Norman L. The Coming Crisis in Israel: Private Faith & Public Policy. 1973. 15.00x (ISBN 0-262-24018-1); pap. 4.95 (ISBN 0-262-74012-5). MIT Pr.

ISRAEL–SOCIAL CONDITIONS

Bentwich, Norman. A New Way of Life: The Collective Settlements of Israel. 1949. 15.00 (ISBN 0-686-17691-X). Quality Lib.

Cohen, Abner. Arab Border-Villages in Israel. 1965. text ed. 28.00x (ISBN 0-7190-0251-6). Humanities.

Curtis, Michael & Chertoff, Mordecai S., eds. Israel: Social Structure & Change. LC 73-78696. (Third World Ser). 460p. 1973. pap. 5.95 (ISBN 0-87855-575-7). Transaction Bks.

Edelman, Lily. Israel. 1958. 20.00 (ISBN 0-686-17232-9). Scholars Ref Lib.

Eisenstadt, Samuel N. & Bar-Yosef, Rivkah. Integration & Development in Israel. 720p. 1971. casebound 24.95 (ISBN 0-87855-178-6). Transaction Bks.

Goldberg, H., ed. Ethnic Groups - Special Topics: Vol. 1, Ethnic Groups in Israeli Society. 52.75 (ISBN 0-677-40065-9). Gordon.

Gratch, Haya, ed. Twenty-Five Years of Social Research in Israel. LC 74-170163. 292p. 1974. 17.50x (ISBN 0-8002-0100-0). Intl Pubns Serv.

Greenberg, Harold I. & Nadler, Samuel. Poverty in Israel: Economic Realities & the Promise of Social Justice. LC 76-58558. (Special Studies). 1977. text ed. 22.95 (ISBN 0-275-24300-1). Praeger.

Henkin, Louis. World Politics & the Jewish Condition. LC 70-190130. 1972. 9.95 (ISBN 0-8129-0265-3). Times Bks.

Inbar, Michael & Adler, Chaim. Ethnic Integration in Israel: A Comparative Study of Moroccan Brothers Who Settled in France & in Israel. LC 76-27933. (Illus.). 1977. lib. bdg. 16.95 (ISBN 0-87855-204-9). Transaction Bks.

Kramer, Ralph M. The Voluntary Service Agency in Israel. LC 76-620011. (Research Ser: No.26). (Illus.). 120p. 1976. pap. 2.50x (ISBN 0-87725-126-6). U of Cal Intl St.

Krausz, Ernest, ed. Studies of Israeli Society. LC 79-93045. 324p. 1980. 29.95 (ISBN 0-87855-414-9); pap. 19.95 (ISBN 0-87855-369-X). Transaction Bks.

Lewis, Arnold. Power, Poverty & Education. 1980. 18.50x (ISBN 965-20-0016-7, Pub. by Turtledove Pub Ltd Israel). Intl Schol Bk Serv.

McNeish, James. Belonging: Conversations in Israel. LC 79-19050. 204p. 1980. 9.95 (ISBN 0-03-046796-9). HR&W.

Mar'I, Sami K. Arab Education in Israel. 1978. 15.00 (ISBN 0-8156-0145-X). Syracuse U Pr.

Marx, Emanuel. The Social Context of Violent Behaviour: A Social Anthropological Study in an Israeli Immigrant Town. (Direct Editions Ser.). (Orig.). 1976. 12.00 (ISBN 0-7100-8420-X). Routledge & Kegan.

NCHS, ed. Multiplicity Study of Marriages & Births in Israel. 1977. pap. 1.95 (ISBN 0-8406-0089-5). Natl Ctr Health Stats.

Samuel, Edwin. The Structure of Society in Israel. 6.00 (ISBN 0-8446-2861-1). Peter Smith.

Segre, Dan V. A Crisis of Identity: Israel & Zionism. 1980. 14.95 (ISBN 0-19-215862-7). Oxford U Pr.

Segre, V. D. Israel: A Society in Transition. 1971. 10.95x (ISBN 0-19-215172-X). Oxford U Pr.

Shama, Avraham & Iris, Mark. Immigration Without Integration: The Status of Third World Jews in Israel. 221p. 1977. text ed. 11.25 (ISBN 0-87073-367-2). Schenkman.

Shokeid, Moshe & Deshen, Shlomo. Distant Relations: Ethnicity & Politics Among Arabs & North African Jews in Israel. 228p. 1981. 21.00x (ISBN 0-89789-021-3). J F Bergin.

Smith, Colin. The Palestinians. (Minority Rights Group Ser.: No. 24). 1975. pap. 2.50 (ISBN 0-89192-110-9). Interbk Inc.

Spender, Stephen. Learning Laughter. (Illus.). Repr. of 1953 ed. lib. bdg. 14.50x (ISBN 0-8371-1958-8, SPLL). Greenwood.

Stern, Geraldine. Israeli Women Speak Out. 1979. 8.95 (ISBN 0-685-93957-X). Har-Row.

Weingrod, Alex. Israel: Group Relations in a New Society. LC 74-9027. (Institute of Race Relations Publications). 1976. Repr. of 1965 ed. lib. bdg. 15.00 (ISBN 0-8371-8884-9, WEIG). Greenwood.

Zweig, Ferdynand. Israel: The Sword & the Harp. LC 74-86291. 326p. 1970. 15.00 (ISBN 0-8386-7534-4). Fairleigh Dickinson.

ISRAEL–SOCIAL LIFE AND CUSTOMS

Cohen, Joseph E. Anarchism & Libertarian Socialism in Israel: A Study of Anti-Statist Movements. 1979. lib. bdg. 42.95 (ISBN 0-686-24784-1). M Buber Pr.

Jarus, A. & Marcus, J. Children & Families in Israel. 634p. 1970. 57.95x (ISBN 0-677-14620-5). Gordon.

Katz, Elihu & Gurevitch, Michael. The Secularization of Leisure: Culture & Communication in Israel. (Illus.). 296p. 1976. 16.50x (ISBN 0-674-79677-2). Harvard U Pr.

Klein, Ralph W. Israel in Exile: A Theological Interpretation. Brueggemann, Walter & Donahue, John R., trs. LC 79-7382. (Overtures to Biblical Theology Ser.). 180p. (Orig.). 1979. pap. 6.95 (ISBN 0-8006-1532-8, 1-1532). Fortress.

Lambert, Lance. Israel: The Unique Land, the Unique People. 256p. 1981. 3.50 (ISBN 0-8423-1771-6). Tyndale.

Manor, Giora & Ingber, Judith B., eds. Israel Dance Annual, 1978-79. (Illus.). 1979. pap. 4.95 (ISBN 0-934682-05-4). Emmett.

Mirsky, Mark J. My Search for the Messiah. LC 76-54910. 1977. 10.95 (ISBN 0-02-585120-9, 58512). Macmillan.

Oliphant, Laurence. Life in the Holy Land. (Illus.). 475p. 1980. 13.95x (ISBN 0-686-64377-1). Behrman.

Pederson, Johannes. Israel: Its Life & Culture, 4 bks. Incl. Bks. 1 & 2. 1973. Repr. of 1926 ed. 59.00x (ISBN 0-19-647899-5). Oxford U Pr.

Rein, Natalie. Daughters of Rachel: Women in Israel. 1980. pap. 4.95 (ISBN 0-14-005731-5). Penguin.

Rennert, Maggie. Shelanu: An Israeli Journal. LC 78-9561. 1979. 12.95 (ISBN 0-13-808808-X). P-H.

Rubin, M. The Walls of Acre: Intergroup Relations & Urban Development in Israel. LC 74-8726. (Case Studies in Cultural Anthropology). 1974. pap. text ed. 5.95 (ISBN 0-03-086299-X, HoltC). HR&W.

Samuel, Edwin. The Structure of Society in Israel. 6.00 (ISBN 0-8446-2861-1). Peter Smith.

Wilson, Edmund. Israel & the Dead Sea Scrolls. 416p. 1978. pap. 4.95 (ISBN 0-374-51341-4). FS&G.

ISRAEL, ELECTION OF

see Jews–Election, Doctrine Of

ISRAEL, TEN LOST TRIBES

see Lost Tribes of Israel

ISRAEL-ARAB BORDER CONFLICTS, 1949-

Aronson, Shlomo. Conflict & Bargaining in the Middle East: An Israeli Perspective. LC 77-10967. 1978. text ed. 18.95x (ISBN 0-8018-2046-4). Johns Hopkins.

Barker, A. J. Arab-Israeli Wars. 1981. 19.95 (ISBN 0-88254-587-6). Hippocrene Bks.

Ben-Dak, Joseph. Systems for Peace. 1980. 25.00x (ISBN 965-20-0007-8, Pub. by Turtledove Pub Ltd Israel). Intl Schol Bk Serv.

DeVore, Ronald M. The Arab-Israeli Conflict: A Historical, Political, Social, & Military Bibliography. LC 76-17575. (War-Peace Bibliography Ser.: No. 4). 273p. 1976. text ed. 32.50 (ISBN 0-87436-229-6). ABC-Clio.

Dupuy, Trevor N. Elusive Victory: The Arab-Israeli Wars, 1947-1974. LC 78-2119. (Illus.). 1978. 25.00 (ISBN 0-06-011112-7, HarpT). Har-Row.

El Shazly, Saad. The Crossing of the Suez. Benson, Susan, ed. (Illus.). 333p. 1980. 15.00 (ISBN 0-9604562-0-1, 80-67107). Am Mideast.

Freedman, Robert O., ed. World Politics & the Arab-Israeli Conflict. (Pergamon Policy Studies). 1979. 39.00 (ISBN 0-08-023380-5). Pergamon.

Gerson, Allan. Israel, the West Bank & International Law. 285p. 1978. 30.00x (ISBN 0-7146-3091-8, F Cass Co). Biblio Dist.

Harkness, Georgia & Kraft, Charles F. The Biblical Backgrounds of the Middle East Conflict. LC 76-22644. (Illus.). 1976. 3.95 (ISBN 0-687-03435-3). Abingdon.

Hawley, Donald. The Trucial States. 13.95 (ISBN 0-685-60149-8, Pub by Twayne). Cyrco Pr.

Heradstveit, Daniel. The Arab-Israeli Conflict: Psychological Obstacles to Peace. 1979. pap. 23.50x (ISBN 82-00-01822-9, Dist. by Columbia U Pr.). Universitet.

Khouri, Fred J. Arab-Israeli Dilemma. 2nd ed. LC 68-20483. 1976. pap. 7.95x (ISBN 0-8156-2178-7). Syracuse U Pr.

Koury, Enver M. The Balance of Military Power: The Arab-Israeli Conflict. LC 76-57912. 111p. 1977. pap. 5.00 (ISBN 0-934484-10-4). Inst Mid East & North Africa.

Lapp, John A. The View from East Jerusalem. LC 79-26122. 1980. pap. 4.95 (ISBN 0-8361-1920-7). Herald Pr.

Malgo, Wim. Israel Shall Do Valiantly. 2.95 (ISBN 0-686-12825-7). Midnight Call.

Novik, Nimrod & Starr, Joyce, eds. Challenges in the Middle East: Regional Dynamics & Western Security. 160p. 1981. 18.95 (ISBN 0-03-059247-X). Praeger.

Polk, William R. The Elusive Peace: The Middle East in the Twentieth Century. LC 79-16393. 1979. 14.50x (ISBN 0-312-24383-9). St Martin.

Pranger, Robert J. & Tahtinen, Dale R. Implications of the 1976 Arab-Israeli Military Status. LC 76-8381. 1976. pap. 4.25 (ISBN 0-8447-3209-5). Am Enterprise.

Rubin, Barry. The Arab States & the Palestine Conflict. LC 81-5829. (Contemporary Issues in the Middle East Ser.). (Illus.). 328p. 1981. text ed. 22.00x (ISBN 0-8156-2253-8); pap. 10.95x (ISBN 0-8156-0170-0). Syracuse U Pr.

Schools Council History 13-16 Project. Arab-Israeli Conflict. (Modern World Problems Ser.). (Illus.). 1979. Repr. of 1977 ed. lib. bdg. 9.95 (ISBN 0-912616-68-7); pap. text ed. 4.45 (ISBN 0-912616-67-9). Greenhaven.

Schuster, Robert L. Israel, The Middle East & the Moral Conscience of the Western World. (The Major Currents in Contemporary World History). (Illus.). 133p. 1981. 47.85 (ISBN 0-89266-301-4). Am Classical Coll Pr.

Senninger, Donald C. The Fraud at Camp David & the Middle East Crisis. (Illus.). 1979. deluxe ed. 39.65 (ISBN 0-930008-27-8). Inst Econ Pol.

Shamir, Moshe. My Life with Ishmael. 222p. 1970. 15.00x (ISBN 0-686-23179-1, Pub. by Vallentine Mitchell England). Biblio Dist.

Tamarin, G. R. The Israeli Dilemma: Essays on a Warfare State. (Publications of Polemological Centre of the Free University of Brussels: Vol. 2). 202p. 1973. pap. text ed. 16.00 (ISBN 90-237-6220-7, Pub. by Swets Serv Holland). Swets North Am.

United Nations. Documents on the Arab Israel Conflict. Wengler, Wilhelm & Tittel, Josef, eds. LC 72-186563. (Resolutions of the United Nations Ser.: Vol. 1). (Illus.). 207p. 1979. pap. 11.25x (ISBN 3-87061-012-3). Intl Pubns Serv.

ISRAEL-ARAB WAR, 1948-1949

Dawidowicz, Lucy S. The War Against the Jews 1933-1945. LC 74-15470. (Illus.). 480p. 1975. 15.00 (ISBN 0-03-013661-X). HR&W.

Dobson, Christopher. Black September: Its Short, Violent History. Griffin, H. W., ed. (Illus.). 160p. 1974. 11.95 (ISBN 0-02-531900-0). Macmillan.

Lorch, Netaniel. Israel's War of Independence, 1947-1949. 2nd ed. Orig. Title: Edge of the Sword. (Illus.). 1969. 12.50 (ISBN 0-87677-011-1). Hartmore.

O'Ballance, Edgar. The Arab-Israeli War, Nineteen Forty-Eight. LC 79-2877. (Illus.). 220p. 1981. Repr. of 1957 ed. 19.75 (ISBN 0-8305-0045-6). Hyperion Conn.

ISRAEL-ARAB WAR, 1956

see Egypt-History-Intervention, 1956; Sinai Campaign, 1956

ISRAEL-ARAB WAR, 1967

Abu-Lughod, Ibrahim, ed. The Transformation of Palestine: An Arab Perspective. 1971. 18.95x (ISBN 0-8101-0345-1). Northwestern U Pr.

Avnery, Uri. Israel Without Zionism: A Plan for Peace in the Middle East. 1971. pap. 1.95 (ISBN 0-02-072050-5, Collier). Macmillan.

Bar-Simon-Tov, Yaacov. The Israeli-Egyptian War of Attrition, Nineteen Sixty-Nine to Nineteen Seventy: A Case-Study of Limited Local War. LC 80-11124. 256p. 1980. 19.50x (ISBN 0-231-04982-X). Columbia U Pr.

Braverman, Libbie L. & Silver, Samuel M. Six-Day Warriors: An Introduction to Those Who Gave Israel Its Vigor and Its Victories. LC 75-78093. (Illus.). (gr. 5-10). 1969. 4.95 (ISBN 0-8197-0199-8). Bloch.

Chomsky, Noam. Peace in the Middle East? Reflections on Justice & Nationhood. LC 74-5000. 1974. pap. 2.45 (ISBN 0-394-71248-X, V-248, Vin). Random.

Feste, Karen. Setups: The Arab-Israeli Conflict, a Decision Making Game. 1977. pap. 3.50 (ISBN 0-915654-20-2). Am Political.

George, Donald E. Israeli Occupation: International Law & Political Realities. 1980. 12.50 (ISBN 0-682-49439-9). Exposition.

Irving, Clifford. Battle of Jerusalem: The Six-Day War of June, 1967. LC 69-11302. (Battle Bks). (Illus.). (gr. 5-8). 1970. 8.95g (ISBN 0-02-747340-6). Macmillan.

Kimche, David & Bawly, Dan. Six-Day War: Prologue & Aftermath. LC 68-25637. (Illus., Orig.). 1971. pap. 4.95 (ISBN 0-8128-1390-1). Stein & Day.

Kimche, Jon. Palestine or Israel: The Untold Story of Why We Failed 1917-1923; 1967-1973. 360p. 1973. 15.00x (ISBN 0-436-23382-7). Intl Pubns Serv.

Lieber, Robert J. Oil & the Middle East War: Europe in the Energy Crisis. LC 75-44689. (Studies in International Affairs: No. 35). (Illus.). 95p. (Orig.). 1976. pap. text ed. 3.45 (ISBN 0-87674-031-X). Harvard U Intl Aff.

Mandle, Bill. Conflict in the Promised Land. (Studies in 20th Century History Ser.). 1976. pap. text ed. 4.50x (ISBN 0-435-31760-1). Heinemann Ed.

Mezerik, Avrahm G. Suez Canal: Nineteen Fifty-Six Crisis Through the 1967 War. 1969. pap. 15.00 (ISBN 0-685-13209-9, 103). Intl Review.

National Lawyers Guild 1977 Middle East Delegation. Treatment of Palestinians in Israeli-Occupied West Bank & Gaza. LC 78-21553. 1978. 12.50 (ISBN 0-9602188-1-5); pap. 4.50 (ISBN 0-9602188-2-3). Natl Lawyers Guild.

O'Ballance, Edgar. No Victor, No Vanquished. LC 76-58756. (Illus.). 1979. 14.95 (ISBN 0-89141-017-1). Presidio Pr.

--The Third Arab-Israeli War. 300p. 1972. 16.50 (ISBN 0-208-01292-3, Archon). Shoe String.

Perlmutter, Amos. Politics & the Military in Israel, 1967-1977. 222p. 1978. 23.50x (ISBN 0-7146-3079-9, F Cass Co). Biblio Dist.

Safran, Nadav. From War to War: The Arab-Israeli Confrontation, 1948-1967. LC 69-27991. (Illus.). 464p. 1969. text ed. 24.50x (ISBN 0-8290-0173-5). Irvington.

--From War to War: The Arab-Israeli Confrontation 1948-1967. LC 68-27991. 1969. pap. 9.95 (ISBN 0-672-63540-2). Pegasus.

Schleifer, Abdullah. The Fall of Jerusalem. LC 79-178713. (Illus.). 256p. 1972. pap. 3.45 (ISBN 0-85345-249-0, PB2490). Monthly Rev.

Skousen, W. Cleon. Fantastic Victory. LC 67-30390. 1967. 5.95 (ISBN 0-685-48243-X). Bookcraft Inc.

Stein, Janice G. & Tanter, Raymond. Rational Decision-Making: Israel's Security Choices, 1967. LC 80-13589. (Illus.). 414p. 1980. 25.00x (ISBN 0-8142-0312-4). Ohio St U Pr.

ISRAEL-ARAB WAR, 1967–DIPLOMATIC HISTORY

Agwani, M. S., ed. West Asian Crisis, Nineteen Sixty-Seven. (Illus.). 1968. 7.00x (ISBN 0-8426-1114-2). Verry.

Bradley, C. Paul. The Camp David Peace Process: A Study of Carter Administration Policies (1977-1980) LC 81-50100. (Illus.). viii, 79p. 1981. pap. text ed. 4.50 (ISBN 0-936988-03-7). Tompson & Rutter.

Brecher, Michael. Decisions in Crisis: Israel 1967 & 1973 (Intl Crisis Behavior Project) LC 78-62850. 1980. 24.95 (ISBN 0-520-03766-9). U of Cal Pr.

Kouri, Fred, et al. The Elusive Peace in the Middle East. Kerr, Malcolm H., ed. LC 75-15581. 350p. 1975. 19.00 (ISBN 0-87395-305-3); pap. 9.95 (ISBN 0-87395-306-1); microfiche 17.00 (ISBN 0-87395-307-X). State U NY Pr.

Mezerik, Avrahm G., ed. Arab-Israel Conflict & U N. 1962. pap. 25.00 (ISBN 0-685-13185-8, 73). Intl Review.

ISRAEL-ARAB WAR, 1967–PERSONAL NARRATIVES

Schleifer, Abdullah. The Fall of Jerusalem. LC 79-178713. (Illus.). 256p. 1972. pap. 3.45 (ISBN 0-85345-249-0, PB2490). Monthly Rev.

Weizman, Ezer. On Eagles' Wings: The Personal Story of the Leading Commander of the Israeli Air Force. 1977. 12.95 (ISBN 0-02-625790-4, 62579). Macmillan.

ISRAEL-ARAB WAR, 1967–PICTORIAL WORKS

Boger, Jan. To Live in the Fire. Seaton, Lionel, tr. from Ger. Orig. Title: Im Feuer Zu Leben. (Illus.). 1978. 9.95 (ISBN 0-89149-036-1); pap. 6.95 (ISBN 0-89149-035-3). Jolex.

ISRAEL-ARAB WAR, 1973

Adan, Avraham. On the Banks of the Suez: Yom Kippur, 1973. LC 80-12322. (Illus.). 1980. 16.95 (ISBN 0-89141-043-0). Presidio Pr.

Carr, Katherine, ed. Israelis & Palestinians: After the October War. LC 74-22055. (International Documentation Ser.: No. 66). 1974. pap. 3.95 (ISBN 0-89021-028-4). IDOC.

Davis, Moshe, ed. The Yom Kippur War: Israel & the Jewish People. LC 74-10466. 381p. 1974. 9.00 (ISBN 0-405-06192-7). Arno.

Dayan, Yael. Three Weeks in October. 1979. 8.95 (ISBN 0-440-07992-6, E Friede). Delacorte.

Golan, Galia. Yom Kippur & After. LC 76-2278. (Soviet & East European Studies). 1977. 38.50 (ISBN 0-521-21090-9). Cambridge U Pr.

Herzog, Chaim. The War of Atonement, October 1973: A Sports Illustrated Book. 1975. 10.95 (ISBN 0-316-35900-9). Little.

Kraut, Florence R. From My Israel Journal. LC 80-80528. 56p. (Orig.). 1980. pap. 2.95 (ISBN 0-939382-00-8). Preston St Pr.

Maghroori, Ray & Gorman, Stephen M. The Yom Kippur War: A Case Study in Crisis Decision Making in American Foreign Policy. LC 80-5811. 98p. 1981. lib. bdg. 14.75 (ISBN 0-8191-1373-5); pap. text ed. 6.75 (ISBN 0-8191-1374-3). U Pr of Amer.

Narayan, B. K. Lessons & Consequences of the October War (The Fourth Arab-Israeli War of October 1973) 1977. 10.50x (ISBN 0-7069-0508-3). Intl Bk Dist.

Palit, D. K. Return to Sinai: The Arab Offensive 1973. LC 74-901203. 172p. 1974. 10.00x (ISBN 0-88386-291-3). South Asia Bks.

Perlmutter, Amos. Politics & the Military in Israel, 1967-1977. 222p. 1978. 23.50x (ISBN 0-7146-3079-9, F Cass Co). Biblio Dist.

Tahtinen, Dale R. The Arab-Israeli Military Balance Since October 1973. 43p. 1974. pap. 3.25 (ISBN 0-8447-3132-3). Am Enterprise.

Van Creveld, Martin. Military Lessons of the Yom Kippur War. LC 75-13845. (The Washington Papers, No. 24). 60p. 1975. 4.00 (ISBN 0-8039-0562-9). Sage.

Wengler, Wilhelm & Tittel, Josef, eds. Documents on the Arab Israel Conflict. (The Resolutions of the United Nations Organization: Vol. 2). (Illus.). 113p. 1978. pap. 11.25x (ISBN 3-87061-112-X). Intl Pubns Serv.

Williams, Louis, ed. Military Aspects of the Israeli-Arab Conflict. LC 76-373116. 1979. 15.00x (ISBN 965-20-0022-1, Pub. by Turtledove Pub Ltd Israel). Intl Schol Bk Serv.

ISRAELI ARCHITECTURE

see Architecture-Israel

ISRAELI ART

see Art, Israeli

ISRAELI FICTION (COLLECTIONS)

Buber, Martin. The Legend of the Baal-Shem. LC 76-86849. 1969. pap. 4.75 (ISBN 0-8052-0233-1). Schocken.

Spicehandler, Ezra & Arnson, Curtis, eds. New Writing in Israel. LC 75-36497. 1976. 10.95x (ISBN 0-8052-3625-2); pap. 4.95 (ISBN 0-8052-0535-7). Schocken.

ISRAELI NATIONAL CHARACTERISTICS

see National Characteristics, Israeli

ISSA, KOBAYASHI, 1763-1827

see Kobayashi, Issa, 1763-1827

ISTANBUL

Asimov, Isaac. Constantinople: The Forgotten Empire. LC 78-122907. (Illus.). (gr. 7 up). 1970. 4.75 (ISBN 0-395-10908-6). HM.

Clement, Clara E. Constantinople. 1977. lib. bdg. 59.95 (ISBN 0-8490-1668-1). Gordon Pr.

Davidson, H. R. The Viking Road to Byzantium. 341p. 1976. 21.50x (ISBN 0-87471-834-1). Rowman.

Istanbul. (Panorama Bks.). (Illus., Fr.). 3.95 (ISBN 0-685-11261-6). French & Eur.

Johnson, Clarence R., ed. Constantinople Today: Or, the Pathfinder Survey of Constantinople, a Study in Oriental Social Life. LC 77-87631. Repr. of 1922 ed. 34.50 (ISBN 0-404-16456-0). AMS Pr.

Kinross, Lord. Hagia Sophia. LC 72-163362. (Wonders of Man Ser). (Illus.). 176p. 1972. 16.95 (ISBN 0-88225-014-0). Newsweek.

Lewis, Bernard. Istanbul & the Civilization of the Ottoman Empire. (Centers of Civilization Ser.: Vol. 9). (Illus.). 1972. 7.95x (ISBN 0-8061-0567-4); pap. 4.95x (ISBN 0-8061-1060-0). U of Okla Pr.

Merani, Shambhu T. The Turks of Istanbul. 1980. 14.95 (ISBN 0-02-584330-3). Macmillan.

Thubron, Colin. Istanbul. new ed. Time-Life Books, ed. (The Great Cities). (Illus.). 1979. 14.95 (ISBN 0-8094-2335-9). Time-Life.

Underwood, Paul A. Kariye Djami, 4 vols. LC 65-10404. (Bollingen Ser.: Vol. 70). (Illus.). 1966. Vols. 1-3. boxed set 85.00 (ISBN 0-691-09777-1); Vol. 4, 1975. 60.00 (ISBN 0-691-09778-X); Vols. 1-4. boxed set 125.00 (ISBN 0-686-57571-7). Princeton U Pr.

ISTANBUL–ANTIQUITIES

Belting, Hans, et al. The Mosaics & Frescoes of St. Mary Pammakaristos (Fethiye Camii) at Istanbul. LC 77-99268. (Dumbarton Oaks Studies: Vol. 15). (Illus.). 118p. 1978. 30.00x (ISBN 0-88402-075-4, Ctr Byzantine). Dumbarton Oaks.

Krischen, Fritz. Die Landmauer von Konstantinopel. Bearbeitet im Auftrage der Deutschen Forschungsgemeinschaft 1. Teil: Zeichnerische Wiederherstellung. Mit Begleitendem Text. (Denkmaeler Antiker Architektur, Hrsg. Vom Deutschen Archaeologischen Institut Vol. 6). (Illus.). viii, 18p. 1974. Repr. of 1938 ed. 117.50x (ISBN 3-11-002238-9). De Gruyter.

ISTANBUL–CHURCH OF THE HOLY APOSTLES

Dvornik, Francis. The Idea of Apostolicity in Byzantium & the Legend of the Apostle Andrew. (Dumbarton Oaks Studies: Vol. 4). 342p. (LC A58-8640). 1958. 25.00x (ISBN 0-88402-004-5, Ctr Byzantine). Dumbarton Oaks.

ISTANBUL–DESCRIPTION

Craven, Elizabeth. Journey Through the Crimea to Constantinople in a Series of Letters. LC 73-115525. (Russia Observed, Series I). 1970. Repr. of 1789 ed. 17.00 (ISBN 0-405-03018-5). Arno.

Evliya, Efendi. Narrative of Travels in Europe, Asia & Africa in the 17th Century, 2 Vols. in 3. (Oriental Translation Fund Ser: No. 32). Repr. of 1834 ed. Set. 46.00 (ISBN 0-384-14895-6). Johnson Repr.

Laiou, Angeliki E. Constantinople & the Latins: The Foreign Policy of Andronicus 2nd, 1282-1328. LC 78-176042. (Historical Studies: No. 88). 1972. 20.00x (ISBN 0-674-16535-7). Harvard U Pr.

Sumner-Boyd, Hilary & Freely, John. Strolling Through Istanbul. (Illus.). 1972. 15.00x (ISBN 0-686-16866-6). Intl Learn Syst.

Thubron, Colin. Istanbul. (The Great Cities Ser.). (Illus.). 1978. lib. bdg. 14.94 (ISBN 0-686-51004-6). Silver.

White, Charles. Three Years in Constantinople: Or, Domestic Manners of the Turks in 1844, 3 vols. LC 77-87638. Repr. of 1845 ed. Set. 82.50 (ISBN 0-404-16910-4). AMS Pr.

ISTANBUL–DESCRIPTION–GUIDEBOOKS

Sumner-Boyd, H. & Freely, J. Istanbul: Strolling Through Istanbul. 2nd ed. (Illus.). 1973. pap. 20.00 (ISBN 0-685-58564-6). Heinman.

ISTANBUL–HISTORY

see also Crusades-Fourth, 1202-1204

Asimov, Isaac. Constantinople: The Forgotten Empire. LC 78-122907. (Illus.). (gr. 7 up). 1970. 4.75 (ISBN 0-395-10908-6). HM.

Baker, B. Granville. The Walls of Constantinople. LC 72-178513. (Medieval Studies Ser.). Repr. of 1910 ed. 22.00 (ISBN 0-404-56509-3). AMS Pr.

Belin, M. A. Histoire de la Latinite de Constantinople. 2nd ed. R. P. Arsene de Chatel, ed. 547p. (Fr.). 1981. Repr. of 1895 ed. lib. bdg. 95.00x (ISBN 0-89241-166-X). Caratzas Bros.

Cameron, Alan. Circus Factions: Blues & Greens at Rome & Byzantium. 1976. 59.00x (ISBN 0-19-814804-6). Oxford U Pr.

Cobham, C. The Patriarchs of Constantinople. 106p. 1974. 10.00 (ISBN 0-89005-028-7). Ares.

De Villehardouin, Geoffroi. De La Conqueste De Constantinoble. Paris, Paulin, ed. 1965. Repr. of 1838 ed. 31.00 (ISBN 0-685-92799-7); pap. 27.00 (ISBN 0-384-64581-X). Johnson Repr.

De Villehardouin, Geoffroy. Conqueste de Constantinople. White, Julian E., Jr., ed. LC 68-16196. (Medieval French Literature Ser). (Orig., Fr.). 1968. pap. text ed. 3.95x (ISBN 0-89197-102-5). Irvington.

Downey, Glanville. Constantinople in the Age of Justinian. LC 60-13473. (The Centers of Civilization Ser.: Vol. 3). (Illus.). 181p. 1981. pap. 3.95 (ISBN 0-8061-1708-7). U of Okla Pr.

Dvornik, Francis. Byzantium & the Roman Primacy. rev. ed. 1979. pap. 6.00 (ISBN 0-8232-0701-3). Fordham.

Evans, David B. Leontius of Byzantium: An Origenist Christology. LC 72-24460. (Dumbarton Oaks Studies: Vol. 13). 206p. 1970. 20.00x (ISBN 0-88402-031-2, Ctr Byzantine). Dumbarton Oaks.

Gerostergios, Asterios. St. Photios the Great. LC 80-82285. 7.00 (ISBN 0-914744-50-X); pap. 5.00 (ISBN 0-914744-51-8). Inst Byzantine.

Godfrey, John. Twelve Hundred & Four - the Unholy Crusade. (Illus.). 196p. 1980. 37.50 (ISBN 0-19-215834-1). Oxford U Pr.

Jacobs, David. Constantinople, City of the Golden Horn. LC 78-81403. (Horizon Caravel Bks.). 154p. (YA) (gr. 7 up). 1969. PLB 12.89 (ISBN 0-06-022799-0, HarpJ). Har-Row.

Jacobs, David & Mango, Cyril A. Constantinople, City on the Golden Horn. LC 78-81403. (Horizon Caravel Bks). (Illus.). 153p. (gr. 6 up). 1969. 9.95 (ISBN 0-8281-5003-6, J037-0); PLB 12.89 (ISBN 0-06-022799-0, Dist. by Har-Row). Am Heritage.

Nelson, Lynn H. & Shirk, Melanie. Liutprand of Cremona, Mission to Constantinople 968 A.D. 62p. 1972. pap. 1.00x (ISBN 0-87291-039-3). Coronado Pr.

Nicol, Donald M. The Last Centuries of Byzantium. 1979. 19.95x (ISBN 0-8464-0103-7). Beekman Pubs.

Pears, E. Destruction of the Greek Empire & the Story of the Capture of Constantinople by the Turks. LC 68-25259. (World History Ser., No. 48). (Illus.). 1969. Repr. of 1903 ed. lib. bdg. 49.95 (ISBN 0-8383-0227-0). Haskell.

Pears, Edwin. Destruction of the Greek Empire & the Story of the Capture of Constantinople by the Turks. LC 69-14032. 1969. Repr. of 1903 ed. lib. bdg. 18.00x (ISBN 0-8371-0612-5, PEGE). Greenwood.

--The Fall of Constantinople. LC 74-11847. 413p. 1974. Repr. of 1885 ed. lib. bdg. 17.50x (ISBN 0-8154-0493-X). Cooper Sq.

Robert Of Clari. Conquest of Constantinople. McNeal, Edgar H., tr. 1966. lib. bdg. 15.50x (ISBN 0-374-95529-8). Octagon.

Rosenthal, Steven T. The Politics of Dependency: Urban Reform in Istanbul. LC 79-7588. (Contributions in Comparative Colonial Studies: No. 3). (Illus.). 1980. lib. bdg. 27.50 (ISBN 0-313-20927-8, RPO/). Greenwood.

Runciman, Steven. Fall of Constantinople, Fourteen Fifty-Three. LC 65-10383. (Illus.). 1969. 32.50 (ISBN 0-521-06165-2); pap. 9.95x (ISBN 0-521-09573-5). Cambridge U Pr.

Talbot, Alice-Mary Maffry, ed. & tr. Correspondence of Athanasius I, Patriarch of Constantinople: Letters to the Emperor Andronicus II, Members of the Imperial Family, & Officials. LC 74-28931. (Dumbarton Oaks Texts: Vol. 3). 518p. 1975. 50.00x (ISBN 0-88402-040-1, Ctr Byzantine). Dumbarton Oaks.

Tsangadas, Byron C. The Fortifications & Defense of Constantinople. (East European Monographs: No. 71). 256p. 1980. 21.50x (ISBN 0-914710-65-6). East Eur Quarterly.

Urbansky, Andrew B. Byzantium & the Danube Frontier. 10.95 (ISBN 0-685-60116-1, Pub by Twayne). Cyrco Pr.

Vasiliev, Alexander A. Russian Attack on Constantinople in 860. 1966. Repr. of 1942 ed. 8.50 (ISBN 0-910956-20-0). Medieval Acad.

Whitting, Philip, ed. Byzantium: An Introduction. LC 76-148056. (Illus.). 1971. 17.50x (ISBN 0-8147-9152-2). NYU Pr.

Wolff, Robert L. Studies in the Latin Empire of Constantinople. 412p. 1980. 60.00x (ISBN 0-902089-99-4, Pub. by Variorum England). State Mutual Bk.

Yenal, Engin. The Ottoman City in Comparative Perspective, Istanbul, 1453-1923: A Selected Bibliography of Urban History. (Architecture Ser.: A 14). 1978. pap. 6.00 (ISBN 0-686-24285-8). Vance Biblios.

ISTANBUL–SERAGLIO

Miller, Barnette. Beyond the Sublime Porte. LC 79-111774. Repr. of 1931 ed. 32.45 (ISBN 0-404-04329-1). AMS Pr.

Penzer, Norman M. The Harem. LC 77-180304. (Illus.). Repr. of 1937 ed. 37.50 (ISBN 0-404-56316-3). AMS Pr.

ISTANBUL–SERAGLIO PALACE SCHOOL

Miller, Barnett. The Palace School of Muhammad the Conqueror. LC 73-6291. (The Middle East Ser.). Repr. of 1941 ed. 15.00 (ISBN 0-405-05349-5). Arno.

ISTANBUL–SOCIAL CONDITIONS

Merani, Shambhu T. The Turks of Istanbul. 1980. 14.95 (ISBN 0-02-584330-3). Macmillan.

ISTANBUL (PATRIARCHATE)–HISTORY

Downey, Glanville. Constantinople in the Age of Justinian. LC 60-13473. (The Centers of Civilization Ser.: Vol. 3). (Illus.). 181p. 1981. pap. 3.95 (ISBN 0-8061-1708-7). U of Okla Pr.

Runciman, Steven. Great Church in Captivity. LC 68-29330. 1968. 42.50 (ISBN 0-521-07188-7). Cambridge U Pr.

Vaporis, Nomikos M. Codex Beta of the Ecumenical Patriarchate of Constantinople: Aspects of the History of the Church of Constantinople. (The Archbishop Iakovos Library of Ecclesiastical & Historical Sources). 1975. pap. 4.95 (ISBN 0-916586-03-0). Holy Cross Orthodox.

--Codex Gamma of the Ecumenical Patriarchate of Constantinople. (The Archbishop Iakovos Library of Ecclesiastical & Historical Sources Ser.). 1974. pap. 4.95 (ISBN 0-916586-01-4). Holy Cross Orthodox.

ISTHMIA

Broneer, Oscar. Terracotta Lamps. LC 76-362971. (Isthmia Ser: Vol. 3). 1977. 25.00x (ISBN 0-87661-933-2). Am Sch Athens.

ISTITUTO PER LA RICOSTRUZIONE INDUSTRIALE, ROME

Deaglio, Mario. Private Enterprise & Public Emulation. (Institute of Economic Affairs, Research Monographs: No. 5). pap. 2.50 (ISBN 0-255-69593-4). Transatlantic.

ISTRIAN PENINSULA–DESCRIPTION AND TRAVEL–GUIDEBOOKS

Berlitz Travel Guide to Istria. 1977. pap. 2.95 (ISBN 0-02-969170-2, Berlitz). Macmillan.

Mesarovic, Jovan, ed. Istria & Kvarnev. Biconic, Sonja, tr. 1.95 (ISBN 0-8184-0120-6). Lyle Stuart.

I.T.A

see Initial Teaching Alphabet

ITALIAN AMERICANS

see also Italians in the United States

Alissi, Albert S. Boys in Little Italy: A Comparison of Their Individual Value Orientations, Family Patterns, & Peer Group Associations. LC 77-90360. 1978. soft cover 10.00 (ISBN 0-88247-495-2). R & E Res Assoc.

American Studies Symposium, 3rd, University of Florence, May 27-29, 1969. Gli Italiani Negli Stati Uniti - Italians in the United States: Proceedings. LC 74-17932. (Italian American Experience Ser). (Illus.). 1975. Repr. 34.00x (ISBN 0-405-06404-7). Arno.

Bacigalupo, Leonard. The Franciscans & Italian Immigration in America. LC 76-50676. 1977. 4.50 (ISBN 0-682-48741-4, University). Exposition.

Bayor, Ronald H. Neighbors in Conflict: The Irish, Germans, Jews & Italians of New York City, 1929-1941. 2nd ed. LC 77-14260. 256p. 1980. pap. 5.95 (ISBN 0-8018-2370-6). Johns Hopkins.

--Neighbors in Conflict: The Irish, Germans, Jews, & Italians of New York City, 1929-1941. LC 77-14260. (Studies in Historical & Political Science, 96th Ser: No. 2). 1978. text ed. 16.00x o. p. (ISBN 0-8018-2024-3); pap. 5.95 (ISBN 0-8018-2370-6). Johns Hopkins.

Biondi, Lawrence. The Italian American Child: His Sociolinguistic Acculturation. LC 75-38898. 160p. 1975. pap. 6.50 (ISBN 0-87840-208-X). Georgetown U Pr.

Briggs, John W. An Italian Passage: Immigrants to Three American Cities, 1890-1930. LC 77-22006. (Illus.). 1978. 25.00x (ISBN 0-300-02095-3). Yale U Pr.

Brizzolara, Andrew. A Directory of Italian & Italian-American Organizations & Community Services in the Metropolitan Area of Greater New York. 1976. pap. 5.00x (ISBN 0-913256-20-X, Dist. by Ozer). Ctr Migration.

Brizzolara, Andrew, compiled by. A Directory of Italian & Italian American Organizations & Community Services in the Metropolitan Area of Greater New York: in the Metropolitan Area of Greater New York, Vol. II. rev. ed. 1980. 9.95x (ISBN 0-913256-44-7). Ctr Migration.

Caroli, Betty B., commentaries by. We Italian Americans: A Pictorial History. (Illus.). 300p. Date not set. 25.00x (ISBN 0-913256-38-2). Ctr Migration.

Caso, Adolph. America's Italian Founding Fathers: 1770-1780. 285p. 1975. 10.00 (ISBN 0-8283-1667-8). Dante U Am.

--Mass Media vs. the Italian Americans. LC 80-66885. (Illus.). 278p. 1980. 12.00 (ISBN 0-8283-1737-2). Branden.

--Mass Media Vs. the Italian Americans. 262p. 1980. 12.00 (ISBN 0-8283-1737-2). Dante U Am.

--They Too Made America Great. (Illus.). 1979. 12.50 (ISBN 0-8283-1699-6). Branden.

Churchill, Charles W. The Italians of Newark. LC 74-17922. (Italian American Experience Ser). (Illus.). 220p. 1975. 18.00x (ISBN 0-405-06395-4). Arno.

Clark, Francis E. Our Italian Fellow Citizens in Their Old Homes & Their New. LC 74-17923. (Italian American Experience Ser). (Illus.). 260p. 1975. Repr. 17.00x (ISBN 0-405-06396-2). Arno.

Cordasco, Francesco, ed. Italian Americans: A Guide to Information Sources. LC 78-4833. (Ethnic Studies Information Guide Ser.: Vol. 2). 1978. 36.00 (ISBN 0-8103-1397-9). Gale.

--Italians in the City: An Original Anthology. LC 74-17933. (Italian American Experience Ser). (Illus.). 1975. Repr. 13.00x (ISBN 0-405-06405-5). Arno.

--Italians in the United States: An Original Anthology. LC 74-17934. (Italian American Experience Ser). (Illus.). 1975. Repr. 39.00x (ISBN 0-405-06406-3). Arno.

D'Angelo, Pascal. Son of Italy. LC 74-17925. (Italian American Experience Ser). 200p. 1975. Repr. 14.00x (ISBN 0-405-06398-9). Arno.

Farmer, George L. The Dilemma of the Italian-American. 1970. 15.00x (ISBN 0-913330-10-8). Sun Dance Bks.

Femminella, Francis X., ed. Power & Class: The Italian American Experience Today. 1971. 2.50 (ISBN 0-686-21888-4). Am Italian.

Ferroni, Charles D. The Italians in Cleveland: A Study in Assimilation. Cordasco, Francesco, ed. LC 80-855. (American Ethnic Groups Ser.). 1981. lib. bdg. 25.00x (ISBN 0-405-13418-5). Arno.

Gabriel, Richard A. The Irish & Italians: Ethnics in City & Suburb. Cordasco, Francesco, ed. LC 80-857. (American Ethnic Groups Ser.). 1981. lib. bdg. 29.00x (ISBN 0-405-13420-7). Arno.

Gallo, Pat, ed. The Urban Experience of Italian Americans. 1977. 5.00 (ISBN 0-686-22157-5). Am Italian.

Garlick, R. C., Jr. & Guidi, Angelo F. Italy & the Italians in Washington's Time. 132p. 1933. 6.50x (ISBN 0-913298-46-8). S F Vanni.

Giovannetti, Alberto. The Italians of America. (Orig.). 1979. pap. 2.50 (ISBN 0-532-25001-X). Woodhill.

Gumina, Deanna P. The Italians of San Francisco, Eighteen Fifty to Nineteen Thirty: (Gli Italiani Di San Francisco, 1850 to 1930) dual language ed. Are, Ennio T., tr. LC 77-89342. 1978. pap. text ed. 9.95x (ISBN 0-913256-28-5, Dist. by Ozer). Ctr Migration.

Iorizzo, Luciano J. & Mondello, Salvatore. The Italian-Americans. rev. ed. (Immigrant Heritage of America Ser.). 1980. lib. bdg. 10.95 (ISBN 0-8057-8416-0). Twayne.

Juliani, Richard N. The Social Organization of Immigration: The Italians in Philadelphia. Cordasco, Francesco, ed. LC 80-868. (American Ethnic Groups Ser.). 1981. lib. bdg. 25.00x (ISBN 0-405-13430-4). Arno.

Kessner, Thomas. The Golden Door: Italian & Jewish Immigrant Mobility in New York City, 1880-1915. 1977. text ed. 14.95 (ISBN 0-19-502116-9); pap. 4.95 (ISBN 0-19-502161-4). Oxford U Pr.

Mangione, Jerre. Mount Allegro: A Memoir of Italian - American Life. 320p. 1981. 17.50x (ISBN 0-231-05330-4); pap. 8.00x (ISBN 0-231-05331-2). Columbia U Pr.

Mariano, John H. The Italian Contribution to American Democracy. LC 74-17938. (Italian American Experience Ser). (Illus.). 336p. 1975. Repr. 19.00x (ISBN 0-405-06409-8). Arno.

--The Italian Immigrant & Our Courts. LC 74-17939. (Italian American Experience Ser). (Illus.). 88p. 1975. Repr. pap. 9.50x (ISBN 0-405-06410-1). Arno.

Meloni, Alberto. Italian Americans: A Study Guide & Resource Book. LC 77-81035. 1977. soft bdg. 6.00 (ISBN 0-88247-482-0). R & E Res Assoc.

Mondello, Salvatore A. The Italian Immigrant in Urban America, 1880-1920, As Reported in the Contemporary Periodiacl Press. Cordasco, Farncesco, ed. LC 80-880. (American Ethnic Groups Ser.). lib. bdg. 25.00x (ISBN 0-405-13441-X). Arno.

Nicandri, David. The Italians of Washington State. LC 77-80592. (Illus.). pap. 5.00 (ISBN 0-917048-08-3). Wash St Hist Soc.

Odencrantz, Louise C. Italian Women in Industry: Study of Conditions in New York City. Stein, Leon, ed. LC 77-70523. (Work Ser.). (Illus.). 1977. Repr. of 1919 ed. lib. bdg. 22.00 (ISBN 0-405-10191-0). Arno.

Panella, Vincent. The Other Side: Growing up Italian in America. LC 78-22346. (Illus.). 192p. 1979. 12.95 (ISBN 0-385-14733-3). Doubleday.

Parenti, Michael J. Ethnic & Political Attitudes. new ed. LC 74-17942. (Italian American Experience Ser). 354p. 1975. 25.00x (ISBN 0-405-06413-6). Arno.

Peroni, Peter A. The Burg: An Italian-American Community at Bay in Trenton. LC 79-63258. 1979. pap. text ed. 8.00 (ISBN 0-8191-0724-7). U Pr of Amer.

Perry, Stewart E. San Francisco Scavengers: Dirty Work & the Pride of Ownership. LC 77-78382. 1978. 14.95 (ISBN 0-520-03518-6). U of Cal Pr.

Pitkin, Thomas M. & Cordasco, Francesco. The Black Hand: A Chapter in Ethnic Crime. (Quality Paperback Ser: No. 333). (Illus.). 1977. pap. 4.95 (ISBN 0-8226-0333-0). Littlefield.

Pozzetta, George, ed. Pane e Lavoro: The Italian American Working Class. 1980. 8.00 (ISBN 0-686-28079-2). Am Italian.

Radin, Paul. The Italians of San Francisco. LC 74-17945. (Italian American Experience Ser). (Illus.). 200p. 1975. Repr. 14.00x (ISBN 0-405-06415-2). Arno.

Rolle, Andrew. The Italian Americans: Troubled Roots. LC 79-6765. 1980. 14.95 (ISBN 0-02-926860-5). Free Pr.

Rose, Philip M. The Italians in America. LC 74-17946. (Italian American Experience Ser). (Illus.). 168p. 1975. Repr. 12.00x (ISBN 0-405-06416-0). Arno.

Scherini, Rose D. The Italian Community of San Francisco: A Descriptive Study. Cordasco, Francesco, ed. LC 80-892. (American Ethnic Groups Ser.). 1981. lib. bdg. 25.00x (ISBN 0-405-13453-3). Arno.

Schiavo, Giovanni. Four Centuries of Italian-American History. (Illus.). 1952. 75.00 (ISBN 0-911574-01-8). Vigo Pr.

--The Italians in America Before the Revolution. 1976. 15.00 (ISBN 0-911574-03-4). Vigo Pr.

--The Italians in Missouri. LC 74-17951. (Italian American Experience Ser). (Illus.). 220p. 1975. Repr. 18.00x (ISBN 0-405-06421-7). Arno.

Schiavo, Giovanni E. Italian-American History. LC 74-17948. (Italian American Experience Ser: Vol. No. 1). (Illus.). 644p. 1975. Repr. 36.00x (ISBN 0-405-06418-7). Arno.

--Italian-American History: The Italian Contribution to the Catholic Church in America. LC 74-17948. (Italian American Experience Ser: Vol. No. 2). (Illus.). 1975. Repr. 64.00x (ISBN 0-405-06429-2). Arno.

--The Italians in America Before the Civil War. LC 74-17949. (Italian American Experience Ser). (Illus.). 420p. 1975. Repr. 23.00x (ISBN 0-405-06419-5). Arno.

--The Italians in Chicago. LC 74-17950. (Italian American Experience Ser). (Illus.). 1975. Repr. 18.00x (ISBN 0-405-06420-9). Arno.

Schiro, George. Americans by Choice: Italians in Utica, New York. LC 74-17953. (Italian American Experience Ser). (Illus.). 192p. 1975. Repr. 11.00x (ISBN 0-405-06422-5). Arno.

Spengler, Paul A. Yankee, Swedish & Italian Acculturation & Economic Mobility in Jamestown, New York from 1860 to 1920. Cordasco, Francesco, ed. LC 80-897. (American Ethnic Groups Ser.). 1981. lib. bdg. 35.00x (ISBN 0-405-13457-6). Arno.

Thompson, Bryan. Cultural Ties As Determinants of Immigrant Settlement in Urban Areas: A Case Study of the Growth of an Italian Neighborhood in Worcestor, Massachusetts, 1875-1922. Cordasco, Francesco, ed. LC 80-901. (American Ethnic Groups Ser.). 1981. lib. bdg. 20.00x (ISBN 0-405-13461-4). Arno.

Tomasi, S. M., ed. Perspectives in Italian Immigration & Ethnicity. LC 77-74178. 1977. pap. text ed. 9.95x (ISBN 0-913256-26-9, Dist. by Ozer). Ctr Migration.

Tomasi, S. M. & Stibili, Edward, eds. Italian-Americans & Religion: An Annotated Bibliography. LC 76-44921. (Bibliographies & Documents Ser.). 1978. lib. bdg. 14.95x (ISBN 0-913256-25-0, Dist. by Ozer). Ctr Migration.

Tomasi, Silvano, ed. The Religious Experience of Italian Americans. 1973. 4.00 (ISBN 0-686-21890-6). Am Italian.

Valletta, Clement L. A Study of Americanization in Carneta. new ed. LC 74-17958. (Italian American Experience Ser). (Illus.). 522p. 1975. 31.00x (ISBN 0-405-06427-6). Arno.

Vecoli, Rudolph J., ed. Italian American Radicalism: Old World Origins & New World Developments. 1972. 2.50 (ISBN 0-686-21889-2). Am Italian.

Workers of the Writer's Program. The Italians of Omaha. LC 74-17940. (Italian American Experience Ser). (Illus.). 138p. 1975. Repr. 12.00x (ISBN 0-405-06411-X). Arno.

Yans-McLaughlin, Virginia. Family & Community: Italian Immigrants in Buffalo, 1880-1930. (Illus.). 1977. 19.50x (ISBN 0-8014-1036-3). Cornell U Pr.

ITALIAN ARCHITECTURE

see Architecture–Italy

ITALIAN ART

see Art, Italian

ITALIAN AUTHORS

see Authors, Italian

ITALIAN BALLADS AND SONGS

see also Songs, Italian

ITALIAN COMPOSERS

see Composers, Italian

ITALIAN DRAMA

see also Commedia Dell'Arte

Chiarelli, Luigi. La Maschera e il Volto. Vena, Michael, ed. (Italian.). 1975. pap. text ed. 4.95x (ISBN 0-89197-840-2). Irvington.

ITALIAN DRAMA (COLLECTIONS)

Cesaresco, Evelyn M., ed. Italian Characters. 1891. 15.00 (ISBN 0-685-43748-5). Norwood Edns.

Fratti, Mario, ed. Nuovo Teatro Italiano: Plays by Nine Modern Young Italian Playwrights. 1972. pap. 2.50x (ISBN 0-913298-25-5). S F Vanni.

ITALIAN DRAMA (COMEDY)–HISTORY AND CRITICISM

Ducharte, P. L. The Italian Comedy. (Illus.). 12.00 (ISBN 0-8446-2002-5). Peter Smith.

ITALIAN DRAMA–BIBLIOGRAPHY

Herrick, Marvin T., compiled by. Italian Plays, 1500-1700, in the University of Illinois Library. LC 66-17248. 1966. 10.00 (ISBN 0-252-72743-6). U of Ill Pr.

ITALIAN DRAMA–HISTORY AND CRITICISM

Collison-Morley, Lacy. Shakespeare in Italy. LC 67-23862. Repr. of 1916 ed. 11.00 (ISBN 0-405-08373-4, Blom Pubns). Arno.

Herrick, Marvin T. Italian Comedy in the Renaissance. LC 60-11659. 1966. pap. 5.50 (ISBN 0-252-72737-1). U of Ill Pr.

Kennard, Joseph S. Italian Theatre, 2 Vols. LC 64-14709. (Illus.). 1932. Set. 30.00 (ISBN 0-405-08692-X, Blom Pubns); 15.00 ea. Vol. 1 (ISBN 0-405-08693-8). Vol. 2 (ISBN 0-405-08694-6). Arno.

McLeod, Addison. Plays & Players in Modern Italy. LC 79-102848. 1970. Repr. of 1912 ed. 15.50 (ISBN 0-8046-0758-3). Kennikat.

Orr, David. Italian Renaissance Drama in England Before 1625. (Studies in Comparative Literature: No. 49). 1970. 11.00x (ISBN 0-8078-7049-8). U of NC Pr.

Parfaict, Francois & Parfaict, Claude. Histoire de l'ancien Theatre italien: Depuis son origine en France jusqu'a sa suppression en l'annee 1697. LC 76-43932. (Music & Theatre in France in the 17th & 18th Centuries). Repr. of 1767 ed. 30.00 (ISBN 0-404-60178-2). AMS Pr.

Solerti, Angelo. Musica, Ballo E Drammatica Alla Corte Medicea Dal 1600 Al 1637. LC 67-12470. (It). 1968. Repr. of 1905 ed. 30.00 (ISBN 0-405-08987-2). Arno.

ITALIAN DRAMA–TRANSLATIONS INTO ENGLISH

Bond, Richard W., ed. Early Plays from the Italian. LC 65-20046. Repr. of 1911 ed. 22.00 (ISBN 0-405-08287-8, Blom Pubns). Arno.

Hosley, Richard, ed. Fedele & Fortunio. (Renaissance Drama Ser.). 1981. lib. bdg. 27.50 (ISBN 0-8240-4461-4). Garland Pub.

Mahaney, William E. & Sherwin, Walter K., eds. Antoninus Bassianus Caracalla: An Edition & Translation. Sherwin, Walter K. & Freyman, Jay M., trs. from Lat. (Salzburg Studies in English Literature, Elizabethan & Renaissance Studies: No. 52). 189p. (Orig.). 1976. pap. text ed. 25.00x (ISBN 0-391-01467-6). Humanities.

Verga, Giovanni, et al. Plays of the Italian Theatre. Goldberg, Isaac, tr. LC 76-40394. (One-Act Plays in Reprint Ser.). 1976. Repr. of 1906 ed. 17.00x (ISBN 0-8486-2009-7). Core Collection.

ITALIAN DRAWINGS

see Drawings, Italian

ITALIAN FICTION

Rotunda, D. P. Motif-Index of the Italian Novella in Prose. LC 72-6778. (Studies in Italian Literature, No. 46). 1972. Repr. of 1942 ed. lib. bdg. 33.95 (ISBN 0-8383-1653-0). Haskell.

ITALIAN FICTION–HISTORY AND CRITICISM

Kennard, Joseph S. Italian Romance Writers. LC 66-25920. Repr. of 1906 ed. 15.00 (ISBN 0-8046-0246-8). Kennikat.

Pacifici, Sergio. The Modern Italian Novel: From Capuana to Tozzi. LC 75-156786. (Crosscurrents-Modern Critiques Ser.). 1973. 10.95 (ISBN 0-8093-0614-X). S Ill U Pr.
--The Modern Italian Novel: From Manzoni to Svevo. LC 67-13047. (Crosscurrents-Modern Critiques Ser.). 215p. 1967. 10.95 (ISBN 0-8093-0267-5). S Ill U Pr.
Stewart, Joan H. The Novels of Mme. Riccoboni. (Studies in the Romance Languages & Literatures Ser: No. 165). 1976. pap. 10.50x (ISBN 0-8078-9165-7). U of NC Pr.
Vittorini, Domenico. Modern Italian Novel. LC 66-27195. 1967. Repr. of 1930 ed. 8.50 (ISBN 0-8462-1034-7). Russell.

ITALIAN FOLK-LORE

see Folk-Lore, Italian

ITALIAN LANGUAGE

Assimil, ed. Italian Without Toil. 1957. 9.50x (ISBN 2-7005-0016-4); 3 cassettes 70.00x (ISBN 0-686-09279-1); 11 records 70.00x (ISBN 0-686-28533-6); book & cassettes 79.00x (ISBN 0-686-28534-4). Intl Learn Syst.
Cardona, Giorgio R. Standard Italian. (Trends in Linguistics, State-of-the-Art Reports Ser.: No. 1). 1976. pap. text ed. 17.00x (ISBN 90-2793-055-4). Mouton.
Cincinnato, Paul D. & Tursi, Joseph A. Italian Two & Three Years. (It.). (gr. 9-12). 1978. pap. text ed. 6.50 (ISBN 0-87720-594-9). AMSCO Sch.
Cioffari, Vincenzo. Beginning Italian. 3rd ed. 1979. text ed. 17.95x (ISBN 0-669-00580-0); wkbk. & lab manual 6.95x (ISBN 0-669-00581-9); tapes-reels 60.00 (ISBN 0-669-00582-7); cassettes 60.00 (ISBN 0-669-00583-5). Heath.
--Spoken Italian. LC 75-15151. (Spoken Language Ser.). 220p. (Prog. Bk.). 1976. pap. 10.00x (ISBN 0-87950-130-8); 6 12 inch lp records (33.3 rpm) 40.00x (ISBN 0-87950-133-2); records with course-bk. 45.00x (ISBN 0-87950-134-0); cassettes 60.00x (ISBN 0-87950-135-9); cassettes with course-bk. 65.00x (ISBN 0-87950-136-7). Spoken Lang Serv.
Ducibella, Joseph W. Phonology of the Sicilian Dialects. LC 77-94206. (Catholic University of America Studies in Romance Languages & Literatures Ser: No. 10). Repr. of 1934 ed. 33.50 (ISBN 0-404-50310-1). AMS Pr.
Frassica, Pietro & Carrara, Antonio. Per Modo Di Dire: A First Course in Italian. 544p. 1981. text ed. 17.95 (ISBN 0-669-02068-0); wkbk. 6.95 (ISBN 0-669-02069-9); cassette 60.00 (ISBN 0-669-02073-7); tapes-reels 60.00 (ISBN 0-669-02072-9); instr's guide 1.95 (ISBN 0-669-02069-9); tapescript (ISBN 0-669-02074-5); demo tape (ISBN 0-669-02075-3). Heath.
Golden, H. H. & Simches, S. O. Modern Italian Languages & Literature: A Bibliography of Homage Studies. LC 59-14742. Repr. of 1959 ed. 16.00 (ISBN 0-527-34320-X). Kraus Repr.
Isaacs, Alan, ed. Multilingual Commercial Dictionary. 1980. 22.50 (ISBN 0-87196-425-2). Facts on File.
Izzo, Herbert J. Tuscan & Etruscan: The Problem of Linguistic Substratum Influence in Central Italy. LC 78-163823. (Romance Ser.). 238p. 1972. 20.00x (ISBN 0-8020-5249-5). U of Toronto Pr.
Jenson, Frede. The Italian Verb. (Studies in the Romance Languages & Literatures: No. 107). 1971. pap. 6.50x (ISBN 0-8078-9107-X). U of NC Pr.
Kelly, Annamaria, et al. Per Tutti i Gusti: Activity Manual. 1980. pap. text ed. 7.95 (ISBN 0-394-32540-0). Random.
Marchetti, Pascale. Le Corse Sans Peine: A Corsican Language Course in French. 1975. 10.50x (ISBN 2-7005-0056-3); Set. 3 cassettes 70.00x (ISBN 0-686-19946-4); 12 records 70.00x (ISBN 0-686-28602-2); bk & cassettes 79.00x (ISBN 0-686-28603-0). Intl Learn Syst.
Mazzola, Michael L. Proto-Romance & Sicilian. 1977. pap. text ed. 11.00x (ISBN 90-316-0088-1). Humanities.
Middleton, W. E., ed. Lorenzo Magalotti at the Court of Charles Ii (His Relazione D'inghilterra 1668) 161p. 1980. text ed. 10.50x (ISBN 0-88920-095-5, Pub. by Laurier U Pr). Humanities.
Ragusa & Cherubini. One Thousand & One Pitfalls in Italian. 1980. pap. 6.95 (ISBN 0-8120-0589-9). Barron.
Rundle, Stanley. Cracking the Language Code: Italian. 1974. 19.95 (ISBN 0-87243-053-7, Pub. by Octavo Pr). Templegate.
Speroni, C. & Golino, C. L. Leggendo E Ripassando. LC 68-13507. (It). (gr. 4-8). 1968. text ed. 12.95 (ISBN 0-03-068795-0, HoltC); tapes 140.00 (ISBN 0-03-068800-0). HR&W.
Whatmough, Joshua. Foundations of Roman Italy. LC 73-122989. (World History Ser., No. 48). 1970. Repr. of 1937 ed. lib. bdg. 43.95 (ISBN 0-8383-1122-9). Haskell.

ITALIAN LANGUAGE–COMPOSITION AND EXERCISES

Absalom, R. N. Passages for Translation from Italian. 1967. pap. 7.50x (ISBN 0-521-09431-3, 431). Cambridge U Pr.
Cagno, Michael. Exercise Book for Italian: Level II. 1977. pap. 1.50x (ISBN 0-913298-00-X). S F Vanni.
--Exercise Book for Italian: Level III. 1977. pap. 1.50x (ISBN 0-913298-01-8). S F Vanni.
Cerutti, Toni. Guide to Composition in Italian. 1966. text ed. 6.50x (ISBN 0-521-04593-2). Cambridge U Pr.
Cioffari, Vincenzo. Italian Review Grammar & Composition. 3rd ed. (Illus.). 1969. text ed. 14.95x (ISBN 0-669-47290-5). Heath.

ITALIAN LANGUAGE–CONVERSATION AND PHRASE BOOKS

see also Italian Language–Self-Instruction; Italian Language–Text-Books for Children

Absalom, R. N. Comprehension of Spoken Italian. LC 76-21015. 1978. limp bdg. 3.95x (ISBN 0-521-29115-1). Cambridge U Pr.
Baran, Elaine A. Modern Spoken Italian: Active Italian Conversation, Part A. 144p. (Orig.). 1981. pap. text ed. 115.00 (ISBN 0-686-73214-6, Z501). J Norton Pubs.
--Modern Spoken Italian: Active Italian Communication, Part B. 144p. (Orig.). 1981. pap. 115.00 (ISBN 0-88432-074-X, Z551). J Norton Pubs.
Berlitz Editors. Italian for Travellers. rev. ed. 1975. pap. 2.95 (ISBN 0-02-963940-9, Berlitz); cassettepak 10.95 (ISBN 0-02-962060-0); cartridgepak 10.95 (ISBN 0-02-968060-3). Macmillan.
Cagno, Michael & D'Arlon, Ben. Rapid Italian for Students & Tourists. 1979. pap. 3.25x (ISBN 0-913298-05-0). S F Vanni.
D'Annunzio, G. Alcyone. Woodhouse, J. R., ed. 200p. 1977. 12.00x (ISBN 0-7190-0684-8, Pub. by Manchester U Pr England). State Mutual Bk.
Deledda, G. Canne al Vento. Meiklejohn, M. F., ed. 230p. 1964. 12.00x (ISBN 0-7190-0198-6, Pub. by Manchester U Pr England). State Mutual Bk.
De Marchi, E. & Speight, K. Cappello del Prete. 262p. 1963. 12.00x (ISBN 0-7190-0199-4, Pub. by Manchester U Pr England). State Mutual Bk.
Ellison, Al. Ellison's Italian Menu Reader. 1977. 2.95 (ISBN 0-930580-02-8). Ellison Ent.
Florio, Giovanni. Florios Second Frutes. LC 72-197. (English Experience Ser.: No. 157). 208p. 1969. Repr. of 1591 ed. 42.00 (ISBN 90-221-0157-6). Walter J Johnson.
Florio, John. Florio His Firste Fruites: A Perfect Induction to the Italian & English Tongues. LC 72-6214. (English Experience Ser.: No. 95). 1969. Repr. of 1578 ed. 42.00 (ISBN 90-221-0095-2). Walter J Johnson.
Gorjanc, Adele A. Italian Conversation: A Practical Guide for Students & Travelers. 7.50 (ISBN 0-8283-1670-8). Branden.
Hamlyn Italian Phrase Book. pap. 2.95 (ISBN 0-600-34900-4, 8146). Larousse.
Hayward, Arthur L. & McFarlane, C. Learn Italian for English Speakers. 8.50 (ISBN 0-87557-046-1, 046-1). Saphrograph.
Holloway Staff. Italian. (Harper Phrase Books for the Traveler Ser.). (Orig.). 1977. pap. 1.00 (ISBN 0-8467-0312-2, Pub. by Two Continents). Hippocrene Bks.
Hughes, Charles A. Grosset's Italian Phrase Book & Dictionary for Travelers. (Orig.). 1971. pap. 2.95 (ISBN 0-448-00653-7). G&D.
Italian in Twenty Lessons. rev. ed. (Cortina Method Language Ser). (Illus.). 6.95 (ISBN 0-385-00101-0). Doubleday.
Italy: A Hugo Phrase Book. (Hugo's Language Courses Ser.: No. 564). 1970. pap. 1.50 (ISBN 0-8226-0564-3). Littlefield.
Lazzarino, Graziana, et al. Prego! An Invitation to Italian. 544p. 1980. text ed. 18.95 (ISBN 0-394-32376-9); wkbk. 6.95 (ISBN 0-394-32538-9); lab manual 6.95 (ISBN 0-394-32539-7); tape program 250.00 (ISBN 0-686-61365-1). Random.
Lennie, Delia & Grego, M. Italian for You. 3rd ed. (Illus.). 1966. pap. text ed. 5.50x (ISBN 0-582-36407-8). Longman.
Leopardi, G. Canti. Whitfield, J. H., ed. 224p. 1967. 15.00x (ISBN 0-7190-0290-7, Pub. by Manchester U Pr England). State Mutual Bk.
Listen & Learn Italian. (Listen & Learn Ser.). 1981. Incl. 3 Cassettes & Manual. 14.95 (ISBN 0-486-99902-5). Dover.
Living Italian, Cassette Ed. 1969. 14.95, with 2 cassettes plus dictionary & manual (ISBN 0-517-00899-8). Crown.
Lo Dica in Italiano. Vols. 1-3. text ed. 7.95 ea.; tapebks. vols. 1 & 2 5.95 ea.; readers vols. 1 & 2 6.75 ea.; cassette sets for vols. 1 & 2 115.00 ea.; tape sets for vols. 1 & 2 225.00 ea. Inst Mod Lang.
Logan, Gerald E. & Banks, Caroline. Italian Conversational Practice. 1977. pap. text ed. 4.95 (ISBN 0-88377-073-3); tchrs.' guide 5.95 (ISBN 0-88377-084-9). Newbury Hse.
Madrigal, Margarita. Invitation to Italian. 1965. 7.95 (ISBN 0-671-38120-2). S&S.
Madrigal, Margarita & Salvadori, Giuseppina. See It & Say It in Italian. (Orig.). pap. 1.75 (ISBN 0-451-09399-2, E9399, Sig). NAL.
Merlonghi, Ferdinando, et al. Oggi in Italia: A First Course in Italian. LC 77-83330. 1978. text ed. 16.50 (ISBN 0-395-26244-5); tchrs'. ed. 17.60 (ISBN 0-395-26243-7); wkbk. 5.50 (ISBN 0-395-26242-9); tapes 148.20 (ISBN 0-395-26245-3). HM.
Negro, Ottavio. Conversational Italian. 1981. 6.00x (ISBN 0-340-23303-6, Pub. by Hodder & Stoughton England). State Mutual Bk.
Norman, Jill & Giorgetti, Pietro. Italian Phrase Book. (Orig., Bilingual). 1968. pap. 2.95 (ISBN 0-14-002707-6). Penguin.
Paolozzi & Sedwick. Conversation in Italian: Points of Departure. 2nd ed. (Illus., Orig.). 1981. pap. text ed. write for info. (ISBN 0-442-24474-6). D Van Nostrand.
Paolozzi, Gabriel J. & Sedwick, Frank. Conversation in Italian: Points of Departure. 1975. 5.95x (ISBN 0-442-26458-5). D Van Nostrand.
R. D. Cortina Company. Conversational Italian in Twenty Lessons. 360p. 1980. pap. 4.95 (ISBN 0-06-463603-8, EH 603). Har-Row.
Ragusa, Olga. Say It in Italian. 1958. lib. bdg. 8.50x (ISBN 0-88307-566-0). Gannon.
Rapaccini, L. Parlo Italiano. (It) 12.10 (ISBN 0-685-20245-3). Schoenhof.
Settar, G. Worldwide Medical Interpreter: Italian, Vol. 6. 1977. pap. 12.00 (ISBN 0-87489-106-X). Med Economics.
Slobodkin, Florence & Slobodkin, Louis. Io Sono (I Am) LC 62-11219. (Illus.). (gr. 3 up). 1962. 4.95 (ISBN 0-8149-0392-4). Vanguard.
Speroni, Charles & Kany, Charles K. Spoken Italian for Students & Travelers. 2nd ed. 1977. pap. text ed. 6.95 (ISBN 0-669-00577-0). Heath.
Tacchi. Conversazioni Italiane per Stranieri. 1976. 6.00x (ISBN 0-686-16883-6). Intl Learn Syst.
Tasso, T. Aminta. Griffiths, C. E., ed. 168p. 1972. 12.00x (ISBN 0-686-63843-3, Pub. by Manchester U Pr). State Mutual Bk.
Vittorini, E. Conversazione in Sicilia. Powell, R., ed. 208p. 1978. 12.00x (ISBN 0-7190-0687-2, Pub. by Manchester U Pr England). State Mutual Bk.
Williamson, Edward. Patterns of Italian Conversation. 1981. pap. 2.25x (ISBN 0-913298-14-X). S F Vanni.

ITALIAN LANGUAGE–DICTIONARIES

Bocchetta, Vittore E., ed. World-Wide Italian Dictionary. 1977. pap. 2.50 (ISBN 0-449-30840-5, Prem). Fawcett.
Dizionario Completo Italiano-Portoghese (Brasiliano)--Portoghese (Brasiliano)-Italiano: Con L'etimologia Delle Voci Itaiane e Portoghesi (Brasiliane), la Loro Esatta Traduzione, Frasi e Modi Di Dire, 2 vols. 1978. Set. 82.00x (ISBN 0-686-70496-7); Vol. 1, 920 Pp. (ISBN 88-203-1010-4); Vol. 2, 1052pp. (ISBN 88-203-0216-0). S F Vanni.
May, Isopel, et al, eds. Putnam's Contemporary Italian Dictionary. (Eng. & It.). 1973. 3.50 (ISBN 0-399-11146-8). Putnam.
Il Nuovissimo Melzi: Dizionario Enciclopedico Italiano, 2 vols. 2970p. 1979. Set. 112.00 (ISBN 0-913298-53-0). S F Vanni.
Purves, John. Italian Dictionary. (Routledge Pocket Dictionaries Ser.). 862p. 1980. pap. 8.95 (ISBN 0-7100-0602-0). Routledge & Kegan.
Reynolds, Barbara. Concise Cambridge Italian Dictionary. 1974. 42.00 (ISBN 0-521-07273-5). Cambridge U Pr.
Scarry, Richard. ABC. (Italian.). 1976. 9.00x (ISBN 0-686-16892-5). Intl Learn Syst.
--Libro Dei Mestieri. (Italian.). 1976. 9.00x (ISBN 0-686-16893-3). Intl Learn Syst.
--Libro Delle Parole. (Italian.). 1976. 9.00x (ISBN 0-686-16890-9). Intl Learn Syst.
--Primo Dizionario. (Italian.). 1976. 9.00x (ISBN 0-686-16891-7). Intl Learn Syst.
Vest-Pocket Italian. pap. 2.95 (ISBN 0-8329-1535-1). New Century.
World-Wide Italian Dictionary: Indexed. 6.95 (ISBN 0-686-31301-1). New Century.
Zingarelli, compiled by. Vocabolario Della Lingua Italiana Zanichelli. 1973. 35.00 (ISBN 0-8478-5257-1). Rizzoli Intl.

ITALIAN LANGUAGE–DICTIONARIES–ENGLISH

Berberi, Dilaver & Berberi, Edel A., eds. Cortina-Grosset Basic Dictionary: Italian. 1977. pap. 2.95 (ISBN 0-448-14030-6). G&D.
Bocchetta, Vittore & Young, Ruth E., eds. Follett Vest-Pocket Italian Dictionary. 1967. 2.50 (ISBN 0-695-81102-9). New Century.
Bocchetta, Vittore E., ed. Follett World-Wide Dictionaries: Italian-English, English-Italian. (Orig.). 6.95 (ISBN 0-695-89696-2). New Century.
Bussi, Luciano & Cognazzo, Maria. Nuovo Dizionario Inglese-Italiano Delle Science Mediche. 864p. 1980. 78.00 (ISBN 0-913298-55-7). S F Vanni.
Cassells. Italian-English Dictionary. 1977. standard 14.95 (ISBN 0-02-052254-1); indexed 16.95 (ISBN 0-02-052253-3). Macmillan.
Cassells, et al. Cassell's Italian Dictionary: Italian-English, English-Italian. LC 77-7405. 1977. index 16.95 (ISBN 0-02-522540-5); plain 14.95 (ISBN 0-02-522530-8). Macmillan.
Cortina. Cortina-Ace Basic Italian Dictionary. (Foreign Language Dictionary Ser.). 384p. 1981. pap. 2.50 (ISBN 0-441-05003-4). Ace Bks.
Denti, Renzo. Dizionario Tecnico Italiano-Inglese--Inglese-Italiano. 9th rev. ed. 1811p. 1979. 44.00x (ISBN 88-203-1052-X). S F Vanni.
English-Italian, Italian-English Dictionary, 1 vol. 17.50 (ISBN 0-685-33020-6, 045-3). Saphrograph.
Florio, John A. Worlde of Wordes: A Sixteenth Century Italian-English Dictionary. 1971. Repr. of 1598 ed. 66.50 (ISBN 3-4870-4227-4). Adler.
Grande Dizionario Hazon-Garzanti Inglese-Italiano Italiano-Inglese. 1976. 45.00x (ISBN 0-686-19963-4). Intl Learn Syst.
Hall, Robert A., ed. The Random House Basic Dictionary Italian. 1981. pap. 1.50 (ISBN 0-345-29618-4). Ballantine.
Hall, Robert A., Jr. Italian Vest Pocket Dictionary. 1957. pap. 2.50 (ISBN 0-394-40060-7). Random.
Hamlyn Italian-English Dictionary. 1977. pap. 3.95 (ISBN 0-600-36566-2, 8089). Larousse.
Hughes, Charles A. Ace's Italian Phrase Book & Dictionary. (Ace's Foreign Phrase Bk). 192p. 1981. pap. 1.95 (ISBN 0-441-37488-3). Ace Bks.
Hugo Pocket Dictionary: Italian-English, English-Italian. 622p. 1971. 3.50 (ISBN 0-8226-0505-8, 505). Littlefield.
Institute for Language Study. Vest Pocket Italian. LC 58-8919. (Illus.). 128p. (Ital.). 1979. pap. 1.95 (ISBN 0-06-464903-2, BN 4900, BN). Har-Row.
Isopel, May, ed. Italian-English, English-Italian Gem Dictionary. (Gem Foreign Language Ser.). 1954. 2.95 (ISBN 0-00-458625-5, G1). Collins Pubs.
Italian-English Dictionary, 1 vol. 17.50 (ISBN 0-685-33019-2, 045-3). Saphrograph.
Jeans Pocket Dictionaries: Italian-English. 224p. (Orig.). 1981. pap. 1.95 (ISBN 0-8437-1727-0). Hammond Inc.
Lipton, Gladys & Colinari, John. Italian Bilingual Dictionary: A Beginner's Guide in Words & Pictures. LC 79-10831. (gr. 9-12). 1980. pap. text ed. 3.50 (ISBN 0-8120-0885-5). Barron.
Lucchesi, Mario. Dizionario Medico Ragionato Inglese-Italiano: Termini, Abbreviazioni, Sigle, Eponimi e Sinonimi Medici, Medico-Biologici e Delle Specializzazionni Mediche. 1490p. 1978. 98.00x (ISBN 0-913298-52-2). S F Vanni.
Marolli, G. Italian-English, English-Italian Technical Dictionary. 10th ed. (Illus.). 75.00 (ISBN 8-8005-1040-X). Heinman.
Melzi, Robert C. The Bantam New College Italian & English Dictionary. 736p. (Orig.). 1976. pap. 2.75 (ISBN 0-553-20267-7). Bantam.
--The New College Italian & English Dictionary. (Orig.). (gr. 7-12). 1976. pap. text ed. 8.50 (ISBN 0-87720-592-2). AMSCO Sch.
Mondadori's Pocket Italian-English English-Italian Dictionary. 1976. pap. 3.50 (ISBN 0-671-80460-X, 80460). PB.
Motta, Giuseppe. Dizionario Commerciale Inglese-Italiano--Italiano-Inglese: Economia, Legge, Finanza, Banca, Etc. 1051p. 1978. 40.00x (ISBN 0-913298-50-6). S F Vanni.
Ragazzini & Gagliardelli. Italian-English, English-Italian Commercial Dictionary. 50.00 (ISBN 0-685-25202-7). Heinman.
Ragazzini, compiled by. Dizionario Inglese-Italiano--Italiano-Inglese Zanichelli. 1972. 35.00 (ISBN 0-8478-5258-X). Rizzoli Intl.
Ragazzini, Giuseppe & Biagi, Adele, eds. Concise English-Italian Italian-English Dictionary. LC 73-17088. 1214p. 1973. pap. text ed. 11.95x (ISBN 0-582-55505-1). Longman.
Reynolds, Barbara. Cambridge Italian Dictionary, 2 vols. LC 74-77384. 1962. Vol. 1. Italian-English 1962. 115.00 (ISBN 0-521-06059-1); Vol. 2, English-italian 1981. 220.00 (ISBN 0-521-08708-2). Cambridge U Pr.
Sansoni. Dizinonario Inglese-Italiano--Italiano-Inglese Sansoni. Macchi, Vladimiro, ed. 1975. 29.95 (ISBN 0-8478-5256-3). Rizzoli Intl.
Settar, G. Worldwide Medical Interpreter: Italian, Vol. 6. 1977. pap. 12.00 (ISBN 0-87489-106-X). Med Economics.
Sezione Grandi Opera Garzanti, compiled by. Dizionario Garzanti (Italiano-Inglese--Inglese-Italiano) 1977. pap. 9.95 (ISBN 0-8478-5255-5). Rizzoli Intl.
Sprudzs, Adolph. Italian Abbreviations & Symbols: Law & Related Subjects. LC 70-95307. 1969. 20.00 (ISBN 0-379-00451-8). Oceana.

ITALIAN LANGUAGE–DICTIONARIES–FRENCH

Dictionnaire Garzanti Francais-Italien, Italien-Francais. 2046p. (Fr.-It.). 1969. 39.95 (ISBN 0-686-57110-X, M-6143). French & Eur.

Ghiotti, et al. Dictionnaire Italien-Francais, Francais-Italien de la Langue d'Aujourd'hui. (Fr.-It.). 1976. 27.50 (ISBN 0-686-57196-7, M-6270). French & Eur.

Larousse And Co. Interprete Larousse, francais-italien et italien-francais. (Fr. & It.). pap. 3.95 (ISBN 0-685-13947-6, 3787). Larousse.

--Larousse de poche, francais-italien et italien-francais. (Fr. & It.). pap. 5.98 (ISBN 0-685-13960-3, 1012). Larousse.

Padovani, G. & Silvestri, R. Dictionnaire bilingue Larousse, francais-italien et italien-francais. (Apollo). (Fr.). 10.50 (ISBN 0-685-13854-2, 3784). Larousse.

Rouede, Pierre & Rouede, Denise. Dictionnaire Italien-Francais et Francais-Italien. 1256p. (Fr.-It.). 1970. 25.00 (ISBN 0-686-57211-4, M-6493). French & Eur.

ITALIAN LANGUAGE–DICTIONARIES–SPANISH

Amador, E. M. Martinez. Diccionario Italiano-Espanol, Espanol-Italiano. 1440p. (Espn. -It.). 50.95 (ISBN 84-303-0133-X, S-12383). French & Eur.

Diccionario Cuyas: Spanish-Italian, Italian-Spanish. 5.50x (ISBN 0-686-00857-X). Colton Bk.

Diccionario Iter Italiano-Espanol, Espanol-Italiano. 712p. (It. -Espn.). leatherette 6.95 (ISBN 84-303-0139-9, S-50434). French & Eur.

Diccionario Iter Italiano-Espanol, Espanol-Italiano. 712p. (It. -Espn.). pap. 5.95 (ISBN 84-303-0138-0, S-50435). French & Eur.

Diccionario Lexicon Italiano-Espanol, Espanol-Italiano. 400p. (Espn. -It.). pap. 3.50 (ISBN 84-303-0136-4, S-31394). French & Eur.

Diccionario Universal Herder Italiano-Espanol, Espanol-Italiano. 5th ed. 364p. (Espn. -It.). 1977. pap. 4.50 (ISBN 84-254-0558-0, S-50433). French & Eur.

Frisoni, Gaetano. Dizionario Moderno Spagnuolo-Italiano--Italiano-Spagnuolo, 2 vols. 1865p. Set. 44.00x (ISBN 0-913298-51-4). S F Vanni.

Ortiz De Burgos, Jose. Diccionario Manual Italiano-Espanol, Spagnuolo-Italiano. 16th ed. 960p. (Espn. -It.). 1977. 5.95 (ISBN 84-7183-045-0, S-50432). French & Eur.

ITALIAN LANGUAGE–EXAMINATIONS, QUESTIONS, ETC.

Coscarelli, Diego, ed. Barron's Regents Exams & Answers. rev ed. 250p. (gr. 10-12). 1981. pap. text ed. 3.95 (ISBN 0-8120-0663-1). Barron.

Rudman, Jack. Italian - Jr. & Sr. H.S. (Teachers License Examination Ser.: T-32). (Cloth bdg. avail. on request). pap. 10.00 (ISBN 0-8373-8032-4). Natl Learning.

ITALIAN LANGUAGE–GLOSSARIES, VOCABULARIES, ETC.

Edler, Florence. Glossary of Mediaeval Terms of Business, 1200-1600. 1934. 22.00 (ISBN 0-527-01690-X). Kraus Repr.

Ragusa, Olga. Italian Verbs - Regular & Irregular. 1971. pap. 2.00x (ISBN 0-913298-27-1). S F Vanni.

ITALIAN LANGUAGE–GRAMMAR

Agard, Frederick B. & Di Pietro, Robert J. The Grammatical Structures of English & Italian. LC 65-25119. (Midway Reprint Ser). 1974. pap. 4.00x (ISBN 0-226-01022-8). U of Chicago Pr.

Bosco, F. J. & Lolli, F. Incontro Con l'Italiano: Primo Corso. 1967. text ed. 17.95 (ISBN 0-471-00040-X); tapes avail. (ISBN 0-471-00041-8). Wiley.

Cascio, Vicenzo L., ed. Italian Linguistic Ninety Seventy Six-Two: On Clitic Pronominalization, No. 2. (Orig.). 1976. pap. text ed. 7.25x (ISBN 0-391-01995-3). Humanities.

Cascio, Vincent, ed. Italian Linguistic Nineteen Seventy-Six-One: Passive & Impersonal Sentences, No. 1. 1976. pap. text ed. 7.25x (ISBN 0-391-01994-5). Humanities.

Cascio, Vincenzo, ed. Italian Linguistics, Nineteen Seventy-Seven-One: Verbi 'modali' an Italiano, No. 3. 1977. pap. text ed. 8.75x (ISBN 0-391-01996-1). Humanities.

Cioffari, Vincenzo. Italian Review Grammar & Composition. 3rd ed. (Illus.). 1969. text ed. 14.95x (ISBN 0-669-47290-5). Heath.

Duff, Charles. Italian for Beginners. 2nd rev ed. 1959. pap. 3.95 (ISBN 0-06-463214-8, EH 214, EH). Har-Row.

Elia, P. I Verbi Italiani Ad Uso Degli Stranieri. (It). 5.25 (ISBN 0-685-20240-2). Schoenhof.

Germano, Joseph & Schmitt, Conrad. Schaum's Outline of Italian Grammar. 2nd ed. (Schaum's Outline Ser.). 288p. 1981. pap. 4.95 (ISBN 0-07-023031-5, SP). McGraw.

Giamatti, Valentine. Minimum of Italian Grammar & Answer Key. 1964. pap. 4.50x (ISBN 0-913298-13-1). S F Vanni.

Hall, Robert A. Descriptive Italian Grammar. LC 74-1556. (Cornell Romance Studies: Vol. 2). 228p. 1974. Repr. of 1948 ed. text ed. 17.00x (ISBN 0-8371-7396-5, HAIG). Greenwood.

Heatwole, O. W. A Comparative Practical Grammar of French, Spanish & Italian. 1977. 8.95x (ISBN 0-913298-39-5); pap. 6.50 (ISBN 0-913298-26-3). S F Vanni.

Italian in Twenty Lessons. rev. ed. (Cortina Method Language Ser). (Illus.). 6.95 (ISBN 0-385-00101-0). Doubleday.

Italian Verbs Simplified. (Hugo's Language Courses Ser.: No. 552). 1970. pap. 1.50 (ISBN 0-8226-0552-X). Littlefield.

Kibler, L. & Noris, M. Giorno per Giorno: Italian in Review. 1971. text ed. 13.95 (ISBN 0-02-362860-X). Macmillan.

Luciani, Vincent. Two Hundred & One Italian Verbs Fully Conjugated in All the Tenses. LC 65-25693. (Orig.). 1966. text ed. 6.50 (ISBN 0-8120-6048-2); pap. text ed. 3.50 (ISBN 0-8120-0228-8). Barron.

Madrigal, Margarita. Invitaton to Italian. 1965. pap. 1.75 (ISBN 0-671-38121-0, Fireside). S&S.

Napolitano, Annamaria & Devine, Maria T. Manuale Di Grammatica Italiana. 1979. pap. text ed. 11.50 (ISBN 0-915838-98-2). Anma Libri.

Notley, Edwin A. A Comparative Grammar of the French, Italian, Spanish & Portuguese Languages. 1977. lib. bdg. 69.95 (ISBN 0-8490-1652-5). Gordon Pr.

Orwen, Gifford. Upgrade Your Italian: A Review Grammar. 1977. pap. 7.75x (ISBN 0-913298-12-3). S F Vanni.

Radford, A., ed. Italian Syntax. LC 77-71424. (Cambridge Studies in Linguistics: No. 21). 1977. 42.50 (ISBN 0-521-21643-5). Cambridge U Pr.

Ragusa, Olga. Essential Italian Grammar. (Orig.). 1963. pap. 2.50 (ISBN 0-486-20779-X). Dover.

--Essential Italian Grammar. LC 63-2911. 1963. lib. bdg. 9.50x (ISBN 0-88307-574-1). Gannon.

Rigal, Waldo A. Shortcut to the Italian Language. (Quality Paperback: No. 165). 1965. pap. 3.50 (ISBN 0-8226-0165-6). Littlefield.

Rossi, Patrizio & Radcliff-Umstead, Douglas. Italiano Oggi: Italian Review Grammar. LC 71-146362. 1976. pap. text ed. 8.95x (ISBN 0-89197-638-8). Irvington.

Saltarelli, Mario. Phonology of Italian in a Generative Grammar. (Janua Linguarum, Ser. Practica: No. 93). (Orig.). 1970. pap. text ed. 22.50x (ISBN 90-2790-737-4). Mouton.

ITALIAN LANGUAGE–HISTORY

Devoto, Giacomo. The Languages of Italy. Katainen, V. Louise, tr. LC 78-3391. (The History & Structure of Languages Ser.). 1978. lib. bdg. 26.00x (ISBN 0-226-14368-6). U of Chicago Pr.

Lepschy, Anna L. & Lepschy, Giulio. The Italian Language Today. (Illus.). 1978. 29.95 (ISBN 0-09-128020-6, Pub. by Hutchinson). Merrimack Bk Serv.

ITALIAN LANGUAGE–IDIOMS, CORRECTIONS, ERRORS

Hall, Robert R., Jr. & Hall, Frances A. Two Thousand & One Italian & English Idioms: 2001 Locuzione Italiane e Inglese. LC 81-66403. 1981. pap. text ed. 9.95 (ISBN 0-8120-0467-1). Barron.

Luciani, Vincent. Italian Idioms with Proverbs. 1981. pap. 6.95 (ISBN 0-913298-15-8). S F Vanni.

ITALIAN LANGUAGE–PHONETICS

Castiglione, Pierina B. Italian Phonetics, Diction & Intonation. 103p. pap. 9.50x (ISBN 0-913298-48-4); castinglone tape set 20.00 (ISBN 0-686-77593-7). S F Vanni.

Colorni, Evelina. Singers' Italian: A Manual of Diction & Phonetics. 1970. pap. text ed. 8.95 (ISBN 0-02-870620-X). Schirmer Bks.

Ducibella, Joseph W. Phonology of the Sicilian Dialects. LC 77-94206. (Catholic University of America Studies in Romance Languages & Literatures Ser: No. 10). Repr. of 1934 ed. 33.50 (ISBN 0-404-50310-1). AMS Pr.

Izzo, Herbert J. Tuscan & Etruscan: The Problem of Linguistic Substratum Influence in Central Italy. LC 78-163823. (Romance Ser.). 238p. 1972. 20.00x (ISBN 0-8020-5249-5). U of Toronto Pr.

Saltarelli, Mario. Phonology of Italian in a Generative Grammar. (Janua Linguarum, Ser. Practica: No. 93). (Orig.). 1970. pap. text ed. 22.50x (ISBN 90-2790-737-4). Mouton.

ITALIAN LANGUAGE–READERS

see also Italian Language–Text-Books for Children

Bernabei, Alfio. Avventura. LC 74-20820. 1974. pap. text ed. 3.95 (ISBN 0-88436-175-6). EMC.

Bernardo, Aldo S. & Mignani, Rigo. Ritratto Dell'Italia. 2nd ed. 1978. text ed. 14.95x (ISBN 0-669-01157-6). Heath.

Borelli, Luigi & Borelli, Mary. Leggende E Racconti Italiani E Quindici Canzoni Popolavi Tradizionali: An Easy Reader for Beginners. 1979. pap. 3.95x (ISBN 0-913298-03-4). S F Vanni.

Campo, Michael R., ed. Pirandello, Moravia & Italian Poetry: Intermediate Readings in Italian. (It). 1968. text ed. 7.95 (ISBN 0-02-318750-6). Macmillan.

Cassola, Carlo. La Ragazza Di Bube. (Easy Readers, C). (Illus.). 1977. pap. text ed. 3.75 (ISBN 0-88436-284-1). EMC.

Fo, Dario. Gli Imbianchini Non Hanno Ricordi. (Easy Readers). 1979. pap. 2.90 (ISBN 0-88436-296-5). EMC.

Galpin, A. M., et al. Beginning Readings in Italian. 1966. text ed. 7.95x (ISBN 0-685-14721-5). Macmillan.

Luciani, Vincent, ed. Betti: Corruzione Al Palazzo di Giustizia. 1980. pap. 4.25x (ISBN 0-913298-20-4). S F Vanni.

--Bracco: Il Piccolo Santo. 1961. pap. 2.95x (ISBN 0-913298-23-9). S F Vanni.

Masella, Aristede B. Leggere Con Piacere. (gr. 7 up). 1976. pap. text ed. 4.83 (ISBN 0-87720-591-4). AMSCO Sch.

Olken, Ilene T., ed. Racconti Del Novecento: Forti E. Deboli. 1966. pap. text ed. 8.95 (ISBN 0-13-750083-1). P-H.

Piero & Chiara. I Giovedi Della Signora Giulia. (Easy Readers, B). 1979. pap. 3.75 (ISBN 0-88436-292-2). EMC.

Pratolini, Vasco. Cronaca Familiare. Olken, Ilene T., ed. LC 73-130788. (Orig., Ital.). 1971. pap. text ed. 8.95x (ISBN 0-89197-117-3). Irvington.

Speroni, C., et al. L' Ialia Oggi: A Basic Reader. LC 75-16245. 1976. pap. text ed. 10.95 (ISBN 0-03-089648-7, HoltC). HR&W.

ITALIAN LANGUAGE–SELF-INSTRUCTION

see also Italian Language–Conversation and Phrase Books

Berlitz, Charles. Italian Step by Step. LC 78-73613. 1979. 9.95 (ISBN 0-89696-028-5). Everest Hse.

Berlitz Schools Of Languages. Self-Teacher: Italian. 1958. 8.95 (ISBN 0-448-01424-6). G&D.

Cagno, Michael & D'Arlon, Ben. Rapid Italian for Students & Tourists. 1979. pap. 3.25x (ISBN 0-913298-05-0). S F Vanni.

Cherel, Albert O. Italiaans Zonder Moeite. 16.95 (ISBN 0-685-11262-4). French & Eur.

--Italian Without Toil. 9.95 (ISBN 0-685-11263-2). French & Eur.

--Italien Sans Peine. 9.95 (ISBN 0-685-11264-0). French & Eur.

--Italienisch Ohne Muhe. 9.95 (ISBN 0-685-11265-9). French & Eur.

Jackson, Eugene & LoPreato, Joseph. Italian Made Simple. 1960. pap. 3.50 (ISBN 0-385-00736-1, Made). Doubleday.

Madrigal, Margarita. Invitation to Italian. 1965. 7.95 (ISBN 0-671-38120-2). S&S.

Madrigal, Margarita & Salvadori, Giuseppina. See It & Say It in Italian. (Orig.). pap. 1.75 (ISBN 0-451-09399-2, E9399, Sig). NAL.

Martin, Genevieve A. & Ciatti, Mario. Living Italian. (YA) (gr. 6-12). 1956. 14.95, with 4 lp records conversation manual & dictionary (ISBN 0-517-00132-2). Crown.

Orwen, Gifford. Introduction to Italian. 1971. 7.75x (ISBN 0-913298-11-5). S F Vanni.

Pei, Mario. New Italian Self-Taught. 336p. (Ital.). 1982. pap. text ed. 5.05 (ISBN 0-06-463616-X, EH 616, BN). Har-Row.

Speight, K. Teach Yourself Italian. (Teach Yourself Ser.). pap. 3.95 (ISBN 0-679-10184-5). McKay.

Stern, A. Z. & Reif, Joseph A., eds. Useful Expressions in Italian. (Useful Expressions Ser.). 64p. (Orig.). 1980. pap. 2.00 (ISBN 0-86628-010-3). Ridgefield Pub.

Teach Yourself Italian Phrase Book. (Teach Yourself Ser.). pap. 3.95 (ISBN 0-679-10236-1). McKay.

ITALIAN LANGUAGE–STUDY AND TEACHING

Absalom, R. N. & Potesta, S. Advanced Italian. LC 74-142964. 1971. pap. text ed. 8.95x (ISBN 0-521-09640-5). Cambridge U Pr.

Agard, Frederick B. & Di Pietro, Robert J. The Sounds of English & Italian. LC 65-25118. (Midway Reprint Ser). 76p. 1974. pap. text ed. 4.00x (ISBN 0-226-01020-1). U of Chicago Pr.

Berlitz, Charles. Passport to Italian. 1974. pap. 1.50 (ISBN 0-451-09694-0, J9694, Sig). NAL.

Cordasco, Francesco, ed. The Italian Community & Its Language in the United States: The Annual Reports of the Italian Teachers Association. 472p. 1975. 27.50x (ISBN 0-87471-585-7). Rowman.

Fucilla, Joseph G. The Teaching of Italian in the United States: A Documentary History. LC 74-17929. 304p. 1975. Repr. 17.00x (ISBN 0-405-06401-2). Arno.

Gimondo, Angelo. Italian First Year. (Orig.). (gr. 7-12). 1975. pap. text ed. 6.00 (ISBN 0-87720-590-6). AMSCO Sch.

Hall, Robert A., Jr. Italian for Modern Living. LC 75-312677. (Spoken Language Ser). xiv, 428p. (Prog. Bk.). 1974. pap. 12.00x (ISBN 0-87950-320-3); cassettes, six dual track 80.00 (ISBN 0-87950-321-1); cassette course, bk. & cassettes 85.00x (ISBN 0-87950-322-X). Spoken Lang Serv.

Simonini, R. C., Jr. Italian Scholarship in Renaissance England. (University of North Carolina Studies in Comparative Literature: No. 3). 1969. Repr. of 1952 ed. 19.50 (ISBN 0-384-55520-9). Johnson Repr.

Thimm, Franz. Italian Without a Teacher. pap. 1.00 (ISBN 0-685-02617-5, 00545260). Stein Pub.

ITALIAN LANGUAGE–TEXT-BOOKS FOR CHILDREN

see also Italian Language–Conversation and Phrase Books

Gimondo, Angelo. Italian First Year. (gr. 8-11). 1978. wkbk. 7.17 (ISBN 0-87720-593-0). AMSCO Sch.

Speroni, C. & Golino, C. L. Leggendo E Ripassando. LC 68-13507. (It). (gr. 4-8). 1968. text ed. 12.95 (ISBN 0-03-068795-0, HoltC); tapes 140.00 (ISBN 0-03-068800-0). HR&W.

ITALIAN LANGUAGE–TEXT-BOOKS FOR FOREIGNERS

Assimil. Assimil Language Courses: For Dutch Speaking People Who Want to Learn Italian - Italiaans Zonder Moeite. 12.95 (ISBN 0-686-56176-7); accompanying records & tapes 75.00 (ISBN 0-686-56177-5). French & Eur.

--Assimil Language Courses: For English Speaking People Who Want to Learn Italian - Italian Without Toil. 11.95 (ISBN 0-686-56146-5); accompanying records & tapes 75.00 (ISBN 0-686-56147-3). French & Eur.

--Assimil Language Courses: For French Speaking People Who Want to Learn Italian - L'Italien Sans Peine. 11.95 (ISBN 0-686-56078-7); accompanying records & tapes 75.00 (ISBN 0-686-56079-5). French & Eur.

--Assimil Language Courses: For Greek Speaking People Who Want to Learn German. 11.95 (ISBN 0-686-56178-3); accompanying records & tapes 75.00 (ISBN 0-686-56179-1). French & Eur.

Bormioli, M. & Pellegrinetti, G. A. Letture Italiane per Stranieri, 2 vols. 1976. Vol. 1. 11.00x (ISBN 0-686-16886-0); Vol. 2. 10.00x (ISBN 0-686-16887-9). Intl Learn Syst.

Bostrom, I. & Moretti, M. Parlate Con Noi. (Illus.). 1971. write for info. Longman.

Calvino, J. Fiabe Italiane. Hall, J., ed. 160p. 1976. 9.00x (ISBN 0-7190-0645-7, Pub. by Manchester U Pr England). State Mutual Bk.

Cioffari, Vincenzo, et al. Graded Italian Reader: Prima Tappa. 2nd ed. 1979. pap. text ed. 6.95 (ISBN 0-669-01955-0). Heath.

Corradini, Claudia. Lab & Excerise Book for Elementary Italian. 2nd ed. 1977. pap. text ed. 8.50 (ISBN 0-8191-0245-8). U Pr of Amer.

Italian in Three Months. (Hugo's Language Courses Ser.: No. 525). 1976. pap. 3.50 (ISBN 0-8226-0525-2). Littlefield.

Roberts, et al. Audio-Active Italian, 2 vols. 1980. Vol. 1, 135 Pgs. 79.00x (ISBN 0-88432-055-3, 1101-1102). Vol. 2, 142 Pgs. J Norton Pubs.

Roncari, A. Corso Preparatorio Di Lingua Italiana per Stranieri. 1976. 9.50x (ISBN 0-686-16881-X). Intl Learn Syst.

--Prime Letture Italiane per Stranieri, 2 vols. 1976. Vol. 1. 4.00x (ISBN 0-686-16884-4); Vol. 2. 4.50x (ISBN 0-686-16885-2). Intl Learn Syst.

Traversa, Vincenzo. Parola E Pensiero: Introduzione Alla Lingua Italiana Moderna. 3rd ed. (Illus.). 437p. 1980. text ed. 18.95 scp (ISBN 0-06-046649-9, HarpC); avail. instrs' manual; wkbk. scp 6.50 (ISBN 0-06-046654-5); tapes 250.00 (ISBN 0-686-77579-1). Har-Row.

Zappala, Stephen. Fsi Italian Programmed Course. (Prog. Bk.). 1976. pap. text ed. 8.50x (ISBN 0-686-10740-3); tchrs. manual 5.00x (ISBN 0-686-10741-1); 23 cassettes 138.00 (ISBN 0-686-10742-X). Intl Learn Syst.

ITALIAN LITERATURE (COLLECTIONS)

Bini, Luciano & Bini, Elzio, eds. Dolci Inizi. 1968. pap. text ed. 8.50x (ISBN 0-435-39630-7). Heinemann Ed.

Brennan, Joseph. Paniolo. 1978. pap. 4.50 (ISBN 0-914916-39-4). Topgallant.

Carducci, Giosue. Od: Barbare. Smith, William F., tr. 1950. 7.50x (ISBN 0-913298-40-9). S F Vanni.

Cavalcanti, Guido. The Sonnets & Ballate of Guido Calvalcanti. LC 78-20454. 1980. Repr. of 1912 ed. 16.00 (ISBN 0-88355-834-3). Hyperion Conn.

Inventario Ceruti, 5 vols. 3616p. (Ital.). 1981. Set. lib. bdg. 750.00 (ISBN 0-88354-164-5, Pub. by Etimar Italy). Vol. 1 (ISBN 0-88354-165-3). Vol. 2 (ISBN 0-88354-166-1). Vol. 3 (ISBN 0-88354-167-X). Vol. 4 (ISBN 0-88354-168-8). Vol. 5 (ISBN 0-88354-169-6). Clearwater Pub.

Picot, Emile. Francais Italianisants Au Seizieme Siecle, 2 Vols. LC 68-56740. (Research & Source Works Ser.: No. 221). (Fr). 1968. Repr. of 1907 ed. 42.50 (ISBN 0-8337-2755-9). B Franklin.
Ragusa, Olga. First Readings in Italian Literature - Letture Facili. 1977. pap. 3.95 (ISBN 0-913298-06-9). S F Vanni.
White, D. M. Zaccaria Seriman: The 'Viaggi de Enrico Wanton': A Contribution to the Study of the Enlightenment in Italy. 178p. 1961. 24.00x (ISBN 0-7190-1218-X, Pub. by Manchester U Pr England). State Mutual Bk.

ITALIAN LITERATURE–BIBLIOGRAPHY

Associazione Italiana Editori, Milan. Italian Books in Print 1979. 3rd ed. Orig. Title: Catologo Dei Libri Italiani in Commercio 1979. (Ital.). for the 3-vol. set 169.00 (ISBN 0-686-62601-X, Pub. by Editrice Bibliografica Italy). Author-titles (ISBN 88-7075-042-6). Subject (ISBN 88-7075-043-4). Bowker.
Cicogna, Emmanuele A. Saggio di Bibliografia Veneziana, 2 vols. Bd. with Bibliografia Veneziana, 2 vols in 1. Sorarzo, Girolamo. Repr. of 1885 ed. 58.50 (ISBN 0-685-23105-4). 1965. Repr. of 1847 ed. Set. 105.50 (ISBN 0-8337-0574-1). B Franklin.
Golden, H. H. & Simches, S. O. Modern Italian Languages & Literature: A Bibliography of Homage Studies. LC 59-14742. Repr. of 1959 ed. 16.00 (ISBN 0-527-34320-X). Kraus Repr.
Harvard University Center for Italian Renaissance Studies at Villa I Tatti (Florence, Italy) Catalogues of the Berenson Library of the Harvard University Center for Italian Renaissance Studies at Villa I Tatti, Florence, Italy, 4 vols. 1973. lib. bdg. 415.00 (ISBN 0-8161-0973-7). G K Hall.
Harvard University Library. Italian History & Literature: Classification Schedule - Author & Title Listing, 2 vols. LC 74-78747. (Widener Library Shelflist: No. 51-52). 1975. Set. text ed. 90.00x (ISBN 0-674-46955-0). Harvard U Pr.
Mortimer, Ruth, compiled by. Italian Sixteenth-Century Books: Harvard College Library, Department of Printing & Graphic Arts: catalog of Books & Manuscripts, 2 vols, Part 2. 1974. Set. text ed. 75.00x (ISBN 0-674-46960-7, Belknap Pr). Harvard U Pr.

ITALIAN LITERATURE–HISTORY AND CRITICISM

Baron, Hans. Humanistic & Political Literature in Florence & Venice at the Beginning of the Quattrocento: Studies in Criticism & Chronology. LC 68-25028. (With a new introduction). 1968. Repr. of 1955 ed. 9.50 (ISBN 0-8462-1139-4). Russell.
Bec, Christian. Les Marchands Ecrivains: Affaires et Humanisme a Florence, 1375-1434. 1967. pap. 48.50 (ISBN 0-686-22141-9). Mouton.
Biasin, Gian-Paolo. Literary Diseases: Theme & Metaphor in the Italian Novel. LC 74-30345. 188p. 1975. 12.50x (ISBN 0-292-74614-8). U of Tex Pr.
Bondanella, Peter, ed. Dictionary of Italian Literature. Bondanella, Julia C. LC 78-4022. 1978. lib. bdg. 39.95x (ISBN 0-313-20421-7, BDI/). Greenwood.
Collins, Joseph. Idling in Italy. facs. ed. LC 77-128226. (Essay Index Reprint Ser). 1920. 17.00 (ISBN 0-8369-1824-X). Arno.
Costa, Dennis. Irenic Apocalypse: Some Uses of Apocalyptic in Dante, Petrarch & Rabelais. (Stanford French & Italian Studies: Vol. 21). 160p. 1981. pap. 20.00 (ISBN 0-915838-18-4). Anma Libri.
Crane, Thomas F. Italian Social Customs of the Sixteenth Century & Their Influence on the Literatures of Europe. LC 70-143873. 1971. Repr. of 1920 ed. 20.00 (ISBN 0-8462-1535-7). Russell.
Dante. Literature in the Vernacular. Purcell, Sally, tr. from Ital. 96p. (Orig.). 1981. pap. 6.95 (ISBN 0-85635-274-8, Pub. by Carcanet New Pr England). Persea Bks.
Diacono, Mario. Vito Acconci: Dal Testo-Azione Al Corpo Come Testo. LC 75-22995. (Illus.). 245p. (Ital.). 1975. 9.95 (ISBN 0-915570-03-3). Oolp Pr.
Dole, Nathan H. Teacher of Dante, & Other Studies in Italian Literature. facs. ed. LC 67-26733. (Essay Index Reprint Ser). 1908. 16.00 (ISBN 0-8369-0383-8). Arno.
Donadoni, Eugenio. A History of Italian Literature, 2 Vols. Monges, Richard, tr. LC 68-13026. (Gotham Library Ser). 1969. o.p. 18.50x set (ISBN 0-8147-0124-8); pap. 7.95 set (ISBN 0-8147-0125-6). NYU Pr.
Foligno, Cesare. Epochs of Italian Literature. LC 78-103223. 1970. Repr. of 1920 ed. 9.00 (ISBN 0-8046-0860-1). Kennikat.
Gardner, Edmund G. Arthurian Legend in Italian Literature. LC 78-120255. 1970. Repr. lib. bdg. 18.50x (ISBN 0-374-92999-8). Octagon.
--The Arthurian Legend in Italian Literature. 1978. Repr. of 1930 ed. lib. bdg. 50.00 (ISBN 0-8274-0001-2). R West.
--Dukes & Poets of Ferrara: A Story in the Poetry, Religion & Politics of Fifteenth & Early Sixteenth Centuries. LC 78-145033. xiv, 578p. 1972. Repr. of 1904 ed. 32.00 (ISBN 0-403-00776-3). Scholarly.
--Italian Literature. 80p. 1980. Repr. of 1927 ed. lib. bdg. 15.00 (ISBN 0-8482-4194-0). Norwood Edns.
--Italian Literature. 1979. Repr. of 1927 ed. 10.00 (ISBN 0-8414-4620-2). Folcroft.
Garnett, Richard. History of Italian Literature. 1973. Repr. of 1898 ed. 45.00 (ISBN 0-8274-1345-9). R West.
Gatt-Rutter, J. A. Writers & Politics in Modern Italy. LC 78-18829. (Writers & Politics Ser.). 1979. 11.50x (ISBN 0-8419-0413-8); pap. text ed. 7.50x (ISBN 0-8419-0416-2). Holmes & Meier.
Grillo, Ernesto. Studies in Modern Italian Literature. 1973. Repr. of 1930 ed. 25.00 (ISBN 0-8274-0203-1). R West.
Heiney, Donald. America in Modern Italian Literature. 278p. 1965. 15.50 (ISBN 0-8135-0471-6). Rutgers U Pr.
Hollander, Robert. Boccaccio's Two Venuses. LC 77-5144. 1977. 20.00x (ISBN 0-231-04224-8). Columbia U Pr.
Lebowitz, Naomi. Italo Svevo. 1978. 16.50 (ISBN 0-8135-0848-7). Rutgers U Pr.
Leone, Michele. L' Industria Nella Letteratura Italiana Contemporanea. (Stanford French & Italian Studies: No. 2). (It.). 1976. pap. 20.00 (ISBN 0-915838-30-3). Anma Libri.
Luciani, Vincent. A Brief History of Italian Literature. 1967. 10.00x (ISBN 0-913298-09-3). S F Vanni.
Marsh, David. The Quattrocento Dialogue: Classical Tradition & Humanist Innovation. LC 79-15625. (Harvard Studies in Comparative Literature: 35). 1980. text ed. 11.50x (ISBN 0-674-74115-3). Harvard U Pr.
Maurino, Ferdinando D. Salvatore Di Giacomo & Neapolitan Dialectal Literature. 1951. 6.50x (ISBN 0-913298-30-1). S F Vanni.
Molinaro, Julius A., ed. Petrarch to Pirandello: Studies in Italian Literature in Honour of Beatrice Corrigan. LC 72-185725. 352p. 1973. 20.00x (ISBN 0-8020-5271-1). U of Toronto Pr.
Pacifici, Sergio. A Guide to Contemporary Italian Literature: From Futurism to Neorealism. LC 72-5472. (Arcturus Books Paperbacks). 352p. pap. 9.95 (ISBN 0-8093-0593-3). S Ill U Pr.
--The Modern Italian Novel: From Pea to Moravia. LC 67-13047. (Crosscurrents Modern Critiques Ser.). 288p. 1979. 16.95 (ISBN 0-8093-0873-8). S Ill U Pr.
Perella, Nicholas J. The Midday in Italian Literature. LC 78-70313. 1979. 22.00x (ISBN 0-691-06389-3). Princeton U Pr.
Phelps, Ruth S. Italian Silhouettes. facs. ed. LC 68-55853. (Essay Index Reprint Ser). 1924. 15.00 (ISBN 0-8369-0786-8). Arno.
Quigley, H. Italy & the Rise of a New Criticism in the Eighteenth Century. (Studies in Comparative Literature: No. 7). 174p. Repr. of 1921 ed. lib. bdg. 15.00x (ISBN 0-87991-509-9). Porcupine Pr.
Ragusa, Olga. Narrative & Drama: Essays in Modern Italian Literature from Verga to Pasolini. (De Proprietatibus Litterarum Series Practica: No. 110). 1976. pap. text ed. 37.50x (ISBN 90-2793-474-6). Mouton.
Riccio, Peter. Italian Authors of Today. LC 75-128298. (Essay Index Reprint Ser). 1938. 15.00 (ISBN 0-8369-1842-8). Arno.
Rimanelli, Giose & Atchity, Kenneth J., eds. Italian Literature: Roots & Branches. LC 75-18182. 480p. 1976. 30.00x (ISBN 0-300-01885-1). Yale U Pr.
Robb, Nesca A. Neoplatonism of the Italian Renaissance. 1968. lib. bdg. 17.00x (ISBN 0-374-96840-3). Octagon.
Rospigliosi, William. The Writer in the Italian Renaissance. (Illus.). 1979. 24.95 (ISBN 0-86033-072-9). Gordon-Cremonesi.
Rotunda, D. P. Motif-Index of the Italian Novella in Prose. LC 72-6778. (Studies in Italian Literature, No. 46). 1972. Repr. of 1942 ed. lib. bdg. 33.95 (ISBN 0-8383-1653-0). Haskell.
Schuyler, Eugene. Italian Influence. 1973. Repr. of 1901 ed. 30.00 (ISBN 0-8274-0921-4). R West.
Seung, T. K. Cultural Thematics: The Formation of the Faustian Ethos. LC 75-43335. 1976. 20.00x (ISBN 0-300-01918-1). Yale U Pr.
Siracusa, Joseph & Laurenti, Josephcompiled by. Literary Relations Between Spain & Italy: A Bibliographic Survey of Comparative Literature (Relaciones Literarias Entre Espana E Italia Ensayo De una Bibliografia De Literature Comparada) 255p. 1972. lib. bdg. 20.00 (ISBN 0-8161-1010-7). G K Hall.
Snell, F. J. Primer of Italian Literature. 1978. Repr. of 1893 ed. lib. bdg. 20.00 (ISBN 0-8274-4140-1). R West.
Symonds, J. A. Italian Literature: From the Beginnings to Ariosto. (Renaissance in Italy Ser). 7.50 (ISBN 0-8446-3041-1). Peter Smith.
Tedeschi, John A. The Literature of the Italian Reformation. 36p. 1971. pap. 1.25 (ISBN 0-685-36218-3). Newberry.
Templer, Margherita D. Itinerario de Amore: Dialettica de Amore e morte nella vita nuova. (Studies in the Romance Languages & Literatures: No. 134). 1973. pap. 10.00x (ISBN 0-8078-9134-7). U of NC Pr.
Thayer, William R. Italica: Studies in Italian Life & Letters. 1973. Repr. of 1908 ed. 25.00 (ISBN 0-8274-0835-8). R West.
Trail, Florence. A History of Italian Literature. LC 72-3466. (Studies in Italian Literature, No. 46). 1972. Repr. of 1903 ed. lib. bdg. 43.95 (ISBN 0-8383-1561-5). Haskell.
Trinkaus, Charles. Adversity's Noblemen. rev. ed. 1965. lib. bdg. 11.50x (ISBN 0-374-97999-5). Octagon.
Vittorini, Domenico. The Age of Dante. LC 75-10219. (Illus.). 188p. 1975. Repr. of 1957 ed. lib. bdg. 16.00x (ISBN 0-8371-8175-5, VIAD). Greenwood.
Wall, Bernard. Alesandro Manzoni. 1954. 24.50 (ISBN 0-686-51343-6). Elliots Bks.
Weinberg, Bernard. A History of Literary Criticism in the Italian Renaissance. LC 60-5470. (Midway Reprint Ser). 656p. 1974. pap. 17.50 ea.; Vol. 1. (ISBN 0-226-88554-2); Vol. 2. (ISBN 0-226-88555-0). U of Chicago Pr.
Whitfield, John H. A Short History of Italian Literature. LC 76-10967. 1976. Repr. of 1960 ed. lib. bdg. 21.25x (ISBN 0-8371-8890-3, WHIL). Greenwood.
Wilkins, Ernest H. A History of Italian Literature. rev. ed. Bergin, Thomas G., rev. by. LC 74-80444. 576p. 1974. text ed. 25.00x (ISBN 0-674-39701-0). Harvard U Pr.
Woodhouse, J. Castiglione: A Reassessment of the Courtier. (Writers of Italy: No. 7). 229p. 1979. 12.50x (ISBN 0-85224-346-4, Pub. by Edinburgh U Pr Scotland). Columbia U Pr.

ITALIAN LITERATURE–TRANSLATIONS INTO ENGLISH

Aristo. The Comedies of Ariosto. Beame, Edmond & Sbrocchi, Leonard G., eds. LC 74-5739. xlvi, 322p. 1975. text ed. 17.50x (ISBN 0-226-02649-3). U of Chicago Pr.
Boccaccio, Giovanni. Filostrato of Giovanni Boccaccio. Griffin, Nathaniel E. & Myrick, Arthur B., trs. LC 72-120232. 1973. Repr. lib. bdg. 27.50x (ISBN 0-374-90730-7). Octagon.
Botteghe Oscure. Anthology of New Italian Writers. Caetani, Marquerite, ed. LC 72-110822. Repr. of 1950 ed. lib. bdg. 18.75x (ISBN 0-8371-3211-8, BOIW). Greenwood.
Capocelli, Ginevra, ed. Outlook on Life of Various Italian Writers. (Illus.). 1963. 4.00 (ISBN 0-87164-124-0). William-F.
Guercio, Francis M., ed. Anthology of Contemporary Italian Prose. LC 79-103226. 1970. Repr. of 1931 ed. 12.50 (ISBN 0-8046-0863-6). Kennikat.
Montale, Eugenio. The Butterfly of Dinard. Singh, G., tr. LC 78-550605. 188p. 1971. 9.00x (ISBN 0-8131-1252-4). U Pr of Ky.
Painter, William. The Palace of Pleasure, 3 Vols. Jacobs, Joseph, ed. 1966. pap. text ed. 4.00 ea.; Vol. 1. pap. text ed. (ISBN 0-486-21691-8); Vol. 2. pap. text ed. (ISBN 0-486-21692-6); Vol. 3. pap. text ed. (ISBN 0-486-21693-4). Dover.
Painter, William M. Palace of Pleasure, 4 Vols. Miles, Hamish, ed. LC 30-20341. Repr. of 1929 ed. Set. 125.00 (ISBN 0-404-04880-3); 31.50 ea. Vol. 1 (ISBN 0-404-04881-1). Vol. 2 (ISBN 0-404-04882-X). Vol. 3 (ISBN 0-404-04883-8). Vol. 4 (ISBN 0-404-04884-6). AMS Pr.
Poliziano, Angelo. A Translation of the Orpheus of Angelo Politian & the Aminta of Torquato Tasso. Lord, Louis E., tr. LC 78-59036. 1979. Repr. of 1931 ed. 16.00 (ISBN 0-88355-708-8). Hyperion Conn.
Speroni, Charles. Wit & Wisdom of the Italian Renaissance. 1964. 30.00x (ISBN 0-520-01199-6). U of Cal Pr.

ITALIAN LITERATURE–TRANSLATIONS INTO ENGLISH–BIBLIOGRAPHY

Scott, Mary A. Elizabethan Translations from the Italian. 1969. 32.50 (ISBN 0-8337-3210-2). B Franklin.
Shields, Nancy C. Italian Translations in America. 59.95 (ISBN 0-8490-0429-2). Gordon Pr.

ITALIAN MUSIC

see Music, Italian

ITALIAN NATIONAL CHARACTERISTICS

see National Characteristics, Italian

ITALIAN PAINTING

see Painting, Italian

ITALIAN PAINTINGS

see Paintings, Italian

ITALIAN PHILOLOGY–BIBLIOGRAPHY

Simon, A. L. Bibliotheca Bacchica, 2 vols. in 1. Repr. of 1927 ed. 60.00x (ISBN 0-685-47435-6). Corner.

ITALIAN POETRY (COLLECTIONS)

Here are entered collections by various authors. For English translations see subdivision Translations into English.

Barkan, Stanley H. & Scammacca, Saverio A., eds. Sicilian Antigruppo. (Illus.). 30p. 1976. 5.00 (ISBN 0-89304-008-8). Cross Cult.
Butler, Arthur J., ed. The Forerunners of Dante: A Selection from Italian Poetry Before 1300. 1977. lib. bdg. 59.95 (ISBN 0-8490-1857-9). Gordon Pr.
Campo, Michael R., ed. Pirandello, Moravia & Italian Poetry: Intermediate Readings in Italian. (It). 1968. text ed. 7.95 (ISBN 0-02-318750-6). Macmillan.
DeLuca, A. Michael & Giuliano, William. Selections from Italian Poetry. LC 66-10394. (Illus.). 128p. (gr. 9 up). 1966. PLB 5.29 (ISBN 0-8178-3792-2). Harvey.
Golino, Carlo L. & Quasimodo, Salvatore, eds. Contemporary Italian Poetry: An Anthology. LC 76-21754. 1977. Repr. of 1962 ed. lib. bdg. 20.75x (ISBN 0-8371-8998-5, GOCI). Greenwood.
Lind, L. R., ed. Twentieth Century Italian Poetry: A Bilingual Anthology. LC 73-11343. (LLA Ser). 432p. 1974. pap. 10.50 (ISBN 0-672-61220-8). Bobbs.
Lucchi, Lorna De, tr. Anthology of Italian Poems, 13th-19th Century. LC 66-30496. (Eng. & Ital.). 1922. 14.00x (ISBN 0-8196-0198-5). Biblo.
Rendel, Romilda. An Anthology of Italian Lyrics. 1926. lib. bdg. 15.00 (ISBN 0-685-84293-2). Folcroft.
--An Anthology of Italian Lyrics from the 13th Century to the Present Day. Repr. of 1926 ed. lib. bdg. 30.00 (ISBN 0-8495-4541-2). Arden Lib.
Schauffler, Robert H., compiled by. Through Italy with the Poets. LC 78-39397. (Granger Index Reprint Ser). Repr. of 1908 ed. 22.00 (ISBN 0-8369-6351-2). Arno.
Smith, William J., ed. Poems from Italy. LC 77-158700. (Poems of the World). (Illus.). (gr. 7-12). 1972. 8.95 (ISBN 0-690-63915-5, TYC-J). Har-Row.

ITALIAN POETRY–HISTORY AND CRITICISM

Cagnone, Nanni. What's Hecuba to Him or He to Hecuba? Verzoni, David, tr. LC 75-4969. 183p. (Eng. & Ital.). 1975. 7.95 (ISBN 0-915570-01-7). Oolp Pr.
Centuori, Walter J. A Concordance to the Poets of the Dolce Stil Novo, 5 vols. LC 77-294. 1977. 185.00 (ISBN 0-8032-0929-0). U of Nebr Pr.
--A Concordance to the Poets of the Dolce Stil Novo, 5 vols. LC 77-294. 1977. 225.00 (ISBN 0-8357-0431-9, IS-00026, Pub. by U of Nebraska Pr.); Vol. 1. (ISBN 0-8032-0929-0); Vol. 2. (ISBN 0-8032-0940-1); Vol.3. (ISBN 0-8032-0941-X); Vol. 4. (ISBN 0-8032-0942-8); Vol. 5. (ISBN 0-8032-0943-6). Univ Microfilms.
Corrigan, Beatrice, ed. Italian Poets & English Critics, 1755-1859: A Collection of Critical Essays. LC 68-54483. (Patterns of Literary Criticism Ser). 1969. 10.50x (ISBN 0-226-11587-9); pap. 3.45 (ISBN 0-226-11588-7, PLC7). U of Chicago Pr.
Howells, William D. Modern Italian Poets. LC 72-6857. (Essay Index Reprint Ser). 1972. Repr. of 1887 ed. 24.00 (ISBN 0-8369-7246-5). Arno.
--Modern Italian Poets: Essays & Versions. LC 72-97534. (Illus.). viii, 370p. 1973. Repr. of 1887 ed. 20.00 (ISBN 0-8462-1709-0). Russell.
Kuhns, Oscar. Great Poets of Italy. facs. ed. LC 75-86767. (Essay Index Reprint Ser). 1903. 22.00 (ISBN 0-8369-1146-6). Arno.
Langley, Ernest. The Poetry of Giacomo Da Lentino: Sicilian Poet of the Thirteenth Century. 1977. lib. bdg. 59.95 (ISBN 0-8490-2448-X). Gordon Pr.
Lipari, Angelo. Dolce Stil Novo According to Lorenzo De'Medici. LC 72-1732. (Yale Romanic Studies: No. 12). Repr. of 1936 ed. 26.75 (ISBN 0-404-53212-8). AMS Pr.
Marchione, Margherita, ed. Twentieth-Century Italian Poetry: A Bilingual Anthology. LC 72-6634. (Illus.). 301p. 1974. 15.00 (ISBN 0-8386-1245-8). Fairleigh Dickinson.
Orwen, Gifford P. Cecco Angiolieri: A Study. (Studies in the Romance Languages & Literatures: No. 215). 104p. 1980. pap. 7.50 (ISBN 0-8078-9215-7). U of NC Pr.
Ozanam, Frederick. Franciscan Poets of the Thirteenth Century. LC 68-26288. 1969. Repr. of 1914 ed. 13.75 (ISBN 0-8046-0342-1). Kennikat.
Rubsamen, Walter H. Literary Sources of Secular Music in Italy: 1500. LC 72-4482. (Music Ser.). 82p. 1972. Repr. of 1943 ed. lib. bdg. 15.00 (ISBN 0-306-70496-X). Da Capo.
Shaw, J. E. Guido Cavalcanti's Theory of Love. LC 50-14715. 1949. 27.50x (ISBN 0-8020-7072-8). U of Toronto Pr.

Slade, Carole A., ed. Approaches to Teaching Dante's Divine Comedy. (Approaches to Teaching Masterpieces of World Literature Ser.: No. 2). 160p. 1981. 14.50x (ISBN 0-87352-477-2); pap. 8.50x (ISBN 0-87352-478-0). Modern Lang.

Smith, Lawrence R., ed. The New Italian Poetry: Nineteen Forty-Five to the Present. 400p. 1981. 28.50 (ISBN 0-520-03859-2); pap. 8.95 (ISBN 0-686-77671-2). U of Cal Pr.

Wordsworth, J. C. Adventures in Literature. 1979. Repr. of 1929 ed. lib. bdg. 25.00 (ISBN 0-8495-5725-9). Arden Lib.

ITALIAN POETRY–TRANSLATIONS INTO ENGLISH

Dante Alighieri. The Inferno: The Divine Comedy of Dante Alighieri, a Verse Translation with Introduction. Mandelbaum, Allen, tr. LC 73-94441. (Illus.). 336p. 1980. 24.95 (ISBN 0-520-02712-4). U of Cal Pr.

Leopardi, Giacomo. A Leopardi Reader. Casale, Ottavio M., ed. LC 80-29068. 246p. 1981. 24.95 (ISBN 0-252-00824-3); pap. 8.95 (ISBN 0-252-00892-8). U of Ill Pr.

Lind, L. R., ed. Twentieth Century Italian Poetry: A Bilingual Anthology. LC 73-11343. (LLA Ser). 432p. 1974. pap. 10.50 (ISBN 0-672-61220-8). Bobbs.

Lucchi, Lorna De, tr. Anthology of Italian Poems, 13th-19th Century. LC 66-30496. (Eng. & Ital.). 1922. 14.00x (ISBN 0-8196-0198-5). Biblo.

Marchione, Margherita, ed. Twentieth-Century Italian Poetry: A Bilingual Anthology. LC 72-6634. (Illus.). 301p. 1974. 15.00 (ISBN 0-8386-1245-8). Fairleigh Dickinson.

Porta, Antonio. As If It Were a Rhythm. Vangelisti, Paul, tr. from Italian. 1978. sewn in wrappers 2.50 (ISBN 0-685-50401-8, Pub by Red Hill). SBD.

Rebay, Luciano, ed. Italian Poetry, a Selection: From St. Francis of Assisi to Salvatore Quasimodo. (Illus., It. & Eng.). 6.00 (ISBN 0-8446-0154-3). Peter Smith.

Rossetti, Dante G. Poems. Doughty, O., ed. 1961. 8.95x (ISBN 0-460-00627-4, Evman). Biblio Dist.

Smith, William J., ed. Poems from Italy. LC 77-158700. (Poems of the World). (Illus.). (gr. 7-12). 1972. 8.95 (ISBN 0-690-63915-5, TYC-J). Har-Row.

Trilussa, pseud. Trilussa: Roman Satirical Poems & Their Translation. Showerman, Grant, tr. & intro. by. 185p. (It. & Eng.). 1945. 6.50x (ISBN 0-913298-47-6). S F Vanni.

ITALIAN POTTERY

see Pottery, Italian

ITALIAN PROSE LITERATURE–HISTORY AND CRITICISM

Baron, Hans. From Petrarch to Leonardo Bruni: Studies in Humanistic & Political Literature. LC 68-16686. 1968. 12.00x (ISBN 0-226-03801-7); pap. 3.25 (ISBN 0-226-03802-5). U of Chicago Pr.

Duisit, Lionel. Satire, Parodie, Calembour. (Stanford French & Italian Studies: No. 11). (Fr.). 1978. pap. 20.00 (ISBN 0-915838-26-5). Anma Libri.

Marcus, Millicent. An Allegory of Form: Literary Self-Conciousness in the "Decameron". (Stanford French & Italian Studies: No. 18). 1979. pap. 20.00 (ISBN 0-915838-21-4). Anma Libri.

ITALIAN SCULPTURE

see Sculpture–Italy

ITALIAN SONGS

see Songs, Italian

ITALIAN TALES

see Tales, Italian

ITALIAN WIT AND HUMOR

Spalding, Henry, ed. Joys of Italian Humor & Folklore. LC 80-13750. 360p. 1980. 16.95 (ISBN 0-8246-0255-2). Jonathan David.

Speroni, Charles. Wit & Wisdom of the Italian Renaissance. 1964. 30.00x (ISBN 0-520-01199-6). U of Cal Pr.

Werner, A. The Humour of Italy. (Illus.). Repr. of 1893 ed. 25.00 (ISBN 0-8274-4182-7). R West.

ITALIAN WOOD-ENGRAVINGS

see Wood-Engravings, Italian

ITALIANS IN AUSTRALIA

Cresciani, Gianfranco. Fascism, Anti-Fascism & Italians in Australia: 1922-1945. LC 78-73567. (Illus.). 262p. 1981. text ed. 26.95 (ISBN 0-7081-1158-0, 0094, Pub. by ANUP Australia). Bks Australia.

Huber, Rina. From Pasta to Pavlova: A Comparative Study of Italian Settlers in Sydney & Griffith. 1977. 19.95x (ISBN 0-7022-1410-8). U of Queensland Pr.

ITALIANS IN ENGLAND

Dorris, George E. Paolo Rolli & the Italian Circle in London, 1715-1744. (Studies in Italian Literature: No. 2). (Orig.). 1967. pap. text ed. 40.75x (ISBN 90-2790-329-8). Mouton.

Einstein, Lewis D. Italian Renaissance in England. LC 77-143671. (Research & Source Works Ser.: No. 26). 1971. Repr. of 1903 ed. 26.50 (ISBN 0-8337-1027-3). B Franklin.

Rudman, Harry. Italian Nationalism & English Letters. LC 72-182707. Repr. of 1940 ed. 17.50 (ISBN 0-404-05450-1). AMS Pr.

Wicks, Margaret C. Italian Exiles in London, Eighteen Sixteen to Eighteen Forty-Eight. facs. ed. LC 68-16987. (Essay Index Reprint Ser). 1937. 17.00 (ISBN 0-8369-0994-1). Arno.

ITALIANS IN FOREIGN COUNTRIES

Boissevain, Jeremy. The Italians of Montreal. LC 74-17921. (Italian American Experience Ser). (Illus.). 104p. 1975. Repr. 9.50x (ISBN 0-405-06394-6). Arno.

Briani, Vittorio. Italian Immigrants Abroad: A Bibliography on the Italian Experience Outside Italy in Europe, the Americas, Australia, & Africa. LC 79-11239. 1979. 25.00 (ISBN 0-87917-069-7). Blaine Ethridge.

Caroli, Betty B., et al, eds. The Italian Immigrant Woman in North America. 1978. 8.00 (ISBN 0-686-25729-4). Am Italian.

Cornelisen, Ann. Strangers & Pilgrims. (McGraw-Hill Paperbacks Ser.). 324p. 1981. pap. 5.95 (ISBN 0-07-013192-9). McGraw.

Foerster, Robert F. Italian Emigration of Our Times. LC 69-18774. (American Immigration Collection Ser., No. 1). 1969. Repr. of 1919 ed. 16.50 (ISBN 0-405-00522-9). Arno.

--Italian Emigration of Our Times. LC 68-15121. (With a new preface by Francesco Cordasco). 1968. Repr. of 1919 ed. 15.00 (ISBN 0-8462-1104-1). Russell.

ITALIANS IN THE UNITED STATES

see also Italian Americans

Assimilation of the Italian Immigrant: An Original Anthology. LC 74-17919. (Italian American Experience Ser). (Illus.). 332p. 1975. Repr. 10.00x (ISBN 0-405-06392-X). Arno.

Bohme, Frederick G. A History of the Italians in New Mexico. LC 74-17920. (Italian American Experience Ser). (Illus.). 304p. 1975. 19.00x (ISBN 0-405-06393-8). Arno.

Brown, Kenny L. The Italians in Oklahoma. LC 79-23342. (Newcomers to a New Land Ser.: Vol. 4). (Illus.). 96p. (Orig.). 1980. pap. 2.95 (ISBN 0-8061-1624-2). U of Okla Pr.

Caliaro, Marco & Francesconi, Mario. John Baptist Scalabrini: Apostle to Emigrants. Zizzamia, Alba I., tr. from It. LC 76-44922. (Illus.). 1977. lib. bdg. 15.00x (ISBN 0-913256-24-2, Dist. by Ozer). Ctr Migration.

Caso, Adolph. America's Italian Founding Fathers. 1975. 10.00 (ISBN 0-8283-1610-4). Branden.

Child, Irvin L. Italian or American? The Second Generation in Conflict. LC 70-121999. 208p. 1970. Repr. of 1943 ed. 11.00 (ISBN 0-8462-1369-9). Russell.

Cinel, Dino. From Italy to San Francisco: The Immigrant Experience. Date not set. price not set. Stanford U Pr.

Cordasco, Francesco. The Italian-American Experience. new ed. LC 74-10922. (Ethnic Bibliographical Guides Ser). (Illus.). xxiii, 183p. 1974. lib. bdg. 14.95 (ISBN 0-89102-028-4). B Franklin.

--Italians in the United States: A Bibliography of Reports, Texts, Critical Studies & Related Materials. LC 78-180898. 1972. 20.00 (ISBN 0-88211-022-5). S A Russell.

Cordasco, Francesco & Bucchioni, Eugene. The Italians: Social Backgrounds of an American Group. LC 74-3151. (Illus.). 1974. lib. bdg. 19.95x (ISBN 0-678-01366-7). Kelley.

Cordasco, Francesco, ed. The Italian Community & Its Language in the United States: The Annual Reports of the Italian Teachers Association. 472p. 1975. 27.50x (ISBN 0-87471-585-7). Rowman.

--La Societa Italiana Di Fronte Alle Prime Migrazioni Di Massa: Italian Society at the Beginnings of the Mass Migrations. LC 74-17954. (Italian American Experience Ser). (Illus.). 524p. 1975. Repr. 29.00x (ISBN 0-405-06423-3). Arno.

--Studies in Italian-American Social History: Essays in Honor of Leonard Covello. (Illus.). 264p. 1975. 27.50x (ISBN 0-87471-705-1). Rowman.

Cornelisen, Ann. Strangers & Pilgrims: The Last Italian Migration. LC 79-3429. 320p. 1980. 12.95 (ISBN 0-03-044285-0). HR&W.

Covello, Leonard. The Social Background of the Italo-American School Child: A Study of the Southern Italian Family Mores and Their Effect on the School Situation in Italy and America. Cordasco, Francesco, ed. xxx, 488p. 1972. Repr. of 1967 ed. 27.50x (ISBN 0-87471-018-9). Rowman.

D'Agostino, Guido. Olives on the Apple Tree. LC 74-17924. (Italian American Experience Ser). 1975. Repr. 17.00x (ISBN 0-405-06397-0). Arno.

De Marco, William M. Ethnics & Enclaves: Boston's Italian North End. Berkhofer, Robert, ed. (Studies in American History & Culture: No. 31). 1981. price not set (ISBN 0-8357-1251-6, Pub. by UMI Res Pr). Univ Microfilms.

Donato, Pietro di. Christ in Concrete. LC 39-10762. 320p. 1975. 8.95 (ISBN 0-672-52161-X); pap. 5.95 (ISBN 0-672-52187-3). Bobbs.

Dondero, Raymond S. The Italian Settlement of San Francisco: Thesis. LC 74-76560. 1974. Repr. of 1950 ed. soft bdg. 8.00 (ISBN 0-88247-284-4). R & E Res Assoc.

Ets, Marie H. Rosa: The Life of an Italian Immigrant. LC 70-110658. 1970. 10.95x (ISBN 0-8166-0574-2). U of Minn Pr.

Gallo, Patrick J. Ethnic Alienation: The Italian-Americans. LC 72-9915. 254p. 1974. 14.50 (ISBN 0-8386-1244-X). Fairleigh Dickinson.

Gambino, Richard. Blood of My Blood: The Dilemma of the Italian Americans. LC 73-11705. 360p. 1974. 4.50 (ISBN 0-686-76996-1). Doubleday.

--Blood of My Blood, the Dilemma of the Italian-Americans. 400p. 1975. pap. 4.50 (ISBN 0-385-07564-2, Anch). Doubleday.

Gans, Herbert J. Urban Villagers. LC 62-15362. 1965. pap. text ed. 7.95 (ISBN 0-02-911120-X). Free Pr.

Grossman, Ronald. Italians in America. rev. ed. LC 66-10149. (In America Bks.). (Illus.). (gr. 5-11). 1979. PLB 6.95g (ISBN 0-8225-0202-X). Lerner Pubns.

Gumina, Deanna P. The Italians of San Francisco, Eighteen Fifty to Nineteen Thirty: (Gli Italiani Di San Francisco, 1850 to 1930) dual language ed. Are, Ennio T., tr. LC 77-89342. 1978. pap. text ed. 9.95x (ISBN 0-913256-28-5, Dist. by Ozer). Ctr Migration.

Iorizzo, John L. Italian Immigration & the Impact of the Padrone System. Cordasco, Francesco, ed. LC 80-866. (American Ethnic Groups Ser.). 1981. lib. bdg. 25.00x (ISBN 0-405-13429-0). Arno.

The Italian American Experience, 39 vols. (Illus.). 1975. 725.00 set (ISBN 0-405-06390-3). Arno.

The Italians of New York City. LC 72-166660. 1938. 32.00 (ISBN 0-403-02215-0). Somerset Pub.

LoGatto, A. F. The Italians in America: A Chronology & Factbook. LC 72-7427. 160p. 1972. 8.50 (ISBN 0-379-00503-4). Oceana.

Lopreato, Joseph. Italian Americans. (Orig.). 1970. pap. text ed. 5.95 (ISBN 0-394-30374-1, RanC). Random.

Lord, Eliot. The Italians in America. 1970. Repr. of 1905 ed. 12.00 (ISBN 0-685-40315-7). R & E Res Assoc.

Lord, Eliot, et al. The Italian in America. facsimile ed. LC 71-130557. (Select Bibliographies Reprint Ser). Repr. of 1905 ed. 16.00 (ISBN 0-8369-5530-7). Arno.

Lovrich, Nicholas P. Yugoslavs & Italians in San Pedro: Political Culture & Civic Involvement. LC 77-75809. 173p. 1977. softcover 8.00 (ISBN 0-918660-01-7). Ragusan Pr.

McBride, Paul. Italians in America: An Interdisciplinary Bibliography. 1975. 2.00 (ISBN 0-686-21892-2). Am Italian.

Mangano, Antonio. Sons of Italy: A Social & Religious Study of the Italians in America. LC 75-180613. (Illus., With a new forward by Francesco Cordasco). 1972. Repr. of 1917 ed. 14.00 (ISBN 0-8462-1621-3). Russell.

--Sons of Italy: A Social & Religious Study of the Italians in America. LC 75-145488. (American Immigration Library). xii, 264p. 1971. Repr. of 1917 ed. lib. bdg. 14.50x (ISBN 0-89198-020-2). Ozer.

Mangione, Jerre. Mount Allegro: A Memoir of Italian American Life. 320p. 1981. 20.00x (ISBN 0-231-05331-2, Pub. by Morningside); pap. 7.95x (ISBN 0-231-05330-4, Pub by Morningside). Columbia U Pr.

Nelli, Humbert S. The Italians in Chicago, 1880-1930: A Study in Ethnic Mobility. (Urban Life in America Ser.). (Illus.). 320p. 1973. pap. text ed. 4.50x (ISBN 0-19-501674-2). Oxford U Pr.

--The Italians in Chicago, 1880-1930: A Study in Ethnic Mobility. (Urban Life in America Ser.). (Illus.). 320p. 1973. pap. text ed. 4.50x (ISBN 0-19-501674-2). Oxford U Pr.

Nicandri, David. The Italians of Washington State. LC 77-80592. (Illus.). pap. 5.00 (ISBN 0-917048-08-3). Wash St Hist Soc.

Rolle, Andrew F. Immigrant Upraised: Italian Adventurers & Colonists in an Expanding America. LC 68-10302. (Illus.). 1968. 17.95x (ISBN 0-8061-0810-X). U of Okla Pr.

Salvemini, Gaetano. Italian Fascist Activities in the United States. Cannistraro, Philip V., intro. by. LC 76-44920. 1977. lib. bdg. 15.00x (ISBN 0-913256-23-4, Dist. by Ozer). Ctr Migration.

Sandler, Gilbert. The Neighborhood. LC 74-75118. (Illus.). 96p. 1974. 5.95 (ISBN 0-910254-06-0); pap. 3.95 (ISBN 0-910254-07-9). Bodine.

Sartorio, Enrico C. Social & Religious Life of Italians in the United States. LC 73-13520. 1974. Repr. of 1918 ed. 13.50x (ISBN 0-678-01364-0). Kelley.

Scarpaci, Jean, ed. The Interaction of Italians & Jews in America. 1974. 4.00 (ISBN 0-686-21891-4). Am Italian.

Scarpaci, Jean A. Italian Immigrants in Louisiana's Sugar Parishes: Recruitment, Labor Conditions, & Community Relations, 1880-1910. Cordasco, Fransecso, ed. LC 80-890. (American Ethnic Groups Ser.). (Illus.). 1981. lib. bdg. 35.00x (ISBN 0-405-13451-7). Arno.

Schiavo, Giovanni. The Italians in America Before the Revolution. 1976. 15.00 (ISBN 0-911574-03-4). Vigo Pr.

Tait, Joseph W. Some Aspects of the Effect of the Dominant American Culture Upon Children of Italian Born Parents. LC 72-81351. (Illus.). Repr. of 1942 ed. lib. bdg. 10.00x (ISBN 0-678-00919-8). Kelley.

--Some Aspects of the Effect of the Dominant American Culture Upon Children of Italian-Born Parents. LC 77-177729. (Columbia University. Teachers College. Contributions to Education: No. 866). Repr. of 1942 ed. 17.50 (ISBN 0-404-55866-6). AMS Pr.

Tomasi, Lydio F., ed. The Italian in America: The Progressive View, 1891-1914. rev. ed. LC 72-80258. (Illus.). 221p. 1978. pap. text ed. 9.95x (ISBN 0-913256-03-X, Dist. by Ozer). Ctr Migration.

Tomasi, S. M., ed. Perspectives in Italian Immigration & Ethnicity. LC 77-74178. 1977. pap. text ed. 9.95x (ISBN 0-913256-26-9, Dist. by Ozer). Ctr Migration.

Tomasi, Silvano M. & Engel, Madeline H. The Italian Experience in the United States. 1970. pap. 9.95x (ISBN 0-913256-01-3, Dist. by Ozer). Ctr Migration.

Ulin, Richard O. The Italo-American Student in the American Public School. LC 74-17957. (Italian American Experience Ser). (Illus.). 226p. 1975. 18.00x (ISBN 0-405-06426-8). Arno.

Villari, Luigi. Gli Stati Uniti d'America et l'Emigrazione Italiana: The United States & Italian Immigration. LC 74-17959. (Italian American Experience Ser). (Illus.). 326p. 1975. Repr. 18.00x (ISBN 0-405-06428-4). Arno.

Whyte, William F. Street Corner Society: The Social Structure of an Italian Slum. rev. ed. LC 55-5152. (Illus.). 1955. 15.00x (ISBN 0-226-89538-6); pap. 4.95x (ISBN 0-226-89539-4). U of Chicago Pr.

Williams, Phyllis H. South Italian Folkways in Europe & America. LC 69-16768. (Illus.). 1969. Repr. of 1938 ed. 8.50 (ISBN 0-8462-1322-2). Russell.

W.P.A. Federal Writers Project. Italians of New York: A Survey. LC 69-18793. (American Immigration Collection Ser., No. 1). (Illus.). 1969. Repr. of 1938 ed. 10.00 (ISBN 0-405-00542-3). Arno.

Wright, Carroll D. Italians in Chicago: A Social & Economic Study. LC 72-129420. (American Immigration Collection, Ser. 2). 1970. Repr. of 1897 ed. 20.00 (ISBN 0-405-00574-1). Arno.

ITALIC INSCRIPTIONS

see Inscriptions, Italic

ITALIC LANGUAGES AND DIALECTS

see also Etruscan Language; Latin Language; Venetic Language

Conway, Robert S. Italic Dialects, 2 Vols. 1967. Repr. of 1897 ed. Set. 80.25 (ISBN 3-4870-1709-1). Adler.

ITALIC WRITING

see Writing, Italic

ITALO-ETHIOPIAN WAR, 1935-1936

Asante, S. K. Pan African Protest: West Africa & the Italo-Ethiopian Crisis, 1934-41. (Legon History Ser.). (Illus.). 1977. text ed. 22.00x (ISBN 0-582-64194-2). Longman.

Baer, George W. Coming of the Italian-Ethiopian War. 1967. 20.00x (ISBN 0-674-14450-3). Harvard U Pr.

--Test Case: Italy, Ethiopia & the League of Nations. new ed. LC 76-20293. (Publications Ser.: No. 159). 384p. 1977. 15.95 (ISBN 0-8179-6591-2). Hoover Inst Pr.

Berkeley, George F. Campaign of Adowa & the Rise of Menelik. LC 76-76477. (Illus.). Repr. of 1902 ed. 20.75x (ISBN 0-8371-1132-3, Pub. by Negro U Pr). Greenwood.

Del Boca, Angelo. Ethiopian War: 1935-1941. Cummins, P. D., tr. LC 71-79562. 1969. 9.50x (ISBN 0-226-14217-5). U of Chicago Pr.

Feis, Herbert. Three International Episodes: Seen from E. A. Orig. Title: Seen from E. 1966. pap. 1.85 (ISBN 0-393-00351-5, Norton Lib). Norton.

Hardie, Frank. The Abyssinian Crisis. 320p. 1974. 18.50 (ISBN 0-208-01435-7, Archon). Shoe String.

Harris, Brice, Jr. The United States & the Italo-Ethiopian Crisis. 1964. 12.50x (ISBN 0-8047-0243-8). Stanford U Pr.

Verich, Thomas W. The European Powers & the Italo-Ethiopian War, 1935-1936: A Diplomatic Study. 1980. 24.95 (ISBN 0-89712-012-4). Documentary Pubns.

ITALY

see also names of cities, towns and geographic areas in Italy

Bishop-Kalla, P. M. Italian Railways. 5.95 (ISBN 0-7153-5168-0). David & Charles.

Ledeen, Michael A. Italy in Crisis. LC 77-72055. (The Washington Papers: No. 43). 80p. 1977. 4.00 (ISBN 0-8039-0792-3). Sage.
Nichols, Peter. Italia, Italia. 1974. 8.95 (ISBN 0-316-60630-8, Pub. by Atlantic Monthly Pr). Little.
Pacifici, Sergio. Italia: Vita E Cultura. 1970. text ed. 13.95x (ISBN 0-394-30463-2, RanC). Random.
Piano d'Azione Come e Stato Approvato dal Convegno Internazionale "l'avvenire delle Alpi". (It.). 1974. pap. 2.50x (ISBN 2-88032-053-4, IUCN55, IUCN). Unipub.
Pulgram, Ernst. Tongues of Italy, Prehistory & History. Repr. of 1958 ed. lib. bdg. 24.75x (ISBN 0-8371-2438-7, PUTI). Greenwood.
Regional Problems & Policies in OECD Countries: Vol. 1, France, Italy, Ireland, Denmark, Sweden, Japan. 1976. 7.00x (ISBN 92-64-11486-6). OECD.
Stael-Holstern, Anne L. Corinne: Or, Italy. Hill, Isabel, tr. LC 77-162890. (Bentley's Standard Novels: No. 24). Repr. of 1833 ed. 17.00 (ISBN 0-404-54424-X). AMS Pr.
Stych, F. S. How to Find Out About Italy. LC 70-123271. 1970. 21.00 (ISBN 0-08-015810-2). Pergamon.
Thayer, William R. Italica: Studies in Italian Life & Letters. facs. ed. LC 77-90684. (Essay Index Reprint Ser). 1908. 17.00 (ISBN 0-8369-1214-4). Arno.
Underwood, F. M. United Italy. LC 79-110927. 1970. Repr. of 1912 ed. 14.50 (ISBN 0-8046-0909-8). Kennikat.
Werner, A. The Humour of Italy. Repr. of 1893 ed. lib. bdg. 30.00 (ISBN 0-8495-5902-2). Arden Lib.
Zariski, R. Italy: The Politics of Uneven Development. LC 78-187769. 1972. pap. text ed. 8.50 (ISBN 0-03-079820-5, HoltC). HR&W.

ITALY–ANTIQUITIES

Alicu, D. & Nemes, E. Roman Lamps from Ulpia Traiana Sarmizegetusa. 1977. 20.00x (ISBN 0-904531-62-7, Pub. by BAR). State Mutual Bk.
Ashby, Thomas. The Roman Campagna in Classical Times. LC 78-12509. (Illus.). 1979. Repr. of 1970 ed. lib. bdg. 15.75x (ISBN 0-313-21115-9, ASRC). Greenwood.
Barker, Graeme. Landscape & Society: Prehistoric Central Italy. (Studies in Archaeology). 288p. 1981. 33.50 (ISBN 0-12-078650-8). Acad Pr.
Barker, Graeme & Hodges, Richard, eds. Archaeology & Italian Society: Prehistoric, Roman & Medeival Studies. 342p. 1981. 70.00x (ISBN 0-86054-120-7, Pub. by BAR). State Mutual Bk.
Blake, H. M., et al. Papers in Italian Archaeology One: Recent Research in Prehistoric, Classical & Medieval Archaeology. 1978. 80.00x (ISBN 0-86054-012-X, Pub. by BAR). State Mutual Bk.
Brown, A. C. Ancient Italy: Before the Romans. 100p. 1979. 15.00x (ISBN 0-900090-65-0, Pub. by Ashmolean Mus Oxford). State Mutual Bk.
Conway, Robert S., et al. Prae-Italic Dialects, 3 Vols. 1967. Repr. of 1933 ed. Set. 175.00 (ISBN 3-4870-1889-6). Adler.
Greece & Italy in the Classical World. 336p. 1979. 36.00x (ISBN 0-9506584-0-5). State Mutual Bk.
Guido, Margaret. Southern Italy: An Archaeological Guide. Daniel, Glyn, ed. LC 72-85245. (Illus.). 1973. 16.00 (ISBN 0-8155-5011-1, NP). Noyes.
Hanson, W. S. & Keppie, L. J. Roman Frontier Studies, Nineteen Seventy-Nine: Papers Presented to the Twelfth International Congress of Roman Frontier Studies. 1980. 160.00x (ISBN 0-86054-080-4, Pub. by BAR). State Mutual Bk.
Herbert, Kevin. Greek & Latin Inscriptions in the Brooklyn Museum. LC 72-139772. (Wilbour Monographs: No. 4). (Illus.). 1972. 8.00 (ISBN 0-913696-13-7). Bklyn Mus.
Hutchinson, G. E., et al. Ianula: An Account of the History & Development of the Lago Di Monterosi, Latium, Italy. LC 70-111462. (Transactions Ser.: Vol. 60, Pt. 4). (Illus.). 1970. pap. 2.50 (ISBN 0-87169-604-5). Am Philos.
Johnson, Jotham. Inscriptions: Republican Magistri. (Excavations at Minturnae Ser.: Vol. 2). (Illus.). 138p. 1933. soft bound 7.00 (ISBN 0-686-11906-1). Univ Mus of U PA.
--Monuments of the Republican Forum. (Excavations at Minturnae Ser.: Vol. 1). (Illus.). 122p. 1935. soft bound 10.00 (ISBN 0-686-11905-3). Univ Mus of U PA.
Kilmer, Martin F. The Shoulder Bust in Sicily & South Central Italy: A Catalogue & Materials for Dating. (Studies in Mediterranean Archaeology Ser.: No. LI). (Illus.). 1977. pap. text ed. 49.00x (ISBN 91-85058-75-0). Humanities.
MacKendrick, Paul. The Mute Stones Speak; The Story of Archaeology in Italy. (Illus.). 384p. 1976. pap. 6.95 (ISBN 0-393-00805-3, Norton Lib). Norton.
Paget, R. F. & Daniel, Glyn, eds. Central Italy: An Archaeological Guide. LC 72-85330. (Illus.). 1973. 16.00 (ISBN 0-8155-5009-X, NP). Noyes.
Randall-MacIver, David. The Iron Age in Italy. LC 74-9221. (Illus.). 243p. 1974. Repr. of 1927 ed. lib. bdg. 27.00x (ISBN 0-8371-7633-6, RAIA). Greenwood.
--Italy Before the Romans. LC 76-145874. (Illus.). 159p. 1972. Repr. of 1928 ed. lib. bdg. 11.00x (ISBN 0-8154-0426-3). Cooper Sq.
Small, A. Monte Irsi, Southern Italy: The Canadian Excavations in the Iron Age & Roman Sites 1971-1972. 1977. 25.00x (ISBN 0-904531-66-X, Pub. by BAR). State Mutual Bk.
Toller, Hugh. Roman Lead Coffins & Ossuaria in Britain. 1977. 10.00x (ISBN 0-904531-73-2, Pub. by BAR). State Mutual Bk.
Trendall, A. D. & Cambitoglou, A. The Red-Figured Vases of Apulia, Vol. I. (Monographs on Classical Archaeology). (Illus.). 1978. 79.00x (ISBN 0-19-813218-2). Oxford U Pr.
Venturi, Abraham. The Most Illustrious Dead Cities of Italy. (Illus.). 1980. 37.85 (ISBN 0-930582-54-3). Gloucester Art.
Whatmough, Joshua. Foundations of Roman Italy. LC 73-122989. (World History Ser., No. 48). 1970. Repr. of 1937 ed. lib. bdg. 43.95 (ISBN 0-8383-1122-9). Haskell.

ITALY–BIBLIOGRAPHY

Cordasco, Francesco. Italian Mass Emigration: The Exodus of a Latin People--A Bibliographical Guide to the "Bollettino Dell'Emigrazione, 1902-1927. (Illus.). 307p. 1980. 47.50x (ISBN 0-8476-6283-7). Rowman.
Harvard University Center for Italian Renaissance Studies at Villa I Tatti (Florence, Italy) Catalogues of the Berenson Library of the Harvard University Center for Italian Renaissance Studies at Villa I Tatti, Florence, Italy, 4 vols. 1973. lib. bdg. 415.00 (ISBN 0-8161-0973-7). G K Hall.
Harvard University Library. Italian History & Literature: Classification Schedule - Author & Title Listing, 2 vols. LC 74-78747. (Widener Library Shelflist: No. 51-52). 1975. Set. text ed. 90.00x (ISBN 0-674-46955-0). Harvard U Pr.
Pubblicita in Italia, 1979-1980. (Illus.). 260p. (Italian.). 1979. 47.50 (ISBN 0-910158-62-2). Art Dir.
Sapori, Armando. Italian Merchant in the Middle Ages. 1970. pap. text ed. 3.95x (ISBN 0-393-09956-3, NortonC). Norton.
Stych, F. S. How to Find Out About Italy. LC 70-123271. 1970. 21.00 (ISBN 0-08-015810-2). Pergamon.

ITALY–BIOGRAPHY

Avery, C. The New Century Italian Renaissance Encyclopedia. 1972. 42.95 (ISBN 0-13-612051-2, Spec). P-H.
Caccamo, Domenico. Eretici Italiani in Moravia, Polonia, Transilvania (1558-1611) LC 72-3474. (Corpus Reformatorum Italicorum & Biblioteca Ser.). (Illus.). 286p. (Latin & It.). 1970. pap. 17.50 (ISBN 0-87580-511-6). N Ill U Pr.
Caponetto, Salvatore, ed. Benedetto Da Mantova: Beneficio Di Cristo. LC 72-3471. (Corpus Reformatorum Italicorum & Biblioteca Ser.). (Illus.). 554p. (Latin & It.). 1972. 40.00x (ISBN 0-87580-035-1). N Ill U Pr.
Caso, Adolph. They Too Made America Great. 175p. 1978. 12.50 (ISBN 0-8283-1699-6). Dante U Am.
De La Sizeranne, Robert. Celebrities of the Italian Renaissance in Florence & in the Louvre. facsimile ed. Jeffery, J. E., tr. LC 73-93354. (Essay Index Reprint Ser). 1926. 22.00 (ISBN 0-8369-1302-7). Arno.
Ginzburg, Carlo, ed. I Costituti Di Don Pietro Manelfi. LC 72-3473. (Corpus Reformatorum Italicorum & Biblioteca Ser.). (Illus.). 100p. 1970. pap. 10.00 (ISBN 0-87580-510-8). N Ill U Pr.
Gonzales, Manuel G. Andrea Costa & the Rise of Socialism in the Romagna. LC 79-6771. 419p. 1980. text ed. 21.75 (ISBN 0-8191-0952-5); pap. text ed. 13.75 (ISBN 0-8191-0953-3). U Pr of Amer.
Groeg, Otto J. Who's Who in Italy. 3rd rev ed. (Who's Who Ser.). 600p. 1980. 126.00x (ISBN 3-921220-16-5, Pub. by Who's Who Germany). Standing Orders.
Hare, Christopher. The Most Illustrious Ladies of the Italian Renaissance. 367p. 1972. Repr. of 1907 ed. 12.50 (ISBN 0-87928-026-3). Corner Hse.
Mattingly, Garrett, et al. Renaissance Profiles. Plumb, J. H., ed. pap. 3.95x (ISBN 0-06-131162-6, TB1162, Torch). Har-Row.
Nicholson, Robert L. Tancred: A Study of His Career & Work. LC 79-29847. Repr. of 1940 ed. 22.50 (ISBN 0-404-15425-5). AMS Pr.
Pettas, William A. The Giunti of Florence. LC 79-25059. 351p. 1980. 45.00 (ISBN 0-9600094-0-X). B M Rosenthal Inc.
Rotondo, Antonio, ed. Camillo Renato: Opere, Documenti E Testimonianze. LC 72-3454. (Corpus Reformatorum Italicorum & Biblioteca Ser.). (Illus.). 380p. (Latin & It.). 1968. 25.00 (ISBN 0-87580-034-3). N Ill U Pr.
Silvan, Matthew. Lazarus, Come Out! The Story of My Life. Moran, Hugh, ed. Giannini, Vera, tr. from It. LC 80-82599. Orig. Title: Quella Violenza Di Dio. 224p. (Orig.). 1981. pap. 5.95 (ISBN 0-911782-36-2). New City.

ITALY–CHURCH HISTORY

Brown, George K. Italy & the Reformation to 1550. LC 70-139908. 1971. Repr. of 1933 ed. 16.00 (ISBN 0-8462-1590-X). Russell.

ITALY–CIVILIZATION

Boulting, William. Tasso & His Times. LC 68-24953. (World History Ser., No. 48). 1969. Repr. of 1907 ed. lib. bdg. 54.95 (ISBN 0-8383-0915-1). Haskell.
Burckhardt, Jacob. Civilization of the Renaissance in Italy, 2 Vols. (Illus.). Set. 16.00 (ISBN 0-8446-1775-X). Peter Smith.
--Civilization of the Renaissance in Italy, 2 Vols. Vol. 1. pap. 3.50 (ISBN 0-06-090459-3, CN459, CN); Vol. 2. pap. 3.50 (ISBN 0-06-090460-7, CN460, CN). Har-Row.
Cagno, Michael. Italian Review & Culture. 1977. pap. 3.95x (ISBN 0-913298-02-6). S F Vanni.
Cultural Policy in Italy. (Studies & Documents on Cultural Policies). 81p. (Orig.). 1972. pap. 5.00 (ISBN 92-3-100921-4, UNESCO). Unipub.
Kent, Maxwell. A Comparative Analysis of the Italians & the Jews: The Two People Who Contributed the Most to the Civilization of Mankind with Strange & Unexpected Conclusions. (Illus.). 1977. 47.75 (ISBN 0-89266-056-2). Am Classical Coll Pr.
Martines, Lauro. Power & Imagination: City-States in Renaissance Italy. LC 78-11666. (Illus.). 1979. 15.95 (ISBN 0-394-50112-8). Knopf.
Sforza, Carlo. Real Italians: A Study of European Psychology. LC 42-14340. Repr. of 1942 ed. 14.50 (ISBN 0-404-05758-6). AMS Pr.
Steel, Ronald, ed. Italy. (Reference Shelf Ser: Vol. 35, No. 6). 1963. 6.25 (ISBN 0-8242-0078-0). Wilson.
Walsh, J. J. What Civilization Owes to Italy. 75.00 (ISBN 0-87968-361-9). Gordon Pr.
Winwar, Frances. The Land & People of Italy. rev. ed. LC 79-38309. (Portraits of the Nations Ser.). (Illus.). (gr. 6 up). 1972. 8.95 (ISBN 0-397-31300-4). Lippincott.

ITALY–COLONIES

Berkeley, George F. Campaign of Adowa & the Rise of Menelik. LC 76-76477. (Illus.). Repr. of 1902 ed. 20.75x (ISBN 0-8371-1132-3, Pub. by Negro U Pr). Greenwood.
Great Britain Foreign Office Historical Section. Spanish & Italian Possessions: Independent States. LC 74-79816. (Illus.). Repr. of 1920 ed. 19.25x (ISBN 0-8371-1473-X, Pub. by Negro U Pr). Greenwood.
Rennell, Francis J. British Military Administration of Occupied Territories in Africa During the Years of 1941-1947. Repr. of 1948 ed. lib. bdg. 27.50x (ISBN 0-8371-4319-5, REBM). Greenwood.

ITALY–DESCRIPTION AND TRAVEL

Amfitheatrof, Erik. The Enchanted Ground: Americans in Italy, 1760-1980. 256p. 1980. 14.95 (ISBN 0-316-03700-1). Little.
Arnold, Howard P. European Mosaic. LC 72-39709. (Essay Index Reprint Ser.). Repr. of 1864 ed. 16.00 (ISBN 0-8369-2740-0). Arno.
Bagot, Richard. The Italian Lakes. 1977. lib. bdg. 59.95 (ISBN 0-8490-2086-7). Gordon Pr.
Banti, Marco, ed. Italy in Colour. LC 73-155752. (Illus.). 254p. 1972. pap. 22.50x (ISBN 0-8002-0834-X). Intl Pubns Serv.
Bartlett, Vernon. Central Italy. (Batsford Countries of Europe Ser). 216p. 1972. 9.95 (ISBN 0-8038-1170-5). Hastings.
Belloc, Hillare. The Path to Rome. 1981. pap. text ed. 5.95 (ISBN 0-89526-884-1). Regnery-Gateway.
Blashfield, Edwin H. & Wilbour, Evangeline. Italian Cities, 2 vols. Repr. of 1900 ed. Set. 30.00 (ISBN 0-8482-7389-3). Norwood Edns.
Brody, Elaine & Brook, Claire. The Music Guide to Italy. LC 78-6846. (Music Guides Ser.). 1978. 10.00 (ISBN 0-396-07436-7). Dodd.
Cesaresco, Evelyn M. Glimpses of Italian Society in the Eighteenth Century from the Journey' of Mrs. Piozzi. 1892. Repr. 25.00 (ISBN 0-8274-2415-9). R West.
Chamberlain, Narcissa G. & Chamberlain, Naricisse. Flavor of Italy. (Illus.). 1965. 9.95 (ISBN 0-8038-2248-0). Hastings.
Dal Maso, Leonardo B. The Villa of Ippolito II D'Este at Tivoli. (Italia Artistica Ser.). (Orig.). 1978. pap. 7.00x (ISBN 0-8002-0026-8). Intl Pubns Serv.
Emmons, Frederick E. & Huntington, T. W., Jr., eds. Traveler's Book of Verse. LC 77-108582. (Granger Index Reprint Ser). 1928. 21.00 (ISBN 0-8369-6110-2). Arno.
Fattorusso, J., ed. Wonders of Italy. 16th rev. ed. 1974. 45.00 (ISBN 0-685-12054-6). Heinman.
Feist, Aubrey. The Italian Lakes. (Batsford Countries Ser.). Date not set. 10.95 (ISBN 0-8038-3398-9). Hastings.
Fernandez, Dominique. The Mother Sea: Travels in South Italy, Sardinia & Sicily. Callum, Michael, tr. 236p. 1967. 5.95 (ISBN 0-8090-7100-2). Hill & Wang.
Garrick, David. Journal of David Garrick Describing His Visit to France & Italy in 1763. Stone, G. W., Jr., ed. 1939. pap. 6.00 (ISBN 0-527-32560-0). Kraus Repr.
Gautier, Theophile. Journeys in Italy. Vermilye, Daniel B., tr. 1902. 20.00 (ISBN 0-8274-2637-2). R West.
Goldring, Douglas. Gone Abroad: A Story of Travel, Chiefly in Italy & the Balearic Isles. 1925. 25.00 (ISBN 0-89984-013-2). Century Bookbindery.
Goldstein, Frances. Children's Treasure Hunt Travel Guide to Italy. LC 79-67280. (Illus., Orig.). (gr. k-12). 1980. pap. 5.95 (ISBN 0-933334-01-X). Paper Tiger Pap.
Guido, Margaret. Southern Italy: An Archaeological Guide. Daniel, Glyn, ed. LC 72-85245. (Illus.). 1973. 16.00 (ISBN 0-8155-5011-1, NP). Noyes.
Harvard Student Agencies. Let's Go, Italy: The Budget Guide 1981 to 1982 Edition. (Illus.). 412p. 1981. pap. 5.95 (ISBN 0-525-93145-7). Dutton.
Highet, Gilbert. Poets in a Landscape. LC 78-12220. 1979. Repr. of 1962 ed. lib. bdg. 25.00x (ISBN 0-313-21208-2, HIPL). Greenwood.
Hunt, Leigh. Lord Byron & Some of His Contemporaries. LC 24-23123. Repr. of 1828 ed. 25.00 (ISBN 0-404-03419-5). AMS Pr.
James, Henry. Italian Hours. LC 77-1427. 1977. Repr. of 1959 ed. lib. bdg. 21.75x (ISBN 0-8371-8474-6, JAIH). Greenwood.
--Italian Hours: Travel Essays. LC 59-5420. 1979. pap. 2.95 (ISBN 0-394-17077-6, B421, BC). Grove.
Lawrence, D. H. D. H. Lawrence & Italy: Twilight in Italy, Sea & Sardinia, Etruscan Places. 1972. 8.95 (ISBN 0-670-27158-6). Viking Pr.
--Twilight in Italy. 1958. 5.00 (ISBN 0-670-73590-6). Viking Pr.
Lechat, Paul. Italy. 1959. 20.00 (ISBN 0-686-17244-2). Scholars Ref Lib.
Mattioli, Renzo & Pellucci, Emanuele. Looking at Fiesole. (Italia Artistica Ser.: No. 23). (Illus., Orig.). 1977. pap. 13.00x (ISBN 0-8002-0027-6). Intl Pubns Serv.
Montaigne, Michel de & Dedeyan, Charles. Journal de Voyage en Italie. 520p. 1946. 13.50 (ISBN 0-686-54777-2). French & Eur.
Moreau, Daniel, ed. L' Italie. (Collection monde et voyages). (Illus.). 159p. (Fr.). 1973. 21.00x (ISBN 2-03-053102-2, 3898). Larousse.
Morton, H. V. A Traveller in Southern Italy. LC 74-86851. (Illus.). 1969. 10.00 (ISBN 0-396-05991-0). Dodd.
Norton, Charles E. Notes of Travel & Study in Italy. 1971. Repr. of 1860 ed. 19.50 (ISBN 0-384-41975-5). Johnson Repr.
O'Faolain, Sean. A Summer in Italy. 5.95 (ISBN 0-8159-6831-0). Devin.
Pereira, Anthony. Naples, Pompeii & Southern Italy. 1977. 24.00 (ISBN 0-7134-0815-4, Pub. by Batsford England). David & Charles.
Pillement, Georges. Unknown Italy, 3 vols. Incl. Vol. 1. The Italian Lakes & the Alpine Regions. 221p. 1965; Vol. 2. The Cities of Central Italy. 239p. 1966; Vol. 3. Southern Italy. 251p. 1968. LC 66-34260. (Unknown Guides Ser). (Illus.). 12.50x ea. Intl Pubns Serv.
Porter, J. The Making of the Central Pennines. 160p. 1980. 20.85x (ISBN 0-903485-80-X, Pub. by Allan Pubs England). State Mutual Bk.
Ricciardi, Lorenzo. The Voyage of the Mir-El-Lah. LC 80-54201. (Illus.). 256p. 1981. 19.95 (ISBN 0-670-74831-5). Viking Pr.
Sandys, George. A Relation of a Journey Begun Anno Domini 1610, 4 bks. LC 72-6028. (English Experience Ser.: No. 554). (Illus.). 316p. 1973. Repr. of 1615 ed. 53.00 (ISBN 90-221-0554-7). Walter J Johnson.
Senior, Nassau W. Journals Kept in France & Italy from 1848 to 1852. LC 70-126608. (Europe 1815-1945 Ser.). 654p. 1973. Repr. of 1871 ed. lib. bdg. 59.50 (ISBN 0-306-70055-7). Da Capo.
Shelley, Mary. Rambles in Germany & Italy in Eighteen Forty, Eighteen Forty-Two, & Eighteen Forty-Three, 2 vols. LC 75-26765. Repr. of 1844 ed. Set. lib. bdg. 75.00 (ISBN 0-8414-7826-0). Folcroft.
Sitwell, Osbert. Discursions on Travel, Art & Life. 1925. lib. bdg. 14.75x (ISBN 0-8371-4336-5, SIDI). Greenwood.
--Winters of Content, & Other Discursions on Mediterranean Art & Travel. LC 75-35029. (Illus.). 1978. Repr. of 1950 ed. lib. bdg. 25.00x (ISBN 0-8371-8570-X, SIWOC). Greenwood.

Smollett, Tobias. Tobias Smollett: Travels Through France & Italy. facsimile ed. Felsenstein, Frank, ed. 45.00x (ISBN 0-19-812611-5). Oxford U Pr.

Stanley, Arthur. Under Italian Skies. 1977. Repr. of 1950 ed. 20.00 (ISBN 0-89984-122-8). Century Bookbindery.

Stendhal. Pages d'Italie. facsimile ed. 1932. 35.00 (ISBN 0-686-55076-5). French & Eur.

Stendhal, pseud. Rome, Naples et Florence. 8.95 (ISBN 0-685-35020-7). French & Eur.

Stendhal. Voyages en Italia: Rome, Naples et Florence (1817 et 1826), L'Italie en 1818, Promenades dans Rome, etc. 1920p. 46.95 (ISBN 0-686-56574-6). French & Eur.

--Voyages en Italie. 1920p. 1973. 45.00 (ISBN 0-686-55085-4). French & Eur.

Sterling Publishing Company Editors. Italy in Pictures. LC 66-16199. (Visual Geography Ser). (Illus., Orig.). (gr. 4-12). 1966. PLB 4.99 (ISBN 0-8069-1071-2); pap. 2.95 (ISBN 0-8069-1070-4). Sterling.

Stych, F. S. How to Find Out About Italy. LC 70-123271. 1970. 21.00 (ISBN 0-08-015810-2). Pergamon.

Tollinchi, Esteban. Arte y Sensualidad: Cincuenta Imagenes Del Hombre y De la Tierra. LC 79-19403. (Illus.). 710p. 1981. write for info. (ISBN 0-8477-2111-6); pap. write for info. (ISBN 0-8477-2112-4). U of PR Pr.

Winwar, Frances. The Land & People of Italy. rev. ed. LC 79-38309. (Portraits of the Nations Ser.). (Illus.). (gr. 6 up). 1972. 8.95 (ISBN 0-397-31300-4). Lippincott.

ITALY–DESCRIPTION AND TRAVEL–GUIDEBOOKS

All Pisa. (Illus.). 64p. 1973. pap. 7.50x (ISBN 0-8002-0652-5). Intl Pubns Serv.

Baedecker. The Baedecker Guide to Italy. (Baedecker Travel Ser.). 1981. 19.95 (ISBN 0-13-055905-9); pap. 11.95 (ISBN 0-13-055897-4). P-H.

Barsali, G. Looking at Pisa. LC 77-459528. (Italia Artistica Ser). (Illus.). 96p. 1974. 12.50x (ISBN 0-8002-1683-0). Intl Pubns Serv.

Blue Guide - Italy, Northern. 1977. 29.95 (ISBN 0-528-84599-3); pap. 22.95 (ISBN 0-528-84600-0). Rand.

Bristow, Philip. Round the Italian Coast. 256p. 1980. 15.00x (ISBN 0-245-52648-X, Pub. by Nautical England). State Mutual Bk.

Chiarelli, Renzo. Rimini & San Marino: Practical Illustrated Guide. (Illus.). 128p. 1973. 6.00x (ISBN 0-8002-1925-2). Intl Pubns Serv.

Daly, Dorothy. Italy. LC 79-89187. (A Rand McNally Pocket Guide). (Illus., Orig.). 1980. pap. 3.95 (ISBN 0-528-84291-9). Rand.

Dollarwise Guide to Italy, 1981-82. 408p. 1981. pap. 5.95 (ISBN 0-671-43033-5). Frommer-Pasmantier.

Evans, Craig. On Foot Through Europe: A Trail Guide to Italy, Greece & E. Europe. Whitney, Stephen, ed. (Illus.). 374p. 1980. lib. bdg. 10.95 (ISBN 0-933710-19-4); pap. 5.95 (ISBN 0-933710-18-6). Foot Trails.

Florence, Pisa, & Siena. LC 73-177329. (Illus.). 80p. 1972. pap. 7.50x (ISBN 0-8002-1425-0). Intl Pubns Serv.

Fodor's Budget Italy 1980. (Fodor's Modern Travel Guides Ser.). 1980. pap. 4.95 (ISBN 0-679-00492-0). McKay.

Fodor's Budget Italy, 1981. 1981. Traveltex 4.95 (ISBN 0-679-00651-6). McKay.

Fodor's Italy, 1981. 1980. 12.95 (ISBN 0-679-00701-6); pap. 9.95 (ISBN 0-679-00702-4). McKay.

Harvard Student Agencies. Let's Go, Italy: The Budget Guide 1980 to 1981 Edition. (Illus.). 1980. pap. 5.50 (ISBN 0-525-93089-2). Dutton.

Italy. 9th ed. 1981. write for info. Michelin.

Micheletti, Emma. Masterpieces of Pitti Palace. (Illus.). 64p. 1973. pap. 7.50x (ISBN 0-8002-1708-X). Intl Pubns Serv.

Michelin Green Travel Guide: Italy. (Illus., Fr. & Eng.). 4.95 (ISBN 0-685-11379-5). French & Eur.

Michelin Guides & Maps. Michelin Red Guide to Italy. (Red Guide Ser.). 1981. 14.95 (ISBN 2-06-006701-4). Michelin.

Michelin Guides & Maps Dept. Michelin Green Guide to Italy. 8th ed. (Green Guide Ser.). (Avail. in Fr., Ger., Ital.). pap. 7.95 (ISBN 2-06-121401-0). Michelin.

Nagel's Encyclopedia Guide: French & Italian Riviera. (Illus.). 640p. 1973. 23.00 (ISBN 2-8263-0045-8). Masson Pub.

Paget, R. F. & Daniel, Glyn, eds. Central Italy: An Archaeological Guide. LC 72-85330. (Illus.). 1973. 16.00 (ISBN 0-8155-5009-X, NP). Noyes.

Rose, Harold. Your Guide to Northern Italy. LC 65-50296. (Your Guide Ser). (Illus.). 1965. 5.25x (ISBN 0-8002-0783-1). Intl Pubns Serv.

Sabin, Francis E. Classical Associations of Places in Italy. 1921. 45.00 (ISBN 0-8274-3977-6). R West.

Whinney, Chris. Backpacker's Italy. (Backpacker's Guide Ser.). (Illus.). 128p. Date not set. pap. 9.95 (ISBN 0-933982-21-6). Bradt Ent.

ITALY–ECONOMIC CONDITIONS

Abulafia, D. The Two Italies. LC 76-11069. (Cambridge Studies in Medieval Life & Thought Ser.: No. 9). (Illus.). 1977. 49.50 (ISBN 0-521-21211-1). Cambridge U Pr.

Cohen, Jon S. Finance & Industrialization in Italy, 1894-1914. Bruchey, Stuart, ed. LC 77-81825. (Dissertations in European Economic History Ser.). (Illus.). 1977. lib. bdg. 18.00x (ISBN 0-405-10777-3). Arno.

Derossi, Flavia. The Technocratic Illusion: A Study of Managerial Power in Italy. Lobello, Susan, tr. from Italian. 225p. 1981. 25.00 (ISBN 0-87332-185-5). M E Sharpe.

Dickinson, Robert E. The Population Problem of Southern Italy: An Essay in Social Geography. LC 76-49087. (Illus.). 1977. Repr. of 1955 ed. lib. bdg. 14.00x (ISBN 0-8371-9337-0, DIPP). Greenwood.

Evans, Robert H. Life & Politics in a Venetian Community. LC 76-21256. (International Studies). 1977. text ed. 15.95x (ISBN 0-268-01256-3); pap. 4.95 (ISBN 0-268-01257-1). U of Notre Dame Pr.

Gerschenkron, Alexander. Economic Backwardness in Historical Perspective: A Book of Essays. LC 62-17217. 1962. 26.00x (ISBN 0-674-22600-3, Belknap Pr). Harvard U Pr.

Hardman, J. B. S. Labor at the Rubicon. Hardman, Virginia M., ed. LC 72-92552. 173p. 1972. 8.95x (ISBN 0-8147-3364-6). NYU Pr.

Hildebrand, George H. Growth & Structure in the Economy of Modern Italy. LC 65-24450. 1965. 22.50x (ISBN 0-674-36450-3). Harvard U Pr.

--Postwar Italy: A Study in Economic Contrasts. 1957. 1.00 (ISBN 0-89215-047-5). U Cal LA Indus Rel.

Hughes, H. Stuart. United States & Italy. 3rd, enl. ed. LC 79-63706. (American Foreign Policy Library). 1979. 17.50x (ISBN 0-674-92545-9). Harvard U Pr.

Kogan, Norman. A Political History of Postwar Italy: From the Old to the New Center Left. 200p. 1981. 22.95 (ISBN 0-03-056653-3). Praeger.

LaPalombara, Joseph. Italy: The Politics of Planning. (National Planning Ser.: No. 7). (Orig.). 1966. pap. 3.95x (ISBN 0-8156-2093-4). Syracuse U Pr.

Lutz, Vera. Italy, a Study in Economic Development. LC 75-3738. (Illus.). 342p. 1975. Repr. of 1962 ed. lib. bdg. 18.75x (ISBN 0-8371-8055-4, LUIT). Greenwood.

Luzzalto, Gino. Economic History of Italy: From the Fall of the Roman Empire to the Beginning of the 16th Century. Jones, Philip, tr. 1961. 8.25 (ISBN 0-7100-1767-7). Routledge & Kegan.

McArdle, Frank. Altopascio: A Study in Tuscan Rural Society, 1587-1784. LC 76-53261. (Cambridge Studies in Early Modern History). (Illus.). 1978. 34.95 (ISBN 0-521-21619-2). Cambridge U Pr.

McGuire, Constantine E. Italy's International Economic Position. LC 27-582. 1971. Repr. of 1926 ed. 38.00 (ISBN 0-384-34804-1, S877). Johnson Repr.

Martellaro, Joseph A. Economic Development in Southern Italy 1950-1960. 1965. 11.95 (ISBN 0-8132-0297-3, Pub. by Cath U Pr). Cath U Pr.

Mountjoy, Alan B. Mezzogiorno. (Problem Regions of Europe Ser). (Illus.). 1973. pap. 7.95x (ISBN 0-19-913100-7). Oxford U Pr.

Pallanti, Giuseppe. La Maremma Senese Nella Crisi Del Seicento. Bruchey, Stuart, ed. LC 80-2820. (Dissertations in European Economic History II). (Illus.). 1981. lib. bdg. 18.00x (ISBN 0-405-14004-5). Arno.

Pareto, Vilfredo. Liberte Economique et les Evenements D'Italie. (Research & Source Works Ser.: No. 199). 1968. Repr. of 1898 ed. 19.50 (ISBN 0-8337-2670-6). B Franklin.

Pucci, Eugenio. Palazzo Vecchio & Piazza Della Signoria. (Illus.). 64p. 1972. pap. 7.50x (ISBN 0-8002-1777-2). Intl Pubns Serv.

Rodgers, Allan. Economic Development in Retrospect: The Italian Model & Its Significance for Regional Planning in Market Oriented Economies. LC 78-20862. (Scripta Series in Geography). 1979. 16.75 (ISBN 0-470-26628-7). Halsted Pr.

Salvemini, Gaetano. Under the Axe of Fascism. LC 68-9589. 1970. Repr. of 1936 ed. 25.00 (ISBN 0-86527-201-8). Fertig.

Sapori, Armando. Italian Merchant in the Middle Ages. 1970. pap. text ed. 3.95x (ISBN 0-393-09956-3, NortonC). Norton.

Saville, Lloyd B. Regional Economic Development in Italy. LC 67-21707. 1967. 11.75 (ISBN 0-8223-0149-0). Duke.

Schmidt, Carl T. Plough & the Sword. LC 38-3030. Repr. of 1938 ed. 16.50 (ISBN 0-404-05608-3). AMS Pr.

Southard, Frank, Jr. The Finances of European Liberation: With Special Reference to Italy. Wilkins, Mira, ed. LC 78-3950. (International Finance Ser.). 1978. Repr. of 1946 ed. lib. bdg. 14.00x (ISBN 0-405-11251-3). Arno.

Steel, Ronald, ed. Italy. (Reference Shelf Ser: Vol. 35, No. 6). 1963. 6.25 (ISBN 0-8242-0078-0). Wilson.

Templeman, Donald C. The Italian Economy. 400p. 1981. 26.95 (ISBN 0-03-057612-1). Praeger.

U. S. Mutual Security Agency. The Structure & Growth of the Italian Economy. LC 78-109870. (Illus.). v, 165p. Repr. of 1953 ed. lib. bdg. 15.00x (ISBN 0-8371-4361-6, SGIE). Greenwood.

Webster, Richard A. Industrial Imperialism in Italy, 1908-1915. LC 74-76393. 480p. 1975. 36.50x (ISBN 0-520-02724-8). U of Cal Pr.

Welk, William G. Fascist Economic Policy. LC 68-10954. (Illus.). 1968. Repr. of 1938 ed. 11.00 (ISBN 0-8462-1056-8). Russell.

Willis, F. Roy. Italy Chooses Europe. 1971 (ISBN 0-19-501383-2). pap. 5.95x (ISBN 0-19-501384-0). Oxford U Pr.

Yver, Georges. Commerce et les Marchands Dans l'Italie Meridionale Au Treizieme et Au Quatorzieme Siecles. (Research & Source Works Ser.: No. 299). (Fr). 1968. Repr. of 1903 ed. 31.50 (ISBN 0-8337-3909-3). B Franklin.

ITALY–EMIGRATION AND IMMIGRATION

Caroli, Betty B. Italian Repatriation from the United States, 1900-1914. LC 73-85825. (Illus.). 117p. 1974. pap. 9.95x (ISBN 0-913256-10-2, Dist. by Ozer). Ctr Migration.

Cordasco, Francesco. Italian Mass Emigration: The Exodus of a Latin People--A Bibliographical Guide to the "Bollettino Dell'Emigrazione, 1902-1927. (Illus.). 307p. 1980. 47.50x (ISBN 0-8476-6283-7). Rowman.

Fenton, Edwin. Immigrants & Unions. LC 74-17926. (Italian American Experience Ser). 672p. 1975. 43.00x (ISBN 0-405-06399-7). Arno.

Foerster, Robert F. Italian Emigration of Our Times. LC 69-18774. (American Immigration Collection Ser., No. 1). 1969. Repr. of 1919 ed. 16.50 (ISBN 0-405-00522-9). Arno.

--Italian Emigration of Our Times. LC 68-15121. (With a new preface by Francesco Cordasco). 1968. Repr. of 1919 ed. 15.00 (ISBN 0-8462-1104-1). Russell.

Iorizzo, John L. Italian Immigration & the Impact of the Padrone System. Cordasco, Francesco, ed. LC 80-866. (American Ethnic Groups Ser.). 1981. lib. bdg. 25.00x (ISBN 0-405-13429-0). Arno.

Stella, Antonio. Some Aspects of Italian Immigration to the United States. LC 74-17956. (Italian American Experience Ser). 178p. 1975. Repr. 14.00x (ISBN 0-405-06425-X). Arno.

ITALY–FOREIGN RELATIONS

Borgese, Giuseppe A. Goliath: The March of Fascism. LC 78-63653. (Studies in Fascism: Ideology & Practice). Repr. of 1937 ed. 37.50 (ISBN 0-404-16909-0). AMS Pr.

Bosworth, R. J. Italy, the Least of the Great Powers. LC 78-18090. (Illus.). 532p. 1980. 69.50 (ISBN 0-521-22366-0). Cambridge U Pr.

Case, Lynn M. Franco-Italian Relations, 1860-1865. LC 75-121289. (BCL Ser. I). Repr. of 1932 ed. 24.50 (ISBN 0-404-01405-4). AMS Pr.

Cassels, Alan. Italian Foreign Policy, Nineteen Eighteen to Nineteen Forty-Five: A Guide to Research & Research Materials. Kimmich, Christoph M., intro. by. LC 80-53890. 275p. 1981. lib. bdg. 17.50 (ISBN 0-8420-2177-9). Scholarly Res Inc.

--Mussolini's Early Diplomacy. LC 72-90944. 1970. 26.50 (ISBN 0-691-05179-8). Princeton U Pr.

Glanville, James L. Italy's Relations with England, 1896-1905. LC 78-64153. (Johns Hopkins University. Studies in the Social Sciences. Fifty-Second Ser. 1934: 1). Repr. of 1934 ed. 18.50 (ISBN 0-404-61263-6). AMS Pr.

Halperin, S. William. Diplomat Under Stress. LC 63-13065. 1963. 7.00x (ISBN 0-226-31441-3). U of Chicago Pr.

Lowe, C. J. & Marzari, F. Italian Foreign Policy. (Foreign Politics of the Great Powers Ser.). 1975. 40.00x (ISBN 0-7100-7987-7). Routledge & Kegan.

Nelli, Humbert, ed. The United States & Italy: The First Two Hundred Years. 1978. 6.50 (ISBN 0-686-22952-5). Am Italian.

Tamagna, Frank M. Italy's Interests & Policies in the Far East. LC 75-30116. (Institute of Pacific Relations). Repr. of 1941 ed. 11.50 (ISBN 0-404-59565-0). AMS Pr.

Thayer, John A. Italy & the Great War: Politics & Culture, 1870-1914. (Illus.). 480p. 1964. 37.50 (ISBN 0-299-03280-9). U of Wis Pr.

Toscano, Mario. Alto Adige-South Tyrol: Italy's Frontier with the German World. Carbone, George A., ed. & tr. from It. LC 75-11349. 304p. 1976. 21.00x (ISBN 0-8018-1567-3). Johns Hopkins.

--Origins of the Pact of Steel. LC 67-24276. 464p. 1968. 25.00x (ISBN 0-8018-0635-6). Johns Hopkins.

Toynbee, Arnold J. & Boulter, V. M. Abyssinia & Italy. Repr. of 1936 ed. pap. 45.00 (ISBN 0-384-61100-1). Johnson Repr.

Turco, Emanuele. The Bilateral Treaties in Force Between the U.S.A. & Italy, 2 vols. 1270p. 1975. text ed. 95.00x (ISBN 0-8377-1201-7). Rothman.

Villari, Luigi. Italian Foreign Policy Under Mussolini. 1956. 7.95 (ISBN 0-8159-5820-X). Devin.

ITALY–HISTORY

see also Austro-Italian War, 1866; Italo-Ethiopian War, 1935-1936; Pavia, Battle of, 1525

Ady, Julia M. Baldassare Castiglione: The Perfect Courtier, His Life & Letters, 1478-1529, 2 Vols. LC 75-154138. (BCL Ser.: No. I). Repr. of 1908 ed. Set. 62.50 (ISBN 0-404-09206-3). AMS Pr.

--Beatrice D'Este, Duchess of Milan, 1475-1497. LC 71-154137. Repr. of 1905 ed. 27.50 (ISBN 0-404-09204-7). AMS Pr.

--Isabella D'Este, Marchioness of Mantua, 1474-1539, 2 Vols. LC 79-154139. Repr. of 1907 ed. Set. 49.50 (ISBN 0-404-09214-4). AMS Pr.

Albrecht-Carrie, Rene. Italy from Napoleon to Mussolini. 9.50 (ISBN 0-8446-1518-8). Peter Smith.

--Italy from Napoleon to Mussolini. LC 49-50178. 302p. 1950. pap. 6.00x (ISBN 0-231-08508-7). Columbia U Pr.

Alfieri, Dino. Dictators Face to Face. Moore, David, tr. LC 78-755. (Illus.). x, 307p. 1978. Repr. of 1954 ed. lib. bdg. 21.75x (ISBN 0-313-20285-0, ALDF). Greenwood.

Armstrong, Edward. Italian Studies. facs. ed. Ady, C. M., ed. LC 67-30172. (Essay Index Reprint Ser). 1934. 18.00 (ISBN 0-8369-0158-4). Arno.

Askew, William C. Europe Italy's Acquisition of Libya, Nineteen Eleven to Nineteen Twelve. LC 73-93628. (Illus.). xi, 317p. Date not set. Repr. of 1942 ed. cancelled (ISBN 0-8462-1783-X). Russell.

Barclay, G. The Rise & Fall of the New Roman Empire. 1973. 8.95 (ISBN 0-312-68320-0). St Martin.

Beales, Derek. The Risorgimento & the Unification of Italy. (Historical Problems: Studies & Documents). 1971. text ed. 18.95x (ISBN 0-04-904004-9); pap. text ed. 8.95x (ISBN 0-04-904005-7). Allen Unwin.

Becker, Marvin B. Medieval Italy: Constraints & Creativity. LC 80-8376. 256p. 1981. 17.50x (ISBN 0-253-15294-1). Ind U Pr.

Berardis, Vincenzo. Italy & Ireland in the Middle Ages. 1977. lib. bdg. 59.95 (ISBN 0-8490-2089-1). Gordon Pr.

Berkeley, C. F. Ialy in the Making, 3 vols. Incl. Vol. 1. Eighteen Fifteen to Eighteen Forty-Six. Repr. of 1932 ed. 38.50 (ISBN 0-521-07427-4); Vol. 2. Eighteen Forty-Six to Eighteen Forty-Eight. Repr. of 1936 ed. 44.50 (ISBN 0-521-07428-2); Vol. 3. January 1, Eighteen Forty-Eight to November 16, Eighteen Forty-Eight. Repr. of 1940 ed. 53.50 (ISBN 0-521-07429-0). (Illus.). 1969. Cambridge U Pr.

Bowsky, William M. Henry Seventh in Italy: The Conflict of Empire & City-State, 1310-1313. LC 74-10014. (Illus.). 301p. 1974. Repr. of 1960 ed. lib. bdg. 20.50x (ISBN 0-8371-7656-5, BOHS). Greenwood.

Bromley, J. S. & Goodwin, A., eds. A Select List of Works on Europe & Europe Overseas, 1715-1815. LC 73-13036. 132p. 1974. Repr. of 1956 ed. lib. bdg. 15.00x (ISBN 0-8371-7102-4, BRLW). Greenwood.

Brunt, P. A. Italian Manpower 225 B.C.-A.D. 14. 1971. 74.00x (ISBN 0-19-814283-8). Oxford U Pr.

Buonarroti, Philippe, ed. Giornale Patriottico Di Corsica: April to November, 1790. (Babeuf & Babouvism Ser.). 1976. Repr. lib. bdg. 72.00x (ISBN 0-8287-1377-4). Clearwater Pub.

Butler, William F. Lombard Communes. LC 68-25226. (World History Ser., No. 48). 1969. lib. bdg. 62.95 (ISBN 0-8383-0923-2). Haskell.

--Lombard Communes: A History of the Republics of North Italy. LC 69-13847. Repr. of 1906 ed. lib. bdg. 22.75x (ISBN 0-8371-2753-X, BULC). Greenwood.

Callmann, Ellen. Apollonio Di Giovanni. (Oxford Studies in the History of Art & Architecture Ser.). (Illus.). 230p. 1974. 59.00x (ISBN 0-19-817196-X). Oxford U Pr.

Carsten, F. L. The Rise of Facism. 2nd ed. LC 80-51592. 1980. 18.50 (ISBN 0-520-04307-3). U of Cal Pr.

Cartwright, Julia. Beatrice D'Este: Duchess of Milan, 1475-1497; a Study of the Renaissance. LC 73-38345. (Select Bibliographies Reprint Ser.). 1899. 20.00 (ISBN 0-8369-6762-3). Arno.

Cassels, Alan. Fascist Italy. LC 68-9740. (AHM Europe Since 1500 Ser.). (Illus.). 1968. pap. 5.95x (ISBN 0-88295-719-8). Harlan Davidson.
Cesaresco, Evelyn M. Liberation of Italy, 1815-1870. LC 72-2563. (Select Bibliographies Reprint Ser.). 1972. Repr. of 1895 ed. 22.00 (ISBN 0-8369-6850-6). Arno.
Chalandon, Ferdinand. Histoire de la domination normande en Italie et en Sicilie, 2 Vols. 1969. Repr. of 1912 ed. Set. 55.50 (ISBN 0-8337-0514-8). B Franklin.
Church, Frederic C. The Italian Reformers, 1534-1564. LC 73-19934. 429p. 1974. Repr. of 1932 ed. lib. bdg. 25.00x (ISBN 0-374-91595-4). Octagon.
Clark, Martin. Antonio Gramsci & the Revolution That Failed. LC 76-49754. 1977. 25.00x (ISBN 0-300-02077-5). Yale U Pr.
Collison-Morley, Lacy. Italy After the Renaissance: Decadence & Display in the Seventeenth Century. LC 77-173510. (Illus.). 1972. Repr. of 1930 ed. 19.00 (ISBN 0-8462-1563-2). Russell.
Colton, Ethan T. Four Patterns of Revolution. facs. ed. LC 79-121456. (Essay Index Reprint Ser). 1935. 17.00 (ISBN 0-8369-1747-2). Arno.
Conway, Robert S. Ancient Italy & Modern Religion. LC 77-27141. (Hibbert Lectures: 1932). Repr. of 1933 ed. 17.00 (ISBN 0-404-60428-5). AMS Pr.
Coughlan, Robert. World of Michelangelo. (Library of Art). (Illus.). 1966. 15.95 (ISBN 0-8094-0232-7). Time-Life.
Davis, John A., ed. Gramsci & Italy's Passive Revolution. LC 79-53440. (Illus.). 1979. text ed. 27.50x (ISBN 0-06-491609-X). B&N.
De Grand, Alexander J. The Italian Nationalist Association & the Rise of Fascism in Italy. LC 77-24633. 1978. 16.50x (ISBN 0-8032-0949-5). U of Nebr Pr.
Delzell, Charles F. Italy in the Twentieth Century. LC 80-71044. (AHA Pamphlets, 428). 80p. (Orig.). (gr. 9-12). 1981. pap. text ed. 3.50 (ISBN 0-87229-024-7). Am Hist Assn.
Diehl, Charles. Etudes sur l'Administration Byzantine dans l'Exarchat de Ravenne (568-751) LC 60-1146. 421p. 1972. Repr. of 1888 ed. 29.50 (ISBN 0-8337-0854-6). B Franklin.
Evola, Niccolo D. Origini e dottrina del fascismo. LC 79-180385. Repr. of 1935 ed. 18.00 (ISBN 0-404-56121-7). AMS Pr.
F., G. B. A. A Discovery of the Great Subtiltie & Wonderful Wisdom of the Italians. LC 74-80221. (English Experience Ser.: No. 656). 1974. Repr. of 1591 ed. 10.50 (ISBN 90-221-0656-X). Walter J Johnson.
Fisher, Herbert A. Medieval Empire, 2 Vols. LC 72-95147. Repr. of 1898 ed. 34.50 (ISBN 0-404-02398-3). AMS Pr.
Forman, Henry J. Grecian Italy. 1978. Repr. of 1927 ed. lib. bdg. 20.00 (ISBN 0-8492-4601-6). R West.
Gardner, E. Saint Catherine of Siena: A Study in the Religion, Literature & History of the Fourteenth Century in Italy. 1976. lib. bdg. 59.95 (ISBN 0-8490-2557-5). Gordon Pr.
Germino, Dante L. The Italian Fascist Party in Power: A Study in Totalitarian Rule. LC 74-80551. 1971. Repr. 22.50 (ISBN 0-86527-108-9). Fertig.
Goad, Harold E. Franciscan Italy. 1979. Repr. of 1926 ed. lib. bdg. 40.00 (ISBN 0-8495-2034-7). Arden Lib.
Gregorovius, Ferdinand. Lucretia Borgia. LC 68-20226. (Illus.). 401p. 1968. Repr. of 1903 ed. 18.00 (ISBN 0-405-08580-X, Blom Pubns). Arno.
Grew, Raymond. Sterner Plan for Italian Unity: The Italian National Society in the Risorgimento. 1963. 32.50x (ISBN 0-691-05155-0). Princeton U Pr.
Griffith, Gwilym O. Mazzini: Prophet of Modern Europe. LC 78-80552. 1970. Repr. 27.50 (ISBN 0-86527-124-0). Fertig.
Hancock, William K. Ricasoli & the Risorgimento in Tuscany. LC 68-9603. 1969. Repr. of 1926 ed. 22.50 (ISBN 0-86527-171-2). Fertig.
Harpur, Brian. Impossible Victory, a Personal Account to the Battle for the River Po. (Illus.). 1981. 19.95 (ISBN 0-88254-518-3). Hippocrene Bks.
Hay, Denys. The Church in Italy in the Fifteenth Century. LC 76-47409. (Birkbeck Lectures: 1971). 1977. 27.50 (ISBN 0-521-21532-3). Cambridge U Pr.
Hearder, H. & Waley, Daniel P. Short History of Italy. (Illus.). 1963. pap. 9.95 (ISBN 0-521-09394-5, 394). Cambridge U Pr.
Hodgkin, Thomas. Italy & Her Invaders, 376-814 A. D, 8 vols. LC 67-16005. (Illus., Repr. of 1880-1889 eds.). 1967. Set. 175.00 (ISBN 0-8462-0835-0). Russell.
Hoffman, Elizabeth. The Sources of Mortality Changes in Italy Since Unification. Bruchey, Stuart, ed. LC 80-2811. (Dissertations in European Economic History II). (Illus.). 1981. lib. bdg. 25.00x (ISBN 0-405-13995-0). Arno.
Hollway-Calthrop, H. C. Petrarch: His Life & Times. LC 75-187413. (Illus.). xi, 319p. 1972. Repr. of 1907 ed. lib. bdg. 13.75x (ISBN 0-8154-0406-9). Cooper Sq.
Homo, Leon P. Primitive Italy & the Beginnings of Roman Imperialism. LC 75-18359. (Illus.). 370p. 1975. Repr. of 1927 ed. lib. bdg. 19.75x (ISBN 0-8371-8326-X, HOPIT). Greenwood.
Ilardi, Vincent, ed. Dispatches with Related Documents of Milanese Ambassadors in France (Mar. 11- June 29 1466, Vol. III. Fata, Frank J., tr. LC 68-20933. 445p. 1980. 35.00 (ISBN 0-87580-069-6). N Ill U Pr.
--Dispatches with Related Documents of Milanese Ambassadors in France & Burgundy 1450-1483. Incl. Vol. I 1450-1460. 390p. 1970 (ISBN 0-8214-0067-3); Vol. II 1460-1461. 486p. 1971 (ISBN 0-8214-0082-7). LC 68-20933. 35.00 ea. N Ill U Pr.
Imerti, Arthur D. Vincenzo Catalani: Neapolitan Jacobin, Jurist, Reformer 1769-1843. (Illus.). 1976. 8.50 (ISBN 0-87291-079-2). Coronado Pr.
Jordan, Edouard. Origines De la Domination Angevine En Italie, 2 Vols. 1967. Repr. of 1909 ed. 50.50 (ISBN 0-8337-1875-4). B Franklin.
Keene, Frances. Neither Liberty nor Bread. LC 76-86029. 1969. Repr. of 1940 ed. 15.00 (ISBN 0-8046-0618-8). Kennikat.
King, Bolton. A History of Italian Unity: Being a Political History of Italy from 1814 to 1871, 2 Vols. rev. ed. LC 66-24716. 1967. Repr. of 1924 ed. Set. 20.00 (ISBN 0-8462-1024-X). Russell.
Krekic, Barisa. Dubrovnik, Italy & the Balkans in the Late Middle Ages. 332p. 1980. 75.00x (ISBN 0-86078-070-8, Pub. by Variorum England). State Mutual Bk.
Lange, Peter & Tarrow, Sidney, eds. Italy in Transition: Conflict & Consensus. 186p. 1980. 25.00x (ISBN 0-7146-3147-7, F Cass Co). Biblio Dist.
Larner, John. Culture & Society in Italy: Twelve Ninety to Fourteen Twenty. 1971. 38.00 (ISBN 0-7134-1521-5, Pub. by Batsford England). David & Charles.
--Italy in the Age of Dante & Petrarch: 1216-1380. LC 79-41509. (Longman History of Italy Ser.). (Illus.). 278p. 1980. text ed. 43.00x (ISBN 0-582-48366-2). Longman.
McArdle, Frank. Altopascio: A Study in Tuscan Rural Society, 1587-1784. LC 76-53261. (Cambridge Studies in Early Modern History). (Illus.). 1978. 34.95 (ISBN 0-521-21619-2). Cambridge U Pr.
Mack Smith, Denis. Italy: A Modern History. rev. & enl. ed. LC 69-15851. (History of the Modern World Ser.). (Illus.). 1969. 12.50x (ISBN 0-472-07051-7). U of Mich Pr.
Mark-Alan, R. Whitecoats Under Fire: With the Italian Espedition Corps in Russia During World War II. LC 71-170800. (Illus.). 1972. 6.50 (ISBN 0-685-37762-8). Helios.
Marraro, Howard. American Opinion on the Unification of Italy, 1846-1861. LC 78-108116. Repr. of 1932 ed. 26.00 (ISBN 0-404-00606-X). AMS Pr.
Marriott, John A. The Makers of Modern Italy: Napoleon to Mussolini. LC 74-30842. (Illus.). 228p. 1975. Repr. of 1931 ed. lib. bdg. 14.75x (ISBN 0-8371-7936-X, MAMA). Greenwood.
Martin, George. Red Shirt & the Cross of Savoy: The Story of Italy's Risorgimento, 1748-1871. LC 68-8279. (Illus.). 1969. 15.00 (ISBN 0-396-05908-2). Dodd.
Martines, Lauro. Power & Imagination: City-States in Renaissance Italy. LC 79-22471. (Illus.). 1980. pap. 6.95 (ISBN 0-394-74384-9, Vin). Random.
Meek, Christine E. The Commune of Lucca Under Pisan Rule, 1342-1369. 1980. cloth 11.00 (ISBN 0-910956-69-3, SAM6); pap. 5.00 (ISBN 0-686-64887-0). Medieval Acad.
Missiroli, Mario. What Italy Owes to Mussolini. 1976. lib. bdg. 59.95 (ISBN 0-8490-2817-5). Gordon Pr.
Muir, Dorothy E. Machiavelli & His Times. LC 74-30928. (Illus.). 262p. 1976. Repr. of 1936 ed. lib. bdg. 22.75 (ISBN 0-8371-7889-4, MUMA). Greenwood.
Munro, Ion S. Through Fascism to World Power: A History of the Revolution in Italy. 1976. lib. bdg. 50.00 (ISBN 0-8490-2748-9). Gordon Pr.
--Through Fascism to World Power: History of the Revolution in Italy. facsimile ed. LC 73-164618. (Select Bibliographies Reprint Ser). Repr. of 1933 ed. 30.00 (ISBN 0-8369-5912-4). Arno.
Mussolini, Benito. Memoirs, 1942-1943. Klibanksy, Raymond, ed. Lobb, Frances, tr. from It. xxviii, 320p. 1975. Repr. of 1949 ed. 25.00 (ISBN 0-86527-126-7). Fertig.
Nissen, Heinrich. Italische Landeskunde, 2 vols. in 3. Finley, Moses, ed. LC 79-4997. (Ancient Economic History Ser.). (Ger.). 1980. Repr. of 1902 ed. Set. lib. bdg. 112.00x (ISBN 0-405-12383-3). Arno.
Osheim, Duane J. An Italian Lordship: The Bishopric of Lucca in the Late Middle Ages. (UCLA Center for Medieval & Renaissance Studies: Vol. 11). 1977. 18.50x (ISBN 0-520-03005-2). U of Cal Pr.
Pareto, Vilfredo. The Ruling Class in Italy Before 1900. LC 73-20130. 143p. 1975. Repr. of 1950 ed. 17.50 (ISBN 0-86527-176-3). Fertig.
Parmele, Mary P. A Short History of Rome & Italy. Repr. of 1908 ed. 20.00 (ISBN 0-685-43324-2). Norwood Edns.
Petit, Paul. Pax Romana. Willis, James, tr. 1976. 32.50x (ISBN 0-520-02171-1). U of Cal Pr.
Petroselli, Francesco. La Vite: Il Lessico Delvignaiolo Nelle Parlate Della Tuscia Viterbese, Vol. I. (Romanic Goteborg: No. 15). (Illus.). 1978. pap. text ed. 28.75x (ISBN 91-7346-001-X). Humanities.
Powell. Renaissance Italy. (Warwick Press Ser.). (gr. 5 up). 1980. PLB 7.60 (ISBN 0-531-09164-3, B34). Watts.
Ragg, Lonsdale. Dante & His Italy. LC 72-2129. (Studies in Dante, No. 9). (Illus.). 1972. lib. bdg. 46.95 (ISBN 0-8383-1462-7). Haskell.
Randall-MacIver, David. Italy Before the Romans. LC 76-145874. (Illus.). 159p. 1972. Repr. of 1928 ed. lib. bdg. 11.00x (ISBN 0-8154-0426-3). Cooper Sq.
Rath, Reuben J. Fall of the Napoleonic Kingdom of Italy 1814. 1971. lib. bdg. 13.50x (ISBN 0-374-96718-0). Octagon.
Rossi, A. The Rise of Italian Fascism, 1918-1922. 75.00 (ISBN 0-87968-435-6). Gordon Pr.
Saladino, Salvatore. Italy from Unification to 1919: Growth & Decay of a Liberal Regime. LC 75-101945. (AHM Europe Since 1500 Ser.). 1970. pap. text ed. 5.95x (ISBN 0-88295-762-7). Harlan Davidson.
Salvatorelli, Luigi. A Concise History of Italy from Prehistoric Times to Our Own Day. Miall, Bernard, tr. LC 75-41239. Repr. of 1940 ed. 36.00 (ISBN 0-404-14596-5). AMS Pr.
Sarti, Roland. Fascism & the Industrial Leadership in Italy, 1919-1940: A Study in the Expansion of Private Power Under Fascism. LC 79-138636. 1971. 27.50x (ISBN 0-520-01855-9). U of Cal Pr.
Sedgwick, Henry D. A Short History of Italy: 476-1900. 1905. Repr. 30.00 (ISBN 0-685-43463-X). Norwood Edns.
Seton-Watson, Christopher. Italy from Liberalism to Fascism, 1870-1925. (Illus.). 1967. text ed. 65.00 (ISBN 0-416-18940-7). Methuen Inc.
Silone, J. Fontamara. Rawson, J., ed. 290p. 1977. 12.00x (ISBN 0-7190-0662-7, Pub. by Manchester U Pr England). State Mutual Bk.
Sismondi, J. C. De. A History of the Italian Republics. 7.50 (ISBN 0-8446-0912-9). Peter Smith.
Society & Politics in Medieval Italy. 1973. 8.95 (ISBN 0-312-73920-6). St Martin.
Solmi, Arrigo. Making of Modern Italy. LC 78-110924. 1970. Repr. of 1925 ed. 11.50 (ISBN 0-8046-0906-3). Kennikat.
Spriano, Paolo. Occupation of the Factories. Williams, Gwyn A., tr. from Ital. 216p. 1980. text ed. 12.00 (ISBN 0-902818-68-6); pap. 5.95 (ISBN 0-902818-67-8). Pluto Pr.
Sprigge, Cecil J. The Development of Modern Italy. 1969. 19.50 (ISBN 0-86527-043-0). Fertig.
Sprigge, Cecil R. The Development of Modern Italy. Repr. of 1943 ed. 20.00 (ISBN 0-685-43281-5). Norwood Edns.
Sweet, John J. Iron Arm: The Mechanization of Mussolini's Army, 1920-1940. LC 79-6825. (Contributions in Military History: No. 23). (Illus.). xxi, 217p. 1980. lib. bdg. 25.00 (ISBN 0-313-22179-0, SWM/). Greenwood.
Tannenbaum, Edward R. & Noether, Emiliana P., eds. Modern Italy: A Topical History Since 1861. LC 73-20031. 395p. 1974. 15.00x (ISBN 0-8147-8156-X). NYU Pr.
Taylor, Frederick L. The Art of War in Italy, 1494-1529. LC 76-84284. (Illus.). 228p. 1973. Repr. of 1921 ed. lib. bdg. 21.50x (ISBN 0-8371-5025-6, TAWI). Greenwood.
Thayer, William R. The Life & Times of Cavour, 2 Vols. LC 68-9634. (Illus.). 1971. Repr. of 1911 ed. Set. 38.50 (ISBN 0-86527-117-8). Fertig.
Thomas, William. The Historie of Italie. LC 77-7434. (English Experience Ser.: No. 895). 1977. Repr. of 1549 ed. lib. bdg. 43.00 (ISBN 90-221-0895-3). Walter J Johnson.
--History of Italy (1549) Parks, George B., ed. (Documents Ser). 1978. 12.95x (ISBN 0-918016-38-X). Folger Bks.
Trease, Geoffrey. Italian Story. LC 64-16262. (Illus.). 1964. 8.95 (ISBN 0-8149-0221-9). Vanguard.
Treves, Paolo. What Mussolini Did to Us. Isolani, Casimiro T., tr. LC 77-180434. Repr. of 1940 ed. 24.50 (ISBN 0-404-56167-5). AMS Pr.
Trollope, Theodosia. Social Aspects of the Italian Revolution, in a Series of Letters from Florence. LC 71-37728. (Women of Letters Ser). Repr. of 1861 ed. 22.50 (ISBN 0-404-56855-6). AMS Pr.
Underwood, F. M. United Italy. LC 79-110927. 1970. Repr. of 1912 ed. 14.50 (ISBN 0-8046-0909-8). Kennikat.
Vaughan, Herbert M. Studies in the Italian Renaissance. LC 66-25951. Repr. of 1930 ed. 10.50 (ISBN 0-8046-0479-7). Kennikat.
Venturi, Franco. Italy & the Enlightenment: Studies in a Cosmopolitan Century. Woolf, Stuart, ed. LC 72-77153. 302p. 1972. 14.50x (ISBN 0-8147-8752-5). NYU Pr.
Villari, P. Life & Time of Niccolo Machiavelli. LC 68-25275. (World History Ser., No. 48). 1969. Repr. of 1892 ed. lib. bdg. 79.95 (ISBN 0-8383-0175-4). Haskell.
Villari, Pasquale. The Barbarian Invasions of Italy, 2 vols. Villari, Linda, tr. LC 70-153607. Repr. of 1902 ed. Set. 22.50 (ISBN 0-404-09275-6). AMS Pr.
--Life & Times of Girolamo Savonarola. 1888. Repr. 35.00 (ISBN 0-8274-2913-4). R West.
--Life & Times of Niccolo Machiavelli, 2 Vols. Villari, Linda, tr. LC 68-31007. (Illus.). 1968. Repr. of 1892 ed. Set. lib. bdg. 41.00x (ISBN 0-8371-0732-6, VINM). Greenwood.
--Mediaeval Italy from Charlemagne to Henry Seventh. Hulton, C., tr. LC 73-153608. (Illus.). Repr. of 1910 ed. 27.50 (ISBN 0-404-09279-9). AMS Pr.
Violante, Cinzio. La Societa Milanese Nell'eta Precomunale. LC 80-2000. Repr. of 1974 ed. 35.00 (ISBN 0-404-18602-5). AMS Pr.
Walbank, F. W. A Historical Commentary on Polybius: Commentary on Books XIX-XL, Vol. 3. 872p. 1979. text ed. 89.00x (ISBN 0-19-814011-8). Oxford U Pr.
Waley, D. Italian City Republics. (Illus., Orig.). 1969. pap. 3.95 (ISBN 0-07-067805-7, SP). McGraw.
Walker, Mack, ed. Plombieres: Secret Diplomacy & the Rebirth of Italy. (Problems in European History Series). (Orig.). 1968. pap. 4.95x (ISBN 0-19-501096-5). Oxford U Pr.
Whittam, J. R. The Politics of the Italian Army 1861-1918. 1976. 18.50 (ISBN 0-208-01597-3, Archon). Shoe String.
Whyte, Arthur J. Evolution of Modern Italy. (Illus.). 1965. pap. 5.95x (ISBN 0-393-00298-5, Norton Lib). Norton.
Winstantley, Lilian. Othello As the Tragedy of Italy. LC 76-40427. 1924. lib. bdg. 20.00 (ISBN 0-8414-9455-X). Folcroft.
Winwar, Frances. The Land & People of Italy. rev. ed. LC 79-38309. (Portraits of the Nations Ser.). (Illus.). (gr. 6 up). 1972. 8.95 (ISBN 0-397-31300-4). Lippincott.
Wiskemann, Elizabeth. Italy Since Nineteen Forty-Five. LC 78-179497. 1972. 17.95 (ISBN 0-312-43925-3). St. Martin.
Woolf, Stuart. A History of Italy Seventeen Hundred to Eighteen Sixty: The Social Constraints of Political Change. 1979. 49.95x (ISBN 0-416-80880-8). Methuen Inc.
Young, Arthur. Travels in France & Italy. Date not set. 8.95x (ISBN 0-460-00720-3, Evman). Biblio Dist.

ITALY-HISTORY-1849-1870

Beales, Derek. The Risorgimento & the Unification of Italy. (Historical Problems: Studies & Documents). 1971. text ed. 18.95x (ISBN 0-04-904004-9); pap. text ed. 8.95x (ISBN 0-04-904005-7). Allen Unwin.
Blakiston, Noel. The Roman Question. 360p. 1980. 35.00 (ISBN 0-89453-150-6). M Glazier.
Marraro, Howard. American Opinion on the Unification of Italy, 1846-1861. LC 78-108116. Repr. of 1932 ed. 26.00 (ISBN 0-404-00606-X). AMS Pr.
Salvadori, M. Cavour & the Unification of Italy. (Anvil Ser.). 191p. 1961. pap. 4.95 (ISBN 0-685-91059-8, Pub. by Van Nostrand Reinhold). Krieger.
Walker, Mack, ed. Plombieres: Secret Diplomacy & the Rebirth of Italy. (Problems in European History Series). (Orig.). 1968. pap. 4.95x (ISBN 0-19-501096-5). Oxford U Pr.
Whittam, J. R. The Politics of the Italian Army 1861-1918. 1976. 18.50 (ISBN 0-208-01597-3, Archon). Shoe String.

ITALY-HISTORY-SOURCES

Beales, Derek. The Risorgimento & the Unification of Italy. (Historical Problems: Studies & Documents). 1971. text ed. 18.95x (ISBN 0-04-904004-9); pap. text ed. 8.95x (ISBN 0-04-904005-7). Allen Unwin.
Mussolini, Benito. The Fall of Mussolini, His Own Story. Ascoli, Max, ed. Frenaye, Frances, tr. from It. LC 75-2699. 212p. 1975. Repr. of 1948 ed. lib. bdg. 18.00x (ISBN 0-8371-8035-X, MUFM). Greenwood.
Salimbene Ognibene Di Guido Di Adamo. Chronik: Des Salimbene Von Parma Nach der Ausgabe der Monuments Germaniae, 2 Vols. Doren, A., ed. Repr. of 1914 ed. pap. 36.50 set (ISBN 0-384-53125-3). Johnson Repr.

ITALY-INTELLECTUAL LIFE

Collison-Morley, Lacy. Italy After the Renaissance: Decadence & Display in the Seventeenth Century. LC 77-173510. (Illus.). 1972. Repr. of 1930 ed. 19.00 (ISBN 0-8462-1563-2). Russell.

Elkin, Felice. Walter Savage Landor: Studies of Italian Life & Literature. LC 74-8062. 1934. lib. bdg. 10.00 (ISBN 0-8414-3938-9). Folcroft.

Grendler, Paul F. Critics of the Italian World, Fifteen Thirty to Fifteen Sixty: Anton Francesco Doni, Nicolo Franco & Ortensio Lando. LC 69-16112. (Illus.). 296p. 1969. 21.50 (ISBN 0-299-05220-6). U. of Wis Pr.

Maniates, Maria R. Mannerism in Italian Music & Culture, Fifteen Thirty to Sixteen Thirty. LC 78-11236. (Illus.). 1979. 29.50x (ISBN 0-8078-1319-2). U. of NC Pr.

ITALY–JUVENILE LITERATURE

Anno, Mitsumasa. Anno's Italy. LC 79-17649. (Illus.). 48p. 1980. 8.95 (ISBN 0-529-05559-7); PLB 8.99 (ISBN 0-529-05560-0). Philomel.

Clark, Ronald & Clark, Pearla. We Go to Northern Italy. LC 66-9246. (We Go to Ser). (Illus.). 1964. 4.00x (ISBN 0-245-57970-2). Intl Pubns Serv.

Fairclough, Chris. Take a Trip to Italy. (Take a Trip to Ser.). (Illus.). 32p. (gr. 1-3). 1981. lib. bdg. 6.90 (ISBN 0-531-04319-3). Watts.

Leech, Michael. Italy. LC 75-44863. (Macdonald Countries). (Illus.). (gr. 6 up). 1976. PLB 7.95 (ISBN 0-382-06107-1, Pub. by Macdonald Ed). Silver.

ITALY–POLITICS AND GOVERNMENT

Alfieri, Dino. Dictators Face to Face. Moore, David, tr. LC 78-755. (Illus.). x, 307p. 1978. Repr. of 1954 ed. lib. bdg. 21.75x (ISBN 0-313-20285-0, ALDF). Greenwood.

Allum, P. A. Italy: Republic Without Government? LC 73-20230. (Comparative Modern Governments Ser.). (Illus.). 267p. 1974. 10.00x (ISBN 0-393-05517-5); pap. 4.95x (ISBN 0-393-09302-6). Norton.

--Politics & Society in Post-War Naples, 1945-1970. LC 75-174259. (Illus.). 1971. 49.95x (ISBN 0-521-08424-5). Cambridge U Pr.

Arthur, William. Italy in Transition. 469p. 1980. Repr. of 1860 ed. lib. bdg. 50.00 (ISBN 0-89760-005-3). Telegraph Bks.

Baer, George W. Test Case: Italy, Ethiopia & the League of Nations. new ed. LC 76-20293. (Publications Ser.: No. 159). 384p. 1977. 15.95 (ISBN 0-8179-6591-2). Hoover Inst Pr.

Barnes, Samuel Henry. Representation in Italy: Institutionalized Tradition & Electoral Choice. LC 76-51819. (Illus.). 1977. 16.00x (ISBN 0-226-03726-6). U. of Chicago Pr.

Baron, Hans. Crisis of the Early Italian Renaissance: Civic Humanism & Republican Liberty in an Age of Classicism & Tyranny. rev. ed. 1966. 30.00 (ISBN 0-691-05114-3); pap. 9.95 (ISBN 0-691-00752-7). Princeton U Pr.

Bayne, E. A. Four Ways of Politics: State & Nation in Italy, Somalia, Israel, Iran. LC 65-14723. 1965. 7.50 (ISBN 0-910116-60-1). Am U Field.

Bonomi, Ivanoe. From Socialism to Fascism: A Study of Contemporary Italy. LC 78-63652. (Studies in Fascism: Ideology & Practice). 168p. Repr. of 1924 ed. 22.50 (ISBN 0-404-16907-4). AMS Pr.

Borgese, Giuseppe A. Goliath: The March of Fascism. LC 78-63653. (Studies in Fascism: Ideology & Practice). Repr. of 1937 ed. 37.50 (ISBN 0-404-16909-0). AMS Pr.

Camiller, Patrick & Rothschild, Jon, eds. Power & Opposition in Post Revolutionary Societies. 288p. 1980. text ed. 17.50x (ISBN 0-906133-18-1); pap. text ed. 9.25x (ISBN 0-906133-19-X). Humanities.

Carsten, F. L. The Rise of Facism. 2nd ed. LC 80-51592. 1980. 18.50 (ISBN 0-520-04307-3). U of Cal Pr.

Caserta, John S. The Red Brigades. 1978. pap. 1.95 (ISBN 0-532-19196-X). Woodhill.

Cassels, Alan. Mussolini's Early Diplomacy. LC 72-90944. 1970. 26.50 (ISBN 0-691-05179-8). Princeton U Pr.

Chabod, Federico. A History of Italian Fascism. Grindrod, Muriel, tr. from It. 192p. 1975. Repr. of 1963 ed. 21.50 (ISBN 0-86527-095-3). Fertig.

Coppa, Frank J. Planning, Protectionism & Politics in Liberal Italy: Economics & Politics in the Giolittian Age. 1971. 11.95 (ISBN 0-8132-0510-7). Cath U Pr.

Dante Alighieri. De Monarchia. LC 74-147412. (Library of War & Peace; Proposals for Peace: a History). lib. bdg. 38.00 (ISBN 0-8240-0210-5). Garland Pub.

De Grand, Alexander J. The Italian Nationalist Association & the Rise of Fascism in Italy. LC 77-24633. 1978. 16.50x (ISBN 0-8032-0949-5). U of Nebr Pr.

De Grazia, Victoria. The Culture of Consent: Mass Organization of Leisure in Fascist Italy. LC 80-24361. (Illus.). 304p. Date not set. price not set (ISBN 0-521-23705-X). Cambridge U Pr.

Del Bo, Dino. Italian Catholics in Crisis. Bricca, John, tr. 1957. 4.95 (ISBN 0-87462-404-5). Marquette.

Di Palma, Giuseppe. Political Syncretism in Italy: Historical Coalition Strategies & the Present Crisis. LC 78-620042. (Policy Papers in International Affairs Ser.: No. 7). 1978. pap. 2.00x (ISBN 0-87725-507-5). U of Cal Intl St.

DiPalma, Guiseppe. Surviving Without Governing: The Italian Parties in Parliament. LC 75-46035. 1977. 24.50x (ISBN 0-520-03195-4). U of Cal Pr.

Di Renzo, Gordon J. Personality, Power & Politics. (Illus.). 1967. 4.00x (ISBN 0-268-00205-3). U of Notre Dame Pr.

DiScala, Spencer. Dilemmas of Italian Socialism: The Politics of Filippo Turati. LC 79-10274. 1980. lib. bdg. 17.50x (ISBN 0-87023-285-1). U of Mass Pr.

Drake, Richard. Byzantium for Rome: The Politics of Nostalgia in Umbertian Italy, 1878-1900. LC 79-16578. 335p. 1980. 20.00x (ISBN 0-8078-1405-9). U of NC Pr.

Ebenstein, William. Fascist Italy. LC 72-84985. (Illus.). 310p. 1973. Repr. of 1939 ed. 18.00 (ISBN 0-8462-1672-8). Russell.

Evans, Robert H. Life & Politics in a Venetian Community. LC 76-21256. (International Studies). 1977. text ed. 15.95x (ISBN 0-268-01256-3); pap. 4.95 (ISBN 0-268-01257-1). U of Notre Dame Pr.

Ferrero, G. Four Years of Fascism. Dickes, E. W., tr. LC 77-180398. Repr. of 1924 ed. 16.00 (ISBN 0-404-56122-5). AMS Pr.

Field, G. Lowell. Syndical & Corporative Institutions of Italian Fascism. (Columbia University. Studies in the Social Sciences: No. 443). Repr. of 1938 ed. 14.00 (ISBN 0-404-51433-2). AMS Pr.

Freeman, Edward A. History of Federal Government in Greece & Italy. 2nd ed. Bury, J. B., ed. LC 72-39670. (Select Bibliographies Reprint Ser). 1972. Repr. of 1893 ed. 28.25 (ISBN 0-8369-9936-3). Arno.

Fritz, Kurt Von. Pythagorean Politics in Southern Italy. 1973. Repr. lib. bdg. 13.00x (ISBN 0-374-92939-4). Octagon.

Gatt-Rutter, J. A. Writers & Politics in Modern Italy. LC 78-18829. (Writers & Politics Ser.). 1979. 11.50x (ISBN 0-8419-0413-8); pap. text ed. 7.50x (ISBN 0-8419-0416-2). Holmes & Meier.

Giglio, Giovanni. Triumph of Barabbas. Mosbacher, E., tr. LC 74-180401. Repr. of 1937 ed. 24.00 (ISBN 0-404-56125-X). AMS Pr.

Giolitti, Giovanni. Memoirs of My Life. LC 72-80619. 472p. 1973. Repr. of 1923 ed. 16.50 (ISBN 0-86527-127-5). Fertig.

Gramsci, Antonio. Antonio Gramsci: Selections from Political Writings, 1910-1920. LC 76-54252. 1977. 13.50 (ISBN 0-7178-0485-2); pap. 4.50 (ISBN 0-7178-0492-5). Intl Pub Co.

--Antonio Gramsci: Selections from Political Writings, 1921-26. 1978. pap. 6.95 (ISBN 0-7178-0555-7). Intl Pub Co.

Gregor, A. James. Italian Fascism & Developmental Dictatorship. LC 79-83992. 1979. 27.50x (ISBN 0-691-05286-7); pap. 9.75 ltd. ed. (ISBN 0-691-10082-9). Princeton U Pr.

Hentze, Margot. Pre-Fascist Italy: The Rise & Fall of the Parliamentary Regime. LC 70-120628. 1970. Repr. of 1939 ed. lib. bdg. 20.00x (ISBN 0-374-93809-1). Octagon.

Hughes, H. Stuart. United States & Italy. 3rd, enl. ed. LC 79-63706. (American Foreign Policy Library). 1979. 17.50x (ISBN 0-674-92545-9). Harvard U Pr.

Isichei, Elizabeth. The Ibo People & the Europeans. LC 73-82826. 200p. 1973. 18.95 (ISBN 0-312-40355-0). St Martin.

Kertzer, David I. Comrades & Christians. LC 79-15313. (Illus.). 1980. 29.95 (ISBN 0-521-22879-4); pap. 7.95x (ISBN 0-521-29700-1). Cambridge U Pr.

Kogan, Norman. A Political History of Postwar Italy: From the Old to the New Center Left. 200p. 1981. 22.95 (ISBN 0-03-056653-3). Praeger.

Longobardi, Cesare. Land-Reclamation in Italy: Rural Revival in the Building of a Nation. LC 78-180410. (Illus.). Repr. of 1936 ed. 22.75 (ISBN 0-404-56134-9). AMS Pr.

Lovett, Clara M. Giuseppe Ferrari & the Italian Revolution. LC 78-24099. 1979. 19.00x (ISBN 0-8078-1354-0). U of NC Pr.

Machiavelli, Niccolo. The History, Political & Diplomatic Writings of Niccolo Machiavelli, 4 vols. 600.00 (ISBN 0-87968-405-4). Gordon Pr.

Marriott, John A. The Makers of Modern Italy: Mazzini, Cavour & Garibaldi. Repr. of 1961 ed. 30.00 (ISBN 0-685-43353-6). Norwood Edns.

Martines, Lauro. Power & Imagination: City-States in Renaissance Italy. LC 78-11666. (Illus.). 1979. 15.95 (ISBN 0-394-50112-8). Knopf.

Matteotti, Giacomo. The Fascisti Exposed: A Year of Fascist Domination. LC 68-9637. 1969. Repr. of 1924 ed. 14.75 (ISBN 0-86527-064-3). Fertig.

Mazzini, Giuseppe. Selected Writings. Gangulee, N., ed. LC 74-9397. (Illus.). 253p. 1974. Repr. of 1945 ed. lib. bdg. 14.00x (ISBN 0-8371-7664-6, MASW). Greenwood.

Molony, John N. The Emergence of Political Catholicism in Italy: Partito Popolare 1919-1926. 225p. 1977. 17.50x (ISBN 0-87471-943-7). Rowman.

Mussolini, Benito. Mussolini As Revealed in His Political Speeches: November 1914-August 1923. Quaranta Di San Severino, B., ed. LC 75-16288. xxviii, 375p. 1977. Repr. of 1923 ed. 27.50 (ISBN 0-86527-134-8). Fertig.

Noether, Emiliana P. Seeds of Italian Nationalism, 1700-1815. LC 79-94926. (Columbia Univ. Social Science Ser.: No. 570). Repr. of 1951 ed. 14.00 (ISBN 0-404-51570-3). AMS Pr.

Penniman, Howard R., ed. Italy at the Polls: The Parliamentary Elections of 1976. 1977. pap. 8.25 (ISBN 0-8447-3268-0). Am Enterprise.

Roskin, Michael. Other Governments of Europe: Sweden, Spain, Italy, Yugoslavia, E. Germany. 1977. pap. text ed. 7.95 (ISBN 0-13-642959-9). P-H.

Salvemini, Gaetano. The Fascist Dictatorship in Italy. 1967. 27.50 (ISBN 0-86527-063-5). Fertig.

Sarti, Roland. Fascism & the Industrial Leadership in Italy, 1919-1940: A Study in the Expansion of Private Power Under Fascism. LC 79-138636. 1971. 27.50x (ISBN 0-520-01855-9). U of Cal Pr.

Schmidt, Carl T. The Corporate State in Action: Italy Under Fascism. LC 72-85008. 173p. 1973. Repr. of 1939 ed. 12.00 (ISBN 0-8462-1676-0). Russell.

Schneider, Herbert W. The Fascist Government of Italy. LC 75-16856. 173p. 1975. Repr. of 1936 ed. lib. bdg. 15.00x (ISBN 0-8371-8273-5, SCFG). Greenwood.

--Making the Fascist State. LC 67-24597. 1968. Repr. 24.50 (ISBN 0-86527-121-6). Fertig.

Seldes, George H. Sawdust Ceaser: The Untold Story of Mussolini & Fascism. LC 70-180277. Repr. of 1935 ed. 23.50 (ISBN 0-404-56197-7). AMS Pr.

Senior, Nassau W. Journals Kept in France & Italy from 1848 to 1852. LC 70-126608. (Europe 1815-1945 Ser.). 654p. 1973. Repr. of 1871 ed. lib. bdg. 59.50 (ISBN 0-306-70055-7). Da Capo.

Serfaty, Simon & Gray, Lawrence, eds. The Italian Communist Party: Yesterday, Today, & Tomorrow. LC 79-6833. (Contributions in Political Science: No. 46). (Illus.). xiii, 256p. 1980. lib. bdg. 29.95 (ISBN 0-313-20995-2, GIT/). Greenwood.

Silj, Alessandro. Never Again Without a Rifle! The Origins of Italian Terrorism. Attanasio, Salvator, tr. from It. LC 78-23640. Orig. Title: Mai Piu Senza Fucile! 1979. 14.95x (ISBN 0-918294-04-5). Karz Pub.

Smith, Denis M. Mussolini's Roman Empire. 1977. pap. 3.95 (ISBN 0-14-003849-3). Penguin.

Southard, Frank, Jr. The Finances of European Liberation: With Special Reference to Italy. Wilkins, Mira, ed. LC 78-3950. (International Finance Ser.). 1978. Repr. of 1946 ed. lib. bdg. 14.00x (ISBN 0-405-11251-3). Arno.

Spencer, Henry R. Government & Politics of Italy. LC 74-137292. Repr. of 1932 ed. 23.50 (ISBN 0-404-06189-3). AMS Pr.

--Government & Politics of Italy. LC 74-137292. Repr. of 1932 ed. 23.50 (ISBN 0-404-06189-3). AMS Pr.

Sprigge, Cecil J. The Development of Modern Italy. 1969. 19.50 (ISBN 0-86527-043-0). Fertig.

Steel, Ronald, ed. Italy. (Reference Shelf Ser: Vol. 35, No. 6). 1963. 6.25 (ISBN 0-8242-0078-0). Wilson.

Steiner, H. Arthur. Government in Fascist Italy. LC 74-12650. 158p. 1975. Repr. of 1938 ed. lib. bdg. 15.00x (ISBN 0-8371-7745-6, STFI). Greenwood.

Thayer, John A. Italy & the Great War: Politics & Culture, 1870-1914. (Illus.). 480p. 1964. 37.50 (ISBN 0-299-03280-9). U of Wis Pr.

Villari, Luigi. The Liberation of Italy. 1960. 10.00 (ISBN 0-8159-6108-1). Devin.

Weinberg, Leonard B. After Mussolini: Italian Neo-Fascism & the Nature of Fascism. LC 79-8511. 1979. pap. text ed. 6.75 (ISBN 0-8191-0870-7). U Pr of Amer.

White, Caroline. Patrons & Partisans: A Study of Politics in Two Southern Italian Comuni. LC 79-53406. (Cambridge Studies in Social Anthropology: No. 31). (Illus.). 1980. 19.95 (ISBN 0-521-22872-7). Cambridge U Pr.

Willis, F. Roy. Italy Chooses Europe. 1971 (ISBN 0-19-501383-2). pap. 5.95x (ISBN 0-19-501384-0). Oxford U Pr.

Young, Wayland H. The Italian Left: A Short History of Political Socialism in Italy. LC 74-33893. (Illus.). 219p. 1975. Repr. of 1949 ed. lib. bdg. 15.25x (ISBN 0-8371-7998-X, HIIL). Greenwood.

Zuckerman, Alan S. The Politics of Faction: Christian Democratic Rule in Italy. 1979. text ed. 20.00 (ISBN 0-300-02285-9). Yale U Pr.

ITALY–POPULATION

Cole, John W. & Wolf, Eric R. The Hidden Frontier: Ecology & Ethnicity in an Alpine Valley. (Studies in Social Discontinuity Ser.). 1974. 27.50 (ISBN 0-12-785132-1). Acad Pr.

Dickinson, Robert E. The Population Problem of Southern Italy: An Essay in Social Geography. LC 76-49087. (Illus.). 1977. Repr. of 1955 ed. lib. bdg. 14.00x (ISBN 0-8371-9337-0, DIPP). Greenwood.

Livi-Bacci, Massimo. A History of Italian Fertility During the Last Two Centuries. LC 76-3271. (Office of Population Research). 1977. text ed. 24.00 (ISBN 0-691-09369-5). Princeton U Pr.

Weissman, Ronald F. Ritual Brotherhood in Renaissance Florence. (Population & Social Structure Advances in Historical Demography Ser.). 1981. price not set (ISBN 0-12-744480-7). Acad Pr.

ITALY–RELATIONS (GENERAL) WITH FOREIGN COUNTRIES

Harney, Martin P. Medieval Ties Between Italy & Ireland. 1963. 1.50 (ISBN 0-8198-0101-1). Dghtrs St Paul.

Woodress, James L. Howells & Italy. Repr. of 1952 ed. lib. bdg. 15.00x (ISBN 0-8371-2393-3, WOHI). Greenwood.

ITALY–SOCIAL CONDITIONS

Alternative Ways of Life: The Italian Case. 29p. 1981. pap. 5.00 (ISBN 92-808-0157-0, TUNU 119, UNU). Unipub.

Arthur, William. Italy in Transition. 469p. 1980. Repr. of 1860 ed. lib. bdg. 50.00 (ISBN 0-89760-005-3). Telegraph Bks.

Banfield, Edward C. & Banfield, L. F. Moral Basis of a Backward Society. LC 58-9398. 1958. 12.95 (ISBN 0-02-901520-0); pap. text ed. 5.95 (ISBN 0-02-901510-3). Free Pr.

Belmonte, Thomas. The Broken Fountain. LC 78-32167. 160p. 1979. 12.50 (ISBN 0-231-04542-5); pap. 6.00x (ISBN 0-231-04543-3). Columbia U Pr.

Evans, Robert H. Life & Politics in a Venetian Community. LC 76-21256. (International Studies). 1977. text ed. 15.95x (ISBN 0-268-01256-3); pap. 4.95 (ISBN 0-268-01257-1). U of Notre Dame Pr.

Fraser, John. Italy: Society in Crisis-Society in Transformation. 288p. 1981. 27.50 (ISBN 0-7100-0771-X). Routledge & Kegan.

Glasser, Ralph. The Net & the Quest: Patterns of Community & How They Can Survive Progress. LC 77-81678. 1978. 15.00x (ISBN 0-87663-726-8, Pica Pr). Universe.

Gross, Feliks. Il Paese: Values & Social Change in an Italian Village. LC 73-145510. (Illus.). 298p. 1973. 15.00x (ISBN 0-8147-2956-8). NYU Pr.

Heitland, William E. Agricola: A Study of Agriculture & Rustic Life in the Greco-Roman World from the Point of View of Labour. Repr. of 1921 ed. lib. bdg. 37.00 (ISBN 0-8371-4088-9, HEAG). Greenwood.

Isichei, Elizabeth. The Ibo People & the Europeans. LC 73-82826. 200p. 1973. 18.95 (ISBN 0-312-40355-0). St Martin.

McArdle, Frank. Altopascio: A Study in Tuscan Rural Society, 1587-1784. LC 76-53261. (Cambridge Studies in Early Modern History). (Illus.). 1978. 34.95 (ISBN 0-521-21619-2). Cambridge U Pr.

Manfredi, John F. Periodical Resources in Italian Sociology since 1945. LC 77-18335. 1977. 15.00 (ISBN 0-8357-0285-5, SS-00049). Univ Microfilms.

Pareto, Vilfredo. The Ruling Class in Italy Before 1900. LC 73-20130. 143p. 1975. Repr. of 1950 ed. 17.50 (ISBN 0-86527-176-3). Fertig.

Whyte, William F. Street Corner Society: The Social Structure of an Italian Slum. 3rd ed. 1981. lib. bdg. 15.00x (ISBN 0-226-89542-4); pap. text ed. 5.95 (ISBN 0-226-89543-2). U of Chicago Pr.

ITALY–SOCIAL LIFE AND CUSTOMS

Belmonte, Thomas. The Broken Fountain. LC 78-32167. 160p. 1979. 12.50 (ISBN 0-231-04542-5); pap. 6.00x (ISBN 0-231-04543-3). Columbia U Pr.

Brizzolara, Andrew, compiled by. A Directory of Italian & Italian American Organizations & Community Services in the Metropolitan Area of Greater New York: in the Metropolitan Area of Greater New York, Vol. II. rev. ed. 1980. 9.95x (ISBN 0-913256-44-7). Ctr Migration.

Brogger, Jan. Montevarese: A Study of Peasant Society & Culture in Southern Italy. 160p. 1971. 19.50x (ISBN 8-200-06143-4, Dist. by Columbia U Pr). Universitet.

Coffin, David R. The Villa in the Life of Renaissance Rome. LC 78-9049. (Monographs in Art & Archaeology: XLIII). 1979. 50.00 (ISBN 0-691-03942-9). Princeton U Pr.

Collison-Morley, Lacy. Italy After the Renaissance: Decadence & Display in the Seventeenth Century. LC 77-173510. (Illus.). 1972. Repr. of 1930 ed. 19.00 (ISBN 0-8462-1563-2). Russell.
Crane, Thomas F. Italian Social Customs of the Sixteenth Century & Their Influence on the Literatures of Europe. LC 70-143873. 1971. Repr. of 1920 ed. 20.00 (ISBN 0-8462-1535-7). Russell.
Ferrari, Robert. Days Pleasant & Unpleasant in the Order Sons of Italy. LC 73-21967. 1974. Repr. of 1926 ed. 13.50x (ISBN 0-678-01363-2). Kelley.
Flower, Raymond. Chianti: The Land, the People & the Wine. LC 78-60736. 1979. 17.50x (ISBN 0-87663-330-0). Universe.
Hauser, Ernest. Italy: A Cultural Guide. LC 81-65998. 1981. 12.95 (ISBN 0-689-11175-4); pap. 7.95 (ISBN 0-689-11233-5). Atheneum.
Heywood, William. Palio & Ponte. LC 68-9004. (Illus.). 1969. Repr. of 1904 ed. 20.00 (ISBN 0-87817-010-3). Hacker.
Jacobitti, Edmund D. Revolutionary Humanism & Historicism in Modern Italy. LC 80-23619. 240p. 1981. text ed. 18.00x (ISBN 0-300-02479-7). Yale U Pr.
Lawrence, D. H. Twilight in Italy. 1958. 5.00 (ISBN 0-670-73590-6). Viking Pr.
Petroselli, Francesco. La Vite: Il Lessico Delvignaiolo Nelle Parlate Della Tuscia Viterbese, Vol. I. (Romanic Goteborg: No. 15). (Illus.). 1978. pap. text ed. 28.75x (ISBN 91-7346-001-X). Humanities.
Pitre, Giuseppe. Bibliografia delle Tradizioni Popolari D'italia, Contre Indici Speciali. LC 72-82380. xx, 603p. 1972. Repr. of 1894 ed. lib. bdg. 43.50 (ISBN 0-8337-2775-3). B Franklin.
Rose, Herbert J. Primitive Culture in Italy. facsimile ed. LC 73-168503. (Select Bibliographies Reprint Ser). Repr. of 1926 ed. 17.00 (ISBN 0-8369-5948-5). Arno.
Ross, Corinne. Christmas in Italy. Lopez, Jadwiga, ed. LC 79-65246. (Round the World Christmas Program Ser.). 1979. 7.95 (ISBN 0-7166-2008-1). World Bk-Childcraft.
Sheedy, Anna T. Bartolus on Social Conditions in the Fourteenth Century. LC 43-3717. (Columbia University. Studies in the Social Sciences: No. 495). Repr. of 1942 ed. 21.00 (ISBN 0-404-51495-2). AMS Pr.
Silverman, Sydel. The Three Bells of Civilization: The Life of an Italian Hill Town. LC 75-15916. (Illus.). 304p. 1975. 17.50x (ISBN 0-231-03804-6); pap. 7.50x (ISBN 0-231-08365-3). Columbia U Pr.
Taylor, L. Ross. Cults of Ostia. 1976. 10.00 (ISBN 0-89005-114-3). Ares.
Villari, Luigi. Italian Life. 1976. lib. bdg. 59.95 (ISBN 0-8490-2087-5). Gordon Pr.
Wharton, Edith. Italian Villas & Thier Gardens. 270p. 1981. Repr. of 1904 ed. lib. bdg. 75.00 (ISBN 0-8495-5832-8). Arden Lib.
Williams, Phyllis H. South Italian Folkways in Europe & America. LC 69-16768. (Illus.). 1969. Repr. of 1938 ed. 8.50 (ISBN 0-8462-1322-2). Russell.
Young, Harben B. & Ferguson, Lucy R. Puberty to Manhood in Italy & America. (Development Psychology Ser.). 294p. 1981. 26.00 (ISBN 0-12-773150-4). Acad Pr.

ITALY IN LITERATURE

Churchill, Kenneth. Italy & English Literature: Seventeen Sixty-Four to Nineteen Thirty. LC 79-55524. 230p. 1980. text ed. 25.00x (ISBN 0-06-491130-6). B&N.
Clarke, Helen A. Browning's Italy. LC 72-3566. (Studies in Browning, No. 4). (Illus.). 1972. Repr. of 1907 ed. lib. bdg. 59.95 (ISBN 0-8383-1546-1). Haskell.

ITASCA STATE PARK, MINNESOTA

Shay, C. Thomas. Itasca Bison Kill Site: An Ecological Analysis. LC 70-148250. (Minnesota Prehistoric Archaeology Ser.: No. 6). (Illus.). 133p. 1971. pap. 5.50 (ISBN 0-87351-063-1). Minn Hist.

ITBAYAT LANGUAGE

see Batan Language

ITEM VETO

see Veto

ITERATIVE METHODS (MATHEMATICS)

Falb, P. L. & De Jong, J. L. Some Successive Approximation Methods in Control & Oscillation Theory. (Mathematics in Science & Engineering Ser.: Vol. 59). 1969. 42.00 (ISBN 0-12-247950-5). Acad Pr.
Hageman, L. A. & Young, D. M. Applied Interactive Methods. (Computer Science & Applied Mathematics Ser.). 1981. write for info. (ISBN 0-12-313340-8). Acad Pr.
Ortega, James M. & Rheinboldt, Werner C. Iterative Solution of Nonlinear Equations in Several Variables. (Computer Science & Applied Mathematics Ser). 1970. 55.50 (ISBN 0-12-528550-7). Acad Pr.
Patterson, W. M. Iterative Methods for the Solution of a Linear Operator Equation in Hilbert Space: A Survey. (Lecture Notes in Mathematics: Vol. 394). 183p. 1974. pap. 15.40 (ISBN 0-387-06805-8). Springer-Verlag.
Rall, Louis B. Computational Solution of Nonlinear Operator Equations. LC 78-2378. 236p. (Orig.). 1979. Repr. of 1969 ed. 13.50 (ISBN 0-88275-667-2). Krieger.
Traub, Joseph F. Iterative Methods for the Solution of Equations. 2nd ed. LC 81-66999. 328p. 1981. text ed. 15.95 (ISBN 0-8284-0312-0). Chelsea Pub.

ITESO LANGUAGE

see Teso Language

ITO JINSAI, 1677-1705

Spae, Joseph J. Ito Jinsai: A Philosopher, Educator & Sinologist. 1967. Repr. of 1948 ed. 8.50 (ISBN 0-8188-0084-4). Paragon.

ITSEKIRI (AFRICAN PEOPLE)

see Gekri (African People)

ITURBIDE, AGUSTIN DE, EMPEROR OF MEXICO, 1783-1824

Caruso, J. A. The Liberators of Mexico. (Illus.). 8.75 (ISBN 0-8446-1105-0). Peter Smith.
Iturbide, Agustin De. The Memoirs of Agustin De Iturbide. lib. bdg. 6.00 (ISBN 0-89712-001-9). Documentary Pubns.
Robertson, William S. Iturbide of Mexico. LC 68-23321. (Illus.). 1968. Repr. of 1952 ed. lib. bdg. 21.00x (ISBN 0-8371-0203-0, ROIM). Greenwood.

ITURI FOREST PYGMIES

see Bambute

IVAN 3RD, CZAR OF RUSSIA, 1462-1505

Grey, Ian. Ivan Third & the Unification of Russia. 1967. pap. 1.25 (ISBN 0-02-032900-8, Collier). Macmillan.
--Ivan Third & the Unification of Russia. (Men & Their Times Ser). 1964. 4.00x (ISBN 0-8426-1282-3). Verry.

IVAN 4TH, THE TERRIBLE, CZAR OF RUSSIA, 1530-1584

Carr, Francis. Ivan the Terrible. (Illus.). 220p. 1981. 18.50x (ISBN 0-389-20150-2). B&N.
Graham, Stephen. Ivan the Terrible: Life of Ivan Fourth of Russia. (Illus.). 1968. Repr. of 1933 ed. 18.50 (ISBN 0-208-00683-4, Archon). Shoe String.
Keenan, Edward L. Kurbskii-Groznyi Apocrypha: The Seventeenth-Century Genesis of the Correspondence Attributed to Prince A. M. Kurbskii & Tsar Ivan Fourth. LC 70-154501. (Russian Research Center Studies: No. 66). (Illus.). 1971. 14.00x (ISBN 0-674-50580-8). Harvard U Pr.
Kurbsky, A. M. History of Ivan Fourth. Fennell, J. L., tr. 1965. 48.00 (ISBN 0-521-05501-6). Cambridge U Pr.
Skrynnikov, R. G. Ivan the Terrible. Graham, Hugh F., ed. (Russian Ser,: No. 32). 1981. 15.00 (ISBN 0-87569-039-4). Academic Intl.
Yanov, Alexander. The Origins of Autocracy: Ivan the Terrible in Russian History. LC 80-39528. 352p. 1981. 22.50x (ISBN 0-520-04282-4). U of Cal Pr.
Yevtushenko, Yevgeny. Ivan the Terrible & Ivan the Fool. LC 79-21282. 1980. 9.95 (ISBN 0-399-90064-0). Marek.

IVAN 4TH, THE TERRIBLE, CZAR OF RUSSIA, 1530-1584–DRAMA

Eisenstein, Sergei M. Ivan the Terrible. (Film Scripts-Classic Ser.). 1969. 3.25 (ISBN 0-671-20447-5, Touchstone Bks). S&S.

IVANOV, VYACHESLAV IVANOVICH, 1866-1949

Slonimskii, Iurii I. Writings on Lev Ivanov. Repr. of 1959 ed. unbound 4.50 (ISBN 0-384-55980-8). Johnson Repr.

IVATAN LANGUAGE

see Batan Language

IVES, CHARLES EDWARD, 1874-1954

Cowell, Henry & Cowell, Sidney. Charles Ives & His Music. (Music Reprint Ser.). x, 253p. 1981. Repr. of 1969 ed. 22.50 (ISBN 0-306-76125-4). Da Capo.
De Lerma, Dominique-Rene. Charles Edward Ives Eighteen Seventy-Four to Nineteen Fifty-Four: A Bibliography of His Music. LC 72-99083. 1970. 10.00x (ISBN 0-87338-057-6). Kent St U Pr.
Hitchcock, H. Wiley. Ives. (Oxford Studies of Composers). 1977. pap. 9.95 (ISBN 0-19-315439-0). Oxford U Pr.
Hitchcock, H. Wiley & Perlis, Vivian, eds. An Ives Celebration: Papers & Panels of the Charles Ives Centennial Festival Conference. LC 77-7987. (Music in American Life Ser). 252p. 1977. 14.95 (ISBN 0-252-00619-4). U of Ill Pr.
Perlis, Vivian. Charles Ives Remembered: An Oral History. LC 74-75288. (Illus.). 228p. 1974. 20.00x (ISBN 0-300-01758-8). Yale U Pr.
--Charles Ives Remembered: An Oral History. (Illus.). 1976. pap. 3.95 (ISBN 0-393-00825-8, Norton Lib). Norton.
Perry, Rosalie S. Charles Ives & the American Mind. LC 74-620003. (Illus.). 200p. 1974. 9.50x (ISBN 0-87338-152-1). Kent St U Pr.
Rossiter, Frank. Charles Ives and His America. (Illus.). 420p. (Orig.). 1975. 15.00 (ISBN 0-87140-610-1). Liveright.
Sive, Helen. Music's Connecticut Yankee: An Introduction to the Life and Music of Charles Ives. LC 76-25000. (Illus.). (gr. 6-9). 1977. 6.95 (ISBN 0-689-30561-3). Atheneum.
Warren, Richard, compiled by. Charles E. Ives: Discography. LC 77-28812. 1978. Repr. of 1972 ed. lib. bdg. 15.00 (ISBN 0-313-20256-7, WAID). Greenwood.

IVORIES

see also Netsukes

Beckwith, John. Ivory Carvings in Early Medieval England. (Illus.). 62.50 (ISBN 0-85602-006-0, Pub. by H Miller England). Heyden.
Bergman, Robert P. The Salerno Ivories: Ars Sacra from Medieval Amalfi. LC 79-22616. (Illus.). 268p. 1981. 37.50x (ISBN 0-674-78528-2). Harvard U Pr.
Curtis, Tony, ed. Ivory. (Illus.). 1978. 3.95 (ISBN 0-902921-85-1). Apollo.
Cust, Anna M. The Ivory Workers of the Middle Ages. LC 70-178523. Repr. of 1902 ed. 16.50 (ISBN 0-404-56537-9). AMS Pr.
Eastham, Barry C. Chinese Art Ivory. rev. & enl. ed. LC 76-23710. (Illus.). 1976. 17.50 (ISBN 0-89344-003-5). Ars Ceramica.
Medieval Ivories in the Walters Art Gallery: A Picture Book. (Illus.). 1969. pap. 3.50 (ISBN 0-685-21830-9). Walters Art.
Wilson, Derek & Ayerst, Peter. White Gold: The Story of African Ivory. LC 76-363. (Illus.). (YA) (gr. 10 up). 1976. 9.95 (ISBN 0-8008-8251-2). Taplinger.
Woodhouse, Charles P. Ivories: The Collector's History & Guide. 1976. 11.50 (ISBN 0-442-29536-7). Van Nos Reinhold.

IVORY–STAINING

see Stains and Staining

IVORY CARVING

see Ivories; Scrimshaws

IVORY COAST

Bernheim, Marc & Bernheim, Evelyne. African Success Story: The Ivory Coast. LC 72-84772. (Illus.). (gr. 7-9). 1970. 6.95 (ISBN 0-15-201650-3, HJ). HarBraceJ.
--Week in Aya's World: The Ivory Coast. LC 70-75391. (Face to Face Bks.). (Illus.). (gr. k-3). 1969. 4.50g (ISBN 0-02-709050-7, CCPr); (CCPr). Macmillan.
Bonnefond, Th. Esquisse Bibliographique Recente en Sciences Humaines du Departement du Centre de la Cote d'Ivoire. (Black Africa Ser.). 50p. (Fr.). 1974. Repr. of 1968 ed. 29.00x (ISBN 0-8287-0106-7, 71-2072). Clearwater Pub.
Cohen, Michael A. Urban Policy & Political Conflict in Africa: A Study of the Ivory Coast. LC 73-90942. 262p. 1974. 16.50x (ISBN 0-226-11223-3). U of Chicago Pr.
Dumestre, G. Atlas Linguistique de Cote d'Ivoire. (Black Africa Ser.). 323p. (Fr.). 1974. Repr. of 1971 ed. lib. bdg. 85.00 (ISBN 0-8287-0296-9, 71-2009). Clearwater Pub.
Editorial Staff, ed. Ivory Coast - in Pictures. LC 76-19802. (Visual Geography Ser.). (Illus.). (gr. 5 up). 1976. PLB 4.99 (ISBN 0-8069-1215-4); pap. 2.95 (ISBN 0-8069-1214-6). Sterling.
Ferrair, Antoine & Thoret, Jacques. Atiekwa: Un Village de Cote d'Ivoire. (Black Africa Ser.). 99p. (Fr.). 1974. Repr. of 1970 ed. lib. bdg. 35.00 (ISBN 0-8287-1331-6, 71-2021). Clearwater Pub.
Foster, Philip & Zolberg, Aristide R., eds. Ghana & the Ivory Coast: Perspectives on Modernization. LC 70-159784. 1971. 12.50x (ISBN 0-226-25752-5). U of Chicago Pr.
Goreux, Louis M. Interdependence in Planning: Multilevel Programming Studies of the Ivory Coast. LC 77-4793. (A World Bank Research Publication Ser.). (Illus.). 1978. text ed. 22.50x (ISBN 0-8018-2001-4); pap. text ed. 7.95x (ISBN 0-8018-2006-5). Johns Hopkins.
Holas, Bohumil. Craft & Culture in the Ivory Coast. LC 79-365220. (Illus.). 148p. 1968. 11.25x (ISBN 0-8002-0726-2). Intl Pubns Serv.
Ivory Coast Today. (Illus.). 240p. 1980. 14.95 (ISBN 0-88254-595-7, Pub. by J. A. Editions France). Hippocrene Bks.
Joshi, Heather, et al. Abidjan: Urban Development & Employment in the Ivory Coast. (A WEP Study). 1976. 17.10 (ISBN 92-2-101391-X); pap. 11.40 (ISBN 9-2210-1390-1). Intl Labour Office.
Masini, Jean, et al. Multinationals in Africa: A Case Study of the Ivory Coast. LC 78-19462. (Praeger Special Studies). 1978. 23.95 (ISBN 0-03-046256-8). Praeger.
Meillassoux, Claude. Anthropologie Economique Des Gouro De Cote-D'ivoire: De L'economie De Subsistance a L'agriculture Commerciale. 3rd ed. (Le Monde D'outre-Mer Passe et Present, Etudes: No. 27). (Illus.). 1974. pap. 38.50x (ISBN 90-2796-298-7). Mouton.
Michotte, J. Etude d'une Experience d'Animation Rurale en Cote d'Ivoire. (Black Africa Ser). 121p. (Fr.). 1974. Repr. of 1967 ed. lib. bdg. 40.00x (ISBN 0-8287-0612-3, 71-2059). Clearwater Pub.
Perl, Lila. Ghana & Ivory Coast, Spotlight on West Africa. LC 74-23106. (Illus.). 160p. (gr. 5-9). 1975. 7.92 (ISBN 0-688-31833-9). Morrow.
Priovolos, Theophilos. Coffee & the Ivory Coast: An Econometric Study. LC 80-8630. (The Wharton Econometric Studies). (Illus.). 240p. 1981. 24.95 (ISBN 0-669-04331-1). Lexington Bks.
Remy, Mylene. La Cote D'Ivoire Aujourd 'hui. (Illus.). 1976. 21.95x (ISBN 2-85258-029-2). Intl Learn Syst.
Richter, Dolores. Art, Economics & Change: The Kulebele of Northern Ivory Coast. (Illus.). 165p. (Orig.). 1980. pap. 8.95 (ISBN 0-932382-01-0). Psych Graphic.
Savonnet, Georges. Les Birifor De Diepla et Sa Region Insulaires Du Rameau Lobi (Haute-Volta) (Atlas Des Structures Agraires Au Sud Du Sahara: No. 12). (Fr.). 1976. pap. text ed. 38.75x (ISBN 90-2797-823-9). Mouton.
Seabrook, Katherine P. Gao of the Ivory Coast. LC 76-106865. (Illus.). Repr. of 1931 ed. 10.00x (ISBN 0-8371-3487-0, Pub. by Negro U Pr). Greenwood.
Soulez. Reflexions sur l'Etude Sociologique des Centres Semi-Urbains de la Cote d'Ivoire. (Black Africa Ser.). 11p. (Fr.). 1974. Repr. of 1967 ed. 20.50 (ISBN 0-8287-1410-X, 71-2056). Clearwater Pub.
Trouchaud, J. P. Bilan de l'Operation Secteurs Pilotes en Moyenne Cote d'Ivoire, 2 vols. (Black Africa Ser.). 415p. (Fr.). 1974. Repr. of 1968 ed. Set. lib. bdg. 562.50 (ISBN 0-8287-0834-7). Vol. 1 (71-2039). Vol. 2 (71-2040). Clearwater Pub.
--Essai de Division Regionale En Cote d'Ivoire. (Black Africa Ser.). 193p. (Fr.). 1974. Repr. of 1968 ed. lib. bdg. 56.00x (ISBN 0-8287-0835-5, 71-2037). Clearwater Pub.
--Propositions pour un Cadre Regional de Planification En Cote d'Ivoire Travaux Preparatoires au Plan, 1971-1975. (Black Africa Ser.). 50p. (Fr.). 1974. Repr. of 1970 ed. lib. bdg. 29.00x (ISBN 0-8287-0836-3, 71-2038). Clearwater Pub.
Weiskel, Timothy C. French Colonial Rule & the Baule Peoples: Resistance & Collaboration, 1889-1911. (Oxford Studies in African Affairs Ser.). (Illus.). 352p. 1981. 49.50x (ISBN 0-19-822715-9). Oxford U Pr.
Wurtz, J. Adiamprikofikro-Douakankro: Etude Geographique D'un Terroir Baoule De Cote-dIvoire. (Atlas Des Structures Agraires Au Sud Du Sahara: No. 5). (Illus.). 1971. pap. 14.50x (ISBN 90-2796-921-3). Mouton.
Zolberg, Aristide R. One-Party Government in the Ivory Coast. rev. ed. 1969. 22.00x (ISBN 0-691-03041-3); pap. 5.95 (ISBN 0-691-00010-7). Princeton U Pr.

IWO JIMA, BATTLE OF, 1945

Gallant, T. Grady. The Friendly Dead. (World at War Ser.: No. 19). 1980. pap. 2.50 (ISBN 0-89083-588-8). Zebra.
Leckie, Robert. Battle for Iwo Jima. (Landmark Ser.). (Illus.). (gr. 5-9). 1967. PLB 5.99 (ISBN 0-394-90418-4, BYR). Random.
Matthews, Allen R. The Assault. LC 80-14926. (Great Classic Stories of World War II Ser.). 1980. 8.95 (ISBN 0-396-07874-5); pap. 5.95 (ISBN 0-396-07875-3). Dodd.
Stein, R. Conrad. The Story of the Battle for Iwo Jima. LC 77-5088. (Cornerstones of Freedom Ser). (Illus.). (gr. 3-5). 1977. PLB 7.95 (ISBN 0-516-04607-1). Childrens.
Wheeler, Keith. The Road to Tokyo. Time-Life Books, ed. (World War Two Ser.). 1980. 14.95 (ISBN 0-8094-2538-6). Time-Life.
Wheeler, Richard. Iwo. 1981. pap. 2.75 (ISBN 0-89083-799-6). Zebra.

IWW

see Industrial Workers of the World

IXODIDAE

see Ticks

J

J U 87 (BOMBERS)

see Stuka (Bombers)

JABHAT AL-TAHRIR AL QUAWMI

Jackson, Henry F. The FLN in Algeria: Party Development in a Revolutionary Society. LC 76-47889. (Contributions in Afro-American & African Studies: No. 30). (Illus.). 1977. lib. bdg. 19.95 (ISBN 0-8371-9401-6, JFA/). Greenwood.
Mezerik, Avrahm G., ed. Algerian Developments. 1960. pap. 15.00 (ISBN 0-685-13184-X, 55). Intl Review.

JABIM LANGUAGE

see also Melanesian Languages

JABOTINSKY, VLADIMIR EUGENEVICH, 1880-1940

Schechtman, Joseph B. Fighter & Prophet: The Vladimir Jabotinsky Story-the Later Years. (Return to Zion Ser.). (Illus.). 643p. Repr. of 1961 ed. lib. bdg. 35.00x (ISBN 0-87991-142-5). Porcupine Pr.

Schechtman, Joseph E. Rebel & Statesman: The Vladimir Jabotinsky Story-the Early Years. (Return to Zion Ser.). (Illus.). 467p. Repr. of 1956 ed. lib. bdg. 27.50x (ISBN 0-87991-143-3). Porcupine Pr.

JACK GAMES

Weigle, Marta. Jacks & Jack Games: Follow My Fancy. Davis, Jessica H., ed. LC 71-81735. (Orig.). (gr. 1-6). 1970. pap. 2.00 (ISBN 0-486-22081-8). Dover.

JACK-RABBITS

see Hares; Rabbits

JACKSON, ANDREW, PRES. U. S., 1767-1845

Baldwin, Joseph G. Party Leaders: Sketches of Thomas Jefferson, Alexander Hamilton, Andrew Jackson, Henry Clay John Randolph of Roanoke; Including Notices of Many Other Distinguished American Statesmen. LC 72-39654. (Essay Index Reprint Ser.). Repr. of 1885 ed. 21.00 (ISBN 0-8369-2741-9). Arno.

Bassett, John S. Life of Andrew Jackson, 2 Vols. in 1. (Illus.). 1967. Repr. of 1931 ed. 29.00 (ISBN 0-208-00175-1, Archon). Shoe String.

Chidsey, Donald B. Andrew Jackson, Hero. LC 76-26025. (gr. 8 up). 1977. 7.95 (ISBN 0-525-66514-5). Elsevier-Nelson.

Curtis, James C. Andrew Jackson & the Search for Vindication. (Library of American Biography). 1976. 7.50 (ISBN 0-316-16554-9); pap. text ed. 4.95 (ISBN 0-316-16553-0). Little.

Davis, Burke. Old Hickory: A Life of Andrew Jackson. 1977. 12.95 (ISBN 0-8037-6548-7). Dial.

Eaton, John H. Life of Andrew Jackson, Major-General in the Service of the United States. LC 77-146393. (First American Frontier Ser). 1971. Repr. of 1824 ed. 21.00 (ISBN 0-405-02846-6). Arno.

Fraser, Hugh R. Democracy in the Making: The Jackson-Tyler Era. LC 38-25891. 1969. Repr. of 1938 ed. 18.00 (ISBN 0-527-31300-9). Kraus Repr.

Hoffmann, William S. Andrew Jackson & North Carolina Politics. 7.00 (ISBN 0-8446-0143-8). Peter Smith.

James, Marquis. Andrew Jackson: The Border Captain. 11.50 (ISBN 0-8446-2309-1). Peter Smith.

Latner, Richard B. The Presidency of Andrew Jackson: White House Politics, 1829-1837. LC 78-18204. 336p. 1979. 20.00 (ISBN 0-8203-0457-3). U of Ga Pr.

Lindsey, David. Jackson & Calhoun. Colegrove, Kenneth, ed. LC 73-2452. (Shapers of History Ser.). (gr. 10 up). 1973. pap. text ed. 3.95 (ISBN 0-8120-0460-4). Barron.

MacDonald, William. Jacksonian Democracy, 1829-1837. Hart, Albert B., ed. LC 74-145154. (Illus.). 1971. 13.00 (ISBN 0-403-00762-3). Scholarly.

Miles, Edwin A. Jacksonian Democracy in Mississippi. LC 78-107415. (American Scene Ser). 1970. Repr. of 1960 ed. lib. bdg. 25.00 (ISBN 0-306-71884-7). Da Capo.

Parton, J. Presidency of Andrew Jackson: From Volume III of the Life of Andrew Jackson. Remini, Robert V., ed. 6.50 (ISBN 0-8446-2709-7). Peter Smith.

Parton, James. Life of Andrew Jackson, 3 Vols. Repr. of 1860 ed. Set. 73.00 (ISBN 0-384-44980-8). Johnson Repr.

Remini, Robert V. Andrew Jackson. 1969. pap. 2.25 (ISBN 0-06-080132-8, P132, PL). Har-Row.

--Andrew Jackson & the Bank War. (Essays in American History Ser.). 1967. pap. 3.95x (ISBN 0-393-09757-9). Norton.

--Andrew Jackson & the Course of American Empire, 1767-1821. LC 77-3766. (Illus.). 1977. 16.95 (ISBN 0-06-013574-3, HarpT). Har-Row.

--Andrew Jackson & the Course of American Freedom: 1822-1832, Vol. 2. LC 80-8694. (Illus.). 416p. 1981. 25.00 (ISBN 0-06-014844-6, HarpT). Har-Row.

--The Election of Andrew Jackson. LC 80-11829. (Critical Periods of History). 232p. 1980. Repr. of 1963 ed. lib. bdg. 19.00x (ISBN 0-313-22396-3, REEJ). Greenwood.

--Election of Andrew Jackson. (Critical Periods of History Ser). (Orig.). 1963. pap. text ed. 6.50 (ISBN 0-397-47040-1, HarpC). Har-Row.

--The Revolutionary Age of Andrew Jackson. 1977. pap. 1.50 (ISBN 0-380-01753-9, 34652). Avon.

Remini, Robert V., ed. The Age of Jackson. LC 72-5337. (Documentary History of the United States Ser). 244p. 1972. 14.95x (ISBN 0-87249-274-5). U of SC Pr.

Rogin, Michael P. Fathers & Children: Andrew Jackson & the Subjugation of the American Indian. LC 76-10814. 1976. pap. 4.95 (ISBN 0-394-71881-X, Vin). Random.

Rowland, Dunbar. Andrew Jackson's Campaign Against the British. facsimile ed. LC 72-146870. (Select Bibliographies Reprint Ser). Repr. of 1926 ed. 23.00 (ISBN 0-8369-5637-0). Arno.

Russo, David J. The Major Political Issues of the Jacksonian Period & the Development of Party Loyalty in Congress 1830-1840. LC 72-76612. (Transactions Ser.: Vol. 62, Pt. 5). 1972. pap. 1.00 (ISBN 0-87169-625-8). Am Philos.

Schlesinger, Arthur M., Jr. Age of Jackson. 1945. 13.95 (ISBN 0-316-77344-1); pap. 4.95 (ISBN 0-316-77343-3, LB18). Little.

Shaw, Ronald. Andrew Jackson, 1767-1845: Chronology, Documents, Bibliographical Aids. LC 71-83748. (Presidential Chronology Ser). 1969. 8.00 (ISBN 0-379-12063-1). Oceana.

Smith, Sam B. & Owsley, Harriet C., eds. The Papers of Andrew Jackson: 1770-1803, Vol. 1. LC 79-15078. (Illus.). 656p. 1980. 25.00 (ISBN 0-87049-219-5). U of Tenn Pr.

Smith, Seba. Letters Written During the President's Tour 'Down East' facs. ed. LC 78-76929. (American Fiction Reprint Ser). 1833. 9.00 (ISBN 0-8369-7008-X). Arno.

Sumner, William. Andrew Jackson As a Public Man. LC 68-24999. (American Biography Ser., No. 32). 1969. Repr. of 1882 ed. lib. bdg. 24.95 (ISBN 0-8383-0244-0). Haskell.

Sumner, William G. Andrew Jackson. LC 80-18576. (American Statesmen Ser.). 405p. 1981. pap. 6.95 (ISBN 0-87754-176-0). Chelsea Hse.

--Andrew Jackson. Morse, John T., Jr., ed. LC 72-128963. (American Statesmen: No. 17). Repr. of 1899 ed. 25.00 (ISBN 0-404-50867-7). AMS Pr.

--Andrew Jackson As a Public Man. LC 4-17072. 1882. 15.00 (ISBN 0-403-00278-8). Scholarly.

--Andrew Jackson As a Public Man: What He Was, What Chances He Had, & What He Did with Them. Repr. of 1882 ed. lib. bdg. 15.50x (ISBN 0-8371-4104-4, SUAJ). Greenwood.

Syrett, Harold C. Andrew Jackson: His Contribution to the American Tradition. LC 75-138600. 1971. Repr. of 1953 ed. lib. bdg. 15.00x (ISBN 0-8371-5802-8, SYAJ). Greenwood.

Taylor, George R., ed. Jackson Versus Biddle's Bank: Struggle Over the Second Bank of the U. S. 2nd ed. (Problems in American Civilization Ser.). 1972. pap. text ed. 4.95x (ISBN 0-669-84491-8). Heath.

Temin, Peter. Jacksonian Economy. (Essays in American History Ser.). 1969. pap. 4.95x (ISBN 0-393-09841-9, NortonC). Norton.

Thompson, Arthur W. Jacksonian Democracy on the Florida Frontier. LC 61-63107. (U of Fla. Social Sciences Monographs Ser.: No. 9). 1961. pap. 3.50 (ISBN 0-8130-0225-7). U Presses Fla.

Van Deusen, Glyndon G. Jacksonian Era: Eighteen Twenty Eight to Eighteen Forty Eight. (New American Nation Ser.). (Illus.). pap. 5.95x (ISBN 0-06-133028-0, TB3028, Torch). Har-Row.

--The Rise & Decline of Jacksonian Democracy. LC 78-11435. (Anvil Ser.). 270p. 1979. pap. 4.95 (ISBN 0-88275-784-9). Krieger.

Ward, John W. Andrew Jackson: Symbol for an Age. (YA) (gr. 9 up). 1962. pap. 4.95 (ISBN 0-19-500699-2, GB). Oxford U Pr.

Wise, W. Harvey, Jr. & Cronin, John W. Bibliography of Andrew Jackson & Martin Van Buren. LC 75-125368. (Bibliography & Reference Ser.: No. 342). 1970. Repr. of 1935 ed. 18.50 (ISBN 0-8337-3831-3). B Franklin.

JACKSON, ANDREW, PRES. U. S., 1767-1845–JUVENILE LITERATURE

Andrist, Ralph K. Andrew Jackson, Soldier & Statesman. LC 63-15123. (American Heritage Junior Library). 154p. (YA) (gr. 7 up). 1963. PLB 12.89 (ISBN 0-06-020106-1, HarpJ). Har-Row.

Coit, Margaret L. Andrew Jackson. (Illus.). (gr. 7-9). 1965. 7.95 (ISBN 0-395-06698-0). HM.

Remini, Robert V. The Revolutionary Age of Andrew Jackson. LC 74-2623. (gr. 7 up). 1976. 8.95 (ISBN 0-06-024856-4, HarpJ); PLB 8.79 (ISBN 0-06-024857-2). Har-Row.

Steele, William O. Andy Jackson's Water Well. LC 59-7282. (Illus.). (gr. 1-5). 4.50 (ISBN 0-15-203364-5, HJ). HarBraceJ.

JACKSON, BARRY VINCENT, b. 1879

Bishop, George W. Barry Jackson & the London Theatre. LC 76-81972. 1933. 15.00 (ISBN 0-405-08272-X, Blom Pubns). Arno.

JACKSON, GEORGE, 1941-1971

Howard, Clark. American Saturday. 1981. 13.95 (ISBN 0-399-90120-5). Marek.

Mann, Eric. Comrade George: An Investigation into the Life, Political Thought & Assassination of George Jackson. 4.50 (ISBN 0-8446-5219-9). Peter Smith.

JACKSON, H. NELSON, 1872-

New England Past: Photographs, 1880 to 1915. (Illus.). 260p. 1981. 37.50 (ISBN 0-8109-1357-7). Abrams.

JACKSON, HELEN MARIA (FISKE) HUNT, MRS., 1831-1885

Banning, Evelyn. Helen Hunt Jackson. LC 73-83038. (gr. 6-10). 1973. 6.95 (ISBN 0-8149-0735-0). Vanguard.

JACKSON, HENRY M.

Ognibene, Peter J. Scoop: The Life & Politics of Henry M. Jackson. LC 75-28238. 1975. 25.00x (ISBN 0-8128-1884-9). Stein & Day.

Stern, Paula. Water's Edge: Domestic Politics & the Making of American Foreign Policy. LC 78-55331. (Contributions in Political Science: No. 15). 1979. lib. bdg. 19.95 (ISBN 0-313-20520-5, SWE/). Greenwood.

JACKSON, JESSE, 1941-

Reynolds, Barbara A. Jesse Jackson: The Man, the Movement, the Myth. LC 74-17813. 416p. 1975. 17.95 (ISBN 0-911012-80-X). Nelson-Hall.

Stone, Eddie. Jesse Jackson: Biography of an Ambitious Man. (Orig.). 1979. pap. 1.95 (ISBN 0-87067-666-0, BH666). Holloway.

Westman, Paul. Jesse Jackson: I Am Somebody. LC 80-20521. (Taking Part Ser.). 48p. (gr. 3 up). 1980. PLB 6.95 (ISBN 0-87518-203-8). Dillon.

JACKSON, MAHALIA, 1911-1972

Cornell, Jean G. Mahalia Jackson: Queen of Gospel Song. LC 73-14713. (Americans All Ser). (Illus.). 96p. (gr. 3-6). 1974. PLB 6.48 (ISBN 0-8116-4581-9). Garrard.

Dunham, Montrew. Mahalia Jackson: Young Gospel Singer. (Childhood of Famous Americans Ser). 1974. 3.95 (ISBN 0-672-51931-3). Bobbs.

Jackson, Jesse. Make a Joyful Noise Unto the Lord: The Life of Mahalia Jackson, Queen of Gospel Singers. LC 72-7549. (Women of America Ser.). (gr. 5-9). 1974. 8.95 (ISBN 0-690-43344-1, TYC-J). Har-Row.

McDearmon, Kay. Mahalia, Gospel Singer. LC 75-33882. (Illus.). 48p. (gr. 2-5). 1976. 5.95 (ISBN 0-396-07280-1). Dodd.

JACKSON, MARY ANNA (MORRISON), 1831-1915–FICTION

Kane, Harnett. The Gallant Mrs. Stonewall. 320p. 1976. Repr. of 1957 ed. lib. bdg. 16.60x (ISBN 0-89244-075-9). Queens Hse.

JACKSON, RACHEL (DONELSON), 1767-1828

Govan, Christine N. Rachel Jackson: Tennessee Girl. (Childhood of Famous Americans Ser). (Illus.). (gr. 3-7). 1955. 3.95 (ISBN 0-672-50152-X). Bobbs.

JACKSON, RACHEL (DONELSON), 1767-1828–FICTION

Stone, Irving. President's Lady. LC 51-6885. 1959. 9.95 (ISBN 0-385-04362-7). Doubleday.

--President's Lady. 1968. pap. 1.95 (ISBN 0-451-07919-1, J7919, Sig). NAL.

JACKSON, REGGIE

Allen, Maury. Mr. October: The Reggie Jackson Story. (Illus.). 1981. 10.95 (ISBN 0-8129-0964-X). Times Bks.

--Reggie Jackson: Three Million Dollar Man. (Star People Ser.). (Illus.). (gr. 4-8). 1978. PLB 5.99 (ISBN 0-8178-5817-2). Harvey.

Burchard, Marshall. Sports Hero: Reggie Jackson. (Sports Hero Ser.). (Illus.). 1975. PLB 6.29 (ISBN 0-399-61014-6). Putnam.

Burchard, S. H. Sports Star: Reggie Jackson. LC 78-20567. (Sports Star Ser). (Illus.). (gr. 1-5). 1979. pap. 2.95 (ISBN 0-15-278024-6, VoyB). HarBraceJ.

Hahn, James & Hahn, Lynn. Reggie Jackson: Slugger Supreme. LC 78-12937. (Champions & Challengers II). (gr. 3-5). 1979. text ed. 5.95 (ISBN 0-88436-449-6); pap. text ed. 3.50 (ISBN 0-88436-475-5). EMC.

Libby, Bill. The Reggie Jackson Story. LC 79-684. (Illus.). (gr. 5 up). 1979. 7.95 (ISBN 0-688-41889-9); PLB 7.63 (ISBN 0-688-51889-3). Lothrop.

Libman, Gary. Reggie Jackson. (Sports Superstars Ser.). (Illus.). (gr. 3-9). 1979. PLB 5.95 (ISBN 0-87191-724-6); pap. 2.95 (ISBN 0-89812-162-0). Creative Ed.

O'Connor, Dick. Reggie Jackson: Yankee Superstar. (gr. 4-6). 1978. pap. 1.25 (ISBN 0-590-05396-5, Schol Pap). Schol Bk Serv.

Stone, Eddie. Reggie Jackson. (Illus.). 96p. (Orig.). 1980. pap. 1.25 (ISBN 0-87067-311-4). Holloway.

Vass, George. Reggie Jackson: From Superstar to Candy Bar. (Sport Stars Ser.). (Illus.). (gr. 2-6). 1979. PLB 7.95 (ISBN 0-516-04303-X); pap. 2.50 (ISBN 0-516-44303-8). Childrens.

JACKSON, ROBERT HOUGHWOUT, 1892-1954

Jackson, R. H., ed. Mr. Justice Jackson: Four Lectures in His Honor. LC 78-89566. 1969. 12.00x (ISBN 0-231-03236-6). Columbia U Pr.

JACKSON, THOMAS JONATHAN (STONEWALL JACKSON), 1824-1863

Cooke, John E. The Life of Stonewall Jackson. facsimile ed. LC 76-179511. (Select Bibliographies Reprint Ser). Repr. of 1863 ed. 18.00 (ISBN 0-8369-6640-6). Arno.

Douglas, Henry K. I Rode with Stonewall. 1940. 12.95 (ISBN 0-8078-0337-5). U of NC Pr.

Harrison, et al. Stonewall Jackson. 35p. (gr. 1-9). 1981. 2.95 (ISBN 0-86575-191-9). Dormac.

Henderson, G. F. Stonewall Jackson & the American Civil War. abr. ed. (Illus.). 10.00 (ISBN 0-8446-1232-4). Peter Smith.

Jackson, Mary A. Memoirs of T. J. (Stonewall) Jackson. (Illus.). 1975. Repr. 35.00 (ISBN 0-685-69614-6). Pr of Morningside.

Tanner, Robert G. Stonewall in the Valley: Thomas J. Stonewall Jackson's Shenandoah Valley Campaign Spring 1862. LC 76-3002. 1976. 13.95 (ISBN 0-385-12148-2). Doubleday.

Vandiver, Frank E. Mighty Stonewall. LC 73-20504. (Illus.). 547p. 1974. Repr. of 1957 ed. lib. bdg. 33.75 (ISBN 0-8371-7331-0, VAMS). Greenwood.

Wheeler, Richard. We Knew Stonewall Jackson. LC 76-58009. (Illus.). 1977. 9.95 (ISBN 0-690-01289-6). T Y Crowell.

JACKSON, THOMAS JONATHAN (STONEWALL JACKSON), 1824-1863–FICTION

Kane, Harnett. The Gallant Mrs. Stonewall. 320p. 1976. Repr. of 1957 ed. lib. bdg. 16.60x (ISBN 0-89244-075-9). Queens Hse.

JACKSON FAMILY

McMillan, Constance V. Randy & Janet Jackson: Ready & Right! LC 77-24073. (So Young, So Far Ser.). (Illus.). 40p. (gr. 3-9). 1977. PLB 5.95 (ISBN 0-88436-404-6); pap. 3.50 (ISBN 0-88436-405-4). EMC.

JACKSON, CALIFORNIA

Sharfman, I. Harold. Jews of Jackson, California. LC 76-79574. (Illus.). 1969. 11.50 (ISBN 0-87062-054-1). A H Clark.

JACKSON, MISSISSIPPI–RIOTS

Report of the President's Commission on Campus Unrest: Including the Killings at Jackson State & Kent State Tragedy. LC 71-139710. 537p. 1970. 5.95 (ISBN 0-405-01712-X). Arno.

JACKSON COUNTY, MISSOURI

History of Jackson County, Missouri. 15.00 (ISBN 0-911208-04-6). Ramfre.

JACKSON HOLE NATIONAL MONUMENT

Anderson, Elisabeth, et al. Cabin Comments: A Journal of Life in Jackson Hole. LC 80-53090. (Illus.). 286p. (gr. 7-12). 1980. 14.75 (ISBN 0-933160-08-9); pap. 7.75 (ISBN 0-933160-09-7). Teton Bkshop.

Betts, Robert B. Along the Ramparts of the Tetons: The Saga of Jackson Hole, Wyoming. LC 77-94083. 1978. 17.50 (ISBN 0-87081-113-4); pap. 7.95 (ISBN 0-87081-117-7). Colo Assoc.

Saylor, David J. Jackson Hole, Wyoming: In the Shadow of the Tetons. (Illus.). 1971. pap. 5.95 (ISBN 0-8061-1424-X). U of Okla Pr.

JACOB, THE PATRIARCH

Jacob. 1979. 0.75 (ISBN 0-8198-0581-5). Dghtrs St Paul.

Lindsay, Gordon. Jacob & His Son, Joseph. (Old Testament Ser.). 1.25 (ISBN 0-89985-129-0). Christ Nations.

--Jacob, The Supplanter Who Became a Prince with God. (Old Testament Ser.). 1.25 (ISBN 0-89985-128-2). Christ Nations.

McGibbon, Lloyd. Annotation on-- Jacob the Man. 1979. 6.95 (ISBN 0-533-03914-2). Vantage.

Molinie, M. D. The Struggle of Jacob. LC 77-78216. Orig. Title: Le Combat De Jacob. 136p. 1977. pap. 1.95 (ISBN 0-8091-2036-4, Deus). Paulist Pr.

Nee, Watchman. Changed into His Likeness. 1969. 3.00 (ISBN 0-87508-411-7); pap. 2.50 (ISBN 0-87508-410-9). Chr Lit.

--Changed into His Likeness. 1978. pap. 1.95 (ISBN 0-8423-0228-X). Tyndale.

Paamoni, Zev. The Adventures of Jacob. (Biblical Ser.). (Illus.). (gr. 5-10). 1970. 6.00 (ISBN 0-914080-26-1). Shulsinger Sales.

Schreiber, Vernon R. Wrestling with God: Messages for Lent & Easter on the Life of Jacob. LC 78-66939. 1979. pap. 3.50 (ISBN 0-8066-1696-2, 10-7360). Augsburg.

Shearburn, Wally M. Jacob's Ladder: A Choral Reading. 1980. 2.25 (ISBN 0-89536-441-7). CSS Pub.

JACOB BEN MOSES, HA-LEVI, 1365-1427

Steiman, Sidney. Custom & Survival. LC 63-19988. 1963. 7.95x (ISBN 0-8197-0186-6). Bloch.

JACOB, MAX, 1876-1944

Levy, Sydney. The Play of the Text: Max Jacob's le Cornet a Des. LC 80-52298. 169p. 1981. 18.00x (ISBN 0-299-08510-4). U of Wis Pr.

Schneider, Judith. Clown at the Altar: The Religious Poetry of Max Jacob. (Studies in the Romance Languages & Literatures: No. 190). (Orig.). 1978. pap. 11.00x (ISBN 0-8078-9190-8). U of NC Pr.

JACOBI, FRIEDRICH HEINRICH, 1743-1819
Wilde, Norman. Friedrich Heinrich Jacobi. LC 3-12361. Repr. of 1894 ed. 14.00 (ISBN 0-404-06946-0). AMS Pr.
JACOBI POLYNOMIALS
see Functions, Orthogonal
JACOBINS
Aulard, Francois V., tr. Societe des Jacobins, 6 Vols. LC 78-161707. (Collection de documents relatifs a l'histoire de Paris pendant la Revolution francaise). Repr. of 1897 ed. Set. 319.50 (ISBN 0-404-52560-1); 53.25 ea. AMS Pr.
Brinton, Crane. The Jacobins: An Essay in the New History. LC 61-13765. 1961. Repr. of 1930 ed. 19.00 (ISBN 0-8462-0137-2). Russell.
Gifford, William, ed. Anti-Jacobin; or, Weekly Examiner. Nos. 1-36. 2 Vols. in 1. LC 68-57996. 1797-1798. lib. bdg. 57.50 (ISBN 0-685-05687-2). AMS Pr.
Kennedy, Michael L. The Jacobin Club of Marseilles 1790-1794. LC 73-8410. (Illus.). 268p. 1973. 22.50x (ISBN 0-8014-0794-X). Cornell U Pr.
--The Jacobin Clubs in the French Revolution: The First Years. LC 81-47138. (Illus.). 360p. 1981. 27.00x (ISBN 0-691-05337-5). Princeton U Pr.
Mallet, George. La Politique Financiere des Jacobins. 449p. (Fr.). 1972. Repr. of 1913 ed. lib. bdg. 29.00 (ISBN 0-8337-2196-8). B Franklin.
Woloch, Isser. Jacobin Legacy: The Democratic Movement Under the Directory. LC 76-83689. 1960. 30.00x (ISBN 0-691-06183-1). Princeton U Pr.
JACOBINS (DOMINICANS)
see Dominicans
JACOBITE CHURCH
Baumstark, Anton. Festbrevier und Kirchenjahr der Syrischen Jakobiten. Repr. of 1910 ed. pap. 18.50 (ISBN 0-384-03575-2). Johnson Repr.
JACOBITE REBELLION, 1715
Hibbert-Ware, Samuel. Lancashire Memorials of the Rebellian 1715, 2 Vols. in 1. 1845. 26.00 (ISBN 0-384-22985-9). Johnson Repr.
Petrie, Charles. The Jacobite Movement. 59.95 (ISBN 0-8490-0432-2). Gordon Pr.
JACOBITE REBELLION, 1745-1746
see also Culloden, Battle of, 1746
Cochrane, Andrew. Cochrane Correspondence Regarding the Affairs of Glasgow. Dennistoun, James, ed. LC 72-1034. (Maitland Club, Glasgow. Publications: No. 37). Repr. of 1836 ed. 20.00 (ISBN 0-404-53009-5). AMS Pr.
Cruickshanks, Eveline. Political Untouchables: The Tories & the '45. LC 79-10340. (Illus.). 1979. text ed. 29.50x (ISBN 0-8419-0511-8). Holmes & Meier.
Graham, Dougal. Collected Writings of Dougal Graham, Skellat Bellman of Glasgow, 2 Vols. LC 69-16478. 1968. Repr. of 1883 ed. Set. 22.00 (ISBN 0-8103-3535-2). Gale.
Lang, Andrew. Pickle the Spy. LC 72-110132. Repr. of 1897 ed. 10.00 (ISBN 0-404-03853-0). AMS Pr.
--Prince Charles Edward. LC 1-25240. Repr. of 1900 ed. 55.00 (ISBN 0-404-03855-7). AMS Pr.
Lenman, Bruce. The Jacobite Rising in Britain Sixteen Eighty-Nine to Seventeen Forty-Six. 1980. text ed. 34.50x (ISBN 0-8419-7004-1). Holmes & Meier.
Maxwell, James. Narrative of Charles Prince of Wales' Expedition to Scotland in the Year 1745. LC 73-173063. (Maitland Club. Glasgow. Publications: No. 53). Repr. of 1841 ed. 20.00 (ISBN 0-404-53035-4). AMS Pr.
JACOBITES
Hill, Patricia K. Oglethorpe Ladies & the Jacobite Conspiracies. LC 76-26441. 1977. bds. 7.95 (ISBN 0-87797-039-4). Cherokee.
Hogg, James. Jacobite Relics of Scotland, 2 Vols. LC 72-144561. Repr. of 1821 ed. Set. 62.50 (ISBN 0-404-08661-6); Vol. 1 (ISBN 0-404-08662-4). Vol. 2 (ISBN 0-404-08663-2). AMS Pr.
JACOBITES-FICTION
Scott, Walter. Redgauntlet. 1957. 10.95x (ISBN 0-460-00141-8, Evman). Biblio Dist.
JACOBITES-POETRY
Campbell, John L. Highland Songs of the Forty-Five. LC 75-173105. Repr. of 1933 ed. 21.00 (ISBN 0-405-08338-6, Blom Pubns). Arno.
JACOBS, HARRIET (BRENT), 1818-1896
Brent, Linda, pseud. Incidents in the Life of a Slave Girl. Child, L. Maria, ed. LC 72-90506. (Illus.). 1973. pap. 4.50 (ISBN 0-15-644350-3, HB245, Harv). HarBraceJ.
JACOBSEN, JTRGEN-FRANTZ, 1900-1938
Bronner, Hedin. Three Faroese Novelists: An Appreciation of Jorgen-Frantz Jacobsen, William Heinesen & Heolin Bru. LC 73-8069. (Library of Scandinavian Literature). 1973. lib. bdg. 12.50x (ISBN 0-8057-3374-4). Irvington.
JACOBY, HELMUT
Walker, Derek, intro. by. Architectural Drawings by Helmut Jacoby, 1968-1976. (Illus.). 1977. 22.95 (ISBN 0-8038-0016-9). Architectural.
JACQUEMONT, VICTOR, 1801-1832
Hamerton, Philip G. Modern Frenchmen: Five Biographies. LC 72-4579. (Essay Index Reprint Ser.). Repr. of 1878 ed. 22.00 (ISBN 0-8369-2947-0). Arno.
JADE
Anderson, Eskil. Asbestos & Jade in the Kobuk River Region of Alaska. facs. ed. 26p. Repr. of 1945 ed. pap. 3.50 (ISBN 0-8466-0037-4, SJS37). Shorey.
Cheng, Te-K'Un. Jade Flowers & Floral Patterns in Chinese Decorative Art. 1969. 15.00 (ISBN 0-685-57074-6). ARS Ceramica.
Chinese Jade. (Illus.). 1981. 50.00x (ISBN 0-686-31469-7, Pub. by Sotheby Parke Bernet England). Biblio Dist.
Chu, Arthur & Chu, Grace. The Collectors Book of Jade. 1978. 11.95 (ISBN 0-517-53150-X). Crown.
Goette, John A. Jade Lore. 2nd ed. LC 76-21489. (Illus.). 1976. 25.00 (ISBN 0-89344-009-4). Ars Ceramica.
Gump, Richard. Jade: Stone of Heaven. LC 62-12100. 1962. 10.95 (ISBN 0-385-01705-7). Doubleday.
Hartman, Joan M. Chinese Jade of Five Centuries. LC 69-12077. (Illus.). 1969. 27.50 (ISBN 0-8048-0099-5). C E Tuttle.
Hemrich, G. Handbook of Jade. pap. 2.50 (ISBN 0-910652-08-2). Gembooks.
Jayne, H. H. Archaic Chinese Jades: Special Exhibition. (Illus.). 58p. 1940. soft bound 2.00 (ISBN 0-686-11896-0). Univ Mus of U PA.
Laufer, Berthold. Jade, a Study in Chinese Archaeology & Religion. (Illus.). 1912. pap. 28.00 (ISBN 0-527-01870-8). Kraus Repr.
--Jade: A Study in Chinese Archaeology & Religion. (Illus.). 11.50 (ISBN 0-8446-5214-8). Peter Smith.
Nott, Stanley C. Chinese Jade Throughout the Ages: A Review of Its Characteristics, Decoration, Folklore & Symbolism. LC 62-8839. (Illus.). 1962. 47.50 (ISBN 0-8048-0100-2). C E Tuttle.
Proskouriakoff, Tatiana. Jades from the Cenote of Sacrifice, Chichen Itza, Yucatan. LC 74-77555. (Peabody Museum Memoirs: Vol. 10, No. 1). 1974. pap. text ed. 40.00 (ISBN 0-87365-682-2). Peabody Harvard.
Schedel, J. J. The Splendor of Jade: Four Thousand Years of the Art of Chinese Jade Carving. LC 74-9855. 1974. 37.50 (ISBN 0-525-49505-3). Dutton.
Schneeberger, Pierre-F. Chinese Jades & Other Hardstones. Watson, Katherine, tr. from Fr. (Illus.). 1976. 225.00 (ISBN 0-7100-0455-9). Routledge & Kegan.
Watt, James C. Chinese Jades from Han to Ch'ing. LC 80-20115. (Illus.). 235p. 1981. 22.50 (ISBN 0-87848-057-9). Weatherhill.
--Chinese Jades from Han to Ch'ing. LC 80-20115. (Illus.). 236p. 1980. 22.50 (ISBN 0-87848-057-9). Asia Soc.
Wills, Geoffrey. Jade of the East. LC 72-78589. (Illus.). 200p. 1972. 38.50 (ISBN 0-8348-1854-X). Weatherhill.
Wobber, Don. Jade Beneath the Sea: A Diving Adventure. (Illus.). 136p. 1975. pap. 3.95 (ISBN 0-910286-44-2). Boxwood.
JAFFRAY, ROBERT ALEXANDER, 1873-1945
Tozer, Aiden W. Let My People Go. pap. 3.50 (ISBN 0-87509-189-X). Chr Pubns.
JAGAN, CHEDDI
Simms, Peter. Trouble in Guyana. (Illus.). 1966. 7.50x (ISBN 0-8002-2114-1). Intl Pubns Serv.
JAGERSTATTER, FRANZ
Zahn, Gordon C. In Solitary Witness: The Life & Death of Franz Jagerstatter. 1981. Repr. of 1964 ed. 18.95x (ISBN 0-03-047535-X). Irvington.
JAGGARD, WILLIAM, 1569-1623
Jaggard, William. Shakespeare & the Tudor Jaggards. 1934. lib. bdg. 6.00 (ISBN 0-8414-5414-0). Folcroft.
Willoughby, Edwin W. Printer of Shakespeare. LC 77-92993. (Studies in Shakespeare, No. 24). 1969. Repr. of 1934 ed. lib. bdg. 39.95 (ISBN 0-8383-1212-8). Haskell.
JAGGAS
see Wachaga
JAGUAR (AUTOMOBILE)
see Automobiles, Foreign-Types-Jaguar
JAHIZ
Pellat, Charles. The Life & Works of Jahiz. Hawke, D. M, tr. (Islamic World Series). 1969. 21.50x (ISBN 0-520-01498-7). U of Cal Pr.
JAI ALAI
see Pelota (Game)
JAIL FEVER
see Typhus Fever
JAILS
see Prisons
JAIME 1ST, KING OF ARAGON, 1208-1276
Burns, Robert I. Islam Under the Crusaders: Colonial Survival in the Thirteenth Century Kingdom of Valencia. (Illus.). 488p. 1974. 35.00x (ISBN 0-691-05207-7). Princeton U Pr.
Jaime I King Of Aragon. The Chronicles of James the First, King of Aragon, 2 vols. Forster, John, tr. LC 78-63501. Repr. of 1883 ed. Set. 69.50 (ISBN 0-404-17190-7). AMS Pr.
JAINA-LITERATURE-HISTORY AND CRITICISM
Lalwani, K. C. Kalpa Sutra. 207p. 1979. 12.95 (ISBN 0-89684-039-5, Pub. by Motilal Banarsidass India). Orient Bk Dist.
Winternitz, Moriz. History of Indian Literature, Vols. 1 & 2. Ketkar, Mrs. S. & Kohn, H., trs. from Ger. LC 73-151559. (1971. Repr. of 1927, 1933 eds.). 60.00 (ISBN 0-8462-1602-7). Russell.
JAINA ISLAND-ANTIQUITIES
Corson, Christopher. Maya Anthropomorphic Figurines from Jaina Island, Compeche. Graham, John A., ed. (Studies in Mesoamerican Art, Archaeology & Ethnohistory: No. 1). (Illus.). 218p. 1976. pap. 7.50 (ISBN 0-87919-053-1). Ballena Pr.
JAINAS
see Jains
JAINISM
Bhargava, Dayanand. Jaina Ethics. 1968. 5.00 (ISBN 0-89684-228-2). Orient Bk Dist.
Bhattacharya, B. C. Jaina Iconography. 2nd, rev. ed. (Illus.). 1974. 17.50 (ISBN 0-686-51809-8). Orient Bk Dist.
Bhattacharyya, Narendra Nath. Jain Philosophy: Historical Outline. 1976. 11.00 (ISBN 0-88386-834-2). South Asia Bks.
Bothra, Pushpa. The Jaina Theory of Perception. 1976. text ed. 9.00x (ISBN 0-8426-0874-5). Verry.
--Jaina Theory of Perception. 1976. 7.50 (ISBN 0-89684-229-0). Orient Bk Dist.
Chatterjee, A. K. A Comprehensive History of Jainism. 1978. 20.00x (ISBN 0-8364-0225-1). South Asia Bks.
Chitrabhanu, Gurudev S. Twelve Facets of Reality: The Jain Path to Freedom. Rosenfeld, Clare, ed. LC 80-16773. 200p. 1980. 8.95 (ISBN 0-396-07902-4). Dodd.
Dwivedi, R. C. Contributions of Jainism to Indian Culture. 1975. 8.95 (ISBN 0-8426-0953-9). Orient Bk Dist.
Dwivedi, R. C., et al. Contribution of Jainism to Indian Culture. 1976. text ed. 13.50x (ISBN 0-8426-0953-9). Verry.
Fischer, Eberhard & Jain, Jyotindra. Art & Rituals: Twenty Five Hundred Years of Jainism in India. LC 78-670055. (Illus.). 1977. 20.00x (ISBN 0-8002-0178-7). Intl Pubns Serv.
Gopalan, S. Outlines of Jainism. LC 73-13196. 205p. 1973. pap. 9.95 (ISBN 0-470-31530-X). Halsted Pr.
Homage to Shravana Belgola. 1981. 28.00x (ISBN 0-8364-0761-X, Pub. by Marg India). South Asia Bks.
Jaini, Jagmandar L. Outlines of Jainism. Thomas, F. W., ed. LC 78-14128. (Illus.). 1981. Repr. of 1940 ed. 19.00 (ISBN 0-88355-801-7). Hyperion Conn.
Jaini, Padmanabh S. The Jaina Path of Purification. LC 77-73496. 1979. 25.00x (ISBN 0-520-03459-7). U of Cal Pr.
Mookerjee, Satkari. The Jaina Philosophy of Non-Absolutism. 1978. 17.50 (ISBN 0-89684-021-2, Pub. by Motilal Banarsidass India). Orient Bk Dist.
--The Jaina Philosophy of Non-Absolutism. 2nd ed. 24.00x (ISBN 0-89684-021-2). South Asia Bks.
Nevaskar, Balwant S. Capitalists Without Capitalism: The Jains of India & the Quakers of the West. LC 72-98709. (Contributions in Sociology: No. 6). 1971. lib. bdg. 14.00 (ISBN 0-8371-3297-5, NCA/). Greenwood.
Pereira, Jose. Monolithic Jinas. 1977. 10.00 (ISBN 0-8426-1027-8, Pub. by Motilal Banarsidass India). Orient Bk Dist.
Sandal, Mohan L. Introduction to the Mimamsa Sutras of Jaimini. LC 73-3821. (Sacred Books of the Hindus: No. 28). Repr. of 1925 ed. 19.00 (ISBN 0-404-57828-4). AMS Pr.
Schubring, Walter. The Doctrine of the Jainas. 1979. 12.50x (ISBN 0-89684-005-0). South Asia Bks.
Schubring, Walther. The Doctrine of the Jainas. Buerlen, Wolfgang, tr. 1978. Repr. 12.50 (ISBN 0-89684-005-0, Pub. by Motilal Banarsidass India). Orient Bk Dist.
Schweitzer, Albert. Indian Thought & Its Development. 1962. 8.25 (ISBN 0-8446-2893-X). Peter Smith.
Singh, R. B. Jainism in Early Medieval Karnataka. 1976. 9.00 (ISBN 0-8426-0981-4). Orient Bk Dist.
--Jainism in Early Medieval Karnataka (c. A. D. 500-1200) 175p. 1976. text ed. 10.50 (ISBN 0-8426-0981-4). Verry.
Umasvati. Tattvarthadhigama Sutra (a Treatise on the Essential Principles of Jainism) Jaini, J. L., ed. & intro. by. LC 73-3836. (Sacred Books of the Jainas: No. 2). Repr. of 1920 ed. 21.50 (ISBN 0-404-57702-4). AMS Pr.
JAINS
Bhattacharya, B. C. The Jaina Iconography. 2nd ed. 171p. 1975. text ed. 21.00x (ISBN 0-685-54201-7). Verry.
Chitrabhanu, Gurudev S. Realize What You Are: The Dynamics of Jain Meditation. Marks, Leonard M., ed. LC 78-9461. (Illus.). 1978. 7.95 (ISBN 0-396-07579-7). Dodd.
Ghoshal, Sarat C., ed. The Sacred Books of the Jainas (Bibliotheca Jainica, 11 vols. Repr. of 1940 ed. 252.50 (ISBN 0-404-57700-8). AMS Pr.
Jain, J. P. Religion & Culture of the Jains. 1976. 7.50x (ISBN 0-88386-741-9). South Asia Bks.
Jain, Muni U. Jaina Sects & Schools. LC 76-900303. 1975. 11.50x (ISBN 0-88386-737-0). South Asia Bks.
Pereira, Jose. Monolithic Jinas: The Iconography of the Jain Temples of Ellora. (Illus.). 1977. text ed. 12.00x (ISBN 0-8426-1027-8). Verry.
JAJA, KING OF OPOBO, 1821-1891
Kaufmann, Herbert. Lost Freedom. Orig. Title: Kings Krokodile. (Illus.). (gr. 7 up). 1969. 6.95 (ISBN 0-8392-3083-4). Astor-Honor.
JALAL AL-DIN RUMI, MAWLANA, 1207-1273
Aflaki. The Whirling Ecstasy. Huart, C., tr. (Illus.). 30p. (Orig.). 1973. pap. 1.50 (ISBN 0-915424-02-9, Prophecy Pressworks). Sufi Islamia-Prophecy.
Chelkowski, Peter J., ed. The Scholar & the Saint: Studies in Commemoration of Abu'l-Rayhan al-Biruni & Jala al-Din al-Rumi. LC 74-29374. 306p. 1975. 28.50x (ISBN 0-8147-1360-2). NYU Pr.
Hakim, Khalifa A. The Metaphysics of Rumi. 157p. 1981. pap. 4.25 (ISBN 0-88004-004-1). Sunwise Turn.
Nicholson, Reynold A., tr. Rumi: Poet & Mystic. (Unwin Paperback Ser.). 1978. pap. 6.50 (ISBN 0-04-891047-3). Allen Unwin.
Schimmel, Annemarie. The Triumphal Sun: A Study of the Works of Jalaloddin Rumi. (Illus.). 1978. 27.50 (ISBN 0-87773-750-9). Great Eastern.
Whinfield, E. H., ed. & tr. Teachings of Rumi, the Masnavi. 1975. pap. 3.95 (ISBN 0-525-47387-4). Dutton.
JALOUX, EDMOND, 1878-1949
Rosenfeld, Marthe. Edmond Jaloux: The Evolution of a Novelist. LC 72-169244. 128p. 1972. 7.50 (ISBN 0-8022-2064-9). Philos Lib.
JAM
Byron, May. Jams & Jellies. 320p. 1975. pap. 3.50 (ISBN 0-486-23130-5). Dover.
Freitus, Joe. Wild Preserves: Illustrated Recipes for Over 100 Natural Jams & Jellies. LC 77-10287. (Illus.). 1977. pap. 6.95 (ISBN 0-913276-22-7). Stone Wall Pr.
Jensen, Margie C. Blue Ribbon Jams & Jellies. (Blue Ribbon Cookbook Ser.). (Illus.). 1976. pap. 3.95 (ISBN 0-686-30951-0). Caroline Hse.
March, Kathryn G. & March, Andrew L. The Quest for Wild Jelly. LC 81-90129. (Illus.). 60p. (Orig.). 1981. pap. 3.95 (ISBN 0-940206-00-5). Meridian Hill.
Mitgutsch, Ali. From Fruit to Jam. LC 81-58. (Carolrhoda Start to Finish Bks.). Orig. Title: Vom Obst Zur Marmelade. (Illus.). 24p. (ps-3). 1981. PLB 5.95 (ISBN 0-87614-154-8). Carolrhoda Bks.
Silitch, Clarissa M., ed. The Forgotten Art of Making Old Fashioned Jellies, Jams, Preserves, Conserves, Marmalades, Butters, Honeys & Leathers. LC 77-83101. (Forgotten Arts Ser.). (Illus.). 1977. pap. 3.95 (ISBN 0-911658-80-7). Yankee Bks.
Vaughan, Beatrice. Jams, Jellies & Marmalades. LC 78-173398. (Harvest Home Cookbooks Ser.). 1971. pap. 1.95 (ISBN 0-8289-0141-4). Greene.
Wejman, Jacqueline & St. Peter, Charles. Jams & Jellies. LC 74-4727. (Illus.). 168p. 1975. pap. 4.95 (ISBN 0-912238-59-3). One Hund One Prods.
JAMAICA
Bridges, G. Wilson. Annals of Jamaica, 2 vols. 1968. Repr. of 1828 ed. Set. 95.00x (ISBN 0-7146-1931-0, F Cass Co). Biblio Dist.
Cargill, Morris. Jamaica Farewell. 1978. 8.95 (ISBN 0-8184-0269-5). Lyle Stuart.
Constitucion De Jamaica, 1962. 100p. (Span.). 1971. pap. 1.00 (ISBN 0-8270-5420-3). OAS.
Cultural Policy in Jamaica. (Studies & Document's on Cultural Policy). 1978. pap. 5.00 (ISBN 92-3-101521-4, U806, UNESCO). Unipub.
Cundall, Frank. Bibliographia Jamaicacensis. LC 72-79229. 83p. 1902. Repr. 9.00 (ISBN 0-403-03320-9). Somerset Pub.
--Bibliographia Jamaicensis. LC 70-168276. (Bibliography & Reference Ser: No. 433). 1971. Repr. of 1902 ed. lib. bdg. 16.50 (ISBN 0-8337-0739-6). B Franklin.
Floyd, Barry. Jamaica: An Island Microcosm. (Illus.). 1979. 14.50x (ISBN 0-312-43953-9). St Martin.

Institute of Jamaica, Kingston, Jamaican National Bibliography, 1964-1974: The Caribbean: Historical & Cultural Perspectives. LC 80-11767. 1981. lib. bdg. 120.00 (ISBN 0-527-45166-5). Kraus Intl.

Jamaica Assembly - 1795-1796. Proceedings: In Regard to the Maroon Negroes. LC 79-111581. Repr. of 1796 ed. 10.50x (ISBN 0-8371-4606-2). Greenwood.

King, David. State & Prospects of Jamaica. 1850. 19.00 (ISBN 0-403-00371-7). Scholarly.

Long, Joseph. Psyche Versus Soma: Traditional Healing Choices in Jamaica. (Traditional Healing Ser.). 1981. 17.50 (ISBN 0-932426-20-4). Trado-Medic.

Manley, Michael. The Politics of Change: A Jamaican Testament. LC 74-34066. 1975. 9.95 (ISBN 0-88258-049-3); pap. 4.50 (ISBN 0-88258-060-4). Howard U Pr.

Phillippo, James M. Jamaica: Its Past & Present State. facs. ed. LC 79-157374. (Black Heritage Library Collection Ser). 1843. 28.25 (ISBN 0-8369-8812-4). Arno.

--Jamaica: Its Past & Present State. LC 70-109998. (Illus.). Repr. of 1843 ed. 23.75x (ISBN 0-8371-4132-X, Pub. by Negro U Pr). Greenwood.

Roberts, George W. The Population of Jamaica. LC 78-23974. 1979. Repr. of 1957 ed. lib. bdg. 25.00 (ISBN 0-527-75865-5). Kraus Repr.

Sterling Publishing Company Editors. Jamaica in Pictures. LC 67-16016. (Visual Geography Ser). (Illus.). (gr. 4-12). 1967. PLB 4.99 (ISBN 0-8069-1085-2); pap. 2.95 (ISBN 0-8069-1084-4). Sterling.

Stone, Carl. Democracy & Clientelism in Jamaica. LC 79-66444. 270p. 1980. text ed. 16.95 (ISBN 0-87855-348-7). Transaction Bks.

Williams, Joseph J. Psychic Phenomena of Jamaica. LC 74-138021. Repr. of 1934 ed. 15.25x (ISBN 0-8371-5669-6). Greenwood.

JAMAICA–DESCRIPTION AND TRAVEL

Bigelow, John. Jamaica in Eighteen-Hundred Fifty: The Effects on Sixteen Years of Freedom on a Slave Colony. LC 72-106880. Repr. of 1851 ed. 12.50x (ISBN 0-8371-3276-2, Pub. by Negro U Pr). Greenwood.

Boot, Adrian & Thomas, Michael. Jamaica: Babylon on a Thin Wire. LC 76-41756. (Illus.). 1977. pap. 6.95 (ISBN 0-8052-0556-X). Schocken.

Clarke, Colin G. & Hodgkiss, Alan G. Jamaica in Maps. LC 74-84659. (Graphic Perspectives of Developing Countries Ser.). (Illus.). 125p. 1975. text ed. 29.50x (ISBN 0-8419-0175-9, Africana). Holmes & Meier.

Duperly, A. Picturesque Jamaica. 1976. lib. bdg. 59.95 (ISBN 0-8490-2443-9). Gordon Pr.

Evans, F. C. A First Geography of Jamaica. 2nd ed. (Illus.). 48p. (gr. 5-8). 1973. 4.75x (ISBN 0-521-20252-3). Cambridge U Pr.

Gurney, Joseph J. Winter in the West Indies, Described in Familiar Letters to Henry Clay, of Kentucky. 2nd ed. LC 69-19356. (Illus.). Repr. of 1840 ed. 13.75x (ISBN 0-8371-1022-X). Greenwood.

Hannau, Hans W. Jamaica. (Panorama Bks.). (Illus., Fr.). 1964. 3.95 (ISBN 0-685-11270-5). French & Eur.

Johnston, James. Jamaica: The New Riviera. 1976. lib. bdg. 59.95 (ISBN 0-8490-2090-5). Gordon Pr.

Lewis, Matthew G. Journal of a West India Proprietor, Kept During a Residence in the Island of Jamaica. LC 74-89041. Repr. of 1834 ed. 19.25x (ISBN 0-8371-1845-X, Pub. by Negro U Pr). Greenwood.

Madden, Richard R. Twelvemonth's Residence in the West Indies, During the Transition from Slavery to Apprenticeship. LC 70-100309. Repr. of 1835 ed. 28.00x (ISBN 0-8371-3232-0). Greenwood.

Mays, Jeb & Wheaton, Philip, eds. Jamaica: Caribbean Challenge. 1979. pap. text ed. 3.50 (ISBN 0-918346-03-7). EPICA.

Olivier, Sydney H. Jamaica: The Blessed Island. LC 71-118339. (Illus.). 1971. Repr. of 1936 ed. 22.50 (ISBN 0-8462-1263-3). Russell.

Pullen-Burry, Bessie. Ethiopia in Exile: Jamaica Revisited. facs. ed. LC 76-157376. (Black Heritage Library Collection Ser). 1905. 16.75 (ISBN 0-8369-8814-0). Arno.

Senior, Bernard M. Jamaica, As It Was, As It Is, & As It May Be. LC 78-82321. Repr. of 1835 ed. 15.25x (ISBN 0-8371-1654-6, Pub. by Negro U Pr). Greenwood.

Stewart, John. Account of Jamaica, & Its Inhabitants. facs. ed. LC 70-157377. (Black Heritage Library Collection Ser). 1808. 18.50 (ISBN 0-8369-8815-9). Arno.

--View of the Past & Present State of the Island of Jamaica. LC 72-94489. Repr. of 1823 ed. 17.75x (ISBN 0-8371-2374-7). Greenwood.

Thome, James A. & Kimball, J. Horace. Emancipation in the West Indies, a Six Months Tour in Antigua, Barbados & Jamaica, in the Year 1837. LC 71-82227. (Anti-Slavery Crusade in America Ser). 1969. Repr. of 1838 ed. 12.00 (ISBN 0-405-00666-7). Arno.

JAMAICA–ECONOMIC CONDITIONS

Ayub, Mahmood A. Made in Jamaica: The Development of the Manufacturing Sector. LC 80-27765. (World Bank Staff Occasional Papers: No. 31). 120p. (Orig.). 1981. pap. text ed. 6.50x (ISBN 0-8018-2568-7). Johns Hopkins.

Bigelow, John. Jamaica in Eighteen-Hundred Fifty: The Effects on Sixteen Years of Freedom on a Slave Colony. LC 72-106880. Repr. of 1851 ed. 12.50x (ISBN 0-8371-3276-2, Pub. by Negro U Pr). Greenwood.

Eisner, Gisela. Jamaica, Eighteen Thirty-Nineteen Thirty: A Study in Economic Growth. LC 73-15054. 399p. 1974. Repr. of 1961 ed. lib. bdg. 23.00x (ISBN 0-8371-7157-1, EIJA). Greenwood.

Higman, B. W. Slave Population & the Economy of Jamaica: 1807-1834. LC 75-28627. (Illus.). 1977. 47.50 (ISBN 0-521-21053-4); pap. 11.50 (ISBN 0-521-29569-6). Cambridge U Pr.

International Bank for Reconstruction & Development. Economic Development of Jamaica. LC 77-86413. Repr. of 1952 ed. 57.50 (ISBN 0-404-60303-3). AMS Pr.

Maunder, W. F. Employment in an Underdeveloped Area. LC 73-19566. (Caribbean Ser.). 215p. 1974. Repr. of 1960 ed. lib. bdg. 15.00 (ISBN 0-8371-7296-9, MAUA). Greenwood.

JAMAICA–HISTORY

Barrett, Leonard E. The Rastafarians: Sounds of Cultural Dissonance. LC 76-48491. (Illus.). 1977. pap. 4.95 (ISBN 0-8070-1115-0, BP559). Beacon Pr.

Bell, Wendell. Jamaican Leaders: Political Attitudes in a New Nation. LC 64-19447. 1964. 22.50x (ISBN 0-520-00103-6). U of Cal Pr.

Brathwaite, Edward. The Development of Creole Society in Jamaica, 1770-1820. 2nd ed. (Illus.). 390p. 1979. pap. 12.95x (ISBN 0-19-823195-4). Oxford U Pr.

Bridges, George W. Annals of Jamaica, 2 Vols. LC 76-106830. Repr. of 1827 ed. 38.00x set (ISBN 0-8371-3452-8, Pub. by Negro U Pr). Greenwood.

Browne, Patrick. Civil & Natural History of Jamaica. LC 71-141130. (Research Library of Colonial Americana). (Illus.). 1972. Repr. of 1756 ed. 50.00 (ISBN 0-405-03276-5). Arno.

Campbell, Mavis C. The Dynamics of Change in a Slave Society: A Sociopolitical History of the Free Colored's of Jamaica, 1800-1865. LC 74-4968. 393p. 1976. 22.00 (ISBN 0-8386-1584-8). Fairleigh Dickinson.

Clarke, Colin G. Kingston, Jamaica: Urban Growth & Social Change, 1692-1962. (Illus.). 1976. 47.50x (ISBN 0-520-02025-1). U of Cal Pr.

Craton, Michael & Walvin, James. Jamaican Plantation: The History of Worthy Park, 1670-1970. 1970. 25.00x (ISBN 0-8020-1727-4). U of Toronto Pr.

Elkins, W. F. Street Preachers, Faith Healers & Herb Doctors in Jamaica, 1890-1925. (Caribbean Studies Ser). 1976. lib. bdg. 69.95 (ISBN 0-87700-241-X). Revisionist Pr.

Fouchard, Jean. The Haitian Maroons: Liberty or Death. Watts, A. Faulkner, tr. from Fr. 500p. 1981. write for info. (ISBN 0-914110-11-X). Blyden Pr.

Gardner, William J. History of Jamaica: From Its Discovery by Christopher Columbus to the Year 1872. 1971. Repr. of 1909 ed. 37.50x (ISBN 0-7146-1938-8, F Cass Co). Biblio Dist.

Long, Edward. History of Jamaica, 3 vols. (Illus.). 1631p. 1970. Repr. of 1774 ed. 250.00x set (ISBN 0-7146-1942-6, F Cass Co). Biblio Dist.

--History of Jamaica: Or, General Survey of the Ancient & Modern State of That Island, 3 Vols. LC 70-141091. (Research Library of Colonial Americana). (Illus.). 1972. Repr. of 1774 ed. Set. 100.00 (ISBN 0-405-03293-5); 34.00 (ISBN 0-405-03294-3); 33.00 (ISBN 0-405-03295-1); 33.00 (ISBN 0-405-03296-X). Arno.

McFarlane, Milton C. Cudjoe the Maroon. (Illus.). 144p. Date not set. pap. 4.95 (ISBN 0-8052-8001-4, Pub. by Allison & Busby England). Schocken.

Manley, Norman. Manley & the New Jamaica. Nettleford, Rex, ed. & intro. by. LC 79-166600. 388p. 1971. text ed. 29.50x (ISBN 0-8419-0084-1, Africana). Holmes & Meier.

Olivier, Sydney H. Jamaica: The Blessed Island. LC 71-118339. (Illus.). 1971. Repr. of 1936 ed. 22.50 (ISBN 0-8462-1263-3). Russell.

Pim, Bedford. Negro & Jamaica. facs. ed. LC 72-157375. (Black Heritage Library Collection Ser). 1866. 10.00 (ISBN 0-8369-8813-2). Arno.

Sells, William. Remarks on the Condition of the Slaves in the Island of Jamaica. 52p. 1972. Repr. of 1823 ed. text ed. 5.50x (ISBN 0-7165-0120-1). Humanities.

Semmel, Bernard. Jamaican Blood & Victorian Conscience: The Governor Eyre Controversy. LC 76-7623. 1976. Repr. of 1963 ed. lib. bdg. 14.00x (ISBN 0-8371-8653-6, SEJB). Greenwood.

Senior, Bernard M. Jamaica, As It Was, As It Is, & As It May Be. LC 78-82321. Repr. of 1835 ed. 15.25x (ISBN 0-8371-1654-6, Pub. by Negro U Pr). Greenwood.

Sterne, Henry. Statement of Facts, Submitted to the Right Hon. Lord Glenelg, His Majesty's Principal Secretary of State for the Colonies. 12.50x (ISBN 0-8371-2714-9, Pub. by Negro U Pr). Greenwood.

Thomas, Mary E. Jamaica & Voluntary Laborers from Africa, 1840-1865. LC 72-93330. (Illus.). 225p. 1974. 12.00 (ISBN 0-8130-0438-1). U Presses Fla.

Underhill, Edward B. Tragedy of Morant Bay: A Narrative of the Disturbances in the Island of Jamaica in 1865. facs. ed. LC 73-157378. (Black Heritage Library Collection Ser). 1895. 16.00 (ISBN 0-8369-8816-7). Arno.

JAMAICA–SOCIAL CONDITIONS

Boot, Adrian & Thomas, Michael. Jamaica: Babylon on a Thin Wire. LC 76-41756. (Illus.). 1977. pap. 6.95 (ISBN 0-8052-0556-X). Schocken.

Brathwaite, Edward. The Development of Creole Society in Jamacia, 1770-1820. 2nd ed. (Illus.). 390p. 1979. pap. 12.95x (ISBN 0-19-823195-4). Oxford U Pr.

Brown, Aggrey. Color, Class & Politics in Jamaica. LC 76-58231. 250p. 1979. text ed. 14.95 (ISBN 0-87855-099-2). Transaction Bks.

Clark, Edith. My Mother Who Fathered Me: A Study of the Family in the Selected Communities in Jamaica. 1976. pap. text ed. 8.95x (ISBN 0-04-573010-5). Allen Unwin.

Curtin, Philip D. Two Jamaicas. LC 69-10082. (Illus.). 1970. pap. 3.95x (ISBN 0-689-70228-0, NL22). Atheneum.

--Two Jamaicas: The Role of Ideas in a Tropical Colony, 1830-1865. LC 69-10082. (Illus.). 1968. Repr. of 1955 ed. lib. bdg. 22.75 (ISBN 0-8371-0055-0, CUTJ). Greenwood.

Dreher, Melanie C. Working Men & Ganja: Marihuana Use in Rural Jamaica. (Illus.). 256p. 1981. text ed. 18.50x (ISBN 0-89727-025-8). Inst Study Human.

Eyre, L. Alan. Geographic Aspects of Population Dynamics in Jamaica. LC 76-151084. 1972. 7.50 (ISBN 0-8130-0440-3). U Presses Fla.

Henriques, Fernando. Family & Colour in Jamaica. 2nd ed. 1968. text ed. 9.00x (ISBN 0-261-62000-2). Humanities.

Kuper, Adam. Changing Jamaica. 160p. 1975. 18.50x (ISBN 0-7100-8241-X). Routledge & Kegan.

Lacey, Terrence J. Violence & Politics in Jamaica, 1960-1970: Internal Security in a Developing Country. 184p. 1977. 25.00x (ISBN 0-7146-6002-7, F Cass Co). Biblio Dist.

Nettleford, Rex. Caribbean Cultural Identity: The Case of Jamaica. Hill, Robert A. & Wilbert, Johannes, eds. LC 79-54305. (Afro-American Culture & Society Monograph: No. 1). Orig. Title: Cultural Action & Social Change: the Case of Jamaica. (Illus.). 239p. 1980. 13.95x (ISBN 0-934934-00-2, Co-Pub by UCLA Lat Am Ctr); pap. 8.00x (ISBN 0-934934-02-9, Co-Pub by UCLA Lat Am Ctr). Ctr Afro-Am Stud.

--Identity, Race, & Protest in Jamaica. 256p. 1972. 7.95 (ISBN 0-688-02854-3). Morrow.

JAMAICA–SOCIAL LIFE AND CUSTOMS

Beckwith, Martha W. Black Roadways: A Study of Jamaican Folk Life. LC 69-16597. (Illus.). Repr. of 1929 ed. 17.75x (ISBN 0-8371-1144-7, Pub. by Negro U Pr). Greenwood.

Heuman, Gad J. Between Black & White: Race, Politics, & the Free Coloreds in Jamaica, 1792-1865. LC 80-661. (Contributions in Comparative Colonial Studies: No. 5). (Illus.). xiii, 231p. 1981. lib. bdg. 35.00 (ISBN 0-313-20984-7, HBW/). Greenwood.

Long, Joseph. Psyche Versus Soma: Traditional Healing Choices in Jamaica. (Traditional Healing Ser.). 300p. 1981. 17.50 (ISBN 0-932426-20-4); pap. 9.95 (ISBN 0-932426-21-2). Conch Mag.

Nettleford, Rex. Caribbean Cultural Identity: The Case of Jamaica. Hill, Robert A. & Wilbert, Johannes, eds. LC 79-54305. (Afro-American Culture & Society Monograph: No. 1). Orig. Title: Cultural Action & Social Change: the Case of Jamaica. (Illus.). 239p. 1980. 13.95x (ISBN 0-934934-00-2, Co-Pub by UCLA Lat Am Ctr); pap. 8.00x (ISBN 0-934934-02-9, Co-Pub by UCLA Lat Am Ctr). Ctr Afro-Am Stud.

Plummer, John. Movement of Jah People: The Growth of the Rastafarians. (Illus., Orig.). (gr. 9-11). 1978. pap. 10.00x (ISBN 0-906507-00-6). Three Continents.

Sells, William. Remarks on the Condition of the Slaves in the Island of Jamaica. 52p. 1972. Repr. of 1823 ed. text ed. 5.50x (ISBN 0-7165-0120-1). Humanities.

Stone, Carl. Democracy & Clientelism in Jamaica. LC 79-66444. 270p. 1980. text ed. 16.95 (ISBN 0-87855-348-7). Transaction Bks.

Williams, Joseph J. Psychic Phenomena of Jamaica. LC 78-32183. 1979. Repr. of 1934 ed. lib. bdg. 19.75x (ISBN 0-8371-5669-6, WPP&). Greenwood.

Wright, Richardson. Revels in Jamaica 1682-1838. LC 78-81202. (Illus.). 1937. Repr. of 1927 ed. 19.00 (ISBN 0-405-09105-2). Arno.

JAMAICAN FOLK-LORE

see Folk-Lore, Jamaican

JAMAICAN FOLK-SONGS

see Folk-Songs, Jamaican

JAMAICAN TALES

see Tales, Jamaican

JAMAL AL-DIN, AL-HUSAINI, AL-AFGHANI, HEY, 1839-1897

Adams, Charles C. Islam & Modernism in Egypt: A Study of the Modern Reform Movement Inaugurated by Muhammed 'Abduh. LC 68-25061. 1968. Repr. of 1933 ed. 18.00 (ISBN 0-8462-1218-8). Russell.

JAMAN, AFRICA–DESCRIPTION AND TRAVEL

Freedman, Richard A. Travels & Life in Ashanti & Jaman. 559p. 1967. 37.50x (ISBN 0-7146-1808-X, F Cass Co). Biblio Dist.

JAMES 1ST, KING OF GREAT BRITAIN, 1566-1625

Akrigg, George P. Jacobean Pageant: The Court of King James First. LC 62-5508. (Illus.). 1967. pap. text ed. 6.95x (ISBN 0-689-70003-2, 103). Atheneum.

Birch, Thomas. Court & Times of James the First, 2 Vols. LC 74-113558. Repr. of 1849 ed. Set. 30.00 (ISBN 0-404-00906-9). AMS Pr.

Chettle, Henry. Englandes Mourning Garment Worne Here by Plaine Shepheardes, in Memorie of Their Mistresse Elizabeth. LC 73-6112. (English Experience Ser.: No. 579). 50p. 1973. Repr. of 1603 ed. 5.00 (ISBN 90-221-0579-2). Walter J Johnson.

Colville, John. Historie & Life of King James the Sext. LC 72-1010. (Bannatyne Club, Edinburgh. Publications: No. 13). Repr. of 1825 ed. 37.50 (ISBN 0-404-52713-2). AMS Pr.

Donne, John. Pseudo-Martyr. LC 74-16215. 450p. 1974. 45.00x (ISBN 0-8201-1140-6). Schol Facsimiles.

Fletcher, Robert. A Briefe & Familiar Epistle Shewing His Maiesties Title to All His Kingdomes. LC 72-5991. (English Experience Ser.: No. 516). 14p. 1973. Repr. of 1603 ed. 6.00 (ISBN 90-221-0516-4). Walter J Johnson.

Fraser, Antonia. King James Sixth & First. 1975. 15.00 (ISBN 0-394-49476-8). Knopf.

Gibson Craig, James T. Papers Relative to the Marriage of King James the Sixth of Scotland with the Princess Anna of Denmark. LC 70-168143. (Bannatyne Club, Edinburgh. Publications: No. 26). Repr. of 1828 ed. 27.50 (ISBN 0-404-52732-9). AMS Pr.

Gordon, John. England & Scotlands Happinesse in Being Reduced to Unitie of Religion. LC 75-38190. (English Experience Ser.: No. 461). 50p. 1972. Repr. of 1604 ed. 7.00 (ISBN 90-221-0461-3). Walter J Johnson.

Houston, S. J. James I. (Seminar Studies in History). 150p. 1974. pap. text ed. 5.50x (ISBN 0-582-35208-8). Longman.

James First-King Of England. Letters to King James the Sixth. Macdonald, Alexander, ed. LC 70-170840. (Maitland Club. Glasgow. Publications: No. 35). Repr. of 1835 ed. 17.50 (ISBN 0-404-53005-2). AMS Pr.

Lee, Maurice, Jr. James First & Henri Fourth: An Essay in English Foreign Policy, 1603-1610. LC 74-100377. (Illus.). 1970. 14.50 (ISBN 0-252-00084-6). U of Ill Pr.

Linklater, Eric. Ben Jonson & King James. LC 74-168250. 1972. Repr. of 1931 ed. 15.00 (ISBN 0-8046-1689-2). Kennikat.

McElwee, William. The Wisest Fool in Christendom. LC 74-7449. (Illus.). 296p. 1974. Repr. of 1958 ed. lib. bdg. 16.00x (ISBN 0-8371-7522-4, MCWF). Greenwood.

--The Wisest Fool in Christendom. LC 74-7449. (Illus.). 296p. 1974. Repr. of 1958 ed. lib. bdg. 16.00x (ISBN 0-8371-7522-4, MCWF). Greenwood.

Nichols, John. Progresses, Processions & Magnificent Festivities of King James First, His Royal Consort, Family & Court, 4 Vols. LC 3-29463. Repr. of 1828 ed. 108.00 (ISBN 0-404-04780-7). AMS Pr.

--Progresses, Processions & Magnificent Festivities of King James the First, His Royal Consort, Family & Court, 4 Vols. (Illus.). 1967. Repr. of 1828 ed. 140.00 (ISBN 0-8337-2537-8). B Franklin.

--Progresses, Processions & Magnificent Festivities of King James First, His Royal Consort, Family & Court, 4 Vols. LC 3-29463. (Illus.). 1968. Repr. of 1828 ed. Set. 108.00 (ISBN 0-527-67170-3). Kraus Repr.

Parsons, Robert. The Judgment of a Catholicke English-Man Living in Banishment for His Religion. LC 57-9033. 1978. Repr. of 1608 ed. 20.00 (ISBN 0-8201-1240-2). Schol Facsimiles.

Williams, Charles W. James First. facsimile ed. LC 77-103673. (Select Bibliographies Reprint Ser). 1934. 24.00 (ISBN 0-8369-5173-5). Arno.

JAMES 2ND, KING OF GREAT BRITAIN, 1633-1701

Ashley, Maurice. James II. (Illus.). 1978. 17.50x (ISBN 0-8166-0826-1). U of Minn Pr.

Belloc, Hilaire. James the Second. facsimile ed. LC 73-165615. (Select Bibliographies Reprint Ser). Repr. of 1928 ed. 18.00 (ISBN 0-8369-5922-1). Arno.

Childs, John. The Army, James II & the Glorious Revolution. 25.00 (ISBN 0-312-04949-8). St Martin.

JAMES 1ST, KING OF SCOTLAND, 1394-1437

James First, King of Scotland: The Kingis Quair. Repr. of 1939 ed. 19.00 (ISBN 0-403-04121-X). Somerset Pub.

Stevenson, Joseph, ed. Life & Death of King James the First of Scotland. LC 76-144432. (Maitland Club. Glasgow. Publications: No. 42). Repr. of 1837 ed. 7.50 (ISBN 0-404-53019-2). AMS Pr.

JAMES 4TH, KING OF SCOTLAND, 1473-1513

Mackie, Robert Laird. King James Fourth of Scotland: A Brief Survey of His Life & Times. LC 76-9098. (Illus.). 1976. Repr. of 1958 ed. lib. bdg. 22.25 (ISBN 0-8371-8145-3, MAKJ). Greenwood.

JAMES 5TH, KING OF SCOTLAND, 1512-1542

James Fifth King Of Scotland. Ad Serenissmum Jacobum Quintum Strena. LC 74-26227. (English Experience Ser.: No. 127). 8p. 1969. Repr. of 1525 ed. 7.00 (ISBN 90-221-0127-4). Walter J Johnson.

Liber Domicilii Regis Jacobi Quinti. Excerpta E Libris Domicilii Domini Jacobi Quinti Regis Scotorum. LC 75-172317. (Bannatyne Club, Edinburgh. Publications: No. 54). Repr. of 1836 ed. 37.50 (ISBN 0-404-52764-7). AMS Pr.

JAMES 6TH, KING OF SCOTLAND

see James 1st, King of Great Britain, 1566-1625

JAMES, ALICE, 1848-1892

James, Alice. Alice James: Her Brothers, Her Journal. Burr, Anna R., ed. LC 77-6980. 1977. Repr. of 1934 ed. lib. bdg. 30.00 (ISBN 0-89341-171-X). Longwood Pr.

Strouse, Jean. Alice James: A Biography. 384p. 1980. 15.00 (ISBN 0-395-27787-6). HM.

Yeazell, Ruth B., ed. The Death & Letters of Alice James: Selected Correspondence. (Illus.). 200p. 1980. 12.95 (ISBN 0-520-03745-6). U of Cal Pr.

JAMES, FRANK, 1844-1915

Baldwin, Margaret & O'Brien, Pat. Wanted! Frank & Jesse James: The Real Story. (Illus.). 192p. (gr. 7 up). 1981. PLB 10.29 (ISBN 0-671-34060-3). Messner.

James, Frank L. Years of Discontent: Dr. Frank L. James in Arkansas, 1877-1878. Baird, W. David, intro. by. LC 76-40025. (Memphis State University Press Primary Source Ser.). 1977. pap. 6.95x (ISBN 0-87870-037-4). Memphis St Univ.

Triplett, Frank. Life, Times & Treacherous Death of Jesse James. Snell, Joseph, ed. LC 70-75734. (Illus.). 344p. 1970. 16.95 (ISBN 0-8040-0187-1, SB); limited ed. 30.00 (ISBN 0-8040-0188-X). Swallow.

JAMES, HENRY, 1811-1882

Babiiha, Thaddeo K. The James-Hawthorne Relation: Biographical Essays. (Scholarly Reference Publications). 1980. lib. bdg. 20.00 (ISBN 0-8161-8431-3). G K Hall.

Daugherty, Sarah B. The Literary Criticism of Henry James. LC 80-36753. xiv, 232p. 1981. 16.95x (ISBN 0-8214-0440-7). Ohio U Pr.

Grattan, C. Hartley. Three Jameses: A Family of Minds: Henry James Sr., William James, Henry James. (Gotham Library). 380p. 1962. pap. 4.95 (ISBN 0-8147-0168-X). NYU Pr.

James, Henry, Sr. The Selected Works of Henry James, Sr, 10 vols. Repr. of 1906 ed. Set. 205.00 (ISBN 0-404-10080-5). AMS Pr.

Le Clair, Robert C. Young Henry James 1813-1876. LC 77-153337. Repr. of 1955 ed. 29.45 (ISBN 0-404-03897-2). AMS Pr.

Monteiro, George. Henry James & John Hay: The Record of a Friendship. LC 65-24094. (Illus.). xiv, 205p. 1965. 10.00 (ISBN 0-87057-091-9, Pub. by Brown U Pr). U Pr of New Eng.

Powers, Lyall H. Henry James & the Naturalist Movement. 200p. 1971. 8.50 (ISBN 0-87013-156-7). Mich St U Pr.

Vientos Gaston, Nilita. Introduccion a Henry James. pap. 1.25 (ISBN 0-8477-3160-X). U of PR Pr.

Warren, Austin. Elder Henry James. LC 75-120675. 1970. Repr. of 1934 ed. lib. bdg. 14.50x (ISBN 0-374-98262-7). Octagon.

--Elder Henry James. facsimile ed. LC 75-107835. (Select Bibliographies Reprint Ser). 1934. 18.00 (ISBN 0-8369-5200-6). Arno.

Young, Frederic H. The Philosophy of Henry James Sr. (Orig.). 1951. 8.50 (ISBN 0-8084-0244-7); pap. 3.45 (ISBN 0-8084-0245-5, P31). Coll & U Pr.

JAMES, HENRY, 1843-1916

Abel, Darrel. Barron's Simplified Approach to James's Turn of the Screw & Other Works. (Orig.). 1964. pap. 1.50 (ISBN 0-8120-0176-1). Barron.

Anderson, Charles R. Person, Place & Thing in Henry James's Novels. LC 77-75619. 1977. 16.75 (ISBN 0-685-86611-4). Duke.

Andreas, Osborn. Henry James & the Expanding Horizon. LC 72-90463. Repr. of 1948 ed. lib. bdg. 15.00 (ISBN 0-8371-2133-7, ANJH). Greenwood.

Appignanesi, Lisa. Femininity & the Creative Imagination: A Study of Henry James, Robert Musil & Marcel Proust. 1973. 12.95x (ISBN 0-8464-0407-9). Beekman Pubs.

Auchincloss, Louis. Reflections of a Jacobite. LC 74-156968. Repr. of 1961 ed. lib. bdg. 12.50x (ISBN 0-678-03571-7). Kelley.

Bea, Harvey D. The Ambassadors Notes. pap. text ed. 1.95 (ISBN 0-8220-0161-6). Cliffs.

Beach, Joseph W. Method of Henry James. rev. ed. 1954. 7.50x (ISBN 0-87556-020-2). Saifer.

Berland, Alwyn. Culture & Conduct in the Novels of Henry James. 225p. 1981. 39.95 (ISBN 0-521-23343-7). Cambridge U Pr.

Bewley, Marius. Complex Fate: Hawthorne, Henry James, & Some American Writers. LC 67-28474. 1967. Repr. of 1954 ed. 9.00 (ISBN 0-87752-008-9). Gordian.

Bosanquet, Theodora. Henry James at Work. (Studies in Henry James, No. 17). 1970. pap. 11.95 (ISBN 0-8383-0009-X). Haskell.

--Henry James at Work. LC 76-13030. 1976. Repr. of 1924 ed. lib. bdg. 7.50 (ISBN 0-8414-3340-2). Folcroft.

Bowden, Edwin T. Themes of Henry James: A System of Observation Through the Visual Arts. (Yale Studies in English Ser.: No. 132). 1969. Repr. of 1956 ed. 15.00 (ISBN 0-208-00723-7, Archon). Shoe String.

Bradbury, Nicola. Henry James: The Later Novels. 236p. 1979. text ed. 39.00x (ISBN 0-19-812096-6). Oxford U Pr.

Brooks, Van Wyck. The Pilgrimage of Henry James. LC 75-159169. vii, 170p. 1972. Repr. of 1925 ed. lib. bdg. 14.00x (ISBN 0-374-91004-9). Octagon.

Buitenhuis, Peter. Grasping Imagination: The American Writings of Henry James. LC 79-149323. 1970. 22.50x (ISBN 0-8020-5244-4); pap. 5.00 (ISBN 0-8020-6225-3). U of Toronto Pr.

Canby, Henry S. Turn West, Turn East: Mark Twain & Henry James. LC 65-23485. 1951. 12.00x (ISBN 0-8196-0154-3). Biblo.

Cary, Elizabeth L. Novels of Henry James: A Study. LC 72-10933. (Studies in Henry James, No. 17). 1969. Repr. of 1905 ed. lib. bdg. 49.95 (ISBN 0-8383-0520-2). Haskell.

Cranfill, Thomas M. & Clark, Robert L., Jr. Anatomy of the Turn of the Screw. LC 78-159037. 1971. Repr. of 1965 ed. text ed. 9.00 (ISBN 0-87752-151-4). Gordian.

Crews, Frederick C. Tragedy of Manners: Moral Drama in the Later Novels of Henry James. LC 77-131376. 1971. Repr. of 1957 ed. 14.50 (ISBN 0-208-01047-5, Archon). Shoe String.

Donadio, Stephen. Nietzsche, Henry James, & the Artistic Will. LC 77-15657. 1978. 16.95x (ISBN 0-19-502358-7). Oxford U Pr.

Dupee, F. W. Henry James. LC 73-16722. 280p. 1974. pap. 2.95 (ISBN 0-688-06776-X). Morrow.

Dupee, F. W., ed. The Question of Henry James. LC 77-159243. 302p. 1973. Repr. of 1945 ed. lib. bdg. 17.50x (ISBN 0-374-92417-1). Octagon.

Dupee, Frederick W. Henry James. LC 72-9047. (American Men of Letters Ser.). (Illus.). 301p. 1973. Repr. of 1951 ed. lib. bdg. 19.25x (ISBN 0-8371-6566-0, DUHE). Greenwood.

Edel, Leon. Henry James in Westminster Abbey: The Address. (Illus.). 24p. 1976. pap. 7.00 (ISBN 0-932136-02-8). Petronium Pr.

--Henry James: The Conquest of London. 1978. pap. 2.95 (ISBN 0-380-39651-3, 39651). Avon.

--Henry James: The Master. 1978. pap. 2.95 (ISBN 0-380-39685-8, 39685). Avon.

--Henry James: The Master 1901-1916. LC 76-163225. (Henry James Ser). (Illus.). 1972. 12.95 (ISBN 0-397-00733-7). Har-Row.

--Henry James: The Middle Years. 1978. pap. 2.95 (ISBN 0-380-39669-6, 39669). Avon.

--Henry James: The Treacherous Years. 1978. pap. 2.95 (ISBN 0-380-39677-7, 39677). Avon.

--Henry James: The Untried Years. 1978. pap. 2.95 (ISBN 0-380-39107-4, 39107). Avon.

Edgar, Pelham. Henry James: Man & Author. LC 64-12141. 1964. Repr. of 1927 ed. 11.00 (ISBN 0-8462-0416-9). Russell.

Egan, Michael, ed. Henry James: The Ibsen Years. 154p. 1972. text ed. 8.00x (ISBN 0-85478-242-7). Humanities.

Fogel, Daniel M. Henry James & the Structure of the Romantic Imagination. LC 81-4824. xvi, 208p. 1981. 17.95 (ISBN 0-8071-0789-1). La State U Pr.

Ford, Ford M. Henry James. 1964. lib. bdg. 13.50x (ISBN 0-374-92775-8). Octagon.

Fox, Hugh. Henry James, a Critical Introduction. LC 65-57412. (Comparative Literature Studies Ser). (Illus.). 109p. 1968. pap. 5.00 (ISBN 0-87423-005-5). Westburg.

Furth, David L. The Visionary Betrayed: Aesthetic Discontinuity in Henry James's The American Scene. (The LeBaron Russell Briggs Prize Honors Essay in English). 1980. pap. text ed. 3.95x (ISBN 0-674-94085-7). Harvard U Pr.

Gale, Robert L. Plots & Characters - James. 280p. 1972. pap. 2.95 (ISBN 0-262-57031-9). MIT Pr.

--Plots & Characters in the Fiction of Henry James. (Plots & Characters Ser.). 1965. 16.00 (ISBN 0-208-00500-5, Archon). Shoe String.

Galloway, David. Henry James: The Portrait of a Lady. (Studies in English Literature). 1973. pap. text ed. 3.95x (ISBN 0-7131-5113-7). Dynamic Learn Corp.

Gard, Roger, ed. Henry James: The Critical Heritage. (The Critical Heritage Ser.). 1976. Repr. of 1968 ed. 38.50x (ISBN 0-7100-6068-8). Routledge & Kegan.

Gervais, David. Flaubert & Henry James: A Study in Contrasts. 1978. text ed. 23.50x (ISBN 0-06-492375-4). B&N.

Grattan, C. Hartley. Three Jameses: A Family of Minds: Henry James Sr., William James, Henry James. (Gotham Library). 380p. 1962. pap. 4.95 (ISBN 0-8147-0168-X). NYU Pr.

Hapgood, Norman. Literary Statesmen & Others: Stendhal, Henry James. 208p. 1981. Repr. of 1897 ed. lib. bdg. 25.00 (ISBN 0-8495-2361-3). Arden Lib.

Hocks, Richard A. Henry James & Pragmatistic Thought: A Study in the Relationship Between the Philosophy of William James & the Literary Art of Henry James. LC 73-16271. (Illus.). 258p. 1974. 22.00x (ISBN 0-8078-1225-0). U of NC Pr.

Holder-Barell, Alexander. Development of Imagery & Its Functional Significance in Henry James's Novels. LC 68-1739. (Studies in Henry James, No. 17). 1969. Repr. of 1959 ed. lib. bdg. 29.95 (ISBN 0-8383-0665-9). Haskell.

Hovanec, Evelyn A. Henry James & Germany. (Costerus: New Ser.: No. XIX). 1979. text ed. 17.25x (ISBN 90-6203-902-2). Humanities.

Hughes, Herbert L. Theory & Practice in Henry James. LC 76-26959. 1926. lib. bdg. 20.00 (ISBN 0-8414-4818-3). Folcroft.

Hyde, H. Montgomery. Henry James at Home. LC 68-14920. (Illus.). 360p. 1969. 6.95 (ISBN 0-374-16944-6). FS&G.

James, Henry. A Bundle of Letters. 64p. 1980. Repr. of 1880 ed. lib. bdg. 10.00 (ISBN 0-8492-5625-9). R West.

--The Letters of Henry James: Vol. 1, 1843-1875. Edel, Leon, ed. LC 74-77181. (Illus.). 493p. 1974. 18.50x (ISBN 0-674-38780-5, Belknap Pr). Harvard U Pr.

--The Letters of Henry James: Vol. 2, 1875-1883. Edel, Leon, ed. LC 74-77181. (Illus.). 438p. 1975. 17.50x (ISBN 0-674-38781-3). Harvard U Pr.

--The Letters of Henry James: 1883-1895, Vol. III. Edel, Leon, ed. LC 74-77181. (Illus.). 601p. 1980. text ed. 20.00x (ISBN 0-674-38782-1). Harvard U Pr.

--The Middle Years. lib. bdg. 35.00 (ISBN 0-8414-9105-4). Folcroft.

--The Tales of Henry James, Vol. 2: 1870-1874. Aziz, Madbool, ed. 1979. 49.00x (ISBN 0-19-812572-0). Oxford U Pr.

James, Henry & Wells, H. G. Henry James & H. G. Wells: A Record of Their Friendship, Their Debate on the Art of Fiction, & Their Quarrel. Edel, Leon & Ray, Gordon N., eds. LC 78-25756. 1979. Repr. of 1958 ed. lib. bdg. 22.50x (ISBN 0-313-20810-7, JAHJ). Greenwood.

Jones, Granville H. Henry James' Psychology of Experience: Innocence, Responsibility & Renunciation in the Fiction of Henry James. LC 74-75036. (De Proprietatibus Litterarum, Ser: No. 79). 310p. 1975. pap. text ed. 48.25x (ISBN 90-2793-292-1). Mouton.

Kappeler, Susanne. Writing & Reading in Henry James. LC 80-18181. 242p. 1980. 22.50x (ISBN 0-231-05198-0). Columbia U Pr.

Kelley, Cornelia P. The Early Development of Henry James. rev. ed. LC 65-19108. (Studies in Language & Literature Ser: Vol. 15). 1965. pap. 6.95 (ISBN 0-252-72385-6). U of Ill Pr.

Kinoian, Vartkis. Monarch Notes on James' Portrait of a Lady. (Orig.). pap. 1.75 (ISBN 0-671-00679-7). Monarch Pr.

--Monarch Notes on James' the American. (Orig.). pap. 1.75 (ISBN 0-671-00678-9). Monarch Pr.

Kirschke, James J. Henry James & Impressionism. LC 80-52732. 357p. 1981. 22.50x (ISBN 0-87875-206-4). Whitston Pub.

Krook, Dorothea. Ordeal of Consciousness in Henry James. (Orig.). 1968. pap. 13.95x (ISBN 0-521-09449-6). Cambridge U Pr.

Lebowitz, Naomi. The Imagination of Loving: Henry James's Legacy to the Novel. LC 65-14595. 1965. 11.95x (ISBN 0-8143-1270-5). Wayne St U Pr.

Lee, Brian. The Novels of Henry James: A Study of Culture & Consciousness. LC 78-16902. 1979. 16.95 (ISBN 0-312-57969-1). St Martin.

Leeming, Glenda. Who's Who in Henry James. LC 75-34783. (Who's Who in Literature Ser.). 224p. 1976. 7.95 (ISBN 0-8008-8268-7). Taplinger.

Liljegren, Sten B. American & European in the Works of Henry James. LC 71-119080. (Studies in Henry James, No. 17). 1970. Repr. of 1919 ed. lib. bdg. 32.95 (ISBN 0-8383-1076-1). Haskell.

Lilly, Katherine A. Portrait of the Artist As a Young Man Notes. (Orig.). pap. 1.75 (ISBN 0-8220-1057-7). Cliffs.

Long, Robert E. The Great Succession: Henry James & the Legacy of Hawthorne. LC 79-922. (Critical Essays in Modern Literature Ser.). 1979. 12.95 (ISBN 0-8229-3398-5). U of Pittsburgh Pr.

Lucas, E. V. Reading, Writing & Remembering: A Literary Record. Meredith, James, Dickens, Thackeray, Conrad, & Hardy. Repr. of 1932 ed. lib. bdg. 30.00 (ISBN 0-8495-3315-5). Arden Lib.

McElderry, Bruce R., Jr. Henry James. (Twayne's United States Authors Ser). 1965. pap. 3.45 (ISBN 0-8084-0152-1, T79, Twayne). Coll & U Pr.

--Henry James. (U. S. Authors Ser.: No. 79). 1965. lib. bdg. 10.95 (ISBN 0-8057-0404-3). Twayne.

MacKenzie, Manfred. Communities of Honor & Love in Henry James. 292p. 1976. 12.50x (ISBN 0-674-15160-7). Harvard U Pr.

Matthiessen, F. O. Henry James: The Major Phase. 1944. 11.95 (ISBN 0-19-501225-9). Oxford U Pr.

Matthiessen, F. O. & Murdock, Kenneth B., eds. The Notebooks of Henry James. xxviii, 426p. 10.95 (ISBN 0-226-51104-9, Phoen). U of Chicago Pr.

Monarch Notes on James the Turn of the Screw & Daisy Miller. 1965. pap. 1.95 (ISBN 0-671-00680-0). Monarch Pr.

Moore, Marianne & Wilson, Edmund. Homage to Henry James. 1971. 9.00 (ISBN 0-911858-17-2). Appel.

Mull, Donald L. Henry James' "Sublime Economy". Money As Symbolic Center in the Fiction. LC 73-6007. 1973. 12.50x (ISBN 0-8195-4064-1, Pub. by Wesleyan U Pr). Columbia U Pr.

Nettels, Elsa. James & Conrad. LC 76-2897. (SAMLA Studies Award Ser.). 289p. 1977. 17.50x (ISBN 0-8203-0408-5). U of Ga Pr.

Norrman, Ralf. The Insecure World of Henry James's Fiction: Intensity & Ambiguity. 1981. 22.50 (ISBN 0-312-41863-9). St Martin.

Perosa, Sergio. Henry James & the Experimental Novel. LC 77-16847. 1978. 12.95x (ISBN 0-8139-0727-6). U Pr of Va.

Peterson, Dale E. The Clement Vision: Poetic Realism in Turgenev & James. (National University Publications Literary Criticism Ser.). 1975. 12.00 (ISBN 0-8046-9107-X, Natl U). Kennikat.

Pirie, Gordon. Henry James. (Literature in Perspective). 152p. 1975. 7.50x (ISBN 0-87471-611-X). Rowman.

Poirer, Richard. Comic Sense of Henry James: A Study of the Early Novels. 1967. pap. 4.95 (ISBN 0-19-500438-8, GB). Oxford U Pr.

Powers, Lyall. Merrill Studies in the Portrait of a Lady. LC 75-116607. 1970. pap. text ed. 2.50x (ISBN 0-675-09357-0). Merrill.

Purdy, Strother B. The Hole in the Fabric: Science, Contemporary Literature, & Henry James. LC 76-6667. (Critical Essays in Modern Literature Ser.). 1977. 12.95 (ISBN 0-686-31717-3). U of Pittsburgh Pr.

Putt, Samuel G. Henry James: A Reader's Guide. LC 66-17350. (YA) (gr. 9-12). 1967. pap. 5.95 (ISBN 0-8014-9027-8). Cornell U Pr.

Ranald, Ralph A. Monarch Notes on James' Washington Square. (Orig.). pap. 2.25 (ISBN 0-671-00846-3). Monarch Pr.

Rimmon, Shlomith. The Concept of Ambiguity: The Example of James. LC 77-2171. 1977. lib. bdg. 19.00x (ISBN 0-226-72010-1). U of Chicago Pr.

Roberts, James L. American Notes. (Orig.). pap. 1.75 (ISBN 0-8220-0164-0). Cliffs.

--Portrait of a Lady Notes. (Orig.). pap. 1.75 (ISBN 0-8220-1066-6). Cliffs.

Roberts, James L., ed. Daisy Miller Notes. Bd. with Turn of the Screw Notes. (Orig.). pap. 2.25 (ISBN 0-8220-0355-4). Cliffs.
Roberts, Morris. Henry James' Criticism. LC 65-26463. (Studies in Henry James, No. 17). 1969. Repr. of 1929 ed. lib. bdg. 28.95 (ISBN 0-8383-0614-4). Haskell.
--Henry James's Criticism. LC 78-120657. 1970. Repr. of 1929 ed. lib. bdg. 11.00x (ISBN 0-374-96855-1). Octagon.
Rowe, John C. Henry Adams & Henry James: The Emergence of a Modern Consciousness. LC 75-16928. 272p. 1976. 19.50x (ISBN 0-8014-0954-3). Cornell U Pr.
Schneider, Daniel J. The Crystal Cage: Adventures of the Imagination in the Fiction of Henry James. LC 77-26894. 1978. 13.00x (ISBN 0-7006-0177-5). Regents Pr KS.
Scholes, James B. Henry James's "the American". A Study Guide. 1978. Repr. of 1963 ed. lib. bdg. 7.50 (ISBN 0-8414-7889-9). Folcroft.
Sharma, J. N. International Fiction of Henry James. 1979. 12.00x (ISBN 0-8364-0498-X, Macmillan India). South Asia Bks.
--The International Fiction of Henry James. 1980. text ed. 12.50x (ISBN 0-333-90300-5). Humanities.
Sheppard, E. A. Henry James & the Turn of the Screw. (Illus.). 304p. 1975. 19.95x (ISBN 0-19-647810-3). Oxford U Pr.
Sicker, Philip. Love & the Quest for Identity in the Fiction of Henry James. LC 79-17311. 1980. 16.00x (ISBN 0-691-06417-2); pap. 8.50 (ISBN 0-691-10092-6). Princeton U Pr.
Siegel, Eli. James & the Children: A Consideration of Henry James's The Turn of the Screw. Baird, Martha, ed. LC 67-31121. (Orig.). 1968. 4.95 (ISBN 0-910492-08-5); pap. 2.45 (ISBN 0-910492-22-0). Definition.
Smalley, Evelyn G. Henry James Year Book. LC 76-29067. 1912. lib. bdg. 12.50 (ISBN 0-8414-7811-2). Folcroft.
Snell, Edwin M. Modern Fables of Henry James. LC 66-27148. 1967. Repr. of 1935 ed. 5.75 (ISBN 0-8462-1030-4). Russell.
Spender, Stephen. Destructive Element. 1970. wrapps 5.00x (ISBN 0-87556-325-2). Saifer.
--Destructive Element: A Study of Modern Writers & Beliefs. 1935. lib. bdg. 25.00 (ISBN 0-8414-7557-1). Folcroft.
Springer, Mary D. A Rhetoric of Literary Character: Some Women of Henry James. LC 78-6699. 1978. lib. bdg. 17.00x (ISBN 0-226-76983-6). U of Chicago Pr.
Stafford, William T. A Name, Title & Place Index to the Critical Writings of Henry James. LC 75-8093. 1975. 23.00 (ISBN 0-910972-47-8). IHS-PDS.
Stafford, William T., ed. Perspectives on James's "The Portrait of a Lady". A Collection of Critical Essays. LC 67-10692. (Gotham Library). (Orig.). 1967. pap. 4.95x (ISBN 0-8147-0400-X). NYU Pr.
Stallman, R. W. The Houses That James Built and Other Literary Studies. LC 77-371844. 256p. 1977. 14.00x (ISBN 0-8214-0362-1); pap. 5.50x (ISBN 0-8214-0363-X). Ohio U Pr.
Stevenson, Elizabeth. The Crooked Corridor. 1980. Repr. of 1949 ed. lib. bdg. 14.00x (ISBN 0-374-97626-0). Octagon.
Stowell, H. Peter. Literary Impressionism, James & Chekhov. LC 78-23737. 286p. 1980. 17.00x (ISBN 0-8203-0468-9). U of Ga Pr.
Tanner, Tony, ed. Henry James. LC 79-125579. (Modern Judgement Ser). 1970. pap. text ed. 2.50 (ISBN 0-87695-099-3). Aurora Pubs.
Tilley, W. H. Background of "The Princess Casamassima". LC 61-6288. (U of Fla. Humanities Monograph Ser.: No. 5). 1961. pap. 3.00 (ISBN 0-8130-0228-1). U Presses Fla.
Veeder, William. Henry James-the Lessons of the Master: Popular Fiction & Personal Style in the Nineteenth Century. LC 75-8957. 1979. 6.95 (ISBN 0-226-85224-5, P848, Phoen). U of Chicago Pr.
--Henry James: The Lessons of the Master. LC 75-8957. (Illus.). xiv, 288p. 1975. lib. bdg. 16.00x (ISBN 0-226-85223-7). U of Chicago Pr.
Vitale, Philip H. Barron's Simplified Approach to James's Portrait of a Lady. LC 70-108019. (gr. 10-12). 1972. pap. 1.50 (ISBN 0-8120-0399-3). Barron.
Waldock, Arthur J. James, Joyce & Others. facs. ed. LC 67-23277. (Essay Index Reprint Ser). 1937. 13.00 (ISBN 0-8369-0963-1). Arno.
Ward, Joseph A. Search for Form: Studies in the Structure of James's Fiction. 1967. 16.00x (ISBN 0-8078-1040-1). U of NC Pr.
Warren, Austin. Elder Henry James. LC 75-120675. 1970. Repr. of 1934 ed. lib. bdg. 14.50x (ISBN 0-374-98262-7). Octagon.
Wegelin, Christof. Image of Europe in Henry James. LC 58-9271. 1958. 5.95 (ISBN 0-87074-122-5). SMU Press.
West, Rebecca. Henry James. LC 73-21774. (Studies in Henry James, No. 17). 1974. lib. bdg. 39.95 (ISBN 0-8383-1833-9). Haskell.
--Henry James. LC 74-8448. 1916. lib. bdg. 12.50 (ISBN 0-8414-9527-0). Folcroft.
Wexford, Jane. Monarch Notes on James' the Aspern Papers. (Orig.). pap. 1.75 (ISBN 0-671-00845-5). Monarch Pr.
Wiesenfarth, Joseph. Henry James & the Dramatic Analogy. LC 63-11901. 1963. 15.00 (ISBN 0-8232-0495-2). Fordham.
Winner, Viola H. Henry James & the Visual Arts. LC 73-109223. (Illus.). 202p. 1970. 10.95x (ISBN 0-8139-0285-1). U Pr of Va.
Yeazell, Ruth B. Language & Knowledge in the Late Novels of Henry James. LC 75-46538. 1976. 10.00x (ISBN 0-226-95094-8). U of Chicago Pr.

JAMES, HENRY, 1843-1916–BIBLIOGRAPHY

Edel, Leon, ed. Henry James: Selected Fiction. 1964. pap. 6.95 (ISBN 0-525-47140-5). Dutton.
James, Henry & Stevenson, Robert Louis. Henry James & Robert Louis Stevenson: A Record of Friendship & Criticism. Smith, Janet A., ed. & intro. by. LC 78-20472. 1980. Repr. of 1948 ed. text ed. 22.50 (ISBN 0-88355-850-5). Hyperion Conn.
McColgan, Kristian P. Henry James, Nineteen Seventeen to Nineteen Fifty-Nine: A Reference Guide. (Reference Bks.). 1979. lib. bdg. 30.00 (ISBN 0-8161-7851-8). G K Hall.
Phillips, Le Roy. Bibliography of the Writings of Henry James. 2nd ed. 1930. 23.50 (ISBN 0-8337-2736-2). B Franklin.
Phillips, Le Roy, ed. A Bibliography of the Writings of Henry James. LC 77-94612. 1979. Repr. of 1906 ed. lib. bdg. 20.00 (ISBN 0-89341-155-8). Longwood Pr.
Ricks, Beatrice. Henry James: A Bibliography of Secondary Works. LC 75-22128. (Author Bibliographies Ser.: No. 24). 1975. 21.00 (ISBN 0-8108-0853-6). Scarecrow.
Scura, Dorothy M. Henry James, Nineteen Sixty to Nineteen Seventy Four: A Reference Guide. (Reference Bks.). 1979. lib. bdg. 40.00 (ISBN 0-8161-7850-X). G K Hall.

JAMES, JESSE WOODSON, 1847-1882

Baldwin, Margaret & O'Brien, Pat. Wanted! Frank & Jesse James: The Real Story. (Illus.). 192p. (gr. 7 up). 1981. PLB 10.29 (ISBN 0-671-34060-3). Messner.
Bradley, Larry C. Jesse James: The Making of a Legend. LC 80-81622. (Illus.). 228p. (Orig.). 1980. pap. 8.95 (ISBN 0-9604370-0-2). Larren Pubs.
Ernst, John. Jesse James. LC 76-10206. (Illus.). (gr. 4-7). 1976. PLB 6.95 (ISBN 0-13-509695-2); pap. 1.95 (ISBN 0-13-509661-8). P-H.
Newmans, Evans. The True Story of the Notorious Jesse James. 1976. 5.00 (ISBN 0-682-48534-9, Lochinvar). Exposition.
Settle, William A., Jr. Jesse James Was His Name: or, Fact & Fiction Concerning the Careers of the Notorious James Brothers of Missouri. LC 76-56786. (Illus.). 1977. pap. 6.50 (ISBN 0-8032-5860-7, BB 640, Bison). U of Nebr Pr.
Triplett, Frank. Life, Times & Treacherous Death of Jesse James. Snell, Joseph, ed. LC 70-75734. (Illus.). 344p. 1970. 16.95 (ISBN 0-8040-0187-1, SB); limited ed. 30.00 (ISBN 0-8040-0188-X). Swallow.
--The Life, Times, & Treacherous Death of Jesse James. 1977. pap. 1.25 (ISBN 0-8439-0432-1, LB432ZK, Leisure Bks). Nordon Pubns.

JAMES, SAINT, APOSTLE

Christensen, Chuck & Christensen, Winnie. James: Faith in Action. LC 75-33442. (Fisherman Bible Study Guides). 1975. pap. 1.95 saddle stitched (ISBN 0-87788-421-8). Shaw Pubs.
King, Georgianna G. The Way of St. James, 3 vols. LC 78-63469. Repr. of 1920 ed. Set. 140.00 (ISBN 0-404-17160-5). AMS Pr.

JAMES, WILL, 1892-1942

Amaral, Anthony A. Will James: The Last Cowboy Legend. rev. ed. LC 80-155. (Lancehead Ser.). (Illus.). xiv, 175p. 1980. 12.00 (ISBN 0-87417-058-3). U of Nev Pr.

JAMES, WILLIAM, 1771-1837

Wilshire, Bruce. William James & Phenomenology: A Study of "the Principles of Psychology". LC 76-6601. Repr. of 1968 ed. 24.00 (ISBN 0-404-15226-0). AMS Pr.

JAMES, WILLIAM, 1842-1910

Allen, Gay W. William James. LC 79-629874. (Pamphlets on American Writers Ser.: No. 88). (Orig.). 1970. pap. 1.25x (ISBN 0-8166-0560-2, MPAW88). U of Minn Pr.
Ayer, Alfred J. Origins of Pragmatism: Studies in the Philosophy of Charles Sanders Peirce & William James. LC 68-21669. 1968. 10.50x (ISBN 0-87735-501-0). Freeman C.
Bergson, Henri. An Introduction to Metaphysics: The Creative Mind. (Quality Paperback: No. 164). 1975. pap. 3.95 (ISBN 0-8226-0164-8). Littlefield.
Bergson, Henri L. Creative Mind. Andison, Mabelle L., tr. LC 68-19264. Repr. of 1946 ed. lib. bdg. 20.75x (ISBN 0-8371-0310-X, BECM). Greenwood.
Brennan, Bernard P. William James. (Twayne's United States Authors Ser). 1968. pap. 3.45 (ISBN 0-8084-0005-3, T131, Twayne). Coll & U Pr.
--William James. (U. S. Authors Ser.: No. 131). 1968. lib. bdg. 10.95 (ISBN 0-8057-0408-6). Twayne.
Browning, Don S. Pluralism & Personality: William James & Some Contemporary Cultures of Psychology. LC 78-75196. 280p. Date not set. 22.50 (ISBN 0-8387-2265-2). Bucknell U Pr.
Clebsch, William A. American Religious Thought. LC 73-82911. (Chicago History of American Religion Ser). 1973. 12.95x (ISBN 0-226-10960-7). U of Chicago Pr.
--American Religious Thought: A History. LC 73-82911. (Chicago History of American Religion Ser.). xxii, 212p. 1975. pap. text ed. 3.95 (ISBN 0-226-10961-5, P638, Phoen). U of Chicago Pr.
Corti, W. The Philosophy of William James. 1977. pap. 25.90 (ISBN 3-7873-0352-9). Adler.
Eisendrath, Craig R. Unifying Moment: The Psychological Philosophy of William James & Alfred North Whitehead. LC 70-135550. 1971. 16.50x (ISBN 0-674-92100-3). Harvard U Pr.
Flournoy, T. Philosophy of William James. LC 78-99658. (Select Bibliographies Reprint Ser). 1917. 22.00 (ISBN 0-8369-5087-9). Arno.
Grattan, C. Hartley. Three Jameses: A Family of Minds: Henry James Sr., William James, Henry James. (Gotham Library). 380p. 1962. pap. 4.95 (ISBN 0-8147-0168-X). NYU Pr.
Hocks, Richard A. Henry James & Pragmatistic Thought: A Study in the Relationship Between the Philosophy of William James & the Literary Art of Henry James. LC 73-16271. (Illus.). 258p. 1974. 22.00x (ISBN 0-8078-1225-0). U of NC Pr.
James, William. In Commemoration of William James, 1842-1942. Repr. of 1942 ed. 7.50 (ISBN 0-404-03550-7). AMS Pr.
--Pragmatism. Kuklick, Bruce, ed. (Philosophical Classics Ser.). 152p. 1980. lib. bdg. 13.50 (ISBN 0-915145-04-9); pap. text ed. 2.95 (ISBN 0-915145-05-7). Hackett Pub.
--Pragmatism & the Meaning of Truth. 1978. 18.50x (ISBN 0-674-69736-7); pap. 6.95 (ISBN 0-674-69737-5). Harvard U Pr.
James, Williams. The Selected Letters of William James. Hardwick, Elizabeth, ed. LC 80-66463. 304p. 1980. pap. 8.95 (ISBN 0-87923-348-6, Nonpareil Bks). Godine.
Kallen, Horace M. William James & Henri Bergson: A Study in Contrasting Theories of Life. LC 75-3213. (Philosophy in America Ser.). Repr. of 1914 ed. 24.50 (ISBN 0-404-59209-0). AMS Pr.
Levinson, Henry S. The Religious Investigations of William James. LC 80-26109. (Studies in Religion). xii, 316p. 1981. 24.00 (ISBN 0-8078-1468-7). U of NC Pr.
--Science, Metaphysics, & the Chance of Salvation: An Interpretation of the Thought of William James. LC 78-7383. 1978. pap. 7.50 (ISBN 0-89130-234-4). Scholars Pr Ca.
Marcell, David W. Progress & Pragmatism: James, Dewey, Beard & the American Idea of Progress. LC 72-818. (Contributions in American Studies: No. 9). 402p. 1974. lib. bdg. 18.50 (ISBN 0-8371-6387-0, MPR/). Greenwood.
Martland, T. R., Jr. Metaphysics of William James & John Dewey. LC 62-12826. 1963. 4.75 (ISBN 0-8022-1073-2). Philos Lib.
Martland, Thomas R. The Metaphysics of William James & John Dewey. LC 73-75586. 224p. Repr. of 1963 ed. lib. bdg. 15.00 (ISBN 0-8371-0563-3, MAME). Greenwood.
Morris, Lloyd R. William James: The Message of a Modern Mind. Repr. of 1950 ed. lib. bdg. 15.00 (ISBN 0-8371-1629-5, MOWJ). Greenwood.
Perry, R. B. In the Spirit of William James. Date not set. 8.00 (ISBN 0-8446-2735-6). Peter Smith.
Perry, Ralph B. Annotated Bibliography of the Writings of William James. LC 72-13946. 1920. lib. bdg. 10.00 (ISBN 0-8414-1321-5). Folcroft.
--In the Spirit of William James. LC 78-31937. 1979. Repr. of 1938 ed. lib. bdg. 17.75x (ISBN 0-313-20715-1, PEIN). Greenwood.
--The Thought & Character of William James, 2 vols. LC 74-5778. (Illus.). 1974. Repr. of 1935 ed. Set. lib. bdg. 78.00x (ISBN 0-8371-7520-8, PEWJ). Greenwood.
Roberts, James D. Faith & Reason: A Comparative Study of Pascal, Bergson & James. 1962. 4.50 (ISBN 0-8158-0176-9). Chris Mass.
Santayana, George. Character & Opinion in the United States. 1967. pap. 3.45x (ISBN 0-393-00389-2, Norton Lib). Norton.
Seigfried, Charlene H. Chaos & Context: A Study in William James. LC 77-86346. xiii, 137p. 1978. 12.95x (ISBN 0-8214-0378-8). Ohio U Pr.
Vanden Burgt, Robert J. The Religious Philosophy of William James. LC 80-22936. 176p. 1981. text ed. 16.95x (ISBN 0-88229-594-2); pap. text ed. 8.95x (ISBN 0-88229-767-8). Nelson-Hall.

JAMES, WILLIAM, 1842-1910–BIBLIOGRAPHY

Perry, Ralph B. Annotated Bibliography of the Writings of William James. 69p. 1980. Repr. of 1920 ed. lib. bdg. 15.00 (ISBN 0-8482-5556-9). Norwood Edns.
--Annotated Bibliography of the Writings of William James. 1968. 12.50x (ISBN 0-911850-06-6). Verbeke.
Skrupskelis, Ignas K. William James: A Reference Guide. (Reference Publications Ser.). 1977. lib. bdg. 18.00 (ISBN 0-8161-7805-4). G K Hall.

JAMES FAMILY

James, Richard. Iter Lancastrense. 1845. 17.00 (ISBN 0-384-26780-7). Johnson Repr.
Matthiessen, F. O. The James Family: A Group Biography, Together with Selections from the Writings of Henry James Senior, William, Henry, & Alice James. LC 79-25952. 1980. pap. 7.95 (ISBN 0-394-74243-5, Vin). Random.

JAMES RIVER AND KANAWHA CANAL

Dunaway, Wayland F. History of the James River & Kanawha Company. (Columbia University. Studies in the Social Sciences: No. 236). Repr. of 1922 ed. 21.00 (ISBN 0-404-51236-4). AMS Pr.
Ellet, Charles, Jr. Essay on the Laws of Trade. LC 65-26363. Repr. of 1839 ed. 15.00x (ISBN 0-678-00202-9). Kelley.

JAMES RIVER AND KANAWHA COMPANY, RICHMOND

Dunaway, Wayland F. History of the James River & Kanawha Company. (Columbia University. Studies in the Social Sciences: No. 236). Repr. of 1922 ed. 21.00 (ISBN 0-404-51236-4). AMS Pr.

JAMESON, ANNA BROWNELL, 1794-1860

Thomas, Clara. Love & Work Enough: The Life of Anna Jameson. LC 67-3186. 1978. pap. 7.50 (ISBN 0-8020-6346-2). U of Toronto Pr.

JAMESON, JOHN FRANKLIN, 1859-1937

Gondos, Victor, Jr. J. Franklin Jameson & the Birth of the National Archives: 1906-1926. LC 80-54050. 1981. 20.00x (ISBN 0-8122-7799-6). U of Pa Pr.

JAMESTOWN, VIRGINIA

Bridenbaugh, Carl. Jamestown, Fifteen Forty-Four to Sixteen Ninity-Nine. (Illus.). 1980. 14.95 (ISBN 0-19-502650-0). Oxford U Pr.
Waring, Gilchrist. Three Ships Come Sailing. 1948. 5.00 (ISBN 0-685-47897-1). Dietz.

JAMESTOWN, VIRGINIA–HISTORY–FICTION

Latham, Jean L. This Dear-Bought Land. LC 59-9439. (Illus.). (gr. 6 up). 1957. PLB 8.79 (ISBN 0-06-023741-4, HarpJ). Har-Row.

JAMESTOWN WEED

see Datura

JAMMES, FRANCIS, 1868-1938

Claudel, Paul. Correspondance avec Francis Jammes et Gabriel Frizeau: 1897-1938. 1952. pap. 7.95 (ISBN 0-686-51969-8). French & Eur.

JAMMING (RADIO)

see Radio–Interference

JAMMU

Charak, Sukhdev Singh. History & Culture of Himalayan States of the Jammu Kingdom, Vol. V, Pt. II. 421p. 1981. text ed. 35.00x (ISBN 0-391-02232-6, Pub. by UBS India). Humanities.

JANACEK, LEOS, 1854-1928

Chisholm, E. Operas of Leos Janacek. 1976. 23.00 (ISBN 0-08-012854-8); pap. 10.75 (ISBN 0-08-012853-X). Pergamon.
Ewans, Michael. Janacek's Tragic Operas. LC 77-93894. 288p. 1978. 15.00x (ISBN 0-253-37504-5). Ind U Pr.
Horsbrugh, Ian. Leos Janacek. (Illus.). 304p. 1981. 28.00 (ISBN 0-7153-8060-5). David & Charles.
Vogt, Richard J. Altering Course. 1979. 10.95 (ISBN 0-393-03230-2). Norton.

JANET, PIERRE, 1859-1947

Mayo, Elton. The Psychology of Pierre Janet. LC 74-106669. 132p. 1952. Repr. lib. bdg. 15.00 (ISBN 0-8371-3362-9, MAPJ). Greenwood.

JANITORS

Arco Editorial Board. Building Custodian. 6th ed. LC 73-83413. 1976. pap. 8.00 (ISBN 0-668-00013-9). Arco.
--Housing Caretaker. 3rd ed. LC 67-16544. (Orig.). 1967. pap. 4.00 (ISBN 0-668-00504-1). Arco.
--Mortuary Caretaker. LC 74-31666. 1975. pap. 6.00 (ISBN 0-668-01354-0). Arco.
Cleaning Consultant Services, Inc. The Comprehensive Custodial Training Manual. 1975. 31.00 (ISBN 0-9601054-1-7). Cleaning Consul.
Gland. Custodial Management Practices in Schools. (Research Bulletin Ser.: No.19). 1975. 2.00 (ISBN 0-685-57425-3). Assn Sch Busn.

Griffin, William R. Instructors Guide to Comprehensive Custodial Training Programs. 1977. tchrs ed 50.00 (ISBN 0-9601054-2-5). Cleaning Consul.
--Supervisors' Guide to Successful Training. (Illus.). 1977. pap. text ed. 6.00 (ISBN 0-9601054-3-3). Cleaning Consul.
Koch, Harry W. Janitorial & Maintenance Examinations. 1975. 5.00 (ISBN 0-913164-54-2). Ken-Bks.
Otfinoski, Steven. Tony the Night Custodian. (People Working Today Ser.). (Illus.). 40p. (gr. 7-12). 1977. pap. text ed. 1.85 (ISBN 0-915510-21-9). Janus Bks.
Reeves, Charles E. An Analysis of Janitor Service in Elementary Schools. LC 77-177185. (Columbia University. Teachers College. Contributions to Education: No. 167). Repr. of 1925 ed. 17.50 (ISBN 0-404-55167-X). AMS Pr.
Robbins, Jerry H. & Williams, Stirling B., Jr. School Custodian's Handbook. 1970. pap. 3.45x (ISBN 0-8134-1129-7, 1129). Interstate.
Rudman, Jack. Assistant Building Custodian. (Career Examination Ser.: C-66). (Cloth bdg. avail. on request). pap. 8.00 (ISBN 0-8373-0066-5). Natl Learning.
--Assistant Buildings Superintendent. (Career Examination Ser.: C-1097). (Cloth bdg. avail. on request). pap. 8.00 (ISBN 0-8373-0071-1). Natl Learning.
--Assistant Custodian. (Career Examination Ser.: C-35). (Cloth bdg. avail. on request). pap. 8.00 (ISBN 0-8373-0035-5). Natl Learning.
--Assistant Custodian-Engineer. (Career Examination Ser.: C-36). (Cloth bdg. avail. on request). pap. 8.00 (ISBN 0-8373-0036-3). Natl Learning.
--Assistant School Custodian-Engineer. (Career Examination Ser.: C-46). (Cloth bdg. avail. on request). pap. 8.00 (ISBN 0-8373-0046-0). Natl Learning.
--Assistant Superintendent of Buildings & Grounds. (Career Examination Ser.: C-937). (Cloth bdg. avail. on request). pap. 10.00 (ISBN 0-8373-0937-9). Natl Learning.
--Borough Supervisor of School Custodians. (Career Examination Ser.: C-1761). (Cloth bdg. avail. on request). 1977. pap. 10.00 (ISBN 0-8373-1761-4). Natl Learning.
--Building Custodian. (Career Examination Ser.: C-99). (Cloth bdg. avail. on request). pap. 8.00 (ISBN 0-8373-0099-1). Natl Learning.
--Chief Custodian. (Career Examination Ser.: C-2555). (Cloth bdg. avail. on request). pap. 12.00 (ISBN 0-8373-2555-2). Natl Learning.
--Custodial Foreman. (Career Examination Ser.: C-970). (Cloth bdg. avail on request). pap. 8.00 (ISBN 0-8373-0970-0). Natl Learning.
--Custodial Work Supervisor. (Career Examination Ser.: C-1231). (Cloth bdg. avail on request). pap. 8.00 (ISBN 0-8373-1231-0). Natl Learning.
--Custodial Worker. (Career Examination Ser.: C-1230). (Cloth bdg. avail on request). pap. 8.00 (ISBN 0-8373-1230-2). Natl Learning.
--Custodian. (Career Examination Ser.: C-175). (Cloth bdg. avail on request). pap. 8.00 (ISBN 0-8373-0175-0). Natl Learning.
--Custodian-Engineer. (Career Examination Ser.: C-176). (Cloth bdg. avail on request). pap. 8.00 (ISBN 0-8373-0176-9). Natl Learning.
--Customs Security Officer (Sky Marshall) (Career Examination Ser.: C-1611). (Coth bdg. avail on request). pap. 8.00 (ISBN 0-8373-1611-1). Natl Learning.
--District Supervisor of School Custodians. (Career Examination Ser.: C-2349). (Cloth bdg. avail. on request). pap. 10.00 (ISBN 0-8373-2349-5). Natl Learning.
--Head Custodian. (Career Examination Ser.: C-1958). (Cloth bdg. avail. on request). pap. 10.00 (ISBN 0-8373-1958-7). Natl Learning.
--Head Janitor. (Career Examination Ser.: C-2066). (Cloth bdg. avail. on request). 1977. pap. 10.00 (ISBN 0-8373-2066-6). Natl Learning.
--Housing Caretaker. (Career Examination Ser.: C-333). (Cloth bdg. avail. on request). pap. 8.00 (ISBN 0-8373-0333-8). Natl Learning.
--Junior Building Custodian. (Career Examination Ser.: C-412). (Cloth bdg. avail. on request). pap. 8.00 (ISBN 0-8373-0412-1). Natl Learning.
--Maintenance (Custodial) Branch Initial-Level Supervisor Examination (U.S.P.S.) (Career Examination Ser.: C-1775). (Cloth bdg. avail. on request). 16.00 (ISBN 0-8373-1775-4). Natl Learning.
--Principal Custodial Foreman. (Career Examination Ser.: C-2560). (Cloth bdg. avail. on request). pap. 12.00 (ISBN 0-8373-2560-9). Natl Learning.
--Railroad Porter. (Career Examination Ser.: C-662). (Cloth bdg. avail. on request). pap. 8.00 (ISBN 0-8373-0662-0). Natl Learning.
--Resident Buildings Superintendent. (Career Examination Ser.: C-675). (Cloth bdg. avail. on request). pap. 10.00 (ISBN 0-685-18356-4). Natl Learning.
--School Custodial Supervisor. (Career Examination Ser.: C-1581). (Cloth bdg. avail. on request). pap. 10.00 (ISBN 0-685-60353-9). Natl Learning.
--School Custodian. (Career Examination Ser.: C-799). (Cloth bdg. avail. on request). pap. 8.00 (ISBN 0-8373-0799-6). Natl Learning.
--School Custodian-Engineer. (Career Examination Ser.: C-701). (Cloth bdg. avail. on request). pap. 8.00 (ISBN 0-8373-0701-5). Natl Learning.
--Senior Building Custodian. (Career Examination Ser.: C-997). (Cloth bdg. avail. on request). pap. 10.00 (ISBN 0-8373-0997-2). Natl Learning.
--Senior Custodial Assistant (Men) (Career Examination Ser.: C-1001a). (Cloth bdg. avail. on request). pap. 8.00 (ISBN 0-8373-1001-6). Natl Learning.
--Senior Custodial Foreman. (Career Examination Ser.: C-2271). (Cloth bdg. avail. on request). 1977. pap. 10.00 (ISBN 0-8373-2271-5). Natl Learning.
--Superintendent Building Service (U.S.P.S.) (Career Examination Ser.: C-1685). (Cloth bdg. avail. on request). pap. 8.00 (ISBN 0-8373-1685-5). Natl Learning.
--Supervising Custodial Foreman. (Career Examination Ser.: C-1044). (Cloth bdg. avail. on request). pap. 10.00 (ISBN 0-8373-1044-X). Natl Learning.
--Supervising Janitor. (Career Examination Ser.: C-2065). (Cloth bdg. avail. on request). 1977. pap. 10.00 (ISBN 0-8373-2065-8). Natl Learning.
--Supervisor of Building Custodians. (Career Examination Ser.: C-1015). (Cloth bdg. avail. on request). pap. 10.00 (ISBN 0-8373-1015-6). Natl Learning.
--Window Cleaner. (Career Examination Ser.: C-893). (Cloth bdg. avail. on request). pap. 6.00 (ISBN 0-8373-0899-2). Natl Learning.

JANSEN, CORNELIUS, 1822-1894

Miller, Betty A. & Miller, Oscar R. Cornelius Jansen Family History, 1822-1973. (Illus.). 73p. 1974. pap. 4.50 (ISBN 0-685-64818-4). O R Miller.

JANSENISTS

see also Old Catholic Church

Clark, Ruth. Strangers & Sojourners at Port Royal. 1972. lib. bdg. 20.00x (ISBN 0-374-91664-0). Octagon.
--Strangers & Sojourners at Port Royal. 1972. lib. bdg. 20.00x (ISBN 0-374-91664-0). Octagon.
De Sainte-Beuve, Charles-Augustin. Port-Royal, 3 tomes. 1953-1955. Set. 79.95 (ISBN 0-685-11502-X). French & Eur.
Mikkelsen, M. A. The Bishop Hill Colony: A Religious, Communistic Settlement in Henry County, Illinois. LC 72-187466. (The American Utopian Adventure Ser.). Repr. of 1892 ed. lib. bdg. 13.50x (ISBN 0-87991-014-3). Porcupine Pr.
--The Bishop Hill Colony, a Religious Communistic Settlement in Henry County, Illinois. pap. 7.00 (ISBN 0-384-38850-7). Johnson Repr.
Neale, John M. A History of the So-Called Jansenist Church of Holland. LC 71-133820. Repr. of 1858 ed. 26.50 (ISBN 0-404-04656-8). AMS Pr.
Pascal, Blaise. Les Provinciales. 4.95 (ISBN 0-686-54852-3). French & Eur.
Pascal, Blaise & Adam, Antoine. Lettres Escrites a un Provincial. 320p. 1967. 4.50 (ISBN 0-686-54847-7). French & Eur.
Saint-Beuve. Port Royal, 3 vols. Vol. 1. 37.50 (ISBN 0-686-56564-9); Vol. 2. 37.50 (ISBN 0-686-56565-7); Vol. 3. 35.95 (ISBN 0-686-56566-5). French & Eur.
Sedgwick, Alexander. Jansenism in Seventeenth-Century France: Voices from the Wilderness. LC 77-2812. 1977. 13.95x (ISBN 0-8139-0702-0). U Pr of Va.

JAPAN

see also names of cities, towns, and geographic areas in Japan

Auer, James E. The Postwar Rearmament of Japanese Maritime Forces 1945-1971. LC 72-83564. (Special Studies in International Politics & Government). 1973. 29.50x (ISBN 0-275-28633-9). Irvington.
Barr, Pat. Japan. (Illus.). 160p. 1980. 24.00 (ISBN 0-7134-0578-3, Pub. by Batsford England). David & Charles.
Beasley, W. G., ed. Modern Japan: Aspects of History, Literature & Society. (Campus Ser.: No. 195). 1977. pap. 7.95x (ISBN 0-520-03495-3). U of Cal Pr.
Bland, John O. China, Japan & Korea. facsimile ed. LC 77-160959. (Select Bibliographies Reprint Ser). Repr. of 1921 ed. 29.00 (ISBN 0-8369-5826-8). Arno.
Bolitho, Harold, ed. A Northern Prospect: Australian Papers on Japan. Rix, Alan. 200p. 1981. pap. text ed. 13.95 (ISBN 0-9594391-0-2, 0099, Pub. by ANUP Australia). Bks Australia.
Bromwell, C. David. Japan Emerges. (Asia Emerges Ser.). 1975. pap. 4.80 (ISBN 0-02-648300-9, 64830); tchr's guide 1.36 (ISBN 0-02-648310-6, 64831). Glencoe.
Burks, Ardath W. Japan: Profile of a Postindustrial Power. (Nations of Contemporary Asia Ser.). (Illus.). 250p. 1980. lib. bdg. 23.25x (ISBN 0-89158-786-1); pap. 9.50x (ISBN 0-86531-040-8). Westview.
Chamberlain, Basil H. Japanese Things: Being Notes on Various Subjects Connected with Japan. LC 76-87791. 1970. pap. 8.50 (ISBN 0-8048-0713-2). C E Tuttle.
Chiang Yee. The Silent Traveller in Japan. 1972. 15.00 (ISBN 0-393-08642-9). Norton.
Craig, Albert M., ed. Japan: A Comparative View. LC 78-70285. 1979. 25.00 (ISBN 0-691-05271-9). Princeton U Pr.
De Moges, Marquis. Recollections of Baron Gros's Embassy to China & Japan in 1857 to 1858. 368p. 1972. Repr. of 1860 ed. 30.00x (ISBN 0-7165-2039-7, Pub. by Irish Academic Pr). Biblio Dist.
De Vos, George A. & Witherall, William O. Japan's Minorities: Burakumin, Koreans, Ainu. (Minority Rights Group: No. 3). 1974. pap. 2.50 (ISBN 0-89192-093-5). Interbk Inc.
Dore, Ronald P. Shinohata: Portrait of a Japanese Village. (Pantheon Village Ser.). 1980. pap. 4.95 (ISBN 0-394-73843-8). Pantheon.
Faure, Elie. The Soul of Japan. lib. bdg. 59.95 (ISBN 0-8490-1089-6). Gordon Pr.
Forbis, William H. Japan Today: People, Places, Power. LC 75-6336. (Illus.). 474p. (YA) 1975. 14.95 (ISBN 0-06-011311-1, HarpT). Har-Row.
Fukuda, Tsuneari, ed. Future of Japan & the Korean Peninsula. Jahng, K., tr. from Japanese. LC 78-71337. (Illus.). 1979. 14.40 (ISBN 0-930878-14-0). Hollym Intl.
Fukui, Eiichir O. The Climate of Japan. LC 76-44473. (Developments in Atmospheric Science: No. 8). 1977. 68.50 (ISBN 0-444-99818-7). Elsevier.
Gibney, Frank. Japan: The Fragile Superpower. rev. ed. 1980. pap. 5.95 (ISBN 0-452-00528-0, F528, Mer). NAL.
Green, William & Swanborough, Gordon. Japanese Army Airforce Fighters. (World War II Aircraft Fact Files Ser.). (Illus.). 1977. pap. 4.95 (ISBN 0-668-04119-6). Arco.
Grossberg, Kenneth A., ed. Japan Today. LC 81-1077. (Orig.). 1981. 12.95 (ISBN 0-89727-018-5); pap. 5.95 (ISBN 0-89727-019-3). Inst Study Human.
Hagoromo Society of Kamikaze Devine Thunderbolt Corps Survivors. Born to Die. Adams, Andrew & Alston, Pat, eds. Asahi, Nobua, tr. LC 73-89817. (Ser. 311). (Illus.). 1973. pap. text ed. 4.50 (ISBN 0-89750-039-3). Ohara Pubns.
Hall, John & Beardsley, R. K. Twelve Doors to Japan. 1965. text ed. 22.00 (ISBN 0-07-025610-1, C). McGraw.
Hall, John W. Japan. 1971. pap. 3.95 (ISBN 0-440-54189-1, Delta). Dell.
Hall, Manly P. Impressions of Modern Japan. pap. 2.50 (ISBN 0-89314-319-7). Philos Res.
Hall, Robert B., Jr. Japan: Industrial Power of Asia. 2nd ed. (New Searchlight Ser). 1976. 4.50x (ISBN 0-442-29752-1). Van Nos Reinhold.
Hall, Robert K. Education for a New Japan. LC 77-136068. 1971. Repr. of 1949 ed. lib. bdg. 21.25x (ISBN 0-8371-5218-6, HAEJ). Greenwood.
Hearn, Lafcadio. Exotics & Retrospectives. LC 72-138069. (Illus.). 1971. pap. 3.50 (ISBN 0-8048-0962-3). C E Tuttle.
--Exotics & Retrospectives. LC 72-96885. (Illus.). Repr. of 1898 ed. lib. bdg. 16.50x (ISBN 0-8398-0774-0). Irvington.
Hinton, Harold C. & Jansen, Marius B., eds. Major Topics on China & Japan: A Handbook for Teachers. LC 78-10673. (Illus.). 1979. Repr. of 1957 ed. lib. bdg. 34.50x (ISBN 0-313-20657-0, HIMT). Greenwood.
Hoffman, Arthur S., ed. Japan & the Pacific Basin. (Atlantic Papers Ser.: No. 40). 68p. 1980. write for info. (ISBN 0-86598-042-X). Allanheld.
Ienago, Saburo. Painting in the Yamato Style. LC 73-3489. (Heibonsha Survey of Japanese Art Ser). Orig. Title: Yamato-E. (Illus.). 168p. 1973. 17.50 (ISBN 0-8348-1016-6). Weatherhill.
Ike, Nobutake. Japan: The New Superstate, a Portable Stanford. pap. text ed. 4.95x (ISBN 0-393-95011-5). Norton.
Japan: A Self-Portrait. 1979. write for info. (ISBN 0-933642-01-6); pap. write for info. (ISBN 0-933642-02-4). Intl Ctr Photo.
Japan Directory - 1981, 3 vols. LC 62-46629. 2100p. 1981. Set. 200.00x (ISBN 0-8002-2790-5). Intl Pubns Serv.
Japan Statistical Yearbook 1979. 29th ed. LC 52-30656. 1979. 60.00x (ISBN 0-8002-2381-0). Intl Pubns Serv.
Japan Times Directory 1979-80. 32nd ed. LC 72-627115. 764p. 1979. pap. 40.00 (ISBN 0-8002-2414-0). Intl Pubns Serv.
Kawabata, Yasunari. Japan, the Beautiful, & Myself. Seidensticker, Edward G., tr. LC 75-90028. 1968. pap. 3.95 (ISBN 0-87011-088-8). Kodansha.
Kenworthy, Leonard. Studying Japan. LC 74-23896. 1975. pap. text ed. 4.25x (ISBN 0-8077-2455-6). Tchrs Coll.
Kublin, Hyman. Japan: Selected Readings. rev. ed. LC 72-84106. (Illus.). 228p. (gr. 6-9). 1973. pap. text ed. 6.60 (ISBN 0-395-13930-9, 2-31046). HM.
Langer, P. F. Japan: Yesterday & Today. (gr. 9 up). 1966. 4.50 (ISBN 0-03-057285-1). HR&W.
Lory, Hillis. Japan's Military Masters: The Army in Japanese Life. LC 72-9367. 256p. 1973. Repr. of 1943 ed. lib. bdg. 16.00x (ISBN 0-8371-6581-4, LOMM). Greenwood.
McNulty, Charles. Japan. (Orig.). (gr. 9-12). 1975. pap. text ed. 4.50 (ISBN 0-87720-616-3). AMSCO Sch.
Mori, S. & Yamamoto, G., eds. Productivity of Communities in Japanese Inland Waters. (Japan International Biological Program Synthetics Ser.: Vol. 10). 1975. pap. 46.50x (ISBN 0-86008-220-2, Pub. by U of Tokyo Pr). Intl Schol Bk Serv.
Morton, W. Scott. Japan: It's History & Culture. (Apollo Eds.). (Illus.). 256p. 1975. pap. 2.95 (ISBN 0-8152-0369-1, A-369). T Y Crowell.
Murakami, Hyoe & Seidensticker, E. G., eds. Guide to Japanese Culture. 224p. 1977. 16.50 (ISBN 0-87040-403-2). Japan Pubns.
Nitobe, Inazo. The Japanese Nation. LC 72-82103. (Japan Library Ser.). (Illus.). 1973. Repr. of 1912 ed. lib. bdg. 21.00 (ISBN 0-8420-1396-2). Scholarly Res Inc.
Numata, M., ed. Ecological Studies in Japanese Grasslands. (Japan International Biological Program Synthetics Ser.: Vol. 13). 1975. pap. 32.50 (ISBN 0-86008-223-7, Pub. by U of Tokyo Pr). Intl Schol Bk Serv.
Ogawa, Dennis, ed. From Japs to Japanese: The Evolution of Japanese-American Stereotypes. LC 76-146315. 1971. 2.20x (ISBN 0-8211-1404-2); text ed. 1.76 (ISBN 0-686-66327-6). McCutchan.
Regamey, Felix. Japan in Art & Industry. Repr. of 1892 ed. 10.00 (ISBN 0-685-76614-4). Norwood Edns.
Regional Problems & Policies in OECD Countries: Vol. 1, France, Italy, Ireland, Denmark, Sweden, Japan. 1976. 7.00x (ISBN 92-64-11486-6). OECD.
Reischauer, Edwin O. The Japanese. (Illus.). 1977. 16.50 (ISBN 0-674-47176-8, Belknap Pr); pap. 6.95 (ISBN 0-674-47178-4). Harvard U Pr.
Richie, Donald. Introducing Japan. LC 77-75966. (Illus.). 1978. 14.95 (ISBN 0-87011-308-9). Kodansha.
Shulman, Frank J. Japan & Korea: An Annotated Bibliography of Doctoral Dissertations in Western Languages, 1877-1969. 360p. 1970. pap. 6.95 (ISBN 0-8389-0085-2). ALA.
Simpson, Colin. Japan: An Intimate View. rev. & enl. ed. LC 69-19966. 1969. 10.00 (ISBN 0-498-07364-5). A S Barnes.
Sterling Publishing Company Editors. Japan in Pictures. rev. ed. LC 60-14338. (Visual Geography Ser). (Orig.). (gr. 6 up). 1978. PLB 4.99 (ISBN 0-8069-1011-9); pap. 2.95 (ISBN 0-8069-1010-0). Sterling.
Strathern, Andrew. Rope of Moka. 26.95 (ISBN 0-521-07987-X); pap. 10.95x (ISBN 0-521-09957-9). Cambridge U Pr.
Tiedemann, Arthur E., ed. An Introduction to Japanese Civilization. 626p. 1974. 27.50x (ISBN 0-231-03651-5). Columbia U Pr.
Titus, David A. Palace & Politics in Pre-War Japan. (Studies of the East Asian Institute, Columbia University). 368p. 1974. 22.50x (ISBN 0-231-03622-1). Columbia U Pr.
Toynbee, Arnold, et al. Introducing Japan. Norbury, Paul, ed. LC 77-3853. (Illus.). 1978. 14.95 (ISBN 0-312-42542-2). St Martin.
Trevor, Hugh. Multi-Channel Japan. 1980. pap. 1.00 (ISBN 0-85363-075-5). OMF Bks.
U. S. Dept. Of State. Japan: Nineteen Thirty-One-Nineteen Forty-One, 2 Vols. 1971. Repr. of 1943 ed. Set. 37.00 (ISBN 0-403-01251-1). Scholarly.
Vogel, Ezra F., ed. Modern Japanese Organization & Decision-Making. 1975. 30.00x (ISBN 0-520-02857-0). U of Cal Pr.
Von Siebold, Philipp F. Nippon. 1975. 2750.00 (ISBN 0-685-82752-6). Johnson Repr.
Webb, Herschel. An Introduction to Japan. 2nd ed. LC 57-9552. 1957. pap. 5.00x (ISBN 0-231-08505-2). Columbia U Pr.
Wheatley, Paul & See, Thomas. From Court to Capital: A Tentative Interpretation of the Origins of the Japanese Urban Tradition. LC 76-25637. (Illus.). 1978. lib. bdg. 15.00x (ISBN 0-226-89430-4). U of Chicago Pr.

JAPAN–AIR FORCE

Davis, Warren J. Japan, the Air Menace of the Pacific. LC 73-111751. (American Imperialism: Viewpoints of United States Foreign Policy, 1898-1941). 1970. Repr. of 1928 ed. 9.00 (ISBN 0-405-02010-4). Arno.

Green, William & Swanborough, Gordon. Japanese Army Fighters, Pt. 2. LC 76-29071. (World War 2 Fact Files Ser.). (Illus.). 1978. pap. 4.95 (ISBN 0-668-04427-6, 4427). Arco.

Thorpe, Donald W. Japanese Army Air Force Camouflage & Markings, World War 2. Oishi, Yasuo, tr. LC 68-54880. (Illus.). 1968. 13.95 (ISBN 0-8168-6575-2); pap. 9.95 (ISBN 0-8168-6579-5). Aero.

JAPAN–ANTIQUITIES

Aikens, C. Melvin & Higuchi, Takayasu. Prehistory of Japan. LC 80-70596. (Studies in Archaeology). 1981. price not set (ISBN 0-12-045280-4). Acad Pr.

Elisseeff, Vadime. Japan. (Archaeologia Mundi Ser.). (Illus.). 200p. 1974. 29.50 (ISBN 0-88254-145-5). Hippocrene Bks.

Groot, Gerard J. The Prehistory of Japan. facsimile ed. Kraus, Bertram S., ed. LC 79-37884. (Select Bibliographies Reprint Ser). Repr. of 1951 ed. 36.00 (ISBN 0-8369-6721-6). Arno.

Munro, Neil G. Prehistoric Japan. (Illus.). 1971. Repr. of 1911 ed. 49.00 (ISBN 0-384-40565-7). Johnson Repr.

Torii, Ryuzo. Ancient Japan in the Light of Anthropology. 59.95 (ISBN 0-87968-627-8). Gordon Pr.

JAPAN–ARMED FORCES

Barker, A. J. Japanese Army Handbook. (Illus.). 128p. 1979. 15.95 (ISBN 0-7110-0833-7, Pub by Ian Allan England). Hippocrene Bks.

Buck, James H., ed. The Modern Japanese Military System. LC 75-14628. (Sage Research Progress Ser. on War, Revolution, & Peacekeeping: Vol. 5). 288p. 1975. 22.50 (ISBN 0-8039-0513-0); pap. 9.95 (ISBN 0-8039-0514-9). Sage.

JAPAN–BIBLIOGRAPHY

Bibliography of European Publications on Japan: Fifteen Forty-Two to Eighteen Fifty-Three. 418p. 1977. Repr. of 1940 ed. 70.00 (ISBN 3-7940-3173-3, Dist. by Gale Research Co). K G Saur.

Borton, Hugh, et al, eds. Selected List of Books & Articles on Japan in English, French & German. rev. & enl. ed. LC 53-5055. (Harvard-Yenching Institute Publications Ser). 1954. 14.00x (ISBN 0-674-79800-7). Harvard U Pr.

Center for Academic Publications Japan. Current Contents of Academic Journals in Japan, 1977: The Humanities & Social Sciences. LC 72-623679. 344p. (Orig.). 1979. pap. 50.00x (ISBN 0-8002-2322-5). Intl Pubns Serv.

Directory of Japanese Scientific Periodicals. 3rd ed. LC 68-5037. 1976. 57.50x (ISBN 0-8002-0761-0). Intl Pubns Serv.

Hall, Robert B. Japanese Geography: A Guide to Japanese Reference & Research Materials. LC 78-5578. (Univ of Michigan Center for Japanese Studies Biblio.: No. 6). 128p. 1978. Repr. of 1956 ed. lib. bdg. 21.75x (ISBN 0-313-20434-9, HAJG). Greenwood.

Ichioka, Yuji, et al, eds. A Buried Past: An Annotated Bibliography of the Japanese American Research Project Collection. LC 73-83063. 1974. 21.75x (ISBN 0-520-02541-5). U of Cal Pr.

Japan Directory, 1980, 3 vols. LC 62-46629. 1971p. 1980. Set. 180.00x (ISBN 0-8002-2687-9). Intl Pubns Serv.

Japan Foundation. An Introductory Bibliography for Japanese Studies, Vol. II, Pt. 1. 1978. 11.50x (ISBN 0-86008-197-4, Pub. by U of Tokyo Pr). Intl Schol Bk Serv.

Japan Foundation, ed. An Introductory Bibliography for Japanese Studies, Vol. 1, Pt. 2. 1976. 11.50x (ISBN 0-86008-155-9, Pub. by U of Tokyo Pr). Intl Schol Bk Serv.

K. B. S. Bibliography of Standard Reference Books for Japanese Studies with Descriptive Notes. Incl. Vol. 1. Generalia. rev. ed. 164p. 1971 (ISBN 0-86008-031-5); Vol. 2. Geography & Travel. 174p. 1966 (ISBN 0-86008-032-3); Vol. 3. History & Biography. 1965. Pt. 1 (ISBN 0-86008-033-1). Pt. 2 (ISBN 0-86008-034-X). Pt. 3 (ISBN 0-86008-035-8); Vol. 4. Religion. 192p. 1966 (ISBN 0-86008-036-6); Vol. 5A. History of Thought. 1965. Pt. 1 (ISBN 0-86008-037-4). Pt. 2 (ISBN 0-86008-038-2); Vol. 5B. Education. 198p. 1966 (ISBN 0-86008-039-0); Vol. 6A. Language. rev. ed. 166p. 1972 (ISBN 0-86008-040-4); Vol. 6B. Literature, 5 pts. 1966-68. Pt. 1 (ISBN 0-86008-041-2). Pt. 3. Edo Period (ISBN 0-86008-043-9). Pt. 4. Modern Period 1 (ISBN 0-86008-044-7). Pt. 5. Modern Period 2 (ISBN 0-86008-045-5); Pt. 7A. Traditional Art & Architecture. rev. ed. 178p. 1971 (ISBN 0-86008-046-3); Vol. 9A. Politics. 188p. 1970 (ISBN 0-86008-049-8); Pt. 9B. Law. 1968-70. Pt. 1 (ISBN 0-86008-050-1). Pt. 2 (ISBN 0-86008-051-X); Vol. 10. Economics. 1969. Pt. 1 (ISBN 0-86008-052-8). Pt. 2 (ISBN 0-86008-053-6); Geography. rev. ed. 234p. 1973. 12.50x (ISBN 0-86008-054-4). 3.50x ea (Pub by U of Tokyo Pr). Intl Schol Bk Serv.

Kerner, Robert J. Northeastern Asia, 2 vols. (Bibliography & Research Ser.: No. 255). 1969. Repr. of 1939 ed. 93.00 (ISBN 0-8337-1914-9). B Franklin.

Nachod, Oscar, et al. Bibliographie Von Japan: 1906-1937, 6 vols. 2696p. (Continued by H. Praesent & W. Haenisch). 1970. Repr. Set. 650.00x (ISBN 3-7772-7025-3). Intl Pubns Serv.

Shinkokai, Kokusai B., compiled by. Current Contents of Academic Journals in Japan, 1970. 208p. 1971. 10.00x (ISBN 0-86008-056-0, Pub. by Japan Sci. Soc.). Intl Schol Bk Serv.

University of Chicago. Catalogs of the Far Eastern Library: Author-Title Catalog, Japanese Catalog, 4 vols. Set. 510.00 (ISBN 0-8161-0130-2). G K Hall.

Wenckstern, Friedrich Von. Bibliography of the Japanese Empire, 2 vols. 976p. 1970. Repr. of 1895 ed. Set. 210.00x (ISBN 3-7772-7032-6). Intl Pubns Serv.

JAPAN–BIOGRAPHY

Fujii, Shinichi. Tenno Seiji: Direct Imperial Rule. (Studies in Japanese History & Civilization). 415p. 1979. Repr. of 1944 ed. 30.00 (ISBN 0-89093-263-8). U Pubns Amer.

Hamada, Kengi. Prince Ito. (Studies Injapanese History & Civilzation). 1979. Repr. of 1936 ed. 22.00 (ISBN 0-89093-267-0). U Pubns Amer.

Harries, Phillip T., tr. from Japanese. The Poetic Memoirs of Lady Daibu. LC 79-65519. 336p. 1980. 17.50x (ISBN 0-8047-1077-5). Stanford U Pr.

Hemphill, Elizabeth. The Least of These: Miki Sawada & Her Children. 176p. 1981. 12.50 (ISBN 0-8348-0155-8, Pub. by John Weatherhill Inc Japan). C E Tuttle.

Huffman, James L. Politics of the Meiji Press: The Life of Fukuchi Gen'ichiro. LC 79-3879. 1980. text ed. 15.00x (ISBN 0-8248-0679-4). U Pr of Hawaii.

Koichi, Marquis K. Diary of Marquis Kido, Nineteen Thirty-One to Nineteen Forty-Five: Selected Translation Selected Translations into English. 500p. 1980. 34.00 (ISBN 0-89093-273-5). U Pubns Amer.

Lifton, Robert J., et al. Six Lives, Six Deaths: Portraits from Modern Japan. Shuichi, Kato & Reich, Michael R., eds. LC 78-11926. (Illus.). 318p. 1980. pap. 7.95 (ISBN 0-300-02600-5). Yale U Pr.

Shiroyama, Saburo. War Criminal: The Life & Death of Hirota Koki. Bester, John, tr. from Japanese. LC 76-9361. Orig. Title: Rakujitsu Moyu. 1980. pap. 4.95 (ISBN 0-87011-368-2). Kodansha.

Sugimoto, Chiyono. But Ships Are Sailing, Sailing. 1960. 4.95 (ISBN 0-89346-058-3, Pub. by Hokuseido Pr). Heian Intl.

Tomita, Kokei. Peasant Sage of Japan: The Life & Work of Sontoku Ninomiya. (Studies in Japanese History & Civilization). 1979. Repr. of 1912 ed. 24.00 (ISBN 0-89093-258-1). U Pubns Amer.

Whitney, Clara A. Clara's Diary: An American Girl in Meiji Japan. LC 80-85385. (Illus.). 356p. 1981. pap. 5.95 (ISBN 0-87011-470-0). Kodansha.

JAPAN–CHURCH HISTORY

Boxer, C. R. The Christian Century in Japan: 1549-1650. (Library Reprint Ser.: No. 51). (Illus.). 552p. 1974. Repr. of 1967 ed. 40.00x (ISBN 0-520-02702-7). U of Cal Pr.

JAPAN–CIVILIZATION

Benedict, Ruth. Chrysanthemum & the Sword: Patterns of Japanese Culture. 1967. pap. 5.95 (ISBN 0-452-00561-2, F561, Mer). NAL.

Boxer, Charles R. Papers on Portugese, Dutch, & Jesuit Influences in 16th & 17th Century Japan: Studies in Japanese History & Civilization. 1979. 29.50 (ISBN 0-89093-255-7). U Pubns Amer.

--Portuguese Embassy to Japan (1644-1647) Bd. with Embassy of Captain Concalo de Siqueria de Souza to Japan in 1644-7. (Studies in Japanese History & Civilization). 172p. 22.00 (ISBN 0-89093-256-5). U Pubns Amer.

Cooper. Introduction to Japanese History & Culture. 1976. pap. 3.94 (ISBN 0-08-017484-1). Pergamon.

Cooper, Michael. This Island of Japon: Joao Rodrigues' Account of 16th Century Japan. LC 72-93533. (Illus.). 354p. 1973. 15.00x (ISBN 0-87011-194-9). Kodansha.

Darr, D. & Giuglaris. Japon Des Realites. (Illus., Fr.). 1965. 12.50x (ISBN 0-685-19322-5). Paragon.

De Becker, Joseph E. Principles & Practice of the Civil Code of Japan: A Complete Theoretical & Practical Exposition of the Motifs of the Japanese Civil Code. (Studies in Japanese Law & Government). 852p. 1979. Repr. of 1921 ed. Set. 60.00 (ISBN 0-89093-216-6). U Pubns Amer.

De Becker, Joseph E., tr. from Japanese. Annotated Civil Code of Japan, 4 vols. (Studies in Japanese Law & Government). 1200p. 1979. 95.00 (ISBN 0-89093-215-8). U Pubns Amer.

Ellwood, Robert S., Jr. An Invitation to Japanese Civilization. (Illus.). 1980. pap. text ed. 6.95 (ISBN 0-87872-237-8). Duxbury Pr.

Embree, John F. The Japanese Nation, a Social Survey. LC 75-8766. (Illus.). 308p. 1975. Repr. of 1945 ed. lib. bdg. 18.00x (ISBN 0-8371-8117-8, EMJN). Greenwood.

Gibney, Frank. Five Gentlemen of Japan: The Portrait of a Nation's Character. LC 74-781480. 1973. pap. 6.95 (ISBN 0-8048-1108-3). C E Tuttle.

Gubbins, John H. The Making of Modern Japan. facsimile ed. LC 73-169760. (Select Bibliographies Reprint Ser). Repr. of 1922 ed. 21.00 (ISBN 0-8369-5980-9). Arno.

Hearn, Lafcadio. Japan: An Attempt at Interpretation. LC 56-249. 1955. pap. 5.50 (ISBN 0-8048-0272-6). C E Tuttle.

--Kokoro: Hints & Echoes of Japanese Inner Life. Repr. of 1896 ed. lib. bdg. 17.00x (ISBN 0-8371-1633-3, HEKO). Greenwood.

--Kokoro: Hints & Echoes of Japanese Inner Life. LC 79-184814. 1972. pap. 5.25 (ISBN 0-8048-1035-4). C E Tuttle.

Hoover, Thomas. Zen Culture. 1978. pap. 3.95 (ISBN 0-394-72520-4, Vin). Random.

Iriye, Akira. Power & Culture: The Japanese-American War, 1941-1945. 22.00 (ISBN 0-686-74484-5). Harvard U Pr.

Ishida, Eiichiro. Japanese Culture: A Study of Origins & Characteristics. Kachi, Teruko, tr. from Japanese. LC 73-92494. Orig. Title: Nihon Bunka Ron. 156p. 1974. 10.00x (ISBN 0-8248-0325-6, Eastwest Ctr). U Pr of Hawaii.

Jansen, Marius B., ed. Changing Japanese Attitudes Toward Modernization. (Studies in the Modernization of Japan). 1965. 25.00 (ISBN 0-691-03007-3). Princeton U Pr.

Japanese Culture Institute. A Hundred Things Japanese. (Illus.). 216p. 1976. 15.00 (ISBN 0-87040-364-8). Japan Pubns.

Kaibara, Ekiken. Way of Contentment. Bd. with Greater Learning for Women. (Studies in Japanese History & Civilization). 1979. Repr. of 1913 ed. 19.00 (ISBN 0-89093-253-0). U Pubns Amer.

Kato, Shuichi. The Japan-China Phenomenon. Chibbett, David, tr. LC 75-11392. 103p. 1974. 8.75x (ISBN 0-87011-260-0). Kodansha.

Kirkwood, Kenneth P. Renaissance in Japan: A Cultural Survey of the Seventeenth Century. LC 72-120389. (Illus.). 1970. Repr. bds. 6.50 (ISBN 0-8048-0916-X). C E Tuttle.

Lebra, Takie S. & Lebra, William P., eds. Japanese Culture & Behavior: Selected Readings. LC 73-78978. 494p. (Orig.). 1974. pap. text ed. 6.95x (ISBN 0-8248-0276-4, Eastwest Ctr). U Pr of Hawaii.

Leonard, Jonathan N. Early Japan. (Great Ages of Man Ser). (Illus.). 1968. 12.95 (ISBN 0-8094-0360-9). Time-Life.

--Early Japan. LC 68-27297. (Great Ages of Man). (Illus.). (gr. 6 up). 1968. PLB 11.97 (ISBN 0-8094-0382-X, Pub. by Time-Life). Silver.

Mackenzie, Donald A. The Myths of China & Japan. LC 77-6878. 1977. Repr. of 1923 ed. lib. bdg. 45.00 (ISBN 0-89341-149-3). Longwood Pr.

Mainichi Newspapers. Japan & the Japanese. new ed. LC 72-95973. 240p. 1974. 7.50 (ISBN 0-87040-223-4); pap. 4.95 (ISBN 0-87040-227-7). Japan Pubns.

Maraini, Fosco. Japan: Patterns of Continuity. LC 76-107610. (Illus.). 240p. 1971. 27.50 (ISBN 0-87011-106-X). Kodansha.

Mason, Richard & Caiger, John. A History of Japan. LC 73-13581. 1973. 10.95 (ISBN 0-02-920290-6). Free Pr.

Matsuhara, Iwao. On Life & Nature in Japan. (Illus.). 1964. 14.95 (ISBN 0-89346-077-X, Pub. by Hokuseido Pr). Heian Intl.

Matsushita, Konosuke. Japan at the Brink. Terry, Charles, tr. from Japanese. LC 75-30180. 136p. 1975. 8.95 (ISBN 0-87011-270-8). Kodansha.

Minear, Richard H. Japanese Tradition & Western Law: Emperor, State, & Law in the Thought of Hozumi Yatsuka. LC 72-115478. (East Asian Ser: No. 48). 1970. 12.50x (ISBN 0-674-47252-7). Harvard U Pr.

Moore, Charles A., ed. Japanese Mind: Essentials of Japanese Philosophy & Culture. LC 67-16704. 1967. pap. text ed. 4.95x (ISBN 0-8248-0077-X). U Pr of Hawaii.

Norman, E. Herbert. Ando Shoeki & the Anatomy of Japanese Feudalism. (Studies in Japanese History & Civilization). 254p. 1979. Repr. of 1949 ed. 26.25 (ISBN 0-89093-224-7). U Pubns Amer.

Ozaki, Robert S. The Japanese: A Cultural Portrait. LC 77-93224. 1978. 15.00 (ISBN 0-8048-1183-0). C E Tuttle.

Pacific Science Congress, 10th, Honolulu 1961. Japanese Culture: Its Development & Characteristics. Smith, Robert J. & Beardsley, Richard K., eds. Repr. of 1962 ed. pap. 15.50 (ISBN 0-384-44400-8). Johnson Repr.

Pyle, Kenneth B. The New Generation in Meiji Japan: Problems of Cultural Identity 1885-1895. LC 69-13183. 1969. 12.50x (ISBN 0-8047-0697-2). Stanford U Pr.

Riesman, David & Riesman, Evelyn T. Conversations in Japan: Modernization, Politics, & Culture. (Midway Reprint Ser.). 1967. pap. 13.00x (ISBN 0-226-71739-9). U of Chicago Pr.

Shively, Donald H., ed. Tradition & Modernization in Japanese Culture. LC 69-18071. (Studies in the Modernization of Japan, No. 5). (Illus.). 1971. 26.00x (ISBN 0-691-03072-3); pap. 9.95 (ISBN 0-691-00020-4). Princeton U Pr.

Spencer, Cornelia. Made in Japan. (Illus.). (gr. 7 up). 1963. PLB 5.99 (ISBN 0-394-91378-7). Knopf.

Stead, Alfred, ed. Japan by the Japanese: A Survey by Its Authorities, 2 vols. (Studies in Japanese History & Civilization). 1979. Repr. of 1904 ed. 55.00 (ISBN 0-89093-264-6). U Pubns Amer.

Suzuki, Daisetz T. Zen & Japanese Culture. (Bollingen Ser.: Vol. 64). (Illus.). 1959. 27.50x (ISBN 0-691-09849-2); pap. 7.95 (ISBN 0-691-01770-0). Princeton U Pr.

Takekoshi, Yosoburo. Economic Aspects of the History of the Civilization of Japan, 3 Vols. 1967. Repr. of 1930 ed. 65.00x (ISBN 0-685-19297-0). Paragon.

Varley, H. Paul. A Syllabus of Japanese Civilization. rev. 2nd ed. LC 68-55815. (Companions to Asian Studies). 120p. 1972. pap. 5.00x (ISBN 0-231-03677-9). Columbia U Pr.

Waley, Arthur. The Originality of Japanese Civilization. 1980. lib. bdg. 60.00 (ISBN 0-8490-3199-0). Gordon Pr.

Wigmore, John H. & Simmons, D. B. Notes on Land Tenure & Local Institutions in Old Japan. (Studies in Japanese History & Civilization). 1979. 21.00 (ISBN 0-89093-223-9). U Pubns Amer.

JAPAN–COMMERCE

Allen, G. C. How Japan Competes. (Institute of Economic Affairs Ser.: Hobart Paper 81). 1979. pap. 5.95 (ISBN 0-255-36113-0). Transatlantic.

Ballon, Robert J. & Lee, Eugene H., eds. Foreign Investment & Japan. LC 72-85427. 340p. 1972. 12.50x (ISBN 0-87011-186-8). Kodansha.

Benjamin, Roger & Ori, Kan. Tradition & Change in Postindustrial Japan: The Roles of the Political Parties. 192p. 1981. 21.95 (ISBN 0-03-059138-4). Praeger.

Business Cycle in Japan: 1950-1970. (Business Cycle Ser: No. 4). 20p. 1971. 10.00x (ISBN 0-901202-24-X). Intl Pubns Serv.

Business Intercommunications, Inc. Handbook on Merchandise Distribution in Japan. 1976. 102.00 (ISBN 0-686-19022-X). A M Newman.

Cocks, Richard. Diary of Richard Cocks, Cape Merchant in the English Factory in Japan: 1615-1622, 2 Vols. Thompson, Edward M., ed. (Hakluyt Society. First Ser.: Nos. 66-67). 1965. Set. 59.00 (ISBN 0-8337-3518-7). B Franklin.

Diamond's Japan Business Directory 1979. LC 74-84890. 1979. 307.50 (ISBN 0-8002-2367-5). Intl Pubns Serv.

East Asian Studies Program-Ohio State University. Business & Society in Japan: Fundamentals for Businessmen. 348p. 1981. 29.95 (ISBN 0-03-059321-2). Praeger.

Farley, Miriam S. The Problem of Japanese Trade Expansion in the Post-War Situation. LC 75-30106. (Institute of Pacific Relations). Repr. of 1940 ed. 11.50 (ISBN 0-404-59523-5). AMS Pr.

Foreign Trade of Japan White Papers 1958-1971, 14 vols. 32.50 ea.; Set. lib. bdg. 455.00 (ISBN 0-685-50591-X). AMS Pr.

Furstenberg, Friedrich. Why the Japanese Have Been So Successful in Business. LC 73-77702. 110p. 1974. 15.00 (ISBN 0-900537-11-6). Hippocrene Bks.

Hattori, Yukimasa. The Foreign Commerce of Japan Since the Restoration, 1869-1900. LC 78-63903. (Johns Hopkins University. Studies in the Social Sciences. Twenty-Second Ser. 1904: 9-10). Repr. of 1904 ed. 13.50 (ISBN 0-404-61156-7). AMS Pr.

Hay, K. A. Friends or Acquaintances? Canada & Japan's Other Trading Partners in the Early 1980's. 52p. 1978. pap. text ed. 3.00x (ISBN 0-920380-15-8, Pub. by Inst Res Pub Canada). Renouf.

Hirschmeier, Johannes & Yui, Tsunehiko. The Development of Japanese Business, 1600-1973. LC 74-82190. 350p. 1975. 16.50x (ISBN 0-674-20045-4). Harvard U Pr.

Ho, Alfred K. Japan's Trade Liberalization in the 1960s' LC 73-75075. (Illus.). 1973. 12.50 (ISBN 0-87332-039-5). M E Sharpe.

Japan Chamber of Commerce & Industry. Standard Trade Index of Japan, 1981-82. 25th ed. LC 55-36368. 1500p. 1981. 130.00x (ISBN 0-8002-2784-0). Intl Pubns Serv.

Japan Fact Book, 1980: Who's Who in Electronics Industry, Almanac of Electronics Industry. (Illus.). 244p. (Orig.). 1980. pap. 30.00x (ISBN 0-8002-2347-0). Intl Pubns Serv.

Japan Telephone Book Yellow Pages: Spring 1979 Issue. 1979. pap. 31.00x (ISBN 0-8002-0407-7). Intl Pubns Serv.

Japan's Community-Based Industries: A Case Study of Small Industry. 300p. 1980. pap. 25.25 (ISBN 0-686-74014-9, APO 100, APO). Unipub.

Japan's Economic Expansion & Foreign Trade, 1955 to 1970. (GATT Studies in International Trade: No. 2). (Orig.). 1971. pap. 2.00 (ISBN 0-685-02938-7, GATT). Unipub.

Kinosita, Yetaro. Past & Present of Japanese Commerce. LC 68-56663. (Columbia University. Studies in the Social Sciences: No. 41). Repr. of 1902 ed. 16.50 (ISBN 0-404-51041-8). AMS Pr.

Labour Market Information for Decision - Making: The Case of Japan. 252p. (Orig.). 1981. pap. text ed. write for info. (ISBN 9-2210-2598-5). Intl Labour Office.

Loutfi, Martha E. The Net Cost of Japanese Foreign Aid. LC 73-28. (Special Studies in International Economics & Development). 1973. 34.00x (ISBN 0-275-28711-4). Irvington.

Magaziner, Ira C. & Hout, Thomas M. Japanese Industrial Policy. LC 81-80791. (Policy Papers in International Affairs: No. 15). (Illus.). 120p. 1981. pap. 5.50x (ISBN 0-87725-515-6). U of Cal Intl St.

Mannari, Hiroshi. The Japanese Business Leaders. LC 74-84827. (Illus.). xxiv, 291p. 1975. 18.50x (ISBN 0-86008-122-2, Pub. by Lotus Pr Japan). Intl Schol Bk Serv.

Massie, Michael R., et al. Alaska-Japan Economic Relations: A Study of the Potential Contribution of Trade with Japan to Alaska's Economic Development. (Joint Institute of Social & Economic Research Ser.: No. 17). 504p. 1968. pap. 8.50 (ISBN 0-295-95114-1). U of Wash Pr.

Matsunaga, Yoshio. Successful Licensing to & from Japan. (Illus.). 1974. 30.00 (ISBN 0-685-51745-4). Sadtler Res.

Mook, Hurbertus J. Van. The Netherlands Indies & Japan. LC 77-179226. Repr. of 1944 ed. 18.00 (ISBN 0-404-54853-9). AMS Pr.

Moulton, Harold G. & Ko, Junichi. Japan: An Economic & Financial Appraisal. LC 77-97886. Repr. of 1931 ed. 38.45 (ISBN 0-404-04507-3). AMS Pr.

Nomura Research Institute. Investing in Japan. (Illus.). 208p. 1980. 25.00x (ISBN 0-85941-067-6). Herman Pub.

Odate, Gyoju. Japan's Financial Relations with the United States. LC 78-57574. (Columbia University. Studies in the Social Sciences: No. 224). Repr. of 1922 ed. 15.00 (ISBN 0-404-51224-0). AMS Pr.

Okada, Barbara T. & Okada, Nancy T. Do's & Don't's for the Japanese Businessman Abroad. 130p. (gr. 10 up). 1973. pap. text ed. 3.95 (ISBN 0-88345-208-1, 18133). Regents Pub.

Paske-Smith, M. Western Barbarians in Japan & Formosa in Tokugawa Days, 1603-1868. LC 68-30741. (Illus.). 1968. Repr. of 1930 ed. 25.00 (ISBN 0-8188-0071-2). Paragon.

Sato, Kazuo, ed. Industry & Business in Japan: An Anthology. LC 79-91904. 1980. text ed. 30.00 (ISBN 0-87332-152-9). M E Sharpe.

Sheldon, Charles D. The Rise of the Merchant Class in Tokugawa Japan, 1600-1868: An Introductory Survey. LC 72-97536. xiv, 220p. (With a new introduction & appendix). 1973. Repr. of 1958 ed. 18.00 (ISBN 0-8462-1725-2). Russell.

Shimaguchi, Mitsuaki. Marketing Channels in Japan. Dufey, Gunter, ed. LC 78-24373. (Research for Business Decisions Ser.: No. 7). 1978. 31.95 (ISBN 0-8357-0960-4, Pub. by UMI Res Pr). Univ Microfilms.

Sueno, Akira. Entrepreneur & Gentleman: The Case History of a Japanese Business. Donner, Neal, tr. LC 76-51611. (Illus.). 1977. 16.50 (ISBN 0-8048-1199-7). C E Tuttle.

Tsurumi, Yoshihiro. Technology Transfer & Foreign Trade: The Case of Japan, 1950 to 1966. rev. ed. Bruchey, Stuart, ed. LC 80-600. (Multinational Corporations Ser.). (Illus.). 1980. lib. bdg. 25.00x (ISBN 0-405-13390-1). Arno.

U. S. Tariff Commission. Postwar Developments in Japan's Foreign Trade. Repr. of 1958 ed. lib. bdg. 17.25x (ISBN 0-8371-2503-0, PODJ). Greenwood.

Yoshitake, Kiyohiko. An Introduction to Public Enterprise in Japan. LC 73-84184. 362p. 1973. 24.00 (ISBN 0-8039-0298-0). Sage.

JAPAN–CONSTITUTIONAL HISTORY

Akita, George. Foundations of Constitutional Government in Modern Japan, 1868-1900. LC 65-13835. (East Asian Ser: No. 23). 1967. 15.00x (ISBN 0-674-31250-3). Harvard U Pr.

Beckmann, George M. The Making of the Meiji Constitution: The Oligarchs & the Constitutional Development of Japan, 1868-1891. LC 72-7963. 158p. 1975. Repr. of 1957 ed. lib. bdg. 15.00 (ISBN 0-8371-6553-9, BEMC). Greenwood.

Fujii, Shinichi. Essentials of Japanese Constitutional Law. (Studies in Japanese Law & Government). 459p. 1979. Repr. of 1940 ed. 32.50 (ISBN 0-89093-214-X). U Pubns Amer.

Henderson, Dan F., ed. Constitution of Japan: Its First Twenty Years, 1947-67. LC 69-20034. (Asian Law Ser: No. 1). 322p. 1969. 13.50 (ISBN 0-295-73836-7). U of Wash Pr.

Ito, Hirobumi. Commentaries on the Constitution of the Empire of Japan. 2nd ed. Ito, Miyoji, tr. from Japanese. LC 74-15166. 1978. Repr. of 1906 ed. lib. bdg. 24.25x (ISBN 0-8371-7810-X, ITEG). Greenwood.

Iyenaga, T. Constitutional Development of Japan: 1853-1881. 1973. Repr. of 1891 ed. pap. 7.00 (ISBN 0-384-26385-2). Johnson Repr.

Maki, John M. Court & Constitution in Japan: Selected Supreme Court Decisions, 1948-60. LC 78-23431. (University of Washington Publications on Asia). 1978. pap. 40.00 (ISBN 0-8357-0335-5, ST-00017, Pub. by U of Wash Pr). Univ Microfilms.

Miller, Frank O. Minobe Tatsukichi: Interpreter of Constitutionalism in Japan. (Center for Japanese & Korean Studies, UC Berkeley). 1965. 27.00x (ISBN 0-520-00865-0). U of Cal Pr.

Nakano, Tomio. Ordinance Power of the Japanese Emperor. LC 71-173009. Repr. of 1923 ed. 16.00 (ISBN 0-404-04650-9). AMS Pr.

Siemes, Johannes. Hermann Roesler - the Making of the Meiji State. LC 68-57055. 1969. 8.50 (ISBN 0-8048-0648-9). C E Tuttle.

Takeuchi, Sterling T. War & Diplomacy in the Japanese Empire. LC 66-27158. 1967. Repr. of 1935 ed. 12.50 (ISBN 0-8462-1013-4). Russell.

JAPAN–COURT AND COURTIERS

Omori, Annie S. & Kochi, Doi, trs. Diaries of Court Ladies of Old Japan. LC 72-111775. Repr. of 1920 ed. 14.50 (ISBN 0-404-04819-6). AMS Pr.

Shonagon, Sei. Pillow Book of Sei Shonagon. Morris, Ivan, tr. (Classics Ser). 1971. pap. 3.95 (ISBN 0-14-044236-7). Penguin.

JAPAN–DESCRIPTION AND TRAVEL

Adachi, Barbara. Living Treasures of Japan. LC 73-80959. (Illus.). 164p. 1973. 22.50 (ISBN 0-87011-204-X). Kodansha.

Alcock, Rutherford. Capital of the Tycoon, 2 Vols. 1863. Set. 49.00 (ISBN 0-403-00241-9). Scholarly.

--Capital of the Tycoon: A Narrative of a Three Years' Residence in Japan, 2 Vols. LC 68-30995. (Illus.). 1968. Repr. of 1863 ed. Set. lib. bdg. 36.50x (ISBN 0-8371-1865-4, ALCT). Greenwood.

American Chamber of Commerce in Japan. Living in Japan. 8th ed. 15.00 (ISBN 0-686-16964-6). A M Newman.

Barthes, Roland. L' Empire des Signes. (Illus.). 152p. 1970. 25.00 (ISBN 0-686-53933-8). French & Eur.

Basho, Matsuo. The Narrow Road to the Deep North & Other Travel Sketches. Yuasa, Nobuyuki, tr. from Japanese. (Classics Ser.). 167p. (Orig.). 1974. pap. 2.95 (ISBN 0-14-044185-9). Penguin.

Bird, Isabella L. Unbeaten Tracks in Japan. LC 75-172002. (Illus.). 1971. pap. 5.95 (ISBN 0-8048-1000-1). C E Tuttle.

Chiang Yee. The Silent Traveller in Japan. 1972. 15.00 (ISBN 0-393-08642-9). Norton.

Chiba, Reiko. Hiroshige's Tokaido in Prints & Poetry. LC 57-11672. (Illus.). 9.50 (ISBN 0-8048-0246-7). C E Tuttle.

Clarke, Joseph I. Japan at First Hand. LC 72-82089. (Japan Library Ser.). (Illus.). 1973. Repr. of 1918 ed. lib. bdg. 32.00 (ISBN 0-8420-1384-9). Scholarly Res Inc.

Cole, Allan B. Yankee Surveyors in the Shogun's Seas: Records of the United States Surveying Expedition to the North Pacific Ocean, 1853-1856. LC 68-55183. (Illus.). 1969. Repr. of 1947 ed. lib. bdg. 15.00x (ISBN 0-8371-0354-1, COYS). Greenwood.

Condon, Jack & Condon, Camy. The Simple Pleasure of Japan. 148p. 1980. pap. 8.50 (ISBN 0-89955-100-9, Pub. by Shufunotomo Japan). Intl Schol Bk Serv.

Dahlgren, E. W. Les Debuts De la Cartographie Du Japon. 1978. text ed. 8.00x (ISBN 90-6041-131-5). Humanities.

Darr, D. & Giuglaris. Japon Des Realites. (Illus., Fr.). 1965. 12.50x (ISBN 0-685-19322-5). Paragon.

Davis, Bob, photos by. Faces of Japan. LC 78-55092. (Illus.). 108p. 1978. 14.95 (ISBN 0-87011-338-0). Kodansha.

De Mente, Boye. Exotic Japan: The Traveler's Wonderland. LC 72-21365. (Illus.). 160p. 1976. pap. 3.95 (ISBN 0-914778-12-9). Phoenix Bks.

--Reading Your Way Around Japan. (Illus.). 1979. pap. 4.95 (ISBN 0-914778-20-X). Phoenix Bks.

--Tourist & the Real Japan: How to Avoid Pitfalls & Get the Most Out of Your Trip. LC 67-15318. (Orig.). 1966. pap. 4.25 (ISBN 0-8048-0593-8). C E Tuttle.

De Moges. Recollections of Baron Gros's Embassy to China & Japan in 1857-1858. LC 72-79818. (China Library Ser.). (Illus.). 1972. Repr. of 1860 ed. lib. bdg. 22.00 (ISBN 0-8420-1366-0). Scholarly Res Inc.

Desiles, Clara. Japan Today. (Illus.). 1979. bds. 14.95 (ISBN 2-8525-8110-8, Pub. by Two Continents). Hippocrene Bks.

Dore, Ronald P. Shinohata: Portrait of a Japanese Village. (Pantheon Village Ser.). 1980. pap. 4.95 (ISBN 0-394-73843-8). Pantheon.

Dresser, Christopher. Japan: Its Art, Architecture, & Art Manufacture. LC 76-17752. (Aesthetic Movement & the Arts & Crafts Movement Ser.: Vol. 5). 1977. Repr. of 1882 ed. lib. bdg. 44.00 (ISBN 0-8240-2454-0). Garland Pub.

Duhamel, Georges. Le Japon. 176p. 1953. 9.95 (ISBN 0-686-55177-X). French & Eur.

Faulds, Henry. Nine Years in Nipon: Sketches of Japanese Life & Manners. LC 72-82092. (Japan Library Ser.). 1973. Repr. of 1885 ed. lib. bdg. 17.00 (ISBN 0-8420-1388-1). Scholarly Res Inc.

Hearn, Lafcadio. Gleanings in Buddha-Fields. LC 73-172539. Repr. of 1897 ed. 17.50 (ISBN 0-405-08609-1). Arno.

--Gleanings in Buddha-Fields: Studies of Hand & Soul in the Far East. LC 72-146523. 1971. pap. 2.75 (ISBN 0-8048-0978-X). C E Tuttle.

--Glimpses of Unfamiliar Japan, 2 Vols. LC 70-101093. Repr. of 1894 ed. 32.50 (ISBN 0-404-03205-2). AMS Pr.

--Glimpses of Unfamiliar Japan, 2 vols. in 1. LC 74-84324. 1974. pap. 5.95 (ISBN 0-8048-1145-8). C E Tuttle.

--Out of the East. LC 72-4161. (Select Bibliographies Reprint Ser.). 1972. Repr. of 1895 ed. 19.00 (ISBN 0-8369-6883-2). Arno.

Inoue, Yasushi. Journey Beyond Samarkand. LC 70-136563. (Illus.). 130p. 1971. 10.00x (ISBN 0-87011-151-5). Kodansha.

Lach, Donald F. Japan in the Eyes of Europe: The Sixteenth Century. LC 64-19848. 1968. pap. 1.45 (ISBN 0-226-46747-3, P295, Phoen). U of Chicago Pr.

Lanier, Alison R. Update -- Japan. LC 80-83913. (Country Orientation Ser.). 1981. pap. text ed. 25.00x (ISBN 0-933662-39-4). Intercult Pr.

Milward, Peter. Oddities in Modern Japan: Observations of an Outsider. (Illus.). viii, 187p. 1980. pap. 11.50 (ISBN 0-89346-183-0, Pub. by Hokuseido Pr). Heian Intl.

Namioka, Lensey. Japan: A Traveller's Companion. LC 78-63639. (Illus.). 1979. 12.95 (ISBN 0-8149-0810-1); pap. 7.95 (ISBN 0-8149-0816-0). Vanguard.

Oliphant, Laurence. Elgin's Mission to China & Japan, 2 Vols. (Oxford in Asia Historical Reprints Ser). 1970. 22.25x (ISBN 0-19-641004-5). Oxford U Pr.

--Narrative of the Lord of Elgin's Mission to China & Japan, 2 Vols. LC 72-77056. Repr. of 1859 ed. 22.00x (ISBN 0-678-00498-6). Kelley.

Perry, Matthew C. Narrative of the Expedition of an American Squadron to the China Seas & Japan, 3 Vols. Hawks, Francis L., ed. LC 1-4228. (Illus.). Repr. of 1856 ed. 200.00 (ISBN 0-404-05060-3). AMS Pr.

Pezeu-Massabuau, Jacques. The Japanese Islands: A Physical & Social Geography. Blum, Paul C., tr. LC 77-82140. (Illus.). 1978. 12.50 (ISBN 0-8048-1184-9). C E Tuttle.

Planck, Charles & Planck, Carolyn. Pacific Paradise on a Low Budget. LC 72-3809. (Illus.). 200p. 1973. pap. 3.50 (ISBN 0-87491-332-2). Acropolis.

Richie, Donald. The Inland Sea. LC 78-157276. (Illus.). 1971. pap. 8.50 (ISBN 0-8348-0138-8). Weatherhill.

Rifkin, Natalie S., ed. Japan: Land of the Golden Fish. LC 77-77892. (National Wildlife Challenge Kit Ser.). 1977. 35.00 (ISBN 0-912186-24-0). Natl Wildlife.

Rundall, Thomas, ed. Memorials of the Empire of Japan, in the Sixteenth & Seventeenth Centuries: The Kingdome of Japonia, Letters of William Adams from 1611 to 1617. (Hakluyt Society First Ser: No. 7). 1965. 24.50 (ISBN 0-8337-3094-0). B Franklin.

Seidensticker, Edward G. This Country, Japan. LC 74-77958. (Illus.). 332p. 1979. 15.00 (ISBN 0-87011-229-5). Kodansha.

Steinmetz, Andrew. Japan & Her People. LC 72-82112. (Japan Library Ser.). (Illus.). 1973. Repr. of 1859 ed. lib. bdg. 31.00 (ISBN 0-8420-1404-7). Scholarly Res Inc.

Sutherland, Mary & Britton, Dorothy. National Parks of Japan. LC 75-30181. 144p. 1981. 17.50 (ISBN 0-87011-250-3). Kodansha.

Svensson, Arne. Japan. LC 72-106899. (Screen Guide Ser). (Illus.). 1970. pap. 4.95 (ISBN 0-498-07654-7). A S Barnes.

Trewartha, Glenn T. Japan: A Geography. rev. ed. (Illus.). 1965. 25.00 (ISBN 0-299-03440-2); pap. 7.95 (ISBN 0-299-03444-5). U of Wis Pr.

Tuttle, Charles E. Incredible Japan. rev. ed. Orig. Title: Japan Unbuttoned. (Illus.). 120p. 1975. pap. 4.50 (ISBN 0-8048-1162-8). C E Tuttle.

White, Trumball. Glimpses of the Orient: or the Manners, Customs, Life & History of the People of China, Japan & Corea. LC 72-82115. (Japan Library Ser.). (Illus.). 1973. Repr. of 1897 ed. lib. bdg. 37.50 (ISBN 0-8420-1408-X). Scholarly Res Inc.

Worswick, Clark, ed. Japan: Photographs, Eighteen Fifty-Four to Nineteen Hundred & Five. LC 79-2215. (Illus.). 1979. 25.00 (ISBN 0-394-50836-X). Knopf.

Yoshida, Kenichi. Japan Is a Circle. LC 75-14731. 149p. 1976. Repr. 7.95 (ISBN 0-87011-262-7). Kodansha.

JAPAN–DESCRIPTION AND TRAVEL–GUIDEBOOKS

Bisignani, J. D. Japan Handbook. LC 81-80991. (Illus.). 450p. (Orig.). 1982. pap. 10.95 (ISBN 0-9603322-2-7, Pub. by Moon Pubns). C E Tuttle.

Cooper, Michael. Exploring Kamakura. LC 79-11997. (Illus.). 1979. pap. 5.95 (ISBN 0-8348-0144-2). Weatherhill.

De Mente, Boye. P's & Cues for Travelers in Japan. 104p. 1980. pap. 5.50 (ISBN 0-89955-114-9, Pub. by Shufunotomo Japan). Intl Schol Bk Serv.

Fodor's Budget Japan, 1981. 1980. pap. 4.95 (ISBN 0-679-00655-9). McKay.

Fodor's Japan & Korea, 1981. 1981. 13.95 (ISBN 0-679-00703-2); pap. 10.95 (ISBN 0-679-00704-0). McKay.

Nagasawa, Kimiki & Condon, Camy. Eating Cheap in Japan. 104p. 1980. pap. 7.50 (ISBN 0-89955-109-2, Pub. by Shufunotomo Japan). Intl Schol Bk Serv.

Nagel Travel Guide to Japan. (Nagel Travel Guide Ser.). (Illus.). 1120p. 1974. 50.00 (ISBN 2-8263-0610-3). Hippocrene Bks.

Nagel's Encyclopedia Guide: Japan. (Illus.). 1120p. 1979. 50.00 (ISBN 0-686-74059-9). Masson Pub.

Sheldon, Walt. Enjoy Japan: A Personal & Highly Unofficial Guide. LC 60-15609. (Illus.). 1961. pap. 4.95 (ISBN 0-8048-0170-3, Tut Bks). C E Tuttle.

Watanabe, Masahiro & Rogers, Bruce. Instant Japan. (Illus.). 202p. 1981. pap. 3.95 (ISBN 0-89346-181-4). Heian Intl.

JAPAN–DICTIONARIES AND ENCYCLOPEDIAS

Papinot, E. Historical & Geographical Dictionary of Japan. LC 71-152116. (Illus.). 1972. pap. 9.50 (ISBN 0-8048-0996-8). C E Tuttle.

JAPAN–DIPLOMATIC AND CONSULAR SERVICE

Miyoshi, Masao. As We Saw Them: The First Japanese Embassy to the United States (1860) LC 78-62851. 1979. 14.95 (ISBN 0-520-03767-7). U of Cal Pr.

JAPAN–ECONOMIC CONDITIONS

Abegglen, James C. The Japanese Factory. rev. ed. LC 80-52878. 200p. 1981. pap. 6.25 (ISBN 0-8048-1372-8). C E Tuttle.

Allen, C. G. A Short Economic History of Modern Japan. 272p. 1980. 19.95 (ISBN 0-312-71771-7). St Martin.

Allen, G. C. Japan's Economic Policy. 1979. text ed. 41.25x (ISBN 0-8419-5063-6). Holmes & Meier.

American Chamber of Commerce in Japan. Manual of Employment Practices in Japan. 1979. 45.00 (ISBN 0-686-16957-3). A M Newman.

Black, Cyril E., et al. The Modernization of Japan & Russia. LC 75-8429. (Perspectives on Modernization Ser.). 1975. 19.95 (ISBN 0-02-906850-9). Free Pr.

Boltho, Andrea. Japan: An Economic Survey 1953-1973. (Economies of the World). (Illus.). 220p. 1975. 24.00x (ISBN 0-19-877036-7). Oxford U Pr.

Business Intercommunications, Inc. White Paper on Japanese Economy, 1978. 1978. 39.00 (ISBN 0-686-19299-0). A M Newman.

--White Paper on Japanese Trade. 1978. 39.00 (ISBN 0-686-11888-X). A M Newman.

Campbell, John C. Contemporary Japanese Budget Politics. LC 73-85782. 1977. 24.50x (ISBN 0-520-02573-3); pap. 7.95x (ISBN 0-520-04087-2, CAMPUS NO. 253). U of Cal Pr.

Clark, Rodney. The Japanese Company. 1979. 27.50x (ISBN 0-300-02310-3); pap. 7.95 (ISBN 0-300-02646-3). Yale U Pr.

Cohen, Jerome B. Japan's Economy in War & Reconstruction. LC 73-11851. 545p. 1973. Repr. of 1949 ed. lib. bdg. 29.50x (ISBN 0-8371-7072-9, COJE). Greenwood.

De Mente, Boye. How to Do Business in Japan. 1974. 12.00 (ISBN 0-914778-15-3). Phoenix Bks.

Denison, Edward F. & Chung, William K. How Japan's Economy Grew So Fast: The Sources of Postwar Expansion. 1976. 14.95 (ISBN 0-8157-1808-X); pap. 5.95 (ISBN 0-8157-1807-1). Brookings.

Desiles, Clara. Japan Today. (Illus.). 1979. bds. 14.95 (ISBN 2-8525-8110-8, Pub. by Two Continents). Hippocrene Bks.

Dodwell Marketing Consultants. Industrial Groupings in Japan, Nineteen Eighty to Nineteen Eighty-One. rev. ed. (Illus.). 503p. (Orig.). 1980. pap. 335.00x (ISBN 0-8002-2817-0). Intl Pubns Serv.

Economic & Foreign Affairs Research Assoc., Tokyo. Statistical Survey of Japan's Economy, 1980. LC 54-43626. (Illus.). 83p. (Orig.). 1981. pap. 17.50x (ISBN 0-8002-2819-7). Intl Pubns Serv.

Economic Planning Agency-Japan, ed. Economic Survey of Japan, 1979-1980. 29th ed. LC 51-61351. (Illus., Orig.). 1980. pap. 45.00x (ISBN 0-8002-2787-5). Intl Pubns Serv.

Economic Survey of Japan: Series One, 7 vols. Set. pap. 85.00x (ISBN 0-8371-9162-9, EC11). Greenwood.

Economic Survey of Japan: Series Two, 10 vols. Set. pap. 120.00x (ISBN 0-8371-9163-7, EC00). Greenwood.

Economic Survey of Japan: 1957-1967, 10 Vols. 1969. Set (ISBN 0-685-01576-9). 20.00x ea. Paragon.

Frank, Isaiah, ed. The Japanese Economy in International Perspective. LC 74-15567. (Committee for Economic Development Ser). (Illus.). 314p. 1975. 20.00x (ISBN 0-8018-1629-7); pap. 5.45x (ISBN 0-8018-1630-0). Johns Hopkins.

Furuya, Seikow Y. Japan's Foreign Exchange & Her Balance of International Payments, with Special Reference to Recent Theories of Foreign Exchange. LC 68-58576. (Columbia University. Studies in the Social Sciences: No. 299). 18.50 (ISBN 0-404-51299-2). AMS Pr.

Gibney, Frank. Japan: The Fragile Superpower. rev. ed. 1979. 12.95 (ISBN 0-393-05704-6). Norton.

Glickman, Norman J. The Growth & Management of the Japanese Urban System. (Studies in Urban Economics Ser.). 1979. 30.50 (ISBN 0-12-286950-8). Acad Pr.

The Growth Pole Approach to Regional Development: A Case Study of Mizushima Industrial Complex, Japan. 136p. 1975. pap. 7.25 (ISBN 0-686-75153-1, CRD009, UNCRD). Unipub.

Haitani, Kanji. The Japanese Economic System: An Institutional Overview. LC 76-11972. 1976. 18.95 (ISBN 0-669-00716-1). Lexington Bks.

Halliday, Jon. A Political History of Japanese Capitalism. LC 74-4774. (Asia Library Ser.). 1975. 15.95 (ISBN 0-394-48391-X). Pantheon.

--A Political History of Japanese Capitalism. 1978. pap. 8.95 (ISBN 0-85345-471-X, PB471X). Monthly Rev.

Halliday, Jon & McCormack, Gavan. Japanese Imperialism Today. LC 72-92027. (Illus.). 272p. 1973. 7.95 (ISBN 0-85345-271-7, CL-2717); pap. 6.50 (ISBN 0-85345-311-X, PB-311X). Monthly Rev.

Hanabusa, Masamichi. Trade Problems Between Japan & Western Europe. LC 79-88567. (Illus.). 138p. 1979. 24.95 (ISBN 0-03-053361-9). Praeger.

Hanley, Susan B. & Yamamura, Kozo. Economic & Demographic Change in Preindustrial Japan, 1600-1868. LC 77-71983. 1978. text ed. 32.50 (ISBN 0-691-03111-8); pap. 12.50 (ISBN 0-691-10055-1). Princeton U Pr.

Harada, Shuichi. Labor Conditions in Japan. (Columbia University Studies in the Social Sciences: No. 301). Repr. of 1928 ed. 22.50 (ISBN 0-404-51301-8). AMS Pr.

Hauser, W. B. Economic Institutional Change in Tokugawa Japan: Osaka & the Kinai Cotton Trade. LC 73-80478. (Illus.). 320p. 1974. 32.50 (ISBN 0-521-20302-3). Cambridge U Pr.

Henderson, Dan F. Foreign Enterprise in Japan: Laws & Policies. LC 72-87493. 592p. 1973. 25.00x (ISBN 0-8078-1210-2). U of NC Pr.

Hirscheier, J. & Yui, T. The Development of Japanese Business. write for info. Allen Unwin.

Ike, Nobutaka. Japanese Politics: Patron-Client Democracy. 2nd ed. 1972. pap. text ed. 4.95 (ISBN 0-394-31695-9). Knopf.

Japan Center for International Exchange, ed. The Silent Power: Japan's Identity & World Role. 1976. 13.50x (ISBN 0-89955-245-5, Pub. by Simul). Intl Schol Bk Serv.

Japan Directory, 1980, 3 vols. LC 62-46629. 1971p. 1980. Set. 180.00x (ISBN 0-8002-2687-9). Intl Pubns Serv.

Japan Economic Yearbook 1979-80. 26th ed. LC 55-40192. (Illus.). 338p. 1979. 32.50x (ISBN 0-8002-2315-2). Intl Pubns Serv.

Japan Institute of International Affairs, ed. White Papers of Japan: Annual Abstract of Official Reports & Statistics of the Japanese Government 1978-79. LC 72-620531. (Illus.). 228p. (Orig.). 1980. pap. 37.50x (ISBN 0-8002-2734-4). Intl Pubns Serv.

Japan Ministry of Foreign Affairs. Statistical Survey of Japan's Economy 1979. LC 54-43626. 1980. 15.00x (ISBN 0-8002-2282-2). Intl Pubns Serv.

Japan's Economic Expansion & Foreign Trade, 1955 to 1970. (GATT Studies in International Trade: No. 2). (Orig.). 1971. pap. 2.00 (ISBN 0-685-02938-7, GATT). Unipub.

Johnson, Chalmers. Japan's Public Policy Companies. 1978. pap. 6.25 (ISBN 0-8447-3272-9). Am Enterprise.

Kahn, Herman. Emerging Japanese Superstate: Challenge & Response. 1971. pap. 2.45 (ISBN 0-13-274670-0, P2, Spec). P-H.

Kahn, Herman & Passin, Herbert. The Japanese Challenge: The Success & Failure of Economic Success. LC 78-69520. 1979. 10.95 (ISBN 0-690-01784-7). T Y Crowell.

Kahn, Herman & Pepper, Thomas. The Japanese Challenge: The Success & Failure of Economic Success. LC 80-15432. 162p. 1980. Repr. of 1979 ed. 4.95 (ISBN 0-688-08710-8, Quill). Morrow.

Kawai, Tatsuo. The Goal of Japanese Expansion. LC 73-3925. (Illus.). 120p. 1973. Repr. of 1938 ed. lib. bdg. 15.00x (ISBN 0-8371-6854-6, KAJE). Greenwood.

Kelley, Allen C. & Williamson, Jeffrey G. Lessons from Japanese Development: An Analytical Economic History. LC 73-90945. 1974. 19.00x (ISBN 0-226-42981-4); pap. text ed. 7.50x (ISBN 0-226-42984-9). U of Chicago Pr.

Kitamura, Hiroshi. Choices for the Japanese Economy: National & International Implications of Economic Growth. 1976. text ed. 18.25x (ISBN 0-905031-01-6). Humanities.

Kojima, Kiyoshi. Direct Foreign Investment: A Japanese Model of Multinational Business Operations. LC 78-61337. (Praeger Special Studies). 1979. 27.95 (ISBN 0-03-047471-X). Praeger.

Kosobud, Richard & Minami, Ryoshin, eds. Econometric Studies of Japan. LC 76-30360. 1977. 29.95 (ISBN 0-252-00255-5). U of Ill Pr.

Kuznets, Simon S., et al, eds. Economic Growth: Brazil, India, Japan. LC 55-9491. 1955. 22.50 (ISBN 0-8223-0103-2). Duke.

Lewin, B. Kleines Woerterbuch der Japanologie. 596p. (Ger. & Japan.). 1968. 38.00 (ISBN 3-447-00530-0, M-7512, Pub. by Harrassowitz). French & Eur.

Lockwood, William W. Economic Development of Japan: Growth & Structural Change, 1868-1938. rev. ed. 28.50 (ISBN 0-691-03014-6). Princeton U Pr.

Maddison, Angus. Economic Growth in Japan & the USSR. LC 70-78065. 1969. pap. text ed. 4.95x (ISBN 0-393-09870-2, NortonC). Norton.

Magaziner, Ira C. & Hout, Thomas M. Japanese Industrial Policy. LC 81-80791. (Policy Papers in International Affairs: No. 15). (Illus.). 120p. 1981. pap. 5.50x (ISBN 0-87725-515-6). U of Cal Intl St.

Mahajan, V. S. Development Planning: Lessons from the Japanese Model. LC 76-52207. 1977. 8.50x (ISBN 0-88386-805-9). South Asia Bks.

Ministry of Finance, Japan. Guide to the Economic Laws of Japan, 2 vols. (Studies in Japanese Law & Government). 1979. Repr. of 1950 ed. Set. 62.50 (ISBN 0-89093-220-4). U Pubns Amer.

Mitsuhashi, Setsuko. Japanese Commodity Flows. LC 78-8319. (Research Papers Ser.: No. 187). (Illus.). 1978. pap. 8.00 (ISBN 0-89065-094-2). U Chicago Dept Geog.

Miyazawa, K. Input-Output Analysis & the Structure of Income Distribution. (Lecture Notes in Economics & Math Systems: Vol. 116). 150p. 1976. pap. 9.90 (ISBN 0-387-07613-1). Springer-Verlag.

Mizuno, Soji. Early Foundations for Japan's Twentieth Century Economic Emergence. 1981. 8.95 (ISBN 0-533-04541-X). Vantage.

Morishima, M., et al. The Working of Econometric Models. LC 79-184901. (Illus.). 300p. 1972. 44.50 (ISBN 0-521-08502-0). Cambridge U Pr.

Moulder, F. V. Japan, China & the Modern World Economy. LC 76-2230. (Illus.). 1977. 24.95 (ISBN 0-521-21174-3); pap. 7.95x (ISBN 0-521-29736-2). Cambridge U Pr.

Moulton, Harold G. & Ko, Junichi. Japan: An Economic & Financial Appraisal. LC 77-97886. Repr. of 1931 ed. 38.45 (ISBN 0-404-04507-3). AMS Pr.

Nakamura, Takafusa. The Postwar Japanese Economy: Its Development & Structure. Rominski, Jacqueline, tr. from Japanese. 284p. 1981. 17.50x (ISBN 0-86008-284-9, Pub. by U of Tokyo Japan). Columbia U Pr.

Norbury, Paul & Bownas, G. Business in Japan: A Guide to Japanese Business Practice & Procedure. LC 74-18421. 351p. 1974. 21.95 (ISBN 0-470-64225-4). Halsted Pr.

Norman, E. Herbert. Japan's Emergence As a Modern State. LC 72-9092. 254p. 1973. Repr. of 1940 ed. lib. bdg. 23.00 (ISBN 0-8371-6573-3, NOJE). Greenwood.

The Occupation of Japan: Economic Policy & Reform. 382p. pap. 6.00 (ISBN 0-686-29519-6). MacArthur Memorial.

Odaka, Kunio. Toward Industrial Democracy: Management & the Workers in Modern Japan. LC 74-82575. (East Asian Monographs: No. 80). 270p. 1975. text ed. 15.00x (ISBN 0-674-89816-8). Harvard U Pr.

Ohkawa & Shinohara. Patterns of Japanese Economic Development. LC 78-23317. 1979. text ed. 34.50 (ISBN 0-300-02183-6). Yale U Pr.

Ohkawa, Kazushi & Rosovsky, Henry. Japanese Economic Growth: Trend Acceleration in the Twentieth Century. LC 72-97203. 352p. 1973. 15.00x (ISBN 0-8047-0833-9). Stanford U Pr.

Okita, Saburo. The Developing Economics of Japan. 284p. 1981. 14.50x (ISBN 0-86008-271-7, Pub. by U of Tokyo Japan). Columbia U Pr.

Olsen, Edward A. Japan: Economic Growth, Resource Scarcity, & Environmental Constraints. LC 77-28013. (A Westview Replica Edition Ser.). 1978. lib. bdg. 18.50x (ISBN 0-89158-064-6). Westview.

Olson, Lawrence. Dimensions of Japan. LC 63-14762. 1963. text ed. 6.50 (ISBN 0-910116-56-3). Am U Field.

Ozawa, Terutomo. Multinationalism, Japanese Style: The Political Economy of Outward Dependency. LC 79-84007. 1979. 20.00x (ISBN 0-691-04221-7). Princeton U Pr.

Patrick, Hugh. Japanese Industrialization & Its Social Consequences. LC 75-7199. 1976. pap. 9.95x (ISBN 0-520-03285-3, CAMPUS 179). U of Cal Pr.

Patrick, Hugh & Rosovsky, Henry, eds. Asia's New Giant: How the Japanese Economy Works. 1976. 24.95 (ISBN 0-8157-6934-2); pap. 14.95 (ISBN 0-8157-6933-4). Brookings.

Raffles, Sir Stanford. Report on Japan to the Secret Committee of the English East India Company. Paske-Smith, M., ed. (Records of Asian History). (Illus.). 1971. text ed. 13.00x (ISBN 0-7007-0003-X). Humanities.

Rebischung, James. Japan: The Facts of Modern Business & Social Life. LC 74-15653. (Illus.). 1975. pap. 4.25 (ISBN 0-8048-1147-4, Tut Bks). C E Tuttle.

Rix, Alan G. Japan's Economic Aid: Policy-Making & Politics. 1980. write for info. (ISBN 0-312-44063-4). St Martin.

Sanderson, Fred. Japan's Food Prospects & Policies. 1978. pap. 3.95 (ISBN 0-8157-7701-9). Brookings.

Sebald, William J. & Spinks, C. Nelson. Japan: Prospects, Options, & Opportunities. 1967. pap. 5.25 (ISBN 0-8447-3056-4). Am Enterprise.

A Selected Bibliography of Socio-Economic Development of Japan: Part B Sixteen Hundred to Nineteen Forty. 156p. 1980. pap. 5.00 (ISBN 92-808-0199-6, TUNU094, UNU). Unipub.

Seminar Summary on "The Role of Japan in Latin America". 19p. 1980. pap. 4.50 (ISBN 0-686-61370-8, COA 40, COA). Unipub.

Smith, Neil S. Materials on Japanese Social & Economic History: Tokugawa, Japan. (Studies in Japanese History & Civilization). 176p. 1979. Repr. of 1937 ed. 19.50 (ISBN 0-89093-262-X). U Pubns Amer.

Sumiya, Mikio & Taira, Koji, eds. Outline of Japanese Economic History Sixteen Three to Nineteen Forty. 1979. 29.50x (ISBN 0-86008-240-7, Pub. by U of Tokyo Pr). Intl Schol Bk Serv.

Suzuki, Yoshio. Money & Banking Contemporary Japan: The Theoretical Setting & Its Application. Greenwood, John G., tr. from Japan. LC 79-23627. 1980. 20.50x (ISBN 0-300-02255-7). Yale U Pr.

Taira, Koji. Economic Development & the Labor Market in Japan. LC 78-111459. (Studies of the East Asian Institute Ser). 1970. 17.50x (ISBN 0-231-03272-2). Columbia U Pr.

Takekoshi, Yosoburo. Economic Aspects of the History of the Civilization of Japan, 3 Vols. 1967. Repr. of 1930 ed. 65.00x (ISBN 0-685-19297-0). Paragon.

Takizawa, Matsuyo. Penetration of Money Economy in Japan & Its Effects Upon Social & Political Institutions. LC 68-54302. (Columbia University. Studies in the Social Sciences: No. 285). Repr. of 1927 ed. 16.50 (ISBN 0-404-51285-2). AMS Pr.

Tanaka, Kakuei. Building a New Japan: A Plan for Remodeling the Japanese Archipelago. 230p. 1973. 14.50 (ISBN 0-89955-241-2, Pub. by Simul). Intl Schol Bk Serv.

Terry, Samuel H. The Retailer's Manual. Assael, Henry, ed. LC 78-316. (Century of Marketing Ser.). 1978. Repr. of 1869 ed. lib. bdg. 24.00x (ISBN 0-405-11179-7). Arno.

Tsuchiya, T. An Economic History of Japan. Singer, Kurt, ed. Shidehara, M., tr. LC 77-24203. (Perspectives in Asian History Ser.: No. 10). (Illus.). 269p. 1977. Repr. of 1937 ed. lib. bdg. 17.50x (ISBN 0-87991-481-5). Porcupine Pr.

Tsuneta Yano Memorial Society (Tokyo), ed. Nippon: A Chartered Survey of Japan, 1980-81. 25th ed. (Illus.). 347p. 1980. 37.50x (ISBN 0-8002-2748-4). Intl Pubns Serv.

Tsuru, S., ed. Economic Growth & Resources: Problems Related to Japan, Vol. V. LC 79-4430. 1979. 37.50x (ISBN 0-312-23318-3). St Martin.

Tsurumi, Yoshi. Japanese Business: A Research Guide with Annotated Bibliography. LC 78-70324. (Praeger Special Studies). 1978. 22.95 (ISBN 0-03-044251-6). Praeger.

U. S. Bureau of Foreign Commerce & Baran, Saul. Investment in Japan: Basic Information for United States Businessmen. Repr. of 1956 ed. lib. bdg. 15.75x (ISBN 0-8371-2267-8, INIJ). Greenwood.

Vogel, Ezra F. Japan As Number One: Lessons for America. LC 79-24059. 1980. pap. 4.95 (ISBN 0-06-090791-6, CN 791, CN). Har-Row.

--Japan As Number One: Lessons for America. LC 78-24059. 1979. 12.50 (ISBN 0-674-47215-2). Harvard U Pr.

Woronoff, Jon. Japan: The Coming Economic Crisis. 300p. 1980. 11.95 (ISBN 0-89955-210-2, Pub. by Lotus Japan). Phoenix Bks.

Yamamura, Kozo. Economic Policy in Postwar Japan: Growth Versus Economic Democracy. (Center for Japanese & Korean Studies, UC Berkeley). 1967. 26.50x (ISBN 0-520-01369-7). U of Cal Pr.

Yoshihara, Kunio. Japanese Economic Development: A Short Introduction. (Illus.). 168p. 1979. text ed. 11.50x (ISBN 0-19-580439-2). Oxford U Pr.

--Japanese Investment in Southeast Asia. LC 77-18017. (Center for Southeast Asian Studies, Kyoto University Monograph Ser). 1978. text ed. 15.00x (ISBN 0-8248-0603-4); pap. text ed. 10.00x (ISBN 0-8248-0604-2). U Pr of Hawaii.

Zepke, Nick. The Hundred Year Miracle: Economic Development in Japan 1918-70. (Studies in 20th Century History Ser.). 1977. pap. text ed. 4.50x (ISBN 0-435-31961-2). Heinemann Ed.

JAPAN–ECONOMIC CONDITIONS–BIBLIOGRAPHY

Remer, Charles F. & Kawai, Saburo. Japanese Economics: A Guide to Japanese Reference & Research Materials. LC 78-5534. (University of Michigan Center for Japanese Studies Bibliographical Ser.: No. 5). 1978. Repr. of 1956 ed. lib. bdg. 16.50x (ISBN 0-313-20435-7, REJE). Greenwood.

Uyehara, Cecil H. Leftwing Social Movements in Japan: An Annotated Bibliography. LC 72-6213. 444p. 1972. Repr. of 1959 ed. lib. bdg. 25.50x (ISBN 0-8371-6472-9, UYLS). Greenwood.

JAPAN–EMPERORS

Akiyama, Aisaburo. Chronological List of Japan & China. 1964. pap. 3.50 (ISBN 0-8188-0000-3). Paragon.

Titus, David A. Palace & Politics in Pre-War Japan. (Studies of the East Asian Institute, Columbia University). 368p. 1974. 22.50x (ISBN 0-231-03622-1). Columbia U Pr.

Webb, Herschel. Japanese Imperial Institution in the Tokugawa Period. LC 68-11912. (East Asian Institute Ser). 1968. 17.50x (ISBN 0-231-03120-3). Columbia U Pr.

JAPAN-FOREIGN RELATIONS

Adams, Louis J. Theory, Law, & Policy of Contemporary Japanese Treaties. LC 73-11245. 256p. 1974. lib. bdg. 21.00 (ISBN 0-379-00021-0). Oceana.

Akagi, Roy. Japan's Foreign Relations, Fifteen Forty-Two to Nineteen Thirty-Six: A Short History. (Studies in Japanese History & Civilization). (Illus.). 560p. 1979. Repr. of 1936 ed. 36.50 (ISBN 0-89093-260-3). U Pubns Amer.

Alcock, Rutherford. Capital of the Tycoon, 2 Vols. 1863. Set. 49.00 (ISBN 0-403-00241-9). Scholarly.

--Capital of the Tycoon: A Narrative of a Three Years' Residence in Japan, 2 Vols. LC 68-30995. (Illus.). 1968. Repr. of 1863 ed. Set. lib. bdg. 36.50x (ISBN 0-8371-1865-4, ALCT). Greenwood.

Allen, Donald M. & Tallman, Warren, eds. The Poetics of the New American Poetry. LC 73-6222. 1973. pap. 3.95 (ISBN 0-394-17801-7, E609, Ever). Grove.

Ballon, Robert J. & Lee, Eugene H., eds. Foreign Investment & Japan. LC 72-85427. 340p. 1972. 12.50x (ISBN 0-87011-186-8). Kodansha.

Beasley, W. G., tr. Select Documents on Japanese Foreign Policy, 1853-1868. 1955. 27.50x (ISBN 0-19-713508-0). Oxford U Pr.

Blaker, Michael. Japanese International Negotiating Style. LC 77-8056. (Studies of the East Asian Institute). 253p. 1977. 17.50x (ISBN 0-231-04130-6). Columbia U Pr.

Borton, Hugh, et al. Japan Between East & West. LC 76-40008. 1976. Repr. of 1957 ed. lib. bdg. 21.50x (ISBN 0-8371-9102-5, BOJE). Greenwood.

Boxer, Charles R. Papers on Portugese, Dutch, & Jesuit Influences in 16th & 17th Century Japan: Studies in Japanese History & Civilization. 1979. 29.50 (ISBN 0-89093-255-7). U Pubns Amer.

--Portuguese Embassy to Japan (1644-1647) Bd. with Embassy of Captain Concalo de Siqueria de Souza to Japan in 1644-7. (Studies in Japanese History & Civilization). 172p. 22.00 (ISBN 0-89093-256-5). U Pubns Amer.

Causton, Eric E. Militarism & Foreign Policy in Japan. LC 78-63658. (Studies in Fascism: Ideology & Practice). Repr. of 1936 ed. 18.00 (ISBN 0-404-16918-X). AMS Pr.

Choi, Woonsang. Fall of the Hermit Kingdom. LC 66-11939. 1967. 10.00 (ISBN 0-379-00277-9). Oceana.

Clyde, Paul H. Japan's Pacific Mandate. LC 67-27586. Repr. of 1935 ed. 11.50 (ISBN 0-8046-0081-3). Kennikat.

Cooper, Michael S. J., compiled by. They Came to Japan: An Anthology of European Reports on Japan, 1543-1640. 1981. pap. 6.95 (ISBN 0-520-04509-2). U of Cal Pr.

Dunn, Frederick S. Peace-Making & the Settlement with Japan. LC 81-6223. xviii, 210p. 1981. Repr. of 1963 ed. lib. bdg. 23.50x (ISBN 0-313-23076-5, DUPM). Greenwood.

Gardiner, C. Harvey. The Japanese & Peru, 1873-1973. LC 75-17371. 202p. 1975. 12.50x (ISBN 0-8263-0391-9). U of NM Pr.

Gerard, Auguste. Ma Mission Au Japan, 1907-1914. LC 72-168109. Repr. of 1919 ed. 29.00 (ISBN 0-404-02713-X). AMS Pr.

Gibney, Frank. Japan: The Fragile Superpower. 1975. 10.95x (ISBN 0-393-05530-2). Norton.

Gubbins, John H. The Making of Modern Japan. facsimile ed. LC 73-169760. (Select Bibliographies Reprint Ser). Repr. of 1922 ed. 21.00 (ISBN 0-8369-5980-9). Arno.

--Progress of Japan, 1853-1871. LC 79-137237. Repr. of 1911 ed. 24.50 (ISBN 0-404-02939-6). AMS Pr.

Hayashi, Tadasu. Secret Memoirs of Count Tadasu Hayashi. Pooley, A. M., ed. LC 72-93536. Repr. of 1915 ed. 21.50 (ISBN 0-404-03159-5). AMS Pr.

Hishida, Seiji G. International Position of Japan As a Great Power. LC 6-23069. (Columbia University. Studies in the Social Sciences: No. 64). Repr. of 1905 ed. 21.50 (ISBN 0-404-51064-7). AMS Pr.

Hoffman, Arthur. Japan & the Pacific Basin, No. 40. (The Atlantic Papers). 68p. 1980. pap. 4.75 (ISBN 0-86598-042-X, Pub. by Atlantic Inst France). Allanheld.

Japan Institute of International Affairs, ed. White Papers of Japan: Annual Abstract of Official Reports & Statistics of the Japanese Government 1978-79. LC 72-620531. (Illus.). 228p. (Orig.). 1980. pap. 37.50x (ISBN 0-8002-2734-4). Intl Pubns Serv.

Jones, F. C. Extraterritoriality in Japan. LC 77-114048. Repr. of 1931 ed. 19.50 (ISBN 0-404-03598-1). AMS Pr.

Kajima, Morinosuke. Emergence of Japan As a World Power, Eighteen Ninety-Five to Nineteen Twenty-Five. LC 68-11079. 1967. 6.60 (ISBN 0-8048-0166-5). C E Tuttle.

--Modern Japan's Foreign Policy. LC 75-77124. (Illus.). 1969. 6.00 (ISBN 0-8048-0658-6). C E Tuttle.

Kasai, Jiuji G. United States & Japan in the Pacific. LC 72-111759. (American Imperialism: Viewpoints of United States Foreign Policy). 1970. Repr. of 1935 ed. 14.00 (ISBN 0-405-02030-9). Arno.

Kase, Toshikazu. Journey to the Missouri. Rowe, David N., ed. 1969. Repr. of 1950 ed. 18.50 (ISBN 0-208-00747-4, Archon). Shoe String.

Kokusaiho, Gakkai. Japan & the United Nations. LC 74-7433. (National Studies on International Organization-Carnegie Endowment for International Peace). 246p. 1974. Repr. of 1958 ed. lib. bdg. 14.00x (ISBN 0-8371-7538-0, KOJU). Greenwood.

Kuno, Yoshi S. Japanese Expansion on the Asiatic Continent, 2 Vols. LC 67-27615. 1968. Repr. of 1940 ed. Set. 32.50x (ISBN 0-8046-0256-5). Kennikat.

Kutakov, Leonid N. Japanese Foreign Policy on the Eve of the Pacific War: A Soviet View. Lensen, George A., ed. LC 77-186316. xii, 244p. 1972. 15.00 (ISBN 0-910512-15-9). Diplomatic Fla.

Kyger, Joanne. Japan & India Journals. 300p. 1981. pap. 10.00 (ISBN 0-939180-01-4). Tombouctou.

Lissington, M. P. New Zealand & Japan, Nineteen Hundred to Nineteen Forty-One. (Illus.). 206p. 1972. 12.00x (ISBN 0-8426-0449-9). Verry.

Manglapus, Raul S. Japan in Southeast Asia: Collision Course. LC 76-14709. 1976. pap. 3.75 (ISBN 0-87003-004-3). Carnegie Endow.

Matsushita, Masatoshi. Japan in the League of Nations. LC 68-58606. (Columbia University. Studies in the Social Sciences: No. 314). Repr. of 1929 ed. 16.50 (ISBN 0-404-51314-X). AMS Pr.

Maxon, Yale C. Control of Japanese Foreign Policy. LC 72-12330. 286p. 1973. Repr. of 1957 ed. lib. bdg. 17.50x (ISBN 0-8371-6728-0, MACJ). Greenwood.

Mendel, Douglas H. Japanese People & Foreign Policy: A Study of Public Opinion in Post-Treaty Japan. LC 74-141277. (Illus.). 1971. Repr. of 1961 ed. lib. bdg. 17.00x (ISBN 0-8371-5882-6, MEJP). Greenwood.

Morley, James W. Japan & Korea: America's Allies in the Pacific. LC 81-4196. (Illus.). 152p. 1981. Repr. of 1965 ed. lib. bdg. 19.50x (ISBN 0-313-23033-1, MOJK). Greenwood.

Morley, James W., ed. Japan's Foreign Policy 1868-1914: A Research Guide. (Studies of the East Asian Institute). 618p. 1973. 27.50x (ISBN 0-231-08966-X). Columbia U Pr.

Morse, Hosea B. & MacNair, Harley F. Far Eastern International Relations, 2 Vols. LC 67-15998. (Illus.). 1967. Repr. of 1928 ed. Set. 35.00 (ISBN 0-8462-0849-0). Russell.

Mueller, Peter G. & Ross, Douglas A. China & Japan: Emerging Global Powers. LC 74-33039. (Special Studies). (Illus.). 240p. 1975. text ed. 24.95 (ISBN 0-275-05400-4); pap. text ed. 11.95 (ISBN 0-275-89390-1). Praeger.

Nish, Ian. Japanese Foreign Policy, 1869-1942: Kasumigaseki to Miyakezaka. (Foreign Policies of the Great Powers Ser.). 1976. 22.00 (ISBN 0-7100-8421-8). Routledge & Kegan.

Nishihara, Masashi. Japanese & Sukarno's Indonesia: Tokyo-Jakarta Relations, 1951-1966. LC 75-35765. (Monographs of the Center for Southeast Asian Studies, Kyoto University). (Illus.). 272p. 1976. text ed. 12.00x (ISBN 0-8248-0458-9, Eastwest Ctr); pap. text ed. 7.50x (ISBN 0-8248-0379-5, Eastwest Ctr). U Pr of Hawaii.

Osgood, Robert E., et al. Japan & the United States in Asia. LC 68-9699. (Studies in International Affairs, No. 8: No. 8). 65p. (Orig.). 1969. pap. 2.95x (ISBN 0-8018-0509-0). Johns Hopkins.

Passin, Herbert & Iriye, Akira, eds. Encounter at Shimoda: Search for a New Pacific Partnership. (Special Studies on China & East Asia). 1979. lib. bdg. 25.75x (ISBN 0-89158-467-6). Westview.

Redman, Vere H. Japan in Crisis: An Englishman's Impressions. LC 72-82107. (Japan Library Ser.). 1973. Repr. of 1935 ed. lib. bdg. 15.00 (ISBN 0-8420-1401-2). Scholarly Res Inc.

Royama, Masamichi. Foreign Policy of Japan: 1914-1939. LC 73-3930. 182p. 1973. Repr. of 1941 ed. lib. bdg. 15.00x (ISBN 0-8371-6853-8, ROFP). Greenwood.

Satow, Ernest M. Diplomat in Japan. Repr. of 1921 ed. 14.50 (ISBN 0-404-05561-3). AMS Pr.

Stockwin, J. A. Japanese Socialist Party & Neutralism. 1968. 18.50x (ISBN 0-522-83838-3, Pub. by Melbourne U Pr). Intl Schol Bk Serv.

Stone, S. Japan & the Third World. LC 75-14397. 1975. 4.00 (ISBN 0-686-11965-7). Bks Intl DH-TE.

Storry, Richard. The Double Patriots: A Study of Japanese Nationalism. 335p. 1973. Repr. of 1957 ed. lib. bdg. 21.50x (ISBN 0-8371-6643-8, STDP). Greenwood.

Takeuchi, Sterling T. War & Diplomacy in the Japanese Empire. LC 66-27158. 1967. Repr. of 1935 ed. 12.50 (ISBN 0-8462-1013-4). Russell.

Weinstein, Franklin B. & Kamiya, Fuji, eds. The Security of Korea: U. S. & Japanese Perspectives on the Nineteen Eighties. (Westview Special Studies in International Relations). 260p. 1980. lib. bdg. 20.00x (ISBN 0-89158-668-7); pap. text ed. 8.50x (ISBN 0-89158-758-6). Westview.

Wu, Y. L. Japan's Search for Oil: A Case Study on Economic Nationalism and International Security. LC 76-41086. (Publications Ser.: No. 165). (Illus.). 1977. pap. 5.95 (ISBN 0-8179-6652-8). Hoover Inst Pr.

Yoshihara, Kunio. Japanese Investment in Southeast Asia. LC 77-18017. (Center for Southeast Asian Studies, Kyoto University Monograph Ser). 1978. text ed. 15.00x (ISBN 0-8248-0603-4); pap. text ed. 10.00x (ISBN 0-8248-0604-2). U Pr of Hawaii.

Young, A. Morgan. Imperial Japan, Nineteen Twenty Six to Nineteen Thirty-Eight. LC 73-17627. 328p. 1974. Repr. of 1938 ed. lib. bdg. 20.25x (ISBN 0-8371-7255-1, YOIJ). Greenwood.

JAPAN-FOREIGN RELATIONS-AUSTRALIA

Crawford, John & Okita, Saburo, eds. Australia & Japan: Issues in the Economic Relationship. (Australia-Japan Economic Relations Research Project Monograph: No. 2). (Illus.). 140p. 1980. pap. text ed. 5.95 (ISBN 0-9596197-1-2). Bks Australia.

Drysdale, Peter & Kojima, Kiyoshi, eds. Australia-Japan Economic Relations in the International Context: Recent Experience & the Prospects Ahead. (Australia-Japan Economic Relations Research Project). 1979. pap. 5.95 (ISBN 0-9596197-0-4, Australis-Japan Economic Relations Research Project). Bks Australia.

Rosecrance, R. N. Australian Diplomacy & Japan, 1945-51. 1962. 14.00x (ISBN 0-522-83722-0, Pub. by Melbourne U Pr). Intl Schol Bk Serv.

JAPAN-FOREIGN RELATIONS-CHINA

Allan, James. Under the Dragon Flag: My Experiences in the Chino-Japanese War. LC 72-82087. (Japan Library Ser.). 1973. Repr. of 1898 ed. lib. bdg. 11.00 (ISBN 0-8420-1383-0). Scholarly Res Inc.

Barnett, A. Doak. China & the Major Powers in East Asia. 1977. 21.95 (ISBN 0-8157-0824-6); pap. 8.95 (ISBN 0-8157-0823-8). Brookings.

Commission on Critical Choices & Hellman, Donald C. China & Japan: A New Balance of Power. LC 75-44730. (Critical Choices for Americans Ser.: Vol. XII). 1976. 19.95 (ISBN 0-669-00426-X). Lexington Bks.

Coox, Alvin D. & Conroy, Hilary, eds. China & Japan: Search for Balance Since World War I. LC 77-10006. 468p. 1978. text ed. 36.50 (ISBN 0-87436-275-X). ABC-Clio.

Jain, R. K. China & Japan Nineteen Forty-Nine to Nineteen Seventy-Six. LC 77-70008. 1977. text ed. 17.50x (ISBN 0-391-00749-1). Humanities.

Jansen, Marius B. Japanese & Sun Yat-Sen. LC 53-8021. (Historical Monographs Ser: No. 27). (Illus.). 1954. 15.00x (ISBN 0-674-47200-4). Harvard U Pr.

--Japanese & Sun Yat-sen. (Illus.). 1954. pap. 3.95 (ISBN 0-8047-0700-6, SP112). Stanford U Pr.

Kawakami, K. K. Manchoukuo: Child of Conflict. LC 79-94317. Repr. of 1933 ed. 10.50 (ISBN 0-404-03639-2). AMS Pr.

Lee, Chae-Jin. Japan Faces China: Political & Economic Relations in the Postwar Era. LC 75-40408. (Illus.). 256p. 1976. 16.00x (ISBN 0-8018-1738-2). Johns Hopkins.

Leng Shao Chuan. Japan & Communist China. LC 75-11893. 166p. 1975. Repr. of 1958 ed. lib. bdg. 15.00x (ISBN 0-8371-8134-8, LEJC). Greenwood.

MacNair, Harley F. Real Conflict Between China & Japan: An Analysis of Opposing Ideologies. (Double-Page Reprint Ser). 1969. Repr. of 1938 ed. 12.75x (ISBN 0-226-50064-0). U of Chicago Pr.

Meng, Chih. China Speaks. LC 74-115205. 1971. Repr. of 1932 ed. 13.50 (ISBN 0-8046-1098-3). Kennikat.

Norton, William F. Tanaka Giichi & Japan's China Policy. LC 79-27570. 330p. 1980. 25.00 (ISBN 0-312-78500-3). St Martin.

Rowe, David N. Informal "Diplomatic Relations". The Case of Japan & the Republic of China, 1972-1974. (Foreign Area Studies: No. 15). 82p. 1975. pap. 10.00 (ISBN 0-685-55011-7, Archon). Shoe String.

Willoughby, Westel W. Sino-Japanese Controversy & the League of Nations. LC 68-54995. (Illus.). 1968. Repr. of 1935 ed. lib. bdg. 26.25x (ISBN 0-8371-0755-5, WISJ). Greenwood.

Yamada, Yosi-Aki & Eastlake, F. Warrington. Heroic Japan: A History of the War Between China & Japan. (Studies in Japanese History & Civilization). 1979. Repr. of 1897 ed. 40.50 (ISBN 0-89093-291-3). U Pubns Amer.

JAPAN-FOREIGN RELATIONS-GERMANY

Morley, James W., ed. Deterrent Diplomacy, Japan, Germany, & the USSR, 1935-1940: Japans Road to the Pacific War. LC 75-25524. (Studies of the East Asian Institute Ser.). 363p. 1976. 20.00x (ISBN 0-231-08969-4). Columbia U Pr.

Presseisen, Ernst L. Germany & Japan: A Study in Totalitarian Diplomacy, 1933-1941. LC 68-57832. 1970. Repr. of 1958 ed. 25.00 (ISBN 0-86527-082-1). Fertig.

JAPAN-FOREIGN RELATIONS-GREAT BRITAIN

Dennis, Alfred L. The Anglo-Japanese Alliance. 1923. pap. 6.00 (ISBN 0-384-11395-8). Johnson Repr.

Fox, Grace. Britain & Japan, 1858-1883. 1969. 22.00x (ISBN 0-19-821374-3). Oxford U Pr.

Ishii, Osamu. Cotton-Textile Diplomacy: Japan, Great Britain & the United States, 1930-1936. Bruchey, Stuart, ed. LC 80-2813. (Dissertations in European Economic History II). 1981. lib. bdg. 45.00x (ISBN 0-405-13996-9). Arno.

Kennedy, Malcolm D. The Estrangement of Great Britain & Japan, 1917-1935. LC 71-77517. (Illus.). 1969. 24.50x (ISBN 0-520-01431-6). U of Cal Pr.

Lowe, Peter. Great Britain & Japan Nineteen Eleven to Nineteen Fifteen: A Study of British Far Eastern Policy. (Illus.). 1969. lib. bdg. 25.00 (ISBN 0-312-34510-0). St Martin.

Nish, Ian H. Alliance in Decline: A Study in Anglo-Japanese Relations 1908-23. (University of London Historical Studies: No. 33). (Illus.). 472p. (Orig.). 1972. text ed. 47.00x (ISBN 0-485-13133-1, Athlone Pr). Humanities.

--The Anglo-Japanese Alliance: The Diplomacy of Two Island Empires. LC 75-16853. 1977. Repr. of 1968 ed. lib. bdg. 28.75x (ISBN 0-8371-8264-6, NIAJ). Greenwood.

Oliphant, Laurence. Elgin's Mission to China & Japan, 2 Vols. (Oxford in Asia Historical Reprints Ser). 1970. 22.25x (ISBN 0-19-641004-5). Oxford U Pr.

--Narrative of the Lord of Elgin's Mission to China & Japan, 2 Vols. LC 72-77056. Repr. of 1859 ed. 22.00x (ISBN 0-678-00498-6). Kelley.

Tilley, John. London to Tokyo. LC 72-82112. (Japan Library Ser.). (Illus.). 1973. Repr. of 1942 ed. lib. bdg. 19.00 (ISBN 0-8420-1405-5). Scholarly Res Inc.

JAPAN-FOREIGN RELATIONS-PHILIPPINE ISLANDS

Saniel, Josefa M. Japan & the Philippines, 1868-1898. LC 72-94983. (Illus.). xvi, 409p. 1973. Repr. of 1969 ed. 21.00 (ISBN 0-8462-1724-4). Russell.

JAPAN-FOREIGN RELATIONS-RUSSIA

Coox, Alvin D. The Anatomy of a Small War: The Soviet-Japanese Struggle for Changkufeng-Khasan, 1938. LC 76-51924. (Contributions in Military History: No. 13). 1977. lib. bdg. 25.00 (ISBN 0-8371-9479-2, CSJ/). Greenwood.

Jain, R. K. The USSR & Japan, Nineteen Forty-Five to Nineteen-Eighty. 400p. 1980. text ed. 24.75x (ISBN 0-391-01898-1). Humanities.

Kirby, E. Stuart. Russian Studies of Japan: An Exploratory Survey. LC 80-18128. 200p. 1981. 22.50 (ISBN 0-312-69610-8). St Martin.

Lensen, George A. Japanese Recognition of the U.S.S.R. Soviet-Japanese Relations, 1921-1930. LC 77-186316. 419p. 1970. 15.00 (ISBN 0-910512-09-4). Diplomatic Fla.

--The Russian Push Toward Japan. LC 75-120640. xv, 553p. 1970. Repr. of 1959 ed. lib. bdg. 30.00x (ISBN 0-374-94936-0). Octagon.

--The Strange Neutrality: Soviet - Japanese Relations During the Second World War, 1941-1945. LC 72-178091. (Illus.). 332p. 1972. 15.00 (ISBN 0-910512-14-0). Diplomatic Fla.

Lensen, George A., compiled by. Japanese Diplomatic & Consular Officials in Russia: A Handbook of Japanese Representatives in Russia from 1874 to 1968. LC 68-26392. 230p. 1968. 15.00 (ISBN 0-910512-05-1). Diplomatic Fla.

Mathieson, Raymond S. Japan's Role in Soviet Economic Growth: Transfer of Technology Since 1965. LC 78-19790. 1979. 21.95 (ISBN 0-03-046481-1). Praeger.

Morley, James W., ed. Deterrent Diplomacy, Japan, Germany, & the USSR, 1935-1940: Japans Road to the Pacific War. LC 75-25524. (Studies of the East Asian Institute Ser.). 363p. 1976. 20.00x (ISBN 0-231-08969-4). Columbia U Pr.

Peterson, Sophia. Sino-Soviet-American Relations: Conflict Communications, & Mutual Threat. LC 78-74238. (Monograph Series in World Affairs: Vol. 16). 1979. pap. 4.00 (ISBN 0-87940-058-7). U of Denver Intl.

Price, Ernest B. Russo-Japanese Treaties of 1907-1916. LC 76-101274. Repr. of 1933 ed. 17.50 (ISBN 0-404-05135-9). AMS Pr.

Vishwanathan, Savitri. Normalization of Soviet - Japanese Relations 1945-1970: An Indian View. LC 70-186317. (Illus.). 190p. 1973. 15.00 (ISBN 0-910512-16-7). Diplomatic Fla.

JAPAN–FOREIGN RELATIONS–UNITED STATES

Adelman, Morris A., et al. Japan-U. S. Assembly: Proceedings of a Conference on the Threat to the World Economic Order, Vol. 2. 1976. 14.25 (ISBN 0-8447-2083-6); pap. 6.25 (ISBN 0-8447-2082-8). Am Enterprise.

Bailey, Thomas A. Theodore Roosevelt & the Japanese-American Crisis. 1964. 8.50 (ISBN 0-8446-1038-0). Peter Smith.

Battistini, Lawrence H. Japan & America from Earliest Times to the Present. LC 76-98210. Repr. of 1954 ed. lib. bdg. 15.00 (ISBN 0-8371-3245-2, BAJA). Greenwood.

Beers, Burton F. Vain Endeavor: Robert Lansing's Attempts to End the American-Japanese Rivalry. LC 61-16907. 1962. 12.75 (ISBN 0-8223-0014-1). Duke.

Borg, Dorothy & Okamoto, Shumpei, eds. Pearl Harbor As History: Japanese-American Relations, 1931-1941. (Studies of the East & Asian Institute). 801p. 1973. 35.00x (ISBN 0-231-03734-1); pap. 14.00x (ISBN 0-231-03890-9). Columbia U Pr.

Chung, Henry. Oriental Policy of the United States. LC 70-111737. (American Imperialism: Viewpoints of United States Foreign Policy, 1898-1941). 1970. Repr. of 1919 ed. 15.00 (ISBN 0-405-02008-2). Arno.

Destler, I. M., et al. Managing an Alliance: The Politics of U. S.-Japanese Relations. 224p. 1976. 14.95 (ISBN 0-8157-1820-9); pap. 6.95 (ISBN 0-8157-1819-5). Brookings.

--The Textile Wrangle: Conflict in Japanese-American Relations, 1969-1971. LC 78-14429. 1979. 25.00x (ISBN 0-8014-1120-3). Cornell U Pr.

Emmerson, John K. The Japanese Thread: A Life in the U.S. Foreign Service. LC 77-26624. (Illus.). 1978. 16.95 (ISBN 0-03-041646-9). HR&W.

Esthus, Raymond A. Theodore Roosevelt & Japan. LC 66-19567. 339p. 1966. 11.50 (ISBN 0-295-74040-X). U of Wash Pr.

Feis, Herbert. Road to Pearl Harbor: The Coming of the War Between the United States & Japan. 1950. 25.00x (ISBN 0-691-05632-3); pap. 6.95 (ISBN 0-691-01061-7). Princeton U Pr.

Friedman, Donald J. Road from Isolation: The Campaign of the American Committee for Non-Participation in Japanese Aggression, 1938-1941. LC 68-4047. (East Asian Monographs Ser: No. 25). (Orig.). 1968. pap. 9.00x (ISBN 0-674-77370-5). Harvard U Pr.

Fry, Varian. War in China: America's Role in the Far East. LC 76-111741. (American Imperialism: Viewpoints of United States Foreign Policy, 1898-1941). 1970. Repr. of 1938 ed. 9.00 (ISBN 0-405-02021-X). Arno.

Grew, Joseph C. Ten Years in Japan: A Contemporary Record. LC 72-4275. (World Affairs Ser.: National & International Viewpoints). (Illus.). 578p. 1972. Repr. of 1944 ed. 27.00 (ISBN 0-405-04600-6). Arno.

--Ten Years in Japan: A Contemporary Record Drawn from the Diaries & Private & Official Papers of Joseph C. Grew, United States Ambassador to Japan, 1932-1942. LC 72-12556. (Illus.). 554p. 1973. Repr. of 1944 ed. lib. bdg. 23.50x (ISBN 0-8371-6723-X, GRTY). Greenwood.

Griffis, William E. Townsend Harris: First American Envoy in Japan. facsimile ed. LC 74-175698. (Select Bibliographies Reprint Ser). Repr. of 1895 ed. 19.00 (ISBN 0-8369-6613-9). Arno.

Hellmann, Donald C. Japanese-American Relations. LC 75-13953. (Orig.). 1975. pap. 3.25 (ISBN 0-8447-2064-X). Am Enterprise.

Herzog, James H. Closing the Open Door: American - Japanese Diplomatic Negotiations 1936-1941. LC 73-82483. 296p. 1973. 14.50 (ISBN 0-87021-728-3). Naval Inst Pr.

Hollerman, Leon, ed. Japan & the United States: Economic & Political Adversaries. LC 79-18646. (Westview Special Studies in International Economics & Business). (Illus.). 245p. 1980. 24.75x (ISBN 0-89158-582-6). Westview.

Iriye, Akira. Pacific Estrangement: Japanese & American Expansion, 1897-1911. LC 72-79307. (Studies in American-East Asian Relations: No. 2). (Illus.). 449p. 1972. 15.00x (ISBN 0-674-65075-1). Harvard U Pr.

Ishii, Osamu. Cotton-Textile Diplomacy: Japan, Great Britain & the United States, 1930-1936. Bruchey, Stuart, ed. LC 80-2813. (Dissertations in European Economic History II). 1981. lib. bdg. 45.00x (ISBN 0-405-13996-9). Arno.

Kaplan, Morton A. & Mushakoji, Kinhide. Japan, America, & the Future World Order. LC 76-15063. 1976. 15.95 (ISBN 0-02-916910-0). Free Pr.

Kasai, Jiuji G. United States & Japan in the Pacific. LC 72-111759. (American Imperialism: Viewpoints of United States Foreign Policy). 1970. Repr. of 1935 ed. 14.00 (ISBN 0-405-02030-9). Arno.

Millis, Walter. This Is Pearl: The United States & Japan, 1941. LC 77-138594. (Illus.). 1971. Repr. of 1947 ed. lib. bdg. 17.25x (ISBN 0-8371-5795-1, MITP). Greenwood.

Miyoshi, Masao. As We Saw Them: The First Japanese Embassy to the United States (1860) LC 78-62851. 1979. 14.95 (ISBN 0-520-03767-7). U of Cal Pr.

Neu, Charles E. An Uncertain Friendship: Theodore Roosevelt & Japan, 1906-1909. LC 67-27091. 1967. 16.50x (ISBN 0-674-92040-6). Harvard U Pr.

Nitobe, Inazo, pseud. The Intercourse Between the U. S. & Japan: An Historical Sketch. LC 72-82102. (Japan Library Ser.). 1973. Repr. of 1891 ed. lib. bdg. 15.00 (ISBN 0-8420-1397-0). Scholarly Res Inc.

Osgood, Robert E. The Weary & the Wary: U. S. & Japanese Security Policies in Transition. LC 71-186510. (School of Advanced International Studies: No. 16). 102p. (Orig.). 1972. 8.50x (ISBN 0-8018-1393-X); pap. 2.95x (ISBN 0-8018-1398-0). Johns Hopkins.

Packard, George R. Protest in Tokyo: The Treaty Crisis of Nineteen Sixty. LC 78-17982. 1978. Repr. of 1966 ed. lib. bdg. 32.25x (ISBN 0-313-20532-9, PAPT). Greenwood.

Peterson, Sophia. Sino-Soviet-American Relations: Conflict Communications, & Mutual Threat. LC 78-74238. (Monograph Series in World Affairs: Vol. 16). 1979. pap. 4.00 (ISBN 0-87940-058-7). U of Denver Intl.

Rappaport, Armin. Henry L. Stimson & Japan: Nineteen Thirty One - Thirty Three. LC 63-18847. 1963. 8.50x (ISBN 0-226-70527-7). U of Chicago Pr.

Reischauer, Edwin O. United States & Japan. 2nd ed. LC 64-8057. (American Foreign Policy Library). 1965. 18.50x (ISBN 0-674-92580-7). Harvard U Pr.

Reischauer, Edwin O., ed. Japan. new ed. LC 74-7767. (Great Contemporary Issues). (Illus.). 1974. 35.00 (ISBN 0-405-04168-3, Co Pub by New York Times). Arno.

Roemer, John E. U. S.-Japanese Competition in International Markets: A Study of the Trade - Investment Cycle in Modern Capitalism. LC 75-620086. (Research Ser.: No. 22). (Illus.). 225p. 1975. pap. 3.95x (ISBN 0-87725-122-3). U of Cal Intl St.

Scalapino, Robert. American-Japanese Relations in a Changing Era. LC 72-6270. (The Washington Papers: No. 2). 128p. 1972. 4.00 (ISBN 0-8039-0276-X). Sage.

Schroeder, Paul W. Axis Alliance & Japanese-American Relations, 1941. LC 72-3451. (Beveridge Award Books Ser.). 245p. 1958. 22.50x (ISBN 0-8014-0371-5). Cornell U Pr.

Shiels, Frederick L. America, Okinawa, & Japan: Case Studies for Foreign Policy Theory. LC 79-5496. 1980. text ed. 18.50 (ISBN 0-8191-0893-6); pap. text ed. 11.25 (ISBN 0-8191-0894-4). U Pr of Amer.

Treat, Payson J. Diplomatic Relations Between the United States & Japan, 1853-1905, 3 vols. 1963. 9.25 ea. (ISBN 0-8446-1450-5). Peter Smith.

--Japan & the United States, 1853-1921. LC 21-19411. Repr. of 1921 ed. 14.50 (ISBN 0-384-61450-7). Johnson Repr.

U. S. Dept. of State. Japan: 1931-1941: Papers Relating to the Foreign Relations of the United States, 2 vols. LC 72-4365. Repr. of 1943 ed. Set. 95.00 (ISBN 0-404-10514-9); 47.50 ea.; Vol. 1. (ISBN 0-404-10515-7); Vol. 2. (ISBN 0-404-10516-5). AMS Pr.

Weinstein, Franklin B. U.S.-Japan Relations & the Security of East Asia: The Next Decade. LC 77-13752. (Special Studies on International Relations & U.S. Foreign Policy Ser.). 1978. pap. text ed. 9.75x (ISBN 0-89158-067-0). Westview.

JAPAN–HISTORY

see also Sino-Japanese Conflict, 1937-1945; United States Naval Expedition to Japan, 1852-1854

Akiyama, Aisaburo. Chronological List of Japan & China. 1964. pap. 3.50 (ISBN 0-8188-0000-3). Paragon.

Asakawa, Kan'ichi. Land & Society in Medieval Japan. 20.00 (ISBN 0-686-09943-5). Far Eastern Pubns.

Asakawa, Kanichi, ed. & tr. The Documents of Iriki, Illustrative of the Development of the Feudal Institutions of Japan. LC 77-136514. (Yale Historical Publications Ser.). (Illus.). xvi, 584p. Repr. of 1929 ed. lib. bdg. 44.00x (ISBN 0-8371-5432-4, ASDI). Greenwood.

Aston, W. G., tr. from Chinese & Japanese. Nihongi: Chronicles of Japan from Earliest Times to A. D. 697. 1969. Repr. of 1924 ed. 14.50 (ISBN 0-8188-0004-6). Paragon.

Ballard, G. A. The Influence of the Sea on the Political History of Japan. 312p. 1972. Repr. of 1921 ed. 25.00x (ISBN 0-7165-2048-6, Pub. by Irish Academic Pr Ireland). Biblio Dist.

Ballard, George A. The Influence of the Sea on the Political History of Japan. LC 74-136516. (Illus.). 311p. 1973. Repr. of 1921 ed. lib. bdg. 17.75x (ISBN 0-8371-5435-9, BAIS). Greenwood.

Beasley, W. G. The Meiji Restoration. LC 72-78868. 436p. 1972. 17.50x (ISBN 0-8047-0815-0). Stanford U Pr.

--The Modern History of Japan. 4th ed. 1981. 27.50 (ISBN 0-312-53999-1). St Martin.

--The Modern History of Japan. 2nd ed. LC 73-7837. 1973. pap. text ed. 10.95 (ISBN 0-03-037931-8, HoltC). HR&W.

Beauchamp, Edward. An American Teacher in Early Meiji Japan. (Asian Studies at Hawaii Ser: No. 17). 176p. 1976. pap. text ed. 6.00x (ISBN 0-8248-0404-X). U Pr of Hawaii.

Bergamini, David. Japan's Imperial Conspiracy. (Illus.). 1971. 14.95 (ISBN 0-688-01905-6). Morrow.

Black, John R. Young Japan: Yokohama & Yedo Eighteen Fifty-Eight to Eighteen Seventy Nine, 2 Vols. (Oxford in Asia Historical Reprints Ser). 1968. Set. 38.00x (ISBN 0-19-641003-7). Oxford U Pr.

Bolitho, H. Meiji Japan. LC 76-54130. (History of Mankind Ser.). (Illus.). 1977. 3.95 (ISBN 0-521-20922-6). Cambridge U Pr.

Borton, Hugh. Japan Since Nineteen Thirty-One, Its Political & Social Developments. LC 73-3922. 168p. 1973. Repr. of 1940 ed. lib. bdg. 15.00x (ISBN 0-8371-6859-7, BOJA). Greenwood.

--Japan's Modern Century--from Perry to 1970. 2nd ed. 610p. 1970. 21.00 (ISBN 0-8260-1220-5). Wiley.

Bowen, Roger W. Rebellion & Democracy in Meiji Japan: A Study of Commoners in the Popular Rights Movement. LC 78-51755. 450p. 1980. 27.50x (ISBN 0-520-03665-4). U of Cal Pr.

Boxer, C. R. The Christian Century in Japan: 1549-1650. (Library Reprint Ser.: No. 51). (Illus.). 552p. 1974. Repr. of 1967 ed. 40.00x (ISBN 0-520-02702-7). U of Cal Pr.

Boxer, Charles R. Papers on Portugese, Dutch, & Jesuit Influences in 16th & 17th Century Japan: Studies in Japanese History & Civilization. 1979. 29.50 (ISBN 0-89093-255-7). U Pubns Amer.

--Portuguese Embassy to Japan (1644-1647) Bd. with Embassy of Captain Concalo de Siqueria de Souza to Japan in 1644-7. (Studies in Japanese History & Civilization). 172p. 22.00 (ISBN 0-89093-256-5). U Pubns Amer.

Brazell, Karen, tr. from Jap. The Confessions of Lady Nijo. 320p. 1973. 12.50x (ISBN 0-8047-0929-7); pap. 5.95 (ISBN 0-8047-0930-0, SP 140). Stanford U Pr.

Brown, Delmer M. Nationalism in Japan: An Introductory Historical Analysis. LC 79-143555. 1971. Repr. of 1955 ed. 28.00 (ISBN 0-8462-1574-8). Russell.

Brown, Keith. Shinjo: The Chronicle of a Japanese Village. LC 78-21493. (Ethnology Monograph: No. 2). (Orig.). 1979. pap. text ed. 11.95 (ISBN 0-916002-37-3, Pub. by U Ctr Intl St). U of Pittsburgh Pr.

Bryan, John T. A History of Japan. LC 78-7683. 1978. Repr. of 1928 ed. lib. bdg. 12.50 (ISBN 0-8414-0264-7). Folcroft.

Cahill, James. Scholar Painters of Japan: The Nanga School. LC 74-27413. (Asia Society Ser.). (Illus.). 1979. Repr. of 1972 ed. lib. bdg. 30.00x (ISBN 0-405-06562-0). Arno.

Caldwell, John C. South of Tokyo. 1978. Repr. of 1957 ed. lib. bdg. 20.00 (ISBN 0-8492-4018-2). R West.

Carnegie Endowment for International Peace, Division of International Law. The Sino-Japanese Negotiations of 1915: Japanese & Chinese Documents & Chinese Official Statement. LC 75-36222. Repr. of 1921 ed. 16.50 (ISBN 0-404-14473-X). AMS Pr.

Chang, Richard T. Historians & Meiji Statesmen. LC 78-631066. (U of Fla. Social Sciences Monographs Ser.: No. 41). (Illus.). 1970. pap. 3.50 (ISBN 0-8130-0307-5). U Presses Fla.

Clarke, Joseph I. Japan at First Hand. LC 72-82089. (Japan Library Ser.). (Illus.). 1973. Repr. of 1918 ed. lib. bdg. 32.00 (ISBN 0-8420-1384-9). Scholarly Res Inc.

Coleman, Frederic. The Far East Unveiled: An Inner History of Events in Japan & China in the Year 1916. LC 72-82090. (Japan Library). 1973. Repr. of 1916 ed. lib. bdg. 17.00 (ISBN 0-8420-1385-7). Scholarly Res Inc.

Collcutt, Martin. Five Mountains: The Rinzai Zen Monastic Institution in Medieval Japan. (Harvard East Asian Monograph: Vol. 85). (Illus.). 450p. 1980. 20.00 (ISBN 0-674-30497-7). Harvard U Pr.

Conroy, Hilary. The Japanese Seizure of Korea, 1868-1910: A Study of Realism & Idealism in International Relations. LC 60-6936. 544p. 1974. pap. 7.50x (ISBN 0-8122-1074-3). U of Pa Pr.

Cooper. Introduction to Japanese History & Culture. 1976. pap. 3.94 (ISBN 0-08-017484-1). Pergamon.

Cooper, Michael S. J., compiled by. They Came to Japan: An Anthology of European Reports on Japan, 1543-1640. 1981. pap. 6.95 (ISBN 0-520-04509-2). U of Cal Pr.

De Bary, W. Theodore & Bloom, Irene, eds. Principle & Practicality: Essays in Neo-Confucianism & Practical Learning. LC 78-11530. (Neo-Confucian Ser. & Studies in Oriental Culture). 1979. 27.50x (ISBN 0-231-04612-X); pap. 12.00x (ISBN 0-231-04613-8). Columbia U Pr.

Decker, Benton W. & Decker, Edwina N. Return of the Black Ships. 1978. 11.95 (ISBN 0-533-03368-3). Vantage.

Dening, Walter. Japan in Days of Yore. (Illus.). 1978. 18.00 (ISBN 0-87773-748-7). Great Eastern.

Desiles, Clara. Japan Today. (Illus.). 1979. bds. 14.95 (ISBN 2-8525-8110-8, Pub. by Two Continents). Hippocrene Bks.

Detwiler, Donald S. & Burdick, Charles B., eds. Japanese Military Studies 1937-1949: Command, Administration, & Special Operations; Japanese & Chinese Studies & Documents. (War in Asia & the Pacific Ser., 1937 to 1949: Vol. 3). 660p. 1980. lib. bdg. 60.50 (ISBN 0-8240-3287-X); lib. bdg. 650.00 set of 15 vols. (ISBN 0-686-77792-1). Garland Pub.

--Japanese Military Studies 1937-1949: China, Manchuria, & Korea, Pt. 1. (War in Asia & the Pacific Ser., 1937 to 1949: Vol. 8). 630p. 1980. lib. bdg. 55.00 (ISBN 0-8240-3292-6); lib. bdg. 650.00 set of 15 vols. (ISBN 0-686-60097-5). Garland Pub.

Dower, John, ed. Origins of the Modern Japanese State: Selected Writings of E. H. Norman. LC 74-4773. 512p. 1975. pap. 5.95 (ISBN 0-394-70927-6). Pantheon.

Duus, Peter. The Rise of Modern Japan. LC 75-33416. (Illus.). 304p. 1976. text ed. 13.50 (ISBN 0-395-20665-0). HM.

Elison, George & Smith, Bardwell L., eds. Warlords, Artists, & Commoners: Japan in the Sixteenth Century. LC 80-24128. (Illus.). 372p. 1981. 20.00x (ISBN 0-8248-0692-1). U Pr of Hawaii.

Fujii, Shinichi. Tenno Seiji: Direct Imperial Rule. (Studies in Japanese History & Civilization). 415p. 1979. Repr. of 1944 ed. 30.00 (ISBN 0-89093-263-8). U Pubns Amer.

Fukuda, Tsuneari, ed. Future of Japan & the Korean Peninsula. Jahng, K., tr. from Japanese. LC 78-71337. (Illus.). 1979. 14.40 (ISBN 0-930878-14-0). Hollym Intl.

Gardiner, C. Harvey. The Japanese & Peru, 1873-1973. LC 75-17371. 202p. 1975. 12.50x (ISBN 0-8263-0391-9). U of NM Pr.

Gibney, Frank. Japan: The Fragile Superpower. rev. ed. 1979. 12.95 (ISBN 0-393-05704-6). Norton.

Gowen, Herbert H. Five Foreigners in Japan. facs. ed. LC 67-28735. (Essay Index Reprint Ser). 1936. 18.00 (ISBN 0-8369-0491-5). Arno.

Griffis, William E. The Makado's Empire, 2 bks. Incl. Bk. 1. History of Japan; Bk. 2. Personal Experiences, Observations, & Studies in Japan. Date not set. Repr. of 1876 ed. Set. 65.00 (ISBN 0-686-20507-3). Quaker City.

Gubbins, John H. The Making of Modern Japan. LC 72-82095. (Japan Library Ser.). (Illus.). 1973. Repr. of 1922 ed. lib. bdg. 20.00 (ISBN 0-8420-1390-3). Scholarly Res Inc.

Hall, John C., tr. from Japanese. Japanese Feudal Law. (Studies in Japanese Law & Government). (Illus.). 266p. 1979. Repr. of 1906 ed. 24.50 (ISBN 0-89093-211-5). U Pubns Amer.

Hall, John W. Japanese History: A Guide to Japanese Reference & Research Materials. LC 73-3013. 165p. 1973. Repr. of 1954 ed. lib. bdg. 19.50x (ISBN 0-8371-6830-9, HAJH). Greenwood.

Hall, John W. & Jansen, Marius B., eds. Studies in the Institutional History of Early Modern Japan. LC 68-15766. 1968. 25.00x (ISBN 0-691-03071-5); pap. 8.95 (ISBN 0-691-00013-1). Princeton U Pr.

Hall, John W. & Mass, Jeffrey P., eds. Medieval Japan: Essays in Institutional History. LC 73-86897. (Illus.). 288p. 1974. 25.00x (ISBN 0-300-01677-8). Yale U Pr.

Hall, John W. & Toyoda, Takeshi, eds. Japan in the Muromachi Age. LC 74-22963. 1977. 27.50x (ISBN 0-520-02888-0); pap. 8.95x (ISBN 0-520-03214-4). U of Cal Pr.

Hall, John W., et al, eds. Japan Before Tokugawa: Political Consolidation & Economic Growth, 1500 to 1650. LC 80-7524. (Illus.). 400p. 1981. 22.50 (ISBN 0-691-05308-1). Princeton U Pr.

Hanley, Susan B. & Yamamura, Kozo. Economic & Demographic Change in Preindustrial Japan, 1600-1868. LC 77-71983. 1978. text ed. 32.50 (ISBN 0-691-03111-8); pap. 12.50 (ISBN 0-691-10055-1). Princeton U Pr.

Haraguchi, Torao, et al, trs. from Jap. The Status System & Social Organization of Satsuma. LC 75-15936. 271p. 1975. text ed. 17.50x (ISBN 0-8248-0390-6). U Pr of Hawaii.

Hayashi, Saburo. Kogun: The Japanese Army in the Pacific War (in Collaboration with Alvin D. Coox) LC 78-756. (Illus.). 1978. Repr. of 1959 ed. lib. bdg. 25.25 (ISBN 0-313-20291-5, HAKO). Greenwood.

Hildreth, Richard. Japan: As It Was & Is. LC 72-82098. (Japan Library Ser.). (Illus.). 1973. Repr. of 1855 ed. lib. bdg. 29.00 (ISBN 0-8420-1392-X). Scholarly Res Inc.

Hishida, Seiji G. International Position of Japan As a Great Power. LC 6-23069. (Columbia University. Studies in the Social Sciences: No. 64). Repr. of 1905 ed. 21.50 (ISBN 0-404-51064-7). AMS Pr.

Huber, Thomas M. The Revolutionary Origins of Modern Japan. LC 79-64214. 272p. 1981. 19.50x (ISBN 0-8047-1048-1). Stanford U Pr.

Hurst, G. Cameron. Insei: Abdicated Sovereigns in the Politics of Late Heian Japan, 1086-1185. LC 75-26574. (Studies of the East Asian Institute). 368p. 1976. 22.50x (ISBN 0-231-03932-8). Columbia U Pr.

Ike, Nobutaka, ed. Japan's Decision for War: Records of the 1941 Policy Conferences. 1967. 18.50x (ISBN 0-8047-0305-1). Stanford U Pr.

Ito, Hirobumi. Commentaries on the Constitution of the Empire of Japan. (Studies in Japanese Law & Government). 310p. 1979. Repr. of 1906 ed. 25.00 (ISBN 0-89093-212-3). U Pubns Amer.

Iyenaga, Toyokichi. The Constitutional Development of Japan. LC 78-63805. (Johns Hopkins University. Studies in the Social Sciences. Ninth Ser. 1891: 9). Repr. of 1891 ed. 11.50 (ISBN 0-404-61068-4). AMS Pr.

Iyenaga, Toyokichi & Sato, Kenosake. Japan & the California Problem. LC 72-82099. (Japan Library Ser.). 1972. Repr. of 1921 ed. lib. bdg. 16.00 (ISBN 0-8420-1393-8). Scholarly Res Inc.

Jansen, Marius B. Japan & Its World: Two Centuries of Change. LC 80-7532. (Illus.). 120p. 1980. 9.50 (ISBN 0-691-05310-3). Princeton U Pr.

--Sakamoto Ryoma & the Meiji Restoration. LC 77-153818. 1961. 18.50x (ISBN 0-8047-0784-7). Stanford U Pr.

Japanese Relocation: Mini-Play. (Multi-Cultural Ser.). (gr. 7 up). 1978. 3.00 (ISBN 0-89550-328-X). RIM.

Jones, F. C. Extraterritoriality in Japan & the Diplomatic Relations Resulting in Its Abolition, Eighteen Fifty-Three to Eighteen Ninety-Nine. 1931. 18.50x (ISBN 0-686-51384-3). Elliots Bks.

Jones, Francis C. Japan's New Order in East Asia: Its Rise & Fall, 1937-45. LC 75-30064. (Institute of Pacific Relations). Repr. of 1954 ed. 40.00 (ISBN 0-404-59535-9). AMS Pr.

Kaempfer, Englebert. History of Japan: Together with a Description of the Kingdom of Siam, 1690-92, 3 Vols. LC 78-137313. (Illus.). Repr. of 1906 ed. Set. 62.50 (ISBN 0-404-03630-9). AMS Pr.

Kaibara, Ekiken. Way of Contentment. Bd. with Greater Learning for Women. (Studies in Japanese History & Civilization). 1979. Repr. of 1913 ed. 19.00 (ISBN 0-89093-253-0). U Pubns Amer.

Kalland, Arne. Shingu: A Japanese Fishing Community. (Scandanavian Institute of Asian Studies Monograph: No. 44). (Orig.). 1980. pap. text ed. 12.50x (ISBN 0-7007-0136-2). Humanities.

Kawasaki, Ichiro. Japan Unmasked. LC 69-13500. (Illus.). 1969. pap. 5.50 (ISBN 0-8048-0277-7). C E Tuttle.

Kennedy, Malcolm D. The Military Side of Japanese Life. LC 72-9091. (Illus.). 367p. 1973. Repr. of 1924 ed. lib. bdg. 27.50x (ISBN 0-8371-6574-1, KEJL). Greenwood.

Ki, Tsurayuki. The Tosa Diary. LC 75-41164. (Eng.). Repr. of 1912 ed. 11.45 (ISBN 0-404-14677-5). AMS Pr.

Kim, Jai-Hyup. The Garrison State in Prewar Japan & Post-War Korea: A Comparative Analysis of Military Politics. LC 77-26344. 1978. 11.25 (ISBN 0-8191-0416-7). U Pr of Amer.

Kim, Key-Hiuk. The Last Phase of the East Asian World Order: Korea, Japan, & the Chinese Empire, 1860-1882. LC 77-83106. 1980. 24.50x (ISBN 0-520-03556-9). U of Cal Pr.

Kinmonth, Earl H. The Self-Made Man in Meija Japanese Thought: From Samurai to Salary Man. LC 80-17984. (Illus.). 400p. 1981. 22.50x (ISBN 0-520-04159-3). U of Cal Pr.

Kiyohara, Michiko. A Checklist of Monographs & Periodicals on the Japanese Colonial Empire. LC 80-84459. (Special Project Ser.: No. 28). 352p. 1981. pap. 11.95 (ISBN 0-8179-4284-X). Hoover Inst Pr.

Krooth, Richard. Japan: Five Stages of Capitalist Development & the Nation's Future. 1976. pap. 3.00 (ISBN 0-939074-02-8). Harvest Pubns.

Kublin, Hyman. Japan: Regional Study. (World Regional Studies): (gr. 7-12). 1973. pap. 6.60 (ISBN 0-395-13830-2, 2-31046). HM.

Kuno, Yoshi S. Japanese Expansion on the Asiatic Continent, 2 Vols. LC 67-27615. 1968. Repr. of 1940 ed. Set. 32.50x (ISBN 0-8046-0256-5). Kennikat.

Lay, Arthur H. Brief Sketch of the History of Political Parties in Japan. Bd. with Political Ideas of Modern Japan: An Interpretation Studies in Japanese Law & Government. Kowakami, Kiyoshi K. 461p. 1979. Repr. of 1902 ed. 22.00 (ISBN 0-89093-222-0). U Pubns Amer.

Lebra, Joyce C., ed. Japan's Greatest East Asia Co-Prosperity Sphere in World War Two: Selected Readings & Documents. 234p. 1975. 27.50x (ISBN 0-19-638265-3). Oxford U Pr.

Lehmann, Jean-Pierre. The Image of Japan: A Changing Society Eighteen Fifty to Nineteen Hundred & Five. (Illus.). 1978. text ed. 21.00x (ISBN 0-04-952013-X). Allen Unwin.

Leonard, Jonathan N. Early Japan. (Great Ages of Man Ser). (Illus.). 1968. 12.95 (ISBN 0-8094-0360-9). Time-Life.

Lifton, Robert J., et al. Six Lives, Six Deaths: Portraits from Modern Japan. Shuichi, Kato & Reich, Michael R., eds. LC 78-11926. (Illus.). 318p. 1980. pap. 7.95 (ISBN 0-300-02600-5). Yale U Pr.

Livingston, Jon, et al. The Japan Reader, 2 vols. LC 73-7015. 1974. Vol. 1. pap. 7.95 (ISBN 0-394-70668-4); Vol. 2. pap. 7.95 (ISBN 0-394-70669-2). Pantheon.

Longford, Joseph H. The Story of Old Japan. LC 72-82101. (Japan Library Ser.). (Illus.). 1973. Repr. of 1910 ed. lib. bdg. 28.00 (ISBN 0-8420-1395-4). Scholarly Res Inc.

Lu, David J. Sources of Japanese History, 2 vols. 696p. 1974. Vol. 1. 13.95 (ISBN 0-07-038902-0, C); Vol. 2. 13.95 (ISBN 0-07-038903-9); Vol. 1. pap. text ed. 9.95 (ISBN 0-07-038904-7); Vol. 2. pap. text ed. 9.95 (ISBN 0-07-038905-5). McGraw.

Lum, Peter. Six Centuries in East Asia: China, Japan & Korea from the 14th Century to 1912. LC 72-12582. (Illus.). 288p. 1973. 10.95 (ISBN 0-87599-183-1). S G Phillips.

McCullough, Helen C., tr. from Japanese. The Taiheiki: A Chronicle of Medieval Japan. LC 79-64824. (Illus.). 1979. pap. 9.50 (ISBN 0-8048-1322-1). C E Tuttle.

McCullough, William H. & McCullough, Helen C., trs. from Japanese. A Tale of Flowering Fortunes: Annals of Japanese Aristocratic Life in the Heian Period, 2 vols. LC 78-66183. (Illus.). 1980. Set. 62.50x (ISBN 0-8047-1039-2). Stanford U Pr.

McNeill, William H. & Sedlar, Jean W., eds. China, India & Japan: The Middle Period. 1971. pap. 4.95x (ISBN 0-19-501439-1). Oxford U Pr.

Mason, Richard & Caiger, John. A History of Japan. LC 73-13581. 1973. 10.95 (ISBN 0-02-920290-6). Free Pr.

Mass, Jeffrey P. The Development of Kamakura Rule, 1180-1250: A History with Documents. LC 78-62271. 1979. 18.50x (ISBN 0-8047-1003-1). Stanford U Pr.

--The Kamakura Bakufu: A Study in Documents. LC 75-39335. (Illus.). 252p. 1976. 17.50x (ISBN 0-8047-0907-6). Stanford U Pr.

Meyer, Milton W. Japan: A Concise History. rev. ed. (Quality Paperback Ser.: No. 318). 1976. pap. 4.50 (ISBN 0-8226-0318-7). Littlefield.

Mitchell, Richard H. Thought Control in Prewar Japan. LC 75-39566. 1976. 17.50x (ISBN 0-8014-1002-9). Cornell U Pr.

Mizuno, Soji. Early Foundations for Japan's Twentieth Century Economic Emergence. 1981. 8.95 (ISBN 0-533-04541-X). Vantage.

Morley, James W., ed. Dilemmas of Growth in Prewar Japan. LC 79-155964. (Studies in the Modernization of Japan). 544p. 1974. 26.00x (ISBN 0-691-03074-X). Princeton U Pr.

Morris, Ivan. The Nobility of Failure. LC 73-3750. 1975. 17.95 (ISBN 0-03-010811-X). HR&W.

--The World of the Shining Prince: Court Life in Ancient Japan. 1979. pap. 4.50 (ISBN 0-14-005479-0, Peregrine). Penguin.

Morse, Edwards S. Japan Day by Day: 1877-78-79, 1882-3. LC 17-28348. (Illus.). 1978. lib. bdg. 35.00 (ISBN 0-910220-93-X). Larlin Corp.

Mounsey, Augustus H. Satsuma Rebellion: An Episode of Modern Japanese History. (Studies in Japanese History & Civilization). 1979p. Repr. of 1879 ed. 24.00 (ISBN 0-89093-259-X). U Pubns Amer.

Murakami, Hyoye & Harper, Thomas J., eds. Great Historical Figures of Japan. (Illus., Orig.). 1978. 18.50 (ISBN 0-87040-431-8). Japan Pubns.

Nish, Ian. The Story of Japan. (Story Ser.). (Illus.). 1968. 6.95 (ISBN 0-571-08440-0, Pub. by Faber & Faber). Merrimack Bk Serv.

Norman, E. Herbert. Ando Shoeki & the Anatomy of Japanese Feudalism. (Studies in Japanese History & Civilization). 254p. 1979. Repr. of 1949 ed. 26.25 (ISBN 0-89093-224-7). U Pubns Amer.

O'Connor, Edmund. Japan's Modernization. Yapp, Malcolm & Killingray, Marget, eds. (World History Ser.). (Illus.). (gr. 10). 1980. Repr. of 1977 ed. lib. bdg. 5.95 (ISBN 0-89908-232-7); pap. text ed. 1.95 (ISBN 0-89908-207-6). Greenhaven.

--The Wealth of Japan. Yapp, Malcolm, et al, eds. (World History Ser.). (Illus.). 32p. (gr. 10). 1980. Repr. of 1977 ed. lib. bdg. 5.95 (ISBN 0-89908-237-8); pap. text ed. 1.95 (ISBN 0-89908-212-2). Greenhaven.

Ogai, Mori. Saiki Koi & Other Stories. Dilworth, David & Rimer, J. Thomas, eds. Dilworth, David & Rimer, J. Thomas, trs. from Japanese. LC 77-4455. 1977. text ed. 12.95x (ISBN 0-8248-0454-6). U Pr of Hawaii.

O'Hara, Betsy. Japan Nineteen Forty-Eight to Nineteen Fifty-Four Through One American's Eyes. Scott, Donald M., ed. Yamakawa, Reiko, tr. 72p. (Orig., English-Japanese.). 16.95x (ISBN 0-9604188-0-6); pap. 12.95x (ISBN 0-9604188-1-4). B O'Hara.

Okuma, Shigenobu. Fifty Years of New Japan, 2 vols. 2nd ed. Repr. of 1910 ed. Set. 34.00 (ISBN 0-527-68280-2). Kraus Repr.

Oxford, Wayne H. Speeches of Fukuzawa. 1973. 24.50 (ISBN 0-89346-094-X, Pub. by Hokuseido Pr). Heian Intl.

Paterson, Katherine. Of Nightingales That Weep. LC 74-8294. (Illus.). (gr. 5 up). 1974. 10.95 (ISBN 0-690-00485-0, TYC-J). Har-Row.

Patric, John. Yankee Hobo in the Orient: Why Japan Was Strong. 1979. 59.95 (ISBN 0-685-96533-3). Revisionist Pr.

Perrin, Noel. Giving up the Gun: Japan's Reversion to the Sword, 1543-1879. (Large Print Bks.). 1979. lib. bdg. 9.95 (ISBN 0-8161-3010-8). G K Hall.

Ponsonby-Fane, Richard A. Fortunes of the Emperors: Studies in Revolution, Exile, Abdication, Usurpation, & Deposition in Ancient Japan. (Studies in Japanese History & Civilization). 1979. 28.00 (ISBN 0-89093-250-6). U Pubns Amer.

--Imperial Cities: The Capitals of Japan from the Oldest Times Until 1229. (Studies in Japanese History & Civilization). 1979. 21.50 (ISBN 0-89093-251-4). U Pubns Amer.

Pratt, Peter, ed. History of Japan: Compiled from the Records of the English East India Company at the Instance of the Court of Directors, 2 vols. (Studies in Japanese History & Civilization). 1979. Repr. of 1931 ed. Set. 62.00 (ISBN 0-89093-261-1). U Pubns Amer.

Pyle, Kenneth B. The Making of Modern Japan: An Introduction. (Civilization & Society Ser.). 1978. pap. text ed. 7.95x (ISBN 0-669-84657-0). Heath.

Reischauer, Edwin O. & Craig, Albert M. Japan: Tradition & Transformation. LC 77-77979. (Illus.). 1978. text ed. 14.25 (ISBN 0-395-25814-6). HM.

Reischauer, Edwin O., ed. Japan. new ed. LC 74-7767. (Great Contemporary Issues). (Illus.). 1974. 35.00 (ISBN 0-405-04168-3, Co Pub by New York Times). Arno.

Reischauer, Robert K. & Reischauer, Jean. Early Japanese History (40 B. C.-A. D. 1167, 2 vols. 19.00 (ISBN 0-8446-1381-9). Peter Smith.

Robinson, B. W. The Arts of the Japanese Sword. (Illus.). 230p. 1979. 38.00 (ISBN 0-571-04723-8, Pub. by Faber & Faber). Merrimack Bk Serv.

Sadler, A. L. The Maker of Modern Japan: The Life of Shogun Tokugawa Ieyasu. LC 78-54935. (Illus.). 1978. pap. 8.50 (ISBN 0-8048-1297-7). C E Tuttle.

Sadler, Arthur L. The Maker of Modern Japan: The Life of Tokugawa Ieyasu. LC 75-41238. Repr. of 1937 ed. 27.50 (ISBN 0-404-14595-7). AMS Pr.

Sansom, George. A History of Japan to 1334. LC 58-11694. (Illus.). 1958. 17.50 (ISBN 0-8047-0522-4); pap. 6.95x (ISBN 0-8047-0523-2). Stanford U Pr.

--A History of Japan, 1334-1615. LC 58-11694. (Illus.). 1961. 17.50 (ISBN 0-8047-0524-0); pap. 6.95x (ISBN 0-8047-0525-9). Stanford U Pr.

--A History of Japan, 1615-1867. LC 58-11694. (Illus.). 1963. 12.50 (ISBN 0-8047-0526-7); pap. 4.95x (ISBN 0-8047-0527-5). Stanford U Pr.

Satow, Ernest M. Diplomat in Japan. Repr. of 1921 ed. 14.50 (ISBN 0-404-05561-3). AMS Pr.

Sawa, Takaaki. Art in Japanese Esoteric Buddhism. Gage, Richard, tr. from Japanese. LC 70-162682. (Heibonsha Survey of Japanese Art Ser). (Illus.). 154p. 1972. 17.50 (ISBN 0-8348-1001-8). Weatherhill.

Shusaku Endo. When I Whistle. Gessel, Van C., tr. from Japanese. LC 79-13183. 1979. 8.95 (ISBN 0-8008-8243-1). Taplinger.

Sinha, S. Aspects of Japan. 6.25x (ISBN 0-210-98193-8). Asia.

Skrzypczak, Edmund, ed. Japan's Modern Century: A Special Issue of Monumenta Nipponica Prepared in Celebration of the Centennial of the Meij Restoration. LC 68-57139. 1968. 11.75 (ISBN 0-8048-0649-7). C E Tuttle.

Sladkovsky, M. I. China & Japan: Past & Present. Price, Robert F., ed. Price, Robert L., tr. from Rus. LC 74-81637. (Forum Asiatica Ser: Vol. 1). (Eng.). 1975. 15.00 (ISBN 0-87569-062-9). Academic Intl.

Smith, Neil S. Materials on Japanese Social & Economic History: Tokugawa, Japan. (Studies in Japanese History & Civilization). 176p. 1979. Repr. of 1937 ed. 19.50 (ISBN 0-89093-262-X). U Pubns Amer.

Smith, Robert J. Kurusu: The Price of Progress in a Japanese Village, 1951-1975. LC 77-79999. (Illus.). 1978. 15.00x (ISBN 0-8047-0962-9); pap. 4.95 (ISBN 0-8047-1060-0, SP-161). Stanford U Pr.

Smith, Thomas C. Nakahara: Family Farming & Population in a Japanese Village, 1717-1830. LC 76-14273. 1977. 10.00x (ISBN 0-8047-0928-9). Stanford U Pr.

Stead, Alfred, ed. Japan by the Japanese: A Survey by Its Authorities, 2 vols. (Studies in Japanese History & Civilization). 1979. Repr. of 1904 ed. 55.00 (ISBN 0-89093-264-6). U Pubns Amer.

Steenstrup, Carl. Hojo Shigetoki (Eleven Ninety-Eight to Twelve Sixty-One) & His Role in the History of Political & Ethical Ideas in Japan. (Scandinavian Institute of Asian Studies Monographs: No. 41). (Orig.). 1980. pap. text ed. 16.50x (ISBN 0-7007-0132-X). Humanities.

Storry, Richard. History of Modern Japan. (Orig.). (YA) (gr. 9 up). 1960. pap. 3.50 (ISBN 0-14-020475-X, Pelican). Penguin.

--Japan & the Decline of the West in Asia. LC 78-31872. (The Making of the Twentieth Century Ser.). 1979. 18.95x (ISBN 0-312-44050-2). St Martin.

Takekoshi, Yosoburo. Economic Aspects of the History of the Civilization of Japan, 3 Vols. 1967. Repr. of 1930 ed. 65.00x (ISBN 0-685-19297-0). Paragon.

Taylor, George. Japanese Sponsored Regime in North China. LC 78-4330. (The Modern Chinese Economy Ser.). 145p. 1980. lib. bdg. 16.50 (ISBN 0-8240-4287-5). Garland Pub.

Thorne, Christopher. Allies of a Kind: The United States, Britain, & the War Against Japan, 1941-1945. LC 79-14921. (Illus.). 1979. pap. 9.95 (ISBN 0-19-520173-6, GB 585, GB). Oxford U Pr.

Tiedemann, Arthur E. Modern Japan: A Brief History. rev. ed. LC 80-13023. (ANVIL Ser.). 192p. (Orig.). 1980. pap. text ed. 4.95 (ISBN 0-89874-204-8). Krieger.

Togo, Shigenori. The Cause of Japan. Togo, Fumihiko & Blakeney, Ben B., eds. LC 76-57155. 1977. Repr. of 1956 ed. lib. bdg. 25.50x (ISBN 0-8371-9432-6, TOCJ). Greenwood.

Toland, John. Rising Sun. (Illus.). 1971. pap. 4.95 (ISBN 0-553-20462-9). Bantam.

Totman, Conrad. Japan Before Perry: A Short History. (Illus.). 275p. 1981. 20.00x (ISBN 0-520-04132-1). U of Cal Pr.

Uyehara, George E. The Political Development of Japan: 1867 to 1909. (Illus.). 296p. 1972. Repr. of 1910 ed. 31.00x (ISBN 0-686-28325-2, Pub. by Irish Academic Pr). Biblio Dist.

Varley, H. Paul. Imperial Restoration in Medieval Japan. LC 73-124573. (Studies of the East Asian Institute of Col. Univ.). 1971. text ed. 17.50x (ISBN 0-231-03502-0). Columbia U Pr.

Von Siebold, Philipp, et al. Manners & Customs of the Japanese in the Nineteenth Century. LC 72-83676. 320p. 1980. pap. 3.50 (ISBN 0-8048-1081-8). C E Tuttle.

Waldmeir, Joseph, ed. Essays in Honor of Russel B. Nye. 1978. 10.00x (ISBN 0-87013-209-1). Mich St U Pr.

Warshaw, Steven, et al. Japan Emerges. LC 73-93980. (Asia Emerges Ser.). 160p. (Orig.). 1974. 6.95 (ISBN 0-87297-016-7, Co-Pub. by Canfield Pr); pap. 5.95 (ISBN 0-685-40097-2). Diablo.

Waswo, Ann. Japanese Landlords: The Decline of a Rural Elite. 1977. 18.75x (ISBN 0-520-03217-9). U of Cal Pr.

Wenckstern, Friedrich Von. Bibliography of the Japanese Empire, 2 vols. 976p. 1970. Repr. of 1895 ed. Set. 210.00x (ISBN 3-7772-7032-6). Intl Pubns Serv.

Wigmore, John H. & Simmons, D. B. Notes on Land Tenure & Local Institutions in Old Japan. (Studies in Japanese History & Civilization). 1979. 21.00 (ISBN 0-89093-223-9). U Pubns Amer.

Wigmore, John H., ed. Law & Justice in Tokugawa Japan: Part VI-B Property: Legal Precedents. 1978. 23.50x (ISBN 0-86008-232-6, Pub. by U of Tokyo Pr). Intl Schol Bk Serv.

--Law & Justice in Tokugawa Japan: Part VI-C Property: Legal Precedents. 1978. 23.50x (ISBN 0-86008-233-4, Pub. by U of Tokyo Pr). Intl Schol Bk Serv.

--Law & Justice in Tokugawa Japan: Part VI-D Property: Legal Precedents. 1978. 23.50x (ISBN 0-86008-234-2, Pub. by U of Tokyo Pr). Intl Schol Bk Serv.

Wildes, Harry E. Aliens in the East: A History of Japan's Foreign Intercourse. LC 72-82117. (Japan Library Ser.). 1973. Repr. of 1937 ed. lib. bdg. 20.00 (ISBN 0-8420-1409-8). Scholarly Res Inc.

Williams, Harold S. Shades of the Past; or, Indiscreet Tales of Japan. LC 63-19394. (Illus.). 352p. 1972. pap. 2.95 (ISBN 0-8048-1050-8). C E Tuttle.

Williams, S. Wells. A Journal of the Perry Expedition to Japan, 1853-1854. LC 72-82118. (Japan Library Ser). 1973. Repr. of 1910 ed. 16.00 (ISBN 0-8420-1410-1). Scholarly Res Inc.

Wilson, Robert A. Genesis of the Meiji Government in Japan, 1868-1871. LC 78-6546. (University of California Publications in History: Vol. 56). 1978. Repr. of 1957 ed. lib. bdg. 18.50x (ISBN 0-8371-9091-6, WIGM). Greenwood.

Yamada, Nakaba. Ghenko: The Mongol Invasion of Japan. (Studies in Japanese History & Civilization). 1979. Repr. of 1916 ed. 25.00 (ISBN 0-89093-254-9). U Pubns Amer.

Yamaguchi, Ken. Kinse Shiriaku: A History of Japan from 1853 to 1869. LC 72-82120. (Japan Library Ser.). 1973. Repr. of 1873 ed. lib. bdg. 12.00 (ISBN 0-8420-1411-X). Scholarly Res Inc.

Yamane, Yuzo. Momoyama Genre Painting. Shields, John, tr. from Japanese. LC 72-92099. (Heibonsha Survey of Japanese Art Ser). (Illus.). 176p. 1973. 17.50 (ISBN 0-8348-1012-3). Weatherhill.

Yanaga, Chitoshi. Japan Since Perry. LC 73-20205. (Illus.). 723p. 1975. Repr. of 1949 ed. lib. bdg. 38.50x (ISBN 0-8371-7330-2, YAJP). Greenwood.

--Japan Since Perry. x, 723p. 1966. Repr. of 1949 ed. 25.00 (ISBN 0-208-00108-5, Archon). Shoe String.

Young, A. Morgan. Imperial Japan, Nineteen Twenty Six to Nineteen Thirty-Eight. LC 73-17627. 328p. 1974. Repr. of 1938 ed. lib. bdg. 20.25x (ISBN 0-8371-7255-1, YOIJ). Greenwood.

--Japan in Recent Times, 1912-1926. LC 76-136554. 347p. 1973. Repr. of 1929 ed. lib. bdg. 18.75x (ISBN 0-8371-5480-4, YOJR). Greenwood.

Zepke, Nick. The Hundred Year Miracle: Economic Development in Japan 1918-70. (Studies in 20th Century History Ser.). 1977. pap. text ed. 4.50x (ISBN 0-435-31961-2). Heinemann Ed.

JAPAN–HISTORY–HISTORIOGRAPHY

Harrison, John A. New Light on Early & Medieval Japanese Historiography. LC 60-62605. (U of Fla. Social Sciences Monographs Ser.: No. 4). 1959. 2.95 (ISBN 0-8130-0104-8). U Presses Fla.

Young, John. The Location of Yamatai: A Case Study in Japanese Historiography, 720-1945. LC 78-64228. (Johns Hopkins University. Studies in the Social Sciences. Seventy-Fifth Ser. 1957: 2). Repr. of 1958 ed. 19.50 (ISBN 0-404-61333-0). AMS Pr.

JAPAN–HISTORY–WAR WITH RUSSIA, 1904-1905

see Russo-Japanese War, 1904-1905

JAPAN–HISTORY–ALLIED OCCUPATION, 1945-1952

Baerwald, Hans H. The Purge of Japanese Leaders Under the Occupation. LC 77-22428. (University of California Publications in Political Science: No. 8). 1977. Repr. of 1959 ed. lib. bdg. 15.00 (ISBN 0-8371-9088-6, BAPJ). Greenwood.

Bakke, E. Wight. Revolutionary Democracy: Challenge & Testing in Japan. 1968. 19.50 (ISBN 0-208-00627-3, Archon). Shoe String.

Blackstock, Graham B. Sojourn in Occupied Japan. 1978. 11.95 (ISBN 0-533-03843-X). Vantage.

Cary, O., et al. War-Wasted Asia: Letters, 1945-46. LC 75-11395. (Illus.). 322p. 1975. 15.00x (ISBN 0-87011-257-0). Kodansha.

Dower, J. W. Empire & Aftermath: Yoshida Shigeru & the Japanese Experience, 1878-1954. (Harvard East Asian Monographs: No. 84). 1979. text ed. 20.00x (ISBN 0-674-25125-3). Harvard U Pr.

Fearey, Robert A. The Occupation of Japan, Second Phase, 1948-50. LC 72-176133. 239p. 1972. Repr. of 1950 ed. lib. bdg. 16.00x (ISBN 0-8371-6271-8, FEOJ). Greenwood.

Feis, Herbert. Contest Over Japan: The Soviet Bid for Power in the Far East, 1945-1952. 1968. pap. 1.85 (ISBN 0-393-00466-X, Norton Lib). Norton.

Gayn, Mark. Japan Diary. LC 80-51196. 530p. 1981. pap. 9.50 (ISBN 0-8048-1369-8). C E Tuttle.

Goodman, Grant K. American Occupation of Japan: A Retrospective View. LC 68-65352. (International Studies: East Asia Ser. No. 2). (Orig.). 1968. pap. 2.50x (ISBN 0-685-19270-9). Paragon.

Johnson, Chalmers. Conspiracy at Matsukawa. LC 73-161998. (Illus.). 1972. 28.50x (ISBN 0-520-02063-4). U of Cal Pr.

Kawai, Kazuo. Japan's American Interlude. LC 59-14111. (Midway Reprint Ser.). 1980. pap. 8.50x (ISBN 0-226-42775-7). U of Chicago Pr.

Klamkin, Mavian. Made in Occupied Japan: A Collector's Guide. (Illus.). 1976. pap. 6.95 (ISBN 0-517-52661-1). Crown.

Martin, Edwin M. The Allied Occupation of Japan. LC 76-169848. 155p. 1972. Repr. of 1948 ed. lib. bdg. 15.00 (ISBN 0-8371-6248-3, MAAO). Greenwood.

Nishi, Toshio. Unconditional Democracy: Education & Politics in Occupied Japan, 1945 to 1952. (Publication Ser.: No. 244). 380p. 1981. 19.95 (ISBN 0-8179-7441-5). Hoover Inst Pr.

The Occupation of Japan: Economic Policy & Reform. 382p. pap. 6.00 (ISBN 0-686-29519-6). MacArthur Memorial.

Oppler, Alfred C. Legal Reform in Occupied Japan: A Participant Looks Back. LC 75-30200. 1976. 26.00 (ISBN 0-691-09234-6). Princeton U Pr.

Perry, John C. Beneath the Eagle's Wings: Americans in Occupied Japan. LC 80-15331. (Illus.). 256p. 1980. 12.95 (ISBN 0-396-07876-1). Dodd.

Piccigallo, Philip R. The Japanese on Trial: Allied War Crimes Operations in the East, 1945-1951. (Illus.). 308p. 1979. text ed. 17.50x (ISBN 0-292-78033-8). U of Tex Pr.

Redford, Lawrence H., ed. The Occupation of Japan & Its Legacy to the Postwar World. 158p. pap. 4.00 (ISBN 0-686-29517-X). MacArthur Memorial.

--The Occupation of Japan: Impact of Legal Refor, 212p. pap. 5.00 (ISBN 0-686-29518-8). MacArthur Memorial.

Textor, Robert B. Failure in Japan: With Keystones for a Positive Policy. LC 70-152610. 262p. 1972. Repr. of 1951 ed. lib. bdg. 15.00x (ISBN 0-8371-6045-6, TEFJ). Greenwood.

U. S. Department of State. Occupation of Japan, Policy & Progress. Repr. of 1946 ed. lib. bdg. 15.00 (ISBN 0-8371-2528-6, OCJA). Greenwood.

Ward, Robert E. & Shulman, Frank J. Allied Occupation of Japan: 1945-52. LC 73-8772. 170p. 1974. pap. text ed. 50.00 (ISBN 0-8389-0127-1). ALA.

Wildes, Henry. Typhoon in Tokyo: The Occupation & Its Aftermath. 1978. Repr. of 1954 ed. lib. bdg. 18.50x (ISBN 0-374-98572-3). Octagon.

Williams, Justin. Japan's Political Revolution Under MacArthur: A Participant's Account. LC 78-5592. (Illus.). 352p. 1979. 16.50 (ISBN 0-8203-0452-2). U of Ga Pr.

Woodard, W. P. The Allied Occupation of Japan 1945-1952 & Japanese Religions. (Illus.). 1972. 40.00 (ISBN 0-685-36170-5). Heinman.

Yoshida, Shigeru. The Yoshida Memoirs: The Story of Japan in Crisis. LC 72-12336. 305p. 1973. Repr. of 1962 ed. lib. bdg. 16.00x (ISBN 0-8371-6733-7, YOYM). Greenwood.

JAPAN–HISTORY, MILITARY

Collier, Basil. Japanese Aircraft of World War Two. LC 78-27558. (Illus.). 1979. 12.50 (ISBN 0-8317-5137-1, Mayflower Bks). Smith Pubs.

Detwiler, Donald S. & Burdick, Charles B., eds. Japanese Military Studies Nineteen Thirty-Seven to Nineteen Forty-Nine, Naval Armament Program & Naval Operations: Japanese & Chinese Studies & Documents, Vol. 4. (War in Asia & the Pacific Ser., 1937 to 1949). 550p. 1980. Part I. lib. bdg. 60.50 (ISBN 0-8240-3288-8); lib. bdg. 650.00 set of 15 vols. (ISBN 0-686-60107-6). Garland Pub.

Morley, James W., ed. The Fateful Choice: Japan's Advance into Southeast Asia, Nineteen Thirty-Nine to Nineteen Forty-One. Burton, Peter A. & Scalapino, Robert A., trs. from Japanese. LC 79-23486. (Studies of the East Asian Institute Ser.). 1980. 25.00x (ISBN 0-231-04804-1). Columbia U Pr.

Mounsey, Augustus H. Satsuma Rebellion: An Episode of Modern Japanese History. (Studies in Japanese History & Civilization). 1979p. Repr. of 1879 ed. 24.00 (ISBN 0-89093-259-X). U Pubns Amer.

Norman, E. Herbert. Soldier & Peasant in Japan: The Origins of Conscription. LC 75-33572. (Institute of Pacific Relations). Repr. of 1943 ed. 12.50 (ISBN 0-404-59549-9). AMS Pr.

Perrin, Noel. Giving up the Gun: Japan's Reversion to the Sword Fifteen Forty-Three to Eighteen Seventy-Nine. LC 80-50744. (Illus.). 122p. 1980. pap. 4.95 (ISBN 0-394-73949-3). Shambhala Pubns.

Tompkins, Tom. Yokosuka: Base of an Empire. (Illus.). 192p. 1981. pap. 12.95 (ISBN 0-89141-088-0). Presidio Pr.

Turnbull, Stephen. The Samurai -- a Military History. LC 76-50595. 1977. 22.95 (ISBN 0-02-620540-8, 62054). Macmillan.

Warner, Philip. Japanese Army of World War Two. LC 73-833380. (Men-at-Arms Ser). (Illus.). 40p. 1973. pap. 7.95 (ISBN 0-88254-163-3). Hippocrene Bks.

Yoshihashi, Takehiko. Conspiracy at Mukden: The Rise of the Japanese Military. LC 80-13747. (Yale Studies in Political Science: No. 9). (Illus.). xvi, 274p. 1980. Repr. of 1963 ed. lib. bdg. 22.50x (ISBN 0-313-22443-9, YOCO). Greenwood.

JAPAN–INDUSTRIES

Abegglen, James C. Management & Worker: The Japanese Solution. LC 72-96130. 200p. 1973. 14.50x (ISBN 0-87011-199-X). Kodansha.

Allen, George C. Japanese Industry: Its Recent Development & Present Condition. LC 75-30093. (Institute of Pacific Relations). Repr. of 1939 ed. 12.50 (ISBN 0-404-59501-4). AMS Pr.

Allinson, Gary D. Japanese Urbanism: Industry & Politics in Kariya, 1872-1972. LC 74-84141. 296p. 1975. 27.50x (ISBN 0-520-02842-2). U of Cal Pr.

Baranson, Jack & Dana, Richard. The Japanese Challenge to the U. S. Industry. LC 80-8889. (Illus.). 1981. write for info. (ISBN 0-669-04402-4). Lexington Bks.

--The Japanese Challenge to U.S. Industry. LC 80-8889. 208p. 1981. 19.95x (ISBN 0-669-04402-4). Lexington Bks.

Broadbridge, Seymour. Industrial Dualism in Japan: A Problem of Economic Growth & Structural Change. 105p. 1966. 27.50x (ISBN 0-7146-1208-1, F Cass Co). Biblio Dist.

The Development of the Bicycle Industry in Japan After World War II. 72p. 1981. pap. 5.00 (ISBN 92-808-0224-0, TUNU144, UNU). Unipub.

The Development of the Eyeglass Industry in Japan. 47p. 1980. pap. 5.00 (ISBN 92-808-0098-1, TUNU 007, UNU). Unipub.

Factors Which Hinder or Help Productivity Improvement: Country Report--Japan. (APO Basic Research Ser.). 111p. 1981. pap. 7.75 (ISBN 92-833-1470-0, APO 94, APO). Unipub.

Henderson, Dan F. Foreign Enterprise in Japan: Laws & Policies. LC 72-87493. 592p. 1973. 25.00x (ISBN 0-8078-1210-2). U of NC Pr.

Hirschmeier, Johannes. Origins of Entrepreneurship in Meiji Japan. LC 64-20973. (East Asian Ser: No. 17). 1964. 17.50x (ISBN 0-674-64475-1). Harvard U Pr.

Imai, Masaaki. Never Take Yes for an Answer: An Inside Look at Japanese Business for Foreign Businessmen. 148p. 1975. pap. 11.00x (ISBN 0-89955-243-9, Pub. by Simul). Intl Schol Bk Serv.

Industrial Groupings in Japan, 1980-81. 1980. pap. 335.00x (ISBN 0-8002-2817-0). Intl Pubns Serv.

Institute of Pacific Relations. Industrial Japan. LC 75-30063. (Institute of Pacific Relations). Repr. of 1941 ed. 26.50 (ISBN 0-404-59534-0). AMS Pr.

Jacobs, Norman. The Origin of Modern Capitalism & Eastern Asia. 243p. 1980. Repr. of 1958 ed. lib. bdg. 17.50x (ISBN 0-374-94140-8). Octagon.

Japan Company Handbook, 2 parts. 1979. 21.00x ea. Pt. 1 (ISBN 0-8002-1604-0). Pt. 2 (ISBN 0-8002-1605-9). Intl Pubns Serv.

Japan Electronics Buyers' Guide - 1981. 1233p. (Orig.). 1981. pap. 65.00x (ISBN 0-8002-2813-8). Intl Pubns Serv.

Japan Motor Industrial Federation. Guide to the Motor Industry of Japan - 1980. 20th ed. LC 73-648715. (Illus.). 250p. (Orig.). 1980. pap. 45.00x (ISBN 0-8002-2816-2). Intl Pubns Serv.

Levine, Solomon B. & Kawada, Hisashi. Human Resources in Japanese Industrial Development. LC 79-19419. 1980. 20.00x (ISBN 0-691-03952-6). Princeton U Pr.

Lockwood, William W. Economic Development of Japan: Growth & Structural Change, 1868-1938. rev. ed. 28.50 (ISBN 0-691-03014-6). Princeton U Pr.

Marsh, Robert M. & Mannari, Hiroshi. Modernization & the Japanese Factory. LC 75-3466. 560p. 1976. 35.00 (ISBN 0-691-09365-2); pap. 12.50 ltd. ed. (ISBN 0-691-10037-3). Princeton U Pr.

Monroe, Wilbur F., et al. The Japanese Industrial Society: Its Organizational, Cultural, & Economic Underpinnings. (Studies in International Business: No. 4). 1977. pap. 5.00 (ISBN 0-87755-268-1). U of Tex Busn Res.

Moulton, Harold G. & Ko, Junichi. Japan: An Economic & Financial Appraisal. LC 77-97886. Repr. of 1931 ed. 38.45 (ISBN 0-404-04507-3). AMS Pr.

Nakayama, Ichiro. Industrialization of Japan. 1965. 3.50x (ISBN 0-8248-0016-8, Eastwest Ctr). U Pr of Hawaii.

Norbury, Paul & Bownas, Geoffrey, eds. Business in Japan: A Guide to Japanese Business Practice & Procedure. (Illus.). 210p. 1980. lib. bdg. 25.00 (ISBN 0-86531-059-9). Westview.

Origin & Development of Iron & Steel Technology in Japan. 81p. 1980. pap. 5.00 (ISBN 92-808-0089-2, TUNU-056, UNU). Unipub.

Science & Technology in Japanese History: University & Society. 10p. 1981. pap. 5.00 (ISBN 92-808-0174-0, TUNU 125, UNU). Unipub.

Smith, Thomas C. Political Change & Industrial Development in Japan: Government Enterprise, 1868-1880. 1955. 10.00x (ISBN 0-8047-0469-4). Stanford U Pr.

Yoshihara, Kunio. Japanese Economic Development: A Short Introduction. (Illus.). 168p. 1979. text ed. 11.50x (ISBN 0-19-580439-2). Oxford U Pr.

--Japanese Investment in Southeast Asia. LC 77-18017. (Center for Southeast Asian Studies, Kyoto University Monograph Ser). 1978. text ed. 15.00x (ISBN 0-8248-0603-4); pap. text ed. 10.00x (ISBN 0-8248-0604-2). U Pr of Hawaii.

JAPAN–INTELLECTUAL LIFE

Center for Academic Publications Japan, ed. Current Contents of Academic Journals in Japan, 1978. 18th ed. LC 72-623679. 392p. (Orig.). 1980. pap. 55.00x (ISBN 0-8002-2740-9). Intl Pubns Serv.

Davis, Sandra T. Intellectual Change & Political Development in Early Modern Japan: Ono Azusa, a Case Study. LC 76-14762. 328p. 1979. 24.50 (ISBN 0-8386-1953-3). Fairleigh Dickinson.

Harrison, John A., ed. Japan: Enduring Scholarship Selected from the Far Eastern Quarterly, the Journal of Asian Studies 1941-1971. LC 72-83062. (Thirtieth Anniversary Commemorative Ser: Vol. 2). 1972. pap. 2.00 (ISBN 0-8165-0362-1). U of Ariz Pr.

Moloney, James C. Understanding the Japanese Mind. LC 68-23316. 1968. Repr. of 1954 ed. lib. bdg. 15.75x (ISBN 0-8371-0172-7, MOJM). Greenwood.

Najita, Tetsuo & Scheiner, Irwin, eds. Japanese Thought in the Tokugawa Period (1600-1868) Methods & Metaphors. LC 78-1463. 1978. lib. bdg. 18.50x (ISBN 0-226-56801-6). U of Chicago Pr.

Okakura, Y. The Japanese Spirit. 59.95 (ISBN 0-8490-0436-5). Gordon Pr.

Pyle, Kenneth B. The New Generation in Meiji Japan: Problems of Cultural Identity 1885-1895. LC 69-13183. 1969. 12.50x (ISBN 0-8047-0697-2). Stanford U Pr.

Roden, Donald T. Schooldays in Imperial Japan: A Study in the Culture of a Student Elite. LC 79-64477. (Illus.). 300p. 1980. 27.50x (ISBN 0-520-03910-6). U of Cal Pr.

Shikaumi, Nobuya. Cultural Policy in Japan. (Studies & Documents on Cultural Policies). (Orig.). 1971. pap. 5.00 (ISBN 92-3-100851-X, U128, UNESCO). Unipub.

Smith, Henry D. Japan's First Student Radicals. LC 72-81276. (East Asian Ser: No. 70). (Illus.). 359p. 1972. 16.00x (ISBN 0-674-47185-7). Harvard U Pr.

JAPAN–JUVENILE LITERATURE

Bolitho, Harold. Meiji Japan. LC 80-7448. (Cambridge Topic Bks.). (Illus.). (gr. 5-10). 1980. PLB 5.95 (ISBN 0-8225-1219-X). Lerner Pubns.

Gidal, Sonia & Gidal, Tim. My Village in Japan. (Illus.). (gr. 4-8). 1966. PLB 5.69 (ISBN 0-394-91908-4). Pantheon.

Hearn, Lafcadio. In Ghostly Japan. LC 79-138068. (Illus.). (gr. 9 up). 1971. pap. 3.50 (ISBN 0-8048-0965-8). C E Tuttle.

Hoare, Sophy. Japan. LC 75-44864. (Macdonald Countries). (Illus.). (gr. 7 up). 1976. PLB 7.95 (ISBN 0-382-06106-3, Pub. by Macdonald Ed). Silver.

Kirk, Ruth. Sigemi: A Japanese Village Girl. LC 65-21699. (Illus.). (gr. 3-5). 1965. 5.95 (ISBN 0-15-274152-6, HJ). HarBraceJ.

Newman, Robert. Japanese: People of the Three Treasures. (Illus.). (YA) (gr. 7 up). 1964. 4.25 (ISBN 0-689-20301-2). Atheneum.

Rosenfeld, Erwin & Geller, Harriet. Japon-Tierra Del Origen Del Sol,Unit 8. Quinones, Nathan & Cesares, Angeles, trs. from Eng. LC 74-16479. (Afro Asian Culture Studies). (Span.). (gr. 9-12). 1975. pap. text ed. 2.50 (ISBN 0-8120-0535-X). Barron.

Ryan, Frank L. & Clark, James I. Windows on Japan. LC 78-60692. (Social Studies Readers Ser.). (Illus., Gr. 4-6). 1978. pap. text ed. 2.80 (ISBN 0-685-94906-0); pap. text ed. 8.48 pkg. of 3 (ISBN 0-395-27183-5); tchr's guide 1.32 (ISBN 0-395-27185-1). HM.

Schloat, G. Warren, Jr. Junichi, a Boy of Japan. (Illus.). (gr. 3-6). 1964. PLB 4.99 (ISBN 0-394-91292-6). Knopf.

Soleillant, Claude. Japan: Activities & Projects in Color. LC 79-91394. (Illus.). 96p. (gr. 2-12). 1980. 9.95 (ISBN 0-8069-4556-7); PLB 9.29 (ISBN 0-8069-4557-5). Sterling.

Sterling Publishing Company Editors. Japan in Pictures. rev. ed. LC 60-14338. (Visual Geography Ser). (Orig.). (gr. 6 up). 1978. PLB 4.99 (ISBN 0-8069-1011-9); pap. 2.95 (ISBN 0-8069-1010-0). Sterling.

Sternberg, Martha. Japan: A Week in Daisuke's World. (Face to Face Bks.). (Illus.). 40p. (gr. k-2). 1973. 4.95g (ISBN 0-02-705560-4, CCPr). Macmillan.

Storry, Richard. Japan. (Countries of Today Ser). (gr. 5-9). 1970. 4.25 (ISBN 0-87250-216-3). D White.

Tames, Richard. Japan in the Twentieth Century. (Twentieth Century World History Ser.). (Illus.). 96p. (gr. 7-10). 1981. 14.95 (ISBN 0-7134-3966-1, Pub. by Batsford England). David & Charles.

Vaughan, Josephine B. The Land & People of Japan. rev. ed. LC 72-38543. (Portraits of the Nations Ser.). (Illus.). (gr. 6 up). 1972. 8.95 (ISBN 0-397-31301-2). Lippincott.

Watson, Jane W. Japan: Islands of the Rising Sun. LC 68-22640. (Living in Today's World Ser). (Illus.). (gr. 3-6). 1968. PLB 7.29 (ISBN 0-8116-6860-6). Garrard.

JAPAN–KINGS AND RULERS

see Japan–Emperors

JAPAN–LEARNED INSTITUTIONS AND SOCIETIES

Kraft, Eva, ed. Japanese Institutions. 611p. (Japanese, Eng.). 1972. text ed. 42.00 (ISBN 3-7940-5041-X, Pub. by K G Saur). Gale.

JAPAN–MILITARY POLICY

Auer, James E. The Postwar Rearmament of Japanese Maritime Forces 1945-1971. LC 72-83564. (Special Studies in International Politics & Government). 1973. 29.50x (ISBN 0-275-28633-9). Irvington.

Buck, James H., ed. The Modern Japanese Military System. LC 75-14628. (Sage Research Progress Ser. on War, Revolution, & Peacekeeping: Vol. 5). 288p. 1975. 22.50 (ISBN 0-8039-0513-0); pap. 9.95 (ISBN 0-8039-0514-9). Sage.

--The Modern Japanese Military System. LC 75-14628. (Sage Research Progress Ser. on War, Revolution, & Peacekeeping: Vol. 5). 288p. 1975. 22.50 (ISBN 0-8039-0513-0); pap. 9.95 (ISBN 0-8039-0514-9). Sage.

Emmerson, John K. & Humphreys, Leonard A. Will Japan Rearm? A Study in Attitudes. (AEI-Hoover Policy Studies). 1973. pap. 6.25 (ISBN 0-8447-3114-5). Am Enterprise.

Kataoka, Tetsuya. Waiting for a "Pearl Harbor". Japan Debates Defense. (Publication Ser.: No. 232). 95p. (Orig.). 1981. pap. 7.95 (ISBN 0-8179-7322-2). Hoover Inst Pr.

Kennedy, Malcolm D. The Military Side of Japanese Life. LC 72-9091. (Illus.). 367p. 1973. Repr. of 1924 ed. lib. bdg. 27.50x (ISBN 0-8371-6574-1, KEJL). Greenwood.

Morley, James W. Forecast for Japan: Security in the 1970's. LC 79-155964. 256p. 1972. 17.50 (ISBN 0-691-03091-X). Princeton U Pr.

Pacific War Research Society, ed. Japan's Longest Day. LC 68-17573. (Illus.). 340p. 1980. pap. 4.95 (ISBN 0-87011-422-0). Kodansha.

Perrin, Noel. Giving up the Gun: Japan's Reversion to the Sword Fifteen Forty-Three to Eighteen Seventy-Nine. LC 80-50744. (Illus.). 122p. 1980. pap. 4.95 (ISBN 0-394-73949-3). Shambhala Pubns.

Smethurst, Richard J. A Social Basic for Prewar Japanese Militarism: The Army & the Rural Community. (Center for Japanese & Korean Studies). 1974. 30.00x (ISBN 0-520-02552-0). U of Cal Pr.

Sunoo, Harold H. Japanese Militarism: Past & Present. LC 74-23366. 170p. 1975. 15.95x (ISBN 0-88229-217-X). Nelson-Hall.

Towle, Philip, ed. Estimating Foreign Military Power. 270p. 1981. text ed. 27.00x (ISBN 0-8419-0736-6). Holmes & Meier.

Zhukov, Y. M., ed. The Rise & Fall of the Gunbatsu. 273p. 1975. 3.90 (ISBN 0-8285-0492-X, Pub. by Progress Pubs Russia). Imported Pubns.

JAPAN–NAVY

Ballard, G. A. The Influence of the Sea on the Political History of Japan. 312p. 1972. Repr. of 1921 ed. 25.00x (ISBN 0-7165-2048-6, Pub. by Irish Academic Pr Ireland). Biblio Dist.

Ballard, George A. The Influence of the Sea on the Political History of Japan. LC 74-136516. (Illus.). 311p. 1973. Repr. of 1921 ed. lib. bdg. 17.75x (ISBN 0-8371-5435-9, BAIS). Greenwood.

Bywater, Hector C. Sea-Power in the Pacific: A Study of the American-Japanese Naval Problem. LC 75-111749. (American Imperialism: Viewpoints of United States Foreign Policy, 1898-1941). 1970. Repr. of 1921 ed. 16.00 (ISBN 0-405-02006-6). Arno.

D'Albas, Andrieu. Death of a Navy. 1957. 7.50 (ISBN 0-8159-5302-X). Devin.

Dingman, Roger. Power in the Pacific: The Origins of Naval Arms Limitation, 1914-1922. LC 75-36402. 1976. lib. bdg. 20.00x (ISBN 0-226-15331-2). U of Chicago Pr.

Jeschura, Hansgeorg & Jung, Dieter. Warships of the Imperial Japanese Navy, 1869-1945. LC 75-43861. 1977. 27.95 (ISBN 0-87021-893-X). Naval Inst Pr.

JAPAN–POLITICS AND GOVERNMENT

Akita, George. Foundations of Constitutional Government in Modern Japan, 1868-1900. LC 65-13835. (East Asian Ser: No. 23). 1967. 15.00x (ISBN 0-674-31250-3). Harvard U Pr.

Arnesen. The Medieval Japanese Daimyo. 1979. text ed. 19.50x (ISBN 0-300-02341-3). Yale U Pr.

Baerwald, H. H. Japan's Parliament: An Introduction. LC 73-90810. 200p. 1974. 19.95x (ISBN 0-521-20387-2). Cambridge U Pr.

Benjamin, Roger & Ori, Kan. Tradition & Change in Postindustrial Japan: The Roles of the Political Parties. 192p. 1981. 21.95 (ISBN 0-03-059138-4). Praeger.

Bergamini, David. Japan's Imperial Conspiracy. (Illus.). 1971. 14.95 (ISBN 0-688-01905-6). Morrow.

Berger, Gordon M. Parties Out of Power in Japan, 1931-1941. LC 76-3243. (Illus.). 1976. text ed. 30.00 (ISBN 0-691-03106-1). Princeton U Pr.

Bhuinya, Niranjan. Parliamentary Democracy in Japan. 1971. 9.00 (ISBN 0-686-20282-1). Intl Bk Dist.

Black, Cyril E., et al. The Modernization of Japan & Russia. LC 75-8429. (Perspectives on Modernization Ser.). 1975. 19.95 (ISBN 0-02-906850-9). Free Pr.

Bolitho, Harold. Treasures Among Men: The Fudai Daimyo in Tokugawa Japan. LC 73-86885. (Yale Historical Publications, Miscellany, No. 101). 304p. 1974. 22.50x (ISBN 0-300-01655-7). Yale U Pr.

Borton, Hugh. Japan Since Nineteen Thirty-One, Its Political & Social Developments. LC 73-3922. 168p. 1973. Repr. of 1940 ed. lib. bdg. 15.00x (ISBN 0-8371-6859-7, BOJA). Greenwood.

Centre for East Asian Cultural Studies, Tokyo, ed. The Meiji Japan Through Contemporary Sources, 3 vols. 758p. 1972. Set. 52.50x (ISBN 0-8002-1716-0). Intl Pubns Serv.

Chang, Richard T. Historians & Meiji Statesmen. LC 78-631066. (U of Fla. Social Sciences Monographs Ser.: No. 41). (Illus.). 1970. pap. 3.50 (ISBN 0-8130-0307-5). U Presses Fla.

Communication Policies in Japan: Communication Policy Studies. 1978. pap. 4.75 (ISBN 92-3-101515-X, U826, UNESCO). Unipub.

Curtis, Gerald L. Election Campaigning: Japanese Style. LC 70-154343. (Studies of the East Asian Institute). 275p. 1971. 16.50x (ISBN 0-231-03512-8). Columbia U Pr.

Davis, Sandra T. Intellectual Change & Political Development in Early Modern Japan: Ono Azusa, a Case Study. LC 76-14762. 328p. 1979. 24.50 (ISBN 0-8386-1953-3). Fairleigh Dickinson.

De Becker, Joseph E. Elements of Japanese Law: Studies in Japanese Law & Government. 1979. Repr. of 1916 ed. 34.00 (ISBN 0-89093-210-7). U Pubns Amer.

--Principles & Practice of the Civil Code of Japan: A Complete Theoretical & Practical Exposition of the Motifs of the Japanese Civil Code. (Studies in Japanese Law & Government). 852p. 1979. Repr. of 1921 ed. Set. 60.00 (ISBN 0-89093-216-6). U Pubns Amer.

De Becker, Joseph E., tr. from Japanese. Annotated Civil Code of Japan, 4 vols. (Studies in Japanese Law & Government). 1200p. 1979. 95.00 (ISBN 0-89093-215-8). U Pubns Amer.

Drea, Edward R. The Nineteen Forty-Two Japanese General Election. (International Studies East Asians Ser.: No. 11). 223p. (Orig.). 1980. pap. 8.00x (ISBN 0-686-64723-8, Ctr E Asian Stud). Paragon.

Duus, Peter. Feudalism in Japan. (Studies in World Civilization). (Orig.). 1969. pap. text ed. 4.95x (ISBN 0-394-31076-4, KnopfC). Knopf.

Fahs, Charles B. Government in Japan: Recent Trends in Its Scope & Operation. LC 75-30105. (Institute of Pacific Relations). Repr. of 1940 ed. 16.00 (ISBN 0-404-59520-0). AMS Pr.

Fujii, Shinichi. Essentials of Japanese Constitutional Law. (Studies in Japanese Law & Government). 459p. 1979. Repr. of 1940 ed. 32.50 (ISBN 0-89093-214-X). U Pubns Amer.

Gerard, Auguste. Ma Mission Au Japan, 1907-1914. LC 72-168109. 867p. Repr. of 1919 ed. 29.00 (ISBN 0-404-02713-X). AMS Pr.

Gresser, Julian, et al. Environmental Law in Japan. (Illus.). 520p. 1981. text ed. 60.00x (ISBN 0-262-07076-6). MIT Pr.

Grew, Joseph C. Ten Years in Japan: A Contemporary Record. LC 72-4275. (World Affairs Ser.: National & International Viewpoints). (Illus.). 578p. 1972. Repr. of 1944 ed. 27.00 (ISBN 0-405-04600-6). Arno.

Grosssberg, Kenneth A. Japan's Renaissance: The Politics of the Muromachi Bakufu. (Harvard East Asian Monographs: No. 99). (Illus.). 260p. 1981. text ed. 15.00x (ISBN 0-674-47251-9). Harvard U Pr.

Gubbins, John H. Progress of Japan, 1853-1871. LC 79-137237. Repr. of 1911 ed. 24.50 (ISBN 0-404-02939-6). AMS Pr.

Hall, John C., tr. from Japanese. Japanese Feudal Law. (Studies in Japanese Law & Government). (Illus.). 266p. 1979. Repr. of 1906 ed. 24.50 (ISBN 0-89093-211-5). U Pubns Amer.

Hall, Robert K., ed. Kokutai No Hongi: Cardinal Principles of the National Entity of Japan. Gauntlett, John O., tr. from Japanese. 200p. 1974. Repr. 12.50x (ISBN 0-89020-008-4). Crofton Pub.

Halliday, Jon. A Political History of Japanese Capitalism. 1978. pap. 8.95 (ISBN 0-85345-471-X, PB471X). Monthly Rev.

Hamada, Kengi. Prince Ito. (Studies Injapanese History & Civilzation). 1979. Repr. of 1936 ed. 22.00 (ISBN 0-89093-267-0). U Pubns Amer.

Hozumi, Nobushige. Ancestor-Worship & Japanese Law. 2nd & rev ed. LC 73-2798. (Select Bibliographies Reprint Ser). 1973. Repr. of 1912 ed. 19.00 (ISBN 0-8369-7163-9). Arno.

Ike, Nobutaka. Beginnings of Political Democracy in Japan. Repr. of 1950 ed. lib. bdg. 16.50x (ISBN 0-8371-1808-5, IKPD). Greenwood.

Iriye, Akira, ed. The Chinese & the Japanese: Essays in Political & Cultural Interactions. LC 79-3215. (Studies in Political Development: No. 10). 1980. 25.00x (ISBN 0-691-03126-6); pap. 9.95 (ISBN 0-691-10086-1). Princeton U Pr.

Irrigation Water Rights Disputes in Japan As Seen in the Asusa River System. 20p. 1980. pap. 5.00 (ISBN 92-808-0087-6, TUNU 080, UNU). Unipub.

Ito, Hirobumi. Commentaries on the Constitution of the Empire of Japan. (Studies in Japanese Law & Government). 310p. 1979. Repr. of 1906 ed. 25.00 (ISBN 0-89093-212-3). U Pubns Amer.

--Commentaries on the Constitution of the Empire of Japan. 2nd ed. Ito, Miyoji, tr. from Japanese. LC 74-15166. 1978. Repr. of 1906 ed. lib. bdg. 24.25x (ISBN 0-8371-7810-X, ITEG). Greenwood.

Itoh, Hiroshi, ed. & tr. Japanese Politics, an Inside View: Readings from Japan. LC 72-12407. (Illus.). 248p. 1973. 22.50x (ISBN 0-8014-0735-4); pap. 7.95 (ISBN 0-8014-9138-X, CP138). Cornell U Pr.

Iwasaki, Uichi. Working Forces in Japanese Politics, 1867-1920. LC 21-7669. (Columbia University. Studies in the Social Sciences: No. 220). Repr. of 1921 ed. 15.00 (ISBN 0-404-51220-8). AMS Pr.

Iyenaga, Toyokichi. The Constitutional Development of Japan. LC 78-63805. (Johns Hopkins University. Studies in the Social Sciences. Ninth Ser. 1891: 9). Repr. of 1891 ed. 11.50 (ISBN 0-404-61068-4). AMS Pr.

Japan Center for International Exchange, ed. The Silent Power: Japan's Identity & World Role. 1976. 13.50x (ISBN 0-89955-245-5, Pub. by Simul). Intl Schol Bk Serv.

Japan Institute of International Affairs, ed. White Papers of Japan: Annual Abstract of Official Reports & Statistics of the Japanese Government 1978-79. LC 72-620531. (Illus.). 228p. (Orig.). 1980. pap. 37.50x (ISBN 0-8002-2734-4). Intl Pubns Serv.

Johnson, Chalmers. Japan's Public Policy Companies. 1978. pap. 6.25 (ISBN 0-8447-3272-9). Am Enterprise.

Lay, Arthur H. Brief Sketch of the History of Political Parties in Japan. Bd. with Political Ideas of Modern Japan: An Interpretation Studies in Japanese Law & Government. Kowakami, Kiyoshi K. 461p. 1979. Repr. of 1902 ed. 22.00 (ISBN 0-89093-222-0). U Pubns Amer.

McLaren, Walter W. Japanese Government Documents: (of the Meiji Era, 2 vols. (Studies in Japanese History & Civilization). 1979. Repr. of 1914 ed. Set. 52.50 (ISBN 0-89093-265-4). U Pubns Amer.

McLaren, Walter Wallace. Political History of Japan During the Meiji Era,1867-1912. new ed. 379p. 1966. 29.50x (ISBN 0-7146-2018-1, F Cass Co). Biblio Dist.

Maki, John M., ed. Japan's Commission on the Constitution: The Final Report. LC 80-50869. (Asian Law Ser.: No. 7). 424p. 1980. 25.00 (ISBN 0-295-95767-0). U of Wash Pr.

Maruyama, Masao & Hane, Mikiso. Studies in the Intellectual History of Tokugawa Japan. LC 70-90954. 350p. 1974. 22.00x (ISBN 0-691-07566-2). Princeton U Pr.

Mason, R. H. Japan's First General Election, Eighteen Ninety. LC 68-23915. (University of Cambridge Oriental Pubns.). 1969. 38.50 (ISBN 0-521-07147-X). Cambridge U Pr.

Mass, Jeffrey P. The Kamakura Bakufu: A Study in Documents. LC 75-39335. (Illus.). 252p. 1976. 17.50x (ISBN 0-8047-0907-6). Stanford U Pr.

--Warrior Government in Early Medieval Japan: A Study of the Kamakur Bakufu, Shugo, & Jito. LC 74-75875. 296p. 1974. 20.00x (ISBN 0-300-01756-1). Yale U Pr.

Matsunami, Niichiro. Japanese Constitution & Politics. (Studies in Japanese Law & Government). 577p. 1979. 38.75 (ISBN 0-89093-217-4). U Pubns Amer.

Maxon, Yale C. Control of Japanese Foreign Policy. LC 72-12330. 286p. 1973. Repr. of 1957 ed. lib. bdg. 17.50x (ISBN 0-8371-6728-0, MACJ). Greenwood.

Military of Justice, Japan. Constitution of Japan & Criminal Statutes. (Studies in Japanese Law & Government). 1979. Repr. of 1957 ed. 38.00 (ISBN 0-89093-221-2). U Pubns Amer.

Mimistry of Finance, Japan. Guide to the Economic Laws of Japan, 2 vols. (Studies in Japanese Law & Government). 1979. Repr. of 1950 ed. Set. 62.50 (ISBN 0-89093-220-4). U Pubns Amer.

Ministry of Labor, Japan. Japan Labor Code, 2 vols. (Studies in Japanese Law & Government). 1979. Repr. of 1953 ed. Set. 56.00 (ISBN 0-89093-217-4). U Pubns Amer.

Mitchell, Richard H. Thought Control in Prewar Japan. LC 75-39566. 1976. 17.50x (ISBN 0-8014-1002-9). Cornell U Pr.

Moore, Frederick. With Japan's Leaders. LC 80-2890. (BCL Ser.: Nos. I & II). Repr. of 1942 ed. 37.50 (ISBN 0-404-18067-1). AMS Pr.

Morley, James W., ed. Dilemmas of Growth in Prewar Japan. LC 79-155964. (Studies in the Modernization of Japan). 544p. 1974. 26.00x (ISBN 0-691-03074-X). Princeton U Pr.

Morse, Ronald A., et al, eds. The Politics of Japan's Energy Strategy. Morse, Ronald A., tr. (Research Papers & Policy Studies). (Orig.). 1981. pap. write for info. (ISBN 0-912966-45-9). IEAS Ctr Chinese Stud.

Najita, Tetsuo. Hara Kei in the Politics of Compromise 1905-1915. LC 67-27090. (East Asian Ser: No. 31). (Illus.). 1967. 16.50x (ISBN 0-674-37250-6). Harvard U Pr.

--Japan: The Intellectual Foundations of Modern Japanese Politics. LC 79-23710. 1980. pap. 4.95 (ISBN 0-226-56803-2, P883). U of Chicago Pr.

Nakamura, Kichisaburo. Formation of Modern Japan: As Viewed from Legal History. 1965. 4.00x (ISBN 0-8248-0015-X, Eastwest Ctr). U Pr of Hawaii.

Norman, E. Herbert. Feudal Background of Japanese Politics... in Preliminary Draft Form. LC 75-30127. (Institute of Pacific Relations). Repr. of 1945 ed. 27.50 (ISBN 0-404-59548-0). AMS Pr.

--Japan's Emergence As a Modern State. LC 72-9092. 254p. 1973. Repr. of 1940 ed. lib. bdg. 23.00 (ISBN 0-8371-6573-3, NOJE). Greenwood.

Notehelfer, F. G. Kotoku Shusui: Portrait of a Japanese Radical. (Illus.). 1971. 42.50 (ISBN 0-521-07989-6). Cambridge U Pr.

OECD. Environmental Policies in Japan. 95p. (Orig.). 1977. pap. 5.00x (ISBN 92-64-11669-9). OECD.

Okamoto, Shumpei. The Japanese Oligarchy & the Russo-Japanese War. LC 74-114259. (Studies of the East Asian Institute of Col. Univ.). 1971. 20.00x (ISBN 0-231-03404-0). Columbia U Pr.

Pempel, T. J. Policy & Politics in Japan: Creative Conservatism. (Policy & Politics in Industrial States Ser.). 295p. 1981. 22.50 (ISBN 0-87722-249-5); pap. 10.95 (ISBN 0-87722-250-9). Temple U Pr.

Ponsonby-Fane, Richard A. Fortunes of the Emperors: Studies in Revolution, Exile, Abdication, Usurpation, & Deposition in Ancient Japan. (Studies in Japanese History & Civilization). 1979. 28.00 (ISBN 0-89093-250-6). U Pubns Amer.

Reischauer, Robert K. Japan, Government-Politics. LC 75-41226. Repr. of 1939 ed. 18.00 (ISBN 0-404-14589-2). AMS Pr.

Richardson, Bradley. The Political Culture of Japan. 1974. pap. 8.95x (ISBN 0-520-03049-4). U. of Cal Pr.

Rinalducci, Ralph J. The Japanese Police Establishment. 388p. 1974. 26.75 (ISBN 0-398-03577-6). C C Thomas.

Sanderson, Fred. Japan's Food Prospects & Policies. 1978. pap. 3.95 (ISBN 0-8157-7701-9). Brookings.

Scalapino, Robert A. Democracy & the Party Movement in Pre-War Japan: The Failure of the First Attempt. (California Library Repr. Ser). 1975. Repr. of 1953 ed. 36.50x (ISBN 0-520-02914-3). U. of Cal Pr.

Sebald, William J., tr. Selection of Japan's Emergency Legislation. (Studies in Japanese Law & Government). 177p. 1979. Repr. of 1937 ed. 16.00 (ISBN 0-89093-219-0). U Pubns Amer.

Steenstrup, Carl. Hojo Shigetoki (Eleven Ninety-Eight to Twelve Sixty-One) & His Role in the History of Political & Ethical Ideas in Japan. (Scandinavian Institute of Asian Studies Monographs: No. 41). (Orig.). 1980. pap. text ed. 16.50x (ISBN 0-7007-0132-X). Humanities.

Storry, Richard. The Double Patriots: A Study of Japanese Nationalism. 335p. 1973. Repr. of 1957 ed. lib. bdg. 21.50x (ISBN 0-8371-6643-8, STDP). Greenwood.

Swearingen, A. Rodger & Langer, Paul. Red Flag in Japan: International Communism in Action, 1919-1951. LC 68-54440. (Illus.). 1968. Repr. of 1952 ed. lib. bdg. 17.50x (ISBN 0-8371-0242-1, SWRF). Greenwood.

Takane, Masaaki. Political Elites in Japan. (Japan Research Monographs: No.1). 180p. 1981. pap. 10.00 (ISBN 0-912966-33-5). IEAS Ctr Chinese Stud.

Takeuchi, Sterling T. War & Diplomacy in the Japanese Empire. LC 66-27158. 1967. Repr. of 1935 ed. 12.50 (ISBN 0-8462-1013-4). Russell.

Tanaka, Kakuei. Building a New Japan: A Plan for Remodeling the Japanese Archipelago. 230p. 1973. 14.50 (ISBN 0-89955-241-2, Pub. by Simul). Intl Schol Bk Serv.

Tanin, O. & Yohan, E. Militarism & Fascism in Japan. LC 72-136553. 320p. 1973. Repr. of 1934 ed. lib. bdg. 16.50x (ISBN 0-8371-5478-2, TAMF). Greenwood.

Tokayer, Marvin & Swartz, Mary. The Fugu Plan: The Untold Story of the Japanese & the Jews in World War II. (Illus.). 1979. 10.95 (ISBN 0-448-23036-4). Paddington.

Totman, Conrad. The Collapse of the Tokugawa Bakufu: Eighteen Sixty-Two to Eighteen Sixty-Eight. LC 79-22094. (Illus.). 1980. text ed. 22.50x (ISBN 0-8248-0614-X). U Pr of Hawaii.

--Politics in the Tokugawa Bakufu, 1600-1843. LC 67-22873. (East Asian Ser: No. 30). (Illus.). 1967. 15.00x (ISBN 0-674-68800-7). Harvard U Pr.

Tsukahira, Toshio G. Feudal Control in Tokugawa Japan: The Sankin Kotai System. LC 67-3532. (East Asian Monographs Ser: No. 20). 1966. pap. 9.00x (ISBN 0-674-29900-0). Harvard U Pr.

Tsurutani, Taketsugu. Political Change in Japan: Response to Postindustrial Challenge. LC 76-58877. (Comparative Studies of Political Life Ser.). 1977. pap. text ed. 10.95x (ISBN 0-582-28183-0). Longman.

Uyehara, George E. The Political Development of Japan: 1867 to 1909. (Illus.). 296p. 1972. Repr. of 1910 ed. 31.00x (ISBN 0-686-28325-2, Pub. by Irish Academic Pr). Biblio Dist.

Vogel, Ezra F. Japan As Number One: Lessons for America. LC 79-24059. 1980. pap. 4.95 (ISBN 0-06-090791-6, CN 791, CN). Har-Row.

Ward, Robert E. Japan's Political System. 2nd ed. (Illus.). 1978. 8.95 (ISBN 0-13-509588-3). P-H.

Ward, Robert E., ed. Five Studies in Japanese Politics. facs. ed. LC 68-58816. (Essay Index Reprint Ser). 1957. 18.00 (ISBN 0-8369-0130-4). Arno.

--Political Development in Modern Japan. (Studies in the Modernization of Japan). 1968. 32.50 (ISBN 0-691-03045-6); pap. 9.95 (ISBN 0-691-00017-4). Princeton U Pr.

Ward, Robert E. & Rustow, Dankwart A., eds. Political Modernization in Japan & Turkey. (Studies in Political Development,: No. 3). 1964. 32.50 (ISBN 0-691-07516-6). Princeton U Pr.

Warshaw, Steven, et al. Japan Emerges. (Illus.). 1974. pap. text ed. 8.50 scp (ISBN 0-06-389132-8, HarpC). Har-Row.

Webb, Herschel. Japanese Imperial Institution in the Tokugawa Period. LC 68-11912. (East Asian Institute Ser). 1968. 17.50x (ISBN 0-231-03120-3). Columbia U Pr.

Wigmore, John H. Law & Justice in Tokugawa Japan: Part VI-H, Legal Precedents. 300p. 1981. 25.00x (ISBN 0-86008-289-X, Pub. by U of Tokyo Japan). Columbia U Pr.

Young, Arthur M. Socialist & Labour Movement in Japan. (Studies in Japanese History & Civilization). 145p. 1979. Repr. of 1921 ed. 18.00 (ISBN 0-89093-268-9). U Pubns Amer.

Yutaka, Hibino. Nippon Shindo Ron; or the National Ideals of the Japanese People. McKenzie, A. P., tr. from Japanese. LC 79-4914. 1980. Repr. of 1928 ed. 19.00 (ISBN 0-88355-964-1). Hyperion Conn.

Zhukov, Y. M., ed. The Rise & Fall of the Gunbatsu. 273p. 1975. 3.90 (ISBN 0-8285-0492-X, Pub. by Progress Pubs Russia). Imported Pubns.

JAPAN–POLITICS AND GOVERNMENT–BIBLIOGRAPHY

Ward, Robert E. & Watanare, Hajime. Japanese Political Science: A Guide to Japanese Reference & Research Materials. LC 78-5925. (University of Michigan Center for Japanese Studies Bibliographical Ser: No. 1). 1978. Repr. of 1961 ed. lib. bdg. 27.75x (ISBN 0-313-20436-5, WAJS). Greenwood.

JAPAN–POLITICS AND GOVERNMENT–1945-

Bakke, E. Wight. Revolutionary Democracy: Challenge & Testing in Japan. 1968. 19.50 (ISBN 0-208-00627-3, Archon). Shoe String.

Blaker, Michael K., ed. Japan at the Polls: The House of Councillors Election of 1974. LC 76-23589. 1976. pap. 6.25 (ISBN 0-8447-3213-3). Am Enterprise.

Ike, Nobutaka. Japanese Politics: Patron-Client Democracy. 2nd ed. 1972. pap. text ed. 4.95 (ISBN 0-394-31695-9). Knopf.

--A Theory of Japanese Democracy. LC 77-8279. (Westview Special Studies on China & East Asia). (Illus.). 178p. 1980. pap. text ed. 8.50x (ISBN 0-89158-932-5). Westview.

Jain, R. K. Japan's Postwar Peace Settlements. 1978. text ed. 16.00x (ISBN 0-391-00870-6). Humanities.

Kosaka, Masataka. One Hundred Million Japanese. LC 72-76298. (Illus.). 282p. 1972. 10.00x (ISBN 0-87011-182-5). Kodansha.

Kurzman, Dan. Kishi & Japan. 1960. 10.00 (ISBN 0-8392-1057-4). Astor-Honor.

Langer, Paul F. Communism in Japan. LC 73-152426. (Studies: No. 30). 112p. 1972. 7.95 (ISBN 0-8179-3301-8). Hoover Inst Pr.

McKean, Margaret A. Environmental Protest & Citizen Politics in Japan. LC 80-12991. 300p. 1981. 18.75x (ISBN 0-520-04115-1). U of Cal Pr.

McNelly, Theodore. Politics & Government in Japan. 2nd ed. LC 74-186377. (Contemporary Government Ser.). (Illus.). 256p. (Orig.). 1972. pap. text ed. 9.50 (ISBN 0-395-12649-5, 3-37419). HM.

Morley, James W. Forecast for Japan: Security in the 1970's. LC 79-155964. 256p. 1972. 17.50 (ISBN 0-691-03091-X). Princeton U Pr.

Morris, I. I. Nationalism & the Right Wing in Japan. LC 73-13034. (Illus.). 476p. 1974. Repr. of 1960 ed. lib. bdg. 22.25x (ISBN 0-8371-7106-7, MONA). Greenwood.

Olson, Lawrence. Dimensions of Japan. LC 63-14762. 1963. text ed. 6.50 (ISBN 0-910116-56-3). Am U Field.

Packard, George R. Protest in Tokyo: The Treaty Crisis of Nineteen Sixty. LC 78-17982. 1978. Repr. of 1966 ed. lib. bdg. 32.25x (ISBN 0-313-20532-9, PAPT). Greenwood.

Pempel, T. John. Policymaking in Contemporary Japan. LC 77-4514. 1977. 22.50x (ISBN 0-8014-1048-7). Cornell U Pr.

Quigley, Harold S. & Turner, John E. The New Japan: Government & Politics. LC 74-10473. (Illus.). 456p. 1974. Repr. of 1956 ed. lib. bdg. 24.00x (ISBN 0-8371-7689-1, QUNJ). Greenwood.

Redford, Lawrence H., ed. The Occupation of Japan: Impact of Legal Refor, 212p. pap. 5.00 (ISBN 0-686-29518-8). MacArthur Memorial.

Scalapino, Robert A. & Masumi, Junnosuke. Parties & Politics in Contemporary Japan. LC 61-14279. 1962. pap. 4.95x (ISBN 0-520-01132-5, CAMPUS69). U of Cal Pr.

Steiner, Kurt, et al, eds. Political Opposition & Local Politics in Japan. LC 80-7555. 480p. 1980. 30.00 (ISBN 0-691-07625-1); pap. 9.95 (ISBN 0-691-10109-4). Princeton U Pr.

Stockwin, J. A. Japan: Divided Politics in a Growth Economy. (Comparative Modern Government Ser). 320p. 1975. text ed. 10.00x (ISBN 0-393-05544-2); pap. text ed. 6.95x (ISBN 0-393-09233-X). Norton.

Supreme Commander For Allied Powers. Political Reorientation of Japan 1945-1948, 2 Vols. 1968. Set. 87.00 (ISBN 0-403-00028-9). Scholarly.

Supreme Commander For The Allied Powers - Government Section. Political Reorientation of Japan, September 1945 to September 1948: Report, 2 Vols. (Illus.). Repr. of 1949 ed. Set. lib. bdg. 78.00x (ISBN 0-8371-3169-3, PROJ). Greenwood.

Swearingen, A. Rodger & Langer, Paul. Red Flag in Japan: International Communism in Action, 1919-1951. LC 68-54440. (Illus.). 1968. Repr. of 1952 ed. lib. bdg. 17.50x (ISBN 0-8371-0242-1, SWRF). Greenwood.

Takayanagi, Shunichi & Miwa, Kimitada, eds. Postwar Trends in Japan. 292p. 1975. 28.00x (ISBN 0-86008-129-X, Pub. by U of Tokyo Pr). Intl Schol Bk Serv.

Takemoto, Toru. Failure of Liberalism in Japan: Shedehara Kijuro's Encounter with Anti-Liberals. LC 78-68695. 1979. pap. text ed. 10.50 (ISBN 0-8191-0698-4). U Pr of Amer.

Thayer, Nathaniel B. How the Conservatives Rule Japan. LC 68-17398. (Studies of the East Asian Institute Ser.). 1969. 25.00x (ISBN 0-691-03029-4); pap. 7.95 (ISBN 0-691-00016-6). Princeton U Pr.

Vogel, Ezra F. Japan As Number One: Lessons for America. LC 78-24059. 1979. 12.50 (ISBN 0-674-47215-2). Harvard U Pr.

Ward, Robert E., ed. Five Studies in Japanese Politics. facs. ed. LC 68-58816. (Essay Index Reprint Ser). 1957. 18.00 (ISBN 0-8369-0130-4). Arno.

Watanuki, Joji. Politics in Postwar Japanese Society. (Illus.). 1978. 12.50x (ISBN 0-86008-190-7, Pub. by U of Tokyo Pr). Intl Schol Bk Serv.

Williams, Justin. Japan's Political Revolution Under MacArthur: A Participant's Account. LC 78-5592. (Illus.). 352p. 1979. 16.50 (ISBN 0-8203-0452-2). U. of Ga Pr.

JAPAN–POPULATION

Dennery, Etienne. Asia's Teeming Millions. LC 70-115201. 1971. Repr. of 1931 ed. 12.50 (ISBN 0-8046-1094-0). Kennikat.

Penrose, Ernest F. Population Theories & Their Application: With Special Reference to Japan. LC 72-136545. 347p. 1973. Repr. of 1934 ed. lib. bdg. 17.50x (ISBN 0-8371-5466-9, PEPO). Greenwood.

Tauber, I. Population in Japan. (Office of Population Research Ser.). 1958. 35.00 (ISBN 0-691-09327-X). Princeton U Pr.

Uyeda, Teijiro. The Growth of Population & Occupational Changes in Japan, 1920-1935. LC 75-30087. Repr. of 1936 ed. 12.50 (ISBN 0-404-59568-5). AMS Pr.

Williams, Harold S. Foreigners in Mikadoland. LC 58-11102. (Illus.). 310p. 1972. pap. 2.95 (ISBN 0-8048-1049-4). C E Tuttle.

JAPAN–RELATIONS (GENERAL) WITH FOREIGN COUNTRIES

Clapp, Priscilla & Halperin, Morton H., eds. United States-Japanese Relations: The 1970's. LC 74-80441. 256p. 1974. text ed. 14.00x (ISBN 0-674-92571-8). Harvard U Pr.

Goldstein, Bernice & Tamura, Kyoko. Japan & America: A Comparative Study in Language & Culture. LC 74-81653. 1975. 7.50 (ISBN 0-8048-1109-1). C E Tuttle.

Goodman, Grant K. Davao: A Case Study in Japanese-Philippine Relations. Wickberg, Edgar, ed. LC 67-65570. (International Studies: East Asian Ser No. 1). (Orig.). 1967. pap. 4.50x (ISBN 0-685-19294-6). Paragon.

Gulick, Sidney L. The American Japanese Problem: A Study of the Racial Relations of the East & the West. LC 77-145483. (The American Immigration Library). x, 372p. 1971. Repr. of 1914 ed. lib. bdg. 18.75x (ISBN 0-89198-014-8). Ozer.

Iriye, Akira. Power & Culture: The Japanese-American War, 1941-1945. 22.00 (ISBN 0-686-74484-5). Harvard U Pr.

Keene, Donald. Japanese Discovery of Europe, 1720-1830. rev. ed. LC 69-13180. (Illus.). 1969. 10.00x (ISBN 0-8047-0668-9); pap. 5.95x (ISBN 0-8047-0669-7). Stanford U Pr.

Neumann, William L. America Encounters Japan: From Perry to MacArthur. (Goucher College Ser). 366p. 1963. Repr. 22.50x (ISBN 0-8018-0485-X). Johns Hopkins.

Scalapino, Robert A. The Foreign Policy of Modern Japan. LC 75-15219. 1977. 21.50 (ISBN 0-520-03196-2); pap. 7.95x (ISBN 0-520-03499-6). U of Cal Pr.

Schwantes, Robert S. Japanese & Americans: A Century of Cultural Relations. LC 76-28326. 1976. Repr. of 1955 ed. lib. bdg. 26.25 (ISBN 0-8371-9101-7, SCJA). Greenwood.

Wildes, Harry E. Aliens in the East: A History of Japan's Foreign Intercourse. LC 72-82117. (Japan Library Ser.). 1973. Repr. of 1937 ed. lib. bdg. 20.00 (ISBN 0-8420-1409-8). Scholarly Res Inc.

Yoshihara, Kunio. Japanese Economic Development: A Short Introduction. (Illus.). 168p. 1979. text ed. 11.50x (ISBN 0-19-580439-2). Oxford U Pr.

JAPAN–RELIGION

Agency for Cultural Affairs. Japanese Religion: A Survey of the Agency for Cultural Affairs. Abe, Yoshiya & Reid, David, trs. from Japanese. LC 80-85384. (Illus.). 276p. 1981. pap. 4.95 (ISBN 0-87011-467-0). Kodansha.

Anesaki, Masaharu. History of Japanese Religion. LC 63-19395. 1963. Repr. of 1930 ed. 19.50 (ISBN 0-8048-0248-3). C E Tuttle.

Basabe, Fernando M. Japanese Religious Attitudes. LC 70-188666. 1972. pap. 2.95x (ISBN 0-88344-227-2). Orbis Bks.

--Religious Attitudes of Japanese Men. LC 68-57415. 1969. bds. 7.65 (ISBN 0-8048-0651-9). C E Tuttle.

Bunce, William K., ed. Religions in Japan. LC 59-9234. 216p. 1981. pap. 5.25 (ISBN 0-8048-0500-8). C E Tuttle.

Cary, Otis. History of Christianity in Japan, Roman Catholic & Greek Orthodox Missions, 2 Vols. 1971. Repr. of 1909 ed. Set. 35.00 (ISBN 0-403-00252-4). Scholarly.

Collcutt, Martin. Five Mountains: The Rinzai Zen Monastic Institution in Medieval Japan. (Harvard East Asian Monograph: Vol. 85). (Illus.). 450p. 1980. 20.00 (ISBN 0-674-30497-7). Harvard U Pr.

Davis, Roy E. Miracle Man of Japan: The Life & Work of Masaharu Taniguchi, One of the Most Influential Spiritual Leaders of Our Time. (Illus., Orig.). pap. 3.00 (ISBN 0-87707-048-2). CSA Pr.

Dogen. A Primer of Soto Zen: A Translation of Dogen's Shobogenzo Zuimonki. Masunaga, Reiho, tr. from Japanese. LC 76-126044. 1971. text ed. 7.50x (ISBN 0-8248-0094-X, Eastwest Ctr). U Pr of Hawaii.

Earhart. Japanese Religion: Unity & Diversity. 2nd ed. LC 73-93288. 1974. pap. 4.95 (ISBN 0-686-66336-5). Duxbury Pr.

--Religion in the Japanese Experience: Sources & Interpretations. LC 73-81295. 1974. pap. 4.95 (ISBN 0-686-66337-3). Duxbury Pr.

Earhart, H. Bryon. Japanese Religion: Unity & Diversity. 2nd ed. 1974. pap. text ed. 8.95x (ISBN 0-8221-0123-8). Dickenson.

--Religion in the Japanese Experience. 1973. pap. text ed. 8.95x (ISBN 0-8221-0104-1). Dickenson.

Earhart, H. Byron. A Religious Study of the Mount Haguro Sect of Shugendo: An Example of Japanese Mountain Religion. LC 79-116596. (Illus.). 214p. 1970. 12.50x (ISBN 0-8002-2434-5). Intl Pubns Serv.

Folk Religion & Spiritual Belief in Modernizing Japan. 22p. 1980. pap. 5.00 (ISBN 92-808-0108-2, TUNU 078, UNU). Unipub.

Griffis, William E. Religions of Japan: From the Dawn of History to the Era of Meiji. facsimile ed. LC 70-37469. (Essay Index Reprint Ser). Repr. of 1895 ed. 21.00 (ISBN 0-8369-2550-5). Arno.

Hashim Amir-Ali. Message of the Qur'an: Presented in Perspective. LC 73-84906. 1974. 25.00 (ISBN 0-8048-0976-3). C E Tuttle.

Hearn, Lafcadio. Glimpses of Unfamiliar Japan, 2 Vols. LC 70-101093. Repr. of 1894 ed. 32.50 (ISBN 0-404-03205-2). AMS Pr.

Heim, Lafcadio. Japan's Religions, Shinto & Buddhism. 1966. 10.00 (ISBN 0-8216-0102-4). Univ Bks.

Holtom, D. C. Modern Japan & Shinto Nationalism. 2nd ed. 1963. 14.00 (ISBN 0-8188-0042-9). Paragon.

Hori, Ichiro. Folk Religion in Japan: Continuity & Change. Kitagawa, Joseph M. & Miller, Alan L., eds. (Haskell Lectures Ser: No. 1). 1968. 6.50x (ISBN 0-226-35333-8). U. of Chicago Pr.

--Folk Religion in Japan: Continuity & Change. Kitagawa, Joseph M. & Miller, Alan L., eds. LC 67-30128. (Haskell Lectures on History of Religions Ser). 1974. pap. 4.25 (ISBN 0-226-35334-6, P607, Phoen). U. of Chicago Pr.

Kitagawa, Joseph M. Religion in Japanese History. LC 65-23669. 475p. 1966. 25.00x (ISBN 0-231-02834-2). Columbia U Pr.

Knox, George W. The Development of Religion in Japan. LC 78-72456. Repr. of 1907 ed. 27.00 (ISBN 0-404-17325-X). AMS Pr.

McFarland, H. Neill. Rush Hour of the Gods. 1967. 9.95 (ISBN 0-02-583200-X). Macmillan.

Morioka, Kiyomi. Religion in Changing Japanese Society. 252p. 1975. 25.00x (ISBN 0-86008-131-1, Pub. by U of Tokyo Pr). Intl Schol Bk Serv.

Nanjio, Bunyiu, tr. from Japanese. Short History of the Twelve Buddhist Sects. (Studies in Japanese History & Civilization). 1979. Repr. of 1886 ed. 19.75 (ISBN 0-89093-252-2). U Pubns Amer.

Norbeck, Edward. Religion & Society in Modern Japan. (Rice University Studies: Vol. 56, No. 1). 232p. 1970. pap. 3.25x (ISBN 0-89263-203-8). Rice Univ.

Okakura, Y. The Japanese Spirit. lib. bdg. 59.95 (ISBN 0-87968-549-2). Krishna Pr.

Ono, Sokyo. Shinto: The Kami Way. LC 61-14033. 1962. 7.50 (ISBN 0-8048-0525-3). C E Tuttle.

Palmer, Aaron H. Documents & Facts Illustrating the Origin of the Mission to Japan. LC 72-82105. (Japan Library Ser.). 1973. Repr. of 1857 ed. lib. bdg. 10.00 (ISBN 0-8420-1399-7). Scholarly Res Inc.

Paske-Smith, Montague, ed. Japanese Traditions of Christianity: Being Some Old Translations from the Japanese, with British Consular Reports of the Persecutions of 1868-1872. (Studies in Japanese History & Civilization). 1979. Repr. of 1930 ed. 17.50 (ISBN 0-89093-257-3). U Pubns Amer.

Pye, Michael. Zen & Modern Japanese Religions. LC 74-155691. (Living Religions Series). (Illus.). 1973. pap. 3.50x (ISBN 0-7062-3148-1). Intl Pubns Serv.

Snider, Lois. Snow Pearl, a Girl of Japan. (Illus.). 1977. pap. 2.45 (ISBN 0-89367-013-8). Light & Life.

Supreme Commander for the Allied Powers. Civil Information & Education Section. Religions in Japan: Buddhism, Shinto, Christianity. LC 77-13855. 1978. Repr. of 1955 ed. lib. bdg. 20.00x (ISBN 0-8371-9874-7, SURJ). Greenwood.

Thomsen, Harry. The New Religions of Japan. LC 77-13846. (Illus.). 1978. Repr. of 1963 ed. lib. bdg. 25.75x (ISBN 0-8371-9878-X, THNR). Greenwood.

Yamamori, Tetsunao. Church Growth in Japan. LC 74-4009. (Illus.). 184p. (Orig.). 1974. pap. 4.95 (ISBN 0-87808-412-6). William Carey Lib.

JAPAN–RELIGION–BIBLIOGRAPHY

Holzman, Donald & Motoyama, Yukihiko. Japanese Religion & Philosophy. LC 74-30052. (University of Michigan Center for Japanese Bibl. Ser.: No. 7). 102p. 1975. Repr. of 1959 ed. lib. bdg. 13.25x (ISBN 0-8371-7910-6, HOJR). Greenwood.

Wheeler, Post, ed. & tr. from Jap. The Sacred Scriptures of the Japanese: With All Authoritative Variants, Chronologically Arranged. LC 75-31427. 562p. 1976. Repr. of 1952 ed. lib. bdg. 41.75 (ISBN 0-8371-8393-6, WHSS). Greenwood.

JAPAN–SOCIAL CONDITIONS

Asahina, K. & Shigiya, R., eds. Physiological Adaptability & Nutritional Status of the Japanese (B) (Japan International Biological Program Synthetics Ser.: Vol. 4). 1975. pap. 32.50x (ISBN 0-86008-214-8, Pub. by U of Tokyo Pr). Intl Schol Bk Serv.

Austin, Lewis, ed. Japan: The Paradox of Progress. LC 75-18163. (Illus.). 1976. 27.50x (ISBN 0-300-01957-2). Yale U Pr.

Bakke, E. Wight. Revolutionary Democracy: Challenge & Testing in Japan. 1968. 19.50 (ISBN 0-208-00627-3, Archon). Shoe String.

Beardsley, Richard K., et al. Village Japan. LC 58-13802. (Illus.). 1959. 14.00x (ISBN 0-226-03997-8). U of Chicago Pr.

Black, Cyril E., et al. The Modernization of Japan & Russia. LC 75-8429. (Perspectives on Modernization Ser.). 1975. 19.95 (ISBN 0-02-906850-9). Free Pr.

Bowring, R. J. Mori Ogai & the Modernization of Japanese Culture. LC 76-11074. (Oriental Publications Ser.: No. 28). (Illus.). 1979. 44.00 (ISBN 0-521-21319-3). Cambridge U Pr.

Cornell, John B. & Smith, Robert J. Two Japanese Villages: Matsunagi, a Japanese Mountain Community, Kurusu, a Japanese Agricultural Community. LC 77-90491. Repr. of 1956 ed. lib. bdg. 18.25x (ISBN 0-8371-2130-2, COJV). Greenwood.

Donoghue, John D. Pariah Persistence in Changing Japan: A Case Study. 1977. pap. text ed. 7.75 (ISBN 0-8191-0170-2). U Pr of Amer.

Dore, R. P. Aspects of Social Change in Modern Japan. (Studies in the Modernization of Japan). 1971. 26.50x (ISBN 0-691-03003-0); pap. 8.95 (ISBN 0-691-00014-X). Princeton U Pr.

East Asian Studies Program-Ohio State University. Business & Society in Japan: Fundamentals for Businessmen. 348p. 1981. 29.95 (ISBN 0-03-059321-2). Praeger.

The Floating World: An Evocation of Old Japan. (Illus.). 1979. pap. 6.95 (ISBN 0-87663-993-7). Universe.

Fukutake, Tadashi. Japanese Society Today. 2nd ed. 180p. 1981. pap. 9.50x (ISBN 0-86008-291-1, Pub. by U of Tokyo Japan). Columbia U Pr.

Hayashi, Yujiro, ed. Perspectives on Postindustrial Society. 240p. 1970. 12.50x (ISBN 0-86008-066-8, Pub by U of Tokyo Pr). Intl Schol Bk Serv.

Ike, Nobutaka. Japanese Politics: Patron-Client Democracy. 2nd ed. 1972. pap. text ed. 4.95 (ISBN 0-394-31695-9). Knopf.

Iritani, Toshio. The Value of Children: a Cross-National Study: Japan, Vol. 6. LC 75-8934. 1979. pap. text ed. 3.00x (ISBN 0-8248-0387-6, Eastwest Ctr). U Pr of Hawaii.

Japan Center for International Exchange, ed. The Silent Power: Japan's Identity & World Role. 1976. 13.50x (ISBN 0-89955-245-5, Pub. by Simul). Intl Schol Bk Serv.

Japan Institute of International Affairs, ed. White Papers of Japan: Annual Abstract of Official Reports & Statistics of the Japanese Government 1978-79. LC 72-620531. (Illus.). 228p. (Orig.). 1980. pap. 37.50x (ISBN 0-8002-2734-4). Intl Pubns Serv.

Kinmonth, Earl H. The Self-Made Man in Meija Japanese Thought: From Samurai to Salary Man. LC 80-17984. (Illus.). 400p. 1981. 22.50x (ISBN 0-520-04159-3). U of Cal Pr.

Kobayashi, Tetzuya. Society, Schools & Progress in Japan. 222p. 1976. text ed. 23.00 (ISBN 0-08-019936-4); pap. text ed. 12.25 (ISBN 0-08-019935-6). Pergamon.

Land Improvement Investment & Agricultural Enterprises in Japan: As Seen in the Azusa River System. 36p. 1980. pap. 5.00 (ISBN 92-808-0088-4, TUNU-059, UNU). Unipub.

Lee, Changsoo & DeVos, George. Koreans in Japan: Ethnic Conflict & Accommodation. LC 80-6053. (Illus.). 448p. 1981. 30.00x (ISBN 0-520-04258-1). U of Cal Pr.

Levy, Howard S. Japanese Sex Crimes in Modern Times. (Asian Folklore & Social Life Monograph: No. 76). 1975. 5.00 (ISBN 0-89986-070-2). E Langstaff.

Maitra, Priyatosh. Underdevelopment Revisited. 1977. 7.00x (ISBN 0-8364-0075-5). South Asia Bks.

Marginalization of Peoples: Racial Oppression in Japan, Political Repression in South Korea, Economic Slavery in Brazil. LC 74-21709. (International Documentation Ser.: No. 65). 1974. pap. 3.95 (ISBN 0-89021-029-2). IDOC.

Minear, Richard. Through Japanese Eyes, Vol. 2: The Present: Coping with Affluence. rev. ed. Clark, Leon E., ed. (Illus.). 156p. (gr. 9-12). 1981. pap. 5.95 (ISBN 0-938960-05-9). CITE.

Minear, Richard H. Through Japanese Eyes, Vol. 1: Past: the Road from Isolation. rev. ed. Clark, Leon E., ed. (Illus.). 156p. (gr. 9-12). 1981. pap. 5.95 (ISBN 0-938960-04-0). CITE.

Mishima, Sumio. The Broader Way: A Woman's Life in the New Japan. LC 74-138596. vi, 247p. Repr. of 1953 ed. lib. bdg. 15.00 (ISBN 0-8371-5797-8, MIBW). Greenwood.

Ogyu Sorai. Political Writings. McEwan, J. R., ed. 1962. 29.95 (ISBN 0-521-05627-6). Cambridge U Pr.

Ohtani, Sueyoshi. Who Is to Be Tried? Incident at Sagamihara. 1979. 15.50 (ISBN 0-932082-00-9, Pub. by ITS Info). Intl Schol Bk Serv.

Olson, Lawrence. Dimensions of Japan. LC 63-14762. 1963. text ed. 6.50 (ISBN 0-910116-56-3). Am U Field.

Pezeu-Massabuau, Jacques. The Japanese Islands: A Physical & Social Geography. Blum, Paul C., tr. LC 77-82140. (Illus.). 1978. 12.50 (ISBN 0-8048-1184-9). C E Tuttle.

Scheiner, Irwin. Christian Converts & Social Protest in Meiji Japan. LC 74-94981. (Center for Japanese & Korean Studies, UC Berkeley). 1970. 22.75x (ISBN 0-520-01585-1). U of Cal Pr.

A Selected Bibliography of Socio-Economic Development of Japan: Part B Sixteen Hundred to Nineteen Forty. 156p. 1980. pap. 5.00 (ISBN 92-808-0199-6, TUNU094, UNU). Unipub.

Sethi, S. Prakash. Japanese Business & Social Conflict: A Comparative Analysis of Response Patterns with American Business. LC 74-22196. 1975. text ed. 18.50 (ISBN 0-88410-274-2). Ballinger Pub.

Shusaku Endo. When I Whistle. Gessel, Van C., tr. from Japanese. LC 79-13183. 1979. 8.95 (ISBN 0-8008-8243-1). Taplinger.

Smith, Thomas C. The Agrarian Origins of Modern Japan. LC 59-7429. 1959. 12.50x (ISBN 0-8047-0530-5); pap. 4.95x (ISBN 0-8047-0531-3). Stanford U Pr.

--Nakahara: Family Farming & Population in a Japanese Village, 1717-1830. LC 76-14273. 1977. 10.00x (ISBN 0-8047-0928-9). Stanford U Pr.

Takizawa, Matsuyo. Penetration of Money Economy in Japan & Its Effects Upon Social & Political Institutions. LC 68-54302. (Columbia University. Studies in the Social Sciences: No. 285). Repr. of 1927 ed. 16.50 (ISBN 0-404-51285-2). AMS Pr.

Tsurumi, Kazuko. Social Change & the Individual: Japan Before & After Defeat in World War 2. 1970. 30.00x (ISBN 0-691-09347-4). Princeton U Pr.

Uyeda, Teijiro. The Growth of Population & Occupational Changes in Japan, 1920-1935. LC 75-30087. Repr. of 1936 ed. 12.50 (ISBN 0-404-59568-5). AMS Pr.

Vogel, Ezra F. Japan's New Middle Class: The Salary Man & His Family in a Tokyo Suburb. new enl. ed. 1971. 24.50x (ISBN 0-520-02092-8); pap. 6.95x (ISBN 0-520-02100-2, CAMPUS72). U of Cal Pr.

White, James W. & Munger, Frank, eds. Social Change & Community Politics in Urban Japan. LC 77-851. (Comparative Urban Studies Monograph: No. 4). (Illus.). 1976. pap. text ed. 4.00 (ISBN 0-89143-047-4). U NC Inst Res Soc Sci.

Yamagata, Hajime. The Ugly Japanese. LC 78-9938. 1979. 7.95 (ISBN 0-533-03828-6). Vantage.

Yazaki, Takeo. Social Change & the City in Japan: From Earliest Times Through the Industrial Revolution. Swain, David L., tr. LC 67-28969. (Illus.). 1968. 19.50 (ISBN 0-87040-117-3). Japan Pubns.

Yoshimura, H. & Kobayashi, S, eds. Physiological Adaptability & Nutritional Status of the Japanese (A) (Japan International Biological Program Synthetics Ser.: Vol. 3). 1975. pap. 32.50x (ISBN 0-86008-213-X, Pub. by U of Tokyo Pr). Intl Schol Bk Serv.

Yutaka, Hibino. Nippon Shindo Ron; or the National Ideals of the Japanese People. McKenzie, A. P., tr. from Japanese. LC 79-4914. 1980. Repr. of 1928 ed. 19.00 (ISBN 0-88355-964-1). Hyperion Conn.

JAPAN–SOCIAL LIFE AND CUSTOMS

Anesaki, Masaharu. Art, Life & Nature in Japan. LC 77-109705. (Illus.). 1971. Repr. of 1933 ed. lib. bdg. 15.00 (ISBN 0-8371-4196-6, ANNJ). Greenwood.

--History of Japanese Religion. LC 63-19395. 1963. Repr. of 1930 ed. 19.50 (ISBN 0-8048-0248-3). C E Tuttle.

Bacon, A. Japanese Girls & Women. 69.95 (ISBN 0-87968-253-1). Gordon Pr.

Beauchamp, Edward R. Learning to Be Japanese: Selected Readings on Japanese Society & Education. 1978. 29.50 (ISBN 0-208-01717-8, Linnet). Shoe String.

Ben-Dasan, Isaiah. The Japanese & the Jews. Gage, Richard L., tr. from Japanese. LC 72-78951. 193p. 1981. pap. 4.95 (ISBN 0-8348-0158-2). Weatherhill.

Benedict, Ruth. Chrysanthemum & the Sword: Patterns of Japanese Culture. 1967. pap. 5.95 (ISBN 0-452-00561-2, F561, Mer). NAL.

Borton, Hugh. Japan Since Nineteen Thirty-One, Its Political & Social Developments. LC 73-3922. 168p. 1973. Repr. of 1940 ed. lib. bdg. 15.00x (ISBN 0-8371-6859-7, BOJA). Greenwood.

Cleaver, Charles G. Japanese & Americans: Cultural Parallels & Paradoxes. 1976. 12.75x (ISBN 0-8166-0761-3). U of Minn Pr.

DeMente, Boye. Bachelor's Japan. LC 67-11428. (Orig.). 1967. pap. 5.95 (ISBN 0-8048-0052-9). C E Tuttle.

DeVos, George A. Socialization for Achievement: Essays on the Cultural Psychology of the Japanese. LC 78-132420. 613p. 1973. pap. 12.95x (ISBN 0-520-02893-7). U of Cal Pr.

Dore, Ronald P. Shinohata: A Portrait of a Japanese Village. LC 78-51791. (Illus.). 1978. 11.95 (ISBN 0-394-46180-0). Pantheon.

--Shinohata: Portrait of a Japanese Village. (Pantheon Village Ser.). 1980. pap. 4.95 (ISBN 0-394-73843-8). Pantheon.

Dunn, Charles J. Everyday Life in Traditional Japan. (Illus.). 1977. pap. 5.25 (ISBN 0-8048-1229-2). C E Tuttle.

Eliot, Alexander. Zen Edge. 1979. 3.95 (ISBN 0-8164-9355-3). Continuum.

Embree, John F. Suye Mura: A Japanese Village. LC 40-1477. (Illus.). 1939. 15.00x (ISBN 0-226-20631-9). U of Chicago Pr.

--Suye Mura: A Japanese Village. LC 40-1477. (Illus.). 1964. pap. 3.25 (ISBN 0-226-20632-7, P173, Phoen). U of Chicago Pr.

Faulds, Henry. Nine Years in Nipon: Sketches of Japanese Life & Manners. LC 72-82092. (Japan Library Ser.). 1973. Repr. of 1885 ed. lib. bdg. 17.00 (ISBN 0-8420-1388-1). Scholarly Res Inc.

The Floating World: An Evocation of Old Japan. (Illus.). 1979. pap. 6.95 (ISBN 0-87663-993-7). Universe.

Fukutake, Tadashi. Japanese Rural Society. Dore, R. P., tr. from Japanese. (Illus.). 230p. 1972. pap. 5.95 (ISBN 0-8014-9127-4, CP127). Cornell U Pr.

--Japanese Society Today. Staff of the Japan Interpreter, tr. from Japanese. 220p. 1974. 12.50x (ISBN 0-86008-113-3, Pub. by U of Tokyo Pr). Intl Schol Bk Serv.

Gunston, David. Finding Out About the Japanese. Date not set. 10.75x (ISBN 0-392-09284-0, SpS). Sportshelf.

Haraguchi, Torao, et al, trs. from Jap. The Status System & Social Organization of Satsuma. LC 75-15936. 271p. 1975. text ed. 17.50x (ISBN 0-8248-0390-6). U Pr of Hawaii.

Havens, Thomas R. Valley of Darkness: The Japanese People & World War Two. (Illus.). 1978. 12.95x (ISBN 0-393-05656-2). Norton.

Hawley, W. M. Mon: The Japanese Family Crest. 1976. 17.50 (ISBN 0-685-65135-5, 910704-57). Hawley.

Hearn, Lafcadio. Kokoro: Hints & Echoes of Japanese Inner Life. Repr. of 1896 ed. lib. bdg. 17.00x (ISBN 0-8371-1633-3, HEKO). Greenwood.

--Kokoro: Hints & Echoes of Japanese Inner Life. LC 79-184814. 1972. pap. 5.25 (ISBN 0-8048-1035-4). C E Tuttle.

Hidaka, Noboru. Japanese Art of Lovemaking. 1980. 10.00 (ISBN 0-533-04490-1). Vantage.

Hidaka, Noburu. Oshun: Japanese Erotica. 128p. 1981. 8.95 (ISBN 0-89962-225-9). Todd & Honeywell.

Ishida, Takeshi. Japanese Society. 7.50 (ISBN 0-8446-4562-1). Peter Smith.

Jippensha, Ikku. Shank's Mare. LC 60-14370. (Illus.). 1960. pap. 8.25 (ISBN 0-8048-0524-5). C E Tuttle.

Jitsupenshva. The Traditional Japanese Annual Brothel Festival. (Asian Folklore & Social Life Monographs: Vol. 99). 1977. 4.50 (ISBN 0-89986-329-9). E Langstaff.

Johnson, Thomas W. Shonendan: Adolescent Peer Group Socialization in Rural Japan. (Asian Folklore & Social Life Monographs: No. 68). 304p. 1975. 7.00 (ISBN 0-89986-063-X). E Langstaff.

Kawasaki, Ichiro. Japanese Are Like That. LC 55-10620. (YA) (gr. 9 up). 1955. pap. 4.95 (ISBN 0-8048-0281-5). C E Tuttle.

Keith, Agnes N. Before the Blossoms Fall: Life & Death in Japan. (352). 1975. 8.95 (ISBN 0-316-48630-2, Pub. by Atlantic Monthly Pr.). Little.

Knox, G. Japanese Life in Town & Country. 59.95 (ISBN 0-8490-0435-7). Gordon Pr.

Koschmann, J. Victor, ed. Authority & the Individual in Japan. 1978. 19.50x (ISBN 0-86008-238-5, Pub. by U of Tokyo Pr). Intl Schol Bk Serv.

Lebra, Takie S. Japanese Patterns of Behavior. LC 76-110392. 1976. pap. text ed. 5.95x (ISBN 0-8248-0460-0, Eastwest Ctr). U Pr of Hawaii.

Levy, Howard S. Oriental Sex Manners. 1978. text ed. 7.50 (ISBN 0-685-67212-3). Langstaff-Levy Ent.

Lewin, B. Kleines Woerterbuch der Japanologie. 596p. (Ger. & Japan.). 1968. 38.00 (ISBN 3-447-00530-0, M-7512, Pub. by Harrassowitz). French & Eur.

Lewis, Brenda R. Growing up in Samarai Japan. (Growing up Ser.). (Illus.). 72p. (gr. 7-10). 1981. 14.95 (ISBN 0-7134-3572-0, Pub. by Batsford England). David & Charles.

Lowell, Percival. Occult Japan. 59.95 (ISBN 0-8490-0750-X). Gordon Pr.

Matsuhara, Iwao. On Life & Nature in Japan. (Illus.). 1964. 14.95 (ISBN 0-89346-077-X, Pub. by Hokuseido Pr). Heian Intl.

Matsuoka, Yoko. Daughter of the Pacific. LC 72-12634. 245p. 1973. Repr. of 1952 ed. lib. bdg. 15.00 (ISBN 0-8371-6683-7, MADP). Greenwood.

Mears, Helen. Year of the Wild Boar. LC 73-7457. 346p. 1973. Repr. of 1942 ed. lib. bdg. 15.75x (ISBN 0-8371-6936-4, MEWB). Greenwood.

Mikes, George. Land of the Rising Yen: Japan. LC 70-118214. (Illus.). 1970. 5.95 (ISBN 0-87645-026-5). Gambit.

Miller, Richard J. Ancient Japanese Nobility: The Kabane Ranking System. (Publications in Occasional Papers, Vol. 7). 1974. pap. 15.75x (ISBN 0-520-09494-8). U of Cal Pr.

Miller, William J. The Japanese World. LC 76-62691. (World of Asia Ser.). (Illus.). 1977. pap. text ed. 3.95x (ISBN 0-88273-501-2). Forum Pr MO.

Milward, Peter. Oddities in Modern Japan: Observations of an Outsider. (Illus.). viii, 187p. 1980. pap. 11.50 (ISBN 0-89346-183-0, Pub. by Hokuseido Pr). Heian Intl.

Morse, Edward S. Japanese Homes & Their Surroundings. (Illus.). 1961. pap. 5.00 (ISBN 0-486-20746-3). Dover.

Morse, Edwards S. Japan Day by Day: 1877-78-79, 1882-3. LC 17-28348. (Illus.). 1978. lib. bdg. 35.00 (ISBN 0-910220-93-X). Larlin Corp.

Munro, Neil G. Prehistoric Japan. (Illus.). 1971. Repr. of 1911 ed. 49.00 (ISBN 0-384-40565-7). Johnson Repr.

Nagai, Kafu. Geisha in Rivalry. Meissner, Kurt, tr. LC 63-7963. (Illus.). 1963. pap. 5.75 (ISBN 0-8048-0204-1). C E Tuttle.

Nakane, Chie. Japanese Society. LC 71-100021. (Center for Japanese & Korean Studies, UC Berkeley). 1970. 17.50x (ISBN 0-520-01642-4); pap. 5.95x (ISBN 0-520-02154-1, CAMPUS74). U of Cal Pr.

Norbeck, Edward. Changing Japan. 2nd ed. LC 76-2709. 1976. pap. text ed. 4.95 (ISBN 0-03-017546-1, HoltC). HR&W.

Norbeck, Edward & Parman, Susan, eds. Study of Japan in the Behavioral Sciences. (Rice University Studies: Vol. 56, No. 4). 309p. 1970. pap. 3.25x (ISBN 0-89263-206-2). Rice Univ.

Ohtani, Sueyoshi. Who Is to Be Tried? Incident at Sagamihara. 1979. 15.50 (ISBN 0-932082-00-9, Pub. by ITS Info). Intl Schol Bk Serv.

Perrin, Noel. Giving up the Gun: Japan's Reversion to the Sword, 1543-1879. LC 78-74252. (Illus.). 1979. 10.00 (ISBN 0-87923-278-1). Godine.
Plath, David W. Long Engagements: Maturity in Modern Japan. LC 79-65181. 248p. 1980. 17.50x (ISBN 0-8047-1054-6). Stanford U Pr.
Rebischung, James. Japan: The Facts of Modern Business & Social Life. LC 74-15653. (Illus.). 1975. pap. 4.25 (ISBN 0-8048-1147-4, Tut Bks). C E Tuttle.
Sansom, George. Japan: A Short Cultural History. rev. ed. LC 77-76152. (Illus.). 1952. 18.75x (ISBN 0-8047-0952-1); pap. 8.95 (ISBN 0-8047-0954-8, SP141). Stanford U Pr.
Shiso-no, Kagako Kenkyo Kai. Japanese Popular Culture. LC 73-1434. (Illus.). 223p. 1973. Repr. of 1959 ed. lib. bdg. 15.00 (ISBN 0-8371-6792-2, SHJP). Greenwood.
Shonagon, Sei. Pillow Book of Sei Shonagon. Morris, Ivan, tr. (Classics Ser). 1971. pap. 3.95 (ISBN 0-14-044236-7). Penguin.
Shusaku Endo. When I Whistle. Gessel, Van C., tr. from Japanese. LC 79-13183. 1979. 8.95 (ISBN 0-8008-8243-1). Taplinger.
Sladen, Douglas. Queer Things About Japan, to Which Is Added a Life of the Emperor of Japan. 4th ed. LC 68-26607. (Illus.). 1968. Repr. of 1913 ed. 24.00 (ISBN 0-8103-3500-X). Gale.
Smith, Neil S. Materials on Japanese Social & Economic History: Tokugawa, Japan. (Studies in Japanese History & Civilization). 176p. 1979. Repr. of 1937 ed. 19.50 (ISBN 0-89093-262-X). U Pubns Amer.
Snider, Lois. Snow Pearl, a Girl of Japan. (Illus.). 1977. pap. 2.45 (ISBN 0-89367-013-8). Light & Life.
Stewart, Basil. A Guide to Japanese Prints & Their Subject Matter. (Illus.). 1979. pap. 10.00 (ISBN 0-486-23809-1). Dover.
Sugimoto, Etsu I. Daughter of the Samurai. LC 66-15849. (gr. 9 up). 1966. 15.50 (ISBN 0-8048-0136-3). C E Tuttle.
--A Daughter of the Samurai. 1934. 20.00 (ISBN 0-685-72785-8). Norwood Edns.
Sutphen, Dick & Sutphen, Trenna. Bushido SST Graduate Manual. 1981. 5.95 (ISBN 0-911842-28-4). Valley Sun.
Suzuki, Takao. Japanese & the Japanese: Words in Culture. Miura, Akira, tr. LC 77-15296. 152p. 1978. 10.95 (ISBN 0-87011-325-9). Kodansha.
Swaan, Wim. Japanese Lantern. LC 67-10333. (Illus.). 1970. 8.95 (ISBN 0-8008-4300-2). Taplinger.
Tames, Richard. Japan Today. Date not set. 12.50x (ISBN 0-7182-0454-9, SpS). Sportshelf.
Vining, Elizabeth G. Windows for the Crown Prince: An American Woman's Four Years As Private Tutor to the Crown Prince of Japan. (Illus.). (gr. 7-9). 1952. 9.95 (ISBN 0-397-00037-5). Lippincott.
Von Siebold, Philipp, et al. Manners & Customs of the Japanese in the Nineteenth Century. LC 72-83676. 320p. 1980. pap. 3.50 (ISBN 0-8048-1081-8). C E Tuttle.
Watanabe, S., et al, eds. Anthropological & Genetic Studies on the Japanese. (Japan International Biological Program Synthetics Ser.: Vol. 2). 1975. pap. 41.00x (ISBN 0-86008-212-1, Pub. by U of Tokyo Pr). Intl Schol Bk Serv.
Whitney, Clara A. Clara's Diary: An American Girl in Meiji Japan. LC 80-85385. (Illus.). 356p. 1981. pap. 5.95 (ISBN 0-87011-470-0). Kodansha.
Williams, Harold S. Foreigners in Mikadoland. LC 58-11102. (Illus.). 310p. 1972. pap. 2.95 (ISBN 0-8048-1049-4). C E Tuttle.
Yamamoto, Yoshiko. The Namahage: A Festival in the Northeast of Japan. LC 78-1500. (Illus.). 1978. text ed. 16.00x (ISBN 0-915980-66-5). Inst Study Human.
Yamamura, Kozo. A Study of Samurai Income & Entrepreneurship. LC 73-87378. (East Asian Ser.: No. 76). 256p. 1974. text ed. 14.00x (ISBN 0-674-85322-9). Harvard U Pr.

JAPAN–SOCIAL LIFE AND CUSTOMS–FICTION

Fraser, Mary. Custom of the Country. LC 70-101811. (Short Story Index Reprint Ser.). 1899. 17.00 (ISBN 0-8369-3199-8). Arno.

JAPAN EXPEDITION OF THE AMERICAN SQUADRON, 1852-1854

see United States Naval Expedition to Japan, 1852-1854

JAPANESE ARCHITECTURE

see Architecture–Japan

JAPANESE ART

see Art, Japanese

JAPANESE ASTRONOMY

see Astronomy, Japanese

JAPANESE BALLADS AND SONGS

see also Folk-Songs, Japanese

JAPANESE BEETLE

Climatic Aspects of the Possible Establishment of the Japanese Beetle in Europe. (Technical Note Ser.). pap. 11.00 (ISBN 0-685-57275-7, WMO). Unipub.

JAPANESE CHESS

see Chinese Chess

JAPANESE-CHINESE CONFLICT, 1937-1945

see Sino-Japanese Conflict, 1937-1945

JAPANESE COLOR PRINTS

see Color Prints, Japanese

JAPANESE DRAMA

see also Kabuki; Kyogen Plays; No Plays

Araki, James T. The Ballad-Drama of Medieval Japan. LC 76-50314. 1977. pap. 4.25 (ISBN 0-8048-1279-9). C E Tuttle.
Edwards, O. Japanese Plays & Playfellows. lib. bdg. 59.95 (ISBN 0-87968-517-4). Krishna Pr.
Ernst, Earle, ed. Three Japanese Plays from the Traditional Theatre. LC 75-31473. (Illus.). 200p. 1976. Repr. of 1959 ed. lib. bdg. 15.00x (ISBN 0-8371-8532-7, ERTJ). Greenwood.
Mushakoji, S. Passion, & Three Other Japanese Plays. Hidaka, Noboru, tr. from Jap. LC 77-98859. 1971. Repr. of 1933 ed. lib. bdg. 15.00 (ISBN 0-8371-3130-8, MUJP). Greenwood.
Pronko, Leonard C. Guide to Japanese Drama. (Reference Bks.). 132p. 1973. lib. bdg. 9.50 (ISBN 0-8161-1108-1). G K Hall.
Takaya, Ted T., tr. from Japanese. Modern Japanese Drama: An Anthology. LC 79-4288. 277p. 1980. pap. 10.00 (ISBN 0-231-04684-7); pap. 9.95 (ISBN 0-231-04685-5). Columbia U Pr.
Yamanobe, T. Noh-Shozoku Monyoshu. (Illus.). 1969. text ed. 90.00x (ISBN 0-8002-1756-X). Intl Pubns Serv.

JAPANESE DRAMA–HISTORY AND CRITICISM

Bowers, Faubion. Japanese Theatre. LC 76-46. (Illus.). 294p. 1976. Repr. of 1952 ed. lib. bdg. 22.50x (ISBN 0-8371-8659-5, BOJT). Greenwood.
Brandon, James R., ed. On Thrones of Gold: Three Javanese Shadow Plays. LC 73-88802. (Illus.). 1970. 20.00x (ISBN 0-674-63775-5). Harvard U Pr.

JAPANESE DRAMA–TRANSLATIONS INTO ENGLISH

Duran, Leo. Plays of Old Japan. LC 73-476. 1973. lib. bdg. 15.00 (ISBN 0-8414-1487-4). Folcroft.
Iwaski, Yozant & Hughes, Glenn, eds. Three Modern Japanese Plays. LC 76-40387. (One-Act Plays in Reprint Ser.). 1976. Repr. of 1923 ed. 12.50x (ISBN 0-8486-2003-8). Core Collection.
Keene, Donald, ed. Twenty Plays of the No Theatre. Tyler, et al, trs. from Japanese. LC 74-121556. (Records of Civilization Sources & Studies & Translations of the Oriental Classics Ser.). 336p. 1970. 22.50x (ISBN 0-231-03454-7); pap. 12.00x (ISBN 0-231-03455-5). Columbia U Pr.
Mushakoji, S. Passion, & Three Other Japanese Plays. Hidaka, Noboru, tr. from Jap. LC 77-98859. 1971. Repr. of 1933 ed. lib. bdg. 15.00 (ISBN 0-8371-3130-8, MUJP). Greenwood.
Noh Drama: Ten Plays from the Japanese. LC 60-11007. 1960. 7.95 (ISBN 0-8048-0428-1). C E Tuttle.
Rimer, J. Thomas, ed. Mask & Sword: Two Plays for the Contemporary Japanese Theater. (Modern Asian Literature Ser.). (Illus.). 1980. 20.00x (ISBN 0-231-04932-3). Columbia U Pr.
Sakanishi, Shio, tr. Japanese Folk Plays: The Ink Smeared Lady & Other Kyogen. (Illus.). 1960. pap. 2.95 (ISBN 0-8048-0297-1). C E Tuttle.

JAPANESE DRAWINGS

see Drawings, Japanese

JAPANESE EMPERORS

see Japan–Emperors

JAPANESE FENCING

see Kendo

JAPANESE FICTION–HISTORY AND CRITICISM

Hibbett, Howard. The Floating World in Japanese Fiction. facsimile ed. LC 70-126238. (Select Bibliographies Ser). Repr. of 1959 ed. 18.00 (ISBN 0-8369-5465-3). Arno.
Kimball, Arthur G. Crisis in Identity & Contemporary Japanese Novels. LC 72-91549. 1972. 6.00 (ISBN 0-8048-1090-7). C E Tuttle.
Morrison, John. Modern Japanese Fiction. LC 75-11954. 1975. Repr. of 1955 ed. lib. bdg. 15.50x (ISBN 0-8371-8053-8, MOMJ). Greenwood.
Rimer, J. Thomas. Modern Japanese Fiction & Its Traditions: An Introduction. LC 68-51188. 1978. text ed. 20.00 (ISBN 0-691-06362-1). Princeton U Pr.

JAPANESE FLOWER ARRANGEMENT

see Flower Arrangement, Japanese

JAPANESE FOLK-LORE

see Folk-Lore, Japanese

JAPANESE FOLK-SONGS

see Folk-Songs, Japanese

JAPANESE IN FOREIGN COUNTRIES

Bailey, Thomas A. Theodore Roosevelt & the Japanese-American Crisis. 1964. 8.50 (ISBN 0-8446-1038-0). Peter Smith.
Canada Department of Labour. Two Reports on Japanese Canadians in World War II, 2 vols. in 1. Daniels, Roger, ed. LC 78-7079. (Asian Experience in North America Ser.). (Illus.). 1979. Repr. of 1947 ed. lib. bdg. 10.00x (ISBN 0-405-11266-1). Arno.
Comissao de Recenseamento da Colonia Japonesa, ed. The Japanese Immigrant in Brazil, 2 vols. 1138p. Set. 63.00x (ISBN 0-86008-069-2, Pub by U of Tokyo Pr). Intl Schol Bk Serv.
Daniels, Roger. The Politics of Prejudice: The Anti-Japanese Movement in California & the Struggle for Japanese Exclusion. 7.00 (ISBN 0-8446-1146-8). Peter Smith.
Daniels, Roger, ed. Two Monographs on Japanese Canadians. LC 78-3222. (Asian Experience in North America Ser.). 1979. lib. bdg. 12.00x (ISBN 0-405-11304-8). Arno.
Gardiner, C. Harvey. Pawns in a Triangle of Hate: The Peruvian Japanese Amd the U. S. LC 81-51278. 248p. 1981. 25.00 (ISBN 0-295-95855-3). U of Wash Pr.
Laviolette, Forrest E. Canadian Japanese & World War Two: A Sociological & Psychological Account. LC 48-11190. 1948. 32.50x (ISBN 0-8020-7052-3). U of Toronto Pr.
Mizuki, John. The Growth of Japanese Churches in Brazil. LC 78-5415. (Illus.). 1978. pap. 8.95 (ISBN 0-87808-323-5). William Carey Lib.
Nakano, Takeo U. & Nakano, Leatrice. Within the Barbed Wire Fence: A Japanese Man's Account of His Internment in Canada. (Illus.). 136p. 1981. 10.00 (ISBN 0-295-95789-1). U of Wash Pr.
Normano, Joao F. The Japanese in South America: An Introductory Survey with Special Reference to Peru. LC 75-30075. (Institute of Pacific Relations). Repr. of 1943 ed. 12.50 (ISBN 0-404-59550-2). AMS Pr.
Samuels, Frederick. The Japanese & the Haoles of Honolulu: Durable Group Interaction. 1970. 6.00 (ISBN 0-8084-0175-0); pap. 2.95 (ISBN 0-8084-0176-9, B50). Coll & U Pr.
Staniford, Philip. Pioneers in the Tropics. (London School of Economics Monographs on Social Anthropology Ser: No. 45). (Illus.). 210p. 1973. text ed. 23.50x (ISBN 0-391-00267-8, Athlone Pr). Humanities.
Sugimoto, Howard H. Japanese Immigration, the Vancouver Riots & Canadian Diplomacy. Daniels, Roger, ed. LC 78-54853. (Asian Experience in North America Ser.). 1979. lib. bdg. 20.00x (ISBN 0-405-11311-0). Arno.
Young, Charles H., et al. The Japanese Canadians. Daniels, Roger, ed. LC 78-54849. (Asian Experience in North America Ser.). 1979. Repr. of 1938 ed. lib. bdg. 22.00x (ISBN 0-405-11300-5). Arno.

JAPANESE IN KOREA

McKenzie, Frederick A. Korea's Fight for Freedom. LC 76-111784. Repr. of 1920 ed. 19.45 (ISBN 0-404-04137-X). AMS Pr.

JAPANESE IN MANCHURIA

Kawakami, K. K. Manchoukuo: Child of Conflict. LC 79-94317. Repr. of 1933 ed. 10.50 (ISBN 0-404-03639-2). AMS Pr.
Meng, Chih. China Speaks. LC 74-115205. 1971. Repr. of 1932 ed. 13.50 (ISBN 0-8046-1098-3). Kennikat.
Morley, James W. The Japanese Thrust into Siberia, 1918. LC 75-38115. (Select Bibliographies Reprint Ser). 1972. Repr. of 1957 ed. 23.00 (ISBN 0-8369-9966-5). Arno.
Rappaport, Armin. Henry L. Stimson & Japan: Nineteen Thirty One - Thirty Three. LC 63-18847. 1963. 8.50x (ISBN 0-226-70527-7). U of Chicago Pr.
Willoughby, Westel W. Sino-Japanese Controversy & the League of Nations. LC 68-54995. (Illus.). 1968. Repr. of 1935 ed. lib. bdg. 26.25x (ISBN 0-8371-0755-5, WISJ). Greenwood.
Young, Carl W. Japan's Special Position in Manchuria. LC 71-175937. Repr. of 1931 ed. 32.75 (ISBN 0-404-07072-8). AMS Pr.

JAPANESE IN THE PHILIPPINE ISLANDS

Goodman, Grant K. Davao: A Case Study in Japanese-Philippine Relations. Wickberg, Edgar, ed. LC 67-65570. (International Studies: East Asian Ser No. 1). (Orig.). 1967. pap. 4.50x (ISBN 0-685-19294-6). Paragon.

JAPANESE IN THE UNITED STATES

Araki, Nancy K. & Horii, Jane. Matsuri! Festival! Japanese American Celebrations & Activities. (Illus., Orig.). 1978. pap. 7.50 (ISBN 0-89346-019-2). Heian Intl.
Asiatic Exclusion League, 1907-1913. Proceedings. Grob, Gerald, ed. LC 76-46064. (Anti-Movements in America Ser). 1977. Repr. of 1907 ed. lib. bdg. 45.00x (ISBN 0-405-09939-8). Arno.
Bailey, Paul. City in the Sun: The Japanese Concentration Camp at Poston, Arizona. (Illus.). 8.50 (ISBN 0-87026-026-X). Westernlore.
Bell, Reginald. Public School Education of Second-Generation Japanese in California. Daniels, Roger, ed. LC 78-54808. (Asian Experience in North America Ser.). 1979. Repr. of 1935 ed. lib. bdg. 10.00x (ISBN 0-405-11264-5). Arno.
Bonacich, Edna & Modell, John. The Economic Basis of Ethnic Solidarity: A Study of Japanese Americans. LC 80-51233. 1980. 18.95x (ISBN 0-520-04155-0). U of Cal Pr.
Broom, Leonard & Riemer, Ruth. Removal & Return: The Socio-Economic Effects of the War on Japanese Americans. (California Library Reprint). 1974. 22.75x (ISBN 0-520-02522-9). U of Cal Pr.
Canada Royal Commission on Chinese & Japanese Immigration. Report of the Royal Commission on Chinese & Japanese Immigration. Daniels, Roger, ed. LC 78-54812. (Asian Experience in North America Ser.). 1979. Repr. of 1902 ed. lib. bdg. 26.00x (ISBN 0-405-11268-8). Arno.
Cole, Chery L. History of the Japanese Community in Sacramento,1883-1972. LC 74-83365. 1975. soft bdg. 10.00 (ISBN 0-685-59167-0). R & E Res Assoc.
Coman, Katherine & Lind, Andrew W. The History of Contract Labor in the Hawaiian Islands & Hawaii's Japanese, 2 vols. in 1. Daniels, Roger, ed. LC 78-54813. (Asian Experience in North America Ser.). (Illus.). 1979. Repr. of 1946 ed. lib. bdg. 22.00x (ISBN 0-405-11269-6). Arno.
Connor, John N. Tradition & Change in Three Generations of Japanese Americans. LC 76-28999. 1977. 21.95x (ISBN 0-88229-288-9). Nelson-Hall.
Connor, John W. Acculturation & the Retention of an Ethnic Identity in Three Generations of Japanese Americans. LC 75-36568. 1977. 8.00 (ISBN 0-88247-458-8). R & E Res Assoc.
Conroy, Hilary. The Japanese Frontier in Hawaii, 1868-1898. Daniels, Roger, ed. LC 78-54840. (Asian Experience in North America). 1979. Repr. of 1953 ed. lib. bdg. 11.00x (ISBN 0-405-11306-4). Arno.
Conroy, Hilary & Miyakawa, T. Scott, eds. East Across the Pacific. LC 72-77825. 322p. 1972. pap. 19.75 (ISBN 0-87436-087-0). ABC-Clio.
Daniels, Roger. The Asian Experience in North America Series: Chinese & Japanese, 47 bks. (Illus.). 1979. Repr. lib. bdg. 1162.00x set (ISBN 0-405-11261-0). Arno.
--Politics of Prejudice: The Anti-Japanese Movement in California & the Struggle for Japanese Exclusion. LC 62-63248. 1968. pap. text ed. 3.95x (ISBN 0-689-70059-8, 116). Atheneum.
--The Politics of Prejudice: The Anti-Japanese Movement in California & the Struggle for Japanese Exclusion. (California Library Reprint Ser). 1978. 18.50x (ISBN 0-520-03412-0); pap. 3.45 (ISBN 0-520-03411-2). U of Cal Pr.
Daniels, Roger, ed. Three Short Works on Japanese Americans. LC 78-3223. (Asian Experience in North America Ser.). 1978. lib. bdg. 23.00x (ISBN 0-405-11261-0). Arno.
Darsie, M. L. Mental Capacity of American-Born Japanese Children. (Comparitive Psychology Monogr.: Vol. 3, No. 15). Repr. of 1926 ed. pap. 6.00 (ISBN 0-527-24850-9). Kraus Repr.
Davis, Daniel S. Behind Barbed Wire: The Imprisonment of Japanese Americans During WWII. (Illus.). 224p. (gr. 4-7). 1981. 11.50 (ISBN 0-525-26320-9). Dutton.
--Behind Barbed Wire: The Imprisonment of Japanese Americans During WWII. (Illus.). 224p. (gr. 4-7). 1981. 11.50 (ISBN 0-525-26320-9). Dutton.
Embree, John F. Acculturation Among the Japanese of Kona, Hawaii. LC 43-1209. (American Anthropological Association Memoirs). pap. 12.00 (ISBN 0-527-00558-4). Kraus Repr.
Flowers, Montaville. The Japanese Conquest of American Opinion. Daniels, Roger, ed. LC 78-54815. (Asian Experience in North America Ser.). 1979. Repr. of 1917 ed. lib. bdg. 17.00x (ISBN 0-405-11271-8). Arno.
Fukei, Budd. The Japanese American Story. LC 75-35578. (Illus.). 160p. 1976. 6.95 (ISBN 0-87518-048-5). Dillon.
Grodzins, Morton. Americans Betrayed. (Midway Reprint Ser). xviii, 445p. 1974. pap. text ed. 17.50x (ISBN 0-226-30940-1). U of Chicago Pr.
Hansen, Arthur A. & Mitson, Betty E., eds. Voices Long Silent: An Oral Inquiry into the Japanese American Evacuation. 1974. 7.95 (ISBN 0-930046-04-8). CSUF Oral Hist.
Hata, Donald T., Jr. Undesirables, Early Immigrants & the Anti-Japanese Movement in San Francisco: 1892-1893. Daniels, Roger, ed. LC 78-54817. (Asian Experience in North American Ser.). 1979. lib. bdg. 14.00x (ISBN 0-405-11273-4). Arno.

Henry, Sheila E. Cultural Persistence & Socio-Economic Mobility: A Comparative Study of Assimilation Among Armenians & Japanese in Los Angeles. LC 77-81011. 1978. soft cover 10.00 (ISBN 0-88247-489-8). R & E Res Assoc.
Herman, Masako. The Japanese in America. LC 74-13106. (Ethnic Chronology Ser.). 160p. (gr. 9-12). 1974. text ed. 8.50 (ISBN 0-379-00512-3). Oceana.
Hosokawa, B. Thirty-Five Years in the Frying Pan. 1978. 10.95 (ISBN 0-07-030435-1, GB). McGraw.
Ichihashi, Yamato. Japanese Immigration: Its Status in California. LC 70-145484. (The American Immigration Library). 78p. 1971. Repr. of 1915 ed. lib. bdg. 7.50x (ISBN 0-89198-015-6). Ozer.
--Japanese in the United States: A Critical Study of the Problems of the Japanese Immigrants & Their Children. LC 69-18780. (American Immigration Collection Ser., No. 1). 1969. Repr. of 1932 ed. 19.00 (ISBN 0-405-00528-8). Arno.
Ishizuka, Karen. The Elder Japanese. LC 77-83483. (Elder Minority Ser). 1978. 3.50x (ISBN 0-916304-36-1). Campanile.
Iyenaga, Toyokichi & Sato, Kenosake. Japan & the California Problem. LC 72-82099. (Japan Library Ser.). 1972. Repr. of 1921 ed. lib. bdg. 16.00 (ISBN 0-8420-1393-8). Scholarly Res Inc.
Japanese General-Consulate. Documental History of Law Cases Affecting Japanese in the United States, 1916-1924, 2 vols. Daniels, Roger, ed. LC 78-54818. (Asian Experience in North America Ser.). 1979. Repr. of 1925 ed. Set. lib. bdg. 85.00x (ISBN 0-405-11274-2). Arno.
Kashima, Tetsuden. Buddhism in America: The Social Organization of an Ethnic Religious Institution. LC 76-57837. (Contributions in Sociology: No. 26). (Illus.). 1977. lib. bdg. 18.95 (ISBN 0-8371-9534-9, KSO/). Greenwood.
Kawakami, Kiyoshi K. The Real Japanese Question. Daniels, Roger, ed. LC 78-54819. (Asian Experience in North America Ser.). 1979. Repr. of 1921 ed. lib. bdg. 17.00x (ISBN 0-405-11275-0). Arno.
Kehr, Eckart. Economic Interest, Militarism, & Foreign Policy: Essays on German History. Craig, Gordon A., ed. Heinz, Grete, tr. from Ger. LC 74-22964. 1977. 21.50x (ISBN 0-520-02880-5). U of Cal Pr.
Kiefer, Christie W. Changing Cultures, Changing Lives: An Ethnographic Study of Three Generations of Japanese Americans. LC 74-3609. (Social & Behavioral Science Ser.). 256p. 1974. 17.95x (ISBN 0-87589-232-9). Jossey-Bass.
Kikomura, Akiko. Michiko: The Story of a Japanese Immigrant Woman. 160p. 1981. 10.00 (ISBN 0-88316-544-9); pap. 5.95 (ISBN 0-88316-543-0). Chandler & Sharp.
Kitagawa, D. Issei & Nisei: The Internment Years. 1967. pap. 3.95 (ISBN 0-8164-9244-1). Continuum.
Kitano, H. H. Japanese Americans: Evolution of a Subculture. 2nd ed. (Ethnic Groups in American Life Ser.). 224p. 1976. Ref. Ed. 11.95 (ISBN 0-13-509430-5); pap. 8.95 (ISBN 0-13-509422-4). P-H.
LaViolette, Forrest E. Americans of Japanese Ancestry. Daniels, Roger, ed. LC 78-54822. (Asian Experience in North America Ser.). 1979. Repr. of 1945 ed. lib. bdg. 13.00x (ISBN 0-405-11278-5). Arno.
Leathers, Noel L. Japanese in America. LC 67-15684. (In America Bks.). (Illus.). (gr. 5-11). 1967. PLB 6.95g (ISBN 0-8225-0211-9). Lerner Pubns.
Levine, Gene M. & Rhodes, Robert C. The Japanese-American Community: A Three-Generation Study. 256p. 1981. 23.95 (ISBN 0-03-055691-0). Praeger.
Lyman, Stanford M. The Asian in North America. LC 77-9095. 299p. 1977. text ed. 17.50 (ISBN 0-87436-254-7). ABC-Clio.
McClatchy, Valentine S. Four Anti-Japanese Pamphlets: An Original Anthology. Daniels, Roger, ed. LC 78-7080. (Asian Experience in North America Ser.). 1979. lib. bdg. 18.00x (ISBN 0-405-11282-3). Arno.
McWilliams, Carey. Prejudice: Japanese-Americans, Symbol of Racial Intolerance. LC 77-122415. 1971. Repr. of 1944 ed. 22.50 (ISBN 0-208-01087-4, Archon). Shoe String.
Matsuda, Mitsugu. Japanese in Hawaii: An Annotated Bibliography. (Social Science & Linguistics Institute Special Publications). 1975. pap. 7.00x (ISBN 0-8248-0290-X). U Pr of Hawaii.
Melendy, H. Brett. The Oriental Americans. 1972. pap. 3.95x (ISBN 0-88254-016-5). Hippocrene Bks.
Millis, H. A. The Japanese Problem in the United States. Daniels, Roger, ed. LC 78-54828. (Asian Experience in North America Ser.). (Illus.). 1979. Repr. of 1915 ed. lib. bdg. 21.00x (ISBN 0-405-11285-8). Arno.
Miyamoto, Kazuo. Hawaii: The End of the Rainbow. LC 63-20213. 1964. pap. 5.25 (ISBN 0-8048-0233-5). C E Tuttle.
Modell, John. The Economics & Politics of Racial Accomodation: The Japanese of Los Angeles, 1900-1942. LC 77-6749. 1977. 12.50 (ISBN 0-252-00622-4). U of Ill Pr.
Montero, Darrel. Japanese Americans: Changing Patterns of Ethnic Affiliation Over Three Generations. LC 79-9428. (Westview Special Studies in Contemporary Social Issues). (Illus.). 172p. 1980. lib. bdg. 20.00 (ISBN 0-89158-595-8). Westview.
Myer, Dillon S. Uprooted Americans: The Japanese Americans & the War Relocation Authority. LC 76-125169. (Illus.). 448p. 1971. pap. 5.95 (ISBN 0-8165-0402-4). U of Ariz Pr.
Naka, Kaizo. Social & Economic Conditions Among Japanese Farmers in California: Thesis. LC 70-155202. 1974. Repr. of 1913 ed. soft bdg. 7.00 (ISBN 0-88247-270-4). R & E Res Assoc.
Nettler, Gwynne. The Relationship Between Attitude & Information Concerning the Japanese in America. Zuckerman, Harriet & Merton, Robert K., eds. LC 79-9016. (Dissertations in Sociology Ser.). 1980. lib. bdg. 16.00x (ISBN 0-405-12984-X). Arno.
O'Brien, Robert W. & Daniels, Roger. The College Nisei. LC 78-54829. (Asian Experience in North America Ser.). (Illus.). 1979. Repr. of 1949 ed. lib. bdg. 10.00x (ISBN 0-405-11286-6). Arno.
Oda, James. Heroic Struggles of Japanese Americans: Partisan Fighters from America's Concentration Camps. 275p. 1980. 14.00 (ISBN 0-686-30106-4); softcover 9.00 (ISBN 0-686-31779-3). Oda.
Ogawa, Dennis M. Jan Ken Po: The World of Hawaii's Japanese Americans. new ed. LC 78-9513. (Illus.). 1978. pap. 3.95 (ISBN 0-8248-0398-1). U Pr of Hawaii.
Ogawa, Dennis M. & Grant, Glen. Kodomo No Tame Ni-for the Sake of the Children: The Japanese American Experience in Hawaii. LC 77-18368. 1978. 15.00 (ISBN 0-8248-0528-3). U Pr of Hawaii.
Penrose, Eldon R. California Nativism: Organized Opposition to the Japanese, 1890-1913. LC 73-82389. lib. bdg. 10.00 (ISBN 0-88247-228-3). R & E Res Assoc.
Smith, Bradford. Americans from Japan. LC 72-12629. (Illus.). 409p. 1974. Repr. of 1948 ed. lib. bdg. 19.25x (ISBN 0-8371-6679-9, SMAJ). Greenwood.
Sone, Monica. Nisei Daughter. LC 79-4921. 1979. pap. 5.95 (ISBN 0-295-95688-7). U of Wash Pr.
Stearns, Marjorie R. The History of the Japanese People in Oregon: Thesis. LC 73-166060. 1974. soft bdg. 8.00 (ISBN 0-88247-251-8). R & E Res Assoc.
Steiner, Jesse F. The Japanese Invasion. Daniels, Roger, ed. LC 78-54831. (Asian Experience in North America Ser.). (Illus.). 1979. Repr. of 1917 ed. lib. bdg. 15.00x (ISBN 0-405-11288-2). Arno.
Strong, Edward K., Jr. Second-Generation Japanese Problem. LC 73-129415. (American Immigration Collection, Ser. 2). 1970. Repr. of 1934 ed. 18.00 (ISBN 0-405-00569-5). Arno.
Thomas, Dorothy S. The Salvage. 1975. Repr. of 1952 ed. 28.50x (ISBN 0-520-02915-1). U of Cal Pr.
Thomas, Dorothy S. & Nishimoto, Richard. The Spoilage: Japanese-American Evacuation & Resettlement During World War Two. (California Library Reprint Ser.). 1974. Repr. 24.75x (ISBN 0-520-02637-3). U of Cal Pr.
U. S. Dept. of State & Morris, Roland. Report on Japanese Immigration & Alleged Discrimatory Legislation Against Japanese Residents in the U. S. Daniels, Roger, ed. LC 78-7081. (Asian Experience in North American Ser.). 1979. Repr. of 1921 ed. lib. bdg. 17.00x (ISBN 0-405-11295-5). Arno.
U.S. House of Representatives, Committee on Immigration & Naturalization. Japanese Immigration. Daniels, Roger, ed. LC 78-54834. (Asian Experience in North America Ser.). 1979. Repr. of 1921 ed. lib. bdg. 86.00x (ISBN 0-405-11292-0). Arno.
Wax, Rosalie H. Doing Fieldwork: Warnings & Advice. 1971. text ed. 15.00x (ISBN 0-226-86949-0, Phoen); pap. 4.95 (ISBN 0-226-86950-4, Phoen). U of Chicago Pr.
Wilson, Robert A. & Hosokawa, Bill. East to America: A History of the Japanese in the United States. LC 80-12139. (Illus.). 352p. 1980. 12.95 (ISBN 0-688-03695-3). Morrow.

JAPANESE LANGUAGE

Akiyama, Nubuo. SR Japanese. (SR Japanese Ser.). 1970. pap. text ed. 4.95 (ISBN 0-88499-125-3); tapebk. 3.95 (ISBN 0-88499-126-1); cassette set 135.00 (ISBN 0-88499-199-7); tape set 295.00 (ISBN 0-88499-198-9). Inst Mod Lang.
Chew, John J., Jr. Transformational Analysis of Modern Colloquial Japanese. (Janua Linguarum Ser. Practica: No. 56). 1974. pap. text ed. 36.25x (ISBN 90-2792-597-6). Mouton.
Fujiwara, Yoichi. A Linguistic Atlas of the Seto & Inland Sea, 2 vols. Incl. Vol. 1. Pronunciation. (Illus.). 142p. 195.00x (ISBN 0-86008-123-0); Vol. 2. Grammar. (Illus.). 150p. 215.00x (ISBN 0-86008-124-9). (Illus., Eng. & Jap.). 1975 (Pub. by U of Tokyo Pr). Intl Schol Bk Serv.
--The Sentence Structure of Japanese: Viewed in the Light of Dialectology. Brannen, Noah & Baird, Scott, trs. from Japanese. LC 73-78976. 156p. 1973. text ed. 9.00x (ISBN 0-8248-0275-6). U Pr of Hawaii.
Gardner, Elizabeth F. Introduction to Literary Japanese. 2.00 (ISBN 0-686-09991-5). Far Eastern Pubns.
Iwaki. Practical Japanese Made Simple. pap. 2.95 (ISBN 0-685-27813-1). Borden.
Karlgren, Bernhard. Analytic Dictionary of Chinese & Sino-Japanese. 10.00 (ISBN 0-8446-5208-3). Peter Smith.
Kawata, Yoshiguki. Let's Speak Japanese. 1977. pap. 5.50 (ISBN 0-912180-29-3). Petroglyph.
Kindaichi, Haruhiko. The Japanese Language. Hirano, Umeyo, tr. LC 77-93226. 1976. pap. 16.50 (ISBN 0-8048-1185-7). C E Tuttle.
Koop, Albert J. & Inada, Hogitaro. Japanese Names & How to Read Them: A Manual for Art-Collectors & Students. 1972. 75.00 (ISBN 0-7100-1707-3). Routledge & Kegan.
Living Japanese: Cassette Edition. (YA) 1969. 14.95, with 2 cassettes plus dictionary & manual (ISBN 0-517-50816-8). Crown.
Miller, Roy A. The Japanese Language. LC 67-16777. (History & Structure of Languages Ser.). 496p. 1980. pap. 16.00x (ISBN 0-226-52718-2, Midway). U of Chicago Pr.
--Japanese Language in Contemporary Japan: Some Sociolinguistic Observations. 1977. pap. 5.25 (ISBN 0-8447-3247-8). Am Enterprise.
--Origins of the Japanese Language. LC 80-50871. (Publications on Asia of the School for International Studies: No. 34). (Illus.). 236p. 1981. 17.50 (ISBN 0-295-95766-2). U of Wash Pr.
Miller, Roy A., ed. Bernard Bloch on Japanese. LC 72-99834. (Linguistic Ser). (Illus.). 1970. 25.00x (ISBN 0-300-01213-6). Yale U Pr.
Peng, Fred C., ed. Language in Japanese Society: Current Issues in Sociolinguistics. (Illus.). 200p. 1976. pap. 8.50x (ISBN 0-86008-149-4, Pub. by U of Tokyo Pr). Intl Schol Bk Serv.
Suzuki, Takao. Japanese & the Japanese: Words in Culture. Miura, Akira, tr. LC 77-15296. 152p. 1978. 10.95 (ISBN 0-87011-325-9). Kodansha.
Taylor. English & Japanese in Contrast. 1979. 6.95 (ISBN 0-88345-356-8). Regents Pub.

JAPANESE LANGUAGE–CONVERSATION AND PHRASE BOOKS

Bonar, Lore S., et al. Say It in Another Language: Phrases in Spanish, French, Japanese, Swahili, & German. (YA) 1976. pap. text ed. 2.50 pkg. of 20 (ISBN 0-88441-414-0, 26-814). GS.
Chaplin, Hamako & Martin, Samuel. Advanced Japanese Conversation. 1976. 7.50 (ISBN 0-686-15389-8); tapes avail. Far Eastern Pubns.
Cortina Company. Conversational Japanese in Twenty Lessons. 256p. 1980. pap. 4.95 (ISBN 0-06-463606-2, EH 606, EH). Har-Row.
Crownover, Richard. Lover's Language Guide to Japan. 1976. pap. 2.00 (ISBN 0-914778-17-X). Phoenix Bks.
De Mente, Boye. Businessman's Language Guide to Japan. 1976. pap. 2.00 (ISBN 0-914778-16-1). Phoenix Bks.
Kai, Miwa. Say It in Japanese. (Orig.). pap. 1.75 (ISBN 0-486-20807-9). Dover.
--Say It in Japanese. LC 55-1925. 1956. lib. bdg. 8.50x (ISBN 0-88307-563-6). Gannon.
Koop, Albert J. & Inada, Hogitaro. Japanese Names & How to Read Them: A Manual for Art-Collectors & Students. 1972. 75.00 (ISBN 0-7100-1707-3). Routledge & Kegan.
Listen & Learn Japanese. (Listen & Learn Ser.). 1981. Incl. 3 Cassettes & Manual. 14.95 (ISBN 0-486-99903-3). Dover.
Maeda, Jun. Let's Study Japanese. LC 64-24949. (Illus.). (gr. 9 up). 1965. pap. 3.25 (ISBN 0-8048-0362-5). C E Tuttle.
Martin, Samuel E. Essential Japanese. LC 59-5072. 12.50 (ISBN 0-8048-0171-1). C E Tuttle.
Murray, D. M. & Wong, T. W. Noodle Words: An Introduction to Chinese & Japanese Characters. LC 79-147179. (Illus.). (gr. 9 up). 1971. pap. 3.75 (ISBN 0-8048-0948-8). C E Tuttle.
Ono, Hideichi. Everyday Expressions in Japanese. 1963. pap. 3.95 (ISBN 0-89346-025-7, Pub. by Hokuseido Pr). Heian Intl.
Sivan, Avraham J. & Ikeda, Yutakada, eds. Useful Expressions in Japanese. (Useful Expressions Ser.). (Illus.). 64p. (Orig.). 1980. pap. 2.00 (ISBN 0-86628-011-1). Ridgefield Pub.
Tazuko Ajiro Monane. Japanese Made Easy. 150p. 1979. pap. 6.95 (ISBN 0-8048-1219-5). C E Tuttle.
Thorlin, Eldora & Brannen, Noah. Everyday Japanese. LC 69-19854. 180p. 1969. 3.95 (ISBN 0-8348-0037-3). Weatherhill.
Thorlin, Eldora S. Japanese Word & Phrase Book for Tourists. LC 76-113904. 1970. flexible leatherette bdg. 5.95 (ISBN 0-8048-0876-7). C E Tuttle.
Watanabe, Masahiro & Nagashima, Kei. Instant Japanese. (Illus.). 188p. 1981. pap. 3.95 (ISBN 0-89346-182-2). Heian Intl.
Young, John & Nakajima, Kimiko. Learn Japanese: College Text, 4 Vols. 1967-69. Vol. 1. pap. text ed. 7.50x (ISBN 0-8248-0061-3, Eastwest Ctr); Vol. 2. pap. 8.50x (ISBN 0-8248-0069-9); Vol. 3. pap. 8.50x (ISBN 0-8248-0073-7); Vol. 4. pap. 9.00x (ISBN 0-8248-0074-5). U Pr of Hawaii.

JAPANESE LANGUAGE–DICTIONARIES–ENGLISH

Ceadel, Eric B. Japanese-English Dictionary, 2 vols. romanized 32.00 (ISBN 0-87557-048-8, 048-8). Saphrograph.
Corwin, Charles, et al. A Dictionary of Japanese & English Idiomatic Equivalents. LC 68-11818. 302p. 1980. 15.00 (ISBN 0-87011-111-6). Kodansha.
Daniels, F. J. Basic English: Writer's Japanese-English Word Book. 1969. 29.95 (ISBN 0-89346-100-8, Pub. by Hokuseido Pr). Heian Intl.
English-Japanese Dictionary (Romanized) 17.50 (ISBN 0-87557-047-X, 048-X). Saphrograph.
Hadamitzky, Wolfgang & Spahn, Mark. Kanji & Kana: A Handbook & Dictionary of the Japanese Writing System. LC 81-50106. 384p. 1981. 11.50 (ISBN 0-8048-1373-6). C E Tuttle.
Institute for Language Study. Vest Pocket Japanese. (Illus.). 240p. (Japanese.). 1979. pap. 2.45 (ISBN 0-686-73493-9, BN 4900, BN). Har-Row.
Japanese-English Dictionary: Romanized. 17.50 (ISBN 0-686-65152-9, 047-X). Saphrograph.
Kai, Hyojun R. All-Romanized English-Japanese Dictionary. LC 73-90232. 1973. pap. 6.95 (ISBN 0-8048-1118-0). C E Tuttle.
Kawamoto, Shigeo & Nishiwaki, Junzaburo, eds. The Kodansha English-Japanese Dictionary. Narita, Shigehisa & Shimizu, Mamoru, trs. 1557p. 1980. pap. 19.50 flexible soft-binding (ISBN 0-87011-420-4). Kodansha.
Kawamoto, Shigeo, et al, eds. The Kodansha Japanese-English Dictionary. Shimizu, Hamoru & Harita, Shigehisa, trs. 1250p. 1980. flexible soft-binding 19.50 (ISBN 0-87011-421-2). Kodansha.
Kikuoka, Tadashi, ed. Japanese Newspaper Compounds: The One Thousand Most Important in Order of Frequency. LC 76-125560. 1970. pap. 4.25 (ISBN 0-8048-0919-4). C E Tuttle.
Koop, Albert J. & Inada, Hogitaro. Japanese Names & How to Read Them: A Manual for Art-Collectors & Students. 1972. 75.00 (ISBN 0-7100-1707-3). Routledge & Kegan.
Marenghi, Guy J. Japanese-English Lingograms. LC 66-26104. (Illus.). 1977. pap. 3.00 (ISBN 0-8048-0289-0). C E Tuttle.
Martin, Samuel. Basic Japanese Conversation Dictionary: English-Japanese & Japanese-English. LC 57-8797. 3.95 (ISBN 0-8048-0057-X). C E Tuttle.
Nelson, Andrew. Modern Reader's Japanese-English Character Dictionary. LC 61-11973. 1962. 35.00 (ISBN 0-8048-0408-7). C E Tuttle.
Parnwell, E. C. Oxford Picture Dictionary of American English: English-Japanese Edition. (Illus.). 96p. (Orig.). 1981. pap. text ed. 6.95x (ISBN 0-19-581877-6). Oxford U Pr.
Rose-Innes, Arthur. Beginners' Dictionary of Chinese-Japanese Characters. 10.00 (ISBN 0-8446-5657-7). Peter Smith.

JAPANESE LANGUAGE–GRAMMAR

American National Standards Institute, Standards Committee Z39 on Library Work, Documentation & Related Publishing Practices. American National Standard System for the Romanization of Japanese. rev. ed. 1978. 4.00 (ISBN 0-686-01888-5, Z39.11). ANSI.
Anderson, Olov B. Bushu: A Key to the 'Radicals' of the Japanese Language. (Scandinavian Institute of Asian Studies). 1980. pap. text ed. 6.50x (ISBN 0-7007-0127-3). Humanities.
Bleiler, E. F. Essential Japanese Grammar. (Orig.). 1963. pap. 2.25 (ISBN 0-486-21027-8). Dover.
Bleiler, Everett F. Essential Japanese Grammer. LC 63-17899. 1963. lib. bdg. 9.50x (ISBN 0-88307-578-4). Gannon.
Clarke, H. D. & Hamamura, Motoko. Colloquial Japanese. (Colloquial Ser.). (Orig.). 1981. pap. 12.50 (ISBN 0-7100-0595-4). Routledge & Kegan.

Collado, Diego. Diego Collado's Grammar of the Japanese Language. Spear, Richard L., ed. (International Studies, East Asian Ser.). 1978. pap. text ed. 12.50x (ISBN 0-685-63619-4). Paragon.

Inamoto, Noboru. Colloquial Japanese. LC 71-133865. 1972. 19.50 (ISBN 0-8048-0741-8). C E Tuttle.

Jorden, Eleanor H. & Chaplin, Hamako I. Beginning Japanese, Pt. 1. (Illus.). 1962. pap. text ed. 8.95x (ISBN 0-300-00135-5). Yale U Pr.

--Beginning Japanese, Pt. 2. (Linguistic Ser). (Illus.). 1963. text ed. 35.00x (ISBN 0-300-00610-1); pap. text ed. 8.95x (ISBN 0-300-00136-3). Yale U Pr.

Kuno, Susumu. The Structure of the Japanese Language. 384p. 1973. 27.50x (ISBN 0-262-11049-0). MIT Pr.

Kuroda, S. Y. Generative Grammatical Studies in the Japanese Language. Hankamer, Jorge, ed. LC 78-66564. (Outstanding Dissertations in Linguistics Ser.). 1979. lib. bdg. 27.50 (ISBN 0-8240-9680-0). Garland Pub.

Lange, Roland A. Two Hundred & One Japanese Verbs Fully Conjugated in All the Forms. LC 76-140634. (Orig.). 1971. pap. text ed. 3.95 (ISBN 0-8120-0391-8). Barron.

Martin, Samuel E. A Reference Grammar of Japanese. LC 74-15211. (Linguistic Ser.). 1250p. 1976. text ed. 50.00x (ISBN 0-300-01813-4). Yale U Pr.

Miller, Roy A. Japanese & Other Altaic Languages. LC 79-151129. (History & Structure of Language Ser). 1971. text ed. 18.50x (ISBN 0-226-52719-0). U of Chicago Pr.

Niwa, Tamako & Matsuda, Mayako. Basic Japanese for College Students. rev. ed. LC 64-22006. (Illus.). 632p. 1966. 16.50 (ISBN 0-295-73714-X); with set of 29 tapes 200.00 (ISBN 0-295-75501-6); of 27 cassettes 200.00 set (ISBN 0-295-75500-8). U of Wash Pr.

Ogawa, Kenji. New Intensive Japanese. rev. ed. 1970. pap. 19.95 (ISBN 0-89346-006-0, Pub. by Hokuseido Pr.). Heian Intl.

Ono, Hideichi. Japanese Grammar. 1973. pap. 19.95 (ISBN 0-89346-004-4, Pub. by Hokuseido Pr.). Heian Intl.

Young, John & Nakajima, Kimiko. Learn Japanese: College Text, 4 Vols. 1967-69. Vol. 1. pap. text ed. 7.50x (ISBN 0-8248-0061-3, Eastwest Ctr); Vol. 2. pap. 8.50x (ISBN 0-8248-0069-9); Vol. 3. pap. 8.50x (ISBN 0-8248-0073-7); Vol. 4. pap. 9.00x (ISBN 0-8248-0074-5). U Pr of Hawaii.

JAPANESE LANGUAGE–GRAMMAR, HISTORICAL

Yokoyama, Masako. Inflection of Eighth Century Japanese. (Language Dissertations: No. 45). 1950. pap. 6.00 (ISBN 0-527-00791-9). Kraus Repr.

JAPANESE LANGUAGE–INFLECTION

Gardner, E. F. Inflections of Modern Literary Japanese. 1950. pap. 6.00 (ISBN 0-527-00792-7). Kraus Repr.

Yokoyama, Masako. Inflection of Eighth Century Japanese. (Language Dissertations: No. 45). 1950. pap. 6.00 (ISBN 0-527-00791-9). Kraus Repr.

JAPANESE LANGUAGE–PHONOLOGY

Martin, Samuel E. Morphophonemics of Standard Colloquial Japanese. 1952. pap. 6.00 (ISBN 0-527-00793-5). Kraus Repr.

Okada, Miyo. Keigo-Honorific Speech in Japanese. 2.00 (ISBN 0-686-09993-1). Far Eastern Pubns.

Wenck, Guenther. The Phonemics of Japanese: Questions & Attempts. LC 67-77983. 104p. 1966. 15.00x (ISBN 3-447-01040-1). Intl Pubns Serv.

JAPANESE LANGUAGE–READERS

Hibbett, Howard S., Jr. & Itasaka, Gen. Modern Japanese: A Basic Reader, 2 vols. 2nd ed. LC 67-22864. (gr. 9 up). 1967. Set. pap. 12.00x (ISBN 0-674-58000-1). Harvard U Pr.

Miller, Roy A. Japanese Reader: Graded Lessons in the Modern Language. LC 62-9359. 1963. bds. 17.50 (ISBN 0-8048-0315-3). C E Tuttle.

Walsh, Len. Read Japanese Today. LC 69-12078. 1969. pap. 4.95 (ISBN 0-8048-0496-6). C E Tuttle.

JAPANESE LANGUAGE–SELF-INSTRUCTION

Inamoto, Norboru. Japanese Primer. 270p. 1974. pap. text ed. 4.50 (ISBN 0-88474-019-6). U of S Cal Pr.

Itasaka, Gen. Modern Japanese: An Advanced Reader, 2 vols. LC 73-89698. 328p. 1974. Set. 12.50x (ISBN 0-87011-222-8). Kodansha.

Jorden, Eleanor H., ed. Japanese Self-Instruction Program, 2 vols. (Japanese.). 1979. Vol. 1, 408p. 8 cassettes incl. 115.00x (ISBN 0-88432-030-8, J401); Vol. 2, 410p. 16 cassettes incl. 98.00x (ISBN 0-88432-031-6, J409). J Norton Pubs.

Kiyooka, Elichi. Japanese in 30 Hours. 1953. pap. 6.95 (ISBN 0-89346-031-1, Pub. by Hokuseido Pr). Heian Intl.

Shirato, Ichiro. Living Japanese. (YA) (gr. 6-12). 1962. 14.95, with 4 lp records conversation manual & dictionary (ISBN 0-517-00997-8). Crown.

JAPANESE LANGUAGE–SYNTAX

Fujiwara, Yoichi. The Sentence Structure of Japanese: Viewed in the Light of Dialectology. Brannen, Noah & Baird, Scott, trs. from Japanese. LC 73-78976. 156p. 1973. text ed. 9.00x (ISBN 0-8248-0275-6). U Pr of Hawaii.

Inoue, Kazuko. Study of Japanese Syntax. LC 68-17883. (Janua Linguarum, Ser. Practica: No. 41). (Orig.). 1969. pap. text ed. 30.00x (ISBN 90-2790-692-0). Mouton.

Jorden, E. H. Syntax of Modern Colloquial Japanese. 1955. pap. 8.00 (ISBN 0-527-00798-6). Kraus Repr.

JAPANESE LANGUAGE–TEXTBOOKS FOR FOREIGNERS

Alfonso, Anthony. Japanese--Book One. (Illus.). (gr. 3-7). 1976. pap. 10.00x (ISBN 0-8048-1233-0). C E Tuttle.

Clarke, H. D. & Hamamura, Motoko. Colloquial Japanese. (Colloquial Ser.). (Orig.). 1981. pap. 12.50 (ISBN 0-7100-0595-4). Routledge & Kegan.

Daub, Edward E., et al. Comprehending Technical Japanese. LC 74-5900. 440p. 1975. 32.50x (ISBN 0-299-06680-0). U of Wis Pr.

Dunn, C. J. & Yanoda, S. Teach Yourself Japanese. (Teach Yourself Ser.). pap. 5.95 (ISBN 0-679-10185-3). McKay.

Gardner, Elizabeth F. & Martin, Samuel E. An Introduction to Modern Japanese Orthography: Kana. 2.00 (ISBN 0-686-09990-7). Far Eastern Pubns.

Japanese Language Research Division of Osaka University. Japanese for Today. LC 73-88140. 1977. 29.95 (ISBN 0-8120-5188-2). Barron.

Jorden, Eleanor H. & Chaplin, Hamako I. Reading Japanese. LC 75-18176. (Linguistic Ser.). 1976. 40.00x (ISBN 0-300-01912-2); pap. text ed. 16.50x (ISBN 0-300-01913-0). Yale U Pr.

Learn Japanese: For English Speakers. pap. 8.50 (ISBN 0-87557-049-6, 049-6). Saphrograph.

Martin, Samuel E. Easy Japanese. LC 57-6763. (YA) (gr. 9 up). 1965. pap. 3.95 (ISBN 0-8048-0157-6). C E Tuttle.

O'Neill, P. G. Essential Kanji. LC 73-2832. 304p. 1973. 8.95 (ISBN 0-8348-0082-9). Weatherhill.

Pye, Michael. The Study of Kanji. 1971. pap. 19.95 (ISBN 0-89346-007-9, Pub. by Hokuseido Pr.). Heian Intl.

Uehara, Toyoaki & Kiyose, Gisaburo N. Fundamentals of Japanese. LC 73-21245. (East Asian Ser.). 608p. 1975. pap. 17.50x (ISBN 0-253-32523-4). Ind U Pr.

Yoshida, Yasuo, et al. Japanese for Beginners. (gr. 12). 1977. 19.95 (ISBN 0-8120-5189-0). Barron.

JAPANESE LANGUAGE–VOCABULARY

Inamoto, Noboru. Colloquial Japanese. LC 71-133865. 1972. 19.50 (ISBN 0-8048-0741-8). C E Tuttle.

Miura, Akira. English Loanwords in Japanese: A Selection. LC 78-65031. 1979. 11.50 (ISBN 0-8048-1248-9). C E Tuttle.

Rose-Innes, A. Vocabulary of Common Japanese Words. 2.00 (ISBN 0-686-09992-3). Far Eastern Pubns.

JAPANESE LANGUAGE–WRITING

Pye, Michael. Everyday Japanese Characters. 1977. pap. 3.95 (ISBN 0-89346-009-5, Pub. by Hokuseido Pr.). Heian Intl.

Rose-Innes, Arthur. Beginners' Dictionary of Chinese-Japanese Characters & Compounds. 1977. pap. 7.95 (ISBN 0-486-23467-3). Dover.

Sakade, Florence, et al. Guide to Reading & Writing Japanese. LC 59-10412. 1959. 9.50 (ISBN 0-8048-0226-2). C E Tuttle.

Yamagiwa, Joseph K. Introduction to Japanese Writing. 1943. 3.25x (ISBN 0-685-21791-4). Wahr.

JAPANESE LEGENDS

see Legends, Japanese

JAPANESE LITERATURE (COLLECTIONS)

see also Short Stories, Japanese

Chibbett, D. G., et al. A Descriptive Catalogue of the Pre-1868 Japanese Books, Manuscripts, & Prints in the Library of the School of Oriental & African Studies. (Illus.). 192p. (Annotated entries). 1976. 34.50x (ISBN 0-19-713586-2). Oxford U Pr.

Daniels, F. J. Japanese Prose. 1944. lib. bdg. 10.00 (ISBN 0-8414-2436-5). Folcroft.

Hirano, Umeyo. Tsustumi Chunogon Monogatari. 1965. pap. 7.95 (ISBN 0-89346-046-X, Pub. by Hokuseido Pr). Heian Intl.

Honda, H. H., tr. Shin Kokinshu: The 13th Century Anthology Edited by Imperial Edict. 1970. 29.50 (ISBN 0-89346-092-3, Pub. by Hokuseido Pr). Heian Intl.

Kato, Genchi & Hoshino, H. Kogoshui: Gleanings from Ancient Stories. (Records of Asian History). (Illus.). 1972. text ed. 8.00x (ISBN 0-7007-0022-6). Humanities.

Kozaki, N. Kitsune: Japan's Fox of Mystery, Romance & Humor. (Illus.). 1961. 9.95 (ISBN 0-89346-071-0, Pub. by Hokuseido Pr). Heian Intl.

Murasaki, Lady. The Tale of Genji-One. LC 50-47132. pap. 2.95 (ISBN 0-385-09275-X, Anch). Doubleday.

Oe, Kenzaburo, et al. The Catch & Other Stories. Bester, John, et al, trs. LC 80-84420. 156p. 1981. pap. 4.95 (ISBN 0-87011-457-3). Kodansha.

Tsuneari, Yukio, et al, eds. Introduction to Contemporary Japanese Literature: Synopses of Major Works 1956-1970. 370p. 1973. 15.00x (ISBN 0-86008-093-5, Pub. by U of Tokyo Pr). Intl Schol Bk Serv.

Watson, Burton, tr. Japanese Literature in Chinese: Poetry and Prose in Chinese by Japanese Writers, 2 vols. 132p. Vol. 1 1975. 12.50x (ISBN 0-231-03986-7); Vol. 2 1976. 15.00x (ISBN 0-231-04146-2). Columbia U Pr.

JAPANESE LITERATURE–BIBLIOGRAPHY

Echols, John M. Preliminary Checklist of Indonesian Imprints During the Japanese Period: March 1962 - August 1945. 1963. pap. 1.50 (ISBN 0-686-62725-3). Cornell Mod Indo.

Fujino, Yukio, ed. Modern Japanese Literature in Translation: A Bibliography. LC 78-66395. 311p. 1979. 15.00 (ISBN 0-87011-339-9). Kodansha.

Japan Foundation. An Introductory Bibliography for Japanese Studies, Vol. II, Pt. 2. 1978. 11.50x (ISBN 0-86008-210-5, Pub. by U of Tokyo Pr). Intl Schol Bk Serv.

Sorimachi, Shigeo, ed. Catalogue of Japanese Illustrated Books & Manuscripts in the Spencer Collection of the New York Public Library. (Illus.). 1978. pap. 35.00 (ISBN 0-87104-306-8, Co-Pub. by Readex Books). NY Pub Lib.

JAPANESE LITERATURE–HISTORY AND CRITICISM

Aston, W. G. History of Japanese Literature. LC 73-157264. 1971. pap. 4.25 (ISBN 0-8048-0997-6). C E Tuttle.

--History of Japanese Literature. 23.00 (ISBN 0-384-02240-5). Johnson Repr.

--A History of Japanese Literature. lib. bdg. 59.95 (ISBN 0-87968-471-2). Krishna Pr.

Braisted, William R. Meiroku: Journal of the Japanese Enlightenment. 1976. 25.00x (ISBN 0-674-54670-9). Harvard U Pr.

Bryan, J. Thomas. Literature of Japan. LC 79-103218. 1970. Repr. of 1929 ed. 11.50 (ISBN 0-8046-0855-5). Kennikat.

Collden, Lisa. Tresors De la Tradition Orale Sakata: Proverbes, Mythes, Legendes, Fabls, Chansons et Devinettes De Sakata. (Uppsala Studies in Cultural Anthropology: No. 2). 446p. (Fr.). 1979. pap. text ed. 40.00x (ISBN 91-554-0898-2). Humanities.

Hibbett, Howard. The Floating World in Japanese Fiction. LC 75-28976. (Illus.). 1974. pap. 5.95 (ISBN 0-8048-1154-7). C E Tuttle.

Hisamatsu, Sen'Ichi. Biographical Dictionary of Japanese Literature. LC 75-14730. (Illus.). 437p. 1976. 35.00x (ISBN 0-87011-253-8). Kodansha.

Ikeda, Daisaku & Nemoto, Makoto. On the Japanese Classics. LC 78-26624. 1979. 13.50 (ISBN 0-8348-0140-X). Weatherhill.

Keene, Dennis. Yokomitsu Riichi, Modernist. LC 79-28532. (Modern Asia Literature Ser.). 1980. 20.00x (ISBN 0-231-04938-2). Columbia U Pr.

Keene, Donald. Appreciations of Japanese Culture. LC 80-85387. (Illus.). 350p. pap. 5.95 (ISBN 0-87011-468-9). Kodansha.

--Japanese Literature: An Introduction for Western Readers. (YA) (gr. 9 up). 1955. pap. 2.25 (ISBN 0-394-17200-0, E9, Ever). Grove.

--Modern Japanese Novels & the West. (Illus.). 1961. 4.95x (ISBN 0-8139-0156-1). U Pr of Va.

--Some Japanese Portraits. LC 76-39679. 228p. 1979. 15.00 (ISBN 0-87011-298-8). Kodansha.

--World Within Walls. LC 75-21484. 1976. 22.95 (ISBN 0-03-013626-1). HR&W.

--World Within Walls: Japanese Literature of the Pre-Modern Era 1600-1867. LC 78-66793. 1979. pap. 9.50 (ISBN 0-394-17074-1, E723, Ever). Grove.

Lippit, Noriko M. Reality & Fiction in Modern Japanese Literature. LC 79-67859. 1980. 20.00 (ISBN 0-87332-137-5). M E Sharpe.

Miyoshi, Masao. Accomplices of Silence: The Modern Japanese Novel. 1975. pap. 3.25 (ISBN 0-520-02744-2). U of Cal Pr.

Petersen, Gwenn B. The Moon in the Water: Understanding Tanizaki, Kawabata, & Mishima. LC 79-14994. 1979. text ed. 14.95x (ISBN 0-8248-0520-8). U Pr of Hawaii.

Putzar, Edward D. Japanese Literature: A Historical Outline. LC 70-189229. 264p. 1973. pap. 6.50x (ISBN 0-8165-0357-5). U of Ariz Pr.

Rimer, J. Thomas. Mori Ogai. LC 74-28163. (World Authors Ser.: No. 355). 1975. lib. bdg. 10.95 (ISBN 0-8057-2636-5). Twayne.

Ryan, Marleigh G., tr. Japan's First Modern Novel. LC 67-15896. 1971. 7.50x (ISBN 0-231-08666-0). Columbia U Pr.

Seidensticker, Edward G. Genji Days. LC 76-44157. 225p. 1977. 15.00 (ISBN 0-87011-296-1). Kodansha.

Takeo, Doi. The Psychological World of Natsume Soseki. (East Asian Monographs: No. 68). 1976. text ed. 15.00x (ISBN 0-674-72116-0). Harvard U Pr.

Ueda, Makoto. Modern Japanese Writers and the Nature of Literature. LC 75-39336. xii, 291p. 1976. 13.50x (ISBN 0-8047-0904-1). Stanford U Pr.

Walker, Janet A. The Japanese Novel of the Meiji Period & the Ideal of Individualism. LC 79-4501. 1979. 22.50x (ISBN 0-691-06400-8). Princeton U Pr.

Yamanouchi, H. The Search for Authenticity in Modern Japanese Literature. LC 77-84815. 214p. 1980. pap. 10.95 (ISBN 0-521-29974-8). Cambridge U Pr.

--The Search for Authenticity in Modern Japanese Literature. LC 77-84815. 1978. 29.95 (ISBN 0-521-21856-X). Cambridge U Pr.

JAPANESE LITERATURE–TRANSLATIONS INTO ENGLISH

Akinari, Veda. Tales of the Spring Rain. Jackman, Barry, tr. from Japanese. Orig. Title: Harusame Mongatari. 270p. 1975. 13.50 (ISBN 0-86008-133-8, Pub. by U of Tokyo Pr). Intl Schol Bk Serv.

Akutagawa Ryunosuke. A Fool's Life. Peterson, Will, tr. (Illus.). 1970. 10.00 (ISBN 0-685-83015-2, Pub. by Mushinsha Bks). SBD.

Henderson, Dan F. Village "Contracts" in Tokugawa Japan: Fifty Specimens with English Translations & Comments. LC 74-31050. (Asian Law Ser.: No. 2). (Illus.). 220p. 1975. 14.50 (ISBN 0-295-95405-1). U of Wash Pr.

Hibbett, Howard. Contemporary Japanese Literature: An Anthology of Fiction, Film, & Other Writing Since 1945. LC 77-4762. 1977. 15.00 (ISBN 0-394-49141-6); pap. 5.95 (ISBN 0-394-73362-2). Knopf.

Ibuse, Masuji. Lieutenant Lookest & Other Stories. Bester, John, tr. from Jap. LC 71-135143. 308p. 1971. 8.95 (ISBN 0-87011-147-7). Kodansha.

Kamo, Chomei. Ten Foot Square Hut & Tales of the Heike. Sadler, Arthur L., ed. Repr. of 1928 ed. lib. bdg. 15.00x (ISBN 0-8371-3114-6, KATF). Greenwood.

Kansuke, Naka. The Silver Spoon. Terasaki, Etsuko, tr. from Japanese. LC 76-21917. 150p. 1977. 10.00 (ISBN 0-914090-14-3); pap. 4.95 (ISBN 0-914090-15-1). Chicago Review.

Keene, Donald, ed. Anthology of Japanese Literature: Earliest Era to Mid-Nineteenth Century. 1955. pap. 7.95 (ISBN 0-394-17221-3, E216, Ever). Grove.

--Modern Japanese Literature: An Anthology. 1956. pap. 7.95 (ISBN 0-394-17254-X, E573, Ever). Grove.

Marks, Alfred H. & Bort, Barry D. Guide to Japanese Prose. (Reference Bks.). 155p. 1975. lib. bdg. 12.00 (ISBN 0-8161-1110-3). G K Hall.

Miner, Earl, tr. Japanese Poetic Diaries. (Center for Japanese & Korean Studies, UC Berkeley). (Illus.). 1969. 22.75x (ISBN 0-520-01466-9); pap. 3.95 (ISBN 0-520-03047-8). U of Cal Pr.

Mishima, Yukio. Sun & Steel. Bester, John, tr. LC 76-100628. Orig. Title: Taiyo to Tetsu. 1970. 10.00 (ISBN 0-87011-117-5). Kodansha.

Reischauer, Edwin O. & Yamagiwa, Joseph K. Translations from Early Japanese Literature. 2nd abr. ed. LC 72-79310. (Harvard-Yenching Institute Studies: No. 29). 352p. 1972. pap. 9.00x (ISBN 0-674-90422-2). Harvard U Pr.

Saikaku, Ihara. Five Women Who Loved Love. De Bary, William T., tr. LC 55-10619. (Illus.). 1955. pap. 4.95 (ISBN 0-8048-0184-3). C E Tuttle.

Seidensticker, Edward G. Genji Days. LC 76-44157. 225p. 1977. 15.00 (ISBN 0-87011-296-1). Kodansha.

Shonagon, Sei. The Pillow Book of Sei Shonagon. (Unwin Bks.). 1928. pap. 2.95 (ISBN 0-04-895005-X). Allen Unwin.

Ury, Marian, tr. Tales of Times Now Past: Sixty-Two Stories from a Medieval Japanese Collection. 1979. 9.95 (ISBN 0-520-03864-9). U of Cal Pr.

Yamagiwa, Joseph K., tr. The Okagami: A Japanese Historical Tale. LC 77-83045. 1977. pap. 5.25 (ISBN 0-8048-1247-0). C E Tuttle.

JAPANESE MATHEMATICS

see Mathematics, Japanese

JAPANESE MUSIC

see Music, Japanese

JAPANESE MYTHOLOGY

see Mythology, Japanese

JAPANESE NATIONAL CHARACTERISTICS

see National Characteristics, Japanese

JAPANESE NEWSPAPERS

Nunn, G. Raymond, compiled by. Japanese Periodicals & Newspapers in Western Languages. 1979. 52.50 (ISBN 0-7201-0934-5, Pub. by Mansell England). Merrimack Bk Serv.

JAPANESE PAINTING

see Painting, Japanese

JAPANESE PAINTINGS

see Paintings, Japanese

JAPANESE PAPER FOLDING

see Origami

JAPANESE PERIODICALS

Japan Chemical Week, ed. Japan Chemical Directory 1981. 19th ed. LC 68-51873. 582p. (Orig.). 1981. pap. 120.00x (ISBN 0-8002-2804-9). Intl Pubns Serv.

Nunn, G. Raymond, compiled by. Japanese Periodicals & Newspapers in Western Languages. 1979. 52.50 (ISBN 0-7201-0934-5, Pub. by Mansell England). Merrimack Bk Serv.

JAPANESE PHILOLOGY

An Introductory Bibliography for Japanese Studies, Vol. III, Pt 1. LC 75-323370. 1978. 11.50x (ISBN 0-86008-236-9, Pub. by U of Tokyo Pr). Intl Schol Bk Serv.

K. B. S. Bibliography of Standard Reference Books for Japanese Studies with Descriptive Notes. Incl. Vol. 1. Generalia. rev. ed. 164p. 1971 (ISBN 0-86008-031-5); Vol. 2. Geography & Travel. 174p. 1966 (ISBN 0-86008-032-3); Vol. 3. History & Biography. 1965. Pt. 1 (ISBN 0-86008-033-1). Pt. 2 (ISBN 0-86008-034-X). Pt. 3 (ISBN 0-86008-035-8); Vol. 4. Religion. 192p. 1966 (ISBN 0-86008-036-6); Vol. 5A. History of Thought. 1965. Pt. 1 (ISBN 0-86008-037-4). Pt. 2 (ISBN 0-86008-038-2); Vol. 5B. Education. 198p. 1966 (ISBN 0-86008-039-0); Vol. 6A. Language. rev. ed. 166p. 1972 (ISBN 0-86008-040-4); Vol. 6B. Literature, 5 pts. 1966-68. Pt. 1 (ISBN 0-86008-041-2). Pt. 3. Edo Period (ISBN 0-86008-043-9). Pt. 4. Modern Period 1 (ISBN 0-86008-044-7). Pt. 5. Modern Period 2 (ISBN 0-86008-045-5); Pt. 7A. Traditional Art & Architecture. rev. ed. 178p. 1971 (ISBN 0-86008-046-3); Vol. 9A. Politics. 188p. 1970 (ISBN 0-86008-049-8); Pt. 9B. Law. 1968-70. Pt. 1 (ISBN 0-86008-050-1). Pt. 2 (ISBN 0-86008-051-X); Vol. 10. Economics. 1969. Pt. 1 (ISBN 0-86008-052-8). Pt. 2 (ISBN 0-86008-053-6); Geography. rev. ed. 234p. 1973. 12.50x (ISBN 0-86008-054-4). 3.50x ea (Pub by U of Tokyo Pr). Intl Schol Bk Serv.

JAPANESE PHILOSOPHY

see Philosophy, Japanese

JAPANESE POETRY (COLLECTIONS)

see also Haiku; Waka

Blyth, R. H. Edo Satirical Verse Anthologies. (Illus.). 1961. 27.50 (ISBN 0-89346-015-X, Pub. by Hokuseido Pr.). Heian Intl.

--Senryu: Japanese Satirical Verses. (Illus.). 1949. 19.95 (ISBN 0-89346-091-5, Pub. by Hokuseido Pr). Heian Intl.

Clack, Robert W. The Soul of Yamato: A History & Anthology of Japanese Poetry, 2 vols. 1975. Set. lib. bdg. 250.00 (ISBN 0-87968-446-1). Gordon Pr.

Davis, A. R., ed. Modern Japanese Poetry. Kirkup, James, tr. from Japanese. (Asian & Pacific Writing Ser). 1979. 14.95x (ISBN 0-7022-1148-6); pap. 8.50x (ISBN 0-7022-1149-4). U of Queensland Pr.

French, J. L. Lotus & Chrysanthemums: An Anthology of Chinese & Japanese Poetry. 59.95 (ISBN 0-8490-0556-6). Gordon Pr.

Hearn, Lafcadio. Japanese Lyrics. LC 76-41848. 1915. lib. bdg. 15.00 (ISBN 0-8414-4943-0). Folcroft.

--Japanese Miscellany. 1954. pap. 5.25 (ISBN 0-8048-0307-2). C E Tuttle.

Japanese Love Poems, Vol. 10. (East Asian Poetry in Translation Ser.). 1977. pap. 4.00 (ISBN 0-89986-323-X). E Langstaff.

Keene, Dennis, tr. from Japanese. The Modern Japanese Prose Poem: An Anthology of Six Poets. LC 79-16809. 1980. 15.00x (ISBN 0-691-06418-0). Princeton U Pr.

Levy, Howard S., tr. Japanese Love Poems, Vol. 9. (East Asian Poetry in Translation Ser.). 1977. pap. 4.00 (ISBN 0-89986-322-1). E Langstaff.

Lotus & Chrysanthemum: An Anthology of Chinese & Japanese Poetry. 1979. Repr. of 1934 ed. lib. bdg. 35.00 (ISBN 0-8492-4635-0). R West.

Miyamori, Asataro, ed. Masterpieces of Japanese Poetry, Ancient & Modern, 2 Vols. Repr. of 1936 ed. Set. lib. bdg. 41.00x (ISBN 0-8371-2944-3, MIJP). Greenwood.

Page, Curtis H. Japanese Poetry. LC 76-67251. 1976. lib. bdg. 25.00 (ISBN 0-8414-6761-7). Folcroft.

Philomene, Marie, ed. Japanese Songs of Innocence & Experience. 1975. 12.95 (ISBN 0-89346-070-2, Pub. by Hokuseido Pr). Heian Intl.

Rexroth, Kenneth & Atsumi, Ikuto, trs. from Japan. The Burning Heart: Women Poets of Japan. 2nd ed. LC 77-1833. 192p. pap. 4.95 (ISBN 0-8164-9332-4). New Directions.

Sato, Hiroaki, tr. Ten Japanese Poets. LC 73-86247. (Illus.). 136p. 1974. pap. 3.00 (ISBN 0-914102-00-1). Granite Pubns.

Sato, Hiroaki & Watson, Burton, trs. From the Country of Eight Islands. LC 80-1077. 480p. 1981. pap. 9.95 (ISBN 0-385-14030-4, Anch). Doubleday.

JAPANESE POETRY–HISTORY AND CRITICISM

Brower, Robert H. & Miner, Earl. Japanese Court Poetry. (Illus.). 1961. 18.50x (ISBN 0-8047-0536-4). Stanford U Pr.

Lee, Peter H. Celebration of Continuity. LC 78-26145. 1979. 17.50x (ISBN 0-674-10457-9). Harvard U Pr.

Levy, Ian H., tr. from Japanese. The Ten Thousand Leaves: A Translation of Man'yoshu, Japan's Premier Anthology of Classical Poetry, Vol. 1. LC 80-8561. (Princeton Library of Asian Translations). (Illus.). 280p. 1981. 25.00 (ISBN 0-691-06452-0). Princeton U Pr.

Miner, Earl. An Introduction to Japanese Court Poetry. LC 68-17138. 1968. 10.00x (ISBN 0-8047-0635-2); pap. 2.95 (ISBN 0-8047-0636-0, SP74). Stanford U Pr.

--Japanese Linked Poetry: An Account with Translations of Renga & Haikai Sequences. LC 78-51182. 400p. 1980. 25.00x (ISBN 0-691-06372-9); pap. 8.50 (ISBN 0-691-01368-3). Princeton U Pr.

Page, Curtis H. Japanese Poetry. LC 76-67251. 1976. lib. bdg. 25.00 (ISBN 0-8414-6761-7). Folcroft.

--Japanese Poetry: An Historical Essay. 1978. Repr. of 1923 ed. lib. bdg. 30.00 (ISBN 0-8495-4350-9). Arden Lib.

Sato, Hiroaki & Watson, Burton, eds. From the Country of Eight Islands: An Anthology of Japanese Poetry. LC 80-1077. 480p. 1981. 17.50 (ISBN 0-295-95798-0). U of Wash Pr.

Stryk, Lucien, et al, trs. from Chinese & Japanese. The Crane's Bill: Zen Poems of China & Japan. LC 80-8949. 208p. 1981. pap. 4.95 (ISBN 0-394-17912-9, B458, BC). Grove.

Taneda, Santoka. Mountain Tasting: The Zen Haiku of Santoka Taneda. Stevens, John, tr. from Japanese. 100p. 1980. pap. 7.95 (ISBN 0-8348-0151-5, Pub. by John Weatherhill Inc Japan). C E Tuttle.

JAPANESE POETRY–TRANSLATIONS INTO ENGLISH

Behn, Harry, tr. More Cricket Songs: Japanese Haiku. LC 77-137755. (Illus., Photos). (gr. 4 up). 1971. 4.50 (ISBN 0-15-255440-8, HJ). HarBraceJ.

Blyth, Reginald H. Senryu: Japanese Satirical Verses. LC 72-98820. Repr. of 1949 ed. lib. bdg. 15.00x (ISBN 0-8371-2958-3, BLSE). Greenwood.

Chiba, Reiko. Hiroshige's Tokaido in Prints & Poetry. LC 57-11672. (Illus.). 9.50 (ISBN 0-8048-0246-7). C E Tuttle.

Erickson, Lois J., tr. Songs from the Land of Dawn. facs. ed. LC 68-58828. (Granger Index Reprint Ser). 1949. 12.00 (ISBN 0-8369-6014-9). Arno.

Hearn, Lafcadio. Shadowings. LC 77-138070. (Illus.). 1971. pap. 5.75 (ISBN 0-8048-0967-4). C E Tuttle.

Henderson, Harold G. Introduction to Haiku. LC 58-11314. (Illus.). 1958. pap. 2.50 (ISBN 0-385-09376-4, A150, Anch). Doubleday.

Ihara, Saikaku. Comrade Loves of the Samurai: Songs of the Geishas. Mathers, Edward P., tr. LC 70-184817. 1972. pap. 4.25 (ISBN 0-8048-1024-9). C E Tuttle.

Kijima Hajime, tr. from Japanese. The Poetry of Postwar Japan. LC 75-17718. (Iowa Translations Ser.). 318p. 1975. 12.50x (ISBN 0-87745-055-2); pap. 7.95 (ISBN 0-87745-063-3). U of Iowa Pr.

Kusano Shimpei. Frogs & Others. Corman, Cid, tr. 1969. shipcase 8.95 (ISBN 0-685-79127-0, Pub. by Mushinska Bks). SBD.

Levy, Howard S. Lesser Known Japanese Poetry Classics, Vol.7. (East Asian Poetry in Translation Ser.). 1976. 4.00 (ISBN 0-89986-302-7). E Langstaff.

Levy, Howard S., tr. Japanese Love Poems, No. 8. (East Asian Poetry in Translation Series). 1976. pap. 4.00 (ISBN 0-89986-304-3). E Langstaff.

--Japan's Best Loved Poetry Classic: Hyakunin Isshu, Vol. 1. 1976. 4.00 (ISBN 0-89986-257-8). E Langstaff.

Lewis, Richard, ed. In a Spring Garden. (Illus.). (gr. 4 up). 6.95 (ISBN 0-8037-4024-7); PLB 6.46 (ISBN 0-8037-4025-5). Dial.

Miner, Earl. An Introduction to Japanese Court Poetry. LC 68-17138. 1968. 10.00x (ISBN 0-8047-0635-2); pap. 2.95 (ISBN 0-8047-0636-0, SP74). Stanford U Pr.

Miyamori, Asataro, ed. Masterpieces of Japanese Poetry, Ancient & Modern, 2 Vols. Repr. of 1936 ed. Set. lib. bdg. 41.00x (ISBN 0-8371-2944-3, MIJP). Greenwood.

Ninomiya, Takamichi & Enright, D. J., eds. The Poetry of Living Japan. LC 78-11863. 1979. Repr. of 1957 ed. lib. bdg. 15.00 (ISBN 0-313-21210-4, NIPL). Greenwood.

Page, Curtis H. Japanese Poetry: An Historical Essay. 1978. Repr. of 1923 ed. lib. bdg. 30.00 (ISBN 0-8495-4350-9). Arden Lib.

Phillipi, Donald L., tr. This Wine of Peace, This Wine of Laughter. LC 68-27534. (Mushinsha Books). (Illus.). 1962. 12.50 (ISBN 0-670-70332-X, Grossman). Viking Pr.

Rexroth, Kenneth, tr. from Japanese. One Hundred More Poems from the Japanese. LC 76-7486. (Illus.). 1976. 8.25 (ISBN 0-8112-0618-1); pap. 3.95 (ISBN 0-8112-0619-X, NDP420). New Directions.

Rexroth, Kenneth, tr. One Hundred Poems from the Japanese. LC 56-2557. (Orig., Jap. & Eng.). 1955. gift ed 11.95 (ISBN 0-8112-0371-9); pap. 2.95 (ISBN 0-8112-0181-3, NDP147). New Directions.

Rimer, J. Thomas & Morrell, Robert E. Guide to Japanese Poetry. (Reference Bks.). 200p. 1976. lib. bdg. 12.00 (ISBN 0-8161-1111-1). G K Hall.

Shiffert, Edith & Sawa, Yuki, trs. Anthology of Modern Japanese Poetry. LC 78-167936. 1971. 6.25 (ISBN 0-8048-0672-1). C E Tuttle.

Stewart, Harold. Chime of Windbells: A Year of Japanese Haiku in English Verse. LC 69-12084. (Illus.). 1969. 17.50 (ISBN 0-8048-0092-8). C E Tuttle.

--Net of Fireflies: Japanese Haiku & Haiku Painting. LC 60-15603. (Illus.). 1960. 17.50 (ISBN 0-8048-0421-4). C E Tuttle.

Stryk, Lucien & Ikemoto, Takashi, eds. The Penguin Book of Zen Poetry. Stryk, Lucien & Ikemoto, Takashi, trs. from Japanese. (Poets Ser.). 1981. pap. 4.95 (ISBN 0-14-042247-1). Penguin.

Teika, Fujiwara. Fujiwara Teika's Superior Poems of Our Time: A Thirteenth Century Poetic Treatise & Sequence. Brower, R. H. & Miner, E., trs. 1967. 10.00x (ISBN 0-8047-0171-7). Stanford U Pr.

Thwaite, Anthony, ed. Penguin Book of Japanese Verse. (Poet Ser.). (Orig.). 1964. pap. 2.95 (ISBN 0-14-042077-0). Penguin.

Watson, Burton, tr. Ryokan: Zen Monk-Poet of Japan. LC 77-11140. (Translations from the Oriental Classics Ser). 1977. 12.50x (ISBN 0-231-04414-3). Columbia U Pr.

Yasuda, Ken. Japanese Haiku: Its Essential Nature, History & Possibilities in English, with Examples. LC 57-8795. pap. 5.95 (ISBN 0-8048-1096-6). C E Tuttle.

JAPANESE POTTERY

see Pottery, Japanese

JAPANESE PRINTS

see Color Prints, Japanese

JAPANESE PROPAGANDA

see Propaganda, Japanese

JAPANESE QUAIL

Fitzgerald, Theodore C. The Coturnix Quail: Anatomy & Histology. (Illus.). 1970. 8.95x (ISBN 0-8138-0356-X). Iowa St U Pr.

JAPANESE-RUSSIAN WAR, 1904-1905

see Russo-Japanese War, 1904-1905

JAPANESE SCIENCE

see Science, Japanese

JAPANESE SCULPTURE

see Sculpture–Japan

JAPANESE SWORDS

see Swords

JAPANESE TALES

see Tales, Japanese

JAPANESE TEA CEREMONY

Castile, Rand. The Way of Tea. LC 70-157271. (Illus.). 1971. 27.50 (ISBN 0-8348-0059-4). Weatherhill.

Chikamatsu, Shigenori. Stories from a Tearoom Window. Mori, Toshiko, ed. Mori, Kozaburo, tr. from Japanese. Orig. Title: Chaso Kanawa. (Illus.). 168p. 1982. 12.50 (ISBN 0-8048-1385-X). C E Tuttle.

Fujioka, Ryoichi. Tea Ceremony Utensils. Cort, Louise, tr. from Japanese. LC 72-11149. (Arts of Japan Ser: No. 3). Orig. Title: Chadogu. (Illus.). 128p. 1973. 15.00 (ISBN 0-8348-2702-6). Weatherhill.

Hayashiya, Tatsusaburo, et al. Japanese Arts & the Tea Ceremony. Macadam, Joseph P., tr. from Japanese. LC 74-76780. (Heibonsha Survey of Japanese Art Ser: Vol. 15). Orig. Title: Cha No Bijutsu. (Illus.). 196p. 1975. 17.50 (ISBN 0-8348-1025-5). Weatherhill.

Lee, Sherman E. Tea Taste in Japanese Art. LC 74-27416. (Asia Society Ser.). (Illus.). 1979. Repr. of 1963 ed. lib. bdg. 26.00x (ISBN 0-405-06565-5). Arno.

Okakura, Kakuzo. Book of Tea. LC 56-13134. (Illus.). bds. 8.50 (ISBN 0-8048-0069-3). C E Tuttle.

--Book of Tea. Bleiler, Everett F., ed. 1906. pap. 1.75 (ISBN 0-486-20070-1). Dover.

Sadler, A. L. Cha-No-Yu: The Japanese Tea Ceremony. LC 62-19787. 1977. pap. 3.95 (ISBN 0-8048-1224-1). C E Tuttle.

Sen, Soshitsu. Chado: The Japanese Way of Tea. LC 78-26503. (Illus.). 1979. 19.50 (ISBN 0-8348-1518-4). Weatherhill.

--Tea Life, Tea Mind. LC 79-10763. (Illus.). 1979. pap. 7.50 (ISBN 0-8348-0142-6). Weatherhill.

Tanaka, Sen'o. Tea Ceremony. LC 73-79766. (Illus.). 214p. 1973. 24.95 (ISBN 0-87011-207-4). Kodansha.

--The Tea Ceremony. (Illus.). 1977. pap. 7.95 (ISBN 0-517-53039-2, Dist. by Crown). Crown.

Tetsuzo Tanikawa & Shufunotomo Editorial Staff, eds. Gendai Chato Taikan: A General View of Contemporary Tea Ceremony & Ceramic Ware, 6 vols. (Illus., Japanese.). 1979. Set. 200.00 (ISBN 0-8048-1343-4, Pub. by Shufunotomo Co Ltd Japan). Vol. 1, 152p. Vol. 2, 164p. Vol. 3, 186p. Vol. 4, 186p. Vol. 5, 186p. Vol. 6, 200p. C E Tuttle.

JAPANESE WIT AND HUMOR

Levy, Howard S., tr. from Jap. & intro. by. Japanese Sex Jokes in Traditional Times. (Sino-Japanese Sexology Classics Translations Ser: Vol. 4). 225p. 1973. pap. 5.25 (ISBN 0-686-02354-4, 910878XX1). Warm-Soft.

Netto, C. & Wagener, G. Japanischer Humor, No. 34. (Asian Folklore & Social Life Monograph). (Ger.). 1901. 6.60 (ISBN 0-89986-034-6). E Langstaff.

JAPANESE WOOD-ENGRAVINGS

see Wood-Engravings, Japanese

JAPANESE WRESTLING

see Sumo

JAPANNING

see also Metals–Finishing; Varnish and Varnishing

JARAMILLO, PEDRO, d. 1907

Hudson, Wilson M., ed. The Healer of Los Olmos & Other Mexican Lore. LC 52-9219. (Texas Folklore Society Publications: No. 24). (Illus.). 1966. Repr. of 1951 ed. 5.95 (ISBN 0-87074-081-4). SMU Press.

JARDINE, MATHESON AND COMPANY, LTD.

Cheong, W. E. Mandarins & Merchants: A China Agency of the Early Nineteenth Century. (Scandinavian Inst. of Asian Studies, Monographs: No. 26). (Illus.). 1977. pap. text ed. 13.00x (ISBN 0-7007-0094-3). Humanities.

LeFevour, Edward. Western Enterprise in Late Ch'ing China: A Selective Survey of Jardine, Matheson & Company's Operations, 1842-1895. LC 73-386. (East Asian Monographs Ser: No. 26). 1968. pap. 9.00x (ISBN 0-674-95010-0). Harvard U Pr.

JARGONS

see Languages, Mixed

JARRELL, RANDALL, 1914-1965

Adams, Charles M. Randall Jarrell. 1978. Repr. of 1958 ed. lib. bdg. 10.00 (ISBN 0-8495-0028-1). Arden Lib.

Ferguson, Suzanne. Poetry of Randall Jarrell. LC 78-166971. (Southern Literary Studies). 1971. 17.50x (ISBN 0-8071-0941-X). La State U Pr.

Quinn O. S. F., Sr. Bernetta. Randall Jarrell. (United States Authors Ser.: No. 398). 1981. lib. bdg. 10.95 (ISBN 0-8057-7266-9). Twayne.

Rosenthal, M. L. Randall Jarrell. (Pamphlets on American Writers Ser: No. 103). pap. 1.25x (ISBN 0-8166-0646-3). U of Minn Pr.

JARRELL, RANDALL, 1914–BIBLIOGRAPHY

Adams, Charles M. Randall Jarrell: A Bibliography. LC 74-8205. Repr. of 1958 ed. lib. bdg. 15.00 (ISBN 0-8414-2977-4). Folcroft.

JARRY, ALFRED, 1873-1907

Jarry: Le Monstre et la marionette. new ed. (Collection themes et textes). 272p. (Orig., Fr.). 1973. pap. 6.75 (ISBN 0-685-39579-0, 2649). Larousse.

LaBelle, Maurice M. Alfred Jarry: Nihilism & the Theatre of the Absurd. LC 79-3009. (The Gotham Library). 1980. 20.00x (ISBN 0-8147-4995-X); pap. 9.50x (ISBN 0-8147-4996-8). NYU Pr.

Shattuck, Roger. Banquet Years. (Orig.). 1968. pap. 3.95 (ISBN 0-394-70415-0, Vin). Random.

--Banquet Years: The Origins of the Avant-Garde in France, 1885 to World War One. rev. ed. LC 79-152213. (Essay Index Reprint Ser.). Repr. of 1968 ed. 35.00 (ISBN 0-8369-2826-1). Arno.

JASPER, JOHN, 1812-1901

Hatcher, W. John Jasper: Negro Philosopher & Preacher. 59.95 (ISBN 0-8490-0452-7). Gordon Pr.

Hatcher, William E. John Jasper, the Unmatched Negro Philosopher & Preacher. LC 71-88413. Repr. of 1908 ed. 11.75x (ISBN 0-8371-1842-5, Pub. by Negro U Pr). Greenwood.

JASPERS, KARL, 1883-1969

Ehrlich, Leonard H. Karl Jaspers: Philosophy As Faith. LC 73-79505. 292p. 1975. 15.00x (ISBN 0-87023-153-7). U of Mass Pr.

Long, Eugene T. Jaspers & Bultmann: A Dialogue Between Philosophy & Theology in the Existentialist Tradition. LC 68-31725. 1968. 9.75 (ISBN 0-8223-0110-5). Duke.
Schilpp, Paul A., ed. & intro. by. The Philosophy of Karl Jaspers. LC 57-14578. (Library of Living Philosophers: Vol. Ix). 918p. 1957. 30.00 (ISBN 0-87548-134-5); pap. 12.00 (ISBN 0-87548-200-7). Open Court.
Wallraff, Charles F. Karl Jaspers: An Introduction to His Philosophy. 1970. 16.00x (ISBN 0-691-07164-0); pap. 6.95 (ISBN 0-691-01971-1). Princeton U Pr.
Young-Bruehl, Elisabeth. Freedom & Karl Jasper's Philosophy. LC 81-40436. 234p. 1981. 20.00x (ISBN 0-300-02629-3). Yale U Pr.

JAUNDICE

Goresky, C. A. & Fisher, M. M., eds. Jaundice. LC 75-8782. (Hepatology: Research & Clinical Issues Ser.: Vol. 2). 422p. 1975. 35.00 (ISBN 0-306-34802-0, Plenum Pr). Plenum Pub.

JAURES, JEAN LEON, 1859-1914

Weinstein, Harold R. Jean Jaures: A Study of Patriotism in the French Socialist Movement. LC 73-3079. 200p. 1973. Repr. of 1936 ed. lib. bdg. 13.50x (ISBN 0-374-98336-4). Octagon.

JAVA

Carey, P. B., ed. The Archive of Yogyakarta, Vol.1. (British Academy Ser.). (Illus.). 254p. Date not set. 79.00x (ISBN 0-19-725997-9). Oxford U Pr.
Chailley-Bert, Joseph. Java et ses habitants. LC 77-86968. Repr. of 1900 ed. 27.50 (ISBN 0-404-16701-2). AMS Pr.
Changes in Community Institutions & Income Distribution in a West Java Village. (IRRI Research Paper Ser.: No. 50). 16p. 1981. pap. 5.00 (ISBN 0-686-69632-8, R131, IRRI). Unipub.
Collier, William L., et al. Income, Employment & Food Systems in Javanese Coastal Villages. LC 77-620017. (Papers in International Studies: Southeast Asia: No. 44). (Illus.). pap. 10.00x (ISBN 0-89680-031-8). Ohio U Ctr Intl.
Forman, Bedrich. Borobudur: The Buddhist Legend in Tone. (Illus.). 1980. 16.95 (ISBN 0-686-70134-8, Mayflower Bks). Smith Pubs.
Geertz, Clifford. The Religion of Java. LC 75-18746. xvi, 396p. 1976. pap. 5.95 (ISBN 0-226-28510-3, P658, Phoen). U of Chicago Pr.
Geraldson, Cornelius. An Addition to the Sea Journal of the Hollanders Unto Java. LC 68-27480. (English Experience Ser.: No. 2). (Illus.). 40p. 1968. Repr. of 1598 ed. 8.00 (ISBN 90-221-0002-2). Walter J Johnson.
Hoadley, M. C. & Hooker, M. B. Introduction to Javanese Law. LC 80-26636. (Monographs of the Association for Asian Studies: No. XXXVII). 1981. text ed. 9.95x (ISBN 0-8165-0727-9). U of Ariz Pr.
Levine, Charles & Hoefer, Hans, eds. Java. (Apa Photo Guides Ser.). (Illus.). 1978. pap. 14.00x (ISBN 0-686-23145-7). Intl Learn Syst.
Moertono, Soemarsaid. State & Statecraft in Old Java: A Study of the Later Mataram Period, 16th to 19th Century. rev. ed. (Monograph Ser.: No. 43). 181p. 1981. 6.50 (ISBN 0-686-72446-1). Cornell Mod Indo.
Palmier, L. H. Social Status & Power in Java. (Monographs on Social Anthropology: No. 20). 1969. pap. text ed. 9.00x (ISBN 0-485-19620-4, Athlone Pr). Humanities.
Ponder, H. W. Javanese Panorama. 1978. lib. bdg. 27.50 (ISBN 0-8495-4317-7). Arden Lib.
Raffles, Stamford. The History of Java, 2 vols. (Asia Historical Reprints Ser.). 1979. Set. 147.00x (ISBN 0-19-580347-7). Oxford U Pr.
Raffles, Thomas S. The History of Java, 2 vols. LC 77-87509. (Illus.). Repr. of 1817 ed. Set. 75.00 (ISBN 0-404-16770-5). AMS Pr.
Technical Progress & Income Distribution in a Rice Village in West Java. (IRRI Research Paper Ser.: No. 55). 11p. 1980. pap. 5.00 (ISBN 0-686-75108-6, R142, IRRI). Unipub.
Weidenreich, Franz. Giant Early Man from Java & South China. LC 76-44798. (American Museum of Natural History. Anthropological Papers: Vol. 40, Pt. 1). Repr. of 1945 ed. 27.50 (ISBN 0-404-15978-8). AMS Pr.
Wessing, Robert. Cosmology & Social Behavior in a West Javanese Settlement: Papers in International Studies. LC 77-620054. (No. 47). 1978. pap. 12.00 (ISBN 0-89680-072-5). Ohio U Ctr Intl.
Woodward, Hiram W., ed. Barabudur: History & Significance of a Buddhist Monument. Gomez, Luis O. 1981. 20.00 (ISBN 0-89581-151-0). Lancaster-Miller.

JAVA-BIBLIOGRAPHY

Van Niel, Robert. Survey of Historical Source Materials in Java & Manila. LC 72-132554. (Asian Studies at Hawaii Ser.: No. 5). (Orig.). 1971. pap. text ed. 7.00x (ISBN 0-87022-841-2). U Pr of Hawaii.

JAVA SEA, BATTLE OF THE, 1942

Oosten, F. C. Van. The Battle of the Java Sea. LC 76-24052. (Sea Battles in Close-up, Ser.: No. 15). 1977. 5.95 (ISBN 0-87021-911-1). Naval Inst Pr.
Van Oosten, F. C. The Battle of the Java Sea. (Sea Battles in Close-up Ser.). (Illus.). 1976. 13.50x (ISBN 0-7110-0615-6). Intl Pubns Serv.
Winslow, Walter G. Ghost of the Java Coast. LC 74-2269. (Illus.). 216p. 1974. 7.95 (ISBN 0-914042-00-9). Coral Reef.

JAVANESE DRAMA-HISTORY AND CRITICISM

Lindsay, Jenny M. Javanese Gamelan. (Illus.). 80p. 1980. pap. 8.95x (ISBN 0-19-580413-9). Oxford U Pr.

JAVANESE LANGUAGE

Horne, Elinor C. Javanese - English Dictionary. (Linguistic Ser). 1974. text ed. 45.00x (ISBN 0-300-01689-1). Yale U Pr.
Rastogi, Navjivan. Krama Tantricism of Kashmir, Vol. 1. 1979. 12.95 (ISBN 0-89684-048-4, Pub. by Motilal Banarsidass India). Orient Bk Dist.
Zurbuchen, Mary S. Introduction to Old Javanese Language and Literature: A Kawi Prose Anthology. LC 76-16235. (Michigan Series in South & Southeast Asian Languages & Linguistics: No. 3). 150p. 1976. pap. 5.00x (ISBN 0-89148-053-6). Ctr S&SE Asian.

JAVANESE MUSIC

see Music, Javanese

JAWBONING

see Wage-Price Policy

JAWORSKI, LEON

Jaworski, Leon & Schneider, Dick. Crossroads. 1981. 10.95 (ISBN 0-89191-289-4). Cook.

JAWS

see also Mastication; Temporomandibular Joint

Bhaskar, S. N. Radiographic Interpretation for the Dentist. 3rd ed. LC 78-31556. 1979. 34.50 (ISBN 0-8016-0690-X). Mosby.
Fried, Lawerence A. Anatomy of the Head, Neck, Face, & Jaws. 2nd ed. LC 80-16800. (Illus.). 299p. 1980. text ed. 17.50 (ISBN 0-8121-0717-9). Lea & Febiger.
Harnisch, Herbert. Clinical Aspects & Treatment of Cysts of the Jaws. (Illus.). 237p. 1974. 38.00 (ISBN 0-686-29201-4). Quint Pub Co.
Harris, Vivian J. Radiology of Jaw Bone Masses in Adults & Children. (Illus.). 280p. 1981. 22.50 (ISBN 0-87527-212-6). Green.
International Society of Geographical Pathology, 11th Conference, Newcastle-Upon-Tyne, August 1972. Oral Pathology, Intestinal Pathology, Hypobaric Pathology: Proceedings. Ruettner, J. R., ed. (Pathologia et Microbiologica: Vol. 39, No. 3-4). 1973. pap. 32.75 (ISBN 3-8055-1370-4). S Karger.
Killey, H. C. & Kay, L. W. Benign Cystic Lesions of the Jaws: Their Diagnosis & Treatment. 3rd ed. (Illus.). 1977. pap. text ed. 16.25 (ISBN 0-443-01616-X). Churchill.
Topazian, Richard G. & Goldberg, Morton H. Management of Infections of the Oral & Maxillofacial Regions. (Illus.). 500p. 1981. text ed. write for info. (ISBN 0-7216-8879-9). Saunders.
Woelfel, Julian B. Permar's Outline for Dental Anatomy. 2nd ed. LC 78-31312. (Illus.). 228p. 1979. pap. 14.50 (ISBN 0-8121-0662-8). Lea & Febiger.

JAWS-SURGERY

Bell, William H., et al. Surgical Correction of Dentofacial Deformities. LC 76-27050. 1979. text ed. 150.00 (ISBN 0-7216-1671-2); Vol. 1. 70.00 (ISBN 0-7216-1675-5); Vol. 2. 80.00 (ISBN 0-7216-1707-7). Saunders.
Robinson, Marsh. Osteotomy of Mandibular Ramus: Prognathism & Allied Problems. (Illus.). 168p. 1977. 19.50 (ISBN 0-398-03610-1). C C Thomas.
Thoma, Kurt H. Oral Surgery, 2 Vols. 5th ed. LC 69-15220. (Illus.). 1969. Set. 79.50 (ISBN 0-8016-4915-3). Mosby.
Whitaker, Linton A. & Randall, Peter, eds. Symposium on Reconstruction of Jaw Deformity. LC 78-4867. (Symposia of the Educational Foundaion of the American Society of Plastic & Reconstructive Surgeons, Inc. Ser.). 1978. text ed. 55.50 (ISBN 0-8016-5610-9). Mosby.

JAY, JOHN, 1745-1829

Jay, William. Life of John Jay, 2 vols. (Select Bibliography Reprint Ser.). 1972. Repr. of 1833 ed. Set. 48.00 (ISBN 0-8369-6858-1). Arno.
Monaghan, Frank. John Jay. LC 74-153339. Repr. of 1935 ed. 24.50 (ISBN 0-404-04647-9). AMS Pr.
Morris, Richard B. John Jay: The Nation & the Court. LC 67-25933. 1967. 7.00x (ISBN 0-8419-8713-0, Pub. by Boston U Pr). Holmes & Meier.
Morris, Richard B., ed. John Jay: The Making of a Revolutionary-Unpublished Papers 1745-1780, Vol. 1. LC 75-6349. (Illus.). 878p. 1975. 27.50 (ISBN 0-06-013080-6, HarpT). Har-Row.
--John Jay: The Winning of the Peace, 1780-1784, Vol. II. LC 79-2644. (Illus.). 1980. 30.00 (ISBN 0-06-013048-2, HarpT). Har-Row.
Pellew, George. John Jay. LC 80-19992. (American Statesmen Ser.). 342p. 1980. pap. 5.95 (ISBN 0-87754-193-0). Chelsea Hse.
--John Jay. Morse, John T., Jr., ed. LC 70-128973. (American Statesmen: No. 9). Repr. of 1898 ed. 19.50 (ISBN 0-404-50859-6). AMS Pr.
Smith, Donald L. John Jay: Founder of a State & Nation. LC 68-57156. (gr. 12 up). 1968. text ed. 8.75x (ISBN 0-8077-2177-8). Tchrs Coll.

JAY, WILLIAM, 1789-1858

Jay, William. Autobiography of William Jay. 1974. 10.95 (ISBN 0-85151-177-5). Banner of Truth.
Tuckerman, Bayard. William Jay & the Constitutional Movement for the Abolition of Slavery. LC 75-108351. (Research & Source Works Ser.: No. 410). 1970. Repr. of 1893 ed. lib. bdg. 17.50 (ISBN 0-8337-4709-6). B Franklin.
--William Jay & the Constitutional Movement for the Abolition of Slavery. LC 69-19000. (Illus.). Repr. of 1893 ed. 12.25x (ISBN 0-8371-4592-9). Greenwood.

JAYS

Pijlman, F. & Heering, P. Jay. (Animal Environment Ser.). (Illus.). 1979. 4.95 (ISBN 0-8120-5302-8). Barron.
Wilmore, Sylvia B. Crows, Jays, Ravens (& Their Relatives) (Illus.). 1979. pap. 6.95 (ISBN 0-87666-878-3, PS-779). TFH Pubns.
--Crows, Jays, Ravens & Their Relatives. LC 77-79245. (Illus.). 1977. 12.95 (ISBN 0-8397-1894-2). Eriksson.

JAY'S TREATY, 1794

Bemis, Samuel F. Jay's Treaty: A Study in Commerce & Diplomacy. LC 75-11844. (Illus.). 1975. Repr. of 1962 ed. lib. bdg. 29.50 (ISBN 0-8371-8133-X, BEJT). Greenwood.
Combs, Jerald A. The Jay Treaty: Political Battleground of the Founding Fathers. LC 70-84044. 1970. 21.50x (ISBN 0-520-01573-8). U of Cal Pr.
Ritcheson, Charles R. Aftermath of Revolution: British Policy Toward the United States, 1783-1795. LC 77-86328. 1969. 12.50 (ISBN 0-87074-100-4). SMU Press.

JAZZ DANCE

Audy, Robert. Jazz Dancing: How to Teach Yourself. 1978. pap. 5.95 (ISBN 0-394-72356-2, Vin). Random.
Czompo, Ann I. Recreational Jazz Dance. 2nd ed. Czompo, Andor, ed. LC 79-26223. (Illus.). 1979. pap. text ed. 9.95 (ISBN 0-935496-00-9). AC Pubns.
Dow, Allen. The Official Guide to Jazz Dancing. LC 79-55238. (Illus.). 96p. 1980. 5.98 (ISBN 0-89196-064-3, Domus Bks). Quality Bks IL.
Stearns, Marshall & Stearns, Jean. Jazz Dance: The Story of American Vernacular Dance. LC 79-2531. (Illus.). 1979. pap. 6.95 (ISBN 0-02-872510-7). Schirmer Bks.

JAZZ MUSIC

see also Blues (Songs, etc.); Gospel Music; Instrumentation and Orchestration

Backus, Rob. Fire Music: A Political History of Jazz. (Illus.). 104p. (Orig.). 1977. pap. 3.95 (ISBN 0-917702-00-X). Vanguard Bks.
Balliett, Whitney. Dinosaurs in the Morning: 41 Pieces on Jazz. LC 78-93. 1978. Repr. of 1962 ed. lib. bdg. 22.25 (ISBN 0-313-20283-4, BADI). Greenwood.
--Improvising: Sixteen Jazz Musicians & Their Art. LC 76-42635. 1977. 12.95 (ISBN 0-19-502149-5). Oxford U Pr.
--New York Notes: A Journal of Jazz in the Seventies. LC 76-51396. (Paperback Ser.). 1977. pap. 4.95 (ISBN 0-306-80037-3). Da Capo.
--Night Creature: A Journal of Jazz, 1975-1980. (Illus.). 275p. 1981. 15.95 (ISBN 0-19-502908-9). Oxford U Pr.
--The Sound of Surprise. LC 77-17852. (Roots of Jazz Ser.). 1978. Repr. of 1961 ed. lib. bdg. 19.50 (ISBN 0-306-77543-3). Da Capo.
Balmforth, Lynn. Rock 'n' Reality. 144p. 1971. pap. 2.50 (ISBN 0-89036-004-9). Hawkes Pub Inc.
Baraka, Amiri, pseud. Black Music. 1967. pap. 3.95 (ISBN 0-688-24344-4). Morrow.
Berendt, Joachim. The Jazz Book: From New Orleans to Rock & Free Jazz. rev. ed. Morgenstern, Dan, ed. & tr. from Ger. LC 73-81750. 480p. 1975. 12.95 (ISBN 0-88208-027-X); pap. 8.95 (ISBN 0-88208-028-8). Lawrence Hill.
--The Jazz Book: From Ragtime to Fusion & Beyond. rev. ed. Morganstern, Dan & Bredigkeit, H. B., trs. from German. 1981. 15.95 (ISBN 0-88208-140-3); pap. 8.95 (ISBN 0-88208-141-1). Lawrence Hill.
Berendt, Joachim E. The Story of Jazz. LC 78-18428. 1978. 12.95 (ISBN 0-13-850248-X, Spec); pap. 6.95 (ISBN 0-13-850230-7). P-H.
Blesh, Rudi. Classic Piano Rags. (Orig.). 1973. pap. 8.95 (ISBN 0-486-20469-3). Dover.
--Shining Trumpets: A History of Jazz. rev. 2nd ed. LC 75-31664. (Roots of Jazz Ser). (Illus.). xxxii, 412p. 1975. lib. bdg. 27.50 (ISBN 0-306-70658-X); pap. 7.95 (ISBN 0-306-80029-2). Da Capo.
Blesh, Rudi & Janis, Harriet. They All Played Ragtime. rev. ed. LC 66-19054. (Illus.). 347p. 1966-71. pap. 7.95 (ISBN 0-8256-0091-X, 000091, Oak). Music Sales.
Blocher, Arlo. Jazz. new ed. LC 75-39816. (Illus.). 32p. (gr. 5-10). 1976. PLB 6.89 (ISBN 0-89375-014-X); pap. 2.50 (ISBN 0-89375-030-1). Troll Assocs.
Brown, Sandy. The McJazz Manuscripts. Binns, David, ed. LC 79-670335. (Illus.). 176p. 1979. 16.95 (ISBN 0-571-11319-2, Pub. by Faber & Faber). Merrimack Bk Serv.
Budds, Michael J. Jazz in the Sixties: The Expansion of Musical Resources & Techniques. LC 78-17438. 1978. 8.95x (ISBN 0-87745-086-2); pap. 4.95x (ISBN 0-87745-087-0). U of Iowa Pr.
Cayou, Dolores K. Modern Jazz Dance. LC 70-126056. 148p. 1971. pap. 5.95 (ISBN 0-87484-139-9). Mayfield Pub.
Charlie Parker Omnibook for E Flat Instruments: Recorded Solos. 1978. 9.95 (ISBN 0-685-90817-8, Atlantic Music Corp.). Criterion Mus.
Charters, Samuel & Kunstadt, Leonard. My Husband Gabrilowitsch: A History of the New York Scene. 27.50 (ISBN 0-306-76055-X). Da Capo.
Chilton, John. Teach Yourself Jazz. 1979. pap. 3.95 (ISBN 0-679-12225-7). McKay.
Clayton, Peter & Gammond, Peter. Fourteen Miles on a Clear Night. LC 78-5685. (Illus.). 1978. Repr. of 1966 ed. lib. bdg. 16.25x (ISBN 0-313-20475-6, CLFM). Greenwood.
Coeuroy, Andre. La Musique Moderne: Le Jazz. 1926. 45.00 (ISBN 0-932062-28-8). Sharon Hill.
Coker, Jerry. The Jazz Idiom. (Illus.). 96p. 1975. 7.95 (ISBN 0-13-509851-3, Spec); pap. 2.95 (ISBN 0-13-509844-0, Spec). P-H.
--Listening to Jazz. (Illus.). 1978. 8.95 (ISBN 0-13-537217-8, Spec); pap. 3.45 (ISBN 0-13-537209-7, Spec). P-H.
Collier, G. Jazz. (Resources of Music Ser.). (Illus.). 200p. 1975. 19.95 (ISBN 0-521-20561-1); pap. 6.95 (ISBN 0-521-09887-4); tape 16.95 (ISBN 0-521-20560-3); record 11.95 (ISBN 0-521-20563-8). Cambridge U Pr.
Collier, James L. The Making of Jazz. 1979. pap. 6.95 (ISBN 0-440-55855-7, Delta). Dell.
--The Making of Jazz: A Comprehensive History. 1978. 20.00 (ISBN 0-395-26286-9). HM.
Condon, Eddie. We Called It Music: A Generation of Jazz. LC 76-110823. Repr. of 1947 ed. lib. bdg. 20.50x (ISBN 0-8371-3223-1, CWCI). Greenwood.
Condon, Eddie & Gehman, Richard, eds. Treasury of Jazz. LC 75-2693. 488p. 1975. Repr. of 1956 ed. lib. bdg. 28.25x (ISBN 0-8371-8032-5, COTJ). Greenwood.
Coryell, Julie & Friedman, Laura. Jazz Rock Fusion, the People, the Music. 1978. pap. 9.95 (ISBN 0-440-54409-2, Delta). Dell.
Dance, Stanley. The World of Swing. LC 79-15249. (Da Capo Quality Paperback Ser.). (Illus.). 436p. 1979. pap. 7.95 (ISBN 0-306-80103-5). Da Capo.
Dankworth, Avril. Jazz: An Introduction to Its Musical Basis. 1968. pap. 6.95x (ISBN 0-19-316501-5). Oxford U Pr.
Dexter, Dave. Jazz Story: From the Nineties to the Sixties. (Illus., Orig.). (gr. 8-10). 1964. pap. 2.95 (ISBN 0-13-509463-1, Spec). P-H.
Dexter, Dave, Jr. Jazz Cavalcade. LC 77-8035. (Roots of Jazz). (Illus.). 1977. Repr. of 1946 ed. lib. bdg. 22.50 (ISBN 0-306-77431-3). Da Capo.
Driggs, Frank & Lewine, Harris. Black Beauty, White Heat: A Pictorial History of Classical Jazz, 1920-1950. (Illus.). 352p. 1981. 35.00 (ISBN 0-688-03771-2); prepub. 29.95 until Dec. 31st (19.50 (ISBN 0-686-73677-X). Morrow.
Erlich, Lillian. What Jazz Is All About. rev. ed. LC 74-30486. (Illus.). 256p. (gr. 7 up). 1975. PLB 8.29 (ISBN 0-671-32731-3). Messner.
Feather, L. Inside Jazz. LC 77-23411. (Roots of Jazz Ser.). (Illus.). 1977. lib. bdg. 17.50 (ISBN 0-306-77437-2); pap. 5.95 (ISBN 0-306-80076-4). Da Capo.
Feather, Leonard. The Book of Jazz. 1976. pap. 1.95 (ISBN 0-440-30680-9, LE). Dell.
--The Encyclopedia of Jazz. Orig. Title: New Edition of the Encyclopedia of Jazz. 1960. 20.00 (ISBN 0-8180-1203-X). Horizon.
--From Satchmo to Miles. LC 70-187311. 1974. pap. 6.95 (ISBN 0-8128-1703-6). Stein & Day.
--The Passion for Jazz. LC 80-15133. (Illus.). 1980. 9.95 (ISBN 0-8180-1221-8). Horizon.
--The Pleasures of Jazz. 1977. pap. 3.95 (ISBN 0-440-56946-X, Delta). Dell.
Feather, Leonard & Tracy, Jack. Laughter from the Hip, the Lighter Side of Jazz. (Paperbacks Ser.). 1979. pap. 5.95 (ISBN 0-306-80092-6). Da Capo.
Finkelstein, Sidney. Jazz: A People's Music. LC 74-23386. (Roots of Jazz Ser). ix, 278p. 1975. Repr. of 1948 ed. lib. bdg. 22.50 (ISBN 0-306-70659-8). Da Capo.

Francis, Andre. Jazz. LC 76-6983. (Roots of Jazz Ser.). 1976. Repr. of 1960 ed. lib. bdg. 19.50 (ISBN 0-306-70812-4). Da Capo.
Gammond, Peter & Fox, Charles. Jazz on Record: A Critical Guide. Morgan, Alun, ed. LC 78-8189. 1978. Repr. of 1960 ed. lib. bdg. 22.00x (ISBN 0-313-20513-2, GAJA). Greenwood.
Giddins, Gary. Riding on a Blue Note: Jazz & American Pop. 330p. 1981. 16.95 (ISBN 0-19-502835-X). Oxford U Pr.
Gillespie, Dizzy & Fraser, Al. To Be or Not to Bop: Memoirs. LC 77-76237. (Illus.). 1979. 15.95 (ISBN 0-385-12052-4). Doubleday.
Goddard, Chris. Jazz Away from Home. LC 79-10542. (Illus.). 1979. 14.95 (ISBN 0-448-22367-8). Paddington.
Goffin, Robert. Jazz: From the Congo to the Metropolitan. Schaap, Walter & Feather, Leonard G., trs. from Fr. LC 74-23384. (Roots of Jazz Ser). xii, 254p. 1975. Repr. of 1944 ed. lib. bdg. 22.50 (ISBN 0-306-70680-6). Da Capo.
Goldberg, Isaac. George Gershwin: A Study in American Music. LC 58-11627. (Illus.). 1958. pap. 5.95 (ISBN 0-8044-6195-3). Ungar.
--Tin Pan Alley. LC 60-63364. (Illus.). 1961. pap. 5.95 (ISBN 0-8044-6196-1). Ungar.
Goldblatt, Burt. Newport Jazz Festival: The Illustrated History. (Illus.). 1977. 14.95 (ISBN 0-8037-6440-5). Dial.
Goldstein, Gil. The Jazz Composer's Companion. (Illus.). 144p. pap. 12.95 (ISBN 0-8256-4207-8). Music Sales.
Gottlieb, Bill. The Golden Age of Jazz. 1979. pap. 7.95 (ISBN 0-671-24730-1). S&S.
Green, Benny. The Reluctant Art: The Growth of Jazz. (New Reprints in Essay & General Literature Index Ser.). 1975. Repr. of 1963 ed. 18.25 (ISBN 0-518-10199-1, 10199). Arno.
Gridley, Mark C. Jazz Styles. (Illus.). 352p. 1978. text ed. 16.95 (ISBN 0-13-509885-8); pap. text ed. 12.95 (ISBN 0-13-509877-7). P-H.
Grossman, William & Farrell, Jack. The Heart of Jazz. LC 76-75730. (Roots of Jazz Ser.). 1976. Repr. of 1956 ed. lib. bdg. 25.00 (ISBN 0-306-70811-6). Da Capo.
Grossman, William L. & Farrell, Jack W. The Heart of Jazz. LC 59-9978. (Illus.). 1956. 12.00x (ISBN 0-8147-0174-4). NYU Pr.
Hadlock, Richard. Jazz Masters of the Twenties. 1965. pap. 2.95 (ISBN 0-02-060770-9). Macmillan.
Harris, Howard C., Jr. & Fielder, William. The Complete Book of Improvisation - Composition & Funk Techniques: Essentials & Augmentations for the Vital Self-Instrument in Jazz Music - Theory, Practices & Life Parallels. (Illus.). 181p. (Orig.). Date not set. price not set spiral bound (ISBN 0-940026-00-7). DeMos Music.
Harrison, Max. Jazz Retrospect. 1977. 11.00 (ISBN 0-8008-4310-X, Crescendo). Taplinger.
Harvey, Eddie. Jazz Piano. (Teach Yourself Ser.). 1974. pap. 5.95 (ISBN 0-679-10369-4). McKay.
Henry, Robert E. The Jazz Ensemble. (Illus.). 144p. 1981. 14.95 (ISBN 0-13-509992-7, Spec); pap. 7.95 (ISBN 0-13-509984-6). P-H.
Hentoff, Nat. Jazz Is. 1978. pap. 2.25 (ISBN 0-380-01858-6, 36558, Discus). Avon.
--The Jazz Life. LC 74-23383. (The Roots of Jazz Ser.). 1975. lib. bdg. 22.50 (ISBN 0-306-70681-4); pap. 5.95 (ISBN 0-306-80088-8). Da Capo.
--Jazz: New Perspectives on the History of Jazz by Twelve of the World's Foremost Jazz Critics & Scholars. McCarthy, Albert J., ed. LC 74-20882. (Roots of Jazz Ser.). xiv, 399p. 1975. pap. 5.95 (ISBN 0-306-80002-0). Da Capo.
Hentoff, Nat & McCarthy, Albert. Jazz: New Perspectives on the History of Jazz. (Music Reprint Ser.). 1974. Repr. of 1959 ed. lib. bdg. 25.00 (ISBN 0-306-70592-3). Da Capo.
Hoare, I., et al. The Soul Book. Frith, S., ed. 1976. pap. 3.95 (ISBN 0-440-58014-5, Delta). Dell.
Hobson, Wilder. American Jazz Music. LC 76-22565. (Roots of Jazz Ser.). 1976. Repr. of 1939 ed. lib. bdg. 19.50 (ISBN 0-306-70816-7). Da Capo.
Hodeir, Andre. Jazz: Its Evolution & Essence. rev. ed. Noakes, David, tr. from French. LC 79-52101. (Illus.). 1980. pap. 3.95 (ISBN 0-394-17525-5, B436, BC). Grove.
--Jazz: Its Evolution & Essence. Noakes, David, tr. from Fr. LC 74-23387. (Roots of Jazz Ser). ix, 295p. 1975. Repr. of 1956 ed. lib. bdg. 22.50 (ISBN 0-306-70682-2). Da Capo.
--Toward Jazz. LC 76-7568. (The Roots of Jazz Ser.). 1976. Repr. of 1962 ed. lib. bdg. 21.50 (ISBN 0-306-70810-8). Da Capo.
--The Worlds of Jazz. Burch, Noel, tr. from Fr. 1972. pap. 2.95 (ISBN 0-394-17770-3, E572, Ever). Grove.
Hodes, Art & Hansen, Chadwick, eds. Selections from the Gutter: Portraits from the Jazz Record. LC 75-7193. 1977. 19.95x (ISBN 0-520-02999-2); pap. 5.95 (ISBN 0-520-03719-7). U of Cal Pr.
Horricks, Raymond. Count Basie & His Orchestra. LC 79-138009. (Illus.). 320p. 1972. Repr. of 1957 ed. 17.00x (ISBN 0-8371-5656-4, Pub. by Negro U Pr). Greenwood.
Jost, Ekkehard. Free Jazz. (Studies in Jazz Research: No. 4). 1975. pap. 27.00 (ISBN 3-7024-0013-3, 51-26654). Eur-Am Music.
Kaufman, Fredrick & Guckin, John P. The African Roots of Jazz. LC 78-8470. 148p. 1979. 14.95 (ISBN 0-88284-065-7); pap. 7.95 (ISBN 0-686-64874-9). Alfred Pub.
Keil, Charles. Urban Blues. LC 66-13876. (Illus.). 1966. 10.00x (ISBN 0-226-42959-8). U of Chicago Pr.
--Urban Blues. LC 66-13876. (Illus.). 1968. pap. 2.45 (ISBN 0-226-42960-1, P291, Phoen). U of Chicago Pr.
Kennington, Donald & Read, Danny L. The Literature of Jazz. 2nd ed. LC 80-19837. 248p. 1981. pap. 11.00 (ISBN 0-8389-0313-4). ALA.
Koerner, Friedrich & Glawischnig, Dieter. Jazz Research (Jazzforschung, Vol. 1. (Ger.). 1970. pap. 49.00 (ISBN 3-7024-0032-X, 51-26601). Eur-Am Music.
--Jazz Research (Jazzforschung, Vol. 2. (Ger.). 1970. pap. 49.00 (ISBN 3-7024-0033-8, 51-26602). Eur-Am Music.
--Jazz Research (Jazzforschung, Vol. 3/4. (Ger.). 1973. pap. 56.00 (ISBN 3-7024-0040-0, 51-26603). Eur-Am Music.
--Jazz Research (Jazzforschung, Vol. 5. (Ger.). 1974. pap. 49.00 (ISBN 3-7024-0072-9, 51-26605). Eur-Am Music.
Kofsky, Frank. Black Nationalism & the Revolution in Music. LC 77-108716. (Illus.). 1970. 14.00 (ISBN 0-87348-149-6); pap. 4.95 (ISBN 0-87348-129-1). Path Pr NY.
Kraehenbuehl, David. Jazz & Blues. Clark, Frances & Goss, Louise, eds. Incl. Book 1. pap. text ed. 3.20 (ISBN 0-87487-111-5); Book 2. pap. text ed. 3.40 (ISBN 0-87487-112-3); Books 5 & 6. 1974. pap. text ed. 3.95 (ISBN 0-87487-113-1). (Frances Clark Library for Piano Students Ser.). 1963. Summy.
Kynaston, Trent & Ricci, Robert. Jazz Improvisation. LC 77-28290. (Illus.). 1978. 15.95 (ISBN 0-13-509315-5, Spec); pap. 9.95 (ISBN 0-13-509307-4). P-H.
Lambert, G. E. Duke Ellington. (Illus.). 1961. pap. 3.95 (ISBN 0-498-04029-1, Prpta). A S Barnes.
Lang, Iain. Jazz in Perspective. LC 76-6985. (Roots of Jazz Ser.). 1976. lib. bdg. 18.50 (ISBN 0-306-70814-0). Da Capo.
Langridge, Derek. Your Jazz Collection. 1970. 12.50 (ISBN 0-208-01061-0, Archon). Shoe String.
Lee, Edward. Jazz: An Introduction. 1977. 7.95 (ISBN 0-8008-4308-8, Crescendo). Taplinger.
Leonard, Neil. Jazz & the White Americans: The Acceptance of a New Art Form. LC 62-19626. 1962. 9.00x (ISBN 0-226-47251-5). U of Chicago Pr.
Locke, Alain. Negro & His Music. Bd. with Negro Art: Past & Present. LC 69-18592. (American Negro-His History & Literature Ser., No.2). 1969. Repr. of 1936 ed. 8.00 (ISBN 0-405-01879-7). Arno.
Longstreet, Stephen. Real Jazz, Old & New. Repr. of 1956 ed. lib. bdg. 15.00x (ISBN 0-8371-2524-3, LORJ). Greenwood.
Lyons, Jimmy & Kamin, Ira. Dizzy, Duke, The Count & Me: The Story of the Monterey Jazz Festival. LC 78-52507. 1978. 19.95 (ISBN 0-89395-005-X); pap. 9.95 (ISBN 0-89395-006-8). Cal Living Bks.
Lyttelton, Humphrey. The Best of Jazz: Basin Street to Harlem. LC 79-13159. (Illus.). 1979. 8.95 (ISBN 0-8008-0727-8, Crescendo). Taplinger.
Lyttleton, Humphrey. Humphrey Lyttelton's Jazz & Big Band Quiz. 1979. 13.50 (ISBN 0-7134-2011-1, Pub. by Batsford England). David & Charles.
McBride, Mary Margaret & Whiteman, Paul. Jazz. LC 74-15753. (Popular Culture in America Ser.). (Illus.). 298p. 1975. Repr. 18.00x (ISBN 0-405-06387-3). Arno.
McCarthy, Albert. Big Band Jazz. (Illus.). 1977. pap. 6.95 (ISBN 0-425-03535-2, Windhover). Berkley Pub.
--Louis Armstrong. (Illus.). 1961. pap. 3.95 (ISBN 0-498-04033-X, Prpta). A S Barnes.
Martinez, Raymond J. Portraits of New Orleans Jazz. 63p. 1971. pap. 2.50 (ISBN 0-911116-93-1). Pelican.
Meeker, David. Jazz in the Movies. 1978. 13.95 (ISBN 0-87000-403-4). Arlington Hse.
Mehegan, John. Jazz Improvisation, 4 vols. Incl. Vol. 1. Tonal & Rhythmic Principles. Bernstein, Leonard, intro. by. 1959 (ISBN 0-8256-4157-8); Vol. 2. Jazz Rhythm & the Improvised Line. Arlen, Harold, intro. by. 1962 (ISBN 0-8256-4158-6); Vol. 3. Swing & Early Progressive Piano Styles. Silver, Horace, intro. by. 1964 (ISBN 0-8256-4159-4); Vol. 4. Contemporary Piano Styles. 1965 (ISBN 0-8256-4160-8). LC 58-13525. (Orig.). pap. 9.95 ea. (Consolidated). Music Sales.
Miller, Paul E. Down Beat's Yearbook of Swing. LC 78-6152. 1978. Repr. of 1939 ed. lib. bdg. 15.00x (ISBN 0-313-20476-4, MIYS). Greenwood.
--Esquire's Jazz Books, 3 vols. Incl. 1944 Jazz Book (ISBN 0-306-79525-6); 1945 Jazz Book (ISBN 0-306-79526-4); 1946 Jazz Book (ISBN 0-306-79527-2). (The Roots of Jazz Ser.). (Repr. of 1944-46 ed.). 1979. Set. 50.00 (ISBN 0-306-79528-0); 19.50 ea. Da Capo.
Morgan, Alun & Horricks, Raymond. Modern Jazz: A Survey of Developments Since 1939. LC 77-8002. 1977. Repr. of 1956 ed. lib. bdg. 20.25 (ISBN 0-8371-9674-4, MOMO). Greenwood.
Nanry, Charles. The Jazz Text. 1979. 10.95 (ISBN 0-442-25904-2). Van Nos Reinhold.
Nanry, Charles, ed. American Music: From Storyville to Woodstock. LC 71-164978. (Culture & Society Ser.). 1975. 12.95 (ISBN 0-87855-007-0); pap. text ed. 4.95x (ISBN 0-87855-506-4). Transaction Bks.
Oakley, Giles. The Devil's Music: A History of the Blues. LC 78-6161. (Illus.). 1978. pap. 6.95 (ISBN 0-15-625586-3, Harv). HarBraceJ.
Oliver, Paul. Bessie Smith. (Illus.). 1961. pap. 3.95 (ISBN 0-498-04031-3, Prpta). A S Barnes.
Osgood, Henry O. So This Is Jazz. LC 77-17859. (Roots of Jazz Ser.). (Illus.). 1978. Repr. of 1926 ed. lib. bdg. 22.50 (ISBN 0-306-77540-9). Da Capo.
Ostransky, Leroy. The Anatomy of Jazz. LC 73-11857. (Illus.). xiii, 362p. 1973. Repr. of 1960 ed. lib. bdg. 18.75x (ISBN 0-8371-7092-3, OSAJ). Greenwood.
--Jazz City: The Impact of Our Cities on the Development of Jazz. LC 78-18492. 1978. 10.95 (ISBN 0-13-509380-5, Spec); pap. 5.95 (ISBN 0-13-509372-4). P-H.
--Understanding Jazz. (Illus.). 352p. 1977. 12.95 (ISBN 0-13-936542-7, Spec); pap. 5.95 (ISBN 0-13-936534-6). P-H.
Panassie, Hughes. Hot Jazz: The Guide to Swing Music. LC 74-135606. Repr. of 1936 ed. 17.75x (ISBN 0-8371-5181-3, Pub. by Negro U Pr). Greenwood.
Panassie, Hugues. The Real Jazz. LC 73-13328. 284p. 1973. Repr. of 1960 ed. lib. bdg. 18.25 (ISBN 0-8371-7123-7, PARJ). Greenwood.
Paul, Elliot H. That Crazy American Music. LC 77-102842. 1970. Repr. of 1957 ed. 14.00 (ISBN 0-8046-0762-1). Kennikat.
Ramsey, Frederic & Smith, Charles E., eds. Jazzmen. LC 78-181233. 360p. 1939. Repr. 27.00 (ISBN 0-403-01654-1). Scholarly.
Ramsey, Frederic, Jr. & Smith, Charles E., eds. Jazzmen. LC 77-4215. (Illus.). 1977. pap. 4.95 (ISBN 0-15-646205-2, Harv). HarBraceJ.
Rich, Allan. Listeners Guide to Jazz. 1980. 9.95 (ISBN 0-671-25444-8). S&S.
Rose, Al & Souchon, Edmond. New Orleans Jazz: A Family Album. rev. ed. LC 77-24076. 1978. 24.95 (ISBN 0-8071-0374-8). La State U Pr.
Rowe, Mike. Chicago Breakdown. (The Roots of Jazz Ser.). (Illus.). 1979. Repr. of 1974 ed. lib. bdg. 21.50 (ISBN 0-306-79532-9). Da Capo.
Russell, Ross. Jazz Style in Kansas City & the Southwest. 1971. 25.00x (ISBN 0-520-01853-2). U of Cal Pr.
Russo, William. Composing for the Jazz Orchestra. 1973. pap. 2.95 (ISBN 0-226-73209-6, P552, Phoen). U of Chicago Pr.
--Jazz Composition & Orchestration. LC 67-20580. (Illus.). xviii, 826p. 1975. pap. 11.95 (ISBN 0-226-73213-4, P635, Phoen). U of Chicago Pr.
Russo, William & Hyams, Reid. Workbook for Composing for the Jazz Orchestra. LC 61-8642. 1979. spiral bdg. 6.95 (ISBN 0-226-73214-2). U of Chicago Pr.
Sargeant, Winthrop. Jazz, Hot & Hybrid. new 3rd ed. LC 74-20823. (Roots of Jazz Ser). 302p. 1975. lib. bdg. 22.50 (ISBN 0-306-70656-3); pap. 4.95 (ISBN 0-306-80001-2). Da Capo.
Schafer, William J. & Allen, Richard B. Brass Bands & New Orleans Jazz. LC 76-58469. 1977. 12.50x (ISBN 0-8071-0280-6); pap. 6.95 (ISBN 0-8071-0282-2). La State U Pr.
Schiedt, Duncan P. The Jazz State of Indiana. LC 77-79202. (Illus.). 1977. pap. 9.95 (ISBN 0-686-00447-7). D Schiedt.
Schuller, Gunther. Early Jazz: Its Roots & Musical Development. (Illus.). 1968. 17.50 (ISBN 0-19-500097-8). Oxford U Pr.
Shapiro, Nat & Hentoff, N. Hear Me Talkin to Ya. 10.00 (ISBN 0-8446-2928-6). Peter Smith.
Shapiro, Nat & Hentoff, Nat, eds. Hear Me Talkin' to Ya: The Story of Jazz by the Men Who Made It. (YA) (gr. 7-12). 1966. pap. 5.00 (ISBN 0-486-21726-4). Dover.
Shaw, Arnold. Fifty Second Street: The Street of Jazz. LC 77-23545. (Paperback Ser.). (Illus.). 1977. pap. 5.95 (ISBN 0-306-80068-3). Da Capo.
--Rock Revolution: What's Happening in Today's Music. LC 69-11109. (Illus.). (gr. 8 up). 1969. 9.95 (ISBN 0-02-782400-4, CCPr). Macmillan.
Sidran, Ben. Black Talk: Roots of Jazz. xvii, 201p. 1981. Repr. of 1971 ed. lib. bdg. 19.50 (ISBN 0-306-76056-8). Da Capo.
Smith, Willie & Hoefer, George. Music on My Mind: The Memoirs of an American Pianist. LC 74-23406. (Roots of Jazz Ser). xvi, 318p. 1975. Repr. of 1964 ed. lib. bdg. 25.00 (ISBN 0-306-70684-9). Da Capo.
Stanton, Kenneth. Introduction to Jazz Theory. 1977. pap. 2.50 (ISBN 0-8008-4202-2, Crescendo). Taplinger.
--Jazz Theory: A Creative Approach. LC 79-9651. 192p. (Orig.). Date not set. pap. 7.95 (ISBN 0-8008-4311-8, Crescendo). Taplinger.
Stearns, Marshall W. Story of Jazz. (Illus.). 1970. pap. 7.95 (ISBN 0-19-501269-0, GB). Oxford U Pr.
--Story of Jazz. 1956. 15.95 (ISBN 0-19-500115-X). Oxford U Pr.
Tanner, Paul & Gerow, Maurice. A Study of Jazz. 4th ed. 225p. 1980. pap. text ed. write for info. (ISBN 0-697-03442-9); instr's manual avail. (ISBN 0-697-03443-7). Wm C Brown.
Terkel, Studs. Giants of Jazz. rev. ed. LC 75-20024. (Illus.). 192p. (gr. 5 up). 1975. 10.95 (ISBN 0-690-00998-4, TYC-J). Har-Row.
Tirro, Frank. Jazz: A History. (Illus.). 1977. 22.95 (ISBN 0-393-02194-7); text ed. 14.95x (ISBN 0-393-09078-7). Norton.
Tomes, Robert. The Americans in Japan: An Abridgment of the Government Narrative of the U.S. Expedition to Japan, Under Commodore Perry. LC 72-82113. (Japan Library Ser.). 1973. Repr. of 1857 ed. lib. bdg. 22.00 (ISBN 0-8420-1406-3). Scholarly Res Inc.
Treadwell, Bill. Jazz: Big Book of Swing. pap. 2.95 (ISBN 0-685-21994-1). Wehman.
Tudor, Dean & Tudor, Nancy. Jazz. LC 78-11737. (American Popular Music on Elpee). 1979. lib. bdg. 22.50 (ISBN 0-87287-148-7). Libs Unl.
Ulanov, Barry. A Handbook of Jazz. LC 74-10018. 248p. 1975. Repr. of 1957 ed. lib. bdg. 17.00x (ISBN 0-8371-7659-X, ULHJ). Greenwood.
--A History of Jazz in America. LC 74-37324. 382p. 1972. Repr. of 1955 ed. lib. bdg. 25.00 (ISBN 0-306-70427-7). Da Capo.
Vian, Boris. Chroniques de Jazz. 288p. 1967. 16.95 (ISBN 0-686-55688-7). French & Eur.
--Chroniques de Jazz. 512p. 1971. pap. 8.95 (ISBN 0-686-55689-5). French & Eur.
White, Mark. Observer's Book of Jazz. (Observer Bks.). (Illus.). 1978. 3.95 (ISBN 0-684-15927-9, ScribT). Scribner.
Williams, Martin, ed. The Art of Jazz: Ragtime to Bebop. (Da Capo Quality Paperbacks Ser.). 248p. 1981. pap. 6.95 (ISBN 0-306-80134-5). Da Capo.
--Jazz Panorama. (The Roots of Jazz Ser.). 1979. Repr. of 1962 ed. lib. bdg. 22.50 (ISBN 0-306-79574-4). Da Capo.
--The Smithsonian Collection of Classic Jazz. 48p. 1973. records & booklet 35.00x (ISBN 0-393-09300-X). Norton.
Williams, Martin T. Jazz Tradition. LC 71-83058. 1970. 14.95 (ISBN 0-19-500664-X). Oxford U Pr.
Wilson, John S. Jazz: The Transition Years, 1940-1960. LC 66-2425. (Illus.). (YA) (gr. 9 up). 1966. 16.95x (ISBN 0-89197-251-X); pap. text ed. 8.95x (ISBN 0-89197-252-8). Irvington.

JAZZ MUSIC–BIBLIOGRAPHY

Blesh, Rudi & Janis, Harriet. They All Played Ragtime. rev. ed. LC 66-19054. (Illus.). 347p. 1966-71. pap. 7.95 (ISBN 0-8256-0091-X, 000091, Oak). Music Sales.
Case, Brian & Britt, Stan. The Illustrated Encyclopedia of Jazz. 1978. 17.95 (ISBN 0-517-53343-X, Harmony); pap. 8.95 (ISBN 0-517-53344-8). Crown.
Hefele, Bernhard, compiled by. Jazz Bibliography: International Literature on Jazz, Blues, Spirituals, Gospel, & Ragtime Music with a Selected List of Works on the Social & Cultural Background from the Beginning to the Present. 368p. 1981. 38.00 (ISBN 0-686-73825-X, Pub. by K G Saur). Shoe String.
Markewich, Reese. The New Expanded Bibliography of Jazz Compositions Based on the Chord Progressions of Standard Tunes. LC 74-84745. 1974. pap. 4.95 (ISBN 0-9600160-5-8). Markewich.
Meadows, Eddie S. Jazz Reference & Research Materials: A Bibliography. 1981. lib. bdg. 25.00 (ISBN 0-8240-9463-8). Garland Pub.
Merriam, Alan P. Bibliography of Jazz. LC 75-127282. (The Roots of Jazz). 1970. Repr. of 1954 ed. lib. bdg. 18.50 (ISBN 0-306-70036-0). Da Capo.
Merriam, Alan P. & Benford, Robert J. Bibliography of Jazz. LC 55-1225. (American Folklore Society Bibliography Ser). Repr. of 1954 ed. 12.00 (ISBN 0-527-01128-2). Kraus Repr.
Ramsey, Frederic, Jr. & Smith, Charles E., eds. Jazzmen. LC 77-4215. (Illus.). 1977. pap. 4.95 (ISBN 0-15-646205-2, Harv). HarBraceJ.

JAZZ MUSIC–DICTIONARIES

Kinkle, Roger D. The Complete Encyclopedia of Popular Music & Jazz 1900-1950, 4 vols. 1974. 75.00 (ISBN 0-87000-229-5). Arlington Hse.

Panassie, Hugues & Gautier, Madeleine. Dictionnaire du Jazz. 363p. (Fr.). 1971. pap. 18.95 (ISBN 0-686-56870-2, M-6648). French & Eur.

--Guide to Jazz. Gurwitch, A. A., ed. Flower, Desmond, tr. from Fr. LC 73-435. (Illus.). 312p. 1973. Repr. of 1956 ed. lib. bdg. 20.50x (ISBN 0-8371-6766-3, PAGJ). Greenwood.

JAZZ MUSIC–DISCOGRAPHY

Blackstone, Orin. Index to Jazz: Jazz Recordings, 1917-1944. LC 77-27076. 1978. Repr. of 1948 ed. lib. bdg. 22.25x (ISBN 0-313-20178-1, BLIJ). Greenwood.

Blesh, Rudi & Janis, Harriet. They All Played Ragtime. rev. ed. LC 66-19054. (Illus.). 347p. 1966-71. pap. 7.95 (ISBN 0-8256-0091-X, 000091, Oak). Music Sales.

Case, Brian & Britt, Stan. The Illustrated Encyclopedia of Jazz. 1978. 17.95 (ISBN 0-517-53343-X, Harmony); pap. 8.95 (ISBN 0-517-53344-8). Crown.

Delauney, Charles. New Hot Discography. 1948. 16.00 (ISBN 0-685-02530-6). Criterion Mus.

Dexter, Dave. Jazz Story: From the Nineties to the Sixties. (Illus., Orig.). (gr. 8-10). 1964. pap. 2.95 (ISBN 0-13-509463-1, Spec). P-H.

Feather, Leonard. The Encyclopedia of Jazz. Orig. Title: New Edition of the Encyclopedia of Jazz. 1960. 20.00 (ISBN 0-8180-1203-X). Horizon.

--Encyclopedia of Jazz in the Sixties. 1967. 20.00 (ISBN 0-8180-1205-6). Horizon.

Feather, Leonard & Gitler, Ira. The Encyclopedia of Jazz in the Seventies. LC 76-21196. (Illus.). 1976. 20.00 (ISBN 0-8180-1215-3). Horizon.

Finkelstein, Sidney. Jazz: A People's Music. LC 74-23386. (Roots of Jazz Ser). ix, 278p. 1975. Repr. of 1948 ed. lib. bdg. 22.50 (ISBN 0-306-70659-8). Da Capo.

Hadlock, Richard. Jazz Masters of the Twenties. 1965. pap. 2.95 (ISBN 0-02-060770-9). Macmillan.

Hodeir, Andre. Jazz: Its Evolution & Essence. Noakes, David, tr. from Fr. LC 74-23387. (Roots of Jazz Ser). ix, 295p. 1975. Repr. of 1956 ed. lib. bdg. 22.50 (ISBN 0-306-70682-2). Da Capo.

Jazz on LP's: A Collector's Guide to Jazz on Decca, Brunswick, London, Felsted, Ducretet-Thomson, Vogue Coral, Telefunken, & Durium Long Playing Records. LC 78-3634. 1978. Repr. of 1956 ed. lib. bdg. 22.75x (ISBN 0-313-20369-5, JALP). Greenwood.

Lomax, Alan. Mr. Jellyroll: The Fortunes of Jellyroll Morton, New Orleans Creole & 'Inventor' 1973. pap. 4.95 (ISBN 0-520-02237-8). U of Cal Pr.

Lyons, Len. The One Hundred & One Best Jazz Albums: A History of Jazz on Records. 1980. 17.95 (ISBN 0-688-03720-8, Quill); pap. 9.95 (ISBN 0-688-08720-5). Morrow.

Panassie, Hugues. The Real Jazz. LC 73-13328. 284p. 1973. Repr. of 1960 ed. lib. bdg. 18.25 (ISBN 0-8371-7123-7, PARJ). Greenwood.

Ramsey, Frederick, Jr. A Guide to Longplay Jazz Records. LC 77-9065. (Roots of Jazz Ser.). (Illus.). 1977. Repr. of 1954 ed. lib. bdg. 25.00 (ISBN 0-306-70891-4). Da Capo.

Reisner, Robert George. The Jazz Titans. LC 76-58559. (Roots of Jazz Ser.). 1977. Repr. of 1960 ed. lib. bdg. 19.50 (ISBN 0-306-70866-3). Da Capo.

Ruppli, Michel, compiled by. The Prestige Label: A Discography. LC 79-8294. (Discographies: No. 3). 1980. lib. bdg. 27.50 (ISBN 0-313-22019-0, RPL/). Greenwood.

Rust, Brian. Jazz Records 1897-1942. 4th ed. 1978. 60.00 (ISBN 0-87000-404-2). Arlington Hse.

Schuller, Gunther. Early Jazz: Its Roots & Musical Development. (Illus.). 1968. 17.50 (ISBN 0-19-500097-8). Oxford U Pr.

Shaw, Arnold. Rock Revolution: What's Happening in Today's Music. LC 69-11109. (Illus.). (gr. 8 up). 1969. 9.95 (ISBN 0-02-782400-4, CCPr). Macmillan.

Smith, Charles E. The Jazz Record Book. LC 78-6147. 1978. Repr. of 1942 ed. lib. bdg. 31.25x (ISBN 0-313-20423-3, SMJR). Greenwood.

Wilson, John S. Jazz: The Transition Years, 1940-1960. LC 66-2425. (Illus.). (YA) (gr. 9 up). 1966. 16.95x (ISBN 0-89197-251-X); pap. text ed. 8.95x (ISBN 0-89197-252-8). Irvington.

JAZZ MUSICIANS

Baxter, Derrick S. Ma Rainey & the Classic Blues Singers. LC 72-120110. (Blues Ser). (Illus.). 1970. pap. 2.95 (ISBN 0-8128-1321-9). Stein & Day.

Berendt, Joachim. The Jazz Book: From Ragtime to Fusion & Beyond. rev. ed. Morganstern, Dan & Bredigkeit, H. B., trs. from German. 1981. 15.95 (ISBN 0-88208-140-3); pap. 8.95 (ISBN 0-88208-141-1). Lawrence Hill.

Berendt, Joachim-Ernst. Jazz: A Photo History. LC 79-7629. (Illus.). 1979. 29.95 (ISBN 0-02-870290-5). Schirmer Bks.

Blesh, Rudi. Combo, U.S.A. Eight Lives in Jazz. (The Roots of Jazz Ser.). 1979. Repr. of 1971 ed. 22.50 (ISBN 0-306-79568-X). Da Capo.

Bruccoli, Matthew J., et al, eds. Conversations with Jazz Musicians. LC 77-9143. (Conversations Ser.: Vol. 2). 1977. 34.00 (ISBN 0-8103-0944-0, A Bruccoli Clark Book). Gale.

Buerkle, Jack V. & Barker, Danny. Bourbon Street Black: The New Orleans Black Jazzman. LC 73-77926. (Illus.). 254p. 1974. pap. 4.95 (ISBN 0-19-501832-X, GB415, GB). Oxford U Pr.

Burton, Jack. Blue Book of Tin Pan Alley, 2 Vols. LC 62-16426. Set. 25.00 (ISBN 0-686-66390-X); Vol. 1. (ISBN 0-87282-014-9); Vol. 2. (ISBN 0-87282-015-7). Century Hse.

Cole, Bill. John Coltrane. LC 76-14289. (Illus.). 1976. 12.95 (ISBN 0-02-870660-9). Schirmer Bks.

Collier, James L. The Great Jazz Artists. LC 77-7212. (Illus.). 192p. (gr. 7 up). 1977. 7.95 (ISBN 0-590-07493-8, Four Winds). Schol Bk Serv.

Danca, Vince. Bunny: A Bio-Discography of Jazz Trumpeter Bunny Berigan. (Illus., Orig.). 1978. pap. 4.95 (ISBN 0-9602390-1-4). V Danca.

Dance, Stanley. The World of Count Basie. 1980. 16.95 (ISBN 0-684-16604-6). Scribner.

Feather, Leonard. The Encyclopedia of Jazz. Orig. Title: New Edition of the Encyclopedia of Jazz. 1960. 20.00 (ISBN 0-8180-1203-X). Horizon.

--Encyclopedia of Jazz in the Sixties. 1967. 20.00 (ISBN 0-8180-1205-6). Horizon.

Feather, Leonard & Gitler, Ira. The Encyclopedia of Jazz in the Seventies. LC 76-21196. (Illus.). 1976. 20.00 (ISBN 0-8180-1215-3). Horizon.

Galster, Robert. Giants of Jazz. Repr. lib. bdg. 13.25x (ISBN 0-89190-145-0). Am Repr-Rivercity Pr.

Gammond, Peter, ed. Duke Ellington: His Life & Music. LC 77-1927. (The Roots of Jazz Ser.). 1977. Repr. of 1958 ed. lib. bdg. 22.50 (ISBN 0-306-70874-4). Da Capo.

Goffin, Robert. Jazz: From the Congo to the Metropolitan. Schaap, Walter & Feather, Leonard G., trs. from Fr. LC 74-23384. (Roots of Jazz Ser). xii, 254p. 1975. Repr. of 1944 ed. lib. bdg. 22.50 (ISBN 0-306-70680-6). Da Capo.

Goldberg, Joe. Jazz Masters of the Fifties. (The Roots of Jazz Ser.). 246p. 1980. Repr. of 1965 ed. lib. bdg. 22.50 (ISBN 0-306-76031-2). Da Capo.

Green, Benny. The Reluctant Art: The Growth of Jazz. (New Reprints in Essay & General Literature Index Ser.). 1975. Repr. of 1963 ed. 18.25 (ISBN 0-518-10199-1, 10199). Arno.

Green, Stanley. Kings of Jazz. LC 74-30980. (Illus.). 1976. 20.00 (ISBN 0-498-01724-9). A S Barnes.

Gridley, Mark C. Jazz Styles. (Illus.). 352p. 1978. text ed. 16.95 (ISBN 0-13-509885-8); pap. text ed. 12.95 (ISBN 0-13-509877-7). P-H.

Guitar Player Magazine, ed. Jazz Guitarists. (Illus.). 120p. 5.95 (ISBN 0-8256-9508-2). Guitar Player.

Hadlock, Richard. Jazz Masters of the Twenties. 1965. pap. 2.95 (ISBN 0-02-060770-9). Macmillan.

Hall, George I. & Kramer, Stephen A., eds. Gene Krupa & His Orchestra. (Jazz Discographies Ser.). 1975. 6.00x (ISBN 0-686-24732-9); 5 or more copies 3.10 (ISBN 0-686-24733-7). Jazz Discographies.

Harris, Sheldon. Blues Who's Who. (Quality Paperbacks Ser.). (Illus.). 775p. 1981. pap. 16.95 (ISBN 0-306-80155-8). Da Capo.

Haskins, James. Scott Joplin: The Man Who Made Ragtime. LC 76-50768. (Illus.). 264p. (Orig.). 1980. pap. 6.95 (ISBN 0-686-64767-X). Stein & Day.

Horricks, Raymond. Count Basie & His Orchestra. LC 79-138009. (Illus.). 320p. 1972. Repr. of 1957 ed. 17.00x (ISBN 0-8371-5656-4, Pub. by Negro U Pr). Greenwood.

Isacoff, Stuart. Thelonious Monk. 64p. pap. 5.95 (ISBN 0-8256-4080-6). Music Sales.

Jewell, Derek. Duke: A Portrait of Duke Ellington. (Illus.). 1977. 12.95 (ISBN 0-393-07512-5). Norton.

Kaminsky, Max & Hughes, V. E. Jazz Band: My Life in Jazz. (Da Capo Quality Paperbacks Ser.). (Illus.). 242p. 1981. pap. 6.95 (ISBN 0-306-80135-3). Da Capo.

Lyttelton, Humphrey. The Best of Jazz: Basin Street to Harlem. LC 79-13159. (Illus.). 1979. 8.95 (ISBN 0-8008-0727-8, Crescendo). Taplinger.

Marquis, Donald M. In Search of Buddy Bolden: First Man of Jazz. (Illus.). xix, 176p. 1980. pap. 5.95 (ISBN 0-306-80130-2). Da Capo.

--In Search of Buddy Bolden: First Man of Jazz. LC 77-10958. 1978. 9.95 (ISBN 0-8071-0356-X). La State U Pr.

Mingus, Charles. Beneath the Underdog. 1980. pap. 3.95 (ISBN 0-14-003880-9). Penguin.

Morgenstern, Dan. Jazz People. LC 76-14462. (Illus.). 1976. 28.50 (ISBN 0-8109-1152-3). Abrams.

--Jazz People. (Illus.). 1978. pap. text ed. 11.95 (ISBN 0-13-511352-0). P-H.

Newton, Francis. The Jazz Scene. LC 75-4748. (Roots of Jazz Ser). 303p. 1975. Repr. of 1960 ed. lib. bdg. 25.00 (ISBN 0-306-70685-7). Da Capo.

Oakley, Giles. The Devil's Music: A History of the Blues. LC 78-6161. (Illus.). 1978. pap. 6.95 (ISBN 0-15-625586-3, Harv). HarBraceJ.

O'Day, Anita & Eells, George. High Times, Hard Times. 320p. 1981. 13.95 (ISBN 0-399-12505-1). Putnam.

Page, Drew. Drew's Blues: A Sideman's Life with the Big Bands. LC 80-12942. (Illus.). 272p. 1980. 14.95 (ISBN 0-8071-0686-0). La State U Pr.

Reisner, Robert George. The Jazz Titans. LC 76-58559. (Roots of Jazz Ser.). 1977. Repr. of 1960 ed. lib. bdg. 19.50 (ISBN 0-306-70866-3). Da Capo.

Rivelli, Pauline & Levin, Robert, eds. Giants of Black Music. 1980. pap. 5.95 (ISBN 0-306-80119-1). Da Capo.

Rose, Al & Souchon, Edmond. New Orleans Jazz: A Family Album. rev. ed. LC 77-24076. 1978. 24.95 (ISBN 0-8071-0374-8). La State U Pr.

Rowe, Mike. Chicago Blues: The City & the Music. (Quality Paperbacks Ser.). (Illus.). 226p. 1981. pap. 6.95 (ISBN 0-306-80145-0). Da Capo.

Schiedt, Duncan P. The Jazz State of Indiana. LC 77-79202. (Illus.). 1977. pap. 9.95 (ISBN 0-686-00447-7). D Schiedt.

Scobey, Jan. He Rambled! 'til Cancer Cut Him Down. LC 76-54444. (Illus.). 1976. 35.00 (ISBN 0-918104-01-7). Pal Pub.

Shapiro, Nat & Hentoff, eds. The Jazz Makers: Essays on the Greats of Jazz. LC 79-15254. (Da Capo Quality Paperback Ser.). 386p. 1979. pap. 6.95 (ISBN 0-306-80105-1). Da Capo.

Shapiro, Nat & Hentoff, Nat, eds. The Jazz Makers. LC 73-11864. 368p. 1975. Repr. of 1957 ed. lib. bdg. 24.25 (ISBN 0-8371-7098-2, SHJM). Greenwood.

Sill, Hal, Jr. Misbehavin' with Fats: A Toby Bradley Adventure. LC 71-10763. (Illus.). 1978. PLB 5.95 (ISBN 0-201-07159-2, A-W Childrens). A-W.

Simon, George T. The Big Bands. rev., enl ed. (Illus.). 600p. 1975. pap. 9.95 (ISBN 0-02-061770-4, Collier). Macmillan.

--Big Bands. 1974. 14.95 (ISBN 0-02-610980-8). Macmillan.

Smith, Charles E. The Jazz Record Book: With Frederic Ramsey Jr., Charles Payne Rogers & William Russell. LC 72-181261. 515p. 1942. Repr. 49.00 (ISBN 0-403-01684-3). Scholarly.

Spellman, A. B. Black Music: Four Lives. LC 66-10410. 1971. pap. 3.95 (ISBN 0-8052-0281-1). Schocken.

Stewart, Rex. Jazz Masters of the Thirties. (The Roots of Jazz Ser.). 223p. 1980. Repr. of 1972 ed. lib. bdg. 22.50 (ISBN 0-306-76030-4). Da Capo.

Surge, Frank. Singers of the Blues. LC 68-30570. (Pull Ahead Books). (Illus.). (gr. 5-12). 1969. PLB 4.95 (ISBN 0-8225-0453-7). Lerner Pubns.

Terkel, Studs. Giants of Jazz. rev. ed. LC 75-20024. (Illus.). 192p. (gr. 5 up). 1975. 10.95 (ISBN 0-690-00998-4, TYC-J). Har-Row.

Ullman, Michael. Jazz Lives: Portraits in Words & Pictures. 244p. 1981. pap. 6.95 (ISBN 0-8256-3253-6, Quick Fox). Music Sales.

Waller, Maurice & Calabrese, Anthony. Fats Waller. LC 77-5208. 1977. 12.95 (ISBN 0-02-872730-4). Schirmer Bks.

Williams, Martin. Jazz Masters in Transition: 1957-1969. (The Roots of Jazz Ser.). 1980. Repr. of 1970 ed. 25.00 (ISBN 0-306-79612-0). Da Capo.

--Jazz Masters of New Orleans. (Paperbacks Ser.). 1979. pap. 6.95 (ISBN 0-306-80093-4). Da Capo.

--Jazz Masters of New Orleans. (The Roots of Jazz Ser.). 1978. Repr. of 1967 ed. lib. bdg. 22.50 (ISBN 0-306-77541-7). Da Capo.

Williams, Martin T. Jazz Tradition. LC 71-83058. 1970. 14.95 (ISBN 0-19-500664-X). Oxford U Pr.

JAZZ MUSICIANS–CORRESPONDENCE, REMINISCENCES, ETC.

see Musicians–Correspondence, Reminiscences, etc.

JAZZ MUSICIANS–PORTRAITS

see Musicians–Portraits

JEALOUSY

see also Envy

Faber, Stuart J. & Levison, Teddi. The Upside-Downs of Jealousy, Possessiveness & Insecurity. 100p. 1975. pap. text ed. 2.95 (ISBN 0-89074-012-7). Good Life.

Hauck, Paul A. Overcoming Jealousy & Possessiveness. LC 81-3040. 1981. pap. 5.95 (ISBN -0664-24374-6). Westminster.

Schoenfeld, Eugene. Jealousy: Taming the Green-Eyed Monster. LC 79-1928. 192p. 1980. 8.95 (ISBN 0-03-044596-5). HR&W.

Tester, Sylvia R. Jealous. (What Does It Mean Ser.). (Illus.). (ps-2). 1980. 7.95g (ISBN 0-516-06446-0). Childrens.

JEAN LE NEVELON, 13TH CENTURY

Armstrong, Edward C. Authorship of the Vengement Alixandre & of the Venjance Alixandre. 1926. pap. 5.00 (ISBN 0-527-02622-0). Kraus Repr.

Jean Le Nevelon & Ham, E. B. Textual Criticism & Jehan le Venelais. LC 47-589. Repr. of 1946 ed. 12.00 (ISBN 0-527-45750-7). Kraus Repr.

JEANNE D'ALBRET, QUEEN OF NAVARRE, 1528-1572

Roelker, Nancy L. Queen of Navarre, Jeanne D'Albret, 1528-1572. LC 68-54024. (Illus.). 1968. 25.00x (ISBN 0-674-74150-1, Belknap Pr). Harvard U Pr.

JEANNE D'ARC, SAINT, 1412-1431

Beaurepaire, Charles De. Notes Sur les Juges et les Assesseurs Du Proces De Condemnation De Jeanne D'arc. 135p. (Fr.). 1981. Repr. of 1890 ed. lib. bdg. 60.00 (ISBN 0-8287-1494-0). Clearwater Pub.

Beevers, John. St. Joan of Arc. LC 59-12615. 1974. pap. 3.50 (ISBN 0-89555-043-1, 153). TAN Bks Pubs.

Clemens, Samuel L. Personal Recollections of Joan of Arc by the Sieur Louis De Conte. LC 80-23663. (Illus.). xiv, 461p. 1980. Repr. of 1906 ed. lib. bdg. 45.00x (ISBN 0-313-22373-4, CLPR). Greenwood.

Cristiani, Leon. St. Joan of Arc, Virgin-Soldier. 1977. 3.95 (ISBN 0-8198-0465-7); pap. 2.95 (ISBN 0-8198-0466-5). Dghtrs St Paul.

De Monstrelet, Enguerrend. Chronique D'Enguerrand De Monstrelet, 6 Vols. Douet D'Arcq, L., ed. 1857-62. Set. 212.50 (ISBN 0-384-39781-6); Set. pap. 185.00 (ISBN 0-384-39780-8). Johnson Repr.

Gies, Frances. Joan of Arc: The Legend & the Reality. LC 80-7900. (Illus.). 256p. 1981. 14.95 (ISBN 0-690-01942-4, HarpT). Har-Row.

Giles, John A., ed. Revolte Du Conte De Warwick Contre le Roi Edward 4e. (Fr). 1849. 24.00 (ISBN 0-8337-1347-7). B Franklin.

Jeanne D'Arc, Saint. Proces De Condamnation et De Rehabilitation De Jeanne D'Arc, 5 Vols. Quicherat, Jules, ed. 1841-1849. 192.00 (ISBN 0-384-27070-0); pap. 154.00 (ISBN 0-384-27071-9). Johnson Repr.

Lucie-Smith, Edward. Joan of Arc. (Illus.). 1977. 10.95 (ISBN 0-393-07520-6). Norton.

Michelet, Jules. Joan of Arc. Guerard, Albert, tr. 1957. pap. 1.95 (ISBN 0-472-06122-4, 122, AA). U of Mich Pr.

Oliphant, Margaret. Jeanne d'Arc. LC 73-14460. (Heroes of the Nations Series). Repr. of 1896 ed. 30.00 (ISBN 0-404-58278-8). AMS Pr.

--Jeanne D'Arc: Her Life & Death. 1896. 30.00 (ISBN 0-8414-6664-5). Folcroft.

Pernoud, Regine. Joan of Arc: By Herself & Her Witnesses. LC 66-24807. 1969. pap. 4.95 (ISBN 0-8128-1260-3). Stein & Day.

Raknem, Ingvald. Joan of Arc in History, Legend & Literature. (Scandinavian University Books). 284p. 1972. 22.00x (ISBN 8-200-02247-1, Dist. by Columbia U Pr). Universitet.

Sabatini, Rafael. Heroic Lives. facs. ed. LC 70-99648. (Essay Index Reprint Ser). 1934. 17.50 (ISBN 0-8369-2071-6). Arno.

Sarmiehto, Lino P. General Joan of Arc. 4.95 (ISBN 0-8062-0725-6). Carlton.

Scott, W. S. Trial of Joan of Arc. 1956. 4.00 (ISBN 0-685-06605-3). Assoc Bk.

Warner, Marina. Joan of Arc: The Image of Female Heroism. LC 80-2720. (Illus.). 1981. 19.95 (ISBN 0-394-41145-5). Knopf.

Weintraub, Stanley, ed. Saint Joan: Fifty Years After, 1923-24 to 1973-74. LC 73-77657. 288p. 1973. 17.50x (ISBN 0-8071-0208-3). La State U Pr.

JEANNE D'ARC, SAINT, 1412-1431–DRAMA

Anouilh, Jean. Alouette. Thomas, Merlin & Lee, Simon, eds. (Orig., Fr.,). 1975. pap. text ed. 8.95x incl. exercises (ISBN 0-89197-005-3). Irvington.

--Alouette. 1963. pap. 3.95 (ISBN 0-685-10991-7, 1153). French & Eur.

--Lark. Fry, Christopher, tr. 1956. 7.95x (ISBN 0-19-500393-4). Oxford U Pr.

Searle, William. The Saint & the Skeptics: Joan of Arc in the Work of Mark Twain, Anatole France, & Bernard Shaw. LC 75-26709. 178p. 1976. text ed. 12.50x (ISBN 0-8143-1541-0). Wayne St U Pr.

Shaw, Bernard. Saint Joan. Bd. with Major Barbara; Androcles & the Lion. 3.95 (ISBN 0-394-60294-3, M294). Modern Lib.

--Saint Joan, a Screenplay. Dukore, Bernard F., ed. LC 68-11039. (Illus.). 224p. 1968. 9.95 (ISBN 0-295-97885-6); pap. 2.45 (ISBN 0-295-95072-2, WP56). U of Wash Pr.

Shaw, George B. Saint Joan. Weintraub, Stanley, ed. LC 76-134308. 1971. pap. 7.50 (ISBN 0-672-61091-4). Bobbs.
--Saint Joan. (Penguin Plays Ser.). (YA) (gr. 9 up). 1958. pap. 1.95 (ISBN 0-14-048005-6). Penguin.
Von Schiller, Friedrich. Maiden of Orleans. 2nd rev. ed. Krumpelmann, John T., tr. LC 63-62703. (North Carolina. University. Studies in the Germanic Languages & Literatures: No. 37). Repr. of 1962 ed. 18.50 (ISBN 0-404-50937-1). AMS Pr.

JEANNE D'ARC, SAINT, 1412-1431-JUVENILE LITERATURE

Boutet de Monvel, Maurice. Joan of Arc. LC 80-5169. (Illus.). 64p. (gr. 7). 1980. Repr. of 1897 ed. 12.95 (ISBN 0-670-40735-6, Studio). Viking Pr.
Daughters Of St. Paul. Wind & Shadows. (Encounter Series). (gr. 4-7). 3.00 (ISBN 0-8198-0174-7); pap. 2.00 (ISBN 0-8198-0175-5). Dghtrs St Paul.
Ready, Dolores. Joan, the Brave Soldier: Joan of Arc. LC 77-86597. (Stories About Christian Heroes). (Illus.). (gr. 1-5). 1977. pap. 1.95 (ISBN 0-03-041666-3). Winston Pr.
Ross, Nancy W. Joan of Arc. (World Landmark Ser: No. 4). (Illus.). (gr. 7-9). 1953. PLB 5.99 (ISBN 0-394-90504-0, BYR). Random.

JEANNERET-GRIS, CHARLES EDOUARD, 1887-1965

Blake, Peter. The Master Builders: Le Corbusier, Mies Van der Rohe, Frank Lloyd Wright. new ed. (Illus.). 432p. 1976. pap. 5.95 (ISBN 0-393-00796-0, N796, Norton Lib). Norton.
De Francieu, Francoise & Fondation le Corbusier, eds. Le Corbusier Sketchbooks: 1954-1957, Vol. 3. 1982. price not set. MIT Pr.
--Le Corbusier Sketchbooks: 1957-1964, Vol. 4. 1982. price not set. MIT Pr.
De Fusco, Renato. Le Corbusier, Designer--Furniture, 1929. LC 77-81368. 1977. 12.95 (ISBN 0-8120-5148-3). Barron.
Eardley, Anthony, et al. Le Corbusier's Firminy Church. (Illus.). 120p. 1981. pap. 17.50 (ISBN 0-8478-0380-5). Rizzoli Intl.
Evenson, Norma. Le Corbusier: The Machine & the Grand Design. LC 60-6079. (Planning & Cities Ser). (Illus., Orig.). 1969. 7.95 (ISBN 0-8076-0514-X); pap. 5.95 (ISBN 0-8076-0518-2). Braziller.
Graves, Michael, intro. by. Le Corbusier: Selected Drawings. (Illus.). 176p. 1981. pap. 15.95 (ISBN 0-8478-0383-X). Rizzoli Intl.
Gropius, et al. Four Great Makers of Modern Architecture: Gropius, le Corbusier, Mies Van der Rohe, Wright. LC 78-130312. (Architecture & Decorative Art Ser.: Vol. 37). 1970. Repr. of 1963 ed. lib. bdg. 29.50 (ISBN 0-306-70065-4). Da Capo.
Henze, Anton. La Tourette: Le Courbusier's Monastery. (Illus.). 1966. 12.50 (ISBN 0-8150-0052-9). Wittenborn.
Jencks, Charles. Le Corbusier & the Tragic View of Architecture. LC 73-84322. (Illus.). 1974. 15.00x (ISBN 0-674-51860-8); pap. 5.95 (ISBN 0-674-51861-6). Harvard U Pr.
Le Corbusier. (Art Library Ser.: Vol. 4). pap. 3.50 (ISBN 0-448-00490-9). G&D.
Le Corbusier Fragments. (Architectural Design Profiles Ser.). (Illus.). 96p. 1980. pap. 12.50 (ISBN 0-8478-5316-0). Rizzoli Intl.
Sekler, Eduard F. & Curtis, William. Le Corbusier at Work: The Genesis of the Carpenter Center for the Visual Arts. LC 77-7315. (Illus.). 1978. 35.00x (ISBN 0-674-52059-9). Harvard U Pr.
Sekler, Mary P. The Early Drawings of Charles Edouard Jeanneret le Corbusier 1902-1908. LC 76-23726. (Outstanding Dissertations in the Fine Arts Ser.). 1978. lib. bdg. 80.00x (ISBN 0-8240-2728-0). Garland Pub.
Turner, Paul V. The Education of le Corbusier. LC 76-23658. (Outstanding Dissertations in the Fine Arts - Twentieth Century). (Illus.). 1977. Repr. of 1971 ed. lib. bdg. 48.00 (ISBN 0-8240-2732-9). Garland Pub.
Von Moos, Stanislaus. Le Corbusier: Elements of a Synthesis. 1979. 32.50x (ISBN 0-262-22023-7). MIT Pr.
Walden, Russell, ed. The Open Hand: Essays on Le Corbusier. LC 76-40046. 1977. 30.00x (ISBN 0-262-23074-7). MIT Pr.

JEANNETTE (SHIP)

Gilder, William H. Ice-Pack & Tundra: An Account of the Search for the Jeanette & a Sledge Journey Through Siberia. LC 74-5838. Repr. of 1883 ed. 24.00 (ISBN 0-404-11643-4). AMS Pr.

JEEP VEHICLE

see Automobiles-Types-Jeep

JEFFCOTT, JOHN, SIR

Hague, R. M. Sir John Jeffcott. 1963. 10.00x (ISBN 0-522-83623-2, Pub. by Melbourne U Pr). Intl Schol Bk Serv.

JEFFERIES, RICHARD, 1848-1887

Besant, Walter. The Eulogy of Richard Jeffries. 1889. Repr. 20.00 (ISBN 0-8274-2319-5). R West.
Looker, S. J. & Porteous, C. Richard Jefferies, Man of the Fields. (Illus.). 1964. 9.00x (ISBN 0-8426-1357-9). Verry.
Salt, H. S. Richard Jefferies: A Study. 1977. Repr. of 1894 ed. lib. bdg. 17.50 (ISBN 0-8495-4817-9). Arden Lib.
Salt, Henry S. Richard Jefferies: His Life & His Ideals. LC 77-113320. 1970. Repr. of 1905 ed. 9.50 (ISBN 0-8046-1033-9). Kennikat.
--Richard Jefferies: His Life & His Ideals. 1973. Repr. of 1905 ed. 20.00 (ISBN 0-8274-1344-0). R West.
--Richard Jeffries: His Life & His Ideals. 1978. Repr. of 1905 ed. lib. bdg. 20.00 (ISBN 0-8414-8168-7). Folcroft.
Thomas, Edward. Richard Jefferies. Gant, Roland, ed. 320p. 1978. 12.95 (ISBN 0-571-11236-6, Pub. by Faber & Faber); pap. 7.95 (ISBN 0-571-11237-4). Merrimack Bk Serv.
--Richard Jefferies: His Life & Work. LC 78-160785. 1971. Repr. of 1909 ed. 15.50 (ISBN 0-8046-1617-5). Kennikat.
--Richard Jefferies: His Life & Work. 1973. lib. bdg. 14.50 (ISBN 0-8414-8043-5). Folcroft.

JEFFERS, ROBINSON, 1887-1962

Adamic, Louis. Robinson Jeffers: A Portrait. LC 73-11375. 1929. lib. bdg. 8.50 (ISBN 0-8414-2881-6). Folcroft.
--Robinson Jeffers: A Portrait. 1978. Repr. of 1929 ed. lib. bdg. 8.50 (ISBN 0-8495-0048-6). Arden Lib.
Alberts, S. S. A Bibliography of the Works of Robinson Jeffers. LC 66-21849. 1966. 25.00 (ISBN 0-685-83031-4). SBD.
Antoninus, Bro. Robinson Jeffers: Fragments of an Older Fury. 1970. 7.50 (ISBN 0-685-04672-9, Pub. by Oyez). SBD.
Beilke, Marlan. Shining Clarity: God & Man in the Works of Robinson Jeffers. LC 77-70786. 1978. separate ed. 100.00x (ISBN 0-918466-01-6). Quintessence.
Bennett, Melba B. Robinson Jeffers & the Sea. LC 73-9. 1971. Repr. of 1936 ed. lib. bdg. 20.00 (ISBN 0-8414-3154-X). Folcroft.
Brophy, Robert J. Robinson Jeffers: Myth, Ritual & Symbol in His Narrative Poems. (Illus.). xxii, 321p. 1976. Repr. of 1973 ed. 19.50 (ISBN 0-208-01574-4, Archon). Shoe String.
Carpenter, Frederic I. Robinson Jeffers. (Twayne's United States Authors Ser). 1962. pap. 3.45 (ISBN 0-8084-0269-2, T22, Twayne). Coll & U Pr.
Coffin, Arthur B. Robinson Jeffers: Poet of Inhumanism. LC 74-121767. 324p. 1971. 25.00 (ISBN 0-299-05840-9). U of Wis Pr.
Gilbert, Rudolph. Shine Perishing Republic. LC 65-15883. (Studies in Poetry, No. 38). 1969. Repr. of 1936 ed. lib. bdg. 49.95 (ISBN 0-8383-0556-3). Haskell.
Harmon, Robert B. The First Editions of Robinson Jeffers. (First Edition Pocket Guides Ser.). 1978. pap. 3.95 (ISBN 0-910720-13-4). Hermes.
Hotchkiss, Bill. Jeffers: The Sivaistic Vision. 1975. 15.00 (ISBN 0-912950-22-6). Blue Oak.
Nolte, William H. Rock & Hawk: Robinson Jeffers & the Romantic Agony. LC 77-22982. 232p. 1978. 15.95x (ISBN 0-8203-0432-8). U of Ga Pr.
Powell, Lawrence C. Robinson Jeffers: The Man & His Work. LC 68-54176. (American Biography Ser., No. 32). (Illus.). 1969. Repr. of 1934 ed. lib. bdg. 33.95 (ISBN 0-8383-0675-6). Haskell.
--Robinson Jeffers: The Man & His Work. 1973. lib. bdg. 59.95 (ISBN 0-8490-0966-9). Gordon Pr.
Vardamis, Alex A. The Critical Reputation of Robinson Jeffers: A Bibliographical Study. (Orig.). 1972. 19.50 (ISBN 0-208-01252-4, Archon). Shoe String.

JEFFERSON, JOSEPH, 1829-1905

Winter, William. Jeffersons. LC 79-81221. (Illus.). 1881. 12.00 (ISBN 0-405-09086-2). Arno.
--Life & Art of Joseph Jefferson. LC 72-78858. 1894. Repr. 20.00 (ISBN 0-403-02098-0). Somerset Pub.
--Wreath of Laurel, Being Speeches on Dramatic & Kindred Occasions. LC 73-130098. (Drama Ser). 1970. Repr. of 1898 ed. lib. bdg. 15.00 (ISBN 0-8337-3828-3). B Franklin.

JEFFERSON, MARTHA (WAYLES) SKELTON, 1748-1782

Adams, W. Howard, ed. Jefferson & the Arts: An Extended View. LC 76-608152. (Illus.). 17.50 (ISBN 0-686-16183-1). Natl Gallery Art.

JEFFERSON, THOMAS, PRES. U. S., 1743-1826

Adams - Jefferson, 2 vols. Incl. Vol. 1. Adams: An American Dynasty. Russell, Francis. LC 76-924. 374p (ISBN 0-8281-0350-X); Jefferson: A Revealing Biography. Smith, Page. LC 76-3593. 310p (ISBN 0-8281-0315-1, Dist. by Scribner). (Illus.). 1976. Boxed Set. 32.50 (ISBN 0-8281-0379-8, 3062D, Dist. by Scribner). Am Heritage.
Adams, Henry. History of the United States of America During the Administrations of Jefferson & Madison, 9 vols. 1980. lib. bdg. 995.00 (ISBN 0-8490-3148-6). Gordon Pr.
Adams, Howard, ed. Jefferson & the Arts: An Extended View. LC 76-21951. 1976. 20.00x (ISBN 0-685-79644-2, National Gallery of Art). U Pr of Va.
Adams, J. Correspondence of John Adams & Thomas Jefferson. LC 25-20253. Repr. of 1925 ed. 14.00 (ISBN 0-527-00460-X). Kraus Repr.
Adams, W. Howard. The Eye of Thomas Jefferson. LC 76-608021. (Illus.). 412p. 1981. Repr. of 1976 ed. 20.00 (ISBN 0-8139-0902-3). U Pr of Va.
Adams, W. Howard, ed. The Eye of Thomas Jefferson. LC 76-608021. (Illus.). pap. 17.95 (ISBN 0-686-16182-3). Natl Gallery Art.
Allison, John M. Adams & Jefferson: The Story of a Friendship. LC 66-13419. (Illus.). 1968. Repr. of 1966 ed. 18.50x (ISBN 0-8061-0705-7). U. of Okla Pr.
Ansley, Delight, compiled by. The Papers of Thomas Jefferson: Index to Volumes 13-18. LC 50-7486. 250p. 1973. pap. text ed. 7.50 (ISBN 0-691-04618-2). Princeton U Pr.
Arrowood, Charles F., ed. Thomas Jefferson & Education in a Republic. LC 70-131611. 1970. Repr. of 1930 ed. 25.00 (ISBN 0-403-00498-5). Scholarly.
--Thomas Jefferson & Education in a Republic. LC 79-136406. (BCL Ser.: No. 1). Repr. of 1930 ed. 12.00 (ISBN 0-404-00406-7). AMS Pr.
Baldwin, Joseph G. Party Leaders: Sketches of Thomas Jefferson, Alexander Hamilton, Andrew Jackson, Henry Clay John Randolph of Roanoke; Including Notices of Many Other Distinguished American Statesmen. LC 72-39654. (Essay Index Reprint Ser.). Repr. of 1885 ed. 21.00 (ISBN 0-8369-2741-9). Arno.
Banning, Lance. The Jeffersonian Persuasion: Evolution of a Party Ideology. LC 77-14666. 1978. 18.50x (ISBN 0-8014-1151-3). Cornell U Pr.
Bear, James A., Jr., ed. Jefferson at Monticello. Incl. Memoirs of a Monticello Slave. Campbell, Isaac; The Private Life of Thomas Jefferson. Pierson, Hamilton W. LC 67-17629. (Illus.). 144p. 1967. pap. 2.95 (ISBN 0-8139-0022-0). U Pr of Va.
Becker, Carl. Declaration of Independence. 6.75 (ISBN 0-8446-1619-2). Peter Smith.
Becker, Carl L. Declaration of Independence: A Study in the History of Political Ideas. 1958. pap. 2.45 (ISBN 0-394-70060-0, V-60, Vin). Random.
Beloff, M. Thomas Jefferson & American Democracy. Rowse, A. L., ed. (Men & Their Time Ser). 4.00x (ISBN 0-8426-1152-5). Verry.
Beloff, Max. Thomas Jefferson & American Democracy. 1962. pap. 1.25 (ISBN 0-02-030620-2, Collier). Macmillan.
Benson, Randolph. Thomas Jefferson As Social Scientist. LC 70-118124. 333p. 1971. 18.00 (ISBN 0-8386-7705-3). Fairleigh Dickinson.
Bestor, Arthur E., et al. Three Presidents & Their Books: The Reading of Jefferson, Lincoln, & Franklin D. Roosevelt. LC 54-12305. (Windsor Ser: No. 5). 1955. pap. 4.95 (ISBN 0-252-72686-3). U of Ill Pr.
Betts, Edwin M., ed. Thomas Jefferson's Farm Book: With Commentary & Relevant Extracts from Other Writings. LC 52-13160. 1977. Repr. of 1953 ed. 20.00x (ISBN 0-8139-0705-5). U Pr of Va.
Boorstin, Daniel J. The Lost World of Thomas Jefferson. LC 80-26835. 320p. 1981. pap. 6.95 (ISBN 0-226-06496-4). U. of Chicago Pr.
--Lost World of Thomas Jefferson. 8.50 (ISBN 0-8446-1701-6). Peter Smith.
Bottorff, William K. Thomas Jefferson. (United States Authors Ser.: No. 327). 1979. lib. bdg. 9.95 (ISBN 0-8057-7260-X). Twayne.
--Thomas Jefferson. (Twayne United States Authors Ser.). 1979. lib. bdg. 8.95 (ISBN 0-8057-7260-X). G K Hall.
Brodie, Fawn M. Thomas Jefferson: An Intimate History. (Illus.). 800p. 1974. 19.95 (ISBN 0-393-07480-3). Norton.
Channing, Edward. Jeffersonian System: Eighteen Hundred & One to Eighteen Eleven. LC 67-30020. 1968. Repr. of 1906 ed. 11.50x (ISBN 0-8154-0049-7). Cooper Sq.
--Jeffersonian System, Eighteen One to Eighteen Eleven. LC 69-13855. Repr. of 1906 ed. lib. bdg. 14.75x (ISBN 0-8371-0995-7, CHJS). Greenwood.
Chinard, Gilbert. Jefferson et les Ideologues. Mayer, J. P., ed. LC 78-67341. (European Political Thought Ser.). (Fr.). 1979. Repr. of 1925 ed. lib. bdg. 18.00x (ISBN 0-405-11685-3). Arno.
--Thomas Jefferson: The Apostle of Americanism. 1957. pap. 5.95 (ISBN 0-472-06013-9, 13, AA). U. of Mich Pr.
Cohen, I. Bernard, ed. Thomas Jefferson & the Sciences: An Original Anthology. LC 79-7970. (Three Centuries of Science in America Ser.). (Illus.). 1980. lib. bdg. 50.00x (ISBN 0-405-12552-6). Arno.
Commager, Henry S. Jefferson, Nationalism, & the Enlightenment: Spread of Enlightment from Old World to New. LC 74-80659. 224p. 1975. 7.50 (ISBN 0-8076-0765-7). Braziller.
Cripe, Helen. Thomas Jefferson & Music. LC 73-81099. (Thomas Jefferson Memorial Foundation Series). (Illus.). 1974. 7.50x (ISBN 0-8139-0504-4); pap. 3.95x (ISBN 0-8139-0547-8). U Pr of Va.
Cunningham, Noble E., Jr. The Image of Thomas Jefferson in the Public Eye: Portraits for the People, 1800-1809. LC 80-22757. (Illus.). 1981. 14.95x (ISBN 0-8139-0821-3). U Pr of Va.
--The Process of Government Under Jefferson. LC 77-85535. (Illus.). 1978. text ed. 25.00 (ISBN 0-691-04651-4). Princeton U Pr.
Dabney, Virginius. The Jefferson Scandals: A Rebuttal. LC 81-1669. (Illus.). 156p. 1981. 8.95 (ISBN 0-396-07964-4). Dodd.
--Mr. Jefferson's University: A History. LC 81-3392. (Illus.). 1981. price not set (ISBN 0-8139-0904-X). U Pr of Va.
Dumbauld, Edward. Thomas Jefferson & the Law. LC 78-5742. (Illus.). 1978. 25.00 (ISBN 0-8061-1441-X). U. of Okla Pr.
Dumbauld, Edward H. Thomas Jefferson, American Tourist. (American Exploration & Travel Ser.: No. 9). (Pap. ed. 1978 reprint of 1946 ed.). 1976. 13.95x (ISBN 0-8061-1345-6); pap. 6.95 (ISBN 0-8061-1353-7). U. of Okla Pr.
Edwards, Everett E., ed. Jefferson & Agriculture: A Sourcebook. LC 75-27636. (World Food Supply Ser). 1976. Repr. of 1943 ed. 10.00x (ISBN 0-405-07778-5). Arno.
Erikson, Erik H. Dimensions of the New Identity: Jefferson Lectures 1973. LC 73-22289. 125p. 1974. 10.95 (ISBN 0-393-05515-9). Norton.
Farr, Naunerle C. George Washington-Thomas Jefferson. (Pendulum Illustrated Biography Ser.). (Illus.). (gr. 4-12). 1979. text ed. 5.00 (ISBN 0-88301-367-3); pap. text ed. 1.95 (ISBN 0-88301-355-X); wkbk. 1.25 (ISBN 0-88301-379-7). Pendulum Pr.
Foley, John P., ed. The Jefferson Encyclopedia. 75.00 (ISBN 0-8490-0441-1). Gordon Pr.
Griggs, Edward H. American Statesmen: An Interpretation of Our History & Heritage. LC 76-121474. (Essay Index Reprint Ser). 1927. 19.50 (ISBN 0-8369-1810-X). Arno.
Henderson, John C. Thomas Jefferson's Views on Public Education. LC 76-137239. Repr. of 1890 ed. 28.00 (ISBN 0-404-03236-2). AMS Pr.
Heslep, Robert D. Thomas Jefferson & Education. 8.00 (ISBN 0-8446-0696-0). Peter Smith.
Honeywell, Roy J. Educational Work of Thomas Jefferson. LC 63-15162. (Illus.). 1964. Repr. of 1931 ed. 8.50 (ISBN 0-8462-0432-0). Russell.
Hook, Sidney. The Paradoxes of Freedom. LC 62-16335. 1962. 12.75x (ISBN 0-520-00568-6); pap. 4.95x (ISBN 0-520-00569-4, CAL100). U of Cal Pr.
Irwin, Frank. Letters of Thomas Jefferson. LC 75-12007. (Sanbornton Bridge Pr Ser.). (Orig.). 1975. 8.95 (ISBN 0-89142-022-3). Sant Bani Ash.
Jackson, Donald. Thomas Jefferson & the Stony Mountains: Exploring the West from Monticello. LC 80-10546. (Illus.). 290p. 1981. 19.95 (ISBN 0-252-00823-5). U. of Ill Pr.
Jacob, John J. Biographical Sketch of the Life of the Late Captain Michael Cresap with Notes & Appendix. LC 73-146404. (First American Frontier Ser). 1971. Repr. of 1826 ed. 10.00 (ISBN 0-405-02863-6). Arno.
The Jefferson Papers of the University of Virginia, 2 pts. enl. ed. Incl. Pt. 1. A Calendar of Manuscripts Acquired Through 1950. Thurlow, Constance E. & Berkeley, Francis L., Jr., eds.; Pt. 2. A Supplementary Calendar of Manuscripts Acquired 1950-1970. Casteen, John & Freudenberg, Anne, eds.. LC 72-91896. 1973. 25.00x (ISBN 0-8139-0414-5). U Pr of Va.
Jefferson, Thomas. Life & Selected Writings. 1944. 3.95 (ISBN 0-394-60234-X, M234). Modern Lib.
--The Living Thought of Thomas Jefferson. 1974. lib. bdg. 29.95 (ISBN 0-685-51297-5). Revisionist Pr.
--Melanges Politiques et Philosophiques Extraits Des Memoires et De la Correspondance De Thomas Jefferson, 2 vols. in one. Mayer, J. P., ed. LC 78-67360. (European Political Thought Ser.). 1979. Repr. of 1833 ed. lib. bdg. 54.00x (ISBN 0-405-11709-4). Arno.
--The Portable Thomas Jefferson. Peterson, Merrill D., ed. (Viking Portable Library: No. 80). 640p. 1977. pap. 5.95 (ISBN 0-14-015080-3). Penguin.
--Thomas Jefferson: Revolutionary Philosopher, a Selection of Writings. Pancake, John S., ed. LC 75-43501. (Orig.). (gr. 10-12). 1976. pap. text ed. 4.50 (ISBN 0-8120-0657-7). Barron.
Johnstone, Robert M., Jr. Jefferson & the Presidency: Leadership in the Young Republic. LC 77-17460. 1978. 19.50x (ISBN 0-8014-1150-5). Cornell U Pr.

Kaplan, Lawrence S. Jefferson & France: An Essay on Politics & Political Ideas. LC 79-27698. (Yale Historical Publications, the Wallace Notestein Essays: No. 5). ix, 175p. 1980. Repr. of 1967 ed. lib. bdg. 17.25x (ISBN 0-313-22154-5, KAJF). Greenwood.
Kimball, Fiske. Thomas Jefferson, Architect. 2nd ed. LC 67-27459. (Architecture & Decorative Art Ser). 1968. lib. bdg. 80.00 (ISBN 0-306-70965-1); pap. 29.50 (ISBN 0-306-70464-1). Da Capo.
Kimball, Marie. Jefferson, the Road to Glory, 1743-1776. LC 76-52415. (Illus.). 1977. Repr. of 1943 ed. lib. bdg. 24.25x (ISBN 0-8371-9444-X, KIJE). Greenwood.
--Jefferson, War & Peace, Seventeen Seventy-Six to Seventeen Eighty-Four. LC 80-12595. (Illus.). ix, 398p. 1980. Repr. of 1947 ed. lib. bdg. 30.25x (ISBN 0-313-22400-5, KIJW). Greenwood.
Klingberg, F. J. & Klingberg, F. W. The Correspondence Between Henry Stephens Randall & Hugh Blair Grigsby 1856-1861. LC 73-37530. (The American Scene Ser). 196p. 1972. Repr. of 1952 ed. lib. bdg. 22.50 (ISBN 0-306-70429-3). Da Capo.
Koch, Adrienne. Jefferson & Madison: The Great Collaboration. 1964. pap. 8.95 (ISBN 0-19-500420-5, GB). Oxford U Pr.
--Jefferson & Madison: The Great Collaboration. 7.50 (ISBN 0-8446-0743-6). Peter Smith.
--Philosophy of Thomas Jefferson. 1972. pap. 2.65 (ISBN 0-8129-6011-4, QP17). Times Bks.
--The Philosophy of Thomas Jefferson. 8.00 (ISBN 0-8446-1270-7). Peter Smith.
Larson, Martin A. The Essence of Jefferson. LC 77-87236. 1977. 10.95 (ISBN 0-89674-001-3). J J Binns.
Levy, Leonard W. Jefferson & Civil Liberties. rev. ed. 225p. 1972. pap. 2.95 (ISBN 0-8129-6228-1). Times Bks.
Linn, William. The Life of Thomas Jefferson. 267p. 1981. Repr. of 1843 ed. lib. bdg. 65.00 (ISBN 0-89760-506-3). Telegraph Bks.
McDonald, Forrest. The Presidency of Thomas Jefferson. LC 76-803. (American Presidency Ser). 1976. 12.00x (ISBN 0-7006-0147-3). Regents Pr KS.
McIlwaine, H. R., ed. The Letters of Thomas Jefferson. LC 27-2700. (Official Letters of the Governors of the State of Virginia Ser: Vol. 2). 1928. 7.50 (ISBN 0-88490-019-3). VA State Lib.
Malone, Dumas. Jefferson & His Time: The Sage of Monticello, Vol. 6. (Illus.). 570p. 1981. 19.95 (ISBN 0-316-54463-9). Little.
--Jefferson & the Ordeal of Liberty, Vol. 3. (Jefferson & His Time). 1969. 17.50 (ISBN 0-316-54475-2); pap. 7.95 (ISBN 0-316-54469-8). Little.
--Jefferson & the Rights of Man, Vol. 2. (Jefferson & His Time). (Illus.). 1951. 17.50 (ISBN 0-316-54473-6); pap. 7.95 (ISBN 0-316-54470-1). Little.
--Jefferson the President: First Term, 1801-1805, Vol. 4. LC 48-5972. (Jefferson & His Time). (Illus.). 1970. 17.50 (ISBN 0-316-54467-1); pap. 7.95 (ISBN 0-316-54466-3). Little.
--Jefferson the President: Second Term, 1805-1809, Vol. 5. (Jefferson & His Time). 1974. 19.95 (ISBN 0-316-54465-5); pap. 8.95 (ISBN 0-316-54464-7). Little.
--Jefferson the Virginian, Vol. 1. (Jefferson & His Time). (Illus.). 1948. 14.50 (ISBN 0-316-54474-4); pap. 4.95 (ISBN 0-316-54472-8, LB78). Little.
--The Sage of Monticello. (Illus.). 512p. 1981. 19.95 (ISBN 0-316-54463-9). Little.
--Thomas Jefferson As Political Leader. LC 78-21568. 1979. Repr. of 1963 ed. lib. bdg. 15.00 (ISBN 0-313-20730-5, MATJ). Greenwood.
Mayo, Bernard. Jefferson Himself. LC 70-87871. pap. 5.95 (ISBN 0-8139-0310-6). U Pr of Va.
Mayo, Bernard, ed. Thomas Jefferson & His Unknown Brother. LC 80-25272. 1981. 7.95x (ISBN 0-8139-0890-6); pap. 3.95x (ISBN 0-8139-0911-2). U Pr of Va.
Miller, John C. The Wolf by the Ears: Thomas Jefferson & Slavery. 1980. pap. 5.95 (ISBN 0-452-00530-2, F530, Mer). NAL.
--The Wolf by the Ears: Thomas Jefferson & Slavery. LC 76-51590. 1977. 15.95 (ISBN 0-02-921500-5). Free Pr.
Morgan, Edmund S. The Meaning of Independence: John Adams, George Washington, Thomas Jefferson. LC 76-8438. 1979. Repr. 8.95x (ISBN 0-8139-0694-6). U Pr of Va.
Morse, John T., Jr. Thomas Jefferson. LC 80-23357. (American Statesmen Ser.). 330p. 1981. pap. 5.95 (ISBN 0-87754-183-3). Chelsea Hse.
Morse, John T., Jr., ed. Thomas Jefferson. LC 77-128975. (American Statesmen: No. 11). Repr. of 1898 ed. 19.50 (ISBN 0-404-50861-8). AMS Pr.
Moscow, Henry. Thomas Jefferson & His World. LC 60-11827. (American Heritage Junior Library). (Illus.). 153p. (gr. 6 up). 1960. 9.95 (ISBN 0-8281-0386-0, J003-0); PLB 12.89 (ISBN 0-06-024346-5, Dist. by Har-Row). Am Heritage.
Mumford, Lewis. South in Architecture. LC 67-27462. (Architecture & Decorative Art Ser). 1967. Repr. of 1941 ed. lib. bdg. 19.50 (ISBN 0-306-70972-4). Da Capo.
Nichols, Frederick D. & Griswold, Ralph E. Thomas Jefferson, Landscape Architect. LC 77-10601. (Illus.). ix, 196p. 1981. pap. 4.95x (ISBN 0-8139-0899-X). U Pr of Va.
--Thomas Jefferson Landscape Architect. LC 77-10601. (Illus.). 1977. 10.95x (ISBN 0-8139-0603-2). U Pr of Va.
Nichols, Frederick D., ed. Thomas Jefferson's Architectural Drawings. 2nd ed. LC 76-163982. (Orig.). 1961. pap. 2.95 (ISBN 0-8139-0328-9). U Pr of Va.
O'Neal, W. B. Jefferson's Fine Arts Library. 1976. 20.00 (ISBN 0-8139-0648-2). Brown Bk.
O'Neal, William B. Jefferson's Fine Arts Library: His Selections for the University of Virginia Together with His Own Architectural Books at Monticello. LC 75-33229. (Illus.). 1976. 20.00x (ISBN 0-8139-0648-2). U Pr of Va.
Padover, Saul K. Jefferson. rev. & abr. ed. 1952. pap. 1.75 (ISBN 0-451-61927-7, MW1927, Ment). NAL.
Pancake, John S. Jefferson & Hamilton. Colegrove, Kenneth, ed. LC 74-750. (Shapers of History Ser). (gr. 10 up). 1974. pap. text ed. 4.95 (ISBN 0-8120-0463-9). Barron.
Parton, James. Life of Thomas Jefferson. LC 76-126604. (American Scene Ser). (Illus.). 1971. Repr. of 1874 ed. lib. bdg. 59.50 (ISBN 0-306-70049-2). Da Capo.
--Life of Thomas Jefferson. 69.95 (ISBN 0-8490-0538-8). Gordon Pr.
Patterson, Caleb P. The Constitutional Principles of Thomas Jefferson. 8.00 (ISBN 0-8446-1340-1). Peter Smith.
--The Constitutional Principles of Thomas Jefferson. facsimile ed. LC 77-157352. (Select Bibliographies Reprint Ser). Repr. of 1953 ed. 16.00 (ISBN 0-8369-5813-6). Arno.
Peterson, Merrill D. Adams & Jefferson: A Revolutionary Dialogue. LC 76-1145. (Illus.). 1978. pap. 3.50 (ISBN 0-19-502355-2, GB533, GB). Oxford U Pr.
--Jefferson Image in the American Mind. 1960. 19.95 (ISBN 0-19-501539-8). Oxford U Pr.
--Thomas Jefferson & the New Nation: A Biography. LC 70-110394. 1970. 35.00 (ISBN 0-19-500054-4). Oxford U Pr.
--Thomas Jefferson & the New Nation: A Biography. LC 70-110394. (Illus.). 1090p. 1975. pap. 9.95 (ISBN 0-19-501909-1, GB436, GB). Oxford U Pr.
Pierson, Hamilton W. Jefferson at Monticello: The Private Life of Thomas Jefferson. facsimile ed. LC 71-154161. (Select Bibliographies Reprint Ser). Repr. of 1862 ed. 20.00 (ISBN 0-8369-5777-6). Arno.
Prescott, F. C. Hamilton & Jefferson. 422p. 1980. Repr. lib. bdg. 40.00 (ISBN 0-8495-4381-9). Arden Lib.
Randall, Henry S. Life of Thomas Jefferson, 3 Vols. facs. ed. LC 72-117890. (Select Bibliographies Reprint Ser). 1857. Set. 90.00 (ISBN 0-8369-5343-6). Arno.
Randall, Henry Stephens. The Life of Thomas Jefferson, 3 vols. LC 79-172011. (The American Scene Ser). (Illus.). 1972. Repr. of 1858 ed. lib. bdg. 65.00 ea.; lib. bdg. 160.00 set (ISBN 0-306-70250-9). Da Capo.
Randolph, Sarah N. Domestic Life of Thomas Jefferson. LC 58-8959. (American Classics Ser.). (Illus.). 12.50 (ISBN 0-8044-1759-8). Ungar.
--The Domestic Life of Thomas Jefferson. LC 78-14312. 1979. 7.50 (ISBN 0-8139-0718-7). U Pr of Va.
Rice, Howard C., Jr., ed. Thomas Jefferson's Paris. LC 75-30203. (Illus.). 160p. 1976. text ed. 22.00 (ISBN 0-691-05232-8); pap. 9.75 (ISBN 0-691-00776-4). Princeton U Pr.
Sanford, Charles B. Thomas Jefferson & His Library. 1977. 16.50 (ISBN 0-208-01629-5, Archon). Shoe String.
Sears, Louis M. Jefferson & the Embargo. 1967. lib. bdg. 18.50x (ISBN 0-374-97220-6). Octagon.
Sheehan, Bernard W. Seeds of Extinction: Jeffersonian Philanthropy & the American Indian. LC 72-85403. (Institute of Early American History & Culture Ser.). 344p. 1973. 19.00x (ISBN 0-8078-1203-X). U of NC Pr.
--Seeds of Extinction: Jeffersonian Philanthropy & the American Indian. 320p. 1974. pap. 5.95 (ISBN 0-393-00716-2). Norton.
Speeches at Full Length in the Cause of the People Against Harry Croswell. LC 78-125716. (American Journalists Ser). 1970. Repr. of 1804 ed. 8.00 (ISBN 0-405-01697-2). Arno.
Stuart, Reginald C. The Half-Way Pacifist: Thomas Jefferson's View of War. LC 78-8232. 1978. 12.50x (ISBN 0-8020-5431-5). U of Toronto Pr.
Swancara, Frank. Thomas Jefferson Versus Religious Oppression. 160p. 1970. 5.95 (ISBN 0-8216-0103-2). Univ Bks.
Thomas Jefferson's Architectural Drawings. 3rd ed. (Massachusetts Historical Society Picture Books Ser.). 1960. 2.00 (ISBN 0-686-21431-5). Mass Hist Soc.
Thurlow, Constance E., et al, eds. The Jefferson Papers of the University of Virginia. LC 72-91896. 1973. 25.00x (ISBN 0-8139-0414-5). U Pr of Va.
Tompkins, Hamilton B. Bibliotheca Jeffersoniana. 12.50 (ISBN 0-8363-0014-9). Jenkins.
Umbreit, Kenneth B. Founding Fathers: Men Who Shaped Our Tradition. LC 68-26228. Repr. of 1941 ed. 13.00 (ISBN 0-8046-0469-X). Kennikat.
Vossler, Otto. Jefferson & the American Revolutionary Ideal. Philippon, Catherine & Wishy, Bernard, trs. LC 79-6726. 1980. pap. text ed. 10.50 (ISBN 0-8191-0941-X); lib. bdg. 18.50 (ISBN 0-8191-0938-X). U Pr of Amer.
Wagoner, Jennings, Jr. Thomas Jefferson & the Education of a New Nation. LC 75-28649. (Fastback Ser.: No. 73). (Orig.). 1976. pap. 0.75 (ISBN 0-87367-073-6). Phi Delta Kappa.
Williams, John S. Thomas Jefferson. LC 13-9744. Repr. of 1913 ed. 18.50 (ISBN 0-404-06985-1). AMS Pr.
Woolery, William K. The Relation of Thomas Jefferson to American Foreign Policy, 1783-1793. LC 78-64123. (Johns Hopkins University. Studies in the Social Sciences. Forty-Fifth Ser. 1927: 2). Repr. of 1927 ed. 13.50 (ISBN 0-404-61237-7). AMS Pr.
--Relation of Thomas Jefferson to American Policy, 1783-1793. LC 70-131863. 1971. Repr. of 1927 ed. 12.00 (ISBN 0-403-00750-X). Scholarly.

JEFFERSON, THOMAS, PRES. U. S., 1743-1826–DRAMA

Green, Paul. The Common Glory. LC 72-11622. (Illus.). 273p. 1973. Repr. of 1948 ed. lib. bdg. 15.25x (ISBN 0-8371-7080-X, GRCH). Greenwood.

JEFFERSON, THOMAS, PRES. U. S., 1743-1826–FICTION

Page, Elizabeth. Tree of Liberty. 1939. 10.00 (ISBN 0-03-029735-4). HR&W.

JEFFERSON, THOMAS, PRES. U. S., 1743-1826–JUVENILE LITERATURE

Barrett, Marvin. Meet Thomas Jefferson. (Step-up Books Ser.). (gr. 2-6). 1967. 3.95 (ISBN 0-394-80067-2, BYR); PLB 4.99 (ISBN 0-394-90067-7). Random.
Harrison, et al. Thomas Jefferson. (Illus.). 35p. (gr. 1-9). 1981. write for info. (ISBN 0-86575-187-0). Dormac.
Johnson, Ann D. Value of Foresight: The Story of Thomas Jefferson. LC 79-19548. (Illus.). (gr. k-6). 1979. 6.95 (ISBN 0-916392-42-2, Dist. by Oak Tree Pubns.). Value Comm.
Richards, Norman. Story of Monticello. LC 70-100699. (Cornerstones of Freedom Ser.). (gr. 4-8). 1970. PLB 7.95 (ISBN 0-516-04627-6). Childrens.
Wayne, Bennett, ed. The Founding Fathers. LC 74-19112. (Target Books Ser). (Illus.). 168p. (gr. 5-12). 1975. PLB 7.29 (ISBN 0-8116-4912-1). Garrard.
Wibberley, Leonard. Young Man from the Piedmont. LC 63-14626. (gr. 7 up). 1963. 3.95 (ISBN 0-374-38712-5). FS&G.

JEFFERSON FAMILY

Betts, Edwin M. & Bear, James A., eds. Family Letters of Thomas Jefferson. LC 66-17954. (Illus.). 1966. 15.00x (ISBN 0-8262-0101-6). U of Mo Pr.
Merrill, Boynton. Jefferson's Nephews. LC 76-3267. 1976. 24.00 (ISBN 0-691-04640-9). Princeton U Pr.

JEFFERSON COUNTY, WISCONSIN

Barrett, Samuel A. Ancient Aztalan. LC 70-11394. Repr. of 1933 ed. lib. bdg. 28.25x (ISBN 0-8371-4624-0, BAAA). Greenwood.

JEFFREY, FRANCIS JEFFREY, LORD, 1773-1850

Cockburn, Henry T. Life of Lord Jeffrey with a Selection from His Correspondence, 2 vols. in 1. LC 70-148763. Repr. of 1857 ed. 41.50 (ISBN 0-404-07297-6). AMS Pr.
Flynn, Philip. Francis Jeffrey. LC 76-27915. 218p. 1978. 13.50 (ISBN 0-87413-123-5). U Delaware Pr.
Gates, Lewis E. Three Studies in Literature: Jeffrey, Newman, Arnold. LC 72-195408. 1899. lib. bdg. 15.00 (ISBN 0-8414-4640-7). Folcroft.
Morgan, P., ed. Jeffrey's Criticism. 200p. 1981. 17.00x (ISBN 0-7073-0300-1, Pub. by Scottish Academic Pr Scotland). Columbia U Pr.
Windham, Kathryn T. Thirteen Mississippi Ghosts & Jeffrey. LC 74-15509. 1974. 7.95 (ISBN 0-87397-047-0). Strode.

JEHOVAH, SERVANT OF

see Servant of Jehovah

JEHOVAH'S WITNESSES

Beckford, James A. The Trumpet of Prophecy: A Sociological Study of Jehovah's Witnesses. LC 75-14432. 246p. 1975. 27.95 (ISBN 0-470-06138-3). Halsted Pr.
Bjornstad, James. Counterfeits at Your Door. LC 78-72864. 1979. pap. text ed. 1.95 (ISBN 0-8307-0610-0, S124254). Regal.
Dencher, Ted. Why I Left Jehovah's Witnesses. 1966. pap. 3.95 (ISBN 0-87508-160-6). Chr Lit.
Gerstner, John H. Teachings of Jehovah's Witnesses. pap. 1.25 (ISBN 0-8010-3718-2). Baker Bk.
Giron, Jose. Testigos De Jehova y Sus Doctrinas. (Spanish Bks.). 1978. 1.50 (ISBN 0-8297-0604-6). Life Pubs Intl.
Gruss, Edmond C. Jehovah's Witnesses & Prophetic Speculation. pap. 3.75 (ISBN 0-8010-3710-7). Baker Bk.
--Jehovah's Witnesses & Prophetic Speculation. pap. 3.75 (ISBN 0-87552-306-4). Presby & Reformed.
--We Left Jehovah's Witnesses. pap. 3.95 (ISBN 0-8010-3696-8). Baker Bk.
--We Left Jehovah's Witnesses: A Non-Prophet Organization. pap. 3.50 (ISBN 0-87552-307-2). Presby & Reformed.
Hewitt, Joe B. I Was Raised a Jehovah's Witness. LC 78-73255. 1979. pap. 3.95 (ISBN 0-89636-018-0). Accent Bks.
Hoekema, Anthony A. The Four Major Cults. 1963. 9.95 (ISBN 0-8028-3117-6). Eerdmans.
--Jehovah's Witnesses. 1974. pap. 1.95 (ISBN 0-8028-1489-1). Eerdmans.
Kern, Herbert. How to Respond to Jehovah's Witnesses. (The Response Ser.). 1977. 1.25 (ISBN 0-570-07679-X, 12-2664). Concordia.
Kirban, Salem. Jehovah's Witnesses. (Illus.). 1972. pap. 2.50 (ISBN 0-912582-03-0). Kirban.
Lambert, O. C. Russellism Unveiled. 1940. pap. 2.00 (ISBN 0-686-21503-6). Firm Foun Pub.
Lewis, Gordon. Bible, Christians & Jehovah's Witnesses. pap. 0.75 (ISBN 0-8010-5568-7). Baker Bk.
Lindsay, Gordon. What About Jehovah's Witnesses? 1.25 (ISBN 0-89985-017-0). Christ Nations.
Manwaring, David R. Render Unto Caesar: The Flag-Salute Controversy. LC 62-13563. 1962. 12.50x (ISBN 0-226-50413-1). U of Chicago Pr.
Martin, Walter. Jehovah's Witnesses. 1969. pap. 1.50 (ISBN 0-87123-270-7, 210270). Bethany Hse.
Martin, Walter & Klann, Norman H. Jehovah of the Watchtower. 1981. pap. 4.95 (ISBN 0-87123-267-7). Bethany Hse.
Martin, Walter R. Jehovah of the Watchtower. rev. ed. 144p. 1974. pap. 3.95 (ISBN 0-8024-4290-0). Moody.
Morey, Robert A. How to Answer a Jehovah's Witness. LC 79-25502. (Orig.). 1980. pap. 2.95 (ISBN 0-87123-206-5, 210206). Bethany Hse.
Oakley, Debbie & Ortega, Helen. Mom & Me: Twenty Years Jehovah's Witnesses. 1978. 5.95 (ISBN 0-533-03385-3). Vantage.
Passantino, Robert, et al. Answers to the Cultist at Your Door. LC 80-83850. 1981. pap. 4.95 (ISBN 0-89081-275-6). Harvest Hse.
Price, E. B. Is It the Watchtower? LC 67-30889. 1967. pap. 0.95 (ISBN 0-8163-0106-9, 09665-1). Pacific Pr Pub Assn.
Rumble, Leslie. The Incredible Creed of the Jehovah Witnesses. 1977. pap. 0.60 (ISBN 0-89555-025-3, 195). TAN Bks Pubs.
Schnell, William J. How to Witness to Jehovah's Witnesses. Orig. Title: Christians, Awake! 160p. 1975. pap. 2.95 (ISBN 0-8010-8048-7). Baker Bk.
--Jehovah's Witnesses Errors Exposed. pap. 4.95 (ISBN 0-8010-8074-6). Baker Bk.
--Thirty Years a Watchtower Slave. (Direction Bks). pap. 1.95 (ISBN 0-8010-7933-0). Baker Bk.

JEKRI (AFRICAN PEOPLE)

Ikime, Obaro. Chief Dogho of Warri. (African Historical Biographies Ser.). (Illus.). 48p. 1977. pap. text ed. 2.75x (ISBN 0-435-94473-8). Heinemann Ed.

JELLYFISH

see Medusae

JEMISON, MARY, 1734-1833

Brush, Edward H. Iroquois Past & Present. LC 74-7944. Repr. of 1901 ed. 12.50 (ISBN 0-404-11831-3). AMS Pr.
Gardner, Jeanne L. Mary Jemison: Seneca Captive. LC 66-23287. (Illus.). (gr. 5-7). 1966. 5.50 (ISBN 0-15-252190-9, HJ). HarBraceJ.
Lenski, Lois. Indian Captive: The Story of Mary Jemison. LC 41-51956. (Illus.). (gr. 7-9). 1941. 10.95 (ISBN 0-397-30072-7, JBL-J). Har-Row.
Seaver, James E. Narrative of the Life of Mrs. Mary Jemison. 7.00 (ISBN 0-8446-2899-9). Peter Smith.

JENGHIS KHAN, 1162-1227
Korostovetz, Iwan J. & Hauer, Erich. Von Cinggis Khan zur Sowjetrepublik: Eine kurze Geschichte der Mongolei unter besonderer Beruecksichtigung der neuesten Zeit. (Illus.). 351p. 1974. Repr. of 1926 ed. 112.00x (ISBN 3-11-002497-7). De Gruyter.
Liddell Hart, Basil. Great Captains Unveiled. facs. ed. LC 67-23240. (Essay Index Reprint Ser). 1928. 19.50 (ISBN 0-8369-0618-7). Arno.
Martin, Henry D. Rise of Chingis Khan & His Conquest of North China. LC 70-120647. 1970. Repr. lib. bdg. 24.00x (ISBN 0-374-95287-6). Octagon.
Vladimirtsov, Boris. Life of Chingis-Khan. Mirsky, D. S., tr. from Rus. LC 76-82003. Repr. of 1930 ed. 12.00 (ISBN 0-405-09048-X). Arno.
Yapp, Malcolm. Chingis Khan & the Mongol Empire. Killingray, Margaret & O'Connor, Edmund, eds. (World History Ser.). (Illus.). 32p. (gr. 10). 1980. Repr. of 1977 ed. lib. bdg. 5.95 (ISBN 0-89908-030-8); pap. text ed. 1.95 (ISBN 0-89908-005-7). Greenhaven.

JENKINS, PAUL, 1923-
Elsen, Albert E. Paul Jenkins. LC 75-101622. (Contemporary Artists Ser.). (Illus.). 284p. 1973. 65.00 (ISBN 0-8109-0215-X). Abrams.

JENNER, BRUCE
Jenner, Bruce & Kiliper, R. Smith. The Olympics & Me. LC 79-7496. (I Want to Know About Ser.). (Illus.). 1980. 6.95a (ISBN 0-385-14928-X); PLB (ISBN 0-385-14929-8). Doubleday.
Soucheray, Joe. Bruce Jenner. (Sports Superstars Ser.). (Illus.). (gr. 3-9). 1979. PLB 5.95 (ISBN 0-87191-723-8); pap. 2.95 (ISBN 0-89812-158-2). Creative Ed.

JENNER, EDWARD, 1749-1823
Saunders, Paul L. Edward Jenner: The Cheltenham Years (Seventeen Ninety-Five to Eighteen Twenty-Three) - Being a Chronicle of the Vaccination Campaign. LC 81-51607. (Illus.). 432p. 1982. 20.00 (ISBN 0-87451-215-8). U Pr of New England.

JENSEN, JOHANNES VILHELM, 1873-1950
Nielsen, Marion L. Denmark's Johannes V. Jensen. 45p. 1955. pap. 3.00 (ISBN 0-87421-019-4). Utah St U Pr.

JENSEN, POVL BANG, 1909-
Flynn, James R. Race, IQ, & Jensen. 320p. 1980. 27.50 (ISBN 0-7100-0651-9). Routledge & Kegan.

JEOPARDY, DOUBLE
see Double Jeopardy

JERBOAS
Kirmiz, John P. Adaptation to Desert Environment: A Study of the Jerboa, Rat & Man. 168p. 1962. 24.50 (ISBN 0-306-30658-1, Plenum Pr). Plenum Pub.

JEREMIAH THE PROPHET
Blank, Sheldon. Jeremiah, Man & Prophet. 1961. 10.00x (ISBN 0-87820-100-9, Pub. by Hebrew Union). Ktav.
Efird, James M. Jeremiah--Prophet Under Siege. LC 79-14837. 1979. pap. 4.95 (ISBN 0-8170-0846-2). Judson.
Holladay, William L. Jeremiah: Spokesman Out of Time. LC 74-7052. 160p. 1974. pap. 3.95 (ISBN 0-8298-0283-5). Pilgrim NY.
Lindsay, Gordon. Isaiah & Jeremiah. (Old Testament Ser.). 1.25 (ISBN 0-89985-155-X). Christ Nations.
Meyer, F. B. Jeremiah. 1972. pap. 2.95 (ISBN 0-87508-355-2). Chr Lit.
Rand, Howard B. Study in Jeremiah. 1947. 5.00 (ISBN 0-685-08816-2). Destiny.
Welch, Adam C. Jeremiah, His Time & His Work. LC 80-17188. vii, 263p. 1980. Repr. of 1928 ed. lib. bdg. 22.50x (ISBN 0-313-22609-1, WEJH). Greenwood.

JEREMIAH THE PROPHET–FICTION
Hyman, Frieda Clark. Jubal & the Prophet. LC 58-11891. (Covenant Ser.). (Illus.). (gr. 6-10). 1958. 3.50 (ISBN 0-8276-0147-6, 274). Jewish Pubn.

JEROME, SAINT (HIERONYMUS, SAINT)
Brewer, James W., Jr. Jerome. 14th ed. (Illus.). 1976. pap. 0.25 (ISBN 0-911408-16-9). SW Pks Mnmts.
Kelly, J. N. His Life, Writings, & Controversies. 353p. 1980. pap. 8.95 (ISBN 0-87061-061-9). Chr Classics.

JEROME, JEROME KLAPKA, 1859-1927
Faurot, Ruth M. Jerome K. Jerome. LC 73-15938. (English Authors Ser.: No. 164). 1974. lib. bdg. 10.95 (ISBN 0-8057-1291-7). Twayne.

JERROLD, DOUGLAS WILLIAM, 1803-1857
Kelly, Richard M. Douglas Jerrold. LC 79-187615. (English Authors Ser.: No. 146). lib. bdg. 10.95 (ISBN 0-8057-1292-5). Twayne.
Stirling, James H. Jerrold, Tennyson & Macaulay, with Other Critical Essays. LC 77-8713. Repr. of 1868 ed. lib. bdg. 22.50 (ISBN 0-8414-7561-X). Folcroft.

JERSEY (PRISON SHIP)
Greene, Albert G. Recollections of the Jersey Prison Ship. 1961. pap. 1.25 (ISBN 0-87091-007-8, AE). Corinth Bks.

JERSEY CITY–POLITICS AND GOVERNMENT
Amato, Matthew F., Jr. Jersey City: A City in Socio-Economic & Political Change. (Illus.). 1979. 5.00 (ISBN 0-682-49511-5). Exposition.

JERUSALEM
Bellow, Saul. To Jerusalem & Back: A Personal Account. LC 76-42198. 192p. 1976. 8.95 (ISBN 0-670-71729-0). Viking Pr.
Benvenisti, Meron. Jerusalem: The Torn City. (Illus.). 1977. 19.50x (ISBN 0-8166-0795-8). U of Minn Pr.
Bovis, H. Eugene. Jerusalem Question: 1917-1968. LC 73-149796. (Studies Ser.: No. 29). (Illus.). 175p. 1971. 9.95 (ISBN 0-8179-3291-7). Hoover Inst Pr.
Collins, Larry & Lapierre, Dominique. O Jerusalem. 1980. pap. 3.95 (ISBN 0-671-83684-6). PB.
Elkins, Dov P., ed. Rejoice with Jerusalem. 1972. pap. 1.95 (ISBN 0-685-30709-3). Prayer BK.
Fischer, Gretl. In Search of Jerusalem: Religion & Ethics in the Writings of A. M. Klein. 288p. 1976. 14.95x (ISBN 0-7735-0227-0). McGill-Queens U Pr.
Hebrew University of Jerusalem, Dept. of Geography. Atlas of Jerusalem. (Illus.). 1973. Boxed. 300.00 (ISBN 3-11-003623-1). De Gruyter.
Kollek, Teddy. Jerusalem. 16p. Date not set. price not set. ADL.
Lillien, E. M. Jerusalem. 25.00 (ISBN 0-87068-471-X). Ktav.
Loti, Pierre. Jerusalem. 15.00 (ISBN 0-685-64788-9). Norwood Edns.
Malgo, Wim. Jerusalem: Focal Point of the World. 2.95 (ISBN 0-686-12827-3). Midnight Call.
Moskin, J. Robert. Report from Jerusalem: City at the Crossroads. LC 77-79877. (Illus.). 1977. pap. 1.50 (ISBN 0-87495-013-9). Am Jewish Comm.
Olson, Nathanael. To Jerusalem, with Love. Kuse, James A., ed. (Illus.). 1979. pap. 1.50 (ISBN 0-89542-463-0). Ideals.
Papas, William. People of Old Jerusalem. LC 80-197. (Illus.). 216p. 1980. 34.95 (ISBN 0-03-057483-8); prepub. 29.95 pre-Jan (ISBN 0-686-77495-7). HR&W.
Prittie, Terrence. Whose Jerusalem? 224p. 1981. 45.00x (ISBN 0-584-10440-5, Pub. by Muller Ltd). State Mutual Bk.
Thubron, Colin. Jerusalem. (Great Cities Ser.). (Illus.). 1976. 14.95 (ISBN 0-8094-2250-6). Time-Life.
Van Till, Cornelius. Jerusalem & Athens. Geehan, Robert, ed. pap. 7.50 (ISBN 0-87552-489-3). Presby & Reformed.
Wilson, Evan M. Jerusalem, Key to Peace. LC 70-119026. (James Terry Duce Ser.: Vol. 2). 1970. 5.95 (ISBN 0-916808-08-4). Mid East Inst.

JERUSALEM–ANTIQUITIES
Dever, William G. Gezer Two. 1974. 35.00x (ISBN 0-685-56198-4). Ktav.
Mare, W. H. The Archeology of the Jerusalem Area. 340p. (Orig.). 1982. pap. price not set (ISBN 0-8010-6126-1). Baker Bk.
Mazar, Benjamin. Beth She'arim: Report of the Excavations During 1936-1940, Vol. 1. (Illus.). 276p. 1973. 30.00x (ISBN 0-8135-0730-8). Rutgers U Pr.
Merrill, Selah. Ancient Jerusalem. Davis, Moshe, ed. LC 77-70724. (America & the Holy Land Ser.). (Illus.). 1977. Repr. of 1908 ed. lib. bdg. 30.00x (ISBN 0-405-10267-4). Arno.
Orlinsky, Harry M., et al. From the Lands of the Bible: Art & Artifacts. (Illus.). 140p. pap. 3.50 (ISBN 0-686-74789-5). Bklyn Mus.
Schaffer, Shaul & Joseph, Asher. Israel's Temple Mount: The Jew's Magnificent Sanctuary. (Illus.). 1975. 10.00 (ISBN 0-685-84975-9). Feldheim.
Siddiqi, I. A. Jerusalem: A Holy City in International Politics. LC 75-14392. 1975. 4.00 (ISBN 0-686-11966-5). Bks Intl DH-TE.
Wilkinson, John. Jerusalem As Jesus Knew It: Archaeology As Evidence. (Illus.). 1978. 8.95 (ISBN 0-500-05031-7). Thames Hudson.
Yadin, Yigael, ed. Jerusalem Revealed: Archeology in the Holy City 1968-1974. LC 75-43338. 1976. 16.95x (ISBN 0-300-01965-3). Yale U Pr.

JERUSALEM–CHURCHES
Bludau, August. Die Pilgerreise der Aetheria. pap. 18.50 (ISBN 0-384-04760-2). Johnson Repr.
Couasnon, Charles. The Church of the Holy Sepulchre in Jerusalem. (British Academy Ser). (Illus.). 80p. 1974. 16.95x (ISBN 0-19-725938-3). Oxford U Pr.
Duckworth, Henry T. The Church of the Holy Sepulchre. LC 78-63361. (BCL Ser.). (Illus.). Repr. of 1922 ed. 25.50 (ISBN 0-404-17014-5). AMS Pr.
Duncan, Alistair. The Noble Heritage: Jerusalem & Christianity - a Portrait of the Church of the Resurrection. 1974. 12.95x (ISBN 0-86685-011-2). Intl Bk Ctr.

JERUSALEM–DESCRIPTION
Adrichem, Christianus van. A Briefe Description of Hierusalem, Also a Mappe. Tymme, T., tr. LC 70-29008. (English Experience Ser.: No. 125). 1969. Repr. of 1595 ed. 21.00 (ISBN 90-221-0125-8). Walter J Johnson.
Avi-Yonah, Michael & Braun, Werner. Jerusalem the Holy. LC 75-24510. (Illus.). 130p. 1976. 10.00 (ISBN 0-8052-3604-X). Schocken.
Barclay, James T. The City of the Great King: Jerusalem As It Was, As It Is, & As It Is to Be. Davis, Moshe, ed. LC 77-70664. (America & the Holy Land Ser.). 1977. Repr. of 1858 ed. lib. bdg. 37.00x (ISBN 0-405-10225-9). Arno.
Cattan, Henry. Jerusalem. 240p. 1981. 25.00 (ISBN 0-312-44182-7). St Martin.
Davis, Moshe, ed. Holy Land Missions & Missionaries: An Original Anthology. LC 77-70703. (America & the Holy Land Ser.). (Illus.). 1977. lib. bdg. 15.00x (ISBN 0-405-10259-3). Arno.
Foster, Dave, ed. Jerusalem: The Christian Herald Photoguide. LC 79-57167. (Illus.). 128p. 1980. 14.95 (ISBN 0-915684-60-8). Christian Herald.
Ganz, Yaffa. Our Jerusalem. (Illus.). (gr. k-2). 1979. pap. 2.50x (ISBN 0-87441-308-7). Behrman.
Geyer, Paul, ed. Itinera Hierosolymitana, Saeculi 3-8. (Corpus Scriptorum Ecclesiasticorum Latinorum Ser: Vol. 39). Repr. of 1898 ed. pap. 33.00 (ISBN 0-384-18270-4). Johnson Repr.
Hopkins, I. W. Jerusalem: A Study in Urban Geography. Pfeiffer, Charles F., ed. (Baker Studies in Biblical Archaeology Ser). 1970. pap. 2.95 (ISBN 0-8010-4000-0). Baker Bk.
Hostetler, Marian. Journey to Jerusalem. (Illus.). (gr. 4-8). 1978. 3.95 (ISBN 0-8361-1847-2); pap. 2.95 (ISBN 0-8361-1848-0). Herald Pr.
Isreal, John & Lundt, Henry. Journal of a Cruize in the U.S. Ship Delaware 74 in the Mediterranean in the Years 1833 & 34. Davis, Moshe, ed. LC 77-70707. (America & the Holy Land Ser.). (Illus.). 1977. Repr. of 1835 ed. lib. bdg. 12.00x (ISBN 0-405-10257-7). Arno.
Johnson, Sarah B. Hadji in Syria: Three Years in Jerusalem. Davis, Moshe, ed. LC 77-70708. (America & the Holy Land Ser.). (Illus.). 1977. Repr. of 1858 ed. lib. bdg. 20.00x (ISBN 0-405-10258-5). Arno.
Kaminker, Sarah F. Footloose in Jerusalem: A Series of Guided Walking Tours. 1981. pap. 4.95 (ISBN 0-517-54294-3). Crown.
Le Strange, Guy, tr. Palestine Under the Moslems. LC 70-180356. Repr. of 1890 ed. 47.50 (ISBN 0-404-56288-4). AMS Pr.
Leymarie, Jean, intro. by. The Jerusalem Windows of Marc Chagall. LC 62-18146. (Illus.). 120p. 1975. 15.00 (ISBN 0-8076-0423-2); pap. 9.95 (ISBN 0-8076-0807-6). Braziller.
Loti, Pierre. Jerusalem. 25.00 (ISBN 0-686-17245-0). Scholars Ref Lib.
Merrill, Selah. Ancient Jerusalem. Davis, Moshe, ed. LC 77-70724. (America & the Holy Land Ser.). (Illus.). 1977. Repr. of 1908 ed. lib. bdg. 30.00x (ISBN 0-405-10267-4). Arno.
Odenheimer, William H. Jerusalem & Its Vicinity: Familiar Lectures on the Sacred Localities Connected with the Week Before the Resurrection. Davis, Moshe, ed. (America & the Holy Land Ser.). (Illus.). 1977. Repr. of 1855 ed. lib. bdg. 15.00x (ISBN 0-405-10272-0). Arno.
Owen, G. Frederick. Jerusalem. (Illus.). 1972. 5.95 (ISBN 0-8341-0215-3, Beacon). Nazarene.
Rosenthal, Gabriella. In & Around Jerusalem with Gabriella Rosenthal. (Illus.). 1978. 19.95 (ISBN 0-685-89708-7); pap. 11.95 (ISBN 0-930430-03-4). Harbor Hse Pub.
Sanger, Richard H. Where the Jordan Flows. LC 63-5019. (Illus.). 1963. 5.75 (ISBN 0-916808-04-1). Mid East Inst.
Schaffer, Shaul & Joseph, Asher. Israel's Temple Mount: The Jew's Magnificent Sanctuary. (Illus.). 1975. 10.00 (ISBN 0-685-84975-9). Feldheim.
Schiller, Ely, ed. The First Photographs of Jerusalem: The Old City. (Illus.). 252p. (Eng. & Heb.). 1978. 30.00x (ISBN 0-8002-2455-8). Intl Pubns Serv.
Thubron, Colin. Jerusalem. (The Great Cities Ser.). (Illus.). (gr. 6 up). 1976. 14.94 (ISBN 0-8094-2251-4, Pub by Time-Life). Silver.
Timberlake, Henry. A True & Strange Discourse of the Travailes of Two English Pilgrimes. LC 74-80228. (English Experience Ser.: No. 699). 28p. 1974. Repr. of 1603 ed. 3.50 (ISBN 90-221-0699-3). Walter J Johnson.
Uris, Leon & Uris, Jill. Jerusalem, Song of Songs. LC 80-2554. (Illus.). 320p. 1981. 39.95 (ISBN 0-385-14863-1). Doubleday.
Vester, Bertha H. Our Jerusalem: An American Family in the Holy City, 1881-1949. Davis, Moshe, ed. LC 77-70752. (America & the Holy Land Ser.). 1977. Repr. of 1950 ed. lib. bdg. 22.00x (ISBN 0-405-10296-8). Arno.
Wallace, Edwin S. Jerusalem the Holy: History of Ancient Jerusalem with an Account of the Modern City & Its Conditions Political, Religious & Social. Davis, Moshe, ed. LC 77-70753. (America & the Holy Land Ser.). (Illus.). 1977. Repr. of 1898 ed. lib. bdg. 22.00x (ISBN 0-405-10298-4). Arno.
Zangwill, Israel. The Voice of Jerusalem. 1976. lib. bdg. 59.95 (ISBN 0-8490-2801-9). Gordon Pr.

JERUSALEM–DESCRIPTION–GUIDEBOOKS
Carta. Jerusalem Guide & Map. rev. ed. (Illus.). 1978. pap. 5.95 (ISBN 0-930038-08-8). Arbit.
Har-El, Menashe. This Is Jerusalem. rev. ed. Zeevy, Rechavam, ed. (Illus.). 368p. 1980. pap. 6.95 (ISBN 0-86628-002-2). Ridgefield Pub.

JERUSALEM–HISTORY
Arbel, Naftali, ed. Jerusalem Past & Present. (Illus.). 1969. 25.00x (ISBN 0-8002-1616-4). Intl Pubns Serv.
Baedeker. Baedeker's Jerusalem. Orig. Title: Palestine & Syria. (Illus.). 1978. Repr. of 1876 ed. 11.75 (ISBN 0-930038-04-5). Arbit.
Bahat, Dan. Historical Atlas of Jerusalem. 1978. 6.95 (ISBN 0-930038-05-3). Arbit.
Baldwin, Marshall W. Raymond III of Tripolis & the the Fall of Jerusalem: 1140-1187. LC 76-29830. Repr. of 1936 ed. 22.50 (ISBN 0-404-15411-5). AMS Pr.
Bernadotte Af Wisborg, Folke G. To Jerusalem. LC 75-6424. (The Rise of Jewish Nationalism & the Middle East Ser.). 280p. 1975. Repr. of 1951 ed. 21.50 (ISBN 0-88355-311-2). Hyperion Conn.
Cattan, Henry. Jerusalem. 240p. 1981. 25.00 (ISBN 0-312-44182-7). St Martin.
Clifford, David. The Two Jerusalems in Prophecy. LC 78-14922. (Illus.). 1978. pap. 3.50 (ISBN 0-87213-081-9). Loizeaux.
Cohen, Gary G. & Runyon, Catherine. Weep Not for Me. 192p. 1980. pap. 2.95 (ISBN 0-8024-4309-5). Moody.
Cohen, Saul B. Jerusalem-A Geopolitical Perspective. 1977. 10.00 (ISBN 0-930832-54-X). Herzl Pr.
Cohen, Yona. Jerusalem Under Siege. Shefer, Dorothea, tr. from Hebrew. (Illus.). 326p. 1981. text ed. 12.00 (ISBN 0-86628-017-0). Ridgefield Pub.
Fink, Henry S., ed. A History of the Expedition to Jerusalem, 1095-1127. Ryan, Sr. Frances R., tr. 1972. pap. text ed. 6.95x (ISBN 0-393-09423-5). Norton.
Ganz, Yaffa. Our Jerusalem. (Illus.). (gr. k-2). 1979. pap. 2.50x (ISBN 0-87441-308-7). Behrman.
Gerlitz, Menaham. The Heavenly City. Weinbach, Sheindel, tr. from Hebrew. 1978. 6.95 (ISBN 0-87306-147-0). Feldheim.
Gilbert, Martin. Jerusalem History Atlas. (Illus.). 1977. 12.95 (ISBN 0-02-543410-1). Macmillan.
Gulston, Charles. Jerusalem: The Tragedy & the Triumph. 1977. 12.95 (ISBN 0-310-35510-9). Zondervan.
Har-El, Menashe. This Is Jerusalem. (Illus.). 350p. 1980. 10.95x (ISBN 0-686-64378-X). Behrman.
Jeremias, Joachim. Jerusalem in the Time of Jesus: An Investigation into Economic & Social Conditions During the New Testament Period. Cave, F. H. & Cave, C. H., trs. from Ger. LC 77-81530. 434p. 1975. pap. 5.95 (ISBN 0-8006-1136-5, 1-1136). Fortress.
Johnson, Alexandra W. Jerusalem Fifteen Hundred. (Illus.). 1981. 12.95 (ISBN 0-930720-66-0). Liberator Pr.
Join-Lambert, Michel. Jerusalem. 1971. 14.95 (ISBN 0-236-30896-3, Pub. by Paul Elek). Merrimack Bk Serv.
Joseph, Dov. Faithful City. 1960. 5.95 (ISBN 0-671-23980-5, 23980); limited deluxe 10.00 (ISBN 0-685-20026-4, 23981). S&S.
Kraemer, Joel L., ed. Jerusalem: Problems & Prospects. 256p. 1980. 24.95 (ISBN 0-03-057733-0); pap. 10.95 (ISBN 0-03-057734-9). Praeger.
Landay, Jerry M. Dome of the Rock. LC 76-178707. (Wonders of Man Ser). (Illus.). 176p. 1972. 16.95 (ISBN 0-88225-018-3). Newsweek.
Lane-Poole, Stanley. Saladin & the Fall of the Kingdom of Jerusalem. LC 73-14453. (Heroes of the Nation Ser.). Repr. of 1926 ed. 30.00 (ISBN 0-404-58270-2). AMS Pr.
Mackowski, Richard M. Jerusalem, City of Jesus. 224p. 1981. 29.95 (ISBN 0-8028-3526-0). Eerdmans.
Newsome, James D., Jr. By the Waters of Babylon: An Introduction to the History & Theology of the Exile. LC 78-5244L 1979. pap. 7.95 (ISBN 0-8042-0016-5). John Knox.
Phillips, John. A Will to Survive: Israel: the Faces of Terror, 1948, the Faces of Hope Today. (Illus.). 1979. pap. 8.95 (ISBN 0-8037-0182-9, J Wade). Dial.

Sanger, Richard H. Where the Jordan Flows. LC 63-5019. (Illus.). 1963. 5.75 (ISBN 0-916808-04-1). Mid East Inst.

Shaffer, E. S. Kubla Khan & the Fall of Jerusalem. LC 79-8492. 362p. 1980. pap. 14.95 (ISBN 0-521-29807-5). Cambridge U Pr.

Smith, George A. Jerusalem: The Topography, Economics & History from the Ancient Times to A. D. 70, 2 Vols. in 1. rev. ed. (Library of Biblical Studies Ser). 1970. 35.00x (ISBN 0-87068-105-2). Ktav.

Vincent, Hughes. Jerusalem, 2 vols. in 4. LC 78-63368. (The Crusades & Military Orders: Second Ser.). Repr. of 1926 ed. Set. 495.00 (ISBN 0-404-17060-9). AMS Pr.

Wight, Fred H. Usos y Costumbres De las Tierras Biblica. 336p. (Span.). 1981. pap. 7.95 (ISBN 0-8024-9043-3). Moody.

Wilkinson, John. Jerusalem Pilgrims Before the Crusades. 225p. 1977. text ed. 44.00x (ISBN 0-85668-078-8, Pub. by Aris & Phillips England). Humanities.

Wilson, Charles W. Jerusalem: The Holy City. (Illus.). 120p. 1979. Repr. of 1880 ed. 20.00x (ISBN 0-8002-2457-4). Intl Pubns Serv.

JERUSALEM–HISTORY–FICTION

Cohen, Gary G. & Runyon, Catherine. Weep Not for Me. 192p. 1980. pap. 2.95 (ISBN 0-8024-4309-5). Moody.

JERUSALEM–HISTORY–LATIN KINGDOM, 1099-1244

Ben-Ami, Aharon. Social Change in a Hostile Environment: The Crusaders' Kingdom of Jerusalem. (Princeton Studies on the Near East Ser.). (Illus.). 1969. 15.00 (ISBN 0-691-09344-X). Princeton U Pr.

Chalandon, Ferdinand. Histoire de la premiere croisade jusqu'a l'election de Godefroi de Bouillon. 380p. 1972. Repr. of 1925 ed. lib. bdg. 25.50 (ISBN 0-8337-0515-6). B Franklin.

Conder, Claude R. The Latin Kingdom of Jerusalem. LC 78-180331. Repr. of 1897 ed. 40.00 (ISBN 0-404-56238-8). AMS Pr.

Dodu, Gaston J. Histoire des institutions monarchiques dans le Royaume latin de Jerusalem, 1099-1291. LC 76-29820. (Fr.). Repr. of 1894 ed. 32.50 (ISBN 0-404-15415-8). AMS Pr.

Enlart, Camille. Les Monuments des Croises dans le Royaume de Jerusalem, 4 vols. LC 78-63336. (The Crusades & Military Orders: Second Ser.). Repr. of 1927 ed. Set. 495.00 (ISBN 0-404-17050-1). AMS Pr.

LaMonte, J. L. Feudal Monarchy in the Latin Kingdom of Jerusalem, 1100-1291. 1932. 18.00 (ISBN 0-527-01685-3). Kraus Repr.

Richard, J. The Latin Kingdom of Jerusalem. (Europe in the Middle Ages Selected Studies: Vol. 11). 1978. 49.00 (ISBN 0-444-85092-9, North-Holland). Elsevier.

Richard, Jean. Le Royaume Latin de Jerusalem. LC 78-63359. (The Crusades & Military Orders: Second Ser.). Repr. of 1953 ed. 28.50 (ISBN 0-404-17029-3). AMS Pr.

Riley-Smith, Jonathan. Feudal Nobility & the Kingdom of Jerusalem, 1174-1277. xiv, 340p. 1973. 19.50 (ISBN 0-208-01348-2, Archon). Shoe String.

Saladin & the Fall of the Kingdom of Jerusalem. 16.00 (ISBN 0-686-18313-4). Kazi Pubns.

JERUSALEM–TEMPLE

see also Tabernacle

Edersheim, Alfred. Temple, Its Ministry & Services. 1950. 3.95 (ISBN 0-8028-8133-5). Eerdmans.

Haran, Menahem. Temples & Temple Service in Ancient Israel: An Inquiry into the Character of Cult Phenomena & the Historical Setting of the Priestly School. (Illus.). 1979. 72.00x (ISBN 0-19-826318-X). Oxford U Pr.

JERWAN, IRAQ

Jacobsen, Thorkild & Lloyd, Seton. Sennacherib's Aqueduct at Jerwan. LC 66-20583. (Oriental Institute Pubns. Ser.: No. 24). (Illus.). 1935. 20.00x (ISBN 0-226-62120-0, OIP24). U of Chicago Pr.

JEST BOOKS

see Chap-Books

JESTERS

see Fools and Jesters

JESTS

see Wit and Humor

JESUITS

Arnauld, Antoine. The Arrainment of the Whole Societie of Jesuites in Fraunce: Holden-the Twelfth & Thirteenth of July, 1594. LC 79-84084. (English Experience Ser.: No. 904). 68p. 1979. Repr. of 1594 ed. lib. bdg. 8.00 (ISBN 0-686-71069-X). Walter J Johnson.

Arrupe, Pedro. Other Apostolates Today: Selected Letters & Addresses - III. Aixala, Jerome, ed. LC 81-80741. 380p. 1981. 9.00 (ISBN 0-912422-81-5); pap. 8.00 smyth sewn (ISBN 0-912422-80-7). Inst Jesuit.

Aveling, J. C. The Jesuits. LC 81-40482. 396p. 1981. 20.00 (ISBN 0-8128-2838-0). Stein & Day.

--The Jesuits. 288p. 1981. 75.00x (ISBN 0-85634-110-X, Pub. by Muller Ltd). State Mutual Bk.

Bangert, William V. A Bibliographical Essay on the History of the Society of Jesus. Ganss, George E., ed. LC 76-12667. (Study Aids on Jesuit Topics Ser.: No. 6). 72p. 1976. pap. 1.50 (ISBN 0-912422-16-5); Smyth Sewn. pap. 2.50 (ISBN 0-912422-21-1). Inst Jesuit.

--A History of the Society of Jesus. LC 78-188687. (Original Studies Composed in English Ser.: No. 3). (Illus.). 570p. 1972. pap. 7.00 (ISBN 0-686-76928-7); Smyth sewn 9.00 (ISBN 0-912422-23-8). Inst Jesuit.

Boehmer, H. The Jesuits. 69.95 (ISBN 0-87968-199-3). Gordon Pr.

Broderick, James. The Economic Morals of the Jesuits. LC 76-38248. (The Evolution of Capitalism Ser.). 168p. 1972. Repr. of 1934 ed. 10.00 (ISBN 0-405-04113-6). Arno.

Brodrick, James. Origin of the Jesuits. LC 70-138604. 1971. Repr. of 1940 ed. lib. bdg. 16.00x (ISBN 0-8371-5523-1, BROJ). Greenwood.

Calvez, J. Y., et al. Conferences on the Chief Decrees of the Jesuit General Congregation XXXII: A Symposium by Some of Its Members. LC 76-2977. (Study Aids on Jesuit Topics Ser.: No. 4). 173p. 1976. smyth sewn 4.50 (ISBN 0-912422-17-3); pap. 3.50 (ISBN 0-912422-13-0). Inst Jesuit.

Campbell, Thomas J. Jesuits: Fifteen Thirty-Four to Nineteen Twenty-One. LC 77-82144. (Reprints Ser). 1970. Repr. of 1921 ed. lib. bdg. 45.00 (ISBN 0-87821-018-0). Milford Hse.

--The Jesuits, 1534-1921, 2 vols. 1977. lib. bdg. 250.00 (ISBN 0-8490-2093-X). Gordon Pr.

Clancy, Thomas H. The Conversational Word of God: A Commentary on the Doctrine of St. Ignatius of Loyola Concerning Spiritual Conversation, with Four Early Jesuit Texts. Ganss, George E., frwd. by. LC 78-51343. (Study Aids on Jesuit Topics: No. 8 in Ser. - IV). 83p. 1978. 5.00 (ISBN 0-912422-33-5); pap. 2.50 smyth sewn (ISBN 0-912422-34-3). Inst Jesuit.

--An Introduction to Jesuit Life: The Constitutions & History Through 435 Years. Ganss, George E., ed. LC 75-46080. (Study Aids on Jesuit Topics Ser.: No. 3). 422p. 1976. 12.00 (ISBN 0-912422-15-7); pap. 5.50 (ISBN 0-912422-12-2). Inst Jesuit.

Cully, Thomas D. Jesuits & Music. 1970. pap. 14.00 (ISBN 0-8294-0335-3). Jesuit Hist.

D'Alembert, Jean. An Account of the Destruction of the Jesuits. 59.95 (ISBN 0-87968-575-1). Gordon Pr.

Dalton, Roy C. Jesuits' Estates Questions, 1760-1888: Study of the Background for the Agitation of 1889. LC 74-393033. (Canadian Studies in History & Government Ser.). 1969. 15.00x (ISBN 0-8020-3217-6). U of Toronto Pr.

De Guibert, Joseph. The Jesuits: Their Spiritual Doctrine & Practice. Young, W. J., tr. LC 64-21430. 717p. 1964. pap. 6.00 (ISBN 0-912422-09-2). Inst Jesuit.

De La Costa, S. J. The Jesuits in the Philippines, Fifteen Eighty-One to Seventeen Sixty-Eight. (Illus.). 715p. 1961. text ed. 25.00x (ISBN 0-674-47400-7). Harvard U Pr.

Egan, Harvey D. The Spiritual Exercises & the Ignatian Mystical Horizon. LC 76-5742. (Study Aids on Jesuit Topics, Series 4: No. 5). xii, 216p. 1976. smyth sewn 7.00 (ISBN 0-912422-18-1); pap. 6.00 (ISBN 0-912422-14-9). Inst Jesuit.

Faase, Thomas P. Making the Jesuits More Modern. LC 81-40388. (Illus.). 478p. (Orig.). 1981. lib. bdg. 24.75 (ISBN 0-8191-1761-7); pap. text ed. 15.75 (ISBN 0-8191-1762-5). U Pr of Amer.

Fulop-Miller, Rene. The Power & Secret of the Jesuits. 1930. 25.00 (ISBN 0-8414-4288-6). Folcroft.

Futrell, John C. Making an Apostolic Community of Love: The Role of the Superior According to St. Ignatius of Loyola. LC 73-139365. (Original Studies Composed in English Ser.). 239p. 1970. smyth sewn 5.00 (ISBN 0-912422-19-X); pap. 4.00 (ISBN 0-912422-08-4). Inst Jesuit.

Ganss, George E., ed. Jesuit Religious Life Today. LC 77-78816. (Jesuit Primary Sources in English Translation Ser.: No. 3). 190p. 1977. pap. 3.00 (ISBN 0-912422-27-0). Inst Jesuit.

Griesinger, Theodor. The Jesuits: A Complete History of Their Open & Secret Proceedings, 2 vols. 1977. Set. lib. bdg. 200.00 (ISBN 0-8490-2092-1). Gordon Pr.

Hughes, Thomas A. Loyola & the Educational Systems of the Jesuits. 1892. 10.00 (ISBN 0-403-00121-8). Scholarly.

Ignatius Of Loyola, St. The Constitutions of the Society of Jesus. Ganss, George E., tr. & commentary by. LC 72-108258. (Jesuit Primary Sources in English Translation Ser.: No. 1). 432p. 1970. 14.50 (ISBN 0-912422-03-3); smyth sewn o.s.i. 6.00 (ISBN 0-912422-20-3); pap. 5.00 (ISBN 0-912422-06-8). Inst Jesuit.

Iparraguirre, Ignacio. Contemporary Trends in Studies on the Constitutions of the Society of Jesus: Annotated Bibliographical Orientations. Ganss, George E., ed. Meenan, Daniel F., tr. from Span. LC 74-77120. (Study Aids on Jesuit Topics Ser: No. 1). 96p. 1974. pap. 1.60 (ISBN 0-912422-10-6). Inst Jesuit.

Laverdiere & Casgrain, eds. Le Journal des Jesuites. (French-Canadian Civilization Ser.). (Fr.). Repr. of 1871 ed. lib. bdg. 28.50x (ISBN 0-697-00050-8). Irvington.

McCabe, Joseph. A Candid History of the Jesuits. 1977. lib. bdg. 59.95 (ISBN 0-8490-1567-7). Gordon Pr.

MacLagan, E. The Jesuits & the Great Mogul. LC 71-159212. 1971. Repr. of 1932 ed. lib. bdg. 20.00x (ISBN 0-374-95248-5). Octagon.

Mitchell, David. The Jesuits. (Illus.). 320p. 1981. 17.50 (ISBN 0-531-09947-4). Watts.

Pascal, Blaise. Provinciales. 1966. 1.95 (ISBN 0-685-11517-8). French & Eur.

--Provinciales. (Documentation thematique). (Illus., Fr.). pap. 2.95 (ISBN 0-685-14062-8, 235). Larousse.

--Les Provinciales. 4.95 (ISBN 0-686-54852-3). French & Eur.

Pascal, Blaise & Adam, Antoine. Lettres Escrites a un Provincial. 320p. 1967. 4.50 (ISBN 0-686-54847-7). French & Eur.

Peters, F. E. Ours: The Making & Unmaking of a Jesuit. 192p. 1981. 11.95 (ISBN 0-399-90113-2). Marek.

Prophecies & Revelations About the Jesuits. 1.95 (ISBN 0-913452-27-0). Jesuit Bks.

Rahner, Karl. The Religious Life Today. 1976. 5.95 (ISBN 0-8245-0371-6). Crossroad NY.

Ronan & Hanisch. Epistolario De Juan Ignacio Molina. (Sp.). 1980. 11.60 (ISBN 0-8294-0360-4). Loyola.

Smith, Gerard, ed. Jesuit Thinkers of the Renaissance. 1939. 8.95 (ISBN 0-87462-431-2). Marquette.

Thompson, R. W. The Footprints of the Jesuits. 1981. lib. bdg. 75.00 (ISBN 0-686-71628-0). Revisionist Pr.

Winterborn, Benjamin. Changing Scenes. 1980. 17.95 (ISBN 0-19-213226-1). Oxford U Pr.

JESUITS–EDUCATION

Ganss, George E. The Jesuit Educational Tradition & Saint Louis University: Some Bearings for the University's Sesquicentennial, 1818-1968. LC 75-87922. (Illus.). 70p. 1969. 3.25 (ISBN 0-912422-02-5). Inst Jesuit.

Owen, Lewis. The Running Register: Recording the State of the English Colledges in All Forraine Parts. LC 68-54654. (English Experience Ser.: No. 19). 118p. 1968. Repr. of 1626 ed. 13.00 (ISBN 90-221-0019-7). Walter J Johnson.

Schwickerat, Robert. Jesuit Education. 59.95 (ISBN 0-8490-0442-X). Gordon Pr.

JESUITS–MISSIONS

see also Catholic Church–Missions

Correia-Afonso, John, ed. Letters from the Mughal Court: The First Jesuit Mission to Akbar (1580-1583) LC 81-81766. (Illus.). 150p. 1981. 9.00 (ISBN 0-912422-57-2). Inst Jesuit.

Du Creux, Francois. History of Canada, or New France, 2 Vols. Conacher, James B., ed. Robinson, Percy J., tr. LC 69-14507. 1969. Repr. of 1951 ed. Vol. 1. lib. bdg. 26.75x (ISBN 0-8371-5070-1, DUHI); Vol. 2. lib. bdg. 25.75x (ISBN 0-8371-5071-X, DUHJ). Greenwood.

Dunne, George H. Generation of Giants. 1962. 9.95x (ISBN 0-268-00109-X). U of Notre Dame Pr.

Dunne, Peter M. Black Robes in Lower California. (California Library Reprint Series: No. 3). (Illus.). 1968. Repr. 26.75x (ISBN 0-520-00362-4). U of Cal Pr.

Graham, Robert B. Vanished Arcadia: Being Some Account of the Jesuits in Paraguay. LC 68-25238. (Studies in Spanish Literature, No. 36). 1969. Repr. of 1901 ed. lib. bdg. 50.95 (ISBN 0-8383-0949-6). Haskell.

The Jesuit Mission of St. Mary's County. 2nd ed. 1976. 15.00 (ISBN 0-686-24147-9). E W Beitzel.

Kenny, Michael. Romance of the Floridas. LC 70-120573. (Illus.). Repr. of 1934 ed. 15.00 (ISBN 0-404-03656-2). AMS Pr.

Le Clercq, Chretien. First Establishment of the Faith in New France, 2 Vols. LC 77-172312. Repr. of 1881 ed. Set. 55.00 (ISBN 0-404-03914-6); 28.00 ea. Vol. 1 (ISBN 0-404-03915-4). Vol. 2 (ISBN 0-404-03916-2). AMS Pr.

McCoy, James C. Jesuit Relations of Canada, 1632-1673: A Bibliography. LC 76-153038. (Illus.). xv, 346p. 1972. Repr. of 1937 ed. lib. bdg. 23.50 (ISBN 0-8337-2314-6). B Franklin.

Menager, Francis M. The Kingdom of the Seal. (Illus.). 1962. 1.80 (ISBN 0-8294-0056-7). Loyola.

Mengarini, Gregory. Recollections of the Flathead Mission. Lothrop, Gloria, ed. LC 74-27573. (Illus.). 1977. 16.95 (ISBN 0-87062-111-4). A H Clark.

Roca, Paul M. Spanish Jesuit Churches in Mexico's Tarahumara. LC 78-14467. 1979. 18.50x (ISBN 0-8165-0651-5); pap. 11.50x (ISBN 0-8165-0572-1). U of Ariz Pr.

Schutte, Josef F. Valignano's Mission Principles for Japan: Vol. I (1573-1582), Pt. I - The Problem (1573-1580) Coyne, John J., tr. from Ger. LC 78-69683. (Modern Scholarly Studies About the Jesuits, in English Translations, Ser. II: No. 3). (Illus.). xxiv, 428p. 1980. 14.00 (ISBN 0-912422-36-X); pap. 12.00 smyth sewn (ISBN 0-912422-35-1). Inst Jesuit.

Shiels, William E. Gonzalo De Tapia, 1561-1594: Founder of the First Permanent Jesuit Mission in North America. LC 74-12835. (U.S. Catholic Historical Society Monograph: No. XIV). 1978. Repr. of 1934 ed. lib. bdg. 18.50x (ISBN 0-8371-7758-8, SHGT). Greenwood.

Taraval, Sigismundo. Indian Uprising in Lower California, 1734-1737. LC 79-137296. Repr. of 1931 ed. 24.00 (ISBN 0-404-06337-3). AMS Pr.

JESUITS IN CANADA

Donnelly, Joseph P. Thwaites' Jesuit Relations, Errata & Addenda. LC 66-27701. (The American West Ser). 1967. 6.95 (ISBN 0-8294-0025-7). Loyola.

McCoy, James C. Jesuit Relations of Canada, 1632-1673: A Bibliography. LC 76-153038. (Illus.). xv, 346p. 1972. Repr. of 1937 ed. lib. bdg. 23.50 (ISBN 0-8337-2314-6). B Franklin.

JESUITS IN CHINA

Borri, Christoforo. Cochin-China: Containing Many Admirable Rarities of That Countrey. LC 71-25710. (English Experience Ser.: No. 223). 1970. Repr. of 1633 ed. 9.50 (ISBN 90-221-0223-8). Walter J Johnson.

D'Orleans, Pierre J. History of the Two Tartar Conquerors of China. LC 75-162706. 1963. Repr. of 1668 ed. 26.00 (ISBN 0-8337-3630-2). B Franklin.

JESUITS IN ENGLAND

Foley, Henry. Records of the English Province of the Society of Jesus, 7 Vols. in 8. (Illus.). Repr. of 1883 ed. 577.50 (ISBN 0-384-16310-6). Johnson Repr.

Law, Thomas G., ed. The Archpriest Controversy, 2 Vols. Repr. of 1898 ed. 44.50 (ISBN 0-384-31730-8). Johnson Repr.

JESUITS IN LATIN-AMERICA

Morner, Magnus. The Political & Economic Activities of the Jesuits in the Plata Region. 1976. lib. bdg. 59.95 (ISBN 0-8490-2451-X). Gordon Pr.

JESUITS IN MEXICO

Dunner, Peter M. Pioneer Jesuits in Northern Mexico. LC 78-10566. (Illus.). 1979. Repr. of 1944 ed. lib. bdg. 20.25x (ISBN 0-313-20653-8, DUPJ). Greenwood.

Ronan, Charles E. Francisco Javier Clavigero, S. J., Figure of the Mexican Enlighment: His Life & Work. 1977. pap. 20.00x (ISBN 0-8294-0347-7). Jesuit Hist.

JESUITS IN NORTH AMERICA

Bolton, Herbert E. Wider Horizons of American History. 1967. pap. 2.25x (ISBN 0-268-00301-7). U of Notre Dame Pr.

Burns, Robert I. Jesuits & the Indian Wars of the Northwest. LC 65-22314. (Western Americana Ser.: No. 11). (Illus.). 1966. 47.00x (ISBN 0-300-00336-6). Yale U Pr.

McCoy, James C. Jesuit Relations of Canada, 1632-1673: A Bibliography. LC 76-153038. (Illus.). xv, 346p. 1972. Repr. of 1937 ed. lib. bdg. 23.50 (ISBN 0-8337-2314-6). B Franklin.

Parkman, Francis. The Jesuits in North America. 586p. 1970. Repr. of 1895 ed. 12.50 (ISBN 0-87928-016-6). Corner Hse.

Polzer, Charles. Rules & Precepts of the Jesuit Missions of Northwestern New Spain. LC 75-8456. 1976. 8.50x (ISBN 0-8165-0551-9); pap. 4.50x (ISBN 0-8165-0488-1). U of Ariz Pr.

JESUITS IN POLAND

Pollard, Alfred F. Jesuits in Poland. LC 76-116799. (Studies in Philosophy, No. 40). 1970. Repr. of 1902 ed. lib. bdg. 27.95 (ISBN 0-8383-1041-9). Haskell.

JESUITS IN THE UNITED STATES

Broderick, James. The Economic Morals of the Jesuits. LC 76-38248. (The Evolution of Capitalism Ser.). 168p. 1972. Repr. of 1934 ed. 10.00 (ISBN 0-405-04113-6). Arno.

Curran, Francis X. The Return of the Jesuits. LC 66-29559. 1966. 3.00 (ISBN 0-8294-0018-4). Loyola.

Delanglez, Jean. The French Jesuits in Lower Louisiana (1700-1763) LC 73-3576. (Catholic University of America. Studies in American Church History: No. 21). Repr. of 1935 ed. 34.50 (ISBN 0-404-57771-7). AMS Pr.

Gache, Louis-Hippolyte. A Frenchman, a Chaplain, a Rebel: The War Letters of Pere Louis-Hippolyte Gache, S. J. Buckley, Cornelius M., tr. 282p. 1981. 8.95 (ISBN 0-8294-0376-0). Loyola.

Gruenberg, Gladys W. Labor Peacemaker: The Life & Works of Father Leo. C. Brown, S. J. Ganss, George E., ed. LC 80-83552. (Original Studies Composed in English Ser.: No. 4). (Illus.). 176p. 1981. 8.50 (ISBN 0-912422-54-8); pap. 7.00 smythsewn paperbound (ISBN 0-912422-53-X); pap. 6.00 (ISBN 0-912422-52-1). Inst Jesuit.

The Jesuit Mission of St. Mary's County. 2nd ed. 1976. 15.00 (ISBN 0-686-24147-9). E W Beitzel.

Lapomarda, Vincent A. The Jesuit Heritage in New England. LC 76-42896. (Illus., Orig.). 1977. 5.00 (ISBN 0-9606294-0-8). Jesuits Holy Cross.

Walsh, J. J. American Jesuits. 59.95 (ISBN 0-87968-605-7). Gordon Pr.

Walsh, James J. American Jesuits. facs. ed. LC 68-29251. (Essay Index Reprint Ser). 1934. 16.25 (ISBN 0-8369-0970-4). Arno.

JESUS, SOCIETY OF

see Jesuits

JESUS CHRIST

see also Antichrist; Atonement; Christianity; Crosses; Incarnation; Logos; Lord's Supper; Mercersburg Theology; Messiah; Millennium; Redemption; Salvation; Second Advent; Trinity

Adams, Jay E. Christ & Your Problems. 1976. pap. 0.75 (ISBN 0-8010-0035-1). Baker Bk.

Agnew, Joseph. Life's Christ Places. 206p. 1911. text ed. 3.95 (ISBN 0-567-02008-8). Attic Pr.

Allen, R. C. Immortal Words of Jesus Christ. 1981. pap. 4.95 (ISBN 0-910228-11-6). Best Bks.

Another Book About Jesus. (ps-3). 3.50 (ISBN 0-685-27824-7, 35-235). Borden.

Augustinus, Aurelius. De Perfectione Ivstitiae Hominis, De Gestis Pelagii, De Gratia Christi et De Peccato Originali Libri Duo. (Corpus Scriptorum Ecclesiasticorum Latinorum Ser: Vol. 42). Repr. of 1902 ed. pap. 41.50 (ISBN 0-384-02495-5). Johnson Repr.

Baird, William. The Quest of the Christ of Faith. LC 77-75461. 1977. 8.95 (ISBN 0-8499-0008-5). Word Bks.

Ball, Barbara. Coffee Talk: Sharing Christ Through Friendly Gatherings. 80p. 1980. pap. 3.50 (ISBN 0-934396-08-6). Churches Alive.

Barrois, Georges. The Face of Christ in the Old Testament. 172p. 1974. pap. 5.95 (ISBN 0-913836-22-2). St Vladimirs.

Barth, Markus. Jesus the Jew. Prussner, Frederick, tr. from Ger. LC 77-15741. 1978. Repr. of 1975 ed. 6.95 (ISBN -08042-0834-4). John Knox.

Beechick, Allen. The Pre-Tribulation Rapture. LC 79-53291. 256p. (Orig.). 1980. pap. 4.95 (ISBN 0-89636-040-7). Accent Bks.

Behnke, John. Stories of Jesus. LC 76-24440. 144p. 1977. 9.95 (ISBN 0-8091-0229-3); pap. 5.95 (ISBN 0-8091-2063-1). Paulist Pr.

Bjerregard, Carl H. Jesus: A Poet, Prophet, Mystic & Man of Freedom. 1976. lib. bdg. 59.95 (ISBN 0-8490-2094-8). Gordon Pr.

Blackwood, Andrew W. Prophets: Elijah to Christ. (Minister's Paperback Library Ser). 1978. pap. 3.95 (ISBN 0-8010-0741-0). Baker Bk.

The Body of Christ. 1978. pap. 0.95 (ISBN 0-686-11132-X, V545). US Catholic.

Boff, Leonardo. Jesus Christ Liberator: A Critical Christology for Our Time. Hughes, Patrick, tr. from Portuguese. LC 78-969. 1978. pap. 9.95 (ISBN 0-88344-236-1). Orbis Bks.

Bonhoeffer, Dietrich. Christ the Center: A New Translation. new ed. LC 78-4747. (Harper's Ministers Paperback Library Ser.). 1978. pap. 3.95 (ISBN 0-06-060815-3, RD 285, HarpR). Har-Row.

Borland, James A. Christ in the Old Testament. 1978. pap. 4.95 (ISBN 0-8024-1391-9). Moody.

Bothwell, Mary D. Christ Jesus. (Christ Our Life Ser.). (Illus.). (gr. 7). 1976. pap. text ed. 3.80 (ISBN 0-8294-0239-X); tchr's ed. 5.95 (ISBN 0-8294-0240-3). Loyola.

Bradlaugh, Charles. Jesus, Shelley, & Malthus. 1978. Repr. of 1877 ed. lib. bdg. 10.00 (ISBN 0-8495-0441-4). Arden Lib.

--Jesus, Shelley & Malthus, or Pious Poverty & Heterodox Happiness. LC 74-180509. 1972. lib. bdg. 5.50 (ISBN 0-8414-3271-6). Folcroft.

Buell, Jon A. & Hyder, O. Quentin. Jesus: God, Ghost or Guru? (Christian Free University Curriculum Ser.). 1978. pap. 4.95 (ISBN 0-310-35761-6). Zondervan.

Bunyan, John. Come & Welcome to Jesus Christ. 1974. pap. 2.50 (ISBN 0-685-52815-4). Reiner.

--Saints Knowledge of Christ's Love. pap. 1.50 (ISBN 0-685-19843-X). Reiner.

Cabasilas, Nicholas. The Life in Christ. Decatanzaro, Carmino J., tr. 229p. 1974. pap. 6.95 (ISBN 0-913836-12-5). St Vladimirs.

Cadoux, C. John. The Historic Mission of Jesus: A Constructive Re-Examination of the Eschatological Teaching in the Synoptic Gospels with an Extensive Bibliography. 1977. lib. bdg. 59.95 (ISBN 0-8490-1955-9). Gordon Pr.

Christ the Vision. 1.95 (ISBN 0-87243-003-0). Templegate.

Christenson, Larry. Christ & His Church. (Trinity Bible Ser.). 1973. pap. 4.95 spiral wkbk. (ISBN 0-87123-550-1, 240550). Bethany Hse.

Clark, Glenn. Three Mysteries of Jesus. 1978. 0.95 (ISBN 0-910924-85-6). Macalester.

Coniaris, Anthony M. The Great I Came's of Jesus. pap. 5.95 (ISBN 0-686-27069-X). Light&Life Pub Co MN.

Cormier, Henri. The Humor of Jesus. Heiman, David, tr. from Fr. LC 77-9887. Orig. Title: L Humour De Jesus. 1977. pap. 4.95 (ISBN 0-8189-0356-2). Alba.

Cottrell, Jack. His Way. LC 78-62710. 96p. (Orig.). 1979. pap. 1.95 (ISBN 0-87239-238-4, 40079). Standard Pub.

Cramer, Raymond L. Psychology of Jesus & Mental Health. pap. 4.95 (ISBN 0-310-22721-6, Pub. by Cowman). Zondervan.

Crawley-Boevey, Mateo. Jesus King of Love. 1978. 5.50 (ISBN 0-8198-0521-1); pap. 3.95 (ISBN 0-8198-0522-X). Dghtrs St Paul.

Crock, Clement H. No Cross No Crown. 1974. Repr. 3.00 (ISBN 0-8198-0510-6). Dghtrs St Paul.

Cullmann, Oscar. The Christology of the New Testament. rev. ed. Guthrie, Shirley C. & Hall, Charles A. M., trs. LC 59-10178. 1980. pap. 11.95 (ISBN 0-664-24351-7). Westminster.

Dahl, Nils A. Jesus in the Memory of the Early Church. LC 76-27072. 1976. pap. 5.95 (ISBN 0-8066-1561-3, 10-3519). Augsburg.

Davies, Chris, et al, eds. Jesus: One of Us. 148p. 1981. pap. 3.95 (ISBN 0-87784-618-9). Inter Varsity.

Dawson, W. J. The Man Jesus Christ. 1977. lib. bdg. 59.95 (ISBN 0-8490-2199-5). Gordon Pr.

De La Fuente, Tomas. La Hermosa Historia De Jesus: Ordenada, Simplificada y Brevemente Explicada. Date not set. pap. price not set (ISBN 0-311-04658-4). Casa Bautista.

Delanghe, Jules A. The Philosophy of Jesus: Real Love. LC 72-96805. 1973. 4.95 (ISBN 0-8059-1821-3). Dorrance.

Demarest, Bruce A. Jesus Christ: The God-Man. 1978. pap. 3.95 (ISBN 0-88207-760-0). Victor Bks.

De Margerie, Bertrand. Human Knowledge of Christ. 1980. 2.95 (ISBN 0-8198-3301-0); pap. 1.50 (ISBN 0-8198-3302-9). Dghtrs St Paul.

Denny, James. Jesus & the Gospel. 1977. lib. bdg. 59.95 (ISBN 0-849C-2095-6). Gordon Pr.

De Pressense, E. Jesus Christ: His Times, Life & Work. 1978. Repr. of 1898 ed. lib. bdg. 50.00 (ISBN 0-8495-1032-5). Arden Lib.

Drane, John. Jesus & the Gospels. LC 77-20448. 1979. pap. 8.95 (ISBN 0-06-062066-8, RD264, HarpR). Har-Row.

Duling, Dennis C. Jesus Christ Through History. 324p. 1979. pap. text ed. 11.95 (ISBN 0-15-547370-0, HC). HarBraceJ.

Dunn, James D. Christology in the Making: A New Testament Inquiry into the Origins of the Doctrine of the Incarnation. LC 80-16968. 1980. pap. 24.50 (ISBN 0-664-24356-8). Westminster.

--Jesus & the Spirit: A Study of the Religious & Charismatic Experience of Jesus & the First Christians as Reflected in the New Testament. LC 75-9802. 1979. soft cover 14.95 (ISBN 0-664-24290-1). Westminster.

Edwards, O. C., Jr. Luke's Story of Jesus. LC 81-43076. 96p. 1981. pap. 3.95 (ISBN 0-8006-1611-1). Fortress.

Endo, Shusaku. A Life of Jesus. Schuchert, Richard, tr. from Japanese. LC 78-61721. 192p. 1980. pap. 2.95 (ISBN 0-8091-2319-3). Paulist Pr.

Evans, David. The Good Book. 96p. 1972. pap. 1.25 (ISBN 0-8431-0129-6). Price Stern.

Fairweather, William. Jesus & the Greeks. 1977. lib. bdg. 59.95 (ISBN 0-8490-2096-4). Gordon Pr.

Finnegan, Robert E. Christ & Satan: A Critical Edition. 169p. 1977. pap. text ed. 11.00 (ISBN 0-88920-041-6, Pub. by Laurier U Pr Canada); pap. text ed. 7.00 (ISBN 0-88920-040-8). Humanities.

Ford, Leighton. New Man... New World. LC 72-88642. 1976. pap. 1.50 (ISBN 0-87680-873-9, 91013, Key Word Bks). Word Bks.

Funk, Robert W. Jesus As Precursor. Beardslee, William A., ed. LC 75-18949. (Semeia Studies). 184p. 1975. pap. 3.95 (ISBN 0-8006-1502-6, 1-1502). Fortress.

Gandhi, Mohandas K. The Message of Jesus Christ. Hingorani, A. T., ed. 121p. (Orig.). 1980. pap. 2.00 (ISBN 0-934676-20-8). Greenlf Bks.

Garrison, R. Benjamin. Are You the Christ? And Other Questions Asked About Jesus. LC 77-11904. 1978. 3.50 (ISBN 0-687-01720-3). Abingdon.

Gatterdam, Vincent J. Have Jesus Visit You. 100p. 1975. 6.95 (ISBN 0-686-11212-1). Evang Authors.

Gautrey, Robert M. The Burning Cataracts of Christ. 1980. Repr. of 1933 ed. lib. bdg. 12.50 (ISBN 0-8482-4193-2). Norwood Edns.

Geisler, Norman L. To Understand the Bible--Look for Jesus. 1979. pap. 2.95 (ISBN 0-8010-3734-4). Baker Bk.

Goodboy, Eadie, ed. Jesus Es el Senor. Fast, Todd H., tr. Orig. Title: Jesus Is Lord. 113p. (Span.). 1979. pap. 3.50 (ISBN 0-930756-50-9, 4230-G01(S)). Women's Aglow.

Greeley, Andrew M. The Jesus Myth. LC 75-160882. 200p. 1973. pap. 2.45 (ISBN 0-385-07865-X, Im). Doubleday.

Grove, Charles. The Incarnations of the Son of God. 1896. 10.00 (ISBN 0-8414-4693-8). Folcroft.

Guillet, J. Religious Experience of Jesus & His Disciples. LC 75-210. (Religious Experience Ser: Vol. 9). 1975. pap. 2.95 (ISBN 0-87029-044-4, 20132). Abbey.

Gunn, George S. Indispensable Christ: Sermons. 266p. 1962. 5.95 (ISBN 0-227-67661-0). Attic Pr.

Habig, Marion. Christ the Prisoner. 1976. pap. 0.25 (ISBN 0-685-77502-X). Franciscan Herald.

Hackwood, F. W. Christ Lore. 59.95 (ISBN 0-87968-861-0). Gordon Pr.

Hagin, Kenneth, Jr. Because of Jesus. 1979. 1.00 (ISBN 0-89276-701-4). Hagin Ministries.

Hall, Charles C. Christ & the Eastern Soul: Oriental Consciousness & Jesus. 1977. lib. bdg. 59.95 (ISBN 0-8490-1613-4). Gordon Pr.

Hartley, Allan. Jesus. (Spire Comics Ser.). (Illus.). 1979. pap. 0.69 (ISBN 0-8007-8538-X). Revell.

Havner, Vance. Jesus Only. rev. ed. 6.95 (ISBN 0-8007-0165-8). Revell.

Haweis, H. R. The Picture of Jesus. 1886. 10.00 (ISBN 0-8414-5022-6). Folcroft.

Heijkoop, H. L. Beginning with Christ. 4.25 (ISBN 0-686-13044-8); pap. 2.95 (ISBN 0-686-13045-6). Believers Bkshelf.

Heline, Corinne. Mystery of the Christos. pap. 6.50 (ISBN 0-87613-016-3). New Age.

Henry, Philip. Christ All in All. 7.95 (ISBN 0-685-88369-8). Reiner.

Hicks, Robert & Bewes, Richard. Jesus Christ. (Understanding Bible Truth Ser.). (Orig.). 1981. pap. 1.50 (ISBN 0-89840-026-0). Heres Life.

Hirst, Edward W. Jesus & the Moralists. 1977. lib. bdg. 59.95 (ISBN 0-8490-2097-2). Gordon Pr.

Hocking, W. J. The Son of His Love. 4.25 (ISBN 0-686-13219-X). Believers Bkshelf.

Holmes, George. He Is Lord. LC 76-20891. (Radiant Life Ser.). 1977. pap. 1.95 (ISBN 0-88243-902-2, 02-0902); teacher's ed 2.50 (ISBN 0-88243-172-2, 32-0172). Gospel Pub.

Horton, Stanley M. Welcome Back Jesus. 1975. pap. 1.25 (ISBN 0-88243-629-5, 02-0629). Gospel Pub.

Hubbard, David A. They Met Jesus. (Trumpet Bks). 1976. pap. 1.25 (ISBN 0-87981-057-2). Holman.

Hubbard, Elbert. Jesus Was an Anarchist. 1974. lib. bdg. 59.95 (ISBN 0-685-50613-4). Revisionist Pr.

Huyssen, Chester & Huyssen, Lucille, eds. Visions of Jesus. 1977. pap. 2.95 (ISBN 0-88270-223-8). Logos.

Imitation of Christ. 1967. 2.95 (ISBN 0-442-82263-4). Peter Pauper.

Inter-Varsity Staff. Christ in You. pap. 0.50 (ISBN 0-87784-175-6). Inter Varsity.

Jefferson, Thomas, ed. Human Jesus. LC 68-27400. (The Life & Morals of Jesus). 1968. 4.95x (ISBN 0-87130-010-9). Eakins.

Jesus. 1974. 6.95 (ISBN 0-671-21715-1). S&S.

Jesus. 1979. 0.75 (ISBN 0-8198-0582-3). Dghtrs St Paul.

Jesus Christ & the Faith: A Collection of Studies by Philippe H. Menoud. LC 78-15551. (Pittsburgh Theological Monographs: No. 18). Orig. Title: Jesus-Christ et la Foi. 1978. pap. 15.95 (ISBN 0-915138-22-0). Pickwick.

Jesus with Us. (gr. 2). 1.92 (ISBN 0-686-67306-9); tchr's manual 2.52 (ISBN 0-02-649360-8). Benziger Pub Co.

Jeter, Hugh. Par Ses Meutrissures. Date not set. 2.50 (ISBN 0-686-76410-2). Life Pubs Intl.

Jeter, Hugo. Por Su Llaga. (Span.). Date not set. 2.50 (ISBN 0-686-76335-1). Life Pubs Intl.

Joyce, Jon L. Aher's Talks About Jesus. 1979. pap. 3.65 (ISBN 0-89536-365-8). CSS Pub.

Jukes, Andrew. Four Views of Christ. 1982. pap. 3.95 (ISBN 0-8254-2953-6). Kregel.

Karris, Robert. Following Jesus: A Guide to the Gospels. (Biblical Ser.). 1973. pap. 1.25 (ISBN 0-8199-0514-3). Franciscan Herald.

Katter, Reuben L. Jesus Christ: The Divine Executive. 1981. write for info. (ISBN 0-911806-04-0). Theotes.

Kee, Howard C. Jesus in History: An Approach to the Study of the Gospels. 2nd ed. LC 77-75349. 1977. pap. text ed. 11.95 (ISBN 0-15-547382-4, HC). HarBraceJ.

Kemois, Thomas A. Imitation of Christ. 1978. plastic bdg. 3.50 (ISBN 0-8198-0533-5); deluxe ed. 5.25 (ISBN 0-8198-0534-3). Dghtrs St Paul.

Kempis, Thomas. Imitation of Christ. Hartmann, Louis F., tr. 1977. 7.95 (ISBN 0-89310-025-0). Carillon Bks.

Knutson, Kent S. His Only Son Our Lord. LC 66-13051. (Orig.). 1966. pap. 1.75 (ISBN 0-8066-9351-7, 10-3040). Augsburg.

Kraeling, Carl H. Anthropos & Son of Man. LC 27-23162. (Columbia University. Oriental Studies: No. 25). Repr. of 1927 ed. 18.50 (ISBN 0-404-50515-5). AMS Pr.

Labadie, Laurance. Jesus As an Anarchist. (Men & Movements in the History & Philosophy of Anarchism Ser.). 1979. lib. bdg. 59.95 (ISBN 0-685-96404-3). Revisionist Pr.

Lacy, Donald C. Mary & Jesus. 1979. pap. 1.95 (ISBN 0-89536-422-0). CSS Pub.

Lagerlof, Selma. Christ Legends. (Illus.). 1977. 10.95 (ISBN 0-903540-06-1, Pub. by Floris Books). St George Bk Serv.

Larsen, Earnest. Jesus Christ: The Gate of Power. LC 76-21589. (Illus.). 1977. pap. 1.75 (ISBN 0-8189-1136-0, Pub. by Alba Bks). Alba.

Latymer de Nedham, Hugh. Juggling with Jesus & His Two-Thousand Year Legacy to Mankind. LC 76-44900. 1977. 10.00 (ISBN 0-682-48651-5, University). Exposition.

Leslie, Robert C. Jesus & Logotherapy. LC 65-11077. (Series AD). 1968. pap. 2.25 (ISBN 0-687-19927-1, Apex). Abingdon.

Lewis, H. Spencer. The Mystical Life of Jesus. 1976. 7.25 (ISBN 0-686-00390-X). AMORC.

Lindars, B. & Smalley, S. S. Christ & Spirit in the New Testament. LC 72-91367. 300p. 1974. 63.00 (ISBN 0-521-20148-9). Cambridge U Pr.

Lindsay, Gordon. Days of Christ & the Apostles. 1.00 (ISBN 0-89985-113-4). Christ Nations.

Lord. Jesus: God's Son, Saviour. pap. 5.50 (ISBN 0-8054-4226-X). Broadman.

Lovasik, Lawrence G. The Lord Jesus. (Illus.). hard bd 3.95 (ISBN 0-686-14285-3, 419/22). Catholic Bk Pub.

McDowell, Josh. More Than a Carpenter. 1977. pap. 1.95 (ISBN 0-8423-4550-7). Tyndale.

Macduff, J. R. The Mind of Jesus. pap. 1.95 (ISBN 0-685-88386-8). Reiner.

McKenna, Megan & Ducote, Darryl. New Testament Understanding of Jesus. LC 78-71529. (Followers of the Way Ser.: Vol. 2). (gr. 9-12). 1979. 22.50 (ISBN 0-8091-9543-7); cassette 7.50 (ISBN 0-8091-7667-X). Paulist Pr.

Mackey, James P. Jesus, the Man & the Myth. LC 78-61627. 311p. 1979. pap. 8.95 (ISBN 0-8091-2169-7). Paulist Pr.

McKinley, Norma A. The Rediscovery of Christ. (Illus.). 1980. deluxe ed. 49.75 (ISBN 0-89266-224-7). Am Classical Coll Pr.

Marxsen, Willi. The Beginnings of Christology, together with The Lord's Supper. Achtemeier, Paul J. & Nieting, Lorenz, trs. from Ger. LC 79-7384. 128p. 1979. pap. 4.95 (ISBN 0-8006-1372-4, 1-1372). Fortress.

Massabki, Charles. Christ: Liberation of the World Today. Mescall, Sr. Eloise T., tr. from Fr. LC 78-12998. 1979. pap. 6.95 (ISBN 0-8189-0374-0). Alba.

Maus, Cynthia P. Christ & the Fine Arts. new ed. LC 76-55286. 1977. pap. 12.95 (ISBN 0-06-065472-4, RD 195, HarpR). Har-Row.

Metcalfe, J. C. Jesus Christ Our Lord. 1970. pap. 1.25 (ISBN 0-87508-919-4). Chr Lit.

Miller, Calvin. Burning Bushes & Moon Walks. LC 77-188065. 1972. pap. 1.95 (ISBN 0-87680-275-7, 90275). Word Bks.

Miller, G. Leslie. Tudo Sobre Anjos. Date not set. 1.20 (ISBN 0-686-76443-9). Life Pubs Intl.

Most, William G. The Consciousness of Christ. 232p. (Orig.). 1980. pap. text ed. 5.95 (ISBN 0-931888-03-4, Chr Coll Pr). Christendom Pubns.

Mowery, Alice L. The Light. 1978. 4.95 (ISBN 0-533-03021-8). Vantage.

Muirhead, L. A. The Times of Christ. (Handbooks for Bible Classes). 179p. 1907. text ed. 3.95 (ISBN 0-567-08133-8). Attic Pr.

Murray, Andrew. Abide in Christ. (Pivot Family Reader Ser.). 192p. 1973. pap. 1.50 (ISBN 0-87983-036-0). Keats.

Murry, John M. The Betrayal of Christ by the Churches. 59.95 (ISBN 0-87968-724-X). Gordon Pr.

My Baby Jesus Pop-up Book. (ps-3). 1.75 (ISBN 0-685-27820-4). Borden.

Nash, Robert. Bringing Christ Back. LC 78-69992. 1978. pap. 3.95 (ISBN 0-87973-642-9). Our Sunday Visitor.

Navone, John. The Jesus Story: Our Life As Story in Christ. rev. ed. 1980. pap. 8.50 (ISBN 0-8146-1048-X). Liturgical Pr.

Nee, T. S. Watchman. Qui Enverrai-Je? Date not set. 1.50 (ISBN 0-686-76412-9). Life Pubs Intl.

Nee, Watchman. Not I,But Christ. Kaung, Stephen, tr. (Basic Lesson Ser.: Vol. 4). 1974. 4.15 (ISBN 0-935008-11-X); pap. 2.75 (ISBN 0-935008-12-8). Christian Fellow Pubs.

Norris, Richard A., Jr. & Rusch, William G., eds. The Christological Controversy. Norris, Richard A., tr. LC 79-8890. (Sources of Early Christian Thought). 176p. 1980. pap. 6.95 (ISBN 0-8006-1411-9, 1-1411). Fortress.
O'Grady, John J. Jesus, Lord & Christ. LC 72-94395. 1973. pap. 4.95 (ISBN 0-8091-1765-7). Paulist Pr.
Our Brother Jesus. (gr. 1). 1.92 (ISBN 0-02-649390-X, 64939); tchr's manual 2.52 (ISBN 0-685-61712-2, 64940). Benziger Pub Co.
Owen, John. The Glory of Christ. 288p. 1980. pap. 7.95 (ISBN 0-8024-2988-2). Moody.
Paramananda, Swami. Christ & Oriental Ideals. 4th ed. 1968. 3.00 (ISBN 0-911564-14-4). Vedanta Ctr.
Patricia. Jesus I, The Man. Morningland Publications, Inc., ed. (Ser. of Three Books Called Jesus). (Illus.). 439p. 1980. pap. 10.00 (ISBN 0-935146-15-6). Morningland.
--Jesus II: The Mission. Morningland Publications, Inc., ed. (Ser. of Three Books Called Jesus). (Illus.). 461p. 1980. pap. 10.00 (ISBN 0-935146-17-2). Morningland.
--Jesus III: The Return. Morningland Publications, Inc., ed. (Ser. of Three Books Called Jesus). (Illus.). 470p. (Orig.). 1980. pap. 10.00 (ISBN 0-935146-18-0). Morningland.
Perrin, Norman. Jesus & the Language of the Kingdom: Symbol & Metaphor in New Testament Interpretation. LC 80-20822. 240p. 1980. pap. 8.95 (ISBN 0-8006-1432-1, 1-1432). Fortress.
Pfeifer, Carl J. Teaching Jesus Today. 144p. 1981. pap. 4.95 (ISBN 0-89622-127-X). Twenty-Third.
Prime, Derek. Tell Me About the Lord Jesus Christ. (Illus., Orig.). (gr. 4-6). 1967. pap. 1.50 (ISBN 0-8024-3618-8). Moody.
Ralph, Margaret. Historias Que Jesus Conto. (Serie Jirafa). Orig. Title: Stories Jesus Told. 1979. 3.60 (ISBN 0-311-38537-0, Edit Mundo). Casa Bautista.
Rawlinson, Alfred E. Christ in the Gospels. Repr. of 1944 ed. lib. bdg. 15.00x (ISBN 0-8371-3736-5, RACG). Greenwood.
Read, E. T. Edgar Cayce on Jesus & His Church. 1970. pap. 2.25 (ISBN 0-446-92693-0). Warner Bks.
Religious Education Staff. Lord & Savior: Friend & Brother, Spirit Masters for The Jesus Book. (To Live Is Christ Ser.). 1979. write for info. (ISBN 0-697-01692-7). Wm C Brown.
Richardson, Don. L' Enfant De Paix. Date not set. 2.25 (ISBN 0-686-76397-1). Life Pubs Intl.
Sanders, J. Oswald. The Incomparable Christ. 256p. 1975. pap. 4.95 (ISBN 0-8024-4081-9). Moody.
Schillebeeck, Edward. Christ: The Experience Oa Jesus As Lord. 900p. 1980. 29.50 (ISBN 0-8245-0005-9). Crossroad NY.
Schillebeeckx, Edward. Jesus: An Experiment in Christology. 1979. 27.50 (ISBN 0-8245-0320-1). Crossroad NY.
Schmaus, Michael. Dogma Three: God & His Christ. (Modern Theology Library Ser.). (Orig.). 1971. pap. 5.95x (ISBN 0-8362-0385-2). Andrews & McMeel.
Schuetze, Armin W. & Habezk, Irwin J. The Shepherd Under Christ. LC 74-81794. 1974. text ed. 14.95 (ISBN 0-8100-0046-6, 15N0351). Northwest Pub.
Schweitzer, Albert. Psychiatric Study of Jesus. 7.50 (ISBN 0-8446-2894-8). Peter Smith.
Shea, John. The Challenge of Jesus. 1977. pap. 2.45 (ISBN 0-385-12439-2, Im). Doubleday.
Sloyan, Gerard S. Is Christ the End of the Law? (Biblical Perspectives on Current Issues). 1978. softcover 4.95 (ISBN 0-664-24190-5). Westminster.
Sobrino, Jon. Christology at the Crossroads: A Latin American Approach. Drury, John, tr. from Span. LC 77-25025. 1978. pap. 12.95 (ISBN 0-88344-076-8). Orbis Bks.
Solomon, Bernard A. The Zaddick Christ: A Suite of Wood Engravings. (Illus.). 1974. 9.95 (ISBN 0-87921-022-2). Attic Pr.
Spurgeon, C. H. Christ Crucified. pap. 0.50 (ISBN 0-686-26193-3). Pilgrim Pubns.
Steiner, Rudolf. Jesus & Christ. pap. 1.50 (ISBN 0-910142-74-2). Anthroposophic.
--Pre-Earthly Deeds of Christ. 1976. pap. 2.75 (ISBN 0-919924-01-8). Anthroposophic.
Stewart, Ed. Here Comes Jesus. 1977. pap. 1.95 (ISBN 0-8307-0553-8, S101-1-57). Regal.
Stott, John R. Understanding Christ. 160p. (Orig.). 1981. pap. 4.95 (ISBN 0-310-41441-5). Zondervan.
Strait, Neil C. The Conquering Christ. 1975. pap. 1.25 (ISBN 0-8341-0273-0). Beacon Hill.
Strange, Roderick. Newman & the Gospel of Christ. (Oxford Theological Monographs). 200p. 1981. 39.00 (ISBN 0-19-826718-5). Oxford U Pr.
Talmage, James E. Jesus the Christ. deluxe ed. 16.50 black leather (ISBN 0-87747-387-0); deluxe ed. 16.50 brown leather (ISBN 0-87747-401-X); deluxe ed. 12.75 pocket ed. black leather (ISBN 0-87747-388-9); deluxe ed. 12.75 pocket ed. brown leather (ISBN 0-87747-402-8). Deseret Bk.
--Jesus the Christ. Bd. with The Articles of Faith. deluxe ed. 15.00 pocket ed. black leather (ISBN 0-87747-392-7); deluxe ed. 15.00 pocket ed. brown leather (ISBN 0-87747-394-3). Deseret Bk.
Tapia, Ralph. Theology of Christ: Commentary. 1971. pap. text ed. 6.95 (ISBN 0-02-829380-0). Glencoe.
Thomas, W. Griffith. Christianity Is Christ. LC 80-85341. (Shepherd Illustrated Classics). (Illus.). 200p. 1981. pap. 5.95 (ISBN 0-87983-238-X). Keats.
Thomas a Kempis. The Imitation of Christ. Rooney, John, tr. 214p. 1980. pap. 5.95 (ISBN 0-87243-097-9). Templegate.
Tippit, Sammy. Reproduced by Permission of the Author. 144p. 1979. pap. 2.50 (ISBN 0-88207-579-9). Victor Bks.
Van Beeck, Frans J. Christ Proclaimed. LC 79-66459. 1979. pap. 8.95 (ISBN 0-8091-2208-1). Paulist Pr.
Vanier, Jean. Followers of Jesus. LC 76-1210. 96p. 1976. pap. 4.95 (ISBN 0-8091-1941-2). Paulist Pr.
Vawter, Bruce. This Man Jesus: An Essay Toward a New Testament Christology. LC 73-78174. 240p. 1975. pap. 2.45 (ISBN 0-385-02797-4, Im). Doubleday.
Von Kietzel, F. Behold the Lamb of God. 3.95x (ISBN 0-686-13090-1). Believers Bkshelf.
Von Wellnitz, Marcus. Christ & the Patriarchs. LC 80-83035. 400p. 1981. 9.95 (ISBN 0-88290-164-8, 2045). Horizon Utah.
Vos, Howard F. Beginnings in the Life of Christ. rev. ed. 220p. 1975. pap. 3.50 (ISBN 0-8024-0608-4). Moody.
Wagner, Clarence M. The Same Jesus. Tru-Faith Publisher's, ed. 72p. (Orig.). 1981. pap. 3.50x (ISBN 0-937498-00-9). Tru-Faith.
Walker, E. Jerry. Seven Who Saw Him. 1978. pap. 4.40 (ISBN 0-89536-299-6). CSS Pub.
Wallis, Arthur. Jesus of Nazareth, Who Is He. 1959. pap. 0.50 (ISBN 0-87508-558-X). Chr Lit.
Walvoord, John F. Jesus Christ Our Lord. 318p. 1974. pap. text ed. 5.95 (ISBN 0-8024-4326-5). Moody.
Watlington, Amanda. Christ Our Lord. LC 78-53844. (Official Catholic Teachings Ser.). 1978. lib. bdg. 20.00 (ISBN 0-8434-0714-X, Pub by Consortium); pap. 15.00 (ISBN 0-8434-0720-4, Pub. by Consortium). McGrath.
Wenham, J. W. Christ & the Bible. LC 72-97950. 187p. 1973. pap. 3.95 (ISBN 0-87784-760-6). Inter-Varsity.
Wenley, R. M. Socrates & Christ. 1977. 59.95 (ISBN 0-8490-2621-0). Gordon Pr.
White, Reginald E. Stranger of Galilee. LC 60-10096. (Pivot Family Reader Ser). 240p. 1975. pap. 2.25 (ISBN 0-87983-108-1). Keats.
Wiersbe, Warren. Meet Your King. 1980. pap. 4.95 (ISBN 0-88207-799-6). Victor Bks.
Wierwille, Victor P. Jesus Christ Our Passover. 327p. 1980. 10.95 (ISBN 0-910068-30-5). Am Christian.
Wilkerson, David. Jesucristo la Roca Firme. (Span.). Date not set. 1.75 (ISBN 0-686-76300-9). Life Pubs Intl.
Wilkins, Ronald J. Focus on Faith in Jesus. (To Live in Christ Ser.). 1980. pap. write for info. (ISBN 0-697-01719-2); parish ed. avail. (ISBN 0-697-01720-6). Wm C Brown.
--The Jesus Book: Short Ed. (To Live Is Christ Ser.). 112p. 1979. pap. write for info. (ISBN 0-697-01695-1); tchr's manual 3.75 (ISBN 0-697-01714-1). Wm C Brown.
Winter, David. Closer Than a Brother. LC 71-181991. 1976. pap. 1.75 (ISBN 0-87788-129-4). Shaw Pubs.
Yamauchi, E. Jesus Zoroaster, Buddha, Socrates, Muhammad. pap. 0.50 (ISBN 0-87784-145-4). Inter-Varsity.
Zenos, A. C. The Son of Man. (Short Course Ser.). 145p. Repr. of 1914 ed. text ed. 3.95 (ISBN 0-567-08312-8). Attic Pr.

JESUS CHRIST-APPEARANCES

see also Theophanies

Detrick, R. Blaine. I Met Jesus When He Ministered. 56p. 1976. pap. 3.55 (ISBN 0-89536-102-7). CSS Pub.
Menendez, Josefa. The Way of Divine Love. LC 79-112493. 1977. pap. 7.50 (ISBN 0-89555-030-X, 104). TAN Bks Pubs.

JESUS CHRIST-ART

see also Bible-Pictures, Illustrations, etc.; Christian Art and Symbolism; Fish (In Religion, Folk-Lore, etc.); Icons

Beauchamp, Virgil. The Life of Christ in the Paintings by Tissot. 1979. deluxe ed. 29.75 (ISBN 0-930582-29-2). Gloucester Art.
Brooks, Neil C. The Sepulchre of Christ in Art & Liturgy. pap. 7.00 (ISBN 0-384-05925-2). Johnson Repr.
Country Beautiful Editors. Love in the Words & Life of Jesus. LC 73-79617. (Illus.). 96p. 1973. 8.95 (ISBN 0-87294-046-2). Country Beautiful.
Emerson, James C., ed. The Life of Christ in the Conception & Expression of Chinese & Oriental Artists. (Illus.). 1978. deluxe ed. 39.75 (ISBN 0-930582-13-6). Gloucester Art.
Henkes, Robert. The Crucifixion in American Painting. 1978. lib. bdg. 79.95 (ISBN 0-8490-1370-4). Gordon Pr.
--The Crucifixion in American Painting. 1978. lib. bdg. 79.95 (ISBN 0-8490-1370-4). Gordon Pr.
Hook, Frances, illus. My Book of Friends. (Illus.). (gr. k-2). 1968. pap. 4.95 board cover (ISBN 0-87239-242-2, 3045). Standard Pub.
Hublow, Karl. The Working of Christ in Man: The Thousand-Year Old Frescoes in the Church of St. George on the Island of Reichenau. (Illus.). 1979. 17.95 (ISBN 0-903540-28-2, Pub. by Floris Books). St George Bk Serv.
Hurll, E. M. The Life of Our Lord in Art. 59.95 (ISBN 0-8490-0534-5). Gordon Pr.
Hurll, Estelle M. Life of Our Lord in Art: With Some Account of the Artistic Treatment of the Life of St. John the Baptist. LC 76-89272. 1969. Repr. of 1898 ed. 22.00 (ISBN 0-8103-3137-3). Gale.
Parker, Elizabeth C. The Descent from the Cross: Its Relation to the Extra-Liturgical Depositio Drama. LC 77-94713. (Outstanding Dissertations in the Fine Arts Ser.). 1978. lib. bdg. 34.00 (ISBN 0-8240-3245-4). Garland Pub.
Phillips, J. B. The Living Gospels. 288p. 1981. 24.95 (ISBN 0-8317-3948-7, Rutledge Pr). Smith Pubs.
Poortvliet, Rien. He Was One of Us. LC 77-16753. 1978. 14.95 (ISBN 0-385-13231-X); Limited edition 100.00 (ISBN 0-385-14742-2). Doubleday.
Sledge, Linda C. Shivering Babe, Victorious Lord: The Nativity in Poetry & Art. 1981. 24.95 (ISBN 0-8028-3553-8). Eerdmans.
Thomas, Denis. The Face of Christ. LC 78-20744. (Illus.). 1979. 7.95 (ISBN 0-385-15306-6). Doubleday.
Weiler, Eugene. Jesus: A Pictorial History of the New Testament. (Illus.). 160p. 1980. pap. 10.95 (ISBN 0-8245-0321-X). Crossroad NY.

JESUS CHRIST-ASCENSION

Benesch, Friedrich. Ascension. 1979. pap. 2.50 (ISBN 0-903540-19-3, Pub. by Floris Books). St George Bk Serv.
Bey, Serapis. Dossier on the Ascension. 1979. pap. 3.95 (ISBN 0-916766-21-7). Summit Univ.
Jesus: His Life & Times. 1979. 22.95 (ISBN 0-8007-1074-6). Revell.
Milligan, William. The Acension of Christ. 1980. 12.50 (ISBN 0-86524-061-2). Klock & Klock.
--The Ascension & Heavenly Priesthood of Our Lord. 1977. Repr. of 1894 ed. 11.95 (ISBN 0-87921-034-6). Attic Pr.
Roddy, Lee. Jesus. 1979. pap. 2.95 (ISBN 0-8007-8380-8, Spire Bks). Revell.
Sherer, Michael L. Ascension Day Dialogue. 1979. pap. 1.90 (ISBN 0-89536-357-7). CSS Pub.
Toon, Peter. Jesus Christ Is Lord. 1979. pap. 4.95 (ISBN 0-8170-0842-X). Judson.

JESUS CHRIST-ATONEMENT

see Atonement

JESUS CHRIST-BAPTISM

Elliott, John R., Jr. & Runnalls, Graham A., eds. The Baptism & Temptation of Christ: The First Day of a Medieval French Passion Play. LC 78-6564. 1978. 17.50x (ISBN 0-300-02199-2). Yale U Pr.

JESUS CHRIST-BEATITUDES

see Beatitudes

JESUS CHRIST-BIOGRAPHY

Andry, Carl F. Jesus & the Four Gospels. LC 78-1128. 1978. pap. 5.95 (ISBN 0-932970-03-6). Prinit Pr.
Ault, Norman. Poets's Life of Christ. LC 72-2513. (Select Bibliographies Reprint Ser). 1972. Repr. of 1922 ed. 20.00 (ISBN 0-8369-6847-6). Arno.
Bailey, Keith M. Learning to Live. 64p. (Orig.). 1978. pap. 0.95 (ISBN 0-87509-158-X). Chr Pubns.
Baldwin, Louis. Jesus of Galilee. LC 79-11587. 1979. pap. 4.95 (ISBN 0-8170-0841-1). Judson.
Bales, James. Jesus the Master Respondent. Date not set. 1.95 (ISBN 0-89315-130-0). Lambert Bk.
Barclay, William. Jesus As They Saw Him. LC 78-18224. 1978. pap. 5.95 (ISBN 0-8028-1775-0). Eerdmans.
--Jesus of Nazareth. 288p. 1981. pap. 10.95 (ISBN 0-8407-5759-X). Nelson.
--Jesus of Nazareth. (Illus.). 1977. 14.95 (ISBN 0-00-250653-X, A1160). Collins Pubs.
--The Life of Jesus for Everyman. LC 75-12282. 96p. 1975. pap. 3.95 (ISBN 0-06-060404-2, RD 319, HarpR). Har-Row.
Barnett, Walter. Jesus: the Story of His Life: A Modern Retelling Based on the Gospels. LC 75-28260. 1976. 14.95 (ISBN 0-88229-308-7). Nelson Hall.
Barrois, George. Jesus Christ & the Temple. LC 80-19700. 164p. 1980. pap. 5.95 (ISBN 0-913836-73-7). St Vladimirs.
Baughman, Ray E. Life of Christ Visualized. (Orig.). 1968. pap. 3.95 (ISBN 0-8024-4726-0). Moody.
Bauman, Edward W. Life & Teaching of Jesus. 1978. softcover 4.95 (ISBN 0-664-24221-9). Westminster.
Bock, Janet L. The Jesus Mystery: Of Lost Years & Unknown Travels. LC 80-67420. (Illus.). 231p. (Orig.). 1980. pap. 6.95 (ISBN 0-937736-00-7). Aura Bks.
Boultwood, Alban. Christ in US: Reflections on Redemption. 160p. (Orig.). 1981. pap. 5.95 (ISBN 0-8146-1234-2). Liturgical Pr.
Bruce, F. F. Paul & Jesus. (Orig.). 1974. pap. 2.95 (ISBN 0-8010-0631-7). Baker Bk.
--Places They Knew - Jesus & Paul. 128p. 1981. 30.00x (ISBN 0-686-75528-6, Pub. by Ark Pub England). State Mutual Bk.
Bultmann, Rudolf. Jesus & the Word. 8.95 (ISBN 0-684-14390-9, ScribT). Scribner.
Carpenter, Humphrey. Jesus. 1980. 7.95 (ISBN 0-8090-6082-5); pap. 2.95 (ISBN 0-8090-1410-6). Hill & Wang.
Cary, Diane M. Master. 1981. 9.95 (ISBN 0-8062-1763-4). Carlton.
Case, Shirley J. Jesus, a New Biography. LC 70-95149. (BCL Ser. II). Repr. of 1927 ed. 17.50 (ISBN 0-404-01406-2). AMS Pr.
--Jesus: A New Biography. LC 68-57594. 1968. Repr. of 1927 ed. lib. bdg. 18.50x (ISBN 0-8371-0342-8, CAJE). Greenwood.
--Jesus, a New Biography. 1928. 30.00 (ISBN 0-932062-36-9). Sharon Hill.
Cassandre. Life When Jesus Was a Boy. 48p. 1981. pap. 5.95 (ISBN 0-8170-0913-2). Judson.
Chambers, Oswald. Bringing Sons Unto Glory. 1973. pap. 1.25 (ISBN 0-87508-104-5). Chr Lit.
Chesterton, G. K. The Everlasting Man. LC 72-11233. 344p. 1974. Repr. of 1925 ed. lib. bdg. 21.75x (ISBN 0-8371-6636-5, CEVM). Greenwood.
Clark, Dennis E. Jesus Christ, His Life & Teaching. 324p. pap. 3.95 (ISBN 0-89191-117-0, 23341). Cook.
Coleman, Robert E. The Mind of the Master. 4.95 (ISBN 0-8007-0880-6). Revell.
Comstock, Jim. Good News, the Story of Jesus. LC 74-32829. 1974. pap. 6.95 (ISBN 0-914440-06-3). EPM Pubns.
Conn, Charles P. The Man from Galilee. LC 74-83547. 1974. pap. 1.35 (ISBN 0-87148-565-6). Pathway Pr.
Converse, Gordon, et al. Come See the Place: The Holy Land Jesus Knew. (Illus.). 1978. 12.95 (ISBN 0-13-152538-7). P-H.
Cornell, George. Behold the Man. LC 74-78044. 1976. pap. 1.95 (ISBN 0-87680-823-2, Key-Word Bks). Word Bks.
Cornwall, Judson. Let Us See Jesus. 1980. pap. 4.95 (ISBN 0-8007-5052-7, Power Bks). Revell.
Culver, Robert D. Life of Christ. LC 76-17967. 272p. 1976. 9.95 (ISBN 0-8010-2379-3). Baker Bk.
Dale, Alan T. Portrait of Jesus. (Illus.). 1979. 6.95 (ISBN 0-8317-7091-0, Mayflower Bks). Smith Pubs.
Daniel-Rops, Henri - Daily Life in the Time of Jesus. O'Brian, Patrick, tr. from Fr. (Illus.). 518p. 1981. pap. 7.95 (ISBN 0-89283-085-9). Servant.
Denney, James. The Death of Christ. LC 81-81100. (The Shephard Illustrated Classics Ser.). (Illus.). 372p. 1981. pap. 6.95 (ISBN 0-87983-258-4). Keats.
DeRosa, Peter. Jesus Who Became Christ. (Fount Religious Paperback Ser.). 1977. pap. 2.95 (ISBN 0-00-624682-6, FA4682). Collins Pubs.
DeVries, Henri. Incarnate Son of God. pap. 2.75 (ISBN 0-87509-095-8). Chr Pubns.
Dickens, Charles. The Life of Our Lord. LC 80-22131. (Illus.). 1981. Repr. of 1934 ed. 8.95 (ISBN 0-664-21382-0). Westminster.
Eaglefort, Alexander. The New Fully Illustrated Family Book on the Life of Christ. (The Most Meaningful Classics in World Culture Ser.). (Illus.). 1979. 47.50 (ISBN 0-89266-190-9). Am Classical Coll Pr.
Edersheim, Alfred. Jesus the Messiah. 1959. pap. 7.95 (ISBN 0-8028-8131-9). Eerdmans.
--Life & Times of Jesus the Messiah. 1972. 18.95 (ISBN 0-8028-8027-4). Eerdmans.
Emmerich, Anne C. Life of Jesus Christ & Biblical Revelations, 4 vols. Schmoeger, C. E., ed. LC 79-90066. 1979. Set. pap. 25.00 (ISBN 0-89555-127-6); Vol. 1. (ISBN 0-89555-123-3); Vol. 2. pap. (ISBN 0-89555-124-1); Vol. 3. (ISBN 0-89555-125-X); Vol. 4. (ISBN 0-89555-126-8). TAN Bks Pubs.

Enslin, Morton S. The Prophet from Nazareth. LC 68-27322. 1969. 6.00x (ISBN 0-8052-3210-9); pap. 1.95 (ISBN 0-8052-0184-X). Schocken.

Farrar, Frederic W. Life of Christ. 1982. lib. bdg. 24.95 (ISBN 0-86524-089-2). Klock & Klock.

--Life of Christ. 1980. 15.00 (ISBN 0-911376-01-1). Fountain Publications Oregon.

Flynn, Cleta. The Parable: A Story of Jesus, Son of Joseph. LC 79-14062. 1979. 7.95 (ISBN 0-915442-81-7, Unilaw); pap. 4.95 (ISBN 0-915442-76-0). Donning Co.

Fosdick, Harry E. The Man from Nazareth: As His Contemporaries Saw Him. LC 78-16469. 1978. Repr. of 1949 ed. lib. bdg. 24.25x (ISBN 0-313-20603-1, FOMN). Greenwood.

Foster, R. C. Studies in the Life of Christ. 1979. Repr. 24.95 (ISBN 0-8010-3452-3). Baker Bk.

Gaddy, C. Welton. Beginning at the End: From Crucifixion to New Life. LC 79-16268. (Orig.). 1980. pap. 3.95 (ISBN 0-687-02760-8). Abingdon.

Galeone, Victor. The Great Drama of Jesus: A Life of Christ for Teens. pap. 5.95 (ISBN 0-686-74586-8, 101-28). Prow Bks-Franciscan.

Genesis Project. Jesus, His Life & Times. LC 79-66457. (Illus.). 1979. 22.95 (ISBN 0-688-03577-9). Morrow.

George, Bill. His Story: The Life of Christ. LC 76-53630. 1977. pap. text ed. 3.50 (ISBN 0-87148-406-4). Pathway Pr.

Giordani, Igino. Christ, Hope of the World. (Illus.). 1964. 8.00 (ISBN 0-8198-0020-1); pap. 7.00 (ISBN 0-8198-0021-X); deluxe ed. 10.00 (ISBN 0-8198-0022-8). Dghtrs St Paul.

Glover, T. R. The Jesus of History. LC 78-25986. 15.00 (ISBN 0-8414-4488-9). Folcroft.

God in Man Made Manifest. 1968. pap. text ed. 0.95 (ISBN 0-570-03533-3, 14-1518, 14-1519). tchr's manual 1.25 (ISBN 0-570-03534-1). Concordia.

Goguel, Maurice. The Life of Jesus. Wyon, Olive, tr. LC 75-41114. Repr. of 1933 ed. 32.50 (ISBN 0-404-14546-9). AMS Pr.

Goodier, A. Public Life of Our Lord Jesus Christ, 2 vols. 1978. Set. 15.95 (ISBN 0-8198-0551-3); Set. pap. 13.95 (ISBN 0-8198-0552-1). Dghtrs St Paul.

Goodspeed, Edgar J. A Life of Jesus. LC 78-21540. 1979. Repr. of 1950 ed. lib. bdg. 18.75x (ISBN 0-313-20728-3, GOLJ). Greenwood.

Gorman, Ralph. Last Hours of Jesus. 1960. 4.50 (ISBN 0-8362-0221-X, Pub. by Sheed). Guild Bks.

Goyen, William. A Book of Jesus. 1974. pap. 1.25 (ISBN 0-451-06217-5, Y6217, Sig). NAL.

Graesser, Erich, et al. Jesus in Nazareth. (Beiheft 40 zur Zeitschrifte fuer die alttestamentliche Wissenschaft). 153p. 1972. 40.00x (ISBN 3-11-004004-2). De Gruyter.

Gray, Donald P. Jesus: The Way to Freedom. LC 79-66823. (Illus.). 1979. pap. text ed. 4.95 (ISBN 0-88489-112-7). St Mary's.

Grollenberg, Lucas. Jesus. Bowden, John, tr. LC 78-13478. 1979. pap. 4.50 (ISBN 0-664-24232-4). Westminster.

Guardini, Romano. Lord. 1978. pap. 9.95 (ISBN 0-89526-909-0). Regnery-Gateway.

Guthrie, Donald. Jesus the Messiah. (Illus.). 1972. 14.95 (ISBN 0-310-25430-2). Zondervan.

--Shorter Life of Christ. LC 71-120039. (Contemporary Evangelical Perspectives Ser). 1970. kivar 4.95 (ISBN 0-310-25441-8). Zondervan.

Hackwood, Frederick W. Christ Lore: Being the Legends, Traditions, Myths, Symbols, Customs, & Superstitions of the Christian Church. LC 69-16064. (Illus.). 1971. Repr. of 1902 ed. 22.00 (ISBN 0-8103-3528-X). Gale.

Harrison, Everett. A Short Life of Christ. (Highlights in the Life of Christ). 1968. pap. 5.95 (ISBN 0-8028-1824-2). Eerdmans.

Hirschmann, Maria A. & Pershing, Betty. Follow Me: A Study of the Life of Christ. LC 79-84331. (Bible Study & Sharing Ser.: No. 2). 224p. (Orig.). 1979. pap. 3.95 (ISBN 0-932878-01-6, HB/01). Hansi.

Hodson, Geoffrey. The Christ Life from Nativity to Ascension. LC 75-4169. 540p. 1975. pap. 5.50 (ISBN 0-8356-0467-5, Quest). Theos Pub Hse.

Horton, Stanley. Maestro: Rustica, No. 1. (Span.). Date not set. 2.75 (ISBN 0-686-76305-X). Life Pubs Intl.

--Maestro: Rustica, No. 2. (Span.). Date not set. 2.75 (ISBN 0-686-76307-6). Life Pubs Intl.

--Maestro: Rustica, No. 3. (Span.). Date not set. 2.75 (ISBN 0-686-76308-4). Life Pubs Intl.

--Maestro: Rustica, No. 4. (Span.). Date not set. 2.75 (ISBN 0-686-76310-6). Life Pubs Intl.

--Maestro: Rustica, No. 5. (Span.). Date not set. 2.75 (ISBN 0-686-76312-2). Life Pubs Intl.

--Maestro: Tela, No. 1. (Span.). Date not set. 3.75 (ISBN 0-686-76306-8). Life Pubs Intl.

--Maestro: Tela, No. 3. (Span.). Date not set. 3.75 (ISBN 0-686-76309-2). Life Pubs Intl.

--Maestro: Tela, No. 4. (Span.). Date not set. 3.75 (ISBN 0-686-76311-4). Life Pubs Intl.

--Maestro: Tela, No. 5. (Span.). Date not set. 3.75 (ISBN 0-686-76313-0). Life Pubs Intl.

Hunt, Marigold. A Life of Our Lord. 191p. 1959. 4.00 (ISBN 0-912414-25-1). Lumen Christi.

Hurll, Estelle M. Life of Our Lord in Art: With Some Account of the Artistic Treatment of the Life of St. John the Baptist. LC 76-89272. 1969. Repr. of 1898 ed. 22.00 (ISBN 0-8103-3137-3). Gale.

Ingraham, F. & Anderson, Eric. Prince of the House of David. Orig. Title: Three Years in the Holy City. 363p. 1980. Repr. text ed. 9.95 (ISBN 0-89841-003-7). Zoe Pubns.

Jacobs, William. Jesus. (Emmaus Book Ser.). 1977. pap. 1.95 (ISBN 0-8091-1986-2). Paulist Pr.

Jefferson, Thomas. The Life & Morals of Jesus of Nazareth. LC 76-17582. 1976. Repr. of 1904 ed. lib. bdg. 25.00 (ISBN 0-8414-5323-3). Folcroft.

--Thomas Jefferson's Life of Jesus. 1976. 2.95 (ISBN 0-87243-056-1). Templegate.

Jesus in the Gospel. (Illus.). 1980. 12.00 (ISBN 0-8198-0618-8). Dghtrs St Paul.

Kahler, Martin. The So Called Historical Jesus & the Historic Biblical Christ. Braaten, Carl E., tr. from Ger. LC 64-12994. 168p. 1964. pap. 3.75 (ISBN 0-8006-1960-9, 1-1960). Fortress.

Kelber, Werner H. Mark's Story of Jesus. LC 78-14668. 96p. 1979. pap. 2.95 (ISBN 0-8006-1355-4, 1-1355). Fortress.

Keller, W. Phillip. Rabboni. 1981. pap. 5.95 (ISBN 0-8007-5053-5, Power Bks). Revell.

--Rabboni. 1977. 9.95 (ISBN 0-8007-0882-2). Revell.

Klausner, Joseph. Jesus of Nazareth: His Life, Times & Teaching. Danby, Herbert, tr. from Hebrew. 1978. 15.95x (ISBN 0-932232-01-9); pap. 12.95 (ISBN 0-932232-02-7). Menorah Pub.

Koch, Rudolph. Life of Jesus. (Illus.). 3.00 (ISBN 0-8159-6110-3). Devin.

Lamsa, George M. Hidden Years of Jesus. 3rd ed. pap. 1.50 (ISBN 0-686-09906-0). Aramaic Bible.

Levi. The Aquarian Gospel of Jesus Christ. 1972. 7.95 (ISBN 0-87516-041-7); pap. 3.50 (ISBN 0-87516-168-5). De Vorss.

Levin, S. Jesus Alias Christ. LC 71-81814. 1969. 5.50 (ISBN 0-8022-2293-5). Philos Lib.

Lewis, E. R. Life & Teaching of Jesus Christ. (London Divinity Ser.). 1977. pap. 4.00 (ISBN 0-227-67519-3). Attic Pr.

Life of Christ, Vols. 1 & 2. 6.49 ea. (0140594). CEF Press.

Lindsay, Gordon. Life & Teachings of Christ, Vol. 1. (Life of Christ & Parable Ser.). pap. 4.00 (ISBN 0-89985-967-4). Christ Nations.

--Life & Teachings of Christ, Vol. 2. (Life of Christ & Parable Ser.). pap. 4.00 (ISBN 0-89985-968-2). Christ Nations.

--Life & Teachings of Christ, Vol. 3. (Life of Christ & Parable Ser.). pap. 4.00 (ISBN 0-89985-969-0). Christ Nations.

--Life of Christ. (Span.). 0.95 (ISBN 0-89985-982-8). Christ Nations.

Ludwig, Emil. Son of Man: The Story of Jesus. (Black & Gold Lib). (Illus.). 1945. 7.95 (ISBN 0-87140-882-1). Liveright.

Maccoby, Hyam. Revolution in Judaea: Jesus & the Jewish Resistance. LC 80-16752. 256p. 1980. 9.95 (ISBN 0-8008-6784-X). Taplinger.

McConkie, Bruce R. The Mortal Messiah: From Bethlehem to Calvary, 4 vols, Bk. 1. LC 79-19606. 536p. 1979. 12.95 (ISBN 0-87747-784-1). Deseret Bk.

--The Mortal Messiah: From Bethlehem to Calvary, Bk. 2. LC 79-19606. 424p. 1980. 11.95 (ISBN 0-87747-803-1). Deseret Bk.

--The Mortal Messiah, from Bethlehem to Calvary, Bk. 3. LC 79-19606. 486p. 1980. 11.95 (ISBN 0-87747-825-2). Deseret Bk.

--The Mortal Messiah: From Bethlehem to Calvary, Bk. 4. LC 79-19606. (The Mortal Messiah Ser.). 447p. 1981. 11.95 (ISBN 0-87747-856-2). Deseret Bk.

Madden, R. Father Madden's Life of Christ. 1960. pap. 1.75 (ISBN 0-685-01125-9, 80424). Glencoe.

Makrakis, Apostolos. The Human Nature of Christ: Growth & Perfection. Orthodox Christian Educational Society, ed. Cummings, D., tr. from Hellenic. 52p. (Orig.). 1965. pap. 1.00x (ISBN 0-938366-28-9). Orthodox Chr.

Martin, Alfred & Martin, Dorothy. The Lord Jesus Christ. (Personal Bible Study Ser.). 64p. 1973. pap. 1.50 (ISBN 0-8024-1103-7). Moody.

Mathews, Basil. A Life of Jesus. (Illus.). 1979. Repr. of 1931 ed. lib. bdg. 25.00 (ISBN 0-8495-3817-3). Arden Lib.

Mauriac, Francois. Life of Jesus. Kernan, Julie, tr. from Fr. (Illus.). 1978. pap. 5.95 (ISBN 0-88347-102-7). Thomas More.

Mauro, Philip. Never Man Spake Like This Man. 32p. 1974. pap. 0.50 (ISBN 0-685-52820-0). Reiner.

Melick, George F., Jr. John Mark & the Origin of the Gospels: A Foundation Document Hypothesis. LC 79-52095. 69p. 1979. 4.95 (ISBN 0-8059-2650-X). Dorrance.

Menendez, Josefa. Christ's Appeal for Love. Keppel, L., tr. from Span. 1975. pap. 2.50 (ISBN 0-89555-013-X, 324). TAN Bks Pubs.

Mills, James R. The Gospel According to Pontius Pilate. 1978. 7.95 (ISBN 0-8007-0953-5). Revell.

Montgomery, Mary & Montgomery, Herb. The Jesus Story. 1974. pupil pack 4.95 (ISBN 0-03-012951-6, 125); tchr's. manual 6.55 (ISBN 0-03-012956-7, 126). Winston Pr.

More, Paul E. Christ of the New Testament. LC 79-88912. Repr. of 1924 ed. lib. bdg. 15.00 (ISBN 0-8371-2323-2, MOCN). Greenwood.

Morgan, G. Campbell. Crises of the Christ. 1954. 11.95 (ISBN 0-8007-0056-2). Revell.

Morrison, Mary C. Jesus: Sketches for a Portrait. rev. & enl. ed. 1979. 2.00 (ISBN 0-686-28782-7). Forward Movement.

Nelson, Carl G. The Prince of Peace. LC 79-63954. (Illus., Ltd. ed-600copies). 1979. 20.00 (ISBN 0-930954-11-4). Tidal Pr.

Nolan, Albert. Jesus Before Christianity. LC 78-6708. 1978. pap. 5.95 (ISBN 0-88344-230-2). Orbis Bks.

Notovich, N. The Unknown Life of Jesus Christ. 69.95 (ISBN 0-87968-073-3). Gordon Pr.

O'Brien, Isidore. Life of Christ. LC 75-5719. 1975. 7.95 (ISBN 0-8198-0489-4); pap. 6.95 (ISBN 0-8198-0490-8). Dghtrs St Paul.

Olson, E. E. The Day of Jesus' Glory. 1973. 1.95 (ISBN 0-89536-052-7). CSS Pub.

Oursler, Fulton. Greatest Story Ever Told. 1949. pap. 3.95 (ISBN 0-385-08028-X, D121, Im). Doubleday.

Padgett, James E. Jesus Birth & Youth As Revealed by Mary, Mother of Jesus. 3.00 (ISBN 0-686-12714-5). Foun Church New Birth.

Phillips, Arnold. One Man's Opinion. 1980. 5.95 (ISBN 0-533-04478-2). Vantage.

Phillips, J. B. The Living Gospels. 288p. 1981. 24.95 (ISBN 0-8317-3948-7, Rutledge Pr). Smith Pubs.

Poortvliet, Rien. He Was One of Us: The Life of Jesus of Nazareth. (Illus.). 1979. pap. 9.95 (ISBN 0-553-01184-7). Bantam.

Powers, Isaias. Nameless Faces in the Life of Jesus. 157p. 1981. pap. 3.95 (ISBN 0-89622-125-3). Twenty-Third.

Ramsey, James. The Education of Christ. LC 80-84438. (Shepherd Classics Ser.). (Illus.). 168p. 1981. pap. 5.95 (ISBN 0-87983-236-3). Keats.

Ramsey, Michael. Jesus & the Living Past. 1980. 8.95 (ISBN 0-19-213963-0). Oxford U Pr.

Robertson, A. T. Epochs in the Life of Jesus. 1974. pap. 3.95 (ISBN 0-8054-1347-2). Broadman.

Roddy, Lee & Sellier, Charles E. In Search of Historic Jesus. 192p. (Orig.). 1979. pap. 2.25 (ISBN 0-553-13588-0). Bantam.

Ross, Pearl, ed. Jesus the Pagan. 84p. 1972. 6.00 (ISBN 0-8022-2097-5). Philos Lib.

Rumble, L. A Brief Life of Christ. (Illus.). 54p. 1974. pap. 0.75 (ISBN 0-89555-096-2, 160). TAN Bks Pubs.

Sanday, W. Outlines of the Life of Christ. 2nd ed. 285p. 1930. Repr. of 1906 ed. text ed. 4.95 (ISBN 0-567-02224-2). Attic Pr.

Savoy, Gene. Jamil: The Child Christ. LC 73-92360. (Sacred Teachings of Light Ser.: Codex I). 118p. 1976. text ed. 25.00 (ISBN 0-936202-00-9). Intl Comm Christ.

Schleiermacher, Friedrich. The Life of Jesus. new ed. Verheyden, Jack C. & Keck, Leander E., eds. MacLean, Gilmour, tr. from Ger. LC 72-87056. (Lives of Jesus Ser.). 542p. 1975. pap. 14.95 (ISBN 0-8006-1272-8, 1-1073). Fortress.

Seeley, John R. Ecce Homo. 1970. 8.95x (ISBN 0-460-00305-4, Evman). Biblio Dist.

Sheed, F. J. To Know Christ Jesus. 1980. pap. 3.95 (ISBN 0-89283-080-8). Servant.

Sheen, Fulton J. Life of Christ. LC 77-81295. 1977. pap. 5.95 (ISBN 0-385-13220-4, Im). Doubleday.

Shepard, John W. Christ of the Gospels. rev. ed. 1946. 7.95 (ISBN 0-8028-1779-3). Eerdmans.

Smith, David. Days of His Flesh, the Earthly Life of Our Lord & Savior, Jesus Christ. (Twin Brooks Ser.). 1976. pap. 8.95 (ISBN 0-8010-8089-4). Baker Bk.

Smyth, Alexander. The True Life of Jesus of Nazareth - the Confessions of St. Paul. (Illus.). 1968. Repr. 7.95 (ISBN 0-932642-15-2); pap. write for info. (ISBN 0-932642-56-X). Unarius.

Spurgeon, Charles H. Christ's Glorious Achievements. (Charles H. Spurgeon Library). 128p. 1975. pap. 3.45 (ISBN 0-8010-8042-8). Baker Bk.

Stalker, J. The Life of Jesus Christ. 2nd ed. (Handbooks for Bible Classes). 157p. 1978. Repr. of 1891 ed. text ed. 7.95 (ISBN 0-567-28130-2). Attic Pr.

Stalker, James. The Story of Jesus. Orig. Title: Life of Christ. (Illus.). 1976. gift ed. 4.95 (ISBN 0-915720-18-3); pap. text ed. 2.25 class ed. (ISBN 0-915720-38-8). Brownlow Pub Co.

--Vida de Jesucristo. 177p. (Span.). 1973. pap. 2.95 (ISBN 0-89922-024-X). Edit Caribe.

Staton, Knofel. Meet Jesus. LC 80-53674. 192p. (Orig.). 1981. pap. 2.95 (ISBN 0-87239-426-3, 40092). Standard Pub.

Stephens, William H. Where Jesus Walked. 1981. soft cover 10.95 (ISBN 0-8054-1138-0). Broadman.

Stewart, James S. The Life & Teaching of Jesus Christ. (Festival Books). 1978. pap. 1.95 (ISBN 0-687-21744-X). Abingdon.

Strauss, David F. Life of Jesus Critically Examined, 2 Vols. Evans, Marian, tr. LC 74-107193. 1970. Repr. of 1860 ed. Set. 44.00 (ISBN 0-403-00238-9). Scholarly.

--The Life of Jesus Critically Examined. Hodgson, Peter C. & Keck, Leander E., eds. LC 72-75655. (The Lives of Jesus Ser.). 832p. 1972. pap. 12.00 (ISBN 0-8006-1271-X, 1-1271). Fortress.

Talmage, James E. Jesus the Christ. 804p. pap. 2.95 (ISBN 0-87747-456-7). Deseret Bk.

Thompson, W. Ian. La Vida Salvadora De Cristo. (Span.). Date not set. 2.00 (ISBN 0-686-76348-3). Life Pubs Intl.

Thurman, Thomas D. The Jesus Years: A Chronological Study of the Life of Christ. LC 77-80314. (Illus.). 1977. pap. 5.95 (ISBN 0-87239-136-1, 40061). Standard Pub.

Treasure, Geoff. The Most Unforgettable Character You'll Ever Meet. 1977. pap. 1.50 (ISBN 0-8024-5625-1). Moody.

Vallotton, Annie. Priority: Jesus' Life in Sixty Drawings. (Illus.). (gr. k-4). 1969. pap. 0.95 (ISBN 0-8361-1901-0). Herald Pr.

Van Dyk, Fay B. His Touch Is Love. (Horizon Ser.). 1978. pap. 4.50 (ISBN 0-8127-0189-5). Review & Herald.

Vermes, Geza. Jesus the Jew. (Fount Religious Paperback Ser.). 1977. pap. 4.95 (ISBN 0-00-624300-2, FA4300). Collins Pubs.

Vines, Jerry. Great Events in the Life of Christ. 1979. pap. 2.95 (ISBN 0-88207-776-7). Victor Bks.

Vos, Geerhardus. The Self-Disclosure of Jesus. 1975. kivar 5.95 (ISBN 0-87552-504-0). Presby & Reformed.

Warschauer, J. The Historical Life of Christ. 1977. lib. bdg. 69.95 (ISBN 0-8490-1960-5). Gordon Pr.

Weatherhead, Leslie D. The Autobiography of Jesus: What He Said About Himself. (Festival Bks.). 1980. pap. 1.95 (ISBN 0-687-02318-1). Abingdon.

Wightman, W. M. Saint Luke's Life of Christ. pap. 1.00x (ISBN 0-685-02586-1). Outlook.

Wilson, Frank E. & Morehouse, Clifford P. Outline Life of Christ. (Orig.). 1947. pap. 1.95 (ISBN 0-8192-1090-0). Morehouse.

Woodson, William, ed. Jesus Christ, Son of God: Freed-Hardeman Lectures. 1973. 10.00 (ISBN 0-89225-108-5); pap. 7.00 (ISBN 0-89225-204-9). Gospel Advocate.

JESUS CHRIST–BIOGRAPHY–APOCRYPHAL AND LEGENDARY LITERATURE

Goodspeed, Edgar J. Strange New Gospels. facsimile ed. LC 70-156652. (Essay Index Reprint Ser). Repr. of 1931 ed. 12.00 (ISBN 0-8369-2364-2). Arno.

--Strange New Gospels. 1979. Repr. of 1931 ed. lib. bdg. 22.50 (ISBN 0-8495-2000-2). Arden Lib.

Goodspeed, Edgar J., ed. Apocrypha. 1959. pap. 4.95 (ISBN 0-394-70163-1, V163, Vin). Random.

Hudson, Thomson J. Physical Manifestations & Philosophy of Christ. 1978. pap. 3.50 deluxe (ISBN 0-87852-003-1). Hudson-Cohan.

Levi. The Aquarian Gospel of Jesus Christ. 1972. 7.95 (ISBN 0-87516-041-7); pap. 3.50 (ISBN 0-87516-168-5). De Vorss.

Life of Christ: A Stanzaic Life of Christ Compiled from Higden's Polychronicon & the Legenda Aurea. (EETS, OS Ser.: No. 166). Repr. of 1926 ed. 22.00 (ISBN 0-527-00163-5). Kraus Repr.

JESUS CHRIST–BIOGRAPHY–HISTORY AND CRITICISM

Bouyer, Louis. The Eternal Son. Inkel, Simone, Sr. & Laughlin, John F., trs. from Fr. LC 77-92090. 431p. 1980. pap. 6.95 (ISBN 0-87973-621-6, 621). Our Sunday Visitor.

Ferguson, John. Jesus in the Tide of Time: An Historical Study. 224p. 1980. 35.00 (ISBN 0-7100-0561-X). Routledge & Kegan.

Herald. Shining Stranger. 3.95 (ISBN 0-916438-29-5). Univ of Trees.

Maccoby, Hyam. Revolution in Judaea: Jesus & the Jewish Resistance. LC 80-16752. 256p. Date not set. pap. 4.95 (ISBN 0-8008-6783-1). Taplinger.

Schillebeeckx, Edward. Interim Report on the Books Jesus & Christ. 160p. 1980. 12.95 (ISBN 0-8245-0029-6). Crossroad NY.

Schweitzer, Albert. Quest of the Historical Jesus. 1968. pap. 6.95 (ISBN 0-02-089240-3). Macmillan.

Smith, Morton. Jesus the Magician. 2nd ed. LC 76-9986. 224p. 1982. pap. 8.95 (ISBN 0-06-067413-X, HarpR). Har-Row.

Steeves, Paul. Getting to Know Jesus. LC 67-28019. Orig. Title: Character & Work of Jesus Christ. pap. 2.25 (ISBN 0-87784-663-4). Inter-Varsity.

Vermes, Geza. Jesus the Jew: A Historian's Reading of the Gospels. LC 80-2381. 288p. 1981. pap. 6.95 (ISBN 0-8006-1443-7, 1-1443). Fortress.

Wise, Melvin J. Survey of the Life of Christ, 2 vols. Date not set. 1.95 ea.; Vol. 1. (ISBN 0-89315-288-9); Vol. 2. (ISBN 0-89315-289-7). Lambert Bk.

JESUS CHRIST–BIOGRAPHY–JUVENILE LITERATURE

see also Jesus Christ–Nativity–Juvenile Literature; Jesus Christ–Parables–Juvenile Literature; Jesus Christ–Resurrection–Juvenile Literature

Berg, Jean H. The Story of Jesus. 32p. (Span.). (gr. k-2). pap. 2.50g (ISBN 0-87510-112-7). Chr Science.

--The Story of Jesus. (Illus.). 32p. (Ger.). (gr. k-2). 1977. pap. 2.75g (ISBN 0-87510-111-9). Chr Science.

Brittain, Grady B. Platty: The Child in Us. (Illus.). 53p. (Orig.). (ps-8). 1981. pap. 1.95 (ISBN 0-86663-761-3). Ide Hse.

Curley, Maureen. Jesus of Nazareth. (Children of the Kingdom Activities Ser.). (gr. 5-10). 1977. 8.95 (ISBN 0-686-13695-0). Pflaum Pr.

Dotts, Maryann J. When Jesus Was Born. LC 79-3958. (Illus.). (ps-3). 1979. 5.95 (ISBN 0-687-45020-9). Abingdon.

Dyer, Heather. Stories Jesus Told. Incl. The Good Samaritan (ISBN 0-89191-286-X); The Good Shepherd (ISBN 0-89191-283-5); The Great Feast (ISBN 0-89191-284-3); The House Built on Sand (ISBN 0-89191-288-6); The Prodigal Son (ISBN 0-89191-285-1); The Rich Man (ISBN 0-89191-287-8). (Illus.). (gr. 1-4). 1980. Repr. 2.50 ea. Cook.

Edwards, David L. Today's Story of Jesus. LC 76-42223. (Illus.). (gr. 4 up). 1976. 7.95 (ISBN 0-529-05331-4, A1152). Collins Pubs.

Egermeier, Elsie E. Egermeier's Picture-Story Life of Jesus. (Illus.). (gr. k-6). 1969. 6.95 (ISBN 0-87162-008-1, D2015). Warner Pr.

Foster, Dorothy F. The Life of Christ Visualized. LC 77-75501. (Illus.). (gr. 3-7). 1977. pap. 5.95 (ISBN 0-87239-155-8, 3005). Standard Pub.

Goddard, Carrie L. Jesus. LC 78-51992. (Illus.). (gr. k-3). 1978. 5.95 (ISBN 0-687-19909-3). Abingdon.

Hayes, Wanda. Jesus Makes Me Happy. (A Happy Day Book). (Illus.). 24p. (gr. k-3). 1979. 0.98 (ISBN 0-686-76812-4, 3620). Standard Pub.

Hill, Dave. Most Wonderful King. (Arch Bks: Set 5). (Illus.). (gr. 3-4). 1968. laminated bdg. 0.79 (ISBN 0-570-06032-X, 59-1145). Concordia.

Hilliard, Dick & Valenti-Hilliard, Beverly. Happenings. (Center Celebration Ser.). (Illus.). 60p. 1981. pap. text ed. 3.95 (ISBN 0-89390-033-8). Resource Pubns.

Jesus & His Friends. (Children of the Kingdom Activities Ser.). (gr. k-4). 1974. 7.95 (ISBN 0-686-13683-7). Pflaum Pr.

Jones, Mary A. Favorite Stories of Jesus. (Rand McNally "Favorite" Ser.). (Illus.). 112p. (ps-2). 1981. 6.95 (ISBN 0-528-82313-2). Rand.

Lorenz, Ed B. Jesus: A Biography. (Illus.). (gr. 3-7). 1977. 4.95 (ISBN 0-89328-011-9). Lorenz Pr.

Mann, C. Stephen. Man for All Time. LC 75-161567. (gr. 8 up). 1971. pap. 2.50 (ISBN 0-8192-1127-3). Morehouse.

Moncure, Jane B. The Gift of Christmas. LC 79-10279. (Bible Story Books). (Illus.). (ps-3). 1979. PLB 5.50 (ISBN 0-89565-083-5). Childs World.

Otting, Rae. When Jesus Was a Lad. (Illus.). (gr. 1-2). 1978. pap. 1.25 (ISBN 0-89508-055-9). Rainbow Bks.

Petersham, Maud & Petersham, Miska. The Christ Child. (Illus.). 64p. (gr. 3-4). 1980. pap. 3.95 (ISBN 0-385-15841-6, Zephyr). Doubleday.

--Story of Jesus. rev. ed. (gr. 2-4). 1967. 6.95g (ISBN 0-02-773850-7). Macmillan.

Raemers, Sidney A. A Teen-Ager's Life of Christ. LC 64-21286. 4.95 (ISBN 0-686-65149-9). Helios.

--Two Books for Teen-Agers. Incl. Christ's Own Stories for Teen-Agers. Dern, Raymond J., frwd. by. 4.50 (ISBN 0-685-22593-3); A Teen-Ager's Life of Christ. Smith, John T., frwd. by. 4.95 (ISBN 0-87037-010-3). (YA) 7.95 set (ISBN 0-685-22592-5). Helios.

Ralph, Margaret. Jesus: Historias de su Vida. LaValle, Teresa, tr. (Serie Jirafa). Orig. Title: The Life of Jesus. 1979. 3.60 (ISBN 0-311-38536-2, Edit Mundo). Casa Bautista.

Richards, Jean H. A Boy Named Jesus. LC 77-71036. (Illus.). (gr. 3-6). 1978. 3.95 (ISBN 0-8054-4415-7). Broadman.

Robertson, Jennny & Parry, Alan. Jesus in Danger. (Ladybird Bible Ser.). (Illus.). 32p. (ps-4). 1980. Repr. 1.95 (ISBN 0-310-42870-X). Zondervan.

Robertson, Jenny. Jesus, the Child. (Ladybird Bible Ser.). (Illus.). 32p. (ps-4). 1980. Repr. 1.95 (ISBN 0-310-42820-3). Zondervan.

--Jesus, the Leader. (Ladybird Bible Ser.). (Illus.). 32p. (ps-4). 1980. Repr. 1.95 (ISBN 0-310-42830-0). Zondervan.

--Jesus, the Storyteller. (Ladybird Bible Ser.). (Illus.). 32p. (ps-4). 1980. Repr. 1.95 (ISBN 0-310-42840-8). Zondervan.

--Paul Meets Jesus. (Ladybird Bible Ser.). (Illus.). 32p. (ps-4). 1980. Repr. 1.95 (ISBN 0-310-42880-7). Zondervan.

Royer, Katherine. Nursery Stories of Jesus. (Illus.). (ps). 1957. pap. 1.25 (ISBN 0-8361-1408-6). Herald Pr.

Schrage, Alice. The King Who Lives Forever. LC 81-50590. (The Life of Jesus Ser.). 128p. 1981. pap. text ed. 1.95 (ISBN 0-8307-0766-2). Regal.

Segraves, Kelly L. The Gift of Love. (Little Talker Ser.). (Illus., Orig.). Date not set. pap. 3.49 (ISBN 0-89293-095-0). Beta Bk.

Sheen, Fulton J. Jesus, Son of Mary: A Book for Children. (Illus.). 32p. 1980. 7.95 (ISBN 0-8164-0470-4). Seabury.

Sockman, Ralph W. Easter Story for Children. (Illus.). (gr. 2-5). 1966. 6.95 (ISBN 0-687-11507-8). Abingdon.

Stevens, Clifford. Man of Galilee. LC 79-88086. (gr. 6-10). 1979. pap. 2.50 (ISBN 0-87973-302-0). Our Sunday Visitor.

Stevenson, J. Sinclair. The Friend of Little Children: Story of Our Lord's Life Told for Children. 1978. Repr. lib. bdg. 25.00 (ISBN 0-8495-4876-4). Arden Lib.

Van Vechten, Schuyler. The Bethlehem Star: Children's Newspaper Reports of the Life of Jesus. (gr. 4 up). 1972. 4.95 (ISBN 0-8027-6097-X). Walker & Co.

JESUS CHRIST–BIOGRAPHY–PASSION WEEK

see Jesus Christ–Passion

JESUS CHRIST–BIOGRAPHY–SERMONS

see also Jesus Christ–Passion–Sermons

Ford, W. Herschel. Simple Sermons About Jesus Christ. pap. 3.95 (ISBN 0-310-24491-9). Zondervan.

JESUS CHRIST–BIOGRAPHY–SOURCES

see also Jesus Christ–Historicity

Bruce, F. F. Jesus & Christian Origins Outside the New Testament. 1974. pap. 3.95 (ISBN 0-8028-1575-8). Eerdmans.

Burkitt, F. Crawford. The Earliest Sources for the Life of Jesus. 1977. lib. bdg. 59.95 (ISBN 0-8490-1736-X). Gordon Pr.

Downing, Francis G. Church & Jesus. (Studies in Biblical Theology, 2nd Ser.: No. 10). 1968. o. p. 9.45x (ISBN 0-8401-4060-6); pap. 6.95x (ISBN 0-8401-3060-0). Allenson-Breckinridge.

Phillips, J. B. Peter's Portrait of Jesus. 1981. 1.95 (ISBN 0-687-30850-X). Abingdon.

JESUS CHRIST–BIOGRAPHY–SOURCES, BIBLICAL

Here are entered works purporting to give a life of Jesus Christ in the words of the four Gospels, harmonized into a continuous narrative.

Beck, William F., tr. Christ of the Gospels. rev. ed. LC 59-11068. 1959. pap. 6.50 (ISBN 0-570-03724-7, 12-2626). Concordia.

Carter, John F. Layman's Harmony of the Gospel. 1961. 8.50 (ISBN 0-8054-1326-X). Broadman.

Dell Isola, Frank. The Good News About Jesus. LC 75-4579. 336p. 1975. pap. 3.95 (ISBN 0-87981-043-2). Holman.

Hodgkin, A. Christ in All the Scriptures. (Direction Bks). 264p. 1976. pap. 2.45 (ISBN 0-8010-4158-9). Baker Bk.

Markve, Arthur. The Witnesses. Orig. Title: A New Harmony of the Gospels. 416p. 1957. kivar 5.95 (ISBN 0-87123-393-2, 210393). Bethany Hse.

Reumann, John. Jesus in the Church's Gospels: Modern Scholarship & the Earliest Sources. LC 68-10983. 564p. 1973. pap. 6.95 (ISBN 0-8006-1091-1, 1-1091). Fortress.

Schaller, John. Biblical Christology. 1981. 10.95 (ISBN 0-8100-0126-8). Northwest Pub.

Shank, Robert, tr. Jesus, His Story: The Four Gospels As One Narrative in Language for Today. LC 62-17864. (Illus.). 256p. 1962. 6.95 (ISBN 0-911620-00-1). Westcott.

Taylor, Kenneth N., ed. Who Is This Man Jesus? Orig. Title: Man Jesus. pap. 1.95 (ISBN 0-8423-4001-7). Tyndale.

What the Gospels Say About Jesus. LC 78-53636. (Journeys Ser). 1978. pap. text ed. 4.50x (ISBN 0-88489-103-8); tchrs' guide 5.00x (ISBN 0-88489-105-4). St Marys.

JESUS CHRIST–BIOGRAPHY–STUDY

Colina, Tessa & Westers, Jacqueline, eds. Jesus & Me Teacher: Primary Study in the Life of Christ. 1978. pap. 6.95 (ISBN 0-87239-165-5, 3243). Standard Pub.

Collins, Stanley N. Man's Only Hope: A Study of the Life & Ministry of Jesus Christ. 1978. 6.00 (ISBN 0-682-49175-6). Exposition.

Elwood, Douglas J. & Magdamo, Patricia L. Christ in the Philippine Context. 1971. wrps. 8.00 (ISBN 0-686-18694-X). Cellar.

Esse, John. The Story of Jesus: An Interpretation. (Illus.). 96p. (Orig.). 1980. pap. 4.95 (ISBN 0-686-29041-0). Pundarika.

Glickman, S. Craig. Knowing Christ. 200p. 1980. pap. 4.95 (ISBN 0-8024-3502-5). Moody.

Hayes, Bernard. To Live As Jesus Did. 128p. (Orig.). 1981. pap. 2.50 (ISBN 0-914544-36-5). Living Flame Pr.

Inter-Varsity Christian Fellowship. Discussions on the Life of Jesus Christ. pap. 2.25 (ISBN 0-87784-402-X). Inter-Varsity.

Owens, Clifford P. A Story of Jesus. 64p. (Orig.). 1963. pap. 2.50 (ISBN 0-87604-022-9). ARE Pr.

Stalker, James M. Life of Jesus Christ. 7.95 (ISBN 0-8007-0177-1). Revell.

Wilkerson, David. Jesucristo, Roca Firme. (Spanish Bks.). (Span.). 1978. 1.60 (ISBN 0-8297-0577-5). Life Pubs Intl.

--Jesus Cristo, a Rocha Firme. (Portuguese Bks.). 1979. 1.40 (ISBN 0-8297-0669-0). Life Pubs Intl.

Wilson, Seth. Learning from Jesus. Gardener, Lynn, ed. LC 77-155407. (The Bible Study Textbook Ser.). (Illus.). 1977. 15.00 (ISBN 0-89900-056-8). College Pr Pub.

JESUS CHRIST–BIRTH

see Jesus Christ–Nativity; Virgin Birth

JESUS CHRIST–CHARACTER

Barton, Bruce. Man Nobody Knows. 1925. pap. 4.95 (ISBN 0-672-50743-9). Bobbs.

Bell, D. Rayford. The Philosophy of Christ. LC 80-67408. 104p. 1980. 6.95 (ISBN 0-9604820-0-8); pap. 4.95 (ISBN 0-9604820-1-6). D R Bell.

Glover, T. R. The Jesus of History. LC 78-25986. 15.00 (ISBN 0-8414-4488-9). Folcroft.

Griffith, Leonard. We Have This Ministry. LC 73-84580. 1977. pap. 3.50 (ISBN 0-8499-2816-8, 2816-8). Word Bks.

Hamilton, Edith. Witness to the Truth: Christ & His Interpreters. rev. ed. 1962. pap. 4.95 (ISBN 0-393-00113-X, Norton Lib). Norton.

Hardy, Edward R. Christology of the Later Fathers. (Library of Christian Classics). 1977. pap. 8.95 (ISBN 0-664-24152-2). Westminster.

Kappen, Sebastian. Jesus & Freedom. LC 76-25927. 1977. 8.95x (ISBN 0-88344-232-9); pap. 3.95x (ISBN 0-88344-233-7). Orbis Bks.

McCaughney, J. D. Diversity & Unity in the New Testament Picture of Christ. (Lectures in Biblical Studies: No. Iii). 1969. pap. 2.00x (ISBN 0-85564-016-2, Pub. by U of W Austral Pr). Intl Schol Bk Serv.

Manson, William. Jesus & the Christian. 1967. 7.50 (ISBN 0-227-67723-4). Attic Pr.

Russell, Chester. Was Jesus a Pacifist. LC 72-145987. 1971. pap. 2.95 (ISBN 0-8054-5511-6). Broadman.

Schuller, Robert H. The Greatest Possibility Thinker That Ever Lived. 1978. 5.95 (ISBN 0-8007-0580-7). Revell.

Simmons, Billy E. The Incomparable Christ. LC 79-52029. 1980. pap. 2.95 (ISBN 0-8054-5171-4). Broadman.

Smail, Thomas A. The Forgotten Father. 1981. pap. 5.95 (ISBN 0-8028-1879-X). Eerdmans.

Ten Boom, Corrie. He Sets the Captive Free. (Jesus Is Victor Ser.). 1978. 6.95 (ISBN 0-8007-0929-2). Revell.

Thomas A Kempis. The Imitation of Christ. 1976. 7.95 (ISBN 0-385-12313-2). Doubleday.

Trueblood, Elton. The Humor of Christ. LC 75-12280. 128p. 1975. pap. 4.95 (ISBN 0-06-068631-6, RD 298, HarpR). Har-Row.

Wahlberg, Rachel C. Jesus According to a Woman. LC 74-27461. 112p. 1975. pap. 2.45 (ISBN 0-8091-1861-0). Paulist Pr.

Williams, Morris. La Justicia De Dios. (Spanish Bks.). (Span.). 1977. 2.50 (ISBN 0-8297-0759-X). Life Pubs Intl.

--Publiez Sa Justice. (French Bks.). (Fr.). 1979. 2.50 (ISBN 0-8297-0839-1). Life Pubs Intl.

JESUS CHRIST–CHILDHOOD

Bangham, Mary D. When Jesus Was Four - or Maybe Five. (Illus., Orig.). (ps). 1968. pap. 2.50 (ISBN 0-8066-0824-2, 10-7058). Augsburg.

Cammaerts, Emile. The Childhood of Christ: As Seen by the Primitive Masters. 1978. Repr. of 1922 ed. lib. bdg. 20.00 (ISBN 0-8495-0766-9). Arden Lib.

Gerlinger, Lorena. Baby Jesus. (Illus.). 12p. 1972. 4.95 (ISBN 0-686-11961-4). L Gerlinger.

Lorber, Jakob. The Three Days Scene at the Temple in Jerusalem. 2nd ed. Von Koerber, Nordewin, tr. from Ger. Date not set. pap. 4.95 (ISBN 0-934616-10-8). Valkyrie Pr.

Otting, Rae. When Jesus Was a Lad. (Illus.). (gr. 1-2). 1978. pap. 1.25 (ISBN 0-89508-055-9). Rainbow Bks.

Petersham, Maud & Petersham, Miska. Christ Child. (gr. 4 up). 1931. 9.95a (ISBN 0-385-07260-0); PLB (ISBN 0-385-07319-4). Doubleday.

JESUS CHRIST–CHRONOLOGY

Hoehner, Harold W. Chronological Aspects of the Life of Christ. 1976. pap. text ed. 3.95 (ISBN 0-310-26211-9). Zondervan.

Jaubert, Annie. Date of the Last Supper. LC 65-17975. 1965. 3.50 (ISBN 0-8189-0036-9). Alba.

Lefgren, John C. April Sixth. LC 80-11199. 71p. 1980. 5.95 (ISBN 0-87747-810-4). Deseret Bk.

Ogg, George. Chronology of the Public Ministry of Jesus. 1980. lib. bdg. 75.00 (ISBN 0-8490-3142-7). Gordon Pr.

JESUS CHRIST–CRUCIFIXION

see also Holy Cross

Adams, Thomas. A Crucifix: A Message on Christ's Sufferings. pap. 0.75 (ISBN 0-685-88372-8). Reiner.

Barbet, Pierre, M.D. Doctor at Calvary. pap. 2.95 (ISBN 0-385-06687-2, D155, Im). Doubleday.

Baxter, Sidlow J. The Master Theme of the Bible. 1975. 5.95 (ISBN 0-8423-4185-4). Tyndale.

Berna, Kurt. Christ Did Not Perish on the Cross: Christ's Body Buried Alive. 1975. 14.50 (ISBN 0-682-48139-4). Exposition.

Bishop, Jim. The Day Christ Died. LC 57-6125. 1978. pap. 2.95 (ISBN 0-06-060786-6, HJ 38, HarpR). Har-Row.

Chappell, Clovis G. Faces About the Cross. (Glovis Chappell Library). pap. 3.95 (ISBN 0-8010-2364-5). Baker Bk.

Cheatham, Dan. That You Might Have Life. 1979. pap. 3.45 (ISBN 0-89536-355-0). CSS Pub.

Cohn, H. The Trial & Death of Jesus. pap. 9.95x (ISBN 0-87068-432-9). Ktav.

Coleman, Robert E. Written in Blood. LC 77-172686. 128p. 1972. pap. 1.95 (ISBN 0-8007-0489-4). Revell.

Coleman, William & Coleman, Patricia. Jesus: His Parables, Death & Resurrection. rev. ed. (Mine Is the Morning Ser.). 160p. (gr. 9-12). 1978. tchrs. manual & duplicator masters 16.95 (ISBN 0-89622-072-9). Twenty-Third.

Coltharp, Bruce R. When They Crucified Our Lord. new ed. LC 74-81762. 80p. 1975. pap. 1.95 (ISBN 0-8054-1929-2, 4219-29). Broadman.

Curtis, Norman E. The Centurion. 1980. 5.70 (ISBN 0-310-22941-3). Zondervan.

Dahl, Nils A. The Crucified Messiah. LC 74-14189. 192p. (Orig.). 1975. pap. 3.95 (ISBN 0-8066-1469-2, 10-1775). Augsburg.

Deedat, A. Was Jesus Crucified. pap. 1.50 (ISBN 0-686-63916-2). Kazi Pubns.

Denny, James. Death of Christ. 1982. lib. bdg. 12.50 (ISBN 0-86524-090-6). Klock & Klock.

Dinsmore, M. H. What Really Happened When Christ Died. LC 79-52539. 1979. pap. 3.95 (ISBN 0-89636-025-3). Accent Bks.

Evans, W. Glynn, ed. Christ Is Victor. LC 77-79774. 1977. pap. 3.95 (ISBN 0-8170-0756-3). Judson.

Fronterhouse, Bob D. Crucifier. 1971. pap. 1.35 (ISBN 0-89536-028-4). CSS Pub.

Goodier, A. Passion & Death of Our Lord Jesus Christ. 1978. 7.50 (ISBN 0-8198-0544-0); pap. 5.95 (ISBN 0-8198-0545-9). Dghtrs St Paul.

Guinness, H. The Man They Crucified. pap. 0.50 (ISBN 0-87784-112-8). Inter-Varsity.

Hanneman-Dijkstra, Maria. The Plot. 1978. 5.50 (ISBN 0-533-03176-1). Vantage.

Harvey, James M., ed. A Letter: The Crucifixion by an Eye Witness. 7th ed. LC 70-186124. (Supplemental Harmonic Ser.: Vol. 4). 107p. 1972. pap. 3.95 (ISBN 0-686-01242-9). Publishers.

Hengel, Martin. Crucifixion: In the Ancient World & the Folly of the Message of the Cross. Bowden, John, tr. from Ger. LC 77-78629. 118p. 1977. pap. 4.50 (ISBN 0-8006-1268-X, 1-1268). Fortress.

Henkes, Robert. The Crucifixion in American Painting. 1978. lib. bdg. 79.95 (ISBN 0-8490-1370-4). Gordon Pr.

Hirsch, David E. Rabbi Emil G. Hirsch: The Reform Advocate. LC 68-24717. 1968. pap. 3.00x (ISBN 0-87655-502-4). Whitehall Co.

Humphreys, Fisher. The Death of Christ. LC 77-90213. 1978. 6.95 (ISBN 0-8054-1617-X). Broadman.

Jesus' Vigil of the Hour "Watch with Me". 1965. 1.95 (ISBN 0-685-79133-5). Summit Univ.

Lightner, Robert P. The Death Christ Died. LC 67-30992. 1975. pap. 3.25 (ISBN 0-87227-012-2). Reg Baptist.

Lindsay, Gordon. Death & Resurrection of Christ. (Span.). 0.95 (ISBN 0-89985-983-6). Christ Nations.

Ludwig, Charles. At the Cross. 1975. pap. 1.25 (ISBN 0-515-03578-5). Jove Pubns.

McAllister, Dawson. A Walk with Christ to the Cross. (Discussion Manual Ser.). 150p. 1981. pap. 7.95 (ISBN 0-8024-9193-6). Moody.

McIntosk & Twyman, trs. The Archko Volume. LC 74-33199. 248p. 1975. 5.95 (ISBN 0-87983-067-0). Keats.

Manson, T. W. Servant-Messiah: A Study of the Public Ministry of Jesus. (Twin Brook Ser). 1977. pap. 3.45 (ISBN 0-8010-6012-5). Baker Bk.
Moltmann, Jurgen. The Crucified God. LC 73-18694. 352p. 1974. 15.95 (ISBN 0-06-065901-7, HarpR). Har-Row.
Moore, Sebastian. The Fire & the Rose Are One. 176p. 1980. 9.95 (ISBN 0-8164-0468-2). Seabury.
Murphy, Richard T. Days of Glory: The Passion, Death, & Resurrection of Jesus Christ. (Orig.). 1980. pap. 4.95 (ISBN 0-89283-082-4). Servant.
Murray, Andrew. The Blood of the Cross. 140p. 1981. pap. 2.50 (ISBN 0-88368-103-X). Whitaker Hse.
Nelson, Carl. Just the Greatest. LC 72-184953. (Illus.). 96p. (Orig.). 1972. pap. 1.25 (ISBN 0-87784-543-3). Inter-Varsity.
Nicholson, William R. Six Miracles of Calvary. 1928. pap. 1.25 (ISBN 0-8024-7834-4). Moody.
Peusch, Leonard. The Three Crosses. 1978. 0.65 (ISBN 0-8199-0723-5). Franciscan Herald.
Rest, Friedrich O. The Cross in Hymns. 1969. bds. 4.95 (ISBN 0-8170-0419-X). Judson.
Schonfield, Hugh. After the Cross. LC 80-27856. 128p. 1981. 7.95 (ISBN 0-498-02549-7). A S Barnes.
Spurgeon, Charles H. Passion & Death of Our Lord. (Treasury of Spurgeon & Life & Work of Our Lord). 13.95 (ISBN 0-8010-8155-6). Baker Bk.
Stewart, John J. The Eternal Gift: The Story of the Crucifixion & Resurrection of Christ. LC 78-52117. 1978. 5.50 (ISBN 0-88290-096-X). Horizon Utah.
Summers, Georgianna. Who Crucifies Him? 1979. pap. 2.35 (ISBN 0-89536-329-1). CSS Pub.
Tozer, A. W. Who Put Jesus on the Cross. 1976. pap. 1.95 (ISBN 0-87509-212-8). Chr Pubns.
Urbano, Paul D. The Marks of the Nails. LC 73-90039. (Illus.). 120p. (Orig.). 1973. pap. 3.50 (ISBN 0-913514-04-7). Am Natl Pub.
White, Reginald E. Beneath the Cross of Jesus. (Pivot Family Reader Ser). 236p. 1975. pap. 2.25 (ISBN 0-87983-109-X). Keats.
Williams, Robert. The Veil. 20p. 1976. pap. 2.10 (ISBN 0-89536-247-3). CSS Pub.
Williams, Sam K. Jesus' Death As Saving Event the Background & Origin of a Concept. LC 75-28341. (Harvard Dissertations in Religion). 1975. pap. 9.00 (ISBN 0-89130-029-5, 020102). Scholars Pr Ca.
Youngdahl, Stephen & Prange, Anton. The King Lives. 12p. 1976. pap. 2.05 (ISBN 0-89536-117-5). CSS Pub.
Zeitlin, Solomon. Who Crucified Jesus? 1976. pap. 4.95 (ISBN 0-8197-0013-4). Bloch.

JESUS CHRIST-CRUCIFIXION-SONGS AND MUSIC

see Passion-Music

JESUS CHRIST-DEVOTIONAL LITERATURE

see also Jesus Christ-Passion-Devotional Literature

Adams, Robert E. Encuentro Con Jesus. (Illus.). Date not set. pap. 1.30 (ISBN 0-311-04657-6). Casa Bautista.
A'Kempis, Thomas. Meditations on Life of Christ. (Summit Bks). 1978. pap. 3.95 (ISBN 0-8010-0123-4). Baker Bk.
Alexander, John W., ed. Believing & Obeying Jesus Christ. 1980. pap. 4.95 (ISBN 0-87784-728-2). Inter-Varsity.
Armstrong, Garner T. The Real Jesus. 1978. pap. 2.25 (ISBN 0-380-40055-3, 40055). Avon.
Berry, Nancee. At Home with Jesus. (Come Unto Me Library). 1979. pap. 1.25 (ISBN 0-8127-0236-0). Review & Herald.
--When Jesus Comes. (Come Unto Me Library). 1979. pap. 1.25 (ISBN 0-8127-0210-7). Review & Herald.
Bjorge, James R. Here Comes Jesus. 100p. (Orig.). 1974. pap. 4.50 (ISBN 0-89536-091-8). CSS Pub.
Boring, Holland, Sr. & Cox, Bill. Gems for His Crown. 1977. pap. 1.65 (ISBN 0-686-21478-1). Firm Foun Pub.
Burt, Donald X. Colors of My Days. 175p. (Orig.). 1980. pap. 3.95 (ISBN 0-8146-1198-2). Liturgical Pr.
The Call of Jesus. (Aglow Bible Study: Bk. 9). 64p. 1976. 1.95 (ISBN 0-930756-19-3, 4220-9). Women's Aglow.
Cannon, William R. A Disciple's Profile of Jesus. LC 75-2956. 1975. 1.95x (ISBN 0-8358-0322-8). Upper Room.
Carter, Edward. The Jesus Experience. LC 76-6701. (Illus.). 1976. pap. 1.75 (ISBN 0-8189-1131-X, Pub. by Alba Bks). Alba.
Cavert, Walter D. With Jesus on the Scout Trail. (Orig.). 1970. pap. 1.50 (ISBN 0-687-45849-8). Abingdon.
Chambers, Oswald. Conformed to His Image. 1971. pap. 1.75 (ISBN 0-87508-133-9). Chr Lit.
Coleman, Bill & Coleman, Patty. Together with Jesus: Family Book. 80p. 1979. pap. 2.95 (ISBN 0-89622-107-5). Twenty-Third.
--Together with Jesus: Kit. (Total Parish Family Program Ser.). 1979. pap. 49.50 (ISBN 0-89622-099-0). Twenty-Third.
Coleman, Robert E. Written in Blood. LC 77-172686. 128p. 1972. pap. 1.95 (ISBN 0-8007-0489-4). Revell.
Coleman, William V. & Coleman, Patricia R. Jesus, Our Brother. (Daybreak Ser.). (Illus.). 1977. tchrs ed. 9.95 (ISBN 0-89622-044-3). Twenty-Third.
Conatser, Howard. I've Got to Find My Father. Martin, Sandra, ed. (Orig.). 1976. pap. 1.50 (ISBN 0-930718-35-6). Harvest Pr Texas.
Criswell, W. A. What a Savior! LC 77-82399. 1978. 6.95 (ISBN 0-8054-5155-2). Broadman.
Cushing, Richard J. Eternal Thoughts from Christ the Teacher, 2 Vols. 1962. 3.50 ea. Vol. 1 (ISBN 0-8198-0606-4). Vol. 2 (ISBN 0-8198-0607-2). Dghtrs St Paul.
Daughters of St. Paul. Alive in the Spirit. rev. ed. (Way, Truth & Life Ser.). (Illus.). (gr. 5). 1974. text ed. 2.25 (ISBN 0-8198-0282-4); tchr's manual 5.25 (ISBN 0-8198-0283-2); activity bk. 1.25 (ISBN 0-8198-0284-0); parents' guide 0.95 (ISBN 0-8198-0285-9). Dghtrs St Paul.
--Christ Lives in Me. rev. ed. (Way, Truth & Life Ser.). (Illus.). (gr. 2). 1973. text ed. 1.50 (ISBN 0-8198-0308-1); teachers manual 5.00 (ISBN 0-8198-0309-X); activity bk. 0.75 (ISBN 0-8198-0310-3); parent guide 0.95 (ISBN 0-8198-0311-1). Dghtrs St Paul.
--Christ: Our Way to the Father. rev. ed. (Way, Truth & Life Ser.). (Illus.). (gr. 3). 1973. text ed. 1.50 (ISBN 0-8198-0300-6); tchrs. manual 5.00 (ISBN 0-8198-0301-4); activity bk. 0.75 (ISBN 0-8198-0302-2); parent guide 0.95 (ISBN 0-8198-0303-0). Dghtrs St Paul.
--Christ's Law of Love. rev. ed. (Way, Truth & Life Ser.). (Illus.). (gr. 4). 1973. text ed. 2.00 (ISBN 0-8198-0296-4); tchrs manual 5.00 (ISBN 0-8198-0297-2); activity bk. 1.25 (ISBN 0-8198-0298-0); parent guide 0.95 (ISBN 0-8198-0299-9). Dghtrs St Paul.
--Drawing Near Him with Confidence. 1976. 3.95 (ISBN 0-8198-0403-7); pap. 2.95 (ISBN 0-8198-0404-5). Dghtrs St Paul.
--God the Father Sent His Son. rev. ed. (Way, Truth & Life Ser.). (Illus.). (gr. 1). 1973. text ed. 1.50 (ISBN 0-8198-0286-7); tchrs. manual 5.00 (ISBN 0-8198-0287-5); activity bk. 0.75 (ISBN 0-8198-0288-3); parent guide 0.95 (ISBN 0-8198-0289-1). Dghtrs St Paul.
--His Saving Love. rev. ed. (Way, Truth & Life Ser.). (Illus.). (gr. 7). 1976. text ed. 2.25 (ISBN 0-8198-0340-5); tchrs. manual 6.50 (ISBN 0-8198-0341-3); activity bk. 1.30 (ISBN 0-8198-0342-1); parent guide 1.25 (ISBN 0-8198-0343-X). Dghtrs St Paul.
--Live the Mass. rev. ed. (Way, Truth & Life Ser.). (Illus.). (gr. 6). text ed. 1.75 (ISBN 0-8198-0272-7); tchrs. manual 3.95 (ISBN 0-8198-0273-5); activity bk. 0.85 (ISBN 0-8198-0274-3); parent guide 0.69 (ISBN 0-8198-0275-1). Dghtrs St Paul.
--Live the Truth-Give the Truth. rev. ed. (Way, Truth & Life Ser.). (Illus.). (gr. 8). 1976. text ed. 2.25 (ISBN 0-8198-0304-9); tchr's manual 6.50 (ISBN 0-8198-0305-7); activity bk. 1.30 (ISBN 0-8198-0306-5); parent guide 1.25 (ISBN 0-8198-0307-3). Dghtrs St Paul.
Daughters St. Paul. Preparing to Recieve Jesus Christ. (Way, Truth & Life Ser.). 1978. 1.00 (ISBN 0-8198-0548-3); tchr's manual 3.00 (ISBN 0-8198-0549-1); activity book 0.75 (ISBN 0-8198-0550-5). Dghtrs St Paul.
DeGiacomo, James, ed. Jesus Who? (Conscience & Concern Ser.: No. 5). 1973. text ed. 1.95 (ISBN 0-03-011771-2, 207); tchr's. guide 0.95 (ISBN 0-03-005941-0, 208). Winston Pr.
De Waters, Lillian. The Christ Within. 5.95 (ISBN 0-686-05717-1). L De Waters.
Di Gangi, Mariano. Spirit of Christ. LC 75-27626. 128p. 1975. 4.95 (ISBN 0-8010-2849-3). Baker Bk.
Edwards, David. Jesus for Modern Man. (Fount Religious Paperbacks Ser). 1976. pap. 1.95 (ISBN 0-00-624000-3, FA4000). Collins Pubs.
Esses, Michael. Jesus in Genesis. LC 74-82565. 1975. pap. 4.95 (ISBN 0-88270-100-2). Logos.
Exley, Richrd D. The Painted Parable. 1978. 5.95 (ISBN 0-533-02995-3). Vantage.
Flack, E. E. Witness of Jesus. 204p. 1973. pap. 2.50 (ISBN 0-89536-255-4). CSS Pub.
Goodboy, Eadie, ed. Jesus Is Lord. 130p. 1977. 3.50 (ISBN 0-930756-27-4, 4230-G01). Women's Aglow.
Goodier, A. Public Life of Our Lord Jesus Christ, 2 vols. 1978. Set. 15.95 (ISBN 0-8198-0551-3); Set. pap. 13.95 (ISBN 0-8198-0552-1). Dghtrs St Paul.
Gratian Of Paris. I Know Christ. (Spirit & Life Ser). 1957. 2.00 (ISBN 0-686-11569-4). Franciscan Inst.
Guyon, Jeanne M. Experiencing the Depths of Jesus Christ. 3rd ed. Edwards, Gene, ed. 1975. pap. 3.95 (ISBN 0-940232-00-6). Christian Bks.
Hayes, Zachary. To Whom Shall We Go: Christ & the Mystery of Man. (Synthesis Ser). 96p. 1975. 0.65 (ISBN 0-8199-0702-2). Franciscan Herald.
Herz, Stephanie M. My Words Are Spirit & Life: Meeting Christ Through Daily Meditation. LC 78-4790. 1979. pap. 3.95 (ISBN 0-385-14258-7, Im). Doubleday.
In Jesus Name We Pray. 1975. 1.25 (ISBN 0-915952-01-7). Lord's Line.
Jackson, Madeline & Jenkins, Jerry. Running for Jesus. LC 76-56483. 176p. 1977. 6.95 (ISBN 0-87680-460-1, 80460). Word Bks.
Jahnsmann, Alan H. It's All About Jesus. LC 74-21233. 160p. (ps-7). 1975. 6.95 (ISBN 0-570-03025-0, 6-1153); pap. 4.95 (ISBN 0-570-03031-5, 6-1157). Concordia.
Jean Du Coeur De Jesus D'elbee. I Believe in Love. 1974. 6.95 (ISBN 0-8199-0545-3). Franciscan Herald.
John Of Landsburg. A Letter of Jesus Christ. LC 81-126. (The Spiritual Classics Ser.). 176p. 1981. 9.95 (ISBN 0-8245-0080-6). Crossroad NY.
Joyce, Jon L. More Conversations About Jesus. 1973. pap. 3.65 (ISBN 0-89536-152-3). CSS Pub.
Judd, Wayne. When Jesus Prayed. (Nugget Ser.). 1979. pap. 0.65 (ISBN 0-8127-0212-3). Review & Herald.
Kasemann, Ernst. The Testament of Jesus: A Study of the Gospel of John in the Light of Chapter 17. LC 78-104781. 96p. (Orig.). 1978. pap. 3.50 (ISBN 0-8006-1399-6, 1-1399). Fortress.
Kempis, Thomas A. The Imitation of Christ. 20.00 (ISBN 0-8274-2557-0). R West.
LaVerdiere, Eugene. Finding Jesus Through the Bible. (Illus.). 40p. 1977. pap. 1.50 (ISBN 0-89570-104-9). Claretian Pubns.
Lense, Esther. A Jesus Happening. 1973. pap. 2.75 (ISBN 0-89536-112-4). CSS Pub.
Lenta, Clementine. What Can I Do for Christ? 5.50 (ISBN 0-910984-17-4). Montfort Pubns.
Liguori, St. Alphonsus. Love Is Prayer - Prayer Is Love. LC 72-97592. 1973. pap. 2.50 (ISBN 0-89243-047-8, 41500). Liguori Pubns.
Lolley, W. Randall & McEachern, Alton H. Bold Preaching About Christ. LC 78-19964. 1978. 3.95 (ISBN 0-8054-1949-7). Broadman.
The Lord Loves His People. 1980. 6.00 (ISBN 0-8198-4400-4). Dghtrs St Paul.
Lovasik, Lawrence. Jesus, Joy of the Suffering. 3.00 (ISBN 0-8198-0641-2); pap. 2.00 (ISBN 0-8198-0642-0). Dghtrs St Paul.
McCauley, Michael F. The Jesus Book. (Illus.). 1978. 13.95 (ISBN 0-88347-094-2). Thomas More.
Marshall, John F. In the Shadow of His Cross. (Spirit & Life Ser). 1969. 2.00 (ISBN 0-686-11577-5). Franciscan Inst.
Martin, Paul. Good Morning, Lord: Devotions for Teens. (Good Morning Lord Ser.). 1962. 3.95 (ISBN 0-8010-5879-1). Baker Bk.
Mauldin, Kenneth L. Table Talk with Jesus. LC 78-13750. 1979. pap. 3.75 (ISBN 0-687-40820-2). Abingdon.
Mead, George R. The Hymn of Jesus. 78p. 1973. pap. 1.00 (ISBN 0-8356-0432-2, Quest). Theos Pub Hse.
Meditations on the Life & Passion of Christ. (EETS, OS Ser.: No. 158). Repr. of 1921 ed. 7.00 (ISBN 0-527-00155-4). Kraus Repr.
Meilach, Michael, ed. There Shall Be One Christ. (Spirit and Life Ser). 1968. 2.50 (ISBN 0-686-11576-7). Franciscan Inst.
Miller, J. R. Come Ye Apart. 378p. 1980. 4.95 (ISBN 0-8407-5217-2). Nelson.
Morton, H. V. In the Steps of the Master. 1935. lib. bdg. 30.00 (ISBN 0-8414-6678-5). Folcroft.
Muggeridge, Malcolm. Jesus Rediscovered. 1979. pap. 4.95 (ISBN 0-385-14654-X, Galilee). Doubleday.
Munger, R. My Heart: Christ's Home. pap. 0.50 (ISBN 0-87784-113-6). Inter-Varsity.
Murray, Donal. Jesus Is Lord: The Gift & the Task of Following Christ. 1.95 (ISBN 0-685-62270-3). M Glazier.
Mustard Seeds & Wineskins: Dramas & Meditations on Seven Parables. LC 79-176471. 1972. pap. 3.50 (ISBN 0-8066-1201-0, 10-4565); drama bklet 1.50 (ISBN 0-8066-1202-9, 10-4566). Augsburg.
Nelson, Wesley. Captivated by Christ. 1974. pap. 1.25 (ISBN 0-87508-433-8). Chr Lit.
Nouwen, Henri J. The Wounded Healer: Ministry in Contemporary Society. 1979. pap. 1.95 (ISBN 0-385-14803-8, Im). Doubleday.
Paone, Anthony J., S.J. My Life with Christ. LC 62-17359. 1962. pap. 2.95 (ISBN 0-385-03361-3, D185, Im). Doubleday.
Papadopoulos, Gerasimos. Orthodoxy, Faith & Life: Christ in the Gospels, Vol. 1. 160p. 1980. 9.50 (ISBN 0-916586-38-3); pap. 4.95 (ISBN 0-916586-37-5). Holy Cross Orthodox.
Paul The Sixth, Pope Who Is Jesus. LC 72-80446. pap. 2.25 (ISBN 0-8198-0325-1). Dghtrs St Paul.
Pennington, M. Basil. Daily We Touch Him: Practical Religious Experiences. 1979. pap. 1.95 (ISBN 0-385-14802-X, Im). Doubleday.
Poovey, W. A. Let Us Adore Him: Dramas & Meditations for Advent, Christmas, Epiphany. LC 72-78563. 128p. 1972. 3.50 (ISBN 0-8066-1229-0, 10-3820); pap. 1.50 (ISBN 0-8066-1230-4, 10-3821). Augsburg.
Powers, Isaias. Quiet Places with Jesus. 128p. 1978. pap. 3.50 (ISBN 0-89622-086-9). Twenty-Third.
Quoist, Michel. I've Met Jesus Christ. LC 73-79643. 160p. 1975. pap. 1.95 (ISBN 0-385-02802-4, Im). Doubleday.
Ragusa, Isa & Green, Rosalie B., eds. Meditations on the Life of Christ: An Illustrated Manuscript of the Fourteenth Century. (Monographs in Art & Archeology: No. 35). (Illus.). 501p. 1975. 32.50x (ISBN 0-691-03829-5); pap. 11.50 (ISBN 0-691-10031-4). Princeton U Pr.
Ramsey, Michael. Jesus & the Living Past. 1980. 8.95 (ISBN 0-19-213963-0). Oxford U Pr.
Reidt, Wilford H. Jesus: God's Way of Healing & Power to Promote Health. 1977. 6.50 (ISBN 0-533-02669-5). Vantage.
Rosage, David E. Linger with Me: Moments Aside with Jesus. (Orig.). 1979. 2.95 (ISBN 0-914544-24-1). Living Flame Pr.
Sanders, J. Oswald. Consider Him. 2nd ed. 1979. pap. write for info. (ISBN 0-85363-123-9). OMF Bks.
Scaer, David P. What Do You Think of Jesus? LC 72-97341. 144p. 1973. pap. 3.75 (ISBN 0-570-03153-2, 12-2538). Concordia.
Schlink, Basilea. Behold His Love. 1973. pap. 1.95 (ISBN 0-87123-039-9). Bethany Hse.
--The Grace of Love. 1977. gift edition 0.50 (ISBN 3-872-09662-1). Evang Sisterhood Mary.
--Those Who Love Him. 96p. 1981. pap. 2.50 (ISBN 0-87123-609-5, 210609). Bethany Hse.
Schroeder, Ruth. Freedom Through Christ. 1979. pap. 3.95 (ISBN 0-8170-0828-4). Judson.
Seashore, Gladys. Let's Talk About Jesus. (Illus.). 1978. pap. 1.75 (ISBN 0-911802-40-1). Free Church Pubns.
Sells, James. Partner with the Living Lord. LC 75-21628. 1975. 1.95x (ISBN 0-8358-0337-6). Upper Room.
Sheldon, Charles M. In His Steps. (Summit Bk Ser). 1978. pap. 2.95 (ISBN 0-8010-8132-7). Baker Bk.
Spurgeon, C. H. Looking Unto Jesus. 1976. pap. 0.10 (ISBN 0-686-16841-0). Pilgrim Pubns.
Stalker, James. The Example of Jesus Christ: Imago Christi. LC 80-82322. (Orig.). 1980. pap. 5.95 (ISBN 0-87983-231-2). Keats.
Steele. Jesus Exultant. pap. 2.95 (ISBN 0-686-12885-0). Schmul Pub Co.
Stewart, James S. King for Ever. 160p. 1975. 6.95 (ISBN 0-687-20883-1). Abingdon.
--Man in Christ. (James S. Stewart Library). 1975. pap. 5.95 (ISBN 0-8010-8045-2). Baker Bk.
Strauss, Lehman. Second Person. 1951. 4.75 (ISBN 0-87213-826-7). Loizeaux.
Summers, Bob. Out Back with Jesus. (Orig.). 1975. pap. 1.75 (ISBN 0-930718-29-1). Harvest Pr Texas.
Ten Boom, Corrie. He Cares, He Comforts. (Jesus Is Victor Ser.). 1977. 6.95 (ISBN 0-8007-0891-1). Revell.
Terry, Lois McBride. By His Side. 1967. gift ed. 4.95 (ISBN 0-915720-08-6); pap. 2.25 class ed. (ISBN 0-915720-37-X). Brownlow Pub Co.
Thomas A Kempis. Of the Imitation of Christ. (Pivot Family Reader Ser). 240p. 1973. pap. 1.25 (ISBN 0-87983-035-2). Keats.
--Of the Imitation of Christ. (Summit Bks). 1977. pap. 1.95 (ISBN 0-8010-0115-3). Baker Bk.
Thomas A Kempis, Saint Imitation of Christ. 1959. 2.25 (ISBN 0-685-43925-9, 80955). Glencoe.
Tollett, T. O., compiled by. We Preach Jesus. 1979. pap. 1.00 (ISBN 0-89114-063-8). Baptist Pub Hse.
Tunink, Wilfrid. Jesus Is Lord. LC 78-19317. 1979. 7.95 (ISBN 0-385-14793-7). Doubleday.
Van De Weyer, Robt. Guru Jesus. 1976. 3.50 (ISBN 0-87243-066-9). Templegate.
Von Balthasar, Hans Urs. The Heart of the World. Leiva, Erasmo, tr. from Ger. LC 79-84879. Orig. Title: Das Herz der Welt. 219p. (Orig.). 1980. pap. 5.95 (ISBN 0-89870-001-9). Ignatius Pr.
Von Trapp, Maria. When King Was Carpenter. LC 75-46021. 1976. pap. 1.95 (ISBN 0-89221-018-4). New Leaf.
Wallis, Reginald. The New Sovereignty. 1974. pap. 1.25 (ISBN 0-87123-391-6, 200391). Bethany Hse.
Weiser, Alfons. The Miracle of Jesus: Then & Now. Karris, Robert, ed. Tiede, David L., tr. (Herald Biblical Bklts.). 1972. pap. 1.25 (ISBN 0-8199-0519-4). Franciscan Herald.
White, Ellen G. Christ in His Sanctuary. LC 70-94869. (Dimension Ser.). 1969. pap. 5.95 (ISBN 0-8163-0128-X, 03254-0). Pacific Pr Pub Assn.

--Steps to Christ. LC 56-7169. 134p. 1956. 4.95 (ISBN 0-8163-0045-3, 19543-8); pap. 0.95 (ISBN 0-8163-0046-1, 19547-9). Pacific Pr Pub Assn.

Wijngaards, Johannes N. Experiencing Jesus. LC 81-52295. 176p. (Orig.). 1981. pap. 4.95 (ISBN 0-87793-235-2). Ave Maria.

Wilson, Everett L. Christ Died for Me. 164p. 1980. pap. 4.50 (ISBN 0-910452-45-8). Covenant.

Womack, David. Alive in Christ. (Radiant Life Ser.). 1975. pap. 1.95 (ISBN 0-88243-888-3, 02-0888, Radiant Books); teacher's ed 2.50 (ISBN 0-88243-162-5, 32-0162). Gospel Pub.

Yungblut, John. Rediscovering the Christ. LC 74-10810. (Orig.). 1977. 7.95 (ISBN 0-8164-1187-5). Pendle Hill.

JESUS CHRIST–DIVINITY

see also Socinianism; Trinity; Unitarianism

Anderson, Robert. The Lord from Heaven. LC 78-9533. (Sir Robert Anderson Library). 1978. pap. 2.95 (ISBN 0-8254-2127-6). Kregel.

Boom, Corrie T. Na Casa De Meu Pai. (Portuguese Bks.). 1979. 1.50 (ISBN 0-8297-0894-4). Life Pubs Intl.

Brown, Raymond E. Jesus, God & Man. LC 67-29587. (Impact Books). 1967. pap. 1.95 (ISBN 0-02-084000-4). Macmillan.

Brungardt, Helen. The Mystical Meaning of Jesus the Christ: Significant Episodes in the Life of the Master. 4.00 (ISBN 0-686-69472-4). Red Earth.

Chemnitz, Martin. Two Natures in Christ. Preus, J. A., tr. LC 74-115465. Orig. Title: De Duabus Naturis in Christo. 1970. 19.95 (ISBN 0-570-03210-5, 15-2109). Concordia.

King, Joseph H. Christ: God's Love Gift. 3.50 (ISBN 0-911866-84-1). Advocate.

Knox, John. Humanity & Divinity of Christ. (Orig.). 18.95 (ISBN 0-521-05486-9); pap. 5.50x (ISBN 0-521-09414-3). Cambridge U Pr.

Liddon, Henry P. The Divinity of Our Lord. 1978. 20.25 (ISBN 0-86524-948-2). Klock & Klock.

McIntosh, Hugh. Is Christ Infallible & the Bible True? 1981. lib. bdg. 27.00 (ISBN 0-86524-076-0). Klock & Klock.

Migne, J. P., ed. Dictionnaires des Preuves de la Divinite de Jesus Christ. (Troisieme et Derniere Encyclopedie Theologique Ser.: Vol. 37). 516p. (Fr.). Date not set. Repr. of 1858 ed. lib. bdg. 66.50x (ISBN 0-89241-316-6). Caratzas Bros.

Nee, Watchman. God's Plan & the Overcomers. Kaung, Stephen, tr. from Chinese. 1977. pap. 1.95 (ISBN 0-935008-19-5). Christian Fellow Pubs.

Santayana, George. The Idea of Christ in the Gospels: Or, God in Man, a Critical Essay. LC 75-3338. Repr. of 1946 ed. 24.50 (ISBN 0-404-59341-0). AMS Pr.

Sullivan, Peter. Christ: The Answer. (Orig.). pap. 1.95 (ISBN 0-8198-0026-0). Dghtrs St Paul.

Tiede, David L. The Charismatic Figure As Miracle Worker. LC 72-87359. (Society of Biblical Literature. Dissertations Ser.: No. 1). (Illus.). pap. 10.50 (ISBN 0-89130-158-5, 060101). Scholars Pr Ca.

Williams, J. Floyd. Christ Jesus: The God-Man. 3.95 (ISBN 0-911866-72-8). Advocate.

JESUS CHRIST–DRAMA

see also Christmas Plays; Easter–Drama

Barker, Kenneth. Seven Dramatic Moments in the Life of Christ: Plays for Church Events. LC 78-52443. 1978. pap. 5.95 (ISBN 0-8042-1432-8). John Knox.

Clark, Dorinda. Jesus Plays for Primary Grades. (Illus.). 48p. 1978. pap. 2.95 (ISBN 0-89622-084-2). Twenty-Third.

Clausen, Robert H. Gift & the Glory. (Orig.). 1966. pap. 0.75 (ISBN 0-8054-9712-9). Broadman.

Dobie, J. Frank, ed. Spur-Of-The-Cock. LC 34-1434. (Texas Folklore Society Publications: No. 11). 1965. Repr. of 1933 ed. 4.95 (ISBN 0-87074-043-1). SMU Press.

Elliott, John R., Jr. & Runnalls, Graham A., eds. The Baptism & Temptation of Christ: The First Day of a Medieval French Passion Play. LC 78-6564. 1978. 17.50x (ISBN 0-300-02199-2). Yale U Pr.

Mustard Seeds & Wineskins: Dramas & Meditations on Seven Parables. LC 79-176471. 1972. pap. 3.50 (ISBN 0-8066-1201-0, 10-4565); drama bklet 1.50 (ISBN 0-8066-1202-9, 10-4566). Augsburg.

Poovey, W. A. Banquets & Beggers: Dramas & Meditations on Six Parables. LC 74-77672. 128p. (Orig.). 1974. pap. 3.25 (ISBN 0-8066-1419-6, 10-0540); drama bklet 1.25 (ISBN 0-8066-1420-X, 10-0541). Augsburg.

Sayers, Dorothy L. The Man Born to Be King. 1970. pap. 6.95 (ISBN 0-8028-1329-1). Eerdmans.

JESUS CHRIST–ETHICS

Bundy, Walter E. The Religion of Jesus. 1929. 10.00 (ISBN 0-8414-2522-1). Folcroft.

JESUS CHRIST–EVANGELISTIC METHODS

Bright, Bill. How to Introduce Others to Christ. (Transferable Concepts Ser.). 64p. 1981. pap. 1.25 (ISBN 0-918956-93-5). Campus Crusade.

--How to Witness in the Spirit. (Transferable Concepts Ser.). 64p. 1981. pap. 1.25 (ISBN 0-918956-92-7). Campus Crusade.

JESUS CHRIST–EXALTATION

Flavel, John. Fountain of Life. (Summit Books). 1977. pap. 3.95 (ISBN 0-8010-3480-9). Baker Bk.

JESUS CHRIST–EXAMPLE

Adams, Jay E. Christ & Your Problems. 1973. pap. 0.40 (ISBN 0-87552-011-1). Presby & Reformed.

Fry, Caroline. Christ Our Example. 155p. 1976. pap. 3.95 (ISBN 0-685-53618-1). Reiner.

Hayes, Bernard. To Live As Jesus Did. 128p. (Orig.). 1981. pap. 2.50 (ISBN 0-914544-36-5). Living Flame Pr.

Hengel, Martin. The Charismatic Leader & His Followers. LC 81-9708. 124p. 1981. 10.95 (ISBN 0-8245-0137-3). Crossroad NY.

Jesus Loves Children. 1981. 6.00 (ISBN 0-8215-9889-9). Sadlier.

Kaung, Stephen. The Splendor of His Ways. Fader, Herbert L., ed. 1974. 4.70 (ISBN 0-935008-42-X); pap. 3.05 (ISBN 0-935008-43-8). Christian Fellow Pubs.

Liddon, H. P. Divinity of Our Lord. 1976. pap. 3.95 (ISBN 0-87508-320-X). Chr Lit.

McConkey, James H. The Way of Victory. 1976. pap. 1.25 (ISBN 0-8024-9232-0). Moody.

McKenna, David L. The Jesus Model. LC 77-83328. 1977. 7.95 (ISBN 0-8499-0036-0). Word Bks.

Sheldon, Charles M. History of in His Steps: "What Would Jesus Do?". commemorative ed. Ripley, John W., ed. write for info. (ISBN 0-685-61842-0). Shawnee County Hist.

Storey, William G. The Week with Christ. LC 81-67742. 112p. 1981. pap. 3.50 (ISBN 0-87793-236-0). Ave Maria.

We Follow Jesus. (gr. 3). 2.82 (ISBN 0-02-649490-6, 64949); tchr's manual 2.52 (ISBN 0-02-649500-7, 64950). Benziger Pub Co.

JESUS CHRIST–FAMILY–ART

see Jesus Christ–Art

JESUS CHRIST–FICTION

Bishop, Jim. Day Christ Died. LC 57-6125. (Illus.). 1957. 12.50 (ISBN 0-06-010345-0, HarpT). Har-Row.

--The Day Christ Died. LC 57-6125. 1978. pap. 2.95 (ISBN 0-06-060786-6, HJ 38, HarpR). Har-Row.

Dostoyevsky, Fedor. Grand Inquisitor on the Nature of Man. Garnett, Constance, tr. 1948. pap. 2.50 (ISBN 0-672-60237-7, LLA63). Bobbs.

Dostoyevsky, Fyodor. The Grand Inquisitor. LC 56-7503. (Milestones of Thought Ser.). pap. 2.45 (ISBN 0-8044-6125-2). Ungar.

Douglas, Lloyd C. Robe. 1942. 10.95 (ISBN 0-395-07635-8). HM.

Gibran, Kahlil. Jesus the Son of Man. (Illus.). 1928. 9.95 (ISBN 0-394-43124-3). Knopf.

Gompertz, Rolf. My Jewish Brother Jesus. LC 76-55591. 1977. 6.95 (ISBN 0-918248-03-5); pap. 3.95 (ISBN 0-918248-02-7). WorDoctor.

Harrell, Sara G. Semo: A Dolphin's Search for Christ. (Illus.). (gr. 5-7). 1977. 5.95 (ISBN 0-570-03458-2, 56-1292); pap. 2.50 (ISBN 0-570-03459-0, 56-1293). Concordia.

Jacobs, Joseph. Jesus As Others Saw Him: A Retrospect A.D. 54. LC 73-2211. (The Jewish People; History, Religion, Literature Ser.). Repr. of 1925 ed. 17.00 (ISBN 0-405-05275-8). Arno.

Lawrence, David H. Saint Mawr. Bd. with The Man Who Died. 1959. pap. 2.45 (ISBN 0-394-70071-6, Vin). Random.

Newcomb, Robert T. Janissa. 1943. 3.00 (ISBN 0-685-08807-3). Destiny.

O'Byrne, Cathal. From Green Hills of Galilee. facsimile ed. LC 71-167464. (Short Story Index Reprint Ser.). Repr. of 1935 ed. 12.00 (ISBN 0-8369-3990-5). Arno.

Wallace, Lew. Ben Hur. (Classics Ser). (YA) (gr. 9 up). pap. 1.95 (ISBN 0-8049-0074-4, CL-74). Airmont.

--Ben-Hur. pap. 2.25 (ISBN 0-451-07847-0, E9148, Sig). NAL.

Wildsmith, Brian. The True Cross. (Illus.). (ps-3). 1978. 7.95 (ISBN 0-19-279718-2). Oxford U Pr.

Ziolkowski, Theodore. Fictional Transfigurations of Jesus. LC 70-39794. 536p. 1972. 20.00 (ISBN 0-691-06235-8); pap. 8.95 (ISBN 0-691-01346-2). Princeton U Pr.

JESUS CHRIST–FICTION, JUVENILE

Ranger, Mary. Benjamin of Nazareth. (Starlight Ser.). (Illus.). (gr. 5-8). 1981. pap. 2.25 (ISBN 0-570-03615-1, 39-1103). Concordia.

--Rebellious Rebecca. (Starlight Ser.). (Illus.). (gr. 5-8). 1977. pap. 2.25 (ISBN 0-570-03612-7, 39-1100). Concordia.

JESUS CHRIST–FORTY DAYS IN THE WILDERNESS

see Jesus Christ–Temptation

JESUS CHRIST–FOUNDATION OF THE CHURCH

see Church–Foundation

JESUS CHRIST–FRIENDS AND ASSOCIATES

Hubbard, David A. They Met Jesus. 1976. pap. 1.25 (ISBN 0-89129-184-9). Jove Pubns.

MacGregor, G. H. & Purdy, A. C. Jew & Greek: Tutors Unto Christ. 59.95 (ISBN 0-8490-0444-6). Gordon Pr.

Malinski, Mieczyslaw. Witnesses to Jesus: The Stories of Five Who Knew Him. 280p. 1982. 12.95 (ISBN 0-8245-0088-1). Crossroad NY.

Marquart, M. Jesus' Second Family. (Arch Book Series Fourteen). (gr. k-2). 1977. pap. 0.79 (ISBN 0-570-06111-3, 59-1229). Concordia.

Ridderbos, N. N. Paul & Jesus. pap. 3.50 (ISBN 0-87552-409-5). Presby & Reformed.

JESUS CHRIST–HISTORICITY

see also Jesus Christ–Biography–Sources

Aulen, Gustaf. Jesus in Contemporary Historical Research. Hjelm, Ingalill H., tr. from Swed. LC 75-36451. 176p. 1976. 7.95 (ISBN 0-8006-0438-5, 1-438). Fortress.

Cullman, Oscar. Christ & Time: The Primitive Christian Conception of Time & History. 1977. lib. bdg. 59.95 (ISBN 0-8490-1614-2). Gordon Pr.

Dahl, Nils A. The Crucified Messiah. LC 74-14189. 192p. (Orig.). 1975. pap. 3.95 (ISBN 0-8066-1469-2, 10-1775). Augsburg.

Goodier, A. Public Life of Our Lord Jesus Christ, 2 vols. 1978. Set. 15.95 (ISBN 0-8198-0551-3); Set. pap. 13.95 (ISBN 0-8198-0552-1). Dghtrs St Paul.

Hiers, Richard H. The Historical Jesus & the Kingdom of God: Present & Future in the Message & Ministry of Jesus. LC 73-2623. (U of Fla. Humanities Monographs: No. 38). 1973. 3.50 (ISBN 0-8130-0386-5). U Presses Fla.

Jeremias, Joachim. Problem of the Historical Jesus. Reumann, John, ed. Perrin, Norman, tr. from Ger. LC 64-23064. (Facet Bks.). 1964. pap. 1.95 (ISBN 0-8006-3015-7, 1-3015). Fortress.

Kautsky, Karl. Foundations of Christianity. Mins, Henry F., tr. LC 53-8294. 1953. 12.00 (ISBN 0-8462-0213-1). Russell.

Kevane, Eugene. The Lord of History. 1980. 4.00 (ISBN 0-8198-0636-6); pap. 3.00 (ISBN 0-8198-0637-4). Dghtrs St Paul.

Latourelle, Rene. Finding Jesus Through the Gospels: History & Hermeneutics. Owen, Aloysius, tr. from Fr. LC 78-25732. 1979. pap. 6.95 (ISBN 0-8189-0379-1). Alba.

Marshall, I. Howard. I Believe in the Historical Jesus. (I Believe Ser). 1977. pap. 3.95 (ISBN 0-8028-1691-6). Eerdmans.

Meyer, Ben F. Man for Others. (Faith & Life Bk). 1970. pap. 3.50 (ISBN 0-02-805200-5). Glencoe.

Murray, Andrew. Secret of Christ Our Life. (Secret Ser.). (Orig.). 1980. pap. 1.25 (ISBN 0-87508-385-4). Chr Lit.

Schultz, Hans J., ed. Jesus in His Time. Watchorn, Brian, tr. from Ger. LC 70-99613. 160p. (Orig.). 1971. pap. 4.95 (ISBN 0-8006-0163-7, 1-163). Fortress.

Schweitzer, Albert. Quest of the Historical Jesus. 1968. pap. 6.95 (ISBN 0-02-089240-3). Macmillan.

JESUS CHRIST–HISTORY OF DOCTRINES

Aulen, Gustaf E. Reformation & Catholicity. Wahlstrom, Eric H., tr. from Swedish. LC 78-25981. 1979. Repr. of 1961 ed. lib. bdg. 17.50x (ISBN 0-313-20809-3, AURC). Greenwood.

Bowman, John W. Which Jesus? LC 74-100953. 1970. pap. 3.75 (ISBN 0-664-24879-9). Westminster.

Burrows, Millar. Jesus in the First Three Gospels. LC 77-3568. 1977. 5.95 (ISBN 0-687-20089-X). Abingdon.

Chesnut, Roberta C. Three Monophysite Christologies: Severus of Antioch, Philoxenus of Mabbug, & Jacob of Sarug. (Oxford Theological Monographs). 1976. 24.95x (ISBN 0-19-826712-6). Oxford U Pr.

Conn, Charles W. Christ & the Gospels. 109p. 1964. 4.75 (ISBN 0-87148-166-9); pap. 3.75 (ISBN 0-87148-150-2). Pathway Pr.

De Jonge, Marinus. Jesus: Stranger from Heaven & Son of God. Steely, John E., ed. LC 77-9984. (Society of Biblical Literature. Sources for Biblical Studies). 1977. pap. 7.50 (ISBN 0-89130-134-8, 060311). Scholars Pr Ca.

Grillmeier, Aloys. Christ in Christian Tradition: From the Apostolic Age to Chalcedon, Vol. 1. rev. ed. Bowden, John S., tr. from Ger. LC 75-13456. 451p. 1975. 28.00 (ISBN 0-8042-0492-6). John Knox.

Hale, Robert. Christ & the Universe. Meilach, Michael, ed. (Theilhard de Chardin & the Universe Ser). 5.50 (ISBN 0-8199-0449-X). Franciscan Herald.

Holladay, Carl R. Theios Aner in Hellenistic-Judaism: A Critique of the Use of This Category in New Testament Christology. LC 77-20712. (Society of Biblical Literature. Dissertation Ser.: No. 40). 1977. pap. 7.50 (ISBN 0-89130-205-0, 060140). Scholars Pr Ca.

Marshall, I. Howard. Origins of New Testament Christology. (Issues in Contemporary Theology Ser.). 1976. pap. 2.95 (ISBN 0-87784-718-5). Inter-Varsity.

Marxsen, Willi. Lord's Supper As a Christological Problem. Reumann, John, ed. Nieting, Lorenz, tr. from Ger. LC 79-81528. (Facet Bks). 64p. 1970. pap. 1.00 (ISBN 0-8006-3059-9, 1-3059). Fortress.

Moule, C. F. The Origin of Christology. LC 76-11087. 1977. 23.95 (ISBN 0-521-21290-1); pap. 7.50x (ISBN 0-521-29363-4). Cambridge U Pr.

O'Collins, Gerald. What Are They Saying About Jesus? LC 77-70640. 1977. pap. 2.45 (ISBN 0-8091-2017-8). Paulist Pr.

Rogers, Jack, et al. Case Studies in Christ & Salvation. LC 76-53765. 1977. pap. 7.95 (ISBN 0-664-24133-6). Westminster.

Talbert, Charles H. & Keck, Leander E., eds. Reimarus: Fragments. Fraser, Ralph S., tr. from German. LC 74-127527. (Lives of Jesus Ser.). 292p. 1970. pap. 4.95 (ISBN 0-8006-0152-1, 1-152). Fortress.

Yamamori, Tetsunao & Taber, Charles R., eds. Christopaganism or Indigenous Christianity? LC 75-6616. (Applied Cultural Anthropology Ser.). 256p. 1975. pap. 5.95 (ISBN 0-87808-423-1). William Carey Lib.

JESUS CHRIST–HOLY SHROUD

see Holy Shroud

JESUS CHRIST–HUMANITY

Brown, Raymond E. Jesus, God & Man. LC 67-29587. (Impact Books). 1967. pap. 1.95 (ISBN 0-02-084000-4). Macmillan.

Chemnitz, Martin. Two Natures in Christ. Preus, J. A., tr. LC 74-115465. Orig. Title: De Duabus Naturis in Christo. 1970. 19.95 (ISBN 0-570-03210-5, 15-2109). Concordia.

Comblin, Jose. Jesus of Nazareth: Meditations on His Humanity. Kabat, Carl, tr. from Port. LC 75-29580. Orig. Title: Jesus De Nazare. 176p. 1976. pap. 4.95 (ISBN 0-88344-239-6). Orbis Bks.

Glover, T. R. Jesus in the Experience of Men. LC 78-23617. 1921. 20.00 (ISBN 0-8414-4616-4). Folcroft.

Johnson, Harry. Humanity of the Saviour. 1962. 8.50x (ISBN 0-8401-1248-3). Allenson-Breckinridge.

Knox, John. Humanity & Divinity of Christ. (Orig.). 18.95 (ISBN 0-521-05486-9); pap. 5.50x (ISBN 0-521-09414-3). Cambridge U Pr.

Lamsa, George M. My Neighbor Jesus. 12th ed. pap. 1.50 (ISBN 0-686-09904-4). Aramaic Bible.

Mackintosh, H. R. The Doctrine of the Person of Jesus Christ. (International Theological Library). 560p. 1978. Repr. text ed. 13.95x (ISBN 0-686-73964-7). Attic Pr.

Murray, Andrew. Secret of Christ Our Life. (Secret Ser.). (Orig.). 1980. pap. 1.25 (ISBN 0-87508-385-4). Chr Lit.

Oligny, Paul, tr. Jesus: in Christian Devotion & Contemplation. LC 73-94170. (Religious Experience Ser.: Vol. 1). 1974. pap. 3.95 (ISBN 0-87029-025-8, 20094). Abbey.

Price, Eugenia. Make Love Your Aim. 192p. 1972. pap. 2.95 (ISBN 0-310-31312-0). Zondervan.

Wierwille, Victor P. Jesus Christ Is Not God. LC 74-25962. 1975. 6.95 (ISBN 0-910068-07-0). Devin.

JESUS CHRIST–ICONOGRAPHY

see Jesus Christ–Art

JESUS CHRIST–INCARNATION

see Incarnation

JESUS CHRIST–INFLUENCE

Calkin, Ruth. Lord, I Keep Running Back to You. 1979. pap. 1.95 pocket (ISBN 0-8423-3820-9). Tyndale.

Carl, Joseph B. Jesus in Our Affluent Society. 208p. 1981. 9.95 (ISBN 0-938234-01-3); pap. 5.95 (ISBN 0-938234-00-5). Ministry Pubns.

Cramer, Raymond L. Psicologia de Jesus y la Salud Mental. Vargas, Carlos A., tr. from Eng. LC 76-16438. 191p. (Orig., Span.). 1976. pap. 3.25 (ISBN 0-89922-074-6). Edit Caribe.

Luccock, Halford E. Jesus & the American Mind. 1930. 10.00 (ISBN 0-8414-5628-3). Folcroft.

Murray, Andrew. Secret of Christ Our Life. (Secret Ser.). (Orig.). 1980. pap. 1.25 (ISBN 0-87508-385-4). Chr Lit.

Schillebeeck, Edward. Christ: The Experience Oa Jesus As Lord. 900p. 1980. 29.50 (ISBN 0-8245-0005-9). Crossroad NY.

JESUS CHRIST–ISLAMIC INTERPRETATIONS

Basetti-Sami, Giulio. Koran in the Light of Christ. 1977. 8.50 (ISBN 0-8199-0713-8). Franciscan Herald.

Miller, William M. Ten Muslims Meet Christ. 1969. pap. 3.95 (ISBN 0-8028-1304-6). Eerdmans.
Parrinder, Geoffrey. Jesus in the Qur'an. 1977. pap. 7.95 (ISBN 0-19-519963-4). Oxford U Pr.
Wismer, Don. The Islamic Jesus: An Annotated Bibliography of Sources in English & French. LC 76-24737. (Reference Library of the Humanities Ser.: Vol. 58). 1977. lib. bdg. 33.00 (ISBN 0-8240-9940-0). Garland Pub.

JESUS CHRIST–JEWISH INTERPRETATIONS

Borowitz, Eugene B. Contemporary Christologies: A Jewish Response. LC 80-81051. 208p. (Orig.). 1980. pap. 7.95 (ISBN 0-8091-2305-3). Paulist Pr.
Buber, Martin. Two Types of Faith: The Interpretation of Judaism & Christianity. pap. 4.50x (ISBN 0-06-130075-6, TB75, Torch). Har-Row.
Dalman, Gustaf. Jesus Christ in the Talmud, Midrash, Zohar, & the Liturgy of the Synagogue. LC 73-2190. (The Jewish People; History, Religion, Literature Ser.). Repr. of 1893 ed. 11.00 (ISBN 0-405-05256-1). Arno.
Hirsch, Emil G. My Religion. Levi, Gerson B., ed. Incl. The Crucifixion Viewed from a Jewish Standpoint (1908. LC 73-2207. (The Jewish People; History, Religion, Literature Ser.). Repr. of 1925 ed. 25.00 (ISBN 0-405-05271-5). Arno.
Lapide, Pinchas. Israelis, Jews, & Jesus. LC 77-82767. 1979. 7.95 (ISBN 0-385-13433-9). Doubleday.
Pawlikowski, John T. Christ in the Light of the Christain-Jewish Dialogue. (Stimulus Bks). 208p. (Orig.). 1982. pap. 7.95 (ISBN 0-8091-2416-5). Paulist Pr.
Sandmel, Samuel. We Jews & Jesus. LC 65-11529. 163p. 1973. pap. 4.95 (ISBN 0-19-501676-9, GB). Oxford U Pr.
Thompson, William M. Jesus, Lord & Savior. LC 80-81052. 304p. 1980. pap. 9.95 (ISBN 0-8091-2306-1). Paulist Pr.
Troki, Isaac A. Faith Strengthened: Hizzuk Emunah. rev. ed. Mocatta, Moses, tr. 1970. 8.95x (ISBN 0-87068-101-X). Ktav.
Umen, Samuel. Pharisaism & Jesus. LC 62-20875. 1962. 3.75 (ISBN 0-8022-1752-4). Philos Lib.
Walker, Thomas T. Jewish Views of Jesus: An Introduction & an Appreciation. LC 73-2229. (The Jewish People; History, Religion, Literature Ser.). Repr. of 1931 ed. 11.00 (ISBN 0-405-05290-1). Arno.
Weiss-Rosmarin, T., ed. Jewish Expressions on Jesus. 9.95x (ISBN 0-87068-470-1). Ktav.

JESUS CHRIST–JUVENILE LITERATURE

see also Jesus Christ–Biography–Juvenile Literature; Jesus Christ–Fiction, Juvenile; Jesus Christ–Nativity–Juvenile Literature; Jesus Christ–Parables–Juvenile Literature; Jesus Christ–Resurrection–Juvenile Literature

Beckmann, Beverly. From. (Illus.). 1980. pap. 3.50 (ISBN 0-570-03489-2, 56-1343). Concordia.
Berg, Jean H. The Story of Jesus. (Illus.). 40p. (ps). 1977. pap. 3.95 (ISBN 0-87510-109-7). Chr Science.
Caffrey, Stephanie & Kenslea, Timothy. The Shepherds Find a King. (Rainbow Books (Bible Story Books for Children)). 16p. 1978. pap. 1.00 (ISBN 0-8192-1232-6). Morehouse.
Carwell, L'Ann. Baby's First Book About Jesus. (Illus.). 1979. 1.00 (ISBN 0-570-08001-0, 56-1326). Concordia.
Cazzola, Gus. A Chisel for Ezekiel. 1979. pap. 1.95 (ISBN 0-570-07975-6, 39-1115). Concordia.
Coleman, William. Jesus, My Forever Friend. (Illus.). (gr. 4-8). 1981. 12.95 (ISBN 0-89191-370-X, 53702). Cook.
Colina, Tessa, ed. Jesus, My Teacher: Pupil Activities Book Two. (Jesus & Me Ser.). (Illus.). 16p. (gr. 1-5). 1978. pap. 1.25 (ISBN 0-87239-269-4, 2441). Standard Pub.
Collins, David R. The Wonderful Story of Jesus. 1980. 6.95 (ISBN 0-570-03490-6, 56-1344); pap. 1.50 (ISBN 0-570-03491-4, 56-1345). Concordia.
D. C. Cook Editors. Jesus, the Friend of Children. LC 77-72722. (Illus.). (gr. k-3). 1977. 8.95 (ISBN 0-89191-077-8). Cook.
Daughters of St. Paul. Always with Jesus. 1973. 3.95 (ISBN 0-8198-0265-4); pap. 2.50 (ISBN 0-8198-0714-1). Dghtrs St Paul.
Dean, Bessie. Let's Learn About Jesus: A Child's Coloring Book of the Life of Christ. (Children's Inspirational Coloring Bk.). (Illus.). (ps-6). 1979. pap. 4.95 (ISBN 0-88290-131-1). Horizon Utah.
Diamond, Lucy. Jesus by the Sea of Galilee. (Ladybird Ser). (Illus.). 1958. bds. 1.49 (ISBN 0-87508-840-6). Chr Lit.
--Jesus Calls His Disciples. (Ladybird Ser). (Illus.). 1959. bds. 1.49 (ISBN 0-87508-842-2). Chr Lit.
--Little Lord Jesus. (Ladybird Ser). (Illus.). 1954. bds. 1.49 (ISBN 0-87508-846-5). Chr Lit.
Dillard, Polly H. Outdoors with Jesus. (gr. k-2). 1980. 5.95 (ISBN 0-8054-4263-4). Broadman.
Downs, Kathy. I'm Not Afraid. LC 81-51000. (Illus.). 16p. (Orig.). (gr. k-3). 1981. pap. 0.98 (ISBN 0-87239-475-1, 2873). Standard Pub.
Dye, Gerald. Growing in Christ. (Double Trouble Puzzles Ser.). 48p. (Orig.). (gr. 6 up). 1981. pap. 1.50 (ISBN 0-87239-447-6, 2837). Standard Pub.
Finley, James & Pennock, Michael. Jesus & You. LC 77-72283. (Illus.). 224p. (gr. 11-12). 1977. pap. text ed. 3.50 (ISBN 0-87793-130-5); tchr's manual 1.95 (ISBN 0-87793-131-3). Ave Maria.
Galusha, David. The First Christmas. (Illus.). 32p. (ps up). 1981. wkbk. 3.95 (ISBN 0-87973-662-3, 662). Our Sunday Visitor.
Haas, Lois J. Tell Me About Jesus Kit: 16 Lessons, Vol. 2. (Tiny Steps of Faith Ser.). (ps). 1967. complete kit 10.95 (ISBN 0-86508-014-3); text only 2.50 (ISBN 0-86508-015-1); color & action book 0.90 (ISBN 0-86508-016-X). BCM Inc.
Hook, Frances, illus. My Jesus Book. (Illus.). (gr. k-2). 1963. pap. 4.95 board cover (ISBN 0-87239-239-2, 3046). Standard Pub.
Jesus Feeds Five Thousand. (Tell-a-Bible Story Ser.). (Illus.). 28p. bds. 0.69 (ISBN 0-686-68645-4, 3689). Standard Pub.
Jesus Is Born. (Tell-a-Bible Story Ser.). (Illus.). 28p. bds. 0.69 (ISBN 0-686-68642-X, 3686). Standard Pub.
The Lost Sheep. (Tell-a-Bible Story Ser.). (Illus.). 28p. bds. 0.69 (ISBN 0-686-68646-2, 3690). Standard Pub.
Maschke, Ruby. Life of Christ Story-N-Puzzle Book. 48p. (Orig.). (gr. 4 up). 1981. pap. 1.50 (ISBN 0-87239-449-2, 2839). Standard Pub.
--Teachings of Christ Story-N-Puzzle Book. 48p. (Orig.). (gr. 4 up). 1981. pap. 1.50 (ISBN 0-87239-451-4, 2842). Standard Pub.
Meu Livro De Jesus. (Portugese Bks.). (Port.). 1979. 3.00 (ISBN 0-8297-0757-3). Life Pubs Intl.
Mi Libro De Jesus. (Spanish Bks.). 1977. 3.50 (ISBN 0-8297-0754-9). Life Pubs Intl.
Mueller, A. C. Jesus & His Friends. (Bible Story Booklets Ser.). (Illus.). (gr. 3-5). 1971. pap. 0.59 (ISBN 0-570-06703-0, 56-1131). Concordia.
--Jesus Helps People. (Bible Story Booklets Ser). (Illus.). (gr. 3-5). 1971. pap. 0.59 (ISBN 0-570-06704-9, 56-1132). Concordia.
--Jesus with Us. (Bible Story Booklets Ser). (Illus., Orig.). (gr. 3-5). 1971. pap. 0.59 (ISBN 0-570-06702-2, 56-1130). Concordia.
Nystrom, Carolyn. Who Is Jesus. (Children's Bible Basics Ser.). 32p. (ps-2). 1980. pap. 3.25 (ISBN 0-8024-5993-5). Moody.
Odor, Ruth. The Baby Jesus: A Surprise Storybook. (Illus.). 16p. (Orig.). (ps-2). 1980. pap. 3.95 (ISBN 0-87239-419-0, 2708). Standard Pub.
Rabens, Neil W. Jesus Loves You. (gr. k-3). 1978. pap. 1.69 (ISBN 0-87239-180-9, 2314). Standard Pub.
The Real Jesus. 128p. (gr. 2-9). pap. 2.95 (ISBN 0-89191-066-2, 08243). Cook.
Richards, Dr. Larry. A Child's Life of Jesus. 1976. pap. 1.29 (ISBN 0-87239-266-X, 2704). Standard Pub.
Roberts, Jim. Jesus Calms the Storm. 1978. 2.49 (ISBN 0-8307-0614-3, 56-057-09). Regal.
--Three in a Furnace. 1978. 2.49 (ISBN 0-8307-0613-5, 56-056-01). Regal.
Rostron, Hilda L. Stories About Jesus the Friend. (Ladybird Ser). (Illus.). (gr. k-1). 1961. bds. 1.49 (ISBN 0-87508-862-7). Chr Lit.
--Stories About Jesus the Helper. (Ladybird Ser). (Illus.). (gr. k-1). 1961. bds. 1.49 (ISBN 0-87508-864-3). Chr Lit.
Royer, Katherine. Nursery Home Books. (Illus.). (ps). 1957. pap. 2.95 (ISBN 0-8361-1002-1). Herald Pr.
Runk, Wesley T. Jesus & the Crowds. (gr. 1-3). 1977. pap. 2.25 (ISBN 0-89536-315-1). CSS Pub.
Schraff, Francis, et al. Learning About Jesus. rev. ed. 80p. (gr. 2-4). 1980. pap. 1.95 (ISBN 0-89243-129-6). Liguori Pubns.
Smith, Mary P. The Story of Jesus. (Illus.). 32p. (Orig.). (ps-2). 1980. pap. 1.95 (ISBN 0-87516-420-X). De Vorss.
Staton, Knofel & Staton, Julia. Jesus & Paul Agree: You Don't Have to Stay the Way You Are. (New Life Ser.). (Illus.). 1976. pap. 2.25 (ISBN 0-87239-108-6, 40039). Standard Pub.
Stifle, J. M. ABC Book About Jesus. 1981. pap. 2.95 (ISBN 0-570-04054-X, 56-1715). Concordia.
Villiers, Marjorie. Jesus Has Come: Based on the French by Martine Douillet & Genevieve Guilhem. 1978. pap. 2.75 (ISBN 0-8170-0810-1). Judson.
--Jesus with Us: Based on the French by Martine Douillet & Genevieve Guilhem. 1978. pap. 2.75 (ISBN 0-8170-0811-X). Judson.
Watson, Elizabeth E. Tell Me About Jesus. 1980. pap. 3.50 (ISBN 0-570-03484-1, 56-1705). Concordia.
Wise Men Visit Jesus. (Tell-a-Bible Story Ser.). (Illus.). 28p. bds. 0.69 (ISBN 0-686-68643-8, 3687). Standard Pub.
Zaccheus Meets J s. (Tell-a-Bible Story Ser.). (Illus.). 28p. b 0.69 (ISBN 0-686-68647-0, 3691). Stand Pub.

JESUS CHRIST–KINGDOM

see also Jesus Christ–Mystical Body

Cribb, C. C. The Coming Kingdom. LC 77-70213. pap. 1.95 (ISBN 0-932046-04-5). Manhattan Ltd NC.
Newbigin, Lesslie. Sign of the Kingdom. 48p. (Orig.). 1981. pap. 1.95 (ISBN 0-8028-1878-1). Eerdmans.
Sauer, Erich. The King of the Earth. 256p. 1979. pap. text ed. 9.50 (ISBN 0-85364-009-2). Attic Pr.

JESUS CHRIST–LANGUAGE

Altizer, Thomas J. Total Presence: The Language of Jesus & the Language of Today. 128p. 1980. 9.95 (ISBN 0-8164-0461-5). Seabury.

JESUS CHRIST–LAST WORDS

see Jesus Christ–Seven Last Words

JESUS CHRIST–LIFE

see Jesus Christ–Biography

JESUS CHRIST–LOGOS DOCTRINE

see Logos

JESUS CHRIST–LORD'S SUPPER

see Lord's Supper

JESUS CHRIST–MEDITATIONS

see Jesus Christ–Devotional Literature

JESUS CHRIST–MESSIAHSHIP

see also Messiah

Anderson, Julian G. The Story of Jesus the Messiah, Four Gospels. LC 76-52054. (A Life of Christ Wkbk). (Illus.). (gr. 6-9). 1977. pap. 3.95x (ISBN 0-9602128-1-7). J G Anderson.
--The Story of Jesus the Messiah, Old Testament. (An Old Testament Wkbk). (Illus.). (gr. 6-9). 1977. pap. 3.95x (ISBN 0-9602128-2-5). J G Anderson.
Blevins, James L. The Messianic Secret in Markan Research, 1901-1976. LC 80-69035. 233p. 1981. lib. bdg. 18.50 (ISBN 0-8191-1606-8); pap. text ed. 9.75 (ISBN 0-8191-1607-6). U Pr of Amer.
Brown, Raymond E. The Birth of the Messiah: A Commentary on the Infancy Narratives in Matthew & Luke. 1979. pap. 6.95 (ISBN 0-385-05405-X, Im). Doubleday.
Edwards, Don. Jesus & The Secret Plan. Graves, Martha, ed. LC 77-94196. 1978. 8.00 (ISBN 0-918566-13-4); pap. 5.00 (ISBN 0-918566-05-3). Excelsior.
Evans, W. Glyn, compiled by. He Has Come! LC 75-18089. 140p. 1975. pap. 2.95 (ISBN 0-8054-1934-9). Broadman.
Grant, F. W. The Crowned Christ. 4.50 (ISBN 0-686-13127-4); pap. 2.75 (ISBN 0-686-13128-2). Believers Bkshelf.
Hall, Willard S. The Lamb of God; the Theme Eternal. 35p. 1974. 4.95 (ISBN 0-87881-033-1). Mojave Bks.
Hugel, Friedrich Von. Essays & Addresses on the Philosophy of Religion. LC 72-9828. 308p. 1974. Repr. of 1921 ed. lib. bdg. 15.25x (ISBN 0-8371-6219-X, HUPR). Greenwood.
Juster, Daniel. Jewishness & Jesus. 1977. pap. 0.50 (ISBN 0-87784-163-2). Inter-Varsity.
McConkie, Bruce R. The Promised Messiah. LC 78-3478. 1978. 12.95 (ISBN 0-87747-702-7). Deseret Bk.
Manson, T. W. Only to the House of Israel? Jesus & the Non-Jews. Reumann, John, ed. LC 64-11860. (Facet Bks). 1964. pap. 1.00 (ISBN 0-8006-3005-X, 1-3005). Fortress.
Miranda, Jose P. Being & the Messiah: The Message of St. John. Eagleson, John, tr. from Span. LC 77-5388. Orig. Title: El Ser y el Mesias. 1977. 8.95x (ISBN 0-88344-027-X); pap. 4.95x (ISBN 0-88344-028-8). Orbis Bks.
Rawlinson, Alfred E. Christ in the Gospels. Repr. of 1944 ed. lib. bdg. 15.00x (ISBN 0-8371-3736-5, RACG). Greenwood.
Shofner, David. Soul Winning. (Illus.). 96p. (Orig.). 1980. pap. 2.95 (ISBN 0-89957-051-8). AMG Pubs.

JESUS CHRIST–MIRACLES

Allen, Charles L. Touch of the Master's Hand: Christ's Miracles for Today. 1956. pap. 1.25 (ISBN 0-8007-8093-0, Spire Bks). Revell.
Bailey, James H. The Miracles of Jesus for Today. LC 76-51202. (Orig.). 1977. pap. 3.95 (ISBN 0-687-27070-7). Abingdon.
Barclay, William. And He Had Compassion. LC 75-28099. 272p. 1976. pap. 5.95 (ISBN 0-8170-0686-9). Judson.
Bruce, A. B. The Miracles of Christ. 1980. 17.25 (ISBN 0-86524-060-4). Klock & Klock.
Cox, Frank L. Miracles of Jesus. pap. 2.25 (ISBN 0-89225-122-0). Gospel Advocate.
--Sermon Notes on the Miracles. pap. 2.50 (ISBN 0-89225-155-7). Gospel Advocate.
Daughters of St. Paul. The Teachings & Miracles of Jesus. 1981. 4.00 (ISBN 0-686-73821-7); pap. 3.00 (ISBN 0-8198-7302-0). Dghtrs St Paul.
Elliot, Elizabeth. Doce Cestas De Mendrugos. (Spanish Bks.). (Span.). 1977. 1.75 (ISBN 0-8297-0804-9). Life Pubs Intl.
Fridrichsen, Anton. Problem of Miracle in Primitive Christianity. Harrisville, Roy A. & Hanson, John S., trs. from Fr. LC 72-176480. 1972. 7.95 (ISBN 0-8066-1211-8, 10-5170). Augsburg.
Habershon, Ada R. Study of the Miracles. LC 62-19174. 1967. 8.95 (ISBN 0-8254-2801-7); pap. 6.95 (ISBN 0-8254-2851-3). Kregel.
Hagin, Kenneth. I Believe in Visions. 128p. 1972. pap. 1.95 (ISBN 0-8007-8376-X, Spire Bks). Revell.
Hatfield, Joyce. The Wedding at Cana. 1981. 1.25 (ISBN 0-89536-471-9). CSS Pub.
Hoefler, Richard C. I Knew You'd Come! The Miracles of Jesus, Ser. A. 80p. (Orig.). 1980. pap. text ed. 4.85 (ISBN 0-89536-444-1). CSS Pub.
Lawson, LeRoy. The Lord of Possibilities-Miracles of Jesus: Student. LC 79-66502. 112p. (Orig.). 1979. pap. 1.95 (ISBN 0-87239-376-3, 39995); instr's. ed. 204p. 2.25 (ISBN 0-87239-375-5, 39994). Standard Pub.
Lindsay, Gordon. Christ the Great Physician. (Divine Healing & Health Ser.). 0.95 (ISBN 0-89985-024-3). Christ Nations.
--The Forgotten Miracles of the Bible. (Miracles in the Bible Ser.: Vol. 6). 0.95 (ISBN 0-89985-183-5). Christ Nations.
--Four Hundred & Fifty-Year Judgment Cycles. (Miracles in the Bible Ser.: Vol. 5). 0.95 (ISBN 0-89985-182-7). Christ Nations.
--Miracles of Christ, 2 parts, Vols. 2 & 3. (Miracles in the Bible Ser.). 0.95 ea. Vol. 2 (ISBN 0-89985-958-5). Vol. 3 (ISBN 0-89985-960-7). Christ Nations.
--Old Testament Healings. (Miracles in the Bible Ser.: Vol. 1). 0.95 (ISBN 0-89985-179-7). Christ Nations.
The Lord of Possibilities-Miracles of Jesus: Instructor. 204p. (Orig.). pap. 2.25 (ISBN 0-87239-375-5, 39994). Standard Pub.
Lovasik, Lawrence G. The Miracles of Jesus. (Saint Joseph Picture Bks.). flexible dg. 0.95 (ISBN 0-686-14289-6, 279). Catholic Bk Pub.
Osborn, T. L. Miracles Proof of God's Power. 96p. (Orig.). 1981. pap. 1.50 (ISBN 0-89274-185-6, HH-185). Harrison Hse.
Pentecost, Dwight. A Harmony of the Words & Works of Jesus Christ. 272p. 1981. pap. price not set (ISBN 0-310-30951-4). Zondervan.
Pentecost, J. Dwight. The Words & Works of Jesus Christ. 576p. 1981. 16.95 (ISBN 0-310-30940-9, 17015). Zondervan.
Spurgeon, Charles H. Miracles of Our Lord I. (Treasury of Spurgeon on Life & Work of Our Lord). 13.95 (ISBN 0-8010-8151-3). Baker Bk.
--Miracles of Our Lord II. (Treasury of Spurgeon on Life & Work of Our Lord). 13.95 (ISBN 0-8010-8152-1). Baker Bk.
Taylor, William M. Miracles of Our Saviour. LC 74-79944. 1975. 10.95 (ISBN 0-8254-3806-3). Kregel.
Trench, R. C. Notes on the Miracles. (Twin Brooks Ser.). pap. 5.95 (ISBN 0-8010-8776-7). Baker Bk.
Weiser, Alfons. The Miracle of Jesus: Then & Now. Karris, Robert, ed. Tiede, David L., tr. (Herald Biblical Bklts.). 1972. pap. 1.25 (ISBN 0-8199-0519-4). Franciscan Herald.
Woolston, Thomas. Discours sur les Miracles de Jesus-Christ, 2 vols. (Holbach & His Friends Ser.). 510p. (Fr.). 1974. Repr. of 1769 ed. lib. bdg. 139.50x (ISBN 0-8287-0885-1, 1538-9). Clearwater Pub.
--Discourses on the Miracles of Our Savior. Wellek, Rene, ed. LC 75-11268. (British Philosophers & Theologians of the 17th & 18th Centuries Ser.: Vol. 67). 565p. 1979. lib. bdg. 42.00 (ISBN 0-8240-1778-1); lib. bdg. 2700.00 set of 101 vols. (ISBN 0-686-60102-5). Garland Pub.

JESUS CHRIST–MIRACLES–JUVENILE LITERATURE

Bergey, Alyce. Beggar's Greatest Wish. (Arch Bks: No. 6). (gr. 4-6). 1969. pap. 0.79 (ISBN 0-570-06040-0, 59-1155). Concordia.
--Fishermen's Surprise. (Arch Bks: Set 4). 1967. laminated cover 0.79 (ISBN 0-570-06028-1, 59-1139). Concordia.
Curley, Maureen. Jesus Miracles. (Children of the Kingdom Acitivities Ser.). (gr. 4-7). 1973. 7.95 (ISBN 0-686-13689-6). Pflaum Pr.
Hill, Dave. Boy Who Gave His Lunch Away. (Arch Bks: Set 4). 1967. laminated bdg. 0.79 (ISBN 0-570-06027-3, 59-1138). Concordia.
Prior, Brenda. Little Sleeping Beauty. (Arch Bks: Set 6). 1969. laminated bdg. 0.79 (ISBN 0-570-06041-9, 59-1156). Concordia.
Warren, Mary P. & Rada. Little Boat That Almost Sank. LC 64-23371. (Arch Bks: Set 2). 1965. pap. 0.79 (ISBN 0-570-06010-9, 59-1111). Concordia.
Warren, Mary P. & Wind, Betty. Lame Man Who Walked Again. (Arch Bks: Set 3). 1966. laminated bdg. 0.79 (ISBN 0-570-06020-6, 59-1129). Concordia.

JESUS CHRIST–MISCELLANEA

Babcock, Winifred. The Palestinian Mystery Play. 1971. pap. 2.95 (ISBN 0-396-06201-6). Dodd.

--The Single Reality. 1971. 9.50 (ISBN 0-396-06206-7); pap. 6.00 (ISBN 0-396-06874-X). Dodd.

Duvall, Sylvanus. Jesus Christ, Earth Guest. LC 78-56841. 1978. 5.95 (ISBN 0-533-03640-2). Vantage.

Elliott, Maurice. The Psychic Life of Jesus. 69.95 (ISBN 0-87968-185-3). Gordon Pr.

Engelsma, David. Marriage: The Mystery of Christ & the Church. LC 74-31902. 1975. pap. 2.95 (ISBN 0-8254-2520-4). Kregel.

McKenna, Megan & Ducote, Darryl. Jesus Living the Father's Values. LC 78-71530. (Followers of the Way Ser.: Vol. 3). (gr. 9-12). 1979. 22.50 (ISBN 0-8091-9544-5); cassette 7.50 (ISBN 0-8091-7668-8). Paulist Pr.

Moran, Carolyn & Moran, Emerson. Grandma, Grandpa & the Jesus Nut. (Orig.). 1980. pap. 3.95 (ISBN 0-88270-445-1). Logos.

Pike, Diane K. Cosmic Unfoldment: The Individualizing Process As Mirrored in the Life of Jesus. LC 76-45344. 99p. 1976. pap. 2.00 (ISBN 0-916192-08-3). L P Pubns.

Rappoport, Angelo S. Mediaeval Legends of Christ. LC 76-15555. 1976. Repr. of 1934 ed. lib. bdg. 30.00 (ISBN 0-8414-7346-3). Folcroft.

Renich, Fred. When Chisel Hits the Rock. 132p. 1980. pap. 3.50 (ISBN 0-88207-218-8). Victor Bks.

Spurgeon, C. H. Remembrance of Christ. 1977. pap. 0.50 (ISBN 0-686-23223-2). Pilgrim Pubns.

Stanley, David M. Jesus in Gethsemane: The Early Church Reflects on the Suffering of Jesus. LC 80-80596. (Orig.). 1980. pap. 7.95 (ISBN 0-8091-2285-5). Paulist Pr.

JESUS CHRIST-MOHAMMEDAN INTERPRETATIONS

see Jesus Christ-Islamic Interpretations

JESUS CHRIST-MYSTICAL BODY

see also Church-Foundation; Communion of Saints; Mystical Union; Priesthood, Universal

Baillie, D. M. God Was in Christ. 232p. 1977. pap. 6.50 (ISBN 0-571-05685-7, Pub. by Faber & Faber). Merrimack Bk Serv.

Collins, John H. Mystical Body of Christ. 1977. 2.00 (ISBN 0-8198-0435-5); pap. 0.95 (ISBN 0-8198-0436-3). Dghtrs St Paul.

Larsen, Earnest. Body of Christ. LC 76-6703. (Illus.). 1976. pap. 1.75 (ISBN 0-8189-1134-4, Pub. by Alba Bks). Alba.

Nee, Watchman. The Body of Christ: A Reality. Kaung, Stephen, tr. 1978. pap. 1.95 (ISBN 0-935008-13-6). Christian Fellow Pubs.

Pelton, Robert S., ed. Church As the Body of Christ. (Cardinal O'Hara Ser.: Vol. 1). 1963. 4.95x (ISBN 0-268-00044-1). U of Notre Dame Pr.

Pius XII, Pope Mystical Body of Christ. pap. 0.25 (ISBN 0-8091-5097-2). Paulist Pr.

Schweizer, Eduard. Church As the Body of Christ. LC 64-16282. (Orig.). 1964. pap. 2.45 (ISBN 0-8042-3376-4). John Knox.

JESUS CHRIST-NAME

see also Servant of Jehovah; Son of Man

Coggan, Donald. Name Above All Names. 48p. 1981. pap. 2.95 (ISBN 0-281-03803-1). Seabury.

Derk, Francis H. Names of Christ: A Pocket Guide. LC 75-44928. 1976. pap. 2.95 (ISBN 0-87123-390-8, 200390). Bethany Hse.

Hausherr, Irenee. The Name of Jesus. Cummings, Charles, tr. LC 77-10559. (Cistercian Studies: No. 44). 1978. 15.95 (ISBN 0-87907-844-8). Cistercian Pubns.

Kramer, Werner. Christ, Lord, Son of God. (Studies in Biblical Theology: No. 50). 1966. 9.45x (ISBN 0-8401-4050-9); pap. 8.95x (ISBN 0-8401-3050-3). Allenson-Breckinridge.

Otis, George. Jesus: 220 Names. pap. 1.50 (ISBN 0-89728-041-5, 533144). Omega Pubns OR.

Rolls, Charles J. His Glorious Name: The Names & Titles of Jesus Christ Beginning with T-W. LC 74-18993. 1975. 4.95 (ISBN 0-87213-729-5). Loizeaux.

Simpson, Albert B. Names of Jesus. pap. 3.00 (ISBN 0-87509-030-3). Chr Pubns.

Spurgeon, Charles H. C. H. Spurgeon's Sermons on Christ's Names & Titles. Cook, Charles T., ed. 1965. Repr. of 1961 ed. 6.95 (ISBN 0-87921-033-8). Attic Pr.

JESUS CHRIST-NATIVITY

see also Christmas; Star of Bethlehem; Virgin Birth

Allen, Charles L. & Wallis, Charles L. Christmas. 1977. 6.95 (ISBN 0-8007-0874-1). Revell.

Bainton, Roland H., tr. Martin Luther Christmas Book with Celebrated Woodcuts by His Contemporaries. LC 59-2930. 80p. 1948. pap. 3.25 (ISBN 0-8006-1843-2, 1-1843). Fortress.

Bishop, Jim. The Day Christ Was Born. LC 60-13444. 1978. pap. 1.95 (ISBN 0-06-060785-8, HJ 37, HarpR). Har-Row.

Brown, Raymond E. The Birth of the Messiah: A Commentary on the Infancy Narratives in Matthew & Luke. LC 76-56271. 1977. 14.95 (ISBN 0-385-05907-8). Doubleday.

Daughters of St. Paul. When Jesus Was Born. (Illus.). 1973. plastic bdg. 2.00 (ISBN 0-8198-0326-X); pap. 1.25 (ISBN 0-8198-0327-8). Dghtrs St Paul.

Gromacki, Robert G. The Virgin Birth of Christ. 200p. 1981. pap. 5.95 (ISBN 0-8010-3765-4). Baker Bk.

Heckman, Theodore, ed. The Nativity of Christ. (Music Ser.). 158p. 1974. pap. 10.00 (ISBN 0-913836-16-8). St Vladimirs.

Jakubowsky, Frank. Jesus Was a Leo. LC 79-65831. 1979. pap. 6.95 (ISBN 0-932588-01-8). Jakubowsky.

Lidden, H. P. & Orr, J. The Birth of Christ. 1980. 13.95 (ISBN 0-86524-058-2). Klock & Klock.

Maier, Paul L. First Christmas: The True & Unfamiliar Story in Words & Pictures. LC 76-163162. (Illus.). 1971. 9.95 (ISBN 0-06-065396-5, HarpR). Har-Row.

Mooney, Patrick. A Child Is Born. (Illus.). 1976. pap. text ed. 1.50 (ISBN 0-89622-013-3). Twenty-Third.

Mudde, Laetitia. Prince Jesus. 1977. 4.50 (ISBN 0-533-02920-1). Vantage.

Northrup, Marguerite. Christmas Story: From the Gospels of Matthew & Luke. LC 65-23504. (Illus.). (gr. 3 up). 1966. 5.95 (ISBN 0-87099-047-0, Pub. by Metro Mus Art). NYGS.

Padgett, James E. Jesus Birth & Youth As Revealed by Mary, Mother of Jesus. 3.00 (ISBN 0-686-12714-5). Foun Church New Birth.

Randegart, Lyle J. Mary's Baby. 1981. 6.75 (ISBN 0-8062-1656-5). Carlton.

Richardson, Don. Hijo De Paz. (Spanish Bks.). (Span.). 1977. 2.45 (ISBN 0-8297-0572-4). Life Pubs Intl.

Schrage, Alice. Birth of the King. LC 80-53874. 128p. 1981. pap. 1.95 (ISBN 0-8307-0765-4). Regal.

Sledge, Linda C. Shivering Babe, Victorious Lord: The Nativity in Poetry & Art. 1981. 24.95 (ISBN 0-8028-3553-8). Eerdmans.

JESUS CHRIST-NATIVITY-ART

see Jesus Christ-Art

JESUS CHRIST-NATIVITY-JUVENILE LITERATURE

Abajian, Diane. The Christmas Story for Children. (Illus.). 16p. (gr. 1-3). 1981. pap. 1.25 (ISBN 0-89622-138-5). Twenty-Third.

Brandt, Catharine. The Story of Christmas for Children. LC 74-79366. (Illus.). 20p. (Orig.). (gr. 1 up). 1974. pap. 4.50 (ISBN 0-8066-1426-9, 10-6040). Augsburg.

Forell, Betty & Wind, Betty. Little Benjamin & the First Christmas. (Arch Bks: Set 1). (Illus.). (ps-3). 1964. laminated bdg. 0.79 (ISBN 0-570-06005-2, 59-1113). Concordia.

Kramer-Lampher, A. H. Baby Born in a Stable. LC 65-15145. (Arch Bks: Set. 2). 1965. pap. 0.79 (ISBN 0-570-06013-3, 59-1118). Concordia.

Laurence, Margaret. The Christmas Birthday Story. LC 79-27159. (Illus.). 32p. (ps-3). 1980. 6.99 (ISBN 0-394-94361-9); pap. 6.95 (ISBN 0-394-84361-4). Knopf.

Lloyd, Mary E. Jesus, the Little New Baby. (gr. k-1). 1951. 3.95 (ISBN 0-687-20203-5). Abingdon.

McCall, Yvonne H. The Man Who Didn't Have Time. (Arch Book Series Fourteen). 1977. pap. 0.79 (ISBN 0-570-06112-1, 59-1231). Concordia.

McNeely, Jeanette & Cunningham, Aline. Led by a Star: Matthew 2: 1-12 for Children. LC 77-6308. (I Can Read a Bible Story Ser: No. 2). (Illus.). (gr. 7-9). 1977. 3.95. (ISBN 0-570-07326-X, 56-1517); pap. 1.95 (ISBN 0-570-07320-0, 56-1417). Concordia.

Make Your Own Nativity Scene. (gr. 2 up). pap. 3.95 (ISBN 0-89191-810-8, 28100). Cook.

Mueller, Virginia. Secret Journey. (Arch Bks: Set 5). (Illus.). (gr. 4-6). 1968. laminated bdg. 0.79 (ISBN 0-570-06037-0, 59-1150). Concordia.

Odor, Ruth. The Very Special Night. Sparks, Judith, ed. (A Happy Day Book). (Illus.). 24p. (gr. k-2). 1980. 0.98 (ISBN 0-87239-405-0, 3637). Standard Pub.

Rostron, Hilda L. Baby Jesus. (Ladybird Ser). (Illus.). 1961. bds. 1.49 (ISBN 0-87508-832-5). Chr Lit.

Trent, Robbie. First Christmas. LC 48-8892. (Illus.). (ps-1). 1948. PLB 6.89 (ISBN 0-06-026121-8, HarpJ). Har-Row.

Wahl, Thomas. How Jesus Came. (Illus.). 48p. (gr. k-3). 1981. 11.95 (ISBN 0-916134-51-2). Pueblo Pub Co.

JESUS CHRIST-NATIVITY-SERMONS

see Christmas Sermons

JESUS CHRIST-NATURES

see also Jesus Christ-Divinity; Jesus Christ-Humanity

Simpson, A. B. El Evangelico Quadruple: Fourfold Gospel, Spanish. Bruchez, Dardo, tr. from Eng. 128p. Date not set. pap. price not set (ISBN 0-87509-268-3). Chr Pubns.

JESUS CHRIST-NEW THOUGHT INTERPRETATIONS

Bostick, W. F. Jesus & Socrates. 59.95 (ISBN 0-8490-0443-8). Gordon Pr.

Colloque De Christologie Tenu a L'universite Laval. Le Christ Hier, Aujourd Hui et Demain: Proceedings. 1977. 19.95x (ISBN 2-7637-6788-5, Pub. by Laval). Intl Schol Bk Serv.

Dunne, Carrin. Buddha & Jesus: Conversations. 1975. pap. 4.95 (ISBN 0-87243-057-X). Templegate.

Fillmore, Charles. Mysteries of John. 1946. 2.95 (ISBN 0-87159-105-7). Unity Bks.

Hayes, John H. Son of God to Superstar: Twentieth-Century Interpretation of Jesus. LC 75-30603. 256p. 1976. 5.95 (ISBN 0-687-39091-5); pap. 6.95 o. p. (ISBN 0-687-39092-3). Abingdon.

Hough, Charles W. The Unique Teacher. 1979. 6.95 (ISBN 0-533-03996-7). Vantage.

Kissinger, Warren S. The Parables of Jesus: A History of Interpretation & Bibliography. (American Theological Library Association (ATLA) Bibliography Ser.: No. 4). 463p. 1979. lib. bdg. 22.00 (ISBN 0-8108-1186-3). Scarecrow.

Moum, Margaret R. Guidebook to the Aquarian Gospel of Jesus the Christ. 93p. 1974. pap. 2.95 (ISBN 0-917200-05-5). ESPress.

Rajneesh, Bhagwan S. The Mustard Seed: Discourses on the Sayings of Jesus from the Gospel According to Thomas. LC 77-20461. 1978. pap. 7.95 (ISBN 0-06-066785-0, RD-255, HarpR). Har-Row.

Smith, Morton. Jesus the Magician. LC 76-9986. (Illus.). 1978. 12.95 (ISBN 0-06-067412-1, HarpR). Har-Row.

Spangler, David. Reflections on the Christ. 144p. 1981. pap. 6.50 (ISBN 0-905249-52-6, Pub. by Findhorn-Thule Scotland). Hydra Bk.

Tiemeyer. Jesus Christ Super Psychic. 1977. pap. 3.95 (ISBN 0-917200-15-2). ESPress.

Vines, Jerry. Interviews with Jesus. 1981. 3.25 (ISBN 0-8054-5180-3). Broadman.

Wilson, Clifford. The Passover Plot Exposed. LC 77-73814. 1977. pap. 2.95 (ISBN 0-89051-032-6, Master Bks). CLP Pubs.

JESUS CHRIST-PARABLES

Barclay, William. And Jesus Said: A Handbook on the Parables of Jesus. 1970. pap. 5.50 (ISBN 0-664-24898-5). Westminster.

Berg, Jean H. The Good Samaritan. (Illus.). 1975. pap. 3.95 (ISBN 0-87510-101-1). Chr Science.

Brewington, Doyle W. The Parables of the Kingdom. 64p. 1981. 4.95 (ISBN 0-8059-2774-3). Dorrance.

Bunyan, John. Barren Fig Tree. pap. 1.25 (ISBN 0-685-19824-3). Reiner.

--Groans of a Lost Soul. LC 68-6571. 1967. pap. 3.25 (ISBN 0-685-19830-8). Reiner.

Buttrick, George A. The Parables of Jesus. (Minister's Paperback Library Ser). 274p. 1973. pap. 5.95 (ISBN 0-8010-0597-3). Baker Bk.

Carlston, Charles E. The Parables of the Triple Tradition. LC 74-26347. 272p. 1975. pap. 14.95 (ISBN 0-8006-0402-4, 1-402). Fortress.

Carpenter, Alton E. The Infinite Thought Projections of Jesus. 1975. 10.00 (ISBN 0-682-48356-7). Exposition.

Chekijian, Vartan S. The Strange Dreams. 109p. 1980. 5.95 (ISBN 0-533-03227-X). Vantage.

Coleman, William & Coleman, Patricia. Jesus: His Parables, Death & Resurrection. rev. ed. (Mine Is the Morning Ser.). 160p. (gr. 9-12). 1978. tchrs. manual & duplicator masters 16.95 (ISBN 0-89622-072-9). Twenty-Third.

Crossan, John. In Parables. LC 73-7067. 160p. 1973. 9.95 (ISBN 0-06-061606-7, HarpR). Har-Row.

Dale, Alan T. God Cares for Everybody, Everywhere. (Rainbow Books (Bible Story Books for Children)). (Orig.). 1978. pap. 1.00 (ISBN 0-8192-1237-7). Morehouse.

David, William & Gibson, Margaret. Reincarnation & the Soul in the Parables of Jesus. 80p. 1980. pap. 4.50 (ISBN 0-87516-412-9). De Vorss.

Dodd, C. H. Parables of the Kingdom. rev. ed. 1961. pap. text ed. 5.95x (ISBN 0-684-15049-2, ScribC). Scribner.

Evans, Colleen. The Vine Life. 120p. 1980. 6.95 (ISBN 0-912376-40-6). Chosen Bks Pub.

Funk, Robert W. Language Hermeneutic, & Word of God. LC 66-20776. (Scholars Press Reprint Ser.: No. 1). 1966. pap. 9.00 (ISBN 0-89130-225-5, 000701). Scholars Pr Ca.

The Good Samaritan. LC 76-47914. (Sunshine Bks.). (Illus.). 1977. pap. 1.00 (ISBN 0-8006-1578-6, 1-1578). Fortress.

Gregory The Great, Saint Parables of the Gospel. 169p. 1960. 5.95 (ISBN 0-933932-12-X). Scepter Pubs.

Gross, Arthur W. Stories Jesus Told. 1981. 6.95 (ISBN 0-570-04059-0, 56YY1352). Concordia.

Hargreaves, John. A Guide to the Parables. LC 74-20518. 144p. 1975. pap. 3.95 (ISBN 0-8170-0653-2). Judson.

Harrington, Wilfrid J. Key to the Parables. (Orig.). 1964. pap. 2.45 (ISBN 0-8091-1612-X, Deus). Paulist Pr.

--Parables Told by Jesus: Contemporary Approach. LC 74-12395. 135p. (Orig.). 1974. pap. 3.95 (ISBN 0-8189-0296-5). Alba.

Hunter, Archibald M. The Parables Then & Now. LC 72-170113. 1972. pap. 5.95 (ISBN 0-664-24940-X). Westminster.

Jeremias, Joachim. Parables of Jesus. rev. ed. LC 63-22114. (Illus.). 1971. pap. 6.95x (ISBN 0-684-16244-X, SL267, ScribC). Scribner.

--Rediscovering the Parables. LC 67-13197. 1966. pap. text ed. 6.95x (ISBN 0-684-15129-4, SL173, ScribC). Scribner.

Jewett, Robert. Jesus Against the Rapture: Seven Unexpected Prophecies. LC 78-31759. 1979. pap. 5.95 (ISBN 0-664-24253-7). Westminster.

Joyce, Jon L. Watermelons from Pumpkin Seeds? 75p. (Orig.). 1975. pap. 3.80 (ISBN 0-89536-250-3). CSS Pub.

Keller, Philip. Bom Pastor E Suas Ovelhas, O. (Port.). Date not set. pap. 1.60 (ISBN 0-686-75283-X). Life Pubs Intl.

--El Buen Pastor y Sus Ovejas. (Span.). Date not set. pap. 1.75 (ISBN 0-686-75313-5). Life Pubs Intl.

Kissinger, Warren S. The Parables of Jesus: A History of Interpretation & Bibliography. (American Theological Library Association (ATLA) Bibliography Ser.: No. 4). 463p. 1979. lib. bdg. 22.00 (ISBN 0-8108-1186-3). Scarecrow.

Kistemaker, Simon. The Parables of Jesus. 264p. 1980. 10.95 (ISBN 0-8010-5423-0). Baker Bk.

Lambrecht, Jan. Once More Astonished: The Parables of Jesus Christ. 262p. 1981. pap. 9.95 (ISBN 0-8245-0093-8). Crossroad NY.

Lawson, LeRoy. Cracking the Code. LC 76-57045. 1977. pap. 1.95 (ISBN 0-87239-125-6, 40042). Standard Pub.

Lightfoot, Neil R. Lessons from the Parables. (Minister's Paperback Library). 184p. 1976. pap. 3.95 (ISBN 0-8010-5564-4). Baker Bk.

--Parables of Jesus, 2 Pts. (Living Word Paperback Ser.). (Orig.). 1963. pap. 2.50 ea. Pt. 1 (ISBN 0-8344-0021-9). Pt. 2 (ISBN 0-8344-0022-7). Sweet.

Lindsay, Gordon. Parables of Christ, Vol. 1. (Span.). 0.95 (ISBN 0-89985-980-1). Christ Nations.

--Parables of Christ, Vol. 2. (Span.). 0.95 (ISBN 0-89985-981-X). Christ Nations.

Loughhead, LaRue A. Sayings & Doings of Jesus. 128p. 1981. pap. 5.95 (ISBN 0-8170-0940-X). Judson.

McFague, Sallie. Speaking in Parables: A Study in Metaphor & Theology. LC 74-26338. 192p. 1975. pap. 4.25 (ISBN 0-8006-1097-0, 1-1097). Fortress.

McQuilkin, Robert C. Our Lord's Parables. 1980. pap. 4.95 (ISBN 0-310-41541-1). Zondervan.

Michaels, J. Ramsey. Servant & Son: Jesus in Parable & Gospel. LC 80-84651. 1981. pap. 8.95 (ISBN 0-8042-0409-8). John Knox.

Millais, John E. The Parables of Our Lord & Savior Jesus Christ. 5.00 (ISBN 0-8446-5225-3). Peter Smith.

Morgan, G. Campbell. Parables & Metaphors of Our Lord. 1956. 10.95 (ISBN 0-8007-0245-X). Revell.

Mustard Seeds & Wineskins: Dramas & Meditations on Seven Parables. LC 79-176471. 1972. pap. 3.50 (ISBN 0-8066-1201-0, 10-4565); drama bklet 1.50 (ISBN 0-8066-1202-9, 10-4566). Augsburg.

Ogilvie, Lloyd J. The Autobiography of God. LC 78-53355. 324p. 1979. 9.95 (ISBN 0-8307-0683-6, 5108101). Regal.

The Parables of Christ. 1980. 12.50 (ISBN 0-86524-059-0). Klock & Klock.

Pentz, Croft M. Outlines on the Parables of Jesus. (Sermon Outline Ser.). (Orig.). 1980. pap. 1.45 (ISBN 0-8010-7055-4). Baker Bk.

Perkins, Pheme. Hearing the Parables of Jesus. LC 80-84508. 228p. (Orig.). 1981. pap. 6.95 (ISBN 0-8091-2352-5). Paulist Pr.

Poovey, W. A. Banquets & Beggers: Dramas & Meditations on Six Parables. LC 74-77672. 128p. (Orig.). 1974. pap. 3.25 (ISBN 0-8066-1419-6, 10-0540); drama bklet 1.25 (ISBN 0-8066-1420-X, 10-0541). Augsburg.

--Prodigals & Publicans: Dramas & Meditations on Six Parables. LC 79-54111. 100p. 1979. pap. 3.75 (ISBN 0-8066-1763-2, 10-5247). Augsburg.

Runk, Wesley T. Parables of Jesus. 1971. 1.85 (ISBN 0-89536-192-2). CSS Pub.

Scott, Bernard B. Jesus, Symbol-Maker for the Kingdom. LC 80-2388. 192p. 1981. 15.95 (ISBN 0-8006-0654-X, 1-654). Fortress.

Seagren, Dan. The Parables. 1978. pap. 3.95 (ISBN 0-8423-4797-6). Tyndale.

Seale, Ervin. Learn to Live. 1966. pap. 5.95 (ISBN 0-911336-08-7). Sci of Mind.

Smith, Charles W. The Jesus of the Parables. LC 74-26816. 255p. 1975. 8.95 (ISBN 0-8298-0267-3). Pilgrim NY.

Spurgeon, Charles H. Parables of Our Lord. (Treasury of Spurgeon on Life & Work of Our Lord). 13.95 (ISBN 0-8010-8154-8). Baker Bk.

Stein, Robert H. An Introduction to the Parables of Jesus. LC 81-3422. 1981. pap. price not set (ISBN 0-664-24390-8). Westminster.
Taylor, William M. Parables of Our Saviour. LC 74-79943. 1975. 10.95 (ISBN 0-8254-3805-5). Kregel.
Tenney, Merrill C. Who's Boss? 1980. text ed. 7.95 (ISBN 0-88207-227-7). Victor Bks.
Thielicke, Helmut. The Waiting Father. Doberstein, J. W., tr. from Ger. 1978. 12.00 (ISBN 0-227-67634-3). Attic Pr.
Trench, R. C. Notes on the Parables of Our Lord. (Twin Brooks Ser). pap. 4.95 (ISBN 0-8010-8774-0). Baker Bk.
Wiersbe, Warren W. Meet Yourself in the Parables. 1979. pap. 3.50 (ISBN 0-88207-790-2). Victor Bks.

JESUS CHRIST-PARABLES-JUVENILE LITERATURE

Bull, Norman J. Stories Jesus Told. LC 76-75402. (Illus.). (gr. 3-7). 1969. 3.50 (ISBN 0-8066-0924-9, 10-6031). Augsburg.
Dale, Alan T. Who's My Friend? (Rainbow Books (Bible Story Books for Children)). 16p. 1978. pap. 1.00 (ISBN 0-8192-1236-9). Morehouse.
--God Cares for Everybody, Everywhere. (Rainbow Books (Bible Story Books for Children)). (Orig.). 1978. pap. 1.00 (ISBN 0-8192-1237-7). Morehouse.
Dean, Bessie. Stories Jesus Told: A Child's Coloring Book of the Parables of Jesus. (Children's Inspirational Coloring Bk.). (Illus.). (ps-6). 1979. pap. 4.95 (ISBN 0-88290-132-X). Horizon Utah.
Diamond, Lucy. Two Stories Jesus Told. (Ladybird Ser). (Illus.). 1959. bds. 1.49 (ISBN 0-87508-870-8). Chr Lit.
Elmer, Irene & Mathews. Boy Who Ran Away. LC 63-23143. (Arch Bks: Set 1). (Illus.). (gr. 3-5). 1964. laminated bdg. 0.79 (ISBN 0-570-06001-X, 59-1104). Concordia.
Hilliard, Dick & Valenti-Hilliard, Beverly. Wonders. (Center Celebration Ser.). (Illus.). 60p. (Orig.). 1981. pap. text ed. 3.95 (ISBN 0-89390-032-X). Resource Pubns.
Kramer, Janice. Sir Abner & His Grape Pickers. (Arch Bks.: Set 7). (Illus., Orig.). (ps-4). 1970. pap. 0.79 (ISBN 0-570-06051-6, 59-1167). Concordia.
--Unforgiving Servant. (Arch Bks: Set 5). (Illus.). (gr. 5). 1968. laminated bdg. 0.79 (ISBN 0-570-06035-4, 59-1148). Concordia.
Kramer, Janice & Mathews. Eight Bags of Gold. LC 64-16985. (Arch Bks: Set 1). (Illus.). 1964. laminated bdg 0.79 (ISBN 0-570-06003-6, 59-1108). Concordia.
--Good Samaritan. LC 63-23369. (Arch Bks: Set 1). (Illus.). 1964. laminated bdg 0.79 (ISBN 0-570-06000-1, 59-1102). Concordia.
--Rich Fool. LC 64-16984. (Arch Bks: Set 1). (Illus.). (gr. 1-3). 1964. 0.79 (ISBN 0-570-06004-4, 59-1109). Concordia.
Latourette, Jane & Mathews. House on the Rock. (Arch Bks: Set 3). 1966. laminated bdg. 0.79 (ISBN 0-570-06019-2, 59-1128). Concordia.
Latourette, Jane & Wind, Betty. Jon & the Little Lost Lamb. LC 65-15145. (Arch Bks: Set 2). 1965. pap. 0.79 (ISBN 0-570-06008-7, 59-1106). Concordia.
Mueller, Virginia. The King's Invitation. (Arch Bks: Set 5). (Illus.). (gr. 3-4). 1968. laminated bdg. 0.79 (ISBN 0-570-06033-8, 59-1146). Concordia.
Raemers, Sidney A. Christ's Own Stories for Teen-Agers. LC 66-29011. 4.50 (ISBN 0-686-65150-2). Helios.
--Two Books for Teen-Agers. Incl. Christ's Own Stories for Teen-Agers. Dern, Raymond J., frwd. by. 4.50 (ISBN 0-685-22593-3); A Teen-Ager's Life of Christ. Smith, John T., frwd. by. 4.95 (ISBN 0-87037-010-3). (YA) 7.95 set (ISBN 0-685-22592-5). Helios.
Reid, John C. Parables from Nature. (ps-6). 1954. 2.95 (ISBN 0-8028-4025-6). Eerdmans.
Scheck, Joan. Two Men in the Temple. (Arch Bks: Set 5). (Illus.). (gr. 5). 1968. laminated bdg. 0.79 (ISBN 0-570-06036-2, 59-1149). Concordia.

JESUS CHRIST-PARABLES-SERMONS

Nelson, Brian A. Hustle Won't Bring the Kingdom of God: Jesus' Parables Interpreted for Today. 1978. pap. 2.95 (ISBN 0-8272-1417-0). Bethany Pr.
St. Bonaventure. What Manner of Man. (Sermons on Christ Ser). 1974. 5.95 (ISBN 0-8199-0497-X). Franciscan Herald.
Thielicke, Helmut. The Waiting Father. LC 75-12284. 192p. 1981. pap. 4.95 (ISBN 0-06-067991-3, RD 364, HarpR). Har-Row.
Tolbert, Mary Ann. Perspectives on the Parables: An Approach to Multiple Interpretations. LC 78-54563. 144p. 1978. 8.95 (ISBN 0-8006-0527-6, 1-527). Fortress.
Ward, C. M. The Playboy Comes Home. LC 75-32603. 112p. (Orig.). 1976. pap. 1.25 (ISBN 0-88243-572-8, 020572). Gospel Pub.

JESUS CHRIST-PASSION

see also Holy Week; Jesus Christ-Relics of the Passion; Lent; Stations of the Cross

Crawford, C. C. Passion of Our Lord. 6.95 (ISBN 0-89225-140-9). Gospel Advocate.
Detrick, R. Blaine. I Met Jesus When He Suffered. 76p. 1976. pap. 3.80 (ISBN 0-89536-103-5). CSS Pub.
Emmerich, Anne C. Dolorous Passion of Our Lord Jesus Christ. 1980. lib. bdg. 64.95 (ISBN 0-8490-3100-1). Gordon Pr.
Jaubert, Annie. Date of the Last Supper. LC 65-17975. 1965. 3.50 (ISBN 0-8189-0036-9). Alba.
Joyce, Jon L. & Sandrock, Alfred G. Lord's Passion. 1977. pap. 13.60 (ISBN 0-89536-143-4). CSS Pub.
Kesich, Veselin. The Passion of Christ. 84p. pap. 1.95 (ISBN 0-913836-80-X). St Vladimirs.
Lacomara, Aelred, ed. The Language of the Cross. 1977. 5.95 (ISBN 0-8199-0617-4). Franciscan Herald.
Maier, Paul L. First Easter: The True & Unfamiliar Story in Words & Pictures. LC 72-81346. (Illus.). 1973. 9.95 (ISBN 0-06-065397-3, HarpR). Har-Row.
Marin, Louis. The Semiotics of the Passion Narratives. Johnson, Alfred M., Jr., tr. (Pittsburgh Theological Monographs: No. 25). 1980. pap. 12.50 (ISBN 0-915138-23-9). Pickwick.
Marison, Fiscar, tr. The Passion of Our Lord. 302p. 1980. pap. 3.95 (ISBN 0-911988-37-8). AMI Pr.
Murphy, Richard T. Days of Glory: The Passion, Death, & Resurrection of Jesus Christ. (Orig.). 1980. pap. 4.95 (ISBN 0-89283-082-4). Servant.
Odenheimer, William H. Jerusalem & Its Vicinity: Familiar Lectures on the Sacred Localities Connected with the Week Before the Resurrection. Davis, Moshe, ed. (America & the Holy Land Ser.). (Illus.). 1977. Repr. of 1855 ed. lib. bdg. 15.00x (ISBN 0-405-10272-0). Arno.
Reid, William. Blood of Jesus. pap. 1.00x (ISBN 0-686-09309-7). Liberty Bell Pr.
Schilder, Klass. The Trilogy, 3 vols. 1978. 48.00 (ISBN 0-86524-940-7). Klock & Klock.
Southwell, Robert. Marie Magdalens Funeral Teares. LC 74-22099. 180p. 1975. 20.00x (ISBN 0-8201-1144-9). Schol Facsimiles.
Spurgeon, Charles H. Passion & Death of Our Lord. (Treasury of Spurgeon & Life & Work of Our Lord). 13.95 (ISBN 0-8010-8155-6). Baker Bk.
Wilson, Ernest C. Week That Changed the World. 1968. 2.95 (ISBN 0-87159-170-7). Unity Bks.
Wright, E. A. Ystoire De la Passion. Repr. of 1944 ed. 11.50 (ISBN 0-384-70484-0). Johnson Repr.

JESUS CHRIST-PASSION-ART

see Jesus Christ-Art

JESUS CHRIST-PASSION-DEVOTIONAL LITERATURE

see also Paschal Mystery

Arrastia, Cecilio. Itinerario De la Pasion: Meditaciones De la Semana Santa. 1981. Repr. of 1978 ed. pap. 2.50 (ISBN 0-311-43036-8). Casa Bautista.
Boevey, Mateo C. Twenty Holy Hours. 1978. pap. 4.00 (ISBN 0-8198-0563-7). Dghtrs St Paul.
Drescher, John M. Testimony of Triumph. 1980. pap. 4.95 (ISBN 0-310-23920-6). Zondervan.
Gariepy, Henry. Footsteps to Calvary. (Orig.). 1977. pap. 2.50 (ISBN 0-89350-014-3). Fountain Pr.
Goodier, A. Passion & Death of Our Lord Jesus Christ. 1978. 7.50 (ISBN 0-8198-0544-0); pap. 5.95 (ISBN 0-8198-0545-9). Dghtrs St Paul.
Locker, Herbert. The Man Who Died for Me. 1979. 6.95 (ISBN 0-8499-0130-8). Word Bks.
Spurgeon, Charles H. Twelve Sermons on the Love of Christ. (Charles H. Spurgeon Library). 1977. pap. 3.45 (ISBN 0-8010-8096-7). Baker Bk.
Symbols of Our Lord's Passion. 1956. pap. 0.25 (ISBN 0-685-18941-4, 06-0518). Northwest Pub.

JESUS CHRIST-PASSION-DRAMA

see Jesus Christ-Drama; Passion-Plays

JESUS CHRIST-PASSION-SERMONS

see also Holy-Week Sermons; Lenten Sermons

Battle, Dennis M. The Gospel Religion of Jesus Christ. LC 80-65198. 52p. 1980. pap. 2.25 (ISBN 0-933464-08-8). D M Battle Pubns.
Joyce, Jon L. Conversations During Christ's Passion. (Orig.). 1977. pap. 3.65 (ISBN 0-89536-047-0). CSS Pub.
Spurgeon, Charles H. Passion & Death of Christ. 1965. pap. 2.95 (ISBN 0-8028-8157-2). Eerdmans.

JESUS CHRIST-PASSION-SONGS AND MUSIC

see Passion-Music

JESUS CHRIST-PERSON AND OFFICES

see also Hypostatic Union

Achebe, Chinua. Arrow of God. LC 75-79409. 1969. pap. 3.50 (ISBN 0-385-01480-5, A698, Anch). Doubleday.
Baillie, Donald M. God Was in Christ. 1948. pap. 3.95 (ISBN 0-684-71704-2, SL111, ScribT). Scribner.
Barclay, William. The Mind of Jesus. LC 61-7332. 352p. 1976. pap. 5.95 (ISBN 0-06-060451-4, RD143, HarpR). Har-Row.
Baxter, Sidlow J. The Master Theme of the Bible. 1975. 5.95 (ISBN 0-8423-4185-4). Tyndale.
Best, W. E. Studies in the Person & Work of Jesus Christ. pap. 2.95 (ISBN 0-8010-0644-9). Baker Bk.
Bornkamm, Gunther. Jesus of Nazareth. LC 61-5256. 240p. 1975. pap. 6.95 (ISBN 0-06-060932-X, RD113, HarpR). Har-Row.
Braun, Herbert. Jesus of Nazareth: The Man & His Time. Kalin, Everett R., tr. from Ger. LC 78-14664. 160p. 1979. 6.95 (ISBN 0-8006-0531-4, 1-531). Fortress.
Buell, Jon A. & Hyder, O. Quentin. Jesus: God, Ghost or Guru? (Christian Free University Curriculum Ser.). 1978. pap. 4.95 (ISBN 0-310-35761-6). Zondervan.
Chemnitz, Martin. Two Natures in Christ. Preus, J. A., tr. LC 74-115465. Orig. Title: De Duabus Naturis in Christo. 1970. 19.95 (ISBN 0-570-03210-5, 15-2109). Concordia.
Chitwood, B. J. Meet the Real Jesus. LC 76-14631. 1977. pap. 2.95 (ISBN 0-8054-1940-3). Broadman.
Cobb, John B., Jr. Christ in a Pluralistic Age. LC 74-820. 1975. 12.50 (ISBN 0-664-20861-4). Westminster.
Conzelmann, Hans. Jesus. Reumann, John, ed. Lord, J. Raymond, tr. from Gr. LC 73-79011. 128p. 1973. pap. 3.50 (ISBN 0-8006-1000-8, 1-1000). Fortress.
Craig, Samuel G. Jesus of Yesterday & Today. kivar 1.95 (ISBN 0-87552-156-8). Presby & Reformed.
Davis, R. M. The Woods: The Human Self & the Realism of Jesus. 79p. 1971. pap. 1.00 (ISBN 0-9600434-0-3, 03). Camda.
Dawe, Donald G. Jesus - Lord for All Times. 128p. 1975. pap. 3.95 (ISBN 0-8042-9066-0); tchrs' ed 3.95 (ISBN 0-8042-9067-9). John Knox.
Dejonge, M. Jesus: Inspiring & Disturbing Presence. Steely, John E., tr. from Dutch. LC 74-10915. 192p. 1974. pap. 4.95 (ISBN 0-687-19920-4). Abingdon.
Dodd, Charles H. Founder of Christianity. LC 73-90222. 1970. pap. 3.95 (ISBN 0-02-084640-1). Macmillan.
Driver, Tom F. Christ in a Changing World: Toward an Ethical Christology. LC 81-5552. 1981. 12.95 (ISBN 0-8245-0105-5). Crossroad NY.
Fisher. Jesus & His Teachings. LC 74-189502. 4.95 (ISBN 0-8054-1333-2). Broadman.
Fitzpatrick, James K. Jesus Christ Before He Became a Superstar. LC 76-8829. 1976. 7.95 (ISBN 0-87000-361-5). Arlington Hse.
Frei, Hans W. The Identity of Jesus Christ: The Hermeneutical Bases of Dogmatic Theology. LC 74-80422. 192p. 1975. 8.95 (ISBN 0-8006-0292-7, 1-292). Fortress.
Guzie, Tad W. Jesus & the Eucharist. LC 73-90069. 1974. pap. 4.95 (ISBN 0-8091-1858-0). Paulist Pr.
Harold, Preston. The Shining Stranger. rev. ed. LC 73-19480. 1974. 9.50 (ISBN 0-396-06931-2, Pub. by Wayfarer Pr); pap. 6.00 (ISBN 0-396-06932-0, Pub. by Wayfarer Pr.). Dodd.
Hengel, Martin. Christ & Power. Kalin, Everett R., tr. from Ger. LC 76-62608. 96p. (Orig.). 1977. pap. 3.25 (ISBN 0-8006-1256-6, 1-1256). Fortress.
--Was Jesus a Revolutionist? Reumann, John, ed. Klassen, William, tr. from Ger. LC 77-157545. (Facet Bks.). 64p. (Orig.). 1971. pap. 1.50 (ISBN 0-8006-3066-1, 1-3066). Fortress.
Hinson, E. Glenn. Jesus Christ. (Faith of Our Fathers Ser.). 1977. 12.50 (ISBN 0-8434-0620-8, Consortium); pap. 6.95 (ISBN 0-686-67856-7). McGrath.
Hooper, John. The Early Writings of John Hooper. 1843. 42.50 (ISBN 0-384-24210-3). Johnson Repr.
Huegel, F. J. Why Jesus? 1970. pap. 1.50 (ISBN 0-87123-635-4, 200635). Bethany Hse.
Jay, E. G. Son of Man, Son of God. 1965. pap. 3.00 (ISBN 0-7735-0029-4). McGill-Queens U Pr.
Johnson, Robert C. The Meaning of Christ. (Layman's Theological Library). 1958. pap. 2.95 (ISBN 0-664-24009-7). Westminster.
Kappen, Sebastian. Jesus & Freedom. LC 76-25927. 1977. 8.95x (ISBN 0-88344-232-9); pap. 3.95x (ISBN 0-88344-233-7). Orbis Bks.
Kasper, Walter. Jesus the Christ. LC 76-20021. 289p. 1977. pap. 6.95 (ISBN 0-8091-2081-X). Paulist Pr.
Ketcham, Charles B. A Theology of Encounter: The Ontological Ground for a New Christology. LC 77-21905. 1978. 14.95x (ISBN 0-271-00520-3). Pa St U Pr.
Koyama, Kosuke. No Handle on the Cross. LC 76-23160. 1977. 7.95x (ISBN 0-88344-338-4); pap. 3.95x (ISBN 0-88344-339-2). Orbis Bks.
Lampe, G. W. God As Spirit: The Bampton Lectures for 1976. 1978. 16.95 (ISBN 0-19-826644-8). Oxford U Pr.
Lane, Dermont A. The Reality of Jesus. LC 77-70635. (Exploration Book Ser.). 180p. 1977. pap. 4.95 (ISBN 0-8091-2020-8). Paulist Pr.
Leivestad, Ragnar. Christ the Conqueror. 1954. 10.00x (ISBN 0-8401-1386-2). Allenson-Breckinridge.
Leuba, Jean-Louis. New Testament Pattern. 1953. 6.00x (ISBN 0-8401-1391-9). Allenson-Breckinridge.
Mackintosh, H. R. The Doctrine of the Person of Jesus Christ. 2nd ed. (International Theological Library). 560p. 1978. Repr. of 1913 ed. pap. text ed. 13.95x (ISBN 0-686-70894-6). Attic Pr.
Maritain, Jacques. De la Grace et de l'Humanite de Jesus. 2nd ed. 156p. 1967. 8.95 (ISBN 0-686-56347-6). French & Eur.
Marshall, I. Howard. The Work of Christ. 1969. pap. 4.50 (ISBN 0-85364-090-4). Attic Pr.
Meilach, M. D. From Order to Omega. pap. 0.95 (ISBN 0-8199-0038-9, L38249). Franciscan Herald.
Meilach, Michael D. Primacy of Christ. 1964. 4.95 (ISBN 0-8199-0087-7, L38655). Franciscan Herald.
Miller, David L. Christs: Meditations on Archetypal Images in Christian Theology. 1981. 12.95 (ISBN 0-8164-0492-5). Seabury.
Moltmann, Jurgen. The Crucified God. LC 73-18694. 352p. 1974. 15.95 (ISBN 0-06-065901-7, HarpR). Har-Row.
More, Paul E. Christ the Word. LC 72-88913. Repr. of 1927 ed. lib. bdg. 14.25x (ISBN 0-8371-2244-9, MOCW). Greenwood.
O'Grady, John F. Models of Jesus. LC 80-1726. 192p. 1981. 10.95 (ISBN 0-385-17320-2). Doubleday.
Pannenberg, Wolfhart. Jesus: God & Man. 2d ed. Wilkins, Lewis L. & Priebe, Duane A., trs. LC 76-26478. 1977. 12.50 (ISBN 0-664-21289-1). Westminster.
Ramsey, A. Michael, et al. The Charismatic Christ. 128p. (Orig.). 1973. pap. 2.50 (ISBN 0-8192-1141-9). Morehouse.
Robinson, O. Preston & Robinson, Christine H. Christ's Eternal Gospel: Do the Dead Sea Scrolls, the Pseudepigrapha, & Other Ancient Records Challenge or Support the Bible? LC 76-44650. (Illus.). 1976. 6.95 (ISBN 0-87747-616-0). Deseret Bk.
Routley, Erik. Man for Others. (Orig.). 1964. pap. 4.95 (ISBN 0-19-500463-9). Oxford U Pr.
Ruether, Rosemary R. To Change the World: Christology & Cultural Criticism. 112p. 1981. 9.95 (ISBN 0-8245-0084-9). Crossroad NY.
Schoonover, Melvin E. What If We Did Follow Jesus? LC 78-2594. 1978. pap. 3.50 (ISBN 0-8170-0791-1). Judson.
Schweizer, Eduard. Jesus. LC 76-107322. 1979. pap. 4.95 (ISBN 0-8042-0331-8). John Knox.
Senior, Donald. Jesus: A Gospel Portrait. 192p. (Orig.). 1975. pap. 2.95 (ISBN 0-8278-9003-6). Pflaum Pr.
Suggs, M. Jack. Wisdom, Christology, & Law in Matthew's Gospel. LC 75-95930. 1970. text ed. 7.95x (ISBN 0-674-95375-4). Harvard U Pr.
Sykes, S. W. & Clayton, J. P. Christ, Faith & History. LC 70-176257. (Cambridge Studies in Christology). (Illus.). 280p. 1972. 44.00 (ISBN 0-521-08451-2); pap. text ed. 10.95x (ISBN 0-521-29325-1). Cambridge U Pr.
Tripole, Martin R. The Jesus Event & Our Response. LC 79-27896. 248p. (Orig.). 1980. pap. 6.95 (ISBN 0-8189-0399-6). Alba.
Trocme, Andre. Jesus & the Nonviolent Revolution. Shenk, Michel, tr. from Fr. LC 73-9934. 296p. 1974. 7.95 (ISBN 0-8361-1719-0). Herald Pr.
Vick, Edward W. H. Jesus. LC 78-10253. (Anvil Ser.). 1979. pap. 4.95 (ISBN 0-8127-0220-4). Review & Herald.
Warfield, B. B. The Person & Work of Christ. 7.95 (ISBN 0-8010-9588-3). Baker Bk.
Warfield, Benjamin B. Person & Work of Christ. 1950. 7.95 (ISBN 0-87552-529-6). Presby & Reformed.
Weiler, Eugene. Jesus: Son of God. 132p. 1975. 12.95 (ISBN 0-685-69891-2). Franciscan Herald.
Wenham, J. W. Christ & the Bible. LC 72-97950. 187p. 1973. pap. 3.95 (ISBN 0-87784-760-6). Inter-Varsity.
Westerman, Claus. Old Testament & Jesus Christ. Kaste, Omar, tr. LC 71-101108. 1970. pap. 3.50 (ISBN 0-8066-1005-0, 10-4736). Augsburg.
Yoder, John H. The Politics of Jesus. 176p. 1972. pap. 4.95 (ISBN 0-8028-1485-9). Eerdmans.

JESUS CHRIST-PERSONALITY

see Jesus Christ-Character

JESUS CHRIST-PICTURES, ILLUSTRATIONS, ETC.

see Jesus Christ-Art

JESUS CHRIST-POETRY

Babin, Lawrence J. Agony in the Garden. LC 75-158476. 1971. deluxe ed. 3.00x (ISBN 0-912492-25-2); pap. 1.00 (ISBN 0-912492-00-7). Pyquag.

Brokering, Herbert F. In Due Season. LC 66-22563. (Illus.). 1966. 6.50 (ISBN 0-8066-0620-7, 10-3209). Augsburg.
Brown, Beatrice. The Southern Passion. LC 74-10772. 1927. 20.00 (ISBN 0-8414-3122-1). Folcroft.
Clark, Thomas C., ed. Master of Men. fascimile ed. LC 72-116396. (Granger Index Reprint Ser). 1930. 15.00 (ISBN 0-8369-6137-4). Arno.
Crow, Martha F. Christ in the Poetry of Today. 1918. lib. bdg. 15.00 (ISBN 0-8414-2420-9). Folcroft.
--Christ in the Poetry of Today: An Anthology from American Poets. 1978. Repr. of 1917 ed. lib. bdg. 25.00 (ISBN 0-8495-0912-2). Arden Lib.
Cynewulf. The Christ of Cynewulf; a Poem in Three Parts: The Advent, the Ascension, & the Last Judgement. Cook, Albert S., ed. LC 73-178524. Repr. of 1900 ed. 20.00 (ISBN 0-404-56538-7). AMS Pr.
De Hojeda, Diego. Christiada: Introduction & Text. Corcoran, Sr. Mary H., ed. LC 35-9384. (Catholic University of America. Studies in Romance Languages & Literatures: No. 11). Repr. of 1935 ed. 38.50 (ISBN 0-404-50311-X). AMS Pr.
Janeway, James. A Token for Children, Being an Exact Account of the Conversion, Holy & Exemplary Lives & Joyful Deaths of Several Young Children, Repr. Of 1676 Ed. Bd. with The Holy Bible in Verse. Harris, Benjamin. Repr. of 1717 ed; History of the Holy Jesus. Repr. of 1746 ed; The School of Good Manners....Rules for Children's Behavior, at the Meeting-House, at Home, at the Table, in Company, in Discourse, at School, Etc. Repr. of 1754 ed; The Prodigal Daughter....Who Because Her Parents Would Not Support Her in All of Her Extravagance, Bargained with the Devil to Poison Them, Etc. Williams, Elizabeth, pref. by. Repr. of 1771 ed. LC 75-32134. (Classics of Children's Literature, 1621-1932: Vol. 2). 1976. PLB 38.00 (ISBN 0-8240-2251-3). Garland Pub.
Marchant, James. Anthology of Jesus. Wiersbe, Warren W., ed. LC 80-25038. 1981. Repr. of 1926 ed. 9.95 (ISBN 0-8254-4015-7). Kregel.
Mims, Edwin. Christ of the Poets. Repr. of 1948 ed. lib. bdg. 15.00 (ISBN 0-8371-2555-3, MICP). Greenwood.
Oetting, R. When Jesus Was a Lad. LC 68-56816. (Illus.). (gr. 2-3). PLB 5.99 (ISBN 0-87783-047-9). Oddo.
Stubbs, Charles W. The Christ of English Poetry. LC 73-1787. 1973. lib. bdg. 20.00 (ISBN 0-8414-2621-X). Folcroft.
Thomas, Joan G. If Jesus Came to My House. (Illus.). (gr. k-3). 1951. 4.95 (ISBN 0-688-40981-4); PLB 5.52 (ISBN 0-688-50981-9). Lothrop.
Vida, Marco G. The Christiad: Latin-English Edition. Drake, Gertrude C. & Forbes, Clarence A., eds. LC 78-1430. 288p. 1978. 9.85x (ISBN 0-8093-0814-2). S Ill U Pr.

JESUS CHRIST–PRAYERS
see also Lord's Prayer
Daughters of St. Paul. I Pray with Jesus. 1978. deluxe ed. 6.00 (ISBN 0-8198-0535-1); imitation leather o.p 3.00 (ISBN 0-8198-0536-X); plastic bdg. 3.00 (ISBN 0-8198-0537-8). Dghtrs St Paul.
Jeremias, Joachim. The Prayers of Jesus. Bowden, John, et al, trs. from Ger. LC 77-10427. 132p. 1978. pap. 3.75 (ISBN 0-8006-1322-8, 1-1322). Fortress.
Jesus Prayer: Selections from the Writings of the Saints. pap. 3.95 (ISBN 0-686-05645-0). Eastern Orthodox.
Macarthur, John, Jr. Jesus' Pattern of Prayer. 200p. 1981. 7.95 (ISBN 0-8024-4961-1). Moody.
Mitchell, Curtis C. Praying Jesus' Way. 1977. 7.95 (ISBN 0-8007-0843-1). Revell.
Poinsett, Brenda. When Jesus Prayed. LC 80-67896. 1981. pap. 3.25 (ISBN 0-8054-5179-X). Broadman.
Rahner, Karl. Watch & Pray with Me: The Seven Last Words. 1977. pap. 4.95 (ISBN 0-8245-0402-X). Crossroad NY.
Sjogren, Per-Olof. The Jesus Prayer. Linton, Sydney, tr. from Swedish. LC 75-18789. 96p. 1975. pap. 3.50 (ISBN 0-8006-1216-7, 1-1216). Fortress.
Stedman, Ray C. Jesus Teaches on Prayer. LC 75-14710. (Discovery Bks.). 1975. 4.95 (ISBN 0-87680-428-8); pap. 5.95 (ISBN 0-87680-988-3, 98040). Word Bks.
Wallis, Arthur. Jesus Prayed. 1966. pap. 0.50 (ISBN 0-87508-559-8). Chr Lit.

JESUS CHRIST–PREACHING
see Jesus Christ–Teaching Methods

JESUS CHRIST–PRE-EXISTENCE
Trakatellis, Demetrius C. The Pre-Existence of Christ in Justin Martyr. LC 76-44913. (Harvard Theological Review Ser.). 1976. pap. 7.50 (ISBN 0-89130-098-8, 020106). Scholars Pr Ca.

JESUS CHRIST–PRIESTHOOD
Bunyan, John. Work of Jesus Christ As an Advocate. pap. 3.95 (ISBN 0-685-19844-8). Reiner.
Milligan, William. The Ascension & Heavenly Priesthood of Our Lord. 1977. Repr. of 1894 ed. 11.95 (ISBN 0-87921-034-6). Attic Pr.

JESUS CHRIST–PRIMACY
see also Jesus Christ–Mystical Body; Logos
Meilach, M. D. From Order to Omega. pap. 0.95 (ISBN 0-8199-0038-9, L38249). Franciscan Herald.

JESUS CHRIST–PROPHECIES
Kirk, David, ed. Quotations from Chairman Jesus. 1979. 4.95 (ISBN 0-87243-091-X). Templegate.
Lucas, DeWitt B. God Tells the World. 1964. pap. 1.50 (ISBN 0-910140-08-1). Anthony.
Promises of Jesus. LC 80-65437. (Illus.). 64p. 1980. 5.95 (ISBN 0-915684-69-1). Christian Herald.
Sapat, Peter. The Return of the Christ & Prophecy. 293p. 1978. 8.95 (ISBN 0-8059-2536-8). Dorrance.
Wallace, Arthur, compiled by. America's Witness for Jesus Christ. 70p. 1978. pap. 1.95 (ISBN 0-937892-04-1). LL Co.
Wilkerson, David. The Pocket Promise Book. gift ed. LC 72-86208. 96p. 1981. imitation leather 3.95 (ISBN 0-8307-0789-1). Regal.

JESUS CHRIST–PROPHETIC OFFICE
Hiers, Richard H. Jesus & the Future: Unsolved Questions on Eschatology. LC 80-82189. 1981. 16.50 (ISBN 0-8042-0341-5); pap. 9.95 (ISBN 0-8042-0340-7). John Knox.
Murray, Andrew. Jesus Christ: Prophet-Priest. 64p. 1967. pap. 1.75 (ISBN 0-87123-271-5, 200271). Bethany Hse.

JESUS CHRIST–RELICS OF THE PASSION
see also Holy Cross; Holy Shroud
Stevenson, Kenneth, ed. Proceedings of the Nineteen Seventy-Seven United States Conference of Research on the Shroud of Turin. (Illus.). 244p. (Orig.). 1980. pap. 10.00 (ISBN 0-9605516-0-3). Shroud of Turin.
Wilson, Ian. The Shroud of Turin: The Burial Cloth of Jesus Christ. LC 79-1942. (Illus.). 1979. pap. 4.50 (ISBN 0-385-15042-3, Im). Doubleday.

JESUS CHRIST–RESURRECTION
see also Easter; Jesus Christ–Appearances; Paschal Mystery
Austin, E. L. C. Earth's Greatest Day. 96p. (Orig.). 1980. pap. 3.95 (ISBN 0-8010-0163-3). Baker Bk.
Barth, Karl. The Resurrection of the Dead. Kastenbaum, Robert, ed. LC 76-19559. (Death and Dying Ser.). 1977. Repr. of 1933 ed. lib. bdg. 17.00x (ISBN 0-405-09555-4). Arno.
Boff, Leonardo. The Question of Faith in the Ressurection of Jesus. Runde, Luis, tr. (Synthesis Ser). 75p. 1972. pap. 0.65 (ISBN 0-8199-0398-1). Franciscan Herald.
Briscoe, Jill. A Time for Living. (Illus.). 1980. pap. 5.95x (ISBN 0-89542-078-3). Ideals.
Brown, Raymond. The Virginal Conception & Bodily Resurrection of Jesus. LC 72-97399. 1973. pap. 2.95 (ISBN 0-8091-1768-1). Paulist Pr.
Chevrot, Georges. On the Third Day. 208p. 1961. 6.95 (ISBN 0-933932-10-3); pap. 2.95 (ISBN 0-933932-11-1). Scepter Pubs.
Coleman, William & Coleman, Patricia. Jesus: His Parables, Death & Resurrection. rev. ed. (Mine Is the Morning Ser.). 160p. (gr. 9-12). 1978. tchrs. manual & duplicator masters 16.95 (ISBN 0-89622-072-9). Twenty-Third.
Craig, William L. The Son Rises. 260p. 1981. 6.95 (ISBN 0-8024-7948-0). Moody.
--The Son Rises: The Historical Evidence for the Resurrection of Jesus. 160p. (Orig.). 1981. pap. 7.95 (ISBN 0-8010-2469-2). Baker Bk.
Drescher, John M. The Way of the Cross & the Resurrection. LC 77-25443. 1978. pap. 4.95 (ISBN 0-8361-1844-8). Herald Pr.
Drillock, David, et al. Pascha: The Resurrection of Christ. (Music Ser.). 274p. 1980. pap. 15.00 (ISBN 0-913836-50-8); 20.00 (ISBN 0-913836-65-6). St Vladimirs.
Emit II. 1.25 (ISBN 0-8423-0686-2). Tyndale.
Fitch, Alger M., Jr. Afterglow of Christ's Resurrection. LC 75-14692. (New Life Bks). (Illus.). 136p. 1975. pap. 3.95 (ISBN 0-87239-055-1, 40030). Standard Pub.
Flynn, Leslie B. Day of Resurrection. (Preaching Helps Ser). 1974. pap. 1.95 (ISBN 0-8010-3467-1). Baker Bk.
Gaffin, Richard B., Jr. Centrality of the Resurrection. (Baker Biblical Monographs). 1978. pap. 4.95 (ISBN 0-8010-3726-3). Baker Bk.
Habermas, Gary. Resurrection of Jesus: An Apologetic. 1980. pap. 5.95 (ISBN 0-8010-4215-1). Baker Bk.
Jansen, John F. The Resurrection of Jesus Christ in New Testament Theology. LC 80-231. 1980. pap. 9.95 (ISBN 0-664-24309-6). Westminster.
Ladd, George E. Creo en la Resurreccion de Jesus. Blanch, Miguel, tr. from Eng. LC 77-79934. (Serie Creo). 204p. (Orig., Span.). 1977. pap. 3.95 (ISBN 0-89922-091-6). Edit Caribe.
Lindsay, Gordon. Death & Resurrection of Christ. (Span.). 0.95 (ISBN 0-89985-983-6). Christ Nations.
Locker, Herbert. The Man Who Died for Me. 1979. 6.95 (ISBN 0-8499-0130-8). Word Bks.
McAllister, Dawson. A Walk with Christ Through the Resurrection. (Discussion Manual Ser.). 150p. 1981. pap. 7.95 (ISBN 0-8024-9192-8). Moody.
McDowell, Josh. The Resurrection Factor. 180p. (Orig.). 1981. cancelled (ISBN 0-918956-71-4, Dist. by Here's Life Publishers Inc.); pap. 4.95 (ISBN 0-918956-72-2). Campus Crusade.
Manson, T. W. Servant-Messiah: A Study of the Public Ministry of Jesus. (Twin Brook Ser). 1977. pap. 3.45 (ISBN 0-8010-6012-5). Baker Bk.
Marxsen, Willi. Resurrection of Jesus of Nazareth. Kohl, Margaret, tr. from Ger. LC 76-120083. 192p. (Orig.). 1970. pap. 4.50 (ISBN 0-8006-0001-0, 1-1). Fortress.
Morison, Frank. Who Moved the Stone. pap. 3.50 (ISBN 0-310-29562-9). Zondervan.
Morpha, Margery C. He Is Risen. 1980. pap. 1.95 (ISBN 0-88479-024-X). Arena Lettres.
Moule, H. C. & Orr, J. The Resurrection of Christ. 1980. 16.95 (ISBN 0-86524-062-0). Klock & Klock.
Mouton, Boyce. By This Shall All Men Know. LC 79-56541. 1980. pap. 2.95 (ISBN 0-89900-139-4). College Pr Pub.
Mumaw, John R. Resurrected Life. LC 65-11460. (Conrad Grebel Lecture Ser.). 1965. 4.00 (ISBN 0-8361-1511-2). Herald Pr.
Murphy, Richard T. Days of Glory: The Passion, Death, & Resurrection of Jesus Christ. (Orig.). 1980. pap. 4.95 (ISBN 0-89283-082-4). Servant.
Nutting, George. Resurrection Is Not a Fairy Tale. 1981. 5.75 (ISBN 0-8062-1649-2). Carlton.
O'Collins, Gerald. The Resurrection of Jesus Christ. LC 73-2613. 160p. 1973. pap. 3.50 (ISBN 0-8170-0614-1). Judson.
--What Are They Saying About the Resurrection? LC 78-51594. 1978. pap. 2.45 (ISBN 0-8091-2109-3). Paulist Pr.
Perrin, Norman. Resurrection According to Matthew, Mark, & Luke. LC 76-47913. 96p. (Orig.). 1977. pap. 3.50 (ISBN 0-8006-1248-5, 1-1248). Fortress.
Richards, H. J. The First Easter. (Fount Religious Paperbacks Ser). 1977. pap. 1.50 (ISBN 0-00-624166-2, FA4166). Collins Pubs.
Riley, James C. Tree of the Resurrection. 1978. pap. 2.00 (ISBN 0-89536-294-5). CSS Pub.
Riss, Richard. The Evidence for the Resurrection of Jesus Christ. LC 76-50978. 1977. pap. 1.95 (ISBN 0-87123-134-4, 200134). Bethany Hse.
Shaw, J. M. The Resurrection of Jesus Christ. 223p. 1920. text ed. 4.95 (ISBN 0-567-02252-8). Attic Pr.
Smith, Judy. The Stone Is Rolled Away. 1979. pap. 2.15 (ISBN 0-89536-372-0). CSS Pub.
Stewart, John J. The Eternal Gift: The Story of the Crucifixion & Resurrection of Christ. LC 78-52117. 1978. 5.50 (ISBN 0-88290-096-X). Horizon Utah.
Urbano, Paul D. The Marks of the Nails. LC 73-90039. (Illus.). 120p. (Orig.). 1973. pap. 3.50 (ISBN 0-913514-04-7). Am Natl Pub.
Wilckens, Ulrich. Resurrection. Stewart, A. M., tr. from Ger. LC 77-15752. Orig. Title: Auferstehung. 1978. 6.95 (ISBN 0-8042-0396-2). John Knox.
Zodhiates, Spiros. Resurrection: True or False? (Illus.). 1978. pap. 2.25 (ISBN 0-89957-524-2). AMG Pubs.

JESUS CHRIST–RESURRECTION–JUVENILE LITERATURE
Bowden, Joan C. Something Wonderful Happened. LC 77-6325. (I Can Read a Bible Story Ser.: No. 2). (Illus.). (gr. 2-4). 1977. 4.95 (ISBN 0-570-07324-3, 56-1515); pap. 1.95 (ISBN 0-570-07318-9, 56-1415). Concordia.
Odor, Ruth S. Happiest Day. LC 79-12184. (Bible Story Bks.). (Illus.). (ps-3). 1979. PLB 5.50 (ISBN 0-89565-085-1). Childs World.

JESUS CHRIST–RESURRECTION–SERMONS
Gordon, John M. Resurrection Messages. (Pocket Pulpit Library Ser.). 1978. pap. 1.95 (ISBN 0-8010-3657-7). Baker Bk.
Spurgeon, Charles H. Twelve Sermons on the Resurrection. (Charles H. Spurgeon Library). pap. 2.95 (ISBN 0-8010-7967-5). Baker Bk.

JESUS CHRIST–SACRED HEART, DEVOTION TO
see Sacred Heart, Devotion To

JESUS CHRIST–SAYINGS
see Jesus Christ–Words

JESUS CHRIST–SECOND ADVENT
see Second Advent

JESUS CHRIST–SERMON ON THE MOUNT
see Sermon on the Mount

JESUS CHRIST–SEVEN LAST WORDS
Allen, R. Earl. Seven Words of Christ: Before the Cross, from the Cross, After the Cross. (Pocket Pulpit Library). Orig. Title: Trials, Tragedies & Triumphs. 160p. 1981. pap. 2.95 (ISBN 0-8010-0175-7). Baker Bk.
Benko, Stephen. My Lord Speaks. LC 68-20433. (Orig.). 1970. pap. 2.50 (ISBN 0-8170-0401-7). Judson.
Blackwood, Andrew W., Jr. The Voice from the Cross. (Minister's Paperback Library Ser.). 1978. pap. 1.95 (ISBN 0-8010-0742-9). Baker Bk.
Chappell, Clovis G. The Seven Words: The Words of Jesus on the Cross Reveal the Heart of the Christian Faith. (Pocket Pulpit Library). 80p. 1976. pap. 1.75 (ISBN 0-8010-2387-4). Baker Bk.
Ford, W. Herschel. Seven Simple Sermons on the Savior's Last Words. pap. 3.95 (ISBN 0-310-24621-0). Zondervan.
--Simple Sermons on Evangelistic Themes. pap. 3.95 (ISBN 0-310-24451-X). Zondervan.
Hooker, Thomas. A Comment Upon Christ's Last Prayer. LC 72-78753. 1656. Repr. 22.00 (ISBN 0-403-08930-1). Somerset Pub.
Pink, Arthur W. Seven Sayings of Our Saviour on the Cross. (Summit Bks). 1977. pap. 2.45 (ISBN 0-8010-7015-5). Baker Bk.
Poovey, W. A. Cross Words: Sermons & Dramas for Lent. LC 68-13421. 1968. pap. 3.95 (ISBN 0-8066-0800-5, 10-1759). Augsburg.
Smith, H. The Last Words. pap. 2.75 (ISBN 0-686-13446-X). Believers Bkshelf.
Spurgeon, C. H. Words of Jesus from the Cross. 1978. pap. 1.95 (ISBN 0-686-23028-0). Pilgrim Pubns.
Spurgeon, Charles H. Christ's Words from the Cross. (Spurgeon Library Ser.). 120p. 1981. pap. 2.95 (ISBN 0-8010-8207-2). Baker Bk.
Stier, Rudolf E. Words of the Risen Christ. 1982. lib. bdg. 8.25 (ISBN 0-86524-088-4). Klock & Klock.
Vowler, Robert M. Meditations on the Seven Last Words. 1979. pap. 1.75 (ISBN 0-89536-360-7). CSS Pub.

JESUS CHRIST–SEVEN LAST WORDS–SONGS AND MUSIC
see Passion-Music

JESUS CHRIST–SIGNIFICANCE
Alexander, John W. Hope for a Troubled World. 32p. 1978. pap. 0.50 (ISBN 0-87784-165-9). Inter-Varsity.
Blanchard, John. Right with God. 1978. pap. 1.95 (ISBN 0-8024-7357-1). Moody.
Brown, Joan W. Every Knee Shall Bow. 1978. 9.95 (ISBN 0-8007-0941-1). Revell.
Cassidy, Richard J. Jesus. Politics, & Society: A Study of Luke's Gospel. LC 78-735. 1978. 15.95 (ISBN 0-88344-238-8); pap. 7.95 (ISBN 0-88344-237-X). Orbis Bks.
Mohr, Victor. The Advent of Christ. 116p. Date not set. pap. 4.95 (ISBN 0-934616-16-7). Valkyrie Pr.
Muggeridge, Malcolm. Jesus. LC 74-28794. 176p. 1976. pap. 7.95 (ISBN 0-06-066042-2, RD149, HarpR). Har-Row.
Sheed, F. J. Christ in Eclipse. 1978. 8.95 (ISBN 0-8362-3302-6). Andrews & McMeel.
Sheldon, Charles M. In His Steps. (Pivot Family Reader Ser). 256p. 1972. pap. 1.95 (ISBN 0-87983-012-3). Keats.
Smith, Joyce Marie. The Significance of Jesus. 1976. pap. 1.75 (ISBN 0-8423-5887-0). Tyndale.
Thomas, Mayor I., tr. Vida Salvadora De Cristo. (Spanish Bks.). (Span.). 1979. 1.90 (ISBN 0-8297-0455-8). Life Pubs Intl.

JESUS CHRIST–SPIRITUALISTIC INTERPRETATION
see also Bible and Spiritualism
Agerskov, Michael, ed. Toward the Light: A Message to Mankind from the Transcendental World. LC 79-9599. Orig. Title: Vandrer Mod Lyset. 348p. 1979. 11.95 (ISBN 87-87871-50-5); pap. 7.95 (ISBN 0-686-27618-3). Toward the Light.
Carroll, Anne W. Christ the King: Lord of History. pap. 7.00 (ISBN 0-686-74591-4, 101-19). Prow Bks-Franciscan.
Lightfoot, Neil R. Jesus Christ Today. pap. 7.95 (ISBN 0-8010-5604-7). Baker Bk.
Montgomery, Ruth. Companions Along the Way. 256p. 1976. pap. 2.25 (ISBN 0-445-08452-9). Popular Lib.
Nee, Watchman. Christ the Sum of All Spiritual Things. Kaung, Stephen, tr. 1973. pap. 2.10 (ISBN 0-935008-14-4). Christian Fellow Pubs.
Richard, Lucien. What Are They Saying About Christ & World Religions? LC 81-80878. 96p. (Orig.). 1981. pap. 3.95 (ISBN 0-8091-2391-6). Paulist Pr.

JESUS CHRIST–TEACHING METHODS
Coleman, William & Coleman, Patricia. Jesus: His Basic Teachings. rev. ed. (Mine Is the Morning Ser.). 160p. (gr. 9-12). 1978. tchrs. manual & duplicator masters 16.95 (ISBN 0-89622-071-0). Twenty-Third.

Horne, Herman H. Teaching Techniques of Jesus. LC 64-16634. 1971. pap. 2.95 (ISBN 0-8254-2804-1). Kregel.

Lum, Ada. Jesus the Disciple Maker. 1974. pap. 1.75 (ISBN 0-87784-444-5). Inter-Varsity.

Stein, Robert H. The Method & Message of Jesus' Teachings. LC 78-16427. 1978. soft cover 7.95 (ISBN 0-664-24216-2). Westminster.

Vanderlip, George. Jesus, Teacher & Lord. 1975. pap. 2.95 (ISBN 0-8170-0318-5). Judson.

JESUS CHRIST-TEACHINGS

Bauman, Edward W. Life & Teaching of Jesus. 1978. softcover 4.95 (ISBN 0-664-24221-9). Westminster.

Bennion, Lowell. Jesus, The Master Teacher. 63p. 1980. 4.95 (ISBN 0-87747-833-3). Deseret Bk.

Boice, James M. The Sermon on the Mount. 328p. (Orig.). 1981. pap. 7.95 (ISBN 0-310-21511-0). Zondervan.

Bruce, F. F. Promise & Fulfilment: Present to Professor S. H. Hooke, by the Society for O. T. Study. 224p. 1979. Repr. of 1963 ed. text ed. 15.50x (ISBN 0-567-02055-X). Attic Pr.

Burtis, Warren D. Jesus: The First Human Behaviorist. 128p. 1981. pap. text ed. 5.95 (ISBN 0-939530-00-7). Burtis Ent.

Butterworth, Eric. Discover the Power Within You. LC 68-17583. 1968. 8.95 (ISBN 0-06-061266-5, HarpR). Har-Row.

Casavis, James N. The Radical Teachings of Jesus: A Study in Perfectionism. LC 77-92375. 1977. pap. 1.00 (ISBN 0-686-23046-9). J N Casavis.

Coniaris, A. M. Christ's Comfort for Those Who Sorrow. 1978. pap. 2.95 (ISBN 0-937032-00-X). Light&Life Pub Co MN.

--The Great I Came's of Jesus. 1980. pap. 5.95 (ISBN 0-686-27069-X). Light&Life Pub Co MN.

--No Man Ever Spoke As This Man. 1969. pap. 3.95 (ISBN 0-937032-18-2). Light&Life Pub Co MN.

Connick, C. Milo. Jesus: The Man, the Mission, & the Message. 2nd ed. (Illus.). 512p. 1974. 18.95 (ISBN 0-13-509521-2). P-H.

Country Beautiful Editors. Love in the Words & Life of Jesus. LC 73-79617. (Illus.). 96p. 1973. 8.95 (ISBN 0-87294-046-2). Country Beautiful.

Cumming, William K. Follow ME. LC 76-47721. 6.95 (ISBN 0-917920-01-5); pap. 1.95 (ISBN 0-917920-00-7). Mustardseed.

Curtis, Donald. The Christ-Based Teachings. LC 75-40657. 1976. 3.95 (ISBN 0-87159-016-6). Unity Bks.

Daughters of St. Paul. The Teachings & Miracles of Jesus. 1981. 4.00 (ISBN 0-686-73821-7); pap. 3.00 (ISBN 0-8198-7302-0). Dghtrs St Paul.

Davis, R. M. The Woods: The Human Self & the Realism of Jesus. 79p. 1971. pap. 1.00 (ISBN 0-9600434-0-3, 03). Camda.

Dean, Bessie. Lessons Jesus Taught. (Children's Inspirational Coloring Books). (Illus.). 72p. (Orig.). (gr. k-5). 1980. pap. 4.95 (ISBN 0-88290-146-X). Horizon Utah.

Deck, Northcote. We Beheld His Glory. pap. 1.25 (ISBN 0-87213-120-3). Loizeaux.

De Vinck, Jose. The Words of Jesus, with Key Readings from New & Old Testaments. 320p. 1977. deluxe ed. 30.00 morocco (ISBN 0-911726-26-8); imitation morocco 12.75x (ISBN 0-911726-27-6); pap. 9.75x (ISBN 0-911726-28-4). Alleluia Pr.

Eller, Vernard. The Simple Life: The Christian Stance Toward Possessions. 1973. pap. 3.95 (ISBN 0-8028-1537-5). Eerdmans.

Fast, Henry A. Jesus & Human Conflict. LC 58-10315. 1959. 6.95 (ISBN 0-8361-1382-9). Herald Pr.

Fisher. Jesus & His Teachings. LC 74-189502. 4.95 (ISBN 0-8054-1333-2). Broadman.

Getz, Gene. Loving One Another. 1979. pap. 3.95 (ISBN 0-88207-786-4). Victor Bks.

Gianaris, Larry. Reality. LC 78-68900. 1980. 5.95 (ISBN 0-533-04184-8). Vantage.

Giordani, Igino. Social Message of Jesus. 1977. 4.50 (ISBN 0-8198-0467-3); pap. 3.50 (ISBN 0-8198-0468-1). Dghtrs St Paul.

Goppelt, Leonard. Theology of the New Testament: Jesus & the Gospels, Vol I. Alsup, John E., tr. LC 80-28947. 316p. 1981. 15.95 (ISBN 0-8028-2384-X). Eerdmans.

Hamerton-Kelly, Robert. God the Father: Theology & Patriarchy in the Teaching of Jesus, No. 4. Brueggemann, Walter & Donahue, John R., eds. LC 78-54551. (Overtures to Biblical Theology Ser.). 144p. 1979. pap. 5.95 (ISBN 0-8006-1528-X, 1-1528). Fortress.

Harrington, Wilfrid. Christ & Life. 160p. 1976. 7.95 (ISBN 0-8199-0571-2). Franciscan Herald.

Hiers, Richard H. The Historical Jesus & the Kingdom of God: Present & Future in the Message & Ministry of Jesus. LC 73-2623. (U of Fla. Humanities Monographs: No. 38). 1973. 3.50 (ISBN 0-8130-0386-5). U Presses Fla.

Hoeksma, Homer C. Voice of Our Fathers. LC 80-8082. 1980. 18.95 (ISBN 0-8254-2841-6). Kregel.

Josephson, Emanuel M. Unheeded Teachings of Christ or Christ Rejected. 1979. write for info. (ISBN 0-685-96472-8). Revisionist Pr.

--Unheeded Teachings of Jesus: Christ Rejected. (Illus.). 7.50 (ISBN 0-685-07976-7); pap. 5.00 (ISBN 0-685-07977-5). Chedney.

Lamont, Daniel. Christ & the World of Thought. 2nd ed. 309p. 1935. text ed. 6.50 (ISBN 0-567-02160-2). Attic Pr.

Lawler, et al. The Teaching of Christ. LC 75-34852. 1976. pap. 7.95 (ISBN 0-87973-858-8). Our Sunday Visitor.

Lawler, Ronald, et al, eds. The Teaching of Christ. abridged ed. LC 79-53070. 1980. pap. 4.95 (ISBN 0-87973-538-4). Our Sunday Visitor.

Lense, Esther. What Does He Offer--This Man Jesus? 1978. pap. 3.35 (ISBN 0-89536-304-6). CSS Pub.

Lewis, E. R. Life & Teaching of Jesus Christ. (London Divinity Ser.). 1977. pap. 4.00 (ISBN 0-227-67519-3). Attic Pr.

Lindsay, Gordon. Life & Teachings of Christ, Vol. 1. (Life of Christ & Parable Ser.). pap. 4.00 (ISBN 0-89985-967-4). Christ Nations.

--Life & Teachings of Christ, Vol. 2. (Life of Christ & Parable Ser.). pap. 4.00 (ISBN 0-89985-968-2). Christ Nations.

--Life & Teachings of Christ, Vol. 3. (Life of Christ & Parable Ser.). pap. 4.00 (ISBN 0-89985-969-0). Christ Nations.

Manson, T. W. Servant-Messiah: A Study of the Public Ministry of Jesus. (Twin Brook Ser). 1977. pap. 3.45 (ISBN 0-8010-6012-5). Baker Bk.

Mathews, Shailer. Jesus on Social Institutions. Cauthen, Kenneth & Keck, Leander E., eds. LC 72-139346. (Lives of Jesus Ser). 232p. 1971. pap. 5.95 (ISBN 0-8006-0156-4, 1-156). Fortress.

Montefiore, Claude G. Some Elements of the Religious Teaching of Jesus According to the Synoptic Ospels. LC 73-2223. (The Jewish People; History, Religion, Literature Ser.). Repr. of 1910 ed. 12.00 (ISBN 0-405-05285-5). Arno.

Murray, Andrew. Money: Christ's Perspective on the Use & Abuse of Money. 1978. pap. 1.50 (ISBN 0-87123-382-7, 200382). Bethany Hse.

--True Vine. pap. 1.95 (ISBN 0-8024-8798-X). Moody.

Mussner, Franz. Christ & the End of the World: A Biblical Study in Eschatology. Von Eroes, Maria, tr. (Contemporary Catechetics Ser). (Orig.). 1965. pap. 0.95x (ISBN 0-268-00040-9). U of Notre Dame Pr.

Neil, William. Why Listen? The Difficult Sayings of Jesus. (Orig.). pap. 1.50 (ISBN 0-89129-227-6). Jove Pubns.

Nicoll, Maurice. The New Man. 160p. 1981. 20.00x (ISBN 0-7224-0194-9, Pub. by Watkins England). State Mutual Bk.

Pearson, Roy. The Hard Commands of Jesus. (Minister's Paperback Library). 128p. 1976. pap. 1.95 (ISBN 0-8010-6992-0). Baker Bk.

Perrin, Norman. Rediscovering the Teachings of Jesus. LC 67-11510. 1976. pap. 4.95x (ISBN 0-06-066493-2, RD 151, HarpR). Har-Row.

Peterson, Ralph H. Did Jesus Know What He Was Talking About. 112p. 1982. 6.95 (ISBN 0-8187-0045-9). Am Developing.

Piper, John. Love Your Enemies. LC 77-95449. (Society for New Testament Studies: No. 38). 1980. 24.50 (ISBN 0-521-22056-4). Cambridge U Pr.

Putnam, Roy C. Those He Came to Save. LC 77-13764. 1978. pap. 4.95 (ISBN 0-687-41862-3). Abingdon.

Rauschenbusch, Walter. The Social Principles of Jesus. LC 76-50566. 1976. Repr. of 1916 ed. lib. bdg. 15.00 (ISBN 0-8414-7308-0). Folcroft.

Robertson, A. T. Keywords in the Teaching of Jesus. 1977. pap. 2.95 (ISBN 0-8054-1366-9, 4213-66). Broadman.

Saraydarian, Torkom. Dialogue with Christ. 1980. pap. 5.00 (ISBN 0-911794-42-5). Aqua Educ.

Sayings of Jesus. 2.95 (ISBN 0-442-82286-3). Peter Pauper.

Sheets, Herchel H. When Jesus Exaggerated. 1977. pap. 4.55 (ISBN 0-89536-307-0). CSS Pub.

Stewart, James S. The Life & Teaching of Jesus Christ. (Festival Books). 1978. pap. 1.95 (ISBN 0-687-21744-X). Abingdon.

Waterman, Leroy. The Religion of Jesus: Christianity's Unclaimed Heritage of Prophetic Religion. LC 78-16405. 1978. Repr. of 1952 ed. lib. bdg. 19.75x (ISBN 0-313-20586-8, WARJ). Greenwood.

Weber, Hans-Ruedi. Jesus & the Children. LC 79-87754. 1980. pap. 4.95 (ISBN 0-8042-1316-X). John Knox.

Welch, Reuben. We Really Do Need to Listen. LC 78-50098. (Illus.). 1978. 5.95 (ISBN 0-914850-30-X); pap. 2.50 (ISBN 0-914850-69-5); pap. text ed. 1.50 study guide (ISBN 0-914850-30-X). Impact Tenn.

Wilder, Amos N. Eschatology & Ethics in the Teaching of Jesus. LC 78-16425. 1978. Repr. of 1950 ed. lib. bdg. 22.75 (ISBN 0-313-20585-X, WIEE). Greenwood.

Wilson, Carl. With Christ in the School of Disciple Building: A Study of Christ's Method of Building Disciples. 1976. pap. 6.95 (ISBN 0-310-34591-X). Zondervan.

Wurmbrand, Richard. Christ on the Jewish Road. (Orig.). 1973. pap. text ed. 3.00 (ISBN 0-88264-015-1). Diane Bks.

JESUS CHRIST-TEMPTATION

Bale, John. Temptation of Christ. LC 74-133636. (Tudor Facsimile Texts. Old English Plays: No. 22). Repr. of 1909 ed. 31.50 (ISBN 0-404-53322-1). AMS Pr.

Kelly, W. Christ Tempted & Sympathizing. 2.75 (ISBN 0-686-13033-2). Believers Bkshelf.

Simpson, Albert B. Christ of the Forty Days. pap. 1.25 (ISBN 0-87509-004-4). Chr Pubns.

Thurman, Howard. Temptations of Jesus. LC 78-74718. 1979. pap. 1.95 (ISBN 0-913408-47-6). Friends United.

JESUS CHRIST-THEOSOPHICAL INTERPRETATIONS

Bailey, Alice A. From Bethlehem to Calvary. 1974. 9.50 (ISBN 0-85330-007-0); pap. 3.75 (ISBN 0-85330-107-7). Lucis.

--Reappearance of the Christ. 1978. 12.00 (ISBN 0-85330-014-3); pap. 3.75 (ISBN 0-85330-114-X). Lucis.

Besant, Annie. Esoteric Christianity. 8th ed. 1966. 6.25 (ISBN 0-8356-7052-X). Theos Pub Hse.

Bonsall, H. Brash. The Person of Christ, Vol. II. 1972. pap. 3.50 (ISBN 0-87508-016-2). Chr Lit.

Saraydarian, Haroutiun. Christ, Avatar of Sacrificial Love. 1974. 8.00 (ISBN 0-911794-38-7); pap. 6.00 (ISBN 0-911794-39-5). Aqua Educ.

Steiner, Rudolf. Christ in Relation to Lucifer & Ahriman. Mollenhauer, Peter, tr. 1978. pap. 1.25 (ISBN 0-910142-77-7). Anthroposophic.

JESUS CHRIST-TRIAL

Bammel, Ernst, ed. Trial of Jesus: Cambridge Studies in Honour of C. F. D. Moule. LC 73-131584. (Studies in Biblical Theology 2nd Ser.: No. 13). (Orig.). 1970. pap. text ed. 8.95x (ISBN 0-8401-3063-5). Allenson Breckinridge.

Brandon, S. G. The Trial of Jesus of Nazareth. LC 68-9206. (Illus.). 1979. pap. 4.95 (ISBN 0-8128-6018-7). Stein & Day.

Cohn, H. The Trial & Death of Jesus. pap. 9.95x (ISBN 0-87068-432-9). Ktav.

Harvey, A. E. Jesus on Trial. LC 77-79588. 1977. Repr. 6.95 (ISBN 0-8042-0335-0). John Knox.

Juel, Donald. Messiah & Temple: The Trial of Jesus in the Gospel of Mark. LC 76-46397. (Society of Biblical Literature. Dissertation Ser.). 1977. pap. 7.50 (ISBN 0-89130-120-8, 060131). Scholars Pr Ca.

Rosadi, Giovanni. The Trial of Jesus. 1977. lib. bdg. 59.95 (ISBN 0-8490-2767-5). Gordon Pr.

Vassilakos, Aristarchus. The Trial of Jesus Christ. Orthodox Christian Educational Society, ed. 64p. (Orig.). 1950. pap. 2.00x (ISBN 0-938366-47-5). Orthodox Chr.

Winter, Paul. On the Trial of Jesus. 2nd ed. Burkill, T. A. & Vermes, G., eds. (Studia Judaica, Vol. 1). 1973. 30.00x (ISBN 3-11-002283-4). De Gruyter.

JESUS CHRIST-TYPOLOGY

see Typology (Theology)

JESUS CHRIST-WORDS

see also Jesus Christ-Seven Last Words

Baldwin, Stanley C. What Did Jesus Say About That? 156p. 1975. pap. 3.95 (ISBN 0-88207-718-X). Victor Bks.

Bartruff, Bryce D. Sayings of Jesus: A Pocket Guide. 1976. pap. 2.95 (ISBN 0-87123-461-0, 200461). Bethany Hse.

Berrigan, Daniel. The Words Our Saviour Gave Us. 1978. pap. 4.95 (ISBN 0-87243-081-2). Templegate.

Brown, John. Discourses & Sayings of Our Lord Jesus Christ, 3 vols. 1981. Set. 45.00 (ISBN 0-88469-142-X). BMH Bks.

Dalman, Gustaf H. Words of Christ. 1981. lib. bdg. 13.50 (ISBN 0-86524-080-9). Klock & Klock.

Garrison, R. Benjamin. Seven Questions Jesus Asked. LC 74-19266. 96p. 1975. pap. 2.75 (ISBN 0-687-38194-0). Abingdon.

Hills, Christopher. The Christ Book: What Did He Really Say? Hills, Norah, ed. LC 80-5865. (Illus.). 224p. 1980. text ed. 10.95 (ISBN 0-916438-37-6). Univ of Trees.

Hunter, Archibald M. The Work & Words of Jesus. rev. ed. LC 73-7559. 1973. pap. 5.95 (ISBN 0-664-24976-0). Westminster.

Kistler, Don. The Arithmetic of God, Vol. 1. 187p. (Orig.). 1976. pap. 3.50 (ISBN 0-940532-00-X). AOG.

--The Father & Sons Shall Be One, Vol. 1. 141p. (Orig.). 1978. pap. 3.50x (ISBN 0-940532-01-8). AOG.

Kline, Leslie L. The Sayings of Jesus in the Pseudo-Clementine Homilies. LC 75-1645. (Society of Biblical Literature. Dissertation Ser.). ix, 198p. 1975. pap. 7.50 (ISBN 0-89130-060-0, 060114). Scholars Pr Ca.

Lindsay, Gordon. Amazing Discoveries in the Words of Jesus. 3.25 (ISBN 0-89985-112-6). Christ Nations.

McClellan, Albert. The Hard Sayings of Jesus. LC 73-83827. 128p. 1975. 4.50 (ISBN 0-8054-1340-5). Broadman.

Manson, T. W. The Sayings of Jesus. LC 79-16611. 1979. pap. 7.95 (ISBN 0-8028-1812-9). Eerdmans.

Michaels, Louis. The Words of Jesus: Arranged for Meditation. 1977. 6.95 (ISBN 0-87243-071-5). Templegate.

Neil, William. The Difficult Sayings of Jesus. 1977. pap. 1.50 (ISBN 0-8028-1668-1). Eerdmans.

Pentecost, Dwight. A Harmony of the Words & Works of Jesus Christ. 272p. 1981. pap. price not set (ISBN 0-310-30951-4). Zondervan.

Pentecost, J. Dwight. The Words & Works of Jesus Christ. 576p. 1981. 16.95 (ISBN 0-310-30940-9, 17015). Zondervan.

Rajneesh, Bhagwan S. Words Like Fire: Discourses on Jesus. LC 80-8343. 288p. (Orig.). 1981. pap. 5.95 (ISBN 0-06-066787-7, RD 347, HarpR). Har-Row.

Sanford, John A. Kingdom Within: A Study of the Inner Meaning of Jesus' Sayings. LC 77-105548. 1970. 10.95 (ISBN 0-397-10101-5). Har-Row.

Stier, Rudolf E. Words of the Risen Christ. 1982. lib. bdg. 8.25 (ISBN 0-86524-088-4). Klock & Klock.

Stuart, Friend. Master Thoughts, 3 vols. 44p. 1981. Set. vinyl 45.00 (ISBN 0-912132-05-1). Dominion Pr.

JESUS CHRIST IN ART

see Jesus Christ-Art

JESUS CHRIST IN FICTION, DRAMA, POETRY, ETC.

Clark, Ira. Christ Revealed: The History of the Neotypological Lyric in the English Renaissance. (Humanities Monographs: No. 51). 1981. pap. write for info. (0-8130-0712-7). U Presses Fla.

Ditsky, John. The Onstage Christ: Studies in the Persistence of a Theme. (Critical Studies Ser.). 188p. 1980. 25.00x (ISBN 0-389-20059-X). B&N.

Eastman, Fred. Christ in the Drama: A Study of the Influence of Christ on the Drama of England & America. facsimile ed. LC 79-167336. (Essay Index Reprints - Shaffer Lectures of Northwestern University, 1946). Repr. of 1947 ed. 15.00 (ISBN 0-8369-2647-1). Arno.

Kremen, Kathryn R. The Imagination of the Resurrection: The Poetic Continuity of a Religious Motif in Donne, Blake, & Yeats. LC 71-168812. 344p. 1972. 18.00 (ISBN 0-8387-7940-9). Bucknell U Pr.

Morrison, George H. Christ in Shakespeare. 142p. 1981. Repr. of 1928 ed. lib. bdg. 30.00 (ISBN 0-89984-342-5). Century Bookbindery.

Roberts, Richard. The Jesus of Poets & Prophets. 1977. Repr. of 1920 ed. lib. bdg. 25.00 (ISBN 0-8492-2312-1). R West.

JESUS CHRIST IN LITERATURE

see Jesus Christ in Fiction, Drama, Poetry, etc.

JESUS CHRIST IN POETRY

see Jesus Christ-Poetry

JESUS MOVEMENT

see Jesus People

JESUS PEOPLE

Enroth, Ronald M., et al. The Story of the Jesus People. 1972. pap. 4.95 (ISBN 0-85364-131-5). Attic Pr.

Kelly, W. Lectures on the Church of God. 3.75 (ISBN 0-686-13516-4). Believers Bkshelf.

Richardson, James T., et al. Organized Miracles: A Study of a Contemporary, Youth, Communal, Fundamentalist Organization. LC 78-55937. 368p. 1979. 16.95 (ISBN 0-87855-284-7). Transaction Bks.

Ryan, John J. Jesus People. 1970. text ed. 2.25 (ISBN 0-914070-03-7). ACTA Found.

Smail, Thomas A. The Forgotten Father. 1981. pap. 5.95 (ISBN 0-8028-1879-X). Eerdmans.

JET FLOW

see Jets-Fluid Dynamics

JET FUEL

see Jet Planes-Fuel

JET PLANES

see also Jet Transports; Heinkel (Fighter Planes)

Boyne, Walter J. & Lopez, Donald S., eds. The Jet Age: Forty Years of Jet Aviation. LC 79-20216. (Illus.). 190p. 1979. 19.95 (ISBN 0-87474-248-X); pap. 8.95 (ISBN 0-87474-247-1). Smithsonian.

Chen, C. J. Vertical Turbulent Buoyant Jets: A Review of Experimental Data. (Heat & Mass Transfer: Vol. 4). (Illus.). 94p. 1979. 28.00 (ISBN 0-08-024772-5). Pergamon.

Christy, Joe. The Lear Jet. (Illus.). 1979. 9.95 (ISBN 0-8306-9870-1); pap. 5.95 (ISBN 0-8306-2246-2, 2246). TAB Bks.
Davies, David P. Handling the Big Jets. 3rd ed. (Illus.). 324p. 1973. 34.95 (ISBN 0-903083-01-9). Pan Am Nav.
Green, William & Cross, Roy. The Jet Aircraft of the World. Gilbert, James, ed. LC 79-7263. (Flight: Its First Seventy-Five Years Ser.). (Illus.). 1979. Repr. of 1956 ed. lib. bdg. 26.00x (ISBN 0-405-12173-3). Arno.
Ingells, Douglas J. Seven Forty-Seven, Story of the Boeing Superjet. LC 78-135055. (Illus.). 1970. 14.95 (ISBN 0-8168-8700-4); pap. 9.95 (ISBN 0-8168-8704-7). Aero.
Jet Planes of the Third Reich. Date not set. price not set (ISBN 0-914144-27-8). Monogram Aviation.
Stevenson, James. Grumman F-14 "Tomcat". LC 75-7465. (Aero Ser.: Vol. 25). 104p. 1975. pap. 7.95 (ISBN 0-8168-0592-X). Aero.
Wooldridge, E. T., Jr. The P-Eighty Shooting Star: Evolution of a Jet Fighter. LC 79-17648. (Famous Aircraft of the National Air & Space Museum Ser.: Bk. 3). (Illus.). 110p. 1979. pap. 6.95 (ISBN 0-87474-965-4). Smithsonian.

JET PLANES–FLIGHT TESTING
Penrose, Harald. No Echo in the Sky. LC 78-169433. (Literature & History of Aviation Ser). 1971. Repr. of 1958 ed. 24.00 (ISBN 0-405-03776-7). Arno.

JET PLANES–FUEL
Factors in Using Kerosine Jet Fuel of Reduced Flash Point. (Special Technical Publications Ser.). 113p. 1979. soft cover 15.00x (ISBN 0-686-76065-4, 688, 04-688000-13). ASTM.

JET PLANES–JUVENILE LITERATURE
Colby, C. B. Jets of the World: New Fighters, Bombers, & Transports. (Illus.). (gr. 4-7). 1966. PLB 5.29 (ISBN 0-698-30202-8). Coward.
Hewish, Mark. The Young Scientist Book of Jets. LC 78-17507. (Young Scientist Ser.). (Illus.). (gr. 4-5). 1978. text ed. 6.95 (ISBN 0-88436-527-1). EMC.

JET PLANES–MOTORS
see Airplanes–Jet Propulsion; Airplanes–Turbojet Engines

JET PLANES, MILITARY
see also B-Fifty-Eight Bomber; B-Fifty-Two Bomber
Brown, Nettie. Alber C-One-Thirty & the Blue Angels A-4 Skyhawk Jets. (Illus.). 64p. 1981. pap. 4.00 (ISBN 0-682-49802-5). Exposition.
Feuchtwanger, E. J. & Mason, R. A. Air Power in the Next Generation. 1979. text ed. 26.00x (ISBN 0-333-23609-2). Humanities.
Holder, William G. Convair F-106 Delta Dart. LC 75-15272. (Aero Ser.: Vol. 27). 104p. 1977. pap. 7.95 (ISBN 0-8168-0600-4). Aero.
Myles, Bruce. Jump Jet: The Revolutionary V-STOL Fighter. LC 78-856. (Illus.). 1978. 9.95 (ISBN 0-89141-021-X). Presidio Pr.

JET PROPELLANTS
see Jet Planes–Fuel

JET PROPELLED AIRPLANES
see Airplanes–Jet Propulsion; Jet Planes

JET PROPULSION
see also Airplanes–Jet Propulsion; Rockets (Aeronautics); Rockets (Ordnance)
Evans, David. Jet Propulsion. 10.75x (ISBN 0-392-07180-0, LTB). Sportshelf.
Lewis, Alexander D. Gas Power Dynamics. LC 77-15095. 544p. 1978. Repr. of 1962 ed. lib. bdg. 29.00 (ISBN 0-88275-629-X). Krieger.

JET STREAM
Harman, J. F. Tropospheric Waves, Jet Streams & United States Weather Patterns. LC 77-182881. (CCG Resource Papers Ser.: No. 11). (Illus.). 1971. pap. text ed. 4.00 (ISBN 0-89291-058-5). Assn Am Geographers.
Reiter, Elmar R. Jet-Stream Meteorology. LC 63-13074. (Illus.). 1963. 25.00x (ISBN 0-226-70967-1). U of Chicago Pr.
--Jet Streams: How Do They Affect Our Weather? LC 78-25793. (Illus.). 1979. Repr. of 1967 ed. lib. bdg. 18.50x (ISBN 0-313-20782-8, REJS). Greenwood.

JET TRANSPORTS
Morgan, Len & Morgan, Terry. Seven-Twenty-Seven Scrapbook. LC 78-72164. 1978. 12.00 (ISBN 0-8168-8344-0); pap. 7.95 (ISBN 0-8168-8349-1). Aero.
Norris, Geoffrey. Jet Adventure. 12.50x (ISBN 0-392-06661-0, SpS). Sportshelf.
Stambler, Irwin. Ocean Liners of the Air. (Illus.). (gr. 6-10). 1969. PLB 4.89 (ISBN 0-399-60495-2). Putnam.

JETS
see also Plasma Jets

JETS–FLUID DYNAMICS
Abramovich, Genrikh N., ed. Turbulent Jets of Air, Plasma, & Real Gas. LC 69-12508. (Illus.). 144p. 1969. 32.50 (ISBN 0-306-10817-8, Consultants). Plenum Pub.
CISM (International Center for Mechanical Sciences), Dept. of Hydro & Gasdynamics, Technical Univ. of Turin, 1970. Fluid Dynamics of Jet Amplifiers. Romiti, A., ed. (CISM Pubns. Ser.: No. 66). (Illus.). 1972. pap. 12.60 (ISBN 0-387-81152-4). Springer-Verlag.
Second Symposium on Jet Pumps & Ejectors & Gas Lift Techniques. Proceedings. 1975. pap. 60.00 (ISBN 0-900983-43-4, Dist. by Air Science Co.). BHRA Fluid.

JETS, PLASMA
see Plasma Jets

JETTATURA
see Evil Eye

JETTIES
see also Shore Protection

JETTISON
see also Salvage; Ships–Cargo

JETTONS
see also Tokens

JEU DE PAUME, PARIS
Magi, Giovanna. Masterpieces of the Louvre & the Jeu De Paume. (Italia Artistica Ser). (Illus.). 62p. 1974. 12.50x (ISBN 0-8002-1709-8). Intl Pubns Serv.

JEUX FLORAUX
see Floral Games

JEWEL, JOHN BP. OF SALISBURY, 1522-1571
Cooper, Thomas. An Answer in Defence of the Truth Against the Apology of Private Mass. 1850. 17.00 (ISBN 0-384-09790-1). Johnson Repr.
Southgate, Wyndham M. John Jewel & the Problem of Doctrinal Authority. LC 62-9430. (Historical Monographs Ser: No. 49). (Illus.). 1962. 10.00x (ISBN 0-674-47750-2). Harvard U Pr.
Weiser, David K. The Prose Style of John Jewel. (Salzburg Studies in English Literature, Elizabethan & Renaissance Studies: No. 9). 194p. 1973. pap. text ed. 25.00x (ISBN 0-391-01562-1). Humanities.

JEWELERS
see also Clock and Watch Makers
Beckman, Elizabeth. Cincinnati Silversmiths, Jewelers, Watch & Clockmakers. LC 75-24983. (Illus.). 170p. 1975. 18.50 (ISBN 0-9600266-6-5). R A Green.
Jacob, Jeffrey R. Court Jewelers of the World. LC 77-82557. (Illus.). 1978. 17.95 (ISBN 0-918924-02-2). Postgrad Intl.

JEWELRY
see also Cameos; Crown Jewels; Gems; Hall-Marks; Jewelry As an Investment; Pins and Needles; Rings
Avons History: President's Club Jewelry. LC 74-32082. (Illus.). 32p. 1976. pap. 3.50 collectors price guide (ISBN 0-913772-05-4). Avons Res.
Bahti, Mark. Collecting Southwestern Native American Jewelry. (Illus.). 1980. pap. 8.95 (ISBN 0-679-50960-7). McKay.
Baker, Lillian. Art Nouveau & Art Deco Jewelry. (Illus.). 1981. 9.95 (ISBN 0-89145-158-7). Collector Bks.
--One Hundred Years of Collectible Jewelry. (Illus.). 1980. pap. 8.95 (ISBN 0-89145-066-1). Collector Bks.
Beck, Horace. Classification & Nomenclature of Beads & Pendants. (Illus.). 80p. 1973. pap. 10.00 (ISBN 0-87387-083-2). Shumway.
Becker, Vivienne. Antique & Twentieth Century Jewellery. 336p. 1981. 50.00x (ISBN 0-7198-0081-1, Pub. by Northwood England). State Mutual Bk.
Bell, Jeanenne. Answers to Questions About Old Jewelry 1840-1950: Identification & Value. (Bks. Americanna). (Illus.). 300p. 1981. pap. 9.95 (ISBN 0-517-54568-3). Crown.
Bennett, Edna M. & Bennett, John F. Turquoise Jewelry of the Indians of the Southwest. (Illus.). 1973. 15.00 (ISBN 0-917834-01-1). Turquoise Bks.
Black, Anderson. The Story of Jewelry. LC 74-5504. Orig. Title: Storia dei Gioielli. (Illus.). 400p. 1974. 29.95 (ISBN 0-688-00308-7). Morrow.
Boehn, Max Von. Ornaments--Lace, Fans, Gloves, Walking-Sticks, Parasols, Jewelry & Trinkets: Modes & Manners Supplement. LC 70-148467. (Illus.). Repr. of 1929 ed. 20.00 (ISBN 0-405-08286-X, Blom Pubns). Arno.
Browne, Miriam. Pewter Jewellery. 1979. 19.95 (ISBN 0-7134-1608-4, Pub. by Batsford England). David & Charles.
Burgess, Frederick W. Antique Jewelry & Trinkets. LC 74-178622. (Illus.). xvi, 399p. 1972. Repr. of 1919 ed. 25.00 (ISBN 0-8103-3863-7). Gale.
Chatt, Orville K. Design Is Where You Find It. LC 79-146932. (Illus.). 116p. 1972. 8.95 (ISBN 0-8138-0415-9). Iowa St U Pr.
Clarke, Patti. Creative Jewelry. LC 77-90127. 1978. 13.95 (ISBN 0-8008-1995-0). Taplinger.
Coutchie, Mariann. Jewelry on Display. (Illus.). 1972. pap. 5.00 (ISBN 0-911380-27-2). Signs of Times.
Cudlipp, Edythe. Jewelry. (Illus.). 1980. pap. 7.95 (ISBN 0-525-93103-1). Dutton.
Curran, Mona. Collecting Antique Jewelry. (Illus.). 8.95 (ISBN 0-87523-149-7). Emerson.
--Treasury of Jewels & Gems. (Illus.). 1962. 9.95 (ISBN 0-87523-139-X). Emerson.
Darling, Ada. Antique Jewelry. (Illus.). 1953. 20.00 (ISBN 0-87282-022-X). Century Hse.
Davis, Mary L. & Pack, Greta. Mexican Jewelry. (Illus.). 1963. 15.00 (ISBN 0-292-73305-4). U of Tex Pr.
Dragsted, Ove. Gems & Jewelry in Color. LC 75-2391. (Illus.). 240p. 1975. 10.95 (ISBN 0-02-533500-6, 53350). Macmillan.
Edwards, I. E. Tutankhamun's Jewelry. LC 76-41859. (Illus.). 1976. pap. 3.95 (ISBN 0-87099-155-8). Metro Mus Art.
Evans, Joan. Magical Jewels of the Middle Ages & the Renaissance. 7.50 (ISBN 0-8446-5572-4). Peter Smith.
--Magical Jewels of the Middle Ages & the Renaissance Particularly in England. LC 75-26288. (Illus.). 288p. 1976. pap. 3.00 (ISBN 0-486-23367-7). Dover.
Ferre, Duane. How to Make Wire Jewelry. (Illus.). 192p. 1980. 13.95 (ISBN 0-8019-6859-3); pap. 7.95 (ISBN 0-8019-6860-7). Chilton.
Gatter, R. S. Gatter & Vallance's "Art Nouveau Jewelry", 2 Vols. pap. 2.95 ea. Vol. 1 (ISBN 0-87282-071-8). Vol. 2 (ISBN 0-87282-115-3). Century Hse.
Geoffroy-Dechaume, Claude. Simple Craft Jewellery. 3rd ed. 76p. 1963. 6.95 (ISBN 0-571-05733-0, Pub. by Faber & Faber). Merrimack Bk Serv.
Gerlach, Martin. Primitive & Folk Jewelry. (Illus.). 1971. pap. 6.50 (ISBN 0-486-22747-2). Dover.
Gill, Joseph O. Gill's Index to Journals, Articles, & Books Relating to Gems & Jewelry. 1978. 24.50 (ISBN 0-87311-009-9). Gemological.
Goldbemberg, Rose. L. Antique Jewelry: A Practical & Passionate Guide. (Illus.). 1976. 8.95 (ISBN 0-517-52653-0); pap. 5.95 (ISBN 0-517-52654-9). Crown.
Hackenbroch, Yvonne. Renaissance Jewellery. (Illus.). 424p. 1980. 135.00 (ISBN 0-85667-056-1, Pub. by Sotheby Parke Bernet England). Biblio Dist.
Hart, Harold H., ed. Jewelry: A Pictorial Archive of Woodcuts & Engravings. (Illus.). 144p. 1981. pap. price not set (ISBN 0-486-24161-0). Dover.
Hejj-Detari, Angela. Old Hungarian Jewelry. (Illus.). 5.00x (ISBN 0-89918-303-4, H303). Vanous.
Henzel, S. Sylvia. Old Costume Jewelry: A Collector's Dream, with Prices. (Illus.). 1978. 7.95 (ISBN 0-87069-228-3). Wallace-Homestead.
Homemade Enamel Jewelry. 1976. pap. 1.50 (ISBN 0-8277-5708-5). British Bk Ctr.
Hornung, C. P., compiled by. A Source Book of Antiques & Jewelry Designs. (Illus.). 1977. pap. 6.95 (ISBN 0-306-80070-5). Da Capo.
Jarvis, Charles A. Jewelry Manufacture & Repair. (Illus.). 3.98 (ISBN 0-517-30587-9). Bonanza.
Jewellery Through 7000 Years. (British Museum Publications Ser.). (Illus.). 1977. pap. 11.95 (ISBN 0-8120-0902-9). Barron.
Kain, Jay D. Cast Pewter Jewelry. LC 75-10493. (Illus.). 96p. 1975. 10.95 (ISBN 0-87192-071-9). Davis Mass.
Kaplan, Arthur G. Official Price Guide to Antique Jewelry. (Collector Ser.). (Illus.). 400p. 1981. pap. 9.95 (ISBN 0-87637-341-4, 341-04). Hse of Collectibles.
Kropt, Wilbur D. Jewelry & the Wedding Band. 1969. 0.90 (ISBN 0-686-30766-6). Rod & Staff.
Kuntzsch, Ingrid. A History of Jewels & Jewelry. (Illus.). 236p. 1981. 27.50 (ISBN 0-312-38088-7). St Martin.
Laffin, Richard F. Jewelers' Inventory Manual. 1981. 24.95 (ISBN 0-931744-04-0). Jewelers Circular.
Liddicoat, Richard T., Jr. & Copeland, L. L. Jewelers' Manual. 2nd ed. 1974. 9.75 (ISBN 0-87311-003-X). Gemological.
Lund, Marsha M. Indian Jewelry: Fact & Fantasy. LC 76-5401. (Illus.). 1976. pap. 6.95 (ISBN 0-87364-052-7, Sycamore Island). Sycamore Island.
--Indian Jewelry: Fact & Fantasy. Lund, Peder C., ed. LC 76-5401. (Illus.). 150p. 1976. pap. 6.95 (ISBN 0-87364-052-7). Paladin Ent.
McNeil, Donald S., ed. Jewelers' Dictionary. 3rd ed. LC 76-26012. 1979. 39.95 (ISBN 0-931744-01-6). Jewelers Circular.
--Who's Who in the Jewelry Industry. LC 79-27501. 1979. 54.95 (ISBN 0-931744-02-4). Jewelers Circular.
Meilach, Dona Z. Ethnic Jewelry: Design & Inspiration for Collectors & Craftsmen. Aymar, Brandt, ed. (Illus.). 192p. 1981. 19.95 (ISBN 0-517-52974-2, Harmony). Crown.
Morton, Philip. Contemporary Jewelry: A Studio Handbook. 2nd ed. LC 75-25851. 1976. pap. 22.95 (ISBN 0-03-089644-4, HoltC). HR&W.
Mourey, Gabriel, et al. Art Nouveau Jewelry & Fans. (Illus.). 150p. 1973. pap. 5.00 (ISBN 0-486-22961-0). Dover.
Muller, Priscilla E. Jewels in Spain, 1500-1800. (Illus.). 260p. 1972. 29.00 (ISBN 0-87535-121-2). Hispanic Soc.
Newman, Harold. An Illustrated Dictionary of Jewelry. (Illustrated Dictionary Ser.). (Illus.). 1981. 29.95 (ISBN 0-500-23309-8). Thames Hudson.
Peter, Mary. Collecting Victorian Jewellery. LC 78-137400. (Illus.). 1971. 9.95 (ISBN 0-87523-174-8). Emerson.
Poynder, Michael. The Price Guide to Jewelery: Three Thousand B.C. to Nineteen Fifty A.D. (Price Guide Ser.). (Illus.). 385p. 1978. 49.50 (ISBN 0-902028-50-2). Antique Collect.
Rosenthal, Renate. Jewelry of the Ancient World. LC 72-10797. (Lerner Archaeology Ser.: Digging up the Past). (gr. 5 up). 1975. PLB 7.95 (ISBN 0-8225-0830-3). Lerner Pubns.
Sarett, Morton R. The Jewelry in Your Life. LC 78-5900. (Illus.). 1979. 27.95 (ISBN 0-88229-367-2). Nelson-Hall.
Smith, M. Clifford. Jewellery. (Illus.). 1973. Repr. of 1908 ed. 29.95x (ISBN 0-8464-0536-9). Beekman Pubs.
Sommer, Elsye. Contemporary Costume Jewelry. LC 73-88268. (Illus.). 224p. 1974. 7.95 (ISBN 0-517-51423-0); pap. 5.95 (ISBN 0-517-51424-9). Crown.
Stillman, Yedida K. Palestinian Costume & Jewelry. LC 78-55711. (Illus.). 1979. pap. 14.95x (ISBN 0-8263-0490-7). U of NM Pr.
Tinkham, Sandra S., ed. Catalog of Textiles, Costume & Jewelry. (Index of American Design Ser.: Pt. 1). (Orig.). 1979. pap. 30.00x (ISBN 0-914146-63-7); incl. color microfiche 690.00x (ISBN 0-914146-62-9). Somerset Hse.
Walters Art Gallery. Jewelry: Ancient to Modern. 1980. 35.00 (ISBN 0-670-40697-X, Studio). Viking Pr.
Weinstein, Michael. World of Jewel Stones. (Illus.). 1958. 22.50 (ISBN 0-911378-29-4). Sheridan.
Wilson, Henry. Silverwork & Jewellery. 1978. pap. 9.95 (ISBN 0-8008-7192-8, Pentalic). Taplinger.
Wruck, Charlotte. Jewels for Their Ears: Why Earrings Are As Popular Today As They Were 10,000 Years Ago. 1979. 8.95 (ISBN 0-533-03935-5). Vantage.

JEWELRY–REPAIRING
Hardy, R. Allen & Bowman, John J. Jewelry Repair Manual. 2nd ed. (Illus.). 1967. 9.95 (ISBN 0-442-03130-0). Van Nos Reinhold.

JEWELRY, ANCIENT
Chandra, Rai G. Indo-Greek Jewelery. 1979. 22.50x (ISBN 0-8364-0320-7). South Asia Bks.
Higgins, Reynold A. Greek & Roman Jewellery. 2nd ed. 1980. 27.50 (ISBN 0-520-03601-8). U of Cal Pr.
Jacka, Jerry D. & Hammack, Nancy S. Indian Jewelry of the Prehistoric Southwest. LC 75-8017. (Illus.). 48p. 1975. pap. 4.95 (ISBN 0-8165-0515-2). U of Ariz Pr.
Jessup, Ronald. Anglo-Saxon Jewellery. (Shire Archaeology Ser.). (Illus.). 96p. 1974. 8.75x (ISBN 0-85263-261-4). Intl Pubns Serv.
Jewellery Through 7000 Years. (British Museum Publications Ser.). (Illus.). 1977. pap. 11.95 (ISBN 0-8120-0902-9). Barron.
L'Orange, Hans P. & Von Gerkan, Arnim. Der Spaetantike Bildschmuck des Konstantinsbogen: Text Vol. & Vol. with Plates. (Studien zur spaetantiken Kunstgeschichte, Vol. 10). (Illus.). 238p. 1978. Repr. of 1939 ed. 323.00x (ISBN 3-11-002249-4). De Gruyter.
Miller, Stella. Two Groups of Thessalian Gold. LC 77-80473. (UC Publications in Classical Studies: Vol. 18). 1979. pap. 14.50x (ISBN 0-520-09580-4). U of Cal Pr.

JEWELRY AS AN INVESTMENT
Darling, Ada W. Antique Jewelry Identification with Price Guide, No. 2. plastic bdg. 6.95 (ISBN 0-87069-098-1). Wallace-Homestead.
Dohrmann, Bernhard. Grow Rich with Diamonds. 228p. 1981. 12.95 (ISBN 0-936602-29-5). Harbor Pub CA.
Freedman, Michael. The Diamond Book: A Practical Guide for Successful Investing. LC 80-70145. 160p. 1981. 14.95 (ISBN 0-87094-223-9). Dow Jones-Irwin.
Sutton, Antony C. The Diamond Connection: A Manual for Investers. LC 78-73799. (Illus.). 1979. 19.95 (ISBN 0-933252-00-5). JD Pr.

JEWELRY MAKING
see also Enamel and Enameling; Goldwork; Jewelry–Repairing; Silverwork
Armstrong, Roger. Beginning Jewelry: A Notebook for Design & Technique. (Illus.). 1979. pap. text ed. 6.95x (ISBN 0-89863-018-5). Star Pub CA.
--Wax & Casting: A Notebook of Process & Technique. (Illus.). 160p. 1982. pap. write for info. (ISBN 0-89863-038-X). Star Pub CA.
Baxter, William T. Jewelry, Gem Cutting & Metalcraft. 3rd ed. 1950. 10.00 (ISBN 0-07-004149-0, GB). McGraw.
Bead Necklaces. 1975. pap. 1.50 (ISBN 0-8277-4464-1). British Bk Ctr.

Bead Threading & Bead Looming. 1975. pap. 1.50 (ISBN 0-8277-4463-3). British Bk Ctr.

Boece De Boodt, Anselme. Le Parfaict Joallier, Ou Histoire Des Pierreries. Repr. of 1644 ed. 207.00 (ISBN 0-8287-0099-0). Clearwater Pub.

Bovin, Murray. Centrifugal or Lost Wax Jewelry Casting for Schools, Tradesmen, Craftsmen. LC 71-135667. (Illus.). 1977. 13.50 (ISBN 0-910280-06-1); pap. 9.95 (ISBN 0-910280-05-3). Bovin.

--Jewelry Making for Schools, Tradesmen, Craftsmen. enl. ed. LC 67-20040. (Illus.). 1979. 15.50 (ISBN 0-910280-02-9); pap. 11.95 (ISBN 0-910280-01-0). Bovin.

Branson, O. T. Indian Jewelry Making, Vol. 1. (Illus.). 1977. pap. 8.95 (ISBN 0-918080-15-0). Treasure Chest.

--Indian Jewelry Making, Vol. 2. (Illus.). 1979. pap. 8.95 (ISBN 0-918080-17-7). Treasure Chest.

--Turquoise: The Gem of the Centuries. new ed. (Illus.). 1975. pap. 7.95 (ISBN 0-918080-01-0). Treasure Chest.

Brynner, Irena. Jewelry As an Art Form. 1979. 12.95 (ISBN 0-442-26114-4). Van Nos Reinhold.

--Modern Jewelry: Design & Technique. 96p. 1968. pap. 6.95 (ISBN 0-442-21141-4). Van Nos Reinhold.

Chamberlain, Marcia. Metal Jewelry Techniques. (Illus.). 200p. 1976. 21.95 (ISBN 0-8230-3036-9). Watson-Guptill.

Choate, Sharr. Creative Casting. (Arts & Crafts Ser). (Illus.). 1966. 12.95 (ISBN 0-517-02445-4). Crown.

Deacon, Eileen. Making Jewelry. LC 77-7942. (Beginning Crafts Ser.). (Illus.). (gr. k-3). 1977. PLB 9.30 (ISBN 0-8393-0116-2). Raintree Child.

DiPasquale, Dominic & Delius, Jean. Jewelry Making: An Illustrated Guide to Technique. (Creative Handcrafts Ser). 1975. 10.95 (ISBN 0-13-509836-X, Spec); pap. 4.95 (ISBN 0-13-509828-9, Spec). P-H.

Edwards, Rod. The Technique of Jewelry. (Illus.). 1977. 17.50 (ISBN 0-684-15309-2, ScribT). Scribner.

Foote, Ted. Jewelry Making: A Guide for Beginners. LC 80-67547. (Illus.). 112p. 1981. 14.95 (ISBN 0-87192-130-8). Davis Mass.

Frank, Larry & Holbrook, Millard J. Indian Silver Jewelry of the Southwest 1868-1930. LC 78-7071. (Illus.). 1979. 29.95 (ISBN 0-8212-0740-7, 417947). NYGS.

Franke, Lois & Udell, William L. Handwrought Jewelry. (gr. 7 up). 1962. text ed. 16.00 (ISBN 0-87345-175-9). McKnight.

French, Bernada. Jewelry Craft Made Easy. (Illus.). 64p. 1976. pap. 2.00 (ISBN 0-910652-22-8). Gembooks.

Garrison, William E. & Dowd, Merle E. Handcrafting Jewelry: Designs & Techniques. LC 77-91199. 1978. pap. 6.95 (ISBN 0-8092-7529-5). Contemp Bks.

Geisinger, Iva L. Jewelry Maker's Handbook. Cox, Jack R., ed. (Illus.). 64p. 1973. pap. 2.00 (ISBN 0-910652-18-X). Gembooks.

Geoffroy-Dechaume, Claude. Craft Jewelery. (Illus.). 144p. 1980. 16.95 (ISBN 0-571-11486-5, Pub. by Faber & Faber); pap. 6.95 (ISBN 0-571-11309-5, Pub. by Faber & Faber). Merrimack Bk Serv.

Gerlach, Martin. Primitive & Folk Jewelry. (Illus.). 9.50 (ISBN 0-8446-0107-1). Peter Smith.

Gibbs, Joan. Jewelry for Everyone: Soft Jewelry to Create at Home from Twine & Wool, Bone & Shell, Fur & Feather, Clay & Leather, Beads, Recyclables, Other Easy-to-Find Materials. (Illus.). 128p. 1981. 15.95 (ISBN 0-916144-74-7); pap. 7.95 (ISBN 0-916144-73-9). Stemmer Hse.

Glass, Fred J. Jewelry Craft. 70p. 1971. pap. 2.95 (ISBN 0-915462-01-X). Paragraph Pr.

Hardy, R. Allen. The Jewelry Engraver's Manual. 1976. pap. 6.95 (ISBN 0-442-20965-7). Van Nos Reinhold.

Howell-Koehler, Nancy. Soft Jewelry: Design Techniques & Materials. LC 77-8984. (Creative Handcraft Ser.). (Illus.). 1977. pap. 6.95 (ISBN 0-13-822528-1, Spec). P-H.

--Soft Jewelry: Design, Techniques, Materials. LC 75-41546. (Illus.). 136p. (gr. 9 up). 1976. 13.00 (ISBN 0-87192-081-6). Davis Mass.

Huckleberry, E. B. How to Make Your Own Wooden Jewelry. (Illus.). 1979. 9.95 (ISBN 0-8306-9852-3); pap. 5.95 (ISBN 0-8306-1075-8, 1075). TAB Bks.

Kallenberg, Lawrence. Modeling in Wax for Jewelry & Sculpture. LC 80-70384. (Illus.). 288p. 1981. 18.50 (ISBN 0-686-69521-6); text ed. 18.50 (ISBN 0-8019-6896-8). Chilton.

Lee, Jerry. Making Wood & Stone Jewelry. LC 77-76499. (Illus.). 1978. 9.95 (ISBN 0-8008-5081-5); pap. 4.95 (ISBN 0-8008-5076-9). Taplinger.

Lerner, Sharon. Making Jewelry. LC 76-13066. (Early Craft Books). (gr. k-3). 1977. PLB 3.95 (ISBN 0-8225-0862-1). Lerner Pubns.

McCreight, Tim. Metalworking for Jewelry: Tools, Materials, Techniques. 1979. 15.95 (ISBN 0-442-26143-8). Van Nos Reinhold.

Macrame Jewellery. 1977. pap. 1.50 (ISBN 0-8277-5738-7). British Bk Ctr.

Meyerowitz, Patricia. Making Jewelry & Sculpture Through Unit Construction. 7.50 (ISBN 0-8446-5794-8). Peter Smith.

--Making Jewelry & Sculpture Through Unit Construction. (Illus.). 1978. pap. 2.75 (ISBN 0-486-23678-1). Dover.

Morton, Philip. Contemporary Jewelry: A Studio Handbook. 2nd ed. LC 75-25851. 1976. pap. 22.95 (ISBN 0-03-089644-4, HoltC). HR&W.

O'Connor, Harold. Creative Jewelry Techniques. (Illus.). 1978. pap. 7.50 (ISBN 0-918820-04-9). Dunconor Bks.

--The Jeweler's Bench Reference. LC 76-53236. (Illus.). 1977. lab manual 8.95 (ISBN 0-918820-03-0). Dunconor Bks.

Pack, Greta. Jewelry Making by the Lost Wax Process. rev. ed. 96p. 1979. pap. 4.95 (ISBN 0-442-25176-9). Van Nos Reinhold.

--Jewelry Making for the Beginning Craftsman. 78p. 1980. pap. 6.95 (ISBN 0-442-20173-7). Van Nos Reinhold.

Pebbles to Pearls. 1975. pap. 1.50x (ISBN 0-8277-4459-5). British Bk Ctr.

Pope, Patricia. Shellcraft Earrings. (Shorttime Projects for Beginners). (Illus.). 32p. 1976. pap. 1.00 (ISBN 0-8200-0508-8). Great Outdoors.

Powers, Bob & Barasch, Marc. Crafting Turquoise Jewelry. LC 78-12277. (Illus.). 192p. 1978. 16.95 (ISBN 0-8117-1803-4). Stackpole.

Pownall, Glen. Jewellery & Gem Craft. (Creative Leisure Ser.). (Illus.). 84p. 1974. 7.50x (ISBN 0-85467-018-1). Intl Pubns Serv.

--Jewellery & Gemcraft. (New Crafts Books Ser.). 1980. 7.50 (ISBN 0-85467-018-1, Pub. by Viking Sevenseas New Zealand). Intl Schol Bk Serv.

Rose, Augustus F. & Cirino, Antonio. Jewelry Making & Design. 4th & rev. ed. (Illus.). 8.25 (ISBN 0-8446-2829-8). Peter Smith.

--Jewelry Making & Design. (Illus.). 1949. pap. 3.50 (ISBN 0-486-21750-7). Dover.

Shoenfelt, Joseph F. Designing & Making Handwrought Jewelry. (Illus.). 1960. pap. 3.50 (ISBN 0-07-057004-3, SP). McGraw.

Smith, Keith. Practical Silver-Smithing & Jewelry. 1975. 12.95 (ISBN 0-442-27791-1). Van Nos Reinhold.

Soukup, Edward J. Jewelry Making for Beginners. Cox, Jack R., ed. (Illus.). 1973. pap. 2.00 (ISBN 0-910652-17-1). Gembooks.

Sprintzen, Alice. Jewelry: Basic Technique & Design. 224p. 1980. 15.95 (ISBN 0-8019-6828-3); pap. 9.95 (ISBN 0-8019-6830-5). Chilton.

Thompson, Brenda & Giesen, Rosemary. Gold & Jewels. LC 76-22437. (First Fact Books Ser). (Illus.). (gr. k-3). 1977. PLB 4.95 (ISBN 0-8225-1356-0). Lerner Pubns.

Trade Marks of the Jewelry & Kindred Trades 1915. (Illus.). 1980. Repr. 9.95 (ISBN 0-915706-20-2). Am Reprints.

Von Neumann, Robert. Design & Creation of Jewelry. rev. ed. LC 72-1500. (Creative Crafts Ser). 1972. 15.00 (ISBN 0-8019-5671-4); pap. 8.95 (ISBN 0-8019-6054-1). Chilton.

Wada, Takashi. The Art of Making Jewelry. (Illus.). 128p. 1975. 11.95x (ISBN 0-442-29149-3). Van Nos Reinhold.

Warwick, James. Beginning Jewelry. (Illus.). 1980. pap. 7.95 (ISBN 0-684-15814-0, ScribT). Scribner.

Wharton, Marshall. How to Make Jewelry Like a Pro. (Illus.). 1977. pap. 4.95 (ISBN 0-8306-6775-X, 775). TAB Bks.

Wigley, Thomas. The Art of the Goldsmith & Jeweler. 1977. lib. bdg. 75.00 (ISBN 0-8490-1455-7). Gordon Pr.

Winnen, Jo. Watermelon Seed Necklaces & Earrings. (Illus.). 26p. 1974. pap. 1.50x (ISBN 0-9603404-0-8). J Winnen.

Zechlin, Katharina. Creative Enamelling & Jewelry-Making. Kuttner, Paul, tr. LC 65-20877. (gr. 10 up). 1965. 6.95 (ISBN 0-8069-5062-5); PLB 6.69 (ISBN 0-8069-5063-3). Sterling.

Ziek, Nona. Making Silver Jewelry. (Illus.). 1977. pap. 2.95 (ISBN 0-425-03486-0, Windhover). Berkley Pub.

JEWELRY TRADE

Ehrhardt, Roy. Trademarks. (Illus.). 1976. Repr. ring bdg. 10.00 (ISBN 0-913902-06-3). Heart Am Pr.

Giacomini, Afton. Trophy Winning Facet Cuts. Cox, Jack R., ed. (Illus.). 32p. 1974. pap. text ed. 2.50 (ISBN 0-910652-19-8). Gembooks.

Schumach, Murray. The Diamond People. (Illus.). 1981. 12.95 (ISBN 0-393-01404-5). Norton.

JEWELS

see Crown Jewels; Gems; Jewelry; Precious Stones

JEWETT, CHARLES COFFIN, 1816-1868

Harris, Michael H., ed. The Age of Jewett: Charles Coffin Jewett & American Librarianship, 1841-1868. LC 75-14205. (Heritage of Librarianship Ser: No. 1). 166p. 1975. lib. bdg. 20.00x (ISBN 0-87287-113-4). Libs Unl.

JEWETT, SARAH ORNE, 1849-1909

Cary, Richard. Sarah Orne Jewett. (Twayne's United States Authors Ser). 1962. pap. 3.45 (ISBN 0-8084-0272-2, T19, Twayne). Coll & U Pr.

Cary, Richard, ed. Appreciation of Sarah Orne Jewett: Twenty-Nine Interpretive Essays. 1973. 11.50 (ISBN 0-910394-11-3). Colby.

Donovan, Josephine L. Sarah Orne Jewett. LC 80-5334. (Modern Literature Ser.). 160p. 1980. 10.95 (ISBN 0-8044-2137-4). Ungar.

Matthiessen, Francis O. Sarah Orne Jewett. 1929. 7.50 (ISBN 0-8446-1305-3). Peter Smith.

Nagel, Gwen L. & Nagel, James, eds. Sarah Orne Jewett: A Reference Guide. (Reference Publications Ser.). 1977. lib. bdg. 15.75 (ISBN 0-8161-7848-8). G K Hall.

Thorp, Margaret F. Sarah Orne Jewett. (Pamphlets on American Writers Ser: No. 61). (Orig.). 1966. pap. 1.25x (ISBN 0-8166-0406-1, MPAW61). U of Minn Pr.

Westbrook, Perry D. Acres of Flint: Sarah Orne Jewett & Her Contemporaries. rev. ed. LC 80-20501. 204p. 1981. 12.50 (ISBN 0-8108-1357-2). Scarecrow.

JEWISH-ARAB RELATIONS

see also Israel-Arab Border Conflicts, 1949-

Alexander, Yonah & Kittrie, Nicholas N. F., eds. Crescent & Star: Arab & Israeli Perspectives on the Middle East Conflict. LC 72-5797. (AMS Studies in Modern Society: Political & Social Issues). 30.00 (ISBN 0-404-10522-X); pap. 11.95 (ISBN 0-404-10523-8). AMS Pr.

Allen, Richard. Imperialism & Nationalism in the Fertile Crescent: Sources & Prospects of the Arab-Israeli Conflict. (Illus.). 400p. 1974. 19.95 (ISBN 0-19-501782-X). Oxford U Pr.

--Imperialism & Nationalism in the Fertile Crescent: Sources & Prospects of the Arab-Israeli Conflict. (Illus.). 1974. pap. 9.95x (ISBN 0-19-501781-1). Oxford U Pr.

Archer, Jules. Legacy of the Desert: Understanding the Arabs. (gr. 7-12). 1976. 8.95 (ISBN 0-316-04965-4). Little.

Beling, Willard A., ed. The Middle East: Quest for an American Policy. LC 73-4281. (Illus.). 364p. 1973. 26.00 (ISBN 0-87395-228-6); microfiche 23.50 (ISBN 0-87395-229-4). State U NY Pr.

Ben-Gurion, David. My Talks with Arab Leaders. LC 72-94298. 342p. 1973. 11.95 (ISBN 0-89388-076-0). Okpaku Communications.

Caplan, Gerald. Arab & Jew in Jerusalem: Explorations in Community Mental Health. LC 79-27832. 1980. text ed. 15.00x (ISBN 0-674-04315-4). Harvard U Pr.

Carmichael, Joel. Open Letter to Moses & Mohammed. LC 68-9705. (Open Letter Ser). (Orig.). 1968. pap. 2.25 (ISBN 0-685-11973-4, 18). Heineman.

Chaim, Bezalel, ed. Toward Jewish-Arab Rapprochement: A History of Ihud. 1979. lib. bdg. 44.95 (ISBN 0-686-24785-X). M Buber Pr.

Chill, Dan S. The Arab Boycott of Israel: Economic Aggression and World Reaction. LC 76-14431. 1976. text ed. 24.95 (ISBN 0-275-56810-5). Praeger.

Davis, John. The Evasive Peace. 1970. pap. 2.95 (ISBN 0-911026-01-0). New World Press NY.

Davis, John H. The Evasive Peace. 2nd ed. LC 79-142227. (Illus.). 1976. text ed. 5.95 (ISBN 0-913228-16-8). Dillon-Liederbach.

Debates of the Israeli Knesset, 1967-1968. 1977. 25.00 (ISBN 0-686-18945-0). Inst Palestine.

Dobson, Christopher. Black September: Its Short, Violent History. Griffin, H. W., ed. (Illus.). 160p. 1974. 11.95 (ISBN 0-02-531900-0). Macmillan.

Ellis, Harry B. Israel: One Land, Two Peoples. LC 73-175104. (Illus.). 210p. 1972. 10.95 (ISBN 0-690-45028-1). T y Crowell.

Elmessiri, Abdelwahab M. The Land of Promise: A Critique of Political Zionism. LC 77-83664. 1977. text ed. 11.95x (ISBN 0-930244-02-8); pap. text ed. 7.95x (ISBN 0-930244-01-X). North American Inc.

Erskine, Beatrice S. Palestine of the Arabs. LC 75-6431. (The Rise of Jewish Nationalism & the Middle East Ser). 255p. 1975. Repr. of 1935 ed. 25.00 (ISBN 0-88355-318-X). Hyperion Conn.

Esco Foundation For Palestine Inc. Palestine: A Study of Jewish, Arab, & British Policies, 2 Vols. LC 47-2569. Repr. of 1947 ed. Set. 120.00 (ISBN 0-527-27750-9). Kraus Repr.

Flapan, Simha. Zionism & the Palestinians. LC 78-26044. (Illus.). 1979. text ed. 24.95x (ISBN 0-06-492104-2). B&N.

Friedlander, Saul & Hussein, Mahmoud. Arabs & Israelis: A Dialogue. Auster, Paul & Davis, Lydia, trs. from Fr. LC 75-9147. 247p. 1975. 17.50x (ISBN 0-8419-0208-9). Holmes & Meier.

Glassman, Jon D. Arms for the Arabs: The Soviet Union & War in the Middle East. LC 75-29254. (Illus.). 254p. 1976. 17.00x (ISBN 0-8018-1747-1). Johns Hopkins.

Goitein, S. D. Jews & Arabs: Their Contacts Through the Ages. 3rd ed. LC 74-9141. 271p. 1974. 10.00x (ISBN 0-8052-3567-1); pap. 4.95 (ISBN 0-8052-0464-4). Schocken.

Harkabi, Y. Arab Attitudes to Israel. 527p. 1972. 20.00x (ISBN 0-85303-157-6, Pub. by Vallentine Mitchell England). Biblio Dist.

Harkabi, Yehoshafat. Arab Attitudes to Israel. 1974. casebound 19.95x (ISBN 0-87855-168-9). Transaction Bks.

--Arab Strategies & Israel's Response. LC 77-70273. 1977. 12.95 (ISBN 0-02-913760-8); pap. 4.95 (ISBN 0-02-913780-2). Free Pr.

Harkness, Georgia & Kraft, Charles F. The Biblical Backgrounds of the Middle East Conflict. LC 76-22644. (Illus.). 1976. 3.95 (ISBN 0-687-03435-3). Abingdon.

Heimler, Eugene. The Storm (the Tragedy of Sinai) Rudolf, Anthony, tr. from Hung. 1976. pap. 3.00 (ISBN 0-685-79253-6, Pub. by Menard Pr). SBD.

Jabber, Paul. Not by War Alone: Security & Arms Control in the Middle East. LC 80-11341. 200p. 1981. 18.50x (ISBN 0-520-04050-3). U of Cal Pr.

Jewish Liberation Project & Committee To Support Middle-East Liberation. Arab-Israeli Debate: Toward a Socialist Solution. (Illus., Orig.). 1971. pap. 1.25 (ISBN 0-87810-007-5). Times Change.

Kazziha, Walid W. Palestine in the Arab Dilemma. LC 78-10543. 1979. text ed. 21.50x (ISBN 0-06-494004-7). B&N.

Kiernan, Thomas. The Arabs: Their History, Aims & Challenge to the Industrialized World. 1975. 12.50 (ISBN 0-316-49201-9). Little.

Kodsy, Ahmad El & Lobel, Eli. Arab World & Israel. LC 70-129571. (Illus.). 1970. pap. 4.50 (ISBN 0-85345-168-0, PB1680). Monthly Rev.

Laqueur, Walter. Confrontation: The Middle East & World Politics. LC 74-79438. 1974. 8.95 (ISBN 0-8129-0454-0). Times Bks.

Lorch, Netanel. One Long War. 1976. 8.00 (ISBN 0-685-82597-3). Herzl Pr.

Magnes, Judah L. & Buber, Martin. Arab-Jewish Unity: Testimony Before the Anglo-American Inquiry for the Ihud (Union) LC 75-7678. (The Rise of Jewish Nationalism & the Middle East Ser). 96p. 1975. Repr. of 1947 ed. 12.00 (ISBN 0-88355-348-1). Hyperion Conn.

Main, Ernest. Palestine at the Crossroads. LC 71-180359. Repr. of 1937 ed. 23.75 (ISBN 0-404-56291-4). AMS Pr.

Mandel, Neville. The Arabs & Zionism Before World War One. LC 73-78545. 1977. pap. 4.95 (ISBN 0-520-03940-8). U of Cal Pr.

Marx, Victor. The Middle East & the Attempt at World Economic Hegemony. (Illus.). 1977. 47.75 (ISBN 0-89266-047-3). Am Classical Coll Pr.

Memmi, Albert. Jews & Arabs. Levieux, Eleanor, tr. from Fr. LC 75-10697. 224p. (Eng.). 1975. 7.95 (ISBN 0-87955-327-8); pap. 4.95 (ISBN 0-87955-328-6). O'Hara.

Merlin, Samuel. The Search for Peace in the Middle East. LC 68-27264. 1969. 9.95 (ISBN 0-498-06878-1, Yoseloff). A S Barnes.

Merlin, Samuel, ed. Big Powers & the Present Crisis in the Middle East. LC 68-8864. 201p. 1968. 12.00 (ISBN 0-8386-7349-X). Fairleigh Dickinson.

Moore, John N., ed. The Arab-Israeli Conflict, 3 vols. LC 72-39792. (American Society of International Law Ser.). 2700p. 1974. Set. 160.00 (ISBN 0-691-05648-X); pap. 13.50 abridged ed. (ISBN 0-691-01066-8). Princeton U Pr.

O'Neill, Bard. Armed Struggle in Palestine: A Political - Military Analysis. LC 78-2285. (Westview Special Studies on the Middle East Ser.). 1978. lib. bdg. 27.75x (ISBN 0-89158-333-5). Westview.

--Revolutionary Warfare in the Middle East: The Israelis vs. the Fedayeen. new ed. LC 74-79038. (Illus.). 1974. 6.00 (ISBN 0-87364-000-4). Paladin Ent.

People's Press Palestine Book Project, et al. Our Roots Are Still Alive: The Story of the Palestinian People. LC 77-10952. (Illus.). 182p. pap. 5.45 (ISBN 0-917654-12-9). IISJ.

Peretz, Don. Israel & the Palestine Arabs. LC 80-1915. Repr. of 1958 ed. 31.00 (ISBN 0-404-18984-9). AMS Pr.

Pfaff, Richard H. Jerusalem: Keystone of an Arab-Israeli Settlement. 1969. pap. 3.75 (ISBN 0-8447-1034-2). Am Enterprise.

Pranger, Robert J. & Tahtinen, Dale R. Nuclear Threat in the Middle East. LC 75-16306. (Orig.). 1975. pap. 4.25 (ISBN 0-8447-3172-2). Am Enterprise.

Rabinovich, I. & Shaked, H., eds. From June to October: The Middle East Between 1967 & 1973. LC 76-45942. 550p. 1977. text ed. 19.95 (ISBN 0-87855-230-8). Transaction Bks.

Reich, Bernard. The Quest for Peace: U. S. - Israeli Relations & the Arab-Israeli Conflict. LC 76-45940. 495p. 1977. text ed. 24.95 (ISBN 0-87855-226-X). Transaction Bks.

Reisman, Michael. Art of the Possible: Diplomatic Alternatives in the Middle East. 1970. 15.00 (ISBN 0-691-05635-8); pap. 6.95 (ISBN 0-691-01059-5). Princeton U Pr.

Safran, Nadav. From War to War: The Arab-Israeli Confrontation, 1948-1967. LC 69-27991. (Illus.). 464p. 1969. text ed. 24.50x (ISBN 0-8290-0173-5). Irvington.

--From War to War: The Arab-Israeli Confrontation 1948-1967. LC 68-27991. 1969. pap. 9.95 (ISBN 0-672-63540-2). Pegasus.

Said, Edward W. The Question of Palestine. LC 80-12146. 288p. 1980. pap. 2.95 (ISBN 0-394-74527-2, Vin). Random.

Sakran, Frank C. Palestine: Still a Dilemma. LC 76-29879. 1976. 6.95 (ISBN 0-87426-042-6). Whitmore.

Schuster, Robert L. Israel, The Middle East & the Moral Conscience of the Western World. (The Major Currents in Contemporary World History). (Illus.). 133p. 1981. 47.85 (ISBN 0-89266-301-4). Am Classical Coll Pr.

Sereni, Ezo H. & Ashery, R. E., eds. Jews & Arabs in Palestine: Studies in a National & Colonial Problem. LC 75-6455. (The Rise of Jewish Nationalism & the Middle East Ser). 416p. 1975. Repr. of 1936 ed. 28.50 (ISBN 0-88355-341-4). Hyperion Conn.

Sheffer, Gabriel. Dynamics of Conflict: A Re-Examination of the Arab-Israel Conflict. (Van Leer Jerusalem Foundation Ser.). 376p. 1975. text ed. 12.50x (ISBN 0-391-00379-8). Humanities.

Sherman, John. Arab-Israeli Conflict, Nineteen Forty-Five to Nineteen Seventy-One: A Bibliography. LC 77-83360. (Reference Library of Social Science Ser.). 1978. lib. bdg. 38.00 (ISBN 0-8240-9829-3). Garland Pub.

Sobel, Lester A., ed. Palestinian Impasse: Arab Guerrillas & International Terror. LC 77-70127. 1977. lib. bdg. 17.50x (ISBN 0-87196-266-7). Facts on File.

Talmon, J. L. Israel Among the Nations. Mandel, To, ed. 1971. 11.95 (ISBN 0-02-616250-4). Macmillan.

Tomeh, George J., ed. United National Resolutions on Palestine, & the Arab-Israeli Conflict,1947-1974. 1977. write for info. (ISBN 0-686-18942-6). Inst Palestine.

Whetten, L. L. The Canal War: Four-Power Conflict in the Middle East. 1974. 25.00x (ISBN 0-262-23069-0). MIT Pr.

Yasser Arafat Palestine Lives. (Illus.). 1975. pap. 0.50 (ISBN 0-914750-03-8). Peoples Pr.

Ziff, William B. The Rape of Palestine. LC 73-97310. (Illus.). 612p. 1975. Repr. of 1938 ed. lib. bdg. 29.25x (ISBN 0-8371-2639-8, ZIRP). Greenwood.

JEWISH-AFRO-AMERICAN RELATIONS
see Afro-Americans-Relations with Jews

JEWISH ART
see Art, Jewish

JEWISH ART AND SYMBOLISM
see also Menorah; Symbolism in the Bible

Altmann, Alexander. Essays in Jewish Intellectual History. LC 80-54471. 336p. 1981. text ed. 20.00x (ISBN 0-87451-192-5). U Pr of New Eng.

Fischman, Joyce. Let's Learn About Jewish Symbols. LC 68-9347. (Illus.). (ps-k). 1969. pap. text ed. 3.50 (ISBN 0-8074-0144-7, 101035). UAHC.

Gutmann, Joseph. Beauty in Holiness: Studies in Jewish Ceremonial Art & Customs. 1970. 35.00x (ISBN 0-87068-012-9). Ktav.

--No Graven Images: Studies in Art & the Hebrew Bible. (Library of Biblical Studies). 1970. 35.00x (ISBN 0-87068-063-3). Ktav.

Halpern, Ben. The Jewish National Home in Palestine. 1970. 25.00x (ISBN 0-87068-050-1). Ktav.

Kanof, Abram. Jewish Ceremonial Art & Religious Observance. 32.50 (ISBN 0-8109-0178-1); pap. 12.50 (ISBN 0-8109-2199-5). Abrams.

Kanof, Abram, intro. by. Ceremonial Art in the Judaic Tradition. LC 75-126321. (Illus.). 92p. 1975. pap. 3.00 (ISBN 0-88259-078-2). NCMA.

Samuel, Edith. Your Jewish Lexicon. (Orig.). 1981. 10.00 (ISBN 0-8074-0054-8); pap. 6.50 (ISBN 0-8074-0061-0). UAHC.

Wigoder, Geoffrey, ed. Jewish Art & Civilization. LC 72-80540. (Illus.). 290p. 1972. boxed ed 95.00 (ISBN 0-8027-0394-1). Walker & Co.

JEWISH AUTHORS
see Authors, Jewish

JEWISH BALLADS AND SONGS
see also Folk-Songs, Jewish; Songs, Jewish

JEWISH CALENDAR
see Calendar, Jewish

JEWISH CHANT
see Chants (Jewish)

JEWISH CHARITIES
see Jews-Charities

JEWISH CHILDREN

Bernard, Jacqueline. The Children You Gave Us. LC 72-87122. (Illus.). 1972. 6.95 (ISBN 0-8197-0356-7). Bloch.

Bial, Morrison D. Your Jewish Child. Syme, Daniel B., ed. 1978. pap. 5.00 (ISBN 0-8074-0012-2, 101200). UAHC.

Birnhack, Sarah. Happy Is the Heart: A Year in the Life of a Jewish Girl. (Illus.). (gr. 5-8). 1976. 5.95 (ISBN 0-87306-131-4). Feldheim.

Donin, Hayim H. To Raise a Jewish Child: A Guide for Parents. LC 76-7679. 1977. 11.95 (ISBN 0-465-08626-8). Basic.

Israel, Richard J. Jewish Identity Games: A How to Do It Book. LC 78-55201. 1978. 3.95 (ISBN 0-9603058-1-5). B'nai B'rith-Hillel.

Wolf, Hannie. Child of Two Worlds. (Illus.). 156p. 1979. 10.00 (ISBN 0-931068-02-9). Purcells.

JEWISH CHRISTIANS
Here are entered works dealing with Christians of Jewish antecedence.
see also Converts from Judaism

Berger, David & Wyschogrod, Michael. Jews & Jewish Christianity. 3.95x (ISBN 0-87068-675-5). Ktav.

Fruchtenbaum, Arnold G. Hebrew Christianity. pap. 2.95 (ISBN 0-8010-3472-8). Baker Bk.

Gartenhaus, Jacob. Famous Hebrew Christians. 1979. pap. 5.95 (ISBN 0-8010-3733-6). Baker Bk.

Jocz, Jakob. The Jewish People & Jesus Christ. 1979. pap. 7.95 (ISBN 0-8010-5085-5). Baker Bk.

Kac, Arthur W. The Messiahship of Jesus. 350p. 1980. pap. 9.95 (ISBN 0-8024-5421-6). Moody.

Longenecker, Richard N. The Christology of Early Jewish Christianity. (Twin Brooks Ser.). 178p. 1981. pap. 5.95 (ISBN 0-8010-5610-1). Baker Bk.

Sobel, B. Z. Hebrew Christianity: The Thirteenth Tribe. LC 74-3351. 428p. 1974. 9.50 (ISBN 0-471-81025-8). Krieger.

JEWISH CHRONOLOGY
see Chronology, Jewish

JEWISH CIVILIZATION
see Jews-Civilization

JEWISH COLONIZATION ASSOCIATION

Winsberg, Morton D. Colonia Baron Hirsch: A Jewish Agricultural Colony in Argentina. LC 64-63523. (U of Fla. Social Sciences Monographs: No. 19). 1963. pap. 3.00 (ISBN 0-8130-0259-1). U Presses Fla.

JEWISH CONVERTS TO CHRISTIANITY
see Converts from Judaism

JEWISH COURTS
see Courts, Jewish

JEWISH CULTUS
see Cultus, Jewish

JEWISH DAY OF ATONEMENT
see Yom Kippur

JEWISH DEFENSE LEAGUE

Lumer, Hyman. Jewish Defense League: A New Face for Reaction. 1971. pap. 0.35 (ISBN 0-87898-072-5). New Outlook.

JEWISH DEVOTIONAL LITERATURE
see also Jews-Prayer-Books and Devotions

Abraham Weiss Jubilee Volume. Date not set. 20.00 (ISBN 0-686-76277-0). Feldheim.

Antidote. Date not set. 3.95 (ISBN 0-87306-173-X). Feldheim.

Anvil of Sinai. Date not set. 9.95 (ISBN 0-686-76479-X). Feldheim.

As a Tree by the Waters. Date not set. 8.95 (ISBN 0-87306-237-X). Feldheim.

Asmussen, Jes P., ed. Jewish-Persian Texts. LC 68-97838. 1968. 7.50x (ISBN 3-447-00447-9). Intl Pubns Serv.

Baal Shem of Michelstadt. Date not set. pap. 3.95 (ISBN 0-686-76481-1). Feldheim.

Because I Believe. Date not set. 12.75 (ISBN 0-686-76482-X). Feldheim.

Beyond the Sun. Date not set. 12.75 (ISBN 0-686-76483-8). Feldheim.

Birkas Hashulchan. Date not set. 5.95 (ISBN 0-686-76484-6); pap. 3.95 (ISBN 0-686-76485-4). Feldheim.

Challenge of Sinai, 2 vols. (Illus.). Date not set. 13.95 (ISBN 0-686-76489-7). Feldheim.

Chumash Koren. Date not set. 5.75 (ISBN 0-686-76491-9). Feldheim.

Chumash with Rashi, 5 vols. Date not set. Set. 17.50 (ISBN 0-686-76492-7); 3.50 ea. Feldheim.

Commentary of Rabbi David. Date not set. price not set. Feldheim.

Concordance. Date not set. Schocken Ed. 22.50 (ISBN 0-686-76495-1); Regular Ed. 14.50 (ISBN 0-686-76496-X). Feldheim.

Dawn of Greatness. Date not set. 6.00 (ISBN 0-686-76503-6). Feldheim.

Days of Awe. Date not set. 6.95 (ISBN 0-686-76504-4). Feldheim.

Duties of the Heart, 2 vols. (Illus.). Date not set. 19.95 (ISBN 0-87306-111-X). Feldheim.

Faith & Courage 230x. 4.95 (ISBN 0-87306-258-2). Feldheim.

Gates of Repentance. Date not set. 8.95 (ISBN 0-87306-252-3). Feldheim.

Gemilath Chasadim. Date not set. 3.95 (ISBN 0-686-76508-7). Feldheim.

Glatzer, Nahum N., ed. A Jewish Reader: In Time & Eternity. 2nd ed. LC 61-14920. 1961. pap. 3.75 (ISBN 0-8052-0016-9). Schocken.

Grace After Meals. Date not set. pap. 0.60 large (ISBN 0-686-76510-9); pap. 0.35 small (ISBN 0-686-76511-7). Feldheim.

Haggadah. Date not set. leatherbound 30.00 (ISBN 0-686-76514-1). Feldheim.

Hashovas Aveida. Date not set. pap. 2.00 (ISBN 0-686-76515-X). Feldheim.

Hertz, Joseph H. Pirke Aboth: Sayings of the Fathers. 1945. pap. 2.95x (ISBN 0-87441-155-6). Behrman.

Hirsch Siddur. Date not set. deluxe leatherbound 45.00 (ISBN 0-686-76517-6). Feldheim.

In Our Father's Ways. Date not set. 7.95 (ISBN 0-686-76519-2). Feldheim.

Joshua Finkel Festschrift. Date not set. 15.00 (ISBN 0-686-76525-7). Feldheim.

Just in Time. Date not set. pap. 4.95 (ISBN 0-87306-257-4). Feldheim.

Kafra Haggadah. Date not set. 25.00 (ISBN 0-686-76527-3). Feldheim.

Knowing Your Tefilen & Hezuzos. Date not set. pap. 2.50 (ISBN 0-686-76528-1). Feldheim.

Koren Tanach. Date not set. small 6.75 (ISBN 0-686-76529-X); medium 12.95 (ISBN 0-686-76530-3); large 75.00 (ISBN 0-686-76531-1). Feldheim.

Lehavin Vlehaskil. Date not set. pap. 5.50 (ISBN 0-686-76535-4). Feldheim.

Leo Jung Jubilee Volume. Date not set. 15.00 (ISBN 0-686-76536-2). Feldheim.

Maaser Kesagim. Date not set. 6.95 (ISBN 0-87306-238-8). Feldheim.

Matter of Return. Date not set. pap. 3.95 (ISBN 0-686-76543-5). Feldheim.

Meditations on the Siddur. Date not set. 9.95 (ISBN 0-686-76545-1). Feldheim.

Mishna Berurah. Date not set. regular ed. 10.95 (ISBN 0-87306-233-7); large ed. 13.95 (ISBN 0-87306-198-5). Feldheim.

Mishnayoth Kehati-Berochoth. Date not set. 3.95 (ISBN 0-686-76548-6). Feldheim.

Mishnayoth Kehati-Sukkoth. Date not set. 3.95 (ISBN 0-686-76549-4). Feldheim.

Mitzvoth. Date not set. 15.95 (ISBN 0-686-76550-8). Feldheim.

Mystical Glory of Shabbos & Pessach. Date not set. pap. 3.95 (ISBN 0-87306-251-5). Feldheim.

Our Sages Showed the Way. Date not set. 6.95 (ISBN 0-87306-200-0). Feldheim.

Path of the Just. Date not set. 7.95 (ISBN 0-87306-239-6). Feldheim.

Practical Guide to Kashruth. Date not set. 5.50 (ISBN 0-686-76247-9). Feldheim.

Prisoner & Other Tales of Faith. Date not set. pap. 3.95 (ISBN 0-87306-243-4). Feldheim.

Providence in the Life of Gersonidies. Date not set. 6.75 (ISBN 0-686-76248-7). Feldheim.

Rabbi's Blessing. Date not set. 7.50 (ISBN 0-686-76249-5). Feldheim.

Road Back. Date not set. pap. 5.95 (ISBN 0-87306-264-7). Feldheim.

Royal Resident. Date not set. 4.95 (ISBN 0-686-76251-7). Feldheim.

Schlink, Basilea. For Jerusalem's Sake I Will Not Rest. 1.45 (ISBN 0-551-00741-9). Evang Sisterhood Mary.

Seder Mincha U'maariv. Date not set. pap. 0.99 (ISBN 0-686-76256-8). Feldheim.

Shemuel Hanagid. Date not set. 5.95 (ISBN 0-87306-220-5). Feldheim.

Sign & Glory. Date not set. 8.95 (ISBN 0-686-76258-4). Feldheim.

The Signs of Omission: The Neglected Child. Date not set. pap. 5.95 (ISBN 0-686-76259-2). Feldheim.

Sparks of the Holy Tongue. Date not set. pap. 2.95 (ISBN 0-87306-240-X). Feldheim.

Taamim Lakorim. Date not set. pap. 6.00 (ISBN 0-686-76267-3); cassette 6.00 (ISBN 0-686-76268-1); book & cassette 10.00 (ISBN 0-686-76269-X). Feldheim.

Taharatti Hamishpacha. Date not set. pap. 2.95 (ISBN 0-87306-100-4). Feldheim.

A Time to Build. Date not set. Vol. 1. 5.95 (ISBN 0-87306-077-6); Vol. 2. 8.95 (ISBN 0-686-76270-3). Feldheim.

Vilna Goan Views Life. Date not set. 4.00 (ISBN 0-686-76275-4). Feldheim.

Weltwende. Date not set. pap. 6.00 (ISBN 0-686-76278-9). Feldheim.

Yossef Mokir Shabbos: Hebrew-English. Date not set. pap. 4.50 (ISBN 0-87306-189-6). Feldheim.

Yossef Mokir Shabbos: Hebrew-French. Date not set. pap. 3.95 (ISBN 0-686-76282-7). Feldheim.

Yossef Mokir Shabbos: Hebrew-Yiddish. Date not set. pap. 3.95 (ISBN 0-686-76283-5). Feldheim.

Zemiros Shabbos. Date not set. pap. 1.25 (ISBN 0-686-76284-3). Feldheim.

JEWISH DRAMA
see also Yiddish Drama

Banki, Judith H. What Viewers Should Know About the Oberammergan Passion Play. 20p. 1980. pap. 1.50 (ISBN 0-87495-024-4). Am Jewish Comm.

Coleman, Edward D. Plays of Jewish Interest on the American Stage. 59.95 (ISBN 0-8490-0842-5). Gordon Pr.

Landis, Joseph C., ed. The Great Jewish Plays. 1974. pap. 3.50 (ISBN 0-380-00123-3, 51573, Bard). Avon.

JEWISH ETHICS
see Ethics, Jewish

JEWISH FASTS AND FEASTS
see Fasts and Feasts-Judaism

JEWISH FOLK-LORE
see Folk-Lore, Jewish

JEWISH FOLK SONGS
see Folk-Songs, Jewish

JEWISH HOLIDAYS
see Fasts and Feasts-Judaism

JEWISH HOLOCAUST (1939-1945)
see Holocaust, Jewish (1939-1945)

JEWISH INSCRIPTIONS
see Inscriptions, Jewish

JEWISH LANGUAGE
see Hebrew Language; Yiddish Language

JEWISH LAW
see also Commandments (Judaism); Commandments, Ten; Courts, Jewish; Jews-Dietary Laws; Responsa

Amram, David W. The Jewish Law of Divorce According to Bible & Talmud. LC 68-23386. 228p. 1975. Repr. of 1896 ed. 7.50 (ISBN 0-87203-008-3). Hermon.

Appel, G. The Concise Code of Jewish Law: Daily Prayers & Religious Observances in the Life-Cycle of the Jew, Vol. 1. 20.00x (ISBN 0-87068-298-9). Ktav.

Associations of Orthodox Jewish Scientists. Proceedings, Vol. 3 & 4. Rosner, Fred, ed. 248p. 1976. pap. 7.95 (ISBN 0-87306-074-1). Feldheim.

Bazak, Jacob. Jewish Law & Jewish Life, 8 bks. in 4 vols. Passamaneck, Stephen M., ed. Incl. Bk. 1. Selected Rabbinical Response (ISBN 0-8074-0034-3, 180210); Bks. 2-4. Contracts, Real Estate, Sales & Usury (180211); Bks. 5-6. Credit, Law Enforcement & Taxation (180212); Bks. 7-8. Criminal & Domestic Relations (ISBN 0-8074-0037-8, 180213). 1978. pap. 12.50 complete vol. (ISBN 0-8074-0038-6, 180218); pap. 5.00 ea. UAHC.

Berkovits, Eliezer. Crisis & Faith. 224p. 1975. 6.95 (ISBN 0-88482-903-0, Sanhedrin Pr). Hebrew Pub.

Blackman, Philip, tr. The Mishnah. 4050p. (Eng. & Hebrew.). 1962. 60.00 (ISBN 0-910818-00-2). Judaica Pr.

Bleich, D. J. Contemporary Halakhic Problems. (The Library of Jewish Law & Ethics: No. 4). 20.00x (ISBN 0-87068-450-7). Ktav.

Boecker, Hans J. Law & the Administration of Justice in the Old Testament & Ancient East. Moiser, Jeremy, tr. LC 80-65556. 224p. 1980. pap. 12.50 (ISBN 0-8066-1801-9, 10-3761). Augsburg.

Cohen, Abraham. Everyman's Talmud. LC 75-10750. 446p. 1975. pap. 9.50 (ISBN 0-8052-0497-0). Schocken.

Cohen, Boaz. Jewish & Roman Law, 2 Vols. 1966. Set. 15.00x (ISBN 0-8381-4100-5). United Syn Bk.

--Law & Tradition in Judaism. 1959. 12.50x (ISBN 0-87068-023-4). Ktav.

Cohn, Haim H. Jewish Law in Ancient & Modern Israel. 1971. 20.00x (ISBN 0-87068-137-0). Ktav.

Corlett, William & Moore, John. Questions of Human Existence As Answered by Major World Religions: The Judaic Law. LC 79-16432. 1980. 8.95 (ISBN 0-87888-152-2). Bradbury Pr.

Dorff, Elliot. Jewish Law & Modern Ideology. 1970. pap. 6.50x (ISBN 0-8381-0209-3). United Syn Bk.

Dresner, Samuel & Siegel, Seymour. Jewish Dietary Laws. rev. ed. pap. 2.95x (ISBN 0-8381-2105-5). United Syn Bk.

Elon, Menachem, ed. The Principles of Jewish Law. 866p. 1975. 50.00 (ISBN 0-87855-188-3). Transaction Bks.

Fairbairn, Patrick. Revelation of Law in Scripture. 1981. 15.95 (ISBN 0-88469-135-7). BMH Bks.

Feldman, David M. Marital Relations, Birth Control, & Abortion in Jewish Law. LC 68-15333. 322p. 1974. pap. 5.95 (ISBN 0-8052-0438-5). Schocken.

Fuss, Abraham, ed. Studies in Jewish Jurisprudence. (Studies in Jewish Jurisprudence Ser.: Vol. 4). 320p. 1975. 14.50 (ISBN 0-87203-058-X). Hermon.

Ganzfried, Solomon & Goldin, Hyman E. Code of Jewish Law. 626p. 1963. 8.95 (ISBN 0-88482-423-3). Hebrew Pub.

Ginsburg, Christian D. Massorah, 4 Vols. rev. ed. (Library of Biblical Studies). 1970. Set. 300.00 (ISBN 0-87068-020-X). Ktav.
Ginzberg, Louis. On Jewish Law & Lore. LC 55-6707. (Temple Bks). 1970. pap. 4.95 (ISBN 0-689-70231-0, T12). Atheneum.
Goldstein, Israel. Jewish Justice & Conciliation. Date not set. 17.50x (ISBN 0-87068-729-8). Ktav.
Guide to Practical Halacha, Vol. 2. Date not set. 10.00 (ISBN 0-686-76512-5); pap. 7.00 (ISBN 0-686-76513-3). Feldheim.
Hayyim, Hafetz, pseud. Ahavath Chesed: The Love of Kindness As Required by G-D. 2nd & rev. ed. Oschry, Leonard, tr. from Hebrew. Orig. Title: Ahavath Hesed. 1976. 8.95 (ISBN 0-87306-110-1). Feldheim.
Herzog, Isaac. Main Institutions of Jewish Law, 2 Vols. Set. 21.00x (ISBN 0-685-01041-4). Bloch.
Herzog, Isaac, et al. Studies in Jewish Jurisprudence. LC 72-136770. (Studies in Jewish Jurisprudence Ser.: Vol. 2). 320p. 1974. 12.50 (ISBN 0-87203-041-5). Hermon.
Jacobs, Louis. Jewish Law. LC 68-27329. (Chain of Tradition Ser). 1968. pap. text ed. 3.95x (ISBN 0-87441-010-X). Behrman.
Kahana, K. Case for Jewish Civil Law in the Jewish State. 6.75x (ISBN 0-685-01037-6). Bloch.
Kahana, Kalman. A Guide for the Year of Sh'mittah. Wengrov, Charles, tr. Orig. Title: Mitzvoth Ha'aretz. 1972. pap. 1.00 (ISBN 0-87306-094-6). Feldheim.
Kaplan, Aryeh. The Story of Tisha B'Av. 160p. (Orig.). 1981. pap. 2.95 (ISBN 0-940118-32-7). Maznaim.
Katz, Mordecai. Protection of the Weak in the Talmud. LC 26-5707. (Columbia University. Oriental Studies: No. 24). Repr. of 1925 ed. 12.50 (ISBN 0-404-50514-7). AMS Pr.
Kirschenbaum, Aaron. Self-Incrimination in Jewish Law. 1970. 8.00x (ISBN 0-8381-3111-5). United Syn Bk.
Klein, Isaac. Responsa & Halakhic Studies. 15.00x (ISBN 0-87068-288-1). Ktav.
Landman, Leo. Jewish Law in the Diaspora. 1968. 15.00x (ISBN 0-685-22505-4). Ktav.
Levine, Aaron. Free Enterprise & Jewish Law: Aspects of Jewish Business Ethics. Date not set. 17.50x (ISBN 0-87068-702-6). Ktav.
Levita, Elijah. Massoreth Ha Massoreth. rev. ed. LC 67-11894. (Library of Biblical Studies). 1969. 25.00x (ISBN 0-87068-081-1). Ktav.
McEleney, Neil J. Law Given Through Moses. (Bible Ser.). pap. 0.50 (ISBN 0-8091-5079-4). Paulist Pr.
Maimonides, Moses. The Code of Maimonides. Incl. Bk. 5. The Book of Holiness. Rabinowitz, Louis I. & Grossman, Philip, trs. xxxiv, 429p. 1965. 35.00x (ISBN 0-300-00846-5); Bk. 6. The Book of Asseverations. Klien, B. D., tr. 273p. 1962. 22.50x (ISBN 0-300-00633-0); Bk. 8. The Book of Temple Service. Lewittes, Mendell, tr. (Illus.). xxvii, 525p. 1957. 40.00x (ISBN 0-300-00717-5); Bk. 9. The Book of Offerings. Danby, Herbert, tr. xxi, 236p. 1950. 20.00x (ISBN 0-300-00398-6); Bk. 10. The Book of Cleanness. Danby, Herbert, tr. (Illus.). xiv, 645p. 1954. 47.50x (ISBN 0-300-00397-8); Bk. 11. The Book of Torts. Klein, Hyman, tr. xvii, 299p. 1954. 22.50x (ISBN 0-300-00632-2); Bk. 12. The Book of Acquisition. Klein, Isaac, tr. xv, 335p. 1951. 25.00x (ISBN 0-300-00631-4); Bk. 13. The Book of Civil Laws. Rabinowitz, Jacob J., tr. xxiv, 345p. 1949. 35.00x (ISBN 0-300-00845-7); Bk. 14. The Book of Judges. Hershman, Abraham M., tr. xxv, 335p. 1949. 25.00x (ISBN 0-300-00548-2). (Judaica Ser.). Yale U Pr.
Marcus, Ralph. Law in the Apocrypha. LC 29-9822. (Columbia University. Oriental Studies: No. 26). Repr. of 1927 ed. 15.00 (ISBN 0-404-50516-3). AMS Pr.
Mayer, Mordecai. Israel's Wisdom in Modern Life: Essays & Interpretations of Religious & Cultural Problems Based on the Talmudic & Midrashic Literature. 22.50 (ISBN 0-87559-147-7). Shalom.
Medical Hulacha for Everyone. Date not set. 8.95 (ISBN 0-87306-218-3). Feldheim.
Meiselman, M. Jewish Woman in Jewish Law. (Library of Jewish Law & Ethics: Vol. 6). 15.00x (ISBN 0-87068-329-2). Ktav.
Meislin, Bernard. Jewish Law in American Trials & Tribunals. 20.00x (ISBN 0-87068-288-1). Ktav.
Narot, Joseph R. A Primer for Temple Life. pap. 1.00 (ISBN 0-686-15808-3). Rostrum Bks.
Neusner, Jacob. The Tosefta, Translated from the Hebrew: Pt. II. Moed. The Order of Appointed Times. 29.50 (ISBN 0-87068-691-7). Ktav.
Popular Halacha I. Date not set. 5.00 (ISBN 0-686-76246-0). Feldheim.
Practical Medical Halacha. Date not set. 5.00 (ISBN 0-87306-221-3). Feldheim.
Quint, Emanuel B. & Hecht, Neil S. Jewish Jurisprudence: Its Sources & Modern Applications, Vol. II. (Jewish Jurisprudence Ser.). 300p. 1981. price not set (ISBN 3-7186-0064-1). Harwood Academic.
Rosenbaum, I. Holocaust & Halakhah. (Library of Jewish Law & Ethics: No. 2). 15.00x (ISBN 0-87068-296-2). Ktav.
Schatz, Elihu A. Proof of the Accuracy of the Bible. LC 73-10726. (Illus.). xxvi, 740p. 1973. 15.00x (ISBN 0-8246-0161-0). Jonathan David.
Schodde, tr. Book of Jubilees. LC 80-53467. 96p. 1980. pap. 3.50 (ISBN 0-934666-08-3). Artisan Sales.
Schreiber, Aaron. Jewish Law & Decision-Making: A Study Through Time. 1980. lib. bdg. 29.50 (ISBN 0-87722-120-0). Temple U Pr.
Schultz, Samuel J. Old Testament Survey: Law & History. rev. ed. LC 64-10037. 1968. pap. text ed. 3.95 (ISBN 0-910566-01-1); instr's. guide 3.95 (ISBN 0-910566-20-8). Evang Tchr.
Siegel, S., ed. Conservative Judaism & Jewish Law. 15.00x (ISBN 0-87068-428-0). Ktav.
Smith, John M. The Origin & History of Hebrew Law. LC 79-1620. 1980. Repr. of 1960 ed. 21.50 (ISBN 0-88355-924-2). Hyperion Conn.
Sonsino, Rifat. Motive Clauses in Hebrew Law: Biblical Forms & Near Eastern Parallels. LC 79-15024. (Society of Biblical Literature Dissertation Ser.: No. 45). 13.50x (ISBN 0-89130-317-0, 060145); pap. 9.00x (ISBN 0-686-29279-0). Scholars Pr CA.
Stylianopoulos, Theodore. Justin Martyr & the Mosaic Law. LC 75-22445. (Society of Biblical Literature. Dissertation Ser.). 1975. pap. 7.50 (ISBN 0-89130-018-X, 060120). Scholars Pr Ca.
Twersky, I. Studies in Jewish Law & Philosophy. 35.00x (ISBN 0-87068-335-7). Ktav.
Zevin, Shlomo Y. The Festivals in Halachah, Vol. II. Kaploon, Uri, ed. Fox-Ashrei, Meir, tr. from Hebrew. (Artscroll Judica Classics Ser.). 336p. 1981. 13.95 (ISBN 0-89906-908-8); pap. 10.95 (ISBN 0-89906-909-6). Mesorah Pubns.

JEWISH LEARNING AND SCHOLARSHIP

see also Jews–Intellectual Life

American Academy for Jewish Research. Harry Austryn Wolfson Jubilee Volume, on the Occasion of His 75th Birthday, 3 vols. (Eng. & Heb., Eng. section 2 vols, Heb. section 1 vol.). Repr. of 1965 ed. Set. 30.00 (ISBN 0-527-02360-4). Kraus Repr.
Berlin, Charles. Index to Festschriften in Jewish Studies. 1971. 50.00x (ISBN 0-87068-133-8). Ktav.
Contemporary Jewish Thinking in Israel, 3 vols. Date not set. Vol. I, Halacha. 2.50 (ISBN 0-686-76497-8); Vol. II, Faith & Knowledge Of God. 2.50 (ISBN 0-686-76498-6); Vol. III, Procreation In The Light Of Halacha. 2.50 (ISBN 0-686-76499-4). Feldheim.
Crenshaw, James L. Studies in Ancient Israelite Wisdom. 1974. 39.50x (ISBN 0-87068-255-5). Ktav.
Friedlander, Gerald, tr. from Heb. Pirke De Rabbi Eliezer (The Chapters of Rabbi Eliezer the Great) LC 80-545920. (The Judaic Studies Library: No. SPH6). 552p. 1981. pap. 12.95 (ISBN 0-87203-095-4). Hermon.
Gamoran, Emanuel. Changing Conceptions in Jewish Education. facsimile ed. LC 74-27986. (Modern Jewish Experience Ser.). 1975. Repr. of 1924 ed. 27.00x (ISBN 0-405-06713-5). Arno.
Gateway to Learning. pap. 2.95 (ISBN 0-87306-253-1). Feldheim.
Goitein, S. D. Letters of Medieval Jewish Traders. LC 72-14025. 316p. 1974. 26.00x (ISBN 0-691-05212-3). Princeton U Pr.
Goldman, Israel. Lifelong Learning Among Jews. 20.00x (ISBN 0-87068-291-1). Ktav.
Gratz, Rebecca. Letters of Rebecca Gratz. facsimile ed. LC 74-27987. (Modern Jewish Experience Ser.). 1975. Repr. of 1929 ed. 29.00x (ISBN 0-405-06714-3). Arno.
Katzman, J. The Jewish Influence on Civilization. LC 74-83940. 1974. 7.95 (ISBN 0-8197-0375-3). Bloch.
Lieberman, Saul. Alexander Marx Jubilee Volume, 2 vols. 1950. 35.00x (ISBN 0-685-31434-0, Pub. by Jewish Theol Seminary). KTAV.
Maimonides. Guide of the Perplexed. Friedlander, tr. 918p. 1972. 12.50 (ISBN 0-88482-878-6). Hebrew Pub.
Mason, Philip P. Directory of Jewish Archival Institutions. LC 75-15504. 72p. 1975. pap. text ed. 3.75x (ISBN 0-8143-1547-X). Wayne St U Pr.
Rossel, Seymour. When a Jew Seeks Wisdom: The Sayings of the Fathers. LC 75-14119. (Jewish Values Ser). (gr. 7). pap. 6.95x (ISBN 0-87441-089-4). Behrman.
Scholarship of Dr. Shmuel Belkin. Date not set. pap. 6.95 (ISBN 0-686-76254-1). Feldheim.
Stearn, Gerald. Some Gentlemen of the Jewish Persuasion. (Illus.). Date not set. cancelled (ISBN 0-914762-03-6); pap. 6.95 (ISBN 0-914762-04-4). Riverwood Pubs.
Tarcov, Edith & Tarcov, Oscar. Illustrated Book of Jewish Knowledge. (Illus.). (gr. 7-9). 1959. 6.00x (ISBN 0-87068-358-6, Pub. by Friendly Hse). Ktav.

JEWISH LEARNING AND SCHOLARSHIP–JUVENILE LITERATURE

Karp, Deborah. Heroes of Jewish Thought. (Illus.). (gr. 5-7). 1965. 6.00x (ISBN 0-87068-538-4). Ktav.
--Heroes of Modern Jewish Thought. (Illus.). (gr. 6-7). 1966. 6.00x (ISBN 0-87068-539-2). Ktav.

JEWISH LEGENDS

see Legends, Jewish

JEWISH LITERATURE (AMERICAN)

see American Literature–Jewish Authors

JEWISH LITERATURE (COLLECTIONS)

see also Apocalyptic Literature; Cabala; Hebrew Literature; Midrash; Rabbinical Literature; Talmud; Yiddish Literature

Alcalay. Basic Encyclopedia of Jewish Proverbs, Quotations, Folk Wisdom. 18.95 (ISBN 0-686-08929-4). Hartmore.
Chutzpah: A Jewish Liberation Anthology. (Chutzpah Collective Ser.). (Illus.). 1978. pap. 5.95 (ISBN 0-912078-53-7). New Glide.
Eisenberg, Azriel. Modern Jewish Life in Literature, 2 Vols. 1952-1968. Vol. 1. 4.50x (ISBN 0-8381-0201-8); Vol. 2. 4.50x (ISBN 0-8381-0207-7). United Syn Bk.
Fleg, Edmond. The Jewish Anthology. Samuel, Maurice, tr. LC 72-142934. 399p. 1975. Repr. of 1925 ed. lib. bdg. 15.75x (ISBN 0-8371-5824-9, FLJA). Greenwood.
Goodman, Philip, ed. Yom Kippur Anthology. LC 72-151312. (Illus.). 1971. 7.50 (ISBN 0-8276-0026-7, 245). Jewish Pubn.
Gordimer, Nadien, et al. South African Jewish Voices. Kalechofsky, Roberta, ed. (Echad 2 Ser.). 300p. 1981. pap. 8.50 (ISBN 0-916288-10-2). Micah Pubns.
Handler, Andrew, ed. & tr. Ararat: A Collection of Hungarian-Jewish Short Stories. LC 75-5244. 153p. 1978. 12.50 (ISBN 0-8386-1733-6). Fairleigh Dickinson.
Howe, Irving, ed. Jewish-American Stories. 1977. pap. 2.50 (ISBN 0-451-61546-8, ME1546, Ment). NAL.
Kabakoff, Jacob. Jewish Book Annual, Vol. 37. 1979. 12.00 (ISBN 0-914820-07-9). JWB Jewish Bk Coun.
Kabakoff, Jacob, ed. Jewish Book Annual, Vol. 38. 1980. 15.00 (ISBN 0-914820-33-8). JWB Jewish Bk Coun.
Kalechofsky, Roberta, ed. Echad: An Anthology of Latin American Jewish Writings. LC 79-88853. 1980. pap. 9.00x (ISBN 0-916288-06-4). Micah Pubns.
Kalechofsky, Roberta, et al. A Micah Anthology. 250p. (Orig.). 1981. pap. 7.00 (ISBN 0-916288-11-0). Micah Pubns.
Magonet, Jonathan, ed. Returning. LC 78-68143. 1978. pap. 3.95 (ISBN 0-8197-0468-7). Bloch.
Mazow, Julia W., ed. The Woman Who Lost Her Names: Selected Writings by American Jewish Women. LC 79-2986. 240p. 1981. pap. text ed. 6.95 (ISBN 0-06-250567-X, HarpR). Harrow.
Mihaly, E. A Song to Creation: A Dialogue with a Text. (Jewish Perspectives Ser.: Vol. 1). 7.50x (ISBN 0-87820-500-4, HUC Pr). Ktav.
Nadel, Max. Portraits of the American Jew: An Anthology of Short Stories by American Jewish Writers. LC 75-34066. 1977. pap. text ed. 3.75 (ISBN 0-8120-0578-3). Barron.
Nemoy, Leon, tr. Karaite Anthology: Excerpts from the Early Literature. (Judaica Ser.: No. 7). 1952. 30.00x (ISBN 0-300-00792-2). Yale U Pr.
Neusner, J. The Tosefta Translated from the Hebrew: The Order of Purities, Pt. 6. 35.00x (ISBN 0-87068-430-2). Ktav.
Newman, Louis I., ed. The Hasidic Anthology: Tales & Teachings of the Hasidim. LC 63-11041. 1963. pap. 6.95 (ISBN 0-8052-0046-0). Schocken.
Nuesner, Jacob. The Tosefta Translated from the Hebrew IV. Nezigin: The Order of Damages. Date not set. 35.00x (ISBN 0-87068-692-5). Ktav.
--The Tosefta Translated from the Hebrew I. Zeraim: The Order of Seeds. Date not set. 35.00x (ISBN 0-87068-693-3). Ktav.
--The Tosefta Translated from the Hebrew V. Qodoshim: The Order of Holy Things. Date not set. 35.00x (ISBN 0-87068-340-3). Ktav.
Patai, Raphael. Gates to the Old City. 928p. 1980. pap. 12.95 (ISBN 0-380-76091-6, 76091). Avon.
--Messiah Texts: An Anthology of Jewish Writings from Three Thousand Years. LC 79-5387. 1979. 17.95x (ISBN 0-8143-1652-2). Wayne St U Pr.
Roth, C., intro. by. The Sarajevo Haggadah. 100.00x (ISBN 0-685-55601-8). Ktav.
Schwartz, Leo W., ed. The Menorah Treasury. LC 64-16760. 1958. slipcase 10.00 (ISBN 0-8276-0021-6). Jewish Pubn.
Schwarz, Leo W., ed. The Jewish Caravan: Great Stories of 25 Centuries. rev. & enl. ed. LC 75-37043. 848p. 1976. pap. 9.95 (ISBN 0-8052-0514-4). Schocken.
Siegel, J. P. The Severus Scroll & 1QIsa. (Society of Biblical Literature Masoretic Studies Ser: No. 2). 10.00x (ISBN 0-89130-028-7). Ktav.
Sonntag, Jacob, ed. Jewish Writing Today. 218p. 1974. 18.00x (ISBN 0-85303-181-9, Pub. by Vallentine Mitchell England). Biblio Dist.
Wallenrod, Reuben. The Literature of Modern Israel. LC 80-12709. 256p. 1980. Repr. of 1956 ed. lib. bdg. 16.00x (ISBN 0-374-98198-1). Octagon.

JEWISH LITERATURE–BIBLIOGRAPHY

An Annotated Bibliography. Date not set. 5.00 (ISBN 0-686-76477-3). Feldheim.
Berliant, Howard M. & Arbit, Bruce, eds. Jewish Literary Marketplace: A Directory of the Press, Periodicals, Publishers, & Booksellers. LC 79-18114. 1979. pap. 7.95 (ISBN 0-930038-16-9). Arbit.
Gittleman, Sol. Sholom Aleichem: A Non-Critical Introduction. (De Proprietatibus Litterarum Ser. Didactica: No. 3). 1974. pap. text ed. 21.25x (ISBN 90-2792-606-9). Mouton.
Grossfeld, B. Bibliography of Targum Literature: Supplement Volume, Vol. 2. (Bibliographica Judaica Ser: No. 8). 29.50x (ISBN 0-87820-905-0, HUC Pr). Ktav.
Kabakoff, Jacob. Jewish Book Annual, Vol. 35. 1977. 10.00 (ISBN 0-914820-05-2). JWB Jewish Bk Coun.
Kabakoff, Jacob, ed. Jewish Book Annual, Vol. 36. 1978. 10.00 (ISBN 0-914820-06-0). JWB Jewish Bk Coun.
Leikind, Miriam, et al. Index to Jewish Periodicals. Per Volume. 50.00 (ISBN 0-686-75688-6). IJP.
New York Public Library, Research Libraries. Dictionary Catalog of Jewish Collection, 14 Vols. 1960. Set. 900.00 (ISBN 0-8161-0409-3). G K Hall.
Rosenbach, A. S. W. American Jewish Bibliography, to 1850. 1926. 17.00 (ISBN 0-527-02373-6). Kraus Repr.

JEWISH LITERATURE–HISTORY AND CRITICISM

Abrahams, Israel. By-Paths in Hebraic Bookland. LC 77-174368. Repr. of 1920 ed. 15.00 (ISBN 0-405-08177-4, Pub by Blom Publications). Arno.
--A Short History of Jewish Literature. 1906. Repr. 20.00 (ISBN 0-8274-3400-6). R West.
Agus, Jacob B., et al, eds. The Jewish People: History, Religion, Literature, 41 bks. 1973. Set. 816.50 (ISBN 0-405-05250-2). Arno.
American Academy for Jewish Research. Louis Ginzberg Jubilee Volume, on the Occasion of His 70th Birthday, 2 Vols. (Eng-Heb). 1945. Set. pap. 28.00 (ISBN 0-527-02359-0). Kraus Repr.
Berenson, Bernard. Contemporary Jewish Fiction. 1976. lib. bdg. 59.95 (ISBN 0-87968-939-0). Gordon Pr.
Bokser, Ben Z. The Jewish Mystical Tradition. LC 80-27627. 280p. 1981. 14.95 (ISBN 0-8298-0435-8); pap. 9.95 (ISBN 0-8298-0451-X). Pilgrim NY.
Davidson, Israel. Parody in Jewish Literature. LC 77-163670. (Columbia University. Oriental Studies: No. 2). Repr. of 1907 ed. 24.50 (ISBN 0-404-50492-2). AMS Pr.
Finkelstein, Louis, ed. The Jews, Vol. 1: Their History. 4th ed. LC 74-107615. 1970. pap. 6.95 (ISBN 0-8052-0271-4). Schocken.
Fletcher, Harris F. Milton's Rabbinical Readings. 1967. Repr. of 1930 ed. 19.50 (ISBN 0-208-00335-5, Archon). Shoe String.
Goldwurm, Hersh, et al. Mishnah-Moed, Vol. 3. (Art Scroll Mishnah Ser.). 1980. 16.95 (ISBN 0-89906-256-3); pap. 13.95 (ISBN 0-89906-257-1). Mesorah Pubns.
Grossfield, B. A Bibliography of Targun Literature, Vol. 1. 1972. 29.50x (ISBN 0-87068-333-0). Ktav.
Guttman, Alexander. Struggle Over Reform in Rabbinic Literature. LC 75-45046. 1977. 13.50 (ISBN 0-8074-0005-X, 382790). UAHC.
Jacobs, Joseph. Jewish Ideals & Other Essays. LC 72-311. (Essay Index Reprint Ser.). Repr. of 1896 ed. 18.00 (ISBN 0-8369-2795-8). Arno.
Kaplan, Aryeh, tr. The Book of Esther. 268p. 8.95 (ISBN 0-686-27543-8); pap. 6.45 (ISBN 0-940118-21-1). Maznaim.
Karpeles, Gustav. Jewish Literature & Other Essays. facsimile ed. LC 78-37159. (Essay Index Reprint Ser). Repr. of 1895 ed. 22.00 (ISBN 0-8369-2512-2). Arno.
Knopp, Josephine Z. The Trial of Judaism in Contemporary Jewish Writing. LC 74-18319. 164p. 1975. 12.50 (ISBN 0-252-00386-1). U of Ill Pr.
Lehrmann, Charles C. Jewish Influences on European Thought. Klin, George & Carpenter, Victor, trs. LC 72-3264. 323p. 1976. 16.50 (ISBN 0-8386-7908-0). Fairleigh Dickinson.

Lvov-Rogachevsky, V. A History of Russian Jewish Literature: Including Russian Literature & the Jews. Levin, Arthur, tr. from Rus. 1979. 15.00 (ISBN 0-88233-271-6); pap. 5.50 (ISBN 0-88233-272-4). Ardis Pubs.
Mann, Jacob. Texts & Studies in Jewish History & Literature, 2 Vols. rev. ed. 1970. Set. 79.50x (ISBN 0-87068-085-4). Ktav.
Oring, Elliott. Israeli Humor & Its Oral Tradition. LC 80-25483. (Modern Jewish Literature & Culture Ser.). 210p. 1981. text ed. 34.00x (ISBN 0-87395-520-X, ORIH); pap. text ed. 9.95x (ISBN 0-87395-521-8, ORIH-P). State U NY Pr.
Pearl, Chaim & Brookes, Reuben. The Guide to Jewish Knowledge. rev. ed. LC 75-187866. 123p. 1973. 4.95 (ISBN 0-87677-046-4). Hartmore.
Philipson, David, et al. Studies in Jewish Literature Issued in Honor of Professor Kaufmann Kohler, Ph.D. Katz, Steven, ed. LC 79-7167. (Jewish Philosophy, Mysticism & History of Ideas Ser.). 1980. Repr. of 1913 ed. lib. bdg. 23.00x (ISBN 0-405-12283-7). Arno.
Pinsker, Sanford. Schlemiel As Metaphor: Studies in the Yiddish & American Jewish Novel. LC 77-132487. (Crosscurrents-Modern Critiques Ser.). 185p. 1971. 6.95 (ISBN 0-8093-0480-5). S Ill U Pr.
Rylaarsdam, J. Coert. Revelation in Jewish Wisdom Literature. (Midway Reprint Ser). xii, 128p. 1974. pap. text ed. 7.00x (ISBN 0-226-73285-1). U of Chicago Pr.
Schwab, Moise. Repertoire des Articles Relatifs a l'Histoire et a la Litterature Juives Parus dans les Periodiques De 1665 a 1900. rev. ed. (Fr.). 1971. 59.50 (ISBN 0-87068-163-X). Ktav.
Steinschneider, Moritz. Gesammelte Schriften. Katz, Steven, ed. LC 79-7152. (Jewish Philosophy, Mysticism & History of Ideas Ser.). 1980. Repr. of 1925 ed. lib. bdg. 48.00x (ISBN 0-405-12289-6). Arno.
Yerushalmi, Yosef H. Haggadah & History. LC 73-21169. 1975. 27.50 (ISBN 0-8276-0046-1, 364). Jewish Pubn.
Zimmels, H. J. The Echo of the Nazi Holocaust in Rabbinic Literature. 22.50x (ISBN 0-87068-427-2). Ktav.
Zinberg, Israel. A History of Jewish Literature, 12 vols. 22.50x (ISBN 0-685-56219-0). Ktav.

JEWISH LITURGICAL MUSIC
see Synagogue Music

JEWISH MIGRATION
see Jews–Migrations

JEWISH MUSIC
see Music, Jewish

JEWISH MYTHOLOGY
see Mythology, Jewish

JEWISH NEW YEAR
see Rosh ha-Shanah

JEWISH NEWSPAPERS
see also Yiddish Newspapers

JEWISH PENTECOST
see Shavu'Oth (Feast of Weeks)

JEWISH PHILOSOPHY
see Philosophy, Jewish

JEWISH POETRY
see also Hebrew Poetry

Benson, Clarence H. Old Testament Survey: Poetry & Prophecy. rev. ed. 1972. pap. text ed. 3.95 (ISBN 0-910566-02-X); instr's. guide by John H. Stoll 3.95 (ISBN 0-910566-21-6). Evang Tchr.
Jason, Heda. Studies in Jewish Ethnopoetry. (Asian Folklore & Social Life Monograph: No. 72). 1975. 7.00 (ISBN 0-89986-068-0). E Langstaff.
Rosenberg, David. Chosen Days: Celebrating Jewish Festivals in Poetry & Art. LC 79-7906. (Illus.). 224p. 1980. 14.95 (ISBN 0-385-14365-6). Doubleday.
Sachs, Michael. Die Religiose Poesie der Juden in Spanien. Katz, Steven, ed. LC 79-7150. (Jewish Philosophy, Mysticism & History of Ideas Ser.). 1980. Repr. of 1901 ed. lib. bdg. 32.00x (ISBN 0-405-12285-3). Arno.
Schwartz, Howard & Rudolf, Anthony, eds. Voices Within the Ark. 1980. pap. 14.95 (ISBN 0-380-76109-2, 76109). Avon.
--Voices Within the Ark: The Modern Jewish Poets. 1980. 39.50 (ISBN 0-916366-11-1); slipcased ed. 50.00 (ISBN 0-686-77603-8). Pushcart Pr.
Smith, George A. The Early Poetry of Israel in the Physical & Social Origins. 1973. Repr. of 1912 ed. 15.00 (ISBN 0-8274-0893-5). R West.

JEWISH PORTRAITS
see Portraits

JEWISH QUESTION
see also Jews–Employment; Marriage, Mixed; Refugees, Jewish; Zionism

Anti-Semitism in America, 1878-1939. An Original Anthology. LC 76-46110. (Anti-Movements in America). (Illus.). 1977. lib. bdg. 35.00 (ISBN 0-405-09981-9). Arno.
Barth. The Modern Jew Faces Eternal Problems. 7.50 (ISBN 0-685-48595-1). Feldheim.
Borochov, Ber. Nationalism & the Class Struggle. LC 70-97268. 205p. 1972. Repr. of 1937 ed. lib. bdg. 15.00x (ISBN 0-8371-2590-1, BONA). Greenwood.
Claudel, Paul. Une Voix sur Israel. 46p. 1950. 2.95 (ISBN 0-686-54445-5). French & Eur.
Dubnow, Simon. Nationalism & History: Essays on Old & New Judaism. Pinson, Koppel S., ed. LC 58-5590. (Temple Bk). 1970. pap. 4.25 (ISBN 0-689-70247-7, T21). Atheneum.
Hendrick, Burton J. The Jews in America. Grob, Gerald, ed. LC 76-46081. (Anti-Movements in America). 1977. Repr. of 1923 ed. lib. bdg. 12.00x (ISBN 0-405-09954-1). Arno.
Herzl, Theodor. Diaries of Theodor Herzl. Lowenthal, ed. 12.50 (ISBN 0-8446-2247-8). Peter Smith.
Heschel, A. J. Kotzk: The Struggle for Integrity, 2 vols. in 1. (Yiddish.). 35.00x (ISBN 0-87068-328-4). Ktav.
Janowsky, Oscar I. Jews & Minority Rights, 1898-1919. LC 33-31678. (Columbia University. Studies in the Social Sciences: No. 384). Repr. of 1933 ed. 24.50 (ISBN 0-404-51384-0). AMS Pr.
Janowsky, Oscar I., ed. American Jew. facs. ed. LC 76-142647. (Essay Index Reprint Ser). 1942. 18.00 (ISBN 0-8369-2166-6). Arno.
Kahane, Meir. Why Be Jewish? Intermarriage, Assimilation & Alienation. LC 77-8774. 1977. 8.95 (ISBN 0-8128-2239-0). Stein & Day.
Leon, Abram. Jewish Question: A Marxist Interpretation. LC 76-108721. 1971. 17.00 (ISBN 0-87348-133-X); pap. 5.45 (ISBN 0-87348-134-8). Path Pr NY.
Lewis, Wyndham. The Jews, Are They Human? LC 72-82188. 1972. Repr. of 1939 ed. lib. bdg. 75.00 (ISBN 0-87968-008-3). Gordon Pr.
Parkes, James. Conflict of the Church & the Synagogue: A Study in the Origins of Antisemitism. LC 61-11472. (Temple Books). 1969. pap. text ed. 6.95x (ISBN 0-689-70151-9, T9). Atheneum.
Pinsker, Lev S. Road to Freedom. LC 70-162734. 142p. 1975. Repr. of 1944 ed. lib. bdg. 15.00x (ISBN 0-8371-6195-9, PIRF). Greenwood.
Poliakov, Leon. The Aryan Myth: A History of Racist & Nationalist Ideas in Europe. 1977. pap. 4.95 (ISBN 0-452-00478-0, F478, Mer). NAL.
Rabinowicz, Oscar K. Winston Churchill on Jewish Problems. LC 74-43. 231p. 1974. Repr. of 1960 ed. lib. bdg. 15.00x (ISBN 0-8371-7357-4, RAWC). Greenwood.
Sartre, Jean-Paul. Anti-Semite & Jew. LC 48-9237. 1965. pap. 3.95 (ISBN 0-8052-0102-5). Schocken.
Steinberg, Milton. Making of the Modern Jew. 1948. 4.95x (ISBN 0-87441-115-7). Behrman.
--A Partisan Guide to the Jewish Problem. (Return to Zion Ser.). 308p. Repr. of 1945 ed. lib. bdg. 20.00x (ISBN 0-87991-135-2). Porcupine Pr.
Tenenbaum, Joseph. Race & Reich: The Story of an Epoch. LC 76-8503. (Illus.). 1976. Repr. of 1956 ed. lib. bdg. 35.25x (ISBN 0-8371-8857-1, TERR). Greenwood.
Timayenis, Telemachus T. The Original Mr. Jacobs: Startling Expose. Grob, Gerald, ed. LC 76-46107. (Anti-Movements in America). 1977. Repr. of 1888 ed. lib. bdg. 18.00x (ISBN 0-405-09978-9). Arno.
Ussher, Arland. The Magic People. 4.95 (ISBN 0-8159-6200-2). Devin.
Weinreich, Max. Hitlers Profesorn. LC 47-42580. (Illus.). 325p. (Yiddish.). 1947. pap. 7.50x (ISBN 0-914512-26-9). Yivo Inst.
--Hitler's Professors. LC 46-5155. (Yivo English Translation Ser.). (Illus.). 291p. 1946. pap. 5.00 (ISBN 0-914512-19-6). Yivo Inst.

JEWISH RABBIS
see Rabbis

JEWISH RELIGIOUS EDUCATION

The Academic Study of Judaism: Essays & Reflections, Third Series. Date not set. 12.50x (ISBN 0-87068-712-3). Ktav.
Ackerman, Walter I. Jewish Religious Education. 19p. 0.25 (ISBN 0-686-74961-8). ADL.
Bessler, Helen. Beresheet: A Kindergarten Guide. LC 68-30816. (Orig.). 1969. pap. text ed. 4.50 (ISBN 0-8074-0130-7, 244310). UAHC.
Bullivant, B. M. The Way of Tradition: Life in an Orthodox Jewish School. (Australian Council for Educational Research Ser.: No. 103). (Illus.). 1979. text ed. 25.00x (ISBN 0-85563-181-3). Verry.
Citron, Samuel J. Dramatics for Creative Teaching. (Illus.). 1961. 9.50x (ISBN 0-8381-0212-3). United Syn Bk.
Dresner, Samuel & Sherwin, Byron. Judaism: The Way of Sanctification. 1978. text ed. 5.95x (ISBN 0-8381-0222-0). United Syn Bk.
Gertman, Stuart A. And You Shall Teach Them Diligently: A Study of the Current State of Religious Education in the Reform Movement. 1977. pap. 5.00 (ISBN 0-8074-0052-1, 383760). UAHC.
Goble, Phillip E., ed. Everything You Need to Grow a Messianic Yeshiva. 312p. (Orig.). Date not set. pap. price not set (ISBN 0-87808-181-X). William Carey Lib.
Golinkin, Noah. Ayn Keloheynn. 128p. 1981. pap. 6.95 (ISBN 0-88400-076-1). Shengold.
Habershon, Ada R. Outline Study of the Tabernacle. LC 73-85298. 1974. pap. 2.50 (ISBN 0-8254-2820-3). Kregel.
Harlow, Jules. Lessons from Our Living Past. LC 72-2055. (Illus.). 128p. (gr. 4-6). 1972. text ed. 6.95x (ISBN 0-87441-085-1). Behrman.
Jick, Leon A. The Teaching of Judaica in American Universities: Proceedings. 1970. 10.00x (ISBN 0-87068-127-3). Ktav.
Krantzler, Harold I. Your Congregation's Adult Jewish Education Committee: A Manual. 1978. pap. 2.50 (ISBN 0-8074-0013-0, 181730). UAHC.
Lepkin, Biela. Creative Drama in the Hebrew School. 1978. pap. 12.95x (ISBN 0-8197-0474-1). Bloch.
Lilmod Ul'lamade: From the Teachings of Our Sages. pap. 5.95 (ISBN 0-87306-207-8). Feldheim.
Lister, Rebecca & Lister, Louis. The Smaller Religious School: A Manual. 1977. pap. text ed. 5.00 (ISBN 0-685-88426-0, 241850). UAHC.
Newman, Shirley & Newman, Louis. A Child's Introduction to Torah. new ed. LC 72-2056. (Illus.). 128p. (gr. k-3). 1972. text ed. 6.95x (ISBN 0-87441-067-3). 1.75x ea., wkbk in 2 pts. Behrman.
Pilch, Judah & Ben-Horin, Meir, eds. Judaism & the Jewish School: Selected Essays on the Direction & Purpose of Jewish Education. LC 66-17947. pap. 4.50 (ISBN 0-685-40446-3). Bloch.
Rosenberg, Amye. Tzedakah. (Jewish Awareness Ser.). (Illus.). (gr. k-1). 1979. pap. text ed. 1.95x (ISBN 0-87441-279-X). Behrman.
Sharon, Ruth. Arts & Crafts the Year Round, 2 Vols. (Illus.). 1965. Set. 29.00x (ISBN 0-8381-0213-1). United Syn Bk.
Tauben, Carol & Abrahams, Edith, eds. Integrating Arts & Crafts in the Jewish School, Vol. I. LC 79-15506. (Illus.). (gr. k-2). 1979. text ed. 9.95x (ISBN 0-87441-288-9). Behrman.

JEWISH SECTS
see also Conservative Judaism; Essenes; Karaites; Orthodox Judaism; Pharisees; Qumran Community; Reconstructionist Judaism; Reform Judaism; Zealots (Jewish Party)

Ashkenazim & Sepharsdim: Their Relations, Differences & Problems As Reflected in the Rabbinical Responsa. 17.50x (ISBN 0-87068-349-7). Ktav.
Blau, Joseph L. Modern Varieties of Judaism. LC 66-10732. (Lectures on the History of Religion Ser.). 217p. 1966. 17.50x (ISBN 0-231-02867-9); pap. 5.00 (ISBN 0-231-08668-7). Columbia U Pr.
Ginzberg, Louis. Unknown Jewish Sect. 1971. 29.50x (ISBN 0-685-31424-3, Pub. by Jewish Theol Seminary). Ktav.
Lightley, John W. Jewish Sects & Parties in the Time of Jesus. 1980. lib. bdg. 75.00 (ISBN 0-8490-3150-8). Gordon Pr.
Porter, Jack N. & Gold, Doris B., eds. Jews & the Cults. LC 81-67448. 50p. 1981. pap. write for info. (ISBN 0-9602036-4-8). Biblio NY.
Simon, Marcel. Jewish Sects at the Time of Jesus. Farley, James H., tr. from Fr. LC 66-25265. 192p. 1980. pap. 5.95 (ISBN 0-8006-0183-1, 1-183). Fortress.

JEWISH SERMONS
see Sermons, Jewish

JEWISH SOCIOLOGY
see Sociology, Jewish

JEWISH SOLDIERS
see also subdivision Jews under names of wars, e.g. World War, 1939-1945–Jews

Rezneck, Samuel. Unrecognized Patriots: The Jews in the American Revolution. LC 74-15160. (Illus.). 1975. lib. bdg. 14.95 (ISBN 0-8371-7803-7, RRJ/). Greenwood.

JEWISH SONGS
see Songs, Jewish

JEWISH SYMBOLISM AND ART
see Jewish Art and Symbolism

JEWISH TALES
see Tales, Jewish

JEWISH THEOLOGY
see also Judaism

Bamberger, Bernard J. The Search for Jewish Theology. new ed. LC 77-28457. 1978. 7.95x (ISBN 0-87441-295-1); pap. 3.95x (ISBN 0-87441-300-1). Behrman.
Blank, S. H. Prophetic Thought: Essays & Addresses. (Jewish Perspectives Ser: Vol. 2). 12.50x (ISBN 0-87820-501-2, HUC Pr). Ktav.
Breuer, Salomon. Chochmo U'Mussar, Vol. 3: Bamidbar-Devarim. Breuer, Jacob, tr. from Ger. Orig. Title: Belehre und Mahnung. 1977. 9.75 (ISBN 0-87306-036-9). Feldheim.
Cohon, S. S. Jewish Theology. 1971. 38.00x (ISBN 90-232-0830-7, Pub by Van Gorcum). Intl Schol Bk Serv.
Commentary Editors. Condition of Jewish Belief. (Orig.). 1967. 10.95 (ISBN 0-02-527260-8). Macmillan.
Epstein, Isidore. Step by Step in the Jewish Religion. PLB 2.95x (ISBN 0-685-01036-8). Bloch.
Friedlander, M. Jewish Religion: Describing & Explaining the Philosophy & Rituals of the Jewish Faith. 22.50 (ISBN 0-87559-117-5). Shalom.
Jacobs, Louis. Jewish Theology. LC 73-17442. 384p. 1973. pap. 8.95x (ISBN 0-87441-248-X). Behrman.
--Theology in the Responsa. (The Littman Library of Jewish Civilization). 1975. 18.75x (ISBN 0-7100-8010-7). Routledge & Kegan.
Kaplan, Aryeh. The Handbook of Jewish Thought. 307p. 13.95 (ISBN 0-940118-27-0). Maznaim.
Katz, Steven T. Jewish Ideas & Concepts. LC 77-75285. 1978. 12.50 (ISBN 0-8052-3664-3). Schocken.
Kaufman, William E. Contemporary Jewish Philosophies. LC 75-30761. 388p. (Orig.). 1976. pap. text ed. 4.95x (ISBN 0-87441-238-2, Jewish Restructionist Press). Behrman.
Kohler, Kaufmann. Jewish Theology Systematically & Historically Considered. rev. ed. LC 67-28641. 1968. Repr. of 1918 ed. 25.00x (ISBN 0-87068-073-0). Ktav.
Kosovesky, Binyamin. Otzar Leshon Ho-Tannaim-Mekilta d'rabi Ishmael, 4 vols. 1965. Set. 60.00x (ISBN 0-685-31425-1, Pub. by Jewish Theol Seminary). Ktav.
Lieberman, Saul. Siphre Zutta. 1968. 10.00x (ISBN 0-685-31431-6, Pub. by Jewish Theol Seminary). Ktav.
--The Tosefta, 13 vols. 125.00 ea. (ISBN 0-685-31430-8, Pub. by Jewish Theol Seminary). KTAV.
Maimonides, Moses. Guide for the Perplexed. Friedlander, M., tr. 1904. pap. 6.00 (ISBN 0-486-20351-4). Dover.
--Guide for the Perplexed: Morah Nevochim. (Heb. & Eng). 28.50 (ISBN 0-87559-079-9). Shalom.
--Guide of the Perplexed, 2 vols. Pines, Shlomo, tr. LC 62-18113. 1963. ea. 15.00 (ISBN 0-686-66551-1); Vol. 1. (ISBN 0-226-50232-5). Vol. 2 (ISBN 0-226-50233-3). U of Chicago Pr.
--The Guide of the Perplexed. Pines, Shlomo, tr. LC 62-18113. 1974. Vol. 1. pap. 10.00 (ISBN 0-226-50230-9, P609, Phoen); Vol. 2. pap. 10.00 (ISBN 0-226-50231-7, P610). U of Chicago Pr.
Mallin, Shlomo & Carmell, Aryeh, trs. The Book of Divine Power. 100p. 1975. pap. 4.95 (ISBN 0-87306-056-3). Feldheim.
Narot, Joseph R. An Introduction to a Faith. pap. 1.00 (ISBN 0-686-15807-5). Rostrum Bks.
--Why I Am a Jew. pap. 0.95 (ISBN 0-686-15802-4). Rostrum Bks.
Nathanael Ibn Al-Fayyumi. Bustan Al-Ukul. Levine, David, tr. LC 8-4311. (American Geographical Society. Oriental Explorations & Studies: No. 6). 20.75 (ISBN 0-404-50496-5). AMS Pr.
Neusner, Jacob. Understanding Jewish Theology. 1973. pap. 8.95x (ISBN 0-87068-215-6). Ktav.
Nickelsburg, George, ed. Studies on the Testament of Moses. LC 73-89039. (Society of Biblical Literature. Septuagint & Cognate Studies). 1973. pap. 7.50 (ISBN 0-89130-167-4, 060404). Scholars Pr Ca.
Pearl, Chaim. The Medieval Jewish Mind. LC 76-184221. 208p. 1973. 7.95 (ISBN 0-87677-043-X). Hartmore.
Rubenstein, Richard J. After Auschwitz: Essays in Contemporary Judaism. (Orig.). 1966. pap. 6.95 (ISBN 0-672-61150-3). Bobbs.
Schechter, Solomon. Aspects of Rabbinic Theology: Major Concepts of the Talmud. LC 61-14919. 1961. pap. 5.95 (ISBN 0-8052-0015-0). Schocken.
Talmage, F., ed. AJS Review, Vol. 1, 1976. 20.00x (ISBN 0-685-55538-0, Pub. by Assoc. for Jewish Studies). Ktav.
--AJS Review, Vol. 2. 1977. 20.00x (ISBN 0-685-55539-9, Pub. by Assoc. for Jewish Studies). Ktav.
Zimmerman, F. The Aramaic Origin of the Four Gospels. 20.00x (ISBN 0-87068-434-5). Ktav.

JEWISH WAY OF LIFE
see also Women, Jewish

Adventures in Living Judaism: Identity, Bk. 1. 1976. Bk. 1. 3.50 (ISBN 0-8074-0030-0, 145050); Survival Bk. 2. 7.50 (ISBN 0-8074-0031-9, 145051). UAHC.
Asheri, Michael. Living Jewish: The Lore & Law of the Practicing Jew. 1978. 14.95 (ISBN 0-89696-003-X). Everest Hse.

Bazak, Jacob. Jewish Law & Jewish Life, 8 bks. in 4 vols. Passamaneck, Stephen M., ed. Incl. Bk. 1. Selected Rabbinical Response (ISBN 0-8074-0034-3, 180210); Bks. 2-4. Contracts, Real Estate, Sales & Usury (180211); Bks. 5-6. Credit, Law Enforcement & Taxation (180212); Bks. 7-8. Criminal & Domestic Relations (ISBN 0-8074-0037-8, 180213). 1978. pap. 12.50 complete vol. (ISBN 0-8074-0038-6, 180218); pap. 5.00 ea. UAHC.
Brand, Sandra. I Dared to Live. LC 78-52142. 1978. 8.95 (ISBN 0-88400-058-3). Shengold.
Bronner, Leah. Gateways to Jewish Life. 1969. 5.00 (ISBN 0-8197-0062-2). Bloch.
Bubis, G. B., ed. Serving the Jewish Family. 20.00x (ISBN 0-87068-439-6). Ktav.
Cohon, S. S. What We Jews Believe & a Guide to Jewish Practice. 1971. 15.00x (ISBN 90-232-0831-5, Pub by Van Gorcum). Intl Schol Bk Serv.
DaCosta, I. Noble Families Among the Sephardic Jews. 1976. lib. bdg. 134.95 (ISBN 0-8490-2349-1). Gordon Pr.
Diller, Jerry V. Ancient Roots & Modern Meanings. LC 77-99196. 1978. 12.50 (ISBN 0-8197-0457-1); pap. 7.95 (ISBN 0-685-27177-3). Bloch.
Donin, Hayim. To Be a Jew. LC 72-89175. 1972. 11.95 (ISBN 0-465-08624-1). Basic.
Elkins, Dov P. Humanizing Jewish Life. LC 75-38456. 1976. 9.95 (ISBN 0-498-01912-8). A S Barnes.
Elkins, Dov P., ed. Being Jewish, Being Human: A Gift Book of Poems & Readings. LC 79-88298. Date not set. softbound 16.50 (ISBN 0-918834-07-4). Growth Assoc.
Gastwirt, Harold P. Fraud Corruption & Holiness: The Controversy Over the Supervision of Jewish Dietary Practice in New York City. LC 74-77649. 1974. 15.00 (ISBN 0-8046-9056-1, Natl U). Kennikat.
Ginsberg, Yona. Jews in a Changing Neighborhood: The Study of Mattapan. LC 74-24368. (Illus.). 1975. 12.95 (ISBN 0-02-911720-8). Free Pr.
Ginsburg, Christian D. Massorah, 4 Vols. rev. ed. (Library of Biblical Studies). 1970. Set. 300.00 (ISBN 0-87068-020-X). Ktav.
Gittelsohn, Roland B. Love, Sex & Marriage: A Jewish View. (Illus.). (gr. 10-12). 1980. pap. 7.95x (ISBN 0-8074-0046-7, 142683). UAHC.
Goldberg, M. Hirsh. Just Because They're Jewish. 1978. 9.95 (ISBN 0-8128-2518-7). Stein & Day.
Greene, Laura. I Am an Orthodox Jew. LC 78-14094. (Illus.). (gr. k-4). 1979. 5.95 (ISBN 0-03-044661-9). HR&W.
Gruber, Samuel. I Chose Life. LC 78-52141. 1978. 8.95 (ISBN 0-88400-055-9). Shengold.
Habel, Norman. When God Told Us His Name: Moses & the Burning Bush. (Purple Puzzle Tree Ser). (Illus., Orig.). (ps-4). 1971. pap. 0.85 (ISBN 0-570-06509-7, 56-1209). Concordia.
--When God Was All Alone. (Purple Puzzle Tree Ser). (Illus., Orig.). (ps-4). 1971. pap. 0.85 (ISBN 0-570-06500-3, 56-1200). Concordia.
Habel, Norman C. When Jacob Buried His Treasure. (Purple Puzzle Tree Ser). (Illus., Orig.). (ps-4). 1971. pap. 0.85 (ISBN 0-570-06508-9, 56-1208). Concordia.
Heilman, Samuel C. Synagogue Life: A Study in Symbolic Interaction. LC 75-36403. 1976. 12.95 (ISBN 0-226-32488-5); pap. 4.95 (ISBN 0-226-32490-7, P824, Phoen). U of Chicago Pr.
Herman, Simon N. Jewish Identity: A Social Psychological Perspective. LC 77-8605. (Sage Library of Social Research: Vol. 48). (Illus.). 263p. 1977. 20.00 (ISBN 0-8039-0874-1); pap. 9.95x (ISBN 0-8039-0875-X). Sage.
Horowitz, George. The Spirit of Jewish Law. LC 53-7535. 1979. Repr. of 1953 ed. text ed. 18.00x (ISBN 0-87632-167-8). Bloch.
Humphreys, W. Lee. Crisis & Story: Introduction to the Old Testament. LC 78-64594. (Illus.). 313p. 1979. 15.95 (ISBN 0-87484-437-1). Mayfield Pub.
Hurwitz, Shimon. Being Jewish. rev. ed. 1979. pap. 4.95 (ISBN 0-87306-196-9). Feldheim.
Janowitz, Morris. Judaism of the Next Generation. pap. 2.00 (ISBN 0-686-15805-9). Rostrum Bks.
The Jewish Experiential Book: The Quest for Jewish Identity. 22.50 (ISBN 0-87068-688-7). Ktav.
Jewish Publication Society of America, ed. The Eternal Light. LC 66-20788. 1977. 12.95 (ISBN 0-8197-0026-6); pap. 6.95 (ISBN 0-8197-0025-8). Bloch.
Joseloff, Samuel H., ed. A Time to Seek: An Anthology of Contemporary Jewish American Poets. 1975. 5.00 (ISBN 0-8074-0199-4, 168000); tchrs'. guide o.p. 5.00 (ISBN 0-685-55043-5, 208001). UAHC.
Jospe, Alfred, ed. Tradition & Contemporary Experience: Essays on Jewish Thought & Life. LC 77-110609. 1970. pap. 3.45 (ISBN 0-8052-0275-7). Schocken.
Kahane, Meir. Why Be Jewish? Intermarriage, Assimilation, & Alienation. LC 77-8774. 264p. 1981. pap. 6.95 (ISBN 0-8128-6129-9). Stein & Day.
Karp, Abraham J. The Jewish Way of Life & Thought. Date not set. 7.95x (ISBN 0-87068-717-4). Ktav.
Kitov, A. E. The Jew & His Home. 10th ed. Bulman, Nathan, tr. LC 63-17660. 233p. 1976. 8.50 (ISBN 0-88400-004-4). Shengold.
Klein, Judith W. Jewish Identity & Self-Esteem: Healing Wounds Through Ethnotherapy. 64p. 1980. write for info. Am Jewish Comm.
Kolatch, Alfred J. The Jewish Book of Why. 1981. 10.95 (ISBN 0-8246-0256-0). Jonathan David.
Lamm, Norman, ed. Treasury of Tradition. Wurzburger, Walter S. 462p. 1967. 7.95 (ISBN 0-88482-434-9). Hebrew Pub.
LaZebnik, Edith. Such a Life. LC 78-759. 1978. 8.95 (ISBN 0-688-03280-X). Morrow.
Lehrman, S. M. The Jewish Design for Living. LC 76-24242. 1976. 8.95 (ISBN 0-88400-003-6). Shengold.
Levita, Elijah. Massoreth Ha Massoreth. rev. ed. LC 67-11894. (Library of Biblical Studies). 1969. 25.00x (ISBN 0-87068-081-1). Ktav.
Liber, Maurice. Rashi: His Life & Works. Szold, Adele, tr. from Fr. LC 70-136767. (Illus.). 1971. Repr. of 1906 ed. 12.50 (ISBN 0-87203-021-0). Hermon.
Lion The Printer. Seven Days a Week. (Illus.). (gr. k-5). 1977. spiral 2.00 (ISBN 0-914080-62-8). Shulsinger Sales.
Maimonodes, Moses. Guide of the Perplexed. abr. ed. Guttman, Julius W., ed. Rabin, Chaim, tr. 1978. pap. text ed. 3.95 (ISBN 0-85222-208-4, East & West Lib). Hebrew Pub.
Mayer, Egon & Sheingold, Carl. Intermarriage & the Jewish Future. LC 79-63378. 46p. 1980. pap. 1.50 (ISBN 0-87495-031-7). Am Jewish Comm.
Narot, Joseph R. For Whom the Rabbi Speaks. pap. 1.65 (ISBN 0-686-15800-8). Rostrum Bks.
--Judaism Without Guilt. pap. 0.75 (ISBN 0-686-15811-3). Rostrum Bks.
--A Preface to Well Being. pap. 1.00 (ISBN 0-686-15806-7). Rostrum Bks.
--What I Believe About God. pap. 0.95 (ISBN 0-686-15803-2). Rostrum Bks.
Nelson, Zev K. The Light Within. LC 78-56774. 1979. 8.95 (ISBN 0-88400-060-5). Shengold.
New Approach to Jewish Life. 4.95 (ISBN 0-87677-142-8). Hartmore.
Oppenheim, Moritz. Pictures of Traditional Jewish Life. 25.00x (ISBN 0-87068-472-8). Ktav.
Podwal, Mark. A Book of Hebrew Letters. LC 78-70076. (Illus.). 1979. pap. 5.95 (ISBN 0-8276-0118-2, 435). Jewish Pubn.
Raphael, Chaim. Encounters with the Jewish People. LC 79-14424. 1979. pap. text ed. 6.95x (ISBN 0-87441-282-X). Behrman.
Reisman, Bernard. The Chavurah: A Contemporary Jewish Experience. 1977. pap. 7.50 (ISBN 0-8074-0048-3, 140050). UAHC.
Rosenthal, Gilbert S., ed. New Directions in the Jewish Family & Community. LC 73-94340. 450p. 1974. 12.50x (ISBN 0-8197-0379-6). Bloch.
Roskies, Diane K. & Roskies, David G. The Shtetl Book. pap. 8.95x (ISBN 0-685-56215-8). Ktav.
Roth, Sol. The Jewish Idea of Community. 1977. 7.95x (ISBN 0-685-84455-2). Bloch.
Rothenberg, Jerome, et al, eds. A Big Jewish Book: Poems & Other Visions of the Jews from Tribal Times to the Present. (Illus.). 1979. pap. 7.95 (ISBN 0-385-02630-7, Anch). Doubleday.
Savitz, Harry A. A Jewish Physician's Harvest. 15.00x (ISBN 0-87068-686-0). Ktav.
Schostak, Zev. Taharath Hamishpacha: Jewish Family Laws. 2.95 (ISBN 0-87306-100-4). Feldheim.
Shapiro. Friendly Society. 6.95 (ISBN 0-686-08930-8). Hartmore.
Shmueli Family, 2 bks. Incl. Bk. 1. A Cartoon Adventure. 5.00x (ISBN 0-685-55046-X, 405310); Bk. 2. More Cartoon Adventures. 5.00x (ISBN 0-685-55047-8, 405311). 1975. UAHC.
Silverman, William B. Rabbinic Wisdom & Jewish Values. rev. ed. Orig. Title: Rabbinic Stories for Christian Ministers & Teachers. 1971. pap. 5.00 (ISBN 0-8074-0190-0, 383210). UAHC.
Sklare, Marshall, et al. Not Quite at Home: How an American Jewish Community Lives with Itself & Its Neighbors. LC 77-81092. (Institute of Human Relations Press Paperback Ser). x, 85p. (Orig.). 1969. pap. 1.00 (ISBN 0-87495-017-1). Am Jewish Comm.
Strassfeld, Michael & Strassfeld, Sharon, eds. The Second Jewish Catalog: Sources & Resources. LC 73-11759. (Illus.). 1976. 7.95 (ISBN 0-8276-0084-4, 391). Jewish Pubn.
Strassfeld, Sharon & Kurzweil, Arthur. Behold a Great Image. LC 78-1168. (Illus.). 1978. 17.50 (ISBN 0-8276-0105-0, 417). Jewish Pubn.
Trepp, Leo. The Complete Book of Jewish Observance. LC 79-1352. (Illus.). 1979. 14.95 (ISBN 0-87441-281-1). Behrman.
Unterman, Alan. Jews: Their Religious Beliefs & Practices. (Library of Religious Beliefs & Practices). 288p. 1981. 22.50 (ISBN 0-7100-0743-4); pap. 13.50 (ISBN 0-7100-0842-2). Routledge & Kegan.
Warshaw, Mal. Tradition: Orthodox Jewish Life in America. (Illus.). 128p. pap. 7.95 (ISBN 0-8052-0555-1). Bklyn Mus.
Weinreich, Uriel. College Yiddish; an Introduction to the Yiddish Language & to Jewish Life & Culture. 5th ed. LC 76-88208. 399p. 1979. 10.00 (ISBN 0-914512-04-8). Yivo Inst.
Zwerin, Raymond A. For One Another: Jewish Organizations That Help Us All. (Illus.). (gr. 6). 1975. text ed. 6.00 (ISBN 0-8074-0136-6, 141420); tchr's. guide o.p. 5.00 (ISBN 0-685-48915-9, 201421). UAHC.

JEWISH WIT AND HUMOR

Ausubel, Nathan, ed. Treasury of Jewish Humor. LC 51-10639. 1951. 13.95 (ISBN 0-385-04499-2). Doubleday.
Bubkis. (Illus.). 160p. 1980. 4.95 (ISBN 0-312-10682-3). St Martin.
Cowan, Lore & Cowan, Maurice. The Wit of the Jews. LC 75-129524. 1970. 2.95 (ISBN 0-87695-114-0). Sherbourne.
Kruger, Mollee. More Unholy Writ: Jewish Verses & Vices. 100p. 1973. pap. 2.25 (ISBN 0-913184-02-0). Maryben Bks.
Landau, Ron. The Book of Jewish Lists. LC 81-40500. 192p. 1981. 11.95 (ISBN 0-8128-2839-9). Stein & Day.
Novak, William & Waldoks, Moshe. The Big Book of Jewish Humor. LC 81-47234. (Illus.). 320p. (Orig.). 1981. pap. 10.95 (ISBN 0-06-090917-X, CN917, CN). Har-Row.
--The Big Book of Jewish Humor. LC 81-47234. (Illus.). 320p. 1981. pap. 10.95 (ISBN 0-06-090917-X, CN917, HarpT): Har-Row.
Olsvanger, Immanuel, ed. Royte Pomerantsen or How to Laugh in Yiddish. 1965. pap. 4.95 (ISBN 0-8052-0099-1). Schocken.
Oring, Elliot. Israeli Humor & Its Oral Tradition. LC 80-25483. (Modern Jewish Literature & Culture Ser.). 250p. 1981. 34.00x (ISBN 0-87395-520-X, ORIH); pap. 9.95x (ISBN 0-87395-521-8, ORIH-P). State U NY Pr.
Pollack, Simon R. Jewish Wit for All Occasions. LC 79-65341. (Orig.). 1979. pap. 5.95 (ISBN 0-89104-153-2). A & W Pubs.
Reik, Theodore. Jewish Wit. 6.00 (ISBN 0-685-45966-7); pap. 2.45 (ISBN 0-685-45967-5). Taplinger.
Rosten, Leo. Joys of Yiddish. 1968. 12.50 (ISBN 0-07-053975-8, GB). McGraw.
--Joys of Yiddish. 1970. pap. 3.95 (ISBN 0-671-78505-2). WSP.
Seaman, Sylvia S. How to Be a Jewish Grandmother. LC 78-22646. 1979. 6.95 (ISBN 0-385-15205-1). Doubleday.
Simon, Solomon. Wise Men of Helm. (gr. 3-7). 1942. pap. 3.95 (ISBN 0-87441-125-4). Behrman.
Spalding, Henry D. A Treasure-Trove of American Jewish Humor. LC 75-40192. 429p. 1976. 12.50 (ISBN 0-8246-0204-8). Jonathan David.
Spalding, Henry D., ed. Encyclopedia of Jewish Humor. LC 68-21429. 1978. 12.50 (ISBN 0-8246-0021-5). Jonathan David.
Weltman, Gershon & Zuckerman, Marvin, trs. Yiddish Sayings Mama Never Taught You. LC 73-79282. (Perivale Translation Ser.: No. 2). 99p. 1976. pap. 4.95 (ISBN 0-912288-04-3). Perivale Pr.

JEWISH WOMEN

see Women, Jewish

JEWISH YOUTH

see Youth, Jewish

JEWITT, JOHN RODGERS, 1783-1821

Jewitt, John R. Narrative of the Adventures & Suffering of John R. Jewitt. 1967. 9.95 (ISBN 0-87770-014-1). Ye Galleon.

JEWS

see also Anglo-Israelism; Falashas; Patriarchs (Bible); Prophets; Sephardim; Youth, Jewish

Agus, Jacob B. Jewish Identity in an Age of Ideologies. LC 76-14230. 1978. 20.00 (ISBN 0-8044-5018-8). Ungar.
Applebaum, Shimon. Jews & Greeks in Ancient Cyrene. (Illus.). 367p. 1980. text ed. 64.00x (ISBN 90-04-05970-9). Humanities.
Belloc, Hilaire. The Jews. 1981. lib. bdg. 69.95 (ISBN 0-8490-3220-2). Gordon Pr.
Bermant, Chaim. The Jews. LC 77-79020. 1977. 12.50 (ISBN 0-8129-0705-1). Times Bks.
Cohen, Arthur A. The Natural & the Supernatural Jew: An Historical and Theological Introduction. LC 79-13038. 1979. Repr. of 1962 ed. pap. text ed. 6.95x (ISBN 0-87441-291-9). Behrman.
Cohen, Bernard L. Jews Among the Nations. LC 77-79171. 1978. 10.00 (ISBN 0-8022-2209-9). Philos Lib.
Davis, Moshe, ed. World Jewry & the State of Israel. LC 77-72730. (Indivual Publications Ser.). 1977. lib. bdg. 12.00x (ISBN 0-405-10305-0). Arno.
Deshen, Solomon. Ethnic Boundaries & Cultural Paradigms: The Case of Southern Tunisian Immigrants in Israel. 35p. 1976. softcover 2.00 (ISBN 0-686-74366-0). ADELANTRE.
Fine, Morris & Himmelfarb, Milton, eds. American Jewish Year Book, 1977, Vol. 77. LC 99-4040. 650p. 1977. 15.00 (ISBN 0-8276-0129-8, 397). Jewish Pubn.
Fishberg, Maurice. The Jews: A Study of Race & Environment. facsimile ed. LC 74-27983. (Modern Jewish Experience Ser.). (Illus.). 1975. Repr. of 1911 ed. 39.00x (ISBN 0-405-06710-0). Arno.
Ford, Henry. The International Jew. 59.95 (ISBN 0-8490-0418-7). Gordon Pr.
Frieman, Donald G. Milestones in the Life of a Jew. LC 65-15710. 1980. pap. 3.95x (ISBN 0-8197-0002-9). Bloch.
Goodspeed, George Stephen. Israel's Messianic Hope. 1900. 12.50 (ISBN 0-8414-4656-3). Folcroft.
Jewish Communities of the World. 7.25x (ISBN 0-8277-0486-0). British Bk Ctr.
Jewish Radicals & Radical Jews. LC 80-41227. 1981. 26.00 (ISBN 0-12-178780-X). Acad Pr.
Judaica in the Houghton Library. 25.00x (ISBN 0-685-56208-5). Ktav.
Kabakoff, Jacob, ed. Jewish Book Annual, Vol. 39. 1981. 15.00 (ISBN 0-914820-34-6). JWB Jewish Bk Coun.
Katz, Jacob. Exclusiveness & Toleranee: Studies in Jewish-Gentile Relations in Medieval & Modern Times. LC 80-12181. (Scripta Judaica: No. III). xv, 200p. 1980. Repr. of 1961 ed. lib. bdg. 19.75x (ISBN 0-313-22387-4, KAEX). Greenwood.
Kautsky, Karl. Are the Jews a Race? LC 72-97288. 255p. 1972. Repr. of 1926 ed. lib. bdg. 16.00x (ISBN 0-8371-2609-6, KAJR). Greenwood.
Kertzer, Morris N. Tell Me, Rabbi. 1978. pap. 2.95 (ISBN 0-02-086340-3, Collier). Macmillan.
--What Is a Jew. rev. ed. LC 73-77280. 217p. 1973. Repr. of 1953 ed. 6.95 (ISBN 0-8197-0299-4). Bloch.
--What Is a Jew? 1978. pap. 2.95 (ISBN 0-02-086350-0, Collier). Macmillan.
Kraines, Oscar. The Impossible Dilemma: Who Is a Jew in the State of Israel? 1976. 6.95 (ISBN 0-8197-0392-3). Bloch.
Levine, Naomi & Hochbaum, Martin, eds. Poor Jews: An American Awakening. LC 73-85097. 275p. 1974. 12.95 (ISBN 0-87855-073-9); pap. 3.95x (ISBN 0-87855-570-6). Transaction Bks.
Lieberman, Saul & Hyman, Arthur, eds. Salo Wittmayer Baron Jubilee Volume: On the Occasion of His Eightieth Birthday, 3 vols. new ed. LC 74-82633. 1533p. 1975. 90.00x set (ISBN 0-685-51945-7); Vol. 1. (ISBN 0-231-03911-5); Vol. 2. (ISBN 0-231-03912-3); Vol. 3. (ISBN 0-231-03913-1). Columbia U Pr.
Memmi, Albert. Liberation of the Jews. Hyun, Judith, tr. LC 66-26539. 1967. 4.95 (ISBN 0-670-42764-0, Grossman). Viking Pr.
Mendes-Flohr, Paul R. & Reinharz, Jehuda. The Jew in the Modern World: A Documentary History. 1980. pap. text ed. 11.95x (ISBN 0-19-502632-2). Oxford U Pr.
Mourant, A. E., et al. The Genetics of the Jews. (Research Monographs on Human Population Biology). (Illus.). 1978. text ed. 39.50x (ISBN 0-19-857522-X). Oxford U Pr.
Otis, George. The Ghost of Hagar. pap. 2.50 (ISBN 0-89728-033-4, 581116). Omega Pubns OR.
Owen, John. Exposition of Hebrews, 7vols. 99.95 (ISBN 0-8010-6673-5). Baker Bk.
Pentz, Croft M. Expository Outlines on Hebrews. (Sermon Outline Ser.). pap. 1.95 (ISBN 0-8010-7045-7). Baker Bk.
Raphael, Chaim. Encounters with the Jewish People. LC 79-14424. 1979. pap. text ed. 6.95x (ISBN 0-87441-282-X). Behrman.
Rosenweig, Bernard. Ashkenazic Jewry in Transition. 173p. 1975. pap. 6.50 (ISBN 0-88920-022-X, Pub. by Laurier U Pr Canada). Humanities.
Samuel, Maurice. Gentleman & the Jew. LC 77-6666. pap. 4.95x (ISBN 0-87441-264-1). Behrman.
Schloss, Ezekiel & Epstein, Morris, eds. More World Over Stories. LC 67-26646. (World Over Anthology for Jewish Youth Ser). (Illus.). (gr. 4-7). 1968. 4.95 (ISBN 0-8197-0255-2). Bloch.
--New World Over Story Book. (Illus.). (gr. 4-7). 4.95 (ISBN 0-8197-0256-0). Bloch.
Seltzer, Sandford. Jews & Non-Jews Falling in Love. 1976. 4.00 (ISBN 0-8074-0098-X, 164050). UAHC.
Set My People Free. (Faith & Life Ser.). 2.10 (ISBN 0-02-655500-X). Benziger Pub Co.

Silberschlag, Eisig, compiled by. An Exhibition of Judaica & Hebraica. (Illus.). 26p. 1973. pap. 3.50 (ISBN 0-87959-034-3). U of Tex Hum Res.

Strassfeld, Michael, et alcompiled by. The Jewish Catalog: A Do-It Yourself Kit. LC 73-11759. (Illus.). 1973. pap. 7.95 (ISBN 0-8276-0042-9, 338). Jewish Pubn.

Strassfeld, Sharon & Strassfeld, Michael, eds. Third Jewish Catalog: Creating Community. LC 80-19818. (Illus.). 416p. 1980. 9.95 (ISBN 0-8276-0183-2, 466). Jewish Pubn.

Szajkowski, Soza. Jews in the French Foreign Legion. 20.00x (ISBN 0-87068-285-7). Ktav.

Wertheimer, Elaine C. Jewish Sources of Spanish Blood Purity Concerns. 28p. 1977. softcover 2.00 (ISBN 0-686-74367-9). ADELANTRE.

Wirth, Louis. Ghetto. LC 56-14116. (Illus.). 1956. pap. 3.95 (ISBN 0-226-90250-1, P7, Phoen). U of Chicago Pr.

JEWS–ADDRESSES, ESSAYS, LECTURES

American Jewish Committee. The Jewish Communities of Nazi-Occupied Europe. 400p. 1981. Repr. of 1944 ed. 28.50x (ISBN 0-86527-337-5). Fertig.

Chiel, Arthur A., ed. Perspectives on Jews & Judaism: Essays in Honor of Wolfe Kelman. 25.00x (ISBN 0-87068-683-6). Ktav.

Dawidowicz, Lucy. The Jewish Presence: Essays on Identity & History. LC 78-6236. 1978. pap. 3.95 (ISBN 0-15-646221-4, Harv). HarBraceJ.

Goldstein, Israel. Toward a Solution. facs. ed. LC 79-128248. (Essay Index Reprint Ser). 1940. 19.00 (ISBN 0-8369-1877-0). Arno.

Gordon, A. D. Selected Essays. LC 73-2201. (The Jewish People; History, Religion, Literature Ser.). Repr. of 1938 ed. 19.00 (ISBN 0-405-05266-9). Arno.

Herzog, Yaacov. A People That Dwells Alone. Louvish, Misha, ed. 282p. 1975. 7.95 (ISBN 0-88482-895-6, Sanhedrin Pr). Hebrew Pub.

Jewish Frontier (Periodical) Anthology, Nineteen Thirty-Four to Nineteen Forty-Four. facsimile ed. LC 76-167370. (Essay Index Reprint Ser). Repr. of 1945 ed. 28.00 (ISBN 0-8369-2459-2). Arno.

Karpeles, Gustav. Jewish Literature & Other Essays. facsimile ed. LC 78-37159. (Essay Index Reprint Ser). Repr. of 1895 ed. 22.00 (ISBN 0-8369-2512-2). Arno.

Malino, Frances & Albert, Phyllis C., eds. Essays in Modern Jewish History: A Tribute to Ben Halpern. LC 80-70585. 500p. 1981. 20.00 (ISBN 0-8386-3095-2). Fairleigh Dickinson.

Wiesel, Elie. A Jew Today. Weisel, Marion, tr. from Fr. LC 79-11251. 1979. pap. 2.50 (ISBN 0-394-74057-2, Vin). Random.

JEWS–ANTHROPOMETRY

Shapiro, Harry L. The Jewish People: A Biological History. LC 76-5851. (Race Question in Modern Science Ser.). 84p. 1976. Repr. of 1960 ed. lib. bdg. 915.00 (ISBN 0-8371-8783-4, SHJE). Greenwood.

Travel's in Jewry. Date not set. 7.50 (ISBN 0-686-76271-1). Feldheim.

JEWS–ANTIQUITIES

see also Ark of the Covenant; Bible–Antiquities; Dancing (In Religion, Folk-Lore, etc.); Menorah; Priests, Jewish–Vestments; Tabernacle

Avi-Yonah, Michael. The Encyclopedia of Archaeological Excavations in the Holy Land, Vol. 4. 1975. 25.00 (ISBN 0-13-275149-6). P-H.

Goodenough, E. R. Jewish Symbols in the Greco-Roman Period, 13 vols. Incl. Vols. 1-3. Archeological Evidence from Palestine & the Diaspora. 1953; Vol. 4. The Problem of Method; Symbols from Jewish Cult. 1954; Vols. 5 & 6. Fish, Bread, & Wine, 2 vols. 1956. o.p. (ISBN 0-691-09754-2); Vols. 7 & 8. Pagan Symbols in Judaism. 1958; Vols. 9-11. Symbolism in the Dura Synagog. 1964. 55.00 (ISBN 0-691-09756-9); Vol. 12. Summary & Conclusions. 1965. 20.00 (ISBN 0-691-09757-7); Vol. 13. General Index & Maps. 1969. (Bollingen Ser.: Vol. 37). Princeton U Pr.

Josephus. Works of Josephus, 9 vols. Warmington, E. H., ed. Incl. Vol. 1. Life; Against Apion (ISBN 0-674-99205-9); Vols 2-3. Jewish War. Vol. 2, Bks 1-3. (ISBN 0-674-99223-7); Vol. 3, Bks. 4-7, Index To Vols. 2 & 3. (ISBN 0-674-99232-6); Vols 4-9. Antiquities. Vol. 4, Bks 1-4. (ISBN 0-674-99267-9); Vol. 5, Bks 5-8. (ISBN 0-674-99310-1); Vol. 6, Bks 9-11. (ISBN 0-674-99360-8); Vol. 7, Bks 12-14. (ISBN 0-674-99402-7); Vol. 8, Bks 15-17. (ISBN 0-674-99451-5); Vol. 9, Bks 18-20, General Index. (ISBN 0-674-99477-9). (Loeb Classical Library: No. 186, 203, 210, 242, 281, 326, 365, 410, 433). 11.00x ea. Harvard U Pr.

Josephus, Flavius. Complete Works of Flavius Josephus. Whiston, William, tr. LC 60-15405. (Orig.). 1974. 15.95 (ISBN 0-8254-2951-X); kivar 11.95 (ISBN 0-8254-2952-8). Kregel.

--Life & Work of Flavius Josephus. Whiston, William, tr. 1957. 16.95 (ISBN 0-03-037015-9). HR&W.

Krauss, Samuel. Talmudische Archaologie, 3 vols. Finley, Moses, ed. LC 79-4988. (Ancient Economic History). (Illus., Ger.). 1980. Repr. of 1912 ed. Set. lib. bdg. 150.00x (ISBN 0-405-12373-6); lib. bdg. 50.00x ea. Vol. 1 (ISBN 0-405-12374-4). Vol. 2 (ISBN 0-405-12375-2). Vol. 3 (ISBN 0-405-12376-0). Arno.

JEWS–APOLOGETICS

see Judaism–Apologetic Works

JEWS–BIBLIOGRAPHY

Baron, Salo W. The Jewish Community, 3 vols. LC 74-97269. 1972. Repr. of 1942 ed. Set. lib. bdg. 53.50x (ISBN 0-8371-3274-6, BAJC). Greenwood.

Berlin, Charles. Studies in Jewish Bibliography, History & Literature: In Honor of I. Edward Kiev. 1971. 50.00x (ISBN 0-87068-143-5). Ktav.

Bloch, ed. Journal of Jewish Bibliography, 4 vols. Set. 29.50 (ISBN 0-685-48593-5). Feldheim.

Eppler, Elizabeth E., ed. International Bibliography of Jewish Affairs 1966-1967: A Select List of Books & Articles Published in the Diaspora. LC 74-84654. 365p. 1976. 35.00x (ISBN 0-8419-0177-5). Holmes & Meier.

--International Bibliograpy on Jewish Affairs: A Selected Annotated List of Books & Articles Published in the Diaspora, 1976-1977. 450p. 1981. lib. bdg. 36.25x (ISBN 0-86531-164-1). Westview.

Liebman, Charles S. & Tabory, Mala. International Jewish Affairs. 1979. 22.00x (ISBN 965-20-0018-3, Pub by Turtledove Pub Ltd Israel). Intl Schol Bk Serv.

New York Public Library, Research Libraries. Dictionary Catalog of Jewish Collection, 14 Vols. 1960. Set. 900.00 (ISBN 0-8161-0409-3). G K Hall.

--Dictionary Catalog of the Jewish Collection, First Supplement, 8 vols. 5424p. 1975. Set. lib. bdg. 750.00 (ISBN 0-8161-0773-4). G K Hall.

Rockland, Mae S. The New Jewish Yellow Pages. (Illus.). 288p. (Orig.). 1981. pap. 9.95 (ISBN 0-89961-016-1). SBS Pub.

Rosenbach, A. S. W. American Jewish Bibliography, to 1850. 1926. 17.00 (ISBN 0-527-02373-6). Kraus Repr.

Wiener Library & Wolff, Ilse. German Jewry: Its History, Life & Culture. LC 75-17202. (Wiener Library Catalogue Series: No. 3). 279p. 1975. Repr. of 1958 ed. lib. bdg. 15.00x (ISBN 0-8371-8292-1, WIGJ). Greenwood.

Yivo Biblyografye 1942-1950: Bibliography of the Publications of the Yiddish Scientific Institute, Vol. 2. LC 47-36672. (Yivo Institute for Jewish Research, Organizatsye Fun der Yidisher Visnshaft: No. 38). 158p. (Yiddish.). 1955. 2.00 (ISBN 0-914512-30-7). Yivo Inst.

JEWS–BIOGRAPHY

see also Rabbis; Women, Jewish; also Jews in Germany; Jews in the United States and similar headings

Abrahams, Robert D. Alfred Mordecai: The Uncommon Soldier. LC 59-5578. (Covenant Ser.). (Illus.). (gr. 6-10). 1959. 3.50 (ISBN 0-8276-0126-3, 283). Jewish Pubn.

--Sir David Salomons: Sound of Bow Bells. LC 62-12320. (Covenant Ser.). (gr. 6-10). 1962. 3.50 (ISBN 0-8276-0159-X, 286). Jewish Pubn.

Agus, Jacob B. High Priest of Rebirth: The Life, Times & Thought of Abraham Isaac Kuk. 2nd ed. 1972. 7.50x (ISBN 0-8197-0281-1). Bloch.

Alexander, Lloyd. August Bondi: Border Hawk. LC 57-11226. (Covenant Ser.). (Illus.). (gr. 6-10). 1958. 3.50 (ISBN 0-8276-0131-X, 279). Jewish Pubn.

Apsler, Alfred. Louis Fleischner: Northwest Pioneer. LC 60-9077. (Covenant Ser.). (Illus.). (gr. 6-10). 1960. 3.50 (ISBN 0-8276-0149-2, 284). Jewish Pubn.

--Samson Wertheimer: The Court Factor. LC 64-16755. (Covenant Ser.). (Illus.). (gr. 6-10). 1964. 3.50 (ISBN 0-8276-0158-1, 272). Jewish Pubn.

Arad, Yitzhak. The Partisan: From the Valley of Death to Mount Zion. LC 78-71299. 1979. 9.95 (ISBN 0-89604-010-0, Pub. by Holocaust Library); pap. 4.95 (ISBN 0-89604-011-9, Pub. by Holocaust Library). Schocken.

Bardin, Shlomo, ed. Self-Fulfillment Through Zionism: A Study in Jewish Adjustment. LC 70-142605. (Biography Index Reprint Ser). Repr. of 1943 ed. 15.00 (ISBN 0-8369-8076-X). Arno.

Berger, Elmer. Memoirs of an Anti-Zionist Jew. 159p. (Orig.). 1978. pap. 5.00x (ISBN 0-911038-87-6, Inst Hist Rev). Noontide.

Bokser, Ben Zion, tr. Abraham Isaac Kook: The Lights of Penitance, Lights of Holiness. the Moral Principles. Essays, Letters & Poems. LC 78-70465. (Classics of Western Spirituality). 448p. 1978. 11.95 (ISBN 0-8091-0278-1); pap. 7.95 (ISBN 0-8091-2159-X). Paulist Pr.

Bolitho, Hector, ed. Twelve Jews. facs. ed. LC 67-23179. (Essay Index Reprint Ser). 1934. 18.00 (ISBN 0-8369-0223-8). Arno.

Chaim, Bezalel. A Bio-Bibliographical Dictionary of Notable Jews Who Perished in German Concentration Camps & Ghettos, Etc. 1980. lib. bdg. 49.50 (ISBN 0-686-59563-7). Revisionist Pr.

--William Zukerman, Voice of Jewish Dissent: The Story of the Jewish Newsletter. 1980. lib. bdg. 49.95 (ISBN 0-686-60056-8). Revisionist Pr.

Czerniakow, Adam. Warsaw Diary of Adam Czerniakow. 1978. 16.95 (ISBN 0-8128-2523-3). Stein & Day.

Doron, P. Nehemiah Kalomiti's War of Truth. 25.00x (ISBN 0-87068-441-8). Ktav.

Dresner. Levi Yitzhak of Berditchev: Portrait of a Hasidic Master. 10.00 (ISBN 0-686-08932-4). Hartmore.

Eckman, Lester. Revered by All. 2nd ed. LC 73-89418. 1976. 10.00 (ISBN 0-88400-002-8). Shengold.

Eisenberg, Azriel. Fill a Blank Page: A Biography of Solomon Schechter. (Illus.). (gr. 6-11). 3.75 (ISBN 0-8381-0730-3, 10-730). United Syn Bk.

Falstein, Louis. The Man Who Loved Laughter: The Story of Sholom Aleichem. LC 68-19608. (Covenant Ser.). (gr. 6-10). 1968. 4.25 (ISBN 0-8276-0033-X, 265). Jewish Pubn.

Feldstein, Janice J. Rabbi Jacob J. Weinstein: Advocate of the People. Date not set. 15.00x (ISBN 0-87068-699-2). Ktav.

Friedlander, Saul. When Memory Comes. 1980. pap. 2.75 (ISBN 0-380-50807-9, 50807, Discus). Avon.

Friedman, Lee M. Jewish Pioneers & Patriots. (Essay Index Reprint Ser.). Repr. of 1942 ed. 24.25 (ISBN 0-518-10146-0). Arno.

Geiger, Abraham. Salomo Gabirol und seine Dichtungen. Katz, Steven, ed. LC 79-7130. (Jewish Philosophy, Mysticism & History of Ideas Ser.). 1980. Repr. of 1867 ed. lib. bdg. 12.00x (ISBN 0-405-12254-3). Arno.

Goldsmith, S. J. Twenty Twentieth Century Jews. LC 70-101827. (Biography Index Reprint Ser). 1962. 18.00 (ISBN 0-8369-8000-X). Arno.

--Twenty Twentieth Century Jews. LC 62-21948. (Illus.). 142p. 1962. 5.95 (ISBN 0-88400-021-4). Shengold.

Gorn, Mordechai M. Journey to Fulfillment. LC 79-50790. (Illus.). 1979. 8.95 (ISBN 0-8197-0471-7). Bloch.

Gray, Bettyanne. Manya's Story. LC 77-92305. (Adult & Young Adult Books). (Illus.). (gr. 5-9). 1978. PLB 7.95 (ISBN 0-8225-0762-5). Lerner Pubns.

Greenberg, Martin H. The Jewish Lists: Physicists & General, Actors & Writers, & Hundreds of Other Lists of Accomplished Jews. LC 79-14349. 1979. 12.95 (ISBN 0-8052-3711-9). Schocken.

Greenberg, Sidney. Likrat Shabbat. LC 72-97593. 7.95x (ISBN 0-686-05619-1). Hartmore.

Gross, David C. Pride of Our People: The Stories of One Hundred Outstanding Jewish Men & Women. LC 77-25592. (Illus.). 448p. 1979. 14.95 (ISBN 0-385-13573-4). Doubleday.

Gumbiner, Joseph H. Leaders of Our People, 2 Bks. (Illus.). (gr. 4-6). Bk. 1. 1963. text ed. 5.00 (ISBN 0-8074-0141-2, 122921); Bk. 2. 1965. text ed. 5.00 (ISBN 0-8074-0142-0, 123921); tchrs'. guide 3.25 (ISBN 0-8074-0143-9, 202922). UAHC.

Hahn, Emily. Isaac Aboab. LC 59-10193. (Covenant Ser.). (Illus.). (gr. 6-10). 1959. 3.50 (ISBN 0-8276-0144-1, 277). Jewish Pubn.

Jordan, Ruth. Daughter of the Waves: Memories of Growing up in Pre-War Palestine. LC 80-39526. (Illus.). 224p. 1982. 10.95 (ISBN 0-8008-2120-3). Taplinger.

Katz, Arthur & Buckingham, Jamie. Ben Israel: A Jewish Intellectual's Conversion to Messianic Judaism. LC 79-95765. 1970. pap. 2.95 (ISBN 0-912106-05-0). Logos.

Kazin, Alfred. New York Jew. LC 77-20359. 1978. 12.95 (ISBN 0-394-49567-5). Knopf.

Kohn, Nahum & Roiter, Howard. A Voice from the Forest: Memoirs of a Jewish Partisan. LC 80-81685. (Illus.). 288p. 1980. 12.95 (ISBN 0-8052-5021-2, Pub. by Holocaust Library); pap. 5.95 (ISBN 0-8052-5020-4). Schocken.

Kohut, Rebekah. His Father's House: The Story of George Alexander Kohut. 1938. 37.50x (ISBN 0-686-51400-9). Elliots Bks.

--My Portion (An Autobiography) 1927. 17.50x (ISBN 0-686-50051-2). Elliots Bks.

Kollek, Teddy & Kollek, Amos. For Jerusalem. (Illus.). 1978. 10.00 (ISBN 0-394-49296-X); limited ed. o.p. 25.00 (ISBN 0-394-50145-4). Random.

Landman, Leo. Rabbi Joseph H. Lookstein Memorial Volume. Date not set. 29.50x (ISBN 0-87068-705-0). Ktav.

Levinger, Elma E. Great Jews Since Bible Times. (Illus.). (gr. 1-4). 2.50x (ISBN 0-87441-053-3). Behrman.

Lewin, Isaac. Unto the Mountains. 160p. 1976. 5.95 (ISBN 0-88482-896-4). Hebrew Pub.

Magnes, Beatrice. Episodes: A Memoir. 10.00 (ISBN 0-686-27358-3). Magnes Mus.

Magnus, Katie. Jewish Portraits. LC 72-3396. (Essay Index Reprint Ser.). Repr. of 1888 ed. 16.00 (ISBN 0-8369-2912-8). Arno.

Marcus, Jacob R. Israel Jacobson: The Founder of the Reform Movement in Judaism. 12.50x (ISBN 0-685-31435-9, Pub. by Hebrew Union). Ktav.

Markell, Jan. Gone the Golden Dream. LC 79-16718. 1979. pap. 3.95 (ISBN 0-87123-049-6, 210049). Bethany Hse.

Men of Distinction, 2 vols. Date not set. 10.00 (ISBN 0-686-76547-8). Feldheim.

Noble, Iris. Nazi Hunter: Simon Wiesenthal. LC 79-15783. 160p. (gr. 7 up). 1979. PLB 7.29 (ISBN 0-671-32964-2). Messner.

Noveck, Simon. Great Jewish Personalities in Ancient & Modern Times. (Pub by B'nai B'rith); pap. 5.95x (ISBN 0-8197-0163-7). Bloch.

--Great Jewish Personalities in Modern Times. (Pub by B'nai B'rith); pap. 5.95x (ISBN 0-8197-0165-3). Bloch.

Portnoy, S. A., ed. & tr. Vladimir Medem: The Life & Soul of a Legendary Jewish Socialist. 25.00x (ISBN 0-87068-332-2). Ktav.

Raisin, Max. Great Jews I Have Known. LC 71-117331. (Biography Index Reprint Ser). 1952. 20.00 (ISBN 0-8369-8023-9). Arno.

Rapoport, Louis. The Lost Jews: Last of the Ethiopian Falashas. LC 79-92340. (Illus.). 264p. 1980. 13.95 (ISBN 0-8128-2720-1). Stein & Day.

Raz, Simcha. A Tzaddik in Our Time. Wengrow, Charles, tr. from Hebrew. Orig. Title: Ish Tzaddik Hayah. (Illus.). 1976. 13.95 (ISBN 0-87306-130-6). Feldheim.

Ribalow, Harold U. Daniel Mendoza: The Fighter from Whitechapel. LC 62-18412. (Covenant Ser.). (Illus.). (gr. 6-10). 1962. 3.50 (ISBN 0-8276-0135-2, 287). Jewish Pubn.

Rogow, Sally. Nurse in Blue: Lillian Wald. LC 66-11719. (Covenant Ser.). (Illus.). (gr. 6-10). 1966. 3.50 (ISBN 0-8276-0030-5, 270). Jewish Pubn.

Rosenbloom, Noah H. Tradition in an Age of Reform: The Religious Philosophy of Samson Raphael Hirsch. LC 75-13438. 490p. 1976. 12.50 (ISBN 0-8276-0070-4, 380). Jewish Pubn.

Rosensaft, Menachem Z. Moshe Sharett. LC 66-25854. 1966. 4.95 (ISBN 0-88400-019-2). Shengold.

Rosenthal, Ludwig. How Was It Possible? 1971. 6.00 (ISBN 0-686-27352-4). Magnes Mus.

Roth, Cecil. Dona Gracia of the House of Nasi. LC 77-92984. 1978. pap. 4.95 (ISBN 0-8276-0099-2, 415). Jewish Pubn.

Rottenberg, Dan. Finding Our Fathers. 1977. 12.95 (ISBN 0-394-40675-3). Random.

Ruderman, David. The World of a Renaissance Jew: The Life & Thought of Abraham Ben Mordecai Faissol. Date not set. 20.00 (ISBN 0-686-73603-6). Ktav.

Sharf, A. The Universe of Shabbetai Donnolo. 20.00x (ISBN 0-87068-485-X). Ktav.

Sherwin, Byron. Abraham Joshua Herschel. LC 78-71051. (Makers of Contemporary Theology Ser.). 1979. pap. 3.45 (ISBN 0-8042-0466-7). John Knox.

Sherwin, Byron L. Mystical Theology & Social Dissent: The Life & Works of Judah Loew of Prague. LC 80-67968. (Littman Library of Jewish Civilization). 340p. 1981. 25.00 (ISBN 0-8386-3028-6). Fairleigh Dickinson.

Shneiderman, S. L. Kafka & His Jewish World. 1980. lib. bdg. 69.95 (ISBN 0-8490-3060-9). Gordon Pr.

Siev, Asher. Rabbi Moses Isserles: His Life, Works & Ideas. 1972. 10.00x (ISBN 0-685-30559-7). Bloch.

Singer, Isaac B. Reaches of Heaven: A Story of the Life of the Baal Shem Tov. 1980. text ed. 15.00 (ISBN 0-374-24733-1). FS&G.

Sputz, David. Generations of Our Sages. 176p. 1980. 7.50 (ISBN 0-9604312-0-9). Sputz.

Sutton, Joseph A. Magic Carpet: Aleppo in Flatbush: The Story of a Unique Ethnic Jewish Community. LC 79-65516. (Illus.). 336p. 1980. text ed. 19.95x (ISBN 0-686-27080-0). Thayer-Jacoby.

Twersky, Isadore. Rabad of Posquieres: A Twelfth-Century Talmudist. LC 79-88696. 1979. pap. 6.95 (ISBN 0-8276-0123-9, 444). Jewish Pubn.

Vineberg, Ethel. Grandmother Came from Dworitz: A Jewish Story. LC 77-89353. (Illus.). (gr. 3-8). 1978. pap. 2.95 (ISBN 0-912766-88-3). Tundra Bks.

Weilerstein, Sadie R. Jewish Heroes, 2 bks. (Illus.). 208p. (gr. 2-3). pap. 4.25x ea. Bk. 1 (ISBN 0-8381-0180-1). Bk. 2 (ISBN 0-8381-0177-1). United Syn Bk.

Zieman, Joseph. The Cigarette Sellers of Three Crosses Square. (YA) (gr. 7-11). 1977. pap. 1.50 (ISBN 0-380-00967-6, 45682). Avon.

JEWS–CABALA

see Cabala

JEWS–CHARITIES

Frisch, Ephraim. Historical Survey of Jewish Philanthropy from the Earliest Times to the Nineteenth Century. LC 79-79197. 196p. Repr. of 1924 ed. 10.00x (ISBN 0-8154-0296-1). Cooper Sq.

Raphael, Marc L. Understanding American Jewish Philanthropy. 17.50 (ISBN 0-87068-689-5). Ktav.

JEWS–CHILDREN

see Jewish Children

JEWS–CHOSEN PEOPLE

see Jews–Election, Doctrine of

JEWS–CIVILIZATION

Alon, Gedaliah. The Jews in Their Land in the Talmudic Age, Vol. 1. Gershon, Levi, tr. from Hebrew. 324p. 1980. text ed. 23.00x (ISBN 965-223-352-8, Pub. by Magnes Israel). Humanities.

Alon, Gedalyahu. Jews, Judaism & the Classical World. Abrahams, Israel, tr. from Hebrew. 499p. 1977. text ed. 34.50x (ISBN 0-686-74316-4, Pub. by Magnes Israel). Humanities.

Barkai, Meyer, ed. Twentieth Century Universal Jewish Encyclopedia. (Illus., Orig.). 1981. pap. write for info. (ISBN 0-86649-024-8). Twentieth Century.

Baron, Salo W. A Social & Religious History of the Jews, 17 vols. 2nd, rev. & enl. ed. Incl. Vol. 1. Ancient Times to the Beginning of the Christian Era. 1952 (ISBN 0-231-08838-8); Vol. 2. Ancient Times: Christian Era: the First Five Centuries. 1952 (ISBN 0-231-08839-6); Vol. 3. High Middle Ages: Heirs of Rome & Persia. 1957 (ISBN 0-231-08840-X); Vol. 4. High Middle Ages: Meeting of the East & West. 1957 (ISBN 0-231-08841-8); Vol. 5. High Middle Ages: Religious Controls & Dissensions. 1957 (ISBN 0-231-08842-6); Vol. 6. High Middle Ages: Laws, Homilies & the Bible. 1958 (ISBN 0-231-08843-4); Vol. 7. High Middle Ages: Hebrew Language & Letters. 1958 (ISBN 0-231-08844-2); Vol. 8. High Middle Ages: Philosophy & Science. 1958 (ISBN 0-231-08845-0); Vol. 9. Late Middle Ages & Era of European Expansion, 1200-1650: Under Church & Empire. 1965 (ISBN 0-231-08846-9); Vol. 10. Late Middle Ages & Era of European Expansion, 1200-1650: On the Empire's Periphery. 1965 (ISBN 0-231-08847-7); Vol. 11. Late Middle Ages & Era of European Expansion, 1200-1650: Citizen or Alien Conjurer. 1967 (ISBN 0-231-08848-5); Vol. 12. Late Middle Ages & Era of European Expansion, 1200-1650: Economic Catalyst. 1967 (ISBN 0-231-08849-3); Vol. 13. Late Middle Ages & Era of European Expansion, 1200-1650: Inquisition, Renaissance & Reformation. 1969 (ISBN 0-231-08850-7); Vol. 14. Late Middle Ages & Era of European Expansion, 1200-1650: Catholic Restoration & Wars of Religion. 1969 (ISBN 0-231-08851-5); Vol. 15. Late Middle Ages & Era of European Expansion, 1200-1650: Resettlement & Exploration. 1973 (ISBN 0-231-08852-3); Index (ISBN 0-231-08877-9). LC 52-404. 27.00x ea. Columbia U Pr.

Blau, Joseph L., ed. Essays on Jewish Life & Thought. LC 57-11757. 458p. 1959. 22.50x (ISBN 0-231-02171-2). Columbia U Pr.

Chouraqui, Andre. The People & the Faith of the Bible. Gugli, William V., tr. LC 74-21237. 224p. 1975. 12.50x (ISBN 0-87023-172-3). U of Mass Pr.

Dawidowicz, L. S., et al, eds. For Max Weinreich on His Seventieth Birthday: Studies in Jewish Language, Literature & Society. 1964. 103.00x (ISBN 0-686-22430-2). Mouton.

Elbogen, Ismar. A Century of Jewish Life. Hadas, Moses, tr. 1944. 6.00 (ISBN 0-8276-0132-8). Jewish Pubn.

Goldin, Judah, ed. & intro. by. The Jewish Expression. LC 75-27866. 512p. 1976. 22.50x (ISBN 0-300-01948-3); pap. 7.95 (ISBN 0-300-01975-0). Yale U Pr.

Horowitz, George. The Spirit of Jewish Law. LC 53-7535. 1979. Repr. of 1953 ed. text ed. 18.00x (ISBN 0-87632-167-8). Bloch.

Hyman, Frieda C. The Jewish Experience: Book I. 1975. 5.25x (ISBN 0-8381-0191-7). United Syn Bk.

Kaplan, Mordecai M. & Cohen, Arthur A. If Not Now, When? Towards a Reconstitution of the Jewish People. LC 72-95901. 1973. 5.95x (ISBN 0-8052-3497-7). Schocken.

Kent, Maxwell. A Comparative Analysis of the Italians & the Jews: The Two People Who Contributed the Most to the Civilization of Mankind with Strange & Unexpected Conclusions. (Illus.). 1977. 47.75 (ISBN 0-89266-056-2). Am Classical Coll Pr.

Lehrmann, Charles C. Jewish Influences on European Thought. Klin, George & Carpenter, Victor, trs. LC 72-3264. 323p. 1976. 16.50 (ISBN 0-8386-7908-0). Fairleigh Dickinson.

Litvin & Hoenig. Jewish Identity. 12.50 (ISBN 0-87306-096-2). Feldheim.

Montefiore, C. G. Ancient Jewish & Greek Consolation. LC 75-184052. 86p. 1973. text ed. 7.95 (ISBN 0-87677-045-6). Hartmore.

Patai, Raphael. The Jewish Mind. LC 76-58040. 1977. 14.95 (ISBN 0-684-14878-1, ScribT); pap. 7.95 (ISBN 0-684-16321-7, SL881, ScribT). Scribner.

Roth, Cecil. The Jewish Contribution to Civilizaton. 1978. pap. 3.95 (ISBN 0-85222-217-3, East & West Lib). Hebrew Pub.

Runes, Dagobert D., ed. The Hebrew Impact on Western Civilization. LC 72-607. 1975. Repr. of 1951 ed. lib. bdg. 43.50x (ISBN 0-8371-6354-4, RUHI). Greenwood.

Scholem, Gershom. From Berlin to Jerusalem: Memories of My Youth. LC 79-25678. (Illus.). 1980. 12.95 (ISBN 0-8052-3738-0). Schocken.

Soloff, Mordecai, et al. Jewish Life. (Sacred Hebrew Ser.). (Illus.). 112p. (Orig.). 1980. pap. 3.50 (ISBN 0-86628-000-6). Ridgefield Pub.

Steinberg, Milton. Making of the Modern Jew. 1948. 4.95x (ISBN 0-87441-115-7). Behrman.

Van Den Haag, Ernest. The Jewish Mystique. LC 76-56974. 1977. 8.95 (ISBN 0-8128-1267-0); pap. 4.95 (ISBN 0-8128-2189-0). Stein & Day.

Voegelin, Eric. Order & History, 4 vols. Incl. Vol. 1. Israel & Revelation. LC 56-11670. xxvi, 534p. 1956 (ISBN 0-8071-0818-9); Vol. 2. The World of the Polis. LC 57-11670. xvii, 390p. 1957 (ISBN 0-8071-0819-7); Vol. 3. Plato & Aristotle. LC 57-11670. xviii, 384p. 1957 (ISBN 0-8071-0820-0); Vol. 4. The Ecumenic Age. LC 56-11670. 1975 (ISBN 0-8071-0081-1). 19.95x ea. La State U Pr.

Weinreich, Uriel. Yidish Launiversitah: Hebrew Edition of "College Yiddish". Bahat, S. & Goldwasser, M., trs. (Illus.). 1977. pap. text ed. write for info. (ISBN 0-914512-35-8). Yivo Inst.

Wigoder, Geoffrey, ed. Jewish Art & Civilization. LC 72-80540. (Illus.). 290p. 1972. boxed ed 95.00 (ISBN 0-8027-0394-1). Walker & Co.

JEWS–COMMERCE

Bloom, Herbert I. Economic Activities of the Jews of Amsterdam in the Seventeenth & Eighteenth Centuries. LC 70-91036. 1969. Repr. of 1937 ed. 15.00 (ISBN 0-8046-0646-3). Kennikat.

Yogev, Gedalia. Diamonds & Coral: Anglo-Dutch Jews & Eighteenth-Century Trade. LC 78-301. 1978. text ed. 28.50x (ISBN 0-8419-0369-7). Holmes & Meier.

JEWS–CONVERTS TO CHRISTIANITY

see Converts from Judaism

JEWS–COURTS

see Courts, Jewish

JEWS–CUSTOMS

see Jews–Social Life and Customs

JEWS–DANCING

see Dancing–Jews

JEWS–DIASPORA

see also Jews–Migrations

Comay, Joan. The Diaspora Story. 19.95 (ISBN 0-394-51644-3). Random.

--The Diaspora Story: The Epic of the Jewish People Among the Nations. 1981. 19.95 (ISBN 0-394-51644-3). Random.

Gellin, William. Moved by Love. LC 80-52633. 272p. 1980. 10.00 (ISBN 0-88400-070-2). Shengold.

Vago, Bela. Jewish Assimilation in Modern Times. 300p. 1981. lib. bdg. 25.75x (ISBN 0-86531-030-0). Westview.

JEWS–DICTIONARIES AND ENCYCLOPEDIAS

see also Judaism–Dictionaries

Ausubel, Nathan. Book of Jewish Knowledge. (Illus.). 1962. 17.95 (ISBN 0-517-09746-X). Crown.

Ben-Asher, Naomi & Leaf, Hayim, eds. Junior Jewish Encyclopedia. 9rev. ed. LC 79-66184. (Illus.). (gr. 9-12). 1979. 14.95 (ISBN 0-88400-066-4). Shengold.

Birnbaum, Philip. Encyclopedia of Jewish Concepts. rev. ed. 1979. pap. 7.95 (ISBN 0-88482-930-8, Sanhedrin Pr). Hebrew Pub.

Bridger & Wolk. The New Jewish Encyclopedia. rev. ed. LC 76-15251. (Illus.). 542p. 1976. 14.95 (ISBN 0-87441-120-3). Behrman.

Encyclopaedia Judaica Editors. Encyclopaedic Dictionary of Judaica. (Illus.). 700p. 1974. 29.95 (ISBN 0-7065-1412-2). L Amiel Pub.

Harkavy, Alexander. Harkavy's Complete Dictionary. 1123p. 1898. 12.50 (ISBN 0-88482-666-X). Hebrew Pub.

Isaacson, Ben. Dictionary of the Jewish Religion. Gross, David C., ed. 208p. 1980. 12.95 (ISBN 0-89961-002-1). SBS Pub.

Jacobs, Joseph. Jewish Encyclopedia: A Guide to Its Contents. 1964. 10.00x (ISBN 0-87068-068-4). Ktav.

Landman, Isaac. Universal Jewish Encyclopedia & Readers Guide, 11 Vols. 1944. 250.00x (ISBN 0-87068-077-3). Ktav.

Markowitz, Endel. The Encyclopedia Yiddishanica. LC 79-89973. (Illus.). 450p. 1980. 19.95 (ISBN 0-933910-02-9); pap. write for info. (ISBN 0-933910-04-5). Haymark.

Rockland, Mae S. & Rockland, Michael A. The Jewish Yellow Pages: A Directory of Goods and Services. LC 76-26524. (Illus.). 1976. pap. 7.95 (ISBN 0-8052-0554-3). Schocken.

Roth, Cecil & Widoger, Geoffrey, eds. The Concise Jewish Encyclopedia. (Orig.). 1980. pap. 8.95 (ISBN 0-452-00526-4, F526, Mer). NAL.

Singer, I., ed. The Jewish Encyclopedia, 12 vols. 1976. Set. lib. bdg. 998.95 (ISBN 0-8490-2101-4). Gordon Pr.

Singer, Isidor. Jewish Encyclopedia, 12 Vols. 1964. Repr. of 1904 ed. Set. 250.00x (ISBN 0-87068-104-4). Ktav.

JEWS–DIETARY LAWS

Cohn, Jacob. The Royal Table: Outline of the Dietary Laws of Israel. 5.95 (ISBN 0-87306-098-9). Feldheim.

Freedman, Seymour E. The Book of Kashrut. LC 74-113870. 1977. pap. 4.95 (ISBN 0-8197-0019-3). Bloch.

Grossman, Bob. The New Chinese-Kosher Cookbook. rev. ed. LC 77-79248. (Illus.). 1978. 5.95 (ISBN 0-8397-6308-5); pap. 4.95 (ISBN 0-8397-6309-3). Eriksson.

Grunfeld. The Jewish Dietary Laws, 2 vols. 1973. Set. 31.50x (ISBN 0-685-32987-9). Bloch.

Munk, Michael L. & Munk, Eli, eds. Shechita: Religious & Historical Research on the Method of Slaughter. (Illus.). 1976. 9.95 (ISBN 0-87306-992-7). Feldheim.

Simon, Bennet. Kosher Konnection: The los Angeles Dining Guide to the Best of Kosher, Delis & Natural Foods. LC 79-67671. (Orig.). 1980. pap. 4.95 (ISBN 0-935618-00-7). Rossi Pubns.

Smith, Hyman. Why Kosher? LC 79-63927. (Illus.). 1980. 8.50 (ISBN 0-533-04289-5). Vantage.

JEWS–DISPERSION

see Jews–Diaspora

JEWS–DIVORCE

see Divorce (Jewish Law)

JEWS–EDUCATION

see also Jewish Religious Education

Dushkin, Alexander M. Jewish Education: Selected Writings. 180p. 1980. text ed. 9.25x (ISBN 965-223-353-6, Pub. by Magnes Israel). Humanities.

Gorelick, Sherry. City College & the Jewish Poor: Education in New York, 1880-1924. (Illus.). 264p. 1981. 14.95 (ISBN 0-8135-0905-X). Rutgers U Pr.

Krantzler, Harold I. Your Congregation's Adult Jewish Education Committee: A Manual. 1978. pap. 2.50 (ISBN 0-8074-0013-0, 181730). UAHC.

Szajkowski, Zosa. Jewish Education in France, Seventeen Eighty-Nine to Nineteen Thirty-Nine. (Conference on Jewish Social Studies Monograph Ser.: No. 2). 1980. 10.00x (ISBN 0-910430-01-2). Columbia U Pr.

Waskow, Arthur I. Godwrestling. LC 78-54389. 208p. 1980. pap. 4.95 (ISBN 0-8052-0645-0). Schocken.

JEWS–ELECTION, DOCTRINE OF

Lacocque, Andre. But As for Me: The Question of Election for God's People Today. LC 78-71042. 1979. 13.00 (ISBN 0-8042-1172-8). John Knox.

Malgo, Wim. Israel's God Does Not Lie. 3.95 (ISBN 0-686-12824-9). Midnight Call.

Manson, T. W. Only to the House of Israel? Jesus & the Non-Jews. Reumann, John, ed. LC 64-11860. (Facet Bks). 1964. pap. 1.00 (ISBN 0-8006-3005-X, 1-3005). Fortress.

Roth, Samuel. Jews Must Live. 1980. lib. bdg. 69.95 (ISBN 0-8490-3204-0). Gordon Pr.

Sandmel, Samuel. The Several Israels. 1971. 10.00x (ISBN 0-87068-160-5). Ktav.

JEWS–EMIGRATION AND IMMIGRATION

see Jews–Migrations

JEWS–EMPLOYMENT

Quinn, Robert P., et al. The Chosen Few: A Study of Discrimination in Executive Selection. LC 68-64118. 49p. 1968. pap. 4.00 (ISBN 0-87944-058-9). Inst Soc Res.

--The Decision to Discriminate: A Study of Executive Selection. LC 68-65536. 162p. 1968. pap. 6.00 (ISBN 0-87944-062-7). Inst Soc Res.

Rogoff, Abraham M. Formative Years of the Jewish Labor Movement in the United States: (1890-1900) LC 78-21163. 1979. Repr. of 1945 ed. lib. bdg. 14.75x (ISBN 0-313-20881-6, ROFJ). Greenwood.

JEWS–ETHICS

see Ethics, Jewish

JEWS–EXODUS

see Exodus, the

JEWS–FASTS AND FEASTS

see Fasts and Feasts–Judaism

JEWS–FOLK-LORE

see Folk-Lore, Jewish

JEWS–GENEALOGY

Alperin, Richard J. Rimmonim Bells: Ten Generations of the Behrman, Drucker, Hahn, Stockler & Sztynberg Families Plus Ten Related Lines. LC 80-65119. (Illus.). 249p. 1980. 39.95x (ISBN 0-9603932-0-X). Junius Inc.

Chamberlain, Mildred & Clarenbach, Laura. Descendants of Hugh Mosher & Rebecca Maxson Through Seven Generations. LC 80-51754. 808p. 1980. 22.50 (ISBN 0-9604142-0-7). M M Chamberlain.

Horowitz, Inge W. & Windmueller, Ida. Windmueller Family Chronicle. 2nd rev. ed. Windmueller, Ida & Grausz, Ilse, trs. from Ger. (Illus.). 320p. Date not set. price not set (ISBN 0-9605242-0-7). Windmill Bks.

Kaganoff, Benzion C. A Dictionary of Jewish Names & Their History. LC 77-70277. 264p. 1980. pap. 5.95 (ISBN 0-8052-0643-4). Schocken.

Kurzweil, Arthur. From Generation to Generation: How to Trace Your Jewish Genealogy & Personal History. LC 79-26466. (Illus.). 1980. 12.95 (ISBN 0-688-03600-7, Quill). Morrow.

JEWS–HISTORY

see also Chronology, Jewish

Adler, Morris. Jewish Heritage Reader. LC 65-17330. 1965. pap. 5.95 (ISBN 0-8008-4376-2). Taplinger.

Agus, Jacob B. The Evolution of Jewish Thought. LC 73-2185. (The Jewish People; History, Religion, Literature Ser.). Repr. of 1959 ed. 22.00 (ISBN 0-405-05251-0). Arno.

Agus, Jacob B., et al, eds. The Jewish People: History, Religion, Literature, 41 bks. 1973. Set. 816.50 (ISBN 0-405-05250-2). Arno.

Ahimaaz Ben Paltiel. Chronicle of Ahimaaz. Salzman, Marcus, tr. LC 79-158233. (Columbia University Oriental Studies: No. 18). Repr. of 1924 ed. 15.75 (ISBN 0-404-50508-2). AMS Pr.

Angel, Marc D., ed. Studies in Sephardic Culture: The David N. Barocas Memorial Volume. LC 79-92737. (Illus.). 190p. 1980. 15.00 (ISBN 0-87203-090-3). Hermon.

Arkin, Marcus. Aspects of Jewish Economic History. LC 75-2847. (Illus.). 271p. 1975. 6.95 (ISBN 0-8276-0063-1, 379). Jewish Pubn.

Ausubel, Nathan. Pictorial History of the Jewish People. rev. ed. (Illus.). 1953. 11.95 (ISBN 0-517-09757-5). Crown.

Bamberger, David. My People: Abba Eban's History of the Jews, Vol. II. (Illus.). 1979. pap. 6.50x (ISBN 0-87441-280-3). Behrman.

--My People: Abba Eban's History of the Jews, Vol. I. LC 77-10667. (Illus.). 1978. pap. text ed. 6.95x (ISBN 0-87441-263-3). Behrman.

Barkai, Meyer, ed. Twentieth Century Universal Jewish Encyclopedia. (Illus., Orig.). 1981. pap. write for info. (ISBN 0-86649-024-8). Twentieth Century.

Baron, Salo W. A Social & Religious History of the Jews, 17 vols. 2nd, rev. & enl. ed. Incl. Vol. 1. Ancient Times to the Beginning of the Christian Era. 1952 (ISBN 0-231-08838-8); Vol. 2. Ancient Times: Christian Era: the First Five Centuries. 1952 (ISBN 0-231-08839-6); Vol. 3. High Middle Ages: Heirs of Rome & Persia. 1957 (ISBN 0-231-08840-X); Vol. 4. High Middle Ages: Meeting of the East & West. 1957 (ISBN 0-231-08841-8); Vol. 5. High Middle Ages: Religious Controls & Dissensions. 1957 (ISBN 0-231-08842-6); Vol. 6. High Middle Ages: Laws, Homilies & the Bible. 1958 (ISBN 0-231-08843-4); Vol. 7. High Middle Ages: Hebrew Language & Letters. 1958 (ISBN 0-231-08844-2); Vol. 8. High Middle Ages: Philosophy & Science. 1958 (ISBN 0-231-08845-0); Vol. 9. Late Middle Ages & Era of European Expansion, 1200-1650: Under Church & Empire. 1965 (ISBN 0-231-08846-9); Vol. 10. Late Middle Ages & Era of European Expansion, 1200-1650: On the Empire's Periphery. 1965 (ISBN 0-231-08847-7); Vol. 11. Late Middle Ages & Era of European Expansion, 1200-1650: Citizen or Alien Conjurer. 1967 (ISBN 0-231-08848-5); Vol. 12. Late Middle Ages & Era of European Expansion, 1200-1650: Economic Catalyst. 1967 (ISBN 0-231-08849-3); Vol. 13. Late Middle Ages & Era of European Expansion, 1200-1650: Inquisition, Renaissance & Reformation. 1969 (ISBN 0-231-08850-7); Vol. 14. Late Middle Ages & Era of European Expansion, 1200-1650: Catholic Restoration & Wars of Religion. 1969 (ISBN 0-231-08851-5); Vol. 15. Late Middle Ages & Era of European Expansion, 1200-1650: Resettlement & Exploration. 1973 (ISBN 0-231-08852-3); Index (ISBN 0-231-08877-9). LC 52-404. 27.00x ea. Columbia U Pr.

Baron, Salo W. & Barzilay, Isaac, eds. Jubilee Volume: The American Academy for Jewish Research, 2 vols. 710p. 1980. text ed. 50.00x (ISBN 0-231-05150-6). Columbia U Pr.

Baron, Salo W., et al. Economic History of the Jews. Gross, Nachum, ed. LC 75-534. (Illus.). 1976. pap. 5.50 (ISBN 0-8052-0538-1). Schocken.

Ben-Gurion, David, ed. The Jews in Their Land. LC 66-11274. 405p. 1974. 9.95 (ISBN 0-385-06152-8). Doubleday.

Ben Horin, Meir. Studies & Essays in Honor of Abraham A. Neuman. 1962. 35.00x (ISBN 0-685-13745-7, Pub. by Dropsie U Pr). Ktav.
Ben-Sasson, H. H. Trial & Achievement: Currents in Jewish History. (Illus.). 327p. 1975. 10.95 (ISBN 0-7065-1420-3). Bloch.
Ben-Sasson, Haim, et al. History of the Jewish People. (Illus.). 1040p. 1976. 45.00 (ISBN 0-674-39730-4). Harvard U Pr.
Bialik, Hayyim N. And It Came to Pass. 281p. 1938. 4.95 (ISBN 0-88482-887-5). Hebrew Pub.
Biberfeld, Philip. Universal Jewish History, 3 vols. Vol. 1. 5.95 (ISBN 0-87306-052-0, Spero Foundation); Vol. 2. 7.95 (ISBN 0-87306-053-9); Vol. 3. 9.95 (ISBN 0-87306-054-7); Set. 22.00 (ISBN 0-87306-051-2). Feldheim.
Bloch, Abraham. Day-by-Day in Jewish History. Date not set. 12.50 (ISBN 0-88482-919-7, Sanhedrin Pr). Hebrew Pub.
Bloch, Abraham P. The Biblical & Historical Backround of Jewish Customs & Ceremonies. Date not set. 20.00x (ISBN 0-87068-658-5). Ktav.
Brown, Jonathan M. Modern Challenges to Halakhah. 1969. pap. 3.95x (ISBN 0-87655-509-1). Whitehall Co.
Carmilly-Weinberger, Moshe. Censorship & Freedom of Expression in Jewish History. LC 77-79828. 1979. pap. 7.50 (ISBN 0-87203-088-1). Hermon.
--Censorship & Freedom of Expression in Jewish History. (LC 77-079828). 1977. 14.50 (ISBN 0-87203-070-9). Hermon.
Chazan, Robert. Medieval Jewish Life: Studies from the Proceedings of the American Academy for Jewish Research. 1974. 35.00x (ISBN 0-87068-253-9). Ktav.
Dawidowicz, Lucy S. The War Against the Jews 1933-1945. LC 74-15470. (Illus.). 480p. 1975. 15.00 (ISBN 0-03-013661-X). HR&W.
Dimont, Max I. The Indestructible Jews. 480p. 1973. pap. 1.95 (ISBN 0-451-07594-3, J7594, Sig). NAL.
Dresner, Samuel H. Between the Generations. pap. 1.75 (ISBN 0-686-02376-5). Hartmore.
Dubnow, Semen M. Jewish History: An Essay in the Philosophy of History. LC 72-5481. (Select Bibliographies Reprint Ser.). 1972. Repr. of 1903 ed. 16.00 (ISBN 0-8369-6903-0). Arno.
Dubnow, Simon. A History of the Jews in Russia & Poland, 3 vols. rev. ed. 1973. 45.00x (ISBN 0-87068-217-2). Ktav.
Duker, A. G. Studies in Polish-Jewish History & Relations. 35.00x (ISBN 0-87068-293-8). Ktav.
Eban, Abba. My People: A History of the Jews. 1968. 25.00 (ISBN 0-394-41431-4). Random.
--My People: The Story of the Jews. LC 68-27328. (Illus.). 1968. 25.00 (ISBN 0-87441-294-3). Behrman.
Edersheim, Alfred. History of the Jewish Nation. 3rd, rev. ed. (Twin Brooks Ser.). 1978. pap. 7.95 (ISBN 0-8010-3335-7). Baker Bk.
Eisenberg, Azriel. Jewish Historical Treasures. LC 68-57432. (Illus.). 1969. 10.00 (ISBN 0-8197-0076-2). Bloch.
Eisenberg, Azriel, ed. Earth, Be Not Silent. 300p. 1979. 12.50 (ISBN 0-88482-911-1, Sanhedrin Pr); pap. 6.95 (ISBN 0-88482-927-8, Sanhedrin Pr). Hebrew Pub.
Eisenberg, Azriel, et al, eds. Eyewitnesses to American Jewish History: 1492 - 1793, Pt. 1. 1976. pap. 5.00 (ISBN 0-686-77106-0, 144060); tchrs'. guide 5.00 (ISBN 0-8074-0019-X, 204061). UAHC.
Ellison, H. L. From Babylon to Bethlehem: The People of God from the Exile to the Messiah. LC 78-71044. (Orig.). 1979. pap. 4.95 (ISBN 0-8042-0034-3). John Knox.
Epstein, Morris. A Picture Parade of Jewish History. 1977. pap. 3.95 (ISBN 0-8197-0024-X). Bloch.
Fackenheim, Emil L. The Jewish Return into History: Reflections in the Age of Auschwitz & a New Jerusalem. LC 77-87861. 312p. 1980. pap. 6.95 (ISBN 0-8052-0649-3). Schocken.
Farmer, William R. Maccabees, Zealots & Josephus. LC 73-15052. 239p. 1974. Repr. of 1956 ed. lib. bdg. 20.25x (ISBN 0-8371-7152-0, FAMA). Greenwood.
Fast, Howard. The Jews: Story of a People. 1978. pap. 2.25 (ISBN 0-440-14444-2). Dell.
Finkelstein, Louis. The Jews: Their History, Culture & Religion, 2 vols. 3rd ed. LC 79-4139. 1979. Repr. of 1960 ed. Set. lib. bdg. 125.00x (ISBN 0-313-21242-2, FIJE). Greenwood.
Finkelstein, Louis, ed. The Jews, Vol. 1: Their History. 4th ed. LC 74-107615. 1970. pap. 6.95 (ISBN 0-8052-0271-4). Schocken.
--The Jews, Vol. 2: Their Religion & Culture. 4th ed. LC 74-107615. 1971. pap. 7.95 (ISBN 0-8052-0272-2). Schocken.
--The Jews, Vol. 3: Their Role in Civilization. 4th ed. LC 74-107615. 1971. pap. 7.95 (ISBN 0-8052-0273-0). Schocken.
Fleg, Edmond. Why I Am a Jew. Wise, Louise W., tr. from Fr. LC 75-4124. 1975. pap. 2.95 (ISBN 0-8197-0009-6). Bloch.
Ford, Henry. The International Jew. 1978. pap. 5.00x (ISBN 0-911038-45-0). Noontide.
The Foundations of Jewish Life: Three Studies. LC 73-2197. (The Jewish People; History, Religion, Literature Ser.). 29.00 (ISBN 0-405-05263-4). Arno.
Franzos, Karl E. The Jews of Barnow. facsimile ed. Macdowall, M. W., tr. from Ger. LC 74-27985. (Modern Jewish Experience Ser.). (Eng.). 1975. Repr. of 1883 ed. 22.00x (ISBN 0-405-06712-7). Arno.
Gill, John, ed. Notices of the Jews & Their Country by the Classic Writers of Antiquity. LC 70-97281. (Judaica Ser). 180p. 1972. Repr. of 1872 ed. lib. bdg. 15.00x (ISBN 0-8371-2603-7, GINJ). Greenwood.
Glanz, Rudolf. Aspects of the Social, Political, & Economic History of the Jews in America. 25.00x (ISBN 0-87068-463-9). Ktav.
Goldberg, Hirsh. The Jewish Connection. LC 75-35914. 1976. 8.95 (ISBN 0-8128-1924-1). Stein & Day.
Goldberg, Israel. Israel: A History of the Jewish People. LC 72-162629. 715p. 1949. Repr. lib. bdg. 29.50x (ISBN 0-8371-6196-7, GOIS). Greenwood.
Gordon, A. D. Selected Essays. LC 73-2201. (The Jewish People; History, Religion, Literature Ser.). Repr. of 1938 ed. 19.00 (ISBN 0-405-05266-9). Arno.
Graetz, Heinrich. The Structure of Jewish History & Other Essays. 20.00x (ISBN 0-87068-466-3); pap. 8.95x (ISBN 0-685-56206-9). Ktav.
Grayzel, Solomon. History of the Jews. rev. ed. (Illus.). 1968. Repr. of 1947 ed. 7.95 (ISBN 0-8276-0142-5, 190). Jewish Pubn.
--A History of the Jews. 768p. 1975. pap. 2.95 (ISBN 0-451-61746-0, ME1746, Ment). NAL.
Heathcote, A. W. From the Death of Solomon to the Captivity of Judah. (London Divinity Ser.). 140p. 1977. pap. 4.50 (ISBN 0-227-67462-6). Attic Pr.
--From the Exile to Herod the Great. (London Divinity Ser). 140p. 1964. 4.50 (ISBN 0-227-67658-0). Attic Pr.
--Israel to the Time of Solomon. (London Divinity Ser). 1965. Repr. of 1960 ed. 4.50 (ISBN 0-227-67505-3). Attic Pr.
Hebrew Union College Annual, 38 Vols. 1969. 650.00x (ISBN 0-87068-065-X). Ktav.
Heller, Celia S. On the Edge of Destruction: Jews of Poland Between the Two World Wars. LC 79-24645. 384p. 1980. pap. 8.95 (ISBN 0-8052-0651-5). Schocken.
Hengel, Martin. Jews, Greeks & Barbarians: Aspects of the Hellenization of Judaism in the Pre-Christian Period. Bowden, John, tr. from Ger. LC 80-8051. 192p. 1980. 9.95 (ISBN 0-8006-0647-7, 1-647). Fortress.
Hoffman, Lawrence A. The Canonization of the Synagogue Service. LC 78-62972. (Studies in Judaism & Christianity in Antiquity: No. 4). 1979. text ed. 15.95 (ISBN 0-268-00727-6). U of Notre Dame Pr.
Howe, Irving & Libo, Kenneth. How We Lived: A Documentary History of Immigrant Jews in America, 1880-1930. (Illus.). 1981. pap. 6.95 (ISBN 0-452-25269-5, Z5269, Plume). NAL.
Huber, Friedrich. Jahwe, Juda und Dieanderen Voelkerbeim Propheten Jesaja. (Beiheft 137 Zur Zeitschrift Fuer die Alttestamentliche Wissenschaft). (Ger.). 1976. 54.50 (ISBN 3-11-005729-8). De Gruyter.
Illustrated History of the Jewish People. LC 72-94297. 1973. 6.95 (ISBN 0-89388-078-7). Okpaku Communications.
Jakobovits, Immanuel. The Timely & the Timeless: Jews, Judaism & Society in a Storm-Tossed Decade. 432p. 1977. 19.50x (ISBN 0-85303-189-4, Pub. by Vallentine Mitchell England). Biblio Dist.
The Jewish Quarterly Review, 1889-1908, 21 Vols. 1966. 400.00x (ISBN 0-87068-070-6). Ktav.
Josephus. Works of Josephus, 9 vols. Warmington, E. H., ed. Incl. Vol. 1. Life; Against Apion (ISBN 0-674-99205-9); Vols 2-3. Jewish War. Vol. 2, Bks 1-3. (ISBN 0-674-99223-7); Vol. 3, Bks. 4-7, Index To Vols. 2 & 3. (ISBN 0-674-99232-6); Vols 4-9. Antiquities. Vol. 4, Bks 1-4. (ISBN 0-674-99267-9); Vol. 5, Bks 5-8. (ISBN 0-674-99310-1); Vol. 6, Bks 9-11. (ISBN 0-674-99360-8); Vol. 7, Bks 12-14. (ISBN 0-674-99402-7); Vol. 8, Bks 15-17. (ISBN 0-674-99451-5); Vol. 9, Bks 18-20, General Index. (ISBN 0-674-99477-9). (Loeb Classical Library: No. 186, 203, 210, 242, 281, 326, 365, 410, 433). 11.00x ea. Harvard U Pr.
Josephus, Flavius. Complete Works of Josephus, 4 vols. Set. 39.95 (ISBN 0-686-12376-X). Church History.
--Great Roman-Jewish War: A.D. 66-70. Whiston, tr. 8.00 (ISBN 0-8446-0729-0). Peter Smith.
--Life & Work of Flavius Josephus. Whiston, William, tr. 1957. 16.95 (ISBN 0-03-037015-9). HR&W.
--Second Jewish Commonwealth: From the Maccabaean Rebellion to the Outbreak of the Judaeo-Roman War. Glatzer, Nahum N., ed. Whitson, William, tr. LC 77-148714. Orig. Title: Antiquities, Books 12-20. 1971. 12.50x (ISBN 0-8052-3395-4); pap. 4.50 (ISBN 0-8052-0296-X). Schocken.
Jospe, Raphael & Wagner, Stanley M. Great Schisms in Jewish History. Date not set. 17.50x (ISBN 0-87068-711-5). Ktav.
Kahler, Erich, et al. Jews Among the Nations: Three Essays. Bd. with The Jews and the Arabs in Palestine. LC 67-16279. vii, 149p. pap. 3.95 (ISBN 0-8044-6333-6). Ungar.
Kedourie, Elie, ed. The Jewish World: History & Culture of the Jewish People. LC 78-31363. (Illus.). 1979. 37.50 (ISBN 0-8109-1154-X). Abrams.
Keller, Werner. Diaspora: The Post-Biblical History of the Jews. LC 68-24393. 1971. pap. 4.95 (ISBN 0-15-626033-6, HB217, Harv). HarBraceJ.
Kellett, E. E. A Short History of the Jews. 1973. lib. bdg. 20.00 (ISBN 0-8414-5556-2). Folcroft.
Kitov, Eliyahu. The Book of Our Heritage, 3 vols. Bulman, Nathan, tr. from Hebrew. Orig. Title: Sefer HaToda'ah. 1978. 29.50 (ISBN 0-87306-151-9); pap. 17.95 (ISBN 0-87306-157-8). Feldheim.
Klaperman, Gilbert & Klaperman, Libby. The Story of the Jewish People, 4 vols. Incl. Vol. 1. From Creation to the Second Temple. pap. text ed. 3.95x (ISBN 0-87441-207-2); Vol. 2. From the Building of the Second Temple Through the Age of the Rabbis. pap. text ed. 3.95x (ISBN 0-87441-208-0); Vol. 3. From the Golden Age in Spain Through the European Emancipation. pap. text ed. 4.50x (ISBN 0-87441-209-9); Vol. 4. From the Settlement of America Through Israel Today. pap. text ed. 4.50x (ISBN 0-87441-210-2). LC 56-12175. (Illus.). (gr. 5-9). 1974. Behrman.
Kobler, Franz. Letters of Jews Through the Ages, Vol. 2. 1978. pap. 5.95 (ISBN 0-85222-213-0, East & West Lib). Hebrew Pub.
Kobler, Franz, ed. Letters of Jews Through the Ages, Vol. 1. 1978. pap. 5.95 (ISBN 0-85222-212-2, East & West Lib). Hebrew Pub.
Kochan, Lionel. The Jew & His History. LC 76-56105. 1977. 15.00x (ISBN 0-8052-3650-3). Schocken.
Kosovsky, Binyamin. Otzar Leshon Ha-Tannaim-Sifra-Tarat Kohanim, 4 vols. 1967. Set. 60.00x (ISBN 0-685-31426-X, Pub. by Jewish Theol Seminary). Ktav.
Kranzler, David. My Jewish Roots: A Practical Guide to Tracing & Recording Your Genealogy & Family History. (Illus.). 1979. pap. 7.95 (ISBN 0-87203-074-1). Hermon.
Kurzman, Dan. The Bravest Battle. 1980. pap. 2.50 (ISBN 0-523-40182-5). Pinnacle Bks.
Lewittes, M. Religious Foundations of the Jewish State: The Concept & Practice of Jewish Statehood from Biblical Times to the Modern State of Israel. 20.00x (ISBN 0-87068-433-7). Ktav.
Lieberman, Saul. Hellenism in Jewish Palestine. 1962. 15.00x (ISBN 0-685-31433-2, Pub. by Jewish Theol Seminary). Ktav.
Lods, Adolphe. Prophets & the Rise of Judaism. Hooke, S. H., tr. LC 77-109772. (Illus.). 1971. Repr. of 1937 ed. lib. bdg. 25.75x (ISBN 0-8371-4262-8, LOPR). Greenwood.
McCarthy, Dennis J. Kings & Prophets. (Contemporary College Theology Ser). 1968. pap. 3.95x (ISBN 0-02-820480-8). Glencoe.
Maier, Johann. Geschichte der juedischen Religion: Von der Zeit Alexanders des Grossen bis zur Aufklaerung. Mit einem Ausblick auf das 19.-20. Jahrhundert. LC 72-77437. xx, 641p. (Ger.). 1972. 36.25x (ISBN 3-11-002448-9). De Gruyter.
Malcioln, Jose. Como los Hebreos Llgaron a Ser Judios. Cordova, Jackie, ed. Malcioln, Jose, tr. from Eng. (Illus.). 1979. pap. 2.00 (ISBN 0-932756-06-9). Polis Pr.
Malino, Frances & Albert, Phyllis C., eds. Essays in Modern Jewish History: A Tribute to Ben Halpern. LC 80-70585. 500p. 1981. 20.00 (ISBN 0-8386-3095-2). Fairleigh Dickinson.
Mann, Jacob. Texts & Studies in Jewish History & Literature, 2 Vols. rev. ed. 1970. Set. 79.50x (ISBN 0-87068-085-4). Ktav.
Marcus, Jacob R. Jew in the Medieval World: A Source Book: 315-1791. LC 60-8666. (Temple Books). 1969. pap. text ed. 6.95x (ISBN 0-689-70133-0, T7). Atheneum.
--Studies in American Jewish History. 1969. 10.00x (ISBN 0-87820-003-7, Pub. by Hebrew Union). Ktav.
Margolis, Max & Marx, Alexander. History of the Jewish People. LC 70-90074. (Temple Books). 1969. pap. text ed. 7.95x (ISBN 0-689-70134-9, T8). Atheneum.
Mauro, Phillip. God's Pilgrims. 192p. 1969. pap. 3.00 (ISBN 0-87509-090-7). Chr Pubns.
Mendelssohn, Sidney. The Jews of Asia: Especially in the Sixteenth & Seventeenth Centuries. LC 77-87612. Repr. of 1920 ed. 21.00 (ISBN 0-404-16436-6). AMS Pr.
Meyer, Michael A., ed. Ideas of Jewish History. LC 73-19960. (Library of Jewish Studies). 384p. 1974. 6.95x (ISBN 0-87441-202-1). Behrman.
Moore, Deborah D. B'nai B'rith & the Challenge of Ethnic Leadership. LC 81-906. (Modern Jewish History Ser.). 292p. 1981. 18.95x (ISBN 0-87395-480-7). State U NY Pr.
Neher, Andre. The Exile of the World: From the Silence of the Bible to the Silence of Auschwitz. 224p. 1980. 17.95 (ISBN 0-8276-0176-X, 465). Jewish Pubn.
Noth, Martin. History of Israel: Biblical History. 2nd ed. LC 58-5195. 1960. 15.00x (ISBN 0-06-066310-3, HarpR). Har-Row.
Patai, Raphael. The Vanished World of Jewry: Pictures by Eugene Rosow & Vivian Kleiman. (Illus.). 192p. 1981. 17.95 (ISBN 0-02-595120-3). Macmillan.
Plastaras, James. Creation & Convenant. 1968. pap. text ed. 3.95 (ISBN 0-685-07626-1, 82470). Glencoe.
Potok, Chaim. Wanderings: Chaim Potok's History of the Jews. LC 78-54915. 1978. 25.00 (ISBN 0-394-50110-1). Knopf.
Rappaport, Solomon. Jew & Gentile: The Philo-Semitic Aspect. LC 79-84854. 1979. 17.50 (ISBN 0-8022-2354-0). Philos Lib.
Reddish, Robert O., Jr. The Burning Burning Bush. LC 73-85938. (Illus.). 1974. 11.95 (ISBN 0-686-05480-6). Rorge Pub Co.
Rischin, Moses, ed. Modern Jewish Experience, 59 vols. 1975. Set. 1643.00x (ISBN 0-405-06690-2). Arno.
Rosenzweig, Rachel. Solidaritae Mit Den Leidenden in Judentum. (Studia Judaica: Vol. 10). 1978. 54.50x (ISBN 3-11-005939-8). De Gruyter.
Roth, Cecil. A History of the Jews: From Earliest Times Through the Six Day War. rev. ed. LC 74-121042. 1970. pap. 7.50 (ISBN 0-8052-0009-6). Schocken.
--Short History of the Jewish People. rev. ed. LC 70-107212. (Illus.). 1970. Repr. of 1969 ed. 14.95 (ISBN 0-87677-004-9). Hartmore.
--A Short History of the Jewish People. rev. ed. (Illus.). 1978. pap. 7.95 (ISBN 0-85222-229-7, East & West Lib). Hebrew Pub.
Rothstein, Raphael. The Story of Masada. (Illus.). 296p. 1981. 10.95 (ISBN 0-89961-012-9). SBS Pub.
Sachar, A. L. History of the Jews. rev. ed. (gr. 6 up). 1967. 20.00 (ISBN 0-394-42871-4); pap. text ed. 14.95 (ISBN 0-394-30482-9). Knopf.
Schauss, Hayyim. Lifetime of a Jew: Throughout the Ages of Jewish History. rev. ed. (Illus.). (YA) (gr. 9 up). 1976. pap. 5.50 (ISBN 0-8074-0096-3, 383473). UAHC.
Schwab, Moise. Repertoire des Articles Relatifs a l'Histoire et a la Litterature Juives Parus dans les Periodiques De 1665 a 1900. rev. ed. (Fr.). 1971. 59.50 (ISBN 0-87068-163-X). Ktav.
Schweitzer, F. History of the Jew Since the First Century A.D. 1971. pap. 1.95 (ISBN 0-02-089260-8). Macmillan.
Shapiro, H. The Jewish People: A Biological History. 1978. lib. bdg. 59.95 (ISBN 0-685-62297-5). Revisionist Pr.
Shapiro, Harry L. The Jewish People: A Biological History. LC 76-5851. (Race Question in Modern Science Ser.). 84p. 1976. Repr. of 1960 ed. lib. bdg. 915.00 (ISBN 0-8371-8783-4, SHJE). Greenwood.
Shneiderman, S. L. The River Remembers. LC 77-93935. (Illus.). 1978. 8.95 (ISBN 0-8180-0821-0). Horizon.
Simon, Marcel. Jewish Sects at the Time of Jesus. Farley, James H., tr. from Fr. LC 66-25265. 192p. 1980. pap. 5.95 (ISBN 0-8006-0183-1, 1-183). Fortress.
Simonsohn, S. History of the Jews in the Duchy of Mantua. 35.00x (ISBN 0-87068-341-1). Ktav.
Singer, Betty J. Friends of the Jews. (Illus.). 1976. pap. text ed. 2.75 (ISBN 0-917400-01-1). Options.
Sputz, David. Generations of Our Sages. 176p. 1980. 7.50 (ISBN 0-9604312-0-9). Sputz.
Stein, Siegfried & Loewe, Raphael, eds. Studies in Jewish Religious & Intellectual History. LC 77-7294. 480p. 1980. 37.50x (ISBN 0-8173-6925-2). U of Ala Pr.
Stern, Shirley. Exploring Jewish History. Date not set. 6.95x (ISBN 0-87068-651-8). Ktav.
Stone, Michael E. Scriptures, Sects & Visions: A Profile of Judaism from Ezra to the Jewish Revolts. LC 78-54151. 160p. 1980. 11.95 (ISBN 0-8006-0641-8, 1-641). Fortress.
Sutton, Joseph A. Magic Carpet: Aleppo in Flatbush: The Story of a Unique Ethnic Jewish Community. LC 79-65516. (Illus.). 336p. 1980. text ed. 19.95x (ISBN 0-686-27080-0). Thayer-Jacoby.

Szjakowski, Soza. Jews, War & Communism. Incl. Vol. 1. The Attitude of American Jews to World War I, the Russian Revolution of 1917, and Communism, 1917 to 1945. 1972. 25.00x (ISBN 0-87068-182-6); Vol. 2. 1974. 25.00x (ISBN 0-87068-239-3). Ktav.
Uchill, Ida L. Pioneers, Peddlers, & Tsadikim: The Story of the Jews in Colorado. 2nd ed. LC 57-57817. 327p. 1979. pap. 10.00 (ISBN 0-9604468-0-X). Uchill.
Universal Jewish History: The Exodous, Vol. 4. Date not set. 8.95 (ISBN 0-686-76273-8). Feldheim.
Usque, Samuel. Samuel Usque's Consolation for the Tribulations of Israel. Cohen, Martin A., tr. LC 77-86706. 1977. pap. 5.95 (ISBN 0-8276-0095-X, 408). Jewish Pubn.
Ussher, Arland. The Magic People. 4.95 (ISBN 0-8159-6200-2). Devin.
Waagenaar, Sam. The Pope's Jews. (Illus.). 500p. 1974. 22.50 (ISBN 0-912050-49-7, Library Pr). Open Court.
Writings on Jewish History: A Selected Annotated Bibliography. 32p. 1974. pap. 0.75 (ISBN 0-87495-029-5). Am Jewish Comm.

JEWS–HISTORY–BIBLIOGRAPHY

Mauro, Phillip. God's Pilgrims. 192p. 1969. pap. 3.00 (ISBN 0-87509-090-7). Chr Pubns.
Wolf, Hannie. Child of Two Worlds. (Illus.). 156p. 1979. 10.00 (ISBN 0-931068-02-9). Purcells.

JEWS–HISTORY–CHRONOLOGY

Kellett, E. E. A Short History of the Jews. 1973. lib. bdg. 20.00 (ISBN 0-8414-5556-2). Folcroft.
Wacholder, Ben Z. Essays on Jewish Chronology & Chronography. Date not set. cancelled (ISBN 0-87068-261-X). Ktav.

JEWS–HISTORY–JUVENILE LITERATURE

Charry, Elias & Segal, Abraham. The Eternal People. (Illus.). 448p. (gr. 9-11). 7.50x (ISBN 0-8381-0206-9, 10-206). United Syn Bk.
Gersh, Harry, et al. Story of the Jew. rev. ed. LC 64-22514. (Illus.). (gr. 8-11). 1965. 5.95x (ISBN 0-87441-019-3). Behrman.
Harlow, Jules. Lessons from Our Living Past. LC 72-2055. (Illus.). 128p. (gr. 4-6). 1972. text ed. 6.95x (ISBN 0-87441-085-1). Behrman.
Pessin, Deborah. Jewish People, 3 Vols. (Illus.). 1951-53. pap. 4.25x ea. Vol. I (ISBN 0-8381-0182-8). Vol. II (ISBN 0-8381-0185-2). Vol. III (ISBN 0-8381-0187-9). pap. 2.50x ea. pupils' activity bks. Vol. I Activity Bk (ISBN 0-8381-0183-6). Vol. II Activity Bk (ISBN 0-8381-0186-0). Vol. III Activity Bk (ISBN 0-8381-0188-7). United Syn Bk.
Rossel, Seymour. Journey Through Jewish History, Vol. 1. Kozodoy, Neil, ed. (Illus.). 128p. (gr. 4-5). 1981. pap. text ed. 5.95x (ISBN 0-87441-335-4). Behrman.
Samuels, Ruth. Pathways Through Jewish History. (Illus.). (gr. 7-10). 1967. pap. 8.00x (ISBN 0-685-13741-4). Ktav.
Wengrov, Charles. The Twelve Tribes of Israel. (Illus.). (ps-3). 1960. pap. 0.99 (ISBN 0-914080-64-4). Shulsinger Sales.

JEWS–HISTORY–PHILOSOPHY

Kann, Kenneth. Joe Rapoport: The Life of a Jewish Radical. (Illus.). 320p. 1980. 17.50x (ISBN 0-87722-208-8). Temple U Pr.
Karp, Abraham J., ed. For Modern Minds & Hearts. pap. 1.95 (ISBN 0-685-23813-X). Prayer Bk.
Kastein, Josef. History & Destiny of the Jews. 1977. Repr. of 1936 ed. lib. bdg. 25.00 (ISBN 0-8495-3003-2). Arden Lib.
Maritain, Jacques. Le Mystere d'Israel. 260p. 1965. 9.95 (ISBN 0-686-56358-1). French & Eur.

JEWS–HISTORY–TO 586 B.C.

see also Exodus, The

Albright, William F. Biblical Period from Abraham to Ezra: A Historical Survey. pap. 3.50x (ISBN 0-06-130102-7, TB102, Torch). Har-Row.
Bright, John. Covenant & Promise: The Prophetic Understanding of the Future in Pre-Exilic Israel. LC 76-13546. 1976. 10.00 (ISBN 0-664-20752-9). Westminster.
Brueggemann, Walter. In Man We Trust: The Neglected Side of Biblical Faith. LC 72-1761. 144p. 1972. 7.50 (ISBN 0-8042-0199-4). John Knox.
Gottwald, Norman K. The Tribes of Yahweh: A Sociology of the Religion of Liberated Israel, 1250-1050 B.C. LC 78-24333. 1979. 29.95 (ISBN 0-88344-498-4); pap. 19.95 (ISBN 0-88344-499-2). Orbis Bks.
Kotker, Norman. The Israelites. (Emergence of Man Ser.). (Illus.). 1975. 9.95 (ISBN 0-8094-1294-2); lib. bdg. avail. (ISBN 0-685-72431-X). Time-Life.
Kraeling, Emil G. Aram & Israel Or, Aramaeans in Syria & Mesopotamia. LC 18-9797. (Columbia University. Oriental Studies: No. 13). Repr. of 1918 ed. 17.00 (ISBN 0-404-50503-1). AMS Pr.
Lindsay, Gordon. The Decline & Fall of Israel & Judah. (Old Testament Ser.). 1.25 (ISBN 0-89985-153-3). Christ Nations.
--Gideon & the Early Judges. (Old Testament Ser.). 1.25 (ISBN 0-89985-135-5). Christ Nations.
Meek, Theophile J. Hebrew Origins. 1960. 8.00 (ISBN 0-8446-2572-8). Peter Smith.
Rattey, B. K. A Short History of the Hebrews: From the Patriarchs to Herod the Great. (Illus.). 1976. pap. 9.50x (ISBN 0-19-832121-X). Oxford U Pr.
Robinson, T. H. Decline & Fall of the Hebrew Kingdoms. LC 74-137284. Repr. of 1926 ed. 21.50 (ISBN 0-404-05376-9). AMS Pr.
Velikovsky, Immanuel. Ages in Chaos. 1952. 12.95 (ISBN 0-385-04897-1). Doubleday.
--Peoples of the Sea. LC 52-5224. 1977. 10.00 (ISBN 0-385-03389-3). Doubleday.
Weippert, Manfred. Settlement of the Israelite Tribes in Palestine. Martin, James, tr. from Ger. (Studies in Biblical Theology, 2nd Ser.: No. 21). (Orig.). 1970. pap. 8.95x (ISBN 0-8401-3071-6). Allenson-Breckinridge.
Wellhausen, Julius. Prolegomena to the History of Ancient Israel. 9.00 (ISBN 0-8446-3147-7). Peter Smith.

JEWS–HISTORY–TO 70 A.D.

Bruce, Frederick F., ed. Israel & the Nations. LC 63-22838. 1963. pap. 5.95 (ISBN 0-8028-1450-6). Eerdmans.
Eller, Meredith F. The Beginnings of the Christian Religion: A Guide to the History & Literature of Judaism & Christianity. 1958. 9.50x (ISBN 0-8084-0392-3); pap. 4.50x (ISBN 0-8084-0393-1, P1). Coll & U Pr.
Grant, Michael. Jews in the Roman World. LC 72-11118. 1973. lib. rep. ed. 20.00x (ISBN 0-684-15494-3, ScribT). Scribner.
Hoenig, Sidney B. The Era of the Second Temple. new ed. LC 74-79271. Orig. Title: Korot Am Olam. 480p. 1974. 10.00 (ISBN 0-88400-009-5). Shengold.
Long Years of Hope. 1968. pap. text ed. 0.85 (ISBN 0-570-03531-7, 14-1516); tchr's man. 1.15 (ISBN 0-570-03532-5, 14-1517). Concordia.
Ringgren, Helmer. Israelite Religion. Green, David E., tr. from Ger. LC 66-10757. 408p. 1975. pap. 6.95 (ISBN 0-8006-1121-7, 1-1121). Fortress.
Smith, George A. Jerusalem: The Topography, Economics & History from the Ancient Times to A. D. 70, 2 Vols. in 1. rev. ed. (Library of Biblical Studies Ser). 1970. 35.00x (ISBN 0-87068-105-2). Ktav.
Zeitlin, Solomon. Studies in the Early History of Judaism. Vol. 3. 35.00x (ISBN 0-87068-278-4); Vol. 4. 25.00 (ISBN 0-87068-454-X). Ktav.
--Studies in the Early History of Judaism, Vol. 1. 1973. 35.00x (ISBN 0-87068-208-3). Ktav.

JEWS–HISTORY–586 B.C.-70 A.D.

see also Maccabees

Bickerman, Elias. From Ezra to the Last of the Maccabees: Foundations of Post-Biblical Judaism. 1962. pap. 2.95 (ISBN 0-8052-0036-3). Schocken.
Gowan, Donald E. Bridge Between the Testaments: Reappraisal of Judaism from the Exile to the Birth of Christianity. 2nd ed. LC 76-49996. (Pittsburgh Theological Monographs: No. 14). 1980. text ed. 13.95 (ISBN 0-915138-47-6). Pickwick.
Guignebert, Charles. Jewish World in the Time of Jesus. 1959. 6.00 (ISBN 0-8216-0033-8). Univ Bks.
Ironside, H. A. Four Hundred Silent Years. pap. 2.75 (ISBN 0-87213-361-3). Loizeaux.
Josephus. Jerusalem & Rome: The Writings of Josephus. Glatzer, Nahum N., ed. 8.00 (ISBN 0-8446-2341-5). Peter Smith.
Josephus, Flavius. Hegesippi Qui Dicitur Historiae, Libri 5. Ussani, V., ed. (Corpus Scriptorum Ecclesiasticorum Latinorum Ser: Vol. 66). 1932. pap. 25.50 (ISBN 0-384-27880-9). Johnson Repr.
--Jewish War. Williamson, Geoffrey A., tr. (Classics Ser.). (Orig.). 1959. pap. 4.95 (ISBN 0-14-044090-9). Penguin.
Pearl, Chaim & Brookes, Reuben. The Guide to Jewish Knowledge. rev. ed. LC 75-187866. 123p. 1973. 4.95 (ISBN 0-87677-046-4). Hartmore.
Pfeiffer, Charles F. Between the Testaments. pap. 3.95 (ISBN 0-8010-6873-8). Baker Bk.
Pfeiffer, Robert H. History of New Testament Times. LC 77-138125. 561p. 1972. Repr. of 1949 ed. lib. bdg. 23.00x (ISBN 0-8371-3559-1, PFNT). Greenwood.
Radin, Max. The Jews Among the Greeks & Romans. LC 73-2224. (The Jewish People; History, Religion, Literature Ser.). Repr. of 1915 ed. 25.00 (ISBN 0-405-05286-3). Arno.
Rattey, B. K. A Short History of the Hebrews: From the Patriarchs to Herod the Great. (Illus.). 1976. pap. 9.50x (ISBN 0-19-832121-X). Oxford U Pr.
Rhoads, David M. Israel in Revolution, 6-74 C.E. A Political History Based on the Writings of Josephus. LC 75-36452. 208p. 1976. 9.95 (ISBN 0-8006-0442-3, 1-442); pap. 5.95 (ISBN 0-8006-1442-9, 1-1442). Fortress.
Russell, D. S. Between the Testaments. LC 77-74742. 176p. 1960. pap. 3.95 (ISBN 0-8006-1856-4, 1-1856). Fortress.
--The Jews from Alexander to Herod. 1967. pap. 11.50x (ISBN 0-19-836913-1). Oxford U Pr.
Schurer, Emil. History of the Jewish People in the Age of Jesus Christ (175 B.C.-A.D. 135, 2 vols. Vermes, Geza, et al, eds. Vol. 1, Repr. Of 1973 Ed., 632p. 46.50x (ISBN 0-567-02242-0); Vol. 2, Repr. Of 1979 Ed., 608p. 46.50x (ISBN 0-567-02243-9). Attic Pr.
--A History of the Jewish People in the Time of Jesus. Glatzer, Nahum N., ed. LC 61-8195. 1961. pap. 5.95 (ISBN 0-8052-0008-8). Schocken.
Tcherikover, Victor. Hellenistic Civilization & the Jews. Applebaum, S., tr. LC 59-8518. (Temple Bk). 1970. pap. 5.95 (ISBN 0-689-70248-5, T22). Atheneum.
The Time Was Right. LC 72-97604. 128p. 1973. 2.95 (ISBN 0-8054-8119-2). Broadman.
Wardle, William L. The History & Religion of Israel. LC 78-11741. (The Clarendon Bible, Old Testament: Vol. I). (Illus.). 1979. Repr. of 1942 ed. lib. bdg. 20.50x (ISBN 0-313-21016-0, WAHR). Greenwood.
Whitley, Charles F. The Exilic Age. LC 74-29795. 160p. 1975. Repr. of 1958 ed. lib. bdg. 15.00 (ISBN 0-8371-8002-3, WHEA). Greenwood.

JEWS–HISTORY–70-1789

Albright, William F. Archaeology of Palestine. rev. ed. 8.00 (ISBN 0-8446-0003-2). Peter Smith.
Bachrach, Bernard S. Jews in Barbarian Europe. 1977. 7.50x (ISBN 0-87291-088-1). Coronado Pr.
Berliner, Abraham. Aus dem Leben der Deuschen Juden im Mittelalter. Katz, Steven, ed. LC.79-7127. (Jewish Philosophy, Mysticism & History of Ideas). 1980. Repr. of 1900 ed. lib. bdg. 12.00x (ISBN 0-405-12241-1). Arno.
Blumenkranz, Bernhard. Juifs et Chretiens Dans le Monde Occidental 430-1096. (Etudes Juives: No. 2). 1960. pap. 29.50 (ISBN 90-2796-111-5). Mouton.
Chazan, Robert. Church, State & Jew in the Middle Ages. new ed. Kozodoy, Neal, ed. LC 78-27221. (Library of Jewish Studies). 1979. pap. text ed. 9.95x (ISBN 0-87441-302-8). Behrman.
Katz, S. Jews in the Visigothic & Frankish Kingdoms of Spain & Gaul. 1937. 14.00 (ISBN 0-527-01697-7). Kraus Repr.
Mann, Jacob. The Jews in Egypt & in Palestine Under the Fatimid Caliphs, 2 Vols. in 1. rev. ed. (Library of Jewish Classics Ser). 1970. 45.00x (ISBN 0-87068-024-2). Ktav.
Marcus, Jacob R. The Jew in the Medieval World: A Source Book, 315-1791. LC 71-97295. 504p. 1975. Repr. of 1938 ed. lib. bdg. 21.50x (ISBN 0-8371-2619-3, MAJM). Greenwood.
Meisl, Josef. Haskalah: Geschichte der Aufklarungsbewegung unter den Juden in Russland. Katz, Stephen, ed. LC 79-7147. (Jewish Philosophy, Mysticism & History of Ideas Ser.). 1980. Repr. of 1919 ed. lib. bdg. 18.00x (ISBN 0-405-12277-2). Arno.
Parkes, James W. The Jew in the Medieval Community. 456p. 1976. pap. 9.75 (ISBN 0-87203-060-1). Hermon.
Poliak, Abraham N. Khazaria: The History of a Jewish Kingdom in Europe. 1978. lib. bdg. 49.95 (ISBN 0-685-62302-5). Revisionist Pr.
Rhoads, David M. Israel in Revolution, 6-74 C.E. A Political History Based on the Writings of Josephus. LC 75-36452. 208p. 1976. 9.95 (ISBN 0-8006-0442-3, 1-442); pap. 5.95 (ISBN 0-8006-1442-9, 1-1442). Fortress.
Roth, Cecil. Gleanings: Essays in Jewish History, Letters & Art. 1967. 7.95 (ISBN 0-8197-0178-5). Bloch.
--The Jews in the Renaissance. LC 59-8516. (Illus.). 1978. pap. 5.25 (ISBN 0-8276-0103-4, 321). Jewish Pubn.
Schurer, Emil. History of the Jewish People in the Age of Jesus Christ (175 B.C.-A.D. 135, 2 vols. Vermes, Geza, et al, eds. Vol. 1, Repr. Of 1973 Ed., 632p. 46.50x (ISBN 0-567-02242-0); Vol. 2, Repr. Of 1979 Ed., 608p. 46.50x (ISBN 0-567-02243-9). Attic Pr.
Steinberg, Milton. Making of the Modern Jew. 1948. 4.95x (ISBN 0-87441-115-7). Behrman.
Szarmach, Paul E., ed. Aspects of Jewish Culture in the Middle Ages. LC 77-29046. (Illus.). 1979. 30.00 (ISBN 0-87395-165-4). State U NY Pr.
Vetulani, A. The Jews of Medieval Poland. 1978. lib. bdg. 59.95 (ISBN 0-685-62298-3). Revisjonist Pr.
Yerushalmi, Y. H. The Lisbon Massacre of 1506 & the Royal Image in the Shebet Yehuda. (Hebrew Union College Annual Supplements: Vol. 1). 7.50x (ISBN 0-87820-600-0, HUC Pr). Ktav.
Zimmer, Eric. Jewish Synods in Germany During the Late Middle Ages (1286-1603) Date not set. 15.00x (ISBN 0-87068-730-1). Ktav.

JEWS–HISTORY–1789-

Adler, Cyrus & Margalith, Aaron M. With Firmness in the Right: American Diplomatic Action Affecting Jews, 1840-1945. Davis, Moshe, ed. LC 77-70651. (America & the Holy Land Ser.). 1977. Repr. of 1946 ed. lib. bdg. 30.00x (ISBN 0-405-10222-4). Arno.
Asch, Sholom. Kiddush Ha-Shem: An Epic of 1648. facsimile ed. Learsi, Rufus, tr. LC 74-27960. (Modern Jewish Experience Ser.). 1975. Repr. of 1926 ed. 14.00x (ISBN 0-405-06691-0). Arno.
Chazan, Robert & Raphael, Marc L., eds. Modern Jewish History: A Source Reader. LC 74-9131. 395p. 1974. pap. text ed. 9.95x (ISBN 0-8052-0462-8). Schocken.
Cholawski, Shalom. Soldiers from the Ghetto: Jewish Armed Resistance in the East, 1941-1945. LC 78-75300. 1980. 9.95 (ISBN 0-498-02382-6). A S Barnes.
Dobroszycki, Lucjan & Kirshenblatt-Gimblett, Barbara. Image Before My Eyes: A Photographic History of Jewish Life in Poland, 1864-1939. LC 75-35448. (Illus.). 1979. pap. 12.50 (ISBN 0-8052-0634-5). Schocken.
Eisenberg, Azriel, et al, eds. Eyewitnesses to American Jewish History: East European Immigration 1881-1920, Pt. 3. (Illus.). 1978. pap. 5.00 (ISBN 0-8074-0017-3, 144061); tchrs'. guide 5.00 (ISBN 0-8074-0021-1, 204063). UAHC.
--Eyewitnesses to American Jewish History: The German Immigration 1800-1875, Pt. 2. (Illus.). 1977. pap. 5.00 (ISBN 0-8074-0016-5, 144059); tchrs'. guide 5.00 (ISBN 0-8074-0020-3, 204062). UAHC.
Grayzel, Solomon. History of the Contemporary Jews from 1900 to the Present. LC 60-15542. (Temple Books). 1969. pap. text ed. 4.95x (ISBN 0-689-70080-6, T3). Atheneum.
Handler, Andrew. Blood Libel at Tiszaeszlar. (East European Monograph: No. 68). 256p. 1980. 20.00x (ISBN 0-914710-62-1). East Eur Quarterly.
Jakobovits, Immanuel. The Timely & the Timeless. 1977. 15.95 (ISBN 0-85303-189-4). Bloch.
Katz, Jacob. Out of the Ghetto: The Social Background of Jewish Emancipation, 1770-1870. 1978. pap. 6.50 (ISBN 0-8052-0601-9). Schocken.
--Tradition & Crisis: Jewish Society at the End of the Middle Ages. LC 61-9168. 1971. pap. 5.95 (ISBN 0-8052-0316-8). Schocken.
Katz, Jacob, ed. The Role of Religion in Modern Jewish History. 10.00x (ISBN 0-87068-297-0, Pub. by an Academic Inst). Ktav.
Kayserling, Meyer. Christopher Columbus & the Participation of Jews in the Spanish & Portugese Discoveries. 189p. 1980. Repr. of 1894 ed. lib. bdg. 25.00 (ISBN 0-8482-1443-9). Norwood Edns.
Klausner, Carla L. & Schultz, Joseph P. From Destruction to Rebirth: The Holocaust & the State of Israel. LC 78-62262. 1978. pap. text ed. 11.25 (ISBN 0-8191-0574-0). U Pr of Amer.
LaZebnik, Edith. Such a Life. LC 78-759. 1978. 8.95 (ISBN 0-688-03280-X). Morrow.
Levin, Nora. While Messiah Tarried: Jewish Socialist Movements, 1871-1917. LC 75-7769. (Illus.). 1979. pap. 10.95 (ISBN 0-8052-0616-7). Schocken.
Marcus, Jacob R. Communal Sick-Care in the German Ghetto. pap. 9.95 (ISBN 0-87820-202-1). Ktav.
Meisl, Josef. Haskalah: Geschichte der Aufklarungsbewegung unter den Juden in Russland. Katz, Stephen, ed. LC 79-7147. (Jewish Philosophy, Mysticism & History of Ideas Ser.). 1980. Repr. of 1919 ed. lib. bdg. 18.00x (ISBN 0-405-12277-2). Arno.
Mendes-Flohr, Paul R. & Reinharz, Jehuda. The Jew in the Modern World: A Documentary History. 1980. 25.00 (ISBN 0-19-502631-4). Oxford U Pr.
Parkes, James W. Emergence of the Jewish Problem, 1878-1939. Repr. of 1946 ed. lib. bdg. 15.00 (ISBN 0-8371-2794-7, PJPR). Greenwood.
Sachar, Howard M. Course of Modern Jewish History. rev ed. 1977. pap. 5.95 (ISBN 0-440-51538-6, Delta). Dell.
Steinberg, Lucien. The Jews Against Hitler. 1978. pap. 8.50 (ISBN 0-86033-061-3). Gordon-Cremonesi.
Weber, Robert & Bertram, Fred. An Epic in Sculpture: The Medallic History of the Jewish People. (Illus.). 180p. 1974. 27.50 (ISBN 0-686-10364-5). Judaic Heritage.
Weinstein, Gregory. The Ardent Eighties: Reminiscences of an Interesting Decade. facsimile ed. LC 74-29529. (Modern Jewish Experience Ser.). (Illus.). 1975. Repr. of 1928 ed. 16.00x (ISBN 0-405-06753-4). Arno.

JEWS–HISTORY, JUVENILE LITERATURE

see Jews–History–Juvenile Literature

JEWS–INTELLECTUAL LIFE

see also Jewish Learning and Scholarship

Crenshaw, James L. Studies in Ancient Israelite Wisdom. 1974. 39.50x (ISBN 0-87068-255-5). Ktav.

Goldsmith, Emanuel S. Architects of Yiddishism at the Beginning of the Twentieth Century: A Study in Jewish Cultural History. LC 73-2894. 309p. 1976. 18.00 (ISBN 0-8386-1384-5). Fairleigh Dickinson.

Klein, Dennis B. Jewish Origins of the Psychoanalytic Movement. 218p. 1981. 26.95 (ISBN 0-03-058642-9). Praeger.

Stein, Siegfried & Loewe, Raphael, eds. Studies in Jewish Religious & Intellectual History. LC 77-7294. 480p. 1980. 37.50x (ISBN 0-8173-6925-2). U of Ala Pr.

Wistrich, Robert S. Revolutionary Jews from Marx to Trotsky. LC 76-12066. (Illus.). 254p. 1976. text ed. 19.50x (ISBN 0-06-497806-0). B&N.

JEWS-KINGS AND RULERS

Johnson, Aubrey R. Sacral Kingship in Ancient Israel. rev. ed. 1967. 18.00 (ISBN 0-7083-0344-7). Verry.

Lindsay, Gordon. The Early Kings of Israel. (Old Testament Ser.). 1.25 (ISBN 0-89985-147-9). Christ Nations.

--The Early Kings of Judah. (Old Testament Ser.). 1.25 (ISBN 0-89985-146-0). Christ Nations.

JEWS-LANGUAGES

see also Hebrew Language; Yiddish Language

Bunis, David M. A Guide to Reading & Writing Judezmo. 49p. 1975. soft cover 5.00 (ISBN 0-917288-01-7). ADELANTRE.

Rayfield, J. R. Languages of a Bilingual Community. LC 73-106457. (Janua Linguarum, Ser. Practica: No. 77). 1970. pap. text ed. 25.00x (ISBN 90-2790-730-7). Mouton.

JEWS-LAW

see Jewish Law

JEWS-LEARNING AND SCHOLARSHIP

see Jewish Learning and Scholarship

JEWS-LEGENDS

see Legends, Jewish

JEWS-LITERATURE

see Hebrew Literature

JEWS-LITURGY AND RITUAL

see also Chants (Jewish); Cultus, Jewish; Worship (Judaism)

Book of Life - Sefer Hachaim. (Heb, & Eng). 15.00 (ISBN 0-87559-102-7). Shalom.

Chanover, Hyman. Haggadah for the School. (Illus.). 1964. pap. 1.75x (ISBN 0-8381-0175-5). United Syn Bk.

Conner, Kevin J. Feasts of Israel. (Illus.). 122p. 1980. pap. 5.95 (ISBN 0-914936-42-5). Bible Pr.

Day of Joy. (Heb. & Eng.). 7.50 (ISBN 0-87559-103-5). Shalom.

Donin, Hayim H. To Pray As a Jew. LC 80-50554. 384p. 1980. 15.00 (ISBN 0-465-08628-4). Basic.

Garfiel, Evelyn. The Service of the Heart: Guide to the Jewish Prayer Book. 1957. 6.95 (ISBN 0-498-07135-9, Yoseloff). A S Barnes.

Gavin, F. Jewish Antecedents of the Christian Sacraments. 1929. 10.00x (ISBN 0-87068-056-0). Ktav.

Gilbert, Arthur. The Passover Seder. (Illus.). 1965. pap. 2.25x (ISBN 0-87068-504-X). Ktav.

Glatzer, Nahum N., ed. Passover Haggadah: Including Readings on the Holocaust: With English Translation, Introduction & Commentary. 3rd ed. LC 69-10846. (Illus., Bilingual ed). 1979. pap. 2.95 (ISBN 0-8052-0624-8). Schocken.

Heinemann, Joseph. Prayer in the Talmud: Forms & Patterns. (Studia Judaica: Vol. 9). 1977. 60.50x (ISBN 3-11-004289-4). De Gruyter.

Hertz, Joseph H. Authorized Daily Prayer Book. (Eng. & Heb.). 1948. 17.50x (ISBN 0-8197-0094-0). Bloch.

Hirsch, Samson R. The Hirsch Siddur. Samson Raphael Hirsch Publication Society Staff, tr. from Ger. 1978. 15.00 (ISBN 0-87306-141-1); compact ed 10.00 (ISBN 0-87306-142-X). Feldheim.

Hynes, Arleen. Passover Meal. LC 76-187207. 1972. pap. 1.95 (ISBN 0-8091-1653-7). Paulist Pr.

Kohler, Kaufmann. The Origins of the Synagogue & the Church. Enelow, H. G., ed. LC 73-2213. (The Jewish People; History, Religion, Literature Ser.). Repr. of 1929 ed. 18.00 (ISBN 0-405-05277-4). Arno.

Lamm, Maurice. Jewish Way in Death & Mourning. rev. ed. LC 69-11684. 1972. 5.95 (ISBN 0-8246-0041-X); pap. 4.95 (ISBN 0-8246-0126-2). Jonathan David.

Levin, Meyer. Israel Haggadah. rev. ed. LC 70-99933. (Illus.). 1977. pap. 4.95 (ISBN 0-8109-2040-9). Abrams.

Mann, Jacob. The Bible As Read & Preached in the Old Synagogue, Vol. 1. rev. ed. (Library of Biblical Studies). 1970. 35.00x (ISBN 0-87068-083-8). Ktav.

--The Bible As Read & Preached in the Old Synagogue, Vol. 2. 1968. 39.50 (ISBN 0-685-22512-7). Ktav.

Millgram, Abraham E. Jewish Worship. LC 77-151316. (Illus.). 1971. 10.95 (ISBN 0-8276-0003-8, 179). Jewish Pubn.

Noth, Martin & Anderson, Berhard W. History of Pentateuchal Traditions. LC 80-24937. (Scholars Press Reproductions Ser.). 1981. pap. 17.50 (ISBN 0-89130-446-0). Scholars Pr CA.

Oesterley, William O. The Jewish Background of the Christian Liturgy. 1925. 8.50 (ISBN 0-8446-1329-0). Peter Smith.

--A Short Survey of the Literature of Rabbinical & Medieval Judaism. LC 72-82352. 328p. 1973. Repr. of 1920 ed. lib. bdg. 24.50 (ISBN 0-8337-3944-1). B Franklin.

Olivestone, Ceil & Olivestone, David. Let's Go to Synagogue. (Illus.). 24p. (ps). 1981. 4.95 (ISBN 0-89961-018-8). SBS Pub.

Otzar Hazmiros. (Heb). 7.50 (ISBN 0-87559-089-6); pap. 5.00 (ISBN 0-87559-088-8). Shalom.

Petuchowski, Jakob J. Prayerbook Reform in Europe: The Liturgy of European Liberal & Reform Judaism. LC 68-8262. 1969. 13.50 (ISBN 0-8074-0091-2, 387580, Pub. by World Union). UAHC.

Pollak, Gabriel, ed. Transliterated Haggadah: Passover Haggadah. (Heb, & Eng). deluxe ed. 18.50 leatherette bdg. (ISBN 0-87559-082-9). Shalom.

Pollak, P. S. Halel vZimrah: Commentary in Hebrew on the Passover Haggadah. (Heb). 7.50 (ISBN 0-87559-100-0); pap. 5.00 (ISBN 0-87559-099-3). Shalom.

--Nefesh Hayah: Commentary & Interpretation on the Passover Haggadah with the Haggadah Text. (Heb.). 7.50 (ISBN 0-87559-091-8). Shalom.

Rossel, Seymour. When a Jew Prays. Borowitz, Eugene B. & Chanover, Hyman, eds. LC 73-1233. (Illus.). 192p. (gr. 4-6). 1973. pap. text ed. 6.95x (ISBN 0-87441-093-2). Behrman.

Silverman, Morris. Torah Readings for the Three Festivals. 3.45 (ISBN 0-685-40682-2). Prayer Bk.

Silverman, Morris & Hillel. Tishah B'av Service. pap. 1.95 (ISBN 0-685-40683-0). Prayer Bk.

Silverman, Morris, ed. Passover Haggadah. rev. ed. (Illus.). 1975. 4.95 (ISBN 0-87677-025-1); pap. 2.45 (ISBN 0-87677-029-4). Prayer Bk.

Stavsky, David. For Thou Art with Me: A Manual of Mourning. 1965. pap. 1.50 (ISBN 0-87306-093-8). Feldheim.

Trepp, Leo. The Complete Book of Jewish Observance. LC 79-1352. (Illus.). 1979. 14.95 (ISBN 0-87441-281-1). Behrman.

Waskow, Arthur I. Godwrestling. LC 78-54389. 208p. 1980. pap. 4.95 (ISBN 0-8052-0645-0). Schocken.

Waskow, Arthur L. Freedom Seder: A New Haggadah for Passover. 1970. pap. 1.50 (ISBN 0-03-084681-1). HR&W.

Werner, Eric. The Sacred Bridge. (Music Reprint Ser.). 1979. Repr. of 1959 ed. lib. bdg. 42.50 (ISBN 0-306-79581-7). Da Capo.

--The Sacred Bridge: Liturgical Parallels in Synagogue & Early Church. abr. ed. LC 75-127818. 1970. pap. 4.95 (ISBN 0-8052-0278-1, Pub. by NLB). Schocken.

Wildman, Joshua A. And Let Us Say Amen. Wengrov, Charles, tr. from Hebrew. 1978. pap. 6.95 (ISBN 0-87306-148-9). Feldheim.

JEWS-MARRIAGE

see Marriage-Jews

JEWS-MIGRATIONS

see also Jews-Diaspora; Refugees, Jewish

Berman, Myron. The Attitude of American Jewry Towards East European Jewish Immigration, 1881-1914. Cordasco, Francesco, ed. LC 80-842. (American Ethnic Groups Ser.). 1981. lib. bdg. 50.00x (ISBN 0-405-13406-1). Arno.

Jacobs, Dan N. & Paul, Ellen F., eds. Studies of the Third Wave: Recent Migration of Soviet Jews to the United States. (Replica Edition Ser.). 176p. 1981. lib. bdg. 20.00x (ISBN 0-86531-143-9). Westview.

Mossek, M. Palestine Immigration Policy Under Sir Herbert Samuel: British, Zionist & Arab Attitudes. 197p. 1978. 25.00x (ISBN 0-7146-3096-9, F Cass Co). Biblio Dist.

Panish, Paul. Exit Visa: The Emigration of the Soviet Jews. 1981. 12.95 (ISBN 0-698-11056-0). Coward.

Shulvass, Moses A. From East to West: The Westward Migration of Jews from Eastern Europe During the Seventeenth & Eighteenth Centuries. LC 72-138314. 1971. text ed. 8.95x (ISBN 0-8143-1437-6). Wayne St U Pr.

Weinberg, A. A. Migration & Belonging: A Study in Mental Health & Personal Adjustment in Israel. LC 62-1150. 1961. 22.50x (ISBN 90-247-0511-8). Intl Pubns Serv.

JEWS-MISCELLANEA

Carlinsky, Dan. The Jewish Quiz Book. LC 77-25580. 1979. pap. 3.95 (ISBN 0-385-13013-9). Doubleday.

Elkins, Dov P., ed. Loving My Jewishness: Jewish Self Pride & Self-Esteem. LC 78-58511. softbound 10.00 (ISBN 0-918834-04-X). Growth Assoc.

Kolatch, Alfred J. Jewish Info. Quiz Book. LC 66-30508. 250p. 1980. 9.95 (ISBN 0-8246-0248-X). Jonathan David.

JEWS-MISSION

see Jews-Election, Doctrine of

JEWS-MUSIC

see Music, Jewish

JEWS-NATIONALISM

see Nationalism-Jews

JEWS-OCCUPATIONS

see Jews-Employment

JEWS-PERSECUTIONS

see also Blood Accusation; Holocaust, Jewish (1939-1945); Refugees, Jewish

Adler, Cyrus & Margalith, Aaron M. With Firmness in the Right: American Diplomatic Action Affecting Jews, 1840-1945. Davis, Moshe, ed. LC 77-70651. (America & the Holy Land Ser.). 1977. Repr. of 1946 ed. lib. bdg. 30.00x (ISBN 0-405-10222-4). Arno.

Arendt, Hannah. Eichmann in Jerusalem: A Report of the Banality of Evil. rev ed. 1977. pap. 3.50 (ISBN 0-14-004450-7). Penguin.

Frydland, Rachmiel. When Being Jewish Was a Crime. LC 78-16689. 1978. pap. 3.95 (ISBN 0-8407-5659-3). Nelson.

Graeber, Isacque & Britt, Steuart H. Jews in a Gentile World: The Problem of Anti-Semitism. LC 78-26329. (Illus.). 1979. Repr. of 1942 ed. lib. bdg. 26.50x (ISBN 0-313-20878-6, GRJE). Greenwood.

Historical Views of Judaism: Four Selections. LC 73-2209. (The Jewish People; History, Religion, Literature Ser.). 35.00 (ISBN 0-405-05273-1). Arno.

Lee, Albert. Henry Ford & the Jews. LC 79-3694. 252p. 1980. 12.95 (ISBN 0-8128-2701-5). Stein & Day.

Poliakov, Leon. The History of Anti-Semitism: From the Time of Christ to the Court Jews. Howard, Richard, tr. LC 65-10228. (Illus.). 340p. 1974. pap. 5.95 (ISBN 0-8052-0443-1). Schocken.

--The History of Anti-Semitism, Vol. 2: From Mohammed to the Marranos. Gerardi, Natalie, tr. from Fr. LC 65-10228. 419p. 1974. 15.00 (ISBN 0-8149-0701-6). Vanguard.

Roth, Cecil. Spanish Inquisition. (Orig.). 1964. pap. 4.95 (ISBN 0-393-00255-1, Norton Lib). Norton.

World Committee For The Relief Of The Victims Of German Fascism. The Reichstag Fire Trial: The Second Brown Book of the Hitler Terror. LC 68-9605. 1969. Repr. of 1934 ed. 22.50 (ISBN 0-86527-165-8). Fertig.

JEWS-PHILOSOPHY

see Philosophy, Jewish

JEWS-POLITICAL AND SOCIAL CONDITIONS

see also Jews-Diaspora; Zealots (Jewish Party); Zionism

Abramov, S. Zalman. Perpetual Dilemma: Jewish Religion in the Jewish State. LC 74-5897. 459p. 1976. 20.00 (ISBN 0-8386-1687-9). Fairleigh Dickinson.

Adler, Cyrus & Margalith, Aaron M. With Firmness in the Right: American Diplomatic Action Affecting Jews, 1840-1945. Davis, Moshe, ed. LC 77-70651. (America & the Holy Land Ser.). 1977. Repr. of 1946 ed. lib. bdg. 30.00x (ISBN 0-405-10222-4). Arno.

Banks, Lynne R. Letters to My Israeli Sons: The Story of Jewish Survival. 240p. 1980. 10.95 (ISBN 0-531-09934-2). Watts.

Baron, Salo W. The Jewish Community, 3 vols. LC 74-97269. 1972. Repr. of 1942 ed. Set. lib. bdg. 53.50x (ISBN 0-8371-3274-6, BAJC). Greenwood.

--A Social & Religious History of the Jews, 17 vols. 2nd, rev. & enl. ed. Incl. Vol. 1. Ancient Times to the Beginning of the Christian Era. 1952 (ISBN 0-231-08838-8); Vol. 2. Ancient Times: Christian Era: the First Five Centuries. 1952 (ISBN 0-231-08839-6); Vol. 3. High Middle Ages: Heirs of Rome & Persia. 1957 (ISBN 0-231-08840-X); Vol. 4. High Middle Ages: Meeting of the East & West. 1957 (ISBN 0-231-08841-8); Vol. 5. High Middle Ages: Religious Controls & Dissensions. 1957 (ISBN 0-231-08842-6); Vol. 6. High Middle Ages: Laws, Homilies & the Bible. 1958 (ISBN 0-231-08843-4); Vol. 7. High Middle Ages: Hebrew Language & Letters. 1958 (ISBN 0-231-08844-2); Vol. 8. High Middle Ages: Philosophy & Science. 1958 (ISBN 0-231-08845-0); Vol. 9. Late Middle Ages & Era of European Expansion, 1200-1650: Under Church & Empire. 1965 (ISBN 0-231-08846-9); Vol. 10. Late Middle Ages & Era of European Expansion, 1200-1650: On the Empire's Periphery. 1965 (ISBN 0-231-08847-7); Vol. 11. Late Middle Ages & Era of European Expansion, 1200-1650: Citizen or Alien Conjurer. 1967 (ISBN 0-231-08848-5); Vol. 12. Late Middle Ages & Era of European Expansion, 1200-1650: Economic Catalyst. 1967 (ISBN 0-231-08849-3); Vol. 13. Late Middle Ages & Era of European Expansion, 1200-1650: Inquisition, Renaissance & Reformation. 1969 (ISBN 0-231-08850-7); Vol. 14. Late Middle Ages & Era of European Expansion, 1200-1650: Catholic Restoration & Wars of Religion. 1969 (ISBN 0-231-08851-5); Vol. 15. Late Middle Ages & Era of European Expansion, 1200-1650: Resettlement & Exploration. 1973 (ISBN 0-231-08852-3); Index (ISBN 0-231-08877-9). LC 52-404. 27.00x ea. Columbia U Pr.

Bauer, Yehuda. The Jewish Emergence from Powerlessness. LC 78-25830. 1979. 10.00x (ISBN 0-8020-2328-2); pap. 6.00 (ISBN 0-8020-6354-3). U of Toronto Pr.

Bernards, Solomon S., ed. Who Is a Jew? 64p. 0.75 (ISBN 0-686-74966-9). ADL.

Borochov, Ber. Nationalism & the Class Struggle. LC 70-97268. 205p. 1972. Repr. of 1937 ed. lib. bdg. 15.00x (ISBN 0-8371-2590-1, BONA). Greenwood.

Dresner, Samuel H. Between the Generations: A Jewish Dialogue. new ed. LC 79-172413. 80p. (YA) 1971. pap. 1.75 (ISBN 0-685-24670-1, Hartmore). Prayer Bk.

Elazar, Daniel J., ed. Kinship & Consent. 1980. 28.00x (ISBN 0-686-66008-0, Pub. by Turtledove Pub Ltd Israel). Intl Schol Bk Serv.

Eldad, Israel. The Jewish Revolution: Jewish Statehood. Schmorak, Hannah, tr. LC 79-163739. 184p. 1971. 7.95 (ISBN 0-88400-037-0). Shengold.

Finkelstein, Louis. Jewish Self-Government in the Middle Ages. LC 74-97277. 390p. 1972. Repr. of 1924 ed. lib. bdg. 20.75x (ISBN 0-8371-2598-7, FIJS). Greenwood.

Fishman, Joshua A., ed. Modern Jewish Social History: Selected Essays from YIVO Annual. 1972. 20.00x (ISBN 0-87068-190-7). Ktav.

Glanz, Rudolf. Aspects of the Social, Political, & Economic History of the Jews in America. 25.00x (ISBN 0-87068-463-9). Ktav.

Goldman, Edward A., ed. Jews in a Free Society: Challenges & Opportunities. 12.50x (ISBN 0-87820-112-2). Ktav.

Henkin, Louis. World Politics & the Jewish Condition. LC 70-190130. 1972. 9.95 (ISBN 0-8129-0265-3). Times Bks.

Henriques, Henry S. Jews & the English Law. LC 73-19744. Repr. of 1908 ed. lib. bdg. 17.50x (ISBN 0-678-01323-3). Kelley.

Hentoff, Nat, ed. Black Anti-Semitism & Jewish Racism. LC 70-89955. 1970. pap. 3.75 (ISBN 0-8052-0280-3). Schocken.

Hinton, Clete A. The Camp David Accords. (Orig.). 1980. pap. 2.95 (ISBN 0-89260-173-6). Hwong Pub.

Horowitz, Irving L. Israeli Ecstacies - Jewish Agonies. 240p. 1974. 12.95 (ISBN 0-19-501747-1). Oxford U Pr.

Isaac, Rael J. Party & Politics in Israel: Three Visions of a Jewish State. (Professional Ser.). (Illus.). 256p. 1980. text ed. 22.50x (ISBN 0-582-28196-2). Longman.

Jakobovits, Immanuel. The Timely & the Timeless. 1977. 15.95 (ISBN 0-85303-189-4). Bloch.

Kautsky, Karl. Foundations of Christianity. Hartmann, Jacob W., tr. from Ger. LC 72-81774. 512p. 1972. pap. 7.95 (ISBN 0-85345-262-8, PB-2628). Monthly Rev.

Kolitz, Zvi. Survival for What. LC 70-75761. 1969. 6.50 (ISBN 0-8022-2272-2). Philos Lib.

Lewittes, M. Religious Foundations of the Jewish State: The Concept & Practice of Jewish Statehood from Biblical Times to the Modern State of Israel. 20.00x (ISBN 0-87068-433-7). Ktav.

Liebman, Arthur. Jews & the Left. LC 78-20871. (Contemporary Religious Movements Ser.). 1979. 21.50 (ISBN 0-471-53433-1, Pub. by Wiley-Interscience). Wiley.
Liebman, Charles S. & Tabory, Mala. International Jewish Affairs. 1979. 22.00x (ISBN 965-20-0018-3, Pub by Turtledove Pub Ltd Israel). Intl Schol Bk Serv.
Marcus, Jacob R. Jew in the Medieval World: A Source Book: 315-1791. LC 60-8666. (Temple Books). 1969. pap. text ed. 6.95x (ISBN 0-689-70133-0, T7). Atheneum.
Novack, George. How Can the Jews Survive: A Socialist Answer to Zionism. pap. 0.25 (ISBN 0-87348-090-2). Path Pr NY.
Ruppin, Arthur. The Jewish Fate & Future. Dickes, E. W., tr. LC 76-97300. (Illus.). 386p. 1972. Repr. of 1940 ed. lib. bdg. 16.00x (ISBN 0-8371-2628-2, RUJF). Greenwood.
--The Jews in the Modern World. LC 73-2225. (The Jewish People; History, Religion, Literature Ser.). Repr. of 1934 ed. 27.00 (ISBN 0-405-05287-1). Arno.
Schneid, Hayyim, ed. The Family. LC 73-11760. (Popular Judaica Library). (Illus.). 1974. pap. 3.95 (ISBN 0-8276-0029-1, 341). Jewish Pubn.
Selzer, Michael. Politics & Jewish Purpose. 45p. 1972. pap. 2.50 (ISBN 0-934676-12-7). Greenlf Bks.
Simon, Rita J. Continuity & Change. LC 77-15090. (ASA Rose Monograph Ser.: No. 6). (Illus.). 1978. 19.95 (ISBN 0-521-21938-8); pap. 6.95x (ISBN 0-521-29318-9). Cambridge U Pr.
Sombart, Werner. Jews & Modern Capitalism. LC 79-80240. (Research & Source Works Ser.: No. 366). 1969. Repr. of 1913 ed. 25.50 (ISBN 0-8337-3318-4). B Franklin.
Starr, Joshua. Jews in the Byzantine Empire. LC 88-101218. (Research & Source Works Ser: No. 386). 1970. Repr. of 1939 ed. text ed. 24.00 (ISBN 0-8337-3374-5). B Franklin.
--Romania: The Jewries of the Levant After the Fourth Crusade. 1943. 10.00x (ISBN 0-685-13744-9). Ktav.
Steinberg, Milton. Making of the Modern Jew. 1948. 4.95x (ISBN 0-87441-115-7). Behrman.
Wirth, Louis. Ghetto. LC 56-14116. (Illus.). 1956. pap. 3.95 (ISBN 0-226-90250-1, P7, Phoen). U of Chicago Pr.

JEWS–PRAYER-BOOKS AND DEVOTIONS

Birnbaum, Philip. Hasiddur Hashalem (Daily Prayer Book) 790p. 1964. 9.00 (ISBN 0-88482-045-9). Hebrew Pub.
Central Conference of American Rabbis. A Passover Haggadah. Baskin, Leonard, ed. (Large Format Ser). (Illus.). 1978. pap. 5.95 (ISBN 0-14-004871-5). Penguin.
Dresner, Samuel. Prayer, Humility & Compassion. 4.95 (ISBN 0-686-02387-0). Hartmore.
Eisenberg, Azriel & Eisenbert, Azriel. The Story of the Prayer Book. 4.95x (ISBN 0-686-02375-7). Hartmore.
Feuer, Avrohom C. Tashlich. (Art Scroll Mesorah Ser.). 64p. 1979. 5.95 (ISBN 0-89906-158-3); pap. 3.95 (ISBN 0-89906-159-1). Mesorah Pubns.
Freedman, Jacob. Polychrome Historical Prayerbook: Siddur 'bet Yosef' (Illus.). 400p. Date not set. 75.00 (ISBN 0-686-12113-9). J Freedman Liturgy.
Ginsberg, Leo. The Comprehensive Supplement to the Machzor. LC 72-85803. 1972. pap. 3.95 (ISBN 0-8197-0294-3). Bloch.
Glatzer, Nahum N., ed. Language of Faith: A Selection from the Most Expressive Jewish Prayers. LC 65-14823. 1974. Eng. Language ed. 4.95 (ISBN 0-8052-3559-0); multilingual ed. 10.00 (ISBN 0-8052-3335-0). Schocken.
Greenberg, Sidney & Sugarman, Allan S. Junior Contemporary Prayer Book for the High Holidays. (gr. 3-8). pap. 2.75 (ISBN 0-87677-054-5). Prayer Bk.
Greenberg, Sidney, ed. Contemporary Prayers & Readings. 1972. pap. 3.95 (ISBN 0-87677-050-2). Prayer BK.
Hirsch. Psalms, 2 vols. Date not set. 22.50 (ISBN 0-87306-025-3). Feldheim.
Hoffman, Lawrence, ed. Gates of Understanding. 1977. 4.95 (ISBN 0-916694-43-7). Central Conf.
Jewish Reconstructionist Foundation. The New Haggadah. 3rd rev. ed. Kaplan, Mordecai M., et al, eds. LC 77-16803. (Illus.). 1978. pap. text ed. 3.50x (ISBN 0-87441-304-4). Behrman.
Judaus. The Baal Shem of Michalstadt. Kuttner, Manfred, tr. (gr. 8 up). 1973. 4.95 (ISBN 0-87306-121-7). Feldheim.
Karff, Samuel E. Agada: The Language of Jewish Faith. 15.00 (ISBN 0-87820-114-9). Ktav.
Kimchi on Psalms. Date not set. 7.50 (ISBN 0-686-76493-5). Feldheim.
Lipman, Zev, illus. Baruch Ata Befi Hataf: Illustrated Prayers & Blessings for Young Children. (Illus.). (ps-1). 3.00 (ISBN 0-685-84974-0). Feldheim.
Lissa, Jacob, et al. The Siddur in Three Volumes. 1971. 20.00 set (ISBN 0-914080-39-3). Shulsinger Sales.
Riemer, Jack, ed. New Prayers for the High Holy Days. Kushner, Harold. pap. 2.95 (ISBN 0-87677-059-6). Prayer Bk.
Silverman, Morris. Junior Prayer Book for Sabbath & Festivals. pap. 3.95x (ISBN 0-685-64875-3). Prayer Bk.
--Junior Prayer Book for the High Holidays. pap. 3.95x (ISBN 0-685-64877-X). Prayer Bk.
--Prayers of Consolation. 1972. 3.95 (ISBN 0-87677-062-6); pap. 2.95 (ISBN 0-87677-063-4). Prayer BK.
Silverman, Morris & Arzt, Max. Selihot Service. rev. ed. pap. 1.95 (ISBN 0-685-40684-9). Prayer Bk.
Silverman, Morris & United Synagogue. High Holiday Prayer Book. 8.95 (ISBN 0-87677-051-0); simulated leather 10.00 (ISBN 0-87677-012-X). Prayer Bk.
--Weekday Prayer Book. 4.45 (ISBN 0-685-40680-6); large ed. 17.50 (ISBN 0-685-40681-4). Prayer Bk.
Soloff, Mordecai, et al. Your Siddur. (Sacred Hebrew Ser.). (Illus.). 175p. 1981. pap. 4.95 (ISBN 0-86628-001-4). Ridgefield Pub.
The Standard Siddur-Prayerbook. 1974. 7.50 (ISBN 0-87306-990-0). Feldheim.
Stern, Chaim. Gates of the House. 1977. 6.95 (ISBN 0-916694-35-6). Central Conf.
Stern, Chaim, ed. Gates of Prayer. pulpit ed. 1975. Hebrew 20.00 (ISBN 0-916694-03-8). Central Conf.
--Gates of Prayer for Weekdays & at a House of Mourning. 1975. pap. 2.00 (ISBN 0-916694-04-6). Central Conf.
--Gates of Prayer: The New Union Prayerbook. 1975. English ed. 10.00 (ISBN 0-916694-01-1); Hebrew ed. 10.00 (ISBN 0-916694-00-3). Central Conf.
Strassfeld, Michael. A Shabbat Haggadah for Celebration & Study. LC 80-83430. 124p. 1980. pap. 5.50 (ISBN 0-87495-025-2). Am Jewish Comm.
Union Home Prayerbook. 1951. 4.00 ea. (ISBN 0-916694-19-4); leatherbound 7.00 ea. (ISBN 0-916694-60-7). Central Conf.
Wenger, Eliezer. Brochos Study Guide: Book One. rev. ed. 52p. 1981. pap. 1.25 (ISBN 0-89655-128-8). BRuach HaTorah.
Wengrow, C., tr. The Hafetz Hayyim on the Siddur. 8.95 (ISBN 0-87306-996-X). Feldheim.

JEWS–PRIESTS

see Priests, Jewish

JEWS–RECREATION

Elkins, Dov P. Experiential Programs for Jewish Groups. LC 78-58512. softcover 10.00 (ISBN 0-918834-05-8). Growth Assoc.

JEWS–RELATIONS WITH AFRO-AMERICANS

see Afro-Americans–Relations with Jews

JEWS–RELIGION

see Judaism

JEWS–RELIGIOUS EDUCATION

see Jewish Religious Education

JEWS–RESTORATION

see also Jews–Diaspora; Zionism

Buber, Martin. On Zion: The History of an Idea. LC 72-88533. 1973. 7.00x (ISBN 0-8052-3485-3). Schocken.
Davis, Moshe, ed. Call to America to Build Zion: An Original Anthology. LC 77-70723. (America & the Holy Land Ser.). 1977. lib. bdg. 15.00x (ISBN 0-405-10306-9). Arno.
--Christian Protagonists for Jewish Restoration: An Orginal Anthology. LC 77-70678. (America & the Holy Land Ser.). 1977. lib. bdg. 15.00x (ISBN 0-405-10221-6). Arno.
--Holy Land Missions & Missionaries: An Original Anthology. LC 77-70703. (America & the Holy Land Ser.). (Illus.). 1977. lib. bdg. 15.00x (ISBN 0-405-10259-3). Arno.
Mehdi, M. T., ed. Palestine & the Bible. LC 71-114557. 1971. pap. 3.00 (ISBN 0-911026-06-1). New World Press NY.
Milton, John P. Prophecy Interpreted. LC 60-6437. 1960. 4.50 (ISBN 0-8066-0001-2, 10-5261). Augsburg.

JEWS–RITES AND CEREMONIES

see also Jewish Way of Life; Bar Mitzvah; Confirmation (Jewish Rite); Menorah

Agnon, Shmuel Y. Days of Awe: A Treasury of Tradition, Legends & Learned Commentaries Concerning Rosh Hashanah, Yom Kippur & the Days Between. LC 48-8316. 1965. 7.50x (ISBN 0-8052-3049-1); pap. 5.95 (ISBN 0-8052-0100-9). Schocken.
Batist, Bessie, ed. A Treasure for My Daughter. pap. 3.95 (ISBN 0-8015-7939-2, Hawthorn). Dutton.
Bloch, Abraham P. The Biblical & Historical Backround of Jewish Customs & Ceremonies. Date not set. 20.00x (ISBN 0-87068-658-5). Ktav.
Chanover, Hyman, adapted by. Service for the High Holy Days Adapted for Youth. new ed. LC 72-2058. 192p. (gr. 8up). 1972. pap. 2.95x (ISBN 0-87441-123-8). Behrman.
Chill, Abraham. The Minhagim: The Customs & Ceremonies of Judaism, Their Origins & Rationale. 2nd corrected ed. LC 78-62153. (Illus.). 339p. 1980. 13.95 (ISBN 0-87203-076-8); pap. 8.75 (ISBN 0-87203-077-6). Hermon.
Cohen, Abraham. Sabbath Sermons. 12.50x (ISBN 0-685-01038-4). Bloch.
Cohon, Beryl D. Judaism in Theory & Practice. 3rd rev. ed. LC 68-57021. 1969. write for info. (ISBN 0-8197-0069-X). Bloch.
Dembitz, Lewis N. Jewish Services in Synagogue & Home. facsimile ed. LC 74-27977. (Modern Jewish Experience Ser.). 1975. Repr. of 1898 ed. 30.00x (ISBN 0-405-06706-2). Arno.
De Sola Pool, David & De Sola Pool, Tamar, eds. The Haggadah of Passover. 123p. pap. 2.25 (ISBN 0-685-58310-4). Bloch.
Donin, Hayim. To Be a Jew. LC 72-89175. 1972. 11.95 (ISBN 0-465-08624-1). Basic.
Edidin, Ben M. Jewish Customs & Ceremonies. 178p. 1940. pap. 4.95 (ISBN 0-88482-438-1). Hebrew Pub.
Epstein, Morris. All About Jewish Holidays & Customs. rev. ed. (gr. 5-6). 1969. pap. 5.95x (ISBN 0-87068-500-7). Ktav.
--Pictorial Treasury of Jewish Holidays. (Illus.). (gr. 7 up). 1959. pap. 9.95x (ISBN 0-87068-360-8). Ktav.
Goldin, Hyman E. Jew & His Duties. 246p. 1953. pap. 4.95 (ISBN 0-88482-429-2). Hebrew Pub.
Gutmann, Joseph. Beauty in Holiness: Studies in Jewish Ceremonial Art & Customs. 1970. 35.00x (ISBN 0-87068-012-9). Ktav.
Israel Ministry. What Is a Jew? 1975. 30.00 (ISBN 0-379-13904-9). Oceana.
Klein, I. A Guide to Jewish Religious Practice. (Moreshet Ser: No. 6). 20.00x (ISBN 0-87334-004-3, Pub. by Jewish Theol Seminary). Ktav.
Kolatch, Alfred J. Family Seder. rev. ed. LC 67-17778. (Illus.). 1972. pap. 2.00 (ISBN 0-8246-0132-7). Jonathan David.
Lauterbach, Jacob Z. Studies in Jewish Law, Custom & Folklore. 1970. 17.50x (ISBN 0-87068-013-7) (ISBN 0-685-13747-3). Ktav.
Levi, Shonie B. & Kaplan, Sylvia R. Guide for the Jewish Homemaker. 2nd ed. LC 59-12039. (Illus.). 1965. pap. 4.95 (ISBN 0-8052-0087-8). Schocken.
Marcus, Ralph. Law in the Apocrypha. LC 29-9822. (Columbia University. Oriental Studies: No. 26). Repr. of 1927 ed. 15.00 (ISBN 0-404-50516-3). AMS Pr.
Maslin, Simeon J., ed. Shaarei Mitzvah: Gates of Mitzvah. (Illus.). 1979. 8.95 (ISBN 0-916694-37-2); pap. 4.95 (ISBN 0-916694-53-4). Central Conf.
Max, Moshen. The Way of G-D. (gr. 6-9). 1968. tchrs' guide 2.50x (ISBN 0-87306-103-9); wkbk 1.50x (ISBN 0-87306-104-7). Feldheim.
Reik, Theodor. Ritual: Psychoanalytic Studies. LC 73-2645. (Illus.). 367p. 1975. Repr. of 1946 ed. lib. bdg. 25.25x (ISBN 0-8371-6814-7, RERI). Greenwood.
Reik, Theodore. Ritual. pap. text ed. 5.95 (ISBN 0-8236-8269-2, 025840). Intl Univs Pr.
Rosenau, William. Jewish Ceremonial Institutions & Customs. rev. ed. 3rd. ed. LC 70-78222. (Illus.). 1971. Repr. of 1925 ed. 19.00 (ISBN 0-8103-3402-X). Gale.
Silverman, Morris. Memorial Service at the Cemetery. pap. 0.50 (ISBN 0-685-64878-8). Prayer Bk.
Sperling, Abraham I. Reasons for Jewish Customs & Traditions. Matts, Abraham, tr. LC 68-31711. 1975. 10.00x (ISBN 0-8197-0184-X); pap. 6.95x (ISBN 0-8197-0008-8). Bloch.
Strassfeld, Michael & Strassfeld, Sharon, eds. The Second Jewish Catalog: Sources & Resources. LC 73-11759. (Illus.). 1976. 7.95 (ISBN 0-8276-0084-4, 391). Jewish Pubn.
Strassfeld, Sharon & Green, Cathy. The Jewish Family Book. 320p. (Orig.). 1981. pap. 9.95 (ISBN 0-553-01339-4). Bantam.
Trepp, Leo. The Complete Book of Jewish Observance. LC 79-1352. (Behrman House Book). (Illus.). 370p. 1980. 14.95 (ISBN 0-671-41797-5). Summit Bks.
--The Complete Book of Jewish Observance. LC 79-1352. (Illus.). 1979. 14.95 (ISBN 0-87441-281-1). Behrman.
--History of the Jewish Experience: Eternal Faith, Eternal People. rev. ed. LC 73-3142. Orig. Title: Eternal Faith, Eternal People: a Journey into Judaism. 296p. 1973. pap. text ed. 6.95x (ISBN 0-87441-072-X). Behrman.
Unterman, Alan. Jews: Their Religious Beliefs & Practices. (Library of Religious Beliefs & Practices). 288p. 1981. 22.50 (ISBN 0-7100-0743-4); pap. 13.50 (ISBN 0-7100-0842-2). Routledge & Kegan.
Weisenberg, David H. Jewish Way. (Illus.). 1969. 5.95 (ISBN 0-8158-0026-6). Chris Mass.

JEWS–RITUAL

see Jews–Liturgy and Ritual; Jews–Social Life and Customs

JEWS–SECTS

see Jewish Sects

JEWS–SOCIAL CONDITIONS

see Jews–Political and Social Conditions

JEWS–SOCIAL LIFE AND CUSTOMS

see also Jewish Way of Life

Abbott, Lyman. The Life & Literature of the Ancient Hebrews. 1976. Repr. of 1901 ed. 39.00 (ISBN 0-403-05671-3, Regency). Scholarly.
Abrahams, Israel. Jewish Life in the Middle Ages. LC 58-11933. (Temple Books). 1969. pap. text ed. 7.95x (ISBN 0-689-70001-6, T1). Atheneum.
Baer, Jean. The Self-Chosen: Our Crowd Is Dead-Long Live Our Crowd! LC 81-66962. 320p. 1982. 12.95 (ISBN 0-87795-330-9). Arbor Hse.
Baron, Salo W. A Social & Religious History of the Jews: Vol. 17, Byzantines, Mameluks & Marghribians. 1980. 30.00x (ISBN 0-231-08853-1). Columbia U Pr.
Ben-Dasan, Isaiah. The Japanese & the Jews. Gage, Richard L., tr. from Japanese. LC 72-78951. 193p. 1981. pap. 4.95 (ISBN 0-8348-0158-2). Weatherhill.
Berger, Elmer. Memoirs of an Anti-Zionist Jew. 1981. lib. bdg. 59.95 (ISBN 0-686-73184-0). Revisionist Pr.
Berliner, Abraham. Aus dem Leben der Deuschen Juden im Mittelalter. Katz, Steven, ed. LC 79-7127. (Jewish Philosophy, Mysticism & History of Ideas). 1980. Repr. of 1900 ed. lib. bdg. 12.00x (ISBN 0-405-12241-1). Arno.
Bloch, Abraham P. The Biblical & Historical Backround of Jewish Customs & Ceremonies. Date not set. 20.00x (ISBN 0-87068-658-5). Ktav.
Bowen, Barbara M. Strange Scriptures That Perplex the Western Mind. 1940. pap. 2.95 (ISBN 0-8028-1511-1). Eerdmans.
Brown, Jonathan M. Modern Challenges to Halakhah. 1969. pap. 3.95x (ISBN 0-87655-509-1). Whitehall Co.
Chagall, Bella. Burning Lights: A Unique Double Portrait of Russian Jewry. LC 46-8515. (Illus., Drawings by Marc Chagall). 1963. pap. 3.95 (ISBN 0-8052-0035-5). Schocken.
DeVaux, Roland. Ancient Israel, Vol. 1. Social Institutions, Vol. 2. Religious Institutions. 1965. Vol. 1, Social Institutions. pap. 4.95 (ISBN 0-07-016599-8, SP); Vol. 2, Religious Institutions. pap. 4.95 (ISBN 0-07-016600-5). McGraw.
Drachman, Bernard. From the Heart of Israel. LC 72-110183. (Short Story Index Reprint Ser.). 1905. 21.00 (ISBN 0-8369-3334-6). Arno.
Dresner, Samuel H. Between the Generations: A Jewish Dialogue. new ed. LC 79-172413. 80p. (YA) 1971. pap. 1.75 (ISBN 0-685-24670-1, Hartmore). Prayer Bk.
Edersheim, Alfred. Sketch of Jewish Social Life. 1974. pap. 4.95 (ISBN 0-8028-8132-7). Eerdmans.
Finkelstein, Louis. The Jews: Their History, Culture & Religion, 2 vols. 3rd ed. LC 79-4139. 1979. Repr. of 1960 ed. Set. lib. bdg. 125.00x (ISBN 0-313-21242-2, FIJE). Greenwood.
Ginsburg, Christian D. Massorah, 4 Vols. rev. ed. (Library of Biblical Studies). 1970. Set. 300.00 (ISBN 0-87068-020-X). Ktav.
Goldberg, M. Hirsh. Just Because They're Jewish: The Incredible, Ironic, Bizarre, Funny, & Provocative in the Way Jews Are Seen by Other People. LC 78-6400. 264p. 1981. pap. 6.95 (ISBN 0-8128-6122-1). Stein & Day.
Goldstein, Andrew & Wikler, Madeline. My Very Own Jewish Home. (Illus.). (ps-4). 1979. pap. 3.50 (ISBN 0-930494-08-3). Kar Ben.
Gonen, Jay Y. A Psychohistory of Zionism. 384p. 1976. pap. 3.95 (ISBN 0-452-00441-1, F441, Mer). NAL.
Goodman, Philip, ed. Jewish Marriage Anthology. Goodman, Hanna. LC 65-17045. (Illus.). 1965. 7.50 (ISBN 0-8276-0145-X, 236). Jewish Pubn.
Grossman, Mendel. With Camera in the Ghetto. Szner, Zvi & Sened, Alexander, eds. LC 76-48815. (Illus., With text from The Chronicle of the Lodz Ghetto, ed. by Lucjan Dobroszycki & Danuta Dombrowska). 1977. 12.95 (ISBN 0-8052-3645-7). Schocken.
Horowitz, George. The Spirit of Jewish Law. LC 53-7535. 1979. Repr. of 1953 ed. text ed. 18.00x (ISBN 0-87632-167-8). Bloch.
The Jewish Family. Date not set. price not set. ADL.
Jung, Leo. Love & Life. LC 79-87873. 1979. 7.50 (ISBN 0-8022-2355-9). Philos Lib.
Kaplan, Benjamin. Jew & His Family. LC 67-21376. 1967. 15.00x (ISBN 0-8071-0545-7). La State U Pr.
Latner, Helen. The Book of Modern Jewish Etiquette: A Guide for All Occasions. LC 80-22537. (Illus.). 416p. 1981. 19.95 (ISBN 0-8052-3757-7). Schocken.
Levi, Shonie B. & Kaplan, Sylvia R. Guide for the Jewish Homemaker. 2nd ed. LC 59-12039. (Illus.). 1965. pap. 4.95 (ISBN 0-8052-0087-8). Schocken.
Levita, Elijah. Massoreth Ha Massoreth. rev. ed. LC 67-11894. (Library of Biblical Studies). 1969. 25.00x (ISBN 0-87068-081-1). Ktav.

Loeb, L., ed. Outcaste: Jewish Life in Southern Iran. 1977. 26.00x (ISBN 0-677-04530-1). Gordon.

Marcus, Jacob R. The Jew in the Medieval World: A Source Book, 315-1791. LC 71-97295. 504p. 1975. Repr. of 1938 ed. lib. bdg. 21.50x (ISBN 0-8371-2619-3, MAJM). Greenwood.

Metzker, Isaac, ed. A Bintel Brief, Vol. II: Letters to the "Jewish Daily Forward," 1950-1980. Metzker, Bella S. & Levy, Diana S., trs. LC 81-50264. 167p. 1981. 10.95 (ISBN 0-670-16671-5). Viking Pr.

Pederson, Johannes. Israel: Its Life & Culture, 4 bks. Incl. Bks. 1 & 2. 1973. Repr. of 1926 ed. 59.00x (ISBN 0-19-647899-5). Oxford U Pr.

Poll, Solomon. The Hasidic Community of Williamsburg: A Study in the Sociology of Religion. 2nd ed. LC 69-19419. 1969. pap. 4.95 (ISBN 0-8052-0209-9). Schocken.

Rockland, Mae S. The Jewish Party Book: A Contemporary Guide to Customs, Crafts, & Foods. LC 78-54387. (Illus.). 1979. 14.95 (ISBN 0-8052-3689-9). Schocken.

Saypol, Judith R. & Wikler, Madeline. My Very Own Rosh Hashanah. (Illus.). (gr. k-6). 1978. pap. 2.50 (ISBN 0-930494-06-7). Kar Ben.

Seltzer, Robert M. Jewish People, Jewish Thought. (Illus.). 1980. text ed. 19.95 (ISBN 0-02-408950-8). Macmillan.

Snyder, Charles R. Alcohol & the Jews: A Cultural Study of Drinking & Sobriety. LC 77-24885. (Arcturus Books Paperbacks). 240p. 1978. pap. 6.95 (ISBN 0-8093-0846-0). S Ill U Pr.

Szarmach, Paul E., ed. Aspects of Jewish Culture in the Middle Ages. LC 77-29046. (Illus.). 1979. 30.00 (ISBN 0-87395-165-4). State U NY Pr.

Unterman, Alan. Jews: Their Religious Beliefs & Practices. (Library of Religious Beliefs & Practices). 288p. 1981. 22.50 (ISBN 0-7100-0743-4); pap. 13.50 (ISBN 0-7100-0842-2). Routledge & Kegan.

Weilerstein, Sadie R. What the Moon Brought. (Illus.). (gr. 1-3). 1942. 4.50 (ISBN 0-8276-0166-2, 261). Jewish Pubn.

Zborowski, Mark & Herzog, Elizabeth. Life Is with People: The Culture of the Shtetl. LC 62-13141. 1962. pap. 6.95 (ISBN 0-8052-0020-7). Schocken.

--Life Is with People: The Jewish Little-Town of Eastern Europe. 1962. text ed. 20.00 (ISBN 0-8236-3020-X). Intl Univs Pr.

JEWS–TEN LOST TRIBES

see Lost Tribes of Israel

JEWS–WOMEN

see Women, Jewish

JEWS–ZIONISM

see Zionism

JEWS, SEPHARDIC

see Sephardim

JEWS, YEMENITE

Brauer, Erich. Ethnologie der Jemenitischen Juden. LC 77-87611. Repr. of 1934 ed. 30.00 (ISBN 0-404-16435-8). AMS Pr.

JEWS AS SOLDIERS

see Jewish Soldiers

JEWS IN AFRICA

Chouraqui, Andre N. Between East & West: A History of the Jews of North Africa. Bernet, Michael M., tr. from Fr. LC 68-19610. (Temple Bks). 1973. pap. 4.65 (ISBN 0-689-70346-5, T26). Atheneum.

Elazar, Daniel J. Jewish Communities in Frontier Societies. 250p. 1981. text ed. 29.00x (ISBN 0-8419-0449-9). Holmes & Meier.

Goldberg, H. E. Cave Dwellers & Citrus Growers. LC 70-174260. (Illus.). 200p. 1972. pap. 23.95 (ISBN 0-521-08431-8). Cambridge U Pr.

Mendelssohn, Sidney. The Jews of Africa, Especially in the 16th & 17th Centuries. 59.95 (ISBN 0-8490-0446-2). Gordon Pr.

Sundkler, Bengt. Zulu Zion & Some Swazi Zionists. (Oxford Studies in African Affairs Ser.). 1976. 48.00x (ISBN 0-19-822707-8). Oxford U Pr.

Weingrod, Alex. Reluctant Pioneers: Village Development in Israel. LC 78-159987. 1971. Repr. of 1966 ed. 12.50 (ISBN 0-8046-1686-8). Kennikat.

Williams, Joseph J. Hebrewisms of West Africa: From Nile to Niger with the Jews. LC 67-19534. (Illus.). 1930. 17.50x (ISBN 0-8196-0194-2). Biblo.

JEWS IN ARABIA

Sassoon, David S. A History of the Jews in Baghdad. LC 77-87645. Repr. of 1949 ed. 24.50 (ISBN 0-404-16427-7). AMS Pr.

Torrey, Charles C. Jewish Foundation of Islam. rev. ed. LC 67-18817. 1968. 15.00x (ISBN 0-87068-117-6). Ktav.

JEWS IN ARGENTINA

Elazar, Daniel J. Jewish Communities in Frontier Societies. 250p. 1981. text ed. 29.00x (ISBN 0-8419-0449-9). Holmes & Meier.

Sofer, Eugene. From Pale to Pampa: The Jewish Immigrant Experience in Buenos Aires. 1981. text ed. 24.00x (ISBN 0-8419-0428-6). Holmes & Meier.

Weisbrot, Robert. The Jews of Argentina: From the Inquisition to Peron. LC 78-62060. (Illus.). 1979. 12.50 (ISBN 0-8276-0114-X, 428). Jewish Pubn.

Winsberg, Morton D. Colonia Baron Hirsch: A Jewish Agricultural Colony in Argentina. LC 64-63523. (U of Fla. Social Sciences Monographs: No. 19). 1963. pap. 3.00 (ISBN 0-8130-0259-1). U Presses Fla.

JEWS IN AUSTRALIA

Elazar, Daniel J. Jewish Communities in Frontier Societies. 250p. 1981. text ed. 29.00x (ISBN 0-8419-0449-9). Holmes & Meier.

Getzler, Israel. Neither Toleration nor Favour: The Australian Chapter of Jewish Emancipation. 153p. 1970. 17.50x (ISBN 0-522-83961-4, Pub. by Melbourne U Pr). Intl Schol Bk Serv.

JEWS IN AUSTRIA

Jewish Life in Austria in the XV Century. Date not set. 9.75 (ISBN 0-686-76522-2). Feldheim.

Pennell, Joseph. The Jew at Home: Impressions of Jewish Life in Russia & Austria. 1976. lib. bdg. 134.95 (ISBN 0-8490-2098-0). Gordon Pr.

Wistrich, Robert S. Socialism & the Jews: The Dialects of Emancipation in Germany & Austria-Hungary. LC 80-70528. 500p. 1981. 35.00 (ISBN 0-8386-3020-0). Fairleigh Dickinson.

JEWS IN AUSTRIA–FICTION

Wolfenstein, Martha. Idyls of the Gass. LC 74-94748. (Short Story Index Reprint Ser.: Vol. 1). 1901. 16.00 (ISBN 0-8369-3128-9). Arno.

JEWS IN BABYLONIA

Mann, Jacob. The Responsa of the Babylonian Geonim As a Source of Jewish History. LC 73-2215. (The Jewish People; History, Religion, Literature Ser.). Repr. of 1921 ed. 17.00 (ISBN 0-405-05279-0). Arno.

JEWS IN CANADA

Marcus, Jacob R. Early American Jewry. 1953. 35.00x (ISBN 0-87068-269-5). Ktav.

JEWS IN CHINA

Kublin, Hyman, ed. & intro. by. Jews in Old China: Some Western Views. 1971. Repr. 14.00 (ISBN 0-8188-0103-4). Paragon.

--Studies of the Chinese Jews: Selected Articles from Journals East & West. 150p. 1971. 12.00 (ISBN 0-8188-0104-2). Paragon.

Leslie, Donald D. The Survival of the Chinese Jews: The Jewish Community of Kaifeng. (Illus.). 270p. 1973. text ed. 54.75x (ISBN 90-040-3413-7). Humanities.

Lord, James H. The Jews in India & the Far East. LC 70-97292. 1976. Repr. of 1907 ed. lib. bdg. 15.00x (ISBN 0-8371-2615-0, LOJI). Greenwood.

Pollak, Michael. Mandarins, Jews & Missionaries: The Jewish Experience in the Chinese Empire. (Illus.). 1979. 14.95 (ISBN 0-8276-0120-4, 438). Jewish Pubn.

Tokayer, Marvin & Swartz, Mary. The Fugu Plan: The Untold Story of the Japanese & the Jews in World War II. (Illus.). 1979. 10.95 (ISBN 0-448-23036-4). Paddington.

White, Willam C. Chinese Jews: A Compilation of Matters Relating to the Jews of K'aifeng Fu. 2nd ed. LC 68-78593. 1966. 32.50x (ISBN 0-8020-1427-5). U of Toronto Pr.

White, William C. Chinese Jews, 3 Vols. in 1. 2nd ed. (Illus.). 1966. Repr. of 1924 ed. 25.00 (ISBN 0-8188-0093-3). Paragon.

--Chinese Jews: A Compilation of Matters Relating to the Jews of K'ai-feng Fu. abr., 2nd ed. cancelled 9.95 (ISBN 0-8037-1252-9). Dial.

JEWS IN COMMUNIST COUNTRIES

Meyer, Peter. Jews in the Soviet Satellites. LC 79-97297. 1971. Repr. of 1953 ed. lib. bdg. 23.00x (ISBN 0-8371-2621-5, MEJS). Greenwood.

Tamir, Vicki. Bulgaria & Her Jews: The History of a Dubious Symbiosis. LC 78-62154. (Illus.). 1979. 14.95 (ISBN 0-87203-075-X). Hermon.

JEWS IN CZECHOSLOVAKIA

Kennan, George F. From Prague After Munich: Diplomatic Papers, 1938-1939. LC 66-26587. 1968. 20.00 (ISBN 0-691-05620-X); pap. 7.95 (ISBN 0-691-01063-3). Princeton U Pr.

Society for the History of Czechoslovak Jews. Jews of Czechoslovakia, Vol. 1. LC 67-12372. 1968. 9.00 (ISBN 0-8276-0146-8, 201). Jewish Pubn.

JEWS IN EGYPT

Aviezer, Golan. Operation Susannah. Peretz, Kidron, tr. from Hebrew. LC 77-3751. (Illus.). 1978. 16.95 (ISBN 0-06-011555-6, HarpT). Har-Row.

Bell, Harold I., ed. Jews & Christians in Egypt. LC 79-97270. (Judaica Ser). (Illus.). 140p. 1972. Repr. of 1924 ed. lib. bdg. 14.00x (ISBN 0-8371-2587-1, BEJA). Greenwood.

Gordon, Benjamin L. New Judea: Jewish Life in Modern Palestine & Egypt. Davis, Moshe, ed. LC 77-70697. (America & the Holy Land Ser.). (Illus.). 1977. Repr. of 1919 ed. lib. bdg. 22.00x (ISBN 0-405-10251-8). Arno.

Landau, Jacob M. Jews in Nineteenth-Century Egypt. LC 69-18282. (Studies in Near Eastern Civilization: No. 2). (Illus.). 1969. 16.00x (ISBN 0-8147-0248-1). NYU Pr.

Mann, Jacob. The Jews in Egypt & in Palestine Under the Fatimid Caliphs, 2 Vols. in 1. rev. ed. (Library of Jewish Classics Ser). 1970. 45.00x (ISBN 0-87068-024-2). Ktav.

Porten, Bezalel. Archives from Elephantine: The Life of an Ancient Jewish Military Colony. (Illus.). 1968. 32.50x (ISBN 0-520-01028-0). U of Cal Pr.

Wasserstein, Bernard. Britain & the Jews of Europe 1939-1945. 1979. 19.95 (ISBN 0-19-822600-4). Oxford U Pr.

JEWS IN ENGLAND

see Jews in Great Britain

JEWS IN EUROPE

Bachrach, Bernard S. Early Medieval Jewish Policy in Western Europe. LC 77-73545. 1977. 17.50x (ISBN 0-8166-0814-8). U of Minn Pr.

Cholawski, Shalom. Soldiers from the Ghetto: Jewish Armed Resistance in the East, 1941-1945. LC 78-75300. 1980. 9.95 (ISBN 0-498-02382-6). A S Barnes.

Dawidowicz, Lucy S., ed. Golden Tradition. pap. 7.95 (ISBN 0-8070-6435-1, BP278). Beacon Pr.

Engelman, Uriah Z. The Rise of the Jew in the Western World. LC 73-2194. (The Jewish People; History, Religion, Literature Ser.). Repr. of 1944 ed. 16.00 (ISBN 0-405-05260-X). Arno.

Fishberg, Maurice. Materials for the Physical Anthropology of the Eastern European Jews. LC 6-2111. 1905. pap. 9.00 (ISBN 0-527-00500-2). Kraus Repr.

Glanz, Rudolf. The Eastern European Jewish Women, Vol. 2. 25.00x (ISBN 0-87068-462-0). Ktav.

Handler, Andrew. Blood Libel at Tiszaeszlar. (East European Monograph: No. 68). 256p. 1980. 20.00x (ISBN 0-914710-62-1). East Eur Quarterly.

Heschel, Abraham J. The Earth Is the Lord's. 109p. 1978. pap. 2.95 (ISBN 0-374-51469-0). FS&G.

Howe, Irving & Greenberg, Eliezer, eds. Voices from the Yiddish: Essays, Memoirs & Diaries. LC 75-10751. 340p. 1975. pap. 4.95 (ISBN 0-8052-0495-4). Schocken.

Imposed Jewish Governing Bodies Under Nazi Rule: Yivo Colloquium Dec. 2-5, 1967. LC 73-150304. 1972. pap. 5.00 (ISBN 0-914512-03-X). Yivo Inst.

Joseph, Samuel. Jewish Immigration to the United States from 1881 to 1910. LC 14-15042. (Columbia University. Studies in the Social Sciences: No. 145). Repr. of 1914 ed. 7.50 (ISBN 0-404-51145-7). AMS Pr.

--Jewish Immigration to the United States from 1881 to 1910. LC 69-18781. (American Immigration Collection Ser., No. 1). (Illus.). 1969. Repr. of 1914 ed. 8.00 (ISBN 0-405-00529-6). Arno.

Katz, Jacob. Jews & Freemasons in Europe, 1723-1939. Oschry, Leonard, tr. from Heb. LC 71-115475. 1970. 16.00x (ISBN 0-674-47480-5). Harvard U Pr.

--Out of the Ghetto: The Social Background of Jewish Emancipation, 1770-1870. LC 72-86386. 1973. 15.00x (ISBN 0-674-64775-0). Harvard U Pr.

Levanon, Yosef. The Jewish Travellers in the Twelfth Century. LC 80-5521. 431p. 1980. lib. bdg. 21.75 (ISBN 0-8191-1122-8); pap. text ed. 13.75 (ISBN 0-8191-1123-6). U Pr of Amer.

Meltzer, Milton. World of Our Fathers: The Jews of Eastern Europe. LC 74-14755. (Illus.). 274p. (gr. 7 up). 1974. 7.95 (ISBN 0-374-38530-0). FS&G.

--World of Our Fathers: The Jews of Eastern Europe. 1976. pap. 1.25 (ISBN 0-440-99422-5, LFL). Dell.

Meyer, Peter. Jews in the Soviet Satellites. LC 79-97297. 1971. Repr. of 1953 ed. lib. bdg. 23.00x (ISBN 0-8371-2621-5, MEJS). Greenwood.

Neugroschel, Joachim, ed. The Shtetl: A Creative Anthology of Jewish Life in Eastern Europe. LC 79-13624. (Illus.). 1979. box ed. 25.00 (ISBN 0-399-90033-0). Marek.

Parkes, James W. The Jew in the Medieval Community. 456p. 1976. pap. 9.75 (ISBN 0-87203-060-1). Hermon.

Philipson, David. Old European Jewries. LC 74-178586. Repr. of 1895 ed. 21.00 (ISBN 0-404-56663-4). AMS Pr.

Poliak, Abraham N. Khazaria: The History of a Jewish Kingdom in Europe. 1978. lib. bdg. 49.95 (ISBN 0-685-62302-5). Revisionist Pr.

Sachs, Abraham S. Worlds That Passed. facsimile ed. Berman, Harold & Joffe, Judah, trs. from Yiddish. LC 74-29521. (Modern Jewish Experience Ser.). (Eng.). 1975. Repr. of 1928 ed. 18.00x (ISBN 0-405-06746-1). Arno.

Trunk, Isaiah. Judenrat. LC 70-173692. 1977. pap. 8.95 (ISBN 0-8128-2170-X). Stein & Day.

Waagenaar, Sam. The Pope's Jews. (Illus.). 500p. 1974. 22.50 (ISBN 0-912050-49-7, Library Pr). Open Court.

Wolf, Hannie. Child of Two Worlds. (Illus.). 156p. 1979. 10.00 (ISBN 0-931068-02-9). Purcells.

Zimmer, Eric. Harmony & Discord: An Analysis of the Decline of Jewish Self-Government in Fifteenth Century Central Europe. 276p. 1970. 5.95x (ISBN 0-685-26214-6, Pub. by Yeshiva U. Pr.). Bloch.

JEWS IN FOLK-LORE

see Folk-Lore, Jewish; Wandering Jew

JEWS IN FOREIGN COUNTRIES

see Jews–Diaspora

JEWS IN FRANCE

Agus, Irving A. Heroic Age of Franco-German Jewry. LC 75-94444. 1969. 15.00x (ISBN 0-8197-0053-3). Bloch.

Albert, Phyllis C. The Modernization of French Jewry: Consistory & Community in the Nineteenth Century. LC 76-50680. (Illus.). 472p. 1977. text ed. 27.50x (ISBN 0-87451-139-9). U Pr of New Eng.

Bensimon-Donath, Doris. L'integration Des Juifs Nord-Africains En France. (Publications De L'institut D'etudes et De Recherches Interethniques et Interculturelles: No. 1). 1971. pap. 10.50x (ISBN 90-2796-930-2). Mouton.

Chazan, Robert. Medieval Jewry in Northern France: A Political & Social History. LC 73-8129. (Ninety-First Series No. 2 (1973)). 249p. 1974. 17.50x (ISBN 0-8018-1503-7). Johns Hopkins.

Count of Coucy. Date not set. 4.95 (ISBN 0-686-76500-1). Feldheim.

Hertzberg, Arthur. French Enlightenment & the Jews. LC 68-18996. 420p. 1968. 22.50x (ISBN 0-231-03049-5). Columbia U Pr.

Inbar, Michael & Adler, Chaim. Ethnic Integration in Israel: A Comparative Study of Moroccan Brothers Who Settled in France & in Israel. LC 76-27933. (Illus.). 1977. lib. bdg. 16.95 (ISBN 0-87855-204-9). Transaction Bks.

Kahn, Leon. Les Juifs De Paris Pendant la Revolution. (Research & Source Works Ser.: No. 198). 1968. Repr. of 1899 ed. 30.50 (ISBN 0-8337-1892-4). B Franklin.

Latour, Anny. The Jewish Resistance in France, 1940-1944. (Illus.). 1981. 12.95 (ISBN 0-8052-5025-5, Pub. by Holocaust Library); pap. 6.95 (ISBN 0-8052-5024-7). Schocken.

Malino, Frances. The Sephardic Jews of Bordeaux: Assimilation & Emancipation in Revolutionary & Napoleonic France. LC 77-22659. (Judaic Studies: Vol. 7). 200p. 1978. 13.95x (ISBN 0-8173-6903-1). U of Ala Pr.

Marrus, Michael R. The Politics of Assimilation: The French Jewish Community at the Time of the Dreyfus Affair. (Illus.). 300p. 1981. pap. 19.95 (ISBN 0-19-822591-1). Oxford U Pr.

Rabinowitz, Louis I. The Social Life of the Jews in Northern France in the 12th-14th Centuries. LC 72-83938. 270p. 1973. Repr. of 1938 ed. 12.50 (ISBN 0-87203-033-4). Hermon.

Shatzmiller, Joseph. Recherches Sur la Communaute Juive De Manosque Au Moyen Age (1241-1329) (Etudes Juives: No. 15). 1973. pap. 19.50x (ISBN 90-2797-188-9). Mouton.

Szajkowski, Soza. Analytical Franco-Jewish Gazetteer, 1939-1945. 1966. 50.00 (ISBN 0-685-13733-3). Ktav.

--Jews & the French Revolution of 1789, 1830 & 1848. 1969. 45.00x (ISBN 0-87068-112-5). Ktav.

Szajkowski, Zosa. Jewish Education in France, Seventeen Eighty-Nine to Nineteen Thirty-Nine. (Conference on Jewish Social Studies Monograph Ser.: No. 2). 1980. 10.00x (ISBN 0-910430-01-2). Columbia U Pr.

Timayenis, Telemachus T. The Original Mr. Jacobs: Startling Expose. Grob, Gerald, ed. LC 76-46107. (Anti-Movements in America). 1977. Repr. of 1888 ed. lib. bdg. 18.00x (ISBN 0-405-09978-9). Arno.

Weinberg, David H. A Community on Trial: The Jews of Paris in the 1930's. LC 77-2999. 1977. 18.50x (ISBN 0-226-88507-0). U of Chicago Pr.

Wilson, Nelly. Bernard-Lazare. LC 77-82524. 1979. 42.00 (ISBN 0-521-21802-0). Cambridge U Pr.

Wilson, Stephen. Ideology & Experience: Antisemitism in France at the Time of the Dreyfus Affair. LC 81-65467. (Illus.). 800p. 1981. 50.00 (ISBN 0-8386-3037-5). Fairleigh Dickinson.

Zuckerman, Arthur J. A Jewish Princedom in Feudal France 768-900. LC 72-137392. (Studies in Jewish History, Culture, & Institutions: No. 2). 435p. 1972. 27.50x (ISBN 0-231-03298-6). Columbia U Pr.

JEWS IN FRANCE–BIBLIOGRAPHY

Szajkowski, Z., ed. Franco Judaica, an Analytical Bibliography of Books, Pamphlets, Decrees, Briefs & Other Printed Documents Pertaining to the Jew in France, 1500-1788. 1962. 18.00 (ISBN 0-527-02385-X). Kraus Repr.

JEWS IN GAUL

Katz, S. Jews in the Visigothic & Frankish Kingdoms of Spain & Gaul. 1937. 14.00 (ISBN 0-527-01697-7). Kraus Repr.

JEWS IN GERMANY

Agus, Irving A. Heroic Age of Franco-German Jewry. LC 75-94444. 1969. 15.00x (ISBN 0-8197-0053-3). Bloch.

--Rabbi Meir of Rothenburg: His Life & Work, 2 Vols. in 1. rev. ed. 1970. 35.00x (ISBN 0-87068-026-9). Ktav.

American Jewish Committee. The Jews in Nazi Germany. 1981. Repr. of 1935 ed. 17.50 (ISBN 0-86527-110-0). Fertig.

Arendt, Hannah. Rahel Varnhagen: The Life of a Jewish Woman. Winston, Richard & Winston, Clara, trs. from Ger. LC 74-6478. (Illus.). 240p. 1974. pap. 3.95 (ISBN 0-15-676100-9, HB287, Harv). HarBraceJ.

--Rahel Varnhagen: The Life of a Jewish Woman. rev ed. Winston, Richard & Winston, Clara, trs. from Ger. LC 74-6478. (Illus.). 224p. 1974. 7.95 (ISBN 0-15-175850-6). HarBraceJ.

Baeck. Studies of the Leo Baeck Institute. Kreutzberger, Max, ed. LC 67-25839. 8.50 (ISBN 0-8044-5047-1). Ungar.

Baker, Leonard. Days of Sorrow & Pain: Leo Baeck & the Berlin Jews. 1978. 14.95 (ISBN 0-02-506340-5). Macmillan.

Bolkosky, Sidney M. The Distorted Image: German Jewish Perceptions of Germans & Germany, 1918-1935. LC 75-8270. 224p. 1975. 13.95 (ISBN 0-444-99014-3). Elsevier.

Cadrain, Linda A., adapted by. The Diary of Anne Frank. (Contemporary Motivators Ser.). (Illus.). 32p. (Orig.). (gr. 4-12). 1979. pap. text ed. 1.95 (ISBN 0-88301-308-8) (ISBN 0-686-65677-6). Pendulum Pr.

Eidelberg, Shlomo, ed. Jews & the Crusaders: The Hebrew Chronicles of the First & Second Crusades. 1977. 17.50 (ISBN 0-299-07060-3). U of Wis Pr.

Gluckel. The Memoirs of Gluckel of Hameln. Lowenthal, Marvin, tr. from Ger. LC 77-75290. 1977. pap. 6.95 (ISBN 0-8052-0572-1). Schocken.

Graupe, Heinz M. The Rise of Modern Judaism: An Intellectual History of German Jewry 1650-1942. LC 77-9059. 344p. 1979. lib. bdg. 19.50 (ISBN 0-88275-395-9). Krieger.

Grunfeld, Frederic V. Prophets Without Honor, a Background to Freud, Kafka, Einstein & Their World. LC 78-31645. (Illus.). 368p. 1979. 15.00 (ISBN 0-03-017871-1). HR&W.

Gutteridge, Richard. Open Thy Mouth for the Dumb! The German Evangelical Church & the Jews, 1879-1950. LC 76-12068. 1976. text ed. 23.50x (ISBN 0-06-492620-6). B&N.

Herz, E. Emil. Before the Fury. LC 66-18484. 1967. 4.50 (ISBN 0-8022-0710-3). Philos Lib.

Historical Views of Judaism: Four Selections. LC 73-2209. (The Jewish People; History, Religion, Literature Ser.). 35.00 (ISBN 0-405-05273-1). Arno.

Horowitz, Inge W. & Windmueller, Ida. Windmueller Family Chronicle. 2nd rev. ed. Windmueller, Ida & Grausz, Ilse, trs. from Ger. (Illus.). 320p. Date not set. price not set (ISBN 0-9605242-0-7). Windmill Bks.

Kaplan, Marion. The Jewish Feminist Movement in Germany: The Campaigns of the Judischer Frauenbund, 1904-1938. LC 78-67567. (Contributions in Women's Studies: No. 8). (Illus.). lib. bdg. 17.50 (ISBN 0-313-20736-4, KGJ/). Greenwood.

Keller, Julius. German Jews Fought Back. 5.95 (ISBN 0-533-01889-7). Vantage.

Kisch, Guido. Jewry-Law in Medieval Germany: Laws & Decisions Concerning Jews. 1949. pap. 14.00 (ISBN 0-527-01137-1). Kraus Repr.

Koehn, Ilse. Mischling, Second Degree: My Childhood in Nazi Germany. LC 77-6189. (gr. 7 up). 1977. 8.95 (ISBN 0-688-80110-2); PLB 8.59 (ISBN 0-688-84110-4). Greenwillow.

Lamberti, Marjorie. Jewish Activism in Imperial Germany: The Struggle for Civil Equality. LC 77-17325. (Yale Historical Publications: No. 119). 1978. 20.00x (ISBN 0-300-02163-1). Yale U Pr.

Low, Alfred D. Jews in the Eyes of the Germans: From the Enlightenment to Imperial Germany. LC 79-334. 1979. 17.50 (ISBN 0-915980-86-X). Inst Study Human.

Lowenthal, Marvin. Jews of Germany: A Story of Sixteen Centuries. LC 75-102516. 1970. Repr. of 1936 ed. 16.50 (ISBN 0-8462-1469-5). Russell.

Marcus, Jacob R. The Rise & Destiny of the German Jew. rev. ed. 1971. 15.00x (ISBN 0-87068-148-6). Ktav.

Mayer, Milton. They Thought They Were Free: The Germans 1933-45. 2nd ed. LC 55-5137. 1966. pap. 5.95 (ISBN 0-226-51192-8, P222, Phoen). U of Chicago Pr.

Mosse, George L. Germans & Jews: The Right, the Left, & the Search for a 'third Force' in Pre-Nazi Germany. LC 68-14552. 1970. 20.00 (ISBN 0-86527-081-3). Fertig.

Niewyk, Donald L. The Jews in Weimar Germany. LC 79-26234. 272p. 1980. 17.50x (ISBN 0-8071-0661-5). La State U Pr.

Poppel, Stephen M. Zionism in Germany 1897-1933: The Shaping of a Jewish Identity. LC 76-14284. 1977. 7.95 (ISBN 0-8276-0085-2, 395). Jewish Pubn.

Reinharz, Jehuda. Fatherland or Promised Land: The Dilemma of the German Jew, 1893-1914. LC 74-25948. (Illus.). 320p. 1975. 12.95 (ISBN 0-472-76500-0). U of Mich Pr.

Robinson, Jacob. Guide to Jewish History Under Nazi Impact. 1974. 35.00x (ISBN 0-87068-231-8). Ktav.

Salomon, Charlotte. Charlotte: Life or Theater?: An Autobiographical Play. Vennewitz, Leila, tr. from Ger. LC 81-24745. (Illus.). 784p. 1981. 75.00 (ISBN 0-670-21283-0, Studio). Viking Pr.

Stanford, Julian C. Reflection: Diary of a German Jew in Hiding. 1965. 4.50 (ISBN 0-686-27350-8). Magnes Mus.

Tal, Uriel. Christians & Jews in Germany: Religion, Politics, & Ideology in the Second Reich, 1870-1914. Jacobs, Noah J., tr. from Hebrew. LC 74-21612. (Illus.). 384p. 1975. 28.50x (ISBN 0-8014-0879-2). Cornell U Pr.

Weinreich, Max. Hitlers Profesorn. LC 47-42580. (Illus.). 325p. (Yiddish.). 1947. pap. 7.50x (ISBN 0-914512-26-9). Yivo Inst.

Wiener Library & Wolff, Ilse. German Jewry: Its History, Life & Culture. LC 75-17202. (Wiener Library Catalogue Series: No. 3). 279p. 1975. Repr. of 1958 ed. lib. bdg. 15.00x (ISBN 0-8371-8292-1, WIGJ). Greenwood.

Wistrich, Robert S. Socialism & the Jews: The Dialects of Emancipation in Germany & Austria-Hungary. LC 80-70528. 500p. 1981. 35.00 (ISBN 0-8386-3020-0). Fairleigh Dickinson.

Zimmer, Eric. Jewish Synods in Germany During the Late Middle Ages (1286-1603) Date not set. 15.00x (ISBN 0-87068-730-1). Ktav.

JEWS IN GREAT BRITAIN

Adler, Hermann. Anglo-Jewish Memories. 59.95 (ISBN 0-87968-636-7). Gordon Pr.

Cobbett, W. Jews & the Jews in England. 1976. lib. bdg. 59.95 (ISBN 0-8490-2103-0). Gordon Pr.

Endelman, Todd M. The Jews of Georgian England, 1714-1830: Tradition & Change in a Liberal Society. LC 78-78390. (Illus.). 1979. 14.50 (ISBN 0-8276-0119-0, 437). Jewish Pubn.

Glassman, Bernard. Anti-Semitic Stereotypes Without Jews: Images of the Jews in England, 1290-1700. LC 75-16391. 218p. 1975. 13.95 (ISBN 0-8143-1545-3). Wayne St U Pr.

Hannam, Charles. Almost an Englishman. (gr. 6 up). 1979. 9.95 (ISBN 0-233-97119-X). Andre Deutsch.

Holmes, Colin. Anti-Semitism & British Society Eighteen Seventy-Six to Nineteen Thirty-Nine. LC 78-21023. 1979. text ed. 45.00x (ISBN 0-8419-0459-6). Holmes & Meier.

Hyamson, Albert M. The Sephardim of England: History of the Spanish & Portugese Jewish Community, 1492-1951. LC 77-87544. Repr. of 1951 ed. 32.50 (ISBN 0-404-16610-5). AMS Pr.

Jacobs, Joseph. The Jews of Angevin England. 75.00 (ISBN 0-87968-406-2). Gordon Pr.

Lipman, V. D., ed. Jewish Life in Britain 1967-77. 250p. 1980. 29.80 (ISBN 0-89664-148-1). K G Saur.

Perry, Thomas W. Public Opinion, Propaganda, & Politics in Eighteenth-Century England: A Study of the Jew Bill of 1753. LC 62-17222. (Historical Monographs Ser: No. 51). 1962. 10.00x (ISBN 0-674-72400-3). Harvard U Pr.

Pollins, Harold. Economic History of the Jews in England. LC 80-70683. (Littman Library of Jewish Civilization). 500p. 1981. 35.00 (ISBN 0-8386-3033-2). Fairleigh Dickinson.

Roth, Cecil. A History of the Jews in England. 3rd ed. 1979. 13.50x (ISBN 0-19-822488-5). Oxford U Pr.

Schoffler, Herbert. Abendland und Altes Testament. Repr. of 1937 ed. pap. 7.00 (ISBN 0-384-54210-7). Johnson Repr.

Webb, Beatrice & Webb, Sidney. Problems of Modern Industry. facsimile new ed. LC 70-37918. (Select Bibliographies Reprint Ser.). Repr. of 1902 ed. 19.00 (ISBN 0-8369-6755-0). Arno.

Webb, Philip C. & Grove, Joseph. The Question Whether a Jew, Born Within the British Dominions, Was, Before the Making of the Late Act of Parliament, a Person Capable by Law, to Purchase & Hold Lands to Him and His Heirs. Berkowitz, David S. & Thorne, Samuel E., eds. LC 77-86671. (Classics of English Legal History in the Modern Era Ser.: Vol. 48). 169p. 1979. lib. bdg. 40.00 (ISBN 0-8240-3097-4). Garland Pub.

Williams, Bill. The Making of Manchester Jewry: 1740-1875. LC 75-43635. (Illus.). 400p. 1976. text ed. 32.50x (ISBN 0-8419-0252-6). Holmes & Meier.

Yidn in England; Studies & Materials, 1880-1940. (Bibliotek Fun Yivo). 302p. (Yiddish.). 1966. 4.50 (ISBN 0-914512-14-5, HE66-1946). Yivo Inst.

JEWS IN INDIA

Barber, Ezekiel. The Bene-Israel of India: Images & Reality. LC 81-40006. (Illus.). 176p. 1981. lib. bdg. 17.75 (ISBN 0-8191-1594-0); pap. text ed. 9.00 (ISBN 0-8191-1645-9). U Pr of Amer.

Kushner, Gilbert. Immigrants From India in Israel: Planned Change in an Administered Community. LC 72-82945. 1973. pap. 2.00 (ISBN 0-8165-0210-2). U of Ariz Pr.

Lord, J. The Jews in India & the Far East. 1976. lib. bdg. 39.95 (ISBN 0-8490-2104-9). Gordon Pr.

Lord, James H. The Jews in India & the Far East. LC 70-97292. 1976. Repr. of 1907 ed. lib. bdg. 15.00x (ISBN 0-8371-2615-0, LOJI). Greenwood.

Musleah, Ezekiel N. On the Banks of the Ganga: The Sojourn of Jews in Calcutta. (Illus.). 555p. 1975. 12.95 (ISBN 0-8158-0313-3). Chris Mass.

JEWS IN IRELAND

Hyman, Louis. The Jews of Ireland. 422p. 1972. 15.00x (ISBN 0-7165-2082-6, Pub. by Irish Academic Pr Ireland). Biblio Dist.

JEWS IN ITALY

Arieti, Silvano. The Parnas. LC 79-1978. 1979. 10.00 (ISBN 0-465-05452-8). Basic.

--The Parnas. LC 79-1978. 1979. 10.00 (ISBN 0-465-05452-8). Basic.

Michaelis, Meir. Mussolini & the Jews: German-Italian Relations & the Jewish Question in Italy 1922-1945. 1979. 59.00x (ISBN 0-19-822542-3). Oxford U Pr.

Roth, Cecil. History of the Jews in Venice. LC 74-26916. (Illus.). 402p. 1975. pap. 6.50 (ISBN 0-8052-0480-6). Schocken.

Yerushalmi, Yosef H. From Spanish Court to Italian Ghetto: Isaac Cardoso, a Study in Seventeenth-Century Marranism & Jewish Apologetics. LC 76-109544. (Illus.). 548p. 1981. pap. 15.00 (ISBN 0-295-95824-3). U of Wash Pr.

JEWS IN HUNGARY

Braham, Randolph L. The Hungarian Jewish Catastrophe; a Selected & Annotated Bibliography. LC 67-4478. (Joint Documentary Projects Bibliographical Ser.: No. 4). 86p. 1962. 5.00 (ISBN 0-914512-21-8). Yivo Inst.

Dicker, Herman. Piety & Perservance: Jews from the Carpathian Mountains. LC 80-54595. (Illus.). 252p. 1981. 14.95 (ISBN 0-87203-094-6); pap. 8.75 (ISBN 0-87203-098-9). Hermon.

JEWS IN JAPAN

Kranzler, David. Japanese, Nazis, & Jews. 2nd ed. (Illus.). 1979. Repr. 17.95 (ISBN 0-686-59888-1). Rabinowitz Hebrew Book.

JEWS IN LATIN AMERICA

Cohen, Martin. Jewish Experience in Latin America, 2 Vols. 1971. Set. 35.00x (ISBN 0-87068-136-2, Pub by Am Jewish Hist Soc). Ktav.

Cohen, Martin A., ed. The Jewish Experience in Latin America, 2 vols. 1972. Set. 35.00 (ISBN 0-87068-136-2, Co-Pub. by KTAV). Am Jewish Hist Soc.

Elkin, Judith L. Jews of the Latin American Republics. LC 79-17394. 1980. 17.00x (ISBN 0-8078-1408-3). U of NC Pr.

Sable, M. H. Latin American Jewry: A Research Guide. (Bibliographica Judaica Ser: No. 6). 45.00x (ISBN 0-87820-904-2, HUC Pr). Ktav.

JEWS IN LITERATURE

Bilik, Dorothy S. Immigrant-Survivors: Post-Holocaust Consciousness in Recent Jewish-American Literature. 295p. 1981. 15.95x (ISBN 0-8195-5046-9). Wesleyan U Pr.

Blackman, Murray. A Guide to Jewish Themes in American Fiction, 1940-1980. LC 80-24953. 271p. 1981. lib. bdg. 15.00 (ISBN 0-8108-1380-7). Scarecrow.

Calisch, Edward N. The Jew in English Literature As Author & Subject. 1980. lib. bdg. 64.95 (ISBN 0-8490-3132-X). Gordon Pr.

Cardozo, Jacob L. The Contemporary Jew in the Elizabethan Drama. (Research & Source Works Ser: No. 175). Repr. of 1925 ed. 15.00 (ISBN 0-8337-0466-4). B Franklin.

Chametzky, Jules. From the Ghetto: The Fiction of Abraham Cahan. LC 76-25047. 1977. 10.00x (ISBN 0-87023-225-8). U of Mass Pr.

Charlton, H. B. Shakespeare's Jew. 1934. lib. bdg. 5.00 (ISBN 0-8414-3560-X). Folcroft.

Coleman, Edward D. Bible in English Drama: An Annotated Bibliography. rev. ed. 1969. 25.00x (ISBN 0-87068-034-X). Ktav.

--Bible in English Drama: An Annotated List of Plays. 1969. 6.95 (ISBN 0-87104-021-2, Co-Pub by Ktav). NY Pub Lib.

--Jew in English Drama: An Annotated Bibliography. rev. ed. LC 67-11901. 1969. 25.00x (ISBN 0-87068-011-0). Ktav.

--Jew in English Drama: An Annotated Bibliography. LC 67-11901. 1968. Repr. of 1943 ed. with The Jew in Western Drama by Edgar Rosenberg 8.95 (ISBN 0-87104-101-4, Co-Pub by Ktav). NY Pub Lib.

Debre, Moses. Image of the Jew in French Literature from 1800 to 1908. Hirschler, Gertrude, tr. 1970. 15.00x (ISBN 0-87068-075-7). Ktav.

Ezrahi, Sidra D. By Words Alone: The Holocaust in Literature. LC 79-56908. 1980. 15.00 (ISBN 0-226-23335-9). U of Chicago Pr.

Fisch, Harold. The Dual Image. 1971. 10.00x (ISBN 0-87068-144-3). Ktav.

Friedlander, Gerald. Shakespeare & the Jew. LC 74-168084. Repr. of 1921 ed. 11.50 (ISBN 0-404-02579-X). AMS Pr.

Gill, John, ed. Notices of the Jews & Their Country by the Classic Writers of Antiquity. LC 70-97281. (Judaica Ser). 180p. 1972. Repr. of 1872 ed. lib. bdg. 15.00x (ISBN 0-8371-2603-7, GINJ). Greenwood.

Goldstein, David I. Dostoyevsky & the Jews. (University of Texas Press Slavic Ser.: No. 3). 256p. 1981. 17.50 (ISBN 0-292-71528-5). U of Tex Pr.

Gross, Theodore L. Literature of American Jews. LC 72-93311. 1973. 12.95 (ISBN 0-02-913190-1). Free Pr.

Harap, Louis. The Image of the Jew in American Literature. LC 74-12887. 608p. 1975. 10.00 (ISBN 0-8276-0054-2, 357). Jewish Pubn.

Kaufmann, David. George Eliot & Judaism. LC 75-130251. (English Literature Ser., No. 33). 1970. Repr. of 1888 ed. lib. bdg. 27.95 (ISBN 0-8383-1141-5). Haskell.

Kayser, Rudolf. The Saints of Qumran: Stories & Essays on Jewish Themes. Zohn, Harry, ed. LC 76-20273. 188p. 1977. 14.50 (ISBN 0-8386-2024-8). Fairleigh Dickinson.

Landa, Myer J. Jew in Drama. LC 68-26290. 1968. Repr. of 1926 ed. 13.75 (ISBN 0-8046-0257-3). Kennikat.

--The Jew in Drama. rev. ed. 1969. 20.00x (ISBN 0-87068-074-9). Ktav.

Lehrmann, C. The Jewish Element in French Literature. LC 75-120998. 295p. 1971. 15.00 (ISBN 0-8386-7725-8). Fairleigh Dickinson.

Lehrmann, Charles C. Jewish Influences on European Thought. Klin, George & Carpenter, Victor, trs. LC 72-3264. 323p. 1976. 16.50 (ISBN 0-8386-7908-0). Fairleigh Dickinson.

Liptzin, Sol. Jew in American Literature. 5.50 (ISBN 0-8197-0152-1). Bloch.

Michelson, Hyman. The Jew in Early English Literature. LC 72-83940. (Illus.). 186p. 1973. Repr. of 1926 ed. 12.50 (ISBN 0-87203-035-0). Hermon.

Naman, Anne A. The Jew in the Victorian Novel: Some Relationships Between Prejudice & Art. LC 79-8634. (AMS Studies in the 19th Century: No. 1). 1980. 16.50 (ISBN 0-404-18023-X). AMS Pr.

Panitz, Esther L. The Alien in Their Midst: Image of Jews in English Literature. LC 78-75183. 192p. 1981. 18.50 (ISBN 0-8386-2318-2). Fairleigh Dickinson.

Philipson, David. Jew in English Fiction. LC 76-42290. 1889. lib. bdg. 15.00 (ISBN 0-8414-6796-X). Folcroft.

--The Jew in English Fiction. LC 76-30568. (English Literature Ser, No. 33). 1977. lib. bdg. 47.95 (ISBN 0-8383-2150-X). Haskell.

Rosenberg, Edgar. From Shylock to Svengali: Jewish Stereotypes in English Fiction. (Illus.). 1960. 15.00x (ISBN 0-8047-0586-0). Stanford U Pr.

Sinsheimer, Hermann. Shylock: The History of a Character. LC 63-23188. (Illus.). Repr. of 1947 ed. 12.00 (ISBN 0-405-08977-5, Pub. by Blom). Arno.

Van Der Veen, H. R. Jewish Characters in Eighteenth Century Fiction & Drama. 1970. 25.00x (ISBN 0-87068-076-5). Ktav.

JEWS IN LITHUANIA

Baron, Salo W. A Social & Religious History of the Jews: Late Middle Ages and Era of European Expansion (1200-1650) Poland-Lithuania 1500-1650, Vol 16. 1976. 27.00x (ISBN 0-231-08853-1). Columbia U Pr.

JEWS IN MEXICO

Liebman, Seymour B. Jews in New Spain: Faith, Flame & the Inquisition. LC 70-91213. (Illus.). 1970. 19.95x (ISBN 0-87024-129-X). U of Miami Pr.

JEWS IN PALESTINE

Chissin, Chaim. A Palestine Diary. 1976. 10.00 (ISBN 0-685-82598-1). Herzl Pr.

Davis, Moshe, ed. Israel: Its Role in Civilization. LC 77-70673. (America & the Holy Land Ser.). 1977. Repr. of 1956 ed. lib. bdg. 23.00 (ISBN 0-405-10241-0). Arno.

--Pioneer Settlement in the Twenties: An Original Anthology. LC 77-70699. (America & the Holy Land Ser.). 1977. lib. bdg. 15.00x (ISBN 0-405-10250-X). Arno.

Eisenstadt, S. N. The Absorption of Immigrants. LC 74-31867. 275p. 1975. Repr. of 1954 ed. lib. bdg. 14.25x (ISBN 0-8371-7947-5, EIAI). Greenwood.

Frankl, Ludwig A. The Jews in the East, 2 vols. Beaton, P., tr. LC 78-97278. 1975. Repr. of 1859 ed. Set. lib. bdg. 28.50x (ISBN 0-8371-2596-0, FRJE). Greenwood.

Friedman, Isaiah. Germany, Turkey, & Zionism, 1897-1918. 1977. 52.50x (ISBN 0-19-822528-8). Oxford U Pr.

Gordon, Benjamin L. New Judea: Jewish Life in Modern Palestine & Egypt. Davis, Moshe, ed. LC 77-70697. (America & the Holy Land Ser.). (Illus.). 1977. Repr. of 1919 ed. lib. bdg. 22.00x (ISBN 0-405-10251-8). Arno.

Hoofien, Sigfried. Report of Mr. S. Hoofien to the Joint Distribution Committee of the American Funds for Jewish War Sufferers,New York. Davis, Moshe, ed. LC 77-70702. (America & the Holy Land Ser.). (Illus.). 1977. Repr. of 1918 ed. lib. bdg. 12.00x (ISBN 0-405-10254-2). Arno.

Lieberman, Saul. Texts & Studies. 1973. 25.50x (ISBN 0-87068-210-5). Ktav.

Mann, Jacob. The Jews in Egypt & in Palestine Under the Fatimid Caliphs, 2 Vols. in 1. rev. ed. (Library of Jewish Classics Ser). 1970. 45.00x (ISBN 0-87068-024-2). Ktav.

Ruppin, Arthur. Three Decades of Palestine: Speeches & Papers on the Upbuilding of the Jewish National Home. LC 70-97301. (Illus.). 342p. 1975. Repr. of 1936 ed. lib. bdg. 16.00x (ISBN 0-8371-2629-0, RUPA). Greenwood.

Segre, V. D. Israel: A Society in Transition. 1971. 10.95x (ISBN 0-19-215172-X). Oxford U Pr.

Sneersohn, Haym Z. Palestine & Roumania: A Description of the Holy Land & the Past & Present State of Roumania & the Roumanian Jews. Davis, Moshe, ed. LC 77-70745. (America & the Holy Land Ser.). 1977. Repr. of 1872 ed. lib. bdg. 12.00x (ISBN 0-405-10291-7). Arno.

JEWS IN POLAND

Banas, Josef. The Scapegoats: The Exodus of the Remnants of Polish Jewry. Szafar, Tadeusz, tr. 1979. text ed. 18.50 (ISBN 0-8419-6303-7). Holmes & Meier.

Baron, Salo W. A Social & Religious History of the Jews: Late Middle Ages and Era of European Expansion (1200-1650) Poland-Lithuania 1500-1650, Vol 16. 1976. 27.00x (ISBN 0-231-08853-1). Columbia U Pr.

Baskerville, B. C. The Polish Jew. 75.00 (ISBN 0-8490-0870-0). Gordon Pr.

Beller, Ilex. Lest My Village Be Forgotten: A Jewish Childhood in Poland. (Illus.). 144p. 50.00 (ISBN 0-933516-30-4). Alpine Fine Arts.

Czerniakow, Adam. Warsaw Diary of Adam Czerniakow. 1978. 16.95 (ISBN 0-8128-2523-3). Stein & Day.

Dobroczcki, L. & Kirshenblatt-Gimblett, B. Image Before My Eyes: A Photographic History of Jewish Life in Poland, 1864-1939. (Illus.). 1977. pap. text ed. write for info. (ISBN 0-914512-38-2). Yivo Inst.

Dobroszycki, Lucjan & Kirshenblatt-Gimblett, Barbara. Image Before My Eyes: A Photographic History of Jewish Life in Poland, 1864-1939. LC 75-35448. (Illus.). 1979. pap. 12.50 (ISBN 0-8052-0634-5). Schocken.

--Image Before My Eyes: A Photographic History of Jewish Life in Poland, 1864-1939. LC 75-35448. (Illus.). 1977. 29.95 (ISBN 0-8052-3607-4). Schocken.

Frydland, Rachmiel. When Being Jewish Was a Crime. LC 78-16689. 1978. pap. 3.95 (ISBN 0-8407-5659-3). Nelson.

Goodhart, Arthur L. Poland & the Minority Races. LC 71-135809. (Eastern Europe Collection Ser). 1970. Repr. of 1920 ed. 9.50 (ISBN 0-405-02751-6). Arno.

Gurdus, Luba K. The Death Train. LC 78-54657. (Illus.). 1979. 10.00 (ISBN 0-89604-005-4, Pub. by Holocaust Library). Schocken.

Heller, Celia. On the Edge of Destruction: Jews in Poland Between the Two World Wars. LC 76-22646. (Illus.). 1977. 20.00x (ISBN 0-231-03819-4). Columbia U Pr.

Heller, Celia S. On the Edge of Destruction: Jews of Poland Between the Two World Wars. LC 79-24645. 384p. 1980. pap. 8.95 (ISBN 0-8052-0651-5). Schocken.

Kallen, Horace M. Frontiers of Hope. Davis, Moshe, ed. LC 77-70711. (America & the Holy Land Ser.). 1977. Repr. of 1929 ed. lib. bdg. 28.00x (ISBN 0-405-10260-7). Arno.

Katsh, Abraham, ed. Scroll of Agony: The Warsaw Diary of Chaim A. Kaplan. 416p. 1981. pap. 6.95 (ISBN 0-02-034000-1). Macmillan.

Kruk, Herman. Togbukh Fun Vilner Geto. Bernstein, Mordecai W., ed. LC 62-56072. (Yivo Institute for Jewish Research, Memoirs Ser.: No. 1). (Illus.). 620p. (Yiddish.). 1961. 6.50 (ISBN 0-914512-29-3). Yivo Inst.

Kurzman, Dan. The Bravest Battle. 1980. pap. 2.50 (ISBN 0-523-40182-5). Pinnacle Bks.

Ringelblum, Emmanuel. Polish-Jewish Relations During the Second World War. Allon, Dafna, et al, trs. LC 76-1394. 330p. 1976. 24.00 (ISBN 0-86527-155-0). Fertig.

Shatzky, Jacob. Geshikhte Fun Yidn in Varshe, 3 vols. LC 48-15791. (Yiddish.). 1953. Set. 10.00 (ISBN 0-914512-27-7); 4.00 ea. Vol. 1 (ISBN 0-914512-32-3). Vol. 2 (ISBN 0-914512-33-1). Vol. 3 (ISBN 0-914512-34-X). Yivo Inst.

Shneiderman, S. L. The River Remembers. LC 77-93935. (Illus.). 1978. 8.95 (ISBN 0-8180-0821-0). Horizon.

Stroop, Jurgen. The Stroop Report: The Jewish Quarter of Warsaw Is No More! LC 79-1900. 1980. 10.00 (ISBN 0-394-50443-7). Pantheon.

Trunk, Isaiah. Lodzher Geto: A Historical & Sociological Study. (Yad Vashem-Yivo Joint Documentary Projects Monographs: No. 1). (Illus.). 528p. (Yiddish.). 1962. 6.00 (ISBN 0-914512-17-X, HE65-1399). Yivo Inst.

Vetulani, A. The Jews of Medieval Poland. 1978. lib. bdg. 59.95 (ISBN 0-685-62298-3). Revisionist Pr.

Vinecour, Earl. Polish Jews: The Final Chapter. LC 77-83266. (Illus.). 1977. 14.50x (ISBN 0-8147-8756-8). NYU Pr.

Vinecour, Earl & Fishman, Charles. Polish Jews: The Final Chapter. (Paperbacks Ser). (Orig.). 1977. pap. 5.95 (ISBN 0-07-067490-6, SP). McGraw.

Vishniac, Roman. Polish Jews: A Pictorial Record. LC 65-25413. (Illus.). 1968. 12.00 (ISBN 0-8052-3205-2); pap. 3.95 (ISBN 0-8052-0360-5). Schocken.

The Warsaw Ghetto in Pictures: Illustrated Catalog. LC 79-26657. (Yivo Institute for Jewish Research Guide & Catalogs Ser.: No. 1). (Illus.). 1970. pap. 3.50 (ISBN 0-914512-08-0). Yivo Inst.

Wiesel, Elie. A Jew Today. Wiesel, Marion, tr. 1978. 10.00 (ISBN 0-394-42054-3). Random.

Zieman, Joseph. The Cigarette Sellers of Three Crosses Square. (YA) (gr. 7-11). 1977. pap. 1.50 (ISBN 0-380-00967-6, 45682). Avon.

Zvi. LC 78-56149. 1978. pap. 2.95 (ISBN 0-915540-23-1). Friends Israel-Spearhead Pr.

JEWS IN PORTUGAL

Barnett, Richard. The Sephardi Heritage. 1971. 35.00x (ISBN 0-685-38387-3, 87068-170-21). Ktav.

Kayserling, Meyer. Bibliotec Espanola-Portugeza-Judaica. rev. ed. 1971. 25.00x (ISBN 0-87068-146-X). Ktav.

Lindo, Elias H. History of the Jews of Spain & Portugal. LC 71-112055. (Research & Source Works Ser: No. 4). (Illus.). 1970. Repr. of 1848 ed. 32.50 (ISBN 0-8337-2109-7). B Franklin.

Singerman, Robert. The Jews in Spain & Portugal: A Bibliography. LC 75-1166. (Reference Library of Social Science: No. 11). 376p. 1975. lib. bdg. 43.00 (ISBN 0-8240-1089-2). Garland Pub.

Yerushalmi, Y. H. The Lisbon Massacre of 1506 & the Royal Image in the Shebet Yehuda. (Hebrew Union College Annual Supplements: Vol. 1). 7.50x (ISBN 0-87820-600-0, HUC Pr). Ktav.

JEWS IN ROME

Radin, Max. The Jews Among the Greeks & Romans. LC 73-2224. (The Jewish People; History, Religion, Literature Ser.). Repr. of 1915 ed. 25.00 (ISBN 0-405-05286-3). Arno.

JEWS IN ROME (CITY)

Katz, R. Black Sabbath. 1969. 7.95 (ISBN 0-02-560780-4). Macmillan.

JEWS IN RUMANIA

Sneersohn, Haym Z. Palestine & Roumania: A Description of the Holy Land & the Past & Present State of Roumania & the Roumanian Jews. Davis, Moshe, ed. LC 77-70745. (America & the Holy Land Ser.). 1977. Repr. of 1872 ed. lib. bdg. 12.00x (ISBN 0-405-10291-7). Arno.

JEWS IN RUSSIA

Ber Of Bolechow. The Memoirs of Ber of Bolechow (1723-1805) LC 73-2186. (The Jewish People; History, Religion, Literature Ser.). Repr. of 1922 ed. 14.00 (ISBN 0-405-05252-9). Arno.

Blaser, Elissa. The Russian Jewry Simulation Game: Exodus. new ed. 36p. (gr. 7 up). 1974. 8.95x (ISBN 0-87441-199-8). Behrman.

Brym, Robert J. The Jewish Intelligentsia & Russian Marxism: A Sociological Study of Intellectual Radicalism & Ideological Divergence. LC 77-14724. 1978. 16.95x (ISBN 0-8052-3685-6). Schocken.

Cang, Joel. Silent Millions: A History of the Jews in the Soviet Union. LC 78-107013. 1970. 7.50 (ISBN 0-8008-7184-7). Taplinger.

Davitt, Michael. Within the Pale: The True Story of Anti-Semetic Persecutions in Russia. facsimile ed. LC 74-27976. (Modern Jewish Experience Ser.). 1975. Repr. of 1903 ed. 19.00x (ISBN 0-405-06705-4). Arno.

Eckman, Lester. Soviet Policy Towards Jews & Israel. LC 73-93237. 1974. 6.95 (ISBN 0-88400-005-2). Shengold.

Errera, Leo A. The Russian Jews: Extermination or Emancipation? Lowy, Bella, tr. LC 70-97276. (Illus.). 206p. 1975. Repr. of 1894 ed. lib. bdg. 15.00x (ISBN 0-8371-2597-9, ERRJ). Greenwood.

Fahey, Dennis. The Rulers of Russia: Jewish Bolshevism and Jewish Influence in the Soviet Government. 1980. lib. bdg. 59.95 (ISBN 0-8490-3098-6). Gordon Pr.

Frankel, Jonathan. Prophecy & Politics: Socialism, Nationalism & the Russian Jews 1862-1917. LC 80-14414. (Illus.). 665p. 1981. 49.50 (ISBN 0-521-23028-4). Cambridge U Pr.

--Prophecy & Politics: Socialism, Nationalism, & the Russian Jews, 1862-1917. LC 80-14414. (Illus.). 816p. 1981. 49.50 (ISBN 0-521-23028-4). Cambridge U Pr.

Frederic, Harold. New Exodus: A Study of Israel in Russia. LC 71-115538. (Russia Observed, Series I). 1970. Repr. of 1892 ed. 14.00 (ISBN 0-405-03027-4). Arno.

Gitelman, Zvi Y. Jewish Nationality & Soviet Politics: The Jewish Sections of the CPSU, 1917-1930. LC 77-154996. (Research Institute on Communist Affairs Ser.). 488p. 1972. 35.00x (ISBN 0-691-07542-5). Princeton U Pr.

Greenberg, Louis. Jews in Russia: The Struggle for Emancipation, 2 Vols. in 1. LC 79-161769. Repr. of 1965 ed. 27.50 (ISBN 0-404-09023-0). AMS Pr.

--The Jews in Russia: The Struggle for Emancipation, 1772-1917, 2 vols. in 1. Wishnitzer, Mark, ed. LC 75-36489. 448p. 1976. pap. 6.95 (ISBN 0-8052-0525-X). Schocken.

Kallen, Horace M. Frontiers of Hope. Davis, Moshe, ed. LC 77-70711. (America & the Holy Land Ser.). 1977. Repr. of 1929 ed. lib. bdg. 28.00x (ISBN 0-405-10260-7). Arno.

Kochan, Lionel, ed. The Jews in Soviet Russia Since 1917. 3rd ed. (Illus.). 1978. pap. 5.95 (ISBN 0-19-281199-1, GB503, GB). Oxford U Pr.

Korey, William. The Soviet Cage: Anti-Semitism in Russia. 384p. 1973. 12.50 (ISBN 0-670-65940-1). Viking Pr.

LaZebnik, Edith. Such a Life. LC 78-759. 1978. 8.95 (ISBN 0-688-03280-X). Morrow.

Lenin, V. I. Lenin on the Jewish Question. Lumer, Hyman, ed. LC 74-6278. 254p. (Eng.). 1974. 7.50 (ISBN 0-7178-0398-8); pap. 2.75 (ISBN 0-7178-0399-6). Intl Pub Co.

Levin, Nora. While Messiah Tarried: Jewish Socialist Movements, 1871-1917. LC 75-7769. (Illus.). 1979. pap. 10.95 (ISBN 0-8052-0616-7). Schocken.

Levin, Shmarya. Youth in Revolt. facsimile ed. Samuel, Maurice, tr. LC 74-27998. (Modern Jewish Experience Ser.). (Eng.). 1975. Repr. of 1930 ed. 18.00x (ISBN 0-405-06725-9). Arno.

Levitats, Isaac. Jewish Community in Russia, 1772-1844. LC 79-120641. 1970. Repr. lib. bdg. 16.50x (ISBN 0-374-94956-5). Octagon.

Meisl, Josef. Haskalah: Geschichte der Aufklarungsbewegung unter den Juden in Russland. Katz, Stephen, ed. LC 79-7147. (Jewish Philosophy, Mysticism & History of Ideas Ser.). 1980. Repr. of 1919 ed. lib. bdg. 18.00x (ISBN 0-405-12277-2). Arno.

Mendelsohn, Ezra. Class Struggle in the Pale. LC 71-96097. 1970. 23.50 (ISBN 0-521-07730-3). Cambridge U Pr.

Orbach, William W. The American Movement to Aid Soviet Jews. LC 78-19696. 1979. 15.00x (ISBN 0-87023-267-3). U of Mass Pr.

Orenstein, Sylvia. Source Book on Soviet Jewry: An Annotated Bibliography. LC 81-65842. 120p. 1980. pap. 3.00 (ISBN 0-87495-019-8). Am Jewish Comm.

--Source Book on Soviet Jewry: An Annotated Bibliography. 1981. 3.00 (ISBN 0-87495-029-5). Am Jewish Comm.

Pennell, Joseph. The Jew at Home: Impressions of Jewish Life in Russia & Austria. 1976. lib. bdg. 134.95 (ISBN 0-8490-2098-0). Gordon Pr.

Porath, Jonathan D. Jews in Russia: The Last Four Centuries. 1973. pap. 3.75x (ISBN 0-8381-0220-4). United Syn Bk.

Raisin, Jacob S. The Haskalah Movement in Russia. LC 79-98740. 355p. 1972. Repr. of 1913 ed. lib. bdg. 17.50x (ISBN 0-8371-2756-4, RAHM). Greenwood.

Rosensaft, Menachem Z. The Legal Status of Soviet Jewry: De Jure Equality & De Facto Discrimination. 30p. 1.00 (ISBN 0-686-74962-6). ADL.

Rothenberg, Joshua. The Jewish Religion in the Soviet Union. 1971. 15.00x (ISBN 0-87068-156-7). Ktav.

Rubin, Ronald I. The Unredeemed: Anti-Semitism in the Soviet Union. (Illus.). 1972. 10.00 (ISBN 0-8129-0500-8). Times Bks.

Rubinow, Isaac M. Economic Conditions of the Jews in Russia. facsimile ed. LC 74-29519. (Modern Jewish Experience Ser.). 1975. Repr. of 1907 ed. 11.00x (ISBN 0-405-06744-5). Arno.

Rybakov, Anatoli. Heavy Sand. Shukman, Harold, tr. from Rus. 384p. 1981. 13.95 (ISBN 0-670-36499-1). Viking Pr.

Sawyer, Thomas E. The Jewish Minority in the Soviet Union. (Special Studies on the Soviet Union & Eastern Europe). 1979. lib. bdg. 28.75x (ISBN 0-89158-480-3). Westview.

Schneersohn, Y. Y. Notations on the Arrest. Levin, Moshe Chaim, ed. Gurevich, David A., tr. from Hebrew. LC 80-21987. (Illus.). 226p. (Orig.). 1980. 11.75 (ISBN 0-86639-100-2). Friends Refugees.

Schroeter, Leonard. The Last Exodus. LC 79-4922. 444p. (Orig.). 1979. pap. 7.95 (ISBN 0-295-95685-2). U of Wash Pr.

Schulman, Elias. A History of Jewish Education in the Soviet Union, 1918-1948. 1971. 12.50x (ISBN 0-87068-145-1). Ktav.

Schwarz, Solomon M. The Jews in the Soviet Union. LC 72-4298. (World Affairs Ser.: National & International Viewpoints). 398p. 1972. Repr. of 1951 ed. 18.00 (ISBN 0-405-04589-1). Arno.

Semenov, E. P. The Russian Government & the Massacres. LC 70-97304. (Judaica Ser). 265p. 1972. Repr. of 1907 ed. lib. bdg. 14.25x (ISBN 0-8371-2632-0, SERG). Greenwood.

Shcharansky, Avital & Ben-Joseph, Ilana. Next Year in Jerusalem. Hoffman, Stefani, tr. LC 79-17494. (Illus.). 1979. 9.95 (ISBN 0-688-03552-3). Morrow.

Shield, 5 vols. in 1. Incl. Vol. 1. Russia & the Jews. Gorky, Maxim; Vol. 2. First Step. Andreyev, Leonid; Vol. 3. Jewish Question in Russia. Milyukov, Paul; Vol. 4. Jewish Question As a Russian Question. Merezhovsky, Dmitry; Vol. 5. Jew, A Story. Artzibashef, Michael. (Eng.). Repr. of 1917 ed. lib. bdg. 15.00 (ISBN 0-8371-2633-9, GOSH). Greenwood.

Stern, Paula. Water's Edge: Domestic Politics & the Making of American Foreign Policy. LC 78-55331. (Contributions in Political Science: No. 15). 1979. lib. bdg. 19.95 (ISBN 0-313-20520-5, SWE/). Greenwood.

Talmon, J. L. Israel Among the Nations. Mandel, To, ed. 1971. 11.95 (ISBN 0-02-616250-4). Macmillan.

Taylor, Telford. Courts of Terror: Soviet Criminal Justice & Jewish Emigration. 1976. pap. 1.95 (ISBN 0-394-71758-9, Vin). Random.

Tobias, Henry J. Jewish Bund in Russia from Its Origins to 1905. LC 75-153820. 1972. 18.50x (ISBN 0-8047-0764-2). Stanford U Pr.

Urussov, Serge D. The Kishinev Pogrom. 1970. Repr. of 1908 ed. text ed. 7.50x (ISBN 0-87503-026-2). Humanities.

Wiesel, Elie. Jews of Silence. Kozodoy, N., tr. LC 66-21622. 1966. 4.95 (ISBN 0-03-060175-4). HR&W.

JEWS IN SOUTH AFRICA

Gordimer, Nadien, et al. South African Jewish Voices. Kalechofsky, Roberta, ed. (Echad 2 Ser.). 300p. 1981. pap. 8.50 (ISBN 0-916288-10-2). Micah Pubns.

Herrman, Louis. A History of the Jews in South Africa from the Earliest Times to 1895. LC 74-97285. (Illus.). 288p. 1975. Repr. of 1935 ed. lib. bdg. 15.00 (ISBN 0-8371-2607-X, HEJS). Greenwood.

Shimoni, Gideon. Jews & Zionism: The South African Experience, 1910-1967. (Illus.). 442p. 1980. 27.50x (ISBN 0-19-570179-8). Oxford U Pr.

Stevens, Richard P. & Elmessiri, Abdelwahab M. Israel & South Africa: The Progression of a Relationship. LC 77-83663. pap. 6.95x (ISBN 0-930244-00-1). North American Inc.

JEWS IN SPAIN

Ashtor, Eliyahu. The Jews of Moslem Spain, Vol. 1. Machlowitz Klein, Aaron, tr. from Heb. LC 73-14081. (Illus.). 470p. 1974. 12.00 (ISBN 0-8276-0017-8, 352). Jewish Pubn.

--The Jews of Moslem Spain, Vol. 2. 1978. 12.00 (ISBN 0-8276-0100-X, 411). Jewish Pubn.

Avni, Haim. Spain, the Jews & Franco. Shimoni, Emanuel, tr. from Hebrew. LC 80-39777. 320p. 1981. 19.95 (ISBN 0-686-73767-9, 469). Jewish Pubn.

Baer, Yitzhak. History of the Jews in Christian Spain, 2 Vols. 1966. pap. 5.95 ea. (ISBN 0-8276-0115-8, 425). Jewish Pubn.

Barnett, Richard. The Sephardi Heritage. 1971. 35.00x (ISBN 0-685-38387-3, 87068-170-21). Ktav.

Beinhart, Haim. Trujillo: A Jewish Community in Extremadura on the Eve of Expulsion from Spain. (Hispania Judaica: No. 2). 372p. 1980. text ed. 23.00x (ISBN 965-223-349-8, Pub. by Magnes Israel). Humanities.

Castro Y Rossi, Aldolfo De. The History of the Jews in Spain: From the Time of Their Settlement in That Country till the Commencement of the Present Century. Kirwan, Edward D., tr. from Span. LC 70-97273. (Judaica Ser). (Illus.). vii, 276p. 1972. Repr. of 1851 ed. lib. bdg. 15.00x (ISBN 0-8371-2593-6, CAJS). Greenwood.

Cohen, Martin A. The Martyr: The Story of a Secret Jew & the Mexican Inquisition in the Sixteenth Century. LC 72-14055. (Illus.). 1973. 7.95 (ISBN 0-8276-0011-9, 327). Jewish Pubn.

Epstein, Isidore. Responsa of Rabbi Simon Ben Zemah & the Responsa of Rabbi Solomon Ben Adreth of Barcelona, 2 Vols. in 1. rev. ed. LC 68-19727. 1968. 12.50x (ISBN 0-87068-039-0). Ktav.

Isaacs, A. Lionel. The Jews of Majorca. 1976. lib. bdg. 59.95 (ISBN 0-8490-2105-7). Gordon Pr.

Katz, S. Jews in the Visigothic & Frankish Kingdoms of Spain & Gaul. 1937. 14.00 (ISBN 0-527-01697-7). Kraus Repr.

Kayserling, Meyer. Bibliotec Espanola-Portugeza-Judaica. rev. ed. 1971. 25.00x (ISBN 0-87068-146-X). Ktav.

Lindo, Elias H. History of the Jews of Spain & Portugal. LC 71-112055. (Research & Source Works Ser: No. 4). (Illus.). 1970. Repr. of 1848 ed. 32.50 (ISBN 0-8337-2109-7). B Franklin.

Mocatta, Frederic D. The Jews of Spain & Portugal & the Inquisition. LC 72-88016. (Illus.). xxii, 106p. 1973. Repr. of 1933 ed. lib. bdg. 8.00x (ISBN 0-8154-0440-9). Cooper Sq.

Moore, Kenneth. Those of the Street: The Catholic-Jews of Mallorca. LC 76-636. 1979. pap. text ed. 4.95x (ISBN 0-268-01836-7). U of Notre Dame Pr.

Neuman, Abraham A. Jews in Spain: Their Social, Political & Cultural Life During the Middle Ages, 2 vols. LC 70-105964. 1970. Repr. of 1942 ed. lib. bdg. 42.00x (ISBN 0-374-96061-5). Octagon.

Roth, Cecil. Spanish Inquisition. (Orig.). 1964. pap. 4.95 (ISBN 0-393-00255-1, Norton Lib). Norton.

Singerman, Robert. The Jews in Spain & Portugal: A Bibliography. LC 75-1166. (Reference Library of Social Science: No. 11). 376p. 1975. lib. bdg. 43.00 (ISBN 0-8240-1089-2). Garland Pub.

JEWS IN THE BYZANTINE EMPIRE

Starr, Joshua. Jews in the Byzantine Empire. LC 88-101218. (Research & Source Works Ser: No. 386). 1970. Repr. of 1939 ed. text ed. 24.00 (ISBN 0-8337-3374-5). B Franklin.

JEWS IN THE ISLAMIC EMPIRE

Fischel, Walter. Jews in the Economic & Political Life of Medieval Islam. rev. ed. LC 68-25719. 1969. Repr. of 1937 ed. 12.50x (ISBN 0-87068-047-1). Ktav.

Goitein, S. D. Jews & Arabs: Their Contacts Through the Ages. 3rd ed. LC 74-9141. 271p. 1974. 10.00x (ISBN 0-8052-3567-1); pap. 4.95 (ISBN 0-8052-0464-4). Schocken.

--A Mediterranean Society: The Jewish Communities of the Arab World As Portrayed in the Documents of the Cairo Geniza. Incl. Vol. I. Economic Foundations. 1968. 30.00x (ISBN 0-520-00484-1); Vol. 2. The Community. 1971. 32.50x (ISBN 0-520-01867-2); Vol. 3. The Family. 1978. 32.50x (ISBN 0-520-03265-9). LC 67-22430. (Near Eastern Center, UCLA). U of Cal Pr.

JEWS IN THE LEVANT

Frankl, Ludwig A. The Jews in the East, 2 vols. Beaton, P., tr. LC 78-97278. 1975. Repr. of 1859 ed. Set. lib. bdg. 28.50x (ISBN 0-8371-2596-0, FRJE). Greenwood.

Starr, Joshua. Romania: The Jewries of the Levant After the Fourth Crusade. 1943. 10.00x (ISBN 0-685-13744-9). Ktav.

JEWS IN THE NEAR EAST

Cohen, Hayyim J. Jews of the Middle East (1860-1972) 224p. 1973. casebound 12.95x (ISBN 0-87855-169-7). Transaction Bks.

Deshen, Shlomo & Shokeid, Moshe. The Predicament of Homecoming: Cultural & Social Life of North African Immigrants in Israel. Turner, Victor, ed. (Symbol, Myth, & Ritual Ser). (Illus.). 251p. 1974. 25.00x (ISBN 0-8014-0885-7). Cornell U Pr.

Goitein, S. D. Letters of Medieval Jewish Traders. LC 72-14025. 316p. 1974. 26.00x (ISBN 0-691-05212-3). Princeton U Pr.

Goldberg, Harvey E., ed. & tr. from Hebrew. The Book of Mordechai: A Study of the Jews of Libya - Selections from the Highid Mordekhai of Mordechai Hakohen. LC 80-11470. 1980. text ed. 19.50x (ISBN 0-89727-005-3). Inst Study Human.

Landshut, Siegfried. The Jewish Communities in the Muslim Countries of the Middle East. LC 75-6443. (The Rise of Jewish Nationalism & the Middle East Ser). 102p. 1976. Repr. of 1950 ed. 14.00 (ISBN 0-88355-330-9). Hyperion Conn.

Woolfson, Marion. Prophets in Babylon: Jews in the Arab World. LC 80-670264. 304p. 1980. 38.00 (ISBN 0-571-11458-X, Pub. by Faber & Faber). Merrimack Bk Serv.

JEWS IN THE NETHERLANDS

Bloom, Herbert I. Economic Activities of the Jews of Amsterdam in the Seventeenth & Eighteenth Centuries. LC 70-91036. 1969. Repr. of 1937 ed. 15.00 (ISBN 0-8046-0646-3). Kennikat.

JEWS IN THE UNITED STATES

see also United States–History–Civil War, 1861-1865–Jews

Altfeld, E. Milton. The Jews Struggle for Religious & Civil Liberty in Maryland. LC 78-99859. (Civil Liberties in American History Ser). 1970. Repr. of 1924 ed. lib. bdg. 25.00 (ISBN 0-306-71859-6). Da Capo.

American Jewish Business Enterprise. (American Jewish Historical Quarterly: Vol. 66, Pt.1). 1976. 8.00 (ISBN 0-911934-03-0). Am Jewish Hist Soc.

Anti-Semitism in America, 1878-1939. An Original Anthology. LC 76-46110. (Anti-Movements in America). (Illus.). 1977. lib. bdg. 35.00 (ISBN 0-405-09981-9). Arno.

Barnard, Harry. Forging of an American Jew: The Life & Times of Judge Julian W. Mack. 1974. 7.95 (ISBN 0-685-52984-3). Herzl Pr.

Bauer, Yehuda. American Jewry & the Holocaust: The American Jewish Joint Distribution Committee, 1939-1945. 550p. 1981. 25.00 (ISBN 0-8143-1672-7). Wayne St U Pr.

Bayor, Ronald H. Neighbors in Conflict: The Irish, Germans, Jews, & Italians of New York City, 1929-1941. LC 77-14260. (Studies in Historical & Political Science, 96th Ser: No. 2). 1978. text ed. 16.00x o. p. (ISBN 0-8018-2024-3); pap. 5.95 (ISBN 0-8018-2370-6). Johns Hopkins.

Berkson, Isaac B. Theories of Americanization: A Critical Study. LC 77-87743. (American Education: Its Men, Institutions & Ideas, Ser. 1). 1969. Repr. of 1920 ed. 15.00 (ISBN 0-405-01387-6). Arno.

--Theories of Americanization: A Critical Study, with Special Reference to the Jewish Group. LC 78-176558. (Columbia University. Teachers College. Contributions to Education: No. 109). Repr. of 1920 ed. 15.00 (ISBN 0-404-55109-2). AMS Pr.

Berlin, William S. On the Edge of Politics: The Roots of Jewish Political Thought in America. (Contributions in Political Science: No. 14). 1978. lib. bdg. 18.95x (ISBN 0-313-20422-5, BEP/). Greenwood.

Berman, Myron. Richmond's Jewry, Seventeen Sixty-Nine to Nineteen Seventy-Six. LC 78-6377. 1979. 12.50x (ISBN 0-8139-0743-8). U Pr of Va.

Bernheimer, Charles S., ed. The Russian Jew in the United States: Studies of Social Conditions in New York, Philadelphia, & Chicago, with a Description of Rural Settlements. LC 79-145470. (The American Immigration Library). 426p. 1971. Repr. of 1905 ed. lib. bdg. 14.95x (ISBN 0-89198-002-4). Ozer.

Blau, Joseph L. Judaism in America: From Curiosity to Third Faith. LC 75-5069. (Chicago History of American Religion Ser.). 1978. pap. 4.95 (ISBN 0-226-05728-3, P761, Phoen). U of Chicago Pr.

Bookstaber, Philip D. Judaism & the American Mind: In Theory & Practice. LC 78-26404. 1979. Repr. of 1939 ed. lib. bdg. 18.75x (ISBN 0-313-20875-1, BOJU). Greenwood.

Bothwell, Etta K. Alienation in the Jewish American Novel of the Sixties. LC 78-3559. 1979. pap. 10.00 (ISBN 0-8477-3191-X). U of PR Pr.

Brooks, Juanita. The History of the Jews in Utah & Idaho, 1853-1950. 252p. 1973. 7.95 (ISBN 0-914740-12-1). Western Epics.

Bunim, Irving M. Ever Since Sinai. Wengrov, Charles, ed. 1978. 12.50 (ISBN 0-87306-138-1). Feldheim.

Cogan, Sara, compiled by. The Jews of San Francisco & the Greater Bay Area: 1849 to 1919. (Western Jewish Americana Ser.: No. 2). 1972. 22.00 (ISBN 0-686-27353-2). Magnes Mus.

--The Jews in los Angeles. (Western Jewish Americana Ser. Publications). 237p. 1980. 24.95 (ISBN 0-686-30816-6); pap. 14.95 (ISBN 0-686-30817-4). Magnes Museum.

Cohen, Emily C. American Jewish Year Book Index. 1968. 20.00x (ISBN 0-87068-040-4). Ktav.

Cohen, Naomi. American Jews & the Zionist Idea. 7.50x (ISBN 0-87068-272-5). Ktav.

Cooper, Elizabeth K. Attitude of Children & Teachers Toward Mexican, Negro & Jewish Minorities. LC 72-86399. pap. 7.00 (ISBN 0-88247-184-8). R & E Res Assoc.

Crawford, Albert G. & Monson, Rela G. Academy & Community: A Study of the Jewish Identity & Involvement of Professors. LC 80-68432. 40p. 1980. pap. 2.00 (ISBN 0-87495-029-5). Am Jewish Comm.

Daly, C. P. Settlement of the Jews in North America. 59.95 (ISBN 0-8490-1027-6). Gordon Pr.

Dawidowicz, Lucy. The Jewish Presence: Essays on Identity & History. LC 78-6236. 1978. pap. 3.95 (ISBN 0-15-646221-4, Harv). HarBraceJ.

Dicker, Herman. Piety & Perservance: Jews from the Carpathian Mountains. LC 80-54595. (Illus.). 252p. 1981. 14.95 (ISBN 0-87203-094-6); pap. 8.75 (ISBN 0-87203-098-9). Hermon.

Dinnerstein, Leonard & Palsson, Mary D., eds. Jews in the South. LC 72-89114. 400p. 1973. 25.00x (ISBN 0-8071-0226-1). La State U Pr.

Eichhorn. Evangelizing the American Jew. LC 77-28975. 1978. 12.50 (ISBN 0-8246-0225-0). Jonathan David.

Eis, Ruth. Torah Binders of the Judah L. Magnes Museum. LC 79-83877. 80p. 1979. pap. 18.00 (ISBN 0-686-30820-4). Magnes Museum.

Elazar, Daniel J. Community & Polity: The Organizational Dynamics of American Jewry. LC 75-8167. (Illus.). 448p. 1976. pap. 6.95 (ISBN 0-8276-0068-2, 377). Jewish Pubn.

Epstein, Benjamin & Forster, Arnold. Some of My Best Friends... LC 75-2694. 274p. 1975. Repr. of 1962 ed. lib. bdg. 15.50x (ISBN 0-8371-8027-9, EPBF). Greenwood.

Epstein, Melech. Jewish Labor in the U. S. A., 1882-1952. rev. ed. 1969. 35.00x (ISBN 0-87068-042-0). Ktav.

Evans, Eli. The Provincials. LC 73-80747. 1976. pap. 7.95 (ISBN 0-689-70532-8, 221). Atheneum.

Farmer, George L. Education: The Dilemma of the Jewish-American. 1969. 15.00x (ISBN 0-913330-11-6). Sun Dance Bks.

Fine, Morris & Himmelfarb, Milton, eds. American Jewish Year Book, 1976, Vol. 76. LC 99-4040. 613p. 1976. 15.00 (ISBN 0-8276-0128-X, 383). Jewish Pubn.

Fine, Morris, et al, eds. The American Jewish Year Book, 1978, Vol. 78. LC 99-4040. (Illus.). 1977. 15.00 (ISBN 0-8276-0130-1, 412). Jewish Pubn.

--American Jewish Year Book 1979, Vol. 79. LC 99-4040. 1979. 15.00 (ISBN 0-8276-0113-1, 429). Jewish Pubn.

Fishman, Joshua A. Yiddish in America: Socio-Linguistic Description & Analysis. LC 65-63395. (General Publications Ser: Vol. 36). (Orig.). 1965. pap. text ed. 5.00x (ISBN 0-87750-110-6). Res Ctr Lang Semiotic.

Ford, Gertrude. Eighty-One Sheriff Street. 272p. 1981. 10.95 (ISBN 0-8119-0343-5). Fell.

Gartner, Lloyd P., ed. Jewish Education in the United States. LC 73-112708. 1970. pap. text ed. 4.25x (ISBN 0-8077-1404-6). Tchrs Coll.

Ginzberg, Eli. American Jews: The Building of a Voluntary Community. (Texts & Studies). 1980. 15.00 (ISBN 0-911934-06-5). Am Jewish Hist Soc.

Glanz, Rudolf. The Jewish Female in America: Two Female Generations, 1820-1929, Vol. 1. 25.00x (ISBN 0-87068-461-2). Ktav.

Glazer, Nathan. American Judaism. rev. ed. LC 57-8574. (Chicago History of American Civilization Ser). 1972. 9.50x (ISBN 0-226-29839-6); pap. 4.50 (ISBN 0-226-29841-8, CHAC7). U of Chicago Pr.

Goldberg, Nathan, et al. The Classification of Jewish Immigrants & Its Implications: A Survey of Opinion. LC 45-6587. (Yivo English Translation Ser.). 154p. 1945. pap. 2.00 (ISBN 0-914512-13-7). Yivo Inst.

Goldman, Jack B. A History of Pioneer Jews in California: Thesis. 1939. 7.00 (ISBN 0-685-40323-8). R & E Res Assoc.

Gordon, Albert I. Jews in Suburbia. LC 73-11749. 264p. 1973. Repr. of 1959 ed. lib. bdg. 15.00x (ISBN 0-8371-7088-5, COJS). Greenwood.

Grossman, Brigite S. Experiencing Jewish Boston. LC 80-85316. (Illus.). 54p. (Orig.). 1981. pap. 3.50 (ISBN 0-9605624-0-0). Jewish Comm Ctr.

Hapgood, Hutchins. Spirit of the Ghetto. facsimile ed. Rischin, Moses, ed. LC 67-12099. (The John Harvard Library). (Illus.). 1967. 16.50x (ISBN 0-674-83265-5). Harvard U Pr.

Hardon, John A. American Judaism. LC 72-148264. (gr. 11 up). 1971. 5.95 (ISBN 0-8294-0199-7). Loyola.

Hartstein, Jacob I. & Miller, Benjamin. Jews in America: Heritage & History. (Illus.). 1978. 6.50 (ISBN 0-686-26239-5). Board Jewish Educ.

Hendrick, Burton J. The Jews in America. Grob, Gerald, ed. LC 76-46081. (Anti-Movements in America). 1977. Repr. of 1923 ed. lib. bdg. 12.00x (ISBN 0-405-09954-1). Arno.

Hertzberg, Arthur. Being Jewish in America: The Modern Experience. LC 78-54390. 320p. 1980. pap. 7.95 (ISBN 0-8052-0654-X). Schocken.

--Being Jewish in America: The Modern Experience. LC 78-54390. 1979. 16.95x (ISBN 0-8052-3692-9). Schocken.

Himmelfarb, Milton & Singer, David, eds. American Jewish Year Book, Vol. 81. LC 99-4040. 450p. 1981. 20.00 (ISBN 0-8276-0185-9, 472). Jewish Pubn.

Hindus, Milton, ed. Old East Side. LC 69-19040. (Illus.). 1969. 6.00 (ISBN 0-8276-0154-9). Jewish Pubn.

Howe, Irving. World of Our Fathers. LC 75-16342. (Illus.). 736p. 1976. 14.95 (ISBN 0-15-146353-0). HarBraceJ.

--World of Our Fathers. LC 76-53818. 1977. pap. 6.95 (ISBN 0-671-22755-6, Touchstone). S&S.

Jacobs, Dan N. & Paul, Ellen F., eds. Studies of the Third Wave: Recent Migration of Soviet Jews to the United States. (Replica Edition Ser.). 176p. 1981. lib. bdg. 20.00x (ISBN 0-86531-143-9). Westview.

Janowsky, Oscar I., ed. American Jew. facs. ed. LC 76-142647. (Essay Index Reprint Ser). 1942. 18.00 (ISBN 0-8369-2166-6). Arno.

Jewish Americana. 1954. 7.50x (ISBN 0-685-38410-1, Pub. by Hebrew Union). Ktav.

Joseph, Samuel. History of the Baron DeHirsch Fund: The Americanization of the Jewish Immigrant. LC 76-52987. (Illus.). Repr. of 1935 ed. lib. bdg. 15.00x (ISBN 0-678-01151-6). Kelley.

--Jewish Immigration to the United States from 1881 to 1910. LC 14-15042. (Columbia University. Studies in the Social Sciences: No. 145). Repr. of 1914 ed. 7.50 (ISBN 0-404-51145-7). AMS Pr.

--Jewish Immigration to the United States from 1881 to 1910. LC 69-18781. (American Immigration Collection Ser., No. 1). (Illus.). 1969. Repr. of 1914 ed. 8.00 (ISBN 0-405-00529-6). Arno.

Kaganoff, Nathan M., ed. Solidarity & Kinship: Essays on American Zionism. (Illus.). 1980. 5.00 (ISBN 0-911934-14-6). Am Jewish Hist Soc.

Kaganoff, Nathan M. & Urofsky, Melvin I., eds. Turn to the South: Essays on Southern Jewry. (Illus.). 1979. 7.95 (ISBN 0-8139-0742-X). Am Jewish Hist Soc.

Karp, Abraham J. To Give Life: The UJA in the Shaping of the American Jewish Community. LC 80-16487. 160p. 1980. 12.95 (ISBN 0-8052-3751-8). Schocken.

Kazin, Alfred. New York Jew. LC 77-20359. 1978. 12.95 (ISBN 0-394-49567-5). Knopf.

Kertzer, Morris N. Tell Me, Rabbi. LC 76-8324. 1976. 7.95 (ISBN 0-8197-0395-8). Bloch.

Kessner, Thomas. The Golden Door: Italian & Jewish Immigrant Mobility in New York City, 1880-1915. 1977. text ed. 14.95 (ISBN 0-19-502116-9); pap. 4.95 (ISBN 0-19-502161-4). Oxford U Pr.

Korn, Bertram W. American Jewry & the Civil War. LC 61-65874. (Temple Bk). 1970. pap. 4.50 (ISBN 0-689-70245-0, T19). Atheneum.

Landesman, Alter E. Brownsville: The Birth, Development & Passing of a Jewish Community in New York. LC 68-57434. 1969. 7.95 (ISBN 0-8197-0151-3). Bloch.

Lavender, Abraham D., ed. A Coat of Many Colors: Jewish Subcommunities in the United States. LC 77-71865. (Contributions in Family Studies: No. 1). 1977. lib. bdg. 17.95x (ISBN 0-8371-9539-X, LCM/). Greenwood.

Learsi, Rufus. The Jew in America: A History. rev. ed. 1972. 8.95x (ISBN 0-87068-177-X). Ktav.

Leiser, Joseph. American Judaism: The Religion & Religious Institutions of the Jewish People in the United States. LC 78-26230. 1979. Repr. of 1925 ed. lib. bdg. 19.75x (ISBN 0-313-20879-4, LEAJ). Greenwood.

Levy, Louis E. The Russian Jewish Refugees in America. 1979. lib. bdg. 59.95 (ISBN 0-685-96468-X). Revisionist Pr.

Lipsky, Louis. Thirty Years of American Zionism, Vol.1. Davis, Moshe, ed. LC 77-70718. (America & the Holy Land Ser.). 1977. Repr. of 1927 ed. lib. bdg. 20.00x (ISBN 0-405-10263-1). Arno.

London, Hannah R. Miniatures & Silhouettes of Early American Jews. LC 78-87797. (Illus.). 1969. Repr. 15.00 (ISBN 0-8048-0657-8). C E Tuttle.

--Portraits of Jews by Gilbert Stuart & Other Early American Artists. LC 69-19613. (Illus.). 1969. Repr. 13.75 (ISBN 0-8048-0459-1). C E Tuttle.

Lopez, Enrique Hank. Eros & Ethos: A Comparative Study of Catholic, Jewish & Protestant Sex Behavior. LC 78-24192. 1979. 9.95 (ISBN 0-13-283432-4). P-H.

Madison, Charles A. Eminent American Jews: 1776 to the Present. LC 74-125967. (Illus.). (gr. 11-12). 1971. text ed. 16.00 (ISBN 0-8044-1576-5). Ungar.

Mailing, Frenkel. American Jewish Organizations Directory. 11th ed. 1978. write for info (ISBN 0-686-21247-9). Frenkel.

Markens, Isaac. The Hebrews in America: A Series of Historical & Biographical Sketches. facsimile ed. LC 74-29504. (Modern Jewish Experiences). 1975. Repr. of 1888 ed. 22.00x (ISBN 0-405-06731-3). Arno.

Mitchell, William E. Mishpokhe: A Study of New York City Jewish Family Clubs. 262p. 1980. text ed. 19.95 (ISBN 90-27976-95-3); pap. text ed. 5.95 (ISBN 0-202-01166-6). Aldine Pub.

Myerhoff, Barbara. Number Our Days. 1980. 5.95 (ISBN 0-671-25430-8, 25430, Touchstone). S&S.

Neusner, Jacob. American Judaism: Adventure in Modernity. pap. 6.95 (ISBN 0-87068-678-X). Ktav.

Orthodox Judaism in America. (American Jewish History Ser.: Vol. 69, Pt. 2). 1980. 6.00 (ISBN 0-911934-13-8). Am Jewish Hist Soc.
Postal, Bernard & Koppman, Lionel. American Jewish Landmarks: A Travel Guide and History, Vol. 1. LC 76-27401. (Orig.). 1977. 18.50 (ISBN 0-8303-0151-8); pap. 10.50 (ISBN 0-8303-0152-6). Fleet.
--American Jewish Landmarks: A Travel Guide & History, the South & Southwest, Vol. II. LC 76-27401. 1979. 15.95 (ISBN 0-8303-0155-0); pap. 7.50 (ISBN 0-8303-0157-7). Fleet.
Ribalow, Harold U. The Jew in American Sports. rev. ed. 1980. 14.95 (ISBN 0-8197-0175-0). Bloch.
Ribalow, Harold U., ed. Autobiographies of American Jews. LC 65-17047. 1965. 6.00 (ISBN 0-8276-0020-8, 227). Jewish Pubn.
Rischin, Moses, ed. The Jews of the West: The Metropolitan Years. (Illus.). 1979. 5.95 (ISBN 0-911934-11-1). Am Jewish Hist Soc.
Roiphe, Anne. Generation Without Memory. 1981. 11.95 (ISBN 0-671-41455-0, Linden). S&S.
Rose, Peter I. Strangers in Their Midst: Small-Town Jews & Their Neighbors. 1977. lib. bdg. 12.95 (ISBN 0-915172-32-1). Richwood Pub.
Rosenbaum, Fred. Architects of Reform: Congregation & Community Leadership, Emanuel of San Francisco. 1849-1980. LC 80-54032. 241p. 1980. 19.95 (ISBN 0-686-30818-2); pap. 9.95 (ISBN 0-686-30819-0). Magnes Museum.
Rosenthal, G. S., ed. The American Rabbi. 12.50x (ISBN 0-87068-327-6). Ktav.
Routtenberg, Max J. Decades of Decision: An Appraisal of American Jewish Life. LC 73-87990. 241p. 1973. 8.95 (ISBN 0-8197-0362-1). Bloch.
Sanders, Ronald. The Downtown Jews: Portrait of an Immigrant Generation. 1977. pap. 2.50 (ISBN 0-451-07284-7, E7284, Sig). NAL.
Sarna, Jonathan D. Jacksonian Jew: The Two Worlds of Mordecai Noah. LC 79-24379. 1981. text ed. 29.50x (ISBN 0-8419-0567-3). Holmes & Meier.
Scarpaci, Jean, ed. The Interaction of Italians & Jews in America. 1974. 4.00 (ISBN 0-686-21891-4). Am Italian.
Sharfman, I. Harold. Jews of Jackson, California. LC 76-79574. (Illus.). 1969. 11.50 (ISBN 0-87062-054-1). A H Clark.
Sherman, C. Bezalel. The Jew Within American Society: A Study in Ethnic Individuality. LC 60-16839. (Waynebooks Ser: No. 19). 1965. pap. 4.95x (ISBN 0-8143-1142-3, WB19). Wayne St U Pr.
Siegel, Steven A., compiled by. Archival Resources. (Jewish Immigrants of the Nazi Period in the USA: Vol. 1). 1979. 55.00 (ISBN 0-89664-027-2, Pub. by K G Saur). Gale.
Sklare, Marshall. America's Jews. 1971. pap. 7.95 (ISBN 0-394-31645-2). Random.
Sklare, Marshall, ed. The Jews: Social Patterns of an American Group. LC 76-49945. 1977. Repr. of 1955 ed. lib. bdg. 40.25 (ISBN 0-8371-9404-0, SKJE). Greenwood.
Sloan, Irving J. The Jews in America: A Chronology & Fact Book. 2nd ed. LC 77-26768. (Ethnic Chronology Ser.). 1978. lib. bdg. 8.50 (ISBN 0-379-00530-1). Oceana.
Strassfeld, Michael & Strassfeld, Sharon, eds. The Second Jewish Catalog: Sources & Resources. LC 73-11759. (Illus.). 1976. 7.95 (ISBN 0-8276-0084-4, 391). Jewish Pubn.
Tebeau, Charlton W. Synagogue in the Central City: Temple Israel of Greater Miami, 1922-1972. LC 71-85107. (Illus.). 144p. 1972. 9.95 (ISBN 0-87024-239-3). U of Miami Pr.
Tobias, Henry J. The Jews in Oklahoma. LC 79-6723. (Newcomers to a New Land Ser.: Vol. 10). (Illus.). 96p. (Orig.). 1980. pap. 3.95 (ISBN 0-8061-1676-5). U of Okla Pr.
Uchill, Ida L. Pioneers, Peddlers, & Tsadikim: The Story of the Jews in Colorado. 2nd ed. LC 57-57817. 327p. 1979. pap. 10.00 (ISBN 0-9604468-0-X). Uchill.
Van Den Haag, Ernest. The Jewish Mystique. LC 76-56974. 1977. 8.95 (ISBN 0-8128-1267-0); pap. 4.95 (ISBN 0-8128-2189-0). Stein & Day.
Wiernik, Peter. History of the Jews in America from the Period of Discovery of the New World to the Present Time. Repr. of 1931 ed. lib. bdg. 15.00 (ISBN 0-8371-2637-1, WIJA). Greenwood.
Winter, Nathan H. Jewish Education in a Pluralist Society: Samson Benderly & Jewish Education in the United States. LC 66-22224. 262p. 1966. 10.00x (ISBN 0-8147-0448-4). NYU Pr.
Wirth, Louis. Ghetto. LC 56-14116. (Illus.). 1956. pap. 3.95 (ISBN 0-226-90250-1, P7, Phoen). U of Chicago Pr.
Wise, Isaac. Reminiscences. Philipson, David, ed. LC 73-2233. (The Jewish People; History, Religion, Literature Ser.). Repr. of 1901 ed. 22.00 (ISBN 0-405-05294-4). Arno.
Wise, James W. Jews Are Like That. facs. ed. LC 70-84348. (Essay Index Reprint Ser). 1928. 14.75 (ISBN 0-8369-1114-8). Arno.
Zagat, Samuel. Jewish Life on New York's Lower East Side: Drawings & Paintings, 1912-1962. Zagat, I. R., ed. (Illus.). 1972. 25.00 (ISBN 0-911268-09-X). Rogers Bk.

JEWS IN THE UNITED STATES–BIOGRAPHY

Alexander, Morris. Israel & Me. LC 76-40091. 1977. 10.00 (ISBN 0-8467-0265-7, Pub. by Two Continents). Hippocrene Bks.
Alofsin, Dorothy. America's Triumph: Stories of American Jewish Heroes. facs. ed. LC 72-148205. (Biography Index Reprint Ser.). 1949. 20.00 (ISBN 0-8369-8052-2). Arno.
Chapman, Abraham, ed. Jewish - American Literature: An Anthology. (Orig.). 1974. pap. 2.25 (ISBN 0-451-61326-0, ME1326, Ment). NAL.
Fishman, Priscilla, ed. The Jews of the United States. LC 73-77033. (The New York Times Library of Jewish Knowledge). 256p. 1974. 8.95 (ISBN 0-8129-0350-1). Times Bks.
Hacker, Louis M. & Hirsch, Mark D. Proskauer, His Life & Times. LC 77-1697. 240p. 1978. 16.25x (ISBN 0-8173-9361-7). U of Ala Pr.
Judah L. Magnes, Pioneer & Prophet on Two Continents: A Pictorial Biography. pap. 5.00 (ISBN 0-686-27357-5). Magnes Mus.
Karp, Abraham J. Golden Door to America: The Jewish Immigrant Experience. LC 77-7998. 1977. pap. 2.95 (ISBN 0-14-004544-9). Penguin.
Kramer, William K., ed. The Western Journal of Isaac Mayer Wise, 1877. 1974. pap. 5.00 (ISBN 0-686-27355-9). Magnes Mus.
Levin, Alexandra L. Dare to Be Different: A Biography of Louis H. Levin of Baltimore. 1972. 7.50x (ISBN 0-8197-0280-3). Bloch.
Levitan, Tina. Jews in American Life. (Illus.). 1969. 6.95 (ISBN 0-88482-891-3). Hebrew Pub.
Lipskay, Louis. Memoirs in Profile. 666p. 1976. 12.00 (ISBN 0-8276-0069-0, 375). Jewish Pubn.
Lotz, Philip H., ed. Distinguished American Jews. LC 78-111842. (Essay Index Reprint Ser). 1945. 12.00 (ISBN 0-8369-1671-9). Arno.
Moddel, Cantor P. Max Helfman: A Biographical Tribute. 1974. 10.00 (ISBN 0-686-28462-3). Magnes Mus.
Rabinowitz, Dorothy. New Lives: Survivors of the Holocaust Living in America. 1976. 10.95 (ISBN 0-394-48573-4). Knopf.
Rezneck, Samuel. The Saga of an American Jewish Family Since the Revolution: A History of the Family of Jonas Phillips. LC 79-6725. 1980. text ed. 17.75 (ISBN 0-8191-0939-8); pap. text ed. 9.50 (ISBN 0-8191-0940-1). U Pr of Amer.
Silverman, Morris. Hartford Jews: Sixteen Fifty-Nine to Nineteen Seventy. (Illus.). 448p. 1970. 17.50x (ISBN 0-940748-21-5). Conn Hist Soc.
Wolf, Hannie. Child of Two Worlds. (Illus.). 156p. 1979. 10.00 (ISBN 0-931068-02-9). Purcells.

JEWS IN THE UNITED STATES - BIBLIOGRAPHY

Alexander, Morris. Israel & Me. (Illus.). 278p. 1977. 12.50x (ISBN 0-87073-204-8). Schenkman.
American Jewish Archives, Cincinnati. Manuscript Catalog of the American Jewish Archives, 4 vols. 1971. Set. lib. bdg. 385.00 (ISBN 0-8161-0899-4). G K Hall.
Brickman, William E., ed. & compiled by. The Jewish Community in America: An Annotated & Classified Bibliographical Guide. (Ethnic Bibliographical Ser: No. 2). 1977. PLB 19.95 (ISBN 0-89102-057-8). B Franklin.
Glanz, Rudolph. German Jew in America: An Annotated Bibliography Including Books, Pamphlets & Articles of Special Interest. 1969. 35.00x (ISBN 0-87068-061-7). Ktav.
Konvitz, Milton R. Judaism & the American Idea. LC 79-14278. 224p. 1980. pap. 5.95 (ISBN 0-8052-0635-3). Schocken.
Marcus, Jacob R. An Index to Articles on American Jewish History. 1971. 20.00x (ISBN 0-87068-139-7). Ktav.
OLSD Committee. Jewish Americans & Their Backgrounds. 32p. 1975. pap. text ed. 1.50x (ISBN 0-8389-5461-8). ALA.
Rubin, Israel. Satmar: An Island in the City. LC 79-182505. 320p. 1972. 8.95 (ISBN 0-8129-0245-9). Times Bks.

JEWS IN THE UNITED STATES–CHARITIES

Berman, Myron. The Attitude of American Jewry Towards East European Jewish Immigration, 1881-1914. Cordasco, Francesco, ed. LC 80-842. (American Ethnic Groups Ser.). 1981. lib. bdg. 50.00x (ISBN 0-405-13406-1). Arno.
Bogen, Boris D. Jewish Philanthropy: An Exposition of Principles & Methods of Jewish Social Service in the United States. LC 69-16225. (Criminology, Law Enforcement, & Social Problems Ser.: No. 86). (With a new intro. by Harry Lurie). 1969. Repr. of 1917 ed. 17.00 (ISBN 0-87585-086-3). Patterson Smith.
Morris, Robert & Freund, Michael, eds. Trends & Issues in Jewish Social Welfare in the United States, 1899-1958. LC 66-17827. 1966. 7.50 (ISBN 0-8276-0163-8, 217). Jewish Pubn.

JEWS IN THE UNITED STATES–HISTORY

America & the Holocaust. (American Jewish History Ser.: Vol. 70, Pt. 3). 1981. 6.00 (ISBN 0-911934-20-0). Am Jewish Hist Soc.
American Jews & the Labor Movement. (American Jewish Historical Quarterly: Vol. 65, Pt.3). 1976. 4.00 (ISBN 0-911934-05-7). Am Jewish Hist Soc.
Baron, Salo W. Steeled in Adversity. (Texts & Studies). (Hebrew.). 1977. 15.00 (ISBN 0-911934-15-4). Am Jewish Hist Soc.
Benjamin, Israel Ben Joseph. Three Years in America: 1859-1862, 2 vols. in 1. facsimile ed. Reznikoff, Charles, tr. from Ger. LC 74-27962. (Modern Jewish Experience Ser.). (Eng.). 1975. Repr. of 1956 ed. 39.00x (ISBN 0-405-06693-7). Arno.
Blau, Joseph L. Judaism in America: From Curiosity to Third Faith. LC 75-5069. (Chicago History of American Religion Ser.). 176p. 1976. 12.95x (ISBN 0-226-05727-5). U of Chicago Pr.
Blau, Joseph L., et al, eds. The Jews of the United States, 1790-1840: A Documentary History, 3 Vols. LC 64-10108. 1034p. 1964. Set. 75.50x (ISBN 0-231-02651-X). Columbia U Pr.
Brandes, Joseph & Douglas, Martin. Immigrants to Freedom: Jewish Communities in Rural New Jersey Since 1882. LC 76-122384. 1971. 20.00x (ISBN 0-8122-7620-5). U of Pa Pr.
Brener, David A. The Jews of Lancaster, Pennsylvania: A Story with Two Beginnings. LC 79-21690. (Illus.). 188p. (Orig.). 1979. 18.00x (ISBN 0-9605482-1-1); pap. 12.00x (ISBN 0-9605482-0-3). Cong Shaarai.
Cahan, Abraham. Fish, Fish, Living Fish! The New Journalism of Abraham Cahan. Rischin, Moses, ed. 600p. 1982. 17.95 (ISBN 0-87754-286-4). Chelsea Hse.
Chotzinoff, Samuel. A Lost Paradise: Early Reminiscences. facsimile ed. LC 74-27970. (Modern Jewish Experience Ser.). 1975. Repr. of 1955 ed. 23.00x (ISBN 0-405-06700-3). Arno.
Cogan, Sara G., compiled by. Pioneer Jews of the California Mother Lode: 1849 to 1880. (Western Jewish Americana Ser.: No. 1). 1968. 7.50 (ISBN 0-686-27351-6). Magnes Mus.
Conference of Historians Convened by the American Jewish Historical Society on the Occasion of the 300th Anniversary of the Settlement of Jews in the U. S. The Writing of American Jewish History: Proceedings. Repr. of 1957 ed. 22.00 (ISBN 0-527-02375-2). Kraus Repr.
Davis, Moshe & Meyer, Isidore S., eds. Writing of American Jewish History. 1957. 6.00 (ISBN 0-911934-18-9). Am Jewish Hist Soc.
Dimont, Max. The Jews in America. 1980. 4.95 (ISBN 0-671-25412-X, Touchstone). S&S.
Dobkowski, Michael N. The Tarnished Dream: The Basis of American Anti-Semitism. LC 78-67655. (Contributions in American History: No. 81). 1979. lib. bdg. 22.50x (ISBN 0-313-20641-4, DDR/). Greenwood.
Ehrmann, E. L. Readings in Jewish History: From the American Revolution to the Present. 7.95x (ISBN 0-87068-447-7). Ktav.
Eisenberg, Azriel, et al, eds. Eyewitnesses to American Jewish History: 1492 - 1793, Pt. 1. 1976. pap. 5.00 (ISBN 0-686-77106-0, 144060); tchrs'. guide 5.00 (ISBN 0-8074-0019-X, 204061). UAHC.
Elovitz, Mark H. A Century of Jewish Life in Dixie: The Birmingham Experience. LC 73-22716. (Judac Studies: No. 5). 256p. 1974. 17.50x (ISBN 0-8173-6901-5). U of Ala Pr.
Elzas, Barnett A. The Jews of South Carolina, from the Earliest Times to the Present Day. LC 77-187364. (Illus.). 352p. 1972. Repr. of 1905 ed. 16.50 (ISBN 0-87152-092-3). Reprint.
Essays in American Jewish History, in Honor of Jacob Rader Marcus. 35.00x (ISBN 0-87068-459-0). Ktav.
Feingold, Henry L. Zion in America. rev. ed. (American Immigrant Ser.). 1981. pap. 10.95 (ISBN 0-88254-592-2). Hippocrene Bks.
Feldman, Abraham J. The American Jew: A Study of Backgrounds. LC 78-26254. 1979. Repr. of 1937 ed. lib. bdg. 15.00x (ISBN 0-313-20876-X, FEAJ). Greenwood.
Feldstein, Stanley. The Land That I Show You. LC 77-76231. 1978. 12.95 (ISBN 0-385-02445-2, Anchor Pr); pap. 7.95 (ISBN 0-385-02983-7). Doubleday.
--Land That I Show You: Three Centuries of Jewish Life in America. (Illus.). 1979. pap. 7.95 (ISBN 0-385-02983-7, Anch). Doubleday.
Fine, Jo Renee & Wolfe, Gerard R. The Synagogues of New York's Lower East Side. LC 75-15126. (Illus.). 1978. 16.95 (ISBN 0-8147-2559-7). NYU Pr.
Friedman, Lee M. Pilgrims in a New Land. LC 78-26208. (Illus.). 1979. Repr. of 1948 ed. lib. bdg. 28.25x (ISBN 0-313-20877-8, FRPI). Greenwood.
Friedman, Saul S. Incident at Massena: The Blood Libel in America. 1978. 9.95 (ISBN 0-8128-2526-8). Stein & Day.
Gartner, L. History of the Jews of Cleveland. 15.00x (ISBN 0-685-55559-3, Pub. by Jewish Theol Seminary). Ktav.
Goldmark, Josephine. Pilgrims of Forty-Eight. facsimile ed. LC 74-27989. (Modern Jewish Experience Ser.). (Illus.). 1975. Repr. of 1930 ed. 21.00x (ISBN 0-405-06716-X). Arno.
Goren, Arthur A. New York Jews & the Quest for Community. LC 76-129961. 1979. 22.50x (ISBN 0-231-03422-9); pap. 10.00x (ISBN 0-231-08368-8). Columbia U Pr.
Handlin, Oscar. American Jews: Their Story. 48p. 1.00 (ISBN 0-686-74960-X). ADL.
Howe, Irving & Libo, Ken. How We Lived: A Documentary History of Immigrant Jews in America, 1880-1930. LC 79-13391. (Illus.). 1979. 22.50 (ISBN 0-399-90051-9). Marek.
Howe, Irving & Libo, Kenneth. How We Lived: A Documentary History of Immigrant Jews in America, 1880-1930. (Illus.). 1981. pap. 6.95 (ISBN 0-452-25269-5, Z5269, Plume). NAL.
Jick, Leon A. The Americanization of the Synagogue, 1820-1870. LC 75-18213. (Illus.). 260p. 1976. text ed. 15.00x (ISBN 0-87451-119-4). U Pr of New Eng.
Kaganoff, Nathan M. & Urofsky, Melvin I., eds. Turn to the South: Essays on Southern Jewry. LC 78-9306. 1979. 7.95x (ISBN 0-8139-0742-X). U Pr of Va.
Karp, Abraham. The Jewish Experience in America, 5 Vols. 1969. Set. 79.50x (ISBN 0-87068-025-0). Ktav.
Karp, Abraham, ed. The Jewish Experience in America, 5 vols. 1969. Set. 59.50 (ISBN 0-685-47699-5, Co-Pub. by KTAV). Vol. 1 (ISBN 0-911934-22-7). Vol. 2 (ISBN 0-911934-23-5). Vol. 3 (ISBN 0-911934-24-3). Vol. 4 (ISBN 0-911934-25-1). Vol. 5 (ISBN 0-911934-26-X). Am Jewish Hist Soc.
Korn, Bertram W. American Jewry: The Formative Years. (Texts & Studies). (Hebrew.). 1971. 10.00 (ISBN 0-911934-04-9). Am Jewish Hist Soc.
Levinson, R. E. The Jews in the California Gold Rush. 20.00x (ISBN 0-87068-436-1). Ktav.
Levinson, Robert. The Jews in the California Gold Rush. 20.00 (ISBN 0-87068-436-1). Magnes Mus.
Marcus, J. R., ed. Jews & the American Revolution: A Bicentennial Documentary. 7.50x (ISBN 0-685-55591-7). Ktav.
Marcus, Jacob R. The American Jewish Woman: A Documentary History. Date not set. 35.00x (ISBN 0-87068-752-2). Ktav.
--Critical Studies in American Jewish History, 3 vols. 1971. 35.00x (ISBN 0-87068-109-5). Ktav.
--Early American Jewry. 1953. 35.00x (ISBN 0-87068-269-5). Ktav.
--An Introduction to Early American Jewish History. (Texts & Studies). (Hebrew.). 1971. 10.00 (ISBN 0-911934-09-X). Am Jewish Hist Soc.
--Memoirs of American Jews: 1775-1865. 1955. 35.00 (ISBN 0-87068-232-6). Ktav.
Marcus, Jacob R., ed. The American Jewish Woman: 1654-1980. 1981. 15.00x (ISBN 0-87068-579-1). Ktav.
Mayer, Egon. From Suburb to Shtetl: The Jews of Boro Park. (Illus.). 1979. 17.50 (ISBN 0-87722-161-8). Temple U Pr.
Meltzer, Milton. Taking Root: Jewish Immigrants in America. LC 76-18169. (Illus.). 256p. (gr. 7 up). 1976. 7.95 (ISBN 0-374-37369-8). FS&G.
Meyer, Isidore S., ed. American Jew in the Civil War. Repr. of 1962 ed. 8.50 (ISBN 0-527-03218-2). Kraus Repr.
--American Jewry in the Civil War. 1961. 5.00 (ISBN 0-685-05621-X); pap. 4.00 (ISBN 0-911934-02-2). Am Jewish Hist Soc.
Mitchell, William E. Mishpokhe: A Study of New York City Jewish Family Clubs. (New Babylon Studies in the Social Sciences Ser.: No. 30). (Illus.). 1978. 19.75x (ISBN 90-279-7695-3). Mouton.
Moore, Deborah D. At Home in America: Second Generation New York Jews. LC 80-18777. (Columbia History of Urban Life Ser.). (Illus.). 280p. 1981. 15.95 (ISBN 0-231-05062-3). Columbia U Pr.
Narrell, Irena. Our City: The Jews of San Francisco. LC 80-21216. 1980. 15.00 (ISBN 0-8310-7122-2). Howell-North.
On Common Ground: The Boston Jewish Community 1649-1980. (Illus.). 1981. 6.00 (ISBN 0-911934-19-7). Am Jewish Hist Soc.
Pessin, Deborah. History of the Jews in America. (Illus.). 1957. pap. 4.95x (ISBN 0-8381-0189-5). United Syn Bk.

Postal, Bernard & Koppman, Lional. Guess Who's Jewish in American History: From Wyatt Earp's Wife to Sandy Koufax. (Illus., Orig.). 1978. pap. 2.25 (ISBN 0-451-08351-2, E8351, Sig). NAL.
Postal, Bernard & Koppman, Lionel. American Jewish Landmarks: A Travel Guide & History, the South & Southwest, Vol. II. LC 76-27401. 1979. 15.95 (ISBN 0-8303-0155-0); pap. 7.50 (ISBN 0-8303-0157-7). Fleet.
--Jewish Landmarks of New York: A Travel Guide & History. LC 76-27400. (Orig.). 1978. 13.95 (ISBN 0-8303-0153-4). Fleet.
Rischin, Moses. The Promised City: New York's Jews, 1870-1914. (Illus.). 342p. 1977. pap. 5.95x (ISBN 0-674-71501-2); text ed. 16.50x (ISBN 0-674-71502-0). Harvard U Pr.
Rischin, Moses, ed. The Jews of the West: The Metropolitan Years. (Illus.). 156p. 1975. pap. 5.95 (ISBN 0-686-27362-1). Magnes Mus.
Rosen, Gladys. Jewish Life in America: Historical Perspectives. 12.50x (ISBN 0-87068-346-2); pap. 6.95 (ISBN 0-686-52683-X). Ktav.
Rosen, Gladys L., ed. Jewish Life in America: Historical Perspectives. LC 78-16560. 198p. 1978. pap. 6.95 (ISBN 0-686-74514-0). Am Jewish Comm.
Sanders, Ronald & Gillon, Edmund V. The Lower East Side: A Guide to Its Jewish Past in Ninety-Nine New Photographs. 10.00 (ISBN 0-8446-5809-X). Peter Smith.
--The Lower East Side: A Guide to Its Jewish Past with Ninety-Nine New Photographs. (Illus.). 1980. pap. 4.50 (ISBN 0-486-23871-7). Dover.
Sarna, Jonathan D., ed. Jews & Judaism in New York. 160p. 1981. text ed. 25.00x (ISBN 0-8419-0707-2); pap. text ed. 14.00x (ISBN 0-8419-0731-5). Holmes & Meier.
Schmier, Louis, ed. Reflections of Southern Jewry: The Letters of Charles Wessolowsky. 1981. 14.95x (ISBN 0-86554-020-9). Mercer Univ Pr.
Silverman, Morris. Hartford Jews: Sixteen Fifty-Nine to Nineteen Seventy. (Illus.). 448p. 1970. 17.50x (ISBN 0-940748-21-5). Conn Hist Soc.
Sklare, Marshall, ed. The Jew in American Society. LC 74-3051. (Library of Jewish Studies). (Illus.). 416p. 1974. text ed. 6.95x (ISBN 0-87441-203-X). Behrman.
--Jewish Community in America. LC 74-8678. (Library of Jewish Studies). (Illus.). 416p. 1974. text ed. 6.95x (ISBN 0-87441-204-8). Behrman.
Stern, M. H. First American Jewish Families: 600 Genealogies 1654-1977. 75.00x (ISBN 0-87068-443-4). Ktav.
Stern, Malcolm H., compiled by. First American Jewish Families: 600 Genealogies 1654-1977. 1978. 75.00 (ISBN 0-87068-443-4). Am Jewish Hist Soc.
Tcherikower, Elias, ed. Geshikhte Fun der Yidisher Arbeterbavegung, Vol.2. LC 45-13072. (Illus., Yiddish.). 1945. 10.00 (ISBN 0-914512-18-8). Yivo Inst.
Trachtenberg, Joshua. Consider the Years: The Story of the Jewish Community of Easton, 1752-1942. (Responsa Ser). (Illus.). 350p. 1973. Repr. of 1944 ed. lib. bdg. 17.50 (ISBN 0-87960-101-9). Hive Pub.
The Two Hundred & Fiftieth Anniversary of the Settlement of the Jews in the United States. LC 6-11670. 1904. pap. 14.00 (ISBN 0-527-02380-9). Kraus Repr.
Wolf, Edwin, 2nd & Whiteman, Maxwell. History of the Jews of Philadelphia: From Colonial Times to the Age of Jackson. (Illus.). 552p. 1975. 8.50 (ISBN 0-8276-0075-5, 372). Jewish Pubn.
Wolf, Hannie. Child of Two Worlds. (Illus.). 156p. 1979. 10.00 (ISBN 0-931068-02-9). Purcells.
Wolf, Simon. The American Jew As Patriot, Soldier, & Citizen. LC 72-8739. (American Revolutionary Ser.). 1979. Repr. of 1895 ed. lib. bdg. 32.00x (ISBN 0-8398-2179-4). Irvington.

JEWS IN THE UNITED STATES–HISTORY–SOURCES

Butwin, Frances. Jews of America: History & Sources. Blecher, Arthur C., ed. LC 73-2253. (Illus.). 160p. (gr. 7-9). 1973. pap. text ed. 3.95x (ISBN 0-87441-062-2). Behrman.
Cowen, Philip. Memories of an American Jew. facsimile ed. LC 74-27974. (Modern Jewish Experience Ser.). (Illus.). 1975. Repr. of 1932 ed. 28.00x (ISBN 0-405-06703-8). Arno.
Karp, Abraham J., intro. by. Beginnings Early American Judaica: A Collection of Ten Publications in facsimile, illustrative of the religious, Communal, Cultural & Political Life of American Jewry, 1761-1845. LC 75-23405. (Illus.). 1975. 20.00 (ISBN 0-8276-0076-3, 376). Jewish Pubn.
Levy, Harriet L. Nine-Twenty O'Farrell Street. facsimile ed. LC 74-29501. (Modern Jewish Experience Ser.). (Illus.). 1975. Repr. of 1947 ed. 17.00x (ISBN 0-405-06728-3). Arno.
Marcus, Jacob R. American Jewry Documents, Eighteenth Century. 1958. 12.50x (ISBN 0-685-13732-5, Pub. by Hebrew Union). Ktav.
Schappes, Morris U., ed. A Documentary History of the Jews in the United States, 1654-1875. 3rd ed. LC 72-122332. 1975. 7.95 (ISBN 0-8052-0488-1). Schocken.
Schoener, Allon. Portal to America: The Lower East Side, 1870-1925. 1967. pap. 7.95 (ISBN 0-03-086712-6). HR&W.

JEWS IN THE UNITED STATES–JUVENILE LITERATURE

Butwin, Frances. Jews in America. rev. ed. LC 68-31501. (In America Bks.). (Illus.). (gr. 5-11). 1980. PLB 6.95g (ISBN 0-686-69988-2). Lerner Pubns.
Karp, Deborah. Heroes of American Jewish History. 1972. 6.00x (ISBN 0-87068-394-2). Ktav.
Schloss, Ezekiel & Epstein, Morris, eds. More World Over Stories. LC 67-26646. (World Over Anthology for Jewish Youth Ser). (Illus.). (gr. 4-7). 1968. 4.95 (ISBN 0-8197-0255-2). Bloch.
--New World Over Story Book. (Illus.). (gr. 4-7). 4.95 (ISBN 0-8197-0256-0). Bloch.

JEWS IN THE UNITED STATES–POLITICAL AND SOCIAL CONDITIONS

American Jews & the Labor Movement. (American Jewish Historical Quarterly: Vol. 65, Pt.3). 1976. 4.00 (ISBN 0-911934-05-7). Am Jewish Hist Soc.
Berman, Myron. The Attitude of American Jewry Towards East European Jewish Immigration, 1881-1914. Cordasco, Francesco, ed. LC 80-842. (American Ethnic Groups Ser.). 1981. lib. bdg. 50.00x (ISBN 0-405-13406-1). Arno.
Conference On Jewish Social Studies. Negro-Jewish Relations in the United States. 1966. pap. 1.50 (ISBN 0-8065-0092-1, 218). Citadel Pr.
Dolgin, Janet L. Jewish Identity & the JDL. LC 76-325. 1977. 16.50 (ISBN 0-691-09368-7). Princeton U Pr.
Doroshkin, Milton. Yiddish in America: Social & Cultural Foundations. LC 72-78612. (Illus.). 281p. 1970. 18.00 (ISBN 0-8386-7453-4). Fairleigh Dickinson.
El Azhary, M. S. Political Cohesion of American Jews in American Politics: A Reappraisal of Their Role in Presidential Elections. LC 80-5317. 70p. 1980. pap. text ed. 6.50 (ISBN 0-8191-1078-7). U Pr of Amer.
Frankel, Jonathan. Prophecy & Politics: Socialism, Nationalism & the Russian Jews 1862-1917. LC 80-14414. (Illus.). 665p. 1981. 49.50 (ISBN 0-521-23028-4). Cambridge U Pr.
Fuchs, Lawrence H. The Political Behavior of American Jews. LC 79-28711. (Illus.). 220p. 1980. Repr. of 1956 ed. lib. bdg. 19.00x (ISBN 0-313-22282-7, FUPB). Greenwood.
Gittler, Joseph. Jewish Life in the United States. 208p. 1981. 19.95 (ISBN 0-8147-2982-7). NYU Pr.
Heitzmann, William R. American Jewish Voting Behavior: A History & Analysis. LC 74-31768. 1975. soft bdg. 8.00 (ISBN 0-88247-337-9). R & E Res Assoc.
Herscher, Uri D. & Chyet, Stanley F. On Jews, America & Immigration: A Socialist Perspective. Date not set. 10.00x (ISBN 0-87820-008-8). Ktav.
Jews & American Liberalism: Studies in Political Behavior. (American Jewish Historical Quarterly: Vol. 66, Pt.2). 1976. 8.00 (ISBN 0-911934-10-3). Am Jewish Hist Soc.
Karpf, Maurice J. Jewish Community Organization in the United States. LC 78-137171. (Poverty U.S.A. Historical Record Ser). 1971. Repr. of 1938 ed. 13.00 (ISBN 0-405-03110-6). Arno.
McWilliams, Carey. A Mask for Privilege: Anti-Semitism in America. LC 78-26197. 1979. Repr. of 1948 ed. lib. bdg. 18.50x (ISBN 0-313-20880-8, MCMP). Greenwood.
Neuringer, Sheldon M. American Jewry & United States Immigration Policy, 1881-1953. Cordasco, Francesco, ed. LC 80-883. (American Ethnic Groups Ser.). 1981. lib. bdg. 45.00x (ISBN 0-405-13444-4). Arno.
Orbach, William W. The American Movement to Aid Soviet Jews. LC 78-19696. 1979. 15.00x (ISBN 0-87023-267-3). U of Mass Pr.
Poll, Solomon. The Hasidic Community of Williamsburg: A Study in the Sociology of Religion. 2nd ed. LC 69-19419. 1969. pap. 4.95 (ISBN 0-8052-0209-9). Schocken.
Rabinowitz, Dorothy. The Other Jews: Portraits in Poverty. LC 77-183251. (Institute of Human Relations Press Paperback Ser). 64p. (Orig.). 1972. 1.25 (ISBN 0-87495-015-5). Am Jewish Comm.
Rogoff, Abraham M. Formative Years of the Jewish Labor Movement in the United States: (1890-1900) LC 78-21163. 1979. Repr. of 1945 ed. lib. bdg. 14.75x (ISBN 0-313-20881-6, ROFJ). Greenwood.
Silcox, Claris E. Catholics, Jews, & Protestants: A Study of Relationships in the United States & Canada. LC 78-21101. 1979. Repr. of 1934 ed. lib. bdg. 22.50x (ISBN 0-313-20882-4, SICJ). Greenwood.
Sklare, Marshall & Greenblum, Joseph. Jewish Identity on the Suburban Frontier: A Study of Group Survival in the Open Society. 2nd ed. LC 78-74165. 1979. lib. bdg. 21.00x (ISBN 0-226-76175-4); pap. 6.95 (ISBN 0-226-76176-2, P808, Phoen). U of Chicago Pr.
Steinitz, Lucy Y. Living After the Holocaust: Reflections by the Post-War Generation in America. Szonyi, David M., ed. LC 76-8322. (Illus.). 1976. 6.95x (ISBN 0-686-77156-7); pap. 4.95 (ISBN 0-8197-0016-9). Bloch.
Strong, Donald S. Organized Anti-Semitism in America: The Rise of Group Prejudice During the Decade 1930-1940. LC 78-26198. 1979. Repr. of 1941 ed. lib. bdg. 16.75x (ISBN 0-313-20883-2, STOA). Greenwood.
Van Den Haag, Ernest. The Jewish Mystique. LC 76-56974. 1977. 8.95 (ISBN 0-8128-1267-0); pap. 4.95 (ISBN 0-8128-2189-0). Stein & Day.

JEWS IN THE UNITED STATES–SOCIAL LIFE AND CUSTOMS

Cohen, Bernard. Sociocultural Changes in American Jewish Life As Reflected in Selected Jewish Literature. LC 75-146162. 282p. 1972. 15.00 (ISBN 0-8386-7848-3). Fairleigh Dickinson.
Cottle, Thomas J. Hidden Survivors: Portraits of Poor Jews in America. LC 79-26718. 1980. 9.95 (ISBN 0-13-387357-9). P-H.
Gittler, Joseph. Jewish Life in the United States. 208p. 1981. 19.95 (ISBN 0-8147-2982-7). NYU Pr.
Hapgood, Hutchins. The Spirit of the Ghetto: Studies of the Jewish Quarter of New York. rev. ed. LC 76-21184. (Illus.). 1976. pap. 4.50 (ISBN 0-8052-0553-5). Schocken.
Heilman, Samuel C. Synagogue Life: A Study in Symbolic Interaction. LC 75-36403. 1976. 12.95 (ISBN 0-226-32488-5); pap. 4.95 (ISBN 0-226-32490-7, P824, Phoen). U of Chicago Pr.
Kaplan, Mordecai M. Judaism As a Civilization: Toward a Reconstruction of American-Jewish Life. LC 81-6057. 601p. 1981. 25.00 (ISBN 0-8276-0193-X, 474); pap. 10.95 (ISBN 0-8276-0194-8, 480). Jewish Pubn.
Mayer, Egon. From Suburb to Shtetl: The Jews of Boro Park. (Illus.). 1979. 17.50 (ISBN 0-87722-161-8). Temple U Pr.
Porter, Jack N., ed. The Sociology of American Jews: A Critical Anthology. 2nd, rev. ed. LC 80-5760. 330p. 1980. pap. text ed. 11.50 (ISBN 0-8191-1236-4). U Pr of Amer.
Wagner, S. M., ed. Traditions of the American Jew. 12.50x (ISBN 0-87068-435-3). Ktav.
Warshaw, Mal. Tradition: Orthodox Jewish Life in America. LC 76-9130. (Illus.). 1976. 14.95 (ISBN 0-8052-3637-6). Schocken.

JEWS IN YEMEN

see also Jews, Yemenite

Goitein, S. D., ed. From the Land of Sheba: Tales of the Jews of Yemen. rev. ed. LC 73-81342. 160p. 1976. pap. 3.45 (ISBN 0-8052-0543-8). Schocken.
Moses Ben Maimon. Epistle to Yemen. 1952. 12.00 (ISBN 0-527-65400-0). Kraus Repr.

JEWS IN YUGOSLAVIA

Freidenreich, Harriet P. The Jews of Yugoslavia: A Quest for Community. LC 79-84733. (Illus.). 1979. 14.95 (ISBN 0-8276-0122-0, 439). Jewish Pubn.

JEZEBEL, WIFE OF AHAB, KING OF ISRAEL–FICTION

Hesky, Olga. Painted Queen. 1962. 10.00 (ISBN 0-8392-1083-3). Astor-Honor.

JEZIDES

see Yezidis

JIB, AL, JORDAN

Pritchard, James B. Gibeon, Where the Sun Stood Still: The Discovery of a Biblical City. 1962. 20.00x (ISBN 0-691-03517-2); pap. 6.95 (ISBN 0-691-00210-X). Princeton U Pr.

JIE (AFRICAN TRIBE)

Gulliver, P. H. Family Herds. (International Library of Sociology). 1972. 22.50x (ISBN 0-7100-3332-X). Routledge & Kegan.
--Family Herds: A Study of Two Pastoral Tribes in East Africa, the Jie & Turkana. LC 79-129943. (Illus.). Repr. of 1955 ed. 15.00x (ISBN 0-8371-5032-9, Pub. by Negro U Pr). Greenwood.
Lamphear, John. The Traditional History of the Jie of Uganda. (Oxford Studies in African Affairs). (Illus.). 1976. 48.00x (ISBN 0-19-821692-0). Oxford U Pr.

JIG (MECHANICAL DEVICE)

see Jigs and Fixtures

JIG SAWS

Brann, Donald R. Scroll Saw Projects, Bk. 756. LC 75-3911. 1975. lib. bdg. 5.95 (ISBN 0-87733-056-5); pap. 3.50 (ISBN 0-87733-756-X). Easi-Bild.

JIGGING

see Ore-Dressing

JIGS AND FIXTURES

American Society Of Tool And Manufacturing Engineers. Handbook of Fixture Design. Wilson, Frank W., ed. 1962. 32.50 (ISBN 0-07-001527-9, P&RB). McGraw.
Boyes, William E., ed. Jigs & Fixtures. LC 79-64915. (Manufacturing Update Ser.). (Illus.). 1979. 29.00 (ISBN 0-87263-051-X). SME.
Hoffman, Edward G. Jig & Fixture Design. 251p. 1980. 10.95 (ISBN 0-442-20162-1). Van Nos Reinhold.
--Jig & Fixture Design, Vol.1. LC 78-55901. 330p. pap. 8.00 (ISBN 0-8273-1694-1); instructor's guide 1.60 (ISBN 0-686-67378-6). Delmar.
Nee, John G. Jig & Fixture Design & Detailing. LC 78-71562. (Illus.). 1979. pap. 14.90x (ISBN 0-911168-41-9). Prakken.
Pollack, Herman. Tool Design. (Illus.). 528p. 1976. 19.95 (ISBN 0-87909-840-6); students manual avail. Reston.
Ryder, G. H. Jigs, Fixtures, Tools & Gauges. 6th ed. Orig. Title: Jigs, Tools & Fixtures. (Illus.). 176p. 1973. text ed. 12.75x (ISBN 0-291-39432-9). Scholium Intl.
Sedlik, Harold. Jigs & Fixtures for Limited Production. LC 74-118842. (Manufacturing Data Ser). (Illus.). 1971. text ed. 12.25 (ISBN 0-87263-025-0). SME.

JIMENEZ, JUAN RAMON, 1881-1958

Crespo, Angel. Juan Ramon Jimenez y la Pintura. (UPREX, Humanidades: No. 26). (Illus.). pap. 1.85 (ISBN 0-8477-0026-7). U of PR Pr.
Gullon, Ricardo, ed. Relaciones Amistosas y Literarias Entre Juan Ramon Jimnez y los Martinez Sierra. pap. 1.55 (ISBN 0-8477-3133-2). U of PR Pr.
Olson, Paul R. Circle of Paradox: Time & Essence in the Poetry of Juan Ramon Jimenez. LC 67-21581. 265p. 1967. 16.50x (ISBN 0-8018-0500-7). Johns Hopkins.
Universidad De Puerto Rico. Homenaje a Juan Ramon Jimnez. pap. 1.00 (ISBN 0-8477-3153-7). U of PR Pr.
Young, Howard T. Juan Ramon Jimenez. LC 67-27361. (Columbia Essays on Modern Writers Ser.: No. 28). (Orig.). 1967. pap. 2.00 (ISBN 0-231-02940-3, MW28). Columbia U Pr.
--The Line in the Margin: Juan Ramon Jimenez & His Readings in Blake, Shelley, & Yeats. LC 79-3963. 242p. 1980. 22.50 (ISBN 0-299-07950-3). U of Wis Pr.
--Victorious Expression: A Study of Four Contemporary Spanish Poets, Unamuno, Machado, Jimenez, & Lorca. 1964. pap. 6.95x (ISBN 0-299-03144-6). U of Wis Pr.

JIMENEZ DE QUESADA, GONZALO, 1500-1579

Arciniegas, German. Knight of El Dorado: The Tale of Don Gonzalo Jimenez De Quesada & His Conquest of New Granada, Now Called Colombia. Adams, Mildred, tr. LC 68-23269. (Illus.). 1968. Repr. of 1942 ed. lib. bdg. 15.00x (ISBN 0-8371-0007-0, AREL). Greenwood.
Graham, R. Cunninghame. Conquest of New Granada: Being the Life of Gonzalo Jimenez De Quesada. LC 66-30734. Repr. of 1922 ed. 13.50x (ISBN 0-8154-0086-1). Cooper Sq.

JIMMA ABBA JIFAR

Lewis, Herbert S. Galla Monarchy: Jimma Abba Jifar, Ethiopia, 1830-1932. (Illus.). 168p. 1965. 17.50x (ISBN 0-299-03690-1). U of Wis Pr.

JIMSON WEED

see Datura

JINNAH, MOHAMMED ALI, 1876-1948

Merriam, Allen H. Gandhi & Jinnah. 1980. 16.00x (ISBN 0-8364-0039-9). South Asia Bks.
Naim, C. M., ed. Iqbal, Jinnah, & Pakistan: The Vision & the Reality. LC 79-25477. (Foreign & Comparative Studies-South Asian Ser: No. 5). 216p. (Orig.). 1979. pap. text ed. 6.50x (ISBN 0-915984-81-4). Syracuse U Foreign Comp.
Ravoofs, A. A. Meet Mr. Jinnah. pap. 3.50 (ISBN 0-686-18315-0). Kazi Pubns.

JIRI Z PODEBRAD, KING OF BOHEMIA, 1420-1471

Odlozilik, Otakar. The Hussite King: Bohemia in European Affairs, 1440-1471. 1965. 22.00 (ISBN 0-8135-0497-X). Rutgers U Pr.

JITNEY BUSES

see Motor Buses

JIU-JITSU

see also Judo

De Pasquale, Michael. Ju-Jitsu. (Monarch Illustrated Guide Ser.). (Illus.). 1977. pap. 2.95 (ISBN 0-671-18777-5). Monarch Pr.
DePasquale, Michael, Jr. Ju-Jitsu. LC 78-10717. (Illus.). 160p. (gr. 7 up). 1978. PLB 7.29 (ISBN 0-671-32963-4). Messner.
Freudenberg, Karl. Natural Weapons: A Manual of Karate, Judo, & Jujitsu Techniques. (Illus., Orig.). 1962. pap. 3.95 (ISBN 0-498-04086-0, Prpta). A S Barnes.
Hall, Nelson. A Complete Course in Super Ju Jitsu. 1958. pap. 14.95 (ISBN 0-911012-38-9). Nelson-Hall.

Hancock, H. Irving & Higashi, Katsukuma. Complete Kano Jiu-Jitsu. (Illus.). 1905. pap. 6.00 (ISBN 0-486-20639-4). Dover.

Jiu Jitsu: Japanese Art of Wrestling. (Illus.). 0.75 (ISBN 0-685-02619-1, 00545296). Stein Pub.

Longhurst, Percy. Ju-Jutsu & Judo. (Illus.). 64p. 1980. softcover 6.00 (ISBN 0-87364-189-2). Paladin Ent.

Moynahan, J. McCauslin, Jr. Police Ju Jitsu. (Illus.). 132p. 1962. 8.75 (ISBN 0-398-01366-7). C C Thomas.

Nakae, K. Jiu Jitsu Complete. 6.95 (ISBN 0-685-21995-X); pap. 3.95 (ISBN 0-686-66565-1). Wehman.

Nakae, Kiyose & Yeager, Charles. Jiu Jitsu Complete. (Illus.). 178p. 1974. pap. 3.95 (ISBN 0-8065-0418-8). Citadel Pr.

Neff, Fred. Fred Neff's Basic Jujitsu Handbook. LC 75-38472. (Fred Neff's Self-Defense Library). (Illus.). 56p. (gr. 5 up). 1976. PLB 5.95g (ISBN 0-8225-1151-7). Lerner Pubns.

Tegner, Bruce. Bruce Tegner's Complete Book of Jujitsu. LC 77-5023. (Illus.). 1977. 6.95 (ISBN 0-87407-516-5, C16); pap. 4.95 (ISBN 0-87407-027-9, T27). Thor.

--Self-Defense Nerve Centers & Pressure Points for Karate, Jujitsu & Atemi-Waza. rev. enlarged ed. LC 78-18169. (Illus.). 1978. 5.95 (ISBN 0-87407-519-X, C-19); pap. 2.95 (ISBN 0-87407-029-5). Thor.

JOACHIM, ABBOT OF FIORE, 1132-1202

Reeves, Marjorie. Joachim of Fiore & the Prophetic Future. (Orig.). 1977. pap. text ed. 4.95x (ISBN 0-06-131924-4, TB1924, Torch). Har-Row.

Reeves, Marjorie & Hirsch-Reich, Beatrice. The Figurae of Joachim of Fiore. (Oxford-Warburg Studies). (Illus.). 374p. 1972. text ed. 36.00x (ISBN 0-19-920038-6). Oxford U Pr.

JOACHIM, JOSEPH, 1831-1907

Bickley, Nora, ed. Letters from & to Joseph Joachim. LC 70-183496. 470p. 1972. Repr. of 1914 ed. 45.00x (ISBN 0-8443-0043-8). Vienna Hse.

JOACHIM DE FLORE

Bett, Henry. Joachim of Flora. (Great Medieval Churchmen Ser). vii, 184p. 1976. Repr. of 1931 ed. lib. bdg. 13.50 (ISBN 0-915172-24-0). Richwood Pub.

JOACHIM MURAT, KING OF NAPLES, 1767-1815

Johnston, Robert M. The Napoleonic Empire in Southern Italy & the Rise of the Secret Societies, 2 vols. LC 77-156852. (Europe 1815-1945 Ser). 640p. 1973. Repr. of 1904 ed. lib. bdg. 49.50 (ISBN 0-306-70558-3). Da Capo.

JOAN, MYTHICAL FEMALE POPE

Durrell, Lawrence. Pope Joan. LC 72-81088. 176p. 1972. Repr. of 1960 ed. 12.95 (ISBN 0-87951-002-1). Overlook Pr.

JOAN OF ARC

see Jeanne D'Arc, Saint, 1412-1431

JOANNES 23RD, POPE, 1881-1963

see John 23rd, Pope, 1881-1963

JOANNES DE JANDUNO, d. 1328

Mokwa, Michael & Permut, Steven, eds. Government Marketing: Theory & Practice. (Public & Nonprofit Sector Marketing Ser.). 400p. 1981. 31.95 (ISBN 0-03-058316-0). Praeger.

JOB, A SLAVE

Grant, Douglas. Fortunate Slave: An Illustration of African Slavery in the Early Eighteenth Century. (Illus.). 1968. 7.50x (ISBN 0-19-215634-9). Oxford U Pr.

JOB, THE PATRIARCH

Besserman, Lawrence L. The Legend of Job in the Middle Ages. LC 78-14936. (Illus.). 1979. 12.50x (ISBN 0-674-52385-7, Belknap Pr). Harvard U Pr.

Gale, Van. Job: A Mini Story in Redemption. 1978. pap. 2.50 (ISBN 0-89274-072-8). Harrison Hse.

Gordis, Robert. The Book of God & Man. LC 65-25126. 1978. pap. 8.95 (ISBN 0-226-30410-8, P771, Phoen). U of Chicago Pr.

Kahn, J. H. Job's Illness: Loss, Grief & Integration; a Psychological Interpretation. 284p. 1975. text ed. 27.00 (ISBN 0-08-018087-6). Pergamon.

Savory, Jerold J. Caged Light. LC 73-2548. 96p. 1973. pap. 2.50 (ISBN 0-8170-0587-0). Judson.

Shestov, Lev. In Job's Balances: On the Sources of the Eternal Truths. Coventry, Camilla & Macartney, C. A., trs. from Ger. LC 73-92902. l, 379p. (Eng.). 1975. 18.00x (ISBN 0-8214-0143-2). Ohio U Pr.

JOB APPLICATIONS

see Applications for Positions

JOB ANALYSIS

see also Job Descriptions; Job Evaluation

Berwitz, Clement J. The Job Analysis Approach to Affirmative Action. LC 75-11660. 327p. 1975. 37.95 (ISBN 0-471-07157-9, Pub. by Wiley-Interscience). Wiley.

Blackler, F. H. & Brown, C. A. Job Redesign & Management Control. LC 78-60430. 1978. 22.95 (ISBN 0-03-046210-X). Praeger.

Bolweg, Joep F. Job Design & Industrial Democracy. (Studies in the Quality of Working Life: No. 3). 1976. lib. bdg. 20.50 (ISBN 90-207-0634-9, Pub. by Martinus Nijhoff Netherlands). Kluwer Boston.

Brown, Ronald. The Practical Manager's Guide to Excellence in Management. 1979. 11.95 (ISBN 0-8144-5520-4). Am Mgmt.

Buchanan, David A. The Development of Job Design Theories & Techniques. LC 79-83808. 180p. 1979. 22.95 (ISBN 0-03-052376-1). Praeger.

Carby, Keith. Job Redesign in Practice. 1976. pap. 6.50x (ISBN 0-85292-138-1). Intl Pubns Serv.

Fogel, Walter, ed. Job Equities - Essays in Honor of Frederic Meyers. (Monograph Ser.: No. 29). 250p. (Orig.). 1981. price not set (ISBN 0-89215-114-5). U Cal LA Indus Rel.

Ford, Robert N. Why Jobs Die & What to Do About It: Job Redesign & Future Productivity. 1979. 15.95 (ISBN 0-8144-5502-6). Am Mgmt.

McCormick, Ernest J. Job Analysis: Methods & Applications. LC 79-7334. (Illus.). 1979. 24.95 (ISBN 0-8144-5504-2). Am Mgmt.

Michalak, Donald F. & Yager, Edwin G. Making the Training Process Work. LC 78-17907. (Continuing Management Education Ser.). 1979. text ed. 13.95 scp (ISBN 0-06-044429-0, HarpC). Har-Row.

National Retail Merch. Assn. Retailing Job Analysis & Job Evaluation. 1975. 17.00 (ISBN 0-685-63847-2, P52215). Natl Ret Merch.

Patterson, T. T. Job Evaluation: A Manual for the Patterson Method, Vol. II. 208p. 1978. text ed. 22.00x (ISBN 0-220-66844-2, Pub. by Busn Bks England). Renouf.

Redford, S. R. Jobmanship: How to Get Ahead by "Psyching Out" Your Boss & Co-Workers. (Illus.). 1979. 9.95 (ISBN 0-02-601410-6). Macmillan.

Shaffer, Dale E. A Guide to Writing Library Job Descriptions: Examples Covering Major Work Areas. 49p. 1981. pap. 4.25 (ISBN 0-915060-17-5). D E Shaffer.

Stewart, V. & Stewart, A. Practical Performance Appraisal. 192p. 1978. text ed. 26.50x (ISBN 0-566-02081-5, Pub by Teakfield Ltd England). Renouf.

Viscusi, W. Kip. Employment Hazards: An Investigation of Market Performance. LC 79-13149. (Harvard Economic Studies: No. 148). (Illus.). 1980. text ed. 20.00x (ISBN 0-674-25176-8). Harvard U Pr.

Wallens, John. Training in Physical Skills. 1975. 22.00x (ISBN 0-8464-0933-X). Beekman Pubs.

Youngman, M. B., et al. Analysing Jobs. 168p. 1978. text ed. 31.50x (ISBN 0-566-02089-0, Pub. by Gower Pub Co England). Renouf.

JOB DESCRIPTIONS

Cooper, Robert. Job Motivation & Job Design. LC 74-192791. (Management in Perspective Ser.). 140p. 1977. pap. 11.50x (ISBN 0-85292-094-6). Intl Pubns Serv.

Davis, Louis E. & Taylor, James C., eds. Design of Jobs. 2nd ed. LC 78-23397. 1979. text ed. 15.95 (ISBN 0-87620-219-9). Goodyear.

Famularo, Joseph J. Organization Planning Manual. rev. ed. (Illus.). 1979. 29.95 (ISBN 0-8144-5538-7). Am Mgmt.

Henderson, Richard I. Job Descriptions - Critical Documents, Versatile Tools. 1976. 4.50 (ISBN 0-8144-6955-8). Am Mgmt.

O'Callaghan, Dorothy. The Job Catalog: Where to Find That Creative Job in Washington - Baltimore. LC 81-80660. 1981. pap. 6.00 (ISBN 0-914694-06-5). Mail Order.

Schreiber, Carol T. Changing Places: Men & Women in Transitional Occupations. 1979. 17.50 (ISBN 0-262-19177-6); pap. 6.95 (ISBN 0-262-69075-6). MIT Pr.

Tourism Education Corp. A Hospitality Industry Guide for Writing & Using Task Unit Job Descriptions. 1976. pap. 14.50 (ISBN 0-8436-2118-4). CBI Pub.

Ulery, John D. Job Descriptions in Manufacturing Industries. 144p. 1981. 21.95 (ISBN 0-8144-5710-X). Am Mgmt.

JOB DISCRIMINATION

see Discrimination in Employment

JOB EVALUATION

see also Job Analysis

Aldag, Ramon J. & Brief, Arthur P. Task Design & Employee Motivation. 1979. pap. text ed. 8.95x (ISBN 0-673-15146-8). Scott F.

Atkinsson, C. Clifford, Jr., et al, eds. Evaluation in the Management of Human Services. 1978. 33.00 (ISBN 0-12-066350-3). Acad Pr.

Azrin, Nathan H. & Besalel, Victoria A. Job Club Counselor's Manual. 224p. 1980. pap. text ed. 14.95 (ISBN 0-8391-1535-0). Univ Park.

Bartley, Douglas. Job Evaluation-Wage & Salary Administration. LC 80-21099. 272p. 1981. text ed. 14.95 (ISBN 0-201-00095-4). A-W.

Burns, Mike. Understanding Job Evaluation. 1978. pap. text ed. 20.00x (ISBN 0-85292-166-7). Intl Pubns Serv.

Committee on Occupational Classification & Analysis. Job Evaluation: An Analytical Review. 1979. pap. 7.00 (ISBN 0-309-02882-5). Natl Acad Pr.

Elizur, Dov. Job Evaluation: A Systematic Approach. 165p. 1980. text ed. 37.25 (ISBN 0-566-02120-X, Pub. by Gower Pub Co England). Renouf.

Evaluation Research & Social Change. 104p. 1981. pap. 11.50 (ISBN 92-3-101699-7, U1083, UNESCO). Unipub.

Henderson, Richard I., et al. Job Pay for Job Worth: Designing & Managing an Equitable Job Classification & Pay System. (Research Monograph: No. 86). 1981. pap. 24.00 (ISBN 0-88406-130-2). Ga St U Busn Pub.

Jaques, Elliott. Measurement of Responsibility: A Study of Work, Payment, & Individual Capacity. 144p. (Orig.). 1972. 8.95 (ISBN 0-435-85480-1). Krieger.

--Progression Handbook. LC 68-13863. (Glacier Project Ser.). (Illus.). 72p. 1968. 7.50x (ISBN 0-8093-0301-9). S Ill U Pr.

Job Evaluation & EEO: The Emerging Issues, Papers Presented at the IRC Colloquium. 1979. spiral bdg. 25.00 (ISBN 0-87330-051-3). Indus Rel.

Levine, Robert A. & Solomon, Marian A., eds. Evaluation Research & Practice: Comparative & International Perspectives. LC 80-26531. (Illus.). 255p. 1981. 20.00 (ISBN 0-8039-1561-6). Sage.

Livy, Brian. Job Evaluation: A Critical Review. (Illus.). 192p. 1975. pap. text ed. 12.50x (ISBN 0-04-658214-2). Allen Unwin.

Montgomery, Gerald W. The Selling of You: A Practical Guide to Job Hunting. new ed. 103p. 1980. 12.95x (ISBN 0-937096-01-6); pap. 9.95x (ISBN 0-937096-00-8). Montgomery Comm.

National Retail Merch. Assn. Retailing Job Analysis & Job Evaluation. 1975. 17.00 (ISBN 0-685-63847-2, P52215). Natl Ret Merch.

National Retail Merchants Assn. Measuring Executive & Employee. 1978. 17.00 (ISBN 0-685-68110-6, P52877). Natl Ret Merch.

Newman, John E. & Hinrichs, John R. Performance Evaluation for Professional Personnal, Bk. 14. LC 80-20739. (Studies in Productivity Highlights of the Literature). 1980. pap. 25.00 (ISBN 0-89361-006-2). Work in Amer.

Otis, Jay L. & Leukart, R. H. Job Evaluation. 2nd ed. 1954. ref. ed. 21.00 (ISBN 0-13-509562-X). P-H.

Patterson, T. T. Job Evaluation: A Manual for the Patterson Method, Vol. II. 208p. 1978. text ed. 22.00x (ISBN 0-220-66844-2, Pub. by Busn Bks England). Renouf.

Rudman, Jack. Position Classification Specialist. (Career Examination Ser.: C-601). (Cloth bdg. avail. on request). 16.00 (ISBN 0-8373-0601-9). Natl Learning.

Schulberg, Herbert C. & Jerrell, Jeanette M., eds. The Evaluator & Management. LC 79-19458. (Sage Research Progress Ser. in Evaluation: Vol. 4). (Illus.). 159p. 1979. 15.00 (ISBN 0-8039-1304-4); pap. 7.50 (ISBN 0-8039-1305-2). Sage.

Universal Training Systems Co. How to Review & Evaluate Employee Performance. 1976. 65.50 (ISBN 0-85013-073-5). Dartnell Corp.

JOB OPENINGS

see Job Vacancies

JOB PERFORMANCE STANDARDS

see Performance Standards

JOB RATING

see Job Evaluation

JOB RESUMES

see Applications for Positions; Resumes (Employment)

JOB SATISFACTION

Bailyn, Lotte & Schein, Edgar H. Living with Technology: Issues at Mid-Career. 160p. 1980. text ed. 15.00x (ISBN 0-262-02153-6). MIT Pr.

Barbash, Jack. Job Satisfaction Attitudes Surveys: Industrial Relations Programme, Special Studies. 1976. 2.00x (ISBN 92-64-11537-4). OECD.

Carnegie, Dale. How to Enjoy Your Life & Your Job. 1977. pap. 2.50 (ISBN 0-671-41761-4). PB.

Carone, Pasquale, et al, eds. Misfits in Industry. 1978. 12.50 (ISBN 0-470-26447-0). Halsted Pr.

Carroll, Bonnie. Job Satisfaction. rev. ed. (Key Issues Ser.: No. 3). 1973. pap. 2.00 (ISBN 0-87546-206-5). NY Sch Indus Rel.

Case Studies in Automation Related to Humanization of Work: Proceedings of the IFAC Workshop, Enschede, the Netherlands, Oct. 1977. 1978. text ed. 18.00 (ISBN 0-08-022012-6). Pergamon.

Cooper, Cary L. & Mumford, Enid, eds. The Quality of Working Life in Western & Eastern Europe. LC 78-27692. (Contributions in Economics & Economic History: No. 25). 1979. lib. bdg. 35.00 (ISBN 0-313-20957-X, CWL/). Greenwood.

Davis, Louis E. & Cherns, Albert B., eds. Quality of Working Life: Cases & Commentary, Vol. 2. LC 74-24370. 1975. 19.95 (ISBN 0-02-907330-8); pap. text ed. 9.95 (ISBN 0-02-907340-5). Free Pr.

De Man, Henri. Joy in Work. Stein, Leon, ed. LC 77-70513. (Work Ser.). 1977. Repr. of 1929 ed. lib. bdg. 15.00 (ISBN 0-405-10182-1). Arno.

Didactic Systems Staff. Job Enrichment - Redesigning Jobs for Motivation. (Simulation Game Ser.). 1971. pap. 6.00 (ISBN 0-89401-045-X); leader's guide & tape avail. (ISBN 0-685-78125-9). Didactic Syst.

Evans, Geraldine & Maas, John M. Job Satisfaction & Teacher Militancy: Some Teacher Attitudes. LC 70-79298. (Illus.). 1969. pap. 2.00x (ISBN 0-8134-1105-X, 1105). Interstate.

Feinstein, Barbara & Brown, Edwin G. New Partnership: Human Services with Business & Industry. 256p. 1981. text ed. 18.95x (ISBN 0-87073-653-1); pap. text ed. 9.95x (ISBN 0-87073-654-X). Schenkman.

Ford, Robert N. Motivation Through the Work Itself. LC 77-77749. 1969. 15.95 (ISBN 0-8144-5173-X). Am Mgmt.

Friedmann, Georges. The Anatomy of Work: Labor, Leisure & the Implications of Automation. LC 78-6171. 1978. Repr. of 1962 ed. lib. bdg. 20.75x (ISBN 0-313-20464-0, FRAW). Greenwood.

Ginzberg, Eli. The Manpower Connection: Education & Work. 288p. 1975. 15.00x (ISBN 0-674-54810-8). Harvard U Pr.

Goldring, Patrick. Multipurpose Man: A New Work Style for the Modern Age. LC 73-18933. 128p. 1974. 6.95 (ISBN 0-8008-5424-1). Taplinger.

Gooding, Judson. The Job Revolution. LC 74-188469. 256p. 1972. 7.95 (ISBN 0-8027-0383-6). Walker & Co.

Gruneberg, Michael M. Understanding Job Satisfaction. LC 78-20782. 1979. 30.95x (ISBN 0-470-26610-4). Halsted Pr.

Gruneberg, Michael M., ed. Job Satisfaction. LC 75-43852. 1976. 32.95 (ISBN 0-470-32911-4). Halsted Pr.

Haldane, Bernard. Career Satisfaction & Success: A Guide to Job Freedom. Olcheski, William, ed. LC 73-85196. 208p. 1974. 10.95 (ISBN 0-8144-5343-0). Am Mgmt.

Hammer, Tove H. & Bacharach, Samuel B., eds. Reward Systems & Power Distribution: Searching for Solutions. (Pierce Ser.: No. 5). 1977. pap. 4.75 (ISBN 0-87546-223-5); pap. 7.75 special hard bdg. (ISBN 0-87546-290-1). NY Sch Indus Rel.

Heisler, William J. & Houck, John W. A Matter of Dignity: Inquiries into the Humanization of Work. LC 76-51620. 1977. pap. text ed. 4.95x (ISBN 0-268-01345-4). U of Notre Dame Pr.

Herzberg, Frederick, et al. Motivation to Work. 2nd ed. 1959. 17.95 (ISBN 0-471-37389-3, Pub. by Wiley-Interscience). Wiley.

Hoppock, Robert. Job Satisfaction. Stein, Leon, ed. LC 77-70505. (Work Ser.). (Illus.). 1977. Repr. of 1935 ed. lib. bdg. 22.00x (ISBN 0-405-10176-7). Arno.

Hubbard, L. Ron. The Problems of Work. 10.00 (ISBN 0-686-30789-5). Church Scient NY.

Hutar, Laddie F. Job Success Dictionary: A Hutar Guide to Becoming a More Valuable Employee & Earning More. (Illus.). pap. 2.00 (ISBN 0-918896-02-9). Hutar.

Johnson, Dale A. & Weiss, Donald J. Middle Management Decision Making & Job Satisfaction. LC 75-166965. 63p. 1971. pap. text ed. 1.25x (ISBN 0-8134-1369-9, 1369). Interstate.

Jones, Rochelle. The Big Switch: New Careers, New Lives After 35. LC 79-24200. 228p. 1980. 10.95 (ISBN 0-07-032810-2). McGraw.

Katzell, Raymond A., et al. Work, Productivity & Job Satisfaction: An Evaluation of Policy-Related Research. LC 75-21726. (Illus.). 445p. (Orig.). 1975. pap. text ed. 7.00 (ISBN 0-15-003082-7, Psych Corp). HarBraceJ.

Kovach, Kenneth A. Organization Size, Job Satisfaction, Absenteeism & Turnover. 148p. 1977. pap. text ed. 7.75 (ISBN 0-8191-0242-3). U Pr of Amer.

Litwin, George H. & Stringer, Robert A., Jr. Motivation & Organizational Climate. LC 68-8417. (Illus.). 1968. 10.00x (ISBN 0-87584-071-X). Harvard Busn.

Maurer, John G. Work Role Involvement of Industrial Supervisors. LC 69-63017. 1969. 6.50 (ISBN 0-87744-067-0). Mich St U Busn.

Morse, Nancy C. Satisfactions in White-Collar Job. Stein, Leon, ed. LC 77-70518. (Work Ser.). (Illus.). 1977. Repr. of 1953 ed. lib. bdg. 16.00x (ISBN 0-405-10187-2). Arno.

Motivation: Key to Good Management. (AMACOM Reprint Collections). 1974. pap. 8.00 (ISBN 0-8144-6938-8). Am Mgmt.

Myers, M. Scott. Every Employee a Manager. Newton, William R., ed. (Illus.). 1981. 16.50 (ISBN 0-07-044269-X, P&RB). McGraw.

Noble, Iris. Life on the Line: Alternative Approaches to Work. (A New Conservation Book). (Illus.). 96p. (gr. 6-8). 1977. PLB 5.49 (ISBN 0-698-30662-7). Coward.
O'Toole, James. Work, Learning, & the American Future. LC 76-50726. (Higher Education Ser.). 256p. 1977. text ed. 15.95x (ISBN 0-87589-304-X). Jossey-Bass.
Palm, Goran. The Flight from Work. Smith, P., tr. LC 77-76077. 1977. 16.95 (ISBN 0-521-21668-0). Cambridge U Pr.
Portigal, Alan H. Towards the Measurement of Work Satisfaction. (OECD Social Indicator Development Programme Ser.). 1976. 1.50x (ISBN 92-64-11516-1). OECD.
Productivity, Quality of Working Life & Labour-Management Relations. 23p. 1976. 2.75 (ISBN 0-686-70977-2, APO62, APO). Unipub.
Quinn, Robert P. & Staines, Graham L. The Nineteen Seventy-Seven Quality of Employment Survey: Descriptive Statistics, with Comparison Data from the 1969-70 & 1972-73 Surveys. LC 78-71659. (Illus.). 1979. pap. text ed. 10.00 (ISBN 0-87944-231-X). Inst Soc. Res.
Reynolds, Lloyd G. & Shister, Joseph. Job Horizons: Study of Job Satisfaction & Labor Mobility. Stein, Leon, ed. LC 77-70526. (Work Ser.). (Illus.). 1977. Repr. of 1949 ed. lib. bdg. 12.00x (ISBN 0-405-10194-5). Arno.
Ronco, William. Jobs: How People Create Their Own. LC 76-48525. (YA) 1977. pap. 4.95 (ISBN 0-8070-2745-6, BP 555). Beacon Pr.
Rosow, Jerome M., ed. The Worker & the Job: Coping with Change. LC 74-765. (An American Assembly Bk.). (Illus.). 224p. 1974. 7.95 (ISBN 0-13-965350-3, Spec); pap. 2.95 (ISBN 0-13-965350-3, Spec). P-H.
Rutler, George W. The Impatience of Job. 1980. pap. 3.95 (ISBN 0-89385-014-4). Sugden.
Sarason, Seymour B. Work, Aging, & Social Change: Professionals and the One Life-One Career Imperative. LC 76-27224. 1977. 14.95 (ISBN 0-02-927860-0). Free Pr.
Srivastva, Suresh. Job Satisfaction and Productivity. LC 77-24063. 1977. Repr. of 1975 ed. 14.50x (ISBN 0-87338-203-X, Pub. by Comp. Adm. Research Inst.). Kent St U Pr.
Stein, Leon, ed. Work or Labor: Original Anthology. LC 77-70551. (Work Ser.). (Illus.). 1977. lib. bdg. 28.00x (ISBN 0-405-10205-4). Arno.
Tannehill, Robert E. Job Enrichment. 1974. 65.50 (ISBN 0-85013-067-0). Dartnell Corp.
Taves, Marvin J., et al. Role Conception & Vocational Success & Satisfaction: A Study of Student & Professional Nurses. (Illus.). 125p. 1963. pap. 3.00x (ISBN 0-87776-112-4, R-112). Ohio St U Admin Sci.
Taylor, Linda K. Not for Bread Alone: An Appreciation of Job Enrichment. 3rd ed. 202p. 1980. pap. 12.25x (ISBN 0-220-67019-6, Pub. by Busn Bks England). Renouf.
Walsh, Ruth M. & Birkin, Stanley J., eds. Job Satisfaction & Motivation: An Annotated Bibliography. LC 78-67915. 1979. lib. bdg. 35.00 (ISBN 0-313-20635-X, WJS/). Greenwood.
Walters, R. W. Job Enrichment for Results: Strategies for Successful Implementation. 320p. 1975. 11.95 (ISBN 0-201-08492-9). A-W.
Warr, P. Personal Goals & Work Design. 1976. 39.50 (ISBN 0-471-92095-9). Wiley.
Weir. Job Satisfaction. 1976. pap. 5.95 (ISBN 0-531-06074-8, Fontana Pap). Watts.
White, Jerry E. & White, Mary E. Your Job: Survival or Satisfaction. 1976. 4.95 (ISBN 0-310-34321-6). Zondervan.
Widick, B. J., ed. Auto Work & Its Discontents. LC 76-16095. (Policy Studies in Employment & Welfare: No. 25). (Illus.). 128p. 1976. 10.00x (ISBN 0-8018-1856-7); pap. 3.95x (ISBN 0-8018-1857-5). Johns Hopkins.
Wilson, John. How to Get Paid for What You've Earned. (Medical Economics Books). 1974. 11.95 (ISBN 0-442-84019-5). Van Nos Reinhold.
Yorks, Lyle. Job Enrichment Revisited. LC 78-21141. 1979. pap. 7.50 (ISBN 0-8144-2226-8). Am Mgmt.
--A Radical Approach to Job Enrichment. LC 75-44481. 176p. 1976. 12.95 (ISBN 0-8144-5412-7). Am Mgmt.

JOB TRAINING
see Occupational Training

JOB VACANCIES
Adams, Robert L. & Noble, John H., III, eds. The Metropolitan New York Job Bank: Including Northern New Jersey, Long Island, Southwestern Connecticut & Westchester. (Job Bank Ser.). 403p. (Orig.). 1981. pap. 9.95 (ISBN 0-937860-03-4). Adams Inc MA.
Basehore, C. J. & Marantette, Carter H. Securing an Executive Position in the Sunbelt. 57p. (Orig.). 1980. pap. 5.95 (ISBN 0-939148-00-5). Exec West.
Bay Area Employer Directory: Nineteen Eighty to Nineteen Eighty-One Edition. 1980. 35.95 (ISBN 0-916210-80-4). Albin.
Davis, Ken & Taylor, Tom. The Adventure of Making Money. LC 79-24749. (Illus., Orig.). (gr. 5-10). 1980. pap. 2.95 (ISBN 0-916392-47-3). Oak Tree Pubns.
Employer Directory: 1981. Date not set. 35.95 (ISBN 0-916210-05-7). Albin.
File, Norman & Howroyd, Bernard. How to Beat the Establishment & Get That Job. LC 70-153840. Date not set. pap. cancelled (ISBN 0-686-11187-7) (ISBN 0-686-11188-5). Laurida.
Gresty, Michael J. Gresty's International Recruitment Guide. 224p. 1980. cancelled (ISBN 0-906071-48-8). Proteus Pub NY.
Hiestand, Dale L. & Morse, Dean W. Comparative Metropolitan Employment Complexes: New York, Chicago, los Angeles, Houston & Atlanta. LC 77-84456. (Conservation of Human Resources Ser.: No. 7). 141p. 1979. text ed. 21.50x (ISBN 0-916672-82-4). Allanheld.
Jew, Wing & Tandy, Carol. Using the Want Ads. (Survival Guides Ser.). (Illus.). 64p. (gr. 7-12). 1977. pap. text ed. 2.85 (ISBN 0-915510-16-2). Janus Bks.
Jobs Versus People: Workers' Education Guide to Population Problems. 1974. 2.85 (ISBN 92-2-101182-8). Intl Labour Office.
Kovach, Kenneth A. Organization Size, Job Satisfaction, Absenteeism & Turnover. 148p. 1977. pap. text ed. 7.75 (ISBN 0-8191-0242-3). U Pr of Amer.
Lathrop, Richard. Who's Hiring Who. new. rev. 3rd ed. LC 75-44412. (Illus.). 1977. 8.95 (ISBN 0-913668-82-6); pap. 5.95 (ISBN 0-913668-55-9). Ten Speed Pr.
Laughlin, Burgess. Job Opportunities in the Black Market. 1981. pap. 7.95 (ISBN 0-686-30637-6). Loompanics.
Lecht, Leonard A. Occupational Choices & Training Needs. LC 76-24356. (Special Studies). 1977. text ed. 23.95 (ISBN 0-275-23960-8). Praeger.
O'Callaghan, Dorothy. The Job Catalog: Where to Find That Creative Job in Washington D. C./Baltimore. 4th ed. LC 81-80660. 1981. pap. 6.00 (ISBN 0-914694-06-5). Mail Order.
Pred, A. R. Major Job-Providing Organizations & Systems of Cities. LC 74-79830. (CCG Resource Papers Ser.: No. 27). (Illus.). 1974. pap. text ed. 4.00 (ISBN 0-89291-074-7). Assn Am Geographers.
Preston, Noreen L. The Help-Wanted Index: Technical Description & Behavioral Trends. LC 77-78974. (Report Ser.: No. 716). (Illus.). 1977. pap. 15.00 (ISBN 0-8237-0150-6). Conference Bd.
Robert Lang Adams & Associates. The Southwest Job Bank. 400p. 1981. pap. 9.95 (ISBN 0-686-30691-0). Adams Inc MA.
Robert Long Adams & Associates. The D.C Baltimore Job Bank. 400p. 1981. pap. 9.95 (ISBN 0-686-30610-4). Adams Inc MA.
Robert Long Adams Associates. The Mid-Atlantic Job Bank. 400p. 1981. pap. 9.95 (ISBN 0-686-30615-5). Adams Inc MA.
--The National Job Bank. 2000p. 1981. pap. 17.50 (ISBN 0-686-30611-2). Adams Inc MA.
--The New England Job Bank. 400p. 1981. pap. 9.95 (ISBN 0-686-30612-0). Adams Inc MA.
--The Northern California Job Bank. 400p. 1981. pap. 9.95 (ISBN 0-686-30613-9). Adams Inc MA.
--The Northwest Job Bank. 400p. 1981. pap. 9.95 (ISBN 0-686-30614-7). Adams Inc MA.
--The Philadelphia Job Bank. 400p. 1981. pap. 9.95 (ISBN 0-686-30616-3). Adams Inc MA.
--The Sun Belt Job Bank. 400p. 1981. pap. 9.95 (ISBN 0-686-30617-1). Adams Inc MA.
--The Texas Job Bank. 400p. 1981. pap. 9.95 (ISBN 0-686-30618-X). Adams Inc MA.
Salmon, Richard D. The Job Hunter's Guide to the Rocky Mountain West. LC 78-74738. 1980. pap. 13.50 (ISBN 0-918938-02-3). Brattle.
Stanat & Reardon. Job Hunting Secrets. pap. 5.95 (ISBN 0-686-31271-6). New Century.
White, Harrison C. Chains of Opportunity: System Models of Mobility in Organizations. LC 78-105374. 1970. 22.50x (ISBN 0-674-10674-1). Harvard U Pr.

JOBS
see Occupations; Professions

JOCKEYS
Ainslie, Tom. Ainslie on Jockeys. rev. ed. LC 74-32023. 160p. 1975. 9.95 (ISBN 0-671-22068-3). S&S.
Fitzgeorge-Parker, Tim. Jockeys of the Seventies. (Illus.). 168p. 1980. 17.95 (ISBN 0-7207-1267-X, Pub. by Michael Joseph). Merrimack Bk Serv.
Haney, Lynn. The Lady Is a Jock. LC 73-11548. (Illus.). 224p. 1973. 5.95 (ISBN 0-396-06870-7). Dodd.
McMillan, Constance V. Steve Cauthen: Million Dollar Baby. LC 77-24072. (So Young, So Far Ser.). (Illus.). 40p. (gr. 3-9). 1977. PLB 5.95 (ISBN 0-88436-406-2); pap. 3.50 (ISBN 0-88436-407-0). EMC.
Mueser, Anne M. The Picture Story of Jockey Steve Cauthen. LC 78-27884. (Illus.). 64p. (gr. 4-6). 1979. PLB 6.97 (ISBN 0-671-32990-1). Messner.
Tuttle, Anthony. Steve Cauthen: Boy Jockey. LC 77-16770. (Illus.). (gr. 3-6). 1978. 7.95 (ISBN 0-399-20631-0). Putnam.

JOGGING
Batten, Jack. The Complete Jogger. (Illus.). 1978. pap. 1.95 (ISBN 0-515-04858-5). Jove Pubns.
--The Complete Jogger. LC 76-55527. (Illus.). 1977. pap. 4.95 (ISBN 0-15-120699-6). HarBraceJ.
Burger, Robert E. The Jogger's Catalog: The Source Book for Runners. LC 78-4271. (Illus.). 192p. 1978. 12.50 (ISBN 0-87131-275-1); pap. 5.95 (ISBN 0-87131-259-X). M Evans.
Cook, Shirley. Diary of a Jogging Housewife. LC 78-72865. 1978. pap. 2.95 (ISBN 0-89636-016-4). Accent Bks.
Daitzman, Reid J. Mental Jogging. LC 79-16602. 1980. 7.95 (ISBN 0-399-90053-5). Marek.
D'Alton, Martina. The Runner's Guide to the U. S. A. LC 78-10315. (Illus.). 1979. 12.95 (ISBN 0-671-40070-3); pap. 6.95 (ISBN 0-671-40022-3). Summit Bks.
Ferstle, Jim. Contemporary Jogging. LC 77-91153. 1978. pap. 3.95 (ISBN 0-8092-7575-9). Contemp Bks.
Fineberg, Robert G. Jogging-the Dance of Death. Ashton, Sylvia, ed. 1980. 12.95 (ISBN 0-87949-174-4). Ashley Bks.
Fisher, A. Garth & Allsen, Philip E. Jogging. (Physical Education Activity Ser.). 96p. 1980. pap. text ed. write for info. (ISBN 0-697-07083-2). Wm C Brown.
Fixx, James F. The Complete Book of Running. (Illus.). 1977. 11.95 (ISBN 0-394-41159-5). Random.
Geline, Robert J. The Practical Runner. (Illus.). 1978. pap. 4.95 (ISBN 0-02-028830-1, Collier). Macmillan.
Harper, Frederick D. Jogotherapy: Jogging As a Therapeutic Strategy. LC 79-55453. 1979. pap. 3.95 (ISBN 0-935392-00-9). Douglass Pubs.
Heinonen, Janet. Sports Illustrated Running for Women. 1979. 8.95 (ISBN 0-397-01330-2); pap. 5.95 (ISBN 0-397-01331-0). Har-Row.
Hochman, Sandra. Jogging: A Love Story. LC 78-21236. 1979. 9.95 (ISBN 0-399-12189-7). Putnam.
Hoffman, Robert & Cantlay, Jed. Running Together: The Family Book of Jogging. LC 79-92135. (West Point Sports Fitness Ser.: Vol. 5). (Illus.). 1980. pap. text ed. 4.95 (ISBN 0-918438-18-7). Leisure Pr.
Kreuter, Gretchen. Running the Twin Cities. (Illus.). 95p. 1980. pap. 3.95 (ISBN 0-931714-08-7). Nodin Pr.
Lovett, C. S. Jogging with Jesus. (Illus.). 1978. pap. 2.95 (ISBN 0-938148-34-6). Personal Christianity.
Lyttle, Richard B. Jogging & Running. (Concise Guides Ser.). (gr. 5 up). 1979. PLB 6.90 s&l (ISBN 0-531-02949-2). Watts.
Sheehan, George. This Running Life. 1980. 10.95 (ISBN 0-671-25608-4). S&S.
Spino, Mike. Beyond Jogging: The Innerspaces of Running. LC 75-28771. 1976. pap. 4.95 (ISBN 0-89087-156-6). Celestial Arts.
Steincrohn, Peter. How to Cure Your Joggermania! LC 79-51020. 1979. 9.95 (ISBN 0-498-02430-X). A S Barnes.
Tyus, Wyomia. Inside Jogging for Women. LC 77-91181. 1978. pap. 4.95 (ISBN 0-8092-7593-7). Contemp Bks.
Zeleznak, Shirley. Jogging. Schroeder, Howard, ed. LC 79-27770. (Back to Nature Ser.). (Illus.). (gr. 3-5). 1979. lib. bdg. 6.95 (ISBN 0-89686-068-X). Crestwood Hse.

JOHN, KING OF ENGLAND, 1167-1216
Jones, J. A. King John & the Magna Carta. (Illus.). 1971. pap. text ed. 5.50x (ISBN 0-582-31463-1). Longman.
Norgate, Kate. John Lackland. LC 76-145212. 303p. 1902. Repr. 14.00 (ISBN 0-403-01129-9). Scholarly.
--John Lackland. 75.00 (ISBN 0-8490-0455-1). Gordon Pr.
Sider, J. W. & Orgel, Stephen, eds. The Troublesome Raigne of John King of England. LC 78-66778. (Renaissance Drama Ser.). 1979. lib. bdg. 31.00 (ISBN 0-8240-9733-5). Garland Pub.
Warren, W. L. King John. rev. ed. (Campus Ser.: No. 209). 1978. o. p. 15.00x (ISBN 0-520-03610-7); pap. 6.95x (ISBN 0-520-03643-3). U of Cal Pr.

JOHN, KING OF ENGLAND, 1167-1216–DRAMA
Bale, John. John Bale's King Johan. Adams, Barry B., ed. LC 67-12048. 1969. 8.50 (ISBN 0-87328-039-3). Huntington Lib.
--Kynge Johan: A Play in Two Parts. Collier, J. Payne, ed. LC 79-160012. (Camden Society, London. Publications, First Ser.: No. 2). Repr. of 1838 ed. 14.00 (ISBN 0-404-50102-8). AMS Pr.
--Kynge Johan, a Play in Two Parts. 15.50 (ISBN 0-384-03130-7). Johnson Repr.
Mattsson, May. Five Plays About King John. 1977. pap. text ed. 19.75x (ISBN 91-554-067-0X). Humanities.
Shakespeare, William. King John. 4th rev. ed. Honingmann, E. A., ed. (Arden Shakespeare Ser.). 1962. Repr. of 1954 ed. 25.95x (ISBN 0-416-47370-9); pap. 5.50 (ISBN 0-416-49620-2). Methuen Inc.
--King John. Quiller-Couch, Arthur, et al, eds. (New Shakespeare Ser). 1969. 23.95 (ISBN 0-521-07540-8). Cambridge U Pr.
--King John. Matchett, William M., ed. pap. 1.95 (ISBN 0-451-50330-9, CJ1899, Sig Classics). NAL.
--King John. Ribner, Irving, ed. (Shakespeare Ser.). 1962. pap. 1.50 (ISBN 0-14-071426-X, Pelican). Penguin.

JOHN 23RD, POPE, 1881-1963
Bonnot, Bernard R. Pope John Twenty-Third: A Clever, Pastoral Leader. LC 79-1770. 1980. 9.95 (ISBN 0-8189-0388-0). Alba.
Calvez, Jean Y. The Social Thought of John Twenty Third: Mater et Magistra. McKenzie, George J., tr. LC 75-40992. 1977. Repr. of 1965 ed. lib. bdg. 15.00 (ISBN 0-8371-8711-7, CASCJ). Greenwood.
Cushing, Richard J. Call Me John. (Illus.). 4.00 (ISBN 0-8198-0014-7). Dghtrs St Paul.
Everybody's Pope: The Life of John 23rd. LC 67-15775. 1966. pap. 1.00 (ISBN 0-911782-06-0). New City.
Kitts, Eustace J. Pope John Twenty-Third & Master John Hus of Bohemia. LC 77-84726. Repr. of 1910 ed. 32.50 (ISBN 0-404-16127-8). AMS Pr.
Lecaro, Giacomo. John Twenty Third: Simpleton or Saint. 1968. 3.50 (ISBN 0-8199-0055-9, L38351). Franciscan Herald.
Pope John XXIII. Journal of a Soul. White, Dorothy, tr. LC 79-7786. (Illus.). 504p. 1980. pap. 5.95 (ISBN 0-385-14842-9, Im). Doubleday.
--Encyclicals & Other Messages of John XXIII. 1976. 6.00 (ISBN 0-8198-0407-X); pap. 5.00 (ISBN 0-8198-0408-8). Dghtrs St Paul.
Zizola, Giancarlo. The Utopia of Pope John XXIII. Barolini, Helen, tr. LC 79-4347. 1979. pap. 9.95 (ISBN 0-88344-520-4). Orbis Bks.

JOHN 23RD, POPE, 1881-1963–JUVENILE LITERATURE
McGravie, Anne. The Boyhood of Pope John XXIII. (Stories About Christian Heroes Ser.). (Illus.). (gr. 1-3). 1979. pap. 1.95 (ISBN 0-03-049446-X). Winston Pr.

JOHN, SAINT, APOSTLE
Barnes, Arthur S. Christianity at Rome in the Apostolic Age. LC 72-114462. (Illus.). 1971. Repr. of 1938 ed. lib. bdg. 15.00 (ISBN 0-8371-4760-3, BACR). Greenwood.
Booth, A. E. Ministry of Peter, John & Paul. Date not set. pap. 0.95 (ISBN 0-686-30739-9). Believers Bkshelf.
Cook, W. Robert. The Theology of John. 1979. 11.95 (ISBN 0-8024-8629-0). Moody.
Culpepper, R. Alan. The Johannine School: An Evaluation of the Johannine-School Hypothesis Based on an Investigation of the Nature of Ancient Schools. LC 75-34235. (Society of Biblical Literature. Dissertation Ser.). 1976. pap. 9.00x (ISBN 0-89130-063-5, 060126). Scholars Pr Ca.
De Vinck, Catherine. Readings: John at Patmos & A Book of Hours. LC 78-55341. 1978. 5.75 (ISBN 0-911726-32-2); pap. 3.75 (ISBN 0-911726-33-0). Alleluia Pr.
Haskell, Stephen N. The Story of the Seer of Patmos. 1977. soft cover 3.95 (ISBN 0-8127-0305-7). Review & Herald.
Helick, R. Martin. The Complex Vision of Philo St. John. LC 75-27035. 1975. 10.00 (ISBN 0-912710-07-1). Regent Graphic Serv.
Johan the Evangelist. LC 71-133689. (Tudor Facsimile Texts. Old English Plays: No. 24). Repr. of 1907 ed. 31.50 (ISBN 0-404-53324-8). AMS Pr.
Laux, Dorothy. John: Beloved Apostle. (Illus.). (gr. 1-6). 1977. bds. 5.50 (ISBN 0-8054-4234-0). Broadman.
Meinardus, Otto F. St. John of Patmos & the Seven Churches of the Apocalypse. LC 78-51245. (In the Footsteps of the Saints Ser.). (Illus.). 1979. lib. bdg. 12.50 (ISBN 0-89241-070-1); pap. 5.95 (ISBN 0-89241-043-4). Caratzas Bros.
Ra, Bo Yin. The Wisdom of St. John. Reichenbach, Bodo A., tr. from Ger. LC 74-15272. 112p. 1975. 5.00 (ISBN 0-915034-01-8). Kober Pr.
Riggs, Robert F. The Apocalypse Unsealed. LC 80-81698. 320p. 1981. 18.95 (ISBN 0-8022-2367-2). Philos Lib.
Robertson, A. T. Epochs in the Life of the Apostle John. 1974. pap. 3.95 (ISBN 0-8054-1349-9). Broadman.
Traylor, Ellen G. John, Son of Thunder. 1978. pap. 5.95 (ISBN 0-8423-1902-6). Tyndale.

JOHN 2ND, COMNENUS, 1088-1143
Kinnamos, John. Deeds of John & Manuel Comnenus. Brand, Charles M., tr. from Greek. LC 76-15317. (Records of Civilization, No. 85). 1976. 20.00x (ISBN 0-231-04080-6). Columbia U Pr.
JOHN HENRY
Felton, Harold W. John Henry & His Hammer. (Illus.). (gr. 5-9). 1950. PLB 5.99 (ISBN 0-394-91291-8). Knopf.
Johnson, Guy B. John Henry, Tracking Down a Negro Legend. LC 75-80720. Repr. of 1929 ed. 12.50 (ISBN 0-404-00177-7). AMS Pr.
Keats, Ezra J. John Henry: An American Legend. (Illus.). (gr. k-3). 1965. PLB 6.99 (ISBN 0-394-91302-7). Pantheon.
JOHN OF GAUNT, DUKE OF LANCASTER, 1340-1399
Hulbert, James R. Chaucer's Official Life. LC 75-93246. 1970. Repr. of 1912 ed. 6.00 (ISBN 0-87753-022-X). Phaeton.
JOHN OF SALISBURY, BP. OF CHARTRES, d. 1180
Lloyd, Roger B. Golden Middle Age. LC 75-90654. (Essay Index Reprint Ser). 1939. 16.00 (ISBN 0-8369-1208-X). Arno.
Pepin, Ronald E. The Entheticus of John of Salisbury: A Critical Text. 1975. pap. 4.00 (ISBN 0-8232-0075-2). Fordham.
Webb, Clement C. John of Salisbury. LC 78-152541. 1971. Repr. of 1932 ed. 13.00 (ISBN 0-8462-1614-0). Russell.
JOHN OF THE CROSS, SAINT, 1542-1591
Brenan, G. St. John of the Cross: His Life & Poetry. Nicholson, Lynda, tr. LC 72-83577. (Illus.). 224p. 1973. 38.50 (ISBN 0-521-20006-7); pap. 8.95x (ISBN 0-521-09953-6). Cambridge U Pr.
Frost, Bede. Saint John of the Cross: Doctor of Divine Love, an Introduction to His Philosophy, Theology & Spirituality. 1977. lib. bdg. 59.95 (ISBN 0-8490-2559-1). Gordon Pr.
Icaza, Sr. Rosa M. Stylistic Relationship Between Poetry & Prose in the Cantico Espiritual of San Juan De la Cruz. LC 76-94191. (Catholic University of America Studies in Romance Languages & Literatures Ser: No. 54). 1969. Repr. of 1957 ed. 16.00 (ISBN 0-404-50354-3). AMS Pr.
Kavanaugh, Kieran & Rodriguez, Otilio, trs. from Span. The Collected Works of St. John of the Cross. 2nd ed. LC 78-65789. 1979. 14.95x (ISBN 0-9600876-5-6); pap. 6.95x (ISBN 0-9600876-7-2). ICS Pubns.
MacDonald, James M. The Life & Writings of St. John of the Cross. 1977. lib. bdg. 59.95 (ISBN 0-8490-2164-2). Gordon Pr.
Mallory, Marilyn M. Christian Mysticism: Transcending Techniques. a Theological Reflection on the Empirical Testing of the Teaching of St. John of the Cross. 1977. pap. text ed. 34.25x (ISBN 90-232-1535-4). Humanities.
Palacios, Miguel A. Saint John of the Cross & Islam. Yoder, Howard W. & Douglas, Elmer H., trs. 1980. 7.95 (ISBN 0-533-04625-4). Vantage.
Peers, E. A. Spirit of Flame: A Study of St. John of the Cross. 1979. pap. 4.95 (ISBN 0-8192-1262-8). Morehouse.
Peers, E. Allison. St. John of the Cross & Other Lectures & Addresses. 1977. lib. bdg. 59.95 (ISBN 0-8490-2558-3). Gordon Pr.
Peers, Edgar A. St. John of the Cross, & Other Lectures & Addresses, 1920-1945. facs. ed. LC 70-136650. (Biography Index Reprint Ser.). 1946. 16.00 (ISBN 0-8369-8045-X). Arno.
JOHN PAUL 2ND, POPE
Annese, Lucius. Pope John Paul II in America. LC 79-56497. (Orig.). 1980. 10.00 (ISBN 0-933402-10-4); pap. 4.95 (ISBN 0-933402-09-0). Charisma Pr.
Castle, Tony, ed. Through the Year with Pope John Paul II: Reading for Every Day of the Year. 288p. 1981. 12.95 (ISBN 0-8245-0041-5). Crossroad NY.
Douglas, Robert W. John Paul II: The Pilgrim Pope. LC 79-24930. (Illus.). 32p. (gr. k up). 1980. PLB 9.25 (ISBN 0-516-03563-0); pap. 2.50 (ISBN 0-516-43563-9). Childrens.
Hebblethwaite, Peter & Kaufmann, Ludwig. John Paul II: A Pictorial Biography. LC 79-53120. (Illus.). 1979. 14.95x (ISBN 0-07-033327-0); pap. 7.95x (ISBN 0-07-033328-9). McGraw.
John Paul II: The Pope's Challenge. 224p. (Orig.). 1979. pap. 4.50 (ISBN 0-933932-33-2). Scepter Pubs.
Karolak, Tadeusz. John Paul II: The Pope from Poland. 2nd, enl. ed. Evans, David, tr. from Polish. LC 80-468695. (Illus.). 176p. 1979. 25.00x (ISBN 83-223-1845-6). Intl Pubns Serv.
--Pope John Paul the Second: The Pope from Poland. Evans, David, tr. from Pol. 175p. 1980. text ed. 25.00 (ISBN 83-223-1845-6). Chicago Review.
Kwiatkowski, Diana, ed. The Poet Pope. 9.50 (ISBN 0-686-74030-0); fine bdg. 4.50 (ISBN 0-686-74031-9). Gusto Pr.
Oram, James. The People's Pope: The Story of Karol Wojtyla of Poland. (Illus.). 1979. pap. 7.95 (ISBN 0-87701-159-1). Chronicle Bks.
Palmer, Russell. John Paul II: A Pictorial Celebration. LC 79-92691. (Illus.). 128p. 1980. 12.95 (ISBN 0-87973-835-9). Our Sunday Visitor.
Pilgrim to Poland: Pope John Paul. 1979. 5.00 (ISBN 0-686-63640-6); pap. 3.50 (ISBN 0-8198-0627-7). Dghtrs St Paul.
Pilgrimage of Peace: Collected Speeches of John Paul II in Ireland & the United States. Date not set. 3.95 (ISBN 0-529-05775-1, RB 5775). Collins Pubs.
Pope John Paul II at the United Nations. Date not set. 9.50 (ISBN 0-686-73270-7); pap. 4.95 (ISBN 0-686-73271-5). UN.
Pope John Paul II: He Came to Us As a Father. (Illus.). 1979. gift edition 14.95 (ISBN 0-8198-0628-5). Dghtrs St Paul.
Pope John Paul. Puebla: A Pilgrimage of Faith. 1979. pap. 2.00 (ISBN 0-8198-0629-3). Dghtrs St Paul.
Pope John Paul, II. Ireland: In the Footsteps of St. Patrick. 1979. 3.95 (ISBN 0-8198-0624-2); pap. 2.95 (ISBN 0-8198-0625-0). Dghtrs St Paul.
--John Paul II in Mexico. (Illus.). 1979. 12.95 (ISBN 0-529-05682-8, 5682). Collins Pubs.
--Turkey: Ecumenical Pilgrimage. 3.50 (ISBN 0-8198-0650-1); pap. 2.50 (ISBN 0-8198-0651-X). Dghtrs St Paul.
--U. S. A. The Message of Justice, Peace & Love. 1979. 5.95 (ISBN 0-8198-0630-7); pap. 4.95 (ISBN 0-8198-0631-5). Dghtrs St Paul.
Pope John Paul II. Africa: Apostolic Pilgrimage. 1980. 8.00 (ISBN 0-8198-0708-7); pap. 7.00 (ISBN 0-8198-0709-5). Dghtrs St Paul.
--Toward a Philosophy of Praxis. Bloch, A. & Czuckza, G. T., eds. LC 80-21239. 152p. 1981. 10.95 (ISBN 0-8245-0033-4). Crossroad NY.
--Words of Certitude: Excerpts from His Talks & Writings As Bishop & Pope. Buono, Anthon, tr. from It. LC 80-81440. 136p. 1980. pap. 2.95 (ISBN 0-8091-2302-9). Paulist Pr.
--You Are My Favorites. 1980. 6.95 (ISBN 0-8198-8701-3). Dghtrs St Paul.
Williams, George H. The Mind of John Paul II: Origins of His Thought & Action. LC 80-19947. 415p. 1981. 26.95 (ISBN 0-8164-0473-9). Seabury.
Wolfe, Rinna. The Singing Pope: The Story of Pope John Paul II. (Illus.). 128p. (gr. 6-8). 1980. 8.95 (ISBN 0-8164-0472-0). Seabury.
JOHN THE BAPTIST, SAINT, ca. 5 B.C.-ca. 30 A.D.
Barton, Peggy. John the Baptist. LC 78-23616. 1978. 3.95 (ISBN 0-87747-727-2). Deseret Bk.
Battersby, W. J. De la Salle: A Pioneer of Modern Education. 236p. 1981. Repr. of 1949 ed. lib. bdg. 40.00 (ISBN 0-89987-065-1). Darby Bks.
Human, Johnnie. John the Baptist: Forerunner of Jesus. (gr. 1-6). 1978. 5.50 (ISBN 0-8054-4240-5). Broadman.
Klug, Ron. Strange Young Man in the Desert: John the Baptist. (Arch Bks: Set 8). (Illus., Orig.). (ps-4). 1971. pap. 0.79 (ISBN 0-570-06057-5, 59-1174). Concordia.
Meyer, F. B. John the Baptist. 1975. pap. 1.75 (ISBN 0-87508-345-5). Chr Lit.
Robertson, A. T. John the Loyal: Studies in the Ministry of John the Baptist. (A. T. Robertston Library). 1977. pap. 3.95 (ISBN 0-8010-7644-7). Baker Bk.
Stowell, Gordon, illus. John the Baptist. 2nd ed. (Little Fish Bks About Bible People). (Illus.). 20p. (ps). 1981. 0.49 (ISBN 0-8307-0336-5, 5600618). Regal.
JOHN THE BAPTIST,-ART
Hurll, Estelle M. Life of Our Lord in Art: With Some Account of the Artistic Treatment of the Life of St. John the Baptist. LC 76-89272. 1969. Repr. of 1898 ed. 22.00 (ISBN 0-8103-3137-3). Gale.
JOHN, AUGUSTUS EDWIN, 1878-1961
Harris, Frank. Contemporary Portraits. (Third Ser.). Repr. of 1920 ed. lib. bdg. 15.00 (ISBN 0-8371-2577-4, HACO). Greenwood.
Holroyd, Michael. Augustus John. LC 74-15489. 1975. 17.95 (ISBN 0-03-013821-3). HR&W.
Holroyd, Michael, intro. by. Augustus John: An Autobiography. 1978. 11.95 (ISBN 0-224-01060-3, Pub. by Chatto Bodley Jonathan). Merrimack Bk Serv.
John, Augustus E. & Rothenstein, John. Augustus John. LC 75-41158. (British Artists Ser.). Repr. of 1945 ed. 34.50 (ISBN 0-404-14560-4). AMS Pr.
Longstreet, Stephen, ed. Drawings of Augustus John. (Master Draughtsman Ser). treasure trove bdg. 6.47x (ISBN 0-685-07237-1); pap. 2.95 (ISBN 0-685-07238-X). Borden.
JOHN, PRESTER
see Prester John
JOHN AND MABEL RINGLING MUSEUM OF ART, SARASOTA, FLORIDA
Craven, Roy C., Jr. Indian Sculpture in the John & Mable Ringling Museum of Art. LC 61-63517. (U of Fla. Humanities Monographs: No. 6). (Illus.). 1961. pap. 2.95 (ISBN 0-8130-0050-5). U Presses Fla.
JOHN BIRCH SOCIETY
Griffin, G. Edward. The Life & Words of Robert Welch, Founder of the John Birch Society. LC 74-3311. (Illus.). 428p. 1975. 12.50 (ISBN 0-912986-07-7). Am Media.
JOHN BROWN RAID
see Harper's Ferry, West Virginia-John Brown Raid, 1859
JOHN F. KENNEDY INTERNATIONAL AIRPORT, IDLEWILD
Jamaica Bay & Kennedy Airport: A Multidisciplinary Environmental Study, 2 vols. 1971. Set. 9.75 (ISBN 0-309-01871-4). Natl Acad Pr.
JOHN MUIR TRAIL, SIERRA NEVADA MOUNTAINS
Roth, Hal. Pathway in the Sky. LC 65-27593. (Illus.). 1965. 15.00 (ISBN 0-8310-7053-6). Howell-North.
Winnett, Thomas. The John Muir Trail. LC 77-88642. (Trail Guide Ser.). (Illus., Orig.). 1978. pap. 5.95 (ISBN 0-911824-64-2). Wilderness.
JOHN NEWBERRY MEDAL BOOKS
see Newbery Medal Books
JOHN QUINN MEMORIAL COLLECTION
Simmonds, Harvey. John Quinn: An Exhibition to Mark the Gift of the John Quinn Memorial Collection. (Illus.). 1968. pap. 2.00 (ISBN 0-87104-224-X). NY Pub Lib.
JOHNS, GEORGE SIBLEY, 1857-1941
Johns, Orrick. Time of Our Lives: The Story of My Father & Myself. 353p. 1973. Repr. of 1937 ed. lib. bdg. 15.00x (ISBN 0-374-94215-3). Octagon.
JOHNS, JASPER, 1930-
Field, Richard S. Jasper Johns: Prints 1970-1977. LC 77-93988. (Illus.). 1978. pap. 10.95 (ISBN 0-931266-00-9, Pub. by Wesleyan U Pr). Columbia U Pr.
Kozloff, Max. Jasper Johns. (Abrams-Meridian Modern Painters Ser). (Illus.). pap. 3.95 (ISBN 0-452-00355-5, FM355, Mer). NAL.
JOHNS, ORRICK, 1887-1946
Johns, Orrick. Time of Our Lives: The Story of My Father & Myself. 353p. 1973. Repr. of 1937 ed. lib. bdg. 15.00x (ISBN 0-374-94215-3). Octagon.
JOHNS HOPKINS HOSPITAL, BALTIMORE
Chesney, Alan M. The Johns Hopkins Hospital & the Johns Hopkins University School of Medicine: A Chronicle, 2 vols. Incl. Vol. 1. 1867-1893. 318p. 1943; Vol. 2. 1893-1905. 499p. 1958. 25.00x (ISBN 0-8018-0113-3); Vol. 3. 1905-1914. 350p. 1963. 20.00x (ISBN 0-8018-0114-1). Johns Hopkins.
Crowe, Samuel J. Halsted of John Hopkins: The Man & His Men. (Illus.). 268p. 1957. ed. spiral bdg. 27.50photocopy (ISBN 0-398-00371-8). C C Thomas.
JOHNS HOPKINS UNIVERSITY-HISTORY
Steiner, B. C. The History of University Education in Maryland. Repr. of 1891 ed. pap. 8.00 (ISBN 0-384-57825-X). Johnson Repr.
JOHNS HOPKINS UNIVERSITY-SCHOOL OF MEDICINE
Chesney, Alan M. The Johns Hopkins Hospital & the Johns Hopkins University School of Medicine: A Chronicle, 2 vols. Incl. Vol. 1. 1867-1893. 318p. 1943; Vol. 2. 1893-1905. 499p. 1958. 25.00x (ISBN 0-8018-0113-3); Vol. 3. 1905-1914. 350p. 1963. 20.00x (ISBN 0-8018-0114-1). Johns Hopkins.
Turner, Thomas B. Heritage of Excellence: The Johns Hopkins Medical Institutions, 1914-1947. LC 73-8131. (Illus.). 656p. 1974. 25.00x (ISBN 0-8018-1504-5). Johns Hopkins.
JOHNSON, ANDREW, PRES. U. S., 1808-1875
Beale, Howard K. Critical Year: A Study of Andrew Johnson & Reconstruction. LC 58-9332. (Illus.). 1958. 20.00 (ISBN 0-8044-1085-2). Ungar.
Benedict, Michael L. A Compromise of Principle: Congressional Republicans & Reconstruction 1863-1869. (Illus.). 1975. 18.95x (ISBN 0-393-05524-8). Norton.
--The Impeachment & Trial of Andrew Johnson. (Norton Essays in American History Ser). 224p. 1973. 6.95x (ISBN 0-393-05473-X); pap. text ed. 3.95x (ISBN 0-393-09418-9). Norton.
Castel, Albert. The Presidency of Andrew Johnson. LC 79-11050. (The American Presidency Ser.). 1979. 15.00x (ISBN 0-7006-0190-2). Regents Pr KS.
Chadsey, Charles E. Struggle Between President Johnson & Congress Over Reconstruction. LC 79-181926. (Columbia University Studies in the Social Sciences: No. 19). Repr. of 1896 ed. 11.50 (ISBN 0-404-51019-1). AMS Pr.
Clemenceau, Georges. American Reconstruction, Eighteen Sixty-Five to Eighteen Seventy. 2nd ed. LC 68-16229. (American Scene Ser). 1969. Repr. of 1928 ed. 25.00 (ISBN 0-306-71010-2). Da Capo.
Dewitt, David M. Impeachment & Trial of Andrew Johnson. LC 66-24686. 1967. Repr. of 1902 ed. 13.50 (ISBN 0-8462-0813-X). Russell.
--The Impeachment & Trial of Andrew Johnson, Seventeenth President of the U.S. 1977. Repr. 55.00 (ISBN 0-403-08179-3). Scholarly.
Dickinson, John N. Andrew Johnson, Eighteen Eight to Eighteen Seventy-Five: Chronology, Documents, Bibliographical Aids. LC 79-116064. (Presidential Chronology Ser). 1970. 8.00 (ISBN 0-379-12075-5). Oceana.
Gerson, Noel B. The Trial of Andrew Johnson. LC 76-58489. (gr. 8 up). 1977. 7.95 (ISBN 0-525-66505-6). Elsevier-Nelson.
Graf, LeRoy P. & Haskins, Ralph W., eds. Papers of Andrew Johnson, 5 vols. Incl. Vol. 1. 1822-1851. (Illus.). 744p. 1967. 20.00x (ISBN 0-87049-079-6); Vol. 2. 1852-1857. (Illus.). 608p. 1970. 20.00x (ISBN 0-87049-098-2); Vol. 3. 1858-1860. (Illus.). 800p. 1972. 20.00x (ISBN 0-87049-141-5); Vol. 4. 1860-1861. 1976. 20.00x (ISBN 0-87049-183-0); Vol. 5. 1861-1862. 1979. text ed. 20.00x (ISBN 0-87049-273-X). LC 67-25733. U of Tenn Pr.
Johnson, Andrew. Trial of Andrew Johnson. LC 69-11326. (Law, Politics, & History Ser). 1970. Repr. of 1868 ed. lib. bdg. 95.00 (ISBN 0-306-71184-2). Da Capo.
Jones, James S. Life of Andrew Johnson, Seventeenth President of the United States. LC 70-170824. Repr. of 1901 ed. 29.50 (ISBN 0-404-04606-1). AMS Pr.
Lomask, Milton. Andrew Johnson: President on Trial. LC 73-9876. 1973. Repr. of 1960 ed. lib. bdg. 17.50x (ISBN 0-374-95082-2). Octagon.
McKitrick, Eric L. Andrew Johnson & Reconstruction. LC 60-5467. 1964. pap. 12.00x (ISBN 0-226-56046-5). U of Chicago Pr.
--Andrew Johnson & Reconstruction. LC 60-5467. 1960. 15.00x (ISBN 0-226-56045-7). U of Chicago Pr.
Mantell, Martin E. Johnson, Grant, & the Politics of Reconstruction. LC 72-13452. 209p. 1973. 15.00x (ISBN 0-231-03507-1). Columbia U Pr.
Nash, Howard P., Jr. Andrew Johnson: Congress & Reconstruction. LC 72-248. 170p. 1972. 10.00 (ISBN 0-8386-1129-X). Fairleigh Dickinson.
Sefton, James E. Andrew Johnson & the Uses of Constitutional Power. (Library of American Biography). 1980. 9.95 (ISBN 0-316-77990-3); pap. 4.95 (ISBN 0-316-77989-X). Little.
Stryker, Lloyd P. Andrew Johnson: A Study in Courage. (Illus.). 1971. Repr. of 1929 ed. 44.00 (ISBN 0-403-01231-7). Scholarly.
Trefousse, Hans L. Impeachment of a President: Andrew Johnson, the Blacks, & Reconstruction. LC 74-29389. 318p. 1975. 12.50x (ISBN 0-87049-164-4). U of Tenn Pr.
United States Congress. The Impeachment & Trial of Andrew Johnson, President of the United States. 8.00 (ISBN 0-8446-5092-7). Peter Smith.
Winston, Robert W. Andrew Johnson: Plebian & Patriot. LC 76-124772. 1970. Repr. of 1928 ed. 24.00 (ISBN 0-404-00240-4). AMS Pr.
JOHNSON, ANDREW, PRES. U. S., 1808-1875-JUVENILE LITERATURE
Paley, Alan L. Andrew Johnson: The President Impeached. Rahmas, D. Steve, ed. LC 74-190248. (Outstanding Personalities Ser: No. 31). 32p. (Orig.). (gr. 7-12). 1972. PLB 2.95 incl. catalog cards (ISBN 0-87157-531-0); pap. 1.50 vinyl laminated covers (ISBN 0-87157-031-9). SamHar Pr.
JOHNSON, BEN CAMPBELL
Leggatt, Alexander. Ben Johnson: His Vision & His Art. 1981. 35.00x (ISBN 0-416-74660-8). Methuen Inc.
Lehrman, Walter D., et al. The Plays of Ben Jonson. 1980. lib. bdg. 36.00 (ISBN 0-8161-8112-8). G K Hall.
JOHNSON, BUSHROD RUST, 1817-1880
Cummings, Charles M. Yankee Quaker Confederate General: The Curious Career of Bushrod Rust Johnson. LC 76-118805. (Illus.). 417p. 1971. 20.00 (ISBN 0-8386-7706-1). Fairleigh Dickinson.
JOHNSON, CHARLES, CAPTAIN, fl. 1724-1736
Gosse, Philip. Bibliography of the Works of Captain Charles Johnson. LC 72-127189. 1970. Repr. of 1927 ed. lib. bdg. 18.50 (ISBN 0-8337-1391-4). B Franklin.
JOHNSON, CLAUDIA ALTA (TAYLOR), 1912-
Pasold, E. W. Ladybird, Ladybird. 720p. 1977. 39.00x (ISBN 0-7190-0682-1, Pub. by Manchester U Pr England). State Mutual Bk.

JOHNSON, EASTMAN, 1824-1906
Hills, Patricia. The Genre Painting of Eastman Johnson: The Sources & Development of His Styles & Themes. LC 76-23627. (Outstanding Dissertations in the Fine Arts - American). (Illus.). 1977. Repr. of 1973 ed. lib. bdg. 48.00 (ISBN 0-8240-2697-7). Garland Pub.
JOHNSON, ESTHER, 1681-1728
Gold, Maxwell B. Swift's Marriage to Stella. LC 66-27085. 1967. Repr. of 1937 ed. 7.50 (ISBN 0-8462-0932-2). Russell.
Hardy, Evelyn. The Conjured Spirit, Swift. LC 70-136933. (Illus.). 266p. 1973. Repr. of 1949 ed. lib. bdg. 14.50x (ISBN 0-8371-5405-7, HACJ). Greenwood.
Le Brocquy, Sybil. Swift's Most Valuable Friend. LC 68-26028. 1968. 7.95 (ISBN 0-8023-1165-2). Dufour.
JOHNSON, FRANKLIN W.
Marriner, Ernest C. Man of Mayflower Hill: A Biography of Franklin W. Johnson. 1967. 5.00 (ISBN 0-910394-05-9). Colby.
JOHNSON, HIRAM WARREN, 1866-1945
Olin, Spencer C., Jr. California's Prodigal Sons: Hiram Johnson & the Progressives. 1968. 16.95 (ISBN 0-520-00973-8). U. of Cal Pr.
JOHNSON, JAMES WELDON, 1871-1938
Bronz, Stephen H. Roots of Negro Racial Consciousness. 1964. 5.00 (ISBN 0-87212-019-8). Libra.
Fleming, Robert E., ed. James Weldon Johnson & Arna Wendell Bontemps. (Reference Publications). 1978. lib. bdg. 15.00 (ISBN 0-8161-7932-8). G K Hall.
Levy, Eugene. James Weldon Johnson: Black Leader, Black Voice. Franklin, John H., ed. LC 72-95134. (Negro American Biographies & Autobiographies Ser). 1973. 18.00x (ISBN 0-226-47603-0). U of Chicago Pr.
--James Weldon Johnson: Black Leader, Black Voice. Franklin, John H., ed. LC 72-95134. (Negro-American Biographies & Autobiographies Ser.). (Illus.). 1976. pap. 5.95 (ISBN 0-226-47604-9, P700, Phoen). U of Chicago Pr.
JOHNSON, JAMES WELDON, 1871-1938–JUVENILE LITERATURE
Egypt, Ophelia S. James Weldon Johnson. LC 73-9521. (Biographies Ser). (Illus.). 40p. (gr. 2-5). 1974. PLB 8.79 (ISBN 0-690-00215-7, TYC-J). Har-Row.
Tarry, Ellen. Young Jim: The Early Years of James Weldon Johnson. LC 67-22194. (Illus.). (gr. 7 up). 1967. 5.95 (ISBN 0-396-05598-2). Dodd.
JOHNSON, JOHN, 1514-1590
Winchester, Barbara. Tudor Family Portrait. (Illus.). 1955. 6.00x (ISBN 0-8426-1597-0). Verry.
JOHNSON, JOHN ALBERT, 1861-1909
Helmes, Winifred. John A. Johnson: The People's Governor. (Illus.). 1949. 9.50x (ISBN 0-8166-0054-6). U. of Minn Pr.
JOHNSON, JOHN ARTHUR, 1878-1946
DeCoy, Robert H. Big Black Fire. (Orig.). 1969. pap. 1.75 (ISBN 0-87067-166-9, BH166). Holloway.
Gilmore, Al-Tony. Bad Nigger! The National Impact of Jack Johnson. LC 74-80590. 1975. 12.95 (ISBN 0-8046-9061-8, Natl U). Kennikat.
Johnson, Jack. Jack Johnson in the Ring & Out. LC 72-162515. (Illus.). ix, 259p. 1975. Repr. of 1927 ed. 19.00 (ISBN 0-8103-4047-X). Gale.
JOHNSON, JOSEPHINE WINSTON, 1910-
Johnson, Josephine W. Seven Houses: A Memoir of Time & Places. (Illus.). 1973. 5.95 (ISBN 0-671-21454-3). S&S.
JOHNSON, LYNDON BAINES, PRES. U. S., 1908-1973
Barton, Thomas F. Lyndon B. Johnson: Young Texan. (Childhood of Famous Americans Ser). (Illus.). (gr. 3-7). 1973. 3.95 (ISBN 0-672-51875-9). Bobbs.
Blum, John M. The Progressive Presidents: Theodore Roosevelt, Woodrow Wilson, Franklin D. Roosevelt, Lyndon B. Johnson. 1981. 11.95 (ISBN 0-393-01330-8). Norton.
The Cumulated Indexes to the Public Papers of the Presidents of the United States: Lyndon B. Johnson, 1963-1969. 1978. lib. bdg. 70.00 (ISBN 0-527-20751-9). Kraus Intl.
Divine, Robert A., ed. Exploring the Johnson Years. (Illus.). 272p. 1981. text ed. 25.00x (ISBN 0-292-72031-9). U of Tex Pr.
Furer, Howard B. Lyndon B. Johnson: Chronology, Documents, Bibliographical Aids. LC 75-95015. (Presidential Chronology Ser). 1971. 8.00 (ISBN 0-379-12077-1). Oceana.
Goldman, Eric F. Tragedy of Lyndon Johnson: A Historian's Personal Interpretation. 1969. 10.00 (ISBN 0-394-44929-0). Knopf.
Harvey, James C. Black Civil Rights During the Johnson Administration. LC 73-80241. 256p. 1973. pap. 5.95x (ISBN 0-87805-021-3). U Pr of Miss.
Johnson, George W., ed. Johnson Presidential Press Conference, 2 vols. LC 78-1869. 1978. 60.00set (ISBN 0-685-87631-4). Vol. 1 (ISBN 0-930576-02-0). Vol. 2 (ISBN 0-930576-05-5). E M Coleman Ent.
Kearns, Doris. Lyndon Johnson & the American Dream. 1977. pap. 2.50 (ISBN 0-451-07609-5, E7609, Sig). NAL.
--Lyndon Johnson & the American Dream. LC 75-42831. 576p. (YA) 1976. 14.95 (ISBN 0-06-012284-6, HarpT). Har-Row.
Kluckhohn, Frank L. Lyndon's Legacy. 1964. 5.95 (ISBN 0-8159-6113-8). Devin.
Miller, Merle. Lyndon: An Oral Biography. 864p. 1981. pap. 9.95 (ISBN 0-345-29652-4). Ballantine.
--Lyndon: An Oral Biography. 1980. 17.95 (ISBN 0-399-12357-1). Putnam.
Mooney, Booth. LBJ: An Irreverent Chronicle. LC 75-33693. 300p. 1976. 9.95 (ISBN 0-690-01089-3). T Y Crowell.
Quill, J. Michael. Lyndon Johnson & the Southern Military Tradition. 1977. pap. text ed. 7.75 (ISBN 0-8191-0354-3). U Pr of Amer.
Redford, Emmette S. & Blissett, Marlan. Organizing the Executive Branch: The Johnson Presidency. LC 81-1142. (An Administrative History of the Johnson Presidency). 1981. lib. bdg. 28.00 (ISBN 0-226-70675-3). U of Chicago Pr.
Rothschild, Eric, ed. The Great Society & Vietnam: 1964-1968. (New York Times School Microfilm Collection Ser.: Guide No. 11). 89p. (gr. 7-12). 1979. pap. 5.50 wkbk. (ISBN 0-667-00560-9). Microfilming Corp.
Rulon, Philip R. The Compassionate Samaritan: The Life of Lyndon Baines Johnson. LC 81-210. 356p. 1981. text ed. 21.95 (ISBN 0-88229-306-0); pap. 10.95 (ISBN 0-88229-787-2). Nelson-Hall.
Schandler, Herbert. The Unmaking of a President: Lyndon Johnson & Vietnam. (Illus.). 1977. text ed. 30.00 (ISBN 0-691-07586-7). Princeton U Pr.
Valenti, Jack. A Very Human President. (Illus.). 402p. 1976. 9.95 (ISBN 0-393-05552-3). Norton.
Wicker, Tom. JFK & LBJ. 1969. pap. 4.95 (ISBN 0-14-021116-0, Pelican). Penguin.
JOHNSON, LYNDON BAINES, PRES. U. S., 1908-1973–JUVENILE LITERATURE
Kurland, Gerald. Lyndon Baines Johnson: President Caught in an Ordeal of Power. Rahmas, D. Steve, ed. LC 76-190243. (Outstanding Personalities Ser: No. 25). 32p. (Orig.). (gr. 7-9). 1972. lib. bdg. 2.95 incl. catalog cards (ISBN 0-87157-525-6); pap. 1.50 vinyl laminated covers (ISBN 0-87157-025-4). SamHar Pr.
Lynch, Dudley. The President from Texas: Lyndon Baines Johnson. LC 74-26817. (Illus.). 192p. (gr. 6 up). 1975. 8.95 (ISBN 0-690-00627-6, TYC-J). Har-Row.
Lyndon B. Johnson: Mini-Play. (President's Choice Ser.). (gr. 8 up). 1978. 3.00 (ISBN 0-89550-318-2). RIM.
Newlon, Clarke. L.B.J. The Man from Johnson City. rev. ed. LC 72-13509. (Illus.). (gr. 9 up). 1976. 5.95 (ISBN 0-396-06199-0). Dodd.
Olds, Helen D. Lyndon Baines Johnson. (Beginning Biographies Ser.). (Illus.). (gr. k-4). 1965. PLB 5.99 (ISBN 0-399-60433-2). Putnam.
JOHNSON, NELSON TRUSLER, 1887-
Buhite, Russell D. Nelson T. Johnson & American Policy Toward China 1925-1941. 1969. 6.00 (ISBN 0-87013-127-3). Mich St U Pr.
JOHNSON, PHILIP CORTELYOU, 1906-
Ciucci, Giorgio, et al. Philip Johnson: Processes. (IAUS Exhibition Catalogues Ser.). (Illus.). 1979. pap. 10.00 (ISBN 0-932628-01-X). IAUS.
Johnson, Philip. Writings. Stern, Robert & Eisenman, Peter, eds. 1979. 29.95 (ISBN 0-19-502378-1); signed & slipcased 75.00 (ISBN 0-19-502573-3). Oxford U Pr.
JOHNSON, REVERLY, 1796-1876
Steiner, Bernard C. Life of Reverdy Johnson. LC 76-81475. (Illus.). 1970. Repr. of 1914 ed. 11.00 (ISBN 0-8462-1384-2). Russell.
JOHNSON, RICHARD MENTOR, 1780-1850
Meyer, Leland W. Life & Times of Colonel Richard M. Johnson of Kentucky. LC 32-11905. (Columbia University. Studies in the Social Sciences: No. 359). Repr. of 1932 ed. 31.50 (ISBN 0-404-51359-X). AMS Pr.
JOHNSON, ROBERT, ca. 1676-1735
Johnson, Robert C. John Heywood. (English Authors Ser.: No. 1260-7). 10.95 (ISBN 0-8057-1260-7). Twayne.
JOHNSON, SAMUEL, 1696-1772
Boswell, James. Everybody's Boswell: Being the Life of Samuel Johnson. abr. ed. Morley, Frank, ed. (Illus.). xvii, 665p. 1981. 24.95x (ISBN 0-7135-1237-7). Ohio U Pr.
Carroll, Peter N. The Other Samuel Johnson: A Psychohistory of Early New England. LC 77-74413. 247p. 1978. 16.50 (ISBN 0-8386-2059-0). Fairleigh Dickinson.
Ellis, Joseph. The New England Mind in Transition: Samuel Johnson of Connecticut, 1696-1772. LC 73-77149. (Historical Publications, Miscellany Ser.: No. 98). (Illus.). 288p. 1973. 17.50x (ISBN 0-300-01615-8). Yale U Pr.
Grant, F. Life of Samuel Johnson. Repr. of 1887 ed. lib. bdg. 20.00 (ISBN 0-8495-1904-7). Arden Lib.
Johnson, Samuel. Samuel Johnson, President of King's College: His Career & Writings, 4 Vols. Schneider, Herbert & Schneider, Carol, eds. LC 72-153333. Repr. of 1929 ed. Set. 150.00 (ISBN 0-404-03600-7); 37.50 ea. AMS Pr.
Jones, Adam L. Early American Philosophers. LC 58-9336. 1958. 8.00 (ISBN 0-8044-5543-0). Ungar.
Kingsmill, Hugh. Samuel Johnson. 1977. Repr. lib. bdg. 30.00 (ISBN 0-8482-1423-4). Norwood Edns.
JOHNSON, SAMUEL, 1709-1784
Alkon, Paul K. Samuel Johnson & Moral Discipline. 1967. 12.95x (ISBN 0-8101-0039-8). Northwestern U Pr.
Ashmun, Margaret. The Singing Swan: An Account of Anna Seward & Her Acquaintance with Dr. Johnson, Etc. 1931. Repr. 20.00 (ISBN 0-8274-3417-0). R West.
Bailey, John. Dr. Johnson & His Circle. 1913. Repr. 15.00 (ISBN 0-8274-2198-2). R West.
Bailey, John C. Dr. Johnson & His Circle. LC 76-9063. 1976. Repr. of 1913 ed. lib. bdg. 15.00 (ISBN 0-8414-3338-0). Folcroft.
Bate, W. Jackson. Samuel Johnson. LC 77-73044. (Illus.). 1977. 19.95 (ISBN 0-15-179260-7). HarBraceJ.
Bate, Walter J. The Achievement of Samuel Johnson. Repr. lib. bdg. write for info. Scholarly.
--The Achievement of Samuel Johnson. LC 78-56308. 1978. pap. 4.95 (ISBN 0-226-03895-5, P804, Phoen). U of Chicago Pr.
Battersby, James L. Rational Praise & Natural Lamentation: Johnson, Lycidas, & Principles of Criticism. LC 77-89774. 288p. 1979. 18.50 (ISBN 0-8386-2148-1). Fairleigh Dickinson.
Biron, Chartres. Sir, Said Dr. Johnson. 1979. Repr. of 1940 ed. lib. bdg. 17.50 (ISBN 0-8414-9843-1). Folcroft.
Bond, W. H., ed. Eighteenth-Century Studies: In Honor of Donald F. Hyde. LC 77-123045. (Illus.). 1970. boxed 30.00x (ISBN 0-8139-0446-3, Dist. by U Pr of Va). Grolier Club.
--Eighteenth-Century Studies: In Honor of Donald F. Hyde. LC 77-123045. (Illus.). xv, 424p. 1970. 30.00x (ISBN 0-8139-0446-3, Grolier Club). U Pr of Va.
Boswell, James. The Journal of a Tour to the Hebrides with Samuel Johnson. Powell, Lawrence F., ed. 1957. 9.95x (ISBN 0-460-00387-9, Evman). Biblio Dist.
--Life of Johnson. (English Library Ser.). 1979. pap. 2.95 (ISBN 0-14-043116-0). Penguin.
--Life of Johnson, 6 vols. Hill, George B. & Powell, L. F., eds. Bd. with Boswell's Journal of a Tour to the Hebrides. Boswell, James; Johnson's Diary of a Journey into North Wales. Johnson, Samuel. Vol. 1-4. 1934 ed. 220.00x (ISBN 0-19-811304-8); Vol. 5-6. 2nd ed. 1965 69.00x (ISBN 0-19-811452-4). Oxford U Pr.
--Life of Samuel Johnson, 2 vols. in 1. 14.95x (ISBN 0-460-10001-7, Evman). Biblio Dist.
--Life of Samuel Johnson. (YA) 1964. pap. 3.95x (ISBN 0-394-30962-6, T62, Mod LibC). Modern Lib.
--Life of Samuel Johnson. abr. ed. Brady, Frank, ed. 1968. pap. 2.50 (ISBN 0-451-51150-6, CE1150, Sig Classics). NAL.
Boulton, James T., ed. Johnson: The Critical Heritage. 1971. 27.95x (ISBN 0-7100-7030-6). Routledge & Kegan.
Brack, O M, Jr. & Kelley, Robert E., eds. The Early Biographies of Samuel Johnson. LC 73-77385. 377p. 1974. text ed. 15.00x (ISBN 0-87745-038-2). U of Iowa Pr.
Bronson, Bertrand H. Johnson Agonistes & Other Essays. Orig. Title: Johnson & Boswell: Three Essays. 1965. pap. 1.50x (ISBN 0-520-00175-3, CAL114). U of Cal Pr.
--Johnson & Boswell. 475p. 1980. Repr. of 1944 ed. lib. bdg. 20.00 (ISBN 0-8495-0397-3). Arden Lib.
--Johnson & Boswell. LC 76-23460. 1944. lib. bdg. 15.00 (ISBN 0-8414-3242-2). Folcroft.
Buono Dello, Carmen J. Rare Early Essays on Johnson & Boswell. 212p. 1981. lib. bdg. 22.50 (ISBN 0-8482-3656-4). Norwood Edns.
Cairns, William T. Religion of Dr. Johnson. facsimile ed. LC 71-93324. (Essay Index Reprint Ser). 1946. 15.00 (ISBN 0-8369-1279-9). Arno.
Carter, Winifred. Dr. Johnson's "Dear Mistress". Repr. 17.50 (ISBN 0-8274-2199-0). R West.
Chandler, Zelphs E. Analysis of the Stylistic Technique of Addison, Johnson, Hazlitt & Pater. 1928. lib. bdg. 10.00 (ISBN 0-8414-3633-9). Folcroft.
Chapman, Robert W. Johnsonian & Other Essays & Reviews. LC 78-158502. Repr. of 1953 ed. 24.00 (ISBN 0-403-01297-X). Scholarly.
--Johnsoniana & Other Essays & Reviews. 1973. Repr. of 1953 ed. 15.00 (ISBN 0-8274-1343-2). R West.
Christiani, Sigyn. Samuel Johnson Als Kritiker Im Lichte Von Pseudoklassizismus und Romantik. 1931. pap. 9.50 (ISBN 0-384-08955-0). Johnson Repr.
Christie, O. F. Johnson, the Essayist: His Opinions of Men, Morals & Manners. LC 68-688. (Studies in Scandinavian Life & Literature, No. 18). 1969. Repr. of 1924 ed. lib. bdg. 33.95 (ISBN 0-8383-0527-X). Haskell.
--Johnson, the Essayist: His Opinions of Men, Morals & Manners. 1924. Repr. 10.75 (ISBN 0-8274-2632-1). R West.
Clifford, James L. Dictionary Johnson. 384p. 1981. pap. 6.95 (ISBN 0-07-011379-3, GB). McGraw.
--Dictionary Johnson: The Middle Years of Samuel Johnson. (Illus.). 1979. 17.95 (ISBN 0-07-011378-5, GB). McGraw.
--Young Sam Johnson. (McGraw-Hill Paperbacks Ser.). (Illus.). 400p. 1981. pap. 6.95 (ISBN 0-07-011381-5). McGraw.
Clifford, James L. & Greene, Donald J. Samuel Johnson: A Survey & Bibliography of Critical Studies. LC 74-109940. 1970. 15.00x (ISBN 0-8166-0572-6). U of Minn Pr.
Conley, C. H. The Reader's Johnson: A Representative Selection of His Writings. 1977. Repr. of 1940 ed. lib. bdg. 30.00 (ISBN 0-8495-0708-1). Arden Lib.
Craig, William H. Doctor Johnson & the Fair Sex: A Study of Contrasts. LC 77-10656. 1977. Repr. of 1895 ed. lib. bdg. 30.00 (ISBN 0-8414-1836-5). Folcroft.
Curley, Thomas M. Samuel Johnson & the Age of Travel. LC 74-30677. (Illus.). 304p. 1976. 18.50x (ISBN 0-8203-0380-1). U of Ga Pr.
Damrosch, Leopold, Jr. Samuel Johnson & the Tragic Sense. LC 72-38514. 284p. 1972. 17.50 (ISBN 0-691-06233-1). Princeton U Pr.
--The Uses of Johnson's Criticism. LC 75-19431. 1976. 13.95x (ISBN 0-8139-0625-3). U Pr of Va.
D'Arblay, Frances. Doctor Johnson & Fanny Burney. LC 70-98806. Repr. of 1911 ed. lib. bdg. 16.25x (ISBN 0-8371-3067-0, ARJF). Greenwood.
Davis, Bertram H. Johnson Before Boswell. LC 72-12309. 222p. 1973. Repr. of 1960 ed. lib. bdg. 15.00x (ISBN 0-8371-6691-8, DAJA). Greenwood.
Dello Buono, Carmen J. Rare Early Essays on Samuel Johnson. 208p. 1981. lib. bdg. 22.50 (ISBN 0-8482-3657-2). Norwood Edns.
Dennis, John. Dr. Johnson. LC 72-10146. 1972. Repr. of 1905 ed. lib. bdg. 10.00 (ISBN 0-8414-0662-6). Folcroft.
De Rose, Peter L. Jane Austen & Samuel Johnson. LC 78-7813. 133p. 1980. lib. bdg. 16.25 (ISBN 0-8191-1073-6); pap. text ed. 7.50 (ISBN 0-8191-1074-4). U Pr of Amer.
Desai, R. W., ed. Johnson on Shakespeare. 1979. text ed. 12.50x (ISBN 0-86131-120-5). Humanities.
Drake, Nathan. Essays: Biographical, Critical & Historical Illustrative of the Rambler, Adventurer & Idler, 2 Vols. (Belles Lettres in English Ser). 1969. Repr. of 1810 ed. Set. 66.50 (ISBN 0-384-12650-2). Johnson Repr.
Edinger, William. Samuel Johnson & Poetic Style. LC 77-5137. 1977. 17.00x (ISBN 0-226-18446-3). U of Chicago Pr.
Einbond, Bernard. Samuel Johnson's Allegory. LC 76-134541. (De Proprietatibus Litterarum, Ser. Practica: No. 24). (Orig.). 1971. pap. text ed. 8.90x (ISBN 0-686-22404-3). Mouton.
Elias, C. F. Doctor Samuel Johnson As Traveler. LC 76-28301. 1937. lib. bdg. 5.50 (ISBN 0-8414-3909-5). Folcroft.
Fan, Tsen-Chung. Dr. Johnson & Chinese Culture. LC 73-15538. 1945. lib. bdg. 6.50 (ISBN 0-8414-4158-8). Folcroft.
Folkenflik, Robert. Samuel Johnson, Biographer. LC 78-58050. 1978. 17.50x (ISBN 0-8014-0968-3). Cornell U Pr.
George, M. Dorothy. England in Johnson's Day. LC 73-16145. 1928. lib. bdg. 20.00 (ISBN 0-8414-4479-X). Folcroft.
Grant, F. Life of Samuel Johnson. LC 70-160756. 1971. Repr. of 1887 ed. 12.00 (ISBN 0-8046-1574-8). Kennikat.
--Life of Samuel Johnson. 1973. Repr. of 1887 ed. 11.50 (ISBN 0-8274-1341-6). R West.
Gray, James. Johnson's Sermons: A Study. (Illus.). 275p. 1972. 22.00x (ISBN 0-19-812033-8). Oxford U Pr.
Hagstrum, Jean H. Samuel Johnson's Literary Criticism. LC 52-12060. 1967. 9.50x (ISBN 0-226-31291-7). U of Chicago Pr.
--Samuel Johnson's Literary Criticism. LC 52-12060. 1967. pap. 1.95 (ISBN 0-226-31292-5, P268, Phoen). U of Chicago Pr.

Hardy, J. P. The Political Writings of Doctor Johnson. 1968. text ed. 7.50x (ISBN 0-391-02026-9). Humanities.
--Samuel Johnson: A Critical Study. 1979. 22.00x (ISBN 0-7100-0291-2). Routledge & Kegan.
Harmsworth, Cecil. Doctor Johnson, a Great Englishman. LC 77-3244. 1923. lib. bdg. 5.00 (ISBN 0-8414-4912-0). Folcroft.
Harper, Charles G. Dr. Johnson's London in a Literary Man's London. 1926. Repr. 30.00 (ISBN 0-8274-2200-8). R West.
Hay, James. Johnson: His Characteristics & Aphorisms. LC 76-16036. 1976. Repr. of 1884 ed. lib. bdg. 25.00 (ISBN 0-8414-4806-X). Folcroft.
Hayley, William. Two Dialogues: Containing a Comparative View of the Lives, Characters, & Writings of Philip, the Late Earl of Chesterfield, & Dr. Samuel Johnson. LC 71-122486. 1970. Repr. of 1787 ed. 28.00x (ISBN 0-8201-1080-9). Schol Facsimiles.
Hayward, A. Doctor Johnson's Mrs. Thrale. 1913. Repr. 25.00 (ISBN 0-8274-3813-3). R West.
Hibbert, Christopher. Personal History of Samuel Johnson. Repr. of 1970 ed. 10.95 (ISBN 0-911660-26-7). Yankee Peddler.
Hill, G. Birkbeck. Wit & Wisdom of Samuel Johnson. LC 78-27082. 1978. lib. bdg. 32.50 (ISBN 0-8414-4969-4). Folcroft.
Hill, George B. Dr. Johnson: His Friends & Critics. 1878. Repr. 30.00 (ISBN 0-8274-2197-4). R West.
--Footsteps of Dr. Johnson - Scotland. LC 77-23040. Repr. of 1890 ed. lib. bdg. 50.00 (ISBN 0-8414-4855-8). Folcroft.
Hilles, Frederick W. Dr. Johnson Rebuked: A Hitherto Unrecorded Incident in His Life As Revealed in a Letter from Dr. Samuel Glasse. LC 72-11538. 1973. lib. bdg. 6.50 (ISBN 0-8414-0762-2). Folcroft.
Hilles, Frederick W., ed. New Light on Dr. Johnson: Essays on the Occasion of His 250th Birthday. 1967. Repr. of 1959 ed. 18.50 (ISBN 0-208-00415-7, Archon). Shoe String.
Hitchcock, Thomas. Unhappy Loves of Men of Genius: Gibbon, Johnson, Goethe, Mozart & Irving. 1979. Repr. of 1892 ed. lib. bdg. 25.00 (ISBN 0-8492-5322-5). R West.
Hollis, Christopher. Dr. Johnson. 1978. Repr. of 1928 ed. lib. bdg. 35.00 (ISBN 0-8492-5249-0). R West.
--Dr. Johnson: 1707-1784. 203p. 1980. Repr. of 1928 ed. lib. bdg. 30.00 (ISBN 0-89987-357-X). Darby Bks.
Hudson, William H. Johnson & Goldsmith & Their Poetry. LC 75-120963. (Poetry & Life Ser.). Repr. of 1918 ed. 7.25 (ISBN 0-404-52515-6). AMS Pr.
--Johnson & Goldsmith & Their Poetry. LC 72-194976. 1918. lib. bdg. 7.50 (ISBN 0-8414-5192-3). Folcroft.
--Johnson & Goldsmith & Their Poetry. 1978. Repr. of 1918 ed. lib. bdg. 8.00 (ISBN 0-8495-2308-7). Arden Lib.
Johnson, Samuel. Catalogue of an Exhibition Commemorative of the Bicentenary of the Birth of Samuel Johnson. LC 73-13673. 1909. Repr. lib. bdg. 15.00 (ISBN 0-8414-5258-X). Folcroft.
--London: A Poem & the Vanity of Human Wishes. 1930. lib. bdg. 5.00 (ISBN 0-685-10261-0). Folcroft.
--Samuel Johnson. LC 76-10963. 1976. Repr. of 1911 ed. lib. bdg. 20.00 (ISBN 0-8414-6143-0). Folcroft.
--Selected Letters of Samuel Johnson. LC 76-29446. Repr. of 1925 ed. 23.00 (ISBN 0-404-15312-7). AMS Pr.
--Selected Writings of Samuel Johnson. LC 77-25885. 1977. 22.00 (ISBN 0-8201-1305-0). Schol Facsimiles.
--Wisdom & Genius of Dr. Samuel Johnson. LC 77-12611. 1977. Repr. of 1875 ed. lib. bdg. 30.00 (ISBN 0-8414-1830-6). Folcroft.
Johnsoniana, 25 vols. Incl. Vol. 1. Early Criticism (ISBN 0-8240-1279-8); Vol. 2. On Johnson's Shakespeare (ISBN 0-8240-1280-1); Vol. 3. Satire on Johnson's Dictionary (ISBN 0-8240-1281-X); Vol. 4. On the False Alarm, Etc (ISBN 0-8240-1282-8); Vol. 5. On Taxation No Tyranny 1 (ISBN 0-8240-1283-6); Vol. 6. On Taxation No Tyranny 2 (ISBN 0-8240-1284-4); Vol. 7. On the Journey to the Western Isles 1 (ISBN 0-8240-1285-2); Vol. 8. On the Journey to the Western Isles 2 (ISBN 0-8240-1286-0); Vol. 9. On the Journey to the Western Isles 3 (ISBN 0-8240-1287-9); Vol. 10. A Johnsonian Testbook (ISBN 0-8240-1288-7); Vol. 11. On the Lives of the Poets 1 (ISBN 0-8240-1289-5); Vol. 12. On the Lives of the Poets 2 (ISBN 0-8240-1290-9); Vol. 13. On the Lives of the Poets 3 (ISBN 0-8240-1291-7); Vol. 14. On the Lives of the Poets 4 (ISBN 0-8240-1292-5); Vol. 15. Biography (ISBN 0-8240-1293-3); Vol. 16. Biography (ISBN 0-8240-1294-1); Vol. 17. Biography (ISBN 0-8240-1295-X); Vol. 18. Biography (ISBN 0-8240-1296-8); Vol. 19. Biography (ISBN 0-8240-1297-6); Vol. 20. Biography (ISBN 0-8240-1298-4); Vol. 21. Biography (ISBN 0-8240-1299-2); Vol. 22. Biography (ISBN 0-8240-1300-X); Vol. 23. Biography (ISBN 0-8240-1301-8); Vol. 24. Biography (ISBN 0-8240-1302-6); Vol. 25. Biography (ISBN 0-8240-1303-4). (The Life & Times of Seven Major British Writers Ser). 1974. lib. bdg. 47.00 ea. Garland Pub.
Kelley, Robert E. & Brack, O M, Jr. Samuel Johnson's Early Biographers. LC 74-151649. (Illus.). 1971. 6.95x (ISBN 0-87745-021-8). U of Iowa Pr.
Kenrick, W. Defence of Mr. Kenrick's Review of Dr. Johnson's Shakespeare. LC 74-144646. Repr. of 1766 ed. 12.50 (ISBN 0-404-03658-9). AMS Pr.
--Review of Doctor Johnson's New Edition of Shakespeare. LC 78-144647. Repr. of 1765 ed. 12.50 (ISBN 0-404-03659-7). AMS Pr.
Kingsmill, Hugh. Johnson Without Boswell: A Contemporary Portrait of Samuel Johnson. 1941. Repr. 30.00 (ISBN 0-8274-2633-X). R West.
--Samuel Johnson. LC 75-42205. (English Literature Ser., No. 33). 1974. lib. bdg. 33.95 (ISBN 0-8383-2018-X). Haskell.
Krutch, Joseph W. Samuel Johnson. 1980. Repr. lib. bdg. 25.00 (ISBN 0-686-71941-7). Scholarly.
List of Books & Articles Relating to Samuel Johnson 1709-1784. (Yale Univ. Library). 1909. pap. 7.50x (ISBN 0-685-89764-8). Elliots Bks.
Lynd, Robert. Dr. Johnson & Company. LC 73-21749. (English Biography Ser., No. 31). 1974. lib. bdg. 49.95 (ISBN 0-8383-1836-3). Haskell.
--Dr. Johnson & Company. 1927. Repr. lib. bdg. 20.00 (ISBN 0-8414-5633-X). Folcroft.
--Dr. Johnson & Company. 1979. Repr. lib. bdg. 22.50 (ISBN 0-8495-3218-3). Arden Lib.
Macaulay, James. Doctor Johnson His Life Works & Table Talk. 156p. 1980. Repr. of 1884 ed. lib. bdg. 20.50 (ISBN 0-8492-1748-2). R West.
Macaulay, Lord. Bibliographies: Bunyan, Goldsmith, & Johnson, with Notes of His Connection with Edinburgh, and Extracts from His Letters & Speeches. 1979. Repr. of 1860 ed. lib. bdg. 25.00 (ISBN 0-8495-3513-1). Arden Lib.
Maclean, Virginia. Much Entertainment: A Visual & Culinary Record of Johnson & Boswell's Tour of Scotland in 1773. 1973. 10.00 (ISBN 0-87140-568-7). Liveright.
McNair, Arnold D. Dr. Johnson & the Law. LC 76-19021. 1976. Repr. of 1948 ed. lib. bdg. 17.50 (ISBN 0-8414-6015-9). Folcroft.
Main, Alexander. Life & Conversations of Dr. Samuel Johnson. 1874. Repr. 40.00 (ISBN 0-8274-2864-2). R West.
Mason, Edward T. Samuel Johnson: His Words & His Ways. LC 72-2104. (Studies in Samuel Johnson, No. 97). 1972. Repr. of 1879 ed. lib. bdg. 37.95 (ISBN 0-8383-1491-0). Haskell.
Mason, J. M. Comments on the Last Edition of Shakespeare's Plays. LC 73-172851. Repr. of 1785 ed. 31.45 (ISBN 0-404-04225-2). AMS Pr.
Meynell, Alice & Chesterton, G. K. Samuel Johnson. Repr. 25.00 (ISBN 0-8274-3320-4). R West.
Miller, C. A. Sir John Hawkins: Samuel Johnson. LC 72-10377. 1951. lib. bdg. 6.00 (ISBN 0-8414-0450-X). Folcroft.
Murphy, Arthur. Lives of Henry Fielding & Samuel Johnson, with Essays from Gray's Inn Journal, 1752-1792. LC 68-24212. 1968. 49.00x (ISBN 0-8201-1035-3). Schol Facsimiles.
Napier, Robina. Johsoniana: Anecdotes of the Late Samuel Johnson. 1884. Repr. 50.00 (ISBN 0-8274-2631-3). R West.
Naugle, Helen H., ed. A Concordance to the Poems of Samuel Johnson. LC 72-13383. (Concordances Ser). 578p. 1973. 32.50x (ISBN 0-8014-0769-9). Cornell U Pr.
Nethercott, Arthur H. Reputation of the Metaphysical Poets During the Age of Johnson & the Romantic Revival. LC 72-98993. (English Literature Ser., No. 33). 1970. pap. 12.95 (ISBN 0-8383-0058-8). Haskell.
Piozzi, Hester L. Anecdotes of the Late Samuel Johnson, L.D: During the Last Twenty Years of His Life. Roberts, S. C., ed. LC 70-95109. 1971. Repr. of 1925 ed. lib. bdg. 15.00x (ISBN 0-8371-3138-3, PIAN). Greenwood.
Piozzi, Hesther L. Anecdotes of Samuel Johnson. Roberts, S. C., ed. LC 75-99668. (Select Bibliographies Reprint Ser). 1925. 17.00 (ISBN 0-8369-5097-6). Arno.
Postgate, Raymond, ed. Conversations of Dr. Johnson. LC 70-121337. 1970. Repr. of 1930 ed. 6.95 (ISBN 0-8008-1814-8). Taplinger.
Quinlan, Maurice J. Samuel Johnson: A Layman's Religion. (Illus.). 256p. 1964. 20.00x (ISBN 0-299-03030-X). U of Wis Pr.
Raleigh, Walter. Samuel Johnson. LC 74-14565. 1907. lib. bdg. 8.50 (ISBN 0-8414-7352-8). Folcroft.
Raleigh, Walter A. Samuel Johnson. 1978. Repr. of 1907 ed. lib. bdg. 6.00 (ISBN 0-8495-4525-0). Arden Lib.
--Six Essays on Johnson. LC 65-13934. 1965. Repr. of 1910 ed. 7.50 (ISBN 0-8462-0517-3). Russell.
Reade, Aleyn L. Johnsonian Gleanings, 11 pts in 10 vols. 1968. Set. lib. bdg. 135.00x (ISBN 0-374-96726-1). Octagon.
Reynolds, Joshua. Johnson & Garrick. LC 74-5045. 1927. Repr. lib. bdg. 10.00 (ISBN 0-8414-7293-9). Folcroft.
Ritson, Joseph. Remarks, Critical & Illustrative, on the Text & Notes of the Last Edition of Shakspeare. LC 73-174324. Repr. of 1783 ed. 14.50 (ISBN 0-404-05348-3). AMS Pr.
Roberts, S. C. Samuel Johnson: Writer. 1926. Repr. 17.50 (ISBN 0-8274-3321-2). R West.
--The Story of Doctor Johnson. LC 73-14816. 1973. lib. bdg. 15.00 (ISBN 0-8414-7205-X). Folcroft.
Roberts, Sidney C. Dr. Johnson & Others. 1973. lib. bdg. 12.50 (ISBN 0-8414-7450-8). Folcroft.
Roberts, Sydney C. Doctor Johnson in Cambridge. LC 77-23775. 1977. Repr. of 1922 ed. lib. bdg. 12.50 (ISBN 0-8414-7393-5). Folcroft.
Roscoe, E. S. Aspects of Doctor Johnson. 1928. Repr. lib. bdg. 30.00 (ISBN 0-8414-7474-5). Folcroft.
Roseberry, Lord. Doctor Johnson. LC 77-22939. 1909. lib. bdg. 6.50 (ISBN 0-8414-7388-9). Folcroft.
Salpeter, Harry. Dr. Johnson & Mr. Boswell. LC 77-9392. 1977. lib. bdg. 30.00 (ISBN 0-8414-7669-1). Folcroft.
Schwartz, Richard B. Samuel Johnson & the New Science. 198p. 1971. 20.00x (ISBN 0-299-06010-1). U of Wis Pr.
--Samuel Johnson & the New Science. 198p. 1971. 20.00x (ISBN 0-299-06010-1). U of Wis Pr.
--Samuel Johnson & the Problem of Evil. LC 74-27314. 128p. 1975. 15.00 (ISBN 0-299-06790-4). U of Wis Pr.
Seccombe, Thomas. The Age of Johnson. 1974. Repr. of 1909 ed. lib. bdg. 15.00 (ISBN 0-8414-8140-7). Folcroft.
Shorter, Clement. Immortal Memories: Dr. Samuel Johnson, William Cowper, George Borrow, George Crabbe. 1978. Repr. of 1907 ed. lib. bdg. 25.00 (ISBN 0-8495-4859-4). Arden Lib.
Smith-Dampier, John L. Who's Who in Boswell? LC 76-102543. 1970. Repr. of 1935 ed. 15.00 (ISBN 0-8462-1471-7). Russell.
Smith-Dampier, Louis L. Who's Who in Boswell. 1935. lib. bdg. 14.95 (ISBN 0-8414-1594-3). Folcroft.
Spittal, John K. Contemporary Criticisms of Doctor Samuel Johnson His Works, & His Biographers. 1923. lib. bdg. 17.00 (ISBN 0-8414-7860-0). Folcroft.
Stephen, Leslie. Samuel Johnson. Morley, John, ed. LC 68-58398. (English Men of Letters Ser). Repr. of 1887 ed. lib. bdg. 12.50 (ISBN 0-404-51729-3). AMS Pr.
--Samuel Johnson. 1979. Repr. of 1878 ed. lib. bdg. 12.50 (ISBN 0-8492-8241-1). R West.
Stock, R. D. Samuel Johnson & Neoclassical Dramatic Theory: The Intellectual Context of the "Preface to Shakespeare". LC 72-77194. xxiv, 226p. 1973. 16.25x (ISBN 0-8032-0819-7). U of Nebr Pr.
Struble, Mildred C. Johnson Handbook. LC 72-190666. 1933. lib. bdg. 20.00 (ISBN 0-8414-0850-5). Folcroft.
Tinker, Chauncey B. Dr. Johnson & Fanny Burney. LC 76-20800. Repr. of 1911 ed. lib. bdg. 35.00 (ISBN 0-685-99243-8). Folcroft.
Trueblood, Elton. Doctor Johnson's Prayers. LC 78-6466. 1947. Repr. 10.00 (ISBN 0-8492-2729-1). R West.
Vesterman, William. Stylistic Life of Samuel Johnson. 1977. 10.00 (ISBN 0-8135-0839-8). Rutgers U Pr.
Voitle, Robert B., Jr. Samuel Johnson the Moralist. LC 61-8842. 1961. 10.00x (ISBN 0-674-78766-8). Harvard U Pr.
Vulliamy, C. E. Ursa Major: A Study of Dr. Johnson & His Friends. 1974. Repr. of 1946 ed. lib. bdg. 25.00 (ISBN 0-8414-9165-8). Folcroft.
Wain, John. Samuel Johnson. 336p. 1976. pap. 4.95 (ISBN 0-07-067715-8, SP). McGraw.
--Samuel Johnson: A Biography. LC 74-6851. (Illus.). 384p. 1975. 12.50 (ISBN 0-670-61671-0). Viking Pr.
Wain, John, ed. Johnson As Critic. (Routledge Critics Ser). 480p. 1973. 35.00x (ISBN 0-7100-7564-2). Routledge & Kegan.
Wallis, John E. Doctor Johnson & His English Dictionary. 1978. Repr. of 1945 ed. lib. bdg. 8.50 (ISBN 0-8495-5643-0). Arden Lib.
Watkins, Walter B. Johnson & English Poetry Before 1660. LC 65-24995. (Princeton Studies in English: No. 13). 1965. Repr. of 1936 ed. 7.50 (ISBN 0-87752-118-2). Gordian.
Werkmeister, Lucyle. Jemmie Boswell & the London Daily Press, 1785-1795. LC 63-15049. (Orig.). 1963. pap. 4.00 (ISBN 0-87104-100-6). NY Pub Lib.
Wieder, Robert. Le Docteur Johnson: Critique Litteraire. 1978. Repr. lib. bdg. 30.00 (ISBN 0-8495-5632-5). Arden Lib.
Wimsatt, William K. Philosophic Words, a Study of Style & Meaning in the Rambler and Dictionary of Samuel Johnson. 1968. Repr. of 1948 ed. 14.50 (ISBN 0-208-00086-0, Archon). Shoe String.
--Prose Style of Samuel Johnson. (Yale Studies in English Ser.: No. 94). 1972. Repr. of 1941 ed. 15.00 (ISBN 0-208-01141-2, Archon). Shoe String.
Young, Karl. Samuel Johnson on Shakespeare. LC 75-37625. (Studies in Shakespeare, No. 24). 1976. lib. bdg. 29.95 (ISBN 0-8383-2109-7). Haskell.

JOHNSON, SAMUEL, 1709-1784–BIBLIOGRAPHY

Bate, W. Jackson. Samuel Johnson. LC 79-10586. (Illus.). 1979. pap. 7.95 (ISBN 0-15-679259-1, Harv). HarBraceJ.
Cahoon, Herbert, compiled by. Samuel Johnson, LL.D., 1709-1784. (Illus.). 1959. 5.00 (ISBN 0-87598-023-6); pap. 5.00 (ISBN 0-87598-024-4). Pierpont Morgan.
Clifford, James L. & Greene, Donald J. Samuel Johnson: A Survey & Bibliography of Critical Studies. LC 74-109940. 1970. 15.00x (ISBN 0-8166-0572-6). U of Minn Pr.
Courtney, William P. A Bibliography of Samuel Johnson. 1977. Repr. 22.00 (ISBN 0-403-07758-3). Scholarly.
Hazen, Allen T. Samuel Johnson's Prefaces & Dedications. LC 72-86538. 228p. 1973. Repr. of 1937 ed. 15.00 (ISBN 0-8046-1749-X). Kennikat.
Johnson, Samuel. Samuel Johnson's Prefaces & Dedications. Hazen, A. T., ed. Repr. of 1937 ed. 20.00 (ISBN 0-403-08935-2). Somerset Pub.
McGuffie, Helen L. Samuel Johnson in the British Press, 1749-1784: A Chronological Checklist. LC 75-24082. (Reference Library of the Humanities: Vol. 29). 348p. 1975. lib. bdg. 37.50 (ISBN 0-8240-9983-4). Garland Pub.
Mathews, Elkin. A Catalogue of Books by or Relating to Dr. Johnson & Members of His Circle. LC 73-16046. 1925. Repr. lib. bdg. 30.00 (ISBN 0-8414-6077-9). Folcroft.
Smith, Frederick M. Some Friends of Doctor Johnson. LC 74-11157. 1974. Repr. of 1931 ed. lib. bdg. 25.00 (ISBN 0-8414-7507-5). Folcroft.

JOHNSON, THOMAS, 1677-1735

Ford, Herbert L. Shakespeare Seventeen-Hundred - Seventeen-Forty. LC 68-56498. 1969. Repr. of 1935 ed. 15.00 (ISBN 0-405-08526-5, Blom Pubns). Arno.

JOHNSON, UWE, 1934-

Boulby, Mark. Uwe Johnson. LC 73-82315. (Modern Literature Ser.). 1974. 10.95 (ISBN 0-8044-2062-9). Ungar.

JOHNSON, WILLIAM, 1771-1834

Morgan, Donald G. Justice William Johnson, the First Dissenter: The Career & Constitutional Philosophy of a Jeffersonian Judge. LC 54-14788. 1954. lib. bdg. 14.95x (ISBN 0-87249-060-2). U of SC Pr.

JOHNSON, WILLIAM MARTIN, d. 1797

Harrison, Gabriel. Life & Writings of John Howard Payne. rev. ed. LC 70-91517. 1885. 21.00 (ISBN 0-405-08600-8). Arno.

JOHNSON, WILLIAM SAMUEL, 1727-1819

Beardsley, E. Edwards. Life & Times of William Samuel Johnson. LC 72-4207. (Select Bibliographies Reprint Ser.). 1972. Repr. of 1876 ed. 16.00 (ISBN 0-8369-6872-7). Arno.
Groce, George C., Jr. William Samuel Johnson: A Maker of the Constitution. LC 37-33132. Repr. of 1937 ed. 14.50 (ISBN 0-404-02936-1). AMS Pr.

McCaughey, Elizabeth P. From Loyalist to Founding Father: The Political Odyssey of William Samuel Johnson. LC 79-17042. 1979. 22.50x (ISBN 0-231-04506-9). Columbia U Pr.

Tyson, Moses & Guppy, Henry. French Journals of Mrs. Thrale & Doctor Johnson. LC 72-1263. (English Literature Ser., No. 33). 1972. Repr. of 1932 ed. lib. bdg. 50.95 (ISBN 0-8383-1430-9). Haskell.

JOHNSON COUNTY, WYOMING–HISTORY

Castelli, Joseph R. Basques in the Western United States: A Functional Approach to Determination of Cultural Presence in the Geographical Landscape. Cordasco, Francesco, ed. LC 80-844. (American Ethnic Groups Ser.). 1981. lib. bdg. 19.00x (ISBN 0-405-13408-8). Arno.

Flagg, Oscar H. Review of the Cattle Business in Johnson County Wyoming, Since 1822, & the Causes That Led to the Recent Invasion. LC 79-90174. (Mass Violence in America Ser). Repr. of 1892 ed. 6.50 (ISBN 0-405-01309-4). Arno.

Hebard, Grace R. Johnson County, Wyoming. LC 71-119876. 15p. 1976. pap. 2.25 (ISBN 0-685-69027-X). Vic.

JOHNSON COUNTY WAR, 1892

Smith, Helena H. War on Powder River. LC 65-28734. (Illus.). 1967. pap. 5.25 (ISBN 0-8032-5188-2, BB 375, Bison). U of Nebr Pr.

JOHNSON FAMILY

Reade, Aleyn L. Johnsonian Gleanings, 11 pts in 10 vols. 1968. Set. lib. bdg. 135.00x (ISBN 0-374-96726-1). Octagon.

JOHNSTON, DENIS WILLIAM, 1901-

Ronsley, Joseph, ed. Denis Johnston: A Retrospective. (Irish Literary Studies: No. 8). 288p. 1981. 23.50x (ISBN 0-389-20233-9). B&N.

JOHNSTON, HENRIETTA (DEERING)

Middleton, Margaret S. Henrietta Johnston of Charles Town, South Carolina: America's First Pastellist. LC 66-25276. (Illus.). 1966. 14.95x (ISBN 0-87249-103-X). U of SC Pr.

JOHNSTON, JOHN, 1822-1900

Thorp, Raymond W. & Bunker, Robert. Crow Killer: The Saga of Liver-Eating Johnson. rev. ed. LC 58-8120. (Illus.). 196p. 1969. 10.95x (ISBN 0-253-11425-X). Ind U Pr.

JOHNSTON, JOSEPH EGGLESTON, 1807-1891

Govan, Gilbert E. & Livingood, James W. A Different Valor, the Story of General Joseph E. Johnston, C.S.A. LC 73-9372. (Illus.). 470p. 1973. Repr. of 1956 ed. lib. bdg. 24.75x (ISBN 0-8371-7012-5, GOVD). Greenwood.

JOHNSTONE, DAVID

Naydler, Merton. The Penance Way. LC 69-13305. (Illus.). 1969. 5.95 (ISBN 0-688-02282-0). Morrow.

JOINERS

see also Cabinet-Workers

JOINERY

see also Cabinet-Work; Carpentry; Furniture Making; Woodwork

Austin, C. K. Contract Joinery. (Illus.). 144p. 1981. 22.50x (ISBN 0-7198-2950-X). Intl Ideas.

Emary, A. B. Handbook of Carpentry & Joinery. LC 81-50984. (Illus., Orig.). 1981. pap. 8.95 (ISBN 0-8069-7536-9). Sterling.

Lavicka, William L., ed. Masonry, Carpentry, Joinery. 280p. (Orig.). 1980. pap. 15.00 (ISBN 0-914090-92-5). Chicago Review.

Rudman, Jack. Joiner. (Career Examination Ser.: C-408). (Cloth bdg. avail. on request). pap. 8.00 (ISBN 0-8373-0408-3). Natl Learning.

Seike, Kiyosi. The Art of Japanese Joinery. Davis, Rebecca, tr. from Japanese. LC 77-9070. (Illus.). 1977. pap. 8.95 (ISBN 0-8348-1516-8). Weatherhill.

JOINT OPERATIONS (MILITARY SCIENCE)

see Amphibious Warfare

JOINT PRODUCTION COMMITTEES

see Works Councils

JOINT TENANCY

see also Condominium (Housing)

JOINT-VENTURE AGREEMENTS

see Foreign Licensing Agreements

JOINTS

see also Ligaments; Pseudarthrosis; also names of anatomical joints, e.g. Elbow

Esch, Dortha & Lepley, Marvin. Evaluation of Joint Motion: Methods of Measurement & Recording. LC 73-93576. (Illus.). 50p. 1974. 5.75x (ISBN 0-8166-0714-1). U of Minn Pr.

Evans, Frances G., ed. Studies on the Anatomy & Function of Bone & Joints. (Illus.). 1966. 31.20 (ISBN 0-387-03677-6). Springer-Verlag.

Ficat, R. P. & Philippe, J., eds. Contrast Arthrography of the Synovial Joints. (Illus.). 200p. 1981. 37.50x (ISBN 0-89352-135-3). Masson Pub.

Guyot, J. Atlas of Human Limb Joints. (Illus.). 252p. 1981. 146.30 (ISBN 0-387-10380-5). Springer-Verlag.

Howorth, Beckett & Bender, Fred. A Doctor's Answer to Tennis Elbow: How to Cure It, How to Prevent It. LC 77-4145. (Illus.). 1977. 7.95 (ISBN 0-87754-054-3). Chelsea Hse.

Kapandji, I. A. Physiology of the Joints, 3 vols. Incl. Vol. 1. Upper Limb. 1970. 14.50 (ISBN 0-443-00654-7); Vol. 2. Lower Limb. (Illus.). 1971. 14.50 (ISBN 0-443-00655-5); Vol. 3. The Truck & Vertebral Column. 2nd ed. 1974. 16.25x (ISBN 0-443-01209-1). (Illus.). Churchill.

Lewis, Raymond W. The Joints of the Extremities: A Radiographic Study. (Illus.). 120p. 1955. photocopy ed. spiral 14.75 (ISBN 0-398-01124-9). C C Thomas.

Lindsey, David C. Bye Bye Backache. LC 81-67080. (Illus.). 208p. 1981. 11.95 (ISBN 0-939342-00-6). DCarlin Pub.

Lodwick, Gwilym S. The Bones & Joints. (Atlas of Tumor Radiology Ser.). (Illus.). 1971. 42.50 (ISBN 0-8151-5625-1). Year Bk Med.

Radin, E. L., et al. Practical Biomechanics for the Orthopedic Surgeon. 168p. 1979. 24.50 (ISBN 0-686-74422-5, Pub. by Wiley Med). Wiley.

Saha, A. K. Theory of Shoulder Mechanism: Descriptive & Applied. (Illus.). 120p. 1961. photocopy ed. spiral 12.50 (ISBN 0-398-01638-0). C C Thomas.

Schaldach, M. & Hohmann, D., eds. Advances in Artificial Hip & Knee Joint Technology. (Engineering in Medicine Ser: Vol. 2). 1976. 36.00 (ISBN 0-387-07728-6). Springer-Verlag.

Simon, William H., ed. The Human Joint in Health & Disease. LC 77-20305. (Illus.). 1978. 25.00x (ISBN 0-8122-7738-4). U of Pa Pr.

Sokoloff, L. The Joints & Synovial Fluid, Vol. 1. Sokoloff, Leon, ed. 1978. 49.50 (ISBN 0-12-655101-4); by subscription 42.00 (ISBN 0-685-80835-1). Acad Pr.

Walker, Peter S. Human Joints & Their Artificial Replacements. (Illus.). 528p. 1978. 64.75 (ISBN 0-398-03615-2). C C Thomas.

Watanabe, M., et al. Atlas of Arthroscopy. 3rd ed. 1979. 75.60 (ISBN 0-387-07674-3). Springer-Verlag.

Wiederanders, Rex E. & Addeo, Edmond G. Biotonics: Stamina Through Six-Second Exercises That Really Work. LC 77-8208. (Funk & W Bk.). (Illus.). 1977. 7.95 (ISBN 0-308-10332-7). T Y Crowell.

Wilson, J. N., ed. Watson-Jones Fractures & Joint Injuries, 2 vols. rev. 5th ed. LC 75-7549. (Illus.). 1976. text ed. 150.00 (ISBN 0-443-01105-2). Churchill.

JOINTS–DISLOCATIONS

see Dislocations

JOINTS–DISEASES

see also Arthritis; Joints–Radiography

Ackerman, Lauren & Spjut, Harlin, eds. Bones & Joints. (International Academy of Pathology Monograph: No. 17). 368p. 1976. 31.00 (ISBN 0-683-00039-X). Williams & Wilkins.

Adams, Ruth & Murray, Frank. All You Should Know About Arthritis. 256p. (Orig.). 1979. pap. 2.25 (ISBN 0-915962-28-4). Larchmont Bks.

American Academy of Orthopaedic Surgeons. Symposium on Anthroscopy & Arthrography of the Knee. LC 78-17015. (Illus.). 1978. text ed. 62.50 (ISBN 0-8016-0056-1). Mosby.

Dihlmann, Wolfgang. Diagnostic Radiology of the Sacroiliac Joints. 2nd ed. (Illus.). 140p. 1980. 42.95 (ISBN 0-8151-2458-9). Year Bk Med.

Feldman, Frieda, ed. Radiology, Pathology & Immunology of Bones & Joints: A Review of Current Concepts. (Illus.). 338p. 1979. 44.50 (ISBN 0-8385-8254-0). ACC.

Ficat, R. P. & Philippe, J., eds. Contrast Arthrography of the Synovial Joints. (Illus.). 200p. 1981. 37.50x (ISBN 0-89352-135-3). Masson Pub.

Forrester, D. M., et al. The Radiology of Joint Disease. 2nd ed. LC 77-27747. 1978. text ed. 37.50 (ISBN 0-7216-3822-8). Saunders.

Grieve, Gregory P., ed. Common Vertebral Joint Problems. (Illus.). 500p. 1981. text ed. 69.00 (ISBN 0-443-02106-6). Churchill.

Hall, Michael C. Luschka's Joint. (Illus.). 160p. 1965. photocopy ed. spiral 16.75 (ISBN 0-398-00760-8). C C Thomas.

Hirohata, Kazushi & Morimoto, Kazuo. Ultrastructure of Bone & Joint Diseases. LC 72-1791. (Illus.). 349p. 1972. 90.50 (ISBN 0-8089-0771-9). Grune.

Huskisson, E. C. & Hart, F. Dudley. Joint Disease-All the Arthropathies. 3rd ed. 1978. 21.50 (ISBN 0-8151-4788-0). Year Bk Med.

Lichtenstein, Louis. Diseases of Bone & Joints. 2nd ed. LC 74-14781. (Illus.). 1975. 38.50 (ISBN 0-8016-3007-X). Mosby.

Luck, J. Vernon. Bone & Joint Diseases: Pathology Correlated with Roentgenological & Clinical Features. (Illus.). 604p. 1950. photocopy ed. spiral 64.00 (ISBN 0-398-04347-7). C C Thomas.

Mennell, John M. Joint Pain: Diagnosis & Treatment Using Manipulative Techniques. 178p. 1964. 14.95 (ISBN 0-316-56668-3). Little.

Morgan, Douglas & Hall, William. Disease of the Temporomandibular Apparatus: A Multidisciplinary Approach. LC 77-3904. (Illus.). 1977. 49.50 (ISBN 0-8016-3487-3). Mosby.

Neviaser, Julius S. Arthrography of the Shoulder: The Diagnosis & Management of the Lesions Visualized. (Illus.). 256p. 1975. photocopy ed. spiral 28.75 (ISBN 0-398-03304-8). C C Thomas.

Panayi, G. S. Rheumatoid Arthritis & Related Conditions, Vol. 2. LC 78-317911. (Annual Research Reviews Ser.). 1978. 19.20 (ISBN 0-88831-022-6). Eden Med Res.

Schajowicz, F. Tumors & Tumor Like Lesions of Bone & Joints. (Illus.). 650p. 165.00 (ISBN 0-387-90492-1). Springer-Verlag.

Solberg, William K. & Clark, Glenn T. Temporomandibular Joint Problems: Biological Diagnosis & Treatment. 177p. 1980. 39.00 (ISBN 0-931386-18-7). Quint Pub Co.

Tzonchev, et al. Radiology of Joint Disease. (Illus.). 1973. 49.95 (ISBN 0-407-90050-0). Butterworth.

JOINTS–RADIOGRAPHY

Dalinka, M. K. Arthrography. (Comprehensive Manuals in Radiology). (Illus.). 209p. 1980. 29.50 (ISBN 0-387-90466-2). Springer-Verlag.

Feldman, Frieda, ed. Radiology, Pathology & Immunology of Bones & Joints: A Review of Current Concepts. (Illus.). 338p. 1979. 44.50 (ISBN 0-8385-8254-0). ACC.

Ficat, R. P. & Philippe, J., eds. Contrast Arthrography of the Synovial Joints. (Illus.). 200p. 1981. 37.50x (ISBN 0-89352-135-3). Masson Pub.

Forrester, D. M., et al. The Radiology of Joint Disease. 2nd ed. LC 77-27747. 1978. text ed. 37.50 (ISBN 0-7216-3822-8). Saunders.

Glinz, Werner. Diagnostic & Operative Arthroscopy of the Knee Joint. Spati-Tuchschmid, Edith, tr. (Illus.). 130p. 1980. text ed. 65.00 (ISBN 3-456-80943-3, Pub. by Hans Huber Switzerland). J K Burgess.

Matzen, Peter-Friedrich & Fleissner, Horst K. Orthopedic Roentgen Atlas. Michaelis, L. S., tr. (Illus.). 300p. 1970. 95.00 (ISBN 0-8089-0634-8). Grune.

Murray, Ronald O. & Jacobson, Harold G. The Radiology of Skeletal Disorders: Exercises in Diagnosis, 4 vols. 2d ed. LC 76-28430. (Illus.). 1977. text ed. 250.00 (ISBN 0-443-01267-9). Churchill.

Tzonchev, et al. Radiology of Joint Disease. (Illus.). 1973. 49.95 (ISBN 0-407-90050-0). Butterworth.

JOINTS–SURGERY

see also Arthroplasty

JOINTS (ENGINEERING)

see also Fasteners

Bickford. An Introduction to the Design & Behavior of Bolted Joints. (Mechanical Engineering Ser.). 632p. 1981. price not set (ISBN 0-8247-1508-X). Dekker.

Davidson, A. Handbook of Precision Engineering, Vol. 5: Joining Techniques. (Illus.). 297p. 1972. 29.50 (ISBN 0-07-015472-4, P&RB). McGraw.

Fisher, John W. & Struik, John H. Guide to Design Criteria for Bolted & Riveted Joints. LC 73-17158. 314p. 1974. 41.00 (ISBN 0-471-26140-8, Pub. by Wiley-Interscience). Wiley.

Symposium on Joining of Materials for Aerospace Systems, Dayton, Ohio. Nov. 15-17, 1965. Proceedings. (Science of Advanced Materials & Process Engineering Ser., Vol. 9). pap. 8.00 (ISBN 0-938994-09-3). Soc Adv Material.

Weiss, Harvey. What Holds It Together? LC 76-54692. (gr. 4-6). 1977. 6.95 (ISBN 0-316-92888-7, Pub by Atlantic Monthly Pr). Little.

JOKES

see Wit and Humor

JOLIET, LOUIS, 1645-1700

Kjelgaard, Jim A. Explorations of Pere Marquette. (Landmark Ser.: No. 17). (Illus.). (gr. 4-6). 1951. PLB 5.99 (ISBN 0-394-90317-X). Random.

Steck, Frances B. The Joliet-Marquette Expedition, 1673. rev. ed. LC 73-5360. (Catholic University of America. Studies in American Church History: No. 6). (Illus.). Repr. of 1928 ed. 27.00 (ISBN 0-404-57756-3). AMS Pr.

Stein, R. Conrad. The Story of Marquette & Jolliet. (Cornerstones of Freedom Ser.). (Illus.). (gr. 3-6). 1981. PLB 7.95 (ISBN 0-516-04630-6); pap. 2.50 (ISBN 0-516-44630-4). Childrens.

JOLIOT-CURIE, FREDERIC, 1900-1958

Goldsmith, Maurice. Frederic Joliot-Curie. 1976. 19.95x (ISBN 0-8464-0426-5). Beekman Pubs.

--Frederic Joliot-Curie. 1976. text ed. 15.75x (ISBN 0-85315-342-6). Humanities.

JOLSON, AL 1886-1950

Oberfirst, Robert. Al Jolson: You Ain't Heard Nothing Yet. LC 80-16736. 1980. 8.95 (ISBN 0-498-02500-4). A S Barnes.

JONAH, THE PROPHET

De Haan, Martin R. Jonah, Fact or Fiction. 1957. pap. 3.95 (ISBN 0-310-23391-7). Zondervan.

Fairbairn, Patrick. Jonah: His Life, Character, & Mission. (Summit Bks.). 248p. 1980. pap. 3.95 (ISBN 0-8010-3498-1). Baker Bk.

Lacocque, Andre & Lacocque, Pierre. Jonah Complex. LC 80-84649. 1981. 14.00 (ISBN 0-8042-0091-2); pap. 7.95 (ISBN 0-8042-0092-0). John Knox.

Martin, Hugh. Prophet Jonah: His Character & Mission to Nineveh. (Giant Summit Books Ser.). 1979. pap. 6.95 (ISBN 0-8010-6072-9). Baker Bk.

Price, Brynmor F. & Nida, Eugene A. A Translators Handbook on the Book of Jonah. (Helps for Translators Ser.). 1978. soft cover 2.80 (ISBN 0-8267-0199-X, 08552). United Bible.

Stowell, Gordon, illus. Jonah. 2nd ed. (Little Fish Bks About Bible People). (Illus.). 20p. (ps). 1981. 0.49 (ISBN 0-8307-0341-1, 5601002). Regal.

JONAH, THE PROPHET–JUVENILE LITERATURE

Bennett, Marian. The Story of Jonah. (Mini Pop-up Books). (Illus.). (gr. k-2). 1978. 2.50 (ISBN 0-87239-221-X, 3607). Standard Pub.

Brem, M. M. The Man Caught by a Fish. (Arch Bks: Set 4). 1967. laminated bdg. 0.79 (ISBN 0-570-06025-7, 59-1136). Concordia.

Brodsky, Beverly. Jonah: An Old Testament Story. LC 77-5925. (gr. 3 up). 1977. 9.95 (ISBN 0-397-31733-6, JBL-J). Har-Row.

Jonah. LC 76-11275. (Sunshine Bks). (Illus.). 20p. 1976. pap. 1.00 (ISBN 0-8006-1577-8, 1-1577). Fortress.

Jonah & the Big Fish. (Tell-a-Bible Story Ser.). (Illus.). 28p. bds. 0.79 (ISBN 0-686-68641-1, 3685). Standard Pub.

New International Version of the Holy Bible. Jonah. (ps up). 9.95 (ISBN 0-686-31565-0). Cornerstone Bks.

Roberts, Jim. Jonah. 1978. pap. 2.49 (ISBN 0-8307-0612-7, 56-055-04). Regal.

JONATHAN (BIBLICAL CHARACTER)

Churgin, Pinchas & Smolar, Leivy. Studies in Targum Jonathan to the Prophets. 39.50x (ISBN 0-87068-109-5). Ktav.

Lindsay, Gordon. Saul & Jonathan. (Old Testament Ser.). 1.25 (ISBN 0-89985-140-1). Christ Nations.

JONES, ALFRED

Davies, P. N. Sir Alfred Jones: Entrepreneur Par Excellence. LC 78-312287. 1978. 15.00x (ISBN 0-905118-17-0). Intl Pubns Serv.

JONES, CHARLES JESSE, 1844-1919

Easton, Robert & Brown, MacKenzie. Lord of Beasts: The Saga of Buffalo Jones. LC 61-14501. (Illus.). 1970. pap. 2.95 (ISBN 0-8032-5727-9, BB 522, Bison). U of Nebr Pr.

--Lord of Beasts: The Saga of Buffalo Jones. LC 61-14501. (Illus.). 1961. 2.00 (ISBN 0-8165-0281-1). U of Ariz Pr.

JONES, DAVID JAMES GWENALLT

Blamires, D. David Jones: Artist & Writer. 234p. 1978. 18.00x (ISBN 0-7190-0730-5, Manchester U Pr England). State Mutual Bk.

Hague, Rene. A Commentary on "The Anathemata" of David Jones. 1978. 17.50x (ISBN 0-8020-2297-9). U of Toronto Pr.

Morgan, Dyfnallt. D. Gwenallt Jones (1899-1968) (Writers of Wales Ser.). 81p. 1973. pap. text ed. 4.50x (ISBN 0-8426-0430-8). Verry.

JONES, DAVID MICHAEL, 1895-1974

Blamires, David. David Jones: Artist & Writer. LC 77-190341. (Illus.). 300p. 1972. 15.00x (ISBN 0-8020-1877-7). U of Toronto Pr.

Hague, Rene. Dai Greatcoat: A Self-Portrait of David Jones in His Letters. LC 80-670267. (Illus.). 320p. 1980. 37.50 (ISBN 0-571-11540-3, Pub. by Faber & Faber). Merrimack Bk Serv.

Hooker, Jeremy. David Jones: An Exploratory Study of His Writings. 1975. 7.50 (ISBN 0-685-72969-9, Pub. by Enitharmon Pr); ltd. ed. 16.00 (ISBN 0-685-72970-2); pap. 4.75 (ISBN 0-685-72971-0). SBD.

Rees, Samuel. David Jones: An Annotated Bibliography & Guide to Research. LC 76-24748. (Reference Library of the Humanities Ser.: Vol. 68). 1977. lib. bdg. 18.00 (ISBN 0-8240-9929-X). Garland Pub.

JONES, GWENALLT D., 1899-1968

Morgan, Dyfnallt. D. Gwenallt Jones (1899-1968) (Writers of Wales Ser.). 81p. 1973. pap. text ed. 4.50x (ISBN 0-8426-0430-8). Verry.

JONES, HENRY ARTHUR, 1851-1929

Cordell, Richard A. Henry Arthur Jones & the Modern Drama. LC 68-26274. 1968. Repr. of 1932 ed. 12.50 (ISBN 0-8046-0089-9). Kennikat.

Jones, Doris A. Life & Letters of Henry Arthur Jones. LC 79-145115. (Illus.). 1971. Repr. of 1930 ed. 49.00 (ISBN 0-403-01053-5). Scholarly.

JONES, INIGO, 1573-1652

Lees-Milne, James. The Age of Inigo Jones. 242p. 1953. Repr. 36.00 (ISBN 0-403-03878-2). Somerset Pub.

Nicoll, Allardyce. Stuart Masques & the Renaissance Stage. LC 63-23186. (Illus.). 1938. 34.00 (ISBN 0-405-08817-5, Pub. by Blom). Arno.
Orgel, Stephen & Strong, Roy. Inigo Jones: The Theatre of the Stuart Court, 2 vols. (Illus.). 1973. Set. 225.00x (ISBN 0-520-02469-9). U of Cal Pr.

JONES, JAMES, 1921-

Giles, James R. James Jones. (United States Authors Ser.: No. 366). 1981. lib. bdg. 9.95 (ISBN 0-8057-7293-6). Twayne.
Hopkins, John & Jones, Jamescompiled by. James Jones: A Checklist. (Illus.). 16.00 (ISBN 0-685-77425-2). Bruccoli.
Hopkins, John R., ed. James Jones: A Checklist. LC 74-20824. (Modern Authors Checklist Ser.). (Illus.). vii, 67p. 1974. 16.00 (ISBN 0-8103-0907-6, Bruccoli Clark Bk). Gale.
Morris, Willie. James Jones: A Friendship. LC 78-4709. (Illus.). 1978. 8.95 (ISBN 0-385-14432-6). Doubleday.
Rosenberg, William G. Liberals in the Russian Revolution: The Constitutional Democratic Party, 1917-1921. LC 73-16765. (Studies of the Russian Institute). 504p. 1974. 38.50x (ISBN 0-691-05221-2); pap. 13.50x (ISBN 0-691-10023-3). Princeton U Pr.

JONES, JESSE HOLMAN, 1874-1956

Timmons, Bascom N. The Man & the Statesman. LC 74-31366. (Illus.). 414p. 1975. Repr. of 1956 ed. lib. bdg. 27.50x (ISBN 0-8371-7925-4, TIJJ). Greenwood.

JONES, JOHN PAUL, 1747-1792

Abbazia, Patrick. John Paul Jones, America's First Naval Hero. Rahmas, D. Steve, ed. (Outstanding Personalities Ser: No. 86). 1976. lib. bdg. 2.95 incl. catalog cards (ISBN 0-686-15816-4); pap. 1.50 vinyl laminated covers (ISBN 0-686-15817-2). SamHar Pr.
Buell, Augustus C. Paul Jones: Founder of the American Navy, 2 vols. facsimile ed. LC 70-157326. (Select Bibliographies Reprint Ser.). Repr. of 1900 ed. Set. 45.00 (ISBN 0-8369-5786-5). Arno.
Fanning, Nathaniel. Fanning's Narrative: Being the Memoirs of Nathaniel Fanning, an Officer of the Revolutionary Navy 1778-1783. Barnes, John S., ed. LC 67-29043. (Eyewitness Accounts of the American Revolution Ser., No. 1). 1968. Repr. of 1912 ed. 12.00 (ISBN 0-405-01105-9). Arno.
Grant, Matthew G. John Paul Jones. LC 73-18212. 1974. PLB 5.95 (ISBN 0-87191-300-3). Creative Ed.
Jones, John Paul. Memoirs of Rear-Admiral Paul Jones. LC 77-166333. (Era of the American Revolution Ser.). (Illus.). 1972. Repr. of 1830 ed. lib. bdg. 45.00 (ISBN 0-306-70247-9). Da Capo.
Lorenz, Lincoln. John Paul Jones, Fighter for Freedom & Glory. 1943. 32.00 (ISBN 0-527-58400-2). Kraus Repr.
Mackenzie, Alexander S. The Life of Paul Jones. facsimile ed. LC 70-160981. (Select Bibliographies Reprint Ser). Repr. of 1848 ed. 18.00 (ISBN 0-8369-5849-7). Arno.
Morison, Samuel E. John Paul Jones: A Sailor's Biography. (Illus.). 453p. 1959. 5.98 (ISBN 0-686-30881-6, Pub. by Faber & Faber). Merrimack Bk Serv.
--John Paul Jones: A Sailor's Biography. (Illus.). 1959. 12.95 (ISBN 0-316-58358-8, Pub. by Atlantic Monthly Pr). Little.
Walsh, Jack. The Night on Fire: The First Complete Account of John Paul Jones' Greatest Battle. LC 77-26762. 1978. 9.95 (ISBN 0-07-067952-5, GB). McGraw.

JONES, JOHN PAUL, 1747-1792–JUVENILE LITERATURE

Poole, Susan. John Paul Jones. LC 78-74129. (Illus.). (gr. 2-5). Date not set. price not set (ISBN 0-89799-180-X); pap. price not set (ISBN 0-89799-179-6). Dandelion Pr.
Worcester, Donald E. John Paul Jones. (gr. 4-6). 1961. 4.36 (ISBN 0-395-01755-6, Piper). HM.

JONES, LE ROI

Benston, Kimberly W. Baraka: The Renegade & the Mask. LC 75-43302. (College Ser.: No. 14). 1976. 20.00x (ISBN 0-300-01958-0). Yale U Pr.
Brown, Lloyd W. Amiri Baraka (le Roi Jones) (United States Authors Ser.: No. 383). 1980. lib. bdg. 9.95 (ISBN 0-8057-7317-7). Twayne.
Hudson, Theodore R. From Leroi Jones to Amiri Baraka: The Literary Works. LC 72-97096. 256p. 1973. 12.75 (ISBN 0-8223-0296-9); pap. 6.75 (ISBN 0-8223-0454-6). Duke.
Lacey, Henry C. To Raise, Destroy, & Create. LC 80-50078. 1981. 15.00x (ISBN 0-87875-185-8). Whitston Pub.
Sollors, Werner. Amiri Baraka - Leroi Jones. 1978. 17.50x (ISBN 0-231-04226-4). Columbia U Pr.

JONES, MARY HARRIS, 1830-1930

Atkinson, Linda. Mother Jones: The Most Dangerous Woman in America. LC 77-15863. (Illus.). (gr. 7 up). 1978. 7.95 (ISBN 0-517-53201-8). Crown.
Bethell, Jean. Three Cheers for Mother Jones. LC 79-28655. (Illus.). 48p. (gr. 2-4). 1980. 6.95 (ISBN 0-03-054831-4). HR&W.
Fetherling, Dale. Mother Jones, the Miners' Angel: A Portrait. LC 73-12444. (Illus.). 280p. 1974. 11.85x (ISBN 0-8093-0643-3). S Ill U Pr.
--Mother Jones, the Miners' Angel: A Portrait. LC 78-16328. (Arcturus Books Paperbacks). (Illus.). 280p. 1979. pap. 8.95 (ISBN 0-8093-0896-7). S Ill U Pr.
Jones, Mary. The Autobiography of Mother Jones. 3rd rev. ed. Parton, Mary F., ed. (Illus.). 288p. 1980. lib. bdg. 10.00 (ISBN 0-88286-023-2); pap. 4.95 (ISBN 0-686-67230-5). C H Kerr.

JONES, ROBERT EDMOND, 1887-1954

Pendleton, Ralph, ed. The Theatre of Robert Edmond Jones. LC 58-5188. (Illus.). 1977. pap. 12.50x (ISBN 0-8195-6053-7, Pub. by Wesleyan U Pr). Columbia U Pr.

JONES, RUFUS MATTHEW, 1863-1948

Hinshaw, David. Rufus Jones, Master Quaker. facsimile ed. LC 74-133522. (Select Bibliographies Reprint Ser.). Repr. of 1951 ed. 19.00 (ISBN 0-8369-5554-4). Arno.

JONES, THOMAS ELSA, 1888-

Jones, Thomas E. Light on the Horizon: The Quaker Pilgrimage of Tom Jones. LC 74-14286. 200p. 1973. 3.95 (ISBN 0-913408-13-1). Friends United.

JONES, WILLIAM, SIR, 1746-1794

Mukherjee, S. N. Sir William Jones. (Cambridge South Asian Studies). (Illus.). 1968. 24.95 (ISBN 0-521-05777-9). Cambridge U Pr.

JONES, WILLIAM, SIR, 1746-1794–BIBLIOGRAPHY

Cannon, Garland. Sir William Jones: A Bibliography of Primary & Secondary Sources. xiv, 73p. 1979. 14.00 (ISBN 90-272-0998-7, LISL 7). Benjamins North Am.

JONGLEURS

see Jugglers and Juggling; Minstrels; Troubadours; Trouveres

JONSBOK

Hermannsson, Halldor. Illuminated Manuscripts of the Jonsbok. LC 42-7225. (Islandica Ser.: Vol. 28). 1940. pap. 9.00 (ISBN 0-527-00358-1). Kraus Repr.

JONSON, BEN, 1573-1637

Bamborough, J. B. Ben Jonson. (English Literature Ser.). 1970. pap. text ed. 4.75x (ISBN 0-09-101691-6, Hutchinson U Lib). Humanities.
Barish, Jonas A. Ben Jonson & the Language of Prose Comedy. 1970. pap. 2.45x (ISBN 0-393-00554-2, Norton Lib). Norton.
Baskervill, Charles R. English Elements in Johnson's Early Comedy. Repr. of 1911 ed. pap. 16.50 (ISBN 0-384-03520-5). Johnson Repr.
--English Elements in Johnson's Early Comedy. LC 67-21711. 1967. Repr. of 1911 ed. 10.00 (ISBN 0-87752-004-6). Gordian.
Bates, Steven L. & Orr, Sidney D. Concordance to the Poems of Ben Jonson. LC 76-25613. xiv, 878p. 1978. 40.00x (ISBN 0-8214-0359-1). Ohio U Pr.
Baum, Helena W. Satiric & the Didactic in Ben Jonson's Comedy. LC 70-139900. 1971. Repr. of 1947 ed. 12.00 (ISBN 0-8462-1550-0). Russell.
Beaurline, Lester A. Jonson & Elizabethan Comedy: Essays in Dramatic Rhetoric. LC 77-75148. (Illus.). 1978. 16.00 (ISBN 0-87328-071-7). Huntington Lib.
Bentley, Gerald E. Shakespeare & Jonson, Their Reputations in the Seventeenth Century Compared, 2 Vols in 1. LC 54-11205. 1965. 20.00x (ISBN 0-226-04269-3). U of Chicago Pr.
Blissett, William, et al, eds. A Celebration of Ben Jonson. LC 73-91241. (Illus.). 1974. 15.00x (ISBN 0-8020-2123-9); pap. 6.50 (ISBN 0-8020-6284-9). U of Toronto Pr.
Boughner, Daniel C. Devils Disciple. LC 67-24571. 1968. 5.95 (ISBN 0-8022-0159-8). Philos Lib.
--The Devil's Disciple: Ben Jonson's Debt to Machiavelli. LC 73-16606. 264p. 1975. Repr. of 1968 ed. lib. bdg. 14.50x (ISBN 0-8371-7183-0, BODD). Greenwood.
Bradley, Jesse F. & Adams, Joseph Q., eds. The Jonson Allusion-Book: A Collection of Allusions to Ben Jonson from 1597 to 1700. LC 76-121998. (Illus.). 466p. 1971. Repr. of 1922 ed. 17.00 (ISBN 0-8462-1353-2). Russell.
--Jonson Allusion-Book: A Collection of Allusions to Ben Jonson from 1597 to 1700. LC 76-144893. 1971. Repr. of 1922 ed. 16.00 (ISBN 0-403-00813-1). Scholarly.
Bryant, J. A., Jr. The Compassionate Satirist: Ben Jonson & His Imperfect World. LC 73-81623. 204p. 1973. 10.00x (ISBN 0-8203-0316-X). U of Ga Pr.
Chalfant, Fran C. Ben Jonson's London: A Jacobean Placename Dictionary. LC 75-32125. 215p. 1978. 16.00 (ISBN 0-8203-0392-5). U of Ga Pr.
Champion, Larry S. Ben Jonson's "Dotages". A Reconsideration of the Late Plays. LC 67-29338. 168p. 1967. 10.00x (ISBN 0-8131-1143-9). U Pr of Ky.
Chan, Mary. Music in the Theatre of Ben Jonson. (Illus.). 344p. 1980. 69.00x (ISBN 0-19-812632-8). Oxford U Pr.
Cruickshank, A. H. Ben Jonson. LC 74-3255. 1912. lib. bdg. 6.50 (ISBN 0-8414-3608-8). Folcroft.
Davis, Joe L. Sons of Ben: Jonsonian Comedy in Caroline England. LC 67-11271. 1967. 10.95x (ISBN 0-8143-1302-7). Wayne St U Pr.
Di Cesare, Mario A. & Fogel, Ephim, eds. A Concordance to the Poems of Ben Jonson. LC 78-59630. (Concordances Ser). 1978. 42.50x (ISBN 0-8014-1217-X). Cornell U Pr.
Dick, Aliki L. Padeia Through Laughter: Jonson's Aristophanic Appeal to Human Intelligence. LC 73-84787. (Studies in English Literature: No. 76). xi, 141p. (Orig.). 1974. pap. text ed. 27.50x (ISBN 90-2792-714-6). Mouton.
Donaldson, Ian. World Upside-Down: Comedy from Jonson to Fielding. (Illus.). 1970. pap. 19.50x (ISBN 0-19-812065-6). Oxford U Pr.
Duncan, D. Ben Jonson & the Lucianic Tradition. LC 78-18093. 1979. 29.95 (ISBN 0-521-22359-8). Cambridge U Pr.
Dunn, Esther C. Ben Jonson's Art. 159p. 1980. Repr. of 1925 ed. lib. bdg. 30.00 (ISBN 0-8495-1122-4). Arden Lib.
Dyce, Alexander. Remarks on Mister J. P. Collier's & Mister C. Knight's Editions of Shakespeare. LC 79-164815. Repr. of 1844 ed. 24.00 (ISBN 0-404-02230-8). AMS Pr.
Enck, John J. Jonson & the Comic Truth. 1957. pap. 4.75x (ISBN 0-299-01604-8). U of Wis Pr.
Evans, Willa M. Ben Jonson & Elizabethan Music. 2nd ed. LC 65-18503. (Music Ser). 1965. Repr. of 1929 ed. 14.50 (ISBN 0-306-70907-4). Da Capo.
Feis, Jacob. Shakspere & Montaigne. LC 73-130615. Repr. of 1884 ed. 17.00 (ISBN 0-404-02375-4). AMS Pr.
Feldman, B. Best of Ben, 5 vols. 1981. Set. 8.95 (ISBN 0-87863-205-0). Farnswth Pub.
Ford, H. L. Collation of the Ben Jonson Folios. LC 73-12916. Repr. of 1932 ed. lib. bdg. 15.00 (ISBN 0-8414-4152-9). Folcroft.
Gilbert, Allan H. Symbolic Persons in the Masques of Ben Jonson. LC 79-85910. (BCL Ser.: I). Repr. of 1948 ed. 23.00 (ISBN 0-404-02759-8). AMS Pr.
Gilchrist, Octavius. Examination of the Charges Maintained by Messrs. Malone, Chalmers & Others, of Ben Jonson's Enmity - Towards Shakspeare. LC 70-168146. Repr. of 1808 ed. 11.50 (ISBN 0-404-02768-7). AMS Pr.
Goldsworthy, Lansdown. Ben Jonson & the First Folio. LC 72-1337. (Studies in Drama, No. 39: English Literature, No. 33). 1972. Repr. of 1931 ed. lib. bdg. 49.95 (ISBN 0-8383-1439-2). Haskell.
Goldsworthy, W. Lansdown. Ben Jonson & the First Folio. LC 72-191959. 1939. lib. bdg. 8.50 (ISBN 0-8414-4493-5). Folcroft.
Gray, Arthur. How Shakespeare Purged Jonson, a Problem Solved. LC 72-153325. Repr. of 1928 ed. 11.50 (ISBN 0-404-02893-4). AMS Pr.
Greg, W. W. Jonson's Masque of Gipsies: In the Burley Belvoir & Windsor Versions. 246p. 1979. 10.00x (ISBN 0-686-26937-3). State Mutual Bk.
Grene, Nicholas. Shakespeare, Jonson, Moliere: The Comic Contract. 246p. 1980. 26.50x (ISBN 0-389-20093-X). B&N.
Hillberry, Clarence B. Ben Jonson's Ethics in Relation to Stoic & Humanistic Ethical Thought. LC 73-12209. 1933. lib. bdg. 5.00 (ISBN 0-8414-4730-6). Folcroft.
Hollis, C. Dr. Jonson. 1928. Repr. 25.00 (ISBN 0-685-43442-7). Norwood Edns.
Hyland, Peter. Disguise & Role-Playing in Ben Jonson's Drama. (Salzburg Studies in English Literature, Jacobean Drama Studies: No. 69). (Orig.). 1977. pap. text ed. 25.00x (ISBN 0-391-01432-3). Humanities.
Johnston, George B. Ben Jonson: Poet. LC 72-120634. 1970. Repr. lib. bdg. 14.00x (ISBN 0-374-94260-9). Octagon.
Jonson, Ben. Ben Jonson's Plays & Masques. Adams, Robert M., ed. (Critical Editions). 1979. 22.95x (ISBN 0-393-04506-4); pap. text ed. 5.95x (ISBN 0-393-09035-3). Norton.
--Timber: or Discoveries. Walker, Ralph S., ed. LC 76-7990. 1976. Repr. of 1953 ed. lib. bdg. 15.00x (ISBN 0-8371-8882-2, WABJ). Greenwood.
Jonson, Benjamin. Jonsonus Virbius; or, the Memorie of Ben Johnson Revived. LC 70-26356. (English Experience Ser.: No. 258). 74p. 1970. Repr. of 1638 ed. 11.50 (ISBN 90-221-0258-0). Walter J Johnson.
Juneja, Renu, et al. Recent Research on Ben Jonson. (Salzburg Studies in English Literature, Jacobean Drama Studies: No.76). 1978. pap. text ed. 25.00x (ISBN 0-391-01441-2). Humanities.
Kerr, Mina. Influence of Ben Johnson on English Comedy, 1598-1642. LC 67-30905. 1967. Repr. of 1912 ed. 7.50 (ISBN 0-87753-024-6). Phaeton.
Knoll, Robert E. Ben Jonson's Plays: An Introduction. LC 64-17220. (Illus.). 1965. 14.50x (ISBN 0-8032-0094-3). U of Nebr Pr.
Linklater, Eric. Ben Jonson & King James. LC 74-168250. 1972. Repr. of 1931 ed. 15.00 (ISBN 0-8046-1689-2). Kennikat.
McEuen, Kathryn A. Classical Influence Upon the Tribe of Ben. 1968. lib. bdg. 15.00x (ISBN 0-374-95472-0). Octagon.
MacLean, Hugh. Ben Jonson & the Cavalier Poets. new ed. (Critical Editions Ser.). 1975. 12.50 (ISBN 0-393-04387-8); pap. 6.95x (ISBN 0-393-09308-5). Norton.
Meagher, John C. Method & Meaning in Jonson's Masques. 1969. pap. 3.50x (ISBN 0-268-00366-1). U of Notre Dame Pr.
Musgrove, S. Shakespeare & Johnson. LC 75-20018. 1957. lib. bdg. 4.95 (ISBN 0-8414-6025-6). Folcroft.
--Shakespeare & Jonson: The Macmillan Brown Lectures. LC 76-38501. Repr. of 1957 ed. 11.50 (ISBN 0-404-04545-6). AMS Pr.
Nason, Arthur H. Heralds & Heraldry in Ben Jonson's Plays, Masques & Entertainments. LC 68-59042. 1968. Repr. of 1907 ed. 8.50 (ISBN 0-87752-076-3). Gordian.
--Heralds & Heraldry in Ben Jonson's Plays: Masques & Entertainments. 1978. Repr. of 1907 ed. lib. bdg. 35.00 (ISBN 0-8495-4004-6). Arden Lib.
--Heralds & Heraldry in Jonson's Plays. LC 73-12356. 1907. lib. bdg. 7.45 (ISBN 0-8414-6250-X). Folcroft.
Nichols, J. G. The Poetry of Ben Jonson. 1969. 18.00x (ISBN 0-7100-6448-9). Routledge & Kegan.
Noyes, Robert G. Ben Jonson on the English Stage, Sixteen Sixty to Seventeen Seventy-Six. LC 65-27916. (Illus.). 1935. 18.00 (ISBN 0-405-08823-X, Pub. by Blom). Arno.
Orgel, Stephen. The Jonsonian Masque. LC 81-6174. (Morningside Bks.). (Illus.). 240p. 1981. 22.50 (ISBN 0-231-05370-3); pap. 8.50x (ISBN 0-686-73339-8). Columbia U Pr.
Parfitt, George. Ben Jonson: Public Poet & Private Man. LC 76-40877. 1976. text ed. 18.50x (ISBN 0-06-495385-8). B&N.
Partridge, A. C. Studies in the Syntax of Ben Jonson's Plays. 1953. text ed. 4.50x (ISBN 0-391-02056-0). Humanities.
Partridge, Edward B. The Broken Compass: A Study of the Major Comedies of Ben Jonson. LC 75-38386. 254p. 1976. Repr. of 1958 ed. lib. bdg. 15.25x (ISBN 0-8371-8662-5, PABC). Greenwood.
Patterson, R. F. Ben Jonson's Conversations with Drummond of Hawthornden. LC 73-22023. (English Literature Ser., No. 33). 1974. lib. bdg. 47.95 (ISBN 0-8383-1835-5). Haskell.
Peterson, Richard S. Imitation & Praise in the Poems of Ben Jonson. LC 80-26261. (Illus.). 280p. 1981. 18.50x (ISBN 0-300-02586-6). Yale U Pr.
Randall, Dale B. Jonson's Gypsies Unmasked: Background & Theme of the Gypsies Metamorphos'd. LC 74-75909. (Illus.). xiii, 200p. 1974. 10.95 (ISBN 0-8223-0322-1). Duke.
Sackton, Alexander H. Rhetoric As a Dramatic Language in Ben Jonson. 1967. Repr. lib. bdg. 13.00x (ISBN 0-374-97011-4). Octagon.
Schelling, Felix E. Ben Jonson & the Classical School. LC 75-2235. (Studies in Drama, No. 39). 1970. Repr. of 1898 ed. lib. bdg. 19.95 (ISBN 0-8383-0346-3). Haskell.
Small, Roscoe A. Stage-Quarrel Between Ben Johnson & the So-Called Poetasters. LC 2-25126. Repr. of 1889 ed. 17.00 (ISBN 0-404-06099-4). AMS Pr.
Smith, G. Gregory. Ben Johnson. LC 71-145306. vi, 310p. 1972. Repr. of 1919 ed. 19.00 (ISBN 0-403-01218-X). Scholarly.
--Ben Jonson. 1919. lib. bdg. 18.50 (ISBN 0-8414-7783-3). Folcroft.
Steel, Byron. O Rare Ben Jonson. 1927. Repr. 30.00 (ISBN 0-685-43441-9). Norwood Edns.
Sturmberger, Ingeborg. The Comic Elements of Ben Jonson's Drama, 2 vols. (Salzburg Studies in English Literature, Jacobean Drama Studies Ser.: Nos. 54-55). 548p. 1975. Set. pap. text ed. 50.25x (ISBN 0-391-01540-0). Humanities.
Summers, Claude J. & Pebworth, Ted-Larry. Ben Jonson. (English Authors Ser.: No. 268). 1979. 12.50 (ISBN 0-8057-6764-9). Twayne.
Swinburne, Algernon C. Study of Ben Jonson. LC 68-24922. (Studies in Drama, No. 39). 1969. Repr. of 1889 ed. lib. bdg. 49.95 (ISBN 0-8383-0245-9). Haskell.
--Study of Ben Jonson. Norland, Howard B., ed. LC 69-12400. 1969. pap. 3.65x (ISBN 0-8032-5709-0, BB 326, Bison). U of Nebr Pr.
Symonds, John A. Ben Jonson. LC 75-128937. Repr. of 1886 ed. 10.00 (ISBN 0-404-06320-9). AMS Pr.
--Ben Jonson. 1973. lib. bdg. 9.95 (ISBN 0-8414-7996-8). Folcroft.

Thayer, Calvin G. Ben Jonson: Studies in the Plays. (Illus.). 1966. Repr. of 1963 ed. 13.95x (ISBN 0-8061-0555-0). U of Okla Pr.

Townsend, Freda L. Apologie for Bartholmew Fayre. 1947. pap. 6.00 (ISBN 0-527-90680-8). Kraus Repr.

Trimpi, Wesley. Ben Jonson's Poems: A Study of the Plain Style. 1962. 15.00x (ISBN 0-8047-0097-4). Stanford U Pr.

Wheeler, Charles F. Classical Mythology in the Plays, Masques, & Poems of Ben Jonson. LC 71-114234. 1970. Repr. of 1938 ed. 11.50 (ISBN 0-8046-1038-X). Kennikat.

Whipple, Thomas K. Martial & English Epigram from Sir Thomas Wyatt to Ben Jonson. LC 70-90362. 1970. Repr. of 1925 ed. 7.50 (ISBN 0-87753-043-2). Phaeton.

Williams, Mary C. Sources of Unity in Ben Jonson's Comedy. (Salzburg Studies in English Literature, Jacobean Drama Studies: No. 22). 230p. 1972. pap. text ed. 25.00x (ISBN 0-391-01572-9). Humanities.

Witt, Robert W. Mirror Within a Mirror: Ben Jonson & the Play-Within. (Salzburg Studies in English Literature Jacobean Drama Studies: No. 46). 154p. 1976. pap. text ed. 25.00x (ISBN 0-391-01574-5). Humanities.

Woodbridge, Elizabeth M. Studies in Jonson's Comedies. LC 66-29470. 1966. Repr. of 1898 ed. 6.00 (ISBN 0-87752-123-9). Gordian.

Young, Richard B., et al. Three Studies in the Renaissance: Sidney, Jonson, Milton. LC 69-15695. (Yale Studies in English Ser.: No. 138). 1969. Repr. of 1958 ed. 19.50 (ISBN 0-208-00780-6, Archon). Shoe String.

Zwager, Nicolaas. Glimpses of Ben Jonson's London. 219p. 1980. Repr. of 1926 ed. lib. bdg. 30.00 (ISBN 0-8495-6205-8). Arden Lib.

JONSON, BEN, 1573-1637–BIBLIOGRAPHY

Brock, D. Heyward & Welsh, James M. Ben Jonson: A Quadricentennial Bibliography, 1947-1972. LC 74-2424. (Author Bibliography Ser.: No. 16). 1974. 10.00 (ISBN 0-8108-0710-6). Scarecrow.

Ford, H. Collation of the Ben Jonson Folios, 1616-31-1640. LC 72-6295. (English Literature Ser., No. 33). 1972. Repr. of 1932 ed. lib. bdg. 41.95 (ISBN 0-8383-1624-7). Haskell.

Ford, H. L. Collation of the Ben Jonson Folios. LC 73-12916. Repr. of 1932 ed. lib. bdg. 15.00 (ISBN 0-8414-4152-9). Folcroft.

JONSON, BEN, 1573-1637–LANGUAGE

Drew-Bear, Annette. Rhetoric in Ben Jonson's Middle Plays: A Study of Ethos, Character Portrayal & Persuasion. (Salzburg Studies in English Literature, Jacobean Drama Studies: No.24). 1973. pap. text ed. 22.75x (ISBN 0-391-01365-3). Humanities.

Gardiner, Judith K. Craftsmanship in Context: The Development of Ben Jonson's Poetry. (Studies in English Literature Ser: No. 110). 208p. 1975. pap. text ed. 23.75x (ISBN 90-2793-191-7). Mouton.

JOPLIN, JANIS, 1943-1970

Caserta, Peggy. Going Down with Janis. 1973. 7.95 (ISBN 0-8184-0156-7). Lyle Stuart.

Caserta, Peggy & Knapp, Dan. Going Down with Janis. 272p. 1974. pap. 1.50 (ISBN 0-440-13194-4). Dell.

Dalton, David. Janis. (Illus.). 320p. 1974. pap. 1.50 (ISBN 0-445-08251-8). Popular Lib.

Freidman, Myra. Buried Alive: The Biography of Janis Joplin. (Illus.). 408p. 1974. pap. 2.95 (ISBN 0-553-14167-8). Bantam.

Friedman, Myra. Buried Alive: The Biography of Janis Joplin. (Illus.). 1973. pap. 4.50 (ISBN 0-688-05160-X). Morrow.

JORDAN, JIM

Johnson, F. Roy. Fabled Doctor Jim Jordan. 1968. 4.95 (ISBN 0-930230-08-6). Johnson NC.

JORDAN, MRS. DOROTHY (BLAND), 1761-1816

Jerrold, Clare A. Story of Dorothy Jordan. LC 70-82555. (Illus.). 1914. 18.00 (ISBN 0-405-08672-5, Blom Pubns). Arno.

JORDAN

Antoun, Richard T. Arab Village: A Social Structural Study of a Transjordanian Peasant Community. LC 70-633555. (Social Science Ser.: No. 29). (Illus.). 210p. 1972. pap. 15.00x (ISBN 0-253-38450-8). Ind U Pr.

Copeland, Paul W. The Land & People of Jordan. rev. ed. LC 72-5362. (Portraits of the Nation Ser.). (Illus.). (gr. 6 up). 1972. 8.95 (ISBN 0-397-31403-5, JBL-J). Har-Row.

Harris, George L., et al. Jordan. LC 58-12701. (Survey of World Cultures Ser). x, 246p. (YA) (gr. 10 up). 1958. 15.00x (ISBN 0-87536-903-0). HRAFP.

International Bank for Reconstruction & Development. Economic Development of Jordan. LC 77-86376. Repr. of 1957 ed. 57.50 (ISBN 0-404-60304-1). AMS Pr.

Kanovsky, Eliyahu. The Economic Development of Jordan. 159p. 1977. pap. 4.95 (ISBN 0-87855-651-6). Transaction Bks.

Lustick, Ian. Israel & Jordan: The Implications of an Adversarial Partnership. LC 78-620041. (Policy Papers in International Affairs Ser.: No. 6). (Illus.). 1978. pap. 2.00x (ISBN 0-87725-506-7). U of Cal Intl St.

Mazur, Michael P. Economic Growth & Development in Jordan. (Special Studies on the Middle East). 1979. lib. bdg. 30.75x (ISBN 0-89158-455-2). Westview.

Poole, Frederick K. Jordan. rev. ed. O'Brien, Linda, ed. (First Bks). (Illus.). (gr. 4-6). 1978. PLB 7.40 s&l (ISBN 0-531-02241-2). Watts.

Shair Management Services, ed. Business Laws and Practices of Jordan. 102p. 1979. 275.00x (ISBN 0-86010-906-2, Pub by Graham & Trotman England). State Mutual Bk.

Sinai, Anne & Pollack, Allen, eds. The Hashemite Kingdom of Jordan & the West Bank. 1977. pap. text ed. 6.95 (ISBN 0-917158-01-6). AAAPME.

JORDAN–ANTIQUITIES

De Hass, Frank S. Buried Cities Recovered: Explorations in Bible Lands. Davis, Moshe, ed. LC 77-70774. (America & the Holy Land). (Illus.). 1977. lib. bdg. 30.00x (ISBN 0-405-10242-9). Arno.

Glueck, Nelson. Deities & Dolphins: The Story of the Nabataeans. (Illus.). 650p. 1965. 15.00 (ISBN 0-374-13668-8). FS&G.

Pritchard, James B. The Bronze Age Cemetery at Gibeon. (Museum Monographs). (Illus.). 123p. 1963. soft bound 3.50 (ISBN 0-934718-17-2). Univ Mus of U PA.

--Hebrew Inscriptions & Stamps from Gibeon. (Museum Monograph). 32p. 1959. 2.00 (ISBN 0-934718-10-5). Univ Mus of U PA.

--The Water System at Gibeon. (Museum Monograph). viii, 34p. 1961. 5.00 (ISBN 0-934718-14-8). Univ Mus of U PA.

--Winery, Defenses, & Soundings at Gibeon. (Museum Monographs). (Illus.). 85p. 1964. soft bound 3.50 (ISBN 0-934718-18-0). Univ Mus of U PA.

JORDAN–DESCRIPTION AND TRAVEL

Nelson, Bryan. Azraq: Desert Oasis. LC 73-92910. (Illus.). xix, 436p. 1973. 16.00x (ISBN 0-8214-0142-4). Ohio U Pr.

JORDAN–HISTORY

Jordan. (Illus.). 1979. 24.95 (ISBN 0-09-133470-5, Pub. by Hutchinson). Merrimack Bk Serv.

Kirkbride, Alec. From the Wings: Amman Memoirs, 1947-1951. 194p. 1976. 25.00x (ISBN 0-7146-3061-6, F Cass Co). Biblio Dist.

Plascov, Avi. The Palestinian Refugees in Jordan 1948-57. 286p. 1981. 45.00x (ISBN 0-7146-3120-5, F Cass Co). Biblio Dist.

Vatikiotis, P. J. Politics & the Military in Jordon: Study of the Arab Legion, 1921-1957. (Illus.). 169p. 1967. 25.00x (ISBN 0-7146-1061-5, F Cass Co). Biblio Dist.

JORDAN–POLITICS AND GOVERNMENT

Antoun, Richard. Low-Key Politics: A Case Study of Local Level Leadership & Change in the Middle East. LC 77-19018. (Illus.). 1979. 29.00 (ISBN 0-87395-373-8). State U NY Pr.

Aresvik, Oddvar. The Agricultural Development of Jordan. LC 75-8399. 1976. 41.95 (ISBN 0-275-00450-3). Praeger.

Faddah, Mohammad I. The Middle East in Transition: A Study of Jordan's Foreign Policy. 1974. 13.95x (ISBN 0-210-22387-1). Asia.

Gubser, Peter. Politics & Change in Al-Karak, Jordan: A Study of a Small Arab Town & Its District. (Middle Eastern Monographs: No. 11). (Illus.). 204p. 1973. 14.50x (ISBN 0-19-215805-8). Oxford U Pr.

Kanovsky, Eliahu. The Economy of Jordan. LC 77-372125. 1979. pap. 9.00x (ISBN 0-686-26883-0, Pub. by Turtledove Pub Ltd Israel). Intl Schol Bk Serv.

Mishal, Shaul. West Bank-East Bank: The Palestinians in Jordan, 1949-1967. LC 77-20692. (Illus.). 1978. 11.00x (ISBN 0-300-02191-7). Yale U Pr.

Schwarz, Philip J. The Jarring Interests. LC 78-3577. (Illus.). 1979. 40.00 (ISBN 0-87395-377-0). State U NY Pr.

JORDAN ALGEBRAS

Faulkner, John R. Octonion Planes Defined by Quadratic Jordan Algebras. LC 52-42839. (Memoirs: No. 104). 1970. pap. text ed. 6.40 (ISBN 0-8218-1804-X, MEMO-104). Am Math.

Jacobson, Nathan. Structure & Representations of Jordan Algebras. LC 67-21813. (Colloquium Pbns. Ser.: Vol. 39). 1968. 33.20 (ISBN 0-8218-1039-1, COLL-39). Am Math.

Racine, Michel L. The Arithmetics of Quadratic Jordan Algebras. LC 73-17270. (Memoirs: No. 136). 1973. pap. 8.40 (ISBN 0-8218-1836-8, MEMO-136). Am Math.

Springer, T. A. Jordan Algebras & Algebraic Groups. LC 72-96718. (Ergebnisse der Mathematik und Ihrer Grenzgebiete: Vol. 75). vii, 169p. 1973. 28.40 (ISBN 0-387-06104-5). Springer-Verlag.

JORDAN RIVER

Sanger, Richard H. Where the Jordan Flows. LC 63-5019. (Illus.). 1963. 5.75 (ISBN 0-916808-04-1). Mid East Inst.

Weingarten, Violet. The Jordan: River of the Promised Land. LC 67-10039. (Rivers of the World Ser.). (Illus.). (gr. 4-7). PLB 3.68 (ISBN 0-8116-6368-X). Garrard.

JORN, ASGER OLUF, 1914-

Atkins, Guy. Jorn, Vol. III. (Asger Jorn Complete Work Ser.). 250p. 1980. write for info. (ISBN 0-8150-0927-5). Wittenborn.

JOS, NIGERIA

Plotnicov, Leonard. Strangers to the City: Urban Man in Jos, Nigeria. LC 67-13928. (Illus.). 1967. pap. 4.95x (ISBN 0-8229-5135-5). U of Pittsburgh Pr.

JOSCELIN 1ST, COUNT OF EDESSA, d. 1131

Nicholson, Robert L. Joscelyn I, Prince of Edessa. LC 78-63352. (The Crusades & Military Orders: Second Ser.). Repr. of 1954 ed. 15.50 (ISBN 0-404-17025-0). AMS Pr.

JOSEPH, CHIEF OF THE NEZ PERCES, 1840-1904

Beal, Merrill D. I Will Fight No More Forever: Chief Joseph & the Nez Perce War. LC 62-13278. (Illus.). 384p. 1963. pap. 6.95 (ISBN 0-295-74009-4). U of Wash Pr.

Chief Joseph's Own Story. facsimile ed. 41p. Repr. of 1879 ed. pap. 4.50 (ISBN 0-8466-4004-X, SJ14). Shorey.

Gidley, M. Kopet: A Documentary Narrative of Chief Joseph's Last Years. LC 80-54428. (Illus.). 168p. 1981. 16.95 (ISBN 0-295-95794-8). U of Wash Pr.

Grant, Matthew G. Chief Joseph. LC 73-9816. 1974. PLB 5.95 (ISBN 0-87191-251-1). Creative Ed.

Haines, Francis. Red Eagles of the Northwest: The Story of Chief Joseph & His People. LC 76-43728. (Illus.). Repr. of 1939 ed. 32.50 (ISBN 0-404-15569-3). AMS Pr.

Howard, Helen Addison. Saga of Chief Joseph. LC 78-16138. (Illus.). 399p. 1978. pap. 5.95 (ISBN 0-8032-7202-2, BB#699, Bison). U of Nebr Pr.

Howard, Oliver O. Nez Perce Joseph. LC 70-39379. (Law, Politics, & History Ser). (Illus.). 274p. 1972. Repr. of 1881 ed. lib. bdg. 37.50 (ISBN 0-306-70461-7). Da Capo.

Jassem, Kate. Chief Joseph, Leader of Destiny. new ed. LC 78-18048. (Illus.). 48p. (gr. 4-6). 1979. PLB 5.89 (ISBN 0-89375-155-3); pap. 1.75 (ISBN 0-89375-145-6). Troll Assocs.

Johnson, R. P. Chief Joseph. LC 74-11467. (Story of an American Indian Ser.). (Illus.). (gr. 5 up). 1974. PLB 6.95 (ISBN 0-87518-062-0). Dillon.

Montgomery, Elizabeth R. Chief Joseph: Guardian of His People. LC 69-12424. (Indians Books Ser.). (Illus.). (gr. 2-5). 1969. PLB 6.09 (ISBN 0-8116-6606-9). Garrard.

Pollock, Dean. Joseph, Chief of the Nez Perce. (Illus.). (gr. 5 up). 1950. 5.95 (ISBN 0-8323-0172-8). Binford.

Wood, Erskine. Days with Chief Joseph: Diary, Recollections & Photos. rev. ed. (Illus.). 42p. 1970. pap. 2.95 (ISBN 0-87595-026-4). Oreg Hist Soc.

JOSEPH 1ST, EMPEROR OF GERMANY, 1678-1711

Ingrao, Charles W. In Quest & Crisis: Emperor Joseph I & the Habsburg Monarchy, LC 77-88358. (Illus.). 1979. 12.95 (ISBN 0-911198-53-9). Purdue.

JOSEPH 2ND, EMPEROR OF GERMANY, 1741-1790

Bernard, Paul P. The Limits of Enlightenment: Joseph II & the Law. LC 79-12030. 1979. 13.50 (ISBN 0-252-00735-2). U of Ill Pr.

Bright, J. Franck. Joseph, Second. LC 78-112795. 1970. Repr. of 1897 ed. 10.50 (ISBN 0-8046-1062-2). Kennikat.

Clayton, Anthony & Savage, Donald C. Government & Labour in Kenya, 1895-1963. 480p. 1974. 35.00x (ISBN 0-7146-3025-X, F Cass Co). Biblio Dist.

Gooch, G. P. Maria Theresa & Other Studies. 1965. Repr. of 1951 ed. 19.50 (ISBN 0-208-00019-4, Archon). Shoe String.

Padover, Saul K. Revolutionary Emperor: Joseph Second of Austria. rev ed. (Illus.). 1967. 19.50 (ISBN 0-208-00236-7, Archon). Shoe String.

Temperly, H. W. Frederick the Great & Kaiser Joseph. 2nd ed. (Illus.). 274p. 1968. 24.00x (ISBN 0-7146-1518-8, F Cass Co). Biblio Dist.

JOSEPH, SAINT

Filas, Francis L. Man Nearest to Christ, St. Joseph. 1947. 10.25 (ISBN 0-234-77036-8). Dufour.

Filas, Joseph. Joseph: The Man Closest to Jesus. 1962. 7.75 (ISBN 0-8198-0070-8). Dghtrs St Paul.

Levy, Rosalie M. Joseph, the Just Man. 4.00 (ISBN 0-8198-3901-9); pap. 3.00 (ISBN 0-8198-3902-7). Dghtrs St Paul.

Life & Glories of St. Joseph. LC 80-53744. 1980. pap. write for info. (ISBN 0-89555-161-6). Tan Bks Pubs.

Lovasik, Lawrence G. Good St. Joseph. (Saint Joseph Picture Bks.). (Illus.). flexible bdg. 0.95 (ISBN 0-686-14272-1, 283). Catholic Bk Pub.

Meyer, F. B. Joseph. 1975. pap. 1.75 (ISBN 0-87508-356-0). Chr Lit.

Nicklesburg, George, ed. Studies on the Testament of Joseph. LC 75-26923. (Society of Biblical Literature. Septurgint & Cognate Studies). 153p. 1975. pap. 7.50 (ISBN 0-89130-027-9, 060405). Scholars Pr Ca.

The Story of Joseph. 79p. pap. 0.50 (ISBN 0-686-29167-0). Faith Pub Hse.

JOSEPH, THE PATRIARCH

Butler, John G. Joseph: Tried, True & Triumphant. 1977. pap. 0.95 (ISBN 0-87227-028-9); tchr's guide 3.95 (ISBN 0-87227-029-7). Reg Baptist.

Flynn, Leslie. Joseph: God's Man in Egypt. 1979. pap. 3.50 (ISBN 0-88207-788-0). Victor Bks.

Joseph. 1979. 0.75 (ISBN 0-8198-0583-1). Dghtrs St Paul.

Lindsay, Gordon. Jacob & His Son, Joseph. (Old Testament Ser.). 1.25 (ISBN 0-89985-129-0). Christ Nations.

--Joseph & His Brethren. (Old Testament Ser.). 1.25 (ISBN 0-89985-130-4). Christ Nations.

JOSEPH, THE PATRIARCH–FICTION

Mann, Thomas. Joseph & His Brothers. (YA) 1948. 17.95 (ISBN 0-394-43132-4). Knopf.

JOSEPH, THE PATRIARCH–JUVENILE LITERATURE

Barrett, Ethel. Joseph. LC 79-65232. (Great Heroes of the Bible Ser.). (gr. 3-9). 1979. pap. 1.95 (ISBN 0-8307-0715-8, 5607701). Regal.

Bergey, Alyce & Wind, Betty. Boy Who Saved His Family. (Arch Bks: Set 3). 1966. laminated cover 0.79 (ISBN 0-570-06017-6, 59-1126). Concordia.

Diamond, Lucy. Story of Joseph. (Ladybird Ser). (Illus.). 1954. bds. 1.49 (ISBN 0-87508-868-6). Chr Lit.

Maniscalco, Joe. Joseph. LC 74-28725. (Bible Hero Stories). (Illus.). 48p. (Orig.). (gr. 3-6). 1975. pap. 2.00 (ISBN 0-87239-332-1, 2737). Standard Pub.

Shimoni, S. Legends of Joseph & His Brothers. (Biblical Ser.). (Illus.). (gr. 1-5). 1975. 5.00 (ISBN 0-914080-11-3). Shulsinger Sales.

Summers, Jester. Joseph: the Forgiver. (Illus.). (gr. 1-6). 1976. bds. 5.50 (ISBN 0-8054-4224-3). Broadman.

JOSEPH NASI, DUKE OF NAXOS, d. 1579

Roth, Cecil. House of Nasi: The Duke of Naxos. Repr. of 1948 ed. lib. bdg. 14.75x (ISBN 0-8371-2387-9, ROHN). Greenwood.

JOSEPH OF ARIMATHEA

Lewis, Lionel S. St. Joseph of Arimathea at Glastonbury. (Illus.). 1964. Repr. of 1955 ed. 8.75 (ISBN 0-227-67600-9). Attic Pr.

JOSEPH OF ARIMATHEA–LEGENDS

Carter, Henry H. The Portuguese Book of Joseph of Arimathea. (Studies in the Romance Languages & Literatures: No. 71). 1968. pap. 19.00x (ISBN 0-8078-9071-5). U of NC Pr.

JOSEPHINE, CONSORT OF NAPOLEON 1ST, 1763-1814

Cole, Hubert. Josephine. 1979. pap. 1.95 (ISBN 0-505-51351-X). Tower Bks.

Epton, Nina. Josephine: The Empress & Her Children. (Illus.). 256p. 1976. 10.95 (ISBN 0-393-07500-1). Norton.

Wilson, R. McNair. Josephine: Portrait of a Woman. 69.95 (ISBN 0-8490-0464-0). Gordon Pr.

JOSEPHUS FLAVIUS

Farmer, William R. Maccabees, Zealots & Josephus. LC 73-15052. 239p. 1974. Repr. of 1956 ed. lib. bdg. 20.25x (ISBN 0-8371-7152-0, FAMA). Greenwood.

Feuchtwanger, Lion. Josephus: A Historical Romance. LC 32-28823. (Temple Bks). 1972. pap. 4.95 (ISBN 0-689-70345-7, T25). Atheneum.

Jackson, F. J. Josephus & the Jews: Religion & History of the Jews Explained by Flavius Josephus. (Twin Brooks Ser.). 320p. 1976. pap. 4.95 (ISBN 0-8010-5069-3). Baker Bk.

Josephus, Flavius. Complete Works of Josephus, 4 vols. 35.00 set (ISBN 0-8010-5056-1). Baker Bk.

Rhoads, David M. Israel in Revolution, 6-74 C.E. A Political History Based on the Writings of Josephus. LC 75-36452. 208p. 1976. 9.95 (ISBN 0-8006-0442-3, 1-442); pap. 5.95 (ISBN 0-8006-1442-9, 1-1442). Fortress.

Thackery, Henry. Josephus: The Man & the Historian. rev. ed. LC 67-18816. 1968. 15.00x (ISBN 0-87068-115-X). Ktav.

Ulrich, Eugene C., Jr. The Qumran Text of Samuel & Josephus. LC 78-15254. (Harvard Semitic Museum. Harvard Semitic Monographs: No. 19). 1978. 10.50 (ISBN 0-89130-256-5, 040019). Scholars Pr Ca.

Whiston, William. The Complete Works of Josephus, 4 vols. 1974. lib. bdg. 35.00 (ISBN 0-8054-7601-6). Broadman.

JOSHUA, SON OF NUN

Auld, A. Graeme. Joshua, Moses & the Land: Tretrateuch-Pentateuch-Hexateuch in a Generation Since 1938. 156p. 1980. Repr. text ed. 20.00x (ISBN 0-567-09306-9). Attic Pr.

Jordan, Bernice C. Fighting Giants: Joshua-Solomon 14 Lessons, Vol. 3. (Footsteps of Faith Ser.). (gr. 3-9). 1957. pap. text ed. 2.50 (ISBN 0-86508-031-3); figures text 11.45 (ISBN 0-86508-032-1). BCM Inc.

Lindsay, Gordon. Joshua, Conqueror of Canaan. (Old Testament Ser.). 1.25 (ISBN 0-89985-134-7). Christ Nations.

Meyer, F. B. Joshua. 1977. pap. 2.95 (ISBN 0-87508-357-9). Chr Lit.

Schaeffer, Francis A. Joshua & the Flow of Biblical History. LC 74-31847. 216p. 1975. pap. text ed. 3.95 (ISBN 0-87784-773-8); 1.50 (ISBN 0-87784-414-3). Inter-Varsity.

Totten, C. A. Joshua's Long Day. 1968. 1.50 (ISBN 0-685-08808-1). Destiny.

JOSHUA, SON OF NUN–JUVENILE LITERATURE

Barrett, Ethel. Joshua. LC 79-65233. (Great Heroes of the Bible Ser.). (gr. 3-9). 1979. pap. 1.95 (ISBN 0-8307-0707-7, 5607000). Regal.

Hill, Dave. Walls Came Tumbling Down. (Arch Bks: Set 4). 1967. laminated bdg 0.79 (ISBN 0-570-06024-9, 59-1135). Concordia.

Shimoni, S. Legends of Joshua. (Biblical Ser.). (Illus.). (gr. 1-5). 1975. 5.00 (ISBN 0-914080-12-1). Shulsinger Sales.

JOSHUA TREE NATIONAL MONUMENT

Mitchell, Roger. Exploring Joshua Tree. rev. ed. (Illus.). 48p. 1974. wrappers 1.95 (ISBN 0-910856-12-5). La Siesta.

JOULE, JAMES PRESCOTT, 1818-1879

Boning, Richard A. Joshua James. (The Incredible Ser.). (Illus.). 48p. (gr. 5-11). 1972. PLB 5.95 (ISBN 0-87966-104-6, Pub. by Dexter & Westbrook). B Loft.

Steffens, H. J. James Prescott Joule & the Concept of Energy. LC 78-31350. 1979. 20.00 (ISBN 0-88202-170-2). N Watson.

Thomson, Thomas. The Scientific Papers of James Prescott Joule, 2 vols. LC 72-170349. 1884-87. Repr. Set. 49.00 (ISBN 0-403-01486-7). Scholarly.

JOURNALISM

see also College and School Journalism; Copy-Reading; Crime and the Press; Editing; Editorials; Foreign News; Government and the Press; Interviewing (Journalism); Journalism, Agricultural; Journalism, Commercial; Journalism, Medical; Journalism, Pictorial; Journalism, Prison; Journalism, Religious; Journalism, Scientific; Journalistic Ethics; Liberty of the Press; Musical Criticism; News-Letters; Newspaper Court Reporting; Newspaper Layout and Typography; Newspaper Publishing; Newspapers; Periodicals; Press; Radio Journalism; Reporters and Reporting; Science News; Sports Journalism; Television Broadcasting of News

Alexander, James P. Programmed Journalism Writing. 1979. pap. text ed. 7.95x (ISBN 0-8138-1020-5). Iowa St U Pr.

Auletta, Ken. Hard Feelings: Reporting on Pols, the Press, People & New York. 1980. 12.95 (ISBN 0-394-50020-2). Random.

Bagdikian, Ben. Bagdikian on Political Reporting: Newspaper Economics, Law & Ethics. 1977. pap. 2.00 (ISBN 0-912646-24-1). Tex Christian.

Baskette, Floyd K. & Sissors, Jack Z. Art of Editing. 2nd ed. 1977. text ed. 18.95x (ISBN 0-02-306270-3, 30627). Macmillan.

Bernstein, Theodore M. Watch Your Language. LC 58-12309. 1965. pap. 4.95 (ISBN 0-689-70531-X, 220). Atheneum.

Berry, Thomas E. Journalism in America: An Introduction to the News Media. (Communication Arts Bks.). 1976. 16.50 (ISBN 0-8038-3712-7); pap. text ed. 8.50x (ISBN 0-8038-3713-5). Hastings.

Bleyer, Willard G. How to Write Special Feature Articles. 1977. Repr. of 1919 ed. lib. bdg. 10.00 (ISBN 0-686-19810-7). Havertown Bks.

--Newspaper Writing & Editing. LC 76-144885. 412p. 1923. Repr. 28.00 (ISBN 0-403-00871-9). Scholarly.

Bowers, David & Plasterer, Nicholas N. On the News Desk: Practical Exercises in Copy Editing. LC 72-94148. 1973. pap. text ed. 7.95x (ISBN 0-8071-0219-9). La State U Pr.

Britt, George, ed. Shoeleather & Printers' Ink. LC 73-90167. 288p. 1974. 9.95 (ISBN 0-8129-0417-6). Times Bks.

Brooks, Brian S., et al. News Reporting & Writing. 542p. (Orig.). 1980. text ed. 16.95x (ISBN 0-312-57201-8); pap. text ed. 10.95x (ISBN 0-312-57202-6); write for info. instructor's manual. St Martin.

Brooks, Charles, ed. Best Editorial Cartoons of the Year: 1979 Edition. (Best Editorial Cartoon Ser.). (Illus.). 1979. 11.95 (ISBN 0-88289-229-0). Pelican.

Brown, Charles H. News Editing & Display. LC 74-109285. (Illus.). 457p. Repr. of 1952 ed. lib. bdg. 21.75x (ISBN 0-8371-3828-0, BRNE). Greenwood.

Callihan, E. L. Grammar for Journalists. 3rd ed. LC 78-22114. 1979. pap. 7.95 (ISBN 0-8019-6823-2). Chilton.

Callihan, E. L., et al. Exercises & Tests for Journalists. 3rd ed. LC 78-22116. 1979. pap. 3.95 (ISBN 0-8019-6824-0, 6824). Chilton.

Canadian Press Association. A History of Canadian Journalism in the Several Portions of the Dominion. LC 75-41047. Repr. of 1908 ed. 24.50 (ISBN 0-404-14745-3). AMS Pr.

Cirino, Robert. Don't Blame the People: How the News Media Uses Bias, Distortion, & Censorship to Manipulate Public Opinion. 1972. pap. 3.95 (ISBN 0-394-71788-0, V788, Vin). Random.

Clark, Ray P., ed. Best Newspaper Writing 1981: Winners of the American Society of Newspaper Editors, Competition. LC 80-646604. (Illus.). 192p. 1981. pap. 5.95 (ISBN 0-935742-03-4). Mod Media Inst.

Clark, Wesley C., ed. Journalism Tomorrow. LC 58-13727. 1958. 8.95x (ISBN 0-8156-0013-5). Syracuse U Pr.

Coblentz, Edmond E., ed. Newsmen Speak: Journalists on Their Craft. facs. ed. LC 68-14900. (Essay Index Reprint Ser). 1954. 15.00 (ISBN 0-8369-0318-8). Arno.

Crawford, Nelson A. The Ethics of Journalism. (American Studies). 1969. Repr. of 1924 ed. 19.50 (ISBN 0-384-10130-5). Johnson Repr.

Crawford, Robert P. The Magazine Article. 1977. Repr. of 1931 ed. lib. bdg. 12.50 (ISBN 0-686-19816-6). Havertown Bks.

Crump, Spencer. Fundamentals of Journalism. (Illus.). 224p. 1974. text ed. 11.95 (ISBN 0-07-014835-X, G). McGraw.

Dana, Charles A. Art of Newspaper Making. LC 71-125689. (American Journalists Ser). 1970. Repr. of 1900 ed. 9.00 (ISBN 0-405-01666-2). Arno.

Darrow, Ralph C. House Journal Editing. LC 73-93505. x, 249p. 1974. pap. text ed. 5.95 (ISBN 0-8134-1628-0, 1628). Interstate.

Dary, David. How to Write News for Broadcast & Print Media. LC 72-94811. 192p. 1973. 9.95 (ISBN 0-8306-3643-9, 643). TAB Bks.

Dennis, Everette, et al. Enduring Issues in Mass Communication. (Mass Communication Ser.). (Illus.). 1978. pap. text ed. 14.95 (ISBN 0-8299-0173-6). West Pub.

Diamond, Edwin. Good News, Bad News. 1978. 14.00x (ISBN 0-262-04057-3); pap. 5.95 (ISBN 0-262-54035-5). MIT Pr.

Duffy, Thomas. Let's Write a Feature, 1969 Edition. (Lucas Text Ser). text ed. 4.00x perfect bdg. (ISBN 0-87543-056-2). Lucas.

English, Earl & Hach, Clarence. Scholastic Journalism. 6th ed. 1978. text ed. 10.50 (ISBN 0-8138-1400-6); pap. text ed. 8.50 (ISBN 0-8138-1390-5). Iowa St U Pr.

Epstein, Edward. News from Nowhere. 1973. 10.00 (ISBN 0-394-46316-1). Random.

Evans, Harold. Handling Newspaper Text. LC 73-11469. 1974. 11.95 (ISBN 0-03-012041-1). HR&W.

Fang, Irving E. Television News, Radio News. 3rd, rev. ed. LC 80-50847. Orig. Title: Television News. (Illus.). 414p. 1980. text ed. 16.95x (ISBN 0-9604212-0-3). Rada Pr.

Finley, John H. Newspaper Reference Methods. 1977. Repr. of 1933 ed. lib. bdg. 15.00 (ISBN 0-686-19824-7). Havertown Bks.

Fishman, Mark. Manufacturing the News. 189p. 1980. text ed. 11.95x (ISBN 0-292-75054-4). U of Tex Pr.

Flippen, Charles C. Liberating the Media: The New Journalism. LC 73-22086. 300p. 1974. 9.95 (ISBN 0-87491-361-6); pap. 5.95 (ISBN 0-87491-362-4). Acropolis.

Fontaine, A. The Art of Writing Nonfiction. 1974. text ed. 12.50 scp (ISBN 0-690-00175-4, HarpC). Har-Row.

Fox, Walter. Writing the News: Print Journalism in the Electronic Age. 1977. 8.95 (ISBN 0-8038-8081-2); pap. text ed. 4.50 (ISBN 0-8038-8082-0). Hastings.

Francois, William E. Beginning News Writing. LC 74-16752. (Journalism & Advertising Ser.). 1975. pap. text ed. 10.95 (ISBN 0-88244-065-9). Grid Pub.

Gans, Herbert J. Deciding What's News: A Study of CBS Evening News, NBC Nightly News, Newsweek & Time. LC 79-22849. 1980. pap. 5.95 (ISBN 0-394-74354-7, Vin). Random.

Glasgow University Media Group. Bad News, Vol. 1. 1976. 22.50x (ISBN 0-7100-8489-7). Routledge & Kegan.

Golden, Hal & Hanson, Kitty. Techniques of Working with the Working Press. LC 62-11972. 1962. 10.00 (ISBN 0-379-00056-3). Oceana.

Golding, Peter & Elliot, Philip. Making the News. LC 78-41006. (Illus.). 241p. 1980. text ed. 35.00x (ISBN 0-582-50460-0). Longman.

Graham, Betsy P. Magazine Article Writing: Substance & Style. LC 79-23249. 224p. (Orig.). 1980. pap. text ed. 10.95 (ISBN 0-03-047156-7, HoltC). HR&W.

Gramling, Oliver. The Story of News. 1977. Repr. of 1940 ed. lib. bdg. 25.00 (ISBN 0-686-19826-3). Havertown Bks.

Greene, Bob. Johnny Deadline Reporter: The Best of Bob Greene. LC 76-6932. 1976. 15.95x (ISBN 0-88229-361-3). Nelson-Hall.

Griffith, John L. & Weston, Edward G. Programed Newswriting. (Basic Skills in Journalism Ser.). (Illus.). 1978. pap. text ed. 6.95 (ISBN 0-13-730630-X). P-H.

Gunther, Max. Writing the Modern Article. 4th ed. 225p. 1981. 12.00 (ISBN 0-87116-128-1). Writer.

--Writing the Modern Magazine Article. rev. ed. 1981. write for info. (ISBN 0-87116-128-1). Writer.

Gutzkow, Karl, ed. Forum der Journal-Literatur: Eine antikritische Quartalsschrift, 2 vols. vol. 1, nos. 1-2 18.00 (ISBN 0-384-16443-9); vol. 2,nos. 1-14 10.00 (ISBN 0-685-30571-6). Johnson Repr.

Hall, Mark W. Broadcast Journalism: An Introduction to News Writing. 2nd rev. ed. 1978. 7.95 (ISBN 0-8038-0781-3); pap. text ed. 4.95x (ISBN 0-8038-0782-1). Hastings.

Hammond, George P. The Californian, Vol. 1. new ed. LC 65-27831. 208p. 1971. 30.00 (ISBN 0-685-24638-8). J Howell.

Harrington, Harry F. Writing for Print. 1977. Repr. of 1929 ed. lib. bdg. 10.00 (ISBN 0-686-19831-X). Havertown Bks.

Harriss, Julian & Johnson, Stanley. The Complete Reporter. 3rd ed. 1977. text ed. 11.95 (ISBN 0-02-350610-5, 35061). Macmillan.

Hart, Jim A. Views on the News: The Developing Editorial Syndrome, 1500-1800. LC 79-112388. (New Horizons in Journalism Ser). 251p. 1970. 8.95x (ISBN 0-8093-0455-4). S Ill U Pr.

Harwood, Dix. Getting & Writing News. 1977. Repr. of 1927 ed. lib. bdg. 12.50 (ISBN 0-686-19807-7). Havertown Bks.

Hellmann, John. Fables of Fact: The New Journalism As New Fiction. LC 80-23881. 175p. 1981. 12.95 (ISBN 0-252-00847-2). U of Ill Pr.

Herzberg, Joseph G., et al. Late City Edition. 1969. Repr. of 1947 ed. 18.50 (ISBN 0-208-00739-3, Archon). Shoe String.

Hill, Evan & Breen, John J. Reporting & Writing the News. 1977. pap. 10.95 (ISBN 0-316-36337-5); instructors manual free (ISBN 0-316-36338-3). Little.

Hinkle, Olin E. & Henry, John. How to Write Columns. Repr. of 1952 ed. lib. bdg. 20.25x (ISBN 0-8371-2295-3, HIWC). Greenwood.

Hohenberg, John. The Professional Journalist. LC 77-8573. 1978. professional ed. 17.95 (ISBN 0-03-040816-4, HoltC). HR&W.

--The Professional Journalist: A Guide to the Practices & Principles of the News Media. 4th ed. LC 77-8573. 1978. 18.95 (ISBN 0-03-018226-3, HoltC). HR&W.

Horton, Philip C., ed. The Third World & Press Freedom. LC 78-17072. (Praeger Special Studies). 1978. 25.95 (ISBN 0-03-045551-0). Praeger.

Host, David, ed. Citizen & the News. 1962. 4.95 (ISBN 0-87462-406-1). Marquette.

Hough, George A. News Writing. 2nd ed. LC 79-91631. (Illus.). 1980. text ed. 14.50 (ISBN 0-395-28636-0); inst. man. 0.75 (ISBN 0-395-28638-7). HM.

Hough, George A., 3rd. Practice Exercises in News Writing. 2nd ed. 1980. pap. text ed. 7.95 (ISBN 0-395-28637-9); instrs'. manual .75 avail. (ISBN 0-395-28638-7). HM.

Hudson, Frederic. Journalism in the U. S. from 1690-1872. 1873. 29.00 (ISBN 0-403-00080-7). Scholarly.

Hughes, Helen M. News & the Human Interest Story. Repr. of 1940 ed. lib. bdg. 15.00x (ISBN 0-8371-0487-4, HUNH). Greenwood.

--News & the Human Interest Story. 1977. Repr. of 1940 ed. lib. bdg. 12.50 (ISBN 0-686-19821-2). Havertown Bks.

Johnson, Michael L. New Journalism: The Underground Press, the Artists of Nonfiction, & Changes in the Established Media. LC 73-165055. 1971. pap. 2.95x (ISBN 0-7006-0085-X). Regents Pr KS.

Julian, James L. Practical News Assignments for Student Reporters. 5th ed. 250p. 1980. write for info. wire coil (ISBN 0-697-04336-3); instructor's manual avail. (ISBN 0-697-04337-1). Wm C Brown.

Kamath, M. V. Professional Journalism. 240p. 1980. text ed. 20.00x (ISBN 0-7069-0990-9, Pub. by Vikas India). Advent NY.

Kennedy, Bruce M. Community Journalism: A Way of Life. 200p. 1973. text ed. 9.50x (ISBN 0-8138-0505-8). Iowa St U Pr.

Kevelson, Roberta. The Inverted Pyramid: An Introduction to a Semiotics of Media Language. LC 77-79845. (Studies in Semiotics: No. 7). 1977. pap. text ed. 14.25x (ISBN 0-87750-203-X). Humanities.

Kobre, Sidney. Backgrounding the News: The Newspaper & the Social Sciences. LC 70-137063. (Illus.). 271p. 1974. Repr. of 1939 ed. lib. bdg. 23.00x (ISBN 0-8371-5526-6, KOBN). Greenwood.

--Press & Contemporary Affairs. Repr. of 1957 ed. lib. bdg. 15.00x (ISBN 0-8371-2526-X, KOPC). Greenwood.

Koenigsberg, Moses. King News. LC 73-39377. (Select Bibliographies Reprint Series). 1972. Repr. of 1941 ed. 20.00 (ISBN 0-8369-9917-7). Arno.

Koral, April. Headlines & Deadlines. LC 80-28173. (Illus.). 64p. (gr. 4-7). 1981. 7.59 (ISBN 0-671-42317-7). Messner.

Krawiec, T. S., ed. A Road Not Taken: The Editorial Opinions of Frederick C. Thorne. 1981. pap. 11.95 (ISBN 0-88422-013-3). Clinical Psych.

Landes, Burton R. A Study of the International Press & Other Media in the Shaping of Public Opinion: The Sarah Churchill Cause. Bd. with The Making of a Senator, 1974: The Biography of Richard S. Schweiker. pap. 2.50 (ISBN 0-915568-06-3). LC 75-7003. 1979. pap. 2.50 (ISBN 0-915568-05-5). B R Landes.

Lattimore, Dan L. & Windhauser, John W. The Editorial Process. 1978. pap. text ed. 8.95x (ISBN 0-89582-003-X). Morton Pub.

Lendvai, Paul. The Bureaucracy of Truth. 350p. 1981. lib. bdg. 24.75 (ISBN 0-86531-142-0). Westview.

Long, Howard R., ed. Main Street Militants: An Anthology from "Grassroots Editor". LC 78-16336. (Arcturus Books Paperbacks Ser.). 178p. 1979. pap. 5.95 (ISBN 0-8093-0894-0). S Ill U Pr.

Long, Joan & Long, Ronald. Writer's & Photographer's Guide to Newspaper Markets. 2nd ed. 175p. 1981. pap. 9.95 (ISBN 0-936940-01-8). Helm Pub.

Lopez De Zuazo Algar, Antonio. Diccionario del Periodismo. 2nd ed. 256p. (Espn.). 1978. leatherette 16.75 (ISBN 84-368-0053-2, S-50177). French & Eur.

Lown, Edward. An Introduction to Technological Changes in Journalism. LC 77-2544. 1977. pap. 10.00 (ISBN 0-8357-0256-1, SS-00031). Univ Microfilms.

MacDougall, Curtis D. Interpretive Reporting. 7th ed. (Illus.). 1977. 18.95 (ISBN 0-02-373110-9). Macmillan.

Machlup, Fritz & Leeson, Kenneth W. Information Through the Printed Word. Incl. Vol. 1. Book Publishing. 28.95 (ISBN 0-03-047401-9); Vol. 2. Journals. 30.95 (ISBN 0-03-047406-X); Vol. 3. Libraries. 25.95 (ISBN 0-03-047411-6). LC 78-19460. 1978. Praeger.

MacLeish, Archibald. Poetry & Journalism. 1973. lib. bdg. 6.50 (ISBN 0-8414-6439-1). Folcroft.

Maloney, Martin & Rubenstein, Paul M. Writing for the Media. 1980. text ed. 15.95 (ISBN 0-13-970558-9). P-H.

Marzio, Peter C. The Men & Machines of American Journalism: A Pictorial Essay. LC 73-5371. (Illus.). 144p. 1973. pap. 4.95 (ISBN 0-87474-629-9). Smithsonian.

Mayer, Andrew, et al, eds. Protect the President: Outrageous Editorials from the Ultra - Right Newspaper Publisher William Loeb. LC 79-87929. (Illus.). 1979. pap. 7.25 (ISBN 0-932400-01-9). Intervale Pub Co.

Mencher, Melvin. News Reporting & Writing. 2nd ed. 624p. 1980. pap. text ed. write for info. (ISBN 0-697-04338-X); student wkbk avail. (ISBN 0-697-04343-6); instr's. manual avail. (ISBN 0-697-04339-8). Wm C Brown.

Mencken, H. L. A Gang of Pecksniffs: And Other Comments on Newspaper Publishers, Editors & Reporters. Lippman, Theo, ed. 1975. 8.95 (ISBN 0-87000-320-8). Arlington Hse.

Merrill, John C. Existential Journalism. (Humanistic Studies in the Communication Arts). 1977. 10.50 (ISBN 0-8038-1928-5); pap. text ed. 4.95x (ISBN 0-8038-1929-3). Hastings.

Metgler, K. Newsgathering. pap. 14.50 (ISBN 0-13-621037-6). P-H.

Meyer, Phillip. Precision Journalism: A Reporter's Introduction to Social Science Methods. 2nd ed. LC 79-2172. (Midland Bks.: No. 232). 448p. 1979. 22.50x (ISBN 0-253-33405-5); pap. 6.95x (ISBN 0-253-20232-9). Ind U Pr.

Mitford, Jessica. Poison Penmanship. LC 78-20560. 1979. 10.00 (ISBN 0-394-50260-4). Knopf.

--Poison Penmanship: The Gentle Art of Muckraking. LC 79-22462. 1980. pap. 3.95 (ISBN 0-394-74269-9, Vin). Random.

Mollenhoff, Clark R. Investigative Reporting. 1980. pap. text ed. 9.95 (ISBN 0-02-381870-0). Macmillan.

Morris, Richard B. & Snyder, Louis L. Treasury of Great Reporting. 1962. pap. 5.95 (ISBN 0-671-75101-8, Fireside). S&S.

Morson, Lillian I. An English Guide for Court Reporters. 9.00 (ISBN 0-533-00947-2). Vantage.

Mott, George F. Survey of Journalism. 1977. Repr. of 1937 ed. lib. bdg. 12.50 (ISBN 0-686-19827-1). Havertown Bks.

Myers, Arthur. Analysis: The Personal Profile Magazine Article. 128p. 1976. pap. 4.95 (ISBN 0-917284-02-X). Foothills Pr.

Nelson, Roy P. Articles & Features. LC 77-85340. (Illus.). 1978. text ed. 14.95 (ISBN 0-395-25517-1). HM.

Newsmen's Privilege Legislation. (Legislative Analyses). 1973. pap. 3.75 (ISBN 0-8447-0155-6). Am Enterprise.

Nieman Reports, ed. Reading, Writing & Newspapers: A Special Issue Devoted Wholly to a Discussion of the Conditions That Affect Newspaper Writing. pap. 4.00 (ISBN 0-384-41560-1). Johnson Repr.

Patterson, Helen M. Writing & Selling Special Feature Articles. 1977. Repr. of 1945 ed. lib. bdg. 12.50 (ISBN 0-686-19830-1). Havertown Bks.

Perry, Murvin H. Newswriting Exercises. 1975. perfect bdg. 5.95 (ISBN 0-8403-1105-2). Kendall-Hunt.

Pollack, Richard, ed. Stop the Presses, I Want to Get off. 337p. 1976. pap. 3.95 (ISBN 0-440-58051-X, Delta). Dell.

Pollock, John C. The Politics of Crisis Reporting: American Journalism & Foreign Affairs. LC 78-19772. (Praeger Special Studies). 1979. 16.95 (ISBN 0-03-044336-9). Praeger.

Porchey, James H. & Carlson, Roger W. Style: A Guide to Journalism Expression. 1979. pap. text ed. 7.95 (ISBN 0-88244-184-1). Grid Pub.

Pray, Isaac C. Memoirs of James Gordon Bennett & His Times. LC 73-125712. (American Journalists). 1970. Repr. of 1855 ed. 24.00 (ISBN 0-405-01693-X). Arno.

Prejean, Blanche & Danielson, Wayne. Programed News Style. (Basic Skills in Journalism Ser.). 1978. pap. text ed. 6.95 (ISBN 0-13-730655-5). P-H.

Quinn, Hestia. Journalism for Beginners. 1979. 6.95x (ISBN 0-85091-052-8, Pub. by Lothian); pap. 3.50x (ISBN 0-85091-049-8). Intl Schol Bk Serv.

Reid, Whitelaw. American & English Studies, 2 Vols. facs. ed. LC 68-29240. (Essay Index Reprint Ser). 1968. Repr. of 1913 ed. 34.00 (ISBN 0-8369-0815-5). Arno.

Rivers, William L. The Mass Media: Reporting, Writing, Editing. 2nd ed. 644p. 1975. text ed. 20.95 scp (ISBN 0-06-045421-0, HarpC). Har-Row.

Rosenhouse, Leo. How to Write Feature Articles on Your Specialty. 20p. 1977. pap. 4.40 (ISBN 0-88409-053-1). Creative Bk Co.

Ross, Charles G. The Writing of News. 1977. Repr. of 1911 ed. lib. bdg. 15.00 (ISBN 0-686-19832-8). Havertown Bks.

Ross, Lillian. Reporting. LC 80-28929. 442p. 1981. 12.95 (ISBN 0-396-07948-2); pap. 8.95 (ISBN 0-396-07949-0). Dodd.

Seldes, George. Never Tire of Protesting. LC 68-18758. 1968. 6.95 (ISBN 0-8184-0060-9). Lyle Stuart.

Shaff, A. L. Student Journalist & the Critical Review. LC 73-92121. (Student Journalist Ser). (Illus.). (gr. 9 up). 1970. PLB 5.97 (ISBN 0-8239-0187-4). Rosen Pr.

Shuman, Edwin. Practical Journalism. 1977. Repr. of 1910 ed. lib. bdg. 10.00 (ISBN 0-686-19825-5). Havertown Bks.

Siebert, Frederick S., et al. Four Theories of the Press: The Authoritarian, Libertarian, Social Responsibility & Soviet Communist Communist Concepts of What the Press Should Be. LC 72-13275. (Essay Index Reprint Ser.). Repr. of 1956 ed. 13.50 (ISBN 0-8369-8173-1). Arno.

Siebert, Fredrick S., et al. Four Theories of the Press: The Authoritarian, Libertarian, Social Responsibility, & Soviet Communist Concepts of What the Press Should Be & Do. LC 56-11881. 1963. pap. 3.95 (ISBN 0-252-72421-6). U of Ill Pr.

Singer, Samuel L. The Student Journalist & Reviewing the Performing Arts. LC 73-80359. (Student Journalist Ser.). (Illus.). 160p. (gr. 7 up). 1974. PLB 7.97 (ISBN 0-8239-0287-0). Rosen Pr.

Smeyak, G. Paul. Broadcast News Writing. LC 76-8811. (Advertising & Journalism Ser.). 1977. pap. text ed. 9.95 (ISBN 0-88244-114-0). Grid Pub.

Smith, C. R. Management of Newspaper Correspondents. 1977. Repr. of 1944 ed. lib. bdg. 12.50 (ISBN 0-686-19818-2). Havertown Bks.

Spencer, M. Lyle. News Writing. 357p. 1980. Repr. of 1917 ed. lib. bdg. 30.00 (ISBN 0-89760-828-3). Telegraph Bks.

--News Writing: The Gathering, Handling & Writing of News Stories. 1978. Repr. of 1917 ed. lib. bdg. 20.00 (ISBN 0-8492-8043-5). R West.

Squire, Elizabeth D. Heroes of Journalism. LC 76-161377. (Heroes of Ser.). (Illus.). 128p. (gr. 9 up). 1973. 7.95 (ISBN 0-8303-0114-3). Fleet.

Steffens, Lincoln. Autobiography of Lincoln Steffens, 2 Vols. LC 67-7897. (Illus.). 1968. Vol. 1. pap. 4.50 (ISBN 0-15-609395-2, HB149, Harv); Vol. 2. pap. 6.75 (ISBN 0-15-609396-0, HB150). HarBraceJ.

Stein, M. L. Reporting Today: The Newswriter's Handbook. rev. ed. (Orig.). 1979. pap. 3.95 (ISBN 0-346-12377-1). Cornerstone.

Stevens, George E. The Student Journalist-Public Opinion Polling. LC 73-82374. 140p. (gr. 7 up). 1974. lib. bdg. 7.97 (ISBN 0-8239-0285-4). Rosen Pr.

Stokke, Olav, ed. Reporting Africa. LC 76-163923. 250p. 1971. text ed. 21.50x (ISBN 0-8419-0090-6, Africana). Holmes & Meier.

Stonecipher, Harry W., et al. Electronic Age News Editing. LC 81-536. 348p. 1981. text ed. 22.95 (ISBN 0-88229-636-1); pap. text ed. 10.95 (ISBN 0-88229-779-1). Nelson-Hall.

Tuchman, Gaye. Making News: A Study in the Construction of Reality. LC 78-53075. 1978. 12.95 (ISBN 0-02-932930-2). Free Pr.

Wall, C. Edward, et al, eds. Media Review Digest, Vol. 10, 1980. 1980. 150.00 (ISBN 0-87650-129-3). Pierian.

Washington Post Writers Group. Writing in Style. 1975. pap. text ed. 8.75 (ISBN 0-395-24018-2). HM.

Waters, Chocolate. To the Man Reporter from the Denver Post. rev. ed. 1980. 3.75 (ISBN 0-935060-05-7). Eggplant Pr.

Wicker, Tom. On Press. 1978. 10.95 (ISBN 0-670-52456-5). Viking Pr.

Williamson, Daniel R. Feature Writing for Newspapers. 1975. 13.50 (ISBN 0-8038-2312-6); pap. text ed. 6.95x (ISBN 0-8038-2313-4). Hastings.

Wingate, Charles F., ed. Views & Interviews on Journalism. LC 78-125724. (American Journalists). 1970. Repr. of 1875 ed. 18.00 (ISBN 0-405-01707-3). Arno.

Wolverton, Mike. And Now...the News. 144p. 1977. 11.95 (ISBN 0-87201-041-4). Gulf Pub.

World Communications: A Two Hundred Country Survey of Press, Radio, Television, Film. 550p. 1975. 27.50 (ISBN 0-89059-001-X). Bowker.

Wrinn, Mary J. Elements of Journalism. 1977. Repr. of 1929 ed. lib. bdg. 15.00 (ISBN 0-686-19805-0). Havertown Bks.

Writers at Work: The Paris Review Interviews. (Third Ser.). 1977. pap. 4.95 (ISBN 0-14-004542-2). Penguin.

Wulfemeyer, K. T. Beginning Broadcast Newswriting: A Self-Instructional Learning Experience. 60p. (Prog. Bk.). 1976. pap. text ed. 5.95 (ISBN 0-8138-0210-5). Iowa St U Pr.

Yates, Edward. Writing for the Mass Media. 250p. 1981. pap. text ed. 7.95 (ISBN 0-89892-042-6). Contemp Pub Co of Raleigh.

JOURNALISM–BIBLIOGRAPHY

Nafziger, Ralph O., compiled by. International News & the Press: An Annotated Bibliography. LC 72-4675. (International Propaganda & Communications Ser.). 223p. 1972. Repr. of 1940 ed. 12.00 (ISBN 0-405-04759-2). Arno.

Price, Warren C. & Pickett, Calder M. Annotated Journalism Bibliography, 1958-1968. LC 70-120810. 1970. 15.00x (ISBN 0-8166-0578-5). U of Minn Pr.

JOURNALISM–BIOGRAPHY

see Journalists

JOURNALISM–HANDBOOKS, MANUALS, ETC.

Alexander, James P. Programmed Journalism Editing. new ed. (Illus.). (gr. 10-12). 1979. pap. text ed. 8.50 (ISBN 0-8138-1040-X). Iowa St U Pr.

Arnold, Edmund C. & Krieghbaum, Hillier. Handbook of Student Journalism: A Guide for Staff & Advisors. LC 75-27047. 335p. 1976. 17.50x (ISBN 0-8147-0557-X). NYU Pr.

Associated Press. The Associated Press Stylebook. 1977. 12.95 (ISBN 0-89328-016-X). Lorenz Pr.

Baker, Bob. Newsthinking: The Secret of Great Newswriting. 206p. 1981. 11.95 (ISBN 0-89879-043-3). Writers Digest.

Berner, R. Thomas. Language Skills for Journalists. LC 78-69584. 1978. pap. text ed. 10.50 (ISBN 0-395-26789-7); inst. manual 0.65 (ISBN 0-395-26790-0). HM.

Bowman, Norman H. Publicity in Print. LC 74-30822. (Illus.). 1974. pap. 6.79x0 (ISBN 0-915716-01-1). Publicity.

Burken, Judith L. Introduction to Reporting. 2nd ed. 240p. 1979. pap. text ed. write for info. (ISBN 0-697-04332-0). Wm C Brown.

Crump, Spencer. The Stylebook for Newswriting: A Manual for Newspapers, Magazines & Radio-TV. LC 79-2440. 1980. 8.95 (ISBN 0-87046-052-8); pap. 2.95 (ISBN 0-87046-051-X). Trans-Anglo.

Evans, Harold. Pictures on a Page. LC 77-15201. (Illus.). 1978. 25.00 (ISBN 0-03-013131-6). HR&W.

Garst, Robert E. & Bernstein, Theodore M. Headlines & Deadlines: A Manual for Copy Editors. 3rd ed. LC 61-7716. 237p. 1961. 17.50x (ISBN 0-231-02450-9); pap. 5.00x (ISBN 0-231-08541-9, 41). Columbia U Pr.

Hage, et al. New Strategies for Public Affairs Reporting: Investigation, Interpretation & Research. (Illus.). 336p. 1976. 13.95 (ISBN 0-13-615831-5). P-H.

Holley, Frederick S., ed. Los Angeles Times Stylebook: A Manual for Writers, Editors, Journalists & Students. 1981. pap. 6.95 (ISBN 0-452-00552-3, F552, Mer). NAL.

Hunter, J. B. How to Win Recognition with a Personal Column. 32p. 1976. pap. 4.40 (ISBN 0-88409-036-1). Creative Bk Co.

Jordan, Lewis. The New York Times Manual of Style & Usage. LC 75-8306. 288p. 1976. 10.00 (ISBN 0-8129-0578-4). Times Bks.

Kent, Ruth. Language of Journalism: A Glossary of Print-Communications Terms. LC 71-100624. (Illus.). 1970. 8.00x (ISBN 0-87338-091-6); pap. 4.00x (ISBN 0-87338-092-4). Kent St U Pr.

Lovell, Ronald P. The Newspaper: An Introduction to Newswriting & Reporting. 1979. pap. text ed. 14.95x (ISBN 0-534-00729-5). Wadsworth Pub.

McGiffert, Robert C. The Art of Editing the News. LC 72-5537. 267p. 1972. pap. text ed. 8.95 (ISBN 0-8019-5734-6). Chilton.

Nordland, Rod. Names & Numbers: A Journalist's Guide to the Most Needed Information Sources & Contacts. LC 78-18903. 560p. 1978. 31.95 (ISBN 0-471-03994-2, Pub. by Wiley-Interscience). Wiley.

Otto, William N. & Marye, Mary E. Journalism for High Schools. 1977. Repr. of 1934 ed. lib. bdg. 10.00 (ISBN 0-686-19814-X). Havertown Bks.

Plasterer, Nicholas N. Assignment Jonesville: A News Reporting Workbook. 2nd ed. xii, 204p. 1966. pap. text ed. 6.95x (ISBN 0-8071-0037-4). La State U Pr.

Reid, Gerene. How to Write News Realeases That Sell. LC 79-66675. (Illus.). 80p. 1980. 7.95x (ISBN 0-931882-09-5). D W Carrey.

Ross, Donald K. Newspaper Correspondent's Manual. 1962. pap. 1.95 (ISBN 0-87462-425-8). Marquette.

Ruehlmann, William. Stalking the Feature Story. 310p. 1978. 9.95 (ISBN 0-911654-51-8). Writers Digest.

Webb, Robert A., ed. The Washington Post Deskbook on Style. 1978. 8.95 (ISBN 0-07-068397-2, GB); pap. 4.95 (ISBN 0-07-068398-0). McGraw.

Williams, W. P. & Van Zandt, Joseph H. How to Write Magazine Articles That Sell. 1979. pap. 3.95 (ISBN 0-8092-7381-0). Contemp Bks.

Wimer, Arthur & Brix, Dale. Workbook for Head Writing & News Editing. 4th ed. 230p. 1978. write for info. wire coil (ISBN 0-697-04328-2). Wm C Brown.

JOURNALISM–HISTORY

Baker, Thomas H. Memphis Commercial Appeal: The History of a Southern Newspaper. LC 74-165066. 1971. 22.50 (ISBN 0-8071-0944-4). La State U Pr.

Barnum, Phineas T. Struggles & Triumphs. LC 77-125677. (American Journalists Ser). 1970. Repr. of 1869 ed. 36.00 (ISBN 0-405-01651-4). Arno.

Bond, Donovan H. & McLeod, W. Reynolds, eds. Newsletters to Newspapers: Eighteenth-Century Journalism. LC 77-81948. 1977. pap. 10.00 (ISBN 0-930362-00-4). West Va U Pr.

Brier, Warren J. & Blumberg, Nathan B., eds. A Century of Montana Journalism. LC 78-169031. 352p. 1971. 10.00 (ISBN 0-87842-023-1). Mountain Pr.

Cappon, Lester J. & Duff, Stella F. Virginia Gazette Index, 2 vols. LC 51-15336. 1314p. 1950. lib. bdg. 65.00 (ISBN 0-910776-00-8). Inst Early Am.

Chalmers, David M. The Muckrake Years. LC 79-22780. 176p. 1980. Repr. of 1974 ed. lib. bdg. 4.95 (ISBN 0-89874-066-5). Krieger.

Cornebise, Alfred. The Amaroc News: The Daily Newspaper of the American Forces in Germany, 1919-1923. LC 80-27275. (New Horizons in Journalism Ser.). 288p. 1981. 24.95 (ISBN 0-8093-1001-5). S Ill U Pr.

Crozier, Emmet. American Reporters on the Western Front, 1914 to 1918. LC 80-19400. (Illus.). xii, 299p. 1980. Repr. of 1959 ed. lib. bdg. 25.75x (ISBN 0-313-22655-5, CRAR). Greenwood.

Desmond, Robert. Windows on the World: World News Reporting Nineteen Hundred to Nineteen Twenty. LC 80-19397. 626p. 1981. text ed. 28.50x (ISBN 0-87745-104-4). U of Iowa Pr.

Diprima, Richard. Headline History of the Sixties. LC 80-71081. 73p. (Orig.). (gr. 6-12). pap. text ed. write for info. (ISBN 0-86652-011-2). Educ Indus.

Dreiser, Theodore. Newspaper Days. (Amer. Newspapermen Ser.: 1790-1933). 502p. 1974. Repr. of 1931 ed. 21.50x (ISBN 0-8464-0023-5). Beekman Pubs.

Emery, Edwin & Emery, Michael. The Press & America. 4th ed. (Illus.). 1978. ref. 19.95 (ISBN 0-13-697979-3). P-H.

Halaas, David F. Boom Town Newspapers: Journalism on the Rocky Mountain Mining Frontier, 1859-1881. (Illus.). 192p. 1981. 14.95 (ISBN 0-8263-0588-1). U of NM Pr.

Hammond, Otis G. Notices from the New Hampshire Gazette 1765-1800. 1970. lib. bdg. 10.00 (ISBN 0-912606-01-0). Hunterdon Hse.

Hart, Jim A. Views on the News: The Developing Editorial Syndrome, 1500-1800. LC 79-112388. (New Horizons in Journalism Ser). 251p. 1970. 8.95x (ISBN 0-8093-0455-4). S Ill U Pr.

Hohenberg, John. The Pulitzer Prize Story II: Award-Winning News Stories, Columns, Editorials, Cartoons, & News Pictures, 1959-1980. (Illus.). 472p. 1980. 17.95 (ISBN 0-231-04978-1). Columbia U Pr.

Jackson, D. K. The Contributors & Contributions to the Southern Literary Messenger 1834-1864. 59.95 (ISBN 0-87968-941-2). Gordon Pr.

Kowalik, Jan. The Polish Press in America. LC 77-90363. 1978. soft cover 8.00 (ISBN 0-88247-498-7). R & E Res Assoc.

Lepidus, Henry. The History of Mexican Journalism. 1976. 59.95 (ISBN 0-8490-1978-8). Gordon Pr.

Luxon, Norval N. Niles' Weekly Register, News Magazine of the Nineteenth Century. LC 72-90550. (Illus.). viii, 337p. Repr. of 1947 ed. lib. bdg. 14.25x (ISBN 0-8371-3045-X, LUNR). Greenwood.

Miller, Orlo. A Century of Western Ontario: The Story of London, the Free Press, & Western Ontario, 1849-1949. LC 71-165443. (Illus.). 289p. 1972. Repr. of 1949 ed. lib. bdg. 15.75x (ISBN 0-8371-6226-2, MIWO). Greenwood.

Payne, George H. History of Journalism in the United States. Repr. of 1920 ed. lib. bdg. 17.25x (ISBN 0-8371-2817-X, PAJU). Greenwood.

Pickett, Calder M. Voices of the Past: Key Documents in the History of American Journalism. LC 76-19674. (Advertising & Journalism). 1977. pap. text ed. 12.95 (ISBN 0-88244-127-2). Grid Pub.

Schroth, Raymond A. The Eagle & Brooklyn: A Community Newspaper, 1841-1955. LC 73-20972. (Contributions in American Studies: No. 13). 304p. 1974. lib. bdg. 15.95 (ISBN 0-8371-7335-3, SBE/). Greenwood.

Smith, Anthony. The Newspaper: An International History. 1979. 14.95 (ISBN 0-500-01204-0). Thames Hudson.

Stansbury, Arthur Joseph. Report of the Trial of James H. Peck. LC 70-38789. (Law, Politics & History Ser). 592p. 1972. Repr. of 1833 ed. lib. bdg. 59.50 (ISBN 0-306-70443-9). Da Capo.

Wallraff, Gunter. The Undesirable Journalist. LC 78-70935. 192p. 1979. 10.00 (ISBN 0-87951-095-1). Overlook Pr.

Whyte, Frederic. The Life of W. T. Stead, 2 vols. 1978. Repr. of 1925 ed. lib. bdg. 65.00 (ISBN 0-8495-5637-6). Arden Lib.

JOURNALISM–JUVENILE LITERATURE

Boy Scouts Of America. Journalism. LC 19-600. (Illus.). 40p. (gr. 6-12). 1976. pap. 0.70x (ISBN 0-8395-3350-0, 3350). BSA.

Farnette, Cherrie. Newspaper Know-How. (Choose-a-Card Ser.). (Illus.). 32p. (gr. 2-6). 1981. pap. text ed. 5.95 (ISBN 0-86530-011-9, IP-119). Incentive Pubns.

Jaspersohn, William. A Day in the Life of a Television News Reporter. (Illus.). 96p. (gr. 5 up). 1981. 9.95 (ISBN 0-316-45813-9). Little.

Lerner, Mark. Careers with a Newspaper. LC 77-72422. (Early Career Bks.). (Illus.). (gr. 2-5). 1977. PLB 4.95 (ISBN 0-8225-0330-1). Lerner Pubns.

Pritchett, Elaine. Student Journalist & the Newsmagazine Format. LC 75-35664. (gr. 7 up). 1976. PLB 7.97 (ISBN 0-8239-0340-0). Rosen Pr.

Reddick, Bryan. Student Journalist & Effective Writing Style. LC 75-44487. (gr. 7 up). 1976. PLB 7.97 (ISBN 0-8239-0352-4). Rosen Pr.

Reque, John. The Student Journalist & Staff Management. (gr. 7-12). 1979. PLB 7.97 (ISBN 0-8239-0442-3). Rosen Pr.

Solomon, Louis. America Goes to Press: The Story of American Newspapers from Colonial Times to the Present. LC 77-103681. (Illus.). (gr. 7-12). 1970. 8.95 (ISBN 0-685-03410-0, CCPr). Macmillan.

Ward, Bill. The Student Journalist As Editor. 160p. (gr. 7-12). 1977. PLB 7.97 (ISBN 0-8239-0373-7). Rosen Pr.

--The Student Journalist: Photographing Sports. (gr. 7-12). 1981. PLB 12.50 (ISBN 0-8239-0413-X). Rosen Pr.

--The Student Journalist: Writing Wit & Humor. (gr. 7-12). Date not set. PLB 7.97 (ISBN 0-8239-0441-5). Rosen Pr.
--The Student Journalist: Writing Wit & Humor. (gr. 7-12). Date not set. PLB 7.97 (ISBN 0-8239-0441-5). Rosen Pr.
Ward, Bill G. Student Journalist & Creative Writing. LC 67-10658. (Illus.). (gr. 7 up). 1971. PLB 5.97 (ISBN 0-8239-0246-3). Rosen Pr.
Webb, Joseph. The Student Journalist & Writing the New Journalism. (Illus.). 160p. (gr. 7-12). 1976. PLB 7.97 (ISBN 0-8239-0367-2); tchrs' manual 1.50 (ISBN 0-8239-0380-X). Rosen Pr.

JOURNALISM–POLITICAL ASPECTS

Ambler, Effie. Russian Journalism & Politics, Eighteen Sixty-One to Eighteen Eighty-One: The Career of Aleksei Suvorin. LC 72-173671. 265p. 1972. 14.50x (ISBN 0-8143-1461-9). Wayne St U Pr.
Anderson, Jack & Boyd, James. Confessions of a Muckraker. 416p. 1980. pap. 2.95 (ISBN 0-345-26025-2). Ballantine.
Auletta, Ken. Hard Feelings: Reporting on Pols, the Press, People & New York. 1980. 12.95 (ISBN 0-394-50020-2). Random.
Aumente, Jerome. Against Misinformation: A Media Action Program for Young People. 126p. pap. 2.50 (ISBN 0-686-74875-1). ADL.
Christian, Harry, ed. The Sociology of Journalism & the Press. (Sociological Review Monograph: No. 29). 1981. 35.00x (ISBN 0-8476-3798-0); pap. 18.95x (ISBN 0-8476-3257-1). Rowman.
Downie, Leonard, Jr. The New Muckrakers. 1978. pap. 2.50 (ISBN 0-451-61628-6, ME1628, Ment). NAL.
Ethnicity & the Media: Race, Ethnicity & the Media... (Illus.). 1978. pap. 25.50 (ISBN 92-3-101454-4, U808, UNESCO). Unipub.
Hoch, Paul. The Newspaper Game. LC 74-192811. 192p. 1979. 10.95 (ISBN 0-7145-0857-8, Pub. by M Boyars); pap. 5.95 (ISBN 0-7145-1125-0, Pub. by M Boyars). Merrimack Bk Serv.
Hulteng, John L. The News Media: What Makes Them Tick? (Topics in Mass Communications Ser.). 1979. ref. 9.95 (ISBN 0-13-621094-5); pap. 8.95 (ISBN 0-13-621086-4). P-H.
Lee, Richard W., Jr., et al. Politics & the Press. LC 72-118670. (Illus.). 1970. 9.95 (ISBN 0-87491-132-X); pap. 6.95 (ISBN 0-87491-315-2). Acropolis.
Merrill, John C. The Imperative of Freedom: A Philosophy of Journalistic Autonomy. (Communication Arts Bks.). (Illus.). 256p. 1974. 11.95 (ISBN 0-8038-3391-1); pap. text ed. 6.75x (ISBN 0-8038-3394-6). Hastings.
Osborn, George C. & Martin, Ron. The Role of the British Press in the 1976 American Presidential Election. LC 80-68861. 187p. 1981. 10.00 (ISBN 0-682-49667-7). Exposition.
Richstad, Jim & Anderson, Michael H., eds. Crisis in International News: Policies & Prospects. LC 81-677. 480p. 1981. 28.50x (ISBN 0-231-05254-5); pap. 12.50 (ISBN 0-231-05255-3). Columbia U Pr.
Rivers, William. Adversaries: Politics & the Press. LC 75-101326. 1971. pap. 2.95 (ISBN 0-8070-6181-6, BP409). Beacon Pr.
Seymour-Ure, Colin. The Political Impact of Mass Media. LC 73-90038. (Communication & Society: Vol. 4). 296p. 1974. 22.50x (ISBN 0-8039-0347-2); pap. 12.50x (ISBN 0-8039-0713-3). Sage.
Stewart, Donald H. Opposition Press of the Federalist Period. LC 69-11319. 1969. 59.00 (ISBN 0-87395-042-9); microfiche 59.00 (ISBN 0-87395-142-5). State U NY Pr.
Tichenor, Philip J., et al. Community Conflict & the Press. LC 79-24401. (People & Communication Ser.: Vol. 8). 240p. 1980. 22.00 (ISBN 0-8039-1425-3); pap. 9.95 (ISBN 0-8039-1426-1). Sage.
Tuchman, Gaye. Making News: A Study in the Construction of Reality. LC 78-53075. (Illus.). 1980. pap. text ed. 8.95 (ISBN 0-02-932960-4). Free Pr.

JOURNALISM–RESEARCH

Kobre, Sidney. Backgrounding the News: The Newspaper & the Social Sciences. LC 70-137063. (Illus.). 271p. 1974. Repr. of 1939 ed. lib. bdg. 23.00x (ISBN 0-8371-5526-6, KOBN). Greenwood.
Nafziger, Ralph O. & Wilerson, Marcus M., eds. Introduction to Journalism Research. LC 68-54429. (Illus.). 1968. Repr. of 1949 ed. lib. bdg. 15.00 (ISBN 0-8371-0588-9, NAJR). Greenwood.

JOURNALISM–SOCIAL ASPECTS

Bird, George L. & Merwin, Frederic E., eds. Press & Society: A Book of Readings. rev. ed. LC 79-147215. 1971. Repr. of 1951 ed. lib. bdg. 23.50x (ISBN 0-8371-5980-6, BIPR). Greenwood.
Breed, Warren. The Newspaperman, News & Society. Zuckerman, Harriet & Merton, Robert K., eds. LC 79-8979. (Dissertations on Sociology Ser.). 1980. lib. bdg. 35.00x (ISBN 0-405-12955-6). Arno.
Cohen, Stanley & Young, Jock, eds. The Manufacture of News: Social Problems, Deviance & the Mass Media. LC 73-87747. (Communication & Society: Vol. 3). 1973. 30.00 (ISBN 0-8039-0325-1); pap. 14.95x (ISBN 0-8039-1174-2). Sage.
Cranfield, Geoffrey A. The Press & Society: From Caxton to Northcliffe. LC 77-21904. (Themes in British Social History). 1978. text ed. 22.00x (ISBN 0-582-48983-0); pap. text ed. 11.50x (ISBN 0-582-48984-9). Longman.
Downie, Leonard, Jr. The New Muckrakers. 1978. pap. 2.50 (ISBN 0-451-61628-6, ME1628, Ment). NAL.
Frady, Marshall. Southerners: A Journalist's Odyssey. 1981. pap. 6.95 (ISBN 0-686-72176-4, F566, Mer). NAL.
Good, Paul. The Trouble I've Seen: White Journalist - Black Movement. LC 74-10923. 354p. 1975. 9.95 (ISBN 0-88258-020-5). Howard U Pr.
Hardt, Hanno. Social Theories of the Press: Early German & American Perspectives. LC 78-31588. (People & Communication: Vol. 6). 1979. 22.00x (ISBN 0-8039-1236-6); pap. 9.95 (ISBN 0-8039-1237-4). Sage.
Joslyn-Scherer, Marcia S. Communication in the Human Services: A Guide to Therapeutic Journalism. LC 79-28653. (Sage Human Services Guides: Vol. 13). 175p. 1980. pap. 8.00 (ISBN 0-8039-1418-0). Sage.
News Values & Principles of Crops-Cultural Communication. (Reports & Papers on Mass Communication: No. 85). 1980. pap. 4.00 (ISBN 92-3-101697-0, U975, UNESCO). Unipub.
Roberge, Gaston. Mediation: The Action of the Media in Our Society. 1980. 24.00x (ISBN 0-8364-0604-4, Pub. by Manohar India). South Asia Bks.
Roshco, Bernard. Newsmaking. LC 75-5076. x, 160p. 1975. 10.00x (ISBN 0-226-72814-5). U of Chicago Pr.
--Newsmaking. LC 75-5076. 1979. pap. 3.95 (ISBN 0-226-72815-3, P823, Phoen). U of Chicago Pr.
Schiller, Dan. Objectivity & the News: The Public & the Right of Commercial Journalism. LC 80-52809. 1981. 20.00x (ISBN 0-8122-7793-7). U of Pa Pr.
Tichenor, Philip J., et al. Community Conflict & the Press. LC 79-24401. (People & Communication Ser.: Vol. 8). 240p. 1980. 22.00 (ISBN 0-8039-1425-3); pap. 9.95 (ISBN 0-8039-1426-1). Sage.

JOURNALISM–STUDY AND TEACHING

Arnold, Edmund C. Student Journalist-Editing the Yearbook. LC 72-94929. (gr. 7-12). 1973. PLB 9.66 (ISBN 0-8239-0279-X). Rosen Pr.
Azzi, Abderrahmane. News Cross Culturally. 1981. 6.95 (ISBN 0-8062-1840-1). Carlton.
Crump, Spencer. Suggestions for Teaching the Fundamentals of Journalism in College. 10.00 (ISBN 0-87046-044-7); pap. 6.00 (ISBN 0-87046-045-5). Trans-Anglo.
Dennis, Everette E. & Ismach, Arnold H. Reporting Processes & Practices: Newswriting for Today's Readers. 400p. 1981. pap. text ed. 14.95x (ISBN 0-534-00941-7). Wadsworth Pub.
Metzler, Ken. Newswriting Exercises. (Illus.). 288p. 1981. pap. text ed. 11.95 (ISBN 0-13-617803-0). P-H.
O'Dell, De Forest. The History of Journalism Education in the United States. LC 78-177129. (Columbia University. Teachers College. Contributions to Education: No. 653). Repr. of 1935 ed. 17.50 (ISBN 0-404-55653-1). AMS Pr.
Ours, Robert M. Journalism at West Virginia University. LC 77-84188. (Illus.). 1977. pap. 3.00 (ISBN 0-930362-01-2). West Va U Pr.
Reddick, DeWitt C. Journalism Exercise & Resource Book. 288p. 1981. pap. text ed. 8.50x (ISBN 0-534-00869-0). Wadsworth Pub.
Singer, Samuel L. The Student Journalist & Reviewing the Performing Arts. LC 73-80359. (Student Journalist Ser.). (Illus.). 160p. (gr. 7 up). 1974. PLB 7.97 (ISBN 0-8239-0287-0). Rosen Pr.
Sutton, Albert A. Education for Journalism in the United States from Its Beginning to 1940. LC 68-54297. (Northwestern University. Humanities Ser.: No. 14). Repr. of 1945 ed. 16.50 (ISBN 0-404-50714-X). AMS Pr.
Telfer, Judie. Training Minority Journalists: A Case Study of the San Francisco Examiner Intern Program. LC 73-4313. 124p. (Orig.). 1973. pap. 4.00x (ISBN 0-87772-169-6). Inst Gov Stud Berk.

JOURNALISM–VOCATIONAL GUIDANCE

Adams, Julian. The Student Journalist & Mass Communication. (Illus.). 190p. 1981. lib. bdg. 8.95 (ISBN 0-8239-0538-1); workbook 1.50 (ISBN 0-8239-0499-7). Rosen Pr.
Bond, F. Fraser. Breaking into Print. 1977. Repr. of 1933 ed. lib. bdg. 15.00 (ISBN 0-686-19798-4). Havertown Bks.
Engeretson, Herschel O. & Gillespie, Jack. Getting Started in Journalism. 92p. (Orig.). 1974. pap. text ed. 4.95 (ISBN 0-89076-003-9); pap. text ed. 3.00 5 or more (ISBN 0-685-51254-1). Educ Impact.
Hicks, Maynard. Where the Jobs Are: Communications. 1977. 7.00 (ISBN 0-682-48949-2). Exposition.
MacNeil, Neil. How to Be a Newspaperman. 1977. lib. bdg. 12.50 (ISBN 0-686-19809-3). Havertown Bks.
Pawlick, Thomas. Exploring Journalism Careers. (Career in Depth Ser.). (Illus.). 1981. lib. bdg. 7.97 (ISBN 0-8239-0515-2). Rosen Pr.
Pitkin, Walter B. Vocational Studies in Journalism. 1977. Repr. of 1931 ed. lib. bdg. 12.50 (ISBN 0-686-19829-8). Havertown Bks.
Swann, Ruth. Financial Aid for Minorities in Journalism & Communications. 50p. 1980. pap. 3.00 (ISBN 0-912048-03-4). Garrett Pk.
Tebbel, John. Opportunities in Journalism. LC 76-14060. (Illus.). (gr. 9 up). 1977. PLB 6.60 (ISBN 0-8442-6541-1); pap. text ed. 4.95 (ISBN 0-8442-6540-3). Natl Textbk.
Trewin, Ion. Journalism. (Profession Ser.). 144p. 1976. 13.50 (ISBN 0-7153-6891-5). David & Charles.
Tyrrell, R. W. The Work of the Television Journalist. (Library of Film & Television Practice). 176p. 1972. 21.95 (ISBN 0-240-51051-8). Focal Pr.
Weber, Ronald, ed. The Reporter As Artist: A Look at the New Journalism Controversy. (Communications Arts Bks.). 312p. 1974. 12.00 (ISBN 0-8038-6330-6); pap. text ed. 6.50 (ISBN 0-8038-6333-0). Hastings.

JOURNALISM–AFRICA

African Book World & Press. 2nd ed. 500p. 1980. 75.00 (ISBN 0-8103-0990-4). Gale.
Barton, Frank. The Press of Africa: Persecution & Perseverence. LC 78-7363. 1979. text ed. 38.50x (ISBN 0-8419-0393-X, Africana). Holmes & Meier.
Driver, C. J. Patrick Duncan. text ed. 65.00x (ISBN 0-435-96200-0). Heinemann Ed.
Potter, Elaine. The Press As Opposition: The Political Role of South African Newspapers. 228p. 1975. 15.00x (ISBN 0-87471-445-1). Rowman.
Rural Journalism in Africa. (Reports & Papers on Mass Communication Ser.: No. 88). 35p. 1981. pap. 5.00 (ISBN 92-3-101752-7, U1098, UNESCO). Unipub.
Switzer, Les & Switzer, Donna. The Black Press in South Africa & Lesotho. (Reference Bks.). 1979. lib. bdg. 28.00 (ISBN 0-8161-8174-8). G K Hall.

JOURNALISM–ASIA

Parker, Elliott S. & Parker, Emelia M. Asian Journalism: A Selected Bibliography of Sources on Journalism in China & Southeast Asia. LC 79-22785. 484p. 1979. 25.00 (ISBN 0-8108-1269-X). Scarecrow.
Schramm, Wilbur & Atwood, L. Erwin. Circulation of News in the Third World: A Study of Asia. 350p. 1981. 25.00 (ISBN 0-295-95870-7, Pub. by Chinese Univ Hong Kong). U of Wash Pr.
--Circulation of News in the Third World: A Study of Asia. 350p. 1981. 22.50 (ISBN 0-295-95870-7). U of Wash Pr.

JOURNALISM–AUSTRALIA

Holden, Willis S. Australia Goes to Press. LC 77-8449. (Illus.). 1977. lib. bdg. 20.75x (ISBN 0-8371-9689-2, HOAU). Greenwood.

JOURNALISM–CHINA

Parker, Elliott S. & Parker, Emelia M. Asian Journalism: A Selected Bibliography of Sources on Journalism in China & Southeast Asia. LC 79-22785. 484p. 1979. 25.00 (ISBN 0-8108-1269-X). Scarecrow.

JOURNALISM–COMMUNIST COUNTRIES

Lendvai, Paul. The Bureaucracy of Truth. 350p. 1981. lib. bdg. 24.75 (ISBN 0-86531-142-0). Westview.
Mickiewicz, Ellen. Media & the Russian Public. 170p. 1981. 19.95 (ISBN 0-03-057681-4); pap. 8.95 (ISBN 0-03-057679-2). Praeger.

JOURNALISM–GERMANY

Fliess, Peter J. Freedom of the Press in the German Republic, 1918-1933. LC 71-90507. Repr. of 1955 ed. lib. bdg. 15.00x (ISBN 0-8371-2208-2, FLFP). Greenwood.

JOURNALISM–GREAT BRITAIN

Andrews, Alexander. History of British Journalism: From the Foundation of the Newspaper Press in England to the Repeal of the Stamp Act, 2 Vols. LC 68-24958. (British History Ser., No. 30). 1969. Repr. of 1859 ed. lib. bdg. 48.95 (ISBN 0-8383-0154-1). Haskell.
--History of British Journalism from the Foundation of the Newspaper Press in England to the Repeal of the Stamp Act in 1855, 2 Vols. 1968. Set. 30.00 (ISBN 0-403-00139-0). Scholarly.
Bourne, Henry R. English Newspapers: Chapters in the History of Journalism, 2 Vols. LC 65-17877. 1966. Repr. of 1887 ed. Set. 25.00 (ISBN 0-8462-0659-5). Russell.
Brodzky, Vivian. Fleet Street: The Inside Story of Journalism. 12.50 (ISBN 0-686-25502-X). British Am Bks.
Cranfield, Geoffrey A. The Development of the Provincial Newspaper, 1700-1760. LC 77-16348. (Illus.). 1978. Repr. of 1962 ed. lib. bdg. 22.50x (ISBN 0-313-20017-3, CRDP). Greenwood.
Curran, James, ed. The British Press: A Manifesto. (Communications & Culture Ser.). 1978. text ed. 27.75x (ISBN 0-333-23459-6). Humanities.
Escott, Thomas H. Masters of English Journalism. LC 74-2282. 1974. Repr. of 1911 ed. lib. bdg. 13.50 (ISBN 0-8414-3937-0). Folcroft.
--Masters of English Journalism: A Study of Personal Forces. LC 74-98834. Repr. of 1911 ed. lib. bdg. 16.00x (ISBN 0-8371-3020-4, ESME). Greenwood.
Ewald, William B., Jr. Rogues, Royalty & Reporters: The Age of Queen Anne Through Its Newspapers. LC 78-17410. 1978. Repr. of 1956 ed. lib. bdg. 22.75x (ISBN 0-313-20506-X, EWRR). Greenwood.
Herd, Harold. The March of Journalism. LC 73-722. (Illus.). 352p. 1973. Repr. of 1952 ed. lib. bdg. 19.75x (ISBN 0-8371-6788-4, HEMG). Greenwood.
Hindle, Wilfrid. The Morning Post, Seventeen Seventy-Two to Nineteen Thirty-Seven: Portrait of a Newspaper. LC 73-16946. (Illus.). 260p. 1974. Repr. of 1937 ed. lib. bdg. 14.25x (ISBN 0-8371-7243-8, HIMP). Greenwood.
Hueston, Robert F. Catholic Press & Nativim, Eighteen Forty to Eighteen Sixty. LC 76-6348. (Irish Americans Ser). 1976. 21.00 (ISBN 0-405-09342-X). Arno.
Miller, Orlo. A Century of Western Ontario: The Story of London, the Free Press, & Western Ontario, 1849-1949. LC 71-165443. (Illus.). 289p. 1972. Repr. of 1949 ed. lib. bdg. 15.75x (ISBN 0-8371-6226-2, MIWO). Greenwood.
Mills, William H. The Manchester Guardian: A Century of History. LC 74-137067. (Illus.). 146p. 1972. Repr. of 1922 ed. lib. bdg. 15.00 (ISBN 0-8371-5530-4, MIMG). Greenwood.
Muddiman, Joseph G. King's Journalist 1659-1689: Studies in the Reign of Charles Second. LC 74-125774. (English Book Trade). (Illus.). Repr. of 1923 ed. 15.00x (ISBN 0-678-00729-2). Kelley.
Nesbitt, George L. Benthamite Reviewing: The First Twelve Years of the Westminister Review, 1824-36. LC 70-181964. Repr. of 1934 ed. 18.50 (ISBN 0-404-04678-9). AMS Pr.
Osborn, George C. & Martin, Don. The Role of the British Press in the 1976 American Presidential Election. 64p. 1981. 10.00 (ISBN 0-682-49667-7). Exposition.
Schults, Raymond L. Crusader in Babylon: W.T. Stead & the "Pall Mall Gazette". LC 71-109603. (Illus.). xvi, 277p. 1972. 17.50x (ISBN 0-8032-0760-3). U of Nebr Pr.
Shaaber, Matthias A. Some Forerunners of the Newspaper in England, 1476-1622. 1966. lib. bdg. 20.00x (ISBN 0-374-97296-6). Octagon.
Thomas, William B. The Story of the Spectator, 1828-1928. LC 79-175711. (Select Bibliographies Reprint Ser.). Repr. of 1928 ed. 18.00 (ISBN 0-8369-6626-0). Arno.
Warner, Philip. The Best of British Pluck: The Boy's Own Paper 1879-1967. (Illus.). 1976. text ed. 19.95x (ISBN 0-8464-0190-8). Beekman Pubs.
Weed, Katherine K. & Bond, Richmond P. Studies of British Newspapers & Periodicals from Their Beginning to 1800. Repr. of 1946 ed. pap. 7.00 (ISBN 0-384-66370-2). Johnson Repr.
Whyte, Frederic. The Life of W. T. Stead, 2 vols. 1978. Repr. of 1925 ed. lib. bdg. 65.00 (ISBN 0-8495-5637-6). Arden Lib.

JOURNALISM–INDIA

Bhattacharjee, Arun. Indian Press: Profession to Industry. 1972. 9.50x (ISBN 0-7069-0084-7). Intl Pubns Serv.
Noorani, A. G., ed. Freedom of the Press in India. 1971. 4.50x (ISBN 0-8426-0250-X). Verry.

JOURNALISM–JAPAN

Asano, Osamu & Ishiwata, Mutsuko, eds. The Japanese Press, 1980. 32nd ed. Henshu-sha, Century E. & Higashi, Shinbu, trs. from Japanese. LC 49-25552. (Illus.). 172p. (Orig.). 1980. pap. 25.00x (ISBN 0-8002-2699-2). Intl Pubns Serv.
Kim, Young C. Japanese Journalists & Their World. LC 80-25720. 233p. 1981. 15.00x (ISBN 0-8139-0877-9). U Pr of Va.

JOURNALISM–LOMBARDY

Greenfield, Kent R. Economics & Liberalism in the Risorgimento: A Study of Nationalism in Lombardy, 1814-1848. LC 78-17674. 1978. Repr. of 1965 ed. lib. bdg. 22.25x (ISBN 0-313-20510-8, GREL). Greenwood.

JOURNALISM–SWITZERLAND

Hartmann, Frederick H. Swiss Press & Foreign Affairs in World War Two. LC 60-62782. (U of Fla. Social Sciences Monographs: No. 5). 1960. pap. 3.25 (ISBN 0-8130-0105-6). U Presses Fla.

JOURNALISM–UNITED STATES

Alter, J. Cecil. Early Utah Journalism. LC 79-98803. Repr. of 1938 ed. lib. bdg. 16.00x (ISBN 0-8371-3065-4, ALUJ). Greenwood.

American Institute of Discussion. Make up Your Own Mind, Bks. 1 & 2. Pollis, Adamantia, ed. Incl. Bk. 1. Contemporary Editorials. 1964. pap. 1.00 (ISBN 0-910092-01-X); Bk. 2. Contemporary Political Issues. 1966. pap. 1.75 (ISBN 0-910092-02-8). Am Inst Disc.

Bailyn, Bernard & Hench, John B., eds. The Press & the American Revolution. 391p. 1981. pap. 9.95 (ISBN 0-930350-30-8). NE U Pr.

Baumgartner, Apollinaris W. Catholic Journalism. LC 75-159997. (BCL Ser. I). Repr. of 1931 ed. 11.50 (ISBN 0-404-00693-0). AMS Pr.

Beasley, Maurine H. & Harlow, Richard R. Voices of Change: Southern Pulitzer Winners. LC 79-52511. 1979. pap. text ed. 8.50 (ISBN 0-8191-0771-9). U Pr of Amer.

Berry, Thomas E. Journalism in America: An Introduction to the News Media. (Communication Arts Bks.). 1976. 16.50 (ISBN 0-8038-3712-7); pap. text ed. 8.50x (ISBN 0-8038-3713-5). Hastings.

Bleyer, Willard G. Main Currents in the History of American Journalism. LC 70-77720. (American Scene Ser). (Illus.). v, 464p. 1973. Repr. of 1927 ed. lib. bdg. 45.00 (ISBN 0-306-71358-6). Da Capo.

Brier, Warren J. & Blumberg, Nathan B., eds. A Century of Montana Journalism. LC 78-169031. 352p. 1971. 10.00 (ISBN 0-87842-023-1). Mountain Pr.

Brucker, Herbert. Communication Is Power: Unchanging Values in a Changing Journalism. 416p. 1973. 12.95 (ISBN 0-19-501599-1). Oxford U Pr.

Campbell, Georgetta M. Extant Collections of Early Black Newspapers: A Research Guide to the Black Press, 1880-1915, with an Index to the Boston Guardian, 1902-1904. LC 80-51418. 433p. 1981. 28.50x (ISBN 0-87875-197-1). Whitston Pub.

Casey, Ralph D., ed. Press in Perspective. LC 63-16657. 1963. 15.00x (ISBN 0-8071-0339-X). La State U Pr.

Conlin, Joseph R. The American Radical Press: 1880-1960, 2 vols. LC 72-9825. 1974. Set. lib. bdg. 35.00x (ISBN 0-8371-6625-X, AMR). Greenwood.

Cornebise, Alfred. The Amaroc News: The Daily Newspaper of the American Forces in Germany, 1919-1923. LC 80-27275. (New Horizons in Journalism Ser.). 288p. 1981. 24.95 (ISBN 0-8093-1001-5). S Ill U Pr.

Culbert, David H. News for Everyman: Radio & Foreign Affairs in Thirties America. LC 75-23862. 238p. 1976. lib. bdg. 14.50 (ISBN 0-8371-8260-3, CRC/). Greenwood.

Doll, Louis W. A History of the Newspapers of Ann Arbor, 1829-1920. LC 59-9322. (Illus.). 1959. pap. 4.95x (ISBN 0-8143-1102-4). Wayne St U Pr.

Dreiser, Theodore. Newspaper Days. (Amer. Newspapermen Ser.: 1790-1933). 502p. 1974. Repr. of 1931 ed. 21.50x (ISBN 0-8464-0023-5). Beekman Pubs.

Emery, Edwin & Emery, Michael. The Press & America. 4th ed. (Illus.). 1978. ref. 19.95 (ISBN 0-13-697979-3). P-H.

Epstein, Edward J. Between Fact & Fiction: The Problem of Journalism. (Orig.). 1975. pap. 3.95 (ISBN 0-394-71396-6, Vin). Random.

Foster, Charles R. Editorial Treatment of Education in the American Press. LC 71-136384. Repr. of 1938 ed. 24.50 (ISBN 0-404-02519-6). AMS Pr.

Gans, Herbert J. Deciding What's News: A Study of CBS Evening News, NBC Nightly News, Newsweek & Time. LC 78-53516. 1979. 12.95 (ISBN 0-394-50359-7). Pantheon.

George Washington University American Studies Program-Rose Bibl. Analytical Guide & Indexes to the Voice of the Negro: 1904-1907. LC 73-15079. 1974. lib. bdg. 54.00x (ISBN 0-8371-7174-1, RBVON). Greenwood.

Green, Laurence. America Goes to Press: The News of Yesterday. LC 79-145060. 1971. Repr. of 1936 ed. 25.00 (ISBN 0-403-01003-9). Scholarly.

Greene, Laurence. America Goes to Press: The News of Yesterday. LC 74-128252. (Essay Index Reprint Ser). 1936. 19.50 (ISBN 0-8369-1929-7). Arno.

Halaas, David F. Boom Town Newspapers: Journalism on the Rocky Mountain Mining Frontier, 1859-1881. (Illus.). 192p. 1981. 14.95 (ISBN 0-8263-0588-1). U of NM Pr.

Hart, Jack R. The Information Empire: The Rise of the los Angeles Times & the Times Mirror Corporation. LC 80-69048. 420p. (Orig.). 1981. lib. bdg. 23.00 (ISBN 0-8191-1580-0); pap. text ed. 14.00 (ISBN 0-8191-1581-9). U Pr of Amer.

Hays, Robert G. Country Editor: Influence of a Weekly Newspaper. LC 73-87423. 83p. 1974. pap. 3.00x (ISBN 0-8134-1617-5, 1617). Interstate.

Hellmann, John. Fables of Fact: The New Journalism As New Fiction. LC 80-23881. 175p. 1981. 12.95 (ISBN 0-252-00847-2). U of Ill Pr.

Hohenberg, John. A Crisis for the American Press. 1978. 15.00 (ISBN 0-231-04578-6). Columbia U Pr.

Hollowell, John. Fact & Fiction: The New Journalism & the Nonfiction Novel. LC 76-20826. 1977. 13.00x (ISBN 0-8078-1281-1). U of NC Pr.

Hooper, Osman C. History of Ohio Journalism, Seventeen Ninety-Three to Nineteen Thirty-Three. 1969. Repr. of 1933 ed. 11.50 (ISBN 0-384-24220-0). Johnson Repr.

Hough, Henry B. Country Editor. LC 40-27604. 1974. pap. 3.95 (ISBN 0-85699-091-4). Chatham Pr.

Hudson, Frederic. Journalism in the United States from 1690 to 1872. LC 68-24985. (American History & Americana Ser., No. 47). 1969. Repr. of 1873 ed. lib. bdg. 52.95 (ISBN 0-8383-0203-3). Haskell.

Irwin, William H. Propaganda & the News, Or, What Makes You Think So. Repr. of 1936 ed. lib. bdg. 15.00x (ISBN 0-8371-2818-8, IRPN). Greenwood.

--Propaganda & the News: Or, What Makes You Think So. (American Studies). 1969. Repr. of 1936 ed. 19.50 (ISBN 0-384-25970-7). Johnson Repr.

Johnson, Gerald W. Peril & Promise. LC 73-14034. 110p. 1974. Repr. of 1958 ed. lib. bdg. 15.00x (ISBN 0-8371-7143-1, JOPP). Greenwood.

Keirstead, Phillip. Journalist's Notebook of Live Radio-TV News. LC 75-41735. (Illus.). 252p. 1976. 12.95 (ISBN 0-8306-6819-5, 819). TAB Bks.

Kerby, William F. A Proud Profession: Memoirs of a Wall Street Journal Reporter, Editor & Publisher. LC 80-740438. 225p. 1981. 12.95 (ISBN 0-87094-235-2). Dow Jones-Irwin.

King, Henry. American Journalism. LC 79-125700. (American Journalists Ser). 1970. Repr. of 1871 ed. 9.00 (ISBN 0-405-01679-4). Arno.

Kingsbury, Susan M., et al. Newspapers & the News, an Objective Measurement of Ethical & Unethical Behavior by Representative Newspapers. Repr. of 1937 ed. lib. bdg. 15.00x (ISBN 0-8371-2967-2, KINN). Greenwood.

--Newspapers & the News: An Objective Measurement of Ethical & Unethical Behavior by Representative Newspapers. (American Studies). 1969. Repr. of 1937 ed. lib. bdg. 19.50 (ISBN 0-384-29480-4). Johnson Repr.

Kirschner, Allen & Kirschner, Linda, eds. Journalism: Readings in the Mass Media. LC 76-158976. 1971. pap. 7.95 (ISBN 0-672-73224-6). Odyssey Pr.

Kobre, Sidney. Foundations of American Journalism. Repr. of 1958 ed. lib. bdg. 16.00x (ISBN 0-8371-3117-0, KOAJ). Greenwood.

Lindstrom, C. E. The Fading American Newspaper. 8.50 (ISBN 0-8446-1282-0). Peter Smith.

Lister, Hal. The Suburban Press: A Separate Journalism. 1975. pap. text ed. 5.25x (ISBN 0-87543-124-0). Lucas.

Lyon, William H., ed. Journalism in the West. 1980. pap. 8.00 (ISBN 0-89745-008-6). Sunflower U Pr.

McPhaul, John J. Deadlines & Monkeyshines. LC 72-6201. (Illus.). 308p. 1973. Repr. of 1962 ed. lib. bdg. 18.00x (ISBN 0-8371-6471-0, MCDM). Greenwood.

Marbut, F. B. News from the Capital: The Story of Washington Reporting. LC 76-132484. (New Horizons in Journalism Ser). (Illus.). 328p. 1971. 12.50x (ISBN 0-8093-0495-3). S Ill U Pr.

Meriwether, James B., ed. South Carolina Journals & Journalists. LC 75-22200. 364p. 1975. 15.00 (ISBN 0-87152-212-8). Reprint.

Miner, Ward L. William Goddard, Newspaperman. LC 62-14873. 1962. 14.75 (ISBN 0-8223-0115-6). Duke.

Mott, Frank L. American Journalism. 3rd ed. (Illus.). 1962. text ed. 16.95x (ISBN 0-685-14611-1). Macmillan.

Murphy, James E. & Murphy, Sharon M. Let My People Know: American Indian Journalism, 1828-1978. LC 80-5941. 300p. 1981. 14.95 (ISBN 0-8061-1623-4). U of Okla Pr.

National Press Club Of Washington. Dateline: Washington, the Story of National Affairs Journalism in the Life & Times of the National Press Club. Phillips, Cabell, et al, eds. Repr. of 1949 ed. lib. bdg. 18.00x (ISBN 0-8371-0183-2, NPCW). Greenwood.

New York, New York: Selections from the Columbia News Service. 1981. write for info. Arno.

Olson, McKinley C., ed. J. W. Gitt's Sweet Land of Liberty. LC 73-88834. (Illus.). 226p. 1975. 8.95x (ISBN 0-89198-113-6). Ozer.

O'Shea, Margaret N. Oldham Paisley: A Community Editor & His Newspapers, the Marion Daily Republican & Marion Weekly Leader. 186p. 1974. pap. 3.75x (ISBN 0-8134-1645-0, 1645). Interstate.

Phillips, Cabel. Dateline Washington. 1977. Repr. of 1949 ed. lib. bdg. 12.50 (ISBN 0-686-19803-4). Havertown Bks.

Prentice, George D. Prenticeana: Or, Wit & Humor in Paragraphs. 306p. 1981. Repr. of 1871 ed. lib. bdg. 30.00 (ISBN 0-8495-4400-9). Arden Lib.

Regier, C. C. The Era of the Muckrakers. 8.00 (ISBN 0-8446-1380-0). Peter Smith.

Roberts, Gene & Jones, David R., eds. Assignment: America. LC 73-79930. (Illus.). 288p. 1974. 8.95 (ISBN 0-8129-0384-6). Times Bks.

Rodechko, James P. Patrick Ford & His Search for America: A Case Study of Irish-American Journalism, 1870-1913. LC 76-6362. (Irish Americans Ser). 1976. 20.00 (ISBN 0-405-09354-3). Arno.

Rosewater, Victor. History of Cooperative News-Gathering in the United States. LC 30-10687. Repr. of 1930 ed. 23.00 (ISBN 0-384-52020-0). Johnson Repr.

Ross, Isabel. Ladies of the Press: The Story of Women in Journalism by an Insider. LC 74-3972. (Women in America Ser). (Illus.). 642p. 1974. Repr. of 1936 ed. 36.00 (ISBN 0-405-06120-X). Arno.

Schlesinger, Arthur M. Prelude to Independence: The Newspaper War on Britain 1764-1776. LC 80-22830. 340p. 1980. pap. text ed. 9.95 (ISBN 0-930350-13-8). NE U Pr.

Schroth, Raymond A. The Eagle & Brooklyn: A Community Newspaper, 1841-1955. LC 73-20972. (Contributions in American Studies: No. 13). 304p. 1974. lib. bdg. 15.95 (ISBN 0-8371-7335-3, SBE/). Greenwood.

Schudson, Michael. Discovering the News: A Social History of American Newspapers. LC 78-54997. 288p. 1981. pap. 5.95 (ISBN 0-465-01666-9). Basic.

Shaw, David. Journalism Today: A Changing Press for a Changing America. LC 77-1738. 1977. text ed. 14.50 scp (ISBN 0-06-160435-6, HarpC) (ISBN 0-06-160432-1, HarpC). Har-Row.

Sinclair, Upton. Brass Check. LC 74-125715. (American Journalists). 1970. Repr. of 1919 ed. 19.00 (ISBN 0-405-01696-4). Arno.

--The Brass Check: A Study of American Journalism. Repr. of 1920 ed. 27.00 (ISBN 0-384-55590-X). Johnson Repr.

Stuart, Mark, ed. & intro. by. In the Record: The "Simeon Stylites" Columns of William A. Caldwell. 1972. 17.00 (ISBN 0-8135-0728-6). Rutgers U Pr.

Sutton, Albert A. Education for Journalism in the United States from Its Beginning to 1940. LC 68-54297. (Northwestern University. Humanities Ser.: No. 14). Repr. of 1945 ed. 16.50 (ISBN 0-404-50714-X). AMS Pr.

Tebbel, John. The Media in America: A Social & Political History. LC 74-9891. 384p. 1975. 11.95 (ISBN 0-690-00500-8). T Y Crowell.

Tinney, James S. & Rector, Justine J. Issues & Trends in Afro-American Journalism. LC 80-6074. 371p. 1980. lib. bdg. 20.75 (ISBN 0-8191-1352-2); pap. text ed. 12.50 (ISBN 0-8191-1353-0). U Pr of Amer.

Villard, Oswald G. Disappearing Daily. facs. ed. LC 69-18939. (Essay Index Reprint Ser). 1944. 17.00 (ISBN 0-8369-0056-1). Arno.

Washington Post Writers Group. The Editorial Page. 1977. pap. text ed. 8.75 (ISBN 0-395-24015-8). HM.

Weinberg, Steve. Trade Secrets of Washington Journalists: How to Get the Facts About What's Going on in Washington. (Illus.). 1981. pap. 7.95 (ISBN 0-87491-085-4). Acropolis.

Wicker, Tom. On Press. 1979. pap. 2.95 (ISBN 0-425-04068-2). Berkley Pub.

Wolfe, Thomas & Johnson, E. W. The New Journalism. 1973. pap. text ed. 11.50 scp (ISBN 0-06-047183-2, HarpC). Har-Row.

JOURNALISM, AFRO-AMERICAN

see Afro-American Press

JOURNALISM, AGRICULTURAL

Evans, James F. & Salcedo, Rodolfo N. Communications in Agriculture: The American Farm Press. (Replica Edition Ser.: No. 4). 276p. 1974. text ed. 7.95x (ISBN 0-8138-0350-0). Iowa St U Pr.

Fox, Rodney. Agricultural & Technical Journalism. LC 79-90509. Repr. of 1952 ed. lib. bdg. 15.00x (ISBN 0-8371-2311-9, FOAT). Greenwood.

Ogilvie, William E. Pioneer Agricultural Journalists: Brief Biographical Sketches of Some of the Early Editors in the Field of Agricultural Journalism. LC 72-89071. (Rural America Ser.). 1973. Repr. of 1927 ed. 11.00 (ISBN 0-8420-1492-6). Scholarly Res Inc.

--Pioneer Agriculture Journalists. (American Newspapermen 1790-1933 Ser.). (Illus.). vii, 128p. 1973. Repr. of 1927 ed. 10.50x (ISBN 0-8464-0010-3). Beekman Pubs.

Ward, William B. Reporting Agriculture Through Newspapers, Magazines, Radio, Television. 2nd ed. (Illus.). 402p. 1959. 18.50x (ISBN 0-8014-0441-X). Comstock.

JOURNALISM, COMMERCIAL

Du Vall, Dean F. Grab Your Share of the Wealth. 1978. 100.00 (ISBN 0-931232-17-1). Du Vall Financial.

Elfenbein, Julien. Business Journalism. 2nd ed. LC 72-91759. Repr. of 1960 ed. lib. bdg. 17.00x (ISBN 0-8371-2433-6, ELBJ). Greenwood.

Elfenbein, Julien, ed. Businesspaper Publishing Practice. Repr. of 1952 ed. lib. bdg. 15.25x (ISBN 0-8371-3090-5, ELBU). Greenwood.

Kirsch, Donald. Documentary Supplement to Financial & Economic Journalism: Analysis, Interpretation & Reporting. LC 78-55415. 1978. pap. 8.00x (ISBN 0-8147-4572-5). NYU Pr.

--Financial & Economic Journalism: Analysis, Interpretation & Reporting. LC 78-55415. 1978. 16.50x (ISBN 0-8147-4569-5). NYU Pr.

Shulman, Joel J. How to Get Published in Business-Professional Journals. (Illus.). 256p. 1980. 14.95 (ISBN 0-8144-5555-7). Am Mgmt.

Simons, Howard, ed. The Media & Business. LC 78-55714. 1979. pap. 4.95 (ISBN 0-394-72741-X, Vin). Random.

Wilbur, L. Perry. How to Write Articles That Sell. LC 80-29098. (Self-Teaching Guides). 217p. 1981. pap. 7.95 (ISBN 0-471-08426-3). Wiley.

JOURNALISM, DAIRY

see Journalism, Agricultural

JOURNALISM, INDUSTRIAL

see Journalism, Technical

JOURNALISM, LEGAL

see also Newspaper Court Reporting

JOURNALISM, MEDICAL

Meiss, Harriet & Jaeger, Doris, eds. Information to Authors: Editorial Guidelines Reprinted from 246 Medical Journals. LC 80-19712. 702p. 1980. pap. 26.00 (ISBN 0-8067-1251-1). Urban & S.

Roueche, Berton. The Medical Detectives. 1980. 15.00 (ISBN 0-8129-0920-8). Times Bks.

JOURNALISM, PICTORIAL

see also Photography, Journalistic

Bilker, Harvey L. Photojournalism: A Freelancer's Guide. (Illus.). 224p. 1981. 14.95 (ISBN 0-8092-5919-2); pap. 7.95 (ISBN 0-8092-5918-4). Contemp Bks.

Evans, Harold & Taylor, Edwin. Pictures on a Page: Photojournalism & Picture Editing. 320p. 1979. text ed. 15.95x (ISBN 0-534-00812-7). Wadsworth Pub.

Geraci, Philip C. Photojournalism: Making Pictures for Publication. 2nd ed. (Illus.). 1978. pap. text ed. 13.95 (ISBN 0-8403-1422-1). Kendall-Hunt.

Popko, Edward S. Transitions: A Photographic Documentary of Squatter Settlements. (Community Development Ser.). (Illus.). 1978. text ed. 28.00 (ISBN 0-07-050467-9, C). McGraw.

Vitray, Laura & Mills, John, Jr. Pictorial Journalism. LC 72-9241. (The Literature of Photography Ser.). Repr. of 1939 ed. 24.00 (ISBN 0-405-04945-5). Arno.

JOURNALISM, PRISON

Langford, J. A. Prison Books & Their Authors. 59.95 (ISBN 0-8490-0892-1). Gordon Pr.

JOURNALISM, RELIGIOUS

Anderson, Margaret J. The Christian Writer's Handbook. LC 73-18706. 1977. pap. 6.95 (ISBN 0-06-060192-2, RD 246, HarpR). Har-Row.

Arnold, Glenn F. Writing Award Winning Articles. LC 79-10863. 1979. pap. 7.95 (ISBN 0-8407-5682-8). Nelson.

Burrell, David B. & Kane, Franzita, eds. Evangelization in the American Context. LC 76-22403. 1976. pap. 2.95x (ISBN 0-268-00902-3). U of Notre Dame Pr.

Marty, Martin E., et al. The Religious Press in America. LC 72-6844. 184p. 1973. Repr. of 1963 ed. lib. bdg. 15.00 (ISBN 0-8371-6500-8, MARP). Greenwood.

Osmer, Harold H. U. S. Religions Journalism & the Korean War. LC 80-5441. 153p. 1980. pap. text ed. 7.50 (ISBN 0-8191-1097-3). U Pr of Amer.

Osteyee, Edith F. Writing for Christian Publications. Repr. of 1953 ed. lib. bdg. 15.00 (ISBN 0-8371-2473-5, OSCP). Greenwood.

Polen, O. W. Editorially Speaking. 1975. pap. 1.25 (ISBN 0-87148-300-9). Pathway Pr.

Thaman, Mary P. Manners & Morals of the Nineteen Twenties: A Survey of the Religious Press. LC 77-8129. 1977. Repr. of 1954 ed. lib. bdg. 15.75x (ISBN 0-8371-9679-5, THMM). Greenwood.

Wintz, Jack, ed. Our Journey in Faith. (Catholic Update Book Ser.). 124p. (Orig.). 1980. pap. 2.25 (ISBN 0-912228-65-2). St Anthony Mess Pr.

JOURNALISM, SCIENTIFIC

Balaban, Miriam, ed. Scientific Information Transfer: The Editor's Role. 1978. lib. bdg. 37.00 (ISBN 90-277-0917-3, Pub. by Reidel Holland). Kluwer Boston.

Burkett, David W. Writing Science News for the Mass Media. 2nd ed. LC 72-84334. 223p. 1973. 11.95 (ISBN 0-87201-924-1). Gulf Pub.

DeBakey, Lois. The Scientific Journal: Editorial Policies & Practices--Guidelines for Editors, Reviewers & Authors. LC 76-6046. 1976. text ed. 13.50 (ISBN 0-8016-1223-3). Mosby.

JOURNALISM, TECHNICAL

see also Handbooks, Vade-Mecums, etc.; House Organs

Beckwith, B. P. Socialist Essays. 1980. 10.00 (ISBN 0-9603262-1-9). Beckwith.

JOURNALISTIC ETHICS

Brucker, Herbert. Freedom of Information. LC 81-1711. 307p. 1981. Repr. of 1951 ed. lib. bdg. 29.75x (ISBN 0-313-22956-2, BRFRI). Greenwood.

Christians, Clifford G. & Covert, Catherine L. Teaching Ethics in Journalism Education. LC 80-10426. (The Teaching of Ethics Ser.). 71p. 1980. pap. 4.00 (ISBN 0-916558-08-8). Hastings Ctr Inst Soc.

Cirino, Robert. Don't Blame the People: How the News Media Uses Bias, Distortion, & Censorship to Manipulate Public Opinion. 1972. pap. 3.95 (ISBN 0-394-71788-0, V788, Vin). Random.

Crawford, Nelson A. Ethics of Journalism. LC 71-131676. 1970. Repr. of 1929 ed. 29.00 (ISBN 0-403-00563-9). Scholarly.

--Ethics of Journalism. LC 74-90493. 1924. lib. bdg. 15.00x (ISBN 0-8371-2155-8, CREJ). Greenwood.

Hulteng, Hung L. Messenger's Motive: Ethical Problems of the News Media. 250p. 1976. pap. 9.95 (ISBN 0-13-577460-8). P-H.

Merril, John C. & Barney, Ralph D., eds. Ethics & the Press: Readings in Mass Media Morality. (Humanistic Studies in Communication Arts). 448p. 1975. 13.95 (ISBN 0-8038-1923-4); pap. text ed. 7.50x (ISBN 0-8038-1924-2). Hastings.

Merrill, John C. The Imperative of Freedom: A Philosophy of Journalistic Autonomy. (Communication Arts Bks.). (Illus.). 256p. 1974. 11.95 (ISBN 0-8038-3391-1); pap. text ed. 6.75x (ISBN 0-8038-3394-6). Hastings.

Simons, Howard & Califano, Joseph A., eds. The Media & the Law. LC 75-19822. (Special Studies). 1976. text ed. 26.95 (ISBN 0-275-55820-7); pap. 11.95 (ISBN 0-275-89530-0). Praeger.

Swain, Bruce M. Reporters' Ethics. 1978. text ed. 10.50 (ISBN 0-8138-1280-1). Iowa St U Pr.

Van Gerpen, Maurice. Privileged Communication & the Press: The Citizen's Right to Know Versus the Law's Right to Confidential News Source Evidence. LC 78-55334. (Contributions in Political Science: No. 19). 1979. lib. bdg. 22.95x (ISBN 0-313-20523-X, VGP/). Greenwood.

Ward, William G. Student Journalist & Editorial Leadership. LC 68-22157. (Student Journalist Ser). (gr. 9 up). PLB 5.97 (ISBN 0-8239-0118-1). Rosen Pr.

JOURNALISTIC LIBRARIES

see Newspaper Office Libraries

JOURNALISTIC PHOTOGRAPHY

see Photography, Journalistic

JOURNALISTS

see also Journalism–Vocational Guidance; War Correspondents; Women Journalists

Aaseng, Nathan. Walter Cronkite. LC 81-3747. (The Achievers Ser.). (Illus.). (gr. 4-9). 1981. PLB 5.95 (ISBN 0-8225-0486-3, AACR2). Lerner Pubns.

A Beckett, Arthur W. A Becketts of Punch. LC 69-17341. 1969. Repr. of 1903 ed. 22.00 (ISBN 0-8103-3518-2). Gale.

American Journalists, 49 Vols. 1971. Repr. Set. 772.00 (ISBN 0-405-01650-6). Arno.

Andrews, Alexander. History of British Journalism: From the Foundation of the Newspaper Press in England to the Repeal of the Stamp Act, 2 Vols. LC 68-24958. (British History Ser., No. 30). 1969. Repr. of 1859 ed. lib. bdg. 48.95 (ISBN 0-8383-0154-1). Haskell.

--History of British Journalism from the Foundation of the Newspaper Press in England to the Repeal of the Stamp Act in 1855, 2 Vols. 1968. Set. 30.00 (ISBN 0-403-00139-0). Scholarly.

Armstrong, William M. E. L. Godkin: A Biography. LC 77-12918. 1978. 35.00 (ISBN 0-87395-371-1). State U NY Pr.

Barry, David S. Forty Years in Washington. (American Newspapermen 1790-1933 Ser.). (Illus.). xi, 349p. 1974. Repr. of 1924 ed. 17.50x (ISBN 0-8464-0031-6). Beekman Pubs.

Bayley, Edwin. Joe McCarthy & the Press. LC 81-50824. 256p. 1981. 18.95 (ISBN 0-299-08620-8). U of Wis Pr.

Begley, Kathleen A. Deadline. (gr. 5 up). 1979. pap. 1.50 (ISBN 0-440-91718-2, LFL). Dell.

--Deadline. LC 77-2550. (gr. 5-8). 1977. 8.95. (ISBN 0-399-20611-6). Putnam.

Blythe, Samuel G. Making of a Newspaper Man. LC 76-95085. Repr. of 1912 ed. lib. bdg. 15.00x (ISBN 0-8371-3075-1, BLNM). Greenwood.

Brewer, George D. The Fighting Editor: Or Warren & the Appeal. (Amer. Newspapermen Ser.: 1790-1933). 1975. Repr. of 1910 ed. 14.50x (ISBN 0-8464-0030-8). Beekman Pubs.

Brown, Marvin L., Jr. Louis Veuillot. LC 77-82882. 1977. 15.00 (ISBN 0-87716-070-8, Pub. by Moore Pub Co). F Apple.

Bryan, Charles V. The Child That Nobody Wanted. LC 57-12228. 284p. 1957. 4.00 (ISBN 0-87004-022-7). Caxton.

Bullard, Frederick L. Famous War Correspondents. (American Newspapermen 1790-1933 Ser.). (Illus.). xii, 437p. 1974. Repr. of 1914 ed. 20.00x (ISBN 0-8464-0029-4). Beekman Pubs.

Buni, Andrew. Robert L. Vann of the Pittsburgh Courier: Politics & Black Journalism. LC 73-7700. 1974. 14.95 (ISBN 0-8229-3274-1). U of Pittsburgh Pr.

Busch, Noel F. Briton Hadden: A Biography of the Co-Founder of Time. LC 75-25253. 236p. 1975. Repr. of 1949 ed. lib. bdg. 14.75x (ISBN 0-8371-8395-2, BUBH). Greenwood.

Carter, Hodding. First Person Rural. LC 77-10014. 1977. Repr. lib. bdg. 18.00x (ISBN 0-8371-9727-9, CAFI). Greenwood.

Chalmers, David M. Social & Political Ideas of the Muckrakers. facs. ed. LC 70-117765. (Essay Index Reprint Ser). 1964. 12.00 (ISBN 0-8369-1745-6). Arno.

Chapin, Charles E. Charles E. Chapin's Story. (Amer. Newspapermen Ser.: 1790-1933). 334p. 1978. Repr. of 1920 ed. 17.50x (ISBN 0-8464-0028-6). Beekman Pubs.

Chapman, John J. William Lloyd Garrison. (American Newspapermen 1790-1933 Ser.). 1974. Repr. 17.50x (ISBN 0-8464-0027-8). Beekman Pubs.

Clark, E. Culpepper. Francis Warrington Dawson & the Politics of Restoration: South Carolina, Eighteen Seventy-Four to Eighteen Eighty-Nine. LC 79-27884. (Illus.). 256p. 1980. 18.95x (ISBN 0-8173-0039-2). U of Ala Pr.

Clark, Mary E. Peter Porcupine in America: The Career of William Cobbett. (American Newspapermen 1790-1933 Ser.). v, 193p. 1974. Repr. of 1939 ed. 11.00x (ISBN 0-8464-0026-X). Beekman Pubs.

Coblentz, Edmond E., ed. Newsmen Speak: Journalists on Their Craft. facs. ed. LC 68-14900. (Essay Index Reprint Ser). 1954. 15.00 (ISBN 0-8369-0318-8). Arno.

Commins, Dorothy. What Is an Editor? Saxe Commins at Work. LC 77-81716. 256p. 5.95 (ISBN 0-226-11428-7, Phoen). U of Chicago Pr.

Davis, Charles B. Adventures & Letters of Richard Harding Davis. (American Newspapermen 1790-1933 Ser.). (Illus.). iii, 417p. 1974. Repr. of 1917 ed. 18.50x (ISBN 0-8464-0024-3). Beekman Pubs.

Davis, Eleanor H. Abraham Fornander: A Biography. LC 78-31368. 1979. 12.95 (ISBN 0-8248-0459-7). U Pr of Hawaii.

Driscoll, Charles B. The Life of O. O. McIntyre. (American Newspaperman 1790-1933 Ser.). (Illus.). 344p. 1974. Repr. of 1938 ed. 17.50x (ISBN 0-8464-0022-7). Beekman Pubs.

Driver, C. J. Patrick Duncan. text ed. 65.00x (ISBN 0-435-96200-0). Heinemann Ed.

Erlanger, Ellen. Dan Rather. LC 81-3697. (The Achievers Ser.). (Illus.). (gr. 4-9). 1981. PLB 5.95 (ISBN 0-8225-0487-1, AACR2). Lerner Pubns.

Escott, Thomas H. Masters of English Journalism: A Study of Personal Forces. LC 74-98834. Repr. of 1911 ed. lib. bdg. 16.00x (ISBN 0-8371-3020-4, ESME). Greenwood.

Ethridge, Willie S. Mark Ethridge: The Life & Times of a Great Newspaperman. (Illus.). 484p. 1981. 20.00 (ISBN 0-8149-0852-7). Vanguard.

Fang, Irving. Those Radio Commentators. (Illus.). 1977. 14.95 (ISBN 0-8138-1500-2); 2 records incl. Iowa St U Pr.

Fisher, Charles. The Columnists. 1977. Repr. of 1944 ed. lib. bdg. 12.50 (ISBN 0-686-19801-8). Havertown Bks.

Flamm, Jerry. Good Life in Hard Times: San Francisco's '20s & '30s. LC 76-30524. (Illus.). 1977. pap. 7.95 (ISBN 0-87701-092-7). Chronicle Bks.

Gettleman, Marvin E. An Elusive Presence: The Discovery of John H. Finley & His America. LC 79-10547. (Illus.). 1979. 18.95x (ISBN 0-88229-312-5); pap. 9.95x (ISBN 0-88229-695-7). Nelson-Hall.

Giles, Frank. The Prince of Journalists: The Life & Times of de Blowitz. 1974. 12.95 (ISBN 0-912050-51-9, Library Pr). Open Court.

Greaves, C. Desmond. Life & Times of James Connolly. (Orig.). 1972. pap. 1.65 (ISBN 0-7178-0330-9). Intl Pub Co.

Hall, Trevor H. Search for Harry Price. (Illus.). 248p. 1979. 28.00 (ISBN 0-7156-1143-7, Pub. by Duckworth England). Biblio Dist.

Harris, H. Wilson. J. A. Spender. 1977. Repr. of 1946 ed. lib. bdg. 8.50 (ISBN 0-686-19811-5). Havertown Bks.

Hauser, Thomas. The Execution of Charles Horman. 272p. 1979. pap. 2.75 (ISBN 0-380-49098-6, 49098, Discus). Avon.

Hearn, Lafcadio. Editorials of Lafacadio Hearn. Hutson, Charles W., ed. (American Newspapermen 1790-1933 Ser.). xx, 356p. 1974. Repr. of 1926 ed. 17.50x (ISBN 0-8464-0020-0). Beekman Pubs.

Herd, Harold. Seven Editors. LC 77-8868. 1977. Repr. of 1955 ed. lib. bdg. 15.00 (ISBN 0-8371-9704-X, HESE). Greenwood.

Hersey, Harold B. Pulpwood Editor. LC 74-4841. 301p. 1974. Repr. of 1937 ed. lib. bdg. 17.00x (ISBN 0-8371-7490-2, HEPE). Greenwood.

Hess, Stephen. The Washington Reporters. LC 80-70077. 275p. 1981. 17.95 (ISBN 0-8157-3594-4); pap. 6.95 (ISBN 0-8157-3593-6). Brookings.

Hibben, Paxton. Henry Ward Beecher: An American Portrait. (American Newspapermen 1790-1933 Ser.). 361p. 1974. Repr. of 1942 ed. 17.50x (ISBN 0-8464-0019-7). Beekman Pubs.

Hohenberg, John. Foreign Correspondence: The Great Reporters & Their Times. LC 64-22762. 1967. 20.00x (ISBN 0-231-02600-5); pap. 6.50x (ISBN 0-231-08579-6). Columbia U Pr.

Hough, Henry B. To the Harbor Light. 1976. Repr. lib. bdg. 10.95 (ISBN 0-8161-6435-5, Large Print Bks). G K Hall.

Hoyt, K. & Leighton, F. Drunk Before Noon: The Behind-the-Scenes Story of the Washington Press Corps. 1979. 12.95 (ISBN 0-13-220830-X). P-H.

Hudson, Derek. British Journalists & Newspapers. 1977. lib. bdg. 8.50 (ISBN 0-686-19799-2). Havertown Bks.

Huffman, James L. Politics of the Meiji Press: The Life of Fukuchi Gen'ichiro. LC 79-3879. 1980. text ed. 15.00x (ISBN 0-8248-0679-4). U Pr of Hawaii.

Ingersoll, Lurton D. Life of Horace Greeley: Founder of the N. Y. Tribune. (American Newspapermen 1790-1933 Ser.). (Illus.). 688p. 1974. Repr. 26.50x (ISBN 0-8464-0018-9). Beekman Pubs.

International Portrait Gallery: Media People Supplement. (International Portrait Gallery Ser.: No. IPG-8). (Illus.). 1978. 150.00 (ISBN 0-8103-1532-7). Gale.

International Portrait Gallery: Vol. 11, Second Media People Supplement. (Illus.). 64p. 1981. 50.00 (ISBN 0-686-69447-3, IPG-11). Gale.

Johnstone, John W., et al. The News People: A Sociological Portrait of American Journalists & Their Work. LC 76-14890. 240p. 1976. 17.50 (ISBN 0-252-00310-1). U of Ill Pr.

Kahn, E. J. About the New Yorker & Me: A Sentimental Journal. LC 78-11497. 1979. 12.95 (ISBN 0-399-12300-8). Putnam.

Landeira, Ricardo. Ramiro De Maeztu. (World Authors Ser.: Spain: No. 484). 1978. lib. bdg. 12.50 (ISBN 0-8057-6325-2). Twayne.

Lorenz, Alfred L. Hugh Gaine: A Colonial Printer-Editor's Odyssey to Loyalism. LC 72-75335. (New Horizons in Journalism Ser.). 205p. 1972. 6.95x (ISBN 0-8093-0588-7). S Ill U Pr.

Luby, James P. James Luby, Journalist. (American Newspapermen 1790-1933 Ser.). 135p. 1974. Repr. of 1930 ed. 11.50x (ISBN 0-8464-0014-6). Beekman Pubs.

Luciw, Wasyl. Ahapius Honcharenko & the Alaska Hearald: The Editor's Life & an Analysis of His Newspaper. LC 65-923. pap. text ed. 6.00 (ISBN 0-918884-10-1). Slavia Lib.

Lucy, Henry. The Diary of a Journalist. 1977. Repr. of 1920 ed. lib. bdg. 7.50 (ISBN 0-686-19804-2). Havertown Bks.

Lyon, William H. Pioneer Editor in Missouri, 1808-1860. LC 64-17647. 1965. 10.00x (ISBN 0-8262-0037-0). U of Mo Pr.

Maddex, Jack P., Jr. The Reconstruction of Edward A. Pollard: A Rebel's Conversion to Postbellum Unionism. LC 74-8961. (The James Sprunt Studies in History & Political Science: Vol. 54). 1974. pap. text ed. 6.50x (ISBN 0-8078-5054-3). U of NC Pr.

Marzio, Peter C. The Men & Machines of American Journalism: A Pictorial Essay. LC 73-5371. (Illus.). 144p. 1973. pap. 4.95 (ISBN 0-87474-629-9). Smithsonian.

Mathews, Joseph J. George W. Smalley: Forty Years a Foreign Correspondent. LC 72-87496. 239p. 1973. 15.50x (ISBN 0-8078-1205-6). U of NC Pr.

Metcalf, Pricilla. James Knowles: Victorian Editor & Architect. (Illus.). 414p. 1980. 44.00x (ISBN 0-19-812626-3). Oxford U Pr.

Miller, Charles G. Don Piatt: His Work & His Ways. (American Newspapermen 1790-1933 Ser.). (Illus.). vi, 381p. 1974. Repr. of 1893 ed. 18.00x (ISBN 0-8464-0013-8). Beekman Pubs.

Mills, George. Harvey Ingham & Gardner Cowles Sr. Bunke, Joan, ed. (Illus.). 1977. 5.95 (ISBN 0-8138-0155-9). Iowa St U Pr.

Mitchell, Burroughs, ed. The Education of an Editor. LC 79-7204. 1980. 8.95 (ISBN 0-385-15032-6). Doubleday.

Morrison, John. The Media Men. (Today's World Ser.). 1978. 14.95 (ISBN 0-7134-0047-1, Pub. by Batsford England). David & Charles.

Noble, Valerie. Hawaiian Prophet: Alexander Hume Ford. (Illus.). 1980. 15.00 (ISBN 0-682-49540-9). Exposition.

Read, Donald. Press & People, Seventeen Ninety to Eighteen Fifty. LC 74-3747. (Illus.). 227p. 1975. Repr. of 1961 ed. lib. bdg. 14.00x (ISBN 0-8371-7465-1, REPP). Greenwood.

Ross, John E. John T. Flynn: Liberal & Conservative. 1980. lib. bdg. 49.95 (ISBN 0-686-59409-6). Revisionist Pr.

Schley, Winfield S. Forty-Five Years Under the Flag. LC 72-78819. 1904. Repr. 20.00 (ISBN 0-403-02020-4). Somerset Pub.

Schoenstein, Ralph. Citizen Paul: A Story of Father & Son. 1978. 8.95 (ISBN 0-374-12385-3). FS&G.

Schorr, Daniel. Clearing the Air. 1978. pap. 2.75 (ISBN 0-425-03903-X). Berkley Pub.

Schurz, Carl. The Reminiscences of Carl Schurz, 3 vols. LC-72-78820. 1907-08. Repr. 69.00 (ISBN 0-403-02021-2). Somerset Pub.

Seitz, Don C. Artemus Ward (Charles Farrar Browne) A Biography & Bibliography. (American Newspapermen 1790-1933 Ser.). (Illus.). 338p. 1974. Repr. of 1919 ed. 20.00x (ISBN 0-8464-0009-X). Beekman Pubs.

Sgard, Jean & Gilot, Michel. Dictionnaire des Journalistes, 1600-1789. 391p. (Fr.). 1976. pap. 75.00 (ISBN 0-686-57221-1, M-6516). French & Eur.

Shipp, Nelson. A Vagabond Newsman. LC 74-79230. 1974. bds. 5.95 (ISBN 0-87797-028-9). Cherokee.

--A Vagabond Newsman. LC 74-79230. 1974. bds. 5.95 (ISBN 0-87797-028-9). Cherokee.

Smith, C. R. Management of Newspaper Correspondents. 1977. Repr. of 1944 ed. lib. bdg. 12.50 (ISBN 0-686-19818-2). Havertown Bks.

Sokolov, Raymond. The Wayward Reporter: The Life of A. J. Liebling. LC 79-3403. (Illus.). 1980. 16.95 (ISBN 0-06-014061-5, HarpT). Har-Row.

Spielmann, M. H. History of Punch. LC 69-16069. 1969. Repr. of 1895 ed. 32.00 (ISBN 0-8103-3553-0). Gale.

Spielmann, Marion H. History of Punch. (Illus.). Repr. of 1895 ed. lib. bdg. 26.50x (ISBN 0-8371-2360-7, SPHP). Greenwood.

Startt, James D. Journalism's Unofficial Ambassador: A Biography of Edward Price Bell 1869-1943. LC 79-17071. (Illus.). xiii, 260p. 1980. 15.95x (ISBN 0-8214-0415-6). Ohio U Pr.

Steel, Ronald. Walter Lippmann & the American Century. (Illus.). 640p. 1980. 19.95 (ISBN 0-316-81190-4). Little.

Syndicated Columnists. 300p. 1979. 32.00 (ISBN 0-686-62481-5). B Klein Pubns.

Terrell, Russell F. A Study of the Early Journalistic Writing of Henry W. Grady. (American Newspapermen 1790-1933 Ser.). 177p. 1974. Repr. of 1927 ed. 14.50x (ISBN 0-8464-0006-5). Beekman Pubs.

Thompson, Slason. Eugene Field: A Study in Heredity & Contradictions, 2 vols. (American Newspapermen 1790-1933 Ser.). (Illus.). 629p. 1973. Repr. of 1901 ed. Set. 37.50x (ISBN 0-8464-0005-7). Beekman Pubs.

Thornbrough, Emma Lou. T. Thomas Fortune: Militant Journalist. LC 73-175305. (Negro American Biographies & Autobiographies Ser). 408p. 1972. 12.50x (ISBN 0-226-79832-1). U of Chicago Pr.

Tunstall, Jeremy. Journalists at Work: Specialist Correspondents; Their News Organizations, News Sources, & Competitor Colleagues. LC 73-87745. (Communication & Society: Vol. 1). 304p. 1974. 22.50x (ISBN 0-8039-0322-7); pap. 10.95 (ISBN 0-8039-1173-4). Sage.

Tyrrell, Robert. Work of the Television Journalist. 2nd ed. LC 80-41970. 200p. 1981. 22.95 (ISBN 0-240-51051-8). Focal Pr.

Van Buren, Abigail. The Best of Dear Abby. 250p. 1981. 9.95 (ISBN 0-8362-7907-7). Andrews & McMeel.

Vanderbilt, Cornelius. A Cub Reporter. (Amer. Newspapermen Ser.: 1870-1933). 1978. 13.50x (ISBN 0-8464-0003-0). Beekman Pubs.

Villard, Oswald G. Some Newspapers & Newspapermen. facs. ed. LC 79-134148. (Essay Index Reprint Ser). 1926. 19.50 (ISBN 0-8369-2206-9). Arno.
Walker, Stanley. City Editor. 1977. Repr. of 1934 ed. lib. bdg. 10.00 (ISBN 0-686-19800-X). Havertown Bks.
Waugh, Evelyn. A Little Order: A Selection from His Journalism. Gallagher, Donat, ed. 224p. 1981. 12.95 (ISBN 0-316-92633-7). Little.
Weiner, Richard. Syndicated Columnists. 3rd ed. LC 78-64585. 1979. 30.00 (ISBN 0-913046-10-8). Public Relations.
White, Theodore H. In Search of History: A Personal Adventure. LC 78-2177. 1978. 12.95 (ISBN 0-06-014599-4, HarpT). Har-Row.
Who Was Who in Journalism, Nineteen Twenty-Five-Nineteen Twenty-Eight. LC 78-13580. (Composite Biographical Dictionary Ser.: No. 4). 1978. 68.00 (ISBN 0-8103-0401-5). Gale.
Whyte, Frederic. The Life of W. T. Stead, 2 vols. 1978. Repr. of 1925 ed. lib. bdg. 65.00 (ISBN 0-8495-5637-6). Arden Lib.
Wicker, Tom. On Press. 1979. pap. 2.95 (ISBN 0-425-04068-2). Berkley Pub.
Wilmer Atkinson: An Autobiography. (American Newspapermen Ser.: 1790-1933). 1976. 21.50x (ISBN 0-8464-0032-4). Beekman Pubs.
Wilson, Nelly. Bernard-Lazare. LC 77-82524. 1979. 42.00 (ISBN 0-521-21802-0). Cambridge U Pr.
Wood, Clement. Bernarr Macfadden: A Study in Success. (American Newspapermen 1790-1933 Ser.). 316p. 1974. Repr. of 1929 ed. 18.00x (ISBN 0-8464-0001-4). Beekman Pubs.
Woods, Donald. Biko. LC 78-55525. (Illus.). 1979. pap. 2.50 (ISBN 0-394-72654-5, Vin). Random.
Writers at Work: The Paris Review Interviews. (Third Ser.). 1977. pap. 4.95 (ISBN 0-14-004542-2). Penguin.
Yates, Norris W. William T. Porter & the Spirit of the Times: Study of the Bear School of Humor. Dorson, Richard M., ed. LC 77-70630. (International Folklore Ser.). 1977. Repr. of 1957 ed. lib. bdg. 14.00x (ISBN 0-405-10134-1). Arno.
Young, John V. Hot Type & Pony Wire: My Life As a California Reporter from Prohibition to Pearl Harbor. LC 80-81419. (Illus.). 165p. 1980. 9.95 (ISBN 0-934136-05-X). Western Tanager.

JOURNALISTS–CORRESPONDENCE, REMINISCENCES, ETC.

see also subdivision Personal Narratives under names of Wars, e.g. World War, 1939-1945–Personal Narratives

Abbot, Willis J. Watching the World Go by. (American Newspapermen 1790-1933 Ser.). (Illus.). 358p. 1974. 17.50x (ISBN 0-8464-0033-2). Beekman Pubs.
Armstrong, William M., ed. The Gilded Age Letters of E. L. Godkin. LC 74-6462. (Illus.). 1974. 39.00 (ISBN 0-87395-246-4); microfiche 39.00 (ISBN 0-87395-247-2). State U NY Pr.
Artken, J. Conversations: The Diary of a Worried Journalist's Trek Across a Divided & Threatened Canada. 1978. pap. 7.95 (ISBN 0-13-172056-2). P-H.
Atkinson, Wilmer. Autobiography. (American Newspapermen 1790-1933). (Illus.). 375p. 1974. Repr. of 1920 ed. 21.50x (ISBN 0-8464-0032-4). Beekman Pubs.
Austin, James C. Fields of the Atlantic Monthly: Letters to an Editor, 1861-1870. LC 53-12551. 1953. 8.50 (ISBN 0-87328-007-5). Huntington Lib.
Bacon, James. Hollywood Is a Four Letter Town. 1977. pap. 1.95 (ISBN 0-380-01671-0, 33399). Avon.
Baillie, Hugh. High Tension. facsimile ed. LC 79-90604. (Essay Index Reprint Ser). 1959. 24.00 (ISBN 0-8369-1543-7). Arno.
Belfrage, Cedric & Aronson, James. Something to Guard: The Stormy Life of the National Guardian. LC 78-3530. 362p. 1978. 25.00x (ISBN 0-231-04510-7). Columbia U Pr.
Bernard, George. Inside the National Enquirer: Confessions of an Undercover Reporter. Hammond, Debbie, ed. LC 76-44613. 1977. 11.95 (ISBN 0-87949-089-6). Ashley Bks.
Bhatia, Prem. All My Yesterdays. (Illus.). 179p. 1972. 6.75x (ISBN 0-685-30444-2). Intl Pubns Serv.
Buckingham, Joseph T. Personal Memoirs & Recollections of Editorial Life. LC 76-125682. (American Journalists Ser). 1970. Repr. of 1852 ed. 20.00 (ISBN 0-405-01657-3). Arno.
Cardus, Neville. Autobiography. LC 75-37825. (Illus.). 288p. 1976. Repr. of 1947 ed. lib. bdg. 17.50x (ISBN 0-8371-8577-7, CAAU). Greenwood.
Carroll, Carroll. My Life with... 1977. pap. 1.95 (ISBN 0-685-76993-3, 3157). Major Bks.
Cassidy, William. Memorial of William Cassidy. LC 73-125684. (American Journalists Ser). 1970. Repr. of 1874 ed. 12.00 (ISBN 0-405-01661-1). Arno.
Clarke, Tom. My Northcliffe Diary. 1977. Repr. of 1931 ed. lib. bdg. 8.50 (ISBN 0-686-19820-4). Havertown Bks.
Cousins, Norman. The Human Options: An Autobiographical Notebook. (Illus.). 1981. 9.95 (ISBN 0-393-01430-4). Norton.
Croffut, William A. American Procession, Eighteen Fifty-Five to Nineteen Fourteen. facs. ed. LC 68-20293. (Essay Index Reprint Ser). 1931. 18.00 (ISBN 0-8369-0352-8). Arno.
Cull, Mervyn. Soviet Assignment. (Illus.). 1974. pap. 4.00x (ISBN 0-340-19510-X). Intl Pubns Serv.
Curtis, George W. Early Letters of George William Curtis to John S. Dwight. Cooke, George W., ed. LC 75-134372. Repr. of 1898 ed. 10.00 (ISBN 0-404-08420-6). AMS Pr.
Daniels, Josephus. Editor in Politics. LC 74-2839. (Illus.). 644p. 1974. Repr. of 1941 ed. lib. bdg. 38.50x (ISBN 0-8371-7439-2, DAEI). Greenwood.
--Tar Heel Editor. LC 74-2840. (Illus.). 544p. 1974. Repr. of 1939 ed. lib. bdg. 34.00x (ISBN 0-8371-7440-6, DATH). Greenwood.
Demaitre, Edmund. Eyewitness: A Journalist Covers the Twentieth Century. (Illus.). 450p. 1981. 17.50 (ISBN 0-8044-1218-9). Ungar.
Elliott, Osborn. The World of Oz. (Illus.). 253p. 1980. 14.95 (ISBN 0-670-78770-1). Viking Pr.
Fischer, Louis. Men & Politics: An Autobiography. LC 73-111498. vi, 672p. Repr. of 1941 ed. lib. bdg. 25.75x (ISBN 0-8371-4641-0, FIMP). Greenwood.
Frady, Marshall. Southerners: A Journalist's Odyssey. 1981. pap. 6.95 (ISBN 0-686-72176-4, F566, Mer). NAL.
Gauvreau, Emile. My Last Million Readers. LC 74-15741. (Popular Culture in America Ser.). 492p. 1975. Repr. 27.00x (ISBN 0-405-06376-8). Arno.
Gayle, Addison, Jr. Wayward Child: A Personal Odyssey. LC 76-42329. 1977. 7.95 (ISBN 0-385-08873-6, Anchor Pr). Doubleday.
Gilmore, Eddy. Me & My Russian Wife. LC 69-10098. (Illus.). 1968. Repr. of 1954 ed. lib. bdg. 16.25x (ISBN 0-8371-0085-2, GIRW). Greenwood.
Greeley, Horace. Recollections of a Busy Life. facs. ed. LC 74-83912. (Black Heritage Library Collection Ser). 1868. 21.00 (ISBN 0-8369-8582-6). Arno.
--Recollections of a Busy Life. LC 74-125695. (American Journalists Ser). 1970. Repr. of 1868 ed. 21.00 (ISBN 0-405-01674-3). Arno.
--Recollections of a Busy Life, 2 Vols. LC 71-137913. (American History & Culture in the Nineteenth Century Ser). 1971. Repr. of 1873 ed. Set. 34.50x (ISBN 0-8046-1481-4). Kennikat.
Hamill, Peter. The Gift. LC 73-3981. 1973. 4.95 (ISBN 0-394-47338-8). Random.
Hauck, Marcus J. Reflections from a Depression: Adolescence to Age Sixty-Two. 80p. 1978. 4.95 (ISBN 0-8059-2542-2). Dorrance.
Havighurst, A. F. Radical Journalist: Henry W. Massingham, 1860-1924. LC 73-83106. (Conference on British Studies Biographical Ser). 368p. 1974. 42.00 (ISBN 0-521-20355-4). Cambridge U Pr.
Healy, George W. Lifetime on Deadline. LC 75-22404. (Illus.). 368p. 1976. 12.50 (ISBN 0-88289-076-X). Pelican.
Herbers, John. No Thank You, Mr. President. 256p. 1976. 7.95 (ISBN 0-393-05570-1). Norton.
Howard, Edwin, ed. The Editorial We: A Posthumous Autobiography by Edward J. Meeman. (Illus.). 238p. 1976. 7.95 (ISBN 0-87870-079-X). Memphis St Univ.
Knoblaufgh, H. Correspondent in Spain. 59.95 (ISBN 0-87968-946-3). Gordon Pr.
Leach, Frank A. Recollections of a Newspaperman: A Record of Life & Events in California. (American Newspapermen 1790-1933 Ser.). (Illus.). 416p. 1974. Repr. of 1917 ed. 20.00x (ISBN 0-8464-0016-2). Beekman Pubs.
Liss, Robert E. Fading Rainbow. LC 79-25812. (Illus.). 1980. 9.95 (ISBN 0-416-00631-0). Methuen Inc.
Lucy, Henry. The Diary of a Journalist. 1979. Repr. of 1920 ed. 20.00 (ISBN 0-8495-3305-8). Arden Lib.
Lyons, Eugene. Assignment in Utopia. LC 76-110271. 1971. Repr. of 1937 ed. lib. bdg. 27.00x (ISBN 0-8371-4497-3, LYAU). Greenwood.
Matthews, Herbert L. The Education of a Correspondent. LC 76-106672. 550p. Repr. of 1946 ed. lib. bdg. 21.50x (ISBN 0-8371-3369-6, MACO). Greenwood.
Mott, Frank L. Time Enough: Essays in Autobiography. 248p. 1972. Repr. of 1962 ed. lib. bdg. 15.00 (ISBN 0-8371-6445-1, MOTE). Greenwood.
Mydans, Carl. More Than Meets the Eye. LC 74-19785. 310p. 1975. Repr. of 1959 ed. lib. bdg. 17.25x (ISBN 0-8371-7808-8, MYME). Greenwood.
Newell, Robert H. Orpheus C. Kerr Papers, 3 Vols. LC 78-169922. Repr. of 1865 ed. Set. 49.50 (ISBN 0-404-03670-8). AMS Pr.
Nichols, Thomas L. Journal in Jail. LC 71-125709. (American Journalists). 1970. Repr. of 1840 ed. 16.00 (ISBN 0-405-01690-5). Arno.
Noble, Gil. Black Is the Color of My TV Tube. (Illus.). 1981. 10.00 (ISBN 0-8184-0297-0). Lyle Stuart.
North, Joseph. No Men Are Strangers. LC 58-11504. 1977. pap. 2.25 (ISBN 0-7178-0462-3). Intl Pub Co.
Noyes, Alexander D. Market Place: Reminiscences of a Financial Editor. Repr. of 1938 ed. lib. bdg. 17.75x (ISBN 0-8371-0592-7, NOMP). Greenwood.
Packard, Reynolds. Rome Was My Beat. LC 74-31665. 1975. 8.95 (ISBN 0-8184-0216-4). Lyle Stuart.
Paine, Philbrook. Squarely Behind the Beavers. (Illus.). 1963. 3.95 (ISBN 0-393-08470-1). Norton.
Pilkington, John, ed. Stark Young, A Life in the Arts: Letters, 1900-1962, 2 vols. LC 73-90874. 1600p. 1976. Set. 65.00x (ISBN 0-8071-0100-1). La State U Pr.
Potter, Jeffrey. Men, Money & Magic: The Story of Dorothy Schiff. (Illus.). 416p. 1976. 9.95 (ISBN 0-698-10666-0). Coward.
Rather, Dan & Herkowitz, Mickey. The Camera Never Blinks: Adventures of a TV Journalist. 1977. 10.00 (ISBN 0-688-03184-6). Morrow.
Rather, Dan & Herskowitz, Mickey. The Camera Never Blinks: Adventures of a TV Journalist. 1978. pap. 2.50 (ISBN 0-345-29025-9). Ballantine.
Reeves, Richard. Jet Lag: The Travels of a Bicoastal Reporter. 250p. 1981. 9.95 (ISBN 0-8362-6207-7). Andrews & McMeel.
Rosten, Leo C. The Washington Correspondents. LC 73-19175. (Politics & People Ser.). 456p. 1974. Repr. 23.00x (ISBN 0-405-05896-9). Arno.
Rutstrum, Calvin. A Columnist Looks at Life. 133p. (Orig.). 1981. pap. 5.95 (ISBN 0-931714-10-9). Nodin Pr.
St. John, Adela R. Honeycomb. 1970. pap. 2.25 (ISBN 0-451-07605-2, E7605, Sig). NAL.
Scripps, Edward W. Damned Old Crank: A Self-Portrait of E. W. Scripps Drawn from His Unpublished Writings. McCabe, Charles R., ed. (Illus.). 1971. Repr. of 1951 ed. lib. bdg. 15.00 (ISBN 0-8371-6159-2, SCDO). Greenwood.
--Damned Old Crank: A Self-Portrait of E. W. Scripps Drawn from His Unpublished Writings. McCabe, Charles R., ed. (Illus.). 1971. Repr. of 1951 ed. lib. bdg. 15.00 (ISBN 0-8371-6159-2, SCDO). Greenwood.
Sedgwick, Ellery. The Happy Profession. LC 78-152604. (Illus.). 343p. 1972. Repr. of 1946 ed. lib. bdg. 16.00x (ISBN 0-8371-6039-1, SEHP). Greenwood.
Sevareid, Eric. Conversations with Eric Sevareid. 1979. 7.00 (ISBN 0-8183-0258-5). Pub Aff Pr.
--Not So Wild a Dream. LC 76-11538. 1978. 15.00 (ISBN 0-689-10741-2); pap. 8.95 (ISBN 0-689-70578-6, 235). Atheneum.
Smith, Harry A. Three Smiths in the Wind: Low Man on a Totem Pole, Life in a Putty Knife Factory, Lost in Horse Latitudes. LC 73-112330. 1971. Repr. of 1946 ed. lib. bdg. 26.50x (ISBN 0-8371-4719-0, SMSW). Greenwood.
Sokal, Michael M., ed. An Education in Psychology: James McKeen Cattell's Journal & Letters from Germany & England 1880-1888. 508p. 1981. text ed. 30.00x (ISBN 0-262-19185-7). MIT Pr.
Stewart, Kenneth N. News Is What We Make It: A Running Story of the Working Press. Repr. of 1943 ed. lib. bdg. 14.75x (ISBN 0-8371-3378-5, STNM). Greenwood.
Stingley, James. Mother, Mother. 224p. 1981. 11.95 (ISBN 0-312-92543-3). St Martin.
Stone, Melville E. Fifty Years a Journalist. facs. ed. LC 76-124259. (Select Bibliographies Reprint Ser). (Illus.). 1921. 21.00 (ISBN 0-8369-5447-5). Arno.
Storke, Thomas M. I Write for Freedom. LC 62-21044. 3.95 (ISBN 0-87461-015-X). McNally.
Stott, Mary. The Woman's Page. Orig. Title: Forgetting's No Excuse. Date not set. lib. bdg. 8.95 (ISBN 0-915864-06-1); pap. 5.00 (ISBN 0-915864-05-3). Academy Chi Ltd.
Strickland, Michael, et al, eds. The Best of Ralph McGill. Selected Columns. LC 80-66816. 213p. 1980. 12.50 (ISBN 0-87797-052-1). Cherokee.
Strong, Anna L. I Change Worlds. LC 79-23128. (Illus.). 468p. 1979. pap. 7.95 (ISBN 0-931188-05-9). Seal Pr WA.
Sullivan, Mark. The Education of an American. LC 38-28922. (American Studies). Repr. of 1938 ed. 23.00 (ISBN 0-384-58770-4). Johnson Repr.
Sulzberger, C. L. An Age of Mediocrity. LC 73-2746. (Illus.). 1000p. 1973. 12.95 (ISBN 0-02-615390-4). Macmillan.
Taylor, Edmond. Awakening from History. LC 69-15947. 1969. 8.95 (ISBN 0-87645-016-8). Gambit.
Thomas, Lowell. Good Evening Everybody. 1977. pap. 2.25 (ISBN 0-380-01777-6, 35105). Avon.
Tibbles, Thomas H. Buckskin & Blanket Days: Memoirs of a Friend of the Indians. LC 57-7289. 1969. pap. 3.95 (ISBN 0-8032-5199-8, BB 503, Bison). U of Nebr Pr.
Timerman, Jacobo. Preso Sin Nombre, Celda Sin Numero. LC 80-2715. (Span.). 1981. 7.95 (ISBN 0-394-74903-0). Knopf.
Vanderbilt, Cornelius, Jr. Personal Experience of a Cub Reporter. (American Newspapermen 1790-1933 Ser.). 212p. 1974. Repr. of 1922 ed. 13.50x (ISBN 0-8464-0003-0). Beekman Pubs.
Ward, Bill G. My Kingdom for Just One Strackeljahn. LC 72-75220. 128p. (gr. 7 up). 1972. PLB 5.97 (ISBN 0-8239-0267-6). Rosen Pr.
Watterson, Henry. Marse Henry: An Autobiography, 2 vols. (American Newspapermen 1790-1933 Ser.). (Illus.). 629p. 1974. Repr. of 1919 ed. Set. 37.00x (ISBN 0-8464-0002-2). Beekman Pubs.
Wechsler, James A. Age of Suspicion. LC 72-152616. 1971. Repr. of 1953 ed. lib. bdg. 15.25x (ISBN 0-8371-6051-0, WEAG). Greenwood.
Weinberg, Steve. The Trade Secrets of Washington Journalists. 1981. 12.50 (ISBN 0-87491-424-8); pap. 7.95 (ISBN 0-87491-085-4). Acropolis.

JOURNALS (MACHINERY)

see Bearings (Machinery)

JOURNEYMAN TAILORS' UNION OF AMERICA

Stowell, Charles J. The Journeymen Tailors' Union of America: A Study in Trade Union Policy. Repr. of 1918 ed. 9.50 (ISBN 0-384-58580-9). Johnson Repr.

JOURNEYS

see Voyages and Travels; Voyages around the World

JOUVENEL, HENRYDE, 1876-1955

Binion, Rudolph. Defeated Leaders: The Political Fate of Caillaux, Jouvenel & Tardieu. LC 75-33933. 425p. 1976. Repr. of 1960 ed. lib. bdg. 22.25x (ISBN 0-8371-8539-4, BIDL). Greenwood.

JOVELLANOS, GASPER MELCHOR DE, 1744-1811

Polt, John H. Gaspar Melchor de Jovellanos. LC 78-147263. (World Authors Ser.). 1971. lib. bdg. 12.95x (ISBN 0-8057-2476-1). Irvington.
--Jovellanos & His English Sources. LC 64-25395. (Transactions Ser.: Vol. 54, Pt. 7). 1964. pap. 1.00 (ISBN 0-87169-547-2). Am Philos.

JOY AND SORROW

see also Church Work with the Bereaved; Happiness; Pleasure

Duquoc, Christian. Gift of Joy. LC 68-59156. (Concilium Ser.: Vol. 39). 172p. pap. 6.95 (ISBN 0-8091-1578-6). Paulist Pr.
Evans, Colleen T. A New Joy. (Orig.). pap. 1.50 (ISBN 0-89129-015-X). Jove Pubns.
Follin. Joy Unspeakable. pap. 0.75 (ISBN 0-686-12887-7). Schmul Pub Co.
Guerra, Cyvette. The Joy Robbers. LC 78-66871. 1979. 4.95 (ISBN 0-914850-05-9, MO579); pap. 2.50 (ISBN 0-914850-39-3, MO575). Impact Tenn.
Hicks, Roy H. He Who Laughs...Lasts...& Lasts...& Lasts. (Orig.). 1976. pap. 1.95 (ISBN 0-89274-003-5). Harrison Hse.
Joy. 186p. 1980. 6.95 (ISBN 0-87747-819-8). Deseret Bk.
McKinney, Donald. Joy Begins with You. LC 74-20523. 96p. 1975. 4.95 (ISBN 0-687-20647-2). Abingdon.
Payne, Richard J. Alive with Joy. (Color Us Wonderful Ser.). (ps). 1971. pap. 0.35 (ISBN 0-8091-6500-7). Paulist Pr.
Pope Paul VI. On Christian Joy. 1975. pap. 0.30 (ISBN 0-8198-0448-7). Dghtrs St Paul.
Powell, Paul W. Why Me, Lord? 120p. 1981. pap. 3.95 (ISBN 0-89693-007-6). Victor Bks.
Schuller, Robert. Transforme Sua Tensao Em Poder. Date not set. 1.20 (ISBN 0-686-76442-0). Life Pubs Intl.
Schutz, William C. Joy: Expanding Human Awareness. 1981. Repr. of 1967 ed. text ed. 18.50x (ISBN 0-8290-0050-X). Irvington.
Trousseau, Marie M. & Citron, Anne M. Joy of Living. (Rejoice Ser.). (gr. 3-6). pap. 0.35 (ISBN 0-8091-6509-0). Paulist Pr.

JOYCE, JAMES, 1882-1941

Adams, Robert M. James Joyce: Common Sense & Beyond. xviii, 232p. 1980. Repr. of 1966 ed. lib. bdg. 15.00x (ISBN 0-374-90053-1). Octagon.
Allt, Peter. Some Aspects of the Life & Works of James Augustine Joyce. 50p. 1980. Repr. of 1942 ed. lib. bdg. 8.50 (ISBN 0-89987-026-0). Darby Bks.
--Some Aspects of the Life & Works of James Augustine Joyce. LC 74-2083. 1952. lib. bdg. 6.00 (ISBN 0-8414-2962-6). Folcroft.

--Some Aspects of the Life & Works of James Augustine Joyce. 1978. Repr. lib. bdg. 7.50 (ISBN 0-8495-0111-3). Arden Lib.

Anderson, Chester G. James Joyce & His World. LC 77-83678. (Illus.). 1978. 9.95 (ISBN 0-684-15510-9, ScribT). Scribner.

--Word Index to James Joyce's Stephen Hero. 185p. 1980. Repr. of 1958 ed. lib. bdg. 35.00 (ISBN 0-8495-0220-9). Arden Lib.

--Words Index to James Joyce's Stephen Hero. LC 76-49592. 1977. lib. bdg. 20.00 (ISBN 0-8414-2961-8). Folcroft.

Andreach, Robert J. Studies in Structure: The Stages of the Spiritual Life in Four Modern Authors. LC 64-24755. 1965. 15.00 (ISBN 0-8232-0630-0). Fordham.

Arnold, Armin. James Joyce. LC 68-31445. (Modern Literature Ser.). 1969. 10.95 (ISBN 0-8044-2007-6); pap. 4.95 (ISBN 0-8044-6008-6). Ungar.

Atherton, J. S. The Books at the Wake: A Study of Literary Allusions in James Joyce's "Finnegans Wake". rev. ed. 15.00 (ISBN 0-911858-26-1). Appel.

Atherton, James S. The Books at the Wake: A Study of Literary Allusions in James Joyce's "Finnegans Wake". LC 74-5407. (Arcturus Books Paperbacks). 308p. 1974. pap. 7.95 (ISBN 0-8093-0687-5). S Ill U Pr.

Barger, James. James Joyce, Modern Irish Writer. new ed. Rahmas, D. Steve, ed. LC 74-14701. (Outstanding Personalities Ser.). 32p. 1974. lib. bdg. 2.95 incl. catalog cards (ISBN 0-686-11492-2); pap. 1.50 vinyl laminated covers (ISBN 0-686-11493-0). SamHar Pr.

Bauerle, Ruth. A Word List to James Joyce's "Exiles". LC 80-8487. 240p. 1981. lib. bdg. 40.00 (ISBN 0-8240-9500-6). Garland Pub.

Beck, Warren. Joyce's Dubliners: Substance, Vision & Art. LC 78-86477. 1969. pap. 8.75 (ISBN 0-8223-0212-8). Duke.

Beckett, Samuel, et al. An Examination of James Joyce. LC 74-1307. (Studies in Joyce, No. 96). 1974. lib. bdg. 39.95 (ISBN 0-8383-2025-2). Haskell.

--James Joyce-Finnegans Wake: a Symposium. LC 44-32829. Orig. Title: Our Exagmination Round His Factification for Incamination of Work in Progress. 202p. 1972. pap. 3.45 (ISBN 0-8112-0446-4, NDP331). New Directions.

Begnal, Michael H. & Eckley, Grace. Narrator & Character in "Finnegans Wake". LC 73-4957. 241p. 1975. 14.50 (ISBN 0-8387-1337-8). Bucknell U Pr.

Begnal, Michael H. & Senn, Fritz, eds. A Conceptual Guide to Finnegans Wake. LC 73-13219. 256p. 1974. 15.95x (ISBN 0-271-01132-7). Pa St U Pr.

Benstock, Bernard. Joyce-Again's Wake: An Analysis of Finnegans Wake. LC 75-3981. (Illus.). 312p. 1975. Repr. of 1966 ed. lib. bdg. 22.00 (ISBN 0-8371-7418-X, BEJW). Greenwood.

Benstock, Shari & Benstock, Bernard. Who's He When He's at Home: A James Joyce Directory. LC 79-17947. 1980. 15.00 (ISBN 0-252-00756-5). U of Ill Pr.

Berrone, Louis, ed. James Joyce in Padua. 1977. 10.00 (ISBN 0-394-40990-6). Random.

Blamires, Harry. The Bloomsday Book: A Guide Through Joyce's Ulysses. (Orig.). 1966. pap. 9.95x (ISBN 0-416-69500-0). Methuen Inc.

Boldereff, Frances M. Hermes to His Son Thoth: Joyce's Use of Giordano Bruno in Finnegans Wake. LC 68-21486. (Illus.). 1968. 10.50 (ISBN 0-9606540-0-3); pap. 4.95 (ISBN 0-9606540-1-1). Classic Nonfic.

Bolt, Sydney. Preface to James Joyce. (Preface Bks.). (Illus.). 1981. text ed. 14.95x (ISBN 0-582-35194-4); pap. text ed. 8.95x (ISBN 0-582-35195-2). Longman.

Bonheim, Helmut. Joyce's Benefictions. LC 64-14725. (Perspectives in Criticism: No. 16). 1964. 18.75x (ISBN 0-520-00147-8). U of Cal Pr.

Bowen, Zack, ed. Irish Renaissance Annual II. 192p. 1981. 12.00 (ISBN 0-87413-185-5). U Delaware Pr.

Bowen, Zack R. Musical Allusions in the Works of James Joyce: Early Poetry Through "Ulysses". LC 74-13314. 1974. 27.50 (ISBN 0-87395-248-0); microfiche 27.50 (ISBN 0-87395-249-9). State U NY Pr.

Boyle, Robert. James Joyce's Pauline Vision: A Catholic Exposition. LC 78-18901. 133p. 1978. 10.95x (ISBN 0-8093-0861-4). S Ill U Pr.

Brandabur, Edward. A Scrupulous Meanness: A Study of Joyce's Early Work. LC 71-131057. 1971. 12.50 (ISBN 0-252-00134-6). U of Ill Pr.

Brennan, J. G. Three Philosophical Novelists. 1964. 9.95 (ISBN 0-02-514930-X). Macmillan.

Brivic, Sheldon R. Joyce Between Freud & Jung. (National University Publications, Literary Criticism Ser.). 1980. 15.00 (ISBN 0-8046-9249-1). Kennikat.

Brown, Homer O. James Joyce's Early Fiction: The Biography of a Form. 1975. Repr. of 1972 ed. 15.00 (ISBN 0-208-01563-9). Shoe String.

Budgen, Frank. James Joyce & the Making of Ulysses. LC 60-50081. (Midland Bks.: No. 26). (Illus.). 352p. 1960. pap. 3.95x (ISBN 0-253-20026-1). Ind U Pr.

Burgess, Anthony. Joysprick: An Introduction to the Language of James Joyce. LC 74-17009. (Illus.). 187p. 1975. pap. 3.95 (ISBN 0-15-646561-2, HB303, Harv). HarBraceJ.

--Re Joyce. 1968. pap. 3.95 (ISBN 0-393-00445-7, Norton Lib). Norton.

Byrne, John F. The Silent Years: An Autobiography with Memoirs of James Joyce & Our Ireland. LC 75-11682. xi, 307p. 1975. Repr. of 1953 ed. lib. bdg. 17.00x (ISBN 0-374-91144-4). Octagon.

Campbell, Joseph & Robinson, Henry M. Skeleton Key to Finnegans Wake. 1977. pap. 5.95 (ISBN 0-14-004663-1). Penguin.

Chace, William M., ed. Joyce: A Collection of Critical Essays. LC 73-18496. (Illus.). 192p. 1974. 10.95 (ISBN 0-13-511303-2, Spec); pap. 4.95 (ISBN 0-13-511295-8, Spec). P-H.

Chatterjee, Sisir. James Joyce: A Study in Technique. 104p. 1981. 8.00x (ISBN 0-86125-128-8, Pub. by Orient Longman India). State Mutual Bk.

--James Joyce, a Study in Technique. 1957. lib. bdg. 12.50 (ISBN 0-8414-3570-7). Folcroft.

Colum, Mary & Colum, Padraic. Our Friend James Joyce. 7.50 (ISBN 0-8446-1122-0). Peter Smith.

Colum, Padraic, et al. Homage to James Joyce. LC 73-14976. 1974. lib. bdg. 10.00 (ISBN 0-8414-3482-4). Folcroft.

Connolly, Thomas E., ed. Joyce's "Portrait". Criticisms & Critiques. LC 62-14861. (Goldentree Books in English Literature). (Orig.). 1962. pap. text ed. 8.95x (ISBN 0-89197-253-6). Irvington.

Conolly, Thomas E. The Personal Library of James Joyce: A Descriptive Bibliography. LC 76-57762. 1974. lib. bdg. 12.50 (ISBN 0-8414-3413-1). Folcroft.

Cope, Jackson I. Joyce's Cities: Archaeologies of the Soul. LC 80-8056. 176p. 1981. text ed. 12.95x (ISBN 0-8018-2543-1). Johns Hopkins.

Costello, Peter. James Joyce. (Gill's Irish Lives Ser.). 135p. 1980. 20.00 (ISBN 0-7171-1077-X, Pub. by Gill & Macmillan Ireland); pap. 6.50 (ISBN 0-7171-0986-0). Irish Bk Ctr.

Cross, Richard K. Flaubert & Joyce: The Rite of Fiction. LC 73-136197. (Princeton Essays Literature Ser.). 1971. 14.00 (ISBN 0-691-06199-8). Princeton U Pr.

Daly, Leo. James Joyce & the Mullingar Connection. (Dolmen Editions: No. 20). 40p. (Demi quarto size). 1975. text ed. 23.00x (ISBN 0-391-00418-2, Dolmen Pr). Humanities.

Davies, Stan G. James Joyce: A Portrait of the Artist. LC 75-11940. (Illus.). 256p. 1976. 25.00x (ISBN 0-8128-1828-8). Stein & Day.

Deming, R. H., ed. James Joyce: Critical Heritage, 2 vols. Incl. Vol. 1. 1907-1927; Vol. 2. 1928-1941. 1970. 35.00 ea. Routledge & Kegan.

Deming, Robert H., ed. James Joyce: The Critical Heritage, 2 vols. (The Critical Heritage Ser.). 1970. Set. 65.00 (ISBN 0-7100-6747-X). Vol. 1, 1907-1927. Vol. 2, 1928-1941. Routledge & Kegan.

Devlin, Laura K. Looking Inward: Studies in James Joyce, E.M. Forster, & the Twentieth Century Novel. 1980. lib. bdg. 59.95 (ISBN 0-87700-269-X). Revisionist Pr.

Duff, Charles. James Joyce & the Plain Reader. LC 78-164027. (Studies in Irish Literature, No. 16). 1971. Repr. of 1932 ed. lib. bdg. 24.95 (ISBN 0-8383-1329-9). Haskell.

--James Joyce & the Plain Reader. LC 72-194752. 1932. lib. bdg. 10.00 (ISBN 0-8414-3713-0). Folcroft.

Edel, Leon. James Joyce: The Last Journey. LC 77-10505. (Studies in Joyce: No. 96). 1977. lib. bdg. 28.95 (ISBN 0-8383-2214-X). Haskell.

Ellman, Richard. Ulysses on the Liffey. 200p. 1972. 13.95 (ISBN 0-19-519665-1). Oxford U Pr.

Ellmann, Richard. The Consciousness of Joyce. 160p. 1981. pap. 4.95 (ISBN 0-19-502898-8, GB 636). Oxford U Pr.

--The Consciousness of Joyce. 1977. 13.95 (ISBN 0-19-519950-2). Oxford U Pr.

--James Joyce. 1959. 27.50 (ISBN 0-19-500541-4). Oxford U Pr.

--James Joyce. pap. 12.95 (ISBN 0-19-500723-9, GB). Oxford U Pr.

--Ulysses on the Liffey. (Illus.). 230p. 1973. pap. 4.95 (ISBN 0-19-501663-7, GB). Oxford U Pr.

Ellmann, Richard, ed. Selected Letters of James Joyce. LC 71-83240. 440p. 1975. 18.95 (ISBN 0-670-63190-6). Viking Pr.

--Selected Letters of James Joyce. LC 71-83240. 1975. pap. 5.95 (ISBN 0-670-00276-3). Penguin.

Epstein, Edmund L. The Ordeal of Stephen Dedalus: The Conflict of the Generations in James Joyce's "A Portrait of the Artist As a Young Man". LC 73-7714. (Arcturus Books Paperbacks). 231p. 1973. pap. 2.65 (ISBN 0-8093-0649-2). S Ill U Pr.

Eruvbetine, Agwonorobo E. Intellectualized Emotions & the Art of James Joyce. 1980. 7.50 (ISBN 0-682-49530-1, University). Exposition.

French, Marilyn. The Book As World: James Joyce's Ulysses. 470p. 1976. 16.50x (ISBN 0-674-07853-5). Harvard U Pr.

Giedion-Welcker, Carola, compiled by. In Memoriam James Joyce. LC 75-13347. 1975. Repr. of 1941 ed. lib. bdg. 10.00 (ISBN 0-8414-4543-5). Folcroft.

Giedion-Welcker, Carols, compiled By. In Memoriam James Joyce. 55p. 1980. Repr. of 1914 ed. lib. bdg. 10.00 (ISBN 0-8495-2043-6). Arden Lib.

Gilbert, Stuart. James Joyce's Ulysses. 1955. pap. 2.95 (ISBN 0-394-70013-9, V13, Vin). Random.

Glasheen, Adaline. A Third Census of Finnegan's Wake. LC 75-3770. 1977. 25.00x (ISBN 0-520-02980-1). U of Cal Pr.

Gluck, Barbara R. Beckett & Joyce: Friendship & Fiction. LC 76-50290. 225p. 1979. 16.00 (ISBN 0-8387-2060-9). Bucknell U Pr.

Golding, Louis. James Joyce. LC 72-196435. 1933. lib. bdg. 8.25 (ISBN 0-8414-4654-7). Folcroft.

Gordon, John. James Joyce's Metamorphoses. 250p. 1981. 22.50x (ISBN 0-389-20167-7). B&N.

Gorman, Herbert. James Joyce. 1972. lib. bdg. 17.50x (ISBN 0-374-93219-0). Octagon.

--James Joyce: His First Forty Years. LC 74-11431. 1924. lib. bdg. 20.00 (ISBN 0-8414-4527-3). Folcroft.

Gorman, Herbert S. James Joyce: His First Forty Years. 1978. Repr. of 1926 ed. lib. bdg. 30.00 (ISBN 0-8495-1927-6). Arden Lib.

Gorman, Herbert W. James Joyce. LC 74-30368. (Studies in Joyce Ser., No. 96). 1974. lib. bdg. 33.95 (ISBN 0-8383-2015-5). Haskell.

Gottfried, Roy K. The Art of Joyce's Syntax in Ulysses. LC 79-10294. 199p. 1980. 15.00x (ISBN 0-8203-0478-6). U of Ga Pr.

Groden, Michael. Ulysses in Progress. LC 77-1217. 1977. text ed. 17.50 (ISBN 0-691-06338-9). Princeton U Pr.

Groden, Michael, ed. Ulysses: "Wandering Rocks," "Sirens," "Cyclops," "Nausicaa": Facsimile of Drafts & Typescripts for Episodes 10-13. LC 77-10196. (James Joyce Archive Ser.). 1978. lib. bdg. 104.00 (ISBN 0-8240-2823-6). Garland Pub.

Grose, Kenneth. James Joyce. (Literature in Perspective Ser.). 150p. 1975. 7.50x (ISBN 0-87471-643-8). Rowman.

Hart, C. James Joyce's Ulysses. (Sydney Studies in Literature). 1968. 6.50x (ISBN 0-424-05620-8, Pub by Sydney U Pr). Intl Schol Bk Serv.

Hart, C. & Senn, F. Wake Digest. (Australian Humanities Research Council Publication). 1968. pap. 5.00x (ISBN 0-424-05610-0, Pub. by Sydney U Pr). Intl Schol Bk Serv.

Hart, Clive. A Concordance to Finnegans Wake. rev. ed. 1963. 35.00 (ISBN 0-911858-27-X). Appel.

Hart, Clive & Hayman, David, eds. James Joyce's Ulysses: Critical Essays. 1974. pap. 6.95 (ISBN 0-520-03275-6). U of Cal Pr.

Hayman, David. Ulysses: The Mechanics of Meaning. LC 79-112692. 1970. pap. text ed. 8.95x (ISBN 0-13-935759-9). Irvington.

Hayman, David & Anderson, Elliott, eds. In the Wake of the "Wake". 216p. 1978. 18.50 (ISBN 0-299-07600-8). U of Wis Pr.

Henke, Suzette & Unkeless, Elaine. Women in Joyce. 235p. 1982. price not set (ISBN 0-252-00891-X). U of Ill Pr.

Henke, Suzette A. Joyce's Moraculous Sindbook: A Study of "Ulysses". LC 77-18049. 1978. 15.00 (ISBN 0-8142-0275-6). Ohio St U Pr.

Herring, Phillip F., ed. Joyce's Notes & Early Drafts for Ulysses: Selections from the Buffalo Collection. LC 76-27362. 1978. 42.50x (ISBN 0-8139-0655-5, Bibliographical Soc., Univ. of Va.). U Pr of Va.

--Joyce's Ulysses Notesheets in the British Museum. LC 70-109222. 1972. 37.50x (ISBN 0-8139-0296-7, Bibliographical Society, University of Virginia). U Pr of Va.

Hodgart, Matthew. James Joyce: A Student's Guide. 1978. 16.00x (ISBN 0-7100-8817-5); pap. 7.95 (ISBN 0-7100-8943-0). Routledge & Kegan.

Hogart, Mathew J. & Worthington, Mabel P. Song in the Works of James Joyce. vi, 217p. 1980. Repr. of 1959 ed. lib. bdg. 14.50x (ISBN 0-374-93922-5). Octagon.

Jones, William P. James Joyce & the Common Reader. rev. ed. LC 55-9624. 1970. 9.95x (ISBN 0-8061-0324-8); pap. 4.95 (ISBN 0-8061-0930-0). U of Okla Pr.

Joyce, James. Dubliners: A Facsimile of Proofs for the 1910 Edition. Groden, Michael, ed. LC 77-22832. (James Joyce Archive Ser.). 1977. lib. bdg. 73.00 (ISBN 0-8240-2804-X). Garland Pub.

--Dubliners: A Facsimile of Proofs for the 1914 Edition. Groden, Michael, ed. LC 77-22835. (James Joyce Archive Ser.). 1977. lib. bdg. 73.00 (ISBN 0-8240-2805-8). Garland Pub.

--Finnegans Wake: A Facsimile of Buffalo Notebooks VI.B.1 - VI.B.4. Groden, Michael, ed. LC 77-11978. (James Joyce Archive Ser.). 1978. lib. bdg. 104.00 (ISBN 0-8240-2828-7). Garland Pub.

--Finnegans Wake: A Facsimile of Buffalo Notebooks VI.B.5 - VI.B.8. Groden, Michael, ed. LC 77-12610. (James Joyce Archive Ser.). 1978. lib. bdg. 104.00 (ISBN 0-8240-2829-5). Garland Pub.

--Finnegans Wake: A Facsimile of Buffalo Notebooks VI.B.9 - VI.B.12. Groden, Michael, ed. LC 77-14619. (James Joyce Archive Ser.). 1978. lib. bdg. 104.00 (ISBN 0-8240-2830-9). Garland Pub.

--Finnegans Wake: A Facsimile of Buffalo Notebooks VI.B. 41-44. LC 78-4174. (James Joyce Archive Ser.). 1978. lib. bdg. 104.00 (ISBN 0-8240-2838-4). Garland Pub.

--Finnegans Wake: Book I: A Facsimile of the Galley Proofs Volume II. Groden, Michael, ed. LC 77-23060. (James Joyce Archive Ser.). 1978. lib. bdg. 104.00 (ISBN 0-8240-2846-5). Garland Pub.

--Finnegans Wake: Book II, Chapter I: A Facsimile of Drafts, Typescripts, & Proofs. Groden, Michael, ed. LC 77-11681. (James Joyce Archive Ser.). 1978. lib. bdg. 104.00 (ISBN 0-8240-2849-X). Garland Pub.

--Finnegans Wake: Book II, Chapter 3: a Facsimile of Drafts, Typescripts, & Proofs, Vol. 1. Groden, Michael, ed. LC 77-10573. (James Joyce Archive Ser.). 1978. lib. bdg. 104.00 (ISBN 0-8240-2850-3). Garland Pub.

--Finnegans Wake: Book III: A Facsimile of the Galley Proofs. Groden, Michael, ed. LC 77-22951. (James Joyce Archive Ser.). 1978. lib. bdg. 104.00 (ISBN 0-8240-2847-3). Garland Pub.

--Finnegans Wake: Book III, Chapter 4: A Facsimile of Drafts, Typescripts, & Proofs. Groden, Michael, ed. LC 78-4465. (James Joyce Archive Ser.). 1978. lib. bdg. 104.00 (ISBN 0-8240-2858-9). Garland Pub.

--Finnegans Wake: Book IV: A Facsimile of Drafts, Typescripts, & Proofs. Groden, Michael, ed. LC 77-22867. (James Joyce Archive Ser.). 1978. lib. bdg. 104.00 (ISBN 0-8240-2848-1). Garland Pub.

--Ulysses: "Aeolus" "Lestrygonians," & "Scylla & Charybdis" a Facsimile of Page Proofs for Episodes 7-9. Groden, Michael, ed. LC 77-14621. (James Joyce Archive Ser.). 1978. lib. bdg. 104.00 (ISBN 0-8240-2817-1). Garland Pub.

--Ulysses: "Circe" & "Eumaeus": A Facsimile of Manuscripts & Typescripts for Episodes 15 (Part II) & 16. Groden, Michael, ed. LC 77-11971. (James Joyce Archive Ser.). 1978. lib. bdg. 104.00 (ISBN 0-8240-2825-2). Garland Pub.

--Ulysses: "Cyclops" & "Nausicaa", & "Oxen of the Sun": a Facsimile of Page Proofs for Episode 12-14. Groden, Michael, ed. LC 77-14655. (James Joyce Archive Ser.). 1978. lib. bdg. 104.00 (ISBN 0-8240-2819-8). Garland Pub.

--Ulysses: "Eumaeus," "Ithaca," & "Penelope": A Facsimile of Page Proofs for Chapters 16-18. Groden, Michael, ed. LC 77-14657. (James Joyce Archive Ser.). 1978. lib. bdg. 104.00 (ISBN 0-8240-2821-X). Garland Pub.

--Ulysses: "Oxen of the Sun," & "Circe": A Facsimile of Drafts, Manuscripts, & Typescripts 14 & 15 (Part 1) Groden, Michael, ed. LC 77-22764. (James Joyce Archive Ser.). 1978. lib. bdg. 104.00 (ISBN 0-8240-2824-4). Garland Pub.

--Ulysses: "Wandering Rocks" & "Sirens" A Facsimile of Page Proofs for Episodes 10-11. Groden, Michael, ed. LC 77-14654. (James Joyce Archive Ser.). 1978. lib. bdg. 104.00 (ISBN 0-8240-2818-X). Garland Pub.

Jung, C. G. Ulysses: A Monologue. LC 76-30789. (Studies in Joyce, No. 96). 1976. lib. bdg. 31.95 (ISBN 0-8383-2117-8). Haskell.

--Ulysses: A Monologue (James Joyce) LC 76-45184. Repr. of 1934 ed. lib. bdg. 7.50 (ISBN 0-8414-5305-5). Folcroft.

Kenner, Hugh. Joyce's Voices. LC 76-38887. (Quantum Book Ser.). 1978. 10.00x (ISBN 0-520-03206-3, CAL 426); pap. 2.95 (ISBN 0-520-03935-1). U of Cal Pr.

Kiely, Robert. Beyond Egotism: The Fiction of James Joyce, Virginia Woolf & D. H. Lawrence. LC 80-14231. 1980. text ed. 14.00x (ISBN 0-674-06896-3). Harvard U Pr.

Knuth, A. M. The Wink of the Word: A Study of James Joyce's Phatic Communication. 1976. pap. text ed. 17.25x (ISBN 0-391-02068-4). Humanities.

Kronegger, Maria E. James Joyce & Associated Image Makers. 1968. 6.00x (ISBN 0-8084-0169-6); pap. 2.95 (ISBN 0-8084-0170-X, L20). Coll & U Pr.
Lane, Gary, ed. A Word-Index to James Joyce's Dubliners. LC 71-183760. (Reference Ser., No. 44). 270p. 1972. lib. bdg. 33.95 (ISBN 0-8383-1384-1). Haskell.
Levin, Harry. James Joyce: A Critical Introduction. LC 60-9222. 1960. pap. 5.95 (ISBN 0-8112-0089-2, NDP87). New Directions.
Litz, A. Walton. Art of James Joyce: Method & Design in Ulysses & Finnegans Wake. 1964. pap. 3.95 (ISBN 0-19-500258-X, GB). Oxford U Pr.
--James Joyce. (English Authors Ser.: No. 31). 1966. lib. bdg. 9.95 (ISBN 0-8057-1300-X). Twayne.
Lyons, J. B. James Joyce's Miltonic Affliction. LC 73-11382. 1974. Repr. lib. bdg. 5.50 (ISBN 0-8414-2284-2). Folcroft.
Lyons, John L. James Joyce's Miltonic Affliction. 52p. 1980. Repr. of 1973 ed. lib. bdg. 8.50 (ISBN 0-8492-1632-X). R West.
MacCabe, Colin. James Joyce & the Revolution of the Word. LC 79-10830. 1979. text ed. 24.50x (ISBN 0-06-494438-7). B&N.
McHugh, Roland. Annotations to Finnegans Wake. LC 79-18419. 638p. 1980. text ed. 32.50x (ISBN 0-8018-2259-9); pap. 9.95x (ISBN 0-8018-2323-4). Johns Hopkins.
--The Finnegans Wake Experience. (Quantum Bks.). 130p. 1981. 10.95x (ISBN 0-520-04298-0). U of Cal Pr.
--The Sigla of "Finnegans Wake". LC 76-13577. 157p. 1976. text ed. 14.95x (ISBN 0-292-77528-8). U of Tex Pr.
MacNicholas, John. James Joyce's Exiles: A Textual Companion. LC 78-67061. (Reference Library Ser.). 1979. lib. bdg. 35.00 (ISBN 0-8240-9781-5). Garland Pub.
Maddox, James H., Jr. Joyce's Ulysses & the Assault Upon Character. 1978. 17.50 (ISBN 0-8135-0851-7). Rutgers U Pr.
Magalaner, Marvin. Time of Apprenticeship: The Fiction of Young James Joyce. facsimile ed. LC 70-140366. (Select Bibliographies Reprint Ser). Repr. of 1959 ed. 15.00 (ISBN 0-8369-5609-5). Arno.
Magalaner, Marvin & Kain, Richard M. Joyce: The Man, the Work, the Reputation. LC 79-17270. 1979. Repr. of 1956 ed. lib. bdg. 24.50x (ISBN 0-313-21258-9, MAJY). Greenwood.
Magalaner, Marvin, ed. James Joyce Miscellany: Third Ser. LC 62-15002. (Illus.). 314p. 1962. 9.95x (ISBN 0-8093-0075-3). S Ill U Pr.
Majault, Joseph. James Joyce. Stewart, Jean, tr. from Fr. 1971. 4.20x (ISBN 0-685-74779-4). Pendragon Hse.
Manganiello, Dominic. Joyce's Politics. 288p. 1980. 27.50 (ISBN 0-7100-0537-7). Routledge & Kegan.
Mason, M. James Joyce: Ulysses. (Studies in English Literature Ser.). 1972. pap. text ed. 3.95x (ISBN 0-7131-5620-1). Dynamic Learn Corp.
Miller-Budnitskaya, R. James Joyce's "Ulysses". LC 78-313. 1973. lib. bdg. 6.50 (ISBN 0-8414-2307-5). Folcroft.
Mink, Louis O. A Finnegans Wake Gazetteer. LC 77-74443. 600p. 1978. 25.00x (ISBN 0-253-32210-3). Ind U Pr.
Mitchell, Breon. James Joyce & the German Novel - 1922-1933. LC 75-36980. xvi, 194p. 1976. 14.00x (ISBN 0-8214-0192-0). Ohio U Pr.
Monarch Notes on Joyce's Ulysses. pap. 1.50 (ISBN 0-671-00564-2). Monarch Pr.
Motz, Reighard. Time As Joyce Tells It. LC 77-22454. 1978. pap. 7.95 (ISBN 0-930144-01-5). Mulford Colebrook.
Murillo, Louis A. Cyclical Night: Irony in James Joyce & Jorge Luis Borges. LC 68-54022. (Illus.). 289p. 1968. 16.00x (ISBN 0-674-18040-2). Harvard U Pr.
Nolan, Brian, et al. James Joyce Essays. LC 73-4183. 1973. lib. bdg. 10.00 (ISBN 0-8414-2355-5). Folcroft.
Norris, Margot. The Decentered Universe of Finnegan's Wake: A Structuralist Analysis. LC 76-25507. 1978. pap. text ed. 3.95 (ISBN 0-8018-2148-7). Johns Hopkins.
Norris, Margot C. The Decentered Universe of Finnegan's Wake: A Structuralist Analysis. 160p. 1977. 11.00x (ISBN 0-8018-1820-6). Johns Hopkins.
O'Brien, Edna. James & Nora: A Portrait of Joyce's Marriage. 50p. 1981. limited signed edition 35.00 (ISBN 0-935716-09-2). Lord John.
O Hehir, Brendan. A Gaelic Lexicon for Finnegans Wake & Glossary for Joyce's Other Works. 1968. 25.00x (ISBN 0-520-00952-5). U of Cal Pr.
O'Hehir, Brendan & Dillon, John M. A Classical Lexicon for Finnegans Wake: A Glossary of the Greek & Latin in Major Works of Joyce. 1977. 34.50x (ISBN 0-520-03082-6). U of Cal Pr.
Peake, C. H. James Joyce: The Citizen & the Artist. LC 76-47985. 1977. 16.95x (ISBN 0-8047-0914-9); pap. 6.95 (ISBN 0-8047-1014-7, SP-151). Stanford U Pr.
Perkins, Jill, ed. Joyce & Hauptmann: Before Sunrise. James Joyce's Translation. LC 77-87870. (Illus.). 1978. text ed. 15.00 (ISBN 0-87328-072-5). Huntington Lib.
Potts, Willard, ed. Portraits of the Artist in Exile: Recollections of James Joyce by Europeans. LC 78-4367. (Illus.). 320p. 1979. 13.95 (ISBN 0-295-95614-3). U of Wash Pr.
Quasha, George. Monarch Notes on Joyce's Portrait of the Artist As a Young Man & Dubliners. (Orig.). pap. 1.95 (ISBN 0-671-00563-4). Monarch Pr.
Raleigh, John H. The Chronicle of Leopold & Molly Bloom: "Ulysses" As Narrative. LC 76-20025. 1978. 20.00x (ISBN 0-520-03301-9). U of Cal Pr.
Reynolds, Mary T. Joyce & Dante: The Shaping Imagination. LC 80-7550. (Illus.). 369p. 1981. 22.50x (ISBN 0-691-06446-6). Princeton U Pr.
Ross, Martin. Music & James Joyce. LC 73-11054. 1936. lib. bdg. 6.00 (ISBN 0-8414-2587-6). Folcroft.
Russell, F. Three Studies in Twentieth Century Obscurity: Joyce, Kafka, Gertrude Stein. LC 68-658. (Studies in Comparative Literature, No. 35). 1969. Repr. of 1954 ed. lib. bdg. 49.95 (ISBN 0-8383-0678-0). Haskell.
Russell, Francis. Three Studies in Twentieth Century Obscurity. 1973. lib. bdg. 69.95 (ISBN 0-87968-046-6). Gordon Pr.
Schlauch, Margaret. The Language of James Joyce. LC 73-2726. 1973. lib. bdg. 6.00 (ISBN 0-8414-2625-2). Folcroft.
Seidel, Michael A. Epic Geography: James Joyce's Ulysses. LC 75-30207. 1976. 20.00 (ISBN 0-691-06303-6). Princeton U Pr.
Senn, Fritz, ed. New Light on Joyce from the Dublin Symposium. LC 72-75638. 224p. 1972. 10.00x (ISBN 0-253-34015-2). Ind U Pr.
Shechner, Mark. Joyce in Nighttown: A Psychoanalytic Inquiry into Ulysses. 1974. 17.50x (ISBN 0-520-02398-6). U of Cal Pr.
Smith, John B. Imagery & the Mind of Stephen Dedalus: A Computer-Assisted Study of James Joyce's A Portrait of the Artist As a Young Man. LC 75-10139. 296p. 1980. 19.50 (ISBN 0-8387-1758-6). Bucknell U Pr.
Smith, Paul J. Key to the Ulysses of James Joyce. pap. 3.00 (ISBN 0-87286-058-2). City Lights.
--Key to the Ulysses of James Joyce. 1927. lib. bdg. 6.50 (ISBN 0-8414-7541-5). Folcroft.
--Key to Ulysses of James Joyce. LC 68-54175. (Studies in Fiction, No. 34). 1969. Repr. of 1934 ed. lib. bdg. 22.95 (ISBN 0-8383-0625-X). Haskell.
Solomon, Margaret C. Eternal Geomater: The Sexual Universe of "Finnegans Wake". LC 69-17107. (Illus.). 176p. 1969. 7.95x (ISBN 0-8093-0392-2). S Ill U Pr.
Sorenson, Dolf. James Joyce's Aesthetic Theory: Its Development & Application. 1977. pap. text ed. 10.50x (ISBN 90-6203-200-1). Humanities.
Spoerri, James F. James Joyce: Books & Pamphlets Relating to the Author & His Works. 1955. lib. bdg. 8.50 (ISBN 0-8414-7923-2). Folcroft.
Staley, Thomas F., ed. James Joyce Today: Essays on the Major Works. LC 79-17222. 1979. Repr. of 1966 ed. lib. bdg. 16.00x (ISBN 0-313-21292-9, STJJ). Greenwood.
--Ulysses: Fifty Years. LC 73-16538. (Illus.). 208p. 1974. 8.50x (ISBN 0-253-36160-5). Ind U Pr.
Staley, Thomas F. & Benstock, Bernard, eds. Approaches to Joyce's Portrait: Ten Essays. LC 76-6670. 1976. 12.95 (ISBN 0-8229-3331-4). U of Pittsburgh Pr.
--Approaches to Ulysses: Ten Essays. LC 76-123093. 1970. 14.95 (ISBN 0-8229-3209-1). U of Pittsburgh Pr.
Steinberg, Erwin R. The Stream of Consciousness & Beyond in Ulysses. LC 72-78932. 1972. 17.95 (ISBN 0-8229-3245-8). U of Pittsburgh Pr.
Stoppard, Tom. Travesties. LC 75-13552. 1975. pap. 2.95 (ISBN 0-394-17884-X, E661, Ever). Grove.
Strong, L. A. The Sacred River. LC 74-7049. (Studies in Joyce, No. 96). 1974. lib. bdg. 32.95 (ISBN 0-8383-1951-3). Haskell.
--The Sacred River: An Approach to James Joyce. LC 74-12261. 176p. 1974. Repr. lib. bdg. 15.50x (ISBN 0-374-97648-1). Octagon.
Sucksmith, H. Joyce: A Portrait of the Artist As a Young Man. (Studies in English Literature Ser.). 1973. pap. text ed. 3.95x (ISBN 0-7131-5717-8). Dynamic Learn Corp.
Svevo, Italo. James Joyce. (Orig.). 1967. pap. 1.25 (ISBN 0-87286-048-5). City Lights.
Thompson, Lawrance. Comic Principle in Sterne, Meredith, Joyce. LC 76-42316. 1954. lib. bdg. 12.50 (ISBN 0-8414-8622-0). Folcroft.
Thornton, Weldon. Allusions in Ulysses: An Annotated List. 1968. 27.00x (ISBN 0-8078-1056-8). U of NC Pr.
Tindall, William. A Readers' Guide to James Joyce. 304p. 1959. pap. 6.95 (ISBN 0-374-50112-2). FS&G.
Tindall, William Y. James Joyce: His Way of Interpreting the Modern World. LC 79-17220. 1979. Repr. of 1950 ed. lib. bdg. 14.75x (ISBN 0-313-22033-6, TIJA). Greenwood.
--The Joyce Country. new ed. LC 72-83501. (Illus.). 174p. 1972. pap. 3.95 (ISBN 0-8052-0347-8). Schocken.
Troy, Mark L. Mummeries of Ressurection: The Cycle of Osiris in Finnegan's Wake. (Studie Anglistica Upsaliensia Ser.: No. 26). 1976. pap. text ed. 10.50x (ISBN 0-685-81615-X). Humanities.
Ussher, Arland. Three Great Irishmen: Shaw, Yeats, Joyce. LC 68-54235. 1953. 9.00x (ISBN 0-8196-0222-1). Biblo.
Waldock, Arthur J. James, Joyce & Others. facs. ed. LC 67-23277. (Essay Index Reprint Ser). 1937. 13.00 (ISBN 0-8369-0963-1). Arno.
Watson, G. J. Irish Identity & the Literary Revival: Synge, Yeats, Joyce & O'Casey. LC 79-54168. 1979. text ed. 27.50x (ISBN 0-06-497495-2). B&N.

JOYCE, JAMES, 1882-1941–BIBLIOGRAPHY
Deming, Robert H., ed. A Bibliography of James Joyce Studies. (Reference Publications Ser.). 1977. lib. bdg. 36.50 (ISBN 0-8161-7969-7). G K Hall.
Giedion-Welcker, Carola, compiled by. In Memoriam James Joyce. LC 75-13347. 1975. Repr. of 1941 ed. lib. bdg. 10.00 (ISBN 0-8414-4543-5). Folcroft.
Groden, Michael. James Joyce's Manuscripts: An Index. LC 78-64575. (Garland Reference Library of the Humanities). 190p. 1980. 25.00 (ISBN 0-8240-9540-5). Garland Pub.
Slocum, John J. A Bibliography of James Joyce: Eighteen Eighty-Two to Nineteen Forty-One. LC 70-138182. 195p. 1972. Repr. of 1953 ed. lib. bdg. 16.25 (ISBN 0-8371-5639-4, SLJJ). Greenwood.
--A Bibliography of James Joyce: Eighteen Eighty-Two to Nineteen Forty-One. LC 70-138182. 195p. 1972. Repr. of 1953 ed. lib. bdg. 16.25 (ISBN 0-8371-5639-4, SLJJ). Greenwood.
Spielberg, Peter, ed. James Joyce's Manuscripts & Letters at the University of Buffalo. LC 62-19657. (Illus.). 1962. 17.00 (ISBN 0-87395-009-7); microfiche 17.00 (ISBN 0-87395-109-3). State U NY Pr.

JOYS FAMILY
Lee, Helen B. Joy Supplement, Two: Descendants of Thomas Joy, Pt.2. LC 76-45277. (Illus.). 1980. pap. 2.50 (ISBN 0-87106-075-2). Globe Pequot.

JUAN, DON
Ballester, Gonzalo T. Don Juan. Lawrence, Sally, tr. 1981. 17.95 (ISBN 0-914366-10-6). Columbia Pub.
Boston, Bruce O., ed. The Sorcerer's Apprentice: A Case Study in the Role of the Mentor. LC 76-21101. 1976. pap. text ed. 2.75 (ISBN 0-86586-075-0). Coun Exc Child.
Castaneda, Carlos. Don Juan Quartet. (Boxed set of Don Juan, A Separate Reality, Journey to Ixtlan & Tales of Power). 1975. pap. 19.95 (ISBN 0-671-22147-7, Touchstone Bks). S&S.
--Journey to Ixtlan. (gr. 10-12). 1976. pap. 2.50 (ISBN 0-671-80424-3, 82768). PB.
--Separate Reality. LC 79-139617. 1971. 11.95 (ISBN 0-671-20897-7). S&S.
--A Separate Reality. (gr. 10-12). 1976. pap. 2.50 (ISBN 0-671-83132-1). PB.
--The Teachings of Don Juan. 1976. pap. 2.50 (ISBN 0-671-82767-7). PB.
--The Teachings of Don Juan: A Yaqui Way of Knowledge. LC 68-17303. 1968. 12.95x (ISBN 0-520-00217-2); pap. 3.95 (ISBN 0-520-02258-0, CAL253). U of Cal Pr.
--The Teachings of Don Juan: A Yaqui Way of Knowledge. 1973. 11.95 (ISBN 0-671-21555-8). S&S.
Colton, C. C. Remarks on Don Juan. 1978. Repr. of 1826 ed. lib. bdg. 10.00 (ISBN 0-8495-0908-4). Arden Lib.
Mandel, Oscar, ed. Theatre of Don Juan: A Collection of Plays & Views, 1630-1963. LC 63-9094. (Illus.). 1963. 18.50x (ISBN 0-8032-0109-5). U of Nebr Pr.
Rank, Otto. The Don Juan Legend. Winter, David G., ed. LC 72-6528. 156p. 1975. 13.00x (ISBN 0-691-08605-2). Princeton U Pr.
Tan, H. G. La Matiere De Don Juan et les Genre Litterairies. (Publications Romanes De L'Universite De Leyde Ser: Vol. 20). 1976. lib. bdg. 21.00 (ISBN 90-6021-215-0, Pub. by Leiden Univ. Holland). Kluwer Boston.
Weinstein, Leo. Metamorphoses of Don Juan. LC 77-12371. (Stanford University. Stanford Studies in Language & Literature: No. 18). 21.50 (ISBN 0-404-51828-1). AMS Pr.

JUAN, DON–FICTION
Mandel, Oscar, ed. Three Classic Don Juan Plays. LC 73-149071. 1971. pap. 3.95x (ISBN 0-8032-5739-2, BB 537, Bison). U of Nebr Pr.

JUAN DE FUCA (STRAIT)
Espinosa y Tello, Jose. Spanish Voyage to Vancouver & the North-West Coast of America. Jane, Cecil, tr. LC 70-136389. (Illus.). Repr. of 1930 ed. 10.00 (ISBN 0-404-02356-8). AMS Pr.
Wagner, Henry R. Spanish Explorations in the Strait of Juan De Fuca. LC 70-137275. Repr. of 1933 ed. 26.50 (ISBN 0-404-06801-4). AMS Pr.

JUAN DE LA CRUZ, SAINT
see John of the Cross, Saint, 1542-1591

JUAN FERNANDEZ ISLANDS
Skottsberg, C. Juan Fernandez & Hawaii: A Phytogeographical Discussion. (BMB Ser.: BMB 16). Repr. of 1925 ed. pap. 5.00 (ISBN 0-527-02119-9). Kraus Repr.

JUAN MANUEL, INFANTE OF CASTILE, 1282-1347
Sturcken, H. Tracy. Don Juan Manuel. (World Authors Ser.: Spain: No. 303). 1974. lib. bdg. 10.95 (ISBN 0-8057-2590-3). Twayne.

JUAREZ, BENITO PABLO, PRES. MEXICO, 1806-1872
Baker, Nina B. Juarez, Hero of Mexico. (Illus.). (gr. 7-9). 1942. 7.95 (ISBN 0-8149-0261-8). Vanguard.
Benito Juarez: Mini-Play. (History of Mexico Ser.). (gr. 5 up). 1978. 3.00 (ISBN 0-89550-374-3). RIM.
Roeder, Ralph. Juarez & His Mexico: A Biographical History, 2 Vols. LC 68-23322. (Illus.). 1968. Repr. of 1947 ed. Set. lib. bdg. 40.75x (ISBN 0-8371-0204-9, ROJM). Greenwood.
Scholes, Walter V. Mexican Politics During the Juarez Regime, 1855-1872. LC 57-63240. 1957. pap. 10.00x (ISBN 0-8262-0581-X). U of Mo Pr.
Smart, Charles A. Viva Juarez! A Biography. LC 74-24588. (Illus.). 444p. 1975. Repr. of 1963 ed. lib. bdg. 28.25 (ISBN 0-8371-6145-2, SMVJ). Greenwood.
Trevino, Elizabeth B. De. Juarez, Man of Law. 160p. (gr. 7 up). 1974. 5.95 (ISBN 0-374-33950-3). FS&G.

JUBILEE INDULGENCES
see Indulgences

JUBILEE SINGERS
Marsh, J. B. Story of the Jubilee Singers with Their Songs. rev. ed. LC 72-165509. (Illus.). Repr. of 1880 ed. 14.00 (ISBN 0-404-04189-2). AMS Pr.
--Story of the Jubilee Singers with Their Songs. rev. ed. LC 72-165509. (Illus.). Repr. of 1880 ed. 14.00 (ISBN 0-404-04189-2). AMS Pr.
--Story of the Jubilee Singers, with Their Songs. rev. ed. LC 79-78583. (Illus.). Repr. of 1881 ed. 15.75x (ISBN 0-8371-1424-1, Pub. by Negro U Pr). Greenwood.
Pike, Gustavus D. Jubilee Singers, & Their Campaign for Twenty Thousand Dollars. LC 72-1692. Repr. of 1873 ed. 18.50 (ISBN 0-404-08329-3). AMS Pr.
--The Singing Campaign for Ten Thousand Pounds. rev. ed. LC 75-164392. (Black Heritage Library Collection). Repr. of 1875 ed. 18.25 (ISBN 0-8369-8851-5). Arno.

JUDAEO-GERMAN
see Yiddish Language

JUDAH, HA-LEVI, 12TH CENTURY
Facets of Medieval Judaism. LC 73-2196. (The Jewish People; History, Religion, Literature Ser.). Repr. of 1973 ed. 14.00 (ISBN 0-405-05262-6). Arno.
Strauss, Leo. Persecution & the Art of Writing. LC 73-1407. 204p. 1973. Repr. of 1952 ed. lib. bdg. 16.75x (ISBN 0-8371-6801-5, STPA). Greenwood.

JUDAICA
see Jews

JUDAISM
Here are entered works on Jewish faith and practice in which the main stream of orthodox Judaism is treated and no cleavage is stressed.
see also Cabala; Circumcision; Commandments, Ten; Cultus, Jewish; Fasts and Feasts–Judaism; Jesus Christ–Jewish Interpretations; Jewish Theology; Jews; Messiah; Mythology, Jewish; Rabbis; Reform Judaism; Sabbath; Synagogues
Abraham Ben Moses Ben Maimon. High Ways to Perfection of Abraham Maimonides. Rosenblatt, Samuel, tr. LC 74-158221. (Columbia University Oriental Studies: No. 27). 1927. 19.00 (ISBN 0-404-50517-1). AMS Pr.
Abravanel, Isaac. Principles of Faith: Rosh Amanah. Kellner, Menachem M., tr. LC 80-67697. 230p. 1981. 20.00 (ISBN 0-8386-3080-4). Fairleigh Dickinson.
ADL Israel Series, 5 vols. (Illus.). Set. pap. 10.00 (ISBN 0-686-74970-7); pap. 2.40 ea. History Until 1880, 275p. History From 1880, 299p. Anti-Semitism, 232p. Holocaust. 214p. Jerusalem, 370p. ADL.

Agus, Jacob B., et al, eds. The Jewish People: History, Religion, Literature, 41 bks. 1973. Set. 816.50 (ISBN 0-405-05250-2). Arno.
Alter, Robert, ed. Modern Hebrew Literature. LC 75-9928. (Library of Jewish Studies). 384p. 1975. text ed. 15.95x (ISBN 0-87441-218-8); pap. text ed. 6.95x (ISBN 0-87441-235-8). Behrman.
Altshuler, David A. Tzedakah: Basic Jewish Ideas Ser. Neusner, Jacob, ed. (Orig.). (gr. 6-8). 1981. pap. 3.95 (ISBN 0-940646-26-9). Rossel Bks.
American Jewish Year Book, 1981, Vol. 81. LC 99-4040. 1980. 20.00 (ISBN 0-8276-0185-9). Am Jewish Comm.
Amsel. Judaism & Psychology. pap. 4.95 (ISBN 0-87306-064-4). Feldheim.
Amsel, Avrohom. Rational Irrational Man: Torah Psychology. 1976. 9.95 (ISBN 0-87306-129-2). Feldheim.
Asheri, Michael. Living Jewish. enl. deluxe ed. 1980. 14.95 (ISBN 0-89696-072-2). Everest Hse.
Baeck, Leo. Essence of Judaism. rev. ed. LC 61-8992. 1961. pap. 5.95 (ISBN 0-8052-0006-1). Schocken.
Bamberger, Bernard J. Story of Judaism. rev. ed. 1970. 6.50 (ISBN 0-8074-0193-5, 959291). UAHC.
Barish, Louis & Barish, Rebecca. Varieties of Jewish Belief. 1979. Repr. 9.95 (ISBN 0-8246-0242-0). Jonathan David.
Baron, David. Rays of Messiah's Glory. 275p. 1979. 7.95 (ISBN 0-88469-147-0). BMH Bks.
Baron, Salo W. A Social & Religious History of the Jews: Vol. 17, Byzantines, Mameluks & Marghribians. 1980. 30.00x (ISBN 0-231-08853-1). Columbia U Pr.
Baynes, David. Catholicism, Judaism, Protestantism & the Decline in American Morality. (Illus.). 1977. 37.55 (ISBN 0-89266-025-2). Am Classical Coll Pr.
Belkin, Samuel. In His Image: The Jewish Philosophy of Man As Expressed in Rabbinic Tradition. LC 78-10192. 1979. Repr. of 1960 ed. lib. bdg. 22.75x (ISBN 0-313-21234-1, BEIH). Greenwood.
Berkovits, Eliezer. God, Man & History. 1979. Repr. of 1959 ed. 9.95 (ISBN 0-8246-0239-0). Jonathan David.
--With God in Hell: Judaism in the Ghettos & Deathcamps. 1979. 7.95 (ISBN 0-88482-937-5, Sanhedrin Pr). Hebrew Pub.
Berman, L. V., et al, eds. The Study of Judaism: Vol. 2. 25.00x (ISBN 0-87068-486-8). Ktav.
Bernstein, Philip S. What the Jews Believe. LC 77-28446. (Illus.). 1978. Repr. of 1951 ed. lib. bdg. 15.00x (ISBN 0-313-20228-1, BEWJ). Greenwood.
Birnbaum, Philip. A Book of Jewish Concepts. 722p. 1964. 12.50 (ISBN 0-88482-876-X). Hebrew Pub.
Blackman, Philip. Ethics of the Fathers. 166p. 1980. pap. 3.95 (ISBN 0-910818-15-0). Judaica Pr.
Blau, Joseph L., ed. Reform Judaism: A Historical Perspective. 1972. 20.00x (ISBN 0-87068-191-5). Ktav.
Bleich, David J. With Perfect Faith. Date not set. 25.00x (ISBN 0-87068-891-X). Ktav.
Bleich, J. David. With Perfect Faith: The Foundations of Jewish Belief. 1980. write for info. (ISBN 0-88482-924-3). Hebrew Pub.
Blue, Lionel. To Heaven with Scribes & Pharisees. 104p. 1976. 7.95 (ISBN 0-19-519831-X). Oxford U Pr.
Bokser, Ben Zion. Judaism & Modern Man. 1958. 3.75 (ISBN 0-8022-0148-2). Philos Lib.
Bookstaber, Philip D. Judaism & the American Mind: In Theory & Practice. LC 78-26404. 1979. Repr. of 1939 ed. lib. bdg. 18.75x (ISBN 0-313-20875-1, BOJU). Greenwood.
Borowitz, Eugene. Understanding Judaism. 1979. 6.00 (ISBN 0-8074-0027-0, 341800). UAHC.
Brafman, Morris & Schimel, David. Trade for Freedom. LC 75-26371. 96p. 1975. 5.95 (ISBN 0-88400-044-3). Shengold.
Breslauer, S. Daniel. The Ecumenical Perspective & the Modernization of Jewish Religion: A Study in the Relationship Between Theology & Myth. 1978. pap. 7.50 (ISBN 0-89130-236-0, 140005). Scholars Pr Ca.
Breuer, Isaac. Concepts of Judaism. Levinger, Jacob S., tr. 1974. 10.00 (ISBN 0-87306-058-X). Feldheim.
Breuer, Jacob. Fundamentals of Judaism. 1969. 8.95 (ISBN 0-87306-041-5); pap. 4.95 (ISBN 0-87306-208-6). Feldheim.
Breuer, Salomon. Chochmah U'mussar, Vol. 2. Breuer, Jacob, tr. 1976. 6.00 (ISBN 0-87306-035-0). Feldheim.
--Chochmo U'Mussar: Bereshith-Shemoth, Vol.1. Breuer, Jacob, tr. 1972. 8.50 (ISBN 0-87306-034-2). Feldheim.
Brod, Max. Paganism - Christianity - Judaism: A Confession of Faith. Wolf, William, tr. LC 78-104937. 220p. 1970. 15.50x (ISBN 0-8173-6700-4). U of Ala Pr.
Buber, Martin. On Judaism. Glatzer, Nahum, ed. LC 67-28091. 242p. 1972. pap. 5.50 (ISBN 0-8052-0343-5). Schocken.
--The Tales of Rabbi Nachman. LC 56-12330. 214p. 1972. 5.95 (ISBN 0-8180-1325-7). Horizon.
Bulka, Reuven P. & Spero, Moshe H. A Psychology-Judaism Reader. (Illus.). 288p. Date not set. price not set (ISBN 0-398-04582-8). C C Thomas.
Carlson, Paul R. O Christian! O Jew! LC 74-78937. 256p. (Orig.). 1974. pap. 1.95 (ISBN 0-912692-39-1). Cook.
Chaim, B., ed. Neturei Karta; Voice of Anti-Zionist Judaism: A Study. 1980. 75.00 (ISBN 0-686-59910-1). Revisionist Pr.
Claudel, Paul. Une Voix sur Israel. 46p. 1950. 2.95 (ISBN 0-686-54445-5). French & Eur.
Cohen, Henry. Why Judaism? a Search for Meaning in Jewish Identity. 192p. 1973. pap. 5.00 (ISBN 0-8074-0077-7, 161901). UAHC.
Cohen, Hermann. Religion of Reason Out of the Sources of Judaism. Kaplan, Simon, tr. LC 79-125962. 1971. 30.00 (ISBN 0-8044-5229-6). Ungar.
Cohen, Seymour J. & Yasher, Sefer Ha. The Book of Righteous. 1973. 15.00x (ISBN 0-87068-197-4). Ktav.
Cohon, Beryl D. Judaism in Theory & Practice. 3rd rev. ed. LC 68-57021. 1969. write for info. (ISBN 0-8197-0069-X). Bloch.
Colodner, Solomon. Concepts & Values. LC 68-58503. 140p. 1968. 4.95 (ISBN 0-88400-020-6). Shengold.
De Fer, Hugo. Jewish Ethics & Catholic Doctrine. LC 78-167699. (Illus.). 32p. 1972. 39.25 (ISBN 0-913314-08-0). Am Classical Coll Pr.
Donin, Hayim H. To Raise a Jewish Child: A Guide for Parents. LC 76-7679. 1977. 11.95 (ISBN 0-465-08626-8). Basic.
Dresner, Samuel H. Zaddik: The Doctrine of the Zaddik According to the Writings of Rabbi Yaakov Yosef of Polnoy. LC 60-7228. 312p. 1974. pap. 3.45 (ISBN 0-8052-0437-7). Schocken.
Duties of the Heart, Chovoth Halevovoth, 2 vols. 1978. Set. pap. 10.95 (ISBN 0-87306-161-6). Feldheim.
Eakin, Frank E. Religion & Western Culture: Selected Issues. 1977. 10.75 (ISBN 0-8191-0256-3). U Pr of Amer.
Edersheim, Alfred. Temple, Its Ministry & Services. 1950. 3.95 (ISBN 0-8028-8133-5). Eerdmans.
Eichenbaum, Sharon & Goldin, Alice. Jewish Awareness Worksheets, 2 vols. pap. 1.95x ea. Vol. 1 (ISBN 0-87441-266-8). Vol. 2 (ISBN 0-87441-270-6). Behrman.
The Emergence of Contemporary Judaism, 4 vols. Incl. Vol. 2. A Survey of Judaism from the 7th to the 17th Centuries. Sigal, Phillip. LC 77-831. (Pittsburgh Theological Monographs: No. 12). 1977. Set. pap. text ed. 11.95 (ISBN 0-915138-14-X). Pickwick.
Epstein, Isidore. Faith of Judaism. 8.25 (ISBN 0-685-01045-7). Bloch.
Essrig, Harry. Judaism. (gr. 11 up). Date not set. pap. text ed. 2.25 (ISBN 0-8120-0309-8). Barron.
Fackenheim, Emil L. Encounters Between Judaism & Modern Philosophy: A Preface to Future Jewish Thought. LC 80-16437. 288p. 1980. pap. 7.95 (ISBN 0-8052-0656-6, Pub. by Holocaust Library). Schocken.
--God's Presence in History: Jewish Affirmations & Philosophical Reflections. LC 79-88135. (Deems Lectureship in Philosophy Ser). 1970. 11.00x (ISBN 0-8147-0142-6). NYU Pr.
Feinsilver, A. Aspects of Jewish Belief. 1973. pap. 4.95x (ISBN 0-87068-225-3). Ktav.
Finegan, Jack. Light from the Ancient Past, 2 vols. 2nd ed. (Illus.). 1959. Vol. 1 2nd Ed. 35.00 (ISBN 0-691-03550-4); Vol. 1 2nd Edition. pap. 8.95 (ISBN 0-691-00207-X); 25.00 (ISBN 0-691-03551-2); Vol. 2. pap. 8.95 (ISBN 0-691-00208-8); Set. 59.50 (ISBN 0-686-76901-5). Princeton U Pr.
Finkelstein, et al. Religions of Democracy. 1941. 4.50 (ISBN 0-8159-6708-X). Devin.
Fishman, Samuel Z. & Saypol, Judyth R., eds. Jewish Studies at American & Canadian Universities: A Catalog of Academic Programs. 2nd ed. LC 79-54250. 1979. pap. 3.95 (ISBN 0-9603058-2-3). B'nai B'rith-Hillel.
Fleg, Edmond. Why I Am a Jew. 2nd facsimile ed. Wise, Louise W., tr. from Fr. LC 74-27984. (Modern Jewish Experience Ser.). (Eng.). 1975. Repr. of 1945 ed. 9.00x (ISBN 0-405-06711-9). Arno.
Forchheimer, Paul. Living Judaism: The Mishneh of Aboth. 1974. 7.95 (ISBN 0-87306-011-3). Feldheim.
Frank, Yakov. Sayings of Yakov Frank. Lenowitz, Harris, tr. from Hebrew. (Tree 6 Ser.: Part One). (Orig.). 1978. pap. 2.50 (ISBN 0-917246-05-5). Maimes.
Frensdorff, Salomon. Ochlah W'Ochlah. 35.00x (ISBN 0-685-38389-X, 87068-194-5). Ktav.
Frey, Jean B. Corpus Inscriptionum Judaicarum. rev. ed. (Library of Biblical Studies). 1970. 100.00x (ISBN 0-87068-103-6). Ktav.
Friedlander, Albert. Out of the Whirlwind. 1968. 7.95 (ISBN 0-8074-0043-2, 959065). UAHC.
Friedlander, G. Jewish Sources of the Sermon on the Mount. 1976. lib. bdg. 59.95 (ISBN 0-8490-2102-2). Gordon Pr.
Friedman, Alexander Z. Wellsprings of Torah. Hirchter, Gertrude, tr. from Yiddish. 584p. 1980. 13.95 (ISBN 0-910818-04-5); pap. 10.95 (ISBN 0-910818-20-7). Judaica Pr.
Gelberman, Joseph H. The Quest. 1976. pap. 2.50 (ISBN 0-89248-002-5). Circle Pr.
Gereboff, Joel. Rabbi Tarfon: The Tradition, the Man & Early Rabbinic Judaism. LC 78-15220. (Brown Judaic Studies: No. 7). 1979. 16.50 (ISBN 0-89130-257-3, 140007); pap. 12.00 (ISBN 0-89130-300-6). Scholars Pr Ca.
Gittelsohn, Roland B. The Modern Meaning of Judaism. LC 78-69972. 1978. 8.95 (ISBN 0-529-05640-2); pap. 5.95 (ISBN 0-529-05486-8, FT5486). Collins Pubs.
Glazer, Nathan. American Judaism. rev. ed. LC 57-8574. (Chicago History of American Civilization Ser). 1972. 9.50x (ISBN 0-226-29839-6); pap. 4.50 (ISBN 0-226-29841-8, CHAC7). U of Chicago Pr.
Goldberg, Louis. Our Jewish Friends. 1977. pap. 3.95 (ISBN 0-8024-6217-0). Moody.
Goldman, Alex J. Judaism Confronts Contemporary Issues. LC 78-54570. 1979. 11.95 (ISBN 0-88400-056-7). Shengold.
Goodman, S. L. The Faith of Secular Jews. (Library of Judaic Learning). 20.00x (ISBN 0-87068-489-2). Ktav.
Gordis, Robert. Root & the Branch: Judaism & the Free Society. LC 62-17133. 1962. 9.00 (ISBN 0-226-30411-6). U of Chicago Pr.
Gottleib. The Fragments. 1974. 7.95 (ISBN 0-87306-105-5). Feldheim.
Green, William S. Approaches to Ancient Judaism II. LC 76-57656. (Brown Judaic Studies). 1980. 15.00 (ISBN 0-89130-447-9); pap. 10.50 (ISBN 0-89130-427-4). Scholars Pr CA.
Gross, David C. The Jewish People's Almanac. LC 79-6864. (Illus.). 600p. 1981. 19.95 (ISBN 0-385-15652-9); pap. 11.95 (ISBN 0-385-15653-7). Doubleday.
--One Thousand & One Questions & Answers About Judaism. LC 76-42330. (Illus.). 1978. 8.95 (ISBN 0-385-11137-1). Doubleday.
Gutmann, Alexander. Studies in Rabbinic Judaism. 20.00x (ISBN 0-87068-013-7). Ktav.
Guttman, Julius. Philosophies of Judaism: The History of Jewish Philosophy from Biblical Times to Franz Rosenzweig. LC 63-11875. 474p. 1973. pap. 7.50 (ISBN 0-8052-0402-4). Schocken.
Halevi, Judah. The Kuzari: An Argument for the Faith of Israel. LC 64-15222. 1966. pap. 4.95 (ISBN 0-8052-0075-4). Schocken.
Halevi, Yehudah. Book of Kuzari. (Heb. & Eng.). 28.50 (ISBN 0-87559-077-2). Shalom.
Harland, Henry. Yoke of the Thorah, by Sidney Luska. Repr. of 1887 ed. 18.50 (ISBN 0-384-21370-7). Johnson Repr.
Haskelevich, B., tr. from Hebrew. The Disputation of Nachmanides: With Introduction & Commentaries. (Rus.). 1981. pap. 3.75 (ISBN 0-938666-00-2). CHAMH.
Herberg, Will. Judaism & Modern Man. LC 59-12913. (Temple Bks). 1970. pap. text ed. 5.95x (ISBN 0-689-70232-9, T13). Atheneum.
Heschel, A. J. Kotzk: The Struggle for Integrity, 2 vols. in 1. (Yiddish.). 35.00x (ISBN 0-87068-328-4). Ktav.
Heschel, Abraham J. Between God & Man, an Interpretation of Judaism. 1965. pap. 7.95 (ISBN 0-02-914510-4). Free Pr.
--God in Search of Man: A Philosophy of Judaism. LC 78-169259. xviii, 438p. 1972. Repr. of 1955 ed. lib. bdg. 22.50x (ISBN 0-374-93878-4). Octagon.
--God in Search of Man: A Philosophy of Judaism. 464p. 1976. pap. 8.95 (ISBN 0-374-51331-7). FS&G.
Hexter, Jack H. The Judaeo Christian Tradition. (Orig.). 1966. pap. text ed. 9.50 scp (ISBN 0-06-042815-5, HarpC). Har-Row.
Hirsch, Emil G. My Religion. Levi, Gerson B., ed. Incl. The Crucifixion Viewed from a Jewish Standpoint (1908. LC 73-2207. (The Jewish People; History, Religion, Literature Ser.). Repr. of 1925 ed. 25.00 (ISBN 0-405-05271-5). Arno.
Hirsch, Richard G. Thy Most Precious Gift: Peace in Jewish Tradition. (Issues of Conscience Ser.). 128p. (Orig.). 1974. pap. 0.50 (ISBN 0-8074-0093-9, 180203). UAHC.
Hirsch, S, R. Judaism Eternal, 2 Vols. Set. 26.50x (ISBN 0-685-01043-0). Bloch.
Hirsch, Samson R. The Nineteen Letters of Ben Uziel on Judaism. Drachman, Bermard, tr. LC 69-131727. 1969. 4.95 (ISBN 0-87306-045-8). Feldheim.
Hirsch, Somson R. Nineteen Letters of Ben Uziel: A Spiritual Presentation of the Principles of Judaism. Drachman, Bernard, tr. (Eng. & Ger., Heb). 22.50 (ISBN 0-87559-076-4). Shalom.
Hirschman, Jack. Kameas. Date not set. 4.00 (ISBN 0-686-13974-7). Tree Bks.
Holmgren, Frederick. The God Who Cares: A Christian Looks at Judaism. LC 78-52445. (Orig.). 1979. pap. 4.95 (ISBN 0-8042-0588-4). John Knox.
Humphreys, W. Lee. Crisis & Story: Introduction to the Old Testament. LC 78-64594. (Illus.). 313p. 1979. 15.95 (ISBN 0-87484-437-1). Mayfield Pub.
Hyams, Ario S. Toward a One World Jewry: An Essay in Jewish Identity. 1979. 10.00 (ISBN 0-682-49503-4). Exposition.
Jakobovits, Immanuel. Jewish Medical Ethics. rev. ed. LC 75-4125. 425p. 1975. 10.00x (ISBN 0-8197-0097-5); pap. 6.95x (ISBN 0-685-53492-8). Bloch.
Jamison, A. Leland, ed. Tradition & Change in Jewish Experience: B.G. Rudolph Lectures in Judaic Studies. 1978. pap. 5.95x (ISBN 0-8156-8097-X). Syracuse U Pr.
Jellicoe, Sidney. Studies in the Septuagint. 1973. 39.50x (ISBN 0-87068-219-9). Ktav.
The Jewish Quarterly Review, 1889-1908, 21 Vols. 1966. 400.00x (ISBN 0-87068-070-6). Ktav.
Jorg, E. W. God's Message to His Chosen Earthly People of Israel. 1978. 6.50 (ISBN 0-533-03165-6). Vantage.
Jung, Leo. The Jewish Library. Incl. Vol. 1. Faith. 9.50x (ISBN 0-685-23058-9); Vol. 2. Folk. 9.50x (ISBN 0-685-23059-7); Vol. 3. Women. 8.00x (ISBN 0-685-23060-0); Vol. 4. Judaism in a Changing World. 9.50x (ISBN 0-685-23061-9); Vol. 5. Panorama of Judaism: Part 1. 9.50x (ISBN 0-685-23062-7); Vol. 6. Panorama of Judaism: Part 2. 9.50x (ISBN 0-685-23063-5). Bloch.
Kagan, Berl. Hebrew Subscription Lists. 50.00x (ISBN 0-87068-282-2, Pub. by Jewish Theol. Seminary). Ktav.
Kalir, Joseph. Introduction to Judaism. LC 79-6758. 170p. 1980. text ed. 17.50 (ISBN 0-8191-0948-7); pap. text ed. 8.50 (ISBN 0-8191-0949-5). U Pr of Amer.
Kaplan, Aryeh. The Handbook of Jewish Thought. 307p. 13.95 (ISBN 0-940118-27-0). Maznaim.
Karp, Abraham J. The Jewish Way of Life & Thought. Date not set. 7.95x (ISBN 0-87068-717-4). Ktav.
Karta, Neturei. Judaism & Zionism: Principles & Definitions. 1980. lib. bdg. 59.95 (ISBN 0-686-68745-0). Revisionist Pr.
Katz, Steven T. Jewish Ideas & Concepts. LC 77-75285. 1979. pap. 6.95 (ISBN 0-8052-0629-9). Schocken.
Katz, Steven T., ed. Jewish Philosophy, Mysticism & History of Ideas Series, 50 bks. (Illus.). 1980. Set. lib. bdg. 2073.00x (ISBN 0-405-12229-2). Arno.
Knopp, Josephine Z. The Trial of Judaism in Contemporary Jewish Writing. LC 74-18319. 164p. 1975. 12.50 (ISBN 0-252-00386-1). U of Ill Pr.
Konvitz, Milton R. Judaism & the American Idea. LC 79-14278. 224p. 1980. pap. 5.95 (ISBN 0-8052-0635-3). Schocken.
Kosovsky, B. Concordance of the Sifrei. 75.00x (ISBN 0-685-56222-0, Pub. by Jewish Theol Seminary). Ktav.
Kukoff, Lydia. Choosing Judaism. (Orig.). 1981. 10.00 (ISBN 0-8074-0151-X); pap. 5.95 (ISBN 0-8074-0150-1). UAHC.
Kushner, Lawrence. The River of Light: Spirituality, Judaism, & the Evolution of Consciousness. LC 80-7738. 192p. (Orig.). 1981. pap. 8.25 (ISBN 0-06-064902-X, HarpR). Har-Row.
--The River of Light: Spirituality, Judaism, & the Evolution of Consciousness. LC 80-7738. 192p. 1981. 12.95 (ISBN 0-940646-00-5). Rossel Bks.
Lachs, Samuel T. & Wachs, Saul P. Judaism. (Illus.). 1978. pap. 3.95 (ISBN 0-89505-023-4). Argus Comm.
Le Deaut, Roger. The Spirituality of Judaism. Barrett, Paul, tr. LC 77-3866. (Religious Experience Ser.: Vol. 11). 1977. pap. 3.95 (ISBN 0-87029-132-7, 20156). Abbey.
Leibowitz. Studies in the Shemoth, 2 vols. 1976. 17.50 (ISBN 0-685-71930-8). Feldheim.
Leiser, Joseph. American Judaism: The Religion & Religious Institutions of the Jewish People in the United States. LC 78-26230. 1979. Repr. of 1925 ed. lib. bdg. 19.75x (ISBN 0-313-20879-4, LEAJ). Greenwood.
Lieberman, Chaim. The Grave Concern. LC 68-58650. 202p. 1968. 3.95 (ISBN 0-88400-016-8). Shengold.
Lipman, Eugene J., compiled by. The Mishnah: Oral Teachings of Judaism. Lipman, Eugene, tr. LC 72-12621. 318p. 1974. pap. 3.95 (ISBN 0-8052-0441-5). Schocken.

Lipman, Eugene J., tr. The Mishnah: Oral Traditions of Judaism. (B'nai B'rith Jewish Heritage Classics Ser). 1973. 7.50 (ISBN 0-670-47856-3). Viking Pr.
Lookstein, Joseph H. Yesterday's Faith for Tomorrow. Date not set. 12.50x (ISBN 0-87068-722-0). Ktav.
Luzatto, Moshe C. Derech HaShem: The Way of G-D. Kaplan, Aryeh, tr. from Hebrew. 1978. 12.95 (ISBN 0-87306-136-5). Feldheim.
Maimonides. Mishneh Torah. Birnbaum, Philip, tr. 334p. 1975. pap. 4.95 (ISBN 0-88482-436-5). Hebrew Pub.
Maimonides, Moses. Code of Maimonides, Bk. 3, Treatise 8, Sanctification Of The New Moon. Gandz, Solomon, tr. (Judaica Ser: No. 11). 1956. 17.50x (ISBN 0-300-00476-1). Yale U Pr.
--Code of Maimonides - Book Three: The Book of Seasons. Gandz, Solomon & Klein, Hyman, trs. (Judaica Ser: No. 14). 1961. 45.00x (ISBN 0-300-00475-3). Yale U Pr.
--Guide for the Perplexed. 2nd ed. 9.50 (ISBN 0-8446-2512-4). Peter Smith.
Mann, Denese B. The Woman in Judaism. 1979. pap. 4.50 (ISBN 0-9603348-0-7). Jonathan Pubns.
Martin, Bernard, ed. Movements & Issues in American Judaism: An Analysis & Sourcebook of Developments Since 1945. LC 77-87971. 1978. lib. bdg. 22.50 (ISBN 0-313-20044-0, MCJ/). Greenwood.
Meiseles, Meir. Judaism, Thought & Legend. Schonfeld-Brand, Rebecca & Newman, Aryeh, trs. from Hebrew. 1978. pap. 7.95 (ISBN 0-87306-140-3). Feldheim.
Menuhin, Moshe. The Decadence of Judaism in Our Time. 1981. lib. bdg. 59.95 (ISBN 0-686-73181-6). Revisionist Pr.
Mills, Lawrence H. Zarathushtra, Philo, the Achaemenids & Israel. LC 74-21261. Repr. of 1906 ed. 34.50 (ISBN 0-404-12815-7). AMS Pr.
Mirsky, Norman B. Unorthodox Judaism. LC 78-8683. 1978. 12.00 (ISBN 0-8142-0283-7). Ohio St U Pr.
Narot, Joseph R. Letters to the Now Generation. pap. 1.95 (ISBN 0-686-15801-6). Rostrum Bks.
--Old Wine in Old Bottles. pap. 0.75 (ISBN 0-686-15809-1). Rostrum Bks.
Neusner. The Way of Torah: An Introduction to Judaism. 3rd ed. LC 73-88121. 1974. pap. 4.95 (ISBN 0-87872-217-3). Duxbury Pr.
Neusner, Jacob. The Academic Study of Judaism: Essays & Reflections I. 12.50x (ISBN 0-87068-281-4). Ktav.
--Between Time & Eternity: The Essentials of Judaism. 1975. pap. 8.95x (ISBN 0-8221-0160-2). Dickenson.
--Judaism: The Evidence of the Mishnah. LC 80-26080. 432p. 1981. 25.00 (ISBN 0-226-57617-5). U of Chicago Pr.
--The Life of Torah: Readings in the Jewish Religious Experience. 1974. pap. text ed. 8.95x (ISBN 0-8221-0124-6). Dickenson.
--Method & Meaning in Ancient Judaism. LC 79-9881. (Brown Judaic Ser.: No. 10). 1979. 13.50 (ISBN 0-89130-281-6, 140010); pap. 9.00 (ISBN 0-89130-300-6). Scholars Pr Ca.
--Understanding American Judaism: Toward the Description of a Modern Religion, 2 vols. Incl. Vol. 1. The Synagogue & the Rabbi (ISBN 0-87068-279-2); Vol. 2. Reform, Orthodoxy, Conservatism, & Reconstructionism (ISBN 0-87068-280-6). pap. 8.95x ea. Ktav.
Neusner, Jacob, ed. Contemporary Judaic Fellowship in Theory of Practice. 1972. 12.50x (ISBN 0-87068-187-7). Ktav.
Newman, Louis I. Jewish Influence on Christian Reform Movements. LC 26-883. (Columbia University. Oriental Studies: No. 23). Repr. of 1925 ed. 45.00 (ISBN 0-404-50513-9). AMS Pr.
--Jewish People, Faith & Life. 1964. 5.95 (ISBN 0-8197-0160-2). Bloch.
Obermann, Julian, ed. Nissim ben Jacob ben Nissim Ibn Shahin (Studies in Islam & Judaism) The Arabic Original of Ibn Shahin's Book of Comfort. LC 78-63561. (Yale Oriental Ser. Researches: No. 17). Repr. of 1933 ed. 72.50 (ISBN 0-404-60287-8). AMS Pr.
O'Dea, Thomas F., et al. Religion & Man: Judiasm, Christianity & Islam. 1972. pap. text ed. 10.95 scp (ISBN 0-06-044893-8, HarpC). Har-Row.
Palliere, Aime. Unknown Sanctuary. 1971. 6.95 (ISBN 0-8197-0271-4). Bloch.
Pearl, Chaim & Brookes, Reuben. The Guide to Jewish Knowledge. rev. ed. LC 75-187866. 123p. 1973. 4.95 (ISBN 0-87677-046-4). Hartmore.
Pearlmutter, Simha. The Tents of Shem. LC 79-56104. 1980. 8.95 (ISBN 0-533-04505-3). Vantage.
Petuchowski, Jakob J. The Theology of Haham David Nieto. 1970. 10.00x (ISBN 0-87068-015-3). Ktav.
Phillips, McCandlish. The Bible, the Supernatural & the Jews. LC 77-92532. 1970. pap. 6.95 (ISBN 0-87123-036-4, 210036). Bethany Hse.
Posner, Zalman I. Think Jewish: A Contemporary View of Judaism, a Jewish View of Today's World. LC 78-71323. 1979. 8.95 (ISBN 0-9602394-0-5); pap. 4.95 (ISBN 0-9602394-1-3). Kesher.
Prager, Dennis & Telushkin, Joseph. Eight Questions People Ask About Judaism. 207p. 1980. 8.95x (ISBN 0-686-64272-4). Tze Ulmad Pr.
--Eight Questions People Ask About Judaism. LC 75-2969. 1976. 7.50 (ISBN 0-685-77698-0). Tze Ulmad Pr.
--Nine Questions People Ask About Judaism. 1981. 11.95 (ISBN 0-671-42593-5). S&S.
Rosenberg, Stuart E. Judaism. (Orig.). 1966. pap. 2.45 (ISBN 0-8091-1608-1, Deus). Paulist Pr.
Rosenthal, Erwin I. Studia Semitica, 2 vols. Incl. Vol. 1. Jewish Themes. 57.00 (ISBN 0-521-07958-6); Vol. 2. Islamic Themes. 45.00 (ISBN 0-521-07959-4). (Oriental Publications Ser.: Nos. 16 & 17). Cambridge U Pr.
Rosenthal, Gilbert S. Four Paths to One God. LC 73-77281. 1973. 8.95 (ISBN 0-8197-0286-2); pap. 5.95x (ISBN 0-8197-0012-6). Bloch.
--The Many Faces of Judaism. Rossel, Seymour, ed. LC 78-25898. 1979. pap. 4.95x (ISBN 0-87441-311-7). Behrman.
Rosenweig, Efraim M. We Jews: Invitation to a Dialogue. LC 77-81359. 1978. 7.95 (ISBN 0-8015-8428-0, Hawthorn). Dutton.
Roth, Leon. Judaism, a Portrait. LC 61-5918. 240p. 1972. pap. 3.75 (ISBN 0-8052-0344-3). Schocken.
Rothenberg, Joshua. The Jewish Religion in the Soviet Union. 1971. 15.00x (ISBN 0-87068-156-7). Ktav.
Rubenstein, Richard J. After Auschwitz: Essays in Contemporary Judaism. (Orig.). 1966. pap. 6.95 (ISBN 0-672-61150-3). Bobbs.
Sanders, James A. Torah & Canon. LC 72-171504. 144p. (Orig.). 1972. pap. 3.25 (ISBN 0-8006-0105-X, 1-105). Fortress.
Sandmel, Samuel. Judaism & Christian Beginnings. 25.00 (ISBN 0-19-502281-5); pap. 7.95x (ISBN 0-19-502282-3). Oxford U Pr.
Schaefer, Peter. Rivalitaet zwischen Engeln und Menschen: Untersuchungen zur rabbinischen Engelvorstellung. (Studia Judaica, Vol. 8). xiv, 280p. 1975. 48.75x (ISBN 3-11-004632-6). De Gruyter.
Schechter, Solomon. Studies in Judaism. LC 58-11934. (Temple Bks). 1970. pap. 3.45 (ISBN 0-689-70233-7, T14). Atheneum.
Schiller, Mayer. The Road Back: A Discovery of Judaism Without Embellishments. new ed. 1978. 8.95 (ISBN 0-87306-164-0). Feldheim.
Schochet, Elijah J. Taz Rabbi David Halevi. 10.00x (ISBN 0-87068-687-9). Ktav.
Schwartz, Charles & Schwartz, Bertie G. A Modern Interpretation of Judaism: Faith Through Reason. LC 75-35447. 208p. 1976. pap. 3.95 (ISBN 0-8052-0526-8). Schocken.
Seltzer, Robert M. Jewish People, Jewish Thought. (Illus.). 1980. text ed. 19.95 (ISBN 0-02-408950-8). Macmillan.
Shafran, Avi. Jewthink: A Guide to Real Judaism for the Thinking Individual. 1977. pap. 3.95 (ISBN 0-87203-064-4). Hermon.
Sharot, Stephen. Judaism: A Sociology. LC 75-37727. 240p. 1976. text ed. 29.50x (ISBN 0-8419-0250-X). Holmes & Meier.
Shunami, S. Bibliography of Jewish Bibliographies. enl. 2nd ed. 1969. 50.00x (ISBN 0-685-27923-5). Ktav.
Sigal, Phillip. Emergence of Contemporary Judaism: Vol. 1, the Foundations of Judaism from Biblical Origins to the Sixth Century A.D. Pt. 1 from the Origins to the Separation of Christianity. (Pittsburgh Theological Monographs: No. 29). 1980. pap. text ed. 17.50 (ISBN 0-915138-30-1). Pickwick.
--New Dimensions in Judaism: A Creative Analysis of Rabbinic Concepts. LC 72-186485. 1972. 10.00 (ISBN 0-682-47429-0, University). Exposition.
Silver, Abba H. Where Judaism Differed. 1956. 5.95 (ISBN 0-02-610690-6); pap. 2.95 (ISBN 0-02-089360-4). Macmillan.
Spero, Moshe H. Judaism & Psychology: Halakhic Perspectives. 17.50x (ISBN 0-87068-693-3). Ktav.
Stadelmann, Luis I. Hebrew Conception of the World. (Analecta Biblica: Vol. 39). 1970. pap. 11.00 (ISBN 0-8294-0313-2). Loyola.
Steinberg, Milton. Basic Judaism. LC 47-30768. 1965. pap. 2.25 (ISBN 0-15-610698-1, HB88, Harv). HarBraceJ.
Steinsaltz, Adin. The Thirteen-Petalled Rose. LC 79-3077. 181p. 1980. 12.95 (ISBN 0-465-08560-1). Basic.
Stitskin, Leon D. Studies in Torah Judaism. LC 68-21858. 1969. 25.00x (ISBN 0-87068-110-9). Ktav.
Studies in Bamidbor. Date not set. 11.50 (ISBN 0-686-76263-0). Feldheim.
Studies in Bereshis. Date not set. 11.50 (ISBN 0-686-76261-4). Feldheim.
Studies in Devorim. Date not set. 11.50 (ISBN 0-686-76264-9). Feldheim.
Studies in Vayikra. Date not set. 11.50 (ISBN 0-686-76262-2). Feldheim.
The Study of Judaism: Vol. 1. 20.00x (ISBN 0-87068-180-X). Ktav.
Taylor, Charles W. Sayings of the Jewish Fathers. 59.95 (ISBN 0-8490-0995-2). Gordon Pr.
Trepp, Leo. Judaism: Development & Life. 2nd ed. 1974. pap. text ed. 8.95x (ISBN 0-8221-0114-9). Dickenson.
Tsa'ar Ba'ale Hayim. 1976. 6.95 (ISBN 0-87306-127-6). Feldheim.
Umen, Samuel. Jewish Concepts & Reflections. LC 62-9774. 1962. 3.75 (ISBN 0-8022-1748-6). Philos Lib.
Walstrom, Gordon J. Revelation of Israel's Messiah: The Seven Churches, Vol. 1. 1980. 11.95 (ISBN 0-533-04581-9). Vantage.
Weininger, O. O. The Psychology of Judaism. (Illus.). 1980. deluxe ed. 41.75 (ISBN 0-89920-002-8). Am Inst Psych.
Weiss-Rosmarin, T. Jewish Survival. 5.95x (ISBN 0-87068-426-4). Ktav.
Wenger, Eliezer. The Jewish Book of Lists & Summaries, Vol. 1. (gr. 5 up). 1978. pap. 1.00 (ISBN 0-89655-140-7). BRuach HaTorah.
Wengrov, Charles, tr. from Hebrew. Sefer Ha'hinnuch, the Book of Education: Genesis-Exodus. (Anonymous Attributed to R. Aharon Halevi). 1978. Vol. 1. 13.95 (ISBN 0-87306-179-9). Feldheim.
Wewers, Gerd S. Geheimnis und Geheimhaltung Im Rabbinischen Judentum. (Religionsgeschichtliche Versuche und Vorarbeiten, Vol. 35). (Ger.). 1975. 42.25x (ISBN 3-11-005858-8). De Gruyter.
Wicks, Henry J. The Doctrine of God in the Jewish Apocryphal & Apocalyptic Literature. Repr. of 1915 ed. 19.95x (ISBN 0-87068-149-4). Ktav.
Williams, Jay G. Judaism. LC 80-51551. 204p. 1981. pap. 5.50 (ISBN 0-8356-0540-X, Quest). Theos Pub Hse.
Wine, Sherwin T. Humanistic Judaism. LC 77-90496. (Library of Liberal Religion). 123p. 1978. 10.95 (ISBN 0-87975-102-9). Prometheus Bks.
Wouk, Herman. This Is My God. LC 79-78741. 1959. 11.95 (ISBN 0-385-02158-5). Doubleday.
Yacovsky, F. Jacob. I & Thy People: As Told by My Son Jacob. LC 78-73355. (Illus.). 1978. pap. 2.50 (ISBN 0-9602130-1-5). Sar Sholem.
Yonah, Rabbeinu. Gates of Repentance, Shaarei Teshuvah. 1976. pap. 5.95 (ISBN 0-87306-112-8). Feldheim.
Zeitlin, Joseph. Disciples of the Wise. LC 71-121517. (Essay Index Reprint Ser). 1945. 17.00 (ISBN 0-8369-1859-2). Arno.
Zeitlin, Solomon. Rise & Fall of the Judaean State. Vol. 3: 66 C.E.-120 C.E. LC 61-11708. 1978. 12.50 (ISBN 0-8276-0094-1, 406). Jewish Pubn.
Zimmermann, Frank. The Book of Tobit. 20.00x (ISBN 0-685-38403-9, Pub. by Dropsie U Pr). Ktav.
Zucker, Norman L. The Coming Crisis in Israel: Private Faith & Public Policy. 1973. 15.00x (ISBN 0-262-24018-1); pap. 4.95 (ISBN 0-262-74012-5). MIT Pr.
Zuckermann, B. A Treatise on the Sabbatical Year & the Jubilee. Lowy, A., tr. from Ger. LC 74-78326. 72p. 1974. Repr. 6.75 (ISBN 0-87203-044-X). Hermon.

JUDAISM–ADDRESSES, ESSAYS, LECTURES

The Academic Study of Judaism: Essays & Reflections, Third Series. Date not set. 12.50x (ISBN 0-87068-712-3). Ktav.
Alexander Kohut Memorial Foundation. Jewish Studies in Memory of Israel Abrahams. Katz, Steven, ed. LC 79-7164. (Jewish Philosophy, Mysticism & History of Ideas Ser.). (Illus.). 1980. Repr. of 1927 ed. lib. bdg. 39.00x (ISBN 0-405-12274-8). Arno.
Appel, Gersion. Samuel K. Mirsky Memorial Volume. 1970. 20.00x (ISBN 0-87068-084-6). Ktav.
Bemporad, J., ed. A Rational Faith: Essays in Honor of Levi A. Olan. 15.00x (ISBN 0-87068-448-5). Ktav.
Ben Horin, Meir. Studies & Essays in Honor of Abraham A. Neuman. 1962. 35.00x (ISBN 0-685-13745-7, Pub. by Dropsie U Pr). Ktav.
Birnbaum, Philip, ed. The New Treasury of Judaism. 1977. 12.50 (ISBN 0-88482-410-1, Sanhedrin Pr); pap. 7.95 (ISBN 0-88482-411-X, Sanhedrin Pr). Hebrew Pub.
Bland, Kalman P. Epistle on the Possibility of Conjunction with the Active Intellect by Ibn Rushd with the Commentary of Moses Narboni. Date not set. 20.00x (ISBN 0-686-73598-6). Ktav.
Brann, M. & Rosenthal, F. Gedenkbuch zur Erinnerung an David Kaufmann. Katz, Steven, ed. LC 79-7142. (Jewish Philosophy, Mysticism & History of Ideas Ser.). 1980. Repr. of 1900 ed. lib. bdg. 60.00x (ISBN 0-405-12292-6). Arno.
Brauner, R. A., ed. Shiv'im: Essays & Studies in Honor of Ira Eisenstein. 20.00x (ISBN 0-87068-442-6). Ktav.
Buber, Martin. Israel & the World: Essays in a Time of Crisis. LC 48-9322. 1963. pap. 5.50 (ISBN 0-8052-0066-5). Schocken.
--Mamre, Essays in Religion. Hort, Greta, tr. LC 72-97271. Repr. of 1946 ed. lib. bdg. 15.00x (ISBN 0-8371-2591-X, BUMA). Greenwood.
Chiel, Arthur A., ed. Perspectives on Jews & Judaism: Essays in Honor of Wolfe Kelman. 25.00x (ISBN 0-87068-683-6). Ktav.
Cohen, Arthur A., ed. The Jew: Essays from Martin Buber's Journal der Jude, 1916-1928. Neugroschel, Joachim, tr. from Ger. LC 79-10610. (Judaic Studies Ser.). 300p. 1980. 25.00x (ISBN 0-8173-6908-2). U of Ala Pr.
Commentary Editors. Condition of Jewish Belief. (Orig.). 1967. 10.95 (ISBN 0-02-527260-8). Macmillan.
Dawidowicz, Lucy. The Jewish Presence: Essays on Identity & History. LC 78-6236. 1978. pap. 3.95 (ISBN 0-15-646221-4, Harv). HarBraceJ.
Dubnow, Simon. Nationalism & History: Essays on Old & New Judaism. Pinson, Koppel S., ed. LC 58-5590. (Temple Bk). 1970. pap. 4.25 (ISBN 0-689-70247-7, T21). Atheneum.
Duker, Abraham G. Joshua Starr Memorial Volume. 1953. 12.50x (ISBN 0-87068-037-4). Ktav.
Eppenstein, Simon, et al. Festschriftum Zum Siebzigsten Geburstage A. Berliner's, 3 vols. Katz, Steven, ed. LC 79-7161. (Jewish Philosophy, Mysticism & History of Ideas Ser.). 1980. Repr. of 1914 ed. Set. lib. bdg. 60.00x (ISBN 0-405-12247-0); lib. bdg. 20.00x ea. Vol. 1 (ISBN 0-405-12248-9). Vol. 2 (ISBN 0-405-12249-7) (ISBN 0-405-12304-3). Arno.
Feldman, Abraham J. Words of My Mouth. LC 74-93294. 1970. 5.95x (ISBN 0-8197-0079-7). Bloch.
Fraenckelscher, Stiftung. Festschrift Seventy Five Jahrigen Bestehen Des Judich-Theologischen Seminars, 2 vols. Katz, Steven, ed. LC 79-7159. (Jewish Philosophy, Mysticism & History of Ideas Ser.). 1980. Repr. of 1929 ed. Set. lib. bdg. 70.00x (ISBN 0-405-12243-8). Arno.
Frank, Luanne T. & George, Emery E., eds. Husbanding the Golden Grain: Studies in Honor of Henry W. Nordmeyer. 337p. 1973. 12.50x (ISBN 0-913950-01-7). M S Rosenberg.
Freiman, A., et al, eds. Festschrift zum Siebzigsten Geburtstage A. Berliner's. LC 79-7165. (Jewish Philosophy, Mysticism & History of Ideas Ser.). 1980. Repr. of 1903 ed. lib. bdg. 39.00x (ISBN 0-405-12252-7). Arno.
Geiger, Abraham. Nachgelassene Schriften, 5 vols. in 3. Katz, Steven, ed. LC 79-7132. (Jewish Philosophy, Mysticism & History of Ideas Ser.). 1980. Repr. of 1875 ed. Set. lib. bdg. 150.00x (ISBN 0-405-12255-1); lib. bdg. 50.00x ea. Vol. 1 (ISBN 0-405-12256-X). Vol. 2 (ISBN 0-405-12257-8). Vol. 3 (ISBN 0-405-12228-4). Arno.
Gesellschaft zur Forderung der Wissenschaft des Judentums. Festschrift Siebzigsten Geburtstage Jakob Guttmanns. Katz, Steven, ed. LC 79-7155. (Jewish Philosophy, Mysticism & History of Ideas Ser.). 1980. Repr. of 1915 ed. lib. bdg. 22.00x (ISBN 0-405-12253-5). Arno.
Gunzburg, D., et al, eds. Festschrift zu Ehren des Dr. A. Harkavy. LC 79-7160. (Jewish Philosophy, Mysticism & History of Ideas Ser.). 1980. Repr. of 1908 ed. lib. bdg. 52.00x (ISBN 0-405-12259-4). Arno.
Ha-am, Achad, pseud. Ten Essays on Zionism & Judaism. LC 73-2202. (The Jewish People; History, Religion, Literature Ser.). Repr. of 1922 ed. 20.00 (ISBN 0-405-05267-7). Arno.
Hilsenrad, Zalman A. My Soul Thirsts. 1976. 8.95 (ISBN 0-87306-128-4). Feldheim.
Hirsch, S. A. Cabalists & Other Essays. LC 74-102572. 1970. Repr. of 1922 ed. 12.00 (ISBN 0-8046-0732-X). Kennikat.
Hoffman, Lawrence, ed. Gates of Understanding. LC 77-23488. 1977. pap. text ed. 4.95 (ISBN 0-8074-0009-2, 142689). UAHC.
Huxley, Thomas H. Science & Hebrew Tradition: Essays. 1979. Repr. of 1894 ed. lib. bdg. 30.00 (ISBN 0-8495-2263-3). Arden Lib.
Jacobs, Louis. Jewish Thought Today. LC 73-116679. (Chain of Tradition Ser). 1970. pap. 3.95x (ISBN 0-87441-014-2). Behrman.
Jung, Leo. Heirloom: Sermons, Lectures & Studies. 1961. 7.50 (ISBN 0-87306-107-1). Feldheim.
Kallen, Horace M. Judaism at Bay: Essays Toward the Adjustment of Judaism to Modernity. LC 74-38451. (Religion in America, Ser. 2). 268p. 1972. Repr. of 1932 ed. 15.00 (ISBN 0-405-04071-7). Arno.
Katsh, Abraham I. & Nemoy, Leon. Essays on the Occasion of the Seventieth Anniversary of Dropsie University: 1909-1979. Date not set. 39.50x (ISBN 0-87068-759-X). Ktav.

Katz, Steven, et al, eds. Judaica Festschrift zu Hermann Cohens Siebzigstem Geburtstage. LC 79-7156. (Jewish Philosophy, Mysticism & History of Ideas Ser.). 1980. Repr. of 1912 ed. lib. bdg. 52.00x (ISBN 0-405-12246-2). Arno.

Kaufman, William E. Contemporary Jewish Philosophies. LC 75-30761. 388p. (Orig.). 1976. pap. text ed. 4.95x (ISBN 0-87441-238-2, Jewish Restructionist Press). Behrman.

Konvitz, Milton R. Judaism & the American Idea. LC 79-14278. 224p. 1980. pap. 5.95 (ISBN 0-8052-0635-3). Schocken.

--Judaism & the American Idea. LC 78-58028. 1978. 13.50x (ISBN 0-8014-1181-5). Cornell U Pr.

Korn, Bertram. A Bicentennial Festschrift for Jacob Rader Marcus. 35.00x (ISBN 0-87068-457-4). Ktav.

Krauss, Samuel & Katz, Steven, eds. Festschrift Adolf Schwarz zum Siebzigsten Geburtstage. LC 79-7162. (Jewish Philosophy, Mysticism & History of Ideas Ser.). (Illus.). 1980. Repr. of 1917 ed. lib. bdg. 50.00x (ISBN 0-405-12275-6). Arno.

Lazarus, Josephine. Spirit of Judaism. facsimile ed. LC 77-38031. (Essay Index Reprint Ser). Repr. of 1895 ed. 16.00 (ISBN 0-8369-2602-1). Arno.

Lehrman, Irving. In the Name of God. LC 79-51518. 1979. 12.00x (ISBN 0-8197-0467-9). Bloch.

Longworth, Philip, ed. Confrontations with Judaism. 1967. 5.50 (ISBN 0-685-06928-1). Bloch.

Mandelbaum, Bernard. Wisdom of Solomon Schechter. 1963. pap. 2.50 (ISBN 0-8381-3103-4). United Syn Bk.

Mirsky, Mark J. My Search for the Messiah. LC 76-54910. 1977. 10.95 (ISBN 0-02-585120-9, 58512). Macmillan.

Modern Jewish Thought: Selected Issues, 1889-1966. LC 73-2221. (The Jewish People; History, Religion, Literature Ser.). 22.00 (ISBN 0-405-05283-9). Arno.

Neusner, Jacob. The Academic Study of Judaism: Essays & Reflections. (Second Ser.). 15.00 (ISBN 0-87068-431-0). Ktav.

--Understanding Jewish Theology. 1973. pap. 8.95x (ISBN 0-87068-215-6). Ktav.

Rosen, Moses. The Paper Bridge: Essays on Judaism. Gottlieb, Wolf, tr. from Romanian. LC 73-88049. 303p. 1975. 11.95 (ISBN 0-914250-02-7). Intl Lib.

Rosenthal, Gilbert S. Generations in Crisis: Judaism's Answers to the Dilemmas of Our Time. LC 79-76231. 1969. 5.95 (ISBN 0-8197-0177-7). Bloch.

Schechter, Solomon. Seminary Addresses. 1959. pap. 2.45 (ISBN 0-8381-2109-8). United Syn Bk.

--Seminary Addresses & Other Papers. LC 79-83435. (Religion in America, Ser. 1). 1969. Repr. of 1915 ed. 14.00 (ISBN 0-405-00260-2). Arno.

Scholem, Gershom. On Jews & Judaism in Crisis: Selected Essays. Dannhauser, Werner J., ed. LC 75-37010. 1978. 16.50 (ISBN 0-8052-3613-9); pap. 7.95 (ISBN 0-8052-0588-8). Schocken.

Simon, Leon, ed. Selected Essays of Ahad Ha-'Am. LC 62-20752. 1970. pap. 3.95 (ISBN 0-689-70246-9, T20). Atheneum.

Slonimsky, Henry. Essays. 7.50x (ISBN 0-685-56216-6). Ktav.

Steinberg, Milton. Believing Jew: The Selected Writings. facsimile ed. LC 76-152215. (Essay Index Reprint Ser). Repr. of 1951 ed. 18.00 (ISBN 0-8369-2256-5). Arno.

Umen, Samuel. Nature of Judaism. LC 60-15964. 1961. 3.75 (ISBN 0-8022-1750-8). Philos Lib.

JUDAISM-APOLOGETIC WORKS

Gudemann, Moritz. Judische Apologetik. Katz, Steven, ed. LC 79-7133. (Jewish Philosophy, Mysticism & History of Ideas Ser.). 1980. Repr. of 1906 ed. lib. bdg. 20.00x (ISBN 0-405-12258-6). Arno.

Kolitz, Zvi. Survival for What. LC 70-75761. 1969. 6.50 (ISBN 0-8022-2272-2). Philos Lib.

Max, Moshe. I Believe. 1978. 8.95 (ISBN 0-87306-155-1). Feldheim.

Rankin, Oliver S. Jewish Religious Polemic. rev. ed. 1969. 17.00x (ISBN 0-87068-007-2). Ktav.

Runes, Dagobert D. Of God, the Devil & the Jews. 1952. 3.00 (ISBN 0-8022-1444-4). Philos Lib.

Troki, Isaac A. Faith Strengthened: Hizzuk Emunah. rev. ed. Mocatta, Moses, tr. 1970. 8.95x (ISBN 0-87068-101-X). Ktav.

Yerushalmi, Yosef H. From Spanish Court to Italian Ghetto: Isaac Cardoso, a Study in Seventeenth-Century Marranism & Jewish Apologetics. LC 76-109544. (Illus.). 548p. 1981. pap. 15.00 (ISBN 0-295-95824-3). U of Wash Pr.

JUDAISM-BIBLIOGRAPHY

Brisman, S. A History & Guide to Judaic Bibliography. (Bibliographica Judaica Ser: No. 7). 29.50x (ISBN 0-87820-900-X, HUC Pr). Ktav.

New York Public Library. The Hebrew-Character Title Catalog of the Jewish Division, the New York Public Library. (Library Catalogs-Supplements Ser.). 1981. lib. bdg. 480.00 (ISBN 0-8161-0373-9). G K Hall.

Oppenheim, Micha F. The Study & Practice of Judaism: A Selected, Annotated List. LC 79-20390. (Orig.). 1979. pap. 4.95 (ISBN 0-9603100-0-2). Torah Res.

JUDAISM-CEREMONIES AND PRACTICES

see Jews-Rites and Ceremonies

JUDAISM-COLLECTIONS

Davis, Moshe. Mordecai M. Kaplan Jubilee Volume, 2 Vols. 1953. Set. 35.00x (ISBN 0-685-13740-6, Pub. by Jewish Theol Seminary). Ktav.

Hirsch, Samson R. The Nineteen Letters of Ben Uziel. Paritzky, Karen, tr. from Ger. 5.95 (ISBN 0-87306-180-2). Feldheim.

Kaufman, William E. Contemporary Jewish Philosophies. LC 75-30761. 388p. (Orig.). 1976. pap. text ed. 4.95x (ISBN 0-87441-238-2, Jewish Restructionist Press). Behrman.

Leslau, Wolf, tr. Falasha Anthology. (Judaica Ser.: No. 6). (Illus.). 1951. 20.00x (ISBN 0-300-00681-0). Yale U Pr.

Millgram, Abraham E. Great Jewish Ideas. pap. 5.95x (ISBN 0-8197-0157-2, Pub by B'nai B'rith). Bloch.

Noveck, Simon. Contemporary Jewish Thought: A Reader. (Pub by B'nai B'rith); pap. 5.95x (ISBN 0-8197-0169-6). Bloch.

--Great Jewish Thinkers in the Twentieth Century. (Pub by B'nai B'rith); pap. 5.95x (ISBN 0-8197-0167-X). Bloch.

Underground Literature, 2 vols. in 1. 80p. 1.95 (ISBN 0-686-74969-3). ADL.

JUDAISM-DEVOTIONAL EXERCISES

see Jews-Prayer-Books and Devotions

JUDAISM-DICTIONARIES

see also Jews-Dictionaries and Encyclopedias

Ausubel, Nathan. Book of Jewish Knowledge. (Illus.). 1962. 17.95 (ISBN 0-517-09746-X). Crown.

Encyclopedia Talmudica, 3 vols. Vol. 1. 20.00 ea. (ISBN 0-87306-209-4). Vol. I (ISBN 0-87306-210-8). Vol. II (ISBN 0-87306-211-6). Vol. III. Feldheim.

Glustrom, Simon. Language of Judaism. rev. ed. 1973. pap. 7.95x (ISBN 0-87068-224-5). Ktav.

Koehler, Ludwig & Baumgartner, Walter. Lexicon in Veteris Testamenti Libros: Hebrew-Aramaic Lexicon, Incl, Supplementum. 1951-53. 49.50 (ISBN 0-8028-2176-6). Eerdmans.

Marwick, Lawrence. Biblical & Judaic Acronyms. 29.50 (ISBN 0-87068-438-8). Ktav.

Runes, Dagobert D., ed. Concise Dictionary of Judaism. LC 77-88933. 124p. Repr. of 1966 ed. lib. bdg. 15.00x (ISBN 0-8371-2109-4, RUDJ). Greenwood.

Schonfield, Hugh J. Popular Dictionary of Judaism. 1966. pap. 1.75 (ISBN 0-8065-0075-1, 232). Citadel Pr.

JUDAISM-EARLY WORKS TO 1900

see Judaism-Works to 1900

JUDAISM-EDUCATION

see Jews-Education

JUDAISM-HISTORY

see also Jews-History-To 70 A.D.

Abrahams, Israel. Jewish Life in the Middle Ages. LC 58-11933. (Temple Books). 1969. pap. text ed. 7.95x (ISBN 0-689-70001-6, T1). Atheneum.

Abramov, S. Zalman. Perpetual Dilemma: Jewish Religion in the Jewish State. 1979. pap. 7.50 (ISBN 0-8074-0088-2, 382500, WUPJ). UAHC.

Ackroyd, Peter R. Israel Under Babylon & Persia. (New Clarendon Bible Ser.). 1970. pap. 11.50x (ISBN 0-19-836917-4). Oxford U Pr.

Albright, William F. Yahweh & the Gods of Canaan: An Historical Analysis of Two Contrasting Faiths. 1978. Repr. of 1968 ed. 9.50x (ISBN 0-931464-01-3). Eisenbrauns.

Anderson, G. W. The History and Religion of Israel. (New Clarendon Bible Ser.). (Illus.). 222p. 1966. pap. 9.95x (ISBN 0-19-836915-8). Oxford U Pr.

Bamberger, Bernard J. Story of Judaism. rev. 3rd ed. LC 64-16463. 1964. pap. 6.50 (ISBN 0-8052-0077-0). Schocken.

Berger, David. The Jewish-Christian Debate in the High Middle Ages: 4th of "Judaica: Texts & Translations". new ed. LC 78-1166. 1978. 25.00 (ISBN 0-8276-0104-2, 416). Jewish Pubn.

Berlin, Charles. Studies in Jewish Bibliography, History & Literature: In Honor of I. Edward Kiev. 1971. 50.00x (ISBN 0-87068-143-5). Ktav.

Bickerman, Elias. From Ezra to the Last of the Maccabees: Foundations of Post-Biblical Judaism. 1962. pap. 2.95 (ISBN 0-8052-0036-3). Schocken.

Bokser, Baruch M. History of Judaism: The Next Ten Years. Neusner, Jacob, ed. LC 80-25501. (Brown Judaic Studies). 1980. 15.00 (ISBN 0-89130-450-9); pap. 10.50 (ISBN 0-89130-451-7). Scholars Pr CA.

--Post Mishnaic Judaism in Transition: Samuel on Berakhot & the Beginnings of Gemara. Neusner, Jacob, ed. LC 80-19702. 1981. 19.50 (ISBN 0-89130-432-0, 14 00 17); pap. 15.00 (ISBN 0-89130-433-9). Scholars Pr CA.

Bokser, Ben Z. Pharisaic Judaism in Transition. LC 73-2189. (The Jewish People; History, Religion, Literature Ser.). Repr. of 1935 ed. 13.00 (ISBN 0-405-05255-3). Arno.

Box, George H. Judaism in the Greek Period, from the Rise of Alexander the Great to the Intervention of Rome. LC 73-109712. Repr. of 1932 ed. lib. bdg. 21.50x (ISBN 0-8371-4288-1, BOJG). Greenwood.

Buchler, Adolph. Studies in Sin & Atonement. rev. ed. (Library of Biblical Studies Ser.). 1967. 25.00x (ISBN 0-87068-031-5). Ktav.

Butwin, Frances. Jews of America: History & Sources. Blecher, Arthur C., ed. LC 73-2253. (Illus.). 160p. (gr. 7-9). 1973. pap. text ed. 3.95x (ISBN 0-87441-062-2). Behrman.

Charles, Robert H. A Critical History of the Doctrine of a Future Life, in Israel, in Judaism, & in Christianity. LC 79-8600. Repr. of 1899 ed. 38.50 (ISBN 0-404-18455-3). AMS Pr.

Cohen, Mark R. Jewish Self-Government in Medieval Egypt: The Origins of the Office of Head of the Jews, Ca. 1065-1125. LC 80-7514. (Princeton Studies on the Near East). 425p. 1980. 27.50 (ISBN 0-691-05307-3). Princeton U Pr.

Collins, John J. Ideal Figures in Ancient Judaism: Profiles & Paradigms. Nickelsburg, George W., ed. LC 80-19878. 1981. 15.00 (ISBN 0-89130-434-7, 060412); pap. 10.50 (ISBN 0-89130-435-5). Scholars Pr CA.

Culi, Yaakov. The Torah Anthology: Mem Lo'ez, 8 vols. Kaplan, Aryeh, tr. Incl. Vol. 1. Beginnings: From Creation Until Abraham. 540p. 14.95 (ISBN 0-940118-01-7); Vol. 2. The Patriarchs: From Abraham Until Jacob. 600p. 15.95 (ISBN 0-940118-02-5); Vol. 3. The Twelve Tribes: From Jacob Until Joseph. 708p; Vol. 4. Israel in Egypt: Subjugation & Prelude to the Exodus. 280p. 12.95 (ISBN 0-940118-04-1); Vol. 5. Redemption: The Exodus from Egypt. 436p. 15.95 (ISBN 0-940118-05-X); Vol. 6. The Ten Commandments: Revelation at Sinai. 534p. 16.95 (ISBN 0-940118-06-8); Vol. 7. The Law: The First Codification. 363p. 13.95 (ISBN 0-940118-07-6). (MeAm Lo'ez Ser.). (Illus.). 1977-1980. Maznaim.

Davies, W. D. The Gospel & the Land: Early Christianity & Jewish Territorial Doctrine. LC 72-82228. 1974. 25.00x (ISBN 0-520-02278-5). U of Cal Pr.

Davis, Moshe. The Emergence of Conservative Judaism: The Historical School in 19th Century America. LC 77-22180. (The Jacob R. Schiff Library of Jewish Contributions to American Democracy: No. 15). (Illus.). 1977. Repr. of 1965 ed. lib. bdg. 36.25x (ISBN 0-8371-9792-9, DAECJ). Greenwood.

Domnitz, Myer. Judaism. (Living Religions Series). (Illus.). 1977. pap. 3.50x (ISBN 0-7062-3596-7). Intl Pubns Serv.

Epstein, Isidore. Judaism. (Orig.). 1959. pap. 4.50 (ISBN 0-14-020440-7, Pelican). Penguin.

L' Esprit du Judaisme ou Examen Raisonne de la Loi de Moise, et de Son Influence sur la Religion Chretienne. (Holbach & His Friends Ser). 227p. (Fr.). 1974. Repr. of 1770 ed. lib. bdg. 63.50x (ISBN 0-8287-1368-5, 1552). Clearwater Pub.

Fairweather, William. The Background of the Gospels or Judaism in the Period Between the Old & New Testaments. 4th ed. 456p. 1961. Repr. text ed. 12.00x (ISBN 0-567-02101-7). Attic Pr.

Fine, Jo Renee & Wolfe, Gerard R. The Synagogues of New York's Lower East Side. LC 75-15126. (Illus.). 1978. 16.95 (ISBN 0-8147-2559-7). NYU Pr.

Finkelstein, Louis, ed. The Jews, Vol. 1: Their History. 4th ed. LC 74-107615. 1970. pap. 6.95 (ISBN 0-8052-0271-4). Schocken.

Fiorenza, Elisabeth S., ed. Aspects of Religious Propaganda in Judaism & Early Christianity. LC 74-27890. 192p. 1976. text ed. 12.95x (ISBN 0-268-00578-8, 85-05786). U of Notre Dame Pr.

Foerster, Werner. From the Exile to Christ: Historical Introduction to Palestinian Judaism. Harris, Gordon E., ed. LC 64-18151. 264p. 1964. pap. 7.50 (ISBN 0-8006-0978-6, 1-978). Fortress.

Fohrer, Georg. History of Israelite Religion. Green, David E., tr. from Ger. LC 72-2010. 416p. 1972. 5.95 (ISBN 0-687-17225-X). Abingdon.

Glatzer, Nahum N. Essays in Jewish Thought. LC 76-51044. (Judaic Studies: Vol. 8). 304p. 1978. 19.50x (ISBN 0-8173-6904-X). U of Ala Pr.

Goldziher, Ignaz. Mythology Among the Hebrews & Its Historical Development. Martineau, Russell, tr. LC 66-2396. Repr. of 1877 ed. 18.50x (ISBN 0-8154-0082-9). Cooper Sq.

Gowan, Donald E. Bridge Between the Testaments: Reappraisal of Judaism from the Exile to the Birth of Christianity. 2nd ed. LC 76-49996. (Pittsburgh Theological Monographs: No. 14). 1980. text ed. 13.95 (ISBN 0-915138-47-6). Pickwick.

Grant, Frederick C. Ancient Judaism & the New Testament. LC 77-18848. 1978. Repr. of 1959 ed. lib. bdg. 17.75x (ISBN 0-313-20204-4, GRAJ). Greenwood.

Graupe, Heinz M. The Rise of Modern Judaism: An Intellectual History of German Jewry 1650-1942. LC 77-9059. 344p. 1979. lib. bdg. 19.50 (ISBN 0-88275-395-9). Krieger.

Green, William S. Approaches to Ancient Judaism: Theory & Practice. LC 76-57656. 1978. pap. 10.50 (ISBN 0-89130-130-5). Scholars Pr Ca.

Guignebert, Charles. Jewish World in the Time of Jesus. 1959. 6.00 (ISBN 0-8216-0033-8). Univ Bks.

Hebrew Union College Annual, 38 Vols. 1969. 650.00x (ISBN 0-87068-065-X). Ktav.

Heschel, Abraham J. Theology of Ancient Judaism, 2 vols. (Heb.). 1973. Set. 23.50x (ISBN 0-685-32988-7). Bloch.

Higgens, Elford. Hebrew Idolatry & Superstition. 1971. Repr. of 1893 ed. 10.00 (ISBN 0-8046-1150-5). Kennikat.

History of the Religion of Israel: From the Babylonian Captivity to the End of the Prophecy, Vol. 4. 39.50x (ISBN 0-685-56209-3). Ktav.

Hyman, Frieda C. The Jewish Experience, Bk. 2. (Illus.). 1978. text ed. 6.95x (ISBN 0-8381-0192-5). United Syn Bk.

Johnson, Paul. Civilizations of the Holy Land. LC 78-73358. (Illus.). 1979. 14.95 (ISBN 0-689-10973-3). Atheneum.

Kaufman, Harriet L. Jews & Judaism Since Jesus: An Introduction. (Illus.). 1978. 3.95 (ISBN 0-9602500-0-X). Kaufman Hse.

Kaufmann, Yehezkel. Religion of Israel. Greenberg, Moshe, tr. LC 60-5466. 1960. 25.00x (ISBN 0-226-42728-5). U of Chicago Pr.

Kedourie, Elie, ed. The Jewish World: History & Culture of the Jewish People. LC 78-31363. (Illus.). 1979. 37.50 (ISBN 0-8109-1154-X). Abrams.

Kent, Charles F. The Messages of Israel's Lawgivers. Sanders, Frank K., ed. 386p. 1981. Repr. of 1916 ed. lib. bdg. 25.00 (ISBN 0-89760-430-X). Telegraph Bks.

Levin, Nora. While Messiah Tarried: Jewish Socialist Movements, 1871-1917. LC 75-7769. (Illus.). 1977. 24.50 (ISBN 0-8052-3615-5). Schocken.

Lods, Adolphe. Prophets & the Rise of Judaism. Hooke, S. H., tr. LC 77-109772. (Illus.). 1971. Repr. of 1937 ed. lib. bdg. 25.75x (ISBN 0-8371-4262-8, LOPR). Greenwood.

Magriso, Yitzchak. Avoth. Barocas, David N., tr. Kaplan, Aryeh, intro. by. & 400p. 15.95 (ISBN 0-940118-22-X). Maznaim.

Markowitz, Sidney L. What You Should Know About Jewish Religion, History, Ethics, & Culture. 226p. 1973. pap. 2.95 (ISBN 0-8065-0028-X). Citadel Pr.

Meek, Theophile J. Hebrew Origins. 1960. 8.00 (ISBN 0-8446-2572-8). Peter Smith.

Meyer, Michael A. The Origins of the Modern Jew: Jewish Identity & European Culture in Germany, 1749-1824. LC 67-12384. (Waynebooks Ser: No. 32). 250p. 1972. 9.95x (ISBN 0-8143-1315-9); pap. 4.95x (ISBN 0-8143-1470-8). Wayne St U Pr.

Meyers, Eric M. & Strange, James F. Archaeology, the Rabbis, & Early Christianity. LC 80-24208. 208p. 1981. pap. 7.95 (ISBN 0-687-01680-0). Abingdon.

Montefiore, Claude J. Lectures on the Origin & Growth of Religion As Illustrated by the Religion of the Ancient Hebrews. 3rd ed. LC 77-27162. (Hibbert Lectures: 1892). Repr. of 1892 ed. 37.50 (ISBN 0-404-60410-2). AMS Pr.

Moore, George F. History of Religions: Judaism, Christianity, Mohammedanism, Vol. II. (International Theological Library). 568p. 1965. Repr. of 1920 ed. text ed. 13.95x (ISBN 0-567-07203-7). Attic Pr.

--Judaism-in the First Centuries of the Christian Era: The Age of the Tannaim, Vol. 2. LC 72-146791. 1971. pap. 7.50 (ISBN 0-8052-0295-1). Schocken.

Muilenburg, James. Way of Israel: Biblical Faith & Ethics. pap. 3.95x (ISBN 0-06-130133-7, TB133, Torch). Har-Row.

Neusner, Jacob. Method & Meaning in Ancient Judaism II. LC 80-21781. (Brown Judaic Studies). Date not set. pap. 27.50 (ISBN 0-89130-418-5). Scholars Pr CA.

--Method & Meaning in Ancient Judiasm III. LC 80-19449. (Brown Judaic Studies). 1981. pap. 27.50 (ISBN 0-89130-418-5). Scholars Pr CA.

--Understanding Rabbinic Judaism: From Talmudic to Modern Times. 1974. pap. 9.95x (ISBN 0-685-56200-X). Ktav.

Noth, Martin & Anderson, Berhard W. History of Pentateuchal Traditions. LC 80-24937. (Scholars Press Reproductions Ser.). 1981. pap. 17.50 (ISBN 0-89130-446-0). Scholars Pr CA.

Oesterley, William O. Jews & Judaism During the Greek Period: The Background of Christianity. LC 74-102580. 1970. Repr. of 1941 ed. 13.00 (ISBN 0-8046-0740-0). Kennikat.

Patai, Raphael. The Hebrew Goddess. 1978. pap. 2.95 (ISBN 0-380-39289-5, 39289, Discus). Avon.

Poliak, Abraham N. The Khazar Conversion to Judaism. 1978. lib. bdg. 39.95 (ISBN 0-685-62299-1). Revisionist Pr.

Raisin, Jacob S. The Haskalah Movement in Russia. 1976. Repr. of 1913 ed. 30.00 (ISBN 0-8274-2471-X). R West.

Rudavsky, David. Modern Jewish Religious Movements. 3rd rev. ed. LC 79-11266. 1979. pap. text ed. 6.95x (ISBN 0-87441-286-2). Behrman.

Russell, D. S. Between the Testaments. LC 77-74742. 176p. 1960. pap. 3.95 (ISBN 0-8006-1856-4, 1-1856). Fortress.

--The Jews from Alexander to Herod. 1967. pap. 11.50x (ISBN 0-19-836913-1). Oxford U Pr.

Sanders, E. P. Paul & Palestinian Judaism: A Comparison of Patterns of Religion. LC 76-62612. 648p. 1977. 25.00x (ISBN 0-8006-0499-7, 1-499). Fortress.

Schechter, Solomon. Studies in Judaism. facsimile ed. LC 78-38775. (Essay Index Reprint Ser). Repr. of 1896 ed. 19.50 (ISBN 0-8369-2670-6). Arno.

Scholem, Gershom. The Messianic Idea in Judaism: And Other Essays on Jewish Spirituality. LC 70-130212. 384p. 1972. 15.00x (ISBN 0-8052-3369-5); pap. 5.95 (ISBN 0-8052-0362-1). Schocken.

Sigal, Phillip. Emergence of Contemporary Judaism: The Foundation of Judaism from Biblical Origins to the Sixth Century A. D, Vol. 1, Pts. 1 & 2. Incl. Pt. 1. From the Origins to the Separation of Christianity. (Pittsburgh Theological Monographs: No. 29). pap. text ed. 17.50 (ISBN 0-686-64852-8); Pt. 2. Rabbinic Judaism. (Pittsburgh Theological Monographs: No. 29a). pap. text ed. 15.75 (ISBN 0-915138-46-8). 1980. pap. text ed. 31.25 set (ISBN 0-915138-46-8). Pickwick.

Silver, Daniel J. & Martin, Bernard. History of Judaism, 2 vols. Incl. Vol. 1. From Abraham to Maimonides. 20.00x (ISBN 0-465-03006-8); pap. 8.95 (ISBN 0-465-03004-1); Vol. 2. Europe & the New World. 20.00x (ISBN 0-465-03007-6); pap. 9.95 (ISBN 0-465-03005-X). LC 73-90131. 1974. Set. 40.00 (ISBN 0-465-03008-4). Basic.

Simpson, Cuthbert A. Revelation & Response in the Old Testament. LC 73-76022. Repr. of 1947 ed. 15.00 (ISBN 0-404-06056-0). AMS Pr.

Steinschneider, Moritz. Gesammelte Schriften. Katz, Steven, ed. LC 79-7152. (Jewish Philosophy, Mysticism & History of Ideas Ser.). 1980. Repr. of 1925 ed. lib. bdg. 48.00x (ISBN 0-405-12289-6). Arno.

--Die Geschichtsliteratur der Juden. Katz, Steven, ed. LC 79-7153. (Jewish Philosophy, Mysticism & History of Ideas Ser.). 1980. Repr. of 1905 ed. lib. bdg. 14.00x (ISBN 0-405-12290-X). Arno.

Surburg, Raymond F. Introduction to the Intertestamental Period. LC 74-33085. 176p. 1975. 8.95 (ISBN 0-570-03237-7, 15-2131). Concordia.

Trepp, Leo. The Complete Book of Jewish Observance. LC 79-1352. (Behrman House Book). (Illus.). 370p. 1980. 14.95 (ISBN 0-671-41797-5). Summit Bks.

--History of the Jewish Experience: Eternal Faith, Eternal People. rev. ed. LC 73-3142. Orig. Title: Eternal Faith, Eternal People: a Journey into Judaism. 296p. 1973. pap. text ed. 6.95x (ISBN 0-87441-072-X). Behrman.

Twersky, Isadore, ed. Studies in Medieval Jewish History & Literature. LC 79-11588. 1979. text ed. 18.50x (ISBN 0-674-85192-7). Harvard U Pr.

Understanding the Jewish Experience. 54p. 2.00 (ISBN 0-686-74981-2). ADL.

Wardle, William L. The History & Religion of Israel. LC 78-11741. (The Clarendon Bible, Old Testament: Vol. I). (Illus.). 1979. Repr. of 1942 ed. lib. bdg. 20.50x (ISBN 0-313-21016-0, WAHR). Greenwood.

Weber, M. Ancient Judaism. LC 52-8156. 1967. pap. text ed. 7.95 (ISBN 0-02-934130-2). Free Pr.

Wellhausen, Julius. Prolegomena to the History of Ancient Israel. 9.00 (ISBN 0-8446-3147-7). Peter Smith.

Yerushalmi, Yosef H. Haggadah & History. LC 73-21169. 1975. 27.50 (ISBN 0-8276-0046-1, 364). Jewish Pubn.

Zeitlin, Solomon. Studies in the Early History of Judaism, Vol. 2. 1973. 35.00x (ISBN 0-87068-209-1). Ktav.

--Studies in the Early History of Judaism, Vol. 4. 35.00x (ISBN 0-87068-454-X). Ktav.

JUDAISM–HISTORY–SOURCES

Ackerman, Walter. Out of Our People's Past: Sources for the Study of Jewish History. 1978. 7.50x (ISBN 0-8381-0221-2). United Syn Bk.

Marcus, Jacob R. An Index to the Picture Collection of the American Jewish Archives. 7.50 (ISBN 0-87820-005-3). Ktav.

Rost, Leonhard. Judaism Outside the Hebrew Canon: An Introduction to the Documents. Green, David E., tr. LC 76-15006. 208p. 1976. 16.95 (ISBN 0-687-20654-5); pap. 5.95 (ISBN 0-687-20653-7). Abingdon.

White, Paul F. Index to the American Jewish Archives, Vols. I-X. 25.00 (ISBN 0-87820-004-5). Ktav.

Zeitlin, Solomon. Studies in the Early History of Judaism, Vol. 1. 1973. 35.00x (ISBN 0-87068-208-3). Ktav.

JUDAISM–HISTORY–TANNAITIC PERIOD, 10-220

see Tannaim

JUDAISM–JUVENILE LITERATURE

Altman, Addie R. Jewish Child's Bible Stories. (gr. 1-3). 1977. 4.50 (ISBN 0-8197-0196-3). Bloch.

Chanover, Hyman, adapted by. Service for the High Holy Days Adapted for Youth. new ed. LC 72-2058. 192p. (gr. 8up). 1972. pap. 2.95x (ISBN 0-87441-123-8). Behrman.

Ehrman, Yocheved. My First Siddur. LC 78-59778. 1979. 6.95 (ISBN 0-8197-0463-6). Bloch.

Geffner, Anne. A Child Celebrates: The Jewish Holidays. rev 2nd ed. Stein, Charlotte M., ed. LC 79-51011. (Illus.). 60p. (Orig.). (gr. k-6). 1980. pap. 4.95 (ISBN 0-916634-08-6). Double M Pr.

Goldman, Alex J. Child's Dictionary of Jewish Symbols. (Illus.). (gr. 1-4). 5.00 (ISBN 0-685-09470-7). Feldheim.

Golomb, Morris. Know Jewish Living & Enjoy It. LC 78-54569. (gr. 3-7). 1981. 10.00 (ISBN 0-88400-054-0). Shengold.

Greenfeld, Howard. Bar Mitzvah. LC 81-5104. (Illus.). 32p. 1981. 6.95 (ISBN 0-03-053861-0). HR&W.

Gumbiner, Joseph H. Leaders of Our People, 2 Bks. (Illus.). (gr. 4-6). Bk. 1. 1963. text ed. 5.00 (ISBN 0-8074-0141-2, 122921); Bk. 2. 1965. text ed. 5.00 (ISBN 0-8074-0142-0, 123921); tchrs'. guide 3.25 (ISBN 0-8074-0143-9, 202922). UAHC.

Jacobs, Louis. Chain of Tradition Series, 5 vols. Incl. Vol. 1. Jewish Law. LC 68-27329. pap. text ed. 3.95x (ISBN 0-87441-211-0); Vol. 2. Jewish Ethics, Philosophy & Mysticism. LC 71-80005. pap. text ed. 3.95x (ISBN 0-87441-212-9); Vol. 3. Jewish Thought Today. LC 73-116679. (Illus.). 1974. pap. text ed. 3.95x (ISBN 0-87441-213-7); Vol. 4. Hasidic Thought; Vol. 5. Jewish Biblical Exegesis. LC 78-1487. (Illus.). (gr. 8 up). 1974. Behrman.

Kripke, Dorothy K. & Levin, Meyer. God & the Story of Judaism. LC 62-17078. (Jewish Heritage Ser: Vol. 1). (gr. 4-6). 1962. 4.95x (ISBN 0-87441-000-2). Behrman.

Levin, Meyer. Beginnings in Jewish Philosophy. LC 76-116677. (Jewish Heritage Ser). (Illus.). 192p. (gr. 9-11). 1971. text ed. 4.95x (ISBN 0-87441-063-0). Behrman.

Levin, Meyer & Kurzband, Toby. Story of the Jewish Way of Life. LC 59-13487. (Jewish Heritage Ser: Vol. 3). (gr. 4-6). 1959. 4.95x (ISBN 0-87441-003-7). Behrman.

Mandel, Morris. Thirteen: A Teenage Guide to Judaism. LC 61-8452. (Illus.). (gr. 7 up). 1961. 10.00 (ISBN 0-8246-0096-7). Jonathan David.

Orovitz, Norma A. Puzzled! The Jewish Word Search. LC 77-83177. 1977. pap. 2.50 (ISBN 0-8197-0022-3). Bloch.

Rossel, Seymour. Judaism. LC 75-31561. (First Bks. Ser.). (Illus.). 72p. (gr. 4-8). 1976. PLB 6.90 (ISBN 0-531-00841-X). Watts.

Schachnowitz, Selig. Light from the West. Leftwich, Joseph, tr. (gr. 7 up). 5.95 (ISBN 0-87306-124-1). Feldheim.

Silverman, William B. Judaism & Christianity. LC 68-27330. pap. 5.95x (ISBN 0-87441-016-9). Behrman.

Simms, Laura & Kozodoy, Ruth. Exploring Our Living Past. Harlow, Jules, ed. (Our Living Past Ser). (Illus.). 1978. pap. 5.95x (ISBN 0-87441-309-5). Behrman.

Singer, Isaac B. The Power of Light: Eight Stories for Hanukkah. (Illus.). (gr. 1 up). 1980. 10.95 (ISBN 0-374-36099-5). FS&G.

Weinbach, Sheindel. Avi Names His Price. (Illus.). (gr. 2-5). 1976. 3.95 (ISBN 0-87306-119-5). Feldheim.

Wenger, Eliezer. Jewish Book of Lists & Summaries, Vol. 2. (gr. 5 up). 1979. pap. 1.00 (ISBN 0-89655-141-5). BRuach HaTorah.

--Loads of Fun in the Spirit of Torah & Judaism, Vol. 2. (Illus.). 32p. (gr. 3 up). 1975. pap. text ed. 1.25 (ISBN 0-89655-151-2). BRuach HaTorah.

JUDAISM–LITURGY AND RITUAL

see Jews–Liturgy and Ritual

JUDAISM–QUOTATIONS, MAXIMS, ETC.

Hertz, Joseph H., ed. A Book of Jewish Thoughts. 1976. Repr. 6.95 (ISBN 0-8197-0252-8). Bloch.

Heschel, Abraham Joshua. The Wisdom of Heschel. 368p. 1975. 10.00 (ISBN 0-374-29124-1); pap. 5.95 (ISBN 0-374-51267-1). FS&G.

Hirsch, Sampson R. From the Wisdom of Mishle. Paritzky-Joshua, Karin, tr. 260p. 1976. 7.95 (ISBN 0-87306-040-7). Feldheim.

Kent, Charles F. The Messages of Israel's Lawgivers. Sanders, Frank K., ed. 386p. 1981. Repr. of 1916 ed. lib. bdg. 25.00 (ISBN 0-89760-430-X). Telegraph Bks.

Zaretsky, David & Wengrov, Charles. The Stories & Parables of the Hafetz Hayyim. Orig. Title: Mishle Hafetz Hayyim. 1976. 8.95 (ISBN 0-87306-132-2). Feldheim.

JUDAISM–RECONSTRUCTIONIST MOVEMENT

see Reconstructionist Judaism

JUDAISM–REFORM MOVEMENT

see Reform Judaism

JUDAISM–RELATIONS

see also Jews–Election, Doctrine Of

Carter, George W. Zoroastrianism & Judaism. LC 70-112489. 1970. Repr. of 1918 ed. 14.00 (ISBN 0-404-01396-1). AMS Pr.

Coggins, R. J. Samaritans & Jews: The Origins of Samaritanism Reconsidered. LC 74-3712. (Growing Points in Theology Ser.). 176p. 1974. pap. 6.95 (ISBN 0-8042-0109-9). John Knox.

Freud, Sigmund. Moses & Monotheism. Jones, Katherine, ed. 1955. pap. 2.45 (ISBN 0-394-70014-7, V14, Vin). Random.

Hengel, Martin. Judaism & Hellenism: Studies in Their Encounter in Palestine During the Early Hellenistic Period. Bowden, John, tr. from Ger. 672p. 1981. Set. 19.95 (ISBN 0-8006-1495-X, 1-1495). Fortress.

McKay, John. Religion in Judah Under the Assyrians. LC 72-97460. (Studies in Biblical Theology, 2nd Ser.: No. 26). 1973. text ed. 9.95x (ISBN 0-8401-4076-2); pap. text ed. 7.45x (ISBN 0-8401-3076-7). Allenson-Breckinridge.

Patai, Raphael. The Jewish Mind. LC 76-58040. 1977. 14.95 (ISBN 0-684-14878-1, ScribT); pap. 7.95 (ISBN 0-684-16321-7, SL881, ScribT). Scribner.

Rowley, Harold H. Prophecy & Religion in Ancient China & Israel. 1956. 8.50x (ISBN 0-8401-2059-1). Allenson Breckinridge.

Schultz, Joseph P. Judaism & the Gentile Faiths: Comparative Studies in Religion. LC 75-5250. 435p. 1976. 19.50 (ISBN 0-8386-1707-7). Fairleigh Dickinson.

JUDAISM–RELATIONS–CHRISTIANITY

Althouse, LaVonne. When Jew & Christian Meet. (Illus.). 1966. pap. 1.50 (ISBN 0-377-36221-2). Friend Pr.

Baeck, Leo. Judaism & Christianity: Essays. Kaufmann, Walter, tr. LC 58-5590. (Temple Bk). 1970. pap. 2.95 (ISBN 0-689-70243-4, T17). Atheneum.

Berger, David. The Jewish-Christian Debate in the High Middle Ages: 4th of "Judaica: Texts & Translations". new ed. LC 78-1166. 1978. 25.00 (ISBN 0-8276-0104-2, 416). Jewish Pubn.

Buber, Martin. Two Types of Faith: The Interpretation of Judaism & Christianity. pap. 4.50x (ISBN 0-06-130075-6, TB75, Torch). Har-Row.

De Lange, N. R. Origin & the Jews. LC 75-36293. (Oriental Publications Ser.: No. 25). 160p. 1977. 36.00 (ISBN 0-521-20542-5). Cambridge U Pr.

DePoncins, Leon V. Judaism & Vatican. 59.95 (ISBN 0-8490-0466-7). Gordon Pr.

L' Esprit du Judaisme ou Examen Raisonne de la Loi de Moise, et de Son Influence sur la Religion Chretienne. (Holbach & His Friends Ser). 227p. (Fr.). 1974. Repr. of 1770 ed. lib. bdg. 63.50x (ISBN 0-8287-1368-5, 1552). Clearwater Pub.

Filthaut, Theodor, ed. Israel in Christian Religious Instruction. (Contemporary Catechetics Ser.: Vol. 3). 1965. pap. 1.25x (ISBN 0-268-00144-8). U of Notre Dame Pr.

Fleischner, Eva. Judaism in German Christian Theology Since 1945: Christianity & Israel Considered in Terms of Mission. LC 75-22374. (ATLA Monograph: No. 8). 1975. 10.00 (ISBN 0-8108-0835-8). Scarecrow.

Grant, Frederick C. Ancient Judaism & the New Testament. LC 77-18848. 1978. Repr. of 1959 ed. lib. bdg. 17.75x (ISBN 0-313-20204-4, GRAJ). Greenwood.

Judaism & Christianity: Selected Accounts, 1892-1962. LC 73-2212. (The Jewish People; History, Religion, Literature Ser.). 22.00 (ISBN 0-405-05276-6). Arno.

Maccoby, Hyam, ed. Judaism on Trial: Jewish-Christian Disputations in the Middle Ages. LC 80-70239. 350p. 1981. 30.00 (ISBN 0-8386-3053-7). Fairleigh Dickinson.

Oesterley, W. O. & Rosenthal, Erwin. Judaism & Christianity, 3 Vols. in 1. rev. ed. LC 68-25717. 1969. 45.00x (ISBN 0-87068-094-3). Ktav.

Oesterley, William O. The Jewish Background of the Christian Liturgy. 1925. 8.50 (ISBN 0-8446-1329-0). Peter Smith.

--Jews & Judaism During the Greek Period: The Background of Christianity. LC 74-102580. 1970. Repr. of 1941 ed. 13.00 (ISBN 0-8046-0740-0). Kennikat.

Parkes, James. Conflict of the Church & the Synagogue: A Study in the Origins of Antisemitism. LC 61-11472. (Temple Books). 1969. pap. text ed. 6.95x (ISBN 0-689-70151-9, T9). Atheneum.

Rosenstock-Huessy, E., et al. Judaism Despite Christianity. LC 68-10993. 203p. 1969. 12.95x (ISBN 0-8173-6606-7). U of Ala Pr.

Rosenstock-Huessy, Eugen, ed. Judaism Despite Christianity: The "Letters on Christianity & Judaism " Between Eugen Rosenstock-Huessy & Franz Rosenzweig. LC 68-10993. 1971. pap. 2.45 (ISBN 0-8052-0315-X). Schocken.

Sandmel, Samuel. A Jewish Understanding of the New Testament. 1974. 12.50x (ISBN 0-87068-262-8); pap. 6.95x (ISBN 0-685-56201-8). Ktav.

Schaeffer, Edith. Christianity Is Jewish. 1975. pap. 2.95 (ISBN 0-8423-0242-5). Tyndale.

Schoffler, Herbert. Abendland und Altes Testament. Repr. of 1937 ed. pap. 7.00 (ISBN 0-384-54210-7). Johnson Repr.

Silcox, Claris E. Catholics, Jews, & Protestants: A Study of Relationships in the United States & Canada. LC 78-21101. 1979. Repr. of 1934 ed. lib. bdg. 22.50x (ISBN 0-313-20882-4, SICJ). Greenwood.

Silver, Abba H. Where Judaism Differed. 1956. 5.95 (ISBN 0-02-610690-6); pap. 2.95 (ISBN 0-02-089360-4). Macmillan.

Silverman, William B. Judaism & Christianity. LC 68-27330. pap. 5.95x (ISBN 0-87441-016-9). Behrman.

Snoek, Johan M. Grey Book: A Collection of Protests Against Anti-Semitism & the Persecution of Jews Issued by Non-Roman Catholic Churches & Church Leaders During Hitler's Rule. 1970. text ed. 12.00x (ISBN 0-391-00004-7). Humanities.

Tal, Uriel. Christians & Jews in Germany: Religion, Politics, & Ideology in the Second Reich, 1870-1914. Jacobs, Noah J., tr. from Hebrew. LC 74-21612. (Illus.). 384p. 1975. 28.50x (ISBN 0-8014-0879-2). Cornell U Pr.

Voss, Carl H. Rabbi & Minister: The Friendship of Stephen S. Wise & John Haynes Holmes. LC 80-7453. (The Library of Liberal Religion). 384p. 1980. pap. 6.95 (ISBN 0-87975-130-4). Prometheus Bks.

Weiss-Rosmarin, Trude. Judaism & Christianity: The Differences. 1965. pap. 2.95 (ISBN 0-8246-0044-4). Jonathan David.

JUDAISM–RELATIONS–ISLAM

Barakat, Ahmad. Muhammad & the Jews: A Re-Examination. 140p. 1980. text ed. 15.00x (ISBN 0-7069-0804-X, Pub. by Vikas India). Advent NY.

Geiger, Abraham. Judaism & Islam. rev. ed. (Library of Jewish Classics). 1970. 15.00x (ISBN 0-87068-058-7). Ktav.

Rabin, Chaim. Qumran Studies. LC 74-26735. 151p. 1975. pap. 3.95 (ISBN 0-8052-0482-2). Schocken.

Torrey, Charles C. Jewish Foundation of Islam. rev. ed. LC 67-18817. 1968. 15.00x (ISBN 0-87068-117-6). Ktav.

JUDAISM–RITUALS

see Jews–Rites and Ceremonies

JUDAISM–WORKS TO 1900

Abrahams, Israel. The Book of Delight & Other Papers. Katz, Steven, ed. LC 79-7124. (Jewish Philosophy, Mysticism & History of Ideas Ser.). 1980. Repr. of 1912 ed. lib. bdg. 23.00x (ISBN 0-405-12238-1). Arno.

Grob, Gerald, ed. A Course of Lectures on the Jews: By Ministers of the Established Church in Glasgow. LC 76-46095. (Anti-Movements in America). 1977. lib. bdg. 28.00x (ISBN 0-405-09968-1). Arno.

Harrington, Daniel J., ed. & tr. from Heb. The Hebrew Fragments of Pseudo-Philo. LC 73-89170. (Socity of Biblical Literature. Texts & Translation-Psuedepigrapha Ser.). 1974. pap. 4.50 (ISBN 0-88414-036-9, 060203). Scholars Pr Ca.

Kraft, Robert A. & Purintun, Ann-Elizabeth. Paraleipomena Jeremiou. LC 72-88436. (Society of Biblical Literature. Texts & Translation-Psuedepigrapha Ser.). 1972. pap. 4.50 (ISBN 0-89130-169-0, 060201). Scholars Pr Ca.

Moses Ben Maimon. Epistle to Yemen. 1952. 12.00 (ISBN 0-527-65400-0). Kraus Repr.

Rosenblatt, Samuel, tr. Saadia Gaon Book of Beliefs & Opinions. (Judaica Ser.: No. 1). 1948. 40.00x (ISBN 0-300-00865-1). Yale U Pr.

JUDAISM–STUDY AND TEACHING

see Jewish Religious Education

JUDAISM, CONSERVATIVE
see Conservative Judaism
JUDAISM, ORTHODOX
see Orthodox Judaism
JUDAISM, RECONSTRUCTIONIST
see Reconstructionist Judaism
JUDAISM, REFORM
see Reform Judaism
JUDAISM AND CHRISTIANITY
see Christianity and Other Religions–Judaism
JUDAISM AND SOCIAL PROBLEMS

Gittelson, Roland B. Modern Jewish Problems. rev. ed. (gr. 9-12). text ed. 5.00 (ISBN 0-8074-0099-8, 163303); tchrs'. guide o.p. 2.50 (ISBN 0-685-04890-X, 203303); wkbk. 1.75 (ISBN 0-685-04891-8, 163312). UAHC.

Miller, Milton G. & Schwartzman, Sylvan D. Our Religion & Our Neighbors. rev. ed. LC 63-14742. (Illus.). (gr. 9). 1971. text ed. 7.50 (ISBN 0-8074-0145-5, 141513); tchrs'. guide 3.50 (ISBN 0-8074-0146-3, 204280). UAHC.

Shapiro, Leon. The History of ORT: A Jewish Movement for Social Change. LC 79-22379. 384p. 1980. 20.00 (ISBN 0-8052-3739-9). Schocken.

Silver, Daniel J. Judaism & Ethics. 1970. 20.00x (ISBN 0-87068-010-2). Ktav.

JUDAS ISCARIOT

Gartner, Bertil. Iscariot. Reumann, John, ed. Gruhn, Victor I., tr. from Ger. LC 73-157544. (Facet Bks.). 64p. (Orig.). 1971. pap. 1.00 (ISBN 0-8006-3065-3, 1-3065). Fortress.

Schaumberg, Ethel L. Judas: The Unforgiven Man. 1981. 2.40 (ISBN 0-686-73784-9). CSS Pub.

JUDD, GERRIT PARMELE, 1803-1873

Judd, Gerrit P. Doctor Judd, Hawaii's Friend: A Biography of Gerrit Parmele Judd, 1803-1873. (Illus.). 1960. 12.00 (ISBN 0-87022-385-2). U Pr of Hawaii.

JUDGE, WILLIAM QUAN, 1851-1896

Judge, William Q. Echoes of the Orient: Collected Writings, Vol. 1. Eklund, Dara, ed. (Illus.). 678p. 1975. 10.00 (ISBN 0-685-62206-1, 913004-28). Point Loma Pub.

JUDGE BAKER GUIDANCE CENTER, BOSTON

Beard, Belle B. Juvenile Probation: An Analysis of the Case Records of Five Hundred Children Studies at the Judge Baker Guidance Clinic & Placed on Probation in the Juvenile Court of Boston. LC 69-16224. (Criminology, Law Enforcement, & Social Problems Ser.: No. 95). 1969. Repr. of 1934 ed. 12.00 (ISBN 0-87585-095-2). Patterson Smith.

Glueck, Sheldon S. & Glueck, Eleanor T. One Thousand Juvenile Delinquents. 1934. 14.00 (ISBN 0-527-34100-2). Kraus Repr.

JUDGE-MADE LAW

Garber, Lyman A. Of Men & Not of Law. 1966. 5.95 (ISBN 0-8159-6400-5). Devin.

Jaffe, Louis L. English & American Judges As Lawmakers. 1969. 16.95x (ISBN 0-19-825193-9). Oxford U Pr.

Murphy, Walter F. Elements of Judicial Strategy. LC 64-24973. 1964. 14.00x (ISBN 0-226-55369-8). U of Chicago Pr.

Murphy, Walter F. & Tanenhaus, Joseph. Comparative Constitutional Law: Cases & Commentaries. LC 76-28119. 1977. text ed. 20.00x (ISBN 0-312-15330-9). St Martin.

Pomorski, Stanislaw. American Common Law & the Principle. 2nd rev., enl. ed. Chodakowska, Elzbieta, tr. from Polish. 1975. pap. 21.25x (ISBN 90-2793-184-4). Mouton.

JUDGE-MADE LAW–GREAT BRITAIN

Jaffe, Louis L. English & American Judges As Lawmakers. 1969. 16.95x (ISBN 0-19-825193-9). Oxford U Pr.

JUDGES
see also Courts; Judgments; Judicial Process; Justice, Administration of; Justices of the Peace; Women Lawyers

Bartholomew, Paul C. The Irish Judiciary. LC 70-175024. 112p. (Orig.). 1972. pap. 3.95x (ISBN 0-268-00457-9). U of Notre Dame Pr.

Bellwood, Sherman J. The Judge: Episodes & Encounters. 1978. 8.95 (ISBN 0-533-03537-6). Vantage.

Berkson, Larry, et al. Judicial Selection in the United States: A Compendium of Provisions. LC 80-70531. 182p. (Orig.). 1981. pap. 7.50 (ISBN 0-938870-02-5, 8565). Am Judicature.

Berkson, Larry C. & Vandenberg, Donna, eds. National Roster of Women Judges, 1980. 120p. (Orig.). 1980. pap. 2.95 (ISBN 0-938870-07-6, 8563). Am Judicature.

Bigelow, Lafayette J. Bench & Bar: A Complete Digest of the Wit, Humor, Asperities & Amenities of the Law. Repr. of 1871 ed. 38.50 (ISBN 0-384-04260-0). Johnson Repr.

Blaustein, Albert P. & Mersky, Roy M. The First One Hundred Justices: Statistical Studies on the Supreme Court of the United States. 1978. 17.50 (ISBN 0-208-01290-7, Archon). Shoe String.

Botein, Bernard. Trial Judge: The Candid, Behind the Bench Story of Justice Bernard Botein. (American Constitutional & Legal History Ser.). 337p. 1974. Repr. of 1952 ed. lib. bdg. 32.50 (ISBN 0-306-70630-X). Da Capo.

Braithwaite, William T. Who Judges the Judges? A Study of Procedures for Removal & Retirement. LC 72-179947. 167p. 1971. pap. 5.00 (ISBN 0-910058-45-8). Am Bar Foun.

Brownlee, Gardner E. Trial Judge's Guide: Objections to Evidence. (Ser. 550). 1974. 15.00 (ISBN 0-686-00407-8). Natl Judicial Coll.

Burkholder, Mark A. & Chandler, D. S. From Impotence to Authority: The Spanish Crown & the American Audienicias, 1687-1808. LC 76-45742. 1977. 15.00x (ISBN 0-8262-0219-5). U of Mo Pr.

Burton, David H. Oliver Wendell Holmes, Jr. (United States Authors Ser.: No. 375). 1980. lib. bdg. 10.95 (ISBN 0-8057-7262-6). Twayne.

Campbell, John C. Lives of the Lord Chancellors & Keepers of the Great Seal of England, 10 Vols. 5th ed. LC 74-39877. Repr. of 1868 ed. Set. 285.00 (ISBN 0-404-01380-5); 28.50 ea. AMS Pr.

Carlen, Pat. Magistrate's Justice. 134p. 1976. 30.50x (ISBN 0-85520-121-5, Pub. by Martin Robertson England). Biblio Dist.

Carney, T. F., ed. John the Lydian, De Magistratibus: On the Magistracies of the Roman Constitution. 127p. 1971. pap. 2.50x (ISBN 0-87291-031-8). Coronado Pr.

Chase, Harold, et al, eds. Biographical Dictionary of the Federal Judiciary. LC 76-18787. (Illus.). 256p. 1976. 65.00 (ISBN 0-8103-1125-9). Gale.

Chase, Harold W. Federal Judges: The Appointing Process. LC 72-189381. 234p. 1972. 13.95x (ISBN 0-8166-0647-1). U of Minn Pr.

Coffin, Frank. The Ways of a Judge: Reflections from the Federal Apellate Bench. 288p. 1980. 10.95 (ISBN 0-395-29461-4). HM.

Dawson, John P. The Oracles of the Law. xix, 520p. 1978. Repr. of 1968 ed. lib. bdg. 40.00x (ISBN 0-313-20260-5, DAOL). Greenwood.

Dawson, Philip. Provinicial Magistrates & Revolutionary Politics in France, 1789-1795. LC 74-182816. (Historical Monographs Ser: No. 66). (Illus.). 416p. 1972. 20.00x (ISBN 0-674-71960-3). Harvard U Pr.

Devlin, Patrick. The Judge. 1979. 22.00x (ISBN 0-19-215949-6). Oxford U Pr.

Douglas, D. Biographical History of Sir William Blackstone. LC 70-112403. Repr. of 1782 ed. lib. bdg. 22.50x (ISBN 0-678-04537-2). Kelley.

Educational Research Council of America. Judge. rev. ed. Ferris, Theodore N. & Marchak, John P., eds. (Real People at Work Ser: G). (Illus.). 1976. pap. text ed. 2.25 (ISBN 0-89247-058-5). Changing Times.

Flory, Thomas. Judge & Jury in Imperial Brazil, 1808-1871: Social Control & Political Stability in the New State. 284p. 1981. text ed. 25.00x (ISBN 0-292-74015-8). U of Tex Pr.

Flynn, Philip. Francis Jeffrey. LC 76-27915. 218p. 1978. 13.50 (ISBN 0-87413-123-5). U Delaware Pr.

Frankfurter, Felix. Felix Frankfurter Reminisces. LC 78-5896. 1978. Repr. of 1960 ed. lib. bdg. 23.50x (ISBN 0-313-20466-7, FRFF). Greenwood.

Fruge, J. C. Biographies of Judges of Louisiana. 1971. 12.50 (ISBN 0-685-42977-6). Claitors.

Gaynor, James K. Lawyers in Heaven. 96p. 1979. 5.95 (ISBN 0-8059-2609-7). Dorrance.

Goldberg, Louis P. Lawless Judges. LC 74-97451. Repr. of 1935 ed. 17.50x (ISBN 0-8371-2696-7, Pub. by Negro U Pr). Greenwood.

Haynes, Evan. The Selection & Tenure of Judges. xix, 308p. 1981. Repr. of 1944 ed. lib. bdg. 30.00x (ISBN 0-8377-0636-X). Rothman.

Higgins, John & Blenerhasset, Thomas. Parts Added to the Mirrour for Magistrates. Campbell, Lily B., ed. LC 76-29439. Repr. of 1946 ed. 35.00 (ISBN 0-404-15319-4). AMS Pr.

Highsaw, Robert B. Edward Douglas White: Defender of the Conservative Faith. LC 80-17874. (Illus.). xvi, 212p. 1981. 20.00 (ISBN 0-8071-0753-0). La State U Pr.

Jaworski, Leon & Schneider, Dick. Crossroads. 1981. 10.95 (ISBN 0-89191-289-4). Cook.

Kennedy, Robert F., Jr. Judge Frank M. Johnson Jr. A Biography. LC 77-27540. 1978. 10.95 (ISBN 0-399-12123-4). Putnam.

Kitchin, William I. Federal District Judges: An Analysis of Judicial Perceptions. LC 77-92607. 1978. pap. 8.70 (ISBN 0-917516-01-X). Collage Pr.

La. Dis. Judges. Judges of Louisiana. 1972. 12.50 (ISBN 0-685-27203-6). Claitors.

Mockler, Anthony. Lions Under the Throne: A Gallery of the Lord Chief Justices of England. 288p. 1981. 45.00x (ISBN 0-584-10437-5, Pub. by Muller Ltd). State Mutual Bk.

National Center for State Courts. Parajudges: Their Role in Today's Court Systems. Prescott, Elizabeth, ed. 1976. pap. 2.00 (ISBN 0-89656-010-4, R0027). Natl Ctr St Courts.

National College of the State Judiciary. Directory of State & Local Judges. (Ser. 175). 1975. 7.50 (ISBN 0-686-00406-X). Natl Judicial Coll.

National Judicial College. Judicial Function Outline. (Ser. 650). 1979. pap. 5.00 (ISBN 0-686-08769-0). Natl Judicial Coll.

Neff, Alan. The United States District Judge Nominating Commissions: Their Members, Procedures & Candidates. LC 80-70512. (Federal Judicial Selection During the Carter Administration Ser.). 204p. (Orig.). 1981. pap. 7.50 (ISBN 0-938870-03-3, 8568). Am Judicature.

Peltason, J. W. Fifty-Eight Lonely Men: Southern Federal Judges & School Desegregation. LC 61-12350. 1971. pap. 6.95 (ISBN 0-252-00175-3). U of Ill Pr.

Perkins, Dexter. Charles Evans Hughes & American Democratic Statesmanship. Handlin, Oscar, ed. LC 78-5919. (The Library of American Biography Ser.). 1978. Repr. of 1956 ed. lib. bdg. 18.00x (ISBN 0-313-20463-2, PECH). Greenwood.

Poldervaart, Arie W. Black-Robed Justice. Cortes, Carlos E., ed. LC 76-1472. (Chicano Heritage Ser.). 1976. Repr. of 1948 ed. lib. bdg. 13.00x (ISBN 0-405-09519-8). Arno.

Reid, T. Wemyss. Life of the Right Honourable William Edward Forster, 2 vols. in 1. LC 73-108853. Repr. of 1888 ed. 27.50x (ISBN 0-678-07763-0). Kelley.

Ryan, John P., et al. American Trial Judges: Their Work Styles & Performance. LC 80-756. (Illus.). 1980. 19.95 (ISBN 0-02-927620-9). Free Pr.

Shetreet, S. Judges on Trial. 1976. 44.00 (ISBN 0-444-10958-7, North-Holland). Elsevier.

Shientag, Bernard L. Moulders of Legal Thought. LC 67-27648. 1968. Repr. of 1943 ed. 11.50 (ISBN 0-8046-0419-3). Kennikat.

Simon, James F. Independent Journey: The Life of William O. Douglas. 512p. 1981. pap. 6.95 (ISBN 0-14-005982-2). Penguin.

Skyrme, Thomas. The Changing Image of the Magistracy: 1974-1977. 1979. text ed. 23.25x (ISBN 0-391-01123-5). Humanities.

Smith, John I. True Stories of Needed Justice: Biography of Judge Henry Smith. (Illus.). 138p. 1979. 5.95 (ISBN 0-914546-14-7). Rose Pub.

Stolz, P. Judging Judges. (Illus.). 545p. 1981. text ed. 19.95 (ISBN 0-02-931670-7). Free Pr.

Trafzer, Clifford E. The Judge: The Life of Robert A. Hefner. (Oklahoma Trackmakers Ser.: No. 1). (Illus.). 275p. 1975. 12.50 (ISBN 0-8061-1307-3). U of Okla Pr.

Ulc, Otto. The Judge in a Communist State: A View from Within. LC 71-141382. xiv, 307p. 1972. 14.00x (ISBN 0-8214-0091-6). Ohio U Pr.

United States Senate, Committee on the Judiciary Ninety-First Congress, 2nd Session. A Judge on Trial: Hearings on the Nomination of George Harrold Carswell: Proceedings. LC 70-3962. (American Constitutional & Legal History Ser.). 467p. 1974. Repr. of 1970 ed. lib. bdg. 27.50 (ISBN 0-306-70209-6). Da Capo.

Vanderbilt, Arthur T. The Challenge of Law Reform. LC 76-3784. 194p. 1976. Repr. of 1955 ed. lib. bdg. 16.75 (ISBN 0-8371-8809-1, VALR). Greenwood.

White, G. Edward. The American Judicial Tradition: Profiles of Leading American Judges. LC 75-32356. 1978. pap. 7.95 (ISBN 0-19-502361-7, GB534, GB). Oxford U Pr.

Williams, David R. Man for a New Country. (Illus.). 360p. 1977. 16.95 (ISBN 0-686-74150-1). Superior Pub.

JUDGES–CORRESPONDENCE, REMINISCENCES, ETC.

Campbell, John L. The Lives of the Chief Justices of England: From the Norman Conquest till the Death of Lord Tenterden, 3 vols. facsimile ed. LC 70-152976. (Select Bibliographies Reprint Ser). Repr. of 1857 ed. Set. 95.00 (ISBN 0-8369-5728-8). Arno.

Cullen, Charles T. & Johnson, Herbert A., eds. The Papers of John Marshall, Vol. 2: Correspondence & Papers, July 1788-Dec. 1795; Account Book, July 1788-Dec. 1795. LC 74-9575. (Institute of Early American History & Culture Ser.). 1977. 22.50x (ISBN 0-8078-1302-8). U of NC Pr.

Douglas, William O. Go East, Young Man. 1974. 10.00 (ISBN 0-394-48834-2). Random.

Field, Stephen J. California Alcalde. (California Heritage Ser.: Vol. 21). 15.00 (ISBN 0-686-12801-X). Sullivan Bks.

Foss, Edward. Judges of England, 9 Vols. LC 76-168126. Repr. of 1864 ed. Set. 287.50 (ISBN 0-404-02580-3). AMS Pr.

Frankfurter, Felix. Felix Frankfurter on the Supreme Court: Extrajudicial Essays on the Court & the Constitution. Kurland, Philip B., ed. LC 70-99518. (Illus.). 1970. 25.00x (ISBN 0-674-29835-7, Belknap Pr). Harvard U Pr.

Goldberg, Louis P. & Levenson, Eleanore. Lawless Judges. LC 73-138498. (Civil Liberties in American History Ser). 1970. Repr. of 1935 ed. lib. bdg. 29.50 (ISBN 0-306-70070-0). Da Capo.

Gollmar, Robert H. Tales of a Country Judge. LC 79-65286. (Illus.). 192p. 1981. 8.95x (ISBN 0-87319-018-1). C Hallberg.

Hayes, Benjamin. Pioneers Notes from the Diaries of Judge Benjain Hayes, 1849-1875. Cortes, Carlos E., ed. LC 76-1274. (Chicano Heritage Ser.). (Illus.). Repr. of 1929 ed. lib. bdg. 19.00x (ISBN 0-405-09506-6). Arno.

Howe, Mark D., ed. Holmes-Laski Letters, the Correspondence of Justice Oliver Wendell Holmes & Harold J. Laski 1916-1935, 2 Vols. LC 63-24385. 1963. pap. 2.65 ea. Vol. 1 (ISBN 0-689-70097-0, 43A). Vol. 2 (ISBN 0-689-70098-9, 43B). Atheneum.

Pollack, Ervin H. The Brandeis Reader: The Life & Contributions of Mr. Justice Louis D. Brandeis. LC 56-12251. (Docket Ser.: No. 7). 1956. pap. 2.50 (ISBN 0-379-11307-4). Oceana.

Sewall, Samuel. Diary of Samuel Sewall, 1674-1729, 3 Vols. LC 77-141102. (Research Library of Colonial Americana). (Illus.). 1972. Repr. of 1878 ed. Set. 100.00 (ISBN 0-405-03311-7); Vol. 1. 34.00 (ISBN 0-405-03312-5); Vol. 2. 33.00 (ISBN 0-405-03313-3); Vol. 3. 33.00 (ISBN 0-405-03314-1). Arno.

Thomason, Ewing. Thomason, the Autobiography of a Federal Judge. 1971. 6.00 (ISBN 0-87404-030-2). Tex Western.

Williams, Dakin. The Bar Bizarre. 270p. 1980. write for info. (ISBN 0-86629-009-5). Sunrise MO.

Williams, O. W. Pioneer Surveyor - Frontier Lawyer. Myres, S. D., ed. (Illus.). 1968. 10.00 (ISBN 0-87404-011-6). Tex Western.

JUDGING (SPORTS)
see Sports Officiating
JUDGMENT
see also Attitude Change; Common Sense

Cohen, Rudolf. Patterns of Personality Judgement. Schaeffer, Dirk L., tr. 1973. 46.00 (ISBN 0-12-178950-0). Acad Pr.

Eiser, J. R. & Strobe, Wolfgang, eds. Categorization & Social Judgment. (European Monographs in Social Psychology Ser.: No. 3). 1973. 28.50 (ISBN 0-12-235350-1). Acad Pr.

Hermeren, Goran. Influence in Art & Literature. LC 73-2466. (Illus.). 340p. 1975. write for info. (ISBN 0-691-07194-2). Princeton U Pr.

Johnson, Donald M. Psychology of Thought & Judgment. LC 70-109292. (Illus.). 1971. Repr. of 1955 ed. lib. bdg. 20.50x (ISBN 0-8371-3835-3, JOTJ). Greenwood.

Keeney, Barnaby C. Judgment by Peers. LC 80-2023. Repr. of 1949 ed. 25.00 (ISBN 0-404-18571-1). AMS Pr.

Kleinmuntz, Benjamin. Formal Representation of Human Judgment. 273p. 1968. 13.50 (ISBN 0-471-49085-7, Pub. by Wiley). Krieger.

Lamont, W. D. Value Judgement. 1955. 6.00 (ISBN 0-8022-0911-4). Philos Lib.

Panichas, George A. The Courage of Judgement: Essays in Criticism, Culture & Society. LC 81-4050. 352p. 1982. text ed. 24.50x (ISBN 0-87049-325-6). U of Tenn Pr.

Rappaport, L. & Summers, D. Human Judgement & Social Interaction. 416p. 1973. 11.50 (ISBN 0-03-085870-4, Pub. by HR&W). Krieger.

Rappoport, Leon & Summers, David, eds. Human Judgement & Social Interaction. LC 72-84872. 1973. 32.50x (ISBN 0-03-085870-4). Irvington.

Sherif, Carolyn W. & Sherif, Muzafer, eds. Attitude, Ego-Involvement, & Change. LC 74-27184. 1976. Repr. of 1967 ed. lib. bdg. 19.75x (ISBN 0-8371-7894-0, SHAE). Greenwood.

Sherif, Muzafer & Hovland, Carl I. Social Judgment: Assimilation & Contrast Effects in Communication & Attitude Change. LC 80-21767. (Yale Studies in Attitude & Communication: Vol. 4). xii, 218p. 1981. Repr. of 1961 ed. lib. bdg. 25.00x (ISBN 0-313-22438-2, SHSO). Greenwood.

JUDGMENT (ETHICS)

Bull, Norman J. Moral Judgement from Childhood to Adolescence. LC 71-101420. 316p. 1970. 17.50 (ISBN 0-8039-0038-4). Sage.

Hudson, Donald. A Century of Moral Philosophy. 1980. 18.95 (ISBN 0-312-12777-4). St Martin.

Perelman, Chaim. Idea of Justice & the Problems of Argument. (International Library of Philosophy & Scientific Method). 1963. text ed. 13.75x (ISBN 0-7100-3610-8). Humanities.

Raphael, David D. Moral Judgment. LC 77-28440. 1978. Repr. of 1955 ed. lib. bdg. 22.25x (ISBN 0-313-20246-X, RAMJ). Greenwood.

Rest, James R. Development in Judging Moral Issues. LC 79-22755. (Illus.). 1979. 19.50x (ISBN 0-8166-0891-1). U of Minn Pr.

JUDGMENT (LOGIC)
see also Fallacies (Logic); Negation (Logic); Reasoning

Anderson, Barry F., et al. Concepts in Judgement & Decision Research. 320p. 1981. 28.95 (ISBN 0-03-059337-9). Praeger.
Barthes, Roland. Mythologies. 1957. 16.95 (ISBN 0-686-53938-9); pap. 5.95 (ISBN 0-686-53939-7). French & Eur.
Bell, David. Frege's Theory of Judgement. 178p. 1979. text ed. 29.95x (ISBN 0-19-827423-8). Oxford U Pr.
Bosanquet, Bernard. Knowledge & Reality. LC 14-924. 1968. Repr. of 1892 ed. 19.00 (ISBN 0-527-10018-8). Kraus Repr.
Husserl, Edmund. Experience & Judgment. Churchill, James S. & Ameriks, Karl, trs. from Ger. LC 72-80566. (Studies in Phenomenology & Existential Philosophy). Orig. Title: Erpahrung und Urteil. 412p. 1973. text ed. 20.95x (ISBN 0-8101-0396-6); pap. 9.95x (ISBN 0-8101-0595-0). Northwestern U Pr.
Kahane, Howard. Logic & Contemporary Rhetoric. 3rd ed. 288p. 1980. pap. text ed. 10.95x (ISBN 0-534-00850-X). Wadsworth Pub.
Kant, Immanuel. Critique of Judgement. Meredith, J. C., tr. 1952. pap. 9.95x (ISBN 0-19-824589-0). Oxford U Pr.
--Critique of Judgment. Bernard, J. H., tr. (Library of Classics Ser: No. 14). pap. text ed. 5.25 (ISBN 0-02-847500-3). Hafner.
--First Introduction to the Critique of Judgment. Haden, James, tr. from German. LC 64-66071. 1965. pap. text ed. 2.95x (ISBN 0-672-60362-4). Irvington.
Piaget, Jean. Judgment & Reasoning in the Child. 1962. Repr. of 1928 ed. text ed. 15.00x (ISBN 0-7100-3065-7). Humanities.

JUDGMENT DAY
see also Second Advent
Battle, Dennis M. Armageddon: Heaven's Holy War on Earth. LC 80-65197. 56p. 1980. pap. 2.50 (ISBN 0-933464-07-X). D M Battle Pubns.
Collins, Adela Y. Apocalypse. Harrington, Wilfrid & Senior, Donald, eds. (New Testament Message Ser.: Vol. 22). 172p. 1979. 9.00 (ISBN 0-89453-145-X); pap. 4.95 (ISBN 0-89453-210-3). M Glazier.
Ford, W. Herschel. Simple Sermons on Heaven, Hell, & Judgment. pap. 3.95 (ISBN 0-310-24481-1). Zondervan.
Hymers, R. L. Holocaust II. 1978. pap. 1.95 (ISBN 0-89728-005-9, 711269). Omega Pubns OR.
Kettler, Wilfried. Das Juengste Gericht Philologische Studienzu Den Wschatologie Vorstellungen in Den Alt-und Fruehmittel Hochdeutschen Denkmaelern. (Quellen und Forschungen Zur Sprach und Kulturgeschichte der Germanischen Voelker: Vol.70). 1977. 51.25x (ISBN 3-11-007345-5). De Gruyter.
Lindsay, Gordon. The Great Day of the Lord. (Revelation Ser.). 1.25 (ISBN 0-89985-037-5). Christ Nations.
--The Great Judgment Throne & the Seven Seals. (Revelation Ser.). 1.25 (ISBN 0-89985-036-7). Christ Nations.
--The Great Trumpets & the Vial Judgments. (End of the Age Ser.: Vol. 6). 0.95 (ISBN 0-89985-072-3). Christ Nations.
--The Judgment Seat of Christ, Vol. 7. (End of the Age Ser.). 0.95 (ISBN 0-89985-073-1). Christ Nations.
--The Vial Judgments or the Seven Last Plagues. (Revelation Ser.). 1.25 (ISBN 0-89985-045-6). Christ Nations.
Miller, John W. Judgment & Hope. 1972. pap. 1.25 (ISBN 0-8361-1700-X). Herald Pr.
Morse, Charlotte C. The Pattern of Judgement in the "Queste" & "Cleanness". LC 77-25158. (Illus.). 1978. 16.50x (ISBN 0-8262-0242-X). U of Mo Pr.
Mussner, Franz. What Did Jesus Teach About the End of the World? (Orig.). 1975. pap. 1.75 (ISBN 0-89283-019-0). Servant.
Prince, Derek. Eternal Judgment. (Foundation Ser.: Bk. VII). 1965-66. pap. 1.50 (ISBN 0-934920-06-0, B-16). Derek Prince.
Sayers, Stanley E. The Nature of Things to Come. 1972. 3.95 (ISBN 0-686-21491-9). Firm Foun Pub.
Swedenborg, Emanuel. Apocalypse Explained, 6 vols. LC 76-46145. student ed. 6.50 ea. Vol. 1 (ISBN 0-87785-000-3). Vol. 2 (ISBN 0-87785-001-1). Vol. 3 (ISBN 0-87785-002-X). Vol. 4 (ISBN 0-87785-003-8). Vol. 5 (ISBN 0-87785-004-6). Vol. 6 (ISBN 0-87785-005-4). student ed. 33.00 set (ISBN 0-87785-006-2). Swedenborg.
Walvoord, John F. & Walvoord, John E. Harmaguedon, le Petrole... Date not set. 2.25 (ISBN 0-686-76403-X). Life Pubs Intl.

JUDGMENTS
see also Judicial Opinions; Jurisdiction; Sentences (Criminal Procedure); Stare Decisis; Supplementary Proceedings
Wasserstrom, Richard A. The Judicial Decision: Toward a Theory of Legal Justification. LC 61-6535. 1961. 10.00x (ISBN 0-8047-0036-2); pap. 3.25 (ISBN 0-8047-0037-0, SP104). Stanford U Pr.

JUDGMENTS BY PEERS
see Jury

JUDICIAL BEHAVIOR
see Judicial Process

JUDICIAL CORRUPTION
Ashman, Charles R. Finest Judges Money Can Buy & Other Forms of Judicial Pollution. LC 73-83520. 1975. 7.95 (ISBN 0-8402-1316-6). Brown Bk.
Bollens, John C. & Schmandt, Henry J. Political Corruption: Power, Money, & Sex. LC 79-88114. 1979. 9.95 (ISBN 0-913530-17-4). Palisades Pub.
Nimmer, Raymond T. Prosecutor Disclosure & Judicial Reform: The Omnibus Hearing in Two Courts. LC 75-13605. 1975. 10.00 (ISBN 0-910058-72-5); pap. 5.00 (ISBN 0-910058-71-7). Am Bar Foun.

JUDICIAL DECISION-MAKING
see Judicial Process

JUDICIAL DISCRETION
see also Administrative Discretion; Law-Interpretation and Construction
Davis, Kenneth C. Discretionary Justice in Europe & America. LC 75-38842. 224p. 1976. 12.50 (ISBN 0-252-00579-1). U of Ill Pr.
Goldstein, Abraham S. The Passive Judiciary: Prosecutorial Discretion & the Guilty Plee. LC 81-11749. 128p. 1982. text ed. 12.95 (ISBN 0-8071-0856-1). La State U Pr.

JUDICIAL DISTRICTS
see also Courts

JUDICIAL ERROR
Borchard, Edwin M. Convicting the Innocent: Errors of Criminal Justice. LC 74-107406. (Civil Liberties in American History Ser). 1970. Repr. of 1932 ed. lib. bdg. 29.50 (ISBN 0-306-71886-3). Da Capo.
Brandon, Ruth & Davies, Christie. Wrongful Imprisonment, Mistaken Convictions & Their Consequences. 296p. 1973. 19.50 (ISBN 0-208-01337-7, Archon). Shoe String.
Downie, Leonard, Jr. Justice Denied. 1972. pap. 2.50 (ISBN 0-14-003457-9). Penguin.
Frank, Jerome & Frank, Barbara. Not Guilty. LC 72-138495. (Civil Liberties in American History Ser.). 1971. Repr. of 1957 ed. lib. bdg. 25.00 (ISBN 0-306-70072-7). Da Capo.
Trebilcock, Dorothy W. Shield of Innocence. 1978. pap. 1.95 (ISBN 0-89041-184-0, 3184). Major Bks.

JUDICIAL INVESTIGATIONS
see Governmental Investigations

JUDICIAL LEGISLATION
see Judge-Made Law

JUDICIAL LAW
see Judge-Made Law

JUDICIAL OFFICERS
see Courts–Officials and Employees

JUDICIAL OPINIONS
see also Advisory Opinions
Bickel, Alexander M. Unpublished Opinions of Mr. Justice Brandeis: The Supreme Court at Work. LC 67-12001. (Court & the Constitution Ser). (Illus.). 1967. pap. 2.45 (ISBN 0-226-04602-8, P259, Phoen). U of Chicago Pr.
Cotton, Joseph P., ed. The Constitutional Decisions of John Marshall, 2 Vols. LC 67-25445. (Law, Politics & History Ser). 1969. Repr. of 1905 ed. 55.00 (ISBN 0-306-70947-3). Da Capo.
Countryman, Vern, ed. The Douglas Opinions. 1977. 17.95 (ISBN 0-394-49795-3). Random.
Douglas, William O. Douglas of the Supreme Court: A Selection of His Opinions. Countryman, Vern, ed. LC 73-19. 401p. 1973. Repr. of 1959 ed. lib. bdg. 24.25x (ISBN 0-8371-6790-6, DODS). Greenwood.
Funston, Richard. Judicial Crises: The Supreme Court in a Changing America. LC 74-2419. 1974. text ed. 14.95 (ISBN 0-470-28780-2); pap. text ed. 5.95x (ISBN 0-470-28781-0). Halsted Pr.
George, Joyce J. Judicial Opinion Writing Handbook. LC 80-84129. xi, 150p. 1981. lib. bdg. 25.00 (ISBN 0-89941-063-4). W S Hein.
Holmes, Oliver W., Jr. Representative Opinions of Mr. Justice Holmes. Lief, Alfred, compiled by. LC 76-156194. 319p. 1972. Repr. of 1931 ed. lib. bdg. 22.50x (ISBN 0-8371-6143-6, HORO). Greenwood.
Rosenbaum, Judith, ed. Judicial Discipline & Disability Digest. LC 81-65601. 600p. 1981. 600.00 (ISBN 0-938870-00-9); lib. bdg. 400.00 (ISBN 0-686-30176-5). Am Judicature.
Schubert, Glendon. Dispassionate Justice: A Synthesis of the Judicial Opinions of Robert H. Jackson. LC 69-13634. 1969. 34.50x (ISBN 0-672-51138-X). Irvington.
--Judicial Mind, Nineteen Forty-Six to Nineteen Sixty-Nine. 1976. codebk. 6.00 (ISBN 0-89138-154-6). ICPSR.
Warren, Earl. The Public Papers of Chief Justice Earl Warren. Christman, Henry M., ed. LC 74-10019. 237p. 1974. Repr. of 1959 ed. lib. bdg. 15.25x (ISBN 0-8371-7654-9, WAPP). Greenwood.

JUDICIAL POWER
see also Courts; Delegation of Powers; Judge-Made Law; Judges; Judicial Review; Separation of Powers
Cohn, Sherman L. Constitutional Law: Part One the Federal Judiciary. 1968. pap. 6.00x (ISBN 0-685-14176-4). Lerner Law.
Fish, Peter G. The Politics of Federal Judicial Administration. LC 76-39785. 488p. 1973. 35.00x (ISBN 0-691-09226-5); pap. 12.50 (ISBN 0-691-10013-6). Princeton U Pr.
Griffith, Kathryn P. Judge Learned Hand & the Role of the Federal Juciciary. LC 72-9254. 363p. 1973. 13.50x (ISBN 0-8061-1071-6); pap. 6.95x (ISBN 0-8061-1369-3). U of Okla Pr.
Haines, Charles G. The American Doctrine of Judicial Supremacy. 2nd ed. LC 59-7256. 1959. 15.00x (ISBN 0-685-33508-9). Boulevard.
Jackson, Robert H. The Struggle for Judicial Supremacy: A Study of a Crisis in American Power Politics. 1979. Repr. lib. bdg. 20.00x (ISBN 0-374-94130-0). Octagon.
Judicial Reform. 1971. pap. 3.75 (ISBN 0-8447-1817-3). Am Enterprise.
League of Women Voters Education Fund. The Growth of Judicial Power: Perspectives on "the Least Dangerous Branch". (Federalist Papers Reexamined: No. 5). 33p. 1977. pap. 1.00 (ISBN 0-89959-041-1, 332). LWV US.
Meigs, W. M. Relation of the Judiciary to the Constitution. LC 73-124896. (American Constitutional & Legal History Ser). 1971. Repr. of 1919 ed. lib. bdg. 29.50 (ISBN 0-306-71988-6). Da Capo.
National Judicial College. Inherent Powers of the Courts. (Illus.). 60p. (Orig.). 1980. pap. 7.50 (ISBN 0-686-28003-2). Natl Judicial Coll.
Radcliffe, James E. The Case or Controversy Provision. LC 77-1683. 1978. text ed. 16.50 (ISBN 0-271-00509-2). Pa St U Pr.
Ransom, William L. Majority Rule & the Judiciary. LC 78-166099. (American Constitutional & Legal History Ser). 1971. Repr. of 1912 ed. pap. 19.50 (ISBN 0-306-70205-3). Da Capo.
Shapiro, David L., ed. The Evolution of a Judicial Philosophy: Selected Opinions & Papers of Justice John M. Harlan. 331p. 1969. text ed. 12.50x (ISBN 0-674-27125-4). Harvard U Pr.
Theberge, Leonard, ed. The Judiciary in a Democratic Society. LC 77-25740. 1979. 16.95 (ISBN 0-669-01508-3). Lexington Bks.

JUDICIAL PROCESS
see also Evidence (Law); Judge-Made Law; Judgments; Law-Interpretation and Construction; Stare Decisis
Abraham, Henry J. The Judicial Process: An Introductory Analysis of the United States, England, & France. 4th ed. 1980. text ed. 16.95x (ISBN 0-19-502612-8); pap. text ed. 9.95x (ISBN 0-19-502613-6). Oxford U Pr.
Ball, Milner S. The Promise of American Law: A Theological, Humanistic View of Legal Process. LC 81-4325. 208p. 1981. text ed. 15.00 (ISBN 0-686-76232-0). U of Ga Pr.
Brockelbank, W. J. Interstate Enforcement of Family Support. 2nd ed. Infausto, Felix, ed. 1971. 13.50 (ISBN 0-672-81529-X, Bobbs-Merrill Law). Michie-Bobbs.
Carbon, Susan B. & Berkson, Larry C. Judicial Retention Elections in the United States. LC 80-69565. 96p. (Orig.). 1980. pap. 4.00 (ISBN 0-938870-01-7, 8566). Am Judicature.
Cardozo, Benjamin N. Nature of the Judicial Process. (Storrs Lectures Ser.). 1921. 15.00x (ISBN 0-300-00346-3); pap. 3.95x (ISBN 0-300-00033-2, Y21). Yale U Pr.
Chian, Nancy & Berkson, Larry. Literature on Judicial Selection. LC 80-69415. 112p. (Orig.). 1980. pap. 4.00 (ISBN 0-938870-05-X, 8564). Am Judicature.
Cohn, Rubin G. To Judge with Justice: History & Politics of Illinois Judicial Reform. LC 72-95002. (Studies in Illinois Constitution Making Ser). 180p. 1973. pap. 5.95 (ISBN 0-252-00332-2). U of Ill Pr.
Cortner, Richard C. The Supreme Court & the Second Bill of Rights: The Fourteenth Amendment & the Nationalization of Civil Liberties. 480p. 1981. 29.50 (ISBN 0-299-08390-X). U of Wis Pr.
Dainow, Joseph, ed. The Role of Judicial Decisions & Doctrine in Civil Law & in Mixed Jurisdictions. LC 73-90871. 350p. 1974. 25.00 (ISBN 0-8071-0080-3). La State U Pr.
Dubois, Philip L. From Ballot to Bench: Judicial Elections & the Quest for Accountability. LC 80-12728. 332p. 1980. text ed. 22.50x (ISBN 0-292-72028-9). U of Tex Pr.
Ehrenzweig, Albert A., et al. Jurisdiction in a Nutshell, State & Federal. 4th ed. LC 80-312. (Nutshell Ser.). 298p. 1980. pap. 6.95 (ISBN 0-8299-2086-2). West Pub.
Eisenstein, James. Politics & the Legal Process. (Danelski Ser.). 356p. 1973. pap. text ed. 10.95 scp (ISBN 0-06-041883-4, HarpC). Har-Row.
Freund, Paul A. On Law & Justice. LC 67-29626. 1968. 12.50x (ISBN 0-674-63550-7, Belknap Pr). Harvard U Pr.
Gluckman, Max. Judicial Process Among the Barotse of Northern Rhodesia. (Rhodes Livingston Institute Bks). 1955. pap. text ed. 15.00x (ISBN 0-7190-1040-3). Humanities.
Goldman, Jerry. Ineffective Justice: Evaluating the Preappeal Conference. LC 79-26333. (Contemporary Evaluation Research: Vol. 3). (Illus.). 125p. 1980. 20.00x (ISBN 0-8039-1266-8); pap. 9.95x (ISBN 0-8039-1267-6). Sage.
Goldstein, Abraham S. The Passive Judiciary: Prosecutorial Discretion & the Guilty Plee. LC 81-11749. 128p. 1982. text ed. 12.95 (ISBN 0-8071-0856-1). La State U Pr.
Grossman, J. B., et al. Social Science Approaches to the Judicial Process. LC 74-153371. (Symposia on Law & Society Ser). 1971. Repr. of 1966 ed. lib. bdg. 14.50 (ISBN 0-306-70135-9). Da Capo.
Grossman, Joel B. & Tanenhaus, Joseph. Frontiers of Judicial Research. 492p. 1969. text ed. 19.50 (ISBN 0-471-32870-7, Pub. by Wiley). Krieger.
Grossman, Joel B. & Wells, Richard S. Constitutional Law & Judicial Policy-Making. 2nd ed. LC 79-20206. 1980. text ed. 27.50 (ISBN 0-471-32849-9). Wiley.
--Supplemental Cases for Constitutional Law & Judicial Policy Making: 1975 Ed. 406p. 1975. pap. text ed. 8.50 (ISBN 0-471-32853-7). Wiley.
Haynes, Evan. The Selection & Tenure of Judges. xix, 308p. 1981. Repr. of 1944 ed. lib. bdg. 30.00x (ISBN 0-8377-0636-X). Rothman.
Hays, Steven W. Court Reform. LC 77-10348. (Illus.). 1978. 16.95 (ISBN 0-669-01841-4). Lexington Bks.
Horowitz, Donald L. The Courts & Social Policy. LC 76-48944. 1977. 14.95 (ISBN 0-8157-3734-3); pap. 5.95 (ISBN 0-8157-3733-5). Brookings.
Hyneman, Charles S. The Supreme Court on Trial. LC 73-20501. 308p. 1974. Repr. of 1963 ed. lib. bdg. 21.75x (ISBN 0-8371-7326-4, HYSC). Greenwood.
Johnson. Judicial Impact. 257p. 1982. pap. text ed. price not set (ISBN 0-87187-222-6). Congr Quarterly.
Keeton, Robert E. Venturing to Do Justice: Reforming Private Law. LC 69-18035. 1969. text ed. 10.00x (ISBN 0-674-93355-9). Harvard U Pr.
Kress, Jack M. Prescripton for Justice: The Theory & Practice of Sentencing Guidelines. 368p. 1980. reference 25.00 (ISBN 0-88410-792-2). Ballinger Pub.
Llewellyn, Karl N. The Common Law Tradition: Deciding Appeals. 565p. 1960. 25.00 (ISBN 0-316-52935-4). Little.
Maddi, Dorothy L. Judicial Performance Polls: 1977 Research Contribution, No. 1. Sikes, Bette, ed. (American Bar Foundation Research Contribution Ser.). (Illus.). 1977. pap. 5.00 (ISBN 0-910058-81-4). Am Bar Foun.
Maki, John M. Court & Constitution in Japan: Selected Supreme Court Decisions, 1948-60. LC 78-23431. (University of Washington Publications on Asia). 1978. pap. 40.00 (ISBN 0-8357-0335-5, ST-00017, Pub. by U of Wash Pr). Univ Microfilms.
Marvell, Thomas B. Appellate Courts & Lawyers: Information Gathering in the Adversary System. LC 77-94743. (Contributions in Legal Studies: No. 4). 1978. lib. bdg. 22.50x (ISBN 0-313-20312-1, MAA/). Greenwood.
Mendelson, Wallace. American Constitution & the Judicial Process. 720p. 1980. 21.95 (ISBN 0-686-73739-3). Dorsey.
Murphy, Walter F. Elements of Judicial Strategy. LC 64-24973. 1964. 14.00x (ISBN 0-226-55369-8). U of Chicago Pr.
--Elements of Judicial Strategy. LC 64-24973. 1973. pap. 6.95 (ISBN 0-226-55370-1, P551, Phoen). U of Chicago Pr.
Murphy, Walter F. & Pritchett, Herman C., eds. Courts, Judges & Politics: An Introduction to the Judicial Process. 3rd ed. LC 78-24033. 1979. text ed. 19.95x (ISBN 0-394-32117-0). Random.
Nagel, Stuart S. & Neef, Marian. Legal Policy Analysis. LC 76-14046. 1977. 23.95 (ISBN 0-669-00731-5). Lexington Bks.
National Center for State Courts. Parajudges: Their Role in Today's Court Systems. Prescott, Elizabeth, ed. 1976. pap. 2.00 (ISBN 0-89656-010-4, R0027). Natl Ctr St Courts.
National Judicial College. Judicial Function Outline. (Ser. 650). 1979. pap. 5.00 (ISBN 0-686-08769-0). Natl Judicial Coll.
Oakley, John B. & Thompson, Robert S. Law Clerks & the Judicial Process: Perceptions of the Qualities & Functions of Law Clerks in American Courts. 150p. 1981. 17.50x (ISBN 0-520-04046-5). U of Cal Pr.
Parker, Kellis E. Modern Judicial Remedies: Cases & Materials. 870p. 1975. 22.75 (ISBN 0-316-69082-1). Little.

Provine, Doris M. Case Selection in the United States Supreme Court. LC 79-25967. 1980. lib. bdg. 18.00x (ISBN 0-226-68468-7). U of Chicago Pr.

Reynolds, William L. Judicial Process in a Nutshell. LC 80-12730. (Nutshell Ser.). 322p. 1980. pap. text ed. 6.95 (ISBN 0-8299-2089-7). West Pub.

Rist, Ray C. & Anson, Ronald J. Education, Social Science, & the Judicial Process. LC 77-962. 1977. pap. text ed. 7.50x (ISBN 0-8077-2532-3). Tchrs Coll.

Rohde, David W. & Spaeth, Harold J. Supreme Court Decision Making. LC 75-25645. (Illus.). 1976. text ed. 18.95x (ISBN 0-7167-0717-9); pap. text ed. 9.95x (ISBN 0-7167-0716-0). W H Freeman.

Schubert, Glendon. Judicial Policy Making: The Political Role of the Courts. rev. ed. 256p. 1974. pap. 6.95x (ISBN 0-673-07914-7). Scott F.

Schubert, Glendon A., ed. Judicial Decision-Making. LC 63-8422. 1963. 14.95 (ISBN 0-02-928230-6). Free Pr.

Starr, Isidore. Great Ideas in the Law-Justice: Due Process of Law. 300p. 1981. pap. text ed. 6.50 (ISBN 0-8299-1020-4). West Pub.

Tesitor, Irene A. & Sinks, Dwight B. Judicial Conduct Organization. 2nd ed. 96p. 1980. pap. 3.75 (ISBN 0-938870-04-1, 8567). Am Judicature.

Thibaut, J. & Walker, L. Procedural Justice: A Psychological Analysis. LC 75-15944. 1975. pap. 4.95 (ISBN 0-470-85869-9). Halsted Pr.

Ulmer, S. S., ed. Courts, Law & Judical Processes. LC 80-1856. (Illus.). 1981. pap. text ed. 12.95 (ISBN 0-02-932970-1). Free Pr.

Wheeler, R. & Whitcomb, H. Judicial Administration: Text & Readings. 1977. text ed. 15.95 (ISBN 0-13-511675-9). P-H.

Zerman, Melvyn B. Beyond a Reasonable Doubt: Inside the America Injury System. (Illus.). 224p. (gr. 7 up). 1981. 9.95 (ISBN 0-690-04094-6, TYC J); PLB 9.89 (ISBN 0-690-04095-4). Har-Row.

JUDICIAL PROCESS–GREAT BRITAIN

Coke, Edward. Lord Coke, His Speech & Charge. LC 79-38167. (English Experience Ser.: No. 444). 64p. 1972. Repr. of 1607 ed. 9.50 (ISBN 90-221-0444-3). Walter J Johnson.

Griffith, J. A. The Politics of the Judiciary. LC 77-88391. (Political Issues of Modern Britain). 1977. text ed. 19.50x (ISBN 0-391-00551-0). Humanities.

JUDICIAL REVIEW

see also Legislative Power; Separation of Powers

Ball, Howard. Judicial Craftsmanship or Fiat? Direct Overturn by the United States Supreme Court. LC 77-91102. (Contributions in Political Science: No. 7). 1978. lib. bdg. 18.95x (ISBN 0-313-20035-1, BJC/). Greenwood.

Berger, Raoul. Congress Vs. the Supreme Court. LC 75-75426. 1969. text ed. 18.50x (ISBN 0-674-16210-2). Harvard U Pr.

Bizzell, William B. Judicial Interpretation of Political Theory: A Study of the Relation of the Courts to the American Party System. LC 73-21602. 1974. Repr. of 1914 ed. lib. bdg. 20.00 (ISBN 0-8337-4819-X). B Franklin.

Black, Charles L., Jr. The People & the Court: Judicial Review in a Democracy. LC 77-8076. 1977. Repr. of 1960 ed. lib. bdg. 20.00x (ISBN 0-8371-9682-5, BLPC). Greenwood.

Cahn, Edmond N., ed. Supreme Court & Supreme Law. LC 68-55629. (Illus.). 1968. Repr. of 1954 ed. lib. bdg. 20.25 (ISBN 0-8371-0335-5, CASC). Greenwood.

Cappelletti. Judicial Review in the Contemporary World. 1971. softbound 6.50 (ISBN 0-672-81757-8, Bobbs-Merrill Law). Michie-Bobbs.

Carr, Robert K. Supreme Court & Judicial Review. LC 74-98215. Repr. of 1942 ed. lib. bdg. 16.50 (ISBN 0-8371-3261-4, CAJR). Greenwood.

Commager, Henry S. Majority Rule & Minority Rights. 5.50 (ISBN 0-8446-1123-9). Peter Smith.

Corwin, Edward S. Court Over Constitution: A Study of Judicial As an Instrument of Popular Government. 7.50 (ISBN 0-8446-1129-8). Peter Smith.

--Doctrine of Judicial Review. 7.50 (ISBN 0-8446-1128-X). Peter Smith.

Davis, Horace A. The Judicial Veto. LC 78-146152. (American Constitutional & Legal History Ser). 1971. Repr. of 1914 ed. lib. bdg. 17.50 (ISBN 0-306-70093-X). Da Capo.

Dean, H. E. Judicial Review & Democracy. 7.75 (ISBN 0-8446-1956-6). Peter Smith.

Dean, Howard E. Judicial Review & Democracy. (Orig.). 1966. pap. text ed. 3.25 (ISBN 0-685-19740-9). Phila Bk Co.

Ely, John H. Democracy & Distrust: A Theory of Judicial Review. LC 79-19859. 1980. 15.00x (ISBN 0-674-19636-8). Harvard U Pr.

Gabin, Sanford B. Judicial Review & the Reasonable Doubt Test. (National University Publications, Multi-Disciplinary Studies in the Law). 1980. 15.00 (ISBN 0-8046-9248-3). Kennikat.

Haines, Charles G. The American Doctrine of Judicial Supremacy. LC 73-250. (American Constitutional & Legal History Ser.). 726p. 1973. Repr. of 1932 ed. lib. bdg. 69.50 (ISBN 0-306-70569-9). Da Capo.

Hidayatullah, M. Democracy in India & the Judicial Process. 1966. 5.00x (ISBN 0-210-22707-9). Asia.

Johnston, Richard E. Effect of Judicial Review on Federal-State Relations in Australia, Canada, & the United States. LC 70-80045. 1969. 22.50x (ISBN 0-8071-0901-0). La State U Pr.

Mayers, Lewis. The Machinery of Justice: An Introduction to Legal Structure & Process. (Quality Paperback: No. 261). 115p. 1976. pap. 2.95 (ISBN 0-8226-0261-X). Littlefield.

Moore, Blaine F. Supreme Court & Unconstitutional Legislation. LC 68-56672. (Columbia University. Studies in the Social Sciences: No. 133). Repr. of 1913 ed. 16.50 (ISBN 0-404-51133-3). AMS Pr.

Nelson, Margaret V. Study of Judicial Review in Virginia, 1789-1928. LC 47-31482. (Columbia University. Studies in the Social Sciences: No. 532). Repr. of 1947 ed. 20.00 (ISBN 0-404-51532-0). AMS Pr.

Nwabueze, B. O. Judicialism in Commonwealth Africa. LC 76-27553. 1977. 22.50x (ISBN 0-312-44695-0). St Martin.

Powell, Thomas R. Vagaries & Varieties in Constitutional Interpretation. LC 74-181973. Repr. of 1956 ed. write for info. (ISBN 0-404-05118-9). AMS Pr.

Pritchett, C. Herman. Political Offender & the Warren Court. LC 66-27194. 1967. Repr. of 1958 ed. 5.00 (ISBN 0-8462-0905-5). Russell.

Provine, Doris M. Case Selection in the United States Supreme Court. LC 79-25967. 1980. lib. bdg. 18.00x (ISBN 0-226-68468-7). U of Chicago Pr.

Rostow, Eugene V. The Sovereign Prerogative. LC 73-17923. 318p. 1974. Repr. of 1962 ed. lib. bdg. 16.50x (ISBN 0-8371-7276-4, RSOP). Greenwood.

Schubert, Glendon A. The Presidency in the Courts. LC 72-8122. (American Constitutional & Legal History Ser). 408p. 1973. Repr. of 1957 ed. lib. bdg. 35.00 (ISBN 0-306-70529-X). Da Capo.

Smith, Franklin A. Judicial Review of Legislation in N.Y. 1906-1938. LC 71-76658. (Columbia University. Studies in the Social Sciences: No. 574). Repr. of 1952 ed. 16.00 (ISBN 0-404-51574-6). AMS Pr.

Tugwell, Rexford G. The Compromising of the Constitution. LC 76-641. 188p. 1976. 8.95x (ISBN 0-268-00714-4). U of Notre Dame Pr.

U. S. Library of Congress Legislative Reference Service. Provisions of Federal Law Held Unconstitutional by the Supreme Court of the United States. Gilbert, Wilfred C., ed. LC 75-35364. (U.S. Government Documents Program Ser.). 148p. 1976. Repr. of 1936 ed. lib. bdg. 15.00 (ISBN 0-8371-8605-6, USPF). Greenwood.

Von Moschzisker, R. Judicial Review of Legislation. LC 78-153372. (American Constitutional & Legal History Ser.). 1971. Repr. of 1923 ed. lib. bdg. 19.50 (ISBN 0-306-70151-0). Da Capo.

JUDICIAL REVIEW–AUSTRALIA

Johnston, Richard E. Effect of Judicial Review on Federal-State Relations in Australia, Canada, & the United States. LC 70-80045. 1969. 22.50x (ISBN 0-8071-0901-0). La State U Pr.

JUDICIAL REVIEW–CANADA

Johnston, Richard E. Effect of Judicial Review on Federal-State Relations in Australia, Canada, & the United States. LC 70-80045. 1969. 22.50x (ISBN 0-8071-0901-0). La State U Pr.

JUDICIAL REVIEW OF ADMINISTRATIVE ACTS

see also Administrative Remedies; Extraordinary Remedies

Henderson, Edith G. Foundations of English Administrative Law. 1963. 6.50x (ISBN 0-678-08033-X). Kelley.

--Foundations of English Administrative Law: Certiorari & Mandamus in the Seventeenth Century. LC 63-11421. (Ames Foundation Publications Ser). 1963. 10.00x (ISBN 0-674-31351-8). Harvard U Pr.

Horowitz, Donald L. The Jurocracy: Government Lawyers, Agency Programs, & Judicial Decisions. LC 76-27921. 1977. 16.95 (ISBN 0-669-00986-5). Lexington Bks.

Ulloth, Dana R. The Supreme Court. new ed. Sterling, Christopher H., ed. LC 78-21744. (Dissertations in Broadcasting Ser.). 1979. lib. bdg. 16.00x (ISBN 0-405-11780-9). Arno.

JUDICIAL SALES

see also Foreclosure

JUDICIAL SEPARATION

see Separation (Law)

JUDICIAL STATISTICS

see also Criminal Statistics

Finkelstein, Michael O. Quantitative Methods in Law: Studies in the Application of Mathematical Probability & Statistics to Legal Problems. LC 77-94081. 1978. 19.95 (ISBN 0-02-910260-X). Free Pr.

Glueck, Sheldon S. & Glueck, Eleanor T. One Thousand Juvenile Delinquents. 1934. 14.00 (ISBN 0-527-34100-2). Kraus Repr.

National Center for State Courts & National Court Statistics Project. State Court Caseload Statistics: Annual Report, 1976. 1980. pap. 12.50 (ISBN 0-89656-044-9, R0052). Natl Ctr St Courts.

JUDICIARY

see Courts; Judicial Power

JUDO

see also Karate

AAU Official Judo Rules 1978-80. (Illus.). 1978. softcover 3.50 (ISBN 0-89710-017-4). AAU Pubns.

Bartlett, E. G. Basic Judo. 2.95 (ISBN 0-685-63743-3). Wehman.

Bruce, Jeannette. Judo: A Gentle Beginning. LC 74-26503. (Illus.). 160p. (gr. 3 up). 1975. 8.95 (ISBN 0-690-00557-1, TYC-J). Har-Row.

Butler, Pat. Judo Complete. (Illus.). 240p. 1971. (Pub. by Faber & Faber); pap. 4.95 (ISBN 0-571-09725-1). Merrimack Bk Serv.

Campbell, B. Championship Judo. 6.95 (ISBN 0-685-63747-6). Wehman.

Clark, Buddy & Davis, Craig. Alone, Unarmed, but Safe! An Illustrated Guide to Judo Defense. (Illus.). 128p. 1981. 8.00 (ISBN 0-682-49712-6); pap. 5.00 (ISBN 0-682-49711-8). Exposition.

Dominy. Judo: Beginner to Black Belt. 6.95 (ISBN 0-685-21999-2). Wehman.

Dominy, Eric. Judo Techniques & Tactics. (Illus.). 1969. pap. 2.50 (ISBN 0-486-22310-8). Dover.

--Judo Techniques & Tactics: Contest Judo. (Illus.). 6.75 (ISBN 0-8446-0586-7). Peter Smith.

--Teach Yourself Judo. (Illus.). 1962. 7.95 (ISBN 0-87523-140-3). Emerson.

Draeger, Donn F. & Otaki, Tadao. Judo Formal Techniques: A Complete Guide to Kodokan Randori No Kata. (Illus.). 1982. 30.00 (ISBN 0-8048-1187-3). C E Tuttle.

Feldenkrais, Moshe. Judo. (Illus.). 1944. 4.95 (ISBN 0-7232-0213-3). Warne.

Freudenberg, Karl. Natural Weapons: A Manual of Karate, Judo, & Jujitsu Techniques. (Illus., Orig.). 1962. pap. 3.95 (ISBN 0-498-04086-0, Prpta). A S Barnes.

Frommer, Harvey. The Martial Arts: Judo & Karate. LC 78-55205. (Illus.). 1978. 7.95 (ISBN 0-689-10908-3). Atheneum.

Gardner, Ruth. Judo for the Gentle Woman. LC 74-147175. (Illus.). 1971. pap. 3.25 (ISBN 0-8048-0660-8). C E Tuttle.

Geesink, A. Go-Kyo: Principles of Judo. 8.95 (ISBN 0-685-63752-2). Wehman.

Glass, George. Competitive Judo: Throwing Techniques & Weight Control. (Illus.). 96p. (Orig.). 1977. pap. 3.95 (ISBN 0-571-10915-2, Pub. by Faber & Faber). Merrimack Bk Serv.

Gleason, G. R. Better Judo. rev. ed. (Better Ser.). (Illus.). 1978. text ed. 15.95x (ISBN 0-7182-0485-9, SpS). Sportshelf.

Gleeson, G. R. Better Judo. LC 72-170800. (Better Sports Ser.). (Illus.). 96p. 1972. 8.50x (ISBN 0-7182-0485-9). Intl Pubns Serv.

Gleeson, Geof. All About Judo. (EP Sports Ser.). (Illus.). 1975. 6.95 (ISBN 0-7158-0590-8). Charles River Bks.

Gleeson, Geoff. All About Judo. (Sports Library). (Illus.). 1979. 12.95 (ISBN 0-8069-9100-3); pap. 6.95 (ISBN 0-8069-9102-X). Sterling.

Goodbody, John. Judo: How to Become a Champ. (Illus.). 1976. pap. 7.50 (ISBN 0-86002-128-9). Transatlantic.

Harrington, Anthony P. Every Boy's Judo. (Illus.). (gr. 7 up). 7.95 (ISBN 0-87523-125-X). Emerson.

--Every Girl's Judo. (Illus.). (gr. 7 up). 7.95 (ISBN 0-87523-127-6). Emerson.

Illustrated Kodokan Judo. (Illus.). 37.00 (ISBN 0-685-21987-9). Wehman.

Inokuma, Isao & Sato, Nobuyuki. Best Judo. LC 79-84656. (Illus.). 256p. 1979. 19.95 (ISBN 0-87011-381-X). Kodansha.

James, Stuart. The Complete Beginner's Guide to Judo. LC 76-56306. (gr. 6-12). 1978. PLB 5.95 (ISBN 0-385-06041-6). Doubleday.

Judo. 1976. pap. 2.50 (ISBN 0-8277-4879-5). British Bk Ctr.

Kim, Daeshik & Shin, Kyung Sun. Judo. 2nd ed. (Physical Education Activities Ser.). 96p. 1977. pap. text ed. write for info. (ISBN 0-697-07069-7). Wm C Brown.

Klinger, Hubert. Judo Self-Taught. pap. 1.95 (ISBN 0-685-22000-1). Wehman.

Kobayashi, K. Sport of Judo. 5.75 (ISBN 0-685-38453-5). Wehman.

Kobayashi, Kiyoshi & Sharp, Harold E. Sport of Judo. LC 57-75. (Illus.). (gr. 9 up). 1957. pap. 6.95 (ISBN 0-8048-0542-3). C E Tuttle.

Kotani, Sumuyuki. Kodokan Judo Revised. 1968. 7.95 (ISBN 0-685-83532-4). Wehman.

Kudo, K. Judo in Action, 2 vols. 4.50 ea. Wehman.

Kudo, Kazuzo. Judo in Action: Grappling Techniques. LC 67-20768. (Illus.). 1967. pap. 5.95 (ISBN 0-87040-074-6). Japan Pubns.

--Judo in Action: Throwing Techniques. LC 67-20768. (Illus.). pap. 5.95 (ISBN 0-87040-073-8). Japan Pubns.

LeBell, Gene & Coughran, L. C. Handbook of Judo. 192p. 1963. pap. 1.95 (ISBN 0-346-12174-4). Cornerstone.

Longhurst, Percy. Ju-Jutsu & Judo. (Illus.). 64p. 1980. softcover 6.00 (ISBN 0-87364-189-2). Paladin Ent.

Neff, Fred. Fred Neff's Manual of Throws for Sport Judo & Self-Defense. LC 75-38476. (Fred Neff's Self-Defense Library). (Illus.). 56p. (gr. 5 up). 1976. PLB 5.95g (ISBN 0-8225-1155-X). Lerner Pubns.

Nishioka, Hayward. Foot Throws. 3.25 (ISBN 0-685-38442-X). Wehman.

--The Judo Textbook. LC 78-65737. (Ser. 210). (Illus.). 1979. pap. 5.95 (ISBN 0-89750-063-6). Ohara Pubns.

Okano, I. & Sato, T. Vital Judo. 14.95 (ISBN 0-685-38458-6). Wehman.

Okano, Isai. Vital Judo: Grappling Techniques. 14.95 (ISBN 0-685-70712-1). Wehman.

Reay, Tony & Hobbs, Geoffrey. The Illustrated Guide to Judo. 1979. pap. 9.95 (ISBN 0-442-26096-2). Van Nos Reinhold.

Rhee, J. Tan-Gun & to-San. 4.95 (ISBN 0-685-38455-1). Wehman.

Robert, Hank. Ketsugo. pap. 1.00 (ISBN 0-686-00695-X). Key Bks.

Science of Judo. 6.95 (ISBN 0-685-88122-9). Wehman.

So, Doshin. What Is Shorinji Kempo. 4.50 (ISBN 0-685-38459-4). Wehman.

Starbrook, Dave. Judo Starbrook Style: Champion's Method. (Illus.). 1978. pap. 14.95x (ISBN 0-8464-0540-7). Beekman Pubs.

Stewart, Paul. Sports Illustrated Judo. LC 75-15827. (Sports Illustrated Ser). (Illus.). 1976. 5.95 (ISBN 0-397-01096-6); pap. 2.95 (ISBN 0-397-01104-0). Lippincott.

Takagaki, S. Technique of Judo. 6.25 (ISBN 0-685-38456-X). Wehman.

Takagaki, Shinzo & Sharp, Harold E. Techniques of Judo. LC 56-13413. (Illus.). 1956. pap. 10.50 (ISBN 0-8048-0569-5). C E Tuttle.

Tegner, Bruce. Bruce Tegner's Complete Book of Judo. rev. ed. LC 75-16441. (Illus.). 224p. (YA) 1975. 6.95 (ISBN 0-87407-512-2, C-12). Thor.

--Judo: Sport Techniques for Physical Fitness & Tournament. LC 76-18090. (Illus.). 144p. 1976. pap. 2.95 (ISBN 0-87407-025-2, T25). Thor.

--Karate & Judo Exercises. rev. ed. LC 81-5251. (Illus.). 1981. pap. 3.95 (ISBN 0-87407-036-8, T-22). Thor.

Wall, Bob. Who's Who in the Martial Arts & Directory of Black Belts. LC 75-22880. (Illus.). 275p. (Orig.). 1975. pap. 7.95 (ISBN 0-685-62677-6). R A Wall.

Watanabe, Jiichi & Avakian, Lindy. Secrets of Judo. LC 59-14089. (Illus.). 1959. 12.95 (ISBN 0-8048-0516-4). C E Tuttle.

JUDSON, ADONIRAM, 1788-1850

Anderson, Courtney. To the Golden Shore: The Life of Adoniram Judson. 1977. pap. 6.95 (ISBN 0-310-36131-1). Zondervan.

Bailey, Faith C. Adoniram Judson. 128p. 1980. pap. 2.50 (ISBN 0-8024-0287-9). Moody.

Brumberg, Joan J. Mission for Life: The Story of the Family of Adoniram Judson. LC 79-54667. (Illus.). 1980. 12.95 (ISBN 0-02-905100-2). Free Pr.

Conant, D. C. The Earnest Man; or the Character & Labors of Adoniram Judson. 1978. Repr. of 1856 ed. lib. bdg. 20.00 (ISBN 0-8492-3943-5). R West.

McElrath, William N. To Be the First. LC 75-14893. (Illus.). 192p. (gr. 5up). 1976. pap. 4.95 (ISBN 0-8054-4318-5). Broadman.

JUDSON, ANN (HASSELTINE) MRS., 1789-1826

Hubbard, Ethel D. Ann of Ava. LC 76-160921. (Biography Index Reprint Ser). Repr. of 1941 ed. 15.25 (ISBN 0-8369-8084-0). Arno.

Pitman, E. R. Ann H. Judson of Burma. 1974. pap. 1.25 (ISBN 0-87508-601-2). Chr Lit.

JUGENDSTIL

see Art Nouveau

JUGGLERS AND JUGGLING

see also Conjuring

Benge, Ken. The Art of Juggling. LC 77-73876. (Illus.). 137p. 1977. pap. 4.95 (ISBN 0-89037-120-2). Anderson World.

Carlo. The Juggling Book. (Illus.). 112p. (Orig.). 1974. pap. 4.95 (ISBN 0-394-71956-5, Vin). Random.

Cassidy, John & Rimbeaux, B. C. Juggling for the Complete Klutz. 2nd ed. (Illus.). 1980. pap. 7.95 (ISBN 0-932592-00-7). Klutz Pr.

Dittrich, R. Juggling Made Easy. 3.00 (ISBN 0-685-38464-0). Wehman.

Dittrich, Rudolf. Juggling Made Easy. pap. 2.00 (ISBN 0-87980-086-0). Wilshire.
Faral, Edmond. Jongleurs En France Au Moyen Age. LC 79-140971. (Reseach & Source Works Ser: No. 606). 1971. Repr. of 1910 ed. 23.50 (ISBN 0-8337-1099-0). B Franklin.
Humphrey, Ron. Juggling for Fun & Entertainment. LC 67-14278. (Illus.). (gr. 6 up). 1967. pap. 3.25 (ISBN 0-8048-1133-4). C E Tuttle.
Mardo, Senor. The Cups & Balls. Date not set. pap. 4.00 (ISBN 0-685-55922-X). Borden.
Meyer, Charles R. How to Be a Juggler. (A Ringling Brothers - Barnum & Bailey Book). (Illus.). (gr. 4-7). 1977. 6.95 (ISBN 0-679-20407-5). McKay.
Ussher, Arland. The Juggler. 88p. 1980. text ed. write for info. (ISBN 0-85105-374-2, Dolmen Pr). Humanities.

JUGOSLAVS
see Yugoslavs

JUGS
see Pitchers

JUGURTHINE WAR, 111-105 B.C.
Sallust. Jugurthine War. Handford, S. A., tr. Bd. with Conspiracy of Catline. (Classics Ser.). 1964. pap. 2.95 (ISBN 0-14-044132-8). Penguin.
--War with Catiline, War with Jugurtha, Etc. (Loeb Classical Library: No. 116). 11.00x (ISBN 0-674-99128-1). Harvard U Pr.

JUJITSU
see Jiu-Jitsu

JUKE FAMILY
Dugdale, Richard L. The Jukes. LC 79-38664. (Foundations of Criminal Justice Ser.). Repr. of 1895 ed. 11.50 (ISBN 0-404-09173-3). AMS Pr.
--Jukes: A Study in Crime, Pauperism, Disease, & Heredity. LC 74-112542. (Rise of Urban America). (Illus.). 1970. Repr. of 1877 ed. 13.00 (ISBN 0-405-02451-7). Arno.

JULIAN THE APOSTATE, EMPEROR OF ROME, 331-363
Athanassiadi-Fowden, Polymnia. Julian & Hellenism: An Intellectual Biography. 248p. 1981. 49.95x (ISBN 0-19-814846-1). Oxford U Pr.
Bowersock, G. W. Julian the Apostate. 1978. 12.50x (ISBN 0-674-48881-4); pap. 5.95x (ISBN 0-674-48882-2). Harvard U Pr.
Gardner, Alice. Julian, Philosopher & Emperor. LC 73-14444. (Heroes of the Nations Ser.). Repr. of 1895 ed. 30.00 (ISBN 0-404-58262-1). AMS Pr.
Partridge, Loren & Starn, Randolph. A Renaissance Likeness: Art & Culture in Raphael's Julius II. LC 79-63549. (Quantum Ser.). (Illus.). 1980. 17.95x (ISBN 0-520-03901-7). U of Cal Pr.
Vidal, Gore. Julian. 1977. pap. 1.95 (ISBN 0-394-72101-2, Vin). Random.

JULIUS 2ND, POPE, 1443-1513
Colledge, Edmund, et al, eds. Julian of Norwich, "Showings". LC 77-90953. (Classics of Western Spirituality). 384p. 1978. 11.95 (ISBN 0-8091-0234-X); pap. 7.95 (ISBN 0-8091-2091-7). Paulist Pr.
Gobineau, Joseph A. Golden Flower. facsimile ed. Redman, B. R., tr. LC 68-54347. (Essay Index Reprint Ser). 1924. 13.00 (ISBN 0-8369-0477-X). Arno.

JULY FOURTH
see Fourth of July

JUMBO (ELEPHANT)–JUVENILE LITERATURE
Denzel, Justin. Jumbo: Giant Circus Elephant. LC 72-9349. (Famous Animal Stories Ser.). (Illus.). 48p. (gr. 2-5). 1973. PLB 6.27 (ISBN 0-8116-4850-8). Garrard.

JUMEL, STEPHEN, 1755-1832
Minnigerode, Meade. Lives & Times. LC 76-121490. (Essay Index Reprint Ser). 1925. 16.00 (ISBN 0-8369-1765-0). Arno.

JUMP ROPE
see Rope Skipping

JUMPING
Ansell, M. P. Jumping. Date not set. 11.00 (ISBN 0-392-08278-0, SpS). Sportshelf.
Bullard, Ernie & Knuth, Larry. Triple Jump Encyclopedia. LC 77-4265. 1977. pap. 8.95 (ISBN 0-87095-057-6). Athletic.
Jarver, Jess, ed. The Jumps. LC 80-54184. (Contemporary Theory, Technique & Training Ser.). (Illus.). 128p. (Orig.). 1981. pap. 7.50 (ISBN 0-911521-00-3). Tafnews.
Ryan, Frank. Jumping for Joy: The High Jump, the Pole Vault, the Long Jump, & the Triple Jump. LC 79-26696. (Illus.). (gr. 4-7). 1980. 7.95 (ISBN 0-684-16337-3). Scribner.
Watts, Denis. Athletics: Jumping & Vaulting. (Pelham Pictorial Sports Instruction Ser.). (Illus.). 1979. 9.95 (ISBN 0-7207-0919-9). Transatlantic.

JUMPING (HORSEMANSHIP)
Batchelor, Vivien. Observer's Book of Show Jumping & Eventing. (Observer Bks.). (Illus.). 1977. 2.95 (ISBN 0-684-15211-8, ScribT). Scribner.
Crago, Judy. Junior Show Jumping. LC 77-102. (Illus.). 1977. 10.95 (ISBN 0-690-01444-9). T Y Crowell.
Froud, Bill. Better Show Jumping. Roberts, Peter, ed. LC 75-317706. (Better Sports Ser.). (Illus.). 1975. 8.50x (ISBN 0-7182-1440-4). Intl Pubns Serv.
Paalman, Anthony. Training Showjumpers. Holstein, G., tr. from Ger. (Illus.). 1978. 38.35 (ISBN 0-85131-260-8, Dist. by Sporting Book Center). J A Allen.
Show Jumping. 1976. pap. 2.50 (ISBN 0-8277-4905-8). British Bk Ctr.
Steinkraus, William. Riding & Jumping. new ed. LC 79-91104. 1969. 7.95 (ISBN 0-385-04816-5). Doubleday.
Williams, Dorian. Great Moments in Sports: Show Jumping. (Illus.). 128p. 1974. 10.95 (ISBN 0-7207-0680-7). Transatlantic.

JUMPING BAIL
see Bail

JUNCTION TRANSISTORS
see also Tunnel Diodes
Milnes, A. G. & Feucht, D. L. Heterojunctions & Metal Semiconductor Junctions. 1972. 55.00 (ISBN 0-12-498050-3). Acad Pr.
Sharma, B. L. & Purohit, R. K. Semiconductor Heterojunctions. LC 73-18449. 1974. text ed. 45.00 (ISBN 0-08-017747-6). Pergamon.
Todd, C. D. Junction Field-Effect Transistors. 285p. 1968. text ed. 14.25 (ISBN 0-471-87650-X, Pub. by Wiley). Krieger.

JUNE DEVOTIONS
see Sacred Heart, Devotion To

JUNG, CARL GUSTAV, 1875-1961
Bennet, E. A. What Jung Really Said. LC 67-13153. (What They Really Said Ser). 1971. pap. 3.95 (ISBN 0-8052-0265-X). Schocken.
Berry, et al. Spring 81: An Annual of Archetypal Psychology & Jungian Thought. (Orig.). 1981. pap. 10.00 (ISBN 0-88214-016-7). Spring Pubns.
Bertine, Eleanor. Jung's Contribution to Our Time. LC 67-17109. 1967. 8.00 (ISBN 0-913430-20-X). C G Jung Foun.
Bickman, Martin. The Unsounded Centre: Jungian Studies in American Romanticism. LC 79-26042. ix, 182p. 1980. 14.50x (ISBN 0-8078-1428-8). U of NC Pr.
Brivic, Sheldon R. Joyce Between Freud & Jung. (National University Publications, Literary Criticism Ser.). 1980. 15.00 (ISBN 0-8046-9249-1). Kennikat.
Brome, Vincent. Jung: Man & Myth. LC 80-25159. 327p. 1981. pap. 7.95 (ISBN 0-689-70588-3, 262). Atheneum.
--Jung: Man & Myth. LC 77-14736. 1978. 11.95 (ISBN 0-689-10853-2). Atheneum.
Brown, Clifford A. Jung's Hermeneutic of Doctrine. LC 80-20795. (American Academy of Religion Dissertation Ser.). 1981. pap. 12.50 (ISBN 0-89130-437-1, 01-01-32). Scholars Pr CA.
Clark, Robert A. Six Talks on Jung's Psychology. (Orig.). 1953. pap. 4.50 (ISBN 0-910286-07-8). Boxwood.
Cohen, Edmund D. C. G. Jung & the Scientific Attitude. LC 73-88705. 1974. 7.50 (ISBN 0-685-48949-3). Philos Lib.
--C. G. Jung & the Scientific Attitude. (Littlefield Adams Quality Paperbacks: No. 322). 167p. 1976. pap. 2.95 (ISBN 0-8226-0322-5). Littlefield.
Corbin, et al. Spring '80: An Annual of Archetypal Psychology & Jungian Thought. Hillman, James, ed. 196p. (Orig.). 1980. pap. text ed. 10.00 (ISBN 0-88214-015-9). Spring Pubns.
Cox, David. Modern Psychology: The Teachings of Carl Gustav Jung. 1968. pap. 2.95 (ISBN 0-06-463231-8, EH 231, EH). Har-Row.
Fordham, Frieda. Introduction to Jung's Psychology. (Orig.). 1953. pap. 2.95 (ISBN 0-14-020273-0, Pelican). Penguin.
--An Introduction to Jung's Psychology. lib. bdg. 9.50x (ISBN 0-88307-354-4). Gannon.
Fordham, Michael, ed. Jungian Psychotherapy: A Study in Analytical Psychology. LC 77-26331. (Wiley Series on Methods in Psychotherapy). 1978. 34.95 (ISBN 0-471-99617-3, Pub. by Wiley-Interscience); pap. 17.50 (ISBN 0-471-99618-1). Wiley.
Frey-Rohn, Liliane. From Freud to Jung. 368p. 1976. pap. 3.95 (ISBN 0-440-54715-6, Delta). Dell.
--From Freud to Jung. LC 73-77114. 1974. 16.00 (ISBN 0-913430-24-2). C G Jung Foun.
Goldbrunner, Josef. Individuation: A Study of the Depth Psychology of Carl Gustav Jung. 1964. pap. 1.25x (ISBN 0-268-00131-6). U of Notre Dame Pr.
Hall, Calvin S. & Nordby, Vernon J. A Primer of Jungian Psychology. 144p. 1973. pap. 1.75 (ISBN 0-451-61865-3, ME1865, Ment). NAL.
--Primer of Jungian Psychology. LC 73-7255. 1973. 7.95 (ISBN 0-8008-6554-5). Taplinger.
Hannah, Barbara. Encounters with the Soul: Active Imagination As Developed by C. G. Jung. LC 81-5316. 264p. 1981. 15.00 (ISBN 0-938434-04-7); pap. 9.50 (ISBN 0-938434-02-0). Sigo Pr.
Heisig, James W. Imago Dei: A Study of C. G. Jung's Psychology of Religion. LC 77-74405. 1978. 18.00 (ISBN 0-8387-2076-5). Bucknell U Pr.
Hillman, et al. Spring 'seventy-Six: An Annual of Archetypal Psychology & Jungian Thought. Hillman, James, ed. 218p. (Orig.). 1976. pap. text ed. 12.00 (ISBN 0-88214-011-6). Spring Pubns.
Hillman, James, ed. An Annual of Archetypal Psychology & Jungian Thought. annual 304p. 1975. pap. 12.00 (ISBN 0-88214-010-8). Spring Pubns.
Homans, Peter. Jung in Context: Modernity & the Making of a Psychology. LC 78-27596. 1979. lib. bdg. 15.00x (ISBN 0-226-35108-4). U of Chicago Pr.
Jacobi, Jolande. Complex-Archetype-Symbol in the Psychology of C. J. Jung. Manheim, R., tr. (Bollingen Series, Vol. 57). (Illus.). 248p. 1959. 15.00 (ISBN 0-691-09720-8); pap. 5.95 (ISBN 0-691-01774-3, 241). Princeton U Pr.
--Psychology of C. G. Jung. new ed. Manheim, Ralph, tr. (Illus.). 1973. 16.50x (ISBN 0-300-01673-5); pap. 5.95 (ISBN 0-300-01674-3, Y75). Yale U Pr.
Jaffe, Aniela. Myth of Meaning. 1975. pap. 2.25 (ISBN 0-14-003990-2). Penguin.
--The Myth of Meaning. LC 73-120093. 1971. 8.00 (ISBN 0-913430-07-2). C G Jung Foun.
Jaffe, Aniela, ed. C. G. Jung: Word & Image. LC 78-17319. (Bollingen Ser. XCVII: 2). (Illus.). 1979. 30.00 (ISBN 0-691-09942-1). Princeton U Pr.
Jung, Carl G. Answer to Job. (Bollingen Ser.: Vol. 20). 1972. pap. 3.95 (ISBN 0-691-01785-9). Princeton U Pr.
--The Visions Seminars. 1976. pap. 25.00 set (ISBN 0-88214-111-2). Spring Pubns.
Jung, Emma & Von Franz, Marie-Louise. The Grail Legend. write for info. (ISBN 0-938434-07-1); pap. write for info. (ISBN 0-938434-08-X). Sigo Pr.
Kaufmann, Walter. Discovering the Mind: Freud Versus Adler & Jung. LC 80-25767. 1981. 14.95 (ISBN 0-07-033313-0). McGraw.
McGuire, William, ed. The Freud-Jung Letters: The Correspondence Between Sigmund Freud & C. G. Jung. Manheim, Ralph & Hull, R. F., trs. LC 76-166373. (Bollingen Ser.: No. 94). 650p. 1974. 30.00 (ISBN 0-691-09890-5); pap. 9.95 (ISBN 0-691-01810-3). Princeton U Pr.
McGuire, William & Hull, R. F., eds. C. G. Jung Speaking: Interviews & Encounters. LC 77-71985. (Bollingen Ser.: No. 98). 1977. 20.00 (ISBN 0-691-09894-8). Princeton U Pr.
Mahoney, Maria F. Meaning in Dreams & Dreaming. 1966. pap. 3.95 (ISBN 0-8065-0095-6). Citadel Pr.
Martin, P. W. Experiment in Depth: A Study of the Work of Jung, Eliot & Toynbee. 1976. pap. 6.95 (ISBN 0-7100-8393-9). Routledge & Kegan.
Mattoon, Mary A. Jungian Psychology in Perspective. LC 81-66603. 288p. 1981. 17.95 (ISBN 0-02-920440-2). Free Pr.
Mattoon, Mary Ann. Applied Dream Analysis: A Jungian Approach. 248p. 1978. 13.95x (ISBN 0-470-26418-7). Halsted Pr.
Meier, Carl A. Jung's Analytical Psychology & Religion. LC 76-48973. (Arcturus Books Paperbacks). 88p. 1977. pap. 2.95 (ISBN 0-8093-0807-X). S Ill U Pr.
Mindell, Arnold. The Dreambody. Sternback-Scott, Sisa, ed. (Orig.). 1981. price not set. (ISBN 0-938434-05-5); pap. price not set. (ISBN 0-938434-06-3). Sigo Pr.
Mooney, Lucindi F. Storming Eastern Temples. LC 76-4903. 1976. 9.75x (ISBN 0-8356-0482-9, Quest); pap. 4.25 (ISBN 0-8356-0479-9). Theos Pub Hse.
Neumann, Erich. The Great Mother: An Analysis of the Archetype. Manheim, Ralph, tr. (Bollingen Ser.: Vol. 47). 628p. 1972. 28.50 (ISBN 0-691-09742-9); pap. 6.95 (ISBN 0-691-01780-8). Princeton U Pr.
Nichols, Sallie. Jung & Tarot: An Archetypal Journey. 1980. 24.95 (ISBN 0-87728-480-6); pap. 9.95 (ISBN 0-87728-515-2). Weiser.
Odajnyk, Volodymyr Walter. Jung & Politics: The Political & Social Ideas of C. G. Jung. LC 76-55153. 1976. 14.50x (ISBN 0-8147-6154-2). NYU Pr.
Olney, James. The Rhizome & the Flower: The Perennial Philosophy--Yeats & Jung. 1980. 26.75x (ISBN 0-520-03748-0). U of Cal Pr.
O'Neill, Timothy R. The Individuated Hobbit: Jung, Tolkien & the Archetypes of Middle-Earth. 1979. 8.95 (ISBN 0-395-28208-X). HM.
Progoff, Ira. Jung, Synchronicity, & Human Destiny. LC 73-84937. 244p. 1975. 6.50 (ISBN 0-517-52767-7). Crown.
--Jung, Synchronicity, & Human Destiny. 192p. 1975. pap. 4.95 (ISBN 0-440-54375-4, Delta). Dell.
Serrano, Miguel. C. G. Jung & Hermann Hesse: A Record of Two Friendships. MacShane, Frank, tr. LC 66-14085. (Illus.). 1968. 7.00x (ISBN 0-8052-3132-3); pap. 2.95 (ISBN 0-686-66533-3). Schocken.
Singer, June. Boundaries of the Soul. LC 72-76205. 520p. 1973. pap. 4.50 (ISBN 0-385-06900-6, Anch). Doubleday.
Staude, John-Raphael. The Adult Development of C. G. Jung. 144p. 1981. 12.95 (ISBN 0-686-76618-0). Routledge & Kegan.
Stern, Paul J. C. G. Jung: The Haunted Prophet. LC 75-37827. 267p. 1976. 8.95 (ISBN 0-8076-0811-4). Braziller.
Ulanov, Ann B. Feminine. 1971. 19.95x (ISBN 0-8101-0351-6); pap. 8.95 (ISBN 0-8101-0608-6). Northwestern U Pr.
Universidad De Puerto Rico.(Rio Piedras Campus) Rectoria. Cuatro Conferencias Conmemorativas: Miguel Angel, Thomas Mann, Rainer Maria Rilke, Carlos Gustavo Jung. LC 77-4452. 1977. pap. 2.50 (ISBN 0-8477-3180-4). U of PR Pr.
Van Der Post, Laurens. Jung & the Story of Our Time. 1977. pap. 3.95 (ISBN 0-394-72175-6, Vin). Random.
Vincie, Joseph F. & Rathbauer-Vincie, Margreta. C. G. Jung & Analytical Psychology: A Comprehensive Bibliography. (Reference Library of Social Science: Vol. 38). (LC 76-052695). 1977. lib. bdg. 32.50 (ISBN 0-8240-9874-9). Garland Pub.
Von Franz, Marie-Louise. C. G. Jung: His Myth in Our Time. Kennedy, William H., tr. LC 73-77115. 355p. 1975. 15.00 (ISBN 0-913430-26-9). C G Jung Foun.
--C. G. Jung: His Myth in Our Time. 1977. pap. 4.95 (ISBN 0-316-90530-5). Little.
--Number & Time. Dykes, Andrea, tr. from Ger. LC 73-86467. (Studies in Jungian Thought). 256p. 1974. 18.95x (ISBN 0-8101-0429-6); pap. 8.95x (ISBN 0-8101-0532-2). Northwestern U Pr.
--Projection & Re-Collection in Jungian Psychology: Reflections of the Soul. Kennedy, William H., tr. from Ger. (The Reality of the Psyche Ser.). Orig. Title: Spiegelungen der Seele: Projektion und Innere Sammlung. 1980. 15.00 (ISBN 0-87548-357-7). Open Court.
--Puer Aeternus. 2nd ed. LC 80-28090. (Illus.). 304p. 1981. 15.00 (ISBN 0-938434-03-9); pap. 10.50 (ISBN 0-938434-01-2). Sigo Pr.
Von Franz, Marie-Louise & Hillman, James. Lecture on Jung's Typology. 150p. 1971. pap. text ed. 7.50 (ISBN 0-88214-104-X). Spring Pubns.

JUNG, JOHANN HEINRICH, 1740-1817
Stecher, Gotthilf. Jung Stilling Als Schriftsteller. Repr. of 1913 ed. 21.50 (ISBN 0-384-57731-8); pap. 18.50 (ISBN 0-384-57730-X). Johnson Repr.

JUNGER, ERNST, 1895-
Junger, Ernst. The Storm of Steel. Creighton, B., tr. from Ger. LC 75-22372. xiii, 319p. 1975. Repr. of 1929 ed. 24.00 (ISBN 0-86527-310-3). Fertig.
Loose, Gerhard. Ernst Junger. (World Authors Ser.: Germany: No. 323). 1974. lib. bdg. 10.95 (ISBN 0-8057-2479-6). Twayne.

JUNGLE ECOLOGY
Anderson, Kenneth. Jungles Long Ago. 1976. 14.95 (ISBN 0-04-799013-9). Allen Unwin.
Ayensu, Edward. Jungles. (Illus.). 208p. 1980. 35.00 (ISBN 0-517-54136-X). Crown.
Jungle. (MacDonald Educational Ser.). (Illus., Arabic.). 3.50 (ISBN 0-686-53079-9). Intl Bk Ctr.
Pope, Joyce. A Closer Look at Jungles. LC 78-4834. (Closer Look at Ser.). (Illus.). (gr. 5 up). 1978. PLB 7.45 s&l (ISBN 0-531-01485-1). Watts.
Seabrook, W. B. Jungle Ways. 1977. Repr. of 1931 ed. lib. bdg. 15.00 (ISBN 0-8414-7935-6). Folcroft.
Selsam, Millicent E. See Through the Jungle. LC 57-5018. 48p. (gr. 3-6). 1957. PLB 8.79 (ISBN 0-06-025366-5, HarpJ). Har-Row.

JUNGLE FAUNA
Booth, Eugene. In the Jungle. LC 77-7947. (A Raintree Spotlight Book). (Illus.). (gr. k-3). 1977. PLB 9.30 (ISBN 0-8393-0104-9). Raintree Child.
Perry, Richard. Life in Forest & Jungle. LC 74-21573. (The Many Worlds of Wildlife Ser). (Illus.). 256p. 1975. 9.95 (ISBN 0-8008-4799-7). Taplinger.
Seabrook, W. B. Jungle Ways. 1977. Repr. of 1931 ed. lib. bdg. 15.00 (ISBN 0-8414-7935-6). Folcroft.

JUNIOR COLLEGE LIBRARIES
Moore, Everett L., ed. Junior College Libraries: Development, Needs, & Perspectives. LC 68-56370. (A.C.R.L. Monograph Ser.: No. 30). (Orig.). 1969. pap. 3.00 (ISBN 0-8389-3090-5). ALA.
Pirie, James W., ed. Books for Junior College Libraries. LC 76-82133. 1970. 35.00 (ISBN 0-8389-0074-7). ALA.

Veit, Fritz. Community College Library. LC 72-843. (Contributions in Librarianship & Information Science Ser.: No. 14). (Illus.). 221p. 1975. lib. bdg. 14.75x (ISBN 0-8371-6412-5, VEJ/). Greenwood.

JUNIOR COLLEGES
see also Community Colleges

Bennett, John E., ed. Building Voluntary Support for the Two-Year College. 1979. pap. 16.50 (ISBN 0-89964-017-6). CASE.

Brawer, Florence B. Personality Characteristics of College & University Faculty: Implications for the Community College. 1968. 3.00 (ISBN 0-87117-076-0). Am Assn Comm Jr Coll.

Bushnell, David S. Priorities for Community Colleges: Organizing for Change. 1973. 14.95 (ISBN 0-07-009311-3, G). McGraw.

Cohen, Arthur M. & Brawer, Florence B. The Two-Year College Instructor Today. LC 77-83482. 1977. 23.95 (ISBN 0-03-039706-5). Praeger.

Cohen, Arthur M., et al. College Responses to Community Demands: The Community College in Challenging Times. LC 74-27912. (Higher Education Ser.). 224p. 1975. 12.95x (ISBN 0-87589-252-3). Jossey-Bass.

The Community, Technical, & Junior College in the United States. 96p. 1978. 3.50 (ISBN 0-686-70761-3, IIE). Unipub.

Drake, Sandra L. Research Report: A Study of Community & Junior College Boards of Trustees. 1977. 6.00 (ISBN 0-87117-080-9). Am Assn Comm Jr Coll.

Eliason, Carol. Women in Community & Junior Colleges: Report of a Study on Access to Occupational Education. 1977. pap. 5.00 (ISBN 0-87117-089-2). Am Assn Comm Jr Coll.

Gleazer, Edmund J., Jr. The Community College: Some Perspectives & Perceptions. 31p. 1974. pap. 1.00 (ISBN 0-87117-000-0). Am Assn Comm Jr Coll.

--Responding to the New Spirit of Learning. 1976. 1.50 (ISBN 0-87117-081-7). Am Assn Comm Jr Coll.

Gleazer, Edmund J., Jr., ed. American Junior Colleges. 8th ed. 1971. 20.00 (ISBN 0-8268-1209-0). ACE.

Harper, William A. Community, Junior, & Technical Colleges: A Public Relations Sourcebook. new ed. LC 77-1993. (Illus.). 1977. text ed. 19.95 (ISBN 0-89116-043-4). Hemisphere Pub.

Hawthorne, Mary E. & Perry, J. Warren. Community Colleges & Primary Health Care: A Study of Allied Health Education Report. 1974. pap. 1.75 (ISBN 0-87117-028-0). Am Assn Comm Jr Coll.

Hoover, Larry T. & Lund, Dennis W. Guidelines for Criminal Justice Programs in Community & Junior Colleges. 1977. 3.00 (ISBN 0-87117-066-3). Am Assn Comm Jr Coll.

Howe, Ray. The Community College Board of Trustees & Negotiations with Faculty. 1973. pap. 3.00 (ISBN 0-87117-007-8). Am Assn Comm Jr Coll.

International Development of the Junior College Idea. 1970. 3.50 (ISBN 0-87117-068-X). Am Assn Comm Jr Coll.

King, Francis P. Benefit Plans in Junior Colleges. 1971. pap. 6.00 (ISBN 0-87117-010-8). Am Assn Comm Jr Coll.

Kintzer, Frederick C. The Multi-Institution Junior College District. (ERIC Monographs Ser). 57p. 1969. pap. 2.00 (ISBN 0-87117-070-1). Am Assn Comm Jr Coll.

Koos, Leonard V. Junior College Movement. LC 72-126660. Repr. of 1925 ed. 17.00 (ISBN 0-404-03775-5). AMS Pr.

--Junior-College Movement. Repr. of 1925 ed. lib. bdg. 17.75x (ISBN 0-8371-3973-2, KOJM). Greenwood.

Korim, Andrew S. Government Careers & the Community College. 1971. pap. 4.00 (ISBN 0-87117-031-0). Am Assn Comm Jr Coll.

--Manpower Training in Community Colleges. 26p. 1974. pap. 2.50 (ISBN 0-87117-033-7). Am Assn Comm Jr Coll.

Morris, John T. Considerations in Establishing a Junior College. LC 79-177085. (Columbia University. Teachers College. Contributions to Education: No. 343). Repr. of 1929 ed. 17.50 (ISBN 0-404-55343-5). AMS Pr.

Myran, Gunder A. Community Services in the Community College. 1969. pap. 3.50 (ISBN 0-87117-013-2). Am Assn Comm Jr Coll.

O'Banion, Terry. Organizing Staff Development Programs That Work. 1978. 5.00 (ISBN 0-87117-074-4). Am Assn Comm Jr Coll.

Roueche, John E., et al. Accountability & the Community College - Directions for the 70's. 42p. 1972. pap. 4.00 (ISBN 0-87117-014-0). Am Assn Comm Jr Coll.

Sessions, H. Douglas & Verhoven, Peter J. Recreation Program Leadership & the Community College: Issues & Perspectives. 32p. 1970. pap. 2.50 (ISBN 0-87117-037-X). Am Assn Comm Jr Coll.

Swift, Joan W. Human Services Career Programs & the Community College. 1971. pap. 4.00 (ISBN 0-87117-039-6). Am Assn Comm Jr Coll.

JUNIOR COLLEGES–DIRECTORIES

Gleazer, Edmund J., Jr., ed. American Junior Colleges. 8th ed. 1971. 20.00 (ISBN 0-8268-1209-0). ACE.

JUNIOR HIGH SCHOOL STUDENTS

Ball, Gerry. Innerchange Conflict Management Resource Set for Junior High. 95.00 (ISBN 0-86584-028-8). Human Dev Train.

JUNIOR HIGH SCHOOLS
see also Middle Schools

Baughman, M. Dale, ed. Administration of the Junior High School. LC 66-28866. 1966. pap. text ed. 2.00x (ISBN 0-8134-6893-0, 6893). Interstate.

--Challenging Talented Junior High School Youth. pap. text ed. 1.50x (ISBN 0-8134-0589-0, 589). Interstate.

--Climate for Learning: Focus on the Teacher. 1964. pap. text ed. 2.00x (ISBN 0-8134-0083-X, 83). Interstate.

--Junior High School Staff Personnel. 1966. pap. text ed. 1.75x (ISBN 0-8134-6874-4, 6874). Interstate.

Beatley, B. Achievement in the Junior High School. Repr. of 1932 ed. pap. 15.50 (ISBN 0-384-03685-6). Johnson Repr.

Billett, Roy O. Teaching in Junior & Senior High School. 327p. 1963. 8.95x (ISBN 0-87471-219-X). Rowman.

--Teaching in Junior & Senior High School. (Quality Paperback: No. 94). (Illus., Orig.). 1967. pap. 3.45 (ISBN 0-8226-0094-3). Littlefield.

Blazier, William H. Lights! Action! Camera! Learn! LC 74-80347. 1974. 10.00 (ISBN 0-686-10561-3). Allison Pubs.

Briggs, Thomas H. The Junior High School. 350p. 1980. Repr. lib. bdg. 20.00 (ISBN 0-89760-045-2, Telegraph). Dynamic Learn Corp.

--The Junior High School. 1978. Repr. of 1920 ed. lib. bdg. 20.00 (ISBN 0-8492-3565-0). R West.

--The Junior High School. 1979. Repr. of 1920 ed. lib. bdg. 20.00 (ISBN 0-8495-0519-4). Arden Lib.

Bruner, Herbert B. The Junior High School at Work. LC 72-176606. (Columbia University. Teachers College. Contributions to Education: No. 177). Repr. of 1925 ed. 17.50 (ISBN 0-404-55177-7). AMS Pr.

Covert, Warren O. Illinois Junior High School - Survey of Practices. LC 74-102879. 1970. pap. text ed. 2.40x (ISBN 0-8134-1141-6, 1141). Interstate.

Cox, John H. The Junior High School & Its Curriculum. (Educational Ser.). 1929. Repr. 10.00 (ISBN 0-685-43509-1). Norwood Edns.

Edwards, Reese. The Middle School Experiment. (Students Library of Education). 112p. 1972. 8.50 (ISBN 0-7100-7329-1). Routledge & Kegan.

Gooch, Wilbur I. Junior High School Costs. LC 75-176813. (Columbia University. Teachers College. Contributions to Education: No. 604). Repr. of 1934 ed. 17.50 (ISBN 0-404-55604-3). AMS Pr.

Gruhn, William T. & Douglass, Harl R. The Modern Junior High School. 3rd ed. LC 78-110549. 424p. 1971. 21.50 (ISBN 0-8260-3695-3, 41985). Wiley.

--The Modern Junior High School. 3rd ed. LC 78-110549. 424p. 1971. 21.50 (ISBN 0-8260-3695-3, 41985). Wiley.

Illinois Junior High School Principals' Association. Go Where the Action Is: Teach in Junior High. 1968. pap. 0.25x (ISBN 0-8134-1068-1, 1068). Interstate.

Koos, Leonard V. The Junior High School. (Educational Ser.). 1921. Repr. 10.00 (ISBN 0-685-43553-9). Norwood Edns.

--Junior High School Trends. Repr. of 1955 ed. lib. bdg. 9.00x (ISBN 0-8371-2874-9, KOJH). Greenwood.

McEwen, E. C., et al. Language Proficiency in the Multiracial Junior School. (Research Reports Ser). 113p. 1975. pap. text ed. 12.50x (ISBN 0-85633-067-1, NFER). Humanities.

Nickerson, Neal C., Jr. Junior High Schools Are on the Way Out. LC 66-23023. 1966. pap. text ed. 1.25x (ISBN 0-8134-6876-0, 6876). Interstate.

Philadelphia Suburban School Study Council - Group B. Junior High School Years. LC 65-23203. 1965. pap. text ed. 1.50x (ISBN 0-8134-6830-2, 6830). Interstate.

Rodgers, Edwin R. The Things We Believe. LC 68-27391. 1968. pap. text ed. 1.00 (ISBN 0-910812-02-0). Johnny Reads.

Sinks, Thomas A. & Hess, John E., eds. Knowledge for What. LC 73-79438. 1969. pap. 2.50x (ISBN 0-8134-1102-5, 1102). Interstate.

Smith, Maurice M. Junior High School Education, Its Principles & Procedures. Repr. of 1942 ed. lib. bdg. 21.00x (ISBN 0-8371-3403-X, SMJH). Greenwood.

South Penn School Study Council. Developing Staff Attitudes in Junior High Schools. LC 68-19798. (Illus.). 32p. 1968. pap. text ed. 1.50x (ISBN 0-8134-1019-3, 1019). Interstate.

Spaulding, F. T. The Small Junior High School. (Harvard Studies in Education: Vol. 9). Repr. of 1927 ed. pap. 15.50 (ISBN 0-384-56950-1). Johnson Repr.

Sweat, Clifford H., ed. Why the Junior High-Middle School: Its Basic Function. 1977. pap. text ed. 3.95x (ISBN 0-8134-1947-6, 1947). Interstate.

Tink, A. Kerby, et al. Junior High Pressure Points in the Seventies. LC 73-82139. 1973. pap. 2.50x (ISBN 0-8134-1578-0, 1578). Interstate.

Van Til, William, et al. Modern Education for the Junior High School Years. 2nd. ed. LC 66-26209. 1967. text ed. 13.50 (ISBN 0-672-60640-2). Bobbs.

Zeller, Dale. The Relative Importance of Factors of Interest in Reading Materials for Junior High School Pupils. LC 77-177607. (Columbia University. Teachers College. Contributions to Education: No. 841). Repr. of 1941 ed. 17.50 (ISBN 0-404-55841-0). AMS Pr.

JUNIPERO, FRAY
see Serra, Junipero, Father, 1713-1784

JUNIPERUS, OF ASISSI, BROTHER, 13TH CENTURY

Benedict, Rex. Oh, Brother Juniper. (Illus.). (gr. 5-6). 1963. PLB 4.99 (ISBN 0-394-91457-0). Pantheon.

JUNIUS, PSEUD., AUTHOR OF THE LETTERS

Cordasco, Francesco. Junius Bibliography. rev ed. 1973. 19.50 (ISBN 0-8337-0664-0). B Franklin.

Ellegard, Alvar. Who Was Junius? LC 78-12218. 1979. Repr. of 1962 ed. lib. bdg. 14.50x (ISBN 0-313-21114-0, ELWJ). Greenwood.

Junius. The Letters of Junius. Cannon, John, ed. (Oxford English Texts Ser.). 1978. 69.00x (ISBN 0-19-812455-4). Oxford U Pr.

JUNK
see Waste Products

JUNK MAIL
see Advertising–Direct-Mail

JUNKERS J U 87 (BOMBERS)
see Stuka (Bombers)

JUPITER (PLANET)

Branley, Franklyn M. Jupiter: King of the Gods, Giant of the Planets. Buckley, Virginia, ed. (Illus.). 96p. 1981. 10.25 (ISBN 0-525-66739-3, 0995-300). Elsevier-Nelson.

Gehrels, T., ed. Jupiter. LC 75-36124. 1976. 38.50x (ISBN 0-8165-0530-6). U of Ariz Pr.

Hunt, Garry & Moore, Patrick. Jupiter. (Rand McNally Library of Astronomical Atlases for Amateur & Professional Observers). (Illus.). 96p. 1981. 14.95 (ISBN 0-528-81542-3). Rand.

Peek, Bertrand M. The Planet Jupiter: The Observer's Handbook. Moore, Patrick, ed. 256p. 1981. price not set (ISBN 0-571-18026-4, Pub. by Faber & Faber). Merrimack Bk Serv.

Shurkin, Joel N. Jupiter: The Star That Failed. LC 78-10885. 1979. 7.95 (ISBN 0-664-32642-0). Westminster.

JURA–DESCRIPTION AND TRAVEL

Michelin Green Travel Guide: Jura. (Fr.). 4.95 (ISBN 0-685-11380-9). French & Eur.

Michelin Guides & Maps. Michelin Green Guide to Jura. 2nd ed. (Green Guide Ser.). (Fr.). 1979. pap. 7.95 (ISBN 2-06-003391-8). Michelin.

JURAK LANGUAGE
see Nenets Language

JURASSIC PERIOD
see Geology, Stratigraphic–Jurassic

JUREIDINI, SAID M., 1866-1952

McRae, Jane C. Photographer in Lebanon: The Story of Said Jureidini. LC 69-19024. (Illus.). (gr. 4-5). 1969. pap. 0.75 (ISBN 0-8054-4313-4). Broadman.

JURIDICAL PSYCHOLOGY
see Psychology, Forensic

JURIEU, PIERRE, 1637-1713

Dodge, Guy H. The Political Theory of the Huguenots of the Dispersion. LC 79-159178. ix, 287p. 1971. Repr. of 1947 ed. lib. bdg. 15.50x (ISBN 0-374-92213-6). Octagon.

JURISDICTION
see also Conflict of Laws; Criminal Jurisdiction; Judgments

Ault, Warren O. Private Jurisdiction in England. LC 80-1998. Repr. of 1923 ed. 37.00 (ISBN 0-404-18550-9). AMS Pr.

Currie, David P. Federal Jurisdiction in a Nutshell. 2nd ed. LC 81-2051. (Nutshell Ser.). 230p. 1981. pap. text ed. write for info. West Pub.

Du Ponceau, Peter S. A Dissertation on the Nature & Extent of the Jurisdiction of the Courts of the U. S., Being a Valedictory Address Delivered... LC 79-37971. (American Law Ser.: The Formative Years). 296p. 1972. Repr. of 1824 ed. 16.00 (ISBN 0-405-04007-5). Arno.

Forrester, Ray & Moye, John E. Federal Jurisdiction & Procedure: Nineteen Eighty-One Supplement to Cases & Materials. 3rd ed. (American Casebook Ser.). 87p. 1981. pap. text ed. 3.95 (ISBN 0-686-71664-7). West Pub.

--Supplement to Federal Jurisdicion & Procedure, Cases, & Materials, 1981. 3rd ed. (American Casebook Ser.). 87p. 1977. pap. text ed. 3.95 (ISBN 0-686-74737-2). West Pub.

Friendly, Henry J. Federal Jurisdiction: A General View. (James Carpenter Lecture Ser.). 199p. 1973. 15.00x (ISBN 0-231-03741-4). Columbia U Pr.

Kelly, John M. Studies on the Civil Judicature of the Roman Empire. 1976. 14.50x (ISBN 0-19-825337-0). Oxford U Pr.

McAlister, Lyle. The Fuero Militar in New Spain 1764-1800. LC 74-6753. 117p. 1974. Repr. of 1957 ed. lib. bdg. 15.00 (ISBN 0-8371-7554-2, MCFM). Greenwood.

Post, C. Gordon. Supreme Court & Political Questions. LC 74-87386. (American History, Politics & Law Ser). 1969. Repr. of 1936 ed. lib. bdg. 19.50 (ISBN 0-306-71610-0). Da Capo.

Pound, Roscoe. Contemporary Juristic Theory. viii, 83p. 1981. Repr. of 1940 ed. lib. bdg. 15.00x (ISBN 0-8377-1008-1). Rothman.

Schussler, Theodore. Federal Courts, Jurisdiction & Practice. (Orig.). 1967. pap. 4.50x (ISBN 0-87526-036-5). Gould.

Wendell, Mitchell. Relations Between Federal & State Courts. LC 68-58637. (Columbia University. Studies in the Social Sciences: No. 555). Repr. of 1949 ed. 22.50 (ISBN 0-404-51555-X). AMS Pr.

JURISDICTION (INTERNATIONAL LAW)
see also Arbitration, International; International Courts

Holt, George C. The Concurrent Jurisdiction of the Federal & State Courts. xxvi, 237p. 1980. Repr. of 1888 ed. lib. bdg. 24.00x (ISBN 0-8377-0630-0). Rothman.

Tomasic, Roman & Feeley, Malcolm, eds. Neighborhood Justice: An Assessment of an Emerging Idea. (Professional Ser.). (Illus.). 320p. 1981. text ed. 27.50x (ISBN 0-582-28253-5). Longman.

JURISDICTION (CANON LAW)
see also Bishops

JURISDICTION, EXTERRITORIAL
see Exterritoriality

JURISDICTION OVER SHIPS AT SEA
see also Search, Right of

JURISPRUDENCE
see also Law; Law–Methodology; Law–Philosophy; Law and Politics; Public Law; Sociological Jurisprudence

Allen, Carleton K. Law in the Making. 7th ed. 1964. pap. 16.95x (ISBN 0-19-881029-6, OPB29). Oxford U Pr.

American Society for Legal History. Essays in Jurisprudence in Honor of Roscoe Pound. Newman, Ralph A., ed. LC 73-10750. (Illus.). 670p. 1973. Repr. of 1962 ed. lib. bdg. 29.50x (ISBN 0-8371-7023-0, EJRP). Greenwood.

Aristotelian Society For The Systematic Study Of Philosophy. Problems in Psychotherapy & Jurisprudence: Proceedings, Supplementary Vol. 29. Repr. of 1955 ed. 14.00 (ISBN 0-384-47979-0); pap. 9.00 (ISBN 0-384-47980-4). Johnson Repr.

Austin, John. Lectures on Jurisprudence, or the Philosophy of Positive Law. 1976. Repr. of 1879 ed. 69.00 (ISBN 0-403-06116-4, Regency). Scholarly.

Bentham, Jeremy. Limits of Jurisprudence Defined. LC 71-100143. Repr. of 1945 ed. lib. bdg. 18.75 (ISBN 0-8371-3249-5, BEJU). Greenwood.

Bodenheimer, Edgar. Jurisprudence: The Philosophy & Method of the Law. rev. ed. LC 74-77182. 1974. text ed. 25.00x (ISBN 0-674-49001-0). Harvard U Pr.

Buckland, W. W. Some Reflections on Jurisprudence. viii, 118p. 1974. Repr. of 1945 ed. 13.50 (ISBN 0-208-01407-1, Archon). Shoe String.

Cahn, Edmond. The Sense of Injustice. (Midland Bks.: No. 55). (Illus.). 200p. 1964. pap. 2.95x (ISBN 0-253-20055-5). Ind U Pr.

Cairns, Huntington. Law & the Social Sciences. LC 69-18855. Repr. of 1935 ed. lib. bdg. 12.00x (ISBN 0-678-04536-4). Kelley.

--Law & the Social Sciences. LC 70-100121. xiv, 279p. 1970. Repr. of 1935 ed. text ed. 12.00x (ISBN 0-8377-2001-X). Rothman.

--Theory of Legal Science. LC 70-100121. Repr. of 1941 ed. 8.00x (ISBN 0-678-04525-9). Kelley.

Caparros, Ernest & Goulet, Jean. Documentation Juridique: Referenceset Abreviations. (Fr.). 1973. 7.50 (ISBN 2-7637-6616-1, Pub. by Laval). Intl Schol Bk Serv.

Cardozo, Benjamin N. Paradoxes of Legal Science. LC 76-104241. Repr. of 1928 ed. lib. bdg. 15.00x (ISBN 0-8371-3263-0, CALS). Greenwood.

Clark, E. C. Practical Jurisprudence: A Comment on Austin. xii, 403p. 1980. Repr. of 1883 ed. lib. bdg. 30.00x (ISBN 0-8377-0427-8). Rothman.
Coffey, Alan R., et al. An Introduction to the Criminal Justice System and Process. (Criminal Justice Ser.). (Illus.). 384p. 1974. ref. ed. 16.95 (ISBN 0-13-481127-5). P-H.
Cohen, Felix S. Legal Conscience, Selected Papers. Cohen, Lucy K., ed. 1970. Repr. of 1960 ed. 27.50 (ISBN 0-208-00813-6, Archon). Shoe String.
Cohn, G. Existentialism & Legal Science. LC 67-14397. 1967. 12.00 (ISBN 0-379-00302-3). Oceana.
Columbia Law Review. Essays on Jurisprudence from the Columbia Law Review. LC 77-10131. 1977. Repr. of 1963 ed. lib. bdg. 29.00x (ISBN 0-8371-9776-7, CLEJ). Greenwood.
Cowan, Thomas A., ed. American Jurisprudence Reader. LC 56-12585. (Orig.). 1956. 7.50 (ISBN 0-379-11308-2); pap. 2.50 (ISBN 0-685-18982-1). Oceana.
De Montesquieu, Charles. Esprit des lois, 2 Vols. (Fr). pap. 2.95 ea. Larousse.
Dhyani, S. N. Jurisprudence: A Study of Indian Legal Theory. 217p. 1972. 9.50x (ISBN 0-8002-1624-5). Intl Pubns Serv.
Fortescue, John. De Natura Legis Naturae, et De Ejus Censura in Succesione Regnorum Suprema: The Works of Sir John Fortescue, London, 1869. (Classics of the Modern Era: Vol. 1). 296p. 1980. lib. bdg. 50.00 (ISBN 0-8240-4600-5). Garland Pub.
Gareis, Karl Von. Introduction to the Science of Law. Kocourek, Albert, tr. LC 68-54749. (Modern Legal Philosophy Ser.: Vol. 1). Repr. of 1911 ed. 18.00x (ISBN 0-678-04513-5). Kelley.
Gorecki, Jan, ed. Sociology & Jurisprudence of Leon Petrazycki. LC 75-38551. (Office of International Programs & Studies Ser). 150p. 1975. 12.50 (ISBN 0-252-00525-2). U of Ill Pr.
Gray, John C. Nature & Sources of the Law. 2nd ed. 8.50 (ISBN 0-8446-2156-0). Peter Smith.
Hall. Foundations of Jurisprudence. 1973. 15.00 (ISBN 0-672-81849-3, Bobbs-Merrill Law). Michie-Bobbs.
Hall, Jerome. Readings in Jurisprudence. 1938. 15.00 (ISBN 0-672-81013-1, Bobbs-Merrill Law). Michie-Bobbs.
Jones, John W. Historical Introduction to the Theory of Law. Repr. of 1940 ed. lib. bdg. 17.50x (ISBN 0-8371-2810-2, JOTL). Greenwood.
--Historical Introduction to the Theory of Law. LC 72-96337. Repr. of 1940 ed. 11.50x (ISBN 0-678-04534-8). Kelley.
Kisch, Guido. Gestalten und Probleme aus Humanismus und Jurisprudenz: Neue Studien und Texte. (Ger). 1969. 40.00x (ISBN 3-11-002566-3). De Gruyter.
Korkunov, Nikolai M. General Theory of Law. rev ed. Hastings, W. G., tr. LC 68-54752. (Modern Legal Philosophy Ser.: Vol. 4). Repr. of 1922 ed. 18.00x (ISBN 0-678-04516-X). Kelley.
Lauterpacht, Hersh. Private Law Sources & Analogies of International Law, with Special Reference to International Arbitration. 1970. Repr. of 1927 ed. 22.50 (ISBN 0-208-00814-4, Archon). Shoe String.
Llewellyn, Karl N. Jurisprudence: Realism in Theory & Practice. LC 62-12634. 1962. 17.50x (ISBN 0-226-48787-3). U of Chicago Pr.
Maloof, A. J. The Layman's Advocate. 1979. 8.95 (ISBN 0-533-03225-3). Vantage.
Mayda, Jaro. Francois Geny & Modern Jurisprudence. LC 78-17864. 1978. 22.50x (ISBN 0-8071-0389-6). La State U Pr.
Mermin, Samuel. Law & the Legal System: An Introduction. 1973. pap. 7.95 (ISBN 0-316-56730-2). Little.
Miller, Perry, ed. Legal Mind in America: From Independence to the Civil War. LC 63-13082. 1970. pap. 5.95 (ISBN 0-8014-9097-9, CP97). Cornell U Pr.
Miller, William G. The Data of Jurisprudence. xiv, 477p. 1980. Repr. of 1903 ed. lib. bdg. 42.50x (ISBN 0-8377-0835-4). Rothman.
Miraglia, Luigi. Comparative Legal Philosophy. Lisle, John, tr. LC 68-54751. (Modern Legal Philosophy Ser.: Vol. 3). Repr. of 1912 ed. 25.00x (ISBN 0-678-04515-1). Kelley.
Montesquieu. The Spirit of Laws: A Compendium of the First English Editon with an English Translation of "an Essay on Causes Affecting Mind & Characters", 1737-1743. Carrithers, David W., ed. (No. 192). 1978. 34.50x (ISBN 0-520-02566-0); pap. 6.95x (ISBN 0-520-03455-4, CAMPUS SER., NO. 192). U of Cal Pr.
Montesquieu, C. de. Spirit of the Laws. (Library of Classic: No. 9). pap. text ed. 5.25 (ISBN 0-02-849270-6). Hafner.
Montesquieu, Charles de. De l'Espirit des Lois: Les Grands Themes. 1970. 4.95 (ISBN 0-686-54781-0). French & Eur.
Montesquieu, Charles-Louis. De L'esprit Des Lois, 2 tomes. Truc, ed. 1962. Set. pap. 13.90 (ISBN 0-685-11129-6). French & Eur.
Morris, Herbert, ed. Freedom & Responsibility: Readings in Philosophy & Law. 1961. 15.00x (ISBN 0-8047-0067-2). Stanford U Pr.
Noonan, John T., Jr. Persons & Masks of the Law: Cardoza, Holmes, Jefferson & Wythe As Makers of the Masks. LC 75-30991. 1976. 10.00 (ISBN 0-374-23076-5); pap. 3.95 (ISBN 0-374-51396-1). FS&G.
Paton, George Whitecross. A Textbook of Jurisprudence. 4th ed. Paton, G. W. & Dorham, David P., eds. 640p. 1972. text ed. 24.00x (ISBN 0-19-825314-1). Oxford U Pr.
Pollack, Ervin H. Jurisprudence: Principles & Applications. LC 78-11627. 1979. 35.00x (ISBN 0-8142-0247-0). Ohio St U Pr.
Pollock, Frederick. First Book of Jurisprudence. 1967. 23.50 (ISBN 0-8337-2803-2). B Franklin.
--Jurisprudence & Legal Essays. LC 77-28352. 1978. Repr. of 1961 ed. lib. bdg. 28.25x (ISBN 0-313-20249-4, POJU). Greenwood.
Pound, Roscoe. Law & Morals. LC 70-96339. Repr. of 1924 ed. 9.00x (ISBN 0-678-04532-1). Kelley.
--Law & Morals. LC 70-96339. ix, 144p. 1970. Repr. of 1924 ed. text ed. 17.50x (ISBN 0-8377-2501-1). Rothman.
Prescot, Julian. Case for Hearing. 13.50x (ISBN 0-392-02514-0, LTB). Soccer.
Schwarz-Liebermann Von Wahlendorf, H. A. Fondements et Principes D'un Ordre Juridique Naissant: Essai De Philosophie Empirique Du Droit. 1972. 47.50x (ISBN 90-2796-957-4). Mouton.
Scott, James B. Law, the State & the International Community. Repr. of 1939 ed. lib. bdg. 38.00x (ISBN 0-8371-2809-9, SCLI). Greenwood.
Sethna, Minocher J., ed. Synthetic Jurisprudence. LC 62-11118. 1962. 10.00 (ISBN 0-379-00113-6). Oceana.
Shartel, Burke. Our Legal System & How It Operates. LC 73-173666. (American Constitutional & Legal History Ser.). 628p. 1972. Repr. of 1951 ed. lib. bdg. 59.50 (ISBN 0-306-70411-0). Da Capo.
Shuchman, Philip. Cohen & Cohen's Readings in Jurisprudence & Legal Philosophy. 2nd ed. 1099p. 1979. text ed. 25.00 (ISBN 0-316-78877-5). Little.
Simpson, Alfred W., ed. Oxford Essays in Jurisprudence, Vol. 2. 315p. 1973. text ed. 45.00x (ISBN 0-19-825313-3). Oxford U Pr.
Smith, Adam. Lectures on Jurisprudence. Meek, R. L. & Raphael, D. D., eds. (The Glasgow Edition of the Works & Correspondence of Adam Smith Ser.). 1978. 75.00x (ISBN 0-19-828188-9). Oxford U Pr.
Stammler, Rudolf. Theory of Justice. Husik, Issac, tr. LC 68-54755. (Modern Legal Philosophy Ser.: Vol. 8). Repr. of 1925 ed. 20.00x (ISBN 0-678-04519-4). Kelley.
Stone, Harlan F. Law & Its Administration. LC 33-17836. Repr. of 1924 ed. 20.00 (ISBN 0-404-06284-9). AMS Pr.
Stone, Julius. Legal System & Lawyers' Reasonings. 1964. 18.75x (ISBN 0-8047-0214-4). Stanford U Pr.
Summers, Robert S. & Howard, C. Law, Its Nature, Functions & Limits. 2nd ed. (Illus.). 1024p. 1972. text ed. 22.95 (ISBN 0-13-526400-6). P-H.
Vinogradoff, Paul. Outlines of Historical Jurisprudence, 2 vols. LC 74-177869. Repr. of 1922 ed. Set. 34.50 (ISBN 0-404-06784-0). AMS Pr.
Wildhorn, Sorrel, et al. Indicators of Justice. LC 76-57898. (Illus.). 1977. 16.00 (ISBN 0-669-01363-3); pap. 7.95 (ISBN 0-669-01361-7). Lexington Bks.

JURISPRUDENCE–HISTORY

Carpenter, William S. Foundations of Modern Jurisprudence. LC 58-5314. 1958. 24.00x (ISBN 0-89197-174-2); pap. text ed. 12.95x (ISBN 0-89197-175-0). Irvington.
Faulkner, Robert K. The Jurisprudence of John Marshall. LC 80-14281. xii, 307p. 1980. Repr. of 1968 ed. lib. bdg. 25.50x (ISBN 0-313-22508-7, FAJU). Greenwood.
Fouillee, A., et al. Modern French Legal Philosophy. Scott, Mrs. Franklin W. & Chamberlin, Joseph P., trs. LC 68-54754. (Modern Legal Philosophy Ser.: Vol. 7). Repr. of 1916 ed. 20.00x (ISBN 0-678-04518-6). Kelley.
--Modern French Legal Philosophy. (Modern Legal Philosophy Ser: Vol. 7). lxvi, 578p. 1969. Repr. of 1916 ed. 20.00x (ISBN 0-8377-2126-1). Rothman.
Haakonssen, Knud. The Science of a Legislator: The Natural Jurisprudence of David Hume & Adam Smith. LC 80-42001. (Illus.). 256p. Date not set. price not set (ISBN 0-521-23891-9). Cambridge U Pr.
Harding, Arthur L., ed. Administration of Justice in Retrospect: Roscoe Pound's 1906 Address in a Half Century of Experience. LC 57-10684. (Studies in Jurisprudence: No. 4). 1957. 4.00 (ISBN 0-87074-066-0). SMU Press.
Lee, Guy C. Historical Jurisprudence: An Introduction to the Systematic Study of the Development of Law. xvi, 517p. 1981. Repr. of 1900 ed. lib. bdg. 37.50x (ISBN 0-8377-0810-9). Rothman.
Prassel, Frank R. The Western Peace Officer: A Legacy of Law & Order. 330p. 1980. pap. 7.95 (ISBN 0-8061-1694-3). U of Okla Pr.
Quint, Emanuel B. & Hecht, Neil S. Jewish Jurisprudence Its Sources & Modern Applications, Vol. 1. 268p. 1980. 31.00 (ISBN 3-7186-0054-4); pap. 11.00 (ISBN 3-7186-0055-2). Harwood Academic.
Reuschlein, Harold G. Jurisprudence: Its American Prophets; a Survey of Taught Jurisprudence. LC 70-158741. 1971. Repr. of 1951 ed. lib. bdg. 25.75x (ISBN 0-8371-6180-0). Greenwood.
Ullmann, Walter. Jurisprudence in the Middle Ages. 390p. 1980. 75.00x (ISBN 0-86078-065-1, Pub. by Variorum England). State Mutual Bk.

JURISPRUDENCE, COMPARATIVE

see Comparative Law

JURISPRUDENCE, DENTAL

see Dental Jurisprudence

JURISPRUDENCE, ETHNOLOGICAL

see Ethnological Jurisprudence

JURISPRUDENCE, MEDICAL

see Medical Jurisprudence

JURISTIC PERSONS

see also Charitable Uses, Trusts and Foundations; Corporation Law; Corporations, Government; Corporations, Nonprofit; Municipal Corporations; Unincorporated Societies

JURISTIC PERSONS (INTERNATIONAL LAW)

see Persons (International Law)

JURISTIC PERSONS, FOREIGN

see Corporations, Foreign

JURISTIC PSYCHOLOGY

see Law–Psychology; Psychology, Forensic

JURISTS

see Lawyers

JURY

see also Grand Jury; Instructions to Juries

Baldwin, John & McConville, Michael. Jury Trials. 1979. 14.95x (ISBN 0-19-825350-8). Oxford U Pr.
Bloomstein, Morris J. Verdict: The Jury System. rev. ed. LC 72-1537. (gr. 9 up). 1972. 5.95 (ISBN 0-396-06608-9). Dodd.
Forsyth, William. History of Trial by Jury. 2nd ed. LC 77-168705. (Research & Source Works Ser.: No. 807). 1971. Repr. of 1878 ed. lib. bdg. 23.50 (ISBN 0-8337-1215-2). B Franklin.
Francis, Philip. How to Serve on a Jury. 2nd ed. LC 53-5766. (Legal Almanac Ser: No. 31). (Orig.). 1979. 5.95 (ISBN 0-379-11122-5). Oceana.
Joiner, Charles W. Civil Justice & the Jury. LC 72-6684. 238p. 1972. Repr. of 1962 ed. lib. bdg. 15.50x (ISBN 0-8371-6495-8, JOCJ). Greenwood.
Justices & Juries in Colonial America: Two Accounts, 1680-1722. LC 77-37968. (American Law Ser.: The Formative Years). 366p. 1972. Repr. of 1972 ed. 18.00 (ISBN 0-405-03995-6). Arno.
Kalven, Harry, Jr. & Zeisel, Hans. American Jury. LC 70-149361. 1971. pap. 7.95 (ISBN 0-226-42317-4, P395, Phoen). U of Chicago Pr.
--The American Jury. 1966. 17.50 (ISBN 0-316-48247-1). Little.
Kroll, John H. Athenian Bronze Allotment Plates. LC 79-162636. (Loeb Classical Monographs Ser). 370p. 1972. 18.50x (ISBN 0-674-05092-4). Harvard U Pr.
Lesser, Maximus. The Historical Development of the Jury System. 1976. lib. bdg. 34.95 (ISBN 0-8490-1957-5). Gordon Pr.
Moore, Lloyd. The Jury: History of the Trial Jury. 1973. 13.50 (ISBN 0-87084-576-4). Anderson Pub C.
National Center for State Courts. Facets of the Jury System: A Survey. Prescott, Elizabeth, ed. 1976. pap. 3.00 (ISBN 0-89656-003-1, R0028). Natl Ctr St Courts.
Parker, L. Craig, Jr. Legal Psychology: Eyewitness Testimony - Jury Behavior. 196p. 1980. 22.75 (ISBN 0-398-04054-0). C C Thomas.
Saks, Michael J. Jury Verdicts: The Role of Group Size & Social Decision Rule. LC 76-44569. 1977. 16.95 (ISBN 0-669-01100-2). Lexington Bks.
Simon, Rita J. The Jury & the Defense of Insanity. 269p. 1967. 16.00 (ISBN 0-316-79149-0). Little.
--The Jury: Its Role in American Society. LC 77-17682. 176p. 1980. 18.95x (ISBN 0-669-02086-9). Lexington Bks.
--The Jury System in America: A Critical Overview. LC 74-82999. (Sage Criminal Justice System Annuals: Vol. 4). 2560p. 1975. 22.50 (ISBN 0-8039-0382-0); pap. 9.95 (ISBN 0-8039-0504-1). Sage.
Spooner, Lysander. Essay on the Trial by Jury. LC 70-166097. (Civil Liberties in American History Ser). 1971. Repr. of 1852 ed. lib. bdg. 25.50 (ISBN 0-306-70320-3). Da Capo.
--Let's Abolish Government: An Original Arno Press Compilation. LC 73-172232. (Right Wing Individualist Tradition in America Ser). 1971. Repr. of 1898 ed. 22.00 (ISBN 0-405-00441-9). Arno.
State Bar of Texas Pattern Jury Charges Committee. Texas Pattern Jury Charges: Vol. 1. 290p. 1969. 26.00 (ISBN 0-938160-00-1, 6307). State Bar TX.
--Texas Pattern Jury Charges: 1973 Cumulation Supplement, Vol. 1. 91p. 1973. pap. 6.50 (ISBN 0-938160-01-X, 6316). State Bar TX.
Van Dyke, Jon M. Jury Selection Procedures: Our Uncertain Commitment to Representative Juries. LC 76-43342. 1977. professional ref. 18.50 (ISBN 0-88410-237-8). Ballinger Pub.
Villasenor, Victor. Jury: The People Vs. Juan Corona. 1977. 8.95 (ISBN 0-316-90300-0). Little.
Zerman, Melvyn B. Beyond a Reasonable Doubt: Inside the America Injury System. (Illus.). 224p. (gr. 7 up). 1981. 9.95 (ISBN 0-690-04094-6, TYC J); PLB 9.89 (ISBN 0-690-04095-4). Har-Row.

JURY–GREAT BRITAIN

Bentham, Jeremy. Elements of the Art of Packing As Applied to Special Juries Particularly in Cases of Libel Law. Berkowitz, David & Thorne, Samuel, eds. LC 77-86672. (Classics of English Legal History in the Modern Era Ser.: Vol. 116). 1979. Repr. of 1821 ed. lib. bdg. 40.00 (ISBN 0-8240-3153-9). Garland Pub.
Spooner, Lysander. Essay on the Trial by Jury. LC 70-166097. (Civil Liberties in American History Ser). 1971. Repr. of 1852 ed. lib. bdg. 25.50 (ISBN 0-306-70320-3). Da Capo.
--Let's Abolish Government: An Original Arno Press Compilation. LC 73-172232. (Right Wing Individualist Tradition in America Ser). 1971. Repr. of 1898 ed. 22.00 (ISBN 0-405-00441-9). Arno.

JUSTICE

see also Due Process of Law; Equality before the Law; Fairness

Ackerman, Bruce A. Social Justice in the Liberal State. LC 80-12618. 408p. 1981. pap. 6.95x (ISBN 0-300-02757-5, Y-401). Yale U Pr.
Arzt, Max. Justice & Mercy. 4.95 (ISBN 0-87677-140-1). Hartmore.
Barry, Brian. The Liberal Theory of Justice: A Critical Examination of the Principal Doctrines in - A Theory of Justice by John Rawls. (Illus.). 180p. 1973. pap. text ed. 4.95x (ISBN 0-19-875032-3). Oxford U Pr.
Bodenheimer, Edgar. Treatise on Justice. LC 67-11987. 1968. 10.00 (ISBN 0-8022-0145-8). Philos Lib.
Bowie, Norman E. & Simon, R. L. The Individual & the Political Order: An Introduction to Social & Political Philosophy. 1977. pap. text ed. 11.95 (ISBN 0-13-457143-6). P-H.
Cahn, Edmond N. Confronting Injustice: The Edmond Cahn Reader. Cahn, Lenore L., ed. LC 72-8525. (Essay Index Reprint Ser.). 1972. Repr. of 1966 ed. 27.00 (ISBN 0-8369-7308-9). Arno.
Cardozo, Benjamin N. Paradoxes of Legal Science. LC 76-104241. Repr. of 1928 ed. lib. bdg. 15.00x (ISBN 0-8371-3263-0, CALS). Greenwood.
Daniels, Norman. Reading Rawls. LC 74-25908. 1975. 15.00x (ISBN 0-465-06854-5); pap. 5.95x (ISBN 0-465-06855-3). Basic.
Eisenhower, Dwight D. Peace with Justice. LC 61-7096. 273p. 20.00x (ISBN 0-231-02472-X). Columbia U Pr.
Fenton, Thomas, ed. Education for Justice (Resource Manual) LC 74-83519. 464p. 1975. pap. 7.95x (ISBN 0-88344-119-5). Orbis Bks.
Fisher, Kenneth P. & Ivie, Charles C. Franchising Justice: The Office of Economic Opportunity Legal Services Program & Traditional Legal Aid. (Legal Services for the Poor Ser). 18p. (Orig.). 1971. pap. 2.00 (ISBN 0-910058-06-7). Am Bar Foun.
Freeman, A. V. International Responsibility of States for Denial of Justice. LC 39-17013. Repr. of 1938 ed. 30.00 (ISBN 0-527-31400-5). Kraus Repr.
Friedrich, Carl J., ed. Justice: Nomos Ser. (No. 6). 336p. 1974. 15.00x (ISBN 0-88311-030-X). Lieber-Atherton.
Galston, William A. Justice & the Human Good. LC 79-25945. 336p. 1980. lib. bdg. 20.00x (ISBN 0-226-27963-4). U of Chicago Pr.
Gard, Wayne. Frontier Justice. (Illus.). 324p. 1981. 17.50 (ISBN 0-8061-0194-6); pap. 8.95 (ISBN 0-8061-1755-9). U of Okla Pr.

Gorman, Walter H. Dynamic Psychiatry & the Sense of Justice. LC 70-96982. (Illus.). 320p. 1974. 17.50 (ISBN 0-87527-106-5). Green.

Harrison, Jonathan. Hume's Theory of Justice. 320p. 1981. 49.50x (ISBN 0-19-824619-6). Oxford U Pr.

Havelock, Eric A. The Greek Concept of Justice: From Its Shadow in Homer to Its Substance in Plato. LC 78-6064. 1978. 18.50x (ISBN 0-674-36220-9). Harvard U Pr.

Hayek, F. A. Law, Legislation, & Liberty: Vol. 2: the Mirage of Social Justice, Vol. 2. LC 73-82488. (Multi-Volumed Set Ser.). 1977. lib. bdg. 15.00x (ISBN 0-226-32082-0); pap. 5.95 (ISBN 0-226-32083-9, P799). U of Chicago Pr.

Hessel, Dieter T. Beyond Survival: Bread & Justice in Christian Perspective. (Orig.). 1977. pap. 4.25 (ISBN 0-377-00068-X). Friend Pr.

Justice in the Modern World. (Franciscan Educational Conferences Ser). 1964. pap. 4.50 (ISBN 0-685-77533-X). Franciscan Herald.

Kaplan, Morton A. Alienation & Identification. LC 76-8146. 1976. 14.95 (ISBN 0-02-916790-6). Free Pr.

--Justice, Human Nature, & Political Obligation. LC 76-8145. 1976. 16.95 (ISBN 0-02-916890-2). Free Pr.

Kelsen, Hans. What Is Justice? & Justice, Law, & Politics in the Mirror of Science. (California Library Reprint Series: No. 20). 1971. 30.00x (ISBN 0-520-01925-3). U of Cal Pr.

Kemenka, Eugene & Tay, Alice E. Justice. LC 79-22174. 1980. 18.50x (ISBN 0-312-44945-3). St Martin.

Kiefer, Howard & Munitz, Milton, eds. Ethics & Social Justice. (Contemporary Philosophic Thought: Vol. 4). 1970. 24.00 (ISBN 0-87395-054-2); microfiche 24.00 (ISBN 0-87395-154-9). State U NY Pr.

Kuhn, Margaret E. Get Out There & Do Something About Injustice. 128p. 1972. pap. 1.95 (ISBN 0-377-02121-0). Friend Pr.

Lehandrus, Lawrence F. The Idea & the Philosophy of Justice. (Illus.). 142p. 1980. 49.85 (ISBN 0-89266-255-7). Am Classical Coll Pr.

Lucas, John R. On Justice. (Illus.). 278p. text ed. 24.95x (ISBN 0-19-824598-X). Oxford U Pr.

McBarnet, Doreen. Conviction: The Law, the State & the Construction of Justice. (Oxford Sociolegal Studies). 1981. text ed. 50.00 (ISBN 0-333-25536-4, Pub. by Macmillan England). Humanities.

McCuen, Gary E., ed. American Justice: Is America a Just Society? (Opposing Viewpoints Ser.: Vol. 9). (Illus.). 1975. lib. bdg. 8.95 (ISBN 0-912616-34-2); pap. text ed. 3.95 (ISBN 0-912616-15-6). Greenhaven.

McGeachy, Pat. Beyond the Facts, Acts. (Orig.). 1973. pap. 1.95 (ISBN 0-377-03051-1). Friend Pr.

Morris, Clarence. Justification of the Law. LC 77-153424. 1971-72. 15.00x (ISBN 0-8122-7639-6); pap. 5.95x (ISBN 0-8122-1030-1, Pa Paperbacks). U of Pa Pr.

Niebuhr, Reinhold. Justice & Mercy. LC 73-18704. 1976. pap. 2.95 (ISBN 0-06-066172-0, RD 191, HarpR). Har-Row.

--Love & Justice: Selections from the Shorter Writings of Reinhold Niebuhr. Robertson, D. B., ed. 6.75 (ISBN 0-8446-2659-7). Peter Smith.

O'Brien, David J. & Shannon, Thomas A., eds. Renewing the Earth: Catholic Documents on Peace, Justice & Liberation. LC 76-52008. 1977. pap. 3.95 (ISBN 0-385-12954-8, Im). Doubleday.

Perelman, Chaim. Idea of Justice & the Problems of Argument. (International Library of Philosophy & Scientific Method). 1963. text ed. 13.75x (ISBN 0-7100-3610-8). Humanities.

Rawls, John. Theory of Justice. LC 73-168432. (Illus.). 1971. 20.00x (ISBN 0-674-88010-2, Belknap Pr); pap. 7.50 (ISBN 0-674-88014-5). Harvard U Pr.

Shoemaker, Dennis E. The Global Connection: Local Action for World Justice. (Orig.). 1977. pap. 3.95 (ISBN 0-377-00069-8). Friend Pr.

Silva, John W., ed. An Introduction to Crime & Justice. LC 72-86200. 1973. 29.00x (ISBN 0-8422-5049-2); pap. text ed. 9.50x (ISBN 0-8422-0223-4). Irvington.

Snyder, Leslie. Justice or Revolution. LC 78-74594. 1979. 12.95 (ISBN 0-916728-20-X). Bks in Focus.

Sokol, Ronald P. Justice After Darwin. LC 75-9170. 141p. 1975. 8.95 (ISBN 0-87215-167-0). Michie-Bobbs.

Stammler, Rudolf. Theory of Justice. (Modern Legal Philosophy Ser: Vol. 8). xli, 591p. 1969. Repr. of 1925 ed. 20.00x (ISBN 0-8377-2603-4). Rothman.

Sterba, James. The Demands of Justice. LC 80-10791. 192p. 1981. text ed. 10.95 (ISBN 0-268-00847-7); pap. text ed. 5.95 (ISBN 0-268-00848-5, NDP-258). U of Notre Dame Pr.

Stone, Julius. Human Law & Human Justice. 1965. 18.75x (ISBN 0-8047-0215-2). Stanford U Pr.

Strick, Anne. Injustice for All: How Our Adversary System of Law Victimizes Us & Subverts True Justice. 1978. pap. 3.95 (ISBN 0-14-005024-8). Penguin.

Susman, Jackwell, ed. Crime & Justice, 2 vols. (An AMS Anthology). 1972-1974. Set. lib. bdg. 60.00 (ISBN 0-404-10200-X); Vol. 1. lib. bdg. 30.00 (ISBN 0-404-10201-8); Vol. 2. lib. bdg. 30.00 (ISBN 0-404-10202-6); Vol. 2. pap. 5.95 (ISBN 0-404-10252-2). AMS Pr.

Tapp, June L. & Levine, Felice. Law, Justice, & the Individual in Society. LC 77-24022. 1977. 18.95 (ISBN 0-03-012156-6, HoltC). HR&W.

Taylor, Telford, et al. Perspectives on Justice. (Julius Rosenthal Memorial Lectures Ser.: 1975). 1975. 9.95x (ISBN 0-8101-0453-9). Northwestern U Pr.

Thomas Aquinas, Saint Political Ideas of St. Thomas Aquinas. Bigongiari, Dino, ed. (Library of Classics Ser.: No. 15). 1973. pap. text ed. 4.95 (ISBN 0-02-840380-0). Hafner.

Thompson, Hugo W. Love-Justice. 1970. 6.95 (ISBN 0-8158-0032-0); pap. 3.95 (ISBN 0-8158-0242-0). Chris Mass.

Tillich, Paul. Love, Power & Justice. 1960. pap. 3.95 (ISBN 0-19-500222-9, GB). Oxford U Pr.

Tomasic, Roman & Feeley, Malcolm M., eds. Neighborhood Justice. (Illus.). 1981. text ed. 27.50x tent. (ISBN 0-582-28253-5). Longman.

Wolff, Robert P. Understanding Rawls: A Reconstruction & Critique of a Theory of Justice. 1977. 16.50 (ISBN 0-691-07218-3); pap. 5.95 (ISBN 0-691-01992-4). Princeton U Pr.

Wright, Elliott. Go Free. 128p. (Orig.). 1973. pap. 1.75 (ISBN 0-377-03011-2). Friend Pr.

JUSTICE, ADMINISTRATION OF

see also Courts; Criminal Justice, Administration of; Due Process of Law; Governmental Investigations; Judges; Judicial Error; Public Defenders; Public Prosecutors

Allen, Francis A. Crimes of Politics: Political Dimensions of Criminal Justice. LC 73-93506. (Oliver Wendell Holmes Lectures: 1973). 128p. 1974. 7.95x (ISBN 0-674-17625-1). Harvard U Pr.

Allen, Henry W. Trial of Henry W. Allen, U. S. Deputy Marshall, for Kidnapping. LC 74-110024. Repr. of 1852 ed. 9.00x (ISBN 0-8371-4108-7). Greenwood.

American Academy Of Political And Social Science. Reform in Administration of Justice. LC 79-156961. (Foundations of Criminal Justice Ser.). Repr. of 1914 ed. 16.00 (ISBN 0-404-09101-6). AMS Pr.

Archer, Jules. You & the Law. LC 78-52812. (gr. 10-12). 1978. 7.95 (ISBN 0-15-299852-7, HJ). HarBraceJ.

Auerbach, Jerold S. Unequal Justice. 1976. 19.95 (ISBN 0-19-501939-3). Oxford U Pr.

Bastiat, Frederic. Law. 76p. 1961. 2.50 (ISBN 0-910614-30-X); pap. 1.00 (ISBN 0-910614-01-6). Foun Econ Ed.

Beeley, Arthur. Bail System in Chicago. LC 27-24082. 1965. Repr. of 1927 ed. 8.00x (ISBN 0-226-04152-2). U of Chicago Pr.

Berry, Mary F. Stability. Security, & Continuity: Mr Justice Burton & Decision-Making in the Supreme Court,1945-1958. LC 77-84772. (Contributions in Legal Studies: No. 1). (Illus.). 1978. lib. bdg. 17.50x (ISBN 0-8371-9798-8, BSS/). Greenwood.

Bonner, Robert J. & Smith, Gertrude S. The Administration of Justice from Homer to Aristotle, 2 vols. LC 70-101917. (BCL Ser.: I). Repr. of 1938 ed. Set. 27.50 (ISBN 0-404-00650-7). AMS Pr.

Bowie, Norman E. Towards a New Theory of Distributive Justice. LC 72-150315. 160p. 1971. 10.00x (ISBN 0-87023-085-9). U of Mass Pr.

Brindze, Ruth. All About Courts & Law. (Allabout Ser.: No. 54). (Illus.). (gr. 6-10). 1964. PLB 5.39 (ISBN 0-394-90254-8, BYR). Random.

Brown, Esther L. Lawyers & the Promotion of Justice. (Russell Sage Foundation Reprint Ser). Repr. of 1938 ed. lib. bdg. 26.00x (ISBN 0-697-00201-2). Irvington.

Buncher, Judith, ed. Crime & Punishment in America. 1978. lib. bdg. 19.95 (ISBN 0-685-59992-2). Facts on File.

Calamandrei, Piero. Procedure & Democracy. Adams, John Clarke, tr. LC 56-10780. 1956. 7.95x (ISBN 0-8147-0068-3). NYU Pr.

Carlsen, Martin, et al. Student Workbook for Introduction to the Administration of Justice. 1978. pap. text ed. 9.95 (ISBN 0-8403-1921-5). Kendall-Hunt.

Chambliss, William J. & Seidman, Robert B. Law, Order & Power. 1971. text ed. 18.95 (ISBN 0-201-00957-9). A-W.

Coffey, Alan R. & Eldefonso, Edward. Process & Impact of Justice. (Criminal Justice Ser.). 1975. pap. text ed. 7.95x (ISBN 0-02-471750-9, 47175). Macmillan.

Cole, George F. Politics & the Administration of Justice. LC 72-84047. (Sage Series on the Legal Order: Vol. 2). 234p. 1973. pap. 9.95 (ISBN 0-8039-0169-0). Sage.

Congressional Quarterly Staff. The Supreme Court, Justice & the Law. 2nd ed. LC 73-20492. 1977. pap. 6.95 (ISBN 0-87187-114-9). Congr Quarterly.

Cook, Joseph G. Constitutional Rights of the Accused: Post-Trial. new ed. LC 75-160369. (Criminal Law Library). 1976. 47.50 (ISBN 0-686-20646-0). Lawyers Co-Op.

Douglas, Jack D, ed. Crime & Justice in American Society. LC 74-126302. 1971. 28.50x (ISBN 0-672-51377-3). Irvington.

Eisenhower, Milton S. Rule of Law: An Alternative to Violence. (Illus.). 7.95 (ISBN 0-87695-025-X); pap. 3.95 (ISBN 0-87695-138-8). Aurora Pubs.

Emery, Lucilius A. Concerning Justice. 1914. 22.50x (ISBN 0-685-69818-1). Elliots Bks.

Engel, A., et al. Justice Game. 1974. pap. 5.95 (ISBN 0-02-472590-0, 47259). Macmillan.

Eymerich, Nicolau. Le Manuel Des Inquisiteurs (Avignon, 1376) Avec les Commentaires De Francisco Pena, Docteur En Droit Canon & En Droit Civil (Rome, 1578. (Le Savoir Historique: No. 8). 1973. pap. 15.50. (ISBN 90-2797-250-8). Mouton.

Fogel, David & Hudson, Joe, eds. Justice As Fairness: Perspectives on the Justice Model. 300p. 1981. pap. text ed. 14.95 (ISBN 0-87084-287-0). Anderson Pub Co.

Frank, Jerome. Courts on Trial: Myth & Reality in American Justice. LC 72-11942. 454p. 1949. 30.00 (ISBN 0-691-09205-2); pap. 6.95 (ISBN 0-691-02755-2). Princeton U Pr.

--Courts on Trial: Myth & Reality in American Justice. LC 72-11942. 454p. 1949. 30.00 (ISBN 0-691-09205-2); pap. 6.95 (ISBN 0-691-02755-2). Princeton U Pr.

Frantz, Albert T. How Courts Decide. LC 68-54164. 1968. lib. bdg. 12.50 (ISBN 0-930342-12-7). W S Hein.

Friedman, Leon, ed. Southern Justice. LC 75-33296. 306p. 1976. Repr. of 1965 ed. lib. bdg. 17.50x (ISBN 0-8371-8489-4, FRSJ). Greenwood.

Garlan, Edwin N. Legal Realism & Justice. xii, 161p. 1981. Repr. of 1941 ed. lib. bdg. 20.00x (ISBN 0-8377-0614-9). Rothman.

Gillers, Stephen. Getting Justice: The Rights of People. 240p. 1973. pap. 1.50 (ISBN 0-451-61227-2, MW1227, Ment). NAL.

Glueck, Sheldon S. Crime & Correction. 1952. 20.00 (ISBN 0-527-34064-2). Kraus Repr.

--Crime & Justice. 1945. 18.00 (ISBN 0-527-34068-5). Kraus Repr.

Goldberg, Louis P. Lawless Judges. LC 74-97451. Repr. of 1935 ed. 17.50x (ISBN 0-8371-2696-7, Pub. by Negro U Pr). Greenwood.

Goldberg, Louis P. & Levenson, Eleanore. Lawless Judges. LC 73-138498. (Civil Liberties in American History Ser). 1970. Repr. of 1935 ed. lib. bdg. 29.50 (ISBN 0-306-70070-0). Da Capo.

Harding, Arthur L., ed. Administration of Justice in Retrospect: Roscoe Pound's 1906 Address in a Half Century of Experience. LC 57-10684. (Studies in Jurisprudence: No. 4). 1957. 4.00 (ISBN 0-87074-066-0). SMU Press.

Harwell, Fred. A True Deliverance. LC 79-2233. 1980. 10.95 (ISBN 0-394-49989-1). Knopf.

Hays, Arthur G. Trial by Prejudice. LC 79-109550. (Civil Liberties in American History Ser). 1970. Repr. of 1933 ed. lib. bdg. 35.00 (ISBN 0-306-71904-5). Da Capo.

Hensley, Thomas R. The Kent State Incident: Impact of Judicial Process on Public Attitudes. LC 80-1712. (Contributions in Political Science Ser.: No. 56). 264p. 1981. lib. bdg. 27.50 (ISBN 0-313-21220-1, HKS/). Greenwood.

Hopkins, Ernest J. Our Lawless Police. LC 74-168829. (Civil Liberties in American History Ser.). 379p. 1972. Repr. of 1931 ed. lib. bdg. 32.50 (ISBN 0-306-70213-4). Da Capo.

Jacob, Herbert. Justice in America: Courts, Lawyers, & the Judicial Process. 3rd ed. 237p. 1978. pap. text ed. 6.95 (ISBN 0-316-45524-5). Little.

--Urban Justice: Law & Order in American Cities. 160p. 1973. pap. 7.95 ref. ed. (ISBN 0-13-938944-X). P-H.

Klein, Fannie J., ed. Federal & State Court Systems: A Guide. LC 76-47480. 1977. 20.00 (ISBN 0-88410-219-X); pap. 9.95 (ISBN 0-88410-795-7). Ballinger Pub.

Knight, Harry & Stevenson, Walter. Communication for Justice Administration: Theory & Skill. 1976. text ed. 7.95 (ISBN 0-87084-503-9). Anderson Pub Co.

Konefsky, Samuel J. The Legacy of Holmes & Brandeis. LC 78-157828. (American Constitutional & Legal History, Ser.). 316p. 1974. Repr. of 1956 ed. lib. bdg. 29.50 (ISBN 0-306-70215-0). Da Capo.

Levin, Leo A. & Wheeler, Russell R., eds. The Pound Conference: Perspectives on Justice in the Future. LC 80-14618. 368p. 1980. text ed. 25.00 (ISBN 0-8299-2096-X). West Pub.

Little, Joseph W. Administration of Justice in Drunk Driving Cases. LC 75-11643. (Social Science Monograph: No. 53). (Illus.). 1975. pap. 6.50 (ISBN 0-8130-0486-1). U Presses Fla.

Logan, Albert B. Justice in Jeopardy: Strategy to Revitalize the American Dream. (Illus.). 260p. 1973. text ed. 12.50 (ISBN 0-398-02694-7); pap. text ed. 8.25 (ISBN 0-398-02764-1). C C Thomas.

Mayhall, P. D. & Geary, D. P. Community Relations & the Administration of Justice. 2nd ed. LC 78-135200. 1979. text ed. 19.95x (ISBN 0-471-04135-1); study guide avail. (ISBN 0-471-05314-7). Wiley.

Murphy, Patrick T. Our Kindly Parent - the State: The Juvenile Justice System & How It Works. LC 73-19322. 192p. 1977. pap. 2.95 (ISBN 0-14-004230-X). Penguin.

National Center for State Courts. Facets of the Jury System: A Survey. Prescott, Elizabeth, ed. 1976. pap. 3.00 (ISBN 0-89656-003-1, R0028). Natl Ctr St Courts.

--Rural Courts: The Effect Ofspace & Distance on the Administration of Justice. (Illus.). 1977. pap. 5.00 (ISBN 0-89656-020-1, R0032). Natl Ctr St Courts.

Naylor, David T. Law, Order, & Justice. (gr. 10 up). 1979. pap. text ed. 5.50x (ISBN 0-8104-6071-8). Hayden.

Nelson, William E. Dispute & Conflict Resolution in Plymouth County, Massachusetts, 1725 - 1825. LC 80-17403. (Studies in Legal History). 240p. 1980. 19.50x (ISBN 0-8078-1454-7). U of NC Pr.

Perelman, Chaim. Justice, Law & Argument: Essays on Moral & Legal Reasoning. (Synthese Library: No. 142). 175p. 1980. lib. bdg. 28.50 (ISBN 90-277-1089-9, Pub. by Reidel Holland); pap. 10.50 (ISBN 90-277-1090-2, Pub. by Reidel Holland). Kluwer Boston.

Perlman, M. & Morris, N. Law & Crime: Essays in Honor of Sir John Barry. 266p. 1972. 30.50x (ISBN 0-677-15270-1). Gordon.

Pettit, Philip. Judging Justice: An Introduction to Contemporary Political Philosophy. 192p. 1980. 25.00x (ISBN 0-7100-0563-6); pap. 11.95 (ISBN 0-7100-0571-7). Routledge & Kegan.

Philadelphia Bureau of Municipal Research. Law Administration & Negro-White Relations in Philadelphia. Repr. of 1947 ed. lib. bdg. 15.00x (ISBN 0-8371-4588-0, PLA&). Greenwood.

Planning in State Courts: Trends & Developments 1976-78. (State Court Planning Capabilities Project Ser.). 1978. pap. 5.50 (ISBN 0-89656-028-7, R0040). Natl Ctr St Courts.

Poldervaart, Arie W. Black-Robed Justice. Cortes, Carlos E., ed. LC 76-1472. (Chicano Heritage Ser.). 1976. Repr. of 1948 ed. lib. bdg. 13.00x (ISBN 0-405-09519-8). Arno.

Posner, Richard A. The Economics of Justice. LC 80-25075. (Illus.). 448p. 1981. text ed. 25.00x (ISBN 0-674-23525-8). Harvard U Pr.

Prassel, Frank R. Criminal Law, Justice & Society. LC 78-12980. 1979. 18.50 (ISBN 0-87620-185-0). Goodyear.

Rees, William, ed. Calendar of Ancient Petitions Relating to Wales, (13th to 16th Century). Public Record Office. (History & Law Ser.: No.28). 1976. text ed. 27.50x (ISBN 0-7083-0566-0). Verry.

Rich, Vernon. Law & the Administration of Justice. 2nd ed. LC 78-31516. 1979. text ed. 19.95 (ISBN 0-471-04961-1). Wiley.

Root, Elihu. Addresses on Government & Citizenship. facs. ed. LC 70-86779. (Essay Index Reprint Ser). 1916. 24.00 (ISBN 0-8369-1190-3). Arno.

Roper, Edith. Skeleton of Justice. LC 73-180425. Repr. of 1941 ed. 21.50 (ISBN 0-404-56159-4). AMS Pr.

Royal Norwegian Ministry of Justice. Administration of Justice in Norway: A Brief Survey. 96p. 1981. pap. 12.00x (ISBN 82-00-05501-9). Universitet.

Sachs, Albie. Justice in South Africa. LC 72-97749. (Perspectives on Southern Africa Ser., No. 12). 1973. 22.75x (ISBN 0-520-02417-6); pap. 3.25 (ISBN 0-520-02624-1). U of Cal Pr.

Samuels, Aaron. Family Court Law & Practice in New York. rev. ed. 1972. 35.00 (ISBN 0-685-05161-7). Acme Law.

Schedler, George. Behavior Modification & "Punishment" of the Innocent: Towards a Justification of the Institution of Legal Punishment. 1977. pap. text ed. 17.25x (ISBN 90-6032-084-0). Humanities.

Schlossman, Steven L. Love & the American Delinquent: The Theory & Practice of "Progressive" Juvenile Justice, 1825-1920. LC 76-17699. (Illus.). 1977. lib. bdg. 15.00x (ISBN 0-226-73857-4). U of Chicago Pr.

Simonsen, Clifford E. & Gordon, Marshall S. Juvenile Justice in America. 1979. text ed. 17.95 (ISBN 0-02-478350-1). Macmillan.

Smith, Bruce. Rural Crime Control. facsimile ed. LC 74-3851. (Criminal Justice in America Ser.). 1974. Repr. of 1933 ed. 18.00x (ISBN 0-405-06182-X). Arno.
Stone, Harlan F. Law & Its Administration. LC 33-17836. Repr. of 1924 ed. 20.00 (ISBN 0-404-06284-9). AMS Pr.
Strick, Anne. Injustice for All. LC 76-41405. 1977. 8.95 (ISBN 0-399-11860-8). Putnam.
Swaton, J. Norman & Morgan, Loren. Administration of Justice. 2nd ed. 1980. text ed. 15.95 (ISBN 0-442-25789-9); instructor's manual 2.50x (ISBN 0-442-25712-0). D Van Nostrand.
Tappan, Paul W. Crime, Justice & Correction. (Sociology Ser.). 1960. text ed. 14.95 (ISBN 0-07-062870-X, C). McGraw.
Taylor, Telford. Grand Inquest: The Story of Congressional Investigations. LC 73-19825. 358p. 1974. Repr. of 1955 ed. lib. bdg. 35.00 (ISBN 0-306-70620-2). Da Capo.
The Third Branch. LC 76-39614. 1976. Repr. lib. bdg. 35.00 (ISBN 0-930342-35-6). W S Hein.
Thornton, William E., et al. Delinquency & Justice. 1981. text ed. 15.95x (ISBN 0-673-15225-1). Scott F.
Vanderbilt, Arthur T. The Challenge of Law Reform. LC 76-3784. 194p. 1976. Repr. of 1955 ed. lib. bdg. 16.75 (ISBN 0-8371-8809-1, VALR). Greenwood.
Walras, Leon. Economie Politique et la Justice. LC 70-132540. (Research & Source Works Ser: No. 558). (Fr). 1970. Repr. of 1860 ed. lib. bdg. 21.00 (ISBN 0-8337-3675-2). B Franklin.
Washburne, George A. Imperial Control of the Administration of Justice in the Thirteen American Colonies 1684-1776. LC 70-109920. (Columbia Univesity. Studies in the Social Sciences: No. 238). Repr. of 1923 ed. 17.50 (ISBN 0-404-51238-0). AMS Pr.
White, G. Edward. The American Judicial Tradition. LC 75-32356. 1976. 19.95 (ISBN 0-19-502017-0). Oxford U Pr.
Williams, Vergil L., et al. Introduction to the Administration of Justice. LC 81-66158. (Administration of Justice Ser). (Illus.). 512p. (Orig.). 1981. text ed. 15.60 (ISBN 0-8273-1755-7); price not set (ISBN 0-8273-1756-5). Delmar.
Willoughby, W. F. Principles of Judicial Administration. xxii, 662p. 1981. Repr. of 1929 ed. lib. bdg. 45.00x (ISBN 0-8377-1312-9). Rothman.
Winstanley, Gerrard. The Law of Freedom in a Platform: Or, True Magistracy Restored. Kenny, Robert W., ed. LC 72-95902. 1973. 12.00x (ISBN 0-8052-3503-5). Schocken.
Wooden, Kenneth. Weeping in the Playtime of Others: The Plight of Incarcerated Children. 1976. 8.95 (ISBN 0-07-071642-0, GB); pap. 4.95 (ISBN 0-07-071643-9). McGraw.
Wren, Brian. Education for Justice: Pedagogical Principles. LC 77-8696. 1977. pap. 4.95x (ISBN 0-88344-110-1). Orbis Bks.
Wunder, John R. Inferior Courts, Superior Justice: A History of the Justices of the Peace on the Northwest Frontier, 1853-1889. LC 78-66720. (Contributions in Legal Studies: No. 7). 1979. lib. bdg. 18.95x (ISBN 0-313-20620-1, WIC/). Greenwood.
Zinn, Howard, ed. Justice in Everyday Life: How It Really Works. 1974. 10.00 (ISBN 0-688-00284-6). Morrow.

JUSTICE, ADMINISTRATION OF-BIBLIOGRAPHY
Klein, Fannie J. The Administration of Justice in the Courts: A Selected Annotated Bibliography, 2 vols. LC 76-2627. 1200p. 1976. text ed. 80.00x set (ISBN 0-379-10137-8); Vol. 1. text ed. (ISBN 0-379-10137-8); Vol. 2. text ed. (ISBN 0-379-10138-6). Oceana.
Klein, Fanny J. Judicial Administration & the Legal Profession: A Bibliography. LC 62-12025. 1963. 50.00 (ISBN 0-379-00153-5). Oceana.

JUSTICE, ADMINISTRATION OF-STATISTICS
see Judicial Statistics

JUSTICE, ADMINISTRATION OF-CHINA
Keeton, George W. The Development of Extraterritoriality in China, 2 Vols. LC 68-9628. 1928. Set. 42.50 (ISBN 0-86527-042-2). Fertig.
Leng, Shao-Chuan. Justice in Communist China: A Survey of the People's Judicial System of the Chinese People's Republic. LC 67-14398. 1967. 15.00 (ISBN 0-379-00305-8). Oceana.
Van Gulik, Robert H., tr. T'ang-Yin-Pi-Shis: Parallel Cases from Under the Pear Tree. LC 79-1605. 1980. Repr. of 1956 ed. 18.00 (ISBN 0-88355-908-0). Hyperion Conn.

JUSTICE, ADMINISTRATION OF-CONFEDERATE STATES OF AMERICA
Robinson, William M., Jr. Justice in Grey: A History of the Judicial System of the Confederate States of America. LC 68-15155. 1968. Repr. of 1941 ed. 20.00 (ISBN 0-8462-1209-9). Russell.

JUSTICE, ADMINISTRATION OF-FRANCE
see also Intendants
Ducoudray, Gustave. Les Origines du Parlement de Paris et la Justice aux Treizieme et Quatorzieme Siecles, 2 vols. 1969. 61.50 (ISBN 0-8337-0938-0). B Franklin.

JUSTICE, ADMINISTRATION OF-GREAT BRITAIN
Cecil, William. Execution of Justice in England. Incl. A True Sincere & Modest Defense of English Catholics. Allen, William. Kingdon, Robert M., ed. (Document Ser). 16.00 (ISBN 0-918016-41-X). Folger Bks.
Jackson, Richard M. The Machinery of Justice in England. 7th ed. LC 77-4401. 1978. 74.50 (ISBN 0-521-21688-5); pap. 24.95 (ISBN 0-521-29231-X). Cambridge U Pr.
Maitland, Frederick W. Justice & Police. LC 79-173540. vi, 176p. 1972. Repr. of 1885 ed. 12.00 (ISBN 0-8462-1657-4). Russell.
Stenton, Doris M. English Justice Between the Norman Conquest & the Great Charter 1066-1215. LC 64-14094. (Memoirs Ser.: Vol. 60). (Illus.). 1964. 4.00 (ISBN 0-87169-060-8). Am Philos.
Vick, R. W. & Schoolbred, C. F. The Administration of Civil Justice in England & Wales. LC 67-31508. 1968. 23.00 (ISBN 0-08-013299-5). Pergamon.
Williams, Roger. Actions of the Low Countries. Davies, D. W., ed. (Documents Ser). 1978. 13.50x (ISBN 0-918016-40-1). Folger Bks.

JUSTICE, ADMINISTRATION OF-GREECE
Bonner, Robert J. & Smith, Gertrude E. Administration of Justice from Homer to Aristotle, 2 Vols. LC 69-13832. (Illus.). 1969. Repr. of 1938 ed. Set. lib. bdg. 55.00x (ISBN 0-8371-0320-7, BOAJ). Greenwood.

JUSTICE, ADMINISTRATION OF-HUNGARY
Kalman, Lajos. Lawyer in Communism. (Illus.). 1960. 3.00 (ISBN 0-8198-0073-2); pap. 2.00 (ISBN 0-8198-0074-0). Dghtrs St Paul.

JUSTICE, ADMINISTRATION OF-INDIA
Mann, T. K. Administration of Justice in India. 1979. text ed. 13.50x (ISBN 0-391-01854-X). Humanities.

JUSTICE, ADMINISTRATION OF-RUSSIA
Berman, Harold J. Justice in the U. S. S. R: An Interpretation of the Soviet Law. rev. ed. LC 63-15045. (Russian Research Center Studies: No. 3). 1963. pap. text ed. 9.00x (ISBN 0-674-49151-3). Harvard U Pr.
Duranty, Walter. Curious Lottery & Other Tales of Russian Justice. LC 78-101805. (Short Story Index Reprint Ser.). 1929. 15.00 (ISBN 0-8369-3193-9). Arno.
Hazard, John N. Settling Disputes in Soviet Society: The Formative Years of Legal Institutions. 1978. Repr. of 1960 ed. lib. bdg. 32.50x (ISBN 0-374-93758-3). Octagon.
Kucherov, Samuel. Courts, Lawyers, & Trials Under the Last Three Tsars. LC 74-20340. 339p. 1975. Repr. of 1953 ed. lib. bdg. 21.00x (ISBN 0-8371-7857-6, KUCL). Greenwood.
Terebilov, Vladimir. The Soviet Court: Guide to the Constitutional Principles of the Administration of Justice in the USSR. 182p. 1973. 12.95x (ISBN 0-8464-0866-X). Beekman Pubs.
Wortman, Richard S. The Development of a Russian Legal Consciousness. LC 76-600. (Illus.). 1976. lib. bdg. 20.00x (ISBN 0-226-90776-7). U of Chicago Pr.

JUSTICE, ADMINISTRATION OF (FRANKISH LAW)
Ganshof, Francois L. Frankish Institutions Under Charlemagne. 1970. pap. 3.95 (ISBN 0-393-00500-3, Norton Lib). Norton.
--Frankish Institutions Under Charlemagne. Lyon, Bryce & Lyon, Mary, trs. LC 68-29166. 107p. 1968. text ed. 12.00x (ISBN 0-87057-108-7, Pub. by Brown U Pr). U Pr of New Eng.

JUSTICE, MISCARRIAGE OF
see Judicial Error

JUSTICE IN LITERATURE
Hamlet, Desmond M. One Greater Man: Justice & Damnation in Paradise Lost. LC 74-27670. 224p. 1976. 14.50 (ISBN 0-8387-1674-1). Bucknell U Pr.

JUSTICES' CLERKS
see Clerks of Court

JUSTICES OF THE PEACE
Beard, Charles A. Office of Justice of the Peace in England in Its Origin & Development. LC 74-18913. (Columbia University Studies in the Social Sciences: No. 52). Repr. of 1904 ed. 10.00 (ISBN 0-404-51052-3). AMS Pr.
--Office of the Justice of the Peace in England in Its Origin and Development. 1962. Repr. of 1904 ed. 15.00 (ISBN 0-8337-0198-3). B Franklin.
--The Office of the Justice of the Peace in England. 1976. Repr. of 1904 ed. 25.00 (ISBN 0-403-06475-9, Regency). Scholarly.
Dalton, Michael. The Countrey Justice, Containing the Practise of the Justices of the Peace Out of Their Sessions. LC 70-37969. (American Law Ser.: The Formative Years). 406p. 1972. Repr. of 1622 ed. 20.00 (ISBN 0-405-03996-4). Arno.
--Countrey Justice, Containing the Practise of the Justices of the Peace Out of Their Sessions. LC 74-28844. (English Experience Ser.: No. 725). 1975. Repr. of 1618 ed. 42.00 (ISBN 90-221-0725-6). Walter J Johnson.
Fitzherbert, Anthony, tr. from Fr. The Newe Boke of Justices of the Peas. LC 72-195. (English Experience Ser.: No. 109). 1969. Repr. of 1538 ed. 21.00 (ISBN 90-221-0109-6). Walter J Johnson.
Lambard, William. Eirenarcha: or, the Office of the Justices of Peace. LC 72-25854. (English Experience Ser.: No. 273). 512p. 1970. Repr. of 1581 ed. 49.00 (ISBN 90-221-0273-4). Walter J Johnson.
Simpson, William. The Practical Justice of the Peace & Parish-Officer, of His Majesty's Province of South Carolina. LC 70-37985. (American Law Ser.: The Formative Years). 288p. 1972. Repr. of 1761 ed. 15.00 (ISBN 0-405-04028-8). Arno.

JUSTICIARS (ENGLAND)
West, F. J. Justiciarship in England 1066-1232. (Cambridge Studies in Medieval Life & Thought: No. 12). 1966. 42.95 (ISBN 0-521-06772-3). Cambridge U Pr.

JUSTIFICATION
see also Assurance (Theology); Faith; Law and Gospel
Anderson, Charles S. Faith & Freedom: The Christian Faith According to the Lutheran Confessions. LC 76-27087. 1977. pap. 3.95 (ISBN 0-8066-1558-3, 10-2170). Augsburg.
Bull, George. Harmony on Justification, Defense of the Nicene Creed, Judgement of the Catholic Church, 5 vols. LC 71-39556. (Library of Anglo-Catholic Theology: No. 4). Repr. of 1855 ed. Set. 150.00 (ISBN 0-404-52070-7). AMS Pr.
Hordern, William. Living by Grace. LC 75-6548. 1975. pap. 5.95 (ISBN 0-664-24763-6). Westminster.
Justification. pap. 1.25 (ISBN 0-686-12888-5). Schmul Pub Co.
Pappas, George S. & Swain, Marshall, eds. Essays on Knowledge & Justification. LC 77-10299. (Illus.). 1978. 25.00x (ISBN 0-8014-1086-X); pap. 8.95x (ISBN 0-8014-9865-1). Cornell U Pr.
Servetus, Michael. Two Treatises of Servetus on the Trinity. Wilbur, Earl M., tr. 1932. pap. 16.00 (ISBN 0-527-01016-2). Kraus Repr.
Wiersbe, Warren W. Be Right. 1977. pap. 3.50 (ISBN 0-88207-729-5). Victor Bks.

JUSTIFICATION (LAW)
see also Consent (Law); Self-Defense (Law)

JUSTIFICATION-HISTORY OF DOCTRINES
Hagglund, Bengt. The Background of Luther's Doctrine of Justification in Late Medieval Theology. Anderson, Charles S., ed. LC 78-152367. (Facet Bks.). 1971. pap. 1.00 (ISBN 0-8006-3063-7, 1-3063). Fortress.
Leaver, Robin A. Luther on Justification. LC 74-11781. 1975. pap. 3.95 (ISBN 0-570-03188-5, 12-2590). Concordia.

JUSTINIANUS 1ST, EMPEROR OF THE EAST, 483-565
Barker, John W. Justinian & the Later Roman Empire. LC 66-11804. 336p. 1966. pap. text ed. 7.95 (ISBN 0-299-03944-7). U of Wis Pr.
Diehl, Charles. Justinien Et La Civilization Byzantine Au Seizieme Siecle, 2 Vols. LC 70-80743. (Research & Source Works Ser: No. 1). 1969. Repr. of 1901 ed. Set. lib. bdg. 47.00 (ISBN 0-8337-0862-7). B Franklin.
Procopius. History of the Wars. Secret History, 7 vols. Incl. Vol. 1, Bks. 1 & 2. Persian War (ISBN 0-674-99054-4); Vol. 2, Bks. 3 & 4. Vandalic War (ISBN 0-674-99090-0); Vols. 3-5, Bks. 5-8. Gothic War. Vol. 3 (ISBN 0-674-99119-2). Vol. 4 (ISBN 0-674-99191-5). Vol. 5 (ISBN 0-674-99239-3); Vol. 6. Anecdota or Secret History (ISBN 0-674-99320-9); Vol. 7. On Buildings; General Index (ISBN 0-674-99378-0). (Loeb Classical Library: No. 48, 81, 107, 173, 217, 290, 343). 11.00x ea. Harvard U Pr.
Rubin, Berthold. Theoderich Und Iustinian. Repr. of 1953 ed. pap. 5.50 (ISBN 0-384-52465-6). Johnson Repr.
Ure, Percy N. Justinian & His Age. LC 78-31752. (Illus.). 1979. Repr. of 1951 ed. lib. bdg. 22.50x (ISBN 0-313-20916-2, URJA). Greenwood.

JUSTUM PRETIUM
see Prices

JUTE
Impact of Synthetics on Jute & Allied Fibers. (Commodity Bulletin Ser.: No. 46). (Orig.). 1969. pap. 10.00 (ISBN 0-685-09390-5, F239, FAO). Unipub.
Intergovernmental Group on Jute, Kenaf & Allied Fibres, 12th Session. Report. 17p. 1977. pap. 7.50 (ISBN 92-5-100125-1, F1121, FAO). Unipub.
Ranjam, T. C. Hanbook on Jute, Vols. 1-3. 1981. 40.00x (ISBN 0-686-76644-X, Pub. by Oxford & IBH India). State Mutual Bk.
Report of the Fourteenth Session of the Intergovernmental Group on Jute, Kenaf, & Allied Fibres. 1979. pap. 7.50 (ISBN 92-5-100669-5, F1533, FAO). Unipub.

JUTES
Evison, Evera I., ed. Angles, Saxons, & Jutes: Essays Presented to J. N. L. Myres. (Illus.). 272p. 1981. 59.00 (ISBN 0-19-813402-9). Oxford U Pr.
Jolliffe, J. E. Pre-Feudal England Jutes. new ed. 122p. 1962. Repr. of 1933 ed. 23.50x (ISBN 0-7146-1484-X, F Cass Co). Biblio Dist.

JUTLAND, BATTLE OF, 1916
Bennett, Geoffrey. Battle of Jutland. 208p. 1980. 14.95 (ISBN 0-7153-5503-1, Pub by David & Charles England). Hippocrene Bks.
Frost, Holloway H. The Battle of Jutland. LC 79-6108. (Navies & Men Ser.). (Illus.). 1980. Repr. of 1964 ed. lib. bdg. 50.00x (ISBN 0-405-13037-6). Arno.

JUVARRA, FILIPP, 1678-1736
Juvarra, Filippo. Filippo Juvarra: Scenografo E Architetto Teatrali. Ferrero, Mercedes V., ed. (Illus.). Repr. of 1969 ed. 60.00 (ISBN 0-405-08684-9, Blom Pubns). Arno.

JUVENAL (DECIMUS JUNIUS JUVENALIS)
Courtney, E. A Commentary on the Satires of Juvenal. 650p. 1981. text ed. 75.00x (ISBN 0-485-11190-X, Athlone Pr). Humanities.
Green, Peter. The Shadow of the Parthenon: Studies in Ancient History & Literature. LC 72-87205. 1973. 22.50x (ISBN 0-520-02322-6). U of Cal Pr.
Juvenal. Thirteen Satires. 1891. 6.95 (ISBN 0-312-80045-2). St Martin.
Tengstrom, Emin. A Study of Juvenal's Tenth Satire. 1981. pap. text ed. 14.00x (ISBN 91-7346-089-3). Humanities.

JUVENILE AUTOMOBILE DRIVERS
see Automobile Drivers

JUVENILE COURTS
see also Probation
Autin, Diana. Young People & the Law. 4th ed. Youth Liberation, ed. (Illus.). 1978. saddle-stitched 2.50 (ISBN 0-918946-05-0). Youth Lib.
Besharov, Douglas J. Juvenile Justice Advocacy: Practice in a Unique Court. 1974. 20.00 (ISBN 0-685-85396-9, C1-1144). PLI.
Bliss, Dennis C. The Effects of the Juvenile Justice System on Self-Concept. LC 76-55465. 1977. soft bdg. 8.00 (ISBN 0-88247-433-2). R & E Res Assoc.
Blomberg, Thomas G. Juvenile Court Reform: Widening the Social Control Net. 256p. 1981. lib. bdg. 20.00 (ISBN 0-89946-087-9). Oelgeschlager.
--Social Control & the Proliferation of Juvenile Court Services. LC 77-90354. 1978. pap. 10.00 perfect bdg. (ISBN 0-88247-504-5). R & E Res Assoc.
Bremner, Robert H. The Juvenile Court: An Original Anthology. LC 74-1688. (Children & Youth Ser.: Vol. 8). 1974. 19.00x (ISBN 0-405-05965-5). Arno.
Carlin, Angela G. & Schwartz, Richard W., eds. Merrick-Rippner Ohio Probate Law: Practice & Forms, Including Juvenile Law Practice & Forms. 3rd rev. ed. (Baldwin's Ohio Practice Ser.). 1978. 95.00 (ISBN 0-8322-0021-2). Banks-Baldwin.
Coffey, Alan R. Juvenile Corrections: Treatment & Rehabilitation. (Criminal Justice Ser). (Illus.). 320p. 1975. ref. ed. 16.95 (ISBN 0-13-514257-1). P-H.
Cox, Steven M. & Conrad, John J. Juvenile Justice: A Guide to Practice & Theory. 1978. wire coil avail. (ISBN 0-697-08206-7); instructor's resource manual 1.00 (ISBN 0-685-50835-8). Wm C Brown.
Dawson, Robert O. Standards Relating to Adjudication. (Juvenile Justice Standards Project Ser.). 1980. softcover 7.95 (ISBN 0-88410-809-0); casebound 12.50 (ISBN 0-88410-236-X). Ballinger Pub.
Eldefonso, Edward & Coffey, Alan. Process & Impact of the Juvenile Justice System. 1976. pap. 9.95x (ISBN 0-02-472490-4). Macmillan.
Emerson, Robert M. Judging Delinquents: Context & Process in Juvenile Court. LC 70-75047. (Law in Action Ser). 1969. 19.95x (ISBN 0-202-23001-5). Aldine Pub.
Empey, LaMar T. The Future of Childhood & Juvenile Justice. LC 79-15129. 1980. 20.00x (ISBN 0-8139-0832-9). U Pr of Va.
Faust, Frederic L. & Brantingham, Paul J. Juvenile Justice Philosophy: Readings, Cases & Comments. 2nd ed. (Criminal Justice Ser.). 1978. pap. text ed. 16.95 (ISBN 0-8299-0179-5). West Pub.
Flammang, C. J. Police Juvenile Enforcement. 284p. 1972. 18.75 (ISBN 0-398-02280-1). C C Thomas.

Fox, Sanford J. Cases & Materials on Modern Juvenile Justice. 2nd ed. (American Casebook Ser.). 970p. 1981. text ed. 22.95 (ISBN 0-686-73868-3). West Pub.

Friday, Paul C. & Stewart, V. Lorne, eds. Youth Crime & Juvenile Justice: International Perspectives. LC 77-7820. (Praeger Special Studies). 1977. text ed. 23.95 (ISBN 0-03-022646-5). Praeger.

Grisso, Thomas. Juveniles Waiver of Righs: Legal & Psychological Competence. (Perspectives in Law & Psychology Ser.: Vol. 3). 285p. 1981. 32.50 (ISBN 0-306-40526-1, Plenum Pr). Plenum Pub.

Hart, Hastings H. Juvenile Court Laws in the United States. (Russell Sage Foundation Reprint Ser). Repr. of 1910 ed. lib. bdg. 21.00x (ISBN 0-697-00202-0). Irvington.

Heaps, Willard A. Juvenile Justice. LC 74-4011. 208p. 1974. 7.95 (ISBN 0-395-28906-8, Clarion). HM.

Hopson, D., Jr., et al. Juvenile Offender & the Law: A Symposium. LC 79-146557. (Symposia on Law & Society Ser). 1968. Repr. lib. bdg. 22.50 (ISBN 0-306-70095-6). Da Capo.

Hurley, Timothy D., compiled by. Origin of the Illinois Juvenile Court Law: Juvenile Courts & What They Have Accomplished. 3rd ed. LC 74-2681. Repr. of 1907 ed. 19.00 (ISBN 0-404-09159-8). AMS Pr.

Hyde, Margaret O. Juvenile Justice & Injustice. (gr. 7 up). 1977. lib. bdg. 7.90 s&l (ISBN 0-531-00122-9). Watts.

International Penal and Prison Commission. Children's Courts in the United States. LC 72-156020. Repr. of 1904 ed. 15.00 (ISBN 0-404-09120-2). AMS Pr.

Kamm, Ernest. Juvenile Law & Procedure in California. 3rd ed. 1981. 11.95 (ISBN 0-686-77434-5); pap. text ed. 9.95x (ISBN 0-02-470790-2). Macmillan.

Klein, Malcolm W., ed. The Juvenile Justice System. LC 75-14632. (Sage Criminal Justice System Annuals: Vol. 5). 287p. 1976. 22.50 (ISBN 0-8039-0450-9); pap. 9.95 (ISBN 0-8039-0451-7). Sage.

Knight, James M. The Juvenile Courts Functions & Relevant Theory. LC 77-90357. 1978. pap. 8.00 perfect bdg. (ISBN 0-88247-515-0). R & E Res Assoc.

Krisberg, Barry & Austin, James, eds. The Children of Ishmael: Critical Perspectives on Juvenile Delinquency. LC 77-89919. 1978. pap. text ed. 13.95 (ISBN 0-87484-387-1). Mayfield Pub.

Lindsey, Ben B. & Borough, Rube. The Dangerous Life. LC 73-11938. (Metropolitan America Ser.). 468p. 1974. Repr. 22.00x (ISBN 0-405-05400-9). Arno.

Lindsey, Ben B. & O'Higgins, Harvey J. The Beast. LC 75-125182. (Americana Library Ser.: No. 19). (Illus.). 368p. 1970. Repr. of 1910 ed. 11.50 (ISBN 0-295-95094-3). U of Wash Pr.

Lou, Herbert H. Juvenile Courts in the United States. LC 77-169394. (Family in America Ser). 297p. 1972. Repr. of 1927 ed. 16.00 (ISBN 0-405-03871-2). Arno.

McCarthy, Francis B. & Carr, James G. Juvenile Law & Its Processes: Cases & Materials. (Contemporary Legal Education Ser.). 700p. 1980. text ed. 21.00 (ISBN 0-686-63197-8). Bobbs.

McCreedy, Kenneth R. Juvenile Justice: System & Procedures. LC 75-6061. 1975. pap. 9.60 (ISBN 0-8273-0437-4); instructor's guide 1.60 (ISBN 0-8273-0438-2). Delmar.

Nyquist, Ola. Juvenile Justice. LC 74-17590. (Cambridge Studies in Criminology: Vol. 12). (Illus.). 302p. 1975. Repr. of 1960 ed. lib. bdg. 19.75x (ISBN 0-8371-7835-5, NYJJ). Greenwood.

Parsloe, Phyllida. Juvenile Justice in Britain & the United States: The Balance of Needs & Rights. (Library of Social Work). 1978. 21.50x (ISBN 0-7100-8772-1). Routledge & Kegan.

Platt, Anthony M. The Child Savers. LC 69-14827. (Phoenix Ser.). 1977. pap. 4.95 (ISBN 0-226-67072-4, P462, Phoen). U of Chicago Pr.

Polier, Justine W. Everyone's Children, Nobody's Child: A Judge Looks at Underprivileged Children in the United States. facsimile ed. LC 74-1698. (Children & Youth Ser.). 370p. 1974. Repr. of 1941 ed. 21.00x (ISBN 0-405-05975-2). Arno.

Riekes, Linda & Ackerly, Sally M. Juvenile Problems & Law. 2nd ed. (Law in Action Ser.). (Illus.). 52p. (gr. 4-6). 1980. pap. text ed. write for info. (ISBN 0-8299-1026-3). West Pub.

--Juvenile Problems & Law. (Law in Action Ser.). (Illus.). (gr. 7-8). 1975. pap. text ed. 3.25 (ISBN 0-8299-1004-2); tchr's manual 3.25 (ISBN 0-8299-1005-0). West Pub.

Rosenheim, Margaret K., ed. Pursuing Justice for the Child. LC 75-43238. (Studies in Crime & Justice). (Illus.). 1976. lib. bdg. 17.00x (ISBN 0-226-72789-0). U of Chicago Pr.

--Pursuing Justice for the Child. LC 75-43238. (Studies in Crime & Justice). (Illus.). 1978. pap. 5.95 (ISBN 0-226-72788-2, P774, Phoen). U of Chicago Pr.

Rubin, H. Ted. Juvenile Justice: Policy Practice & Law. new ed. 1979. pap. text ed. 10.95 (ISBN 0-87620-502-3). Goodyear.

Rubin, Sol. Law of Juvenile Justice: With a New Model Juvenile Court Act. LC 76-4526. (Legal Almanac Ser: No. 22). 1976. lib. bdg. 5.95 (ISBN 0-379-11105-5). Oceana.

Ryerson, Ellen. The Best-Laid Plans: America's Juvenile Court Experiment. 1978. pap. 4.95 (ISBN 0-8090-0135-7). Hill & Wang.

Sandhu, Harjit S. & Heasley, Wayne C. Improving Juvenile Justice. 240p. 1981. text ed. 24.95x (ISBN 0-89885-033-9); pap. text ed. 11.95x (ISBN 0-686-76243-6). Human Sci Pr.

Schlossman, Steven L. Love & the American Delinquent: The Theory & Practice of "Progressive" Juvenile Justice 1825-1920. LC 76-17699. 304p. 1981. pap. price not set (ISBN 0-226-73858-2). U of Chicago Pr.

--Love & the American Delinquent: The Theory & Practice of "Progressive" Juvenile Justice, 1825-1920. LC 76-17699. (Illus.). 1977. lib. bdg. 15.00x (ISBN 0-226-73857-4). U of Chicago Pr.

Senna & Siegel. Cases & Comments on Juvenile Law. (Criminal Justice Ser.). 600p. 1976. pap. text ed. 18.50 (ISBN 0-8299-0629-0). West Pub.

Simonsen, Clifford & Gordon, Marshall. Juvenile Justice in America. 2nd ed. 1982. text ed. 17.95 (ISBN 0-686-75038-1). Macmillan.

Simonsen, Clifford E. & Gordon, Marshall S. Juvenile Justice in America. 1979. text ed. 17.95 (ISBN 0-02-478350-1). Macmillan.

Sprowls, James T. Discretion & Lawlessness: Compliance in Juvenile Court. LC 79-6735. 144p. 1980. 14.95x (ISBN 0-669-03540-8). Lexington Bks.

Stapleton, W. Vaughan & Teitelbaum, Lee E. In Defense of Youth: A Study of the Role of Counsel in American Juvenile Courts. LC 72-83837. 1972. 11.95 (ISBN 0-87154-833-X). Russell Sage.

Stewart, V. Lorne, ed. The Changing Faces of Juvenile Justice. LC 77-87578. 1978. 16.50x (ISBN 0-8147-7788-0). NYU Pr.

Streib, Victor L. Juvenile Justice in America. (National University Pubns. Multi-Disciplinary Studies in the Law). 1978. 12.50 (ISBN 0-8046-9212-2). Kennikat.

Teitelbaum, Lee E. & Gough, Aidan, eds. Beyond Control: Status Offenders in the Juvenile Court. LC 76-30285. 1977. 17.50 (ISBN 0-88410-202-5); pap. text ed. 7.95 (ISBN 0-88410-212-2). Ballinger Pub.

Turner, Kenneth A. Juvenile Justice: Juvenile Court Problems, Procedures & Practices in Tennessee. 1969. 20.00 (ISBN 0-87215-121-2). Michie-Bobbs.

Twentieth Century Fund. Confronting Youth Crime: Report of the Twentieth Century Fund Task Force on Sentencing Policy Toward Young Offenders. LC 78-3612. (Illus.). 1978. text ed. 16.50x (ISBN 0-8419-0381-6). Holmes & Meier.

United States Children's Bureau. Standards for Specialized Courts Dealing with Children. LC 78-10186. 1978. Repr. of 1954 ed. lib. bdg. 15.00 (ISBN 0-313-20678-3, CBSS). Greenwood.

U.S. Children's Bureau. Juvenile Courts at Work. LC 76-38674. (Foundations of Criminal Justice Ser.). Repr. of 1925 ed. 24.50 (ISBN 0-404-09188-1). AMS Pr.

U.S. Senate, Juvenile Court of the District of Columbia. Message from the President of the United States Transmitting a Letter from the Judge of the Juvenile Court of the District of Columbia: A Report Covering the Work of the Juvenile Court During the Period from July 1, 1906 to June 30, 1926. LC 73-11937. (Metropolitan America Ser.). 174p. 1974. Repr. 12.00x (ISBN 0-405-05431-9). Arno.

Van Waters, Miriam. Youth in Conflict. LC 70-120218. Repr. of 1925 ed. 22.50 (ISBN 0-404-06754-9). AMS Pr.

Wheeler, Gerald R. Counterdeterrence: A Report on Juvenile Sentencing & Effects of Prisonization. LC 77-26975. 208p. 1978. 17.95x (ISBN 0-88229-315-X). Nelson-Hall.

Wies, Louis B. A Guide to Juvenile Court. 1977. pap. text ed. 8.50 (ISBN 0-88450-565-0, 1715-B). Lawyers & Judges.

Young, Pauline V. Social Treatment in Probation & Delinquency. 2nd ed. LC 69-14955. (Criminology, Law Enforcement, & Social Problems Ser.: No. 47). 1969. Repr. of 1952 ed. 24.00 (ISBN 0-87585-047-2). Patterson Smith.

JUVENILE COURTS–GREAT BRITAIN

Anderson, Richard. Representation in the Juvenile Court. (Direct Editions Ser). (Orig.). 1978. pap. 10.00 (ISBN 0-7100-8578-8). Routledge & Kegan.

Davis, Samuel M. Rights of Juvenile: The Juvenile Justice System. LC 74-84201. 1980. 45.00 (ISBN 0-87632-104-X). Boardman.

Grunhut, Max. Juvenile Offenders Before the Courts. LC 77-27073. (Illus.). 1978. Repr. of 1956 ed. lib. bdg. 14.00x (ISBN 0-313-20194-3, GRJU). Greenwood.

Morris, Allison & McIsaac, Mary. Juvenile Justice? (Cambridge Studies in Criminology). 1978. text ed. 30.95x (ISBN 0-435-82601-8). Heinemann Ed.

Parsloe, Phyllida. Juvenile Justice in Britain & the United States: The Balance of Needs & Rights. (Library of Social Work). 1978. 21.50x (ISBN 0-7100-8772-1). Routledge & Kegan.

Priestley, Philip, et al. Justice for Juveniles: The Nineteen Hundred Sixty-Nine Children & Young Persons Act-A Case for Reform? (Library of Social Work). 1978. 13.00 (ISBN 0-7100-8703-9). Routledge & Kegan.

JUVENILE DELINQUENCY

see also Child Welfare; Church Work with Juvenile Delinquents; Gangs; Juvenile Courts; Juvenile Detention Homes; Narcotics and Youth; Police Services for Juveniles; Reformatories; Rehabilitation of Juvenile Delinquents; Runaway Children; Social Work with Delinquents and Criminals

Abbott, Grace, ed. Child & State: Select Documents, 2 Vols. LC 68-57587. (Illus.). 1968. Repr. of 1938 ed. Set. lib. bdg. 53.75x (ISBN 0-8371-0279-0, ABCS). Greenwood.

Abstracts on Crime & Juvenile Delinquency, 1976: An Index to the Microform Collection. 82p. 1978. 15.00 (ISBN 0-667-00518-8). Microfilming Corp.

Abstracts on Crime & Juvenile Delinquency 1977: An Index to the Microform Collection. 79p. 1978. 15.00 (ISBN 0-667-00548-X). Microfilming Corp.

Adams, Gary B., et al. Juvenile Justice Management. (Illus.). 660p. 1973. 25.00 (ISBN 0-398-02773-0). C C Thomas.

Addams, Jane, et al. Child, the Clinic, & the Court. LC 72-137577. 1971. Repr. lib. bdg. 10.00 (ISBN 0-384-08782-5). Johnson Repr.

Agee, Vicki L. Treatment of the Violent Incorrigible Adolescent. LC 78-24653. (Illus.). 1979. 17.95 (ISBN 0-669-02811-8). Lexington Bks.

Aichhorn, August. Delinquency & Child Guidance: Selected Papers of August Aichhorn. Fleischmann, Otto, et al, eds. LC 64-8751. (Menninger Foundation Monograph Ser.: No. 1). 1967. text ed. 15.00 (ISBN 0-8236-1160-4). Intl Univs Pr.

Alissi, Albert S. Boys in Little Italy: A Comparison of Their Individual Value Orientations, Family Patterns, & Peer Group Associations. LC 77-90360. 1978. soft cover 10.00 (ISBN 0-88247-495-2). R & E Res Assoc.

Altieri de Barreto, Carmen G. El Lexico De la Delincuencia En Puerto Rico. (UPREX, C. Sociales: No. 18). pap. 1.85 (ISBN 0-8477-0018-6). U of PR Pr.

Altman, Michael L. Standards Relating to Juvenile Records & Information Systems. (Juvenile Justice Standards Project Ser.). 1980. softcover 7.95 (ISBN 0-88410-819-8); casebound 16.50 (ISBN 0-88410-247-5). Ballinger Pub.

An Annotated Bibliography of Works on Juvenile Delinquency in America & Britain in the Nineteenth Century. 1980. lib. bdg. 25.00 (ISBN 0-8414-7288-2). Folcroft.

Areen, Judith. Standards Relating to Youth Service Agencies. (Juvenile Justice Standards Project Ser.). 1980. softcover 7.95 (ISBN 0-88410-804-X); casebound 16.50 (ISBN 0-88410-756-6). Ballinger Pub.

Arnold, William R. Juveniles on Parole: A Sociological Perspective. 1970. text ed. 6.95 (ISBN 0-394-30001-7). Phila Bk Co.

Bakal, Yitzhak & Polsky, Howard W. Reforming Corrections for Juvenile Offenders. LC 73-11680. 1979. 17.95 (ISBN 0-669-90209-8). Lexington Bks.

Bartollas, Clemens & Miller, Stuart J. The Juvenile Offender: Control, Correction & Treatment. 1978. text ed. 19.95 (ISBN 0-205-06069-2, 826069-9). Allyn.

Beard, Belle B. Juvenile Probation: An Analysis of the Case Records of Five Hundred Children Studies at the Judge Baker Guidance Clinic & Placed on Probation in the Juvenile Court of Boston. LC 69-16224. (Criminology, Law Enforcement, & Social Problems Ser.: No. 95). 1969. Repr. of 1934 ed. 12.00 (ISBN 0-87585-095-2). Patterson Smith.

Belkin, Alison. The Criminal Child. (Belkin Ser.). 1978. pap. text ed. 6.95 (ISBN 0-8403-1852-9). Kendall-Hunt.

Bennett, James. Oral History & Delinquency: The Rhetoric of Criminology. LC 81-7514. 1981. lib. bdg. 28.50x (ISBN 0-226-04245-6). U of Chicago Pr.

Bing, Stephen & Brown, Larry. Standards Relating to Monitoring. (Juvenile Justice Standards Project Ser.). 1980. softcover 7.95 (ISBN 0-88410-805-8); casebound 16.50 (ISBN 0-88410-753-1). Ballinger Pub.

Bittner, Egon & Krantz, Sheldon. Standards Relating to Police Handling of Juvenile Problems. (Juvenile Justice Standards Project Ser.). 1980. softcover 7.95 (ISBN 0-88410-806-6); final casebound 16.50 (ISBN 0-88410-755-8). Ballinger Pub.

Bloch, Herbert A. & Niederhoffer, Arthur. The Gang: A Study in Adolescent Behavior. LC 76-6517. 1976. Repr. of 1958 ed. lib. bdg. 15.75x (ISBN 0-8371-8865-2, BLTG). Greenwood.

Blumer, Herbert & Hauset, Philip M. Movies, Delinquency, & Crime. 1933. 30.00 (ISBN 0-685-72808-0). Norwood Edns.

Bovet, Lucien, Psychiatric Aspects of Juvenile Delinquency, a Study. LC 74-98747. Repr. of 1951 ed. lib. bdg. 15.00x (ISBN 0-8371-3019-0, BOPA). Greenwood.

Boyle, Hugh. Delinquency & Crime. new ed. Burnes, Alan J., ed. (Urban America Ser). (Illus.). 61p. (Orig.). 1970. pap. 0.95 (ISBN 0-88301-013-5). Pendulum Pr.

Breckinridge, Sophonisba P. & Abbott, Edith. Delinquent Child & the Home. LC 70-112525. (Rise of Urban America). 1970. Repr. of 1912 ed. 17.00 (ISBN 0-405-02438-X). Arno.

Brodsky, Stanley L. & Smitherman, O'Neal. Handbook of Scales for Research in Crime & Delinquency. (Perspectives in Law & Psychology Ser.: Vol. 5). 530p. 1982. text ed. 42.50 (ISBN 0-306-40792-2, Plenum Pr). Plenum Pub.

Buckle, Leonard & Buckle, Suzann. Standards Relating to Planning for Juvenile Justice. (Juvenile Justice Standards Project Ser.). 1980. softcover 7.95 (ISBN 0-88410-807-4); final casebound 16.50 (ISBN 0-88410-754-X). Ballinger Pub.

Burgess, Ernest W. Ernest W. Burgess on Community, Family & Delinquency. Cottrell, Leonard S., Jr., et al, eds. LC 73-83572. (Illus.). 1977. pap. 4.45 (ISBN 0-226-08058-7, P715, Phoen). U of Chicago Pr.

--On Community, Family & Delinquency. Cottrell, Leonard S., Jr., et al, eds. (Heritage of Sociology Ser). 1974. 15.00x (ISBN 0-226-08057-9). U of Chicago Pr.

Caldwell, Robert G. & Black, James A. Juvenile Delinquency. LC 79-153805. 358p. 1971. 16.50 (ISBN 0-686-74195-1). Krieger.

Carpenter, Mary. Juvenile Delinquents, Their Condition & Treatment. LC 76-108224. (Criminology, Law Enforcement, & Social Problems Ser.: No. 107). (With essay by Katharine Lenroot & index added). 1970. Repr. of 1953 ed. lib. bdg. 15.00 (ISBN 0-87585-107-X). Patterson Smith.

--Reformatory Schools for the Children of the Perishing & Dangerous Classes & for Juvenile Offenders. LC 72-108223. (Criminology, Law Enforcement, & Social Problems Ser.: No. 106). 1970. Repr. of 1851 ed. lib. bdg. 15.00 (ISBN 0-87585-106-1). Patterson Smith.

Carter, Robert M. & Klein, Malcolm. Back on the Street: The Diversion of Juvenile Offenders. (Illus.). 400p. 1976. pap. 12.95 (ISBN 0-13-055319-0). P-H.

Cavan, Ruth S. & Ferdinand, Theodore N. Juvenile Delinquency. 4th ed. 448p. 1981. text ed. 17.50 scp (ISBN 0-06-041206-2, HarpC). Har-Row.

Cavan, Ruth S., ed. Readings in Juvenile Delinquency. 3rd ed. LC 74-26560. 1975. pap. text ed. 14.50 scp (ISBN 0-397-47318-4, HarpC). Har-Row.

Chirol, Yves, et al. Delinquance Juvenile et Developpement Socio-Economique. (Publication Du Centre De Europeen De Coordination De Recherche et De Documentation En Sciences Sociales: No. 6). (Illus.). pap. 35.00x (ISBN 90-2797-882-4). Mouton.

Cloward, Richard A. & Ohlin, Lloyd E. Delinquency & Opportunity: A Theory of Delinquent Gangs. LC 60-10892. 1966. 17.95 (ISBN 0-02-905600-4); pap. text ed. 5.95 (ISBN 0-02-905590-3). Free Pr.

Coates, Robert B. & Miller, Alden D. Diversity in a Youth Correctional System: Handling Delinquents in Massachusetts. LC 78-7311. 1979. reference 17.50 (ISBN 0-88410-787-6). Ballinger Pub.

Coffey, Alan R. Juvenile Justice As a System: Law Enforcement to Rehabilitation. (Criminal Justice Ser). 1974. ref. ed. 12.95 (ISBN 0-13-514372-1). P-H.

--The Prevention of Crime & Delinquency. (Illus.). 400p. 1975. 16.95 (ISBN 0-13-699157-2). P-H.

Cohen, A. K. Delinquent Boys. LC 55-7337. 1955. 14.95 (ISBN 0-02-905760-4); pap. text ed. 4.95 (ISBN 0-02-905770-1). Free Pr.

Cottle, Thomas J. Children in Jail. LC 75-77440. 1977. 9.95 (ISBN 0-8070-0492-8); pap. 4.95 (ISBN 0-8070-0493-6, BP589). Beacon Pr.

Cromwell, Paul F., Jr., et al. Introduction to Juvenile Delinquency: Text & Readings. (Criminal Justice Ser.). 1978. pap. text ed. 14.50 (ISBN 0-8299-0153-1). West Pub.

Crow, Lester D. & Crow, Alice. Our Teen-Age Boys & Girls. facs. ed. LC 68-58783. (Essay Index Reprint Ser). 1945. 16.50 (ISBN 0-8369-1030-3). Arno.

De Fleur, Lois B. Delinquency in Argentina: A Study of Cordoba Youth. (Illus., Orig.). 1970. pap. 4.00 (ISBN 0-87422-003-3). Wash St U Pr.

Deutsch, Albert. Our Rejected Children. LC 74-1680. (Children & Youth Ser.: Vol. 29). 316p. 1974. Repr. of 1950 ed. 19.00x (ISBN 0-405-05958-2). Arno.

Donohue, John K. Baffling Eyes of Youth. LC 74-9578. 251p. 1974. Repr. of 1957 ed. lib. bdg. 15.00x (ISBN 0-8371-7601-8, DOBY). Greenwood.

Doshay, Lewis J. Boy Sex Offender & His Later Career. LC 69-14921. (Criminology, Law Enforcement, & Social Problems Ser.: No. 59). 1969. Repr. of 1943 ed. 12.00 (ISBN 0-87585-059-6). Patterson Smith.

Drucker, Saul & Hexter, Maurice-Beck. Children Astray. LC 74-1681. (Children & Youth Ser.: Vol. 28). 450p. 1974. Repr. of 1923 ed. 25.00x (ISBN 0-405-05959-0). Arno.

Eldefonso, Edward. Law Enforcement & the Youthful Offender. 3rd ed. LC 77-13331. 363p. 1978. 18.95 (ISBN 0-471-03234-4); tchrs. manual avail. (ISBN 0-471-03769-9). Wiley.

Elliott, Desmond & Voss, Harwin L. Delinquency & Dropout. 224p. 1974. 19.95 (ISBN 0-669-91934-9). Lexington Bks.

Empey, LaMar T. & Lubeck, Stephen G. Explaining Delinquency: Construction, Test & Reformulation of a Sociological Theory. 1971. 16.95x (ISBN 0-669-74641-X). Lexington Bks.

Evans, David J. Geographical Perspectives in Juvenile Delinquency. 132p. 1980. text ed. 27.75x (ISBN 0-566-00351-1, Pub. by Gower Pub Co England). Renouf.

Fabricant, Michael. Deinstitutionalizing Delinquent Youth. 222p. 1980. text ed. 15.50x (ISBN 0-87073-866-6); pap. text ed. 9.95x (ISBN 0-87073-892-5). Schenkman.

Falkin, Gregory R. Reducing Delinquency. (Illus.). 240p. 1979. 21.95 (ISBN 0-669-02318-3). Lexington Bks.

Ferdinand, Theodore N., ed. Juvenile Delinquency: Little Brother Grows up. LC 77-81152. (Sage Research Progress Series in Criminology: Vol. 2). (Illus.). 160p. 1977. 15.00 (ISBN 0-8039-0916-0); pap. 7.50 (ISBN 0-8039-0911-X). Sage.

Ferracuti, Franco, et al. Delinquents & Nondelinquents in the Puerto Rican Slum Culture. LC 75-16465. 1975. 15.00 (ISBN 0-8142-0239-X). Ohio St U Pr.

Finestone, Harold. Victims of Change: Juvenile Delinquents in American Society. LC 76-5327. (Contributions in Sociology: No. 20). (Illus.). 256p. 1976. lib. bdg. 22.50 (ISBN 0-8371-8897-0, FTD/). Greenwood.

Flammang, C. J. Police Juvenile Enforcement. 284p. 1972. 18.75 (ISBN 0-398-02280-1). C C Thomas.

Frankenstein, C. Varieties of Juvenile Delinquency. 1970. 37.50x (ISBN 0-677-02820-2). Gordon.

Friday, Paul C. & Stewart, V. Lorne, eds. Youth Crime & Juvenile Justice: International Perspectives. LC 77-7820. (Praeger Special Studies). 1977. text ed. 23.95 (ISBN 0-03-022646-5). Praeger.

Friedlander, Kate. Psychoanalytical Approach to Juvenile Delinquency: Theory, Case Studies, Treatment. 1960. text ed. 17.50 (ISBN 0-8236-4400-6). Intl Univs Pr.

Fyvel, T. R. Troublemakers: Rebellious Youth in an Affluent Society. LC 62-13142. 1964. pap. 2.25 (ISBN 0-8052-0073-8). Schocken.

Garabedian, Peter G. & Gibbons, Don C., eds. Becoming Delinquent: Young Offenders & the Correctional Process. LC 73-91727. (Illus.). 1970. text ed. 19.95x (ISBN 0-202-30103-6). Aldine Pub.

Gardiner, Muriel. The Deadly Innocents: Portraits of Children Who Kill. LC 75-36379. 192p. 1976. 13.95x (ISBN 0-465-01583-2). Basic.

Giallombardo, Rose. Juvenile Delinquency. 4th ed. 600p. 1982. pap. text ed. 9.95 (ISBN 0-471-08344-5). Wiley.

Giallombardo, Rose, ed. Juvenile Delinquency: A Book of Readings. 3rd ed. LC 75-35887. 1976. pap. text ed. 16.95 (ISBN 0-471-29726-7). Wiley.

Gittler, Josephine. Standards Relating to Juvenile Probation Function: Intake & Predisposition Investigative Services. (Juvenile Justice Standards Project Ser.). 1980. softcover 7.95 (ISBN 0-88410-828-7); casebound 14.50 (ISBN 0-88410-248-3). Ballinger Pub.

Glueck, Sheldon & Glueck, Eleanor. Toward a Typology of Juvenile Offenders: Implications for Therapy & Prevention. LC 71-115014. 200p. 1970. 29.00 (ISBN 0-8089-0648-8). Grune.

Glueck, Sheldon & Glueck, Eleanor T. Delinquents & Nondelinquents in Perspective. LC 68-25609. 1968. 15.00x (ISBN 0-674-19600-7). Harvard U Pr.

Glueck, Sheldon S. & Glueck, Eleanor T. Juvenile Delinquents Grown Up. 1940. 19.00 (ISBN 0-527-34084-7). Kraus Repr.

--One Thousand Juvenile Delinquents. 1934 14.00 (ISBN 0-527-34100-2). Kraus Repr.

--Physique & Delinquency. 1956. 28.00 (ISBN 0-527-34104-5). Kraus Repr.

Gold, Martin. Status Forces in Delinquent Boys. 229p. 1963. pap. 5.00 (ISBN 0-87944-035-X). Inst Soc Res.

Goldberg, Harriet L. Child Offenders: A Study in Diagnosis & Treatment. LC 69-14928. (Criminology, Law Enforcement, & Social Problems Ser.: No. 75). 1969. Repr. of 1948 ed. 15.00 (ISBN 0-87585-075-8). Patterson Smith.

Goldberg, Jacob A. & Goldberg, Rosamond W. Girls on the City Streets: A Study of 1400 Cases of Rape. LC 74-3952. (Women in America Ser). 384p. 1974. Repr. of 1935 ed. 22.00x (ISBN 0-405-06099-8). Arno.

Goshen, Charles E. Society & the Youthful Offender. (American Lectures in Behavioral Science & Law Ser.). (Illus.). 192p. 1974. 14.50 (ISBN 0-398-02934-2). C C Thomas.

Gough, Aidan. Standards Relating to Non-Criminal Misbehavior. (Juvenile Justice Standards Project Ser.). Date not set. softcover 6.95 (ISBN 0-88410-832-5). Ballinger Pub.

Griffin, Brenda S. & Griffin, Charles T. Juvenile Delinquency in Perspective. (Illus.). 1978. text ed. 18.95 scp (ISBN 0-06-042512-1, HarpC). Har-Row.

Grimm, Fred. No Time for Fairy Tales. LC 80-81759. 158p. 1980. pap. 3.95 (ISBN 0-914850-44-X). Impact Tenn.

Hackler, James C. The Prevention of Youthful Crime: The Great Stumble Forward. 1979. pap. 10.90x (ISBN 0-416-60001-8). Methuen Inc.

Hahn, Paul H. The Juvenile Offender & the Law. 2nd ed. (Criminal Justice Text Ser). 1978. text ed. 17.95 (ISBN 0-87084-337-0). Anderson Pub Co.

Hardy, Richard E. & Cull, John G., eds. Climbing Ghetto Walls: Disadvantagement, Delinquency & Rehabilitation. (American Lectures in Social & Rehabilitation Psychology Ser.). (Illus.). 210p. 1973. 12.75 (ISBN 0-398-02865-6). C C Thomas.

--Fundamentals of Juvenile Criminal Behavior & Drug Abuse. 276p. 1975. 18.50 (ISBN 0-398-03162-2). C C Thomas.

--Problems of Adolescents: Social & Psychological Approach. (Amer. Lec. in Social & Rehabilitation Psychology Ser.). (Illus.). 296p. 1974. 19.75 (ISBN 0-398-03163-0). C C Thomas.

--Psychological & Vocational Rehabilitation of the Youthful Delinquent. (American Lectures in Social Rehabilitation Psychology Ser.). (Illus.). 264p. 1974. 16.50 (ISBN 0-398-03154-1). C C Thomas.

Hart, Hastings H. Preventive Treatment of Neglected Children with Special Papers by Leading Authorities. LC 70-137169. (Poverty U.S.A. Historical Record Ser). 1971. Repr. of 1910 ed. 20.00 (ISBN 0-405-03107-6). Arno.

Hawes, Joseph M. Children in Urban Society: Juvenile Delinquency in Nineteenth-Century America. (Urban Life in America Ser). 1971. 13.95 (ISBN 0-19-501410-3). Oxford U Pr.

Healy, William. Individual Delinquent, a Text-Book of Diagnosis & Prognosis for All Concerned in Understanding Offenders. LC 69-16238. (Criminology, Law Enforcement, & Social Problems Ser.: No. 85). (Illus.). 1969. Repr. of 1915 ed. 30.00 (ISBN 0-87585-085-5). Patterson Smith.

Healy, William & Bronner, Augusta F. Delinquents & Criminals: Their Making & Unmaking. Repr. of 1926 ed. 10.00 (ISBN 0-404-03197-8). AMS Pr.

--Delinquents & Criminals, Their Making & Unmaking, Studies in Two American Cities. LC 69-14931. (Criminology, Law Enforcement, & Social Problems Ser.: No. 69). (With an intro added). 1969. Repr. of 1926 ed. 12.00 (ISBN 0-87585-069-3). Patterson Smith.

--New Light on Delinquency & Its Treatment. Repr. of 1936 ed. lib. bdg. 15.00 (ISBN 0-8371-2253-8, HENL). Greenwood.

Hindelang, Michael J., et al. Measuring Delinquency. (Sage Library of Social Research). 248p. 20.00 (ISBN 0-8039-1598-5); pap. 9.95 (ISBN 0-8039-1599-3). Sage.

Hirschi, Travis. Causes of Delinquency. LC 69-16508. 1969. 22.75x (ISBN 0-520-01487-1); pap. 5.95x (ISBN 0-520-01901-6, CAMPUS47). U of Cal Pr.

Hirschi, Travis & Selvin, Hanan C. Principles of Survey Analysis. LC 67-15058. Orig. Title: Delinquency Research. 1973. pap. text ed. 5.95 (ISBN 0-02-914740-9). Free Pr.

Hoenig, Gary. Reaper: The Inside Story of a Gang Leader. LC 73-22673. 192p. 1975. 6.95 (ISBN 0-672-51896-1). Bobbs.

Hyde, Margaret O. Juvenile Justice & Injustice. (gr. 7 up). 1977. lib. bdg. 7.90 s&l (ISBN 0-531-00122-9). Watts.

Index to Abstracts on Crime & Juvenile Delinquency: 1968-1975. 201p. 1977. 25.00 (ISBN 0-667-00293-6). Microfilming Corp.

Jensen, Gary F. Sociology of Delinquency: Current Issues. (Sage Research Progress Series in Criminology: Vol. 22). 160p. 1981. 15.00 (ISBN 0-8039-1696-5); pap. 7.50 (ISBN 0-8039-1697-3). Sage.

Jensen, Gary F. & Rojek, Dean G. Readings in Juvenile Delinquency. 448p. 1982. pap. text ed. 12.95 (ISBN 0-669-03763-X). Heath.

Johnson, R. E. Juvenile Delinquency & Its Origins. LC 78-67263. (ASA Rose Monograph). (Illus.). 1979. 19.95 (ISBN 0-521-22477-2); pap. 6.95 (ISBN 0-521-29516-5). Cambridge U Pr.

Jones, Vernon F. Adolescents with Behavior Problems: Strategies for Teaching, Counseling & Parent Involvement. 353p. 1979. 19.95 (ISBN 0-205-06801-4). Allyn.

Junker, John M. Standards Relating to Juvenile Delinquency & Sanctions. (Juvenile Justice Standards Project Ser.). 1980. softcover 5.95 (ISBN 0-88410-829-5); casebound 12.50 (ISBN 0-88410-235-1). Ballinger Pub.

Kamm, Ernest, et al. Juvenile Law & Procedure in California. 2nd ed. (California Handbook Ser). 1971. pap. text ed. 7.95x (ISBN 0-02-474690-8, 47469). Macmillan.

Klewpuer, Jack & Parker, Rodger. Juvenile Delinquency & Juvenile Justice. 384p. 1981. 14.95 (ISBN 0-686-73912-4, New Viewpoints). Watts.

Konopka, Gisela. Young Girls: A Portrait of Adolescence. 8.95 (ISBN 0-13-977215-4, Spec); pap. 3.45 (ISBN 0-13-977207-3, Spec). P-H.

Kornhauser, Ruth R. Social Sources of Delinquency: An Appraisal of Analytic Models. LC 78-3776. (Illus.). 1978. lib. bdg. 18.00x (ISBN 0-226-45113-5). U of Chicago Pr.

Kratcoski, P. & Kratcoski, L. Juvenile Delinquency. 1979. 16.95 (ISBN 0-13-514281-4). P-H.

Kupperstein, Leonore R. & Caldee, Jaime Toro. Delincuencia Juvenil En Puerto Rico. pap. 5.00 (ISBN 0-8477-2478-6). U of PR Pr.

Kvaraceus, William & Miller, Walter B. Delinquent Behavior, 2 vols. in 1. LC 76-2585. 1976. Repr. of 1959 ed. lib. bdg. 28.25x (ISBN 0-8371-8794-X, KVDB). Greenwood.

Lamson, Amy. Psychology of Juvenile Crime. 1982. in prep. (ISBN 0-89885-060-6). Human Sci Pr.

Lander, Bernard. Towards an Understanding of Juvenile Delinquency. LC 72-120208. (Columbia University. Studies in the Social Sciences: No. 578). Repr. of 1954 ed. 11.50 (ISBN 0-404-51578-9). AMS Pr.

Langer, Sidney. Scared Straight: Fear in the Deterrence of Delinquency. LC 80-5859. 141p. 1981. lib. bdg. 15.50 (ISBN 0-8191-1494-4); pap. text ed. 6.75 (ISBN 0-8191-1495-2). U Pr of Amer.

Lerman, Paul. Community Treatment & Social Control: A Critical Analysis of Juvenile Correctional Policy. LC 74-11629. (Studies in Crime & Justice). 1977. pap. 4.95 (ISBN 0-226-47308-2, P735, Phoen). U of Chicago Pr.

LeShan, Eda. The Roots of Crime: What You Need to Know About Crime & What You Can Do About It. LC 80-69999. 192p. (gr. 7 up). 1981. 8.95 (ISBN 0-590-07532-2, Four Winds). Schol Bk Serv.

Levine, Phyllis. Delinquency Proneness: A Comparison of Delinquent Tendencies in Minors Under Court Supervision. LC 77-90356. 1978. pap. 8.00 perfect bdg. (ISBN 0-88247-516-9). R & E Res Assoc.

Lewis, Dorothy O. & Balla, David A. Delinquency & Psychopathology. LC 76-44883. 1976. 29.50 (ISBN 0-8089-0976-2). Grune.

Lewis, Dorothy O., ed. Vulnerabilities to Delinquency. 343p. 1981. text ed. 30.00 (ISBN 0-89335-136-9). Spectrum Pub.

Liu, Jin-An. Sino-American Juvenile Justice System. LC 80-67051. (Scholarly Monographs). 340p. 1980. pap. 27.50 (ISBN 0-8408-0512-8). Carrollton Pr.

McClintock, F. H. & Bottoms, A. E. Criminals Coming of Age. (Cambridge Studies in Criminology). 1973. text ed. 20.95 (ISBN 0-435-82580-1). Heinemann Ed.

McPartland, James M. & McDill, Edward L., eds. Violence in Schools: Perspectives, Programs & Positions. 1977. 17.95 (ISBN 0-669-01082-0). Lexington Bks.

Malmquist, Carl. Handbook of Adolescence. LC 78-53819. 1978. 40.00x (ISBN 0-87668-270-0). Aronson.

Mannheim, Hermann. Juvenile Delinquency in an English Middletown. LC 73-108226. (Criminology, Law Enforcement, & Social Problems Ser.: No. 109). (Illus., With intro. added). 1970. Repr. of 1948 ed. 9.00 (ISBN 0-87585-109-6). Patterson Smith.

Marohn, Richard C., et al. Juvenile Delinquents: Psychodynamic Assessment & Hospital Treatment. LC 80-18398. 300p. 1980. 22.50 (ISBN 0-87630-239-8). Brunner-Mazel.

Martin, F. M., et al, eds. Children Out of Court. 320p. 1981. 27.00x (ISBN 0-7073-0287-0, Pub. by Scottish Academic Pr Scotland). Columbia U Pr.

Martinez, Emanuel J. Aggression & Criminality of Adolescence. 1979. 7.50 (ISBN 0-682-49224-8, University). Exposition.

Matza, D. Deliquency & Drift. LC 64-18135. 1964. pap. text ed. 9.95x (ISBN 0-471-57708-1). Wiley.

Mennel, Robert M. Thorns & Thistles: Juvenile Delinquents in the United States, 1825-1940. LC 72-95187. 259p. 1973. text ed. 15.00x (ISBN 0-87451-070-8). U Pr of New Eng.

Meyer, Henry J., et al. Girls at Vocational High: An Experiment in Social Work Intervention. LC 65-16221. 1965. 7.95 (ISBN 0-87154-601-9). Russell Sage.

Moore, Jim. Flip Line. 300p. (Orig.). 1981. pap. 2.95 (ISBN 0-686-28992-7). Tuppence.

Moore, Joan, et al. Homeboys: Gangs, Drugs & Prison in the Barrios of Los Angeles. LC 78-11808. (Illus.). 1979. 19.50x (ISBN 0-87722-121-9); pap. 8.95 (ISBN 0-87722-114-6). Temple U Pr.

Morrison, William D. Juvenile Offenders. LC 75-156029. Repr. of 1897 ed. 10.00 (ISBN 0-404-09130-X). AMS Pr.

--Juvenile Offenders. LC 70-172589. (Criminology, Law Enforcement, & Social Problems Ser.: No. 179). 1975. 12.50 (ISBN 0-87585-179-7). Patterson Smith.

Mueller, Gerhard O., et al. Delinquency & Puberty Examination of a Juvenile Delinquency Fad. (New York University Criminal Law Education & Research Center Monograph: No. 5). (Illus.). 123p. (Orig.). 1971. pap. text ed. 8.50x (ISBN 0-8377-0830-3). Rothman.

Murray, Charles A. & Cox, Louis A., Jr. Beyond Probation: Juvenile Corrections & the Chronic Delinquent. LC 79-17859. (Sage Library of Social Research: Vol. 94). (Illus.). 235p. 1979. 20.00x (ISBN 0-8039-1336-2); pap. 9.95 (ISBN 0-8039-1337-0). Sage.

Murrell, Mary & Lester, David. Juvenile Delinquency. 1981. pap. 9.95x (ISBN 0-02-478790-6). Macmillan.

Offer, Daniel, et al. The Psychological World of the Juvenile Delinquent. LC 78-53813. 1979. text ed. 15.00x (ISBN 0-465-06674-7). Basic.

Palmer, Ted & Lewis, Roy V. An Evaluation of Juvenile Diversion. LC 80-14818. 384p. 1980. text ed. 22.50 (ISBN 0-89946-020-8). Oelgeschlager.

Parizeau, Alice. Parenting & Delinquent Youth. LC 79-47982. 208p. 1980. 22.95x (ISBN 0-669-03620-X). Lexington Bks.

Parker, Howard, et al. Receiving Juvenile Justice: Adolescents & State Care & Control. 256p. 1981. 19.95x (ISBN 0-631-12727-5, Pub. by Basil Blackwell England); pap. 9.95x (ISBN 0-631-12745-3). Biblio Dist.

Peirce, Bradford K. Half Century with Juvenile Delinquents, or the New York House of Refuge & Its Times. LC 69-16242. (Criminology, Law Enforcement, & Social Problems Ser.: No. 91). (Illus., With intro. added). 1969. Repr. of 1869 ed. 18.00 (ISBN 0-87585-091-X). Patterson Smith.

Perez, Joseph F. Family Roots of Adolescent Delinquency. 1978. text ed. 16.95x (ISBN 0-442-26535-2). Van Nos Reinhold.

Phelps, Thomas R. Juvenile Delinquency: A Contemporary View. LC 74-31511. 300p. 1976. text ed. 19.95 (ISBN 0-87620-500-7). Goodyear.

Phillipson, Michael. Understanding Crime & Delinquency: A Sociological Introduction. LC 73-84934. (Law in Action Ser.). 204p. 1974. text ed. 9.95x (ISBN 0-202-23013-9). Beresford Bk Serv.

Pickett, Robert S. House of Refuge: Origins of Juvenile Reform in New York State, 1815-1857. LC 69-19745. (New York State Studies). (Illus.). 1969. 10.95x (ISBN 0-8156-2138-8). Syracuse U Pr.

Platt, Anthony M. The Child Savers. LC 69-14827. (Phoenix Ser.). 1977. pap. 4.95 (ISBN 0-226-67072-4, P462, Phoen). U of Chicago Pr.

--The Child Savers: The Invention of Delinquency. 2nd, enl. ed. LC 69-14827. 1980. Repr. of 1969 ed. 12.50x (ISBN 0-226-67073-2). U of Chicago Pr.

Powers, Edwin & Witmer, Helen. Experiment in the Prevention of Delinquency: The Cambridge - Somerville Youth Study. LC 70-172573. (Criminology, Law Enforcement, & Social Problems Ser.: No. 159). 1972. Repr. of 1951 ed. 18.50 (ISBN 0-87585-159-2). Patterson Smith.

Ramos, Nancy P., ed. Delinquent Youth & Learning Disabilities. 1978. pap. text ed. 4.00x (ISBN 0-87879-190-6). Acad Therapy.

Ravielli, Anthony. What Are Street Games? LC 80-22657. 1981. 9.95 (ISBN 0-689-30838-8). Atheneum.

Reckless, Walter C. & Dinitz, Simon. The Prevention of Juvenile Delinquency: An Experiment. LC 72-6750. 1972. 12.00 (ISBN 0-8142-0182-2). Ohio St U Pr.

Redl, Fritz & Wineman, David. Children Who Hate: The Disorganization & Breakdown of Behavior Controls. LC 51-13784. 1965. pap. 4.95 (ISBN 0-02-925960-6). Free Pr.

Reifen, David. The Juvenile Court in a Changing Society: Young Offenders in Israel. LC 73-178000. 280p. 1973. 10.00x (ISBN 0-8122-7649-3). U of Pa Pr.

Reiner, Beatrice S. & Kaufman, Irving. Character Disorders in Parents of Delinquents. LC 59-15631. 1959. pap. 5.00x (ISBN 0-87304-089-9). Family Serv.

Richards, Pamela, et al. Crime As Play: Delinquency in a Middle Class Suburb. LC 79-12772. 1979. 20.00 (ISBN 0-88410-798-1). Ballinger Pub.

Robison, Sophia. Can Delinquency Be Measured? LC 73-9635. 304p. 1973. Repr. of 1936 ed. 25.00 (ISBN 0-527-76040-4). Kraus Repr.

Robison, Sophia Moses. Can Delinquency Be Measured? LC 75-129307. (Criminology, Law Enforcement, & Social Problems Ser.: No. 129). (Illus.). 312p. (With intro. added). 1972. Repr. of 1936 ed. 15.00 (ISBN 0-87585-129-0). Patterson Smith.

Roman, Melvin. Reaching Delinquents Through Reading. (American Lecture Psychology). (Illus.). 144p. 1957. photocopy ed. spiral 14.50 (ISBN 0-398-04407-4). C C Thomas.

Rosenquist, Carl M. & Megargee, Edwin I. Delinquency in Three Cultures. (Hogg Foundation Research Ser). (Illus.). 570p. 1969. 17.50x (ISBN 0-292-78415-5). U of Tex Pr.

Rossman, Parker. After Punishment What? Discipline & Reconciliation. 1980. 8.95 (ISBN 0-529-05734-4, RB5734). Collins Pubs.

Roucek, Joseph S., ed. Juvenile Delinquency. LC 70-128306. (Essay Index Reprint Ser). 1958. 22.00 (ISBN 0-8369-1848-7). Arno.

--Sociology of Crime. Repr. of 1961 ed. lib. bdg. 23.75x (ISBN 0-8371-2105-1, ROSC). Greenwood.

Rubenfeld, Seymour. Family of Outcasts. LC 65-20000. 1965. 12.95 (ISBN 0-02-927580-6). Free Pr.

Sanders, Wiley B. Negro Child Welfare in North Carolina. LC 68-55782. (Criminology, Law Enforcement, & Social Problems Ser.: No. 18). (Illus.). 1968. Repr. of 1933 ed. 15.00 (ISBN 0-87585-018-9). Patterson Smith.

Sanders, Wiley B., ed. Juvenile Offenders for a Thousand Years: Selected Readings from Anglo-Saxon Times to 1900. LC 76-97012. 1970. 24.00x (ISBN 0-8078-1127-0). U of NC Pr.

Sanders, William. Juvenile Delinquency: An Introduction. 448p. 1980. pap. text ed. cancelled (ISBN 0-03-040776-1, HoltC). HR&W.

Sanders, William B. Juvenile Delinquency. LC 74-15685. 238p. 1976. pap. text ed. 6.95 (ISBN 0-03-038311-0, HoltC). HR&W.

--Juvenile Delinquency: Causes, Patterns, & Reactions. 1981. text ed. 16.96 (ISBN 0-03-040776-1, HoltC). HR&W.

Sandhu, Harjit. Juvenile Delinquency-Causes, Control & Prevention. (Illus.). 1977. text ed. 14.50 (ISBN 0-07-054650-9, G); instructor's manual 3.50 (ISBN 0-07-054651-7). McGraw.

Schauss, Alexander. Diet, Crime & Delinquency. 3.95 (ISBN 0-686-29957-4). Cancer Bk Hse.

Schlossman, Steven L. Love & the American Delinquent: The Theory & Practice of "Progressive" Juvenile Justice 1825-1920. LC 76-17699. 304p. 1981. pap. price not set (ISBN 0-226-73858-2). U of Chicago Pr.

Schur, Edwin M. Radical Nonintervention: Rethinking the Delinquency Problem. 192p. 1973 (ISBN 0-13-750422-5, Spec). pap. 3.95 (ISBN 0-13-750414-4, Spec). P-H.

Scrivenger, Mark. In Trouble with the Law. (New Citizen Books). (Illus.). 80p. 1973. 10.00x (ISBN 0-85340-226-4). Intl Pubns Serv.

Sellin, Thorsten & Wolfgang, Marvin E. The Measurement of Delinquency. (Criminology, Law Enforcement, & Social Problems Ser.: No. 209). 433p. 1975. Repr. of 1964 ed. 20.00 (ISBN 0-87585-209-2). Patterson Smith.

Sellin, Thorsten & Wolfgang, Marvin E., eds. Delinquency: Selected Studies. 161p. 1969. 9.00 (ISBN 0-471-77568-1, Pub. by Wiley). Krieger.

Shaw, Clifford R. Jack-Roller: A Delinquent Boy's Own Story. LC 66-23698. 1966. pap. 2.95 (ISBN 0-226-75126-0, P241, Phoen). U of Chicago Pr.

--Natural History of a Delinquent Career. LC 68-56042. (Illus.). 1968. Repr. of 1931 ed. lib. bdg. 16.75x (ISBN 0-8371-0654-0, SHDC). Greenwood.

Shaw, Clifford R. & McKay, Henry D. Juvenile Delinquency & Urban Areas. rev. ed. LC 69-14511. 1972. pap. 3.95 (ISBN 0-226-75127-9, P448, Phoen). U of Chicago Pr.

Shaw, Clifford R. & McKay, Henry D., eds. Juvenile Delinquency & Urban Areas. rev. ed. LC 69-14511. 1969. 14.75x (ISBN 0-226-75125-2). U of Chicago Pr.

Shaw, Clifford R., et al. Brothers in Crime. LC 38-38001. 1967. 12.50x (ISBN 0-226-75123-6). U of Chicago Pr.

Shichor, David & Kelly, Delos H., eds. Critical Issues in Juvenile Delinquency. LC 77-18579. (Illus.). 368p. 1980. 29.95x (ISBN 0-669-02103-2). Lexington Bks.

Short, James F., Jr. & Strodtbeck, Fred L. Group Process & Gang Delinquency. LC 65-14434. xxvi, 296p. 1974. pap. 3.45 (ISBN 0-226-75465-0, P585, Phoen). U of Chicago Pr.

Short, James F., Jr., ed. Delinquency, Crime, & Society. LC 75-27895. (Illus.). 1978. pap. 5.95 (ISBN 0-226-75469-3, P772, Phoen). U of Chicago Pr.

Shukla, K. S. Adolescent Thieves. 1979. text ed. 15.00x (ISBN 0-391-01925-2). Humanities.

Siegel, Larry J. & Senna, Joseph J. Juvenile Delinquency: Theory, Practice & Law. (Criminal Justice Ser.). (Illus.). 554p. 1981. text ed. 19.95 (ISBN 0-8299-0414-X). West Pub.

Smith, William C. Reactions to Delinquency. LC 78-70859. 1978. pap. text ed. 7.50 (ISBN 0-8191-0649-6). U Pr of Amer.

Sorrentino, Anthony. The Delinquent & His Neighbors. 250p. 1977. pap. text ed. 9.50 (ISBN 0-8191-0069-2). U Pr of Amer.

--How to Organize the Neighborhood for Delinquency Prevention. LC 79-1279. 1979. 22.95 (ISBN 0-87705-391-X); pap. 10.95 (ISBN 0-87705-413-4). Human Sci Pr.

--Organizing Against Crime: Redeveloping the Neighborhood. LC 76-21840. 1977. 24.95 (ISBN 0-87705-301-4). Human Sci Pr.

Spergel, Irving. Racketville, Slumtown, Haulburg: An Exploratory Study of Delinquent Subcultures. LC 64-17165. (Midway Reprint Ser). 1973. pap. 7.00x (ISBN 0-226-76934-8). U of Chicago Pr.

Sterne, Richard S. Delinquent Conduct & Broken Homes. 1964. 4.00x (ISBN 0-8084-0101-7); pap. 1.95 (ISBN 0-8084-0102-5, B35). Coll & U Pr.

Stott, D. H. Delinquency: The Problem & Its Prevention. LC 80-25928. 521p. 1981. text ed. 25.00 (ISBN 0-686-73344-4). SP Med & Sci Bks.

--Saving Children from Delinquency. 1954. 4.75 (ISBN 0-8022-1658-7). Philos Lib.

Strang, Ruth. Juvenile Delinquency & the Schools. LC 48-6850. (National Society for the Study of Education Yearbooks Ser: No. 47, Pt. 1). 1948. 5.50x (ISBN 0-226-60000-9). U of Chicago Pr.

Strasburg, Paul A. Violent Delinquents. LC 77-17819. (Illus.). 1978. pap. 8.95 (ISBN 0-671-18346-X). Monarch Pr.

Stratton, John R. & Terry, Robert M. Prevention of Deliquency: Problems & Programs. (Orig.). 1968. text ed. 6.95x (ISBN 0-02-417930-2). Macmillan.

Stumphauzer, Jerome S. Behavior Therapy with Delinquents. (Illus.). 376p. 1973. photocopy ed. spiral 34.75 (ISBN 0-398-02668-8). C C Thomas.

Swanson, Guy E. Emotional Disturbances & Juvenile Delinquency. Zuckerman, Harriet & Merton, Robert K., eds. LC 79-9033. (Dissertations on Sociology Ser.). 1980. lib. bdg. 18.00x (ISBN 0-405-13000-7). Arno.

Tappan, Paul W. Delinquent Girls in Court: A Study of the Wayward Minor Court of New York. LC 69-14950. (Criminology, Law Enforcement, & Social Problems Ser.: No. 67). 1969. Repr. of 1947 ed. 15.00- (ISBN 0-87585-067-7). Patterson Smith.

Thomas, William I. The Unadjusted Girl: With Cases & Standpoint for Behavior Analysis. 1967. lib. bdg. 13.50x (ISBN 0-88307-267-X). Gannon.

Thomas, William I. & Thomas, Dorothy S. The Child in America, Behavior Problems & Programs. (Social Welfare Ser). Repr. of 1928 ed. 27.00 (ISBN 0-384-60178-2). Johnson Repr.

Thornton, William E., et al. Delinquency & Justice. 1981. text ed. 15.95x (ISBN 0-673-15225-1). Scott F.

Thorpe, D. H., et al. Out of Care: The Community Support of Juvenile Offenders. (Illus.). 224p. 1980. text ed. 27.50x (ISBN 0-04-364018-4); pap. text ed. 10.95x (ISBN 0-04-364019-2). Allen Unwin.

Troanowicz, Robert C. Juvenile Delinquency: Concepts & Control. 2nd ed. (Illus.). 1978. ref. ed. 16.95 (ISBN 0-13-514331-4). P-H.

Twentieth Century Fund. Confronting Youth Crime: Report of the Twentieth Century Fund Task Force on Sentencing Policy Toward Young Offenders. LC 78-3612. (Illus.). 1978. text ed. 16.50x (ISBN 0-8419-0381-6). Holmes & Meier.

Tyler, Gus, ed. Organized Crime in America: A Book of Readings. 1962. pap. 5.95 (ISBN 0-472-06127-5, 127, AA). U of Mich Pr.

U. S. Congress - Senate Committee on the Judiciary. Juvenile Delinquency: National, Federal & Youth-Serving Agencies. LC 68-55115. (Illus.). 1968. Repr. of 1954 ed. lib. bdg. 32.00 (ISBN 0-8371-0699-0, JUDA). Greenwood.

--Juvenile Delinquency, Youth Employment. LC 68-55117. (Illus.). 1968. Repr. of 1955 ed. lib. bdg. 15.00 (ISBN 0-8371-0700-8, JUDY). Greenwood.

Vachss, Andrew H. & Bakal, Yitzhak. The Life-Style Violent Juvenile. LC 77-2520. 1979. 25.95 (ISBN 0-669-01515-6). Lexington Bks.

Van Waters, Miriam. Youth in Conflict. LC 70-120218. Repr. of 1925 ed. 22.50 (ISBN 0-404-06754-9). AMS Pr.

Vedder, Clyde B. Juvenile Offenders. rev., 6th ed. (Illus.). 368p. 1979. text ed. 14.25 (ISBN 0-398-03844-9). C C Thomas.

Wadsworth, Michael. The Roots of Delinquency: Infancy, Adolescence & Crime. 1979. text ed. 23.50x (ISBN 0-06-497305-0). B&N.

Walker, Robert N. Psychology of the Youthful Offender. 2nd ed. 164p. 1973. 14.75 (ISBN 0-398-02859-1). C C Thomas.

Wallenstein, Nehemiah. Character & Personality of Children from Broken Homes. LC 70-177664. (Columbia University. Teachers College. Contributions to Education: No. 721). Repr. of 1937 ed. 17.50 (ISBN 0-404-55721-X). AMS Pr.

Wattenberg, William W., ed. Social Deviancy Among Youth. LC 66-2248. (National Society for the Study of Education Yearbooks Ser: No. 65, Pt. 1). 1966. 8.00x (ISBN 0-226-60081-5). U of Chicago Pr.

Webb, G. L. Young First Offenders: Their Criminal Careers. LC 78-72958. 1979. 9.95 (ISBN 0-933012-03-9). Coker Pub.

Weber, George H. Child-Menders. LC 79-4244. 223p. 1979. 17.50x (ISBN 0-8039-1184-X). Sage.

Wenk, Ernst A., ed. Delinquency Prevention & the Schools: Emerging Perspectives. LC 76-41104. (Sage Contemporary Social Science Issues: Vol. 29). 1976. pap. 5.95x (ISBN 0-8039-0730-3). Sage.

Williams, L. Weinberg. Our Runaway. LC 78-15132. 1979. pap. 2.95 (ISBN 0-8170-0813-6). Judson.

Wilson, Paul R., ed. Delinquency in Australia: A Critical Appraisal. 1977. text ed. 25.00 (ISBN 0-7022-1372-1); pap. text ed. 12.95x (ISBN 0-7022-1371-3). U of Queensland Pr.

Winslow, Robert W. Juvenile Delinquency in a Free Society. 3rd ed. 1976. pap. text ed. 9.95x (ISBN 0-8221-0177-7). Dickenson.

Wolfgang, Marvin, et al. Deliquency in a Birth Cohort. LC 75-187929. (Studies in Crime & Justice). 1979. pap. text ed. 11.00x (ISBN 0-226-90554-3, Midway Reprint). U of Chicago Pr.

Youth in Trouble: Problems, Issues, & Programs in Texas. (Policy Research Project Report: No. 26). 1978. 3.00 (ISBN 0-89940-619-X). LBJ Sch Public Affairs.

JUVENILE DELINQUENCY–BIBLIOGRAPHY

Cabot, Philippe S., ed. Juvenile Delinquency: A Critical Annotated Bibliography. LC 75-138580. 1971. Repr. of 1946 ed. lib. bdg. 15.75x (ISBN 0-8371-5779-X, CAJD). Greenwood.

Crime & Juvenile Delinquency: A Bibliographic Guide to the Basic Microform Collection. LC 77-3702. 416p. 1977. 95.00 (ISBN 0-667-00292-8). Microfilming Corp.

Crime & Juvenile Delinquency: A Bibliographic Guide to the 1976 Documents Update. 99p. 1978. 50.00 (ISBN 0-667-00545-5). Microfilming Corp.

Crime & Juvenile Delinquency: A Bibliographic Guide to the 1978 Documents Update. 1981. pap. write for info. (ISBN 0-667-00571-4). Microfilming Corp.

Crime & Juvenile Delinquency: A Bibliographic Guide to the 1979 Documents Update. 1981. pap. write for info. (ISBN 0-667-00588-9). Microfilming Corp.

Remick, Cecile P. An Annotated Bibliography of Works on Juvenile Delinquency in America & Britain in the Nineteenth Century. 1978. Repr. of 1976 ed. lib. bdg. 12.50 (ISBN 0-8492-2291-5). R West.

U. S. Congress - Senate Committee on the Judiciary. Juvenile Delinquency. 1955-1956. Repr. lib. bdg. 38.75 (ISBN 0-8371-2774-2, JUDE). Greenwood.

JUVENILE DELINQUENCY–GREAT BRITAIN

Boss, Peter. Social Policy & the Young Delinquent. (Library of Social Policy & Administration). (Orig.). 1967. text ed. 5.25x (ISBN 0-7100-4030-X); pap. text ed. 2.75x (ISBN 0-7100-4029-6). Humanities.

Gath, Dennis, et al. Child Guidance & Delinquency in a London Borough. (Maudsley Monographs: No. 24). (Illus.). 1977. text ed. 15.75x (ISBN 0-19-712146-2). Oxford U Pr.

Grunhut, Max. Juvenile Offenders Before the Courts. LC 77-27073. (Illus.). 1978. Repr. of 1956 ed. lib. bdg. 14.00x (ISBN 0-313-20194-3, GRJU). Greenwood.

Halloran, J. D., et al. Television & Delinquency. (Television Research Committee Working Papers: No. 3). 1970. pap. text ed. 13.00x (ISBN 0-7185-1088-7, Leicester). Humanities.

McDonald, Lynn. Social Class & Delinquency. 1969. 17.50 (ISBN 0-208-00835-7, Archon). Shoe String.

Morgan, Patricia. Delinquent Fantasies. LC 78-309292. 1979. 18.50 (ISBN 0-85117-116-8). Transatlantic.

Parker, Howard J. View from the Boys: A Sociology of Downtown Adolescents. LC 74-76184. (People, Plans & Problems Ser.). 1974. 17.95 (ISBN 0-7153-6456-1). David & Charles.

West, Donald J. Young Offender. 1967. text ed. 17.50 (ISBN 0-8236-7020-1). Intl Univs Pr.

JUVENILE DELINQUENCY–MEXICO

Rosenquist, Carl M. & Megargee, Edwin I. Delinquency in Three Cultures. (Hogg Foundation Research Ser). (Illus.). 570p. 1969. 17.50x (ISBN 0-292-78415-5). U of Tex Pr.

JUVENILE DETENTION HOMES

Amos, William E. & Manella, Raymond L. Readings in the Administration of Institutions for Delinquent Youth. 228p. 1965. photocopy ed. spiral 18.75 (ISBN 0-398-00041-7). C C Thomas.

Amos, William E. & Manella, Raymond L., eds. Delinquent Children in Juvenile Correctional Institutions: State Administered Reception & Diagnostic Centers. (Illus.). 176p. 1973. ed. spiral bdg. 14.75photocopy (ISBN 0-398-00040-9). C C Thomas.

Bartollas, C., et al. Juvenile Victimization: The Institutional Paradox. LC 76-3476. 324p. 1976. 18.95 (ISBN 0-470-05490-5). Halsted Pr.

Bartollas, Clemens, et al. Juvenile Victimization: The Institutional Paradox. LC 76-3476. 324p. 1976. 17.50 (ISBN 0-470-05490-5, Pub. by Wiley). Krieger.

Clements, Bruce & Clements, Hanna. Coming Home to a Place You've Never Been Before. LC 75-26716. 192p. (gr. 7 up). 1975. 6.95 (ISBN 0-374-31530-2). FS&G.

De Lopez, Awilda P. & Ortiz, Ernesto R. En la Calle Estabas: La Vida En una Institucion De Menores. 2nd ed. 3.75 (ISBN 0-8477-2415-8); pap. 3.40 (ISBN 0-8477-2416-6). U of PR Pr.

Eldefonso, E. & Hartinger, W. Control Treatment & Rehabilitation of Juvenile Offenders. 1976. 14.95x (ISBN 0-02-474160-4, 47416). Macmillan.

Fabricant, Michael. Deinstitutionalizing Delinquent Youth. 222p. 1980. text ed. 15.50x (ISBN 0-87073-866-6); pap. text ed. 9.95x (ISBN 0-87073-892-5). Schenkman.

Feld, Barry C. Neutralizing Inmate Violence: Juvenile Offenders in Institutions. LC 77-21389. (CCJ Series on Massachusetts Youth Correctional Reform). 1977. 16.50 (ISBN 0-88410-790-6). Ballinger Pub.

Hawes, Joseph M. Children in Urban Society: Juvenile Delinquency in Nineteenth-Century America. (Urban Life in America Ser). 1971. 13.95 (ISBN 0-19-501410-3). Oxford U Pr.

Hood, Roger. Homeless Borstal Boys. 103p. 1966. pap. text ed. 5.00x (ISBN 0-686-70847-4, Pub. by Bedford England). Renouf.

McEwen, Craig A. Designing Correctional Organizations for Youth: Dilemmas of Subcultural Development. LC 77-27488. 1978. 18.00 (ISBN 0-88410-789-2). Ballinger Pub.

Moseley, Sr. Riccarda & James, Howard. Knock On Our Door: A Home for Troubled Girls. LC 79-65849. 1979. 11.95 (ISBN 0-89526-683-0). Regnery-Gateway.

Mukherjee, S. K. Administration of Juvenile Correctional Institutions. 272p. 1974. text ed. 15.00x (ISBN 0-8426-0688-2). Verry.

O'Connor, Zena C. The Runaway Boy in the Correctional School. LC 74-177128. (Columbia University. Teachers College. Contributions to Education: No. 742). Repr. of 1938 ed. 17.50 (ISBN 0-404-55742-2). AMS Pr.

Ohlin, Lloyd E. & Coates, Robert B. Reforming Youth Corrections: The Massachusetts Experience in the Nineteenth & Twentieth Centuries. 1980. reference 16.00 (ISBN 0-88410-788-4). Ballinger Pub.

Polsky, Howard W. Cottage Six: Social System of Delinquent Boys in Residential Treatment. LC 76-50144. (Illus.). 192p. 1977. pap. text ed. 4.95 (ISBN 0-88275-475-0). Krieger.

Polsky, Howard W., et al. Dynamics of Residential Treatment: A Social System Analysis. 1968. 15.00x (ISBN 0-8078-1069-X). U of NC Pr.

JUVENILE DETENTION HOMES–GREAT BRITAIN

Mayers, Michael O. The Hard-Core Delinquent: An Experiment in Control & Care in a Community Home with Education. 1980. 17.95 (ISBN 0-566-00318-X, 03297-2, Pub. by Saxon Hse England). Lexington Bks.

Tutt, Norman. Care or Custody: Community Homes & the Treatment of Delinquency. LC 74-9318. 240p. 1975. 9.00x (ISBN 0-87586-049-4). Agathon.

Walter, J. A. Sent Away: A Study of Young Offenders in Care. 193p. 1978. text ed. 26.50x (ISBN 0-566-00199-3, Pub by Teakfield Ltd England). Renouf.

JUVENILE DRINKING

see Alcohol and Youth

JUVENILE ENCYCLOPEDIAS

see Children's Encyclopedias and Dictionaries

JUVENILE LITERATURE

see Children's Literature (Collections); also subdivisions under Children's Literature

JUVENILE VOYAGES AND TRAVELS

see Voyages and Travels, Juvenile

K

K-MESONS

see Mesons

K-THEORY

Bak, A. K-Theory of Forms. LC 80-7847. (Annals of Mathematics Studies: No. 98). 220p. 1980. 20.00x (ISBN 0-691-08274-X); pap. 8.50x (ISBN 0-691-08275-8). Princeton U Pr.

Bass, Hyman. Introduction to Some Methods of Algebraic K-Theory. LC 73-19925. (CBMS Regional Conference Series in Mathematics: No. 20). 1974. pap. 8.20 (ISBN 0-8218-1670-5, CBMS-20). Am Math.

Bott, Raoul. Lectures on K(X) (Math Lecture Notes Ser.: No. 22). 1969. 17.50 (ISBN 0-8053-1050-9, Adv Bk Prog). Benjamin-Cummings.

Friedlander, E. M. & Stein, M. R., eds. Algebraic K-Theory: Proceedings. (Lecture Notes in Mathematics Ser.: Vol. 854). 517p. 1981. pap. 27.00 (ISBN 0-387-10698-7). Springer-Verlag.

Hilton, Peter J. General Cohomology Theory & K. Theory. (London Mathematics Society Lecture Note Ser.: No. 1). 1970. text ed. 11.95 (ISBN 0-521-07976-4). Cambridge U Pr.

Hodgkin, L. H. Topics in K-Theory: Two Independent Contributions. LC 75-41435. (Lecture Notes in Mathematics: Vol. 496). 1975. pap. 15.30 (ISBN 0-387-07536-4). Springer-Verlag.

Karoubi, M. K-Theory: An Introduction. LC 77-23162. (Gsundlehsen Des Mathematischen Wissenschaften: Band 226). (Illus.). 1978. 45.10 (ISBN 0-387-08090-2). Springer-Verlag.

Moss, R. M. F. & Thomas, C. B. Algebraic K-Theory & Its Geometric Applications. LC 74-97991. (Lecture Notes in Mathematics). 1969. pap. 10.70 (ISBN 0-387-04627-5). Springer-Verlag.

Snaith, V. P. Algebraic Cobordism & K-Theory. LC 79-17981. (Memoirs Ser.: No. 221). 1979. 9.60 (ISBN 0-8218-2221-7). Am Math.

Swan, R. G. & Evans, E. G. K-Theory of Finite Groups & Orders. LC 75-133576. (Lecture Notes in Mathematics: Vol. 149). 1970. pap. 11.20 (ISBN 0-387-04938-X). Springer-Verlag.

KABAIL

see Kabyles

KABBALA

see Cabala

KABUKI

Brandon, James R., et al. Studies in Kabuki: Its Acting, Music, & Historical Context. LC 77-5336. 1978. pap. 6.50x (ISBN 0-8248-0452-X, Eastwest Ctr). U Pr of Hawaii.

Ernst, Earle. The Kabuki Theatre. (Illus.). 368p. 1974. pap. 4.95 (ISBN 0-8248-0319-1, Eastwest Ctr). U Pr of Hawaii.

Halford, Aubrey S. & Halford, Giovanna M. Kabuki Handbook: A Guide to Understanding & Appreciation. LC 55-10618. (Illus.). 1955. pap. 6.75 (ISBN 0-8048-0332-3). C E Tuttle.

Inoura, Yoshinobu & Kawatake, Toshio. Traditional Theatre of Japan. (Illus.). 200p. 1981. 20.00 (ISBN 0-8348-0161-2, Pub. by John Weatherhill Inc Tokyo). C E Tuttle.

Kincaid, Zoe. Kabuki: The Popular Stage of Japan. LC 65-19617. (Illus.). Repr. of 1925 ed. 25.00 (ISBN 0-405-08703-9). Arno.

Leiter, Samuel L. The Art of Kabuki: Famous Plays in Performance. LC 77-83107. 1979. 16.95 (ISBN 0-520-03555-0). U of Cal Pr.

--Kabuki Encyclopedia: An English-Language Adaptation of Kabuki Jiten. LC 78-73801. (Illus.). 1979. lib. bdg. 39.95 (ISBN 0-313-20654-6, LKE). Greenwood.

Malm, William P. Nagauta: The Heart of Kabuki Music. LC 73-6260. (Illus.). 344p. 1973. Repr. of 1963 ed. lib. bdg. 24.25 (ISBN 0-8371-6900-3, MANA). Greenwood.

KABUKI KYOGEN PLAYS

see Kyogen Plays

KABUKI PLAYS–TRANSLATIONS INTO ENGLISH

Brandon, James R. Kabuki: Five Classic Plays. LC 74-82192. (Illus.). 448p. 1975. 22.50x (ISBN 0-674-30485-3). Harvard U Pr.

Richie, Donald & Watanabe, Miyoko, trs. Six Kabuki Plays. 1963. pap. 5.50 (ISBN 0-89346-041-9, Pub. by Hokuseido Pr). Heian Intl.

KABYLES

see also Berbers

Bourdieu, P. Algeria Nineteen Sixty. LC 78-4237. (Studies in Modern Capitalism). (Illus.). 1979. 19.95 (ISBN 0-521-22090-4). Cambridge U Pr.

--Outline of a Theory of Practice. LC 76-11073. (Studies in Social Anthropology: No. 16). (Illus.). 1977. 29.95 (ISBN 0-521-21178-6); pap. 9.95x (ISBN 0-521-29164-X). Cambridge U Pr.

Bousquet-Lefevre, Laure M. Recherches sur la condition de la femme Kabyle: La coutume et l'oeuvre francaise. LC 77-87660. Repr. of 1939 ed. 18.50 (ISBN 0-404-16404-8). AMS Pr.

Hanoteau, A. & Letourneux, A. La Kabylie et les Kabyles, 3 vols. 2nd ed. LC 77-87661. Repr. of 1893 ed. Set. 110.00 (ISBN 0-404-16410-2). AMS Pr.

Terhorst, Bernd. With the Riff Kabyles. LC 69-18998. (Illus.). Repr. of 1926 ed. 13.75x (ISBN 0-8371-4948-7). Greenwood.

KACHIN TRIBES

Leach, E. R. Political Systems of Highland Burma: A Study of Kachin Social Structure. (Monographs on Social Anthropology Ser: No. 44). 1977. text ed. 15.00x (ISBN 0-391-00147-7, Athlone Pr); pap. text ed. 14.50x (ISBN 0-391-00975-3). Humanities.

KACHINAS

see Katcinas

KAESTNER, ERICH, 1899-

Last, R. W. Erich Kastner. (Modern German Authors Ser: No. 3). (Illus.). 128p. 1974. text ed. 7.25x (ISBN 0-85496-051-1). Humanities.

KAFFIR LANGUAGE

see Xosa Language

KAFFRARIA

Brownlee, Frank, ed. Transkeian Native Territories: Historical Records. LC 75-129942. Repr. of 1923 ed. 14.25x (ISBN 0-8371-1611-2). Greenwood.

Kay, Stephan. Travels & Researches in Caffraria. 1834. 32.00 (ISBN 0-403-00374-1). Scholarly.

KAFFRARIA–POLITICS AND GOVERNMENT

Callaway, Godfrey. Sketches of Kafir Life. LC 79-77192. (Illus.). Repr. 12.75x (ISBN 0-8371-1277-X). Greenwood.

KAFIR WARS

see South Africa–History

KAFIRS (AFRICAN PEOPLE)

see also Pondos; Thonga Tribe; Xosa; Zulus

Brownlee, Charles P. Reminiscences of Kafir Life & History & Other Papers. (Killie Campbell Africana Library Reprint Ser: No. 1). (Illus.). 1977. text ed. 25.00 (ISBN 0-86980-104-X). Verry.

Hewat, Matthew L. Bantu Folk Lore. LC 77-129948. Repr. of 1906 ed. 10.00x (ISBN 0-8371-4992-4, Pub. by Negro U Pr). Greenwood.

Kidd, Dudley. Kafir Socialism & the Dawn of Individualism. LC 69-18985. Repr. 14.25x (ISBN 0-8371-1024-6, Pub. by Negro U Pr). Greenwood.

--Savage Childhood: A Study of Kafir Children. LC 75-76482. Repr. of 1906 ed. 19.25x (ISBN 0-8371-1135-8). Greenwood.

McKay, J. Reminiscences of the Last Kaffir War. (Africa Collectanea Ser.: No. 36). Repr. 19.00x (ISBN 0-8426-1363-3). Verry.

Maclean. Colonel. Compendium of Kaffir Laws & Customs. (Illus.). 171p. 1968. Repr. of 1858 ed. 29.50x (ISBN 0-7146-1907-8, F Cass Co). Biblio Dist.

Shooter, Joseph. Kafirs of Natal & the Zulu Country. LC 77-82073. (Illus.). Repr. of 1857 ed. 19.25x (ISBN 0-8371-1538-8, Pub. by Negro U Pr). Greenwood.

KAFIRS (KAFRISTAN)

Robertson, Sir George S. The Kafirs of the Hindu-Kush. LC 15-25146. 1971. Repr. of 1896 ed. 54.00 (ISBN 0-384-13850-0). Johnson Repr.

KAFKA, FRANZ, 1883-1924

Alberes, Rene M. Kafka: Torment of Man. LC 67-11570. 1968. 4.75 (ISBN 0-8022-0014-1). Philos Lib.

Alberes, Rene M. & De Boisdeffre, Pierre. Kafka: The Torment of Man. Baskin, Wade, tr. 1968. pap. 1.95 (ISBN 0-8065-0109-X, 275). Citadel Pr.

Albright, Daniel. Representation & the Imagination: Beckett, Kafka, Nabokov, & Schoenberg. LC 80-26975. (Chicago Originals Ser.). 256p. 1981. lib. bdg. 20.00x (ISBN 0-226-01252-2). U of Chicago Pr.

Baumer, Franz. Franz Kafka. Farbstein, Abraham, tr. from Ger. LC 68-3144. (Modern Literature Ser.). 1971. 10.95 (ISBN 0-8044-2024-6); pap. 4.95 (ISBN 0-8044-6014-0). Ungar.

Beck, Evelyn T. Kafka & the Yiddish Theater: Its Impact on His Work. LC 75-143763. 1971. 19.50 (ISBN 0-299-05881-6). U of Wis Pr.

Brod, Max. Franz Kafka: A Biography. 2nd ed. LC 60-14601. (gr. 7-12). 1963. pap. 4.95 (ISBN 0-8052-0047-9). Schocken.

Carrouges, Michel. Kafka Versus Kafka. Parker, Emmett, tr. LC 68-10990. 141p. 1968. 10.50x (ISBN 0-8173-6604-0). U of Ala Pr.

Corngold, Stanley. The Commentators' Despair: The Interpretation of Kafka's Metamorphosis. LC 72-189558. 1973. 15.00 (ISBN 0-8046-9017-0, Natl U); pap. 7.95 (ISBN 0-8046-9051-0). Kennikat.

Czermak, Herberth. The Trial Notes. 1976. pap. text ed. 1.95 (ISBN 0-8220-1304-5). Cliffs.

Emrich, Wilhelm. Franz Kafka: A Critical Study of His Writings. Buehne, Sheema Z., tr. LC 68-12121. 1968. 22.00 (ISBN 0-8044-2168-4). Ungar.

Flores, Angel. The Problem of the Judgment: Eleven Approaches to Kafka's Story. LC 76-48958. 1977. 12.50 (ISBN 0-87752-210-3). Gordian.

Flores, Angel, ed. The Kafka Debate: New Perspectives for Our Time. LC 77-2699. 1977. 18.50 (ISBN 0-87752-211-1). Gordian.

--The Kafka Problem: An Anthology of Criticism About Franz Kafka. LC 77-2699. 1976. Repr. of 1963 ed. 17.50 (ISBN 0-87752-204-9). Gordian.

Flores, Angel & Swander, Homer, eds. Franz Kafka Today. LC 77-23982. 1977. Repr. of 1958 ed. 12.00x (ISBN 0-87752-207-3). Gordian.

Friedman, Maurice. Problematic Rebel: Melville, Dostoievsky, Kafka, Camus. rev. ed. LC 72-101360. 1970. pap. 3.95 (ISBN 0-226-26396-7, P358, Phoen). U of Chicago Pr.

Gray, Ronald D. Francis Kafka. LC 72-83576. 192p. 1973. 36.00 (ISBN 0-521-20007-5); pap. 10.50x (ISBN 0-521-09747-9). Cambridge U Pr.

Grunfeld, Frederic V. Prophets Without Honor: A Background to Freud, Kafka, Einstein & Their World. 1980. pap. 5.95x (ISBN 0-07-025087-1). McGraw.

Hall, Calvin S. & Lind, Richard E. Dreams, Life & Literature: A Study of Franz Kafka. 1970. 10.50x (ISBN 0-8078-1129-7). U of NC Pr.

Hamalian, Leo, ed. Franz Kafka. 160p. (Orig.). 1974. pap. 2.25 (ISBN 0-07-025702-7, SP). McGraw.

Hayman, Ronald. Kafka: A Biography. (Illus.). 384p. 1982. 19.95 (ISBN 0-19-520279-1). Oxford U Pr.

Heller, Peter. Dialectics & Nihilism: Essays on Lessing, Nietzsche, Mann & Kafka. LC 65-26240. 1969. Repr. of 1966 ed. 15.00x (ISBN 0-87023-019-0). U of Mass Pr.

Hubben, William. Dostoevsky, Kierkegaard, Nietzsche & Kafka. Orig. Title: Four Prophets of Our Destiny. 1962. pap. 1.95 (ISBN 0-02-065750-1, Collier). Macmillan.

Hughes, Kenneth, ed. Franz Kafka: An Anthology of Marxist Criticism. LC 81-51611. (Illus.). 432p. 1982. text ed. 20.00 (ISBN 0-87451-206-9). U Pr of New Eng.

Jaffe, Adrian. Process of Kafka's Trial. vii, 160p. 1967. 4.50 (ISBN 0-87013-112-5). Mich St U Pr.

Janouch, Gustav. Conversations with Kafka. rev. ed. Rees, Goronwy, tr. LC 74-156976. 1971. 8.50 (ISBN 0-8112-0295-X). New Directions.

Kafka, Franz. Letters to Friends, Family, & Editors. Winston, Richard & Winston, Clara, trs. from Ger. LC 77-3136. 1977. 24.50x (ISBN 0-8052-3662-7); pap. 7.95 (ISBN 0-8052-0429-6). Schocken.

--Letters to Ottla & the Family. Glatzer, N. N., ed. Winston, Richard & Winston, Clara, trs. (Illus.). 160p. 1982. 15.95 (ISBN 0-8052-3772-0). Schocken.

Levi, M. Franz Kafka & Anarchism. 59.95 (ISBN 0-685-26309-6). Revisionist Pr.

Marson, Eric, et al. Kafka's Trial: The Case Against Josef K. 353p. 1975. text ed. 21.00x (ISBN 0-7022-0890-6). Humanities.

Neumeyer, Peter F., ed. Twentieth Century Interpretations of The Castle. 1969. pap. 1.25 (ISBN 0-13-120378-9, Spec). P-H.

Politzer, Heinz. Franz Kafka: Parable & Paradox. rev. & enl. ed. LC 62-20733. (Illus.). 432p. (YA) (gr. 9-12). 1966. 25.00x (ISBN 0-8014-0341-3); pap. 6.95 (ISBN 0-8014-9022-7, CP22). Cornell U Pr.

Rajan, B. & Pearse, Andrew. Focus One (Symposium on Kafka, Rex Warner & Dos Passos) Repr. of 1945 ed. lib. bdg. 15.00 (ISBN 0-8414-1275-8). Folcroft.

Rhein, Phillip H. Urge to Live: A Comparative Study of Franz Kafka's Der Prozess & Albert Camus L'etranger. (Germanic Languages & Literatures Studies: No. 45). 9.00x (ISBN 0-8078-8045-0). U of NC Pr.

Robert, Marthe. The Old & the New: From Don Quixote to Kafka. Cosman, Carol, tr. 1977. 24.00x (ISBN 0-520-02509-1). U of Cal Pr.

Rolleston, James. Kafka's Narrative Theater. LC 73-6881. 228p. 1974. 16.50x (ISBN 0-271-01121-1, Penn State). Pa St U Pr.

Roy, Gregor. Monarch Notes on Kafka's the Trial, the Castle & Other Works. (Orig.). pap. 1.95 (ISBN 0-671-00847-1). Monarch Pr.

Russell, F. Three Studies in Twentieth Century Obscurity: Joyce, Kafka, Gertrude Stein. LC 68-658. (Studies in Comparative Literature, No. 35). 1969. Repr. of 1954 ed. lib. bdg. 49.95 (ISBN 0-8383-0678-0). Haskell.

Russell, Francis. Three Studies in Twentieth Century Obscurity. 1973. lib. bdg. 69.95 (ISBN 0-87968-046-6). Gordon Pr.

Shneiderman, S. L. Kafka & His Jewish World. 1980. lib. bdg. 69.95 (ISBN 0-8490-3060-9). Gordon Pr.

Sokel, Walter H. Franz Kafka. LC 66-26005. (Columbia Essays on Modern Writers Ser.: No. 19). (Orig.). 1966. pap. 2.00 (ISBN 0-231-02751-6, MW19). Columbia U Pr.

Spann, Meno. Franz Kafka. LC 75-26548. (World Authors Ser.: Austria: No. 381). 1976. lib. bdg. 9.95 (ISBN 0-8057-6182-9). Twayne.

Spilka, Mark. Dickens & Kafka; a Mutual Interpretation. 7.75 (ISBN 0-8446-0928-5). Peter Smith.

Stern, J. P. The World of Kafka. (Illus.). 256p. 1980. 18.95 (ISBN 0-03-051366-9). HR&W.

Sussman, Henry. Franz Kafka: Geometrician of Metaphor. LC 78-13450. (Illus.). 181p. 1979. 10.95 (ISBN 0-930956-02-8); pap. 4.95 (ISBN 0-930956-03-6). Coda Pr.

Tauber, H. Franz Kafka. 75.00 (ISBN 0-8490-0192-7). Gordon Pr.

Thorlby, Anthony. Kafka: A Study. 101p. 1972. 6.00x (ISBN 0-87471-121-5). Rowman.

Tiefenbrun, Ruth. Moment of Torment: An Interpretation of Franz Kafka's Short Stories. LC 72-8911. (Crosscurrents-Modern Critiques Ser.). 176p. 1973. 6.95 (ISBN 0-8093-0620-4). S Ill U Pr.

Urzidil, Johannes. There Goes Kafka. Basilius, Harold A., tr. from Ger. LC 68-21544. Orig. Title: Da Geht Kafka. 1969. 9.95x (ISBN 0-8143-1353-1). Wayne St U Pr.

Weinberg, Helen A. New Novel in America: The Kafkan Mode in Contemporary Fiction. LC 70-87011. 1970. 22.50x (ISBN 0-8014-0537-8). Cornell U Pr.

Zyla, Wolodymyr T., ed. Franz Kafka: His Place in World Literature. (Proceedings of the Comparative Literature Symposium: Vol. IV). (Illus., Orig.). 5.00 (ISBN 0-89672-046-2). Tex Tech Pr.

KAFKA, FRANZ, 1883-1924–BIBLIOGRAPHY

Flores, Angel. A Kafka Bibliography 1908-1976. LC 76-21333. 256p. 1976. 15.00 (ISBN 0-87752-206-5). Gordian.

KAGAWA, TOYOHIKO, 1888-1960

Davey, Cyril. Saint in the Slums (Kagawa of Japan) 1968. pap. 1.50 (ISBN 0-87508-620-9). Chr Lit.

KAHANAMOKU, DUKE

Brennan, Joe. Duke Kahanamoku - Hawaii's Golden Man. O'Connell, Pat, ed. (Hawaii Cultural Heritage Ser.: Vol. 3). (Illus.). 64p. (gr. 4 up). 1974. pap. 2.50 (ISBN 0-911776-26-5). Hogarth.

KAHN, LOUIS I., 1901-

Johnson, Nell E., compiled by. Light Is the Theme: Louis I Kahn & the Kimbell Art Museum. LC 78-61163. (Illus.). 1975. pap. 5.00 (ISBN 0-912804-03-3). Kimbell Art.

Komendant, August E. Eighteen Years with Architect Louis I. Kahn. LC 75-14437. (Illus.). 208p. 1975. text ed. 15.00 (ISBN 0-913690-06-6). Aloray.

Lobell, John. Between Silence & Light: Spirit in the Architecture of Louis I. Kahn. LC 78-65437. (Illus.). 1979. pap. 7.95 (ISBN 0-394-73687-7). Shambhala Pubns.

Robb, David M. Louis I. Kahn: Sketches for the Kimbell Art Museum. LC 78-55375. (Illus.). pap. 4.95 (ISBN 0-912804-02-5). Kimbell Art.

Ronner, H., et al, eds. Complete Works 1935-74: Louis I Kahn. (Illus.). 456p. 1976. 98.00 (ISBN 3-7643-0900-8). Birkhauser.

Wurman, Richard S. & Feldman, Eugene, eds. The Notebooks & Drawings of Louis I. Kahn. 2nd ed. 1974. 19.95 (ISBN 0-262-23065-8). MIT Pr.

KAILA

see Falashas

KAISER, GEORG, 1878-1945

Schurer, Ernst. Georg Kaiser. (World Authors Ser.: Germany: No. 196). lib. bdg. 10.95 (ISBN 0-8057-2480-X). Twayne.

KAIULANI, PRINCESS OF HAWAII, 1785-1899
Hoyt, Helen P. The Princess Kaiulani. LC 75-16523. (Illus.). (gr. 1-7). 1974. 4.95 (ISBN 0-89610-016-2). Island Her.
KAKKE
see Beri-Beri
KALAHARI DESERT
Dornan, S. S. Pygmies & Bushmen of the Kalahare. LC 71-140807. (Illus.). Repr. of 1925 ed. 17.25x (ISBN 0-8371-3668-7). Greenwood.
Kuper, Adam. Kalahari Village Politics: An African Democracy. LC 70-112470. (Studies in Social Anthropology). (Illus.). 1970. 19.95 (ISBN 0-521-07863-6). Cambridge U Pr.
Luard, Nicholas. The Last Wilderness: A Journey Across the Great Kalahari Desert. 1981. 14.95 (ISBN 0-671-41264-7). S&S.
Russell, Margo & Russell, M. Afrikaners of the Kalahari. LC 77-85693. (African Studies: No. 24). (Illus.). 1979. 19.95 (ISBN 0-521-21897-7). Cambridge U Pr.
Silberbauer, George B. Hunter & Habitat in the Central Kalahari Desert. LC 80-16768. (Illus.). 288p. 1981. 39.50 (ISBN 0-521-23578-2); pap. 14.95 (ISBN 0-521-28135-0). Cambridge U Pr.
Thomas, Elizabeth M. Harmless People. (Illus.). 1959. 8.95 (ISBN 0-394-42779-3). Knopf.
--Harmless People. 1965. pap. 2.95 (ISBN 0-394-70289-1, Vin). Random.
Van Der Post, Laurens. The Lost World of the Kalahari. LC 77-4292. (Illus.). 1977. pap. 3.95 (ISBN 0-15-653706-0, Harv). HarBraceJ.
KALAM
see Islamic Theology
KALAMBO FALLS SITE
Clark, J. Desmond. Kalambo Falls Prehistoric Site, 2 vols. LC 68-25084. (Illus.). 1973. Vol. 1. 75.00 (ISBN 0-521-06962-9); Vol. 2. 125.00 (ISBN 0-521-20009-1). Cambridge U Pr.
KALB, JEAN, BARON DE, ORIGINALLY JOHANN KALB, 1721-1780
Kapp, Friedrich. Life of John Kalb, Major-General in the Revolutionary Army. LC 72-78762. 1884. Repr. 21.00 (ISBN 0-403-02036-0). Somerset Pub.
KALEVALA (EPIC POEMS)
Lonnrot, Elias, ed. Kalevala: Poems of the Kaleva District. Magoun, Francis P., Jr., tr. LC 63-19142. (Illus.). 1963. 20.00x (ISBN 0-674-50000-8). Harvard U Pr.
KALI
Kinsley, David R. The Sword & the Flute - Kali & Krsna: Dark Visions of the Terrible & the Sublime in Hindu Mythology. LC 73-91669. 175p. 1975. 20.00x (ISBN 0-520-02675-6); pap. 2.95 (ISBN 0-520-03510-0). U of Cal Pr.
KALIDASA, fl. 5TH CENTURY A.D.
Narang, S. P. Kalidasa Bibliography. LC 76-900614. 475p. 1976. 20.00x (ISBN 0-88386-762-1). South Asia Bks.
Sabnis, S. A. Kalidasa, His Style & His Times. LC 68-9972. 480p. 1966. 9.00x (ISBN 0-8002-1625-3). Intl Pubns Serv.
Singh, A. D., ed. Kalidasa: A Critical Study. 1977. 15.00x (ISBN 0-88386-989-6). South Asia Bks.
KALINGAS
Barton, Roy F. Kalingas, Their Institutions & Custom Law. LC 72-161778. Repr. of 1949 ed. 18.00 (ISBN 0-404-09015-X). AMS Pr.
Dozier, Edward P. Mountain Arbiters: The Changing Life of a Philippine Hill People. LC 66-18530. (Illus.). 1966. 10.00x (ISBN 0-8165-0061-4). U of Ariz Pr.
KALLEN, GUNNAR, 1926-1968
Kaellen, G. Quantum Electrodynamics. Iddings, C. & Mizushima, M., trs. from Ger. LC 76-172529. 230p. 1972. 29.50 (ISBN 0-387-05574-6). Springer-Verlag.
KAMBA LANGUAGE
see also Kikuyu Language
KAMBA TRIBE
Lindblom, Gerhard. Akamba in British East Africa: An Ethnographic Monograph. LC 76-97406. Repr. of 1920 ed. 27.00x (ISBN 0-8371-2625-8, Pub. by Negro U Pr). Greenwood.
Middleton, J. Kikuyu & Kamba of Kenya. 1972. 10.50x (ISBN 0-85302-016-7). Intl Pubns Serv.
Munro, J. Forbes. Colonial Rule & the Kamba: Social Change in the Kenya Highlands 1889-1939. (Oxford Studies in African Affairs). (Illus.). 288p. 1975. 19.50x (ISBN 0-19-821699-8). Oxford U Pr.
KAMCHATKA
De Lesseps, Jean. Travels in Kamtschatka, During the Years 1787 & 1788. LC 72-115557. (Russia Observed, Series I). 1970. Repr. of 1790 ed. 25.00 (ISBN 0-405-03043-6). Arno.
Golovnin, V. N. Around the World on the "Kamchatka," 1817-1819. Wiswell, Ella L., tr. from Rus. LC 79-15230. (Illus.). 1979. text ed. 20.00x (ISBN 0-8248-0640-9). U Pr of Hawaii.
Kennan, George. Tent Life in Siberia: A New Account of an Old Undertaking Adventures Among the Koraks & Other Tribes in Kamchatka & Northern Asia. LC 79-115572. (Russia Observed, Series I). 1970. Repr. of 1910 ed. 22.00 (ISBN 0-405-03037-1). Arno.
Krasheninnikov, Stepan P. Explorations of Kamchatka: North Pacific Scimitar. Crownhart-Vaughan, E. A., tr. LC 72-79116. (North Pacific Studies Ser.: No. 1). (Illus.). 408p. 1972. 14.95 (ISBN 0-87595-033-7). Oreg Hist Soc.
KAMEHAMEHA 1ST, THE GREAT, KING OF THE HAWAIIAN ISLANDS, d. 1819
Day, A. Grove. Kamehameha, First King of Hawaii. Hazama, Dorothy, ed. (Vol. 5): (Illus.). 64p. (gr. 4 up). 1974. pap. 2.50 (ISBN 0-911776-25-7). Hogarth.
Gowen, Herbert H. The Napoleon of the Pacific, Kamehameha the Great. LC 75-35193. Repr. of 1919 ed. 26.00 (ISBN 0-404-14221-4). AMS Pr.
KAMES, LORD
see Home, Henry, Lord Kames, 1696-1782
KAMIKAZE AIRPLANES
Aeronautical Staff of Aero Publishers. Kamikaze. LC 66-19666. (Aero Ser: Vol. 7). 1966. pap. 3.00 (ISBN 0-8168-0524-5). Aero.
KAMMERER, PAUL, 1880-1926
Koestler, Arthur. The Case of the Midwife Toad. 192p. 1973. pap. 2.45 (ISBN 0-394-71823-2, Vin). Random.
KAMUTI
see Bonsai
KANADA LANGUAGE
see Kannada Language
KANARA (DISTRICT)
Palakshappa, T. C. The Siddhis of North Kanara. 1976. text ed. 9.00x (ISBN 0-8426-0890-7). Verry.
KANARESE LANGUAGE
see Kannada Language
KANDINSKY, WASSILY, 1866-1944
Kandinsky, Wassily. Concerning the Spiritual in Art. 6.75 (ISBN 0-8446-5588-0). Peter Smith.
Lacoste, Michel C. Kandinsky. (Crown QLP Ser.). (Illus.). 1979. 6.95 (ISBN 0-517-53884-9). Crown.
Long, Rose-Carol. Kandinsky: The Development of an Abstract Style. (Studies in the History of Art & Architecture). (Illus.). 308p. 1980. 98.00x (ISBN 0-19-817311-3). Oxford U Pr.
Overy, Paul. Kandinsky: The Language of the Eye. 1969. pap. 17.50 (ISBN 0-236-17770-2, Pub. by Paul Elek). Merrimack Bk Serv.
Roethel, Hans K. & Benjamin, Jean K. Kandinsky. LC 79-12966. (Illus.). 1979. 35.00 (ISBN 0-933920-00-8). Hudson Hills.
Tower, Beeke S. Klee & Kandinsky in Munich & at the Bauhans. Foster, Stephen, ed. (Studies in Fine Arts--the Avant-Garde: No. 16). 1981. write for info. (ISBN 0-8357-1179-X, Pub. by UMI Res Pr). Univ Microfilms.
Weiss, Peg. Kandinsky in Munich: The Formative Jugendstil Years. LC 78-51203. (Illus.). 1979. text ed. 35.00 (ISBN 0-691-03934-8). Princeton U Pr.
KANE, ELISHA KENT, 1820-1857
Corner, George W. Dr. Kane of the Arctic Seas. LC 72-88531. 330p. 1972. 17.50x (ISBN 0-87722-022-0). Temple U Pr.
Elder, Williams. Biography of Elisha Kent Kane. LC 72-78696. 1857. Repr. 16.00 (ISBN 0-403-02077-8). Somerset Pub.
Mirsky, Jeannette. Elisha Kent Kane & the Seafaring Frontier. LC 71-148639. (Illus.). 1971. Repr. of 1954 ed. lib. bdg. 15.00 (ISBN 0-8371-6004-9, MIEK). Greenwood.
--Elisha Kent Kane & the Seafaring Frontier. LC 71-148639. (Illus.). 1971. Repr. of 1954 ed. lib. bdg. 15.00 (ISBN 0-8371-6004-9, MIEK). Greenwood.
KANE, MARGARET (FOX) 1836-1893
Davenport, Reuben B. The Death-Blow to Spiritualism: Being the True Story of the Fox Sisters. LC 75-36836. (Occult Ser.). 1976. Repr. of 1888 ed. 14.00x (ISBN 0-405-07949-4). Arno.
KANG, YU-WEI, 1858-1927
Hsiao, Kung-Chuan. A Modern China & a New World: K'ang Yu-Wei, Reformer & Utopian, 1858-1927. LC 74-28166. (Publications on Asia of School of International Studies: No. 25). 680p. 1975. 26.50 (ISBN 0-295-95385-3). U of Wash Pr.
Lo, Jung-Pang. K'ang Yu-Wei: A Biography & a Symposium. LC 66-20911. (Association for Asian Studies Monograph: No. 23). 1967. 14.50x (ISBN 0-8165-0152-1). U of Ariz Pr.
KANGAROOS
Coerr, Eleanor B. Biography of a Kangaroo. LC 75-20468. (Nature Biography Ser.). (Illus.). 64p. (gr. 2-4). 1976. PLB 6.59 (ISBN 0-399-60967-9). Putnam.
Edwards, Bruce. Kangaroos & Wallabies. (Young Nature Library). (Illus.). 36p. (gr. 6 up). 1974. Repr. of 1972 ed. 2.95 (ISBN 0-88359-002-6). R Curtis Bks.
Frith, H. J. & Calaby, J. H. Kangaroos. 1969. text ed. 17.50x (ISBN 0-391-02073-0). Humanities.
Glendinning, Sally. Little Blue & Rusty: Red Kangaroos. LC 80-13935. (Young Animal Adventures Ser.). 40p. (gr. 2). 1980. PLB 6.48 (ISBN 0-8116-7502-5). Garrard.
Hogan, Paula Z. The Kangaroo. LC 79-13660. (Life Cycles). (Illus.). (gr. k-3). 1979. PLB 11.15 (ISBN 0-8172-1504-2). Raintree Pubs.
Hurd, Edith. The Mother Kangaroo. (Illus.). (gr. 1-3). 1976. 5.95g (ISBN 0-316-38326-0). Little.
Pape, Donna L. Where Is My Little Joey? LC 78-1022. (Imagination Ser.). (Illus.). (gr. 1-4). 1978. PLB 6.18 (ISBN 0-8116-4411-1). Garrard.
Rau, Margaret. The Gray Kangaroo at Home. LC 77-14942. (gr. 5-8). 1978. PLB 5.95 (ISBN 0-394-83451-8); 5.95 (ISBN 0-394-93451-2). Knopf.
Stonehouse, Bernard. Kangaroos. LC 77-60872. (Animals of the World Ser.). (Illus.). (gr. 4-8). 1978. PLB 11.95 (ISBN 0-8172-1079-2). Raintree Pubs.
Time Life Books Editors. Kangaroos & Other Creatures from Down Under. (Wild, Wild World of Animals). (Illus.). 1978. 10.95 (ISBN 0-913948-17-9). Time-Life.
Townsend, Anita. The Kangaroo. LC 78-68536. (First Look at Nature Ser.). (Illus.). (gr. 2-4). 1979. 2.50 (ISBN 0-531-09141-4); PLB 6.45 s&l (ISBN 0-531-09152-X). Watts.
Williamson, H. D. The Year of the Kangaroo. encore ed. LC 77-13362. (Illus.). (gr. 4-7). 1977. 2.95 (ISBN 0-684-16368-3, ScribT). Scribner.
KANKRIN, EGOR FRANTSOVICH, 1774-1845
Pintner, Walter M. Russian Economic Policy Under Nicholas First. LC 67-23067. 1967. 22.50x (ISBN 0-8014-0337-5). Cornell U Pr.
KANNADA LANGUAGE
Bean, Susan S. Symbolic & Pragmatic Semantic: A Kannada System of Address. LC 77-18198. (Illus.). 1978. lib. bdg. 17.00x (ISBN 0-226-03989-7). U of Chicago Pr.
McCormack, William & Krishnamurthi, M. G. Kannada: A Cultural Introduction to the Spoken Styles of the Language. 216p. 1966. text ed. 17.50 (ISBN 0-299-03840-8). U of Wis Pr.
KANNA'IM
see Zealots (Jewish Party)
KANO, NIGERIA (CITY)
Fika, Adamu M. The Kano Civil War & British Over-Rule: Eighteen Eighty-Two to Nineteen Forty. (Illus.). 1979. 33.00x (ISBN 0-19-575448-4). Oxford U Pr.
Trevallion, B. A. Metropolitan Kano, 2 vols. 1967. Set. 75.00 (ISBN 0-08-012635-9). Pergamon.
KANO, AMINU, 1920-
Feinstein, Alan. African Revolutionary. LC 72-91378. (Illus.). 320p. 1973. 9.95 (ISBN 0-8129-0321-8). Times Bks.
KANSAS
see also names of cities, towns, counties, etc. in Kansas
Baughman, Robert W. Kansas in Maps. LC 60-63876. (Illus.). 1961. 9.95 (ISBN 0-87726-006-0). Kansas St Hist.
Bell, Jonathan W., ed. The Kansas Art Reader. LC 80-621211. (Kansas Studies). 437p. (Orig.). 1976. pap. text ed. 6.75 (ISBN 0-936352-02-7, B926). U of KS Ind Stud Div.
Euler, Harrison L. County Unification in Kansas. LC 74-176758. (Columbia University. Teachers College. Contributions to Education: No. 645). Repr. of 1935 ed. 17.50 (ISBN 0-404-55645-0). AMS Pr.
Federal Writers' Project. Kansas: A Guide to the Sunflower State. 538p. 1939. Repr. 49.00 (ISBN 0-403-02167-7). Somerset Pub.
Hale, Edward E. Kansas & Nebraska. facsimile ed. LC 75-37595. (Black Heritage Library Collection). Repr. of 1854 ed. 17.75 (ISBN 0-8369-8971-6). Arno.
Kansas. 28.00 (ISBN 0-89770-040-6). Curriculum Info Ctr.
Koch, William E. Folklore from Kansas: Customs, Beliefs, & Superstitions. LC 79-20197. (Illus.). 1980. 20.00 (ISBN 0-7006-0192-9). Regents Pr KS.
Miller, Nyle H., et al. Kansas in Newspapers. LC 63-63786. 1963. 9.95 (ISBN 0-87726-007-9). Kansas St Hist.
Richmond, Robert. Kansas a Land of Contrast. rev ed. LC 74-77390. 1979. pap. text ed. 10.95x (ISBN 0-686-70276-X). Forum Pr MO.
Robinson, Sara T. Kansas: Its Interior & Exterior Life. facsimile ed. LC 77-160991. (Select Bibliographies Reprint Ser). Repr. of 1856 ed. 21.00 (ISBN 0-8369-5859-4). Arno.
Rydjord, John. Kansas Place-Names. 613p. 1980. pap. 12.50 (ISBN 0-8061-1638-2). U of Okla Pr.
Self, Huber. Environment & Man in Kansas: A Geographical Analysis. LC 77-5867. (Illus.). 1978. 18.00x (ISBN 0-7006-0162-7). Regents Pr KS.
State Industrial Directory Corp. Kansas State Industrial Directory, 1980. 1980. pap. 35.00 (ISBN 0-89910-002-3). State Indus Dir.
KANSAS-DESCRIPTION AND TRAVEL
Alinder, et al. Kansas Album. Enyeart, James L., ed. LC 77-23657. (Illus.). 1977. 18.00 (ISBN 0-89169-024-7). Addison Hse.
Federal Writers' Project. Kansas: A Guide to the Sunflower State. 538p. 1939. Repr. 49.00 (ISBN 0-403-02167-7). Somerset Pub.
Fradin, Dennis. Kansas: In Words & Pictures. LC 80-12576. (Young People's Stories of Our States Ser.). (Illus.). 48p. (gr. 2-5). 1980. PLB 9.25 (ISBN 0-516-03916-4). Childrens.
Hart, Herbert M. Tour Guide to Old Forts of Texas, Kansas, Nebraska, Oklahoma, Vol. 4. (Illus.). 65p. (Orig.). 1981. pap. 3.95 (ISBN 0-87108-583-6). Pruett.
Kansas State Historical Society Staff & Miller, Nyle H. Kansas: The Thirty-Fourth Star. LC 76-4385. (Illus.). 1977. 6.00 (ISBN 0-87726-003-6). Kansas St Hist.
Lyle, Wes & Fisher, James. Kansas Impressions: Photographs & Words. LC 75-171529. (Illus.). 1972. 7.50 (ISBN 0-7006-0084-1). Regents Pr KS.
Self, Huber. Environment & Man in Kansas: A Geographical Analysis. LC 77-5867. (Illus.). 1978. 18.00x (ISBN 0-7006-0162-7). Regents Pr KS.
Shortridge, James R. Kaw Valley Landscapes: A Guide to Eastern Kansas. 1977. pap. 8.50x (ISBN 0-87291-091-1). Coronado Pr.
Stinson, Pat & Richmond, Robert. Take a Look at Kansas. (Illus.). (gr. 2-5). 1979. text ed. 4.95x (ISBN 0-88273-003-7). Forum Pr MO.
Wislizenus, Frederick A. Tour to Northern Mexico with Col. Doniphan, 1846-1847. LC 74-85495. (Beautiful Rio Grande Classic Ser). (Illus.). 160p. 1969. Repr. of 1848 ed. lib. bdg. 10.00 (ISBN 0-87380-003-6). Rio Grande.
Yost, Nellie S. Medicine Lodge: The Story of a Kansas Frontier Town. LC 79-132588. (Illus.). 237p. 1970. (SB); pap. 5.95 (ISBN 0-8040-0199-5). Swallow.
KANSAS-HISTORY
Anderson, George L. Essays in Kansas History: In Memorium. Williams, Burton J., ed. 1977. 7.50x (ISBN 0-87291-086-5). Coronado Pr.
Athearn, Robert G. In Search of Canaan: Black Migration to Kansas, 1879-80. LC 78-2343. (Illus.). 1978. 14.00x (ISBN 0-7006-0171-6). Regents Pr KS.
Barry, Louise. The Beginning of the West: Annals of the Kansas Gateway to the American West 1540-1854. LC 78-172252. (Illus.). 1972. 14.75 (ISBN 0-87726-001-X). Kansas St Hist.
--Comprehensive Index to Publications 1875-1930. 1959. 5.00 (ISBN 0-87726-011-7). Kansas St Hist.
Bird, Roy. Topeka: A Pictorial History. Friedman, Donna R., ed. LC 80-39669. (Illus.). 208p. 1981. pap. 12.95 (ISBN 0-89865-114-X). Donning Co.
Bird, Roy D. & Wallace, Douglass W. Witness of the Times, a History of Shawnee County. Richmond, Robert W., ed. LC 76-4390. 1976. 7.95 (ISBN 0-685-72361-5); pap. 4.95 (ISBN 0-685-72362-3). Shawnee County Hist.
Blackburn, Forrest R., et al, eds. Kansas & the West: Bicentennial Essays in Honor of Nyle H. Miller. LC 76-20097. (Illus.). 1976. 8.95 (ISBN 0-87726-002-8). Kansas St Hist.
Blackmar, Frank W. The Life of Charles Robinson: The First State Governor of Kansas. facsimile ed. LC 70-169751. (Select Bibliographies Reprint Ser). Repr. of 1901 ed. 21.00 (ISBN 0-8369-5971-X). Arno.
Brewerton, G. Douglas. The War in Kansas. facsimile ed. LC 74-164381. (Black Heritage Library Collection). Repr. of 1856 ed. 24.00 (ISBN 0-8369-8840-X). Arno.
Brownlee, Richard S. Gray Ghosts of the Confederacy: Guerrilla Warfare in the West, 1861-65. LC 58-14213. (Illus.). 1958. 17.50 (ISBN 0-8071-0333-0). La State U Pr.
Burritt, Orrin U. The Sun Rides High: Pioneering Days in Oklahoma, Kansas & Missouri. 1974. 8.95 (ISBN 0-89015-022-2). Eakin Pubns.
Calhoun, William G. Fort Scott: A Pictorial History. LC 77-93303. (Illus., Orig.). pap. 8.50 (ISBN 0-9601568-1-X). Historic Pres Bourbon.
Castel, Albert E. A Frontier State at War: Kansas, Eighteen Sixty-One to Eighteen Sixty-Five. LC 78-26281. 1979. Repr. of 1958 ed. lib. bdg. 21.00x (ISBN 0-313-20863-8, CAFS). Greenwood.
Coe, Edith C. Hertzler Heritage. Vandergriff, James, ed. LC 75-32001. (Illus.). 172p. 1975. 7.50x (ISBN 0-686-13109-6); pap. 5.80x (ISBN 0-686-13110-X). Emporia State.
Davis, Kenneth S. Kansas: A Bicentennial History. (States & the Nation Ser). (Illus.). 1976. 12.95 (ISBN 0-393-05593-0, Co-Pub by AASLH). Norton.
Ebbutt, Percy G. Emigrant Life in Kansas. facsimile ed. LC 75-96. (Mid-American Frontier Ser.). (Illus.). 1975. Repr. of 1886 ed. 15.00x (ISBN 0-405-06862-X). Arno.

Fradin, Dennis. Kansas: In Words & Pictures. LC 80-12576. (Young People's Stories of Our States Ser.). (Illus.). 48p. (gr. 2-5). 1980. PLB 9.25 (ISBN 0-516-03916-4). Childrens.

Gates, Paul W. Fifty Million Acres. Bruchey, Stuart, ed. LC 76-56733. (Management of Public Lands in the U. S. Ser.). (Illus.). 1979. Repr. of 1954 ed. lib. bdg. 22.00x (ISBN 0-405-11332-3). Arno.

Gihon, John H. Geary & Kansas. facsimile ed. LC 74-165634. (Select Bibliographies Reprint Ser). Repr. of 1857 ed. 20.00 (ISBN 0-8369-5943-4). Arno.

Gladstone, T. H. Englishman in Kansas; or, Squatter Life & Border Warfare. LC 74-155700. 1971. 21.50x (ISBN 0-8032-0800-6); pap. 3.95 (ISBN 0-8032-5742-2, BB 536, Bison). U of Nebr Pr.

Gower, Calvin W. Kansas Towns & Trade from Pike's Peak Gold Seekers, 1858-1860. 1980. pap. text ed. 8.00 (ISBN 0-89126-097-8). MA-AH Pub.

History of Kansas Newspapers. (Illus.). pap. 1.00 (ISBN 0-87726-012-5). Kansas St Hist.

Ise, John. Sod & Stubble: The Story of a Kansas Homestead. LC 37-10937. (Illus.). xvi, 326p. 1967. 19.50x (ISBN 0-8032-0087-0); pap. 3.50 (ISBN 0-8032-5098-3, BB 372, Bison). U of Nebr Pr.

Isely, M. D. Arkansas Valley Interurban. (Special Ser.: No. 19). (Illus.). 1977. pap. 6.00 (ISBN 0-916374-29-7). Interurban.

Jackson, Ronald V. & Teeples, Gary R. Kansas Census Index 1855. LC 77-85930. (Illus.). lib. bdg. 22.00 (ISBN 0-89593-043-9). Accelerated Index.

Johnson, Samuel A. The Battle Cry of Freedom: New England Emigration Aid Company in the Kansas Crusade. LC 77-11619. (Illus.). 1977. Repr. of 1954 ed. lib. bdg. 25.00x (ISBN 0-8371-9813-5, JOBC). Greenwood.

Kansas: The Story Told in Pictures. (Illus.). 1967. pap. 0.75 (ISBN 0-87726-013-3). Kansas St Hist.

Lee, Lawrence B. Kansas & the Homestead Act: 1862-1905, 2 vols. in one. Bruchey, Stuart, ed. LC 78-36703. (Management of Public Lands in the U. S. Ser.). (Illus.). 1979. lib. bdg. 40.00x (ISBN 0-405-11341-2). Arno.

Lee, Wayne C. Trails of the Smoky Hill. LC 79-67199. (Illus.). 235p. (Orig.). 1980. cancelled (ISBN 0-87004-288-2); pap. 12.95 (ISBN 0-87004-276-9). Caxton.

McNemar, Richard. The Kentucky Revival; or, a Short History of the Late Extraordinary Out-Pouring of the Spirit of G Od in the Western States of America. LC 72-2990. Repr. of 1846 ed. 16.00 (ISBN 0-404-10752-4). AMS Pr.

Malin, James. John Brown & the Legend of Fifty-Six. LC 70-117588. (Studies in History & Culture, No. 54). 1970. Repr. of 1942 ed. lib. bdg. 79.95 (ISBN 0-8383-1021-4). Haskell.

Malin, James C. Doctors, Devils & the Woman: Fort Scott, Kansas 1870-1890. 122p. 1975. 8.50x (ISBN 0-87291-074-1). Coronado Pr.

Mays, William E. Sublette Revisited: Stability & Change in a Rural Kansas Community After a Quarter of a Century. 142p. 1968. pap. 3.95x (ISBN 0-912598-03-4). Florham.

Miller, Nyle H. Kansas. LC 65-13610. 1965. pap. 2.95 (ISBN 0-8077-1812-2). Tchrs Coll.

Miller, Nyle H. & Snell, Joseph W. Great Gunfighters of the Kansas Cowtowns, 1867-1886. LC 63-63480. (Illus.). 1967. 22.50x (ISBN 0-8032-0123-0); pap. 4.50 (ISBN 0-8032-5137-8, BB 333, Bison). U of Nebr Pr.

Miner, H. Craig & Unrau, William E. The End of Indian Kansas: A Study of Cultural Revolution, 1854-1871. LC 77-4410. (Illus.). 1977. 12.50x (ISBN 0-7006-0161-9). Regents Pr KS.

Muilenburg, Grace & Swineford, Ada. Land of the Post Rock: Its Origins, History & People. LC 74-23833. (Illus.). 1979. pap. 9.50 (ISBN 0-7006-0194-5). Regents Pr KS.

Oliva, Leo E. Fort Hays, Frontier Army Post, 1865-1889. LC 80-82227. (Illus.). 66p. 1980. pap. 2.00 (ISBN 0-87726-020-6). Kansas St Hist.

Owen, Jennie S. The Annals of Kansas, 1886-1925, 2 vols. Mechem, Kirke, ed. Incl. Vol. 1. 1954. 4.00 (ISBN 0-87726-009-5); Vol. 2. 1956. 4.00 (ISBN 0-87726-010-9). LC 55-62029. (Illus.). 7.50 set (ISBN 0-87726-008-7). Kansas St Hist.

Parker, Martha J. & Laird, Betty A. Soil of Our Souls: Histories of the Clinton Lake Area Communities, Kansas. 1976. pap. 4.95 (ISBN 0-87291-080-6). Coronado Pr.

Phillips, William. The Conquest of Kansas, by Missouri & Her Allies. facsimile ed. LC 76-161271. (Black Heritage Library Collection). Repr. of 1856 ed. 21.50 (ISBN 0-8369-8830-2). Arno.

Rawley, James A. Race & Politics: Bleeding Kansas & the Coming of the Civil War. LC 79-14856. (Illus.). xvi, 304p. 1979. 18.95x (ISBN 0-8032-3854-1); pap. 4.95 (ISBN 0-8032-8901-4, BB 714, Bison). U of Nebr Pr.

--Race & Politics: Bleeding Kansas & the Coming of the Civil War. LC 73-85110. (Illus.). 1969. 5.95 (ISBN 0-397-00600-4); pap. text ed. 2.95 (ISBN 0-397-47194-7). Har-Row.

Rich, Everett. The Heritage of Kansas. 1960. pap. 6.95 (ISBN 0-686-14877-0). Flint Hills.

Rich, Everett, ed. The Heritage of Kansas. 1960. pap. 5.00 (ISBN 0-686-00367-5). AG Pr.

Robertson, Clara H. Kansas Territorial Settlers of 1860 Who Were Born in Tennessee, Virginia, North Carolina & South Carolina. LC 76-13287. 1976. 17.50 (ISBN 0-8063-0697-1). Genealog Pub.

Robinson, Charles. The Kansas Conflict. facsimile ed. LC 70-37599. (Black Heritage Library Collection). Repr. of 1892 ed. 25.00 (ISBN 0-8369-8975-9). Arno.

Robley, T. F. History of Bourbon County, Kansas: To the Close of 1865. 1976. Repr. of 1894 ed. soft bdg. 8.50 (ISBN 0-686-25559-3). Historic Pres Bourbon.

Ropes, Hannah A. Six Months in Kansas, by a Lady. facsimile ed. LC 76-38020. (Black Heritage Library Collection). Repr. of 1856 ed. 15.50 (ISBN 0-8369-8987-2). Arno.

Smeal, Lee. Kansas Historical & Biographical Index. LC 78-53696. (Illus.). Date not set. lib. bdg. price not set (ISBN 0-89593-181-8). Accelerated Index.

Socolofsky, Homer & Self, Huber. Historical Atlas of Kansas. 1972. 12.95x (ISBN 0-8061-1022-8); pap. 8.95 (ISBN 0-8061-1032-5). U of Okla Pr.

Spring, Leverett W. Kansas: The Prelude to the War for the Union. LC 72-3757. (American Commonwealths: No. 6). Repr. of 1907 ed. 24.50 (ISBN 0-404-57206-5). AMS Pr.

Stockwell, Nancy. Out Somewhere & Back Again: The Kansas Stories. 1978. pap. write for info. (ISBN 0-9601714-0-1). Medusa.

Tower, Philo. Slavery Unmasked. LC 74-104585. Repr. of 1856 ed. lib. bdg. 15.50x (ISBN 0-8398-1971-4). Irvington.

--Slavery Unmasked, Being a Truthful Narrative of a Three Years' Residence & Journeying in Eleven Southern States. LC 69-16563. (Illus.). Repr. of 1856 ed. 19.75x (ISBN 0-8371-1131-5). Greenwood.

Vestal, Stanley. Queen of Cowtowns: Dodge City. LC 51-11962. (Illus.). 1972. pap. 3.45 (ISBN 0-8032-5758-9, BB 551, Bison). U of Nebr Pr.

Vexler, R. I. Kansas Chronology & Factbook, Vol. 16. 1978. 8.50 (ISBN 0-379-16141-9). Oceana.

Whittemore, Margaret. Historic Kansas. 1954. pap. 5.95 (ISBN 0-686-14876-2). Flint Hills.

--Historic Kansas: A Centenary Sketchbook. 1954. pap. 5.00 (ISBN 0-686-00370-5). AG Pr.

Wilder, Daniel W. Annals of Kansas: 1541-1885. facsimile ed. LC 75-130. (Mid-American Frontier Ser.). 1975. Repr. of 1886 ed. 66.00x (ISBN 0-405-06895-6). Arno.

Yost, Nellie S. Medicine Lodge: The Story of a Kansas Frontier Town. LC 79-132588. (Illus.). 237p. 1970. (SB); pap. 5.95 (ISBN 0-8040-0199-5). Swallow.

Zornow, William F. Kansas: A History of the Jayhawk State. (Illus.). 1971. Repr. of 1957 ed. 14.95 (ISBN 0-8061-0379-5). U of Okla Pr.

KANSAS–IMPRINTS

Historical Records Survey: Check List of Kansas Imprints, 1854-1876. 1939. pap. 31.00 (ISBN 0-527-01907-0). Kraus Repr.

KANSAS–JUVENILE LITERATURE

Bailey, Bernadine. Picture Book of Kansas. rev. ed. LC 65-29625. (Illus.). (gr. 3-5). 1969. 5.50g (ISBN 0-8075-9518-7). A Whitman.

Carpenter, Allan. Kansas. LC 79-12433. (New Enchantment of America State Bks.). (Illus.). (gr. 4 up). 1979. PLB 10.60 (ISBN 0-516-04116-9). Childrens.

KANSAS–POETRY

Wattles, Willard, compiled by. Sunflowers. facs. ed. LC 78-133077. (Granger Index Reprint Ser). 1916. 14.00 (ISBN 0-8369-6207-9). Arno.

KANSAS–POLITICS AND GOVERNMENT

Brown, George W. Reminiscences of Gov. R. J. Walker: With the True Story of the Rescue of Kansas from Slavery. LC 73-137230. Repr. of 1902 ed. 12.75x (ISBN 0-8371-1605-8). Greenwood.

--Reminiscences of Gov. R. J. Walker: With the True Story of the Rescue of Kansas from Slavery. facsimile ed. LC 79-38010. (Black Heritage Library Collection). Repr. of 1902 ed. 15.50 (ISBN 0-8369-8978-3). Arno.

Drury, James W. The Government of Kansas. 3rd rev. ed. (Illus.). 600p. (Orig.). 1980. pap. 17.50x (ISBN 0-7006-0205-4). Regents Pr KS.

Gaeddart, Gustave R. The Birth of Kansas. LC 73-18442. (Perspectives in American History Ser.: No. 9). (Illus.). 232p. Repr. of 1940 ed. lib. bdg. 15.00x (ISBN 0-87991-335-5). Porcupine Pr.

Harder, Marvin A. & Davis, Raymond G. The Legislature As an Organization: A Study of the Kansas Legislature. (Illus.). 1979. pap. 11.50x (ISBN 0-7006-0187-2). Regents Pr KS.

Miller, Benjamin S. Ranch Life in Southern Kansas & the Indian Territory, As Told by a Novice: How a Fortune Was Made in Cattle. facsimile ed. LC 75-111. (Mid-American Frontier Ser.). 1975. Repr. of 1896 ed. 12.00x (ISBN 0-405-06878-6). Arno.

Nugent, Walter T. Tolerant Populists: Kansas Populism & Nativism. LC 63-13069. 1963. 10.50x (ISBN 0-226-60739-9). U of Chicago Pr.

Rawley, James A. Race & Politics: Bleeding Kansas & the Coming of the Civil War. LC 73-85110. (Illus.). 1969. 5.95 (ISBN 0-397-00600-4); pap. text ed. 2.95 (ISBN 0-397-47194-7). Har-Row.

Seward, William H. Admission of Kansas: A Speech. facs. ed. 16p. Repr. of 1860 ed. pap. 2.75 (ISBN 0-8466-0056-0, SJS56). Shorey.

Sumner, Charles. Crime Against Kansas, the Apologies for the Crime, the True Remedy. LC 78-82226. (Anti-Slavery Crusade in America Ser). 1969. Repr. of 1856 ed. 12.00 (ISBN 0-405-00665-9). Arno.

Wilder, Daniel W. Annals of Kansas: 1541-1885. facsimile ed. LC 75-130. (Mid-American Frontier Ser.). 1975. Repr. of 1886 ed. 66.00x (ISBN 0-405-06895-6). Arno.

KANSAS, UNIVERSITY OF–HISTORY

Carey, James C. Kansas State University: The Quest for Identity. LC 77-392. (Illus.). 1977. 10.95x (ISBN 0-7006-0156-2). Regents Pr KS.

Griffin, Clifford S. The University of Kansas: A History. LC 73-12349. (Illus.). 808p. 1974. 20.00x (ISBN 0-7006-0106-6). Regents Pr KS.

KANSAS CAVALRY, 11TH REGIMENT, 1862-1865

Vaughn, Jesse W. The Battle of Platte Bridge. (Illus.). 1964. 9.95 (ISBN 0-8061-0592-5). U of Okla Pr.

KANSAS CITY, MISSOURI

Briggs, John W. An Italian Passage: Immigrants to Three American Cities, 1890-1930. LC 77-22006. (Illus.). 1978. 25.00x (ISBN 0-300-02095-3). Yale U Pr.

Brown, A. Theordore & Dorsett, Lyle W. K.C. A History of Kansas City, Missouri. (Western Urban History Ser.). (Illus.). 1978. 13.50 (ISBN 0-87108-526-7); pap. 6.95 (ISBN 0-87108-563-1). Pruett.

Dorsett, Lyle W. The Pendergast Machine. LC 80-11581. (Illus.). xvi, 163p. 1980. 13.50x (ISBN 0-8032-1655-6); pap. 3.95 (ISBN 0-8032-6554-9, BB 744, Bison). U of Nebr Pr.

Gilbert, Bill. This City, This Man: The Cookingham Era in Kansas City. LC 78-13401. (Illus.). 1978. 16.00 (ISBN 0-87326-021-X). Intl City Mgt.

Moffett, Virginia & Jacobson, Rosalyn. Greater Kansas Caity's Successful Single Man. (Illus.). 203p. 1981. pap. 8.95 (ISBN 0-940772-00-0). Jinro Pub.

Rieger, James & Mathews, Boots. Dining in Kansas City. (Dining In Ser.). 200p. (Orig.). 1980. pap. 7.95 (ISBN 0-89716-041-X). Peanut Butter.

Stolurow, Lawrence M. & Hildebrand, Myrene R. LEA Evaluation of Resources: North Kansas City School District. (Resource Task Force Report: No. 1). 21p. (Orig.). 1981. pap. text ed. 2.50 (ISBN 0-939984-02-4). U IA Ctr Ed Experiment.

Unell, Barbara. Kansas City Kids Catalog. 96p. (Orig.). (gr. 4 up). 1980. pap. 6.00 (ISBN 0-8309-0286-4). Independence Pr.

KANSAS CITY FOOTBALL TEAM (AMERICAN LEAGUE)

May, Julian. The Kansas City Chiefs. (The NFL Today Ser.). (gr. 4-8). 1980. lib. bdg. 6.45 (ISBN 0-87191-729-7); pap. 2.95 (ISBN 0-89812-232-5). Creative Ed.

--Kansas City Chiefs. LC 74-2301. (Superbowl Champions Ser). (gr. 4-8). 1974. PLB 6.45 (ISBN 0-87191-353-4); pap. 2.95 (ISBN 0-89812-087-X). Creative Ed.

KANSAS-NEBRASKA BILL

Ray, P. Orman. Repeal of the Missouri Compromise. 1965. Repr. of 1909 ed. 12.50x (ISBN 0-910324-07-7). Canner.

Wolff, Gerald. Kansas-Nebraska Bill: Party, Section, & the Origin of the Civil War. 1980. lib. bdg. 75.00 (ISBN 0-87700-255-X). Revisionist Pr.

KANSAS RIVER AND VALLEY

Streeter, Floyd B. The Kaw: Heart of a Nation. facsimile ed. LC 75-124. (Mid-American Frontier Ser.). (Illus.). 1975. Repr. of 1941 ed. 21.00x (ISBN 0-405-06889-1). Arno.

KANSU, CHINA

Chu, Wen-Djang. Moslem Rebellion in Northwest China, 1862-1878. (Central Asiatic Studies: No. 5). 1966. pap. text ed. 48.75x (ISBN 90-2790-017-5). Mouton.

Farrer, Reginald. The Rainbow Bridge. LC 76-47496. (Illus.). 1976. Repr. of 1921 ed. 15.00 (ISBN 0-913728-15-2). Theophrastus.

Farrer, Reginald J. On the Eaves of the World, 2 Vols. LC 79-136386. (BCL Ser.: I). Repr. of 1917 ed. Set. 57.50 (ISBN 0-404-02368-1). AMS Pr.

KANT, IMMANUEL, 1724-1804

Adickes, Erich. German Kantian Bibliography, 3 pts. in 1 vol. 1967. Repr. of 1896 ed. 40.50 (ISBN 0-8337-0017-0). B Franklin.

Al-Azm, Sadik. Kant's Theory of Time. LC 67-17632. 1967. 3.95 (ISBN 0-8022-0013-3). Philos Lib.

Al-Azm, Sadik J. Origins of Kant's Arguments in the Antinomies. 1972. 15.95x (ISBN 0-19-824375-8). Oxford U Pr.

Aune, Bruce. Kant's Theory of Morals. LC 79-17938. 1980. 16.50x (ISBN 0-691-07238-8); pap. 4.95 (ISBN 0-691-02006-X). Princeton U Pr.

Beck, Lewis W. Commentary on Kant's Critique of Practical Reason. LC 60-5464. 1960. pap. 6.00x (ISBN 0-226-04075-5, P114, Phoen). U of Chicago Pr.

--Early German Philosophy: Kant & His Predecessors. LC 79-75427. 1969. 25.00x (ISBN 0-674-22125-7, Belknap Pr). Harvard U Pr.

--Essays on Kant & Hume. LC 77-19999. 1978. 17.50x (ISBN 0-300-02170-4). Yale U Pr.

Beck, Lewis W., ed. Kant Studies Today. LC 68-57207. ix, 507p. (Orig.). 1969. 22.50 (ISBN 0-87548-028-4). Open Court.

Bennett, Jonathan. Kant's Analytic. (Orig.). 1966. 35.50 (ISBN 0-521-04157-0); pap. 9.95x (ISBN 0-521-09389-9, 389). Cambridge U Pr.

--Kant's Dialectic. LC 73-89762. 290p. 1974. 38.50 (ISBN 0-521-20420-8); pap. 9.95x (ISBN 0-521-09849-1). Cambridge U Pr.

Bernstein, John A. Shaftsbury, Rousseau & Kant: An Introduction to the Conflict Between Aesthetic & Moral Values in Modern Thought. LC 78-75190. 192p. 1980. 17.50 (ISBN 0-8386-2351-4). Fairleigh Dickinson.

Bird, Graham. Kant's Theory of Knowledge: An Outline of One Central Argument in the Critique of Pure Reason. (International Library of Philoaophy & Scientific Method Ser.). 1973. Repr. of 1962 ed. text ed. 10.00x (ISBN 0-391-00316-X). Humanities.

Bowne, Borden P. Kant & Spencer, a Critical Exposition. LC 66-25898. Repr. of 1912 ed. 14.50 (ISBN 0-8046-0037-6). Kennikat.

Brittan, Gordon G., Jr. Kant's Theory of Science. LC 77-85531. 1978. 17.50 (ISBN 0-691-07221-3). Princeton U Pr.

Broad, O. D. Kant: An Introduction. Lewy, C., ed. LC 77-80829. 1978. 47.50 (ISBN 0-521-21755-5); pap. 11.50 (ISBN 0-521-29265-4). Cambridge U Pr.

Carus, Paul. Kant & Spencer. 59.95 (ISBN 0-8490-0468-3). Gordon Pr.

Cassirer, Ernst. Kant's Life & Thought. Haden, James, tr. from Ger. LC 81-3354. 464p. 1981. 24.50x (ISBN 0-300-02358-8). Yale U Pr.

--Rousseau, Kant, & Goethe. 1970. 15.00 (ISBN 0-691-07168-3); pap. 4.95 (ISBN 0-691-01970-3). Princeton U Pr.

Cassirer, H. W. Kant's First Critique: An Appraisal of the Significance of Kant's Critique of Pure Reason. (Muirhead Library of Philosophy Ser.). 1978. Repr. of 1954 ed. text ed. 17.50x (ISBN 0-391-00868-4). Humanities.

Chamberlain, H. S. Immanuel Kant, 2 vols. 250.00 (ISBN 0-8490-0387-3). Gordon Pr.

Coleman, Francis X. The Harmony of Reason: A Study in Kant's Aesthetics. LC 74-4520. 1974. 12.95x (ISBN 0-8229-3282-2). U of Pittsburgh Pr.

Collins, James. Interpreting Modern Philosophy. LC 70-160259. 1972. 28.50 (ISBN 0-691-07179-9); pap. 8.95 (ISBN 0-691-01985-1). Princeton U Pr.

Crawford, Donald W. Kant's Aesthetic Theory. LC 73-15259. 200p. 1974. 19.50x (ISBN 0-299-06510-3, 651). U of Wis Pr.

Decleve. Heidegger und Kant. (Phaenomenologica Ser: No. 40). 1970. lib. bdg. 45.00 (ISBN 90-247-5016-4, Pub. by Martinus Nijhoff Netherlands). Kluwer Boston.

Despland, Michel. Kant on History & Religion. 368p. 1973. text ed. 20.00x (ISBN 0-7735-0125-8). McGill-Queens U Pr.

De Vleeschauwer, H. J. La Deduction Transcendentale Dans L'oeuvre De Kant, 3 vols. Beck, Lewis W., ed. LC 75-32049. (Philosophy of Immanuel Kant Ser.). 1976. Set. lib. bdg. 100.00 (ISBN 0-8240-2326-9). Garland Pub.

Dufrenne, Mikel. The Notion of the A Priori. Casey, E. S., tr. (Studies in Phenomenology & Existential Philosophy). 1966. 13.95x (ISBN 0-8101-0082-7). Northwestern U Pr.

Ewing, Alfred C. Kant's Treatment of Causality. 1969. Repr. of 1924 ed. 16.50 (ISBN 0-208-00733-4, Archon). Shoe String.

--Short Commentary on Kant's Critique of Pure Reason. LC 39-13499. 1965. 11.00x (ISBN 0-226-22777-4). U of Chicago Pr.

--Short Commentary on Kant's Critique of Pure Reason. 2nd ed. LC 39-13499. 1967. pap. 3.95 (ISBN 0-226-22778-2, P265, Phoen). U of Chicago Pr.

Findlay, J. N. Kant & the Transcendental Object. 400p. 1981. 24.95x (ISBN 0-19-824638-2). Oxford U Pr.

Fischer, Kuno. A Commentary on Kant's Critick of Pure Reason. Beck, Lewis W., ed. LC 75-32039. (The Philosophy of Immanuel Kant Ser.: Vol. 3). 1977. Repr. of 1866 ed. lib. bdg. 26.00 (ISBN 0-8240-2327-7). Garland Pub.

Funke, Gerhard, ed. Akten Des Vierten Internationalen Kant-Kongresses Mainz 6-10, April 1974: Part II, 1 & 2 Sektionen, 2 vols. xxx, 986p. (Ger.). 1974. 162.25x (ISBN 3-11-004371-8). De Gruyter.

--Akten Des Vierten Internationalen Kant-Kongresses Mainz, 6.-10. April 1974: Part I, Kan-Studien Sunderhoft Symposien. viii, 310p. 1974. pap. 40.00x (ISBN 3-11-004369-6). De Gruyter.

Galston, William A. Kant & the Problem of History. LC 74-11620. xiv, 290p. 1975. 13.50x (ISBN 0-226-28044-6). U of Chicago Pr.

Garnett, Christopher B. Kantian Philosophy of Space. LC 65-27117. 1965. Repr. of 1939 ed. 12.50 (ISBN 0-8046-0163-1). Kennikat.

Gauchhwal, B. S. Concept of Perfection in the Teachings of Kant & the Gita. 1967. 4.50 (ISBN 0-89684-186-3). Orient Bk Dist.

Gloy, Karen. Die Kantische Theorie der Naturwissenschaft. 1976. 42.25x (ISBN 3-11-006569-X). De Gruyter.

Grayeff, Victor. Kant's Theoretical Philosophy: A Commentary to the Central Part of the Critique of Pure Reason. 240p. 1970. 30.00x (ISBN 0-7190-0406-3, Pub. by Manchester U Pr England); pap. 15.00x (ISBN 0-7190-0441-1). State Mutual Bk.

Guyer, Paul. Kant & the Claims of Taste. LC 78-19179. 1979. text ed. 20.00x (ISBN 0-674-50020-2). Harvard U Pr.

Hegel. Glauben und Wissen (Faith & Knowledge) Cerf, Walter & Harris, H. S., eds. Cerf, Walter & Harris, H. S., trs. from Ger. LC 76-10250. 1977. 19.00 (ISBN 0-87395-338-X); microfiche o.p. 17.00 (ISBN 0-87395-339-8). State U NY Pr.

Heidegger, Martin. Kant & the Problem of Metaphysics. 6.50 (ISBN 0-8446-2233-8). Peter Smith.

Hendel, Charles W. The Philosophy of Kant & Our Modern World. LC 81-4693. vii, 132p. 1981. Repr. of 1957 ed. lib. bdg. 19.75x (ISBN 0-313-23051-X, HEPK). Greenwood.

Hintikka, Jaakko. Logic, Language-Games, & Information: Kantian Themes in the Philosophy of Logic. (Illus.). 305p. 1973. 45.00x (ISBN 0-19-824364-2). Oxford U Pr.

Hoffman, W. Michael. Kant's Theory of Freedom: A Metaphysical Inquiry. LC 78-70860. 1978. pap. text ed. 7.50 (ISBN 0-8191-0651-8). U Pr of Amer.

Hossenfelder, Malte. Kants Konstitutionstheorie und Die Transzendentale Deduktion. (Quellen und Studien Zur Philosophie: Vol. 12). 1978. 40.00 (ISBN 3-11-005969-X). De Gruyter.

Howard, Claud. Coleridge's Idealism. LC 72-191125. 1924. lib. bdg. 17.50 (ISBN 0-8414-5131-1). Folcroft.

Hutchings, Patrick. Kant on Absolute Value. LC 75-174669. 296p. 1972. text ed. 11.50x (ISBN 0-8143-1459-7). Wayne St U Pr.

Janke, Wolfgang. Historische Dialektik: Destruktion Dialektrischer Grundformen Von Kant Bis Marx. 1977. 84.00x (ISBN 3-11-007286-6). De Gruyter.

Jaspers, Karl. Kant, Taken from Vol. 1 Great Philosophers. Manheim, Ralph, tr. LC 66-88121. Orig. Title: Great Philosophers, Vol. 1 (Pt. 3) 1966. pap. 3.50 (ISBN 0-15-646685-6, HB101, Harv). HarBraceJ.

Kant, Immanuel. Educational Theory of Immanuel Kant. 1981. Repr. lib. bdg. 25.00 (ISBN 0-403-00040-8). Scholarly.

--Kant's Cosmogony: As in His Essay on Retardation of the Rotation of the Earth. Hastie, W., tr. (Contributions in Philosophy, No. 1). 1968. lib. bdg. 15.95 (ISBN 0-8371-1500-0, KAH/). Greenwood.

--Kant's Political Writings. Reiss, H., ed. 1970. pap. 8.95x (ISBN 0-521-29212-3). Cambridge U Pr.

Kantindex Allgemeiner zu Kants Gesammelten Schriften, 21 vols. Incl. Vols. 16 & 17. Wortindex Zu Band 1-9. viii, 1100p. 1967. 123.25x (ISBN 3-11-005180-X); Vol. 20, Sect. 3. Personenindex zu Kants Gesammelten Schriften. Holger, Katharina, et al, eds. viii, 142p. 1969. 26.50x (ISBN 3-11-002557-4). (Ger.). De Gruyter.

Kants Werke. 1977. Vol. A. 15.25x (ISBN 3-11-006995-4); Vol. B. 13.75x (ISBN 3-11-007017-0). De Gruyter.

Kaufmann, Walter. Discovering the Mind, Vol. 1: Goethe, Kant, & Hegel. LC 79-18004. 1980. 14.95 (ISBN 0-07-033311-4). McGraw.

Kaulbach, Friedrich. Immanuel Kant. (Sammlung Goeschen, Vols. 536 & 536A). (Ger.). 1969. 5.00x (ISBN 3-11-002748-8). De Gruyter.

--Das Prinzip Handling in der Philosophie Kants. 1978. 60.00x (ISBN 3-11-007219-X). De Gruyter.

Kemp, John. The Philosophy of Kant: Opus. 1978. pap. text ed. 5.95 (ISBN 0-19-888036-7). Oxford U Pr.

Kemp-Smith, Norman. Commentary to Kant's Critique of Pure Reason. 2nd ed. 1962. text ed. 20.00x (ISBN 0-391-00457-3). Humanities.

Knox, Israel. Aesthetic Theories of Kant, Hegel & Schopenhauer. 1978. Repr. of 1936 ed. text ed. 12.50x (ISBN 0-391-00929-X). Humanities.

Lehmann, Gerhard. Beitraege zur Geschichte und Interpretation der Philosophie Kants. (Ger). 1969. 45.00x (ISBN 3-11-002561-2). De Gruyter.

Lindsay, A. D. Kant. 1978. Repr. of 1934 ed. lib. bdg. 40.00 (ISBN 0-8492-1573-0). R West.

Lindsay, Alexander D. Kant. LC 76-109970. Repr. of 1934 ed. lib. bdg. 14.25x (ISBN 0-8371-4473-6, LIKA). Greenwood.

Loew, Reinhard. Philosophie Des Lebendigen Kants Begriff Des Organischen, Seine Wurzlen und Seine Aktualiat. 360p. 1980. text ed. 31.20 (ISBN 0-686-64717-3, 3-518-7499, Pub. by Suhrkamp Verlag Germany); pap. 22.40 quality paper (ISBN 3-518-07540-3). Suhrkamp.

Macmillan, R. A. The Crowning Phase of the Critical Philosophy: A Study in Kant's Critique of Judgment. Beck, Lewis W., ed. LC 75-32041. (The Philosophy of Immanuel Kant Ser.: Vol. 4). 1977. Repr. of 1912 ed. lib. bdg. 33.00 (ISBN 0-8240-2328-5). Garland Pub.

Maier, Josef. On Hegel's Critique of Kant. LC 39-31564. Repr. of 1939 ed. 16.45 (ISBN 0-404-04168-X). AMS Pr.

Martin, Gottfried. Arithmetik und Kombinatorik bei Kant. 148p. (Ger.). 1972. 33.75x (ISBN 3-1100-3593-6). De Gruyter.

--Kant's Metaphysics & Theory of Science. Lucas, P. G., tr. LC 73-15053. 218p. 1974. Repr. of 1955 ed. lib. bdg. 15.00 (ISBN 0-8371-7154-7, MAKM). Greenwood.

Martin, Gottfried & Loewisch, Dieter-Juergen, eds. Sachindex zu Kants Kritik der reinen Vernunft. (Ger). 1967. 24.00x (ISBN 3-11-005179-6). De Gruyter.

May, J. A. Kant's Concept of Geography & Its Relation to Recent Historical Thought. 1970. pap. 7.50x (ISBN 0-8020-3260-5). U of Toronto Pr.

Melnick, Arthur. Kant's Analogies of Experience. 1974. 10.95x (ISBN 0-226-51964-3). U of Chicago Pr.

Michalson, G. E. The Historical Dimensions of Rational Faith: The Role of History in Kant's Religious Thought. 1977. 9.50 (ISBN 0-8191-0308-X). U Pr of Amer.

Mohanty, J. N. & Shahan, Robert W. Essays on Kant's Critique of Pure Reason. LC 81-40295. 208p. 1981. 12.95 (ISBN 0-8061-1782-6). U of Okla Pr.

Monarch Notes in Kant's Philosophy. (gr. 7-12). pap. 1.95 (ISBN 0-671-00530-8). Monarch Pr.

Monarch Notes on Kant, The Philosophy. pap. 1.95 (ISBN 0-671-00530-8). Monarch Pr.

Murphy, Jefferie G. Kant: The Philosophy of Right. (Philosophers in Perspective Ser). 1970. pap. 5.50 (ISBN 0-312-44975-5). St Martin.

Nell, Onora. Acting on Principle: An Essay in Kantian Ethics. LC 74-20647. 155p. 1975. 15.00x (ISBN 0-231-03848-8). Columbia U Pr.

Nitsch, Friedrich A. A General & Introductory View of Professor Kant's Principles. Wellek, Rene, ed. LC 75-11240. (British & Theologians of the 17th & 18th Centuries: Vol. 40). 1977. Repr. of 1796 ed. lib. bdg. 42.00 (ISBN 0-8240-1792-7). Garland Pub.

Nolen, Desire. La Critique De Kant et la Metaphysique De Leibniz: histoire et theorie De leurs rapports... 476p. 1981. Repr. of 1875 ed. lib. bdg. 185.00 (ISBN 0-8287-1485-1). Clearwater Pub.

Novak, David. Suicide & Morality: The Theories of Plato, Aquinas & Kant & Their Relevance for Suicidology. LC 75-37543. x, 136p. 1976. lib. bdg. 7.50 (ISBN 0-685-69079-2). Scholars Studies.

Orsini, Gian N. Coleridge & German Idealism: A Study in the History of Philosophy. with Unpublished Material from Coleridge's Manuscripts. LC 69-11512. 320p. 1969. 10.00x (ISBN 0-8093-0363-9). S Ill U Pr.

Paton, H. J. The Categorical Imperative: A Study in Kant's Moral Philosophy. 1971. pap. 5.95x (ISBN 0-8122-1023-9, Pa Paperbks). U of Pa Pr.

Paton, Herbert J. Kant's Metaphysics of Experience, 2 Vols. (Muirhead Library of Philosophy). 1976. Repr. of 1961 ed. Set. text ed. 42.50x (ISBN 0-391-00673-8). Humanities.

Peddle, Frank. Thought & Being: Hegel's Criticism of Kant's System of Cosmological Ideas. LC 79-9695. 204p. 1980. text ed. 17.75 (ISBN 0-8191-0987-8); pap. text ed. 9.50 (ISBN 0-8191-0988-6). U Pr of Amer.

Pelegrinis, Theodosius N. Kant's Conceptions of the Categorical Imperative & the Will. 236p. 1980. text ed. 32.50x (ISBN 0-391-01922-8). Humanities.

The Philosophy of Immanuel Kant Series, 14 vols. 1977. lib. bdg. 350.00 set (ISBN 0-685-83865-X). Garland Pub.

Prauss, Gerold. Erscheinung Bei Kant: Ein Problem der Kritik der reinen Vernunft. (Quellen und Studien Zur Philosophie, 1). (Ger). 1971. 48.75x (ISBN 3-11-006427-8). De Gruyter.

Prichard, H. A. Kant's Theory of Knowledge. Beck, Lewis W., ed. LC 75-32042. (The Philosophy of Immanuel Kant Ser.: Vol. 5). 1977. Repr. of 1909 ed. lib. bdg. 26.00 (ISBN 0-8240-2329-3). Garland Pub.

Rainer, Enskat. Kants Theorie Des Geometrischen Gegenstandes. (Quellen & Studien Zur Philosophie: Vol. 13). 1978. 53.50x (ISBN 3-11-007644-6). De Gruyter.

Raschke, Carl A. Moral Action, God, & History in the Thought of Immanuel Kant. LC 75-11787. (American Academy of Religion. Dissertation Ser.). xiv, 236p. 1975. pap. 7.50 (ISBN 0-89130-003-1, 010105). Scholars Pr Ca.

Roettgers, Kurt. Kritik und Praxis: Zur Geschichte Des Kritikbegriffs Von Kant Bis Marx. LC 73-93165. (Quellen und Studien zur Philosophie, Vol. 8). x, 302p. 1974. 57.25x (ISBN 3-11-004604-0). De Gruyter.

Ross, Sir William D. Kant's Ethical Theory: A Commentary on the Grundlegung zur Metaphysid ser Sitten. LC 78-6730. 1978. Repr. of 1954 ed. lib. bdg. 15.00x (ISBN 0-8371-9059-2, ROKE). Greenwood.

Saner, Hans. Kant's Political Thought. Ashton, E. B., tr. from Gr. 1973. 13.50x (ISBN 0-226-73475-7). U of Chicago Pr.

Scheler, Max. Formalism in Ethics & Non-Formal Ethics of Values: A New Attempt Toward the Foundation of an Ethical Personalism. Frings, Manfred S. & Funk, Roger L., trs. from Ger. LC 72-97416. (Studies in Phenomenology & Existential Philosophy). Orig. Title: Der Formalismus der Ethik und die Materiale Wertethik. 750p. 1973. text ed. 25.95x (ISBN 0-8101-0415-6); pap. 11.95 (ISBN 0-8101-0620-5). Northwestern U Pr.

Schilpp, Paul A. Kant's Pre-Critical Ethics. 2nd ed. Beck, Lewis W., ed. LC 75-32043. (The Philosophy of Immanuel Kant Ser.: Vol. 6). 1977. Repr. of 1960 ed. lib. bdg. 24.00 (ISBN 0-8240-2330-7). Garland Pub.

Sellars, Wilfrid. Science & Metaphysics: Variations on Kantian Themes. LC 68-12258. (International Library of Philosophy & Scientific Method). 1968. text ed. 21.00x (ISBN 0-7100-3501-2). Humanities.

Seth, Andrew. The Development from Kant to Hegel, with Chapters on the Philosophy of Religion. Beck, Lewis W., ed. LC 75-32044. (The Philosophy of Immanuel Kant Ser.: Vol. 7). 1977. Repr. of 1882 ed. lib. bdg. 20.00 (ISBN 0-8240-2331-5). Garland Pub.

Seth Pringle Pattison, Andrew. The Development from Kant to Hegel. 1975. lib. bdg. 49.95 (ISBN 0-8490-0020-3). Gordon Pr.

Shell, Susan M. The Rights of Reason: A Study of Kant's Philosophy & Politics. LC 79-19801. 1979. 15.00x (ISBN 0-8020-5462-5). U of Toronto Pr.

Sherover, Charles M. Heidegger, Kant & Time. LC 74-135011. 344p. 1971. 15.00x (ISBN 0-253-32720-2). Ind U Pr.

Sidgwick, Henry. Lectures on the Philosophy of Kant & Other Philosophical Lectures & Essays. Ward, James, ed. LC 5-35670. 1968. Repr. of 1905 ed. 26.00 (ISBN 0-527-82818-1). Kraus Repr.

Smith, Alic H. Kantian Studies. LC 73-9266. 196p. 1974. Repr. of 1947 ed. lib. bdg. 15.00 (ISBN 0-8371-7003-6, SMKS). Greenwood.

Sontag, Frederick. Existentialist Prolegomena: To a Future Metaphysics. LC 68-11315. 1969. 9.00x (ISBN 0-226-76819-8). U of Chicago Pr.

Stevens, Rex P. Kant on Moral Practice. LC 81-9489. x, 181p. 1981. 15.95x (ISBN 0-86554-012-8). Mercer Univ Pr.

Stockhammer, Morris. Kant Dictionary. LC 76-155974. 1971. 10.00 (ISBN 0-8022-1649-8). Philos Lib.

Storrs, Margaret. Relations of Carlyle to Kant & Fichte. LC 77-9971. 1929. lib. bdg. 12.50 (ISBN 0-8414-7562-8). Folcroft.

Strawson, P. F. The Bounds of Sense: An Essay on Kant's Critique of Pure Reason. 296p. 1966. 24.00x (ISBN 0-416-29100-7); pap. 9.95x (ISBN 0-416-83560-0). Methuen Inc.

Stuhlmann-Laeisz, Rainer. Kants Logik: Eine Interpretation auf der Grundlage von Vorlesungen, veroeffentlichten Werken und Nachlass. (Quellen und Studien zur Philosophie: Vol. 9). 124p. 1976. 32.50x (ISBN 3-11-005840-5). De Gruyter.

Teale, A. E. Kantian Ethics. LC 74-30981. 328p. 1975. Repr. of 1951 ed. lib. bdg. 17.50x (ISBN 0-8371-7940-8, TEKE). Greenwood.

Third International Kant Congress. Kant's Theory of Knowledge: Selected Papers. Beck, L. W., ed. LC 74-83006. 217p. 1974. pap. 16.00 (ISBN 90-277-0529-1, Pub. by Reidel Holland). Kluwer Boston.

Tuschling, Burkhard. Metaphysische und transzendentale Dynamik in Kant opus postumum. (Quellen und Studien Zur Philosophie, 3). 224p. 1971. 33.50x (ISBN 3-11-001889-6). De Gruyter.

Vaihinger, Hans. Commentar Zu Kants Kritik der Reinen Vernunft, 2 vols. Beck, Lewis W., ed. Incl. Vol. 1. Stuttgart 1881; Vol. 2. Stuttgart & Berlin 1892. LC 75-32048. (Philosophy of Immanual Kant Ser.: Vol. 8). 1976. Repr. of 1892 ed. Set. lib. bdg. 66.00 (ISBN 0-8240-2332-3). Garland Pub.

Walker, Ralph C. Kant. (The Arguments of the Philosophers Ser.). 1978. 22.00x (ISBN 0-7100-8994-5). Routledge & Kegan.

Wallace, W. Kant. 219p. 1980. Repr. of 1899 ed. lib. bdg. 22.50 (ISBN 0-89984-503-7). Century Bookbindery.

Wallace, William. Kant. LC 72-4162. (Select Bibliographies Reprint Ser.). 1972. Repr. of 1882 ed. 16.00 (ISBN 0-8369-6894-8). Arno.

--Kant. 1882. Repr. 30.00 (ISBN 0-8274-2642-9). R West.

Walsh, W. H. Kant's Criticism of Metaphysics. 1976. pap. 4.50 (ISBN 0-226-87215-7, P688, Phoen). U of Chicago Pr.

Ward, James. A Study of Kant. Beck, Lewis W., ed. Bd. with Immanual Kant (Seventeen Twenty-Four to Eighteen Hundred Four) The British Academy Annual Philosophical Lecture. LC 75-32045. (Philosophy of Immanuel Kant Ser.: Vol. 9). 1977. Repr. of 1922 ed. lib. bdg. 24.00 (ISBN 0-8240-2333-1). Garland Pub.

Watson, John. Kant & His English Critics: A Comparison of Critical & Empirical Philosophy. Beck, Lewis W., ed. LC 75-32046. (The Philosophy of Immanuel Kant Ser.: Vol. 10). 1977. Repr. of 1881 ed. lib. bdg. 37.00 (ISBN 0-8240-2334-X). Garland Pub.

--The Philosophy of Kant Explained. 515p. 1981. Repr. of 1908 ed. lib. bdg. 40.00 (ISBN 0-8495-5659-7). Arden Lib.

--The Philosophy of Kant Explained. 515p. 1980. Repr. of 1908 ed. lib. bdg. 40.00 (ISBN 0-8482-7060-6). Norwood Edns.

--The Philosophy of Kant Explained. LC 78-14918. 1978. Repr. of 1908 ed. lib. bdg. 50.00 (ISBN 0-8414-9708-7). Folcroft.

--The Philosophy of Kant Explained. Beck, Lewis W., ed. LC 75-32047. (Philosophy of Immanual Kant Ser.: Vol. 11). 1977. Repr. of 1908 ed. lib. bdg. 40.00 (ISBN 0-8240-2335-8). Garland Pub.

Webb, C. J. Kant's Philosophy of Religion. Repr. of 1926 ed. 11.00 (ISBN 0-527-94912-4). Kraus Repr.

Wenley, R. M. Kant & His Philosophical Revolution. 1910. Repr. 35.00 (ISBN 0-8274-2643-7). R West.

Wenley, Robert M. Kant & His Philosophical Revolution. facsimile ed. Smeaton, Oliphant, ed. LC 78-169780. (Select Bibliographies Reprint Ser.). Repr. of 1910 ed. 19.00 (ISBN 0-8369-6600-7). Arno.

Werkmeister, W. H. Kant: The Architectonic & Development of His Philosophy. 1980. 15.00 (ISBN 0-87548-345-3). Open Court.

--Kant's Silent Decade. LC 78-31668. (A Florida State University Bk.). 15.75 (ISBN 0-8130-0606-6, IS-00071, University Presses of Florida). Univ Microfilms.

Werkmeister, William H., ed. Reflections on Kant's Philosophy. LC 75-20376. 180p. 1975. 8.00 (ISBN 0-8130-0541-8). U Presses Fla.

Whitney, G. T. & Fogel, P. H. Introduction to Kant's Critical Philosophy. 69.95 (ISBN 0-8490-0419-5). Gordon Pr.

Wilbur, James B., ed. The Worlds of Hume & Kant. rev. ed. Allen, Harold J. 196p. 1981. pap. text ed. 7.95 (ISBN 0-87975-163-0). Prometheus Bks.

Wilkerson, T. E. Kant's Critique of Pure Reason: A Commentary for Students. 256p. 1976. text ed. 24.00x (ISBN 0-19-824548-3); pap. text ed. 6.95x (ISBN 0-19-824549-1). Oxford U Pr.

Wilm, E. C. Immanuel Kant: 1724-1924. LC 78-15740. 1978. Repr. of 1925 ed. lib. bdg. 20.00 (ISBN 0-8414-9569-6). Folcroft.

Wilm, Emil C. Immanuel Kant, Seventeen Hundred Twenty-Four to Nineteen Twenty-Four. 88p. 1980. Repr. of 1925 ed. lib. bdg. 20.00 (ISBN 0-8482-7062-2). Norwood Edns.

Wolff, Robert P. Kant: A Collection of Critical Essays. 1968. 10.95x (ISBN 0-268-00148-0). U of Notre Dame Pr.

--Kant's Theory of Mental Activity, a Commentary on the Transcendental Analytic of the Critique of Pure Reason. 8.00 (ISBN 0-8446-4054-9). Peter Smith.

Wood, Allen W. Kant's Moral Religion. LC 74-98065. 283p. 1970. 20.00x (ISBN 0-8014-0548-3). Cornell U Pr.

--Kant's Rational Theology. LC 78-58059. 1979. 14.50x (ISBN 0-8014-1200-5). Cornell U Pr.

Yovel, Yirmiahu. Kant & the Philosophy of History. LC 79-84024. (Illus.). 1979. 18.50x (ISBN 0-691-07225-6). Princeton U Pr.

Zeldin, Mary-Barbara. Freedom & the Critical Undertaking: Essays on Kant's Later Critiques. LC 80-17553. (Sponsor Ser.). 346p. (Orig.). 1980. pap. 21.75 (ISBN 0-8357-0525-0, SS-00143). Univ Microfilms.

KANTOROWICZ, ERNST

Evans, Arthur R., Jr., ed. On Four Modern Humanists: Hofmannsthal, Gundolf, Curtius, Kantorowicz. LC 76-90945. (Princeton Essays Literature). 1970. 16.00 (ISBN 0-691-06174-2). Princeton U Pr.

KANURI LANGUAGE

Koelle, Sigismund W. African Native Literature: Or, Proverbs, Tales, Fables & Historical Fragments in the Kanuri or Bornu Language. facs. ed. LC 75-133158. (Black Heritage Library Collection Ser). 1854. 17.25 (ISBN 0-8369-8713-6). Arno.

Lukas, Johannes. Study of the Kanuri Language. LC 68-87331. (African Languages & Linguistics Ser). 1967. 11.25x (ISBN 0-7129-0146-9). Intl Pubns Serv.

KAONS

see Mesons

KAPAUKU (PAPUAN PEOPLE)

Pospisil, Leopold. Kapauku Papuan Economy. LC 78-188171. (Yale University Publications in Anthropology Reprints Ser: No. 67). 502p. 1972. pap. 15.00x (ISBN 0-87536-526-4). HRAFP.

--Kapauku Papuans & Their Law. LC 64-20560. (Yale University Publications in Anthropology Reprints Ser: No. 54). 296p. 1964. pap. 10.00x (ISBN 0-87536-502-7). HRAFP.

Pospisil, Leopold J. The Kapauku Papuans of West New Guinea. 2nd ed. LC 77-25981. 1978. pap. 6.95 (ISBN 0-03-041621-3, HoltC). HR&W.

KAPAUKU LAW

see Law, Kapauku

KAPLAN, MORDECAI MENAHEM, 1881-

Davis, Moshe. Mordecai M. Kaplan Jubilee Volume, 2 Vols. 1953. Set. 35.00x (ISBN 0-685-13740-6, Pub. by Jewish Theol Seminary). Ktav.

KAPODISTRIAS, IOANNES ANTONIOS, KOMES, 1776-1831

Woodhouse, C. M. Capodistria: The Founder of Greek Independence. new ed. (Illus.). 560p. 1973. 32.00x (ISBN 0-19-211196-5). Oxford U Pr.

KAPOSI'S SARCOMA

Bluefarb, Samuel M. Kaposi's Sarcoma: Multiple Idiopathic Hemorrhagic Sarcoma. (American Lecture Dermatology). (Illus.). 192p. 1957. ed. spiral bdg. 16.50photocopy (ISBN 0-398-00175-8). C C Thomas.

Olweny, Ch. L., et al, eds. Kaposi's Sarcoma. (Antibiotics Chemotherapy: Vol. 29). (Illus.). 200p. 1981. 53.50 (ISBN 3-8055-2076-X). S Karger.

KAPPUS, FRANZ XAVER, 1883-

Rilke, Rainer M. Letters to a Young Poet. rev. ed. 1963. pap. 2.95 (ISBN 0-393-00158-X, Norton Lib). Norton.

KARAGEORGEVICH, ALEXANDER

see Alexander 1st, of Yugoslavia, 1888-1934-Assassination

KARACHI

Streefland, Pieter. The Sweepers of Slaughterhouse: A Study of Conflict & Survival in a Karachi Neighbourhood. (Studies of Developing Countries Ser.: No. 23). 1979. pap. text ed. 14.25x (ISBN 90-232-1665-2). Humanities.

KARADZIC, VUK STEFANOVIC, 1787-1864

Koljevic, Svetozar. The Epic in the Making. (Illus.). 392p. 1980. 69.00x (ISBN 0-19-815759-2). Oxford U Pr.

KARAITES

Al-Qirqisani, Ya'Qub. Kitab Al-Anwar Wal-Maraoib: Code of Karaite Law, 3 vols. Incl. Vol. 1. First Discourse - Historical Introduction; Second Discourse - Philosophical & Theological Principles of Juris Prudence; Vol. 2. Third Discourse - Criticism of Sectarian Doctrines; Fourth Discourse - Methods of Construction & Interpretation of Law; Vol. 3. Fifth Discourse - Circumcion - Sabbath; Sixth Discourse - Civil & Criminal Law Liturgy. pap. 37.50 ea.; Set. pap. 100.00x (ISBN 0-686-52167-6). Elliots Bks.

Ankori, Zvi. Karaites in Byzantium: The Formative Years, 970-1100. LC 71-158258. (Columbia University Studies in the Social Sciences: No. 597). Repr. of 1959 ed. 28.50 (ISBN 0-404-51597-5). AMS Pr.

Mann, Jacob. Texts & Studies in Jewish History & Literature, 2 Vols. rev. ed. 1970. Set. 79.50x (ISBN 0-87068-085-4). Ktav.

Nemoy, Leon, tr. Karaite Anthology: Excerpts from the Early Literature. (Judaica Ser.: No. 7). 1952. 30.00x (ISBN 0-300-00792-2). Yale U Pr.

Schecter, Solomon. Documents of Jewish Sectaries, 2 Vols. in 1. rev. ed. (Library of Biblical Studies Ser). (Illus.). 1970. 35.00x (ISBN 0-87068-016-1). Ktav.

KARAMZIN, NIKOLAY MIKHAILOVICH, 1765-1826

Black, J. L. Nicholas Karamzin & Russian Society in the 19th Century: A Study in Russian Political & Historical Thought. LC 75-20146. 1975. 25.00x (ISBN 0-8020-5335-1). U of Toronto Pr.

Black, J. L., ed. Essays on Karamzin: Russian Man of Letters, Political Thinker, Historian, 1766-1826. (Slavistic Printings & Reprints: No.309). 232p. 1975. pap. text ed. 43.50x (ISBN 90-2793-251-4). Mouton.

Kochetkova, Natalya. Nikolay Karamazin. (World Authors Ser.: Russia: No. 250). 1974. lib. bdg. 12.50 (ISBN 0-8057-2488-5). Twayne.

KARATE

see also T'ai Chi Ch'Uan

Adams, Andrew. Ninja, the Invisible Assasins. Alston, Pat, ed. LC 75-130760. (Ser. 302s). (Illus.). 1970. 6.95 (ISBN 0-89750-030-X). Ohara Pubns.

Adams, B. Medical Implications of Karate Blows. 7.95 (ISBN 0-685-63768-9). Wehman.

Adams, Brian. Medical Implications of Karate Blows. LC 68-27195. (Illus.). 1969. 10.95 (ISBN 0-498-06786-6). A S Barnes.

--Medical Implications of Karate Blows. LC 68-27195. (Illus.). 1978. pap. 7.95 (ISBN 0-498-02300-1). A S Barnes.

Anderson, Dan. American Freestyle Karate. LC 81-50512. (Illus.). 200p. 1981. pap. 7.95 (ISBN 0-86568-021-3). Unique Pubns.

Anton & St. Denise. Bruce Lee's Guide to Savage Street Fighting. 1977. 1.95 (ISBN 0-685-83172-8). Wehman.

--Bruce Lee's My Martial Arts Training Manual. 1977. 1.95 (ISBN 0-685-83173-6). Wehman.

Armstrong. Seisan Kata Karate. 1976. 4.95 (ISBN 0-685-83534-0). Wehman.

Arneil, Steve & Dowler, Bryan. Better Karate: The Key to Better Technique. (Better Bks.). (Illus.). 98p. 1980. text ed. 15.95x (ISBN 0-7182-1444-7, SpS). Sportshelf.

Arvanitis, Jim. Mu Tau: The Modern Greek Karate. (Illus.). 1979. pap. 15.00 (ISBN 0-89200-035-X). Atlantis-by-the-Sea.

--Mu Tau: The Modern Greek Karate. (Illus.). 272p. (Orig.). 1979. pap. 15.00 (ISBN 0-89962-001-9). Todd & Honeywell.

Barnes, Steve. Ki: How to Generate the Dragon Spirit. Goodman, David, ed. (Sendo Martial Arts: No. 1). (Illus.). 51p. 1976. 2.95 (ISBN 0-686-15598-X); pap. 1.00 (ISBN 0-686-15599-8). Senseis DoJo.

Bartlett, E. G. Basic Karate. (Illus.). 96p. 1980. 13.95 (ISBN 0-571-11435-0, Pub. by Faber & Faber); pap. 6.95 (ISBN 0-571-11436-9, Pub. by Faber & Faber). Merrimack Bk Serv.

Benko, James S. Taekwon-Do Hyungs for Blue & Red Belt Levels. LC 81-82100. (Illus.). 112p. (Orig.). 1981. 13.95 (ISBN 0-937314-05-6); pap. 8.95 (ISBN 0-937314-04-8). Midwest Taekwon-Do.

--Taekwon-Do Hyungs for White, Yellow & Green Belt Levels. LC 81-81353. (Illus.). 118p. (Orig.). 1981. 13.95 (ISBN 0-937314-03-X); pap. 8.95 (ISBN 0-937314-02-1). Midwest Taekwon-Do.

--Taekwon-Do: Self Defense Against Weapons. LC 80-82015. (Illus.). 108p. (Orig.). 1980. pap. 8.95 (ISBN 0-686-27630-2). Midwest Taekwon-Do.

Brinkley, F. Samurai, the Invincible Warriors. Lucas, Charles, ed. LC 75-42567. (Series 316). 1975. pap. text ed. 4.50 (ISBN 0-89750-043-1). Ohara Pubns.

Burns, Donald J. An Introduction to Karate for Student & Teacher. 1977. pap. text ed. 6.95 (ISBN 0-8403-1692-5). Kendall-Hunt.

Chang, W. Mind Force Principles of Authentic Chinese Kung-Fu. 15.95 (ISBN 0-685-70691-5). Wehman.

Chen, Y. K. Tai-Chi-Ch'uan: Effects & Practical Applications. 9.95 (ISBN 0-685-70710-5). Wehman.

Chin, D. & Staples, M. Hop Gar Kung Fu. 1976. 4.95 (ISBN 0-685-83526-X). Wehman.

Chin, David & Staples, Michael. Hop Gar Kung Fu. (Illus.). 94p. 1976. pap. 4.50 (ISBN 0-86568-030-2). Unique Pubns.

Cho, S. H. Korean Karate. 13.50 (ISBN 0-685-22014-1). Wehman.

Cho, Sihak H. Korean Karate: Free Fighting Techniques. LC 68-18608. (Illus.). 1968. 25.50 (ISBN 0-8048-0350-1). C E Tuttle.

--Self-Defense Karate. LC 71-84824. (Illus.). 1969. 7.95 (ISBN 0-87396-005-X); pap. 3.95 (ISBN 0-87396-006-8). Stravon.

Chow, David & Spangler, Richard. Kung Fu, History, Philosophy, & Techniques. LC 73-14043. (Illus.). 220p. 1980. pap. 10.95 (ISBN 0-86568-011-6). Unique Pubns.

Chun, Richard. Tae Kwon Do: The Korean Martial Art & National Sport. LC 74-1799. (Illus.). 544p. 1976. 35.00 (ISBN 0-06-010779-0, HarpT). Har-Row.

Crompton, Paul. Karate Training Methods. 1971. 10.95 (ISBN 0-7207-0897-4, Pub. by Michael Joseph). Merrimack Bk Serv.

Crompton, Paul H. Kung Fu: Theory & Practice. (Illus.). 1975. 6.95 (ISBN 0-919364-94-2, ADON 3554). Pagurian.

--Kung-Fu Theory & Practice. 7.50 (ISBN 0-685-63765-4). Wehman.

Demura, F. Shito-Ryu Karate. 3.25 (ISBN 0-685-38450-0). Wehman.

Demura, Fumio. Advanced Nunchaku. 1976. 5.95 (ISBN 0-685-88116-4). Wehman.

--Nunchaku. 4.95 (ISBN 0-685-38448-9). Wehman.

--Nunchaku Karate Weapon of Self-Defense. LC 78-183341. (Ser. 111). (Illus.). 1971. pap. text ed. 6.95 (ISBN 0-89750-006-7). Ohara Pubns.

--Sai Karate Weapon of Self-Defense. LC 74-83597. (Ser. 115). (Illus.). 1974. pap. text ed. 6.95 (ISBN 0-89750-010-5). Ohara Pubns.

--Shito-Ryu Karate. LC 74-169720. (Ser. 110). (Illus.). 1971. pap. text ed. 5.95 (ISBN 0-89750-005-9). Ohara Pubns.

Demura, Fumio & Allee, John G. Bo, Karate Weapon of Self Defense. 5.95 (ISBN 0-685-70670-2). Wehman.

Demura, Fumio & Ivan, Dan. Advanced Nunchaku. Johnson, Gilbert & Adachi, Geraldine, eds. LC 76-40816. (Ser. 126). (Illus.). 1976. pap. text ed. 5.95 (ISBN 0-89750-021-0). Ohara Pubns.

Demura, Funio. Bo Karate Weapon of Self-Defense. Johnson, Gil & Adachi, Geraldine, eds. LC 76-13757. (Ser. 124). (Illus.). 1976. pap. text ed. 6.95 (ISBN 0-89750-019-9). Ohara Pubns.

Demure, F. Sai: Karate Weapon of Self-Defense. 4.95 (ISBN 0-685-63776-X). Wehman.

Dennis, F. & Simmons, P. Beginner's Guide to Kung-Fu. 2.50 (ISBN 0-685-63746-8). Wehman.

Dobson, Terry & Miller, Victor. Giving in to Get Your Way. 1978. 8.95 (ISBN 0-440-03247-4). Delacorte.

Dominy, Eric. Teach Yourself Karate. (Illus.). 1968. 7.95 (ISBN 0-87523-163-2). Emerson.

Draeger, Donn F. & Nakayama, Masatoshi. Practical Karate, 6 vols. LC 63-11828. (Illus.). 1963-65. pap. 4.75 ea.; Vol. 1. pap. 5.95 (ISBN 0-8048-0481-8); Vol. 2. pap. 4.75 (ISBN 0-8048-0482-6); Vol. 3. pap. 4.75 (ISBN 0-8048-0483-4); Vol. 4. pap. 4.75 (ISBN 0-8048-0484-2); Vol. 5. pap. 4.75 (ISBN 0-8048-0485-0); Vol. 6. pap. 4.75 (ISBN 0-8048-0486-9). C E Tuttle.

Droeger, D. Pentjak Silat. 8.95 (ISBN 0-685-38449-7). Wehman.

Dynamic Kicks. 1976. 2.95 (ISBN 0-685-88119-9). Wehman.

Egami, S. Way of Karate. 1976. 12.95 (ISBN 0-685-83542-1). Wehman.

Egami, Shigeru. The Heart of Karate-Do. LC 80-82529. (Illus.). 127p. 1981. 14.95 (ISBN 0-87011-437-9). Kodansha.

Fong, L. Power Training in Kung-Fu & Karate. 6.95 (ISBN 0-685-63773-5). Wehman.

Fong, L. T. Sil Lum Kung-Fu. 5.95 (ISBN 0-685-38451-9). Wehman.

Fong, Leo T. Choy Lay Fut Kung-Fu. Alston, Pat, ed. LC 70-181999. (Series 307). (Illus.). 1972. pap. text ed. 6.95 (ISBN 0-89750-035-0). Ohara Pubns.

Freudenberg, Karl. Natural Weapons: A Manual of Karate, Judo, & Jujitsu Techniques. (Illus., Orig.). 1962. pap. 3.95 (ISBN 0-498-04086-0, Prpta). A S Barnes.

Frommer, Harvey. The Martial Arts: Judo & Karate. LC 78-55205. (Illus.). 1978. 7.95 (ISBN 0-689-10908-3). Atheneum.

Fu, Leong. Shaolin Kung Fu: Chinese Art of Self Defense. 15.95 (ISBN 0-685-70703-2). Wehman.

Funakoshi, G. Karate-Do Kyohan. 19.95 (ISBN 0-685-38447-0). Wehman.

Funakoshi, Gichin. Karate-Do-Kyohan: The Master Text. Ohshima, Tsutomu, tr. from Japanese. LC 72-90228. (Illus.). 370p. 1973. 22.50 (ISBN 0-87011-190-6). Kodansha.

--Karate-Do, My Way of Life. LC 74-29563. (Illus.). 127p. 1975. 8.95 (ISBN 0-87011-241-4). Kodansha.

--Karate-Do, My Way of Life. 6.95 (ISBN 0-685-63759-X). Wehman.

Gambordella, Theodore. The Complete Book of Karate Weapons. (Illus.). 256p. 1981. 24.95 (ISBN 0-87364-206-6). Paladin Ent.

Glaessner, Verina. Kung-Fu: Cinema of Vengeance. 4.95 (ISBN 0-685-70686-9); pap. 2.95 (ISBN 0-686-67481-2). Wehman.

Goldstein, Frances. Karate for Kids. LC 76-4105. 1977. 8.95 (ISBN 0-668-04122-6). Arco.

Golomb, Robert. Karate for Beginners. (Do-It-Yourself Ser). (Illus.). pap. 3.50 (ISBN 0-910294-05-4). Brown Bk.

Gwon, Pu G. Dynamic Art of Breaking. 1977. 4.50 (ISBN 0-685-88118-0). Wehman.

Haines, B. A. Karate: History & Tradition. 5.95 (ISBN 0-685-63760-3). Wehman.

Haines, Bruce A. Karate's History & Traditions. LC 68-25893. (Illus.). 1968. 8.95 (ISBN 0-8048-0341-2). C E Tuttle.

Han, Bong Soo. Hapkido Korean Art of Self-Defense. Cocoran, John, ed. LC 74-15500. (Ser. 116). (Illus.). 1974. pap. text ed. 5.95 (ISBN 0-89750-011-3). Ohara Pubns.

Harrington, A. P. Defend Yourself with Kung Fu. LC 75-40969. 1976. 7.95 (ISBN 0-87523-189-6). Emerson.

Harrison, E. J. Manual of Karate. LC 66-16205. (Illus.). 160p. (gr. 7 up). 1975. 6.95 (ISBN 0-8069-4092-1); PLB 6.69 (ISBN 0-8069-4093-X). Sterling.

Harrison, Ernest J. Manual of Karate. 6.95 (ISBN 0-685-22028-1). Wehman.

Hassell, Randall G. The Karate Experience: A Way of Life. LC 80-53429. 124p. 1981. 9.95 (ISBN 0-8048-1348-5). C E Tuttle.

Hisataka, Masayuki. Scientific Karate. 19.95 (ISBN 0-685-70701-6). Wehman.

Hisatake, Masayuki. Scientific Karatedo: Spiritual Development of Individuality in Mind and Body. (Illus.). 256p. 1976. 25.00 (ISBN 0-87040-362-1). Japan Pubns.

Inosanto. Jeet Kune Do, Art & Philosophy of Bruce Lee. 1976. 13.95 (ISBN 0-685-83528-6); pap. 10.95 (ISBN 0-685-83529-4). Wehman.

Jee, J. M. Hapkido: Elementary. 7.95 (ISBN 0-685-63754-9). Wehman.

--Hapkido: Introduction. 7.95 (ISBN 0-685-63755-7). Wehman.

Kei Hua, E. Kung-Fu Meditations. 1.95 (ISBN 0-685-63764-6). Wehman.

Kim, Daeshik & Leland, Tom W. Karate. 2nd ed. (Physical Education Activities Ser.). 96p. 1978. pap. text ed. write for info. (ISBN 0-697-07079-4). Wm C Brown.

Kim, Richard. The Weaponless Warriors. Scurra, John, ed. LC 74-21218. (Ser. 313). (Illus.). 1974. pap. text ed. 5.95 (ISBN 0-89750-041-5). Ohara Pubns.

Kong, B. Hung Gar Kung-Fu. 4.95 (ISBN 0-685-38444-6). Wehman.

Kong, Bucksam & Ho, Eugene H. Hung Gar Kung-Fu Chinese Art of Self-Defense. Scurra, John, ed. LC 73-75551. (Ser. 310). 1973. pap. text ed. 6.95 (ISBN 0-89750-038-5). Ohara Pubns.

Kozuki, Russel. Junior Karate. (Illus.). (gr. 4-6). 1977. pap. 1.50 (ISBN 0-686-68483-4). PB.

Kozuki, Russell. Junior Karate. LC 71-167665. (Illus.). (gr. 3 up). 1971. 6.95 (ISBN 0-8069-4446-3); PLB 6.69 (ISBN 0-8069-4447-1). Sterling.

--Junior Karate. (gr. 4-6). 1977. pap. 1.75 (ISBN 0-671-42065-8). Archway.

--Karate for Young People. LC 73-93590. (Athletic Institute Ser.). (Illus.). 128p. (gr. 3 up). 1974. 6.95 (ISBN 0-8069-4074-3); PLB 6.69 (ISBN 0-8069-4075-1). Sterling.

--Karate for Young People. 128p. 1975. pap. 1.95 (ISBN 0-346-12186-8). Cornerstone.

--The Karate Road to Power. LC 69-19478. (Illus.). 192p. 1973. pap. 3.95 (ISBN 0-02-029130-2, Collier). Macmillan.

Kubota, Takayuki. Gosoku Ryu Karate: Kumite I. LC 80-53036. (Illus.). 160p. (Orig.). 1980. pap. 6.95 (ISBN 0-86568-010-8). Unique Pubns.

Kurban, Roy. Kicking Techniques. LC 79-65639. (Ser. 211). (Illus.). 1979. pap. 5.95 (ISBN 0-89750-065-2). Ohara Pubns.

Lee, Bruce. Bruce Lee's Fighting Method, 4 vols. 1976. 6.25 ea. (ISBN 0-685-83515-4); Set. 24.95 (ISBN 0-686-77314-4). Wehman.

--Bruce Lee's Training Method, 4 vols. 1977. Set. 24.95 (ISBN 0-685-83171-X). Wehman.

--Tao of Teet Kune Do. 10.95 (ISBN 0-685-63784-0). Wehman.

Lee, Bruce & Uyehara, M. Bruce Lee's Fighting Method, 4 vols. LC 78-71205. (Ser. 406 H). 1978. 29.95 (ISBN 0-89750-062-8). Ohara Pubns.

--Bruce Lee's Fighting Method: Advanced Techniques. LC 77-92737. (Ser. 405: Vol. 4). (Illus.). 1977. pap. 5.50 (ISBN 0-89750-053-9). Ohara Pubns.

--Bruce Lee's Fighting Method: Basic Training, Vol. II, No. 403. Shelrud, Doris, ed. LC 77-79057. (Illus.). 1977. pap. text ed. 5.50 (ISBN 0-89750-051-2). Ohara Pubns.

--Bruce Lee's Fighting Method: Skill in Techniques. LC 77-81831. (Ser. 404: Vol. 3). (Illus.). 1977. pap. 5.50 (ISBN 0-89750-052-0). Ohara Pubns.

Lee, Bruce & Uyehara, Mitoshi. Bruce Lee's Fighting Method: Self-Defense Techniques, Vol. 1. LC 76-51476. (Series 402: Vol. 1). (Illus.). 1976. pap. text ed. 5.50 (ISBN 0-89750-050-4). Ohara Pubns.

Lee, Chong. Dynamic Kicks: Essentials for Free Fighting. Johnson, Gilbert, ed. LC 75-36052. (Ser. 122). (Illus.). 1975. pap. text ed. 5.95 (ISBN 0-89750-017-2). Ohara Pubns.

Lee, J. Yimm. Wing Chun Kung-Fu. 6.95 (ISBN 0-685-38460-8). Wehman.

--Wing Chun Kung-Fu. LC 72-87863. (Ser. 309). (Illus.). 1972. pap. 7.95 (ISBN 0-89750-037-7). Ohara Pubns.

Lee, Joo B. HWA Rang Do. LC 78-52313. (Ser. 131). 1979. pap. 6.95 (ISBN 0-89750-070-9). Ohara Pubns.

Lee Ying-Arng. Pa-Kua Chang for Self-Defense. 7.95 (ISBN 0-685-63771-9). Wehman.
Lew, J. Art of Stretching & Kicking. 1977. 4.50 (ISBN 0-685-83170-1). Wehman.
Lewis, Tom G. Karate for Kids. 120p. (Orig.). 1980. pap. 3.95 (ISBN 0-89826-005-1). Natl Paperback.
Lin, Willy. T'ien Shan P'ai Kung Fu. Adachi, Geraldine, ed. LC 76-15348. (Ser. 319). (Illus.). 1976. pap. text ed. 5.95 (ISBN 0-89750-045-8). Ohara Pubns.
--Tien Shan Pai Kung Fu. 1976. 4.95 (ISBN 0-685-83540-5). Wehman.
Linick, Andrew S. Nunchaku, Karate's Deadliest Fighting Sticks. LC 75-6144. (Illus.). 124p. 1974. 19.95 (ISBN 0-917098-01-3); pap. 12.95 (ISBN 0-917098-00-5). LKA Inc.
Long, Harold & Wheeler, Allen. Dynamics of Isshinryu Karate Black & Brown Belt, Bk. 3. Condry, Steve, ed. (Isshinryu Karate Ser.). (Illus.). 146p. (Orig.). 1980. pap. 3.95 (ISBN 0-89826-006-X). Natl Paperback.
--Dynamics of Isshinryu Karate Blue & Green Belt, Bk. 2. Condry, Steve, ed. (Illus., Orig.). 1979. pap. 2.95 (ISBN 0-89826-004-3). Natl Paperback.
Lowe, Bobby. Mas Oyama's Karate. LC 64-10376. (Illus.). 224p. 1973. pap. 1.95 (ISBN 0-668-01140-8). Arco.
Mack, C. J. Karate Test Techniques. 91p. 1971. 6.95 (ISBN 0-7207-0441-3, Pub. by Michael Joseph). Merrimack Bk Serv.
Madeiros, E. C. History & Philosophy of Kung-Fu. 8.50 (ISBN 0-685-63756-5). Wehman.
Marchini, Ron & Fong, Leo. Power Training in Kung-Fu & Karate. Cocoran, John & Scurra, John, eds. LC 74-14128. (Ser.400). (Illus.). 1974. pap. text ed. 7.95 (ISBN 0-89750-047-4). Ohara Pubns.
Mart, Harry. Kung Fu Bible. (Illus.). 1981. 4.95 (ISBN 0-89962-008-6). Todd & Honeywell.
--Kung Fu Bible. (Illus.). 1979. 4.95 (ISBN 0-89200-036-8). Atlantis-by-the-Sea.
Maslak, Paul. Strategy in Unarmed Combat. (Illus.). 136p. 1980. pap. 6.95 (ISBN 0-86568-025-6). Unique Pubns.
--What the Masters Know. (Illus.). 108p. 1980. pap. 6.95 (ISBN 0-86568-026-4). Unique Pubns.
Masters, Robert V., compiled by. Complete Book of Karate & Self-Defense. (Illus.). 542p. (gr. 10 up). 1974. 12.95 (ISBN 0-8069-4084-0); PLB 11.69 (ISBN 0-8069-4085-9). Sterling.
Mattson, George E. Uechiryu Karate Do. LC 75-5978. 1974. 15.00 (ISBN 0-686-10569-9). Peabody Pub.
--Way of Karate. LC 62-14116. (Illus.). 1963. 10.00 (ISBN 0-8048-0624-1). C E Tuttle.
--Way of Karate. 10.00 (ISBN 0-685-22157-1). Wehman.
Minick, H. Kung-Fu Exercise Book: Health Secrets of Ancient China. 3.95 (ISBN 0-685-63763-8). Wehman.
Morris, P. M. The Illustrated Guide to Karate. 1979. pap. 9.95 (ISBN 0-442-26095-4). Van Nos Reinhold.
Nagamine, S. Essence of Okinawan Karate Do. 1976. 19.50 (ISBN 0-685-83525-1). Wehman.
--Okinawan Karate Do. 1976. 15.00 (ISBN 0-685-83533-2). Wehman.
Nagamine, Shoshin. The Essence of Okinawan Karate - Do. LC 75-28717. (Illus.). 1976. 19.50 (ISBN 0-8048-1163-6). C E Tuttle.
Nakayama & Draeger. Karate Practico. Incl. Fundamentos; Defensa Contra un Asaltante Desarmado. 6.95 ea. Wehman.
Nakayama, M. Dynamic Karate. Kauz, Herman, tr. LC 66-28954. (Illus.). 308p. 1966. 22.50 (ISBN 0-87011-037-3). Kodansha.
--Dynamic Karate. (Illus.). 1966. 19.95 (ISBN 0-685-21935-6). Wehman.
--Karate Kata, 5 vols. (Japan Karate Association Ser). (Illus.). 1969. pap. 5.95 ea. (Pub. by Kodansha). Wehman.
--Karate Kata: Heian 1, Tekki 1. LC 70-100629. (Karate Kata Ser.). (Illus., Orig.). 1970. pap. 5.95 (ISBN 0-87011-105-1). Kodansha.
--Karate Kata: Heian 4. LC 68-26559. (Karate Kata Ser.). (Illus., Orig.). 1968. pap. 5.95 (ISBN 0-87011-097-7). Kodansha.
--Karate Kata: Heian 5. LC 69-16365. (Karate Kata Ser.). (Illus., Orig.). 1969. pap. 5.95 (ISBN 0-87011-078-0). Kodansha.
--Karate Kata: Tekki 2-Tekki 3. LC 70-134605. (Karate Kata Ser). (Illus., Orig.). 1970. pap. 5.95 (ISBN 0-87011-144-2). Kodansha.
Nakayama, Masatoshi. Best Karate: 1 Comprehensive. LC 77-74829. (Best Karate Ser.: Vol. 1). (Illus.). 1977. pap. 6.95 (ISBN 0-87011-317-8). Kodansha.
--Best Karate: 2 Fundamentals. LC 77-74829. (Best Karate Ser.: Vol. 2). (Illus.). 1978. pap. 6.95 (ISBN 0-87011-324-0). Kodansha.
--Best Karate: 3 Kumite I. LC 77-74829. (Best Karate Ser: Vol. 3). (Illus.). 1978. pap. 6.95 (ISBN 0-87011-332-1). Kodansha.
--Best Karate: 5 Kata: Heian & Tekki. LC 77-74829. (Best Karate Ser.: Vol. 5). 1979. pap. 6.95 (ISBN 0-87011-379-8). Kodansha.
--Best Karate: 6 Kata: Bassai & Kanku. LC 77-74829. (Best Karate Ser.: Vol. 6). (Illus., Orig.). 1980. pap. 6.95 (ISBN 0-87011-383-6). Kodansha.
--Best Karate: 7 Kata: Jutte, Hangetsu, Empi. LC 77-74829. (Best Karate Ser.: Vol. 7). (Illus.). 144p. 1981. pap. 6.95 (ISBN 0-87011-390-9). Kodansha.
--Best Karate: 8 Kata: Gankaku, Jion. LC 77-74829. (Best Karate Ser.: Vol. 8). (Illus.). 144p. (Orig.). 1981. pap. 6.95 (ISBN 0-87011-402-6). Kodansha.
Nakayama, Masatoshi & Draeger, Donn F. Karate Practico: Vol. 1. (Illus., Orig., Span.). 1964. pap. 3.05 (ISBN 0-8048-0335-8). C E Tuttle.
--Karate Practico: Vol. 2. (Illus., Orig., Span.). 1965. pap. 2.75 (ISBN 0-8048-0336-6). C E Tuttle.
--Karate Pratique: Vol. 3. (Illus., Orig., Fr.). 1966. pap. 2.75 (ISBN 0-8048-0339-0). C E Tuttle.
Nakayama, Masatoshi N. Best Karate: 4 Kumite 2. LC 77-74829. (Best Karate Ser.: Vol. 4). (Illus.). 1979. pap. 6.95 (ISBN 0-87011-359-3). Kodansha.
Neff, Fred. Fred Neff's Basic Karate Handbook. LC 75-38471. (Fred Neff's Self-Defense Library). (Illus.). 56p. (gr. 5 up). 1976. PLB 5.95g (ISBN 0-8225-1150-9). Lerner Pubns.
--Karate Is for Me. LC 79-16900. (Sports for Me Bks.). (Illus.). (gr. 2-5). 1980. PLB 5.95g (ISBN 0-8225-1090-1). Lerner Pubns.
Nishiyama, H. & Brown. Karate. 12.75 (ISBN 0-685-22002-8). Wehman.
Nishiyama, Hidetaka & Brown, Richard C. Karate: Art of Empty Hand Fighting. LC 59-10409. (Illus.). (gr. 9 up). 1960. 22.50 (ISBN 0-8048-0340-4). C E Tuttle.
Nitobe, Inazo. Bushido, the Warrior's Code. Lucas, Charles, ed. LC 75-21718. (Ser. 303s). (Illus.). 1975. pap. text ed. 4.95 (ISBN 0-89750-031-8). Ohara Pubns.
Norris, C. Winning Tournament Karate. 4.50 (ISBN 0-685-63791-3). Wehman.
Norris, Chuck. Winning Tournament Karate. Cocoran, John, ed. LC 75-5497. (Ser. 121). (Illus.). 1975. pap. text ed. 5.95 (ISBN 0-89750-016-4). Ohara Pubns.
Ohara Publications. Dear Bruce Lee. (Series 407). pap. 7.95 (ISBN 0-89750-069-5). Ohara Pubns.
Okazaki, Teruyuki & Stricevc, Milorad. The Textbook of Modern Karate. LC 80-84478. (Illus.). 350p. Date not set. 27.50 (ISBN 0-87011-461-1). Kodansha.
Okinawa Goju-Ryu: Fundamentals of Shorei-Kan Karate. 4.95 (ISBN 0-685-70694-X). Wehman.
O'Malley, Martin J. The Lun Yu of Kung Fu. LC 75-19749. 20p. 1975. pap. 1.00 (ISBN 0-9606610-0-X). M J O'Malley.
Oyama, M. Advanced Karate. (Illus.). 1970. 25.00 (ISBN 0-685-21871-6, Pub. by Japan Pubns). Wehman.
--Mastering Karate. 4.95 (ISBN 0-685-47571-9). Wehman.
Oyama, Mas. Boy's Karate. (Illus.). 1969. pap. 4.95 (ISBN 0-685-00903-3). Wehman.
--Mas Oyama's Essential Karate. LC 77-79509. (Illus.). 1979. pap. 7.95 (ISBN 0-8069-8844-4). Sterling.
--Mas Oyama's Essential Karate. LC 77-79509. (Illus.). 1978. 14.95 (ISBN 0-8069-4120-0); lib. bdg. 14.99 (ISBN 0-8069-4121-9). Sterling.
--This Is Karate. 25.00 (ISBN 0-685-22138-5). Wehman.
--What Is Karate. 19.50 (ISBN 0-685-22160-1). Wehman.
Oyama, Masutatsu. The Kyokushin Way. LC 79-1961. 1979. 8.95 (ISBN 0-87040-460-1). Japan Pubns.
--Mastering Karate. 1969. pap. 7.95 (ISBN 0-448-01747-4). G&D.
--This Is Karate. rev. ed. LC 65-17218. (Illus.). 368p. 1973. boxed 32.00 (ISBN 0-87040-254-4). Japan Pubns.
--Vital Karate. LC 67-19867. (Illus.). pap. 5.95 (ISBN 0-87040-143-2). Japan Pubns.
--Vital Karate. (Illus.). 1967. pap. 4.50 (ISBN 0-685-22152-0). Wehman.
Parker, E. Secrets of Chinese Karate. 8.95 (ISBN 0-685-41911-8). Wehman.
Parker, Ed. Secrets of Chinese Karate. (Funk & W Bk.). (Illus.). 1968. pap. 2.95 (ISBN 0-308-90041-3, F23). T Y Crowell.
Parker, Edmund K. Secrets of Chinese Karate. 1963. 8.95 (ISBN 0-13-797852-9); pap. 5.95 (ISBN 0-13-797845-6). P-H.
Patterson, C. T. Wado-Ryu Karate. 2.95 (ISBN 0-685-63788-3). Wehman.
Pfluger, A. Karate: Basic Principles. 1970. pap. 2.95 (ISBN 0-06-463307-1, EH 307, EH). Har-Row.
--Karate: Basic Principles. Kuttner, Paul & Cunningham, Dale S., trs. LC 67-27760. (Illus.). (gr. 8 up). 1969. Repr. of 1967 ed. 6.95 (ISBN 0-8069-4432-3); PLB 7.49 (ISBN 0-8069-4433-1). Sterling.
Phillips, James M. Nunchaku Two. LC 75-18740. (Illus.). 278p. 1975. 6.95 (ISBN 0-932572-01-4). J M Phillips.
Plee, H. D. Karate: Beginner to Black Belt. (Illus.). 1967. 7.95 (ISBN 0-685-22003-6). Wehman.
--Karate by Pictures. 5.95 (ISBN 0-685-22004-4). Wehman.
Practical Karate, 6 Vols. 4.75 ea. Wehman.
Pu Gill Gwon. Dynamic Breaking Techniques. LC 77-89191. (Ser. 128). 1977. pap. 6.95 (ISBN 0-89750-023-7). Ohara Pubns.
Radlauer, Ed. Some Basics About Karate. (Gemini Ser.). (Illus.). (gr. 3 up). 1981. PLB 9.25 (ISBN 0-516-07694-9); pap. 2.95 (ISBN 0-516-47694-7). Childrens.
Rhee, J. Hwa-Rang Chung-Mu: Taekwondo. 4.95 (ISBN 0-685-38445-4). Wehman.
--Won-Hyo & Yul-Kok. 4.95 (ISBN 0-685-38461-6). Wehman.
Rhee, Jhoon. Chon-Ji of Tae Kwon Do Hyung. Alvarez, Roberto, tr. LC 74-120124. (Series 102). (Illus., Sp. & Eng.). 1970. pap. text ed. 5.95 (ISBN 0-89750-000-8). Ohara Pubns.
--Chung-Gun & Toi Gye of Tae Kwon Do Hyung. LC 76-163381. (Series 108). (Illus.). 1971. pap. text ed. 5.95 (ISBN 0-89750-003-2). Ohara Pubns.
--Hwa-Rang & Chung-Mu of Tae Kwon Do Hyung. LC 77-163382. (Ser. 109). (Illus.). 1971. pap. text ed. 5.95 (ISBN 0-89750-004-0). Ohara Pubns.
--Tan-Gun & to-San of Tae Kwon Do. LC 71-150320. (Ser. 100S: No. 106). (Illus.). 1971. pap. text ed. 5.95 (ISBN 0-89750-001-6). Ohara Pubns.
--Won-Hyo & Yul-Kok of Tae Kwon Do Hyung. LC 70-157046. (Ser. 107). (Illus.). 1971. pap. text ed. 5.95 (ISBN 0-89750-002-4). Ohara Pubns.
Roth, Jordan. Black Belt Karate. LC 73-87677. (Illus.). 1970. 35.00 (ISBN 0-8048-0065-0). C E Tuttle.
--Black Belt Karate. 27.50 (ISBN 0-685-47545-X). Wehman.
Russell, Scott. Karate: Energy Connection. 1976. 7.95 (ISBN 0-685-83530-8). Wehman.
Sawar, K. Essence of Kung Fu: Tai-Ki Ken. 6.95 (ISBN 0-685-70680-X). Wehman.
Schroeder, Charles R. & Wallace, Bill. Karate: Basic Concepts & Skills. LC 75-12101. (Illus.). 176p. 1976. text ed. 6.95 (ISBN 0-201-06837-0). A-W.
Scott, W. Chinese Kung Fu (Kenpo) 1976. 12.50 (ISBN 0-685-83522-7). Wehman.
Scott, William D. Chinese Kung Fu (Kenpo) An Introduction. LC 75-33438. (Illus.). 1976. 13.50 (ISBN 0-8048-1157-1). C E Tuttle.
Serizawa, Katsusuke. Tsubo: Vital Points for Oriental Therapy. (Illus.). 256p. 1976. 22.00 (ISBN 0-87040-350-8). Japan Pubns.
Shin Duk Kung. One-Step Sparring. LC 78-60159. (Ser. 132). 1978. pap. 5.50 (ISBN 0-89750-057-1). Ohara Pubns.
Singer, Kurt. Karate-Do. LC 80-84423. (Illus.). 176p. 1981. pap. 4.95 (ISBN 0-87011-460-3). Kodansha.
Siou, Lily. Chi Kung. 1976. 14.50 (ISBN 0-685-83521-9). Wehman.
Smith, J. Basic Karate Katas. 1973. 10.00 (ISBN 0-685-83516-2). Wehman.
Smith, Robert W. Secrets of Shaolin Temple Boxing. LC 64-22002. (Illus.). 1964. 7.95 (ISBN 0-8048-0518-0). C E Tuttle.
Son, Duk S. & Clark, R. Korean Karate: The Art of Tae Kwan Do. LC 68-17527. 1968. 11.95 (ISBN 0-13-516815-5). P-H.
Son, Duk Sung. Korean Karate. 10.95 (ISBN 0-685-41909-6). Wehman.
Soo, K. P. Palgue (4, 5, 6) of Tae Kwon Do. 4.95 (ISBN 0-685-63772-7). Wehman.
SooHan, B. Hapkido: Korean Self-Defense. 4.95 (ISBN 0-685-63753-0). Wehman.
Staples, M. Tibetan Kung Fu. 1976. 3.75 (ISBN 0-685-83539-1). Wehman.
Staples, M. P. White Crane Gung-Fu. 3.25 (ISBN 0-685-41916-9). Wehman.
Staples, Michael P. Tibetan Kung-Fu: The Way of the Monk. (Illus.). 80p. 1976. pap. 3.75 (ISBN 0-86568-029-9). Unique Pubns.
Stockman. Kickboxing. 1976. 2.95 (ISBN 0-685-83531-6). Wehman.
Sugano, J. Basic Karate for Women: Health & Self-Defense. 9.95 (ISBN 0-685-70669-9). Wehman.
Suzuki, Tatsuo. Karate-Do. 160p. 1967. 14.95 (ISBN 0-7207-0144-9, Pub. by Michael Joseph). Merrimack Bk Serv.
Tackett, T. Hsing-I Kung-Fu. 4.95 (ISBN 0-685-63757-3). Wehman.
Tackett, Tim. Hsing-I Kung-Fu. Johnson, Gil, ed. LC 75-24802. (Ser. 306). (Illus.). 1975. pap. text ed. 5.95 (ISBN 0-89750-034-2). Ohara Pubns.
Tang, P. The New Manual of Kung Fu. 7.95 (ISBN 0-685-63786-7). Wehman.
Tegner, Bruce. Bruce Tegner's Complete Book of Karate. 256p. 1973. pap. 2.95 (ISBN 0-553-20079-8, 20079-8). Bantam.
--Bruce Tegner's Complete Book of Karate: Self-Defense & Sport. 2nd rev ed. LC 70-126632. (Illus.). 1970. 6.95 (ISBN 0-87407-502-5, C-2). Thor.
--Karate & Judo Exercises. rev. ed. LC 81-5251. (Illus.). 1981. pap. 3.95 (ISBN 0-87407-036-8, T-22). Thor.
--Karate: Self Defense & Traditional Sport Forms. LC 73-9742. (Illus.). 160p. (Orig.). 1973. pap. 2.95 (ISBN 0-87407-023-6). Thor.
--Kung Fu & Tai Chi: Chinese Karate & Classical Exercises. rev. ed. LC 80-27516. (Illus.). 127p. 1981. pap. 3.95 (ISBN 0-87407-035-X, T-15). Thor.
--Self-Defense Nerve Centers & Pressure Points for Karate, Jujitsu & Atemi-Waza. rev. enlarged ed. LC 78-18169. (Illus.). 1978. 5.95 (ISBN 0-87407-519-X, C-19); pap. 2.95 (ISBN 0-87407-029-5). Thor.
Tegner, Bruce & McGrath, Alice. Solo Forms of Karate, Tai Chi, Aikido & Kung Fu. (Illus.). 112p. 1981. pap. 3.95 (ISBN 0-87407-034-1, T-34). Thor.
Thomas, Raymond. Diccionario del Budo: Artes Marciales. 128p. (Span., Japanese, Chinese, Korean, & Other Oriental Languages.). 1978. pap. 4.50 (ISBN 84-203-0069-1, S-50092). French & Eur.
Tohei, K. Book of Ki. 1976. 6.95 (ISBN 0-685-83517-0). Wehman.
Tohei, Koichi. The Book of "Ki". Co-Ordinating Body and Mind in Daily Life. LC 76-29340. (Illus.). 128p. 1976. pap. 7.95 (ISBN 0-87040-379-6). Japan Pubns.
--Ki in Daily Life. Orig. Title: Aikido in Daily Life. 1978. pap. 10.95 (ISBN 0-87040-436-9). Japan Pubns.
Trias, Robert A. The Hand Is My Sword: A Karate Handbook. LC 72-88098. 1973. 10.00 (ISBN 0-8048-1077-X). C E Tuttle.
Tueleners, T. Beginning Karate. 4.50 (ISBN 0-685-63744-1). Wehman.
Tulleners, Tonny. Beginning Karate. Corcoran, John, ed. LC 74-78904. (Ser. 206s). (Illus.). 1974. pap. text ed. 6.95 (ISBN 0-89750-027-X). Ohara Pubns.
Un, S. H. Pak-Mei Kung Fu. 8.00 (ISBN 0-685-63774-3). Wehman.
Unique Publications Staff. Bruce Lee: The Untold Story. (Illus.). 80p. 1980. pap. 3.50 (ISBN 0-86568-009-4). Unique Pubns.
Urban, P. Karate Dojo. 5.95 (ISBN 0-685-22005-2). Wehman.
Urban, Peter. Karate Dojo: Traditions & Tales of a Martial Art. LC 67-20952. 1967. 7.75 (ISBN 0-8048-0334-X). C E Tuttle.
Uyehara, Mitoshi. Bruce Lee--Farewell, My Friend. LC 76-25359. (Collectors Ser.: No. 907). (Illus.). 1976. 3.95 (ISBN 0-89750-054-7). Ohara Pubns.
Van Clief, Ron. The Manual of the Martial Arts: An Introduction to the Combined Techniques of Karate, Kung-Fu, Tae Kwon Do, & Aiki-Jitsu for Everyone. (Illus.). 1981. 14.95 (ISBN 0-89256-204-8); pap. 9.95 (ISBN 0-89256-204-8). Rawson Wade.
Ventresca, Peter. Shoto-Kan Karate: The Ultimate in Self-Defense. LC 71-104205. (Illus.). 1970. 12.50 (ISBN 0-8048-0529-6). C E Tuttle.
Wall, Bob. Who's Who in the Martial Arts & Directory of Black Belts. LC 75-22880. (Illus.). 275p. (Orig.). 1975. pap. 7.95 (ISBN 0-685-62677-6). R A Wall.
Wills, Jay T. Advanced Kenpo Karate. (Illus.). 116p. (Orig.). 1980. pap. 5.95 (ISBN 0-86568-008-6). Unique Pubns.
Wong, D. L. Kung-Fu: The Way of Life. 4.95 (ISBN 0-685-70687-7). Wehman.
Wong, Douglas L. The Deceptive Hands of Wing Chu. LC 76-55613. (Illus.). 112p. 1977. pap. 5.95 (ISBN 0-86568-027-2). Unique Pubns.
--Kung-Fu: The Way of Life. LC 76-55617. (Illus.). 112p. 1975. pap. 5.50 (ISBN 0-86568-028-0). Unique Pubns.
--Shaolin Fighting. LC 76-55613. (Illus.). 1975. pap. 5.50 (ISBN 0-86568-031-0). Unique Pubns.
Wong, G. Wing Chun Kung-Fu. 8.00 (ISBN 0-685-63793-X). Wehman.
Yamaguchi, Gosei. The Fundamentals of Goju-Ryu Karate. Alston, Pat, ed. LC 72-80830. (Ser.112). (Illus.). 1972. pap. text ed. 7.95 (ISBN 0-89750-007-5). Ohara Pubns.
--Goju-Ryu Karate, 2 vols. 5.95 ea. Wehman.
Yamashita, T. Shorin Ryu Karate. 1976. 4.50 (ISBN 0-685-83536-7). Wehman.
Ying-Arng, Lee. Iron Palm in One Hundred Days. 7.95 (ISBN 0-685-63758-1). Wehman.
--Lee's Modified Tai Chi for Health. 10.95 (ISBN 0-685-70688-5). Wehman.
Yuen, K. Beginning Kung-Fu. 4.95 (ISBN 0-685-63745-X). Wehman.
Yuen, Kam. Beginning Kung-Fu. Johnson, Gilbert, ed. LC 75-21721. (Ser. 314). (Illus.). 1975. pap. text ed. 6.95 (ISBN 0-89750-042-3). Ohara Pubns.
--Three Sectional Staff. LC 79-87639. (Ser. 332). (Illus.). 1979. pap. 5.95 (ISBN 0-89750-064-4). Ohara Pubns.

KARATEPE, CILICIA

Obermann, Julian. Discoveries at Karatepe: A Phoenician Royal Inscription from Cilicia. (Supplements: 9). (Illus.). 1948. pap. 1.00 (ISBN 0-686-00045-5). Am Orient Soc.

KARIBA DAM

Colson, Elizabeth. Social Consequences of Resettlement: The Impact of the Kariba Resettlement Upon the Gwembe Tonga. (Kariba Studies: No. 4). 1971. pap. text ed. 6.50x (ISBN 0-7190-1033-0). Humanities.

KARL 5TH, EMPEROR OF GERMANY, 1500-1558

Brandi, Karl. The Emperor Charles V: The Growth & Destiny of a Man & of a World-Empire. Wedgwood, C. V., tr. from Ger. 655p. 1980. Repr. lib. bdg. 35.00 (ISBN 0-8492-3751-3). R West.

Robertson, William. The History of the Reign of the Emperor Charles V, 3 vols. LC 78-67539. Repr. of 1769 ed. Set. 185.00 (ISBN 0-404-17530-9). AMS Pr.

Seaver, Henry L. Great Revolt in Castile: A Study of the Comunero Movement of 1520-1521. 1967. lib. bdg. 18.00x (ISBN 0-374-97239-7). Octagon.

KARL 12TH, KING OF SWEDEN, 1682-1718

Bain, Robert N. Charles Twelfth & the Collapse of the Swedish Empire, 1682-1719. facsimile ed. LC 70-95062. (Select Bibliographies Reprint Ser). 1895. 30.00 (ISBN 0-8369-5064-X). Arno.

Voltaire. Histoire de Charles XII. Malhos, Georges, ed. 256p. 1968. 3.95 (ISBN 0-686-55746-8). French & Eur.

KARL 12TH, KING OF SWEDEN, 1682-1718–DRAMA

Strindberg, August. Queen Christina, Charles XII, Gustav III. Johnson, Walter, tr. LC 55-7573. (American-Scandinavian Foundation Scandinavian Studies). (Illus.). 293p. 1968. 11.50 (ISBN 0-295-73899-5); pap. 2.95 (ISBN 0-295-78570-5, WP45). U of Wash Pr.

KARL 12TH, KING OF SWEDEN, 1682-1718–FICTION

Von Heidenstam, Verner. Charles Men, 2 Vols. Stork, Charles W., tr. from Swedish. LC 72-122718. (Short Story Index Reprint Ser). 1920. Set. 32.00 (ISBN 0-8369-3551-9). Arno.

--King & His Campaigners. Tegnier, Axel, tr. LC 70-113676. (Short Story Index Reprint Ser.). 1902. 15.00 (ISBN 0-8369-3405-9). Arno.

KARLOFF, BORIS, 1887-1969

Bojarski, Richard & Beale, Kenneth. The Films of Boris Karloff. LC 71-147832. (Illus.). 256p. 1974. 12.00 (ISBN 0-8065-0396-3). Citadel Pr.

Bojarsky, Richard & Beale, Kenneth. The Films of Boris Karloff. (Illus.). 288p. 1976. pap. 6.95 (ISBN 0-8065-0516-8). Citadel Pr.

Glut, Donald F. The Frankenstein Legend: A Tribute to Mary Shelley & Boris Karloff. LC 73-944. (Illus.). 1973. 13.50 (ISBN 0-8108-0589-8). Scarecrow.

KARMA

see also Anthroposophy

Abhedananda, Swami. Doctrine of Karma. 4.50 (ISBN 0-87481-608-4). Vedanta Pr.

Besant, Annie. Karma. 10th ed. 1975. 3.25 (ISBN 0-8356-7035-X). Theos Pub Hse.

Bhikshu, Yogi. Karma Yoga. 1928. 6.00 (ISBN 0-911662-20-0). Yoga.

Birdsong, Robert E. Physical Experience & Karmic Liability. (Aquarian Academy Monograph: Ser. A, Lecture No. 6). 38p. 1977. pap. 1.50 (ISBN 0-917108-20-5). Sirius Bks.

Carus, Paul. Karma; Nirvana: Two Buddhist Tales. LC 73-82781. (Illus.). 160p. 1973. 12.95 (ISBN 0-87548-249-X); pap. 4.95 (ISBN 0-686-76973-2). Open Court.

Duke, Philip S. The Law of Karma with Biblical Quotations & a Karmic Bibliography. 1978. pap. 2.00 (ISBN 0-685-59611-7). Duke Pr IL.

Grahek, Margaret L. Astrological Insight to Your Karma. 1978. 6.95 (ISBN 0-533-03645-3). Vantage.

Hanson, Virginia, ed. Karma. 2nd rev. ed. Stewart, Rosemarie. LC 80-53951. 200p. 1980. pap. 4.95 (ISBN 0-8356-0543-4). Theos Pub Hse.

Iswarananda, Swami. Does the Soul Reincarnate? 1964. pap. 1.00 (ISBN 0-87481-478-2). Vedanta Pr.

Karma: Your Whispering Wisdom. 2.95 (ISBN 0-686-12817-6). Lotus Ashram.

Leo, Alan. The Key to Your Own Nativity. 1978. pap. 6.95 (ISBN 0-685-62086-7). Weiser.

Rama, Swami. Freedom from the Bondage of Karma. 2nd ed. 1977. pap. 3.95 (ISBN 0-89389-031-6). Himalayan Intl Inst.

Saraydarian, Torkom. Questioning Traveller & Karma. 1979. pap. 2.50 (ISBN 0-911794-45-X). Aqua Educ.

Schulman, Martin. Karmic Astrology: Joy & the Part of Fortune, Vol. 3. 1978. pap. 4.95 (ISBN 0-87728-346-X). Weiser.

--Karmic Astrology: The Karma of the Now, Vol. 4. 1978. pap. 4.95 (ISBN 0-686-77109-5). Weiser.

Sivananda, Swami. Practice of Karma Yoga. 324p. 1974. text ed. 6.00x (ISBN 0-8426-0675-0). Verry.

Steiner, Rudolf. Karmic Relationships, 8 vols. Incl. Vol. 1; Vol. 2. 12.50 (ISBN 0-685-36128-4); Vol. 3. 12.95 (ISBN 0-685-36129-2); Vol. 4; Vol. 5; Vol. 6. 9.75 (ISBN 0-685-36132-2); Vol. 7. 9.95 (ISBN 0-685-36133-0); Vol. 8. 9.95 (ISBN 0-685-36134-9). Anthroposophic.

Van Pelt, Gertrude W. The Doctrine of Karma. Small, W. Emmett & Todd, Helen, eds. (Theosophical Manual: No. 3). 64p. 1975. pap. 1.75 (ISBN 0-685-52027-7, 913004-16). Point Loma Pub.

Woodward, Mary Ann. Edgar Cayce's Story of Karma. 1972. pap. 1.95 (ISBN 0-425-03781-9, Medallion). Berkley Pub.

KARNAK, EGYPT

Epigraphic Survey - Reliefs & Inscriptions at Karnak, 3 vols. Incl. Vol. 1. Ramses the Third's Temple Within the Great Inclosure of Amon, Part One. Nelson, Harold H. (Oriental Institute Pubns. Ser: No. 25). 1936. 60.00x (ISBN 0-226-62121-9); Vol. 2. Ramses the Third's Temple Within the Inclosure of Amon, Part Two, & Ramses the Third's Temple in the Precinct of Mut. (Oriental Institute Pubns. Ser: No. 35). 1936. 60.00x (ISBN 0-226-62132-4); Vol. 3. The Bubastic Portal. Hughes, George R. (Oriental Institute Pubns. Ser: No. 74). 1954. 50.00x (ISBN 0-226-62175-8). LC 36-11240. U of Chicago Pr.

Epigraphic Survey. The Temple of Khonsu: Vol. 2, Scenes & Inscriptions in the Court & the First Hypostyle Hall. LC 80-82999. (Oriental Institute Publications Ser.: Vol. 103). 1981. pap. price not set incl. 97 plates in portfolio (ISBN 0-918986-29-X). Oriental Inst.

Parker, Richard A., et al. The Edifice of Taharqa by the Sacred Lake of Karnak. Crozier-Brelot, Claude, tr. LC 77-76345. (Brown Egyptological Studies: No. 8). (Illus.). x, 100p. 1979. 60.00x (ISBN 0-87057-151-6, Pub. by Brown U Pr). U Pr of New Eng.

KARPOV, ANATOLI EVAGENEVICH, 1951-

Botvinnik, Mikhael M. Anatoly Karpov: His Road to the World Championship. Neat, Kenneth P., tr. LC 77-30655. 1978. text ed. 15.00 (ISBN 0-08-021139-9); pap. text ed. 8.00 (ISBN 0-08-021138-0). Pergamon.

Karpov, Anatoly. My Best Games. Russell, Hanon, tr. from Rus. LC 77-94938. pap. 9.95 (ISBN 0-89058-036-7). R H M Pr.

Karpov's Collected Games. LC 74-29703. 11.95 (ISBN 0-89058-204-1); pap. 9.95 (ISBN 0-89058-005-7). R H M Pr.

KARST

Herak, M. & Stringfield, V. T., eds. Important Karst Regions of the Northern Hemisphere. LC 74-151736. (Illus.). 565p. 1971. 95.25 (ISBN 0-444-40849-5). Elsevier.

Jakucs, Laszlo. The Morphogenesis of Karst Regions: Variants of Karst Evolution. LC 76-40003. 1977. 63.95 (ISBN 0-470-98952-1). Halsted Pr.

Jennings, J. N. Karst. (Introduction to Systematic Geomorphology Ser). 1971. 15.00x (ISBN 0-262-10011-8). MIT Pr.

Sweeting, Marjorie M. Karst Landforms. LC 72-172813. (Illus.). 380p. 1973. 30.00x (ISBN 0-231-03623-X). Columbia U Pr.

KARTING

Kart Magazine. Complete Book of Karting. Day, Dick, ed. 1961. 14.95 (ISBN 0-13-157487-6). P-H.

Leonard, Jerry. Kart Racing. LC 79-26985. (Illus.). 160p. (gr. 7 up). 1980. PLB 8.29 (ISBN 0-671-34033-6). Messner.

McFarland, Kenton & Sparks, James C., Jr. Midget Motoring & Karting. (Illus.). (gr. 7 up). 1961. 10.95 (ISBN 0-525-34880-8). Dutton.

Martin, Gary. Competitive Karting. LC 80-83189. (Illus.). 144p. 1980. pap. 9.95 (ISBN 0-9605068-0-2). Martin Motorsports.

Smith, Leroi. Karting. LC 70-77893. (Illus.). 1970. lib. bdg. 7.95 (ISBN 0-668-01939-5). Arco.

Washington, Rosemary G. Karting: Racing's Fast Little Cars. LC 80-12385. (Superwheels & Thrill Sports Bks.). (Illus.). (YA) (gr. 4 up). 1980. PLB 6.95g (ISBN 0-8225-0435-9). Lerner Pubns.

KARYOKINESIS

see also Chromosomes; Meiosis

Guern, J. & Peaud-Lenoel, C., eds. Metabolism & Molecular Activities of Cytokinins: Proceedings. (Proceedings in Life Sciences Ser.). (Illus.). 370p. 1981. 59.00 (ISBN 0-387-10711-8). Springer-Verlag.

Hsu, T. C. & Benirschke, K. Atlas of Mammalian Chromosomes, Vols. 1-6. LC 67-19307. (Illus.). 1968-71. Vol. 1. loose-leaf boxed 21.70 (ISBN 0-387-03878-7); Vol. 3. loose-leaf boxed 21.70 (ISBN 0-387-04563-5); Vol. 4. loose-leaf boxed 31.20 (ISBN 0-387-04882-0); Vol. 5. loose-leaf boxed 31.20 (ISBN 0-387-05280-1); Vol. 6. 29.00 (ISBN 0-387-05590-8). ring binder for indiv. vols. 7.50 ea. (ISBN 0-387-90005-5); ring binder for indiv. vols. 6.80 ea. (ISBN 0-387-90005-5). Springer-Verlag.

Symposium on the Cell in Mitosis. Proceedings. Levine, Lawrence, ed. 1963. 38.00 (ISBN 0-12-444950-6). Acad Pr.

Valleron, A. J. & Macdonald, P. D., eds. Biomathematics & Cell Kinetics. (Developments in Cell Biology Ser.: Vol. 2). 1978. 67.50 (ISBN 0-444-80059-X, DCB 2, North Holland). Elsevier.

KARYOTYPES

see also Chromosome Abnormalities

Benirschke, K. & Hsu, T. C., eds. Chromosome Atlas: Fish, Amphibians, Reptiles & Birds, Vol. 1. LC 73-166079. (Illus.). 225p. 1972. loose leaf 16.30 (ISBN 0-387-05507-X). Springer-Verlag.

Buckton, K. E. & Evans, H. J. Methods for the Analysis of Human Chromosome Aberrations. (Also avail. in French & Russian). 1973. 4.80 (ISBN 92-4-154031-1). World Health.

International Conference on Comparative Mammalian Cytogenetics, Dartmouth Medical School, 1968. Proceedings. Benirschke, K., ed. (Illus.). 1969. 59.80 (ISBN 0-387-04442-6). Springer-Verlag.

Kaplan, Barbara. Preparation of the Normal Karyotype. LC 78-720409. (Illus.). 1979. 55.00 (ISBN 0-89189-057-2, 21-9-015-00); student ed. 9.00 (ISBN 0-89189-071-8, 21-9-015-20). Am Soc Clinical.

KASAK, NIKOLAI

Kasak, Nikoli. Art of Kasak. (Illus.). 14.75 (ISBN 0-8079-0140-7). October.

KASANDSI LANGUAGE

see Bangala Language

KASHMIR

Aslam, Mohd. Social Implications of Technological Change in Rural Kashmir. 147p. 1981. text ed. 15.75x (ISBN 0-391-02377-2, Pub. by Concept India). Humanities.

Fujiwara, Shinya. Kashmir. LC 77-75973. (This Beautiful World Ser.: Vol. 60). (Illus.). 1977. pap. 4.95 (ISBN 0-87011-310-0). Kodansha.

Gupta, Sisir. Kashmir: A Study of India-Pakistan Relations. 1967. 14.00x (ISBN 0-210-22625-0). Asia.

Hassnain, F. M. Buddhist Kashmir. 1974. text ed. 9.00x (ISBN 0-8426-0642-4). Verry.

Kapur, M. L. Kashmir, Sold & Snatched. 1968. 6.75x (ISBN 0-8426-1329-3). Verry.

Khan, R. Kashmir & the United Nations. 1969. 8.25x (ISBN 0-8426-1332-3). Verry.

Raza, Moonis, et al. The Valley of Kashmir: The Land, Vol. 1. LC 77-93391. 1978. 23.95 (ISBN 0-89089-058-7). Carolina Acad Pr.

Singh, Mala. Kashmir. (Nehru Library for Children). (Illus.). (gr. 1-10). 1979. pap. 1.50 (ISBN 0-89744-177-X). Auromere.

KASHMIR–HISTORY

Bamzai, Prithivi N. A History of Kashmir, Political, Social, Cultural: From the Earliest Times to the Present Day. rev. 2nd ed. LC 72-908048. (Illus.). 866p. 1973. 32.50x (ISBN 0-8002-0905-2). Intl Pubns Serv.

Hassnain, F. M. British Policy Towards Kashmir (Prior to 1974) 1974. 9.00x (ISBN 0-8426-0690-4). Verry.

Kalhana. Kalhana's Rajatarangini, 2 vols, Vol. I. Stein, Aurel, tr. from Sanskrit. 1979. Repr. of 1900 ed. Vol. 1, 402p (ISBN 0-89684-101-4, Pub. by Motilal Banarsidass India). Vol. 2, 555p (ISBN 0-89684-102-2). Set. 34.50 (ISBN 0-686-77507-4). Orient Bk Dist.

KASHMIR–POLITICS AND GOVERNMENT

Bazaz, Prem N. Democracy Through Intimidation & Terror: The Untold Story of Kashmiri Politics. 1978. 12.00x (ISBN 0-8364-0270-7). South Asia Bks.

Hayes, Louis D. Impact of U. S. Policy on the Kashmir Conflict. LC 77-135900. (Institute of Government Research Ser). 59p. 1971. pap. 1.50x (ISBN 0-8165-0291-9). U of Ariz Pr.

Korbel, Josef. Danger in Kashmir. 1954. 22.00 (ISBN 0-691-07505-0); pap. 6.95 (ISBN 0-691-02153-8). Princeton U Pr.

KASHMIRI TALES

see Tales, Kashmiri

KASHUBIAN LANGUAGE

Perkowski, Jan L. Kashubian Idiolect in the United States. LC 68-64529. (Language Science Monographs Ser: Vol. 2). 1969. pap. text ed. 11.50x (ISBN 0-87750-135-1). Res Ctr Lang Semiotic.

KASTNER, ERICH, 1899-

see Kaestner, Erich, 1899-

KASTRIOTES, GEORGIOS, CALLED SCANDERBEG, PRINCE OF EPIRUS, d. 1467

Cambini, Andrea. Two Very Notable Commentaries, of the Originall of Turcks, Etc. Shute, J., tr. LC 75-25772. (English Experience Ser.: No. 235). 1970. Repr. of 1562 ed. 28.00 (ISBN 90-221-0235-1). Walter J Johnson.

KASUBE LANGUAGE

see Kashubian Language

KATANGA, CONGO (PROVINCE)–HISTORY

Lefever, Ernest W. Crisis in the Congo: A U.N. Force in Action. 1965. 11.95 (ISBN 0-8157-5198-2); pap. 4.95 (ISBN 0-8157-5197-4). Brookings.

Valahu, Mugar. Katanga Circus. 6.00 (ISBN 0-8315-0039-5). Speller.

KATANGA, CONGO (PROVINCE)–POLITICS AND GOVERNMENT

Fabian, Johannes. Jamaa: A Charismatic Movement in Katanga. 1971. 13.95x (ISBN 0-8101-0339-7). Northwestern U Pr.

KATATONIA

see Catatonia

KATAYAMA DISEASE

see Schistosomiasis

KATCINAS

Colton, Harold S. Hopi Kachina Dolls with a Key to Their Identification. rev ed. LC 59-5480. (Illus.). 150p. 1971. pap. 6.95 (ISBN 0-8263-0180-0). U of NM Pr.

Earle, Edwin & Kennard, Edward A. Hopi Kachinas. 2nd ed. LC 71-139867. (Illus.). 1971. 12.50 (ISBN 0-934490-11-2). Mus Am Ind.

Gilhodes, Charles. The Kachins: Religion & Customs. LC 77-87035. Repr. of 1922 ed. 28.50 (ISBN 0-404-16820-5). AMS Pr.

Hanson, Ola. The Kachins: Their Customs & Traditions. LC 77-87038. Repr. of 1913 ed. 24.00 (ISBN 0-404-16826-4). AMS Pr.

The Kachina Doll Book 1. 1972. pap. 2.50 (ISBN 0-918858-00-3). Fun Pub.

The Kachina Doll Book 2. 1973. pap. 2.50 (ISBN 0-918858-01-1). Fun Pub.

Museum Staff. Introduction to Hopi Kachinas. (Illus.). 1977. pap. 1.50 (ISBN 0-89734-004-3). Mus Northern Ariz.

Wright, Barton. Hopi Kachinas: The Complete Guide to Collecting Kachina Dolls. LC 76-52581. (Illus.). 1977. pap. 8.95 (ISBN 0-87358-161-X). Northland.

--Kachinas: A Hopi Artist's Documentary. LC 73-75204. (Illus.). 272p. 1973. 40.00 (ISBN 0-87358-110-5). Northland.

KATHMANDU–DESCRIPTION

Fleming, Robert L. & Fleming, Linda L. Kathmandu Valley. LC 77-15371. (This Beautiful World Ser.: No. 61). (Illus.). 1978. pap. 4.95 (ISBN 0-87011-328-3). Kodansha.

Lamplugh, Barbara. Kathmandu by Truck. (Illus.). 1976. pap. 4.95 (ISBN 0-903909-03-0, Roger Lascelles). Bradt Ent.

Raj, Prakash A. Kathmandu & the Kingdom of Napel. 3rd ed. (Travel Paperbacks Ser.). (Illus.). 160p. 1981. pap. 5.95 (ISBN 0-908086-24-5, Pub. by Lonely Planet Australia). Hippocrene Bks.

Ripley, S. Dillon. A Naturalist's Adventure in Nepal: Search for the Spiny Babbler. (Illus.). 301p. 1981. Repr. of 1953 ed. 12.50 (ISBN 0-87474-810-0). Smithsonian.

Slusser, Mary S. Nepal Mandala: A Cultural Study of the Kathmandu Valley, 2 vols. LC 80-36662. (Illus., Vol.1, 580pp.; vol2, 350pp.). 1982. Set. 75.00x (ISBN 0-691-03128-2). Princeton U Pr.

KATMAI, MOUNT

Alaska Travel Publications Editors. Exploring Katmai National Monument & the Valley of Ten Thousand Smokes. LC 74-84798. (Illus.). 1975. 7.50 (ISBN 0-914164-02-3). Alaska Travel.

Bohn, Dave. Rambles Through an Alaskan Wild: Katmai & the Valley of the Smokes. (Illus.). 1979. 20.00 (ISBN 0-88496-125-7, Noel Young Bk). Capra Pr.

KATSUSHIKA, HOKUSAI, 1760-1849

see Hokusai, Katsushika, 1760-1849

KATYN FOREST MASSACRE, 1940

FitzGibbon, Louis. Katyn. (Illus.). 285p. Date not set. 12.00 (ISBN 0-911038-25-6); pap. 8.00 (ISBN 0-911038-60-4). Inst Hist Rev.

--Katyn. (Illus.). 1979. Repr. of 1971 ed. 12.00 (ISBN 0-911038-25-6, Inst Hist Rev); pap. 8.00 (ISBN 0-911038-60-4). Noontide.

Zawodny, J. K. Death in the Forest: The Story of the Katyn Forest Massacre. LC 62-16639. (Illus.). 235p. 1980. text ed. 14.00 (ISBN 0-268-00849-3); pap. text ed. 7.95 (ISBN 0-268-00850-7). U of Notre Dame Pr.

KAUAI

Bennett, W. C. Archaeology of Kauai. Repr. of 1931 ed. pap. 16.00 (ISBN 0-527-02186-5). Kraus Repr.

Col, Dora J. & Wichman, Juliet R. Early Kauai Hospitality: A Family Cookbook of Receipts, 1820-1920. 1977. write for info. Kauai Museum.

Gleasner, Bill & Gleasner, Diana. Kauai Traveler's Guide. (Illus.). 1978. pap. 4.00 (ISBN 0-932596-03-7, Pub. by Oriental). Intl Schol Bk Serv.

Smith, Robert. Hiking Kauai: The Garden Isle. 2nd ed. Winnett, Thomas, ed. LC 79-63922. (Wilderness Press Trail Guide Ser.). (Illus.). 112p. 1979. pap. 4.95 (ISBN 0-911824-89-8). Wilderness Pr.

KAUFMAN, GEORGE SIMON, 1889-1961

Goldstein, Malcolm. George S. Kaufman: His Life, His Theater. (Illus.). 1979. 25.00 (ISBN 0-19-502623-3). Oxford U Pr.

KAUFMANN, PETER

Easton, Loyd D. Hegel's First American Followers: The Ohio Hegelians. LC 66-20062. ix, 353p. 1966. 17.00 (ISBN 0-8214-0026-6). Ohio U Pr.

KAUS LANGAUGE
see Coos Language
KAUTALYA–ARTHASASTRA
Rao, M. V. Studies in Kautilya. rev. ed. 1958. 5.50x (ISBN 0-8426-1486-9). Verry.
KAUTSKY, KARL, 1854-1938
Lenin, Vladimir I. Proletarian Revolution & the Renegade Kautsky. 1965. pap. 1.95 (ISBN 0-8351-0279-3). China Bks.
Luxemburg, Rosa. Letters to Karl & Luise Kautsky 1896-1918. 75.00 (ISBN 0-87968-190-X). Gordon Pr.
Salvadori, Massimo. Karl Kautsky & the Socialist Revolution: Eighteen Eighty-Nineteen Thirty-Eight. 1979. 19.95 (ISBN 0-86091-015-6, Pub. by NLB). Schocken.
Trotsky, Leon. Terrorism & Communism. Orig. Title: Defense of Terrorism & Dictatorship Vs Democracy. 1961. pap. 2.45 (ISBN 0-472-06056-2, 56, AA). U of Mich Pr.
KAVANAGH, ARTHUR MACMORROUGH, 1831-1889
McCormick, Donald. Incredible Mister Kavanagh. 1961. 6.95 (ISBN 0-8159-5810-2). Devin.
KAVANAGH, PATRICK
Kavanagh, Patrick. By Night Unstarred: An Autobiographical Novel. LC 76-57462. 1978. 25.00 (ISBN 0-914612-07-7). Kavanagh.
--Lapped Furrows: Corresp. 1933-1967. 300p. 1969. 25.00 (ISBN 0-914612-02-6). Kavanagh.
Kavanagh, Peter. Garden of the Golden Apples: A Bibliography of Patrick Kavanagh. 1972. pap. 5.00 (ISBN 0-914612-05-0). Kavanagh.
--Love Is Tortured Headland: A Continuation of Lapped Furrows. 1978. 15.00 (ISBN 0-914612-10-7). Kavanagh.
--Sacred Keeper: A Biography of Patrick Kavanagh. (Illus.). 404p. 1980. text ed. 21.00x (ISBN 0-904984-48-6). Humanities.
Nemo, John. Patrick Kavanagh. (English Authors Ser.: No. 267). 1979. lib. bdg. 14.50 (ISBN 0-8057-6770-3). Twayne.
O'Brien, Darcy. Patrick Kavanaugh. (Irish Writers Ser.). 72p. 1975. 4.50 (ISBN 0-8387-7884-4); pap. 1.95 (ISBN 0-8387-7985-9). Bucknell U Pr.
KAVANAUGH, EDWARD, 1795-1844
Lucey, William L. Edward Kavanagh, Catholic, Statesman, Diplomat from Maine, 1795-1844. 1947. 3.50 (ISBN 0-8338-0042-6). M Jones.
KAVERIN, V. A.
Oulanoff, Hongor. The Prose Fiction of Veniamin A. Kaverin. 1976. soft cover 9.95 (ISBN 0-89357-032-X). Slavica.
KAVIRONDO (AFRICAN PEOPLE)
see also Gisu (Bantu Tribe)
KAWASAKI MOTORCYCLE
Chilton's Automotive Editorial Department. Chilton's Repair & Tune-up Guide for Kawasaki, 1966-1972. LC 72-6444. (Illus.). 171p. 1972. 8.95 (ISBN 0-8019-5696-X); pap. 8.95 (ISBN 0-8019-6044-4). Chilton.
Chilton's Repair & Tune-up Guide for Kawasaki 900-1000, 1973-1977. (Repair & Tune-up Guides Ser.). (Illus.). 1978. pap. 8.95 (ISBN 0-8019-6605-1). Chilton.
Collett, George. Kawasaki Owners Workshop Manual: 900zi & Zib '73-79. (Owners Workshop Manuals Ser.: No. 222). 1979. 8.50 (ISBN 0-686-14951-3, Pub. by J H Haynes England). Haynes Pubns.
Darlington, Mansur. Kawasaki Owner's Workshop Manual: Kz 400 Twins '74-76. (Owners Workshop Manuals Ser.: No. 281). 1979. 8.50 (ISBN 0-85696-281-3, Pub. by J H Haynes England). Haynes Pubns.
Jorgensen, Eric, ed. Kawasaki Kz650 Fours Nineteen Seventy-Six to Nineteen Eighty Service, Repair, Performance. (Illus.). pap. 9.95 (ISBN 0-89287-296-9, M358). Clymer Pubns.
Meek, Frank. Kawasaki Owners Workshop Manual: 250 & 400 3 Cyl '72-79. (Owners Workshop Manuals Ser.: No. 134). 1979. 8.50 (ISBN 0-85696-134-5, Pub. by J H Haynes England). Haynes Pubns.
Robinson, Jeff, ed. Kawasaki Service - Repair Handbook: 250 & 350cc Twins, All Years. (Illus.). pap. text ed. 9.95 (ISBN 0-89287-016-8, M352). Clymer Pubns.
--Kawasaki Service--Repair Handbook: 80-450cc Singles, 1966-1977. (Illus.). pap. 9.95 (ISBN 0-89287-152-0, M350). Clymer Pubns.
--Kawasaki Service & Repair Handbook: Kz400 Twins, 1974-1979. (Illus.). pap. 9.95 (ISBN 0-89287-138-5, M355). Clymer Pubns.
Wilkins, Stewart. Kawasaki Owners Workshop Manual: 500 & 750 3 Cyl Thru '76. (Owners Workshop Manuals Ser.: No. 325). 1979. 8.50 (ISBN 0-85696-325-9, Pub. by J H Haynes England). Haynes Pubns.
KAYAKS
see Canoes and Canoeing
KAZAKH LANGUAGE
Shnitnikov, Boris N. Kazakh-English Dictionary. (Orig.). 1966. pap. text ed. 45.00x (ISBN 90-2790-367-0). Mouton.
KAZAKHSTAN–HISTORY
Demko, George J. Russian Colonization of Kazakhstan, 1896-1916. (Uralic & Altaic Ser.: No. 99). (Orig.). 1969. pap. text ed. 10.50x (ISBN 0-87750-082-7). Res Ctr Lang Semiotic.
KAZAKS
Hudson, Alfred E. Kazak Social Structure. LC 64-24363. (Yale University Publications in Anthropology Reprints Ser.: No. 20). 109p. 1964. pap. 6.00x (ISBN 0-87536-508-6). HRAFP.
Kazak Folk Art Designs. 1981. 45.00 (ISBN 0-8351-0758-2). China Bks.
KAZANTZAKIS, NIKOS, 1885-1957
Bien, Peter. Kazantzakis & Linguistic Revolution in Greek Literature. LC 79-154991. (Princeton Essays in Literature Ser.). 1972. 17.50 (ISBN 0-691-06206-4). Princeton U Pr.
Kazantzakis, Nikos. The Suffering God: Selected Letters to Galatea & to Papastephanou. Ramp, Philip & Rooke, Katerina, trs. LC 78-75133. 1979. 12.50 (ISBN 0-89241-088-4). Caratzas Bros.
Lea, James. Kazantzakis: The Politics of Salvation. LC 78-8644. 220p. 1979. 15.50x (ISBN 0-8173-7002-1). U of Ala Pr.
Levitt, Morton P. The Cretan Glance: The World & Art of Nikos Kazantzakis. LC 79-23990. 1980. 12.50 (ISBN 0-8142-0304-3). Ohio St U Pr.
McDonough, B. T. Nietzsche & Kazantzakis. LC 78-61302. 1978. pap. text ed. 7.25 (ISBN 0-8191-0607-0). U Pr of Amer.
Nelson, Bonnie. Monarch Notes on Kazantzakis' Zorba the Greek & Other Works. 1975. pap. 1.50 (ISBN 0-671-00918-4). Monarch Pr.
KEAN, EDMUND, 1787-1833
Hawkins, Frederick W. Life of Edmund Kean, 2 vols in 1. LC 76-82831. 1869. 30.00 (ISBN 0-405-08603-2, Blom Pubns). Arno.
Hillebrand, Harold N. Edmund Kean. LC 77-181904. Repr. of 1933 ed. 27.00 (ISBN 0-404-03269-9). AMS Pr.
MacQueen-Pope, W. Edmund Kean: The Story of an Actor. 1975. Repr. of 1960 ed. 25.00 (ISBN 0-8274-3997-0). R West.
Playfair, Giles. Kean. LC 73-10878. (Illus.). 346p. 1973. Repr. of 1939 ed. lib. bdg. 18.50x (ISBN 0-8371-7047-8, PLKE). Greenwood.
Procter, Bryan W. Life of Edmund Kean, 2 Vols. in 1. LC 70-82840. Repr. of 1835 ed. 22.00 (ISBN 0-405-08864-7, Pub. by Blom). Arno.
KEAN, ROBERT GARLICK HILL, 1828-1898
Kean, Robert G. Inside the Confederate Government: The Diary of Robert Garlick Kean. Younger, Edward, ed. LC 73-11863. (Illus.). 241p. 1974. Repr. of 1957 ed. lib. bdg. 15.00x (ISBN 0-8371-7097-4, KECG). Greenwood.
KEARNY'S EXPEDITION, 1846
Hughes, John T. Doniphan's Expedition: Containing an Account of the Conquest of New Mexico. LC 72-9453. (The Far Western Frontier Ser.). (Illus.). 156p. 1973. Repr. of 1847 ed. 13.00 (ISBN 0-405-04981-1). Arno.
Turner, Henry S. The Original Journals of Henry Smith Turner: With Stephen Watts Kearny to New Mexico & California. Clarke, Dwight L., ed. (American Exploration & Discovery Ser.: No. 51). 1967. pap. 4.95 (ISBN 0-8061-1157-7). U of Okla Pr.
KEATON, BUSTER, 1895-1966
Blesh, Rudi. Keaton. 1966. 8.95 (ISBN 0-02-511570-7). Macmillan.
Dardis, Tom. Keaton: The Man Who Wouldn't Lie Down. (Illus.). 352p. 1980. pap. 4.95 (ISBN 0-14-005701-3). Penguin.
Moews, Daniel. Keaton: The Silent Features Close up. 1977. 15.95 (ISBN 0-520-03126-1); pap. 4.50 (ISBN 0-520-03155-5, CAL 338). U of Cal Pr.
Wead, George. Buster Keaton & the Dynamics of Visual Wit. Lowett, Garth S., ed. LC 75-21437. (Dissertations on Film Ser.). 1976. lib. bdg. 22.00x (ISBN 0-405-07538-3). Arno.
Wead, George & Lellis, George. The Film Career of Buster Keaton. Gottesman, Ronald, ed. (Three Director Set). 1978. pap. 7.80 (ISBN 0-913178-57-8). Redgrave Pub Co.
Wead, George & Lellis, George, eds. The Film Career of Buster Keaton. (Reference Publications Ser.). 1977. lib. bdg. 15.00 (ISBN 0-8161-7923-9). G K Hall.
KEATS, JOHN, 1795-1821
Arnold, Matthew. John Keats in "Essays in Criticism". Second Series. Repr. 15.00 (ISBN 0-8274-2625-9). R West.
Askwith, Betty. Keats. 288p. 1980. Repr. of 1924 ed. lib. bdg. 25.00 (ISBN 0-8495-0072-9). Arden Lib.
--Keats. LC 76-43959. 1976. lib. bdg. 25.00 (ISBN 0-8414-2892-1). Folcroft.
Baldwin, Dane L. & Broughton, L. N. Concordance to the Poems of John Keats. 1963. 37.50 (ISBN 0-8446-1044-5). Peter Smith.
Bate, W. Jackson. John Keats. LC 63-17194. (Harvard Paperback Ser.: No. 142). (Illus.). 1979. 25.00x (ISBN 0-674-47800-2, Belknap Pr); pap. 10.00 (ISBN 0-674-47825-8, Belknap Pr). Harvard U Pr.
Bate, Walter J. Negative Capability: The Intuitive Approach in Keats. LC 75-28991. Repr. of 1939 ed. 14.50 (ISBN 0-404-14002-5). AMS Pr.
Bate, Walter J., ed. Keats: A Collection of Critical Essays. (Orig.). 1964. pap. 2.95 (ISBN 0-13-514745-X, STC43, Spec). P-H.
Bayley, John. Keats & Reality. LC 73-16442. 1962. lib. bdg. 6.50 (ISBN 0-8414-9877-6). Folcroft.
Beaudry, Harry R. The English Theatre & John Keats. (Salzburg Studies in English Literature, Poetic Drama & Poetic Theory: No. 13). 240p. 1973. pap. 25.00x (ISBN 0-391-01321-1). Humanities.
Becker, et al. The Garland Dickens Bibliographies: A Concordance to the Poems of John Keats. 1981. lib. bdg. 90.00 (ISBN 0-8240-9807-2). Garland Pub.
Becker, Michael G., et al. A Concordance to the Poems of John Keats. LC 78-68264. (Garlnd Reference Library of the Humanities: No. 137). 1979. lib. bdg. 50.00 (ISBN 0-8240-9807-2). Garland Pub.
Beyer, Werner W. Keats & the Daemon King. LC 76-86270. 1969. Repr. of 1947 ed. lib. bdg. 20.00x (ISBN 0-374-90627-0). Octagon.
Bhattacherje, M. M. Keats & Spenser. LC 73-9720. 1944. lib. bdg. 15.00 (ISBN 0-8414-3123-X). Folcroft.
Blackstone, Bernard. The Consecrated Urn: An Interpretation of Keats in Terms of Growth & Form. LC 78-13773. 1979. Repr. of 1966 ed. lib. bdg. 25.00x (ISBN 0-313-20628-7, BLCU). Greenwood.
Blunden, Edmund. Shelley & Keats As They Struck Their Contemporaries. LC 70-174689. (English Literature Ser., No. 33). 1971. Repr. of 1925 ed. lib. bdg. 32.95 (ISBN 0-8383-1341-8). Haskell.
--Shelley & Keats As They Struck Their Contemporaries. LC 74-16306. 1925. lib. bdg. 15.00 (ISBN 0-8414-9878-4). Folcroft.
Bridges, Robert. A Critical Introduction to Keats. 1929. Repr. 10.00 (ISBN 0-8274-2119-2). R West.
--John Keats. LC 72-1976. (Studies in Keats, No. 19). 1972. Repr. of 1895 ed. lib. bdg. 29.95 (ISBN 0-8383-1453-8). Haskell.
Broughton, L. N. & Baldwin, D. C. Concordance to Poems of John Keats. 59.95 (ISBN 0-87968-922-6). Gordon Pr.
Brown, Charles A. Life of John Keats. LC 74-3172. 1937. lib. bdg. 17.50 (ISBN 0-8414-3116-7). Folcroft.
Brown, Leonard. Genesis, Growth & Meaning of Endymion. LC 74-3369. 1933. lib. bdg. 5.00 (ISBN 0-8414-3107-8). Folcroft.
Bryon-Shelley-Keats: Prize Essays by Competitors. 50.00 (ISBN 0-8495-6282-1). Arden Lib.
Byron, May. A Day with John Keats. Repr. 7.50 (ISBN 0-8274-2151-6). R West.
Caldwell, James R. John Keats' Fancy. 1965. lib. bdg. 14.00x (ISBN 0-374-91197-5). Octagon.
Carmichael, Katherine. Critical Edition of the Early Poems of John Keats with a Philosophical Supplement. 1944. lib. bdg. 7.50 (ISBN 0-8414-3533-2). Folcroft.
Chatterjee, Bhabatosh. John Keats: His Mind & Work. 504p. 1981. 30.00x (ISBN 0-86125-129-6, Pub. by Orient Longman India). State Mutual Bk.
Church, Richard. John Keats: An Introduction & Selection. 1948. Repr. 20.00 (ISBN 0-8274-2623-2). R West.
Colvin, S. John Keats: His Life & Poetry. 59.95 (ISBN 0-8490-0453-5). Gordon Pr.
Colvin, Sidney. John Keats: His Life & Poetry, His Friends. LC 73-96155. 1970. Repr. lib. bdg. 36.00x (ISBN 0-374-91881-3). Octagon.
--Keats. Morley, John, ed. LC 68-58373. (English Men of Letters). Repr. of 1889 ed. lib. bdg. 12.50 (ISBN 0-404-51706-4). AMS Pr.
--Keats. 1978. Repr. of 1887 ed. lib. bdg. 15.00 (ISBN 0-8495-0734-0). Arden Lib.
--Keats. 1979. Repr. of 1906 ed. lib. bdg. 15.00 (ISBN 0-8482-7575-6). Norwood Edns.
Colvin, Sidney, et al. Keats. 1902. lib. bdg. 12.00 (ISBN 0-8414-2371-7). Folcroft.
Dello Buono, Carmen J. Rare Early Essays on John Keats. 208p. 1980. lib. bdg. 22.50 (ISBN 0-8482-3675-0). Norwood Edns.
Dickstein, Morris. Keats & His Poetry: A Study in Development. LC 74-136019. 1971. 14.00x (ISBN 0-226-14795-9). U of Chicago Pr.
--Keats & His Poetry: A Study in Development. LC 74-136019. 288p. 1974. pap. 4.25 (ISBN 0-226-14796-7, P599, Phoen). U of Chicago Pr.
Downer, Arthur C. Odes of Keats. LC 72-194427. 1897. lib. bdg. 8.50 (ISBN 0-8414-3858-7). Folcroft.
Ellershaw, Henry. Keats Poetry & Prose: With Essays by Charles Lamb, Leigh Hunt, Robert Bridges, & Others. 1922. Repr. 20.00 (ISBN 0-8274-2645-3). R West.
Ende, Stuart A. Keats & the Sublime. LC 76-8420. 1976. 16.50x (ISBN 0-300-02010-4). Yale U Pr.
Enscoe, Gerald. Eros & the Romantics. LC 67-30548. (Studies in English Literature: Vol. 45). 1967. text ed. 28.75x (ISBN 90-2790-282-8). Mouton.
Erlande, Albert. The Life of John Keats. 1929. lib. bdg. 45.00 (ISBN 0-8414-3990-7). Folcroft.
Evans, B. I. Keats. LC 74-6371. (Studies in Keats, No. 19). 1974. lib. bdg. 31.95 (ISBN 0-8383-1858-4). Haskell.
Evans, Benjamin. Keats: A Critical Biographical Study. LC 77-131699. 1971. Repr. of 1934 ed. 19.00 (ISBN 0-403-00586-8). Scholarly.
Evans, Benjamin I. Keats. LC 74-16285. 1974. Repr. of 1934 ed. lib. bdg. 10.50 (ISBN 0-8414-3987-7). Folcroft.
Evert, Walter H. Aesthetic & Myth in the Poetry of Keats. 1964. 20.00 (ISBN 0-691-06001-0). Princeton U Pr.
Fausett, H. I. Keats, a Study in Development. 1966. Repr. of 1922 ed. 13.50 (ISBN 0-208-00188-3, Archon). Shoe String.
Finney, Claude L. Evolution of Keats's Poetry, 2 vols in 1. LC 63-11029. (Illus.). 1963. Repr. of 1936 ed. 50.00 (ISBN 0-8462-0372-3). Russell.
Fogle, Richard H. Imagery of Keats & Shelley: A Comparative Study. 1949. Repr. of 1949 ed. 19.50x (ISBN 0-8078-0568-8). U of NC Pr.
Ford, Newell F. The Prefigurative Imagination of John Keats: A Study of the Beauty-Truth Identification & Its Implications. LC 74-24643. (Stanford University. Stanford Studies in Language & Literature: No. 2). Repr. of 1951 ed. 14.50 (ISBN 0-404-51818-4). AMS Pr.
Forman, Maurice B. John Keats & His Family. LC 77-1149. 1973. lib. bdg. 6.50 (ISBN 0-8414-4198-7). Folcroft.
Garrod, H. W. Keats. 157p. 1980. Repr. of 1926 ed. lib. bdg. 15.00 (ISBN 0-8495-1952-7). Arden Lib.
Gilbert, Elliot. Monarch Notes on Keats' Poetry. (Orig.). pap. 1.75 (ISBN 0-671-00785-8). Monarch Pr.
Gillham, D. G. Keats-Poems of Eighteen Twenty. 224p. 1969. pap. text ed. 9.95x (ISBN 0-7121-0141-1, Pub. by Macdonald & Evans England). Intl Ideas.
Gittings, Robert. John Keats: The Living Year Twenty-One September Eighteen Eighteen to Twenty-One September Eighteen Nineteen. LC 78-6098. (Illus.). 247p. 1978. Repr. of 1968 ed. lib. bdg. 21.00x (ISBN 0-313-20390-3, GIJK). Greenwood.
--The Mask of Keats. 174p. 1979. Repr. lib. bdg. 25.00 (ISBN 0-89987-303-0). Darby Bks.
Gittings, Robert, ed. Selected Poems & Letters of Keats. (The Poetry Bookshelf). 1966. pap. text ed. 3.95x (ISBN 0-435-15045-6). Heinemann Ed.
Gorell, Lord. John Keats: The Principle of Beauty. LC 73-13743. 1948. lib. bdg. 12.50 (ISBN 0-8414-4434-X). Folcroft.
Gorell, Ronald. Keats: The Principle of Beauty. LC 72-122978. (Studies in Keats, No. 19). 1970. Repr. of 1948 ed. lib. bdg. 27.95 (ISBN 0-8383-1110-5). Haskell.
Gorell, Ronald G. John Keats: The Principle of Beauty. 126p. 1980. Repr. of 1948 ed. lib. bdg. 15.00 (ISBN 0-8495-2044-4). Arden Lib.
Gradman, Barry. Metamorphosis in Keats. LC 79-3756. 160p. 1980. 18.50x (ISBN 0-8147-2977-0); pap. 9.00x (ISBN 0-8147-2978-9). NYU Pr.
Graham, William. Last Links with Byron, Shelley & Keats. LC 72-196918. 1898. lib. bdg. 15.00 (ISBN 0-8414-4666-0). Folcroft.
Green, David B. & Wilson, Edwin G., eds. Keats, Shelley, Byron, Hunt & Their Circles: A Bibliography, July 1, 1950-June 30, 1962. LC 64-15181. 1964. 15.00x (ISBN 0-8032-0059-5). U of Nebr Pr.
Hale-White, William. Keats As Doctor & Patient. 96p. 1980. Repr. of 1938 ed. lib. bdg. 10.50 (ISBN 0-8495-2297-8). Arden Lib.
--Keats As Doctor & Patient. LC 72-193726. 1938. lib. bdg. 6.45 (ISBN 0-8414-4868-X). Folcroft.
Hancock, Albert E. John Keats: A Literary Biography. 1979. Repr. of 1908 ed. lib. bdg. 35.00 (ISBN 0-8495-2291-9). Arden Lib.
Harwell, Thomas M. Keats & the Critics, 1848-1900. (Salzburg Studies in English Literature, Romantic Reassessment: No. 2). 1972. pap. text ed. 25.00x (ISBN 0-391-01399-8). Humanities.
Hewlett, Dorothy. A Life of John Keats. 1979. Repr. of 1937 ed. lib. bdg. 45.00 (ISBN 0-8495-2290-0). Arden Lib.
Hirst, Wolf Z. John Keats. (English Author Ser.: No. 334). 1981. lib. bdg. 11.95 (ISBN 0-8057-6821-1). Twayne.

Hogg, James, ed. Keats Criticism Since Nineteen Fifty-Four: A Bibliography, Vol. 3. (Salzburg Studies - Romantic Reassessment: No. 83). 52p. 1981. pap. text ed. 25.00x (ISBN 0-391-02341-1, Pub. by Salzburg Austria). Humanities.
Houghton, Richard M. Life & Letters of John Keats. 1954. 8.95x (ISBN 0-460-00801-3, Evman). Biblio Dist.
Huang, Tsokan. The Magazine Reviews of Keats's Lamia Volume (1820) (Salzburg Studies in English Literature, Romantic Reassessment: No. 26). 123p. 1973. pap. text ed. 25.00x (ISBN 0-391-01424-2). Humanities.
Hudson, William H. Keats & His Poetry. LC 71-120962. (Poetry & Life Ser.). Repr. of 1919 ed. 7.25 (ISBN 0-404-52516-4). AMS Pr.
--Keats & His Poetry. LC 72-194444. 1911. lib. bdg. 7.50 (ISBN 0-8414-5193-1). Folcroft.
--Keats & His Poetry. 1978. Repr. of 1911 ed. lib. bdg. 8.00 (ISBN 0-8495-2236-6). Arden Lib.
Hunt, Kenneth. Studies in Romanticism. 1980. Set. 60.00 (ISBN 0-915042-18-5). Lib Soc Sci.
Inglis, Fred. Keats. LC 69-16156. (Literary Critiques Ser.). (Illus.). 1969. Repr. lib. bdg. 4.95 (ISBN 0-668-01885-2). Arco.
Jones, James L. Adam's Dream: Mythic Consciousness in Keats & Yeats. LC 73-88362. 234p. 1975. 15.00x (ISBN 0-8203-0340-2). U of Ga Pr.
Kauvar, Gerald B. Other Poetry of Keats. LC 69-18836. 238p. 1970. 15.00 (ISBN 0-8386-7434-8). Fairleigh Dickinson.
Keats, John. John Keats. (Pocket Poets Ser.). pap. 1.10 (ISBN 0-289-27745-0). Dufour.
--John Keats in "the English Poets", Vol. 4. Ward, T. H., ed. Repr. 25.00 (ISBN 0-8274-2624-0). R West.
--The Keats Letters Papers & Other Relics. Forman, H. Buxton, ed. LC 72-4861. 1973. lib. bdg. 45.00 (ISBN 0-8414-0004-0). Folcroft.
--Keats: Poetical Works. (Oxford Standard Author Ser.). (Illus.). 1979. leatherbound 49.50 (ISBN 0-19-192832-1). Oxford U Pr.
Keats-Shelley Memorial House, Rome. Catalog of Books & Manuscripts at the Keats-Shelley Memorial House in Rome. 1969. lib. bdg. 50.00 (ISBN 0-8161-0856-0). G K Hall.
Keats-Wilde-Morley-Rosenbach. 1977. pap. 4.50 (ISBN 0-939084-03-1). Rosenbach Mus and Lib.
Leoff, Eve. A Study of Keats's Isabella. (Salzburg Studies in English Literature, Romantic Reassessment: No. 17). 217p. 1972. pap. text ed. 25.00x (ISBN 0-391-01457-9). Humanities.
Little, Judy. Keats As a Narrative Poet: A Test of Invention. LC 74-81365. viii, 165p. 1975. 12.50x (ISBN 0-8032-0846-4). U of Nebr Pr.
Lowell, Amy. John Keats, 2 Vols. (Illus.). 1969. Repr. of 1925 ed. Set. 45.00 (ISBN 0-208-00698-2, Archon). Shoe String.
McCabe, Victoria, ed. John Keats's Porridge: Favorite Recipes of American Poets. LC 75-8612. 120p. (Orig.). 1975. pap. 2.95 (ISBN 0-87745-058-7). U of Iowa Pr.
MacEachen, Dougald B. Keats & Shelley Notes. (Orig.). 1971. pap. 2.25 (ISBN 0-8220-0702-9). Cliffs.
Masson, David. Wordsworth, Shelley, Keats, & Other Essays. LC 68-58239. (Research & Source Ser.: No. 489). 1970. Repr. of 1875 ed. lib. bdg. 18.50 (ISBN 0-8337-2292-1). B Franklin.
Matthews, G. M., ed. Keats: The Critical Heritage. 1971. 36.00x (ISBN 0-7100-7147-7). Routledge & Kegan.
Mayhead, Robin. John Keats. (British Authors Ser). (Orig.). 1967. 23.95 (ISBN 0-521-05706-X); pap. 7.95x (ISBN 0-521-09419-4). Cambridge U Pr.
Muir, Kenneth, ed. John Keats: A Reassessment. 1979. Repr. of 1969 ed. lib. bdg. 35.00 (ISBN 0-8495-3847-5). Arden Lib.
Murchie, Guy. The Spirit of Place in Keats: Sketches of Persons & Places Known by Him, & His Reaction to Them. LC 78-11851. 1978. Repr. of 1955 ed. lib. bdg. 30.00 (ISBN 0-8414-6327-1). Folcroft.
--The Spirit of Place in Keats: Sketches of Persons & Places Known by Him, & His Reaction to Them. 1979. Repr. of 1955 ed. lib. bdg. 25.00 (ISBN 0-8495-3779-7). Arden Lib.
Murry, J. Middleton. Keats. 1976. Repr. of 1955 ed. lib. bdg. 15.50x (ISBN 0-374-96027-5). Octagon.
Murry, John M. Keats & Shakespeare: A Study of Keats Poetic Life from 1816-1820. LC 78-15430. 1978. Repr. of 1951 ed. lib. bdg. 23.00 (ISBN 0-313-20581-7, MUKS). Greenwood.
--Studies in Keats. LC 78-185023. (Studies in Keats, No. 19). 1969. Repr. of 1930 ed. lib. bdg. 31.95 (ISBN 0-8383-0671-3). Haskell.
--Studies in Keats, New & Old. LC 74-9966. 1939. 15.00 (ISBN 0-8414-6150-3). Folcroft.
Notcutt, H. Clement. Interpretation of Keat's Endymion. LC 72-193155. 1919. lib. bdg. 10.00 (ISBN 0-8414-6661-0). Folcroft.
O'Neill, Judith, ed. Critics on Keats. LC 68-54476. (Readings in Literary Criticism Ser: No. 1). 1968. 5.95x (ISBN 0-87024-097-8). U of Miami Pr.
Owen, Frances. John Keats: A Study. LC 72-191835. 1880. lib. bdg. 20.00 (ISBN 0-8414-0862-9). Folcroft.
Owen, Frances M. John Keats, A Study. LC 75-30009. 1976. Repr. of 1880 ed. write for info. (ISBN 0-404-14015-7). AMS Pr.
Patterson, Charles I., Jr. The Daemonic in the Poetry of John Keats. LC 71-94399. 1970. 15.00 (ISBN 0-252-00079-X). Lib Soc Sci.
Perkins, David. Quest for Permanence: Symbolism of Wordsworth, Shelley, & Keats. 1959. 15.00x (ISBN 0-674-74200-1). Harvard U Pr.
Raymond, Ernest. Two Gentlemen of Rome: Keats & Shelley. 69.95 (ISBN 0-8490-1238-4). Gordon Pr.
--Two Gentlemen of Rome: Keats & Shelley. 1973. 10.50 (ISBN 0-8274-1073-5). R West.
Read, W. A. Keats & Spenser. 1897. lib. bdg. 15.00 (ISBN 0-8414-7344-7). Folcroft.
Regester, F. A. Keats' Fragments & Finales. LC 76-16030. 1936. Repr. lib. bdg. 15.00 (ISBN 0-8414-7220-3). Folcroft.
Regester, Frederic A. Keats' Fragments & Finales. LC 78-6905. 1979. Repr. of 1936 ed. lib. bdg. 15.00 (ISBN 0-8495-4615-X). Arden Lib.
Richardson, Joanna. Fanny Brawne. 190p. 1980. Repr. lib. bdg. 22.50 (ISBN 0-89987-705-2). Darby Bks.
Ricks, Christopher. Keats & Embarrassment. 232p. 1974. 28.00x (ISBN 0-19-812055-9); pap. 4.95x (ISBN 0-19-281190-8, O*P*B). Oxford U Pr.
Robertson, Graham. Keats. (Jackdaw Ser: No. 118). 1974. 6.95 (ISBN 0-670-41194-9, Grossman). Viking Pr.
Rogers, Neville. Keats, Shelley & Rome. LC 72-186989. Repr. of 1949 ed. lib. bdg. 20.00 (ISBN 0-8414-0352-X). Folcroft.
--Keats, Shelley & Rome. LC 75-22076. (English Literature Ser, No. 33). 1975. lib. bdg. 29.95 (ISBN 0-8383-2080-5). Haskell.
Rossetti, William M. Life of John Keats. LC 75-122695. Repr. of 1887 ed. 14.00 (ISBN 0-404-05428-5). AMS Pr.
--Life of John Keats. 1972. lib. bdg. 30.00 (ISBN 0-8414-7481-8). Folcroft.
Ryan, R. M. Keats: The Religious Sense. 1976. 18.50 (ISBN 0-691-06316-8). Princeton U Pr.
Saito, Takeshi. Keats' View of Poetry. LC 72-187210. 1929. lib. bdg. 12.50 (ISBN 0-8414-7509-1). Folcroft.
--Keats' View of Poetry (Plus an Essay on English Literature in Japan by Blunden, E. LC 75-29567. Repr. of 1929 ed. 11.00 (ISBN 0-404-14017-3). AMS Pr.
Schwartz, Lewis M. Keats Reviewed by His Contemporaries: A Collection of Notices for the Years 1816-1821. LC 72-12779. 1973. 13.50 (ISBN 0-8108-0577-4). Scarecrow.
Sharp, Ronald A. Keats, Skepticism, & the Religion of Beauty. LC 78-21463. 208p. 1979. 14.00x (ISBN 0-8203-0470-0). U of Ga Pr.
Shelley, Percy B. Adonais, an Elegy on the Death of John Keates. Wise, Thomas J., ed. LC 74-30284. (Shelley Society, Second Ser.: No. 1). 1886. Repr. 12.50 (ISBN 0-404-11503-9). AMS Pr.
Sperry, Stuart M., Jr. Keats the Poet. LC 72-6516. 328p. 1973. 25.00x (ISBN 0-691-06220-X). Princeton U Pr.
Stillinger, Jack. Hoodwinking of Madeline & Other Essays on Keats's Poems. LC 70-147924. 1971. 12.50 (ISBN 0-252-00174-5). U of Ill Pr.
--The Texts of Keat's Poems. LC 73-86940. 320p. 1974. text ed. 15.00x (ISBN 0-674-87511-7). Harvard U Pr.
Stillinger, Jack, ed. The Poems of John Keats. LC 78-4490. 1978. 30.00x (ISBN 0-674-67730-7, Belknap Pr). Harvard U Pr.
Suddard, S. Mary. Keats, Shelley & Shakespeare. LC 76-23214. 1912. lib. bdg. 15.00 (ISBN 0-8414-7731-0). Folcroft.
Thomas, Edward. Keats. LC 72-192911. lib. bdg. 8.50 (ISBN 0-8414-8040-0). Folcroft.
Thorpe, Clarence D. Mind of John Keats. LC 64-18603. 1964. Repr. of 1926 ed. 18.00 (ISBN 0-8462-0489-4). Russell.
Tighe, Mary B. Keats & Mary Tighe: The Poems of Mary Tighe with Parallel Passages from Work of John Keats. Weller, E. V., ed. 1928. pap. 20.00 (ISBN 0-527-90120-2). Kraus Repr.
Villard, Leonie. The Influence of Keats on Tennyson & Rosetti. 94p. 1980. Repr. of 1914 ed. lib. bdg. 20.00 (ISBN 0-8482-2830-8). Norwood Edns.
--The Influence of Keats on Tennyson & Rossetti. LC 78-12646. 1978. Repr. of 1914 ed. lib. bdg. 20.00 (ISBN 0-8414-9191-7). Folcroft.
Wasserman, Earl R. The Finer Tone: Keats' Major Poems. LC 53-5494. 236p. 1953. 15.00x (ISBN 0-8018-0657-7); pap. 3.95 (ISBN 0-8018-0658-5). Johns Hopkins.
Wigod, Jacob. The Darkening Chamber: The Growth of Tragic Consciousness in Keats. (Salzburg Studies in English Literature, Romantic Reassessment: No. 22). 231p. 1972. pap. text ed. 25.00x (ISBN 0-391-01567-2). Humanities.
Zillman, Lawrence J. John Keats & the Sonnet Tradition. LC 66-18035. 1966. Repr. lib. bdg. 13.50x (ISBN 0-374-98854-4). Octagon.

KEATS, JOHN, 1795-1821-FICTION

Hale-White, William. Keats As Doctor & Patient. 1972. lib. bdg. 11.00x (ISBN 0-374-93376-6). Octagon.
Walsh, William. Introduction to Keats. 1981. 16.00x (ISBN 0-416-30490-7); pap. 6.95x (ISBN 0-416-30500-8). Methuen Inc.

KEBLE, JOHN, 1792-1866

Coleridge, John T. A Memoir of the Rev. John Keble, 2 vols. in 1. 2nd rev. ed. LC 75-30019. Repr. of 1869 ed. 38.50 (ISBN 0-404-14024-6). AMS Pr.
Donaldson, Augustas B. Five Great Oxford Leaders: Keble, Newman, Pusey, Liddon & Church. 1978. Repr. of 1900 ed. lib. bdg. 35.00 (ISBN 0-8495-1036-8). Arden Lib.
Lock, Walter. John Keble. 1895. Repr. 20.00 (ISBN 0-8274-2626-7). R West.
--John Keble. 1977. Repr. of 1895 ed. lib. bdg. 20.00 (ISBN 0-8495-3221-3). Arden Lib.
Martin, Brian W. John Keble: Priest, Professor & Poet. 191p. 1976. 25.00x (ISBN 0-85664-381-5, Pub. by Croom Helm Ltd England). Biblio Dist.
Shairp, J. C. Studies in Poetry & Philosophy. LC 70-113345. 1970. Repr. of 1868 ed. 14.50 (ISBN 0-8046-1052-5). Kennikat.
Warren, Wm. T., ed. Kebleland: Keble's Home at Hursley, Incidents in His Life, Extracts from His Poetical Works, Keble's Churches, Keble College, Oxford, with Notes on the Neighbouring Villages; Also a Short Life of Richard Cromwell, of Merdon, & Other Character Sketches. 1979. Repr. of 1900 ed. lib. bdg. 35.00 (ISBN 0-8492-2989-8). R West.
Wood, Edward L. John Keble: Leaders of the Church 1800-1900. Russell, George W., ed. 1909. Repr. 25.00 (ISBN 0-8274-2627-5). R West.

KECHUA LANGUAGE

see Quechua Language

KEELEY CURE

see Alcoholism–Treatment

KEEPSAKES (BOOKS)

see Gift-Books (Annuals, etc.)

KEESHOND

see Dogs–Breeds–Keeshond

KEFAUVER, ESTES, 1903-1963

Fontenay, Charles L. Estes Kefauver: A Biography. LC 79-28299. (Illus.). 432p. 1980. 18.50 (ISBN 0-87049-262-4). U of Tenn Pr.
Gorman, Joseph B. Kefauver: A Political Biography. 1971. 15.95 (ISBN 0-19-501481-2). Oxford U Pr.
Moore, William H. The Kefauver Committee & the Politics of Crime 1950-1952. LC 72-93923. 320p. 1974. 15.00x (ISBN 0-8262-0145-8). U of Mo Pr.

KELANTAN

Firth, Rosemary. Housekeeping Among Malay Peasants. 2nd ed. (Monographs on Social Anthropology: No. 7). 1966. text ed. 18.75x (ISBN 0-485-19507-0, Athlone Pr). Humanities.
Kessler, Clive S. Islam & Politics in a Malay State: Kelantan, 1838-1969. LC 77-14682. (Illus.). 1978. 20.00x (ISBN 0-8014-1103-3). Cornell U Pr.
Roff, William R., ed. Kelantan: Religion, Society & Politics in a Malay State. 392p. 1974. 25.50x (ISBN 0-19-638239-4). Oxford U Pr.

KELL, JOHN MCINTOSH, 1823-1900

Delaney, Norman C. John McIntosh Kell of the Raider Alabama. LC 72-7349. 1973. 20.50x (ISBN 0-8173-5106-X). U of Ala Pr.

KELLER, GOTTFRIED, 1819-1890

Hauch, Edward F. Gottfried Keller As a Democratic Idealist. LC 16-6640. (Columbia University. Germanic Studies, Old Series: No. 20). Repr. of 1916 ed. 15.00 (ISBN 0-404-50420-5). AMS Pr.
Lindsay, James M. Gottfried Keller: Life & Works. LC 9-14390. 9.95 (ISBN 0-8023-1205-5). Dufour.
Preitz, M. Gottfried Kellers Dramatische Bestrebungen. Repr. of 1909 ed. pap. 15.50 (ISBN 0-384-47670-8). Johnson Repr.
Reichert, Herbert W. Basic Concepts in the Philosophy of Gottfried Keller. LC 49-11614. (North Carolina. University. Studies in the Germanic Languages & Literatures: No. 1). Repr. of 1949 ed. 18.50 (ISBN 0-404-50901-0). AMS Pr.
Roessing-Hager, Monika & Soerensen, Niels, eds. Wortindex zu Gottfried Keller, Die Leute von Seldwyla, 2 Pts. (Deutsche Wortindices, No. 2). (Ger). 1971. 136.75x (ISBN 3-11-006441-3). De Gruyter.
Schrader, Edda, ed. Wortindex zu Gottfried Keller. der gruene Heinrich: Erste Fassung, 2 vols. (Deutsche Wortindices, 3). 1255p. 1971. 168.00x (ISBN 3-11-003354-2). De Gruyter.

KELLER, HELEN ADAMS, 1880-1968

Hanks, Geoffrey. Helen: The Story of Helen Keller. 1978. pap. 1.55 (ISBN 0-08-021235-2). Pergamon.
Johnson, Ann D. The Value of Determination: The Story of Helen Keller. 2nd ed. LC 76-54762. (Valuetales Ser). (Illus.). (gr. k-6). 1976. 6.95 (ISBN 0-916392-07-4, Dist. by Oak Tree Pubns.). Value Comm.
Johnson, Patty T. Helen Keller. 1980. 4.95 (ISBN 0-87397-170-1). Strode.
Keller, Helen. Story of My Life. (Classics Ser). (gr. 8 up). pap. 0.95 (ISBN 0-8049-0070-1, CL-70). Airmont.
--Story of My Life. LC 54-11951. 1954. 12.95 (ISBN 0-385-04453-4). Doubleday.
--Story of My Life. English Language Services, ed. (English Readers Ser). pap. 1.40 (ISBN 0-02-971390-0). Macmillan.
--The Story of My Life. (gr. 7-12). 1973. pap. 1.25 (ISBN 0-590-01488-9, Schol Pap). Schol Bk Serv.
Lash, Joseph P. Helen & Teacher: The Story of Helen Keller & Anne Sullivan Macy. 1980. 17.95 (ISBN 0-440-03654-2). Delacorte.

KELLER, HELEN ADAMS, 1880-1968 - JUVENILE LITERATURE

Bigland, Eileen. Helen Keller. LC 67-22810. (Illus.). (gr. 7-10). 1967. 9.95 (ISBN 0-87599-134-3). S G Phillips.
Davidson, Margaret. Helen Keller: Centennial Edition. new ed. 128p. (gr. 6-10). 1980. cancelled (ISBN 0-8038-3015-7). Hastings.
Graff, Stewart & Graff, Polly A. Helen Keller. (Illus.). (gr. 2-7). 1966. pap. 1.25 (ISBN 0-440-43566-8, YB). Dell.
--Helen Keller: Toward the Light. LC 65-14550. (Discovery Books Ser). (gr. 2-5). 1965. PLB 6.09 (ISBN 0-8116-6288-8). Garrard.
Hickock, L. A. The Story of Helen Keller. 1980. pap. 1.50 (ISBN 0-448-17149-X, Tempo). Ace Bks.
Kelton, Nancy. The Finger Game Miracle. LC 76-46408. (When They Were Young Ser.). (Illus.). (gr. k-3). 1977. PLB 8.95 (ISBN 0-8172-0452-0). Raintree Pubs.
Peare, Catherine O. Helen Keller Story. LC 59-10979. (gr. 5 up). 1959. 9.95 (ISBN 0-690-37520-4, TYC-J). Har-Row.
Waite, Helen E. Valiant Companions. (gr. 7-11). 1959. 6.25 (ISBN 0-8255-9060-4). Macrae.
Wayne, Bennett, ed. Four Women of Courage. LC 74-13482. (Target Books Ser). (Illus.). 168p. (gr. 5-12). 1975. PLB 7.29 (ISBN 0-8116-4911-3). Garrard.

KELLEY, FLORENCE, 1859-1932

Goldmark, Josephine C. Impatient Crusader: Florence Kelley's Life Story. LC 76-23383. 217p. 1976. Repr. of 1953 ed. lib. bdg. 16.25x (ISBN 0-8371-9011-8, GOIM). Greenwood.

KELLOGG, FRANK BILLINGS, 1856-1937

Ellis, Lewis E. Frank B. Kellogg & American Foreign Relations, 1925-1929. LC 74-10636. 303p. 1974. Repr. of 1961 ed. lib. bdg. 22.00 (ISBN 0-8371-7651-4, ELFK). Greenwood.
Ferrell, Robert H. Frank B Kellogg (1925-29) & Henry L. Stimson (1929-33) (American Secretaries of State & Their Diplomacy, New Ser.: Vol. 11). 1963. 12.00x (ISBN 0-8154-0069-1). Cooper Sq.
Neubeck, Deborah K. Guide to the Microfilm Edition of The Frank B. Kellogg Papers. LC 78-63612. 56p. 1978. pap. 2.00 (ISBN 0-87351-126-3). Minn Hist.

KELLOGG TREATY, PARIS, AUG. 27, 1928

Myers, Denys P. Origin & Conclusion of the Paris Pact. Bd. with Renunciation of War. Page, Kirby. LC 75-147608. (Library of War & Peace; Kellogg Pact & the Outlawry of War). lib. bdg. 38.00 (ISBN 0-8240-0368-3). Garland Pub.

KELLY, ELLSWORTH, 1923-

Goossen, E. C. Kelly. (Derriere le Miroir: No. 110). (Illus.). 1978. pap. 19.95 (ISBN 0-8120-2000-6). Barron.
McConathy, Dale. Ellsworth Kelly. (Illus.). 1964. deluxe ed. 300.00x wrappers, bds. & slipcase (ISBN 0-915346-35-4). A Wofsy Fine Arts.

KELLY, GENE, 1912-

Thomas, Tony. The Films of Gene Kelly. (Illus.). 1976. pap. 6.95 (ISBN 0-8065-0543-5). Citadel Pr.
--Song & Dance Man: The Films of Gene Kelly. LC 73-90949. (Illus.). 256p. 1974. 12.00 (ISBN 0-8065-0400-5). Citadel Pr.

KELLY, GEORGE ALEXANDER, 1905-

Bannister, Donald & Mair, John M., eds. Evaluation of Personality Constructs. 1968. 37.50 (ISBN 0-12-077950-1). Acad Pr.

KELOTOMY

see Hernia

KELP

Brown, Joseph E. Wonders of the Kelp Forest. LC 74-2601. (Wonders Ser.). (Illus.). 80p. (gr. 3-7). 1974. 5.95 (ISBN 0-396-06967-3). Dodd.

Lauber, Patricia. Sea Otters & Seaweed. LC 76-17796. (Good Earth Bks). (Illus.). 64p. (gr. 2-6). 1976. lib. bdg. 6.57 (ISBN 0-8116-6106-7). Garrard.

Powell, Eric. Kelp, the Health Giver. 1980. pap. 1.95 (ISBN 0-87904-041-6). Lust.

Powell, Eric F. Kelp the Health Giver. 1980. 15.00x (ISBN 0-85032-195-6, Pub. by Daniel Co England). State Mutual Bk.

--Kelp the Health Giver. 1980. 2.25 (ISBN 0-8464-1028-1). Beekman Pubs.

KELSEN, HANS, 1881-

Ebenstein, William. Pure Theory of Law. LC 79-96336. Repr. of 1945 ed. 9.50x (ISBN 0-678-04535-6). Kelley.

Moore, Ronald. Legal Norms & Legal Science: A Critical Study of Kelsen's Pure Theory of Law. LC 77-12392. 1978. text ed. 12.00x (ISBN 0-8248-0516-X). U Pr of Hawaii.

KELVIN, WILLIAM THOMSON, BARON, 1824-1907

Gray, Andrew. Lord Kelvin: An Account of His Scientific Life & Work. LC 73-113129. (Illus.). 326p. 1973. Repr. of 1908 ed. text ed. 9.95 (ISBN 0-8284-0264-7). Chelsea Pub.

Sharlin, Harold & Sharlin, Tiby. Lord Kelvin: The Dynamic Victorian. LC 78-50771. (Illus.). 1979. 18.75 (ISBN 0-271-00203-4). Pa St U Pr.

Thompson, Silvanus P. The Life of Lord Kelvin, 2 vols. 2nd ed. LC 75-45133. (Illus.). 1977. text ed. 39.50 set (ISBN 0-8284-0292-2). Chelsea Pub.

KEMBLE, CHARLES, 1775-1854

Williamson, Jane. Charles Kemble: Man of the Theatre. LC 69-19105. (Illus.). 1970. 16.95x (ISBN 0-8032-0727-1). U of Nebr Pr.

KEMBLE, FRANCES ANNE, 1809-1893

Driver, Leota S. Fanny Kemble. LC 76-97449. Repr. of 1933 ed. 10.00x (ISBN 0-8371-2697-5, Pub. by Negro U Pr). Greenwood.

Furnas, J. C. Fanny Kemble: Leading Lady of the Nineteenth Century Stage. 516p. 1982. 15.95 (ISBN 0-385-27208-1, Dist. by Doubleday). Dial.

Rushmore, Robert. Fanny Kemble. LC 70-95176. (gr. 7 up). 1970. 9.95 (ISBN 0-02-777920-3, CCPr). Macmillan.

Scott, John A. Fanny Kemble's America. LC 72-7557. (Women of America Ser). (Illus.). 168p. (gr. 5-9). 1973. 8.95 (ISBN 0-690-28911-1, TYC-J). Har-Row.

Wister, Fanny K. Fanny, the American Kemble: Her Journals & Unpublished Letters. LC 72-80474. 227p. 1972. 10.00x (ISBN 0-932068-00-6). South Pass Pr.

KEMBLE, JOHN PHILIP, 1757-1823

Baker, Herschel C. John Philip Kemble: The Actor in His Theatre. LC 76-90701. Repr. of 1942 ed. lib. bdg. 15.25x (ISBN 0-8371-2279-1, BAJK). Greenwood.

Boaden, James. Memoirs of the Life of John Philip Kemble, 2 vols. LC 77-89713. 1825. 40.00 (ISBN 0-405-08276-2, Blom Pubns). Arno.

Fitzgerald, Percy. Kembles, 2 Vols. LC 73-89712. (Illus.). 1871. Set. 28.00 (ISBN 0-405-08516-8, Blom Pubns); 14.00 ea. Vol. 1 (ISBN 0-405-08517-6). Vol. 2 (ISBN 0-405-08518-4). Arno.

Kelly, Linda. The Kemble Era: John Philip Kemble, Sarah Siddons & the London Stage. (Illus.). 1980. 12.95 (ISBN 0-394-41034-3). Random.

Shattuck, Charles H., ed. John Philip Kemble Promptbooks, 11 vols. (Facsimiles Ser). 1978. Set. 220.00 (ISBN 0-8139-0558-3). Folger Bks.

KEMBLE FAMILY

Fitzgerald, Percy. Kembles, 2 Vols. LC 73-89712. (Illus.). 1871. Set. 28.00 (ISBN 0-405-08516-8, Blom Pubns); 14.00 ea. Vol. 1 (ISBN 0-405-08517-6). Vol. 2 (ISBN 0-405-08518-4). Arno.

KEMPE, MARGERY (BURNHAM), b. 1373

Cholmeley, Katharine. Margery Kempe, Genius & Mystic. LC 78-7811. 1978. Repr. of 1947 ed. lib. bdg. 17.50 (ISBN 0-8414-0296-5). Folcroft.

Watkins, E. I. On Julian of Norwich, & in Defence of Margery Kempe. rev. ed. 65p. 1979. pap. text ed. 4.50x (ISBN 0-85989-054-6, Pub. by U Exeter England). Humanities.

KEMPER COUNTY, MISSISSIPPI

Lynch, James D. Kemper County Vindicated, & a Peep at Radical Rule in Mississippi. LC 70-91663. Repr. of 1879 ed. 20.00x (ISBN 0-8371-2069-1, Pub. by Negro U Pr). Greenwood.

KEMPER COUNTY, MISSISSIPPI-HISTORY

The Eighteen Seventy-Six Catalogue of the Kemper Family School for Boys & Young Men, Boonville, Missouri. 1975. pap. 5.00 (ISBN 0-916440-00-1). VKM.

Wells, James M. Chisholm Massacre. LC 73-95454. (Studies in Black History & Culture, No. 54). 1970. Repr. of 1877 ed. lib. bdg. 38.95 (ISBN 0-8383-1210-1). Haskell.

--Chisolm Massacre: A Picture of Home Rule in Mississippi. LC 77-77217. (Illus.). Repr. of 1877 ed. 15.25x (ISBN 0-8371-1285-0, Pub. by Negro U Pr). Greenwood.

KEN, THOMAS, BP. OF BATH AND WELLS, 1637-1711

Marston, E. Thomas Ken & Izaak Walton: A Sketch of Their Lives & Family Connection. 1908. Repr. 35.00 (ISBN 0-8274-3613-0). R West.

Rice, Hugh A. L. Thomas Ken: Bishop & Non-Juror. 1958. pap. 7.50x (ISBN 0-8401-2008-7). Allenson-Breckinridge.

KENDALL, GEORGE WILKINS, 1809-1867

Copeland, Fayette. Kendall of the "Picayune". Being His Adventures in New Orleans, on the Texas Santa Fe Expedition, in the Mexican War & in the Colonization of the Texas Frontier. (Illus.). 1970. Repr. of 1943 ed. 9.95 (ISBN 0-8061-0851-7). U of Okla Pr.

KENDO

AJK Foundation. Fundamental Kendo. 13.95 (ISBN 0-685-41904-5). Wehman.

Kammer, Reinhard, ed. Zen & Confucius in the Art of Swordsmanship(the Tengu-Geijutsu-Ron of Chozan Shissai) Fitzgerald, Betty, tr. (Illus.). 1978. cased 16.00 (ISBN 0-7100-8737-3). Routledge & Kegan.

Sasamori & Warner. This Is Kendo. 15.00 (ISBN 0-685-22139-3). Wehman.

Warner, Gordon & Sasamori, Junzo. This Is Kendo: The Art of Japanese Fencing. LC 64-22900. 1964. 16.50 (ISBN 0-8048-0574-1). C E Tuttle.

KENNEBEC RIVER AND VALLEY

Everson, Jennie. Tidewater Ice of the Kennebec River. LC 68-11102. (Maine Heritage Ser.: No. 1). (Illus.). 1971. 9.95 (ISBN 0-913764-03-5). Maine St Mus.

The Kennebec-Boothbay Harbor Steamboat Album. 1974. pap. 3.25 (ISBN 0-89272-004-2). Down East.

Willoughby, Charles C. Indian Antiquities of the Kennebec Valley. Spiess, Arthur E., ed. (Occasional Publications in Maine Archaeology: No. 1). (Illus.). 160p. 1980. 22.00 (ISBN 0-913764-13-2). Maine St Mus.

--Indian Antiquities of the Kennebec Valley. (Illus.). 1980. 22.00 (ISBN 0-913764-13-2). Maine St Mus.

KENNEBUNKPORT, MAINE

Butler, Joyce. Kennebunkport Scrapbook. (Illus., Orig.). 1977. pap. 5.95 (ISBN 0-932006-01-9). Durrell.

KENNEDY, EDWARD MOORE, 1932-

Aschburner, Steve. Ted Kennedy: The Politician & the Man. LC 79-27299. (Illus.). 48p. (gr. 4-8). 1980. PLB 7.95 (ISBN 0-8172-0430-X). Raintree Pubs.

Burns, James M. Edward Kennedy & the Camelot Legacy. (Illus.). 384p. 1976. 11.95 (ISBN 0-393-07501-X). Norton.

Hersh, Burton. The Education of Edward Kennedy: A Family Biography. (Illus.). 1972. 10.95 (ISBN 0-688-00075-4). Morrow.

Honan, William H. Ted Kennedy: Profile of a Survivor. (Illus.). 192p. 1972. pap. 1.25 (ISBN 0-532-12130-9). Woodhill.

Lerner, Max. Ted & the Kennedy Legend: A Study in Character & Destiny. write for info. St Martin.

Levin, Murray B. & Repak, T. A. Edward Kennedy: The Myth of Leadership. 1980. 10.95 (ISBN 0-395-29249-2). HM.

Lippman, Theo, Jr. Senator Ted Kennedy: The Career Behind the Image. (Illus.). 1976. 9.95 (ISBN 0-393-05568-X). Norton.

Olsen, Jack. The Bridge at Chappaquidick. 1980. pap. 1.95 (ISBN 0-441-07958-X). Ace Bks.

Schapp, Dick. Ted. LC 79-91296. (Illus., Orig.). 1980. cancelled (ISBN 0-448-16551-1). G&D.

Tedrow, Richard L. & Tedrow, Thomas. Death at Chappaquiddick. rev. ed. LC 79-21703. 240p. 1980. pap. 5.95 (ISBN 0-88289-249-5). Pelican.

Tedrow, Richard L. & Tedrow, Thomas L. Death at Chappaquiddick. LC 76-3349. (Illus.). 240p. 1976. 9.95 (ISBN 0-916054-28-4). Green Hill.

Willis, Larryanne. Chappaquiddick Decision. (Illus., Orig.). 1980. pap. 2.95 (ISBN 0-937980-00-5). Better Bks.

KENNEDY, JACQUELINE

see Onassis, Jacqueline Kennedy, 1929-

KENNEDY, JOHN FITZGERALD, PRES. U. S., 1917-1963

Bradlee, Benjamin C. Conversations with Kennedy. (Illus.). 251p. 1975. 7.95 (ISBN 0-393-08722-0). Norton.

Brauer, Carl M. John F. Kennedy & the Second Reconstruction. LC 76-57686. (Contemporary American History Ser.). 396p. 1977. 20.00x (ISBN 0-231-03862-3); pap. 8.00x (ISBN 0-231-08367-X). Columbia U Pr.

Country Beautiful Editors. America the Beautiful in the Words of John F. Kennedy. LC 64-18166. (America the Beautiful Ser). (Illus.). 1964. 9.95 (ISBN 0-87294-002-0). Country Beautiful.

Crown, James Tracy. The Kennedy Literature: A Bibliographical Essay on John F. Kennedy. LC 68-29428. 1968. 14.50x (ISBN 0-8147-0109-4). NYU Pr.

Davis, Bill & Tree, C. The Kennedy Library. (Illus.). 144p. 1980. pap. 9.95 (ISBN 0-916838-36-6). Schiffer.

Dollen, Charles. John F. Kennedy American. (Illus., Orig.). 1965. 5.00 (ISBN 0-8198-0068-6); pap. 4.00 (ISBN 0-8198-0069-4). Dghtrs St Paul.

Dulles, Eleanor L. The Wall: A Tragedy in Three Acts. LC 78-189022. (Studies in International Affairs: No. 9). 106p. 1972. 5.95x (ISBN 0-87249-267-2). U of SC Pr.

Gromyko, Anatolii A. Through Russian Eyes: President Kennedy's One Thousand Thirty-Six Days. Garon, Philip A., ed. LC 73-75637. 239p. 1973. 11.95 (ISBN 0-914250-00-0). Intl Lib.

Halberstam, David. The Best & the Brightest. 832p. 1973. pap. 3.50 (ISBN 0-449-24033-9, Crest). Fawcett.

John -- the Man Who Would Be President. LC 79-93341. 1979. 9.95 (ISBN 0-89387-040-4). Sat Eve Post.

Johnson, George W., ed. Kennedy Presidential Press Conferences, Vol. 1. LC 78-1869. 1978. text ed. 35.00 (ISBN 0-930576-01-2). E M Coleman Ent.

Lasky, Victor. J F K: The Man & the Myth. 1966. 12.95 (ISBN 0-87000-016-0). Arlington Hse.

Latham, Earl. J. F. Kennedy & Presidential Power. 1972. pap. text ed. 4.95x (ISBN 0-669-82099-7). Heath.

Menendez, Alfred. John F. Kennedy: Catholic & Humanist. LC 78-68139. 144p. 1979. 12.95 (ISBN 0-87975-109-6). Prometheus Bks.

Miroff, Bruce. Pragmatic Illusions: The Presidential Politics of John F. Kennedy. LC 76-7554. 1976. 9.95x (ISBN 0-679-30298-0); pap. text ed. 8.95x (ISBN 0-582-28130-X). Longman.

Newcomb, Joan I. John F. Kennedy: An Annotated Bibliography. LC 77-7568. 1977. 10.00 (ISBN 0-8108-1042-5). Scarecrow.

O'Donnell, Kenneth P. & Powers, David. Johnny, We Hardly Knew Ye: Memories of John Fitzgerald Kennedy. 448p. 1972. 10.00 (ISBN 0-316-71625-1). Little.

Paper, Lewis J. John F. Kennedy: The Promise & the Performance. xi, 408p. 1980. pap. 7.95 (ISBN 0-306-80114-0). Da Capo.

Parmet, Herbert S. Jack: The Struggles of John F. Kennedy. 1980. 14.95 (ISBN 0-8037-4452-8). Dial.

Ray, John. Roosevelt & Kennedy. 1970. pap. text ed. 3.95x (ISBN 0-435-31757-1). Heinemann Ed.

Rothschild, Eric, ed. John F. Kennedy & the New Frontier: 1960-1963. (New York Times School Microfilm Collection Ser.: Guide No. 10). 37p. (gr. 7-12). 1978. pap. 5.50 wkbk (ISBN 0-667-00559-5). Microfilming Corp.

Schlesinger, Arthur M., Jr. Thousand Days. 1977. pap. 3.50 (ISBN 0-449-30852-9, Prem). Fawcett.

Schneidman, J. Lee. John F. Kennedy. (World Leaders Ser: No. 28). 1974. lib. bdg. 9.95 (ISBN 0-8057-3696-4). Twayne.

Shank, Alan. Presidential Policy Leadership: Kennedy & Social Welfare. LC 80-8278. 309p. 1980. lib. bdg. 19.75 (ISBN 0-8191-1265-8); pap. text ed. 11.50 (ISBN 0-8191-1266-6). U Pr of Amer.

Shepard, Tazewell, Jr. John F. Kennedy: Man of the Sea. LC 65-26256. (Illus.). 162p. 1965. 15.95 (ISBN 0-87294-018-7). Country Beautiful.

Smith, Malcolm E. John F. Kennedy's Thirteen Great Mistakes in the White House. 240p. 1980. 9.95 (ISBN 0-936066-01-6). Suffolk Hse.

Stone, Ralph A., ed. John F. Kennedy, 1917-1963: Chronology, Documents, Bibliographical Aids. LC 75-116063. (Presidential Chronology Ser). 1971. 8.00 (ISBN 0-379-12076-3). Oceana.

Stoughton, Cecil & Clifton, Chester V. The Memories: JFK 1961-1963. (Illus.). 208p. 1980. pap. 7.95 (ISBN 0-393-00985-8). Norton.

Toscano, Vincent L. Since Dallas: Images of John F. Kennedy in Popular & Scholarly Literature, 1963-1973. LC 77-81013. 1978. soft cover 10.00 (ISBN 0-88247-493-6). R & E Res Assoc.

Webb, Lucas. The Attempted Assassination of John F. Kennedy. LC 76-40282. 1976. lib. bdg. 8.95x (ISBN 0-89370-104-1); pap. 2.95 (ISBN 0-89370-204-8). Borgo Pr.

Wicker, Tom. JFK & LBJ. 1969. pap. 4.95 (ISBN 0-14-021116-0, Pelican). Penguin.

Wofford, Harris. Of Kennedys & Kings: Making Sense of the Sixties. 496p. 1980. 17.50 (ISBN 0-374-22432-3). FS&G.

Wood, James. The Life & Words of John F. Kennedy. LC 64-24582. (Illus.). 82p. 1964. 9.95 (ISBN 0-87294-019-5). Country Beautiful.

Wszelaki, Jan, ed. John F. Kennedy & Poland, a Selection of Texts & Documents. 140p. 1965. pap. 5.00 (ISBN 0-686-09131-0). Polish Inst Arts.

KENNEDY, JOHN FITZGERALD, PRES. U. S., 1917-1963–ASSASSINATION

see also United States President's Commission on the Assassination of President John F. Kennedy

Bales, James. Communism Killed Kennedy but Did America Learn? 3.95 (ISBN 0-89315-015-0). Lambert Bk.

Bane, Bernard M. The Bane in Kennedy's Existence. LC 66-30557. 169p. 1967. soft bdg. 4.95 (ISBN 0-9600164-0-6). BMB Pub Co.

--Is President John F. Kennedy Alive...and Well? LC 76-218107. 161p. 1981. soft cover 5.95 (ISBN 0-930924-08-8). BMB Pub Co.

Belin, David. November Twenty-Second, 1963: You Are the Jury. LC 73-82479. 1973. 12.50 (ISBN 0-8129-0374-9). Times Bks.

Bugge, Brian K. The Mystique of Conspiracy: Oswald, Castro, & the CIA. 1978. pap. 2.95 (ISBN 0-9601708-1-2). B K Bugge.

Canfield, Michael & Weberman, Alan J. Coup D'etat in America: The CIA & the Assassination of John F. Kennedy. LC 75-4360. (Illus.). 336p. 1975. 12.95 (ISBN 0-89388-204-6). Okpaku Communications.

Eddowes, Michael. The Oswald File. (Illus.). 1977. 10.00 (ISBN 0-517-53055-4). Crown.

Epstein, Edward J. The Legend: Secret World of Lee Harvey Oswald. 1978. 12.95 (ISBN 0-07-019539-0, GB). McGraw.

Fensterwald, Bernard. Coincidence or Conspiracy? (Illus.). 1977. pap. 2.50 (ISBN 0-89083-232-3). Zebra.

Greenberg, Bradley S. & Parker, Edwin B., eds. Kennedy Assassination & the American Public: Social Communication in Crisis. 1965. 18.75x (ISBN 0-8047-0257-8). Stanford U Pr.

Guth, DeLloyd J. & Wrone, David R.compiled By. The Assassination of John F. Kennedy: A Comprehensive Historical & Legal Bibliography, 1963-1979. LC 79-6184. (Illus.). lvi, 442p. 1980. lib. bdg. 37.50 (ISBN 0-313-21274-0, GJK/). Greenwood.

Hayman, Leroy. The Assassinations of John & Robert Kennedy. (gr. 7 up). 1977. pap. 1.25 (ISBN 0-590-01377-7, Schol Pap). Schol Bk Serv.

Hoch, Paul L., et al. The Assassinations: Dallas & Beyond - A Guide to Cover-ups & Investigations. Stetler, Russell & Scott, Peter D., eds. 1976. 15.00 (ISBN 0-394-40107-7). Random.

James, Rosemary & Wardlaw, Jack. Plot or Politics: The Garrison Case & Its Cast. (Illus.). 1967. pap. 2.95 (ISBN 0-911116-11-7). Pelican.

Jenkins, John H. Neither the Fanatics nor the Fainthearted: The Tour Leading to President Kennedy's Death & the Two Speeches He Could Not Give. 25.00 (ISBN 0-685-13277-3); pap. 4.50 wrappers (ISBN 0-685-13278-1). Jenkins.

Kantor, Seth. The Ruby Cover Up. 1980. pap. 2.95 (ISBN 0-89083-680-9). Zebra.

Kurland, Gerald. Assassination of President John F. Kennedy. Rahmas, D. Steve, ed. (Events of Our Times Ser.: No. 10). 32p. 1973. lib. bdg. 2.95 incl. catalog cards (ISBN 0-87157-707-0); pap. 1.50 vinyl laminated covers (ISBN 0-87157-207-9). SamHar Pr.

Lattimer, John K. Lincoln & Kennedy: Medical & Ballistic Comparisons of Their Assassinations. LC 80-7963. 1980. 19.95 (ISBN 0-15-152281-2). HarBraceJ.

Lifton, David S. Best Evidence: Deception & Disguise in the Assassination of John F. Kennedy. 1981. 16.95 (ISBN 0-02-571870-3). Macmillan.

McDonald, Hugh & Moore, Robin. LBJ & the JFK Conspiracy. LC 78-71413. 1978. pap. 2.25 (ISBN 0-89516-056-0). Condor Pub Co.

McDonald, Hugh C. Appointment in Dallas: The Final Solution to the Assassination of JFK. (Illus.). 210p. (Orig.). pap. 1.95 (ISBN 0-89083-100-9). Zebra.

McKnight, Janet, ed. Three Assassinations: The Deaths of John & Robert Kennedy & Martin Luther King. LC 77-154630. (Illus.). 1971. Repr. 17.50x (ISBN 0-87196-190-3). Facts on File.

Manchester, William. Death of a President - November Twentieth to November Twenty-Fifth, Nineteen Sixty-Three. LC 67-10496. 1967. 20.00 (ISBN 0-06-012762-7, HarpT). Har-Row.

Meagher, Sylvia. Accessories After the Fact: The Warren Commission, the Authorities & the Report. 1976. pap. 5.95 (ISBN 0-394-71630-2, Vin). Random.

Meagher, Sylvia & Owens, Gary. Master Index to the J. F. K. Assassination Investigation: The Reports & Supporting Volumes of the House Select Committee on Assassinations & the Warren Commission. LC 80-17494. xii, 435p. 1980. 20.00 (ISBN 0-8108-1331-9). Scarecrow.

Model, Peter F. J. F. K. the Case for Conspiracy. 224p. (Orig.). 1975. pap. 1.50 (ISBN 0-532-19137-4). Woodhill.

Oglesby, Carl. The Yankee & the Cowboy War. 1977. pap. 1.95 (ISBN 0-425-03493-3, Medallion). Berkley Pub.

Roffman, Howard. Presumed Guilty: Lee Harvey Oswald in the Assassinaion of President Kennedy. LC 74-1119. (Illus.). 297p. 1975. 15.00 (ISBN 0-8386-1526-0). Fairleigh Dickinson.

Summers, Anthony. Conspiracy. (McGraw-Hill Paperbacks Ser.). (Illus.). 656p. 1981. pap. 7.95 (ISBN 0-07-062400-3). McGraw.

--Conspiracy. LC 79-25474. 372p. 1980. 17.95 (ISBN 0-07-062392-9). McGraw.

Weisberg, Harold. Post Mortem: JFK Assassination Cover-Up Smashed! 1975. 10.00x (ISBN 0-911606-05-X). Weisberg.

--Whitewash Four: Top Secret JFK Assassination Transcript. 1974. 6.00x (ISBN 0-911606-07-6). Weisberg.

--Whitewash: The Report on the Warren Report. 1965. 6.00x (ISBN 0-911606-01-7). Weisberg.

--Whitewash Two: The FBI-Secret Service Cover-Up. 1966. 6.00x (ISBN 0-911606-02-5). Weisberg.

Wilber, Charles G. Medicolegal Investigation of the President John F. Kennedy Murder. (Illus.). 336p. 1978. 19.50 (ISBN 0-398-03679-9). C C Thomas.

Wrone, David R., ed. The Legal Proceedings of Harold Weisberg v. General Services Administration Civil Action 2052-73 Together with the January 22 & 27 Warren Commission Transcripts. (Freedom of Information Act & Political Assassinations Ser.: Vol. 1). (Illus., Orig.). pap. 8.95 (ISBN 0-932310-00-1, Foundation Pr.). U of Wis-Stevens Point.

KENNEDY, JOHN FITZGERALD, PRES. U. S., 1917-1963–FUNERAL AND MEMORIAL SERVICES

Manchester, William. Death of a President - November Twentieth to November Twenty-Fifth, Nineteen Sixty-Three. LC 67-10496. 1967. 20.00 (ISBN 0-06-012762-7, HarpT). Har-Row.

KENNEDY, JOHN FITZGERALD, PRES. U. S., 1917-1963–JUVENILE LITERATURE

Campling, Elizabeth. Kennedy. (Leaders Ser.). (Illus.). 80p. (gr. 9-12). 1980. 14.95 (ISBN 0-7134-1920-2, Pub. by Batsford England). David & Charles.

Graves, Charles P. John F. Kennedy. (Illus.). (gr. 1-7). 1966. pap. 0.95 (ISBN 0-440-44242-7, YB). Dell.

--John F. Kennedy: New Frontiersman. LC 65-10509. (Discovery Books Ser). (Illus.). (gr. 2-5). 1965. PLB 6.09 (ISBN 0-8116-6287-X). Garrard.

John F. Kennedy: Mini Play. (President's Choice Ser.). (gr. 9 up). 1977. 3.00 (ISBN 0-89550-372-7). RIM.

Martin, Patricia M. John Fitzgerald Kennedy. (See & Read Biographies). (Illus.). (gr. k-4). 1964. PLB 5.99 (ISBN 0-399-60319-0). Putnam.

Tregaskis, Richard. John F. Kennedy & PT-109. (Landmark Ser: No. 99). (gr. 7-8). 1962. PLB 5.99 (ISBN 0-394-90399-4, BYR). Random.

White, Nancy B. Meet John F. Kennedy. (Step-up Books Ser). (Illus.). (gr. 2-5). 1965. 3.95 (ISBN 0-394-80059-1, BYR); PLB 4.99 (ISBN 0-394-90059-6). Random.

KENNEDY, JOHN FITZGERALD, PRES. U. S., 1917-1963–MONUMENTS, ETC.

Goldman, Alex J. John Fitzgerald Kennedy: The World Remembers. LC 68-23981. (Illus.). (gr. 4-9). 1968. 12.00 (ISBN 0-8303-0065-1). Fleet.

Runnymede Memorial. pap. 1.20x (ISBN 0-8277-0104-7). British Bk Ctr.

KENNEDY, JOHN FITZGERALD, PRES. U. S., 1917-1963–POETRY

Berry, Wendell. November 26, 1963. LC 64-19345. (Illus.). 1964. 5.00 (ISBN 0-8076-0263-9). Braziller.

Chinmoy, Sri. Kennedy: The Universal Heart. 30p. 1973. pap. 1.00 (ISBN 0-88497-033-7). Aum Pubns.

KENNEDY, JOHN PENDLETON, 1795-1870

Bohner, Charles H. John Pendleton Kennedy: Gentleman from Baltimore. 288p. 1961. 18.50x (ISBN 0-8018-0083-8). Johns Hopkins.

Ridgely, Joseph V. John Pendleton Kennedy. (Twayne's United States Authors Ser). 1966. pap. 3.45 (ISBN 0-8084-0190-4, T102, Twayne). Coll & U Pr.

Tuckerman, Henry T. The Life of John Pendleton Kennedy. 490p. 1980. lib. bdg. 65.00 (ISBN 0-89987-813-X). Darby Bks.

KENNEDY, JOSEPH PATRICK, 1888-1969

Beschloss, Michael R. Kennedy & Roosevelt: The Uneasy Alliance. (Illus.). 1980. 14.95 (ISBN 0-393-01335-9). Norton.

KENNEDY, ROBERT F., 1925-1968

Brown, Stuart G. Presidency on Trial: Robert Kennedy's 1968 Campaign & Afterwards. 1972. 9.00x (ISBN 0-8248-0202-0). U Pr of Hawaii.

Christian, John & Turner, William. The Assassination of Robert F. Kennedy: The Conspiracy & the Cover-up, 1968-1978. 1978. 12.95 (ISBN 0-394-40273-1). Random.

Country Beautiful Editors. America the Beautiful in the Words of Robert F. Kennedy. LC 68-58164. (America the Beautiful Ser). (Illus.). 98p. 1968. 9.95 (ISBN 0-87294-004-7). Country Beautiful.

Graves, Charles P. Robert F. Kennedy: Man Who Dared to Dream. LC 76-101302. (Americans All Ser). (Illus.). (gr. 3-6). 1970. PLB 6.48 (ISBN 0-8116-4557-6). Garrard.

Halberstam, David. Unfinished Odyssey of Robert Kennedy. LC 69-14435. Orig. Title: Traveling with Robert Kennedy. 1969. 4.95 (ISBN 0-394-45025-6). Random.

Hannibal, Edward & Boris, Robert. Blood Feud. 1979. 10.00 (ISBN 0-345-28100-4). Ballantine.

Hayman, Leroy. The Assassinations of John & Robert Kennedy. (gr. 7 up). 1977. pap. 1.25 (ISBN 0-590-01377-7, Schol Pap). Schol Bk Serv.

Kurland, Gerald. Assassination of Robert Kennedy. Rahmas, D. Steve, ed. LC 72-89219. (Events of Our Times Ser.: No. 2). 32p. (Orig.). (gr. 7-12). 1973. lib. bdg. 2.95 incl. catalog cards (ISBN 0-87157-702-X); pap. 1.50 vinyl laminated covers (ISBN 0-87157-202-8). SamHar Pr.

McKnight, Janet, ed. Three Assassinations: The Deaths of John & Robert Kennedy & Martin Luther King. LC 77-154630. (Illus.). 1971. Repr. 17.50x (ISBN 0-87196-190-3). Facts on File.

Mehdi, Mohammad T. Kennedy & Sirhan, Why. LC 68-57262. (Illus., Orig.). pap. 4.00 (ISBN 0-911026-04-5, KSW). New World Press NY.

Navasky, Victor S. Kennedy Justice. LC 77-145633. 1977. pap. 5.95 (ISBN 0-689-70543-3, 231). Atheneum.

Newfield, Jack. Robert F. Kennedy: A Memoir. 1978. pap. 2.50 (ISBN 0-425-04047-X, Dist. by Putnam). Berkley Pub.

Ross, Douglas. Robert F. Kennedy Apostle of Change. 1968. 7.95 (ISBN 0-671-27013-3). Trident.

Salinger, Pierre, et al, eds. Honorable Profession: A Tribute to Robert F. Kennedy. LC 68-55381. (Illus.). 1968. 100.00 (ISBN 0-385-07159-0). Doubleday.

Schlesinger, Arthur M., Jr. Robert Kennedy & His Times. 1978. 19.95 (ISBN 0-395-24897-3); ltd. ed. 100.00 (ISBN 0-395-27394-3). HM.

Wofford, Harris. Of Kennedys & Kings: Making Sense of the Sixties. 496p. 1980. 17.50 (ISBN 0-374-22432-3). FS&G.

KENNEDY, ROSE FITZGERALD, 1890-

Church, Carol B. Rose Kennedy: No Time for Tears. Bender, David L. & Mc Cuen, Gary E., eds. (Focus on Famous Women Ser.). (Illus.). (gr. 3-9). 1976. 6.95 (ISBN 0-912616-44-X); read-along cassette 9.95 (ISBN 0-89908-243-2). Greenhaven.

Eldred, Patricia M. Rose Kennedy. LC 75-1119. (Creative Education Closeup Bks.). (Illus.). 32p. (gr. 3-6). 1975. PLB 5.95 (ISBN 0-87191-423-9). Creative Ed.

Kennedy, Rose Fitzgerald. Times to Remember. LC 73-79682. 552p. 1974. 12.50 (ISBN 0-385-01625-5). Doubleday.

KENNEDY FAMILY

Adler, Bill. The Kennedy Children: Triumphs & Tragedies. 320p. 1980. 13.95 (ISBN 0-531-09933-4). Watts.

Allen, Gary. Ted Kennedy: In Over His Head. 144p. Date not set. pap. 4.95 (ISBN 0-686-31147-7). Concord Pr.

Aschbumer, Steve. Ted Kennedy. 1981. lib. bdg. 7.95 (ISBN 0-8172-0430-X). Raintree Pubs.

Brown, Gene, ed. The Kennedys: A New York Times Profile. LC 80-10744. (Illus.). 256p. 1980. lib. bdg. 12.98 (ISBN 0-405-13142-9). Arno.

Rust, Zad. Teddy Bare: The Last of the Kennedy Clan. LC 79-25329. 1971. pap. 4.95 (ISBN 0-88279-109-5). Western Islands.

KENNEDY ROUND, GENEVA, 1964-1967

Evans, John W. Kennedy Round in American Trade Policy: The Twilight of the GATT? LC 77-139725. (Center for International Affairs Ser). 1971. 18.50x (ISBN 0-674-50275-2). Harvard U Pr.

Preeg, Ernest H. Traders & Diplomats: An Analysis of the Kennedy Round of Negotiations Under the General Agreement on Tariffs & Trade. LC 69-19693. 1970. 12.95 (ISBN 0-8157-7176-2). Brookings.

KENNELLY-HEAVISIDE LAYER

see Ionosphere

KENNELS

Unkelbach, Kurt. How to Make Money in Dogs. LC 74-2591. (Illus.). 128p. (gr. 5 up). 1974. 5.95 (ISBN 0-396-06969-X). Dodd.

KENNET AND AVON CANAL

Clew, Kenneth R. The Kennet & Avon Canal. (Inland Waterways Histories Ser.). (Illus.). 1973. 16.95 (ISBN 0-7153-5939-8). David & Charles.

KENNETT, WHITE, BP. OF PETERBOROUGH, 1660-1728

Bennett, Gareth V. White Kennett, 1660-1728. LC 57-2086. (Church Historical Society Ser.: No. 69). 1957. 17.50x (ISBN 0-8401-5069-5). Allenson-Breckinridge.

KENNY, ELIZABETH, 1886-1952

Cohn, Victor. Sister Kenny: The Woman Who Challenged the Doctors. LC 75-15401. (Illus.). 320p. 1976. 16.50 (ISBN 0-8166-0755-9). U of Minn Pr.

KENOSIS (THEOLOGY)

see Incarnation

KENSINGTON, ENGLAND

Borer, Mary C. Two Villages: Story of Chelsea & Kensington. (Illus.). 288p. 1974. 12.50 (ISBN 0-491-01061-3). Transatlantic.

KENSINGTON RUNE STONE

Blegen, Theodore C. Kensington Rune Stone: New Light on an Old Riddle. LC 68-66739. (Illus.). 212p. 1968. 7.50 (ISBN 0-87351-044-5). Minn Hist.

Holand, Hjalmar R. Norse Discoveries & Explorations in North America, Leif Ericson to the Kensington Stone. LC 68-14764. Orig. Title: Westward from Vinland. 1969. pap. 4.50 (ISBN 0-486-22014-1). Dover.

KENT, JAMES, 1763-1847

Horton, John T. James Kent: A Study in Conservatism, 1763-1847. LC 76-84189. (American Scene, Comments & Commentators Ser.). 1969. Repr. of 1939 ed. lib. bdg. 35.00 (ISBN 0-306-71502-3). Da Capo.

Kent, James. Memoirs & Letters of James Kent. Kent, William, ed. LC 78-99481. (American Public Figures Ser). 1970. Repr. of 1898 ed. lib. bdg. 32.50 (ISBN 0-306-71847-2). Da Capo.

KENT, CONNECTICUT–HISTORY

Grant, Charles S. Democracy in the Connecticut Frontier Town of Kent. LC 77-120201. (Columbia University. Studies in the Social Sciences: No. 601). Repr. of 1961 ed. 12.50 (ISBN 0-404-51601-7). AMS Pr.

--Democracy in the Connecticut Frontier Town of Kent. 1972. pap. 2.95 (ISBN 0-393-00639-5, Norton Lib). Norton.

KENT, ENGLAND

Glover, Judith. The Place Names of Kent. 1976. 19.95 (ISBN 0-7134-3069-9, Pub. by Batsford England). David & Charles.

Whyman, John & Bruchey, Stuart, eds. Aspects of Holidaymaking & Resort Development with in the Isle of Thanet, with Particular Reference to Margate, Circa 1736 to Circa 1840. LC 80-2834. (Dissertations in European Economic History II). (Illus.). 1981. lib. bdg. 75.00x two vols. (ISBN 0-405-14018-5). Arno.

KENT, ENGLAND–DESCRIPTION AND TRAVEL

Glover, Judith. Batsford Colour Book of Kent. 1976. 11.95 (ISBN 0-7134-3153-9, Pub. by Batsford England). David & Charles.

Hall, Hammond. Mr. Pickwick's Kent. LC 74-28420. 1899. 17.50 (ISBN 0-8414-4707-1). Folcroft.

Hughes, Pennethorne. Kent: A Shell Guide. (Shell Guide Ser.). (Illus.). 176p. 1969. 7.95 (ISBN 0-571-09091-5, Pub. by Faber & Faber). Merrimack Bk Serv.

Winbolt, S. E. Kent. Repr. of 1929 ed. 20.00 (ISBN 0-89987-031-7). Darby Bks.

KENT, ENGLAND–HISTORY

Crouch, Marcus & Bergess, Wyn. Victorian & Edwardian Kent. 1974. 19.95 (ISBN 0-7134-2886-4, Pub. by Batsford England). David & Charles.

Larking, Lambert B., ed. Proceedings Principally in the County of Kent, in Connection with the Parliaments Called in 1640, & Especially with the Committee of Religion Appointed in That Year. (Camden Society, London. Publications, First Series: No. 80a). Repr. of 1862 ed. 28.00 (ISBN 0-404-50180-X). Ams Pr.

Roake, Margaret. Essays in Kentish History. Whyman, John, ed. (Illus.). 315p. 1973. 25.00x (ISBN 0-7146-2956-1, F Cass Co). Biblio Dist.

Sandys, Charles. A History of Gavelkind & Other Remarkable Customs in the County of Kent. xvi, 352p. 1981. Repr. of 1851 ed. lib. bdg. 35.00x (ISBN 0-8377-1117-7). Rothman.

Witney, K. P. The Jutish Forest: A Study of the Weald of Kent from 450 to 1380 AD. (Illus.). 1976. text ed. 37.75x (ISBN 0-485-11165-9, Athlone Pr). Humanities.

KENT STATE UNIVERSITY

Aptheker, Bettina, et al. Kent State Ten Years After. Bills, Scott, ed. (Illus.). 88p. (Orig.). 1980. pap. 3.95 (ISBN 0-933522-04-5). Kent Popular.

Davies, Peter. The Truth About Kent State. (Illus.). 241p. 1973. 10.00 (ISBN 0-374-27938-1). FS&G.

Hensley, Thomas R. & Lewis, Jerry M. Kent State & May 4th: A Social Science Perspective. 1978. pap. text ed. 8.95 (ISBN 0-8403-1856-1). Kendall-Hunt.

Kelner, Joseph & Munves, James. The Kent State Cover up. LC 77-11813. (Illus.). 1980. 15.00 (ISBN 0-06-012282-X, HarpT). Har-Row.

Michener, James A. Kent State: What Happened & Why. (Illus.). 1978. pap. 2.75 (ISBN 0-449-23869-5, Crest). Fawcett.

O'Neil, Robert M., et al. No Heroes, No Villains: New Perspectives on Kent State & Jackson State. LC 72-6044. (Higher Education Ser.). 1972. 13.95x (ISBN 0-87589-145-4). Jossey-Bass.

Payne, J. Gregory. Mayday - Kent State. 208p. 1981. pap. text ed. 8.95 (ISBN 0-8403-2393-X). Kendall-Hunt.

Report of the President's Commission on Campus Unrest: Including the Killings at Jackson State & Kent State Tragedy. LC 71-139710. 537p. 1970. 5.95 (ISBN 0-405-01712-X). Arno.

Tompkins, Phillip K. & Anderson, Elaine V. Communication Crisis at Kent State: A Case Study. LC 77-161215. (Illus.). 186p. 1971. 22.50x (ISBN 0-677-03970-0). Gordon.

Whitney, R. W. The Kent State Massacre. new ed. Rahmas, D. Steve, ed. (Events of Our Times Ser.). 32p. 1975. lib. bdg. 2.95 incl. catalog cards (ISBN 0-686-11233-4); pap. 1.50 vinyl laminated covers (ISBN 0-686-11234-2). SamHar Pr.

KENTON, SIMON, 1755-1836

Eckert, Allan W. The Frontiersmen. 1967. 17.50 (ISBN 0-316-20856-6). Little.

Jahns, Patricia. Violent Years. 8.50 (ISBN 0-8038-7726-9). Hastings.

Kenton, Edna. Simon Kenton, His Life & Period, 1755-1836. LC 70-146406. (First American Frontier Ser). (Illus.). 1971. Repr. of 1930 ed. 21.00 (ISBN 0-405-02865-2). Arno.

Wilkie, Katharine E. Simon Kenton: Young Trail Blazer. LC 60-8882. (Childhood of Famous Americans Ser.). (Illus.). (gr. 3-7). 1960. 3.95 (ISBN 0-672-50166-X). Bobbs.

KENTON, STAN

Easton, Carol. Straight Ahead: The Story of Stan Kenton. (Quality Paperbacks Ser.). (Illus.). 252p. 1981. pap. 7.95 (ISBN 0-306-80152-3). Da Capo.

Lee, William F. Stan Kenton: Artistry in Rhythm. (Illus.). 832p. 29.95 (ISBN 0-686-72145-4). Creative Pr.

KENTUCKY

see also names of cities, towns, counties etc. in Kentucky

Boles, John B. Religion in Antebellum Kentucky. LC 76-4434. (Kentucky Bicentennial Bookshelf Ser.). 160p. 1976. 6.95 (ISBN 0-8131-0227-8). U Pr of Ky.

Bowman, Mary J. & Haynes, W. Warren. Resources & People in East Kentucky: Problems & Potentials of a Lagging Economy. LC 77-86389. (Resources for the Future, Inc. Publications). Repr. of 1963 ed. 47.50 (ISBN 0-404-60328-9). AMS Pr.

Clark, Thomas D. Agrarian Kentucky. LC 77-73703. (Kentucky Bicentennial Bookshelf Ser.). (Illus.). 152p. 1977. 6.95 (ISBN 0-8131-0237-5). U Pr of Ky.

Collins, Lewis. Historical Sketches of Kentucky Embracing Its History, Antiquities, & Natural Curiosities, Geographical, Statistical, & Geological Description. LC 77-146385. (First American Frontier Ser). (Illus.). 1971. Repr. of 1848 ed. 27.00 (ISBN 0-405-02836-9). Arno.

Edmonds, Thomas & Ramey, Walter. Kentucky Pre-License Real Estate Manual. 2nd ed. 1977. pap. text ed. 12.00 (ISBN 0-89493-001-X). Realty Train.

Ellis, John H. Medicine in Kentucky. LC 76-51156. (Kentucky Bicentennial Bookshelf Ser.). (Illus.). 112p. 1977. 5.95 (ISBN 0-8131-0232-4). U Pr of Ky.

Federal Writers' Project. Kentucky: A Guide to the Bluegrass State. 492p. 1939. Repr. 45.00 (ISBN 0-403-02168-5). Somerset Pub.

Giles, Janice H. The Kentuckians. 1980. lib. bdg. 15.95 (ISBN 0-8161-3050-7, Large Print Bks). G K Hall.

Harvey, Curtis E. The Economics of Kentucky Coal. LC 76-51160. (Illus.). 192p. 1977. 13.00x (ISBN 0-8131-1358-X). U Pr of Ky.

Kentucky. 28.00 (ISBN 0-89770-093-7). Curriculum Info Ctr.

McMurtrie, D. C. Check List of Kentucky Imprints, 1811-1820, with Notes in Supplement to the Check List of 1787-1810. Allen, A. H., ed. Repr. of 1939 ed. 12.00 (ISBN 0-527-01903-8). Kraus Repr.

Wagstaff, Ann. Index to the Eighteen Ten Census of Kentucky. LC 80-66547. 230p. 1980. 18.50 (ISBN 0-8063-0896-6). Genealog Pub.

Woods, Lewis C., Jr., ed. Index of Kentucky & Virginia Maps, 1562 to 1900. LC 76-3233. 1976. 15.00 (ISBN 0-916968-04-9). Kentucky Hist.

KENTUCKY–ANTIQUITIES

Dunnell, R. C. The Prehistory of Fishtrap, Kentucky. LC 72-90078. (Publications in Anthropology: No. 75). 1972. pap. 7.00 (ISBN 0-685-64463-4). Yale U Anthro.

Knight, Thomas A. & Greene, Nancy L. Country Estates of the Blue Grass. 1973. Repr. of 1904 ed. 15.95 (ISBN 0-87642-010-2). Henry Clay.

KENTUCKY-DESCRIPTION AND TRAVEL

Allen, James L. Blue-Grass Region of Kentucky: And Other Kentucky Articles. LC 74-39712. (Essay Index Reprint Ser.). Repr. of 1892 ed. 23.00 (ISBN 0-8369-2734-6). Arno.

Beckman, Tom. Central Kentucky Companion. 135p. 1980. pap. 4.95 (ISBN 0-937204-02-1). T Beckman & Assoc.

Coleman, J. Winston. Historic Kentucky. 1968. 9.95 (ISBN 0-87642-000-5). Henry Clay.

Collins, Lewis. Historical Sketches of Kentucky Embracing Its History, Antiquities, & Natural Curiosities, Geographical, Statistical, & Geological Description. LC 77-146385. (First American Frontier Ser). (Illus.). 1971. Repr. of 1848 ed. 27.00 (ISBN 0-405-02836-9). Arno.

Dilamarter, Ronald R. & Hoffman, Wayne L., eds. Field Trip Guide: Nineteen Eighty AAG Louisville Meeting. LC 80-65645. (Illus.). 96p. 1980. pap. 2.00 (ISBN 0-89291-140-9). Assn Am Geographers.

Mendes, Guy, ed. Local Light, Photographs Made in Kentucky. (Illus.). 1976. pap. 5.00 (ISBN 0-917788-02-8). Gnomon Pr.

Owen, Kathryn. Old Graveyards of Clark Co, Ky. (Illus.). 1975. 10.00 (ISBN 0-686-20888-9). Polyanthos.

Sehlinger, Bob & Underwood, Wes. A Guide to the Float Fishing Streams of Kentucky. (Illus., Orig.). 1980. pap. 9.95 (ISBN 0-89732-006-9). Thomas Pr.

State Industrial Directories Corp. Kentucky State Industrial Directory, Nineteen Eighty-One. Date not set. pap. price not set (ISBN 0-89910-042-2). State Indus D.

Trabue, Daniel. Westward into Kentucky: The Narrative of Daniel Trabue. Young, Raymond C., ed. LC 80-51022. (Illus.). 1981. 17.00 (ISBN 0-8131-1410-1). U Pr of Ky.

Wharton, Mary E. & Bowen, Edward L. The Horse World of the Bluegrass, Vol. 1. Denbo, Bruce F. & Wharton, Mary E., eds. 246p. 1980. 30.00 (ISBN 0-934554-00-5). Host Assoc.

White, Sheryl. Beautiful Kentucky. Shangle, Robert D., ed. LC 80-25924. (Illus.). 72p. 1980. 14.95 (ISBN 0-915796-67-8); pap. 7.95 (ISBN 0-915796-66-X). Beautiful Am.

KENTUCKY-DESCRIPTION AND TRAVEL-GUIDEBOOKS

Federal Writers' Project. Kentucky: A Guide to the Bluegrass State. 492p. 1939. Repr. 45.00 (ISBN 0-403-02168-5). Somerset Pub.

Lander, Arthur B., Jr. A Guide to the Backpacking & Day Hiking Trails of Kentucky. LC 79-16188. (Orig.). 1979. pap. 9.95 (ISBN 0-89732-002-6). Thomas Pr.

--A Guide to the Kentucky Outdoors. LC 78-71189. (Orig.). 1978. pap. 9.95 (ISBN 0-89732-001-8). Thomas Pr.

Osler, Jack. Fifty Best Mini-Trips for Kentucky. (Illus.). 1977. pap. 2.50 (ISBN 0-89645-001-5). Media Ventures.

Sehlinger, Bob. A Canoeing & Kayaking Guide to the Streams of Kentucky. LC 78-9837. (Illus.). 1978. pap. 12.95 (ISBN 0-89732-000-X). Thomas Pr.

Strode, William. The Complete Guide to Kentucky Horse Country. LC 80-67138. (Orig.). 1980. 4.95 (ISBN 0-937222-00-3). Classic Pub.

KENTUCKY-GENEALOGY

Ardery, Mrs. William B. Kentucky Court & Other Records, Vol. 2: Wills, Deeds, Orders, Suits, Church Minutes, Marriages, Old Bibles & Tombstone Inscriptions. LC 65-24115. 1979. Repr. of 1932 ed. 12.50 (ISBN 0-8063-0510-X). Genealog Pub.

Clift, G. Glenn. Kentucky Marriages, 1797-1865. LC 66-27027. 1978. Repr. of 1940 ed. 15.00 (ISBN 0-8063-0076-0). Genealog Pub.

Clift, Glenn G. Kentucky Obituaries, 1787-1854. LC 76-57789. 1979. 15.00 (ISBN 0-8063-0758-7). Genealog Pub.

Davis, Elsie S. Descendants of Jacob Young of Shelby County, Kentucky: Including President Harry S. Truman. LC 80-70981. (Illus.). 171p. (Orig.). 1980. 16.00 (ISBN 0-9605618-1-1); pap. 9.00 (ISBN 0-9605618-0-3). E S Davis.

Donnelly, Sr. Mary L. The Buckman Family of Maryland & Kentucky. LC 79-90465. (Illus.). 530p. 1979. 32.00 (ISBN 0-939142-04-X). Donnelly.

--Genealogy of Thomas Hill & Rebecca Miles. LC 79-31237. (Illus.). 380p. 1971. 25.00 (ISBN 0-939142-00-7). Donnelly.

--Rapier, Hayden & Allied Families: Colonial Maryland & Kentucky. LC 78-656670. (Illus.). 595p. 1978. 30.00 (ISBN 0-939142-03-1). Donnelly.

Donnelly, Sr. Mary Louise. Imprints Sixteen Hundred Eight to Nineteen Eighty, Hamilton, Allied Families. LC 80-84574. (Illus.). 660p. 1980. 38.00 (ISBN 0-939142-05-8). Donnelly.

Fowler, Ila E. Kentucky Pioneers & Their Descendants. LC 67-16864. 1978. Repr. of 1951 ed. 17.50 (ISBN 0-8063-0150-3). Genealog Pub.

Hall, C. Mitchel, ed. Jenny Wiley Country, Vol. III. LC 72-79119. (Illus.). 1979. 22.95 (ISBN 0-685-39469-7). C M Hall.

Hathaway, Beverly W. Genealogical Research Sources in Kentucky. LC 77-87435. (Illus.). lib. bdg. 10.00 (ISBN 0-89593-161-3). Accelerated Index.

Heinemann, Charles B. First Census of Kentucky, 1790. LC 66-16627. (Illus.). 1976. Repr. of 1940 ed. 10.00 (ISBN 0-8063-0175-9). Genealog Pub.

Jackson, Ronald V. & Teeples, Gary R. Index to Kentucky Wills to 1851: The Testators. LC 77-86052. lib. bdg. 28.00 (ISBN 0-89593-156-7). Accelerated Index.

--Kentucky Census Index 1810. LC 77-85932. (Illus.). lib. bdg. 29.00 (ISBN 0-89593-044-7). Accelerated Index.

--Kentucky Census Index 1820. LC 77-85933. (Illus.). lib. bdg. 32.00 (ISBN 0-89593-045-5). Accelerated Index.

--Kentucky Census Index 1830. LC 77-85934. (Illus.). lib. bdg. 36.00 (ISBN 0-89593-046-3). Accelerated Index.

--Kentucky Census Index 1840. LC 77-85936. (Illus.). lib. bdg. 57.00 (ISBN 0-89593-047-1). Accelerated Index.

--Kentucky Census Index 1850. LC 77-85937. (Illus.). lib. bdg. 61.00 (ISBN 0-89593-048-X). Accelerated Index.

Kozee, William C. Early Families of Eastern & Southeastern Kentucky & Their Descendants. LC 73-9089. (Illus.). 1979. Repr. of 1961 ed. 30.00 (ISBN 0-8063-0577-0). Genealog Pub.

Quisenberry, Anderson C. Revolutionary Soldiers in Kentucky. LC 68-22328. 1974. Repr. of 1896 ed. 13.50 (ISBN 0-8063-0283-6). Genealog Pub.

Railey, William E. History of Woodford County, Kentucky. LC 74-21773. (Illus.). 449p. 1975. Repr. of 1938 ed. 18.50 (ISBN 0-8063-7999-5). Regional.

Rice, Phillip A., et al, eds. Early Marriage Records of Casey Co., Ky. 1807-1915, Vols. 1 & 2. 1977. 17.50 (ISBN 0-686-22209-1). Polyanthos.

Roberts, Leonard. Sang Branch Settlers: Tales & Songs of an Eastern Kentucky Family. text ed. 12.00 (ISBN 0-933302-05-3); pap. text ed. 7.95 (ISBN 0-933302-06-1). Pikeville Coll.

Slone, Verna M. What My Heart Wants to Tell. LC 78-31688. (Illus.). 1980. pap. 1.95 (ISBN 0-06-080510-2, P510, PL). Har-Row.

KENTUCKY-HISTORY

Abernethy, Thomas P. Three Virginia Frontiers. 6.50 (ISBN 0-8446-1001-1). Peter Smith.

Ardery, Mrs. William B. Kentucky Court & Other Records, Vol. 1. LC 65-24115. 206p. 1977. Repr. of 1926 ed. 12.00 (ISBN 0-8063-0005-1). Genealog Pub.

Baker, Jim. Forts in the Forest: Kentucky in the Year of the Bloody Sevens. LC 75-39915. (Illus.). 48p. (Orig.). 1975. pap. 1.95 (ISBN 0-914482-11-4). Ohio Hist Soc.

Boultinghouse, Marquis E. Silversmiths, Jewelers, Clock & Watchmakers of Kentucky 1785-1900. (Illus.). 368p. 1980. 39.95x (ISBN 0-9604358-0-8). M E Boultinghouse.

Brashers, Charles. A Snug Little Purchase: How Richard Henderson Bought Kaintuckee from the Cherokees in 1775. LC 78-74150. (Illus.). 1979. 7.95 (ISBN 0-933362-01-3); pap. 4.95 (ISBN 0-933362-02-1). Assoc Creative Writers.

Channing, Steven A. Kentucky. (The States & the Nation Ser.). (Illus.). 1977. 12.95 (ISBN 0-393-05654-6, Co-Pub by AASLH). Norton.

Clark, Thomas D. Historic Maps of Kentucky. LC 79-4003. (Illus.). 1979. 27.50 (ISBN 0-8131-0097-6). U Pr of Ky.

--Kentucky. LC 65-23498. 1965. pap. 2.95 (ISBN 0-8077-1164-0). Tchrs Coll.

--The Kentucky. (Rivers of America Ser.). (Illus.). 7.95 (ISBN 0-87642-004-8). Henry Clay.

Clift, G. Glenn. Second Census of Kentucky: 1800. LC 66-19191. 1976. Repr. of 1954 ed. 17.50 (ISBN 0-8063-0077-9). Genealog Pub.

Coleman, J. Winston, Jr. Kentucky: A Pictorial History. 2nd ed. LC 74-160043. (Illus.). 256p. 1972. 20.00 (ISBN 0-8131-0092-5). U Pr of Ky.

Coleman, John W., Jr. Slavery Times in Kentucky. LC 40-31785. (Basic Afro-American Reprint Library Ser). (Illus.). 1970. Repr. of 1940 ed. 18.50 (ISBN 0-384-09535-6). Johnson Repr.

Collins, Lewis. Historical Sketches of Kentucky Embracing Its History, Antiquities, & Natural Curiosities, Geographical, Statistical, & Geological Description. LC 77-146385. (First American Frontier Ser). (Illus.). 1971. Repr. of 1848 ed. 27.00 (ISBN 0-405-02836-9). Arno.

--History of Kentucky. (Illus.). 1968. Repr. of 1847 ed. buckram 12.50 (ISBN 0-87642-001-3). Henry Clay.

Collins, Lewis & Collins, Richard H. A History of Kentucky. Set. 80.00 (ISBN 0-89308-168-X); Vol. 1, 683 Pp. (ISBN 0-89308-166-3); Vol. 2, 804 Pp. (ISBN 0-89308-167-1). Southern Hist Pr.

Coulter, E. Merton. The Civil War & Readjustment in Kentucky. 1926. 8.50 (ISBN 0-8446-1131-X). Peter Smith.

Crowe-Carraco, Carol. Big Sandy. LC 78-58126. (Kentucky Bicentennial Bookshelf Ser.). (Illus.). 152p. 1979. 6.95 (ISBN 0-8131-0234-0). U Pr of Ky.

Evans, Herndon J. The Newspaper Press in Kentucky. LC 76-24340. (Kentucky Bicentennial Bookshelf Ser.). (Illus.). 138p. 1976. 6.95 (ISBN 0-8131-0221-9). U Pr of Ky.

Fairhurst, Richard E. The Fairhurst Essays: A Public Look at a Private Memoir. (Illus.). 404p. 1981. 14.95 (ISBN 0-935284-20-6). Patrice Pr.

Filson, John. Discovery, Settlement & Present State of Kentucke. 7.00 (ISBN 0-8446-2058-0). Peter Smith.

Fuson, Henry H. Ballads of the Kentucky Highlands. 219p. 1980. Repr. of 1931 ed. text ed. 25.00 (ISBN 0-8492-4706-3). R West.

Green, Thomas M. The Spanish Conspiracy: A Review of Early Spanish Movements in the South-West. Repr. of 1891 ed. 7.50 (ISBN 0-8446-1207-3). Peter Smith.

Hall, C. Mitchel, ed. Jenny Wiley Country, Vol. III. LC 72-79119. (Illus.). 1979. 22.95 (ISBN 0-685-39469-7). C M Hall.

Hammack, James W., Jr. Kentucky & the Second American Revolution: The War of 1812. LC 75-41986. (Kentucky Bicentennial Bookshelf Ser.). (Illus.). 132p. 1976. 6.95 (ISBN 0-8131-0216-2). U Pr of Ky.

Harding, Margery, compiled by. George Rogers Clark & His Men: Military Records, 1778-1784. LC 80-82439. 225p. 1981. 25.00 (ISBN 0-916968-09-X). Kentucky Hist.

Harrison, Lowell. The Civil War in Kentucky. LC 75-3545. (The Kentucky Bicentennial Bookshelf Ser.). (Illus.). 136p. 1980. Repr. of 1975 ed. 6.95 (ISBN 0-8131-0209-X). U Pr of Ky.

Harrison, Lowell H. The Antislavery Movement in Kentucky. LC 77-92923. (Kentucky Bicentennial Bookshelf Ser.). 136p. 1978. 6.95 (ISBN 0-8131-0243-X). U Pr of Ky.

Harrison, Lowell H. & Dawson, Nelson L., eds. A Kentucky Sampler: Essays from the Filson Club History Quarterly, 1926 to 1976. LC 77-76471. 452p. 1980. Repr. of 1977 ed. 20.00x (ISBN 0-8131-1360-1). U Pr of Ky.

Heck, Frank H. Proud Kentuckian: John C. Breckinridge, 1821-1875. LC 76-9502. (Kentucky Bicentennial Bookshelf Ser.). 184p. 1976. 6.95 (ISBN 0-8131-0217-0). U Pr of Ky.

Heinemann, Charles B. First Census of Kentucky, 1790. LC 66-16627. (Illus.). 1976. Repr. of 1940 ed. 10.00 (ISBN 0-8063-0175-9). Genealog Pub.

History of Fayette & Hardeman Counties. 1979. Repr. 22.50 (ISBN 0-89308-112-4). Southern Hist Pr.

Hood, Fred J., ed. Kentucky: Its History & Heritage. LC 77-82469. (Illus., Orig.). 1978. pap. text ed. 6.95x (ISBN 0-88273-019-3). Forum Pr MO.

Horton, John B. Not Without Struggle. 1978. 6.95 (ISBN 0-533-03649-6). Vantage.

Ireland, Robert M. The County Courts in Antebellum Kentucky. LC 71-160045. 208p. 1972. 14.00x (ISBN 0-8131-1257-5). U Pr of Ky.

--The County in Kentucky History. LC 76-4436. (Kentucky Bicentennial Bookshelf Ser.). (Illus.). 104p. 1976. 6.95 (ISBN 0-8131-0229-4). U Pr of Ky.

--Little Kingdoms: The Counties of Kentucky, 1850-1891. LC 76-24341. (Illus.). 200p. 1977. 13.00x (ISBN 0-8131-1351-2). U Pr of Ky.

Irvin, Helen D. Women in Kentucky. LC 77-92924. (Ketucky Bicentennial Bookshelf Ser.). (Illus.). 144p. 1979. 6.95 (ISBN 0-8131-0239-1). U Pr of Ky.

Jillson, Willard R. Kentucky Land Grants: A Systematic Index to All of the Land Grants Recorded in Frankfort Ky. 1782-1924, 2 vols. LC 75-148534. (Filson Club Publications Ser.: No. 33). (Illus.). 1971. Repr. of 1925 ed. Set. 60.00 (ISBN 0-8063-0477-4). Genealog Pub.

Johnson, Lewis F. Famous Kentucky Trails & Tragedies: 1915 Study of Famous Trials in the 1800's. 1972. Repr. of 1915 ed. 9.95 (ISBN 0-87642-008-0). Henry Clay.

Johnson, William S. River Boy from Kentucky. 1978. 12.50 (ISBN 0-533-03132-X). Vantage.

Kelly, Mary Ann. My Old Kentucky Home, Good night. 1978. 15.00 (ISBN 0-682-49143-8). Exposition.

Kozee, William C. Pioneer Families of Eastern & Southeastern Kentucky. LC 73-9090. 1980. Repr. of 1957 ed. 15.00 (ISBN 0-8063-0576-2). Genealog Pub.

Lafferty, Maude W. Lure of Kentucky: A Historical Guide Book. LC 71-153018. (Illus.). 1971. Repr. of 1939 ed. 22.00 (ISBN 0-8103-3344-9). Gale.

Lyons, John A. Historical Sketches of Parish of St. Bernard of Clairvaux on Casey Creek, Kentucky. (Illus.). 1979. pap. 5.00 (ISBN 0-934906-02-5). R J Liederbach.

McAdams, Mrs. Harry K. Kentucky Pioneer & Court Records. LC 67-28612. 1975. Repr. of 1929 ed. 15.00 (ISBN 0-8063-0217-8). Genealog Pub.

M'Clung, John A. Sketches of Western Adventure. LC 76-90184. (Mass Violence in America Ser). Repr. of 1832 ed. 13.00 (ISBN 0-405-01326-4). Arno.

McKee, Lewis W. & Bond, Lydia K. History of Anderson County: Kentucky. LC 75-15200. (Illus.). 1975. Repr. of 1937 ed. 13.50 (ISBN 0-8063-8004-7). Regional.

McMurtry, Richard K. John McMurtry & the American Indian: A Frontiersman in the Struggle for the Ohio Valley. LC 80-7469. (Illus., Orig.). 1980. pap. 9.95 (ISBN 0-936012-05-6). Current Issues.

Mattingly, M. R. The Catholic Church on the Kentucky Frontier: 1785-1812. LC 73-3579. (Catholic University of America. Studies in American Church History: No. 25). Repr. of 1936 ed. 21.45 (ISBN 0-404-57775-X). AMS Pr.

Owen, Kathryn. Old Graveyards of Clark Co, Ky. (Illus.). 1975. 10.00 (ISBN 0-686-20888-9). Polyanthos.

Perrin, W. H. History of Christian County, Kentucky, Historical & Biographical. 656p. 1979. 32.50 (ISBN 0-89308-165-5). Southern Hist Pr.

--History of Fayette County, Kentucky, with an Outline Sketch of the Bluegrass Region. 905p. 1979. 40.00 (ISBN 0-89308-163-9). Southern Hist Pr.

--History of Todd County, Kentucky. Battle, J. H., ed. 385p. 1979. Repr. of 1884 ed. 30.00 (ISBN 0-89308-162-0). Southern Hist Pr.

--History of Trigg County, Historical & Biographical. (Illus.). 293p. 1979. 27.50 (ISBN 0-89308-164-7). Southern Hist Pr.

Perrin, W. H., et al. Kentucky, a History of the State, 10 vols. Incl. The General History. (Illus.). 632p. Repr. of 1885 ed. 37.50 (ISBN 0-89308-132-9); The First Edition. (Illus.). 342p. Repr. of 1885 ed. 32.50 (ISBN 0-89308-133-7); The Second Edition. (Illus.). 421p. Repr. of 1885 ed. 37.50 (ISBN 0-89308-134-5); The Third Edition. (Illus.). 511p. Repr. of 1886 ed. 37.50 (ISBN 0-89308-135-3); The Fourth Edition. (Illus.). 415p. Repr. of 1887 ed. 35.00 (ISBN 0-89308-136-1); The Fifth Edition. (Illus.). 234p. Repr. of 1887 ed. 25.00 (ISBN 0-89308-137-X); The Sixth Edition. (Illus.). 244p. Repr. of 1887 ed. 22.50 (ISBN 0-89308-138-8); The Seventh Edition. (Illus.). 283p. Repr. of 1887 ed. 32.50 (ISBN 0-89308-139-6); The Eighth Edition-A, 2 pts. (Illus.). Repr. of 1888 ed. Pt. A. 25.00 (ISBN 0-89308-140-X); Pt. B, 286p. 35.00 (ISBN 0-89308-141-8). 1979. Repr. of 1886 ed. Southern Hist Pr.

Perrin, William H. & Peter, Robert. History of Bourbon, Scott, Harrison, & Nicholas Counties, with a Brief Synopsis of the Bluegrass Region. (Illus.). 815p. 1979. Repr. of 1882 ed. 45.00 (ISBN 0-89308-142-6). Southern Hist Pr.

Railey, William E. History of Woodford County, Kentucky. LC 74-21773. (Illus.). 449p. 1975. Repr. of 1938 ed. 18.50 (ISBN 0-8063-7999-5). Regional.

Ranck, George W. Boonesborough: Its Founding, Pioneer Struggles, Indian Experiences, Transylvania Days, & Revolutionary Annals. LC 70-146414. (First American Frontier Ser). (Illus.). 1971. Repr. of 1901 ed. 17.00 (ISBN 0-405-02878-4). Arno.

Reed, Rufus M. Conquerors of the Dark Hills. 1978. 6.95 (ISBN 0-533-03701-8). Vantage.

Rice, Otis K. Frontier Kentucky. LC 75-3550. (Kentucky Bicentennial Bookshelf Ser.). (Illus.). 152p. 1975. 6.95 (ISBN 0-8131-0212-X). U Pr of Ky.

Roberts, Leonard. South from Hell-Fer Sartin. 287p. 1964. pap. 2.95 (ISBN 0-933302-13-4). Pikeville Coll.

Robertson, James R. Petitions of the Early Inhabitants of Kentucky to the General Assembly of Virginia, 1769 to 1792. 292p. 1981. Repr. of 1914 ed. 25.00 (ISBN 0-89308-206-6). Southern Hist.

--Petitions of the Early Inhabitants of Kentucky to the General Assembly of Virginia, 1769 to 1792. LC 74-146415. (First American Frontier Ser). 1971. Repr. of 1914 ed. 14.00 (ISBN 0-405-02879-2). Arno.

Roosevelt, Theodore. Winning of the West. Wish, Harvey, ed. & intro. by. 8.00 (ISBN 0-8446-2827-1). Peter Smith.

Scalf, Henry P. Kentucky's Last Frontier. 565p. 1972. Repr. of 1966 ed. 12.00 (ISBN 0-933302-11-8). Pikeville Coll.

Schulman, Robert. John Sherman Cooper: The Global Kentuckian. LC 76-9514. (Kentucky Bicentennial Bookshelf Ser.). (Illus.). 124p. 1976. 6.95 (ISBN 0-8131-0220-0). U Pr of Ky.

Shaler, Nathaniel S. Kentucky, a Pioneer Commonwealth. LC 72-3759. (American Commonwealths: No. 4). Repr. of 1885 ed. 28.75 (ISBN 0-404-57204-9). AMS Pr.

Smeal, Lee. Kentucky Historical & Biographical Index. LC 78-53697. (Illus.). Date not set. lib. bdg. price not set (ISBN 0-89593-182-6). Accelerated Index.

Sonne, Niels H. Liberal Kentucky, 1780-1828. LC 39-20412. 300p. 1968. pap. 5.00x (ISBN 0-8131-0119-0). U Pr of Ky.

Sprague, Stuart & Perkins, Elizabeth. Frankfort: A Pictorial History. LC 80-23571. (Illus.). 1980. 16.95 (ISBN 0-89865-003-8); ltd. ed. 24.95 (ISBN 0-89865-001-1). Donning Co.

Stone, Richard G., Jr. A Brittle Sword: The Kentucky Militia, 1776-1912. LC 77-76330. (Kentucky Bicentennial Bookshelf Ser.). (Illus.). 136p. 1977. 6.95 (ISBN 0-8131-0242-1). U Pr of Ky.

--Kentucky Fighting Men: 1861-1945. LC 79-57561. 1982. 6.95 (ISBN 0-8131-0249-9). U Pr of Ky.

Stuart, Jesse. Trees of Heaven. LC 80-51020. 344p. 1980. 19.50 (ISBN 0-8131-1446-2); pap. 7.00 (ISBN 0-8131-0150-6). U Pr of Ky.

Tachau, Mary K. Federal Courts in the Early Republic: Kentucky, 1789-1816. LC 78-51196. 1978. text ed. 17.50 (ISBN 0-691-04661-1). Princeton U Pr.

Tapp, Hambleton & Klotter, James C. Kentucky: Decades of Discord, 1865-1900. LC 75-30400. 1977. members only 12.50 (ISBN 0-916968-05-7); non-members 17.50 (ISBN 0-685-75668-8). Kentucky Hist.

Tapp, Hambleton & Klotter, James C., eds. The Union, the Civil War & John W. Tuttle: A Kentucky Captains Account. LC 79-89244. 1980. 20.00 (ISBN 0-916968-08-1). Kentucky Hist.

Taylor, Philip F. A Calendar of the Warrants for Land in Kentucky, Granted for Service in the French & Indian War. LC 67-28596. (Illus.). 1975. Repr. of 1917 ed. 7.50 (ISBN 0-8063-0327-1). Genealog Pub.

Vexler, R. I. Kentucky Chronology & Factbook, Vol. 17. 1978. 8.50 (ISBN 0-379-16142-7). Oceana.

Warren, Robert P. Jefferson Davis Gets His Citizenship Back. LC 80-51023. 120p. 1980. 8.75 (ISBN 0-8131-1445-4). U Pr of Ky.

Watlington, Patricia. The Partisan Spirit: Kentucky Politics, 1779-1792. (Institute of Early American History & Culture Ser.). 276p. 1972. 17.00x (ISBN 0-8078-1218-8). U of NC Pr.

Webb, Ross A. Kentucky in the Reconstruction Era. LC 78-58148. (Kentucky Bicentennial Bookshelf Ser.). 112p. 1979. 6.95 (ISBN 0-8131-0247-2). U Pr of Ky.

KENTUCKY-HISTORY-FICTION, JUVENILE

Thurman, Evelyn. A Pioneer Civil War Story for Molly & Ben. (Illus.). 1979. 4.50 (ISBN 0-533-03848-0). Vantage.

KENTUCKY-IMPRINTS

Townsend, J. W., ed. Historical Records Survey: Supplemental Check List of Kentucky Imprints, 1788-1820, Including the Original Printing of the Original Kentucky Copyright Ledger, 1800-1854. 1942. pap. 12.00 (ISBN 0-527-01925-9). Kraus Repr.

KENTUCKY-JUVENILE LITERATURE

Bailey, Bernadine. Picture Book of Kentucky. rev. ed. LC 55-8828. (Illus.). (gr. 3-5). 1967. 5.50g (ISBN 0-8075-9519-5). A Whitman.

Carpenter, Allan. Kentucky. LC 79-12696. (New Enchantment of America State Bks.). (Illus.). (gr. 4 up). 1979. PLB 10.60 (ISBN 0-516-04117-7). Childrens.

Fradin, Dennis. Kentucky: In Words & Pictures. LC 80-25810. (Young People's Stories of Our States Ser.). (Illus.). 48p. (gr. 2-5). 1981. PLB 9.25 (ISBN 0-516-03917-2). Childrens.

Steele, William O. Old Wilderness Road: An American Journey. LC 68-25197. (Illus.). (gr. 7-9). 1968. 5.95 (ISBN 0-15-257847-1, HJ). HarBraceJ.

KENTUCKY-POLITICS AND GOVERNMENT

Baldwin's Kentucky Revised Statutes, with Rules of Practice Annotated, 9 vols. 4th ed. 1969. Set. 430.00 (ISBN 0-8322-0004-2). Banks-Baldwin.

Bodley, Temple, ed. Littell's Political Transactions in & Concerning Kentucky. Bd. with Letter of George Nicholas to His Friend in Virginia; General Wilkinson's Memorial. LC 70-146375. (First American Frontier Ser). 322p. 1971. Repr. of 1926 ed. 16.00 (ISBN 0-405-02826-1). Arno.

Brickey, Kathleen F. Kentucky Criminal Law: A Treatise on Criminal Law Under the New Kentucky Penal Code. (Baldwin's Law Books). 1974. 45.00 (ISBN 0-8322-0012-3). Banks-Baldwin.

Coward, Joan W. Kentucky in the New Republic: The Process of Constitution Making. LC 77-92920. (Illus.). 232p. 1979. 17.00x (ISBN 0-8131-1380-6). U Pr of Ky.

Criminal Law of Kentucky Annotated. 1978. 35.00 (ISBN 0-8322-0020-4). Banks-Baldwin.

Dukeminier, Jesse, Jr. Perpetuities Law in Action: Kentucky Case Law & the 1960 Reform Act. LC 62-13459. (Illus.). 180p. 1962. 8.50x (ISBN 0-8131-1070-X). U Pr of Ky.

Gilmer, Wesley, ed. Kentucky Legal Forms, 6 vols. 1975. Set. 260.00 (ISBN 0-8322-0016-6). Banks-Baldwin.

Hathaway, Beverly W. Inventory of County Records of Kentucky. LC 77-87434. (Illus.). Date not set. lib. bdg. price not set (ISBN 0-89593-162-1). Accelerated Index.

Ireland, Robert M. The County in Kentucky History. LC 76-4436. (Kentucky Bicentennial Bookshelf Ser.). (Illus.). 104p. 1976. 6.95 (ISBN 0-8131-0229-4). U Pr of Ky.

Jewell, Malcolm E. Kentucky Votes: U. S. House Primary & General Elections, 1920-1960, Vol. 3. LC 63-12390. 104p. 1963. pap. 2.25x (ISBN 0-8131-0083-6). U Pr of Ky.

Kendall, Amos. Autobiography. Stickney, ed. 10.00 (ISBN 0-8446-1261-8). Peter Smith.

Kentucky Financial Institutions & Securities Law Annotated. 1975. 37.50 (ISBN 0-8322-0014-X). Banks-Baldwin.

Kentucky Revised Statutes, 21 vols. 1971. write for info (ISBN 0-672-83035-3, Bobbs-Merrill Law); 1980 suppl. avail. (ISBN 0-87215-349-5). Michie-Bobbs.

Landy, Marc Karnis. The Politics of Environmental Reform: Controlling Kentucky Strip Mining. LC 76-15907. (Resources for the Future Working Papers Ser.). 1976. pap. 8.95x (ISBN 0-8018-1888-5). Johns Hopkins.

Lyons, W. E. The Politics of City-County Merger: The Lexington-Fayette County Experience. LC 77-73706. (Illus.). 192p. 1977. 14.00x (ISBN 0-8131-1363-6). U Pr of Ky.

Meyer, Leland W. Life & Times of Colonel Richard M. Johnson of Kentucky. LC 32-11905. (Columbia University. Studies in the Social Sciences: No. 359). Repr. of 1932 ed. 31.50 (ISBN 0-404-51359-X). AMS Pr.

Murrell, David E. Kentucky Criminal Practice: A Treatise on Criminal Practice & Procedure. (Baldwin's Law Books). 1975. 45.00 (ISBN 0-8322-0013-1). Banks-Baldwin.

Nunn, Louie B. The Public Papers of Governor Louie B. Nunn, 1967-1971. Sexton, Robert F., ed. LC 74-18938. (Public Papers of the Governors of Kentucky). 640p. 1975. 28.00x (ISBN 0-8131-0601-X). U Pr of Ky.

KENTUCKY-SOCIAL LIFE AND CUSTOMS

Kinder, Alice J. Papa's Neighbors. 120p. 1979. pap. 2.50 (ISBN 0-8341-0581-0, Beacon). Nazarene.

Plunkett, H. Dudley & Bowman, Mary J. Elites & Change in the Kentucky Mountains. LC 76-160049. (Illus.). 216p. 1973. 13.50x (ISBN 0-8131-1275-3). U Pr of Ky.

Schwarzweller, Harry K., et al. Mountain Families in Transition: A Case Study of Appalachian Migration. LC 71-138090. 1971. 14.95x (ISBN 0-271-01149-1). Pa St U Pr.

Share, Allen J. Cities in the Commonwealth: Two Centuries of Urban Life in Kentucky. LC 81-51015. (Kentucky Bicentennial Bookshelf Ser.). 1982. 6.95 (ISBN 0-8131-0252-9). U Pr of Ky.

Spalding, Martin. Sketches of the Early Catholic Missions of Kentucky; from Their Commencement in 1787 to the Jubilee of 1826-7. LC 70-38548. (Religion in America, Ser. 2). 328p. 1972. Repr. of 1844 ed. 18.00 (ISBN 0-405-04087-3). Arno.

Stuart, Jesse. Trees of Heaven. LC 80-51020. 344p. 1980. 19.50 (ISBN 0-8131-1446-2); pap. 7.00 (ISBN 0-8131-0150-6). U Pr of Ky.

Thomas, Jean. Devil's Ditties: Being Stories of the Kentucky Mountain People, Told by Jean Thomas, with the Songs They Sing. LC 75-16369. (Illus.). viii, 180p. 1976. Repr. of 1931 ed. 26.00 (ISBN 0-8103-3999-4). Gale.

Tischendorf, Alfred P. & Taylor, Elisha P., eds. Diary & Journal of Richard Clough Anderson Jr., 1814-1826. LC 64-19178. 1964. 14.75 (ISBN 0-8223-0179-2). Duke.

KENTUCKY, UNIVERSITY OF

Talbert, Charles G. The University of Kentucky: The Maturing Years. LC 65-11827. (Illus.). 224p. 1965. 8.00 (ISBN 0-8131-1095-5). U Pr of Ky.

KENTUCKY AND VIRGINIA RESOLUTIONS OF 1798

see also Alien and Sedition Laws, 1798

Warfield, Ethelbert D. Kentucky Resolutions of 1798. facsimile ed. LC 69-16850. (Select Bibliographies Reprint Ser). 1894. 15.00 (ISBN 0-8369-5017-8). Arno.

KENTUCKY CAVALRY, 1ST REGIMENT, 1861-1864

Tarrant, Eastham. Wild Riders of the First Kentucky Calvary: Reprint of 1894 Union Calvalry Record. (Illus.). 1969. 12.50 (ISBN 0-87642-005-6). Henry Clay.

KENTUCKY RIFLE

Lindsay, Merrill. The Kentucky Rifle. LC 72-78520. (Illus.). 1976. 15.00 (ISBN 0-8079-0185-7). Arma Pr.

Nation Muzzle Loading Rifle Association. Muzzle Blasts: Early Years Plus Vol. I & II 1939-41. LC 74-11637. 352p. 1974. pap. 18.00 softbound (ISBN 0-87387-069-7). Shumway.

KENTUCKY VALLEY-HISTORY

Young, Chester R., ed. Westward into Kentucky: The Narrative of Daniel Trabue. Humphreys, David K. LC 80-51022. (Illus.). 224p. 1981. 17.00x (ISBN 0-8131-1410-1). U Pr of Ky.

KENYA

Bolton, Kenneth. Harambee Country: A Guide to Kenya. (Illus.). 1970. 10.50x (ISBN 0-7138-0266-9). Intl Pubns Serv.

De Veen, J. J. The Rural Access Roads Programme: Apropriate Technology in Kenya. International Labour Office, Geneva, ed. (Illus.). 175p. (Orig.). 1980. pap. 11.40 (ISBN 92-2-102204-8). Intl Labour Office.

Diesfeld, H. J. & Hecklau, H. K. Kenya - A Geomedical Monograph. (Geomedical Monograph: Vol. 5). (Illus.). 1978. 46.10 (ISBN 0-387-08729-X). Springer-Verlag.

Farrand, William R., et al. An Archaeological Investigation on the Loboi Plain, Baringo District, Kenya. (Technical Reports Ser.: No. 4). (Illus.). 1976. pap. 3.50x (ISBN 0-932206-13-1). U Mich Mus Anthro.

Leaky, L. S. Stone Age Cultures of Kenya Colony. 1971. Repr. of 1931 ed. 29.50x (ISBN 0-7146-2465-9, F Cass Co). Biblio Dist.

Leys, Norman. Kenya. 4th rev. ed. 437p. 1973. 32.50x (ISBN 0-7146-1688-5, F Cass Co). Biblio Dist.

Mockerie, Parmenas G. An African Speaks for His People. LC 74-15068. Repr. of 1934 ed. 12.50 (ISBN 0-404-12110-1). AMS Pr.

Rhoades, John. Linguistic Diversity & Language Belief in Kenya: The Special Position of Swahili. LC 77-20016. (Foreign & Comparative Studies-African Ser.: No. 26). 127p. 1977. pap. text ed. 6.00x (ISBN 0-915984-23-7). Syracuse U Foreign Comp.

Soja, Edward W. Geography of Modernization in Kenya: A Spatial Analysis of Social, Economic, & Political Growth. LC 67-26922. (Geographical Ser.: No. 2). (Illus.). 1968. 13.95x (ISBN 0-8156-2120-5). Syracuse U Pr.

Wa-Githumo, Mwangi. Land & Nationalism: The Impact of Land Expropriation & Land Grievances Upon the Rise & Development of Nationalist Movements in Kenya, 1885-1939. LC 80-5589. 502p. 1981. lib. bdg. 24.50 (ISBN 0-8191-1491-X); pap. text ed. 16.50 (ISBN 0-8191-1492-8). U Pr of Amer.

KENYA-DESCRIPTION AND TRAVEL

Belshaw, Roger. Kenya Map & Photo Studies. (Illus.). 32p. 5.00x (ISBN 0-8002-1628-8). Intl Pubns Serv.

Fletcher, Colin. The Winds of Mara. (Illus.). (gr. 7 up). 1972. 12.95 (ISBN 0-394-47091-5). Knopf.

Jones, David K. Faces of Kenya. (Illus.). 1978. 25.00 (ISBN 0-8317-3130-3, Mayflower Bks). Smith Pubs.

Lusigi, W. Planning Human Activities on Protected Natural Ecosystems. (Dissertationes Botanica: No. 48). (Illus.). 1979. pap. 20.00x (ISBN 3-7682-1214-9). Lubrecht & Cramer.

Mollison, Simon. Kenya's Coast: An Illustrated Guide. LC 72-981806. (Illus.). 159p. (Orig.). 1971. pap. 5.00x (ISBN 0-8002-1629-6). Intl Pubns Serv.

Naipaul, Shiva. North of South: An African Journey. 1980. pap. 3.95 (ISBN 0-14-004894-4). Penguin.

Robson, Peter. Mountains of Kenya. (Illus.). 1969. 6.00x (ISBN 0-8002-1732-2). Intl Pubns Serv.

Tichy, Herbert, ed. Kenya: The Magical World of Kenya. (Illus.). 1981. 29.95 (ISBN 0-686-73419-X). Ungar.

KENYA-ECONOMIC CONDITIONS

Amsden, Alice H. International Firms & Labour in Kenya: 1945-1971. 1971. 35.00x (ISBN 0-7146-2581-7). Intl Pubns Serv.

--International Firms & Labour in Kenya, 1945-1970. 186p. 1971. 26.00x (ISBN 0-7146-2581-7, F Cass Co). Biblio Dist.

Bigsten, Arne. Regional Inequality & Development: A Case Study of Kenya. 191p. 1980. text ed. 44.00x (ISBN 0-566-00382-1, Pub. by Gower Pub Co England). Renouf.

Ghai, Dharam, et al. Planning for Basic Needs in Kenya: Performance, Policies & Prospects. International Labour Office, Geneva, ed. (Illus.). 166p. (Orig.). 1979. pap. 11.40 (ISBN 9-22-102171-8). Intl Labour Office.

Harbeson, John W. Nation-Building in Kenya: The Role of Land Reform. LC 72-80567. 421p. 1973. text ed. 15.75x (ISBN 0-8101-0389-3). Northwestern U Pr.

Hazlewood, Arthur. The Economy of Kenya: The Kenyatta Era. (Economies of the World Ser.). (Illus.). 242p. 1979. text ed. 29.95x (ISBN 0-19-877101-0); pap. text ed. 12.95x (ISBN 0-19-877102-9). Oxford U Pr.

Heyer, Judith, ed. Agricultural Development in Kenya: An Economic Assessment. Senga, W. M. & Maitha, J. K. (Illus.). 1977. 17.95x (ISBN 0-19-572377-5). Oxford U Pr.

Kaplinsky, Raphael, ed. Readings on the Multinational Corporation in Kenya. 326p. 1978. text ed. 24.95x (ISBN 0-19-572446-1). Oxford U Pr.

King, John R. Stabilization Policy in an African Setting Nineteen Sixty-Three to Seventy-Three. LC 79-670197. (Studies in the Economics of Africa). 1979. text ed. 25.95x (ISBN 0-435-97375-4); pap. text ed. 10.95x (ISBN 0-686-65420-X). Heinemann Ed.

Kitching, Gavin. Class & Economic Change in Kenya: The Making of an African Petite Bourgeoisie, 1905-1970. LC 79-21804. 448p. 1980. text ed. 39.50x (ISBN 0-300-02385-5). Yale U Pr.

Langdon, Steven W. Multinational Corporations in the Political Economy of Kenya. 220p. 1981. 27.50x (ISBN 0-312-55254-8). St Martin.

Leys, Colin. Underdevelopment in Kenya: The Political Economy of Neo-Colonialism, 1964-71. LC 74-76387. 1975. 20.00x (ISBN 0-520-02731-0); pap. 7.95x (ISBN 0-520-02770-1). U of Cal Pr.

Marris, Peter & Somerset, Anthony. African Businessmen: A Study of Entrepreneurship & Development in Kenya. (Illus.). 228p. (Orig.). 1971. pap. 10.00x (ISBN 0-7100-6958-8). Intl Pubns Serv.

Norcliffe, Glen, ed. Planning African Development: The Kenya Experience. Pinfold, Tom. 224p. 1981. lib. bdg. 28.25x (ISBN 0-86531-161-7). Westview.

Oyugi, Walter O. Rural Development Administration: A Kenyan Experience. 192p. 1981. text ed. 20.00x (ISBN 0-7069-1131-8, Pub. by Vikas India). Advent NY.

Rempel, Henry & Hourse, William J. The Kenyan Employment Problem. 1978. 21.50x (ISBN 0-19-572453-4). Oxford U Pr.

Sandbrook, R. Proletarians & African Capitalism: The Kenyan Case, 1960-1972. LC 73-91818. (Perspectives on Development: No. 4). 288p. 1975. 34.95 (ISBN 0-521-20428-3). Cambridge U Pr.

Swainson, Nicola. The Development of Corporate Capitalism in Kenya, Nineteen Eighteen to Nineteen Seventy-Seven. 1980. 20.00 (ISBN 0-520-03988-2); pap. 8.95 (ISBN 0-520-04019-8). U of Cal Pr.

Von Haugwitz, Hans-Wilhelm & Thorwart, Hermann. Some Experiences with Smallholder Settlement in Kenya 1963-64 to 1966-67. LC 74-175541. (Afrika Studien: No. 72). (Illus.). 94p. 1972. text ed. 10.50x (ISBN 3-8039-0058-1). Humanities.

World Bank. Kenya: Into the Second Decade, World Bank Country Economic Report. LC 75-10895. (Illus.). 548p. 1975. 25.00x (ISBN 0-8018-1754-4); pap. 6.95x (ISBN 0-8018-1755-2). Johns Hopkins.

Zwanenberg, R. M. van & King, Anne. An Economic History of Kenya & Uganda 1800-1970. new ed. (Illus.). 256p. 1975. text ed. 25.00x (ISBN 0-391-00400-X). Humanities.

KENYA-HISTORY

Clayton, Anthony. Counter-Insurgency in Kenya, 1952-1960: A Study of Military Operations Against the Mau Mau. (Transafrica Historical Papers: No. 4). (Illus.). 1976. pap. 5.00x (ISBN 0-8002-0203-1). Intl Pubns Serv.

Cone, L. Winston & Lipscomb, J. F. The History of Kenya Agriculture. LC 72-178470. (Illus.). 160p. 1972. 8.50x (ISBN 0-8002-0606-1). Intl Pubns Serv.

Fadiman, Jeffrey A. The Moment of Conquest: Meru, Kenya, 1907. LC 79-10870. (Papers in International Studies: Africa: No. 36). 1979. pap. 5.50 (ISBN 0-89680-081-4). Ohio U Ctr Intl.

Farrant, Leda. The Legendary Grogan: Kenya's Controversial Pioneer. (Illus.). 220p. 1981. 35.00 (ISBN 0-241-10592-7, Pub. by Hamish Hamilton England). David & Charles.

Frost, Richard. Race Against Time: Human Relations & Politics in Kenya Before Independence. (Illus.). 292p. 1978. 24.50x (ISBN 0-8476-3102-8). Rowman.

Gregoy, Robert G., et al. The Guide to the Kenya National Archives. (Foreign & Comparative Studies-Eastern African Bibliographic Ser.: No. 3). 452p. 1969. 16.00 (ISBN 0-686-70996-9). Syracuse U Foreign Comp.

Hazlewood, Arthur. The Economy of Kenya: The Kenyatta Era. (Economies of the World Ser.). (Illus.). 242p. 1979. text ed. 29.95x (ISBN 0-19-877101-0); pap. text ed. 12.95x (ISBN 0-19-877102-9). Oxford U Pr.

Hobley, C. W. Kenya from Chartered Company to Crown Colony. 2nd ed. (Illus.). 252p. 1970. 28.50x (ISBN 0-7146-1679-6, F Cass Co). Biblio Dist.

Hohnel, L. Von & Bell, N., trs. Discovery of Lakes Rudolf & Stefanie. (Illus.). 1968. Repr. of 1894 ed. 85.00x (ISBN 0-7146-1814-4, F Cass Co). Biblio Dist.

Kenyatta, Jomo. The Challenge of Uhuru: The Progress of Kenya, 1968-70. (Illus.). 52p. 1971. pap. 3.00x (ISBN 0-8002-0513-8). Intl Pubns Serv.
King, Kenneth & Salim, Admed. Kenya Historical Biographies. (Nairobi Historical Studies Ser: No. 2). 192p. 1971. 15.00x (ISBN 0-8002-1627-X). Intl Pubns Serv.
Mbithi, Philip M. & Rasmusson, Rasmus. Self Reliance in Kenya: The Case of Harambee. (Scandinavian Institute of African Studies, Uppsala). (Illus.). 1978. pap. text ed. 11.75 (ISBN 0-8419-9729-2). Holmes & Meier.
Munro, J. Forbes. Colonial Rule & the Kamba: Social Change in the Kenya Highlands 1889-1939. (Oxford Studies in African Affairs). (Illus.). 288p. 1975. 19.50x (ISBN 0-19-821699-8). Oxford U Pr.
Ogot, Bethwell A. Historical Dictionary of Kenya. LC 81-1815. (African Historical Dictionaries Ser.: No. 29). 299p. 1981. 16.00 (ISBN 0-8108-1419-6). Scarecrow.
Ross, W. McGregor. Kenya from Within: A Short Political History. new ed. (Illus.). 486p. 1968. 25.00x (ISBN 0-7146-1715-6, F Cass Co). Biblio Dist.
Tignor, R. Colonial Transformation of Kenya: The Kamba, Kikuyu, & Maasai from 1900-1939. 1975. 30.00x (ISBN 0-691-03103-7). Princeton U Pr.
Waruhiu Itote. Mau Mau General. LC 68-80463. (Illus.). 297p. 1967. pap. 5.00x (ISBN 0-8002-0607-X). Intl Pubns Serv.

KENYA–JUVENILE LITERATURE

Jacobs, Francine. Africa's Flamingo Lake. LC 79-13117. (Illus.). 96p. (gr. 4-6). 1979. 5.95 (ISBN 0-688-22197-1); PLB 5.71 (ISBN 0-688-32197-6). Morrow.

KENYA–MAPS

National Atlas of Kenya. 3rd ed. (Illus.). 103p. 1970. 35.00x (ISBN 0-8002-0624-X). Intl Pubns Serv.

KENYA–NATIVE RACES

Huxley, Elspeth & Perham, Margery. Race & Politics in Kenya. LC 75-11878. (Illus.). 302p. 1975. Repr. of 1956 ed. lib. bdg. 20.00x (ISBN 0-8371-7914-9, HURPK). Greenwood.
Massam, J. A. Cliff Dwellers of Kenya. (Illus.). 268p. 1968. Repr. of 1927 ed. 25.00x (ISBN 0-7146-1697-4, F Cass Co). Biblio Dist.

KENYA–POLITICS AND GOVERNMENT

Barkan, Joel D. & Okumu, John J. Politics & Public Policy in Kenya & Tanzania. LC 78-19470. 1979. 27.95 (ISBN 0-03-023206-6); pap. 10.95 student edition (ISBN 0-03-052336-2). Praeger.
Buijtenhuijs, Robert. Mau Mau: Twenty Years After, the Myth & the Survivors. (Publications of the Afrika-Studiecentrum, Leiden). (Illus.). 1973. pap. 27.25x (ISBN 90-2797-245-1). Mouton.
Cell, John W., ed. By Kenya Possessed: The Correspondence of J. H. Oldham & Norman Leys, 1918-1926. LC 75-27894. (Studies in Imperialism Ser). 382p. 1976. lib. bdg. 20.00x (ISBN 0-226-09971-7). U of Chicago Pr.
Coe, Richard L. The Kenya National Youth Service: A Governmental Response to Young Political Activists. LC 73-620220. (Papers in International Studies: Africa: No. 20). pap. 4.00 (ISBN 0-89680-053-9). Ohio U Ctr Intl.
Gertzel, C. J., et al, eds. Government & Politics in Kenya. (East African Publishing House Political Studies Ser: No. 10). (Illus.). 611p. 1969. 17.50x (ISBN 0-8002-1463-3). Intl Pubns Serv.
Heyer, Judith, ed. Agricultural Development in Kenya: An Economic Assessment. Senga, W. M. & Maitha, J. K. (Illus.). 1977. 17.95x (ISBN 0-19-572377-5). Oxford U Pr.
Holm, John D., et al. A Comparative Study of Political Involvement in Three African States: Botswana, Ghana & Kenya. LC 78-14731. (Foreign & Comparative Studies-African Ser.: No. 30). 139p. 1978. pap. 6.50x (ISBN 0-915984-52-0). Syracuse U Foreign Comp.
Huxley, Elspeth & Perham, Margery. Race & Politics in Kenya. LC 75-11878. (Illus.). 302p. 1975. Repr. of 1956 ed. lib. bdg. 20.00x (ISBN 0-8371-7914-9, HURPK). Greenwood.
Kariuki, Josiah M. Mau Mau Detainee: The Account by a Kenya African of His Experiences in Detention Camps 1953-1960. (Illus.). 214p. 1975. pap. 7.00x (ISBN 0-19-572381-3). Oxford U Pr.
Karp, Ivan. Fields of Change Among the Iteso of Kenya. (International Library of Anthropology). 1978. 21.00x (ISBN 0-7100-8863-9). Routledge & Kegan.
Kassam, Shirin, et al. A Bibliography on Kenya. (Foreign & Comparative Studies-Eastern African Bibliographic Ser.: No. 2). 461p. 1967. pap. 8.00x (ISBN 0-686-70995-0). Syracuse U Foreign Comp.
Kitching, Gavin. Class & Economic Change in Kenya: The Making of an African Petite Bourgeoisie, 1905-1970. LC 79-21804. 448p. 1980. text ed. 39.50x (ISBN 0-300-02385-5). Yale U Pr.
Lamb, Geoff. Peasant Politics: Conflict & Development in Murang'a. LC 74-77270. 172p. 1974. 16.95 (ISBN 0-312-59990-0). St Martin.
Leys, Colin. Underdevelopment in Kenya: The Political Economy of Neo-Colonialism, 1964-71. LC 74-76387. 1975. 20.00x (ISBN 0-520-02731-0); pap. 7.95x (ISBN 0-520-02770-1). U of Cal Pr.
Maxon, R. M. John Ainsworth & the Making of Kenya. LC 80-8165. 472p. 1980. lib. bdg. 23.50 (ISBN 0-8191-1155-4); pap. text ed. 15.00 (ISBN 0-8191-1156-2). U Pr of Amer.
Roelker, Jack R. Mathu of Kenya: A Political Study. LC 76-20294. (Publication Ser.: No. 157). 1976. 11.95 (ISBN 0-8179-6571-8). Hoover Inst Pr.
Ross, W. McGregor. Kenya from Within: A Short Political History. new ed. (Illus.). 486p. 1968. 25.00x (ISBN 0-7146-1715-6, F Cass Co). Biblio Dist.
Saberwal, Satish. The Traditional Political System of the Embu of Central Kenya. (East African Studies Ser: No. 35). (Illus.). 107p. 1973. 10.00x (ISBN 0-8002-2094-3). Intl Pubns Serv.
Stren, Richard E. Housing the Urban Poor in Africa: Policy, Politics, & Bureaucracy in Mombasa. LC 78-620001. (Research Ser: No. 34). (Illus.). 1978. pap. 5.95x (ISBN 0-87725-134-7). U of Cal Intl St.
Wasserman, G. B. Politics of Decolonization. LC 75-2735. (African Studies: No. 17). (Illus.). 224p. 1976. 27.50 (ISBN 0-521-20838-6). Cambridge U Pr.
Wolff, Richard D. The Economics of Colonialism: Britain & Kenya, 1870-1930. (Economic History Ser.). 1974. 17.50x (ISBN 0-300-01639-5). Yale U Pr.

KENYA–SOCIAL CONDITIONS

Cooper, Frederick. From Slaves to Squatters: Plantation Labor & Agriculture in Zanibar & Coastal Kenya, 1890-1925. LC 80-5391. 352p. 1981. text ed. 25.00x (ISBN 0-300-02454-1). Yale U Pr.
Frost, Richard. Race Against Time: Human Relations & Politics in Kenya Before Independence. (Illus.). 292p. 1978. 24.50x (ISBN 0-8476-3102-8). Rowman.
Heyer, Judith & Ireri, Dunstan. Rural Development in Kenya. (East African Rural Development Studies Ser: No. 6). (Illus.). 132p. 1973. 10.00x (ISBN 0-8002-0504-9). Intl Pubns Serv.
Huxley, Elspeth. A New Earth. LC 72-12318. (Illus.). 288p. 1973. Repr. of 1960 ed. lib. bdg. 17.25x (ISBN 0-8371-6688-8, HUNE). Greenwood.
Hyden, Goran, et al. Development Administration: The Kenyon Experience. (Illus.). 384p. 1970. text ed. 12.95x (ISBN 0-686-70607-2). Oxford U Pr.
Karp, Ivan. Fields of Change Among the Iteso of Kenya. (International Library of Anthropology). 1978. 21.00x (ISBN 0-7100-8863-9). Routledge & Kegan.
Kitching, Gavin. Class & Economic Change in Kenya: The Making of an African Petite Bourgeoisie, 1905-1970. LC 79-21804. 448p. 1980. text ed. 39.50x (ISBN 0-300-02385-5). Yale U Pr.
Lipscomb, J. F. White Africans. LC 74-3746. 172p. 1974. Repr. of 1955 ed. lib. bdg. 15.00x (ISBN 0-8371-7469-4, LIWA). Greenwood.
Munro, J. Forbes. Colonial Rule & the Kamba: Social Change in the Kenya Highlands 1889-1939. (Oxford Studies in African Affairs). (Illus.). 288p. 1975. 19.50x (ISBN 0-19-821699-8). Oxford U Pr.
Potholm, Christian P. & Fredland, Richard A., eds. Integration & Disintegration in East Africa. LC 80-5914. 229p. 1980. lib. bdg. 17.75 (ISBN 0-8191-1298-4); pap. text ed. 9.75 (ISBN 0-8191-1299-2). U Pr of Amer.
Stren, Richard E. Housing the Urban Poor in Africa: Policy, Politics, & Bureaucracy in Mombasa. LC 78-620001. (Research Ser: No. 34). (Illus.). 1978. pap. 5.95x (ISBN 0-87725-134-7). U of Cal Intl St.
Zwanenberg, R. M. van & King, Anne. An Economic History of Kenya & Uganda 1800-1970. new ed. (Illus.). 256p. 1975. text ed. 25.00x (ISBN 0-391-00400-X). Humanities.

KENYA–SOCIAL LIFE AND CUSTOMS

Court, David & Ghai, Dharam, eds. Education, Society & Development: New Perspectives from Kenya. (Illus.). 356p. 1975. pap. 8.95x (ISBN 0-19-572345-7). Oxford U Pr.
Frontera, Ann. Persistence & Change: A History of Taveta. 1978. 8.00 (ISBN 0-918456-19-3, Crossroads). African Studies Assn.
Langley, Myrtle S. The Nandi of Kenya: Life Crisis Rituals in a Period of Change. LC 78-31186. 1979. 18.95x (ISBN 0-312-55884-8). St Martin.
Ross-Larson. Bajun & the Sea. LC 77-190183. (Illus.). (gr. 4-8). 1972. PLB 6.95 (ISBN 0-87191-208-2). Creative Ed.
Strayer, R. Inquiry into World Cultures - Kenya: Focus on Nationalism. 1974. pap. text ed. 5.28 (ISBN 0-13-498998-8). P-H.
Wolf, J. Differentiation & Integration in Western Kenya. 1977. 19.50x (ISBN 90-279-7672-4). Mouton.

KENYATTA, JOMO

Delf, George. Jomo Kenyatta: Towards Truth About "the Light of Kenya". LC 75-17469. 215p. 1975. Repr. of 1961 ed. lib. bdg. 14.50x (ISBN 0-8371-8307-3, DEJK). Greenwood.
Murray-Brown, Jeremy. Kenyatta. 2nd ed. (Illus.). 1979. 17.95 (ISBN 0-04-920059-3). Allen Unwin.

KENYON COLLEGE, GAMBIER, OHIO

Caswall, Henry. America, & the American Church. LC 77-83413. (Religion in America Ser). 1969. Repr. of 1839 ed. 16.00 (ISBN 0-405-00234-3). Arno.

KEPAUKOE (PAPUAN PEOPLE)

see Kapauku (Papuan People)

KEPLER, JOHANNES, 1571-1630

Dow, T. W. Repeal Kepler's Laws. LC 60-13372. 1960. 5.00 (ISBN 0-910340-02-1). Celestial Pr.
Koyre, Alexandre. The Astronomical Revolution. (Illus.). 532p. 1973. 32.50x (ISBN 0-8014-0776-1). Cornell U Pr.
Lear, John. Kepler's Dream: With the Full Text & Notes of Somnium Sive Astronomia Lunaris, Joannis Kepleri. Kirkwood, Patrica F., tr. LC 64-21775. 1965. 18.00x (ISBN 0-520-00716-6). U of Cal Pr.
Palter, Robert, compiled by. Johannes Kepler, 1571-1630: An Exhibit of Books, Manuscripts, & Related Materials. LC 70-180652. (Illus.). 1971. pap. 6.00 (ISBN 0-87959-014-9). U of Tex Hum Res.
Tiner, John H. Johannes Kepler: Giant of Faith & Science. LC 77-558. (Sowers Ser). (Illus.). (gr. 3-6). 1977. pap. 4.25 (ISBN 0-915134-11-X). Mott Media.

KEPLER'S LAWS

see Orbits

KERALA, INDIA (STATE)

Alexander, P. C. Buddhism in Kerala. LC 78-72369. Repr. of 1949 ed. 37.50 (ISBN 0-404-17216-4). AMS Pr.
Jones, Clifford & Jones, Betty T. Kathakali: An Introduction to the Dance-Drama of Kerala. LC 70-131488. (Illus.). 1970. pap. 6.95 (ISBN 0-87830-530-0). Theatre Arts.
Koshy, M. J. Last Days of Monarchy in Kerala. 1973. 14.00x (ISBN 0-8364-0425-4). South Asia Bks.
Mammen, P. M. Communalism Vs. Communism: A Study of the Socio-Religious Communities & Political Parties in Kerala, 1892-1970. 1981. 18.50x (ISBN 0-8364-0041-0). South Asia Bks.
Miller, Roland. Mapilla Muslims of Kerala: A Study of Islamic Trends. LC 76-901758. 1976. 14.00x (ISBN 0-88386-080-5). South Asia Bks.
Panikkar, K. K. Community Development Administration in Kerala. 250p. 1974. text ed. 12.00x (ISBN 0-8426-0644-0). Verry.
Puthenkalam, J. Marriage & Family in Kerala. 1981. 16.00x (ISBN 0-8364-0687-7, Pub. by U Calgary India). South Asia Bks.
Splendours of Kerala. 1981. 28.00x (ISBN 0-686-72862-9, Pub. by Marg India). South Asia Bks.

KERAMICS

see Ceramics

KERATIN

Fraser, R. D., et al. Keratins: Their Composition, Structure & Biosynthesis. (Amer. Lec. Living Chemistry Ser.). (Illus.). 320p. 1972. 24.75 (ISBN 0-398-02283-6). C C Thomas.
Leon, N. H. Chemical Reactivity & Modification of Keratin Fibres. 81p. 1975. 70.00x (ISBN 0-686-63750-X). State Mutual Bk.
Parakkal, P. F. & Alexander, Nancy J. Keratinization - a Survey of Vertebrate Epithelia. (Monographs on the Ultrastructure of Cells & Organisms). 1972. 19.50 (ISBN 0-12-454140-2). Acad Pr.

KERES, PAUL

Keres, Paul. Grandmaster of Chess: The Complete Games of Paul Keres. Golombeck, Harry, tr. LC 72-642. 1972. pap. 2.95 (ISBN 0-668-02645-6). Arco.

KERESAN INDIANS

see Indians of North America–Southwest, New

KERMA, EGYPT

Reisner, G. A. Excavations at Kerma, Pts. I-V. Hooton, E. A. & Bates, Natica I., eds. (Harvard African Studies: Vol. 5). Pts. I-III. lib. bdg. 81.00 set (ISBN 0-527-01028-6); Pts. IV-V. lib. bdg. 69.00 set (ISBN 0-527-01029-4). Kraus Repr.

KERN, JEROME, 1885-1945

Bordman, Gerald. Jerome Kern: His Life & Music. (Illus.). 1980. 20.00 (ISBN 0-19-502649-7). Oxford U Pr.
Freedland, Michael. Jerome Kern. (Illus.). 182p. 1978. 13.25x (ISBN 0-8476-3126-5). Rowman.
--Jerome Kern: A Biography. LC 80-6160. 200p. 1981. 12.95 (ISBN 0-8128-2776-7). Stein & Day.

KERN RIVER VALLEY, CALIFORNIA

Powers, Bob. North Fork Country. LC 74-84608. (Illus.). 1974. 18.95 (ISBN 0-87026-034-0). Westernlore.
--South Fork Country. LC 72-180832. (Illus.). 1972. 18.95 (ISBN 0-87026-020-0). Westernlore.
The Rough & the Righteous. (Illus.). 1979. limited ed. 700 copies 14.00 (ISBN 0-686-73992-2). Acoma Bks.
Walker, Ardis M. Kern River Valley Vignettes. (Illus.). 72p. 1975. wrappers 1.95 (ISBN 0-910856-14-1). La Siesta.

KEROUAC, JOHN, 1922-1969

Blouet, Brian W. & Stitcher, Teresa L., eds. The Origins of Academic Geography in the United States. 1981. 37.50 (ISBN 0-208-01881-6, Archon). Shoe String.
Cassady, Carolyn. Heart Beat: My Life with Jack & Neal. LC 76-12732. (Illus.). 1976. pap. 4.00 (ISBN 0-916870-03-0). Creative Arts Bk.
Charters, Ann. Jack Kerouac. 2nd rev. ed. LC 75-30147. (Phoenix Bibliographies Ser.). (Illus.). 1975. 10.00 (ISBN 0-916228-06-1); pap. 3.50 (ISBN 0-916228-07-X). Phoenix Bk Shop.
--Kerouac. (Illus.). 416p. 1974. pap. 2.50 (ISBN 0-446-81331-1). Warner Bks.
Feied, Frederick. No Pie in the Sky: The Hobo As American Cultural Hero in the Works of Jack London, John Dos Passos, & Jack Kerouac. (Orig.). 1964. pap. 1.50 (ISBN 0-8065-0088-3, 170). Citadel Pr.
Gifford, Barry. Kerouac's Town. rev. ed. LC 76-50838. (Modern Authors Monograph Ser.: No. 2). (Illus.). 1977. pap. 3.50 (ISBN 0-916870-07-3). Creative Arts Bk.
Gifford, Barry & Lee, Lawrence. Jack's Book: An Oral Biography of Jack Kerouac. 1979. pap. 4.50 (ISBN 0-14-005269-0). Penguin.
--Jack's Book: An Oral Biography of Jack Kerouac. LC 77-15824. (Illus.). 1978. 10.95 (ISBN 0-312-43942-3). St Martin.
Hipkiss, Robert A. Jack Kerouac, Prophet of the New Romanticism: A Critical Study of the Published Works of Kerouac & a Comparison of Them to Those of J. D. Salinger, James Purdy, John Knowles & Ken Kesey. LC 76-14817. 1976. 10.50x (ISBN 0-7006-0151-1). Regents Pr KS.
Huebel, Harry R. Jack Kerouac, No. 39. LC 79-53652. (Western Writers Ser.). (Illus.). 48p. (Orig.). 1979. pap. 2.00 (ISBN 0-88430-063-3). Boise St Univ.
Hunt, Tim. Kerouacs Crooked Road: The Development of a Fiction. xvii, 262p. 1981. 19.50 (ISBN 0-208-01871-9, Archon). Shoe String.
Jarvis, Charles E. Visions of Kerouac: The Life of Jack Kerouac. LC 75-24815. (Illus.). 1975. pap. 4.95 (ISBN 0-915940-00-0). Ithaca Pr MA.
McNally, Dennis. Desolate Angel: Jack Kerouac, the Beats, & America. LC 78-23786. (Illus.). 1979. 15.00 (ISBN 0-394-50011-3). Random.
Milewski, Robert J., et al. Jack Kerouac: An Annotated Bibliography of Secondary Sources, 1944-1979. LC 80-24477. (Author Bibliographies Ser.: No. 52). 237p. 1981. 12.50 (ISBN 0-8108-1378-5). Scarecrow.
Tytell, John. Naked Angels: The Lives & Literature of the Beat Generation. LC 75-22206. 260p. 1976. 10.00 (ISBN 0-07-065723-8, GB). McGraw.

KERR, STANLEY ELPHINSTONE

Kerr, Stanley E. The Lions of Marash: Personal Experiences with American Near East Relief, 1919-1922. LC 75-38001. 122p. 1973. 23.00 (ISBN 0-87395-200-6); microfiche 23.00 (ISBN 0-87395-201-4). State U NY Pr.

KERR CELL SHUTTERS

see also Geodimeter

KERRY BLUE TERRIERS

see Dogs–Breeds–Kerry Blue Terriers

KERTESZ, ANDRE

Kismark, Carole. Andre Kertesz, No. 6. LC 77-70070. (Aperture History of Photography Ser.). 1977. pap. 8.95 (ISBN 0-912334-96-7). Aperture.

KERYGMA

Althaus, Paul. Fact & Faith in the Kerygma of Today. Cairas, David, tr. 89p. 1978. Repr. of 1959 ed. lib. bdg. 15.00 (ISBN 0-313-20446-2, ALFA). Greenwood.
Grasso, Domenico. Proclaiming God's Message: A Study in the Theology of Preaching. (Liturgical Studies Ser.: No. 8). 1965. 7.95x (ISBN 0-268-00222-3); pap. 2.75x (ISBN 0-268-00376-9). U of Notre Dame Pr.
McBride, Alfred. Catechetics: A Theology of Proclamation. (Orig.). 1966. pap. 2.25 (ISBN 0-685-07616-4, 80450). Glencoe.
McDonald, J. H. Kerygma & Didache: The Articulation & Structure of the Earliest Christian Message. LC 77-95446. (Society for New Testament Studies Monograph: No. 37). 1980. 19.95 (ISBN 0-521-22055-6). Cambridge U Pr.
Oden, Thomas C. Kerygma & Counseling. LC 77-20456. 1978. pap. 4.95 (ISBN 0-06-066346-4, RD-253, HarpR). Har-Row.

KESEY, KEN

Gatto, John. Monarch Notes on Kesey's One Flew Over the Cuckoos Nest. 1975. pap. 1.75 (ISBN 0-671-00966-4). Monarch Pr.

Holland, Thomas R. One Flew Over the Cuckoo's Nest Notes. 65p. (Orig.). 1974. pap. text ed. 1.75 (ISBN 0-8220-0962-5). Cliffs.

Leeds, Barry H. Ken Kesey. LC 81-40466. (Modern Literature Ser.). 160p. 1981. 10.95 (ISBN 0-8044-2497-7). Ungar.

KESWICK MOVEMENT

Bundy, David D. Keswick: A Bibliographic Introduction to the Higher Life Movements. LC 76-369083. (Occasional Bibliographic Papers of the B. L. Fisher Library: No. 3). 89p. 1975. 3.00 (ISBN 0-914368-03-6). Asbury Theological.

KETONES

D'Angelo, Jean. Ketone Enolates: Regiospecific Preparation & Synthetic Uses. 1977. text ed. 12.75 (ISBN 0-08-021587-4). Pergamon.

Patai, Saul. Chemistry of Ketenes, Allenes & Related Compounds, 2 pts. (Chemistry of Functional Groups Ser.). 1980. 96.25 ea. (Pub. by Wiley-Interscience). Pt. 1 (ISBN 0-471-99713-7). Pt. 2 (ISBN 0-471-27670-7). Wiley.

Preston, S. T., Jr. & Pankratz, Ronald. A Guide to the Analysis of Ketones by Gas Chromatography. 2nd rev. ed. 1975. spiral 25.00 (ISBN 0-913106-07-0). PolyScience.

Soling, H. D. & Seufert, C. D., eds. Biochemical & Clinical Aspects of Ketone Body Metabolism. LC 76-52978. (Illus.). 280p. 1978. 34.50 (ISBN 0-88416-144-7). Wright-PSG.

KETTELER, WILHELM EMANUEL, FREIHERR VON, BP., 1811-1877

Bock, Edward C. Wilhelm Von Ketteler, Bishop of Mainz: His Life, Times & Ideas. 287p. 1977. pap. text ed. 10.25 (ISBN 0-8191-0270-9). U Pr of Amer.

KETTERING, CHARLES FRANKLIN, 1876-1958

Boyd, Thomas A. Professional Amateur: The Biography of Charles Franklin Kettering. LC 72-5036. (Technology & Society Ser.). (Illus.). 242p. 1972. Repr. of 1957 ed. 13.00 (ISBN 0-405-04689-8). Arno.

KETTLEDRUM

see also Drum

Altenburg, J. Ernst. Trumpeters' & Kettledrummers' Art (1795) new ed. Tarr, Edward H., tr. from Ger. LC 74-4026. (Illus.). 168p. 1974. 11.00 (ISBN 0-914282-01-8). Brass Pr.

KEW-ROYAL GARDENS

Blunt, Wilfrid. In for a Penny: A Prospect of Kew Gardens. (Illus.). 1978. 27.00 (ISBN 0-241-89823-4, Pub. by Hamish Hamilton England). David & Charles.

Bringham, Madeleine. The Making of Kew. (Folio Miniature Ser.). 48p. 1975. 4.95 (ISBN 0-7181-1304-7, Pub. by Michael Joseph). Merrimack Bk Serv.

Daniels, G. Artists from the Royal Botanic Gardens, Kew. (Illus.). 1974. pap. 8.00x (ISBN 0-913196-17-7). Hunt Inst Botanical.

KEY, FRANCIS SCOTT, 1779-1843

Silkett, John T. Francis Scott Key & the History of the Star Spangled Banner. LC 76-2141. (Illus.). 1978. pap. 2.75 (ISBN 0-932330-50-9). Vintage Am.

KEY, FRANCIS SCOTT, 1779-1843–JUVENILE LITERATURE

Lowitz, Sadyebeth & Lowitz, Anson. Mr. Key's Song. 1979. pap. 0.95 (ISBN 0-440-45884-6, YB). Dell.

KEY DEER

see White-Tailed Deer

KEY WEST, FLORIDA

Browne, Jefferson B. Key West: The Old & the New. LC 72-14327. (Bicentennial Floridiana Facsimile & Reprint Ser.). (Illus.). 266p. 1973. Repr. of 1912 ed. 8.50 (ISBN 0-8130-0367-9). U Presses Fla.

Sherrill, Chris & Aiello, Roger. Key West the Last Resort. (Illus.). 171p. 1980. pap. 5.95 (ISBN 0-916224-61-9). Banyan Bks.

Warnke, James R. Balustrades & Gingerbread: Key West's Handcrafted Homes & Buildings. LC 78-15247. (Illus.). 1978. pap. 7.95 (ISBN 0-916224-43-0). Banyan Bks.

Windhorn, Stan & Langley, Wright. Yesterday's Key West. LC 73-80596. (Historic Cities Ser: No. 4). (Illus.). 144p. 1973. 8.95 (ISBN 0-912458-25-9). E A Seemann.

KEYBOARD HARMONY

see Harmony, Keyboard

KEYNES, GEOFFREY LANGDON, SIR, 1887-

Browne, Thomas. Selected Writings. Keynes, Geoffrey, ed. LC 68-55536. 1969. 12.00x (ISBN 0-226-07635-0). U of Chicago Pr.

Buchanan, James M. & Wagner, Richard E. Democracy in Deficit: The Political Legacy of Lord Keynes. 1977. 14.50 (ISBN 0-12-138850-6). Acad Pr.

KEYNES, JOHN MAYNARD, 1883-1946

Buchanan, J. M., et al. The Consequences of Mr. Keynes: An Analysis of the Misuse of Economic Theory for Political Profiteering, with Proposals for Constitutional Disciplines. (Hobart Papers Ser.: No. 78). 1978. pap. 5.95 (ISBN 0-255-36110-6). Transatlantic.

Crabtree, Derek & Thirlwall, A. P., eds. Keynes & the Bloomsbury Group. 1980. text ed. 30.00x (ISBN 0-8419-5066-0). Holmes & Meier.

Dobbs, Zygmund. Keynes at Harvard. rev. & enl ed. 3.75 (ISBN 0-685-46997-2). Veritas.

Fender, John. Understanding Keynes: An Analysis of the General Theory. LC 81-3385. 192p. 1981. 29.95 (ISBN 0-470-27197-3). Halsted Pr.

Harrod, Roy F. Life of John Maynard Keynes. 2nd ed. LC 68-30524. Repr. of 1952 ed. 19.50x (ISBN 0-678-00459-5). Kelley.

Johnson, Elizabeth S. & Johnson, Harry G. The Shadow of Keynes: Understanding Keynes, Cambridge, & Keynesian Economics. LC 78-56338. 1979. 15.00 (ISBN 0-226-40148-0). U of Chicago Pr.

Keynes, John M. The Collected Writings, 23 vols. Incl. Vol. 1. Indian Currency & Finance. 184p. 1971. Repr. of 1913 ed (ISBN 0-521-22093-9); Vol. 2. The Economic Consequences of the Peace. LC 76-133449. 192p. 1971. Repr. of 1919 ed (ISBN 0-521-22094-7); Vol. 3. Revision of the Treaty. LC 76-133449. 158p. 1972 (ISBN 0-521-22095-5); Vol. 4. Tract on Monetary Reform. LC 76-133449. 172p. 1972 (ISBN 0-521-22096-3); Vol. 5. Pt. 1. Treatise on Money, the Pure Theory of Money. 336p. 1972 (ISBN 0-521-22097-1); Vol. 6, Pt.2. Treatise on Money, the Applied Theory of Money. 390p. 1972 (ISBN 0-521-22098-X); Vol. 7. The General Theory of Employment, Interest, & Money. 428p. 1973 (ISBN 0-521-22099-8). pap. 7.95 (ISBN 0-521-29382-0); Vol. 8. Treatise on Probability. 514p. 1972 (ISBN 0-521-22100-5); Vol. 9. Essays & Persuasions. 451p. 1972 (ISBN 0-521-22101-3); Vol. 10. Essays in Biography. 460p. 1972 (ISBN 0-521-22102-1); Vol. 13. The General Theory & After, Pt. One: Preparation. 653p. 1973 (ISBN 0-521-22103-X); Vol. 14. The General Theory & After, Pt. Two: Defence & Development. 584p. 1973 (ISBN 0-521-22104-8); Vol. 15. Activities: Nineteen-Six to Nineteen-Fourteen: India & Cambridge. 312p. 1971 (ISBN 0-521-22105-6); Vol. 16. Activities, Nineteen-Fourteen to Nineteen-Nineteen: The Treasury & Versailles. 488p. 1971 (ISBN 0-521-22106-4); Vol. 17. Activities Nineteen Twenty to Twenty-Two: Treaty Revision & Reconstruction. 1978 (ISBN 0-521-21874-8); Vol. 18. Activities Nineteen Twenty-Two to Thirty-Two: The End of Reparations. 1978 (ISBN 0-521-21875-6); Vol. 19. Activities Nineteen Thirty-Nine to Forty-Five: Internal War Finance. 519p. 1978 (ISBN 0-521-23071-3); Vol. 20. Activities Nineteen Forty to Forty-Three: External War Finance. 330p. 1979 (ISBN 0-521-23072-1); Vol. 21. Activities Nineteen Forty-Four to Forty-Six: The Transition to Peace. 688p. 1979 (ISBN 0-521-23073-X); Vol. 22. Activities Nineteen Forty-Three to Forty-Six: Shaping the Post War World: the Clearing Union (ISBN 0-521-21876-4); Vol. 23. Activities Nineteen Forty-Three to Forty-Six: Shaping the Postwar World: Bretton Woods & Reparations. 368p. 1980 (ISBN 0-521-22016-5); Vol. 24. Activities Nineteen Forty to Forty-Six: Shaping the Post-War World: Employment & Commodities (ISBN 0-521-22017-3). 42.50 ea. Cambridge U Pr.

Keynes, Milo, ed. Essays on John Maynard Keynes. LC 74-12975. (Illus.). 1980. pap. 11.95 (ISBN 0-521-29696-X). Cambridge U Pr.

Langlois, Wilfred V. Keynes & the Economic Bankruptcy of the United States. (Illus.). 139p. 1980. deluxe ed. 59.45 (ISBN 0-918968-71-2). Inst Econ Finan.

Leijohnufvud, Axel. Keynes & the Classics. (Institute of Economic Affairs, Occasional Papers Ser.: No. 30). pap. 2.50 (ISBN 0-255-27601-X). Transatlantic.

Lekachman, Robert. The Age of Keynes. LC 66-12014. 336p. 1975. pap. 3.95 (ISBN 0-07-037154-7, SP). McGraw.

Mattick, Paul. Marx & Keynes: The Limits of the Mixed Economy. LC 69-15526. (Extending Horizons Ser.). 1973. pap. 3.45 (ISBN 0-87558-069-6). Porter Sargent.

Moggridge, D. E., ed. Keynes: Aspects of the Man & His Work. 112p. 1974. 16.95 (ISBN 0-312-45185-7). St Martin.

Moggridge, D. F. John Maynard Keynes. (Modern Masters Ser). 1976. pap. 2.95 (ISBN 0-14-004319-5). Penguin.

Patinkin, Don. Keynes' Monetary Thought: A Study of Its Development. LC 75-40630. 1976. 11.50 (ISBN 0-8223-0360-4). Duke.

Patinkin, Don & Leith, J. Clark. Keynes, Cambridge & the General Theory. 1978. 22.50x (ISBN 0-8020-2296-0). U of Toronto Pr.

Thirlwall, A. P., ed. Keynes & International Monetary Relations: The Second Keynes Seminar Held at University of Kent at Canterbury, 1974. LC 75-44515. 115p. 1976. 15.95 (ISBN 0-312-45255-1). St. Martin.

Victor, R. F. John Maynard Keynes: Father of Modern Economics. Rahmas, D. Steve, ed. (Outstanding Personalities Ser: No. 17). 32p. (Orig.). (gr. 7-12). 1972. lib. bdg. 2.95 incl. catalog cards (ISBN 0-87157-517-5); pap. 1.50 vinyl laminated covers (ISBN 0-87157-017-3). SamHar Pr.

KEYNESIAN ECONOMICS

Collected Economic Papers of Joan Robinson, 5 vols. 1980. Set. text ed. 125.00x (ISBN 0-262-18099-5); text ed. 25.00x ea. Vol. 1 (ISBN 0-262-18093-6). Vol. 2 (ISBN 0-262-18094-4). Vol. 3 (ISBN 0-262-18095-2). Vol. 4 (ISBN 0-262-18096-0). Vol. 5 (ISBN 0-262-18097-9). Index. text ed. 12.50x (ISBN 0-262-18098-7). MIT Pr.

Collins, Robert M. The Business Response to Keynes, 1929-1964. LC 81-3898. (Contemporary American History Ser.). 320p. 1981. 20.00x (ISBN 0-231-04486-0). Columbia U Pr.

Cumes, J. W. The Indigent Rich: A Theory of General Equilibrium in a Keynesian System. 224p. 1972. 16.50 (ISBN 0-08-017534-1). Pergamon.

Fujino, Shozaburo. A Neo-Keynesian Theory of Income, Prices & Economic Growth. LC 75-327752. (Illus.). 1975. 15.00x (ISBN 0-8002-0318-6). Intl Pubns Serv.

Hansen, Alvin H. Guide to Keynes. (Illus.). 1953. pap. 3.95 (ISBN 0-07-026046-X, SP). McGraw.

Harris, Seymour E., ed. New Economics. LC 65-19642. Repr. of 1947 ed. 19.50x (ISBN 0-678-00074-3). Kelley.

Harrod, Roy F. Life of John Maynard Keynes. 2nd ed. LC 68-30524. Repr. of 1952 ed. 19.50x (ISBN 0-678-00459-5). Kelley.

Hayek, F. A. A Tiger by the Tail: the Keynesian Legacy of Inflation. (Hobart Paperbacks). 1972. pap. 5.95 (ISBN 0-255-36029-0). Transatlantic.

Hayek, Friedrich A. A Tiger by the Tail: The Keynesian Legacy of Inflation. (The Cato Papers Ser.: No. 6). 178p. 1979. pap. 4.00x (ISBN 0-932790-06-2). Cato Inst.

Hazlitt, Henry, ed. The Critics of Keynesian Economics. 1977. Repr. of 1960 ed. 11.00 (ISBN 0-87000-401-8). Arlington Hse.

Hicks, John. The Crisis in Keynesian Economics. LC 74-79284. 85p. 1975. text ed. 10.00 (ISBN 0-465-01480-1). Basic.

Hines, A. G. On the Reappraisal of Keynesian Economics. 85p. 1972. pap. 7.95x (ISBN 0-85520-004-9, Pub. by Martin Robertson England). Biblio Dist.

Hutt, W. H. The Keynesian Episode. 1981. 10.00 (ISBN 0-913966-60-6); pap. 4.50 (ISBN 0-913966-61-4). Liberty Fund.

--The Keynesian Episode: A Reassessment. LC 79-4150. 1980. 10.00 (ISBN 0-913966-60-6, Liberty Press); pap. 4.50 (ISBN 0-913966-61-4). Liberty Fund.

Johnson, Elizabeth S. & Johnson, Harry G. The Shadow of Keynes: Understanding Keynes, Cambridge, & Keynesian Economics. LC 78-56338. 1979. 15.00 (ISBN 0-226-40148-0). U of Chicago Pr.

Keynes, John M. The Collected Writings, 23 vols. Incl. Vol. 1. Indian Currency & Finance. 184p. 1971. Repr. of 1913 ed (ISBN 0-521-22093-9); Vol. 2. The Economic Consequences of the Peace. LC 76-133449. 192p. 1971. Repr. of 1919 ed (ISBN 0-521-22094-7); Vol. 3. Revision of the Treaty. LC 76-133449. 158p. 1972 (ISBN 0-521-22095-5); Vol. 4. Tract on Monetary Reform. LC 76-133449. 172p. 1972 (ISBN 0-521-22096-3); Vol. 5. Pt. 1. Treatise on Money, the Pure Theory of Money. 336p. 1972 (ISBN 0-521-22097-1); Vol. 6, Pt.2. Treatise on Money, the Applied Theory of Money. 390p. 1972 (ISBN 0-521-22098-X); Vol. 7. The General Theory of Employment, Interest, & Money. 428p. 1973 (ISBN 0-521-22099-8). pap. 7.95 (ISBN 0-521-29382-0); Vol. 8. Treatise on Probability. 514p. 1972 (ISBN 0-521-22100-5); Vol. 9. Essays & Persuasions. 451p. 1972 (ISBN 0-521-22101-3); Vol. 10. Essays in Biography. 460p. 1972 (ISBN 0-521-22102-1); Vol. 13. The General Theory & After, Pt. One: Preparation. 653p. 1973 (ISBN 0-521-22103-X); Vol. 14. The General Theory & After, Pt. Two: Defence & Development. 584p. 1973 (ISBN 0-521-22104-8); Vol. 15. Activities: Nineteen-Six to Nineteen-Fourteen: India & Cambridge. 312p. 1971 (ISBN 0-521-22105-6); Vol. 16. Activities, Nineteen-Fourteen to Nineteen-Nineteen: The Treasury & Versailles. 488p. 1971 (ISBN 0-521-22106-4); Vol. 17. Activities Nineteen Twenty to Twenty-Two: Treaty Revision & Reconstruction. 1978 (ISBN 0-521-21874-8); Vol. 18. Activities Nineteen Twenty-Two to Thirty-Two: The End of Reparations. 1978 (ISBN 0-521-21875-6); Vol. 19. Activities Nineteen Thirty-Nine to Forty-Five: Internal War Finance. 519p. 1978 (ISBN 0-521-23071-3); Vol. 20. Activities Nineteen Forty to Forty-Three: External War Finance. 330p. 1979 (ISBN 0-521-23072-1); Vol. 21. Activities Nineteen Forty-Four to Forty-Six: The Transition to Peace. 688p. 1979 (ISBN 0-521-23073-X); Vol. 22. Activities Nineteen Forty-Three to Forty-Six: Shaping the Post War World: the Clearing Union (ISBN 0-521-21876-4); Vol. 23. Activities Nineteen Forty-Three to Forty-Six: Shaping the Postwar World: Bretton Woods & Reparations. 368p. 1980 (ISBN 0-521-22016-5); Vol. 24. Activities Nineteen Forty to Forty-Six: Shaping the Post-War World: Employment & Commodities (ISBN 0-521-22017-3). 42.50 ea. Cambridge U Pr.

Keynes, M., ed. Essays on John Maynard Keynes. LC 74-12975. (Illus.). 304p. 1975. 38.50 (ISBN 0-521-20534-4). Cambridge U Pr.

Leijonhufvud, Axel. On Keynesian Economics & the Economics of Keynes: A Study in Monetary Theory. 1968. text ed. 12.95x (ISBN 0-19-500948-7). Oxford U Pr.

Lekachman, Robert. The Age of Keynes. LC 66-12014. 336p. 1975. pap. 3.95 (ISBN 0-07-037154-7, SP). McGraw.

McKenna, Joseph P. Aggregate Economic Analysis. 5th ed. LC 76-19362. 1977. text ed. 19.95 (ISBN 0-03-089707-6). Dryden Pr.

Mantoux, Etienne. The Carthaginian Peace or the Economic Consequences of Mr. Keynes. Wilkins, Mira, ed. LC 78-3936. (International Finance Ser.). 1978. Repr. of 1946 ed. lib. bdg. 15.00x (ISBN 0-405-11237-8). Arno.

Mattick, Paul. Marx & Keynes: The Limits of the Mixed Economy. LC 69-15526. (Extending Horizons Ser). 1969. 6.95 (ISBN 0-87558-045-9). Porter Sargent.

Mehta, Ghanshyan. The Structure of the Keynesian Revolution. LC 77-91864. 1979. 17.95x (ISBN 0-312-76770-6). St Martin.

Minsky, Hyman P. John Maynard Keynes. (Essays on the Great Economists). 181p. 1975. 17.50x (ISBN 0-231-03616-7); pap. 5.00x (ISBN 0-231-03917-4). Columbia U Pr.

Moggridge, D. E., ed. Keynes: Aspects of the Man & His Work. 112p. 1974. 16.95 (ISBN 0-312-45185-7). St Martin.

Morgan, Brian. Monetarists & Keynesians: Their Contributions to Monetary Theory. 1980. pap. text ed. 12.95x (ISBN 0-470-26885-9). Halsted Pr.

Murad, Anatol. What Keynes Means. 1962. pap. 2.45 (ISBN 0-8084-0320-6, B18). Coll & U Pr.

Robinson, Joan. Economic Heresies: Some Old-Fashioned Questions in Economic Theory. LC 71-147012. 1971. pap. 5.95x (ISBN 0-465-09515-1, TB5016). Basic.

--Essays in the Theory of Employment. LC 78-14138. (Illus.). 1981. Repr. of 1950 ed. 18.50 (ISBN 0-88355-812-2). Hyperion Conn.

Timlin, Mabel F. Keynesian Economics. LC 43-2023. 1948. 16.50x (ISBN 0-8020-7044-2). U of Toronto Pr.

Tobin, James. The New Economics One Decade Older. (Eliot Janeway Lectures in Historical Economics). 100p. 1974. 11.50 (ISBN 0-691-04205-5). Princeton U Pr.

Turner, Carl B. Analysis of Soviet Views on John Maynard Keynes. LC 70-79236. 1969. 12.75 (ISBN 0-8223-0211-X). Duke.

Weintraub, Sidney. Keynes, Keynesians, & Monetarists. LC 77-20307. (Illus.). 1978. pap. 9.95x (ISBN 0-8122-7741-4). U of Pa Pr.
Wright, David M. Keynesian System. LC 62-15667. (Millar Lecture Ser: No. 4). 1962. 7.50 (ISBN 0-8232-0455-3). Fordham.

KEYS
see Locks and Keys

KEYSERLING, EDUARD HEINRICH NIKOLAUS, GRAF VON, 1855-1918
Knoop, K. Die Erzaehlungen Eduard Von Keyserlings. Repr. of 1929 ed. pap. 7.00 (ISBN 0-384-29980-6). Johnson Repr.

KEYSTONE FILM COMPANY
Lahue, Kalton C. & Brewer, Terry. Kops & Custards: The Legend of Keystone Films. (Illus.). 1968. 9.95 (ISBN 0-8061-0765-0); pap. 4.95 (ISBN 0-8061-1045-7). U of Okla Pr.

KGALAGADI (AFRICAN PEOPLE)
Kuper, Adam. Kalahari Village Politics: An African Democracy. LC 70-112470. (Studies in Social Anthropology). (Illus.). 1970. 19.95 (ISBN 0-521-07863-6). Cambridge U Pr.

KHAJRAHO, INDIA–DESCRIPTION
Mitra, S. K. The Early Rulers of Khajuraho. 2nd rev. ed. 1977. 10.00 (ISBN 0-8426-0913-X, Pub. by Motilal Banarsidass India). Orient Bk Dist.

KHALIFAT
see Caliphate

KHALIFS
see Caliphs

KHANTY
see Ostiaks

KHARTOUM RELIEF EXPEDITION, 1884-1885
Preston, Adrian, ed. In Relief of Gordon: Lord Wolseley's Campaign Journal of the Khartoum Relief Expedition, 1884-1885. LC 79-92562. 267p. 1970. 15.00 (ISBN 0-8386-7572-7). Fairleigh Dickinson.

KHAS LANGUAGE
see Nepali Language

KHASI LANGUAGE
see also Mon-Khmer Languages

KHAUSTOV, VIKTOR ALEKSANDROVICH, 1938-
Litvinov, Pavel. Demonstration in Pushkin Square: The Trial Records with Commentary & an Open Letter. Harari, Manya, tr. from Rus. LC 77-91996. 1969. 5.95 (ISBN 0-87645-009-5). Gambit.

KHAZARS
Golb, Norman & Pritsak, Omeljan. Khazarian Hebrew Documents of the Tenth Century. 1981. 25.00 (ISBN 0-8014-1221-8). Cornell U Pr.
Koestler, Arthur. The Thirteenth Tribe: The Khazar Empire & Its Heritage. 1976. 8.95 (ISBN 0-394-40284-7). Random.
Kutschera, Hugo F. The Khazars. 1978. lib. bdg. 44.95 (ISBN 0-685-62303-3). Revisionist Pr.
Landau, A. The Present Position of the Khazar Problem. 1978. lib. bdg. 59.95 (ISBN 0-685-62304-1). Revisionist Pr.
Poliak, Abraham N. The Khazar Conversion to Judaism. 1978. lib. bdg. 39.95 (ISBN 0-685-62299-1). Revisionist Pr.
--Khazaria: The History of a Jewish Kingdom in Europe. 1978. lib. bdg. 49.95 (ISBN 0-685-62302-5). Revisionist Pr.
Weinryb, B. The Khazars: An Annotated Bibliography. 1979. lib. bdg. 59.95 (ISBN 0-686-59410-X). Revisionist Pr.
Zajaczkowski, A. The Khazar Culture & Its Heirs. 1978. lib. bdg. 59.95 (ISBN 0-685-62300-9). Revisionist Pr.
--The Problem of the Language of the Khazars. 1978. lib. bdg. 59.95 (ISBN 0-685-62305-X). Revisionist Pr.

KHILAFAT
see Caliphate

KHITA
see Hittites

KHIVA–DESCRIPTION AND TRAVEL
Burnaby, Fred. Ride to Khiva: Travels & Adventures in Central Asia. LC 79-115513. (Russia Observed, Ser., No. 1). 1970. Repr. of 1877 ed. 15.00 (ISBN 0-405-03010-X). Arno.
Murav'Yov, Nikolay. Journey to Khiva Through the Turkoman Country. 1977. text ed. 25.50x (ISBN 0-905820-00-2). Humanities.

KHIVA–POLITICS AND GOVERNMENT
Becker, Seymour. Russia's Protectorates in Central Asia: Bukhara & Khiva, 1865-1924. LC 67-30825. (Russian Research Center Studies: No. 54). (Illus.). 1968. 18.50x (ISBN 0-674-78360-3). Harvard U Pr.

KHMER LANGUAGE
English-Khmer Phrasebook with Useful Word List: For Cambodians. LC 80-66143. 140p. 1980. pap. text ed. 4.00x (ISBN 0-87281-115-8). Ctr Appl Ling.
FSI Cambodian Basic Course: Units 1-45. 1966. pap. text ed. 6.30x (ISBN 0-686-10700-4); 19 cassettes 114.00x (ISBN 0-686-10701-2). Intl Learn Syst.
FSI Cambodian Basic Course: Units 46-90. 1970. pap. text ed. 6.50x (ISBN 0-686-10702-0); 29 cassettes 174.00x (ISBN 0-686-10703-9). Intl Learn Syst.
Huffman, Franklin E. & Im Proum. Intermediate Cambodian Reader. 1972. pap. text ed. 12.00x (ISBN 0-300-01552-6). Yale U Pr.
Huffman, Franklin E. & Proum, Im. Cambodian-English Glossary. LC 76-50539. (Linguistic Ser.). 160p. 1981. pap. 5.95x (ISBN 0-300-02070-8). Yale U Pr.
--Cambodian Literary Reader & Glossary. LC 76-50538. (Linguistic Ser.). 1977. pap. text ed. 21.50x (ISBN 0-300-02069-4). Yale U Pr.
Huffman, Franklin E., et al. Cambodian System of Writing & Beginning Reader. LC 78-104614. 1970. text ed. 30.00x (ISBN 0-300-01199-7). Yale U Pr.
--Modern Spoken Cambodian. LC 71-104615. 1970. text ed. 35.00x (ISBN 0-300-01315-9); pap. text ed. 12.00x (ISBN 0-300-01316-7). Yale U Pr.
Jacob, Judith. A Concise Cambodian-English Dictionary. 277p. 1974. 59.00x (ISBN 0-19-713574-9). Oxford U Pr.
Noss, Richard B. & Purtle, Dale. Spoken Cambodian, Bk. II. 363p. 1980. pap. 10.00x (ISBN 0-87950-667-9); cassettes i & iI 145.00x (ISBN 0-87950-669-5); bk. II & cassettes II 150.00x (ISBN 0-87950-671-7); bks. I & II & cassettes I & II 240.00x (ISBN 0-87950-672-5). Spoken Lang Serv.
Noss, Richard B., et al. Spoken Cambodian, Bk. I. 449p. 1980. pap. 10.00x (ISBN 0-87950-666-0); cassettes i 19 dual track 95.00x (ISBN 0-87950-668-7); book i & cassettes i 100.00x (ISBN 0-87950-670-9); books i & iI & cassettes i & iI 240.00 (ISBN 0-87950-672-5). Spoken Lang Serv.

KHMERS
American National Standards Institute, Standards Committee Z39 on Library Work, Documentation & Related Publishing Practices. American National Standard System for the Romanization of Lao, Khmer, & Pali, Z39.35. 1979. 4.50 (ISBN 0-686-28238-8). ANSI.

KHOI-KHOIN (AFRICAN PEOPLE)
see Hottentots

KHOMEINI, AYATOLLAH
see Khumayni, Ruh Allah

KHOMIAKOV, ALEXEI STEPANOVICH, 1804-1860
Zernov, Nicholas. Three Russian Prophets: Khomiakov, Dostoevsky, Soloviev. 3rd ed. LC 72-97040. (Russian Ser.: Vol. 43). 1974. Repr. of 1944 ed. 14.50 (ISBN 0-87569-050-5). Academic Intl.

KHOTAN
Bailey, H. W. Dictionary of Khotan Saka. LC 77-80825. 1979. 210.00 (ISBN 0-521-21737-7). Cambridge U Pr.
Stein, M. Aurel. Ancient Khotan: Detailed Report of Archaeological Explorations in Chinese Turkestan, 2 vols. in 1. LC 73-86329. 1975. Repr. of 1907 ed. 120.00 (ISBN 0-87817-146-0). Hacker.

KHOTANESE LANGUAGE
Bailey, H. W. Khotanese Buddhist Texts. rev. ed. LC 80-41425. (University of Cambridge Oriental Publications Ser.: No. 31). 168p. Date not set. price not set (ISBN 0-521-23717-3). Cambridge U Pr.
Bailey, Harold W. Khotanese Texts, 4 bks. 1961-1967. Vols. 1-3. 156.00 (ISBN 0-521-06961-0); Vol. 4. 75.00 (ISBN 0-521-04080-9); Vol. 5. 136.00 (ISBN 0-521-04081-7); Vol. 6. 150.00 (ISBN 0-521-07113-5). Cambridge U Pr.

KHRUSHCHEV, NIKITA SERGEEVICH, 1894-1971
Frankland, Mark. Khrushchev. LC 67-16690. 1969. pap. 4.95 (ISBN 0-8128-1234-4). Stein & Day.
Hoxha, Enver. The Khrushchevites-Memoirs. (Illus.). 135p. 1980. pap. 3.00 (ISBN 0-86714-011-9). Marxist-Leninist.
Kurland, Gerald. Nikita Sergeievich Khrushchev: Modern Dictator of the USSR. Rahmas, D. Steve, ed. LC 74-185668. (Outstanding Personalities Ser.: No. 12). 32p. 1972. lib. bdg. 2.95 incl. catalog cards (ISBN 0-87157-512-4); pap. 1.50 vinyl laminated covers (ISBN 0-87157-012-2). SamHar Pr.
Linden, Carl A. Khrushchev & the Soviet Leadership, 1957-1964. 278p. (Orig.). 1966. 17.50x (ISBN 0-8018-0374-8); pap. 4.95x (ISBN 0-8018-0375-6). Johns Hopkins.
McCauley, Martin. Khrushchev & the Development of Soviet Agriculture: The Virgin Land Program, 1953-1964. LC 76-14411. 1976. text ed. 32.50x (ISBN 0-8419-0283-6). Holmes & Meier.
Marcum, James. Khruschev & the Legacy of Stalinism. Date not set. pap. 9.95 (ISBN 0-8120-5279-X). Barron.
Medvedev, Roy A. & Medvedev, Zhores A. Khrushchev: The Years in Power. LC 76-19104. 197p. 1976. 15.00x (ISBN 0-231-03939-5). Columbia U Pr.
--Khrushchev: The Years in Power. 1978. pap. 4.95 (ISBN 0-393-00879-7). Norton.
--N. S. Khrushchev: The Years in Power. LC 75-37259. (Rus., Sponsored by Columbia Univ. Ress). 1975. 18.00 (ISBN 0-8357-0154-9, SS-08003). Univ Microfilms.
Slusser, Robert M. Berlin Crisis of Nineteen Sixty-One: Soviet-American Relations & the Struggle for Power in the Kremlin, June-November,1961. LC 72-4025. 525p. 1973. 27.00x (ISBN 0-8018-1404-9); pap. 8.50x (ISBN 0-8018-1459-6). Johns Hopkins.
Tolstoy, A. Nikita's Childhood. 197p. 1977. 2.70 (ISBN 0-8285-1213-2, Pub. by Progress Pubs Russia). Imported Pubns.

KHUMAYNI, RUH ALLAH
Stone, Eddie. Khomeini, the Shah, the Ayatollah, the Shi'ite Explosion. 224p. 1980. pap. 1.95 (ISBN 0-87067-677-6, 677). Holloway.

KHURRIANS
see Hurrians

KHWAJA ASIM, 1672-1738
Malik, Zahiruddin. A Mughal Statesman of the Eighteenth Century: Khan-I-Dauran Mir Bashshi of Mumammad Shah 1719-1739. 120p. 1973. 2.75x (ISBN 0-210-40544-9). Asia.

KHWALISSES
see also Khazars

KI-KONGO LANGUAGE
see Congo Language

KIANGSI, CHINA (PROVINCE)
Kim, Ilpyong. The Politics of Chinese Communism: Kiangi Under Soviet Rule. LC 73-76101. 1974. 23.50x (ISBN 0-520-02438-9). U of Cal Pr.
Wright, Stanley. Kiangsi Native Trade & Its Taxation. LC 78-74332. (The Modern Chinese Economy Ser.). 201p. 1980. lib. bdg. 22.00 (ISBN 0-8240-4258-1). Garland Pub.

KIBBUTZ
see Collective Settlements

KICKAPOO INDIANS
see Indians of North America–The West

KICKING (FOOTBALL)
Gogolak, Pete. Kicking the Football Soccer Style. Siegener, Ray, ed. 1972. pap. 1.25 (ISBN 0-689-70406-2, Aladdin). Atheneum.
--Kicking the Football Soccer Style with Tips on Playing Soccer. Siegener, Ray, ed. LC 73-190403. (Illus.). 1972. 4.95 (ISBN 0-689-10502-9). Atheneum.
Sullivan, George. Pro Football's Kicking Game. LC 73-1653. (Illus.). (gr. 5 up). 1973. 5.95 (ISBN 0-396-06800-6). Dodd.

KIDD, WILLIAM, d. 1701
Marsh, Angela. Pirate Treasure. LC 78-26275. (Raintree Great Adventures). (Illus.). (gr. 3-6). 1979. PLB 10.25 (ISBN 0-8393-0155-3). Raintree Child.

KIDDER, ALFRED VINCENT, 1885-1963
Woodbury, Richard B. Alfred V. Kidder. LC 72-10082. (Leaders of Modern Anthropology Ser.). 225p. 1973. 15.00x (ISBN 0-231-03484-9); pap. 5.00x (ISBN 0-231-03485-7). Columbia U Pr.

KIDNAPPING
see also Abduction
Alix, Ernest K. Ransom Kidnapping in America, 1874-1974: The Creation of a Capital Crime. LC 78-1985. 256p. 1980. pap. 7.95 (ISBN 0-8093-0976-9). S Ill U Pr.
--Ransom Kidnapping in America, 1874-1974: The Creation of a Capital Crime. LC 78-1985. (Perspectives in Sociology Ser.). 256p. 1978. 15.00 (ISBN 0-8093-0849-5). S Ill U Pr.
Baugh, Jack W. & Morgan, Jefferson. Why Have They Taken Our Children. 1979. pap. 2.25 (ISBN 0-440-19468-7). Dell.
Cassidy, William. Political Kidnapping. 1978. pap. 6.00 (ISBN 0-87364-141-8). Sycamore Island.
Cassidy, William L. Political Kidnapping. 70p. 1978. pap. 6.00 (ISBN 0-87364-141-8, Sycamore Island). Paladin Ent.
Clutterbuck, Richard. Kidnap & Ransom: The Response. 192p. 1978. (Pub. by Faber & Faber); pap. 7.95 (ISBN 0-571-11327-3). Merrimack Bk Serv.
Cole, Richard B. Executive Security: A Corporate Guide to Effective Response to Abduction & Terrorism. LC 80-14662. 323p. 1980. 27.95 (ISBN 0-471-07736-4, Pub. by Wiley Interscience). Wiley.
Enzinga, Netfa, et al. I Was Kidnapped by Idi Amin. (Orig.). 1979. pap. 1.95 (ISBN 0-87067-662-8, BH662). Holloway.
Katz, Robert. Days of Wrath. LC 79-7050. 1980. 12.95 (ISBN 0-385-14910-7). Doubleday.

KIDNEY, ARTIFICIAL
see Artificial Kidney

KIDNEY FAILURE
see Renal Insufficiency

KIDNEY FUNCTION TESTS
Duarte, Cristobal G. Renal Function Tests. (Laboratory Medicine Ser.). 1980. text ed. 27.50 (ISBN 0-316-19398-4). Little.
International Symposium on Unilateral Renal Function Studies, 1st, Montecatini Terme, May 1977, et al. Unilateral Renal Function Studies: Proceedings. Giovannetti, S. & Thomas, S., eds. (Contrubutions to Nephrology: Vol. 11). (Illus.). 1978. 46.75 (ISBN 3-8055-2858-2). S Karger.

KIDNEYS
see also Adrenal Glands; Diuretics and Diuresis; Nephrology; Urinary Organs; Urine;
also headings beginning with the word Renal
Albini, B., et al. Immunopathology of the Kidney. (Current Topics in Immunology Ser.: Vol. 2). (Illus., Orig.). 1979. pap. 19.95 (ISBN 0-8151-0104-X). Year Bk Med.
Bastron, R. Dennis & Deutsch, Stanley. Anesthesia & the Kidney. LC 76-41193. (Scientific Basis of Clinical Anesthesia). (Illus.). 128p. 1976. 22.75 (ISBN 0-8089-0974-6). Grune.
Bauman, John W. & Chinard, Francis P. Renal Function: Physiological & Medical Aspects. LC 74-28278. 1975. pap. 10.45 (ISBN 0-8016-0509-1). Mosby.
Berlyne, G. H., ed. Reprinted Selected Top Articles Published 1976 - 1977. (Kargar Highlights, Nephrology One). (Illus.). 1978. pap. 9.00 (ISBN 3-8055-2938-4). S Karger.
Brenner, Barry M. & Rector, Floyd C., eds. The Kidney, 2 vols. LC 74-25474. (Illus.). 1500p. 1976. Set. text ed. 95.00 (ISBN 0-7216-1965-7). Vol. 1 (ISBN 0-7216-1966-5). Saunders.
Brod, J. The Kidney. (Illus.). 750p. 1973. 75.00 (ISBN 0-407-23900-6). Butterworth.
Coburn, J. W. & Massry, S. G., eds. Uses & Actions of 1,25 Dihyroxyvitamin D3 in Uremia. (Contributions to Nephrology: Vol. 18). (Illus.). 1980. 48.50 (ISBN 3-8055-3064-1). S Karger.
Dalton, A. J. & Haguenau, Francis. Ultrastructure of the Kidney. (Ultrastructure in Biological Systems). 1967. 40.00 (ISBN 0-12-200956-8). Acad Pr.
Deetjen, P., et al. Physiology of the Kidney & of Water Balance. LC 72-85949. (Illus.). 145p. 1974. pap. 12.50 (ISBN 0-387-90048-9). Springer-Verlag.
Edwards, K. D. & Stokes, G. S., eds. Drugs Affecting the Renin-Angiotensin-Aldosterone System Use of Angiotensin Inhibitors: Proceedings. (Progress in Biochemical Pharmacology: Vol. 12). 1977. 85.25 (ISBN 3-8055-2410-2). S Karger.
Eisenbach, G. M. & Brod, J., eds. Kidney & Pregnancy. (Contributions to Nephrology Ser.: Vol. 25). (Illus.). vi, 170p. 1981. pap. 57.00 (ISBN 3-8055-1798-X). S Karger.
Eisenbach, G. M. & Brod, Jan, eds. Non-Vasoactive Renal Hormones. (Contributions to Nephrology: Vol. 13). (Illus.). 1978. pap. 40.75 (ISBN 3-8055-2895-7). S Karger.
Epstein, M., ed. The Kidney in Liver Disease. 1978. 32.50 (ISBN 0-444-00240-5, North Holland). Elsevier.
Fillastre, Jean-Paul, ed. Nephrotoxicity: Interaction of Drugs with Membranes Systems Mitochondria-Lysosomes. (Illus.). 332p. 1978. 55.00x (ISBN 0-89352-032-2). Masson Pub.
Finlayson, Birdwell & Thomas, William C., Jr., eds. Colloquium on Renal Lithiasis. LC 77-7779. (Illus.). 1977. 25.00 (ISBN 0-8130-0566-3). U Presses Fla.
Fleisch, H., et al, eds. Urolithiasis Research. LC 76-47019. 582p. 1976. 49.50 (ISBN 0-306-30988-2, Plenum Pr). Plenum Pub.
Gerrick, David J. Anatomy of the Sheep Kidney: Clinical Implications. (Illus.). 1978. pap. text ed. 15.00 (ISBN 0-916750-04-3). Dayton Labs.
Giebisch, Gerhard H. & Purcell, Elizabeth F., eds. Renal Function. LC 77-99173. (Illus.). 1978. text ed. 10.00 (ISBN 0-914362-24-0). J Macy Foun.
Gilmore, Joseph P. Renal Physiology. LC 72-77317. 132p. 1972. pap. 9.50 (ISBN 0-683-03622-X). Krieger.
Gonick, Harvey C., ed. Current Nephrology, Vol. 1. (Illus.). 1977. 48.00 (ISBN 0-471-09482-X, Pub. by Wiley Med). Wiley.
--Current Nephrology, Vol. 3. 1979. 48.00 (ISBN 0-471-09484-6, Pub. by Wiley Med). Wiley.
Hamburger, Jean, et al. Structure & Function of the Kidney. LC 72-151678. (Organ Physiology Ser.). (Illus.). 1971. 7.00 (ISBN 0-7216-4490-2). Saunders.
--Structure & Function of the Kidney. LC 72-151678. (Organ Physiology Ser.). (Illus.). 1971. 7.00 (ISBN 0-7216-4490-2). Saunders.
Hamburger, Jean, et al, eds. Advances in Nephrology, Vol 6. (Illus.). 1976. 45.00 (ISBN 0-8151-4115-7). Year Bk Med.
--Advances in Nephrology, Vol. 7. (Illus.). 1978. 43.95 (ISBN 0-8151-4116-5). Year Bk Med.
--Advances in Nephrology, Vol. 8. (Illus.). 1979. 44.95 (ISBN 0-8151-4117-3). Year Bk Med.
Harrington, Avery R. & Zimmerman, Stephen W. Renal Pathophysiology. (Wiley Pathophysiology Ser.). 240p. 1982. 17.95 (ISBN 0-471-07815-8, Pub. by Wiley Med). Wiley.

Heptinstall, Robert H. Pathology of the Kidney, 2 vols. 2nd ed. LC 73-17664. 1200p. 1974. 80.00 set (ISBN 0-316-35795-2). Little.

Horton, R. & Dunn, M. J., eds. Prostaglandins & the Kidney. (Journal: Mineral & Electrolyte Metabolism Ser.: Vol. 6, No. 1-2). (Illus.). 104p. 1981. pap. write for info. (ISBN 3-8055-3406-X). S Karger.

International Committee for Nomenclature & Nosology of Renal Disease. A Handbook of Kidney Nomenclature & Nosology. LC 73-17665. 400p. 1975. text ed. 19.95 (ISBN 0-316-41920-6). Little.

International Congress of Nephrology, 5th. Mexico, 1972. Nephrology: Proceedings, 3 vols. Villarreal, H., ed. Incl. Vol. 1. Morphology & Pathology (ISBN 3-8055-1742-4); Vol. 2. Physiology (ISBN 3-8055-1743-2); Vol. 3. Clinic (ISBN 3-8055-1744-0). 1974. 37.25 ea.; Set. 96.00 (ISBN 3-8055-1423-9). S Karger.

International Congress of Nephrology, 7th, Montreal, June 18-23, 1978. Proceedings. Bergerson, Michael, ed. 1978. 89.25 (ISBN 3-8055-2915-5). S Karger.

International Congress, 6th, Florence, June 1975. Advances in Nephrology: Proceedings. Giovannetti, S. & Bonomini, V., eds. (Illus.). 800p. 1976. 107.25 (ISBN 3-8055-2287-8). S Karger.

International Symposium on Unilateral Renal Function Studies, 1st, Montecatini Terme, May 1977, et al. Unilateral Renal Function Studies: Proceedings. Giovannetti, S. & Thomas, S., eds. (Contributions to Nephrology: Vol. 11). (Illus.). 1978. 46.75 (ISBN 3-8055-2858-2). S Karger.

Jamison, Rex L. & Kriz, Wilhelm. Urinary Concentrating Mechanism: Structure & Function. (Illus.). 425p. 1981. text ed. 35.00x (ISBN 0-19-502801-5). Oxford U Pr.

Jenis, Edwin H. & Lowenthal, David T. Kidney Biopsy Interpretation. LC 76-30870. (Illus.). 1977. text ed. 27.50 (ISBN 0-8036-4990-8). Davis Co.

Kaissling, B. & Kriz, W. Structural Analysis of the Rabbit Kidney. (Advances in Anatomy, Embryology & Cell Biology: Vol. 56). (Illus.). 1979. pap. 28.10 (ISBN 0-387-09145-9). Springer-Verlag.

Kobayashi, K., et al, eds. Renal Research: Clinical & Experimental Contributions from Japan. (Contributions to Nephrology: Vol. 6). 1977. 41.50 (ISBN 3-8055-2402-1). S Karger.

Kurtzman, Neil A. & Martinez-Maldonado, Manuel. Pathophysiology of the Kidney. (Illus.). 1104p. 1977. 99.50 (ISBN 0-398-03600-4). C C Thomas.

Leaf, Alexander & Cotran, Ramzi. Renal Pathophysiology. 2nd ed. (Illus.). 448p. 1980. text ed. 18.95x (ISBN 0-19-502688-8); pap. text ed. 11.95x (ISBN 0-19-502689-6). Oxford U Pr.

Lindheimer, Marshall D. & Katz, Adrian I. Kidney Function & Disease in Pregnancy. LC 76-30312. (Illus.). 241p. 1977. text ed. 15.00 (ISBN 0-8121-0593-1). Lea & Febiger.

McCrory, Wallace W. Developmental Nephrology. LC 72-75399. (Commonwealth Fund Publications Ser). (Illus.). 314p. 1972. 12.00x (ISBN 0-674-20275-9). Harvard U Pr.

Maeda, K., et al, eds. Recent Advances in Renal Research: Contributions from Japan. (Contributions to Nephrology: Vol. 9). (Illus.). 1978. 29.50 (ISBN 3-8055-2826-4). S Karger.

Mandal, Anil K. & Bohman, Sven-Olof, eds. The Renal Papilla and Hypertension. (Illus.). 230p. 1980. 27.50 (ISBN 0-306-40506-7, Plenum Med Bk). Plenum Pub.

Marsh, Donald J. Renal Physiology. 1981. write for info. (ISBN 0-89004-465-1, 519). Raven.

Massry, Shaul G. & Fleisch, Herbert, eds. Renal Handling of Phosphate. (Illus.). 400p. 1980. 37.50 (ISBN 0-306-40368-4, Plenum Pr). Plenum Pub.

Maude, David L. Kidney Physiology & Kidney Disease. LC 76-50093. (Illus.). 1977. 19.50 (ISBN 0-397-52079-4, JBL-Med-Nursing). Har-Row.

Maunbach, A. N., et al, eds. Functional Ultrastructure of the Kidney. 1981. 96.00 (ISBN 0-12-481250-3). Acad Pr.

Moffat, D. B. The Control of Water Balance by the Kidney. rev. ed. Head, J. J., ed. LC 76-62967. (Carolina Biology Readers Ser.). (Illus.). (gr. 11 up). 1978. pap. 1.65 (ISBN 0-89278-214-5, 45-9614). Carolina Biological.

--The Mammalian Kidney. LC 74-82590. (Biological Structure & Function Ser.: No. 5). (Illus.). 272p. 1975. 53.50 (ISBN 0-521-20599-9). Cambridge U Pr.

Mota-Hernandez, F., ed. Seminar on Kidney Diseases in Children. (Journal: Paediatrician Ser.: Vol. 8, No. 5-6, 1979). 1979. pap. 39.75 (ISBN 3-8055-0344-X). S Karger.

Muth, Robert G. Renal Medicine. (Illus.). 300p. 1978. 21.75 (ISBN 0-398-03711-6). C C Thomas.

Ono, J., et al, eds. Vitamin D & Calcium Metabolism in the Renal Diseases. (Contributions to Nephrology: Vol. 22). (Illus.). 1980. soft cover 42.00 (ISBN 3-8055-0389-X). S Karger.

O'Reilly, P H & Shields. Nuclear Medicine in Urology & Nephrology. (Illus.). 1979. text ed. 44.95 (ISBN 0-407-00151-4). Butterworth.

Peters, G., ed. Renal Adaptation to Nephron Loss. (Yale Journal of Biology & Medicine: Vol. 51, No. 3). (Illus.). 1979. pap. 39.75 (ISBN 3-8055-3024-2). S Karger.

Pitts, Robert F. Physiology of the Kidney & Body Fluids. 3rd ed. (Illus.). 307p. 1974. pap. 12.95 (ISBN 0-8151-6703-2). Year Bk Med.

Rector, Barry M. & Rector, Floyd C., eds. The Kidney, 2 vols. 2nd ed. 1981. Vol. 1. text ed. write for info. (ISBN 0-7216-1967-3); Vol. 2. text ed. write for info. (ISBN 0-7216-1968-1); Set. text ed. write for info. (ISBN 0-7216-1969-X). Saunders.

Riegel, J. A. Comparative Physiology of Renal Excretion. (University Reviews in Biology Ser.). (Illus.). 1972. pap. 7.95 (ISBN 0-02-850920-X). Hafner.

Robinson, Brian. Dialysis, Transplantation, Nephrology: Proceedings, European Dialysis & Transplant Asso., Volume 14. (Illus.). 1978. 49.95x (ISBN 0-8464-0329-3). Beekman Pubs.

Robinson, Brian, ed. Dialysis, Transplantation, Nephrology: Proceedings European Dialysis & Transplant Assoc. Volume 13. (Illus.). 1977. 59.95x (ISBN 0-8464-0328-5). Beekman Pubs.

Robinson, J. W. Intestinal Ion Transport. (Illus.). 1976. 39.50 (ISBN 0-8391-0876-1). Univ Park.

Ross, D. B. & Guder, W. G., eds. Biochemical Aspects of Renal Function: Proceedings of a Symposium Held in Honour of Professor Sir Hans Krebs FRS, at Merton College, Oxford, 16-19 September 1979. (Illus.). 340p. 1980. pap. 55.00 (ISBN 0-08-025517-5). Pergamon.

Rouiller, C. & Muller, A., eds. The Kidney: Morphology, Biochemistry, Physiology. Incl. Vols. 1-2. 1969. 78.00 (ISBN 0-686-76968-6). Vol. 1 (ISBN 0-12-598801-X). Vol. 2. 78.00 (ISBN 0-12-598802-8); Vols. 3-4. 1971. 59.00 ea. Vol. 3 (ISBN 0-12-598803-6). Vol. 4 (ISBN 0-12-598804-4). Set. 225.00 (ISBN 0-686-66787-5). Acad Pr.

Schillings, P. H. & Schuurmans Steloven, H. J. Atlas of Glomerular Histopathology. (Illus.). 1980. 58.75 (ISBN 3-8055-0201-X). S Karger.

Schumann, G. Berry & Weiss, Mark. Atlas of Renal & Urinary Tract Cytology & Its Histopathologic Bases. (Illus.). 240p. 1981. text ed. 55.00 (ISBN 0-397-50443-8, JBL-Med-Nursing). Har-Row.

Schwartz, Allan B. Nephrology for the Practicing Physician. 168p. 1975. 29.50 (ISBN 0-8089-0915-0). Grune.

Sideman, Samuel & Chang, T. M., eds. Hemoperfusion: Kidney & Liver Support Detoxification, Pt. 2. 1982. text ed. price not set (ISBN 0-89116-211-9). Hemisphere Pub.

Sies, H. & Wondel, A., eds. Functions of Glutathione in Liver & Kidney. (Proceedings in Life Sciences). (Illus.). 1979. 34.10 (ISBN 0-387-09127-0). Springer-Verlag.

Silbernagel, S., ed. Abstracts of the International Conference on Renal Transport of Organic Substances Held in Innsbruck, July, 1980. (Journal: Renal Physiology: Vol. 2, No. 3). (Illus.). 62p. 1980. pap. 17.00 (ISBN 3-8055-1641-X). S Karger.

Smith, Homer W. Kidney: Structure & Functions in Health & Disease. (Illus.). 1951. 35.00x (ISBN 0-19-501140-6). Oxford U Pr.

Stein, Jay H. Nephrology. (The Science & Practice of Clinical Medicine Ser.). 496p. 1980. 39.50 (ISBN 0-8089-1246-1). Grune.

Stokes, G. S. & Mahony, J. H., eds. Hormones & the Kidney. (Progress in Biochemical Pharmacology: Vol. 17). (Illus.). viii, 298p. 1981. 98.25 (ISBN 3-8055-1090-X). S Karger.

Sullivan, Lawrence P. Physiology of the Kidney. LC 73-8851. (Illus.). 149p. 1974. pap. 6.50 (ISBN 0-8121-0461-7). Lea & Febiger.

Symposium, Montreal, June 17, 1978. A New Class of Renally Active Compounds with Antihypertensive, Diuretic, Uricosuric Properties. Lemieux, G. & Steele, T. H., eds. (Nephron: Vol. 23 Suppl. 1). (Illus.). 1979. pap. 22.25 (ISBN 3-8055-3002-1). S Karger.

Tager, J. M., et al, eds. Use of Isolated Liver Cells & Kidney Tabules in Metabolic Studies: Proceedings. 1976. 58.75 (ISBN 0-444-10925-0, North-Holland). Elsevier.

Thurau, K. Kidney & Urinary Tract Physiology, Vol. III. 1982. 39.50 (ISBN 0-686-76800-0). Univ Park.

--Kidney & Urinary Tract Physiology. (MTP International Review of Science-Physiology Ser.: Vol. 6). 1974. 29.50 (ISBN 0-8391-1055-3). Univ Park.

--Kidney & Urinary Tract Physiology, II. (International Review of Physiology: Vol. II). 1976. 29.50 (ISBN 0-8391-1060-X). Univ Park.

Uhlschmid, G. K. Analysis of Three Hundred & Thirty-Three Necro-Kidney-Allografts. (European Surgical Research: Vol. 11, Suppl. 1). (Illus.). 1979. pap. 15.00 (ISBN 3-8055-3004-8). S Karger.

Valtin, Heinz. Renal Functions: Mechanisms Preserving Fluid & Solute Balance in Health. 1973. pap. 12.95 (ISBN 0-316-89556-3). Little.

Vander, Arthur J. Renal Physiology. 2nd ed. (Illus.). 1980. pap. text ed. 9.95 (ISBN 0-07-066958-9). McGraw.

Vogel, H. G. & Ullrich, K. J., eds. New Aspects of Renal Function: Proceedings of the Sixth Workshop Conference Hoechst, Schloss Reisensburg, July 1977. (International Congress Ser: No. 422). 1978. 36.75 (ISBN 0-444-90025-X, Excerpta Medica). Elsevier.

Wesson, L. Recent Advances in Renal Physiology & Pharmacology. 1974. 39.50 (ISBN 0-8391-0682-3). Univ Park.

Wesson, Laurence G., Jr. Physiology of the Human Kidney. LC 68-29036. (Illus.). 736p. 1969. 89.00 (ISBN 0-8089-0524-4). Grune.

Williams, Arthur V., Jr., et al, eds. Self-Assessment of Current Knowledge in Nephrology. 2nd ed. 1976. 14.00 (ISBN 0-87488-280-X). Med Exam.

KIDNEYS–DISEASES

see also Calculi, Urinary; Kidney Function Tests; Proteinuria; Renal Hypertension; Renal Insufficiency; Uremia

Allen, Arthur C. The Kidney: Medical & Surgical Diseases. 2nd ed. LC 61-17894. (Illus.). 1962. 112.75 (ISBN 0-8089-0008-0). Grune.

Allen, D. E. & Dowling, J. P. Techniques for Nephropathology. 144p. 1981. 49.95 (ISBN 0-8493-5791-8). CRC Pr.

Anderson, Robert J. & Schrier, Robert W. Clinical Uses of Drugs in Patients with Kidney & Liver Disease. (Illus.). 368p. Date not set. text ed. price not set (ISBN 0-7216-1239-3). Saunders.

Becker, E. Lovell, et al, eds. Nephrology - Cornell Seminars. 138p. 1971. pap. 7.50 (ISBN 0-683-00493-X, Pub. by Williams & Wilkins). Krieger.

Bennett, William M., et al. Drugs & Renal Disease. (Monographs in Clinical Pharmacology: Vol. 2). 1978. text ed. 19.50 (ISBN 0-443-08004-6). Churchill.

Beregi, Edit & Varga, I. Renal Biopsy in Glomerular Diseases. Goemoeri, P., ed. De Catel, R., tr. (Illus.). 335p. 1978. 35.00x (ISBN 963-05-1356-0). Intl Pubns Serv.

Bianchi, G. The Kidney in Arterial Hypertension. 181p. pap. text ed. 24.50 (ISBN 0-8391-1482-6). Univ Park.

Bookstein, Joseph J. & Clark, Richard L. Renal Microvascular Disease. 1980. text ed. 42.50 (ISBN 0-316-10237-7). Little.

Brundage, Dorothy J. Nursing Management of Renal Problems. 2nd ed. LC 80-11720. (Illus.). 1980. pap. text ed. 10.45 (ISBN 0-8016-0849-X). Mosby.

--Nursing Management of Renal Problems. LC 75-22149. (Illus.). 204p. 1976. pap. text ed. 8.95 (ISBN 0-8016-0850-3). Mosby.

Buckalew, Vardaman M. & Moore, Micahel A. Renal Tubular Dysfunction. LC 79-92915. (Discussions in Patient Management Ser.). 1980. pap. 13.50 (ISBN 0-87488-889-1). Med Exam.

Butt, Arthur J. Etiologic Factors in Renal Lithiasis. (Illus.). 416p. 1956. photocopy spiral ed. 39.75 (ISBN 0-398-04374-4). C C Thomas.

Cameron, Stewart. Kidney Disease: The Facts. (The Facts Ser.). (Illus.). 250p. 1981. text ed. 11.95x (ISBN 0-19-261329-4). Oxford U Pr.

Cheigh, Jhoong S., et al, eds. Manual of Clinical Nephrology of the Rogosin Kidney Center. (Developments in Nephrology: No. 1). (Illus.). 470p. 1981. PLB 65.00 (ISBN 90-247-2397-3, Pub. by Martinus Nijhoff Netherlands). Kluwer Boston.

Churg, Jacob, et al. Kidney Disease: Present Status. (International Academy of Pathology Monograph Ser.: No. 20). 1979. 43.00 (ISBN 0-683-01671-7). Williams & Wilkins.

Cost, Jacquelyn S. Dietary Management of Renal Disease: A Controlled Protein, Sodium & Potassium Cookbook. LC 75-18657. 1975. 9.00x (ISBN 0-913590-27-4). C B Slack.

Darmady, E. M. & MacIver, A. Renal Pathology. LC 79-42838. (Postgraduate Pathology Ser.). 560p. 1980. 99.95 (ISBN 0-407-00119-0). Butterworth.

Davison, Alex M. A Synopsis of Renal Diseases. (Illus.). 196p. 1981. pap. text ed. 20.00 (ISBN 0-7236-0569-6). Wright-PSG.

De Wardener, H. E. The Kidney: An Outline of Normal & Abnormal Structure & Function. 4th ed. LC 73-175548. (Illus.). 440p. 1973. text ed. 27.50x (ISBN 0-443-01027-7). Churchill.

Dunnill, Michael. Pathological Basis of Renal Disease. LC 76-26775. (Illus.). 1976. text ed. 40.00 (ISBN 0-7216-3230-0). Saunders.

Dzhavad-Zade, M. D. Surgery of Kidney & Ureteral Anomalies. 1980. 12.75 (ISBN 0-686-74526-4, Pub. by Mir Pubs Russia). Imported Pubns.

Earley, Lawrence E. & Gottschalk, Carl W. Strauss & Welt's Diseases of the Kidney, 2 vols. 3rd ed. 1979. text ed. 95.00 (ISBN 0-316-20314-9). Little.

Edelmann, Chester., Jr. Pediatric Kidney Disease. 1978. text ed. 75.00 (ISBN 0-316-21070-6). Little.

Fortner-Frazier, Carrie L. Social Work & Dialysis: The Medical & Psychosocial Aspects of Kidney Disease. LC 78-51754. 224p. 1981. 17.50x (ISBN 0-520-03674-3). U of Cal Pr.

Freedman, Philip, et al. Nephrology. (Medical Examination Review Book: Vol. 34). 1976. spiral bdg. 15.00 (ISBN 0-87488-176-5). Med Exam.

Friedman, Eli A. & L'Esperance, Frances, eds. Diabetic Renal-Retinal Syndrome. (Illus.). 480p. 1980. 39.50 (ISBN 0-8089-1302-6). Grune.

Gabriel, Roger. Renal Medicine: Concise Medical Textbook. 2nd ed. (Illus.). 288p. 1981. pap. text ed. write for info. (ISBN 0-02-857780-9). Macmillan.

Germuth, Frederick G., Jr. & Rodriguez, Eugene. Immunopathology of the Renal Glomerulus: Immune Complex Deposit & Antibasement Membrane Disease. (Illus.). 1973. 28.50 (ISBN 0-316-30839-0). Little.

Golden, Abner. The Kidney. 2nd ed. LC 76-30733. 222p. 1977. 19.50 (ISBN 0-686-74090-4). Krieger.

Griffiths, Harry J. Radiology of Renal Failures: SMCR-9. LC 74-17754. (Illus.). 1976. text ed. 24.00 (ISBN 0-7216-4283-7). Saunders.

Hamburger, Jean, et al, eds. Advances in Nephrology, Vol 6. (Illus.). 1976. 45.00 (ISBN 0-8151-4115-7). Year Bk Med.

Harrington, Avery R. & Zimmerman, Stephen W. Renal Pathophysiology. (Wiley Pathophysiology Ser.). 240p. 1982. 17.95 (ISBN 0-471-07815-8, Pub. by Wiley Med). Wiley.

Hodson, C. John & Kincaid-Smith, Priscilla, eds. Reflux Nephropathy. LC 79-84477. (Illus.). 366p. 1979. text ed. 43.50x (ISBN 0-89352-044-6). Masson Pub.

Hook, Jerry B., ed. Toxicology of the Kidney. (Target Organ Toxicology Ser.). 288p. 1981. 32.50 (ISBN 0-89004-475-9). Raven.

International Congress of Nephrology, 4th, Stockholm, 1969. Proceedings, 3 vols. Alwall, N., et al, eds. Incl. Vol. 1. Embryology, Ultrastructure, Physiology (ISBN 3-8055-0950-2); Vol. 2. Endocrinology, Metabolic Aspects (ISBN 3-8055-0951-0); Vol. 3. Clinical Nephrology Immunology (ISBN 3-8055-0952-9). 1970. Set. 90.00 (ISBN 3-8055-0953-7). S Karger.

Jackle, Mary & Rasmussen, Claire. Renal Problems: A Critical Care Nursing Focus. LC 79-9498. (Illus.). 356p. 1979. pap. text ed. 16.95 (ISBN 0-87619-408-0). R J Brady.

Jepson, Joanne H. Hematologic Problems in Renal Disease. LC 78-60829. 1979. 38.50 (ISBN 0-201-03481-6, Med-Nurse). A-W.

Jones, Norman F. Recent Advances in Renal Diseases, No. 1. LC 74-33158. (Illus.). 1975. text ed. 35.00x (ISBN 0-443-01288-1). Churchill.

Kagan, Lynn W. Renal Disease: A Manual of Patient Care. (Illus.). 1979. text ed. 17.95 (ISBN 0-07-033190-1, HP). McGraw.

Kirschenbaum, M. A. Practical Diagnosis: Renal Disease. 253p. 1978. pap. 22.00 (ISBN 0-471-09485-4). Wiley.

Kirschenbaum, Michael A. Practical Diagnosis: Renal Disease. (Illus.). 1978. kroydenflex 22.00 (ISBN 0-471-09485-4, Pub. by Wiley Med). Wiley.

Klahr, Saulo. Essentials of Renal Pathophysiology. 1982. 10.95 (ISBN 0-8036-5377-8). Davis Co.

Knox, Franklyn G., ed. Textbook of Renal Pathophysiology. (Illus.). 1978. text ed. 23.00x (ISBN 0-06-141450-6, Harper Medical). Har-Row.

Krawitt, Laura P. & Weinberger, Emily K. Practical Low Protein Cookery. (Illus.). 128p. 1971. pap. 10.50 (ISBN 0-398-01049-8). C C Thomas.

Kurtzman, Neil A. & Martinez-Maldonado, Manuel. Pathophysiology of the Kidney. (Illus.). 1104p. 1977. 99.50 (ISBN 0-398-03600-4). C C Thomas.

Lancaster, Larry E. The Patient with End Stage Renal Disease. LC 78-23659. 349p. 1979. 21.00 (ISBN 0-471-03564-5, Pub. by Wiley Medical). Wiley.

Laszlo, F. A. Renal Cortical Necrosis. (Contributions to Nephrology Ser.: Vol. 28). (Illus.). viii, 216p. 1981. pap. 45.00 (ISBN 3-8055-2109-X). S Karger.

Leaf, Alexander & Cotran, Ramzi. Renal Pathophysiology. 2nd ed. (Illus.). 448p. 1980. text ed. 18.95x (ISBN 0-19-502688-8); pap. text ed. 11.95x (ISBN 0-19-502689-6). Oxford U Pr.

Leaf, Alexander, et al, eds. Renal Pathophysiology - Recent Advances. 293p. 1980. text ed. 35.50 (ISBN 0-89004-399-X). Raven.
Lindheimer, Marshall D. & Katz, Adrian I. Kidney Function & Disease in Pregnancy. LC 76-30312. (Illus.). 241p. 1977. text ed. 15.00 (ISBN 0-8121-0593-1). Lea & Febiger.
Loehr, E., ed. Renal & Adrenal Tumors. (Illus.). 1980. 114.40 (ISBN 0-387-09192-0). Springer-Verlag.
McClusky & Andres. Immunologically Mediated Renal Diseases. (Immunology Ser.: Vol. 10). 1978. 19.50 (ISBN 0-8247-6779-9). Dekker.
McDonald. Clinical Kidney Disease & Hypertension. LC 80-14107. 1980. 32.00 (ISBN 0-913258-91-1). Thieme Stratton.
McGiven, A. R., ed. Immunological Investigation of Renal Disease. (Practical Methods in Clinical Immunology Ser.: Vol. 1). (Illus.). 160p. 1980. text ed. 39.50 (ISBN 0-443-01899-5). Churchill.
Mandal, Anil K. Electron Microscopy of the Kidney in Renal Disease & Hypertension: A Clinicopathological Approach. LC 78-24409. (Illus.). 472p. 1978. 32.50 (ISBN 0-306-40110-X, Plenum Pr). Plenum Pub.
Massry, S. G., ed. Kidney in Systemic Diseases. (Contributions to Nephrology: Vol. 7). (Illus.). 1977. 58.75 (ISBN 3-8055-2445-5). S Karger.
Massry, Shaul G. & Ritz, Eberhard, eds. Homeostasia of Phosphate & Other Minerals. LC 78-5709. (Advances in Experimental Medicine & Biology Ser.: Vol. 103). 552p. 1978. 49.50 (ISBN 0-306-40008-1, Plenum Pr). Plenum Pub.
Maude, David L. Kidney Physiology & Kidney Disease. LC 76-50093. (Illus.). 1977. 19.50 (ISBN 0-397-52079-4, JBL-Med-Nursing). Har-Row.
Meadows, Robert. Renal Histopathology: A Light, Electron, & Immunofluorescent Microscopy Study of Renal Disease. 2nd ed. (Illus.). 1978. text ed. 65.00x (ISBN 0-19-261213-1). Oxford U Pr.
Meeting on Hemoperfusion, Kidney & Liver Supports & Detoxification, Haifa, Aug 25-26, 1979. Hemoperfusion: Kidney & Liver Support & Detoxification, Pt. 1. Sideman, Samuel & Chang, T. M., eds. LC 80-14154. 496p. 1980. text ed. 49.50 (ISBN 0-89116-152-X). Hemisphere Pub.
Merrill, John P. The Treatment of Renal Failure. 2nd ed. LC 65-15272. (Illus.). 400p. 1965. 49.75 (ISBN 0-8089-0318-7). Grune.
Nowinski, W. W. & Goss, R. J., eds. Compensatory Renal Hypertrophy. 1970. 48.00 (ISBN 0-12-522750-7). Acad Pr.
Parrish, Alvin E. Kidney Disease Case Studies. 2nd. ed. 1979. 14.75 (ISBN 0-87488-022-X). Med Exam.
Pathophysiology of Renal Disease. (Contributions to Nephrology Ser.: Vol. 23). (Illus.). vi, 234p. 1980. pap. 58.75 (ISBN 3-8055-0943-X). S Karger.
Ranyi-Vamos, F. & Balogh, F. Pyelonephritis. 1979. 18.40 (ISBN 0-9960010-1-8, Pub. by Kiado Hungary). Heyden.
Reidenberg, Marcus. Renal Function & Drug Action. LC 74-135334. 1971. 7.50 (ISBN 0-7216-7538-7). Saunders.
Reissigl, H., et al, eds. Infusionstherapie bei Volumenmangel und bei rheologischen Indikationen. (Beitraege Zu Infusionstherapie und Klinische Ernaehrung: Band 2). 1979. pap. 12.00 (ISBN 3-8055-3014-5). S Karger.
Remuzzi, Giuseppe, et al, eds. Hemostasis, Prostaglandins & Renal Disease. (Monographs of the Mario Negri Institute for Pharmacological Research). 475p. 1980. text ed. 52.50 (ISBN 0-89004-484-8). Raven.
Renal Stone Research Symposium, Madrid, Sept. 1972. Urinary Calculi: Recent Advances in Aetiology, Stone Structure & Treatment, Proceedings. Cifuentes Delatte, L., et al, eds. (Illus.). 1973. 78.00 (ISBN 3-8055-1618-5). S Karger.
Renyi-Vamos, F. & Balogh, F. Pyelonephritis. (Illus.). 191p. 1979. 20.00x (ISBN 963-05-1724-8). Intl Pubns Serv.
Rieselbach, Richard E. & Garnick, Marc B. Cancer & the Kidney. (Illus.). 700p. 1981. write for info. (ISBN 0-8121-0804-3). Lea & Febiger.
Rose, Burton D. Pathophysiology of Renal Disease. (Illus.). 1981. 23.95 (ISBN 0-07-053616-3); pap. text ed. 23.95 (ISBN 0-07-053615-5). McGraw.
Rosenthal, J. & Franz, H. E., eds. Medical & Surgical Aspects of Renovascular Hypertension. (Contributions to Nephrology: Vol. 3). (Illus.). 200p. 1976. 38.50 (ISBN 3-8055-2341-6). S Karger.
Rossmann, P. & Jirka, I. Rejection Nephropathy. 1977. 66.00 (ISBN 0-444-80032-8, North-Holland). Elsevier.
Schreiner, G. E. Controversies in Nephrology. (Illus.). 722p. 1979. 49.50x (ISBN 0-686-77785-9). Masson Pub.
Schrier, Robert W., ed. Renal & Electrolyte Disorders. 2nd ed. 500p. 1980. text ed. 22.95 (ISBN 0-316-77476-6). Little.
Seelig, Mildred S., ed. Magnesium Deficiency in the Pathogenesis of Disease. (Topics in Bone & Mineral Disorders Ser.). 500p. 1980. 39.50 (ISBN 0-306-40202-5, Plenum Pr). Plenum Pub.
Spaeth, Gudrun. Hinweise Zur Konservativen Behandlung des Akuten Nierenversagens. (Illus.). 1977. 8.50 (ISBN 3-8055-2749-7). S Karger.
Spargo, Benjamin H., et al. Renal Biopsy Pathology with Diagnostic & Therapeutic Implications. 1979. 47.50 (ISBN 0-471-03119-4, Pub. by Wiley-Interscience). Wiley.
Sunderman, F. William & Sunderman, F. William, Jr. Laboratory Diagnosis of Kidney Diseases. LC 73-76164. (Illus.). 604p. 1970. 29.50 (ISBN 0-87527-077-8). Green.
Symposium on Natriuretic Hormone, Czechoslovakia, June, 1969. Regulation of Body Fluid Volumes by the Kidney: Proceedings. Cort, J. H. & Lichardus, B., eds. (Illus.). 192p. 1970. 40.75 (ISBN 3-8055-0772-0). S Karger.
Uldall, Robert. Renal Nursing. 2nd ed. (Blackwell Scientific Pubns.). 1977. 16.00 (ISBN 0-632-00086-4). Mosby.
Valtin, Heinz. Renal Dysfunction: Mechanisms Involved in Fluid & Solute Imbalance. 1979. text ed. 17.95 (ISBN 0-316-89553-9); pap. text ed. 12.95 (ISBN 0-316-89554-7). Little.
Verrier-Jones, John. Immunological Aspects of Kidney Disease. (Illus.). Date not set. text ed. write for info. (ISBN 0-443-08023-2). Churchill.
Weller, John M. Fundamentals of Nephrology. (Illus.). 1979. pap. text ed. 19.95 (ISBN 0-06-142655-5, Harper Medical). Har-Row.
Williams, G. Atlas des Maladies Renales. Levy, Micheline, tr. (Atlas Karger en Couleur: No. 4). (Illus.). 240p. 1974. 39.00 (ISBN 3-8055-1639-8). S Karger.
Williams, George. Color Atlas of Renal Diseases. (Year Book Color Atlas Ser.). 1973. 29.50 (ISBN 0-8151-9300-9). Year Bk Med.
Wills, M. R. Biochemical Consequences of Chronic Renal Failure. (Illus.). 218p. 1972. 24.50 (ISBN 0-8391-0583-5). Univ Park.
Wilson, Curtis B., et al, eds. Immunologic Mechanisms of Renal Disease. (Contemporary Issues in Nephrology: Vol. 3). (Illus.). 1979. text ed. 29.00 (ISBN 0-443-08018-6). Churchill.

KIDNEYS–DISEASES–DIAGNOSIS

Beregi, Edit & Varga, I. Renal Biopsy in Glomerular Diseases. Goemoeri, P., ed. De Catel, R., tr. (Illus.). 335p. 1978. 35.00x (ISBN 963-05-1356-0). Intl Pubns Serv.
Brun & Olsen. Atlas of Renal Biopsy. (Illus.). 266p. text ed. write for info. (ISBN 0-7216-2164-3). Saunders.
Chaussy, Charles, et al. Beruehrungsfreie Nierensteinzertruemmerung durch extrakorporal erzeugte, fokussierte Stosswelle. (Beitraege zur Urology Ser.: Vol. 2). vi, 94p. 1980. pap. 36.00 (ISBN 3-8055-1901-X). S Karger.
Coe, Fredric L. Nephrolithiasis: Pathogenesis & Treatment. (Illus.). 1978. 29.50 (ISBN 0-8151-1799-X). Year Bk Med.
Gabriel, Roger. Renal Medicine. (Concise Medical Textbook Ser.). (Illus.). 1978. pap. text ed. 11.95 (ISBN 0-02-857810-4). Macmillan.
Kirschenbaum, M. A. Practical Diagnosis: Renal Disease. 253p. 1978. pap. 22.00 (ISBN 0-471-09485-4). Wiley.
Klahr, M. D., et al. Differential Diagnosis of Renal & Electrolyte Disorders. LC 77-10321. (Illus.). pap. text ed. 12.00x (ISBN 0-668-04063-7, 4063). Arco.
Lang, Erich K. Roentgenographic Diagnosis of Renal Mass Lesions. LC 70-125008. (Illus.). 190p. 1971. 12.50 (ISBN 0-87527-047-6). Green.
Risdon, R. A. & Turner, D. R. Atlas of Renal Pathology, Vol. 2. (Current Histopathology Ser.). (Illus.). 150p. 1981. text ed. 42.50 (ISBN 0-397-50452-7, JBL-Med-Nursing). Har-Row.
Rosenfield, Arthur T., et al, eds. Diagnostic Imaging in Renal Disease. (Illus.). 332p. 1979. 37.50 (ISBN 0-8385-1690-4). ACC.
Rouiller, C. & Muller, A., eds. The Kidney: Morphology, Biochemistry, Physiology. Incl. Vols. 1-2. 1969. 78.00 (ISBN 0-686-76968-6). Vol. 1 (ISBN 0-12-598801-X). Vol. 2. 78.00 (ISBN 0-12-598802-8); Vols. 3-4. 1971. 59.00 ea. Vol. 3 (ISBN 0-12-598803-6). Vol. 4 (ISBN 0-12-598804-4). Set. 225.00 (ISBN 0-686-66787-5). Acad Pr.
Valenzuela, Rafael & Deodhar, Sharad D. Interpretation of Immunofluorescent Patterns in Renal Diseases. LC 80-26598. (Illus.). 144p. 1981. text ed. 45.00 (ISBN 0-89189-079-3, 16-A-003-00); text & atlas 140.00 (ISBN 0-89189-098-X, 15-A-003-00). Am Soc Clinical.
Zollinger, H. U., et al. Renal Pathology in Biopsy: Light, Electron & Immunofluorescent Microscopy & Clinical Aspects. Castagnoli, E., tr. LC 77-23922. (Illus.). 1977. 108.00 (ISBN 0-387-08382-0). Springer-Verlag.

KIDNEYS–RADIOGRAPHY

Davidson, Alan J. Radiologic Diagnosis of Renal Parenchymal Disease. LC 76-20086. (Monograhs in Clinical Radiology: No. 11). (Illus.). 1977. text ed. 30.00 (ISBN 0-7216-2925-3). Saunders.
Evans, John A. & Bosniak, Morton. The Kidney. (Atlas of Tumor Radiology Ser.). (Illus.). 1971. 43.00 (ISBN 0-8151-3164-X). Year Bk Med.
Rosenfield, Arthur T., et al, eds. Diagnostic Imaging in Renal Disease. (Illus.). 332p. 1979. 37.50 (ISBN 0-8385-1690-4). ACC.
Weill, F. S., et al, eds. Renal Sonography. (Illus.). 140p. 1981. 76.00 (ISBN 0-387-10398-8). Springer-Verlag.

KIDNEYS–TRANSPLANTATION

Casciani, C. U. & Adorno, D., eds. Tissue Typing & Kidney Transplantation, 1978 Report. (Illus.). 57p. 1980. 20.00 (ISBN 8-8212-0032-9, Pub. by Piccin Italy). J K Burgess.
Chatterjee, S. N., et al. Manual of Renal Transplantation. 1979. 31.30 (ISBN 0-387-90337-2). Springer-Verlag.
Chatterjee, Satya N., ed. Renal Transplantation. 1980. 26.50 (ISBN 0-89004-308-6). Raven.
Corry, Robert J. & Thompson, John S. Renal Transplantation Case Studies. 1977. spiral bdg. 14.00 (ISBN 0-87488-015-7). Med Exam.
European Dialysis & Transplant Assoc., 1974, Tel Aviv. Dialysis, Transplantation & Nephrology: Proceedings, Vol. 11. Moorhead, John, ed. (Illus.). 600p. 1975. 45.00x (ISBN 0-8464-0326-9). Beekman Pubs.
European Dialysis & Transplant Assoc. Dialysis, Transplantation & Nephrology: Proceedings, Vol. 12. Moorhead, J. F., ed. (Illus.). 1976. text ed. 49.00x (ISBN 0-8464-0327-7). Beekman Pubs.
Hamburger, Jean, et al. Renal Transplantation: Theory & Practice. 2nd ed. (Illus.). 384p. 1981. 45.00 (ISBN 0-686-77747-6, 3872-9). Williams & Wilkins.
Iwasaki, Yoji, ed. Cadaveric Renal Transplantation. (Illus.). 1974. 40.00 (ISBN 0-89640-019-0). Igaku-Shoin.
Microsymposium, Nijmegen, 1977. Radiological Aspects of Renal Transplantation: Proceedings. Penn, William, ed. (Radiologia Clinica: Vol. 47, No. 1). (Illus.). 1977. 11.75 (ISBN 3-8055-2844-2). S Karger.
Morris, P. J. Kidney Transplantation: Principles & Practice. 328p. 1979. 47.00 (ISBN 0-8089-1142-2). Grune.
Robinson, Brian. Dialysis, Transplantation, Nephrology: Proceedings, European Dialysis & Transplant Asso., Volume 14. (Illus.). 1978. 49.95x (ISBN 0-8464-0329-3). Beekman Pubs.
Robinson, Brian, ed. Dialysis, Transplantation, Nephrology: Proceedings European Dialysis & Transplant Assoc. Volume 13. (Illus.). 1977. 59.95x (ISBN 0-8464-0328-5). Beekman Pubs.
Rossmann, P. & Jirka, I. Rejection Nephropathy. 1977. 66.00 (ISBN 0-444-80032-8, North-Holland). Elsevier.
Sachs, Bonnie L. Renal Transplantaton - A Nursing Perspective. 1977. spiral bdg. 9.50 (ISBN 0-87488-358-X). Med Exam.
Simmons, Roberta G., et al. Gift of Life: The Social & Psychological Impact of Organ Transplantation. LC 77-2749. (Health, Medicine & Society Ser.). 1977. 32.95 (ISBN 0-471-79197-0, Pub by Wiley-Interscience). Wiley.
Touraine, J. L., et al, eds. Transplantation & Clinical Immunology, Vol. IX. (International Congress Ser: No. 423). 1978. 47.00 (ISBN 0-444-90013-6, Excerpta Medica). Elsevier.

KIELY, BENEDICT, 1919-

Casey, Daniel. Benedict Kiely. (Irish Writers Ser.). 107p. 1975. 4.50 (ISBN 0-8387-7936-0); pap. 1.95 (ISBN 0-8387-7970-0). Bucknell U Pr.
Eckley, Grace. Benedict Kiely. LC 72-187616. (English Authors Ser.: No. 145). lib. bdg. 10.95 (ISBN 0-8057-1304-2). Twayne.

KIERKEGAARD, SOREN AABYE, 1813-1855

Anderson, Barbara. Kierkegaard: A Fiction. 1974. 11.95x (ISBN 0-8156-0100-X). Syracuse U Pr.
Arbaugh, George E. & Arbaugh, George B. Kierkegaard's Authorship: A Guide to the Writings of Kierkegaard. LC 68-2512. (Augustana College Library Ser.: No. 32). 1968. 6.95 (ISBN 0-910182-32-9). Augustana Coll.
Attwater, Donald, ed. Modern Christian Revolutionaries. facsimile ed. LC 76-156608. (Essay Index Reprint Ser). Repr. of 1947 ed. 23.00 (ISBN 0-8369-2304-9). Arno.
Bain, J. A. Soren Kierkegaard: His Life & Religious Teaching. Repr. of 1935 ed. 13.00 (ISBN 0-527-04400-8). Kraus Repr.
Becker, Ernest. The Denial of Death. LC 73-1860. 1973. 12.95 (ISBN 0-02-902150-2); pap. 3.95 (ISBN 0-02-902310-6). Free Pr.
Bedell, George C. Kierkegaard & Faulkner: Modalities of Existence. LC 71-181356. 262p. 1972. 20.00 (ISBN 0-8071-0043-9). La State U Pr.
Burgess, Andrew J. Passion, Knowing How, & Understanding: An Essay on the Concept of Faith. LC 75-31550. (American Academy of Religion. Dissertation Ser.). 1975. pap. 7.50 (ISBN 0-89130-044-9, 010109). Scholars Pr Ca.
Bykhovskii, Bernard. Kierkegaard. (Philosophical Currents Ser: No. 16). 122p. 1976. pap. text ed. 16.50x (ISBN 90-6032-070-0). Humanities.
Colette. Histoire et Absolu: Essai Sur Kierkegaard. 19.95 (ISBN 0-686-54575-3). French & Eur.
Crites, Stephen. In the Twilight of Christendom: Hegel Vs. Kierkegaard on Faith & History. LC 77-188905. (American Academy of Religion. Studies in Religion). 1972. pap. text ed. 7.50 (ISBN 0-89130-154-2, 010002). Scholars Pr Ca.
Diem, Hermann. Kierkegaard's Dialectic of Existence. Knight, Harold, tr. from German. LC 77-18886. 1978. Repr. of 1959 ed. lib. bdg. 21.00x (ISBN 0-313-20220-6, DIKD). Greenwood.
Duncan, Elmer H. Soren Kierkegaard. Patterson, Bob E., ed. LC 76-2862. (Markers of the Modern Theological Mind Ser.). 1976. 7.95 (ISBN 0-87680-463-6, 80463). Word Bks.
Eller, Vernard. The Simple Life: The Christian Stance Toward Possessions. 1973. pap. 3.95 (ISBN 0-8028-1537-5). Eerdmans.
Elrod, J. W. Being & Existence in Kierkegaard's Pseudonymous Works. 1975. 19.50 (ISBN 0-691-07204-3). Princeton U Pr.
Elrod, John W. Kierkegaard & Christendom. LC 80-8547. 384p. 1981. 22.50x (ISBN 0-691-07261-2). Princeton U Pr.
Fenger, Henning. Kierkegaard, the Myths & Their Origins: Studies in the Kierkegaardian Papers & Letters. Schoolfield, George C., tr. from Swedish. LC 80-277. 256p. 1980. 19.50x (ISBN 0-300-02462-2). Yale U Pr.
George, A. G. First Sphere: An Introduction to Kierkegaardian Aesthetics. 5.25x (ISBN 0-210-27137-X). Asia.
Harper, Ralph. The Seventh Solitude: Metaphysical Homelessness in Kierkegaard, Dostoevsky, & Nietzsche. LC 65-11662. 163p. 1965. 11.50x (ISBN 0-8018-0256-3); pap. 3.95 (ISBN 0-8018-0257-1). Johns Hopkins.
Heiss, Robert. Hegel, Kierkegaard, Marx. 448p. 1975. pap. 3.95 (ISBN 0-440-53529-8, Delta). Dell.
Heschel, Abraham J. A Passion for Truth. 336p. 1973. 8.95 (ISBN 0-374-22992-9); pap. 5.95 (ISBN 0-374-51184-5). FS&G.
Hohlenberg, Johannes. Soren Kierkegaard. 1978. Repr. of 1954 ed. lib. bdg. 17.50x (ISBN 0-374-93923-3). Octagon.
Hubben, William. Dostoevsky, Kierkegaard, Nietzsche & Kafka. Orig. Title: Four Prophets of Our Destiny. 1962. pap. 1.95 (ISBN 0-02-065750-1, Collier). Macmillan.
Jaspers, Karl. Reason & Existenz. Earle, William, tr. from Ger. pap. 3.95 (ISBN 0-374-50060-6, N117). FS&G.
Kern, Edith. Existential Thought & Fictional Technique: Kierkegaard, Sartre, Beckett. LC 79-81422. 1970. 20.00x (ISBN 0-300-01203-9). Yale U Pr.
Kierkegaard, Soren. Kierkegaard's Writings: Vol. XIV, Two Ages, The Age of Revolution & The Present Age. Hong, Howard V. & Hong, Edna H., eds. LC 77-71986. 1978. text ed. 14.00 (ISBN 0-691-07226-4). Princeton U Pr.
--Letters & Documents. Rosenmeier, Henrik, tr. from Danish. LC 77-85897. (Kierkegaard's Writings Ser.: No. XXV). 584p. 1978. 27.50x (ISBN 0-691-07228-0). Princeton U Pr.
--Soren Kierkegaard's Journals & Papers, 7 vols. Hong, Howard V. & Hong, Edna H., eds. Incl. Vol. 1. A-E. 572p. 1967. 25.00x (ISBN 0-253-18240-9); Vol. 2. F-K. 640p. 1970. 35.00x (ISBN 0-253-18241-7); Vol. 3. L-R. 944p. 1976. 40.00x (ISBN 0-253-18242-5); Vol. 4. S-Z. 800p. 1976. 40.00x (ISBN 0-253-18243-3); Vol. 5. Autobiographical, Part One, 1829-1848. 576p. 1978. 27.50x (ISBN 0-253-18244-1); Vol. 6. Autobiographical, Part Two, 1848-1855. 648p. 1978. 35.00x (ISBN 0-253-18245-X); Vol. 7. Index & Composite Collation. 160p. 1978. 20.00x (ISBN 0-253-18246-8). LC 67-13025. Set. 175.00x (ISBN 0-253-18239-5). Ind U Pr.
Klemke. Studies in the Philosophy of Kiekegaard. 1976. pap. 16.00 (ISBN 90-247-1852-X, Pub. by Martinus Nijhoff Netherlands). Kluwer Boston.
Kuehnhold, Christa. Der Begriff De Sprunges und der Weg De Sprachdenkens: Eine Einfuehrung in Kierkegaard. xii, 183p. (Ger.). 1975. 42.25x (ISBN 3-11-004965-1). De Gruyter.
Lapointe, Francois H., compiled by. Soren Kierkegaard & His Critics: An International Bibliography of Criticism. LC 80-783. viii, 430p. 1980. lib. bdg. 37.50 (ISBN 0-313-22333-5, LKI/). Greenwood.

Lawson, Lewis A., ed. Kierkegaard's Presence in Contemporary American Life: Essays from Various Disciplines. LC 76-142237. 1971. 10.00 (ISBN 0-8108-0358-5). Scarecrow.

Lowrie, Walter. Kierkegaard, 2 vols. Set. 18.00 (ISBN 0-8446-0778-9). Peter Smith.

--Short Life of Kierkegaard. 1942. 14.50 (ISBN 0-691-07163-2); pap. 5.95 (ISBN 0-691-01957-6). Princeton U Pr.

Mackey, Louis. Kierkegaard: A Kind of Poet. LC 75-157050. (Orig.). 1971. 19.95x (ISBN 0-8122-7641-8); pap. 6.95x (ISBN 0-8122-1042-5). U of Pa Pr.

McKinnon, A., ed. Kierkegaard in Translation. LC 77-855336. (Kierkegaard Indices to Kierkegaard's Samlede Vaerker Ser.: Vol. I). 155p. 1979. 14.00x (ISBN 0-691-07248-5). Princeton U Pr.

McKinnon, Alastair, ed. Computational Analysis of Kierkegaard's Samlede Vaerker. LC 76-354264. (The Kierkegaard Indices to Kierkegaard's Samlede Vaerker Ser.). 1095p. 1979. 195.00x (ISBN 0-691-07251-5); Set, Vols. I-VI. 495.00 (ISBN 0-686-75220-1). Princeton U Pr.

--Index Verborum Til Kierkegaard's Samlede Vaerker. LC 74-306005. (The Kierkegaard Indices to Kierkegaard's Samlede Vaerker Ser.: Vol. III). 1338p. 1979. 170.00x (ISBN 0-691-07250-7). Princeton U Pr.

--Konkordians Til Kierkegaard's Samlede Vaerker. LC 72-181002. (Kierkegaard Indices to Kierkegaard's Samlede Vaerker Ser.: Vol. II). 1153p. 1979. 170.00 (ISBN 0-691-07249-3). Princeton U Pr.

Malantschuk, Gregor. The Controversial Kierkegaard. McKinnon, Alastair, ed. Hong, Howard V. & Hong, Edna H., trs. (The Kierkegard Monograph). 82p. 1980. pap. text ed. 7.50 (ISBN 0-88920-093-9, Pub. by Laurier U Pr Canada). Humanities.

--Kierkegaard's Thought. Hong, Howard V. & Hong, Edna H., trs. from Dan. LC 77-155000. 400p. (Eng.). 1974. 28.00 (ISBN 0-691-07166-7, 317); pap. 7.95 (ISBN 0-691-01982-7). Princeton U Pr.

--Kierkegaard's Thought. Hong, Howard V. & Hong, Edna H., trs. from Dan. LC 77-155000. 400p. (Eng.). 1974. 28.00 (ISBN 0-691-07166-7, 317); pap. 7.95 (ISBN 0-691-01982-7). Princeton U Pr.

Manheimer, Ronald J. Kierkegaard As Educator. LC 76-24587. 1978. 17.50x (ISBN 0-520-03312-4). U of Cal Pr.

Mullen, John D. Kierkegaard's Philosophy: Self-Deception & Cowardice in the Present Age. (Orig.). 1981. pap. 2.95 (ISBN 0-451-61945-5, ME1945, Ment). NAL.

Nordentoft, Kresten. Kierkegaard's Psychology. Kirmmse, Bruce, tr. from Danish. (Psychological Ser.: Vol. 7). 1978. text ed. 20.00x (ISBN 0-391-00661-4). Duquesne.

Ostenfeld, Ib. Soren Kierkegaard's Psychology. McHinnon, Alastair, ed. (The Kierkargaard Monograph). 68p. 1978. pap. text ed. 6.95 (ISBN 0-88920-121-8). Humanities.

Paley, Alan L. Soren Kierkegaard: Modern Philosopher & Existentialist. LC 72-81903. 32p. 1972. lib. bdg. 2.95 incl. catalog cards (ISBN 0-87157-550-7); pap. 1.50 vinyl laminated covers (ISBN 0-87157-050-5). SamHar Pr.

Perkins, Robert L., ed. Kierkegaard's Fear & Trembling: Critical Appraisals. LC 79-16984. xii, 251p. 1981. text ed. 24.75x (ISBN 0-8173-0028-7). U of Ala Pr.

Shestov, Lev. Kierkegaard & the Existential Philosophy. Hewitt, Elinor, tr. LC 68-29656. vii, 314p. 1969. 20.00 (ISBN 0-8214-0060-6). Ohio U Pr.

Shmueli, Adi. Kierkegaard & Consciousness. LC 70-132241. 1971. 15.00 (ISBN 0-691-07143-8). Princeton U Pr.

Smith, Joseph H., ed. Kierkegaard's Truth: The Disclosure of the Self. LC 80-26983. (Psychiatry & the Humanities: Vol. 5). (Illus.). 456p. 1981. 36.50x (ISBN 0-300-02621-8). Yale U Pr.

Sontag, Frederick. A Kierkegaard Handbook. LC 79-87741. 1980. pap. 6.95 (ISBN 0-8042-0654-6). John Knox.

Sponheim, Paul R. Kierkegaard on Christ & Christian Coherence. LC 75-3999. (Illus.). 332p. 1976. Repr. of 1968 ed. lib. bdg. 19.75x (ISBN 0-8371-7455-4, SPKC). Greenwood.

Stack, George J. Kierkegaard's Existential Ethics. LC 75-16344. (Studies in Humanities: No. 16). 240p. 1977. 15.00x (ISBN 0-8173-6624-5); pap. 5.50 (ISBN 0-8173-6626-1). U of Ala Pr.

--On Kierkegaard: Philosophical Fragments. (Eclipse Bks.). 160p. 1976. pap. text ed. 5.00x (ISBN 0-391-00586-3). Humanities.

Stendahl, Brita K. Soren Kierkegaard. LC 76-6860. (World Authors Ser.: Denmark: No. 392). 1976. lib. bdg. 10.95 (ISBN 0-8057-6234-5). Twayne.

Sullivan, F. Russell. Faith & Reason in Kierkegaard. LC 78-60695. 1978. pap. text ed. 7.50 (ISBN 0-8191-0559-7). U Pr of Amer.

Taylor, Mark C. Journeys to Selfhood: Hegel & Kierkegaard. 264p. 1981. 22.50x (ISBN 0-520-04167-4); pap. 7.95 (ISBN 0-520-04176-3, CAL 483). U of Cal Pr.

--Kierkegaard's Pseudonymous Authorship: A Study in Time & the Self. 404p. 1975. 28.00 (ISBN 0-691-07202-7). Princeton U Pr.

Thomte, Reidar. Kierkegaard's Philosophy of Religion. Repr. of 1948 ed. lib. bdg. 15.00x (ISBN 0-8371-0979-5, THKI). Greenwood.

Thulstrup, Niels. Kierkegaard's Relation to Hegel. Stengren, George L., tr. LC 79-3233. 1980. 27.50x (ISBN 0-691-07243-4); pap. 10.75 limited ed. (ISBN 0-691-10079-9). Princeton U Pr.

Tian-Min Lin, Timothy. The Life & Thought of Soren Kierkegaard. 1974. 7.00x (ISBN 0-8084-0376-1); pap. 2.95x (ISBN 0-8084-0377-X, P15). Coll & U Pr.

Ussher, Arland. Journey Through Dread. LC 68-54234. 1955. 9.00x (ISBN 0-8196-0221-3). Biblo.

Walker, Jeremy. To Will One Thing: Reflections on Kierkegaard's Purity of Heart. 1972. 11.00 (ISBN 0-7735-0084-7). McGill-Queen's U. Pr.

Warnock, Mary. Existentialist Ethics. (Orig.). 1967. pap. 4.50 (ISBN 0-312-27510-2, E73250). St Martin.

Zuidema, S. U. Kierkegaard. pap. 1.25 (ISBN 0-87552-585-7). Presby & Reformed.

KIFIOTI LANGUAGE

see Congo Language

KIKUYU LANGUAGE

Armstrong, Lilias E. Phonetic & Tonal Structure of Kikuyu. (African Language & Lingustics Ser). 1967. 25.00x (ISBN 0-7129-0204-X). Intl Pubns Serv.

Barlow, A. R. English-Kikuyu Dictionary. Benson, T. G., tr. 340p. 1975. 24.95x (ISBN 0-19-864407-8). Oxford U Pr.

Benson, T. G., ed. Kikuyu-English Dictionary. 1964. 24.95x (ISBN 0-19-864405-1). Oxford U Pr.

KIKUYU TRIBE

Bulpett, C. W., ed. King of the Wa-Kikuyu. (Illus.). 320p. 1968. Repr. of 1911 ed. 27.50x (ISBN 0-7146-1638-9, F Cass Co). Biblio Dist.

Kenyatta, Jomo. Facing Mount Kenya. 1962. pap. 3.95 (ISBN 0-394-70210-7, Vin). Random.

--Facing Mount Kenya: The Tribal Life of Gikuyu. LC 75-41161. Repr. of 1953 ed. 18.50 (ISBN 0-404-14676-7). AMS Pr.

Leaky, L. S. B., et al. The Southern Kikuyu Before 1903, 3 vols. Ensminger, J. & Beecher, G. S. B., eds. 1978. Vol. 1. 74.00 (ISBN 0-12-439901-0); Vol. 2. 74.00 (ISBN 0-12-439902-9); Vol. 3. 74.00 (ISBN 0-12-439903-7). Acad Pr.

Middleton, J. Kikuyu & Kamba of Kenya. 1972. 10.50x (ISBN 0-85302-016-7). Intl Pubns Serv.

Mockerie, Parmenas G. An African Speaks for His People. LC 74-15068. Repr. of 1934 ed. 12.50 (ISBN 0-404-12110-1). AMS Pr.

Muriuki, Godfrey. A History of the Kikuyu 1500-1900. (Illus.). 168p. 1974. text ed. 10.50x (ISBN 0-19-572314-7). Oxford U Pr.

Prins, Adriaan H. East African Age-Class Systems: An Inquiry into the Social Order of Galla, Kipsigis & Kikuyu. LC 72-106785. (Illus.). Repr. of 1953 ed. 10.00x (ISBN 0-8371-3538-9). Greenwood.

Routledge, W. S. & Routledge, K. With a Prehistoric People: A Kikuyu of British East Africa. (Illus.). 392p. 1968. Repr. of 1910 ed. 29.50x (ISBN 0-7146-1716-4, F Cass Co). Biblio Dist.

KILARI LANGUAGE

see Congo Language

KILAUEA

Stone, J. B. Products & Structure of Kilavea. Repr. of 1926 ed. pap. 7.00 (ISBN 0-527-02136-9). Kraus Repr.

KILGALLEN, DOROTHY

Israel, Lee. Kilgallen. (Illus.). 1979. 12.95 (ISBN 0-440-04522-3). Delacorte.

KILIMANJARO

Dundas, Charles. Kilimanjaro & Its People. (Illus.). 349p. 1968. Repr. of 1924 ed. 27.50x (ISBN 0-7146-1659-1, F Cass Co). Biblio Dist.

Edberg, Rolf. The Dream of Kilimanjaro. Bradfield, Keith, tr. LC 78-20415. (Illus.). 1979. 8.95 (ISBN 0-394-50384-8). Pantheon.

KILKENNY CONFEDERATION

see Irish Confederation, 1642-1648

KILLIGREW, THOMAS, 1612-1683

Harbage, Alfred. Thomas Killigrew, Cavalier Dramatist. LC 67-23854. 1967. Repr. of 1930 ed. 14.00 (ISBN 0-405-08597-4). Arno.

Summers, Montague. Playhouse of Pepys. 1964. text ed. 20.00x (ISBN 0-391-00470-0). Humanities.

KILLILEA, KAREN, 1940-

Killilea, Marie. Karen. 1962. 8.95 (ISBN 0-13-514638-0). P-H.

KILLING, MERCY

see Euthanasia

KILLY, JEAN CLAUDE

Hahn, James & Hahn, Lynn. Killy! The Sports Career of Jean-Claude Killy. Schroeder, Howard, ed. (Sports Legends Ser.). (Illus.). 48p. (gr. 3 up). 1981. PLB 6.95 (ISBN 0-89686-132-5); pap. text ed. 3.25 (ISBN 0-89686-147-3). Crestwood Hse.

KILMER, ALFRED JOYCE, 1886-1918

Cargas, Harry. I Lay Down My Life. 1964. 2.50 (ISBN 0-8198-0063-5); pap. 1.50 (ISBN 0-8198-0064-3). Dghtrs St Paul.

KILNS

see also Drying Apparatus; Furnaces

Bachrich, Jack L. Dry Kiln Handbook. (Illus.). 273p. 1980. 50.00 (ISBN 0-87930-087-6, Pub. by H A Simons Intl Canada). Miller Freeman.

Colson, Frank. Kiln Building with Space-Age Materials. 128p. 1975. 12.95x (ISBN 0-442-21641-6). Van Nos Reinhold.

Colson, Frank A. Kiln Building with Space-Age Materials. 127p. 1980. pap. 7.95 (ISBN 0-442-24423-1). Van Nos Reinhold.

Fournier, Robert. Electric Kiln Construction for Potters. (Illus.). 1977. 11.95 (ISBN 0-442-30134-0). Van Nos Reinhold.

Gregory, Ian. Kiln Building: A Ceramic Skillbook. (Illus.). 1977. 9.95 (ISBN 0-8230-0590-9). Watson-Guptill.

Olsen, Frederick. The Kiln Book. 2nd ed. 276p. 1981. 19.95 (ISBN 0-686-30226-5). Chilton.

Peray, K. & Waddell, J. J. The Rotary Cement Kiln. (Illus.). 1972. 18.50 (ISBN 0-8206-0237-X). Chem Pub.

Rhodes, Daniel. Kilns, Design, Construction, & Operation. 2nd ed. LC 80-70262. 256p. 1981. 21.50 (ISBN 0-8019-7064-4). Chilton.

--Kilns: Design, Construction & Operation. LC 68-57512. (Creative Crafts Ser). (Illus.). 1968. 12.95 (ISBN 0-8019-5358-8). Chilton.

Riegger, Hal. Electric Kiln Ceramics. 1978. 14.95 (ISBN 0-442-26961-7); pap. 8.95 (ISBN 0-442-26958-7). Van Nos Reinhold.

Ritchie, Ralph W. How to Get the Most Heat from Your Fuel, No. 1. LC 81-90069. (Energy Conservation in the Crafts - a Craft Monograph). (Illus.). 36p. (Orig.). 1979. pap. 4.00 (ISBN 0-939656-00-0). Studios West.

--How to Recover & Re-Use Heat from Kilns & Furnaces. LC 81-90073. (Energy Conservation in the Crafts - a Craft Monograph: No. 5). (Illus.). 52p. (Orig.). 1981. pap. 4.00 (ISBN 0-939656-04-3). Studios West.

--Kiln & Furnace Stacks, No. 2. LC 81-90070. (Energy Conservation in the Crafts - a Craft Monograph). (Illus.). 46p. (Orig.). 1980. pap. 4.00 (ISBN 0-939656-01-9). Studios West.

--Understanding & Using Burners. LC 81-90072. (Energy Conservation in the Crafts - a Craft Monograph: No. 4). (Illus.). 60p. (Orig.). 1981. pap. 4.00 (ISBN 0-939656-03-5). Studios West.

--User's Fuel Handbook. LC 81-90075. (Energy Conservation in the Crafts - a Craft Monograph: No. 7). (Illus., Orig.). 1981. pap. 4.00 (ISBN 0-939656-06-X). Studios West.

Ritchie, Ralph W. & Ritchie, Fern J. Electric Kiln Handbook, Vol. 6. LC 81-90074. (Energy Conservation in the Crafts-a Craft Monograph). (Illus.). 60p. (Orig.). 1981. pap. 4.00 (ISBN 0-939656-05-1). Studios West.

KILPATRICK, WILLIAM HEARD, 1871-1965

Perry, L., ed. Bertrand Russell, A. S. Neill, Homer Lane, W. H. Kilpatrick: Four Progressive Educators. 1968. pap. text ed. 1.95x (ISBN 0-02-975150-X). Macmillan.

KIMBERLEY, WESTERN AUSTRALIA (DIVISION)–DESCRIPTION AND TRAVEL

Douglas, Malcolm. Kimberly in Colour. LC 73-178763. (Colourful Australia Ser). (Illus.). 32p. 1973. 6.50x (ISBN 0-85179-454-8). Intl Pubns Serv.

KIN KLETSO (PUEBLO)

Vivian, Gordon, et al. Kin Kletso, a Pueblo Three Community in Chaco Canyon, New Mexico, & Tree-Ring Dating of the Archeological Sites in the Chaco Canyon Region, New Mexico, Vol. 6, Pts. 1&2. LC 42-40993. (Illus.). 1973. pap. 4.00x (ISBN 0-911408-15-0). SW Pks Mnmts.

KINCAID, TREVOR, 1872-1970

Guberlet, Muriel L. Windows to His World: The Story of Trevor Kincaid. LC 73-91594. (Illus.). 1975. 9.95 (ISBN 0-87015-210-6). Pacific Bks.

KINDERGARTEN

see also Creative Activities and Seatwork; Education, Preschool; Montessori Method of Education; Nursery Schools; Object-Teaching

Adams, Anne, et al. Success in Kindergarten Reading & Writing. (gr. k). 1980. text ed. 12.95 (ISBN 0-8302-8420-6). Goodyear.

Baranoff, Timy. Kindergarten Minute by Minute. LC 78-72076. 1979. pap. 6.50 (ISBN 0-8224-4100-4). Pitman Learning.

Boegehold, Betty. Education Before Five. 1978. pap. 7.50x (ISBN 0-8077-2557-9). Tchrs Coll.

Collier, et al. Kids' Stuff: Kindergarten - Nursery School. (The Kids' Stuff Set). (ps-k). 1969. pap. 10.95 (ISBN 0-913916-00-5, IP005). Incentive Pubns.

A Curriculum on Cards for Kindegarten. Date not set. price not set (ISBN 0-939418-02-9). Ferguson-Florissant.

The Extended Day Kindergarten. Date not set. price not set (ISBN 0-939418-35-5). Ferguson-Florissant.

Fairchild, Thomas N., et al. Kindergarten Primer. 1975. 3.75 (ISBN 0-89301-023-5). U Pr of Idaho.

Forcelledo-Derodriguez, Maria. El Kindergarten Como Parte De la Escuela Elemental. 2nd ed. 3.75 (ISBN 0-8477-2708-4). U of PR Pr.

Forte, Imogene. Think About It-Kindergarten. LC 80-84619. (Think About It Ser.). (Illus.). 80p. (ps-k). 1981. pap. text ed. 5.95 (ISBN 0-913916-96-X, IP-96X). Incentive Pubn.

Froebel, Friedrich. Mother's Songs, Games & Stores: Froebel's Mutter-und Rose-Lieder Rendered in English. LC 75-35068. (Studies in Play & Games). (Illus.). 1976. Repr. 20.00x (ISBN 0-405-07919-2). Arno.

Hahn, Julia L. Critical Evaluation of a Supervisory Program in Kindergarten - Primary Grades. LC 74-176829. (Columbia University. Teachers College. Contributions to Education: No. 495). Repr. of 1931 ed. 17.50 (ISBN 0-404-55495-4). AMS Pr.

Harris, Esther K. Responsiveness of Kindergarten Children to the Behavior of Their Fellows. 1946. pap. 10.00 (ISBN 0-527-01538-5). Kraus Repr.

Headley, Keith E. Education in the Kindergarten. 4th ed. (Illus.). 1966. text ed. 14.95x (ISBN 0-442-21642-4). Van Nos Reinhold.

Holland, Bernice C. How to Individualize Kindergarten Teaching: New Approaches Learning the Key Sensory Modes. 1974. 11.95 (ISBN 0-13-413211-4). P-H.

Kalinina, V. Going to Kindergarten. 19p. 1974. pap. 0.75 (ISBN 0-8285-1153-5, Pub. by Progress Pubs Russia). Imported Pubns.

Learning Activities for Kindergarten & Grade One: Language. Date not set. price not set (ISBN 0-939418-11-8). Ferguson-Florissant.

Learning Activities for Kindergarten & Grade One: Math. Date not set. price not set (ISBN 0-939418-12-6). Ferguson-Florissant.

Lewallen, Joyce. Galaxy of Games & Activities for the Kindergarten. (Illus.). 1978. 11.95 (ISBN 0-13-346106-8, Parker). P-H.

Massey, James O. Readiness for Kindergarten. 1975. pap. 1.25 (ISBN 0-89106-014-6, 1281). Consulting Psychol.

Miller, Mabel E. Kindergarden Teacher's Activities Desk Book. 1974. 11.95 (ISBN 0-13-515254-2, Parker). P-H.

Nale, Nell, et al. Kindergarten Keys. rev. ed. 1975. tchr's guidebk. 85.50 (ISBN 0-87892-655-0). Economy Co.

Paley, Vivian G. White Teacher. LC 78-9841. 1979. text ed. 8.95x (ISBN 0-674-95185-9). Harvard U Pr.

Petrone, Fred R. The Developmental Kindergarten: Individualized Instruction Through Diagnostic Grouping. (Illus.). 240p. 1976. 18.75 (ISBN 0-398-03506-7). C C Thomas.

Priestman, Barbara. Frobel Education Today. 59.95 (ISBN 0-8490-0202-8). Gordon Pr.

Ramsey, Marjorie E. & Bayless, Kathleen. Kindergarten: Program & Practices. LC 80-11478. (Illus.). 1980. pap. text ed. 13.95 (ISBN 0-8016-4076-8). Mosby.

Read, Katherine & Patterson, June. Nursery School & Kindergarten. 4th ed. LC 79-25455. 419p. 1980. text ed. 18.95 (ISBN 0-03-055221-4, HoltC). HR&W.

Schickedanz, et al. Strategies for Teaching Young Children. (Early Childhood Series). 1977. text ed. 16.95 (ISBN 0-13-851105-5). P-H.

Siglin, Lynne. Prepare Your Child for Kindergarten. 24p. 1977. pap. 0.95 (ISBN 0-87227-017-3). Reg Baptist.

Skill Checklists & Criteria for Kindergarten: Language. Date not set. price not set (ISBN 0-939418-09-6). Ferguson-Florissant.

Skill Checklists & Criteria for Kindergarten: Math. Date not set. price not set (ISBN 0-939418-10-X). Ferguson-Florissant.

Snyder, Agnes. Dauntless Women in Childhood Education, 1856-1931. LC 72-80018. (Illus.). 1972. pap. 9.50x (ISBN 0-87173-021-9). ACEI.

Weber, Evelyn. Kindergarten: Its Encounter with Educational Thought in America. LC 70-75202. 1969. pap. 8.25x (ISBN 0-8077-2315-0). Tchrs Coll.

Wolf, Theta. The Effect of Praise & Competition on the Persisting Behavior of Kindergarten Children. LC 76-141552. (Univ. of Minnesota Institute of Child Welfare Monographs: No. 15). (Illus.). 138p. 1975. Repr. of 1938 ed. lib. bdg. 15.00x (ISBN 0-8371-5899-0, CWWP). Greenwood.

Zeitlin, Shirley. Kindergarten Screening. (Illus.). 304p. 1976. 19.75 (ISBN 0-398-03574-1). C C Thomas.

KINDERGARTEN–METHODS AND MANUALS

Barbe, Walter B. Resource Book for the Kindergarten Teacher. (Illus.). 1980. 34.95 (ISBN 0-88309-103-8). Zaner-Bloser.

Barbe, Walter B., et al. Basic Skills in Kindergarten: Foundations for Formal Learning. 1980. 10.00 (ISBN 0-88309-104-6). Zaner-Bloser.

Barry, James C. & Treadway, Charles F., eds. Kindergarten Resource Book. LC 65-15333. 1965. pap. 5.75 (ISBN 0-8054-3205-1). Broadman.

Boning, Richard A. We Study Word Shapes, Bks. K-A. (gr. k-1). 1969. 3.75 ea. (Pub. by Dexter & Westbrook); Bk. K. (ISBN 0-87966-056-2); Bk. A. (ISBN 0-87966-057-0). B Loft.

Cohen, Dorothy H. & Rudolph, Marguerita. Kindergarten & Early Schooling. (Illus.). 352p. 1977. text ed. 18.95 (ISBN 0-13-515239-9). P-H.

Launch: A Handbook of Classroom Ideas to Motivate the Teaching of Preschool & Kindergarten. (The Spice Ser). 1972. 6.50 (ISBN 0-89273-111-7). Educ Serv.

Lucas, Virginia H., et al. Kindergarten Program. (Illus.). 1980. pupil bk. 2.97 (ISBN 0-88309-101-1); tchr's guide 4.97 (ISBN 0-88309-102-X). Zaner-Bloser.

Newbury, Josephine. More Kindergarten Resources. LC 73-5349. 264p. (Orig.). 1974. pap. 7.95 (ISBN 0-8042-1360-7). John Knox.

Oxley, Mary B. Illustrated Guide to Individualized Kindergarten Instruction. 1976. 11.95 (ISBN 0-13-450957-9, Parker). P-H.

Robison, Helen F. New Directions in the Kindergarten. LC 65-22438. (Orig.). 1966. pap. 7.00x (ISBN 0-8077-2045-3). Tchrs Coll.

Romer, Terry L. Complete Kindergarten Handbook. (Illus.). 1979. 12.95 (ISBN 0-13-161331-6, Parker). P-H.

KINDERGARTEN–MUSIC

see also Games with Music; Nursery Schools–Music; Singing Games

Cradock, Eveline. Musical Appreciation in an Infant School. (Illus.). 50p. (Orig.). 1977. pap. text ed. 6.75 (ISBN 0-19-321055-X). Oxford U Pr.

Daniel, Katinka S. Kodaly in Kindergarten 50 Lesson Plans Curriculum Song Collection. (Illus.). 190p. (Orig.). 1981. wire bdg. 17.50 (ISBN 0-916656-15-2, MF-15). Mark Foster Mus.

Pape, Mary. Growing up with Music: Musical Experiences in the Infant School. 1970. 4.75x (ISBN 0-19-317410-3). Oxford U Pr.

Zeitlin, Patty. A Song Is a Rainbow: Body Movement, Music, & Rythym Instruments in the Nursery School & Kindergarten. 336p. (Orig.). pap. 12.95 (ISBN 0-8302-8196-7). Goodyear.

KINDERGARTENS

Murray, Rebecca, ed. History of the Public School Kindergarten in North Carolina. 91p. 1974. pap. text ed. 7.95x (ISBN 0-8422-0414-8). Irvington.

Vandewalker, Nina C. The Kindergarten in American Education. LC 75-165732. (American Education, Ser. 2). 1972. Repr. of 1908 ed. 19.00 (ISBN 0-405-03721-X). Arno.

KINDNESS

Chaim, Chafetz, pseud. Ahavath Chesed: The Love of Kindness As Required by G-D. Oschry, Leonard, tr. from Hebrew. 1978. pap. 4.95 (ISBN 0-87306-167-5). Feldheim.

Moncure. Kindness: Values to Live by. Date not set. lib. bdg. 7.95 (ISBN 0-516-06524-6). Childrens.

Moncure, J. B. Kindness. LC 80-15286. (What Does the Bible Say? Ser.). (Illus.). 32p. (ps-2). 1980. PLB 4.95 (ISBN 0-89565-167-X). Childs World.

Moncure, Jane B. Kindness. (Values to Live by Ser.). (Illus.). (ps-3). 1981. PLB 8.65 (ISBN 0-516-06524-6). Childrens.

Sempe, Jean-Jacques. Displays of Affection. LC 81-40504. 96p. 1981. 3.95 (ISBN 0-89480-194-5). Workman Pub.

KINDNESS TO ANIMALS

see Animals, Treatment Of

KINEMATICS

see also Hodograph; Mechanical Movements; Mechanics; Motion; Quaternions; Relativistic Kinematics; Screws, Theory of

Clagett, Marshall, tr. Nicole Oresme & the Medieval Geometry of Qualities & Motions. (Medieval Science Pubns., No. 12). (Illus.). 728p. 1968. 50.00x (ISBN 0-299-04880-2). U of Wis Pr.

Endrenyi, Laszlo, ed. Kinetic Data Analysis: Design & Analysis of Enzyme & Pharmacokinetic Experiments. 427p. 1981. 47.50 (ISBN 0-306-40724-8, Plenum Pr). Plenum Pub.

Hardison, Thomas B. Introduction to Kinematics. (Illus.). 1979. text ed. 18.95 (ISBN 0-8359-3228-1); students manual avail. Reston.

Kepler, Harold B. Basic Graphical Kinematics. 2nd ed. (Illus.). 384p. 1973. text ed. 17.95 (ISBN 0-07-034171-0, G); problems 4.95 (ISBN 0-07-034173-7); solutions for problems 3.00 (ISBN 0-07-034172-9); solutions manual 3.00 (ISBN 0-07-034174-5). McGraw.

Patton, William J. Kinematics. (Illus.). 1979. text ed. 18.95 (ISBN 0-8359-3693-7); students manual avail. (ISBN 0-8359-3694-5). Reston.

Pimenov, R. I. Kinematic Spaces. LC 69-20126. (Seminars in Mathematics Ser.: Vol. 6). 185p. 1970. 27.50 (ISBN 0-306-18806-6, Consultants). Plenum Pub.

KINEMATICS OF MACHINERY

see Machinery, Kinematics of

KINESICS

see Nonverbal Communication

KINESIOLOGY

see also Human Locomotion; Human Mechanics; Motor Ability

Barham, Jerry N. Mechanical Kinesiology. LC 77-23969. (Illus.). 1978. 18.95 (ISBN 0-8016-0476-1). Mosby.

Barton, John & Barton, Margaret. Quick Ready Reference. (Encyclopedia of Mind & Body Ser.: Vol. 3). (Illus.). 250p. (Orig.). 1981. pap. text ed. 25.00 (ISBN 0-937216-06-2). J&M Barton.

Basmajian, J. V. & MacConaill, M. A. Muscles & Movements: A Basis for Human Kinesiology. rev. ed. LC 76-6883. 412p. 1977. 21.50 (ISBN 0-88275-398-3). Krieger.

Brunnstrom. Clinical Kinesiology. rev. 3rd ed. (Illus.). 1979. text ed. 15.95 (ISBN 0-8036-1301-6). Davis Co.

Cooper, John M., et al. Kinesiology. 5th ed. LC 81-11116. (Illus.). 512p. 1981. text ed. 20.50 (ISBN 0-8016-1040-0). Mosby.

Diamond, John. Your Body Doesn't Lie. 1980. pap. 2.50 (ISBN 0-446-91118-6). Warner Bks.

Esch, Dortha & Lepley, Marvin. Musculoskeletal Function: An Anatomy & Kinesiology Laboratory Manual. LC 73-93577. (Illus.). 112p. 1974. text ed. 6.50x (ISBN 0-8166-0716-8). U of Minn Pr.

Gowitzke, Barbara & Milner, Morris. Understanding the Scientific Bases of Human Movement. 2nd ed. (Illus.). 376p. 1980. pap. 28.50 (ISBN 0-683-03592-4). Williams & Wilkins.

Grenlee, Geraldine, et al. Kinesiology. Kneer, Marian, ed. (Basic Stuff Ser.: No. I, 2 of 6). (Illus.). 90p. (Orig.). 1981. pap. text ed. 5.95 (ISBN 0-686-30220-6). AAHPERD.

Harris, Ruth. Kinesiology: Workbook & Laboratory Manual. (Illus.). 1977. 10.95 (ISBN 0-395-20668-5). HM.

Haywood, Kathleen, et al. Motor Development. Kneer, Marian, ed. (Basic Stuff Ser.). (Illus.). 55p. (gr. k up). 1981. pap. text ed. 5.95 (ISBN 0-686-30221-4). AAHPERD.

Hinson, Marilyn M. Kinesiology. 2nd ed. 336p. 1981. text ed. write for info. (ISBN 0-697-07173-1). Wm C Brown.

Jensen, Clayne R. & Schultz, Gordon W. Applied Kinesiology. 2nd ed. (McGraw-Hill Ser. in Health Ed., Phys. Ed., & Recreation). (Illus.). 1976. text ed. 15.95 (ISBN 0-07-032463-8, C). McGraw.

Logan, Gene A. & McKinney, Wayne C. Anatomic Kinesiology. 2nd ed. 304p. 1977. text ed. write for info. (ISBN 0-697-07140-5). Wm C Brown.

Omura, Yoshiaki. A New Approach to Self-Diagnosis: Introducing Applied Kinesiology. LC 79-89345. (Illus.). Date not set. 9.95 (ISBN 0-87040-468-7). Japan Pubns.

Pangrazi & Dauer. Movement in Early Childhood & Primary Education. LC 80-69535. 1981. 19.95x (ISBN 0-8087-3314-1). Burgess.

Payton, Otto, et al, eds. Scientific Bases for Neurophysiological Approaches to Therapeutic Exercise: An Anthology. LC 76-53831. 290p. 1977. pap. text ed. 10.00 (ISBN 0-8036-6795-7). Davis Co.

Piscope, John. Kinesiology: The Science of Movement. LC 80-21545. 619p. 1981. text ed. 19.95 (ISBN 0-471-03483-5). Wiley.

Rasch, Philip J. & Burke, Roger K. Kinesiology & Applied Anatomy: The Science of Human Movement. 6th ed. LC 78-8765. (Illus.). 496p. 1978. text ed. 18.50 (ISBN 0-8121-0619-9). Lea & Febiger.

Rothstein, Anne, et al. Motor Learning. Kneer, Marian, ed. (Basic Stuff Ser.: No. I, 3 of 6). (Illus.). 109p. (Orig.). 1981. pap. text ed. 5.95 (ISBN 0-686-30222-2). AAHPERD.

Schotland, Donald L. Diseases of the Motor Unit. (Illus.). 1981. write for info. (ISBN 0-89289-410-5). HM.

Schutz, Noel W., Jr. Kinesiology: the Articulation of Movement. (Pdr Press Publication in Nonverbal Behavior Ser.: No. 2). (Illus.). 1976. pap. text ed. 3.50x (ISBN 903-1600-84-9). Humanities.

Spence, Dale W. Essentials of Kinesiology: A Laboratory Manual. LC 74-673. (Health Education, Physical Education, & Recreation Ser.). (Illus.). 120p. 1975. pap. 7.50 (ISBN 0-8121-0492-7). Lea & Febiger.

Thompson, Clem W. Manual of Structural Kinesiology. 9th ed. LC 81-1675. (Illus.). 142p. 1981. pap. text ed. 13.95 (ISBN 0-8016-4940-4). Mosby.

--Manual of Structural Kinesiology. 8th ed. LC 76-46400. (Illus.). 1977. pap. text ed. 11.95 (ISBN 0-8016-4939-0). Mosby.

Winnick, Joseph P. Early Movement Experiences & Development Habitation & Remediation. LC 78-57921. (Illus.). 1979. text ed. 16.95 (ISBN 0-7216-9465-9). HR&W.

KINESIOTHERAPY

see Exercise Therapy

KINETIC ART

Compton, Michael. Optical & Kinetic Art. (Tate Gallery: Little Art Book Ser.). 1977. pap. 1.95 (ISBN 0-8120-0859-6). Barron.

Malina, Frank J., ed. Kinetic Art: Selections from the Journal Leonardo. (Illus.). 1974. pap. 6.50 (ISBN 0-486-21284-X). Dover.

Marks, Mickey K. Op-Tricks: Creating Kinetic Art. LC 79-38550. (gr. 5-9). 1972. PLB 7.89 (ISBN 0-397-31217-2). Har-Row.

Tovey, John. The Technique of Kinetic Art. 1971. 19.95 (ISBN 0-7134-2518-0, Pub. by Batsford England). David & Charles.

KINETIC THEORY OF GASES

see Gases, Kinetic Theory of

KINETIC THEORY OF LIQUIDS

see Liquids, Kinetic Theory of

KINETICS

see Dynamics; Mechanics, Analytic; Motion

KINETICS, CHEMICAL

see Chemical Reaction, Rate Of

KINETOGRAPH

Knust, Albrecht. Dictionary of Kinetography Laban, 2 vols. 1980. 57.00x (ISBN 0-7121-0416-X, Pub. by Macdonald & Evans). Vol. 1, 448pp. Vol. 2, 168pp. State Mutual Bk.

KINETOSCOPE

Dickson, W. K. & Dickson, Antonia. History of the Kinetograph, Kinetoscope & Kinetophonograph. LC 79-124005. (Literature of Cinema, Ser. 1). Repr. of 1895 ed. 6.00 (ISBN 0-405-01611-5). Arno.

KING, B. B.

Sawyer, Charles. The Arrival of B. B. King: The Authorized Biography. LC 79-6085. (Illus.). 288p. 1980. 14.95 (ISBN 0-385-15929-3). Doubleday.

KING, BILLIE JEAN

Burchard, Marshall & Burchard, Sue. Sports Hero: Billie Jean King. LC 74-16623. (Sports Hero Ser.). 96p. (gr. 3-5). 1975. PLB 6.29 (ISBN 0-399-60907-5). Putnam.

Church, Carol B. Billie Jean King: Queen of the Courts. Bender, David L. & Mc Cuen, Gary E., eds. (Focus on Famous Women Ser). (Illus.). (gr. 3-9). 1976. 6.95 (ISBN 0-912616-41-5); read-along cassette 9.95 (ISBN 0-89908-240-8). Greenhaven.

Hahn, James & Hahn, Lynn. King! The Sports Career of Billie Jean King. Schroeder, Howard, ed. (Sports Legends Ser.). (Illus.). 48p. (gr. 3 up). 1981. PLB 6.95 (ISBN 0-89686-134-1); pap. text ed. 3.25 (ISBN 0-89686-149-X). Crestwood Hse.

Morse, A. R. Tennis Champion: Billie Jean King. (Allstars Ser.). (Illus.). (gr. 2-6). 1976. PLB 5.95 (ISBN 0-87191-479-4); pap. 2.95 (ISBN 0-89812-202-3). Creative Ed.

Olsen, James T. Billie Jean King. LC 76-12090. (Creative Superstars Ser.). 1974. PLB 5.95 (ISBN 0-87191-275-9); pap. 2.95 (ISBN 0-89812-177-9). Creative Ed.

KING, CHARLES, 1844-1933–BIBLIOGRAPHY

Dornbusch, Charles E. Charles King, American Army Novelist: A Bibliography. 1963. pap. 3.00 (ISBN 0-910746-05-2). Hope Farm.

KING, CORETTA SCOTT, 1927-

Patterson, Lillie. Coretta Scott King. LC 76-19077. (American All Ser.). (Illus.). (gr. 3-6). 1977. lib. bdg. 6.48 (ISBN 0-8116-4585-1). Garrard.

Taylor, Paula. Coretta Scott King. LC 74-17360. (Illus.). (gr. 4-8). 1975. PLB 5.95 (ISBN 0-87191-410-7). Creative Ed.

Wofford, Harris. Of Kennedys & Kings: Making Sense of the Sixties. 496p. 1980. 17.50 (ISBN 0-374-22432-3). FS&G.

KING, CLARENCE, 1842-1901

Shebl, James M. King of the Mountains. (Western American Ser.: No. 5). 1974. 4.50 (ISBN 0-686-25563-1). Holt Atherton.

KING, MARTIN LUTHER, 1929-1968

Alico, Stella H. Benjamin Franklin - Martin Luther King Jr. (Pendulum Illustrated Biography Ser.). (Illus.). (gr. 4-12). 1979. text ed. 5.00 (ISBN 0-88301-365-7); pap. text ed. 1.95 (ISBN 0-88301-353-3); wkbk 1.25 (ISBN 0-88301-377-0). Pendulum Pr.

Bennett, Lerone, Jr. What Manner of Man: A Biography of Martin Luther King Jr, 1929-1968. 1968. 9.95 (ISBN 0-87485-027-4). Johnson Chi.

Crawford, Fred R., et al. Certain Reactions by the Atlanta Public to the Death of the Rev. Dr. Martin Luther King Jr. LC 73-85669. 1969. pap. 3.00 (ISBN 0-89937-023-3). Ctr Res Soc Chg.

Davis, Lenwood G. I Have a Dream: The Life & Times of Martin Luther King, Jr. LC 70-154202. 303p. 1973. Repr. of 1969 ed. lib. bdg. 17.00x (ISBN 0-8371-5977-6, DHD&). Greenwood.

Ebony Editors. Martin Luther King, Jr. (Ebony Picture Biography Ser). (Illus., Orig.). 1968. pap. 1.50 (ISBN 0-87485-025-8). Johnson Chi.

Fisher, William H. Free at Last: A Bibliography of Martin Luther King, Jr. LC 77-22202. 1977. 10.00 (ISBN 0-8108-1081-6). Scarecrow.

Garrow, David J. The FBI and Martin Luther King, Jr. 1981. 15.95 (ISBN 0-393-01509-2). Norton.

Hoyt, Robert G. Martin Luther King, Jr. LC 70-124086. (Illus.). 1970. 9.95 (ISBN 0-87294-028-4). Country Beautiful.

Lewis, David L. King: A Biography. 2nd ed. (Blacks in the New World Ser.). 1978. 17.50 (ISBN 0-252-00679-8); pap. 5.95 (ISBN 0-252-00680-1). U of Ill Pr.

Lincoln, C. Eric. Martin Luther King, Jr: A Profile. LC 69-16828. (American Profiles Ser). 232p. 1969. pap. 4.95 (ISBN 0-8090-0209-4). Hill & Wang.

Lomax, Louis. To Kill a Black Man. LC 68-8400. (Orig.). 1968. pap. 0.95 (ISBN 0-87067-160-X, BH160). Holloway.

Luther, Martin & Kepler, Thomas S., eds. Table Talk of Martin Luther. (Summit Bks.). 1979. pap. 3.95 (ISBN 0-8010-5408-7). Baker Bk.

McKnight, Janet, ed. Three Assassinations: The Deaths of John & Robert Kennedy & Martin Luther King. LC 77-154630. (Illus.). 1971. Repr. 17.50x (ISBN 0-87196-190-3). Facts on File.

Newton, Michael. A Case of Conspiracy. (Orig.). 1980. pap. 2.25 (ISBN 0-87067-003-4, BH003). Holloway.

Paris, Peter J. Black Leaders in Conflict: Joseph H. Jackson, Martin Luther King Jr., Malcolm X, Adam Clayton Powell Jr. LC 78-3833. 1978. pap. 6.95 (ISBN 0-8298-0336-X). Pilgrim NY.

Philosophy of Non-Violence: Martin Luther King-Mini-Play. (People of Conscience Ser). (gr. 8 up). 1978. 3.00 (ISBN 0-89550-313-1). RIM.

Schulke, Flip, ed. Martin Luther King, Jr. A Documentary...Montgomery to Memphis. (Illus.). 224p. 1976. 19.95 (ISBN 0-393-07487-0); limited ed. o.p. 100.00 (ISBN 0-685-62030-1); pap. 9.95 (ISBN 0-393-07492-7). Norton.

Scruggs, Julius R. Baptist Preachers with Social Consciousness: A Comparative Study of Martin Luther King Jr. & Harry Emerson Fosdick. 72p. 1979. 5.00 (ISBN 0-8059-2501-5). Dorrance.

Smith, Ervin. The Ethics of Martin Luther King, Jr. (Studies in American Religion: Vol. 2). 1982. soft cover 24.95x (ISBN 0-88946-974-1). E Mellen.

Smith, Kenneth L. & Zepp, Ira G., Jr. Search for the Beloved Community: The Thinking of Martin Luther King, Jr. LC 73-10777. 160p. 1974. 6.95 (ISBN 0-8170-0611-7). Judson.

Spruill, Robert. Death & Life of Dr. Martin Luther King. 1980. 4.00 (ISBN 0-8062-1174-1). Carlton.

Walton, Hanes, Jr. Political Philosophy of Martin Luther King Jr. LC 76-111260. (Contributions in Afro-American & African Studies: No. 10). 1971. text ed. 13.95 (ISBN 0-8371-4661-5); pap. 4.95 (ISBN 0-8371-8931-4). Greenwood.

Weisberg, Harold. Frame-up: The Martin Luther King-James Earl Ray Case. LC 70-149057. 10.00x (ISBN 0-911606-06-8). Weisberg.

Wilson, Beth P. Giants for Justice: Bethune, Randolph & King. LC 77-88971. (gr. 5 up). 1978. 6.95 (ISBN 0-15-230781-8, HJ). HarBraceJ.

Wofford, Harris. Of Kennedys & Kings: Making Sense of the Sixties. 496p. 1980. 17.50 (ISBN 0-374-22432-3). FS&G.

KING, MARTIN LUTHER, 1929-1968–JUVENILE LITERATURE

Behrens, June. Martin Luther King, Jr. The Story of a Dream. (Holiday Play Bks). (Illus.). (gr. k-4). 1979. PLB 8.65 (ISBN 0-516-08879-3, Golden Gate). Childrens.

Clayton, Ed. Martin Luther King: The Peaceful Warrior. (gr. 4-6). 1969. pap. 1.50 (ISBN 0-671-29932-8). PB.

Clayton, Edward. Martin Luther King: The Peaceful Warrior. 3rd ed. (Illus.). (gr. 4-7). 1968. PLB 5.95 (ISBN 0-13-559765-X). P-H.

De Kay, James T. Meet Martin Luther King Jr. LC 78-79789. (Step-up Books Ser.). (gr. 3-6). 1969. 3.95 (ISBN 0-394-80055-9, BYR); PLB 4.99 (ISBN 0-394-90055-3). Random.

Faber, Doris & Faber, Howard. The Assassination of Martin Luther King, Jr. LC 78-1726. (Focus Bks.). (Illus.). 1978. lib. bdg. 6.90 s&l (ISBN 0-531-02465-2). Watts.

Haskins, James. The Life & Death of Martin Luther King, Jr. LC 77-3157. (Illus.). (gr. 5 up). 1977. PLB 6.96 (ISBN 0-688-51802-8). Lothrop.
Martin Luther King Jr: Mini Play. (Black Americans Ser.). (gr. 5 up). 1977. 3.00 (ISBN 0-89550-363-8). RIM.
Patterson, Lillie. Martin Luther King, Jr: Man of Peace. LC 69-19152. (Americans All Ser). (Illus.). (gr. 3-6). 1969. PLB 6.48 (ISBN 0-8116-4555-X). Garrard.
Preston, Edward. Martin Luther King: Fighter for Freedom. LC 68-8391. (gr. 7-8). 1970. 5.95 (ISBN 0-385-08923-6). Doubleday.
Wilson, Beth P. Martin Luther King, Jr. (See & Read Biographies). (Illus.). (gr. k-3). 1971. PLB 5.99 (ISBN 0-399-60452-9). Putnam.
Young, Margaret B. Picture Life of Martin Luther King, Jr. LC 67-20866. (Picture Life Bks). (Illus.). (gr. k-3). 1968. PLB 7.40 (ISBN 0-531-00981-5). Watts.

KING, RUFUS, 1755-1827
Ernst, Robert. Rufus King: American Federalist. LC 68-15747. (Institute of Early American History & Culture Ser.). 1968. 24.50x (ISBN 0-8078-1070-3). U of NC Pr.
King, Rufus. The Life & Correspondence of Rufus King, 6 vols. King, Charles R., ed. LC 69-16653. (American Public Figures Ser.). 1971. Repr. of 1894 ed. Set. lib. bdg. 245.00 (ISBN 0-306-71125-7). Da Capo.

KING, THOMAS BUTLER, 1800-1864
Steel, Edward M., Jr. T. Butler King of Georgia. LC 64-17061. 204p. 1964. 10.00 (ISBN 0-8203-0174-4). U of Ga Pr.

KING, WILLIAM, 1812-1895
Jamieson, Annie S. William King, Friend & Champion of Slaves. LC 76-91662. Repr. of 1925 ed. 12.75x (ISBN 0-8371-2074-8). Greenwood.

KING, WILLIAM LYON MACKENZIE, 1874-1950
Esbery, Joy E. Knight of the Holy Spirit: A Study of William Lyon Mackenzie King. 336p. 1980. 20.00 (ISBN 0-8020-5502-8). U of Toronto Pr.
Hardy, Henry R. Mackenzie King of Canada: A Biography. LC 77-135245. (Illus.). xii, 390p. Repr. of 1949 ed. lib. bdg. 17.75x (ISBN 0-8371-5164-3, HAMK). Greenwood.
Pickersgill, J. W., ed. The Mackenzie King Record, 4 vols. Incl. Vol. 1. 1939-1944. 1960. 25.00x (ISBN 0-8020-1129-2); Vol. 2. 1944-1945. Forster, D. F., ed. 1968. 25.00x (ISBN 0-8020-1525-5); Vol. 3. 1945-1946. Forster, D. F., ed. 1970. 25.00x (ISBN 0-8020-1655-3); Vol. 4. 1947-1948. Forster, D. F., ed. 1970. 25.00x (ISBN 0-8020-1686-3). LC 60-51004. 65.00x set (ISBN 0-8020-1693-6). U of Toronto Pr.
William Lyon Mackenzie King, 3 vols. Incl. Vol. 1. A Political Biography, 1874-1923. Dawson, Robert M. LC 59-347. (Illus.). 1958. 30.00x (ISBN 0-8020-1083-0); Vol. 2. The Lonely Heights, 1924-1932. Neatby, H. Blair. LC 67-9143. 1980. Repr. of 1963 ed. 50.00x (ISBN 0-8020-7109-0); Vol. 3. The Prism of Unity, 1932-1939. Neatby, H. Blair. LC 59-347. (Illus.). 1976. 25.00 (ISBN 0-8020-5381-5). 52.50 set (ISBN 0-8020-2259-6). U of Toronto Pr.

KING FAMILY (SINGING GROUP)
Perrin, Nigel, et al. The King's Singers: A Self-Portrait. (Illus.). 160p. 1980. 17.50x (ISBN 0-8476-3685-2). Rowman.

KING PHILIP'S WAR, 1675-1676
Drake, Samuel G., ed. The Old Indian Chronicle. LC 74-7963. Repr. of 1867 ed. 26.00 (ISBN 0-404-11850-X). AMS Pr.
Ellis, George W. & Morris, John E. King Philip's War. LC 76-43697. Repr. of 1906 ed. 28.50 (ISBN 0-404-15529-4). AMS Pr.
Geller, L. D. Traditional Murder Test of King Philip's War. Date not set. 0.25 (ISBN 0-686-30044-0). Pilgrim Hall.
The History of King Phillip's War. LC 72-78674. 1867. Repr. 20.00 (ISBN 0-403-08929-8). Somerset Pub.
Leach, Douglas E. Flintlock & Tomahawk: New England in King Philip's War. 1966. pap. 4.95 (ISBN 0-393-00340-X, Norton Lib). Norton.
Leach, Douglas E., ed. A Rhode Islander Reports on King Philip's War. 1963. 10.00 (ISBN 0-685-67673-0). RI Hist Soc.
Lincoln, Charles H., ed. Narratives of the Indian Wars, Sixteen Seventy-Five to Sixteen Ninety-Nine. (Original Narratives). 1959. Repr. of 1913 ed. 18.50x (ISBN 0-06-480540-9). B&N.
Slotkin, Richard & Folsom, James K., eds. So Dreadful a Judgement: Puritan Responses to King Philip's War, 1676-1677. 1978. 25.00x (ISBN 0-8195-6058-8); pap. 10.00x (ISBN 0-686-77485-X). Wesleyan U Pr.

KING PHILIP'S WAR, 1675-1676–FICTION
Cooper, James F. Wept of Wish Ton-Wish, 2 Vols in 1. LC 74-107169. 1971. Repr. of 1829 ed. 17.00 (ISBN 0-403-00432-2). Scholarly.
--Wept of Wish-Ton-Wish, 2 vols. in one. (BCL I). Repr. of 1829 ed. 18.00 (ISBN 0-404-01715-0). AMS Pr.

KING RANCH, TEXAS
Denhardt, Robert M. The King Ranch Quarter Horses: And Something of the Ranch & the Men That Bred Them. LC 73-123340. (Illus.). 1978. Repr. of 1970 ed. 16.95 (ISBN 0-8061-0924-6). U of Okla Pr.
Frissell, Toni. The King Ranch, 1939-1944: A Photographic Essay. LC 75-4187. (Illus.). 144p. 1975. 15.00 (ISBN 0-87100-086-5). Morgan.

KING SALMON
see Chinook Salmon

KING SNAKES
Davis, Burke. Biography of a King Snake. LC 74-16625. (Nature Biography Ser.). (Illus.). (gr. 3-5). 1975. PLB 6.59 (ISBN 0-399-60919-9). Putnam.

KING WILLIAM COUNTY, VIRGINIA
Clarke, Peyton N. Old King William Homes & Families: An Account of Some of the Old Homesteads & Families of King William County, Virginia, from Its Earliest Settlement. LC 64-21422. (Illus.). 1976. Repr. of 1897 ed. 12.50 (ISBN 0-8063-7956-1). Genealog Pub.

KING WILLIAM'S WAR, 1689-1697
see United States–History–King William's War, 1689-1697

KINGALA LANGUAGE
see Congo Language

KINGDOM OF GOD
see also Covenants (Theology)
Allchin, A. M. The Kingdom of Love & Knowledge. 224p. (Orig.). 1982. pap. 7.95 (ISBN 0-8164-2354-7). Seabury.
Augustine, Saint City of God, 2 Vols. Tasker, R. V., ed. Healey, John, tr. 1957. 8.95x ea. (ISBN 0-686-66408-6, Evman). Vol. 1 (ISBN 0-460-00982-6). Vol. 2 (ISBN 0-460-00983-4). Biblio Dist.
Augustine, St. City of God, Bks. 1-7. (Fathers of the Church Ser.: Vol. 8). 24.00 (ISBN 0-8132-0008-3). Cath U Pr.
Augustine, Saint City of God Against the Pagans, 7 vols. (Loeb Classical Library: No. 411-417). 11.00x ea. Harvard U Pr.
--On the Two Cities: Selections from the City of God. Strothmann, F. W., ed. LC 57-13344. (Milestones of Thought Ser.). 4.50 (ISBN 0-8044-5827-8); pap. 2.75 (ISBN 0-8044-6791-9). Ungar.
Augustinus, Saint Aurelius. De Civitate Dei Libri 22: Sec. 5, 2 pts, Pts. 1 & 2. (Corpus Scriptorum Ecclesiasticorum Latinorum Ser: Vol. 40). Repr. of 1899 ed. pap. 41.50 ea. (ISBN 0-384-02370-3). Johnson Repr.
Christenson, Larry. The Kingdom. (Trinity Bible Ser.). 1972. pap. 4.95 (ISBN 0-87123-548-X, 240548). Bethany Hse.
Cripe, Earl. What, When, & Where Is the Kingdom of God. 1975. write for info. (ISBN 0-912314-14-1); pap. write for info. (ISBN 0-912314-16-8). Academy Pr-Santa.
Godsey, John D. Preface to Bonhoeffer: The Man & Two of His Shorter Writings. LC 79-7378. 80p. 1979. pap. 2.95 (ISBN 0-8006-1367-8, 1-1367). Fortress.
Hansen, Klaus J. Quest for Empire: The Political Kingdom of God & the Council of Fifty in Mormon History. x, 300p. 1967. 7.50 (ISBN 0-87013-106-0). Mich St U Pr.
Hunter, A. M. Christ & the Kingdom: What Scripture Says About Living in the Kingdom of God. 120p. 1980. pap. 3.95 (ISBN 0-89283-092-1). Servant.
Jabay, Earl. Kingdom of Self. LC 73-89494. 1974. pap. 3.95 (ISBN 0-88270-062-6). Logos.
Kraybill, Donald B. The Upside-Down Kingdom. LC 78-9435. 1978. pap. 5.95 (ISBN 0-8361-1860-X). Herald Pr.
Ladd, George E. Crucial Questions About the Kingdom of God. 1952. pap. 2.95 (ISBN 0-685-09270-4). Eerdmans.
--Gospel of the Kingdom. 1959. pap. 2.95 (ISBN 0-8028-1280-5). Eerdmans.
--The Presence of the Future: The Eschatology of Biblical Realism. 1973. pap. 7.95 (ISBN 0-8028-1531-6). Eerdmans.
McClain, Alva J. The Greatness of the Kingdom. 10.95 (ISBN 0-88469-011-3). BMH Bks.
Millet, Robert. Perfected Millenial Kingdom. 1974. pap. 2.00 (ISBN 0-89036-034-0). Hawkes Pub Inc.
Mumford, Bob. The King & You. 256p. 1974. pap. 3.50 (ISBN 0-8007-0672-2). Revell.
Niebuhr, H. Richard. Kingdom of God in America. pap. 4.95x (ISBN 0-06-130049-7, TB49, Torch). Har-Row.
Pannenberg, Wolfhart. Theology & the Kingdom of God. LC 69-12668. 1969. pap. 3.95 (ISBN 0-664-24842-X). Westminster.
Rand, Howard B. Digest of the Divine Law. 1943. 3.00 (ISBN 0-685-08802-2). Destiny.
Talese, Gay. The Kingdom & the Power. 1981. pap. 3.25 (ISBN 0-440-14397-7). Dell.
Tolstoy, Leo. Kingdom of God, & Peace Essays. Maude, Aylmer, tr. 17.95 (ISBN 0-19-250445-2). Oxford U Pr.
Trombley, Charles. Chasse Du Royaume! Date not set. 2.00 (ISBN 0-686-76390-4). Life Pubs Intl.
--Expulsado Del Reino. (Span.). Date not set. 2.25 (ISBN 0-686-76287-8). Life Pubs Intl.
Weiss, Johannes. Jesus' Proclamation of the Kingdom of God. Keck, Leander E., ed. Hiers, Richard H. & Holland, David L., trs. from Ger. LC 79-135267. (Lives of Jesus Ser). 160p. (Orig.). 1971. pap. 3.95 (ISBN 0-8006-0153-X, 1-153). Fortress.

KINGDOM OF GOD–BIBLICAL TEACHING
Dodd, C. H. Parables of the Kingdom. rev. ed. 1961. pap. text ed. 5.95x (ISBN 0-684-15049-2, ScribC). Scribner.
Kelber, Werner H. The Kingdom in Mark: A New Place & a New Time. LC 73-88353. 190p. 1974. 10.95 (ISBN 0-8006-0268-4, 1-268). Fortress.
McClain, Alva J. The Greatness of the Kingdom. 10.95 (ISBN 0-88469-011-3). BMH Bks.
Ribberbos, Herman N. Coming of the Kingdom. pap. 7.50 (ISBN 0-87552-408-7). Presby & Reformed.
Stephens, Julius H. The Churches & the Kingdom. LC 78-5676. 1978. Repr. of 1959 ed. lib. bdg. 15.00x (ISBN 0-313-20488-8, STCK). Greenwood.
Wilder, Amos N. Eschatology & Ethics in the Teaching of Jesus. LC 78-16425. 1978. Repr. of 1950 ed. lib. bdg. 22.75 (ISBN 0-313-20585-X, WIEE). Greenwood.

KINGLAKE, ALEXANDER WILLIAM, 1809-1891
De Gaury, Gerald. Travelling Gent: Life of Alexander Kinglake 1809-1891. (Illus.). 224p. 1972. 10.95 (ISBN 0-7100-7310-0). Routledge & Kegan.
Ince, Richard B. Calverley & Some Cambridge Wits of the Nineteenth Century. LC 74-28333. 1929. lib. bdg. 17.50 (ISBN 0-8414-0887-4). Folcroft.
Jewett, Iran B. Alexander W. Kinglake. (English Authors Ser.: No. 324). 1981. lib. bdg. 13.95 (ISBN 0-8057-6812-2). Twayne.

KINGS AND RULERS
see also Caliphate; Caliphs; Courts and Courtiers; Despotism; Dictators; Divine Right of Kings; Emperors; Prerogative, Royal; Roman Emperors; also subdivision Kings and Rulers under names of countries, e.g. Great Britain–Kings and Rulers
Allen, C. G., ed. Rulers & Government of the World: 1977-1978, 3 vols. Incl. Vol. 1. Earliest Times to 1491. Ross, Martha, compiled by. LC 77-72342. 1978 (ISBN 0-85935-021-5); Vol. II. 1492 to 1929. Spuler, Bertold, compiled by. LC 77-70294. 1977 (ISBN 0-85935-009-6); Vol. III. 1930 to 1975. Spuler, Bertold, compiled by. LC 77-72339. 1978 (ISBN 0-85935-056-8). 49.50 ea.; Set. 135.00 (ISBN 0-85935-051-7). Bowker.
Bolingbroke, Viscount. The Idea of a Patriot King. Jackman, Sydney W., ed. LC 64-66066. 1965. pap. text ed. 1.25x (ISBN 0-672-60433-7). Irvington.
Boyd, William K. Ecclesiastical Edicts of the Theodosian Code. LC 70-77991. (Columbia University. Studies in the Social Sciences: No. 63). Repr. of 1905 ed. 14.50 (ISBN 0-404-51063-9). AMS Pr.
Broadhurst, R. J. A History of the Ayyubid Sultans of Egypt. (International Studies & Translations Program-Arabic Literature Ser.). 1980. lib. bdg. 22.00 (ISBN 0-8057-8168-4). Twayne.
Brook, Christopher. Saxon & Norman Kings. 1978. 28.00 (ISBN 0-7134-1534-7, Pub. by Batsford England). David & Charles.
Burns, Eugene. Last King of Paradise. LC 72-10607. (Select Bibliographies Reprint Ser.). 1973. Repr. of 1952 ed. 19.00 (ISBN 0-8369-7102-7). Arno.
Canning, John, ed. One Hundred Great Kings, Queens & Rulers of the World. LC 68-23429. 1978. pap. 7.95 (ISBN 0-8008-5776-3). Taplinger.
Castelot, Andre. King of Rome. LC 74-6778. (Illus.). 396p. 1974. Repr. of 1960 ed. lib. bdg. 19.75x (ISBN 0-8371-7571-2, CAKR). Greenwood.
Constant, Stephen. Foxy Ferdinand: Tsar of Bulgaria. 352p. 1980. 17.50 (ISBN 0-531-09930-X). Watts.
Conti, Flavio. Homes of the Kings: The Grand Tour. LC 77-88245. (Illus.). 1978. 14.95 (ISBN 0-15-142165-X). HarBraceJ.
Day, U. N. The Government of the Sultanate. LC 72-901571. 219p. 1972. 7.50x (ISBN 0-8002-0639-8). Intl Pubns Serv.
DeFelice, Gerald T. Death in Egypt. 400p. (Orig.). 1981. pap. 29.95 (ISBN 0-686-30237-0). Une Pub.
Egan, E. W., et al, eds. Kings, Rulers & Statesmen. LC 67-16020. (Illus.). 1976. 20.00 (ISBN 0-8069-0050-4); lib. bdg. 17.59 (ISBN 0-8069-0051-2). Sterling.
Elyot, Thomas. The Boke Named the Governor, 2 Vols. Croft, Herbert S., ed. 1967. 55.50 (ISBN 0-8337-1058-3). B Franklin.
--Four Political Treatises, 1533-1541. LC 67-10273. 1967. 44.00x (ISBN 0-8201-1015-9). Schol Facsimiles.
--The Governor. 1962. 8.95x (ISBN 0-460-00227-9, Evman). Biblio Dist.
Erasmus, Desiderius. Education of a Christian Prince. Born, Lester K., tr. 1965. lib. bdg. 21.00x (ISBN 0-374-92603-4). Octagon.
Ferdowsi. The Epic of the Kings: Shah- nama. (Persian Heritage Ser). 1973. 30.00 (ISBN 0-7100-1367-1). Routledge & Kegan.
Ferrarius Montanus, Joannes. A Work Touching the Good Ordering of a Common Weal. Bauande, William, tr. 430p. Repr. of 1559 ed. 37.00 (ISBN 0-384-15509-X). Johnson Repr.
Franklin, Julian H., ed. & tr. Constitutionalism & Resistance in the Sixteenth Century: Three Treatises by Heltman, Beza & Mornay. LC 71-77131. (Orig.). 1969. pap. 4.95 (ISBN 0-672-63519-4). Pegasus.
Franklin, Julian H., ed. Constitutionalism & Resistance in the Sixteenth Century: Three Treatises by Holtman, Beza & Mornay. LC 71-77131. 1969. 22.50x (ISBN 0-672-53519-X). Irvington.
Furio Ceriol, Fadrique. Of Councils & Counselors, 1570: An English Reworking by Thomas Blundeville of el Consejo I Consejeros Del Principe, 1559. LC 63-7083. 1963. 20.00x (ISBN 0-8201-1018-3). Schol Facsimiles.
Ghazali. Book of Counsel for Kings. I, Jalal Huma & Isaacs, H. D., eds. Bagley, F. R., tr. 1964. 24.95x (ISBN 0-19-713129-8). Oxford U Pr.
Gurney, Gene. Kingdoms of the World: An Illustrated Encyclopedia of Ruling Monarchs from Ancient Times to the Present. (Illus.). 800p. 1981. 25.00 (ISBN 0-517-54395-8). Crown.
Hocart, A. M. Kings & Councillors: An Essay in the Comparative Anatomy of Human Society. Needham, Rodney, ed. LC 71-101297. (Classics in Anthropology Ser). 1972. pap. 3.95 (ISBN 0-226-34568-8, P368, Phoen). U of Chicago Pr.
--Kings & Councillors: An Essay in the Comparative Anatomy of Human Society. Needham, Rodney, ed. LC 71-101297. (Classics in Anthropology Ser). 1970. lib. bdg. 17.50x (ISBN 0-226-34566-1). U of Chicago Pr.
Irstam, Tor V. King of Ganda: Studies in the Institutions of Sacral Kingship in Africa. LC 70-106885. Repr. of 1944 ed. 18.00x (ISBN 0-8371-3281-9, Pub. by Negro U Pr). Greenwood.
Kaggwa, Apolo. The Kings of Buganda. Kiwanuka, M. S., tr. LC 75-981559. (Historical Texts of Eastern & Central Africa Ser.). (Illus.). 256p. 1971. 12.50x (ISBN 0-8002-1633-4). Intl Pubns Serv.
Kantorowicz, Ernest H. King's Two Bodies: A Study of Medieval Political Theology. 1957. 40.00 (ISBN 0-691-07120-9). Princeton U Pr.
Klonsky, Milton. The Fabulous Ego: Absolute Power in History. LC 74-77951. (Illus.). 512p. 1974. 15.00 (ISBN 0-8129-0490-7). Times Bks.
Kuper, Hilda. Sobhuza II: Ngwenyama & King of Swaziland. LC 78-2356. 1978. text ed. 38.00x (ISBN 0-8419-0383-2, Africana). Holmes & Meier.
Major, John M., ed. Sir Thomas Elyot's: The Book Named the Governor. LC 75-108883. 1970. text ed. 9.75 (ISBN 0-8077-1796-7); pap. 4.25x (ISBN 0-8077-1795-9). Tchrs Coll.
Mechoulan, Henri, ed. Raison et Alterite Chez Fadrique Furio Ceriol, Philosphe Pollitique Espagnol Du XVIe Siecle. 1973. pap. 22.50x (ISBN 90-2797-194-3). Mouton.
Mornay, Philippe. Defense of Liberty Against Tyrants. Laski, Harold, ed. 6.75 (ISBN 0-8446-1316-9). Peter Smith.
Myers, Henry A. & Wolfram, Herwig. Medieval Kingship. 520p. 1981. text ed. 25.95x (ISBN 0-88229-633-7); pap. text ed. 13.95x (ISBN 0-88229-782-1). Nelson-Hall.
Richter, Gustav. Studien Zur Geschichte der Alteren Arabischen Furstenspiegel. (Ger). 1932. pap. 9.50 (ISBN 0-384-50770-0). Johnson Repr.
Sawyer, P. H. & Wood, I. N., eds. Early Medieval Kingship. 193p. 1977. pap. 9.50x (ISBN 0-8476-2359-9). Rowman.
Schnittkind, Henry T. & Schnittkind, Thomas D. Living Biographies of Famous Rulers. facsimile ed. LC 72-38752. (Essay Index Reprint Ser). Repr. of 1940 ed. 24.00 (ISBN 0-8369-2671-4). Arno.
Sirjean, Gaston & Cuny, Hubert. Encyclopedic Genealogique des Maisons Souveraines du Monde, 13 vols. (Fr.). 1966-76. 275.00 (ISBN 0-686-56773-0, M-6519). French & Eur.
Sturdza, Michel. Betrayal by Rulers. LC 73-92437. 1976. pap. 4.00 (ISBN 0-88279-122-2). Western Islands.

KINGS AND RULERS–EDUCATION
see Education of Princes

KINGS AND RULERS–GENEALOGY
see also Royal Descent, Families of
Allstroem, Carl M. Dictionary of Royal Lineage of Europe & Other Countries. 1976. 55.00 (ISBN 0-685-71106-4, Regency). Scholarly.

Bennet, Daphne. Queen Victoria's Children. (Illus.). 139p. 1980. 12.50 (ISBN 0-312-66006-5). St Martin.
McNaughton, Arnold. The Book of Kings: A Royal Genealogy, 3 vols. LC 72-77538. 1000p. 1973. 125.00 (ISBN 0-8129-0280-7). Times Bks.
Sturluson, Snorri. Heims Kringla, History of the Kings of Norway. Hollander, Lee M., tr. from Old Norse. LC 64-10460. (Illus.). 1977. Repr. of 1964 ed. 32.50x (ISBN 0-89067-040-4). Am Scandinavian.

KINGS AND RULERS–JUVENILE LITERATURE

Coen, Rena N. Kings & Queens in Art. LC 64-8042. (Fine Arts Bks). (Illus.). (gr. 5-11). 1965. PLB 4.95 (ISBN 0-8225-0155-4). Lerner Pubns.

KINGS AND RULERS (IN RELIGION, FOLK-LORE, ETC.)

see also Emperor Worship

Capt, E. Raymond. Jacob's Pillar. (Illus.). 96p. 1977. pap. 3.00 (ISBN 0-934666-03-2). Artisan Sales.
Chaney, William A. The Cult of Kingship in Anglo-Saxon England: The Transition from Paganism to Christianity. LC 72-79041. 1970. 21.50x (ISBN 0-520-01401-4). U of Cal Pr.
Frankfort, Henri. Kingship & the Gods: A Study of Ancient Near Eastern Religion As the Integration of Society & Nature. LC 48-5158. 1978. pap. 7.95 (ISBN 0-226-26011-9, P766, Phoen). U of Chicago Pr.
Hadfield, P. Traits of Divine Kingship in Africa. LC 78-32120. 1979. Repr. of 1949 ed. lib. bdg. 14.00x (ISBN 0-8371-5189-9, HDK&). Greenwood.
Roheim, Geza. Animism, Magic & the Divine King. LC 78-190281. 390p. 1972. Repr. of 1930 ed. text ed. 30.00 (ISBN 0-8236-0150-1). Intl Univs Pr.

KING'S EVIL

see Scrofula

KINGS MOUNTAIN, BATTLE OF, 1780

Draper, Lyman C. King's Mountain & Its Heroes: History of the Battle of King's Mountain, October 7th 1780 & the Events Which Led to It. LC 67-25801. (Illus.). 1967. Repr. of 1881 ed. 15.00 (ISBN 0-87152-035-4). Reprint.
--King's Mountain & Its Heroes: History of the Battle of Kings Mountain, October 7th 1780 & the Events Which Led to It. LC 67-28623. (Illus.). 612p. 1978. Repr. of 1881 ed. 17.50 (ISBN 0-8063-0097-3). Genealog Pub.
Messick, Hank. King's Mountain: The Epic of the Blue Ridge Mountain Men in the American Revolution. 1976. 9.95 (ISBN 0-316-56796-5). Little.
White, Katherine K. King's Mountain Men: The Story of the Battle with Sketches of the American Soldiers Who Took Part. LC 66-30368. 1977. Repr. of 1924 ed. 12.50 (ISBN 0-8063-0383-2). Genealog Pub.

KINGSLEY, CHARLES, 1819-1875

Brown, W. Henry. Charles Kingsley. LC 73-12770. 1924. lib. bdg. 17.50 (ISBN 0-8414-3231-7). Folcroft.
Clare, Maurice. A Day with Charles Kingsley. Repr. 10.00 (ISBN 0-8274-2148-6). R West.
Downes, David. The Temper of Victorian Belief: Studies in the Religious Novels of Pater, Kingsley & Newman. 8.95 (ISBN 0-685-60146-3, Pub by Twayne). Cyrco Pr.
Ellis, James J. Charles Kingsley. 1890. Repr. 25.00 (ISBN 0-8274-3799-4). R West.
Harris, Styron. Charles Kingsley: A Reference Book. (Reference Books Ser.). 1981. 26.00 (ISBN 0-8161-8166-7). G K Hall.
Kaufmann, M. Charles Kingsley: Christian Social Reformer. LC 77-20677. 1892. Repr. 30.00 (ISBN 0-8492-1416-5). R West.
--Charles Kingsley: Christian Socialist & Social Reformer. 1978. Repr. of 1892 ed. lib. bdg. 25.00 (ISBN 0-8495-3010-5). Arden Lib.
Kendall, Guy. Charles Kingsley & His Ideas. LC 72-6679. (English Biography Ser., No. 31). 195p. 1972. Repr. of 1937 ed. lib. bdg. 33.95 (ISBN 0-8383-1639-5). Haskell.
Kingsley, Charles. Charles Kingsley: His Letters & Memories of His Life, 2 Vols. LC 74-148803. (Illus.). Repr. of 1877 ed. Set. 37.50 (ISBN 0-404-08869-4); 19.00 ea. Vol. 1 (ISBN 0-404-08870-8). Vol. 2 (ISBN 0-404-08871-6). AMS Pr.
--Charles Kingsley, His Letters & Memories of His Life. 1908. 30.00 (ISBN 0-932062-97-0). Sharon Hill.
--Life & Works, 28 Vols. 1969. Repr. of 1880 ed. Set. 1200.00 (ISBN 3-4870-2156-0). Adler.
Pope-Hennessy, Una. Canon Charles Kingsley, a Biography. LC 73-9669. (Illus.). 320p. 1973. Repr. of 1949 ed. 27.00 (ISBN 0-527-71900-5). Kraus Repr.
Seaver, George. Charles Kingsley: Poet. LC 73-1252. 1973. lib. bdg. 6.00 (ISBN 0-8414-1540-4). Folcroft.
Stubbs, Charles W. Charles Kingsley & the Christian Social Movement. LC 70-148310. Repr. of 1899 ed. 17.50 (ISBN 0-404-08914-3). AMS Pr.
Thorp, Margaret F. Charles Kingsley, 1819-1875. LC 70-96170. 1969. Repr. of 1937 ed. lib. bdg. 14.00x (ISBN 0-374-97942-1). Octagon.
Uffelman, Larry K. Charles Kingsley. (English Authors Ser.: No. 273). 1979. 13.50 (ISBN 0-8057-6752-5). Twayne.

KINGSTON, ONTARIO

Angus, Margaret. Kingston General Hospital: A Social & Institutional History. 1973. write for order info 10.00 (ISBN 0-7735-0173-8). McGill-Queens U Pr.
--The Old Stones of Kingston: Its Buildings Before Eighteen Sixty-Seven. LC 66-6913. (Illus.). 1980. pap. 12.50 (ISBN 0-8020-6419-1). U of Toronto Pr.
Tulchinsky, Gerald, ed. To Preserve & Defend: Essays on Kingston in the Nineteenth Century. (Illus.). 448p. 1976. 18.00x (ISBN 0-7735-0214-9). McGill-Queens U Pr.

KINGSTON, ONTARIO–QUEEN'S UNIVERSITY

Wallace, Robert C., ed. Some Great Men of Queen's. facs. ed. LC 79-86792. (Essay Index Reprint Ser). 1941. 12.00 (ISBN 0-8369-1200-4). Arno.

KINIASSA LANGUAGE

see Nyanja Language

KININS

see also Hypotensive Agents; Vasodilators

Back, Nathan, et al, eds. Kinins: Pharmacodynamics & Biological Rules. LC 76-7006. (Advances in Experimental Medicine & Biology Ser.: Vol. 70). 398p. 1976. 42.50 (ISBN 0-306-39070-1, Plenum Pr). Plenum Pub.
Fujii, Setsuro, et al, eds. Kinins IIA: Biochemistry, Pathophysiology, & Clinical Aspects. LC 79-9079. (Advances in Experimental Medicine & Biology: Vol. 120A). 622p. 1979. 59.50 (ISBN 0-306-40196-7, Plenum Pr). Plenum Pub.
--Kinins IIB: Systemic Proteases & Cellular Function. LC 79-9079. (Advances in Experimental Medicine & Biology: Vol. 120B). 733p. 1979. 69.50 (ISBN 0-306-40197-5, Plenum Pr). Plenum Pub.

KINKEL, JOHANN GOTTFRIED, 1815-1882

De Jonge, Alfred R. Gottfried Kinkel As Political & Social Thinker. LC 70-163695. (Columbia University. Germanic Studies, Old Ser.: No. 30). Repr. of 1926 ed. 21.00 (ISBN 0-404-50430-2). AMS Pr.

KINLOSS ABBEY

Ferrerio, Giovanni. Ferrerii Historia Abbatum De Kynlos. LC 78-168018. (Bannatyne Club, Edinburgh. Publications: No. 63). Repr. of 1839 ed. 15.00 (ISBN 0-404-52774-4). AMS Pr.

KINMONT, JILL

Valens, Evans G. A Long Way up: The Story of Jill Kinmont. (Illus.). 1966. 10.95 (ISBN 0-06-014483-1, HarpT). Har-Row.

KINNERSLEY, EBENEZER, 1711-1778

Crum, Bartley C. Behind the Silken Curtain: A Personal Account of Anglo-American Diplomacy in Palestine & the Middle East. LC 68-8246. 1969. Repr. of 1947 ed. 11.50 (ISBN 0-8046-0093-7). Kennikat.

KINO, EUSBIUS FRANCISCO, 1644-1711

Bolton, Herbert E. Padre on Horseback. LC 63-13248. (Illus.). 1963. Repr. of 1962 ed. 3.00 (ISBN 0-8294-0003-6). Loyola.
Kelly, Annamaria. Kino Alla Conquista Dell 'America. LC 80-53508. (Illus.). 148p. (Orig.). 1980. pap. 6.50 (ISBN 0-915076-05-5). SW Mission.

KINSALE, IRELAND–SIEGE, 1601-1602

Silke, John J. Kinsale: The Spanish Intervention in Ireland at the End of the Elizabethan Wars. LC 77-96148. (Illus.). 1970. 25.00 (ISBN 0-8232-0865-6). Fordham.

KINSELLA, THOMAS, 1928-

Harmon, Maurice. The Poetry of Thomas Kinsella. 126p. 1975. text ed. 8.50x (ISBN 0-391-00386-0); pap. text ed. 4.95x (ISBN 0-391-00387-9). Humanities.

KINSEY, ALFRED CHARLES, 1894-1956

Bohn, Dave & Petschek, Rodolfo. Kinsey, Photographer: A Half Century of Negatives by Darius & Tabitha May Kinsey. (Illus.). 320p. 1975. boxed set 150.00 (ISBN 0-685-52668-2, Pub. by Scrimshaw Calif); Vol. 1. (ISBN 0-937106-01-1); Vol. 2. (ISBN 0-937106-02-X). Ross Valley.
Cochran, William G., et al. Statistical Problems of the Kinsey Report on Sexual Behavior in the Human Male: A Report of the American Statistical Association Committee to Advise the National Research Council Committee for Research in Problems of Sex. LC 68-57595. (Illus.). 1968. Repr. of 1954 ed. lib. bdg. 15.00x (ISBN 0-8371-7377-9, AMKR). Greenwood.

KINSHIP

see also Clans and Clan System; Consanguinity; Family; Tribes and Tribal System

Allen, Graham A. Sociology of Friendship & Kinship. (Studies in Sociology Ser.). (Orig.). 1979. text ed. 22.50x (ISBN 0-04-301104-7); pap. text ed. 8.95x (ISBN 0-04-301105-5). Allen Unwin.
Ballonoff, Paul A. Mathematical Foundations of Social Anthropology. (Publications of the Maison Des Sciences De L'homme). (Illus.). 131p. 1976. pap. text ed. 16.25x (ISBN 90-2797-934-0). Mouton.
Barnes, J. A. Three Styles in the Study of Kinship. LC 74-142057. 1972. 19.50x (ISBN 0-520-01879-6); pap. 6.95x (ISBN 0-520-02481-8). U of Cal Pr.
Brady, Ivan A., ed. Transactions in Kinship: Adoption & Fosterage in Oceania. LC 76-10342. (Association for Social Anthropology in Oceania Monograph: No.4). 320p. 1976. text ed. 16.00x (ISBN 0-8248-0478-3). U Pr of Hawaii.
Coale, Ansley J., et al, eds. Aspects of the Analysis of Family Structure. 1965. 18.50 (ISBN 0-691-09306-7). Princeton U Pr.
Cordell, Linda S. & Beckerman, Stephen, eds. The Versatility of Kinship. LC 80-525. (Studies in Anthropology). 1980. 40.00 (ISBN 0-12-188250-0). Acad Pr.
Cuisenier, Jean. Economie et Parente: Leurs Affinites De Structure Dans le Domaine Turc et Dans le Domaine Arabe. (Le Monde D'outre-Mer Passe & Present, Etudes: No. 60). (Illus.). 1975. pap. 80.00x (ISBN 90-2797-675-9). Mouton.
Davis, Kingsley. A Structural Analysis of Kinship: Prolegomena to the Sociology of Kinship. Zuckerman, Harriet & Merton, Robert K., eds. LC 79-8990. (Dissertations on Sociology Ser.). 1980. lib. bdg. 33.00x (ISBN 0-405-12962-9). Arno.
Djamour, Judith. Malay Kinship & Marriage in Singapore. (Monographs on Social Anthropology: No. 21). (Orig.). 1959. pap. text ed. 10.50x (ISBN 0-485-19621-2, Athlone Pr). Humanities.
Evans-Pritchard, Edward E. Kinship & Marriage Among the Nuer. (Illus.). 1951. 24.00x (ISBN 0-19-823104-0). Oxford U Pr.
Farber, Bernard. Comparative Kinship Systems: A Method of Analysis. 147p. 1968. text ed. 7.75 (ISBN 0-471-25477-0, Pub. by Wiley). Krieger.
Firth, Raymond. We, the Tikopia. (Illus.). 1963. pap. 6.95x (ISBN 0-8070-4695-7, BP164). Beacon Pr.
Firth, Raymond, et al. Families & Their Relatives, Kinship in a Middle-Class Sector of London: An Anthropological Study. (International Library of Sociology & Social Reconstruction). 1970. text ed. 16.25x (ISBN 0-7100-6431-4). Humanities.
Fortes, Meyer. Kinship & the Social Order: The Legacy of Lewis Henry Morgan. LC 80-67927. (Lewis Henry Morgan Lectures). 368p. Date not set. cancelled; pap. cancelled (ISBN 0-521-28211-X). Cambridge U Pr.
Freedman, M. Chinese Lineage & Society: Fukien & Kwangtung. (Monographs on Social Anthropology: No. 33). (Illus.). 206p. 1971. pap. text ed. 10.00x (ISBN 0-391-00199-X, Athlone Pr). Humanities.
Freedman, Maurice. Lineage Organization in Southeastern China. rev. ed. (Monographs on Social Anthropology: No. 18). 1965. pap. text ed. 9.50x (ISBN 0-485-19618-2, Athlone Pr). Humanities.
Goody, Jack. Comparative Studies in Kinship. LC 73-76227. 1969. 15.00x (ISBN 0-8047-0678-6). Stanford U Pr.
Gray, Robert F. & Gulliver, P. H., eds. The Family Estate in Africa: Studies in the Role of Property in Family Structure & Lineage Continuity. LC 64-19442. 1964. 9.50x, USA (ISBN 0-8147-0169-8). NYU Pr.
Harris, C. C. Readings in Kinship in Urban Society. 1970. 23.00 (ISBN 0-08-016039-5); pap. 12.75 (ISBN 0-08-016038-7). Pergamon.
Hart, Donn V. Compadrinazgo: Ritual Kinship in the Philippines. LC 75-15015. (Illus.). 240p. 1976. 15.00 (ISBN 0-87580-062-9). N Ill U Pr.
Hsu, F. L. Iemoto: The Heart of Japan. LC 74-5352. 260p. 1975. text ed. 11.25 (ISBN 0-470-41755-2); pap. text ed. 7.95x (ISBN 0-470-41756-0). Halsted Pr.
Hsu, Francis K., ed. Kinship & Culture. LC 72-75050. 1971. 18.95x (ISBN 0-202-01078-3). Beresford Bk Serv.
--Kinship & Culture. LC 72-75050. 1971. 18.95x (ISBN 0-202-01078-3). Beresford Bk Serv.
Ianni, Francis A. & Ianni, Elizabeth R. A Family Business: Kinship & Social Control in Organized Crime. LC 72-75320. 1972. 10.00 (ISBN 0-87154-396-6). Russell Sage.
Inden, Ronald B & Nicholas, Ralph W. Kinship in Bengali Culture. LC 76-25639. 1977. 15.50x (ISBN 0-226-37835-7). U of Chicago Pr.
Kohler, Josef. On the Prehistory of Marriage. Barnes, R. H., ed. LC 74-11626. (Classics in Anthropology Ser). x, 298p. 1975. pap. text ed. 12.50x (ISBN 0-226-45025-2, Midway Reprint). U of Chicago Pr.
Korn, Francis. Elementary Structures Reconsidered: Levi-Strauss on Kinship. LC 73-78212. 1973. 20.00x (ISBN 0-520-02476-1). U of Cal Pr.
Labby, David. The Demystification of Yap: Dialectics of Culture on a Micronesian Island. LC 75-21270. (Illus.). 176p. 1976. lib. bdg. 12.95x (ISBN 0-226-46711-2). U of Chicago Pr.
Leach, Edmund R. Pul Eliya: A Village in Ceylon. 1961. 22.50 (ISBN 0-521-05524-5). Cambridge U Pr.
Leichter, Hope J. & Mitchell, William E. Kinship & Casework. LC 66-24898. 1967. 11.00 (ISBN 0-87154-522-5). Russell Sage.
Lichtman, Allan J. & Challinor, Joan R. Kin & Communities: Families in America. LC 78-24246. (Illus.). 335p. 1979. text ed. 19.95x (ISBN 0-87474-608-6); pap. text ed. 8.95x (ISBN 0-87474-609-4). Smithsonian.
Linant De Bellefonds, Y. Traite De Droit Musulman Compare: Filiation - Incapacites - Liberalites Entre Vifs, Tome 3. (Recherches Mediterraneennes: No. 9). 1973. pap. 47.75x (ISBN 90-2797-199-4). Mouton.
Nakane, Chie. Kinship & Economic Organization in Rural Japan. (Monographs on Social Anthropology: No. 32). 1967. text ed. 9,50x (ISBN 0-485-19532-1, Athlone Pr). Humanities.
Nukunya, G. K. Kinship & Marriage Among the Anlo Ewe. LC 68-18054. (Monographs on Social Anthropology Ser: No. 37). 1969. text ed. 23.50x (ISBN 0-485-19537-2, Athlone Pr). Humanities.
Nutini, H. G. & Bell, B. Ritual Kinship: The Structure & Historical Development of the Compadrazgo System in Rural Tlaxcala. 1980. 28.50 (ISBN 0-691-09382-2); pap. 11.50 (ISBN 0-691-10093-4). Princeton U Pr.
Nutini, Hugo G., et al, eds. Essays on Mexican Kinship. LC 75-9124. (Pitt Latin American Ser.). (Illus.). 1976. 14.95x (ISBN 0-8229-3307-1). U of Pittsburgh Pr.
Parry, J. P. Caste & Kinship in Kangra. (International Library of Anthropology Ser.). (Illus.). 1978. 31.50x (ISBN 0-7100-0012-X). Routledge & Kegan.
Pasternak, Burton. Introduction to Kinship & Social Organization. (Illus.). 208p. 1976. Ref. Ed. pap. 8.95 (ISBN 0-13-485466-7). P-H.
Peristiany, J. G., ed. Mediterranean Family Structure. LC 75-20833. (Cambridge Studies in Social Anthropology: No. 13). (Illus.). 434p. 1976. 39.95 (ISBN 0-521-20964-1). Cambridge U Pr.
Pinxten, Rik. On Going Beyond Kinship, Sex & the Tribe. (Philosophy & Anthropology Ser.: No. 1). 1980. text ed. 19.00x (ISBN 90-6439-182-3). Humanities.
Radcliff-Brown, Alfred R., ed. African Systems of Kinship & Marriage. 1950. pap. 14.95x (ISBN 0-19-724147-6). Oxford U Pr.
Rivers, William H. Kinship & Social Organization: Together with the Genealogical Method of Anthropological Enquiry. LC 67-17557. (Monographs on Social Anthropology). (Illus.). 1968. text ed. 10.75x (ISBN 0-485-19534-8, Athlone Pr). Humanities.
Schneider, David M. American Kinship: A Cultural Account. LC 79-18185. 1980. lib. bdg. 16.00x (ISBN 0-226-73929-5); pap. 4.50 (ISBN 0-226-73930-9, P878, Phoen). U of Chicago Pr.
Schneider, David M. & Smith, Raymond T. Class Differences in American Kinship. LC 77-17676. (Anthropology Ser.). 1977. pap. 12.25 (ISBN 0-472-02700-X, IS-00038, Univ. of Michigan Press). Univ Microfilms.
Schneider, David M. & Gough, Kathleen, eds. Matrilineal Kinship. (California Library Reprint Ser.). 1974. 42.50x (ISBN 0-520-02587-3); pap. 10.95x (ISBN 0-520-02529-6, CAMPUS 103). U of Cal Pr.
Schusky, Ernest L. Variation in Kinship. LC 73-7898. (Studies in Anthropological Method). 1974. pap. 4.95 (ISBN 0-03-091312-8, HoltC). HR&W.
Schwarzweller, Harry K., et al. Mountain Families in Transition: A Case Study of Appalachian Migration. LC 71-138090. 1971. 14.95x (ISBN 0-271-01149-1). Pa St U Pr.
Shaw, Daniel, ed. Kinship Studies in Papua, New Guinea. 246p. 1974. 5.00x (ISBN 0-7263-0245-7). Summer Inst Ling.
Soliday, Gerald L., ed. History of the Family & Kinship: A Select International Bibliography. LC 80-11782. 1980. lib. bdg. 50.00 (ISBN 0-527-84451-9). Kraus Intl.
Thomas, Northcote W. Kinship Organizations & Group Marriage in Australia. 1966. Repr. of 1906 ed. text ed. 8.25x (ISBN 0-7146-1961-2). Humanities.

Turner, Christopher. Family & Kinship in Modern Britain. (Students Library of Sociology). 1969. pap. text ed. 1.50x (ISBN 0-7100-6347-4). Humanities.

Van Velsen, J. The Politics of Kinship: A Study in Social Manipulation Among the Lakeside Tonga of Malawi. (Institute for African Studies). (Illus.). 338p. 1964. pap. text ed. 13.75x (ISBN 0-7190-1036-5). Humanities.

Vreeland, Herbert H., 3rd. Mongol Community & Kinship Structure. LC 72-12334. (Illus.). 327p. 1973. Repr. of 1962 ed. lib. bdg. 17.50x (ISBN 0-8371-6734-5, VRMC). Greenwood.

Witherspoon, Gary. Navajo Kinship & Marriage. LC 74-21340. (Illus.). xii, 138p. 1975. lib. bdg. 9.50x (ISBN 0-226-90419-9). U of Chicago Pr.

Young, Michael & Willmott, Peter. Family & Kinship in East London. 1957. text ed. 12.00x (ISBN 0-7100-3911-5). Humanities.

KIOSKS

see Pavilions

KIOWA INDIANS

see Indians of North America–The West

KIPLING, RUDYARD, 1865-1936

Amis, Kingsley. Kipling & His World. LC 75-29827. 1976. 8.95 (ISBN 0-684-14550-2, ScribT). Scribner.

Bateson, Vaughan. Kipling & the Doctors. LC 73-15769. 1929. lib. bdg. 6.50 (ISBN 0-8414-3294-5). Folcroft.

Beresford, G. C. Schooldays of Kipling. 1936. Repr. 35.00 (ISBN 0-8274-3335-2). R West.

Birkenhead, Lord. Rudyard Kipling. 1978. 15.00 (ISBN 0-394-50315-5). Random.

Braybrooke, Patrick. Kipling & His Soldiers. LC 72-3229. (English Literature Ser., No. 33). 1972. Repr. of 1926 ed. lib. bdg. 32.95 (ISBN 0-8383-1506-2). Haskell.

Bridges, Robert. Wordsworth & Kipling in Collected Essays, Papers, Etc, Vol. 11. Repr. 10.00 (ISBN 0-8274-3750-1). R West.

Brown, Hilton. Rudyard Kipling. LC 74-7017. (English Literature Ser., No. 33). 1974. lib. bdg. 49.95 (ISBN 0-8383-1853-3). Haskell.

--Rudyard Kipling. 1945. Repr. 25.00 (ISBN 0-685-43445-1). Norwood Edns.

--Rudyard Kipling, a New Appreciation. LC 74-12167. 1974. Repr. of 1945 ed. lib. bdg. 14.75 (ISBN 0-8414-3213-9). Folcroft.

Charles, Cecil. Rudyard Kipling: His Life & Works. 1973. lib. bdg. 8.50 (ISBN 0-8414-0903-X). Folcroft.

--Rudyard Kipling, His Life & Works. 1978. Repr. of 1911 ed. lib. bdg. 12.50 (ISBN 0-8495-0838-X). Arden Lib.

Chevrillon, Andre. Three Studies in English Literature, Kipling, Galsworthy & Shakespeare. LC 67-27585. Repr. of 1923 ed. 11.00 (ISBN 0-8046-0077-5). Kennikat.

Clemens, Cyril. A Chat with Rudyard Kipling. 1943. lib. bdg. 6.50 (ISBN 0-8414-3042-X). Folcroft.

Clemens, Will M. A Ken of Kipling: Being a Biographical Sketch of Rudyard Kipling, with an Appreciation and Some Anecdotes. 1899. Repr. 15.00 (ISBN 0-8274-2648-8). R West.

Croft-Cooke, Rupert. Rudyard Kipling. LC 74-7100. (English Biography Ser., No. 31). 1974. lib. bdg. 29.95 (ISBN 0-8383-1856-8). Haskell.

Durand, R. A. A Handbook to the Poetry of Rudyard Kipling. Repr. of 1914 ed. 20.00 (ISBN 0-527-25900-4). Kraus Repr.

Falls, Cyril. Rudyard Kipling: A Critical Study. LC 72-13996. 1915. lib. bdg. 20.00 (ISBN 0-8414-1312-6). Folcroft.

Falls, Cyril B. Rudyard Kipling: A Critical Study. 208p. 1980. Repr. of 1915 ed. lib. bdg. 20.00 (ISBN 0-8495-1710-9). Arden Lib.

Farwell, Byron. Mr. Kipling's Army. (Illus.). 1981. 13.95 (ISBN 0-393-01386-3). Norton.

Gilbert, Elliot L. The Good Kipling. LC 73-122098. ix, 216p. 1970. 13.50x (ISBN 0-8214-0085-1). Ohio U Pr.

Gilbert, Elliot L., ed. Kipling & the Critics. LC 65-13208. (Gotham Library). 183p. (Orig.). 1965. 10.00x (ISBN 0-8147-0161-2); pap. 3.95x (ISBN 0-8147-0162-0). NYU Pr.

Green, Roger L., ed. Kipling: The Critical Heritage. 1971. 33.75x (ISBN 0-7100-6978-2). Routledge & Kegan.

Grosse, John, ed. Age of Kipling. 1972. 12.95 (ISBN 0-671-21405-5). S&S.

Hart, Walter M. Kipling the Story-Writer. LC 73-4428. 1918. lib. bdg. 20.00 (ISBN 0-8414-2084-X). Folcroft.

Hopkins, R. Thurston. Rudyard Kipling: A Literary Appreciation. LC 78-13606. 1978. Repr. of 1916 ed. lib. bdg. 35.00 (ISBN 0-8414-4871-X). Folcroft.

--Rudyard Kipling's World. 1977. Repr. of 1925 ed. lib. bdg. 25.00 (ISBN 0-8495-2224-2). Arden Lib.

Hopkins, Robert T. Rudyard Kipling: The Story of a Genius. LC 77-10659. 1977. lib. bdg. 250.00 (ISBN 0-8414-4956-2). Folcroft.

Hopkins, Thurston. Kipling's Sussex. 1921. Repr. 30.00 (ISBN 0-8274-3853-2). R West.

--Kipling's Sussex: Revisited. 1929. Repr. 30.00 (ISBN 0-8274-3854-0). R West.

--Rudyard Kipling: A Character Study. 1915. Repr. 30.00 (ISBN 0-8274-3911-3). R West.

--Rudyard Kipling's World. 1925. Repr. 30.00 (ISBN 0-8274-3910-5). R West.

Islam, Shamsul. Kipling's Law: A Study of His Philosophy of Life. LC 75-24793. 300p. 1975. 18.95 (ISBN 0-312-45675-1). St Martin.

Jerome, Jerome K., intro. by. My First Book: The Experiences of Rudyard Kipling, A. Conan Doyle & Robert Louis Stevenson. 1978. Repr. of 1894 ed. 35.00 (ISBN 0-8492-5601-1). R West.

Kernahan, Coulson. Nothing Quite Like Kipling Had Happened Before: Some Little Memories of a Great Man. 1977. Repr. of 1944 ed. lib. bdg. 17.50 (ISBN 0-8414-5469-8). Folcroft.

Kipling, Rudyard. Letters of Travel (1892-1913) Repr. lib. bdg. 15.70x (ISBN 0-88411-820-7). Amereon Ltd.

Knowles, Frederic L. Kipling Primer. LC 73-17092. (English Literature Ser., No. 33). 1974. lib. bdg. 33.95 (ISBN 0-8383-1729-4). Haskell.

--A Kipling Primer. 1977. Repr. of 1899 ed. lib. bdg. 25.00 (ISBN 0-8414-5471-X). Folcroft.

LeGallienne, Richard. Rudyard Kipling. LC 73-21739. (English Literature Ser, No. 33). 1974. lib. bdg. 39.95 (ISBN 0-8383-1838-X). Haskell.

Lyon, James K. Bertolt Brecht & Rudyard Kipling: A Marxist's Imperialist. LC 73-94231. (Studies in General & Comparative Literature: No. 3). 138p. 1975. pap. text ed. 20.00x (ISBN 90-2793-411-8). Mouton.

McClure, John A. Kipling & Conrad: The Colonial Fiction. LC 81-4117. 208p. 1981. text ed. 16.50 (ISBN 0-674-50529-8). Harvard U Pr.

Mac Munn, George. Kipling's Women. Repr. 30.00 (ISBN 0-8274-2654-2). R West.

MacMunn, George F. Rudyard Kipling: Craftsman. LC 74-14563. 1974. Repr. of 1937 ed. lib. bdg. 10.00 (ISBN 0-8414-6102-3). Folcroft.

Monkshood, G. F. Rudyard Kipling: An Attempt at Appreciation. 1899. Repr. 30.00 (ISBN 0-8274-3310-7). R West.

Palmer, J. Rudyard Kipling. LC 73-21706. (English Literature Ser., No. 33). 1974. lib. bdg. 39.95 (ISBN 0-8383-1830-4). Haskell.

Palmer, John. Rudyard Kipling. LC 73-13777. 1973. Repr. of 1915 ed. lib. bdg. 10.00 (ISBN 0-8414-6717-X). Folcroft.

Rao, K. Bhaskara. Rudyard Kipling's India. 1967. pap. 5.95x (ISBN 0-8061-1243-3). U of Okla Pr.

Rather, Lois. West Is West: Rudyard Kipling in San Francisco. (Illus.). 1976. ltd. ed. 20.00 (ISBN 0-686-20624-X). Rather Pr.

Rice, Howard C. Rudyard Kipling in New England. LC 72-6747. (English Biography Ser., No. 31). 39p. 1972. Repr. of 1936 ed. lib. bdg. 40.95 (ISBN 0-8383-1635-2). Haskell.

Roberton, W. T. The Kipling Guide Book. limited ed. 1899. lib. bdg. 20.00 (ISBN 0-8414-7447-8). Folcroft.

Rudyard Kipling. 128p. 1980. Repr. of 1915 ed. lib. bdg. 15.00 (ISBN 0-8492-2168-4). R West.

The Rudyard Kipling Calendar. Repr. 20.00 (ISBN 0-8274-3311-5). R West.

Rutherford, Andrew, ed. Kipling's Mind & Art: Selected Critical Essays. 1964. 15.00x (ISBN 0-8047-0212-8); pap. 3.95 (ISBN 0-8047-0213-6, SP12). Stanford U Pr.

Shahane, Vasant A. Rudyard Kipling: Activist & Artist. LC 73-9536. (Crosscurrents-Modern Critiques Ser.). 172p. 1973. 6.95 (ISBN 0-8093-0622-0). S Ill U Pr.

Shanks, Edward. Rudyard Kipling: A Study in Literature & Political Ideas. LC 71-126931. (Illus.). 1971. Repr. of 1940 ed. 12.00x (ISBN 0-8154-0344-5). Cooper Sq.

Stewart, J. I. Rudyard Kipling. LC 66-22906. (Illus.). 1966. 5.00 (ISBN 0-396-05408-0). Dodd.

Thomas, J. M. Veiled Being: On Kipling. LC 74-23855. 1917. lib. bdg. 8.50 (ISBN 0-8414-8512-7). Folcroft.

Van Dewater, F. F. Rudyard Kipling's Vermont Feud. LC 74-1100. (English Literature Ser., No. 33). 1974. lib. bdg. 46.95 (ISBN 0-8383-2024-4). Haskell.

Wilson, Angus. The Strange Ride of Rudyard Kipling. (Illus.). 1979. pap. 5.95 (ISBN 0-14-005122-8). Penguin.

--The Strange Ride of Rudyard Kipling. 1978. 17.50 (ISBN 0-670-67701-9). Viking Pr.

Younge, W. A. A Kipling Dictionary. 75.00 (ISBN 0-8490-0473-X). Gordon Pr.

KIPLING, RUDYARD, 1865-1936–BIBLIOGRAPHY

Livingston, Flora. Bibliography of the Works of Rudyard Kipling. (Library of Literature, Drama & Criticism). 1970. Repr. of 1927 ed. 38.50 (ISBN 0-384-32980-2). Johnson Repr.

Livingston, Flora V. Bibliography of the Works of Rudyard Kipling, 2 Vols. (Illus.). Repr. of 1927 ed. Set. 43.00, incl. suppl (ISBN 0-8337-2128-3). B Franklin.

Martindell, E. W. A Bibliography of the Works of Rudyard Kipling. LC 72-3118. (English Literature Ser., No. 33). 1972. Repr. of 1922 ed. lib. bdg. 33.95 (ISBN 0-8383-1514-3). Haskell.

Tompkins, J. M. The Art of Rudyard Kipling. LC 65-26135. 1965. pap. 3.95x (ISBN 0-8032-5200-5, BB 332, Bison). U of Nebr Pr.

Young, William A. Dictionary of the Characters & Scenes in the Stories & Poems of Rudyard Kipling. LC 73-104696. (Bibliography & Reference Ser.: No. 291). 1970. text ed. 22.50 (ISBN 0-8337-3901-8). B Franklin.

KIPLING, RUDYARD, 1865-1936–JUVENILE LITERATURE

Manley, Seon. Rudyard Kipling: Creative Adventurer. LC 65-10230. (Illus.). (gr. 7 up). 7.95 (ISBN 0-8149-0360-6). Vanguard.

KIPSIGIS

Peristiany, Jean G. Social Institutions of the Kipsigis. 4th ed. text ed. 15.75x (ISBN 0-7100-1946-7). Humanities.

Prins, Adriaan H. East African Age-Class Systems: An Inquiry into the Social Order of Galla, Kipsigis & Kikuyu. LC 72-106785. (Illus.). Repr. of 1953 ed. 10.00x (ISBN 0-8371-3538-9). Greenwood.

Saltman, Michael. The Kipsigis: A Case Study in Changing Customary Law. 128p. 1978. text ed. 13.50x (ISBN 0-87073-560-8). Schenkman.

KIRCHNER, ERNEST LUDWIG, 1880-1938

Gordon, Donald E. Ernst Ludwig Kirchner. LC 68-25610. (Illus.). 1968. 40.00x (ISBN 0-674-26100-3). Harvard U Pr.

North Carolina Museum Of Art, ed. E. L. Kirchner, German Expressionist: A Loan Exhibition. LC 59-2148. (Illus.). 1958. pap. 1.50x (ISBN 0-88259-002-2). NCMA.

KIRGHIZ

Atkinson, Thomas W. Oriental & Western Siberia: A Narrative of Seven Years' Explorations & Adventures in Siberia, Mongolia, the Kirghissteppes, Chinese Tartary & Part of Central Asia. LC 75-115504. (Russia Observed, Ser., No. 1). 1970. Repr. of 1858 ed. 19.00 (ISBN 0-405-03002-9). Arno.

Shahrani, M. Nazif Mohib. The Kirghiz & Wakhi of Afghanistan: Adaptation to Closed Frontiers. LC 79-11665. (Publications on Ethnicity & Nationality of the School of International Studies). (Illus.). 288p. 1979. 16.50 (ISBN 0-295-95669-0). U of Wash Pr.

KIRGHIZ-KAISSAK LANGUAGE

see Kazakh Language

KIRGHIZ-KAZAKS

see Kazaks

KIRK, JOHN, SIR, 1832-1922

Coupland, Reginald. Kirk on the Zambesi: A Chapter of African History. Repr. of 1928 ed. 15.25x (ISBN 0-8371-2916-8, Pub. by Negro U Pr). Greenwood.

KIRKLAND, CAROLINE MATILDA (STANSBURY), 1801-1864

Osborne, William S. Caroline M. Kirkland. (U. S. Authors Ser.: No. 207). lib. bdg. 10.95 (ISBN 0-8057-0424-8). Twayne.

KIRKLAND, JOSEPH, 1830-1894

Henson, Clyde E. Joseph Kirkland. (Twayne's United States Authors Ser). 1962. pap. 3.45 (ISBN 0-8084-0193-9, T13, Twayne). Coll & U Pr.

--Joseph Kirkland. LC 61-18071. (United States Authors Ser.). 1962. lib. bdg. 12.95x (ISBN 0-8057-0428-0); pap. text ed. 2.95x (ISBN 0-8290-0001-1). Irvington.

KIRKSTALL ABBEY

Hope, William H. Architectural Description of Kirkstall Abbey. 1907. pap. 28.00 (ISBN 0-384-24260-X). Johnson Repr.

KIRLIAN PHOTOGRAPHY

Dakin, H. S. High-Voltage Photography. 3rd ed. LC 74-77233. 1978. pap. 4.95 (ISBN 0-685-82476-4). H S Dakin.

Kirlian Electrophotography: Data Package A. (Illus.). 97p. 1974. pap. 3.95 (ISBN 0-917200-06-3). ESPress.

Krippner, Stanley & Rubin, Daniel, eds. The Energies of Consciousness: Exploration in Acupuncture, Auras & Kirlian Photography. new ed. (Social Change Ser). 266p. 1975. 29.25x (ISBN 0-677-05190-5). Gordon.

--Galaxies of Life: The Human Aura in Acupuncture & Kirlian Photography. (Social Change Ser.). 1973. 27.00x (ISBN 0-677-15480-1). Gordon.

Steiner, Lee R. Psychic Self-Healing for Psychological Problems. LC 76-56849. (Illus.). 176p. 1977. 8.95 (ISBN 0-13-732677-7). P-H.

KIRSTEIN, LINCOLN, 1907-

Kirstein, Lincoln. New York City Ballet. 1973. 30.00 (ISBN 0-394-46652-7). Knopf.

KISCH, FREDERICK HERMANN, 1888-1943

Kisch, Frederick H. Palestine Diary. LC 73-180354. Repr. of 1938 ed. 31.45 (ISBN 0-404-56286-8). AMS Pr.

KISHAMBALA LANGUAGE

see Shambala Language

KISHI, NOBUSU, 1896

Kurzman, Dan. Kishi & Japan. 1960. 10.00 (ISBN 0-8392-1057-4). Astor-Honor.

KISHIDA, KUNIO, 1890-1954

Rimer, J. Thomas. Toward a Modern Japanese Theatre: Kishida Kunio. LC 72-6521. 428p. 1974. text ed. 23.00x (ISBN 0-691-06249-8). Princeton U Pr.

KISII (BANTU TRIBE)

see Gusii (Bantu Tribe)

KISSING

The Kiss. LC 76-5091. (Illus.). 96p. (Orig.). 1976. pap. 4.95 (ISBN 0-87663-947-3). Universe.

Morris, Hugh. The Art of Kissing. LC 76-40626. 1977. pap. 1.95 (ISBN 0-385-12630-1, Dolp). Doubleday.

Nyrop, Christopher. Kiss & Its History. Harvey, William F., tr. LC 68-22040. 1968. Repr. of 1901 ed. 19.00 (ISBN 0-8103-3512-3). Gale.

Nyrop, K. The Kiss & Its History. 59.95 (ISBN 0-87968-330-9). Gordon Pr.

Perella, Nicolas J. The Kiss Sacred & Profane: An Interpretative History of Kiss Symbolism & Related Religio-Erotic Themes. LC 75-83292. (Illus.). 1969. 32.50x (ISBN 0-520-01392-1). U of Cal Pr.

Richey, David. The Small-Boat Handbook. LC 78-3315. 224p. pap. 3.95 (ISBN 0-06-463535-X, EH 535, EH). Har-Row.

KISSINGER, HENRY ALFRED, 1923-

Allen, Gary. Kissinger. 1976. 6.95 (ISBN 0-89245-003-7). Devin.

--The Kissinger: The Secret Side of the Secretary of State. LC 76-14012. (Orig.). 1976. pap. 1.50 (ISBN 0-685-65508-3). Seventy-Six.

Allen, Gary, tr. from Ger. Kissinger: The Secret Side of the Secretary of State. 200p. Date not set. softbound 5.00 (ISBN 0-686-31311-9); pap. 1.50 (ISBN 0-686-31312-7). Concord Pr.

Bell, Coral. The Diplomacy of Detente: The Kissinger Era. LC 77-82634. 1977. 14.95x (ISBN 0-312-21122-8). St Martin.

Blumenfeld, Ralph & Staff & Editors of the New York Post. Henry Kissinger: The Private & Public Story. (Illus., Orig.). 1974. pap. 1.75 (ISBN 0-451-06343-0, E6343, Sig). NAL.

Brown, Seyom. The Crises of Power: Foreign Policy in the Kissinger Years. LC 79-15796. 1979. 12.50 (ISBN 0-231-04264-7). Columbia U Pr.

Catlin, George. Kissinger's Atlantic Charter. 144p. 1974. 13.50x (ISBN 0-87471-694-2). Rowman.

Dickson, P. Kissinger & the Meaning of History. LC 78-5633. 1978. 19.95 (ISBN 0-521-22113-7). Cambridge U Pr.

Golan, Matti. The Secret Conversations of Henry Kissinger. LC 75-36262. 288p. 1976. 8.95 (ISBN 0-8129-0608-X). Times Bks.

Graubard, Stephen R. Kissinger: Portrait of a Mind. new ed. 288p. 1973. text ed. 9.95 (ISBN 0-393-05481-0); pap. text ed. 5.95x (ISBN 0-393-09278-X). Norton.

Hanna, David. Kissinger: His Rise and...? 1975. pap. 1.50 (ISBN 0-532-15152-6). Woodhill.

Kirban, Salem. Kissinger, Man of Peace? (Illus.). 1974. pap. 1.50 (ISBN 0-912582-18-9). Kirban.

The Kissenger Years, 3 vols. 1981. write for info. Arno.

Kissinger, Henry. The White House Years. (Illus.). 1979. 22.50 (ISBN 0-316-49661-8). Little.

Liska, George. Beyond Kissinger: Ways of Conservative Statecraft. LC 75-10838. (Studies in International Affairs: No.26). 176p. 1975. pap. 2.95x (ISBN 0-8018-1764-1). Johns Hopkins.

Mazlish, Bruce. Kissinger: The European Mind in American Policy. LC 76-9340. (Illus.). 1976. 13.50 (ISBN 0-465-03727-5). Basic.

Nutter, G. Warren. Kissinger's Grand Design. 1975. pap. 5.25 (ISBN 0-8447-3186-2). Am Enterprise.

Sobel, Lester A., ed. Kissinger & Detente. 202p. 1975. lib. bdg. 17.50 (ISBN 0-87196-243-8). Facts on File.

Statement of the Honorable Henry A. Kissinger with Respect to the Treaty on Strategic Arms Limitation Before the Committee on Foreign Relations of the U. S. Senate, July 31, 1979. (Significant Issues Ser.: Vol. I, No. 4). 35p. 1979. pap. 5.00 (ISBN 0-686-68798-1, CSIS005, CSIS). Unipub.

Stoessinger, John G. Henry Kissinger: The Anguish of Power. 1976. 8.95 (ISBN 0-393-05589-2). Norton.

--Henry Kissinger: The Anguish of Power. LC 76-22585. 1977. pap. text ed. 3.95x (ISBN 0-393-09153-8). Norton.

Taylor, Paula. Henry Kissinger. LC 74-32470. (Creative Education Closeup Bk.). (Illus.). 32p. (gr. 3-6). 1975. PLB 5.95 (ISBN 0-87191-422-0). Creative Ed.

Valeriani, Richard. Travels with Henry. 1979. 12.95 (ISBN 0-395-27091-X). HM.

Winston, Henry. The Moynihan-Kissinger Doctrine & the "Third World". 1975. pap. 0.50 (ISBN 0-87898-116-0). New Outlook.

KISVALHELI LANGUAGE
Krapf, Johann L. Outline of the Elements of the Kisua'heli Language with Special Reference to the Kinika Dialect. 142p. 1970. Repr. of 1850 ed. 16.50x (ISBN 0-8002-1771-3). Intl Pubns Serv.
KISWAHILI LANGUAGE
see Swahili Language
KITA, IKKI, 1883-1937
Wilson, George W. Radical Nationalist in Japan: Kita Ikki, 1883-1937. LC 69-12740. (East Asian Ser: No. 37). (Illus.). 1969. 12.50x (ISBN 0-674-74590-6). Harvard U Pr.
KITAGAWA, UTAMARO
see Utamaro, Kitagawa, 1754-1806
KITARA
see Banyoro
KITCHEN CABINETS
Geary, Donald. How to Build Kitchen Cabinets, Counters, & Vanities. (Illus.). 1979. 10.95 (ISBN 0-8359-2933-7). Reston.
Haynie, Paul J. Cabinetmaking. (Illus.). 272p. 1976. 15.95 (ISBN 0-13-110239-7). P-H.
How to Re-Do Your Kitchen Cabinets & Counter Tops. (Home Care Guides Ser.). (Illus.). 1981. pap. 2.50 (ISBN 0-686-71124-6). S&S.
Langer, Steven, ed. Salaries & Fringe Benefits in the Kitchen Cabinet Industry. 1977. pap. 125.00 (ISBN 0-916506-16-9). Abbott Langer Assocs.
Russell, James E. Advanced Kitchens. Horowitz, Shirley M., ed. (Illus.). 144p. 1981. 17.95 (ISBN 0-932944-43-4); pap. 6.95 (ISBN 0-932944-44-2). Creative Homeowner.
Stevenson, Robert P. How to Build & Buy Cabinets for the Modern Kitchen. 3rd ed. LC 66-15142. 1974. 10.00 (ISBN 0-668-03454-8). Arco.
Sunset Editors. Kitchen Storage. LC 81-81380. (Illus.). 80p. (Orig.). 1981. pap. 3.95 (ISBN 0-376-01571-3, Sunset Bks.). Sunset-Lane.
KITCHEN-GARDENS
see Vegetable Gardening
KITCHEN-MIDDENS
see also Mounds
Wyman, Jeffries. Fresh Water Shell Mounds of the St. John's River, Florida. LC 72-5002. (Harvard University. Peabody Museum of Archaeology & Ethnology. Antiquities of the New World: No. 7). (Illus.). Repr. of 1875 ed. 25.00 (ISBN 0-404-57307-X). AMS Pr.
KITCHEN UTENSILS
see also Blenders (Cookery); Food Processor Cookery
American Institute of Physics. The Pressure Cooker. (Phyics of Technology Project Ser.). 1975. 4.00 (ISBN 0-07-001730-1, G). McGraw.
Barons, Richard I., ed. American Hearth: Colonial and Post-Colonial Cooking Tools Ed. (Illus.). 1977. pap. 6.00 (ISBN 0-89062-085-7, Pub. by Roberson Ctr). Pub Ctr Cult Res.
Campbell, Susan. Cooks' Tools: The Complete Manual of Kitchen Implements & How to Use Them. LC 80-81456. (Illus.). 288p. 1980. 14.95 (ISBN 0-688-03682-1). Morrow.
Conran, Terence. The Kitchen Book. (Illus.). 1977. 35.00 (ISBN 0-517-53131-3). Crown.
Culinary Institute of America. The Professional Chef's Knife. LC 77-26689. (Illus.). 1978. pap. 9.95 (ISBN 0-8436-2125-7). CBI Pub.
Curtis, Tony, ed. Kitchen Equipment. (Illus.). 1978. 3.95 (ISBN 0-902921-41-X). Apollo.
De Groot, Roy A. Cooking with the Cuisinart Food Processor. LC 76-46586. 1977. 12.95 (ISBN 0-07-016273-5, GB). McGraw.
Felt, Joseph B. Customs of New England. 1967. Repr. of 1853 ed. 19.00 (ISBN 0-8337-1105-9). B Franklin.
Folsom, Leroi A. How to Master the Tools of Your Trade: The French Knife. (Illus.). 42p. 1970. pap. 7.50 (ISBN 0-685-04743-1). Radio City.
Franklin, Linda C. From Hearth to Cookstove. LC 73-93247. (Collector Ser.). (Illus.). 1978. 15.00 (ISBN 0-87637-339-2, 339-02). Hse of Collectibles.
--Three Hundred Years of Kitchen Collectibles: Identification & Values for Collectors. (Illus.). 400p. 1981. pap. 9.95 (ISBN 0-517-54410-5, Americana). Crown.
Heck, Anne. The Complete Kitchen. new ed. LC 74-84299. (Finder's Guide Ser.: No. 3). (Illus.). 320p. (Orig.). 1974. pap. 2.95 (ISBN 0-914400-02-9). Oliver Pr.
Heckmann, Manfred. Corkscrews: An Introduction to Their Appreciation. Sullivan, Maurice, ed. (Illus.). 124p. 1981. 12.95 (ISBN 0-686-69566-6). Wine Appreciation.
Heyn, Ernest & Shuldner, Herbert. Popular Science Book of Gadgets. 256p. 1981. 16.95 (ISBN 0-517-54280-3); pap. 9.95 (ISBN 0-517-54443-1). Crown.
Kanzaki, Noritake. Form & Function: Japanese Teapots. LC 78-71255. (Form & Function Ser.: Vol. 4). (Illus.). 1981. pap. 8.95 (ISBN 0-87011-392-5). Kodansha.
Punchard, Lorraine. Playtime Dishes. (Illus.). 1978. softbound 9.95 (ISBN 0-87069-212-7). Wallace-Homestead.
Russell, Loris. Handy Things to Have Around the House: Old-Time Domestic Appliances of Canada & the United States. (Illus.). 1979. 19.95 (ISBN 0-07-082781-8). McGraw.
Stewart, Regina & Cosentino, Geraldine. Kitchenware. (Golden Handbook of Collectibles Ser.). 1977. lib. bdg. 9.15 (ISBN 0-307-64344-1, Golden Pr). Western Pub.
Studley, Vance. The Woodworker's Book of Wooden Kitchen Utensils. LC 80-22124. (Illus.). 128p. 1981. 15.95 (ISBN 0-442-24726-5). Van Nos Reinhold.
Sunset Editors. Food Processor Cook Book. LC 77-90721. (Illus.). 80p. 1978. pap. 3.95 (ISBN 0-376-02402-X, Sunset Bks.). Sunset-Lane.
Vapor Removal from Cooking Equipment. (Eighty-Ninety Ser). 1973. pap. 2.00 (ISBN 0-685-58163-2, 96). Natl Fire Prot.
Watney, Bernard W. & Babbidge, Homer D., Jr. Corkscrews for Collectors. (Illus.). 1981. 35.00 (ISBN 0-85667-113-4, Pub. by Sotheby Parke Bernet England). Biblio Dist.
Weiss, Jeffrey. Kitchen Antiques. LC 80-7831. (Illus.). 128p. (Orig.). 1980. pap. 8.95 (ISBN 0-06-090813-0, CN 813, CN). Har-Row.
Wolf, Ray. Build-It-Yourself Rodale Plans: Home Soyfood Equipment. (Illus.). 80p. (Orig.). Date not set. pap. 14.95 (ISBN 0-87857-361-5). Rodale Pr Inc.
KITCHENER, HORATIO HERBERT, 1ST EARL, 1850-1916
Wilkinson-Latham, R. J. Kitchener. (Clarendon Biography Ser.). (Illus.). 1973. pap. 3.50 (ISBN 0-912728-68-X). Newbury Bks.
KITCHENS
see also Kitchen Cabinets
Better Homes & Gardens Editors. Better Homes & Gardens Kitchen Projects You Can Build. (Illus.). 1977. 5.95 (ISBN 0-696-00250-7). Meredith Corp.
Brett, James. The Kitchen. (Illus.). 1977. 25.00 (ISBN 0-8230-7320-3, Whitney Lib). Watson-Guptill.
Broughton, K. F. Better Kitchencraft. LC 78-670079. (Better Sports Ser.). (Illus.). 1973. 8.50x (ISBN 0-7182-0493-X). Intl Pubns Serv.
Conran, Terence. The Kitchen Book. (Illus.). 1977. 35.00 (ISBN 0-517-53131-3). Crown.
Consumer Guide Editors. Whole Kitchen Catalog. 1979. 14.95 (ISBN 0-671-24830-8); pap. 7.95 (ISBN 0-671-24145-1). S&S.
Cook, George A. How to Remodel Your Kitchen & Save Dollars. 200p. 1975. 5.95 (ISBN 0-385-09738-7, Dolp). Doubleday.
Creative Educational Society Editors. How to Have Fun Making a Kite. LC 73-12514. (Creative Craft Bks.). (Illus.). 32p. (gr. 2-5). 1973. PLB 5.90 (ISBN 0-87191-273-2). Creative Ed.
Douglas, Peter. Kitchen Planning & Design. (Case Studies Ser.: Vol. 2). (Illus.). 128p. 1980. 19.95 (ISBN 0-7137-0982-0, Pub. by Blandford Pr England); pap. 14.95 (ISBN 0-7137-1034-9). Sterling.
--Kitchen Planning & Design Theory, Vol. 1. (Illus.). 112p. 1980. 19.95 (ISBN 0-7137-0981-2, Pub. by Blandford Pr England); pap. 14.95 (ISBN 0-7137-1033-0, Pub. by Blandford Pr England). Sterling.
Galvin, Patrick J. Book of Successful Kitchens. 2nd ed. LC 77-25375. (Illus.). 136p. 1978. 13.95 (ISBN 0-912336-58-7); pap. 6.95 (ISBN 0-912336-59-5). Structures Pub.
--Kitchen Planning Guide: For Builders & Architects. 2nd ed. LC 77-25423. 1978. 24.95 (ISBN 0-912336-57-9). Structures Pub.
Geary, Donald. How to Build Kitchen Cabinets, Counters, & Vanities. (Illus.). 1979. 10.95 (ISBN 0-8359-2933-7). Reston.
Guide to Bathroom & Kitchen Remodeling. (Home Improvement Ser.). 1980. pap. 3.95 (ISBN 0-07-045968-1). McGraw.
Habeeb, Virginia & Treves, Ralph. Remodeling Your Kitchen & Building Your Own Cabinets. LC 79-33571. (Popular Science Skill Bks.). (Orig.). 1980. pap. 4.95 (ISBN 0-06-090781-9, CN 781, CN). Har-Row.
Hines, Millie, ed. Easy Ways to Decorate Your Kitchen. (Illus.). 96p. (Orig.). 1981. pap. 2.00 (ISBN 0-918178-24-X). Simplicity.
Housing Press. The House & Home Kitchen Planning Guide. (Illus.). 1978. 18.95 (ISBN 0-07-030472-6, P&RB). McGraw.
How to Re-Do Your Kitchen Cabinets & Counter Tops. (Home Care Guides Ser.). (Illus.). 1981. pap. 2.50 (ISBN 0-686-71124-6). S&S.
Hylton, William H., ed. Build Your Harvest Kitchen. (Illus.). 640p. 1980. 24.95 (ISBN 0-87857-316-X). Rodale Pr Inc.
Modi, John. The Best Kitchen Remodeling Workbook. LC 77-91162. 1978. o. p. 12.95 (ISBN 0-8092-7927-4); pap. 7.95 (ISBN 0-8092-7541-4). Contemp Bks.
Nunn, Richard V. Easy Kitchen Remodeling. LC 75-12124. (Family Guidebooks Ser.). (Illus.). 96p. 1975. pap. 1.95 (ISBN 0-8487-0387-1). Oxmoor Hse.
Piene, Otto. More Sky. 1973. pap. 3.95 (ISBN 0-262-66017-2). MIT Pr.
Pinkham, Mary E. Mary Ellen's Best of Helpful Kitchen Hints. (Illus., Orig.). 1980. pap. 4.50 (ISBN 0-446-97212-6). Warner Bks.
Russell, James E. Advanced Kitchens. Horowitz, Shirley M., ed. (Illus.). 144p. 1981. 17.95 (ISBN 0-932944-43-4); pap. 6.95 (ISBN 0-932944-44-2). Creative Homeowner.
Ser-Vol-Tel Institute. Kitchen Sanitation. (Foodservice Career Education Ser.). 1974. pap. 4.95 (ISBN 0-8436-2005-6). CBI Pub.
Shapiro, Cecile, et al. Better Kitchens. Horowitz, Shirley M., ed. LC 80-67151. (Illus.). 160p. (Orig.). 1980. 17.95 (ISBN 0-932944-23-X); pap. 6.95 (ISBN 0-932944-24-8). Creative Homeowner.
Sumichrast, Michael J., et al. Kitchen Appliances & Other Equipment in New Homes. (Illus.). 86p. 1979. 20.00 (ISBN 0-86718-063-3). Natl Assn Home Builders.
Sunset Editors. Kitchens: Planning & Remodeling. 5th ed. LC 76-7663. (Illus.). 80p. 1976. pap. 3.95 (ISBN 0-376-01337-0, Sunset Bks.). Sunset-Lane.
Time-Life Books, ed. Kitchens & Bathrooms. (Home Repair Ser.). (Illus.). 1977. 10.95 (ISBN 0-8094-2386-3). Time-Life.
Weiss, Jeffery. Great Kitchens. 96p. 1981. pap. 9.95 (ISBN 0-312-34605-0). St Martin.
Wise, Herbert H. Kitchen Detail. (Illus.). 160p. 1980. 27.50 (ISBN 0-8256-3204-8, Quick Fox); pap. 12.95 (ISBN 0-8256-3198-X). Music Sales.
Yarwood, Doreen. The British Kitchen. (Illus.). 192p. 1981. 28.95 (ISBN 0-7134-1430-8, Pub. by Batsford England). David & Charles.
KITES
Bahadur, Dinesh. Kite Flying & Kite Fighting. (Illus.). (gr. 6 up). 1979. pap. cancelled (ISBN 0-671-33026-8). Wanderer Bks.
Brummitt, Wyatt. Kites. (Golden Guide Ser). (Illus.). 1971. PLB 10.38 (ISBN 0-307-64344-1, Golden Pr); pap. 1.95 (ISBN 0-686-76849-3). Western Pub.
Dolan, Edward F., Jr. The Complete Beginnger's Guide to Making & Flying Kites. LC 75-36585. (gr. 4-7). 1977. PLB 6.95 (ISBN 0-385-04937-4). Doubleday.
--Go Fly a Kite: The Complete Guide to Making & Flying Kites. (Illus.). 1979. pap. 2.95 (ISBN 0-346-12376-3). Cornerstone.
Downer, Marion. Kites: How to Make & Fly Them. LC 58-14497. (Illus.). (gr. 4-6). 1959. PLB 7.44 (ISBN 0-688-51227-5). Lothrop.
Dyson, John & Dyson, Kate. Fun with Kites. LC 77-71707. 1977. Repr. 3.95 (ISBN 0-8120-5139-4). Barron.
Hart, Clive. Your Book of Kites. (gr. 7 up). 1964. 6.50 (ISBN 0-571-04712-2). Transatlantic.
Hunt, Leslie. Twenty-Five Kites That Fly. (Illus.). 1971. pap. 1.75 (ISBN 0-486-22550-X). Dover.
Hunt, Leslie L. Twenty-Five Kites That Fly. (Illus.). 6.00 (ISBN 0-8446-0151-9). Peter Smith.
Jordan, John W. Make Your Own Kite. (Illus.). 96p. (Orig.). 1981. 7.95 (ISBN 0-918464-35-8); pap. 4.95 (ISBN 0-918464-34-X). D Armstrong.
Jue, David F. Chinese Kites: How to Make & Fly Them. LC 67-16412. (Illus.). (gr. 6 up). 1967. 6.50 (ISBN 0-8048-0101-0). C E Tuttle.
Lloyd, Ambrose, et al. Kites: How to Fly Them, How to Build Them. LC 75-37220. 1976. 5.95 (ISBN 0-03-042891-2); pap. 3.95 (ISBN 0-685-93206-0). HR&W.
Marks, Burton & Marks, Rita. Kites for Kids. LC 79-22559. (Illus.). (gr. 3 up). 1980. 6.95 (ISBN 0-688-41930-5); PLB 6.67 (ISBN 0-688-51930-X). Lothrop.
Mitton, Bruce H. Kites, Kites, Kites: The Ups & Downs of Making & Flying Them. LC 78-57062. (Illus.). (gr. 3 up). 1978. pap. 5.95 (ISBN 0-8069-8460-0). Sterling.
Moulton, Ron. Kites. (Illus.). 1979. 24.95 (ISBN 0-7207-0829-X). Transatlantic.
Neal, Harry E. Story of the Kite. LC 52-11121. (Illus.). (gr. 4-9). 1954. 6.95 (ISBN 0-8149-0373-8). Vanguard.
Newman, Lee S. & Newman, Jay H. Kite Craft. LC 73-91154. (Arts & Crafts Ser.). (Illus.). 224p. 1974. pap. 4.95 (ISBN 0-517-51471-0). Crown.
Newnham, Jack. Kites to Make & Fly. (Practical Ser.). (Illus.). (gr. 2-7). 1977. pap. 1.95 (ISBN 0-14-049149-X, Puffin). Penguin.
Nicklaus, Carol. Flying, Gliding, and Whirling: Making Things That Fly. (Easy-Read Activity Bks.). (Illus.). 32p. (gr. 1-3). 1981. lib. bdg. 8.90 (ISBN 0-531-04313-4). Watts.
Olney, Ross R. & Bush, Chan. Better Kite Flying for Boys & Girls. LC 80-14817. (Better Sports Ser.). (Illus.). 64p. (gr. 4 up). 1980. PLB 5.95 (ISBN 0-396-07853-2). Dodd.
Pelham, David. The Penguin Book of Kites. (Illus.). 224p. 1976. pap. 4.95 (ISBN 0-14-004117-6). Penguin.
Schmitz, Dorothy C. Kite Flying. Schroeder, Howard, ed. LC 78-6876. (Funseekers Ser.). (Illus.). (gr. 3-4). 1978. PLB 6.95 (ISBN 0-913940-92-5); pap. 3.25 (ISBN 0-89686-013-2). Crestwood Hse.
Streeter, Tal. The Art of the Japanese Kite. LC 74-76102. (Illus.). 184p. 1980. pap. 9.95 (ISBN 0-8348-0157-4). Weatherhill.
Wagenvoord, James. Flying Kites. 1969. pap. 2.95 (ISBN 0-02-082660-5, Collier). Macmillan.
Wier, Delight B. Delight Wier's Kitchen. (Illus.). pap. 6.95 (ISBN 0-87069-283-6). Wallace-Homestead.
Yolen, Jane. World on a String: The Story of Kites. (Illus.). (gr. 5 up). 1975. PLB 5.91 (ISBN 0-529-00394-5). Philomel.
KITES (METEOROLOGY)
see also Atmosphere, Upper
KITTYHAWK (FIGHTER PLANES)
see P-Forty (Fighter Planes)
KITUBA LANGUAGE
see Congo Language
KIVAS
Hibben, Frank C. Kiva Art of the Anasazi at Pottery Mound, N.M. DenDooven, Gweneth R., ed. LC 75-19742. (Illus.). 1975. 35.00 (ISBN 0-916122-16-6); signed, limited ed. 100.00 (ISBN 0-685-60911-1). KC Pubns.
Vivian, Gordon & Reiter, Paul. The Great Kivas of Chaco Canyon & Their Relationships. (School of American Research Monograph: No. 22). (Illus.). 112p. 1980. pap. 7.95 (ISBN 0-8263-0297-1). U of NM Pr.
KIWAI (PAPUAN PEOPLE)
Landtman, G. Kiwai Papuans of British New Guinea. LC 28-13873. (Landmarks in Anthropology Ser). (Illus.). 1970. Repr. of 1927 ed. 46.00 (ISBN 0-384-31270-5). Johnson Repr.
KIYONAGA
see Toric Kiyonaga, 1752-1815
KLAJ, JOHANN, 1616-1656
Franz, A. Johann Klaj. pap. 15.50 (ISBN 0-384-16740-3). Johnson Repr.
KLEBSIELLA
Kauffmann, F. The Differentiation of Escherichia & Klebsiella Types. (American Lecture Tests & Techniques). 56p. 1951. photocopy ed. spiral 10.50 (ISBN 0-398-04304-3). C C Thomas.
KLEE, PAUL, 1879-1940
Geelhaar, Christian. Klee, Paul. (Pocket Art Ser.). (Illus.). 112p. (gr. 9-12). 1982. pap. 3.50 (ISBN 0-8120-2186-X). Barron.
--Paul Klee. (Pocket Art Ser.). 1982. pap. 3.50 (ISBN 0-8120-2186-X). Barron.
Klee "Livres Archives". Date not set. price not set (5343). Barron.
Klee, Paul. Drawings of Paul Klee. Huggler, Max, ed. (Master Draughtsman Ser). (Illus., Orig.). treasure trove bdg. 6.47x (ISBN 0-685-07281-9); pap. 2.95 (ISBN 0-685-07282-7). Borden.
--Klee, Notebooks of Paul Klee, Vol. 1: The Thinking Eye. Spiller, Jurg, ed. (Documents of Modern Art: V0l. 15). 1978. Repr. 40.00 (ISBN 0-8150-0039-1). Wittenborn.
--Paul Klee. Grohmann, Will, ed. (Library of Great Painters Ser). 1967. 40.00 (ISBN 0-8109-0228-1). Abrams.
Pierce, James S. Paul Klee & Primitive Art. LC 75-23807. (Outstanding Dissertations in the Fine Arts - 20th Century). 1976. lib. bdg. 31.00 (ISBN 0-8240-2001-4). Garland Pub.
Plant, Margaret. Paul Klee: Figures & Faces. (Illus.). 1978. 27.50 (ISBN 0-500-23274-1). Thames Hudson.
Raboff, Ernest. Paul Klee. LC 68-26550. (gr. 3-7). 1968. 6.95a (ISBN 0-385-04916-1); PLB (ISBN 0-385-05113-1). Doubleday.
Svendsen, Louise A. Klee at the Guggenheim Museum. (Illus.). 1977. pap. 6.95 (ISBN 0-89207-006-4). S R Guggenheim.
Tower, Beeke S. Klee & Kandinsky in Munich & at the Bauhans. Foster, Stephen, ed. (Studies in Fine Arts--the Avant-Garde: No. 16). 1981. write for info. (ISBN 0-8357-1179-X, Pub. by UMI Res Pr). Univ Microfilms.
A Tribute to Paul Klee Eighteen Seventy-Nine to Nineteen Forty. (Illus.). 1979. pap. 19.95 (ISBN 0-88884-381-X, 56523-8, Pub. by Natl Gallery Canada). U of Chicago Pr.
Wheeler, M., pref. by. Paul Klee: Three Exhibitions: 1930, 1941, 1949. LC 68-57298. (Museum of Modern Art Publications in Reprint Ser). (Illus.). 1970. Repr. 18.00 (ISBN 0-405-01518-6). Arno.
Whitford, Frank. Paul Klee. 1981. 36.00x (ISBN 0-906379-35-0, Pub. by Jupiter England). State Mutual Bk.
KLEIN, MELANIE
Salzberger-Wittenberg, Isca. Psycho-Analytic Insight & Relationships: A Kleinian Approach. (Library of Social Work). 1970. cased 12.50 (ISBN 0-7100-6835-2). Routledge & Kegan.
Segal. Introduction to the Work of Melanie Klein. 2nd ed. LC 73-89899. 1974. text ed. 11.50x (ISBN 0-465-03583-3). Basic.
Segal, Hanna. Introduction to the Work of Melanie Klein. 2nd ed. LC 73-91077. 144p. 1980. pap. 3.95 (ISBN 0-465-03584-1). Basic.

--Melanie Klein. 1981. pap. 3.95 (ISBN 0-14-005926-1). Penguin.
--Melanie Klein. (Modern Masters Ser.). 204p. 1980. 12.95 (ISBN 0-670-46474-0). Viking Pr.
--The Work of Hanna Segal: A Kleinian Approach to Clinical Practice. 240p. 1981. write for info. Aronson.

KLEINHOLZ, FRANK

Cole, Sylvan, Jr., compiled by. Kleinholz-Graphics 1940-1975. LC 74-31266. (Illus.). 1975. pap. 7.50 (ISBN 0-916224-18-X). Banyan Bks.
Freundlich, August L. Frank Kleinholz-The Outsider. LC 73-75849. 1969. 10.00 (ISBN 0-916224-19-8). Banyan Bks.

KLEIST, HEINRICH VON, 1777-1811

Burckhardt, Sigurd. The Drama of Language: Essays on Goethe & Kleist. LC 77-97492. 183p. 1970. 12.00x (ISBN 0-8018-1049-3). Johns Hopkins.
Dyer, Denys. The Stories of Kleist: A Critical Study. LC 76-58356. 1977. text ed. 26.50x (ISBN 0-8419-0303-4). Holmes & Meier.
Ellis, John M. Heinrich Von Kleist: Studies in the Character & Meaning of His Writing. (Studies in the Germanic Languages & Literatures). 1979. 13.50x (ISBN 0-8078-8094-9). U of NC Pr.
Fricke, Gerhard. Gefuehl und Schicksal Bei Heinrich V. Kleist. LC 70-149657. Repr. of 1929 ed. 19.50 (ISBN 0-404-02578-1). AMS Pr.
Gearey, John. Heinrich Von Kleist: A Study in Tragedy & Anxiety. LC 67-26224. 1968. 12.00x (ISBN 0-8122-7557-8). U of Pa Pr.
Gundolf, Friedrich. Heinrich Von Kleist. LC 72-112914. Repr. of 1922 ed. 18.50 (ISBN 0-404-02962-0). AMS Pr.
Helbling, Robert E. Heinrich von Kleist: The Major Works. LC 74-26509. 224p. 1975. 13.50 (ISBN 0-8112-0563-0); pap. 3.95 (ISBN 0-8112-0564-9, NDP390). New Directions.
Kleist, Heinrich von. An Abyss Deep Enough: The Letters of Heinrich Von Kleist with a Selection of Essays & Anecdotes. Miller, Philip B., ed. & tr. 288p. Date not set. 17.50 (ISBN 0-525-05479-0); pap. 8.95 (ISBN 0-525-03008-5). Dutton.
Maass, Joachim. Kleist. Manheim, Ralph, tr. from Ger. 1981. 17.95 (ISBN 0-374-18162-4). FS&G.
Richardson, Frank C. Kleist in France. LC 62-64205. (North Carolina. University. Studies in the Germanic Languages & Literatures: No. 35). Repr. of 1962 ed. 18.50 (ISBN 0-404-50935-5). AMS Pr.
Silz, Walter. Heinrich Von Kleist: Studies in His Works & Literary Character. LC 77-21871. 1977. Repr. of 1962 ed. lib. bdg. 20.75x (ISBN 0-8371-9796-1, SIHV). Greenwood.

KLEY, HEINRICH, 1863-

Kley, Heinrich. Drawings of Heinrich Kley. Weeks, Donald, ed. (Master Draughtsman Ser). treasure trove bdg. 6.47x (ISBN 0-685-07259-2); pap. 2.95 (ISBN 0-685-07260-6). Borden.
--More Drawings by Heinrich Kley. (Illus.). 1923. pap. 3.75 (ISBN 0-486-20041-8). Dover.

KLICKITAT-HISTORY

Neils, Selma M. So This Is Klickitat. (Illus.). 1967. 8.95 (ISBN 0-8323-0193-0). Binford.

KLIMT, GUSTAV

Comini, Alessandra. Gustav Klimt. LC 75-10965. (Illus.). 112p. 1975. pap. 8.95 (ISBN 0-8076-0806-8). Braziller.
Gustav Klimt. 1976. pap. 5.95 (ISBN 0-517-52648-4, Harmony). Crown.
Hofmann, Werner. Gustav Klimt. LC 70-186455. (Illus.). 182p. 1972. 37.50 (ISBN 0-8212-0452-1, 332518). NYGS.
Hofstatter, Hans H. Gustav Klimt: Erotic Drawings. (Illus.). 88p. 1980. 145.00 (ISBN 0-686-62690-7, 1203-1). Abrams.
Kallir, Jane, ed. Gustav Klimt - Egon Schiele. 1980. pap. 10.95 (ISBN 0-517-54234-X, Michelman Books). Crown.
Klimt, Gustav. Twenty Five Drawings. 1964. 105.00x (ISBN 0-685-29649-0); Bound. 105.00 (ISBN 3-201-00373-5). Intl Pubns Serv.
Novotny, Fritz & Dobai, Johannes. Gustav Klimt. LC 68-19809. (Illus.). 1976. 175.00 (ISBN 0-8212-0669-9, 332496). NYGS.

KLINE, FRANZ

Hess, Thomas B. & Feldman, Morton. Six Painters: Mondrian, DeKooning, Guston, Kline, Pollock, Rothko. LC 67-30452. (Illus.). 1968. pap. 3.00 (ISBN 0-914412-22-1). Inst for the Arts.

KLONDIKE GOLD FIELDS

Adney, Edwin T. The Klondike Stampede. 1976. Repr. of 1900 ed. 66.00 (ISBN 0-403-05805-8, Regency). Scholarly.
Becker, Ethel A. Klondike Ninety Eight: E. A. Hegg's Gold Rush Album. rev. ed. LC 67-27689. 1967. 12.50 (ISBN 0-8323-0000-4). Binford.
Berton, Pierre. Klondike Fever: The Life & Death of the Last Great Stampede. (Illus.). 1958. 12.95 (ISBN 0-394-43206-1). Knopf.
Black, Martha L. My Ninety Years. Whyard, Flo, ed. LC 76-3117. (Northern History Library). (Illus.). 1976. pap. 7.95 (ISBN 0-88240-062-2). Alaska Northwest.
Bolotin, Norm. Klondike Lost: A Decade of Photographs by Kinsey & Kinsey. (Illus.). 1980. album style 12.95 (ISBN 0-88240-130-0). Alaska Northwest.
Bronson, William. The Last Grand Adventure. LC 77-2616. (Illus.). 1977. 24.95 (ISBN 0-07-008014-3, GB). McGraw.
Cadell, H. M. Klondike & Yukon Goldfield in 1913. facs. ed. 20p. Repr. pap. 3.75 (ISBN 0-8466-0027-7, SJS27). Shorey.
Cohen, Stan B. The Streets Were Paved with Gold: A Pictorial History of the Klondike Gold Rush 1896-99. LC 77-80011. (Illus.). 192p. 1977. pap. 7.95 (ISBN 0-933126-03-4). Pictorial Hist.
Green, Lewis. The Gold Hustlers. LC 77-7341. (Illus.). 1977. pap. 7.95 (ISBN 0-88240-088-6). Alaska Northwest.
Klondike News, Vol. 1. facs. ed. 40p. Repr. of 1898 ed. 12.00 (ISBN 0-8466-0140-0, SJS140). Shorey.
London, Jack. Economics of the Klondike. 8p. Repr. of 1903 ed. pap. 3.00 (ISBN 0-8466-0178-8, SJS178). Shorey.
Lucia, Ellis. Klondike Kate. 1978. pap. 2.25 (ISBN 0-89174-024-4). Comstock Edns.
Martinsen, Ella L. Trail to North Star Gold. LC 70-98194. (Illus.). 1969. 8.95 (ISBN 0-8323-0190-6). Binford.
Poynter, Margaret. Gold Rush! The Yukon Stampede of 1898. LC 78-14503. (Illus.). (gr. 5 up). 1979. 7.95 (ISBN 0-689-30694-6). Atheneum.
Webb, John S. Rush to the Klondike Over the Mountain Pass. Bd. with River Trip to the Klondike. 36p. Repr. of 1898 ed. pap. 5.95 (ISBN 0-8466-0180-X, SJS180). Shorey.

KLOPSTOCK, FRIEDRICH GOTTLIEB, 1724-1803

Hamburger Klopstock-Ausgabe Briefe, Vol. 1. 1978. 44.00x (ISBN 3-11-007257-2). De Gruyter.
Hurlebusch, Klaus, ed. Arbeitstagebuch, Section Agenda, Vol. 2. LC 74-81088. (Ger.). 1977. 154.50x (ISBN 3-11-005713-1). De Gruyter.
Hurlebusch, Rose-Marie, ed. Friedrich Gottlieb Klopstock Werke und Brief Historisch-Kritische Ausgabe Sect. Werke: Die Gelehrtenrepublik Part 1, Text, Vol. 7. LC 74-81088. vi, 246p. 1975. text ed. 55.00x (ISBN 3-11-006538-X). De Gruyter.
Klopstock, F. G. Klopstock, Friedrich Gottlieb: Werke und Briefe Historisch-kritische Ausgabe, 30 vols. Gronemeyer, Horst, et al, eds. (Sect. Werke, Pt. 4, der Messias, Vol. 1, Text). 1974. 51.25x (ISBN 3-11-004895-7). De Gruyter.
--Klopstock, Friedrich Gottlieb: Werke und Briefe. Historisch-Kritische Ausgabe. Hoepker-Herberg, Elizabeth, ed. (Sect. Werke, Pt. 4, Der Messias, Vol. 2, Text). vi, 227p. 1975. 60.00x (ISBN 3-11-005848-0). De Gruyter.
Tombo, Rudolf. Ossian in Germany. LC 73-144434. (Columbia University. Germanic Studies, Old Ser.: No. 2). Repr. of 1901 ed. 19.00 (ISBN 0-404-50402-7). AMS Pr.

KLUCKHOHN, CLYDE, 1905-1960

Taylor, Walter W., et al, eds. Culture & Life: Essays in Memory of Clyde Kluckhohn. LC 70-188702. 239p. 1973. 9.95x (ISBN 0-8093-0582-8). S Ill U Pr.

KLUGER, RUTH, 1914-

Kluger, Ruth & Mann, Peggy. The Secret Ship. LC 76-2804. (gr. 7 up). 1978. 5.95 (ISBN 0-385-11328-5). Doubleday.

KLYSTRONS

Hamilton, Donald R., et al. Klystons & Microwave Triodes. (Illus.). 6.75 (ISBN 0-8446-2195-1). Peter Smith.
Hamilton, Donald R., et al, eds. Klystrons & Microwave Triodes. (Illus.). 1966. pap. text ed. 4.50 (ISBN 0-486-61558-8). Dover.

KNAPP, SEAMAN ASAHL, 1833-1911

Bailey, Joseph C. Seaman A. Knapp: Schoolmaster of American Agriculture. LC 73-165702. (American Education, Ser. 2). 1971. Repr. of 1945 ed. 17.00 (ISBN 0-405-03691-4). Arno.

KNATHS, KARL, 1891-

Eaton, Charles, intro. by. Karl Knaths: Five Decades of Painting. LC 73-82318. (Illus.). 160p. 1973. pap. 8.00 (ISBN 0-88397-056-2). Intl Exhibit Foun.

KNEADING MACHINERY

see Mixing Machinery

KNEE

American Academy of Orthopaedic Surgeons. Symposium on Anthroscopy & Arthrography of the Knee. LC 78-17015. (Illus.). 1978. text ed. 62.50 (ISBN 0-8016-0056-1). Mosby.
--Symposium on Reconstructive Surgery of the Knee. LC 78-6486. (Illus.). 1978. 52.50 (ISBN 0-8016-0132-0). Mosby.
--Symposium on the Athlete's Knee: Surgical Repair & Reconstruction. LC 80-19414. (Illus.). 218p. 1980. text ed. 40.50 (ISBN 0-8016-0077-4). Mosby.
Cailliet, Rene. Knee Pain & Disability. (Illus.). 160p. 1973. 7.95 (ISBN 0-8036-1620-1). Davis Co.
Dandy, David J. Arthroscopic Surgery of the Knee. (Illus.). 150p. 1981. text ed. 50.00 (ISBN 0-443-02047-7). Churchill.
Eikelaar, H. Arthroscopy of the Knee. (Illus.). 1976. 65.00 (ISBN 0-685-77087-7). Univ Park.
Freeman, M. A., ed. Arthritis of the Knee. (Clinical Features & Surgical Management Ser.). (Illus.). 320p. 1980. 110.00 (ISBN 0-387-09699-X). Springer-Verlag.
Glinz, Werner. Diagnostic & Operative Arthroscopy of the Knee Joint. Spati-Tuchschmid, Edith, tr. (Illus.). 130p. 1980. text ed. 65.00 (ISBN 3-456-80943-3, Pub. by Hans Huber Switzerland). J K Burgess.
Hastings, D. E., ed. The Knee: Ligament & Articular Cartilage Injuries. (Progress in Orthopedic Surgery: Vol. 3). (Illus.). 1978. 22.00 (ISBN 0-387-08679-X). Springer-Verlag.
Henche, H. R. Arthroscopy of the Knee Joint. Casey, P. A., tr. from Ger. (Illus.). 1979. 73.30 (ISBN 0-387-09314-1). Springer-Verlag.
Hungerford, D. S., ed. Leg Length Discrepancy: The Injured Knee. 1977. 22.40 (ISBN 0-387-08037-6). Springer-Verlag.
Jackson, Robert W. & Dandy, D. J., eds. Arthroscopy of the Knee. (Modern Orthopedic Monographs). (Illus.). 144p. 1976. 30.50 (ISBN 0-8089-0947-9). Grune.
Johnson, Lanny L. Comprehensive Arthroscopic Examination of the Knee. LC 77-21646. (Illus.). 1977. 47.50 (ISBN 0-8016-2534-3). Mosby.
Kennedy, John C. The Injured Adolescent Knee. (Illus.). 1979. 29.95 (ISBN 0-683-04594-6). Williams & Wilkins.
Klein, Karl K. The Knees. 6.95 (ISBN 0-8363-0060-2). Jenkins.
The Knee. 1980. pap. 5.00 (ISBN 0-912452-27-7). Am Phys Therapy Assn.
Maquet, P. G. Biomechanics of the Knee: With Application to the Pathogenesis & the Surgical Treatment of Osteoarthritis. (Illus.). 1976. 91.60 (ISBN 0-387-07882-7). Springer-Verlag.
O'Connor, Richard L. Arthroscopy. LC 77-4908. 1977. 49.50 (ISBN 0-397-50371-7, JBL-Med-Nursing). Har-Row.
Ritter, Merrill A. & Gosling, Craig. The Knee: A Guide to the Examination & Diagnosis of Ligament Injuries. (Illus.). 1979. pap. 6.00 (ISBN 0-398-03901-1). C C Thomas.
Roche, Alex F., et al. Skeletal Maturity: The Knee Joint As a Biological Indicator. 374p. 1975. 35.00 (ISBN 0-306-30900-9, Plenum Pr). Plenum Pub.
Schaldach, M. & Hohmann, D., eds. Advances in Artificial Hip & Knee Joint Technology. (Engineering in Medicine Ser: Vol. 2). 1976. 36.00 (ISBN 0-387-07728-6). Springer-Verlag.
Schulitz, K. P., et al, eds. Late Reconstructions of Injured Ligaments of the Knee. (Illus.). 1978. 31.20 (ISBN 0-387-08720-6). Springer-Verlag.
Smillie, I. S. Diseases of the Knee Joint. 2nd ed. (Illus.). 1980. text ed. 79.50 (ISBN 0-443-01382-9). Churchill.
--Injuries of the Knee Joint. 5th ed. (Illus.). 1979. text ed. 79.50 (ISBN 0-443-01381-0). Churchill.

KNEE-RADIOGRAPHY

Pyle, S. Idell & Hoerr, Normand L. Radiographic Atlas of Skeletal Development of the Knee: A Standard of Reference. (Illus.). 96p. 1955. photocopy ed. spiral 10.75 (ISBN 0-398-01529-5). C C Thomas.
--A Radiographic Standard of Reference for the Growing Knee. (Illus.). 152p. 1969. photocopy ed. spiral 15.75 (ISBN 0-398-01530-9). C C Thomas.
Thijn, C. J. Arthrography of the Knee Joint. (Illus.). 1979. 56.60 (ISBN 0-387-09129-7). Springer-Verlag.

KNEE JERK

see Reflexes

KNEIPP CURE

see Hydrotherapy

KNIAZ, POTEMKIN TAVRICHESKII (ARMOURED CRUISER)-DRAMA

Hough, Richard. The Potemkin Mutiny. LC 75-3797. (Illus.). 190p. 1975. Repr. of 1960 ed. lib. bdg. 14.50x (ISBN 0-8371-8075-9, HOPM). Greenwood.

KNIEVEL, EVEL, 1938-

Batson, Larry. Evel Knievel. LC 74-18302. (Sports Superstars Ser). (Illus.). 32p. (gr. 3-6). 1974. PLB 5.95 (ISBN 0-87191-385-2); pap. 2.75 o. p. (ISBN 0-89812-191-4). Creative Ed.
Schmitz, Dorothy C. Evel Knievel: Motorcycle Daredevil. LC 77-70889. (Pros Ser.). (Illus.). (gr. 2). 1977. PLB 6.45 (ISBN 0-913940-61-5). Crestwood Hse.
Spiegel, Marshall. Evel Knievel: The Cycle Jumper. (gr. 7 up). 1978. pap. 1.25 (ISBN 0-590-11846-3, Schol Pap). Schol Bk Serv.
Taylor, Paula. World's Daredevil: Evel Knievel. (Allstars Ser.). (Illus.). (gr. 2-6). 1976. PLB 5.95 (ISBN 0-87191-478-6); pap. 2.95 (ISBN 0-89812-201-5). Creative Ed.

KNIFE-THROWING

Collins, Blackie. Knife Throwing: Sport..Survival..Defense. (Illus.). 31p. (Orig.). 1978. pap. 3.00 (ISBN 0-940362-03-1). Knife World.
Echanis, Michael D. Knife Fighting, Knife Throwing for Combat. LC 77-93069. (Ser. 129). (Illus.). 1978. pap. 7.95 (ISBN 0-89750-058-X). Ohara Pubns.
McEvoy, H. K. Knife-Throwing. 3.95 (ISBN 0-685-63762-X). Wehman.
McEvoy, Harry K. For Knife Lovers Only. (Illus.). 69p. (Orig.). 1979. pap. 4.95 (ISBN 0-940362-05-8). Knife World.
--Knife Throwing: A Practical Guide. LC 72-91550. (Illus.). 1973. pap. 3.95 (ISBN 0-8048-1099-0). C E Tuttle.

KNIGHT, JOHN, d. 1606

Lancaster, James. Voyages of Sir James Lancaster, Kt., to the East Indies. Markham, Clements R., ed. LC 78-134713. (Hakluyt Society First Ser: No. 56). 1970. Repr. of 1877 ed. lib. bdg. 32.00 (ISBN 0-8337-1995-5). B Franklin.

KNIGHT, OLIVER

Scripps, Edward W. I Protest: Selected Disquisitions of E. W. Scripps. Knight, Oliver, ed. (Illus.). 816p. 1966. 22.00x (ISBN 0-299-03990-0). U of Wis Pr.

KNIGHTS AND KNIGHTHOOD

see also Chivalry; Heraldry; Honor; Templars; Teutonic Knights; Tournaments

Barber, Richard. The Knight & Chivalry. 2nd ed. (Illus.). 400p. 1975. 17.50x (ISBN 0-87471-653-5). Rowman.
--The Reign of Chivalry. (Illus.). 208p. 1980. 27.50 (ISBN 0-312-66994-1). St Martin.
Boalt, Gunnar, et al. European Orders of Chivalry. LC 70-151002. 153p. 1971. 7.50x (ISBN 0-8093-0506-2). S Ill U Pr.
Bornstein, Diane. Mirrors of Courtesy. (Illus.). 158p. (Orig.). 1975. 16.50 (ISBN 0-208-01501-9, Archon). Shoe String.
Bumke, Joachim. The Concept of Knighthood in the Middle Ages. Jackson, W. T. & Jackson, Ericka, trs. from Ger. LC 79-8840. (AMS Studies in the Middle Ages). Orig. Title: Studien Zum Ritterbegriff Im 12. und 13. Jahrhundert. (Illus.). 1981. 24.95 (ISBN 0-404-18033-7). AMS Pr.
--The Concept of Knighthood in the Middle Ages. Jackson, Erika, tr. from Ger. LC 79-8840. (AMS Studies in the Middle Ages Ser.: No. 2). 1981. 24.95 (ISBN 0-404-18034-5). AMS Pr.
Clyomon & Clamydes. LC 76-133737. (Tudor Facsimile Texts. Old English Plays: No. 85). Repr. of 1913 ed. 31.50 (ISBN 0-404-53385-X). AMS Pr.
Cook, Albert S. Historical Background of Chaucer's Knight. LC 68-1564. (Studies in Chaucer, No. 6). 1969. Repr. of 1916 ed. lib. bdg. 23.95 (ISBN 0-8383-0531-8). Haskell.
De La Tour-Landry, Geoffroy. The Book of the Knight of la Tour-Landry. Taylor, G. S., ed. LC 79-8366. Repr. 24.50 (ISBN 0-404-18350-6). AMS Pr.
Diaz, De Gamez. The Unconquered Knight: A Chronicle of the Deeds of Don Pero Nino. Evans, Joan, tr. LC 78-63494. Repr. of 1928 ed. 27.50 (ISBN 0-404-17143-5). AMS Pr.
Forster, C. Thornton. The Life & Letters of Ogier Ghiselin de Busberg, Seigneur of Bausbecque, Knight, Imperial Ambasador, 2vols. 1971. Repr. of 1881 ed. Set. 60.00x (ISBN 0-8002-1297-5). Intl Pubns Serv.
Generides. Royal Historie of the Excellent Knight Generides. Furnivall, Frederick J., ed. LC 70-147837. (Research & Source Works Ser.: No. 727). 1971. Repr. 25.50 (ISBN 0-8337-1252-7). B Franklin.
Hall, Louis B. The Knightly Tales of Sir Gawain. LC 76-17866. (Illus.). 192p. 1976. 14.95x (ISBN 0-88229-350-8); pap. 8.95x (ISBN 0-88229-407-5). Nelson-Hall.
Liu, James J. Chinese Knight Errant. LC 66-14112. 1967. 10.50x (ISBN 0-226-48688-5). U of Chicago Pr.
Major, Charles. When Knighthood Was in Flower. LC 70-126656. Repr. of 1898 ed. 24.00 (ISBN 0-404-04169-8). AMS Pr.
Mifsud, Alfred. Knights Hospitallers of the Venerable Tongue of England in Malta. LC 78-63348. (The Crusades & Military Orders: Second Ser.). (Illus.). Repr. of 1914 ed. 34.50 (ISBN 0-404-17009-9). AMS Pr.
Moorman, Charles. A Knyght There Was: The Evolution of the Knight in Literature. LC 67-17846. 180p. 1967. 12.00x (ISBN 0-8131-1133-1). U Pr of Ky.
Robinson, Gertrude. David Urquhart: Some Chapters in the Life of a Victorian Knight Errant of Justice & Liberty. LC 78-110120. Repr. of 1920 ed. 15.00x (ISBN 0-678-00609-1). Kelley.

Shaw, William A. Knights of England: A Complete Record from the Earliest Time to the Present Day of the Knights of All the Orders of Chivalry in England, Scotland & Ireland, & of Knights Bachelor, 2 Vols. LC 74-129966. 1971. Repr. of 1906 ed. Set. 42.50 (ISBN 0-8063-0443-X). Genealog Pub.

KNIGHTS AND KNIGHTHOOD–JUVENILE LITERATURE

Buehr, Walter. Knights, Castles & Feudal Life. (Illus.). (gr. 4-6). 1957. PLB 5.29 (ISBN 0-399-60341-7). Putnam.

Glubok, Shirley. Knights in Armor. LC 69-10208. (Illus.). (gr. 3-7). 1969. PLB 8.79 (ISBN 0-06-022038-4, HarpJ). Har-Row.

The Knights. LC 79-10211. (The Living Past Ser.). (Illus.). (gr. 4 up). 1979. 6.95 (ISBN 0-668-04785-2, 4785-2). Arco.

Koenig, Alma J. Gudrun. Bell, Anthea, tr. LC 79-917. (gr. 7 up). 1979. 8.25 (ISBN 0-688-41899-6); PLB 7.92 (ISBN 0-688-51899-0). Lothrop.

KNIGHTS OF LABOR

Foner, Philip S. & Lewis, Ronald L., eds. Black Worker: The Era of the AFL, the Railroad Brotherhoods & the UMW, 1880-1903, Vol. IV. LC 78-2875. 1979. 22.50 (ISBN 0-87722-139-1). Temple U Pr.

--Black Worker: The Era of the Knights of Labor & the Colored Farmers' Alliance, Eighteen Eighty to Eighteen Ninety, Vol. III. LC 78-2875. 1979. 22.50 (ISBN 0-87722-138-3). Temple U Pr.

McLaurin, Melton A. The Knights of Labor in the South. LC 77-87916. (Contributions in Labor History: No. 4). (Illus.). 1978. lib. bdg. 18.95 (ISBN 0-313-20033-5, MCK/). Greenwood.

Powderly, Terence V. Path I Trod. LC 77-181971. Repr. of 1940 ed. 31.50 (ISBN 0-404-05098-0). AMS Pr.

--Thirty Years of Life & Labor, 1859-1889. rev. ed. LC 66-21692. Repr. of 1890 ed. 17.50x (ISBN 0-678-00249-5). Kelley.

Scontras, Charles A. Organized Labor & Labor Politics in Maine, 1880-1890. 1966. pap. 1.50 (ISBN 0-89101-013-0). U Maine Orono.

Turcheneske, John A., Jr., ed. Terence Vincent Powderly Papers, 1864-1937 & John William Hayes Papers, 1880-1921, the Knights of Labor: A Guide to the Microfilm Edition. LC 75-16251. 60p. 1975. pap. 25.00 (ISBN 0-88455-148-2). Microfilming Corp.

Ware, Norman. The Labor Movement in the United States 1860-1895. 1959. 8.00 (ISBN 0-8446-1466-1). Peter Smith.

KNIGHTS OF MALTA

Cavaliero, Roderick. The Last of the Crusaders. LC 78-63337. (The Crusades & Military Orders: Second Ser.). Repr. of 1960 ed. 27.50 (ISBN 0-404-17006-4). AMS Pr.

Knights of Malta. The Rule Statutes & Customs of the Hospitallers, 1099-1310. LC 78-63347. (The Crusades & Military Orders: Second Ser.). 272p. Repr. of 1934 ed. 29.00 (ISBN 0-404-16246-0). AMS Pr.

Mifsud, Alfred. Knights Hospitallers of the Venerable Tongue of England in Malta. LC 78-63348. (The Crusades & Military Orders: Second Ser.). (Illus.). Repr. of 1914 ed. 34.50 (ISBN 0-404-17009-9). AMS Pr.

Peyrefitte, Roger. Knights of Malta. LC 59-12194. 1959. 12.95 (ISBN 0-87599-087-8). S G Phillips.

Philippus De Thame. Knights Hospitallers in England. Repr. of 1857 ed. 31.00 (ISBN 0-384-46330-4). Johnson Repr.

Riley-Smith, J. Knights of St. John in Jerusalem & Cyprus: 1050-1310. (Illus.). 1967. 22.50 (ISBN 0-312-45850-9, K83500). St Martin.

Schembri, H. C. Coins & Medals of the Knights of Malta. 1966. 18.00 (ISBN 0-685-51537-0, Pub by Spink & Son England). S J Durst.

Schermerhorn, Elizabeth W. Malta of the Knights. LC 76-29838. Repr. of 1929 ed. 32.00 (ISBN 0-404-15429-8). AMS Pr.

KNIGHTS OF SAINT CRISPIN

Lescohier, Don D. Knights of St. Crispin, Eighteen Sixty-Seven to Eighteen Seventy-Four. LC 77-89748. (American Labor from Conspiracy to Collective Bargaining, Ser. 2). 101p. 1969. Repr. of 1910 ed. 10.00 (ISBN 0-405-02136-4). Arno.

KNIGHTS TEMPLARS (MASONIC)

see Freemasons–Knights Templars

KNIGHTS TEMPLARS (MONASTIC AND MILITARY ORDER)

see Templars

KNIT GOODS

Allen, Virginia P. Beyond the Pattern: A Guide to Creative Sewing & Design with Knit Fabrics. LC 73-91225. 1973. softcover 9.95 (ISBN 0-686-09884-6); lib. bdg. 15.95 (ISBN 0-686-09885-4). Spinning Spool.

Haigh, D. Dyeing & Finishing Knitted Goods. 14.00 (ISBN 0-87245-496-7). Textile Bk.

Reichman, C., et al. Knitted Fabric Primer. 20.00 (ISBN 0-87245-269-7). Textile Bk.

Reichman, Charles. Guide to the Manufacture of Sweaters, Knit Shirts & Swimwear. (Illus.). 1963. 10.00 (ISBN 0-87245-266-2). Textile Bk.

Wright, Ja. Sewing Magic with Knits. LC 72-85681. (Illus.). 192p. 1973. lib. bdg. 6.95 (ISBN 0-668-02719-3). Arco.

KNIT GOODS INDUSTRY

Burnip, M. S. & Thomas, J. H. The Production and Properties of Knitted and Woven Fabrics. 139p. 1969. 70.00x (ISBN 0-686-63783-6). State Mutual Bk.

Davison's Knit Goods Trade. 1981. 40.00 (ISBN 0-686-67904-0). Davison.

Gottlieb, N. The Production & Properties of Warp-Knitted Fabrics. 100p. 1975. 70.00x (ISBN 0-686-63786-0). State Mutual Bk.

Henson, Gravenor. History of the Framework Knitters, Vol. 1. LC 70-97974. Repr. of 1831 ed. lib. bdg. 19.50x (ISBN 0-678-05671-4). Kelley.

Herbert, R. W. The Organization of a Seasonal Range of Knitted Fabrics. 1979. 60.00x (ISBN 0-686-63779-8). State Mutual Bk.

Smirfitt, J. A. The Production & Properties of Weft-Knitted Fabrics. 113p. 1973. 70.00x (ISBN 0-686-63787-9). State Mutual Bk.

Turner, J. D. The Production & Properties of Knitted Fabrics. 159p. 1971. 70.00x (ISBN 0-686-63782-8). State Mutual Bk.

KNITTING

see also Beadwork; Knit Goods

Abbey, Barbara. The Complete Book of Knitting. LC 79-168526. (Illus.). 224p. 1972. 12.95 (ISBN 0-670-23399-4, Studio). Viking Pr.

American School of Needlework. The Great Afghan Book. Thomas, Mary, ed. LC 80-68389. (Illus.). 160p. 1981. 16.95 (ISBN 0-8069-5444-2, Columbia Hse). Sterling.

Better Homes & Gardens Books, ed. Better Homes & Gardens Crocheting & Knitting. (Illus.). 1977. 5.95 (ISBN 0-696-00155-1). Meredith Corp.

Bray, Bonita. Afghans: Traditional & Modern. (Illus.). 1977. 9.95 (ISBN 0-517-53104-6); pap. 5.95 (ISBN 0-517-53105-4). Crown.

Burnham, Nellie. Knitted Toys & Dolls: Complete Instructions for 17 Easy-to-Do Projects. (Illus.). 32p. (Orig.). 1981. pap. price not set (ISBN 0-486-24148-3). Dover.

Carroll, Alice. Knitting & Crocheting Your Own Fashions of the Forties. Orig. Title: Complete Guide to Modern Knitting & Crocheting. (Illus.). 5.50 (ISBN 0-8446-5013-7). Peter Smith.

Compton, Rae. The Craft of Knitting. 1976. 6.95 (ISBN 0-09-124810-8, Pub. by Hutchinson); pap. 3.95 (ISBN 0-09-124811-6). Merrimack Bk Serv.

Cone, Ferne. Knit Art. 1975. 10.50 (ISBN 0-442-21655-6); pap. 6.95 (ISBN 0-442-21656-4). Van Nos Reinhold.

Cone, Ferne G. Knit with Style. LC 79-13744. (Connecting Threads Ser.). (Illus.). 1979. pap. 8.95 (ISBN 0-914842-38-2). Madrona Pubs.

--Knutty Knitting for Kids. LC 76-50323. (Illus.). (gr. 4 up). 1977. 6.95 (ISBN 0-695-80739-0); lib. bdg. 6.99 (ISBN 0-695-40739-2). Follett.

Creative Educational Society Editors. How to Have Fun Knitting. LC 73-12471. (Creative Craft Bks.). (Illus.). 32p. (gr. 2-5). 1973. PLB 5.95 (ISBN 0-87191-274-0). Creative Ed.

Dale Yarn Co. Knit Your Own Norwegian Sweaters. LC 73-94350. (Illus.). 64p. 1974. pap. 3.25 (ISBN 0-486-23031-7). Dover.

Dawson, Pat. Knitting. (Monarch Illustrated Guide Ser.). 1977. pap. 6.95 (ISBN 0-671-18769-4). Monarch Pr.

Dittrick, Mark, ed. Design Knitting. LC 78-53411. 1979. 14.95 (ISBN 0-8015-2021-5, Hawthorn). Dutton.

Drysdale, Rosemary. Miniature Crocheting & Knitting for Dollhouses. (Illus.). 50p. Date not set. pap. price not set (ISBN 0-486-23964-0). Dover.

Dubane, Janet & Friend, Diane, eds. Knit & Crochet. (Illus.). 64p. (Orig.). 1980. pap. 2.00 (ISBN 0-918178-21-5). Simplicity.

Duncan, Ida R. Complete Book of Progressive Knitting. rev. ed. LC 70-149630. 1971. pap. 3.45 (ISBN 0-87140-043-X). Liveright.

Editors of Time-Life Books. Shortcuts to Elegance. LC 73-91757. (The Art of Sewing). (Illus.). (gr. 6 up). 1974. PLB 11.97 (ISBN 0-8094-1711-1, Pub. by Time-Life). Silver.

Halevy, Robyne. Knitting & Crocheting Pattern Index. LC 76-50550. 1977. 10.00 (ISBN 0-8108-0998-2). Scarecrow.

Hamilton, Gail & Brown, Gail. The Super-Sweater Idea Book. LC 77-92584. (Illus.). 1978. pap. 6.95 (ISBN 0-8329-0179-2). New Century.

Harste, Patricia. The Knitting Book: Techniques, Patterns, Projects. (Creative Handcrafts Ser.). (Illus.). 320p. 1980. 22.95 (ISBN 0-13-516617-9, Spec); pap. 12.95 (ISBN 0-13-516609-8). P-H.

Hedin, Solweig. Knit Sweaters the Easy Way. LC 81-43044. (Illus.). 128p. 1981. 11.95 (ISBN 0-385-17180-3). Doubleday.

Hollis, Nesta & Rickwood, Winifred. Knitted Outfits for Teenage Dolls. (Illus.). 134p. 1975. 14.00 (ISBN 0-571-10453-3). Transatlantic.

Hubert, Margaret. One-Piece Knits That Fit: How to Knit & Crochet One-Piece Garments. 1978. 15.95 (ISBN 0-442-23567-4). Van Nos Reinhold.

Hurlburt, Regina. Left-Handed Knitting. 1977. pap. 5.95 (ISBN 0-442-23585-2). Van Nos Reinhold.

Jeffs, Angela, ed. Wild Knitting. LC 79-51988. (Illus.). 1979. 19.95 (ISBN 0-89479-054-4). A & W Pubs.

Kinzel, Marianne. First Book of Modern Lace Knitting. LC 72-86063. (Illus.). 96p. 1973. pap. 3.50 (ISBN 0-486-22904-1). Dover.

--First Book of Modern Lace Knitting. (Illus.). 5.50 (ISBN 0-8446-4762-4). Peter Smith.

--Second Book of Modern Lace Knitting. rev. ed. LC 72-86064. (Illus.). 128p. 1973. pap. 4.00 (ISBN 0-486-22905-X). Dover.

--Second Book of Modern Lace Knitting. (Illus.). 5.50 (ISBN 0-8446-4763-2). Peter Smith.

Knitting. (Good Housekeeping Library of Needle Arts). 128p. 1982. 8.95 (ISBN 0-87851-054-0). Hearst Bks.

Knitting Encyclopedia of the National Knitted Outerwear Association. 34.95 (ISBN 0-87245-445-2). Textile Bk.

Lindberg Press. Knitting for Babies. 1980. pap. 2.75 (ISBN 0-486-23953-5). Dover.

Lorant, Tessa. Hand & Machine Knitting. 1981. 19.95 (ISBN 0-684-16770-0, ScribT). Scribner.

McGregor, Sheila. The Complete Book of Traditional Fair Isle Knitting. (Illus.). 144p. 1981. 22.50 (ISBN 0-7134-1432-4, Pub. by Batsford England). David & Charles.

Mayfield, A., intro. by. Odhams Knitting Encyclopaedia. (Illus.). 1971. 8.95 (ISBN 0-600-72123-X). Transatlantic.

Meyers, Belle. Knitting Know-How: An Illustrated Encyclopedia. LC 80-7857. (Illus.). 208p. 1981. 14.95 (ISBN 0-06-014905-1, HarpT). Har-Row.

Mon Tricot. Knitting Dictionary: Stitches & Patterns. 3rd ed. (Illus.). 210p. (YA) 1975. pap. 2.50 (ISBN 0-517-52206-3). Crown.

Mon Tricot Editors. Knit & Crochet, Vol. 1. (Mon Tricot Ser.). 1976. pap. 7.95 (ISBN 0-517-52537-2). Crown.

--Knit & Crochet, Vol. 2. (Mon Tricot Ser.). 1976. pap. 1.98 (ISBN 0-517-52800-2). Crown.

Odhams Knitting Encylopedia. 1970. 8.95 (ISBN 0-87245-243-3). Textile Bk.

Ondori Publishing Company Staff. Illustrated Basic Crochet & Knit. (Illus.). 48p. 1977. pap. 2.95 (ISBN 0-87040-389-3). Japan Pubns.

Parkinson, Francesca. Knit & Crochet Your Own Designs. LC 76-41163. (Illus.). 1979. lib. bdg. 14.95 (ISBN 0-668-04126-9, 4126). Arco.

Phillips, Mary W. Creative Knitting: A New Art Form. 128p. 1980. pap. 9.95 (ISBN 0-442-26224-8). Van Nos Reinhold.

Rubenstone, Jessie. Knitting for Beginners. LC 73-6755. (gr. 3-4). 1973 (JBL-J). pap. 2.95 (ISBN 0-397-31474-4). Har-Row.

Sara, Dorothy. Key to Basic Knitting. pap. 2.00 (ISBN 0-686-00696-8). Key Bks.

Smirfitt, J. A. Introduction to Weft Knitting. 1975. 13.00 (ISBN 0-87245-567-X). Textile Bk.

Somers, Lucy. How to Crochet a High Fashion Wardrobe. 1978. 12.50 (ISBN 0-682-49027-X). Exposition.

Sommer, Elyse & Sommer, Mike. A New Look at Knitting: An Easier & More Creative Approach. 1977. 12.95 (ISBN 0-517-52860-6). Crown.

Step by Step to Better Knitting & Crochet. LC 81-67434. (Illus.). 288p. 1982. write for info. (ISBN 0-668-05343-7, 5343). Arco.

Sunset Editors. Knitting. LC 76-7659. (Illus.). 80p. 1976. pap. 2.95 (ISBN 0-376-04432-2, Sunset Bks). Sunset-Lane.

Taylor, Gertrude. America's Knitting Book. LC 68-54833. (Encore Edition). (Illus.). 1974. 5.95 (ISBN 0-684-15464-1, ScribT). Scribner.

Thomas, D. G. Introduction to Warp Knitting. 1971. 13.00 (ISBN 0-87245-410-X). Textile Bk.

Thomas, M. Knitting Patterns. 316p. 18.50 (ISBN 0-87559-111-6). Shalom.

Thomas, Mary. Mary Thomas's Book of Knitting Patterns. (Illus.). 340p. 1972. pap. 4.50 (ISBN 0-486-22818-5). Dover.

--Mary Thomas's Book of Knitting Patterns. (Illus.). 8.00 (ISBN 0-8446-4611-3). Peter Smith.

--Mary Thomas's Knitting Book. (Illus.). 269p. (gr. 6-12). 1972. pap. 3.50 (ISBN 0-486-22817-7). Dover.

--Mary Thomas's Knitting Book. (Illus.). 6.75 (ISBN 0-8446-4617-2). Peter Smith.

Von Wartburg, Ursula. The Workshop Book of Knitting. LC 71-157313. (Illus.). 160p. (gr. 3 up). 1973. 9.95 (ISBN 0-689-20696-8); pap. 4.95 (ISBN 0-689-70564-6). Atheneum.

Walker, Barbara. Barbara Walker's Learn to Knit Afghan Book. LC 73-10906. (Encore Edition). (Illus.). 1976. pap. 1.95 (ISBN 0-684-16929-0, SL666, ScribT). Scribner.

Walker, Barbara G. Mosaic Knitting. LC 75-22311. (Encore Edition). (Illus.). 224p. 1976. 7.95 (ISBN 0-684-15961-9, ScribT). Scribner.

--Treasury of Knitting Patterns. LC 67-24064. (Illus.). 1968. 10.00 (ISBN 0-684-10627-2, ScribT). Scribner.

Wilson, Sherry. Creative Knitting. 96p. Date not set. price not set (Pub. by Reed Books Australia). C E Tuttle.

Workbasket Magazine, ed. Aunt Ellen's Knitting Handbook: A Treasury of Techniques & Projects. LC 81-82242. (Illus.). 64p. (Orig.). 1981. pap. 2.95 (ISBN 0-86675-326-5, 3265). Mod Handcraft.

Wright, Mary. Cornish Guernsey & Knit-Frocks. 72p. 1980. 10.00x (ISBN 0-906720-05-2, Pub. by Hodge England). State Mutual Bk.

Zimmerman, Elizabeth. Elizabeth Zimmerman's Knitter's Almanac: Projects for Each Month of the Year. Orig. Title: Knitter's Almanac. (Illus.). 152p. 1981. pap. price not set (ISBN 0-486-24178-5). Dover.

--Knitting Without Tears. LC 70-140776. (Illus.). 1973. pap. 7.95 (ISBN 0-684-13505-1, SL466, ScribT). Scribner.

KNITTING–PATTERNS

Bindingarmynstur, Foroysk. Faroese Knitting Patterns. 60p. 1980. pap. 10.95 (ISBN 0-906191-17-3, Pub. by Thule Pr England). Intl Schol Bk Serv.

Chatterton, Pauline. Scandinavian Knitting Designs. LC 76-27879. (Encore Edition). (Illus.). 1977. 5.95 (ISBN 0-684-16538-4, ScribT). Scribner.

Dale Yarn Co. Knit Your Own Norwegian Sweaters: Complete Instructions for 50 Authentic Sweaters, Hats, Mittens, Gloves, Caps, Etc. (Illus.). 8.00 (ISBN 0-8446-5175-3). Peter Smith.

Hollingworth, Shelagh. Knitting & Crochet for the Physically Handicapped & Elderly. (Illus.). 120p. 1981. 22.00 (ISBN 0-7134-3340-X, Pub. by Batsford England). David & Charles.

Hubert, Margaret & Gusick, Dorothy D. Weekend Knitting Projects. 1979. 15.95 (ISBN 0-442-23572-0). Van Nos Reinhold.

Ladies Home Journal Editors. Knitting. 1977. 13.50 (ISBN 0-442-80474-1); pap. 8.95 (ISBN 0-442-80476-8). Van Nos Reinhold.

Mariano, Linda. The Encyclopedia of Knitting & Crochet Stitch Patterns. 1976. 15.95 (ISBN 0-442-25117-3). Van Nos Reinhold.

Mon Tricot Staff. Two-Hundred Fifty Patterns to Knit & Crochet. (Illus.). 1977. pap. 2.50 (ISBN 0-517-53065-1). Crown.

Morgan, Gwyn. Traditional Knitting Patterns of Ireland, Scotland, & England. (Illus.). 128p. 1981. 13.95 (ISBN 0-686-72591-3); pap. 8.95 (ISBN 0-312-81314-7). St Martin.

Norbury, James. Traditional Knitting Patterns from Scandinavia, the British Isles, France, Italy & Other European Countries. LC 73-79490. (Illus.). 240p. 1973. pap. 4.50 (ISBN 0-486-21013-8). Dover.

--Traditional Knitting Patterns from Scandinavia, the British Isles, France, Italy & Other European Countries. (Illus.). 8.50 (ISBN 0-8446-5071-4). Peter Smith.

The Pattern Library: Knitting. 96p. 1981. pap. 4.95 (ISBN 0-345-29595-1). Ballantine.

Thompson, Gladys. Patterns for Guernseys, Jerseys & Arans: Fishermans' Sweaters from the British Isles. (Illus.). 1971. pap. 4.50 (ISBN 0-486-22703-0). Dover.

Vale, Nancy. Knitting Nineteen Twenties & Nineteen Thirties Originals. (Illus.). 104p. 1980. pap. 8.95 (ISBN 0-686-61417-8, Pub. by Mills & Boon England). Hippocrene Bks.

Walker, Barbara G. A Second Treasury of Knitting Patterns. 1981. pap. 14.95 (ISBN 0-684-16938-X, ScribT). Scribner.

KNITTING, MACHINE

Critser, James R., Jr. Knitting Machinery (1975) (Ser. 9-75). 1976. 50.00 (ISBN 0-914428-39-X). Lexington Data.

Gartshore, Linda. The Craft of Machine Knitting. 1978. 7.95 (ISBN 0-09-131660-X, Pub. by Hutchinson); pap. 3.95 (ISBN 0-09-131661-8). Merrimack Bk Serv.

Holbourne, David. The Basic Book of Machine Knitting. 1979. 12.95 (ISBN 0-442-23482-1). Van Nos Reinhold.

Lorant, Tessa. Hand & Machine Knitting. 1981. 19.95 (ISBN 0-684-16770-0, ScribT). Scribner.

Mendelson, Linda & Dittrick, Mark. Creative Machine Knitting. (Illus.). 1979. 17.50 (ISBN 0-8015-1810-5, Hawthorn). Dutton.

Reichman, Charles. Guide to the Manufacture of Sweaters, Knit Shirts & Swimwear. (Illus.). 1963. 10.00 (ISBN 0-87245-266-2). Textile Bk.

--Knitted Stretch Technology. (Knitting Production Ser). 10.00 (ISBN 0-87245-268-9). Textile Bk.

--Wool & Synthetic Knitwear Handbook. (Knitting Production Ser). 12.00 (ISBN 0-87245-272-7). Textile Bk.

Reisfeld, A. Warp Knit Engineering. 1966. 24.00 (ISBN 0-87245-275-1). Textile Bk.
Reisfeld, A., et al. Fundamentals of Raschel Knitting. (Illus.). 1958. 5.75 (ISBN 0-87245-274-3). Textile Bk.
Shinn, W. E. Flat Knitting. (Knitting Technology Ser). 20.00 (ISBN 0-87245-303-0). Textile Bk.

KNIVES
see also Knife-Throwing
Barney, Richard W., et al. How to Make Knives. Beinfeld, Wallace, ed. 182p. 1977. 13.95 (ISBN 0-917714-13-X). Beinfeld Pub.
Blandford, Percy. How to Make Your Own Knives. (Illus.). 1979. pap. 6.95 (ISBN 0-8306-1130-4, 1130). TAB Bks.
Boye, David. Step-by-Step Knifemaking. LC 77-22383. 1977. 12.95 (ISBN 0-87857-180-9); pap. 9.95 (ISBN 0-87857-181-7). Rodale Pr Inc.
Cassidy, William. Knife Digest. 2nd ed. (Illus.). 1976. pap. 7.95 (ISBN 0-87364-058-6). Sycamore Island.
Cassidy, William L. The Complete Book of Knife Fighting. Lund, Peder C., ed. LC 75-25207. (Illus.). 130p. 1975. 12.95 (ISBN 0-87364-029-2). Paladin Ent.
--Knife Digest: Second Annual Edition. (Illus.). 178p. 1976. pap. 7.95 (ISBN 0-87364-058-6, Sycamore Island). Paladin Ent.
Ehrhardt, Larry. Encyclopedia of Pocket Knives, Bk. 3: Winchester-Marbles - Knives & Hardware. (Illus.). 1974. plastic ring bdg. 6.95 (ISBN 0-913902-08-X). Heart Am Pr.
Ehrhardt, Roy & Ferrell, J. Encyclopedia of Pocket Knives: Book One & Two Price Guide. rev. ed. (Illus.). 1977. plastic ring bdg. 6.95 (ISBN 0-913902-02-0). Heart Am Pr.
Hardin, Albert N., Jr. & Hedden, Robert W. Light but Efficient: A Study of the M1880 Hunting & M1890 Intrenching Knives & Scabbards. LC 73-90405. (Illus.). 1973. 7.95 (ISBN 0-9601778-0-9). Hardin.
Hughes, B. R. Modern Handmade Knives. Date not set. price not set (ISBN 0-913150-44-4). Pioneer Pr.
Ingber-Irvin, Beth. Knifemakers Guild Directory. (Illus.). 200p. 1981. pap. 12.95 (ISBN 0-917714-32-6). Beinfeld Pub.
Knife World Publications. The Best of Knife World, Vol. I. (Illus.). 92p. 1980. pap. 3.95 (ISBN 0-940362-04-X). Knife World.
Latham, Sid. Knifecraft. LC 78-16825. (Illus.). 240p. 1978. 18.95 (ISBN 0-8117-0927-2). Stackpole.
--Knives & Knifemakers. 1973. 17.50 (ISBN 0-87691-109-2). Winchester Pr.
--Knives & Knifemakers. (Illus.). 160p. 1974. pap. 7.95 (ISBN 0-02-011750-7, Collier). Macmillan.
Levine, Bernard R. Knifemakers of Old San Francisco. LC 77-18529. (Illus.). 1978. 12.95 (ISBN 0-930478-01-0). Badger Bks.
Lewis, Jack & Hughes, B. R. Gun Digest Book of Folding Knives. (Illus.). 288p. 1977. pap. 7.95 (ISBN 0-695-80839-7). DBI.
McEvoy, Harry K. For Knife Lovers Only. (Illus.). 69p. (Orig.). 1979. pap. 4.95 (ISBN 0-940362-05-8). Knife World.
Mayes, Jim. How to Make Your Own Knives. LC 78-57407. (Illus.). 1979. 10.95 (ISBN 0-89696-018-8); pap. 7.95 (ISBN 0-89696-146-X). Everest Hse.
Parker, James F. & Voyles, J. Bruce. The Official Nineteen Eighty One Price Guide to Collector Knives. 4th ed. 1982. pap. 9.95 (ISBN 0-87637-179-9). Hse of Collectibles.
Perteron, Harold L. American Knives. 1980. 15.00 (ISBN 0-88227-016-8). Gun Room.
Peterson, Harold L. American Knives. LC 58-7523. 1975. pap. 6.95 (ISBN 0-684-14440-9, SL611, ScribT). Scribner.
Schreier, Konrad F., Jr. Marbles, Knives & Axes. LC 78-15942. 70p. 1978. pap. 4.50 (ISBN 0-917714-19-9). Beinfeld Pub.
Steele, David E. Secrets of Modern Knife Fighting. LC 75-37196. (Illus.). 1975. 15.95 (ISBN 0-685-16327-X); pap. 9.95 (ISBN 0-685-16328-8). Phoenix Assocs.
Stephens, Frederick J. Fighting Knives. LC 80-10699. (Illus.). 144p. 1980. 14.95 (ISBN 0-668-04955-3, 4955-3). Arco.
Tappan, Mel, ed. A Guide to Handmade Knives & the Official Directory of the Knifemaker's Guild. LC 77-9199. (Illus., Orig.). 1977. pap. 9.50 (ISBN 0-916172-03-1). Janus Pr.
--Guide to Handmade Knives & the Official Directory of the Knifemakers Guild. 1977. limited ed. 19.50 (ISBN 0-916172-06-6). Janus Pr.
Warner, Ken. The Practical Book of Knives. 1976. 12.95 (ISBN 0-87691-218-8). Winchester Pr.
Warner, Ken, ed. Knives Eighty One. 192p. 1980. pap. 5.95 (ISBN 0-910676-15-1). DBI.
--Knives 'Eighty-Two. (Illus.). 192p. 1981. pap. 6.95 (ISBN 0-910676-34-8). DBI.

KNOSSOS (CRETE)
Chadwick, John, et al. Knossos Tables: A Transliteration. 4th ed. (Illus.). 1971. 53.00 (ISBN 0-521-08085-1). Cambridge U Pr.
Evans, Arthur. Palace of Minos, 4 Vols. in 7. LC 63-18048. 1921. 500.00x (ISBN 0-8196-0129-2). Vol. 1 (ISBN 0-8196-0130-6). Vol. 2, Pt. 1 (ISBN 0-8196-0131-4). Vol. 2, Pt. 2 (ISBN 0-8196-0141-1). Vol. 3 (ISBN 0-8196-0132-2). Vol. 4, Pt. 1 (ISBN 0-8196-0133-0). Vol. 4, Pt. 2 (ISBN 0-8196-0134-9). Index (ISBN 0-8196-0135-7). Biblo.
Horwitz, Sylvia. The Find of a Lifetime: Sir Arthur Evans & the Discovery of Knossos. LC 80-36851. (Illus.). 288p. 1981. 14.95 (ISBN 0-670-13575-5). Viking Pr.

KNOT THEORY
Birman, Joan S. Braids, Links & Mapping Class Groups. LC 74-2961. (Annals of Mathematics Studies: No. 82). 300p. 1974. 16.00x (ISBN 0-691-08149-2). Princeton U Pr.
Crowell, H. R. & Fox, H. R. Introduction to Know Theory. 4th ed. LC 77-22776. (Graduate Texts in Mathematics: Vol. 57). (Illus.). 1977. Repr. of 1963 ed. 16.30 (ISBN 0-387-90272-4). Springer-Verlag.
Hausman, J. C., ed. Knot Theory: Proceedings, Plans-Sur-Bex, Switzerland 1977. (Lecture Note in Mathematics Ser.: Vol. 685). 1979. 18.50 (ISBN 0-387-08952-7). Springer-Verlag.
Levine, J. P. Algebraic Structure of Knot Modules. (Lecture Notes in Mathematics: Vol. 772). 104p. 1980. pap. 9.80 (ISBN 0-387-09739-2). Springer-Verlag.
Murasugi, Kunio. On Closed 3 Braids. LC 74-17176. (Memoirs: No. 151). 1974. pap. 8.80 (ISBN 0-8218-1851-1, MEMO-151). Am Math.
Neuwirth, L. P., ed. Knots, Groups, & 3-Manifolds: Papers Dedicated to the Memory of R. H. Fox. LC 75-5619. (Annals of Mathematics Studies: No. 84). 345p. 1975. 24.00 (ISBN 0-691-08170-0); pap. 9.50 (ISBN 0-691-08167-0). Princeton U Pr.
Ocken, Stanley. Parametrized Knot Theory. LC 76-3641. (Memoirs: No. 170). 1976. pap. 12.00 (ISBN 0-8218-1870-8, MEMO-170). Am Math.
Rolfsen, Dale. Knots & Links. LC 76-15514. (Mathematics Lecture Ser: No. 7). (Illus.). 1976. pap. 15.00 (ISBN 0-914098-16-0). Publish or Perish.
Stoltzfus, N. Unraveling the Integral Knot Concordance Group. LC 77-10133. (Memoirs Ser.: No. 192). 1977. 10.80 (ISBN 0-8218-2192-X, MEMO 192). Am Math.
Takahashi, Moto-O. Two-Bridge Knotts Have Property P. LC 80-26113. (MEMO: No. 239). Date not set. 7.20 (ISBN 0-8218-2239-X). Am Math.

KNOTS (TOPOLOGY)
see Knot Theory

KNOTS AND SPLICES
see also Macrame
Ashley, Clifford W. Ashley Book of Knots. 1944. 19.95 (ISBN 0-385-04025-3). Doubleday.
Belash, C. A. Braiding & Knotting: Techniques & Projects. LC 74-75266. 1974. pap. 2.00 (ISBN 0-486-23059-7). Dover.
Belash, Constantine A. Braiding & Knotting: Techniques & Projects. (Illus.). 3.75 (ISBN 0-8446-5002-1). Peter Smith.
Berthier, Marc P. G. The Art of Knots. 1977. 6.95 (ISBN 0-385-11464-8). Doubleday.
Blandford, Percy W. Knots & Splices. LC 65-25270. (Orig.). 1967. pap. 1.25 (ISBN 0-668-01331-1). Arco.
--Practical Knots & Ropework. (Illus., Orig.). 1980. 14.95 (ISBN 0-8306-9956-2); pap. 9.95 (ISBN 0-8306-1237-8, 1237). TAB Bks.
Boy Scouts of America. Knots & How to Tie Them. (Illus.). pap. text ed. 0.55x (ISBN 0-8395-3170-2, 3170). BSA.
Brown, Terry & Hunter, Rob. The Book of Knots. (Illus.). 1977. pap. 2.95 (ISBN 0-7715-9373-2). Vanguard.
Day, Cyrus L. Art of Knotting & Splicing. 3rd rev. ed. LC 55-10028. (Illus.). 1970. 17.95 (ISBN 0-87021-083-1). Naval Inst Pr.
--Knot & Splices. 1977. 5.95 (ISBN 0-8286-0071-6). De Graff.
Fiber: A Bibliography (Knotting, Stitchery & Surface Design) 1979. 5.70 (ISBN 0-88321-039-8). Am Craft.
Gibson, Charles E. Handbook of Knots & Splices: & Other Work with Hempen & Wire Rope. (Illus.). (gr. 7 up). 8.95 (ISBN 0-87523-146-2). Emerson.
Gibson, Walter. Fell's Official Guide to Knots & How to Tie Them. LC 61-9266. 127p. 1961. pap. 4.95 (ISBN 0-8119-0369-9). Fell.
Grainger, Stuart E. Creative Ropecraft. (Illus.). 1977. 10.95 (ISBN 0-393-08746-8). Norton.
Graumont, Raoul. Handbook of Knots. LC 45-11362. (Illus.). 1945. pap. 3.00 (ISBN 0-87033-030-6). Cornell Maritime.
Graumont, Raoul & Hensel, John. Encyclopedia of Knots & Fancy Rope Work. 4th ed. (Illus.). 1952. 22.50 (ISBN 0-87033-021-7). Cornell Maritime.
--Splicing Wire & Fiber Rope. LC 45-3379. (Illus.). 1945. pap. 5.00 (ISBN 0-87033-118-3). Cornell Maritime.
Graumont, Raoul & Wenstrom, Elmer. Fisherman's Knots & Nets. LC 48-423. (Illus.). 1948. pap. 6.50 (ISBN 0-87033-024-1). Cornell Maritime.
Harrison, P. P. The Harrison Book of Knots. 1981. 25.00x (ISBN 0-85174-346-3, Pub. by Nautical England). State Mutual Bk.
Hensel, John. The Book of Ornamental Knots. (Encore Edition). (Illus.). 1978. pap. 2.95 (ISBN 0-684-16900-2, ScribT); 12.50 (ISBN 0-684-13409-8). Scribner.
Irving, J. & Searl, C. Knots, Ties & Splices: A Handbook for Seafarers, Travellers, & All Who Use Cordage. rev. ed. 1978. pap. 4.50 (ISBN 0-7100-8671-7). Routledge & Kegan.
Jarman, Colin & Beavis, Bill. Modern Rope Seamanship. LC 76-20290. (Illus.). 1979. 15.00 (ISBN 0-87742-074-2). Intl Marine.
Lane, Maggie. Maggie Lane's Book of Beads. (Illus., Orig.). 1979. pap. 5.95 (ISBN 0-684-16234-2, SL 874, ScribT). Scribner.
MacLean, William P. Modern Marlinspike Seamanship. LC 79-7354. (Illus.). 1979. 16.95 (ISBN 0-672-52606-9). Bobbs.
McNally, Tom. Complete Book of Fisherman's Knots. (Illus.). 1975. 7.95 (ISBN 0-686-75268-6); pap. 4.95 (ISBN 0-89149-020-5). Jolex.
Montgomery, Edward. Useful Knots for Everyone. LC 73-2551. (Illus.). 128p. 1973. pap. 3.50 (ISBN 0-684-13393-8, SL447, ScribT). Scribner.
Russell, John. The Arco Book of Useful Knots. LC 81-10977. (Illus.). 96p. 1982. pap. 4.95 (ISBN 0-668-05372-0, 5372). Arco.
Shaw, George R. Knots: Useful & Ornamental. 3rd ed. (Illus.). 1972. pap. 4.95 (ISBN 0-02-082030-5, Collier). Macmillan.
Smallman, Robert E. Knots & Lashing. (Campcraft Skills Ser.). (Illus.). (gr. 5-12). 1976. pap. text ed. 0.95 (ISBN 0-88441-423-X, 26-213). GS.
Smith, Hervey G. Marlinspike Sailor. rev. ed. LC 77-143856. (Illus.). 1969. 10.00 (ISBN 0-8286-0044-9). De Graff.
Snyder, Paul & Snyder, Arthur. Knots & Lines Illustrated. LC 73-107462. 1970. 7.95 (ISBN 0-8286-0046-5). De Graff.
Spencer, Chas. L. Knots, Splices & Fancy Work. 1981. 25.00x (ISBN 0-85174-157-6, Pub. by Nautical England). State Mutual Bk.
Svensson, Sam. Handbook of Seaman's Ropework. LC 74-173886. (Illus.). 190p. 1972. 9.95 (ISBN 0-396-06475-2). Dodd.
Toghill, Jeff. Knots & Splices. (Illus.). 64p. (Orig.). 1979. pap. 3.50 (ISBN 0-589-50079-1, Pub. by Reed Books Australia). C E Tuttle.
Waller, Irene. Knots & Netting. LC 76-55911. (Illus.). 1977. 8.95 (ISBN 0-8008-4484-X). Taplinger.
Wheelock, Walt. Ropes, Knots & Slings for Climbers. rev. ed. (Illus.). 1967. wrappers 1.50 (ISBN 0-910856-00-1). La Siesta.

KNOTT, WALTER, 1889?-
Kooiman, Helen. Walter Knott - Keeper of the Flame. LC 73-83770. (Illus.). 224p. 1973. 7.95x (ISBN 0-916434-07-9). Plycon Pr.

KNOW-HOW ASSISTANCE AGREEMENTS
see Foreign Licensing Agreements

KNOW-NOTHING PARTY
see American Party

KNOWABLENESS OF GOD
see God-Knowableness

KNOWLEDGE, BOOKS OF
see Encyclopedias and Dictionaries

KNOWLEDGE, CLASSIFICATION OF
see Classification; Classification of Sciences

KNOWLEDGE, REFLEXIVE
see Self-Knowledge, Theory of

KNOWLEDGE, SOCIOLOGY OF
Ackermann, Robert J. Theories of Knowledge: A Critical Introduction. 1965. 14.95 (ISBN 0-07-000180-4, C). McGraw.
Bannister, Robert C. Social Darwinism: Science & Myth in Anglo-American Social Thought. Davis, Allen F., ed. LC 79-615. (American Civilization Ser.). 1979. lib. bdg. 17.50x (ISBN 0-87722-155-3). Temple U Pr.
Benge, Ronald. Communication & Identity. 208p. 1972. 17.50 (ISBN 0-208-01178-1, Linnet). Shoe String.
Berger, Peter L. & Luckmann, Thomas. Social Construction of Reality: A Treatise in the Sociology of Knowledge. LC 66-14925. pap. 3.95 (ISBN 0-385-05898-5, A589, Anch). Doubleday.
DeGre, Gerard. Society & Ideology: An Inquiry into the Sociology of Knowledge. Coser, Lewis A. & Powell, Walter W., eds. LC 79-6991. (Perennial Works in Sociology Ser.). 1979. Repr. of 1943 ed. lib. bdg. 13.00x (ISBN 0-405-12091-5). Arno.
Erikson, Bjorn. Problems of an Empirical Sociology of Knowledge. (Acta Univ. Upsaliensis Studies Sociologica: No. 10). 171p. 1975. pap. 13.00x (ISBN 91-554-0258-5). Humanities.
Fuhrman, Ellsworth R. The Sociology of Knowledge in America, Eighteen Eighty-Three to Nineteen Fifteen. LC 79-14829. 1980. 20.00x (ISBN 0-8139-0785-3). U Pr of Va.
Havelock, Ronald G., et al. Bibliography on Knowledge Utilization & Dissemination. rev. ed. LC 75-184872. 217p. 1972. pap. 6.00 (ISBN 0-87944-061-9). Inst Soc Res.
Horowitz, Irving L. Philosophy, Science & the Sociology of Knowledge. LC 76-27756. 1976. Repr. of 1961 ed. lib. bdg. 16.75x (ISBN 0-8371-9051-7, HOPS). Greenwood.
Jones, Robert A. & Kuklick, Henrika, eds. Research in Sociology of Knowledge, Sciences & Art, Vol. 2. (Orig.). 1979. lib. bdg. 32.50 (ISBN 0-89232-123-7). Jai Pr.
Krishnamurti, Jiddu. Beyond Violence. LC 72-9875. 176p. 1973. pap. 3.95 (ISBN 0-06-064839-2, RD 61, HarpR). Har-Row.
Langrish, J., et al. Wealth from Knowledge. 1972. 27.95 (ISBN 0-470-51721-2). Halsted Pr.
Machlup, Fritz. Knowledge: Its Creation, Distribution, & Economic Significance, Vol. 1, Knowledge & Knowledge Production. LC 80-7544. 264p. 1980. 17.50 (ISBN 0-691-04226-8). Princeton U Pr.
Malcolm, Norman. Thought & Knowledge: Essays. LC 76-25647. 1977. 17.50x (ISBN 0-8014-1074-6). Cornell U Pr.
Mannheim, Karl. Essays on the Sociology of Knowledge. 2nd ed. Kecskemeti, Paul, ed. 1952. 24.50x (ISBN 0-19-519159-5). Oxford U Pr.
Mulkay, Michael. Science & the Sociology of Knowledge. (Controversies in Sociology Ser.). 1979. text ed. 19.95x (ISBN 0-04-301093-8); pap. text ed. 7.95x (ISBN 0-04-301094-6). Allen Unwin.
Outhwaite, William. Understanding Social Life: The Method Called Verstehen. LC 75-26783. 127p. 1976. text ed. 12.00x (ISBN 0-8419-0239-9). Holmes & Meier.
Piepe, Anthony. Knowledge & Social Order. 1971. text ed. 5.00x (ISBN 0-435-82685-9). Heinemann Ed.
Regelous, K. J., ed. The Sociology of Knowledge. 1980. 30.00x (ISBN 0-905484-14-2, Pub. by Nafferton England). State Mutual Bk.
Remmling, Gunter W. The Sociology of Karl Mannheim: Chaos or Planning? With a Bibliographical Guide to the Sociology of Knowledge, Ideological Analysis, & Social Planning. (International Library of Sociology). 1974. text ed. 15.75x (ISBN 0-391-00376-3). Humanities.
Remmling, Gunter W., ed. Towards the Sociology of Knowledge: Origin & Development of a Sociological Thought Style. (International Library of Sociology). (Illus.). 463p. 1974. text ed. 32.50x (ISBN 0-391-00291-0). Humanities.
Sahay, Arun. Sociological Analysis. (International Library of Sociology). 220p. 1972. 17.50x (ISBN 0-7100-7363-1). Routledge & Kegan.
Schutz, Alfred & Luckmann, Thomas. The Structures of the Life-World. Zaner, Richard & Engelhardt, Tristram, Jr., trs. from Ger. (Studies in Phenomenology & Existential Philosophy). 1973. text ed. 18.95x (ISBN 0-8101-0395-8); pap. 8.95 (ISBN 0-8101-0622-1). Northwestern U Pr.
Schwartz, Barry. Vertical Classification: A Study in Structuralism & the Sociology of Knowledge. LC 80-24207. (Chicago Original Paperback Ser.). 244p. 1981. pap. 18.00x (ISBN 0-226-74208-3). U of Chicago Pr.
Shils, Edward. The Calling of Sociology: And Other Essays on the Pursuit of Learning. LC 79-15048. 1980. lib. bdg. 25.00x (ISBN 0-226-75323-9). U of Chicago Pr.
Silverman, David. Reading Castaneda: A Prologue to the Social Sciences. 1975. 15.00 (ISBN 0-7100-8145-6); pap. 7.95 (ISBN 0-7100-8146-4). Routledge & Kegan.
Wilson, Patrick. Public Knowledge, Private Ignorance: Toward a Library & Information Policy. LC 76-52327. (Contributions in Librarianship & Information Sciences: No. 10). 1977. lib. bdg. 15.00x (ISBN 0-8371-9485-7, WPN/). Greenwood.
Zand, Dale. Information, Organization, & Power: Effective Management in the Knowledge Society. LC 80-22160. (Illus.). 224p. 1981. 13.95 (ISBN 0-686-73412-2, P&RB). McGraw.

KNOWLEDGE, THEORY OF
see also A Priori; Analogy; Apperception; Belief and Doubt; Cognition; Common Sense; Comprehension; Concepts; Error; Experience; Fictions, Theory of; Gestalt Psychology; Identity; Ideology; Intellect; Intuition; Judgment; Knowledge, Sociology of; Objectivity; Perception; Personality (Theory of Knowledge); Pragmatism; Rationalism; Reality; Self-Knowledge, Theory of; Sense Data; Senses and Sensation; Sufficient Reason; Truth; Uniformity of Nature; Universals (Philosophy); Values
Aaron, Richard I. Knowing & the Function of Reason. 286p. 1971. 22.00x (ISBN 0-19-824351-0). Oxford U Pr.
Afnan, Ruhi. The Revelation of Baha'u'llah & the Bab: Descartes Theory of Knowledge, Bk. 1. LC 75-109166. 1970. 7.50 (ISBN 0-8022-2307-9). Philos Lib.

Alexander, Hartley B. The Problem of Metaphysics & the Meaning of Metaphysical Explanation. LC 72-38480. Repr. of 1902 ed. 14.00 (ISBN 0-404-00322-2). AMS Pr.

Allison, Henry E., ed. The Kant-Eberhard Controversy. LC 73-8113. 208p. 1974. 14.00x (ISBN 0-8018-1456-1). Johns Hopkins.

Armstrong, Allen. Belief, Truth & Knowledge. LC 72-83586. 240p. 1973. 35.50 (ISBN 0-521-08706-6); pap. 10.50x (ISBN 0-521-09737-1). Cambridge U Pr.

Armstrong, David M. Perception & the Physical World. (International Library of Philosophy & Scientific Method). 1961. text ed. 15.50x (ISBN 0-7100-3603-5). Humanities.

Arner, Douglas G. Perception, Reason, & Knowledge: An Introduction to Epistemology. 180p. 1972. pap. 6.95x (ISBN 0-673-05897-2). Scott F.

Aune, B. A. Knowledge, Mind & Nature. 1979. lib. bdg. 22.00 (ISBN 0-917930-27-4); pap. text ed. 7.50x (ISBN 0-917930-07-X). Ridgeview.

Austin, John L. Sense & Sensibilia. Warnock, Geoffrey J., ed. 1962. pap. 3.95x (ISBN 0-19-500307-1). Oxford U Pr.

Ayer, Alfred J. Language, Truth & Logic. 7.00 (ISBN 0-8446-1571-4). Peter Smith.

--Language, Truth & Logic. 2nd ed. 1936. pap. 2.00 (ISBN 0-486-20010-8). Dover.

--Problem of Knowledge. (Orig.). 1957. pap. 2.95 (ISBN 0-14-020377-X, Pelican). Penguin.

Baldwin, James M. Thought & Things: A Study of the Development & Meaning of Thought or Genetic Logic, 3 vols. LC 75-3029. (Philosopy in America Ser.). Repr. of 1911 ed. 97.00 set (ISBN 0-404-59025-X). AMS Pr.

Baroja, Pio. The Tree of Knowledge. Bell, Aubrey F., tr. from Span. 329p. 1975. Repr. of 1928 ed. 21.50 (ISBN 0-86527-316-2). Fertig.

Barry, Frederick. Scientific Habit of Thought. Repr. of 1927 ed. 26.00 (ISBN 0-404-00666-3). AMS Pr.

Bateson, Gregory. Step to an Ecology of Mind. 1975. pap. 3.50 (ISBN 0-345-29351-7). Ballantine.

Berdiaev, Nikolai. Solitude & Society. Reavey, George, tr. from Rus. LC 70-98211. 207p. 1976. Repr. of 1938 ed. lib. bdg. 15.25x (ISBN 0-8371-3250-9, BESS). Greenwood.

Berger, Gaston. Recherches Sur les Conditions De la Connaissance Essai D'une Theoretique Pure. Natanson, Maurice, ed. LC 78-66755. (Phenomenology Ser.: Vol. 1). 194p. 1979. lib. bdg. 20.00 (ISBN 0-8240-9569-3). Garland Pub.

Berkeley, George. The Principles of Human Knowledge. (Fount Religious Paperbacks Ser.). 1976. pap. 2.95 (ISBN 0-00-632756-7, FA2756). Collins Pubs.

--The Principles of Human Knowledge & Three Dialogues Between Hylas & Philonous. 8.00 (ISBN 0-8446-5833-2). Peter Smith.

--Treatise Concerning the Principles of Human Knowledge. Turbayne, Colin M., ed. LC 57-1290. 1957. pap. 3.50 (ISBN 0-672-60225-3, LLA53). Bobbs.

--A Treatise Concerning the Principles of Human Knowledge. McCormack, Thomas J., ed. & pref. by. xv, 128p. 1963. 9.95 (ISBN 0-87548-071-3); pap. 3.95 (ISBN 0-87548-072-1). Open Court.

--A Treatise Concerning the Principles of Human Knowledge: Text & Critical Essays. Turbayne, Colin M., ed. LC 69-16531. (Text & Critical Essays Ser). 1970. pap. 6.95 (ISBN 0-672-61115-5, TC2). Bobbs.

Bijalwan, C. D. Indian Theory of Knowledge Based Upon Jayana's Nyayamanjari. 1977. 16.00 (ISBN 0-88386-947-0). South Asia Bks.

Blyth, John W. Whitehead's Theory of Knowledge. LC 73-9672. 112p. 1973. Repr. of 1941 ed. 18.00 (ISBN 0-527-09100-6). Kraus Repr.

Boas, George. Inquiring Mind: An Introduction to Epistemology. LC 58-6815. vi, 428p. 1959. 19.95 (ISBN 0-87548-099-3). Open Court.

Bois, J. Samuel. The Art of Awareness: A Textbook on General Semantics & Epistemics. 3rd ed. 360p. 1978. text ed. write for info. (ISBN 0-697-04279-0). Wm C Brown.

--Epistemics: The Science-Art of Innovating. LC 71-93028. 1972. pap. text ed. 4.50x (ISBN 0-918970-09-1). Intl Gen Semantics.

Bradley, Francis H. Appearance & Reality: A Metaphysical Essay. 1930. 32.50x (ISBN 0-19-824109-7). Oxford U Pr.

Brandt, Richard B. Philosophy of Schleiermacher: The Development of His Theory of Scientific & Religious Knowledge. LC 68-19265. 1968. Repr. of 1941 ed. lib. bdg. 16.75x (ISBN 0-8371-0027-5, BRPS). Greenwood.

Brentano, Franz C. True & the Evident. Kraus, Oskar, ed. (International Library of Philosophy & Scientific Method). 1971. text ed. 16.25x (ISBN 0-391-00183-3). Humanities.

Brockman, John, ed. About Bateson: An Introduction to Gregory Bateson. LC 77-4971. 1977. pap. 4.95 (ISBN 0-525-47469-2). Dutton.

Bronowski, Jacob. The Origins of Knowledge & Imagination. LC 77-13209. (Silliman Lectures Ser.). 1978. 12.50 (ISBN 0-300-02192-5); pap. 3.95 (ISBN 0-300-02409-6). Yale U Pr.

Bruner, Jerome S. On Knowing: Essays for the Left Hand. expanded ed. LC 62-13264. (Paperback Ser.: No. 143). (Illus.). 1979. 10.00x (ISBN 0-674-63475-6, Belknap Pr); pap. 3.95 (ISBN 0-674-63525-6, Belknap Pr). Harvard U Pr.

Bruner, Jerome S., et al. Contemporary Approaches to Cognition: A Symposium Held at the University of Colorado. LC 57-12963. (Illus.). 1957. 12.50x (ISBN 0-674-16650-7). Harvard U Pr.

Butchvarov, Panayot. Concept of Knowledge. LC 78-107608. (Publications in Analytical Philosophy Ser). 1970. text ed. 14.95x (ISBN 0-8101-0319-2). Northwestern U Pr.

Carnap, Rudolf. The Logical Structure of the World & Pseudoproblems in Philosophy. George, Rolf A., tr. LC 66-13604. Orig. Title: Logische Aufbau der Welt. 1967. pap. 9.95x (ISBN 0-520-01417-0, CAL184). U of Cal Pr.

Cassirer, Ernst. Essay on Man: An Introduction to a Philosophy of Human Culture. 1962. pap. 5.45 (ISBN 0-300-00034-0, Y52). Yale U Pr.

--The Philosophy of Symbolic Forms, Vol. 3, The Phenomenolgy Of Knowledge. Manheim, Ralph, tr. 1965. pap. 7.95 (ISBN 0-300-00039-1, Y148). Yale U Pr.

--Problem of Knowledge: Philosophy, Science, & History Since Hegel. Woglom, William H. & Hendel, Charles W., trs. 1950. 24.00x (ISBN 0-300-00356-0); pap. 5.95 1969 (ISBN 0-300-01098-2, Y211). Yale U Pr.

--Substance & Function & Einstein's Theory of Relativity. 9.00 (ISBN 0-8446-1822-5). Peter Smith.

Childe, Vere G. Society & Knowledge. LC 72-10690. 131p. 1973. Repr. of 1956 ed. lib. bdg. 15.00x (ISBN 0-8371-6620-9, CHSK). Greenwood.

Chisholm, Roderick. Theory of Knowledge. 2nd ed. (Foundations of Philosophy Ser.). 1977. text ed. 13.50 (ISBN 0-13-914168-5); pap. text ed. 7.95 (ISBN 0-13-914150-2). P-H.

Chisholm, Roderick M. Perceiving: A Philosophical Study. LC 74-7639. (Contemporary Philosophy Ser.). 214p. 1957. 17.50x (ISBN 0-8014-0077-5). Cornell U Pr.

Chomsky, Noam. Problems of Knowledge & Freedom: The Russell Lectures. 1972. pap. 1.65 (ISBN 0-394-71815-1, V815, Vin). Random.

Churchland, P. M. Scientific Realism & the Plasticity of Mind. LC 78-73240. (Cambridge Studies in Philosophy). (Illus.). 1979. 22.50 (ISBN 0-521-22632-5). Cambridge U Pr.

Coffey, Peter. Epistemology, 2 vols. 9.00 ea. (ISBN 0-8446-1118-2). Peter Smith.

Cornman, James W. Skepticism, Justification, & Explanation. (Philosophical Studies Series in Philosophy: No. 18). 368p. 1980. lib. bdg. 39.50 (ISBN 90-277-1041-4, Pub. by Reidel Holland). Kluwer Boston.

Cournot, Antoine A. An Essay on the Foundations of Our Knowledge. Moore, M. H., tr. 1956. pap. 3.95 (ISBN 0-672-60400-0). Bobbs.

Coursault, Jesse H. The Learning Process: Educational Theory Implied in Theory of Knowledge. LC 76-176674. (Columbia University. Teachers College. Contributions to Education: No. 16). Repr. of 1907 ed. 17.50 (ISBN 0-404-55016-9). AMS Pr.

Cowan, Philip. Piaget: With Feeling. LC 78-993. 1978. pap. 12.95 (ISBN 0-03-039856-8, HoltC). HR&W.

Crowell, Norton B. Triple Soul: Browning's Theory of Knowledge. 235p. 1963. text ed. 26.50x (ISBN 0-8290-0228-6). Irvington.

D'Arcy, Martin C. The Nature of Belief. facsimile ed. (Select Bibliographies Reprint Ser). Repr. of 1931 ed. 19.00 (ISBN 0-8369-5930-2). Arno.

D'Arcy, Martin S. The Nature of Belief. LC 72-10693. 236p. 1976. Repr. of 1958 ed. lib. bdg. 16.75x (ISBN 0-8371-6616-0, DANB). Greenwood.

De Condillac, Etienne B. Essay on the Origin of Human Knowledge. Nugent, Thomas, tr. LC 74-147960. Repr. of 1756 ed. 21.50 (ISBN 0-404-08210-6). AMS Pr.

De Fer, Hugo. The Metaphysics of Inventiveness. (Illus.). 200p. 1976. 34.15 (ISBN 0-913314-72-2). Am Classical Coll Pr.

De Santillana, Giorgio & Von Dechend, Hertha. Hamlet's Mill: An Essay on Myth & the Frame of Time. LC 69-13267. (Illus.). 1969. 15.00 (ISBN 0-87645-008-7). Gambit.

Dewey, John & Bentley, Arthur F. Knowing & the Known. LC 75-31432. 334p. 1976. Repr. of 1949 ed. lib. bdg. 25.00x (ISBN 0-8371-8498-3, DEKK). Greenwood.

Drake, D., et al. Essays in Critical Realism. LC 67-30877. 1967. Repr. of 1920 ed. 9.00 (ISBN 0-87752-028-3). Gordian.

Dretske. Knowledge. Date not set. 18.50x (ISBN 0-262-04063-8, Pub. by Bradford). MIT Pr.

Dretske, Fred I. Knowledge & the Flow of Information. LC 81-21633. (Illus.). 288p. 1981. text ed. 18.50x (ISBN 0-262-04063-8, Pub. by Bradford). MIT Pr.

--Seeing & Knowing. LC 68-31658. 1969. 12.00x (ISBN 0-226-16244-3). U of Chicago Pr.

Earle, William. Objectivity: An Essay in Phenomenological Ontology. 1968. pap. 2.45 (ISBN 0-8129-6060-2, QP109). Times Bks.

Ebersole, Frank B. Things We Know: Fourteen Essays on Problems of Knowledge. LC 68-63599. 1967. 7.50 (ISBN 0-87114-016-0). U of Oreg Bks.

Eddington, Arthur. Philosophy of Physical Science. 1958. pap. 3.95 (ISBN 0-472-06020-1, 20, AA). U of Mich Pr.

Eliot, T. S. Knowledge & Experience in the Philosophy of F. H. Bradley. 1964. 4.50 (ISBN 0-374-18176-4). FS&G.

Elliott, John G. Matter, Life & Evolution. LC 77-74876. (Orig.). 1977. 4.95 (ISBN 0-918892-01-5); pap. 2.95 (ISBN 0-918892-02-3). Gibson Hiller.

Elyot, Sir Thomas. Of the Knowledge Which Maketh a Wise Man. Howard, Edwin J., ed. 1942. limited to 200 copies 15.00x (ISBN 0-686-17396-1). R S Barnes.

Evans, J. L. Knowledge & Infallibility. 1979. 17.95 (ISBN 0-312-45906-8). St Martin.

Falco, Maria J., ed. Through the Looking Glass: Epistemology & the Conduct of Inquiry, an Anthology. LC 79-66471. 1979. pap. text ed. 14.00 (ISBN 0-8191-0841-3). U Pr of Amer.

Fay, Cornelius R. & Tiblier, Henry. Epistemology. 1967. pap. text ed. 3.95 (ISBN 0-02-827300-1). Glencoe.

Firsoff, V. Axel. At the Crossroads of Knowledge. 146p. 8.95 (ISBN 0-86025-812-2). Ross-Erikson.

Frank, S. L. Reality & Man: An Essay in the Metaphysics of Human Nature. LC 66-12950. 1966. 6.00 (ISBN 0-8008-6650-9). Taplinger.

French, Peter A., et al, eds. Studies in Epistemology. (Midwest Studies in Philosophy: Vol. 5). 1980. 35.00x (ISBN 0-8166-0944-6); pap. 15.00x (ISBN 0-8166-0947-0). U of Minn Pr.

Frey, Gerhard, ed. Bela Juhos: Selected Papers. Foulkes, Paul, tr. LC 76-17019. (Vienna Circle Collection Ser: No. 7). 1976. lib. bdg. 55.00 (ISBN 90-277-0686-7, Pub. by Reidel Holland); pap. 28.95 (ISBN 90-277-0687-5). Kluwer Boston.

Fullerton, George S. System of Metaphysics. LC 68-23290. Repr. of 1968 ed. lib. bdg. 32.00x (ISBN 0-8371-0079-8, FUSM). Greenwood.

--System of Metaphysics. 1968. Repr. of 1904 ed. 31.00 (ISBN 0-403-00125-0). Scholarly.

Furnivall, F. J., ed. The Fyrst Boke of the Introduction of Knowledge. (EETS, ES Ser.: No. 10). Repr. of 1870 ed. 21.00 (ISBN 0-527-00224-0). Kraus Repr.

Gallagher, Kenneth T. Philosophy of Knowledge. 1964. text ed. 6.95 (ISBN 0-8362-0373-9). Andrews & McMeel.

Garforth, Francis W., ed. John Locke's of the Conduct of the Understanding. LC 66-20498. 1966. text ed. 8.75 (ISBN 0-8077-1401-1); pap. text ed. 4.00x (ISBN 0-8077-1398-8). Tchrs Coll.

Gellner, E. Legitimation of Belief. LC 74-14337. 240p. 1975. 29.95 (ISBN 0-521-20467-4). Cambridge U Pr.

Ginet, C. Knowledge, Perception, & Memory. LC 75-8602. (Philosophical Studies: No. 5). 207p. 1975. 39.50 (ISBN 90-277-0574-7, Pub. by Reidel Holland). Kluwer Boston.

Ginsburg, Herbert & Opper, Sylvia. Piaget's Theory of Intellectual Development. 2nd ed. (Illus.). 1979. 14.95 (ISBN 0-13-675140-7); pap. 9.95 (ISBN 0-13-675132-6). P-H.

Goodall, Blake. The Homilies of St. John Chrysostom on the Letters of St. Paul to Titus & Philemon. (Univ. of California Publications in Classical Studies: Vol. 20). 1979. 12.00x (ISBN 0-520-09596-0). U of Cal Pr.

Goodman, Nelson. Languages of Art. 2nd, new ed. LC 68-31825. (Illus.). 1976. 17.50 (ISBN 0-915144-35-2); pap. text ed. 8.50 (ISBN 0-915144-34-4). Hackett Pub.

Gregg, Lee W., ed. Knowledge & Cognition. LC 74-16105. (Carnegie Mellon U. Cognition Ser.). 320p. 1974. 16.50 (ISBN 0-470-32657-3). Halsted Pr.

Grene, Marjorie. The Knower & the Known. 1974. pap. 3.95x (ISBN 0-520-02765-5). U of Cal Pr.

Grene, Marjorie, ed. The Anatomy of Knowledge. LC 68-19672. 1969. 15.00x (ISBN 0-87023-043-3). U of Mass Pr.

--Interpretations of Life & Mind: Essays Around the Problem of Reduction. LC 76-150237. 1971. text ed. 8.75x (ISBN 0-391-00144-2). Humanities.

Griffiths, A. Philips, ed. Knowledge & Belief. 1967. pap. 4.95x (ISBN 0-19-500328-4). Oxford U Pr.

Gruber, Howard & Voneche, Jacques, eds. The Essential Piaget. LC 76-9337. (Illus.). 1977. text ed. 35.00x (ISBN 0-465-02058-5). Basic.

Habermas, Jurgen. Knowledge & Human Interests. Shapiro, Jeremy J., tr. from Ger. LC 72-136230. 1971. pap. 5.95 (ISBN 0-8070-1541-5, BP422). Beacon Pr.

Haldane, Viscount. The Reign of Relativity. 434p. 1981. Repr. lib. bdg. 35.00 (ISBN 0-8495-2354-0). Arden Lib.

Hamilton, Peter. Knowledge & Social Structure: An Introduction to the Classical Argument in the Sociology of Knowledge. (International Library of Sociology). 174p. 1974. 16.50x (ISBN 0-7100-7746-7); pap. 7.95 (ISBN 0-7100-7786-6). Routledge & Kegan.

Hamlyn, D. W. Experience & the Growth of Understanding. (International Library of the Philosophy of Education). 1980. pap. 7.50 (ISBN 0-7100-0336-6). Routledge & Kegan.

--The Theory of Knowledge. (Modern Introductions to Philosophy Ser.). 308p. 1980. pap. text ed. 8.50 (ISBN 0-333-11548-1). Humanities.

Handy, Rollo & Harwood, E. C. Useful Procedures of Inquiry. LC 72-93865. (Orig.). 1973. 10.00x (ISBN 0-913610-00-3). Behavioral Mass.

--Useful Procedures of Inquiry. LC 72-93865. (Orig.). 1973. 10.00x (ISBN 0-913610-00-3). Behavioral Mass.

Harman, Gilbert H. Thought. LC 72-4044. 232p. 1973. 16.50 (ISBN 0-691-07188-8); pap. 5.95 (ISBN 0-691-01986-X). Princeton U Pr.

Harris, Kevin. Education & Knowledge: The Structured Misrepresentation of Reality. 1979. 22.00x (ISBN 0-7100-0137-1); pap. 9.95 (ISBN 0-7100-0140-1). Routledge & Kegan.

Highet, Gilbert. Man's Unconquerable Mind. LC 54-6133. 138p. 1954. 11.00x (ISBN 0-231-02016-3); pap. 3.95 (ISBN 0-231-08501-X). Columbia U Pr.

Hintikka, Jaakko. Knowledge & Belief: An Introduction to the Logic of the Two Notions. LC 74-7639. (Contemporary Philosophy Ser.). 189p. 1962. 17.50x (ISBN 0-8014-0187-9). Cornell U Pr.

--Knowledge & the Known: Historical Perspectives in Epistemology. LC 74-76473. (Synthese Historical Library: No. 11). xii, 235p. 1974. lib. bdg. 18.50 (ISBN 90-277-0455-4, Pub. by Reidel Holland). Kluwer Boston.

Hirst, Paul Q. Durkheim, Bernard, & Epistemology. 1980. pap. 7.95 (ISBN 0-7100-0384-6). Routledge & Kegan.

--Durkheim, Bernard & Epistemology. 1975. 18.50 (ISBN 0-7100-8071-9). Routledge & Kegan.

Hobhouse, Leonard T. Theory of Knowledge. LC 74-101094. Repr. of 1896 ed. 28.00 (ISBN 0-404-03278-8). AMS Pr.

Horstmann, Rolf-Peter, et al, eds. Transcendental Arguments & Science. (Synthese Library: No. 133). 1979. lib. bdg. 34.00 (ISBN 90-277-0963-7, Pub. by Reidel Holland); pap. 16.00 (ISBN 90-277-0964-5). Kluwer Boston.

Hubig, Chr. & Rahden, W. Van, eds. Kritischer Wissenschafts-Theorie. (De Gruyter Studienbuch). 1978. 19.00x (ISBN 3-11-007079-0). De Gruyter.

Hume, David. An Enquiry Concerning Human Understanding: & from a Gentleman to His Friend in Edinburgh. new ed. Steinberg, Eric, ed. LC 77-2600. 1977. lib. bdg. 12.50 (ISBN 0-915144-17-4); pap. text ed. 2.75x (ISBN 0-915144-16-6). Hackett Pub.

--Enquiry Concerning Human Understanding. 2nd ed. McCormack, Thomas J. & Calkins, Mary W., eds. 280p. 1966. 17.50 (ISBN 0-87548-015-2); pap. 6.95 (ISBN 0-87548-362-3). Open Court.

--Inquiry Concerning Human Understanding: An Abstract of a Treatise of Human Nature. Hendel, Charles W., ed. LC 59-11685. 1955. pap. 5.50 (ISBN 0-672-60218-0, LLA49). Bobbs.

--Treatise of Human Nature, Bks. 2 & 3. (Fount Religious Paperbacks Ser.). 1976. pap. 2.95 (ISBN 0-00-632744-3, FA2744). Collins Pubs.

--Treatise of Human Nature, Book One. (Fount Religious Paperbacks Ser.). 1976. pap. 2.95 (ISBN 0-00-632909-8, FA2909). Collins Pubs.

Joachim, H. Henry. Nature of Truth: An Essay. Repr. of 1906 ed. lib. bdg. 15.00x (ISBN 0-8371-0931-0, JONT). Greenwood.

Joske, W. D. Material Objects. 1967. 17.95 (ISBN 0-312-52150-2). St Martin.

Kant, Immanuel. Critique of Practical Reason & Other Writings in Moral Philosophy. Beck, Lewis W., tr. LC 75-32038. (The Philosophy of Immanuel Kant Ser.: Vol. 1). 1977. Repr. of 1949 ed. lib. bdg. 35.00 (ISBN 0-8240-2325-0). Garland Pub.

--Critique of Pure Reason. 2nd ed. 1979. 8.95x (ISBN 0-460-00909-5, Evman); pap. 4.95x (ISBN 0-460-01909-0, Evman). Biblio Dist.

--Critique of Pure Reason. pap. 3.95 (ISBN 0-385-07534-0, A551, Anch). Doubleday.

--Critique of Pure Reason. Smith, Norman K., ed. 1969. 19.95 (ISBN 0-312-45045-1); pap. 7.50x (ISBN 0-312-45010-9). St Martin.

--Prolegomena to Any Future Metaphysics. rev. ed. LC 51-10279. 1950. pap. 3.95 (ISBN 0-672-60187-7, LLA27). Bobbs.
--Prolegomena to Any Future Metaphysics That Will Be Able to Come Forward As Science. new ed. Ellington, J. W., ed. Carus, Paul, tr. LC 76-51051. 1977. 12.50 (ISBN 0-915144-33-6); pap. 2.50 (ISBN 0-915144-25-5). Hackett Pub.
Kaplan, Morton A. On Historical & Political Knowing: An Inquiry into Some Problems of Universal Law & Human Freedom. LC 79-131879. 1971. 7.50x (ISBN 0-226-42420-0). U of Chicago Pr.
Kaufman, Gordon D. Relativism, Knowledge & Faith. LC 59-11620. 1960. 8.00x (ISBN 0-226-42682-3). U of Chicago Pr.
Keil, Frank C. Semantic & Conceptual Development: An Ontological Perspective. LC 79-10491. 1979. 16.50x (ISBN 0-674-80100-8). Harvard U Pr.
Klauder, Francis J. The Wonder of Intelligence. LC 73-79083. (Illus.). 144p. 1973. 6.95 (ISBN 0-8158-0307-9). Chris Mass.
Klein, Jacob. Plato's Trilogy: Theaetetus the Sophist & the Statesman. LC 76-25642. 1977. 16.00x (ISBN 0-226-43951-8). U of Chicago Pr.
Klein, Peter D. Certainty: A Refutation of Scepticism. 256p. 1981. 20.00x (ISBN 0-8166-0995-0); pap. 8.95 (ISBN 0-8166-0998-5). U of Minn Pr.
Knorr, Karin D. The Manufacture of Knowledge: An Essay on the Constructivist & Contextual Nature of Science. 200p. Date not set. 39.01 (ISBN 0-08-025777-1); pap. 19.21 (ISBN 0-08-025778-X). Pergamon.
Kruse, Frederik V. The Foundation of Human Thought: The Problem of Science & Ethics. LC 73-17928. 404p. 1975. Repr. of 1949 ed. lib. bdg. 22.50x (ISBN 0-8371-7273-X, KRFH). Greenwood.
Ladd, George T. Knowledge, Life & Reality. 1918. 34.50x (ISBN 0-685-69836-X). Elliots Bks.
--Philosophy of Knowledge: An Inquiry into the Nature, Limits & Validity of Human Cognitive Faculty. LC 75-3223. Repr. of 1897 ed. 42.50 (ISBN 0-404-59219-8). AMS Pr.
Laird, John. Knowledge, Belief & Opinion. 515p. 1972. Repr. of 1930 ed. 25.00 (ISBN 0-208-01215-X, Archon). Shoe String.
Lakatos, Imre. Philosophical Papers: Mathematics, Science & Epistemology, Vol. 2. Worrall, J. & Currie, G., eds. LC 77-14374. 295p. 1980. pap. 13.50 (ISBN 0-521-28030-3). Cambridge U Pr.
--Philosophical Papers: Mathematics, Science & Epistology, Vol. 2. Worrall, J. & Currie, G., eds. LC 77-71415. 1978. 32.50 (ISBN 0-521-21769-5). Cambridge U Pr.
Lazaro, Jose M. Iniciacion Al Estudio Del Conocimiento. 3.75 (ISBN 0-8477-2803-X). U of PR Pr.
Lee, Harold N. Percepts, Concepts & Theoretic Knowledge: A Study in Epistemology. new ed. LC 72-82796. 288p. 1973. 12.95x (ISBN 0-87870-014-5). Memphis St Univ.
Lehrer, Keith. Knowledge. 1979. pap. 11.50x (ISBN 0-19-824416-9). Oxford U Pr.
Lenzen, Victor F. Procedures of Empirical Science. LC 71-131570. (Foundations of the Unity of Science Ser: Vol. 1, No. 5). 1938. pap. 1.95x (ISBN 0-226-57580-2, P404, Phoen). U of Chicago Pr.
Levi, Isaac. The Enterprise of Knowledge: An Essay on Knowledge, Credal Probability, & Chance. 1980. text ed. 27.50x (ISBN 0-262-12082-8). MIT Pr.
Lewis, Clarence I. Analysis of Knowledge & Valuation. LC 47-20878. (Paul Carus Lecture Ser.). xxi, 578p. 1971. 25.00 (ISBN 0-87548-093-4); pap. 9.75 (ISBN 0-87548-094-2). Open Court.
--Mind & the World Order. 1924. pap. 6.50 (ISBN 0-486-20359-X). Dover.
Lindblom, Charles E. & Cohen, Davis K. Usable Knowledge. 1979. 14.50x (ISBN 0-300-02335-9); pap. 4.45x (ISBN 0-300-02336-7). Yale U Pr.
Locke, John. An Essay Concerning Human Understanding. Nidditch, Peter H., ed. 776p. 1979. pap. text ed. 12.95x (ISBN 0-19-824595-5). Oxford U Pr.
--Essay Concerning Human Understanding, 2 Vols. Fraser, Alexander C., ed. Set. 22.00 (ISBN 0-8446-2478-0). Peter Smith.
--Essay Concerning Human Understanding, 2 Vols. Fraser, Alexander C., ed. (Illus.). 1894. Vol. 1. pap. 8.00 (ISBN 0-486-20530-4); Vol. 2. pap. 7.00 (ISBN 0-486-20531-2). Dover.
--An Essay Concerning Human Understanding. abr. ed. Pringle-Pattison, A. S., ed. 1978. Repr. of 1924 ed. text ed. 12.50x (ISBN 0-391-00573-1). Humanities.
--An Essay Concerning Human Understanding. (Fount Religious Paperback Ser.). 1977. pap. 2.95 (ISBN 0-00-641040-5, FA1040). Collins Pubs.
Lonergan, Bernard. Insight. 1957. pap. 10.00 (ISBN 0-8022-0994-7). Philos Lib.
Lovejoy, Arthur O. Revolt Against Dualism. 2nd ed. (Paul Carus Lecture Ser.). 405p. 1960. 19.95 (ISBN 0-87548-106-X); pap. 7.95 (ISBN 0-87548-107-8). Open Court.
Luce, Arthur A. Sence Without Matter; or Direct Perception. LC 72-12498. 165p. 1973. Repr. of 1954 ed. lib. bdg. 15.00 (ISBN 0-8371-6739-6, LUSM). Greenwood.
Lukes, S. Development of the Sociology of Knowledge. (Studies in Sociology). 1980. pap. text ed. write for info. (ISBN 0-391-01130-8). Humanities.
McGarry, Kevin J. & Burrell, T. W. Logic & Semantics in the Organization of Knowledge. (Programmed Texts in Library & Information Science Ser). 1972. 13.50 (ISBN 0-208-01172-2, Linnet). Shoe String.
Mack, Robert D. Appeal to Immediate Experience. facs. ed. LC 68-58803. (Essay Index Reprint Ser). 1945. 12.00 (ISBN 0-8369-0085-5). Arno.
Macloed, Roy, ed. Days of Judgement. 1980. 50.00x (ISBN 0-686-64955-9, Pub. by Nafferton England). State Mutual Bk.
Malcolm, Norman. Knowledge & Certainty: Essays & Lectures. LC 63-10529. 256p. 1975. pap. 5.95 (ISBN 0-8014-9154-1). Cornell U Pr.
Mandelbaum, Maurice. Philosophy, Science, & Sense Perception: Historical and Critical Studies. 288p. 1964. 18.50x (ISBN 0-8018-0450-7); pap. 3.45x (ISBN 0-8018-0451-5). Johns Hopkins.
Maquet, J. P. The Sociology of Knowledge. Locke, John F., tr. from Fr. LC 70-168963. 318p. 1973. Repr. of 1951 ed. lib. bdg. 17.75x (ISBN 0-8371-6236-X, MASK). Greenwood.
Maritain, Jacques. Distinguer Pour Unir: Les Degres du Savoir. 8th ed. 946p. 1959. 32.50 (ISBN 0-686-56350-6). French & Eur.
Marti, Fritz. The Unconditional in Human Knowledge: Four Early Essays (1794-1796) by F. W. J. Schelling. Schelling, F. W., tr. LC 77-74407. 272p. 1980. 18.50 (ISBN 0-8387-2020-X). Bucknell U Pr.
Masaryk, Thomas G. Masaryk on Thought & Life. LC 78-135840. (Eastern Europe Collection Ser). 1970. Repr. of 1938 ed. 11.00 (ISBN 0-405-02782-6). Arno.
Mattessich, Richard. Instrumental Reasoning & Systems Methodology. (Theory & Decision Library: No. 15). 1978. lib. bdg. 45.00 (ISBN 90-277-0837-1, Pub. by Reidel Holland); pap. 20.00 (ISBN 0-686-28628-6, Pub. by Reidel Holland). Kluwer Boston.
Mead, George H. Philosophy of the Act. Morris, Charles W., ed. LC 38-15971. 1938. 15.00x (ISBN 0-226-51666-0). U of Chicago Pr.
Merleau-Ponty, Maurice. Visible & the Invisible. Lingis, Alphonso, tr. LC 68-30125. (Studies in Phenomenology & Existential Philosophy Ser). 1969. 17.95x (ISBN 0-8101-0026-6); pap. 7.95x (ISBN 0-8101-0457-1). Northwestern U Pr.
Mill, J. S. John Stuart Mill's Philosophy of Scientific Method. (Library of Classics Ser.: No. 12). 1950. pap. text ed. 4.25 (ISBN 0-02-849250-1). Hafner.
Miller, Wilma H. Sight Word Knowledge Activity Sheets. (Corrective Reading Skills Activity File Ser.). (Orig.). 1977. pap. 11.95x (ISBN 0-87628-220-6). Ctr Appl Res.
Mischel, Theodore. Cognitive Development & Epistemology. 1971. 46.00 (ISBN 0-12-498640-4). Acad Pr.
Montague, William P. The Way of Knowing. 1962. Repr. of 1978 ed. text ed. 17.50x (ISBN 0-391-00568-5). Humanities.
Moore, Addison W. The Functional Versus the Representational Theories of Knowledge in Locke's Essay. LC 75-3629. Repr. of 1902 ed. 16.00 (ISBN 0-404-59002-0). AMS Pr.
Morris, Charles R. Idealistic Logic. LC 76-102578. 1970. Repr. of 1933 ed. 14.00 (ISBN 0-8046-0738-9). Kennikat.
Morris, Charles W. Six Theories of Mind. 1932. 10.50x (ISBN 0-226-54004-9). U of Chicago Pr.
Murphy, Richard T. Hume & Husserl: Towards Radical Subjectivism. 156p. 1980. lib. bdg. 34.00 (ISBN 90-247-2172-5, Pub. by Martinus Nijhoff Netherlands). Kluwer Boston.
Nathan, N. M. Evidence & Assurance. LC 79-50505. (Cambridge Studies in Philosophy). 1980. 29.50 (ISBN 0-521-22517-5). Cambridge U Pr.
Newman, John H. The Uses of Knowledge: Selections from the Idea of the University. Ward, Leo L., ed. LC 48-8929. (Crofts Classics Ser.). 1948. pap. text ed. 2.95x (ISBN 0-88295-063-0). Harlan Davidson.
Norman, Richard. Hegel's Phenomenology. LC 76-12235. 1976. 15.95x (ISBN 0-312-36680-9). St Martin.
Norris, John. Christian Blessedness (with) Reflections Upon a Late Essay Concerning Human Understanding. Wellek, Rene, ed. LC 75-11241. (British Philosophers & Theologians of the 17th & 18th Centuries Ser.). 1978. Repr. of 1690 ed. lib. bdg. 42.00 (ISBN 0-8240-1793-5). Garland Pub.
--An Essay Towards the Theory of the Ideal or Intelligible World, 2 Vols., 1701 & 1704. Wellek, Rene, ed. LC 75-11243. (British Philosophers & Theologians of the 17th & 18th Centuries Ser.). 1978. Set. lib. bdg. 42.00 (ISBN 0-8240-1795-1). Garland Pub.
Oman, John W. The Natural & the Supernatural. LC 79-39696. (Select Bibliographies Reprint Ser). 1972. Repr. of 1931 ed. 20.75 (ISBN 0-8369-9941-X). Arno.
O'Neill, Reginald, ed. Readings in Epistemology. LC 61-18427. 1979. pap. text ed. 11.95x (ISBN 0-89197-604-3). Irvington.
O'Neill, Reginald F. Theories of Knowledge: With a New Preface. 242p. 1980. Repr. of 1959 ed. text ed. 28.50x (ISBN 0-8290-0227-8); pap. text ed. 12.95x (ISBN 0-8290-0386-X). Irvington.
Papanoutsos, Evangelos P. Foundations of Knowledge. Anton, John P., ed. Coukis, Basil P. & Anton, John P., trs. LC 68-19533. Orig. Title: Gnosiology. 1968. 23.00 (ISBN 0-87395-034-8); microfiche 23.00 (ISBN 0-87395-134-4). State U NY Pr.
Pappas, George, ed. Justification & Knowledge: New Studies in Epistemology. (Philosophical Studies Series in Philosophy: No. 17). 1980. lib. bdg. 29.00 (ISBN 90-277-1023-6, Pub. by Reidel Holland); pap. 10.50 (ISBN 90-277-1024-4, Pub. by Reidel Holland). Kluwer Boston.
Pappas, George S. & Swain, Marshall, eds. Essays on Knowledge & Justification. LC 77-10299. (Illus.). 1978. 25.00x (ISBN 0-8014-1086-X); pap. 8.95x (ISBN 0-8014-9865-1). Cornell U Pr.
Peifer, John F. Mystery of Knowledge. Orig. Title: Concept in Thomism. 1964. pap. 5.00x (ISBN 0-87343-013-1). Magi Bks.
Piaget, Jean. Genetic Epistemology. Duckworth, Eleanor, tr. 1971. pap. 3.95 (ISBN 0-393-00596-8, Norton Lib.). Norton.
Piaget, Jean, et al. Epistemology & Psychology of Functions. Castellanos, Javier & Anderson, Vivian, trs. (Synthese Library: No. 83). 1977. lib. bdg. 45.00 (ISBN 90-277-0804-5, Pub. by Reidel Holland). Kluwer Boston.
Piaser, Antonio. Pour une Sociologie Scientifiques: Epsitemlogie Compare de le Analyse Conceptuelle. (Interaction - l'Homme et Son Environment Social: No. 9). (Fr.). 1976. pap. text ed. 41.25x (ISBN 90-2797-563-9). Mouton.
Polanyi, Michael. Knowing & Being. Grene, Marjorie, ed. LC 76-77151. 1969. 10.50x (ISBN 0-226-67284-0). U of Chicago Pr.
--Study of Man. LC 59-4021. 1963. pap. 3.50 (ISBN 0-226-67292-1, P128, Phoen). U of Chicago Pr.
--Tacit Dimension. LC 66-21015. 1967. pap. 2.50 (ISBN 0-385-06988-X, A540, Anch). Doubleday.
Pollock, John L. Knowledge & Justification. LC 74-2974. 352p. 1975. 25.00x (ISBN 0-691-07203-5). Princeton U Pr.
Pols, Edward. Recognition of Reason. LC 63-14296. (Philosophical Exploration Ser.). 269p. 1963. 9.95x (ISBN 0-8093-0111-3). S Ill U Pr.
Polyani, Michael. Knowing & Being. Green, Marjorie, ed. LC 76-77151. 264p. 1973. pap. text ed. 4.95 (ISBN 0-226-67285-9, P539, Phoen). U of Chicago Pr.
Popper, Karl R. Conjectures & Refutations: The Growth of Scientific Knowledge. 1968. pap. 7.50x (ISBN 0-06-131376-9, TB1376, Torch). Har-Row.
--Objective Knowledge: An Evolutionary Approach. 360p. 1972. pap. text ed. 7.95x (ISBN 0-19-875024-2). Oxford U Pr.
Potter, Karl, ed. Indian Metaphysics & Epistemology: The Tradition of Nyaya-Vaisesika up to Gangesa. Encyclopedia of Indian Philosophies. LC 77-85558. 1977. 35.00 (ISBN 0-691-07183-7). Princeton U Pr.
Powell, Betty. Knowledge of Actions. 1967. text ed. 5.00x (ISBN 0-04-121004-2). Humanities.
Quine, Willard V. Ontological Relativity & Other Essays. LC 72-91121. (John Dewey Lectures Ser.: No. 1). 1969. 15.00x (ISBN 0-231-03307-9); pap. 5.00x (ISBN 0-231-08357-2). Columbia U Pr.
Rahner, Karl. Spirit in the World. Lynch, William, tr. LC 67-29676. 1968. 13.50 (ISBN 0-8164-1122-0). Crossroad NY.
Rand, Ayn. An Introduction to Objectivist Epistemology. (Orig.). 1979. pap. 2.50 (ISBN 0-451-62001-1, ME2001, Ment). NAL.
Regis, Louis-Marie. Saint Thomas & Epistemology. (Aquinas Lecture Ser.). 1946. 6.95 (ISBN 0-87462-110-0). Marquette.
Reichenbach, Hans. Experience & Prediction: An Analysis of the Foundations & the Structure of Knowledge. (Midway Reprint Ser.). 1976. pap. 16.00x (ISBN 0-226-70748-2). U of Chicago Pr.
Rescher, Nicholas. Cognitive Systematization: A Systems-Theoretic Approach to a Coherentist Theory of Knowledge. 211p. 1979. 18.50x (ISBN 0-8476-6094-X). Rowman.
--Dialectics: A Controversy-Oriented Approach to the Theory of Knowledge. LC 77-9542. 1977. 19.00 (ISBN 0-87395-372-X). State U NY Pr.
--Methodological Pragmatism: A Systems-Theoretic Approach to the Theory of Knowledge. LC 76-54605. 315p. 1977. usa 22.50x (ISBN 0-8147-7371-0). NYU Pr.
Rescher, Nicholas, ed. Studies in Epistemology. (Monograph Ser.: Vol. 9). 168p. 1975. pap. 15.00x (ISBN 0-631-11530-7, Pub. by Basil Blackwell). Biblio Dist.
--Studies in the Theory of Knowledge. (Monograph Ser.: No. 4). 132p. 1970. pap. 19.00x (ISBN 0-631-11480-7, Pub. by Basil Blackwell). Biblio Dist.
Rich, Robert F. The Knowledge Cycle. (Sage Focus Editions: Vol. 35). 232p. 1981. 20.00 (ISBN 0-8039-1686-8); pap. 9.95 (ISBN 0-8039-1687-6). Sage.
Royce, J. R. & Rozeboom, W. W., eds. The Psychology of Knowing. LC 75-138363. 504p. 1972. 83.75x (ISBN 0-677-13850-4). Gordon.
Russell, Bertrand. Analysis of Mind. 1978. Repr. of 1921 ed. text ed. 11.50x (ISBN 0-391-00922-2). Humanities.
--Human Knowledge: Its Scope & Limits. (Orig.). (YA) (gr. 9 up). 1962. pap. 6.95 (ISBN 0-671-20145-X, Touchstone Bks). S&S.
--Inquiry into Meaning & Truth. 1940. text ed. 18.00x (ISBN 0-04-121007-7). Humanities.
Russell, James. The Acquisition of Knowledge. LC 78-6881. 1978. 20.00x (ISBN 0-312-00273-4). St Martin.
Schaeffer, Francis. He Is There & He Is Not Silent. pap. 2.95 (ISBN 0-8423-1413-X). Tyndale.
Scheffler, Israel. Conditions of Knowledge: An Introduction to Epistemology & Education. LC 78-54987. 1978. pap. 3.95 (ISBN 0-226-73668-7, P789, Phoen). U of Chicago Pr.
--Science & Subjectivity. LC 67-27839. (Orig.). 1967. pap. 4.95 (ISBN 0-672-60724-7). Bobbs.
Schlick, M. General Theory of Knowledge. Blumberg, A. E., tr. from Ger. LC 73-80988. (Library of Exact Philosophy: Vol. 11). 450p. 1974. 46.10 (ISBN 0-387-81160-5). Springer-Verlag.
Schofield, Malcolm, et al, eds. Doubt & Dogmatism: Studies in Hellenistic Epistemology. 354p. 1980. text ed. 37.50x (ISBN 0-19-824601-3). Oxford U Pr.
Schopenhauer, Arthur, et al. The World As Will & Idea, 3 vols. Haldane, R. B. & Kemp, J., trs. from Ger. LC 75-41243. Repr. of 1896 ed. 87.50 set (ISBN 0-404-15060-8). AMS Pr.
Segerstedt, Torgny, ed. The Frontiers of Human Knowledge: Lectures Held at the Quincentenary Celebrations of Uppsala University 1977. (Illus.). 1978. pap. 31.00x (ISBN 91-554-0791-9). Humanities.
Sellars, Wilfrid. Philosophical Perspectives: Metaphysics & Epistemology. 1979. lib. bdg. 21.00 (ISBN 0-917930-25-8); pap. text ed. 6.50x (ISBN 0-917930-05-3). Ridgeview.
Shaffer, Jerome A. Reality, Knowledge, & Value: A Basic Introduction to Philosophy. 1971. pap. text ed. 6.95x (ISBN 0-394-31267-8, RanC). Random.
Shuchman, Philip. Problems of Knowledge in Legal Scholarship. LC 79-80252. 136p. 1979. pap. text ed. 8.95 (ISBN 0-939328-00-3). U Conn Sch Law.
Simmel, Georg. The Problems of the Philosophy of History: An Epistemological Essay. Oakes, Guy, tr. LC 76-51588. 1977. 14.95 (ISBN 0-02-928890-8). Free Pr.
Simms, James R. Measure of Knowledge. LC 71-118312. 1970. 8.75 (ISBN 0-8022-2347-8). Philos Lib.
Sokolowski, Robert. Presence & Absence: A Philosophical Investigation of Language & Being. LC 77-23628. (Studies in Phenomenology & Existential Philosophy Ser.). 192p. 1978. 15.00x (ISBN 0-253-34600-2). Ind U Pr.
Sowell, Thomas. Knowledge & Decisions. LC 79-7347. 1979. 18.50x (ISBN 0-465-03736-4). Basic.
Spence, Larry D. The Politics of Social Knowledge. LC 77-10543. 1978. 17.75x (ISBN 0-271-00521-1). Pa St U Pr.
Spier, J. M. Introduction to Christian Philosophy. Freeman, D. H., tr. 1954. pap. 4.50 (ISBN 0-934532-25-7). Presby & Reformed.
Stace, Walter T. Theory of Knowledge & Existence. Repr. of 1932 ed. lib. bdg. 18.50x (ISBN 0-8371-4343-8, STTK). Greenwood.

Stark, Werner. Sociology of Knowledge: An Essay in Aid of a Deeper Understanding of the History of Ideas. (International Library of Sociology & Social Reconstruction Ser.). 1958. pap. text ed. 13.00x (ISBN 0-7100-6554-X). Humanities.

Stegmueller, W. The Structure & Dynamics of Theories. Wohlhueter, W., tr. from Ger. LC 75-28364. 352p. 1975. 39.60 (ISBN 0-387-07493-7). Springer-Verlag.

Steiner, Rudolf. Philosophy of Freedom. Wilson, Michael, tr. from Ger. 226p. 1973. pap. 5.50 (ISBN 0-910142-52-1). Anthroposophic.

--Truth & Knowledge: Introduction to "Philosophy of Spiritual Activity". 2nd ed. Allen, Paul M., ed. Stebbing, Rita, tr. from Ger. LC 62-22389. (The Major Writings of Rudolf Steiner in English Translation Ser.: The Centennial Edition). 112p. 1981. Repr. of 1963 ed. 10.00x (ISBN 0-8334-0740-6, Steinerbooks). Multimedia.

Stich, Stephen P., ed. Innate Ideas. 1975. 22.75x (ISBN 0-520-02822-8); pap. 6.95x (ISBN 0-520-02961-5). U of Cal Pr.

Stroll, Avrum, ed. Epistemology: New Essays in the Theory of Knowledge. LC 78-31395. (Sources in Contemporary Philosophy). 1979. Repr. of 1967 ed. lib. bdg. 19.25x (ISBN 0-313-20967-7, STEM). Greenwood.

Strong, Charles A. A Theory of Knowledge. LC 75-3405. Repr. of 1923 ed. 11.00 (ISBN 0-404-59399-2). AMS Pr.

Swain, Marshall. Reasons & Knowledge. LC 80-69825. 1981. 22.50x (ISBN 0-8014-1378-8). Cornell U Pr.

Swartz, Robert J., ed. Perceiving, Sensing & Knowing: A Book of Readings from Twentieth-Century Sources in the Philosophy of Perception. LC 75-3778. 560p. 1977. pap. 7.95x (ISBN 0-520-02986-0, CAMPUS 151). U of Cal Pr.

Sweeeney, Francis, ed. The Knowledge Explosion: Liberation & Limitations. 249p. 1969. 4.95 (ISBN 0-374-18204-3). FS&G.

Tennessen, Herman. Problems of Knowledge. 88p. 1980. pap. text ed. 10.25x (ISBN 90-232-1762-4). Humanities.

Thomas, Stephen N. The Formal Mechanics of Mind. LC 77-3128. 1978. 25.00x (ISBN 0-8014-1034-7). Cornell U Pr.

Tipton, I. C., ed. Locke on Human Understanding: Selected Essays. 1977. pap. text ed. 5.95x (ISBN 0-19-875039-0). Oxford U Pr.

Toulmin, Stephen. Human Understanding, Vol. 1, the Collective Use & Evolution of Concepts. LC 73-166391. 500p. 1972. 30.00x (ISBN 0-691-07185-3); pap. 7.95 (ISBN 0-691-01996-7). Princeton U Pr.

Towner, George. The Architecture of Knowledge. LC 80-5127. 220p. 1980. text ed. 17.75 (ISBN 0-8191-1049-3); pap. text ed. 9.50 (ISBN 0-8191-1050-7). U Pr of Amer.

Unger, Roberto M. Knowledge & Politics. LC 74-15369. (Illus.). 1975. 12.95 (ISBN 0-02-932840-3). Free Pr.

Valle, Ronald S. & Eckartsberg, Rolf Von, eds. The Metaphors of Consciousness. 500p. 1981. 25.00 (ISBN 0-306-40520-2, Plenum Pr). Plenum Pub.

Varadi, Emery Y. Functional Human Universalism. 1981. 8.95 (ISBN 0-533-04869-9). Vantage.

Wallraff, Charles F. Philosophical Theory & Psychological Fact: An Attempt at Synthesis. LC 61-15392. 1961. 2.00 (ISBN 0-8165-0071-1). U of Ariz Pr.

Weigel, Gustave & Madden, Arthur G. Knowledge, Its Values & Limits. 118p. 1973. Repr. of 1961 ed. lib. bdg. 15.00 (ISBN 0-8371-6627-6, WENN). Greenwood.

Weiss, Paul A., ed. Knowledge in Search of Understanding: The Frensham Papers. LC 75-24542. 1975. 15.00 (ISBN 0-87993-071-3). Futura Pub.

Weissman, David. Dispositional Properties. LC 65-11655. (Philosophical Explorations Ser). 231p. 1965. 8.95x (ISBN 0-8093-0163-6). S Ill U Pr.

--Eternal Possibilities: A Neutral Ground for Meaning & Existence. LC 77-23246. (Philosophical Explorations Ser.). 228p. 1977. 12.50x (ISBN 0-8093-0799-5). S Ill U Pr.

Werkmeister, William H. Basis & Structure of Knowledge. LC 68-23337. (Illus.). 1968. Repr. of 1948 ed. lib. bdg. 21.50x (ISBN 0-8371-0265-0, WEBK). Greenwood.

Whitehead, Alfred N. Concept of Nature. 32.95 (ISBN 0-521-06787-1); pap. 8.95x (ISBN 0-521-09245-0). Cambridge U Pr.

Wilke, John T. A Neuropsychological Model of Knowing. LC 81-40175. 88p. (Orig.). 1981. lib. bdg. 16.50 (ISBN 0-8191-1768-4); pap. text ed. 6.75 (ISBN 0-8191-1769-2). U Pr of Amer.

Williams, Michael. Groundless Belief: An Essay on the Possibilities of Epistemology. LC 76-52338. 1977. 15.00x (ISBN 0-300-02128-3). Yale U Pr.

Windelband, Wilhelm. Theories in Logic. LC 61-15253. 1962. 2.75 (ISBN 0-8022-1899-7). Philos Lib.

Wisdom, John. Problems of Mind & Matter. (Orig.). pap. 6.95x (ISBN 0-521-09197-7). Cambridge U Pr.

Wolgast, Elizabeth. Paradoxes of Knowledge. LC 77-3130. 1977. 19.50x (ISBN 0-8014-1090-8). Cornell U Pr.

Woozley, A. D. Theory of Knowledge: An Introduction. (Repr. of 1949 ed). 1964. pap. text ed. 11.25x (ISBN 0-09-044571-6, Hutchinson U Lib). Humanities.

World Philosophy Conference, Dec. 28, 1975-Jan. 3, 1976. Knowledge, Culture & Value: Proceedings. Pandeya, R. C. & Bhatt, S. R., eds. 1976. text ed. 37.50x (ISBN 0-8426-0850-8). Verry.

Ziman, J. M. The Force of Knowledge. LC 75-23529. (Illus.). 368p. 1976. 41.50 (ISBN 0-521-20649-9); pap. 14.95x (ISBN 0-521-09917-X). Cambridge U Pr.

KNOWLEDGE, THEORY OF–DICTIONARIES

Battro, A. M. Dictionnaire d'Epistemologie Genetique. 188p. (Fr.). 1966. 29.00 (ISBN 90-277-0002-8, Pub. by Reidel Holland). Kluwer Boston.

Meyers Standardlexikon Des Gesamten Wissens. (Ger.). 1975. 15.95 (ISBN 3-411-01346-X, M-7562, Pub. by Bibliographisches Institut). French & Eur.

Miers, Horst E. Lexikon des Geheimwissens. (Ger.). leatherette 68.00 (ISBN 3-7626-0028-7, M-7214). French & Eur.

KNOWLEDGE, THEORY OF (RELIGION)

see also Faith and Reason; God–Knowableness

Apczynski, John V. Doers of the Word. LC 76-51640. (American Academy of Religion. Dissertation Ser.). 1977. pap. 7.50 (ISBN 0-89130-128-3, 010118). Scholars Pr Ca.

Biardeau, Madeleine. Theorie De la Connaissance et Philosophie De la Parole Dans le Brahmanisme Classique. (Le Monde D'outre-Mer Passe et Present, Etudes: No. 23). 1963. pap. 51.20x (ISBN 90-2796-178-6). Mouton.

Brandt, Richard B. Philosophy of Schleiermacher: The Development of His Theory of Scientific & Religious Knowledge. LC 68-19265. 1968. Repr. of 1941 ed. lib. bdg. 16.75x (ISBN 0-8371-0027-5, BRPS). Greenwood.

Furse, Margaret L., et al. The Problem of Religious Knowledge. (Rice University Studies: Vol. 60, No. 1). 129p. 1974. pap. 3.25x (ISBN 0-89263-219-4). Rice Univ.

Lynch, John E. The Theory of Knowledge of Vital Du Four. (Philosophy Ser). 1972. 15.00 (ISBN 0-686-11546-5). Franciscan Inst.

Nature of Religious Experience: Essays in Honor of Douglas Clyde Macintosh. facsimile ed. LC 78-152202. (Essay Index Reprint Ser). Repr. of 1937 ed. 13.75 (ISBN 0-8369-2286-7). Arno.

Nee, Watchman. Spiritual Knowledge. Kaung, Stephen, tr. 1973. 3.75 (ISBN 0-935008-36-5); pap. 2.35 (ISBN 0-935008-37-3). Christian Fellow Pubs.

Pearlman, Myer. Knowing the Doctrines of the Bible. 1937. 5.95 (ISBN 0-88243-534-5, 02-0534). Gospel Pub.

Reymond, Robert. The Justification of Knowledge. 1976. kivar 4.50 (ISBN 0-87552-406-0). Presby & Reformed.

Santoni, Ronald E., ed. Religious Language & the Problem of Religious Knowledge. LC 68-27352. 384p. 1968. pap. 3.95x (ISBN 0-253-35001-8). Ind U Pr.

Thomas Aquinas, Saint Providence & Predestination: Questions 5 & 6 of "Truth". Mulligan, Robert W., tr. pap. 3.95 (ISBN 0-89526-937-6). Regnery-Gateway.

Van Til, Cornelius. S Survey of Christian Epistemology. syllabus 4.50 (ISBN 0-87552-495-8). Presby & Reformed.

Warfield, Benjamin B. Studies in Tertullian & Augustine. Repr. of 1930 ed. lib. bdg. 29.00x (ISBN 0-8371-4490-6, WATT). Greenwood.

KNOWLEDGE OF GOD

see God–Knowableness

KNOWLEDGE OF SELF, THEORY OF

see Self-Knowledge, Theory of

KNOWLES, JOHN

Monarch Notes on Knowles' a Separate Peace. (Orig.). pap. 1.75 (ISBN 0-671-00889-7). Monarch Pr.

Roberts, James L. & Carey, Gary. Separate Peace Notes. (Orig.). pap. 1.75 (ISBN 0-8220-1183-2). Cliffs.

KNOX, HENRY, 1750-1806

Belliveau, James E. K Equals X, & Then Some. (Robert Charles Billings Fund Publication Pamphlet Ser.: No. 2). (Illus., Orig.). 1965. pap. 1.00 (ISBN 0-934552-23-1). Boston Athenaeum.

Brooks, Noah. Henry Knox, a Soldier of the Revolution. LC 74-8496. (Era of the American Revolution Ser). (Illus.). xiv, 286p. 1974. Repr. of 1900 ed. lib. bdg. 25.00 (ISBN 0-306-70617-2). Da Capo.

Drake, Francis S. Life & Correspondence of Henry Knox. LC 72-78690. 1873. Repr. 25.00 (ISBN 0-403-08919-0). Somerset Pub.

KNOX, JOHN, 1505-1572

Cowan, Henry. John Knox: The Hero of the Scottish Reformation. LC 70-133817. (Illus.). Repr. of 1905 ed. 27.50 (ISBN 0-404-01788-6). AMS Pr.

Edwards, Charles. John Knox, Bold One for God. LC 78-61733. (Destiny Ser.). 1979. pap. 4.95 (ISBN 0-8163-0238-3). Pacific Pr Pub Assn.

Greaves, Richard L. Theology & Revolution in the Scottish Reformation. 336p. 1980. pap. 10.95 (ISBN 0-8028-1847-1, Chr Univ Pr). Eerdmans.

Harland, Marion. John Knox. 1900. 25.00 (ISBN 0-686-19912-X). Quaker City.

Innes, A. Taylor. John Knox. 1978. Repr. of 1896 ed. lib. bdg. 17.50 (ISBN 0-8414-5057-9). Folcroft.

Lang, Andrew. John Knox & the Reformation. LC 66-25923. Repr. of 1905 ed. 13.50 (ISBN 0-8046-0258-1). Kennikat.

Muir, Edwin. John Knox: Portrait of a Calvinist. 1978. Repr. of 1930 ed. lib. bdg. 30.00 (ISBN 0-8414-6246-1). Folcroft.

--John Knox: Portrait of a Calvinist. LC 78-159096. 1971. Repr. of 1929 ed. 14.00 (ISBN 0-8046-1639-6). Kennikat.

--John Knox: Portrait of a Calvinist. facsimile ed. LC 76-148892. (Select Bibliographies Reprint Ser). Repr. of 1929 ed. 19.00 (ISBN 0-8369-5656-7). Arno.

Murray, Iain. John Knox. 1976. pap. 0.50 (ISBN 0-686-70959-4). Banner of Truth.

Pearce, G. R. John Knox. 1936. Repr. 25.00 (ISBN 0-8274-3855-9). R West.

Percy, Eustace. John Knox. LC 65-11937. 1965. 6.95 (ISBN 0-8042-0924-3). John Knox.

--John Knox. 1964. 8.95 (ISBN 0-227-67510-X). Attic Pr.

Preedy, George R. The Life of John Knox. 1940. Repr. 35.00 (ISBN 0-8274-2933-9). R West.

Reid, W. Stanford. Trumpeter of God: A Biography of John Knox. 372p. 1981. pap. 7.95 (ISBN 0-8010-7708-7). Baker Bk.

KNOX, RONALD ARBUTHNOTT, 1888-1957

Fitzgerald, Penelope. The Knox Brothers. LC 77-22621. (Illus.). 1978. 10.95 (ISBN 0-698-10860-4). Coward.

KNOX, WILLIAM, 1732-1810

Bellot, Leland J. William Knox: The Life & Thought of an Eighteenth-Century Imperialist. LC 76-44006. 276p. 1977. text ed. 14.95x (ISBN 0-292-79007-4). U of Tex Pr.

KNOX COLLEGE, GALESBURG, ILLINOIS

Calkins, Earnest E. They Broke the Prairie: Being Some Account of the Settlement of the Upper Mississippi Valley by Religious & Educational Pioneers, Told in Terms of One City, Galesburg, & of One College, Knox. LC 75-138103. 1971. Repr. of 1937 ed. lib. bdg. 19.50x (ISBN 0-8371-5679-3, CABP). Greenwood.

KNOX COUNTY, KENTUCKY–SOCIAL LIFE AND CUSTOMS

Fetterman, John. Stinking Creek: The Portrait of a Small Mountain Community in Appalachia. 1970. pap. 3.95 (ISBN 0-525-47266-5). Dutton.

KNOXVILLE, TENNESSEE

Creekmore, Betsey B. Knoxville. 3rd ed. LC 66-21195. (Illus.). 1976. 10.00 (ISBN 0-87049-204-7). U of Tenn Pr.

Isenhour, Judith C. Knoxville: A Pictorial History. LC 78-1489. (Illus.). 1978. pap. 12.95 (ISBN 0-915442-46-9). Donning Co.

Kirkham, E. Bruce. The Building of Uncle Tom's Cabin. LC 76-49637. (Illus.). 1977. 14.00x (ISBN 0-87049-205-5). U of Tenn Pr.

Proudfoot, Merrill. Diary of a Sit-In. 1962. pap. 1.95 (ISBN 0-8084-0106-8, B21). Coll & U Pr.

KOALAS

Eberle, Irmengarde. Koalas Live Here. LC 67-17779. (gr. 1-3). 1967. 6.95 (ISBN 0-385-08719-5). Doubleday.

Hunt, Patricia. Koalas. LC 80-13717. (A Skylight Bk.). (Illus.). 48p. (gr. 2-5). 1980. PLB 4.95 (ISBN 0-396-07849-4). Dodd.

Noguere, Suzanne, et al. Little Koala. LC 78-17112. (Illus.). (gr. k-2). 1979. 6.95 (ISBN 0-03-044041-6). HR&W.

KOAN

Becker, Karen, illus. Every End Exposed: The One Hundred Perfect Koans of Master Kido with the Answers of Hakuin-Zen. Hoffmann, Yoel, tr. from Japanese. LC 77-74891. (Illus.). 1977. 7.95 (ISBN 0-394-42069-1); pap. 3.95 (ISBN 0-394-73428-9). Autumn Pr.

Kubose, Gyomay. Zen Koans. LC 72-11183. (Illus.). 256p. 1973. pap. 4.95 (ISBN 0-8092-9065-0). Contemp Bks.

Miura, Isshu & Sasaki, Ruth F. Zen Koan. LC 65-19104. (Illus.). 1966. pap. 2.95 (ISBN 0-15-699981-1, HB112, Harv). HarBraceJ.

Sekida, Katsuki, tr. from Chinese. Two Zen Classics: Mumonkan & Hekiganroku. LC 77-2398. 1977. 13.50 (ISBN 0-8348-0131-0); pap. 8.95 (ISBN 0-8348-0130-2). Weatherhill.

KOASATI INDIANS

see Indians of North America–Eastern States

KOBAYASHI, ISSA, 1763-1827

Lewis, Richard, ed. Of This World: A Poet's Life in Poetry. LC 68-28739. (Illus.). (gr. 7-12). 1968. PLB 4.58 (ISBN 0-8037-6551-7). Dial.

KOCH, ROBERT, 1843-1910

Mechnikov, et al. Founders of Modern Medicine. facs. ed. Berger, D., tr. LC 78-142669. (Essay Index Reprint Ser). 1939. 19.00 (ISBN 0-8369-2111-9). Arno.

KOCH'S LYMPH

see Tuberculin

KOCHTITZKY, OTTO

Kochtitzky, Otto. Story of a Busy Life. (Illus.). 1957. 4.00 (ISBN 0-911208-16-X). Ramfre.

KODAK CAMERA

see Cameras–Types–Kodak

KODALY, ZOLTAN, 1882-1967

Choksy, Lois. Kodaly Context. 1981. 15.95 (ISBN 0-13-516674-8); pap. 10.95 (ISBN 0-13-516666-7). P-H.

--The Kodaly Method: Comprehensive Music Education from Infant to Adult. LC 73-18316. (Illus.). 224p. 1974. 15.95 (ISBN 0-13-516765-5); pap. 11.50 (ISBN 0-13-516757-4). P-H.

Daniel, Katinka S. Kodaly Approach Workbooks. 1973. Wkbk No. 1. 3.32 (ISBN 0-8224-9050-1); Wkbk. No.2. 3.68 (ISBN 0-8224-9051-X); Wkbk No. 3. 3.68 (ISBN 0-8224-9052-8); tchrs' manual 1.60 (ISBN 0-8224-9053-6). Pitman Learning.

Eosze, Laszlo. Zoltan Kodaly: His Life & Work. LC 77-77170. 1969. 7.50 (ISBN 0-8008-8789-1, Crescendo). Taplinger.

Kodaly, Zoltan. Selected Writings of Zoltan Kodaly. 239p. 1974. 9.50 (ISBN 0-85162-021-3). Boosey & Hawkes.

Szonyi, Erzsebet. Kodaly's Principles in Practice. Weissman, John & Alston, Raymond, trs. 1974. pap. text ed. 3.50 (ISBN 0-85162-009-4). Boosey & Hawkes.

Young, Percy M. Zoltan Kodaly, a Hungarian Musician. LC 75-45268. (Illus.). 231p. 1976. Repr. of 1964 ed. lib. bdg. 17.75x (ISBN 0-8371-8650-1, YOZK). Greenwood.

Zemke, Sr. Lorna. Kodaly Concept: Its History, Philosophy, Development. 2nd ed. LC 77-78027. (Orig.). 1977. pap. text ed. 9.95 (ISBN 0-916656-08-X). Mark Foster Mus.

KODIAK, ALASKA

Hrdlicka, Ales. The Anthropology of Kodiak Island. LC 74-5848. Repr. of 1944 ed. 60.50 (ISBN 0-404-11653-1). AMS Pr.

KOENIGGRATZ, BATTLE OF, 1866

Craig, Gordon A. The Battle of Koniggratz: Prussia's Victory Over Austria, 1866. LC 75-35334. (Illus.). 211p. 1976. Repr. of 1964 ed. lib. bdg. 16.25x (ISBN 0-8371-8563-7, CRBK). Greenwood.

Wagner, Arthur L. The Campaign of Koniggratz: A Study of the Austro-Prussian Conflict in the Light of the American Civil War. LC 68-54814. (Military Ser.). (Illus.). 121p. 1972. Repr. of 1889 ed. lib. bdg. 15.00 (ISBN 0-8371-5028-0, WACK). Greenwood.

KOESTLER, ARTHUR, 1905-

Calder, Jenni. Chronicles of Conscience: A Study of George Orwell & Arthur Koestler. LC 69-12146. (Critical Essays in Modern Literature Ser). 1969. pap. 5.95 (ISBN 0-8229-5205-X). U of Pittsburgh Pr.

Fitzpatrick, W. J. Monarch Notes on Koestler's Darkness at Noon. (Orig.). pap. 2.25 (ISBN 0-671-00849-8). Monarch Pr.

Merrill, Reed B. & Frazier, Thomas, eds. Arthur Koestler: An International Bibliography. (Illus.). 1979. 20.00 (ISBN 0-88233-333-X). Ardis Pubs.

Pearson, Sidney A., Jr. Arthur Koestler. (English Authors Ser.: No. 228). 1978. lib. bdg. 12.50 (ISBN 0-8057-6699-5). Twayne.

Sperber, Murray, ed. Arthur Koestler: A Collection of Critical Essays. (Twentieth Century View Ser.). 10.95 (ISBN 0-13-049213-2, Spec). P-H.

KOETSCHAV, PAUL, 1857

Origen. On First Principles: Being Koetschau's Text of the De Principiis. Butterworth, G. W., tr. 7.50 (ISBN 0-8446-2685-6). Peter Smith.

KOHLBERG, ALFRED, 1887-1960

Hersh, Richard H., et al. Promoting Moral Growth: From Piaget to Kohlberg. LC 78-19945. 256p. 1979. pap. text ed. write for info (ISBN 0-582-28057-5). Longman.

KOHLER, KAUFMANN, 1843-1926

Kohler, Kaufmann. The Origins of the Synagogue & the Church. Enelow, H. G., ed. LC 73-2213. (The Jewish People; History, Religion, Literature Ser.). Repr. of 1929 ed. 18.00 (ISBN 0-405-05277-4). Arno.

KOHLER STRIKE, KOHLER, WISCONSIN, 1954-1960

Petro, Sylvester. Kohler Strike. (Americanist Classics Ser). 1965. pap. 1.00 pocketsize (ISBN 0-88279-004-8). Western Islands.

KOKOSCHA, OSCAR, 1886-

Oskar Kokoschka. (Illus.). 1958. pap. 5.00 (ISBN 0-910810-09-5). Johannes.

Rathenau, Ernest G., compiled by. Oskar Kokoschka - Drawings 1906-1965. LC 76-129665. (Illus.). 1970. 19.95 (ISBN 0-87024-176-1). U of Miami Pr.

KOLBE, EMMA ELIZA (COE) 1850-1913

Dutton, Geoffrey. Queen Emma of the South Seas. LC 77-71162. 1978. 8.95 (ISBN 0-312-65992-X). St Martin.

KOLBE, MAXIMILLAN

Manteau-Bonamy, H. M. Immaculate Conception & the Holy Spirit: The Marian Teachings of Father Kolbe. Geiger, Bernard M., ed. Arnandez, Richard, tr. from Fr. LC 77-93104. (Illus.). 1977. pap. 4.00 (ISBN 0-913382-00-0, 101-20). Prow Bks-Franciscan.

Maria Was His Middle Name. (Illus.). 1978. 5.00 (ISBN 0-686-10180-4). Benziger Sis.

Winowska, Maria. The Death Camp Proved Him Real: The Life of Father Maximilian Kolbe, Franciscan. rev. ed. Bowers, Jacqueline & Geiger, Bernard M., trs. from Fr. LC 71-178762. (Illus.). 1971. pap. 3.95 (ISBN 0-913382-03-5, 101-3). Prow Bks-Franciscan.

KOLLWITZ, JOHANNES

Kollwitz. Drawings of Kollwitz. Longstreet, Stephen, ed. (Master Draughtsman Ser). (Illus., Orig.). treasure trove bdg. 6.47x (ISBN 0-685-07269-X); pap. 2.95 (ISBN 0-685-07270-3). Borden.

KOLLWITZ, KATHE, 1867-1945

Kearns, Martha. Kaethe Kollwitz: Woman & Artist. (Biography Ser.: No. 5). (Illus.). 256p. (Orig.). 1975. 6.95 (ISBN 0-912670-15-0). Feminist Pr.

Klein, Mina C. & Klein, Arthur H. Kathe Kollwitz: Life in Art. LC 75-10858. (Illus.). 208p. 1975. pap. 6.95 (ISBN 0-8052-0504-7). Schocken.

Kollwitz, Kathe. Prints & Drawings of Kathe Kollwitz. (Illus.). 12.50 (ISBN 0-8446-0745-2). Peter Smith.

--Prints & Drawings of Kathe Kollwitz. Zigrosser, Carl, ed. LC 73-76286. 1969. pap. 6.00 (ISBN 0-486-22177-6). Dover.

St. Etienne, Galerie. Kaethe Kollwitz. (Illus.). 1976. pap. 7.00 (ISBN 0-910810-18-4). Johannes.

KOLS

see Mundas

KOLUSCHAN LANGUAGE

see Tlingit Language

KOMMUNISTICHESKAIA PARTIIA SOVETSKOGO SOIUZA

see Communist Party of Russia

KOMMUNISTIKA STRANA CESKOSLOVENSKA

see Communist Party of Czechoslovakia

KON-TIKI EKSPEDISJONEN, 1947

Engel, Dolores. Voyage of the Kon-Tiki. LC 78-26766. (Raintree Great Adventures). (Illus.). (gr. 3-6). 1979. PLB 10.25 (ISBN 0-8393-0151-0). Raintree Child.

Heyerdahl, Thor. Kon-Tiki. LC 50-9489. (Illus.). (gr. 7 up). 1950. 10.00 (ISBN 0-528-81865-1). Rand.

--Kon Tiki. (gr. 11 up). 1977. pap. 2.25 (ISBN 0-671-82796-0). PB.

KONARAK, INDIA-TEMPLE

Ebersole, Robert. Black Pagoda. LC 57-12929. (Illus.). 1957. 8.50 (ISBN 0-8130-0070-X). U Presses Fla.

KONDE TRIBES

see Makonde (Bantu Tribe); Nyakyusa (African Tribe)

KONGO

see Congo

KONICA CAMERA

see Cameras–Types–Konica

KONIGGRATZ, BATTLE OF, 1866

see Koeniggratz, Battle of, 1866

KONUNGS SKUGGSIJA

Flom, George T. The Language of the Konungs Skuggsja Speculum Regale, 2 Vols. 1921-1923. Vol. 7. 9.50 ea. (ISBN 0-384-16060-3); Vol. 8. (ISBN 0-384-16070-0). Johnson Repr.

KOOK, ABRAHAM ISAAC, 1865-1935

Agus, Jacob B. High Priest of Rebirth: The Life, Times & Thought of Abraham Isaac Kuk. 2nd ed. 1972. 7.50x (ISBN 0-8197-0281-1). Bloch.

KOOLAH

see Koalas

KOPECHNE, MARY JO, 1941-1969

Tedrow, Richard L. & Tedrow, Thomas L. Death at Chappaquiddick. LC 76-3349. (Illus.). 240p. 1976. 9.95 (ISBN 0-916054-28-4). Green Hill.

KORAES, ADAMANTIS, 1748-1833

Chaconas, Stephen G. Adamantios Korais: A Study in Greek Nationalism. LC 68-58555. (Columbia University Studies in the Social Sciences: No. 490). Repr. of 1942 ed. 22.50 (ISBN 0-404-51490-1). AMS Pr.

KORAN

Ahmad, Mufassir M. The Koran. LC 81-52147. (Illus.). 600p. 1981. pap. 3.95 (ISBN 0-940368-04-8). Tahrike Tarsile Quran.

Ali, A. A. Holy Qur'an, 2 Vols. 25.50x (ISBN 0-87902-038-5). Orientalia.

Ali, M. M. Introduction to the Study of the Holy Qur'an. 4.95x (ISBN 0-87902-040-7). Orientalia.

Ali, S. V., tr. from Arabic. The Holy Qur'an. 550p. 1981. text ed. 6.95 (ISBN 0-940368-08-0); pap. 3.95 (ISBN 0-940368-07-2). Tahrike Tarsile Quran.

Ali, Yousuf. The Holy Quran with Arabic Text Commentary & Translation. 15.95 (ISBN 0-686-18528-5); deluxe ed. 19.95 (ISBN 0-686-18529-3). Kazi Pubns.

--An Interpretation of the Holy Quran with Arabic Text. 9.95 (ISBN 0-686-18338-X). Kazi Pubns.

Ali, Yusuf. The Holy Qur'an. LC 77-78098. 1977. 12.00 (ISBN 0-89259-006-8). Am Trust Pubns.

As-Said, Labib. Recited Koran: A History of the First Recorded Version. Weiss, Bernard, ed. LC 73-20717. (Illus.). 156p. 1975. 10.00 (ISBN 0-87850-024-3). Darwin Pr.

Azizullah. Glimpses of the Holy Quran. pap. 3.95 (ISBN 0-686-18517-X). Kazi Pubns.

Basetti-Sami, Giulio. Koran in the Light of Christ. 1977. 8.50 (ISBN 0-8199-0713-8). Franciscan Herald.

Baydun, M. Quran. (Arabic.). 30.00x (ISBN 0-86685-133-X). Intl Bk Ctr.

--Quran. (Arabic.). medium sized. 25.00x (ISBN 0-86685-134-8). Intl Bk Ctr.

--Quran. (Arabic.). 10.00x (ISBN 0-86685-135-6). Intl Bk Ctr.

--Quran. (Arabic.). pocket sized 6.00x (ISBN 0-86685-136-4). Intl Bk Ctr.

Bell, Richard, tr. The Qur'an: A New Translation with a Critical Rearrangement of the Surahs, 2 vols. 12.50 ea. Vol. 1 (ISBN 0-567-02027-4). Vol. 2 (ISBN 0-567-02028-2). Attic Pr.

Bucaille, Maurice. The Bible, the Qur'an & Science. Beg, Anwer, ed. Bucaille, Maurice & Pannell, Alastair D., trs. from Fr. LC 77-90336. 1978. 11.95 (ISBN 0-89259-010-6). Am Trust Pubns.

Burton, J. The Collection of the Qur'an. LC 76-27899. 1977. 38.50 (ISBN 0-521-21439-4); pap. 12.95 (ISBN 0-521-29652-8). Cambridge U Pr.

Chipa, A. K. Beauty & Wisdom of the Holy Qur'an. 1971. 2.50x (ISBN 0-87902-159-4). Orientalia.

Cross, Frank M. & Talmon, Shemaryahu, eds. Qumran & the History of the Biblical Text. LC 75-12529. 415p. 1975. text ed. 18.50x (ISBN 0-674-74360-1); pap. text ed. 8.95x (ISBN 0-674-74362-8). Harvard U Pr.

Eckman, J. Middle Turkic Glosses of Rylands Interlinear Koran Translation. 1976. 27.50x (ISBN 963-05-0984-9). Intl Pubns Serv.

Eckmann. Mid. Turkic Glosses of Rylands Interlinear Koran Translation. 1976. 29.00 (ISBN 0-9960008-3-6, Pub. by Kaido Hungary). Heyden.

Faruqi, I. Azad. The Tarouman Al-Quar'n: A Critical Analysis of Maulana Abul Kalam Azad's Approach to the Understanding of the Qura'n. 128p. 1981. text ed. 15.00x (ISBN 0-7069-1342-6, Pub. by Vikas India). Advent NY.

Gatje, Helmut. The Qur'an & Its Exegesis: Selected Texts with Classical & Modern Muslim Interpretations. Welch, Alford T., ed. LC 74-82847. (Islamic World Ser). 1977. 29.75x (ISBN 0-520-02833-3). U of Cal Pr.

Gauhar, Altaf. Translation from the Quran. 5.95 (ISBN 0-686-18511-0). Kazi Pubns.

Geiger, Abraham. Judaism & Islam. rev. ed. (Library of Jewish Classics). 1970. 15.00x (ISBN 0-87068-058-7). Ktav.

Hafiz, M. Virtues of the Holy Quran. pap. 3.50 (ISBN 0-686-18508-0). Kazi Pubns.

Hamidullah, D. M. Holy Quran, 2 vols. (Arabic, Fr.). 1981. Set. french & arabic 35.00 (ISBN 0-686-77430-2). Kazi Pubns.

Hingora. The Prophecies of the Holy Quran. pap. 3.00 (ISBN 0-686-18509-9). Kazi Pubns.

The Holy Quran. (Arabic.). 14.95 (ISBN 0-686-18522-6). Kazi Pubns.

Husain, S. A. The Message of Quran. 6.95 (ISBN 0-686-18483-1). Kazi Pubns.

Izutsu, Toshihiko. God & Man in the Koran. LC 79-52554. (Islam Ser.). 1980. Repr. of 1964 ed. lib. bdg. 20.00x (ISBN 0-8369-9262-8). Arno.

Jang, N. An Approach to the Study of the Quran. pap. 3.00 (ISBN 0-686-18520-X). Kazi Pubns.

Jeffery, Arthur. The Qur'an As Scripture. LC 79-52555. (Islam Ser.). 1980. lib. bdg. 12.00x (ISBN 0-8369-9263-6). Arno.

--The Qur'an As Scripture. LC 80-1924. Repr. of 1952 ed. 18.00 (ISBN 0-404-18970-9). AMS Pr.

Jeffery, Arthur, ed. Materials for the History of the Text of the Qur'an. LC 79-180350. Repr. of 1937 ed. 57.50 (ISBN 0-404-56282-5). AMS Pr.

Jung, N. An Approach to the Study of the Qur'an. 1970. 2.95x (ISBN 0-87902-168-3). Orientalia.

Jung, Nizamat. An Approach to the Study of the Qur'an. 84p. (Orig.). 1981. pap. 3.25 (ISBN 0-88004-002-5). Sunwise Turn.

Karim, A. Beauty & Wisdom of the Holy Quran. 3.00 (ISBN 0-686-18519-6). Kazi Pubns.

Katsh, Abraham I. Judaism in Islam: Biblical & Talmudic Background of the Koran & Its Commentaries. 3rd ed. LC 80-50001. 1980. pap. 7.95 (ISBN 0-87203-086-5). Hermon.

Khalifa, Rashad. English Transliteration of the Qur'an, 3bks. in 1. 1978. 19.00 (ISBN 0-934894-00-0). Islamic Prods.

--Quran: The Final Scripture. 600p. (Orig.). 1981. 19.00 (ISBN 0-934894-19-1). Islamic Prods.

Khalifa, Rashad, tr. from Arabic. The Glorious Qur 'an: Standard Translation, 12 vols. set. 1st ed. 1978. 19.00set (ISBN 0-934894-01-9). Islamic Prods.

Khalifa, Rashad A. Miracle of the Qur'an: Significance of the Mysterious Alphabets. (Illus.). 200p. 1973. 6.85 (ISBN 0-934894-02-7). Islamic Prods.

Kur'An. Here Begynneth a Lytell Treatyse of the Turkes Lawe Called Alcaron. LC 77-7411. (English Experience Ser.: No. 876). 1977. Repr. of 1519 ed. lib. bdg. 3.50 (ISBN 90-221-0876-7). Walter J Johnson.

Latif, S. A. The Mind Al-Quran Builds. 4.95 (ISBN 0-686-18510-2). Kazi Pubns.

Maudadi, A. A. Tafhimul - Quaran: Urdu Translation & Commentary. 48.00 (ISBN 0-686-18523-4). Kazi Pubns.

Maududi, A. A. The Meaning of the Quran, 8 vols. 5.00 ea. Kazi Pubns.

Muhajir. Lessons from the Stories of the Quran. pap. 5.25 (ISBN 0-686-18515-3). Kazi Pubns.

Muhajir, A. M. Lessons from the Stories of the Qur'an. 1969. 6.75x (ISBN 0-87902-066-0). Orientalia.

Nadui, S. M. A Geographical History of the Qur'an. 1970. 5.50x (ISBN 0-87902-300-7). Orientalia.

Nadvi. A Geographical History of the Quran. 4.50 (ISBN 0-686-18521-8). Kazi Pubns.

The Object of Life According to the Holy Qur'an. 1972. 3.00x (ISBN 0-87902-181-0). Orientalia.

Penrice, John. Dictionary & Glossary of the Koran. (Eng. & Arabic.). 18.00 (ISBN 0-86685-088-0). Intl Bk Ctr.

--Dictionary & Glossary of the Koran, with Copious Grammatical References & Explanations. LC 70-90039. 1969. Repr. of 1873 ed. 17.50x (ISBN 0-8196-0252-3). Biblo.

--A Dictionary & Glossary of the Koran with Grammatical References & Explanations. 1980. lib. bdg. 55.00 (ISBN 0-8490-3123-0). Gordon Pr.

Pickthall. The Holy Quran: Text & Explanatory Translation. 15.95 (ISBN 0-686-18527-7). Kazi Pubns.

--The Meaning of the Glorious Quran. pap. 2.95 (ISBN 0-686-18531-5). Kazi Pubns.

Pickthall, M. M., ed. Holy Quran with English Translation. 1976. Repr. 16.00x (ISBN 0-8364-0415-7). South Asia Bks.

Pickthall, M. M., tr. The Meaning of the Illustrious Qur'an: Arabic & English. 1970. 4.00x (ISBN 0-87902-182-9). Orientalia.

Pickthall, Marmaduke, ed. The Glorious Koran. bilingual ed. 1696p. 1976. text ed. 50.00x (ISBN 0-04-297036-9). Allen Unwin.

Pickthall, Mohammed M., tr. Meaning of the Glorious Koran. pap. 2.95 (ISBN 0-451-61924-2, ME1924, Ment). NAL.

Pickthall, Muhammed M., tr. from Arabic. The Glorious Koran. 1979. deluxe ed. 50.00 (ISBN 0-87773-713-4). Great Eastern.

Pikthall, Marmaduke. The Meaning of the Glorious Koran. leather-bound deluxe ed. Pickthall, Marmaduke, tr. from Arabic. 693p. 1981. text ed. 100.00x (ISBN 0-7069-1330-2, Pub. by Vikas India). Advent NY.

Quasem, M. A. The Jewels of the Qur'an: Al-Ghazali's Theory. 244p. 1980. 13.95x (ISBN 0-89955-204-8, Pub. by M A Quasem Malaysia); pap. 7.95x (ISBN 0-89955-205-6). Intl Schol Bk Serv.

--The Recitation & Interpretation of the Qur'an. 121p. 1980. 9.95x (ISBN 0-89955-206-4, Pub. by M A Quasem Malaysia); pap. 6.95x (ISBN 0-89955-207-2). Intl Schol Bk Serv.

Quasem, Muhammad A. The Jewels of the Qur'an: Al-Ghazali's Theory. 1977. 12.00 (ISBN 0-686-23467-7). Quasem.

Rahman, Fazlur. Major Themes of the Qur'an. LC 79-54189. 1980. 22.00x (ISBN 0-88297-026-7). Bibliotheca.

Rodwell, J. M., ed. & tr. Koran. 1953. pap. 3.50x (ISBN 0-460-01380-7, Evman). Biblio Dist.

Sales, George & Wherry, E. M., eds. Comprehensive Commentary on the Qur'an, 4 Vols. LC 79-153620. Repr. of 1896 ed. Set. 110.00 (ISBN 0-404-09520-8); 27.50 ea. Vol. 1 (ISBN 0-404-09521-6). Vol. 2 (ISBN 0-404-09522-4). Vol. 3 (ISBN 0-404-09523-2). Vol. 4 (ISBN 0-404-09524-0). AMS Pr.

Sarwar, H. G. Philosophy of the Qur'an. 1969. 6.25x (ISBN 0-87902-187-X). Orientalia.

--Philosophy of the Quran. 3.50 (ISBN 0-686-18604-4). Kazi Pubns.

Seale, M. S. Qur'an & Bible: Studies in Interpretation & Dialogue. 124p. 1978. 20.00x (ISBN 0-85664-818-3, Pub. by Croom Helm Ltd England). Biblio Dist.

Shah, A. Miftah-ul-Quran: Glossary of Quran, 2 vols. 16.50 (ISBN 0-686-18525-0). Kazi Pubns.

Siddigi, K. N. The Qur'An & the World Today. 295p. 1971. 6.25x (ISBN 0-87902-249-3). Orientalia.

Siddiqui, A. H. The Holy Quran: Text, Translation & Explanatory Notes, I-Viii. (Avail. in sep. parts). pap. 3.00 ea. Kazi Pubns.

Stanton, H. U. Teaching of the Qur'An, with an Account of Its Growth & Subject Index. LC 74-90040. 1969. Repr. 12.50x (ISBN 0-8196-0253-1). Biblo.

Tariq, M. A. Holy Quran Made Easy. 1968. 4.85x (ISBN 0-87902-070-9). Orientalia.

Torrey, Charles C. Jewish Foundation of Islam. rev. ed. LC 67-18817. 1968. 15.00x (ISBN 0-87068-117-6). Ktav.

Watt, W. Montgomery. Companion the the Qur'an: Based on the Arberry Translation. 1967. text ed. 17.95x (ISBN 0-04-297019-9). Allen Unwin.

Yusuf, A. The Holy Quran. (Arabic & Eng.). 14.95x (ISBN 0-86685-167-4). Intl Bk Ctr.

KORAN-LAW

see Islamic Law

KORBUT, OLGA

Jacobs, Linda. Olga Korbut, Girl of Tears & Triumph. LC 74-2384. (Women Who Win Ser.). 1974. 5.95 (ISBN 0-88436-124-1). EMC.

Smith, Jay H. Olga Korbut. LC 74-19169. (Creative Education Sports Superstars Ser.). (Illus.). 32p. (gr. 3-6). 1974. PLB 5.95 (ISBN 0-87191-384-4); pap. 2.95 (ISBN 0-89812-190-6). Creative Ed.

Taylor, Paula. Gymnastics' Happy Superstar: Olga Korbut. (The Allstars Ser.). (Illus.). (gr. 2-6). 1977. PLB 5.95 (ISBN 0-87191-581-2); pap. 2.95 (ISBN 0-89812-197-3). Creative Ed.

KORDOFAN

Macmichael, H. A. Tribes of Northern & Central Kordofan. 260p. 1967. Repr. of 1912 ed. 40.00x (ISBN 0-7146-1113-1, F Cass Co). Biblio Dist.

KOREA

American Chamber of Commerce in Korea. Living in Korea: 1978 Ed. 1978. 13.00 (ISBN 0-686-23876-1). A M Newman.

Bland, John O. China, Japan & Korea. facsimile ed. LC 77-160959. (Select Bibliographies Reprint Ser). Repr. of 1921 ed. 29.00 (ISBN 0-8369-5826-8). Arno.

Butler, Lucius A. & Youngs, Chaesoon T.compiled by. Films for Korean Studies. LC 77-86325. (Occasional Papers Ser.: No. 8). 167p. 1978. pap. 6.00x (ISBN 0-917536-12-6). Ctr Korean U HI at Manoa.

Center for Korean Studies. Korean Studies, Vol. I. (Korean Studies). 1977. pap. text ed. 13.50x (ISBN 0-8248-0560-7). U Pr of Hawaii.

Clark, Charles A. Religions of Old Korea: New York, 1932. LC 78-74297. (Oriental Religions Ser.: Vol. 14). 295p. 1981. lib. bdg. 33.00 (ISBN 0-8240-3916-5). Garland Pub.

Fukuda, Tsuneari, ed. Future of Japan & the Korean Peninsula. Jahng, K., tr. from Japanese. LC 78-71337. (Illus.). 1979. 14.40 (ISBN 0-930878-14-0). Hollym Intl.

Grad, Andrew J. Modern Korea. 1979. Repr. of 1944 ed. lib. bdg. 18.00x (ISBN 0-374-93226-3). Octagon.

Harrison, John A., ed. Japan: Enduring Scholarship Selected from the Far Eastern Quarterly, the Journal of Asian Studies 1941-1971. LC 72-83062. (Thirtieth Anniversary Commemorative Ser: Vol. 2). 1972. pap. 2.00 (ISBN 0-8165-0362-1). U of Ariz Pr.

Hazard, B. H., ed. Korean Studies Guide. LC 74-9394. (University of California, Institute of Asiatic Studies Ser). (Illus.). 220p. 1975. Repr. of 1954 ed. lib. bdg. 14.00x (ISBN 0-8371-7662-X, MAKS). Greenwood.

Hiu Lie. Die Mandschu-Sprachkunde in Korea. (Uralic & Altaic Ser.: No. 114). (Illus.). 276p. 1973. pap. text ed. 42.50x (ISBN 0-686-27752-X). Mouton.

Kim, Young C. & Halpern, Abraham M., eds. The Future of the Korean Peninsula. LC 77-24407. (Praeger Special Studies). 1977. text ed. 25.95 (ISBN 0-03-021846-2). Praeger.

Kim Byong Sik. Modern Korea. Perlo, Victor, ed. Haga, Takeshi, tr. LC 70-130866. 8.95 (ISBN 0-7178-0291-4, 137, NW). Intl Pub Co.

Korea Annual 1980. 17th ed. LC 64-6162. (Illus.). 732p. 1980. pap. 30.00x (ISBN 0-8002-2733-6). Intl Pubns Serv.

The Korea Directory 1980. 23rd ed. LC 68-57222. (Illus.). 1416p. (Orig.). 1980. pap. 45.00x (ISBN 0-8002-2436-1). Intl Pubns Serv.

Korea Telephone & Telex Directory 1981. 1548p. (Orig.). 1981. pap. 57.50x (ISBN 0-8002-2823-5). Intl Pubns Serv.

Korean Repository, 5 Vols. (Illus.). 1964. Repr. of 1898 ed. Set. 175.00x (ISBN 0-8188-0056-9). Paragon.

Lie, Hiu. Die Mandschu-Sprachkunde in Korea. LC 70-635028. (Uralic & Altaic Ser: Vol. 114). (Illus., Orig.). 1972. pap. text ed. 16.00x (ISBN 0-87750-162-9). Res Ctr Lang Semiotic.

McCann, David R., et al, eds. Studies on Korea in Transition. LC 78-67859. (Occasional Papers Ser.: No. 9). 245p. 1979. pap. 8.00x (ISBN 0-917536-13-4). Ctr Korean U HI at Manoa.

McCormack, Gavan & Selden, Mark, eds. Korea, North & South: The Deepening Crisis. LC 78-4503. 1978. 12.50 (ISBN 0-85345-448-5, CL-4485). Monthly Rev.

Occasional Papers, 2 pts. Incl. Parental Encouragement & College Plans of High School Students in Korea. Yang, Choon & Won, George.; Gains & Costs of Postwar Industrialization in South Korea. Lim, Youngil. 51p. 1973. pap. 3.50 (ISBN 0-917536-00-2). Ctr Korean U HI at Manoa.

Osgood, Cornelius. The Koreans & Their Culture. (Illus.). 1951. 24.95 (ISBN 0-471-06943-4). Ronald Pr.

Price, Ernest B. Russo-Japanese Treaties of 1907-1916. LC 76-101274. Repr. of 1933 ed. 17.50 (ISBN 0-404-05135-9). AMS Pr.

Traverso, E. Korea & the Limits of Limited War. Brown, Richard H. & Halsey, Van R., eds. (Amherst Ser.). (gr. 9-12). 1970. pap. text ed. 4.52 (ISBN 0-201-07582-2, Sch Div); tchrs' manual 1.92 (ISBN 0-201-07584-9). A-W.

Warring, R. H. Know Your Model Aero Engine. (Illus., Orig.). 1979. pap. 8.50x (ISBN 0-85242-607-0). Intl Pubns Serv.

Weinstein, Franklin B. & Kamiya, Fuji, eds. The Security of Korea: U. S. & Japanese Perspectives on the Nineteen Eighties. (Westview Special Studies in International Relations). 260p. 1980. lib. bdg. 20.00x (ISBN 0-89158-668-7); pap. text ed. 8.50x (ISBN 0-89158-758-6). Westview.

KOREA–BIBLIOGRAPHY

Courant, Maurice A. Bibliographie Coreenne, Tableau Litteraire De la Coree, 4 vols in 3. (Incl. suppl). Repr. of 1894 ed. Set. 177.00 (ISBN 0-8337-0692-6). B Franklin.

Koh, Hesung C. & Steffens, Joan, eds. Korea: An Analytical Guide to Bibliographies. LC 70-125119. (Behavior Science Bibliographies Ser.). xviii, 344p. 1971. 18.00x (ISBN 0-87536-241-9). HRAFP.

Shulman, Frank J. Japan & Korea: An Annotated Bibliography of Doctoral Dissertations in Western Languages, 1877-1969. 360p. 1970. pap. 6.95 (ISBN 0-8389-0085-2). ALA.

KOREA–DESCRIPTION AND TRAVEL

Adams, Edward B. Korea Guide. (Illus.). 1979. pap. 12.00 (ISBN 0-89860-026-X). Eastview.

Bartz, Patricia M. South Korea. (Illus.). 248p. 1972. 24.95x (ISBN 0-19-874008-5). Oxford U Pr.

Chung, Chong-Wha, ed. Meetings & Farewells: Modern Korean Studies. LC 80-506. 1980. write for info. (ISBN 0-312-52855-8). St Martin.

Fodor's Japan & Korea, 1981. 1981. 13.95 (ISBN 0-679-00703-2); pap. 10.95 (ISBN 0-679-00704-0). McKay.

Kim, Edward. Korea: Beyond the Hills. LC 79-91523. (Illus.). 184p. 1980. 26.00 (ISBN 0-87011-411-5). Kodansha.

Lanier, Alison R. Update -- South Korea. LC 80-83919. (Country Orientation Ser.). 1980. pap. text ed. 25.00x (ISBN 0-933662-33-5). Intercult Pr.

Moore, Robin, et al. Suzi: The Korean Connection. LC 78-66724. pap. 2.25 (ISBN 0-89516-052-8). Condor Pub Co.

Wallis, Kathleen. Let's Look at Korea. 1977. pap. 1.25 (ISBN 0-85363-118-2). OMF Bks.

KOREA–ECONOMIC CONDITIONS

Adelman, Irma, ed. Practical Approaches to Development Planning: Korea's Second Five-Year Plan. LC 69-19467. 320p. 1969. 22.50x (ISBN 0-8018-1061-2). Johns Hopkins.

Adleman, Irma & Robinson, Sherman. Income Distribution Policy in Developing Countries: A Case Study of Korea. LC 76-14269. 1978. 12.50x (ISBN 0-8047-0925-4). Stanford U Pr.

Bartz, Patricia M. South Korea. (Illus.). 248p. 1972. 24.95x (ISBN 0-19-874008-5). Oxford U Pr.

Brown, Gilbert T. Korean Pricing Policies & Economic Development in the 1960s. LC 73-8121. (Illus.). 328p. 1974. 22.50x (ISBN 0-8018-1479-0). Johns Hopkins.

Chung, Joseph S. The North Korean Economy: Structure & Development. LC 75-187263. (Publications Ser.: No. 132). (Illus.). 212p. 1974. 9.95 (ISBN 0-8179-6321-9). Hoover Inst Pr.

Cole, David, et al. The Korean Economy: Issues of Development. LC 79-620015. (Korea Research Monographs: No. 1). 1979. pap. 3.50 (ISBN 0-912966-20-3). IEAS Ctr Chinese Stud.

Cole, David C., et al. Korean Development: The Interplay of Politics & Economics. LC 75-131468. (Center for International Affairs Ser). (Illus.). 1971. 16.50x (ISBN 0-674-50563-8). Harvard U Pr.

Factors Which Hinder or Help Productivity Improvement: Country Report--Korea. (APO Basic Research Ser.). 115p. 1980. pap. 7.75 (ISBN 92-833-1465-4, APO 99, APO). Unipub.

Frank, Charles R. & Kim, Kwang Suk. South Korea, Vol. 7. Bhagwati, Jagdish N. & Krueger, Anne O., eds. (Foreign Trade Regimes & Economic Development). 250p. 1975. 15.00x (ISBN 0-87014-507-X, Dist by Columbia Pr). Natl Bur Econ Res.

Hong, Wontack. Factor Supply & Factor Intensity of Trade in Korea. 1976. text ed. 10.00x (ISBN 0-8248-0539-9). U Pr of Hawaii.

--Trade, Distortions & Employment Growth in Korea. 410p. 1979. 15.00x (ISBN 0-8248-0678-6, Korea Devel Inst). U Pr of Hawaii.

Hong, Wontack & Krueger, Anne O., eds. Trade & Development in Korea. 1975. text ed. 10.00x (ISBN 0-8248-0536-4). U Pr of Hawaii.

Jones, Leroy & Sakong, Il. Government, Business, & Entrepreneurship in Economic Development: The Korean Case. (East Asian Monographs: No. 91). 1979. 15.00x (ISBN 0-674-35791-4). Harvard U Pr.

Kim, Chuk Kyo, ed. Industrial & Social Development Issues: Essays on the Korean Economy, Vol.2. 1977. text ed. 12.00x (ISBN 0-8248-0547-X, Korea Development Institute Bk). U Pr of Hawaii.

--Planning Model & Macroeconomic Policy Issues: Essays on the Korean Economy, Vol.1. 1977. text ed. 14.00x (ISBN 0-8248-0546-1, Korea Development Institute Bk). U Pr of Hawaii.

Kim, Youn-Soo, ed. The Economy of the Korean Democratic People's Republic, 1945-1977. (Monographie der Deutschen Korea-Studien Gruppe: No. 2). 1979. pap. text ed. 18.00x (ISBN 0-8188-0139-5). Paragon.

Korea Development Institute. Long-Term Prospect for Economic & Social Development of Korea, 1977-1991. 310p. 1979. pap. text ed. 10.00x (ISBN 0-8248-0641-7, Korea Devel Inst). U Pr of Hawaii.

Korean Traders Association. Korean Trade Directory, 1979 to 1980. 21st ed. LC 60-45910. 579p. 1979. 35.00x (ISBN 0-8002-2520-1). Intl Pubns Serv.

Kuznets, Paul W. Economic Growth & Structure in Republic of Korea. LC 76-45407. (Illus.). 1977. 20.00x (ISBN 0-300-02019-8). Yale U Pr.

Lim, Youngil. Government Policy & Private Enterprise: Korean Experience. (Korea Research Monographs: No. 6). 1981. pap. price not set (ISBN 0-912966-36-X). IEAS Ctr Chinese Stud.

Mason, Edward S. The Economic & Social Modernization of the Republic of Korea. (Harvard East Asian Monographs: Vol. 92). 500p. 1980. 20.00x (ISBN 0-674-23175-9). Harvard U Pr.

Park, Chong Kee. Social Security in Korea: An Approach to Socio-Economic Development. 1975. text ed. 10.00x (ISBN 0-8248-0537-2). U Pr of Hawaii.

Park, Chong Kee, ed. Essays on the Korean Economy: Vol. III--Macroeconomic & Industrial Development in Korea. 402p. 1981. text ed. 15.00x (ISBN 0-8248-0754-5). U Pr of Hawaii.

--Essays on the Korean Economy: Vol. IV--Human Resources & Social Development in Korea. 372p. 1981. text ed. 15.00x (ISBN 0-8248-0755-3). U Pr of Hawaii.

Repetto, Robert, et al. Economic Development, Population Policy & Demographic Trsnsition in the Republic of Korea. (Harvard East Asian Monographs: No. 93). 200p. 1981. text ed. 15.00x (ISBN 0-674-23311-5). Harvard U Pr.

Sang Chul Suhgro. Growth & Structural Changes in the Korean Economy, 1910-1940. (Harvard East Asian Monograph: No. 83). 1978. 15.00x (ISBN 0-674-36439-2). Harvard U Pr.

U. S. Department Of State - Office Of Public Affairs. Korea, Nineteen Forty-Five to Nineteen Forty-Eight: A Report on Political Development & Economic Resources with Selected Documents. LC 68-55125. (Illus.). 1968. Repr. of 1948 ed. lib. bdg. 14.00x (ISBN 0-8371-1731-3, KORE). Greenwood.

Wade, L. L. & Kim, B. S. The Economic Development of South Korea: The Political Economy of Success. LC 78-2665. (Praeger Special Studies). 1978. 25.95 (ISBN 0-03-043591-9). Praeger.

World Bank. Korea: Problems & Issues in a Rapidly Growing Economy. LC 76-17238. (A World Bank Country Economic Report Ser). (Illus.). 296p. 1976. 17.50x (ISBN 0-8018-1864-8). Johns Hopkins.

KOREA–FOREIGN RELATIONS

Baldwin, Frank, ed. Without Parallel: The American-Korean Relationship Since 1945. LC 73-18718. 1974. pap. 3.95 (ISBN 0-394-70642-0). Pantheon.

Barnds, William J., ed. The Two Koreas in East Asian Affairs. LC 75-27379. 216p. 1976. 15.00x (ISBN 0-8147-0988-5). NYU Pr.

Boettcher, Robert & Freedman, Gordon L. Gifts of Deceit: Sun Myung Moon, Tongsun Park & the Korean Scandal. LC 79-20192. 408p. 1980. 14.95 (ISBN 0-03-044576-0). HR&W.

Buss, Claude A. The United States & the Republic of Korea: Background to Policy. (Publication Ser.: No. 254). (Illus.). 240p. 1982. pap. price not set (ISBN 0-8179-7542-X). Hoover Inst Pr.

Chai, Nam-Yearl, et al. Korean International Law. (Korean Research Monographs: No. 4). 80p. 1981. pap. price not set (ISBN 0-912966-40-8). IEAS Ctr Chinese Stud.

Choi, Woonsang. Fall of the Hermit Kingdom. LC 66-11939. 1967. 10.00 (ISBN 0-379-00277-9). Oceana.

Chung, Chin O. Pyongyang Between Peking & Moscow: North Korea's Involvement in the Sino-Soviet Dispute, 1958-1975. LC 76-44261. 1978. 16.75x (ISBN 0-8173-4728-3). U of Ala Pr.

Deuchler, Martina. Confucian Gentlemen & Barbarian Envoys: The Opening of Korea, 1875-1885. LC 76-57228. (Royal Asiatic Society Ser.). 324p. 1978. 22.50 (ISBN 0-295-95552-X). U of Wash Pr.

Fukuda, Tsuneari, ed. Future of Japan & the Korean Peninsula. Jahng, K., tr. from Japanese. LC 78-71337. (Illus.). 1979. 14.40 (ISBN 0-930878-14-0). Hollym Intl.

Head, Richard G., et al. Crisis Resolution: Presidential Decision Making in the Mayaguez & Korean Confrontations. (A Westview Special Study). 1978. lib. bdg. 27.75x (ISBN 0-89158-163-4). Westview.

Kim, Kie-Taek & Kaulins, Andis, eds. The Foreign Policies & Foreign Trade of the German Democratic Republic & the Korean Democratic People's Republic. (German Korea Studies Group Ser.). 144p. 1980. pap. 15.00 (ISBN 0-8188-0117-4, Pub. by German Korea Stud Germany). Paragon.

Lee, Yur-Bok. Diplomatic Relations Between the United States & Korea 1866-1887. 1970. text ed. 7.50x (ISBN 0-391-00084-5). Humanities.

McCune, G. M. & Harrison, J. A. Korean-American Relations, Vol. 1. LC 51-111. Repr. of 1951 ed. 14.00 (ISBN 0-527-59200-5). Kraus Repr.

Morley, James W. Japan & Korea: America's Allies in the Pacific. LC 81-4196. (Illus.). 152p. 1981. Repr. of 1965 ed. lib. bdg. 19.50x (ISBN 0-313-23033-1, MOJK). Greenwood.

Nelson, Melvin F. Korea & the Old Orders in Eastern Asia. LC 66-27132. 1967. Repr. of 1945 ed. 8.50 (ISBN 0-8462-0851-2). Russell.

Pearson, Roger, ed. Korea in the World Today. 1976. pap. 10.00 (ISBN 0-685-79962-X). Coun Am Affairs.

Stueck, William W., Jr. The Road to Confrontation: American Policy Toward China & Korea, 1947 - 1950. LC 80-11818. (Illus.). ix, 326p. 1981. 20.00x (ISBN 0-8078-1445-8); pap. 10.00x (ISBN 0-8078-4080-7). U of NC Pr.

Sunoo, Harold H. America's Dilemma in Asia: The Case of South Korea. LC 78-24029. 224p. 1979. 17.95x (ISBN 0-88229-357-5). Nelson-Hall.

Swartout, Robert R., Jr. Mandarins, Gunboats, & Power Politics: Owen Nickerson Denny & International Rivalries in Korea. LC 79-22242. 1980. text ed. 9.75x (ISBN 0-8248-0681-6). U Pr of Hawaii.

KOREA–HISTORY

see also Korean War, 1950-1953

Choe Ching Young. The Rule of the Taewon'gun, 1864-1873: Restoration in Yi Korea. LC 73-183975. (East Asian Monographs Ser: No. 45). 1972. pap. 9.00x (ISBN 0-674-78030-2). Harvard U Pr.

Choi, Woonsang. Fall of the Hermit Kingdom. LC 66-11939. 1967. 10.00 (ISBN 0-379-00277-9). Oceana.

Choy, Bong-Youn. Korea: A History. LC 73-147180. (Illus.). 1971. 13.75 (ISBN 0-8048-0249-1). C E Tuttle.

Chung, Kyung C. Korea: The Third Republic. 1971. 10.95 (ISBN 0-02-525560-6). Macmillan.

Detwiler, Donald S. & Burdick, Charles B., eds. Japanese Military Studies 1937-1949: China, Manchuria, & Korea, Pt. 1. (War in Asia & the Pacific Ser., 1937 to 1949: Vol. 8). 630p. 1980. lib. bdg. 55.00 (ISBN 0-8240-3292-6); lib. bdg. 650.00 set of 15 vols. (ISBN 0-686-60097-5). Garland Pub.

Deuchler, Martina. Confucian Gentlemen & Barbarian Envoys: The Opening of Korea, 1875-1885. LC 76-57228. (Royal Asiatic Society Ser.). 324p. 1978. 22.50 (ISBN 0-295-95552-X). U of Wash Pr.

Ginsburgs, George K. & Kim, Roy U. Calendar of Diplomatic Affairs Democratic People's Republic of Korea 1945-1975. 1977. 27.50 (ISBN 0-918542-00-6). Symposia Pr.

Goodrich, Leland M. Korea: A Study of U. S. Policy in the United Nations. LC 78-24120. 1979. Repr. of 1956 ed. lib. bdg. 18.75x (ISBN 0-313-20825-5, GOKO). Greenwood.

Griffis, William E. Corea, the Hermit Nation. rev. ed. 9th ed., enl ed. LC 74-158615. Repr. of 1911 ed. 34.50 (ISBN 0-404-02916-7). AMS Pr.

Gupta, Alka. UN Peacekeeping Activities in Korea: A Study of India's Role, 1947-1953. 1977. 11.00x (ISBN 0-88386-850-4). South Asia Bks.

Han, Woo-Keun. The History of Korea. Mintz, Grafton K., ed. Lee, Kyung-Shik, tr. from Korean. (Illus.). 568p. 1971. (Eastwest Ctr); pap. text ed. 8.95x (ISBN 0-8248-0334-5). U Pr of Hawaii.

Harvey, Youngsook K. Six Korean Women: The Socialization of Shamans. (American Ethnological Society Ser). (Illus.). 1979. text ed. 20.95 (ISBN 0-8299-0243-0). West Pub.

Henthorn, William E. History of Korea. LC 75-143511. 1971. 14.95 (ISBN 0-02-914460-4); pap. text ed. 7.95 (ISBN 0-02-914610-0). Free Pr.

Hong, Wontack & Krueger, Anne O., eds. Trade & Development in Korea. 1975. text ed. 10.00x (ISBN 0-8248-0536-4). U Pr of Hawaii.

Hulbert, Homer B. History of Korea, 2 Vols. rev. ed. Weems, C. N., ed. 1962. Set. text ed. 30.00x (ISBN 0-391-00521-9). Humanities.

Hwang, In K. The Korean Reform Movement of the 1880's: Transition in Intra-Asian Relations. LC 78-290. 1978. text ed. 16.25 (ISBN 0-87073-974-3). Schenkman.

Kim, Jai-Hyup. The Garrison State in Prewar Japan & Post-War Korea: A Comparative Analysis of Military Politics. LC 77-26344. 1978. 11.25 (ISBN 0-8191-0416-7). U Pr of Amer.

Kim, Jeong-Hak. The Prehistory of Korea. Pearson, Richard J. & Pearson, Kazue, trs. from Japanese. LC 77-28056. 1979. text ed. 17.50x (ISBN 0-8248-0552-6). U Pr of Hawaii.

Kim, Joungwon A. Divided Korea: The Politics of Development, 1945-1972. LC 74-24936. (East Asian Monographs Ser: No. 59). 330p. 1975. text ed. 15.00x (ISBN 0-674-21287-8). Harvard U Pr.

Kim, Key-Hiuk. The Last Phase of the East Asian World Order: Korea, Japan, & the Chinese Empire, 1860-1882. LC 77-83106. 1980. 24.50x (ISBN 0-520-03556-9). U of Cal Pr.

Lum, Peter. Six Centuries in East Asia: China, Japan & Korea from the 14th Century to 1912. LC 72-12582. (Illus.). 288p. 1973. 10.95 (ISBN 0-87599-183-1). S G Phillips.

McKenzie, Frederick A. Korea's Fight for Freedom. LC 76-111784. Repr. of 1920 ed. 19.45 (ISBN 0-404-04137-X). AMS Pr.

Nahm, Andrew C. & Berton, Peter A. Japanese Penetration of Korea. (Bibliographies Ser.: No. 5). 1959. pap. 5.95 (ISBN 0-8179-2052-8). Hoover Inst Pr.

Nelson, Sarah M. Han River Chulmuntogi: A Study of Early Neolithic Korea. LC 76-2391. (Program in E. A. Studies: No. 9). 1975. pap. 5.00 (ISBN 0-914584-09-X). West Wash Univ.

Song, Minako I. & Matsui, Masato, eds. Japanese Sources on Korea in Hawaii. LC 79-55927. (Occassional Papers Ser.: No. 10). 251p. (Orig.). 1980. pap. 8.00 (ISBN 0-917536-14-2). Ctr Korean U HI at Manoa.

Swartout, Robert R., Jr. Mandarins, Gunboats, & Power Politics: Owen Nickerson Denny & International Rivalries in Korea. LC 79-22242. 1980. text ed. 9.75x (ISBN 0-8248-0681-6). U Pr of Hawaii.

U. S. Congress,(Senate), Committee on Foreign Relations. The United States & the Korean Problem Documents, 1943-1953. LC 72-38089. Repr. of 1953 ed. 10.00 (ISBN 0-404-56962-5). AMS Pr.

Wagner, Edward W. The Literati Purges: Political Conflict in Early Yi Korea. LC 74-21777. (East Asian Monographs: No. 58). 200p. 1975. text ed. 15.00x (ISBN 0-674-53618-5). Harvard U Pr.

Yi Kyu-Tae. Modern Transformation of Korea. (Illus.). 1970. 12.50x (ISBN 0-685-33016-8). Paragon.

KOREA–JUVENILE LITERATURE

Solberg, S. E. The Land & People of Korea. rev. ed. LC 73-602. (Portraits of the Nations Series). (Illus.). 1973. 8.95 (ISBN 0-397-31405-1). Lippincott.

Sterling Publishing Company Editors. Korea in Pictures. LC 68-8767. (Visual Geography Ser). (Illus., Orig.). (gr. 4-12). 1968. pap. 2.95 (ISBN 0-8069-1104-2). Sterling.

KOREA–POLITICS AND GOVERNMENT

Brandt, Vincent S. A Korean Village: Between Farm & Sea. LC 73-162857. (East Asian Ser: No. 65). (Illus.). 224p. 1972. 14.00x (ISBN 0-674-50565-4). Harvard U Pr.

Chong-Sik Lee, ed. & tr. from Korean. Materials on Korean Communism, 1945-1947. LC 77-80003. (Occasional Papers Ser.: No. 7). 268p. 1977. pap. 6.00x (ISBN 0-917536-11-8). Ctr Korean U HI at Manoa.

Chung, Kyung C. Korea: The Third Republic. 1971. 10.95 (ISBN 0-02-525560-6). Macmillan.

Cole, David C., et al. Korean Development: The Interplay of Politics & Economics. LC 75-131468. (Center for International Affairs Ser). (Illus.). 1971. 16.50x (ISBN 0-674-50563-8). Harvard U Pr.

Cultural Policy in the Republic of Korea. (Studies & Documents on Cultural Policies). (Illus.). 1977. pap. 5.00 (ISBN 92-3-101384-X, U130, UNESCO). Unipub.

Han, Sungjoo. The Failure of Democracy in South Korea. LC 73-76100. 1974. 21.50x (ISBN 0-520-02437-0). U of Cal Pr.

Hanson, Eric O. Catholic Politics in China & Korea. LC 79-27206. (Orig.). 1980. pap. 9.95 (ISBN 0-88344-084-9). Orbis Bks.

Hasan, Parvez, et al. Korea: Policy Issues for Long-Term Development. LC 78-21399. 1979. 25.00 (ISBN 0-8018-2228-9); pap. 9.50 (ISBN 0-8018-2229-7). Johns Hopkins.

Henderson, Gregory. Korea: The Politics of the Vortex. LC 68-25611. (Center for International Affairs Ser). (Illus.). 1968. 25.00x (ISBN 0-674-50550-6). Harvard U Pr.

Hwang, In K. The Neutralized Unification of Korea in Perspective. LC 79-19108. 192p. 1980. 16.95x (ISBN 0-87073-827-5); pap. 8.95 (ISBN 0-87073-828-3). Schenkman.

Jones, Leroy & Sakong, Il. Government, Business, & Entrepreneurship in Economic Development: The Korean Case. (East Asian Monographs: No. 91). 1979. 15.00x (ISBN 0-674-35791-4). Harvard U Pr.

Kim, Chong Lim, ed. Political Participation in Korea: Democracy, Mobilization & Stability. (Studies in International & Comparative Politics: No. 15). (Illus.). 238p. 1980. text ed. 28.50 (ISBN 0-87436-296-2). ABC-Clio.

Kim, Chuk Kyo, ed. Industrial & Social Development Issues: Essays on the Korean Economy, Vol.2. 1977. text ed. 12.00x (ISBN 0-8248-0547-X, Korea Development Institute Bk). U Pr of Hawaii.

--Planning Model & Macroeconomic Policy Issues: Essays on the Korean Economy, Vol.1. 1977. text ed. 14.00x (ISBN 0-8248-0546-1, Korea Development Institute Bk). U Pr of Hawaii.

Kim, Se-Jin. Politics of Military Revolution in Korea. LC 71-123101. (Illus.). 1971. 16.50x (ISBN 0-8078-1168-8). U of NC Pr.

Kim, Youn-Soo. Korea & Germany: The Status & Future Prospects of Divided Nations. Bussen, Friedrich, ed. (Monograph of the German Korean-Studies Group: No. I). (Orig.). 1979. pap. text ed. 15.00x (ISBN 0-685-97140-6). Paragon.

Kim Il Sung. For the Independent, Peaceful Reunification of Korea. LC 75-9985. (Orig.). 1975. pap. 3.25 (ISBN 0-7178-0427-5). Intl Pub Co.

Lee, Hahn-Been. Korea: Time, Change & Administration. LC 67-28036. (Illus.). 1968. 12.00x (ISBN 0-8248-0072-9, Eastwest Ctr). U Pr of Hawaii.

Lim, Youngil. Government Policy & Private Enterprise: Korean Experience. (Korea Research Monographs: No. 6). 1981. pap. price not set (ISBN 0-912966-36-X). IEAS Ctr Chinese Stud.

McCormack, Gavan, et al, eds. Korea, North & South: The Deepening Crisis. LC 78-4503. 1980. pap. 5.50 (ISBN 0-85345-531-7, PB5317). Monthly Rev.

Marginalization of Peoples: Racial Oppression in Japan, Political Repression in South Korea, Economic Slavery in Brazil. LC 74-21709. (International Documentation Ser.: No. 65). 1974. pap. 3.95 (ISBN 0-89021-029-2). IDOC.

Oliver, Robert T. Syngman Rhee. LC 72-13864. (Illus.). 380p. 1973. Repr. of 1954 ed. lib. bdg. 18.50x (ISBN 0-8371-6759-0, OLSR). Greenwood.

Palais, James B. Politics & Policy in Traditional Korea, 1864-1876. (East Asian Monographs). 288p. 1976. text ed. 18.00x (ISBN 0-674-19058-0). Harvard U Pr.

Park, Chong Kee. Social Security in Korea: An Approach to Socio-Economic Development. 1975. text ed. 10.00x (ISBN 0-8248-0537-2). U Pr of Hawaii.

Reeve, W. D. The Republic of Korea: A Political & Economic Study. LC 79-9857. 1979. Repr. of 1963 ed. lib. bdg. 18.50x (ISBN 0-313-21265-1, RERK). Greenwood.

Suh, Dae-Sook & Lee, Chae-Jin, eds. Political Leadership in Korea. LC 76-5480. (Publications on Asia of the Institute for Comparative & Foreign Area Studies: No. 27). 276p. 1976. 11.50 (ISBN 0-295-95437-X). U of Wash Pr.

Sunoo, Harold H. America's Dilemma in Asia: The Case of South Korea. LC 78-24029. 224p. 1979. 17.95x (ISBN 0-88229-357-5). Nelson-Hall.

T. K. Letters from South Korea. Sekai Magazine, ed. Swain, David L., tr. from Japanese. LC 76-22836. (International Documentation Ser.: No. 72). 428p. 1976. pap. 7.95 (ISBN 0-89021-040-3). IDOC.

U. S. Department Of State - Office Of Public Affairs. Korea, Nineteen Forty-Five to Nineteen Forty-Eight: A Report on Political Development & Economic Resources with Selected Documents. LC 68-55125. (Illus.). 1968. Repr. of 1948 ed. lib. bdg. 14.00x (ISBN 0-8371-1731-3, KORE). Greenwood.

Wade, L. L. & Kim, B. S. The Economic Development of South Korea: The Political Economy of Success. LC 78-2665. (Praeger Special Studies). 1978. 25.95 (ISBN 0-03-043591-9). Praeger.

Weems, Benjamin. Reform, Rebellion & the Heavenly Way. LC 64-17267. (Association for Asian Studies Monograph: No. 15). 1964. 3.75x (ISBN 0-8165-0144-0). U of Ariz Pr.

Wright, Edward R., ed. Korean Politics in Transition. LC 74-34070. (Illus.). 412p. 1975. 13.50 (ISBN 0-295-95422-1). U of Wash Pr.

KOREA-RELIGION

Blair, William & Hunt, Bruce. The Korean Pentecost & the Sufferings Which Followed. 1977. pap. 2.95 (ISBN 0-85151-244-5). Banner of Truth.

Lee, Jung Y. Korean Shamanistic Rituals. (Religion & Society Ser.). 1979. text ed. 44.50x (ISBN 90-279-3378-2). Mouton.

KOREA-SOCIAL LIFE AND CUSTOMS

Griffis, William E. Corea, the Hermit Nation. rev. ed. 9th ed., enl ed. LC 74-158615. Repr. of 1911 ed. 34.50 (ISBN 0-404-02916-7). AMS Pr.

Harvey, Youngsook K. Six Korean Women: The Socialization of Shamans. (American Ethnological Society Ser). (Illus.). 1979. text ed. 20.95 (ISBN 0-8299-0243-0). West Pub.

Hong, Sawon. Community Development & Human Reproductive Behavior. 196p. 1979. text ed. 10.00x (ISBN 0-8248-0685-9, Korea Devel Inst). U Pr of Hawaii.

Kardoss. An Outline History of Korean Drama. 1966. 2.00 (ISBN 0-913252-01-8). LIU Univ.

Kim, Young-Pyoung. A Strategy for Rural Development: Saemaeul Undong in Korea. 1980. pap. 5.00 (ISBN 0-89249-032-2). Intl Development.

Korea Development Institute. Long-Term Prospect for Economic & Social Development of Korea, 1977-1991. 310p. 1979. pap. text ed. 10.00x (ISBN 0-8248-0641-7, Korea Devel Inst). U Pr of Hawaii.

Lee, Sung Jin. The Value of Children: a Cross-National Study: Korea, Vol. 7. LC 75-8934. 1979. pap. text ed. 3.00x (ISBN 0-8248-0388-4, Eastwest Ctr). U Pr of Hawaii.

Mason, Edward S. The Economic & Social Modernization of the Republic of Korea. (Harvard East Asian Monographs: Vol. 92). 500p. 1980. 20.00x (ISBN 0-674-23175-9). Harvard U Pr.

Michaud, Roland & Michaud, Sabrina. Korea. Alens, Gregory, tr. from Fr. (Illus.). 144p. 1981. 45.00 (ISBN 0-86565-020-9). Vendome.

Osgood, C. The Koreans & Their Culture. 387p. 1951. 24.95 (ISBN 0-471-06943-4, Pub. by Wiley-Interscience). Wiley.

T. K. Letters from South Korea. Sekai Magazine, ed. Swain, David L., tr. from Japanese. LC 76-22836. (International Documentation Ser.: No. 72). 428p. 1976. pap. 7.95 (ISBN 0-89021-040-3). IDOC.

Traditional Performing Arts of Korea. (Illus.). 1978. pap. 13.75 (ISBN 0-685-86541-X, UNESCO). Unipub.

Yoon, Hong-Key. Geomantic Relationship Between Culture & Nature in Korea. (Asian Folklore & Social Life Monographs: Vol. 88). 7.50 (ISBN 0-89986-297-7). E Langstaff.

KOREA (DEMOCRATIC PEOPLE'S REPUBLIC)

Barnds, William J., ed. The Two Koreas in East Asian Affairs. LC 75-27379. 216p. 1976. 15.00x (ISBN 0-8147-0988-5). NYU Pr.

Brun, Ellen & Hersh, Jacques. Socialist Korea: A Case Study in the Strategy of Economic Development. LC 76-1651. (Illus.). 1977. 16.50 (ISBN 0-85345-386-1, CL-386-1). Monthly Rev.

Ginsburgs, George. Calendar of Diplomatic Affairs, Democratic People's Republic of Korea. Kim, Roy U., ed. LC 77-71677. 1978. lib. bdg. 25.00 (ISBN 0-379-20354-5). Oceana.

Kim, Ilpyong J. Communist Politics in North Korea. LC 72-92887. (Special Studies). 130p. 1975. text ed. 24.95 (ISBN 0-275-09190-2). Praeger.

Kim Il Sung. Revolution & Socialist Construction in Korea: Selected Writings of Kim Il Sung. LC 75-152910. 1971. 7.50 (ISBN 0-7178-0324-4); pap. 2.95 (ISBN 0-7178-0325-2). Intl Pub Co.

Kiyosaki, Wayne S. North Korea's Foreign Relations: The Politics of Accomodation, 1945-75. LC 76-19548. (Special Studies). 1976. 24.95 (ISBN 0-275-23490-8). Praeger.

Nam, Koon Woo. The North Korean Communist Leadership, 1945-1965: A Study of Factionalism & Political Consolidation. LC 73-13433. 224p. 1974. 15.50x (ISBN 0-8173-4723-2). U of Ala Pr.

Paige, Glenn D. Korean People's Democratic Republic. LC 65-27783. (Studies Ser.: No. 11). 1966. pap. 4.95 (ISBN 0-8179-3112-0). Hoover Inst Pr.

KOREAN ART

see Art, Korean

KOREAN LANGUAGE

Basic Korean Course, Vol. 1. 553p. 1980. plus 18 audio-cassettes 145.00x (ISBN 0-88432-047-2, Q800). J Norton Pubs.

Chin-W Kim, ed. Papers in Korean Linguistics. 1979. pap. text ed. 6.75 (ISBN 0-685-96323-3). Hornbeam Pr.

Eun, Lee & Blyth, R. H. First Book of Korean. 1962. pap. 9.95 (ISBN 0-89346-026-5, Pub. by Hokuseido Pr). Heian Intl.

Foreign Service Institute. Basic Korean Course, Vol. 2. 560p. 1980. plus 16 audio-cassettes 135.00x (ISBN 0-88432-048-0, Q850). J Norton Pubs.

Grant, Bruce K. A Guide to Korean Characters: Reading & Writing Hangul & Hanja. 400p. 1979. 18.50 (ISBN 0-930878-13-2). Hollym Intl.

Martin, Samuel E. Korean in a Hurry: A Quick Approach to Spoken Korean. LC 60-8363. 1954. pap. 3.50 (ISBN 0-8048-0349-8). C E Tuttle.

Martin, Samuel E. & Lee, Young-Sook C. Beginning Korean. LC 69-15452. (Linguistic Ser.). 1969. pap. text ed. 17.50x (ISBN 0-300-00285-8). Yale U Pr.

Martin, Samuel E., et al. Korean-English Dictionary. (Linguistic Ser.). 1967. text ed. 75.00x (ISBN 0-300-00753-1). Yale U Pr.

Park, B. Nam & Kay, Chunghwa T. FSI Korean Basic Course, Units 1-18. 1975. pap. text ed. 15.00x (ISBN 0-686-10747-0); 18 cassettes 108.00x (ISBN 0-686-10748-9). Intl Learn Syst.

--FSI Korean Basic Course, Units 19-47. 1975. pap. text ed. 5.80x (ISBN 0-686-10749-7); 16 cassettes 96.00x (ISBN 0-686-10750-0). Intl Learn Syst.

Pong, K. Lee & Chi, Sik R. Let's Talk in Korean. LC 78-72953. 1978. 4.50 (ISBN 0-930878-10-8). Hollym Intl.

Ramstedt, G. J. A Korean Grammar. 1979. Repr. of 1939 ed. text ed. 22.00x (ISBN 0-391-00954-0). Humanities.

Rockwell, Coralie. Kagok: A Traditional Korean Vocal Form. LC 72-87568. (D (Monographs), No. 3). (Illus.). 312p. (Orig.). 1972. pap. text ed. 7.50x (ISBN 0-913360-05-8). Asian Music Pub.

Shin Jo Joo Hwang. Korean Clause Structure. (Publications in Linguistics & Related Fields Ser: No. 50). 1976. pap. 4.50x (ISBN 0-88312-060-7); microfiche 1.00 (ISBN 0-686-67551-7). Summer Inst Ling.

Sohn, Ho-Min, ed. The Korean Language: Its Structure & Social Projection. LC 76-355151. (Occasional Papers Ser: No.6). 126p. 1975. pap. 4.50x (ISBN 0-917536-04-5). Ctr Korean U HI at Manoa.

Thorlin, Eldora & Henthorn, Taesoon. Everyday Korean. LC 71-183519. 180p. 1972. 3.95 (ISBN 0-8348-0069-1). Weatherhill.

KOREAN LANGUAGE-READERS

Chang, Choo-Un. An Intermediate Korean Reader. (Korean & Eng.). 4.25 (ISBN 0-686-09939-7). Far Eastern Pubns.

Chang, Sung-Un. Korean Newspaper Readings. 4.25 (ISBN 0-686-09938-9). Far Eastern Pubns.

Chang, Sung-Un & Martin, Samuel E. Readings in Contemporary Korean. 2.75 (ISBN 0-686-09941-9). Far Eastern Pubns.

KOREAN LITERATURE (COLLECTIONS)

In-Sob, Zong, ed. & tr. Folk Tales from Korea. LC 53-12953. 1979. 6.95 (ISBN 0-394-17096-2, E738, Ever). Grove.

Lee, Peter H., ed. Anthology of Korean Literature: From Early Times to the Nineteenth Century. 448p. 1981. 24.00x (ISBN 0-8248-0739-1); pap. 12.00x (ISBN 0-8248-0756-1). U Pr of Hawaii.

KOREAN LITERATURE-BIBLIOGRAPHY

Courant, Maurice A. Bibliographie Coreenne, Tableau Litteraire De la Coree, 4 vols in 3. (Incl. suppl). Repr. of 1894 ed. Set. 177.00 (ISBN 0-8337-0692-6). B Franklin.

KOREAN LITERATURE-HISTORY AND CRITICISM

Kim, Han-Kyo, ed. Studies on Korea: A Scholar's Guide. LC 79-26491. 576p. 1980. text ed. 25.00x (ISBN 0-8248-0673-5). U Pr of Hawaii.

Lee, Peter H. Songs of Flying Dragons. LC 73-92866. (Harvard-Yenching Institute Monographs Ser: No. 22). 352p. 1975. text ed. 16.95x (ISBN 0-674-82075-4). Harvard U Pr.

Lee, Peter H., ed. Anthology of Korean Literature: From Early Times to the Nineteenth Century. 448p. 1981. lib. bdg. 24.00x (ISBN 0-8248-0739-1); pap. text ed. 12.00x (ISBN 0-8248-0756-1). U Pr of Hawaii.

KOREAN PAINTING

see Painting, Korean

KOREAN POETRY-TRANSLATIONS INTO ENGLISH

Barkan, Stanley H., compiled by. South Korean Poets of Resistance. Ko Won, tr. LC 79-90037. (Cross-Cultural Review Ser.: No. 4). (Illus., Korean-Eng.). 1980. 10.00x (ISBN 0-89304-606-X, CCC124); pap. 4.00x (ISBN 0-89304-607-8). Cross Cult.

Grigsby, Joan S. Orchid Door: Ancient Korean Poems. 1970. 7.00 (ISBN 0-8188-0009-7). Paragon.

Ko Won, tr. from Korean. Contemporary Korean Poetry. LC 74-113487. (Iowa Translations Ser). 1970. 6.95 (ISBN 0-87745-002-1). U of Iowa Pr.

Lee, Peter H., ed. & tr. from Korean. Poems from Korea: A Historical Anthology. rev. ed. LC 73-80209. 196p. 1974. 8.50x (ISBN 0-8248-0263-2, Eastwest Ctr). U Pr of Hawaii.

Lee, Peter H., ed. The Silence of Love: Twentieth-Century Korean Poetry. LC 80-21999. 368p. 1980. text ed. 17.95x (ISBN 0-8248-0711-1); pap. 8.95 (ISBN 0-8248-0732-4). U Pr of Hawaii.

KOREAN POTTERY

see Pottery, Korean

KOREAN REUNIFICATION QUESTION (1945-)

Barnds, William J., ed. The Two Koreas in East Asian Affairs. LC 75-27379. 216p. 1976. 15.00x (ISBN 0-8147-0988-5). NYU Pr.

KOREAN TALES

see Tales, Korean

KOREAN WAR, 1950-1953

see also Chongchongang, Battle of, 1950

Acheson, Dean. Korean War. 1971. pap. text ed. 2.95x (ISBN 0-393-09978-4). Norton.

--Korean War. 1971. pap. text ed. 2.95x (ISBN 0-393-09978-4). Norton.

Caridi, Ronald J. Korean War & American Politics: The Republican Party As a Case History. LC 68-9738. 1969. 12.00 (ISBN 0-8122-7581-0). U of Pa Pr.

Cheng, Peter P. C. Truce Negotiations Over Korea & Quemoy. 1977. pap. text ed. 8.75 (ISBN 0-8191-0290-3). U Pr of Amer.

Clark, Mark W. From the Danube to the Yalu. LC 72-12495. (Illus.). 369p. 1973. Repr. of 1954 ed. lib. bdg. 23.00x (ISBN 0-8371-6742-6, CLDY). Greenwood.

Cumings, Bruce. The Origins of the Korean War: Liberation & the Emergence of Separate Regimes, 1945-1947. LC 80-8543. (Illus.). 552p. 1981. 40.00x (ISBN 0-691-09383-0); pap. 14.50x (ISBN 0-686-77439-6). Princeton U Pr.

Fehrenbach, T. R. Crossroads in Korea. (gr. 9-12). 1968. 8.95 (ISBN 0-02-734380-4). Macmillan.

Fincher, E. B. The War in Korea. (First Bks.). (Illus.). 72p. (gr. 4 up). 1981. lib. bdg. 7.40 (ISBN 0-531-04330-4). Watts.

Geneva - Conference - 1954. Nineteen Fifty-Four Geneva Conference Indo-China & Korea. LC 68-57791. Repr. of 1954 ed. lib. bdg. 20.50x (ISBN 0-8371-0652-4, GECO). Greenwood.

George, Alexander L. The Chinese Communist Army in Action: The Korean War & Its Aftermath. LC 67-12659. 1967. 20.00x (ISBN 0-231-03020-7); pap. 7.50x (ISBN 0-231-08595-8). Columbia U Pr.

Goodrich, Leland M. Korea: A Study of U. S. Policy in the United Nations. LC 78-24120. 1979. Repr. of 1956 ed. lib. bdg. 18.75x (ISBN 0-313-20825-5, GOKO). Greenwood.

Hammel, Eric. Chosin: Heroic Ordeal of the Korean War. 512p. 1981. 22.50 (ISBN 0-8149-0856-X). Vanguard.

Harris, W. W. Puerto Rico's Fighting Sixty-Fifth U. S. Infantry: From San Juan to Chorwan. LC 79-26889. (Illus.). 1980. 12.95 (ISBN 0-89141-056-2). Presidio Pr.

Heller, Francis H., ed. The Korean War: A 25-Year Perspective. LC 77-4003. (Illus.). 1977. 13.00x (ISBN 0-7006-0157-0). Regents Pr KS.

Kirkendall, Richard S. Harry S. Truman: A Decision to Intervene. LC 75-37090. (The Forum Ser.). (Illus.). 1975. pap. text ed. 1.60x (ISBN 0-88273-071-1). Forum Pr MO.

Kurland, Gerald. The Korean War. (Events of Our Times Ser.: No. 13). 32p. lib. bdg. 2.95 incl. catalog cards (ISBN 0-686-07222-7); pap. 1.50 vinyl laminated covers (ISBN 0-686-07223-5). SamHar Pr.

Lyons, Gene M. Military Policy & Economic Aid: The Korean Case, 1950-1953. LC 61-7301. 1961. 4.50 (ISBN 0-8142-0088-5). Ohio St U Pr.

O'Ballance, Edgar. Korea: Nineteen Fifty to Nineteen Fifty-Three. 1969. 15.00 (ISBN 0-208-00831-4, Archon). Shoe String.

Ridgway, Matthew B., General, U.S. Army, Retired. Korean War. LC 67-11172. 1967. 8.95 (ISBN 0-385-03507-1). Doubleday.

Riley, John W., Jr. & Schramm, Wilbur. The Reds Take a City: The Communist Occupation of Seoul, with Eyewitness Accounts. Cynn, Hugh H., tr. LC 72-12118. (Illus.). 210p. 1973. Repr. lib. bdg. 15.00x (ISBN 0-8371-6711-6, RIRT). Greenwood.

Rothschild, Eric, ed. The Korean War, Civil Rights, & Sputnik: 1950-1959. (New York Times School Microfilm Collection Ser.: Guide No. 9). 70p. (gr. 7-12). 1978. pap. 5.50 wkbk (ISBN 0-667-00558-7). Microfilming Corp.
Simmons, Robert R. The Strained Alliance: Peking, P'yongyang, Moscow & the Politics of the Korean Civil War. LC 74-4891. 1975. 10.95 (ISBN 0-02-928880-0). Free Pr.
Spanier, John W. Truman-MacArthur Controversy & the Korean War. 1965. pap. 4.95 (ISBN 0-393-00279-9, Norton Lib). Norton.
Stairs, Denis. The Diplomacy of Constraint: Canada, the Korean War, & the United States. LC 72-95814. 1974. 20.00x (ISBN 0-8020-5282-7). U of Toronto Pr.
Stone, I. F. Hidden History of the Korean War. rev. ed. LC 79-81788. 1969. pap. 6.50 (ISBN 0-85345-161-3, PB-1613). Monthly Rev.
Traverso, E. Korea & the Limits of Limited War. Brown, Richard H. & Halsey, Van R., eds. (Amherst Ser.). (gr. 9-12). 1970. pap. text ed. 4.52 (ISBN 0-201-07582-2, Sch Div); tchrs' manual 1.92 (ISBN 0-201-07584-9). A-W.
Vatcher, William H., Jr. Panmunjom: The Story of the Korean Military Armistice Negotiations. LC 72-14001. (Illus.). 322p. 1973. Repr. of 1958 ed. lib. bdg. 16.50x (ISBN 0-8371-6743-4, VAPA). Greenwood.
--Panmunjom: The Story of the Korean Military Armistice Negotiations. LC 72-14001. (Illus.). 322p. 1973. Repr. of 1958 ed. lib. bdg. 16.50x (ISBN 0-8371-6743-4, VAPA). Greenwood.
Whiting, Allen S. China Crosses the Yalu: The Decision to Enter the Korean War. LC 68-13744. 1960. 12.50x (ISBN 0-8047-0627-1); pap. 3.95 (ISBN 0-8047-0629-8, SP86). Stanford U Pr.

KOREAN WAR, 1950-1953–AERIAL OPERATIONS
Allward, Maurice. F-Eighty Six Sabre. (Illus.). 1978. 9.95 (ISBN 0-684-15883-3, ScribT). Scribner.
Stewart, James T. & Gilbert, James, eds. Airpower: The Decisive Force in Korea. LC 79-7298. (Flight: Its First Seventy-Five Years Ser.). (Illus.). 1979. Repr. of 1957 ed. lib. bdg. 28.00x (ISBN 0-405-12204-7). Arno.

KOREAN WAR, 1950-1953–CAMPAIGNS
Heinl, Robert D., Jr. Victory at High Tide: The Inchon-Seoul Campaign. LC 79-90111. (Illus.). 307p. 1979. Repr. of 1968 ed. 17.95 (ISBN 0-933852-03-7). Nautical & Aviation.
Langley, Michael. Inchon Landing: MacArthur's Last Triumph. LC 78-20688. 1979. 10.00 (ISBN 0-8129-0821-X). Times Bks.
--Inchon: Macarthur's Last Triumph. 1979. 24.00 (ISBN 0-7134-3346-9, Pub. by Batsford England). David & Charles.

KOREAN WAR, 1950-1953–FICTION
Franklin, Edward. It's Cold in Pongo-Ni. LC 65-17368. 1965. 6.95 (ISBN 0-8149-0100-X). Vanguard.
Michener, James A. Bridges at Toko-Ri. (gr. 10 up). 1953. 12.95 (ISBN 0-394-41780-1). Random.

KOREAN WAR, 1950-1953–NAVAL OPERATIONS
Cagle, Malcolm W. & Manson, Frank A. The Sea War in Korea. LC 79-6104. (Navies & Men Ser.). (Illus.). 1980. Repr. of 1957 ed. lib. bdg. 50.00x (ISBN 0-405-13033-3). Arno.
Langley, Michael. Inchon Landing: MacArthur's Last Triumph. LC 78-20688. 1979. 10.00 (ISBN 0-8129-0821-X). Times Bks.

KOREAN WAR, 1950-1953–PERSONAL NARRATIVES, AMERICAN
Goodman, Allen E., ed. Negotiating While Fighting: The Diary of Admiral C. Turner Joy at the Korean Armistice Conference. LC 77-77565. (Publication Ser No. 175). (Illus.). 1978. 22.50 (ISBN 0-8179-6751-6). Hoover Inst Pr.
Griffin, Bobby. The Search. pap. 1.75 (ISBN 0-686-12739-0). Grace Pub Co.
Russ, Martin. The Last Parallel. LC 73-438. (Illus.). 333p. 1973. Repr. of 1957 ed. lib. bdg. 17.75x (ISBN 0-8371-6770-1, RULP). Greenwood.

KOREAN WAR, 1950-1953–PRISONERS AND PRISONS
Bradbury, William C. Mass Behavior in Battle & Captivity: The Communist Soldier in the Korean War. Meyers, Samuel M. & Biderman, Albert D., eds. LC 68-16705. 1968. 15.00x (ISBN 0-226-06996-6). U of Chicago Pr.
Dean, William F. General Dean's Story. LC 72-12310. (Illus.). 305p. 1973. Repr. of 1954 ed. lib. bdg. 18.00x (ISBN 0-8371-6690-X, DEDS). Greenwood.
Weintraub, Stanley. War in the Wards. LC 76-51509. (Illus.). 1977. 8.95 (ISBN 0-89141-012-0). Presidio Pr.
White, William L. The Captives of Korea: An Unofficial White Paper on the Treatment of War Prisoners; Our Treatment of Theirs: Their Treatment of Ours. LC 78-14347. 1979. Repr. of 1957 ed. lib. bdg. 23.50x (ISBN 0-313-20631-7, WHCK). Greenwood.

KOREAN WAR, 1950-1953–REGIMENTAL HISTORIES
Marshall, Samuel L. River & the Gauntlet: Defeat of the Eighth Army by the Chinese Communist Forces, November 1950. Repr. of 1953 ed. lib. bdg. 21.25x (ISBN 0-8371-3011-5, MARG). Greenwood.
U. S. Marine Corps. U. S. Marine Operations in Korea, 4 Vols. 1968. Repr. Set. 98.00 (ISBN 0-403-03719-0); 25.00 ea. Scholarly.

KOREANS IN FOREIGN COUNTRIES
Choy, Bong-Yong. Koreans in America. LC 79-9791. 1979. 19.95x (ISBN 0-88229-352-4). Nelson-Hall.
Givens, Helen L. The Korean Community in Los Angeles: Thesis. LC 74-76511. 1974. soft bdg. 7.00 (ISBN 0-88247-253-4). R & E Res Assoc.
Hurh, Won M. Comparative Study of Korean Immigrants in the United States: A Typological Approach. LC 76-55959. 1977. soft bdg. 8.00 (ISBN 0-88247-439-1). R & E Res Assoc.
Hurh, Won M. & Kim, Hei C. Assimilation Patterns of Immigrants in the United States: A Case Study of Korean Immigrants in the Chicago Area. LC 78-59860. (Illus.). 1978. pap. text ed. 7.75 (ISBN 0-8191-0553-8). U Pr of Amer.
Hyung-Chan Kim. The Koreans in America. LC 77-73741. (In America Bks). (Illus.). (gr. 5 up). 1977. PLB 6.95g (ISBN 0-8225-0230-5). Lerner Pubns.
Kim, Hyung-Chan. The Koreans in America. LC 74-13732. (Ethnic Chronology Ser.). 160p. (gr. 9-12). 1974. text ed. 8.50 (ISBN 0-379-00513-1). Oceana.
Kim, Hyung-chan, ed. The Korean Diaspora: Historical & Sociological Studies of Korean Immigration & Assimilation in North America. LC 77-7080. (Illus.). 268p. 1977. text ed. 31.50 (ISBN 0-87436-250-4). ABC-Clio.
Kim, Illsoo. New Urban Immigrants: The Korean Community in New York. LC 80-8556. 352p. 1981. 26.50x (ISBN 0-691-09355-5). Princeton U Pr.
Kim, Sangho J. A Study of the Korean Church & Her People in Chicago, Illinois. LC 75-18129. 1975. soft bdg. 8.00 (ISBN 0-88247-357-3). R & E Res Assoc.
Lee, Changsoo & DeVos, George. Koreans in Japan: Ethnic Conflict & Accommodation. LC 80-6053. (Illus.). 448p. 1981. 30.00x (ISBN 0-520-04258-1). U of Cal Pr.
Lee, Don C. Acculturation of Korean Residents in Georgia. LC 75-18126. 1975. soft bdg. 8.00 (ISBN 0-88247-360-3). R & E Res Assoc.
Melendy, H. Brett. Asians in America: Filipinos, Koreans, & East Indians. (Immigrant Heritage of America Ser.). 1977. lib. bdg. 10.95 (ISBN 0-8057-8414-4). Twayne.
Mitchell, Richard H. The Korean Minority in Japan. (Center for Japanese & Korean Studies, UC Berkeley). 1967. 21.50x (ISBN 0-520-00870-7). U of Cal Pr.
Skim, Steve S. Korean Immigrant Churches Today in Southern California. LC 76-24724. 1977. soft bdg. 9.00 (ISBN 0-88247-426-X). R & E Res Assoc.

KORINA
see Limba

KOSCIUSZKO, ANDRZEJ BONAWENTURA, 1746-1817
Haiman, Miecislaus. Kosciuszko in the American Revolution. LC 72-10782. (Library of Polish Studies: Vol. 4). 1975. Repr. of 1943 ed. text ed. 7.50 (ISBN 0-917004-09-4). Kosciuszko.
--Kosciuszko: Leader & Exile. LC 76-17926. (Library of Polish Studies: Vol. V). (Illus.). 1977. Repr. text ed. 7.50 (ISBN 0-917004-10-8). Kosciuszko.
Johns, Joseph P. Kosciuszko. (Illus.). 1965. 3.00 (ISBN 0-685-09285-2). Endurance.
Kopczewski, Jan S. Kosciuszko & Pulaski. (Illus.). 1976. 40.00x (ISBN 0-8002-1637-7). Intl Pubns Serv.

KOSHER FOOD
see Jews–Dietary Laws

KOSSUTH, LAJOS, 1802-1894
Deak, Istvan. The Lawful Revolution: Louis Kossuth & the Hungarians, 1848-1849. LC 78-22063. Orig. Title: Reluctant Rebels. (Illus.). 416p. 1979. 20.00x (ISBN 0-231-04602-2). Columbia U Pr.
Garrison, William L., et al. Letter to Louis Kossuth, Concerning Freedom & Slavery in the United States in Behalf of the American Anti-Slavery Society. LC 76-82204. (Anti-Slavery Crusade in America Ser). 1969. Repr. of 1852 ed. 9.00 (ISBN 0-405-00630-6). Arno.
Headley, Phineas C. The Life of Louis Kossuth, Governor of Hungary. facsimile ed. LC 78-154152. (Select Bibliographies Reprint Ser). Repr. of 1852 ed. 23.00 (ISBN 0-8369-5768-7). Arno.
Pulszky, Ferencz A. White, Red, Black, 2 Vols. in One. LC 72-107853. 1971. Repr. of 1853 ed. 43.00 (ISBN 0-384-48250-3). Johnson Repr.
Pulszky, Ferencz A. & Pulszky, Terezia W. White, Red, Black, Sketches of Society in the United States During the Visit of Their Guest, 3 Vols. LC 68-58066. Repr. of 1853 ed. Set. 33.00x (ISBN 0-8371-0627-3). Greenwood.
Zarek, Otto. Kossuth. Hudson, Lynton, tr. LC 78-112823. 1970. Repr. of 1937 ed. 12.50 (ISBN 0-8046-1090-8). Kennikat.

KOTA LANGUAGE
see also Tamil Language

KOTOKO LANGUAGE
Lebeuf, Jean P. Etudes Kotoko. (Cahiers De L'homme Nouvelle Ser: No. 16). 107p. 1976. pap. text ed. 17.25x (ISBN 90-2797-932-4). Mouton.

KOTURK INSCRIPTIONS
see Inscriptions, Turkish (Old)

KOUSSEVITZKY, SERGEI ALEKSANDROVICH, 1874-1951
Leichtentritt, Hugo. Serge Koussevitsky, the Boston Symphony Orchestra & the New American Music. LC 75-41172. Repr. of 1946 ed. 16.45 (ISBN 0-404-14680-5). AMS Pr.
Lourie, Arthur. Sergei Koussevitsky & His Epoch. LC 78-121287. Repr. of 1931 ed. 17.50 (ISBN 0-404-04036-5). AMS Pr.
--Sergei Koussevitzky & His Epoch. Pring, S. W., tr. LC 78-94276. (Select Bibliographies Reprint Ser). 1931. 22.00 (ISBN 0-8369-5050-X). Arno.

KOVALY, HEDA
Kovaly, Heda & Kohak, Erazim. The Victors & the Vanquished. 320p. 1973. 8.95 (ISBN 0-8180-1603-5). Horizon.

KOZLOV, IVAN ANDREYEVICH, 1888-1957
Barratt, Glynn. Ivan Kozlov: A Study & a Setting. LC 72-78019. 1972. 18.00 (ISBN 0-88866-516-4). Samuel Stevens.

KPELLE
Bellman, Beryl L. Village of Curers & Assassins: On the Production of Fala Kpelle Cosmological Categories. LC 73-76893. (Approaches to Semiotics: No. 39). 196p. 1975. text ed. 44.10x (ISBN 90-2793-042-2). Mouton.
Bledsoe, Caroline H. Women & Marriage in Kpelle Society. LC 78-66170. (Illus.). 233p. 1980. 16.50x (ISBN 0-8047-1019-8). Stanford U Pr.
Gay, John. Mathematics & Logic in the Kpelle Language & a First Course in Kpelle. 1971. 10.00x (ISBN 0-8002-1711-X). Intl Pubns Serv.

KRAMER, REUBEN, 1909-
Kramer, Reuben. Art of Reuben Kramer. Low, Theodore L., ed. (Illus.). 1963. bds. 10.00 (ISBN 0-685-21822-8). Walters Art.

KRAUS, KARL, 1874-1936
Grimstad, Kari. Masks of the Prophet: The Theatrical World of Karl Kraus. 280p. 1981. 20.00x (ISBN 0-8020-5522-2). U of Toronto Pr.
Iggers, Wilma A. Karl Kraus: A Viennese Critic of the Twentieth Century. 1967. 12.50x (ISBN 0-685-59659-1). M S Rosenberg.
Szasz, Thomas. Karl Kraus & the Soul-Doctors: A Pioneer Critic & His Criticism of Psychiatry & Psychoanalysis. LC 76-17004. 1976. 12.50x (ISBN 0-8071-0196-6). La State U Pr.
Zohn, Harry. Karl Kraus. LC 71-120020. 1980. Repr. 10.95 (ISBN 0-8044-2990-1). Ungar.

KRAUTH, CHARLES PORTERFIELD, 1823-1883
Spaeth, Adolph. Charles Porterfield Krauth. LC 78-83440. (Religion in America, Ser. 1). 1969. Repr. of 1898 ed. 37.00 (ISBN 0-405-00265-3). Arno.

KREISLER, FRITZ, 1875-1962
Lochner, Louis P. Fritz Kreisler. LC 76-181203. 1951. Repr. 40.00 (ISBN 0-403-01613-4). Scholarly.

KRETZER, MAX, 1854-1941
Keil, Gunther. Max Kretzer: A Study in German Nationalism. LC 54-171550. Repr. of 1928 ed. 14.00 (ISBN 0-404-50433-7). AMS Pr.

KRIEGSSPIEL
see War Games

KRISHNA
Banerjee, Priyatosh. The Life of Krishna in Indian Art. LC 79-905410. (Illus.). 384p. 1978. 57.50x (ISBN 0-8002-2317-9). Intl Pubns Serv.
Bhaktivedanta, Swami A. C. Krsna: The Supreme Personality of Godhead, 3 vols. LC 74-118081. (Illus.). 1970. Set. pap. 6.95 (ISBN 0-912776-30-7); pap. 2.95 ea.; Vol. 1. pap. (ISBN 0-912776-31-5); Vol. 2. pap. (ISBN 0-912776-32-3); Vol. 3. pap. (ISBN 0-912776-33-1). Bhaktivedanta.
--Krsna: The Supreme Personality of Godhead, 3 vols. LC 74-118081. (Illus.). 1970. Set. 24.95 (ISBN 0-912776-60-9); 9.95 ea. Vol. 1 (ISBN 0-912776-57-9). Vol. 2 (ISBN 0-912776-58-7). Vol. 3 (ISBN 0-912776-59-5). Bhaktivedanta.
Bhaktivendanta, Swami A. C. Srimad Bhagavatam: Ninth Canto, 3 vols. LC 73-169353. (Illus., Sanskrit & Eng.). 1977. 9.95 ea. Vol. 1 (ISBN 0-912776-94-3). Vol. 2 (ISBN 0-912776-95-1). Vol. 3 (ISBN 0-912776-96-X). Bhaktivedanta.
Choudhary, Bani R. The Story of Krishna. (Illus.). (gr. 3-10). 1979. 6.00 (ISBN 0-89744-134-6). Auromere.
Daner, F. J. The American Children of Krsna: Case Studies in Cultural Anthrology. LC 75-15616. 1976. pap. text ed. 4.95 (ISBN 0-03-013546-X, HoltC). HR&W.
Dasi, Krsnastuta. Agha the Terrible Demon. LC 77-10612. (gr. 1-4). 1977. PLB 5.95 (ISBN 0-89213-007-5). Bala Bks.
Frith, Nigel. The Legend of Krishna. LC 75-35449. 1976. 7.95 (ISBN 0-8052-3611-2). Schocken.
Goswami, Satsvarupa D. A Handbook for Krishna Consciousness. LC 79-97. 1979. pap. 6.95 (ISBN 0-89647-008-3). Bala Bks.
Greene, Joshua, retold by. Krishna, Master of All Mystics. (Illus.). 16p. (gr. 1-4). 1981. pap. 2.95 (ISBN 0-89647-010-5). Bala Bks.
Hawley, John S. At Play with Krishna: Pilgrimage Dramas from Brindavan. LC 80-8552. (Illus.). 400p. 1981. 27.50x (ISBN 0-691-06470-9). Princeton U Pr.
Hiltebeitel, Alf. The Ritual of Battle: Krishna in the Mahabharata. LC 75-18496. 1975. 27.50x (ISBN 0-8014-0970-5). Cornell U Pr.
Hutchins, Francis G. Young Krishna. LC 80-66834. (Illus.). 1980. 29.50 (ISBN 0-935100-01-6). Amarta Pr.
Kinsby, David R. The Divine Player: A Study of Krishna Lila. 1979. 20.00x (ISBN 0-89684-019-0). South Asia Bks.
Kinsley, David R. The Sword & the Flute - Kali & Krsna: Dark Visions of the Terrible & the Sublime in Hindu Mythology. LC 73-91669. 175p. 1975. 20.00x (ISBN 0-520-02675-6); pap. 2.95 (ISBN 0-520-03510-0). U of Cal Pr.
Pal, P. Krishna: The Cowherd King. LC 70-185825. 1972. pap. 4.95 (ISBN 0-87587-048-1). LA Co Art Mus.
Poddar, Hanumanprasad. Gopis' Love for Sri Krishna. (Illus.). 51p. 1981. pap. 9.95 (ISBN 0-913922-51-X). Dawn Horse Pr.
Prabhavananda, Swami. Srimad Bhagavatam: The Wisdom of God. 1978. Repr. of 1943 ed. 5.95 (ISBN 0-87481-483-9). Vedanta Pr.
Saradananda, Swami. Sri Ramakrishna: The Great Master, Part I. new, rev. ed. Swami Jagadananda, tr. (Illus.). 563p. pap. 8.50x (ISBN 0-87481-495-2). Vedanta Pr.
Satsvarupa dasa Goswami. A Lifetime in Preparation: Srila Prabhupada-lilamrta, Vol. 1. (Illus.). 357p. 1980. 9.95 (ISBN 0-686-71685-X). Bhaktivedanta.
--Planting the Seed. (Srila Prabhupada Lilamrta Ser.: Vol. II). (Illus.). 331p. 1980. 9.95 (ISBN 0-89213-106-3). Bhaktivedanta.
Singer, Milton, ed. Krishna: Myths, Rites, & Attitudes. LC 65-20585. 1969. pap. 5.95 (ISBN 0-226-76101-0, P329, Phoen). U of Chicago Pr.
Singer, Milton B., ed. Krishna: Myths, Rites, & Attitudes. LC 80-29194. xvii, 277p. 1981. Repr. of 1966 ed. lib. bdg. 27.50x (ISBN 0-313-22822-1, SIKR). Greenwood.
Singh, Bhagat. The Story of Krishna. (Illus.). 20p. (Orig.). (ps-5). 1976. pap. 1.25 (ISBN 0-89744-135-4, Pub. by Hemkunt India). Auromere.
Swami, Shri P., tr. The Geeta. 96p. (Orig.). 1965. pap. 4.95 (ISBN 0-571-06157-5, Pub. by Faber & Faber). Merrimack Bk Serv.
Wilson, Frances, ed. & tr. The Love of Krishna: The Krsnakarnamrta of Lilasuka Bilvamangala. LC 74-153426. (Haney Foundation Ser.). 448p. 1975. 20.00x (ISBN 0-8122-7655-8). U of Pa Pr.

KRISHNA IN ART, LITERATURE, ETC.
Dimock, Edward C., Jr. & Levertov, Denise, trs. In Praise of Krishna: Songs from the Bengali. (Illus.). xii, 96p. 4.50 (ISBN 0-226-15231-6, Phoen). U of Chicago Pr.
Lewis, Samuel L. The Rejected Avatar. (Illus.). 24p. (Orig.). 1968. pap. 1.25 saddlestitched (ISBN 0-915424-00-2, Prophecy Pressworks). Sufi Islamia-Prophecy.
White, Charles S., ed. The Caurasi Pad of Sri Hit Harivams: Introduction, Translation, Notes, & Edited Hindi Text. LC 76-54207. (Asian Studies at Hawaii Ser: No. 16). 1977. pap. text ed. 9.50x (ISBN 0-8248-0359-0). U Pr of Hawaii.

KRISHNAMURTI, JIDDU, 1895-
Fouere, Rene. Krishnamurti: The Man & His Teaching. 1974. lib. bdg. 69.95 (ISBN 0-8490-0477-2). Gordon Pr.
Krishnamurti, J. Early Writings of Krishnamurti, 2 vols. 1974. lib. bdg. 250.00 (ISBN 0-87968-533-6). Krishna Pr.
Mehta, Rohit. The Nameless Experience: A Comprehensive Discussion of J. Krishnamurti's Approach to Life. 2nd ed. 1977. text ed. 16.50x (ISBN 0-8426-0928-8). Verry.
Methorst-Kuiper, A. J. Krishnamurti: A Biography. 1974. lib. bdg. 69.95 (ISBN 0-87968-545-X). Krishna Pr.
Shringy, R. K. Philosophy of J. Krishnamurti: A Systematic Study. LC 78-670076. 1977. 20.00x (ISBN 0-8002-0245-7). Intl Pubns Serv.

--Philosophy of J. Krishnamurti: A Systematic Study. 1977. 20.00x (ISBN 0-8364-0113-1). South Asia Bks.
Suares, Carlo. Krishnamurti & the Unity of Man. 1974. lib. bdg. 69.95 (ISBN 0-8490-0476-4). Gordon Pr.
KRISTINA, QUEEN OF SWEDEN, 1626-1689
Goldsmith, Margaret. Christina of Sweden: A Psychological Biography. 1977. Repr. of 1935 ed. lib. bdg. 25.00 (ISBN 0-8492-1041-0). R West.
KRISTINA, QUEEN OF SWEDEN, 1626-1689-DRAMA
Strindberg, August. Queen Christina, Charles XII, Gustav III. Johnson, Walter, tr. LC 55-7573. (American-Scandinavian Foundation Scandinavian Studies). (Illus.). 293p. 1968. 11.50 (ISBN 0-295-73899-5); pap. 2.95 (ISBN 0-295-78570-5, WP45). U of Wash Pr.
KROEBER, ALFRED LOUIS, 1876-1960
Kroeber, Theodora. Alfred Kroeber: A Personal Configuration. LC 71-94983. (Illus.). 1970. 15.95 (ISBN 0-520-01598-3); pap. 4.95 (ISBN 0-520-03720-0). U of Cal Pr.
Steward, Julian. Alfred Kroeber. LC 72-8973. (Leaders of Modern Anthropology Ser.). 225p. 1973. 15.00x (ISBN 0-231-03489-X); pap. 6.00x (ISBN 0-231-03490-3). Columbia U Pr.
KRONSTADT, RUSSIA-HISTORY-REVOLT, 1921
Avrich, Paul. Kronstadt Nineteen Twenty-One. 288p. 1974. pap. 4.95x (ISBN 0-393-00724-3, Norton Lib). Norton.
Petrov-Skitaletz, E. Kronstadt Thesis. 1964. 4.00 (ISBN 0-8315-0040-9). Speller.
KROPOTKIN, PETR ALEKSEEVICH, 1842-1921
Avrich, Paul, ed. The Anarchists in the Russian Revolution. LC 72-13386. (Documents of Revolution Ser.). 180p. 1973. pap. 4.95 (ISBN 0-8014-9141-X, CP141). Cornell U Pr.
Kropotkin, Peter. Kropotkin's Revolutionary Pamphlets. Baldwin, Roger, ed. 6.75 (ISBN 0-8446-0748-7). Peter Smith.
Miller, Martin A. Kropotkin. LC 75-20885. 1979. pap. 5.95 (ISBN 0-226-52594-5, P818, Phoen). U of Chicago Pr.
Munoz, V. Kropotkin: A Chronology. Johnson, W. Scott, tr. (Libertarian & Anarchist Chronology Ser.). 1979. lib. bdg. 59.95 (ISBN 0-8490-3022-6). Gordon Pr.
Osofsky, Stephen. Peter Kropotkin. (World Leaders Ser.: No. 77). 1979. lib. bdg. 13.50 (ISBN 0-8057-7724-5). Twayne.
--Peter Kropotkin. (Twayne World Authors Ser.). 1979. lib. bdg. 11.95 (ISBN 0-8057-7724-5). G K Hall.
Read, Herbert. Meet Kropotkin, the Master. 59.95 (ISBN 0-8490-0602-3). Gordon Pr.
Woodcock, G. & Avakumovic, I. Anarchist Prince, a Biographical Study of Peter Kropotkin. Repr. of 1950 ed. 18.00 (ISBN 0-527-97900-7). Kraus Repr.
KRUEDENER, BARBARA JULIANE VON, 1764-1824
Knapton, Ernest J. Lady of the Holy Alliance: The Life of Julie De Krudener. LC 39-14081. Repr. of 1939 ed. 22.45 (ISBN 0-404-03732-1). AMS Pr.
KRUGER, STEPHANUS JOHANNES PAULUS, PRES. SOUTH AFRICAN REPUBLIC, 1825-1904
Hillegas, Howard C. Oom Paul's People: A Narrative of the British-Boer Troubles in South Africa. LC 69-18653. (Illus.). Repr. of 1899 ed. 15.75x (ISBN 0-8371-4946-0). Greenwood.
KRULEWITCH, MELVIN L., 1895-
Taylor, Telford. Nuremberg & Vietnam: An American Tragedy. LC 74-138904. (Orig.). 1972. pap. 1.95 (ISBN 0-686-66332-2, QP308). Times Bks.
KRUPP FAMILY
Manchester, William. Arms of Krupp: 1587-1968. 1970. pap. 3.95 (ISBN 0-553-06470-3, J13149-4). Bantam.
--The Arms of Krupp, 1587-1968. LC 68-24450. (Illus.). 1968. 19.95 (ISBN 0-316-54490-6). Little.
KRUPP VON BOHLEN UND HALBACK, ALFRIED, 1907-1967
Manchester, William. The Arms of Krupp, 1587-1968. LC 68-24450. (Illus.). 1968. 19.95 (ISBN 0-316-54490-6). Little.
KRUPP'SCHE GUSSTAHLFABRIK, ESSEN
Manchester, William. The Arms of Krupp, 1587-1968. LC 68-24450. (Illus.). 1968. 19.95 (ISBN 0-316-54490-6). Little.
KRUSENSTERN, ADAM JOHAN VON, 1770-1846
Von Krusenstern, Adam J. Memoir of the First Russian Circumnavigator. facs. ed. Bernhardi, Charlotte, ed. (Illus.). Repr. of 1856 ed. pap. 8.50 (ISBN 0-8466-0053-6, SJS53). Shorey.
KRUTCH, JOSEPH WOOD, 1893-1970
Harris, Markham. The Case for Tragedy, Being a Challenge to Those Who Deny the Possibility of a Tragic Spirit in the Modern World. LC 72-84990. 196p. 1973. Repr. of 1932 ed. 14.00 (ISBN 0-8462-1693-0). Russell.
Krutch, Joseph W. A Krutch Omnibus: Forty Years of Social & Literary Criticism. LC 80-14794. 342p. 1980. 6.95 (ISBN 0-688-00389-3, Quill). Morrow.
Margolis, John D. Joseph Wood Krutch: A Writer's Life. LC 80-182. (Illus.). 288p. 1980. 14.50 (ISBN 0-87049-292-6). U of Tenn Pr.
KRYLOV, IVAN ANDREYEVICH, 1768-1844
Stepanov, Nikolai L. Ivan Krylov. (World Authors Ser.: Russia: No. 247). lib. bdg. 10.95 (ISBN 0-8057-2504-0). Twayne.
KU KLUX KLAN
Annual Meeting, 1st, North Carolina,July 1923. Papers Read at the Meeting of Grand Dragons Knights of the Ku Klux Klan. Grob, Gerald, ed. LC 76-46086. (Anti-Movements in America Ser). 1977. Repr. of 1923 ed. lib. bdg. 12.00x (ISBN 0-405-09959-2). Arno.
Beard, James M. K.K.K. Sketches, Humorous & Didactic, Treating the More Important Events of the Ku-Klux-Klan Movement in the South with a Discussion of the Causes Which Gave Rise to It & the Social & Political Issues Emanating from It. 1976. Repr. of 1877 ed. 25.00 (ISBN 0-403-06477-5, Regency). Scholarly.
Bermanzohn, Paul & Bermanzohn, Sally. The True Story of the Greensboro Massacre. (Illus.). 256p. 1981. pap. text ed. 3.95 (ISBN 0-686-30430-6). Cauce Pubs.
Brown, W. G. Lower South in American History. LC 68-24973. (American History & Americana Ser., No. 47). 1969. Repr. of 1902 ed. lib. bdg. 33.95 (ISBN 0-8383-0919-4). Haskell.
Brown, William G. Lower South in American History. LC 69-13843. Repr. of 1902 ed. lib. bdg. 15.00x (ISBN 0-8371-0925-6, BRO&). Greenwood.
Chalmers, David M. Hooded Americanism: The History of the Ku Klux Klan. 512p. 1980. 13.95 (ISBN 0-531-09931-8). Watts.
--Hooded Americanism: The History of the Ku Klux Klan. 2nd ed. 1981. pap. 7.95 (ISBN 0-531-05632-5). Watts.
Cooke, Fred J. Ku Klux Klan: America's Recurring Nightmare. LC 80-19325. (Illus.). 160p. (YA) (gr. 7 up). 1981. PLB 9.29 (ISBN 0-671-34055-7). Messner.
Damer, Eyre. When the Ku Klux Rode. LC 70-106882. Repr. of 1912 ed. 10.25x (ISBN 0-8371-3278-9). Greenwood.
--When the Ku Klux Rode. facsimile ed. LC 79-37588. (Black Heritage Library Collection). Repr. of 1912 ed. 13.25 (ISBN 0-8369-8964-3). Arno.
Disraeli, Benjamin. Lothair. LC 78-115230. 1971. Repr. 14.00x (ISBN 0-403-00458-6). Scholarly.
Fisher, William H. The Invisible Empire: A Bibliography of the Ku Klux Klan. LC 80-10133. 212p. 1980. lib. bdg. 10.00 (ISBN 0-8108-1288-6). Scarecrow.
Frost, Stanley. Challenge of the Klan. LC 75-94227. Repr. of 1924 ed. 15.00 (ISBN 0-404-00160-2). AMS Pr.
--Challenge of the Klan. (Illus.). Repr. of 1924 ed. 19.00x (ISBN 0-8371-2192-2, Pub. by Negro U Pr). Greenwood.
Fry, Henry P. Modern Ku Klux Klan. LC 74-88411. Repr. of 1922 ed. 10.50x (ISBN 0-8371-1929-4, Pub. by Negro U Pr). Greenwood.
Goldberg, Robert A. Hooded Empire: The Ku Klux Klan in Colorado. LC 81-7625. (Illus.). 264p. 1981. 14.95 (ISBN 0-252-00848-0). U of Ill Pr.
Horn, Stanley F. Invisible Empire, Story of the Ku Klux Klan, 1866-1871. LC 68-24983. (American History & Americana Ser., No. 47). 1969. Repr. of 1939 ed. lib. bdg. 32.95 (ISBN 0-8383-0927-5). Haskell.
--Invisible Empire: Story of the Ku Klux Klan. 75.00 (ISBN 0-87968-013-X). Gordon Pr.
--Invisible Empire, the Story of the Ku Klux Klan, 1866-1871. 2nd, enl. ed. LC 69-16239. (Criminology, Law Enforcement, & Social Problems Ser.: No. 81). (Illus.). 1969. 15.00 (ISBN 0-87585-081-2). Patterson Smith.
Ingalls, Robert P. Hoods: The Story of the Ku Klux Klan. LC 78-11596. (Illus.). (gr. 6 up). 1979. 8.95 (ISBN 0-399-20658-2). Putnam.
Jackson, Kenneth T. Ku Klux Klan in the City, 1915-1930. (Urban Life in America Ser.). 1967. pap. text ed. 5.95x (ISBN 0-19-500918-5). Oxford U Pr.
Leland, John A. A Voice from South Carolina. facsimile ed. LC 72-37310. (Black Heritage Library Collection). Repr. of 1879 ed. 15.50 (ISBN 0-8369-8947-3). Arno.
Lester, J. C. & Wilson, D. L. Ku Klux Klan. LC 71-114758. (Civil Liberties in Amer. History Ser.). (Illus.). 208p. 1973. Repr. of 1905 ed. lib. bdg. 22.50 (ISBN 0-306-71927-4). Da Capo.
--Ku Klux Klan, Its Origin, Growth & Disbandment. LC 70-144650. Repr. of 1905 ed. 12.50 (ISBN 0-404-00195-5). AMS Pr.
--Ku Klux Klan, Its Origin, Its Growth & Disbandment. LC 72-131766. 1973. Repr. of 1905 ed. 8.00 (ISBN 0-403-00653-8). Scholarly.
Lowe, David. KKK: The Invisible Empire. (Illus.). 1967. 11.95 (ISBN 0-393-05307-5). Norton.
Mars, Florence. Witness in Philadelphia. LC 76-50660. 1977. 10.00 (ISBN 0-8071-0265-2). La State U Pr.
Mecklin, John M. Ku Klux Klan: A Study of the American Mind. LC 63-15172. 1963. Repr. of 1924 ed. 15.00 (ISBN 0-8462-0384-7). Russell.
Monteval, Marion. Klan Inside Out. LC 76-111583. Repr. of 1924 ed. 10.25x (ISBN 0-8371-4609-7, Pub. by Negro U Pr). Greenwood.
Owens, Don B., Jr. I Am a Black Hooded Klansman. LC 79-128047. (Orig.). 1970. pap. 5.98 (ISBN 0-911734-06-6). Commonsense.
Rice, Arnold S. The Ku Klux Klan in American Politics. LC 72-1152. (Southern Literature & History Ser., No. 65). 1972. Repr. of 1962 ed. lib. bdg. 49.95 (ISBN 0-8383-1427-9). Haskell.
Sims, Patsy. The Klan. LC 77-2335. (Illus.). 384p. 1981. pap. 8.95 (ISBN 0-8128-6096-9). Stein & Day.
--The Klan. 1978. 12.50 (ISBN 0-8128-2268-4). Stein & Day.
Tourgee, Albion W. Fool's Errand. Franklin, John H., ed. LC 61-13744. (The John Harvard Library). 1961. pap. 4.50x (ISBN 0-674-30751-8). Harvard U Pr.
--Fool's Errand: A Novel of the South During Reconstruction. Fredrickson, George M., ed. pap. 5.95x (ISBN 0-06-133074-4, TB3074, Torch). Har-Row.
Trelease, Allen W. White Terror: The Ku Klux Klan Conspiracy & Southern Reconstruction. LC 78-12864. 1979. Repr. of 1972 ed. lib. bdg. 34.00x (ISBN 0-313-21168-X, TRWT). Greenwood.
U. S. Circuit Court Fourth Circuit. Proceedings in the Ku Klux Klan Trials, at Columbia S. C. in the United States Circuit Court, November Term 1871. LC 72-184818. Repr. of 1872 ed. 32.50x (ISBN 0-8371-1997-9). Greenwood.
U. S. Congress. Report of the Joint Select Committee to Inquire into the Condition of Affairs in the Late Insurrectionary States. Ku Klux Conspiracy Report, 13 Vols. Senate Report 41. LC 35-31867. Repr. of 1872 ed. Set. 400.00 (ISBN 0-404-00180-7); 31.00 ea. AMS Pr.
U.S. House of Representatives. Affairs in the Late Insurrectionary States. LC 71-90199. (Mass Violence in America Ser.). Repr. of 1872 ed. 22.00 (ISBN 0-405-01321-3). Arno.
--Ku Klux Klan: 67th Congress, First Session, House Committee on Rules Hearings. LC 72-90203. (Mass Violence in America Ser). Repr. of 1921 ed. 15.25 (ISBN 0-405-01315-9). Arno.
KU KLUX KLAN-FICTION
Dixon, Thomas, Jr. The Clansman: An Historical Romance of the Ku Klux Klan. LC 71-104761. (Novel As American Social History Ser.). 392p. 1970. pap. 8.00x (ISBN 0-8131-0126-3). U Pr of Ky.
KUANUA (MELANESIAN PEOPLE)
see Tolai (Melanesian People)
KUBA (BANTU TRIBE)
Vansina, Jan. The Children of Woot: A History of the Kuba Peoples. LC 77-91061. (Illus.). 406p. 1978. 30.00 (ISBN 0-299-07490-0). U of Wis Pr.
KUBIN, ALFRED, 1877-1959
Kubin, Alfred. Kubin's Dance of Death & Other Drawings. LC 72-81285. Orig. Title: Die Blatter Mit Dem Tod. (Illus.). 1973. pap. 3.00 (ISBN 0-486-22884-3). Dover.
KUBLAI KHAN, 1216-1294
Shaffer, E. S. Kubla Khan & the Fall of Jerusalem. LC 79-8492. 362p. 1980. pap. 14.95 (ISBN 0-521-29807-5). Cambridge U Pr.
KUBO-FUTURISM
see Futurism
KUBRICK, STANLEY
Coyle, Wallace. Stanley Kubrick: A Guide to Reference & Resources. 1980. lib. bdg. 24.00 (ISBN 0-8161-8058-X). G K Hall.
Phillips, Gene D. Stanley Kubrick: A Film Odyssey. (Illus.). 1977. pap. 3.95 (ISBN 0-445-08414-6). Popular Lib.
Walker, Alexander. Stanley Kubrick Directs. enl. ed. LC 77-153692. (Illus.). 304p. 1972. pap. 5.95 (ISBN 0-15-684892-9, HB242, Harv). HarBraceJ.
KUCHEAN LANGUAGE
see Tokharian Language
KUDURRU INSCRIPTIONS
see Boundary Stones, Babylonian
KUHAULUA, JESSE, 1944-
Kuhaulua, Jesse & Wheeler, John. Takamiyama: The World of Sumo. LC 72-96129. (Illus.). 176p. 1973. 12.95 (ISBN 0-87011-195-7). Kodansha.
KUHN, ISOBEL
Kuhn, Isobel. By Searching. 1959. pap. 1.95 (ISBN 0-8024-0053-1). Moody.
Reason, Joyce. Searcher for God (Isabel Kuhn) 1963. pap. 1.50 (ISBN 0-87508-621-7). Chr Lit.
KUHN, WALT, 1880-1949
Adams, Philip R. Walt Kuhn: A Classic Revival. (Illus.). 1978. pap. 1.00 (ISBN 0-88360-030-7). Amon Carter.
--Walt Kuhn, Painter: His Life & Work. LC 78-3502. (Illus.). 1978. 35.00 (ISBN 0-8142-0258-6). Ohio St U Pr.
Bartlett, Fred S., frwd. by. Walt Kuhn: An Imaginary History of the West. LC 64-+012. (Illus.). 52p. 1964. pap. 2.50 (ISBN 0-88360-008-0). Amon Carter.
KUITSCH LANGUAGE
Frachtenberg, Leo J. Lower Umpqua Texts & Notes on the Kusan Dialects. LC 72-82341. (Columbia Univ. Contributions to Anthropology Ser.: Vol. 4). 1969. Repr. of 1914 ed. 16.50 (ISBN 0-404-50554-6). AMS Pr.
KUKAI, 774-835
Hakeda, Yoshita S., tr. from Japanese. Kukai: Major Works, Translated with an Account of His Life & a Study of His Thought. LC 72-3124. (Records of Civilization, Sources, Studies & Translations of the Oriental Classics Ser.). 303p. 1972. 17.50x (ISBN 0-231-03627-2). Columbia U Pr.
KULIKOVO, BATTLE OF, 1380
Jakobson, Roman & Worth, Dean S., eds. Sofonija's Tale of the Russian-Tatar Battle on the Kulikovo Field. (S P R Ser: No. 51). 1963. text ed. 20.00x (ISBN 90-2790-196-1). Mouton.
KUMRAN COMMUNITY
see Qumran Community
KUNDALI YOGA
see Yoga, Hatha
KUNG, AI-LING (SUNG), 1888-
Hahn, Emily. Soong Sisters. Repr. of 1941 ed. lib. bdg. 17.00x (ISBN 0-8371-4429-9, HASI). Greenwood.
KUNG, HANS, 1928-
Costanzo, Joseph F. The Historical Credibility of Hans Kung. 1979. 12.95 (ISBN 0-8158-0370-2). Chris Mass.
Nowell, Robert. A Passion for Truth: Hans Kung & His Theology. 376p. 1981. 17.50 (ISBN 0-8245-0039-3). Crossroad NY.
KUNG (AFRICAN PEOPLE)
see Bushmen
KUNG-CH'AN-TANG
Compton, Boyd, ed. & tr. Mao's China: Party Reform Documents, 1942-44. LC 51-12273. (Publications on Asia of the International Studies: No. 1). (Illus.). 332p. 1966. pap. 2.95 (ISBN 0-295-74011-6). U of Wash Pr.
KUNG-FU
see Karate
KUNIYOSHI, UTAGAWA
see Utagawa, Kuniyoshi, 1798-1861
KUOMINTANG
see Chung-Kuo Kuo Min Tang
KUPKA, FRANTISEK
Kupka, Karel & Breton, Andre. Un Art a L'etat Brut: Peintures et Sculptures Des Aborigenes d'Australie. (Illus.). 195p. (Fr.). 1962. lib. bdg. 14.95 (ISBN 0-87817-285-8, Pub. by Guilde Du Livre Switzerland). Hacker.
KURCHATOV, IGOR VASIL'EVICH, 1903-1960
Golovin, I. N. Kurchatov, I. V., Biography of the Soviet Nuclear Scientist. Dougherty, William H., tr. LC 68-58753. 1968. pap. 4.00 (ISBN 0-911706-11-9). Selbstverlag.
KURDISH LANGUAGE
Mokri, M. Al-Hadiyati 'l-Hamidiyah: Kurdish-Arabic Dictionary. 1975. 28.00x (ISBN 0-86685-126-7). Intl Bk Ctr.
KURDISTAN-SOCIAL CONDITIONS
Barth, Fredrik. Principles of Social Organization in Southern Kurdistan. LC 77-87641. Repr. of 1953 ed. 16.50 (ISBN 0-404-16423-4). AMS Pr.
Daniel, Elton L. The Political & Social History of Khurasan Under Abbasid Rule 747-820. LC 79-53302. 1979. 28.00x (ISBN 0-88297-025-9). Bibliotheca.
Hamilton, Archibald M. Road Through Kurdistan. LC 70-180345. Repr. of 1937 ed. 26.00 (ISBN 0-404-56275-2). AMS Pr.
Hansen, Henny H. The Kurdish Woman's Life: Field Research in a Muslim Society, Iraq. (Ethnographical Ser.: No. 7). (Illus.). 1961. pap. text ed. 28.75x (ISBN 87-480-6231-6). Humanities.
KURDS
Behn, Wolfgang. Kurds in Iran: A Selected & Annotated Bibliography. 1977. pap. 12.50 (ISBN 0-7201-0700-8, Pub. by Mansell England). Merrimack Bk Serv.
Chaliand, Gerard, ed. & intro. by. People Without a Country: The Kurds & Kurdistan. 292p. (Orig.). 1980. 19.95 (ISBN 0-905762-69-X, Pub. by Zed Pr); pap. 8.50 (ISBN 0-905762-74-6). Lawrence Hill.

Kahn, Margaret. Children of the Jinn: In Search of the Kurds & Their Country. LC 79-66069. (Illus.). 288p. 1980. pap. 6.95 (ISBN 0-87223-627-7, Dist. by Har-Row). Wideview Bks.

--Children of the Jinn: In Search of the Kurds & Their Country. LC 79-66069. (Illus.). 1980. 10.95 (ISBN 0-87223-564-5, Dist. by Har-Row). Seaview Bks.

O'Ballance, Edgar. Kurdish Revolt, Nineteen Sixty-One to Nineteen Seventy. 189p. 1973. 15.00 (ISBN 0-208-01395-4, Archon). Shoe String.

Short, Martin & McDermott, Anthony. The Kurds. (Minority Rights Group: No. 23). 1975. pap. 2.50 (ISBN 0-89192-109-5). Interbk Inc.

KURILE ISLANDS

Gorshkov, G. S. Volcanism & the Upper Mantle: Investigations in the Kurile Island Arc. LC 69-12530. (Monographs in Geoscience Ser.). 385p. 1970. 39.50 (ISBN 0-306-30407-4, Plenum Pr). Plenum Pub.

Krasheninnikov, Stepan P. Explorations of Kamchatka: North Pacific Scimitar. Crownhart-Vaughan, E. A., tr. LC 72-79116. (North Pacific Studies Ser.: No. 1). (Illus.). 408p. 1972. 14.95 (ISBN 0-87595-033-7). Oreg Hist Soc.

Stephan, John J. The Kuril Islands: Russo-Japanese Frontier in the Pacific. (Illus.). 256p. 1975. 37.50x (ISBN 0-19-821563-0). Oxford U Pr.

KURMANJI LANGUAGE

see Kurdish Language

KURNAI TRIBE

Fison, Lorimer & Howitt, Alfred W. Kamilaroi & Kurnai: Group Marriage & Relationship, & Marriage by Elopement, the Kurnai Tribe: Their Customs in Peace & War. (Maps). 1967. pap. text ed. 15.50x (ISBN 90-6234-053-9). Humanities.

KUROSAWA, OKIRA, 1910-

Richie, Donald. The Films of Akira Kurosawa. (Illus.). 1965. pap. 9.95 (ISBN 0-520-01781-1, CAL198). U of Cal Pr.

KUSAN LANGUAGES

Frachtenberg, Leo J. Lower Umpqua Texts & Notes on the Kusan Dialects. LC 72-82341. (Columbia Univ. Contributions to Anthropology Ser.: Vol. 4). 1969. Repr. of 1914 ed. 16.50 (ISBN 0-404-50554-6). AMS Pr.

KUSANA

see Kushans

KUSHANS

Kumar, Baldev. The Early Kusanas. (Illus.). 329p. 1973. text ed. 17.50x (ISBN 0-8426-0544-4). Verry.

Rosenfield, John M. The Dynastic Arts of the Kushans. (California Studies in the History of Art: No. V). 1967. 60.00x (ISBN 0-520-01091-4). U of Cal Pr.

KUT ET AMARA-SIEGE, 1915-1916

Litvinov, Pavel. Demonstration in Pushkin Square: The Trial Records with Commentary & an Open Letter. Harari, Manya, tr. from Rus. LC 77-91996. 1969. 5.95 (ISBN 0-87645-009-5). Gambit.

KUTENAI INDIANS

see Indians of North America-Northwest, Pacific

KUWAIT, ARABIA (STATE)

Abraham, Nicholas A. Doing Business in Kuwait. Prinz, Karl E., ed. (Doing Business in the Middle East: Vol. 3). (Illus.). 280p. (Orig.). 1981. pap. text ed. 79.95x (ISBN 0-934592-02-0). Trade Ship Pub Co.

Alessa, S. Y. Manpower Problems in Kuwait. 160p. 1981. price not set (ISBN 0-7103-0009-3). Routledge & Kegan.

Al-Sabah, Y. S. F. The Oil Economy of Kuwait. 176p. 1981. 29.95 (ISBN 0-7103-0003-4). Routledge & Kegan.

Bidwell, Robin, ed. Affairs of Kuwait: 1896-1905, 2 vols. new ed. 1971. Set. 99.50x (ISBN 0-7146-2692-9, F Cass Co). Biblio Dist.

Chisholm, A. H. First Kuwait Oil Concession: Record of the Negotiations, 1911-1934. 272p. 1975. 35.00x (ISBN 0-7146-3002-0, F Cass Co). Biblio Dist.

Demir, Soliman. The Kuwait Fund & the Political Economy of Arab Regional Development. LC 75-45305. (Special Studies). (Illus.). 160p. 1976. text ed. 24.95 (ISBN 0-275-22980-7). Praeger.

Dickson, Violet. Forty Years in Kuwait. 1971. 21.00 (ISBN 0-04-920032-1). Allen Unwin.

Eid, Nimr. Legal Aspects of Marketing Behavior in Lebanon & Kuwait. 8.00x (ISBN 0-86685-013-9). Intl Bk Ctr.

El Mallakh, Ragaei. Economic Development & Regional Cooperation: Kuwait. LC 68-20512. (Publications of the Center for Middle Eastern Studies Ser.). 1968. 11.50x (ISBN 0-226-20157-0). U of Chicago Pr.

--Kuwait: Trade & Investment. (Special Studies in International Economics & Business). 1979. lib. bdg. 33.75x (ISBN 0-89158-375-0). Westview.

El Mallakh, Ragai & Atta, Jacob K. The Absorptive Capacity of Kuwait: Domestic & International Perspectives. LC 81-47026. (Illus.). 1981. 21.95 (ISBN 0-669-04541-1). Lexington Bks.

Felber, John E. Kuwait Welcomes Commerce. (Illus.). 48p. 1962. pap. 2.00 (ISBN 0-910794-04-9). Intl Intertrade.

Freeth, Zahra. A New Look at Kuwait. 1972. 16.50 (ISBN 0-04-953008-9). Allen Unwin.

Freeth, Zahra & Winstone, Victor. Kuwait: Prospect & Reality. (Illus.). 1972. 27.50 (ISBN 0-04-953007-0). Allen Unwin.

Kabeel, Saroya M. Selected Bibliography on Kuwait & the Arabian Gulf. LC 70-17777. 118p. 1969. 18.50x (ISBN 0-8002-1966-X). Intl Pubns Serv.

Karam, N. H. Business Laws & Practices of Kuwait. 350p. 1980. 297.00x (ISBN 0-86010-224-6, Pub. by Graham & Trotman England). State Mutual Bk.

Karam, N. H., tr. Banking Laws of Kuwait. 275p. 1979. 22.00x (ISBN 0-86010-139-8, Pub.by Graham & Trotman England). State Mutual Bk.

Lanier, Alison R. Update -- Kuwait. LC 80-83923. (Country Orientation Ser.). 1980. pap. text ed. 25.00x (ISBN 0-933662-29-7). Intercult Pr.

Mezerik, Avrahm G., ed. Kuwait-Iraq Dispute. 1961. pap. 15.00 (ISBN 0-685-13204-8, 66). Intl Review.

Oliver, R. A. & Lewis, D. G. The Content of Sixth-Form General Studies. 144p. 1974. 12.00x (ISBN 0-7190-0586-8, Pub. by Manchester U Pr England). State Mutual Bk.

State of Kuwait. Kuwaiti Commercial Law. Law Offices of Simon Siksek, Edouard Hanna, & Antoine Abboud, tr. from Arabic. 588p. 1975. lib. bdg. 150.00x (ISBN 0-88206-202-6). Caravan Bks.

Sterling Publishing Company Editors. Kuwait in Pictures. LC 73-126858. (Visual Geography Ser). (Illus., Orig.). (gr. 6 up). 1970. PLB 4.99 (ISBN 0-8069-1132-8); pap. 2.95 (ISBN 0-8069-1133-6). Sterling.

KWA LANGUAGES

see also Ewe Language; Fanti Language; Gonja Language; Ibo Language; Twi Language; Yoruba Language

Thomas, Elaine. A Grammatical Description of the Engenni Language. (Publications in Linguistics & Related Fields: No. 60). 1978. pap. 9.60 (ISBN 0-88312-074-7); microfiche write for info. Summer Inst Ling.

KWAKIUTAL INDIANS

see Indians of North America-Northwest, Pacific

KWAKIUTL LANGUAGE

Boas, Franz. Bella Bella Texts. (Columbia Univ. Contributions to Anthropology Ser.: No. 5). Repr. of 1928 ed. 24.00 (ISBN 0-404-50555-4). AMS Pr.

--Contributions to the Ethnology of the Kwakiutl. LC 77-82353. (Columbia Univ. Contributions to Anthropology Ser.: Vol. 3). Repr. of 1925 ed. 27.00 (ISBN 0-404-50553-8). AMS Pr.

--Geographical Names of the Kwakiutl Indians. LC 77-82361. (Columbia Univ. Contributions to Anthropology Ser.: No. 20). 1969. Repr. of 1934 ed. 25.00 (ISBN 0-404-50570-8). AMS Pr.

--Kwakiutl Grammar - with a Glossary of Suffixes. LC 74-7939. Repr. of 1947 ed. 24.50 (ISBN 0-404-11826-7). AMS Pr.

--Kwakiutl Indian Language. pap. 13.50 (ISBN 0-8466-4027-9, SJI27). Shorey.

--Kwakiutl Tales. LC 70-82343. (Columbia University. Contributions to Anthropology: No. 2). Repr. of 1910 ed. 34.50 (ISBN 0-404-50552-X). AMS Pr.

--Kwakiutl Tales: New Series, 2 Vols. LC 79-82367. (Columbia Univ. Contributions to Anthropology Ser.: Vol. 26). 1969. Repr. of 1943 ed. Set. 40.00 (ISBN 0-404-50576-7); 20.00 ea. Vol. 1 (ISBN 0-404-50596-1). Vol. 2 (ISBN 0-404-50597-X). AMS Pr.

--Religion of the Kwakiutl Indians, 2 Vols. LC 72-82368. (Columbia Univ. Contributions to Anthropology Ser.: No. 10). Repr. of 1930 ed. Set. 45.00 (ISBN 0-404-50560-0); 22.50 ea. AMS Pr.

KYANIZING

see Wood-Preservation

KYD, THOMAS, 1558-1595?

Kyd, Thomas. The Spanish Tragedy. Mulryne, J. R., ed. (New Mermaids Ser.). pap. 2.95x (ISBN 0-393-90017-7). Norton.

Murray, Peter B. Thomas Kyd. (English Authors Ser.: No. 88). 10.95 (ISBN 0-8057-1308-5). Twayne.

KYDD, SAM

Kydd, Sam. For You, the War Is Over. 1974. 9.50 (ISBN 0-85974-005-6). Transatlantic.

KYOGEN PLAYS

Ken, Kiribatake. Kyogen Costume. (Illus.). 224p. 1980. 175.00 (ISBN 0-500-01243-1). Thames Hudson.

Sakanishi, Shio, tr. Japanese Folk Plays: The Ink Smeared Lady & Other Kyogen. (Illus.). 1960. pap. 2.95 (ISBN 0-8048-0297-1). C E Tuttle.

KYOTO

Bayrd, Edwin. Kyoto. LC 73-87150. (Wonders of Man Ser.). (Illus.). 176p. 1974. 16.95 (ISBN 0-88225-085-X). Newsweek.

Cole, Wendell. Kyoto in the Momoyama Period. (Centers of Civilization Ser.: Vol. 22). 166p. 1967. 5.95x (ISBN 0-8061-0748-0). U of Okla Pr.

Ishikawa, T. Imperial Villas of Kyoto. LC 79-128690. (This Beautiful World Ser.: Vol. 21). (Illus.). 146p. (Orig.). 1970. pap. 4.95 (ISBN 0-87011-133-7). Kodansha.

Karhu, Clifton. Kyoto Rediscovered: A Portfolio of Woodblock Prints. LC 80-17382. (Illus.). 216p. 1981. 125.00 (ISBN 0-8348-1521-4). Weatherhill.

Mosher, Gouverneur. Kyoto: A Contemplative Guide. rev. ed. LC 64-24951. (Illus.). 1978. pap. 8.50 (ISBN 0-8048-1294-2). C E Tuttle.

Plutschow, Herbert. Introducing Kyoto. LC 79-51164. (Illus.). 1979. 14.95 (ISBN 0-87011-384-4). Kodansha.

Stewart, Harold. By the Old Walls of Kyoto. (Illus.). 544p. 1981. 22.50 (ISBN 0-8348-0154-X). Weatherhill.

L

L DEVELOPMENTAL LANGUAGES

see L Systems

L SYSTEMS

Lindenmayer, A. & Rosenberg, G. Automata, Languages, Development. 1976. 58.75 (ISBN 0-444-11118-2, North-Holland). Elsevier.

Rozenberg, G. & Salomaa, A., eds. L Systems. (Lecture Notes in Computer Science: Vol. 15). vi, 338p. 1974. pap. 19.00 (ISBN 0-387-06867-8). Springer-Verlag.

Rozenberg, Grzegorz & Salomaa, Arto. The Mathematical Theory of L Systems. LC 79-25254. (Pure & Applied Mathematics Ser.). 1980. 43.50 (ISBN 0-12-597140-0). Acad Pr.

LAADI LANGUAGE

see Congo Language

LABADISTS

Danckaerts, Jasper. Journal of Jasper Danckaerts, Sixteen Seventy-Nine to Sixteen Eighty. James, B. B. & Jameson, J. Franklin, eds. (Original Narratives). 1969. Repr. of 1913 ed. 18.50x (ISBN 0-06-480422-4). B&N.

James, B. B. Labadist Colony in Maryland. 1973. Repr. of 1899 ed. pap. 7.00 (ISBN 0-384-26744-0). Johnson Repr.

James, Barlett B. The Labadist Colony in Maryland. LC 78-63870. (Johns Hopkins University. Studies in the Social Sciences. Seventeenth Ser. 1899: 6). Repr. of 1899 ed. 11.50 (ISBN 0-404-61126-5). AMS Pr.

Labadie, Laurance. Laurance Labadie: Individualist, Anarchist & Mutualist, Vol. 1. (Men & Movements in the History & Philosophy of Anarchism). 1976. lib. bdg. 59.95 (ISBN 0-685-66199-7). Revisionist Pr.

LABARGE, JOSEPH, 1815-1899

Chittenden, Hiram M. Early Steamboat Navigation on the Missouri River. Repr. 12.50 (ISBN 0-87018-009-6). Ross.

LABELS

see also Cigar Bands and Labels

Bracken, Carolyn. Super Stickers for Kids: One Hundred & Twenty-Eight Fun Labels. (Illus.). 16p. (Orig.). 1981. pap. 2.25 (ISBN 0-486-24092-4). Dover.

Hendler, Muncie. Mailing Labels & Postal Stickers: 120 Handy Gummed & Perforated Forms & Notices. 1981. pap. 2.75 (ISBN 0-486-24086-X). Dover.

Lawson, R. G. Advertising & Labelling Laws in the Common Market. 1975. looseleaf bdg. 67.50x (ISBN 0-85308-040-2); 1978 supplement. Rothman.

Organization for Economic Cooperation & Development. Compulsory Labelling of Prepackaged Consumer Products. 43p. 1974. 2.50 (ISBN 92-64-11247-2). OECD.

Sibbett, Ed. Gourmet Kitchen Labels. 16p. 1981. pap. 2.75 (ISBN 0-486-24087-8). Dover.

LABOR (OBSTETRICS)

see also Childbirth; Natural Childbirth; Obstetrics; Puerperium

Cartwright, Ann. The Dignity of Labour? A Study of Childbearing & Induction. 1979. 23.95x (ISBN 0-422-76690-9). Methuen Inc.

Elder, M. G. & Hendricks, C. H. Obstetrics & Gynecology: Preterm Labor, Vol. 1. (Butterworths International Medical Reviews Ser.). 1981. text ed. 29.95 (ISBN 0-407-02300-3). Butterworth.

Engelmann, George J. Labor Among Primitive Peoples, Showing the Development of the Obstetric Science of Today. LC 75-23705. (Illus.). Repr. of 1882 ed. 20.00 (ISBN 0-404-13257-X). AMS Pr.

Friedman, Emanuel A. Labor: Clinical Evaluation & Management. 2nd ed. (Illus.). 512p. 1978. 34.00 (ISBN 0-8385-5580-2). ACC.

Gunn, Alexander. Questions & Answers on Labour and Birth. 160p. (Orig.). 1980. pap. 6.50x (ISBN 0-85242-697-6). Intl Pubns Serv.

Keirse, Marc J., et al, eds. Human Parturition: New Concepts & Developments. (Boerhaave Series for Postgraduate Medical Education: No. 15). 1980. lib. bdg. 45.00 (ISBN 9-0602-1445-5, Leiden U Pr). Kluwer Boston.

Klopper, A. & Gardner, J., eds. Endocrine Factors in Labour. LC 73-80474. (Memoirs of the Society for Endocrinology: No. 20). (Illus.). 200p. 1973. 42.50 (ISBN 0-521-20158-6). Cambridge U Pr.

Moir, Donald. Pain Relief in Labour. 3rd ed. (Illus.). 1978. 6.50 (ISBN 0-443-01527-9). Churchill.

Oxorn, Harry. Oxorn-Foote Human Labor & Birth. 4th ed. (Illus.). 726p. 1980. 18.95 (ISBN 0-8385-7664-8). ACC.

Parfitt, Rebecca R. The Birth Primer: A Source Book of Traditional & Alternative Methods in Labor & Delivery. (Illus.). 1980. pap. 2.50 (ISBN 0-451-09070-5, E9070, Sig). NAL.

Rydberg, Erik. The Mechanism of Labour. (American Lecture Gynecology & Obstetrics). (Illus.). 192p. 1954. photocopy ed. spiral 19.50 (ISBN 0-398-01636-4). C C Thomas.

Sumner, Phillip E. & Phillips, Celeste R. Birthing Rooms: Concepts & Reality. LC 81-993. (Illus.). 213p. 1981. pap. text ed. 12.95 (ISBN 0-8016-4873-4). Mosby.

Todd, Linda. Labor & Birth: A Guide for You. (Illus.). 50p. 1980. write for info. (ISBN 0-934024-03-0). ICEA.

LABOR (OBSTETRICS)-PROGRAMMED INSTRUCTION

Stenchever, Morton A. & Kitay, David Z. Labor: A Workbook in Obstetrics & Gynecology. (Illus.). 1969. pap. 12.95 (ISBN 0-8151-8195-7). Year Bk Med.

LABOR, COMPLICATED

see also Anesthesia in Obstetrics; Forceps, Obstetric; Hemorrhage, Uterine; Placenta

Reid, Duncan E., et al. Principles & Management of Human Reproduction. LC 70-118593. (Illus.). 1972. 25.00 (ISBN 0-7216-7532-8). Saunders.

LABOR, COMPULSORY

see Forced Labor

LABOR, CONSCRIPTION OF

see Service, Compulsory Non-Military

LABOR, COOLIE

see Chinese in Foreign Countries

LABOR, DIVISION OF

see Division of Labor

LABOR, FORCED

see Forced Labor

LABOR, HOURS OF

see Hours of Labor

LABOR, MIGRANT

see Migrant Labor

LABOR, ORGANIZED

see Trade-Unions

LABOR, PAINLESS (OBSTETRICS)

see Natural Childbirth

LABOR, SKILLED

see Skilled Labor

LABOR ABSENTEEISM

see Absenteeism (Labor)

LABOR AGREEMENTS

see Collective Labor Agreements

LABOR AND CAPITAL

see Industrial Relations

LABOR AND LABORING CLASSES

see also Absenteeism (Labor); Alien Labor; Apprentices; Arbitration, Industrial; Artisans; Capital; Children-Employment; Church and Labor; Collective Bargaining; Commuting; Contract Labor; Convict Labor; Cost and Standard of Living; Discrimination in Employment; Division of Labor; Employees, Dismissal of; Employees, Rating of; Employees' Representation in Management; Employment Agencies; Factory System; Forced Labor; Friendly Societies; Gilds; Home Labor; Hours of Labor; Industrial Relations; International Labor Activities; Job Satisfaction; Machinery in Industry; Middle Classes; Migrant Labor; Occupations; Old Age Pensions; Open and Closed Shop; Part-Time Employment; Peasantry; Pension Trusts; Poor; Professions; Proletariat; Sabotage; Serfdom; Servants; Skilled Labor; Slave Labor; Slavery; Socialism; Strikes and Lockouts; Sunday Legislation; Supplementary Employment; Syndicalism; Trade-Unions; Unemployed; Wages; Welfare Work in Industry; Women-Employment; World War, 1939-1945-Manpower; Youth-Employment

also classes of laborers, e.g. Coal-Miners, Railroads-Employees; subdivisions Economic Conditions and Social Conditions under names of countries, cities, etc., e.g. U. S.-Economic Conditions

Abarbanel, Jerome. Redefining the Environment. (Key Issues Ser.: No. 9). 1972. pap. 2.00 (ISBN 0-87546-200-6). NY Sch Indus Rel.

Abel, I. W. Labor's Role in Building a Better Society. (Distinguished Lecturers Ser.: No. 2). 18p. 1972. pap. 1.00 (ISBN 0-87755-174-X). U of Tex Busn Res.

Adamic, Louis. My America. LC 76-2050. (FDR & the Era of the New Deal). 1976. Repr. of 1938 ed. lib. bdg. 49.50 (ISBN 0-306-70801-9). Da Capo.
Addams, Jane. Newer Ideals of Peace. LC 71-137523. (Peace Movement in America Ser). xviii, 243p. 1972. Repr. of 1907 ed. lib. bdg. 14.25x (ISBN 0-89198-050-4). Ozer.
--Newer Ideals of Peace. Repr. of 1911 ed. 20.00 (ISBN 0-685-72767-X). Norwood Edns.
Addison, John & Siebert, W. S. The Market for Labor: An Analytical Treatment. LC 78-10976. (Illus.). 1979. text ed. 17.95 (ISBN 0-87620-558-9). Goodyear.
Adlam, Diana, et al, eds. Politics & Power: Problems in Labour Politics. (Politics & Power Ser.). 220p. (Orig.). 1981. pap. 17.50 (ISBN 0-7100-0716-7). Routledge & Kegan.
Akabas, Sheila H. & Kurzman, Paul. Work, Workers, & Work Organizations: A View from Social Work. 272p. 1982. 18.95 (ISBN 0-13-965335-X). P-H.
Allen, Henry J. & Gompers, Samuel. Party of the Third Part: The Story of the Kansas Industrial Relations Court. LC 74-156401. (American Labor Ser., No. 2). 1971. Repr. of 1920 ed. 16.00 (ISBN 0-405-02911-X). Arno.
American Labor Conference on International Affairs. Modern Review, Vols. 1-3, No. 2. 1947-50. Repr. lib. bdg. 57.50x (ISBN 0-8371-9203-X, MR00). Greenwood.
American Labor: From Conspiracy to Collective Bargaining, Ser 1, 60 vols. 1969. Repr. 945.50 set (ISBN 0-405-02100-3). Arno.
American Labor: From Conspiracy to Collective Bargaining, Ser. 2, 45 vols. 1971. 796.00 set (ISBN 0-405-02910-1). Arno.
American Workers Party. Labor Age, Vols. 1-22, No. 1. 1913-33. Repr. lib. bdg. 360.00x (ISBN 0-8371-9130-0, LB00). Greenwood.
Anderson, William A. & Dynes, Russell R. Social Movements, Violence, & Change: The May Movement in Curacao. LC 75-6769. (Illus.). 1975. 12.50 (ISBN 0-8142-0240-3). Ohio St U Pr.
Aronson, Charles N. In the Labor Pool. LC 77-78227. (Eagle Ser.: No. 4). (Illus.). 1977. 12.00 (ISBN 0-915736-13-6); pap. 8.00 (ISBN 0-915736-14-4). C N Aronson.
Auerbach, Jerold S., ed. American Labor: The Twentieth Century. LC 69-14822. (American Heritage Ser). 1969. pap. 9.50 (ISBN 0-672-60128-1, 78). Bobbs.
Aveling, Edward B. & Aveling, Eleanor M. Working Class Movement in America. LC 78-89716. (American Labor, from Conspiracy to Collective Bargaining Ser., No. 1). 239p. 1969. Repr. of 1891 ed. 11.50 (ISBN 0-405-02102-X). Arno.
Ayusawa, Iwao F. International Labor Leglistation. LC 75-82214. (Columbia University Studies in the Social Sciences: No. 208). Repr. of 1920 ed. 16.50 (ISBN 0-404-51208-9). AMS Pr.
Backman, Jules, ed. Labor, Technology & Productivity in the Seventies. LC 74-13004. (Key Issues Ser). 144p. 1974. 10.00x (ISBN 0-8147-0981-8); pap. 3.95x (ISBN 0-8147-0982-6). NYU Pr.
Bairoch, P. Working Population & Its Structure. 1969. 52.75x (ISBN 0-677-61130-7). Gordon.
Baker, Ray S. New Industrial Unrest: Reasons & Remedies. LC 78-156402. (American Labor Ser., No. 2). 1971. Repr. of 1920 ed. 12.00 (ISBN 0-405-02912-8). Arno.
Bakke, E. Wight. Citizens Without Work: A Study of the Effects of Unemployment Upon the Workers' Social Relations & Practices. LC 70-85913. 1969. Repr. of 1940 ed. 19.50 (ISBN 0-208-00810-1, Archon). Shoe String.
Barnes, Charles B. The Longshoremen. Stein, Leon, ed. LC 77-70482. (Work Ser.). (Illus.). 1977. Repr. of 1915 ed. lib. bdg. 25.00x (ISBN 0-405-10156-2). Arno.
Barnes, William E., ed. Labor Problem: Plain Questions & Practical Answers. LC 75-156404. (American Labor Ser., No. 2). 1971. Repr. of 1886 ed. 14.00 (ISBN 0-405-02914-4). Arno.
Barnett, George E. Chapters on Machinery & Labor. LC 68-25563. (Arcturus Books Paperbacks). 191p. 1969. pap. 2.25 (ISBN 0-8093-0398-1). S Ill U Pr.
Bayod Serrat, Ramon. Diccionario Laboral. 546p. (Espn.). 1969. pap. 6.95 (ISBN 84-290-0937-X, S-50139). French & Eur.
Beal, Fred E. Proletarian Journey. LC 70-146158. (Civil Liberties in American History Ser). 1971. Repr. of 1937 ed. lib. bdg. 39.50 (ISBN 0-306-70096-4). Da Capo.
--Proletarian Journey: New England, Gastonia, Moscow. facsimile ed. LC 73-179505. (Select Bibliographies Reprint Ser). Repr. of 1937 ed. 22.00 (ISBN 0-8369-6634-1). Arno.
Beard, Mary. The American Labor Movement. LC 71-89717. (American Labor Ser. 1). 206p. 1969. Repr. of 1931 ed. 9.50 (ISBN 0-405-02103-8). Arno.
Bedford, Henry F. Socialism & the Workers in Massachusetts, 1886-1912. LC 66-15794. (Illus.). 1966. 12.50x (ISBN 0-87023-010-7). U of Mass Pr.
Bellamy, Joyce M. & Saville, John, eds. Dictionary of Labour Biography, 5 vols. LC 78-185417. 414p. 1972. Vol. 1. lib. bdg. 37.50x (ISBN 0-678-07008-3); Vol. 2. lib. bdg. 47.50x (ISBN 0-678-07018-0); Vols. 3. lib. bdg. 37.50x (ISBN 0-333-14415-5); Vol. 4. lib. bdg. 37.50x (ISBN 0-333-19704-6); Vol. 5. lib. bdg. 37.50x (ISBN 0-333-22015-3). Kelley.
Belloc, Hilaire. The Servile State. LC 77-2914. 1977. 8.00 (ISBN 0-913966-31-2, Liberty Classics); pap. 2.00 (ISBN 0-913966-32-0). Liberty Fund.
Bing, Alexander M. War-Time Strikes & Their Adjustment. LC 79-156405. (American Labor Ser., No. 2). 1971. Repr. of 1921 ed. 17.00 (ISBN 0-405-02915-2). Arno.
Blackburn, R. M. & Mann, Michael. The Working Class in the Labour Market. (Cambridge Studies in Sociology). 1979. text ed. 25.00x (ISBN 0-333-24325-0). Humanities.
Blake, Fay M. The Strike in the American Novel. LC 72-623. 1972. 10.00 (ISBN 0-8108-0481-6). Scarecrow.
Blyakhman, L. & Shkaratan, O. Man at Work. 306p. 1977. 3.75 (ISBN 0-8285-0242-0, Pub. by Progress Pubs Russia). Imported Pubns.
Boggs, James. American Revolution: Pages from a Negro Worker's Notebook. LC 63-20103. (Orig.). 1963. pap. 2.95 (ISBN 0-85345-015-3, PB0153). Monthly Rev.
Bok, Derek C. & Dunlop, John T. Labor & the American Community. 1970. pap. 6.95 (ISBN 0-671-20415-7, Touchstone Bks). S&S.
Brennan, Mary E., ed. Public Employees Conference, Dec. 7-10, 1980, Monterey, CA: Proceedings. 114p. (Orig.). 1981. pap. 10.00 (ISBN 0-89154-151-9). Intl Found Employ.
--Pulic Employees Conference, Dec. 5-8, 1979, Hollywood, Fla. Proceedings. 160p. 1980. pap. 10.00 (ISBN 0-89154-126-8). Intl Found Employ.
Bromley, Ray & Gerry, Chris, eds. Casual Work & Poverty in Third World Cities. LC 78-11329. 1979. 47.25 (ISBN 0-471-99731-5, Pub. by Wiley-Interscience). Wiley.
Brownson, Orestes A. The Laboring Classes. LC 78-17952. 1978. Repr. of 1840 ed. 22.00 (ISBN 0-8201-1314-X). Schol Facsimiles.
Buchanan, Joseph R. The Story of a Labor Agitator. LC 70-88521. (Illus.). xi, 460p. Repr. of 1903 ed. lib. bdg. 19.25x (ISBN 0-8371-4973-8, BULA). Greenwood.
--The Story of a Labor Agitator. facsimile ed. LC 75-148873. (Select Bibliographies Reprint Ser.). 1972. Repr. of 1903 ed. 24.00 (ISBN 0-8369-5644-3). Arno.
Burawoy, Michael. Manufacturing Consent: Changes in the Labor Process Under Monopoly Capitalism. LC 79-10188. 1980. lib. bdg. 20.00x (ISBN 0-226-08037-4). U of Chicago Pr.
Burtt, Everett. Labor in the American Economy. LC 78-73037. 1979. text ed. 14.95x (ISBN 0-312-46248-4). St Martin.
Butler, Elizabeth B. Women & the Trades. LC 70-89757. (American Labor, from Conspiracy to Collective Bargaining Ser., No. 1). 440p. 1969. Repr. of 1909 ed. 18.00 (ISBN 0-405-02108-9). Arno.
Byington, Margaret F. Homestead: The Households of a Mill Town. LC 70-89757. (American Labor, from Conspiracy to Collective Bargaining, Ser. 1). 307p. 1969. Repr. of 1910 ed. 16.00 (ISBN 0-405-02109-7). Arno.
Cahn, William. A Pictorial History of American Labor. (Illus.). 12.50 (ISBN 0-517-50040-X). Crown.
Calkins, Clinch. Spy Overhead: The Story of Industrial Espionage. LC 70-156408. (American Labor Ser., No. 2). 1971. Repr. of 1937 ed. 24.00 (ISBN 0-405-02917-9). Arno.
Campbell, Alan & Bowyer, John. Trade Unions & the Individual. 480p. 1981. 54.00x (ISBN 0-906214-05-X, Pub. by ESC Pub England). State Mutual Bk.
Cantor, Milton, ed. American Workingclass Culture: Explorations in American Labor & Social History. LC 78-59260. (Contributions in Labor History: No. 7). 1979. lib. bdg. 27.50 (ISBN 0-313-20611-2, CAW/). Greenwood.
Carey, Henry C. Essay of the Rate of Wages. LC 77-119647. Repr. of 1835 ed. 7.00 (ISBN 0-404-01392-9). AMS Pr.
--Essay on the Rate of Wages. LC 64-66155. Repr. of 1835 ed. 6.75x (ISBN 0-678-00081-6). Kelley.
--Slave Trade: Domestic & Foreign. LC 67-18574. Repr. of 1853 ed. 17.50x (ISBN 0-678-00248-7). Kelley.
Carnegie, Andrew. Problems of to-Day: Wealth - Labor - Socialism. 1908. 10.00 (ISBN 0-686-17693-6). Quality Lib.
--Problems of To-Day: Wealth-Labor-Socialism. 1908. 10.00 (ISBN 0-685-72817-X). Norwood Edns.
Carnegie Endowment for International Peace. American Labor in a Changing World Economy. LC 78-15545. (Praeger Special Studies). 1978. 31.95 (ISBN 0-03-045281-3). Praeger.
Carpenter, Niles. Nationality, Color, & Economic Opportunity in the City of Buffalo. LC 70-107480. Repr. of 1927 ed. 18.75x (ISBN 0-8371-3782-9, Pub. by Negro U Pr). Greenwood.
Case, John, et al, eds. Workers' Control: A Reader on Labor & Social Change. pap. 3.95 (ISBN 0-394-71862-3, V-862, Vin). Random.
Cass, Eugene L. & Zimmer, Frederick G., eds. Man & Work in Society. 313p. 1980. pap. text ed. 9.95 (ISBN 0-442-21929-6). Van Nos Reinhold.
Cayton, Horace R. & Mitchell, George S. Black Workers & the New Unions. LC 71-129941. 473p. 1939. Repr. 21.00x (ISBN 0-8371-3355-6, Pub. by Negro U Pr). Greenwood.
Chaikin, Sol C. A Labor Viewpoint. LC 80-12784. (Illus.). 250p. (Orig.). 1980. pap. 10.95 (ISBN 0-912526-26-2). Lib Res.
Chamberlain, Neil W. & Cullen, D. E. The Labor Sector. 2nd ed. Orig. Title: The Firm: Microeconomic Planning & Action. 1972. 17.95 (ISBN 0-07-010428-X, C). McGraw.
Champion Labor Monthly, Vols. 1-3, No. 10. 1936-38. Repr. lib. bdg. 125.00 (ISBN 0-8371-9140-8, C100). Greenwood.
Chenery, William L. Industry & Human Welfare. Stein, Leon, ed. LC 77-70487. (Work Ser.). 1977. Repr. of 1922 ed. lib. bdg. 15.00x (ISBN 0-405-10159-7). Arno.
Chernikov, G. The Crisis of Capitalism and the Condition of the Working People. 1980. 6.00 (ISBN 0-8285-1775-4, Pub. by Progress Pubs Russia). Imported Pubns.
Child, Nellise. If I Come Home. LC 74-29041. (The Labor Movement Fiction & Non-Fiction Ser.). Repr. of 1943 ed. 23.00 (ISBN 0-404-58522-1). AMS Pr.
Chipeta, Chinyamata. Economics of Indigenous Labor. 1981. 9.95 (ISBN 0-533-04995-4). Vantage.
Clarke, J., et al, eds. Working Class Culture: Studies in History & Theories. 1980. 19.95x (ISBN 0-312-88978-X). St Martin.
Cohen, Robin & Gutkind, C. W., eds. Peasants & Proletarians: The Struggles of Third World Workers. LC 79-10020. 1980. pap. text ed. 7.50 (ISBN 0-85345-505-8, PB5058). Monthly Rev.
Cohen, Sanford. Labor in the United States. 5th ed. (Economics Ser.). 1979. text ed. 19.95 (ISBN 0-675-08299-4). Merrill.
Cole, Robert E. Work, Mobility, & Participation: A Comparative Study of American & Japanese Industry. LC 77-80468. 1979. 22.50x (ISBN 0-520-03542-9); pap. 7.95x (ISBN 0-520-04204-2). U of Cal Pr.
Coles, Robert & Coles, Jane. Women of Crisis. 1979. pap. 6.95 (ISBN 0-440-59683-1, Delta). Dell.
Commons, John R. Industrial Goodwill. LC 75-89726. (American Labor, from Conspiracy to Collective Bargaining, Ser. 1). 213p. 1969. Repr. of 1919 ed. 12.00 (ISBN 0-405-02113-5). Arno.
--Labor & Administration. LC 64-17404. Repr. of 1913 ed. 19.50x (ISBN 0-678-00035-2). Kelley.
Commons, John R., ed. Trade Unionism & Labor Problems. LC 66-21664. Repr. of 1905 ed. 22.50x (ISBN 0-678-00221-5). Kelley.
--Trade Unionism & Labor Problems, 2nd Series. LC 66-21665. Repr. of 1921 ed. 27.50x (ISBN 0-678-00287-8). Kelley.
Conference of Socialist Economists, ed. Labour Process & Class Strategies. pap. 4.95 (ISBN 0-686-24150-9, Pub. by Stage One). Carrier Pigeon.
Conference of the Universities. Aspects of Labor Economics: Proceedings. LC 75-19698. (National Bureau of Economic Research Ser.). (Illus.). 1975. Repr. 20.00x (ISBN 0-405-07578-2). Arno.
Connell, John & Lipton, Michael. Assessing Village Labour Situations in Developing Countries. 1977. 7.50x (ISBN 0-19-560794-5). Oxford U Pr.
Coombs, Whitney. Wages of Unskilled Labor in Manufacturing Industries in the United States, 1890-1924. LC 76-76686. (Columbia University Studies in the Social Sciences: No. 283). Repr. of 1926 ed. 16.50 (ISBN 0-404-51283-6). AMS Pr.
Cooperation & the Working Class: Theoretical Contributions, 1827-1834. LC 72-2521. (British Labour Struggles Before 1850 Ser). (4 pamphlets). 1972. 10.00 (ISBN 0-405-04414-3). Arno.
Cowling, Maurice. Impact of Labour, Nineteen Twenty-Twenty-Four: The Beginning of Modern British Politics. LC 73-127236. (Studies in History & Theory of Politics). 1971. 49.95 (ISBN 0-521-07969-1). Cambridge U Pr.
Crisis & National Co-Operative Trade Union Gazette, Vols. 1-4, No. 20. 1832-34. Repr. lib. bdg. 59.00x (ISBN 0-8371-9156-4, CU00). Greenwood.
Curtin, Richard T. Income Equity Among U. S. Workers: The Bases & Consequences of Deprivation. LC 76-24349. (Praeger Special Studies). 1977. 22.95 (ISBN 0-275-23780-X). Praeger.
Dacus, Joseph A. Annals of the Great Strikes in the United States. LC 72-89728. (American Labor, from Conspiracy to Collective Bargaining, Ser. 1). 480p. 1969. Repr. of 1877 ed. 19.00 (ISBN 0-405-02115-1). Arno.
Davis, Louis E. & Cherns, Albert B., eds. The Quality of Working Life: Problems, Prospects & the State of the Art, Vol.1. LC 74-24369. 1975. 19.95 (ISBN 0-02-907390-1); pap. text ed. 9.95 (ISBN 0-02-907380-4). Free Pr.
Dealtry, William. The Laborer: A Remedy for His Wrongs. LC 76-89729. (American Labor, from Conspiracy to Collective Bargaining Ser). 420p. 1969. Repr. of 1869 ed. 16.50 (ISBN 0-405-02116-X). Arno.
De Caux, Len. The Living Spirit of the Wobblies. LC 76-1865. 1978. 7.50 (ISBN 0-7178-0431-3); pap. 2.95 (ISBN 0-7178-0432-1). Intl Pub Co.
De Man, Henri. Joy in Work. Stein, Leon, ed. LC 77-70513. (Work Ser.). 1977. Repr. of 1929 ed. lib. bdg. 15.00 (ISBN 0-405-10182-1). Arno.
Deutsch, Arnold. The Human Resources Revolution: Communicate or Litigate. (Illus.). 1979. 13.50 (ISBN 0-07-016593-9, P&RB). McGraw.
Dewitt, Sherri. Worker Participation & the Crisis of Liberal Democracy. (Westview Replica Edition Ser.). 150p. 1980. lib. bdg. 18.00x (ISBN 0-89158-922-8). Westview.
D'Ignazio, Fred. Working Robots. Buckley, Virginia, ed. (Illus.). 160p. 1981. 11.50 (ISBN 0-525-66740-7, 01117-330). Elsevier-Nelson.
Dion, Gerard. Dictionnaire Canadien des Relations du Travail: Francais-Anglais. 682p. (Eng.-Fr.). 1976. 49.95 (ISBN 0-686-57118-5, M-6163). French & Eur.
Dixon, Marlene. In Defense of the Working Class. 1980. pap. 3.00 (ISBN 0-89935-007-0). Synthesis Pubns.
Douglas, Paul H. Real Wages in the United States, 1890-1926. LC 66-21671. (Illus.). Repr. of 1930 ed. 19.50x (ISBN 0-678-00171-5). Kelley.
Douglas, Paul H., et al. The Worker in Modern Economic Society. LC 70-89730. (American Labor, from Conspiracy to Collective Bargaining Ser., No. 1). 929p. 1969. Repr. of 1923 ed. 35.00 (ISBN 0-405-02117-8). Arno.
Dubofsky, Melvyn. Industrialism & the American Worker: 1865-1920. LC 74-7326. (American History Ser.). 1975. pap. 4.95x (ISBN 0-88295-726-0). Harlan Davidson.
--When Workers Organize: New York City in the Progressive Era. LC 68-19669. 1968. 12.00x (ISBN 0-87023-042-5). U of Mass Pr.
Dubreuil, Hyacinth. Robots or Men: French Workman's Experience in American Industry. Stein, Leon, ed. LC 77-70491. (Work Ser.). 1977. Repr. of 1930 ed. lib. bdg. 18.00x (ISBN 0-405-10163-5). Arno.
Editorial Research Reports on Jobs for Americans. LC 77-18994. 1978. pap. text ed. 6.95 (ISBN 0-87187-120-3). Congr Quarterly.
Ehrenberg, Ronald, ed. Research in Labor Economics, Vol. 2. 381p. 1979. 37.50 (ISBN 0-89232-097-4). Jai Pr.
Ellis, Susan J. & Noyes, Katherine H. No Excuses: The Team Approach to Volunteer Management. (Volunteer Energy Ser.: No. 2). (Illus.). 65p. 1981. pap. 7.50 (ISBN 0-940576-04-X). Energize.
--Proof Positive: Developing Significant Volunteer Recordkeeping Systems. LC 80-69647. (Volunteer Energy Ser.: No. 1). (Illus.). 50p. 1980. pap. 7.50 (ISBN 0-940576-03-1). Energize.
Elson, Diane, ed. Value: The Representation of Labour in Capitalism. 1980. text ed. 30.00x (ISBN 0-906336-07-4); pap. text ed. 12.50x (ISBN 0-906336-08-2). Humanities.
Ely, Richard T. Labor Movement in America. LC 74-89731. (American Labor, from Conspiracy to Collective Bargaining, Ser. 1). 399p. 1969. Repr. of 1890 ed. 14.00 (ISBN 0-405-02119-4). Arno.
Emergency Program Branches of the I. W. W. Industrial Unionist, Vols. 1-2. Repr. lib. bdg. 140.00x (ISBN 0-8371-9165-3, IN00). Greenwood.
Enciclopedia Labor: La Enciclopedia Organica de Nuestro Tiempo, 12 vols. 3rd ed. 10000p. (Espn.). 1976. Set. 600.00 (ISBN 84-335-0310-3, S-12295). French & Eur.
Enciclopedia Labor 3, 3 vols. 2nd ed. 1193p. (Espn.). 1972. Set. 92.00 (ISBN 84-335-0306-5, S-12294). French & Eur.

Engels, Friedrich. El Papel Del Trabajo En la Transformacion Del Mono En Hombre. 18p. (Span.). 1977. pap. 0.50 (ISBN 0-8285-1354-6, Pub. by Progress Pubs Russia). Imported Pubns.
--El Sistema De Trabajo Asalariado. 62p. (Span.). 1976. pap. 0.75 (ISBN 0-8285-1674-X, Pub. by Progress Pubs Russia). Imported Pubns.
Epstein, Melech. Jewish Labor in the U. S. A., 1882-1952. rev. ed. 1969. 35.00x (ISBN 0-87068-042-0). Ktav.
Erickson, Charlotte J. American Industry & the European Immigrant, 1860-1885. LC 66-27065. 1967. Repr. of 1957 ed. 18.00 (ISBN 0-8462-0922-5). Russell.
Fearn. Labor Economics: The Emerging Synthesis. 1981. 18.95 (ISBN 0-686-72663-4). P-H.
Fink, Gary M. Labor's Search for Political Order: The Political Behavior of the Missouri Labor Movement, 1890-1940. LC 73-80582. 1973. 12.00x (ISBN 0-8262-0149-0). U of Mo Pr.
Fink, Gary M. & Cantor, Milton, eds. Biographical Dictionary of American Labor Leaders. LC 74-9322. 1974. lib. bdg. 25.00 (ISBN 0-8371-7643-3, FAL/). Greenwood.
Fiscal Measures for Employment Promotion in Developing Countries. 3rd ed. 1974. 14.25 (ISBN 92-2-100160-1). Intl Labour Office.
Foner, Moe & Vassil, Pamela, eds. Images of Labor. LC 80-28820. (Illus.). 94p. 1981. 29.95 (ISBN 0-8298-0433-1); pap. 16.95 (ISBN 0-686-72684-7). Pilgrim NY.
Foner, P., ed. Formation of the Workingmen's Party of the U. S. 1876. (Occasional Papers: No.18). 1976. 1.25 (ISBN 0-89977-017-7). Am Inst Marxist.
Foner, Philip S., ed. We, the Other People: Alternative Declarations of Independence, by Labor Groups, Farmers, Woman's Rights Advocates, Socialists, & Blacks, 1829-1975. LC 76-10736. 1976. 10.00 (ISBN 0-252-00623-2); pap. 2.95 (ISBN 0-252-00624-0). U of Ill Pr.
Foner, Philip S. & Lewis, Ronald L., eds. Black Worker: The Era of the AFL, the Railroad Brotherhoods & the UMW, 1880-1903, Vol. IV. LC 78-2875. 1979. 22.50 (ISBN 0-87722-139-1). Temple U Pr.
--Black Worker: The Era of the Knights of Labor & the Colored Farmers' Alliance, Eighteen Eighty to Eighteen Ninety, Vol. III. LC 78-2875. 1979. 22.50 (ISBN 0-87722-138-3). Temple U Pr.
Foner, Phillip S. Labor & the American Revolution. LC 76-18034. 1976. lib. bdg. 17.95 (ISBN 0-8371-9003-7, FLA/). Greenwood.
Foster, William Z. More Pages from a Worker's Life. Zipser, Arthur, ed. (Occasional Papers: No. 32). 1979. 1.50 (ISBN 0-89977-026-6). Am Inst Marxist.
--Pages from a Worker's Life. LC 72-130864. 1970. 7.50 (ISBN 0-7178-0297-3); pap. 3.25 (ISBN 0-7178-0149-7). Intl Pub Co.
Fried, Marc. The World of the Urban Working Class. LC 73-81673. 432p. 1973. text ed. 20.00x (ISBN 0-674-96195-1). Harvard U Pr.
Furniss, Edgar S. & Guild, Laurence R. Labor Problems: A Book of Materials for Thir Study. LC 71-89733. (American Labor, from Conspiracy to Collective Bargaining, Ser. 1). 621p. 1969. Repr. of 1925 ed. 25.00 (ISBN 0-405-02122-4). Arno.
Galarza, Ernesto. Merchants of Labor: The Mexican Bracero Story. (gr. 9-12). 1966. text ed. 10.00 (ISBN 0-87461-023-0); pap. text ed. 5.95 (ISBN 0-87461-024-9). McNally.
Galenson, Walter. Primer on Employment & Wages. 1970. pap. text ed. 3.25x (ISBN 0-394-30720-8). Phila Bk Co.
--Rival Unionism in the United States. LC 66-13170. 1966. Repr. of 1940 ed. 8.50 (ISBN 0-8462-0720-6). Russell.
Galenson, Walter, ed. Labor in Developing Economics. LC 76-3786. 299p. 1976. Repr. of 1962 ed. lib. bdg. 18.50x (ISBN 0-8371-8817-2, GALD). Greenwood.
Gallie, D. In Search of the New Working Class. LC 77-80834. (Studies in Sociology: No. 9). (Illus.). 1978. 36.00 (ISBN 0-521-21771-7); pap. 10.95x (ISBN 0-521-29275-1). Cambridge U Pr.
Garson, Barbara. All the Livelong Day: The Meaning & Demeaning of Routine Work. 1977. pap. 2.95 (ISBN 0-14-004381-0). Penguin.
Gaskell, Peter. Artisans & Machinery: Moral & Physical Condition of the Manufacturing Population. new ed. 399p. 1968. 37.50x (ISBN 0-7146-1395-9, F Cass Co). Biblio Dist.
Gelder, L. van, et al. Enciclopedia Juvenil Labor, 3 vols. 592p. (Espn.). 1977. Set. leatherette 54.00 (ISBN 84-335-0333-2, S-50474). French & Eur.
George, Henry. Labor Question. abr. ed. Orig. Title: Condition of Labor. 47p. 1959. Repr. of 1891 ed. pap. 0.25 (ISBN 0-911312-22-6). Schalkenbach.
Gilbert, James B. Work Without Salvation: America's Intellectual & Industrial Alienation, 1880-1910. LC 74-2249. 256p. 1977. 16.50x (ISBN 0-8018-1954-7). Johns Hopkins.
Gilfillan, Harriet W. I Went to Pit College. LC 74-25389. (The Labor Movement in Fiction & Non-Fiction Ser.). Repr. of 1934 ed. 21.50 (ISBN 0-404-58494-2). AMS Pr.
Ginzberg, Eli. The Manpower Connection: Education & Work. 288p. 1975. 15.00x (ISBN 0-674-54810-8). Harvard U Pr.
Gladden, Washington T. Working People & Their Employers. LC 75-89734. (American Labor: From Conspiracy to Collective Bargaining Ser., No. 1). 1969. Repr. of 1876 ed. 11.00 (ISBN 0-405-02123-2). Arno.
Glasser, Carrie. Wage Differentials. LC 77-76638. (Columbia University Studies in the Social Sciences: No. 476). (Illus.). 1969. Repr. of 1940 ed. 16.50 (ISBN 0-404-51476-6). AMS Pr.
Gohre, Paul. Three Months in a Workshop: A Practical Study. LC 74-38277. (Evolution of Capitalism Ser.). 236p. 1972. Repr. of 1895 ed. 19.00 (ISBN 0-405-04121-7). Arno.
Golden, Clinton S. & Ruttenberg, Harold J. The Dynamics of Industrial Democracy. LC 72-2372. (FDR & the Era of the New Deal Ser). 388p. 1973. Repr. of 1942 ed. lib. bdg. 27.50 (ISBN 0-306-70472-2). Da Capo.
Gompers, Samuel. Labor & the Common Welfare. Robbins, Hayes, ed. LC 70-102240. (Select Bibliographies Reprint Ser). 1919. 24.00 (ISBN 0-8369-5125-5). Arno.
--Labor & the Common Welfare. LC 79-89735. (American Labor, from Conspiracy to Collective Bargaining, Ser. 1). 306p. 1969. Repr. of 1919 ed. 13.00 (ISBN 0-405-02124-0). Arno.
--Labor & the Employer. LC 79-156413. (American Labor Ser., No. 2). 1971. Repr. of 1929 ed. 21.00 (ISBN 0-405-02921-7). Arno.
--Seventy Years of Life & Labour, 2 Vols. LC 66-21674. Repr. of 1925 ed. Set. 45.00x (ISBN 0-678-00213-4). Kelley.
Gordon, David M. The Working Poor: Towards a State Agenda. Barker, Michael, ed. LC 79-67382. (Studies in State Development Policy: Vol. 4). 1980. pap. 8.95 (ISBN 0-934842-03-5). Coun State Plan.
Gordon, L. & Klopov, E. Man After Work. 306p. 1975. 2.10 (ISBN 0-8285-0274-9, Pub. by Progress Pubs Russia). Imported Pubns.
Gould, Elgin R. The Social Condition of Labor. 1973. Repr. of 1893 ed. pap. 7.00 (ISBN 0-384-19420-6). Johnson Repr.
--The Social Condition of Labor. LC 78-63816. (Johns Hopkins University. Studies in the Social Sciences. Eleventh Ser. 1893: 1). Repr. of 1893 ed. 11.50 (ISBN 0-404-61079-X). AMS Pr.
Graham, Bob. Workdays: Finding Florida on the Job. Mahoney, Lawrence, ed. LC 78-4177. (Illus.). 1978. pap. 5.95 (ISBN 0-916224-34-1). Banyan Bks.
Green, Gil. Whats Happening to Labor. LC 76-14861. 312p. 1976. 12.00 (ISBN 0-7178-0465-8); pap. 4.50 (ISBN 0-7178-0464-X). Intl Pub Co.
Greenslade, Roy. Goodbye to the Working Class. LC 76-373483. 192p. 1979. 11.95 (ISBN 0-7145-2511-1, Pub. by M Boyars); pap. 6.95 (ISBN 0-7145-2523-5). Merrimack Bk Serv.
Greenstone, J. David. Labor in American Politics. 1977. pap. 5.95 (ISBN 0-226-30715-8, P728, Phoen). U of Chicago Pr.
Gutman, Herbert G. Work Culture & Society in Industrializing America: Essays in America's Working Class & Social History. 1977. pap. 4.95 (ISBN 0-394-72251-5, Vin). Random.
Hagburg, Eugene C. & Levine, Marvin J. Labor Relations: An Integrated Perspective. 1978. text ed. 19.95 (ISBN 0-8299-0168-X). West Pub.
Hall, Gus. Labor up Front. (Orig.). 1980. pap. 1.00 (ISBN 0-7178-0565-4). Intl Pub Co.
--Steel & Metal Workers - It Takes a Fight to Win! 2nd ed. (Illus.). 64p. 1972. pap. 0.25 (ISBN 0-87898-094-6). New Outlook.
Hammer, Tove H. & Bacharach, Samuel B., eds. Reward Systems & Power Distribution: Searching for Solutions. (Pierce Ser.: No. 5). 1977. pap. 4.75 (ISBN 0-87546-223-5); pap. 7.75 special hard bdg. (ISBN 0-87546-290-1). NY Sch Indus Rel.
Hapgood, Hutchins. The Spirit of Labor. LC 74-22787. Repr. of 1907 ed. 24.50 (ISBN 0-404-58436-5). AMS Pr.
Hardman, J. B., ed. American Labor Dynamics. LC 72-89736. (American Labor Ser. 1). 432p. 1969. Repr. of 1928 ed. 17.00 (ISBN 0-405-02125-9). Arno.
Hardman, Jacob B., ed. American Labor Dynamics in the Light of Post-War Developments. LC 68-25675. (Illus.). 1968. Repr. of 1928 ed. 12.00 (ISBN 0-8462-1146-7). Russell.
Harris, Herbert. Labor's Civil War. Repr. of 1940 ed. lib. bdg. 15.00 (ISBN 0-8371-2285-6, HALC). Greenwood.
Haseler, Stephen. The Tragedy of Labour. (Mainstream Ser.). 262p. 1981. pap. 7.95x (ISBN 0-631-12836-0, Pub. by Basil Blackwell England). Biblio Dist.
Haynes, George E. Negro at Work in New York City: A Study in Economic Progress. LC 68-28999. (American Negro: His History & Literature Ser., No. 1). 1968. Repr. of 1912 ed. 7.00 (ISBN 0-405-01818-5). Arno.
Hedges, Marion H. Iron City. LC 74-26114. (The Labor Movement in Fiction & Non-Fiction Ser.). Repr. of 1919 ed. 23.50 (ISBN 0-404-58439-X). AMS Pr.
Heisler, William J. & Houck, John W. A Matter of Dignity: Inquiries into the Humanization of Work. LC 76-51620. 1977. pap. text ed. 4.95x (ISBN 0-268-01345-4). U of Notre Dame Pr.
Helmer, John. The Deadly Simple Mechanics of Society. LC 73-6417. 288p. 1974. 9.95 (ISBN 0-8164-9162-3). Continuum.
Helps, Arthur. The Claims of Labour. (The Development of Industrial Society Ser.). 288p. 1971. Repr. of 1845 ed. 21.00x (ISBN 0-686-28329-5, Pub. by Irish Academic Pr). Biblio Dist.
Henderson, Charles R. Social Spirit in America. LC 77-39378. (Select Bibliographies Reprint Series). 1972. Repr. of 1897 ed. 16.50 (ISBN 0-8369-9911-8). Arno.
Herald to the Trades Advocate & Cooperative Journal, Nos. 1-36. 1830-31. Repr. lib. bdg. 29.00x (ISBN 0-8371-9380-X, HA00). Greenwood.
Herbst, Josephine. The Executioner Waits. LC 74-26115. (The Labor Movement Fiction & Non-Fiction Ser.). Repr. of 1934 ed. 27.00 (ISBN 0-404-58440-3). AMS Pr.
Heron, Alexander R. Why Men Work. Stein, Leon, ed. LC 77-70502. (Work Ser.). 1977. Repr. of 1948 ed. lib. bdg. 15.00x (ISBN 0-405-10174-0). Arno.
Hiley, Michael. Victorian Working Women. LC 79-92110. (Illus.). 144p. 1980. 18.95 (ISBN 0-87923-324-9). Godine.
Hillquit, Morris, et al. Double Edge of Labor's Sword: Discussion & Testimony on Socialism & Trade Unionism Before the Commission on Industrial Relations. LC 70-156419. (American Labor Ser., No. 2). 1971. Repr. of 1914 ed. 12.00 (ISBN 0-405-02927-6). Arno.
Hine, Lewis W. Men at Work. LC 76-50337. (Illus.). 1977. pap. 3.00 (ISBN 0-486-23475-4). Dover.
--Men at Work: Photographic Modern Men & Machines. 7.50 (ISBN 0-8446-5585-6). Peter Smith.
Hourwich, Isaac A. Immigration & Labor. rev. ed. 2nd ed. LC 70-170055. Repr. of 1922 ed. 27.50 (ISBN 0-404-03348-2). AMS Pr.
--Immigration & Labor: The Economic Aspects of European Immigration to the United States. LC 69-18779. (American Immigration Collection Ser., No. 1). (Illus.). 1969. Repr. of 1912 ed. 16.50 (ISBN 0-405-00527-X). Arno.
Howe, Irving, ed. The World of the Blue-Collar Worker. LC 77-190132. 312p. 1973. 8.95 (ISBN 0-8129-0251-3); pap. 3.50 (ISBN 0-8129-0402-8). Times Bks.
Howell, Joseph T. Hard Living on Clay Street: Portraits of Blue Collar Families. 6.00 (ISBN 0-8446-5202-4). Peter Smith.
Huberman, Leo. Labor Spy Racket. LC 77-139201. (Civil Liberties in American History Ser). (Illus.). 1971. Repr. of 1937 ed. lib. bdg. 22.50 (ISBN 0-306-70080-8). Da Capo.
Hughes, Henry. Treatise on Sociology, Theoretical & Practical. LC 68-58060. (Illus.). Repr. of 1854 ed. 15.50x (ISBN 0-8371-0488-2). Greenwood.
Humpherys, Anne. Travels into the Poor Man's Country: The Work of Henry Mayhew. LC 76-15346. 240p. 1977. 16.00 (ISBN 0-8203-0416-6). U of Ga Pr.
Hunter, Robert. Violence & the Labor Movement. LC 71-90180. (Mass Violence in America Ser). Repr. of 1914 ed. 14.00 (ISBN 0-405-01320-5). Arno.
Hurwitz, Howard L. Theodore Roosevelt & Labor in New York State, 1880-1900. LC 68-58592. (Columbia University. Studies in the Social Sciences: No. 500). Repr. of 1943 ed. 18.00 (ISBN 0-404-51500-2). AMS Pr.
Husband, J. I. Labour Administration: A General Introduction. 1980. pap. 17.10 (ISBN 9-2210-2349-4); pap. 11.40 (ISBN 9-2210-2350-8). Intl Labour Office.
ILO Thesaurus: Labour, Employment & Training Terminology. 2nd ed. 223p. 1980. 13.70 (ISBN 92-2-001982-5). Intl Labour Office.
Independent Labour League of America. Workers Age, Vols. 1-9, No. 42. 1932-41. Repr. lib. bdg. 530.00x (ISBN 0-8371-9270-6, WA00). Greenwood.
Industrial Union Party. Industrial Unionist, Ser. 1: Vols. 1-8, No. 3; Ser. 2, Nos. 1-4, 1941; Ser. 3, Nos. 1-6, 1949-50. 1932-50. Repr. lib. bdg. 147.50x (ISBN 0-8371-9181-5, IU00). Greenwood.
Industrial Workers of the World. Industrial Pioneer, Ser. 1: Vol. 1, Ser. 2: Vol. 1-4, No. 5. 1921-26. Repr. lib. bdg. 150.00x (ISBN 0-8371-9179-3, IP00). Greenwood.
--Industrial Union Bulletin (Industrial Workers of the World, Vols. 1-2, No. 31. 1907-09. Repr. lib. bdg. 145.00x (ISBN 0-8371-9180-7, IB00). Greenwood.
--Industrial Worker, Vols. 1-5, No. 21. 1909-13. Repr. lib. bdg. 395.00x (ISBN 0-8371-9182-3, IW00). Greenwood.
--One Big Union Monthly, Ser. 1: Vols. 1-3, No. 1, Ser. 2: Vols. 1-2, No. 6. 1919-28. Repr. lib. bdg. 125.00x (ISBN 0-8371-9183-1, OB00). Greenwood.
Innis, Harold A., ed. Labor in Canadian-American Relations: The History of Labor Interaction, by Norman J. Ware, & Labor Costs & Labor Standards, by H. A. Logan. LC 74-102505. (Relations of Canada & the U. S. Ser). (Illus.). 1970. Repr. of 1937 ed. 12.00 (ISBN 0-8462-1368-0). Russell.
International Class Struggle, Nos. 1-3. 1936-37. Repr. lib. bdg. 15.00x (ISBN 0-8371-9151-3, IC00). Greenwood.
International Labor Office Conference. Living & Working Conditions of Indigenous Populations in Independent Countries, 2 vols. in 1. LC 74-2685. 1974. Repr. of 1956 ed. lib. bdg. 19.75x (ISBN 0-8371-7424-4, INLW). Greenwood.
International Labor Profiles: Comprehensive Reports on the Labor Forces of Forty Key Nations. (Country Labor Profiles Ser.). 304p. 1981. 48.00 (ISBN 0-8103-0429-5). Gale.
International Labour Code, 1951, 2 Vols. 1952. Set. 28.50 (ISBN 92-2-100146-6). Intl Labour Office.
International Labour Conference, 60th Session, 1975. Making Work More Human: Working Conditions & Environment,Offprint from the Report of the Director-General. 2nd ed. 1978. 10.00 (ISBN 9-2210-1514-9). Intl Labour Office.
International Labour Office, ed. Equal Opportunities & Equal Treatment for Men & Women Workers: Workers with Family Responsibilities, Report V (1) 84p. (Orig.). 1980. pap. 10.00 (ISBN 92-2-102405-9). Intl Labour Office.
Jelley, Symmes M. Voice of Labor. LC 78-89740. (American Labor, from Conspiracy to Collective Bargaining Ser., No. 1). 401p. 1969. Repr. of 1888 ed. 17.50 (ISBN 0-405-02129-1). Arno.
Jones, Alfred W. Life, Liberty & Property. 1964. lib. bdg. 18.00x (ISBN 0-374-94294-3). Octagon.
Jones, Gwilym P. Workers Abroad. LC 74-22747. Repr. of 1939 ed. 14.00 (ISBN 0-404-58499-3). AMS Pr.
Jones, Lamar B. Mexican-American Labor Problems in Texas. LC 73-163941. 1972. pap. 7.00 (ISBN 0-88247-150-3). R & E Res Assoc.
Jones, Samuel M. The New Right: A Plea for Fair Play Through a More Just Social Order. LC 75-327. (The Radical Tradition in America Ser.). (Illus.). 479p. 1975. Repr. of 1899 ed. 29.50 (ISBN 0-88355-231-0). Hyperion Conn.
Kelley, Florence. Modern Industry: In Relation to the Family, Health, Education, Morality. LC 75-329. (The Radical Tradition in America Ser.). 147p. 1975. Repr. of 1914 ed. 15.00 (ISBN 0-88355-233-7). Hyperion Conn.
--Some Ethical Gains Through Legislation. LC 75-89742. (American Labor, from Conspiracy to Collective Bargaining Ser., No. 1). 341p. 1969. Repr. of 1905 ed. 14.00 (ISBN 0-405-02131-3). Arno.
Kellogg, Edward. Labor & Other Capital. LC 68-27853. Repr. of 1849 ed. 17.50x (ISBN 0-678-00803-5). Kelley.
Kellogg, Paul U., ed. Wage-Earning Pittsburgh, Vol. 6. LC 73-11906. (Metropolitan America Ser.). (Illus.). 726p. 1974. Repr. 37.00x (ISBN 0-405-05398-3). Arno.
Kelly, Edmond. A Practical Program for Workingmen. LC 75-332. (The Radical Tradition in America Ser). 240p. 1975. Repr. of 1906 ed. 19.00 (ISBN 0-88355-235-3). Hyperion Conn.
Kerr, Clark. Migration to the Seattle Labor Market Area, 1940-1942. Repr. of 1942 ed. lib. bdg. 15.00x (ISBN 0-8371-3058-1, KEMS). Greenwood.
Kerr, Clark & Rosow, Jerome M., eds. Work in America: The Decade Ahead. (Work in America Ser.). 1979. text ed. 15.95 (ISBN 0-442-20372-1). Van Nos Reinhold.
Kilpatrick, John A. The Changing Labor Content of American Foreign Trade: Nineteen Seventy to Nineteen Seventy-Five. Dufey, Gunter, ed. (Research for Business Decisions: Vol. 19). 93p. 1980. 21.95 (ISBN 0-8357-1103-X, Pub. by UMI Res Pr). Univ Microfilms.
Klein, Stuart M. Workers Under Stress: The Impact of Work Pressure on Group Cohesion. LC 75-160046. (Illus.). 136p. 1971. 9.50x (ISBN 0-8131-1253-2). U Pr of Ky.

Knight, Charles. Capital & Labor: Including the Results of Machinery. LC 76-38272. (The Evolution of Capitalism Ser.). 254p. 1972. Repr. of 1845 ed. 18.00 (ISBN 0-405-04125-X). Arno.

Koch, Harry W. Eligibility Worker Examinations. 1981. 6.00 (ISBN 0-913164-86-0). Ken-Bks.

Koenig, Allen E., ed. Broadcasting & Bargaining: Labor Relations in Radio & Television. 358p. 1970. 25.00 (ISBN 0-299-05521-3). U of Wis Pr.

Kornblum, William. Blue Collar Community. LC 74-5733. (Studies of Urban Society Ser). 1976. pap. 6.50 (ISBN 0-226-45038-4, P699, Phoen). U of Chicago Pr.

Krader, Lawrence. A Treatise of Social Labor. (Dialectic & Society: No. 7). 1979. text ed. 46.75x (ISBN 90-232-1692-X). Humanities.

Labor Fact Book: Combined Serial Index to Vol. 1 to 17. LC 72-83656. 1972. 6.00 (ISBN 0-88211-033-0). S A Russell.

Labor Research Assn. Labor Fact Book, Vol. 1. LC 72-83656. (Labor Fact Books). 224p. 1972. Repr. of 1931 ed. 8.50 (ISBN 0-88211-025-X). S A Russell.

--Labor Fact Book, Vol. 2. LC 72-83656. (Labor Fact Bks.). 224p. 1972. Repr. of 1934 ed. 8.50 (ISBN 0-88211-026-8). S A Russell.

--Labor Fact Book, Vol. 3. LC 72-83656. (Labor Fact Bks.). 224p. 1972. Repr. of 1936 ed. 8.50 (ISBN 0-88211-027-6). S A Russell.

--Labor Fact Book, Vol. 4. LC 72-83656. (Labor Fact Bks.). 224p. 1972. Repr. of 1938 ed. 8.50 (ISBN 0-88211-028-4). S A Russell.

--Labor Fact Book, Vol. 5. LC 72-83656. (Labor Fact Bks.). 224p. 1972. Repr. of 1941 ed. 8.50 (ISBN 0-88211-029-2). S A Russell.

Labor Research Front. Labor Bulletin, Vols. 1-2, No. 1. 1936-38. Repr. lib. bdg. 30.00x (ISBN 0-8371-9187-4, LP00). Greenwood.

Labour Administration: A General Introduction. 88p. 1980. pap. 12.75 (ISBN 92-2-102350-8, ILO145, ILO). Unipub.

Labour & Population. (Population Profiles: No. 5). 47p. 1977. pap. 1.50 (ISBN 0-685-81708-3, UNFPA). Unipub.

Labour Force Statistics 1976-1977. 1979. 21.25 (ISBN 92-64-01928-6). OECD.

Labour Inspection: Purposes & Practice. 2nd ed. 1976. 10.00 (ISBN 92-2-100963-7). Intl Labour Office.

Labourer: A Monthly Magazine of Politics, Literature, & Poetry, Vols. 1-4. 1847-48. Repr. lib. bdg. 55.00x (ISBN 0-8371-9188-2, LE00). Greenwood.

Lafargue, Paul. The Right to Be Lazy. 69.95 (ISBN 0-87968-039-3). Gordon Pr.

LaFollette, Robert M., ed. The Making of America: Labor. LC 72-89744. (American Labor, from Conspiracy to Collective Bargaining, Ser. 1). 433p. 1969. Repr. of 1906 ed. 23.00 (ISBN 0-405-02132-1). Arno.

Lancashire & Yorkshire Co-Operator & Useful Classes Advocate, Ser. 1: Nos. 1-6, Ser. 2: Nos. 1-12, Ser. 3: Nos. 1-10. 1831-32. Repr. lib. bdg. 18.00x (ISBN 0-8371-9189-0, LY00). Greenwood.

Lanfear, Vincent W. Business Fluctuations & the American Labor Movement, 1915-1922. LC 68-57572. (Columbia University. Studies in the Social Sciences: No. 247). Repr. of 1924 ed. 15.00 (ISBN 0-404-51247-X). AMS Pr.

Langdon, Emma F. Cripple Creek Strike: A History of Industrial Wars in Colorado 1903-4-5. LC 75-90402. (Mass Violence in America). Repr. of 1905 ed. 28.00 (ISBN 0-405-01322-1). Arno.

Lasso de La Vega, Javier & Rubert Candau, Jose M., eds. Diccionario Enciclopedias Labor, 9 vols. 7th ed. 6500p. (Span., Fr., Port., Eng. & Ger.). 1978. Set. leatherette 470.00 (ISBN 84-335-0322-7, S-12269). French & Eur.

Lauck, W. Jett & Sydenstricker, Edgar. Conditions of Labor in American Industries. LC 70-89746. (American Labor, from Conspiracy to Collective Bargaining, Ser. 1). 404p. 1969. Repr. of 1917 ed. 17.50 (ISBN 0-405-02134-8). Arno.

League for Industrial Democracy. Industrial Democracy, Vols. 1-6, No. 6. 1932-38. Repr. lib. bdg. 125.00x (ISBN 0-8371-9268-4, ID00). Greenwood.

League for Industrial Democracy: New York L. I. D. Monthly, Vols. 1-10, No. 8. 1922-32. Repr. lib. bdg. 46.50x (ISBN 0-8371-9269-2, LG00). Greenwood.

Lees-Smith, Hastings B., ed. The Encyclopaedia of the Labour Movement, 3 vols. 7th ed. LC 73-167033. xxv, 1132p. 1972. Repr. of 1928 ed. Set. 125.00 (ISBN 0-8103-3028-8). Gale.

LeMasters, E. E. Blue Collar Aristocrats: Life Styles at a Working Class Tavern. LC 74-27309. 228p. 1975. 17.50 (ISBN 0-299-06550-2); pap. 5.95 (ISBN 0-299-06554-5). U of Wis Pr.

Lenin, V. I. El Poder Sovietico y la Situacion Del Campesinado. 113p. (Span.). 1979. pap. 1.05 (ISBN 0-8285-1487-9, Pub. by Progress Pubs Russia). Imported Pubns.

Lenin, Vladimir I. Declaration of Rights of the Working & Exploited People. 1980. pap. 0.75 (ISBN 0-8285-1867-X, Pub. by Progress Pubs Russia). Imported Pubns.

Levasseur, Emile. The American Workman. Marburg, Theodore, ed. Adams, Thomas S., tr. LC 78-64267. (Johns Hopkins University. Studies in the Social Sciences. Extra Volumes: 22). Repr. of 1900 ed. 38.00 (ISBN 0-404-61369-1). AMS Pr.

--The American Workman. Stein, Leon & Marburg, Theodore, eds. Adams, Thomas S., tr. LC 77-70510. (Work Ser.). lib. bdg. 33.00 (ISBN 0-405-10180-5). Arno.

Levison, Andrew. The Working Class Majority. 1975. pap. 3.95 (ISBN 0-14-004084-6). Penguin.

Lewin, David, et al. Public Sector Labor Relations: Analysis & Readings. LC 77-3021. 1977. 14.95 (ISBN 0-685-58421-6); pap. 8.95 (ISBN 0-913878-12-X). T Horton & Dghts.

Lewis, W., et al. Wharton Assembly Addresses 1937. facsimile ed. LC 79-157969. (Essay Index Reprint Ser). Repr. of 1937 ed. 10.00 (ISBN 0-8369-2258-1). Arno.

Lightfoot, Claude & Patterson, William L. Four Score Years in Freedom's Fight. 16p. 1972. pap. 0.35 (ISBN 0-87898-081-4). New Outlook.

Lincoln, Jonathan T. The City of the Dinner-Pail. Stein, Leon, ed. LC 77-70511. (Work Ser.). 1977. Repr. of 1909 ed. lib. bdg. 15.00x (ISBN 0-405-10181-3). Arno.

Lippi, Marco. Value & Naturalism in Marx. 160p. 1980. 12.50 (ISBN 0-8052-7076-0, Pub. by NLB). Schocken.

Lloyd, Henry D. Men, the Workers. Withington, Anne & Stallbohen, Caroline, eds. LC 79-89751. (American Labor, from Conspiracy to Collective Bargaining Ser., No. 1). 280p. 1969. Repr. of 1909 ed. 14.00 (ISBN 0-405-02138-0). Arno.

London Co-Operative Magazine, Vols. 1-4, No. 3. 1826-30. Repr. lib. bdg. 65.00x (ISBN 0-8371-9191-2, LM00). Greenwood.

Lorwin, Lewis L. Labor & Internationalism. (Brookings Institution Reprint Ser). lib. bdg. 29.50x (ISBN 0-697-00164-4); pap. 6.95x (ISBN 0-89197-820-8). Irvington.

Loveridge, R. & Mok, A. L. Theories of Labour Market Segmentation. 1979. lib. bdg. 44.00 (ISBN 90-207-0859-7, Pub. by Martinus Nijhoff). Kluwer Boston.

Lunn, Kenneth, ed. Hosts, Immigrants & Minorities: Historical Responses to Newcomers in British Society 1870-1914. 1980. 25.00 (ISBN 0-312-39238-9). St Martin.

McCourt, Kathleen. Working-Class Women & Grass-Roots Politics. LC 76-26340. 256p. 1977. 10.00x (ISBN 0-253-36650-X). Ind U Pr.

McCulloch, John R. Treatise on the Circumstances Which Determine the Rate of Wages & the Conditions of the Labouring Classes. LC 64-56231. Repr. of 1851 ed. 11.50x (ISBN 0-678-00005-0). Kelley.

McIntyre, John T. Ferment. LC 74-26117. (The Labor Movement in Fiction & Non-Fiction Ser.). Repr. of 1937 ed. 27.00 (ISBN 0-404-58448-9). AMS Pr.

McKelvey, Jean T., ed. The Duty of Fair Representation. 1977. 10.95 (ISBN 0-87546-260-X); pap. 6.95 (ISBN 0-87546-234-0). NY Sch Indus Rel.

McKenney, Ruth. Industrial Valley. Repr. of 1939 ed. lib. bdg. 17.00x (ISBN 0-8371-0585-4, MCIV). Greenwood.

McNeill, George E., ed. Labor Movement. LC 66-21683. Repr. of 1887 ed. 22.50x (ISBN 0-678-00713-6). Kelley.

Mallet, Serge. Essays on the New Working Class. Howard, Dick & Savage, Dean, eds. Howard, Dick, tr. from Fr. LC 75-34904. 240p. (Orig.). 1975. 12.00 (ISBN 0-914386-13-1); pap. 4.50 (ISBN 0-914386-14-X). Telos Pr.

Man in His Working Environment. 142p. 1980. pap. 7.00 (ISBN 92-2-102060-6, ILO-139, ILO). Unipub.

Mann, Michael. Consciousness & Action Among the Western Working Class. (Studies in Sociology). 80p. (Orig.). 1975. pap. 6.75x (ISBN 0-333-13773-6). Humanities.

Manpower Assessment & Planning Projects in the Arab Region - Current Issues & Perspectives. 31p. 1980. pap. 6.50 (ISBN 92-2-102173-4, ILO146, ILO). Unipub.

Marx, Karl. Trabajo Asalariado y Capital. 42p. (Span.). 1979. pap. 0.60 (ISBN 0-8285-1357-0, Pub. by Progress Pubs Russia). Imported Pubns.

Maurer, Harry. Not Working. 1981. pap. 6.95 (ISBN 0-452-25272-5, Z5272, Plume). NAL.

Meador, Bruce S. Wetback Labor in the Lower Rio Grande Valley. LC 73-76012. pap. 9.00 (ISBN 0-88247-215-1). R & E Res Assoc.

Meier, August & Rudwick, Elliott. Black Detroit & the Rise of the UAW. (Illus.). 1979. 17.95 (ISBN 0-19-502561-X). Oxford U Pr.

Menger, Anton. Right to the Whole Produce of Labour. LC 68-54737. Repr. of 1899 ed. lib. bdg. 17.50x (ISBN 0-678-00714-4). Kelley.

Millen, Bruce H. The Political Role of Labor in Developing Countries. LC 79-29735. x, 148p. 1980. Repr. of 1963 ed. lib. bdg. 18.75x (ISBN 0-313-22286-X, MIPO). Greenwood.

Mitchell, Broadus. Rise of Cotton Mills in the South. 2nd ed. LC 68-8128. (American Scene Ser). 1968. Repr. of 1921 ed. lib. bdg. 27.50 (ISBN 0-306-71141-9). Da Capo.

Mitchell, Broadus & Mitchell, George. Industrial Revolution in the South. LC 75-100818. Repr. of 1930 ed. 14.00 (ISBN 0-404-00201-3). AMS Pr.

Mitchell, Charlene. Fight to Free Angela Davis: Its Importance for the Working Class. 12p. 1972. pap. 0.25 (ISBN 0-87898-085-7). New Outlook.

Mitchell, John. Organized Labor. LC 68-56263. Repr. of 1903 ed. 19.50x (ISBN 0-678-00733-0). Kelley.

Montgomery, David. Workers' Control in America. LC 78-32001. (Illus.). 1979. 16.95 (ISBN 0-521-22580-9). Cambridge U Pr.

Moore, Wilbert E. & Feldman, Arnold S., eds. Labor Commitment & Social Change in Developing Areas. LC 60-53440. 1960. pap. 8.00 (ISBN 0-527-03305-7). Kraus Repr.

More, Louise B. Wage Earners' Budgets: A Study of Standards & Cost of Living in New York City. LC 73-137178. (Poverty U.S.A. Historical Record Ser). 1971. Repr. of 1907 ed. 15.00 (ISBN 0-405-03116-5). Arno.

Mosely Industrial Commission. Reports of the Delegates of the Mosely Industrial Commission to the United States of America, Oct.-Dec., 1902. LC 73-2526. (Big Business; Economic Power in a Free Society Ser.). Repr. of 1903 ed. 14.00 (ISBN 0-405-05105-0). Arno.

New England Offering: A Magazine of Industry, Vols. 1-3. Repr. of 1848 ed. lib. bdg. 30.25x (ISBN 0-8371-9214-5, NEOO). Greenwood.

Newcomb, Simon. Plain Man's Talk on the Labor Question. LC 77-89756. (American Labor, from Conspiracy to Collective Bargaining, Ser. 1). 195p. 1969. Repr. of 1886 ed. 9.50 (ISBN 0-405-02143-7). Arno.

Newland, Kathleen. Women, Men & the Division of Labor. LC 80-51662. (Worldwatch Papers). 1980. pap. 2.00 (ISBN 0-916468-36-4). Worldwatch Inst.

Nicholson, J. Shield. The Effects of Machinery on Wages. LC 72-38263. (The Evolution of Capitalism Ser.). 160p. 1972. Repr. of 1892 ed. 12.00 (ISBN 0-405-04129-2). Arno.

Noble, Iris. Life on the Line: Alternative Approaches to Work. (A New Conservation Book). (Illus.). 96p. (gr. 6-8). 1977. PLB 5.49 (ISBN 0-698-30662-7). Coward.

Northup, Herbert R. Restrictive Labor Practices in the Supermarket Industry, No. 44. 1967. 7.50x (ISBN 0-8122-7555-1). U of Pa Pr.

Novack, George & Mandel, Ernest. The Revolutionary Potential of the Working Class. LC 74-75357. (Illus.). 80p. 1974. 8.00 (ISBN 0-87348-363-4); pap. 2.25 (ISBN 0-87348-364-2). Path Pr NY.

O'Connell, Donald W., ed. Public Sector Labor Relations in Maryland: Issues & Prospects. LC 72-92069. (PSLRCB Publication No. 1). (Illus., Orig.). 1972. pap. 5.00 (ISBN 0-913400-00-9). Pub Sect Lab Rel.

OECD. Labour Force Statistics Nineteen Sixty-Seven to Nineteen Seventy-Eight. (Illus.). 437p. (Orig.). 1980. pap. text ed. 21.25x (ISBN 92-64-02092-6, 30-80-02-3). OECD.

O'Higgins, Paul. Workers' Rights. 1976. pap. 1.95 (ISBN 0-09-911890-4, Pub. by Hutchinson). Merrimack Bk Serv.

Olivier, Sydney H. White Capital & Coloured Labour. LC 74-132079. Repr. of 1910 ed. 10.75x (ISBN 0-8371-4681-X). Greenwood.

Orear, Leslie F., ed. On the Job in Illinois. 60p. 1976. 8.00 (ISBN 0-916884-04-X); pap. 2.50 (ISBN 0-916884-02-3). C H Kerr.

--On the Job in Illinois, Then & Now. (Illus.). 1976. 8.00 (ISBN 0-916884-04-X); pap. 2.50 (ISBN 0-916884-02-3). Ill Labor Hist Soc.

O'Toole, James. Work, Learning, & the American Future. LC 76-50726. (Higher Education Ser.). 256p. 1977. text ed. 15.95x (ISBN 0-87589-304-X). Jossey-Bass.

Owen. Working Hours: An Economic Analysis. LC 78-22287. (Illus.). 1979. 21.95 (ISBN 0-669-02740-5). Lexington Bks.

Parker, Carleton H. Casual Laborer & Other Essays. LC 67-19916. 1967. Repr. of 1920 ed. 7.50 (ISBN 0-8462-0946-2). Russell.

Parmer, J. Norman. Colonial Labor Policy & Administration 1910-1941. 6.00 (ISBN 0-685-71735-6). J J Augustin.

Parnes, Herbert S. Work & Retirement: A Longitudinal Study of Men. (Illus.). 320p. 1981. text ed. 27.50x (ISBN 0-262-16079-X). MIT Pr.

Participation by Employers & Workers Organisations in Economic & Social Planning: A General Introduction. 1971. 9.00 (ISBN 92-2-100129-6). Intl Labour Office.

People: Their Rights & Liberties, Their Duties & Their Interests Ser. 1: Vols. 1-3, Ser. 2: Vols. 1-2. 1848-52. Repr. lib. bdg. 155.00x (ISBN 0-8371-9382-6, PE00). Greenwood.

Perlman, Selig. A Theory of the Labor Movement. LC 79-9092. pap. 6.95x (ISBN 0-87991-818-7). Porcupine Pr.

--Theory of the Labor Movement. LC 66-18323. Repr. of 1928 ed. 15.00x (ISBN 0-678-00025-5). Kelley.

Perlo, Victor. American Labor Today. 1968. pap. 0.25 (ISBN 0-87898-029-6). New Outlook.

Pfeffer, Richard. Working for Capitalism. 1979. 22.50x (ISBN 0-231-04426-7); pap. 8.00x (ISBN 0-231-04427-5). Columbia U Pr.

Pflug, Warner W. A Guide to the Archives of Labor History & Urban Affairs, Wayne State University. LC 73-6004. 224p. 1974. text ed. 8.95x (ISBN 0-8143-1501-1). Wayne St U Pr.

Pioneer: Or Grand National Consolidated Trades Union Magazine, Nos. 1-44. Repr. of 1833 ed. lib. bdg. 26.00x (ISBN 0-8371-9384-2, PI00). Greenwood.

Politics for the People, Nos. 1-17. LC 69-13752. Repr. of 1848 ed. 20.00x (ISBN 0-678-00663-6). Kelley.

Poole, Michael. Workers Participation in Industry. 1975. 13.50x (ISBN 0-7100-8004-2). Routledge & Kegan.

--Workers' Participation in Industry. rev ed. 1978. pap. 6.50 (ISBN 0-7100-8824-8). Routledge & Kegan.

Poor Man's Advocate & Workman's Guide, Nos. 1-50. 1832-33. Repr. of 1832 ed. lib. bdg. 20.00x (ISBN 0-8371-9230-7, PW00). Greenwood.

Poor Man's Guardian, Nos. 1-238. 1831-35. Repr. of 1831 ed. lib. bdg. 145.00x (ISBN 0-8371-9231-5, PG00). Greenwood.

Pope, Jesse E., ed. Clothing Industry in New York. 1970. text ed. 24.00 (ISBN 0-8337-2808-3). B Franklin.

Portes, Alejandro & Walton, John. Labor, Class, & the International System. 1981. 19.50 (ISBN 0-12-562020-9). Acad Pr.

Powderly, Terence V. Path I Trod. LC 77-181971. Repr. of 1940 ed. 31.50 (ISBN 0-404-05098-0). AMS Pr.

Powell, Jim. Work Study. 1976. pap. 1.95 (ISBN 0-09-911910-2, Pub. by Hutchinson). Merrimack Bk Serv.

Praktische Betriebswirt, Vols. 1-26, No. 6. Repr. of 1921 ed. lib. bdg. 1475.00x (ISBN 0-8371-9232-3, PS00). Greenwood.

Pratt, Edward E. Industrial Causes of Congestion of Population in New York City. LC 68-56682. (Columbia University. Studies in the Social Sciences: No. 109). Repr. of 1911 ed. 21.00 (ISBN 0-404-51109-0). AMS Pr.

Preis, Art. Labor's Giant Step: Twenty Years of the CIO. rev. ed. LC 72-79771. pap. 7.95 (ISBN 0-87348-263-8). Path Pr NY.

Proctor, Roscoe. Black Workers & the Class Struggle. 40p. 1972. pap. 0.45 (ISBN 0-87898-078-4). New Outlook.

Randall, John H., Jr. Problem of Group Responsibility to Society. LC 72-89760. (American Labor, from Conspiracy to Collective Bargaining Ser., No. 1). 296p. 1969. Repr. of 1922 ed. 12.00 (ISBN 0-405-02145-3). Arno.

Rice, Stuart A. Farmers & Workers in American Politics. LC 78-82242. (Columbia University. Studies in the Social Sciences: No. 253). Repr. of 1924 ed. 20.00 (ISBN 0-404-51253-4). AMS Pr.

Rifkin, Bernard. American Labor Sourcebook. 1980. 39.95 (ISBN 0-07-052830-6, P&RB). McGraw.

Ritzer, George. Working: Conflict & Change. 2nd ed. (Illus.). 1977. text ed. 19.95 (ISBN 0-13-967638-4). P-H.

Roberts, Kenneth. Working Class. 1978. pap. text ed. 10.50x (ISBN 0-582-48935-0). Longman.

Robinson, Terry. Staff Status for Manual Workers. 1972. 11.00x (ISBN 0-85038-012-X). Intl Pubns Serv.

Roney, Frank. Frank Roney: Irish Rebel & California Labor Leader. LC 74-22758. (The Labor Movement in Fiction & Non-Fiction Ser.). Repr. of 1931 ed. 36.75 (ISBN 0-404-58511-6). AMS Pr.

--Irish Rebel & California Labor Leader: An Autobiography. Cross, Ira B., ed. LC 76-6363. (Irish Americans Ser.). (Illus.). 1976. Repr. of 1931 ed. 37.00 (ISBN 0-405-09355-1). Arno.

Rosow, Jerome M., ed. The Worker & the Job: Coping with Change. LC 74-765. (An American Assembly Bk.). (Illus.). 224p. 1974. 7.95 (ISBN 0-13-965350-3, Spec); pap. 2.95 (ISBN 0-13-965350-3, Spec). P-H.

Roth, Rainer. Lexikon der Arbeits und Soziallere. (Ger.). 1976. 26.00 (ISBN 3-403-00593-3, M-7278). French & Eur.

Rowe, William E., ed. Studies in Labor Theory & Practice: Papers from the Fifth Midwst Marxist Scholars Conference. (Studies in Marxism: Vol. 12). 100p. (Orig.). 1981. 10.50 (ISBN 0-930656-23-7); pap. 3.95 (ISBN 0-930656-24-5). Marxist Educ.
Rubin, Lillian. Worlds of Pain: Life in the Working Class Family. LC 76-21648. 1977. pap. 4.95x (ISBN 0-465-09724-3, CN-5024). Basic.
Rubin, Lillian B. Worlds of Pain: Life in the Working Class Family. LC 76-7677. 1976. 12.95x (ISBN 0-465-09245-4). Basic.
Rudman, Jack. Senior Labor Specialist. (Career Examination Ser.: C-2351). (Cloth bdg. avail. on request). pap. 12.00 (ISBN 0-8373-2351-7). Natl Learning.
Ryan, John A. Declining Liberty, & Other Papers. facs. ed. LC 68-8491. (Essay Index Reprint Ser). 1927. 18.00 (ISBN 0-8369-0845-7). Arno.
Saposs, David, ed. Readings in Trade Unionism, LC 70-89762. (American Labor, from Conspiracy to Collective Bargaining Ser., No. 1). 415p. 1969. Repr. of 1926 ed. 17.00 (ISBN 0-405-02147-X). Arno.
Sargant, William L. Economy of the Labouring Classes. LC 68-20177. Repr. of 1857 ed. 19.50x (ISBN 0-678-00393-9). Kelley.
Scarborough, Dorothy. Can't Get a Red Bird. LC 74-26120. (The Labor Movement in Fiction & Non-Fiction Ser.). Repr. of 1929 ed. 27.50 (ISBN 0-404-58468-3). AMS Pr.
Schmidman, John. Unions in Post-Industrial Society. LC 78-112229. 1979. text ed. 13.95 (ISBN 0-271-00209-3). Pa St U Pr.
Schofer, Lawrence. The Formation of a Modern Labor Force: Upper Silesia 1865-1914. LC 73-90658. 1975. 24.00x (ISBN 0-520-02651-9). U of Cal Pr.
Schrank, Robert. Ten Thousand Working Days. LC 77-14521. 1978. 15.00x (ISBN 0-262-19169-5); pap. 4.95 (ISBN 0-262-69064-0). MIT Pr.
Schrank, Robert, ed. American Workers Abroad. 1979. 15.00 (ISBN 0-262-19178-4). MIT Pr.
Scoresby, William. American Factories & Their Female Operatives: With an Appeal on Behalf of the British Factory Population & Suggestions for the Improvement of Their Condition. (Research & Source Works Ser.: No. 184). 1967. Repr. of 1845 ed. 19.00 (ISBN 0-8337-3206-4). B Franklin.
Seager, Henry R. Labor, & Other Economic Essays. facs. ed. Gulick, Charles A., Jr., ed. LC 68-22943. (Essay Index Reprint Ser). 1968. Repr. of 1931 ed. 19.50 (ISBN 0-8369-0859-7). Arno.
Seaton, Douglas P. Catholics & Radicals: The Association of Catholic Trade Unionists & the American Labor Movement, from Depression to Cold War. 272p. 1981. 22.50 (ISBN 0-8387-2193-1). Bucknell U Pr.
Seifer, Nancy. Absent from the Majority: Working Class Women in America. (Illus.). 1973. pap. 2.25 (ISBN 0-87495-016-3). Am Jewish Comm.
Senior, Clarence. Santiago Iglesias: Apostol de los Trabajadores. Benitez, Jesus, tr. LC 72-91601. (Illus.). 110p. (Orig., Eng.). 1972. 5.00 (ISBN 0-913480-01-0); pap. 2.95 (ISBN 0-913480-03-7). Inter Am U Pr.
--Santiago Iglesias: Labor Crusader. Zebrowski, John, ed. Benitez, Jesus, tr. from Eng. LC 72-91601. (Illus.). 98p. (Orig.). 1972. 5.00 (ISBN 0-913480-00-2); pap. 2.95 (ISBN 0-913480-02-9). Inter Am U Pr.
Sheppard, Harold L. & Herrick, Neal Q. Where Have All the Robots Gone? Worker Dissatisfaction in the Seventies. LC 72-77285. 1972. 7.95 (ISBN 0-02-928600-X); pap. text ed. 3.95 (ISBN 0-02-928590-9). Free Pr.
Shostak, Arthur B. Blue Collar Stress. LC 79-16531. (A-W Occupational Stress Ser.). 1979. pap. text ed. 6.50 (ISBN 0-201-07688-8). A-W.
Silverman, Bertram & Yanowitch, Murray. The Worker in Post-Industrial Capitalism: Liberal & Radical Responses. LC 73-14431. (Illus.). 1974. pap. text ed. 8.95 (ISBN 0-02-928770-7). Free Pr.
Simkhovitch, Mary K. City Worker's World in America. LC 70-156424. (American Labor Ser., No. 2). 1971. Repr. of 1917 ed. 14.00 (ISBN 0-405-02942-X). Arno.
Slichter, Sumner H. Union Policies & Industrial Management. LC 73-89763. (American Labor, from Conspiracy to Collective Bargaining Ser., No.1). 611p. 1969. Repr. of 1941 ed. 24.00 (ISBN 0-405-02148-8). Arno.
Socialist Publishing Society. The Accused, the Accusers. LC 74-89715. (American Labor: from Conspiracy to Collective Bargaining Ser., No. 1). 188p. 1969. Repr. of 1887 ed. 9.00 (ISBN 0-405-02149-6). Arno.
Socialist Union Party. Labor Power, Vols. 1-2. 1939-41. Repr. lib. bdg. 27.50x (ISBN 0-8371-9242-0, LC00). Greenwood.
Somers, Gerald G., ed. Labor, Management, & Social Policy: Essays in the John R. Commons Tradition. 318p. 1963. 27.50 (ISBN 0-299-02870-4). U of Wis Pr.
Spalding, John L. Socialism & Labor, & Other Arguments Social, Political & Patriotic. facs. ed. LC 67-28768. (Essay Index Reprint Ser). 1902. 15.00 (ISBN 0-8369-0893-7). Arno.
Spencer, Charles. Blue Collar. 2nd ed. LC 76-50937. 242p. 1978. pap. 4.95 (ISBN 0-917702-05-0). Vanguard Bks.
--Blue Collar: An Internal Examination of the Workplace. LC 76-50937. 1977. pap. 4.95 (ISBN 0-918206-01-4). Lakeside Chart.
--Blue Collar: An Internal Examination of the Work Place. 2nd ed. LC 76-50937. 242p. 1978. pap. 4.95 (ISBN 0-917702-05-0). Vanguard Bks.
Squire, Lyn. Labor Force, Employment, & Labor Markets in the Course of Economic Development. (World Bank Research Publications Ser.). 208p. 1981. 16.95 (ISBN 0-19-520266-X); pap. 7.95 (ISBN 0-19-520267-8). Oxford U Pr.
Standing, Guy. Labour Force Participation & Development. 1978. 22.80 (ISBN 92-2-101769-9); limp cover 18.55 (ISBN 92-2-101770-2). Intl Labour Office.
Standing, Guy & Sheehan, Glen, eds. Labour Force Participation in Low-Income Countries. 1978. 18.55 (ISBN 92-2-101811-3); pap. 12.85 limp cover (ISBN 92-2-101812-1). Intl Labour Office.
Stead, William T. Chicago To-Day: Or, the Labour War in America. LC 76-90192. (Mass Violence in America). Repr. of 1894 ed. 13.00 (ISBN 0-405-01337-X). Arno.
Stein, Leon, ed. Work or Labor: Original Anthology. LC 77-70551. (Work Ser.). (Illus.). 1977. lib. bdg. 28.00x (ISBN 0-405-10205-4). Arno.
Stein, Leon & Taft, Philip, eds. Workers Speak: Self-Portraits, 1902-1906. LC 70-156433. (American Labor Ser., No. 2). 1971. 12.00 (ISBN 0-405-02956-X). Arno.
Stilwell, Hart. Border City. LC 74-22818. (The Labor Movement in Fiction & Non-Fiction Ser.). Repr. of 1945 ed. 23.00 (ISBN 0-404-58477-2). AMS Pr.
Stimson, Frederic. Labor in Its Relations to Law. LC 72-2675. (Select Bibliographies Reprint Ser). 1972. Repr. of 1895 ed. 14.00 (ISBN 0-8369-6865-4). Arno.
Sullivan, Teresa A. Marginal Workers, Marginal Jobs: The Underutilization of American Workers. 245p. 1980. pap. 9.95x (ISBN 0-292-75055-2). U of Tex Pr.
Sullivan, William A. The Industrial Worker in Pennsylvania, 1800-1840. 1971. Repr. of 1955 ed. 18.50 (ISBN 0-384-58775-5). Johnson Repr.
Summers, Clyde & Rabin, Robert. The Rights of Union Members. 1979. pap. 2.25 (ISBN 0-380-46193-5, 46193, Discus). Avon.
Swinton, John. Momentous Question: The Respective Attitudes of Labor & Capital. LC 71-157155. (Research & Source Works Ser.: No. 721). 1971. Repr. of 1895 ed. lib. bdg. 29.00 (ISBN 0-8337-4441-0). B Franklin.
--A Momentous Question: The Respective Attitudes of Labor & Capital. LC 77-89764. (American Labor, from Conspiracy to Collective Bargaining, Ser. 1). 498p. 1969. Repr. of 1895 ed. 19.00 (ISBN 0-405-02155-0). Arno.
Swinton, John, et al. Striking for Life: Labor's Side of the Labor Question. 59.95 (ISBN 0-8490-1143-4). Gordon Pr.
Taft, Donald. Two Portuguese Communities in New England. LC 69-18792. (American Immigration Collection Ser., No. 1). 1969. Repr. of 1923 ed. 10.50 (ISBN 0-405-00541-5). Arno.
Tannenbaum, Frank. Labor Movement: Its Conservative Functions & Social Consequences. LC 70-89765. (American Labor: From Conspiracy to Collective Bargaining Ser., No. 1). Repr. of 1921 ed. 12.50 (ISBN 0-405-02153-4). Arno.
Taylor, Paul S. Mexican Labor in the United States, 3 Vols. Repr. of 1934 ed. Set. pap. 61.00 (ISBN 0-384-59626-6). Johnson Repr.
Tcherikower, Elias, ed. Geshikhte Fun der Yidisher Arbeterbavegung, Vol.2. LC 45-13072. (Illus., Yiddish.). 1945. 10.00 (ISBN 0-914512-18-8). Yivo Inst.
Tead, Ordway. Instincts in Industry. LC 73-89766. (American Labor, from Conspiracy to Collective Bargaining, Ser. 1). 222p. 1969. Repr. of 1918 ed. 10.00 (ISBN 0-405-02154-2). Arno.
Terkel, Studs. Working. 1975. pap. 3.50 (ISBN 0-380-00259-0, 55731). Avon.
Thompson, Herbert M. The Theory of Wages: And Its Application to the Eight Hour Question & Other Labour Problems. LC 79-51868. 1981. Repr. of 1892 ed. 16.50 (ISBN 0-88355-960-9). Hyperion Conn.
Thompson, William. Labor Rewarded. LC 66-21695. Repr. of 1827 ed. 12.50x (ISBN 0-678-00299-1). Kelley.
--Labour Rewarded: The Claims of Labor & Capital Conciliated or How to Secure to Labor the Whole Products of Its Exertions. 1971. Repr. of 1827 ed. lib. bdg. 13.00 (ISBN 0-8337-3528-4). B Franklin.
Thornton, William T. On Labour: Its Wrongful Claims & Rightful Dues: Its Actual Present & Possible Future. 2nd ed. (The Development of Industrial Society Ser.). 499p. 1971. Repr. of 1870 ed. 35.00x (ISBN 0-7165-1788-4, Pub. by Irish Academic Pr). Biblio Dist.
Todd, Arthur J. Industry & Society: Sociological Appraisal of Modern Industrialism. Stein, Leon, ed. LC 77-70540. (Work Ser.). 1977. Repr. of 1933 ed. lib. bdg. 39.00x (ISBN 0-405-10209-7). Arno.
Topham, Tony. The Organized Worker. 1975. pap. 1.95 (ISBN 0-09-910200-5, Pub. by Hutchinson). Merrimack Bk Serv.
Los Trabajadores y Su Papel Esencial. Orig. Title: Labor up-Front. 120p. (Span.). 1980. 1.00 (ISBN 0-7178-0574-3). Intl Pub Co.
Tronti, Mario, et al, eds. Working Class Autonomy & the Crisis. 1981. text ed. 33.75x (ISBN 0-391-01811-6); pap. text ed. write for info. (ISBN 0-391-01812-4). Humanities.
Twentieth Century Fund. Labor & Government: An Investigation. Bernheim, Alfred L. & Van Doren, Dorothy, eds. LC 35-9534. 1935. 22.00 (ISBN 0-527-02808-8). Kraus Repr.
Union: A Monthly Record of Moral, Social, & Educational Progress, Nos. 1-10. 1842-43. Repr. lib. bdg. 23.00x (ISBN 0-8371-9255-2, UN00). Greenwood.
U. S. Bureau Of Labor. Index to All Reports Issued by Bureaus of Labor Statistics in the United States Prior to March 1, 1902. Wright, Carroll D., ed. Repr. of 1902 ed. 15.50 (ISBN 0-384-62750-1). Johnson Repr.
--Regulations & Restriction of Output. 1971. Repr. of 1904 ed. 59.00 (ISBN 0-403-01246-5). Scholarly.
United States Bureau of Labor Statistics. The Gift of Freedom: A Study of the Economic & Social Status of Wage Earners in the United States. LC 78-10339. (Illus.). 1978. Repr. of 1949 ed. lib. bdg. 15.75x (ISBN 0-313-20687-2, USGF). Greenwood.
U. S. Bureau of Labor Statistics. Techniques of Preparing Major BLS Statistical Ser. Lipstein, Benjamin, ed. Repr. of 1954 ed. lib. bdg. 15.00 (ISBN 0-8371-2273-2, TESS). Greenwood.
U. S. Department of Labor. The American Workers' Fact Book. Repr. of 1960 ed. lib. bdg. 17.25x (ISBN 0-8371-2274-0, AMWF). Greenwood.
United Workers Party. New Essays, Vols. 1-6, No. 4. Repr. of 1934 ed. lib. bdg. 130.00x (ISBN 0-8371-9215-3, NC00). Greenwood.
Unwin, George. Industrial Organization in the Sixteenth & Seventeenth Centuries. LC 68-58854. Repr. of 1904 ed. 24.00x (ISBN 0-678-05000-7). Kelley.
Velasco, Gustavo R. Labor Legislation from an Economic Point of View. Rogge, Benjamin A., ed. LC 73-86984. 76p. 1973. 3.00x (ISBN 0-913966-02-9). Liberty Fund.
Vetrova, N. & Lipkin, R. El Crecimiento Del Militarismo y la Explotacion Fiscal De los Trabajadores En EE. UU. 159p. (Span.). 1978. pap. 2.15 (ISBN 0-8285-1413-5, Pub. by Progress Pubs Russia). Imported Pubns.
Vincent, Henry. Story of the Commonweal. LC 70-90194. (Mass Violence in America Ser). Repr. of 1894 ed. 9.00 (ISBN 0-405-01339-6). Arno.
Vorse, Mary H. Labor's New Millions. LC 71-89768. (American Labor, from Conspiracy to Collective Bargaining, Ser. 1). 312p. 1969. Repr. of 1938 ed. 13.00 (ISBN 0-405-02156-9). Arno.
Walling, William E. American Labor & American Democracy. LC 75-89769. (American Labor Ser., No. 2). 1971. Repr. of 1926 ed. 19.00 (ISBN 0-405-02947-0). Arno.
Ware, Norman J. Labor in Modern Industrial Society. LC 68-25052. 1968. Repr. of 1935 ed. 12.00 (ISBN 0-8462-1184-X). Russell.
Watkins, Gordon S. Labor Problems & Labor Administration in the United States During the World War. 15.50 (ISBN 0-384-66000-2). Johnson Repr.
Webb, John N. Migratory-Casual Worker. LC 73-165690. (FDR & the Era of the New Deal Ser.). 1971. Repr. of 1937 ed. lib. bdg. 15.00 (ISBN 0-306-70339-4). Da Capo.
Who's Who in Labor. LC 75-7962. 1976. 65.00 (ISBN 0-405-06651-1). Arno.
Williams, Whiting. What's on the Worker's Mind: By One Who Put on Overalls to Find Out. LC 73-156441. (American Labor Ser., No. 2). 1971. Repr. of 1920 ed. 18.00 (ISBN 0-405-02949-7). Arno.
Willis, Paul. Learning to Labor: How Working Class Kids Get Working Class Jobs. (Morningside Bks.). 224p. 1981. pap. 8.50x (ISBN 0-231-05357-6). Columbia U Pr.
Wilson, Walter. Forced Labor in the United States. LC 76-144704. Repr. of 1933 ed. 18.00 (ISBN 0-404-00239-0). AMS Pr.
Winston, Henry. Build the Communist Party - the Party of the Working Class. 1969. pap. 0.35 (ISBN 0-87898-039-3). New Outlook.
Winter, J. M., ed. R. H. Tawney: The American Labour Movement & Other Essays. 1979. 25.00x (ISBN 0-312-66124-X). St Martin.
Wootton, Graham. Workers, Unions & the State. LC 67-12612. 1967. 6.00x (ISBN 0-8052-3295-8). Schocken.
Workers Party of the United States. Labor Action, Vols. 4, 6-22, No. 19. 1940-58. Repr. lib. bdg. 1275.00x (ISBN 0-8371-9262-5, LAP1). Greenwood.
Working Man: A Weekly Record of Social & Industrial Progress Ser. 1: Nos. 1-26, Ser. 2: Nos. 1-25. 1866. Repr. lib. bdg. 135.00x (ISBN 0-8371-9264-1, WM00). Greenwood.
Wright, Carroll. The Industrial Evolution of the United States. (History of American Economy Ser). Repr. 13.00 (ISBN 0-384-69425-X). Johnson Repr.
Wyckoff, Walter A. A Day with a Tramp & Other Days. LC 74-173129. Repr. of 1901 ed. 10.50 (ISBN 0-405-09108-7). Arno.
Year Book of Labour Statistics 1980. 687p. 1981. 63.50 (ISBN 92-2-002526-4, ILO 173, ILO). Unipub.
Yearbook of Labour Statistics 1979. 711p. 1980. pap. 60.25 (ISBN 92-2-002249-4, ILO 143, ILO). Unipub.
Yellen, Samuel. American Labor Struggles. LC 73-93633. (Illus.). 416p. 1974. pap. 5.45 (ISBN 0-913460-33-8, Dist. by Pathfinder Pr. N.Y.). Monad Pr.
Young, John & Newton, Jan. Capitalism & Human Obsolescence: Corporate Control vs. Individual Survival in Rural America. LC 78-71099. (LandMark Study). 272p. 1980. text ed. 21.50 (ISBN 0-916672-22-0). Allanheld.
Zahler, Helene S. Eastern Workingmen & National Land Policy 1829-1862. Repr. of 1941 ed. lib. bdg. 15.00x (ISBN 0-8371-1868-9, ZAEW). Greenwood.
Zieger, Robert H. Republicans & Labor, 1919-1929. LC 77-80087. 320p. 1969. 20.00x (ISBN 0-8131-1180-3). U Pr of Ky.
Zipser, Arthur. Working Class Giant: The Life of William Z. Foster. (Orig.). 1981. 11.00 (ISBN 0-7178-0590-5); pap. 4.25 (ISBN 0-7178-0582-4). Intl Pub Co.

LABOR AND LABORING CLASSES–ACCIDENTS

see Industrial Accidents

LABOR AND LABORING CLASSES–BIBLIOGRAPHY

Bibliography on Women Workers: Bibliography on Women Workers: Eighteen Sixty One to Nineteen Sixty-Five. 2nd ed. (Bibliographical Contributions Ser.: No. 26). 1974. 4.55 (ISBN 92-2-000936-6). Intl Labour Office.
Co-operative Bibliography: Supplement No. 1 to Co-operative Information. 1973. 11.40 (ISBN 92-2-100951-3). Intl Labour Office.
Diccionario Enciclopedico Labor, 8 vols. & 2 supplements. (Span.). 1975. 485.00 (ISBN 0-8277-3009-8). Maxwell Sci Intl.
McBrearty, James C. American Labor History & Comparative Labor Movements: A Selected Bibliography. LC 78-190624. 1973. pap. 2.00 (ISBN 0-8165-0504-7). U of Ariz Pr.
Slobodek, Mitchell. A Selective Bibliography of California Labor History. 1964. 6.00 (ISBN 0-89215-045-9). U Cal LA Indus Rel.
Smith, Harold, ed. British Labor Movement to Nineteen Seventy: A Bibliography. 268p. 1981. text ed. 70.00 (ISBN 0-7201-0924-8, Pub. by Mansell England). Merrimack Bk Serv.
Stein, Emanuel. The Labor Boycott: A Bibliography. 111p. 1974. Repr. 14.00x (ISBN 0-89020-005-X). Crofton Pub.
Subject Guide to Publications of the International Labour Office, with Geographical Index, 1919-1964. 1968. Set. 4.55 (ISBN 92-2-100930-0). Intl Labour Office.
United States Bureau of Labor Statistics. Subject Index of Bulletins Published by the Bureau of Labor Statistics: Consisting of "Subject Index of the Publications of the United States Bureau of Labor Statistics up to May 1, 1915" (Issued in 1915) & "Subject Index of Bulletins Published by the Bureau of Labor Statistics, 1915-1959" (Issued in 1960, 2 vols. in 1. LC 78-10739. 1978. Repr. of 1915 ed. lib. bdg. 28.50x (ISBN 0-313-20688-0, USSI). Greenwood.
U. S. Department of Labor. Washington D. C. Catalog of the United States Department of Labor Library (Washington, D.C., 38 vols. 1975. Set. lib. bdg. 3800.00 (ISBN 0-8161-1165-0). G K Hall.

LABOR AND LABORING CLASSES–CHILD LABOR

see Children–Employment

LABOR AND LABORING CLASSES–DISCIPLINE

see Labor Discipline

LABOR AND LABORING CLASSES–DWELLINGS

see also Cottages; Garden Cities; Housing; Labor Camps; Slums; Tenement Houses

Bauer, Catherine. Modern Housing. LC 73-11908. (Metropolitan America Ser.). (Illus.). 380p. 1974. Repr. 19.00x (ISBN 0-405-05386-X). Arno.

Fuller, Millard. Bokotola. 1977. pap. 3.95 (ISBN 0-8096-1924-5). New Century.

Kaufman, M. The Housing of the Working Classes & of the Poor. 146p. 1975. Repr. of 1907 ed. 9.50x (ISBN 0-87471-706-X). Rowman.

Tarn, J. N. Working Class Housing in Nineteenth Century Britain. (Architectural Association Papers Ser: No. 7). (Illus., Orig.). 1971. pap. 15.00x (ISBN 0-8150-0179-7). Wittenborn.

Taylor, Graham R. Satellite Cities: A Study of Industrial Suburbs. LC 70-112576. (Rise of Urban America). (Illus.). 1970. Repr. of 1915 ed. 18.00 (ISBN 0-405-02478-9). Arno.

Walker, Mabel L. Urban Blight & Slums: Economic & Legal Factors in Their Origin, Reclamation & Prevention. LC 70-139943. (Illus.). 1971. Repr. of 1938 ed. 20.00 (ISBN 0-8462-1546-2). Russell.

LABOR AND LABORING CLASSES–EDUCATION

Carnoy, Martin. Education & Employment: A Critical Appraisal. (Fundamentals of Educational Planning Ser: No. 26). 1978. pap. 4.75 (ISBN 92-803-1078-X, U779, UNESCO). Unipub.

Colquhoun, P. A New & Appropriate System of Education for the Labouring People. 98p. 1971. Repr. of 1806 ed. 15.00x (ISBN 0-7165-1773-6, Pub. by Irish Academic Pr Ireland). Biblio Dist.

Cook, John H. A Study of the Mill Schools of North Carolina. LC 73-176668. (Columbia University. Teachers College. Contributions to Education: No. 178). Repr. of 1925 ed. 17.50 (ISBN 0-404-55178-5). AMS Pr.

Curoe, Philip R. Educational Attitudes & Policies of Organized Labor in the United States. LC 76-89169. (American Education: Its Men, Institutions & Ideas, Ser. 1). 1969. Repr. of 1926 ed. 14.00 (ISBN 0-405-01407-4). Arno.

--Educational Attitudes & Policies of Organized Labor in the United States. LC 76-176702. (Columbia University. Teachers College. Contributions to Education: No. 201). Repr. of 1926 ed. 7.50 (ISBN 0-404-55201-3). AMS Pr.

Davidson, Thomas. Education of the Wage-Earners: Contribution Toward Solution of Educational Problems of Democracy. Bakewell, Charles M., ed. LC 77-160419. (Research & Source Works Ser.: No. 722). 1971. Repr. of 1904 ed. lib. bdg. 20.50 (ISBN 0-8337-0778-7). B Franklin.

Doeringer, Peter B., ed. Workplace Perspectives on Education & Training. (Boston Studies in Applied Economics). 184p. 1981. lib. bdg. 17.50 (ISBN 0-89838-054-5, Pub. by Martinus Nijhoff). Kluwer Boston.

Dwyer, Richard E. Labor Education in the U. S. An Annotated Bibliography. LC 77-21572. 1977. 14.50 (ISBN 0-8108-1058-1). Scarecrow.

The Factory Education Bill of Eighteen Forty Three. LC 72-2526. (British Labour Struggles Before 1850 Ser.). (6 pamphlets). 10.00 (ISBN 0-405-04419-4). Arno.

Fieldhouse, Roger. Workers' Educational Association: Aims & Achievements 1903-1977. (Landmarks & New Horizons Ser.: No. 4). 1977. pap. 3.50 (ISBN 0-87060-072-9). Syracuse U Cont Ed.

Hansome, Marius. World Workers' Educational Movements, Their Social Significance. LC 68-58587. (Columbia University. Studies in the Social Sciences: No. 338). Repr. of 1931 ed. 37.50 (ISBN 0-404-51338-7). AMS Pr.

Hole, James. Light, More Light. LC 76-5888. (Social History of Education). Repr. of 1860 ed. 15.00x (ISBN 0-678-08455-6). Kelley.

--Light, More Light: On the Present State of Education Amongst Working Classes of Leeds & How It Can Best Be Improved. (First Ser. in Social History of Education: No. 4). 1969. Repr. of 1860 ed. 18.00x (ISBN 0-7130-0005-8, Pub. by Woburn Pr England). Biblio Dist.

How to Improve Worker's Education. v, 112p. 1976. 6.85 (ISBN 92-2-101277-8). Intl Labour Office.

Kakkar, N. K. Workers' Education in India. 1973. 12.00x (ISBN 0-8426-0616-5). Verry.

Kay, Joseph. Social Condition & Education of the People in England & Europe, 2 Vols. LC 72-141318. Repr. of 1850 ed. lib. bdg. 50.00x (ISBN 0-678-00144-8). Kelley.

Kerrison, Irvine L. & Levine, Herbert A. Labor Leadership Education: A Union-University Approach. LC 73-9255. 188p. 1973. Repr. of 1960 ed. lib. bdg. 15.00x (ISBN 0-8371-6996-8, KELE). Greenwood.

Marot, Helen. Creative Impulse in Industry: A Proposition for Educators. Stein, Leon, ed. LC 77-70514. (Work Ser.). 1977. Repr. of 1918 ed. lib. bdg. 12.00x (ISBN 0-405-10183-X). Arno.

The Role of Universities in Workers' Education. 1974. 8.55 (ISBN 92-2-101096-1). Intl Labour Office.

Scoggins, Will. Labor in Learning: Public School Treatment of the World of Work. 1966. 2.00 (ISBN 0-89215-050-5). U Cal LA Indus Rel.

Silver, Pamela & Silver, Harold. The Education of the Poor: The History of a National School 1824-1974. (Routledge Library in the History of Education). 208p. 1974. 22.00x (ISBN 0-7100-7804-8). Routledge & Kegan.

Simon, Brian. Education & the Labour Movement: Studies in the History of Education, Vol. 2. 387p. 1965. 15.00x (ISBN 0-8464-0353-6); pap. 9.95x (ISBN 0-8464-0354-4). Beekman Pubs.

Stoikov, V. The Economics of Recurrent Education & Training: A WEP Study. viii, 115p. 1975. 14.25 (ISBN 92-2-101223-9); pap. 8.75 (ISBN 0-685-52514-7). Intl Labour Office.

Symons, Jelinger C. School Economy. LC 71-78973. (Social History of Education). Repr. of 1852 ed. 15.00x (ISBN 0-678-08460-2). Kelley.

Willis, Paul E. Learning to Labour: How Working Class Kids Get Working Class Jobs. (Illus.). 1977. 21.00 (ISBN 0-566-00150-0, 00730-7, Pub. by Saxon Hse England). Lexington Bks.

Worker's Education & Its Techniques: Worker's Education Manual. 1976. 10.00 (ISBN 92-2-100195-4). Intl Labour Office.

LABOR AND LABORING CLASSES–HISTORY

Here are entered general works and works dealing with the United States in particular. Works dealing with the history of labor and laboring classes in other specific areas will be found in the geographical subdivisions which follow.

Adamic, Louis. Dynamite, the Story of Class Violence in America. (Illus.). 1959. 8.75 (ISBN 0-8446-1002-X). Peter Smith.

Adams, Donald R., Jr. Wage Rates in Philadelphia, Seventeen Ninety to Eighteen Thirty. facsimile ed. LC 75-2572. (Dissertations in American Economic History). (Illus.). 1975. Repr. of 1975 ed. 21.00x (ISBN 0-405-07253-8). Arno.

Adelman, William. Pilsen & the West Side. (Illus.). 112p. 1981. pap. 4.50 (ISBN 0-916884-07-4). Ill Labor Hist Soc.

Albert, Peter J. American Federation of Labor Records: the Samuel Gompers Era: Guide to a Joint Microfilm Publication. Miller, Harold L., ed. 67p. 1981. pap. 5.00 (ISBN 0-87020-190-5). State Hist Soc Wis.

Allmendinger, Susan. The American People in the Industrial City. new ed. Allmendinger, David, Jr., ed. LC 72-95872. (American People Ser.). (Illus.). 224p. (gr. 9-12). 1973. PLB 7.95 (ISBN 0-88301-090-9); pap. 2.50 (ISBN 0-88301-074-7). Pendulum Pr.

Alman, David. World Full of Strangers. LC 74-29040. (The Labor Movement in Fiction & Non-Fiction). Repr. of 1949 ed. 24.00 (ISBN 0-404-58521-3). AMS Pr.

American Jews & the Labor Movement. (American Jewish Historical Quarterly: Vol. 65, Pt.3). 1976. 4.00 (ISBN 0-911934-05-7). Am Jewish Hist Soc.

Aptheker, Herbert. Unfolding Drama. Aptheker, Bettina, ed. LC 78-21025. 1979. 11.00 (ISBN 0-7178-0560-3); pap. 3.50 (ISBN 0-7178-0501-8). Intl Pub Co.

Aronowitz, Stanley. False Promises: The Shaping of American Working-Class Consciousness. LC 73-5679. 480p. 1973. 12.50 (ISBN 0-07-002315-8, GB); pap. 4.95 (ISBN 0-07-002316-6). McGraw.

Barkin, Solomon, ed. Worker Militancy & Its Consequences, 1965-75: New Directions in Western Industrial Relations. LC 75-3745. (Illus.). 448p. 1975. text ed. 31.95 (ISBN 0-275-07410-2); pap. 11.95 (ISBN 0-275-89440-1). Praeger.

Bimba, Anthony. History of the American Working Class. 3rd ed. LC 68-30818. (Illus.). 1968. Repr. of 1936 ed. lib. bdg. 25.00x (ISBN 0-8371-0020-8, BIWC). Greenwood.

Boyer, Richard & Morais, Herbert. Labor's Untold Story. 380p. 1955. 4.50 (ISBN 0-916180-01-8). United Elec R&M.

Brecher, Jeremy. Strike! new ed. LC 77-82654. (Illus.). 1977. pap. 6.50 (ISBN 0-8467-0364-5). South End Pr.

Brestensky, Dennis F., et al. Patch-Work Voices. LC 78-23824. (Orig.). 1978. pap. text ed. 3.95 (ISBN 0-916002-36-5, Pub. by U Ctr Intl St). U of Pittsburgh Pr.

Brody, David. Workers in Industrial America: Essays on the 20th Century Struggle. 1979. text ed. 14.95x (ISBN 0-19-502490-7); pap. text ed. 3.95x (ISBN 0-19-502491-5). Oxford U Pr.

Brooks, John G. Labor's Challenge to the Social Order. LC 74-137931. (Economic Thought, History & Challenge Ser). 1971. Repr. of 1920 ed. 16.00 (ISBN 0-8046-1437-7). Kennikat.

Brooks, Thomas. Toil & Trouble. 2nd ed. 1971. 7.95 (ISBN 0-440-08975-1). Delacorte.

Buchanan, Joseph R. The Story of a Labor Agitator. facsimile ed. LC 75-148873. (Select Bibliographies Reprint Ser.). 1972. Repr. of 1903 ed. 24.00 (ISBN 0-8369-5644-3). Arno.

Burn, James D. Three Years Among the Working-Classes in the United States During the War. LC 74-22735. Repr. of 1865 ed. 18.50 (ISBN 0-404-58487-X). AMS Pr.

Buxton, L. H. Primitive Labour. LC 70-115315. 1971. Repr. of 1924 ed. 12.50 (ISBN 0-8046-1106-8). Kennikat.

Bythell, Duncan. The Sweated Trades: Outwork in the Nineteenth Century. 1978. 50.00 (ISBN 0-7134-1259-3, Pub. by Batsford England). David & Charles.

Cahn, William. Lawrence Nineteen Twelve: The Bread & Roses Strike. LC 80-10878. (Illus.). 1980. pap. 6.95 (ISBN 0-8298-0390-4). Pilgrim NY.

--A Pictorial History of American Labor. (Illus.). 12.50 (ISBN 0-517-50040-X). Crown.

Calkins, Robert G. Distribution of Labor: The Illuminators of the Hours of Catherine of Cleves & Their Workshop. LC 79-51537. (Transactions Ser.: Vol. 69, Pt. 5). 1979. 10.00 (ISBN 0-87169-695-9). Am Philos.

Carlson, Douglas W., et al. Guide to the Papers in the John Hunter Walker Collection, 1911-1953. LC 80-16678. (Robert B. Downs Publication Fund Ser.: No. 6). 114p. 1980. pap. 15.00 (ISBN 0-87845-056-4). U of Ill Lib Info Sci.

Cloward, Richard & Piven, Frances. Poor People's Movements: Why They Succeed, How They Fail. LC 77-5298. 1977. 12.95 (ISBN 0-394-48840-7). Pantheon.

Colton, Calvin. The Junius Tracts. (The Neglected American Economists Ser.). 1974. lib. bdg. 50.00 (ISBN 0-8240-1009-4). Garland Pub.

Commons, John R., et al. History of Labor in the United States, 4 Vols. LC 66-18557. Repr. of 1918 ed. 85.00x (ISBN 0-678-00142-1); 25.00 ea. Vol. 1 (ISBN 0-678-04036-2). Vol. 2 (ISBN 0-678-04037-0). Vol. 3 (ISBN 0-678-04038-9). Vol. 4 (ISBN 0-678-04039-7). Kelley.

Commons, John R., et al, eds. Documentary History of American Industrial Society, 10 Vols. 2nd ed. LC 58-7086. (Illus., 1958. new prefaces. repr. of 1909-11 ed). Set. 250.00 (ISBN 0-8462-0155-0). Russell.

Cross, Ira B. A History of the Labor Movement in California. (Illus.). 1935. pap. 21.50 (ISBN 0-384-10245-X). Johnson Repr.

--A History of the Labor Movement in California. (California Library Reprint Ser.). 1974. Repr. 25.75x (ISBN 0-520-02646-2). U of Cal Pr.

Cumbler, John T. Working-Class Community in Industrial America: Work, Leisure, & Struggle in Two Industrial Cities, 1880-1930. LC 78-57768. (Contributions in Labor History: No. 8). 1979. lib. bdg. 22.95 (ISBN 0-313-20615-5, CWC/). Greenwood.

Dacus, Joseph A. Annals of the Great Strikes in the United States: A Reliable History & Graphic Description of the Causes & Thrilling Events of the Labor Strikes & Riots of 1877. LC 68-57902. (Research & Source Works Ser.: No. 306). (Illus.). 1969. Repr. of 1877 ed. 25.50 (ISBN 0-8337-0755-8). B Franklin.

David, Henry. History of the Haymarket Affair. 2nd ed. LC 58-7136. 1958. Repr. of 1936 ed. 25.00 (ISBN 0-8462-0163-1). Russell.

The Democrats & Labor in Rhode Island, Nineteen Fifty-Two to Nineteen Sixty-Two: Changes in the Old Alliance. LC 67-26817. (Illus.). xii, 154p. 1967. 10.00x (ISBN 0-87057-104-4, Pub. by Brown U Pr). U Pr of New Eng.

Derber, M. & Young, E., eds. Labor & the New Deal. LC 70-169656. (Fdr & the Era of the New Deal Ser.). 394p. 1972. Repr. of 1957 ed. lib. bdg. 29.50 (ISBN 0-306-70364-5). Da Capo.

De Robertis, Francesco M. & Norr, Dieter. Lavoroe Lavoratori Nel Mondo Romano & Zur Sozialen und Rechtlichen Bewertung der Freien Arbeit in Rom. Francesco M. Finley, Moses, ed. LC 79-4967. (Ancient Economic History Ser.). (Ger. & It.). 1980. Repr. of 1965 ed. lib. bdg. 34.00x (ISBN 0-405-12355-8). Arno.

De Witt, Howard. Violence in the Fields: California Filipino Farm Labor Unionization During the Great Depression. LC 79-65249. 125p. 1980. 9.00 (ISBN 0-86548-008-7). Century Twenty One.

Dickinson, Joan Y., ed. The Role of the Immigrant Woman in the U.S. Labor Force 1890-1910. Cordasco, Francesco. LC 80-852. (American Ethnic Groups Ser.). 1981. lib. bdg. 22.00x (ISBN 0-405-13415-0). Arno.

Dubofsky, Melvyn. We Shall Be All: A History of the Industrial Workers of the World. LC 75-78306. 576p. 1972. 17.50 (ISBN 0-8129-0089-8); pap. 5.95 (ISBN 0-8129-6234-6). Times Bks.

Dulles, Foster R. Labor in America: A History. LC 66-19224. 1968. pap. 8.95x (ISBN 0-88295-729-5). Harlan Davidson.

Dunlop, John, ed. Labor in the Twentieth Century. (Studies in Labor Economics Ser.). 1978. 24.50 (ISBN 0-12-224350-1). Acad Pr.

Edwards, Richard C. Contested Terrain: The Transformation of the Workplace in America. LC 78-19942. 1979. 12.95 (ISBN 0-465-01412-7). Basic.

Ellis, Susan J. & Noyes, Katherine H. By the People: A History of Americans As Volunteers. LC 78-60156. (Illus.). 308p. 1978. 8.95 (ISBN 0-940576-00-7); pap. 5.75 (ISBN 0-940576-01-5). Energize.

Engels, Friedrich. The Part Played by Labour in the Transition from Ape to Man. 16p. 1972. pap. 0.50 (ISBN 0-8285-0044-4, Pub. by Progress Pubs Russia). Imported Pubns.

Epstein, Melech. Jewish Labor in the U. S. A., 1882-1952. rev. ed. 1969. 35.00x (ISBN 0-87068-042-0). Ktav.

Evans, George E. Tools of Their Trades: An Oral History of Men at Work, 1900. LC 74-134282. 1971. 10.00 (ISBN 0-8008-7747-0). Taplinger.

Feichtinger, Kristine. You Never Hear About Any Struggles. 2nd ed. 36p. 1981. pap. 2.00 (ISBN 0-916884-06-6). Ill Labor Hist Soc.

Foner, Philip S. Great Labor Uprising of 1877. LC 77-80725. 1978. 17.00 (ISBN 0-913460-56-7); pap. 5.45 (ISBN 0-913460-57-5). Monad Pr.

--History of the Labor Movement in the United States, 4 vols. Incl. Vol. 1. From Colonial Times to the Founding of the American Federation of Labor. 576p. 1947. 15.00 (ISBN 0-7178-0091-1); pap. 3.95 (ISBN 0-7178-0376-7); Vol. 2. From the Founding of the American Federation of Labor to the Emergence of American Imperialism. 480p. 1955. 15.00 (ISBN 0-7178-0092-X); pap. 4.95 (ISBN 0-7178-0388-0); Vol. 3. Policies & Practices of the A. F. of L. 1900-1909. 480p. 1964. 15.00 (ISBN 0-7178-0093-8); pap. 3.95 (ISBN 0-7178-0389-9); Vol. 4. Industrial Workers of the World. 608p. 1965. 15.00 (ISBN 0-7178-0094-6); pap. 4.95 (ISBN 0-7178-0396-1). LC 47-19381. Intl Pub Co.

--History of the Labor Movement in the United States: The AFL in the Progressive Era (1910-1915, Vol. 5. 15.00 (ISBN 0-7178-0570-0); pap. 4.95 (ISBN 0-7178-0562-X). Intl Pub Co.

--Women & the American Labor Movement: From World War I to the Present. LC 80-753. (Illus.). 1980. 22.50 (ISBN 0-02-910380-0). Free Pr.

Foner, Philip S. & Chamberlin, Brewster, eds. Friedrich A. Sorge's Labor Movement in the United States: A History of the American Working Class from Colonial Times to 1890. LC 76-15319. (Illus.). 1977. lib. bdg. 25.00 (ISBN 0-8371-9028-2, FLM/). Greenwood.

Foster, John. Class Struggle & the Industrial Revolution. LC 74-19888. 352p. 1975. 19.95 (ISBN 0-312-14280-3). St Martin.

Fujita, Kuniko. Black Worker's Struggles in Detroit's Auto Industry 1935-1975. LC 79-93300. 125p. 1980. 10.00 (ISBN 0-86548-010-9). Century Twenty One.

Fusfeld, Daniel R. Rise and Repression of Radical Labor, U. S. A., Eighteen Seventy Seven to Nineteen Eighteen. (Illus., Orig.). 1979. pap. text ed. 2.00 (ISBN 0-88286-050-X). C H Kerr.

Ginzberg, Eli & Berman, H. American Worker in the Twentieth Century. LC 63-10647. 1963. 14.95 (ISBN 0-02-911730-5). Free Pr.

Gray, James. The American Civil Liberties Union of Southern California & Imperial Valley Agricultural Labor Disturbances,1930,1934. LC 77-75491. 1977. 13.00 (ISBN 0-685-82439-X). R & E Res Assoc.

Greeley, Horace, ed. The American Laborer, Devoted to the Cause of Protection to Home Industry, Embracing the Arguments, Reports & Speeches of the Ablest Civilians of the United States in Favor of the Policy of Protection to American Labor. (The Neglected American Economists Ser.). 1974. lib. bdg. 50.00 (ISBN 0-8240-1005-1). Garland Pub.

Green, James R. The World of the Worker: Labor in Twentieth Century America. Foner, Eric, ed. 1978. 8.95 (ISBN 0-8090-9830-X); pap. 4.95 (ISBN 0-8090-0132-2). Hill & Wang.

Green, James R. & Donahue, Hugh C. Boston's Workers: A Labor History. (Illus.). 1978. write for info. (ISBN 0-89073-056-3). Boston Public Lib.

Green, Marguerite. The National Civic Federation & the American Labor Movement. LC 73-9337. 537p. 1973. Repr. of 1956 ed. lib. bdg. 23.00x (ISBN 0-8371-7007-9, GRCF). Greenwood.

Griffen, Clyde & Griffen, Sally. Natives & Newcomers: The Ordering of Opportunity in Mid-Nineteenth-Century Poughkeepsie. (Studies in Urban History). 1977. 18.50x (ISBN 0-674-60325-7). Harvard U Pr.
Gruenberg, Gladys W. Labor Peacemaker: The Life & Works of Father Leo. C. Brown, S. J. Ganss, George E., ed. LC 80-83552. (Original Studies Composed in English Ser.: No. 4). (Illus.). 176p. 1981. 8.50 (ISBN 0-912422-54-8); pap. 7.00 smythsewn paperbound (ISBN 0-912422-53-X); pap. 6.00 (ISBN 0-912422-52-1). Inst Jesuit.
Gutman, Herbert. Work Culture & Society in Industrializing America. 1976. 12.50 (ISBN 0-394-49694-9). Knopf.
Ham, F. Gerald & Hedstrom, Margaret, eds. Guide to Labor Papers in the State Historical Society of Wisconsin. LC 78-23820. (Illus.). 1978. pap. 5.00 (ISBN 0-87020-177-8). State Hist Soc Wis.
Hammond, J. L. & Hammond, Barbara. The Town Labourer, Seventeen Sixty - Eighteen Thirty-Two: The New Civilisation. 1979. Repr. of 1917 ed. lib. bdg. 25.00 (ISBN 0-8495-2258-7). Arden Lib.
--The Town Labourer: The New Civilization 1760-1832. 7.50 (ISBN 0-8446-2197-8). Peter Smith.
Hammond, John L. The Skilled Labourer, 1760-1832. LC 66-22626. Repr. of 1919 ed. 17.50x (ISBN 0-678-00264-9). Kelley.
--Town Labourer, Seventeen Sixty to Eighteen Thirty-Two: The New Civilization. LC 66-22627. Repr. of 1917 ed. 17.50x (ISBN 0-678-00265-7). Kelley.
Haskins, Jim. The Long Struggle: The Story of American Labor. LC 76-23379. (gr. 7 up). 1976. 7.50 (ISBN 0-664-32602-1). Westminster.
Hirsch, Susan E. Roots of the American Working Class: The Industrialization of Crafts in Newark, 1800-1860. LC 78-51784. (Illus.). 1978. 18.00x (ISBN 0-8122-7747-3). U of Pa Pr.
Kerry, Tom. Workers, Bosses, & Bureaucrats: A Socialist View of the Labor Movement in the 1930's. 300p. 1980. lib. bdg. 17.00 (ISBN 0-87348-604-8); pap. 5.45 (ISBN 0-87348-603-X). Path Pr NY.
Kirstein, Peter N. Anglo Over Bracero: A History of the Mexican Worker in the United States from Roosevelt to Nixon. LC 76-56554. 1977. soft bdg. 9.00 (ISBN 0-88247-442-1). R & E Res Assoc.
Kuczynski, Jurgen. The Rise of the Working Class. (Illus., Orig.). 1968. pap. 3.95 (ISBN 0-07-035580-0, SP). McGraw.
Labor Movement in Fiction & Non-Fiction, 114 vols. Repr. of 1952 ed. Set. write for info (ISBN 0-404-58400-4). AMS Pr.
Labor Publishing Company. Labor: Its Rights & Wrongs. LC 75-334. (The Radical Tradition in America Ser.). 321p. 1975. Repr. of 1886 ed. 23.50 (ISBN 0-88355-237-X). Hyperion Conn.
Labour Problems Before the Industrial Revolution: 1727-1745. LC 72-2532. (British Labour Struggles Before 1850 Ser). (4 pamphlets). 1972. 10.00 (ISBN 0-405-04425-9). Arno.
Laurie, Bruce. Working People of Philadelphia, Eighteen Hundred to Eighteen Fifty. 1980. 19.50 (ISBN 0-87722-168-5). Temple U Pr.
Lenin, V. I. Letter to American Workers. Letter to the Workers of Europe & America. 32p. 1972. pap. 0.50 (ISBN 0-8285-0136-X, Pub. by Progress Pubs Russia). Imported Pubns.
Lipsitz, George. Class & Culture in Cold War America: A Rainbow at Midnight. 256p. 1981. 24.95 (ISBN 0-03-059207-0). Praeger.
McBrearty, James C. American Labor History & Comparative Labor Movements: A Selected Bibliography. LC 78-190624. 1973. pap. 2.00 (ISBN 0-8165-0504-7). U of Ariz Pr.
MacCarthy, James P. Rise of Dennis Hathnaught: Life of the Common People Across the Ages. LC 77-170961. (History, Economics & Social Science Ser.: No. 289). 1971. Repr. of 1915 ed. lib. bdg. 20.00 (ISBN 0-8337-2161-5). B Franklin.
McLaughlin, Doris B. Michigan Labor: A Brief History from 1818 to the Present. LC 73-633304. (Orig.). 1970. 9.50x (ISBN 0-87736-312-9); pap. 4.50x (ISBN 0-87736-333-1). U of Mich Inst Labor.
McNeill, George E., ed. Labor Movement. LC 66-21683. Repr. of 1887 ed. 22.50x (ISBN 0-678-00713-6). Kelley.
Meier, August & Rudwick, Elliott. Black Detroit & the Rise of the UAW. (Illus.). 304p. 1981. pap. 6.95 (ISBN 0-19-502895-3, GB 632). Oxford U Pr.
Meltzer, Milton. Bread & Roses: The Struggle of American Labor, 1865-1911. (RL 7). 1977. pap. 1.75 (ISBN 0-451-61574-3, ME1574, Ment). NAL.
Mikhailov, B. Y., ed. Recent History of the Labor Movement in the U.S. (1939-1965) 616p. 1979. 11.50 (ISBN 0-8285-1582-4, Pub. by Progress Pubs Russia). Imported Pubns.
Miller, Marc S., ed. Working Lives: The "Southern Exposure" History of Labor in the South. (Illus.). 1981. 17.95 (ISBN 0-394-50912-9); pap. 7.95 (ISBN 0-394-73965-5). Pantheon.
Mills, C. Wright. New Men of Power. LC 68-56261. Repr. of 1948 ed. 15.00x (ISBN 0-678-00715-2). Kelley.
Milton, David. The Politics of U. S. Labor: From the Great Depression to the New Deal. LC 80-8934. 352p. 1981. 18.00 (ISBN 0-85345-569-4, CL5694). Monthly Rev.
Montgomery, David. Beyond Equality: Labor & the Radical Republicans, 1862-1872. LC 80-24434. 550p. 1981. pap. 9.95 (ISBN 0-252-00869-3). U of Ill Pr.
--Workers' Control in America: Studies in History of Work, Technology, & Labor Struggles. 1980. 5.95 (ISBN 0-521-28006-0). Cambridge U Pr.
Morris, Richard B. Government & Labor in Early America. 557p. 1981. pap. 9.95x (ISBN 0-930350-24-3). NE U Pr.
--Government & Labor in Early America. 1965. lib. bdg. 32.50x (ISBN 0-374-95890-4). Octagon.
Moskin, L. The Working Class & Its Allies. 1980. 7.00 (ISBN 0-8285-1850-5, Pub by Progress Pubs Russia). Imported Pubns.
Murray, Tom. Waterfront Supercargo. (Singlejack Little Bks.). 59p. (Orig.). 1980. pap. 1.95 (ISBN 0-917300-10-6). Miles & Weir.
Myers, Gustavus. The History of American Idealism. LC 74-26126. (The Labor Movement in Fiction & Non-Fiction Ser.). Repr. of 1925 ed. 26.00 (ISBN 0-404-58506-X). AMS Pr.
New York State Joint Legislative Committee Investigating Seditious Activities. Revolutionary Radicalism, 8 vols. LC 78-12114. (Civil Liberties in American History Ser.). 1971. Repr. of 1920 ed. Set. lib. bdg. 250.00 (ISBN 0-306-71974-6). Da Capo.
O'Connor, Harvey. Revolution in Seattle: A Memoir by Harvey O' Connor. LC 81-80332. (Illus.). 300p. (Orig.). 1981. pap. 7.50 (ISBN 0-939306-01-8). Left Bank.
Oneal, James. Workers in American History. 32nd ed. LC 78-156437. (American Labor Ser., No. 2). 1971. Repr. of 1912 ed. 12.00 (ISBN 0-405-02935-7). Arno.
Parsons, Lucy E. Life of Albert R. Parsons. LC 68-56561. Repr. of 1889 ed. 17.50x (ISBN 0-678-01219-9). Kelley.
Pelling, Henry. American Labor. LC 60-7247. (Chicago History of American Civilization Ser). (Illus.). 1960. 10.50x (ISBN 0-226-65392-7); pap. 3.95 (ISBN 0-226-65393-5, CHAC16). U of Chicago Pr.
The People Make History: The Practice of the Democratic Workers' Party, Rebel Worker Organization & Grass Roots Alliance. 62p. (Orig.). 1980. pap. 3.95 (ISBN 0-89935-014-3). Synthesis Pubns.
Perkins, Frances & St Sure, J. Paul. Two Views of American Labor. 1965. 1.00 (ISBN 0-89215-048-3). U Cal LA Indus Rel.
Pessen, Edward. Most Uncommon Jacksonians: The Radical Leaders of the Early Labor Movement. LC 67-63761. 1967. 15.00 (ISBN 0-87395-029-1); pap. 7.95 (ISBN 0-87395-066-6); microfiche 15.00 (ISBN 0-87395-129-8). State U NY Pr.
Piven, Frances F. & Cloward, Richard A. Poor People's Movements: Why They Succeed, How They Fail. LC 78-54652. 1979. pap. 4.95 (ISBN 0-394-72697-9, Vin). Random.
Ramirez, Bruno. When Workers Fight: The Politics of Industrial Relations in the Progressive Era, 1898-1916. LC 77-83895. (Contributions in Labor History: No. 2). 1978. lib. bdg. 18.95 (ISBN 0-8371-9826-7, RAW/). Greenwood.
Rodgers, Daniel T. The Work Ethic in Industrial America: 1850-1920. LC 77-81737. 1978. lib. bdg. 15.00x (ISBN 0-226-72351-8). U of Chicago Pr.
Rogoff, Abraham M. Formative Years of the Jewish Labor Movement in the United States: (1890-1900) LC 78-21163. 1979. Repr. of 1945 ed. lib. bdg. 14.75x (ISBN 0-313-20881-6, ROFJ). Greenwood.
Rule, John. The Experience of Labour in Eighteenth Century Industry. 1980. 25.00 (ISBN 0-312-27664-8). St Martin.
Schluter, Herman. Lincoln, Labor & Slavery. LC 65-17920. 1965. Repr. of 1913 ed. 7.50 (ISBN 0-8462-0570-X). Russell.
Schnapper, M. B. American Labor: A Pictorial History. 576p. 1979. pap. 20.00 (ISBN 0-8183-0253-4). Pub Aff Pr.
Simonds, J. C. The Story of Manual Labor in All Lands & Ages. 59.95 (ISBN 0-8490-1135-3). Gordon Pr.
Simonds, John C. & McEnnis, John T. The Story of Manual Labor. LC 70-16983. (Management History Ser.: No. 8). 715p. 1972. Repr. of 1886 ed. 23.75 (ISBN 0-87960-007-1). Hive Pub.
Singal, Daniel J. Southern Tenant Farmers Union Papers, 1934-1970: Guide to the Microform Edition. 236p. 1971. pap. 50.00 (ISBN 0-667-00656-7). Microfilming Corp.
Sokolsky, George E. Labor's Fight for Power. LC 72-137979. (American History & Culture in the Twentieth Century Ser). 1971. Repr. of 1934 ed. 13.50 (ISBN 0-8046-1434-2). Kennikat.
Soviet Authors Group. Recent History of the Labor Movement in the United States, 1917-1939. Mikailov, B. Y., ed. 533p. 1977. 8.00 (ISBN 0-8285-9041-9, Pub. by Progress Pubs Russia). Imported Pubns.
Stein, Leon & Taft, Philip, eds. Religion, Reform & Revolution: Labor Panaceas in the Nineteenth Century. LC 79-89743. (American Labor, from Conspiracy to Collective Bargaining Ser., No. 1). 581p. 1969. 24.00 (ISBN 0-405-02151-8). Arno.
--Wages, Hours & Strikes: Labor Panaceas in the Twentieth Century. LC 79-89743. (American Labor, from Conspiracy to Collective Bargaining Ser., No. 1). 528p. 1969. 30.00 (ISBN 0-405-02152-6). Arno.
Taylor, Paul S. Labor on the Land: Collected Writings 1936-1970. 1981. write for info. Arno.
Thomas, Mary E. Jamaica & Voluntary Laborers from Africa, 1840-1865. LC 72-93330. (Illus.). 225p. 1974. 12.00 (ISBN 0-8130-0438-1). U Presses Fla.
Thomson, Fred & Murfin, Patrick. IWW: First 70 Years (1905-1975) the History of an Effort to Organize the Working Class. LC 75-27589. Orig. Title: IWW First 50 Years. (Illus.). lib. bdg. 15.00 (ISBN 0-917124-03-0); pap. 4.95 (ISBN 0-917124-04-9). Indus Workers World.
Tilgher, Adriano. Work: What It Has Meant to Men Through the Ages. Stein, Leon, ed. Fisher, Dorothy C., tr. from Italian. LC 77-70538. (Work Ser.). 1977. Repr. of 1930 ed. lib. bdg. 16.00x (ISBN 0-405-10208-9). Arno.
Tuckett, J. D. A History of the Past & Present State of the Labouring Population, 2 vols. 916p. 1971. Repr. of 1846 ed. 60.00x (ISBN 0-7165-1572-5, Pub. by Irish Academic Pr Ireland). Biblio Dist.
Turcheneske, John A., Jr., ed. The John Mitchell Papers, 1885-1919: A Guide to the Microfilm Edition. LC 75-9921. 114p. 1975. pap. 25.00 (ISBN 0-88455-197-0). Microfilming Corp.
Turner, Steve. Night Shift in a Pickle Factory. (Singlejack Little Bks.). 61p. 1980. pap. 1.95 (ISBN 0-917300-13-0). Miles & Weir.
U. S. Bureau of Labor & Wright, Carroll D. Index of All Reports Issued by Bureaus of Labor Statistics in the United States Prior to March 1,1902. LC 75-45446. (U.S. Government Documents Program Ser.). 287p. 1976. Repr. lib. bdg. 15.00 (ISBN 0-8371-8717-6, USIN). Greenwood.
U. S. Bureau of Statistics. Labor in Europe & America. LC 70-88493. (Illus.). vi, 864p. Repr. of 1875 ed. lib. bdg. 28.50x (ISBN 0-8371-4962-2, USLE). Greenwood.
Vincent, David. Bread, Knowledge & Freedom: A Study of Nineteenth-Century Working Class Autobiography. 221p. 1981. 45.00x (ISBN 0-905118-55-3). Intl Pubns Serv.
Walkowitz, Daniel J. Worker City, Company Town: Iron & Cotton-Worker Protest in Troy & Cohoes, New York, 1855-84. LC 78-18305. (The Working Class in American History Ser.). 1978. 14.00 (ISBN 0-252-00667-4). U of Ill Pr.
Ward, Cyrenus O. Ancient Lowly: A History of the Ancient Working People from the Earliest Known Period to the Adoption of Christianity by Constantine, 2 Vols. LC 77-114817. 1970. Set. text ed. 49.00 (ISBN 0-8337-3685-X). B Franklin.
Ware, Norman. Industrial Worker, Eighteen Forty - Eighteen Sixty: The Reaction of American Industrial Revolution. 1964. pap. 2.95 (ISBN 0-8129-6017-3, QP13). Times Bks.
--The Labor Movement in the United States 1860-1895. 1959. 8.00 (ISBN 0-8446-1466-1). Peter Smith.
Wearmouth, R. F. Some Working-Class Movements of the Nineteenth Century. 1977. lib. bdg. 59.95 (ISBN 0-8490-2630-X). Gordon Pr.
Winter, J. M., ed. R. H. Tawney: The American Labour Movement & Other Essays. 1979. 25.00x (ISBN 0-312-66124-X). St Martin.
Wright, Carroll D. Industrial Evolution of the United States. LC 67-19917. (Illus.). 1967. Repr. of 1895 ed. 8.50 (ISBN 0-8462-0911-X). Russell.
Yearley, Clifton K. Britons in American Labor: A History of the Influence of the United Kingdom Immigrants on American Labor, 1820-1914. LC 78-64227. (Johns Hopkins University. Studies in the Social Sciences. Seventy-Fifth Ser. 1957: 1). Repr. of 1957 ed. 15.50 (ISBN 0-404-61329-2). AMS Pr.
Yearley, Clifton K., Jr. Britons in American Labor. LC 73-13822. (Studies in Historical & Political Science Ser. 75: Ser. 75, No. 1). 332p. 1974. Repr. of 1957 ed. lib. bdg. 16.00x (ISBN 0-8371-7120-2, YEBA). Greenwood.
Yellowitz, Irwin. Industrialization & the American Labor Movement, 1850-1900. 1976. 15.00 (ISBN 0-8046-9150-9, National University Pub). Kennikat.
Zagladin, V. V. The Working Class: The Leading Force of the World Revolutionary Process. 190p. 1976. pap. 2.00 (ISBN 0-8285-0414-8, Pub by Progress Pubs Russia). Imported Pubns.

LABOR AND LABORING CLASSES–INSURANCE

see Insurance, Accident; Insurance, Health; Old Age Pensions; Insurance, Unemployment

LABOR AND LABORING CLASSES–JUVENILE LITERATURE

Famous American Labor Leaders. (Famous American Heroes & Leaders Ser.). 80p. (gr. 5-9). PLB 3.50 (ISBN 0-513-01200-1). Denison.
The Ludlow Massacre: Mini-Play. (Labor Studies). (gr. 8 up). 1978. 3.00 (ISBN 0-89550-321-2). RIM.
Morgen, Linda. Heroes of American Labor. new ed. (Heroes of... Ser). 140p. (gr. 6 up). Date not set. 6.95 (ISBN 0-8303-0145-3). Fleet.
Neigoff, Anne. The Energy Workers. Rubin, Caroline, ed. LC 74-23973. (Career Awareness Community Helpers Ser.). (Illus.). 32p. (gr. k-2). 1975. 5.25g (ISBN 0-8075-2049-7). A Whitman.
Sandler, Martin. The Way We Lived: A Photographic Record of Work in a Vanished America. (Illus.). (gr. 3-7). 1977. 8.95 (ISBN 0-316-77020-5). Little.
Selvin, David F. Champions of Labor. LC 67-16836. (Illus.). (gr. 7 up). 1967. 7.95 (ISBN 0-200-71723-5, B13020, AbS-J). Har-Row.
Shissler, Barbara. Worker in Art. LC 72-84409. (Fine Art Ser). (Illus.). (gr. 5-11). 1970. PLB 4.95 (ISBN 0-8225-0167-8). Lerner Pubns.

LABOR AND LABORING CLASSES–MEDICAL CARE

see also Medicine, Industrial; Nurses and Nursing; Occupational Diseases; Welfare Work in Industry

Collis, Edgar L. & Greenwood, Major. The Health of the Industrial Worker. Stein, Leon, ed. LC 77-70489. (Work Ser.). (Illus.). 1977. Repr. of 1921 ed. lib. bdg. 29.00x (ISBN 0-405-10161-9). Arno.
Egdahl, R. H., ed. Background Papers on Industry's Changing Role in Health Care Delivery. LC 77-13611. (Springer Series on Industry & Health Care: No. 3). 1977. 36.10 (ISBN 0-387-90290-2). Springer-Verlag.
Encyclopaedia of Occupational Health & Safety, 2 Vols. 5th ed. 1976. Set. 89.95 (ISBN 92-2-101000-7, Dist. in U. S. by McGraw Hill N. Y.). Intl Labour Office.
Foote, Andrea & Erfurt, John C. Occupational Employee Assistance Programs for Substance Abuse & Mental Health Problems. 1977. pap. 3.50x (ISBN 0-87736-327-7). U of Mich Inst Labor.
International Labour Organization. Encyclopedia of Occupational Health, 2 vols. LC 74-39329. (Illus.). 1972. Set. 68.50 (ISBN 0-07-079555-X, P&RB). McGraw.
Melville, Mary H. The Temporary Worker in the Nuclear Power Industry: An Equity Analysis. LC 81-65590. (CENTED Monographs: No. 1). (Illus.). 60p. 1981. pap. text ed. 5.00 (ISBN 0-939436-00-0). Ctr Tech Environ.
Schwartz, Rosalind, ed. Health Care & Industrial Relations: Costs, Conflicts & Controversy. (Monograph Ser.: No. 28). 90p. 1981. 7.50 (ISBN 0-89215-112-9). U Cal LA Indus Rel.

LABOR AND LABORING CLASSES–PERIODICALS

see also Employees' Magazines, Handbooks, etc.

Harrison, Royden, et al. The Warwick Guide to British Labour Periodicals: 1790-1970: a Checklist. 1977. text ed. 60.00x (ISBN 0-391-00589-8). Humanities.
International Labor Office - Geneva. Yearbook of Labor Statistics 1980. 40th ed. (Illus.). 690p. 1980. 67.50x (ISBN 92-2-002526-4). Intl Pubns Serv.

LABOR AND LABORING CLASSES–SONGS AND MUSIC

see also Lumbermen–Songs and Music; also similar headings

Foner, Philip S., ed. American Labor Songs of the Nineteenth Century. LC 74-20968. (Music in American Life Ser.). (Illus.). 600p. 1975. 17.50 (ISBN 0-252-00187-7). U of Ill Pr.
George, Mary D. England in Transition: Life & Work in the 18th Century. LC 75-41110. Repr. of 1931 ed. 19.50 (ISBN 0-404-14544-2). AMS Pr.
Leopold, Vincent, illus. The Alliance & Labor Songster. facsimile ed. LC 74-30660. (American Farmers & the Rise of Agribusiness Ser.). 1975. Repr. of 1891 ed. 9.50x (ISBN 0-405-06837-9). Arno.

LABOR AND LABORING CLASSES–WAGES

see Wages

LABOR AND LABORING CLASSES–1914-

Anderson, Nels. Men on the Move. LC 74-7427. (FDR & the Era of the New Deal Ser.). xii, 357p. 1974. Repr. of 1940 ed. lib. bdg. 37.50 (ISBN 0-306-70588-5). Da Capo.

Botsch, Robert E. We Shall Not Overcome: Populism & Southern Blue-Collar Workers. LC 80-11567. xv, 237p. 1981. 19.50x (ISBN 0-8078-1444-X). U of NC Pr.

Bould-Vantil, Sally. Work & the Culture of Poverty: The Labor Force Activity of Poor Men. LC 75-38300. 1976. softbound 10.00 (ISBN 0-88247-409-X). R & E Res Assoc.

Braatoy, Bjarne. Labour & War: The Theory of Labour Action to Prevent War. LC 77-147508. (Library of War & Peace; Labor, Socialism & War). lib. bdg. 38.00 (ISBN 0-8240-0303-9). Garland Pub.

Cobb, Jonathan & Sennett, Richard. Hidden Injuries of Class. 1973. pap. 2.95 (ISBN 0-394-71940-9, V940, Vin). Random.

Coleman, John R. Blue-Collar Journal: A College President's Sabbatical. LC 73-21902. 1974. 8.95 (ISBN 0-397-01030-3). Har-Row.

Duncan, K. D., et al, eds. Changes in Working Life. LC 80-40129. 1981. 71.95 (ISBN 0-471-27777-0, Pub. by Wiley-Interscience). Wiley.

Green, Marguerite. The National Civic Federation & the American Labor Movement. LC 73-9337. 537p. 1973. Repr. of 1956 ed. lib. bdg. 23.00x (ISBN 0-8371-7007-9, GRCF). Greenwood.

Hollander, Jacob H. The Abolition of Poverty. LC 75-17226. (Social Problems & Social Policy Ser.). 1976. Repr. of 1914 ed. 7.00x (ISBN 0-405-07496-4). Arno.

King, William L. Industry & Humanity. LC 72-95460. (Social History of Canada Ser.). 1973. 17.50x (ISBN 0-8020-1947-1); pap. 7.50 (ISBN 0-8020-6174-5). U of Toronto Pr.

Kornhauser, Arthur & Sheppard, Harold. When Labor Votes. LC 76-2533. (Illus.). 352p. 1976. Repr. of 1956 ed. lib. bdg. 23.75x (ISBN 0-8371-8787-7, KOWL). Greenwood.

Labor Research Associates. Labor Fact Book, Vols. 6-10. LC 72-836566. 1973. Repr. of 1943 ed. 8.50 ea. Vol. 6 (ISBN 0-88211-036-5). Vol. 7 (ISBN 0-88211-037-3). Vol. 8 (ISBN 0-88211-038-1). Vol. 9 (ISBN 0-88211-039-X). Vol. 10 (ISBN 0-88211-040-3). S A Russell.

--Labor Facts Book, Vols. 11-17. LC 72-836566. 1973. 8.50 ea. Vol. 11 (ISBN 0-88211-056-X). Vol. 12 (ISBN 0-88211-057-8). Vol. 13 (ISBN 0-88211-058-6). Vol. 14 (ISBN 0-88211-059-4). Vol. 15 (ISBN 0-88211-060-8). Vol. 16 (ISBN 0-88211-061-6). Vol. 17 (ISBN 0-88211-062-4). S A Russell.

Larrowe, Charles P. Harry Bridges: The Rise & Fall of Radical Labor in the United States. rev. ed. LC 72-78321. 416p. 1977. pap. 8.95 (ISBN 0-88208-001-6). Lawrence Hill.

Low-Beer, J. R. Protest & Participation. LC 77-8084. (ASA Rose Monograph Ser.: No. 4). (Illus.). 1978. 19.95 (ISBN 0-521-21782-2); pap. 6.95x (ISBN 0-521-29277-8). Cambridge U Pr.

MacKenzie, G. The Aristocracy of Labor. LC 73-80484. (Studies in Sociology). (Illus.). 208p. 1973. pap. 9.95x (ISBN 0-521-09825-4). Cambridge U Pr.

Petersen, Arnold. Capital & Labor. 7th ed. 1975. pap. text ed. 0.50 (ISBN 0-935534-06-7). NY Labor News.

Rosmer, Alfred. Le Mouvement Ouvrier Pendant la Premiere Guerre Mondiale: De Zimmerwald a la Revolution Russe, Vol. 2. (Societe, Mouvements Sociaux & Ideologies, Documents & Temoignages: No. 1). 1959. pap. 22.75x (ISBN 90-2796-241-3). Mouton.

Seidman, Joel. American Labor from Defense to Reconversion. (Midway Reprint Ser.). 1953. pap. 11.50x (ISBN 0-226-74530-9). U of Chicago Pr.

Terkel, Studs. Working: People Talk About What They Do All Day & How They Feel About What They Do. LC 73-18037. 1974. 10.00 (ISBN 0-394-47884-3). Pantheon.

Warne, Frank J. The Workers at War. LC 74-22762. (Labor Movement in Fiction & Non-Fiction). Repr. of 1920 ed. 20.00 (ISBN 0-404-58515-9). AMS Pr.

Woytinsky, W. S., et al. Employment & Wages in the United States. LC 75-22869. (America in Two Centuries Ser). 1976. Repr. of 1953 ed. 49.00x (ISBN 0-405-07734-3). Arno.

LABOR AND LABORING CLASSES–AFRICA

Barnum, H. N. Migration, Education & Urban Surplus Labour: The Case of Tanzania. (Employment Ser.: No. 13). 1976. 5.50x (ISBN 92-64-11531-5). OECD.

Beling, Willard A., ed. Role of Labor in African Nation-Building. 15.00 (ISBN 0-685-37307-X). Univ Place.

Berger, Elena L. Labour, Race & Colonial Rule: The Copperbelt from 1924 to Independence. (Oxford Studies in African Affairs). 272p. 1974. 29.50x (ISBN 0-19-821690-4). Oxford U Pr.

The Conditions of the Black Worker. 298p. (Orig.). 1975. pap. text ed. 6.00 (ISBN 0-89192-067-6). Interbk Inc.

Cooper, Frederick. From Slaves to Squatters: Plantation Labor & Agriculture in Zanibar & Coastal Kenya, 1890-1925. LC 80-5391. 352p. 1981. text ed. 25.00x (ISBN 0-300-02454-1). Yale U Pr.

Gray, Paul S. Unions & Leaders in Ghana: A Model of Labor & Development. LC 80-18482. 1981. 35.00 (ISBN 0-914970-57-7); pap. text ed. 17.50 (ISBN 0-914970-58-5). Conch Mag.

Gutkind, Peter C., et al, eds. African Labor History. LC 78-6635. (Sage Ser. on African Modernization & Development: Vol. 2). 280p. 1978. 22.50x (ISBN 0-8039-1063-0); pap. 9.95 (ISBN 0-8039-1064-9). Sage.

Indicus. Labor & Other Questions in South Africa. LC 75-77203. Repr. of 1930 ed. 10.00x (ISBN 0-8371-1298-2, Pub. by Negro U Pr). Greenwood.

Industrial Relations & Personnel Management in English-Speaking Africa. (Labour-Management Relations Ser: No. 40). 204p. 1972. 7.15 (ISBN 92-2-100168-7). Intl Labour Office.

Koloko, Massiye E. The Manpower Approach to Planning: Theoretical Issues & Evidence from Zambia. (Monograph Ser. in World Affairs). 94p. (Orig.). 1980. pap. 5.00 (ISBN 0-87940-064-1). U of Denver Intl.

Nzula, A., et al. Forced Labour in Colonial Africa. Cohen, Robin, ed. 218p. (Orig.). 1979. 16.95 (ISBN 0-905762-30-4, Pub. by Zed Pr); pap. 6.95 (ISBN 0-905762-31-2). Lawrence Hill.

Olivier, Lord. The Anatomy of African Misery. facsimile ed. LC 74-38017. (Black Heritage Library Collection). Repr. of 1927 ed. 15.50 (ISBN 0-8369-8984-8). Arno.

Orde Browne, G. St. The African Labourer. 240p. 1967. Repr. of 1933 ed. 24.00x (ISBN 0-686-26224-7, F Cass Co). Biblio Dist.

Sandbrook, Richard & Cohen, Robin. The Development of an African Working Class. 1976. pap. 10.00 (ISBN 0-686-77167-2). U of Toronto Pr.

South African Native Races Committee, ed. South African Natives, Their Progress & Present Condition. LC 71-82077. Repr. of 1908 ed. 13.00x (ISBN 0-8371-1539-6). Greenwood.

Van Der Horst, Shelia T. Native Labour in South Africa. 340p. 1971. Repr. of 1942 ed. 28.50x (ISBN 0-7146-1781-4, F Cass Co). Biblio Dist.

Wilson, Francis. Labour in the South African Gold Mines 1936-1969. LC 77-161290. (African Studies: No. 6). 1972. 38.50 (ISBN 0-521-08303-6). Cambridge U Pr.

LABOR AND LABORING CLASSES–ALGERIA

Bourdieu, Pierre, et al. Travail et Travailleurs En Algerie. (Recherches Mediterraneennes Documents). 1963. pap. text ed. 40.50x (ISBN 90-279-6224-3). Mouton.

LABOR AND LABORING CLASSES–ANGOLA

Cadbury, William A. Labour in Portuguese West Africa. 2nd ed. LC 73-75542. (Illus.). Repr. of 1910 ed. 12.50x (ISBN 0-8371-0982-5, Pub. by Negro U Pr). Greenwood.

LABOR AND LABORING CLASSES–ASIA

Labour Market Information in Asia: Present Issues & Tasks for the Future. 116p. 1980. pap. 6.50 (ISBN 92-2-102168-8, ILO147, ILO). Unipub.

Role of Employer's Organisations in Asian Countries. (Labour-Management Relations Ser.: No. 39). 1971. 9.00 (ISBN 92-2-100133-4). Intl Labour Office.

LABOR AND LABORING CLASSES–AUSTRALASIA

Brissenden, Paul F. The Settlement of Labor Disputes on Rights in Australia. (Monograph Ser.: No.13). 1966. 5.00 (ISBN 0-89215-014-9). U Cal LA Indus Rel.

Clark, Victor S. Labour Movement in Australasia: A Study in Social Democracy. LC 77-122222. (Research & Source Ser.: No. 506). 1970. Repr. of 1906 ed. lib. bdg. 23.50 (ISBN 0-8337-0583-0). B Franklin.

Miller, John. The Workingman's Paradise. Wilding, Michael, ed. 272p. 1980. 18.50x (ISBN 0-424-00057-1, Pub.by Sydney U Pr Australia). Intl Schol Bk Serv.

LABOR AND LABORING CLASSES–AUSTRALIA

Bordow, Allan, ed. The Worker in Australia: A Behavioral Science Perspective. (Illus.). 1978. text ed. 24.95x (ISBN 0-7022-1473-6); pap. text ed. 14.95x (ISBN 0-7022-1474-4). U of Queensland Pr.

Ebbels, R. N. The Australian Labor Movement: Eighteen Fifty to Nineteen Seven. 15.00x (ISBN 0-392-07633-0, SpS). Sportshelf.

Harris, Joe. The Bitter Fight: A Pictorial History of the Australian Labor Movement. (Illus.). 1970. 20.50x (ISBN 0-7022-0613-X). U of Queensland Pr.

Manning, Ian. The Journey to Work. LC 78-57601. 1978. text ed. 17.95x (ISBN 0-86861-192-1); pap. text ed. 9.50x (ISBN 0-86861-200-6). Allen Unwin.

Parnaby, Owen W. Britain & the Labor Trade in the Southwest Pacific. LC 64-13987. 1964. 12.50 (ISBN 0-8223-0129-6). Duke.

Salter, Moira Joan. Studies in the Immigration of the Highly Skilled: Immigrants in Australia, No. 7. LC 77-94940. 1978. text ed. 12.95 (ISBN 0-7081-0722-2). Bks Australia.

Sheridan, T. Mindful Militants. LC 74-17503. 352p. 1976. 35.50 (ISBN 0-521-20680-4). Cambridge U Pr.

Wawn, William T. The South Sea Islanders & the Queensland Labour Trade. new ed. Corris, Peter, ed. & intro. by. LC 73-78979. (Pacific History Ser.: No. 5). 529p. 1973. text ed. 17.50x (ISBN 0-8248-0282-9). U Pr of Hawaii.

West & Holmes. Socialism or Nationalism? Which Road for the Australian Labor Movement? (Illus.). 1980. pap. 3.25 (ISBN 0-909196-06-0). Path Pr NY.

LABOR AND LABORING CLASSES–CANADA

Cross, Michael S., ed. The Workingman in the Nineteenth Century. 336p. 1974. pap. 9.95x (ISBN 0-19-540220-0). Oxford U Pr.

Horowitz, Gad. Canadian Labour in Politics. LC 68-101781. 1968. pap. 6.50 (ISBN 0-8020-6155-9). U of Toronto Pr.

Kealey, Gregory S. Toronto Workers Respond to Industrial Capitalism, 1867-1892. 1980. 27.50x (ISBN 0-8020-5488-9); pap. 12.50 (ISBN 0-8020-6393-4). U of Toronto Pr.

MacEwen, Paul. Miners & Steelworkers: Trade Unions in Cape Breton. 1976. 14.95 (ISBN 0-88866-533-4). Samuel Stevens.

Ostry, Sylvia & Zaidi, Mahmood. Labor Economics in Canada. 3rd ed. 418p. 1979. pap. 12.95x (ISBN 0-7705-1728-5, Pub. by Macmillan of Canada). NYU Pr.

Thompson, T. Philips. The Politics of Labor. LC 75-9924. (Social History of Canada Ser.). 1975. pap. 6.50 (ISBN 0-8020-6270-9). U of Toronto Pr.

LABOR AND LABORING CLASSES–CHINA

Aijmer, Goran. Economic Man in Sha Tin: Vegetable Gardeners in a Hong Kong Valley. (Scandanavian Institute of Asian Studies Monograph: No. 43). (Orig.). 1980. pap. text ed. 11.00x (ISBN 0-7007-0135-4). Humanities.

Andors, Stephen, ed. Workers & Workplaces in Revolutionary China. Mathews, Jay, et al, trs. LC 76-53710. (The China Book Project Ser.). 1977. 25.00 (ISBN 0-87332-094-8). M E Sharpe.

Bennett, H. C. Chinese Labor: A Lecture Delivered Before the San Francisco Mechanic's. 1976. Repr. of 1870 ed. 25.00 (ISBN 0-403-06648-4, Regency). Scholarly.

Chan, Ming K. Historiography of the Chinese Labor Movement. LC 80-8323. (Bibliographical Ser.: No. 60). 1981. 35.00 (ISBN 0-8179-2601-1). Hoover Inst Pr.

Chesneaux, Jean. Chinese Labor Movement, 1919-1927. Wright, H. M., tr. 1968. 25.00x (ISBN 0-8047-0644-1). Stanford U Pr.

Cuban Economic Research Project, University of Miami. Labor Conditions in Communist Cuba. LC 63-21349. 1963. pap. 2.95x (ISBN 0-87024-303-9). U of Miami Pr.

Epstein, Israel. Notes on Labor Problems in Nationalist China. LC 78-74341. (The Modern Chinese Economy Ser.). 159p. 1980. lib. bdg. 16.50 (ISBN 0-8240-4281-6). Garland Pub.

Fang, Fu-An. Chinese Labour: An Economic & Statistical Survey of the Labour Conditions & Labour Movements in China. LC 78-22780. (The Modern Chinese Economy Ser.: Vol. 34). 185p. 1980. lib. bdg. 20.00 (ISBN 0-8240-4282-4). Garland Pub.

Goldwasser, Janet & Dowty, Stuart. Huan-Ying: Workers' China. LC 74-7790. (Modern Reader Paperback Ser). 1976. pap. 5.95 (ISBN 0-85345-389-6, PB3896). Monthly Rev.

Hoffmann, Charles. The Chinese Worker. LC 74-3053. 1974. 19.00 (ISBN 0-87395-238-3); microfiche 19.00 (ISBN 0-87395-239-1). State U NY Pr.

Lowe, Chuan-Hua. Facing Labor Issues in China. (Studies in Chinese History & Civilization). 1977. Repr. of 1938 ed. 17.50 (ISBN 0-89093-082-1). U Pubns Amer.

Ridker, Ronald. Employment in South Asia: Problems, Prospects & Prescriptions. (Occasional Papers: No. 1). 74p. 1971. 1.00 (ISBN 0-686-28697-9). Overseas Dev Council.

Shih Kuo-Heng. China Enters the Machine Age: A Study of Labor in Chinese War Industry. Fei Hsiao-T'Ung & Hsu Lang-Kuang, eds. LC 68-23327. 1968. Repr. of 1944 ed. lib. bdg. 15.00 (ISBN 0-8371-0222-7, SHCL). Greenwood.

Tawney, R. H. Land & Labor in China. LC 77-72070. 1977. Repr. of 1932 ed. pap. 6.95 (ISBN 0-87332-106-5). M E Sharpe.

Tsiang, Tingfu F. Labor & Empire. 1971. lib. bdg. 14.50x (ISBN 0-374-98029-2). Octagon.

Tso, Shih K. The Labor Movement in China. LC 79-2842. 230p. 1981. Repr. of 1928 ed. 19.75 (ISBN 0-8305-0018-9). Hyperion Conn.

Turner, H. A. The Last Colony: But Whose?; a Study of the Labour Movement, Labour Market & Labour Relations in Hong Kong. LC 80-41112. (Department of Applied Economics Papers in Industrial Relations & Labour: No. 5). (Illus.). 1981. 24.95 (ISBN 0-521-23701-7). Cambridge U Pr.

Wagner, Augusta. Labor Legislation in China. LC 78-22780. (The Modern Chinese Economy Ser.). 301p. 1980. lib. bdg. 33.00 (ISBN 0-8240-4283-2). Garland Pub.

Wales, Nym, pseud. The Chinese Labor Movement. LC 71-119947. (Select Bibliographies Reprint Ser.). Repr. of 1945 ed. 17.00 (ISBN 0-8369-5390-8). Arno.

LABOR AND LABORING CLASSES–COMMONWEALTH OF NATIONS

Roberts, Benjamin C. Labour in the Tropical Territories of the Commonwealth. LC 64-25334. 1964. 18.75 (ISBN 0-8223-0145-8). Duke.

LABOR AND LABORING CLASSES–EUROPE

Abendroth, Wolfgang. A Short History of the European Working Class. Jacobs, Nicholas, et al, trs. from Ger. LC 72-81766. 208p. 1972. pap. 5.95 (ISBN 0-85345-289-X, PB-289X). Monthly Rev.

Alessa, S. Y. Manpower Problems in Kuwait. 160p. 1981. price not set (ISBN 0-7103-0009-3). Routledge & Kegan.

Callesen, Gerd & Logue, John. Social-Demokraten & Internationalism: The Copenhagen Social Democratic Newspaper's Coverage of International Labor Affairs, 1871-1958. (U. of Gothenburg (Sweden), Research Section Post-War History Publications: No. 8). (Illus.). 1979. pap. 2.95 (ISBN 0-933522-00-2). Kent Popular.

Chiplin, Brian, et al. Can Workers Manage? (Hobart Papers Ser.: No. 77). 1978. pap. 5.75 (ISBN 0-255-36103-3). Transatlantic.

Cooper, Cary L. & Mumford, Enid, eds. The Quality of Working Life in Western & Eastern Europe. LC 78-27692. (Contributions in Economics & Economic History: No. 25). 1979. lib. bdg. 35.00 (ISBN 0-313-20957-X, CWL/). Greenwood.

Dimitrov, Georgi. The Working Class Against Fascism. LC 78-63662. (Studies in Fascism: Ideology & Practice). Repr. of 1935 ed. 17.00 (ISBN 0-404-16925-2). AMS Pr.

Dolleans, Edouard. Histoire du Mouvement Ouvrier, 3 vols. in two. Mayer, J. P., ed. LC 78-67350. (European Political Thought Ser.). (Fr.). 1979. Repr. of 1953 ed. Set. lib. bdg. 72.00x (ISBN 0-405-11693-4); Vols. 1 & 2. lib. bdg. 36.00x (ISBN 0-405-11694-2); Vol. 3. 36.00x (ISBN 0-405-11696-9). Arno.

Dovring, Folke. Land & Labour in Europe in the 20th Century: A Comparative Survey of Recent Agrarian History. LC 66-6949. 522p. 1965. 30.00x (ISBN 0-8002-1640-7). Intl Pubns Serv.

Engels, Friedrich. El Problema Campesino en Francia y en Alemania. 29p. (Span.). 1979. pap. 0.70 (ISBN 0-8285-1673-1, Pub. by Progress Pubs Russia). Imported Pubns.

Fitzgerald, Mark J. Common Market's Labor Programs. 1966. 9.95x (ISBN 0-268-00053-0). U of Notre Dame Pr.

Geary, Dick. European Labour Protest. 1981. price not set (ISBN 0-312-26974-9). St Martin.

Gross, Feliks. The Polish Worker: Study of a Social Stratum. LC 77-87525. Repr. of 1945 ed. 22.00 (ISBN 0-404-16602-4). AMS Pr.

Haraszti, Miklos. A Worker in a Worker's State. LC 77-88841. 176p. 1981. pap. 4.95 (ISBN 0-87663-561-3). Universe.

International Council for the Quality of Working Life. Working on the Quality of Working Life. (International Ser. on the Quality of Working Life: Vol. 8). 1979. lib. bdg. 36.75 (ISBN 0-89838-001-4, Pub. by Martinus Nijhoff Netherlands). Kluwer Boston.

Kennedy, M. Thomas. European Labor Relations: Text & Cases. LC 78-14155. 448p. 1980. 29.95x (ISBN 0-669-02663-8). Lexington Bks.

Korpi, Walter. The Working Class in Welfare Capitalism. (International Library of Sociology). 1978. 28.00x (ISBN 0-7100-8848-5). Routledge & Kegan.

Krane, Ronald E. International Labor Migration in Europe. LC 78-19746. (Praeger Special Studies). 1979. 24.95 (ISBN 0-03-022361-X). Praeger.

Lenin, V. I. Differences in the European Labor Movement. 10p. 1975. pap. 0.50 (ISBN 0-8285-0127-0, Pub. by Progress Pubs Russia). Imported Pubns.

Magarelli, Clyde. Crisis of Convergence: Military Professionalism & Working Class Struggle, Portuguese Case Study, March 16,1974-November 25,1975. LC 81-40362. (Illus.). 332p. (Orig.). 1981. lib. bdg. 22.50 (ISBN 0-8191-1792-7); pap. text ed. 12.25 (ISBN 0-8191-1793-5). U Pr of Amer.

Perlman, Selig. Theory of the Labor Movement. LC 66-18323. Repr. of 1928 ed. 15.00x (ISBN 0-678-00025-5). Kelley.

Power, Jonathan. Western Europe's Migrant Workers. (Minority Rights Group: No. 28). 1976. pap. 2.50 (ISBN 0-89192-085-4). Interbk Inc.

Royaume de Belgique. Ministere de l'Interieur. Enquete sur la Condition des Classes Ouvrieres et sur le Travail des Enfants, 3 vols. (Conditions of the 19th Century French Working Class Ser.). (Fr.). 1974. Repr. of 1846 ed. Set. lib. bdg. 503.00x (ISBN 0-8287-0743-X). Vol. 1 (1157). Vol. 2 (1158). Vol. 3 (1159). Clearwater Pub.

Saunders & Marsden. Pay Inequalities in the European Community. 1981. text ed. price not set (ISBN 0-408-10727-8). Butterworth.

Scase, Richard. Social Democracy in Capitalist Society: Working-Class Politics in Britain & Sweden. 184p. 1977. 17.50x (ISBN 0-87471-948-8). Rowman.

Stearns, Peter N. Lives of Labor: Work in a Maturing Industrial Society. LC 74-28298. 1975. text ed. 34.50x (ISBN 0-8419-0192-9). Holmes & Meier.

Triska, Jan F. & Gati, Charles, eds. Blue-Collar Workers in Eastern Europe. (Illus.). 320p. 1981. text ed. 37.50x (ISBN 0-04-321027-9); pap. text ed. 12.95x (ISBN 0-04-321028-7). Allen Unwin.

Wallerstein, Immanual, ed. On the European Workers' Movement. (Contemporary Marxism Ser.). 100p. 1980. pap. 5.001311 (ISBN 0-686-70057-0). Synthesis Pubns.

Watillon, Leon. The Knights of Labor in Belgium. Meyers, Frederic, tr. (Monograph Ser.: No. 3). 1959. 3.50 (ISBN 0-89215-005-X). U Cal LA Indus Rel.

Watson, Philippa, ed. Social Security Law of the European Communities. (Studies in Labour & Social Law). 292p. 1981. text ed. 38.50 (ISBN 0-7201-0926-4, Pub. by Mansell England). Merrimack Bk Serv.

Weinberg, Paul J. European Labor & Multinationals. LC 78-9449. (Praeger Special Studies). 1978. 21.95 (ISBN 0-03-044256-7). Praeger.

Workers' Management in Yugoslavia. (Studies & Reports, New Ser.: No. 64). 1962. 9.00 (ISBN 92-2-100991-2). Intl Labour Office.

LABOR AND LABORING CLASSES–FINLAND

Knoellinger, Carl E. Labor in Finland. LC 60-7996. (Wertheim Publications in Industrial Relations Ser). 1960. 15.00x (ISBN 0-674-50650-2). Harvard U Pr.

LABOR AND LABORING CLASSES–FRANCE

Agulhon, Maurice. Une Ville Ouvriere au Temps du Socialisme Utopique: Toulon De 1815 a 1851. 2nd ed. (Civilisations et Societes: No. 18). 1977. pap. 24.70 (ISBN 90-2796-287-1). Mouton.

Aminzade, Ronald. Class, Politics, & Early Industrial Capitalism: A Study of Mid-Nineteenth-Century Toulouse, France. LC 80-28284. (European Social History Ser.). (Illus.). 230p. 1981. 29.50x (ISBN 0-87395-528-5, AMCS); pap. 9.95x (ISBN 0-87395-529-3, AMCS-P). State U NY Pr.

Apercu sur la Condition des Classes Ouvrieres et Critique de l'Ouvrage de M. Buret, par le Pce D.S. (Condition of the 19th Century French Working Class Ser). 107p. (Fr.). 1974. Repr. of 1844 ed. lib. bdg. 37.00 (ISBN 0-8287-1328-6, 1062). Clearwater Pub.

Arnaud, Camille. Du Livret d'Ouvrier. (Conditions of the 19th Century French Working Class Ser.). 103p. (Fr.). 1974. Repr. of 1856 ed. lib. bdg. 36.00x (ISBN 0-8287-0036-2, 1096). Clearwater Pub.

Audiganne, A. Memoires d'un Ouvrier de Paris, 1871-1872. (Conditions of the 19th Century French Working Class Ser.). 320p. (Fr.). 1974. Repr. of 1873 ed. lib. bdg. 84.00x (ISBN 0-8287-0176-8, 1092). Clearwater Pub.

--Les Ouvriers a Present et la Nouvelle Economie du Travail. (Conditions of the 19th Century French Working Class Ser.). 492p. (Fr.). 1974. Repr. of 1865 ed. lib. bdg. 118.00 (ISBN 0-8287-0041-9, 1103). Clearwater Pub.

--Les Ouvriers en Famille,Cinqueime Edition Augmentee d'un Manuel Elementaire des Societes de Secours Mutuel. (Conditions of the 19th Century French Working Class Ser.). 263p. (Fr.). 1974. Repr. of 1858 ed. lib. bdg. 71.25x (ISBN 0-8287-0042-7, 1039). Clearwater Pub.

--Les Populations Ouvrieres et les Industries de la France, 2 vols. (Conditions of the 19th Century French Working Class Ser.). 860p. (Fr.). 1974. Repr. of 1860 ed. Set. lib. bdg. 217.00x (ISBN 0-8287-0043-5). Vol. 1 (1168). Vol. 2 (1169). Clearwater Pub.

--Le Travail et les Ouvriers sous la Troisieme Republique. (Conditions of the 19th Century French Working Class Ser). 36p. (Fr.). 1974. Repr. of 1873 ed. 26.00x (ISBN 0-8287-1424-X, 1086). Clearwater Pub.

Audiganne, Armand. Les Populations ouvrieres et les industries de la France, 2 Vols. 2nd ed. (Research & Source Works Ser., History, Economics & Social Science). 1971. Repr. of 1860 ed. lib. bdg. 48.00 (ISBN 0-8337-0124-X). B Franklin.

Barberet, J. Les Greves et la Loi sur les Coalitions. (Conditions of the 19th Century French Working Class Ser.). 189p. (Fr.). 1974. Repr. of 1873 ed. lib. bdg. 55.00x (ISBN 0-8287-0055-9, 1104). Clearwater Pub.

--Le Travail en France, Monographies Professionnelles, 7 vols. (Conditions of the 19th Century French Working Class Ser.). (Fr.). 1974. Repr. of 1866 ed. Set. lib. bdg. 860.00x, order nos. 1176-1182 (ISBN 0-8287-1423-1). Clearwater Pub.

Benoiston De Chateauneuf. Recherches sur les Consommations de Tout Genre de la Ville de Paris-Comparees a Ce Qu'Elles Etaient en 1789. (Conditions of the 19th Century French Working Class Ser.). 157p. (Fr.). 1974. Repr. of 1821 ed. lib. bdg. 48.00x (ISBN 0-8287-0079-6, 1120). Clearwater Pub.

Bernstein, Samuel. Beginnings of Marxian Socialism in France. LC 65-25426. (With a new preface). 1965. Repr. of 1933 ed. 8.50 (ISBN 0-8462-0654-4). Russell.

Bonaparte, Louis-Napoleon. Extinction du Pauperisme. (Conditions of the 19th Century French Working Class Ser.). 31p. (Fr.). 1974. Repr. of 1848 ed. 22.50x (ISBN 0-8287-1375-8, 1116). Clearwater Pub.

Bouquet, Louis. Le Travail des Enfants et des Filles Mineures dans l'Industrie. (Conditions of the 19th Century French Working Class Ser.). 356p. (Fr.). 1974. Repr. of 1885 ed. lib. bdg. 93.50x (ISBN 0-8287-0129-6, 1106). Clearwater Pub.

Boyer, Adolphe. De l'Etat des Ouvriers et de Son Amelioration par l'Organisation du Travail. (Conditions of the 19th Century French Working Class Ser.). 141p. (Fr.). 1974. Repr. of 1841 ed. lib. bdg. 44.50x (ISBN 0-8287-0133-4, 1105). Clearwater Pub.

Buret, Eugene. De la Misere Des Classes Laborieuses en Angleterre et en France, 2 vols. (Conditions of the 19th Century French Working Class Ser.). 924p. (Fr.). 1974. Repr. of 1840 ed. lib. bdg. 234.00x set (ISBN 0-8287-0152-0). Vol. 1 (1170). Vol. 2 (1171). Clearwater Pub.

Cere, Paul. Les Population Dangereuses et les Miseres Sociales. (Conditions of the 19th Century French Working Class Ser.). 378p. (Fr.). 1974. Repr. of 1872 ed. lib. bdg. 104.75x (ISBN 0-8287-0173-3, 1093). Clearwater Pub.

Cerfbeer, Auguste-Edouard. Des Societes De Bienfaisance Mutuelle. (Conditions of the 19th Century French Working Class Ser.). 113p. (Fr.). 1974. Repr. of 1836 ed. lib. bdg. 38.00x (ISBN 0-8287-0174-1, 1059). Clearwater Pub.

Chamborant, C. G. De. Du Pauperisme, Ce Qu'Il Etait dans L'antiquite et Ce Qu'Il Est de Nos Jours. (Conditions of the 19th Century French Working Class Ser.). 496p. (Fr.). 1974. Repr. of 1842 ed. lib. bdg. 127.00 (ISBN 0-8287-0177-6, 1097). Clearwater Pub.

Chambre de Commerce de Paris. Enquete sur les Conditions de Travail en France pendant l'Annee 1872. (Conditions of the 19th Century French Working Class Ser.). 323p. (Fr.). 1974. Repr. of 1875 ed. lib. bdg. 85.00x (ISBN 0-8287-1342-1, 1021). Clearwater Pub.

Chambre de Commerce de Paris. Statistique de l'Industrie a Paris, Resultant de l'Enquete Faite par la Chambre de Commerce pour les Annees 1847-1848: Resultats Generaux. (Conditions of the 19th Century French Working Class Ser.). 420p. (Fr.). 1974. Repr. of 1851 ed. lib. bdg. 106.00 (ISBN 0-8287-1343-X, 1142). Clearwater Pub.

Cherbuliez, A. E. Etudes sur les Causes de la Misere. (Conditions of the 19th Century French Working Class Ser). 352p. (Fr.). 1974. Repr. of 1853 ed. lib. bdg. 91.00x (ISBN 0-8287-0185-7, 1082). Clearwater Pub.

--Richesse ou Pauvrete. Exposition des Causes et des Effets de la Distribution Actuelle des Richesses Sociales. (Conditions of the 19th Century French Working Class Ser.). 184p. (Fr.). 1974. Repr. of 1841 ed. lib. bdg. 56.00x (ISBN 0-8287-0186-5, 1056). Clearwater Pub.

Chevalier, Michel. Questions des Travailleurs: L'amelioration du Sort des Ouvriers. Les Salaires, l'Organisation du Travail. (Conditions of the 19th Century French Working Class Ser.). 32p. (Fr.). 1974. Repr. of 1848 ed. lib. bdg. 23.00x (ISBN 0-8287-0189-X, 1001). Clearwater Pub.

Chevallier, Emile. Les Salaires au Dix-Neuvieme Siecle. (Conditions of the 19th Century French Working Class Ser.). 299p. (Fr.). 1974. Repr. of 1887 ed. lib. bdg. 79.50x (ISBN 0-8287-0190-3, 1094). Clearwater Pub.

Clement, Ambroise. Recherches sur les Causes de l'Indigence. (Conditions of the 19th Century French Working Class Ser.). 368p. (Fr.). 1974. Repr. of 1846 ed. lib. bdg. 95.00x (ISBN 0-8287-0204-7, 1002). Clearwater Pub.

Cochin, Augustin. La Condition des Ouvriers Francais d'apres les Dernier Travaux. (Conditions of the 19th Century French Working Class Ser.). 48p. (Fr.). 1974. Repr. of 1862 ed. lib. bdg. 24.50x (ISBN 0-8287-0208-X, 1107). Clearwater Pub.

Compagnon, A. Les Classes Laborieuses, Leur Condition Actuelle, Leur Avenir par la Reorginisation du Travail. (Conditions of the 19th Century French Working Class Ser.). 354p. (Fr.). 1974. Repr. of 1858 ed. lib. bdg. 91.50x (ISBN 0-8287-0215-2, 1076). Clearwater Pub.

Corbon, Anthime. De l'Enseignement Professionnel, quatrieme edition. (Conditions of the 19th Century French Working Class Ser.). 192p. (Fr.). 1974. Repr. lib. bdg. 55.50x (ISBN 0-8287-0226-8, 1144). Clearwater Pub.

--Le Secret du Peuple de Paris. (Conditions of the 19th Century French Working Class Ser.). 412p. (Fr.). 1974. Repr. of 1863 ed. lib. bdg. 95.50x (ISBN 0-8287-0227-6, 1084). Clearwater Pub.

Coste, Adolphe. Hygiene Sociale contre le Pauperisme. (Conditions of the 19th Century French Working Class Ser.). 543p. (Fr.). 1974. Repr. of 1882 ed. lib. bdg. 134.00x (ISBN 0-8287-0228-4, 1085). Clearwater Pub.

Dale, Leon A. French Labor: A Bibliography. LC 72-95163. 1969. 42.50x (ISBN 0-678-00543-5). Kelley.

Daubie, Julie. La Femme Pauvre Au Dix-Neuvieme Siecle. Condition Economique. Condition Professionnelle, 3 vols. (Conditions of the 19th Century French Working Class Ser.). (Fr.). 1974. Repr. of 1869 ed. Set. lib. bdg. 205.00x (ISBN 0-8287-0249-7). Vol. 1 (1139). Vol. 2 (1140). Vol. 3 (1141). Clearwater Pub.

De Cellier, Florent. Histoire des Classes Ouvrieres en France depuis la Conquete de la Gaule jusqu'a Nos Jours. (Conditions of the 19th Century French Working Class Ser.). 486p. (Fr.). 1974. Repr. of 1859 ed. lib. bdg. 121.00 (ISBN 0-8287-0252-7, 1004). Clearwater Pub.

De La Farelle, F. F. Du Progres Social au Profit des Classes Populaires ou Indigentes. (Conditions of the 19th Century French Working Class Ser.). 514p. (Fr.). 1974. Repr. of 1847 ed. lib. bdg. 127.50x (ISBN 0-8287-0482-1, 1095). Clearwater Pub.

Delesalle, Paul. Les Conditions de Travail Chez les Ouvriers en Instruments de Precision de Paris. (Conditions of the 19th Century French Working Class Ser.). 35p. (Fr.). 1974. Repr. of 1899 ed. lib. bdg. 21.00 (ISBN 0-8287-0255-1, 1122). Clearwater Pub.

De Madre, Ad. Des Ouvriers et Des Moyens D'ameliorer Leur Condition Dans les Villes. (Conditions of the 19th Century French Working Class Ser.). 140p. (Fr.). 1974. Repr. of 1863 ed. lib. bdg. 44.00x (ISBN 0-8287-0257-8, 1087). Clearwater Pub.

De Melun, Armand. De l'Intervention de la Societe pour Prevenir et Soulager la Misere. (Conditions of the 19th Century French Working Class Ser.). 71p. (Fr.). 1974. Repr. of 1849 ed. lib. bdg. 30.00 (ISBN 0-8287-0598-4, 1063). Clearwater Pub.

De Morogues, Bigot. De la Misere des Ouvriers et de la Marche a Suivre Pour y Remedier. (Conditions of the 19th Century French Working Class Ser.). 135p. (Fr.). 1974. Repr. of 1832 ed. lib. bdg. 43.00x (ISBN 0-8287-0643-3, 1029). Clearwater Pub.

--Du Pauperisme, de la Mendicite et des Moyens d'en Prevenir les Funestes Effects. (Conditions of the 19th Century French Working Class Ser.). 683p. (Fr.). 1974. Repr. of 1834 ed. lib. bdg. 165.00x (ISBN 0-8287-0644-1, 1030). Clearwater Pub.

--Recherches des Causes de la Richesse et de la Misere des Peuples Civilises. (Conditions of the 19th Century French Working Class Ser.). 649p. (Fr.). 1974. Repr. of 1834 ed. lib. bdg. 156.00x (ISBN 0-8287-0645-X, 1031). Clearwater Pub.

De Villeneuve-Bargemont, Alban. Economie Politique Chretienne, 3 vols. (Conditions of the 19th Century French Working Class Ser.). 1780p. (Fr.). 1974. Repr. of 1834 ed. lib. bdg. 437.50x (ISBN 0-8287-0865-7, 1034-6). Clearwater Pub.

Du Cellier, Florent. Les Classes Ouvrieres en France depuis 1789. (Conditions of the 19th Century French Working Class Ser.). 96p. (Fr.). 1974. Repr. of 1857 ed. lib. bdg. 34.50 (ISBN 0-8287-0284-5, 1003). Clearwater Pub.

Duchatel, M. T. La Charite dans ses Rapports avec l'Etat Moral, et le Bien-Etre des Classes Inferieures de la Societe. (Conditions of the 19th Century French Working Class Ser.). 431p. (Fr.). 1974. Repr. of 1829 ed. lib. bdg. 108.50 (ISBN 0-8287-0285-3, 1005). Clearwater Pub.

Ducpetiaux, Edouard. De la Condition Physique et Morale des Jeunes Ouvriers et des Moyens de l'Ameliorer. (Conditions of the 19th Century French Working Class Ser.). 472p. (Fr.). 1974. Repr. of 1843 ed. lib. bdg. 118.00 (ISBN 0-8287-0287-X, 1161). Clearwater Pub.

Du Maroussem. Ministere du Commerce, de l'Industrie et des Colonies. Office du Travail. La Petite Industrie. Salaires et Duree du Travail, 2 vols. (Conditions of the 19th Century French Working Class Ser.). (Fr.). 1974. Repr. of 1873 ed. Set. lib. bdg. 251.50x (ISBN 0-8287-1387-1). Vol. 1 (1127). Vol. 2 (1128). Clearwater Pub.

Du Maroussem, P. La Question Ouvriere, 4 vols. (Conditions of the 19th Century French Working Class Ser.). (Fr.). 1974. Repr. of 1891 ed. Set. lib. bdg. 282.00x (ISBN 0-8287-0292-6). Vol. 1 (1183). Vol. 2 (1184). Vol. 3 (1185). Vol. 4 (1186). Clearwater Pub.

Du Mesnil. L' Hygenie a Paris. l'Habitation du Pauvre. (Conditions of the 19th Century French Working Class Ser.). 233p. (Fr.). 1974. Repr. of 1890 ed. lib. bdg. 65.00x (ISBN 0-8287-0700-6, 1172). Clearwater Pub.

Du Mesnil & Mangenot. Etude d'Hygiene et d'Economie Sociale. Enquete sur les Logements, Professions, Salaires et Budgets. (Conditions of the 19th Century French Working Class Ser.). 166p. (Fr.). 1974. Repr. of 1899 ed. lib. bdg. 50.00x (ISBN 0-8287-0295-0, 1114). Clearwater Pub.

Dumont, A. A. Les Habitations Ouvrieres dans les Grands Centre Industries et Plus Particulierments dans la Region du Nord. (Conditions of the 19th Century French Working Class Ser.). 268p. (Fr.). 1974. Repr. of 1905 ed. lib. bdg. 72.50x (ISBN 0-8287-0297-7, 1054). Clearwater Pub.

Dupin, Charles. Du Travail des Enfants Qu'Emploient les Ateliers, les Usines, et les Manufactures. (Conditions of the 19th Century French Working Class Ser.). (Fr.). 1974. Repr. of 1847 ed. lib. bdg. 84.00x (ISBN 0-8287-0301-9, 1118). Clearwater Pub.

--Des Forces Productives et Commerciales De la France. (Conditions of the 19th Century French Working Class Ser.). (Fr.). 1974. Repr. of 1827 ed. lib. bdg. 180.50x (ISBN 0-8287-0300-0, 1153). Clearwater Pub.

Dupont. Les Ouvriers. Histoire Populaire Illustree des Travailleurs au Dix-Neuvieme Siecle. (Conditions of the 19th Century French Working Class Ser.). 600p. (Fr.). 1974. Repr. of 1890 ed. lib. bdg. 146.00x (ISBN 0-8287-0302-7, 1151). Clearwater Pub.

Dupont-White, Charles. Essai sur les Relations du Travail avec le Capital. (Conditions of the 19th Century French Working Class Ser.). 444p. (Fr.). 1974. Repr. of 1846 ed. lib. bdg. 111.00 (ISBN 0-8287-0303-5, 1007). Clearwater Pub.

Durand. De la Conditions des Ouvriers de Paris de 1789 jusqu'en 1841. (Conditions of the 19th Century French Working Class Ser.). 287p. (Fr.). 1974. Repr. of 1841 ed. lib. bdg. 77.00x (ISBN 0-8287-0305-1, 1009). Clearwater Pub.

Dutens, J. M. Essai Comparatif sur la Formation et la Distribution du Revenu de la France en 1815 et 1835. (Conditions of the 19th Century French Working Class Ser.). 182p. (Fr.). 1974. Repr. of 1842 ed. lib. bdg. 53.50x (ISBN 0-8287-0307-8, 1010). Clearwater Pub.

Dutouquet, H. E. De la Condition des Classes Pauvres a la Campagne, des Moyens les plus Efficaces de l'Ameliorer. (Conditions of the 19th Century French Working Class Ser.). 112p. (Fr.). 1974. Repr. of 1846 ed. lib. bdg. 38.00x (ISBN 0-8287-0308-6, 1011). Clearwater Pub.

Ehrmann, Henry W. French Labor from Popular Front to Liberation. LC 72-151548. 1971. Repr. of 1947 ed. 16.00 (ISBN 0-8462-1596-9). Russell.

Enquete sur les Conseils de Prud'hommes et les Livrets d'Ouvriers, 3 vols. (Conditions of the 19th Century French Working Class Ser.). (Fr.). 1974. Repr. of 1869 ed. Set. lib. bdg. 465.00x (ISBN 0-8287-0315-9). Vol. 1 (1042). Vol. 2 (1043). Vol. 3 (1044). Clearwater Pub.

Esterno, F. C. De la Misere, de Ses Causes, de Ses Remedies. (Conditions of the 19th Century French Working Class Ser.). 259p. (Fr.). 1974. Repr. of 1842 ed. lib. bdg. 83.00x (ISBN 0-8287-0319-1, 1012). Clearwater Pub.
Fagniez, Gustave C. Etudes sur l'Industrie et la Classe Industrielle a Paris aux 13e et au 14e Siecle. LC 73-126393. (Research & Source Works: No. 566). (Fr). 1970. Repr. of 1877 ed. 32.50 (ISBN 0-8337-1096-6). B Franklin.
Fix, Theodore. Observations sur l'Etat des Classes Ouvrieres. (Conditions of the 19th Century French Working Class Ser.). 416p. (Fr.). 1974. Repr. of 1846 ed. lib. bdg. 105.50 (ISBN 0-8287-0343-4, 1013). Clearwater Pub.
Fodere, F. E. Essai Historique et Moral sur la Pauvrete des Nations, la Population, la Mendicite, les Hospitaux et les Enfants Trouves. (Conditions of the 19th Century French Working Class Ser.). 628p. (Fr.). 1974. Repr. of 1825 ed. lib. bdg. 152.50x (ISBN 0-8287-0347-7, 1014). Clearwater Pub.
Fregier, H. A. Des Classes Dangereuses De la Societe Dans les Grandes Villes et Des Moyens De les Rendre Meilleures, 2 vols. (Conditions of the 19th Century French Working Class Ser.). (Fr.). 1974. Repr. of 1840 ed. Set. lib. bdg. 115.00 (ISBN 0-8287-0354-X, 1015, 1037). Clearwater Pub.
Gatti de Gamond, Zoe. Pauperisme et Association. (Conditions of the 19th Century French Working Class Ser.). 176p. (Fr.). 1974. Repr. of 1847 ed. lib. bdg. 52.00x (ISBN 0-8287-0366-3, 1058). Clearwater Pub.
Gerando, J. M. De la Bienfaisance Publique, 4 vols. (Conditions of the 19th Century French Working Class Ser.). (Fr.). 1974. Repr. of 1839 ed. lib. bdg. 950.00x set (ISBN 0-8287-0372-8). Vol. 1 (1188). Vol. 2 (1189). Vol. 3 (1190). Vol. 4 (1191). Clearwater Pub.
Gerando, J. M. de. Le Visiteur du Pauvre. (Conditions of the 19th Century French Working Class Ser.). 170p. (Fr.). 1974. Repr. of 1820 ed. lib. bdg. 51.00x (ISBN 0-8287-0373-6, 1017). Clearwater Pub.
Gillet. Quelques Reflexions sur l'Emploi des Enfants dans les Fabriques et sur les Moyens d'en Prevenir les Abus. (Conditions of the 19th Century French Working Class Ser.). 84p. (Fr.). 1974. Repr. of 1840 ed. lib. bdg. 31.50x (ISBN 0-8287-0377-9, 1150). Clearwater Pub.
Girardin, Emile de. L' Abolition de la Misere par l'Elevation des Salaires. (Conditions of the 19th Century French Working Class). 160p. (Fr.). 1974. Repr. of 1850 ed. lib. bdg. 48.50 (ISBN 0-8287-0251-9, 1018). Clearwater Pub.
Granier, Camille. Essai de Bibliographie Charitable. (Conditions of the 19th Century French Working Class Ser.). 458p. (Fr.). 1974. Repr. of 1891 ed. lib. bdg. 115.00 (ISBN 0-8287-0392-2, 1090). Clearwater Pub.
Guepin, Ange. Nantes au Dix-Neuvieme Siecle. Statistique Topographique, Industrielle et Morale: Hygenie Physique et Morale. (Conditions of the 19th Century French Working Class Ser.). 203p. (Fr.). 1974. Repr. of 1835 ed. lib. bdg. 58.00x (ISBN 0-8287-0402-3, 1187). Clearwater Pub.
Guerry, Andre-Michel. Essai sur la Statistique Morale de la France. (Conditions of the 19th Century French Working Class Ser.). 90p. (Fr.). 1974. Repr. of 1833 ed. lib. bdg. 33.00x (ISBN 0-8287-0403-1, 1152). Clearwater Pub.
Hamilton, Richard F. Affluence & the French Worker in the Fourth Republic. (Center of International Studies Ser.). 1967. 22.00x (ISBN 0-691-09300-8). Princeton U Pr.
Hanagan, Michael P. The Logic of Solidarity: Artisans & Industrial Workers in Three French Towns, 1871-1914. LC 79-13181. (The Working Class in European History Ser.). (Illus.). 280p. 1980. 15.00 (ISBN 0-252-00758-1). U of Ill Pr.
Hennequin, Amedee. De l'Organisation de la Statistique du Travail et du Placement des Ouvriers. (Conditions of the 19th Century French Working Class Ser.). 44p. (Fr.). 1974. Repr. of 1848 ed. lib. bdg. 23.50 (ISBN 0-8287-0423-6, 1019). Clearwater Pub.
Hubbard, G. De l'Organisation des Societes de Prevoyances ou de Secours Mutuel. (Conditions of the 19th Century French Working Class Ser.). 317p. 1974. Repr. of 1852 ed. lib. bdg. 84.00x (ISBN 0-8287-0453-8, 1020). Clearwater Pub.
Hubert-Valleroux, P. Les Associations Cooperatives en France et a l'Etranger. (Conditions of the 19th Century French Working Class Ser.). 480p. (Fr.). 1974. Repr. of 1884 ed. lib. bdg. 120.00 (ISBN 0-8287-0454-6, 1160). Clearwater Pub.
Husson, Armand. Les Consommations de Paris. (Conditions of the 19th Century French Working Class Ser.). 531p. (Fr.). 1974. Repr. of 1856 ed. lib. bdg. 131.00 (ISBN 0-8287-0456-2, 1065). Clearwater Pub.
Des Institutions Ouvriers Au Dix-Neuvieme Siecle. (Conditions of the 19th Century French Working Class Ser.). 295p. (Fr.). 1974. Repr. of 1866 ed. lib. bdg. 78.50x (ISBN 0-8287-1063-5, 1100). Clearwater Pub.
Jourdain, Victor. La Legislation Francaise sur les Coalitions Ouvrieres, son Evolution au 19th Siecle (These) (Conditions of the 19th Century French Working Class Ser.). 180p. (Fr.). 1974. Repr. of 1898 ed. lib. bdg. 53.00x (ISBN 0-8287-0466-X, 1119). Clearwater Pub.
Laboulaye, Charles. Les Droits des Ouvries: Etude sur l'Ordre dans l'Industrie. (Conditions of the 19th Century French Working Class Ser.). 117p. (Fr.). 1974. Repr. of 1873 ed. lib. bdg. 39.00x (ISBN 0-8287-0476-7, 1121). Clearwater Pub.
Lallemand, Leon. La Question des Enfants Abandonnes et Delaisses au 19th Siecle. (Conditions of the 19th Century French Working Class Ser.). 238p. (Fr.). 1974. Repr. of 1885 ed. lib. bdg. 66.00x (ISBN 0-8287-0494-5, 1064). Clearwater Pub.
Lefort, Joseph. Etudes sur la Moralisation et le Bien-Etre des Classes Ouvrieres. (Conditions of the 19th Century French Working Class Ser.). 362p. (Fr.). 1974. Repr. of 1875 ed. lib. bdg. 94.00x (ISBN 0-8287-0519-4, 1164). Clearwater Pub.
Le Play, Frederic. Les Ouvriers Europeens, 6 vols. (Conditions of the 19th Century French Working Class Ser.). (Fr.). 1974. lib. bdg. 967.00 (ISBN 0-8287-0536-4, 1067-72). Clearwater Pub.
Leroy-Beaulieu, P. La Travail des Femmes au 19th Siecle. (Conditions of the 19th Century French Working Class Ser.). 464p. (Fr.). 1974. Repr. of 1873 ed. lib. bdg. 116.00 (ISBN 0-8287-0538-0, 1099). Clearwater Pub.
Levasseur, Emile. Histoire Des Classes Ouvrieres et De L'industrie En France De 1789-1870, 2 Vols. 2nd ed. LC 78-92175. (Fr). Repr. of 1904 ed. Set. 105.00 (ISBN 0-404-03977-4). AMS Pr.
Lorain. Tableau de l'Instruction Primaire en France. (Conditions of the 19th Century French Working Class Ser.). 410p. 1974. Repr. of 1837 ed. lib. bdg. 104.00 (ISBN 0-8287-0553-4, 1124). Clearwater Pub.
Losseau, Leon. De la Reparation des Accidents de Travail. (Conditions of the 19th Century French Working Class Ser.). 376p. (Fr.). 1974. Repr. of 1897 ed. lib. bdg. 97.00x (ISBN 0-8287-0555-0, 1091). Clearwater Pub.
Maignen, Maurice. Scenes et Croquis De la Vie Ouvriere. 183p. 1981. Repr. lib. bdg. 80.00 (ISBN 0-8287-1559-9). Clearwater Pub.
Mann, Michael. Consciousness & Action Among the Western Working Class. (Studies in Sociology). 80p. (Orig.). 1975. pap. 6.75x (ISBN 0-333-13773-6). Humanities.
Marbeau, J. B. Des Creches Ou Moyen De Diminuer la Misere En Augmentant la Population. (Conditions of the 19th Century French Working Class Ser.). 139p. (Fr.). 1974. Repr. of 1845 ed. lib. bdg. 44.00x (ISBN 0-8287-0570-4, 1113). Clearwater Pub.
--Du Pauperisme En France et Des Moyens D'y Remedier, Ou Principes D'economie Charitable. (Conditions of the 19th Century French Working Class Ser.). 195p. (Fr.). 1974. Repr. of 1847 ed. lib. bdg. 56.00x (ISBN 0-8287-0571-2, 1022). Clearwater Pub.
Marchand, P. R. Du Pauperisme. (Conditions of the 19th Century Working Class Ser.). 536p. (Fr.). 1974. Repr. of 1845 ed. lib. bdg. 132.00x (ISBN 0-8287-0573-9, 1023). Clearwater Pub.
Ministere de l'Agriculture, du Commerce et des Travaux Publics, Enquete sur les Societes de Cooperation. (Conditions of the 19th Century French Working Class Ser.). 690p. (Fr.). 1974. Repr. of 1866 ed. lib. bdg. 179.50x (ISBN 0-8287-0617-4, 1045). Clearwater Pub.
Ministere de l'Instruction Publique et des Beaux-Arts. Commission d'Enquete sur la Situation des Ouvrieres et des Industries d'Art. (Conditions of the 19th Century French Working Class Ser.). 540p. (Fr.). 1974. Repr. of 1884 ed. lib. bdg. 133.00x (ISBN 0-8287-0618-2, 1081). Clearwater Pub.
Ministere de l'Interieur. Enquete de la Commission Extra-Parlementaire des Associations Ouvrieres, 2 vols. (Conditions of the 19th Century French Working Class Ser.). 790p. (Fr.). 1974. Repr. of 1888 ed. Set. lib. bdg. 201.50x (ISBN 0-8287-0619-0). Vol. 1 (1125). Vol. 2 (1126). Clearwater Pub.
Modeste, Victor. Du Pauperisme en France: Etat Actuel Causes, Remedes Possibles. (Conditions of the 19th Century French Working Class Ser.). 589p. (Fr.). 1974. Repr. of 1858 ed. lib. bdg. 144.00x (ISBN 0-8287-0627-1, 1024). Clearwater Pub.
Molher, Edmond. Sur l'Amelioration du Sort des Travailleurs. (Conditions of the 19th Century French Working Class Ser.). 129p. 1974. Repr. of 1849 ed. lib. bdg. 42.00x (ISBN 0-8287-0630-1, 1073). Clearwater Pub.
Mollot. Le Contrat d'Apprentissage Explique aux Maitres et aux Apprentis. (Conditions of the 19th Century French Working Class Ser.). 108p. (Fr.). 1974. Repr. of 1847 ed. lib. bdg. 37.50 (ISBN 0-8287-0631-X, 1145). Clearwater Pub.
Moreau-Christophe, L. M. Du Probleme de la Misere et de sa Solution Chez le Peuples Anciens et Modernes, Tome 3: Peuples Modernes. (Conditions of the 19th Century French Working Class Ser.). 580p. (Fr.). 1974. Repr. of 1851 ed. lib. bdg. 142.00x (ISBN 0-8287-0635-2, 1027). Clearwater Pub.
Moss, Bernard H. The Origins of the French Labor Movement. LC 75-3775. 1976. 16.00x (ISBN 0-520-02982-8). U of Cal Pr.
Organization for Economic Cooperation & Development & Kennedy-Brenner, C. Foreign Workers & Immigration Policy: The Case of France. (Development Center Studies). (Illus.). 106p. (Orig.). 1980. pap. text ed. 6.00x (ISBN 92-64-11964-7, 41 79 04 1). OECD.
Parent-Duchatelet, A. J. Hygiene Publique, 2 vols. (Conditions of the 19th Century French Working Class Ser.). 1510p. (Fr.). 1974. Repr. of 1836 ed. lib. bdg. 330.00x (ISBN 0-8287-0047-8, 1131-2). Clearwater Pub.
Perreymond. Le Bilan de la France, ou la Misere et le Travail. (Conditions of the 19th Century French Working Class Ser.). 117p. (Fr.). 1974. Repr. of 1849 ed. lib. bdg. 39.00 (ISBN 0-8287-0681-6, 1032). Clearwater Pub.
Perrot, Michelle. Enquetes sur la Condition Ouvriere au Dix-Neuvieme Siecle. (Conditions of the 19th Century French Working Class Ser.). 110p. (Fr.). 1974. pap. text ed. 11.50x (ISBN 0-8287-0682-4, 1000). Clearwater Pub.
Prince De Monaco. Du Pauperisme en France et des Moyens de le Detruire. (Conditions of the 19th Century French Working Class Ser.). 260p. (Fr.). 1974. Repr. of 1839 ed. lib. bdg. 71.00x (ISBN 0-8287-0632-8, 1146). Clearwater Pub.
Rapport Fait au Nom de la Commission d'Enquete Parlementaire sur les Conditions de Travail en France. (Conditions of the 19th Century French Working Class Ser.). 355p. (Fr.). 1974. Repr. of 1877 ed. lib. bdg. 92.00x (ISBN 0-8287-1403-7, 1138). Clearwater Pub.
Rapport Presente a la Commission d'Enquete Parlementaire sur la Situation des Ouvriers de L'agriculture et de l'Industrie en France et sur la Crise Parisiene. (Conditions of the 19th Century French Working Class Ser.). 220p. (Fr.). 1974. Repr. of 1885 ed. lib. bdg. 62.00x (ISBN 0-8287-1405-3, 1166). Clearwater Pub.
Rapport Presente a la Commission d'Enquete Parlementaire sur la Situation des Ouvriers de l'Agriculture et de l'Industrie en France. (Conditions of the 19th Century French Working Class Ser.). 199p. (Fr.). 1974. Repr. of 1885 ed. lib. bdg. 57.00x (ISBN 0-8287-1406-1, 1167). Clearwater Pub.
Republique Francaise. Ministere du Commerce, De l'Industrie, des Postes et Telegraphes. Office du Travail. Salaires et Duree du Travail dans l'Industrie Francaise, 5 vols. (Conditions of the 19th Century French Working Class Ser.). (Fr.). 1974. Repr. of 1894 ed. Set. lib. bdg. 635.00x, order nos. 1133-1137 (ISBN 0-8287-1412-6). Clearwater Pub.
Republique Francaise Ministere du Commerce, De l'Industrie, des Postes et des Telegraphes. Office du Travail. les Associations Professionnelles Qvrietes, 4 vols. (Conditions of the 19th Century French Working Class Ser.). (Fr.). 1974. Repr. of 1899 ed. Set. lib. bdg. 785.00x, order nos. 1049-1052 (ISBN 0-8287-1413-4). Clearwater Pub.
Republique Francaise. Ministere du Commerce et de l'Industrie. Office Du Travail. Le Placement des Employes, Ouvriers et Domestiques en France. (Conditions of the 19th Century French Working Class Ser.). 740p. (Fr.). 1974. Repr. of 1893 ed. lib. bdg. 195.00x (ISBN 0-8287-0715-4, 1053). Clearwater Pub.
Republique Francaise. Ministere du Travail et de la Prevoyance Sociale. Statistique Generale de la France. Salaires et Cout de l'Existence a Diverses Epoques jusqu'en 1910. (Conditions of the 19th Century French Working Class Ser.). 527p. (Fr.). 1974. Repr. of 1911 ed. lib. bdg. 142.00x (ISBN 0-8287-0716-2, 1046). Clearwater Pub.
Reybaud, Louis. Le Fer et la Houille. (Conditions of the 19th Century French Working Class Ser.). 454p. (Fr.). 1974. Repr. of 1874 ed. lib. bdg. 114.00 (ISBN 0-8287-0729-4, 1175). Clearwater Pub.
--La Laine. (Conditions of the 19th Century French Working Class Ser.). 466p. (Fr.). 1974. Repr. of 1867 ed. lib. bdg. 116.50 (ISBN 0-8287-0730-8, 1174). Clearwater Pub.
Rigaudias-Weiss, Hilde. Las Enquetes Ouvrieres En France Entre 1830 et 1848: The Working Class Surveys in France Between 1830 & 1848. LC 74-25777. (European Sociology Ser.). 270p. 1975. Repr. 18.00x (ISBN 0-405-06531-0). Arno.
Rougier, J. Paul. Les Associations Ouvrieres. (Conditions of the 19th Century French Working Class Ser.). 472p. (Fr.). 1974. Repr. of 1864 ed. lib. bdg. 118.00 (ISBN 0-8287-0740-5, 1149). Clearwater Pub.
Saposs, David J. Labor Movement in Post-War France. LC 77-180619. (Illus.). 1972. Repr. of 1931 ed. 18.00 (ISBN 0-8462-1627-2). Russell.
Scott, Joan W. The Glassworkers of Carmaux. LC 73-83423. (Studies in Urban History). 256p. 1974. text ed. 12.50x (ISBN 0-674-35440-0); pap. 5.95x (ISBN 0-686-76999-6). Harvard U Pr.
Sewell, W. H., Jr. Work & Revolution in France. LC 80-12103. (Illus.). 336p. 1980. 35.95 (ISBN 0-521-23442-5); pap. 8.95 (ISBN 0-521-29951-9). Cambridge U Pr.
Stearns, Peter N. Lives of Labor: Work in a Maturing Industrial Society. LC 74-28298. 1975. text ed. 34.50x (ISBN 0-8419-0192-9). Holmes & Meier.
Tallon, Eugene & Gustave, Maurice. Legislation sur le Travail des Enfants dans les Manufactures. (Conditions of the 19th Century French Working Class Ser.). 600p. (Fr.). 1974. Repr. of 1875 ed. lib. bdg. 146.00x (ISBN 0-8287-0802-9, 1066). Clearwater Pub.
Terme, J. F. & Monfalcon, J. B. Histoire des Enfants Trouves, Nouvelle Edition Revue et Augmentee. (Conditions of the 19th Century French Working Class Ser.). 497p. 1974. Repr. of 1840 ed. lib. bdg. 124.00 (ISBN 0-8287-0811-8, 1163). Clearwater Pub.
Veron, Eugene. Les Institutions Ouvrieres de Mulhouse et des Environs. (Conditions of the 19th Century French Working Class Ser.). 399p. (Fr.). 1974. Repr. of 1866 ed. lib. bdg. 101.50 (ISBN 0-8287-0857-6, 1083). Clearwater Pub.
Villerme, Louis-Rene. Des Associations Ouvrieres. (Conditions of the 19th Century French Working Class Ser.). 104p. 1974. Repr. of 1849 ed. lib. bdg. 36.00 (ISBN 0-8287-0866-5, 1101). Clearwater Pub.
--Sur les Cites Ouvrieres. (Conditions of the 19th Century French Working Class Ser.). 32p. (Fr.). 1974. Repr. of 1850 ed. lib. bdg. 23.50x (ISBN 0-8287-0868-1, 1111). Clearwater Pub.
--Tableau de l'Etat Physique et Moral des Ouvriers Employes dans les Manufactures de Cotton, de Laine et ! De Soie, 2 vols. (Conditions of the 19th Century French Working Class Ser.). 455p. 1974. Repr. of 1840 ed. lib. bdg. 249.75x (ISBN 0-8287-0869-X, 1060-1). Clearwater Pub.
Vincard, Pierre. Les Ouvriers de Paris: Alimentation. (Conditions of the 19th Century French Working Class Ser.). 381p. (Fr.). 1974. Repr. of 1863 ed. lib. bdg. 97.50x (ISBN 0-8287-0873-8, 1075). Clearwater Pub.
Walras, L. Les Associations Populaires de Consommation, de Production et de Credit. (Conditions of the 19th Century French Working Class Ser.). 300p. (Fr.). 1974. Repr. of 1865 ed. lib. bdg. 80.00 (ISBN 0-8287-0879-7, 1077). Clearwater Pub.

LABOR AND LABORING CLASSES–GERMANY

Anderson, Evelyn. Hammer or Anvil. LC 72-92773. 200p. 1973. Repr. of 1945 ed. 10.00 (ISBN 0-88211-043-8). S A Russell.
Comfort, Richard A. Revolutionary Hamburg: Labor Politics in the Early Weimar Republic. 1966. 15.00x (ISBN 0-8047-0284-5). Stanford U Pr.
De Man, Henri. Joy in Work. Stein, Leon, ed. LC 77-70513. (Work Ser.). 1977. Repr. of 1929 ed. lib. bdg. 15.00 (ISBN 0-405-10182-1). Arno.
Gohre, Paul. Three Months in a Workshop: A Practical Study. LC 74-38277. (Evolution of Capitalism Ser.). 236p. 1972. Repr. of 1895 ed. 19.00 (ISBN 0-405-04121-7). Arno.
Grebing, Helga. The History of the German Labour Movement. Korner, Edith, tr. from Ger. 240p. 1981. pap. text ed. 18.75x (ISBN 0-85496-139-9, Pub. by Wolff England). Humanities.
Guillebaud, C. W. The Social Policy of Nazi Germany. LC 71-80553. 1971. Repr. 16.50 (ISBN 0-86527-183-6). Fertig.
Homze, Edward L. Foreign Labor in Nazi Germany. 1967. 20.00 (ISBN 0-691-05118-6). Princeton U Pr.
Kele, Max H. Nazis & Workers: National Socialist Appeals to German Labor, 1919-1933. LC 77-174786. 288p. 1972. 16.50x (ISBN 0-8078-1184-X). U of NC Pr.
Kuczynski, Jurgen. Germany: Economic & Labour Conditions Under Fascism. LC 68-30824. (Illus.). 1968. Repr. of 1945 ed. lib. bdg. 15.50x (ISBN 0-8371-0519-6, KUGE). Greenwood.
Maehl, William H. August Bebel: Shadow Emperor of the German Workers. LC 79-51544. (Memoirs Ser.: Vol. 138). 1980. 20.00 (ISBN 0-87169-138-8). Am Philos.

Oppenheimer-Bluhm, Hilde. Standard of Living of German Labor Under Nazi Rule. (Social Research Suppl.: No. 5). 1943. pap. 4.00 (ISBN 0-527-00865-6). Kraus Repr.

Peltzer, Martin. Labour Management Relations Act: Federal Republic of Germany. 300p. (Ger. & Eng.). 1977. 33.50x (ISBN 3-7819-2806-3). Intl Pubns Serv.

Peltzer, Martin & Boer, Rolf. German Labour Management Relations Act. 384p. 1980. 66.00x (ISBN 0-7121-5515-5, Pub. by Macdonald & Evans). State Mutual Bk.

Schneider, Hannes & Hellwig, Hans-Jurgen, eds. German Labour Law. 196p. 1980. 45.00x (ISBN 0-7121-5496-5, Pub. by Macdonald & Evans). State Mutual Bk.

Wendel, Hugo C. Evolution of Industrial Freedom in Prussia 1845-1849. facsimile ed. LC 74-109636. (Select Bibliographies Reprint Ser). 1921. 15.00 (ISBN 0-8369-5245-6). Arno.

LABOR AND LABORING CLASSES–GREAT BRITAIN

Aftermath of the Lost Labourers' Revolt: 1830-1831. LC 72-2518. (British Labour Struggles Before 1850 Ser). (14 pamphlets). Repr. of 1972 ed. 23.00 (ISBN 0-405-04411-9). Arno.

Askham, Janet. Fertility & Deprivation. LC 75-2718. (Papers in Sociology Ser.: No. 5). (Illus.). 192p. 1975. 24.95 (ISBN 0-521-20795-9). Cambridge U Pr.

Baernreither, Joseph M. English Associations of Working Men. Taylor, A., tr. LC 66-28040. 1966. Repr. of 1889 ed. 26.00 (ISBN 0-8103-3078-4). Gale.

Bamford, Samuel. Autobiography. Chaloner, W. H., ed. 1967. Vol. 1. 25.00x (ISBN 0-7146-1055-0, F Cass Co); Vol. 2. 27.50x (ISBN 0-7146-1056-9). Biblio Dist.

--Walks in South Lancashire & on Its Borders. LC 72-80019. 288p. Repr. of 1844 ed. lib. bdg. 15.00x (ISBN 0-678-08023-2). Kelley.

Bell, Florence E. At the Works: A Study of a Manufacturing Town. LC 69-10847. 1907. 15.00x (ISBN 0-678-05510-6). Kelley.

Besant, Walter. East London. LC 79-56945. (The English Working Class Ser.). 1980. lib. bdg. 32.00 (ISBN 0-8240-0100-1). Garland Pub.

Black, Clementina. Married Women's Work: Being the Report of an Inquiry Undertaken by the Women's Industrial Council. LC 79-56947. (The Englishworking Class Ser.). 1980. lib. bdg. 25.00 (ISBN 0-8240-0102-8). Garland Pub.

Booth, Charles. Charles Booth on the City: Physical Pattern & Social Structure. Pfautz, Harold W., ed. LC 67-28466. (Heritage of Sociology Ser). (Illus.). 1967. pap. 3.45 (ISBN 0-226-06551-0, P282, Phoen). U of Chicago Pr.

--Life & Labour of the People of London, First Series: Poverty, 5 Vols. rev. ed. LC 68-55487. (Illus.). Repr. of 1902 ed. Set. 95.00x (ISBN 0-678-00455-2). Kelley.

Bray, John F. Labour's Wrongs & Labour's Remedy. LC 66-21656. Repr. of 1839 ed. 12.50x (ISBN 0-678-00283-5). Kelley.

Bray, Reginald A. Boy Labour & Apprenticeship. LC 79-56952. (The English Working Class Ser.). 1980. lib. bdg. 22.00 (ISBN 0-8240-0106-0). Garland Pub.

Briggs, Asa. Chartist Studies. 1959. pap. 9.95 (ISBN 0-312-13125-9, Papermac). St Martin.

Briggs, Asa & Saville, John, eds. Essays in Labour History, 1886-1923. 1971. 22.50 (ISBN 0-208-01239-7, Archon). Shoe String.

--Essays in Labour History: 1918-1939. 1977. 18.00 (ISBN 0-208-01641-4, Archon). Shoe String.

British Labourer's Protector & Factory Child's Friend, Nos. 1-31. 1832-33. Repr. lib. bdg. 15.00x (ISBN 0-8371-9373-7, BP00). Greenwood.

Brown, Ernest H. The Growth of British Industrial Relations. LC 74-14024. (Illus.). 414p. 1975. Repr. of 1959 ed. lib. bdg. 26.00x (ISBN 0-8371-7781-2, BRBI). Greenwood.

Brown, K. D., ed. Essays in Anti-Labour History: Responses to the Rise of Labour in Britain. viii, 408p. (Orig.). 1974. 25.00 (ISBN 0-208-01335-0, Archon). Shoe String.

Brown, Kenneth D. Labour & Unemployment, 1900-1914. 219p. 1971. 12.50x (ISBN 0-87471-039-1). Rowman.

Bulmer, Martin. Working-Class Images of Society. (Direct Editions Ser.). (Orig.). 1975. 10.95 (ISBN 0-7100-8308-4). Routledge & Kegan.

Buret, Eugene. De la Misere Des Classes Laborieuses en Angleterre et en France, 2 vols. (Conditions of the 19th Century French Working Class Ser.). 924p. (Fr.). 1974. Repr. of 1840 ed. lib. bdg. 234.00x set (ISBN 0-8287-0152-0). Vol. 1 (1170). Vol. 2 (1171). Clearwater Pub.

Burgess, Keith. The Challenged of Labour: Shaping British Society, 1850-1930. LC 80-10251. 224p. 1980. 19.95 (ISBN 0-312-12805-3). St Martin.

Butler, C. V. Domestic Service. LC 79-56953. (The English Working Class Ser.). 1980. lib. bdg. 15.00 (ISBN 0-8240-0107-9). Garland Pub.

Cadbury, Edward, et al. Women's Work & Wages. LC 79-56954. (The English Working Class). 1980. lib. bdg. 30.00 (ISBN 0-8240-0108-7). Garland Pub.

Carpenter, Kenneth E., ed. British Labour Struggles: Contemporary Pamphlets, 1727-1850, 32 bks. 1972. Set. 500.00 (ISBN 0-405-04410-0). Arno.

Citrine, W. M. Men & Work: An Autobiography. LC 75-36094. (Illus.). 1976. Repr. of 1964 ed. lib. bdg. 24.00x (ISBN 0-8371-8613-7, CIMW). Greenwood.

Clark, Alice. Working Life of Women in the Seventeenth Century. 328p. 1968. 26.00x (ISBN 0-7146-1291-X, F Cass Co). Biblio Dist.

Cole, G. D. & Postgate, Raymond. The Common People: 1746-1946. 4th ed. 1961. pap. 15.95x (ISBN 0-416-67720-7). Methuen Inc.

Cole, George D. Labour in the Commonwealth: Book for the Younger Generation. facsimile ed. LC 75-157330. (Select Bibliographies Reprint Ser). Repr. of 1918 ed. 16.00 (ISBN 0-8369-5790-3). Arno.

Cole, George D. & Filson, A. W. British Working Class Movements: Select Documents. 1951. pap. 9.95 (ISBN 0-312-10570-3, Papermac). St Martin.

Conditions of Work & Living: The Reawakening of the English Conscience, 1838-1844. LC 72-2520. (British Labour Struggles Before 1850 Ser). (5 pamphlets). 1972. Repr. 11.00 (ISBN 0-405-04413-5). Arno.

Craig, Gary, et al, eds. Jobs & Community Action. (Community Work Studies). 1979. pap. 14.25 (ISBN 0-7100-0241-6). Routledge & Kegan.

Davis, W. Hints to Philanthropists. 176p. 1971. Repr. of 1821 ed. 20.00x (ISBN 0-7165-1564-4, Pub. by Irish Academic Pr Ireland). Biblio Dist.

Dean, Andrew. Wages & Earnings. (Reviews of United Kingdom Statistical Sources Ser.: Vol. XIII). 1980. 45.00 (ISBN 0-08-024060-7). Pergamon.

Dodd, William. Factory System Illustrated. LC 67-28260. (Illus.). Repr. of 1842 ed. 24.00x (ISBN 0-678-05043-0). Kelley.

--Labouring Classes of England. LC 68-55703. Repr. of 1847 ed. 13.50x (ISBN 0-678-00961-9). Kelley.

Dore, Ronald P. British Factory - Japanese Factory: The Origins of National Diversity in Employment Relations. LC 72-78948. 1973. 18.50x (ISBN 0-520-02268-8); pap. 7.95x (ISBN 0-520-02495-8, CAMPUS96). U of Cal Pr.

Eastwood, Gerry. Skilled Labor Shortages in the United Kingdom: With Particular Reference to the Engineering Industry. 52p. 1976. 3.00 (ISBN 0-902594-28-1). Natl Planning.

Engels, Frederick. Condition of the Working Class in England. 351p. 1973. 14.95x (ISBN 0-8464-1082-6). Beekman Pubs.

--The Condition of the Working Class in England. (Illus.). 336p. 1979. pap. 4.95 (ISBN 0-586-02880-3, Pub. by Granada England). Academy Chi Ltd.

Engels, Friedrich. The Condition of the Working Class in England. 351p. 1973. 2.50 (ISBN 0-8285-0020-7, Pub. by Progress Pubs Russia). Imported Pubns.

--The Condition of the Working Class in England. Henderson, W. O. & Chaloner, W. H., trs. (Illus.). 1958. 15.00x (ISBN 0-8047-0633-6); pap. 6.95x (ISBN 0-8047-0634-4). Stanford U Pr.

Fay, Charles R. Life & Labour in the Nineteenth Century. LC 73-90143. Repr. of 1920 ed. lib. bdg. 14.25x (ISBN 0-8371-2165-5, FALL). Greenwood.

Foner, Philip S. British Labor & the American Civil War. LC 80-26162. 130p. 1981. text ed. 19.50x (ISBN 0-8419-0671-8). Holmes & Meier.

Forester, Tom. The British Labour Party & the Working Class. LC 75-19474. 225p. 1976. 17.50x (ISBN 0-8419-0217-8). Holmes & Meier.

Freeman, Arnold. Boy Life & Labour: The Manufacture of Inefficiency. LC 79-56956. (The English Working Class Ser.). 1980. lib. bdg. 25.00 (ISBN 0-8240-0110-9). Garland Pub.

Furniss, Edgar S. Position of the Laborer in a System of Nationalism. LC 58-3121. Repr. of 1920 ed. 15.00x (ISBN 0-678-00093-X). Kelley.

Gaskell, Peter. Artisans & Machinery. LC 68-28259. Repr. of 1836 ed. 30.00x (ISBN 0-678-05047-3). Kelley.

--The Manufacturing Population of England. LC 73-38266. (The Evolution of Capitalism Ser.). 374p. 1972. Repr. of 1833 ed. 19.00 (ISBN 0-405-04120-9). Arno.

Gillespie, Frances E. Labor & Politics in England: 1850-1867. 1967. lib. bdg. 15.00x (ISBN 0-374-93078-3). Octagon.

Gorman, John. To Build Jerusalem. 208p. 1980. 50.00x (ISBN 0-905906-26-8); pap. 26.00x (ISBN 0-905906-27-6). State Mutual Bk.

Gray, Robert Q. The Labour Aristocracy in Victorian Edinburgh. (Illus.). 1976. text ed. 45.00x (ISBN 0-19-822442-7). Oxford U Pr.

Gupta, Partha S. Imperialism & the British Labour Movement 1914-1964. LC 74-28203. 438p. 1975. text ed. 35.00x (ISBN 0-8419-0191-0). Holmes & Meier.

Hall, Richard J. British Labour Costs 1975-1980. LC 76-35345. 1975. pap. 90.00x (ISBN 0-8002-0736-X). Intl Pubns Serv.

Hammond, J. L. & Hammond, Barbara. Age of the Chartists from Eighteen Thirty-Two to Eighteen Fifty-Four: A Study of Discontent. 1962. Repr. of 1930 ed. 22.50 (ISBN 0-208-00060-7, Archon). Shoe String.

Hammond, John L. The Village Labourer, 1760-1832: A Study in the Government of England Before the Reform Bill. new ed. LC 66-22628. Repr. of 1913 ed. 17.50x (ISBN 0-678-00266-5). Kelley.

Hayek, Friedrich A., ed. Capitalism & the Historians. 1954. 9.00x (ISBN 0-226-32071-5). U of Chicago Pr.

--Capitalism & the Historians. 1963. pap. 3.95 (ISBN 0-226-32072-3, P120, Phoen). U of Chicago Pr.

Hearn, Francis. Domination, Legitimation, & Resistance: The Incorporation of the Nineteenth-Century English Working Class. LC 77-84753. (Contributions in Labor History: No. 3). 1978. lib. bdg. 19.95 (ISBN 0-8371-9847-X, HDL/). Greenwood.

Hepple, B. A., et al. Labour Law in Great Britain & Ireland to Nineteen Seventy Eight. 1981. text ed. 35.00 (ISBN 0-7201-1624-4, Pub. by Mansell England). Merrimack Bk Serv.

Hill, Richard L. Toryism & the People 1832-1846. LC 75-25724. (Perspectives in European Hist. Ser.: No. 8). xiii, 278p. Repr. of 1929 ed. lib. bdg. 17.50x (ISBN 0-87991-614-1). Porcupine Pr.

Hill, Stephen. The Dockers: Class & Tradition in London. 1976. text ed. 37.00x (ISBN 0-435-82416-3). Heinemann Ed.

Hobson, John A. Problems of Poverty. 8th ed. LC 67-29506. Repr. of 1913 ed. 13.50x (ISBN 0-678-00755-1). Kelley.

Hodgskin, Thomas. Labour Defended Against the Claims of Capital. LC 68-54736. Repr. of 1922 ed. 9.50x (ISBN 0-678-00004-2). Kelley.

Hole, James. Light, More Light. LC 76-5888. (Social History of Education). Repr. of 1860 ed. 15.00x (ISBN 0-678-08455-6). Kelley.

--Light, More Light: On the Present State of Education Amongst Working Classes of Leeds & How It Can Best Be Improved. (First Ser. in Social History of Education: No. 4). 1969. Repr. of 1860 ed. 18.00x (ISBN 0-7130-0005-8, Pub. by Woburn Pr England). Biblio Dist.

Hollis, Patricia, ed. Class & Conflict in Nineteenth-Century England, 1815-1850. (Birth of Modern Britain Ser). 402p. 1973. 20.00x (ISBN 0-7100-7419-0); pap. 10.00 (ISBN 0-7100-7420-4). Routledge & Kegan.

Huggett, Frank E. A Day in the Life of a Victorian Factory Worker. (Victorian Day Ser.). 1973. pap. text ed. 5.95x (ISBN 0-04-942113-1). Allen Unwin.

Hunt, E. H. British Labour History, Eighteen Fifteen to Nineteen Fourteen. 428p. 1981. text ed. 48.25x (ISBN 0-391-02209-1, Pub. by Weidenfeld England). Humanities.

Hunter, Lawrence C. & Robertson, D. J. Economics of Wages & Labour. LC 70-83359. (Illus.). 1969. 17.50x (ISBN 0-678-07002-4). Kelley.

Hutchins, B. L. Women in Modern Industry. LC 79-56959. (The English Working Class Ser.). 1980. lib. bdg. 28.00 (ISBN 0-8240-0112-5). Garland Pub.

Jevons, William S. State in Relation to Labour. 4th ed. Hirst, Francis, ed. LC 67-16344. Repr. of 1910 ed. 13.50x (ISBN 0-678-00434-X). Kelley.

Johnston, Thomas. History of the Working Classes in Scotland. 4th ed. 410p. 1974. Repr. of 1946 ed. 15.00x (ISBN 0-87471-460-5). Rowman.

Jordan, Bill. Automatic Poverty: The Ricardo Phenomenon. 208p. 1981. 22.50 (ISBN 0-7100-0824-4); pap. 12.95 (ISBN 0-7100-0825-2). Routledge & Kegan.

Kapp, Yvonne. Eleanor Marx, Vols. 1 & 2. LC 77-77538. 1977. Vol.1. 10.00 (ISBN 0-394-42143-4); Vol. 2. 17.95 (ISBN 0-394-42151-5); Vol. 1. pap. 4.95 (ISBN 0-394-73456-4); Vol. 2. pap. 6.95 (ISBN 0-394-73457-2). Pantheon.

Kay-Shuttleworth, J. P. Moral & Physical Condition of the Working Classes in the Cotton Manufacture in Manchester. 2nd ed. 120p. 1970. 23.50x (ISBN 0-7146-2425-X, F Cass Co). Biblio Dist.

Kay-Shuttleworth, James P. Moral & Physical Condition of the Working Classes in the Cotton Manufacture in Manchester. LC 79-96379. Repr. of 1832 ed. lib. bdg. 18.50x (ISBN 0-678-05107-0). Kelley.

Kellogg, Paul U. & Gleason, Arthur. British Labour & the War: Reconstruction for a New World. LC 70-147517. (Library of War & Peace; Labor, Socialism & War). lib. bdg. 38.00 (ISBN 0-8240-0306-3). Garland Pub.

Kingsford, P. W. Victorian Railwaymen: Emergence & Growth of Railway Labour, 1830-1870. (Illus.). 198p. 1970. 25.00x (ISBN 0-7146-1331-2, F Cass Co). Biblio Dist.

Knight, Charles. Capital & Labor: Including the Results of Machinery. LC 76-38272. (The Evolution of Capitalism Ser.). 254p. 1972. Repr. of 1845 ed. 18.00 (ISBN 0-405-04125-X). Arno.

Knowles, Lillian C. Industrial & Commercial Revolutions in Great Britain During the Nineteenth Century. 4th ed. LC 67-27704. Repr. of 1961 ed. 17.50x (ISBN 0-678-06518-7). Kelley.

Kydd, Samuel. History of the Factory Movement from the Year Eighteen Hundred Two to the Enactment of the Ten Hours Bill in Eighteen Forty Seven, 2 vols. in 1. 1965. Repr. of 1857 ed. 30.50 (ISBN 0-8337-1967-X). B Franklin.

Kydd, Samuel A. History of the Factory Movement, 2 Vols. in 1. LC 66-18320. Repr. of 1857 ed. 25.00x (ISBN 0-678-00163-4). Kelley.

Kynaston, David. King Labour: The British Working Class, 1850-1914. 184p. 1976. 13.00x (ISBN 0-87471-891-0). Rowman.

Laqueur, Thomas W. Religion & Respectability: Sunday Schools & English Working Class Culture, 1780-1850. LC 74-29728. 1976. 30.00x (ISBN 0-300-01859-2). Yale U Pr.

Lees-Smith, Hastings B., ed. The Encyclopaedia of the Labour Movement, 3 vols. 7th ed. LC 73-167033. xxv, 1132p. 1972. Repr. of 1928 ed. Set. 125.00 (ISBN 0-8103-3028-8). Gale.

Leventhal, F. M. Respectable Radical: George Howell & Victorian Working Class Politics. LC 77-135190. 1971. 15.00x (ISBN 0-674-76540-0). Harvard U Pr.

Levitt, Ian & Smout, Christopher. The State of the Scottish Working Class in Eighteen Forty-Three. (Illus.). 290p. 1980. text ed. 15.00x (ISBN 0-7073-0247-1, Pub. by Scottish Academic Pr). Columbia U Pr.

Loane, M. From Their Point of View. LC 79-56961. (The English Working Class Ser.). 1980. lib. bdg. 27.00 (ISBN 0-8240-0113-3). Garland Pub.

Lovell, John C. Stevedores & Dockers: A Study of Trade Unionism in the Port of London, 1870-1914. LC 74-99263. (Illus.). 1969. 15.00x (ISBN 0-678-07003-2). Kelley.

The Luddites: Eighteen Twelve to Eighteen Thirty-Nine. LC 72-2533. (British Labour Struggles Before 1850 Ser). 18.00 (ISBN 0-405-04426-7). Arno.

Ludlow, John M. & Jones, Lloyd. Progress of the Working Classes, 1832-1867. LC 72-77050. Repr. of 1867 ed. 17.50x (ISBN 0-678-00909-0). Kelley.

Lunn, Kenneth, ed. Hosts, Immigrants & Minorities: Historical Responses to Newcomers in British Society 1870-1914. 1980. 25.00 (ISBN 0-312-39238-9). St Martin.

Lynd, Robert. Passion of Labour. facs. ed. LC 73-76909. (Essay Index Reprint Ser). 1920. 15.00 (ISBN 0-8369-0025-1). Arno.

Macdonald, J. Ransay, ed. Women in the Printing Trades: A Sociological Study. LC 79-56961. (The English Working Class Ser.). 1980. lib. bdg. 18.00 (ISBN 0-8240-0114-1). Garland Pub.

McKenzie, Robert & Silver, Allan. Angels in Marble: Working Class Conservatives in Urban England. LC 67-30555. (Studies in Urban Society Ser.). 1968. 12.50x (ISBN 0-226-56017-1). U of Chicago Pr.

Mann, Michael. Consciousness & Action Among the Western Working Class. (Studies in Sociology). 80p. (Orig.). 1975. pap. 6.75x (ISBN 0-333-13773-6). Humanities.

Marcus, Steven. Engels, Manchester & the Working Class. pap. 2.95 (ISBN 0-394-71406-7, V-406, Vin). Random.

Masterman, C. F. From the Abyss. of Its Inhabitants by One of Them. LC 79-56963. (The English Working Class Ser.). 1980. lib. bdg. 12.00 (ISBN 0-8240-0115-X). Garland Pub.

Mayhew, Henry. London Labour & the London Poor, 4 vols. (Illus.). 1967. 165.00x (ISBN 0-7146-1148-4, F Cass Co). Biblio Dist.

Meacham, Standish. A Life Apart: The English Working Class, 1890-1914. 1977. 15.00x (ISBN 0-674-53075-6). Harvard U Pr.

Morton, Arthur L. & Tate, George. British Labour Movement, 1770-1920. 313p. 1974. pap. 9.95x (ISBN 0-8464-0215-7). Beekman Pubs.

--The British Labour Movement, 1770-1920: A Political History. LC 74-25892. 313p. 1975. Repr. of 1973 ed. lib. bdg. 17.50x (ISBN 0-8371-7865-7, MOBL). Greenwood.
--The British Labour Movement, 1770-1920: A Political History. LC 74-25892. 313p. 1975. Repr. of 1973 ed. lib. bdg. 17.50x (ISBN 0-8371-7865-7, MOBL). Greenwood.
Mountford, Alan. English in Workshop Practice. (English in Focus Ser.). 1975. pap. text ed. 6.95x (ISBN 0-19-437511-0); tchrs'. ed. 9.25x (ISBN 0-19-437502-1). Oxford U Pr.
Mudie-Smith, Richard, ed. Handbook of the Daily News Sweated Industries Exhibition. LC 79-56964. (The English Working Class Ser.). 1980. lib. bdg. 16.00 (ISBN 0-8240-0116-8). Garland Pub.
Orwell, George. The Road to Wigan Pier. LC 58-10888. 232p. 1972. pap. 2.95 (ISBN 0-15-676750-3, HB240, Harv). HarBraceJ.
Paterson, Alexander. Across the Bridges or Life by the South London River-Side. LC 79-56967. (The English Working Class Ser.). 1980. lib. bdg. 25.00 (ISBN 0-8240-0118-4). Garland Pub.
Peel, Frank. Risings of the Luddites, Chartists & Plug-Drawers. 3rd ed. LC 68-21440. (Illus.). Repr. of 1895 ed. 25.00x (ISBN 0-678-05013-9). Kelley.
Pelling, Henry. Popular Politics & Society in Late Victorian Britain. LC 68-29377. 1968. 17.95 (ISBN 0-312-63070-0). St Martin.
Pemer Reeves, M. S. Round About a Pound a Week. LC 79-56968. (The English Working Class Ser.). 1980. lib. bdg. 25.00 (ISBN 0-8240-0119-2). Garland Pub.
Pinchbeck, Ivy. Women Workers & the Industrial Revolution, 1750-1850. 2nd & rev. ed. 342p. 1969. 27.50x (ISBN 0-7146-1351-7, F Cass Co). Biblio Dist.
Pritt, D. N. Law, Class & Society, 4 vols. 174p. 1970. 44.00x set (ISBN 0-8464-0547-4). Beekman Pubs.
Razzell, Peter. Victorian Working Class: Selections from the "Morning Chronicle". Wainwright, R. W, ed. (Illus.). 380p. 1973. 27.50x (ISBN 0-7146-2957-X, F. Cass Co). Biblio Dist.
Redford, A. Labour Migration in England Eighteen Hundred to Eighteen Fifty. Chaloner, W. H., ed. 210p. 1976. 18.00x (ISBN 0-686-63739-9, Pub. by Manchester U Pr England). State Mutual Bk.
Redford, Arthur. Labour Migration in England, 1800-1850. 2nd rev. ed. Chaloner, W. H., ed. LC 68-6093. 1964. 12.50x (ISBN 0-678-06766-X). Kelley.
Richmond, Alexander B. Narrative of the Condition of the Manufacturing Population. LC 68-56571. Repr. of 1824 ed. 15.00x (ISBN 0-678-00676-8). Kelley.
Rountree, B. Seebohm. Poverty: A Study of Town Life. 2nd ed. LC 79-56969. (The English Working Class Ser.). 1980. lib. bdg. 38.00 (ISBN 0-8240-0120-6). Garland Pub.
Routh, Guy. Occupation & Pay in Great Britain. 2nd, rev. ed. 269p. 1981. text ed. 37.50x (ISBN 0-333-28417-8, Pub.by Macmillan England); pap. text ed. 20.00x (ISBN 0-333-28653-7). Humanities.
Sargant, William L. Economy of the Labouring Classes. LC 68-20177. Repr. of 1857 ed. 19.50x (ISBN 0-678-00393-9). Kelley.
Scase, Richard. Social Democracy in Capitalist Society: Working-Class Politics in Britain & Sweden. 184p. 1977. 17.50x (ISBN 0-87471-948-8). Rowman.
Senior, Nassau W. Three Lectures on the Rate of Wages. 2nd ed. LC 65-25863. Repr. of 1831 ed. 9.50x (ISBN 0-678-00126-X). Kelley.
Smelser, Neil J. Social Change in the Industrial Revolution. LC 59-10743. (Illus.). 1959. 12.00x (ISBN 0-226-76311-0). U of Chicago Pr.
Smith, Harold, ed. British Labor Movement to Nineteen Seventy: A Bibliography. 268p. 1981. text ed. 70.00 (ISBN 0-7201-0924-8, Pub. by Mansell England). Merrimack Bk Serv.
Sturt, George B. Change in the Village. LC 75-86314. Repr. of 1912 ed. 12.50x (ISBN 0-678-08001-1). Kelley.
Taylor, William C. Notes of a Tour in the Manufacturing Districts of Lancashire. LC 67-131562. Repr. of 1842 ed. 17.50x (ISBN 0-678-05088-0). Kelley.
Thakur, Manab & Naylor, Michael. White Collar Unions. LC 76-372318. (Information Report Ser.: No. 22). (Orig.). 1976. pap. 17.50x (ISBN 0-85292-130-6). Intl Pubns Serv.
Tholfsen, Trygve. Working Class Radicalism in Mid-Victorian England. LC 76-43323. 1977. 22.50x (ISBN 0-231-04234-5). Columbia U Pr.
Thompson, Edward P. Making of the English Working Class. 1966. pap. 5.95 (ISBN 0-394-70322-7, Vin). Random.
Thornley, Jenny. Worker's Co-Operatives: Jobs & Dreams. 1981. text ed. 45.00x (ISBN 0-435-83890-3). Heinemann Ed.
Toynbee, Arnold J. Lectures on the Industrial Revolution in England. LC 68-59517. Repr. of 1884 ed. 15.00x (ISBN 0-678-05636-6). Kelley.
Urwick, E. J., ed. Study of Boy Life in Our Cities. LC 79-56942. (The English Working Class Ser.). 1980. lib. bdg. 28.00 (ISBN 0-8240-0125-7). Garland Pub.
Van Den Bergh, T. Trade Unions, What Are They? LC 79-97952. 1970. 19.50 (ISBN 0-08-006517-1); pap. 9.75 (ISBN 0-08-006516-3). Pergamon.
Vincent, David, ed. Testaments of Radicalism: Memoirs of Working Class Politicians 1790-1885. LC 77-377253. 1977. 17.50 (ISBN 0-905118-01-4). Intl Pubns Serv.
Wade, John. History of the Middle & Working Classes. LC 66-18321. Repr. of 1833 ed. 25.00x (ISBN 0-678-00173-1). Kelley.
Wearmouth, Robert F. Methodism & the Working-Class Movements of England 1800-1850. LC 73-139523. Repr. of 1937 ed. 15.00x (ISBN 0-678-00829-9). Kelley.
Webb, Beatrice & Webb, Sidney. Problems of Modern Industry. facsimile new ed. LC 70-37918. (Select Bibliographies Reprint Ser.). Repr. of 1902 ed. 19.00 (ISBN 0-8369-6755-0). Arno.
Weir, David. Men & Work in Modern Britain. 1974. pap. 2.95 (ISBN 0-531-06052-7, Fontana Pap). Watts.
Williams, Alfred. Life in a Railway Factory. LC 79-56941. 1980. lib. bdg. 28.00 (ISBN 0-8240-0126-5). Garland Pub.
Willis, Paul E. Learning to Labour: How Working Class Kids Get Working Class Jobs. (Illus.). 1977. 21.00 (ISBN 0-566-00150-0, 00730-7, Pub. by Saxon Hse England). Lexington Bks.
Wilson, Alexander. Chartist Movement in Scotland. LC 72-130604. 1970. lib. bdg. 15.00x (ISBN 0-678-06782-1). Kelley.
Wright, Thomas. Great Unwashed. LC 72-118122. Repr. of 1868 ed. 17.50x (ISBN 0-678-00659-8). Kelley.
--Our New Masters. LC 69-20019. Repr. of 1873 ed. 17.50x (ISBN 0-678-00482-X). Kelley.
--Some Habits & Customs of the Working Classes by Journeyman Engineer. LC 67-19960. Repr. of 1867 ed. 17.50x (ISBN 0-678-00268-1). Kelley.
Wunderlich, Frieda. British Labor & the War. (Social Research Suppl.: No. 3). 1941. pap. 4.00 (ISBN 0-527-00863-X). Kraus Repr.

LABOR AND LABORING CLASSES–GREECE

Kintis, Andreas A. The Demand for Labour in Greek Manufacturing. LC 76-369094. (Research Monograph Ser.). 179p. 1973. pap. 7.50x (ISBN 0-8002-0034-9). Intl Pubns Serv.
Taylor, David. Work in Acient Greece & Rome. (Greek & Roman Topics Ser.). 1975. pap. text ed. 3.95x (ISBN 0-04-930005-9). Allen Unwin.
Ward, Cyrenus O. Ancient Lowly: A History of the Ancient Working People from the Earliest Known Period to the Adoption of Christianity by Constantine, 2 Vols. LC 77-114817. 1970. Set. text ed. 49.00 (ISBN 0-8337-3685-X). B Franklin.

LABOR AND LABORING CLASSES–HUNGARY

Kabos. Studies on History of Hungarian Trade-Union Movement. 1977. 30.00 (ISBN 0-9960006-0-7, Pub. by Kaido Hungary). Heyden.
Nemes, Dezso, ed. History of the Revolutionary Workers Movement in Hungary (1944-1962) Racz, Eva, tr. from Hungarian. 1972. 14.95x (ISBN 0-8464-0485-0). Beekman Pubs.
Timar, Janos. Planning the Labor Force in Hungary. LC 66-20465. 1966. 20.00 (ISBN 0-87332-015-8). M E Sharpe.
Vass. Studies on History of Hungarian Working-Class Movement. 1975. 29.00 (ISBN 0-9960006-1-5, Pub. by Kaido Hungary). Heyden.

LABOR AND LABORING CLASSES–INDIA

Agarwal, Rajesh K. & Nangia, Sudesh. Economic & Employment Potential of Archaeological Monuments in India. (Illus.). 90p. 1974. 5.95x (ISBN 0-210-40553-8). Asia.
Aziz, Abdul. Organizing Agricultural Labourers in India. 1980. 7.50x (ISBN 0-8364-0651-6, Pub. by Minerva India). South Asia Bks.
Beidelman, Thomas O. A Comparitive Analysis of the Jajmani System. 2.50 (ISBN 0-685-71736-4). J J Augustin.
Dadi, M. M. Income Share of Factory Labour in India. LC 74-900715. 119p. 1973. 7.50x (ISBN 0-8002-0058-6). Intl Pubns Serv.
Ghosh, Moni. Our Struggle: A Short History of Trade Union Movement in Tisco Industry at Jamshedpur. LC 74-900968. 278p. 1973. 10.00x (ISBN 0-88386-514-9). South Asia Bks.
Gupta, R. D. Wage Flexibility & Full Employment. 1971. 4.50x (ISBN 0-686-20323-2). Intl Bk Dist.
Karnik, V. B. Indian Labour: Problems & Prospects. LC 74-902109. 250p. 1974. 11.00 (ISBN 0-88386-436-3). South Asia Bks.
Mies, M. The Lace Makers of Narsapur: Indan Housewives in the World Market. 144p. 1981. pap. 7.95 (ISBN 0-86232-032-1, Pub. by Zed Pr England). Lawrence Hill.
Pandhe, M. K., ed. Bonded Labour in India. LC 76-901994. 1976. 10.00x (ISBN 0-88386-764-8). South Asia Bks.
Rastogi, S. R. Wage Regulation in India. 1979. text ed. 13.50x (ISBN 0-8426-1620-9). Verry.
Sen, Sukomal. Working Class of India: History of Emergence & Movement, 1930-1970. 1977. 14.00x (ISBN 0-8364-0002-X). South Asia Bks.
Sharma, Baldev R. Indian Industrial Worker: Issues in Perspective. 1974. 9.00 (ISBN 0-686-20255-4). Intl Bk Dist.
Sharma, Ursula. Woman, Work & Property in North-West India. 1980. 25.00x (ISBN 0-422-77120-1, Pub. by Tavistock). Methuen Inc.
Vaid, K. N. Gheraos & Labour Unrest in West Bengal. 252p. 1972. 11.25x (ISBN 0-8002-0641-X). Intl Pubns Serv.
--Labour Welfare in India. (Illus.). 392p. 1970. 17.50x (ISBN 0-8002-1639-3). Intl Pubns Serv.

LABOR AND LABORING CLASSES–IRELAND

Clarkson, J. Dunsmore. Labour & Nationalism in Ireland. LC 78-12024. (Columbia University Studies in the Social Sciences: No. 266). Repr. of 1925 ed. 31.50 (ISBN 0-404-51266-6). AMS Pr.
Crumpe, Samuel. Essay on the Best Means of Providing Employment for the People. 2nd. ed. LC 67-29499. Repr. of 1795 ed. 19.50x (ISBN 0-678-00410-2). Kelley.
Ellis, P. Beresford. The History of the Irish Working Class. LC 72-86716. 352p. 1973. 8.95 (ISBN 0-8076-0654-5). Braziller.
Ellis, P. Berresford, ed. James Connolly: Selected Writings. LC 73-90071. (Modern Reader Paperbacks Ser.). 320p. 1976. 11.95 (ISBN 0-85345-326-8, PB-3527); pap. 5.95 (ISBN 0-85345-348-9). Monthly Rev.
Hepple, B. A., et al. Labour Law in Great Britain & Ireland to Nineteen Seventy Eight. 1981. text ed. 35.00 (ISBN 0-7201-1624-4, Pub. by Mansell England). Merrimack Bk Serv.
Mitchell, Arthur. Labour in Irish Politics: Eighteen Ninty to Nineteen Thirty: the Irish Labor Movement in an Age of Revolution. (Illus.). 317p. 1974. 20.00x (ISBN 0-686-28343-0, Pub. by Irish Academic Pr). Biblio Dist.

LABOR AND LABORING CLASSES–ISRAEL

Daniel, Abraham. Labor Enterprises in Israel: The Cooperative Economy, Vol. 1. 312p. 1976. pap. text ed. 5.95 (ISBN 0-87855-638-9). Transaction Bks.
--Labor Enterprises in Israel: The Institutional Economy, Vol. 2. 232p. 1976. pap. text ed. 4.95 (ISBN 0-87855-639-7). Transaction Bks.
Lefkowitz, Jerome. Public Employee Unionism in Israel. LC 78-634400. (Comparative Studies in Public Employment Labor Relations Ser.). 1971. 6.00x (ISBN 0-87736-017-0); pap. 3.00x (ISBN 0-87736-018-9). U of Mich Inst Labor.

LABOR AND LABORING CLASSES–ITALY

Cornelisen, Ann. Strangers & Pilgrims. (McGraw-Hill Paperbacks Ser.). 324p. 1981. pap. 5.95 (ISBN 0-07-013192-9). McGraw.
Griffiths, Trevor. Occupations. new ed. 74p. 1981. pap. 7.50 (ISBN 0-571-11667-1, Pub. by Faber & Faber). Merrimack Bk Serv.
Haider, Carmen. Capital & Labor Under Fascism. LC 68-58586. (Columbia University. Studies in the Social Sciences: No. 318). Repr. of 1930 ed. 25.00 (ISBN 0-404-51318-2). AMS Pr.
Low-Beer, J. R. Protest & Participation. LC 77-8084. (ASA Rose Monograph Ser.: No. 4). (Illus.). 1978. 19.95 (ISBN 0-521-21782-2); pap. 6.95x (ISBN 0-521-29277-8). Cambridge U Pr.
Mann, Michael. Consciousness & Action Among the Western Working Class. (Studies in Sociology). 80p. (Orig.). 1975. pap. 6.75x (ISBN 0-333-13773-6). Humanities.
Neufeld, Maurice F. Italy: School for Awakening Countries. LC 73-22507. (Cornell International Industrial & Labor Relations Reports: No. 5). (Illus.). 589p. 1974. Repr. of 1961 ed. lib. bdg. 34.00x (ISBN 0-8371-6339-0, NEIT). Greenwood.
Spriano, Paolo. Occupation of the Factories. Williams, Gwyn A., tr. from Ital. 216p. 1980. text ed. 12.00 (ISBN 0-902818-68-6); pap. 5.95 (ISBN 0-902818-67-8). Pluto Pr.
Williams, Gwyn A. Proletarian Order. 368p. 1980. text ed. 15.00 (ISBN 0-902818-66-X); pap. 7.95 (ISBN 0-902818-65-1). Pluto Pr.

LABOR AND LABORING CLASSES–JAPAN

Abegglen, James C. Management & Worker: The Japanese Solution. LC 72-96130. 200p. 1973. 14.50x (ISBN 0-87011-199-X). Kodansha.
Cole, Robert E. Japanese Blue Collar: The Changing Tradition. LC 77-107656. 1971. pap. 8.95x (ISBN 0-520-02354-4, CAMPUS86). U of Cal Pr.
--Work, Mobility, & Participation: A Comparative Study of American & Japanese Industry. LC 77-80468. 1979. 22.50x (ISBN 0-520-03542-9); pap. 7.95x (ISBN 0-520-04204-2). U of Cal Pr.
Dore, Ronald P. British Factory - Japanese Factory: The Origins of National Diversity in Employment Relations. LC 72-78948. 1973. 18.50x (ISBN 0-520-02268-8); pap. 7.95x (ISBN 0-520-02495-8, CAMPUS96). U of Cal Pr.
Harada, Shuichi. Labor Conditions in Japan. (Columbia University Studies in the Social Sciences: No. 301). Repr. of 1928 ed. 22.50 (ISBN 0-404-51301-8). AMS Pr.
Labour Market Information for Decision - Making: The Case of Japan. 252p. (Orig.). 1981. pap. text ed. write for info. (ISBN 9-2210-2598-5). Intl Labour Office.
Large, Stephen S. Organized Workers & Socialist Politics in Interwar Japan. LC 80-42158. 304p. Date not set. price not set (ISBN 0-521-23675-4). Cambridge U Pr.
Ministry of Labor, Japan. Japan Labor Code, 2 vols. (Studies in Japanese Law & Government). 1979. Repr. of 1953 ed. Set. 56.00 (ISBN 0-89093-217-4). U Pubns Amer.
Nishikawa, Shunsaku, ed. The Labor Market in Japan. 277p. 1980. 17.50x (ISBN 0-86008-262-8, Pub. by Univ Tokyo Pr Japan). Intl Schol Bk Serv.
Young, Arthur M. Socialist & Labour Movement in Japan. (Studies in Japanese History & Civilization). 145p. 1979. Repr. of 1921 ed. 18.00 (ISBN 0-89093-268-9). U Pubns Amer.

LABOR AND LABORING CLASSES–LATIN AMERICA

Alba, Victor. Politics & the Labor Movement in Latin America. 1968. 17.50x (ISBN 0-8047-0193-8). Stanford U Pr.
Anderson, Rodney D. Outcasts in Their Own Land: Mexican Industrial Workers 1906-1911. Perry, Laurens B., ed. LC 74-28896. (The Origins of Modern Mexico Ser.). (Illus.). 407p. 1976. 17.50 (ISBN 0-87580-054-8). N Ill U Pr.
Chaplin, David. Peruvian Industrial Labor Force. 1967. 23.00 (ISBN 0-691-09324-5). Princeton U Pr.
Clark, M. R. Organized Labor in Mexico. 1976. lib. bdg. 59.95 (ISBN 0-8490-2381-5). Gordon Pr.
Hart, John M. Anarchism & the Mexican Working Class, 1860-1931. LC 77-16210. (Illus.). 259p. 1978. 20.00x (ISBN 0-292-70331-7). U of Tex Pr.
Hemphill, Grace F. The Political, Economic & Labor Climate in Colombia. 1980. pap. 15.00 (ISBN 0-89546-025-4). Indus Res Unit-Wharton.
Kepner, Charles D. Social Aspects of the Banana Industry. LC 36-20189. (Columbia University. Studies in the Social Sciences: No. 414). Repr. of 1936 ed. 20.00 (ISBN 0-404-51414-6). AMS Pr.
Lora, G. A History of the Bolivian Labour Movement 1848-1971. Whitehead, L., ed. Whitehead, Christine, tr. LC 76-22988. (Latin American Studies: No. 27). 1977. 44.50 (ISBN 0-521-21400-9). Cambridge U Pr.
Mantero, Francisco. Manual Labor in S. Thome & Principe. LC 71-90121. (Port). Repr. of 1910 ed. 34.00x (ISBN 0-8371-2035-7, Pub. by Negro U Pr). Greenwood.
Ramos, Joseph R. Labor & Development in Latin America. LC 74-108095. (Institute of Latin American Studies). (Illus.). 1970. 20.00x (ISBN 0-231-03250-1). Columbia U Pr.
Ruiz, Ramon Eduardo. Labor & the Ambivalent Revolutionaries: Mexico 1911-1923. LC 75-29087. 154p. 1976. 12.00x (ISBN 0-8018-1728-5). Johns Hopkins.
Spalding, Hobart. Organized Labor in Latin America. 1977. pap. 5.95x (ISBN 0-06-131923-6, TB1923, Torch). Har-Row.

LABOR AND LABORING CLASSES–OCEANICA

Decker, John A. Labor Problems in the Pacific Mandates. LC 75-30053. (Institute of Pacific Relations). Repr. of 1940 ed. 24.50 (ISBN 0-404-59517-0). AMS Pr.
Parnaby, Owen W. Britain & the Labor Trade in the Southwest Pacific. LC 64-13987. 1964. 12.50 (ISBN 0-8223-0129-6). Duke.

LABOR AND LABORING CLASSES–PERU

Chaplin, David. Peruvian Industrial Labor Force. 1967. 23.00 (ISBN 0-691-09324-5). Princeton U Pr.
Payne, James L. Labor & Politics in Peru. LC 65-22335. 1980. Repr. of 1965 ed. 9.00 (ISBN 0-915728-05-2). Lytton Pub.
Stephens, Evelyne H. The Politics of Workers' Participation: The Peruvian Approach in Comparative Perspective. (Studies in Social Discontinuity). 1980. 29.50 (ISBN 0-12-666250-9). Acad Pr.

LABOR AND LABORING CLASSES-PHILIPPINE ISLANDS

Kurihara, Kenneth K. Labor in the Philippine Economy. LC 78-161766. Repr. of 1945 ed. 14.75 (ISBN 0-404-09027-3). AMS Pr.

Ramos, Elias T. Philippine Labor Movement in Transition. 1976. wrps. 5.75x (ISBN 0-686-09445-X). Cellar.

LABOR AND LABORING CLASSES-PUERTO RICO

Quintero-Rivera, Angel. Workers' Struggle in Puerto Rico: A Documentary History. Belfrage, Cedric, tr. from Span. LC 76-40343. 1977. 11.95 (ISBN 0-85345-392-6, CL-3926). Monthly Rev.

Silvestrini De Pacheco, Blanca. Los Trabajadores Puertoriquenos y el Partido Socialista, 1932 a 1940. Orig. Title: Puerto Rican Workers & the Socialist Party, 1932-1940. (Illus., Sp.). 1979. pap. 7.50 (ISBN 0-8477-0858-6). U of PR Pr.

LABOR AND LABORING CLASSES-ROME

Taylor, David. Work in Acient Greece & Rome. (Greek & Roman Topics Ser.). 1975. pap. text ed. 3.95x (ISBN 0-04-930005-9). Allen Unwin.

Ward, Cyrenus O. Ancient Lowly: A History of the Ancient Working People from the Earliest Known Period to the Adoption of Christianity by Constantine, 2 Vols. LC 77-114817. 1970. Set. text ed. 49.00 (ISBN 0-8337-3685-X). B Franklin.

LABOR AND LABORING CLASSES-RUSSIA

Atholl, Katherine. Conscription of a People. LC 73-161703. Repr. of 1931 ed. 17.00 (ISBN 0-404-00414-8). AMS Pr.

Borisova, Y. S. Outline History of the Soviet Working Class. 387p. 1973. 5.40 (ISBN 0-8285-0488-1, Pub. by Progress Pubs Russia). Imported Pubns.

Borisova, Y. S., et al. Outline History of the Soviet Working Class. 387p. 1975. 18.00x (ISBN 0-8464-0695-0). Beekman Pubs.

Brinton, Maurice. The Bolsheviks & Worker's Control. 1975. pap. 1.50 (ISBN 0-934868-05-0). Black & Red.

Freeman, Joseph. The Soviet Worker. LC 73-841. (Russian Studies: Perspectives on the Revolution Ser.). 408p. 1973. Repr. of 1932 ed. 27.50 (ISBN 0-88355-036-9). Hyperion Conn.

Gordon, Manya. Workers Before & After Lenin. LC 74-22743. Repr. of 1941 ed. 31.50 (ISBN 0-404-58495-0). AMS Pr.

Heldman, Dan C. Trade Unions & Labor Relations in the USSR. 1977. pap. 10.00 (ISBN 0-685-85742-5). Coun Am Affairs.

Iorchuk, M. T. & Kogan, L. N., eds. The Cultural Life of the Soviet Worker: A Sociological Study. 207p. 1975. 2.25 (ISBN 0-8285-0268-4, Pub. by Progress Pubs Russia). Imported Pubns.

Kahan, Arcadius & Ruble, Blair A. Industrial Labor in the USSR. (Pergamon Policy Studies). 1979. 42.00 (ISBN 0-08-023701-0); pap. 13.00 (ISBN 0-08-023899-8). Pergamon.

Kaplan, Frederick I. Bolshevik Ideology & the Ethics of Soviet Labor. LC 67-17636. 1969. 10.00 (ISBN 0-8022-2256-0). Philos Lib.

Keep, John. The Russian Revolution: A Study in Mass Mobilization. (Revolutions in the Modern World Ser.). 1977. 19.50x (ISBN 0-393-05616-3). Norton.

Koenker, Diane. Moscow Workers & the Nineteen Seventeen Revolution. LC 80-8557. (Studies of the Russian Institute, Columbia University). (Illus.). 456p. 1981. 30.00x (ISBN 0-691-05323-5). Princeton U Pr.

Lane, David & O'Dell, Felicity. The Soviet Industrial Worker: Social Class, Education & Control. LC 78-60509. 1978. 16.95 (ISBN 0-312-74841-8). St Martin.

Livshitz, R. & Nikitinsky, V. An Outline of Soviet Labour Law. 207p. 1970. pap. 2.75 (ISBN 0-8285-0342-7, Pub. by Progress Pubs Russia). Imported Pubns.

McAulay, Alastair. Women's Work & Wages in the Soviet Union. 248p. 1981. text ed. 28.50x (ISBN 0-04-339020-X). Allen Unwin.

Mendelsohn, Ezra. Class Struggle in the Pale. LC 71-96097. 1970. 23.50 (ISBN 0-521-07730-3). Cambridge U Pr.

Schapiro, Leonard & Godson, Joseph, eds. The Soviet Worker: Illusion & Realities. Date not set. price not set (ISBN 0-312-74923-6). St Martin.

Tiurin, Sergei P. From Peter the Great to Lenin. LC 68-13720. Repr. of 1935 ed. 24.00x (ISBN 0-678-05091-0). Kelley.

Turnin, S. P. From Peter the Great to Lenin: A History of the Russian Labour Movement with Special Reference to Trade Unionism. 216p. 1968. Repr. 24.00x (ISBN 0-7146-1364-9, F Cass Co). Biblio Dist.

Weltner, Andor. Fundamental Traits of Socialist Labour Law with Special Regard to Hungarian Legislation. LC 72-187654. 218p. 1970. 7.50x (ISBN 0-8002-1439-0). Intl Pubns Serv.

Yanowitch, Murray, ed. Soviet Work Attitudes: The Issue of Participation in Management. Vale, Michel, tr. LC 79-4871. 1979. 17.50 (ISBN 0-87332-147-2). M E Sharpe.

Zelnik, Reginald E. Labor & Society in Tsarist Russia: The Factory Workers of St. Petersburg, 1855-1870. LC 73-130832. 1971. 20.00x (ISBN 0-8047-0740-5). Stanford U Pr.

LABOR AND LABORING CLASSES-SOUTH AFRICA

Olivier, Sydney H. Anatomy of African Misery. LC 76-90125. Repr. of 1927 ed. 12.25x (ISBN 0-8371-2019-5, Pub. by Negro U Pr). Greenwood.

Thomas, Wolfgang H., ed. Labour Perspective on South Africa. 259p. 1974. pap. 6.00x (ISBN 0-8476-2395-5). Rowman.

LABOR AND LABORING CLASSES-WEST INDIES

Sewell, William. Ordeal of Free Labour in the West Indies. 2nd ed. LC 67-31561. Repr. of 1862 ed. 19.50x (ISBN 0-678-05097-X). Kelley.

LABOR AND THE CHURCH

see Church and Labor

LABOR ARBITRATION

see Arbitration, Industrial

LABOR CAMPS

Bradwin, Edmund W. Bunkhouse Man: A Study of Work & Pay in the Camps of Canada, 1903-14. LC 79-163834. (Social History of Canada Ser.). 1972. pap. 7.50 (ISBN 0-8020-6135-4). U of Toronto Pr.

--Bunkhouse Man: A Study of Work & Play in the Camps of Canada, 1903-1914. LC 68-57564. (Columbia University Studies in the Social Sciences: No. 296). Repr. of 1928 ed. 12.50 (ISBN 0-404-51296-8). AMS Pr.

Hathway, Marion. The Migratory Worker & Family Life. LC 77-169386. (Family in America Ser). 258p. 1972. Repr. of 1934 ed. 13.00 (ISBN 0-405-03863-1). Arno.

Kyu, Kwak B. The Land of Eternal Darkness: Memories of Siberian Labor Camps. 1978. 10.00 (ISBN 0-533-03149-4). Vantage.

LABOR COLONIES

see Agricultural Colonies

LABOR CONTRACT

see also Collective Bargaining; Collective Labor Agreements; Employees, Dismissal Of; Grievance Procedures; Temporary Employment; Discrimination in Employment-Law and Legislation; Wages

Annual Research Conference, 11th & 12th, UCLA, 1968-1969. Problems in Contract Negotiation & Problems & Goals in Manpower Policy: Proceedings. 1970. 2.00 (ISBN 0-89215-030-0). U Cal LA Indus Rel.

Ferguson, Robert H. Cost-of-Living Adjustments in Union-Management Agreements. LC 76-21445. (ILR Bulletin: No. 65). 1976. pap. 2.50 (ISBN 0-87546-214-6). NY Sch Indus Rel.

Seldman, Joel I. The Yellow Dog Contract. LC 78-64146. (Johns Hopkins University. Studies in the Social Sciences. Fiftieth Ser. 1932: 4). Repr. of 1932 ed. 14.50 (ISBN 0-404-61257-1). AMS Pr.

Stone, Morris. Labor-Management Contracts at Work: Analysis of Awards Reported by the American Arbitration Association. LC 78-31591. 1979. Repr. of 1961 ed. lib. bdg. 22.50x (ISBN 0-313-20966-9, STLW). Greenwood.

LABOR COSTS

see also Non-Wage Payments; Wages

Accounting for Labor Costs & Labor-Related Costs. 3.95 (ISBN 0-686-09811-0, 5715). Natl Assn Accts.

Brechling, Frank. Investment & Employment Decisions. 110p. 1975. 12.50x (ISBN 0-87471-751-5). Rowman.

Granof, Michael H. How to Cost Your Labor Contract. LC 73-77273. 158p. 1973. 10.00 (ISBN 0-87179-191-9). BNA.

LABOR COURTS

see also Arbitration, Industrial

Aaron, Benjamin, ed. Labor Courts & Grievance Settlement in Western Europe. LC 72-123628. 1971. 32.50x (ISBN 0-520-01757-9). U of Cal Pr.

Braun, Kurt. Labor Disputes & Their Settlement. LC 73-13320. 343p. 1974. Repr. of 1955 ed. lib. bdg. 16.50x (ISBN 0-8371-7121-0, BRDS). Greenwood.

Wunderlich, Frieda. German Labor Courts. LC 73-86731. (Illus.). x, 252p. Date not set. Repr. of 1946 ed. 13.00 (ISBN 0-8462-1750-3). Russell.

LABOR DISCIPLINE

see also Employee Rules

Grote, R. Positive Discipline. 1979. leader's guide 125.00 (ISBN 0-07-025007-3, T&D); 3-ring binder 40.00 (ISBN 0-07-025006-5). McGraw.

Staff of Didactic Systems. Constructive Discipline. 2nd ed. (Simulation-Game Ser.). 1978. pap. 24.90 (ISBN 0-89401-123-5); Two Or More Sets. 21.50 (ISBN 0-685-08735-2). Didactic Syst.

--Positive Discipline. (Study Units Ser.). 1978. pap. 9.00 (ISBN 0-89401-122-7). Didactic Syst.

LABOR DISPUTES

see also Arbitration, Industrial; Boycott; Collective Bargaining; Labor Courts; Strikes and Lockouts

Berman, Edward. Labor Disputes & the President of the United States. LC 75-76691. (Columbia University Studies in the Social Sciences: No. 249). Repr. of 1924 ed. 20.00 (ISBN 0-404-51249-6). AMS Pr.

Cooling, W. Colebrook. Arbitration Presentation: Box Seat at a Labor Management Dispute. 1978. manual 20.00 (ISBN 0-89806-006-0, 122); play package 80.00 (ISBN 0-89806-008-7, 152). Am Inst Indus Eng.

Cooper, Jerry M. The Army & Civil Disorder: Federal Military Intervention in Labor Disputes, 1877-1900. LC 79-7064. (Contributions in Military History: No. 19). 1980. lib. bdg. 22.50 (ISBN 0-313-20958-8, CAD/). Greenwood.

Hartmann, George W. & Newscomb, Theodore, eds. Industrial Conflict: Psychological Interpretation. LC 77-182. (Work Ser.). (Illus.). 1977. Repr. of 1939 ed. lib. bdg. 38.00x (ISBN 0-405-10173-2). Arno.

Kornhauser, Arthur, et al, eds. Industrial Conflict. LC 77-70509. (Work Ser.). 1977. Repr. of 1954 ed. lib. bdg. 34.00x (ISBN 0-405-10179-1). Arno.

Labour Disputes in the Early Days of the Industrial Revolution: 1758-1780. LC 72-2530. (British Labour Struggles Before 1850 Ser). 1972. 10.00 (ISBN 0-405-04423-2). Arno.

Labour Disputes in the Mines: 1831-1844. LC 72-2531. (British Labour Struggles Before 1850 Ser). (8 pamphlets). 1972. 10.00 (ISBN 0-405-04424-0). Arno.

Quin, Mike. The Big Strike. (Illus.). 1979. pap. 2.95 (ISBN 0-7178-0504-2). Intl Pub Co.

Witte, Edwin E. The Government in Labor Disputes. LC 70-89770. (American Labor, from Conspiracy to Collective Bargaining, Ser. 1). 352p. 1969. Repr. of 1932 ed. 15.00 (ISBN 0-405-02157-7). Arno.

LABOR ECONOMICS

see also Human Capital; Industrial Relations; Labor and Laboring Classes

Appleton, J. D. Labour Economics. 2nd ed. (Illus.). 240p. 1979. pap. text ed. 9.95 (ISBN 0-7121-1246-4, Pub. by Macdonald & Evans England). Intl Ideas.

Azevedo, Ross. Labor Economics: A Guide to Information Sources. LC 73-17568. (Economics Information Guide Ser.: Vol. 8). 1978. 36.00 (ISBN 0-8103-1297-2). Gale.

Beckerman, Wilfred, ed. The Labour Government's Economic Record: 1964-1970. LC 72-184050. 1972. 20.00x (ISBN 0-7156-0608-5). Intl Pubns Serv.

Bellante, Donald & Jackson, Mark. Labor Economics: Choice in Labor Markets. (Illus.). 1979. text ed. 14.95 (ISBN 0-07-004397-3, C); instructor's manual 3.50 (ISBN 0-07-004398-1). McGraw.

Bloch, Farrell, ed. Research in Labor Economics, Supplement 1: Evaluating Manpower Training Programs. 1979. lib. bdg. 37.50 (ISBN 0-89232-046-X). Jai Pr.

Blum, Solomon. Labor Economics. LC 79-89719. (American Labor from Conspiracy to Collective Bargaining, Ser. 1). 579p. 1969. Repr. of 1925 ed. 22.00 (ISBN 0-405-02105-4). Arno.

Bowen, William G. & Ashenfelter, Orley, eds. Labor & the National Economy. rev. ed. (Problems of the Modern Economy Ser). 1975. 8.95x (ISBN 0-393-05456-X); pap. 4.95x (ISBN 0-393-09996-2). Norton.

Carnegie Endowment for International Peace. American Labor in a Changing World Economy. LC 78-15545. (Praeger Special Studies). 1978. 31.95 (ISBN 0-03-045281-3). Praeger.

Chamberlain, Neil, et al. The Labor Sector. 3rd rev. ed. (Illus.). 1979. text ed. 17.95 (ISBN 0-07-010435-2); instr's. manual 7.95 (ISBN 0-07-010436-0). McGraw.

Cochrane, James L. Industrialism & Industrial Man in Retrospect: A Critical Review of the Ford Foundation's Support for the Inter-University Study of Labor. LC 79-18897. 196p. 1979. 14.75 (ISBN 0-916584-12-7, IS-00091, Pub. by Ford Found). Univ Microfilms.

Conference of the Universities. Aspects of Labor Economics: Proceedings. LC 75-19698. (National Bureau of Economic Research Ser.). (Illus.). 1975. Repr. 20.00x (ISBN 0-405-07578-2). Arno.

Ehrenberg, Ronald & Smith, Robert S. Modern Labor Economics: Analysis & Public Policy. 1982. text ed. 19.95 (ISBN 0-673-15365-7). Scott F.

Ehrenberg, Ronald, ed. Research in Labor Economics, Vol. 3. 410p. 1980. lib. bdg. 37.50 (ISBN 0-89232-157-1). Jai Pr.

Ehrenberg, Ronald G. The Regulatory Process & Labor Earnings. LC 79-6953. (Studies in Labor Economics). 1979. 19.00 (ISBN 0-12-233250-4). Acad Pr.

Ehrenberg, Ronald G., ed. Research in Labor Economics, Vol. 1. (Orig.). 1977. lib. bdg. 37.50 (ISBN 0-89232-017-6). Jai Pr.

--Research in Labor Economics, Vol. 4. 350p. 1981. 37.50 (ISBN 0-89232-243-8). Jai Pr.

Fearn. Labor Economics: The Emerging Synthesis. 1981. 18.95 (ISBN 0-686-72663-4). P-H.

Finegan, T. A. & Bowen, W. G, Economics of Labor Force Participation. LC 69-17396. (Illus.). 1969. 38.50 (ISBN 0-691-04193-8). Princeton U Pr.

Fischer, Malcolm R. Economic Analysis of Labour. 1972. 18.95 (ISBN 0-312-22680-2). St Martin.

Fleisher, Belton M. & Kniesner, Thomas J. Labor Economics: Theory, Evidence & Policy. 2nd ed. (Illus.). 1980. text ed. 21.00 (ISBN 0-13-517433-3). P-H.

Freeman, Richard B. Labor Economics. 2nd ed. (Foundations of Economics Ser.). (Illus.). 1979. text ed. 14.95 (ISBN 0-13-517482-1); pap. text ed. 9.95 (ISBN 0-13-517474-0). P-H.

Furniss, Edgar S. Position of the Laborer in a System of Nationalism. LC 58-3121. Repr. of 1920 ed. 15.00x (ISBN 0-678-00093-X). Kelley.

Galenson, Walter. Primer on Employment & Wages. 1970. pap. text ed. 3.25x (ISBN 0-394-30720-8). Phila Bk Co.

Galenson, Walter, ed. Labor in Developing Economics. LC 76-3786. 299p. 1976. Repr. of 1962 ed. lib. bdg. 18.50x (ISBN 0-8371-8817-2, GALD). Greenwood.

Ginzberg, Eli. The Human Economy. 1976. 13.95 (ISBN 0-07-023283-0). McGraw.

Hall, Richard J. British Labour Costs 1975-1980. LC 76-35345. 1975. pap. 90.00x (ISBN 0-8002-0736-X). Intl Pubns Serv.

Heldman, Dan C., et al. Deregulating Labor Relations. LC 79-56315. 200p. (Orig.). 1981. 11.95 (ISBN 0-933028-14-8); pap. 6.95 (ISBN 0-933028-13-X). Fisher Inst.

Helfgott, Roy B. Labor Economics. 2nd ed. 674p. 1981. text ed. 19.95 (ISBN 0-394-32325-4). Random.

Hicks, John R. Theory of Wages. 2nd ed. (International Economic Assn. Ser). 1963. 25.00 (ISBN 0-312-79870-9). St Martin.

Hildebrand, George H. American Unionism: An Historical & Analytical Survey. LC 78-74685. (Perspectives on Economics Ser.). 1979. pap. text ed. 6.95 (ISBN 0-201-08368-X). A-W.

Hunter, Lawrence C. & Robertson, D. J. Economics of Wages & Labour. LC 70-83359. (Illus.). 1969. 17.50x (ISBN 0-678-07002-4). Kelley.

King, J. E., ed. Readings in Labour Economics. (Illus.). 454p. 1980. text ed. 39.50x (ISBN 0-19-877132-0); pap. text ed. 13.95x (ISBN 0-19-877133-9). Oxford U Pr.

Kreps, Juanita M., et al. Contemporary Labor Economics & Labor Relations. 2nd ed. 496p. 1980. text ed. 21.95x (ISBN 0-534-00810-0). Wadsworth Pub.

Levitan, Sar A., et al. Human Resources & Labor Markets: Employment and Training in the American Economy. 3rd ed. 576p. 1981. text ed. 21.50 scp (ISBN 0-06-044074-0, HarpC). Har-Row.

McNulty, Paul J. The Origins & Development of Labor Economics. 320p. 1980. text ed. 17.50x (ISBN 0-262-13162-5). MIT Pr.

Marshall, F. Ray, et al. Labor Economics: Wages, Employment & Trade Unionism. 4th ed. 1980. 20.95x (ISBN 0-256-02334-4). Irwin.

Martin, Donald L. An Ownership Theory of the Trade Union: A New Approach. LC 80-13147. 160p. 1981. 19.50x (ISBN 0-520-03884-3). U of Cal Pr.

The New Private Sector Initiative Program: A Source of Funds for Training Workers. LC 79-57737. Date not set. pap. 7.00 (ISBN 0-89834-009-8, 6036). Chamber Comm US.

Okun, Arthur M., ed. Battle Against Unemployment. rev. ed. (Problems of the Modern Economy Ser). 1972. 7.95x (ISBN 0-393-05446-2); pap. 4.95x (ISBN 0-393-09846-X). Norton.

Patton, John A. Indirect Labor Measurement & Control. 73p. 1980. wkbk. 50.00 (ISBN 0-89806-010-9). Am Inst Indus Eng.

Phelps, Orme W. Introduction to Labor Economics. 4th ed. LC 78-15720. 572p. 1978. Repr. of 1967 ed. lib. bdg. 21.50 (ISBN 0-88275-676-1). Krieger.

Rees, Albert. The Economics of Work & Pay. 2nd ed. (Illus.). 1979. text ed. 16.50 scp (ISBN 0-06-045354-0, HarpC). Har-Row.

Reynolds, Lloyd G. Labor Economics & Labor Relations. 8th ed. (Illus.). 656p. 17.95 (ISBN 0-13-517680-8). P-H.

--Labor Economics & Labor Relations. 7th ed. (Illus.). 1978. ref. 20.95 (ISBN 0-13-517706-5). P-H.

Reynolds, Lloyd G., et al. Readings in Labor Economics & Labor Relations. 2nd ed. (Illus.). 1978. pap. text ed. 12.95 (ISBN 0-13-761569-8). P-H.

Robinson, James W., et al, eds. Introduction to Labor. 1975. pap. 11.95 (ISBN 0-13-485490-X). P-H.
Rosen, Sherwin, ed. Studies in Labor Markets. (National Bureau of Economic Research Ser.: Universities-Nat'l Conference Series No. 31). (Illus.). 400p. 1981. lib. bdg. 34.00x (ISBN 0-226-72628-2). U of Chicago Pr.
Rowan, Richard L. Readings in Labor Economics & Labor Relations. 4th ed. 1980. 12.95x (ISBN 0-256-02367-0). Irwin.
Scheuch, Richard. Labor in the American Economy: Labor Problems & Union-Management Relations. 621p. 1981. text ed. 21.50 scp (ISBN 0-06-045774-0, HarpC). Harper Row.
Silverman, Bertram & Yanowitch, Murray. The Worker in Post-Industrial Capitalism: Liberal & Radical Responses. LC 73-14431. (Illus.). 1974. pap. text ed. 8.95 (ISBN 0-02-928770-7). Free Pr.
Somers, Gerald G., ed. Labor, Management, & Social Policy: Essays in the John R. Commons Tradition. 318p. 1963. 27.50 (ISBN 0-299-02870-4). U of Wis Pr.
Squire, Lyn. Labor Force, Employment, & Labor Markets in the Course of Economic Development. (World Bank Research Publications Ser.). 208p. 1981. 16.95 (ISBN 0-19-520266-X); pap. 7.95 (ISBN 0-19-520267-8). Oxford U Pr.
Wilson, Maurice. Growing on the Job. Herr, Edwin L., ed. (Cooperative Work Experience Education for Careers Program). (Illus.). (gr. 11-12). 1976. pap. text ed. 5.04 (ISBN 0-07-028337-0, G); tchrs manual 2.75 (ISBN 0-07-028338-9). McGraw.

LABOR EXCHANGES
see Employment Agencies

LABOR FORCE
see Labor Supply

LABOR GRIEVANCES
see Grievance Procedures

LABOR LAWS AND LEGISLATION
see also Alien Labor; Boycott; Children–Employment; Employees, Dismissal Of; Factory Laws and Legislation; Freedom of Movement; Hours of Labor; Labor Contract; Mining Law; Strikes and Lockouts; Sunday Legislation; Trade-Unions; Unfair Labor Practices; Workmen's Compensation; Works Councils;
also subdivision Legal Status, Laws, etc. under names of professions, e.g. Teachers–Legal Status, Laws, etc.

Aboud, Grace S. & Doherty, Robert E. Practices & Procedures Under the Taylor Law: A Practical Guide in Narrative Form. 1974. pap. 2.00 (ISBN 0-87546-203-0). NY Sch Indus Rel.
Administrative Justice & the Unemployed. (Studies in Labour & Social Law: Vol. 1). 1978. lib. bdg. 23.00 (ISBN 0-7201-0555-2, Pub. by Mansell England). Merrimack Bk Serv.
American Chamber of Commerce in Korea. Korean Labor Laws. 1977. 10.00 (ISBN 0-686-23280-1). A M Newman.
Anderson, Howard J. Major Labor-Law Principles Established by the NLRB & the Courts: December 1964-December 1975. LC 73-93852. 188p. 1976. 15.00 (ISBN 0-87179-231-1). BNA.
Anderson, Nels. The Right to Work. LC 70-136835. (Illus.). 152p. 1973. Repr. of 1938 ed. lib. bdg. 15.00 (ISBN 0-8371-5264-X, ANRW). Greenwood.
Annual Research Conference, 8th, UCLA, 1965. Research Conference on Labor Relations: Proceedings. 2.00 (ISBN 0-89215-028-9). U Cal LA Indus Rel.
Baker, Elizabeth. Protective Labor Legislation, with Special Reference to Women in the State of New York. LC 76-82239. (Columbia University Studies in the Social Sciences: No. 259). Repr. of 1925 ed. 20.00 (ISBN 0-404-51259-3). AMS Pr.
Bellace, Janice R., et al. The Landrum-Griffin Act: Twenty Years of Federal Protection of Union Members' Rights. LC 79-2465. (Labor Relations & Public Policy Ser.: No. 19). 1979. pap. 15.00 (ISBN 0-89546-014-9). Indus Res Unit-Wharton.
Bercusson, Brian. Fair Wages Resolutions. (Studies in Labour & Social Law: Vol. 2). 1977. lib. bdg. 30.50 (ISBN 0-7201-0709-1, Pub. by Mansell England). Merrimack Bk Serv.
Bioff, Allan L., et al, eds. The Developing Labor Law: The Board, the Courts, & the National Labor Relations Act, 1977 Supplement. 340p. 1978. pap. 7.50 (ISBN 0-87179-286-9). BNA.
--The Developing Labor Law: The Board, the Courts, and the National Labor Relations Act, 1976 Supplement. 358p. 1977. pap. 5.00 (ISBN 0-87179-249-4). BNA.
--Developing Labor Law: The Board, the Courts, & the National Relations Act, 1971-75 Cumulative Supplement. LC 76-54726. 614p. 1976. 10.00 (ISBN 0-87179-240-0). BNA.
Blackburn, Jack. The Rodda Act--One Year Later. (IPA Training Manual). 1977. 8.00 (ISBN 0-89215-072-6). U Cal LA Indus Rel.
Blanpain, R., ed. Bulletin of Comparative Labour Relations, No. 10. 1979. pap. 31.50 (ISBN 90-312-0091-3, Pub. by Kluwer Law Netherlands). Kluwer Boston.
Blum, Solomon. Labor Economics. LC 79-89719. (American Labor from Conspiracy to Collective Bargaining, Ser. 1). 579p. 1969. Repr. of 1925 ed. 22.00 (ISBN 0-405-02105-4). Arno.
Bradlaugh, Charles. Labor & Law. LC 68-55490. Repr. of 1891 ed. 15.00x (ISBN 0-678-00888-4). Kelley.
Brandeis, Louis D. & Goldmark, Josephine. Women in Industry. LC 73-89720. (American Labor, from Conspiracy to Collective Bargaining Ser., No. 1). 121p. 1969. Repr. of 1907 ed. 10.00 (ISBN 0-405-02106-2). Arno.
Brown, Ralph S., Jr. Loyalty & Security: Employment Tests in the United States. LC 79-151417. (Civil Liberties in American History Ser). 522p. 1972. Repr. of 1958 ed. lib. bdg. 47.50 (ISBN 0-306-70218-5). Da Capo.
Butsch, Charlotte. American Labor Movement, Student Syllabus. 30p. 1976. pap. text ed. 3.95 (ISBN 0-89420-078-X, 330011); cassette recording 24.30 (ISBN 0-89420-206-5, 330000). Natl Book.
Cabot, Stephen J. Labor Management Relations Act Manual. 1st ed. 1978. 44.00 (ISBN 0-88262-208-0, 78-60446). Warren.
California Labor Code. 1981. 12.00 (ISBN 0-911110-29-1). Parker & Son.
Chafee, Zechariah. The Inquiring Mind. LC 74-699. (American Constitutional & Legal History Ser.). 276p. 1974. Repr. of 1928 ed. lib. bdg. 27.50 (ISBN 0-306-70641-5). Da Capo.
Cogley, Thomas S. The Law of Strikes, Lockouts & Labor Organizations. xiv, 377p. 1981. Repr. of 1894 ed. lib. bdg. 32.50x (ISBN 0-8377-0435-9). Rothman.
Colberg, Marshall R. The Consumer Impact of Repeal of 14(B) LC 77-17061. 1978. 3.00 (ISBN 0-89195-021-4). Heritage Found.
Commons, John R. & Andrews, John B. Principles of Labor Legislation. 4th ed. LC 66-22620. Repr. of 1936 ed. 19.50x (ISBN 0-678-00207-X). Kelley.
--Principles of Labor Legislation. 1916. 15.00 (ISBN 0-686-17721-5). Quest Edns.
Construction Industry Labor Relations, 1979. (Litigation Course Handbook Ser., 1978-79: Vol. 138). 1979. pap. 20.00 (ISBN 0-686-50957-9, H4-3893). PLI.
Cox, Archibald. Law & the National Labor Policy. (Monograph Ser.: No. 5). 1960. 5.00 (ISBN 0-89215-007-6). U Cal LA Indus Rel.
Cox, Sarah. Down the Road: Unemployment & the Fight for the Right to Work. (Illus.). 124p. 8.95 (ISBN 0-904613-43-7); pap. 2.95 (ISBN 0-904613-35-6). Writers & Readers.
Davies, Paul & Freedland, Mark. Labour Law: Text & Materials with 1980 Supplement. (Law in Context Ser.). xliv, 766p. 1979. 50.00x (ISBN 0-297-77591-X, Pub. by Weidenfeld & Nicolson England); pap. 4.00 suppl., 1980, 32p. (ISBN 0-297-77888-9). Rothman.
--Labour Law: Text & Materials with 1980 Supplement. (Law in Context Ser.). xliv, 766p. 1979. 50.00x (ISBN 0-297-77591-X, Pub. by Weidenfeld & Nicolson England); suppl., 1980 32 pgs. 4.00x (ISBN 0-297-77888-9). Rothman.
Dawson, W. A. Introductory Guide to Central Labour Legislation. 10.00x (ISBN 0-210-27188-4). Asia.
Eaves, Lucile. A History of California Labor Legislation. 1910. pap. 31.00 (ISBN 0-384-13760-1). Johnson Repr.
Eggert, Gerald G. Steelmasters & Labor Reform, Eighteen Eighty-Six to Nineteen Twenty-Three. LC 81-50636. 256p. 1981. 17.50 (ISBN 0-8229-3801-4). U of Pittsburgh Pr.
Ehrenberg, Ronald G. & Schumann, Paul L. Longer Hours or More Jobs? An Investigation of Amending Hours Legislation to Create Unemployment. (Cornell Studies in Industrial & Labor Relations: No. 22). 160p. 1981. write for info. (ISBN 0-87546-090-9); pap. write for info. (ISBN 0-87546-091-7). NY Sch Indus Rel.
Epp, David. Labor Law. new & rev. ed. LC 76-26109. (Legal Almanac Ser.: No. 7). 1976. lib. bdg. 5.95 (ISBN 0-379-11102-0). Oceana.
Estey, Marten S., ed. Labor Relations Policy in an Expanding Economy: American Academy of Political & Social Science. LC 74-10648. 152p. 1974. Repr. of 1961 ed. lib. bdg. 15.00x (ISBN 0-8371-7645-X, ESLR). Greenwood.
Feldacker, Bruce S. Labor Guide to Labor Law. (Illus.). 1980. ref. ed. 24.95 (ISBN 0-686-77691-7); text ed. 16.95 (ISBN 0-8359-3921-9). Reston.
Fisher, Thomas R. Industrial Disputes & Federal Legislation. LC 68-58571. (Columbia University. Studies in the Social Sciences: No. 467). Repr. of 1940 ed. 26.00 (ISBN 0-404-51467-7). AMS Pr.
Foner, Philip S., ed. Fellow Workers & Friends: I.W.W. Free-Speech Fights As Told by Participants. LC 80-23621. (Contributions in American History Ser.: No. 92). 224p. 1981. lib. bdg. 29.95 (ISBN 0-313-20660-0, FFW/). Greenwood.
Foster, G. W., Jr. Jurisdiction, Rights, & Remedies for Group Wrongs Under the Fair Labor Standards Act: Special Federal Questions. (Research Contributions Ser: No. 10). 1975. pap. 2.00 (ISBN 0-685-64483-9). Am Bar Foun.
Frankfurter, Felix & Greene, Nathan. The Labor Injunction. 1963. 8.75 (ISBN 0-8446-1190-5). Peter Smith.
Goldman, A. L. Labour Law & Industrial Relations in the U. S. A. 1979. pap. 36.00 (ISBN 90-312-0097-2, Pub. by Kluwer Law Netherlands). Kluwer Boston.
Goldman, Alvin L. The Supreme Court & Labor-Management Relations Law. LC 75-42953. 1976. 19.95 (ISBN 0-669-00496-0). Lexington Bks.
Gregory, Charles O. & Katz, Harold A. Labor & the Law. 3rd ed. 1979. 35.00 (ISBN 0-393-01208-5); pap. text ed. 10.95x (ISBN 0-393-09995-4). Norton.
Groat, George G. Attitude of American Courts in Labor Cases. LC 78-77993. (Columbia University. Studies in the Social Sciences: No. 108). Repr. of 1911 ed. 27.50 (ISBN 0-404-51108-2). AMS Pr.
--Trade Unions & the Law in New York: A Study of Some Legal Phases of Labor Organizations. LC 68-56659. (Columbia University. Studies in the Social Sciences: No. 51). Repr. of 1905 ed. 16.50 (ISBN 0-404-51051-5). AMS Pr.
Grodin, Joseph R. Union Government & the Law: British & American Experiences. (Monograph Ser: No. 8). 1961. 6.00 (ISBN 0-89215-010-6). U Cal LA Indus Rel.
Hanslowe, Kurt L., et al. Union Security in Public Employment: Of Free Riding & Free Association. LC 78-620002. (Institute of Public Employment Monograph: No.8). 1978. pap. 3.25 (ISBN 0-87546-065-8). NY Sch Indus Rel.
Harris, R., et al. Job "Creation"-or Destruction? Six Essays on the Effects of Government Intervention in the Labor Market. (Institute of Economic Affairs Readings Ser.: No. 20). (Orig.). 1979. 10.95 (ISBN 0-255-36121-1). Transatlantic.
Higgins, George C. Voluntarism in Organized Labor in the United States, 1930-40. LC 76-89737. (American Labor: From Conspiracy to Collective Bargaining Ser., No. 1). 1969. Repr. of 1944 ed. 9.00 (ISBN 0-405-02126-7). Arno.
Hill, Myron G., et al. Smith's Review of Labor Law & Employment Discrimination, for Law School, Bar & College Examinations. 2nd ed. LC 79-23934. (Legal Gem Ser.). 235p. 1980. pap. text ed. 9.95 (ISBN 0-8299-2069-2). West Pub.
Janner, Greville. Janner's Compendium of Employment Law. 759p. 1979. text ed. 45.50x (ISBN 0-220-66363-7, Pub. by Busn Bks England). Renouf.
--Janner's Employment Forms. 397p. 1979. text ed. 61.25x (ISBN 0-220-67027-7, Pub. by Busn Bks England). Renouf.
Jenness, Linda, et al. Affirmative Action Versus Seniority: Last Hired, First Fired. pap. 0.50 (ISBN 0-87348-375-8). Path Pr NY.
Keenan, Denis. Principles of Employment Law. 192p. 1980. 49.74x (ISBN 0-906501-05-9, Pub. by Keenan England); paper 24.75x (ISBN 0-906501-04-0). State Mutual Bk.
Kelley, Florence. Some Ethical Gains Through Legislation. LC 75-89742. (American Labor, from Conspiracy to Collective Bargaining Ser., No. 1). 341p. 1969. Repr. of 1905 ed. 14.00 (ISBN 0-405-02131-3). Arno.
Kingsbury, Susan M., et al, eds. Labor Laws & Their Enforcement. LC 71-156446. (American Labor Ser., No. 2). (Illus.). 1971. Repr. of 1911 ed. 29.00 (ISBN 0-405-02930-6). Arno.
Labor Law Group. Labor Relations & Social Problems: A Course Book. 3rd. ed. Incl. Unit Five. Cases & Materials on Negotiation. Peck, Cornelius J., ed. 200p. 1972; Unit Seven. Labor Relations & Social Problems: A Course Book. Goldman, Alvin L. & Labor Law Group, eds. 275p. 1972. 5.00x (ISBN 0-87179-157-9); Unit Nine. Individuals & Unions. Dunsford, John E., et al, eds. 1973; Unit Two. Labor Relations & Social Problems: A Course Book. 2nd ed. Covington, Robert N. & Labor Law Group, eds. 227p. 1974. 5.00 (ISBN 0-87179-163-3); Unit Three. Discrimination in Employment. Covington, Robert N., et al, eds. 1976. text ed. 9.50x (ISBN 0-87179-235-4). LC 77-166518. BNA.
Lauchheimer, Malcolm H. The Labor Law of Maryland. LC 78-63969. (Johns Hopkins University. Studies in the Social Sciences. Thirty-Seventh Ser. 1919: 2). Repr. of 1919 ed. 18.00 (ISBN 0-404-61215-6). AMS Pr.
Lee, R. Alton. Truman & Taft-Hartley: A Question of Mandate. LC 80-17251. viii, 254p. 1980. Repr. of 1966 ed. lib. bdg. 22.50x (ISBN 0-313-22618-0, LETT). Greenwood.
Leslie, Douglas. Cases & Materials on Labor Law. 1979. 22.00 (ISBN 0-316-52157-4); pap. 4.95 statutory supplement (ISBN 0-316-52158-2). Little.
Leslie, Douglas L. Labor Law in a Nutshell. LC 79-158396. (Nutshell Ser.). 403p. 1979. pap. text ed. 6.95 (ISBN 0-8299-2053-6). West Pub.
Lingenfelter, Richard E. The Hardrock Miners: A History of the Mining Labor Movement in the American West, 1863-1893. 1974. 16.95 (ISBN 0-520-02468-0). U of Cal Pr.
Lynd, Staughton. Labor Law for the Rank & Filer. LC 77-95429. (Singlejack Little Book Ser.). 1978. 6.95x (ISBN 0-917300-05-X); pap. 1.95 (ISBN 0-917300-04-1). Miles & Weir.
McClintock, Michael C. NLRB General Counsel: Unreviewable Power to Refuse to Issue an Unfair Labor Practice Complaint. LC 80-67049. (Scholarly Monographs). 180p. 1980. pap. 15.00 (ISBN 0-8408-0510-1). Carrollton Pr.
McCrea, Joan. Texas Labor Laws. 3rd ed. 100p. 1978. pap. 4.95 (ISBN 0-87201-414-2). Gulf Pub.
MacKenzie, Susan T. Group Legal Services. (Key Issues Ser.: No. 18). 1975. pap. 3.00 (ISBN 0-87546-231-6). NY Sch Indus Rel.
McNeill, George E., ed. Labor Movement. LC 66-21683. Repr. of 1887 ed. 22.50x (ISBN 0-678-00713-6). Kelley.
Mason, Alpheus T. Organized Labor & the Law. LC 73-89755. (American Labor, from Conspiracy to Collective Bargaining, Ser. 1). 265p. 1969. Repr. of 1925 ed. 12.00 (ISBN 0-405-02142-9). Arno.
Millis, Harry A. & Brown, Emily C. From the Wagner Act to Taft-Hartley. LC 50-7091. 1950. 27.50x (ISBN 0-226-52937-1). U of Chicago Pr.
Mitchell, E. Employer's & Personnel Manager's Handbook of Draft Letters of Employment Law. 1977. Repr. 39.50x (ISBN 0-8464-0373-0). Beekman Pubs.
Morris, Charles J., ed. The Developing Labor Law, the Board, the Courts, & the National Labor Relations Act. rev ed. 1981. text ed. price not set (ISBN 0-87179-360-1). BNA.
Morris, Charles J., et al, eds. Developing Labor Law: The Board, the Courts, & the National Labor Relations Act. LC 74-106074. 1104p. 1971. 24.85 (ISBN 0-87179-051-3). BNA.
Morris, Victor P. Oregon's Experience with Minimum Wage Legislation. LC 68-58609. (Columbia University. Studies in the Social Sciences: No. 320). Repr. of 1930 ed. 20.00 (ISBN 0-404-51320-4). AMS Pr.
Morse, Sanford M., ed. Reporter Services & Their Use. 164p. 1979. pap. 5.00 (ISBN 0-87179-314-8). BNA.
Murphy, D. J. Labor in Politics: The State Labor Parties in Australia 1880-1920. 1975. 20.00x (ISBN 0-7022-0939-2). U of Queensland Pr.
Myers & Twomey. Labor Law & Legislation. 5th ed. 1968. text ed. 11.60 (ISBN 0-538-12970-0). SW Pub.
Newhouse, Wade J. Public Sector Labor Relations Law in New York State. LC 78-50698. 1978. lib. bdg. 24.50 (ISBN 0-930342-57-7). W S Hein.
Oxfeld, Eric J., ed. Analysis of Workers Compensation Laws, Nineteen Eighty. LC 60-36379. (Orig.). 1980. pap. 6.00 (ISBN 0-89834-019-5, 6174). Chamber Comm US.
The People Make History: The Practice of the Democratic Workers' Party, Rebel Worker Organization & Grass Roots Alliance. 62p. (Orig.). 1980. pap. 3.95 (ISBN 0-89935-014-3). Synthesis Pubns.
Putnam, Bertha H., ed. Enforcement of the Statutes of Labourers During the First Decade After the Black Death, 1349-59. LC 70-127447. (Columbia University Social Science Studies: No. 85). Repr. of 1908 ed. 20.00 (ISBN 0-404-51085-X). AMS Pr.
Reed, Merl E., et al, eds. Southern Workers & Their Unions, Eighteen Eighty to Nineteen Seventy-Five: Selected Papers, the Second Southern Labor History Conference, 1978. LC 80-24724. (Contributions in Economics & Economic History Ser.: No. 39). (Illus.). 256p. 1981. lib. bdg. 29.95 (ISBN 0-313-22701-2, RSW/). Greenwood.
Rice, Charles E. An Idea Whose Time Has Gone: Compulsory Unionism in the Eighties. 1980. cancelled (ISBN 0-89651-350-5). Icarus.
Schlossberg, Stephen I. & Sherman, Fredrick E. Organizing & the Law. 2nd ed. LC 70-140189. 320p. 1971. 10.00 (ISBN 0-87179-116-1); pap. 7.50 (ISBN 0-87179-117-X). BNA.

Scoville, John W. Labor Monopolies, or Freedom. LC 71-172229. (Right Wing Individualist Tradition in America Ser). 1972. Repr. of 1946 ed. 11.00 (ISBN 0-405-00437-0). Arno.

Seyfarth, Shaw, Fairweather, & Geraldson. Labor Relations & the Law in Belgium & the United States. (Michigan International Labor Studies: No. 2). 455p. 1969. 15.00 (ISBN 0-87712-110-9). U Mich Busn Div Res.

Seyfarth, Shaw, Fairweather & Geraldson. Labor Relations & the Law in France & the United States. (Michigan International Labor Studies: No. 5). 648p. 1972. 15.00 (ISBN 0-87712-113-3). U Mich Busn Div Res.

Seyfarth, Shaw, Fairweather, & Geraldson. Labor Relations & the Law in Italy & the United States. (Michigan International Labor Studies: No. 4). 626p. 1970. 15.00 (ISBN 0-87712-112-5). U Mich Busn Div Res.

Seyfarth, Shaw, Fairweather & Geraldson. Labor Relations & the Law in the United Kingdom & the United States. (Michigan International Labor Studies: No. 1). 634p. 1968. 15.00 (ISBN 0-87712-109-5). U Mich Busn Div Res.

--Labor Relations & the Law in West Germany & the United States. (Michigan International Labor Studies: No. 3). 606p. 1969. 15.00 (ISBN 0-87712-111-7). U Mich Busn Div Res.

Siegel, Abraham J. & Lipsky, David B., eds. Unfinished Business: An Agenda for Labor, Management, & the Public. 1978. 9.95x (ISBN 0-262-19175-X). MIT Pr.

Simmons & Smith. Wage & Hour Manual for California Employees. 1979. pap. 45.00 (ISBN 0-917386-28-0). Exec Ent.

Special Committee of the Section of Labor Relations Law, ABA, ed. The Developing Labor Law: The Board, the Courts, & the National Labor Relations Act, 1978 Supplement. 298p. 1979. 7.50 (ISBN 0-87179-312-1). BNA.

Stokes, McNeill. Labor Law in Contractors' Language. 1979. write for info. (ISBN 0-07-061650-7, P&RB). McGraw.

Swann, James P., Jr. NLRB Elections: A Guidebook for Employers. 150p. (Orig.). 1980. pap. 10.00 (ISBN 0-87179-322-9). BNA.

Taylor, Benjamin & Witney, Fred. Labor Relations Law. 3rd ed. 1979. text ed. 23.95 (ISBN 0-13-519645-0). P-H.

Weltner, Andor. Fundamental Traits of Socialist Labour Law with Special Regard to Hungarian Legislation. LC 72-187654. 218p. 1970. 7.50x (ISBN 0-8002-1439-0). Intl Pubns Serv.

Werne, Benjamin. The Law & Practice of Public Employment Labor Relations, 3 vols. LC 74-79539. 1607p. 1974. 100.00 (ISBN 0-87215-168-9). Michie-Bobbs.

Willoughby, William F. State Activities in Relation to Labor in the United States. LC 78-63880. (Johns Hopkins University. Studies in the Social Sciences. Nineteenth Ser. 1901: 4-5). Repr. of 1901 ed. 14.50 (ISBN 0-404-61135-4). AMS Pr.

Wilson, Wesley M. Labor Law Handbook. 1963. with 1981 suppl. 25.00 (ISBN 0-672-82866-9, Bobbs-Merrill Law); 1981 suppl. 15.00 (ISBN 0-672-84386-2). Michie-Bobbs.

Witte, Edwin E. The Government in Labor Disputes. LC 70-89770. (American Labor, from Conspiracy to Collective Bargaining, Ser. 1). 352p. 1969. Repr. of 1932 ed. 15.00 (ISBN 0-405-02157-7). Arno.

--The Government in Labor Disputes. LC 70-89770. (American Labor, from Conspiracy to Collective Bargaining, Ser. 1). 352p. 1969. Repr. of 1932 ed. 15.00 (ISBN 0-405-02157-7). Arno.

Wootton, Graham. Workers, Unions & the State. LC 67-12612. 1967. 6.00x (ISBN 0-8052-3295-8). Schocken.

Yeiser, Ted M., Jr. The De-Certification Casebook. 1980. 14.95 (ISBN 0-686-27479-2). Management Pr.

--How to De-Certify a Union. 1979. 8.95 (ISBN 0-686-27480-6). Management Pr.

Zepke, Brent E. Labor Law. (Littlefield Adams Quality Paperbacks: No. 325). (Orig.). 1977. pap. 3.95 (ISBN 0-8226-0325-X). Littlefield.

LABOR LAWS AND LEGISLATION–BIBLIOGRAPHY

Arluck, Mary S., ed. Papers of the American Association for Labor Legislation, 1905-1943: Guide to the Microfilm Edition. 73p. 1974. pap. 25.00 (ISBN 0-667-00527-7). Microfilming Corp.

Hepple, B. A., et al. A Bibliography of the Literature on British & Irish Labour Law. LC 74-76298. 1975. 31.50 (ISBN 0-7201-0447-5, Pub. by Mansell England). Merrimack Bk Serv.

LABOR LAWS AND LEGISLATION–CASES

Cox, Archibald, et al. Cases & Materials on Labor Law. 9th ed. (University Casebook Ser.). 1184p. 1981. text ed. write for info. (ISBN 0-88277-027-6). Foundation Pr.

Leslie, Douglas L. Cases & Materials on Labor Law: 1981 Supplement. 1981. text ed. write for info. (ISBN 0-316-52159-0). Little.

Meltzer, Bernard D. Labor Law: Cases, Materials, & Problems. 1980. pap. 7.25 suppl. (ISBN 0-316-56637-3). Little.

--Labor Law: Cases, Materials & Problems. 2nd ed. 1221p. 1977. 27.50 (ISBN 0-316-56644-6); statutory appendix 1977 pap. o.p. 3.50 (ISBN 0-316-56645-4). Little.

LABOR LAWS AND LEGISLATION–AUSTRALIA

Harris, Joe. The Bitter Fight: A Pictorial History of the Australian Labor Movement. (Illus.). 1970. 20.50x (ISBN 0-7022-0613-X). U of Queensland Pr.

LABOR LAWS AND LEGISLATION–BELGIUM

Seyfarth, Shaw, Fairweather, & Geraldson. Labor Relations & the Law in Belgium & the United States. (Michigan International Labor Studies: No. 2). 455p. 1969. 15.00 (ISBN 0-87712-110-9). U Mich Busn Div Res.

LABOR LAWS AND LEGISLATION–CANADA

American Bar Association, Committee on International Labor Law Section of Labor Relations Law. The Labor Relations Law of Canada. LC 77-23122. 258p. 1977. 15.00 (ISBN 0-87179-247-8). BNA.

Craven, Paul. An Impartial Umpire: Industrial Relations & the Canadian State, 1900-1911. (The State & Economic Life Ser.). 560p. 1980. 27.50x (ISBN 0-8020-5505-2); pap. 13.50x (ISBN 0-8020-6401-9). U of Toronto Pr.

Murg, Gary E. & Fox, John C. Labor Relations Law: Canada, Mexico, & Western Europe, 2 vols. LC 78-58374. 1978. text ed. 40.00 (ISBN 0-685-65702-7, H6-2942). PLI.

Stewart, Bryce M. Canadian Labor Laws & the Treaty. LC 77-76689. (Columbia University. Studies in Social Sciences: No. 278). 1969. Repr. of 1926 ed. 32.50 (ISBN 0-404-51278-X). AMS Pr.

LABOR LAWS AND LEGISLATION–CHINA

Wagner, Augusta. Labor Legislation in China. LC 78-22780. (The Modern Chinese Economy Ser.). 301p. 1980. lib. bdg. 33.00 (ISBN 0-8240-4283-2). Garland Pub.

Wagner, Augusta B. Labor Legislation in China. LC 79-2843. 302p. 1980. Repr. of 1938 ed. 22.50 (ISBN 0-8305-0019-7). Hyperion Conn.

LABOR LAWS AND LEGISLATION–COLOMBIA

Urrutia, Miguel. Development of the Colombian Labor Movement. LC 70-81433. (Illus.). 1969. 25.00x (ISBN 0-300-01153-9). Yale U Pr.

LABOR LAWS AND LEGISLATION–CZECHOSLOVAK REPUBLIC

Bloss, Esther. Labor Legislation in Czechoslovakia. LC 79-76641. (Columbia University Studies in the Social Sciences: No. 446). Repr. of 1938 ed. 18.50 (ISBN 0-404-51446-4). AMS Pr.

LABOR LAWS AND LEGISLATION–EUROPE

Kennedy, M. Thomas. European Labor Relations: Text & Cases. LC 78-14155. 448p. 1980. 29.95x (ISBN 0-669-02663-8). Lexington Bks.

Murg, Gary E. & Fox, John C. Labor Relations Law: Canada, Mexico, & Western Europe, 2 vols. LC 78-58374. 1978. text ed. 40.00 (ISBN 0-685-65702-7, H6-2942). PLI.

Schneider, Hannes & Hellwig, Hans-Jurgen, eds. German Labour Law. 196p. 1980. 45.00x (ISBN 0-7121-5496-5, Pub. by Macdonald & Evans). State Mutual Bk.

Seyfarth, Shaw, Fairweather & Geraldson. Labor Relations & the Law in France & the United States. (Michigan International Labor Studies: No. 5). 648p. 1972. 15.00 (ISBN 0-87712-113-3). U Mich Busn Div Res.

Seyfarth, Shaw, Fairweather, & Geraldson. Labor Relations & the Law in Italy & the United States. (Michigan International Labor Studies: No. 4). 626p. 1970. 15.00 (ISBN 0-87712-112-5). U Mich Busn Div Res.

Seyfarth, Shaw, Fairweather & Geraldson. Labor Relations & the Law in the United Kingdom & the United States. (Michigan International Labor Studies: No. 1). 634p. 1968. 15.00 (ISBN 0-87712-109-5). U Mich Busn Div Res.

--Labor Relations & the Law in West Germany & the United States. (Michigan International Labor Studies: No. 3). 606p. 1969. 15.00 (ISBN 0-87712-111-7). U Mich Busn Div Res.

Unemployment Compensation & Related Employment Policy Measures: General Report & County Studies. (Document Ser.). 286p. 1979. 17.50x (ISBN 92-64-11909-4). OECD.

Wage Policies & Collective Bargaining Developments in Finland, Ireland & Norway. 110p. 1979. 7.25x (ISBN 92-64-11915-9). OECD.

LABOR LAWS AND LEGISLATION–GREAT BRITAIN

Askwith, George R. Industrial Problems & Disputes. facsimile ed. LC 72-179502. (Select Bibliographies Reprint Ser). Repr. of 1920 ed. 24.00 (ISBN 0-8369-6631-7). Arno.

Bradlaugh, Charles. Labor & Law. LC 68-55490. Repr. of 1891 ed. 15.00x (ISBN 0-678-00888-4). Kelley.

Hepple, B. A., et al. A Bibliography of the Literature on British & Irish Labour Law. LC 74-76298. 1975. 31.50 (ISBN 0-7201-0447-5, Pub. by Mansell England). Merrimack Bk Serv.

Jevons, William S. State in Relation to Labour. 4th ed. Hirst, Francis, ed. LC 67-16344. Repr. of 1910 ed. 13.50x (ISBN 0-678-00434-X). Kelley.

Ludlow, John M. & Jones, Lloyd. Progress of the Working Classes, 1832-1867. LC 72-77050. Repr. of 1867 ed. 17.50x (ISBN 0-678-00909-0). Kelley.

Mason, Alpheus T. Organized Labor & the Law. LC 73-89755. (American Labor, from Conspiracy to Collective Bargaining, Ser. 1). 265p. 1969. Repr. of 1925 ed. 12.00 (ISBN 0-405-02142-9). Arno.

Miliband, Ralph. Parliamentary Socialism: A Study in the Politics of Labour. 2nd ed. 1972. lib. bdg. 12.50x (ISBN 0-678-08066-6). Kelley.

National Association for the Promotion of Social Science Trades' Societies Committee. Trades' Societies & Strikes. LC 67-20514. Repr. of 1860 ed. 22.50x (ISBN 0-678-00347-5). Kelley.

Pritt, D. N. Law, Class & Society, 4 vols. 174p. 1970. 44.00x set (ISBN 0-8464-0547-4). Beekman Pubs.

Putnam, Bertha H., ed. Enforcement of the Statutes of Labourers During the First Decade After the Black Death, 1349-59. LC 70-127447. (Columbia University Social Science Studies: No. 85). Repr. of 1908 ed. 20.00 (ISBN 0-404-51085-X). AMS Pr.

Seyfarth, Shaw, Fairweather & Geraldson. Labor Relations & the Law in the United Kingdom & the United States. (Michigan International Labor Studies: No. 1). 634p. 1968. 15.00 (ISBN 0-87712-109-5). U Mich Busn Div Res.

Webb, Beatrice & Webb, Sidney. Problems of Modern Industry. facsimile new ed. LC 70-37918. (Select Bibliographies Reprint Ser.). Repr. of 1902 ed. 19.00 (ISBN 0-8369-6755-0). Arno.

LABOR LAWS AND LEGISLATION–LATIN AMERICA

Meyers, Frederic. Mexican Industrial Relations Viewed from the Perspective of the Mexican Labor Court. (Monograph: No. 24). 1979. 5.00 (ISBN 0-89215-104-8). U Cal LA Indus Rel.

LABOR LAWS AND LEGISLATION–INDIA

Vaid, K. N. State & Labour in India. 10.00x (ISBN 0-210-26949-9). Asia.

LABOR LAWS AND LEGISLATION–JAPAN

Hanami, T. A. Labour Law & Industrial Relations in Japan. 1979. lib. bdg. 37.00 (ISBN 90-312-0099-9, Pub. by Kluwer Law Netherlands); pap. 20.00 (ISBN 90-312-0095-6, Pub. by Kluwer Law Netherlands). Kluwer Boston.

Harari, Ehud. The Politics of Labor Legislation in Japan: National-International Interaction. LC 72-78945. 1973. 24.50x (ISBN 0-520-02264-5). U of Cal Pr.

LABOR LAWS AND LEGISLATION–MEXICO

Murg, Gary E. & Fox, John C. Labor Relations Law: Canada, Mexico, & Western Europe, 2 vols. LC 78-58374. 1978. text ed. 40.00 (ISBN 0-685-65702-7, H6-2942). PLI.

LABOR LAWS AND LEGISLATION–RUSSIA

McAulay, Alastair. Women's Work & Wages in the Soviet Union. 248p. 1981. text ed. 28.50x (ISBN 0-04-339020-X). Allen Unwin.

LABOR LAWS AND LEGISLATION, INTERNATIONAL

see also Alien Labor

Ayusawa, Iwao F. International Labor Leglistation. LC 75-82214. (Columbia University Studies in the Social Sciences: No. 208). Repr. of 1920 ed. 16.50 (ISBN 0-404-51208-9). AMS Pr.

Bar-Niv, Zvi H., et al. International Labour Law Reports, Vol. 3: 1976 - 1977. 420p. 1981. 40.00 (ISBN 90-286-2711-1). Sijthoff & Noordhoff.

Conventions & Recommendations, 1919-1966. (With suppls. 1967-81). 22.80 (ISBN 92-2-100935-1). Intl Labour Office.

International Labour Conference, 67th Session, 1981. Minimum Age, Report III: Summary of Reports on Convention Number 138 & Recommendation Number 146 (Article 19 of the Constitution, Pt. 2. (Illus.). 162p. (Orig.). 1981. pap. 12.85 (ISBN 0-686-30178-1). Intl Labour Office.

Joyce, James A. World Labour Rights & Their Protection. 192p. 1980. 22.50x (ISBN 0-312-89137-7). St Martin.

Landy, E. A. Effectiveness of International Supervision: Three Decades of I. L. O. Experience. LC 66-11877. 1966. 20.00 (ISBN 0-379-00283-3). Oceana.

Vaidyanathan, N. International Labour Standards: A Handbook. 1977. 12.50x (ISBN 0-88386-843-1). South Asia Bks.

Valticos, N. International Labour Law. 1979. lib. bdg. 37.00 (ISBN 90-312-0101-4, Pub. by Kluwer Law Netherlands); pap. 20.00 (ISBN 90-312-0096-4, Pub. by Kluwer Law Netherlands). Kluwer Boston.

LABOR-MANAGEMENT RELATIONS

see Industrial Relations

LABOR MARKET

see Labor Supply

LABOR MOBILITY

see also Labor Supply; Labor Turnover

Adams, Leonard P. & Aronson, Robert L. Workers & Industrial Change. LC 73-22502. (Cornell Studies in Industrial & Labour Relations, Vol. 8). (Illus.). 209p. 1974. Repr. of 1957 ed. lib. bdg. 15.00 (ISBN 0-8371-6373-0, ADIC). Greenwood.

Aliboni, Roberto, ed. Arab Industrialization & Economic Integration. LC 78-10632. 1979. 23.95 (ISBN 0-312-04702-9). St Martin.

Gitelman, Howard M. Workingmen of Waltham: Mobility in American Urban Industrial Development, 1850-1890. LC 74-6822. (Illus.). 208p. 1974. 14.00x (ISBN 0-8018-1570-3). Johns Hopkins.

Hansen, Niles M. Location Preferences, Migration, & Regional Growth: A Study of the South & Southwest United States. LC 72-76449. (Special Studies in U.S. Economic, Social, & Political Issues). 1973. 34.00x (ISBN 0-275-06650-9). Irvington.

History Task Force, Centro De Estudios Puertorriquenos. Labor Migration Under Capitalism: The Puerto Rican Experience. LC 78-13918. (Modern Reader Paperback Ser.). (Illus.). 287p. 1980. pap. 6.50 (ISBN 0-85345-494-9). Monthly Rev.

Jaffe, A. & Carleton, R. O. Occupational Mobility in the United States, 1930-1960. LC 73-16947. (Illus.). 105p. 1974. Repr. of 1954 ed. lib. bdg. 15.00x (ISBN 0-8371-7248-9, JAOM). Greenwood.

Jennings, Eugene E. Routes to the Executive Suite. LC 70-134596. (McGraw-Hill Paperbacks). 1976. pap. 4.95 (ISBN 0-07-032444-1, SP). McGraw.

Jones, Donald W. Migration & Urban Unemployment in Dualistic Economic Development. LC 75-35772. (Research Papers Ser: No. 165). (Illus.). 1975. pap. 8.00 (ISBN 0-89065-072-1). U Chicago Dept Geog.

Kirchner, John A. Sugar & Seasonal Labor Migration: The Case of Tucuman, Argentina. LC 80-11605. (Research Papers Ser.: No. 192). (Illus.). 168p. 1980. pap. 8.00 (ISBN 0-89065-099-3). U Chicago Dept Geog.

Mueller, Charles. The Economics of Labor Migration. (Studies in Urban Economic Ser.). 1981. price not set (ISBN 0-12-509580-5). Acad Pr.

Niejolt, G. Thomas-Lycklama. On the Road for Work: Migratory Workers on the East Coast of the United States. (Ser. on the Development of Societies: Vol. VII). 224p. 1980. lib. bdg. 16.00 (ISBN 0-89838-043-X). Kluwer Boston.

Palmer, Gladys L. & Brainerd, Carol P. Labor Mobility in Six Cities. LC 54-9679. 1954. 8.75 (ISBN 0-527-03308-1); pap. 3.75 (ISBN 0-527-03309-X). Kraus Repr.

Parnes, Herbert S. Research on Labor Mobility. LC 54-9681. 1954. pap. 4.25 (ISBN 0-527-03292-1). Kraus Repr.

Piore, Michael J. Birds of Passage: Migrant Labor & Industrial Societies. LC 78-12067. (Illus.). 192p. 1980. pap. 6.95 (ISBN 0-521-28058-3). Cambridge U Pr.

Ramachandran, P. Some Aspects of Labor Mobility in Bombay City. LC 74-900696. 139p. 1974. 9.50x (ISBN 0-8002-0051-9). Intl Pubns Serv.

Reynolds, Lloyd G. Structure of Labor Markets: Wage & Labor Mobility in Theory & Practice. LC 73-109302. (Illus.). 1971. Repr. of 1951 ed. lib. bdg. 26.50x (ISBN 0-8371-3845-0, RELM). Greenwood.

--Structure of Labor Markets: Wage & Labor Mobility in Theory & Practice. LC 73-109302. (Illus.). 1971. Repr. of 1951 ed. lib. bdg. 26.50x (ISBN 0-8371-3845-0, RELM). Greenwood.

Reynolds, Lloyd G. & Shister, Joseph. Job Horizons: Study of Job Satisfaction & Labor Mobility. Stein, Leon, ed. LC 77-70526. (Work Ser.). (Illus.). 1977. Repr. of 1949 ed. lib. bdg. 12.00x (ISBN 0-405-10194-5). Arno.

Tenebaum, Marcel. A Demographic Analysis of Interstate Labor Growth Rate Differentials: United States, 1890-1900 to 1940-1950. Bruchey, Stuart, ed. LC 76-54119. (Nineteen Seventy-Seven Dissertations Ser.). (Illus.). 1977. lib. bdg. 22.00x (ISBN 0-405-09930-4). Arno.

Van Hoek, F. J. Migration of High Level Manpower from Developing to Developed Countries. (Institute of Social Studies Publications Ser). (Orig.). 1970. pap. text ed. 6.70x (ISBN 90-2791-623-3). Mouton.

White, Harrison C. Chains of Opportunity: System Models of Mobility in Organizations. LC 78-105374. 1970. 22.50x (ISBN 0-674-10674-1). Harvard U Pr.

LABOR MOBILITY-AFRICA

Bourdieu, Pierre, et al. Travail et Travailleurs En Algerie. (Recherches Mediterraneennes Documents). 1963. pap. text ed. 40.50x (ISBN 90-279-6224-3). Mouton.

Mabogunje, Akin L. Regional Mobility & Resource Development in West Africa. (Keith Callard Lectures Ser.). 160p. 1972. 5.00 (ISBN 0-7735-0120-7); pap. 2.50 (ISBN 0-7735-0129-0). McGill-Queens U Pr.

LABOR MOBILITY-GREAT BRITAIN

Mackay, D. I. Geographical Mobility & the Brain Drain: A Case Study of Aberdeen University Graduates, 1860-1960. 1970. 12.00 (ISBN 0-8426-1362-5). Verry.

LABOR NEGOTIATIONS

see Arbitration, Industrial; Collective Bargaining

LABOR ORGANIZATIONS

see Gilds; Trade-Unions

LABOR OUTPUT

see Labor Productivity

LABOR PARTY (GREAT BRITAIN)

see Labour Party (Great Britain)

LABOR POLICY

see also Labor Laws and Legislation; Manpower Policy

Bernstein, Irving. The New Deal Collective Bargaining Policy. LC 75-8997. (FDR & the Era of the New Deal Ser.). xi, 178p. 1975. Repr. of 1950 ed. lib. bdg. 20.00 (ISBN 0-306-70703-9). Da Capo.

Carmichael, John, Jr. & Bulmer, Charles. Labor & Employment Policy. (Orig.). 1979. pap. 5.00 (ISBN 0-918592-35-6). Policy Studies.

Chaim, Bezalel V. Francis Parker Yockey's Imperium & the Program of the U. S. Labor Party: A Comparative Analysis of Hamiltonian Economic & Political Philosophies. 1980. lib. bdg. 44.95 (ISBN 0-686-59575-0). Revisionist Pr.

Cohen, Sanford. Issues in Labor Policy. new ed. (Economics). 1977. pap. text ed. 11.95 (ISBN 0-675-08517-9). Merrill.

Collins, Doreen. Social Policy of the European Economic Community. LC 75-22282. 286p. 1975. 30.95 (ISBN 0-470-16583-9). Halsted Pr.

Deutscher, Isaac. Soviet Trade Unions: Their Place in Soviet Labour Policy. LC 73-837. (Russian Studies: Perspectives on the Revolution Ser.). 156p. 1973. Repr. of 1950 ed. 16.00 (ISBN 0-88355-033-4). Hyperion Conn.

Frankel, Jonathan. Prophecy & Politics: Socialism, Nationalism & the Russian Jews 1862-1917. LC 80-14414. (Illus.). 665p. 1981. 49.50 (ISBN 0-521-23028-4). Cambridge U Pr.

Horowitz, Ruth L. Political Ideologies of Organized Labor: The New Deal Era. LC 76-58229. 260p. 1978. text ed. 19.95 (ISBN 0-87855-208-1). Transaction Bks.

Jackson, Gordon E. How to Stay Union Free. LC 78-61773. 1978. 8.95 (ISBN 0-686-14631-X). Management Pr.

LaFollette, Robert M., ed. The Making of America: Labor. LC 72-89744. (American Labor, from Conspiracy to Collective Bargaining, Ser. 1). 433p. 1969. Repr. of 1906 ed. 23.00 (ISBN 0-405-02132-1). Arno.

McClure, Arthur F. The Truman Administration & the Problems of Postwar Labor 1945-1948. LC 68-57718. 267p. 1969. 15.00 (ISBN 0-8386-6999-9). Fairleigh Dickinson.

Martin, George. Madam Secretary: Frances Perkins. 1976. 16.95 (ISBN 0-395-24293-2). HM.

Mills, Daniel Q. Government, Labor & Inflation: Wage Stabilization in the United States. LC 75-9685. viii, 312p. 1976. lib. bdg. 16.50x (ISBN 0-226-52951-7). U of Chicago Pr.

Panitch, L. Social Democracy & Industrial Militancy. LC 75-16869. (Illus.). 306p. 1976. 34.95 (ISBN 0-521-20779-7). Cambridge U Pr.

Perlman, Richard. Labor Theory. LC 80-12286. 250p. 1981. Repr. of 1969 ed. lib. bdg. write for info. (ISBN 0-89874-163-7). Krieger.

Ruiz, Ramon Eduardo. Labor & the Ambivalent Revolutionaries: Mexico 1911-1923. LC 75-29087. 154p. 1976. 12.00x (ISBN 0-8018-1728-5). Johns Hopkins.

Taira, Koji. Economic Development & the Labor Market in Japan. LC 78-111459. (Studies of the East Asian Institute Ser). 1970. 17.50x (ISBN 0-231-03272-2). Columbia U Pr.

Warne, Frank J. The Workers at War. LC 74-22762. (Labor Movement in Fiction & Non-Fiction). Repr. of 1920 ed. 20.00 (ISBN 0-404-58515-9). AMS Pr.

Watkins, Gordon S. Labor Problems & Labor Administration in the United States During the World War. 15.50 (ISBN 0-384-66000-2). Johnson Repr.

LABOR PRODUCTIVITY

see also Machinery in Industry; Production Standards

Adam, Nabil R. & Dogramaci, Ali, eds. Productivity Analysis at the Organizational Level. (Productivity Analysis Studies). 192p. 1981. lib. bdg. 21.00 (ISBN 0-89838-038-3, Pub. by Martinus Nijhoff). Kluwer Boston.

Alexander Hamilton Institute, Inc. Como Aumentar a Productividade. Jenks, James M., ed. (Illus.). 69p. (Span.). 1979. pap. 58.75 (ISBN 0-86604-025-0). Hamilton Inst.

--Como Aumentar la Productividad. Jenks, James M., ed. (Illus.). 77p. (Orig., Span.). 1977. pap. 47.75 (ISBN 0-86604-024-2). Hamilton Inst.

Bergson, Abram. Productivity & the Social System - The USSR & the West. LC 77-15493. 1978. 17.50x (ISBN 0-674-71165-3). Harvard U Pr.

Bhattasali, B. N. Productivity & Economic Development. LC 76-186285. 121p. 1972. 11.75 (ISBN 92-833-1015-2, APO 60, APO). Unipub.

Blake, Robert R. & Mouton, Jane S. Productivity & Creativity: A Social Dynamics Approach. 143p. 1981. 9.95 (ISBN 0-8144-5692-8). Am Mgmt.

Bodkin, Ronald G. Wage-Price-Productivity Nexus. LC 64-24502. 1966. 10.00x (ISBN 0-8122-7470-9). U of Pa Pr.

Buehler, Vernon M. & Shetty, Y. Krishna, eds. Productivity Improvement: Case Studies of Proven Practice. 304p. 1981. 19.95 (ISBN 0-8144-5701-0). Am Mgmt.

Burnham, Donald C. Productivity Improvement. LC 72-97978. (Benjamin Fairless Memorial Lectures Ser). 73p. 1973. 7.50x (ISBN 0-231-03755-4). Columbia U Pr.

Carvajal, Manuel J., ed. Population Growth & Human Productivity. LC 75-39576. 1976. 8.25 (ISBN 0-8130-0553-1). U Presses Fla.

Chorafas, Dimitris N. Office Automation: The Productivity Challenge. (Illus.). 304p. 1982. text ed. 24.95 (ISBN 0-13-631028-1). P-H.

Communication Strategies for Productivity Improvement. 236p. 1980. 24.50 (ISBN 92-833-1053-5, APO 86, APO). Unipub.

Conference On Research In Income And Wealth. Output, Input & Productivity Measurement. (Studies in Income & Wealth: No. 25). 1961. 16.00x (ISBN 0-87014-181-3, Dist. by Princeton U Pr). Natl Bur Econ Res.

Cummings, Thomas G. & Molloy, Edmond S. Improving Productivity & the Quality of Work Life. LC 76-24348. (Praeger Special Studies). 1977. text ed. 29.95 (ISBN 0-275-56870-9); pap. 10.95 (ISBN 0-03-022601-5). Praeger.

Dessler, Gary. Human Behavior: Improving Productivity at Work. (Illus.). 480p. 1980. text ed. 19.95 (ISBN 0-8359-2994-9); instrs' manual avail. Reston.

Eilon, Samuel, et al. Applied Productivity Analysis for Industry. 206p. 1976. text ed. 30.00 (ISBN 0-08-020507-0); pap. text ed. 17.50 (ISBN 0-08-020506-2). Pergamon.

Fabricant, Solomon. Employment in Manufacturing, 1899-1939: An Analysis of Its Relation to the Volume of Production. LC 75-19711. (National Bureau of Economic Research Ser.). (Illus.). 1975. Repr. 21.00x (ISBN 0-405-07591-X). Arno.

--A Primer on Productivity. 7.50 (ISBN 0-8446-0616-2). Peter Smith.

Fein, Mitchell. Rational Approaches to Raising Productivity. 1974. pap. text ed. 10.00 (ISBN 0-89806-029-X, 26). Am Inst Indus Eng.

Fuchs, Victor R., ed. Production & Productivity in the Service Industries. (Studies in Income & Wealth Ser.: No. 34). 208p. 1975. Repr. of 1969 ed. 17.50x (ISBN 0-87014-489-8, Dist. by Columbia U Pr). Natl Bur Econ Res.

Galenson, Walter. Labor Productivity in Soviet & American Industry. LC 76-49596. 1977. Repr. of 1955 ed. lib. bdg. 18.00x (ISBN 0-8371-9370-2, GALPS). Greenwood.

Gellerman, Saul W. Motivation & Productivity. LC 63-16332. 1963. 15.95 (ISBN 0-8144-5084-9). Am Mgmt.

Goldmark, Josephine & Hopkins, Mary D. Comparison of an Eight-Hour Plant & a Ten-Hour Plant: U.S. Public Health Bulletin, No. 106. Stein, Leon, ed. LC 77-70495. (Work Ser.). 1977. Repr. of 1920 ed. lib. bdg. 15.00x (ISBN 0-405-10168-6). Arno.

Greenberg, Leon. A Practical Guide to Productivity Measurement. LC 73-75981. 78p. 1973. pap. 5.00 (ISBN 0-87179-190-0). BNA.

A Guide to Worker Productivity Experiments in the United States, 1971-1975. 186p. 1981. 17.50 (ISBN 0-86670-003-X). Moffat Pub.

Haggard, Howard W. & Greenberg, Leon A. Diet & Physical Efficiency: Influence of Frequency of Meals Upon Physical Efficiency & Industrial Productivity. Stein, Leon, ed. LC 77-70500. (Work Ser.). (Illus.). 1977. lib. bdg. 15.00x (ISBN 0-405-10171-6). Arno.

Heaton, Herbert. Productivity in Service Organizations: Organizing for People. (Illus.). 1977. 16.95 (ISBN 0-07-027705-2, P&RB). McGraw.

Hinrichs, John R. Practical Management for Productivity. 1978. 15.95 (ISBN 0-442-20370-5). Van Nos Reinhold.

Houery, N. Mesurer la Productivite: Les Comptes de Surplus. 160p. (Fr.). 1979. pns (M-6320). French & Eur.

Ingle, Sud. Quality Circles Master Guide: Increasing Productivity with People Power. 224p. 1981. 24.95 (ISBN 0-13-745018-4); pap. text ed. 14.95 (ISBN 0-13-745000-1). P-H.

Kendrick, John W. Productivity Trends in the United States. LC 75-19715. (National Bureau of Economic Research Ser.). (Illus.). 1975. Repr. 38.00x (ISBN 0-405-07595-2). Arno.

Kendrick, John W. & Vaccara, Beatrice N., eds. New Developments in Productivity Measurement & Analysis. LC 79-20399. (Studies in Income & Wealth: No. 44). 1980. lib. bdg. 52.00x (ISBN 0-226-43080-4). U of Chicago Pr.

Knox, Frank M. Managing Paperwork: The Key to Productivity. LC 80-19685. 1980. 16.95 (ISBN 0-444-00452-1, Thomond Pr). Elsevier.

Koch, H. William, Jr. Employee Handling Magic That Fires People up to Boost Company Profits. 1976. 74.50 (ISBN 0-13-274860-6). Exec Reports.

Levidow, Les & Young, Bob, eds. Science, Technology & the Labour Process. (Marxist Studies: Vol. 1). 1981. text ed. 31.25x (ISBN 0-906336-20-1, Pub. by CSE Bks England); pap. text ed. 10.50x (ISBN 0-906336-21-X, Pub. by CSE Bks England). Humanities.

Luke, Hugh D. Automation for Productivity. 298p. 1972. 16.50 (ISBN 0-471-55400-6, Pub. by Wiley). Krieger.

Mackenzie, Susan T. Noise & Office Work. (Key Issues Ser.: No. 19). 1975. pap. 3.00 (ISBN 0-87546-232-4). NY Sch Indus Rel.

Maximizing Employee Productivity. 1977. pap. 8.00 (ISBN 0-685-86704-8, P53277). Natl Ret Merch.

Measurement & Interpretation of Productivity. 1980. 18.00 (ISBN 0-309-02898-1). Natl Acad Pr.

Miller, R. B., ed. Participative Management: Quality of Worklife & Job Enrichment. LC 77-85661. (Management Review Ser.: No. 1). (Illus.). 1978. 18.00 (ISBN 0-8155-0683-X). Noyes.

Myers, Charles A., ed. Wages, Prices, Profits & Productivity. LC 59-12574. 1959. pap. 2.00 (ISBN 0-936904-07-0). Am Assembly.

Prasad, P. H. Growth with Full Employment. 51p. 1970. 3.00x (ISBN 0-8188-1155-2). Paragon.

Prendergast, Curtis, ed. Productivity: The Link to Economic & Social Progress. LC 76-19833. (Swedish-American Exchange of Views Ser.). 1976. pap. text ed. 3.50 (ISBN 0-89361-000-3). Work in Amer.

Productivity Measurement: A Symposium for the Seventies. LC 72-180945. 50p. 1971. 5.00x (ISBN 0-85292-029-6). Intl Pubns Serv.

Productivity, Quality of Working Life & Labour-Management Relations. 23p. 1976. 2.75 (ISBN 0-686-70977-2, APO62, APO). Unipub.

Ross, Joe. Productivity, People & Profits. 150p. 1981. text ed. 17.95 (ISBN 0-8359-5473-0); pap. 10.95 (ISBN 0-8359-5472-2). Reston.

Rubin, Irwin M., et al. Task-Oriented Team Development. (Illus.). 1978. 50.00 (ISBN 0-07-054197-3, T&D); 3-ring binder 75.00 (ISBN 0-07-054196-5); facilitator manual 15.00 (ISBN 0-07-054197-3). McGraw.

Rudman, Jack. Supervising Labor Specialist. (Career Examination Ser.: C-2382). (Cloth bdg. avail. on request). pap. 12.00 (ISBN 0-8373-2382-7). Natl Learning.

Salter, W. E. Productivity & Technical Change. (Cambridge Department of Applied Economics Monographs: No. 6). (Illus.). 1969. pap. 12.95x (ISBN 0-521-09568-9). Cambridge U Pr.

Seddon, David, ed. Relations of Production: Marxist Approaches to Economic Anthropology. 414p. 1978. 29.50x (ISBN 0-7146-3000-4, F Cass Co); pap. 11.50x (ISBN 0-7146-4024-7). Biblio Dist.

Sen, Amartya K. Choice of Techniques: An Aspect of the Theory of Planned Economic Development. 3rd ed. LC 68-3220. 1968. 12.50x (ISBN 0-678-06266-8). Kelley.

Shapiro, Eli & White, William L., eds. Capital for Productivity & Jobs. 1977. 11.95 (ISBN 0-13-113498-1); pap. 5.95 (ISBN 0-13-113480-9). Am Assembly.

Siegel, Irving. Productivity Measurement: An Evolving Art, Vol. 16. (Studies in Productivity-Highlights of the Literature). (Orig.). 1980. pap. 25.00 (ISBN 0-89361-023-2). Work in Amer.

Siegel, Irving H. Company Productivity: Measurement for Improvement. LC 80-11930. 1980. pap. text ed. 3.50 (ISBN 0-911558-60-8). Upjohn Inst.

Smith, I. G. The Measurement of Productivity. 1973. 21.00x (ISBN 0-8464-0623-3). Beekman Pubs.

Staff of Didactic Systems. Planning & Assigning Work. (Study Units Ser.). 1978. pap. 9.00 (ISBN 0-89401-121-9). Didactic Syst.

Stern, David. The Art of Full Employment. 200p. 1981. 19.95 (ISBN 0-86569-097-9). Auburn Hse.

Studies in Productivity Series: Highlights of the Literature. (Entire series). write for info. (ISBN 0-89361-006-2). Work in Amer.

Suojanen, Waino W., et al, eds. Perspectives on Job Enrichment & Productivity. LC 75-31553. 276p. 1975. pap. 9.95 (ISBN 0-88406-008-X). Ga St U Busn Pub.

Survey of Workers: Attitude Toward Productivity. Date not set. pap. 10.00 (ISBN 0-89834-026-8). Chamber Comm US.

Sutermeister. People & Productivity. 3rd ed. (Management Ser). 1976. text ed. 15.50 (ISBN 0-07-062367-8, C); pap. text ed. 10.95 (ISBN 0-07-062371-6). McGraw.

Titus, Parvin S. & Graham, Ben S., Jr. The Amazing Oversight: Total Participation for Productivity. LC 79-10070. 1979. 13.95 (ISBN 0-8144-5510-7). Am Mgmt.

Ullmann, John E., ed. The Improvement of Productivity: Myths & Realities. 24.95 (ISBN 0-03-055301-6). Praeger.

U.S. House of Representatives, Committee on Labor, Sixty-Third Congress. The Stop Watch & Bonus System in Government Work: Proceedings. Stein, Leon, ed. LC 77-70542. (Work Ser.). 1977. Repr. of 1914 ed. lib. bdg. 12.00x (ISBN 0-405-10211-9). Arno.

Vernon, Horace M. Industrial Fatigue & Efficiency. Stein, Leon, ed. LC 77-70543. (Work Ser.). (Illus.). 1977. Repr. of 1921 ed. lib. bdg. 18.00x (ISBN 0-405-10212-7). Arno.

Voydanoff, Patricia. Implications of Work-Family Relationships for Productivity, Vol. 13. (Studies in Productivity-Highlights of the Literature). (Orig.). 1980. pap. 25.00 (ISBN 0-89361-020-8). Work in Amer.

Wage Increases & Labour Productivity in Japanese Smaller Business. 34p. 1972. 2.75 (ISBN 0-686-70985-3, APO11, APO). Unipub.

Yarrington, Roger, ed. Employee Training for Productivity. (Orig.). 1980. pap. 5.00 (ISBN 0-87117-102-3). Am Assn Comm Jr Coll.

LABOR PRODUCTIVITY-ACCOUNTING

see Productivity Accounting

LABOR PRODUCTIVITY-BIBLIOGRAPHY

Kubr, Milan, et al, eds. Management, Administration & Productivity: International Directory of Institutions & Information Sources. 2nd ed. xiii, 305p. (Orig., Eng., Fr., Span.). 1981. pap. 18.55 (ISBN 92-2-002468-3). Intl Labour Office.

U. S. Bureau of Labor Statistics. Productivity: A Bibliography, November, 1957. Spatz, Laura, ed. LC 75-16611. 182p. 1975. Repr. of 1958 ed. lib. bdg. 15.25x (ISBN 0-8371-8255-7, SPPR). Greenwood.

Work in America Insititute. Work in America Institute Studies in Productivity Highlights of the Literature, 6 bks. Incl. Bk. 1. Mid-Career Perspectives: The Middle-Aged & Older Population. LC 78-51006 (ISBN 0-89361-011-9); Bk. 2. Productivity & the Quality of Working Life. LC 78-51009 (ISBN 0-89361-014-3); Bk. 3. Trends in Product Quality & Worker Attitude. LC 78-51012 (ISBN 0-89361-016-X); Bk. 4. Managerial Productivity. LC 78-51010 (ISBN 0-89361-010-0); Bk. 5. Worker Alienation. LC 78-51011 (ISBN 0-89361-017-8); Bk. 6. Human Resource Accounting. LC 78-51007 (ISBN 0-89361-008-9). 1978. Set. 110.00 (ISBN 0-686-67163-5); 25.00 ea. Work in Amer.

LABOR PRODUCTIVITY-GREAT BRITAIN

Pratten, C. F. Labour Productivity Differentials Within International Companies. LC 76-8294. (Department of Applied Economics. Occasional Papers: No. 50). (Illus.). 1976. pap. 15.95x (ISBN 0-521-29102-X). Cambridge U Pr.

LABOR RELATIONS

see Industrial Relations

LABOR REPRESENTATION IN REGULATION OF INDUSTRY

see Employees' Representation in Management

LABOR SUPPLY

see also Absenteeism (Labor); Children-Employment; Employment Agencies; Human Capital; Job Vacancies; Labor Mobility; Manpower; Manpower Policy; Occupational Retraining; Unemployed; World War, 1939-1945-Manpower; Youth-Employment

Adams, Leonard P. & Aronson, Robert L. Workers & Industrial Change. LC 73-22502. (Cornell Studies in Industrial & Labour Relations, Vol. 8). (Illus.). 209p. 1974. Repr. of 1957 ed. lib. bdg. 15.00 (ISBN 0-8371-6373-0, ADIC). Greenwood.

Altman, Ralph. Availability for Work, a Study in Unemployment Compensation. LC 68-8935. (Illus.). 1968. Repr. of 1950 ed. lib. bdg. 17.25x (ISBN 0-8371-0004-6, ALAW). Greenwood.

Anderson, Terry L. The Economic Growth of Seventeenth Century New England: A Measurement of Regional Income. LC 75-2574. (Dissertations in American Economic History). (Illus.). 1975. 16.00x (ISBN 0-405-07255-4). Arno.

Ashenfelter, Orley C. & Oates, Wallace, eds. Essays in Labor Market Analysis. LC 77-9421. 229p. 1978. 46.95 (ISBN 0-470-99222-0). Halsted Pr.

Bancroft, Gertrude. American Labor Force: Its Growth & Changing Composition. LC 73-86717. (Census Monograph). (Illus.). xvi, 256p. 1975. Repr. of 1958 ed. 18.00 (ISBN 0-8462-1760-0). Russell.

Basche, James R., Jr. & Duerr, Michael G. Experience with Foreign Production Work Forces. (Report Ser.: No. 661). 35p. (Orig.). 1975. pap. 15.00 (ISBN 0-8237-0080-1). Conference Bd.

Berg, Ivar, ed. Sociological Perspectives on Labor Markets. (Quantitative Studies in Social Relations). 1981. 31.00 (ISBN 0-12-089650-8). Acad Pr.

Berg, Mark R., et al. Jobs & Energy in Michigan: The Next Twenty Years. LC 80-24884. (Illus.). 210p. 1981. 19.95 (ISBN 0-87944-264-6); pap. 11.95 (ISBN 0-87944-263-8). Inst Soc Res.

Beveridge, William H. Causes & Cures of Unemployment. LC 76-9030. 1976. Repr. of 1931 ed. lib. bdg. 15.50x (ISBN 0-8371-8893-8, BEVCC). Greenwood.

Birks, J. S. & Sinclair, C. A. Arab Manpower. LC 80-12416. 450p. 1980. 45.00 (ISBN 0-312-04708-8). St Martin.

Brown, C. V. Taxation & the Incentive to Work. (Illus.). 128p. 1980. 29.95x (ISBN 0-19-877134-7); pap. 11.95x (ISBN 0-19-877135-5). Oxford U Pr.

Brown, C. V., ed. Taxation & Labour Supply. (Illus.). 304p. 1981. text ed. 35.00x (ISBN 0-04-336073-4). Allen Unwin.

Cain, Glen G. & Watts, Harold W., eds. Income Maintenance & Labor Supply. 1973. 22.50 (ISBN 0-12-154950-X). Acad Pr.

Clark, Harold F. Economic Theory & Correct Occupational Distribution. Stein, Leon, ed. LC 77-70488. (Work Ser.). 1977. Repr. of 1931 ed. lib. bdg. 14.00x (ISBN 0-405-10160-0). Arno.

Committee of the President's Conference on Unemployment. Business Cycles & Unemployment: Proceedings. LC 75-19697. (National Bureau of Economic Research Ser.). (Illus.). 1975. Repr. 25.00x (ISBN 0-405-07577-4). Arno.

Disadvantaged Groups on the Labour Market & Measures to Assist Them. (Document Ser.). 70p. 1979. 4.50x (ISBN 92-64-12012-2). OECD.

Doeringer, Peter B. & Piore, Michael J. Internal Labor Markets & Manpower Analysis. 1971. 13.95 (ISBN 0-669-63529-4). Lexington Bks.

Durand, J. B. Labor Force in the United States (1890-1960) (Demographic Monographs Ser.). 1968. 44.50x (ISBN 0-677-01550-X). Gordon.

Durand, John D. The Labor Force in Economic Development: A Comparison of International Census Data, 1946-1966. LC 75-2988. 288p. 1975. 19.50x (ISBN 0-691-04207-1). Princeton U Pr.

Easterlin, Richard A. Population, Labor Force & Long Swings in Economic Growth: The American Experience. (General Ser: No. 86). (Illus.). 1968. 15.00x (ISBN 0-87014-474-X, Dist. by Columbia U Pr). Natl Bur Econ Res.

Editorial Research Reports on Jobs for Americans. LC 77-18994. 1978. pap. text ed. 6.95 (ISBN 0-87187-120-3). Congr Quarterly.

Ginzberg, Eli. Good Jobs, Bad Jobs, No Jobs. LC 79-10706. 1979. 15.00x (ISBN 0-674-35710-8). Harvard U Pr.

--Human Resources: The Wealth of a Nation. LC 73-9263. 183p. 1973. Repr. of 1958 ed. lib. bdg. 15.00x (ISBN 0-8371-6999-2, GIHR). Greenwood.

--Manpower Agenda for America. 1968. 8.50 (ISBN 0-07-023278-4, C). McGraw.

Gordon, David M. The Working Poor: Towards a State Agenda. Barker, Michael, ed. LC 79-67382. (Studies in State Development Policy: Vol. 4). 1980. pap. 8.95 (ISBN 0-934842-03-5). Coun State Plan.

Gordon, Margaret S. Employment Expansion & Population Growth: The California Experience. LC 76-5893. 192p. 1976. Repr. of 1954 ed. lib. bdg. 14.75x (ISBN 0-8371-8805-9, GOEE). Greenwood.

Greenfield, Harry I. Manpower & the Growth of Producer Services. LC 66-28265. 144p. 1967. 20.00x (ISBN 0-231-03028-2). Columbia U Pr.

Groat, H. Theodore, et al. Labor Force Participation & Family Formation Among Currently Married Women 15-44 Years of Age. Olmstead, Mary, ed. (United States Ser.: No. 9). 1981. pap. text ed. 1.75 (ISBN 0-8406-0233-2). Natl Ctr Health Stats.

Hansen, Niles M. Improving Access to Economic Opportunity: Nonmetropolitan Labor Markets in an Urban Society. LC 75-38800. 280p. 1976. text ed. 16.50 (ISBN 0-88410-289-0). Ballinger Pub.

Hellinger, Stephen H. & Hellinger, Douglas A. Unemployment & the Multinationals: A Strategy for Technological Change in Latin America. 1976. 13.95 (ISBN 0-8046-9126-6, National University Pub). Kennikat.

Herman, Bohuslav. The Optimal International Division of Labour: A WEP Study. 1975. 17.10 (ISBN 92-2-101286-7); pap. 11.40 (ISBN 92-2-101285-9). Intl Labour Office.

Hiestand, Dale L. Economic Growth & Employment Opportunities for Minorities. LC 64-20359. 127p. 1964. 17.50x (ISBN 0-231-02729-X). Columbia U Pr.

Hiestand, Dale L. & Morse, Dean W. Comparative Metropolitan Employment Complexes: New York, Chicago, los Angeles, Houston & Atlanta. LC 77-84456. (Conservation of Human Resources Ser.: No. 7). 141p. 1979. text ed. 21.50x (ISBN 0-916672-82-4). Allanheld.

Jakubauskas, Edward B. & Palomba, Neil A. Manpower Economics. LC 79-186208. 1973. text ed. 15.95 (ISBN 0-201-03284-8). A-W.

Keeley, Michael C. Labor Supply & Public Policy: A Critical Review. LC 80-2338. (Studies in Labor Economics Ser.). 1981. 22.50 (ISBN 0-12-403920-0). Acad Pr.

Kerr, Clark. Labor Markets & Wage Determination: The Balkanization of Labor Markets & Other Essays. LC 75-17291. 1977. 18.50x (ISBN 0-520-03070-2). U of Cal Pr.

Knox, Francis. Labour Supply in Economic Development. 1979. text ed. 31.25x (ISBN 0-566-00238-8, Pub. by Gower Pub Co England). Renouf.

Krumm, Ronald J. The Impact of the Minimum Wage on Regional Labor Markets. 1981. 11.25 (ISBN 0-8447-3425-X); pap. 4.25 (ISBN 0-8447-3426-8). Am Enterprise.

Labour Force Estimates & Projections, 1950-2000: Asia, Africa, Latin America, Europe, Northern America, Oceania, USSR, World Summary; Methodological Supplement, Pts. 1-6. 1977. 45.60 (ISBN 9-2210-1672-2). Intl Labour Office.

Lenderink, R. S. & Siebrand, J. C. A Disequalibrium of the Labour Market. 1979. text ed. 19.00x (ISBN 90-237-2277-9, Pub. by Gower Pub Co England). Renouf.

Lester, Richard A. Manpower Planning in a Free Society. 244p. 1966. 18.00 (ISBN 0-691-04143-1); pap. 6.95 (ISBN 0-691-00355-6). Princeton U Pr.

Levitan, Sar & Belous, Richard. Shorter Hours, Shorter Weeks: Spreading the Work to Reduce Unemployment. LC 77-4787. (Policy Studies in Employment & Welfare: No. 30). (Illus.). 1977. pap. text ed. 4.50x (ISBN 0-8018-1999-7). Johns Hopkins.

Levitan, Sar A. & Taggart, Robert, 3rd. Employment & Earnings Inadequacy: A New Social Indicator. LC 74-6831. (Policy Studies in Employment & Welfare: No. 19). (Illus.). 128p. 1974. 9.00x (ISBN 0-8018-1623-8); pap. 3.50x (ISBN 0-8018-1624-6). Johns Hopkins.

Levitan, Sar A., et al. Human Resources & Labor Markets: Labor & Manpower in the American Economy. 2nd ed. 631p. 1976. text ed. 24.50 scp (ISBN 0-06-043999-8, HarpC). Har-Row.

Maddox, James G. The Advancing South: Manpower Prospects & Problems. Repr. of 1967 ed. 8.00 (ISBN 0-527-02827-4). Kraus Repr.

Mesics, Emil A. Education & Training for Effective Manpower Utilization: An Annotated Bibliography. (Bibliography Ser.: No. 9). 1969. pap. 2.50 (ISBN 0-87546-023-2). NY Sch Indus Rel.

Mieszkowski, P. & Peterson, G., eds. Public Sector Lavor Markets. 216p. 1981. pap. 10.00 (ISBN 0-87766-285-1, 29100). Urban Inst.

Mitchell, Daniel J. B. Labor Issues of American International Trade & Investment. LC 76-7052. (Policy Studies in Employment & Welfare: No. 24). (Illus.). 128p. 1976. 8.50x (ISBN 0-8018-1848-6); pap. 3.95x (ISBN 0-8018-1849-4). Johns Hopkins.

Myers, Charles A. & Schultz, George P. The Dynamics of a Labor Market: A Study the Impact of Employment Changes on Labor Mobility, Job Satisfactions, & Company & Union Policies. LC 75-36100. 219p. 1976. Repr. of 1951 ed. lib. bdg. 16.25x (ISBN 0-8371-8620-X, MYLM). Greenwood.

Organization for Economic Cooperation & Development. Statistics of the Occupational & Educational Structure of the Labour Force in 53 Countries. bilingual ed. 288p. 1969. 7.00x (ISBN 0-686-14806-1). OECD.

Orr, Larry L. Income, Employment & Urban Residential Location. (Institute for Research on Poverty Monograph Ser). 1975. 12.00 (ISBN 0-12-528440-3). Acad Pr.

Perlman, Mark, ed. Human Resources in the Urban Economy: Papers Presented at a Conference of the Human Resources Sub-Committee of the Committee on Urban Economics, Resources for the Future, (1962) Plus an Earlier Working Paper. LC 76-2041. 265p. 1976. Repr. of 1963 ed. lib. bdg. 21.00x (ISBN 0-8371-8756-7, PEHR). Greenwood.

Peterson, Wallace C. Income, Employment & Economic Growth. 3rd ed. (Illus.). 500p. 1974. text ed. 10.95x (ISBN 0-393-09279-8). Norton.

Pierson, John H. Full Employment Without Inflation. LC 79-5446. 254p. 1980. text ed. 18.50 (ISBN 0-916672-39-5). Allanheld.

Piore, Michael J. Birds of Passage: Migrant Labor & Industrial Societies. LC 78-12067. (Illus.). 192p. 1980. pap. 6.95 (ISBN 0-521-28058-3). Cambridge U Pr.

Pissarides, C. A. Labour Market Adjustment. LC 75-21035. 1976. 44.50 (ISBN 0-521-21064-X). Cambridge U Pr.

Rees, Albert & Shultz, George P. Workers & Wages in an Urban Labor Market. LC 75-110114. (Studies in Business & Society Ser). 1970. 12.50x (ISBN 0-226-70705-9). U of Chicago Pr.

Rima, Ingrid. Labor Markets, Wages, & Employment. (Illus.). 1980. 14.95 (ISBN 0-393-95058-1). Norton.

Rodgers, John M. State Estimates of Outputs, Employment & Payrolls 1947, 1958, 1963. LC 72-5759. (Multiregional Input-Output Study: Vol. 2). (Illus.). 1972. 25.95 (ISBN 0-669-73494-2). Lexington Bks.

Schofer, Lawrence. The Formation of a Modern Labor Force: Upper Silesia 1865-1914. LC 73-90658. 1975. 24.00x (ISBN 0-520-02651-9). U of Cal Pr.

Schultz, T. W. Investment in Human Capital. LC 77-122273. 1971. 14.95 (ISBN 0-02-928220-9). Free Pr.

Smith, A. D. Concepts of Labour Force Underutilization. (Employment Research Papers). 1972. 3.40 (ISBN 92-2-100108-3). Intl Labour Office.

Smith, Allen W. Understanding Inflation & Unemployment. 2nd ed. LC 75-29492. 176p. 1981. text ed. 15.95x (ISBN 0-88229-276-5); pap. text ed. 7.95x (ISBN 0-88229-492-X). Nelson-Hall.

Stanback, Thomas M. & Knight, Richard V. Metropolitan Economy. LC 77-133492. 1970. 20.00x (ISBN 0-231-03426-1). Columbia U Pr.

Strong, Merle E., ed. Developing the Nation's Work Force. (AVA Yearbook Ser.: 5). 347p. 1975. 10.00 (ISBN 0-89514-018-7, 01975). Am Voc Assn.

Structural Determinants of Employment & Unemployment, Vol. II. (Document Ser.). 344p. 1979. 18.75x (ISBN 92-64-11940-X). OECD.

Swanson, Gordon I. & Michaelson, Jon, eds. Manpower Research & Labor Economics. LC 79-11162. 332p. 1979. 22.50 (ISBN 0-8039-1268-4); pap. 12.50 (ISBN 0-8039-1269-2). Sage.

Taylor, Milton & Peppard, Donald. Jobs for the Jobless: Detroit's Unresolved Dilemma. 1975. 2.50 (ISBN 0-686-16217-X). MSU-Inst Comm Devel.

Tenebaum, Marcel. A Demographic Analysis of Interstate Labor Growth Rate Differentials: United States, 1890-1900 to 1940-1950. Bruchey, Stuart, ed. LC 76-54119. (Nineteen Seventy-Seven Dissertations Ser.). (Illus.). 1977. lib. bdg. 22.00x (ISBN 0-405-09930-4). Arno.

Thomas, Barry & Deaton, David. Labour Shortage & Economic Analysis: A Study of Occupational Labour Markets. (Warwick Studies in Industrial Relations Ser.). 220p. 1977. 36.00x (ISBN 0-631-18310-8, Pub by Basil Blackwell England). Biblio Dist.

Thompson, Wilbur R. & Mattila, John M. An Econometric Model of Postwar State Industrial Development. LC 73-9132. (Illus.). 716p. 1973. Repr. of 1959 ed. lib. bdg. 15.00x (ISBN 0-8371-6988-7, THEC). Greenwood.

Trebous, Madeleine. Migration & Development, the Case of Algeria. 244p. 1970. 4.00x (ISBN 0-686-14668-9). OECD.

U. S. Department of Health, Education, & Welfare. Work in America: Report of a Special Task Force to the Secretary of Health, Education, & Welfare. 262p. 1973. pap. 4.95 (ISBN 0-262-58023-3). MIT Pr.

Vincens, Jean & Robinson, Derek. Research into Labour Market Behaviour. 148p. 1974. 4.50x (ISBN 92-64-11203-0). OECD.

Weintraub, Sidney. Capitalism's Inflation & Unemployment Crisis. LC 77-73955. (Economics Ser.). (Illus.). 7.95 (ISBN 0-201-08502-X). A-W.

Williams, Gareth, et al. The Academic Labour Market: Economic & Social Aspects of a Profession. LC 73-85231. (Studies on Education Ser: Vol. 3). (Illus.). 566p. 1974. 18.95 (ISBN 0-444-41154-2). Elsevier.

Woytinsky, W. S., et al. Employment & Wages in the United States. LC 75-22869. (America in Two Centuries Ser). 1976. Repr. of 1953 ed. 49.00x (ISBN 0-405-07734-3). Arno.

Yoder, Dale. Demands for Labor: Opportunities for Research. LC 49-7101. 1948. pap. 1.00 (ISBN 0-527-03297-2). Kraus Repr.

Zopf, Paul E., Jr. A Demographic & Occupational Profile of State Planning Region G. LC 74-20614. 325p. 1974. pap. text ed. 4.00 (ISBN 0-89055-111-1). Carolina Pop Ctr.

LABOR SUPPLY–AFRICA

Doxey, G. V. The Industrial Colour Bar in South Africa. LC 73-11865. 205p. 1974. Repr. of 1961 ed. lib. bdg. 15.00x (ISBN 0-8371-7099-0, DOCB). Greenwood.

Sanyal, Bikas C., et al. Higher Education & the Labour Market in Zambia: Expectations & Performance. (Illus.). 373p. 1976. pap. 15.00 (ISBN 92-803-1072-0, U286, UNESCO). Unipub.

LABOR SUPPLY–CANADA

Dodge, William. Skilled Labour Supply Imbalances: The Canadian Experience. LC 77-93071. 56p. 1977. 3.00 (ISBN 0-902594-31-1). Natl Planning.

Hartle, Douglas G. Employment Forecast Survey. LC 62-4588. (Canadian Studies in Economics). (Illus.). 1962. 7.50x (ISBN 0-8020-3075-0). U of Toronto Pr.

Menten, Theodore, ed. Ancient Egyptian Cut & Use Stencils. (Illus.). 1978. pap. 3.25 (ISBN 0-486-23626-9). Dover.

LABOR SUPPLY–GREAT BRITAIN

Bowers, J. The Anatomy of Regional Activity Rates. Bd. with Regional Social Accounts for the U.K. Woodward, V. H. (Economic & Social Research Ser. No. 1). 1971. 13.95 (ISBN 0-521-07719-2). Cambridge U Pr.

Webb, A. E. & Weeden, R. Unemployment, Vacancies & the Rate of Change of Earnings: Regional Rates of Growth of Employment. (National Inst. of Economic & Social Research, Regional Papers: No. 3). 1974. pap. 13.95 (ISBN 0-521-09895-5). Cambridge U Pr.

LABOR SUPPLY–INDIA

Agarwal, S. P. Manpower Demand. 1970. 13.25x (ISBN 0-8426-0238-0). Verry.

Bhardwaj, Ramesh C. Employment & Unemployment in India. LC 68-27099. 1969. text ed. 5.00x (ISBN 0-391-00631-2). Humanities.

LABOR SUPPLY–JAPAN

Abegglen, James C. The Japanese Factory. rev. ed. LC 80-52878. 200p. 1981. pap. 6.25 (ISBN 0-8048-1372-8). C E Tuttle.

Changes in Japan's Labour Market During High-Rate Economic Growth. (Productivity Ser.: No. 9). (Illus.). 1976. pap. 5.50 (ISBN 92-833-3001-3, APO 15, APO). Unipub.

LABOR SUPPLY–PERU

Payne, James L. Labor & Politics in Peru. LC 65-22335. 1980. Repr. of 1965 ed. 9.00 (ISBN 0-915728-05-2). Lytton Pub.

LABOR SUPPLY–PUERTO RICO

Holbik, Karel & Swan, Philip L. Industrialization & Employment in Puerto Rico, 1950-1972. (Studies in Latin American Business: No. 16). (Orig.). 1975. pap. 4.00 (ISBN 0-87755-208-8). U of Tex Busn Res.

LABOR SUPPLY–TURKEY

Paine, Suzanne. Exporting Workers. LC 74-19528. (Department of Applied Economics, Occasional Papers Ser.: No. 41). 224p. 1974. 34.95 (ISBN 0-521-20631-6); pap. 15.95x (ISBN 0-521-09879-3). Cambridge U Pr.

Robinson, Richard D. High-Level Manpower in Economic Development: The Turkish Case. LC 67-25400. (Middle Eastern Monographs Ser: No. 17). 5.95x (ISBN 0-674-39050-4). Harvard U Pr.

LABOR TURNOVER

see also Employment Agencies; Employment Stabilization; Labor Mobility

Becker, Joseph. Experience Rating in Unemployment Insurance: An Experiment in Competitive Socialism. LC 72-4026. (Illus.). 419p. 1972. 25.00x (ISBN 0-8018-1429-4). Johns Hopkins.

Hinrichs, John R. Controlling Absenteeism & Turnover, Vol. 17. (Studies in Productivity-Highlights of the Literature). (Orig.). pap. 25.00 (ISBN 0-89361-024-0). Work in Amer.

Pettman, Barrie O., ed. Labour Turnover & Retention. LC 75-18452. 204p. 1976. 24.95 (ISBN 0-470-68448-8). Halsted Pr.

Price, James L. The Study of Turnover. 1977. text ed. 8.95x (ISBN 0-8138-1645-9). Iowa St U Pr.

Woytinsky, Wladimir S. Three Aspects of Labor Dynamics. LC 73-16650. (Illus.). 249p. 1974. Repr. of 1942 ed. lib. bdg. 15.00x (ISBN 0-8371-7215-2, WOLD). Greenwood.

LABOR-UNIONS

see Trade-Unions

LABORATORIES

see also Biological Laboratories; Chemical Laboratories; Chemical Engineering Laboratories; Language Laboratories; Medical Laboratories; Radioisotope Laboratories

Archenhold, W. F., et al. Social Science Laboratories: A Handbook of Design, Management & Organisation. 303p. 1980. 35.00x (ISBN 0-7195-3436-4, Pub. by Murray Pubs England). State Mutual Bk.

Armitage, Philip. Laboratory Safety: A Science Teacher's Source Book. 1977. pap. text ed. 6.50x (ISBN 0-435-57050-1). Heinemann Ed.

Berger, Melvin. Police Lab. LC 75-33198. (Illus.). 1976. PLB 9.89 (ISBN 0-381-99620-4, JD-J). Har-Row.

Bourne, John R. Laboratory Minicomputing. 1981. price not set (ISBN 0-12-119080-3). Acad Pr.

Cheney, Ray E. Equipment Specifications for High Schools, Their Use & Imporvement: A New Aproach. LC 73-176641. (Columbia University. Teachers College. Contributions to Education: No. 612). Repr. of 1934 ed. 17.50 (ISBN 0-404-55612-4). AMS Pr.

Commission for the European Communities, Directorate-General for Research, Science & Education, ed. Inventory of Major Research Facilities in the European Community, 2 vols. 1561p. 1977. text ed. 120.00 (ISBN 3-7940-3019-2, Pub. by K G Saur). Gale.

Conference on Clinically Oriented Documentation of Laboratory Data, Buffalo, 1971. Clinically Oriented Documentation of Laboratory Data. Gabrieli, E. R., ed. 1972. 47.00 (ISBN 0-12-271850-X). Acad Pr.

Creedy, John. A Laboratory Manual for Schools & Colleges. (Illus.). 1977. text ed. 34.00x (ISBN 0-435-57130-3). Heinemann Ed.

Fire Protection for Laboratories Using Chemicals. 1974. pap. 2.50 (ISBN 0-685-58204-3, 45-T). Natl Fire Prot.

Fuscaldo, Anthony A., et al, eds. Laboratory Safety: Theory & Practice. LC 80-762. 1980. 39.50 (ISBN 0-12-269980-7). Acad Pr.

Gadad, M. G. & Hiregoudar, H. R. Experimental Errors & Their Treatment. 220p. 1981. 20.00x (ISBN 0-86125-064-8, Pub. by Orient Longman India). State Mutual Bk.

Grover, F & Wallace, P. Laboratory Organization & Management. (Illus.). 1979. text ed. 19.95 (ISBN 0-408-70793-3). Butterworth.

Huston, Norman E., ed. Management Systems for Laboratory Instrument Services. 712p. 1980. pap. text ed. 35.00x (ISBN 0-87664-486-8). Instru Soc.

Safety Aspects of the Design & Equipment of Hot Laboratories. (Safety Ser.: No. 30). 1969. pap. 9.75 (ISBN 92-0-123069-9, ISP169, IAEA). Unipub.

Steere, Norman V. Handbook of Laboratory Safety, CRC. 2nd ed. LC 67-29478. (Handbook Ser). 1971. 59.95 (ISBN 0-8493-0352-4). CRC Pr.

Westlake, G., ed. Automation & Management in the Clinical Laboratory. (Illus.). 1975. 19.50 (ISBN 0-8391-0627-0). Univ Park.

LABORATORIES–APPARATUS AND SUPPLIES

Holum J. R. 5th ed. 182p. 1979. lab manual 10.95 (ISBN 0-471-04751-1). Wiley.

Lee, Leslie. Elementary Principles of Laboratory Instruments. 4th ed. LC 77-12913. (Illus.). 1978. text ed. 18.95 (ISBN 0-8016-2917-9). Mosby.

Morgan-Grampian Books, ed. Laboratory Equipment Directory, 1981. 250p. 1981. 75.00x (ISBN 0-686-75508-1, Pub. by Morgan-Grampian Bk). State Mutual Bk.

Taub, Howard. Basic Laboratory Skills for Laboratory Assistants: Measurements, Inventory of Supplies, Collecting Specimens, Specimen Processing, Media Preparation. (Illus.). 612p. 1980. spiral (lexotone) 38.00 (ISBN 0-398-04132-6). C C Thomas.

LABORATORIES, ATOMIC ENERGY RESEARCH

see Atomic Energy Research–Laboratories

LABORATORIES, BIOLOGICAL

see Biological Laboratories

LABORATORIES, CHEMICAL

see Chemical Laboratories

LABORATORIES, CHEMICAL ENGINEERING

see Chemical Engineering Laboratories

LABORATORIES, LANGUAGE

see Language Laboratories

LABORATORIES, MEDICAL

see Medical Laboratories

LABORATORIES, RADIOISOTOPE

see Radioisotope Laboratories

LABORATORY ANIMALS

Agricultural Board. Nutrient Requirements of Laboratory Animals. rev. 3rd ed. LC 54-60841. (Illus.). 128p. 1978. pap. 6.75 (ISBN 0-309-02767-5). Natl Acad Pr.

Altman, Philip L. & Katz, Dorothy D., eds. Inbred & Genetically Defined Strains of Laboratory Animals. Incl. Pt. 1. Mouse & Rat. 65.00 (ISBN 0-913822-12-4); Pt. 2. Hamster, Guinea Pig, Rabbit & Chicken. 50.00 (ISBN 0-913822-13-2). LC 78-73555. (Biological Handbooks: Vol. 3). (Illus.). 1979. Set. 100.00 (ISBN 0-913822-14-0). FASEB.

Andersen, A. C., ed. Beagle As an Experimental Dog. LC 79-83321. (Illus.). 1970. 19.50x (ISBN 0-8138-0169-9). Iowa St U Pr.

Animal Welfare Institute. Comfortable Quarters for Laboratory Animals. 7th ed. (Illus.). 108p. 1979. pap. text ed. 3.00 (ISBN 0-938414-01-1). Animal Welfare.

Arrington, L. R. Introductory Laboratory Science: The Breeding, Care & Management of Experimental Animals. 2nd ed. LC 77-78419. (Illus.). 1978. 13.00 (ISBN 0-8134-1963-8, 1963). Interstate.

Barnes, C. D. & Eltherington, L. G. Drug Dosage in Laboratory Animals: A Handbook. 2nd rev. & enl. ed. 1973. 30.00x (ISBN 0-520-02273-4). U of Cal Pr.

Cass, Jules S. Laboratory Animals: An Annotated Bibliography. 1971. 20.75 (ISBN 0-02-842640-1). Hafner.

Coates, Marie E. Germ-Free Animal in Research. LC 68-24698. (Illus.). 1968. 46.00 (ISBN 0-12-177150-4). Acad Pr.

Comber, L. & Hogg, M. Animals in Schools: Vol. 2, Terrestrial Invertebrates. LC 79-670193. (Orig.). 1980. pap. text ed. 9.50x (ISBN 0-435-59401-X). Heinemann Ed.

Conference on Marmosets in Experimental Medicine, Oak Ridge Tenn., March 16-18, 1977. Marmosets in Experimental Medicine: Proceedings. Moor-Jankowski, J., et al, eds. (Primates in Medicine: Vol. 10). (Illus.). 1977. 91.75 (ISBN 3-8055-2750-0). S Karger.

Cook, Margaret J. The Anatomy of the Laboratory Mouse. 1965. 26.00 (ISBN 0-12-186956-3). Acad Pr.

Crispens, Charles G., Jr. Handbook on the Laboratory Mouse. 278p. 1975. pap. 14.75 spiral (ISBN 0-398-03403-6). C C Thomas.

Diner, Jeff. Physical & Mental Suffering of Experimental Animals. Animal Welfare Institute, ed. 195p. (Orig.). 1979. pap. text ed. 4.00 (ISBN 0-938414-03-8). Animal Welfare.

Fogh, Jorgen & Giovanella, Beppino, eds. The Nude Mouse in Experimental & Clinical Research. 1978. 44.50 (ISBN 0-12-261860-2). Acad Pr.

Foster, Henry L., et al, eds. The Mouse in Biomedical Research: History Genetics & Wild Mice, Vol. 1. (ACLAM Ser.). 1981. price not set (ISBN 0-12-262501-3). Acad Pr.

Gay, W. I., ed. Methods of Animal Experimentation, 5 vols. Vol. 1. 1965. 50.00 (ISBN 0-12-278001-9); Vol. 2. 1965. 56.50 (ISBN 0-12-278002-7); Vol. 3. 1968. 61.00 (ISBN 0-12-278003-5); Vol. 4. 1973. 56.00 (ISBN 0-12-278004-3); Vol. 5. 1974. 56.00 (ISBN 0-12-278005-1). Acad Pr.

Gay, William, ed. Methods of Animal Experimentation, Vol 6. 1981. price not set (ISBN 0-12-278006-X). Acad Pr.

Gershwin, M. E. & Merchant, B., eds. Immunologic Defects in Laboratory Animals, 2 vols. (Vol. 1 357 pp.;vol. 2 379 pp.). 1981. Vol. 1. 37.50 (ISBN 0-306-40668-3, Plenum Pr); Vol. 2. 42.50 (ISBN 0-306-40673-X); Set. 72.50 (ISBN 0-686-73235-9). Plenum Pub.

Hafez, E. S., ed. Reproduction & Breeding Techniques for Laboratory Animals. LC 70-98498. (Illus.). 375p. 1970. text ed. 21.00 (ISBN 0-8121-0295-9). Lea & Febiger.

Hebel, Rudolph & Stromberg, Melvin W. Anatomy of the Laboratory Rat. 1976. 26.50 (ISBN 0-683-03950-4). Williams & Wilkins.

Hime, Malcolm. Handbook of Diseases of Laboratory Animals. 1979. pap. text ed. 37.95 (ISBN 0-433-14723-7). Intl Ideas.

Hombuger, F. & Trentin, J. J., eds. Oncogenesis & Natural Immunity in Syrian Hamsters. (Progress in Experimental Tumor Research: Vol. 23). (Illus.). 1978. 58.75 (ISBN 3-8055-2824-8). S Karger.

Inglis, J. K. Laboratory Animal Technology. 1980. 48.00 (ISBN 0-08-023772-X); pap. 23.00 (ISBN 0-08-023771-1). Pergamon.

Institute for Laboratory Animal Resources. Animals for Research. 10th ed. 1979. pap. 6.25 (ISBN 0-309-02920-1). Natl Acad Pr.

Institute of Laboratory Animal Resources. Amphibians: Guidelines for the Breeding, Care & Management of Laboratory Animals. (Illus.). 160p. 1974. pap. 10.75 (ISBN 0-309-02210-X). Natl Acad Pr.

--Animal Models for Biomedical Research, No. 3. LC 76-607190. (Illus.). 1970. pap. 5.75 (ISBN 0-309-01854-4). Natl Acad Pr.

Institute of Laboratory Animal Resources, National Research Council. Laboratory Animal Housing. 1979. pap. text ed. 12.00x (ISBN 0-309-02790-X). Natl Acad Pr.

Institute of Laboratory Animal Resources. Research in Zoos & Aquariums. 1975. pap. 10.00 (ISBN 0-309-02319-X). Natl Acad Pr.

--Ruminants: Cattle, Sheep & Goats, Guidelines for Breeding, Care & Management of Laboratory Animals. (Illus.). 76p. 1974. pap. 5.50 (ISBN 0-309-02149-9). Natl Acad Pr.

Laboratory Training Manual on the Use of Nuclear Techniques in Animal Research. (Technical Reports Ser.: No. 193). 1979. pap. 40.75 (ISBN 92-0-115179-9, IDC 193, IAEA). Unipub.

Laidler, Kieth. The Talking Ape. LC 80-5388. (Illus.). 160p. 1980. 11.95 (ISBN 0-8128-2731-7). Stein & Day.

Lane-Petter, W., ed. Animals for Research: Principles of Breeding & Management. 1963. 78.00 (ISBN 0-12-435750-4). Acad Pr.

Lane-Petter, W. & Pearson, A. E., eds. The Laboratory Animal: Principles & Practices. 1972. 46.50 (ISBN 0-12-435760-1). Acad Pr.

Lewis, William M. Maintaining Fishes for Experimental & Instructional Purposes. LC 62-15001. 109p. 1963. 5.95x (ISBN 0-8093-0077-X). S Ill U Pr.

McGiffin, Heather & Brownley, Nancie, eds. Animals in Education. 160p. (Orig.). (gr. 9-12). 1980. pap. 9.95 (ISBN 0-937712-00-0). Inst Study Animal.

McSheehy, T., ed. Control of the Animal House Environment. 335p. 1981. 41.25x (ISBN 0-901334-06-5, Pub. by Lab Animals England). State Mutual Bk.

Mayer, et al. Perspectives on the Educational Use of Animals. (Illus.). 77p. 1981. pap. 3.00 (ISBN 0-913098-38-8). Myrin Institute.

Melby, Edward C., Jr. & Altman, Norman H., eds. Handbook of Laboratory Animal Science, CRC, 2 vols. LC 74-19795. (Handbook Ser.). Vol. 1, 1974, 451 Pgs. 59.95 (ISBN 0-8493-0341-9); Vol. 2, 523 Pgs. 64.95 (ISBN 0-8493-0342-7). CRC Pr.

Mitruka, Brij M. & Rawnsley, Howard M. Clinical Biochemical & Hematological Reference Values in Normal Experimental Animals. LC 77-84608. (Illus.). 286p. 1977. 28.75x (ISBN 0-89352-006-3). Masson Pub.

Mitruka, Brij M., et al. Animals for Medical Research: Models for the Study of Human Disease. LC 80-11455. 608p. 1981. Repr. of 1976 ed. lib. bdg. write for info. (ISBN 0-89874-156-4). Krieger.

Nathanielsz, Peter W., ed. Fetal Endocrinology: An Experimental Approach. LC 76-22194. 1976. 41.50 (ISBN 0-7204-0582-3, North-Holland). Elsevier.

Porter, George & Lane-Petter, William, eds. Notes for Breeders of Common Laboratory Animals. 1964. 33.00 (ISBN 0-12-562750-5). Acad Pr.

Pratt, Dallas. Alternatives to Pain in Experiments on Animals. LC 79-51889. 1980. pap. 3.95 (ISBN 0-916858-05-7). Argus Archives.

Price, Edward O. & Stokes, Allen W. Animal Behavior in Laboratory & Field. 2nd ed. (Illus.). 1975. pap. text ed. 9.95x (ISBN 0-7167-0762-4); tchr's manual avail. W H Freeman.

Prince, Jack H. The Rabbit in Eye Research. (Illus.). 672p. 1964. photocopy ed. spiral 66.75 (ISBN 0-398-01525-2). C C Thomas.

Seamer, J. H. Safety in the Animal House. Wood, Margery, ed. 106p. 1981. 12.50x (ISBN 0-901334-09-X, Pub. by Lab Animals England). State Mutual Bk.

Shifrine, Moshe & Wilson, Floyd D., eds. The Canine As a Biomedical Research Model: Immunological, Hematological & Oncological Aspects. LC 80-24174. 35p. 1980. 14.50 (ISBN 0-686-75554-5). DOE.

Silverman, Paul. Animal Behavior in the Laboratory. LC 77-88842. (Illus.). 1978. text ed. 29.50x (ISBN 0-87663-727-6, Pica Pr). Universe.

Smyth, D. H. Alternatives to Animal Experiments. 1978. (Pub. by Scolar Pr England); pap. 5.95 (ISBN 0-85967-396-0). Biblio Dist.

Sos, J. Diets for Animal Experiments. (Illus.). 168p. 1974. 13.50x (ISBN 963-05-0253-4). Intl Pubns Serv.

Sperlinger, David. Animals in Research: New Perspectives in Animal Experimentation. 384p. 1980. 46.50 (ISBN 0-471-27843-2, Pub. by Wiley-Interscience). Wiley.

Stolte, H. & Alt, Jeannette. Research Animals & Experimental Design in Nephrology. (Contributions to Nephrology: Vol. 19). (Illus.). x, 250p. 1980. soft cover 49.25 (ISBN 3-8055-3075-7). S Karger.

Symposium on the Syrian Hamster in Toxicology & Carcinogenesis Research, Boston, November 30-December 2, 1977. The Syrian Hamster in Toxicology & Carcinogenesis: Proceedings. Homburger, F., ed. (Progress in Experimental Tumor Research: Vol. 24). (Illus.). 1979. 97.75 (ISBN 3-8055-2890-6). S Karger.

Universities Federation for Animal Welfare. Handbook on the Care & Management of Laboratory Animals. 5th ed. (Illus.). 1976. text ed. 47.50 (ISBN 0-443-01404-3). Churchill.

Vyvyan, John. In Pity & in Anger: A Study in the Use of Animals in Science. 1972. 7.50 (ISBN 0-7181-0719-5). Transatlantic.

Weisbroth, Stephen H., et al, eds. The Biology of the Laboratory Rabbit. 1974. 67.50 (ISBN 0-12-742150-5). Acad Pr.

LABORATORY ANIMALS–DISEASES

Baker, Henry J., et al, eds. The Laboratory Rat: Vol. I: Biology & Diseases. LC 79-51688. (American College of Laboratory Animal Medicine Ser.). 1979. 55.50 (ISBN 0-12-074901-7); Set. 88.00 (ISBN 0-686-66199-0). Acad Pr.

Flynn, Robert J. Parasites of Laboratory Animals. LC 77-171165. (Illus.). 827p. 1973. 35.00x (ISBN 0-8138-0470-1). Iowa St U Pr.

Harkness, John E. & Wagner, Joseph E. The Biology & Medicine of Rabbits & Rodents. LC 76-23136. (Illus.). 152p. 1977. pap. 8.00 (ISBN 0-8121-0576-1). Lea & Febiger.

LABORATORY OF SOCIAL HYGIENE, BEDFORD HILLS, NEW YORK

Spaulding, Edith R. Experimental Study of Psychopathic Delinquent Women. LC 69-14947. (Criminology, Law Enforcement, & Social Problems Ser.: No. 60). (Illus.). 1969. Repr. of 1923 ed. 17.00 (ISBN 0-87585-060-X). Patterson Smith.

LABORATORY SCHOOLS

Cole, Mary I. Cooperation Between the Faculty of the Campus Elementary Training School & the Other Departments of Teachers Colleges & Normal Schools. LC 76-176658. (Columbia University. Teachers College. Contributions to Education: No. 746). Repr. of 1939 ed. 17.50 (ISBN 0-404-55746-5). AMS Pr.

Lindsey, Margaret, et al. Inquiry into Teaching Behavior of Supervisors in Teacher Education Laboratories. LC 79-106358. (Illus.). 1969. pap. 5.00 (ISBN 0-8077-1693-6). Tchrs Coll.

Marshall Kaplan, Gans & Kahn. Children & the Urban Environment: Evaluation of the WGBH-TV Educational Project. LC 70-187397. (Special Studies in U. S. Economic, Social & Political Issues). 1973. 28.00x (ISBN 0-275-28687-8). Irvington.

Williams, Edward I. The Actual & Potential Use of Laboratory Schools in State Normal Schools & Teachers Colleges. (Columbia University. Teachers College. Contributions to Education: No. 846). Repr. of 1942 ed. 17.50 (ISBN 0-404-55846-1). AMS Pr.

LABORATORY TECHNICIANS

see also Medical Technologists

Casciero, Albert J. & Roney, Raymond G. Introduction to AV for Technical Assistants. (Library Science Text). (Illus.). 250p. 1981. lib. bdg. 23.50x (ISBN 0-87287-232-7). Libs Unl.

Holum J. R. 5th ed. 182p. 1979. lab manual 10.95 (ISBN 0-471-04751-1). Wiley.

Morgan, Seth A. Manual for the Laboratory Assistant. pap. 4.95 (ISBN 0-89741-007-6). Roadrunner Tech.

Oppenheim, Irwin A. Textbook for Laboratory Assistants. 3rd ed. LC 80-26455. (Illus.). 187p. 1981. pap. text ed. 13.50 (ISBN 0-8016-3722-8). Mosby.

Rudman, Jack. Certified Laboratory Assistant. (Career Examination Ser.: C-179). (Cloth bdg. avail. on request). pap. 8.00 (ISBN 0-8373-0179-3). Natl Learning.

--Instrumentation Technician. (Career Examination Ser.: C-2366). (Cloth bdg. avail. on request). pap. 10.00 (ISBN 0-685-60428-4). Natl Learning.

--Laboratory Aide. (Career Examination Ser.: C-430). (Cloth bdg. avail. on request). pap. 8.00 (ISBN 0-8373-0430-X). Natl Learning.

--Laboratory Assistant. (Career Examination Ser.: C-1879). (Cloth bdg. avail. on request). 1977. pap. 10.00 (ISBN 0-8373-1879-3). Natl Learning.

--Laboratory Equipment Specialist. (Career Examination Ser.: C-2297). (Cloth bdg. avail. on request). 1977. pap. 8.00 (ISBN 0-8373-2297-9). Natl Learning.

--Laboratory Helper (Man) (Career Examination Ser.: C-446). (Cloth bdg. avail. on request). pap. 8.00 (ISBN 0-8373-0446-6). Natl Learning.

--Laboratory Helper (Women) (Career Examination Ser.: C-447). (Cloth bdg. avail. on request). pap. 8.00 (ISBN 0-8373-0447-4). Natl Learning.

--Laboratory Technician. (Career Examination Ser.: C-1734). (Cloth bdg. avail. on request). pap. 10.00 (ISBN 0-8373-1734-7). Natl Learning.

--Laboratory Technician. (Career Examination Ser.: C-1587). (Cloth bdg. avail. on request). pap. 8.00 (ISBN 0-686-53357-7). Natl Learning.

--Laboratory Technician - Secondary Schools. (Teachers License Examination Ser.: T-36). (Cloth bdg. avail. on request). pap. 10.00-(ISBN 0-8373-8036-7). Natl Learning.

--Registered Technologist - R.T.(AR-RT) (Career Examination Ser.: C-680). (Cloth bdg. avail. on request). pap. 10.00 (ISBN 0-8373-0680-9). Natl Learning.

Schapiro, Melvin & Kuritsky, Joel. The Gastroenterology Assistant: A Laboratory Manual. 2nd ed. LC 81-50268. (Illus.). 150p. 1981. 22.50x (ISBN 0-9605718-3-3). Valley Presbyterian.

Taub, Howard. Basic Laboratory Skills for Laboratory Assistants: Measurements, Inventory of Supplies, Collecting Specimens, Specimen Processing, Media Preparation. (Illus.). 612p. 1980. spiral (lexotone) 38.00 (ISBN 0-398-04132-6). C C Thomas.

LABORERS

see Labor and Laboring Classes

LA BOULAYE, MAXIMILLEN ECHALARD, MARQUIS DE, 1612-1668

De Beauvais-Nangis, Nicolas D. Memoires Du Marquis De Beauvais-Nangis et Journal Du Proces Du Marquis De La Boulaye. 1862. 35.50 (ISBN 0-384-03695-3); pap. 31.00 (ISBN 0-685-13509-8). Johnson Repr.

LABOULBENIACEAE

Benjamin, Richard K. Introduction & Supplement to Thaxter's Contribution Towards a Monograph of the Laboulbeniacea. 1971. 16.00 (ISBN 3-7682-0708-0). Lubrecht & Cramer.

Thaxter, R. Contribution Towards a Monograph of the Laboulbeniaceae. (Illus.). 1971. 200.00 (ISBN 3-7682-0708-0). Lubrecht & Cramer.

LABOUR PARTY (GREAT BRITAIN)

Cline, Catherine A. Recruits to Labour: The British Labour Party, 1914-1931. LC 63-13888. 1963. 12.95x (ISBN 0-8156-2046-2). Syracuse U Pr.

Cole, G. D. A History of the Labour Party: New Impression. 1978. Repr. of 1958 ed. 40.00x (ISBN 0-7100-6628-7). Routledge & Kegan.

Cole, George D. History of the Labour Party from 1914. LC 73-90407. Repr. of 1948 ed. 19.50x (ISBN 0-678-06505-5). Kelley.

Cole, Harry B. The British Labour Party: A Functioning Participatory Democracy. 1977. pap. text ed. 5.75 (ISBN 0-08-021811-3). Pergamon.

Cook, Chris & Taylor, Ian. The Labour Party. (Illus.). 208p. 1980. text ed. 25.00x (ISBN 0-582-49038-3); pap. text ed. 9.95x (ISBN 0-582-49039-1). Longman.

Cowling, Maurice. Impact of Labour, Nineteen Twenty-Twenty-Four: The Beginning of Modern British Politics. LC 73-127236. (Studies in History & Theory of Politics). 1971. 49.95 (ISBN 0-521-07969-1). Cambridge U Pr.

Currie, Robert. Industrial Politics. LC 78-40480. 1979. 45.00x (ISBN 0-19-827419-X). Oxford U Pr.

Drucker, H. M. Doctrine & Ethos in the Labour Party. 1979. text ed. 17.95x (ISBN 0-04-329026-4); pap. text ed. 7.50x (ISBN 0-04-329027-2). Allen Unwin.

Eatwell, Roger. The Labour Governments Nineteen Forty-Five to Nineteen Fifty-One. 1979. 40.00 (ISBN 0-7134-0262-8, Pub. by Batsford England); pap. 14.95 (ISBN 0-7134-0263-6). David & Charles.

Foot, Michael. Debts of Honour: Profiles in Autobiography. LC 81-47227. 240p. 1981. 13.95 (ISBN 0-06-039001-8, HarpT). Har-Row.

Forester, Tom. The British Labour Party & the Working Class. LC 75-19474. 225p. 1976. 17.50x (ISBN 0-8419-0217-8). Holmes & Meier.

Gordon, Michael R. Conflict & Consensus in Labour's Foreign Policy, 1914-1965. 1969. 15.00x (ISBN 0-8047-0686-7). Stanford U Pr.

Haseler, Stephen. The Tragedy of Labour. (Mainstream Ser.). 249p. 1980. 19.50x (ISBN 0-631-11341-X, Pub. by Basil Blackwell). Biblio Dist.

Hatfield, Michael. The House That Left Built: Inside Labour Policy Making, 1970-1975. 1978. text ed. 25.00x (ISBN 0-575-02471-2). Verry.

Hobhouse, L. T. The Labour Movement. 3rd rev. ed. (Society & the Victorians). 1974. text ed. 10.00x (ISBN 0-901759-24-4). Humanities.

Howell, David. British Social Democracy: A Study in Development & Decay. 2nd ed. 340p. 1980. 28.50 (ISBN 0-312-10536-3). St Martin.

--British Social Democracy: A Study in Development & Decay. LC 76-11701. 1976. 18.95 (ISBN 0-312-10535-5). St Martin.

Jarman, T. L. Socialism in Britain: From the Industrial Revolution to the Present Day. LC 73-185255. 217p. 1972. 6.50 (ISBN 0-8008-7240-1). Taplinger.

Jenkins, Hugh. Rank & File. 181p. 1980. 25.00x (ISBN 0-7099-0331-6, Pub by Croom Helm Ltd England). Biblio Dist.

Jones, Bill. The Russia Complex: The British Labour Party & the Soviet Union. 229p. 1977. 21.50x (ISBN 0-8476-6082-6). Rowman.

Kellogg, Paul U. & Gleason, Arthur. British Labour & the War: Reconstruction for a New World. LC 70-147517. (Library of War & Peace; Labor, Socialism & War). lib. bdg. 38.00 (ISBN 0-8240-0306-3). Garland Pub.

Lees-Smith, Hastings B., ed. The Encyclopaedia of the Labour Movement, 3 vols. 7th ed. LC 73-167033. xxv, 1132p. 1972. Repr. of 1928 ed. Set. 125.00 (ISBN 0-8103-3028-8). Gale.

Middleton, Lucy, ed. Women in the Labour Movement: The British Experience. 224p. 1977. 16.50x (ISBN 0-87471-942-9). Rowman.

Minkin, Lewis. The Labour Party Conference: A Study in the Politics of Intra-Party Democracy. 448p. 1981. 36.00x (ISBN 0-686-73061-5, Pub. by Manchester U Pr England). State Mutual Bk.

Morgan, Janet P. The House of Lords & the Labour Government, 1964-1970. (Illus.). 270p. 1975. text ed. 45.00x (ISBN 0-19-827191-3). Oxford U Pr.

Panitch, L. Social Democracy & Industrial Militancy. LC 75-16869. (Illus.). 306p. 1976. 34.95 (ISBN 0-521-20779-7). Cambridge U Pr.

Pelling, Henry. The Origins of the Labour Party, 1880-1900. 2nd ed. 1965. pap. 7.95x (ISBN 0-19-881110-1). Oxford U Pr.

--A Short History of the Labour Party. 5th ed. LC 76-40726. 1977. 15.95x (ISBN 0-312-72030-0); pap. text ed. 6.95x (ISBN 0-312-71995-7). St Martin.

Perelman, Chaim. Justice, Law & Argument: Essays on Moral & Legal Reasoning. (Synthese Library: No. 142). 175p. 1980. lib. bdg. 28.50 (ISBN 90-277-1089-9, Pub. by Reidel Holland); pap. 10.50 (ISBN 90-277-1090-2, Pub. by Reidel Holland). Kluwer Boston.

Pimlott, B. Labour & the Left in the 1930's. LC 76-27906. 1977. 19.95 (ISBN 0-521-21448-3). Cambridge U Pr.

Simpson, Bill. Labour, the Unions & the Party: A Study of the Trade Unions & the British Labour Movement. (Ruskin House Series in Trade Union Studies). 1973. text ed. 12.50x (ISBN 0-04-331057-5). Allen Unwin.

Sinclair, William A. Socialism & the Individual: Notes on Joining the Labour Party. LC 77-18930. 1978. Repr. of 1955 ed. lib. bdg. 15.75x (ISBN 0-313-20199-4, SISO). Greenwood.

Stansky, Peter, ed. Left & War: The British Labour Party & World War 1. (Problems in European History Ser). (Orig.). 1969. pap. 5.95x (ISBN 0-19-501066-3). Oxford U Pr.

Strauss, Patricia. Bevin & Co. LC 71-128317. (Essay Index Reprint Ser). 1941. 17.00 (ISBN 0-8369-1896-7). Arno.

Tawney, Richard H. British Labor Movement. LC 68-57646. (Illus.). 1969. Repr. of 1925 ed. lib. bdg. 15.00x (ISBN 0-8371-0677-X, TABL). Greenwood.

Tracey, Herbert, ed. The Book of the Labour Party: Its History, Growth, Policy, & Leaders, 3 vols. facsimile ed. LC 79-160997. (Select Bibliographies Reprint Ser.). Repr. of 1925 ed. Set. 75.00 (ISBN 0-8369-5865-9). Arno.

Turner, John E. Labour's Doorstep Politics in London. LC 77-99160. 1978. 19.50x (ISBN 0-8166-0843-1). U of Minn Pr.

Williamson, Rene & Greene, Lee, eds. Five Years of British Labour. 1950. pap. 2.00 (ISBN 0-910824-05-3). Kallman.

Windrich, Elaine. British Labour's Foreign Policy. LC 73-147227. 1971. Repr. of 1952 ed. lib. bdg. 15.00x (ISBN 0-8371-5992-X, WIBL). Greenwood.

Wyatt, Woodrow. What's Left of the Labour Party? 1977. 16.95x (ISBN 0-8464-0969-0). Beekman Pubs.

LABRADOR

Cartwright, George. A Journal of Transactions & Events, During a Residence of Nearly 16 Years on the Coast of Labrador, 3 vols. LC 74-5829. Repr. of 1792 ed. Set. 165.00 (ISBN 0-404-11632-9); Vol. 1. (ISBN 0-404-11633-7); Vol. 2. (ISBN 0-404-11634-5); Vol. 3. (ISBN 0-404-11635-3). AMS Pr.

Grenfell, Wilfred T. Down North on the Labrador. LC 70-122712. (Short Story Index Reprint Ser). 1911. 15.00 (ISBN 0-8369-3545-4). Arno.

--Labrador, the Country & the People. LC 74-5843. Repr. of 1909 ed. 41.50 (ISBN 0-404-11648-5). AMS Pr.

Kerr, James L. Wilfred Grenfell, His Life & Work. LC 73-21177. 1977. lib. bdg. 19.50x (ISBN 0-8371-6068-5, KEWG). Greenwood.

Laird, M. Bibliography of the Natural History of Newfoundland & Labrador. 1980. 66.50 (ISBN 0-12-434050-4). Acad Pr.

McLean, John. Notes of a Twenty-Five Years' Service in the Hudson's Bay Territory. Wallace, W. S., ed. LC 68-28607. 1968. Repr. of 1932 ed. lib. bdg. 29.50x (ISBN 0-8371-5057-4, MCNS). Greenwood.

Packard, Alpheus S. The Labrador Coast: A Journal of Two Summer Cruises to That Region. LC 74-5862. Repr. of 1891 ed. 32.50 (ISBN 0-404-11668-X). AMS Pr.

Stewart, Robert. Labrador. (The World's Wild Places Ser.). (Illus.). 1977. lib. bdg. 11.97 (ISBN 0-686-51020-8). Silver.

--Labrador. (World's Wild Places Ser.). (Illus.). 1977. 12.95 (ISBN 0-8094-2065-1). Time-Life.

Tuck, James A. Newfoundland & Labrador Prehistory. 1976. pap. 8.50x (ISBN 0-442-29889-7). Van Nos Reinhold.

Universite Laval,Centre d'Etudes Nordiques, Quebec. Bibliographie de la Peninsule du Quebec-Labrador, 2 Vols. Cooke, Alan & Caron, Fabien, eds. 1968. Set. 190.00 (ISBN 0-8161-0758-0). G K Hall.

LABRADOR DOGS

see Dogs–Breeds–Labrador Dogs

LABRADOR RETRIEVERS

see Dogs–Breeds–Labrador Dogs

L'ABRI, SWITZERLAND

Schaeffer, Edith. L'Abri. 1969. pap. 3.95 (ISBN 0-8423-2101-2). Tyndale.

LA BRUYERE, JEAN DE, 1645-1696

Gosse, Edmund W. Three French Moralists & the Gallantry of France. facs. ed. LC 67-23223. (Essay Index Reprint Ser). 1918. 13.00 (ISBN 0-8369-0489-3). Arno.

Knox, Edward. Jean de la Bruyere. (World Authors Ser.: France: No. 298). 1973. lib. bdg. 10.95 (ISBN 0-8057-2507-5). Twayne.

Koppisch, Michael S. The Dissolution of Character: Changing Perspectives in La Bruyere's Caracteres. LC 80-70808. (French Forum Monographs: No.24). 120p. (Orig.). 1981. pap. 10.50 (ISBN 0-917058-23-2). French Forum.

La Bruyere, Jean de. Maximes et Pensees. 4.95 (ISBN 0-686-54264-9). French & Eur.

Van Delft. La Bruyers Moraliste: Quatre Etudes sur "Les Caracteres". (Coll. Hist. des Idees et Crit. Litt.). 13.50 (ISBN 0-685-34229-8). French & Eur.

LABYRINTH (EAR)

see also Corti's Organ; Equilibrium (Physiology); Meniere's Disease

Duverney, Guichard J. A Treatise of the Organ of Hearing. LC 77-147969. Repr. of 1737 ed. 21.50 (ISBN 0-404-08221-1). AMS Pr.

Hammer, Gunnar. A Quantitative Cytochemical Study of Shock Wave Effects on Spiral Ganglion Cells. 1956. pap. 9.00 (ISBN 0-384-21250-6). Johnson Repr.

Hoshino, T. Beitraege Zur Funktion Des Kleinhirnwurmes Beim Kaninchen. 1921. pap. 9.00 (ISBN 0-384-24365-7). Johnson Repr.

Kornhuber, H. H., ed. Handbook of Sensory Physiology: Vestibular System, Psychophysics, Applied Aspects & General Interpretations. (Vol. 6, Pt. 2). (Illus.). viii, 680p. 1975. 129.60 (ISBN 0-387-06864-3). Springer-Verlag.

Lombard, R. E. Comparative Morphology of the Inner Ear in Salamanders: Caudata-Amphibia. (Contributions to Vertebrate Evolution: Vol. 2). 1977. 45.00 (ISBN 3-8055-2408-0). S Karger.

Wersall, Jan. Studies in the Structure & Innervation of the Sensory Epithelium of the Cristae Ampullares in the Guinea Pig. Repr. of 1956 ed. pap. 9.00 (ISBN 0-384-66900-X). Johnson Repr.

LABYRINTHS

see also Hiding-Places (Secret Chambers, etc.); Maze Tests

Lockridge, Ross F. The Labyrinth. LC 75-336. (The Radical Tradition in America Ser). (Illus.). 94p. 1975. Repr. of 1941 ed. 13.50 (ISBN 0-88355-239-6). Hyperion Conn.

Matthews, W. H. Mazes & Labyrinths. LC 70-75946. 1969. Repr. of 1922 ed. 22.00 (ISBN 0-8103-3839-4). Gale.

--Mazes & Labyrinths: Their History & Development. (Illus.). 7.50 (ISBN 0-8446-0790-8). Peter Smith.

--Mazes & Labyrinths: Their History & Development. (Illus.). 1970. pap. 3.50 (ISBN 0-486-22614-X). Dover.

Shepherd, Walter. Big Book of Mazes & Labyrinths. (Illus.). 6.50 (ISBN 0-8446-4815-9). Peter Smith.

LACE AND LACE MAKING

see also Macrame; Tatting

Arnold, Eunice. Teach Yourself Torchon Lace: Six Basic Lessons in Bobbin Lace with Workcards. 1980. 9.95 (ISBN 0-686-27276-5). Robin & Russ.

Bath, Virginia C. Lace. (Handbooks Ser). (Illus.). 1979. pap. 9.95 (ISBN 0-14-046378-X). Penguin.

Biedermann, Gertrude, et al. Traditional Bobbin Lace: Pictoral Patterns. Kliot, Jules, ed. 1977. pap. 10.00 (ISBN 0-916896-10-2). Lacis Pubns.

Boehn, Max Von. Ornaments--Lace, Fans, Gloves, Walking-Sticks, Parasols, Jewelry & Trinkets: Modes & Manners Supplement. LC 70-148467. (Illus.). Repr. of 1929 ed. 20.00 (ISBN 0-405-08286-X, Blom Pubns). Arno.

Brooke, Margaret L. Lace in the Making. 1975. Repr. of 1923 ed. 11.95 (ISBN 0-686-11142-7). Robin & Russ.

Bullock, Alice-May. Lace & Lacemaking. LC 81-81037. (Illus.). 168p. 1981. 19.95 (ISBN 0-88332-261-7, 8193). Larousse.

Clifford, C. R., ed. Lace Dictionary: Including Historic & Commercial Terms, Technical Terms, Native & Foreign. (Illus.). 156p. 1981. Repr. of 1913 ed. 20.00 (ISBN 0-8103-4311-8). Gale.

Cook, Bridget M. & Stott, Geraldine. The Book of Bobbin Lace Stitches. (Illus.). 144p. 1980. 18.50 (ISBN 0-8231-5057-7). Branford.

Dawson, Amy. Bobbin Lacemaking for Beginners. (Illus.). 1978. 6.95 (ISBN 0-7137-0817-4, Pub by Blandford Pr England). Sterling.

Doyle, Mary. Carrickamacross Lace. (Illus., Orig.). 1978. 2.50 (ISBN 0-913664-11-1). Thresh Pubns.

Felkin, William. History of the Machine-Wrought Hosiery & Lace Manufactures. (Illus.). 1967. Repr. of 1867 ed. 23.50 (ISBN 0-8337-1104-0). B Franklin.

--History of the Machine-Wrought Hosiery & Lace Manufactures. LC 67-89041. Repr. of 1867 ed. 16.50x (ISBN 0-678-05685-4). Kelley.

Fish, Harriet U. Creative Lace-Making with Thread & Yarn. LC 72-81039. (Little Craft Book Ser.). (Illus.). 50p. 1972. 5.95 (ISBN 0-8069-5216-4); lib. bdg. 6.69 (ISBN 0-8069-5217-2). Sterling.

Gubser, Elsie. Bobbin Lace. (Illus.). 5.00 (ISBN 0-686-09828-5). Robin & Russ.

Guide to Lace-Making. Repr. 3.50 (ISBN 0-686-09833-1). Robin & Russ.

Jackson, Emily. The History of Hand Made Lace: Dealing with the Origin of Lace, the Growth of the Great Lace Centres, Etc. LC 70-136558. (Tower Bks.). (Illus.). xiv, 245p. 1972. Repr. of 1900 ed. 32.00 (ISBN 0-8103-3935-8). Gale.

Jourdain, M. Old Lace: A Handbook for Collectors; an Account of the Different Styles of Lace, Their History, Characteristics & Manufacture. (Illus.). 121p. 1981. Repr. of 1908 ed. 20.00 (ISBN 0-8103-4310-X). Gale.

Kinzel, Marianne. First Book of Modern Lace Knitting. LC 72-86063. (Illus.). 96p. 1973. pap. 3.50 (ISBN 0-486-22904-1). Dover.

Kliot, Jules & Kliot, Kaethe. Honiton Bobbin Lace: Designs for Prickling from Traditional Pieces. 1979. pap. 8.95 (ISBN 0-916896-16-1). Lacis Pubns.

Kliot, Jules, ed. Irish Crochet Lace. Kliot, Kaethe. 68p. 1980. pap. 5.95 (ISBN 0-916896-17-X). Lacis Pubns.

Kliot, Jules & Kliot, Kaethe, eds. Bobbin Lace Patterns in Torchon: A Student's Work Book. 1979. pap. 7.95 (ISBN 0-916896-15-3). Lacis Pubns.

--Honiton Bobbin Lace: Designs for Pricking from Traditional Pieces. 1979. pap. 8.95 (ISBN 0-916896-16-1). Lacis Pubns.

--Needle Laces: Battenberg, Point & Reticella. (Illus.). 1981. pap. 5.95 (ISBN 0-916896-18-8). Lacis Pubns.

Kliot, Kaethe & Kliot, Jules. Bobbin Lace: Form by the Twisting of Cords. (Arts & Crafts Ser.). (Illus.). 264p. 1973. pap. 4.95 (ISBN 0-517-50593-2). Crown.

Die Kloppelspitzen. (Second Ser.). (Illus., Ger.). Date not set. 28.00 (ISBN 0-8103-4313-4). Gale.

Knight, Pauline. The Technique of Filet Lace. (Illus.). 144p. 1980. 19.95 (ISBN 0-7134-1698-X, Pub. by Batsford England). David & Charles.

Lawrence, Ellen. Bobbin Lace: Designs & Instruction. Kliot, Jules, ed. Kliot, Kaethe. 1979. pap. 3.95 (ISBN 0-916896-14-5). Lacis Pubns.

Lovesey, Nenia. The Technique of Needlepoint Lace. LC 80-80099. (Illus.). 144p. 1980. 15.95 (ISBN 0-88332-249-8, 8057). Larousse.

Luxton, Elsie. The Technique of Honiton Lace. (Illus.). 168p. 1979. 11.50 (ISBN 0-8231-5051-8). Branford.

McPeek, Mary, tr. & intro. by. Bobbin Lace, First Series: Les Dentelles Aux Fuseaux, 3 pts. rev. ed. LC 73-18373. (Illus.). 255p. 1974. Repr. Set. 48.00 (ISBN 0-8103-3955-2); 25 corner patterns incl. (ISBN 0-685-49538-8). Gale.

Maidment, Margaret. Manual of Handmade Bobbin Lace Work. (Illus.). 12.50 (ISBN 0-686-09831-5). Robin & Russ.

May, F. L. Catalogue of Laces & Embroideries in the Collection. (Illus.). 1936. 5.00 (ISBN 0-87535-038-0). Hispanic Soc.

May, Florence L. Hispanic Lace & Lacemaking. 1980. 12.00 (ISBN 0-87535-048-8). Hispanic Soc.

Milroy, M. E., ed. Church Lace: Being Eight Ecclesiastical Patterns in Pillow Lace. (Illus.). 121p. 1981. Repr. of 1920 ed. 24.00 (ISBN 0-8103-3014-8). Gale.

Mincoff & Marriage. Pillow Lace: A Practical Handbook. Date not set. 19.95 (ISBN 0-903585-10-3). Robin & Russ.

Moody, Penderel, ed. Devon Pillow Lace: Its History & How to Make It. (Illus.). 160p. 1981. Repr. of 1907 ed. 24.00 (ISBN 0-8103-3031-8). Gale.

Nieuwhoff, Constance. Contemporary Lace Making. (Illus.). 1975. 9.95 (ISBN 0-442-30071-9). Van Nos Reinhold.

Nottingham, Pamela. Complete Book of English Bobbin Lace. Date not set. 14.95 (ISBN 0-442-26063-6). Robin & Russ.

--Complete Book of English Bobbin Lace. (Illus.). 1976. 14.95 (ISBN 0-442-26063-6). Van Nos Reinhold.
--Technique of Bobbin Lace. 1976. 27.00 (ISBN 0-7134-3230-6, Pub. by Batsford England). David & Charles.
Palliser, Mrs. Bury. History of Lace. Jourdain, M. & Dryden, Alice, eds. (Illus.). 1977. Repr. of 1902 ed. 49.00x (ISBN 0-7158-1183-5). Charles River Bks.
Palliser, Fanny M. History of Lace. LC 75-78219. (Illus.). x, 454p. 1972. Repr. of 1875 ed. 37.00 (ISBN 0-8103-3941-2). Gale.
Powys, Marian. Lace & Lace Making. (Illus.). 219p. 1981. Repr. of 1955 ed. 28.00 (ISBN 0-8103-4312-6). Gale.
Rotenstein, C. Lace Manufacturing on Raschel Machines. 7.95 (ISBN 0-87245-284-0). Textile Bk.
Saulpaugh, Dassah. The Lace with the Delicate Air. (Illus.). 28p. pap. 0.75 (ISBN 0-87273-014-X). Bklyn Mus.
Sharp, Mary. Point & Pillow Lace: A Short Account of Various Kinds, Ancient & Modern, & How to Recognize Them. LC 72-141752. (Tower Bks). (Illus.). 1971. Repr. of 1905 ed. 22.00 (ISBN 0-8103-3912-9). Gale.
Simeon, Margaret. The History of Lace. (Illus.). 144p. 1979. 32.50x (ISBN 0-8476-6263-2). Rowman.
Southard, Doris. Bobbin Lacemaking. LC 77-2240. (Encore Edition). (Illus.). 1977. 4.95 (ISBN 0-684-16555-4, ScribT). Scribner.
Stillwell, Alexandra. Teneriffe Lace. (Illus.). 144p. 1980. 16.95 (ISBN 0-8231-5056-9). Branford.
Vinciolo, Federico. Renaissance Patterns for Lace & Embroidery. (Illus.). 1971. pap. 2.75 (ISBN 0-486-22438-4). Dover.
Wright, Doreen. Bobbin Lace Making. (Illus.). 1971. 9.75 (ISBN 0-8231-5033-X). Branford.

LACERTIDAE
Boulenger, George A. Monograph of the Lacertidae, 2 Vols. (Illus.). 1920-1921. Set. 61.50 (ISBN 0-384-05305-X). Johnson Repr.

LACERTILIA
see Lizards

LACHAISE, GASTON
Holland, Vyvyan B. Time Remembered After Pere Lachaise. LC 79-8064. Repr. of 1966 ed. 22.50 (ISBN 0-404-18375-1). AMS Pr.
Kramer, et al. Sculpture of Gaston Lachaise. LC 67-17017. (Illus., Orig.). 1967. 15.00x (ISBN 0-87130-016-8); pap. 9.00x (ISBN 0-87130-017-6). Eakins.
Nordland, Gerald. Gaston Lachaise: The Man & His Work. LC 74-80661. (Illus.). 1974. 15.00 (ISBN 0-8076-0761-4). Braziller.

LACKAWANNA VALLEY, PENNSYLVANIA
Folsom, Burton W., Jr. Urban Capitalists: Entrepreneurs & City Growth in Pennsylvania's Lackawanna & Lehigh Valleys, 1800-1920. LC 80-8864. (Studies in Industry & Society: No. 1). (Illus.). 208p. 1981. text ed. 16.50x (ISBN 0-8018-2520-2). Johns Hopkins.

LACLOS, PIERRE AMBROISE FRANCOIS CHODERLOS, 1741-1803
Michael, Colette V. Choderlos De Laclos, the Man, His Works, & His Critics: An Annotated Bibliography. 1981. lib. bdg. 35.00 (ISBN 0-8240-9363-1). Garland Pub.
Rosbottom, Ronald C. Choderlos de Laclos. (World Authors Ser.: France: No. 502). 1978. 13.95 (ISBN 0-8057-6343-0). Twayne.
Thody, P. M. Laclos: Les Liasons Dangereuses. (Studies in French Literature). 1970. pap. text ed. 3.95x (ISBN 0-7131-5499-3). Dynamic Learn Corp.
Versini. Laclos et la Tradition: Essai sur les Sources et la Technique des Liaisons Dangereuses. 43.75 (ISBN 0-685-34039-2). French & Eur.

LACORDANCE, JEAN BAPTISTE HENRI DOMINIQUE DE, 1802-1861
Spencer, Philip. Politics of Belief in Nineteenth-Century France. LC 77-80592. 284p. 1973. Repr. of 1954 ed. 22.50 (ISBN 0-86527-156-9). Fertig.

LACQUER AND LACQUERING
see also Metals-Finishing; Varnish and Varnishing
Boyer, Martha. Japanese Lacquers in the Walters Art Gallery. (Illus.). 1970. bds. 30.00 (ISBN 0-685-21828-7). Walters Art.
Gaynes, Norman I. Formulation of Organic Coatings. (Illus.). 1967. 16.95x (ISBN 0-442-02627-7). Van Nos Reinhold.
Huth, Hans. Lacquer of the West: The History of a Craft & an Industry, 1600-1950. LC 73-130185. (Illus.). 1971. 25.00 (ISBN 0-226-36315-5). U of Chicago Pr.
Newell, Adnah C. Coloring, Finishing & Painting Wood. Holtrop, ed. (gr. 9-12). 1972. text ed. 18.00 (ISBN 0-87002-124-9). Bennett IL.
Pekarik, Andrew J. Japanese Lacquer, 1600-1900: Selections from the Charles A. Greenfield Collection. Wasserman, Rosanne, ed. (Illus.). 146p. 1980. 19.95 (ISBN 0-87099-247-3). Metro Mus Art.
Yonemura, Ann. Japanese Lacquer. LC 79-19719. (Illus.). 1979. pap. 12.00 (ISBN 0-934686-35-1). Freer.

LACRIMAL ORGANS
see also Aqueous Humor
Yamaguchi. Recent Advances on the Lacrimal System. 1981. 47.50 (ISBN 0-89352-140-X). Masson Pub.

LACROSSE
Boyd, Margaret. Lacrosse. (Illus.). 1959. 6.95 (ISBN 0-498-08156-7). A S Barnes.
Brackenridge, Celia. Women's Lacrosse. LC 77-93733. (gr. 9-12). 1978. 4.95 (ISBN 0-8120-5152-1). Barron.
Delano, Anne. Lacrosse for Girls & Women. (Physical Education Activities Ser.). 80p. 1970. pap. text ed. write for info. (ISBN 0-697-07018-2); tchrs.' manual avail. (ISBN 0-686-66583-X). Wm C Brown.
Evans, G. Heberton & Anderson, Robert E. Lacrosse Fundamentals. (Illus.). 1966. 10.00 (ISBN 0-498-06371-2). A S Barnes.
Flanagan, Henry E., Jr. & Gardner, Robert. Basic Lacrosse Strategy: An Introduction for Young Players. (Illus.). 1979. 7.95 (ISBN 0-385-14001-0). Doubleday.
Fusting, Eugene M. Star-Sticks. LC 79-64888. (Illus.). 242p. (gr. 5 up). 1980. pap. text ed. 9.95 (ISBN 0-935736-27-1). Summer House.
Hanna, Mike, et al. Lacrosse for Men & Women: Skills & Strategies for the Athlete & Coach. (Illus.). 160p. 1981. pap. 9.95 (ISBN 0-8015-4372-X, Hawthorn). Dutton.
James, Stuart. Lacrosse for Beginners. LC 80-27810. (Illus.). 128p. (gr. 7 up). 1981. PLB 8.79 (ISBN 0-671-34050-6). Messner.
Kurtz, Agnes B. Women's Lacrosse for Coaches & Players. LC 77-85214. (Illus.). 1979. pap. text ed. 8.95 (ISBN 0-9601420-1-0). ABK Pubns.
Lacrosse. 1976. pap. 2.50 (ISBN 0-8277-4882-5). British Bk Ctr.
Lacrosse: A Know the Game Handbook. Date not set. pap. 2.95x (ISBN 0-7158-0276-3, SpS). Sportshelf.
Lacrosse Guide Nineteen Eighty-One to Eighty Three. 1981. 3.50 (ISBN 0-685-67030-9, 243-81681). AAHPERD.
Scott, Bob. Lacrosse: Technique & Tradition. LC 76-17223. (Illus.). 232p. 1976. 14.95 (ISBN 0-8018-1873-7); pap. 4.95 (ISBN 0-8018-2060-X). Johns Hopkins.
Walker, Jay. How to Play Winning Lacrosse. 1980. 9.95 (ISBN 0-671-96131-4); pap. 3.50 (ISBN 0-346-12393-3). Cornerstone.
Weyand, Alexander M. & Roberts, Milton R. The Lacrosse Story. LC 65-22885. (Illus.). 1965. 8.50 (ISBN 0-910718-01-6). H & A Herman.

LACTAMS
Manhas, Maghar S. Chemistry of Penicillins & Other Beta-Lactams. LC 78-27100. 248p. 1981. Repr. of 1971 ed. write for info. (ISBN 0-88275-830-6). Krieger.

LACTARIA
Hesler, L. R. & Smith, Alexander H. North American Species of Lactarius. (Illus.). 856p. 1979. text ed. 25.00x (ISBN 0-472-08440-2). U of Mich Pr.

LACTATION
see also Breast Feeding
Aebi & Whitehead, eds. Maternal Nutrition During Pregnancy & Lactation. (Nestle Foundation Publication Ser.: No. 1). (Illus.). 354p. 1980. text ed. 31.00 (ISBN 3-456-80945-X, Pub. by Hans Huber Switzerland). J K Burgess.
Cowie, A. T., et al. Hormonal Control of Lactation. (Monographs on Endocrinology: Vol. 15). (Illus.). 320p. 1980. 52.00 (ISBN 0-387-09680-9). Springer-Verlag.
Ebrahim, G. J. Breast Feeding: The Biological Option. LC 78-13096. 1980. text ed. 10.95x (ISBN 0-8052-3701-1). Schocken.
Falconer, Ian R., ed. Lactation. LC 70-159524. (Illus.). 443p. 1971. 24.50x (ISBN 0-271-01140-8). Pa St U Pr.
Fulkerson, W. J. Hormonal Control of Lactation, Vol. 1. Horrobin, D. F., ed. (Annual Research Reviews). 1980. 18.00 (ISBN 0-88831-061-7). Eden Med Res.
Fulkerson, William J. Hormonal Control of Lactation: Vol. 2. Horrobin, David F., ed. (Annual Research Reviews). 84p. 1981. 14.00 (ISBN 0-88831-087-0). Eden Med Res.
Hirschman, Charles & Hendershot, Gerry E. Trends in Breast Feeding Among American Mothers. Shipp, Audrey, ed. (Ser. 23: No. 3). 1979. pap. text ed. 1.75 (ISBN 0-8406-0159-X). Natl Ctr Health Stats.
Horrobin, David F. Prolactin, Vol. 7. LC 77-369577. (Annual Research Reviews Ser.). 126p. 1980. 18.00 (ISBN 0-88831-069-2). Eden Med Res.
International Symposium, Basel, March 1978. Lactate in Acute Conditions. Bossart, H. & Perret, C., eds. (Illus.). 1979. 53.50 (ISBN 3-8055-2968-6). S Karger.
Jelliffe, Derrick B. & Jelliffe, E. F. Human Milk in the Modern World: Psychosocial, Nutritional & Economic Significance. (Illus.). 1978. Repr. of 1978 ed. 17.95 (ISBN 0-19-264921-3). Oxford U Pr.
Josimovich, John B., et al, eds. Lactogenic Hormones, Fetal Nutrition, & Lactation. LC 73-12542. 483p. 1974. 34.50 (ISBN 0-471-45091-X, Pub. by Wiley). Krieger.
Kon, S. K. & Cowie, Alfred T., eds. Milk: The Mammary Gland & Its Secretion, 2 Vols. (Illus.). 1961. Vol. 1. 56.00 (ISBN 0-12-418701-3); Vol. 2. 56.00 (ISBN 0-12-418702-1); Set. 92.00 (ISBN 0-685-05135-8). Acad Pr.
Larson, Bruce L. & Smith, Vearl R., eds. Lactation: A Comprehensive Treatise. Incl. Vol. 1, 1974. Development, Lactogenesis. 63.50 (ISBN 0-12-436701-1); subscription 63.50 (ISBN 0-686-77185-0); Vol. 2. 1974. 48.75, by subscription 41.75 (ISBN 0-12-436702-X); Vol. 3. Milk, Nutrution & Maintenance. 1974. 56.00, by subscription 56.00 (ISBN 0-12-436703-8); Vol. 4. 1978. 66.50, by subscription 66.50 (ISBN 0-12-436704-6). Acad Pr.
Moret, P. R., et al, eds. Lactate: Physiologic, Methodologic & Pathologic Approach. (Illus.). 270p. 1980. pap. 24.00 (ISBN 0-387-09829-1). Springer-Verlag.
Pasteels, J. L., et al, eds. Human Prolactin: Proceedings. (International Congress Ser.: No. 308). 1974. 55.25 (ISBN 0-444-15061-7, Excerpta Medica). Elsevier.
Patton, Stuart & Jensen, Robert G. Biomedical Aspects of Lactation. 1976. pap. text ed. 13.25 (ISBN 0-08-020192-X). Pergamon.
Sulman, F. G. Hypothalamic Control of Lactation. LC 70-125281. (Monographs on Endocrinology: Vol. 3). (Illus.). 1970. 34.40 (ISBN 0-387-04973-8). Springer-Verlag.
Symposium, Campione, Sept 1973. Milk & Lactation: Proceedings. Kretchmer, N., et al, eds. (Modern Problems in Paediatrics: Vol. 15). (Illus.). 250p. 1975. 58.75 (ISBN 3-8055-2056-5). S Karger.
Whittemore, Colin T. Lactation of the Dairy Cow. LC 79-40442. (Longman Handbooks in Agriculture Ser.). (Illus.). 94p. 1980. pap. text ed. 9.95x (ISBN 0-582-45079-9). Longman.
Worthington, Bonnie S. & Williams, Sue R. Nutrition in Pregnancy & Lactation. LC 76-57760. (Illus.). 1977. pap. text ed. 9.95 (ISBN 0-8016-5237-5). Mosby.

LACTONES
Yoshioka, Hirosuke, et al, eds. Sesquiterpene Lactones: Chemistry, NMR & Plant Distribution. 1973. 49.50x (ISBN 0-86008-075-7, Pub. by U of Tokyo Pr). Intl Schol Bk Serv.

LACY FAMILY
Ferne, John. The Blazon of Gentrie. LC 72-5986. (English Experience Ser.: No. 513). (Illus.). 488p. 1973. Repr. of 1586 ed. 70.00 (ISBN 90-221-0513-X). Walter J Johnson.
Wightman, Wilfred E. The Lacy Family in England & Normandy, 1066-1194. LC 80-2206. Repr. of 1966 ed. 37.50 (ISBN 0-404-18794-3). AMS Pr.

LADAK
Ahluwalia, H. P. The Hermit Kingdom: Ladakh. (Illus.). 180p. 1981. text ed. 75.00x (ISBN 0-7069-1022-2, Pub. by Vikas India). Advent NY.
Harrer, Heinrich. Ladakh: Gods & Mortals Behind the Himalayas. (Illus.). 1981. 29.95 (ISBN 0-686-73111-5). Ungar.
Heber, A. Reeve & Heber, Kathleen. Himalayan Tibet & Ladakh. LC 76-91103. (Illus.). 1976. Repr. of 1903 ed. 13.50x (ISBN 0-8002-0251-1). Intl Pubns Serv.
Koshal, Samyukta. Ladakhi Grammar. 1979. 22.95 (ISBN 0-89684-052-2, Pub. by Motilal Banarsidass India). Orient Bk Dist.
Snellgrove, D. L. & Skorupski, T. The Cultural Heritage of Ladakh, - Two: Zangskar & the Cave Temples of Ladakh. 166p. 1981. text ed. 45.00x (ISBN 0-85668-148-2, Pub. by Aris & Phillips England). Humanities.
Snellgrove, David L. & Skorupski, Tadeusz. The Cultural Heritage of Ladakh, Vol. 1. (Illus.). 1977. 30.00 (ISBN 0-87773-700-2, Prajna). Great Eastern.
Tsering, Nawang. Buddhism in Ladakh. 112p. 1979. text ed. 7.95 (ISBN 0-89684-263-0, Pub. by Sterling India). Orient Bk Dist.
Wahid, Siddiq. Ladakh: Between Heaven & Earth. (Illus.). 1981. 27.50 (ISBN 2-88001-101-9). Norton.

LADD, WILLIAM, 1778-1841
Hemmenway, John. The Apostle of Peace: Memoir of William Ladd. LC 70-137544. 272p. 1972. Repr. of 1872 ed. lib. bdg. 15.95x (ISBN 0-89198-072-5). Ozer.

LADIN LANGUAGE
see Raeto-Romance Language

LADING, BILLS OF
see Bills of Lading

LADO ENCLAVE
Stigand, C. H. Equatoria: The Lado Enclave. new ed. (Illus.). 253p. 1968. 26.00x (ISBN 0-7146-1722-9, F Cass Co). Biblio Dist.

LADYBIRDS
Ali, Mohamed. Ecological & Physiological Studies: Alfalfa Ladybird. 1979. 20.00 (ISBN 0-9960015-8-1, Pub. by Kaido Hungary). Heyden.
--Ecological & Physiological Studies on the Alfalfa Ladybird. 1981. 50.00x (ISBN 0-569-08553-5, Pub. by Collet's). State Mutual Bk.
Conklin, Gladys. Lucky Ladybugs. (Illus.). (gr. k-3). 1968. reinforced bdg. 7.95 (ISBN 0-8234-0072-7). Holiday.
Gage, John H. The Larvae of the Coccinellidae. (Illinois Biological Monographs: Vol. 6, No. 4). pap. 6.00 (ISBN 0-384-17550-3). Johnson Repr.
Hawes, Judy. Ladybug, Ladybug, Fly Away Home. LC 67-15399. (A Let's-Read-&-Find-Out Science Bk). (Illus.). (gr. k-3). 1967. (TYC-J); PLB 8.79 (ISBN 0-690-48384-8); filmstrip with record 11.95 (ISBN 0-690-48385-6); filmstrip with cassette 14.95 (ISBN 0-690-48387-2). Har-Row.
--Ladybug, Ladybug, Fly Away Home. LC 67-15399. (Crocodile Paperbacks Ser.). (Illus.). (ps-3). 1973. pap. 2.95 (ISBN 0-690-00200-9, TYC-J). Har-Row.
McClung, Robert M. Ladybug. (Illus.). (gr. k-3). pap. 3.80 (ISBN 0-688-35010-0). Morrow.
Mohamed Ali. Ecological & Physiological Studies of the Alfalfa Ladybird. (Illus.). 200p. 1979. 22.50x (ISBN 9-6305-1702-7). Intl Pubns Serv.
Wong, Herbert H. & Vessel, Matthew F. My Ladybug. LC 69-15802. (Illus.). (gr. k-2). 1969. PLB 6.95 (ISBN 0-201-08721-9, A-W Childrens) (ISBN 0-685-05058-0). A-W.

LAETRILE
Bradford, R. & Culbert, M. Laetrile Program Handbook. 3.50 (ISBN 0-686-29869-1). Cancer Bk Hse.
Commission of Freedom of Choice. Sloan-Ketttering (Laetrile) Studies. 3.50 (ISBN 0-686-29895-0). Cancer Bk Hse.
Culbert, M. L. Vitamin B-17: Forbidden Weapon Against Cancer. 1974. 8.95 (ISBN 0-87000-279-1). Arlington Hse.
Culbert, Michael L. Freedom from Cancer. new ed. LC 76-43206. (Illus.). 1976. pap. 2.95 (ISBN 0-89245-007-X). Seventy-Six.
Culbert, Mike. Vitamin B17, the Fight for Laetrile. 8.95 (ISBN 0-686-29898-5). Cancer Bk Hse.
Griffin, G. Edward. World Without Cancer: The Story of Vitamin B 17. LC 74-83649. (Illus., Orig.). 1974. 14.95 (ISBN 0-912986-08-5); pap. 4.95 (ISBN 0-912986-09-3). Am Media.
Halstead, Bruce. Amygdalin (Laetrile) Therapy. 3.00 (ISBN 0-686-29936-1). Cancer Bk Hse.
Halstead, Bruce W. Amgydalin (Laetrile) Therapy. (Illus.). 1977. pap. 3.00 (ISBN 0-933904-06-1). Gold Quill Pubs CA.
--Laetrile Poisoning & Cancer Politics. LC 79-54034. (Illus.). 1981. pap. 8.95 (ISBN 0-933904-05-3). Gold Quill Pubs CA.
Joyce, Florence. Laetrile Diet Cook Book. 4.95 (ISBN 0-686-29765-2). Cancer Bk Hse.
Kell, George. Laetrile vs. Cancer. 2.00 (ISBN 0-686-29766-0). Cancer Bk Hse.
Kittler, Glenn D. Laetrile Control for Cancer. updated ed. 3.95 (ISBN 0-686-29772-5). Cancer Bk Hse.
--Laetrile Control for Cancer. 1963. 8.95 (ISBN 0-8392-1059-0). Astor-Honor.
McNaughton Foundation. Laetrile-Nitrilosides-in Prevention & Control of Cancer. 3.50 (ISBN 0-686-29805-5). Cancer Bk Hse.
Markle, Gerald E. & Petersen, James C., eds. The Laetrile Phenomenon: Politics, Science, & Cancer. LC 80-13466. 208p. 1980. 20.00 (ISBN 0-89158-854-X); pap. 9.75 (ISBN 0-86531-046-7). Westview.
Markle, Gerald E. & Peterson, James C., eds. Politics, Science, & Cancer: The Laetrile Phenomenon. (AAAS Selected Symposium: No. 46). 250p. 1980. lib. bdg. 20.00 (ISBN 0-89158-854-X); pap. 9.50 (ISBN 0-86531-046-7). Westview.
Miniutti, Denise & Brecher, Amy. Laetrile: Special Report. (Illus.). 1977. pap. 1.50 (ISBN 0-89552-012-5). DMR Pubns.
Prince, Patricia. Contreras Clinic Laetrile Cookbook. 9.95 (ISBN 0-686-29941-8). Cancer Bk Hse.
--The Contreras Clinic Laetrile Cookbook. LC 79-89609. (Illus.). 248p. 1979. pap. 10.00 (ISBN 0-8159-5221-X, Pub. by ESP Inc). Devin.
Richardson, J. & Griffin, P. Laetrile Case Histories. 5.95 (ISBN 0-686-29952-3). Cancer Bk Hse.
Richardson, John & Griffin, Patricia. Laetrile Case Histories: The Richardson Cancer Clinic Experience. new ed. 1977. pap. 5.95 (ISBN 0-912986-03-4). Am Media.
Richardson, John A. Laetrile Case Histories. 316p. pap. 4.00 (ISBN 0-686-31152-3). Concord Pr.
Timms, Moira & Zar, Zachariah. Natural Sources: Vitamin B-17--Laetrile. LC 77-90009. (Illus.). 1978. pap. text ed. 4.95 (ISBN 0-89087-217-1). Celestial Arts.

LA FARGE, JOHN, 1880-

Cortissoz, Royal. John Lafarge.A Memoir &A Study. LC 70-87508. (Library of American Art Ser). (Illus.). 1971. Repr. of 1911 ed. lib. bdg. 25.00 (ISBN 0-306-71405-1). Da Capo.

Weinberg, H. Barbara. The Decorative Work of John la Farge. LC 76-23654. (Outstanding Dissertations in the Fine Arts - 2nd Series - American). (Illus.). 1977. Repr. of 1972 ed. lib. bdg. 84.00 (ISBN 0-8240-2736-1). Garland Pub.

LA FAYETTE, MARIE ADRIENNE FRANCOISE (DE NOAILLES), d. 1807

Maurois, Andre. Adrienne ou la Vie de Madame de La Fayette. 15.90 (ISBN 0-685-34312-X). French & Eur.

LAFAYETTE, MARIE JOSEPH PAUL YVES ROCH GILBERT DU MOTIER, MARQUIS DE, 1757-1834

Beahrs, Virginia O. The Fire & the Glory: Lafayette & America's Fight for Freedom. LC 76-5848. 1976. 8.95 (ISBN 0-664-32592-0). Westminster.

Fish, Hamilton. Lafayette in America During & After the Revolutionary War: And Other Essays on Franco-American Relations. 1977. 6.95 (ISBN 0-533-02314-9). Vantage.

Gerson, Noel B. Statue in Search of a Pedestal: A Biography of the Marquis de Lafayette. 1976. 7.95 (ISBN 0-396-07341-7). Dodd.

Gottschalk, Louis. Lafayette & the Close of the American Revolution. LC 42-12337. (Midway Reprint Ser). xiv, 458p. 1974. pap. 17.50x (ISBN 0-226-30538-4). U of Chicago Pr.

--Lafayette Between the American & French Revolution: 1783-1789. LC 50-5286. (Midway Reprint Ser). xii, 461p. 1974. pap. 17.50x (ISBN 0-226-30536-8). U of Chicago Pr.

--Lafayette Comes to America. LC 35-15130. (Midway Reprint Ser). xiv, 184p. 1974. pap. 9.50x (ISBN 0-226-30540-6). U of Chicago Pr.

--Lafayette Joins the American Army. LC 37-38848. (Midway Reprint Ser). 400p. 1974. pap. 15.00x (ISBN 0-226-30542-2). U of Chicago Pr.

Gottschalk, Louis & Maddox, Margaret. Lafayette in the French Revolution: From the October Days Through the Federation. LC 69-12572. 1973. 22.00x (ISBN 0-226-30547-3). U of Chicago Pr.

--Lafayette in the French Revolution, Through the October Days. LC 69-12572. 1969. 15.00x (ISBN 0-226-30545-7). U of Chicago Pr.

Gottschalk, Louis & Bill, Shirley, eds. The Letters of Lafayette to Washington 1777-1799. 2nd rev. ed. LC 76-8599. (Memoirs Ser.: Vol. 115). 1976. 10.00 (ISBN 0-87169-115-9). Am Philos.

Gottschalk, Louis, et al, eds. Lafayette: A Guide to the Letters, Documents, & Manuscripts in the United States. LC 75-18724. 296p. 1975. 45.00x (ISBN 0-8014-0953-5). Cornell U Pr.

Idzerda, Stanley J. & Smith, Roger E., eds. Lafayette in the Age of the American Revolution: Selected Letters & Papers, 1776-1790, Vol. I. LC 76-50268. (Lafayette Papers Ser.). (Illus.). 1977. 25.00x (ISBN 0-8014-1031-2). Cornell U Pr.

Idzerda, Stanley J., et al, eds. Lafayette in the Age of the American Revolution: Selected Letters & Papers, 1776 to 1790, Vol. 4, April 1, 1781 to December 23, 1781. (Illus.). 600p. 1981. 38.50 (ISBN 0-8014-1336-2). Cornell U Pr.

--Lafayette in the Age of the American Revolution: Selected Letters & Papers, 1776-1790 Vol. III: April 27, 1780-March 29, 1781. LC 76-50268. (The Lafayette Papers). (Illus.). 584p. 1981. 35.00x (ISBN 0-8014-1335-4). Cornell U Pr.

--Lafayette in the Age of the American Revolution, Selected Letters & Papers, 1776-1790: April 1, 1781-December 23, 1781, Vol. IV. LC 76-50268. (The Lafayette Papers Ser.). (Illus.). 1981. 38.50x (ISBN 0-8014-1336-2). Cornell U Pr.

--Lafayette in the Age of the American Revolution, Vol. II, Selected Letters & Papers 1776-1790. LC 76-50268. (Illus.). 1979. 25.00x (ISBN 0-8014-1246-3). Cornell U Pr.

Jackson, Stuart W. La Fayette: A Bibliography. 1930. 21.50 (ISBN 0-8337-1813-4). B Franklin.

Loveland, Anne C. Emblem of Liberty: Image of Lafayette in the American Mind. LC 70-142336. 1971. 15.00x (ISBN 0-8071-0804-9). La State U Pr.

Nolan, James B. Lafayette in America Day by Day. LC 72-1709. Repr. of 1934 ed. 16.00 (ISBN 0-404-52427-3). AMS Pr.

Sedgwick, Henry D. La Fayette. 432p. 1981. Repr. of 1928 ed. lib. bdg. 30.00 (ISBN 0-8495-5045-9). Arden Lib.

Tower, Charlemagne. The Marquis de La Fayette in the American Revolution, 2 vols. facsimile ed. LC 70-169778. (Select Bibliographies Reprint Ser.). Repr. of 1894 ed. Set. 56.00 (ISBN 0-8369-5998-1). Arno.

--Marquis De Lafayette in the American Revolution with Some Account of the Attitude of France Toward the War of Independence, 2 Vols. LC 79-112310. (Era of the American Revolution Ser). 1970. Repr. of 1901 ed. lib. bdg. 75.00 (ISBN 0-306-71914-2). Da Capo.

Tuckerman, Bayard. Life of General Lafayette, 2 Vols. LC 72-177575. Repr. of 1889 ed. Set. 45.00 (ISBN 0-404-07187-2). Vol. 1 (ISBN 0-404-07188-0). Vol. 2 (ISBN 0-404-07189-9). AMS Pr.

Whitman, Walt. Lafayette in Brooklyn. LC 73-4023. 1973. lib. bdg. 15.00 (ISBN 0-8414-2840-9). Folcroft.

LAFAYETTE, MARIE JOSEPH PAUL YVES ROCH GILBERT DU MOTIER, MARQUIS DE, 1757-1834-JUVENILE LITERATURE

Grant, Matthew G. Lafayette. LC 73-18155. 1974. PLB 5.95 (ISBN 0-87191-301-1). Creative Ed.

Holbrook, Sabra. Lafayette: Man in the Middle. LC 77-2553. (gr. 7 up). 1977. 7.95 (ISBN 0-689-30585-0). Atheneum.

Tuckerman, Bayard. Life of General Lafayette, 2 Vols. LC 72-177575. Repr. of 1889 ed. Set. 45.00 (ISBN 0-404-07187-2). Vol. 1 (ISBN 0-404-07188-0). Vol. 2 (ISBN 0-404-07189-9). AMS Pr.

LAFAYETTE, MARIE MADELEINE PIOCHE DE LA VERGNE, COMTESSE DE, 1634-1693

Burkart, Rosemarie. Die Kunst Des Masses in Mme de Lafayette's "Princesse de Cleves". 1933. pap. 14.00 (ISBN 0-384-06545-7). Johnson Repr.

Haig, Stirling. Madame de Lafayette. LC 71-79207. (World Authors Ser.). 1970. lib. bdg. 12.95x (ISBN 0-8057-2508-3). Irvington.

Kaps, Helen K. Moral Perspective in La Princesse De Cleves. LC 79-4661. 1968. 5.00 (ISBN 0-87114-021-7). U of Oreg Bks.

Kuizenga, Donna. Narrative Strategies in "la Princesse de Cleves". LC 76-17258. (Monographs: No.2). 160p. (Orig.). 1976. pap. 9.50x (ISBN 0-917058-01-1). French Forum.

LAFAYETTE ESCADRILLE

see France–Army–Lafayette Escadrille

LAFEVER, MINARD

Landy, Jacob. Architecture of Minard Lafever. LC 69-19461. (Illus.). 313p. 1970. 22.50x (ISBN 0-231-03132-7). Columbia U Pr.

LAFITTE, JEAN, 1782-1854

Gayarre, Charles. Historical Sketch of Pierre & Jean Lafitte, the Famous Smugglers of Louisiana. pap. 4.50 wrappers (ISBN 0-685-13272-2). Jenkins.

Gonzalez, Catherine T. Lafitte: The Terror of the Gulf. (Stories for Young Americans Ser.). (Illus.). 64p. 1981. 5.95 (ISBN 0-89015-284-5). Eakin Pubns.

Ingraham, Joseph H. Lafitte: The Pirate of the Gulf, 2 vols in 1. 1972. Repr. of 1836 ed. 29.50 (ISBN 0-8422-8078-2). Irvington.

Ray, Cyril. Lafite. LC 69-17938. 1969. 25.00x (ISBN 0-8128-1214-X). Stein & Day.

LAFITTE, JEAN, 1782-1854–FICTION

Ingraham, Joseph H. Lafitte: The Pirate of the Gulf, 2 vols. LC 72-78759. 1836. Repr. 49.00 (ISBN 0-686-01344-1). Somerset Pub.

LA FOLLETTE, ROBERT MARION, 1855-1925

Greenbaum, Fred. Robert Marion La Follette. LC 74-26675. (World Leaders Ser: No. 44). 1975. lib. bdg. 12.50 (ISBN 0-8057-3057-5). Twayne.

Ham, F. Gerald & Mattern, Carolyn J., eds. The Papers of Robert M. LaFollette at the State Historical Society of Wisconsin: Guide to a Microfilm Edition. LC 72-619621. (Guides to Historical Resources Ser.). 1972. pap. 3.00 (ISBN 0-87020-121-2). State Hist Soc Wis.

La Follette, Robert M. La Follette's Autobiography: A Personal Narrative of Political Experiences. 362p. 1960. pap. 5.25 (ISBN 0-299-02194-7). U of Wis Pr.

Maney, Patrick J. Young Bob La Follette: A Biography of Robert M. La Follette, Jr. 1895-1953. LC 77-24991. 1978. 18.00x (ISBN 0-8262-0230-6). U of Mo Pr.

Maxwell, Robert, ed. La Follette. LC 69-15341. (Great Lives Observed Ser.). 1969. pap. 1.95 (ISBN 0-13-522433-0, Spec). P-H.

Thelen, David P. The Early Life of Robert M. la Follette, 1855-1884. LC 66-11931. (Illus.). 1966. 2.95 (ISBN 0-8294-0078-8). Loyola.

--Robert La Follette & the Insurgent Spirit. 208p. 1976. 7.50 (ISBN 0-316-83927-2); pap. 4.95 (ISBN 0-316-83925-6). Little.

Torelle, Ellen, ed. The Political Philosophy of Robert M. LaFollette. LC 75-348. (The Radical Tradition in America Ser). (Illus.). 426p. 1975. Repr. of 1920 ed. 28.50 (ISBN 0-88355-252-3). Hyperion Conn.

LA FONTAINE, JEAN DE, 1621-1695

Collinet. Le Monde Litteraire de La Fontaine. 33.95 (ISBN 0-685-34231-X). French & Eur.

Giraudoux, Jean. Les Cinq Tentations de la Fontaine. 303p. 1958. 7.95 (ISBN 0-686-54000-X). French & Eur.

Hamel, Frank. Jean De La Fontaine. LC 70-113313. (Illus.). 1970. Repr. of 1911 ed. 15.00 (ISBN 0-8046-0996-9). Kennikat.

Lapp, John C. Esthetics of Negligence: La Fontaine's Contes. LC 72-142130. 1971. 42.00 (ISBN 0-521-08067-3). Cambridge U Pr.

Mackay, Agnes E. La Fontaine & His Friends. LC 73-79049. (Illus.). 228p. 1973. 8.95 (ISBN 0-8076-0694-4). Braziller.

March, Edward. Fables de-la Fontaine. LC 81-67110. (Illus.). 32p. 1981. 45.00 (ISBN 0-940032-00-7); prepub. 37.50 until december 31, 1981 (ISBN 0-686-76559-1). Alphabet Pr.

Regnier, Henri M. Lexique De la Langue De Jean De la Fontaine: Avec une Introduction Grammaticale, 2 vols. LC 72-82402. 1140p. (Fr.). 1973. Repr. of 1892 ed. Set. 65.00 (ISBN 0-8337-4768-1). B Franklin.

Rochambeau, Eugene A. Bibliographie Des Oeuvres De la Fontaine. LC 70-123603. (Bibliography & Reference Ser.: No. 365). 1970. Repr. of 1911 ed. 40.50 (ISBN 0-8337-3032-0). B Franklin.

Sutherland, Monica. La Fontaine: The Man & His Work. LC 74-7095. 1974. Repr. of 1953 ed. lib. bdg. 20.00 (ISBN 0-8414-7754-X). Folcroft.

--La Fontaine: The Man & His Work. 1973. Repr. of 1953 ed. 20.00 (ISBN 0-8274-1407-2). R West.

Tyler, J. Allen & Parrish, Stephen M., eds. A Concordance to the Fables & Tales of Jean De la Fontaine. LC 73-8388. (Concordances Ser.). 1104p. (Fr. & Eng.). 1974. 42.50x (ISBN 0-8014-0811-3). Cornell U Pr.

Wadsworth, Philip A. Young La Fontaine. LC 78-128943. (Northwestern Humanities Ser.: No. 29). 1970. Repr. of 1952 ed. 21.50 (ISBN 0-404-50729-8). AMS Pr.

LAFORGUE, JULES

Arkell, David. Looking for Laforgue: An Informal Biography of Jules Laforgue. LC 79-89449. 1979. 20.00 (ISBN 0-89255-042-2). Persea Bks.

Collie, Michael. Jules Laforgue. (Athlone French Poets Ser). 160p. 1977. text ed. 18.75x (ISBN 0-485-14606-1, Athlone Pr); pap. text ed. 6.25x (ISBN 0-485-12206-5). Humanities.

Laforgue, Jules. Lettres a un ami: 1880-1886, avec le Fac-Simile d'Une Lettre Inedite a Stephane Mallarme. LC 77-10274. 240p. Repr. of 1941 ed. 29.00 (ISBN 0-404-16326-2). AMS Pr.

Ramsey, Warren, ed. Jules Laforgue: Essays on a Poet's Life & Work. LC 69-11503. (Crosscurrents-Modern Critiques Ser.). 224p. 1969. 7.95 (ISBN 0-8093-0346-9). S Ill U Pr.

LAG, CULTURAL

see Cultural Lag

LAGARDE, PAUL ANTON DE, 1827-1891

Stern, Fritz R. The Politics of Cultural Despair: A Study in the Rise of the Germanic Ideology. (California Library Reprint Ser.). 1974. 26.75x (ISBN 0-520-02643-8); pap. 7.95x (ISBN 0-520-02626-8). U of Cal Pr.

LAGERKVIST, PAR FABIAN, 1891-

Sjoberg, Leif. Par Lagerkvist. (Columbia Essays on Modern Writers Ser.: No. 74). 1976. pap. 2.00 (ISBN 0-231-03103-3). Columbia U Pr.

Spector, Robert D. Par Lagerkvist. (World Authors Ser.: Sweden: No. 267). 1973. lib. bdg. 10.95 (ISBN 0-8057-2509-1). Twayne.

White, Ray L. Par Lagerkvist in America. 157p. 1980. text ed. 19.25x (ISBN 91-22-00362-2). Humanities.

LAGERLOF, SELMA OTTILIANA LOUISA, 1858-1940

Berendsohn, Walter A. Selma Lagerlof, Her Life & Work. LC 67-27576. (Illus.). 1931. Repr. 9.00 (ISBN 0-8046-0027-9). Kennikat.

Lagerloef, Selma O. The Diary of Selma Lagerloef. Howard, Velma S., tr. LC 36-30959. 1975. Repr. of 1936 ed. 16.00 (ISBN 0-527-54000-5). Kraus Repr.

--Memories of My Childhood: Further Years at Marbacka. Howard, Velma S., tr. LC 34-27093. 1975. Repr. of 1934 ed. 17.00 (ISBN 0-527-54010-2). Kraus Repr.

Larsen, Hanna A. Selma Lagerloef. LC 36-27415. 1975. Repr. of 1936 ed. 13.00 (ISBN 0-527-54880-4). Kraus Repr.

LAGOS (CITY)

Baker, Pauline H. Urbanization & Political Change: The Politics of Lagos, 1917-1967. LC 70-162001. 1975. 31.95x (ISBN 0-520-02066-9). U of Cal Pr.

Cole, P. D. Modern & Traditional Elites in the Politics of Lagos. LC 74-76578. (African Studies: No. 12). 264p. 1975. 28.95 (ISBN 0-521-20439-9). Cambridge U Pr.

Echeruo, Michael J. Victorian Lagos: Aspects of Nineteenth Century Lagos Life. (Illus.). 1978. text ed. 16.50x (ISBN 0-8419-5031-8). Holmes & Meier.

Folami, Takiu. The History of Lagos, Nigeria: The Shaping of an African City. (Illus.). 256p. 1981. 8.50 (ISBN 0-682-49772-X). Exposition.

Lagos: Urban Development & Employment. 109p. 1980. pap. 11.25 (ISBN 92-2-101997-7, ILO 102, ILO). Unipub.

Marris, Peter. Family & Social Change in an African City: A Study of Rehousing in Lagos. (African Studies Ser.: No. 8). (Illus.). 1962. 9.95x (ISBN 0-8101-0156-4). Northwestern U Pr.

LAGRANGE EQUATIONS

Kilmister, C. W. Lagrangian Dynamics: An Introduction for Students. LC 68-28883. 136p. 1968. 22.50 (ISBN 0-306-30368-X, Plenum Pr). Plenum Pub.

Wells, Dare A. Lagrangian Dynamics. (Schaum's Outline Ser). (Orig.). 1967. pap. 6.95 (ISBN 0-07-069258-0, SP). McGraw.

LAGRANGIAN FUNCTIONS

Edelen, D. G. Lagrangian Mechanics of Nonconservative Nonholonomic Systems. (Mechanics: Dynamical Systems Ser.: No. 2). 314p. 1977. 30.00x (ISBN 90-286-0077-9). Sijthoff & Noordhoff.

Leray, Jean. Lagrangian Analysis & Quantum Mechanics. Schroeder, Carolyn, tr. from Fr. 288p. 1981. 35.00x (ISBN 0-262-12087-9). MIT Pr.

Pierre, Donald A. & Lowe, Michael J. An Introduction with Computer Programs. (Applied Mathematics & Computation: No. 9). 464p. 1975. text ed. 24.50 (ISBN 0-201-05796-4); pap. text ed. 14.50 (ISBN 0-201-05797-2). A-W.

LAGUARDIA, FIORELLO HENRY, 1882-1947

Heckscher, August & Robinson, Phyllis. When LaGuardia Was Mayor: New York's Legendary Years. (Illus.). 1978. 17.50 (ISBN 0-393-07534-6). Norton.

Kamen, Gloria. Fiorello. LC 81-2282. (Illus.). 64p. (gr. 3-6). 1981. price not set (ISBN 0-689-30869-8). Atheneum.

Kurland, Gerald. Fiorello la Guardia: The People's Mayor of New York. Rahmas, D. Steve, ed. LC 77-190238. (Outstanding Personalities Ser: No. 20). 32p. (Orig.). (gr. 7-12). 1972. lib. bdg. 2.95 incl. catalog cards (ISBN 0-87157-520-5); pap. 1.50 vinyl laminated covers (ISBN 0-87157-020-3). SamHar Pr.

Mann, Arthur. La Guardia: A Fighter Against His Times, 1882-1933. 1969. pap. 2.95 (ISBN 0-226-50330-5, P330, Phoen). U of Chicago Pr.

--La Guardia Comes to Power, Nineteen Thirty Three. 1969. pap. 1.95 (ISBN 0-226-50331-3, P331, Phoen). U of Chicago Pr.

Meltzer, Ida. Fiorello LaGuardia. 1979. of 10 6.75 set (ISBN 0-87594-188-5). Book Lab.

Moses, Robert. Laguardia: A Salute & a Memoir. 1957. 2.50 (ISBN 0-671-40620-5). S&S.

Zinn, Howard. La Guardia in Congress. LC 72-4007. 288p. 1972. Repr. of 1959 ed. lib. bdg. 15.25x (ISBN 0-8371-6434-6, ZILG). Greenwood.

--LaGuardia in Congress. 1969. pap. 2.35x (ISBN 0-393-00488-0, Norton Lib). Norton.

LAING, RONALD DAVID

Boyers, Robert & Orrill, Robert, eds. R. D. Laing & Anti-Psychiatry. 304p. 1974. Repr. of 1971 ed. lib. bdg. 16.00x (ISBN 0-374-90906-7). Octagon.

Collier, Andrew. R.D. Laing: The Philosophy & Politics of Psychotherapy. LC 76-62705. 1977. 10.00 (ISBN 0-394-41130-7); pap. 3.95 (ISBN 0-394-73353-3). Pantheon.

Friedenberg, Edgar Z. R. D. Laing. (Modern Masters Ser.). 128p. 1974. 5.95 (ISBN 0-670-58984-5). Viking Pr.

Howarth-Williams, Martin. R.D. Laing: His Work & Its Relevance to Sociology. (Direct Editions Ser.). (Orig.). 1977. pap. 14.50 (ISBN 0-7100-8624-5). Routledge & Kegan.

LAISSEZ-FAIRE

see also Competition; Industry and State; Manchester School of Economics

Adams, Henry C. Two Essays: Relation of the State to Industrial Action & Economics & Jurisprudence. Dorfman, Joseph, ed. LC 75-76510. (Reprints of Economic Classics). Repr. of 1954 ed. 15.00x (ISBN 0-678-00494-3). Kelley.

Aronson, Charles N. Free Enterprise. LC 78-73546. (Eagle Ser.: No. 5). (Illus.). 1979. 25.00 (ISBN 0-915736-15-2); pap. 18.00 (ISBN 0-915736-16-0). C N Aronson.

Brown, K. W. & Warner, A. R. Free Enterprise: Fundamentals of the American System. 1981. 13.32 (ISBN 0-07-067501-5); tchr's. manual & key 4.50 (ISBN 0-07-067502-3). McGraw.

Burns, Arthur F. Reflections of an Economic Policy Maker: Speeches & Congressional Statements, 1969-1978. 1978. 17.25 (ISBN 0-8447-3319-9); pap. 9.25 (ISBN 0-8447-3333-4). Am Enterprise.

Cunningham, William. The Growth of English Industry & Commerce, 3 vols. in 2. Incl. Vol. 1. Early & Middle Ages. 5th ed; Vol. 2. Modern Times: the Mercantile System. 4th ed; Vol. 3. Modern Times: Laissez Faire. 4th ed. LC 66-21667. Repr. of 1907 ed. Set. 50.00x (ISBN 0-678-00288-6). Kelley.

Dahlberg, Arthur. How to Save Free Enterprise. LC 74-75390. (Illus.). 374p. 1975. 12.95 (ISBN 0-8159-5708-4). Devin.

Fine, Sidney. Laissez Faire & the General-Welfare State: A Study of Conflict in American Thought, 1865-1901. 1964. pap. 4.95x (ISBN 0-472-06086-4, 86, AA). U of Mich Pr.
Greene, Leonard. Free Enterprise Without Poverty. 1981. 12.95 (ISBN 0-393-01470-3). Norton.
Hirst, Francis W., ed. Free Trade & Other Fundamental Doctrines of the Manchester School. LC 68-27674. Repr. of 1903 ed. 19.50x (ISBN 0-678-00403-X). Kelley.
Jewkes, John. A Return to Free Market Economics? 1978. text ed. 32.50x (ISBN 0-8419-5028-8). Holmes & Meier.
Keynes, John M. The End of Laissez-Faire. (Reprints in History). 1927. lib. bdg. 16.50x (ISBN 0-697-00040-0); pap. 8.95x (ISBN 0-89197-747-3). Irvington.
Luker, William, et al. Hard Choices: The American Free Enterprise System at Work. (Illus.). (gr. 12). 1979. text ed. 9.95 (ISBN 0-88408-128-1); pap. text ed. 7.95 (ISBN 0-88408-123-0); tchrs.' manual avail. Sterling Swift.
McKenzie, Richard B. Bound for Freedom. (Publication Ser.: No. 255). 210p. 1982. 15.95 (ISBN 0-8179-7551-9). Hoover Inst Pr.
Meyer, Herbert E. The War Against Progress. 1979. 11.95 (ISBN 0-935166-00-9). Storm King.
Paul, Ellen F. Moral Revolution & Economic Science: The Demise of Laissez-Faire in Nineteenth Century British Political Economy. LC 78-73797. (Contributions in Economics & Economic History: No. 23). 1979. lib. bdg. 25.00 (ISBN 0-313-21055-1, PMR/). Greenwood.
Read, Leonard E. Free Market & Its Enemy. 75p. 1965. 1.75 (ISBN 0-910614-39-3); pap. 0.50 (ISBN 0-910614-09-1). Foun Econ Ed.
--Having My Way. xiii, 176p. 1974. 3.00 (ISBN 0-910614-49-0). Foun Econ Ed.
--Then Truth Will Out. 177p. 1971. 3.00 (ISBN 0-910614-27-X); pap. 1.00 (ISBN 0-910614-26-1). Foun Econ Ed.
Robillard, Raymond A. Interdependence of Free Enterprise & Governments in the Global Marketplace. LC 79-66832. 1979. pap. text ed. 9.00 (ISBN 0-8191-0852-9). U Pr of Amer.
Soble, Ronald L. Whatever Became of Free Enterprise? (Orig.). 1977. pap. 1.75 (ISBN 0-451-07542-0, E7542, Sig). NAL.
Society Without Government. LC 74-172235. (Right Wing Individualist Tradition in America Ser). 1972. Repr. of 1971 ed. 15.00 (ISBN 0-405-00440-0). Arno.
Taylor, Arthur J. Laissez-Faire & State Intervention in Nineteenth-Century Britain. (Studies in Economic & Social History). 64p. (Orig.). 1972. pap. text ed. 4.00x (ISBN 0-333-09925-7). Humanities.
Waligorski, Conrad & Hone, Thomas, eds. Anglo-American Liberalism: A Collection of Readings in Political Economy. LC 81-4008. 330p. 1981. text ed. 20.95x (ISBN 0-88229-617-5); pap. text ed. 10.95x (ISBN 0-88229-785-6). Nelson-Hall.

LAITY

see also Fish Movement (Christianity); Lay Readers; Priesthood, Universal

Barta, Russell, ed. Challenge to the Laity. LC 79-92441. (Illus.). 144p. 1980. pap. 2.95 (ISBN 0-87973-532-5, 532). Our Sunday Visitor.
Bucy, Ralph D. The New Laity: Between Church & World. 1978. pap. 7.95 (ISBN 0-8499-2833-8). Word Bks.
Cross, Claire. Church & People, 1450-1600. LC 76-25005. (Fontana Library of English History). 288p. 1976. text ed. 18.25x (ISBN 0-391-00649-5). Humanities.
Duquoc, Christian, ed. Spirituality in Church & World. LC 65-28868. (Concilium Ser.: Vol. 9). 174p. 6.95 (ISBN 0-8091-0139-4). Paulist Pr.
Hall, Cameron P. Lay Action: The Church's Third Force. (Orig.). 1974. pap. 3.50 (ISBN 0-377-00018-3). Friend Pr.
Keller, Philip W. Un Laica Exam: El Padrenuestro. (Span.). Date not set. 2.00 (ISBN 0-686-76344-0). Life Pubs Intl.
Lindgren, Alvin J. & Shawchuck, Norman. Let My People Go: Empowering Laity for Ministry. LC 80-16035. 144p. (Orig.). 1980. pap. 5.95 (ISBN 0-687-21377-0). Abingdon.
Marney, Carlyle. Priests to Each Other. LC 73-16787. 128p. (Orig.). 1974. pap. 2.95 (ISBN 0-8170-0628-1). Judson.
Portillo, Alvaro del. Faithful & Laity in the Church. 200p. pap. 3.75 (ISBN 0-933932-40-5). Scepter Pubs.
Schillebeeck, Edward. Layman in the Church. 1963. 1.95 (ISBN 0-8189-0073-3). Alba.
Schillebeeckx, Edward. Definition of the Christian Layman. (Synthesis Ser). 1970. pap. 0.65 (ISBN 0-8199-0380-9). Franciscan Herald.
Southard, Samuel. Comprehensive Pastoral Care: Enabling the Laity to Share in Pastoral Ministry. 128p. 1975. pap. 3.50 (ISBN 0-8170-0655-9); pap. 9.95 with casette (ISBN 0-8170-0692-3). Judson.
Thompson, James W. The Literacy of the Laity in the Middle Ages. Repr. of 1939 ed. pap. 14.00 (ISBN 0-384-60270-3). Johnson Repr.
Vaillancourt, Jean-Guy. Papal Power: A Study of Vatican Control Over Lay Catholic Elites. 375p. 1980. 16.95 (ISBN 0-520-03733-2). U of Cal Pr.

LA JOLLA, CALIFORNIA

Dorn, Edward. Hello, La Jolla. LC 78-50780. 1978. 12.50 (ISBN 0-914728-24-5); signed ed 35.00 (ISBN 0-914728-25-3); pap. 3.50 (ISBN 0-914728-23-7). Wingbow Pr.

LAKANAL, JOSEPH, 1762-1845

Dawson, John C. Lakanal the Regicide. facs. ed. (Select Bibliographies Reprint Ser). 1948. 17.00 (ISBN 0-8369-5520-X). Arno.

LAKE CHAMPLAIN

see Champlain, Lake

LAKE DISTRICT, ENGLAND

Abraham, Ashley P. Some Portraits of the Lake Poets & Their Homes. 1978. Repr. of 1914 ed. lib. bdg. 20.00 (ISBN 0-8495-0129-6). Arden Lib.
Bouch, Charles M. & Jones, G. P. Short Economic & Social History of the Lake Counties, 1500-1830. LC 67-8870. (Illus.). 1962. 15.00x (ISBN 0-678-06786-4). Kelley.
Bunting, James. The Lake District. (Batsford Britain Ser.). Date not set. 9.95 (ISBN 0-8038-4287-2). Hastings.
Colourmaster. Lake District (Cumberland, Lancashire, Westmoreland) (Travel in England Ser.). (Illus.). 96p. 1975. Repr. 7.95 (ISBN 0-85933-006-0). Transatlantic.
Hardy, Eric. The Naturalist in Lakeland. (Regional Naturalist Ser.). (Illus.). 1973. 2.95 (ISBN 0-7153-5745-X). David & Charles.
Lake District. (Red Guides Ser). 1973. 7.50x (ISBN 0-7063-1374-7). Intl Pubns Serv.
Marshall, J. D. & Davies-Shiel, M. The Lake District at Work: Past & Present. (Industrial History in Pictures Ser.). (Illus.). 1971. 5.95 (ISBN 0-7153-5104-4). David & Charles.
Nicholson, Norman. Greater Lakeland. (Illus.). 1969. 10.50x (ISBN 0-7091-0951-2). Intl Pubns Serv.
--Portrait of the Lakes. LC 64-4949. (Portrait Bks.). (Illus.). 1964. 10.50x (ISBN 0-7091-2897-5). Intl Pubns Serv.
Pearsall, W. H. & Pennington, W. The Lake District: A Landscape History. (The New Naturalist Ser.). (Illus.). 320p. 1974. 11.95x (ISBN 0-8008-4534-X). Taplinger.
Rice, H. A. Lake Country Towns. LC 74-171442. (Portrait Bk.). (Illus.). 189p. 1974. 10.50x (ISBN 0-7091-4450-4). Intl Pubns Serv.
Trent, Christopher. Lakeland. LC 67-93536. (Motoring on Regional Byways Ser). (Illus.). 1967. 6.25x (ISBN 0-8002-0888-9). Intl Pubns Serv.
Wordsworth, William. Guide Through the District of the Lakes in the North of England, with a Description of the Scenery for the Use of Tourists & Residents. LC 68-55639. (Illus.). 1968. Repr. of 1952 ed. lib. bdg. 15.00x (ISBN 0-8371-0764-4, WOLE). Greenwood.
--Guide to the Lakes. De Selincourt, Ernest, ed. (Illus.). 1977. pap. 5.95x (ISBN 0-19-281219-X, OPB387). Oxford U Pr.

LAKE-DWELLERS AND LAKE-DWELLINGS

Cresson, H. T. Report Upon Pile-Structures in Naaman's Creek, Near Claymont, Delaware. (Harvard University Peabody Museum of Archaeology & Ethnology Papers Ser: HU. PMP Vol. 1, No. 4). Repr. of 1892 ed. pap. 4.00 (ISBN 0-527-01186-X). Kraus Repr.

LAKE ERIE, BATTLE OF, 1813

see Erie, Lake, Battle Of, 1813

LAKE GENEVA

see Geneva, Lake

LAKE GEORGE

see George, Lake

LAKE LUCERNE

see Lucerne, Lake

LAKE POETS

Abraham, Ashley P. Some Portraits of the Lake Poets, & Their Homes. LC 75-28026. 1975. Repr. of 1914 ed. lib. bdg. 20.00 (ISBN 0-8414-2874-3). Folcroft.
--Some Portraits of the Lake Poets & Their Homes. 1978. Repr. of 1914 ed. lib. bdg. 20.00 (ISBN 0-8495-0129-6). Arden Lib.
Bald, R. C. Literary Friendships in the Age of Wordsworth. 1968. lib. bdg. 17.50x (ISBN 0-374-90342-5). Octagon.
Brandl, Alois. Samuel Taylor Coleridge & the English Romantic School. LC 68-757. (Studies in Coleridge, No. 7). 1969. Repr. of 1887 ed. lib. bdg. 49.95 (ISBN 0-8383-0512-1). Haskell.
De Quincy, Thomas. Recollections of the Lakes & the Lake Poets. (English Library Ser.). 1971. pap. 3.95 (ISBN 0-14-043056-3). Penguin.
Robinson, Henry C. Blake, Coleridge, Wordsworth, Lamb, Etc., Being Selections from the Remains of Henry Crabb Robinson. Morley, Edith J., ed. LC 23-6630. Repr. of 1922 ed. 10.00 (ISBN 0-404-05364-5). AMS Pr.

LAKE SUPERIOR

see Superior, Lake

LAKE TAHOE

see Tahoe, Lake

LAKE TANGANYIKA

see Tanganyika, Lake

LAKE TSANA

see Tsana Lake

LAKES

see also Limnology; Thermal Pollution of Rivers, Lakes, etc.;

also names of lakes e.g. Superior Lake

Ackermann, William C., et al, eds. Man-Made Lakes: Their Problems and Environmental Effects. LC 73-86486. (Geophysical Monograph Ser.: Vol. 17). (Illus.). 1973. 30.00 (ISBN 0-87590-017-8). Am Geophysical.
Bennett, George W. Management of Lakes & Ponds. 2nd ed. (Illus.). 1971. 21.95x (ISBN 0-442-15668-5). Van Nos Reinhold.
Bloomfield, J. A., ed. The Lakes of New York State, 2 vols. Incl. Vol. 1. Ecology of the Finger Lakes. 34.50, by subscription 34.50 (ISBN 0-12-107301-7); Vol. 2. The Lakes of Western New York. 31.00, by subscription 31.00 (ISBN 0-12-107302-5). 1978. Acad Pr.
Bloomfield, Jay A., ed. Lakes of New York State, Vol. 3: Ecology of the Lakes of East-Central New York. 1980. 29.50, subscription 29.50 (ISBN 0-12-107303-3). Acad Pr.
Britt, N. Wilson, et al. Limmological Studies of the Island Area of Western Lake Erie. 1973. 3.00 (ISBN 0-686-30328-8). Ohio Bio Survey.
Dokulil, M., et al, eds. Shallow Lakes: Contributions to Their Limnology. (Developmrnts in Hydrobiology Ser.: No. 3). 218p. 1981. PLB 59.50 (ISBN 0-686-28842-4, Pub. by Junk Pubs Netherlands). Kluwer Boston.
Dussart, Bernard H. Man-Made Lakes As Modified Ecosystems: Scope Report 2. (Scientific Committee on Problems of the Environment Ser.). 1978. pap. 8.00 (ISBN 0-471-99595-9, Pub. by Wiley-Interscience). Wiley.
Forel, Francois A. Handbuch der Seenkunde,Allgemeine Limnologie: Handbook of Lake Studies. Egerton, Frank N., 3rd, ed. LC 77-74225. (History of Ecology Ser.). 1978. Repr. of 1901 ed. lib. bdg. 15.00x (ISBN 0-405-10395-6). Arno.
Gaines, David. Mono Lake Guidebook. (Illus.). 120p. (Orig.). 1981. pap. 3.95 (ISBN 0-939716-00-3). Mono Lake Comm.
Gibbs, R. J. & Shaw, R. P., eds. Transport Processes in Lakes & Oceans. (Marine Science Ser.: Vol. 7). 296p. 1977. 27.50 (ISBN 0-306-35507-8, Plenum Pr). Plenum Pub.
Goetz, Delia. Lakes. LC 72-7226. (Illus.). 64p. (gr. 3-7). 1973. 6.75 (ISBN 0-688-21866-0). Morrow.
Graf, W. H. & Mortimer, C. H., eds. Hydrodynamics of Lakes: Proceeding of the Symposium, Switzerland, Oct. 1978. LC 79-17492. (Developments in Water Science Ser.: Vol. 11). 360p. 1979. 61.00 (ISBN 0-444-41827-X). Elsevier.
Hakanson, Lars. A Manual of Lake Morphometry. (Illus.). 78p. 1981. pap. 13.90 (ISBN 0-387-10480-1). Springer-Verlag.
Hanna, Alfred & Hanna, Kathryn. Lake Okeechobee. new ed. LC 48-5872. (Lakes of America Ser). (Illus.). 400p. 1973. 18.00 (ISBN 0-910220-44-1). Larlin Corp.
Hohnel, L. Von & Bell, N., trs. Discovery of Lakes Rudolf & Stefanie. (Illus.). 1968. Repr. of 1894 ed. 85.00x (ISBN 0-7146-1814-4, F Cass Co). Biblio Dist.
Jaques, Florence P. Canoe Country. LC 38-27731. (Illus.). 1938. 7.95 (ISBN 0-8166-0024-4); pap. 5.95 (ISBN 0-8166-0922-5). U of Minn Pr.
Jenkins, S. H., ed. Eutrophication of Deep Lakes: Proceedings of Seminar Held in Oslo, Norway June 1978. (Progress in Water Technology Ser.: Vol. 12, No. 2). (Illus.). 208p. 1980. pap. 47.00 (ISBN 0-08-026024-1). Pergamon.
Jorgensen, S. E, ed. Lake Management. (Water Development, Supply & Management). 1980. 42.00 (ISBN 0-08-022432-6). Pergamon.
Lerman, A., et al, eds. Lakes: Chemistry, Geology, Physics. LC 78-17842. (Illus.). 1978. 46.00 (ISBN 0-387-90322-4). Springer-Verlag.
Loehr, Raymond C., ed. Phosphorus Management Strategies for Lakes. LC 79-55150. (Illus.). 1980. 39.95 (ISBN 0-250-40332-3). Ann Arbor Science.
Macam, T. T. & Worthington, E. B. Life in Lakes & Rivers. 1972. pap. 2.25 (ISBN 0-531-06040-3, Fontana Pap). Watts.
Murray, John & Pullar, Laurence. Bathymetrical Survey of the Scottish Fresh Water Lochs, Vol. 1. Egerton, Frank N., 3rd, ed. LC 77-74243. (History of Ecology Ser.). (Illus.). 1978. Repr. of 1910 ed. lib. bdg. 49.00x (ISBN 0-405-10412-X). Arno.
Neal, James T., ed. Playas & Dried Lakes: Occurrence & Development. LC 74-31134. (Benchmark Papers in Geology Ser: No. 20). 411p. 1975. 52.50 (ISBN 0-12-787110-1). Acad Pr.
Nute, Grace L. Voyageur's Highway: Minnesota's Border Lake Land. LC 65-63529. (Illus.). 113p. 1976. pap. 3.75 (ISBN 0-87351-006-2). Minn Hist.
Preston, William L. Vanishing Landscapes: Land & Life in the Tulare Lake Basin. LC 80-6055. (Illus.). 290p. 1981. 18.95 (ISBN 0-520-04053-8). U of Cal Pr.
Przhevalskii, Nikolai M. From Kulja, Across the Tian Shan to Lob-Nor. Morgan, E. Delmar, tr. Repr. of 1879 ed. lib. bdg. 15.00x (ISBN 0-8371-3856-6, PRFK). Greenwood.
Ramsbottom, A. E. Depth Charts of the Cumbrian Lakes. 1976. 11.00x (ISBN 0-900386-25-8, Pub. by Freshwater Bio). State Mutual Bk.
Scavia, Donald & Robertson, Andrew, eds. Perspectives on Lake Ecosystem Modeling. LC 77-93388. 1979. 39.95 (ISBN 0-250-40248-3). Ann Arbor Science.
Serruya, Colette. Lake Kinneret: Lake of Tiberias, Sea of Galilee. (Monographiae Biologicae: No.32). 1978. lib. bdg. 68.50 (ISBN 90-619-3085-5, Pub. by Junk Pubs Netherlands). Kluwer Boston.
Stanley, N. F. & Alpers, M. Man Made Lakes & Human Health. 1975. 78.50 (ISBN 0-12-663550-1). Acad Pr.
Temple, Philip. Patterns of Water: The Great Southern Lakes of New Zealand. LC 75-323384. (Illus.). 136p. 1974. 23.50x (ISBN 0-7233-0405-X). Intl Pubns Serv.
Thomas, Bill & Thomas, Phyllis. Lakeside Recreation Areas. LC 76-54716. (Illus.). 160p. 1977. pap. 6.95 (ISBN 0-8117-2104-3). Stackpole.
Tourbier, Joachim & Westmacott, Richard. Lakes & Ponds. LC 76-19607. (Technical Bulletin Ser.: No. 72). (Illus.). 70p. 1976. pap. 14.50 (ISBN 0-87420-072-5). Urban Land.
Verduin, J. Field Guide to Lakes. (Earth Science Curriculum Project Pamphlet Ser). 288p. 1971. pap. 3.20 (ISBN 0-395-02622-9, 2-14608). HM.
Wilcoxson, Kent H. Angler's Guide to Freshwater Fishing in New York State. 2nd ed. LC 76-42142. (Angler's Guide Ser.). (Illus.). 160p. 1977. pap. 4.50 (ISBN 0-89046-064-7). Herman Pub.

LAKES, FREEZING AND OPENING OF

see Ice on Rivers, Lakes, Etc.

LAKISTS

see Lake Poets

LA LYRE

Drawings of La Lyre. (Master Draughtsman Ser). (Illus.). treasure trove bdg. 6.47x (ISBN 0-685-07271-1); pap. 2.95 (ISBN 0-685-07272-X). Borden.

LAMAISM

see also Bon (Tibetan Religion)

Avedon, John F. An Interview with the Dalai Lama. LC 80-83015. (Illus.). 83p. (Orig.). 1980. pap. 6.95 (ISBN 0-937896-00-4). Littlebird.
Chapman, F. Spencer. Lhasa the Holy City. facsimile ed. LC 75-37875. (Select Bibliographies Reprint Ser). Repr. of 1940 ed. 32.00 (ISBN 0-8369-6712-7). Arno.
David-Neel, Alexandra. Magic & Mystery in Tibet. 1971. pap. 4.25 (ISBN 0-486-22682-4). Dover.
--Magic & Mystery in Tibet. (Illus.). 1965. 7.50 (ISBN 0-8216-0110-5). Univ Bks.
--Secret Oral Teachings in Tibetan Buddhist Sects. 1967. pap. 3.00 (ISBN 0-87286-012-4). City Lights.
Ekvall, Robert B. The Lama Knows: A Tibetan Legend Is Born. (Illus.). 144p. 1981. pap. 5.95 (ISBN 0-88316-541-4). Chandler & Sharp.
Ellam, J. E. The Religion of Tibet: Study of Lamaism. 59.95 (ISBN 0-8490-0940-5). Gordon Pr.
Evans-Wentz, W. Y., ed. Tibet's Great Yogi, Milarepa. 2nd ed. (Illus.). 1951. 15.95 (ISBN 0-19-501436-7). Oxford U Pr.
Hoffmann, Helmut. The Religions of Tibet. LC 78-11420. (Illus.). 1979. Repr. of 1961 ed. lib. bdg. 17.50x (ISBN 0-313-21120-5, HORT). Greenwood.
Lessing, Ferdinand D. Ritual & Symbol: Essays on Lainaisin & Chinese Symbolism, Vol. 91. (Asian Folklore & Social Life Monographs). (Ger.). 1976. 5.00 (ISBN 0-89986-305-1). E Langstaff.
Pozdneyev, Aleksei M. Religion & Ritual in Society: Lamaist Buddhism in Late 19th-Century Mongolia. Krueger, John R., ed. Raun, Alo & Raun, Linda, trs. from Rus. (Occasional Papers Ser.: No. 10). Orig. Title: Ocherki Byta Buddiiskikh Monastyrei. pap. 15.00 (ISBN 0-910980-50-0). Mongolia.
Rampa, T. Lobsang. Third Eye. 1974. pap. 2.50 (ISBN 0-345-29023-2). Ballantine.
Schlagintweit, Emil. Buddhism in Tibet. LC 73-426191. (Illus.). Repr. of 1863 ed. 35.00x (ISBN 0-678-07263-9). Kelley.
Waddell, Austine. Tibetan Buddhism with Its Mystic Cults, Symbolism & Mythology, & in Its Relation to Indian Buddhism. (Illus.). 598p. 1972. pap. 6.00 (ISBN 0-486-20130-9). Dover.

LAMAR, LUCIUS QUINTUS CINCINNATUS, 1825-1893

Cate, Wirt A. Lucius Q. C. Lamar: Secession & Reunion. LC 68-25674. (Illus.). 1969. Repr. of 1935 ed. 15.00 (ISBN 0-8462-1194-7). Russell.

Mayes, Edward. Lucius Q. C. Lamar: His Life, Times & Speeches, 1825-1893. LC 70-173065. Repr. of 1896 ed. 47.50 (ISBN 0-404-04613-4). AMS Pr.

Murphy, James B. L. Q. C. Lamar: Pragmatic Patriot. LC 72-94150. (Southern Biography Ser.). 320p. 1973. 20.00x (ISBN 0-8071-0217-2). La State U Pr.

LAMAR COUNTY, TEXAS–SOCIAL LIFE AND CUSTOMS

Lombard, Charles M. Lamartine. (World Authors Ser.: France: No. 254). 1973. lib. bdg. 10.95 (ISBN 0-8057-2510-5). Twayne.

LAMARCK, JEAN BAPTISTE PIERRE ANTOINE DE MONET DE, 1744-1820

Burkhardt, Richard W., Jr. The Spirit of System: Lamarck & Evolutionary Biology. 1977. 16.50x (ISBN 0-674-83317-1). Harvard U Pr.

Cannon, H. Graham. Lamarck & Modern Genetics. LC 75-10211. 152p. 1975. Repr. of 1959 ed. lib. bdg. 16.50x (ISBN 0-8371-8173-9, CALA). Greenwood.

Packard, Alpheus S. Lamarck: The Founder of Evolution; His Life & Work; with Translations of His Writings on Organic Evolution. Cohen, I. Bernard, ed. LC 79-7980. (Three Centuries of Science in America Ser.). (Illus.). 1980. Repr. of 1901 ed. lib. bdg. 34.00x (ISBN 0-405-12562-3). Arno.

LAMARR, HEDDY

Young, Christopher. The Films of Hedy Lamarr. (Illus.). 1980. pap. 6.95 (ISBN 0-8065-0698-9). Citadel Pr.

LAMARTINE, ALPHONSE MARIE LOUIS DE PRAT DE, 1790-1869

Duclaux, Agnes M. French Ideal. facs. ed. LC 67-23209. (Essay Index Reprint Ser). 1911. 16.00 (ISBN 0-8369-0393-5). Arno.

George, Albert J. Lamartine & Romantic Unanimism. LC 71-168106. Repr. of 1940 ed. 18.50 (ISBN 0-404-02712-1). AMS Pr.

Hamlet-Metz, Mario. La Critique Litteraire De Lamartine. (Studies in French Literature: No. 21). 1974. pap. 45.00x (ISBN 90-2792-694-8). Mouton.

Pirazzini, Agide. Influence of Italy on the Literary Career of Alphonse De Lamartine. LC 18-2055. (Columbia University. Studies in Romance Philology & Literature). Repr. of 1917 ed. 17.50 (ISBN 0-404-50622-4). AMS Pr.

Whitehouse, Henry R. Life of Lamartine, 2 Vols. facsimile ed. LC 73-103672. (Select Bibliographies Reprint Ser). 1918. 56.00 (ISBN 0-8369-5172-7). Arno.

LAMAZE METHOD OF CHILDBIRTH

see Natural Childbirth

LAMB, CAROLINE (PONSONBY), LADY, 1785-1828

Cecil, David. Melbourne. LC 76-138583. 1971. Repr. of 1954 ed. lib. bdg. 19.25x (ISBN 0-8371-5782-X, CEME). Greenwood.

LAMB, CHARLES, 1775-1834

Ainger, Alfred. Charles Lamb. 186p. 1980. Repr. of 1888 ed. lib. bdg. 15.00 (ISBN 0-8495-0175-X). Arden Lib.

--Charles Lamb. LC 77-131605. 1970. Repr. of 1901 ed. 19.00 (ISBN 0-403-00492-6). Scholarly.

--Charles Lamb. Morley, John, ed. LC 68-58369. (English Men of Letters). Repr. of 1888 ed. lib. bdg 10.00 (ISBN 0-404-51701-3). AMS Pr.

--Charles Lamb. 1888. Repr. 9.95 (ISBN 0-8274-2038-2). R West.

--Charles Lamb: English Men of Letters. 186p. 1981. Repr. of 1882 ed. lib. bdg. 15.00x (ISBN 0-89760-010-X). Telegraph Bks.

Anthony, Katherine. The Lambs: A Study of Pre-Victorian England. LC 72-7815. (Illus.). 256p. 1973. Repr. of 1948 ed. lib. bdg. 14.50x (ISBN 0-8371-6523-7, ANLA). Greenwood.

Baily, F. E. The Perfect Age. 187p. 1981. Repr. of 1946 ed. lib. bdg. 30.00 (ISBN 0-89987-064-3). Darby Bks.

Barnett, George L. Charles Lamb. (English Author Ser.). 1976. lib. bdg. 12.50 (ISBN 0-8057-6668-5). Twayne.

--Charles Lamb: The Evolution of Elia. LC 72-6858. (English Literature Ser., No. 33). 1972. Repr. of 1964 ed. lib. bdg. 37.95 (ISBN 0-8383-1652-2). Haskell.

Bensusan, S. L. Charles Lamb: His Homes & Haunts. LC 79-14593. 1979. Repr. lib. bdg. 10.00 (ISBN 0-8414-9834-2). Folcroft.

Bensusan, Samuel L. Charles Lamb: His Homes & Haunts. 81p. 1980. Repr. of 1910 ed. lib. bdg. 10.00 (ISBN 0-8495-0606-9). Arden Lib.

Birkhoff, Barbara. As Between Friends: Criticism of Themselves & One Another in the Letters of Coleridge, Wordsworth & Lamb. LC 73-10246. 1930. lib. bdg. 10.00 (ISBN 0-8414-3181-7). Folcroft.

Blunden, E. Charles Lamb & His Life: Recorded by His Contemporaries. 59.95 (ISBN 0-87968-841-6). Gordon Pr.

Blunden, Edmund. Charles Lamb & His Contemporaries. 1967. Repr. of 1933 ed. 17.50 (ISBN 0-208-00461-0, Archon). Shoe String.

--Charles Lamb: His Life Recorded by His Contemporaries. 1934. Repr. 35.00 (ISBN 0-8274-2039-0). R West.

Brewer, Luther A. Some Lamb & Browning Letters to Leigh Hunt. LC 72-196923. 1924. lib. bdg. 6.50 (ISBN 0-8414-2541-8). Folcroft.

Brown, John M. The Portable Charles Lamb. LC 75-11488. 594p. 1975. Repr. of 1949 ed. lib. bdg. 28.25x (ISBN 0-8371-8202-6, LAPCL). Greenwood.

Craddock, Thomas. Charles Lamb. 216p. 1979. Repr. of 1867 ed. lib. bdg. 25.00 (ISBN 0-686-60117-3). Norwood Edns.

--Charles Lamb. 1867. lib. bdg. 25.00 (ISBN 0-8414-9984-5). Folcroft.

--Charles Lamb. 1979. Repr. of 1867 ed. lib. bdg. 25.00 (ISBN 0-8495-0937-8). Arden Lib.

Daniel, George. Recollections of Charles Lamb. LC 74-9598. 1927. lib. bdg. 10.00 (ISBN 0-8414-3745-9). Folcroft.

Dobell, Bertram. Sidelights on Charles Lamb. LC 76-43277. 1976. Repr. of 1903 ed. lib. bdg. 30.00 (ISBN 0-8414-3702-5). Folcroft.

Fitzgerald, Percy. Charles Lamb: His Friends, His Haunts & His Books. LC 78-2784. Repr. of 1866 ed. lib. bdg. 30.00 (ISBN 0-8414-4359-9). Folcroft.

Fitzgerald, Percy H. Charles Lamb: His Friends, His Haunts & His Books. 228p. 1980. Repr. of 1866 ed. lib. bdg. 30.00 (ISBN 0-8492-4629-6). R West.

--Charles Lamb: His Friends, His Haunts & His Books. 228p. 1979. Repr. of 1866 ed. lib. bdg. 30.00 (ISBN 0-8482-0849-8). Norwood Edns.

Frank, Robert. Don't Call Me Gentle Charles: Discourses on Charles Lambs' Essays of Elia. (Oregon State Studies in Literature: No. 2). 144p. 1976. 7.95 (ISBN 0-87071-082-6). Oreg St U Pr.

Gordon, ed. Charles Lamb: Prose & Poetry with Essays. 1978. Repr. of 1921 ed. lib. bdg. 17.50 (ISBN 0-8414-5750-6). Folcroft.

Gordon, George. Charles Lamb, Prose & Poetry. LC 74-9967. 1937. 17.50 (ISBN 0-8414-4517-6). Folcroft.

Hazlitt, W. Carew. Mary & Charles Lamb: Poems, Letters, & Remains. 1978. Repr. of 1874 ed. lib. bdg. 50.00 (ISBN 0-8495-2335-4). Arden Lib.

Hazlitt, William C. Lambs, Their Lives, Their Friends & Their Correspondence: New Particulars & New Materials. Repr. of 1897 ed. 17.50 (ISBN 0-404-07369-7). AMS Pr.

Hine, Reginald L. Charles Lamb & His Hertfordshire. 374p. 1981. Repr. lib. bdg. 45.00 (ISBN 0-89984-284-4). Century Bookbindery.

--Charles Lamb & His Hertfordshire. LC 73-13023. 374p. 1974. Repr. of 1949 ed. lib. bdg. 18.50x (ISBN 0-8371-7111-3, HICL). Greenwood.

--Charles Lamb & His Hertfordshire. 1949. Repr. 40.00 (ISBN 0-8274-2040-4). R West.

Howe, Will D. Charles Lamb & His Friends. LC 72-6196. 364p. 1972. Repr. of 1944 ed. lib. bdg. 18.00x (ISBN 0-8371-6454-0, HOCL). Greenwood.

Ireland, A. List of Works of Charles Lamb. Repr. of 1868 ed. 21.00 (ISBN 0-403-04152-X). Somerset Pub.

Ireland, Alexander. List of the Writings of William Hazlitt, Leigh Hunt & Charles Lamb. LC 70-102856. (Bibliography & Reference Ser: No. 299). 1970. Repr. of 1868 ed. lib. bdg. 13.00 (ISBN 0-8337-1806-1). B Franklin.

Iseman, John S. Perfect Sympathy, Charles Lamb & Sir Thomas Browne. LC 73-6735. 1937. lib. bdg. 10.00 (ISBN 0-8414-2106-4). Folcroft.

Jerrold, Walter. Charles Lamb. 1978. Repr. of 1905 ed. lib. bdg. 10.00 (ISBN 0-8495-2737-6). Arden Lib.

Lake, Bernard. A General Introduction to Charles Lamb. 91p. 1980. Repr. of 1903 ed. lib. bdg. 15.00 (ISBN 0-8492-1627-3). R West.

--General Introduction to Charles Lamb-with a Special Study of His Relation to Robert Burton Author of the Anatomy of Melancholy. LC 77-7515. 1903. lib. bdg. 12.50 (ISBN 0-8414-5815-4). Folcroft.

Lamb, Charles. Lamb As Critic. Park, Roy, ed. LC 78-73572. xii, 367p. 1980. 21.50x (ISBN 0-8032-8700-3). U of Nebr Pr.

Law, Marie H. English Familiar Essay in the Early Nineteenth Century: The Elements Old & New Which Went into Its Making, As Exemplified in the Writings of Hunt, Hazlitt & Lamb. LC 65-17906. 1965. Repr. of 1934 ed. 7.50 (ISBN 0-8462-0580-7). Russell.

Lucas, E. V. Charles Lamb & the Lloyds. 1898. Repr. 30.00 (ISBN 0-8274-2041-2). R West.

--Life of Charles Lamb. 5th rev. ed. LC 68-59324. Repr. of 1921 ed. 22.50 (ISBN 0-404-04059-4). AMS Pr.

--Life of Charles Lamb. 59.95 (ISBN 0-8490-0528-0). Gordon Pr.

--The Life of Charles Lamb. 1978. Repr. of 1905 ed. lib. bdg. 50.00 (ISBN 0-8492-1590-0). R West.

McKenna, Wayne. Charles Lamb & the Theatre. LC 77-82139. 1978. 19.50x (ISBN 0-06-494707-6). B&N.

Marrs, Edwin W., Jr., ed. The Letters of Charles & Mary Lamb, 3 vols. 45.00x ea. Vol. I, 1975 (ISBN 0-8014-0930-6). Vol. II-1976 (ISBN 0-8014-0977-2). Vol. III-1978 (ISBN 0-8014-1129-7). Cornell U Pr.

Martin, Benjamin E. In the Footprints of Charles Lamb. 1891. Repr. lib. bdg. 30.00 (ISBN 0-8414-6479-0). Folcroft.

May, James L. Charles Lamb. 1978. Repr. of 1934 ed. lib. bdg. 25.00 (ISBN 0-8492-6710-2). R West.

--Charles Lamb: A Study. LC 72-12907. 1973. lib. bdg. 25.00 (ISBN 0-8414-1015-1). Folcroft.

Morley, F. V. Lamb Before Elia. LC 73-12357. 1932. Repr. lib. bdg. 27.50 (ISBN 0-8414-5995-9). Folcroft.

North, Ernest D. The Wit & Wisdom of Charles Lamb. 267p. 1980. Repr. of 1892 ed. lib. bdg. 25.00 (ISBN 0-8495-4109-3). Arden Lib.

--The Wit & Wisdom of Charles Lamb. LC 74-2110. Repr. lib. bdg. 25.00 (ISBN 0-8414-6266-6). Folcroft.

Procter, B. Waller. Charles Lamb: A Memoir. LC 73-12285. Repr. of 1896 ed. lib. bdg. 25.00 (ISBN 0-8414-3429-8). Folcroft.

Randel, Fred V. The World of Elia: Charles Lamb's Essayistic Romanticism. (National University Publications Literary Criticism Ser.). 1975. 12.95 (ISBN 0-8046-9118-5, Natl U). Kennikat.

Roff, Renee, compiled by. Bibliography of the Writings of Charles & Mary Lamb. LC 79-54867. (Illus.). 1979. 22.00x (ISBN 0-935164-01-4). N T Smith.

Ross, Ernest C. Charles Lamb & Emma Isola. 1950. lib. bdg. 10.00 (ISBN 0-8414-2579-5). Folcroft.

Stoddard, Richard H. Personal Recollections of Lamb, Hazlitt, & Others. 1978. Repr. of 1875 ed. lib. bdg. 30.00 (ISBN 0-8492-2584-1). R West.

Ward, A. C. Frolic & the Gentle: A Centenary Study of Charles Lamb. LC 78-103215. 1970. Repr. of 1934 ed. 10.50 (ISBN 0-8046-0852-0). Kennikat.

Wherry, George. Cambridge & Charles Lamb. 90p. 1980. Repr. of 1925 ed. lib. bdg. 15.00 (ISBN 0-8482-7059-2). Norwood Edns.

Williams, Orlo. Charles Lamb. 143p. 1980. Repr. of 1934 ed. lib. bdg. 15.00 (ISBN 0-8495-5675-9). Arden Lib.

--Charles Lamb. LC 73-12608. 1934. lib. bdg. 12.50 (ISBN 0-8414-9408-8). Folcroft.

LAMB, EDWARD OLIVER

Stoddard, Richard H. Personal Recollections of Lamb, Hazlitt, & Others. 1978. Repr. of 1875 ed. lib. bdg. 30.00 (ISBN 0-8492-2584-1). R West.

LAMB, MARY ANN, 1764-1847

Anthony, Katherine. The Lambs: A Study of Pre-Victorian England. LC 72-7815. (Illus.). 256p. 1973. Repr. of 1948 ed. lib. bdg. 14.50x (ISBN 0-8371-6523-7, ANLA). Greenwood.

Baily, F. E. The Perfect Age. 187p. 1981. Repr. of 1946 ed. lib. bdg. 30.00 (ISBN 0-89987-064-3). Darby Bks.

Gilchrist, Anne. Mary Lamb. LC 78-148784. Repr. of 1883 ed. 25.00 (ISBN 0-404-07348-4). AMS Pr.

Gilchrist, Mrs. Mary Lamb. 1883. 25.00 (ISBN 0-932062-63-6). Sharon Hill.

Hazlitt, W. Carew. Mary & Charles Lamb: Poems, Letters, & Remains. 1978. Repr. of 1874 ed. lib. bdg. 50.00 (ISBN 0-8495-2335-4). Arden Lib.

Marrs, Edwin W., Jr., ed. The Letters of Charles & Mary Lamb, 3 vols. 45.00x ea. Vol. I, 1975 (ISBN 0-8014-0930-6). Vol. II-1976 (ISBN 0-8014-0977-2). Vol. III-1978 (ISBN 0-8014-1129-7). Cornell U Pr.

Roff, Renee, compiled by. Bibliography of the Writings of Charles & Mary Lamb. LC 79-54867. (Illus.). 1979. 22.00x (ISBN 0-935164-01-4). N T Smith.

LAMBAS

Doke, Clement M. Lambas of Northern Rhodesia: A Study of Their Customs & Beliefs. LC 74-107473. (Illus.). Repr. of 1931 ed. 23.00x (ISBN 0-8371-3751-9, Pub. by Negro U Pr). Greenwood.

LAMBETH CONFERENCE

Curtis, William R. Lambeth Conferences: The Solution for Pan-Anglican Organization. LC 68-58565. (Columbia University Studies in the Social Sciences: No. 488). Repr. of 1942 ed. 24.50 (ISBN 0-404-51488-X). AMS Pr.

Marrett, Michael M. The Lambeth Conferences & Women Priests: The Historical Background of the Lambeth Conferences & Their Impact on the Episcopal Church in America. 208p. 1981. 12.50 (ISBN 0-682-49765-7). Exposition.

Stephenson, Alan M. First Lambeth Conference. (Church Historical Society Ser.: No. 88). 1967. 17.50x (ISBN 0-8401-5088-1). Allenson-Breckinridge.

LAMDAN, ISAAC

Yudkin, L. Isaac Lamdan: A Study in Twentieth-Century Hebrew Poetry. Patterson, David, ed. LC 72-127781. (Studies in Modern Hebrew Literature). 1971. 16.50x (ISBN 0-8014-0597-1). Cornell U Pr.

LAMELLIBRANCHIATA

see also Oysters; Pearls

Arkell, W. J. The Corallian Lamellibranchia, Vols. 1-10. Set. pap. 89.50 (ISBN 0-384-02030-5). Johnson Repr.

Ellis, A. E. British Freshwater Bivalve Mollusca: Keys & Notes for the Identification of the Species. (A Volume in the Synopses of the British Fauna Ser.). 1978. pap. 8.50 (ISBN 0-12-236950-5). Acad Pr.

Hayami, Itaru. A Systematic Survey of the Mesozoic Bivalvia from Japan. (Illus.). 1976. 34.50x (ISBN 0-86008-152-4, Pub by U of Tokyo Pr). Intl Schol Bk Serv.

Newell, Norman D. Late Paleozoic Pelecypods: Pectinacea & Mytilacea, State Geological Survey of Kansas, Vol. 10, Pts. 1 & 2. Gould, Stephen J., ed. LC 79-8337. (The History of Paleontology Ser.). (Illus.). 1980. Repr. of 1937 ed. lib. bdg. 21.00x (ISBN 0-405-12722-7). Arno.

Stanley, Steven M. Relation of Shell Form to Life Habits in the Bivalvia. LC 71-111441. (Memoir: No. 125). (Illus.). 1970. 14.00x (ISBN 0-8137-1125-8). Geol Soc.

Stenzel, H. B., et al. Pelecypoda from the Type Locality of the Stone City Beds (Middle Eocene) of Texas. (Illus.). 237p. 1957. 3.75 (ISBN 0-686-29361-4, PUB 5704). Bur Econ Geology.

Trueman, A. E. & Weir, J. The British Carboniferous Non-Marine Lamellibranchia, Pts. I-IX. 1946-56. Set. pap. 62.50 (ISBN 0-384-61750-6). Johnson Repr.

Waine, Peter R. Culture of Bivalue Molluses. 1978. 20.00 (ISBN 0-685-63398-5). State Mutual Bk.

LAMENTATIONS

see Elegaic Poetry

LAMERIE, PAUL DE, 1688-1751

Phillips, Philip A. Paul De Lamerie, Citizen & Goldsmith of London 1688-1751. 75.00x (ISBN 0-87556-510-7). Saifer.

LAME'S FUNCTIONS

see also Harmonic Functions

Hobson, Ernest W. Spherical & Ellipsoidal Harmonics. LC 55-233. 1955. 14.95 (ISBN 0-8284-0104-7). Chelsea Pub.

Strutt, Max J. Lame, Mathieu Funktionen. LC 66-23757. (Ger). 8.50 (ISBN 0-8284-0203-5). Chelsea Pub.

LAMINAR FLOW

Betchov, Robert & Criminale, William O., Jr. Stability of Parallel Flows. (Applied Mathematics & Mechanics Ser.: Vol. 10). 1967. 54.00 (ISBN 0-12-093750-6). Acad Pr.

Faizullaev, Dzharulla F. Laminar Motion of Multiphase Media in Conduits. LC 69-12511. 144p. 1969. 32.50 (ISBN 0-306-10816-X, Consultants). Plenum Pub.

Moore, Franklin K., ed. Theory of Laminar Flows. (High Speed Aerodynamics & Jet Propulsion Ser.: Vol. 4). 1964. 62.50 (ISBN 0-691-08051-8). Princeton U Pr.

Phillips, G. B. & Runkle, R. S. Biomedical Applications of Laminar Airflow. LC 72-95698. (Uniscience Ser.). 1973. 49.95 (ISBN 0-8493-5006-9). CRC Pr.

Taylor, C. & Morgan, K., eds. Numerical Methods in Laminar & Turbulent Flow. LC 78-16077. 1978. 75.95x (ISBN 0-470-26462-4). Halsted Pr.

LAMINATED MATERIALS

see also Laminated Wood; Sandwich Construction

Calcote, Lee R. Analysis of Laminated Composite Structures. (Illus.). 1969. 16.95x (ISBN 0-442-15628-6). Van Nos Reinhold.

LAMINATED METALS

see also Thermostat

LAMINATED WOOD

see also Plywood; Veneers and Veneering

Castle, Wendell & Edman, David. Wendell Castle Book of Wood Lamination. 192p. 1980. 18.95 (ISBN 0-442-21478-2). Van Nos Reinhold.

LAMONT, BARBARA

Goldreich, Gloria & Goldreich, Esther. What Can She Be? A Newscaster. LC 73-4940. (What Can She Be? Ser.). (Illus.). 48p. (gr. k-5). 1973. PLB 7.20 (ISBN 0-688-51540-1). Lothrop.

LAMONT, CORLISS

Lamont, Corliss. Yes to Life: Memoirs of Corliss Lamont. (Illus.). 1981. 14.95 (ISBN 0-8180-0232-8). Horizon.

LAMP SHADES

see Lampshades

LAMPREYS
Hardisty, M. W. & Potter, I., eds. Biology of Lampreys, 2 vols. 1972. Vol. 1. 67.00 (ISBN 0-12-324801-9); Vol. 2. 68.00 (ISBN 0-12-324802-7). Acad Pr.

LAMPS
see also Electric Lamps; Lampshades
Allphin, Willard. Primer of Lamps & Lighting. 3rd ed. LC 72-12250. (Illus.). 240p. 1973. 12.50 (ISBN 0-201-00170-5). A-W.
Broneer, Oscar. Terracotta Lamps. LC 76-362971. (Isthmia Ser: Vol. 3). 1977. 25.00x (ISBN 0-87661-933-2). Am Sch Athens.
Courter, J. W. Aladdin, the Magic Name in Lamps. 17.50 (ISBN 0-87069-001-9). Wallace-Homestead.
Freeman, Larry. New Light on Old Lamps. 6th ed. LC 68-12854. Orig. Title: Light on Old Lamps. (Illus.). 1968. 15.00 (ISBN 0-87282-051-3). Century Hse.
Holbrook, Wallace W. Contemporary Lamps. (gr. 9 up). 1968. text ed. 13.28 (ISBN 0-87345-029-9). McKnight.
Howland, Richard H. Greek Lamps & Their Survivals. (Athenian Agora Ser: Vol. 4). (Illus.). 1966. Repr. of 1958 ed. 17.50x (ISBN 0-87661-204-4). Am Sch Athens.
Little, Ruth. Old Lamps & New: Restoring & Decorating. LC 64-17394. (Illus.). 15.00 (ISBN 0-685-22811-8). R Little.
Luciano. Stained Glass Lamps & Terrariums. (Illus.). 112p. 1981. pap. 3.95 (ISBN 0-8256-3800-3, Hidden Hse). Music Sales.
Luciano & Colson. Stained Glass Lamp Art. (Illus.). 144p. 1981. pap. 6.95 (ISBN 0-8256-3812-7, Hidden Hse). Music Sales.
Luciano & Miller, Judy. Stained Glass Lamp Patterns. 88p. 1981. pap. 4.95 (ISBN 0-8256-3837-2, Hidden Hse). Music Sales.
McDonald, Ann G. Evolution of the Night Lamp. (Illus.). 1979. 19.95 (ISBN 0-87069-270-4). Wallace-Homestead.
Martens, Rachel. The How-to Book of Repairing, Rewiring, & Restoring Lamps & Lighting Fixtures. LC 78-66997. (Illus.). 192p. 1980. 13.95 (ISBN 0-385-17261-3). Doubleday.
--The How-to Book of Repairing, Rewiring & Restoring Lamps & Lighting Fixtures. LC 78-66997. (Illus.). 1979. pap. 5.95 (ISBN 0-385-14747-3, Dolp). Doubleday.
Martin, Jeani H. Carbide Mine Lamps. LC 77-84577. (Illus.). 1979. 17.50 (ISBN 0-498-02116-5). A S Barnes.
Murphy, Bruce. Lampmaking. LC 76-16360. (Illus.). 192p. 1976. 14.95 (ISBN 0-8069-5420-5); lib. bdg. 13.29 (ISBN 0-8069-5421-3). Sterling.
Murphy, Bruce & Lopo, Ana. Lampmaking. rev. ed. LC 76-16360. (Illus.). 192p. 1980. pap. 7.95 (ISBN 0-8069-8462-7). Sterling.
Paton, James. Lamps: A Collector's Guide. (Illus.). 1979. 12.50 (ISBN 0-684-16054-4, ScribT). Scribner.
Perlzweig, Judith. Lamps from the Athenian Agora. (Excavations of the Athenian Agora Picture Bks.: No. 9). (Illus.). 1964. pap. 1.50x (ISBN 0-87661-609-0). Am Sch Athens.
--Lamps of the Roman Period, First to Seventh Century After Christ. (Athenian Agora Ser: Vol. 7). (Illus.). 1971. Repr. of 1961 ed. 17.50x (ISBN 0-87661-207-9). Am Sch Athens.
Thuro, Catherine. Oil Lamps: The Kerosene Era in America. 1976. 29.95 (ISBN 0-87069-121-X). Wallace-Homestead.
--Price Guide to Oil Lamps. 1976. 1.50 (ISBN 0-87069-170-8). Wallace-Homestead.

LAMPSHADES
Colquhoun, Robert. Life Begins at Midnight. Date not set. 12.95 (ISBN 0-392-08555-0, SpS). Sportshelf.
Fishburn, Angela. Making Lampshades. LC 77-7729. (Illus.). 1977. pap. 5.95 (ISBN 0-8069-8494-5). Sterling.
Making Lampshades. 1976. pap. 1.50 (ISBN 0-8277-5725-5). British Bk Ctr.
Montagna, Pier. How to Make Lampshades & Draperies. pap. 2.00 (ISBN 0-686-00708-5). Key Bks.
Neustadt, Egon. The Lamps of Tiffany. LC 78-142102. (Illus.). 224p. 1970. 165.00 (ISBN 0-913158-01-1); Museum Edition. 205.00 (ISBN 0-685-26779-2). Fairfield.
Rourke, Margaret. Lampshades. Date not set. 4.50 (ISBN 0-392-12444-0, SpS). Sportshelf.

LANARKSHIRE, SCOTLAND–HISTORY
Campbell, Alan B. The Lanarkshire Miners: A Social History of Their Trade Unions, 1775-1874. 1980. text ed. 46.75x (ISBN 0-85976-048-0). Humanities.
Hamilton, William. Descriptions of the Sheriffdoms of Lanark & Renfrew. LC 75-168237. (Maitland Club, Glasgow. Publications: No. 12). Repr. of 1831 ed. 34.50 (ISBN 0-404-52943-7). AMS Pr.

LANCASHIRE, ENGLAND
Aikin, J. Description of the Country from Thirty to Forty Miles Round Manchester. LC 67-19706. (Illus.). Repr. of 1795 ed. 24.50x (ISBN 0-678-00340-8). Kelley.
Bagley, J. J. Lancashire. (Batsford Britain Ser.). Date not set. 9.95 (ISBN 0-8038-4280-5). Hastings.
Bagley, John J. History of Lancashire. rev. ed. (County History Ser.). (Illus.). 1961. 10.95 (ISBN 0-85208-047-6). Dufour.
Baines, Edward. History, Directory & Gazetteer of the County Palatine of Lancaster, 2 Vols. LC 68-26160. Repr. of 1824 ed. lib. bdg. 35.00x (ISBN 0-678-05554-8). Kelley.
Bell, Peter S., ed. Victorian Lancashire. (Illus.). 200p. 1974. 4.95 (ISBN 0-7153-6213-5). David & Charles.
Broxap, E. The Great Civil War in Lancashire: 1642-51. (Illus.). xv, 226p. Repr. of 1910 ed. lib. bdg. 13.50x (ISBN 0-678-06792-9). Kelley.
Elbourne, Roger. Music & Tradition in Early Industrial Lancashire: Seventeen Eighty to Eighteen Forty. (Folklore Society Mistletoe Ser.). 177p. 1980. 26.00x (ISBN 0-8476-6244-6). Rowman.
Gooderson, P. J. A History of Lancashire. (Illus.). 144p. 1980. 17.95 (ISBN 0-7134-2588-1, Pub. by Batsford England). David & Charles.
Harland, John & Wilkinson, T. T. Lancashire Legends. LC 73-13529. (Folklore Ser). 15.00 (ISBN 0-88305-262-8). Norwood Edns.
Hibbert-Ware, Samuel. Lancashire Memorials of the Rebellian 1715, 2 Vols. in 1. 1845. 26.00 (ISBN 0-384-22985-9). Johnson Repr.
Holt, John. General View of the Agriculture of the County of Lancaster. LC 68-13155. (Illus.). Repr. of 1795 ed. 20.00x (ISBN 0-678-05602-1). Kelley.
Hornyold-Strickland, H. Biographical Sketches of the Members of Parliament of Lancashire, 1290-1550. 1935. 13.00 (ISBN 0-384-24340-1). Johnson Repr.
Hughes, Glyn. Millstone Grit. 1975. text ed. 14.50x (ISBN 0-575-01941-7). Verry.
Langton, J. Geographical Change & Industrial Revolution. LC 78-67428. (Cambridge Geographical Studies: No. 11). (Illus.). 1980. 53.50 (ISBN 0-521-22490-X). Cambridge U Pr.
Lofthouse, Jessica. Portrait of Lancashire. LC 67-92282. (Portrait Bks.). (Illus.). 1967. 10.50x (ISBN 0-7091-6359-2). Intl Pubns Serv.
Makepease, C. E. Lancashire in the Twenties & Thirties. 1977. 19.95 (ISBN 0-7134-0439-6, Pub. by Batsford England). David & Charles.
Marshall, J. D. Lancashire (England) LC 74-76198. 1975. 4.95 (ISBN 0-7153-6653-X). David & Charles.
Marshall, J. D., ed. A History of Lancashire County Council 1889-1974. 456p. 1977. bds. 36.00x (ISBN 0-85520-215-7, Pub. by Martin Robertson England). Biblio Dist.
Midwinter, E. C. Social Administration in Lancashire, 1830-60. 200p. 1969. 27.95x (ISBN 0-7190-0369-5, Pub. by Manchester U Pr England). State Mutual Bk.
Ormerod, George, ed. Tracts Relating to Military Proceedings in Lancashire During the Great Civil War. 1844. 29.00 (ISBN 0-384-43700-1). Johnson Repr.
Taylor, William C. Notes on Tour in the Manufacturing Districts of Lancashire. 3rd ed. 331p. 1968. 27.50x (ISBN 0-7146-1408-4, F Cass Co). Biblio Dist.
Walker, Frank. Historical Geography of Southwest Lancashire Before the Industrial Revolution. Repr. of 1939 ed. 13.00 (ISBN 0-384-65560-2). Johnson Repr.

LANCASHIRE, ENGLAND–BIBLIOGRAPHY
Whitaker, Harold. Descriptive List of the Printed Maps of Lancashire, 1577-1900. (Chetham Society New Ser: Vol. 101). 19.50 (ISBN 0-384-68000-3). Johnson Repr.

LANCASHIRE AND YORKSHIRE RAILWAY COMPANY
Marshall, John. Lancashire & Yorkshire Railway, Vol. 1. (Railway History Ser.). 1970. 12.50 (ISBN 0-7153-4352-1). David & Charles.
--The Lancashire & Yorkshire Railway, Vol. 2. (Railway History Ser.). (Illus.). 327p. 1970. 14.95 (ISBN 0-7153-4906-6). David & Charles.
--The Lancashire & Yorkshire Railway, Vol. 3. (Railway History Ser.). (Illus.). 288p. 1972. 14.50 (ISBN 0-7153-5320-9). David & Charles.
--The Lancashire & Yorkshire Railway in Pictures. 13.50 (ISBN 0-7153-7478-8). David & Charles.

LANCASTER, JAMES, SIR, d. 1618
Lancaster, James. Voyages of Sir James Lancaster, Kt., to the East Indies. Markham, Clements R., ed. LC 78-134713. (Hakluyt Society First Ser: No. 56). 1970. Repr. of 1877 ed. lib. bdg. 32.00 (ISBN 0-8337-1995-5). B Franklin.

LANCASTER, JOSEPH, 1778-1838
Kaestle, Carl F. Joseph Lancaster & the Monitorial School Movement: A Documentary History. LC 72-97206. 200p. 1973. text ed. 12.00 (ISBN 0-8077-2375-4); pap. text ed. 5.50x (ISBN 0-8077-2380-0). Tchrs Coll.

LANCASTER, PENNSYLVANIA
Walker, Joseph E., ed. Lancaster County During the American Revolution, 7 vols. 1976. pap. 13.00 set (ISBN 0-915010-14-3). Sutter House.

LANCASTER COUNTY, VIRGINIA
Duvall, Lindsay O. Lancaster County, Virginia Records, Vol. 2. (Virginia Colonial Abstracts, Series II). 1979. Repr. 17.50 (ISBN 0-89308-063-2). Southern Hist Pr.
Holcomb, Brent H. Lancaster County, S. C., Deed Abstracts, 1787 to 1811. 200p. 1981. 20.00 (ISBN 0-89308-213-9). Southern Hist.
Wood, Stacy B. & Kramer, Stephen E. Clockmakers of Lancaster County & Their Clocks: 1750-1850. 1977. 17.95 (ISBN 0-442-29531-6). Van Nos Reinhold.

LANCASTRIAN SYSTEM
see Monitorial System of Education

LANCELOT
App, August J. Lancelot in English Literature. LC 65-21392. (Arthurian Legend & Literature Ser., No. 1). 1969. Repr. of 1929 ed. lib. bdg. 28.95 (ISBN 0-8383-0504-0). Haskell.
Cross, Tom P. & Nitze, William N. Lancelot & Guenevere: A Study of the Origins of Courtly Love. LC 79-91348. 1970. Repr. of 1922 ed. 7.50 (ISBN 0-87753-010-6). Phaeton.
Fuehrer, Sr. Mary R. Study of the Relation of the Dutch Lancelot & the Flemish Perchevael Fragments to the Manuscripts of Chretien's Conte del Graal. LC 73-140025. (Catholic University Studies in German Ser.: No. 14). Repr. of 1939 ed. 17.50 (ISBN 0-404-50234-2). AMS Pr.
Paton, Lucy A. Sir Lancelot of the Lake. LC 74-8340. 1929. lib. bdg. 50.00 (ISBN 0-8414-6774-9). Folcroft.
Pyle, Howard. The Story of the Champions of the Round Table. (Illus.). (ps-4). 1968. pap. 5.00 (ISBN 0-486-21883-X). Dover.
Sommer, H. Oskar, ed. Livre De Lancelot Del Lac, Pt. 1. (Vulgate Version of the Arthurian Romances: No. 3). Repr. of 1910 ed. 57.50 (ISBN 0-404-17633-X). AMS Pr.
--Livre De Lancelot Del Lac, Pt. 2. (Vulgate Version of the Arthurian Romances: No. 4). Repr. of 1911 ed. 57.50 (ISBN 0-404-17634-8). AMS Pr.
--Livre De Lancelot Del Lac, Pt. 3. (Vulgate Version of the Arthurian Romances: No. 5). Repr. of 1912 ed. 57.50 (ISBN 0-404-17635-6). AMS Pr.
Weigand, Hermann J. Three Chapters on Courtly Love in Arthurian France & Germany. LC 56-58693. (North Carolina. University. Studies in the Germanic Languages & Literatures: No. 17). Repr. of 1956 ed. 18.50 (ISBN 0-404-50917-7). AMS Pr.
Weston, Jessie. Three Days Tournament: Study in Romance & Folk-Lore. LC 65-26456. (Studies in Comparative Literature, No. 35). 1969. Repr. of 1902 ed. lib. bdg. 42.95 (ISBN 0-8383-0563-8). Haskell.
Weston, Jessie L. Legend of Sir Lancelot Du Lac: Studies Upon Its Origin, Development, & Position in the Arthurian Romantic Cycles. LC 78-144525. (Grimm Library: No. 12). Repr. of 1901 ed. 12.50 (ISBN 0-404-53555-0). AMS Pr.

LAND
see Land Use

LAND–VALUATION
see Farms–Valuation; Real Property–Valuation

LAND, CONDEMNATION OF
see Eminent Domain

LAND, LIABILITY FOR CONDITION AND USE OF
see Liability for Condition and Use of Land

LAND, NATIONALIZATION OF
see also Land Tenure; Real Property
Bazant, Jan. Alienation of Church Wealth in Mexico. (Cambridge Latin American Studies: No. 11). 33.00 (ISBN 0-521-07872-5). Cambridge U Pr.
Lillich, Richard B., ed. The Valuation of Nationalized Property in International Law, Vol. 2. LC 70-177376. (Virginia Legal Studies). 200p. 1973. 15.00x (ISBN 0-8139-0465-X). U Pr of Va.

LAND, RECLAMATION OF
see Reclamation of Land

LAND CONSOLIDATION
see Consolidation of Land Holdings

LAND CREDIT
see Agricultural Credit

LAND DRAINAGE
see Drainage

LAND FORMS
see Landforms

LAND-GRANT COLLEGES
see State Universities and Colleges

LAND GRANTS
see also Church Lands; Railroad Land Grants; School Lands
also subdivision Public Lands under names of countries, e.g. United States–Public Lands
Ackerman, Robert K. South Carolina Colonial Land Policies. LC 74-16184. (Tricentennial Studies: No. 9). 1977. 14.95x (ISBN 0-87249-254-0). U of SC Pr.
Avina, Rose H. Spanish & Mexican Land Grants in California. LC 73-76003. pap. 7.00 (ISBN 0-88247-205-4). R & E Res Assoc.
--Spanish & Mexican Land Grants in California. Cortes, Carlos E., ed. LC 76-1231. (Chicano Heritage Ser.). (Illus.). 1976. 11.00x (ISBN 0-405-09483-3). Arno.
Bowden, J. J. Spanish & Mexican Land Grants in the Chihuahuan Acquisition. 1971. 12.00 (ISBN 0-87404-031-0). Tex Western.
--Spanish & Mexican Land Grants in the Chihuahuan Acquisition. 1971. 12.00 (ISBN 0-87404-031-0). Tex Western.
Brayer, Herbert O. Pueblo Indian Land Grants of the "Rio Abajo", New Mexico. Bruchey, Stuart, ed. LC 78-56700. (Management of Public Lands in the U. S. Ser.). 1979. Repr. of 1938 ed. lib. bdg. 10.00x (ISBN 0-405-11320-X). Arno.
Burgner, Goldene F. North Carolina Land Grants in Greene County, Tennessee. 160p. Date not set. 20.00 (ISBN 0-89308-204-X). Southern Hist.
--North Carolina Land Grants in Tennessee, 1778 to 1791. 200p. Date not set. 20.00 (ISBN 0-89308-205-8). Southern Hist.
Cortes, Carlos E., ed. Spanish & Mexican Land Grants. LC 73-14216. (The Mexican American Ser.). (Illus.). 1974. Repr. 25.00x (ISBN 0-405-05690-7). Arno.
Cripps, Arthur S. Africa for Africans. LC 79-98716. (Illus.). Repr. of 1927 ed. 11.75x (ISBN 0-8371-2764-5, Pub. by Negro U Pr). Greenwood.
Dyer, Albion M. First Ownership of Ohio Lands. LC 69-18897. 1978. Repr. of 1911 ed. 7.50 (ISBN 0-8063-0098-1). Genealog Pub.
Gahn, Bessie W. Original Patentees of Land at Washington Prior to 1700. LC 77-77982. 1969. Repr. of 1936 ed. 8.50 (ISBN 0-8063-0155-4). Genealog Pub.
Harrison, Fairfax. Virginia Lands Grants. Bruchey, Stuart, ed. LC 78-56669. (Management of Public Lands in the U. S. Ser.). 1979. Repr. of 1925 ed. lib. bdg. 12.00x (ISBN 0-405-11335-8). Arno.
Index to the Headright & Bounty Grants in Georgia from 1756-1909. 1970. 35.00 (ISBN 0-89308-017-9). Southern Hist Pr.
Jillson, Willard R. Old Kentucky Entries & Deeds: A Complete Index to All of the Earliest Land Entries, Military Warrants, Deeds & Wills of the Commonwealth of Kentucky. LC 73-86808. (Filson Club Publications Ser: No. 34). (Illus.). 1978. Repr. of 1926 ed. 20.00 (ISBN 0-8063-0193-7). Genealog Pub.
Kaylor, Peter C. & Chappelear, George W. Abstract of Land Grant Surveys of Augusta & Rockingham Cos., Virginia, 1761-1791. LC 76-16887. 1976. Repr. of 1938 ed. 12.50 (ISBN 0-8063-0725-0). Genealog Pub.
Kehoe, Dalton, et al, eds. Public Land Ownership. LC 75-41925. 1976. 21.95 (ISBN 0-669-00486-3). Lexington Bks.
La Potin, Armand S. The Minisink Patent. Bruchey, Stuart, ed. LC 78-56697. (Management of Public Lands in the U. S. Ser.). 1979. lib. bdg. 20.00x (ISBN 0-405-11340-4). Arno.
Lerner, Craig A., ed. Grants Register, 1981 to 1983. 7th ed. LC 77-12055. 782p. 32.50 (ISBN 0-686-75646-0). St Martin.
Miller, Thomas L. Bounty & Donation Land Grants of Texas, 1835-1888. 908p. 1967. 40.00x (ISBN 0-292-73672-X). U of Tex Pr.
Nugent, Nell M. Cavaliers & Pioneers: Abstracts of Virginia Land Patents & Grants, 1666-1695, Vol. 2. 1977. 20.00 (ISBN 0-88490-009-6). VA State Lib.
O'Callaghan, Edmund B. History of New Netherland: Or, New York Under the Dutch, 2 Vols. LC 66-25099. (Illus.). 1967. Repr. of 1846 ed. Vol. 1. 20.00 (ISBN 0-87152-033-8); Vol. 2. 25.00 (ISBN 0-87152-034-6); Set. 45.00 (ISBN 0-87152-332-9). Reprint.
Robinson, W. Stitt, Jr. Mother Earth: Land Grants in Virginia, 1607-1699. (Illus.). 1957. pap. 1.95x (ISBN 0-8139-0136-7). U Pr of Va.
Ross, Ivy B. The Confirmation of Spanish & Mexican Land Grants in California: Thesis. LC 73-82384. 1974. soft bdg. 8.00 (ISBN 0-88247-265-8). R & E Res Assoc.
Smith, Clifford N. Federal Land Series, Vol. 2. LC 73-3863. (Illus.). 1973. 20.00 (ISBN 0-8389-0144-1). ALA.
--Federal Land Series: A Calendar of Archival Materials on the Land Patents Issued by the United States Government, with Subject, Tract, & Name Indexes, 1810 to 1814, Vol. 3. LC 72-3238. 382p. 1980. 45.00 (ISBN 0-8389-0278-2). ALA.
Van Ness, John R. & Van Ness, Christine M., eds. Spanish & Mexican Land Grants in New Mexico & Colorado. 1980. pap. 8.00 (ISBN 0-89745-012-4). Sunflower U Pr.
Whitelaw, Ralph T. Virginia's Eastern Shore: A History of Northampton & Accomack Counties, 2 vols. (Illus.). 40.00 (ISBN 0-8446-1478-5). Peter Smith.

Wirth, Fremont P. The Discovery & Exploitation of the Minnesota Iron Lands. Bruchey, Stuart, ed. LC 78-53544. (Development of Public Lands in the U. S. Ser.). 1979. Repr. of 1937 ed. lib. bdg. 16.00x (ISBN 0-405-11393-5). Arno.

LAND PATENTS
see Land Grants

LAND QUESTION
see Land Tenure

LAND RECLAMATION
see Reclamation of Land

LAND REFORM
Here are entered works on land distribution combined with the socio-economic policy relating to the population of that area of distribution.
see also Agriculture and State; Land Tenure

Agrarian Reform & Rural Development. (Terminology Billetin Ser.: No. 35). 120p. 1979. pap. 8.25 (ISBN 92-5-000755-8, F1822, FAO). Unipub.
Ahmad, Saghir. Class & Power in a Punjabi Village. LC 76-1663. 1977. 8.95 (ISBN 0-85345-385-3, CL-3853). Monthly Rev.
Ahmed, Iftikhar. Technological Change & Agrarian Structure: A Study of Bangladesh. International Labour Office, ed. xvi, 136p. (Orig.). 1981. pap. 8.55 (ISBN 92-2-102543-8). Intl Labour Office.
Ahmed, Zahir. Land Reforms in Southeast Asia. LC 75-907992. 1975. 9.50x (ISBN 0-88386-709-5, Orient Longman). South Asia Bks.
Bell, A., et al. Land & Water Resources. (Place & People Ser.: No. 6). 1977. pap. text ed. 4.95x (ISBN 0-435-34698-9). Heinemann Ed.
Blanco, Hugo. Land or Death: The Peasant Struggle in Peru. LC 73-186689. 192p. 1972. 14.00 (ISBN 0-87348-265-4); pap. 3.95 (ISBN 0-87348-266-2). Path Pr NY.
Cohen, Suleiman. Agrarian Structures & Agrarian Reform. (Studies in Development & Planning: Vol. 8). 1978. lib. bdg. 15.50 (ISBN 90-207-0764-7, Pub. by Martinus Nijhoff Netherlands). Kluwer Boston.
Eckholm, Erik. The Dispossessed of the Earth: Land Reform & Sustainable Development. LC 79-65740. (Worldwatch Papers). 1979. pap. 2.00 (ISBN 0-916468-29-1). Worldwatch Inst.
Handelman, Howard, ed. The Politics of Agrarian Change in Asia & Latin America. LC 81-47565. (Illus.). 148p. 1981. 22.50x (ISBN 0-253-34548-0). Ind U Pr.
Harbeson, John W. Nation-Building in Kenya: The Role of Land Reform. LC 72-80567. 421p. 1973. text ed. 15.75x (ISBN 0-8101-0389-3). Northwestern U Pr.
Hewes, Lawrence I., Jr. Japan-Land & Men. LC 74-8262. (Illus.). 154p. 1974. Repr. of 1955 ed. lib. bdg. 11.50x (ISBN 0-8371-7574-7, HEJA). Greenwood.
Hirschman, Albert O. Journeys Toward Progress: Studies of Economic Policy-Making in Latin America. (Illus.). 320p. 1973. pap. 3.45x (ISBN 0-393-00693-X, Norton Lib). Norton.
Koo, Anthony Y. Land Market Distortion & Tenure Reform. (Illus.). 184p. 1982. text ed. 14.50 (ISBN 0-8138-1076-0). Iowa St U Pr.
Kravchinskii, Sergiel M. The Russian Peasantry: Their Agrarian Condition, Social Life, & Religion. LC 75-39055. (Russian Studies: Perspectives on the Revolution Ser). vi, 401p. 1977. Repr. of 1888 ed. 29.50 (ISBN 0-88355-435-6). Hyperion Conn.
Land Reform. (Land Settlement & Cooperatives 1975: No. 1). 125p. 1976. pap. 8.25 (ISBN 0-685-66309-4, F1013, FAO). Unipub.
Land Reform. (Land Settlement & Cooperatives 1977: No. 2). 1979. pap. 7.50 (ISBN 0-685-94191-4, F1540, FAO). Unipub.
Land Reform: Land Settlement & Co-Operatives, 1974, No. 1 & 2. 147p. 1975. pap. 11.50 (ISBN 0-685-62392-0, F1012, FAO). Unipub.
Land Reform: Land Settlement & Cooperatives, 1978, No. 1. 124p. 1979. pap. 8.50 (ISBN 0-685-96674-7, F1567, FAO). Unipub.
Land Reform: Land Settlement & Cooperatives, 1976, No. 2. (Illus.). 1978. pap. 7.50 (ISBN 0-685-86538-X, FAO). Unipub.
Land Reform, Nineteen Seventy-Eight, No. 2. 1979. pap. 7.50 (ISBN 0-686-59752-4, F1647, FAO). Unipub.
Land Tenure Center, University of Wisconsin - Madison. Land Tenure & Agrarian Reform in Africa & the Near East: An Annotated Bibliography. (Ser. Seventy). 1976. lib. bdg. 22.00 (ISBN 0-8161-7921-2). G K Hall.
Lichfield, Nathaniel & Darin-Drabkin, Haim. Land Policy in Planning. (Urban & Regional Studies: No. 8). (Illus.). 334p. 1981. text ed. 39.95 (ISBN 0-04-333017-7). Allen Unwin.
Lin, Sein. Land Reform Inplementation: A Comparative Perspective. 1974. pap. 3.00 (ISBN 0-686-17292-2). Lincoln Inst Land.
Lin, Sein, ed. Readings in Land Reform. 374p. 1970. pap. 2.50 (ISBN 0-686-01013-2). Lincoln Inst Land.
Loveman, Brian. Struggle in the Countryside: Politics & Rural Labor in Chile, 1919-1973. LC 74-6521. (International Development Research Center, Studies in Development: No. 10). (Illus.). 480p. 1976. 15.00x (ISBN 0-253-35565-6). Ind U Pr.
Melville, T. & Melville, M. Guatemala: The Politics of Land Ownership. LC 70-143523. 1971. 12.95 (ISBN 0-02-920840-8). Free Pr.
Preston, David A. Environment, Society & Rural Change in Latin America: The Past, Present & Future in the Country. LC 79-41481. 256p. 1980. 41.75 (ISBN 0-471-27713-4, Pub. by Wiley-Interscience). Wiley.
Ramakrishnan, S., ed. Land Policies in Developing Countries: Select Bibliography on Land Reform (1973-1977) 1978. pap. 3.00 (ISBN 0-686-23888-5). Lincoln Inst Land.
Ratcliffe, John. Land Policy. 1976. 7.95 (ISBN 0-09-127070-7, Pub. by Hutchinson); pap. 3.95 (ISBN 0-09-127071-5). Merrimack Bk Serv.
Roll, Charles R., Jr. The Distribution of Rural Incomes in China: A Comparison of the 1930's & 1950's. LC 78-74301. (The Modern Chinese Economy Ser.: Vol. 13). 223p. 1980. lib. bdg. 22.00 (ISBN 0-8240-4288-3). Garland Pub.
Salamini, Heather F. Agrarian Radicalism in Veracruz, 1920-38. LC 77-26106. (Illus.). 1978. 16.50x (ISBN 0-8032-0952-5). U of Nebr Pr.
Sanderson, Steven E. Agrarian Populism & the Mexican State: The Struggle for Land in Sonora. LC 80-14262. 1981. 22.75 (ISBN 0-520-04056-2). U of Cal Pr.
Skar, Harald O. The Warm Valley People. 304p. 1981. 26.00 (ISBN 82-00-05682-1). Universitet.
Steenland, Kyle. Agrarian Reform Under Allende: Peasant Revolt in the South. LC 76-57540. (Illus.). 241p. 1977. pap. 6.50x (ISBN 0-8263-0450-8). U of NM Pr.
Sturgess, Roy. The Rural Revolution in an English Village. (Cambridge Introduction to the History of Mankind). (Illus.). 48p. Date not set. pap. price not set (ISBN 0-521-22800-X). Cambridge U Pr.
Tai, Hung-chao. Land Reform & Politics: A Comparative Analysis. 1974. 45.00x (ISBN 0-520-02337-4). U of Cal Pr.
Walinsky, Louis & Ladejinsky, Wolf. Agrarian Reform As Unfinished Business: The Selected Papers of Wolf Ladejinsky. (World Bank Research Publications Ser.). 1977. 32.50x (ISBN 0-19-920095-5); pap. 10.95x (ISBN 0-19-920098-X). Oxford U Pr.
Whetham, E. H. Co-Operation, Land Reform & Land Settlement: Report on a Survey in Kenya, Uganda, Sudan, Ghana, Nigeria & Iran. Plunkett Foundation for Co-Operative Studies, ed. 1968. 13.00x (ISBN 0-686-75619-3, Pub. by Plunkett Found England). State Mutual Bk.
Wilkie, James W. Measuring Land Reform. LC 74-620145. (Supplements to the Statistical Abstract of Latin America, V. 5). (Illus., Orig.). 1974. pap. text ed. 8.50 (ISBN 0-87903-226-X). UCLA Lat Am Ctr.

LAND RESEARCH

Gibson, W. L., Jr., et al, eds. Methods for Land Economics Research. LC 66-19269. 1967. pap. 3.95x (ISBN 0-8032-5225-0, BB 352, Bison). U of Nebr Pr.
Salter, Leonard A., Jr. Critical Review of Research in Land Economics. 1967. pap. 5.75x (ISBN 0-299-04424-6). U of Wis Pr.

LAND SCRIP (U. S.)
see Bounties, Military-United States

LAND SETTLEMENT
see also Agricultural Colonies; Colonization; Migration, Internal

Ashmore, Wendy, ed. Lowland Maya Settlement Patterns. (School of American Research Advanced Seminar Ser.). 464p. 1981. 30.00x (ISBN 0-8263-0556-3). U of NM Pr.
Bartlett, R. P. Human Capital: The Settlement of Foreigners in Russia, 1762-1804. LC 78-68337. 1980. 53.00 (ISBN 0-521-22205-2). Cambridge U Pr.
Bathke, W. L. & Haney, W. A., eds. Land Management in the Seventies: Concepts & Models. (Illus.). 1972. 10.00 (ISBN 0-911302-19-0). San Francisco Pr.
Bayard, Charles J. The Development of the Public Land Policy, 1783-1820, with Special Reference to Indiana. Bruchey, Stuart, ed. LC 78-53556. (Development of Public Lands Law in the U. S. Ser.). 1979. lib. bdg. 24.00x (ISBN 0-405-11364-1). Arno.
Bell, Gwen, ed. Strategies for Human Settlements: Habitat & Environment. LC 76-5416. (Illus.). 200p. (Orig.). 1976. (Eastwest Ctr); pap. 3.95 (ISBN 0-8248-0469-4). U Pr of Hawaii.
Bibliography on Land Settlement. 1977. pap. 17.00 (ISBN 92-5-000221-1, F1729, FAO). Unipub.
Chisholm, Michael. Rural Settlement & Land Use: An Essay in Location. 1966. text ed. 16.25x (ISBN 0-09-063001-7, Hutchinson U Lib). Humanities.
Clawson, Marion. Resettlement Experience on Nine Selected Resettlement Projects. 1979. pap. 4.00 (ISBN 0-87461-021-4). McNally.
Collier, David. Squatters & Oligarchs: Authoritarian Rule & Policy Change in Peru. LC 75-34112. (Illus.). 200p. 1976. 12.00x (ISBN 0-8018-1748-X). Johns Hopkins.
Eidt, Robert C. Pioneer Settlement in Northeast Argentina. LC 71-138058. 294p. 1971. 22.50x (ISBN 0-299-05920-0). U of Wis Pr.
Emmons, David M. Garden in the Grasslands: Boomer Literature of the Central Great Plains. LC 70-125100. (Illus.). xiv, 220p. 1971. 15.50x (ISBN 0-8032-0753-0). U of Nebr Pr.
Foweraker, J. The Struggle for Land. (Illus.). 304p. Date not set. 39.50 (ISBN 0-521-23555-3). Cambridge U Pr.
Garstin, Crosbie. Sunshine Settlers. 240p. 1972. 12.50x (ISBN 0-8426-1267-X). Verry.
Godfrey, Marie H. Early Settlers of Barbour County, Ala, Vol. 2. 200p. 1976. pap. 12.00 (ISBN 0-686-65628-8). Southern Hist Pr.
Hadfield, Alice M. The Chartist Land Company. 2nd ed. (Illus.). 248p. 1970. 8.95 (ISBN 0-7153-4872-8); pap. 3.95 (ISBN 0-7153-5809-X). David & Charles.
Harbeson, John W. Nation-Building in Kenya: The Role of Land Reform. LC 72-80567. 421p. 1973. text ed. 15.75x (ISBN 0-8101-0389-3). Northwestern U Pr.
Heathcote, R. L. Back of Bourke. 1965. 18.50x (ISBN 0-522-83887-1, Pub. by Melbourne U Pr). Intl Schol Bk Serv.
Hegen, Edmund E. Highways into the Upper Amazon Basin. LC 66-64732. (Latin American Monographs: Ser. 2, No. 2). (Illus.). 1966. pap. 3.75 (ISBN 0-8130-0109-9). U Presses Fla.
Holley, Donald. Uncle Sam's Farmers: The New Deal Communities in the Lower Mississippi Valley. LC 75-20091. 1975. 19.95 (ISBN 0-252-00510-4). U of Ill Pr.
Keyes, Dale L. Land Development & the Natural Environment: Estimating Impacts. (Land Development Impact Ser.). 128p. 1976. pap. 4.95 (ISBN 0-685-99523-2, 13500). Urban Inst.
Land Reform, Land Settlements & Cooperatives, 1975, Vol. 2. 1976. pap. 11.50 (ISBN 0-685-71578-7, F1014, FAO). Unipub.
Lee, Lawrence B. Kansas & the Homestead Act: 1862-1905, 2 vols. in one. Bruchey, Stuart, ed. LC 78-36703. (Management of Public Lands in the U. S. Ser.). (Illus.). 1979. lib. bdg. 40.00x (ISBN 0-405-11341-2). Arno.
Lonsdale, Richard E. & Holmes, John H., eds. Settlement Systems in Sparsely Populated Regions: The United States & Australia. LC 80-27278. (Pergamon Policy Studies on Urban Affairs; Comparative Rural Transformation Ser.). (Illus.). 360p. 1981. 40.00 (ISBN 0-08-023111-X). Pergamon.
McCready, K. J. The Land Settlement Association: Its History & Present Form. Plunkett Foundation for Co-Operative Studies, ed. 135p. 1974. 20.00x (ISBN 0-85042-006-7, Pub. by Plunkett Found England). State Mutual Bk.
Meyer, Iain R. Geography: Theory in Practice, Bk. 1, Settlements. 201p. (Orig.). pap. text ed. 9.50 (ISBN 0-06-318096-0, Pub. by Har-Row Ltd England). Har-Row.
Mitchell, Robert D. Commercialism & Frontier: Perspectives on the Early Shenandoah Valley. LC 76-26610. (Illus.). 1977. 13.95x (ISBN 0-8139-0661-X). U Pr of Va.
Muller, Thomas. Economic Impacts of Land Development: Employment, Housing & Property Values. (Land Development Impact Ser.). 148p. 1976. pap. 3.95 (ISBN 0-87766-173-1, 15800). Urban Inst.
Nelson, Michael. The Development of Tropical Lands: Policy Issues in Latin America. LC 72-12363. (Resources for the Future Ser). 323p. 1973. 22.00x (ISBN 0-8018-1488-X). Johns Hopkins.
O'Callaghan, Jerry A. The Disposition of the Public Domain in Oregon. Bruchey, Stuart, ed. LC 78-53563. (Development of Public Lands in the U. S. Ser.). 1979. Repr. of 1960 ed. lib. bdg. 10.00x (ISBN 0-405-11382-X). Arno.
Ramsey, Robert W. Carolina Cradle: Settlement of the Northwest Carolina Frontier, 1747-1762. 1964. 12.95 (ISBN 0-8078-0934-9). U of NC Pr.
Roberts, Brian K. Rural Settlement in Britain. (Studies in Historical Geography Ser.). (Illus.). 1977. 18.50 (ISBN 0-208-01621-X, Archon). Shoe String.
Rollins, George W. The Struggle of the Cattleman, Sheepman & Settler for Control of Lands in Wyoming, 1867-1910. Bruchey, Stuart, ed. LC 78-56671. (Management of Public Lands in the U. S. Ser.). (Illus.). 1979. lib. bdg. 28.00x (ISBN 0-405-11353-6). Arno.
Treadgold, Donald W. The Great Siberian Migration. LC 75-25498. 1976. Repr. of 1957 ed. lib. bdg. 19.00x (ISBN 0-8371-8427-4, TRSM). Greenwood.
United Nations Conference on Human Settlements. Aspects of Human Settlement Planning. LC 77-9877. (Habitat Ser.). 350p. 1978. 52.00 (ISBN 0-08-022011-8). Pergamon.
Wacker, Peter O. Land & People: A Cultural Geography of Preindustrial New Jersey-- Origins & Settlement Patterns, Vol. 1. 520p. 1975. 35.00 (ISBN 0-8135-0742-1). Rutgers U Pr.
Wagstaff, J. M. The Development of Rural Settlements: A Study of the Helos Plain in Southern Greece. 1981. 60.00x (ISBN 0-86127-302-8, Pub. by Avebury Pub England). State Mutual Bk.
Weis, Dieter. Die Grossstadt Essen. pap. 15.50 (ISBN 0-384-66570-5). Johnson Repr.
Whetham, E. H. Co-Operation, Land Reform & Land Settlement: Report on a Survey in Kenya, Uganda, Sudan, Ghana, Nigeria & Iran. Plunkett Foundation for Co-Operative Studies, ed. 1968. 13.00x (ISBN 0-686-75619-3, Pub. by Plunkett Found England). State Mutual Bk.

LAND SLIDES
see Landslides

LAND SUBDIVISION

Accounting for Retail Land Sales. 1973. pap. 3.50 (ISBN 0-685-36116-0). Am Inst CPA.
Allan, Leslie, et al. Promised Lands 1: Subdivisions in Deserts & Mountains, Vol. 1. LC 76-46735. (Promised Lands). (Illus.). 1976. pap. 20.00x (ISBN 0-918780-04-7). Inform.
Browning, Frank. The Vanishing Land: The Corporate Theft of America. 8.00 (ISBN 0-8446-5166-4). Peter Smith.
Costonis, John & DeVoy, Robert. The Puerto Rico Plan: Environmental Protection Through Development Rights Transfer. LC 75-15460. (Illus.). 90p. 1975. 9.00 (ISBN 0-87420-561-1). Urban Land.
Peters, William E. Ohio Lands & Their History. 3rd. ed. Bruchey, Stuart, ed. LC 78-53541. (Development of Public Land Law in the U. S. Ser.). (Illus.). 1979. Repr. of 1930 ed. lib. bdg. 23.00x (ISBN 0-405-11383-8). Arno.
Simko, Patricia A. The Insider's Guide to Owning Land in Subdivisions: How to Buy, Appraise & Get Rid of Your Lot. (Illus., Orig.). 1979. pap. 2.50 (ISBN 0-918780-17-9). Inform.
Thrower, Norman J. Original Survey & Land Subdivision. LC 66-13454. (Monograph: No. 4). 3.95 (ISBN 0-89291-083-6). Assn Am Geographers.

LAND SUBDIVISION–LAW AND LEGISLATION
see also Zoning Law

Lefcoe, George. Land Development Law. 2nd ed. (Contemporary Legal Education Ser). 1974. 21.00 (ISBN 0-672-81942-2, Bobbs-Merrill Law). Michie-Bobbs.
Platt, Rutherford H. Land Use Control: Interface of Law & Geography. Natoli, Salvatore J., ed. LC 76-18389. (Resource Papers for College Geography Ser.). (Illus.). 1976. pap. text ed. 4.00 (ISBN 0-89291-109-3). Assn Am Geographers.

LAND SURVEYING
see Surveying

LAND TAX
see Land Value Taxation; Real Property Tax

LAND TENURE
see also Administration of Estates; Agricultural Colonies; Decentralization in Government; Elections; Mayors; Metropolitan Government; Municipal Government; Public Administration; Special Districts; Villages

Akagi, R. H. Town Proprietors of the New England Colonies. 1963. 8.50 (ISBN 0-8446-1012-7). Peter Smith.
Banks, Enoch M. Economics of Land Tenure in Georgia. LC 68-56647. (Columbia University, Studies in the Social Sciences Ser.: No. 58). Repr. of 1905 ed. 16.50 (ISBN 0-404-51058-2). AMS Pr.
Bayard, Charles J. The Development of the Public Land Policy, 1783-1820, with Special Reference to Indiana. Bruchey, Stuart, ed. LC 78-53556. (Development of Public Lands Law in the U. S. Ser.). 1979. lib. bdg. 24.00x (ISBN 0-405-11364-1). Arno.
Bertrand, Alvin L. & Corty, Floyd L., eds. Rural Land Tenure in the United States: A Socioeconomic Approach to Problems, Programs, & Trends. LC 62-16212. (Illus.). 1962. 22.50x (ISBN 0-8071-0325-X). La State U Pr.
Bogue, Margaret B. Patterns from the Sod: Land Use & Tenure in the Grand Prairie, 1850-1900. (Illinois Historical Collections Ser.: Vol. 34). 1959. 2.50 (ISBN 0-912154-14-4). Ill St Hist Lib.
Bond, Beverley W. The Quit-Rent System in the American Colonies. 1919. 8.00 (ISBN 0-8446-1082-8). Peter Smith.
Brooks, Robert P. The Agrarian Revolution in Georgia, 1865-1912. LC 72-181919. Repr. of 1914 ed. 15.00 (ISBN 0-404-00007-X). AMS Pr.

Cantor, Louis. Prologue to the Protest Movement: The Missouri Sharecropper Roadside Demonstrations of 1939. LC 70-86480. 1969. 12.75 (ISBN 0-8223-0215-2). Duke.

Chinen, Jon J. Great Mahele: Hawaii's Land Division of 1848. LC 57-14473. (Orig.). 1958. pap. 1.50x (ISBN 0-87022-125-6). U Pr of Hawaii.

Clawson, Marion. Land System of the United States: An Introduction to the History & Practice of Land Use & Land Tenure. LC 68-10250. (Illus.). 1968. 10.95x (ISBN 0-8032-0016-1). U of Nebr Pr.

Coles, Harry L. A History of the Administration of Federal Land Policies & Land Tenure in Louisiana, 1803-1860. Bruchey, Stuart, ed. LC 78-56718. (Management in Public Lands in the U. S. Ser.). (Illus.). 1979. lib. bdg. 25.00x (ISBN 0-405-11327-7). Arno.

Committee on Taxation, Resources, & Economic Development. Land Use & Public Policy. Lynn, Arthur D., Jr., ed. 268p. 1976. 22.50x (ISBN 0-299-06920-6). U of Wis Pr.

Copp, Henry N. Public Land Laws. Bruchey, Stuart, ed. LC 78-53559. (Development of Public Land Law in the U. S. Ser.). 1979. Repr. of 1875 ed. lib. bdg. 55.00x (ISBN 0-405-11372-2). Arno.

--United States Mineral Lands. Bruchey, Stuart, ed. LC 78-53539. (Development of Public Land Law in the U. S. Ser.). 1979. Repr. of 1882 ed. lib. bdg. 39.00x (ISBN 0-405-11373-0). Arno.

Currie, J. M. The Economic Theory of Agricultural Land Tenure. LC 80-41114. (Illus.). Date not set. 32.50 (ISBN 0-521-23634-7). Cambridge U Pr.

Dana, Samuel T. & Krueger, Myron. California Lands. Bruchey, Stuart, ed. LC 78-53561. (Development of Public Lands Law in the U. S. Ser.). (Illus.). 1979. Repr. of 1958 ed. lib. bdg. 21.00x (ISBN 0-405-11374-9). Arno.

Diller, Robert. Farm Ownership, Tenancy, & Land Use in the Nebraska Community. Bruchey, Stuart, ed. LC 78-56629. (Management of Public Lands in the U. S. Ser.). 1979. Repr. of 1932 ed. lib. bdg. 15.00x (ISBN 0-405-11339-0). Arno.

Egle, William H. Early Pennsylvania Land Records: Minutes of the Board of Property of the Province of Pennsylvania. LC 76-15827. 1976. Repr. of 1893 ed. 25.00 (ISBN 0-8063-0723-4). Genealog Pub.

Egleston, Melville. The Land System of the New England Colonies. 1973. pap. 7.00 (ISBN 0-384-13963-9). Johnson Repr.

Ellis, David M. Landlords & Farmers in the Hudson-Mohawk Region, 1790-1850. 1967. lib. bdg. 17.50x (ISBN 0-374-92546-1). Octagon.

Farnam, Henry W. Chapters in the History of Social Legislation in the United States to 1860. LC 73-111778. Repr. of 1938 ed. 22.50 (ISBN 0-404-00157-2). AMS Pr.

Gates, Paul W. Landlords & Tenants on the Prairie Frontier: Studies in American Land Policy. (Illus.). 338p. 1973. 22.50x (ISBN 0-8014-0763-X). Cornell U Pr.

Gates, Paul W., et al. Four Persistent Issues: Essays on California's Land Ownership Concentration, Water Deficits, Sub-State Regionalism, & Congressional Leadership. LC 78-17964. 1978. pap. 5.75x (ISBN 0-87772-257-9). Inst Gov Stud Berk.

Gould, Clarence P. Land System in Maryland, 1720-1765. Bruchey, Stuart, ed. LC 78-53540. (Development of Public Land in the U. S. Ser.). 1979. Repr. of 1913 ed. lib. bdg. 10.00x (ISBN 0-405-11376-5). Arno.

Harris, Marshall D. Origin of the Land Tenure System in the United States. Repr. of 1953 ed. lib. bdg. 18.25x (ISBN 0-8371-3731-4, HATS). Greenwood.

Hibbard, Benjamin H. History of the Public Land Policies. 608p. 1965. pap. 9.95x (ISBN 0-299-03494-1). U of Wis Pr.

Ingle, E. Local Institutions of Virginia. 1973. Repr. of 1885 ed. pap. 11.00 (ISBN 0-384-25741-0). Johnson Repr.

Jacoby, Erich H. Agrarian Reconstruction. 1968. pap. 4.75 (ISBN 0-685-09369-7, FAO). Unipub.

Kammer, Jerry. The Second Long Walk: The Navajo-Hopi Land Dispute. 1980. 14.95 (ISBN 0-8263-0549-0). U of NM Pr.

La Potin, Armand S. The Minisink Patent. Bruchey, Stuart, ed. LC 78-56697. (Management of Public Lands in the U. S. Ser.). 1979. lib. bdg. 20.00x (ISBN 0-405-11340-4). Arno.

Lindholm, Richard W. & Lin, Sein, eds. Henry George & Sun Yat-Sen: Application & Evolution of Their Land Use Doctrine (Centenary of Progress & Poverty) LC 77-94219. 1977. pap. text ed. 5.00 (ISBN 0-686-05023-1). Lincoln Inst Land.

Livermore, Shaw. Early American Land Companies. 1968. lib. bdg. 16.50x (ISBN 0-374-95073-3). Octagon.

Longnon, Jean & Topping, Peter. Documents Sur le Regime Des Terres Dans la Principaute De Moree Au XIVe Siecle. (Documents et Recherches Sur L'economie Des Pays Byzantins, Islamiques et Slaves et Leurs Relations Commerciales Au Moyen Age: No. 9). 1969. pap. 51.25x (ISBN 90-2796-261-8). Mouton.

McAuslan, Patrick. Land, Law & Planning. (Law in Context Ser.). xxix, 736p. 1975. text ed. 37.50x (ISBN 0-297-76880-8). Rothman.

Macy, J. Institutional Beginnings in a Western State: Iowa. pap. 7.00 (ISBN 0-384-34942-0). Johnson Repr.

Maris, Paul V. Land Is Mine: From Tenancy to Family Farm Ownership. Repr. of 1950 ed. lib. bdg. 24.50x (ISBN 0-8371-1871-9, MALM). Greenwood.

Mills, Edwin S. & Oates, Wallace E. Fiscal Zoning & Land Use Controls. LC 74-21877. 224p. 1975. 19.95 (ISBN 0-669-96685-1). Lexington Bks.

Morris, Richard B. Studies in the History of American Law. 2nd ed. 1964. lib. bdg. 18.50x (ISBN 0-374-95909-9). Octagon.

Ortiz, Roxanne D. Roots of Resistance: Land Tenure in New Mexico, Sixteen Eighty to Nineteen Eighty. LC 80-18935. 202p. (Orig.). 1980. 14.95 (ISBN 0-89551-052-9); pap. 9.95 (ISBN 0-89551-050-2). UCLA Chicano Stud.

Probyn, John W., ed. Systems of Land Tenure in Various Countries. facs. new ed. LC 75-153000. (Select Bibliographies Reprint Ser). Repr. of 1881 ed. 25.00 (ISBN 0-8369-5752-0). Arno.

Raper, Arthur F. Preface to Peasantry: A Tale of Two Black Belt Counties. LC 72-137183. (Poverty U.S.A. Historical Record Ser). 1971. Repr. of 1936 ed. 25.00 (ISBN 0-405-03121-1). Arno.

--Preface to Peasantry: A Tale of Two Black Belt Counties. LC 68-16417. (Studies in American Negro Life). (Illus.). 1968. pap. 4.95 (ISBN 0-689-70163-2, NL5). Atheneum.

Rollins, George W. The Struggle of the Cattleman, Sheepman & Settler for Control of Lands in Wyoming, 1867-1910. Bruchey, Stuart, ed. LC 78-56671. (Management of Public Lands in the U. S. Ser.). (Illus.). 1979. lib. bdg. 28.00x (ISBN 0-405-11353-6). Arno.

Sakolski, A. M. Land Tenure & Land Taxation in America. 316p. 1957. 2.00 (ISBN 0-911312-32-3). Schalkenbach.

Simpson, S. R. Land Law & Registration. LC 74-16994. 700p. 1976. 90.00 (ISBN 0-521-20628-6). Cambridge U Pr.

Stewart, Charles L. Land Tenure in United States, with Special Reference to Illinois. (Illus.). Repr. of 1916 ed. 9.50 (ISBN 0-384-58160-9). Johnson Repr.

Thornton, William T. Plea for Peasant Proprietors. LC 68-58028. Repr. of 1848 ed. 15.00x (ISBN 0-678-00569-9). Kelley.

Tuma, Elias H. Twenty-Six Centuries of Agrarian Reform: A Comparative Analysis. (Near Eastern Center, UCLA). 1965. 24.75x (ISBN 0-520-01286-0). U of Cal Pr.

Wa-Githumo, Mwangi. Land & Nationalism: The Impact of Land Expropriation & Land Grievances Upon the Rise & Development of Nationalist Movements in Kenya, 1885-1939. LC 80-5589. 502p. 1981. lib. bdg. 24.50 (ISBN 0-8191-1491-X); pap. text ed. 16.50 (ISBN 0-8191-1492-8). U Pr of Amer.

Wilhelm, L. W. Local Institutions of Maryland. Repr. of 1885 ed. pap. 11.00 (ISBN 0-384-68479-3). Johnson Repr.

Wirth, Fremont P. The Discovery & Exploitation of the Minnesota Iron Lands. Bruchey, Stuart, ed. LC 78-53544. (Development of Public Lands in the U. S. Ser.). 1979. Repr. of 1937 ed. lib. bdg. 16.00x (ISBN 0-405-11393-5). Arno.

Woodard, Florence M. Town Proprietors in Vermont. LC 68-58646. (Columbia University. Studies in the Social Sciences: No. 418). Repr. of 1936 ed. 16.50 (ISBN 0-404-51418-9). AMS Pr.

Woofter, Thomas J. Negro Migration: Changes in Rural Organization & Population of the Cotton Belt. LC 70-144705. Repr. of 1920 ed. 7.50 (ISBN 0-404-00243-9). AMS Pr.

--Negro Migration, Changes in Rural Organization & Population of the Cotton Belt. LC 76-89063. Repr. of 1920 ed. 10.00x (ISBN 0-8371-1943-X, Pub. by Negro U Pr). Greenwood.

Zahler, Helene S. Eastern Workingmen & National Land Policy 1829-1862. Repr. of 1941 ed. lib. bdg. 15.00x (ISBN 0-8371-1868-9, ZAEW). Greenwood.

LAND TENURE–BIBLIOGRAPHY

Land Tenure Center. Land Tenure & Agrarian Reform in Asia: An Annotated Bibliography. 1980. lib. bdg. 45.00 (ISBN 0-8161-8221-3). G K Hall.

Ross, Denman W. Early History of Landholding Among the Germans. LC 73-168704. (Research & Source Works Ser: No. 814). 1971. Repr. of 1883 ed. lib. bdg. 21.50 (ISBN 0-8337-3058-4). B Franklin.

LAND TENURE–LAW

see also Contracts, Agricultural; Conveyancing; Copyhold; Farm Tenancy; Feudal Law; Homestead Law; Inclosures; Land Titles; Landlord and Tenant; Leases; Mortmain; Real Property; Riparian Rights

Abrams, Charles. Revolution in Land. Bruchey, Stuart, ed. LC 78-56679. (Management of Public Lands in the U. S. Ser.). (Illus.). 1979. Repr. of 1939 ed. lib. bdg. 22.00x (ISBN 0-405-11316-1). Arno.

Avina, Rose H. Spanish & Mexican Land Grants in California. Cortes, Carlos E., ed. LC 76-1231. (Chicano Heritage Ser.). (Illus.). 1976. 11.00x (ISBN 0-405-09483-3). Arno.

Bernard, Michael M. Constitutions, Taxation, & Land Policy: Vol. II, Discussion & Analysis of Federal & State Constitutional Constraints on the Use of Taxation As an Instrument of Land-Planning Policy. LC 78-24792. (Lincoln Institute of Land Policy Bk). 144p. 1980. 16.95x (ISBN 0-669-03462-2). Lexington Bks.

Bogue, Margaret B. Patterns from the Sod. Bruchey, Stuart, ed. LC 78-56691. (Management of Public Lands Law in the U. S. Ser.). (Illus.). 1979. Repr. of 1959 ed. lib. bdg. 21.00x (ISBN 0-405-11318-8). Arno.

Bosselman, Fred P., et al. Federal Land Use Regulation. new ed. LC 76-46667. 1977. text ed. 20.00 (ISBN 0-685-88298-5, N1-1306). PLI.

Browning, Frank. The Vanishing Land: The Corporate Theft of America. 8.00 (ISBN 0-8446-5166-4). Peter Smith.

Chao Kuo-Chun. Agrarian Policy of the Chinese Communist Party, Nineteen Twenty-One to Nineteen Fifty-Nine. LC 77-14587. 1977. Repr. of 1960 ed. lib. bdg. 31.25x (ISBN 0-8371-9861-5, CHAP). Greenwood.

Johnson, A. H. The Disappearance of the Small Landowner. LC 79-14625. (Illus.). xiii, 164p. 1979. Repr. of 1909 ed. lib. bdg. 13.50x (ISBN 0-678-08077-1). Kelley.

Libecap, Gary. Locking up the Range: Federal Land Controls & Grazing. (Pacific Institute for Public Policy Research Ser.). Date not set. price not set professional reference (ISBN 0-88410-382-X). Ballinger Pub.

Mandelker, Daniel R. Environmental & Land Controls Legislation. 1976. 30.00 (ISBN 0-672-82486-8, Bobbs-Merrill Law); 1980 suppl. 10.00 (ISBN 0-672-84303-X). Michie-Bobbs.

LAND TENURE–AFRICA

Allan, William. Land Holding & Land Usage Among the Plateau Tonga of Mazabuka District, a Reconnaissance Survey, 1945. LC 76-129937. (Illus.). Repr. of 1948 ed. 12.50x (ISBN 0-8371-0305-3, Pub. by Negro U Pr). Greenwood.

Bohannan, Paul. Tiv Farm & Settlement. pap. 8.00 (ISBN 0-384-04959-1). Johnson Repr.

Hayford, Casely. Truth About the West African Land Question. LC 75-78767. Repr. of 1913 ed. 12.00x (ISBN 0-8371-1393-8). Greenwood.

Hekken, P. M. Land Scarcity & Rural Inequality in Tanzania: Some Case Studies from Rungwe District. (Communications: No. 3). (Illus.). 1972. pap. 10.50x (ISBN 90-2796-984-1). Mouton.

Hill, Polly. Migrant Cocoa Farmers of Southern Ghana. 42.95 (ISBN 0-521-05264-5). Cambridge U Pr.

James, R. W. Land Tenure & Policy in Tanzania. LC 76-185718. 375p. 1971. pap. 6.50x (ISBN 0-8020-1808-4). U of Toronto Pr.

Land Tenure Center, University of Wisconsin - Madison. Land Tenure & Agrarian Reform in Africa & the Near East: An Annotated Bibliography. (Ser. Seventy). 1976. lib. bdg. 22.00 (ISBN 0-8161-7921-2). G K Hall.

Meek, Charles K. Colonial Law, a Bibliography with Special Reference to Native African Systems of Law & Land Tenure. LC 78-14383. 1978. lib. bdg. 15.00 (ISBN 0-313-21011-X, MECL). Greenwood.

Palmer, Robin. Land & Racial Domination in Rhodesia. LC 76-14300. (Illus.). 1977. 24.50x (ISBN 0-520-03255-1). U of Cal Pr.

Plaatje, Solomon T. Native Life in South Africa, Before & Since the European War & the Boer Rebellion. 2nd ed. LC 76-78585. (Illus.). 1916. 18.25x (ISBN 0-8371-1420-9, Pub. by Negro U Pr). Greenwood.

Sheddick, V. G. Land Tenure in Basutoland. Repr. of 1954 ed. pap. 23.00 (ISBN 0-384-54985-3). Johnson Repr.

Wasserman, G. B. Politics of Decolonization. LC 75-2735. (African Studies: No. 17). (Illus.). 224p. 1976. 27.50 (ISBN 0-521-20838-6). Cambridge U Pr.

West, Henry W. Land Policy in Buganda. LC 73-152635. (African Studies: No. 3). 1972. 32.50 (ISBN 0-521-08116-5). Cambridge U Pr.

Whetham, E. H. Co-Operation, Land Reform & Land Settlement: Report on a Survey in Kenya, Uganda, Sudan, Ghana, Nigeria & Iran. Plunkett Foundation for Co-Operative Studies, ed. 1968. 13.00x (ISBN 0-686-75619-3, Pub. by Plunkett Found England). State Mutual Bk.

LAND TENURE–ASIA

Chambliss, William. Chiarajima Village: Land Tenure, Taxation, & Local Trade, 1818-1884. LC 64-17266. (Association for Asian Studies Monograph: No. 19). 1965. 5.00x (ISBN 0-8165-0148-3). U of Ariz Pr.

Hinton, William. Fanshen: A Documentary of Revolution in a Chinese Village. LC 66-23525. (gr. 9-12). 1967. 15.00 (ISBN 0-85345-046-3, CL-0463). Monthly Rev.

Hogbin, I. & Lawrence, P. Studies in New Guinea Land Tenure. 1967. pap. 5.00x (ISBN 0-424-05230-X, Pub. by Sydney U Pr). Intl Schol Bk Serv.

Leach, Edmund R. Pul Eliya: A Village in Ceylon. 1961. 22.50 (ISBN 0-521-05524-5). Cambridge U Pr.

Obeyesekere, Gananath. Land Tenure in Village Ceylon. (Cambridge South Asian Studies: No. 4). 1967. 29.95 (ISBN 0-521-05854-6). Cambridge U Pr.

Rahman, Mushtaqur & Iowa State University Research Foundation. Agrarian Egalitarianism, Land Tenures & Land Reforms in South Asia. 224p. 1980. pap. text ed. 9.95 (ISBN 0-8403-2343-3). Kendall-Hunt.

Roth, Dennis M. The Friar Estates of the Philippines. LC 76-21550. 1977. 12.00x (ISBN 0-8263-0429-X). U of NM Pr.

Sansom, Robert L. Economics of Insurgency in the Mekong Delta of Vietnam. 1970. 15.00x (ISBN 0-262-19064-8). MIT Pr.

Singh, Baljit & Misra, Shridhar. Study of Land Reforms in Uttar Pradesh. (Illus.). 1965. 10.00x (ISBN 0-8248-0020-6, Eastwest Ctr). U Pr of Hawaii.

Singh, Tarlok. Poverty & Social Change: With a Reappraisal. 2nd ed. LC 74-33899. 352p. 1975. Repr. of 1969 ed. lib. bdg. 18.75x (ISBN 0-8371-8000-7, SIPO). Greenwood.

Smith, Thomas C. The Agrarian Origins of Modern Japan. LC 59-7429. 1959. 12.50x (ISBN 0-8047-0530-5); pap. 4.95x (ISBN 0-8047-0531-3). Stanford U Pr.

Stokes, E. T. The Peasant & the Raj. LC 77-77731. (South Asian Studies: No. 23). 1978. 37.50 (ISBN 0-521-21684-2). Cambridge U Pr.

Wigmore, John H. & Simmons, D. B. Notes on Land Tenure & Local Institutions in Old Japan. (Studies in Japanese History & Civilization). 1979. 21.00 (ISBN 0-89093-223-9). U Pubns Amer.

Yang, Martin M. Socio-Economic Results of Land Reform in Taiwan. 1970. 17.50x (ISBN 0-8248-0091-5, Eastwest Ctr). U Pr of Hawaii.

LAND TENURE–AUSTRALIA

Roberts, Sir Stephen H. History of Australian Land Settlement 1788-1920. 1968. Repr. of 1924 ed. 23.00 (ISBN 0-384-51450-2). Johnson Repr.

LAND TENURE–CANADA

Harris, Richard C. Seigneurial System in Early Canada. (Illus.). 264p. 1966. 20.00x (ISBN 0-299-03980-3). U of Wis Pr.

Munro, William B., ed. Documents Relating to the Seigniorial Tenure in Canada, 1598-1854. LC 68-28598. 1968. Repr. of 1908 ed. lib. bdg. 30.50x (ISBN 0-8371-5042-6, MUDS). Greenwood.

LAND TENURE–CHILE

Loveman, Brian. Struggle in the Countryside: Politics & Rural Labor in Chile, 1919-1973. LC 74-6521. (International Development Research Center, Studies in Development: No. 10). (Illus.). 480p. 1976. 15.00x (ISBN 0-253-35565-6). Ind U Pr.

LAND TENURE–CHINA

Beattie, Hilary J. Land & Lineage in China. LC 77-91080. (Cambridge Studies in Chinese History, Literature & Institutions). 1979. 34.95 (ISBN 0-521-21974-4). Cambridge U Pr.

Buck, John L. Three Essays on Chinese Farm Economy. LC 78-74308. (Modern Chinese Economy Ser.: Vol. 10). 155p. 1980. lib. bdg. 20.00 (ISBN 0-8240-4259-X). Garland Pub.

Hinton, William. Fanshen: A Documentary of Revolution in a Chinese Village. 1968. pap. 5.95 (ISBN 0-394-70465-7, Vin). Random.

LAND TENURE–EGYPT

Gadalla, Saad M. Land Reform in Relation to Social Development, Egypt. LC 62-14208. 1962. 10.00x (ISBN 0-8262-0592-5). U of Mo Pr.

Hardy, Edward R., Jr. Large Estates of Byzantine Egypt. LC 68-58589. (Columbia University Studies in the Social Sciences: No. 354). 16.50 (ISBN 0-404-51354-9). AMS Pr.

LAND TENURE–ETHIOPIA

Hoben, Allan. Land Tenure Among the Amhara of Ethiopia: The Dynamics of Cognatic Descent. 1973. 12.00x (ISBN 0-226-34548-3). U of Chicago Pr.

LAND TENURE–EUROPE

Bloch, Marc. French Rural History: An Essay on Its Basic Characteristics. Sondheimer, Janet, tr. LC 66-15483. (Illus.). 1966. 25.00x (ISBN 0-520-00127-3); pap. 7.95x (ISBN 0-520-01660-2, CAMPUS28). U of Cal Pr.

Emmons, Terence. Russian Landed Gentry & the Peasant Emancipation of 1861. LC 68-29654. 1968. 41.95 (ISBN 0-521-07340-5). Cambridge U Pr.

Jones, Michael. Finland, Daughter of the Sea. (Studies in Historical Geography). (Illus.). 1977. 19.50 (ISBN 0-208-01623-6, Archon). Shoe String.

Kieniewicz, Stefan. Emancipation of the Polish Peasantry. LC 79-92684. 1970. 12.50x (ISBN 0-226-43524-5). U of Chicago Pr.

Leslie, Thomas E. Land Systems & Industrial Economy of Ireland, England, & Continental Countries. LC 67-18570. Repr. of 1870 ed. 19.50x (ISBN 0-678-00346-7). Kelley.

Owen, Launcelot A. Russian Peasant Movement, 1906-1917. LC 62-16196. (Illus.). 1963. Repr. of 1937 ed. 7.50 (ISBN 0-8462-0332-4). Russell.

Roberts, Henry L. Rumania: Political Problems of an Agrarian State. (Illus.). 1969. Repr. of 1951 ed. 20.00 (ISBN 0-208-00651-6, Archon). Shoe String.

Robinson, Geroid T. Rural Russia Under the Old Regime: A History of the Landlord-Peasant World & a Prologue to the Peasant Revolution of 1917. 1967. pap. 7.95 (ISBN 0-520-01075-2). U of Cal Pr.

Ross, Denman W. Early History of Landholding Among the Germans. LC 73-168704. (Research & Source Works Ser: No. 814). 1971. Repr. of 1883 ed. lib. bdg. 21.50 (ISBN 0-8337-3058-4). B Franklin.

Russian Agriculture During the War. Bd. with Rural Economy. Antisferov, Alexis N; Land Settlement. Blimovich, Alexander B. LC 68-57638. Orig. Title: Land Settlement. (Illus.). xvii, 394p. 1969. Repr. of 1930 ed. lib. bdg. 18.25x (ISBN 0-8371-0286-3, ANRA). Greenwood.

LAND TENURE–GERMANY

Inoki, Takenori. Aspects of German Peasant Emigration to the United States 1815-1914: A Reexamination of Some Behavioral Hypotheses in Migration Theory. Bruchey, Stuart, ed. LC 80-2812. (Dissertations in European Economic History II). (Illus.). 1981. lib. bdg. 25.00x (ISBN 0-405-13997-7). Arno.

LAND TENURE–GREAT BRITAIN

Ault, Warren O. Open-Field Husbandry & the Village Community: A Study of Agrarian By-Laws in Medieval England. LC 65-27426. (Transactions Ser.: Vol. 55, Pt. 7). 1965. pap. 1.00 (ISBN 0-87169-557-X). Am Philos.

Battle Abbey. Custumals of Battle Abbey, in the Reigns of Edward I & Edward II: 1283-1312. Scargill-Bird, S. R., ed. 22.50 (ISBN 0-384-03545-0). Johnson Repr.

Bowen, H. C. & Fowler, P. J. Early Land Allotment in the British Isles: A Survey of Recent Work. 1978. 24.00x (ISBN 0-86054-015-4, Pub. by BAR). State Mutual Bk.

Brodrick, George C. English Land & English Landlords. LC 67-29495. Repr. of 1881 ed. 19.50x (ISBN 0-678-00360-2). Kelley.

Caird, James. Landed Interest & the Supply of Food. 4th ed. LC 67-16346. Repr. of 1880 ed. 15.00x (ISBN 0-678-05034-1). Kelley.

--Landed Interests & the Supply of Food. 5th rev ed. 184p. 1967. 24.00x (ISBN 0-7146-1042-9, F Cass Co). Biblio Dist.

Calthorpe, Charles. The Relation Betweene the Lord of a Mannor & the Coppy-Holder His Tenent, Etc. LC 74-38163. (English Experience Ser.: No. 440). 100p. 1972. Repr. of 1635 ed. 15.00 (ISBN 90-221-0440-0). Walter J Johnson.

Cheyney, Edward P. Social Changes in England in the Sixteenth Century As Reflected in Contemporary Literature. LC 76-168055. (Illus.). Repr. of 1895 ed. 12.50 (ISBN 0-404-01523-9). AMS Pr.

Chibnall, A. C. Sherington: Fiefs & Fields of a Buckinghamshire Village. 1966. 57.50 (ISBN 0-521-04637-8). Cambridge U Pr.

Davenport, Frances G. A Classified List of Printed Original Materials for English Manorial & Agrarian History During the Middle Ages. (Radcliffe College Monographs: No. 6). 1964. Repr. of 1894 ed. 20.00 (ISBN 0-8337-0774-4). B Franklin.

--Economic Development of a Norfolk Manor, 1085-1585. LC 67-16349. (Illus.). Repr. of 1906 ed. 19.50x (ISBN 0-678-05041-4). Kelley.

Geary, Frank. Land Tenure & Unemployment. LC 77-81147. Repr. of 1925 ed. 15.00x (ISBN 0-678-00509-5). Kelley.

Gonner, Edward C. Common Land & Inclosure. 2nd ed. (Illus.). Repr. of 1912 ed. 27.50 (ISBN 0-678-05050-3). Kelley.

Hone, Nathaniel J. Manor & Manorial Records. LC 73-137947. (Economic Thought, History & Challenge Ser). 1971. Repr. of 1906 ed. 17.00 (ISBN 0-8046-1449-0). Kennikat.

Jeudwine, John W. The Foundation of Society & the Land. rev. ed. LC 74-25760. (European Sociology Ser.). 509p. 1975. 30.00x (ISBN 0-405-06514-0). Arno.

Johnson, A. H. The Disappearance of the Small Landowner. LC 79-14625. (Illus.). 1979. Repr. of 1909 ed. lib. bdg. 13.50 (ISBN 0-678-08077-1). Kelly.

Leslie, Thomas E. Land Systems & Industrial Economy of Ireland, England, & Continental Countries. LC 67-18570. Repr. of 1870 ed. 19.50x (ISBN 0-678-00346-7). Kelley.

Madox, Thomas. Baronia Anglica. LC 79-8369. Repr. of 1841 ed. 78.50 (ISBN 0-404-18358-1). AMS Pr.

Moore, Margaret F. Two Select Bibliographies of Medieval Historical Study. 1912. 21.00 (ISBN 0-8337-2452-5). B Franklin.

Ogilvie, William. Birthright in Land. LC 68-57110. Repr. of 1891 ed. 19.50x (ISBN 0-678-00597-4). Kelley.

Round, Horace. King's Serjeants & Officers of State: With Their Coronation Service. (Genealogy Ser.: No. 3). 416p. 1971. Repr. of 1911 ed. 35.00x (ISBN 0-7130-0026-0, Pub. by Woburn Pr England). Biblio Dist.

Rudkin, Olive D. Thomas Spence & His Connections. LC 65-26376. Repr. of 1927 ed. 13.50x (ISBN 0-678-00178-2). Kelley.

Shrimpton, Colin. The Landed Society & the Farming Community of Essex in the Late 18th & Early 19th Centuries. Bruchey, Stuart, ed. LC 77-77185. (Dissertations in European Economic History Ser.). 1977. lib. bdg. 29.00x (ISBN 0-405-10798-6). Arno.

Simpson, Alfred W. Introduction to the History of the Land Law. 1961. 29.50x (ISBN 0-19-825150-5). Oxford U Pr.

Tupling, George H. The Economic History of Rossendale. Repr. of 1927 ed. 15.50 (ISBN 0-384-61970-3). Johnson Repr.

Vinogradoff, Paul. English Society in the Eleventh Century: Essays in English Medieval History. 1968. Repr. of 1908 ed. 43.00 (ISBN 0-403-00047-5). Scholarly.

Worcester Cathedral. Registrum, Sive, Liber Irrotularius et Consuetudinarius Prioratus Beatae Mariae Wigorniensis. 31.00 (ISBN 0-384-69240-0). Johnson Repr.

Young, Charles R. The Royal Forests of Medieval England. LC 78-65109. (The Middle Ages Ser.). (Illus.). 1979. 15.00x (ISBN 0-8122-7760-0). U of Pa Pr.

LAND TENURE–GREECE

Woodhouse, William J. Solon the Liberator. 1965. lib. bdg. 14.50x (ISBN 0-374-98721-1). Octagon.

LAND TENURE–INDIA

Baden-Powell, Baden H. The Land-Systems of British India: Being a Manual of the Land-Tenures & of the Systems of Land-Revenue Administration Prevalent in the Several Provinces, 3 Vols. LC 8-13098. Repr. of 1892 ed. Set. lib. bdg. 123.00 (ISBN 0-384-03034-3). Johnson Repr.

--The Origin & Growth of Village Communities in India. LC 1-18996. (Landmarks in Anthropology Ser). Repr. of 1899 ed. 13.00 (ISBN 0-384-03035-1). Johnson Repr.

Franda, Marcus F. West Bengal & the Federalizing Process in India. LC 68-10391. 1968. 19.00x (ISBN 0-691-03068-5). Princeton U Pr.

Frykenberg, Robert. Land Tenure & Peasant in South Asia. 1979. 16.00x (ISBN 0-8364-0347-9, Orient Longman). South Asia Bks.

Frykenberg, Robert E., ed. Land Control & Social Structure in Indian History. LC 69-16111. 278p. 1969. 21.50x (ISBN 0-299-05240-0). U of Wis Pr.

Merillat, H. C. Land & the Constitution in India. LC 79-127362. (Studies of the South Asian). 321p. 1970. 20.00x (ISBN 0-231-03362-1). Columbia U Pr.

Mishra, R. R. Effects of Land Reforms in Saurashtra. (New Delhi Research Planning Commission - 1961). 1961. 6.75x (ISBN 0-8426-1387-0). Verry.

Mukherjee, N. Ryotwari System in Madras, 1792-1827. 1962. 6.75x (ISBN 0-8426-1441-9). Verry.

Neale, Walter C. Economic Change in Rural India: Land Tenure & Reform in Uttar Pradish, 1800-1955. LC 72-85284. 352p. 1973. Repr. of 1962 ed. 17.50 (ISBN 0-8046-1704-X). Kennikat.

LAND TENURE–IRELAND

Balfour, Arthur J., et al. Against Home Rule. Rosenbaum, S., ed. LC 75-102591. (Irish Culture & History Ser). (Illus.). 1970. Repr. of 1912 ed. 14.50 (ISBN 0-8046-0768-0). Kennikat.

Butler, William F. Confiscation in Irish History. LC 76-102594. (Irish Culture & History Ser). 1970. Repr. of 1917 ed. 12.50 (ISBN 0-8046-0771-0). Kennikat.

Conditions to Be Observed by British Undertakers of the Escheated Lands in Ulster. LC 74-38139. (English Experience Ser.: No. 490). 1972. Repr. of 1610 ed. 5.00 (ISBN 90-221-0490-7). Walter J Johnson.

Godkin, James. Land-War in Ireland. LC 72-102605. (Irish Culture & History Ser). 1970. Repr. of 1870 ed. 22.50 (ISBN 0-8046-0782-6). Kennikat.

Palmer, Norman D. The Irish Land League Crisis. 340p. 1976. Repr. of 1940 ed. lib. bdg. 16.50x (ISBN 0-374-96196-4). Octagon.

--Irish Land League Crisis: Misc. 37. (Yale Hist. Pubs. Ser.). 1940. 14.50x (ISBN 0-686-51406-8). Elliots Bks.

Solow, Barbara L. Land Question & the Irish Economy, 1870-1903. LC 78-158431. (Economic Studies: No. 139). (Illus.). 1971. 10.00x (ISBN 0-674-50875-0). Harvard U Pr.

Steele, E. D. Irish Land & British Politics: Tenant-Right & Nationality, 1865-1870. LC 73-91618. (Illus.). 352p. 1974. 41.00 (ISBN 0-521-20421-6). Cambridge U Pr.

LAND TENURE–LATIN AMERICA

Brading, D. A. Haciendas & Ranchos in the Mexican Bajio Leon 1700-1860. LC 77-90203. (Cambridge Latin American Studies: No. 32). (Illus.). 1979. 41.50 (ISBN 0-521-22200-1). Cambridge U Pr.

Ford, Thomas R. Man & Land in Peru. LC 76-152538. (Illus.). 1971. Repr. of 1955 ed. 11.00 (ISBN 0-8462-1611-6). Russell.

Handelman, Howard. Struggle in the Andes: Peasant Political Mobilization in Peru. (Latin American Monographs: No. 35). 321p. 1975. 14.95x (ISBN 0-292-77513-X). U of Tex Pr.

Harris, Charles H., 3rd. The Sanchez Navarros: A Socio-Economic Study of a Coahuilan Latifundio 1846-1853. 1964. 3.50 (ISBN 0-8294-0034-6). Loyola.

McBride, George M. Chile: Land & Society. LC 71-154618. 1971. Repr. of 1936 ed. lib. bdg. 25.00x (ISBN 0-374-95429-1). Octagon.

--Chile: Land & Society. LC 72-123494. 1971. Repr. of 1936 ed. 17.50 (ISBN 0-8046-1381-8). Kennikat.

--Land Systems of Mexico. LC 78-154617. 1971. Repr. of 1923 ed. lib. bdg. 16.50x (ISBN 0-374-95430-5). Octagon.

Melville, T. & Melville, M. Guatemala: The Politics of Land Ownership. LC 70-143523. 1971. 12.95 (ISBN 0-02-920840-8). Free Pr.

Senior, Clarence. Land Reform & Democracy. LC 74-8261. (Illus.). 269p. 1974. Repr. of 1958 ed. lib. bdg. 14.75x (ISBN 0-8371-7563-1, SELR). Greenwood.

Shaw, R. Paul. Land Tenure & the Rural Exodus in Chile, Colombia, Costa Rica, & Peru. LC 75-40048. (Latin American Monograph: Ser. 2, No. 19). (Illus.). 1976. 11.50 (ISBN 0-8130-0528-0). U Presses Fla.

Tannenbaum, Frank. Mexican Agrarian Revolution. 1968. Repr. of 1929 ed. 25.00 (ISBN 0-208-00709-1, Archon). Shoe String.

Taylor, William B. Landlord & Peasant in Colonial Oaxaca. LC 70-153819. (Illus.). 1972. 15.00x (ISBN 0-8047-0796-0). Stanford U Pr.

Whetten, Nathan L. Rural Mexico. LC 48-8023. (Illus.). 1948. 20.00x (ISBN 0-226-89439-8). U of Chicago Pr.

LAND TENURE–NEAR EAST

Granovsky, Abraham. Land Policy in Palestine. LC 75-6436. (The Rise of Jewish Nationalism & the Middle East Ser). 208p. 1975. Repr. of 1940 ed. 18.00 (ISBN 0-88355-323-6). Hyperion Conn.

Land Tenure Center, University of Wisconsin - Madison. Land Tenure & Agrarian Reform in Africa & the Near East: An Annotated Bibliography. (Ser. Seventy). 1976. lib. bdg. 22.00 (ISBN 0-8161-7921-2). G K Hall.

Warriner, Doreen. Land Reform & Development in the Middle East. LC 75-31476. (Illus.). 238p. 1976. Repr. of 1962 ed. lib. bdg. 15.25x (ISBN 0-8371-8530-0, WALR). Greenwood.

LAND TENURE–NEW GUINEA

Hutchins, Edwin. Culture & Inference: A Trobriand Case Study. LC 80-13280. (Cognitive Science Ser.: No. 2). (Illus.). 153p. 1980. text ed. 14.00x (ISBN 0-674-17970-6). Harvard U Pr.

LAND TENURE–OCEANIA

Lundsgaarde, Henry P., ed. Land Tenure in Oceania. LC 73-90854. (Association for Social Anthropology in Oceania Monographs: No. 2). 320p. 1974. text ed. 14.00x (ISBN 0-8248-0321-3). U Pr of Hawaii.

LAND TENURE–ROME

Clausing, Roth. Roman Colonate: The Theories of Its Origin. LC 70-78011. (Columbia University Studies in the Social Sciences: No. 260). 1969. Repr. of 1925 ed. 27.50 (ISBN 0-404-51260-7). AMS Pr.

LAND TENURE–RUSSIA

Emmons, T. L., ed. Emancipation of the Russian Serfs. 128p. 1970. pap. text ed. 5.50 (ISBN 0-03-077360-1, Pub. by HR&W). Krieger.

Field, Daniel. The End of Serfdom: Nobility & Bureaucracy in Russia, 1855-1861. LC 75-32191. (Russian Research Center Studies: No. 75). 496p. 1976. 25.00x (ISBN 0-674-25240-3). Harvard U Pr.

Hourwich, Isaac A. Economics of the Russian Village. LC 76-127451. (Columbia University Studies in the Social Sciences: No. 5). Repr. of 1892 ed. 16.50 (ISBN 0-404-51005-1). AMS Pr.

LAND TENURE (MAORI LAW)

Kawharu, Ian H. Maori Land Tenure: Studies of a Changing Institution. 1977. 59.00x (ISBN 0-19-823177-6). Oxford U Pr.

LAND TENURE (PRIMITIVE LAW)–AFRICA

Mifsud, Frank M. Customary Land Law in Africa. (FAO Legislative Ser.: No. 7). (Orig.). 1967. pap. 4.75 (ISBN 0-685-09374-3, F 106, FAO). Unipub.

LAND TITLES

see also Adverse Possession; Conveyancing; Deeds; Leases; Mortgages; Real Covenants; Real Property; Vendors and Purchasers

Gahn, Bessie W. Original Patentees of Land at Washington Prior to 1700. LC 77-77982. 1969. Repr. of 1936 ed. 8.50 (ISBN 0-8063-0155-4). Genealog Pub.

Jillson, Willard R. Old Kentucky Entries & Deeds: A Complete Index to All of the Earliest Land Entries, Military Warrants, Deeds & Wills of the Commonwealth of Kentucky. LC 73-86808. (Filson Club Publications Ser: No. 34). (Illus.). 1978. Repr. of 1926 ed. 20.00 (ISBN 0-8063-0193-7). Genealog Pub.

Laurence, Edward. The Duty & Office of a Land Steward: Represented Several Plain & Distinct Articles. Chandler, Alfred D., ed. LC 79-7549. (History of Management Thought & Practice Ser.). 1980. Repr. of 1731 ed. lib. bdg. 24.00x (ISBN 0-405-12333-7). Arno.

Madsen, George F. Iowa Title Opinions & Standards, Annotated. 2nd ed. 1978. text ed. 35.00 (ISBN 0-87473-107-0). A Smith Co.

Parham, Sydney F. A Virginia Title Examiners' Manual. rev. ed. 517p. 1973. 35.00 (ISBN 0-87215-151-4); 1977 suppl 15.00 (ISBN 0-87215-290-1). Michie-Bobbs.

Rhode Island Historical Society. Rhode Island Land Evidences, Vol. 1: 1648-1696. LC 79-77882. 1970. Repr. of 1921 ed. 15.00 (ISBN 0-8063-0391-3). Genealog Pub.

Rudman, Jack. Commission of Deeds. (Career Examination Ser.: C-157). (Cloth bdg. avail. on reqqest). pap. 10.00 (ISBN 0-8373-0157-2). Natl Learning.

--Senior Title Searcher. (Career Examination Ser.: C-2086). (Cloth bdg. avail. on request). 1977. write for info. (ISBN 0-8373-2086-0). Natl Learning.

--Title Examiner. (Career Examination Ser.: C-809). (Cloth bdg. avail. on request). pap. 8.00 (ISBN 0-8373-0809-7). Natl Learning.

--Title Searcher. (Career Examination Ser.: C-1516). (Cloth bdg. avail. on request). pap. 8.00 (ISBN 0-8373-1516-6). Natl Learning.

Salley, A. S. & Olsberg, R. Nicholas, eds. Warrants for Lands in South Carolina, 1672-1711. LC 73-9542. 724p. 1973. 27.50x (ISBN 0-87249-938-3). U of SC Pr.

Shick, Blair C. & Plotkin, Irving H. Torrens in the United States. 18.95 (ISBN 0-669-02666-2). Lexington Bks.

Smathers, George H. The History of Land Titles in Western North Carolina. Bruchey, Stuart, ed. LC 78-53566. (Development of Public Land Law in the U. S. Ser.). 1979. Repr. of 1938 ed. lib. bdg. 11.00x (ISBN 0-405-11385-4). Arno.

Spence, Thomas, et al. Pioneers of Land Reform. 34.95 (ISBN 0-8490-0838-7). Gordon Pr.

Sullivan, James. The History of Land Titles in Massachusetts. LC 75-37989. (American Law Ser.: The Formative Years). 396p. 1972. Repr. of 1801 ed. 17.00 (ISBN 0-405-04034-2). Arno.

Woodward, M. K. & Hobbs, Robert. Cases & Materials on Texas Land Titles. rev. ed. 1977. pap. text ed. 18.50 (ISBN 0-88408-105-2). Sterling Swift.

LAND TRUSTS

Laurence, Edward. The Duty & Office of a Land Steward: Represented Several Plain & Distinct Articles. Chandler, Alfred D., ed. LC 79-7549. (History of Management Thought & Practice Ser.). 1980. Repr. of 1731 ed. lib. bdg. 24.00x (ISBN 0-405-12333-7). Arno.

LAND USE

see also Agriculture; Church Lands; Eminent Domain; Feudalism; Open Spaces; Real Estate Business; Real Property; Reclamation of Land; Rent; School Lands; Waste Lands; Zoning

Allensworth, Don T. Land Planning Law. 272p. 1981. 23.95 (ISBN 0-03-057039-5). Praeger.

American Society of Civil Engineers, compiled by. Land Application of Residual Materials. 192p. 1977. pap. text ed. 10.00 (ISBN 0-87262-081-6). Am Soc Civil Eng.

Andrews, Richard N., ed. Land in America. LC 77-14735. (Illus.). 1979. 21.00 (ISBN 0-669-01989-5). Lexington Bks.

Barlowe, Raleigh. Land Resource Economics: The Economics of Real Estate. 3rd ed. (Illus.). 1978. ref. ed. 22.95 (ISBN 0-13-522532-9). P-H.

Bartelli, L. J., et al, eds. Soil Surveys & Land Use Planning. (Illus.). 1966. 3.00 (ISBN 0-89118-002-8). Am Soc Agron.

Baxter, R., et al. Urban Development Models. (Land Use & Built Form Models: Vol. 3). 1975. text ed. 38.00x (ISBN 0-904406-11-3). Longman.

Beardsley, John. Probing the Earth: Contemporary Land Projects. LC 77-12419. (Illus.). 112p. 1978. 17.50 (ISBN 0-87474-232-3). Smithsonian.

Beatty, M. T., et al, eds. Planning the Uses & Management of Land. (Illus.). 1981. 30.00 (ISBN 0-89118-058-3). Am Soc Agron.

Berger, Curtis J. Land Ownership & Use: Cases, Statutes & Other Materials. 2nd ed. 1975. 25.00 (ISBN 0-316-09152-9). Little.

Berry, Wendell. The Gift of Good Land: Further Essays Cultural & Agricultural. LC 81-81507. 304p. 1981. 15.00 (ISBN 0-86547-051-0); pap. 7.50 (ISBN 0-86547-052-9). N Point Pr.

Boley, Robert E., ed. Land: Recreation & Leisure. LC 78-123466. (Special Report Ser). (Orig.). 1970. pap. 4.75 (ISBN 0-87420-554-9). Urban Land.

Bosselman, Fred, et al. The Permit Explosion. LC 76-55844. (Management & Control of Growth Ser.). 86p. 1976. pap. text ed. 11.00 (ISBN 0-87420-570-0). Urban Land.

Breimyer, Harold F. A Form, Food & Land Use Policy for the Future. LC 75-42815. (Agriculture Committee Ser.). 36p. 1976. pap. 1.50 (ISBN 0-89068-004-3). Natl Planning.

Cesaretti, C. A. & Commins, Stephen, eds. Let the Earth Bless the Lord: A Christian Perspective on Land Use. 160p. (Orig.). 1981. pap. 5.95 (ISBN 0-8164-2296-6). Seabury.

Chisholm, Michael. Rural Settlement & Land Use: An Essay in Location. 1966. text ed. 16.25x (ISBN 0-09-063001-7, Hutchinson U Lib). Humanities.

Christensen, Kathleen. Social Impact of Land Development: An Initial Approach for Estimating Impacts on Neighborhood Usages & Perceptions. (Land Development Impact Ser.). 144p. 1966. pap. 3.95 (ISBN 0-87766-171-5, 15700). Urban Inst.

Clark, Colin. Population Growth & Land Use. 2nd ed. LC 77-78978. (Illus.). 1977. 21.50 (ISBN 0-312-63141-3). St Martin.

Clawson, Marion, et al. Land for the Future. (Resources for the Future Ser). (Illus.). 570p. 1960. 28.50x (ISBN 0-8018-0123-0). Johns Hopkins.

Coates, Donald R., ed. Urban Geomorphology. LC 76-4242. (Special Paper: No. 174). (Illus., Orig.). 1976. pap. 15.00x (ISBN 0-8137-2174-1). Geol Soc.

Collier, William L. Social & Economic Aspects of Tidal Swamp Land Development in Indonesia. (Development Studies Centre-Occasional Paper: No. 15). 71p. (Orig.). 1980. pap. 3.95 (ISBN 0-909150-90-7, 0567, Pub. by ANUP Australia). Bks Australia.

Committee On Agricultural Land Use And Wildlife Resources. Land Use & Wildlife Resources. LC 70-607553. (Orig.). 1970. pap. 9.25 (ISBN 0-309-01857-9). Natl Acad Pr.

Conkling, Edgar C. & Yeates, Maurice H. Man's Economic Environment. (Geography Ser.). 1976. text ed. 17.50 (ISBN 0-07-012408-6, C). McGraw.

Conversion of Tropical Moist Forests. 1980. 12.50 (ISBN 0-309-02945-7). Natl Acad Pr.

Darin-Drabkin, H. Land Policy & Urban Growth. LC 76-39912. 1977. text ed. 23.00 (ISBN 0-08-020401-5). Pergamon.

Davis, Kenneth P. Land Use. 1976. text ed. 17.95 (ISBN 0-07-015534-8, C). McGraw.

De Chiara, Joseph. Site Planning Standards. (Illus.). 1977. 27.50 (ISBN 0-07-016216-6, P&RB). McGraw.

Denman, D. R. & Prodano, Sylvio. Land Use: An Introduction to Proprietary Land Use Analysis. 1972. text ed. 25.00x (ISBN 0-04-333013-4). Allen Unwin.

Ecological Land Classification in Urban Areas. (Ecological Land Class Ser: No. 3). 1978. pap. 7.50 (ISBN 0-660-01415-7, SSC 104, SSC). Unipub.

Ellickson, Robert C. & Tarlock, A. Dan. Land Use Controls. 1239p. 1981. 25.00 (ISBN 0-316-23299-8). Little.

Fabos, Julius G. Planning the Total Landscape: A Guide to Intelligent Land Use. (Illus.). 1979. lib. bdg. 20.00x (ISBN 0-89158-172-3). Westview.

FAO Production Yearbook 1978. 287p. 1980. 24.50 (ISBN 92-5-000766-3, F1837, FAO). Unipub.

Farm Foundation & Resources for the Future, Inc. Land Economics Research: Papers Presented at a Symposium Held at Lincoln, Nebraska, June 16-23, 1961. Ackerman, Joseph, et al, eds. LC 77-86388. (Resources for the Future, Inc. Publications). Repr. of 1962 ed. 32.50 (ISBN 0-404-60327-0). AMS Pr.

Food & Agriculture Organization. FAO-UNDP Land & Water Resources Survey in the Jebel Marra Area-the Sudan. (Orig.). 1968. 15.00 (ISBN 0-685-27886-7, FAO). Unipub.

Forest Land Use: An Annotated Bibliography of Policy, Economic, & Management Issues, 1970-1980. 62p. (Orig.). 1981. pap. 7.00 (ISBN 0-89164-067-3). Conservation Foun.

Foth, Henry & Schafer, John. Soil Geography & Land Use. LC 79-27731. 484p. 1980. text ed. 28.95 (ISBN 0-471-01710-8). Wiley.

Fustel De Coulanges, Numa D. The Origin of Property in Land. Ashley, Margaret, tr. LC 52-45494. 153p. 1891. Repr. 22.50 (ISBN 0-8337-0803-1). B Franklin.

Gardiner, John A. & Lyman, Theodore R. Decisions for Sale: Corruption & Reform in Localland-Use & Building Regulation. LC 78-19758. 1978. 23.95 (ISBN 0-03-044691-0). Praeger.

Garrison, William L., et al. Studies of Highway Development & Geographic Change. (Illus.). Repr. of 1959 ed. lib. bdg. 18.75x (ISBN 0-8371-2096-9, SHD). Greenwood.

Gerrard, John. Soils & Landforms. (Illus.). 256p. 1981. text ed. 35.00x (ISBN 0-04-551048-2); pap. text ed. 16.95x (ISBN 0-04-551049-0). Allen Unwin.

Gitelman, Morton & Wright, Robert R. Cases & Materials on Land Use. 3rd ed. (American Casebook Ser.). 1100p. 1981. price not set. West Pub.

Gold, Steven D. Property Tax Relief. LC 79-1723. 352p. 1979. 29.95 (ISBN 0-669-02917-3). Lexington Bks.

Graham, Edward H. Natural Principles of Land Use. Repr. of 1944 ed. lib. bdg. 15.25x (ISBN 0-8371-2394-1, GRLU). Greenwood.

Haimes, Y. & Kindler, J., eds. Water & Related Land Resource Systems: Proceedings of the IFAC Symposium, Cleveland, Ohio, U. S. A., 28-31 May 1980. LC 80-41690. (IFAC Proceedings Ser.). (Illus.). 550p. 1981. 120.00 (ISBN 0-08-027307-6). Pergamon.

Harrison, A. J. Economics & Land Use Planning. LC 76-62533. 1977. 22.50x (ISBN 0-312-23432-5). St Martin.

Healy, Robert G. & Rosenberg, John. Land Use & the States. 2nd ed. LC 79-4864. (Resources for the Future Ser.). 1978. 18.00x (ISBN 0-8018-2284-X); pap. 4.95x (ISBN 0-8018-2285-8). Johns Hopkins.

Hite, James C. Room & Situation: The Political Economy of Land-Use Policy. LC 79-11691. 1979. 21.95x (ISBN 0-88229-479-2); pap. 11.95x (ISBN 0-88229-700-7). Nelson-Hall.

Jackson, John N. Surveys for Town & Country Planning. LC 76-7580. 1976. Repr. of 1963 ed. lib. bdg. 16.25x (ISBN 0-8371-8866-0, JAST). Greenwood.

Johnson, A. H. The Disappearance of the Small Landowner. 1977. lib. bdg. 59.95 (ISBN 0-8490-1727-0). Gordon Pr.

Keyes, Dale L. Land Development & the Natural Environment: Estimating Impacts. (Land Development Impact Ser.). 128p. 1976. pap. 4.95 (ISBN 0-685-99523-2, 13500). Urban Inst.

Khartoum Workshop on Arid Lands Management: Proceedings. 97p. 1980. pap. 11.00 (ISBN 92-808-0044-2, TUNU 040, UNU). Unipub.

Koenigsberger, Otto, et al, eds. Review of Land Policies. 200p. 1981. 50.00 (ISBN 0-08-026078-0). Pergamon.

Lal, R. & Russell, E. W. Tropical Agricultural Hydrology: Watershed Management & Land Use. LC 80-41590. 448p. 1981. 69.00 (ISBN 0-471-27931-5, Pub. by Wiley-Interscience). Wiley.

Land Development Manual. LC 74-193156. 356p. 1974. pap. 7.50x (ISBN 0-686-15221-2). Natl Assn Home.

Land Use Policy & Planning Bills. (Legislative Analyses). 1973. pap. 3.75 (ISBN 0-8447-0158-0). Am Enterprise.

Lassey, William R. Planning in Rural Environments. (McGraw-Hill Publications in the Agricultural Sciences). 1977. text ed. 16.95 (ISBN 0-07-036580-6, C). McGraw.

LBJ School of Public Affairs, 3rd. Advanced Seminar in Economic Development. Land Use Planning & Economic Developement: Proceedings. LC 75-620077. 1975. 3.00 (ISBN 0-89940-050-7). LBJ Sch Public Affairs.

Lefcoe, George. Land Development in Crowded Places: Lessons from Abroad. LC 79-54201. 151p. 1979. 13.50 (ISBN 0-89164-056-8). Conservation Foun.

--Tax Policies to Achieve Land-Use Goals. (Lincoln Institute Monograph: Nos. 78-8). (Orig.). pap. text ed. 6.00 (ISBN 0-686-25119-9). Lincoln Inst Land.

--When Governments Become Land Developers: Notes on the Public-Sector Experience in the Netherlands & California. 1978. pap. 5.00 (ISBN 0-686-12251-8). Lincoln Inst Land.

Lefcoe, George, ed. Respective Roles of State & Local Governments in Land Policy & Taxation. (Lincoln Institute Monograph: No. 80-7). 271p. 1980. pap. text ed. 12.00 (ISBN 0-686-31827-7). Lincoln Inst Land.

Lemire, Robert A. Creative Land Development: Bridge to the Future. 1979. 8.95 (ISBN 0-395-28590-9). HM.

Lenin. El Problema De la Tierra y la Lucha Por la Libertad. 151p. (Span.). 1979. pap. 1.50 (ISBN 0-8285-1399-6, Pub. by Progress Pubs Russia). Imported Pubns.

Lin, Sein & Ramakrishnan, S., eds. Land Management Issues & Development Strategies in Developing Countries. (Lincoln Institute Monograph: No. 78-4). (Orig.). 1979. pap. text ed. 4.00 (ISBN 0-686-25118-0). Lincoln Inst Land.

McClellan, Grant S., ed. Land Use in the United States. (Reference Shelf Ser: Vol. 43, No. 2). 1971. 6.25 (ISBN 0-8242-0447-6). Wilson.

Mandelker, Daniel R. Environment & Equity: A Regulatory Challenge. (Regulation of American Business & Industry (RABI) Ser.). 240p. 1981. 24.95 (ISBN 0-07-039864-X, P&RB). McGraw.

Mandelker, Daniel R. & Cunningham, Roger A. Planning & Control of Land Development Cases & Materials. (Contemporary Legal Education Ser). 1200p. 1979. text ed. 23.00 (ISBN 0-672-83416-2). Bobbs.

Muller, Thomas. Economic Impacts of Land Development: Employment, Housing & Property Values. (Land Development Impact Ser.). 148p. 1976. pap. 3.95 (ISBN 0-87766-173-1, 15800). Urban Inst.

Muth, Richard F. Cities & Housing: The Spatial Pattern of Urban Residential Land Use. LC 69-13201. (Studies in Business & Society Ser). (Illus.). 1969. 19.00x (ISBN 0-226-55413-9). U of Chicago Pr.

Nelson, Robert H. Zoning & Property Rights. 1977. pap. 5.95 (ISBN 0-262-64019-8). MIT Pr.

Netter, Edith, ed. Land Use Law: Issues for the Eighties. 230p. (Orig.). 1981. pap. price not set (ISBN 0-918286-24-7). Planners Pr.

O'Mara, W. Paul, et al. Adaptive Use. LC 78-56054. (Illus.). 246p. 1978. 29.25 (ISBN 0-87420-582-4). Urban Land.

Patterson, T. William. Land Use Planning: Techniques of Implementation. (Environmental Engineering Ser.). 1979. text ed. 22.50 (ISBN 0-442-24203-4). Van Nos Reinhold.

Pereira, H. C. Land Use & Water Resources. LC 72-85437. (Illus.). 180p. (Orig.). 1973. 39.00 (ISBN 0-521-08677-9); pap. 10.95x (ISBN 0-521-09750-9). Cambridge U Pr.

Perin, Constance. Everything in Its Place: Social Order & Land Use in America. LC 77-72133. 1977. text ed. 20.00 (ISBN 0-691-09372-5); pap. 6.95 (ISBN 0-691-02819-2). Princeton U Pr.

Peskin, Sarah. Guiding Growth & Change: A Handbook for the Massachusetts Citizen. (Illus.). 1978. pap. 6.95 (ISBN 0-910146-15-2). Appalach Mtn.

Popper, Frank. The Politics of Land-Use Reform. 327p. 1981. 20.00 (ISBN 0-299-08530-9); pap. text ed. 7.50 (ISBN 0-299-08534-1). U of Wis Pr.

Preston, Edward. How to Buy Land Cheap. 1981. pap. 4.95 (ISBN 0-686-30633-3). Loompanics.

Pronin, Monica, ed. Land Use Planning Abstracts, Seventy-Eight-Seventy-Nine: A Select Guide to Land & Water Resources Information. LC 74-28044. 1979. 95.00 (ISBN 0-89947-002-5). Environ Info.

Ratcliff, Richard U. Urban Land Economics. LC 71-135608. (Illus.). 533p. 1972. Repr. of 1949 ed. lib. bdg. 34.25x (ISBN 0-8371-5195-3, RAUL). Greenwood.

Report of the Workshop on Arid Lands Management. 22p. 1980. pap. 7.50 (ISBN 0-686-61621-9, TUNU 043, UNU). Unipub.

Report on the FAO-UNFPA Expert Consultation on Land Resources for Population of the Future. 1979. pap. 7.50 (ISBN 92-5-100653-9, F1532, FAO). Unipub.

Rhind, D. & Hudson, R. Land Use. 1980. 26.00x (ISBN 0-416-71780-2); pap. 12.95x (ISBN 0-416-71790-X). Methuen Inc.

Sampson, R. Neil. Farmland or Wasteland: A Time to Choose. Ebenreck, Sara, ed. (Illus.). 1981. 14.95 (ISBN 0-87857-366-6). Rodale Pr Inc.

Schaemnan, Philip S. Using an Impact Measurement System to Evaluate Land Development. (Land Development Impact Ser.). 106p. 1976. pap. 3.95 (ISBN 0-685-99522-4, 15500). Urban Inst.

Schnidman, Frank. Agricultural Land Preservation: Serious Land Policy Concern or Latest "Public Interest" Ploy. (Lincoln Institute Monograph: No. 81-1). 1981. pap. text ed. 5.00 (ISBN 0-686-30620-1). Lincoln Inst Land.

Sopher, Charles D. & Baird, Jack V. Soils & Soil Management. (Illus.). 1978. text ed. 15.95 (ISBN 0-87909-801-5); instrs'. manual avail. Reston.

Strom, Frederic A. Land Use & Environment Law Review: Annual. Incl. 1975 (ISBN 0-87632-116-3); 1976 (ISBN 0-87632-117-1); 1977 (ISBN 0-87632-118-X); 1978 (ISBN 0-87632-119-8); 1979 (ISBN 0-87632-120-1). 1980 45.00, (ISBN 0-87632-121-X). LC 70-127585. 42.50 ea. Boardman.

Strong, Ann L. Land Banking: European Reality, American Prospect. LC 78-11804. (Johns Hopkins Studies in Urban Affairs Ser.). 1979. text ed. 22.50x (ISBN 0-8018-2169-X). Johns Hopkins.

Strunk, W. The Great American Land Swindle. 69.95 (ISBN 0-685-26319-3). Revisionist Pr.

Symposium on Land Subsidence, Tokyo, 1969. Land Subsidence, 2 vols. (Illus., Orig.). 1970. Set. pap. 46.25 (ISBN 92-3-000832-X, U347, UNESCO). Unipub.

Timmons, John F. & Murray, William G., eds. Land Problems & Policies. LC 72-2870. (Use & Abuse of America's Natural Resources Ser). 312p. 1972. Repr. of 1950 ed. 16.00 (ISBN 0-405-04537-9). Arno.

Trends in Research & in the Application of Science & Technology for Arid Zone Development. (MAB Technical Note Ser.: No. 10). 1979. pap. 7.00 (ISBN 92-3-101597-4, U907, UNESCO). Unipub.

Vink, A. P. Land Use in Advancing Agriculture. LC 74-31006. (Advanced Series in Agricultural Sciences, Vol. 1). (Illus.). 450p. 1975. 32.80 (ISBN 0-387-07091-5). Springer-Verlag.

Walker, B. J., ed. Management of Semi-Arid Ecosystems. (Dev. in Agricultural & Managed-Forest Ecology Ser.: Vol. 7). 398p. 1980. 78.00 (ISBN 0-686-62656-7). Elsevier.

Walker, Francis A. Land & Its Rent. LC 79-1595. 1981. Repr. of 1883 ed. 18.50 (ISBN 0-88355-900-5). Hyperion Conn.

Water & Land-Use Development & the Aquatic Environment: Problems & Solutions. (FAO Fisheries Technical Papers: No.141). 10p. 1976. pap. 7.50 (ISBN 0-685-66352-3, F871, FAO). Unipub.

Wegner, Robert, ed. Land Development Decision-Making: Special Training in Zoning, Teamwork, Policy Making, Land Management, Citizen Participation, & Land Development Planning. 1979. 120.00 (ISBN 0-686-28437-2). Inst Urban Studies.

Wendt, P. F., ed. Forecasting Transportation Impacts Upon Land Use. (Studies in Applied Regional Science: No. 2). 1976. pap. 15.00 (ISBN 90-207-0627-6, Pub. by Martinus Nijhoff Netherlands). Kluwer Boston.

Western Resources Conference - 1968. Public Land Policy: Proceedings. Foss, Phillip O., ed. LC 70-109923. 1969. pap. 9.50 (ISBN 0-87081-001-4). Colo Assoc.

Woodruff, A. M., et al, eds. International Seminar on Land Taxation, Land Tenure & Land Reform in Developing Countries. LC 67-30788. (Orig.). 1966. pap. text ed. 3.65 (ISBN 0-686-00917-7). Lincoln Inst Land.

Zube, Ervin H. & Zube, Margaret J., eds. Changing Rural Landscapes. LC 76-46599. 1977. 10.00x (ISBN 0-87023-228-2); pap. 5.50x (ISBN 0-87023-235-5). U of Mass Pr.

LAND USE–BIBLIOGRAPHY

Bernard, Michael M., ed. Annotated Bibliography on Taxation As an Instrument of Land Planning Policy. (Lincoln Institute Monograph: No. 80-8). 90p. 1980. pap. text ed. 4.00 (ISBN 0-686-29504-8). Lincoln Inst Land.

Niemann, Bernard J., Jr. & Mladenoff, David J. An Annotated Bibliography of Land Planning & Land Information Systems. (Public Administration Ser.: Bibliography P-308). 1979. pap. 13.00 (ISBN 0-686-26360-X). Vance Biblios.

LAND USE–CLASSIFICATION

Fisher, Kenneth P. & Moyer, D. David. Land Parcel Identifiers for Information Systems. LC 73-91110. 1973. 15.00 (ISBN 0-910058-59-8); pap. 7.50 (ISBN 0-685-39801-3). Am Bar Foun.

Mandelker, Daniel R. New Developments in Land Use & Environmental Controls. (Contemporary Legal Education Ser). 1974. 5.50 (ISBN 0-672-81964-3, Bobbs-Merrill Law). Michie-Bobbs.

LAND USE–TAXATION

see Land Value Taxation; Real Property Tax

LAND USE–AFRICA

Development Projects in the Sudan: An Analysis of Their Reports with Implications for Research & Training in Arid Land Management. 58p. 1980. pap. 5.00 (ISBN 92-808-0042-6, TUNU 019, UNU). Unipub.

Duly, Leslie C. British Land Policy at the Cape, Seventeen Ninety-Five-Eighteen Forty-Four: A Study of Administrative Procedures in the Empire. LC 67-29574. 1968. 9.75 (ISBN 0-8223-0048-6). Duke.

Ecological Management of Arid & Semi-Arid Rangeland II: Volume VIII, Sudan. 41p. 1979. pap. 7.50 (ISBN 92-5-100677-6, F1589, FAO). Unipub.

Ecological Management of Arid & Semi-Arid Rangelands of Africa, the Near & Middle East. Emarar - Phase II: Vol. VII, Near East Grassland Education & Training. 55p. 1979. pap. 7.50 (ISBN 92-5-100680-6, F1619, FAO). Unipub.

Ecological Management of Arid & Semi-Arid Rangeland: Volume IX, the Countries of North Africa; Education & Training in the Rangeland Sector; Components of a Strategy. 42p. 1979. pap. 7.75 (ISBN 0-686-52638-4, F1590, FAO). Unipub.

Harbeson, John W. Nation-Building in Kenya: The Role of Land Reform. LC 72-80567. 421p. 1973. text ed. 15.75x (ISBN 0-8101-0389-3). Northwestern U Pr.

O'Keefe, Phil & Wisner, Ben, eds. Land Use & Development. (African Environment: Special Report Ser.: No. 5). (Illus.). 1977. pap. 16.50x (ISBN 0-85302-058-2). Intl Pubns Serv.

Prothero, R. Mansell, ed. People & Land in Africa South of the Sahara: Readings in Social Geography. (Illus.). 1972. pap. text ed. 9.95x (ISBN 0-19-501287-9). Oxford U Pr.

The Sahel: Ecological Approaches to Land Use. (MAB Technical Notes). (Illus.). 99p. 1975. pap. 6.25 (ISBN 92-3-101237-1, U565, UNESCO). Unipub.

Third Meeting of the Eastern African Sub Committee for Soil Correlation & Land Evaluation. (World Soil Resources Report: No. 51). 170p. 1981. pap. 11.50 (ISBN 92-5-100902-3, F2082, FAO). Unipub.

LAND USE–ASIA

Thalen, D. C. Ecology & Utilization of Desert Shrub Rangelands in Iraq. (Illus.). 1979. lib. bdg. 77.50 (ISBN 90-6193-593-8, Pub. by Junk Pubs Netherlands). Kluwer Boston.

LAND USE–AUSTRALIA

Austin, M. P. & Cocks, K. D. Land Use on the South Coast of New South Wales. 129p. 1981. 40.00x (ISBN 0-643-00248-0, Pub. by CSIRO Australia). State Mutual Bk.

--Land Use on the South Coast of New South Wales: Bio-Physical Background Studies, Vol. 2. 119p. 1981. 40.00x (ISBN 0-643-00249-9, Pub. by CSIRO Australia). State Mutual Bk.

--Land Use on the South Coast of New South Wales: Land Function Studies, Vol. 4. 209p. 1981. 50.00x (ISBN 0-643-00251-0, Pub. by CSIRO Australia). State Mutual Bk.

--Land Use on the South Coast of New South Wales: Socio-Economic Background Studies, Vol. 3. 107p. 1981. 40.00x (ISBN 0-643-00250-2, Pub. by CSIRO Australia). State Mutual Bk.

Cannon, Michael. Land Boomers. 1973. pap. 9.00x (ISBN 0-522-83788-3, Pub. by Melbourne U Pr). Intl Schol Bk Serv.

Grant, K. Terrain Analysis & Classification for Engineering & Conservation Purposes of the Port Clinton Area, Old-Including the Shoalwater Bay Military Training Area. 1980. 10.00x (ISBN 0-643-00321-5, Pub. by CSJRO Australia). State Mutual Bk.

The Potential for Liquid Fuels from Agriculture & Forestry in Australia. 147p. 1979. pap. 9.00 (ISBN 0-686-71840-2, CO 25, CSIRO). Unipub.

Principles of a Balanced Land-Use Policy for Australia. 30p. 1976. pap. 6.00 (ISBN 0-686-71839-9, CO 43, CSIRO). Unipub.

Principles of a Balanced Land-Use Policy for Australia. 30p. 1976. pap. 6.00 (ISBN 0-686-71839-9, CO 43, CSIRO). Unipub.

LAND USE–CANADA

Frankena, M. W. & Scheffman, D. T. Economic Analysis of Provincial Land Use Policies in Ontario. (Ontario Economic Council Research Studies). 1980. pap. 7.50 (ISBN 0-8020-3364-4). U of Toronto Pr.

LAND USE–CHINA

Brown, James R. & Woodruff, A. M., eds. Land for the Cities of Asia. LC 77-161842. 416p. 1971. pap. 3.00 (ISBN 0-686-01012-4). Lincoln Inst Land.

Liang Fang-Chung. Single-Whip Method of Taxation in China. Wang Yu-Ch'Uan, tr. LC 56-4991. (East Asian Monographs Ser: No. 1). 1956. pap. 9.00x (ISBN 0-674-80895-9). Harvard U Pr.

Lippit, Victor D. Land Reform & Economic Development in China: A Study of Institutional Change & Development Finance. LC 74-15391. 172p. 1975. 20.00 (ISBN 0-87332-064-6). M E Sharpe.

Tawney, R. H. Land & Labor in China. LC 77-72070. 1977. Repr. of 1932 ed. pap. 6.95 (ISBN 0-87332-106-5). M E Sharpe.

LAND USE–GREAT BRITAIN

Baker, Alan R. & Harley, J. B., eds. Man Made the Land: Essays in English Historical Geography. LC 73-5602. (Illus.). 208p. 1973. 23.50x (ISBN 0-87471-184-3). Rowman.

Gilg, Andrew W. Countryside Planning: The First Three Decades 1945-76. (Illus.). 1979. pap. 8.95x (ISBN 0-416-72340-3). Methuen Inc.

Land Use Mapping by Local Authorities in Britain: Experimental Cartography Unit. 1978. 25.00 (ISBN 0-85139-333-0). Nichols Pub.

Moore, Margaret F. Lands of the Scottish Kings in England. LC 70-91997. Repr. of 1915 ed. lib. bdg. 13.50x (ISBN 0-678-00728-4). Kelley.

Moss, Graham. Britain's Wasting Acres: Land Use in a Changing Society. 240p. 1981. 33.50 (ISBN 0-85139-078-1). Nichols Pub.

Ravensdale, J. R. Liable to Floods: Village Landscape on the Edge of Fens. LC 73-80473. (Illus.). 254p. 1974. 31.95 (ISBN 0-521-20285-X). Cambridge U Pr.

Royal Scottish Geographical Society Symposium, Held in the University of Edinburgh, May 1979. Land Assessment in Scotland: Proceedings. Thomas, M. F. & Coppock, J. T., eds. (Illus.). 156p. 1980. text ed. 20.00 (ISBN 0-08-025716-X, Pub. by Aberdeen Scotland). Pergamon.

Wibberley, Gerald & Davidson, Joan. Planning & the Rural Environment. 1977. text ed. 26.00 (ISBN 0-08-020527-5); pap. text ed. 13.25 (ISBN 0-08-020526-7). Pergamon.

Yelling, James A. Common Field & Enclosure in England,1450-1850. (Illus.). 1977. 19.50 (ISBN 0-208-01698-8, Archon). Shoe String.

LAND USE–INDIA

Gosal, Gurdev S. & Ojha, B. S. Agricultural Land-Use in Punjab: A Spatial Analysis. (Illus.). 87p. 1967. 7.50x (ISBN 0-8002-0430-1). Intl Pubns Serv.

Mayer, Adrian C. Land & Society in Malabar. LC 73-13032. 158p. 1974. Repr. of 1952 ed. lib. bdg. 15.00x (ISBN 0-8371-7103-2, MASM). Greenwood.

Patel, M. L. Changing Land Problems of Tribal India. LC 74-900800. 160p. 1974. 9.50x (ISBN 0-8002-0531-6). Intl Pubns Serv.

Vashishta, H. B. Land Revenue & Public Administration in Maratha Administration. LC 75-901880. 1975. 11.00x (ISBN 0-88386-606-4). South Asia Bks.

LAND USE–IRAN

Gharatchedaghi, Cyrus. Distribution of Land in Varamin: An Opening Phase of the Agrarian Reform in Iran. 179p. 1967. 20.00x (ISBN 3-8100-0087-6). Intl Pubns Serv.

Iran: Concepts of Biotic Community Conservation. (Illus.). 1976. pap. 7.50x (ISBN 2-88032-048-8, IUCN56, IUCN). Unipub.

LAND USE–IRELAND

Petty, William. History of the Survey of Ireland, Commonly Called the Down Survey. Larcom, Thomas A., ed. LC 67-20090. Repr. of 1851 ed. 19.50x (ISBN 0-678-00341-6). Kelley.

Simms, John G. The Williamite Confiscation in Ireland, 1690-1703. LC 76-44839. (Studies in Irish History: Vol. 7). (Illus.). 1977. Repr. of 1956 ed. lib. bdg. 16.00x (ISBN 0-8371-9306-0, SIWI). Greenwood.

LAND USE–ITALY

Longobardi, Cesare. Land Reclamation in Italy. 1976. lib. bdg. 34.95 (ISBN 0-8490-2127-8). Gordon Pr.

Metraux, Guy P. Western Greek Land: Use & City-Planning in the Archaic Period. LC 77-94709. (Outstanding Dissertations in the Fine Arts Ser.). 1978. lib. bdg. 21.00x (ISBN 0-8240-3241-1). Garland Pub.

LAND USE–KOREA

Yi Hun-Gu. Land Utilization & Rural Economy in Korea. LC 68-57650. (Illus.). 1968. Repr. of 1936 ed. lib. bdg. 17.50x (ISBN 0-8371-0975-2, YILU). Greenwood.

LAND USE–LATIN AMERICA

Hirschman, Albert O. Journeys Toward Progress: Studies of Economic Policy-Making in Latin America. LC 68-8620. (Illus.). 1968. Repr. of 1963 ed. lib. bdg. 16.00x (ISBN 0-8371-0106-9, HIJP). Greenwood.

Nelson, Michael. The Development of Tropical Lands: Policy Issues in Latin America. LC 72-12363. (Resources for the Future Ser). 323p. 1973. 22.00x (ISBN 0-8018-1488-X). Johns Hopkins.

Skar, Harald O. The Warm Valley People. 304p. 1981. 26.00 (ISBN 82-00-05682-1). Universitet.

Taylor, William B. Landlord & Peasant in Colonial Oaxaca. LC 70-153819. (Illus.). 1972. 15.00x (ISBN 0-8047-0796-0). Stanford U Pr.

LAND USE–NEAR EAST

Ecological Management of Arid & Semi-Arid Rangelands of Africa, the Near & Middle East. Emarar - Phase II: Vol. VII, Near East Grassland Education & Training. 55p. 1979. pap. 7.50 (ISBN 92-5-100680-6, F1619, FAO). Unipub.

Report of the Fifth Session of the Regional Commission on Land & Water Use in the Near East. (Land & Water Development Document: No. 13). 32p. 1976. pap. 7.50 (ISBN 92-5-100238-X, F2090, FAO). Unipub.

LAND USE–NEW GUINEA

Lands of the Ramu-Mandang Area, Papua New Guinea. (Land Research Ser.: No. 37). (Illus.). 135p. 1976. pap. 13.50 (ISBN 0-643-00175-1, CO18, CSIRO). Unipub.

LAND USE–UNITED STATES

Abrams, Charles. Revolution in Land. Bruchey, Stuart, ed. LC 78-56679. (Management of Public Lands in the U. S. Ser.). (Illus.). 1979. Repr. of 1939 ed. lib. bdg. 22.00x (ISBN 0-405-11316-1). Arno.

Abstract of the Original Titles of Record in the General Land Office of Texas. Repr. of 1838 ed. 17.50 (ISBN 0-685-13268-4). Jenkins.

Andrews, Richard B. Urban Land Economics & Public Policy. LC 77-122281. 1971. 12.95 (ISBN 0-02-900710-0). Free Pr.

Barlowe, Raleigh. Sac & Fox Lands: Appraisal of Portions in Royce Area 50 in Wisconsin, Illinois & Missouri, 1805. (Library of American Indian Affairs). 70p. 1974. lib. bdg. 28.50 (ISBN 0-8287-1218-2). Clearwater Pub.

Bernard, Michael M. Constitutions, Taxations, & Land Policy: Vol. I, Abstract of Federal & State Constitutional Constraints on the Power of Taxation Relating to Land Planning Policy. (Lincoln Institute of Land Policy Book). (Illus.). 176p. 1979. 16.95 (ISBN 0-669-02823-1). Lexington Bks.

Birkelbach, Aubrey W., Jr. & Wassall, Gregory H. The Case Against the Sale of Development Rights of Connecticut's Agricultural Land. 1975. pap. text ed. 1.00 (ISBN 0-686-23012-4). Lincoln Inst Land.

Bjork, Gordon C. Life, Liberty, & Property: The Economics & Politics of Land-Use Planning & Environmental Controls. LC 80-8038. 160p. 1980. 16.50x (ISBN 0-669-03952-7). Lexington Bks.

Bogue, Margaret B. Patterns from the Sod. Bruchey, Stuart, ed. LC 78-56691. (Management of Public Lands Law in the U. S. Ser.). (Illus.). 1979. Repr. of 1959 ed. lib. bdg. 21.00x (ISBN 0-405-11318-8). Arno.

--Patterns from the Sod: Land Use & Tenure in the Grand Prairie, 1850-1900. (Illinois Historical Collections Ser.: Vol. 34). 1959. 2.50 (ISBN 0-912154-14-4). Ill St Hist Lib.

Brooks, Thomas B. The Augusta Tract: Map & Manual, 1858. LC 72-78924. (Illus.). 100p. 1972. 9.95 (ISBN 0-912526-03-3). Lib Res.

Carlson, Theodore L. The Illinois Military Tract. Bruchey, Stuart, ed. LC 78-56707. (Management of Public Lands in the U. S. Ser.). (Illus.). 1979. Repr. of 1951 ed. lib. bdg. 15.00 (ISBN 0-405-11322-6). Arno.

Carstensen, Vernon. Farms of Forests. Bruchey, Stuart, ed. LC 78-36706. (Management of Public Lands in the U. S. Ser.). (Illus.). 1979. Repr. of 1958 ed. lib. bdg. 10.00x (ISBN 0-405-11323-4). Arno.

Chapman, Jeffrey I. Proposition Thirteen & Land Use: A Case Study of Fiscal Limits in California. LC 79-3749. 1981. 22.95x (ISBN 0-669-03471-1). Lexington Bks.

Chisholm, Roger K. Appraisal of Land in Royce Area 163 & 164. 61p. 1974. lib. bdg. 27.00 (ISBN 0-8287-0919-X). Clearwater Pub.

Clawson, Marion. America's Land & Its Uses. LC 70-167985. (Resources for the Future Ser.). (Illus.). 166p. 1972. 12.50x (ISBN 0-8018-1343-3); pap. 3.95x (ISBN 0-8018-1330-1). Johns Hopkins.

--Land System of the United States: An Introduction to the History & Practice of Land Use & Land Tenure. LC 68-10250. (Illus.). 1968. 10.95x (ISBN 0-8032-0016-1). U of Nebr Pr.

--Suburban Land Conversion in the United States: An Economic & Governmental Process. LC 70-149239. (Resources for the Future Ser). (Illus.). 400p. 1971. 22.50x (ISBN 0-8018-1313-1). Johns Hopkins.

Clawson, Marion, ed. Modernizing Urban Land Policy. LC 72-12365. (Resources for the Future Ser). (Illus.). 255p. 1973. 16.50x (ISBN 0-8018-1491-X). Johns Hopkins.

Cooley, Richard A. Alaska: A Challenge in Conservation. (Illus.). 186p. (YA) (gr. 9-12). 1966. pap. 4.00x (ISBN 0-299-04024-0). U of Wis Pr.

Cowing, Sheila. Our Wild Wetlands. LC 80-17600. (Illus.). 96p. (gr. 4-6). 1980. PLB 7.79 (ISBN 0-671-33089-6). Messner.

De Neufville, Judith I., ed. The Land Use Policy Debate in the United States. (Environment, Development, & Public Policy - Environmental Policy & Planning Ser.). 315p. 1981. text ed. 29.50 (ISBN 0-306-40718-3, Plenum Pr). Plenum Pub.

Duck, Berkley W. Appraisal Report on a Tract of Ground Located in Central Indiana & Extending Eastward into Ohio. (Library of American Indian Affairs). 179p. 1974. lib. bdg. 55.00 (ISBN 0-8287-0949-1). Clearwater Pub.

Elmquist, Gordon E. Appraisal of the Lands of the Lower Sioux Community in Minnesota. (Library of American Indian Affairs). 142p. 1974. lib. bdg. 46.00 (ISBN 0-8287-0936-X). Clearwater Pub.

Englehorn, Vern A. Appraisal Report on Brunot Land, Wyoming, Sold by Shoshone Tribe. (Library of American Indian Affairs). 199p. 1974. lib. bdg. 60.00 (ISBN 0-8287-0950-5). Clearwater Pub.

Ervin, David E, et al. Land Use Control: Evaluating Economic & Political Effects. LC 76-51214. 1977. 17.50 (ISBN 0-88410-062-6). Ballinger Pub.

Ford, Amelia C. Colonial Precedents of Our National Land System As It Existed in 1800. LC 76-54887. (Perspectives in American History Ser.: No. 44). 157p. Repr. of 1910 ed. lib. bdg. 15.00x (ISBN 0-87991-368-1). Porcupine Pr.

Gibbons, Boyd. Wye Island: Outsiders, Insiders & Resistance to Change. LC 76-47399. (Resources for the Future Ser.). (Illus.). 248p. 1977. 15.00x (ISBN 0-8018-1936-9). Johns Hopkins.

Hall, Richard B. Appraisal of Lands in Northern Oklahoma, Cherokee Outlet, 1893. 96p. 1974. lib. bdg. 39.00 (ISBN 0-8287-0922-X). Clearwater Pub.

Hansen, William & Bigelow, Bo. Lake Management Case Study: Westlake Village California. LC 77-79282. (No. 73). 1976. 17.00 (ISBN 0-87420-073-3). Urban Land.

Harrison, T. S. & Harrison, J. W. Appraisal of Oil & Gas Lands of the Portion of Wind River Basin, Wyoming Ceded by the Brunot Agreement of September 26, 1872. (Library of American Indian Affairs). 84p. 1974. lib. bdg. 32.00 (ISBN 0-8287-0924-6). Clearwater Pub.

Harwood, Corbin C. Using Land to Save Energy. 352p. 1977. professional reference 22.50x (ISBN 0-88410-061-8). Ballinger Pub.

Hatfield, James. Tillamook-Nehalem Lands. (Library of American Indian Affairs). 142p. 1974. lib. bdg. 46.00 (ISBN 0-8287-1277-8). Clearwater Pub.

Holbrook, M. J., et al. Appraisal Report of the Warm Springs Reservation in Oregon, 1859, 3 vols. (Library of American Indian Affairs). 682p. 1974. lib. bdg. 197.50 (ISBN 0-8287-0947-5). Clearwater Pub.

Hoyt, Homer. Emigrant New York Lands in Northeastern Wisconsin & Northwestern Michigan: Appraisal. (Library of American Indian Affairs). 135p. 1974. lib. bdg. 45.00 (ISBN 0-8287-1031-7). Clearwater Pub.

--Miami Tribe: Appraisal of Lands in North Central Indiana, Royce Areas 192-199, 251-256, & 258. (Library of American Indian Affairs). 294p. 1974. lib. bdg. 82.50 (ISBN 0-8287-1122-4). Clearwater Pub.

Jackson, Richard H. Land Use in America. LC 80-20184. (Scripta Ser. in Geography). 224p. 1981. 29.95 (ISBN 0-470-27063-2). Halsted Pr.

Kentucky Historical Society. Certificate Book of the Virginia Land Commission, 1779 to 1780: The Register for 1923. 416p. 1981. Repr. of 1923 ed. 27.50 (ISBN 0-89308-207-4). Southern Hist.

Kolesar, John & Scholl, Jaye. Saving Farmland. 1975. 3.50 (ISBN 0-686-23336-0). Ctr Analysis Public Issues.

Land Planning Committee, U.S. National Resources Board. Report of the Land Planning Committee, Pt. 2. LC 75-26322. (World Food Supply Ser). (Illus.). 1976. Repr. of 1934 ed. 13.00x (ISBN 0-405-07798-X). Arno.

Land Study Bureau, Univ. of Hawaii. Compensible Regulations: Their Potential for Land Use & Development Control in Hawaii. (Land Study Bureau Report: No. 7). 55p. 1968. pap. 3.00x (ISBN 0-8248-0316-7). U Pr of Hawaii.

--Detailed Land Classification. Incl. Island of Hawaii. (No. 6). 763p. 1965; Island of Kauai. (No. 9). 151p. 1967. pap. 9.00x (ISBN 0-8248-0309-4); Island of Lanai. (No. 8). (Illus.). 60p. 1967. pap. 3.00x (ISBN 0-8248-0310-8); Island of Maui. (No. 7). (Illus.). 167p. 1967. pap. 9.50x (ISBN 0-8248-0312-4); Island of Molokai. (No. 10). (Illus.). 95p. 1968. pap. 5.00x (ISBN 0-8248-0308-6); Island of Oahu. rev. ed. (No. 11). 320p. 1973. pap. 17.00x (ISBN 0-8248-0320-5). (Land Study Bureau Bulletin). U Pr of Hawaii.

--Kauai Lands Classified by Physical Qualities for Urban Usage. (Land Study Bureau Circular: No. 17). (Illus.). 38p. 1973. pap. 15.00x (ISBN 0-8248-0348-5). U Pr of Hawaii.
--Land Use & Productivity Data, State of Hawaii, 1968. (Land Study Bureau Circular: No. 15). 95p. 1969. pap. 5.00x (ISBN 0-8248-0314-0). U Pr of Hawaii.
--Maui Lands Classified by Physical Qualities for Urban Usage. (Land Study Bureau Circular: No. 16). (Illus.). 52p. 1970. pap. 18.00x (ISBN 0-8248-0317-5). U Pr of Hawaii.
--Molokai: Present & Potential Land Use. (Land Study Bureau Bulletin: No. 1). (Illus.). 90p. 1960. pap. 5.00x (ISBN 0-8248-0313-2). U Pr of Hawaii.
League of Women Voters of Pennsylvania. Land Use. 1976. pap. 3.00 spiral bdg. (ISBN 0-931374-01-4). LWVPA.
Lemon, James T. The Best Poor Man's Country: A Geographical Study of Early Southeastern Pennsylvania. LC 77-165352. (Illus.). 320p. 1972. 19.50x (ISBN 0-8018-1189-9). Johns Hopkins.
Little, C. Challenge of the Land. 1969. 12.25 (ISBN 0-08-006913-4). Pergamon.
McEntyre, John G. Land Survey Systems. LC 78-8551. 1978. text ed. 28.95 (ISBN 0-471-02492-9). Wiley.
Mandelker, Daniel R. Environment & Equity: A Regulatory Challenge. 162p. 1981. 24.95 (ISBN 0-07-039864-X). McGraw.
Marsh, William M. Environmental Analysis: For Land-Use & Site Planning. (Illus.). 1977. 24.50 (ISBN 0-07-040490-9, P&RB). McGraw.
Moriarty, Barry M. Industrial Location & Community Development. LC 79-16029. 1980. 20.00x (ISBN 0-8078-1400-8); pap. 10.95x (ISBN 0-8078-4064-5). U of NC Pr.
Mosk, Sanford A. Land Tenure Problems in the Santa Fe Railroad Grant Area. Bruchey, Stuart, ed. LC 80-1333. (Railroads Ser.). (Illus.). 1981. Repr. of 1944 ed. lib. bdg. 12.00x (ISBN 0-405-13807-5). Arno.
Murray, Henry T. Klamath & Modoc Tribes & the Yahooskin Band of Snake Indians: Appraisal Report of Lands in Oregon. (Library of American Indian Affairs). 275p. 1974. lib. bdg. 78.00 (ISBN 0-8287-1094-5). Clearwater Pub.
--Kootenai Tribe in Idaho: Appraisal, As of March 8, 1859. (Library of American Indian Affairs). 220p. 1974. lib. bdg. 64.50 (ISBN 0-8287-1100-3). Clearwater Pub.
Murray, William G. Omaha Tract in Nebraska, 1854: Appraisal. (Library of American Indian Affairs). 143p. 1974. lib. bdg. 46.50 (ISBN 0-8287-1155-0). Clearwater Pub.
--Osage Nation Land Cession in Missouri & Arkansas, 1810: Appraisal. (Library of American Indian Affairs). 196p. 1974. lib. bdg. 59.00 (ISBN 0-8287-1166-6). Clearwater Pub.
--Pawnee Tracts in Nebraska & in Kansas: Appraisal, 2 vols. (Library of American Indian Affairs). 480p. 1974. lib. bdg. 159.00 (ISBN 0-8287-1188-7). Clearwater Pub.
--Seminole Lands in Florida: Appraisal. (Library of American Indian Affairs). 220p. 1974. lib. bdg. 64.50 (ISBN 0-8287-1237-9). Clearwater Pub.
Muske, William H. Sisseton & Wahpeton Tribes of North Dakota: Appraisal of Lands Disposed of Under the Act of April 27, 1904. (Library of American Indian Affairs). 100p. 1974. lib. bdg. 36.00 (ISBN 0-8287-1254-9). Clearwater Pub.
Myers, Donald D. & Kleinman, Frank R., Jr. Western Bands of Shoshone: Appraisal of Lands in Nevada & California, 2 vols. (Library of American Indian Affairs). 1974. lib. bdg. 151.50 (ISBN 0-8287-1301-4). Clearwater Pub.
Myers, Donald D., et al. Appraisal of the Lands of the Fort McDowell Mohave-Apache & the Yavapai-Apache Communities in Arizona, 2 vols. (Library of American Indian Affairs). 394p. 1974. lib. bdg. 106.50 (ISBN 0-8287-0932-7). Clearwater Pub.
Myers, Phyllis. So Goes Vermont. 39p. 1974. pap. 1.50 (ISBN 0-89164-021-5). Conservation Foun.
Neutze, Max. The Suburban Apartment Boom: Case Study of a Land Use Problem. LC 69-10889. (Resources for the Future Ser). 170p. (Orig.). 1968. pap. 5.00x (ISBN 0-8018-0490-6). Johns Hopkins.
Ottoson, Howard W., ed. Land Use Policy & Problems in the United States. LC 63-9096. (Illus.). 1963. 22.50x (ISBN 0-8032-0139-7). U of Nebr Pr.
Palmer, M. A. Appraisal of the Former Malheur Reservation in Eastern Oregon. (Library of American Indian Affairs). 95p. 1974. lib. bdg. 43.50 (ISBN 0-8287-0929-7). Clearwater Pub.
Passell, Peter. Essays in the Economics of Nineteenth Century American Land Policy. LC 75-2590. (Dissertations in American Economic History). (Illus.). 1975. 12.00x (ISBN 0-405-07212-0). Arno.
Pelham, Thomas G. State Land-Use Planning & Regulation: Florida, the Model Code, & Beyond. LC 79-2390. (Lincoln Institute of Land Policy Books). 224p. 1979. 23.95 (ISBN 0-669-03062-7). Lexington Bks.
Plummer, Norman B. Appraisal Report of Chelan County, Washington. (Library of American Indian Affairs). 131p. 1974. lib. bdg. 43.50 (ISBN 0-8287-0944-0). Clearwater Pub.
Raney, Frank R. & Raney, Chase W. Steilacoom, Nisqually & Squaxtin Tracts in Western Washington: Appraisal As of March 3, 1855. 176p. 1974. lib. bdg. 54.00 (ISBN 0-8287-1267-0). Clearwater Pub.
Raup, Philip M. The Federal Dynamic in Land Use. 32p. (Orig.). 1981. pap. 4.00 (ISBN 0-89068-054-X). Natl Planning.
Robinson, Shepard D. Land Use Guide for Builders, Developers, & Planners. LC 77-9380. 1977. 20.00 (ISBN 0-912336-54-4). Structures Pub.
Robinson, W. W. Land in California: The Story of Mission Lands, Ranchos, Squatters, Mining Claims, Railroad Grants, Land Scrip, Homesteads. (Illus.). 1979. pap. 4.95 (ISBN 0-520-03875-4, CAL. NO. 419). U of Cal Pr.
Robinson, William W. Land in California. Bruchey, Stuart, ed. LC 78-56665. (Management of Public Lands in the U. S. Ser.). (Illus.). 1979. Repr. of 1948 ed. lib. bdg. 18.00x (ISBN 0-405-11352-8). Arno.
Rosenbaum, Nelson M. Citizen Involvement in Land Use Governance: Issues & Methods. 82p. 1976. pap. 3.50 (ISBN 0-87766-140-5, 11500). Urban Inst.
Sakolski, Aaron M. Great American Land Bubble. (Illus.). Repr. of 1932 ed. 19.00 (ISBN 0-384-53100-8). Johnson Repr.
Salter, Leonard A., Jr. Critical Review of Research in Land Economics. 1967. pap. 5.75x (ISBN 0-299-04424-6). U of Wis Pr.
Sato, Shosuke. History of the Land Question in the United States. LC 78-63765. (Johns Hopkins University. Studies in the Social Sciences. Fourth Ser. 1886: 7-9). Repr. of 1886 ed. 14.00 (ISBN 0-404-61032-3). AMS Pr.
Schmid, A. Allan. Converting Land from Rural to Urban Uses. LC 68-16166. (Resources for the Future Ser.). (Illus.). 103p. (Orig.). 1968. pap. 4.00x (ISBN 0-8018-0578-3). Johns Hopkins.
Schnepf, Max, ed. Farmland, Food & the Future. LC 79-5490. (Illus.). 214p. (Orig.). 1980. pap. 8.00 (ISBN 0-935734-03-1). Soil Conservation.
Schwarz, Philip J. The Jarring Interests. LC 78-3577. (Illus.). 1979. 40.00 (ISBN 0-87395-377-0). State U NY Pr.
Scifres, Charles J. Brush Management: Principles & Practices for Texas & the Southwest. LC 79-7407. (Illus.). 376p. 1980. 17.50 (ISBN 0-89096-080-1). Tex A&M Univ Pr.
Sears, Roscoe H. & Garret, H. J. Sac & Fox Tract Indian Territory: Appraisal. (Library of American Indian Affairs). 160p. 1974. lib. bdg. 50.00 (ISBN 0-8287-1223-9). Clearwater Pub.
Shomon, Joseph James. Open Land for Urban America: Acquisition, Safekeeping, & Use. LC 70-147367. (Illus.). 176p. 1971. 12.00x (ISBN 0-8018-1217-8); pap. 2.95x (ISBN 0-8018-1435-9). Johns Hopkins.
Siegan, Bernard H. Land Use Without Zoning. LC 72-4936. (Illus.). 1972. 14.50 (ISBN 0-669-82040-7). Lexington Bks.
Society of American Foresters. Land-Use Allocation: Processes, People, Politics, Professionals. Evans, H. H., ed. (SAF Convention Proceedings Ser.). (Illus.). 298p. (Orig.). 1981. pap. 17.00 (ISBN 0-939970-07-4). Soc Am Foresters.
Strong, Ann L. Private Property & the Public Interest: The Brandywine Experience. LC 74-24390. (Illus.). 232p. 1975. 15.00x (ISBN 0-8018-1662-9). Johns Hopkins.
Sullivan, John J., ed. Explorations in Urban Land Economics. LC 79-119693. 122p. 1970. pap. 2.50 (ISBN 0-686-01014-0). Lincoln Inst Land.
Surratt, Marshall E. Land Values in Texas Cities. LC 72-94747. 12.50 (ISBN 0-686-11958-4). Land Values.
Susskind, Lawrence, ed. The Land Use Controversy in Massachusetts: Case Studies & Policy Options. 150p. 1976. 15.00x (ISBN 0-262-69056-X). MIT Pr.
Timmons, John F. & Murray, William G., eds. Land Problems & Policies. LC 72-2870. (Use & Abuse of America's Natural Resources Ser). 312p. 1972. Repr. of 1950 ed. 16.00 (ISBN 0-405-04537-9). Arno.
Tondro, Terry J. Connecticut Land Use Regulation. LC 79-68712. 356p. (Orig.). 1979. pap. text ed. write for info. (ISBN 0-939328-02-X). U Conn Sch Law.
Vasu, Michael L. Politics & Planning: A National Study of American Planners. LC 78-10440. (Institute for Research in Social Science Ser.). 1979. 17.00x (ISBN 0-8078-1342-7). U of NC Pr.
Watson, J. W. & O'Riordan, T. American Environment: Perceptions & Policies. LC 73-21939. 352p. 1976. 38.45 (ISBN 0-471-92221-8, Pub. by Wiley-Interscience); pap. 22.25 (ISBN 0-471-92222-6). Wiley.
Williamson, M. J. Creek Nation East of the Mississippi: Appraisal of Lands in Georgia & Alabama As of August 9, 1814. (Library of American Indian Affairs). 21p. 1974. lib. bdg. 17.00 (ISBN 0-8287-1023-6). Clearwater Pub.
Windsor, Duane. Fiscal Zoning in Suburban Communities. LC 78-20632. (Illus.). 208p. 1979. 21.00 (ISBN 0-669-02751-0). Lexington Bks.
Wolf, Peter. Land in America: Its Value, Use & Control. Date not set. 20.00 (ISBN 0-394-50437-2). Pantheon.

LAND USE, URBAN-PLANNING
see City Planning

LAND VALUATION
see Farms–Valuation; Real Property–Valuation

LAND VALUE TAXATION
see also Single Tax

Bernard, Michael M. Constitutions, Taxation, & Land Policy: Vol. II, Discussion & Analysis of Federal & State Constitutional Constraints on the Use of Taxation As an Instrument of Land-Planning Policy. LC 78-24792. (Lincoln Institute of Land Policy Bk). 144p. 1980. 16.95x (ISBN 0-669-03462-2). Lexington Bks.
Bernard, Michael M., ed. Annotated Bibliography on Taxation As an Instrument of Land Planning Policy. (Lincoln Institute Monograph: No. 80-8). 90p. 1980. pap. text ed. 4.00 (ISBN 0-686-29504-8). Lincoln Inst Land.
Brown, Harry G. Selected Articles by Harry Gunnison Brown: The Case for Land Value Taxation. 245p. 1980. 12.50 (ISBN 0-911312-50-1). Schalkenbach.
Church, Albert M., ed. Non-Renewable Resource Taxation in the Western States. 1977. pap. text ed. 10.00 (ISBN 0-686-20037-3). Lincoln Inst Land.
Computer Assisted Mass Appraisal-Assessment Ratio Bibliography. 1977. pap. 0.75 (ISBN 0-686-20036-5). Lincoln Inst Land.
Conference on Federal Taxation & Land Use. Proceedings. (Lincoln Institute Monograph: 78-7). (Orig.). 1978. pap. text ed. 5.00 (ISBN 0-686-25526-7). Lincoln Inst Land.
Douglas, F. C. Land-Value Rating. 76p. 1961. pap. 0.75 (ISBN 0-685-46967-0). Schalkenbach.
Huang Han Liang. Land Tax in China. LC 76-76706. (Columbia University. Studies in the Social Sciences: No. 187). Repr. of 1918 ed. 16.50 (ISBN 0-404-51187-2). AMS Pr.
Kolesar, John & Scholl, Jaye. Saving Farmland. 1975. 3.50 (ISBN 0-686-23336-0). Ctr Analysis Public Issues.
Liang Fang-Chung. Single-Whip Method of Taxation in China. Wang Yu-Ch'Uan, tr. LC 56-4991. (East Asian Monographs Ser: No. 1). 1956. pap. 9.00x (ISBN 0-674-80895-9). Harvard U Pr.
Lindholm, Richard W., ed. Land Value Taxation: The "Progress & Poverty" Centenary. LC 80-52299. (Taxation, Resources & Economic Development (TRED) Ser.). 304p. 1981. 20.00x (ISBN 0-299-08520-1). U of Wis Pr.
Proposition Thirteen: A First Anniversary Assessment. (Lincoln Institute Monograph: No. 80-5). (Illus.). 1980. pap. text ed. 5.00 (ISBN 0-686-29506-4). Lincoln Inst Land.
Sakolski, A. M. Land Tenure & Land Taxation in America. 316p. 1957. 2.00 (ISBN 0-911312-32-3). Schalkenbach.
State Taxation of Forest & Land Resources: Symposium Proceedings. (Lincoln Institute Monograph: No. 80-6). 149p. 1980. pap. text ed. 12.00 (ISBN 0-686-29507-2). Lincoln Inst Land.
Viegas, Leslie A. The Feasibility of Contracting Separately for Data Collection in a Revalution Project. 1977. pap. 1.50 (ISBN 0-686-20035-7). Lincoln Inst Land.
Wang, Yeh-Chien. Land Taxation in Imperial China, 1750-1911. LC 73-80024. (East Asian Ser: No. 73). 192p. 1974. 10.00x (ISBN 0-674-50860-2). Harvard U Pr.
Wang, Yeh chin. An Estimate of the Land Tax Collection in China, 1753 & 1908. LC 73-80025. (East Asian Monographs Ser: No. 52). 192p. 1973. pap. text ed. 9.00x (ISBN 0-674-26825-3). Harvard U Pr.
Williams, Percy R. The Pittsburgh Graded Tax Plan. 71p. 1964. pap. 0.50 (ISBN 0-911312-38-2). Schalkenbach.
Young, Wylie. Antidote for Madness: What Every High School Student Should Know. 123p. 1976. pap. 2.00 (ISBN 0-911312-55-2). Schalkenbach.

LAND-WARRANTS
see Land Titles

LANDAU, LEV DAVIDOVICH, 1908-

Livanova. L. D. Landau. Sykes, J., tr. 1980. 26.00 (ISBN 0-08-023076-8). Pergamon.

LANDAUER, GUSTAV, 1870-1919

Fishman, Sterling. Prophets, Poets & Priests: Gustav Landauer, Kurt Eisner, Eric Muhsam & the Bavarian Revolution of 1919. 1974. lib. bdg. 39.95 (ISBN 0-685-51298-3). Revisionist Pr.
Hyman, Ruth L. Gustav Landauer: Philosopher of Utopia. LC 76-49585. 1977. 25.00 (ISBN 0-915144-27-1). Hackett Pub.
Lunn, Eugene. Prophet of Community: The Romantic Socialism of Gustav Landauer. LC 70-186105. 1973. 28.50x (ISBN 0-520-02207-6). U of Cal Pr.
Maurer, Charles B. Call to Revolution: The Mystical Anarchism of Gustav Landauer. LC 75-148270. 1971. text ed. 9.50x (ISBN 0-8143-1441-4). Wayne St U Pr.
Munoz, V. Gustav Landauer: A Chronology. Johnson, W. Scott, tr. (Libertarian & Anarchist Chronology Ser.). 1979. lib. bdg. 59.95 (ISBN 0-8490-3029-3). Gordon Pr.

LANDFORMS
see also names of topographical features e.g. Mountains; Plains

Adams, George F. & Wyckoff, Jerome. Landforms. (Golden Guide Ser). (Illus.). 1971. 1.95 (ISBN 0-307-24350-8, Golden Pr); PLB 10.38 (ISBN 0-307-63550-3). Western Pub.
Atlas of Landforms. 2nd ed. LC 73-14921. (Illus.). 144p. 1974. text ed. 22.50 (ISBN 0-471-03628-5). Wiley.
Brandon, P. F. & Millman, R. N., eds. Historic Landscapes: Observer's & Recorder's Handbook. 1981. 40.00x (ISBN 0-86127-306-0, Pub. by Avebury Pub England). State Mutual Bk.
Coburn, Doris K. A Spit Is a Piece of Land: Landforms in the U. S. A. LC 77-17605. (Illus.). 128p. (gr. 4-6). 1978. PLB 7.79 (ISBN 0-671-32844-1). Messner.
Crickmay, C. H. The Work of the River. LC 74-21703. 271p. 1974. 35.00 (ISBN 0-444-19515-7). Elsevier.
Douglas, Ian. Humid Landforms. (Illus.). 1977. text ed. 16.00x (ISBN 0-262-04054-9). Mit Pr.
Heyl, James & Brook, George. Introduction to Landforms. 2nd ed. 220p. 1979. pap. text ed. 11.95 (ISBN 0-89892-008-6). Contemp Pub Co Raleigh.
Isachenko, A. G. Principles of Landscape Science & Physical-Geographic Regionalization. Massey, John S. & Rosengren, N. J., eds. Zatorski, R. J., tr. from Rus. 332p. 1973. 27.50x (ISBN 0-522-84046-9, Pub. by Melbourne U Pr). Intl Schol Bk Serv.
Jones, David, ed. The Shaping of Southern England. LC 80-40888. (Special Publications of the Institute of British Geographers: Vol.2). 1981. 35.50 (ISBN 0-12-388950-2). Acad Pr.
King, Cuchlaine, ed. Landforms & Geomorphology: Concepts & History. LC 76-3489. (Benchmark Papers in Geology Ser.: Vol. 28). 400p. 1976. 51.00 (ISBN 0-12-786845-3). Acad Pr.
Lind, Aulis O. Coastal Landforms of Cat Island, Bahamas: A Study of Holocene Accretionary Topography & Sea Level Change. LC 76-77892. (Research Papers Ser.: No. 122). 156p. 1969. pap. 8.00 (ISBN 0-89065-029-2). U Chicago Dept Geog.
Melhorn, W. N. & Flemal, R. C., eds. Theories of Landform Development. (Binghamton Symposia in Geomorphology: International Ser.: No. 6). (Illus.). 312p. 1980. text ed. 20.00x (ISBN 0-04-551039-3). Allen Unwin.
Mitchell, Colin. Terrain Evaluation. Houston, J., ed. LC 74-158517. (Illus.). 224p. 1974. pap. text ed. 10.95x (ISBN 0-582-48426-X). Longman.
Morisawa, M. Theories of Landform Development. Melhorn, W. & Flemal, R., eds. (Geomorphology Symposium: 6th). 1976. 10.00 (ISBN 0-686-10458-7). Pubns Geomorphology.
Pearl, Richard M. Landforms of Colorado. 1975. pap. 2.75 (ISBN 0-686-14942-4). Earth Science.
--Nature's Names for Colorado Communities. 1975. pap. 1.00 (ISBN 0-686-14943-2). Earth Science.
Penck, Walther. Morphological Analysis of Land Forms: A Contribution to Physical Geology. Czech, Hella & Boswell, Katharine Cumming, trs. from Ger. Orig. Title: Die Morphologische Analyse. 443p. 1972. Repr. of 1953 ed. 21.75 (ISBN 0-02-850130-6). Hafner.
Thompson, Betty F. The Shaping of America's Heartland: The Landscape of the Middle West. (Naturalist's America Ser.: Vol. 4). 1977. 11.95 (ISBN 0-395-24760-8). HM.
Tuttle, Sherwood D. Landforms & Landscapes. 3rd ed. 160p. 1980. pap. text ed. write for info. (ISBN 0-697-05020-3). Wm C Brown.
Twidale, C. R. Structural Landforms. (Geomorphology Ser.: Vol. 5). 1971. 17.50x (ISBN 0-262-20018-X). MIT Pr.
Yoshikawa, Torao, et al. The Landforms of Japan. (Illus.). 270p. 1981. 39.50x (ISBN 0-86008-283-0, Pub. by U of Tokyo Japan). Columbia U Pr.

LANDING AIDS (AERONAUTICS)
see also Airplanes–Electric Equipment; Airplanes–Electronic Equipment; Electronics in Aeronautics

LANDING OPERATIONS
Here are entered general works on the landing of waterborne or airborne troops on hostile territory, including the tactics of transporting, landing and establishing such troops and their supplies, and combat during the landing phase. Works on the joint operation of air, land and sea forces to establish troops on shore, as developed in World War II, are entered under Amphibious Warfare.
see also Amphibious Warfare

LANDLORD AND TENANT
see also Apartment Houses; Leases; Rent; Tenement Houses

Abrams, Kathleen & Abrams, Lawrence. Successful Landlording. Case, Virginia, ed. LC 80-36678. (Successful Ser.). (Illus.). 144p. 1980. 15.95 (ISBN 0-89999-006-1); pap. 6.95 (ISBN 0-89999-007-X). Structures Pub.

Blumberg, Richard E. & Grow, James R. The Rights of Tenants. 1979. pap. 1,95 (ISBN 0-380-41780-4, 41780). Avon.

Davidow, Mike. Life Without Landlords. 32p. 1973. pap. 0.40 (ISBN 0-87898-100-4). New Outlook.

Faber, Stuart J. Handbook of Landlord-Tenant Law. pap. 22.50 (ISBN 0-89074-053-4). Lega Bks.

--How to Outsmart Your Landlord (If You're a Tenant) or How to Outsmart Your Tenant (If You're a Landlord) rev. ed. 90p. (Orig.). 1978. pap. 4.45 (ISBN 0-89074-057-7). Good Life.

--Landlord - Texas Problems: Texas Edition. 1978. pap. 7.95 (ISBN 0-89074-059-3). Lega Bks.

Greenleaf, Barbara K. America Fever: The Story of American Immigration. (RL 7). 1974. pap. 1.95 (ISBN 0-451-61279-5, MJ1279, Ment). NAL.

Harper, Michael. Landlord Vs. Tenant. 1978. 15.00 (ISBN 0-7045-0264-X). State Mutual Bk.

Harris, Doris E. Delaware Landlord-Tenant Handbook. 260p. 1980. 12.50 (ISBN 0-87215-314-2). Michie-Bobbs.

Hill, David S. Landlord & Tenant Law in a Nutshell. LC 79-11051. (Nutshell Ser.). 319p. 1979. pap. text ed. 6.95 (ISBN 0-8299-2039-0). West Pub.

How to Pin Your Landlord to the Mat: The Legal Guide for Tenants. LC 80-65096. 1981. write for info. (ISBN 0-89648-072-0); pap. write for info. (ISBN 0-89648-073-9). Citizens Law.

Isenhour, Barbara A., et al. Tenants' Rights: A Guide for Washington State. rev. ed. LC 77-73312. (Illus.). 132p. 1981. pap. 6.95 (ISBN 0-295-95844-8). U of Wash Pr.

--Tenants' Rights: A Guide for Washington State. rev. ed. LC 77-73312. (Illus.). 1981. pap. 6.95 (ISBN 0-295-95844-8). U of Wash Pr.

Jessup, Libby F. Landlord & Tenant. rev., 4th ed. LC 74-11396. (Legal Almanacs Ser.). 128p. 1974. 5.95 (ISBN 0-379-11089-X). Oceana.

Kane, Andy. Care & Feeding of Tenants. (Illus.). 120p. 1981. pap. 8.95 (ISBN 0-87364-240-6). Paladin Ent.

Kass, Louis A. Landlord - Tenant (N.Y.) 1964. pap. 2.00x (ISBN 0-87526-043-8). Gould.

Kim, Sung B. Landlord & Tenant in Colonial New York: Manorial Society, 1664-1775. LC 77-24423. (Institute of Early American History & Culture Ser.). (Illus.). 1978. 22.50x (ISBN 0-8078-1290-0). U of NC Pr.

Knight, Willys R. The Postwar Rent Control Controversy. LC 62-64129. (Research Monograph: No. 23). 1962. spiral bdg 5.00x (ISBN 0-88406-009-8). Ga St U Busn Pub.

Lomnicki, A. J. Summary of Landlord & Tenant Law. 1975. 25.00 (ISBN 0-7134-2923-2, Pub. by Batsford England); pap. 14.95 (ISBN 0-7134-2924-0). David & Charles.

Moskovitz, et al. California Tenant's Handbook. 6th ed. 1981. pap. 7.95 (ISBN 0-917316-36-3). Nolo Pr.

Ozanne, Larry & Struyk, Raymond J. Housing from the Existing Stock: Comparative, Economic Analyses of Owner-Occupants & Landlords. (An Institute Paper). 196p. 1976. pap. 5.50 (ISBN 0-87766-168-5, 14900). Urban Inst.

Partington, Martin. Landlord & Tenant: Text & Materials on Housing & Law. 2nd ed. (Law in Context Ser.). xxxviii, 554p. 1981. 54.00x (ISBN 0-297-77790-4, Pub. by Weidenfeld & Nicolson England). Rothman.

Rhunka, John C. Housing Justice in Small Claims Courts. 1979. 6.00 (ISBN 0-89656-031-7, R0043). Natl Ctr St Courts.

Robinson, Leigh. The Eviction Book for California. 112p. (Orig.). 1980. pap. text ed. 10.00 (ISBN 0-932956-02-5). Express.

--Landlording: A Handy Manual for Scrupulous Landlords & Landladies How Do It Themselves. 3rd ed. 272p. 1980. pap. text ed. 15.00 (ISBN 0-932956-01-7); pap. text ed. 17.50 Canadian edition (ISBN 0-932956-03-3). Express.

Rose, Jerome G. Landlords & Tenants. LC 72-82194. 380p. 1973. 12.95 (ISBN 0-87855-042-9); pap. 3.95 (ISBN 0-87855-538-2). Transaction Bks.

Schoshinski, Robert. American Law of Landlords & Tenant, Vol. 1. LC 80-81653. 1980. 60.00 (ISBN 0-686-29238-3). Lawyers Co-Op.

Simons, Jim, et al. Texas Tenants' Handbook. 1980. pap. price not set (ISBN 0-201-08302-7). A-W.

Striker, John M. & Shapiro, Andrew O. Super Tenant: New York City Tenant Handbook. LC 77-72336. 1978. 8.95x (ISBN 0-03-021101-8); pap. 4.95x (ISBN 0-03-021096-8). HR&W.

Taylor-Moore, Suzanne. Landlords Are People Too. 48p. 1980. pap. 2.50 (ISBN 0-686-28086-5). MTM Pub Co.

--Taylor-Moore Lodge. 1981. pap. 2.50 (ISBN 0-686-28090-3). MTM Pub Co.

Thypin, Marilyn & Glasner, Lynne. Leases & Landlords. LC 79-9391. (Consumer Education Ser.: No. 2). (Orig.). (gr. 9-12). 1980. pap. text ed. 3.50 (ISBN 0-88436-515-8). EMC.

Woofter, Thomas J. Landlord & Tenant on the Cotton Plantation. LC 74-75537. (Illus.). Repr. of 1936 ed. 14.25x (ISBN 0-8371-1035-1, Pub. by Negro U Pr). Greenwood.

LANDLORD AND TENANT–GREAT BRITAIN

Greve, John. Private Landlords in England. 54p. 1965. pap. text ed. 3.75x (ISBN 0-686-70855-5, Pub. by Bedford England). Renouf.

Walton, John K. The Blackpool Landlady: A Social History. (Illus.). 229p. 1978. 18.50x (ISBN 0-8476-2265-7). Rowman.

LANDMARKS (BOUNDARIES)
see Boundaries (Estates)

LANDMARKS, LITERARY
see Literary Landmarks

LANDMARKS, PRESERVATION OF
see Natural Monuments

LANDON, ALFRED MOSSMAN, 1887-

McCoy, Donald R. Landon of Kansas. LC 65-16190. (Landmark Edition). (Illus.). 1966. 34.50x (ISBN 0-8032-0116-8). U of Nebr Pr.

LANDOR, WALTER SAVAGE, 1775-1864

Bradley, William. Early Poems of Walter Savage Landor. LC 72-192844. 1914. lib. bdg. 15.00 (ISBN 0-8414-3195-7). Folcroft.

Colvin, Sidney. English Men of Letters, Walter Savage Landor. Morley, John, ed. 224p. 1980. Repr. of 1881 ed. lib. bdg. 15.00 (ISBN 0-89760-117-3). Telegraph Bks.

--Landor. 1979. Repr. of 1881 ed. lib. bdg. 15.00 (ISBN 0-89987-100-3). Darby Bks.

--Landor. Morley, John, ed. LC 68-58374. (English Men of Letters). Repr. of 1888 ed. lib. bdg. 12.50 (ISBN 0-404-51705-6). AMS Pr.

--William Savage Landor. (English Men of Letters Ser). 1978. Repr. lib. bdg. 12.50 (ISBN 0-8414-1849-7). Folcroft.

Elkin, Felice. Walter Savage Landor: Studies of Italian Life & Literature. LC 74-8062. 1934. lib. bdg. 10.00 (ISBN 0-8414-3938-9). Folcroft.

Evans, Edward W. Walter Savage Landor: A Critical Study. LC 74-22322. 1974. Repr. of 1907 ed. lib. bdg. 7.45 (ISBN 0-8414-3929-X). Folcroft.

Evans, Edward W., Jr. Walter Savage Landor: A Critical Study. LC 74-103186. 1970. Repr. of 1892 ed. 12.50 (ISBN 0-8046-0823-7). Kennikat.

Forster, John. Walter Savage Landor: A Biography, 8 Bks. LC 79-115241. 1971. Repr. of 1869 ed. 42.00 (ISBN 0-403-00407-1). Scholarly.

--Walter Savage Landor: A Biography, 2 vols. 1979. Repr. of 1869 ed. lib. bdg. 100.00 (ISBN 0-8492-4612-1). R West.

Landor, Walter S. Landor As Critic. Proudfit, Charles L., ed. LC 78-55580. 1979. 19.95x (ISBN 0-8032-3654-9). U of Nebr Pr.

Pinsky, Robert. Landor's Poetry. LC 68-26760. 1968. 7.00x (ISBN 0-226-66942-4). U of Chicago Pr.

Sidgwick, J. B. The Shorter Poems of Walter Savage Landor. LC 73-13982. 1974. Repr. of 1946 ed. lib. bdg. 10.00 (ISBN 0-8414-7652-7). Folcroft.

Super, Robert H. Walter Savage Landor: A Biography. LC 77-10142. (Illus.). 1977. Repr. of 1954 ed. lib. bdg. 37.25x (ISBN 0-8371-9783-X, SUWL). Greenwood.

Whiting, Lillian. The Florence of Landor. 1905. Repr. 35.00 (ISBN 0-8274-2350-0). R West.

LANDSCAPE
see also Mountains in Literature; Natural Monuments; Nature (Esthetics); Nature in Literature; Sea in Literature

Appleton, Jay H. The Experience of Landscape. LC 73-20899. 293p. 1975. 47.25 (ISBN 0-471-03256-5, Pub. by Wiley-Interscience). Wiley.

Brandon, P. F. & Millman, R. N., eds. Historic Landscapes: Observer's & Recorder's Handbook. 1981. 40.00x (ISBN 0-86127-306-0, Pub. by Avebury Pub England). State Mutual Bk.

Burton, Robert. Exploring Hills & Moors. (Countryside Leisure Ser.). (Illus.). 1978. 9.95 (ISBN 0-7158-0468-5). Charles River Bks.

Countryside Books, ed. Home Landscaping. (Illus.). 144p. 7.95 (ISBN 0-88453-002-7). Berkshire Traveller.

Cozens, Alexander. A New Method of Landscape. LC 76-30518. (Masterpieces of the Illustrated Book Ser.). (Illus.). 1977. pap. 4.95 (ISBN 0-448-22120-9). Paddington.

Dirr, Michael. Manual of Woody Landscape Plants. 2nd ed. (Illus.). 1977. 17.80 (ISBN 0-87563-144-4); pap. text ed. 13.80 (ISBN 0-87563-137-1). Stipes.

Home Landscaping. (Illus.). 1974. pap. 7.95 (ISBN 0-88453-002-7). Countryside Bks.

Litton, R. Burton, Jr., et al. Water & Landscape: An Aesthetic Overview of the Role of Water in the Landscape. LC 74-79147. (Illus.). 314p. 1974. pap. text ed. 15.00 (ISBN 0-912394-10-2). Water Info.

The Man-Made Landscape. (Museums & Monuments Ser.: Vol. XVI). 1978. pap. 15.75 (ISBN 92-3-101455-2, U815, UNESCO). Unipub.

Manwaring, Elizabeth W. Italian Landscape in Eighteenth Century England. LC 66-10419. (Illus.). 1965. Repr. of 1925 ed. 10.00 (ISBN 0-8462-0705-2). Russell.

Manwaring, Elizabeth Wheeler. Italian Landscape in Eighteenth Century England. (Illus.). 243p. 1965. Repr. 25.00x (ISBN 0-7146-2069-6, F Cass Co). Biblio Dist.

Meinig, D. W., ed. The Interpretation of Ordinary Landscapes. (Illus.). 1979. pap. text ed. 6.95 (ISBN 0-19-502536-9). Oxford U Pr.

Monkhouse, F. J. & Hardy, A. V. The Man-Made Landscape. (Illus.). 96p. 1974. text ed. 5.75x (ISBN 0-521-20365-1). Cambridge U Pr.

New American Landscapes. (Illus.). 1973. pap. 1.50 (ISBN 0-89192-018-8). Interbk Inc.

Price, Colin. Landscape Economics. (Illus.). 1979. text ed. 34.00x (ISBN 0-8419-5049-0). Holmes & Meier.

Sugden, D. E. & John, B. S. Glaciers & Landscape: A Geomorphological Approach. LC 76-11014. 1976. 21.95x (ISBN 0-470-15113-7). Halsted Pr.

Tietze, W., ed. Man-Made Landscape. 100p. 1975. pap. text ed. 24.00 (ISBN 0-08-019667-5). Pergamon.

Tunnard, Christopher. A World with a View: An Inquiry into the Nature of Scenic Values. LC 77-13729. (Illus.). 1978. 19.50x (ISBN 0-300-02157-7). Yale U Pr.

Tuttle, Sherwood D. Landforms & Landscapes. 3rd ed. 160p. 1980. pap. text ed. write for info. (ISBN 0-697-05020-3). Wm C Brown.

Vance, Mary. Landscape, Landscape Architecture & Landscape Gardening: A Selective List of Books. (Architecture Ser.: Bibliography A-197). 61p. 1980. pap. 6.50 (ISBN 0-686-29057-7). Vance Biblios.

Van Dresser, Peter. A Landscape for Humans. LC 72-86154. 1976. 12.00 (ISBN 0-89016-006-6); pap. 6.95 (ISBN 0-89016-005-8). Lightning Tree.

Whitlock, Ralph. Exploring Rivers, Lakes & Canals. (Countryside Leisure Ser.). (Illus.). 1978. 9.95 (ISBN 0-7158-0467-7). Charles River Bks.

LANDSCAPE ARCHITECTURE
see also Decks (Architecture, Domestic); Garden Lighting; Garden Ornaments and Furniture; Garden Walks; Landscape Gardening; Landscape Protection; Parks; Patios; Perennials; Plants, Ornamental; Shrubs; Topiary Work; Trees; Urban Beautification; Woody Plants

Anderson, Paul. Regional Landscape Analysis. LC 80-6837. 1980. pap. 19.50 (ISBN 0-918436-11-7). Environ Des VA.

Arnold, Henry F. Trees in Urban Design. 192p. 1979. text ed. 24.50 (ISBN 0-442-20336-5). Van Nos Reinhold.

Boy Scouts Of America. Landscape Architecture. LC 19-600. (Illus.). 48p. (gr. 6-12). 1969. pap. 0.70x (ISBN 0-8395-3355-1, 3355). BSA.

Brainerd, John W. Working with Nature: A Practical Guide. (Illus.). 550p. 1973. 24.95x (ISBN 0-19-501667-X). Oxford U Pr.

Campbell, Craig S. Water in Landscape Architecture. 1978. 15.95 (ISBN 0-442-21459-6). Van Nos Reinhold.

Carpenter, et al. Plants in the Landscape. 1975. 18.50 (ISBN 0-7167-0778-0). Thomson Pub CA.

Carver, Humphrey. Compassionate Landscape. LC 75-22280. (Illus.). 1975. pap. 7.50 (ISBN 0-8020-6269-5). U of Toronto Pr.

Chang, Ching-Yu, ed. Landscape Architecture. (Stylos: Architecture International Ser.: No. 2). (Illus.). 1979. pap. 18.50 (ISBN 0-89860-030-8). Eastview.

Colloquium on the History of Landscape Architecture, 6 vols. Incl. Vol. 1. The Italian Garden. Coffin, David, ed. LC 72-93722. (Illus.). 114p. 1972; Vol. 2. The Picturesque Garden & Its Influence Outside the British Isles. Pevsner, Nikolaus, ed. LC 74-196954. (Illus.). 1974. o. p. 10.00x (ISBN 0-88402-050-9); Vol. 3. The French Formal Garden. MacDougall, Elisabeth B. & Hazlehurst, F. Hamilton, eds. LC 75-318945. (Illus.). 1974. 12.50x (ISBN 0-88402-052-5); Vol. 4. The Islamic Garden. MacDougall, Elisabeth B. & Ettinghausen, Richard, eds. LC 76-468. (Illus.). 100p. 1976. o. p. 15.00x (ISBN 0-88402-064-9). Ctr Landscape Arch). Dumbarton Oaks.

Colvin, Brenda. Land & Landscape: Evolution, Design & Control. 2nd ed. (Illus.). 1970. 21.00x (ISBN 0-7195-1800-8). Intl Pubns Serv.

Cotton, Lin. All About Landscaping. Ortho Books Editorial Staff, ed. LC 80-66347. (Illus.). 96p. (Orig.). 1981. pap. 4.95 (ISBN 0-917102-87-8). Ortho.

Couston, Brian, ed. Landscape Design with Plants. 470p. 1980. 39.95 (ISBN 0-442-26197-7). Van Nos Reinhold.

Cowell, F. R. The Garden As Fine Art. 1978. 20.00 (ISBN 0-395-27065-0). HM.

Crowe, Sylvia & Miller, Zvi, eds. Shaping Tomorrow's Landscape, 2 vols. Incl. Vol. 1. The Landscape Architect's Role in Conservation. 1964. text ed. 24.00x (ISBN 0-686-22476-0); Vol. 2. The Landscape Architect's Role in the Changing Landscape. 1964. text ed. 32.75 (ISBN 0-686-22477-9). (Illus.). Mouton.

Downing, M. E. Landscape Construction. 247p. 1977. text ed. 22.95x (ISBN 0-419-10890-4, Pub. by E & FN Spon England). Methuen Inc.

Eckbo, Garrett. Urban Landscape Design. (Illus.). 1964. 27.50 (ISBN 0-07-018880-7, P&RB). McGraw.

Eliot, Charles. Charles Eliot, Landscape Architect. facsimile ed. LC 72-190971. (Select Bibliographies Reprint Ser). Repr. of 1902 ed. 60.00 (ISBN 0-8369-5839-X). Arno.

Ferguson, Bruce K. Landscape Literature of the Twentieth Century Books Reviewed in "Landscape Architecture" Magazine, 1910-1979. (Architecture Ser.: Bibliography A-259). 84p. 1980. pap. 9.00 (ISBN 0-686-29058-5). Vance Biblios.

Floyd, John A., Jr. Trees & Shrubs: Ground Covers Vines. LC 79-92605. (Illus.). 256p. 1980. 17.95 (ISBN 0-8487-0512-2). Oxmoor Hse.

A Guide to Estimating Landscape Costs. LC 79-55474. 1979. pap. 19.50 (ISBN 0-918436-09-5). Environ Des VA.

Hannenbaum, L. Landscape Design: A Practical Approach. 1981. text ed. 19.95 (ISBN 0-8359-3934-0); instr's. manual o.p. free (ISBN 0-8359-5578-8). Reston.

Hoover, Norman K. Approved Practices in Beautifying the Home Grounds. 5th ed. (Illus.). (gr. 9-12). 1979. 14.00 (ISBN 0-8134-2042-3, 2042). Interstate.

Ingels, Jack E. Landscaping: Principles & Practices. LC 76-51686. 1978. pap. text ed. 11.24 (ISBN 0-8273-1634-8); instructor's guide 1.60 (ISBN 0-8273-1635-6). Delmar.

--Landscaping Principles & Practices. 1978. 14.95 (ISBN 0-442-23634-4). Van Nos Reinhold.

Jackson, John B. American Space: The Centennial Years, 1865-1876. (Illus.). 256p. 1972. 7.95 (ISBN 0-393-06321-6); pap. 4.95x (ISBN 0-393-09382-4). Norton.

Jakle, John A. & Oliver, Virginia. Past Landscapes: A Bibliography for Historic Preservationists. rev. ed. (Architecture Ser.: Bibliography A-314). 68p. 1980. pap. 7.50 (ISBN 0-686-29063-1). Vance Biblios.

Kerr, Kathleen W., et al. Cost Data for Landscape Construction: March 1981 Edition. rev. ed. (Cost Data for Landscape Construction Ser.). (Illus.). 244p. 1981. pap. 24.95 (ISBN 0-937890-01-4). Kerr Assoc.

Kimball, Theodora, Jr. Forty Years of Landscape Architecture: Professional Papers of Fredrick Law Olmsted, Vol 2 Central Park. Olmsted, Frederick L., Jr., ed. 1973. pap. 5.95 (ISBN 0-262-65006-1). MIT Pr.

Kirby, Rosina G. Mexican Landscape Architecture-from the Street & From Within. LC 72-83818. 167p. 1972. 27.50 (ISBN 0-8165-0327-3). U of Ariz Pr.

Landphair, H. C. & Klatt, F., Jr. Landscape Architecture Construction. 1979. 24.95 (ISBN 0-444-00264-2, North Holland). Elsevier.

Landscape Architecture Magazine. Home Landscape Nineteen Eighty-One. Clay, Grady & Johnson, Norman, eds. (Landscape Architecture Magazine Ser.). 168p. 1981. 7.95 (ISBN 0-07-036193-2). McGraw.

--Landscapes for Living. (Illus.). 1980. 19.95 (ISBN 0-07-036191-6). McGraw.

--Water & Landscape. (Illus.). 1979. 24.50 (ISBN 0-07-036190-8, P&RB). McGraw.

Laurie, Michael. An Introduction to Landscape Architecture. LC 74-3728. (Illus.). 224p. 1975. 27.00 (ISBN 0-444-00146-8, North Holland); pap. text ed. 14.95 (ISBN 0-444-00171-9). Elsevier.
Lees, Carlton B. New Budget Landscaping. LC 78-10546. (Illus.). 1979. 10.95 (ISBN 0-03-016851-1); pap. 5.95 (ISBN 0-03-016846-5). HR&W.
Litton, R. Burton, Jr., et al. Water & Landscape: An Aesthetic Overview of the Role of Water in the Landscape. LC 74-79147. (Illus.). 314p. 1974. pap. text ed. 15.00 (ISBN 0-912394-10-2). Water Info.
Lovejoy, Derek, et al, eds. Spon's Landscape Price Book. 2nd ed. 1981. 35.00x (ISBN 0-686-77445-0, Pub. by E & FN Spon). Methuen Inc.
McCurdy, Dwight R., et al. How to Choose Your Tree: A Guide to Parklike Landscaping in Illinois, Indiana, & Ohio. LC 74-156791. (Illus.). 255p. 1972. 10.00x (ISBN 0-8093-0514-3). S Ill U Pr.
MacDougall, Elisabeth B. & Miller, Naomi. Fons Sapientiae: Garden Fountains in Illustrated Books, Sixteen-Eighteenth Centuries. LC 77-76011. (Illus.). 1977. pap. 5.00x (ISBN 0-88402-073-8, Ctr Landscape Arch). Dumbarton Oaks.
McLaughlin, Charles Capen, ed. The Papers of Frederick Law Olmsted, Vol. 1: The Formative Years, 1822-1852. LC 76-47378. (The Papers of Frederick Law Olmsted Ser). (Illus.). 448p. 1977. 22.50x (ISBN 0-8018-1798-6). Johns Hopkins.
Marlowe, Olwen C. Outdoor Design: A Handbook for the Architect & Planner. (Illus.). 1977. 37.50 (ISBN 0-8230-7405-6, Whitney Lib). Watson-Guptill.
Moffat, Anne & Schiller, Marc. Landscape Design That Saves Energy. LC 80-85098. (Illus.). 224p. 1981. 17.95 (ISBN 0-688-00031-2, Quill); pap. 9.95 (ISBN 0-688-00395-8). Morrow.
Morris, Robert & King County Arts Commision, eds. Earthworks: Land Reclamation As Sculpture. 71p. 1980. pap. text ed. 5.95 (ISBN 0-932216-04-8). Seattle Art.
Munson, Albe E. Construction Design for Landscape Architects. (Illus.). 212p. 1974. 19.95 (ISBN 0-07-044046-8, P&RB). McGraw.
Nathan, Kurt. Basic Site Engineering for Landscape Designers. 1973. pap. text ed. 12.95x (ISBN 0-8422-0354-0). Irvington.
Nelson, William R. Planting Design: A Manual of Theory & Practice. (Illus.). 1979. text ed. 14.00x (ISBN 0-87563-174-6); pap. text ed. 9.00x (ISBN 0-87563-172-X). Stipes.
Newton, Norman T. Design on the Land: The Development of Landscape Architecture. LC 70-134955. (Illus.). 1971. 30.00x (ISBN 0-674-19870-0, Belknap Pr). Harvard U Pr.
Nichols, Frederick D. & Griswold, Ralph E. Thomas Jefferson Landscape Architect. LC 77-10601. (Illus.). 1977. 10.95x (ISBN 0-8139-0603-2). U Pr of Va.
Office Landscaping. 12.00 (ISBN 0-686-05204-8). Busn Pr.
Reimann, et al. Landscape Architecture Uniform National Examination Seminar Leader's Manual. LC 78-55458. 1978. pap. 15.00 (ISBN 0-918436-05-2). Environ Des VA.
--Uniform National Examination in Landscape Architecture: Candidate Review Manual. LC 78-55457. 1978. pap. 25.00 (ISBN 0-918436-04-4). Environ Des VA.
Repton, Humphry. The Art of Landscape Gardening. LC 76-51839. (Illus.). Date not set. Repr. of 1907 ed. 25.00 (ISBN 0-913728-20-9). Theophrastus.
Robinette, Gary O. Landscape Architectural Site Construction Details. LC 76-55519. 1977. pap. 20.00 (ISBN 0-918436-01-X). Environ Des VA.
--Landscape Design & Management for Water Conservation. (Illus.). 96p. 1981. pap. 20.00 (ISBN 0-918436-17-6). Environ Des VA.
--Landscape Planning for Energy Conservation. LC 76-57857. 1977. pap. 20.00 (ISBN 0-918436-03-6). Environ Des VA.
--Off the Board - into the Ground. (Illus.). 1977. plastic comb bdg. 14.95 (ISBN 0-8403-0136-7). Kendall-Hunt.
--Parking Lot Landscape Development. LC 76-55514. (Illus.). 1977. pap. 15.00 (ISBN 0-918436-00-1). Environ Des VA.
--Roofscape. LC 76-57856. 1977. pap. 20.00 (ISBN 0-918436-02-8). Environ Des VA.
Rudman, Jack. Senior Landscape Architect. (Career Examination Ser.: C-1479). (Cloth bdg. avail. on request). pap. 10.00 (ISBN 0-8373-1479-8). Natl Learning.
Rutledge, A. J. Anatomy of a Park Plan: The Essentials of Recreation Area Design. 1971. 22.95 (ISBN 0-07-054347-X, P&RB). McGraw.
Simonds, J. O. Landscape Architecture. 1961. 26.50 (ISBN 0-07-057391-3, P&RB). McGraw.
Smith, Michael A. Landscapes 1975-1979, 2 vols. (Illus.). 1981. Set. 275.00 (ISBN 0-9605646-0-8). Vol. 1, 116pgs (ISBN 0-9605646-1-6). Vol. II, 52pgs (ISBN 0-9605646-2-4). Lodima.
Smith, Ronald C. Landscape Contracting. LC 79-51504. 1979. pap. 15.00 (ISBN 0-918436-07-9). Environ Des VA.
Staff of Center for Landscape Architectural Education & Research, ed. Manual of Site Management. LC 78-55459. (Illus.). 630p. 1981. pap. 49.95 (ISBN 0-918436-16-8). Environ Des VA.
--Manual of Site Management. LC 78-55459. 1978. 85.00 (ISBN 0-918436-06-0). Environ Des VA.
Stevenson, Elizabeth. Park-Maker: A Life of Frederick Law Olmsted. (Illus.). 1977. 19.95 (ISBN 0-02-614440-9, 61444). Macmillan.
Tandy, Clifford. The Landscape of Industry. LC 75-28033. 314p. 1975. 61.95 (ISBN 0-470-84440-X). Halsted Pr.
Tandy, Clifford R., ed. Landscape & Human Life: The Impact of Landscape Architecture Upon Human Activities. 1966. text ed. 36.25x (ISBN 0-686-22440-X). Mouton.
Tobey, G. B. A History of Landscape Architecture. LC 72-87211. 320p. 1973. 25.00 (ISBN 0-444-00131-X, North Holland). Elsevier.
Trained & Sculptured Plants. 1.95 (ISBN 0-686-21132-4). Bklyn Botanic.
Tree & Shrub Forms-Their Landscape Use. 1.95 (ISBN 0-686-21157-X). Bklyn Botanic.
Turner, Richard A. The Vision of Landscape in Renaissance Italy. LC 66-11977. (Illus.). 336p. 1974. 31.00x (ISBN 0-691-03849-X, 319); pap. 7.95 (ISBN 0-691-00307-6, 319). Princeton U Pr.
Untermann, Richard. Principles & Practices of Grading, Drainage & Road Alignment: An Ecological Approach. (Illus.). 1978. ref. ed. 21.95 (ISBN 0-87909-641-1); instrs'. manual avail. Reston.
Vance, Mary. Landscape, Landscape Architecture & Landscape Gardening: A Selective List of Books. (Architecture Ser.: Bibliography A-197). 61p. 1980. pap. 6.50 (ISBN 0-686-29057-7). Vance Biblios.
Weddle, A. E., ed. Landscape Techniques: Incorporating Techniques of Landscape Architecture. 265p. 1980. 35.00 (ISBN 0-442-25627-2). Van Nos Reinhold.
Wolgensinger, Bernard. The Personal Garden: Its Architecture & Design. (Illus.). 164p. 1975. 30.00 (ISBN 0-442-29569-3). Van Nos Reinhold.

LANDSCAPE ARCHITECTURE–EXAMINATION, QUESTIONS, ETC.

Rudman, Jack. Assistant Landscape Architect. (Career Examination Ser.: C-42). (Cloth bdg. avail. on request). pap. 8.00 (ISBN 0-8373-0042-8). Natl Learning.
--Assistant Landscape Engineer. (Career Examination Ser.: C-43). (Cloth bdg. avail. on request). pap. 8.00 (ISBN 0-8373-0043-6). Natl Learning.
--Junior Landscape Architect. (Career Examination Ser.: C-401). (Cloth bdg. avail. on request). pap. 8.00 (ISBN 0-8373-0401-6). Natl Learning.
--Landscape Architect. (Career Examination Ser.: C-2392). pap. 10.00 (ISBN 0-685-60440-3). Natl Learning.
--Senior Landscape Architect. (Career Examination Ser.: C-1479). (Cloth bdg. avail. on request). pap. 10.00 (ISBN 0-8373-1479-8). Natl Learning.

LANDSCAPE ARCHITECTURE–ITALY

Wharton, Edith. Italian Villas & Their Gardens. LC 76-10659. (Architecture & Decorative Arts Ser.). 1976. lib. bdg. 39.50 (ISBN 0-306-70817-5); pap. 8.95 (ISBN 0-306-80048-9). Da Capo.

LANDSCAPE ARCHITECTURE AS A PROFESSION

Frazier, John & Julin, Richard. Your Future in Landscape Architecture. LC 67-14523. (Careers in Depth Ser). (Illus.). (gr. 8-12). 1967. PLB 5.97 (ISBN 0-8239-0043-6). Rosen Pr.
Griswold, Ralph E. Opportunities in Landscape Architecture. 2nd ed. LC 78-58665. (Illus.). (gr. 8 up). 1978. lib. bdg. 6.60 (ISBN 0-685-92739-3); pap. 4.95 (ISBN 0-8442-6477-6). Natl Textbk.

LANDSCAPE DRAWING

Blake, Wendon. Landscape Drawing. (Artist's Painting Library Ser.). (Illus.). 80p. (Orig.). 1981. pap. 5.95 (ISBN 0-8230-2593-4). Watson-Guptill.
Harris, John. A Catalogue of British Drawings for Architecture, Decoration, Sculpture & Landscape Gardening: 1550-1900, in American Collections. LC 75-93124. (Illus.). 1971. lib. bdg. 98.00x (ISBN 0-8398-0766-X). Irvington.
Kemnitz, Milton N. Ann Arbor Now & Then: A Book of Personal Drawings. 4th ed. (Illus.). 120p. 1972. 10.00 (ISBN 0-89824-010-7). Trillium Pr.
Kenfield, Warren G. Wild Gardener in the Wild Landscape. (Illus.). 1972. 12.00 (ISBN 0-02-847800-2). Hafner.
La Dell, Edwin. Your Book of Landscape Drawing. (Your Book Ser.). (Illus.). 62p. 1964. 7.95 (ISBN 0-571-05888-4, Pub. by Faber & Faber). Merrimack Bk Serv.
Perard, Victor. Sketching Landscape. (Grosset Art Instruction Ser.: Vol. 25). pap. 2.95 (ISBN 0-448-00534-4). G&D.
Pitz, Henry C. Drawing Outdoors. 1977. pap. 7.95 (ISBN 0-8230-1417-7). Watson-Guptill.
Rembrandt, Van Rijn. Rembrandt Landscape Drawings. (Dover Art Library). (Illus.). 64p. (Orig.). 1981. pap. price not set (ISBN 0-486-24160-2). Dover.
Robinette, Gary O., ed. Evergreen Form Studies. (Illus.). 320p. 1981. pap. 20.00 (ISBN 0-918436-18-4). Environ Des VA.
Zaidenberg, Arthur. How to Draw Landscapes, Seascapes & Cityscapes. LC 63-10467. (How to Draw Ser). (Illus.). (gr. 5-10). 1963. PLB 8.79 (ISBN 0-200-00074-8, B38431, AbS-J). Har-Row.

LANDSCAPE GARDENING

see also Espaliers; Grounds Maintenance; Landscape Architecture

Ahern, John H. Miniature Landscape Modelling. (Illus.). 136p. 7.50x (ISBN 0-85344-104-9). Intl Pubns Serv.
Arco Editorial Board. Gardener--Assistant Gardener. 2nd ed. LC 75-27588. (Orig.). 1975. pap. 8.00 (ISBN 0-668-01340-0, 1340). Arco.
Bailey, Leo L. A Step-by-Step Guide to Landscaping & Gardening. LC 74-84421. 1974. 10.00 (ISBN 0-682-48084-3, Banner). Exposition.
Ballard, Edward B., et al, eds. A Technical Glossary of Horticultural & Landscape Terminology. LC 78-165521. 1971 (ISBN 0-686-26652-8). text ed. 9.95 (ISBN 0-935336-00-1); tchrs' ed. 6.00 (ISBN 0-935336-00-1). Horticult Research.
Bright, James L. Outdoor Recreation Projects. LC 77-28410. 1978. 13.95 (ISBN 0-912336-62-5); pap. 6.95 (ISBN 0-912336-63-3). Structures Pub.
Carpenter, et al. Plants in the Landscape. 1975. 18.50 (ISBN 0-7167-0778-0). Thomson Pub CA.
Carpenter, Philip L., et al. Plants in the Landscape. LC 74-32292. (Illus.). 1975. text ed. 24.95x (ISBN 0-7167-0778-0). W H Freeman.
Clouston, Brian, ed. Landscape Design with Plants. (Illus.). 1977. 50.00x (ISBN 0-434-36650-1). Intl Ideas.
Cotton, Lin. All About Landscaping. Ortho Books Editorial Staff, ed. LC 80-66347. (Illus.). 96p. (Orig.). 1981. pap. 4.95 (ISBN 0-917102-87-8). Ortho.
Couston, Brian, ed. Landscape Design with Plants. 470p. 1980. 39.95 (ISBN 0-442-26197-7). Van Nos Reinhold.
Crockett, James U. Landscape Gardening. (Encyclopedia of Gardening Ser). (Illus.). 1971. 12.95 (ISBN 0-8094-1089-3); lib. bdg. avail. (ISBN 0-685-04842-X). Time-Life.
--Landscape Gardening. LC 64-140420. (Time-Life Encyclopedia of Gardening). (Illus.). (gr. 6 up). 1971. lib. bdg. 11.97 (ISBN 0-8094-1090-7, Pub. by Time-Life). Silver.
Crowe, Sylvia. Garden Design. 1959. 8.95 (ISBN 0-8208-0043-0). Hearthside.
DeGraaf, Richard M. & Witman, Gretchin M. Trees, Shrubs, & Vines for Attracting Birds: A Manual for the Northeast. LC 78-19698. (Illus.). 14.00x (ISBN 0-87023-266-5). U of Mass Pr.
Dieckelmann, John & Schuster, Robert M. Natural Landscaping: Designing with Native Plant Communities. (Illus.). 264p. 1982. 18.95 (ISBN 0-07-016813-X, P&RB). McGraw.
Downing, Andrew J. Rural Essays. Curtis, George W., ed. LC 69-13713. (Architecture & Decorative Art Ser). 640p. 1978. Repr. of 1854 ed. lib. bdg. 39.50 (ISBN 0-306-71035-8). Da Capo.
--A Treatise on the Theory & Practice of Landscape Gardening Adapted to North America. (Illus.). Date not set. Repr. of 1875 ed. 20.00 (ISBN 0-913728-23-3). Theophrastus.
DuPont, Elizabeth N. Landscaping with Native Plants in the Middle-Atlantic Region. Williams, Wick, ed. LC 78-21194. (Illus.). 1978. 6.95 (ISBN 0-940540-02-9). Brandywine Conserv.
Earle, Alice M. Old Time Gardens, Newly Set Forth. LC 68-31219. (Illus.). 1968. Repr. of 1901 ed. 22.00 (ISBN 0-8103-3429-1). Gale.
Eckbo, Garrett. Art of Home Landscaping. 1956. 16.95 (ISBN 0-07-018878-5, P&RB). McGraw.
--Home Landscape: The Art of Home Landscaping. rev. & enl. ed. (Illus.). 1978. 13.95 (ISBN 0-07-018879-3, P&RB). McGraw.
--Landscape We See. 1967. 28.50 (ISBN 0-07-018882-3, P&RB). McGraw.
Favretti, Rudy J. & Favretti, Joy P. Landscapes & Gardens for Historic Buildings: A Handbook for Reproducing & Creating Authentic Landscape Settings. LC 78-17200. (Illus.). 1979. pap. 10.00 (ISBN 0-910050-34-1). AASLH.
Felice, Raymond. Successful Landscaping. LC 77-16624. (Illus.). 1978. 13.95 (ISBN 0-912336-55-2); pap. 6.95 (ISBN 0-912336-56-0). Structures Pub.
Fortune. Guide to Landscaping. LC 64-472. (Illus.). 1963. pap. 1.95 (ISBN 0-8200-0403-0). Great Outdoors.
Givens, Harold. Landscape It Yourself. LC 76-14436. (Illus.). 1977. pap. 8.95 (ISBN 0-15-147689-6, Harv). HarBraceJ.
Grounds, Roger. Ornamental Grasses. 216p. 1981. 16.95 (ISBN 0-442-24707-9). Van Nos Reinhold.
Guide to Landscape & Lawn Care. (McGraw-Hill Paperbacks Home Improvement Ser.). (Illus.). 112p. 1980. pap. 3.95 (ISBN 0-07-045972-X). McGraw.
Guide to Landscape & Lawn Care. (McGraw-Hill Paperbacks Home Improvement Ser.). (Illus.). 112p. 1980. pap. 3.95 (ISBN 0-07-045972-X). McGraw.
Halfacre, R. Gordon & Shawcroft, Anne. Carolina Landscape Plants. (Illus.). write for info. (ISBN 0-916822-00-1). Sparks Pr.
Hannebaum, Leroy G. Landscape Operations: Management, Methods, & Materials. (Illus.). 1980. text ed. 17.95 (ISBN 0-8359-3937-5); instrs' manual avail. Reston.
Hazlehurst, F. Hamilton. Gardens of Illusion: The Genius of Andre Le Nostre. (Illus.). 448p. 1981. 39.95 (ISBN 0-8265-1209-7). Vanderbilt U Pr.
Helmer, Jane. Pictorial Library of Landscape Plants. 3rd ed. LC 81-82113. (Northern Hardiness Zones One Through Six: Vol. 1). (Illus.). 352p. 1981. text ed. 65.00 (ISBN 0-89484-027-4). Merchants Pub.
House & Garden, ed. Twentieth Century Decorating Architecture & Gardens. LC 80-12593. (Illus.). 320p. 1980. 34.95 (ISBN 0-03-047581-3); pre-Jan. 29.95 (ISBN 0-686-77496-5). HR&W.
Ingels, Jack E. Landscaping Principles & Practices. 1978. 14.95 (ISBN 0-442-23634-4). Van Nos Reinhold.
Ireys, Alice R. How to Plan & Plant Your Own Property. LC 67-19689. (Illus.). 1967. pap. 7.95 (ISBN 0-688-06831-6, Barrows & Co). Morrow.
--Small Gardens for City & Country: A Guide to Designing & Planting Your Own Property. (Illus.). 1978. (Spec); pap. 8.95 (ISBN 0-13-813055-8, Spec). P-H.
Landscape Design for the Middle East: Proceedings. 1979. pap. 15.95 (ISBN 0-900630-68-X, Pub. by RIBA). Intl Schol Bk Serv.
Landscape Planning for Small Gardens. pap. 7.50x (ISBN 0-392-06854-0, ABC). Sportshelf.
Landscaping Your Home. LC 73-91440. (Family Guide Book Ser). (Illus.). 1974. pap. 2.95 (ISBN 0-8487-0285-9). Oxmoor Hse.
Larke, Stan. Gardening in Towns & Cities. 160p. 1975. pap. 3.95 (ISBN 0-07-082247-6, GB). McGraw.
Lees, Carlton B. New Budget Landscaping. LC 78-10546. (Illus.). 1979. 10.95 (ISBN 0-03-016851-1); pap. 5.95 (ISBN 0-03-016846-5). HR&W.
McDonald, Elvin. Easy Gardens: A Weed Eater Book. LC 77-89551. (Illus.). 1978. 8.95 (ISBN 0-916752-20-8). Dorison Hse.
Nelson, William R. Planting Design: A Manual of Theory & Practice. (Illus.). 1979. text ed. 14.00x (ISBN 0-87563-174-6); pap. text ed. 9.00x (ISBN 0-87563-172-X). Stipes.
New, Earl H. The New Look in Home Landscaping. 1975. pap. 12.00 (ISBN 0-686-19191-9). Thomson Pub CA.
Newcomb, Duane. Mobile Home Gardening Manual. (Illus.). 3.95 (ISBN 0-87593-030-1). Trail-R.
Perry, Robertc. Trees & Shrubs for Dry California Landscapes. (Illus.). 184p. 1981. 24.50 (ISBN 0-9605988-0-4); text ed. 24.50 (ISBN 0-9605988-1-2). Land Design.
Prendergast, Curtis. Easy Gardens. Time-Life Books, ed. (Encyclopedia of Gardening Ser.). (Illus.). 1979. 12.95 (ISBN 0-8094-2637-4). Time-Life.
Repton, Humphry. The Art of Landscape Gardening. LC 76-51839. (Illus.). Date not set. Repr. of 1907 ed. 25.00 (ISBN 0-913728-20-9). Theophrastus.
Robinette, Gary O. Off the Board - into the Ground. (Illus.). 1977. plastic comb bdg. 14.95 (ISBN 0-8403-0136-7). Kendall-Hunt.
--Plant Form Studies: Design Characteristics of Plant Materials. LC 80-68358. (Illus.). 244p. pap. text ed. 19.50 (ISBN 0-918436-12-5). Environ Des VA.

Rose, Graham. Landscape with Weeds. (Illus.). 160p. 1980. 14.95 (ISBN 0-241-10353-3, Pub. by Hamish Hamilton England). David & Charles.
Schmutz, Ervin M., ed. Landscaping with Native Arizona Plants. LC 73-76309. (Illus.). 1973. pap. 4.95x (ISBN 0-8165-0385-0). U of Ariz Pr.
Smith, Ken. Western Home Landscaping. LC 78-51897. (Illus.). 1978. pap. 7.95 (ISBN 0-89586-003-1). H P Bks.
Spangler, Ronald L. & Ripperda, Jerry. Landscape Plants: For Central & Northeastern U.S. Including Lower & Eastern Canada. LC 77-86016. 1977. pap. text ed. 16.95x (ISBN 0-8087-4532-8). Burgess.
Sunset Editors. Landscaping & Garden Remodeling. LC 77-82872. (Illus.). 80p. 1978. pap. 3.95 (ISBN 0-376-03455-6, Sunset Bks.). Sunset-Lane.
Vance, Mary. Landscape, Landscape Architecture & Landscape Gardening: A Selective List of Books. (Architecture Ser.: Bibliography A-197). 61p. 1980. pap. 6.50 (ISBN 0-686-29057-7). Vance Biblios.
Watkins, John V. & Sheehan, Thomas J. Florida Landscape Plants: Native & Exotic. rev. ed. LC 75-22365. (Illus.). 1975. 11.95 (ISBN 0-8130-0529-9). U Presses Fla.
Weber, Nelva M. How to Plan Your Own Home Landscape. LC 75-33535. (Illus.). 1979. pap. 10.95 (ISBN 0-672-52599-2). Bobbs.
--How to Plan Your Own Home Landscape. LC 75-33535. (Illus.). 320p. 1976. 13.95 (ISBN 0-685-62625-3). Bobbs.
Whitcomb, Carl E. Know It & Grow It: A Guide to the Identification & Use of Landscape Plants in the Southern States. rev. ed. (Illus.). 1976. 19.95x (ISBN 0-686-22363-2). Whitcomb Pubns.
Wilkes, Lyall. John Dobson, Architect & Landscape Gardener. 144p. 1980. 30.00 (ISBN 0-85362-181-0). Routledge & Kegan.
Workman, Richard W. Growing Native: Native Plants for Landscape Use in Coastal South Florida. (Illus.). 137p. 1980. pap. 9.95 (ISBN 0-916224-60-0). Banyan Bks.

LANDSCAPE GARDENING–HISTORY

Colvin, Brenda. Land & Landscape: Evolution, Design & Control. 2nd ed. (Illus.). 1971. 28.00 (ISBN 0-7195-1800-8). Transatlantic.

LANDSCAPE GARDENING–GREAT BRITAIN

Blomfield, Reginald T. Formal Garden in England. 3rd ed. LC 77-181912. (BCL Ser. I). Repr. of 1901 ed. 15.00 (ISBN 0-404-00898-4). AMS Pr.
Clifford, J. Capability Brown. (Clarendon Biography Ser.). (Illus.). 1974. pap. cancelled (ISBN 0-912728-84-1). Newbury Bks.
Manwaring, Elizabeth W. Italian Landscape in Eighteenth Century England. LC 66-10419. (Illus.). 1965. Repr. of 1925 ed. 10.00 (ISBN 0-8462-0705-2). Russell.
Manwaring, Elizabeth Wheeler. Italian Landscape in Eighteenth Century England. (Illus.). 243p. 1965. Repr. 25.00x (ISBN 0-7146-2069-6, F Cass Co). Biblio Dist.
Sanecki, K. Humphrey Repton. (Clarendon Biography Ser.). 1974. pap. 2.50 (ISBN 0-912728-73-6). Newbury Bks.

LANDSCAPE GARDENING–JAPAN

Japanese Gardens & Miniature Landscapes. 1.95 (ISBN 0-686-21133-2). Bklyn Botanic.

LANDSCAPE IN ART

Barcham, William L. The Imaginary View Scenes of Antonio Canaletto. LC 76-23603. (Outstanding Dissertations in the Fine Arts - 18th Century). (Illus.). 1977. Repr. of 1974 ed. lib. bdg. 63.00 (ISBN 0-8240-2677-2). Garland Pub.
Brommer, Gerald F. Landscapes. Horn, George F., ed. LC 76-50508. (Insights to Art Ser.). (Illus.). 1977. 10.50 (ISBN 0-87192-086-7). Davis Mass.
Carli, Enzo. The Landscape in Art: From Three Thousand B.C. to Today. Cinotti, Mia, ed. Fitton, Mary, tr. from Ital. LC 80-81667. Orig. Title: Il Paesaggio. (Illus.). 320p. 1980. 35.00 (ISBN 0-688-03678-3). Morrow.
Novak, Barbara. Nature & Culture: American Landscape & Painting 1825-1875. (Out-of-Ser. Paperback). (Illus.). 336p. 1981. pap. 18.95 (ISBN 0-19-502935-6). Oxford U Pr.
Russell, Ronald. Guide to British Topographical Prints. LC 79-53737. (Illus.). 1979. 32.00 (ISBN 0-7153-7810-4). David & Charles.
Stein, Roger B. Susquehanna: Images of the Settled Landscape. Bothwell, Lawrence B., ed. LC 81-50681. (Illus.). 150p. 1981. pap. 10.00 (ISBN 0-937318-08-6, Pub. by Roberson Ctr). Pub Ctr Cult Res.

LANDSCAPE IN LITERATURE

see Nature in Literature

LANDSCAPE PAINTING

see also Barbizon School

Battarbee, Rex & Battarbee, Bernice. Modern Aboriginal Paintings. (Illus.). 1972. 5.00x (ISBN 0-85179-269-3). Verry.
Bazarov, Konstantine. Landscape Painting. (Illus.). 224p. (YA) 1981. 25.00 (ISBN 0-7064-1230-3, Mayflower Bks). Mayflower Bks.
Blake, Wendon. Landscape Painting in Oil. (Illus.). 152p. 1976. 19.95 (ISBN 0-8230-2609-4). Watson-Guptill.
Born, Wolfgang. American Landscape Painting: An Interpretation. LC 71-100222. Repr. of 1948 ed. lib. bdg. 27.50x (ISBN 0-8371-3253-3, BOAL). Greenwood.
Carlson, John F. Carlson's Guide to Landscape Painting. (Illus.). 144p. 1973. pap. 4.00 (ISBN 0-486-22927-0). Dover.
Cikovsky, Nicolai, Jr. The Life & Work of George Inness. LC 76-23605. (Outstanding Dissertations in the Fine Arts - American). (Illus.). 1977. Repr. of 1965 ed. lib. bdg. 70.00 (ISBN 0-8240-2679-9). Garland Pub.
Clark, Kenneth. Landscape into Art. rev. & enl. ed. (Icon Editions). (Illus.). 1978. pap. 8.95 (ISBN 0-06-430088-9, IN-88, HarpT). Har-Row.
--Landscape into Art. rev. & enl. ed. LC 75-23876. (Illus.). 320p. 1976. 19.95 (ISBN 0-06-010781-2, HarpT). Har-Row.
Czestochowski, Joseph. The American Landscape Tradition: A Study & Gallery of Paintings. Nelson, Cyril I., ed. (Illus.). 160p. 1982. 30.00 (ISBN 0-525-93206-2); pap. 20.75 (ISBN 0-525-47674-1). Dutton.
De Reyna, Rudy. Magic Realist Landscape Painting: Techniques in Oil, Watercolor, Egg Tempera, & Acrylic. (Illus.). 168p. 1976. 19.95 (ISBN 0-8230-2955-7). Watson-Guptill.
Grant, Maurice H. A Dictionary of British Landscape Painters: From the 16th to the 20th Century. (Illus.). 236p. 1970. 40.00x (ISBN 0-85317-250-1). Intl Pubns Serv.
Home Book of the Picturesque: Or American Scenery, Art, & Literature. LC 67-10179. 1967. Repr. of 1852 ed. 20.00x (ISBN 0-8201-1029-9). Schol Facsimiles.
Irving, Washington, et al. A Landscape Book, by American Artists & American Authors. Weinberg, H. Barbara, ed. LC 75-28865. (Art Experience in Late 19th Century America Ser.: Vol. 1). (Illus.). 1977. Repr. of 1868 ed. lib. bdg. 44.00 (ISBN 0-8240-2225-4). Garland Pub.
Jeffares, Bo. Landscape Painting. LC 78-25573. (Mayflower Gallery). (Illus.). 1979. 12.50 (ISBN 0-8317-5413-3). Smith Pubs.
Kautzky, Ted. Painting Trees & Landscapes in Watercolor. 1981. pap. 9.95 (ISBN 0-442-21918-0). Van Nos Reinhold.
Lassiter, Barbara Babcock. American Wilderness: The Hudson River School of Painting. LC 73-13089. (gr. 7 up). 1978. 8.95a (ISBN 0-385-08192-8); PLB (ISBN 0-385-04376-7). Doubleday.
Lindquist-Cock, Elizabeth. The Influence of Photography on American Landscape Painting, 1839-1880. LC 76-23608. (Outstanding Dissertations in the Fine Arts - 2nd Series - American). (Illus.). 1977. Repr. of 1967 ed. lib. bdg. 48.00 (ISBN 0-8240-2680-2). Garland Pub.
McShine, Kynaston, ed. Natural Paradise: Painting in America 1800-1950. LC 76-23513. (Illus.). 1977. 19.95 (ISBN 0-87070-505-9, Pub. by Museum Mod Art). NYGS.
Nevius, Blake. Cooper's Landscapes: An Essay on the Picturesque Vision. LC 74-77730. (Quantum Bks). 1976. 15.75x (ISBN 0-520-02751-5). U of Cal Pr.
Novak, Barbara. Nature & Culture: American Landscape & Painting Eighteen Twenty-Five to Eighteen Seventy-Five. (Illus.). 1980. 35.00 (ISBN 0-19-502606-3). Oxford U Pr.
--Nature & Culture: American Landscape & Painting 1825-1875. (Out-of-Ser. Paperback). (Illus.). 336p. 1981. pap. 18.95 (ISBN 0-19-502935-6). Oxford U Pr.
Pellen, John C. Acrylic Landscape Painting. (Illus.). 160p. 1976. pap. 9.95 (ISBN 0-8230-0051-6). Watson-Guptill.
Pleasants, Jacob H. Four Late Eighteenth Century Anglo-American Landscape Painters. LC 78-128288. (Essay Index Reprint Ser). 1943. 16.00 (ISBN 0-8369-1894-0). Arno.
R. W. Norton Art Gallery. Louisiana Landscape & Genre Paintings of the 19th Century. LC 81-50951. (Illus.). 48p. 1981. pap. 5.75x (ISBN 0-913060-19-4). Norton.
Reff, Theodore, ed. Exhibitions of Barbizon & Landscape Art. (Modern Art in Paris 1855 to 1900 Ser.). 449p. 1981. lib. bdg. 44.00 (ISBN 0-8240-4737-0). Garland Pub.
Richard Clague: 1821-1873. LC 74-25157. (Illus.). 128p. 1974. pap. 5.00x (ISBN 0-685-57002-9, New Orleans Museum of Art). Norton Art.
Rowbotham, Theodore. The Art of Landscape Painting with a Detailed Analysis of the Colours to Use in Watercolouring. 1979. deluxe ed. 39.35 (ISBN 0-930582-21-7). Gloucester Art.
Rowbotham, Thomas. The Art of Landscape Painting in Watercolors. LC 77-94619. 1979. Repr. of 1865 ed. lib. bdg. 10.00 (ISBN 0-89341-351-8). Longwood Pr.
Sawin, Martica. Wolf Kahn: Landscape Painter. LC 81-51081. (Illus.). 96p. 1981. 14.95 (ISBN 0-8008-8420-5); pap. 8.95 (ISBN 0-8008-8421-3). Taplinger.
Sheaks, Barclay. Drawing & Painting the Natural Environment. LC 74-78390. (Illus.). 136p. 1974. 13.95 (ISBN 0-87192-060-3). Davis Mass.
Springfield Museum of Fine Arts. Landscapes in Recent Paintings. (Illus.). 1981. write for info. (ISBN 0-916746-05-4). Springfield Lib & Mus.
Szabo, Zoltan. Landscape Painting in Watercolor. 1971. 19.95 (ISBN 0-8230-2620-5). Watson-Guptill.
Telepy, Katalin. Landscapes in the Hungarian National Gallery. LC 75-331273. (Illus.). 108p. 1973. 9.00x (ISBN 0-8002-0842-0). Intl Pubns Serv.

LANDSCAPE PAINTING–TECHNIQUE

Ballinger, Harry R. Painting Landscapes. new enl. ed. (Illus.). 192p. 1973. 19.95 (ISBN 0-8230-3651-0). Watson-Guptill.
Battershill, Norman. Painting Landscapes in Oils. (Leisure Arts Painting Ser.). (Illus.). 32p. 1980. pap. 2.50 (ISBN 0-8008-6202-3, Pentalic). Taplinger.
Betts, Edward. Creative Landscape Painting. (Illus.). 1978. 17.95 (ISBN 0-8230-1080-5). Watson-Guptill.
Blake, Wendon. Complete Guide to Landscape Painting in Oil. rev. ed. (Illus.). 192p. (Orig.). 1981. 22.50 (ISBN 0-8230-0808-8). Watson-Guptill.
--Landscapes in Acrylic. (Artist's Painting Library). (Illus.). 80p. 1980. pap. 5.95 (ISBN 0-8230-2599-3). Watson-Guptill.
--Landscapes in Watercolor. (The Artist's Painting Library). (Illus.). 1979. pap. 5.95 (ISBN 0-8230-2621-3). Watson-Guptill.
Blake, Wendon & Cherepov, George. Landscapes in Oil. (The Artist's Painting Library). (Illus.). 1979. pap. 5.95 (ISBN 0-8230-2598-5). Watson-Guptill.
Borgman, Harry. Landscape Painting with Markers. (Illus.). 1979. pap. text ed. 9.95 (ISBN 0-8230-2636-1). Watson-Guptill.
Burridge, Jan. Painting Landscapes in Watercolour. (The Leisure Arts Painting Ser.). 1981. pap. 2.50 (ISBN 0-8008-6198-1, Pentalic). Taplinger.
Caddell, Foster. Keys to Successful Landscape Painting. (Illus.). 160p. 1976. 19.95 (ISBN 0-8230-2579-9). Watson-Guptill.
Carrington, Joanna. Landscape Painting for Beginners. LC 79-84664. (Start to Paint Ser.). (Illus.). 1979. pap. 3.95 (ISBN 0-8008-4543-9, Pentalic). Taplinger.
Hayes, Colin. A Practical Guide to Landscape Painting. 120p. 1981. 15.95 (ISBN 0-8230-0322-1). Watson-Guptill.
Hill, Adrian. How to Paint Landscapes & Seascapes. (Illus.). 1964. 5.95 (ISBN 0-7137-0182-X, Pub by Blandford Pr England). Sterling.
Jones, Franklin. Painting Nature: Solving Landscape Problems. LC 77-93216. (Illus.). 1978. 16.95 (ISBN 0-89134-013-0, Pub. by Van Nostrand Reinhold). North Light Pub.
Kinstler, Everett R. Painting Faces, Figures & Landscapes. 144p. 1981. 22.50 (ISBN 0-8230-3625-1). Watson-Guptill.
Landscapes - Seascapes. treasure trove bdg. 4.47 (ISBN 0-685-07361-0); pap. 1.00 (ISBN 0-685-07362-9). Borden.
Meyer, Susan E., ed. Twenty Landscape Painters & How They Work. (Illus.). 1977. 21.95 (ISBN 0-8230-5490-X). Watson-Guptill.
Parramon, J. M. Landscape Paintings in Oils: How to Set About It. (Improve Your Painting & Drawing Ser.). (Illus.). 128p. (Orig.). 1980. pap. 12.50x (ISBN 0-85242-707-7). Intl Pubns Serv.
Pellew, John C. Painting Maritime Landscapes. (Illus.). 1979. pap. 9.95 (ISBN 0-8230-3696-0). Watson-Guptill.
Richmond, Leonard. Landscape Painting in Oils. (Grosset Art Instruction Ser.: Vol. 37). pap. 2.95 (ISBN 0-448-00546-8). G&D.
--Landscape Painting Step-by-Step. (Illus.). 1978. pap. 9.95 (ISBN 0-8230-2616-7). Watson-Guptill.
Savage, Ernest. Painting Landscape in Pastel. (Illus.). 1978. pap. 9.95 (ISBN 0-8230-3652-9). Watson-Guptill.
Schmid, Richard. Richard Schmid Paints Landscapes: Creative Techniques in Oil. (Illus.). 144p. 1975. 18.50 (ISBN 0-8230-4862-4). Watson-Guptill.
Strisik, Paul & Movalli, Charles. The Art of Landscape Painting. (Illus.). 144p. (gr. 9-12). 1980. 21.95 (ISBN 0-8230-0273-X). Watson-Guptill.
Waugh, Coulton. Landscape Painting with a Knife. (Illus.). 1979. pap. 9.95 (ISBN 0-8230-2633-7). Watson-Guptill.

LANDSCAPE PAINTING–CHINA

Contag, Victoria. Zwei Meister Chinesischer Landschhafts Malerei. 1955. 15.00 (ISBN 0-685-57326-5). Paragon.
Lee, Sherman E. Chinese Landscape Painting. rev. ed. (Icon Editions). (Illus.). 1971. pap. 5.95 (ISBN 0-06-430010-2, IN-10, HarpT). Har-Row.
Maeda, Robert J. Two Sung Texts on Chinese Painting & the Landscape Styles of the 11th & 12th Centuries. LC 77-94706. (Outstanding Dissertations in the Fine Arts Ser.). 1978. lib. bdg. 27.50 (ISBN 0-8240-3238-1). Garland Pub.
Sullivan, Michael. Chinese Landscape Painting in the Sui & T'ang Dynasties. (Illus.). 1980. 38.50 (ISBN 0-520-03558-5). U of Cal Pr.
--Symbols of Eternity: The Art of Landscape Painting in China. LC 78-65393. (Illus.). 1979. 18.50 (ISBN 0-8047-1025-2). Stanford U Pr.

LANDSCAPE PAINTING–GREAT BRITAIN

Barrell, J. The Dark Side of the Landscape. LC 78-72334. (Illus.). 1980. 34.00 (ISBN 0-521-22509-4). Cambridge U Pr.
Vandervell, Anthony & Coles, Charles. Game & the English Landscape. LC 80-5358. (Illus.). 160p. 1980. 40.00 (ISBN 0-670-33391-3, Debrett's Peerage). Viking Pr.
Wark, Robert R. British Landscape Drawings & Watercolors, 1750-1850: Twenty-Four Examples from the Huntington Collection. LC 81-121. (Illus.). 51p. 5.00 (ISBN 0-87328-116-0). Huntington Lib.

LANDSCAPE PAINTING–ITALY

Manwaring, Elizabeth W. Italian Landscape in Eighteenth Century England. LC 66-10419. (Illus.). 1965. Repr. of 1925 ed. 10.00 (ISBN 0-8462-0705-2). Russell.
Manwaring, Elizabeth Wheeler. Italian Landscape in Eighteenth Century England. (Illus.). 243p. 1965. Repr. 25.00x (ISBN 0-7146-2069-6, F Cass Co). Biblio Dist.
Turner, Richard A. The Vision of Landscape in Renaissance Italy. LC 66-11977. (Illus.). 336p. 1974. 31.00x (ISBN 0-691-03849-X, 319); pap. 7.95 (ISBN 0-691-00307-6, 319). Princeton U Pr.

LANDSCAPE PAINTING–NETHERLANDS

Czobor, A. Dutch Landscapes. (Illus.). 1967. 8.00x (ISBN 963-13-7044-5). Intl Pubns Serv.
Stechow, Wolfgang. Dutch Landscape Painting of the Seventeenth Century. LC 81-66148. (Cornell Paperbacks; Cornell-Phaidon Bks; Landmarks in Art History). (Illus.). 504p. 1981. pap. 9.95 (ISBN 0-8014-9228-9, Pub. by Phaidon England). Cornell U Pr.
--Dutch Landscape Painting of the Seventeenth Century. (Illus.). 494p. 1981. pap. 9.95 (ISBN 0-8014-9228-9). Cornell U Pr.

LANDSCAPE PHOTOGRAPHY

see Photography–Landscapes

LANDSCAPE PROTECTION

see also Landscape Architecture; Monuments–Preservation; Regional Planning

Brainerd, John W. Working with Nature: A Practical Guide. (Illus.). 550p. 1973. 24.95x (ISBN 0-19-501667-X). Oxford U Pr.
Hasler, A. D., ed. Coupling of Land & Water Systems. LC 74-8931. (Ecological Studies: Vol. 10). (Illus.). xviii, 336p. 1975. 31.30 (ISBN 0-387-06707-8). Springer-Verlag.
Hutnik, Russell & Davis, Grant, eds. Ecology & Reclamation of Devastated Land, 2 vols. LC 76-122849. (Illus.). 1040p. 1973. Vol. 1. 77.00x (ISBN 0-677-15580-8); Vol. 2. 77.00x (ISBN 0-677-15590-5); Set. 125.50x (ISBN 0-677-15600-6). Gordon.
Jackson, J. B. The Necessity for Ruins, & Other Topics. LC 79-23212. 1980. lib. bdg. 10.00x (ISBN 0-87023-291-6); pap. 5.50x (ISBN 0-87023-292-4). U of Mass Pr.
Tandy, Clifford R., ed. Landscape & Human Life: The Impact of Landscape Architecture Upon Human Activities. 1966. text ed. 36.25x (ISBN 0-686-22440-X). Mouton.
Zube, E. H., et al, eds. Landscape Assessment: Values, Perceptions & Resources. LC 74-13331. (Community Development Ser: Vol. 11). 367p. 1975. 40.00 (ISBN 0-87933-147-X). Dh&R.

LANDSLIDES

Annual Summary of Information on Natural Disasters: Earthquakes, Tsunamis, Volcanic Eruptions, Landslides, Avalanches, Vol. 9, 1974. (Illus.). 99p. 1976. pap. 7.00 (ISBN 92-3-001369-2, U30, UNESCO). Unipub.
Coates, Donald R., ed. Reviews in Engineering Geology, Vol. 3: Landslides. LC 62-51690. (Illus.). 1977. pap. 27.00x (ISBN 0-8137-4103-3). Geol Soc.
Shreve, Ronald L. Blackhawk Landslide. LC 68-29062. (Special Paper: No. 108). (Illus., Orig.). 1968. pap. 6.00x (ISBN 0-8137-2108-3). Geol Soc.
Voight, B. Rockslides & Avalanches: Engineering Sites, Pt. 2. (Developments in Geotechnical Engineering Ser.: Vol. 14b). Date not set. 117.00 (ISBN 0-444-41508-4). Elsevier.
--Rockslides & Avalanches: Natural Phenomena, Pt. 1. (Development in Geotechnical Engineering Ser.: Vol. 14a). 1978. 117.00 (ISBN 0-444-41507-6). Elsevier.

LANE, FITZHUGH, 1804-1865
Wilmerding, John. Fitz Hugh Lane, 1804-1865: American Marine Painter. (Illus.). 1967. 6.50 (ISBN 0-8446-1480-7). Peter Smith.
LANE, HOMER TYRRELL, 1876-1925
Bazeley, E. T. Homer Lane & the Little Commonwealth. LC 69-19624. 1969. pap. 1.95 (ISBN 0-8052-0221-8). Schocken.
Perry, L., ed. Bertrand Russell, A. S. Neill, Homer Lane, W. H. Kilpatrick: Four Progressive Educators. 1968. pap. text ed. 1.95x (ISBN 0-02-975150-0). Macmillan.
LANE, JOSEPH, 1801-1881
Hendrickson, James E. Joe Lane of Oregon: Machine Politics & the Sectional Crisis, 1849-1861. (Western Americana Ser: No. 16). (Illus.). 1967. 22.50x (ISBN 0-300-00547-4). Yale U Pr.
LANE, LUNSFORD, 1803-
Hawkins, William G. Lunsford Lane: Or, Another Helper from North Carolina. LC 76-91260. Repr. of 1863 ed. 14.25x (ISBN 0-8371-2059-4, Pub. by Negro U Pr). Greenwood.
LANE, ROSE (WILDER), 1887-1968
MacBride, Roger L. The Lady & the Tycoon. LC 72-78366. 1973. 5.95 (ISBN 0-87004-234-3). Caxton.
LANFRANC, ABP. OF CANTERBURY, 1005-1089 DECRETA
Gibson, Margaret. Lanfranc of Bec. 1978. 40.00x (ISBN 0-19-822462-1). Oxford U Pr.
Lanfranc. The Letters of Lanfranc, Archbishop of Canterbury. Clover, Helen & Gibson, Margaret, eds. (Oxford Medieval Texts Ser.). (Illus.). 218p. 1979. text ed. 59.00x (ISBN 0-19-822235-1). Oxford U Pr.
Macdonald, Allan J. Lanfranc, a Study of His Life, Work & Writing. LC 80-2223. Date not set. Repr. of 1926 ed. 37.50 (ISBN 0-404-18768-4). AMS Pr.
LANG, ANDREW, 1844-1912
Falconer, C. M. The Writings of Andrew Lang. LC 73-13899. 1894. lib. bdg. 6.50 (ISBN 0-8414-4156-1). Folcroft.
Green, Roger L. Andrew Lang. 1946. Repr. lib. bdg. 20.00 (ISBN 0-8414-4679-2). Folcroft.
Grierson, Herbert. Lang, Lockhart & Biography. LC 73-14791. 1834. Repr. lib. bdg. 6.00 (ISBN 0-8414-4444-7). Folcroft.
Langstaff, Eleanor D. Andrew Lang. (English Authors Ser.: No. 241). 1978. 12.50 (ISBN 0-8057-6719-3). Twayne.
Ormerod, James. Poetry of Andrew Lang. LC 74-28468. 1943. lib. bdg. 8.50 (ISBN 0-8414-6502-9). Folcroft.
LANG, FRITZ, 1890-
Armour, Robert. Fritz Lang. (Theatrical Art Ser.). 1978. 12.50 (ISBN 0-8057-9259-7). Twayne.
Eisner, Lotte. Fritz Lang. LC 76-41081. (Illus.). 1977. 25.00 (ISBN 0-19-519912-X). Oxford U Pr.
Jenkins, Stephen. Fritz Lang. (Illus.). 168p. 1981. 24.95 (ISBN 0-85170-108-6, BFI); pap. 14.95 (ISBN 0-85170-109-4). NY Zoetrope.
Kaplan, E. Ann. Fritz Lang: A Guide to References & Resources. (Scholarly Reference Publications Ser.). 1981. lib. bdg. 45.00 (ISBN 0-8161-8035-0). G K Hall.
Weinberg, Herman G. Fritz Lang. (Film Ser.). 1979. lib. bdg. 59.95 (ISBN 0-8490-2923-6). Gordon Pr.
LANGBEIN, JULIUS, 1851-1907
Stern, Fritz R. The Politics of Cultural Despair: A Study in the Rise of the Germanic Ideology. (California Library Reprint Ser.). 1974. 26.75x (ISBN 0-520-02643-8); pap. 7.95x (ISBN 0-520-02626-8). U of Cal Pr.
LANGDON, JOHN, 1741-1819
Mayo, Lawrence S. John Langdon of New Hampshire. LC 75-120884. (American Bicentennial Ser). 1970. Repr. of 1937 ed. 15.00 (ISBN 0-8046-1277-3). Kennikat.
LANGE, DOROTHEA
Lange, Dorothea, photos by. Dorothea Lange. (Aperture History of Photography Ser.: Vol. 17). (Illus.). 96p. 1981. 9.95 (ISBN 0-89381-078-9). Aperture.
Meltzer, Milton. Dorothea Lange: A Photographer's Life. LC 78-5509. 384p. 1978. 15.00 (ISBN 0-374-14323-4). FS&G.
Ohrn, Karin B. Dorothea Lange & the Documentary Tradition. LC 79-20841. (Illus.). 1980. 27.50x (ISBN 0-8071-0551-1). La State U Pr.
LANGERHANS, ISLANDS OF
see Pancreas
LANGLAND, WILLIAM, 1330-1400
Aers, David. Chaucer, Langland & the Creative Imagination. 1980. 25.00x (ISBN 0-7100-0351-X). Routledge & Kegan.
Anderson, Judith H. The Growth of a Personal Voice: Piers Plowman & "the Faerie Queene". LC 75-43300. 1976. 19.50x (ISBN 0-300-02000-7). Yale U Pr.
Blanch, Robert J., ed. Style & Symbolism in Piers Plowman: A Modern Critical Anthology. LC 69-20115. (Illus., Orig.). 1969. 11.00x (ISBN 0-87049-093-1); pap. text ed. 4.95x (ISBN 0-87049-101-6). U of Tenn Pr.
Chadwick, Dorothy. Social Life in the Days of Piers Plowman. LC 73-77669. 1969. Repr. of 1922 ed. 7.00 (ISBN 0-8462-1342-7). Russell.
Chambers, R. W. Poets & Their Critics: Langland & Milton. 1942. lib. bdg. 6.50 (ISBN 0-685-10478-8). Folcroft.
--Text of Piers Plowman. LC 72-195253. lib. bdg. 6.50 (ISBN 0-8414-3015-2). Folcroft.
Chambers, R. W. & Grattan, J. H. The Text of Piers Plowman. 1978. Repr. of 1931 ed. lib. bdg. 8.50 (ISBN 0-8495-0825-8). Arden Lib.
Coghill, Nevill. Pardon of Piers Plowman. LC 73-4674. 1945. lib. bdg. 6.50 (ISBN 0-8414-3350-X). Folcroft.
--The Pardon of Piers Plowman. 1978. Repr. of 1946 ed. lib. bdg. 8.50 (ISBN 0-8495-0907-6). Arden Lib.
Colaianne, A. J. Piers Plowman: An Annotated Bibliography of Editions & Criticism, 1550-1977. LC 78-7631. (Garland Reference Library of the Humanities: Vol. 121). 1978. lib. bdg. 18.00 (ISBN 0-8240-9822-6). Garland Pub.
Connolly, Terence L. An Introduction to Chaucer & Langland. LC 76-40470. 1925. lib. bdg. 12.50 (ISBN 0-8414-3586-3). Folcroft.
Dunning, T. P. Piers Plowman: An Interpretation of the A-Text. LC 72-186986. 1937. lib. bdg. 25.00 (ISBN 0-8414-3876-5). Folcroft.
Dunning, Thomas P. Piers Plowman: An Interpretation of the A-Text. LC 73-95095. 1971. Repr. of 1937 ed. lib. bdg. 15.00x (ISBN 0-8371-3088-3, DUPP). Greenwood.
Fowler, David C. Piers the Plowman: Literary Relations of the A & B Texts. LC 61-11575. (Publications in Language & Literature: No. 16). 260p. 1961. 10.50 (ISBN 0-295-73879-0). U of Wash Pr.
Hort, Greta. Piers Plowman & Contemporary Religious Thought. LC 72-193685. lib. bdg. 15.00 (ISBN 0-8414-5129-X). Folcroft.
Iijima, Ikuzo. Langland & Chaucer. LC 75-170059. Repr. of 1925 ed. 19.50 (ISBN 0-404-03482-9). AMS Pr.
--Langland & Chaucer: A Study of the Two Types of Genius in English Poetry. 1978. Repr. lib. bdg. 25.00 (ISBN 0-8492-1219-7). R West.
Jusserand, Jean A. Les Anglais au Moyen Age: L'Epopee Mystique in William Langland. 275p. 1980. Repr. of 1893 ed. lib. bdg. 30.00 (ISBN 0-8495-2755-4). Arden Lib.
--Piers Plowman: A Contribution to the History of English Mysticism. Richards, Marion & Richards, Elise, trs. LC 65-13959. (Illus.). 1965. Repr. of 1894 ed. 10.00 (ISBN 0-8462-0548-3). Russell.
Kane, George & Donaldson, E. Talbot, eds. Piers Plowman: The B Version. (Piers Plowman: The Three Versions Ser). 681p. 1975. text ed. 72.50x (ISBN 0-485-13502-7, Athlone Pr). Humanities.
Manley, J. M. Piers Plowman & Its Sequence. LC 74-31198. 1926. lib. bdg. 6.00 (ISBN 0-8414-5982-7). Folcroft.
Mitchell, A. G. Lady Meed - the Art of 'Piers Plowman. facs. ed. LC 72-148891. (Select Bibliographies Reprint Ser). 1956. 10.00 (ISBN 0-8369-5679-6). Arno.
Murtaugh, Daniel M. Piers Plowman & the Image of God. LC 77-25544. 1978. 8.50 (ISBN 0-8130-0534-5). U Presses Fla.
Robertson, Durant W., Jr. & Huppe, Bernard F. Piers Plowman & Scriptural Tradition. 1970. lib. bdg. 14.50x (ISBN 0-374-96859-4). Octagon.
Smith, A. H. Piers Plowman & the Pursuit of Poetry. 1950. lib. bdg. 7.50 (ISBN 0-8414-7704-3). Folcroft.
Taitt, Peter S. Incubus & Ideal: Ecclesiastical Figures in Chaucer & Langland. (Salzburg Studies in English Literature, Elizabethan & Renaissance Studies Ser.: No. 44). 228p. (Orig.). 1975. pap. text ed. 25.00x (ISBN 0-391-01544-3). Humanities.
LANGLEY, THOMAS, BP. OF DURHAM, d. 1437
Storey, Robert L. Thomas Langley & the Bishopric of Durham. (Church Historical Society: No. 80). 1961. 11.50x (ISBN 0-8401-5080-6). Allenson Breckinridge.
LANGMUIR, IRVING, 1881-1957
Rosenfeld, A. The Quintescence of Irving Langmuir. 1966. 15.00 (ISBN 0-08-011049-5); pap. 7.50 (ISBN 0-08-011048-7). Pergamon.
LANGO (AFRICAN TRIBE)
Curley, Richard T. Elders, Shades, & Women: Ceremonial Change in Lango, Uganda. LC 70-634788. 1973. 19.50x (ISBN 0-520-02149-5). U of Cal Pr.
Hayley, Thomas T. Anatomy of Lango Religion & Groups. LC 74-100263. Repr. of 1947 ed. 13.75x (ISBN 0-8371-2871-4, Pub. by Negro U Pr). Greenwood.
Tosh, John. Clan Leaders & Colonial Chiefs in Lango: The Political History of an East African Stateless Society, 1800-1939. (Studies in African Affairs). (Illus.). 1979. 52.50x (ISBN 0-19-822711-6). Oxford U Pr.
LANGTON, STEPHEN, CARDINAL, d. 1228
Powicke, F. M. Stephen Langton. Repr. of 1927 ed. lib. bdg. 10.00x (ISBN 0-678-08060-7). Kelley.
LANGTRY, LILLIE (EMILY CHARLOTTE LE BRETON), 1852-1929
Birkett, Jeremy & Richardson, John. Lillie Langtry: Her Life in Words & Pictures. (Illus.). 64p. 1980. pap. 3.95 (ISBN 0-7137-1073-X, Pub. by Blandford Pr England). Sterling.
Langtry, Lillie. The Days I Knew. LC 79-8067. Repr. of 1925 ed. 29.50 (ISBN 0-404-18378-6). AMS Pr.
LANGUAGE, INTERNATIONAL
see Language, Universal
LANGUAGE, LEGAL
see Law-Language
LANGUAGE, PHILOSOPHY OF
see Languages-Philosophy
LANGUAGE, PSYCHOLOGY OF
see Psycholinguistics
LANGUAGE, UNIVERSAL
see also ALGOL (Computer Program Language)
Collinson, William E. & Morris, A. V. Indication: A Study of Demonstratives, Articles & Other Indicators. 1937. pap. 6.00 (ISBN 0-527-00821-4). Kraus Repr.
Fraser, Russell. The Language of Adam: On the Limits and Systems of Discourse. LC 77-3528. 288p. 1977. 17.50x (ISBN 0-231-04256-6). Columbia U Pr.
Greenberg, Joseph H., et al, eds. Universals of Human Language, 4 vols. Incl. Vol. I. Method & Theory. 15.00x (ISBN 0-8047-0965-3); Vol. II. Phonology. 25.00x (ISBN 0-8047-0966-1); Vol. III. Word Structure. 25.00x (ISBN 0-8047-0968-8); Vol. IV. Syntax. 25.00x (ISBN 0-8047-0969-6). LC 77-89179. 1978. Set. 90.00x (ISBN 0-8047-1012-0). Stanford U Pr.
Guerard, Albert L. A Short History of the International Language Movement. LC 78-14124. 1979. Repr. of 1922 ed. 21.50 (ISBN 0-88355-796-7). Hyperion Conn.
Knowlson, James R. Universal Language Schemes in England & France 1600-1800. LC 73-81759. (Romance Ser: No. 29). 328p. 1975. 25.00x (ISBN 0-8020-5296-7). U of Toronto Pr.
Pei, Mario. One Language for the World & How to Achieve It. LC 68-56449. 1958. 10.00x (ISBN 0-8196-0218-3). Biblo.
Salmon, Vivian. The Works of Francis Lodwick: A Study of His Writings in the Intellectual Context of the Seventeenth Century. (The Classics of Linguistics Ser.). (Illus.). 263p. 1972. text ed. 24.00x (ISBN 0-582-52494-6). Longman.
Wainscott, Elisabeth. Uni- the New International Language. (Illus.). 346p. 1974. 10.95 (ISBN 0-912904-00-3); pap. 5.95 (ISBN 0-912904-01-1). Uniline Div.
Weilgart, W. John. The Language of Space (Dedicated to Cosmic-Conscious Youth) 4th ed. (Illus.). 342p. 1974. pap. 8.00 (ISBN 0-912038-08-X). Cosmic Comm.
LANGUAGE ACQUISITION
see Children-Language
LANGUAGE AND LANGUAGES
Here are entered works on language in general, works on the origin and history of language, and surveys of languages; Works dealing with the scientific study of human speech, including phonetics, phonemics, morphology and syntax, are entered under Linguistics. Works on the philosophy and psychology of language are entered under Languages-Philosophy, and Languages-Psychology, respectively.
see also Bilingualism; Children-Language; Communication; Conversation; Formal Languages; Judgment; Languages-Philosophy; Linguistic Research; Linguistics; Literature; Mathematical Linguistics; Multilingualism; Philology; Programming Languages (Electronic Computers); Psycholinguistics; Rhetoric; Semantics; Semantics (Philosophy); Sociolinguistics; Speech; Translating and Interpreting; Voice; Writing
also names of particular languages or groups of cognate languages, e.g. English Language, Semitic Languages
ACTFL Nineteen Seventy Nine: Abstracts of Presented Papers. (Language in Education Ser.: No. 25). 1980. pap. 6.50x (ISBN 0-87281-113-1). Ctr Appl Ling.
Adler, Mortimer. Some Questions About Language. LC 75-1221. 203p. 1976. 12.95 (ISBN 0-87548-320-8). Open Court.
Akmajian, Adrian, et al. Linguistics: An Introduction to Language & Communication. (Illus.). 1979. text ed. 17.50x (ISBN 0-262-01058-5); pap. 9.95x (ISBN 0-262-51019-7). MIT Pr.
Allen, H. A. & Borge, E. Focusing on Language. 1975. pap. 4.50 (ISBN 0-685-52283-0). Tech Pub.
Anderson, W. L. & Stageberg, N. C., eds. Introductory Readings on Language. 4th ed. LC 74-16229. 1975. pap. text ed. 12.95 (ISBN 0-03-089578-2, HoltC); instructor's manual avail., write for info. (ISBN 0-03-089660-6). HR&W.
Barfield, Owen. Owen Barfield & the Origin of Language. 1979. pap. 1.95 (ISBN 0-916786-42-0). St George Bk Serv.
Bauer, F. L. & Samelson, K., eds. Language Hierarchies & Interfaces. (Lectures in Computer Science Ser.: Vol. 46). 1976. soft cover 19.40 (ISBN 0-387-07994-7). Springer-Verlag.
Beattie, James. Theory of Language, Pts. 1 & 2. LC 78-147953. Repr. of 1788 ed. 36.50 (ISBN 0-404-08201-7). AMS Pr.
Behrens, Sophia. Directory of Foreign Language Service Organizations. (Language in Education Ser.: No. 1). 1978. pap. 4.25x (ISBN 0-87281-077-1). Ctr Appl Ling.
Bell & Howell Audio-Visual Products Division. Master It! with the Language Master. LC 78-52959. 1978. pap. 5.95 (ISBN 0-8224-4409-7). Pitman Learning.
Benjamin, Robert L. Semantics & Language Analysis. 128p. pap. text ed. 3.95x (ISBN 0-8290-0330-4). Irvington.
Berry, Jack, ed. Language & Education in the Third World. (International Journal of Thesociology of Language: No. 8). 1976. pap. 20.00x (ISBN 90-2797-851-4). Mouton.
Bickerton, Derek. Roots of Language. (Illus.). 300p. 1981. 24.95x (ISBN 0-89720-044-6). Karoma.
Bishop, G. Reginald, Jr., ed. Culture in Language & Learning. Incl. An Anthropological Concept of Culture. Friedl, Ernestine; Language As Culture. Welmers, William E; Teaching of Classical Cultures. Kibbe, Doris E; Teaching of Western European Cultures. Wade, Ira; Teaching of Slavic Cultures. Twarog, Leon I. 1960. pap. 7.95x (ISBN 0-915432-60-9). NE Conf Teach Foreign.
Black, M. & Smalley, W. A., eds. On Language, Culture & Religion: In Honor of Eugene A. Nida. (Approaches to Semiotics Ser: No. 56). (Illus.). 386p. 1974. text ed. 45.90x (ISBN 90-2793-236-0). Mouton.
Black, Max. Critical Thinking. 2nd ed. 1952. text ed. 16.95 (ISBN 0-13-194092-9). P-H.
Blau, Ulrich. Dreiwertige Logik der Sprache Ihre Syntax, Semantik und Anwendung in der Sprachanalyse. (Grundlagen der Kommunikation). 1977. 40.00x (ISBN 3-11-006989-X). De Gruyter.
Bloom, Lois, ed. Readings in Language Development. LC 77-10717. (Communications Disorders Ser.). 1978. text ed. 22.50 (ISBN 0-471-08221-X). Wiley.
Bloomfield, L. Language. 1963. text ed. 15.95 (ISBN 0-03-004885-0, HoltC). HR&W.
Bobrinskoy, George V., ed. Languages & Areas: Studies Presented to George V. Bobrinskoy. 1969. 10.50x (ISBN 0-226-06271-6). U of Chicago Pr.
Bolinger, Dwight & Sears, Donald A. Aspects of Language. 3rd ed. 352p. 1981. pap. text ed. 9.95 (ISBN 0-15-503872-9). HarBraceJ.
Born, Warren C., ed. Language: Acquisition, Application, Appreciation. Incl. Language Acquisition. Cintas, Pierre F; Language Application. Elaster, Kenneth; Language Appreciation. Bure, Germaine. 1977. pap. 7.95x (ISBN 0-915432-77-3). NE Conf Teach Foreign.
Brerewood, Edward. Enquieries Touching the Diversity of Languages & Religions Through the Cheif Parts of the World. (Bound with French translation). 1972. Repr. 55.00x (ISBN 0-8002-1267-3). Intl Pubns Serv.
Brod, Richard I., ed. Language Study for the Nineteen Eighties: Reports of the MLA-ACLS Language Task Forces. LC 79-87582. 106p. 1980. pap. 8.50x (ISBN 0-87352-088-2). Modern Lang.
Brod, Richard I. & Neel, Jasper P., eds. Profession 77. 60p. 1977. pap. 4.00x (ISBN 0-87352-312-1). Modern Lang.
Brown, Roger. Words & Things. LC 58-9395. 1968. 15.95 (ISBN 0-02-904800-1); pap. text ed. 7.95 (ISBN 0-02-904810-9). Free Pr.
Burling, R. Man's Many Voices: Language in Its Cultural Context. LC 78-111258. 1970. text ed. 11.95 (ISBN 0-03-081001-9, HoltC). HR&W.
Burnet, James L. Origin & Progress of Language, 6 vols. (Linguistics 13th-18th Century Ser.). (Fr.). 1974. Repr. of 1792 ed. lib. bdg. 792.50x set, order nos. are 71-5032 to 71-5037 (ISBN 0-8287-0154-7). Clearwater Pub.
Burnett, James. Of the Origin & Progress of Language, 6 vols. 1975. Repr. 302.00 set (ISBN 3-4870-5432-9). Adler.
Carroll, John B. Language & Thought. (Orig.). 1964. pap. 7.95 ref. ed. (ISBN 0-13-522706-2). P-H.
Cassirer, Ernst. Language & Myth. 6.75 (ISBN 0-8446-1820-9). Peter Smith.

--Language & Myth. Langer, Susanne K., tr. 1946. pap. 2.00 (ISBN 0-486-20051-5). Dover.

--Philosophy of Symbolic Forms, Vol. 1, Language. Manheim, Ralph, tr. 1965. pap. 5.95 (ISBN 0-300-00037-5, Y146). Yale U Pr.

Chao, Yuen-Ren. Language & Symbolic Systems. (Orig.). 1968. 29.95 (ISBN 0-521-04616-5); pap. 10.95x (ISBN 0-521-09457-7, 457). Cambridge U Pr.

Chapey, Roberta. Language Intervention Strategies in Adult Aphasia. (Illus.). 381p. 1981. 32.00 (ISBN 0-686-69565-8, 1511-7). Williams & Wilkins.

Chaplin, A. The Romance of Language. 1920. 12.50 (ISBN 0-8274-3302-6). R West.

Chaplin, Alethea. The Romance of Language. 1978. Repr. of 1920 ed. lib. bdg. 25.00 (ISBN 0-89760-106-8, Telegraph). Dynamic Learn Corp.

Chase, Stuart. Tyranny of Words. LC 38-27108. 1959. pap. 4.95 (ISBN 0-15-692394-7, HB26, Harv). HarBraceJ.

Chase, Stuart & Chase, Marian T. Power of Words. LC 54-5980. 1954. 9.95 (ISBN 0-15-173487-9). HarBraceJ.

Clark, Virginia P., et al, eds. Language: Introductory Readings. 3rd ed. 650p. 1981. pap. 9.95x (ISBN 0-312-46796-6). St Martin.

The Colloquial Faculty for Languages. 1886. 15.00 (ISBN 0-8274-2073-0). R West.

Conference on Communication, Language & Sex, 1st Annual. Communication, Language, & Sex: Proceedings. Berryman, Cynthia & Eman, Virginia, eds. 1980. pap. text ed. 13.95 (ISBN 0-88377-136-5). Newbury Hse.

Cooper, Robert L. Language Attitudes, II. (International Journal of the Sociology of Language Ser.: No. 6). (Illus.). 1975. pap. 20.00x (ISBN 90-2797-974-X). Mouton.

Cooper, Robert L., ed. Language Attitudes, I. (International Journal of the Sociology of Language Ser.: No. 3). 1974. pap. 20.00x (ISBN 90-2797-645-7). Mouton.

Costello, Nancy A. Katu Vocabulary. 1971. pap. 2.00x (ISBN 0-88312-778-4). Summer Inst Ling.

Cressey, William W. & Napoli, Donna J., eds. Linguistic Symposium on Romance Languages, No. 9. (Orig.). 1981. pap. text ed. 8.95x (ISBN 0-87840-081-8). Georgetown U Pr.

Cripwell, Kenneth. Language. Yapp, Malcolm, et al, eds. (World History Ser.). (Illus.). (gr. 10). 1980. Repr. of 1977 ed. lib. bdg. 5.95 (ISBN 0-89908-146-0); pap. text ed. 1.95 (ISBN 0-89908-121-5). Greenhaven.

Dale, Philip S. Language Development: Structure & Function. 2nd ed. LC 75-43640. 358p. 1976. pap. text ed. 12.95 (ISBN 0-03-089705-X, HoltC). HR&W.

Davies, Alan, ed. Problems of Language & Learning. 1975. text ed. 12.95x (ISBN 0-435-10190-0). Heinemann Ed.

Denis, Ernest. La Boheme Depius la Montagne-Blanche, 2 vols. 1981. Repr. Set. lib. bdg. 59.00 (ISBN 0-686-71907-7). Scholarly.

Denton, David E. Language of Ordinary Experience. LC 72-100580. 1970. 5.00 (ISBN 0-8022-2312-5). Philos Lib.

De Villiers, Jill G. & De Villiers, Peter A. Language Acquisition. 1978. 12.50x (ISBN 0-674-50931-5). Harvard U Pr.

Diack, Hunter. Language for Teaching. 1967. 4.75 (ISBN 0-8022-0392-2). Philos Lib.

Diamond, Arthur S. History & Origin of Language. 1965. pap. 1.95 (ISBN 0-8065-0127-8, 207). Citadel Pr.

DiBlasi, Augustine. Word Derivation Made Simple: Did You Know - Word Derivation Made Simple. 1980. 6.95 (ISBN 0-87164-043-0). William-F.

Dobson, M. J. & Hughes, P. J. In Other Words. (Winston Mine Editions). 1967. text ed. 4.96 (ISBN 0-685-33412-0). HR&W.

Dodge, James W., ed. Other Words, Other Worlds: Language in Culture. 1972. pap. 7.95x (ISBN 0-915432-72-2). NE Conf Teach.

Dorion, Henri, ed. Les Noms De Lieux et Le Contact Des Langues. 1972. 12.00x (ISBN 2-7637-6642-0, Pub by Laval). Intl Schol Bk Serv.

Dressler, Wolfgang & Wodak-Leodolter, Ruth. Language Death. 1977. 17.25x (ISBN 90-279-7704-6). Mouton.

Ducrot, Oswald & Todorov, Tzvetan. Encyclopedic Dictionary of the Sciences of Language. Porter, Catherine, tr. LC 78-23901. 1979. text ed. 19.95x (ISBN 0-8018-2155-X). Johns Hopkins.

Duke, Richard. Gaming: The Future's Language. LC 74-14522. 223p. 1974. 13.50 (ISBN 0-470-22405-3). Halsted Pr.

Eckenstein, Lina. Spell of Words: Studies in Language Bearing on Custom. 1932. 8.25 (ISBN 0-8274-3491-X). R West.

Eckman, Fred R. & Hastings, Ashley, eds. Studies in First & Second Language Acquisition. 1979. pap. text ed. 13.95 (ISBN 0-88377-119-5). Newbury Hse.

Elliot, Alison J. Child Language. (Cambridge Textbooks in Linguistics). 180p. 1981. text ed. 29.95 (ISBN 0-521-22518-3); pap. text ed. 8.95 (ISBN 0-521-29556-4). Cambridge U Pr.

Elton, William. Aesthetics & Language. 1967. 5.75 (ISBN 0-8022-0451-1). Philos Lib.

Elton, William, ed. Aesthetics & Language. 186p. 1970. 24.00x (ISBN 0-631-04610-0, Pub. by Basil Blackwell). Biblio Dist.

Ervin-Tripp, Susan M. Language Development. (Master Lectures on Developmental Psychology: Manuscript No. 1336). 4.00 (ISBN 0-912704-24-1). Am Psychol.

Esau, Helmut, et al. Language & Communication. 1980. pap. 8.75 (ISBN 0-686-70677-3). Hornbeam Pr.

Ewton, Ralph W., Jr. & Ornstein, Jacob. Studies in Language & Linguistics, 1969-70. pap. 5.00 (ISBN 0-87404-019-1). Tex Western.

Falk, Julia S. Linguistics & Language: A Survey of Basic Concepts & Implications. 2nd ed. LC 77-22927. 1978. pap. text ed. 15.95 (ISBN 0-471-02529-1). Wiley.

Fasold, Ralph & Shuy, Roger, eds. Analyzing Variation in Language. LC 75-15973. 327p. 1975. pap. 6.95 (ISBN 0-87840-207-1). Georgetown U Pr.

Faust, Norma W. Gramatica Cocama: Lecciones para el Apprendizaje del Idoma Cocama. (Peruvian Linguistic Ser.: No. 6). 1972. pap. 3.00x (ISBN 0-88312-766-0). Summer Inst Ling.

Ferguson, C. A., et al, eds. Language in the U. S. A. 650p. Date not set. price not set (ISBN 0-521-23140-X); pap. price not set (ISBN 0-521-29834-2). Cambridge U Pr.

Ferguson, Charles A. Language Structure & Language Use: Essays by Charles A. Ferguson. Dil, A. S., ed. LC 79-150322. (Language Science & National Development Ser). 1971. 15.00x (ISBN 0-8047-0780-4). Stanford U Pr.

Firth, J. R. The Tongues of Man. 1937. 20.00 (ISBN 0-8274-3639-4). R West.

Fisher, Dexter, ed. Minority Language & Literature: Retrospective & Perspective. 160p. 1977. pap. 6.50x (ISBN 0-87352-350-4). Modern Lang.

Fishman, Joshua A., ed. Advances in Language Planning. LC 73-85456. (Contributions to the Sociology of Language Ser.: Vol. 5). 590p. (Orig.). 1974. pap. text ed. 37.25x (ISBN 90-2792-618-2). Mouton.

Florian, David J. The Phenomenon of Language: Tabula Latina. (Illus.). 243p. (Orig.). (gr. 6-9). 1979. 5.50x (ISBN 0-88334-124-7). Ind Sch Pr.

Flowers, Ann M. Big Book of Language Through Sounds. 2nd ed. LC 79-92515. 1980. pap. text ed. 6.95x (ISBN 0-8134-2114-4, 2114). Interstate.

Fodor, Jerry & Katz, J. J. Structure of Language. 1964. 20.95 (ISBN 0-13-854703-3). P-H.

Fowler, Roger, et al. Language & Control. (Illus.). 1979. 22.50x (ISBN 0-7100-0288-2). Routledge & Kegan.

Friedrich, Johannes. Extinct Languages. 12.00 (ISBN 0-8022-0546-1). Philos Lib.

Fromkin, Victoria A. & Rodman, R. An Introduction to Language. 2nd ed. LC 77-16616. 1978. pap. text ed. 15.95 (ISBN 0-03-089947-8, HoltC). HR&W.

Fry, I. A Key to Language. 1926. 12.50 (ISBN 0-8274-2649-6). R West.

Gaeng, Paul A. Introduction to the Principles of Language. 1971. pap. text ed. 16.50 scp (ISBN 0-06-042218-1, HarpC). Har-Row.

Gans, Eric. The Origin of Language: A Formal Theory of Representation. LC 80-19653. 1981. 19.95x (ISBN 0-520-04202-6). U of Cal Pr.

Gere, Anne R. & Smith, Eugene. Attitudes, Language, & Change. LC 79-20099. (Orig.). 1979. pap. 6.65 (ISBN 0-8141-0217-4). NCTE.

Gleason, Henry A., Jr. Introduction to Descriptive Linguistics. rev. ed. LC 61-8588. 1961. text ed. 14.95 (ISBN 0-03-010465-3, HoltC); wkbk. 9.95 (ISBN 0-03-005585-7). HR&W.

Gochnour, Elizabeth A. & Smith, Theresa B. Language of Life. 2nd ed. (Illus.). 1981. pap. 6.50x (ISBN 0-8134-2162-4, 2162). Interstate.

Goldberg, Isaac. Wonder of Words: An Introduction to Language for Every Man. LC 74-164294. 1971. Repr. of 1938 ed. 26.00 (ISBN 0-8103-3777-0). Gale.

Goodenough, Ward. Language, Culture & Society. 2nd ed. 1981. 9.95 (ISBN 0-8053-3341-X); pap. 5.95 (ISBN 0-686-69658-1). Benjamin-Cummings.

Goshgarian, Gary, ed. Exploring Language. 2nd ed. 457p. 1980. pap. text ed. 9.95 (ISBN 0-316-32148-6); tchr's manual free (ISBN 0-316-32149-4). Little.

Green, Judith & Wallat, Cynthia, eds. Ethnography & Language in Educational Settings, Vol. 5. (Advances in Discourse Processes Ser.). 368p. 1981. text ed. 29.50 (ISBN 0-89391-035-X); pap. 16.50 (ISBN 0-89391-078-3). Ablex Pub.

Greenberg, Joseph H. Language Universals: With Special References to Feature Hierarchies. (Janua Linguarum Ser. Minor: No. 59). (Orig.). 1966. pap. text ed. 15.75x (ISBN 0-686-22444-2). Mouton.

Greenberg, Joseph H., ed. Universals of Language. 2nd rev. ed. 1966. pap. 7.95x (ISBN 0-262-57008-4). MIT Pr.

Gregor, D. B. Friulan: Language & Literature. (Illus.). 1975. 15.00 (ISBN 0-902675-39-7). Oleander Pr.

Gregory, Michael & Carroll, Susanne. Language & Situation: Language Varieties & Their Social Contexts. (Language & Societay Ser). 1978. 12.50x (ISBN 0-7100-8756-X); pap. 7.95 (ISBN 0-7100-8773-X). Routledge & Kegan.

Grimes, Barbara F. Ethnologue. 338p. 1978. pap. 9.60 (ISBN 0-88312-909-4); microfiche 3.40 (ISBN 0-88312-597-8). Summer Inst Ling.

Guillaume, Gustave. Langage et Science Du Langage. (Fr). 1969. pap. 7.00x (ISBN 2-7637-6574-2, Pub. by Laval). Intl Schol Bk Serv.

Haas, Mary R. Prehistory of Languages. LC 76-75689. (Janua Linguarum, Ser. Minor: No. 57). 1978. pap. text ed. 14.50 (ISBN 90-279-0681-5). Mouton.

Hall, S., et al, eds. Culture, Media, Language. 311p. 1981. text ed. 28.00x (ISBN 0-09-142070-9, Hutchinson U Lib); pap. text ed. 8.75x (ISBN 0-09-142071-7, Hutchinson U Lib). Humanities.

Harnad, Stevan, et al, eds. Origins & Evolution of Language & Speech, Vol. 280. (Annals of the New York Academy of Sciences). 914p. 1976. 59.00x (ISBN 0-89072-026-6). NY Acad Sci.

Harris, James. Hermes: Or a Philosophical Inquiry Concerning Universal Grammar. 1871. 75.00 (ISBN 0-8274-2490-6). R West.

Hatten, John T. & Hatten, Pequetti. Natural Language. 1975. pap. 5.95 (ISBN 0-88450-002-0, 2026-B). Communication Skill.

Haugen, E., et al, eds. Minority Language Today. 224p. 1981. 22.50x (ISBN 0-85224-421-5, Pub. by Edinburgh U Pr Scotland). Columbia U Pr.

Hayden, Donald E., et al, eds. Classics in Linguistics. LC 67-11571. 1968. 10.00 (ISBN 0-8022-0694-8). Philos Lib.

Hayes, Curtis W., et al. ABC's of Languages & Linguistics. LC 77-75915. 1977. pap. text ed. 9.95 (ISBN 0-88499-066-4). Inst Mod Lang.

Heatherington, M. How Language Works. 288p. 1980. pap. 9.95 (ISBN 0-87626-333-3). Winthrop.

Herdan, G. Language As Choice & Chance. 15.00 (ISBN 0-8022-0709-X). Philos Lib.

Hersov, L. A., et al, eds. Language & Language Disorders in Childhood. 1980. 21.00 (ISBN 0-08-025206-0); pap. 9.00 (ISBN 0-08-025205-2). Pergamon.

Hevesi, J. L., ed. Essays on Language & Literature by Proust, Valery, Sartre & Others. LC 67-27608. 1967. Repr. of 1947 ed. 12.00 (ISBN 0-8046-0202-6). Kennikat.

Hjelmslev, Louis. Language: An Introduction. Whitfield, Francis J., tr. from Danish. LC 70-98119. Orig. Title: Sproget. 158p. 1970. 15.00 (ISBN 0-299-05640-6). U of Wis Pr.

--Prolegomena to a Theory of Language. rev. ed. Whitfield, Francis J., tr. 152p. 1961. 15.00x (ISBN 0-299-02470-9). U of Wis Pr.

--Resume of a Theory of Language. Whitfield, Francis J., tr. 312p. 1975. 25.00x (ISBN 0-299-07040-9). U of Wis Pr.

Hoenigswald, H. M. Studies in Formal Historical Linguistics. LC 72-95891. (Formal Linguistics Ser: No. 3). 63p. 1973. lib. bdg. 16.00 (ISBN 90-277-0270-5, Pub. by Reidel Holland). Kluwer Boston.

Howell, Richard W. & Vetter, Harold J. Language in Behavior. LC 74-8363. 400p. 1976. text ed. 29.95 (ISBN 0-87705-157-7); pap. text ed. 12.95 (ISBN 0-87705-351-0). Human Sci Pr.

Hoy, James F. & Somer, John, eds. The Language Experience. 288p. 1974. pap. 2.95 (ISBN 0-440-54640-0, Delta). Dell.

Huizinga, Abel H. Analogy in the Semitic Languages. 59.95 (ISBN 0-87968-618-9). Gordon Pr.

Humez, Alexander & Humez, Nicholas. Alpha to Omega: The Life & Times of the Greek Alphabet. 1981. 13.95 (ISBN 0-87923-377-X). Godine.

Hutson, Charles. The Story of Language. 1897. 20.00 (ISBN 0-8274-3518-5). R West.

Hymes, Dell, ed. Language in Culture & Society: A Reader in Linguistics & Anthropology. 1964. text ed. 31.95 scp (ISBN 0-06-043030-3, HarpC). Har-Row.

Imagine That Language Workbook. tchrs guide 2.98 (ISBN 0-917186-23-0); stu. ed. 5.00 (ISBN 0-917186-24-9). McQueen.

Instructors of Introduction to Language the Ohio State University. Language Files: An Introduction to Language. Geoghegan, Shelia, et al, eds. 218p. 1980. pap. text ed. 8.65 (ISBN 0-89894-031-1). Advocate Pub Group.

The Insult Dictionary: How to Get What You Want in Five Nasty Languages. 1981. pap. 4.95 (ISBN 0-686-29649-4). Natl Textbk.

Jackson, K. H. Language & History in Early Britain. 1953. 42.50 (ISBN 0-85224-116-X, Pub. by Edinburgh U Pr Scotland). Columbia U Pr.

Jakobson, Roman. Selected Writings, 6 vols. Incl. Vol. 1. Phonological Studies. 2nd ed. 1971 (ISBN 90-2791-662-4); Vol. 2. Word & Language. 1971; Vol. 3. The Grammar of Poetry & the Poetry of Grammar; Vol. 4. Slavic Epic Studies. 1966 (ISBN 90-2791-003-0); Vol. 5. Verse, Its Masters & Explorers; Vol. 6. Slavic Literary Ties & Traditions. text ed. 80.00x ea. Mouton.

Jakobson, Roman & Halle, Morris. Fundamentals of Language. 2nd rev. ed. (Janua Linguarum, Ser. Minor: No. 1). (Orig.). 1971. pap. text ed. 6.70x (ISBN 90-2793-074-0). Mouton.

Jenkins, Frances. Language Development in Elementary Grades. (Educational Ser.). Repr. of 1936 ed. 12.50 (ISBN 0-685-43660-8). Norwood Edns.

Jespersen, Otto. Language: Its Nature, Development & Origin. 1980. Repr. of 1922 ed. lib. bdg. 50.00 (ISBN 0-89341-480-8). Longwood Pr.

--Language: Its Nature, Development & Origin. 1922. text ed. 16.50x (ISBN 0-04-400007-3). Allen Unwin.

Johnson, Alexander B. Meaning of Words. Repr. of 1862 ed. lib. bdg. 14.25x (ISBN 0-8371-0501-3, JOMW). Greenwood.

--Treatise on Language. Rynin, David, ed. LC 68-25841. 1969. pap. text ed. 4.00 (ISBN 0-486-22019-2). Dover.

--A Treatise on Language. Rynin, David, ed. (With critical essays on Johnson's philosophy of language by the editor). 5.50 (ISBN 0-8446-2331-8). Peter Smith.

Johnson, Nancy A. Current Topics in Language: Introductory Readings. (Illus.). 1976. pap. text ed. 9.95x (ISBN 0-87626-169-1). Winthrop.

Jones, Morris V. Language Development: The Key to Learning. 336p. 1972. photocopy ed. spiral 31.75 (ISBN 0-398-02324-7). C C Thomas.

Kasanin, J. S., ed. Language & Thought in Schizophrenia. 1964. pap. 2.95 (ISBN 0-393-00252-7, Norton Lib). Norton.

Kelling, George W. Language: Mirror, Tool & Weapon. LC 74-10511. 274p. 1974. 18.95x (ISBN 0-911012-85-0). Nelson-Hall.

Kerr, J. Y., ed. Oral Practice in the Language Laboratory. 91p. 1981. pap. 29.75x (ISBN 0-85633-193-7, NFER). Humanities.

Keyan, Rostam. The Evolution of Language. LC 77-93256. 1979. 6.00 (ISBN 0-685-86324-7). Philos Lib.

Keyser, S. Jay. Recent Transformational Studies in European Languages. (Linguistic Inquiry Monograph Ser.: No. 3). 1978. pap. 12.00x (ISBN 0-262-61024-8). MIT Pr.

Kinneavy, James L. Theory of Discourse. 496p. 1980. pap. 8.95x (ISBN 0-393-00919-X). Norton.

Kittredge, Richard & Lehrberger, John, eds. Sublanguage: Studies on Language in Restricted Semantic Domains. (Foundations of Communications Ser.). 240p. 1980. text ed. 52.50x (ISBN 3-11-008244-6). De Gruyter.

Kolbe, F. W. Language-Study Based on Bantu. facs. ed. LC 78-154081. (Black Heritage Library Collection Ser). 1888. 12.75 (ISBN 0-8369-8792-6). Arno.

Kostelanetz, Richard, ed. Language & Structure in North America. (Illus.). 1978. Repr. of 1975 ed. pap. 4.00 (ISBN 0-932360-19-X). RK Edns.

Kristeva, Julia. Desire in Language: A Semoitic Approach to Literature & Art. Roudiez, Leon S., ed. Jardine, Alice & Gora, Thomas, trs. from Fr. LC 80-10689. (European Perspectives Ser.). (Illus.). 336p. 1980. 16.95 (ISBN 0-231-04806-8). Columbia U Pr.

Kurtz, Paul. Language & Human Nature. LC 73-108782. 264p. 1971. 17.50 (ISBN 0-87527-022-0). Fireside Bks.

Laird, Charlton. Language in America. 560p. 1972. pap. 4.95 (ISBN 0-13-522722-4, Spec). P-H.

Langacker, Ronald W. Language & Its Structure: Some Fundamental Linguistic Concepts. 2nd ed. LC 68-27167. 1973. pap. text ed. 13.95 (ISBN 0-15-549192-X, HC). HarBraceJ.

Language, Man & Society, 23 titles in 31 vols. Repr. of 1916 ed. Set. 927.50 (ISBN 0-404-08490-7); sep. vols. avail. (ISBN 0-685-02384-2). AMS Pr.

Language Workbook. tchrs guide 2.98 (ISBN 0-917186-15-X); stu. ed. 5.00 (ISBN 0-917186-16-8). McQueen.

Larson, Arlene & Logan, Carolyn. How Does Language Work? 208p. (Orig.). 1980. pap. text ed. 11.95 (ISBN 0-8403-2199-6). Kendall-Hunt.

Lass, Norman J., ed. Speech & Language: Advances in Basic Research & Practice, Vol. 1. (Serial Publication). 1979. 30.00 (ISBN 0-12-608601-X). Acad Pr.

--Speech & Language: Advances in Basic Research & Practice, Vol. 3. (Serial Publication). 1980. 29.50 (ISBN 0-12-608603-6). Acad Pr.
--Speech & Language: Advances in Basic Research & Practice, Vol. 5. (Serial Publication). 1981. price not set (ISBN 0-12-608605-2). Acad Pr.
--Speech & Language: Advances in Basic Research & Practice, Vol. 2. (Serial Publication). 1979. 30.00 (ISBN 0-12-608602-8). Acad Pr.
Lawson, Chester A. Language, Thought, & the Human Mind. vii, 117p. 1958. 4.50 (ISBN 0-87013-035-8). Mich St U Pr.
Lee, Victor. Language Development. LC 78-9081. 1979. 24.95x (ISBN 0-470-26432-2). Halsted Pr.
Lehmann, Winfred P., et al. Introduction to Scholarship in Modern Languages & Literatures. Gibaldi, Joseph, ed. LC 81-1254. xi, 143p. 1981. 11.75x (ISBN 0-87352-092-0); pap. 6.25x (ISBN 0-87352-093-9). Modern Lang.
Levitt, John & Levitt, Joan. Spell of Words. Repr. of 1959 ed. lib. bdg. 15.00x (ISBN 0-8371-2087-X, LESW). Greenwood.
Lewis, Michael & Rosenblum, Leonard, eds. Interaction, Conversation, & the Development of Language. LC 76-49037. (Origins of Behavior: Vol. 5). 1977. 30.95 (ISBN 0-471-02526-7, Pub. by Wiley-Interscience). Wiley.
Linguistic Association of Canada & the U. S. Fifth LACUS Forum: Proceedings. Woelck, Wolfgang & Garvin, Paul L., eds. 1979. pap. text ed. 10.95 (ISBN 0-685-96325-X). Hornbeam Pr.
Linsky, Leonard, ed. Semantics & the Philosophy of Language. 2nd ed. LC 52-10465. 1969. pap. 5.95 (ISBN 0-252-00093-5). U of Ill Pr.
Lohrli, Anne, ed. Household Words: A Weekly Journal, 1850-1859, Conducted by Charles Dickens. LC 71-185722. 1973. 65.00x (ISBN 0-8020-1912-9). U of Toronto Pr.
The Lover's Dictionary: How to Be Amorous in Five Delectable Languages. 1981. pap. 4.95 (ISBN 0-686-29648-6). Natl Textbk.
Lowell, Edgar L. Play It by Ear! 1963. Repr. of 1960 ed. spiral bound 5.20 (ISBN 0-9606312-0-8). John Tracy Clinic.
Macaulay, R. S. Language, Social Class, & Education. 1978. 10.00x (ISBN 0-85224-320-0, Pub. by Edinburgh U Pr Scotland). Columbia U Pr.
McCormack, William & Wrum, Stephen A., eds. Approaches to Language. (World Anthropology Ser.). 1978. 73.70 (ISBN 0-202-90073-8). Beresford Bk Serv.
McCormack, William & Wurm, Stephen A., eds. Language & Thought: Anthropological Issues. (World Anthropology Ser.: Vol. 55). 1978. 41.00 (ISBN 0-202-90055-X). Beresford Bk Serv.
McNeill, David. The Conceptual Basis of Language. LC 78-32105. 306p. 1979. 19.95 (ISBN 0-470-26663-5). Halsted Pr.
Maher, J. Peter. Papers on Language Theory & History I: Creation & Tradition in Language. xx, 171p. 1977. 23.00 (ISBN 90-272-0904-9, CILT 3). Benjamins North Am.
Margalis, Joel. An Awareness of Language. 1975. pap. 7.95x (ISBN 0-87626-050-4). Winthrop.
Martinet, Andre. Le Langage. (Methodique Ser.). 1544p. 46.95 (ISBN 0-686-56443-X). French & Eur.
Mathews, William. Words: Their Use & Abuse. facsimile ed. LC 70-37792. (Essay Index Reprint Ser). Repr. of 1876 ed. 21.00 (ISBN 0-8369-2611-0). Arno.
Mead, George H. Mind, Self, & Society: From the Standpoint of a Social Behaviorist. Morris, Charles W., ed. 1967. lib. bdg. 15.00x (ISBN 0-226-51667-9, P272, Phoen); pap. 4.95 (ISBN 0-226-51668-7). U of Chicago Pr.
Mepham, Michael S. Computation in Language Text Analysis. (Illus.). 232p. 1974. pap. 10.95x (ISBN 2-7637-6691-9, Pub. by Laval). Intl Schol Bk Serv.
Michaelis, Johann D. Dissertation on the Influence of Opinions on Language & of Language on Opinions. LC 72-147981. Repr. of 1769 ed. 25.00 (ISBN 0-404-08236-X). AMS Pr.
Michigan Oral Language Series: ACTFL, 9 bks. Set. pap. 100.00x (ISBN 0-87352-072-6). Modern Lang.
Miller, George A. Communication, Language & Meaning: Psychological Perspectives. LC 70-174815. 320p. 1973. 12.50x (ISBN 0-465-12833-5); pap. 5.95x (ISBN 0-465-09721-9, CN-5021). Basic.
--Language & Speech. LC 80-27018. (Illus.). 1981. text ed. 13.00x (ISBN 0-7167-1297-0); pap. text ed. 5.95x (ISBN 0-7167-1298-9). W H Freeman.
Mitchell, Richard. Less Than Words Can Say. LC 79-15484. 1979. 9.95 (ISBN 0-316-57506-2); pap. 5.95 (ISBN 0-316-57507-0). Little.
Modern Language Association of America, Center for Scholarly Editions. The Center for Scholarly Editions: An Introductory Statement. 1977. pap. 3.00x (ISBN 0-87352-022-X). Modern Lang.
Muma, John R. Language Handbook: Concepts, Assessment, Intervention. (Illus.). 1978. 19.95 (ISBN 0-13-522755-0). P-H.
Murane, Elizabeth. Daga Grammar. (Publications in Linguistics & Related Fields: No. 43). 1974. pap. 14.00x (ISBN 0-88312-053-4); microfiche 3.40 (ISBN 0-88312-453-X). Summer Inst Ling.
Nalimov, V. V. In the Labyrinths of Language: A Mathematician's Journey. Colodny, Robert G., ed. (Illus.). 246p. 1981. 22.50 (ISBN 0-89495-007-X). ISI Pr.
Narasimham, R. Modelling Language Behavior. (Springer Series in Language & Communication: Vol. 10). (Illus.). 220p. 1981. 29.40 (ISBN 0-387-10513-1). Springer-Verlag.
Nash, Walter. Our Experience of Language. LC 76-165542. (Griffin Paperbacks Ser). 1974. pap. 5.95 (ISBN 0-312-59045-8). St Martin.
Neustupny, J. V. Post-Structural Approaches to Language: Language Theory in a Japanese Context. 1978. pap. 9.50 (ISBN 0-86008-194-X, Pub. by U of Tokyo Pr). Intl Schol Bk Serv.
Nida, Eugene A. Language Structure & Translation: Essays by Eugene A. Nida. Dil, A. S., ed. LC 75-183. (Language Science & National Development Ser). 300p. 1975. 12.95x (ISBN 0-8047-0885-1). Stanford U Pr.
Nyffenegger, Eugen. Cristan der Kuchimaister, Nuewe Casus Monasterii Sancti Galli: Edition & Sprachgeschichtliche Einordnung. (Quellen & Forschungen Zur Sprach-und Kulturgeschichte der Germanischen Voelker N. F. 60). (Ger.). 1974. 77.25x (ISBN 3-11-004098-0). De Gruyter.
Parret, Herman. Contexts of Understanding. vii, 109p. 1980. pap. 14.00 (ISBN 90-272-2509-5, P & B 6). Benjamins North Am.
Pecheux, Michael. Language, Semantics & Ideology. 1981. 25.00x (ISBN 0-312-46915-2). St Martin.
Pei, Mario. All About Language. (Illus.). (gr. 7-9). 1954. 10.95 (ISBN 0-397-30263-0). Har-Row.
--One Language for the World & How to Achieve It. LC 68-56449. 1958. 10.00x (ISBN 0-8196-0218-3). Biblo.
--Story of Language. rev. ed. pap. 2.25 (ISBN 0-451-61782-7, ME1782, Ment). NAL.
Pei, Mario A. Voices of Man. LC 71-173940. Repr. of 1962 ed. 15.00 (ISBN 0-404-07928-8). AMS Pr.
Peterson, Carole W. Conversation Starters for Speech & Language Pathology. 1981. pap. 2.75 (ISBN 0-8134-2186-1, 2186). Interstate.
Petty, Walter, et al. Experiences in Language: Tools & Techniques for Language Arts Methods. 3rd ed. 544p. 1980. pap. text ed. 18.95 (ISBN 0-205-07176-7, 237176-6). Allyn.
Pierce, Joe E. Languages & Linguistics: An Introduction. (Janua Linguarum Series Didactica: No. 4). 188p. (Orig.). 1975. pap. text ed. 35.00x (ISBN 90-2793-371-5). Mouton.
--The Nature of Natural Languages. (Orig.). 1979. pap. 8.95 (ISBN 0-913244-20-1). Hapi Pr.
Postal, Paul, et al. Language & Learning: Investigations & Interpretations. (Reprint Ser.: No. 7). 4.50 (ISBN 0-916690-07-5). Harvard Educ Rev.
Ptacek, Paul H., et al. Index to Speech, Language & Hearing Journal Titles, 1954-78. LC 79-20058. 305p. 1979. text ed. 25.00 (ISBN 0-933014-54-6). College-Hill.
Revesz, Geza. The Origins & Prehistory of Language. Butler, J., tr. from Ger. LC 78-138128. 240p. Repr. of 1956 ed. lib. bdg. 15.00x (ISBN 0-8371-4167-2, RELA). Greenwood.
Rosen, Victor. Style Character & Language. Jucovy, Milton & Atkin, Samuel, eds. LC 77-70332. 1977. 25.00x (ISBN 0-87668-251-4, 2514). Aronson.
Rosenthal, Joseph H. The Neuropsychopathology of Written Language. LC 77-2825. 1977. 18.95x (ISBN 0-88229-382-6). Nelson-Hall.
Rousseau, Jean-Jacques. Essai sur l'Origine des Langues. 1976. 13.95 (ISBN 0-686-55347-0); pap. 3.95 (ISBN 0-686-55348-9). French & Eur.
Rubin, Joan. Directory of Language Planning Organizations. LC 79-22330. 1980. pap. text ed. 3.50x (ISBN 0-8248-0687-5, Eastwest Ctr). U Pr of Hawaii.
Russell, C. V. Post O-Level Studies in Modern Languages. 1971. 17.25 (ISBN 0-08-016194-4). Pergamon.
Safire, William. On Language. 1980. 12.95 (ISBN 0-8129-0937-2). Times Bks.
St. Clair, Robert N. & Giles, Howard, eds. The Social & Psychological Contexts of Language. LC 79-28232. 352p. 1980. text ed. 24.95x (ISBN 0-89859-021-3). L Erlbaum Assocs.
Salomaa, Arto. Jewels of Formal Language Theory. (Illus.). 1981. text ed. 24.95 (ISBN 0-914894-69-2). Computer Sci.
Samuels, M. L. Linguistic Evolution with Special Reference to English. LC 72-176255. (Cambridge Studies in Linguistics: No. 5). (Illus.). 256p. 1973. 32.50 (ISBN 0-521-08385-0); pap. 9.95x (ISBN 0-521-09913-7). Cambridge U Pr.
Sapir. Language. 1980. text ed. 10.50x (ISBN 0-246-11074-0). Humanities.
Sapir, Edward. Culture, Language, & Personality: Selected Essays. Mandelbaum, David G., ed. 1949. pap. 6.95x (ISBN 0-520-01116-3, CAL5). U of Cal Pr.
--Language: An Introduction to the Study of Speech. LC 21-20134. 1955. pap. 2.45 (ISBN 0-15-648233-9, HB7, Harv). HarBraceJ.
--Selected Writings of Edward Sapir in Language, Culture, & Personality. Mandelbaum, David G., ed. 1949. 32.50x (ISBN 0-520-01115-5). U of Cal Pr.
Sapir, Edward & Swadesh, M. Expression of the Ending-Point Relation in English, French, & German. 1932. pap. 6.00 (ISBN 0-527-00814-1). Kraus Repr.
Sayce, Archibald H. Introduction to the Science of Language, 2 vols. 1980. lib. bdg. 200.00 (ISBN 0-8490-3163-X). Gordon Pr.
Schiefelbusch. Language Intervention Strategies. 1978. 19.50 (ISBN 0-8391-1238-6). Univ Park.
Schiefelbusch, Richard L. & Hollis, John H., eds. Language Intervention from Ape to Child. (Language Intervention Ser.). 552p. 1979. text ed. 24.95 (ISBN 0-8391-1413-3). Univ Park.
Schuh, Russell G. A Dictionary of Ngizim, Vol. 99. (U.C. Publications in Linguistics). 1981. pap. 10.00x (ISBN 0-520-09636-3). U of Cal Pr.
Schulz, Renate A. Options for Undergraduate Foreign Language Programs: Four-Year & Two-Year Colleges. LC 78-71999. (Options for Teaching Ser.: No. 3). 97p. 1979. pap. 7.00x (ISBN 0-87352-302-4). Modern Lang.
Shaw, George B. On Language. Tauber, A., ed. (Orig.). pap. 1.85 (ISBN 0-685-19409-4, 111, WL). Citadel Pr.
Shepard, Mary & Shepard, Ray. Vegetable Soup Activities. 96p. 1975. text ed. 6.95 (ISBN 0-590-07443-1, Citation); pap. text ed. 2.25 (ISBN 0-590-09603-6). Schol Bk Serv.
Shopen, Timothy. Languages & Their Speakers. (Illus.). 1979. text ed. 14.95 (ISBN 0-87626-483-6). Winthrop.
--Languages & Their Status. (Illus.). 1979. text ed. 14.95 (ISBN 0-87626-485-2). Winthrop.
Shuy, Roger W. & Fasold, Ralph W., eds. Language Attitudes: Current Trends & Prospects. LC 72-97143. 201p. 1973. pap. 5.50 (ISBN 0-87840-203-9). Georgetown U Pr.
Silverman, David & Torode, Brian. The Material Word: Some Theories of Language & Its Limits. (Illus.). 1980. 24.50 (ISBN 0-7100-0398-6); pap. 14.95 (ISBN 0-7100-0399-4). Routledge & Kegan.
Sinclair, A., et al. The Child's Conception of Language. (Springer Ser. in Language & Communication: Vol. 2). (Illus.). 1979. 22.50 (ISBN 0-387-09153-X). Springer-Verlag.
Singh, Jagjit. Great Ideas in Information Theory, Language & Cibernetics. 7.00 (ISBN 0-8446-2946-4). Peter Smith.
Singh, S. Diagnostic Procedures in Hearing, Language & Speech. 1978. 29.50 (ISBN 0-8391-1217-3). Univ Park.
Skinner, B. F. Verbal Behavior. 1957. 21.00 (ISBN 0-13-941591-2). P-H.
Skinner, Paul H. & Shelton, Ralph L. Speech, Language & Hearing: Normal Processes & Disorders. LC 77-73956. (Speech Pathology & Audiology Ser.). 1978. text ed. 16.95 (ISBN 0-201-07461-3); instr's man. price not set (ISBN 0-201-07462-1). A-W.
Smith, Barbara H. On the Margins of Discourse: The Relation of Literature to Language. LC 78-18274. 1979. 14.00x (ISBN 0-226-76452-4). U of Chicago Pr.
Sparke, William & McKowen, Clark. Montage: Investigations in Language. (Illus.). 1970. text ed. 13.50x (ISBN 0-02-414220-4). Macmillan.
Stam, James H. Inquiries into the Origin of Language: The Fate of a Question. (Studies in Language Ser.). 320p. 1976. text ed. 22.95 scp (ISBN 0-06-046403-8, HarpC). Har-Row.
Stross, Brian. The Origin & Evolution of Language. (Elements of Anthropology Ser.). 96p. 1976. pap. text ed. write for info. (ISBN 0-697-07544-3). Wm C Brown.
Sweet, Henry. The History of Language. LC 74-16090. 1974. Repr. of 1930 ed. lib. bdg. 15.00 (ISBN 0-8414-7804-X). Folcroft.
Thomson, David. Language. (Human Behavior Ser.). 9.95 (ISBN 0-8094-1966-1). Time-Life.
Tidwell, Mary S. John Tracy Clinic Language Guide. 1976. 10.30 (ISBN 0-9606312-1-6). John Tracy Clinic.
Tollefson, Stephen & Davis, Kim. Reading & Writing About Language. 1979. pap. text ed. 8.95x (ISBN 0-534-00617-5). Wadsworth Pub.
Tursi, Joseph A., ed. FLS & the 'new' Student. 1970. pap. 7.95x (ISBN 0-915432-70-6). NE Conf Teach.
Tyberg, Judith M. The Language of the Gods. 1976. 8.95 (ISBN 0-930736-00-1). E-W Cultural Ctr.
Tylor, Edward B. Researches into the Early History of Mankind & the Development of Civilization. abr. ed. Bohannan, Paul, ed. LC 64-23416. 1964. 12.50x (ISBN 0-226-82121-8). U of Chicago Pr.
--Researches into the Early History of Mankind & the Development of Civilization. abr. ed. LC 64-23416. (Classics in Anthropology Ser.). (Orig.). 1964. pap. 2.95 (ISBN 0-226-82122-6, P175, Phoen). U of Chicago Pr.
Vandamme, Fernard J. Simulation of Natural Language. (Janua Linguarum, Ser Major: No. 50). 1972. text ed. 40.00x (ISBN 90-2792-106-7). Mouton.
Vendryes, Joseph. Language: A Linguistic Introduction to History. Radin, Paul, tr. LC 78-59048. 1979. Repr. of 1925 ed. 27.50 (ISBN 0-88355-720-7). Hyperion Conn.
Von Slagle, Uhlan. Language, Thought & Perception. LC 72-94506. (Janua Linguarum, Ser. Major: No. 98). 60p. 1974. pap. text ed. 13.75x (ISBN 90-2793-023-6). Mouton.
Vossler, Karl. The Spirit of Language in Civilization. Oeser, Oscar, tr. LC 75-41285. Repr. of 1932 ed. 17.00 (ISBN 0-404-14625-2). AMS Pr.
Ward, Martha C. Them Children: A Study in Language Learning. Spindler, George & Spindler, Louise, eds. (Case Studies in Education & Culture). 112p. pap. text ed. 6.95x (ISBN 0-8290-0323-1). Irvington.
Warfel, Harry R. Language: A Science of Human Behavior. LC 62-9619. 1962. 19.00x (ISBN 0-8201-1047-7). Schol Facsimiles.
Watson, George. Universe of Language. 1979. Repr. of 1878 ed. lib. bdg. 50.00 (ISBN 0-8492-2963-4). R West.
Weekly, Ernest. Something About Words. 1977. Repr. lib. bdg. 20.00 (ISBN 0-8495-5607-4). Arden Lib.
Welby, V. Significs & Language: The Articulate Form of Our Expressive & Interpretative Resources. 105p. 1981. Repr. of 1911 ed. lib. bdg. 30.00 (ISBN 0-89984-507-X). Century Bookbindery.
Wells, Gordon, et al. Learning Through Interaction: The Study of Language Development. LC 80-41113. (Language at Home & at School Ser.). (Illus.). 200p. 1981. text ed. 39.50 (ISBN 0-521-23774-2); pap. text ed. 10.95 (ISBN 0-521-28219-5). Cambridge U Pr.
Wescott, Roger W., ed. Language Origins. LC 74-25443. 1974. pap. 6.50x (ISBN 0-932130-04-6). Linstok Pr.
West, Fred. The Way of Language: An Introduction. 250p. (Orig.). 1975. pap. text ed. 9.95 (ISBN 0-15-595130-0, HC). HarBraceJ.
Wheeler, Benjamin I. Analogy & the Scope of Its Application in Language. 5.00 (ISBN 0-384-67840-8). Johnson Repr.
Whitney, William. The Life & Growth of Language. 1875. 25.00 (ISBN 0-8274-2865-0). R West.
Whitney, William D. Language & the Study of Language. 6th ed. LC 78-137305. Repr. of 1901 ed. 31.50 (ISBN 0-404-06942-8). AMS Pr.
--Language & the Study of Language: Twelve Lectures on the Principle of Linguistics Science. Repr. of 1901 ed. 53.00 (ISBN 3-4870-4754-3). Adler.
--Life & Growth of Language: An Outline of Linguistic Science. 1977. Repr. of 1875 ed. lib. bdg. 30.00 (ISBN 0-685-81476-9). Norwood Edns.
Widdowson, H. G. Teaching Language As Communication. 1978. pap. text ed. 9.00x (ISBN 0-19-437077-1). Oxford U Pr.
Wilson, John. Language & the Pursuit of Truth. 1956. pap. 4.95x (ISBN 0-521-09421-6). Cambridge U Pr.
Wolf, Maryanne, et al, eds. Thought & Language - Language & Reading. (Reprint Ser.: No. 14). Date not set. 14.95 (ISBN 0-916690-15-6). Harvard Educ Rev.
Young, Thomas. Miscellaneous Works of the Late Thomas Young, 3 vols. Repr. of 1855 ed. Set. 92.50 (ISBN 0-384-40420-0). Johnson Repr.
Zale, Eric M., ed. Proceedings of the Conference on Language & Language Behavior. LC 68-28144. 1968. 30.00x (ISBN 0-89197-906-9). Irvington.
Zierer, Ernesto. Formal Logic & Linguistics. LC 78-134547. (Janua Linguarum, Ser. Minor: No. 102). 92p. (Orig.). 1972. pap. text ed. 13.75x (ISBN 90-2792-009-5). Mouton.

LANGUAGE AND LANGUAGES–ADDRESSES, ESSAYS, LECTURES

Aarsleff, Hans. From Locke to Saussure: Essays on the Study of Language. LC 81-10428. 474p. 1981. 29.50x (ISBN 0-8166-0964-0); pap. 12.95x (ISBN 0-8166-0967-5). U of Minn Pr.

Achtert, Walter S. & Fisher, John H., eds. MLA Abstracts of Articles in Scholarly Journals, 1970. 252p. 1972. 25.00x (ISBN 0-87352-200-1). Modern Lang.
Achtert, Walter S., compiled by. MLA Abstracts of Articles in Scholarly Journals, 1971. 417p. 1973. 25.00x (ISBN 0-87352-217-6). Modern Lang.
--MLA Abstracts of Articles in Scholarly Journals, 1973. 409p. 1975. 35.00x (ISBN 0-87352-229-X). Modern Lang.
Achtert, Walter S., et al, eds. MLA Abstracts of Articles in Scholarly Journals, 1974. 407p. 1976. 35.00x (ISBN 0-87352-237-0). Modern Lang.
Anshen, Ruth N., ed. Language: An Enquiry into Its Meaning & Function. LC 75-91040. (Essay & General Literature Index Reprint Ser). 1971. Repr. of 1957 ed. 14.25 (ISBN 0-8046-1396-6). Kennikat.
Black, Max, ed. Importance of Language. 1968. pap. 4.95 (ISBN 0-8014-9077-4, CP77). Cornell U Pr.
Bloomfield, Morton W. Essays & Explorations: Studies in Ideas, Language, & Literature. LC 70-106956. (Illus.). x, 321p. 1970. 16.50x (ISBN 0-674-26425-8). Harvard U Pr.
Bright, William. Variation & Change in Language: Essays by William Bright. Dil, A. S., ed. LC 76-23370. (Language Science & National Development Ser.). 304p. 1976. 10.95x (ISBN 0-8047-0926-2). Stanford U Pr.
Carroll, John B., ed. Language, Thought & Reality: Selected Writings of Benjamin Lee Whorf. 1956. 17.00x (ISBN 0-262-23003-8); pap. 4.95 (ISBN 0-262-73006-5, 5). MIT Pr.
Casselman, Barry. Language, a Magical Enterprise, the Body. (Paperplay Mini-Bks.: Vol. 7). (Illus.). 16p. 1978. saddle-stitched 2.50 (ISBN 0-939044-13-7). Lingua Pr.
Escholz, Paul A., et al, eds. Language Awareness. 2nd ed. LC 77-86011. 1978. pap. text ed. 6.95x (ISBN 0-312-46691-9). St Martin.
Foucault, Michel. Language, Counter-Memory, Practice: Selected Essays & Interviews. Bouchard, Donald F., ed. Simon, Sherry, tr. from Fr. LC 77-4561. (Cornell Paperbacks Ser.). 240p. 1980. pap. 5.95 (ISBN 0-8014-9204-1). Cornell U Pr.
Gaburo, Kenneth, et al, eds. Allos: 41 Writings by 41 Writers. LC 80-80809. (Illus.). 448p. 1980. soft cover 18.95 (ISBN 0-939044-26-9). Lingua Pr.
Grace, George. An Essay on Language. 1981. 14.50 (ISBN 0-686-77715-8); pap. 9.95 (ISBN 0-686-77716-6). Hornbeam Pr.
Greenberg, Joseph H. Language, Culture, & Communication: Essays by Joseph H. Greenberg. Dil, A. S., ed. LC 72-150323. (Language Science & National Development Ser). 1971. 15.00x (ISBN 0-8047-0781-2). Stanford U Pr.
Grimshaw, Allen D. Language As Social Resource: Essays by Allen D. Grimshaw. Dil, Anwar S., ed. LC 81-50704. (Language Science & National Development). 400p. 1981. 18.75x (ISBN 0-8047-1108-9). Stanford U Pr.
Halliday, Michael A. Explorations in the Functions of Language. new ed. LC 76-57229. 1977. 8.95 (ISBN 0-444-00201-4, North Holland). Elsevier.
Hamilton, G. Rostrevor. Guides & Marshals: An Essay on Words & Imaginative Order. 1956. lib. bdg. 20.00 (ISBN 0-8482-9971-X). Norwood Edns.
Henle, Paul, ed. Language, Thought & Culture. 1958. pap. 2.45 (ISBN 0-472-06097-X, 97, AA). U of Mich Pr.
Hockett, C. F. The View from Language: Selected Essays, 1948-1974. LC 75-3818. 360p. 1977. 20.00x (ISBN 0-8203-0381-X). U of Ga Pr.
Kachru, Braj B., et al, eds. Issues in Linguistics: Papers in Honor of Henry & Renee Kahane. LC 72-88807. 940p. 1973. 32.50 (ISBN 0-252-00246-6). U of Ill Pr.
Kramarae, Cheris, ed. The Voices & Words of Women & Men. 195p. 1981. 29.50 (ISBN 0-08-026106-X). Pergamon.
Lambert, Wallace E. Language, Psychology, & Culture: Essays by Wallace E. Lambert. Dil, A. S., ed. LC 71-183890. (Language Science & National Development Ser.). xvi, 368p. 1972. 15.00x (ISBN 0-8047-0803-7). Stanford U Pr.
Lock, Andrew, ed. Action, Gesture & Symbol: The Emergence of Language. 1979. 66.50 (ISBN 0-12-454050-3). Acad Pr.
MacBeth, John W. The Might & Mirth of Literature: A Treatise on Figurative Language. 1875. 45.00 (ISBN 0-8495-6257-0). Arden Lib.
Mackesy, Eileen M., compiled by. MLA Abstracts of Articles in Scholarly Journals, 1975. 555p. 1977. 40.00x (ISBN 0-87352-249-4). Modern Lang.
Mackillop, James & Cross, Donna W. Speaking of Words: A Language Reader. LC 77-14952. 1978. pap. 10.95 (ISBN 0-03-018056-2, HoltC). HR&W.
McQuown, Norman A. Language, Culture, & Education: Essays by Norman A. McQuown. Dil, Anwar S., ed. LC 81-50705. (Language Science & National Development Ser.). 256p. 1981. 15.95x (ISBN 0-8047-1122-4). Stanford U Pr.
Michaels, Leonard & Ricks, Christopher, eds. The State of the Language. 1980. 14.95 (ISBN 0-520-03763-4); pap. 8.95 (ISBN 0-520-04400-2). U of Cal Pr.
Mueller, Friedrich M. The Science of Language, 2 vols. LC 73-18817. Repr. of 1891 ed. 74.50 (ISBN 0-404-11441-5). AMS Pr.
--Selected Essays on Language, Mythology & Religion, 2 vols. LC 73-18814. Repr. of 1881 ed. 67.50 set (ISBN 0-404-11456-3). AMS Pr.
Partridge, Eric. From Sanskrit to Brazil: Vignettes & Essays Upon Language. 1977. Repr. of 1952 ed. lib. bdg. 15.00 (ISBN 0-8482-2153-2). Norwood Edns.
--Words at War, Words at Peace: Essays on Language in General & Particular Words. facsimile ed. LC 76-117911. (Select Bibliographies Reprint Ser). Repr. of 1948 ed. 16.00 (ISBN 0-8369-5364-9). Arno.
--Words, Words, Words! facsimile ed. LC 70-117912. (Select Bibliographies Reprint Ser). Repr. of 1933 ed. 19.00 (ISBN 0-8369-5365-7). Arno.
--The World of Words: An Introduction to Language in General & to English & American in Particular. facsimile 3rd ed. LC 73-117913. (Select Bibliographies Reprint Ser). Repr. of 1948 ed. 20.00 (ISBN 0-8369-5366-5). Arno.
Pittman, Richard & Kerr, Harland, eds. Papers on the Languages of the Australian Aborigines. 166p. 1964. pap. 2.00x (ISBN 0-88312-795-4). Summer Inst Ling.
Rich, Adrienne. On Lies, Secrets & Silence: Selected Prose 1966-1978. 1979. 15.95 (ISBN 0-393-01233-6); pap. 3.95 (ISBN 0-393-00942-4). Norton.
Smith, Frank & Miller, George, eds. Genesis of Language: A Psycholinguistic Approach. 1966. pap. 4.95 (ISBN 0-262-69022-5). MIT Pr.
Symposia in Applied Mathematics - New York - 1960. Structure of Language & Its Mathematical Aspects: Proceedings, Vol. 12. Jakobson, R., ed. LC 50-1183. 1980. Repr. of 1961 ed. 22.00 (ISBN 0-8218-1312-9, PSAPM-12). Am Math.
Titone, Renzo. Teaching Foreign Languages: An Historical Sketch. LC 68-22774. 128p. 1968. pap. 3.15 (ISBN 0-87840-158-X). Georgetown U Pr.

LANGUAGE AND LANGUAGES–BIBLIOGRAPHY

Asher, J. A. Amis et Amiles: An Exploratory Survey. 1978. Repr. of 1952 ed. lib. bdg. 8.50 (ISBN 0-8482-0120-5). Norwood Edns.
Brewer, Annie, ed. Abbreviations, Acronyms, Ciphers & Signs:...a Reference Source for Identifying Books in Many Languages Which Concern Themselves with Short Forms of Cummunication. 315p. 1981. 40.00 (ISBN 0-8103-0529-1). Gale.
Dingwall, William O. Language & the Brain, 2 vols. LC 80-8491. 1981. lib. bdg. 100.00 (ISBN 0-8240-9495-6). Garland Pub.
Hewes, Gordon W., ed. Language Origins: A Bibliography Part One A-K Part Two L-Z. (Approaches to Semiotics Ser.: No. 44). 890p. 1975. text ed. 161.25x (ISBN 90-2793-401-0). Mouton.
Meserole, Harrison T., compiled by. MLA International Bibliography of Books & Articles on the Modern Languages & Literatures, 1970. 754p. 1972. 150.00x (ISBN 0-87352-202-8). Modern Lang.
--MLA International Bibliography of Books & Articles on the Modern Languages & Literatures, 1971. 834p. 1973. 150.00x (ISBN 0-87352-213-3). Modern Lang.
--MLA International Bibliography of Books & Articles on the Modern Languages & Literatures, 1972. 955p. 1974. 150.00x (ISBN 0-87352-221-4). Modern Lang.
--MLA International Bibliography of Books & Articles on the Modern Languages & Literatures, 1973. 871p. 1975. 150.00x (ISBN 0-87352-233-8). Modern Lang.
MLA Directory of Periodicals: A Guide to Journals & Series in Languages & Literatures. 541p. 1979. 65.00x (ISBN 0-87352-414-4). Modern Lang.
MLA International Bibliography of Books & Articles on the Modern Languages & Literatures, 1980. LC 64-20773. 1050p. 1981. 150.00x (ISBN 0-87352-422-5). Modern Lang.
MLA International Bibliography of Books & Articles on the Modern Languages & Literatures, 1978. LC 64-20773. 1045p. 1979. 150.00x (ISBN 0-87352-413-6). Modern Lang.
MLA International Bibliography of Books & Articles on the Modern Languages & Literatures, 1977. LC 64-20773. 879p. 1978. 150.00x (ISBN 0-87352-408-X). Modern Lang.
MLA International Bibliography of Books & Articles on the Modern Languages & Literatures, 1976. LC 64-20773. 902p. 1978. 150.00x (ISBN 0-87352-403-9). Modern Lang.
Rubin, Joan & Jernudd, Bjorn H. References for Students of Language Planning. LC 79-17656. 1979. pap. text ed. 3.50 (ISBN 0-8248-0686-7, Eastwest Ctr). U Pr of Hawaii.
Wertheimer, Leonard. Books in Other Languages. 4th ed. 1979. pap. 45.00 (ISBN 0-89664-147-3, Pub. by K G Saur). Gale.

LANGUAGE AND LANGUAGES–CLASSIFICATION

Breton, Roland J. Atlas Geographique Des Langues et Des Ethnics De L'inde et Du Subcontinent. (Illus., Fr.). 1977. 30.00x (ISBN 2-7637-6760-5, Pub. by Laval). Intl Schol Bk Serv.
Dyen, Isidore, ed. Lexicostatistics in Genetic Linguistics: Proceedings of the Yale Conference, Yale University, April 3-4, 1971. (Janua Linguarum Series Maior: No. 69). 1973. 36.25x (ISBN 0-686-21262-2). Mouton.
Uspensky, B. Principles of Structural Typology. LC 68-17893. (Janua Linguarum, Ser. Minor). (Orig.). 1968. pap. text ed. 15.75x (ISBN 90-2790-590-8). Mouton.
Voegelin, Charles F. & Voegelin, Florence M. Classification & Index of the World's Languages. LC 74-19546. (Foundations of Linguistics Ser.). 576p. 1976. 50.00 (ISBN 0-444-00155-7, North Holland). Elsevier.

LANGUAGE AND LANGUAGES–DATA PROCESSING

see Linguistics–Data Processing

LANGUAGE AND LANGUAGES–DICTIONARIES

see also Dictionaries, Polyglot; Polyglot Glossaries, Phrase Books, etc.

Aman, Reinhold, ed. Maledicta 1978. LC 77-649633. (Maledicta: International Journal of Verbal Aggression Ser.: Vol. 2, No. 1-2). (Illus.). 1979. pap. 20.00 (ISBN 0-916500-52-7). Maledicta.
Aschmann, Herman & Aschmann, Bessie. Diccionario Totonaco De Papantla. (Vocabularios Indigenas Ser.: No. 16). 1973. pap. 5.00 (ISBN 0-88312-750-4); microfiche 2.20 (ISBN 0-88312-585-4). Summer Inst Ling.
Castell, Edmund. Lexicon Heptaglotton, 2 vols. LC 70-870022. 1544p. 1970. Repr. of 1686 ed. Set. 175.00x (ISBN 3-201-00074-4). Intl Pubns Serv.
Douglas, W. H. Illustrated Topical Dictionary of the Western Desert Language: 1959. 2nd rev. ed. (AIAS Research Regional Studies: No. 11). 1977. pap. text ed. 3.50x (ISBN 0-85575-061-8). Humanities.
Graham, John. Shetland Dictionary. 160p. 1980. 12.95 (ISBN 0-906191-33-5, Pub. by Findhorn-Thule Scotland). Hydra Bk.
Guinagh, Kevin, ed. & tr. Dictionary of Foreign Phrases & Abbreviations. 2nd ed. 1972. 12.00 (ISBN 0-8242-0460-3). Wilson.
Hartmann, R. R. & Stork, F. C., eds. Dictionary of Language & Linguistics. LC 72-6251. 1976. 36.95 (ISBN 0-470-35667-7); pap. 29.95 (ISBN 0-470-15200-1). Halsted Pr.
Laita, Luis M. Cortina-Grosset Basic Spanish Dictionary. Berberi, Dilaver & Berberi, Edel A., eds. LC 73-18525. 384p. 1975. 3.95 (ISBN 0-448-11559-X). G&D.
Lithgow, David & Lithgow, Daphne. Muyuw Dictionary. 1974. pap. 2.50 (ISBN 0-7263-0205-8). Summer Inst Ling.
Living Language Dictionaries & Manuals. (Living Language Course Ser). pap. 2.00 ea. Crown.
Marcy, Teresa & Marcy, Michel. Cortina-Grosset Basic French Dictionary. Berberi, Dilaver & Berberi, Edel A., eds. LC 73-18522. 384p. 1975. pap. 3.50 (ISBN 0-448-14031-4). G&D.
Pensinger, Brenda. Diccionario Mixteco del Este De Jamiltepec. (Vocabularios Indigenas Ser.: No. 18). 1974. 8.00 (ISBN 0-88312-751-2); microfiche 1.60 (ISBN 0-88312-586-2). Summer Inst Ling.
Pipics, Z. The Librarian's Practical Dictionary in Twenty-Two Languages. 386p. 1980. 90.00x (ISBN 0-686-72094-6, Pub. by Collet's). State Mutual Bk.
Smith, Josefa J., et al, eds. Cortina-Grosset Basic German Dictionary. LC 73-18523. 384p. 1975. pap. 3.50 (ISBN 0-448-14029-2). G&D.
Stark, Frederick. Phrase Dictionaries for the American Tourist, 6 bks. Incl. German for the American Tourist. pap. (ISBN 0-8326-2409-8, 6570); Spanish for the English-Speaking Tourist. pap. (ISBN 0-8326-2410-1, 6571); French for the English-Speaking Tourist. pap. (ISBN 0-8326-2411-X, 6572); Italian for the English-Speaking Tourist. pap. (ISBN 0-8326-2412-8, 6573); Greek for the English-Speaking Tourist. pap. (ISBN 0-8326-2413-6, 6574); Russian for the English-Speaking Tourist. pap. (ISBN 0-8326-2414-4, 6575). 128p. (Orig.). 1981. pap. 1.95 ea. Delair.
Stoudt, Betty. Vocabulario Mixteco de San Miguel el Grande. (Vocabularios Indigenas Ser.: No. 12). 1965. pap. 3.00 (ISBN 0-88312-660-5); write for info. microfiche (ISBN 0-88312-580-3). Summer Inst Ling.
Todorov, Tzvetan. Enzyklopaedisches Woerterbuch der Sprachwissenschaften. 420p. (Ger.). 1975. 69.50 (ISBN 3-7997-0162-1, M-7087). French & Eur.
Urdang, Laurance, ed. Allusions: Cultural, Literary, Biblical, & Historical: A Thematic Dictionary. 1981. 45.00 (ISBN 0-8103-1124-0). Gale.
Varios. Diccionario Enciclopedico De las Ciencias Del Lenquaje. (Span.). 32.95 (ISBN 0-686-56652-1, S-30990). French & Eur.
Walford, Alberto J. & Screen, J. E., eds. A Guide to Foreign Language Courses & Dictionaries. LC 77-26283. 1978. lib. bdg. 22.50 (ISBN 0-313-20100-6, WGL/). Greenwood.
Zlotnicki, T. Lexicon Medicum. 1603p. 1980. 150.00x (ISBN 0-569-07372-3, Pub. by Collet's). State Mutual Bk.

LANGUAGE AND LANGUAGES–ETYMOLOGY

see also Names;
also subdivision Etymology under names of languages

Bergren, Ann L. The Etymology & Usage of Peirar in Early Greek Poetry. (American Philological Association, American Classical Studies). 1975. pap. 6.00 (ISBN 0-89130-242-5, 400402). Scholars Pr Ca.
Cohane, John P. The Key. (Illus.). 256p. 1969. 7.95 (ISBN 0-517-50733-1). Crown.
Conde, Judith S. Poridat de las Poridades: Vocabulario Etimologico. LC 81-4531. (Applied Literature Press Medieval Studies: Vol. 6). 1981. 14.25 (ISBN 0-8357-0583-8, IS-00133, Pub. by Applied Lit Pr). Univ Microfilms.
Fishman, J. Advances in the Creation & Revision of Writing Systems. 1977. 53.50 (ISBN 90-279-7552-3). Mouton.
Hunt, Cecil. A Dictionary of Word Makers: Pen Pictures of the People Behind Our Language. LC 72-13203. Repr. of 1949 ed. lib. bdg. 15.00 (ISBN 0-8414-1153-0). Folcroft.
Johannesson, Alex. Islaendisches Etymologisches Woerterbuch. 1406p. (Ice. -Ger.). 1956. 232.00 (ISBN 3-7720-0429-6, M-7485, Pub. by Francke). French & Eur.
Lokotsch, Karl. Etymologisches Woerterbuch der Europaeischen Woerter Orientalischen Ursprungs. 2nd ed. (Ger.). 1975. pap. 43.50 (ISBN 3-533-02427-X, M-7369, Pub. by Carl Winter). French & Eur.
Malkiel, Yakov. Etymological Dictionaries: A Tentative Typology. LC 75-11866. 160p. 1976. lib. bdg. 19.00x (ISBN 0-226-50292-9). U of Chicago Pr.
Pokorny, Julius. Indogermanisches Etymologisches Woerterbuch, 2 vols, Vols. 1 & 2. 1648p. 1969. 240.00 set (ISBN 3-7720-0526-8, M-7478, Pub. by Francke). French & Eur.
Rensch, Calvin R. Comparative Otomanuean Phonology. (Language Science Monographs: No. 14). 1976. pap. text ed. 15.00x (ISBN 0-87750-178-5). Res Ctr Lang Semiotic.
Richardson, Henry B. Etymological Vocabulary to the Libro De Buen Amor of Juan Ruiz, Arcipreste De Hita. LC 72-1684. (Yale Romanic Studies: No. 2). Repr. of 1930 ed. 14.50 (ISBN 0-404-53202-0). AMS Pr.
Smith, W. B. De la Toponymie Bretonne, Dictionnaire Etymologique. Repr. of 1940 ed. 6.00 (ISBN 0-527-00824-9). Kraus Repr.
Taylor, Isaac. Words & Places: Or, Etymological Illustrations of History, Ethnology & Geography. 1977. Repr. of 1888 ed. lib. bdg. 30.00 (ISBN 0-8492-2607-4). R West.
Train, John. Remarkable Words: With Astonishing Origins, Remarkable Ser. (Clarkson N. Potter Bks.). 1980. 5.95 (ISBN 0-517-54185-8). Potter.
Wartburg, Walter von. Franzoesisch Etymologisches Woerterbuch. 2nd ed. (Fr.). 1948. 38.50 (ISBN 3-16-926772-8, M-7414, Pub. by Francke). French & Eur.
Word Origins. 1980. pap. 3.95 (ISBN 0-686-65070-0). Lyle Stuart.

LANGUAGE AND LANGUAGES–EXAMINATIONS, QUESTIONS, ETC.

Blank, Marion, et al. Preschool Language Assessment Instrument: Language of Learning in Practice. 116p. 1978. 18.50 (ISBN 0-8089-1072-8); record forms 11.25 (ISBN 0-8089-1107-4). Grune.
Cohen, Andrew D. Testing Language Ability in the Classroom. 1981. pap. text ed. 10.95 (ISBN 0-88377-155-1). Newbury Hse.
Finocchiaro, Mary & Sako, Sydney. Foreign Language Testing: A Practical Approach. 1981. pap. text ed. 9.95 (ISBN 0-88345-362-2). Regents Pub.
Flowers, Ann M. Language Building Cards: Matching of Color & Form. 1968. text ed. 11.00 (ISBN 0-8134-1007-X). Interstate.

--Language-Building Cards: Serial Speech. 1968. text ed. 11.00 (ISBN 0-8134-1006-1). Interstate.

Kirk, Samuel, et al. Illinois Test of Psycholinguistic Abilities. rev. ed. 1968. 110.00 (ISBN 0-252-78420-0); examiner's manual 6.50x (ISBN 0-252-00059-5); pckg. of record forms & visual closure picture strips 12.50 (ISBN 0-252-00060-9). U of Ill Pr.

Oller, John W., Jr. Language Tests at School: A Pragmatic Approach. (Applied Linguistics & Language Study Ser.). (Illus.). 1979. text ed. 18.75x (ISBN 0-582-55365-2); pap. text ed. 12.25x (ISBN 0-582-55294-X). Longman.

Rudman, Jack. Foreign Languages Chairman - Jr. H.S. (Teachers License Examination Ser.: CH-8). (Cloth bdg. avail. on request). pap. 12.00 (ISBN 0-8373-8158-4). Natl Learning.

--Graduate School Foreign Language Test (GSFLT) (Admission Test Ser.: ATS-28). (Cloth bdg. avail. on request). pap. 13.95 (ISBN 0-686-67282-8). Natl Learning.

Savard, Jean-Guy. Bibliographie Analytique De Tests De Langue: Analytical Bibliography of Language Tests. 2nd, rev. ed. (Fr. & Eng.). 1977. 29.00x (ISBN 2-7637-6438-X, Pub. by Laval). Intl Schol Bk Serv.

Spolsky, Bernard, ed. Approaches to Language Testing. LC 78-62080. (Advances in Language Testing Ser.: No. 2). 1978. pap. text ed. 5.50x (ISBN 0-87281-075-5). Ctr Appl Ling.

--Some Major Tests. LC 78-60576. (Advances in Testing Ser.: No. 1). 1979. pap. text ed. 6.00x (ISBN 0-87281-074-7). Ctr Appl Ling.

Thorum, Arden R. Language Assessment Instruments: Infancy Through Adulthood. 320p. 1980. text ed. 19.75 (ISBN 0-398-04107-5). C C Thomas.

Toronto, Allen S., et al. Del Rio Language Screening Test. (Illus.). 1975. test manual, paper, bound with flash cards 18.00 (ISBN 0-916542-04-1, 15FT). NELP.

LANGUAGE AND LANGUAGES-FOREIGN ELEMENTS

Steiger, Arnaldo. Origin & Spread of Oriental Words in European Languages. 1963. 7.50x (ISBN 0-913298-32-8). S F Vanni.

Weiman, R. Native & Foreign Elements in Language. LC 75-35649. 1940. lib. bdg. 15.00 (ISBN 0-8414-9439-8). Folcroft.

LANGUAGE AND LANGUAGES-GRAMMAR, COMPARATIVE

see Grammar, Comparative and General

LANGUAGE AND LANGUAGES-JUVENILE LITERATURE

Adler, Irving & Adler, Joyce. Language & Man. LC 78-109148. (Reason Why Ser). (Illus.). (gr. 3-6). 1970. lib. bdg. 8.79 (ISBN 0-381-99978-5, A42100, JD-J). Har-Row.

Gallant, Roy A. Man Must Speak: The Story of Language. (Illus.). (gr. 7-10). 1969. PLB 5.69 (ISBN 0-394-91532-1, BYR). Random.

Lambert, Eloise. Our Language: The Story of the Words We Use. LC 55-10444. (gr. 6 up). 1955. 8.25 (ISBN 0-688-41607-1). Lothrop.

Schwartz, Alvin. The Cat's Elbow & Other Secret Languages. (Illus.). 96p. (gr. 3 up). 1981. 9.95 (ISBN 0-374-31224-9). FS&G.

LANGUAGE AND LANGUAGES-PHILOSOPHY

see Languages-Philosophy

LANGUAGE AND LANGUAGES-PHONETIC TRANSCRIPTIONS

Akers, Glenn A. Phonological Variation in the Jamaican Continuum. 158p. 1981. pap. 8.50 (ISBN 0-89720-038-1). Karoma.

Dew, Donald & Jensen, Alfred D. Phonetic Transcription. 2nd ed. 1979. text ed. 7.95 (ISBN 0-675-08309-5); instructors manual 3.95 (ISBN 0-686-67278-X). Merrill.

Pierssens, Michel. Tower of Babel: A Study of Logophilia. Lovitt, Carl R., tr. from Fr. Orig. Title: Tour De Babil. 144p. 1980. Repr. of 1976 ed. 20.00x (ISBN 0-7100-0373-0). Routledge & Kegan.

Pike, Kenneth L. Phonemics: A Technique for Reducing Language to Writing. 1947. pap. 6.50x (ISBN 0-472-08732-0). U of Mich Pr.

LANGUAGE AND LANGUAGES-POLITICAL ASPECTS

see Languages-Political Aspects

LANGUAGE AND LANGUAGES-PRINTING

see Printing-Style Manuals

LANGUAGE AND LANGUAGES-PROGRAMMED INSTRUCTION

Blumberg, Harris M. A Program of Sequential Language Development: A Theoretical & Practical Guide for Remediation of Language, Reading & Learning Disorders. (Illus.). 108p. 1975. 12.75 (ISBN 0-398-03320-X). C C Thomas.

Boyd-Bowman, Peter. Self-Instructional Language Programs. (Occasional Publication). 1973. pap. 1.50 (ISBN 0-89192-139-7). Interbk Inc.

Bung, K. Toward a Theory of Programmed Learning Foreign Language. (Janua Linguarum Ser. Didactica: No. 1). 1973. text ed. 17.00x (ISBN 90-2792-383-3). Mouton.

Johnson, Rita B. & Johnson, Stuart R. Assuring Learning With Self-Instructional Packages, or Up the Up Staircase. 1973. pap. text ed. 9.95 (ISBN 0-201-03327-5). A-W.

Motley. Orientations to Language & Communication. Applbaum, Ronald & Hart, Roderick, eds. LC 77-12329. (MODCOM - Modules in Speech Communication). 1978. pap. text ed. 2.50 (ISBN 0-574-22534-X, 13-5534). SRA.

O'Donnell, Mabel, et al. Programmed Studies in the Language Arts. Incl. Critical Reading Skills. text ed. 4.08 (ISBN 0-06-510318-1); tchrs' ed. 8.16 (ISBN 0-06-510418-8); pre-test & post-tests 0.40 (ISBN 0-685-28886-2); Literary Style. text ed. 4.08 (ISBN 0-06-510319-X); tchrs' ed. 8.16 (ISBN 0-06-510419-6); pre-tests & post-tests 0.40 (ISBN 0-685-28887-0). (Design for Reading Ser). (gr. 7-8, SchDept). Har-Row.

Winitz, Harris, ed. The Learnables, Vol. 1. 64p. (Orig.). 1978. pap. 2.50 (ISBN 0-939990-09-1, SR 10-365); used with language cassette 4.00 (ISBN 0-686-30251-6). Intl Linguistics.

--The Learnables, Vol. 2. 64p. (Orig.). 1978. pap. 2.50 (ISBN 0-939990-10-5, SR 10-365); used with language cassette 4.00 (ISBN 0-686-30252-4). Intl Linguistics.

--The Learnables, Vol. 3. 64p. (Orig.). 1978. pap. 2.50 (ISBN 0-939990-11-3, SR 10-365); used with language cassette 4.00 (ISBN 0-686-30253-2). Intl Linguistics.

--The Learnables, Vol. 4. 64p. (Orig.). 1978. pap. 2.50 (ISBN 0-939990-12-1, SR 10-365); used with language cassette 4.00 (ISBN 0-686-30254-0). Intl Linguistics.

--The Learnables, Vol. 5. 64p. (Orig.). 1978. pap. 2.50 (ISBN 0-686-30255-9, SR 10-365); used with language cassette 4.00 (ISBN 0-686-30256-7). Intl Linguistics.

--The Learnables, Vol. 6. 64p. (Orig.). 1978. pap. 2.50 (ISBN 0-939990-14-8, SR 10-365); used with language cassette 4.00 (ISBN 0-686-30257-5). Intl Linguistics.

--The Learnables, Vol. 7. 64p. (Orig.). 1978. pap. 2.50 (ISBN 0-939990-15-6, SR 10-365); used with language cassette 4.00 (ISBN 0-686-30258-3). Intl Linguistics.

--The Learnables, Vol. 8. 64p. (Orig.). 1978. pap. 2.50 (ISBN 0-939990-16-4, SR 10-365); used with language cassette 4.00 (ISBN 0-686-30259-1). Intl Linguistics.

--The Learnables, Vol. 9. 64p. (Orig.). 1978. pap. 2.50 (ISBN 0-939990-17-2, SR 10-365); used with language cassette 4.00 (ISBN 0-686-30260-5). Intl Linguistics.

--The Learnables, Vol. 10. 64p. (Orig.). 1978. pap. 2.50 (ISBN 0-939990-18-0, SR 10-365); used with language cassette 4.00 (ISBN 0-686-30261-3). Intl Linguistics.

--The Learnables, Vol. 11. 64p. (Orig.). 1978. pap. 2.50 (ISBN 0-939990-19-9, SR 10-365); used with language cassette 4.00 (ISBN 0-686-30262-1). Intl Linguistics.

--The Learnables, Vol. 12. 64p. (Orig.). 1978. pap. 2.50 (ISBN 0-939990-20-2, SR 10-365); used with language cassette 4.00 (ISBN 0-686-30263-X). Intl Linguistics.

--The Learnables, Vol. 13. 64p. (Orig.). 1978. pap. 2.50 (ISBN 0-939990-21-0, SR 10-365); used with language cassette 4.00 (ISBN 0-686-30264-8). Intl Linguistics.

--The Learnables, Vol. 14. 64p. (Orig.). 1978. pap. 2.50 (ISBN 0-939990-22-9, SR 10-365); used with language cassette 4.00 (ISBN 0-686-30265-6). Intl Linguistics.

--The Learnables, Vol. 15. 64p. (Orig.). 1978. pap. 2.50 (ISBN 0-939990-23-7, SR 10-365); used with language cassette 4.00 (ISBN 0-686-30266-4). Intl Linguistics.

--The Learnables, Vol. 16. 64p. (Orig.). 1978. pap. 2.50 (ISBN 0-939990-24-5, SR 10-365); used with language cassette 4.00 (ISBN 0-686-30267-2). Intl Linguistics.

--The Learnables, Vol. 17. 64p. (Orig.). 1978. pap. 2.50 (ISBN 0-939990-25-3, SR 10-365); used with language cassette 4.00 (ISBN 0-686-30268-0). Intl Linguistics.

--The Learnables, Vol. 18. 64p. (Orig.). 1978. pap. 2.50 (ISBN 0-939990-26-1, SR 10-365); used with language cassette 4.00 (ISBN 0-686-30269-9). Intl Linguistics.

--The Learnables, Vol. 19. 64p. (Orig.). 1978. pap. 2.50 (ISBN 0-939990-27-X, SR 10-365); used with language cassette 4.00 (ISBN 0-686-30270-2). Intl Linguistics.

--The Learnables, Vol. 20. 64p. (Orig.). 1978. pap. 2.50 (ISBN 0-939990-28-8, SR 10-365); used with language cassette 4.00 (ISBN 0-686-30271-0). Intl Linguistics.

LANGUAGE AND LANGUAGES-PSYCHOLOGY

see Psycholinguistics

LANGUAGE AND LANGUAGES-RELIGIOUS ASPECTS

see Religion and Language

LANGUAGE AND LANGUAGES-RESEARCH

see Linguistic Research

LANGUAGE AND LANGUAGES-STATISTICAL METHODS

see Mathematical Linguistics

LANGUAGE AND LANGUAGES-STUDY AND TEACHING

see also Language and Languages-Vocational Guidance; Linguistic Research

Aarsleff, Hans. From Locke to Saussure: Essays on the Study of Language. LC 81-10428. 474p. 1981. 29.50x (ISBN 0-8166-0964-0); pap. 12.95x (ISBN 0-8166-0967-5). U of Minn Pr.

Alatis, James E., et al, eds. The Second Language Classroom: Directions for the 1980's. Altman, Howard B. & Alatis, Penelope M. (Illus.). 304p. 1981. text ed. 14.95x (ISBN 0-19-502928-3); pap. text ed. 7.95x (ISBN 0-19-502929-1). Oxford U Pr.

Alexander, Christopher, et al. A Pattern Language: Towns, Buildings, Construction. LC 74-22874. (Illus.). 1440p. 1977. 39.50 (ISBN 0-19-501919-9). Oxford U Pr.

Allen, Edward D. & Valette, Rebecca M. Classroom Techniques: Foreign Languages & English As a Second Language. (Orig.). 1977. pap. text ed. 10.95 (ISBN 0-15-507674-4, HC). HarBraceJ.

Allen, Jerry & Allen, Janice. Halia Language Course. 68p. 1965. pap. 1.00x (ISBN 0-88312-771-7). Summer Inst Ling.

Anchor: A Handbook of Classroom Ideas to Motivate the Teaching of Intermediate Language Arts. (The Spice Ser). 1970. 6.50 (ISBN 0-89273-109-5). Educ Serv.

Andersen, Roger W., ed. New Dimensions in Second Language Acquisition Research. (Illus.). 280p. (Orig.). 1981. pap. text ed. 14.95 (ISBN 0-88377-180-2). Newbury Hse.

Anderson, Iona L. The Effectiveness of an Open Classroom Approach on Second Language Acquisition. LC 78-62238. 1978. soft cover 10.00 (ISBN 0-88247-541-X). R & E Res Assoc.

Anderson, Paul S. Linguistics in the Classroom. 1971. pap. text ed. 7.95 (ISBN 0-02-303280-4, 30328). Macmillan.

Arendt, Jermaine D., et al, eds. Foreign Language Learning, Today & Tomorrow: Essays in Honor of Emma M. Birkmaier. 1979. 19.25 (ISBN 0-08-024628-1). Pergamon.

Bartz, Walter H. Testing Oral Communication in the Foreign Language Classroom. (Language in Education Ser.: No. 17). 1979. pap. 3.25x (ISBN 0-87281-103-4). Ctr Appl Ling.

Baughman, M. Dale, ed. Foreign Language Instruction in the Junior High School Grades. pap. text ed. 1.50x (ISBN 0-8134-0590-4, 590). Interstate.

Bearth, Thomas. L' Enonce Toura (Cote d'Ivoire) (Publications in Linguistics & Related Fields Ser.: No. 30). 481p. (Fr.). 1971. microfiche 3.00 (ISBN 0-88312-432-7). Summer Inst Ling.

Bell, Roger T. An Introduction to Applied Linguistics: Approaches & Methods in Language Teaching. 1981. 25.00x (ISBN 0-312-42547-3). St Martin.

Bellack, Arno A., et al. Language of the Classroom. LC 66-22926. 1966. pap. 7.50 (ISBN 0-8077-1063-6). Tchrs Coll.

Bendor-Samuel, David. Hierarchical Structures in Guajajara. (Publications in Linguistics & Related Fields, No. 37). 214p. 1972. pap. 4.50x (ISBN 0-88312-039-9); microfiche 2.20 (ISBN 0-88312-439-4). Summer Inst Ling.

Benseler, David P. & Schultz, Renate A. Intensive Foreign Language Courses. (Language in Education Ser.: No. 18). 55p. 1979. pap. 5.50x (ISBN 0-87281-104-2). Ctr Appl Ling.

Bernstein, Basil. Class, Codes, & Control: Theoretical Studies Towards a Sociology of Language. LC 74-9130. 252p. 1975. pap. 4.95 (ISBN 0-8052-0458-X). Schocken.

Berry, Mildred F. Teaching Linguistically Handicapped Children. 1980. text ed. 18.95 (ISBN 0-13-893545-9). P-H.

Blood, Henry F. A Reconstruction of Proto-Mnong. 110p. 1968. pap. 4.00 (ISBN 0-88312-641-9). Summer Inst Ling.

Born, Warren C., ed. The Foreign Language Teacher in Today's Classroom Environment. 1979. pap. 7.95x (ISBN 0-915432-79-X). NE Conf Teach.

Bottiglia, William F., ed. Current Issues in Language Teaching. Incl. Linguistics & Language Teaching. Hall, Robert A., Jr; Programmed Learning. Hayes, Alfred S; A Survey of FLES Practices. Alkons, Nancy V. & Biophy, Mary A.. 1962. 7.95x (ISBN 0-915432-62-5). NE Conf Teach Foreign.

--Language Learning: The Intermediate Phase. Incl. The Continuum: Listening & Speaking. Belasco, Simon; Reading for Meaning. Sherer, George; Writing an Expression. Prochoroff, Marina. 85p. 1963. pap. 9.95 (ISBN 0-915432-63-3). NE Conf Teach Foreign.

Bradley, C. Henry. A Linguistic Sketch of Jicaltepec Mixtec. (Publications in Linguistics & Related Fields Ser.: No. 25). 97p. 1970. pap. 3.00x (ISBN 0-88312-027-5); microfiche 1.60 (ISBN 0-686-66936-3). Summer Inst Ling.

Brewer, Forrest & Brewer, Jean. Vocabulario Mexicano de Tetelcingo. (Vocabularios Indigenas Ser.: No. 8). 274p. 1962. pap. 4.00x (ISBN 0-88312-658-3); microfiche 2.20 (ISBN 0-88312-363-0). Summer Inst Ling.

Brewster, E. Thomas & Brewster, Elizabeth S. Language Acquisition Made Practical (LAMP) new ed. LC 75-43377. (Illus.). 1976. 12.00 (ISBN 0-916636-00-3); tape 3.50 (ISBN 0-685-63929-0); bk. & tape 15.00 (ISBN 0-685-63930-4). Lingua Hse.

Britton, James. Language & Learning. LC 74-137564. 1971. 11.95x (ISBN 0-87024-186-9). U of Miami Pr.

Brod, Richard I. & Fisher, Dexter, eds. Profession 1981. 60p. (Orig.). 1981. pap. 4.00x (ISBN 0-87352-316-4). Modern Lang.

Brod, Richard I. & Neel, Jasper P., eds. Profession 79. 60p. 1979. pap. 4.00x (ISBN 0-87352-314-8). Modern Lang.

Brown, H. Douglas. Principles of Language Learning & Teaching. (Illus.). 1980. pap. text ed. 9.95 (ISBN 0-13-709295-4). P-H.

Bruce, R. Teach Yourself Cantonese. (Teach Yourself Ser). 1971. pap. 4.95 (ISBN 0-679-10208-6). McKay.

Bush, Wilma J. & Giles, Marian T. Aids to Psycholinguistic Teaching. 2nd ed. (Special Education Ser.). 1977. text ed. 19.95 (ISBN 0-675-08525-X). Merrill.

Casad, Eugene. Dialect Intelligibility Tests. (Publications in Linguistics & Related Fields Ser.: No. 38). 1974. pap. 8.00x (ISBN 0-88312-040-2); microfiche 2.20 (ISBN 0-88312-440-8). Summer Inst Ling.

Cashdan, Asher. Language Reading & Learning. 171p. pap. text ed. 11.95 (ISBN 0-8391-1365-X). Univ Park.

Cates, G. Truett & Swaffar, Janet K. Reading a Second Language. (Language in Education Ser.: No. 20). 1979. pap. 3.25x (ISBN 0-87281-106-9). Ctr Appl Ling.

Clark, Raymond C. Language Teaching Techniques. LC 80-84109. (Pro Lingua Language Resource Handbook Ser.: No. 1). (Illus.). 128p. (Orig.). 1980. pap. 5.50 (ISBN 0-86647-000-X). Pro Lingua.

Cohen, Andrew D. Testing Language Ability in the Classroom. 1981. pap. text ed. 10.95 (ISBN 0-88377-155-1). Newbury Hse.

Cooper, Jean, et al. Helping Language Development. LC 77-27524. 1978. 10.95 (ISBN 0-312-36757-0). St Martin.

Coulthard, Malcolm. Introduction to Discourse Analysis. (Applied Linguistics & Language Study Ser.). 1978. pap. text ed. 9.00x (ISBN 0-582-55087-4). Longman.

Creber, J. W. Lost for Words: Language & Educational Failure. lib. bdg. 8.50x (ISBN 0-88307-328-5). Gannon.

Crescimbeni, Joseph. Language Enrichment Activities for the Elementary School. (Illus.). 1979. 13.95 (ISBN 0-13-522987-1, Parker). P-H.

Derbyshire, Desmond. Textos Hixkaryana. 206p. 1965. pap. 2.75 (ISBN 0-88312-649-4). Summer Inst Ling.

Dickerson, Wayne B. & Dickerson, Lonna J. Tips on Taping: Language Recording in Social Sciences. LC 76-50023. (Applied Cultural Anthropology Ser.). 1977. pap. 4.95x (ISBN 0-87808-147-X). William Carey Lib.

Diller, Karl C. Individual Differences & Universals in Language Learning Aptitude. (Orig.). 1981. pap. text ed. 15.95 (ISBN 0-88377-164-0). Newbury Hse.

--The Language Teaching Controversy. rev ed. LC 78-7021. 1978. pap. text ed. 6.95 (ISBN 0-88377-114-4). Newbury Hse.

Elkins, Richard E. Major Grammatical Patterns of Western Bukidnon Manobo. (Publications in Linguistics & Related Fields Ser.: No. 26). 76p. 1970. pap. 2.00x (ISBN 0-88312-028-3). Summer Inst Ling.

Ericson, Carol. Learning Predictable Language. LC 73-78323. 1973. pap. 7.00x (ISBN 0-87879-046-2). Acad Therapy.

Fisiak, Jacek. Contrastive Linguistics & the Language Teacher. 160p. 1981. pap. 9.95 (ISBN 0-08-027230-4). Pergamon.

Flaxman, Seymour L., ed. Modern Language Teaching in Schools & Colleges. 72p. 1961. pap. 7.95x (ISBN 0-915432-61-7). NE Conf Teach Foreign.

Flowers, Ann M. Language Development Through Perceptual-Motor Activities. 1975. text ed. 9.95 (ISBN 0-8134-1761-9). Interstate.

Francis, Hazel. Language in Teaching & Learning. (Unwin Education Books). 1978. text ed. 14.95x (ISBN 0-04-407003-9); pap. text ed. 6.50x (ISBN 0-04-407004-7). Allen Unwin.

Freed, Barbara F. From the Community to the Classroom: Gathering Second Language Speech Samples. (Language in Education Ser.: No. 6). 1978. pap. 3.25x (ISBN 0-87281-085-2). Ctr Appl Ling.

Freeman, Gerald G. Speech & Language Services & the Classroom Teacher. 1978. pap. text ed. 3.75 (ISBN 0-86586-078-5). Coun Exc Child.

Freeman, Stephen A. Middlebury College Foreign Language Schools, Nineteen Fifteen to Nineteen Seventy: The Story of a Unique Idea. (Orig.). 1975. pap. 5.95x (ISBN 0-910408-17-3). Coll Store.

Freudenstein, Reinhold, ed. Teaching Foreign Languages to the Very Young. LC 79-42885. (Pergamon Institute of English - Symposium). (Illus.). 112p. 1979. 7.50 (ISBN 0-08-024576-5). Pergamon.

Freudenstein, Reinhold, et al. Language Incorporated: Teaching Foreign Languages in Industry. LC 80-42188. (Illus.). 128p. 1981. pap. 13.95 (ISBN 0-08-024578-1). Pergamon.

Gahagan, D. M. & Gahagan, G. A. Talk Reform: Exploration in Language for Infant School Children. LC 74-158824. (Primary Socialization, Language & Education: Vol. 3). 147p. 1971. 12.50x (ISBN 0-8039-0122-4). Sage.

Garfinkel, Alan & Hamilton, Stanley. Designs for Foreign Language Teacher Education. LC 76-20755. (Innovations in Foreign Language Education Ser). 1976. pap. text ed. 7.95 (ISBN 0-88377-062-8). Newbury Hse.

Gattegno, Caleb. The Common Sense of Teaching Foreign Languages. (The Common Sense of Teaching Ser.). 1976. 5.95 (ISBN 0-87825-071-9). Ed Solutions.

--Teaching Foreign Languages in Schools: The Silent Way. 144p. 1972. pap. text ed. 4.95 (ISBN 0-87825-046-8). Ed Solutions.

Geno, Thomas H., ed. Foreign Language & International Studies: Toward Cooperation & Integration. LC 55-34379. 200p. 1981. pap. 7.95 (ISBN 0-915432-81-1). NE Conf Teach Foreign.

--Our Profession: Present Status & Future Directions. 1980. pap. 7.95x (ISBN 0-915432-80-3). NE Conf Teach.

Gerdel, Florence & Slocum, Marianna. Vocabulario Tzeltal de Bachajon. (Vocabularios Indigenas Ser.: No. 13). 215p. 1965. pap. 3.25 (ISBN 0-88312-667-2); 2.20 (ISBN 0-88312-589-7). Summer Inst Ling.

Gibaldi, Joseph & Mirollo, James V., eds. The Teaching Apprentice Program in Language & Literature. LC 81-1159. (Options for Teaching Ser.: No. 4). vi, 133p. (Orig.). 1981. pap. 7.00x (ISBN 0-87352-303-2). Modern Lang.

Gingras, Rosario C., ed. Second-Language Acquisition & Foreign Language Teaching. LC 78-74014. 1978. pap. text ed. 7.95x (ISBN 0-87281-090-9). Ctr Appl Ling.

Grittner, Frank M. Teaching Foreign Languages. 2nd ed. 1977. text ed. 19.50 scp (ISBN 0-06-042524-5, HarpC); instructor's manual free (ISBN 0-06-362515-6). Har-Row.

Haggitt, T. W. Working with a Language. (Illus.). 9.50x (ISBN 0-392-01959-0, Sps). Sportshelf.

Hall, Robert A., Jr. New Ways to Learn a Foreign Language. LC 73-15154. viii, 180p. 1980. pap. 6.00x (ISBN 0-87950-293-2). Spoken Lang Serv.

Handschin, Charles H., et al. Methods for Teaching Modern Language. (Educational Ser.). 1905. Repr. 15.00 (ISBN 0-685-43490-7). Norwood Edns.

Hawkins, Eric. Modern Languages in the Curriculum. (Illus.). 200p. 1981. 29.95 (ISBN 0-521-23211-2). Cambridge U Pr.

Healev, F. G. Foreign Language Teaching in the Universities. 290p. 1967. 30.00x (ISBN 0-686-63738-0, Pub. by Manchester U Pr England). State Mutual Bk.

Healey, Alan, ed. Language Learner's Field Guide. 500p. 1975. pap. 7.95x (ISBN 0-7263-0356-9). Summer Inst Ling.

Heckleman, R. G. Perceptual Auditory Learning Series Kit (Pals) 1975. manual & boxed cards 35.00x (ISBN 0-87879-101-9). Acad Therapy.

Hodge, Virginia. Personality & Second Language Learning. (Language in Education Ser.: No. 12). 1978. pap. 3.25x (ISBN 0-87281-086-0). Ctr Appl Ling.

Hodgson, F. M. Language Learning Material. 41p. 1961. pap. 1.40 (ISBN 0-685-46936-0). Ed Solutions.

Holec, Henri. Autonomy & Foreign Language Learning. LC 80-41849. 64p. 1981. pap. 4.95 (ISBN 0-08-025357-1). Pergamon.

Honig, Lucille J. & Brod, Richard I. Foreign Languages & Careers. 2nd ed. (Orig.). 1979. pap. 1.25x (ISBN 0-87352-087-4). Modern Lang.

Hornsey, Alan W., ed. Handbook for Modern Language Teachers. 1972. 35.00x (ISBN 0-423-89690-3). Methuen Inc.

Hudelson, Sarah, ed. Learning to Read in Different Languages. LC 80-36878. (Linguistics & Literacy Ser.: No. 1). 1981. pap. 7.95x (ISBN 0-87281-118-2). Ctr Appl Ling.

Hunt, L. C., ed. The Making of a Book. (Satellite Books Ser). (Level 14). pap. 2.92 (ISBN 0-03-084624-2, HoltE). HR&W.

Hurd, Conrad & Hurd, Phyllis. Nasioi Language Course. 283p. 1966. pap. 1.00x (ISBN 0-88312-791-1). Summer Inst Ling.

Huse, H. R. The Psychology of Foreign Language Study. (Educational Ser.). 1931. Repr. 20.00 (ISBN 0-685-43477-X). Norwood Edns.

Izzo, Sue. Second Language Learning: A Review of Related Studies. (Orig.). 1981. pap. write for info. (ISBN 0-89763-058-0). Natl Clearinghse Bilingual Ed.

Jankowsky, Kurt R., ed. Georgetown University Round Table on Languages & Linguistics: Language & International Studies. LC 58-31607. (1969). 238p. (GURT 1973). pap. 4.50 (ISBN 0-87840-108-3). Georgetown U Pr.

Jarvis, Gilbert A. Responding to New Realities. (ACTFL Review Ser.: Vol. 5). 1973. 15.00 (ISBN 0-8442-9349-0). Natl Textbk.

Jarvis, Gilbert A. & Adams, Shirley J. Evaluating a Second Language Program. (Language in Education Ser.: No. 19). 1979. pap. 3.25x (ISBN 0-87281-105-0). Ctr Appl Ling.

Johnson, Dora E., et al, eds. A Survey of Materials for the Study of the Uncommonly Taught Languages No. 2: Eastern Europe & the Soviet Union. LC 76-44589. 1976. pap. 4.95x (ISBN 0-87281-053-4). Ctr Appl Ling.

--A Survey of Materials for the Study of the Uncommonly Taught Languages No. 4: South Asia. LC 76-44592. 1976. pap. 4.95x (ISBN 0-87281-054-2). Ctr Appl Ling.

--A Survey of Materials for the Study of the Uncommonly Taught Languages No. 5: Eastern Asia. LC 76-44593. 1976. pap. 4.95x (ISBN 0-87281-055-0). Ctr Appl Ling.

--A Survey of Materials for the Study of the Uncommonly Taught Languages: Middle East, No. 3. LC 76-44591. 1976. pap. 4.95x (ISBN 0-87281-056-9). Ctr Appl Ling.

Johnson, Kieth. Notional Syllabuses & Communicative Language Teaching. Date not set. pap. 7.95 (ISBN 0-08-025355-5). Pergamon.

Jones, Morris V. Speech & Language Problems: An Overview. (Am. Lec. Special Education Ser.). (Illus.). 420p. 1979. 22.75 (ISBN 0-398-03790-6). C C Thomas.

Joyce, William W. & Banks, James A., eds. Teaching the Language Arts to Culturally Different Children. LC 78-136123. (Education Ser). 1971. pap. 6.95 (ISBN 0-201-03403-4). A-W.

Kellerman, Marcelle. The Forgotten Third Skill: Reading a Foreign Language. LC 80-41029. (Language Teaching Methodology Ser.). 96p. 1981. 11.95 (ISBN 0-08-024599-4); pap. 7.95 (ISBN 0-08-024598-6). Pergamon.

Kelly, Louis G. Twenty Five Centuries of Language Teaching. 1969. pap. 11.95 (ISBN 0-912066-00-8). Newbury Hse.

Key, Harold. Fonotacticas del Cayuvava. (Notas Linguisticas De Bolivia Ser.: No. 4). 72p. 1962. pap. 0.75 (ISBN 0-88312-764-4). Summer Inst Ling.

Kitzhaber, Albert R. Language Paperbacks. Incl. Blueprint for Language. (gr. 7). pap. text ed. 4.96 (ISBN 0-03-010821-7); Inside Language. (gr. 8). pap. text ed. 4.88 (ISBN 0-03-010826-8); Language - Beneath the Surface. (gr. 9). pap. text ed. 5.28 (ISBN 0-03-010841-1); Language - Putting It All Together. (gr. 10). pap. text ed. 5.28 (ISBN 0-03-010846-2); Language - Parts Within Parts. (gr. 11). pap. text ed. 5.28 (ISBN 0-03-010851-9). (gr. 7-11). 1974. tchr's guides for ea. book 2.64 (ISBN 0-685-42778-1, HoltE). HR&W.

Klooster, W. G. The Structure Underlying Measure Phrase Sentences. LC 76-188003. (Foundations of Language Supplementary Ser: No. 17). 247p. 1972. lib. bdg. 39.50 (ISBN 90-277-0229-2, Pub. by Reidel Holland). Kluwer Boston.

Krashen, Stephen. Second Language Acquisition & Second Language Learning. (Language Teaching Methodology Ser.). 176p. 1981. pap. 9.95 (ISBN 0-08-025338-5). Pergamon.

Krashen, Stephen D., et al, eds. Child-Adult Differences in Second Language Acquisition. (Issues in Second Language Research Ser.). 336p. 1982. pap. text ed. 16.95 (ISBN 0-88377-206-X). Newbury Hse.

Kratoville, Betty L. Listen, My Children, & You Shall Hear, Bk. 1. LC 68-29770. 1968. pap. 3.25x (ISBN 0-8134-1044-4, 1044); pkg. of 20 extra grading sheets 0.75 (ISBN 0-8134-1045-2, 1045). Interstate.

Lado, Robert. Lado English Series, Bk. 5. (Illus.). 198p. (gr. 7-12). 1980. pap. text ed. 3.95 (ISBN 0-88345-307-X, 18749); tchr's manual 4.95 (ISBN 0-88345-344-4); wkbk., 132 pp. 2.50 (ISBN 0-88345-338-X, 18755). Regents Pub.

--Lado English Series, Bk. 6. (Illus.). 1980. pap. text ed. 3.95 (ISBN 0-88345-333-9); tchr's manual 4.95 (ISBN 0-88345-345-2); wkbk. 2.50 (ISBN 0-88345-339-8). Regents Pub.

--Language Teaching, a Scientific Approach. 1964. pap. text ed. 9.95 (ISBN 0-07-035740-4, C). McGraw.

Larson, Donald N. & Smalley, William A. Becoming Bilingual: A Guide to Language Learning. LC 74-8839. (Applied Cultural Anthropology Ser.). 425p. (Orig.). 1974. pap. 6.95x (ISBN 0-87808-718-4). William Carey Lib.

Larson, Mildred. Studies in Peruvian Indian Languages One. (Publications in Linguistics & Related Fields Ser.: No. 9). 220p. 1963. pap. 1.50x (ISBN 0-88312-009-7); microfilm 1.60 (ISBN 0-88312-409-2). Summer Inst Ling.

Larson, Mildred L. Vocabulario Aguaruna de Amazonas. (Peruvian Linguistic Ser: No. 3). 1966. pap. 3.00x (ISBN 0-88312-653-2). Summer Inst Ling.

Leach, Ilo M. Vocabulario Ocaina. (Peruvian Linguistic Ser: No. 4). 176p. 1969. pap. 2.50x (ISBN 0-88312-662-1); microfiche 1.60 (ISBN 0-88312-364-9). Summer Inst Ling.

Learning in Language & Literature. Incl. Insistent Tasks in Language Learning. MacKinnon, A. R. (Burton Lectures Ser: 1962); The Developing Imagination. Frye, Northrop. (Inglis Lectures Ser: 1962). LC 63-13811. 62p. 1963. 5.95x (ISBN 0-674-52000-9). Harvard U Pr.

Leeming, Ken, et al. Teaching Language & Communication to the Mentally Retarded. 1979. 32.50x (ISBN 0-416-60051-4). Methuen Inc.

Leeson, Richard. Fluency & Language Teaching. (Applied Linguistics & Language Study Ser.). 1976. pap. text ed. 9.00x (ISBN 0-582-55078-5). Longman.

Lewis, E. Glyn. Linguistics & Second Language Pedagogy: A Theoretical Study. LC 73-79891. (Janua Linguarum, Ser. Didactica: No. 10). 137p. (Orig.). 1974. pap. text ed. 20.75x (ISBN 90-2792-707-3). Mouton.

Lind, Carolyn P., pseud. One Hundred Four Ideas for Improving Your Young Child's Language Skills. (Illus.). 80p. (Orig.). 1980. pap. 10.00 (ISBN 0-9604940-0-6). Lindell Pubs.

Lindskoog, John & Lindskoog, Carrie. Vocabulario Cayapa. (Vocabularios Indigenas Ser.: No. 9). 129p. 1964. pap. 2.50 (ISBN 0-88312-654-0). Summer Inst Ling.

Linguistic Circle of Saigon & Summer Institute of Linguistics. Mon-Khmer Studies, No. 1-4. Incl. No. 1. Banker, John, et al. 163p. 1964. microfiche 1.60 (ISBN 0-88312-541-2); No. 2. Thomas, David, et al, eds. 111p. 1966. microfiche 1.60 (ISBN 0-88312-542-0); No. 3. Burton, Eva, et al. 147p. 1969. microfiche 1.60 (ISBN 0-685-41028-5); No. 4. Thomas, David D. & Hoa, Nguyen D. 1973. pap. 5.00 (ISBN 0-685-41029-3); microfiche 1.60 (ISBN 0-88312-357-6). Summer Inst Ling.

Llamzon, Teodoro A. A Handbook for Second Language Teaching. wrps. 7.25x (ISBN 0-686-09507-3). Cellar.

Love, William & Honig, Lucille, eds. Options & Perspectives: A Sourcebook of Innovative Foreign Language Programs in Action, K-12. 361p. (Orig.). 1973. pap. 7.50x (ISBN 0-87352-070-X). Modern Lang.

McElhannon, Kenneth. Selepet Phonology. (Pacific Linguistics, Ser. B: No. 14). 47p. 1970. pap. 1.50 (ISBN 0-88312-644-3). Summer Inst Ling.

McGivern, A. B., et al. Language Stories: Teaching Language to Developmentally Disabled Children. LC 76-27347. (John Day Bk.). 1978. 29.95x (ISBN 0-381-98108-8). T y Crowell.

Mackey, W. F. Language Teaching Analysis. LC 67-20424. (Studies in the History & Theory of Linguistics). 576p. 1967. 15.00x (ISBN 0-253-33215-X). Ind U Pr.

Madsen, Harold S. & Bowen, J. Donald. Adaptation in Language Teaching. 1978. pap. text ed. 9.95 (ISBN 0-88377-105-5). Newbury Hse.

Mandel, Barrett J., ed. Three Language-Arts Curriculum Models: Pre-Kindergarten Through College. 1980. pap. 8.50 (ISBN 0-8141-5458-1). NCTE.

Mann, Lynne. The EARLI Program, 2 vols. 1981. Set. pap. 29.90 (ISBN 0-89334-029-4). Humanics Ltd.

Markova, A. K. The Teaching & Mastery of Language. Szekely, Beatrice B., ed. Vale, Michel, tr. from Rus. LC 78-65595. 1979. 25.00 (ISBN 0-87332-131-6). M E Sharpe.

Martin, Samuel E. Language Study Techniques. 1.50 (ISBN 0-686-09959-1). Far Eastern Pubns.

Material Development Needs in the Uncommonly Taught Languages: Priorities for the Seventies. 1975. pap. text ed. 2.50 (ISBN 0-87281-048-8). Ctr Appl Ling.

Meader, Robert E. Iranxe: Notas Gramaticais e Lista Vocabular. 139p. 1967. pap. 2.00x (ISBN 0-88312-777-6). Summer Inst Ling.

Medlin, D. M. The Verbal Art of Jean Francois Regnard, Vol. 1. 156p. 1966. pap. 7.00 (ISBN 0-912788-00-3). Tulane Romance Lang.

Meech, D. W. Learn That Language. 1976. pap. 3.00 (ISBN 0-88312-782-2). Summer Inst Ling.

Melear, John. Conceptual Oral Language Activities (COLA) Kit. 1973. pap. 25.00x set (ISBN 0-87879-062-4). Acad Therapy.

Merrifield, William R. Palantla Chinantec Grammar. 127p. 1968. pap. 1.50x (ISBN 0-88312-794-6); microfiche 1.60 (ISBN 0-88312-359-2). Summer Inst Ling.

Milewski, Tadeusz. Introduction to the Study of Language. 1973. pap. text ed. 32.50x (ISBN 90-2792-598-4). Mouton.

Minor, Eugene E. & Minor, Dorothy. Vocabulario Huitoto Muinane. (Peruvian Linguistic Ser: No. 5). 139p. 1970. pap. 3.00x (ISBN 0-88312-656-7); microfiche 1.60 (ISBN 0-88312-362-2). Summer Inst Ling.

Modern Language Association of America, Advisory Committee on the Job Market. Guide for Job Candidates & Department Chairmen in English & Foreign Languages. 2nd ed. 1978. pap. 4.50x (ISBN 0-87352-009-2). Modern Lang.

Moerk, E. Pragmatic & Semantic Aspects of Early Language Development. 1977. 18.50 (ISBN 0-8391-1118-5). Univ Park.

Moskowitz, Gertrude. Caring & Sharing in the Foreign Language Class: A Sourcebook on Humanistic Techniques. 1978. pap. 13.95 (ISBN 0-88377-098-9). Newbury Hse.

Munby, J. Communicative Syllabus Design. LC 77-90216. (Illus.). 1978. 19.95x (ISBN 0-521-22071-8). Cambridge U Pr.

National Education Association. Source Materials for Teachers of Foreign Languages: An Annotated Bibliography. rev. ed. LC 74-8934. 1974. pap. 2.50 (ISBN 0-8106-1319-0). NEA.

Nemoianu, Anca M. The Boat's Gonna Leave: A Study of Children Learning a Second Language from Conversations with Other Children. vi, 116p. 1980. pap. 14.00 (ISBN 90-272-2507-9). Benjamins North Am.

Nuchelmans, G. Theories of the Proposition. (Linguistics Ser.: Vol. 8). 1973. 31.75 (ISBN 0-444-10513-1, North-Holland); pap. 24.50 (ISBN 0-444-10522-0). Elsevier.

Oliver, Thomas E. The Modern Language Teacher's Handbook. 1978. Repr. of 1935 ed. lib. bdg. 50.00 (ISBN 0-8482-2041-2). Norwood Edns.

Oller, John & Perkins, Kyle. Language in Education: Testing the Tests. LC 78-2676. 1978. pap. text ed. 9.95 (ISBN 0-88377-104-7). Newbury Hse.

Oller, John W., Jr. & Richards, Jack R., eds. Focus on the Learner: Pragmatic Perspectives for the Language Teacher. 1973. pap. text ed. 9.95 (ISBN 0-912066-67-9). Newbury Hse.

Omaggio, Alice C. Games & Simulations in the Foreign Language Classroom. (Language in Education Ser. No. 13). (Orig.). 1979. pap. text ed. 6.50x (ISBN 0-87281-099-2). Ctr Appl Ling.

Oskarsson, Mats. Approaches to Self-Assessment in Foreign Language Learning. (PIE Council of Europe Language Learning Ser.). 1980. pap. 4.95 (ISBN 0-08-024594-3). Pergamon.

Palmer, Harold E. & Redman, H. Vere. The Language-Learning Business. 219p. 1981. Repr. of 1932 ed. lib. bdg. 30.00 (ISBN 0-89760-711-2). Telegraph Bks.

--This Language-Learning Business. (Educational Ser.). 1932. Repr. 25.00 (ISBN 0-685-43591-1). Norwood Edns.

Patterson, W. R. Language - Students Manual. 59.95 (ISBN 0-8490-0485-3). Gordon Pr.

PIE Seminar,Papers, Oxford, April 1979. Foreign Language Learning: Meeting Individual Needs. Altman, Howard B., ed. 128p. pap. 7.95 (ISBN 0-08-024604-4). Pergamon.

Pierce, Joe E. Languages & Linguistics. 2nd ed. 188p. 1980. pap. 11.95 (ISBN 0-913244-23-6). Hapi Pr.

Pillet, Roger A. Foreign-Language Study. LC 73-84194. 1974. 8.00x (ISBN 0-226-66826-6). U of Chicago Pr.

Pimsleur, Paul & Quinn, Terence, eds. Psychology of Second Language Learning. (Illus.). 1971. 27.50 (ISBN 0-521-08236-6). Cambridge U Pr.

Posner, R. The Romance Languages: A Linguistic Introduction. 7.75 (ISBN 0-8446-0853-X). Peter Smith.

Pride, Leslie & Pride, Kitty. Vocabulario Chatino de Tataltepec. (Vocabularios Indigenas Ser.: No. 15). 103p. 1970. pap. 3.00 (ISBN 0-88312-655-9). Summer Inst Ling.

Ramos, Maximo, et al. Determination & Implementation of Language Policy. LC 68-28747. (Philippine Center for Language Study Monographs: No. 2). 1968. 8.25 (ISBN 0-379-12152-2). Oceana.

Raskin, Bruce, ed. Mud Puddles, Rainbows & Asparagus Tips: Learning's Best Language Arts Ideas. LC 78-74910. (Learning Ideabooks Ser.). 1979. pap. 10.95 (ISBN 0-8224-1911-4). Pitman Learning.

Richards, Jack C., ed. Understanding Second & Foreign Language Learning. LC 78-24457. 1978. pap. text ed. 10.95 (ISBN 0-88377-124-1). Newbury Hse.

Risko, Victoria. Testing-Teaching Module of Auditory Discrimination. 1975. pap. 7.50x manual (ISBN 0-87879-099-3); Set. 25 diagnostic tests 6.00 (ISBN 0-87879-099-3). Acad Therapy.

Ritchie, William C., ed. Second Language Acquisition Research: Issues & Implications. (Perspectives in Neurolinguistics & Psycholinguistics Ser.). 1978. 19.50 (ISBN 0-12-589550-X). Acad Pr.

Rivers, Wilga M. The Psychologist & the Foreign Language Teacher. LC 64-15809. 1977. pap. 4.95 (ISBN 0-226-72094-2, P741, Phoen). U of Chicago Pr.

--Teaching Foreign Language Skills. 2nd, rev. ed. LC 80-24993. 1981. lib. bdg. 22.00x (ISBN 0-226-72098-5); pap. 12.50x (ISBN 0-226-72097-7). U of Chicago Pr.

Robbins, Frank E. Quiotepec Chinantec Grammar. 150p. 1968. pap. 1.50x (ISBN 0-88312-799-7). Summer Inst Ling.

Ross, Dorothea M. & Ross, Sheila A. Fundamental Skills & Concepts 1: Language Arts Lessons for Grades 1-3. (Makemaster Bk.). 1981. pap. 14.95 (ISBN 0-8224-0291-2). Pitman Learning.

--Fundamental Skills & Concepts 2: Arithmetic Lessons for Grades 1-3. (Makemaster Bk.). 1981. pap. 14.95 (ISBN 0-8224-0292-0). Pitman Learning.

Roulet, E. Linguistic Theory, Linguistic Description & Language Teaching. Candlin, Christopher N., tr. LC 75-326964. (Applied Linguistics & Language Study Ser.). 112p. 1975. pap. text ed. 9.00x (ISBN 0-582-55075-0). Longman.

Ruddell, R. Reading-Language Instruction: Innovative Practices. 1973. 20.95 (ISBN 0-13-753285-7). P-H.

Sanborn, Donald A. The Language Process: Toward a Holistic Schema with Implications for an English Curriculum Theory. LC 70-182464. (Janua Linguarum, Ser. Minor: No. 103). (Illus.). 168p. (Orig.). 1971. pap. text ed. 20.75x (ISBN 90-2791-893-7). Mouton.

Sayre, Joan M. Teaching Language Through Sight & Sound - Set 1. 1980. 29.75x (ISBN 0-8134-2077-6). Interstate.

Schoenhals, Alvin & Schoenhals, Louise. Vocabulario Mixe de Totontepec. (Vocabularios Indigenas Ser.: No. 14). 353p. 1965. pap. 5.00x (ISBN 0-88312-659-1). Summer Inst Ling.

Schumann, John H. & Stenson, Nancy. New Frontiers in Second Language Learning. 1975. pap. 9.95 (ISBN 0-912066-84-9). Newbury Hse.

Schweitzer, Sydney C. Winning with Deception & Bluff. LC 78-25798. 1979. 8.95 (ISBN 0-13-961276-9). P-H.

Shane, Harold G. & Walden, James, eds. Classroom-Relevant Research in the Language Arts. LC 78-56931. 1978. pap. text ed. 7.50 (ISBN 0-87120-090-2, 611-78140). Assn Supervision.

Spolsky, Bernard & Cooper, Robert L., eds. Case Studies in Bilingual Education. 1978. pap. text ed. 15.95 (ISBN 0-88377-092-X). Newbury Hse.

Staubach, Charles N. How to Study Languages. 1952. 1.00x (ISBN 0-685-21789-2). Wahr.

Stemmer, Nathan. An Empiricist Theory of Language Acquisition. LC 73-81546. (Janua Linguarum, Ser. Minor: No. 173). 147p. 1974. pap. text ed. 27.50x (ISBN 90-2792-485-6). Mouton.

Stevick, Earl W. Teaching Languages: A Way & Ways. (Orig.). 1980. pap. text ed. 11.95 (ISBN 0-88377-147-0). Newbury Hse.

Titone, Renzo. Teaching Foreign Languages: An Historical Sketch. LC 68-22774. 128p. 1968. pap. 3.15 (ISBN 0-87840-158-X). Georgetown U Pr.

Trail, Ronald L. A Grammar of Lamani. (Publications in Linguistics & Related Fields Ser.: No. 24). 225p. 1970. pap. 4.50x (ISBN 0-88312-026-7); microfiche 2.20 (ISBN 0-88312-426-2). Summer Inst Ling.

United Nations Educational Scientific & Cultural Organization. The Use of Vernacular Languages in Education. Cordasco, Francesco, ed. LC 77-90566. (Bilingual-Bicultural Education in the U. S. Ser.). 1978. Repr. of 1953 ed. lib. bdg. 14.00x (ISBN 0-405-11105-3). Arno.

Vallette, Rebecca M. Modern Language Testing: A Handbook. 2nd ed. LC 76-49392. (Orig.). 1977. pap. text ed. 9.95 (ISBN 0-15-561926-8, HC). HarBraceJ.

Van Ek, J. A. The Threshold Level for Modern Language Learning in Schools. (Applied Linguistics & Language Study Ser.). 1978. pap. text ed. 9.00x (ISBN 0-582-55700-3). Longman.

Van Wynen, Donald & Van Wynen, Mabel. Fonemas Tacana Vy Modelos de Acentuacion. (Notas Linguisticas De Bolivia Ser.: No. 6). 32p. 1962. pap. 0.75 (ISBN 0-88312-763-6). Summer Inst Ling.

The Verb Be & Its Synonyms. Incl. Part 1. Classical Chinese, Athapaskan, Mundari. Verhaar, J. W., ed. 100p. 1967. lib. bdg. 16.00 (ISBN 90-277-0032-X); Part 2. Eskimo, Hindi, Zuni, Modern Greek, Malayalam, Kurukh. Verhaar, J. W., ed. 148p. 1968. lib. bdg. 18.50 (ISBN 90-277-0033-8); Part 3. Japanese, Kashmiri, Armenian, Hungarian, Sumerian, Shona. Verhaar, J. W., ed. 125p. 1968. lib. bdg. 18.50 (ISBN 90-277-0034-6); Part 4. Twi, Modern Chinese, Arabic. Verhaar, J. W., ed. 125p. 1969. lib. bdg. 18.50 (ISBN 90-277-0035-4); Part 5. Urdu, Turkish, Beugali, Amharic, Indonesian, Telegu, Estonian. Verhaar, J. W., ed. LC 79-159659. 233p. 1972. lib. bdg. 31.50 (ISBN 90-277-0217-9); Part 6. Ancient Greek. Kahn, C. H., ed. LC 74-183367. 486p. 1973. lib. bdg. 63.00 (ISBN 90-277-0222-5); pap. 29.00 (ISBN 90-277-0313-2). (Foundations of Language Supplementary Ser., Pub. by Junk Pubs Netherlands). Kluwer Boston.

Walford, Alberto J. & Screen, J. E., eds. A Guide to Foreign Language Courses & Dictionaries. LC 77-26283. 1978. lib. bdg. 22.50 (ISBN 0-313-20100-5, WGL/). Greenwood.

Webb, David. Teaching Modern Languages. LC 74-82025. (Teaching Ser.). 1975. 8.95 (ISBN 0-7153-6858-3). David & Charles.

Weinberg, Michael A. Teach Your Babies & Toddlers Foreign Languages. 100p. 1981. write for info. Weinberg.

Wilkinson, Andrew. Foundations of Language: Talking & Reading in Young Children. (Orig.). 1971. pap. text ed. 6.50x (ISBN 0-19-911016-6). Oxford U Pr.

--Language & Education. (Oxford Studies in Education Ser.). 1977. pap. text ed. 6.50x (ISBN 0-19-911101-4). Oxford U Pr.

Winitz, Harris. Language Through Pictures, 8 vols. (gr. 2-12). pap. 39.95 (ISBN 0-939990-38-5). Intl Linguistics.

Winitz, Harris & Reeds, James. Comprehension & Problem Solving As Strategies for Language Training. (Janua Linguarum Series Didactica). (Illus.). 100p. (Orig.). 1975. pap. text ed. 20.75x (ISBN 90-2793-103-8). Mouton.

--Comprehension & Problem Solving As Strategies in Language. LC 73-76893. (Illus.). 100p. 1981. pap. 8.50 (ISBN 0-939990-29-6). Intl Linguistics.

Winitz, Harris, ed. The Comprehension Approach to Foreign Language Instruction. (Illus.). 352p. (Orig.). 1981. pap. text ed. 15.95 (ISBN 0-88377-181-0). Newbury Hse.

Winn-Bell, Judy E. Communication Starters: Techniques for the Language Classroom. 2nd ed. Lee, William R., ed. (Language Teaching Methodology Ser.). (Illus.). 96p. 1981. pap. 6.50 (ISBN 0-08-025360-1). Pergamon.

Wise, Mary R. Identification of Participants in Discourse: A Study of Aspects of Form & Meaning in Nomatsiguenga. (Publications in Linguistics & Related Fields Ser.: No. 28). 244p. 1971. pap. 4.50x (ISBN 0-88312-030-5); microfiche 2.20 (ISBN 0-88312-430-0). Summer Inst Ling.

Wise, Mary R. & Shell, Olive. Grupos Idiomaticos del Peru. 46p. 1971. pap. 2.00 (ISBN 0-88312-769-5). Summer Inst Ling.

Wood, Barbara S. Children & Communication: Verbal & Nonverbal Language Development. 2nd ed. (Illus.). 320p. 1981. text ed. 15.95 (ISBN 0-13-131920-5). P-H.

Wright, A., et al. Games for Language Learning. pap. 7.95 (ISBN 0-521-22170-6). Cambridge U Pr.

Wright, Andrew. Visual Materials for the Language Teacher. (Longman Handbooks for Language Teachers). (Illus.). 192p. 1975. pap. text ed. 7.50x (ISBN 0-582-52267-6). Longman.

Young, R. A. The Verb in Bena-Bena: Its Form & Function. v, 68p. 1971. pap. 1.85x (ISBN 0-88312-651-6). Summer Inst Ling.

Zimmerman, et al. Preschool Language Scale Forms. 2nd ed. 1979. text ed. 9.50 (ISBN 0-675-08261-7). Merrill.

LANGUAGE AND LANGUAGES–STUDY AND TEACHING–BIBLIOGRAPHY

Hesse. Approaches to Teaching Foreign Languages. 1975. 29.50 (ISBN 0-444-11006-2, North-Holland). Elsevier.

Johnson, Dora E., et al, eds. A Survey of Materials for the Study of the Uncommonly Taught Languages No. 6: Sub-Saharan Africa. LC 76-44594. 1977. pap. 4.95x (ISBN 0-87281-058-5). Ctr Appl Ling.

--A Survey of Materials for the Study of the Uncommonly Taught Languages No. 7: Southeast Asia & the Pacific. LC 76-44595. 1977. pap. 4.95x (ISBN 0-87281-057-7). Ctr Appl Ling.

--A Survey of Materials for the Study of the Uncommonly Taught Languages No. 8: North, Central & South America. LC 76-44596. 1977. pap. 4.95x (ISBN 0-87281-059-3). Ctr Appl Ling.

LANGUAGE AND LANGUAGES–SYNTAX

see also Grammar, Comparative and General–Syntax

Callahan, J. J. Science of Language. 1938. 15.00 (ISBN 0-8274-3338-7). R West.

Chafe, Wallace L. Meaning & Structure of Language. LC 79-114855. x, 360p. 1975. pap. 7.50x (ISBN 0-226-10056-1, Phoen). U of Chicago Pr.

Cooper, William S. Set Theory & Syntactic Description. (Janua Linguarum, Ser. Minor: No. 34). 52p. 1974. pap. text ed. 10.65x (ISBN 90-2792-704-9). Mouton.

Culicover, Peter W. Syntax: Internatonal Edition. 1977. 13.50 (ISBN 0-12-199230-6). Acad Pr.

Gattegno, Caleb. A Thousand Sentences. 87p. 1974. pap. 2.20 (ISBN 0-87825-007-7). Ed Solutions.

Gopnik, Myrna. Linguistic Structures in Scientific Texts. (Janua Linguarum, Ser. Minor: No. 129). 1972. text ed. 23.75x (ISBN 90-2792-295-0). Mouton.

Heil, John. Logic & Language: An Introduction to Elementary Logic & the Theory of Linguistic Descriptions. 1978. pap. text ed. 16.75 (ISBN 0-8191-0396-9). U Pr of Amer.

Hirst, D. Intonative Features: A Syntactic Approach to English Intonation. 1977. 20.00x (ISBN 90-279-7536-1). Mouton.

International Symposium on Functional Sentence Perspective, 1st, Marienbad, Czechoslovakia. Papers on Functional Sentence Perspective. Danes, F., ed. (Janua Linguarum, Ser. Minor: No. 147). 222p. (Eng. & Czech.). 1974. pap. text ed. 25.50x (ISBN 90-2793-202-6). Mouton.

Kiefer, F., ed. Studies in Syntax & Semantics. (Foundations of Language Supplementary Ser: No. 10). 242p. 1969. lib. bdg. 34.00 (ISBN 90-277-0027-3, Pub. by Reidel Holland); pap. 21.00 (ISBN 90-277-0597-6). Kluwer Boston.

Lee, Laura L. The Northwestern Syntax Screening Test. (Illus.). 1969. Set. 19.95x (ISBN 0-8101-9796-0); 200 record forms 14.95 (ISBN 0-8101-9795-2). Northwestern U Pr.

Marcus, Mitchell. Theory of Syntactic Recognition for Natural Language. (A. I. Ser.). 352p. 1980. text ed. 25.00x (ISBN 0-262-13149-8). MIT Pr.

Matthews, Brander. Parts of Speech. 1901. 25.00 (ISBN 0-8274-3102-3). R West.

Perez-Sala, Paulino. Interferencia Linguistica Del Ingles En el Espanol Hablado En Puerto Rico. LC 72-93776. 132p. (Span.). 1973. 7.50 (ISBN 0-913480-10-X). Inter Am U Pr.

Platt, J. T. Grammatical Form & Grammatical Meaning. LC 72-166313. (Linguistic Ser.: Vol. 5). 1973. pap. 19.50 (ISBN 0-444-10510-7, North-Holland). Elsevier.

Salmond. A Generative Syntax of Luangiua. (Janua Linguarum, Ser. Practica: No. 152). (Illus.). 256p. 1974. pap. text ed. 51.25x (ISBN 90-2792-721-9). Mouton.

Schneider, Clarence E. Syntax & Style. LC 72-97330. 342p. 1974. pap. 7.95x (ISBN 0-88316-019-6). Chandler & Sharp.

Sommerfelt, Ay. Diachronic & Synchronic Aspects of Language. (Janua Linguarum, Ser. Major: No. 7). 1971. text ed. 52.50x (ISBN 90-2791-922-4). Mouton.

LANGUAGE AND LANGUAGES–TESTING

see Language and Languages–Examinations, Questions, etc.

LANGUAGE AND LANGUAGES–VOCATIONAL GUIDANCE

Bourgoin, Edward. Foreign Languages & Your Career. rev. 2nd ed. iii, 74p. 1981. pap. text ed. 6.00 (ISBN 0-9604126-1-1). Columbia Lang Serv.

Brod, Richard I., et al, eds. English & Foreign Languages: Employment & the Profession. 77p. 1976. pap. 5.00x (ISBN 0-87352-311-3). Modern Lang.

Foreign Language Careers. 1980. text ed. 7.95 (ISBN 0-686-65127-8, 63887); pap. text ed. 5.95 (ISBN 0-686-65128-6, 63885). Natl Textbk.

Freudenstein, Reinhold, et al. Language Incorporated: Teaching Foreign Languages in Industry. LC 80-42188. (Illus.). 128p. 1981. pap. 13.95 (ISBN 0-08-024578-1). Pergamon.

Huebener, Theodore. Opportunities in Foreign Language Careers. rev. ed. LC 75-3792. 1975. PLB 6.60 (ISBN 0-8442-6445-8); pap. text ed. 4.95 (ISBN 0-8442-6443-1). Natl Textbk.

Sherif, June L. Careers in Foreign Languages: A Handbook. rev. ed. 228p. (gr. 9-12). 1975. pap. 3.95 (ISBN 0-88345-250-2). Regents Pub.

LANGUAGE AND LOGIC

see Logical Positivism

LANGUAGE AND RELIGION

see Religion and Language

LANGUAGE AND SOCIETY

see Sociolinguistics

LANGUAGE ARTS

see also Communication; English Language; Literature–Study and Teaching; Reading; Speech

Adams, Anne, et al. Mainstreaming Language Arts & Social Studies: Special Activities for the Whole Class. LC 76-13164. (Illus.). 1977. text ed. 12.95 (ISBN 0-87620-591-0). Goodyear.

Allen, Roach V. Language Experience Activities. LC 75-31012. (Illus.). 384p. 1976. pap. text ed. 10.95 (ISBN 0-395-18626-9). HM.

Aquino, John. Film in the Language Arts Class. 56p. 1976. pap. 2.75 (ISBN 0-686-63668-6, 1811-7-06). NEA.

Ashby-Davis, Claire & Francks, Olive R., eds. Tapestry: The Interrelationships of the Arts in Reading & Language Development. 1979. pap. text ed. 9.50 (ISBN 0-686-62268-5). Collegium Bk Pubs.

Bannatyne, Alexander. Language, Reading & Learning Disabilities: Psychology, Neuropsychology, Diagnosis & Remediation. (Illus.). 800p. 1976. 21.50 (ISBN 0-398-02182-1). C C Thomas.

Berner, R. Thomas. Language Skills for Journalists. LC 78-69584. 1978. pap. text ed. 10.50 (ISBN 0-395-26789-7); inst. manual 0.65 (ISBN 0-395-26790-0). HM.

Biedenharn, Norma W. Basic Language: Messages & Meanings 1978, Level 4. (gr. 10). 1978. 11.96 (ISBN 0-06-530109-9, SchDept); tchr's guide 11.16 (ISBN 0-06-530209-5). Har-Row.

Biedenharn, Norma W., et al. Basic Language: Messages & Meanings, Level 3. (gr. 9). 1978. 11.96 (ISBN 0-06-530108-0, SchDept); tchr's guide 11.16 (ISBN 0-06-530208-7). Har-Row.

--Basic Languages: Messages & Meanings 1978, Level 5. (gr. 11). 1978. 11.96 (ISBN 0-06-530110-2, SchDept); tchr's guide 11.16 (ISBN 0-06-530210-9). Har-Row.

--Basic Languages: Messages & Meanings 1978, Level 6. (gr. 12). 1978. 11.96 (ISBN 0-06-530111-0, SchDept); tchr's guide 11.16 (ISBN 0-06-530211-7). Har-Row.

Blatt, Gloria T. It's Your Move: Expressive Movement in the Language Arts Reading Class. (Orig.). 1981. lib. bdg. 22.50 (ISBN 0-8077-2687-7); pap. 14.95x (ISBN 0-8077-2640-0). Tchrs Coll.

Blockcolsky, V. D., et al. Speech & Language Development. rev. ed. 1977. pap. 8.00 (ISBN 0-88450-173-6, 2040-B). Communication Skill.

Booth, Jack, ed. Inside Outside. (Language Patterns Impressions). (Illus.). 1978. text ed. 9.00 (ISBN 0-03-920023-X, HR&W Canada); reading skill 4.25 (ISBN 0-03-920027-2); tchr's guide ed 11.88 (ISBN 0-03-920029-9); language skills wkbk. 4.10 (ISBN 0-03-920025-6). HR&W.

Boyd. Teaching Communication Skills in the Elementary Schools. 2nd ed. 1977. text ed. 17.95x (ISBN 0-442-20737-9). Van Nos Reinhold.

Braun, C. & Froese, V. An Experience Based Approach to Language & Reading. 1977. 18.75 (ISBN 0-8391-1146-0). Univ Park.

Brod, Richard I. & Neel, Jasper P., eds. Profession 78. 60p. 1978. pap. 4.00x (ISBN 0-87352-313-X). Modern Lang.

Burnham, Philip & Lederer, Richard. Basic Verbal Skills for the Middle School. (gr. 6-9). 1976. pap. text ed. 5.25x (ISBN 0-88334-098-4); wkbk. 2.50x (ISBN 0-88334-074-7). Ind Sch Pr.

Burns, Paul C. Assessment & Correction of Language Arts Difficulties. (Elementary Education Ser.: No. C22). 312p. 1980. pap. text ed. 9.95 (ISBN 0-675-08198-X). Merrill.

Burns, Paul C. & Broman, Betty L. The Language Arts in Childhood Education. 4th ed. LC 81-80802. (Illus.). 1979. text ed. 16.95 (ISBN 0-395-30571-3); instructor's manual free (ISBN 0-528-61041-4). HM.

Cambio, Edward P. The International Federation of Library Associations & Institutions: A Selected List of References. 51p. 1977. 10.25 (ISBN 3-7940-4431-2, Pub. by K G Saur). Shoe String.

Canario, Jack. The Big Hassle: Getting Along with Authority. (Read on! - Write on! Ser.). (Illus.). 64p. (gr. 6-12). 1980. 2.85 (ISBN 0-915510-38-3). Janus Bks.

--The Put-Down Pro: Getting Along with Friends. (Read on! - Write on! Ser.). (Illus.). 64p. (gr. 6-12). 1980. 2.85 (ISBN 0-915510-39-1). Janus Bks.

Chaney, Betty B. Stimulating Language Development in Early Childhood. 80p. 1977. pap. text ed. 6.50 (ISBN 0-8191-0031-5). U Pr of Amer.

Chappel, Bernice M. Independent Language Arts Activities: Seatwork for the Primary Grades. 2nd ed. LC 66-26670. 1973. pap. 3.95 (ISBN 0-8224-4215-9). Pitman Learning.

Chenfeld, Mimi B. Teaching Language Arts Creatively. (Illus.). 1978. pap. text ed. 11.95 (ISBN 0-15-588807-2, HC). HarBraceJ.

Clapp, Ouida, ed. Classroom Practices in Teaching English, 1977-1978: Teaching the Basics--Really! LC 77-21003. 1977. pap. 7.00 (ISBN 0-8141-0687-0). NCTE.
Cleary, Donna M., ed. Thinking Thursdays: Language Arts in the Reading Lab. 1978. pap. text ed. 3.00 (ISBN 0-87207-223-1). Intl Reading.
Cohen, Sandra B. & Plaskon, Stephen P. Language Arts for the Mildly Handicapped. (Special Education Ser.). 544p. 1980. text ed. 17.95x (ISBN 0-675-08131-9). Merrill.
Cole, Martha L. & Cole, Jack T. Effective Intervention with the Language Impaired Child. LC 80-28037. 291p. 1981. text ed. 26.95 (ISBN 0-89443-344-X). Aspen Systems.
Costinett, Sandra. Advanced Readings & Conversations. 1973. pap. text ed. 4.95 (ISBN 0-88499-050-8). Inst Mod Lang.
Cowe, Eileen G. A Study of Kindergarten Activities for Language Development. LC 74-83368. 8.00 (ISBN 0-88247-301-8). R & E Res Assoc.
Dale, E., et al. Techniques of Teaching Vocabulary. 1971. text ed. 11.95 (ISBN 0-8464-1101-6). Benjamin-Cummings.
Decker, Randall E. Patterns of Exposition Seven. 388p. 1980. pap. text ed. 7.95 (ISBN 0-316-17921-3); instructor's manual free (ISBN 0-316-17922-1). Little.
DeHaven, Edna P. Teaching & Learning the Language Arts. 1979. text ed. 17.95 (ISBN 0-316-17933-7); tchrs' manual free (ISBN 0-316-17934-5). Little.
Diederich, Paul B. Measuring Growth in English. LC 74-84480. 112p. 1974. pap. 4.50 (ISBN 0-8141-3109-3). NCTE.
Di Pietro, Robert J., et al, eds. The First Delaware Symposium on Language Studies: Selected Papers. LC 80-71116. 420p. 1981. 35.00 (ISBN 0-87413-190-1). U Delaware Pr.
Donoghue, Mildred R. & Kunkle, John F. Second Languages in Primary Education. 1979. pap. text ed. 6.95 (ISBN 0-88377-132-2). Newbury Hse.
Ducrot, O. & Todorov, T. Dictionnaire Encyclopedique des Sciences du Langage. 476p. (Fr.). 1972. 26.50 (ISBN 0-686-57296-3, F-132840). French & Eur.
Elliott, Fred T. Language Is You, Bks. 1 & 2. 2nd ed. (gr. 7-9). 1977. pap. text ed. (Sch Div); Bk. 1. pap. text ed. 5.36 (ISBN 0-201-41511-9); Bk. 2. pap. text ed. 5.36 (ISBN 0-201-41513-5); tchr's eds. 5.68 ea.; Bk. 1 Tchr's Ed. (ISBN 0-201-41512-7); Bk. 2 Tchr's Ed. 5.68 (ISBN 0-201-41514-3). A-W.
Evans, Zelia S. Tricks of the Trade for Teachers of Language Arts. LC 74-84424. 1974. 6.50 (ISBN 0-682-48070-3, University). Exposition.
Flanigan, Michael G. & Boone, Robert S. Using Media in the Language Arts. LC 76-9550. (Language Arts for Children Ser). 1977. pap. text ed. 4.95 (ISBN 0-87581-194-9). Peacock Pubs.
Flood, James E. & Lapp, Diane. Language-Reading Instruction for the Young Child. (Illus.). 1981. text ed. 16.95 (ISBN 0-02-338470-0). Macmillan.
Fowler, H. Ramsey & Little, Brown Editors. The Little, Brown Handbook. 555p. 1980. text ed. 9.95 (ISBN 0-316-28961-2); 5.95 (ISBN 0-316-28964-7). Little.
Frank, Marjorie S. & Hutchins, P. J. Building Language Power with Cloze: Level C. (Skillbooster Ser.). 64p. (gr. 3). 1981. write for info. wkbk. (ISBN 0-87895-516-X). Modern Curr.
--Building Language Power with Cloze: Level D. (Skillbooster Ser.). 64p. (gr. 4). 1981. write for info. (ISBN 0-87895-517-8). Modern Curr.
--Building Language Power with Cloze: Level E. (Skillbooster Ser.). 64p. (gr. 5). 1981. write for info. wkbk. (ISBN 0-87895-518-6). Modern Curr.
Froese, Victor & Straw, Stanley B., eds. Research in the Language Arts. 336p. 1981. pap. text ed. 24.50 (ISBN 0-8391-1609-8). Univ Park.
Frontier Press Company. Lincoln Library of Language Arts, 2 vols. 5th ed. LC 80-54173. 1981. Set. 54.95 (ISBN 0-912168-06-4). Frontier Pr Co.
Graham, Frances. Language Skills, Intermediate Written & Oral Communications. McConahay, Gleeda, ed. 1976. lib. bdg. 4.50 (ISBN 0-917030-35-4); wkbk 4.50 (ISBN 0-686-17627-8); 24 duplicating masters & tchr's guide incl. (ISBN 0-686-17628-6). Graham Educ.
--Language Skills, Primary Written & Oral Communications. McConahay, Gleeda, ed. 1976. lib. bdg. 4.50 (ISBN 0-917030-36-2); 24 duplicating masters & tchr's guide incl. (ISBN 0-686-17629-4). Graham Educ.
Granowsky, Alvin & Mumford, Janice H. Building Life Skills, Level D. (Skillbooster Ser.: Bk. 1). 64p. (gr. 4). 1981. write for info. wkbk. (ISBN 0-87895-418-X). Modern Curr.
--Building Life Skills, Level E. (Skillbooster Ser.: Bk. 2). 64p. (gr. 5). 1981. write for info. (ISBN 0-87895-523-2). Modern Curr.
--Building Life Skills, Level F. (Skillbooster Ser.: Bk. 3). 64p. (gr. 6). 1981. write for info. wkbk. (ISBN 0-87895-617-4). Modern Curr.
Guth, Hans P. & Schuster, E. H. American English Today, Bk. 11: The Uses of Language. 2nd rev. ed. LC 75-4772. (gr. 11). 1977. text ed. 11.16 (ISBN 0-07-025337-4). McGraw.
Guthrie, John T. Cognition, Curriculum & Comprehension. 1977. pap. 8.50 (ISBN 0-87207-520-6). Intl Reading.
Hansen-Krening, Nancy. Competency & Creativity in Language Arts: A Multi-Ethnic Focus. LC 78-18632. (Education Ser.). (Illus.). 1979. pap. text ed. 7.95 (ISBN 0-201-02802-6). A-W.
Hendrickson, Robert. The Literary Life & Other Curiosities. LC 81-65262. (Illus.). 352p. 1981. 20.00 (ISBN 0-670-43029-3). Viking Pr.
Hodge, Ben, Sr. Language Arts Play & Study Guide. 1976. pap. 2.50 (ISBN 0-912122-16-1). Football Hobbies.
Hoffman, Marvin. Vermont Diary: Language Arts in the Open Classroom. LC 78-16429. 1978. pap. 4.00 (ISBN 0-915924-07-2). Tchrs & Writers Coll.
Hunter, William F., et al. Continuing Language Skills. (Learning Skills Ser: Language Arts). (Illus.). 1978. pap. text ed. 4.52 (ISBN 0-07-031333-4, W); tchr's manual 6.32 (ISBN 0-07-031335-0). McGraw.
--Directing Language Skills. (Learning Skill Ser: Lanugage Arts). (Illus.). 1978. pap. text ed. 4.52 (ISBN 0-07-031334-2, W); tchr's manual 6.32 (ISBN 0-07-031335-0). McGraw.
Ideas for Teaching Language Arts. pap. 25.00 ea. Multi Media TX.
Kelly, Lou. From Dialogue to Discourse: An Open Approach to Competence & Creativity. 371p. 1972. pap. 5.95x (ISBN 0-673-07821-3). Scott F.
Kerby, Maude L. Independent Language Arts Activities: Language Use & Comprehension for the Intermediate Grades. 2nd ed. LC 68-58362. 1973. pap. 4.50 (ISBN 0-8224-4216-7). Pitman Learning.
Koops, Willem & Weider, Joachim, eds. IFLA's First Fifty Years. 158p. 1977. 22.50 (ISBN 3-7940-4430-4, Pub. K G Saur). Shoe String.
Koops, Willem, et al, eds. IFLA's Annual Nineteen Seventy-Eight: Annual Report. 197p. 1979. 30.00 (ISBN 3-598-20659-3, Pub. by K G Saur). Shoe String.
Language Arts Books: Bk. 1. 1980. 5.95 (ISBN 0-88488-194-6, 80201). Creative Pubns.
Language Arts Books: Bk. 2. 1980. 5.95 (ISBN 0-88488-195-4, 80202). Creative Pubns.
Language Arts Books: Bk. 3. 1980. 5.95 (ISBN 0-88488-196-2, 80203). Creative Pubns.
Language Arts Books: Bk. 4. 1980. 5.95 (ISBN 0-88488-197-0, 80204). Creative Pubns.
Language Arts Books: Bk. 5. 1980. 5.95 (ISBN 0-88488-198-9, 80205). Creative Pubns.
Language Arts Books: Bk. 6. 1980. 5.95 (ISBN 0-88488-199-7, 80206). Creative Pubns.
Lee, Dorris & Rubin, Joseph B. Children & Language. 1979. text ed. 18.95x (ISBN 0-534-00686-8). Wadsworth Pub.
Loban, Walter. Language Development: Kindergarden Through Grade 12. LC 76-41007. (Research Report: No. 18). (Orig.). (gr. k-12). 1976. pap. 6.00 (ISBN 0-8141-2654-5). NCTE.
Lock, Andrew. The Guided Reinvention of Language. LC 79-41518. 1980. 34.00 (ISBN 0-12-453950-5). Acad Pr.
Logan, L., et al. Creative Communication: Teaching the Language Arts. 1972. text ed. 15.95 (ISBN 0-07-092672-7, C). McGraw.
Malmstrom, Jean. Understanding Language: A Primer for Language Arts Teachers. LC 76-28138. 1977. 15.95x (ISBN 0-312-83090-4); pap. text ed. 5.95x (ISBN 0-312-83125-0). St Martin.
Marcus, Marie. Diagnostic Teaching of the Language Arts. LC 76-52400. 1977. text ed. 24.95x (ISBN 0-471-56854-6). Wiley.
Markoff, Annabelle M. Teaching Low Achieving Children Reading, Spelling & Handwriting: Developing Perceptual Skills with the Graphic Symbols of the Language. (Illus.). 320p. 1976. 22.75 (ISBN 0-398-03483-4). C C Thomas.
Mattam, Donald. Vital Approach. 2nd ed. 1973. text ed. 16.50 (ISBN 0-08-017700-X); pap. text ed. 7.00 (ISBN 0-08-017701-8). Pergamon.
May, Jill P. Films & Filmstrips for Language Arts: An Annotated Bibliography. 1981. pap. price not set (ISBN 0-8141-1726-0, 17260). NCTE.
Mellon, John C., ed. National Assessment & the Teaching of English. LC 75-28674. 127p. (Orig.). 1975. pap. 6.30 (ISBN 0-8141-3223-5). NCTE.
Milton, Octavia. Assist Three: For Consonant Blends of L, R, & S. 50p. 1981. pap. text ed. 13.00 (ISBN 0-88450-729-7). Communication Skill.
Minsheu, John. Ductor in Linguas: The Guide into Tongues. LC 78-14754. 600p. 1978. Repr. of 1617 ed. lib. bdg. 120.00x (ISBN 0-8201-1321-2). Schol Facsimiles.
Moffett, James & Wagner, Betty J. Student Centered Language Arts & Reading, K-13: A Handbook for Teachers. 2nd ed. LC 76-11920. (Illus.). 640p. 1976. 19.50 (ISBN 0-395-20630-8). HM.
Moldenhauer, Janice. Developing Dictionary Skills. (gr. 3-8). 1979. 5.95 (ISBN 0-916456-48-X, GA120). Good Apple.
National Association of Independent Schools. A Teacher's Notebook: Language Arts, K-4. 1972. pap. 3.25 (ISBN 0-934338-00-0). NAIS.
Neidecker, Elizabeth. School Programs in Speech-Language: Organization & Management. (Illus.). 1980. text ed. 17.95 (ISBN 0-13-794321-0). P-H.
Nierman, J. Harris. Preparing Your Research Paper. (Illus.). 23p. (Orig.). (gr. 10 up). 1979. pap. 1.95 (ISBN 0-935770-00-3). Creative Res & Educ.
Norton, Donna E. The Effective Teaching of Language Arts. (Elementary Education Ser.: No. C22). 512p. 1980. text ed. 17.95 (ISBN 0-675-08196-3); instructor's manual 3.95 (ISBN 0-686-63186-2). Merrill.
--Language Arts Activities for Children. (Elementary Education Ser.: No. C22). 416p. 1980. pap. text ed. 9.95 (ISBN 0-675-08134-3). Merrill.
Oller, John & Perkins, Kyle. Research in Language Testing. 1980. pap. text ed. 14.95 (ISBN 0-88377-131-4). Newbury Hse.
Patterson, William R. Language-Student's Manual. 1981. Repr. of 1917 ed. lib. bdg. 25.00 (ISBN 0-89987-650-1). Darby Bks.
Petty & Jansen. Developing Children's Language. 512p. 1980. text ed. 19.95 (ISBN 0-205-06868-5, 2368684). Allyn.
Pilon, A. Barbara. Teaching Language Arts Creatively in the Elementary Grades. LC 77-23508. 1978. 14.50 (ISBN 0-471-68980-7). Wiley.
Pollio, H. R., et al. Psychology & the Poetics of Growth: Figurative Language in Psychology, Psychotherapy, & Education. LC 77-9880. 1977. 16.50 (ISBN 0-470-99158-5). Halsted Pr.
Price, Glanville & Wells, David A., eds. The Year's Work in Modern Language Studies, 1979, Vol. 41. LC 31-32540. 1260p. 1980. 107.50x (ISBN 0-900547-73-1). Intl Pubns Serv.
Raskin, Bruce, ed. Mud Puddles, Rainbows & Asparagus Tips: Learning's Best Language Arts Ideas. LC 78-74910. (Learning Ideabooks Ser.). 1979. pap. 10.95 (ISBN 0-8224-1911-4). Pitman Learning.
Rieke, Jane, et al. Teaching Strategies for Language Development. 136p. 1977. pap. 15.50 (ISBN 0-8089-0996-7). Grune.
Roos, Anne D., et al. Using Our Language: Level 1 of 6. LC 76-12418. (Illus.). (gr. 1). 1977. pap. text ed. 3.18 (ISBN 0-8372-9301-4); 3.90 (ISBN 0-8372-9302-2, C406-1). Bowmar-Noble.
Rossi-Landi, Ferruccio. Language As Work & Trade. 320p. 1981. 22.95 (ISBN 0-89789-022-1). J F Bergin.
Rothwell, J. Dan. Telling It Like It Isn't: What We Can Do About Language Misuse & Malpractice. 240p. 1981. 10.95 (ISBN 0-13-903161-8); pap. 5.95 (ISBN 0-13-903153-7). P-H.
Rubin, Dorothy. The Intermediate-Grade Teacher's Language Arts Handbook. LC 80-12689. (Orig.). (gr. 4-8). 1980. wkbk. 14.95 (ISBN 0-03-053781-9). HR&W.
--The Primary-Grade Teacher's Language Arts Handbook. LC 80-12723. (Orig.). (gr. 1-4). 1980. wkbk. 14.95 (ISBN 0-03-053776-2). HR&W.
Ruddell, Robert B., et al. Resources in Reading-Language Instruction. (Illus.). 480p. 1974. pap. text ed. 10.95 (ISBN 0-13-774943-0). P-H.
Schaff, Joanne. New Dimensions in English. LC 78-8318. (Illus.). 1978. pap. text ed. 10.95 (ISBN 0-87620-612-7). Goodyear.
Schiltman, Maria J., ed. The International Exchange of Publications. 135p. 1973. 15.00 (ISBN 3-7940-4311-1, Pub. by K G Saur). Shoe String.
Singer, Harry & Donlan, Dan. Reading & Learning from Text. 543p. 1980. text ed. 16.95 (ISBN 0-316-79274-8). Little.
Smith, E. Brooks, et al. Language & Thinking in School. 2nd ed. LC 75-11519. 1976. text ed. 18.95 (ISBN 0-03-089248-1, HoltC). HR&W.
Smith, James A. Classroom Organization for the Language Arts. LC 76-9555. 1977. pap. text ed. 4.95 (ISBN 0-87581-195-7). Peacock Pubs.
Sonderman, Judith C. & Zwitman, Daniel H. Articulation Skills Carryover Stories. 1976. pap. 16.50 (ISBN 0-88450-760-2, 2029-B). Communication Skill.
Squire, James R., ed. The Teaching of English: 76th Yearbook, Part I. LC 76-44918. (The National Society for the Study of Education). (Illus.). 1977. lib. bdg. 12.00x (ISBN 0-226-60122-6). U of Chicago Pr.
Stubbs, Marcia & Barnet, Sylvan. The Little, Brown Reader. 2nd ed. (Illus.). 600p. 1980. pap. text ed. 9.95 (ISBN 0-316-82002-4); instructor's manual free (ISBN 0-316-82003-2). Little.
Tannen, Deborah, ed. Georgetown University Round Table on Languages & Linguistics 1981: Analyzing Discourse - Text & Talk. (Orig.). 1981. pap. text ed. price not set (ISBN 0-87840-116-4). Georgetown U Pr.
Van Der Geest, A. J. Some Aspects of Communicative Competence & Their Implications. 272p. 1975. pap. text ed. 20.75x (ISBN 90-232-1261-4). Humanities.
Wanat, Stanley F., ed. Language & Reading Comprehension. LC 77-80380. (Linguistics & Reading Ser.: No. 2). 1977. pap. text ed. 6.00x (ISBN 0-87281-061-5). Ctr Appl Ling.
Waugh, Linda R. Melody of Language. 378p. text ed. 29.50 (ISBN 0-8391-1557-1). Univ Park.
Webber, Margaret S. Communication Skills for Exceptional Learners. LC 80-28094. 275p. 1981. text ed. 24.95 (ISBN 0-89443-343-1). Aspen Systems.
Yawkey, Thomas D., et al. Language Arts & the Young Child. LC 80-52447. 259p. 1981. pap. text ed. 8.50 (ISBN 0-87581-263-5). Peacock Pubs.
Zijderveld, Anton C. On Cliches: The Supersedure of Meaning by Function in Modernity. (International Library of Sociology). 1979. 18.00 (ISBN 0-7100-0186-X). Routledge & Kegan.

LANGUAGE ARTS–SIMULATION METHODS

Mann, Lynne. The EARLI Program, Vol. I. 180p. pap. 14.95 (ISBN 0-89334-067-7). Humanics Ltd.
--The EARLI Program, Vol. II. 180p. pap. 14.95 (ISBN 0-89334-074-X). Humanics Ltd.
Troyka, Lynn Q. & Nudelman, Jerrold. Taking Action: Writing, Reading, Speaking & Listening Through Simulation Games. (Illus.). 176p. 1975. pap. text ed. 7.95 (ISBN 0-13-882571-8). P-H.

LANGUAGE ARTS–STUDY AND TEACHING

see Language Arts

LANGUAGE ARTS (ELEMENTARY)

Beveridge, Agnes. Expressive Language Remediation for the Older Elementary Child. LC 75-16935. 1976. text ed. 2.95x (ISBN 0-8134-1744-9, 1744). Interstate.
Brown. Skillbooster Series, Level D. Incl. Building Word Power. pap. text ed. 1.92 (ISBN 0-87895-411-2); Increasing Comprehension. pap. text ed. 1.92 (ISBN 0-87895-412-0); Organizing Information. pap. text ed. 1.92 (ISBN 0-87895-414-7); Using References. pap. text ed. 1.92 (ISBN 0-87895-415-5); Working with Facts & Details. pap. text ed. 1.92 (ISBN 0-87895-413-9). (gr. 4). 1976. Modern Curr.
--Skillbooster Series, Level E. Incl. Building Word Power. pap. text ed. 1.92 (ISBN 0-87895-511-9); Increasing Comprehension. pap. text ed. 1.92 (ISBN 0-87895-512-7); Organizing Information. pap. text ed. 1.92 (ISBN 0-87895-514-3); Using References. pap. text ed. 1.92 (ISBN 0-87895-515-1); Working with Facts & Details. pap. text ed. 1.92 (ISBN 0-87895-513-5). (gr. 5). 1976. Modern Curr.
--Skillbooster Series, Level F. Incl. Building Word Power. pap. text ed. 1.92 (ISBN 0-87895-611-5); Increasing Comprehension. pap. text ed. 1.92 (ISBN 0-87895-612-3); Organizing Information. pap. text ed. 1.92 (ISBN 0-87895-614-X); Using References. pap. text ed. 1.92 (ISBN 0-87895-615-8); Working with Facts & Details. pap. text ed. 1.92 (ISBN 0-87895-613-1). (gr. 6). 1976. Modern Curr.
Buckley, Lillian A. & Cullum, Albert. Picnic of Sounds: A Playful Approach to Reading. LC 74-28490. (Illus.). 138p. 1975. pap. 3.95 (ISBN 0-590-09595-1, Citation). Schol Bk Serv.
Burney, Susan L. Prime Time Rhyme Time. (Illus.). 36p. (gr. 2). 1981. pap. 4.95 (ISBN 0-89305-039-3). Anna Pub.
Disney Practice Workbooks. Incl. Phonics (ISBN 0-448-16120-6); Spelling & Dictionary Skills (ISBN 0-448-16121-4); Creative Writing (ISBN 0-448-16122-2); Reading Comprehension (ISBN 0-448-16123-0); Numbers: Addition & Subtraction (ISBN 0-448-16124-9); Number: Multiplication (ISBN 0-448-16125-7). (Mickey's Practice Workbooks Ser.). (Illus.). (gr. k-3). 1978. pap. 1.25 ea. G&D.
Foster, Lawrençe J., et al. Teaching Preschool Language Arts. (Illus.). 272p. 1981. pap. text ed. 15.95 (ISBN 0-8425-1933-5). Brigham.
Gittings, Elisa. Shape Books. (Illus., Orig.). (gr. k-3). 1974. pap. 2.50 (ISBN 0-918932-40-8). Activity Resources.

Greene, Gordon. Development of the Language Arts: From Birth Through Elementary School. LC 73-85548. (Professional Education Ser). 78p. 1973. pap. text ed. 1.75 (ISBN 0-88224-050-1). Cliffs.

Hastings, Phyllis & Hayes, Bessie. Encouraging Language Development. (Special Education Ser.). (Illus.). 80p. 1981. pap. 11.00x (ISBN 0-7099-0287-5, Pub. by Croom Helm Ltd England). Biblio Dist.

Hatten, John T., et al. Emerging Language Two. 1976. pap. 6.95 (ISBN 0-88450-003-9, 2028-B). Communication Skill.

Hutchcroft, Diana M., et al. Making Language Work: A Practical Approach to Literacy for Teachers of 5 to 13 Year Old Children. 264p. 1981. pap. 18.50x (ISBN 0-07-084119-5). Nichols Pub.

Jenkins, Frances. Language Development in Elementary Grades. 256p. 1981. Repr. of 1936 ed. lib. bdg. 30.00 (ISBN 0-8495-2762-7). Arden Lib.

Kean, John M. & Personke, Carl R. The Language Arts: Teaching & Learning in the Elementary Schools. LC 75-38020. 450p. 1976. text ed. 18.95 (ISBN 0-312-46620-X). St Martin.

Klein, Marvin L. Talk in the Language Arts Classroom. LC 77-1765. 1977. pap. 5.00 (ISBN 0-8141-5004-7). NCTE.

Kruse, Ramona. Sociolinguistics & Reading: How Parents Can Contribute to the Development of Children's Language & Reading Ability. LC 81-51218. 30p. 1981. perfect bound 3.50 (ISBN 0-88247-598-3). R & E Res Assocs.

MacDonald, James & Horstmeier, Deanna. Environmental Language Intervention Program. (Special Education Ser.). 1978. 59.95 (ISBN 0-675-08379-6); instructor's manual 3.95 (ISBN 0-686-67977-6). Merrill.

McNichols, Joan & Purkiss, Gerri. Word Ways. (Math Is Everywhere Ser.). (Illus., Orig.). (gr. 1-9). 1974. pap. 4.95 (ISBN 0-918932-44-0). Activity Resources.

Moxley, Roy. Writing & Reading in Early Childhood: A Functional Approach. LC 81-9686. (Illus.). 290p. 1982. price not set (ISBN 0-87778-180-X). Educ Tech Pubns.

Prevo, Helen R. My Language Arts Book. 1973. pap. 2.50x (ISBN 0-88323-113-1, 201). Richards Pub.

Reynell, Joan. Language Development & Assessment. (Studies in Developmental Pediatrics Ser.: Vol. 1). 178p. 1980. text ed. 16.50 (ISBN 0-88416-377-6). Wright-PSG.

Rubin, Dorothy. Teaching Elementary Language Arts. 2nd ed. LC 79-20044. 480p. 1980. text ed. 19.95 (ISBN 0-03-053236-1, HoltC). HR&W.

Savage, John F. Effective Communication: Language Arts in the Elementary School. LC 76-47700. 448p. 1977. text ed. 14.95 (ISBN 0-574-23090-4, 13-6090). SRA.

Schaff, Joanne D. The Language Arts Idea Book: Classroom Activities for Children. LC 75-16597. 1976. 10.95 (ISBN 0-87620-520-1); pap. text ed. 9.95 (ISBN 0-87620-519-8). Goodyear.

Sloan, Glenna. The Child As Critic: Teaching Literature in the Elementary School. LC 75-23360. 1975. pap. text ed. 6.50x (ISBN 0-8077-2482-3). Tchrs Coll.

Southwest Educational Development Laboratory. Concepts & Language. (gr. k). 1973. 468.00 set (ISBN 0-685-85512-0, 03BA). NELP.

Taylor, Joy. Reading & Writing in the First School. (Unwin Education Bks.). 1973. text ed. 16.50x (ISBN 0-04-372005-6); pap. text ed. 8.95x (ISBN 0-04-372006-4). Allen Unwin.

Thompson, Richard A. Treasury of Teaching Activities for Elementary Language Arts. 1975. 11.95 (ISBN 0-13-930446-0). P-H.

Tiedt. Language Arts Activities for the Classroom. 1978. text ed. 17.95 (ISBN 0-205-05896-5); pap. text ed. 11.50 (ISBN 0-205-05912-0). Allyn.

LANGUAGE DATA PROCESSING

see Linguistics–Data Processing

LANGUAGE GAMES

see Literary Recreations

LANGUAGE GEOGRAPHY

see Linguistic Geography

LANGUAGE LABORATORIES

see also Languages, Modern–Study and Teaching–Audio-Visual Aids

Green, Peter S., ed. The Language Laboratory in School: Performance & Prediction, an Account of the York Study. LC 75-23183. (Illus.). 1976. text ed. 16.50x (ISBN 0-05-002870-7). Longman.

Stack, Edward M. Language Laboratory & Modern Language Teaching. 3rd ed. 1971. text ed. 8.95x (ISBN 0-19-501388-3). Oxford U Pr.

LANGUAGE QUESTION IN THE CHURCH

see also Bible–Versions; Latin Language–Church Latin

LANGUAGES–PHILOSOPHY

see also Analysis (Philosophy)

Aarsleff, Hans. Study of Language in England, Seventeen Eighty to Eighteen Sixty. LC 78-13573. 1979. Repr. of 1967 ed. lib. bdg. 19.75x (ISBN 0-313-21046-2, AASL). Greenwood.

Alexander, Hubert G. The Language & Logic of Philosophy. LC 72-80755. (Illus.). 368p. 1972. pap. 4.95x (ISBN 0-8263-0248-3). U of NM Pr.

Alston, William P. Philosophy of Language. (Orig.). 1964. pap. 7.95x ref. ed. (ISBN 0-13-663799-X). P-H.

Altieri, Charles. Act & Quality: A Theory of Literary Meaning & Humanistic Understanding. LC 81-2147. 352p. 1981. lib. bdg. 27.50x (ISBN 0-87023-327-0). U of Mass Pr.

Ambrose, Alice & Lazerowitz, Morris, eds. Ludwig Wittgenstein: Philosophy & Language. (Muirhead Library of Philosophy). 1972. text ed. 26.00x (ISBN 0-391-00190-6). Humanities.

Anscombe, G. E. Introduction to Wittgenstein's Tractatus. 3rd ed. 1967. pap. text ed. 4.00 (ISBN 0-09-051131-X, Hutchinson U Lib). Humanities.

Ayer, Alfred J. Language, Truth & Logic. 7.00 (ISBN 0-8446-1571-4). Peter Smith.

--Language, Truth & Logic. 2nd ed. 1936. pap. 2.00 (ISBN 0-486-20010-8). Dover.

Bar-Hillel, Y., ed. Pragmatics of Natural Languages. LC 77-159653. (Synthese Library: No. 41). 231p. 1971. lib. bdg. 31.50 (ISBN 90-277-0194-6, Pub. by Reidel Holland); pap. 18.50 (ISBN 90-277-0599-2, Pub. by Reidel Holland). Kluwer Boston.

Bar-Hillel, Yehoshua. Aspects of Language: Essays & Lectures on Philosophy of Language, Linguistic Philosophy & Methodology of Linguistics. 1970. text ed. 30.00x (ISBN 0-7204-6033-6, Pub. by North Holland). Humanities.

Black, Max. Language & Philosophy: Studies in Method. LC 81-6206. (Illus.). xiii, 264p. 1981. Repr. of 1949 ed. lib. bdg. 27.50x (ISBN 0-313-23082-X, BLLP). Greenwood.

--Margins of Precision: Essays in Logic & Language. LC 75-128369. 288p. 1970. 19.50x (ISBN 0-8014-0602-1). Cornell U Pr.

--Models & Metaphors: Studies in Language & Philosophy. 267p. 1962. 18.50x (ISBN 0-8014-0041-4). Cornell U Pr.

Bogen, James. Wittgenstein's Philosophy of Language: Some Aspects of Its Development. (International Library of Philosophy & Scientific Method). 1972. text ed. 15.00x (ISBN 0-391-00227-9). Humanities.

Bolinger, Dwight. Language: The Loaded Weapon. (Longman Linguistics Library). (Illus.). 240p. 1980. text ed. 25.00x (ISBN 0-582-29107-0); pap. text ed. 11.95x (ISBN 0-582-29108-9). Longman.

Boretz, Benjamin. Language, As a Music: Six Marginal Pretexts for Composition. LC 80-80807. (Illus.). 88p. 1980. lib. bdg. 13.95 (ISBN 0-939044-20-X). Lingua Pr.

Born, Warren C., ed. Language & Culture: Heritage & Horizons. 1976. pap. 7.95x (ISBN 0-915432-76-5). NE Conf Teach Foreign.

Botwinick, Aryeh. Wittgenstein & Historical Understanding. LC 80-5968. 65p. (Orig.). 1981. pap. text ed. 5.00 (ISBN 0-8191-1431-6). U Pr of Amer.

Bronowski, Jacob. The Origins of Knowledge & Imagination. LC 77-13209. (Silliman Lectures Ser.). 1978. 12.50 (ISBN 0-300-02192-5); pap. 3.95 (ISBN 0-300-02409-6). Yale U Pr.

Capdevila Font, Juan. Diccionario Ideologico Manual de la Lengua Espanola. 900p. (Espn.). 1976. 18.75 (ISBN 84-85117-22-0, S-50264). French & Eur.

Casares, Julio. Diccionario Ideologico De la Lengua Espanola. 2nd ed. 1444p. (Espn.). 1977. leatherette 54.00 (ISBN 0-686-77259-8, S-11920). French & Eur.

Casares Sanchez, Julio. Diccionario Ideologico De la Lengua Espanola. 2nd ed. 1444p. (Espn.). 1977. pap. 50.95 (ISBN 84-252-0126-8, S-50270). French & Eur.

Chappell, V. C., ed. Ordinary Language: Essays in Philosophical Method. 128p. 1981. pap. 2.75 (ISBN 0-486-24082-7). Dover.

Chomsky, Noam. Language & Responsibility. LC 78-53921. 1978. 10.00 (ISBN 0-394-42650-9); pap. 3.95 (ISBN 0-394-73619-2). Pantheon.

--Problems of Knowledge & Freedom: The Russell Lectures. 1972. pap. 1.65 (ISBN 0-394-71815-1, V815, Vin). Random.

Cook, Daniel. Language in the Philosophy of Hegel. (Janua Linguarum, Ser. Minor: No. 135). 198p. (Orig.). 1973. pap. text ed. 28.75x (ISBN 90-2792-402-3). Mouton.

Cordemoy, Geraud de. A Philosophicall Discourse Concerning Speech (1668) & a Discourse Written to a Learned Frier (1670) LC 72-6400. (History of Psychology Ser.). 224p. 1972. Repr. 23.00x (ISBN 0-8201-1106-6). Schol Facsimiles.

Cowan, Daniel A. Language & Negation: The Two-Level Structure That Prevents Paradox. LC 76-21954. 112p. 1980. pap. 6.00 (ISBN 0-915878-03-8). Joseph Pub Co.

Cowan, J. L., ed. Studies in Thought & Language. LC 75-89620. 220p. 1970. 2.00 (ISBN 0-8165-0189-0). U of Ariz Pr.

Crick, Malcolm. Explorations in Language & Meaning: Towards a Semantic Anthropology. LC 76-17290. 1977. text ed. 30.95 (ISBN 0-470-15144-7). Halsted Pr.

Crosby, Donald A. Horace Bushnell's Theory of Language: In the Context of Other Nineteenth-Century Philosophies of Language. (Studies in Philosophy: No. 22). 300p. 1975. text ed. 52.50x (ISBN 90-2793-044-9). Mouton.

Danford, John W. Wittgenstein & Political Philosophy: A Re-Examination of the Foundation of Social Science. LC 78-6716. 1978. lib. bdg. 17.00x (ISBN 0-226-13593-4). U of Chicago Pr.

Davis, Steven. Philosophy & Language. LC 75-15910. (Traditions in Philosophy Ser.). 1976. pap. 7.95 (ISBN 0-672-63674-3). Pegasus.

Derrida, Jacques. Of Grammatology. Spivak, Gayatri C., tr. LC 76-17226. (Illus.). 446p. 1977. 22.50 (ISBN 0-8018-1841-9); pap. 6.95 (ISBN 0-8018-1879-6). Johns Hopkins.

Diccionario Ilustrado Danae de la Lengua Espanola. (Espn.). pns leatherette (ISBN 84-7060-397-3, S-50207). French & Eur.

Donnelly, John, ed. Language, Metaphysics, & Death. LC 76-18463. 1978. 20.00 (ISBN 0-8232-1016-2); pap. 8.00 (ISBN 0-8232-1017-0). Fordham.

Dowty, David R. Word Meaning & Montague Grammar. (Synthese Language Library: No. 7). 1979. lib. bdg. 47.00 (ISBN 90-277-1008-2, Pub. by Reidel Holland); pap. 18.00 (ISBN 90-277-1009-0). Kluwer Boston.

Dufrenne, Mikel. Language & Philosophy. Veatch, Henry B., tr. LC 68-55630. (Illus.). 1968. Repr. of 1963 ed. lib. bdg. 15.00x (ISBN 0-8371-0396-7, DULP). Greenwood.

Dummett, Michael. The Interpretation of Frege's Philosophy. LC 77-12777. 1980. text ed. 40.00x (ISBN 0-674-45975-X). Harvard U Pr.

Ebersole, Frank B. Language & Perception: Essays in the Philosophy of Language. LC 79-88305. 1979. pap. text ed. 11.00 (ISBN 0-8191-0776-X). U Pr of Amer.

--Meaning & Saying: Essays in the Philosophy of Language. LC 79-88304. 1979. pap. text ed. 10.00 (ISBN 0-8191-0775-1). U Pr of Amer.

Edie, James M. Speaking & Meaning: The Phenomenology of Language. LC 75-28909. (Studies in Phenomenology & Existential Philosophy). 288p. 1976. 22.50x (ISBN 0-253-35425-0). Ind U Pr.

Ferre, Frederick. Language, Logic, & God. LC 77-9060. 1977. Repr. of 1961 ed. lib. bdg. 18.25x (ISBN 0-8371-9716-3, FELL). Greenwood.

Finch, Henry L. Wittgenstein-the Later Philosophy: An Exposition of the Philosophical Investigations. LC 76-46421. 1977. text ed. 16.00x (ISBN 0-391-00680-0). Humanities.

Fodor, Jerry & Katz, J. J. Structure of Language. 1964. 20.95 (ISBN 0-13-854703-3). P-H.

Forrester, Mary G. Moral Language. 224p. 1981. 22.50 (ISBN 0-299-08630-5). U of Wis Pr.

Foucault, Michel. Language, Counter-Memory, Practice: Selected Essays and Interviews. Bouchard, Donald F., ed. & tr. from Fr. LC 77-4561. (Illus.). 1977. 18.50x (ISBN 0-8014-0979-9). Cornell U Pr.

Fraser, Russell. The Language of Adam: On the Limits and Systems of Discourse. LC 77-3528. 288p. 1977. 17.50x (ISBN 0-231-04256-6). Columbia U Pr.

French, Peter A., et al, eds. Contemporary Perspectives in the Philosophy of Language. (Midwest Studies in Philosophy). 1977. 25.00x (ISBN 0-8166-0865-2); pap. 8.95x (ISBN 0-8166-0866-0). U of Minn Pr.

Ganz, Joan S. Rules: A Systematic Study. (Janua Linguarum, Ser. Minor: No. 96). (Illus.). 144p. (Orig.). 1972. pap. text ed. 20.75x (ISBN 90-2791-853-8). Mouton.

Gass, William. On Being Blue: A Philosophical Inquiry. LC 75-43103. 1978. pap. 5.95 (ISBN 0-87923-237-4). Godine.

George, F. H. Precision, Language & Logic. 224p. 1977. text ed. 29.00 (ISBN 0-08-019650-0). Pergamon.

Graham, Keith. J. L. Austin: A Critique of Ordinary Language Philosophy. 1977. text ed. 22.25x (ISBN 0-391-00747-5). Humanities.

Guenthner, F. & Guenthner-Reutter, M., eds. Meaning & Translation: Phlosophical & Linquistic Approaches. LC 78-57003. 1978. cusa 35.00x (ISBN 0-8147-2974-6). NYU Pr.

Haller, R. & Grassl, W., eds. Language, Logic & Philosophy. (Proceedings of the International Wittgenstein Synposia: No. 4). 550p. 1980. pap. 52.50 (ISBN 0-686-27692-2, Pub. by Reidel Holland). Kluwer Boston.

Hamm, Victor M. Language, Truth & Poetry. (Aquinas Lecture). 1960. 6.95 (ISBN 0-87462-125-9). Marquette.

Hardwick, Charles S. Language Learning in Wittgenstein's Later Philosophy. LC 71-159464. (Janua Linguarum, Ser. Minor: No. 104). 152p. 1971. pap. text ed. 18.75x (ISBN 90-2791-839-2). Mouton.

Hardy, William G. Language, Thought & Experience: A Tapestry of the Dimensions of Meaning. 1978. 29.50 (ISBN 0-8391-1213-0). Univ Park.

Harrison, Bernard. An Introduction to the Philosophy of Language. LC 79-28463. 340p. 1980. 25.00x (ISBN 0-312-43109-0). St Martin.

Hartnack, Justus. Language & Philosophy. 140p. 1972. pap. text ed. 20.75x (ISBN 90-2792-361-2). Mouton.

Heidegger, Martin. Poetry, Language, Thought. Hofstadter, Albert, tr. from Ger. 1975. pap. 3.95 (ISBN 0-06-090430-5, CN430, CN). Har-Row.

Heintz, John. Subjects & Predicables. LC 73-81805. (Janua Linguarum, Ser. Minor: No. 79). 103p. 1973. pap. text ed. 20.00x (ISBN 90-2792-539-9). Mouton.

Hookway, C. & Pettit, P., eds. Action & Interpretation. LC 77-7875. 178p. 1980. 22.95 (ISBN 0-521-21740-7); pap. 9.95x (ISBN 0-521-29908-X). Cambridge U Pr.

Ishiguro, Hide. Leibniz's Philosophy of Logic & Language. LC 72-2357. 165p. 1972. 19.50x (ISBN 0-8014-0737-0). Cornell U Pr.

Israel, Joachim. The Language of Dialectics & Dialectics of Language. 1979. text ed. 25.00x (ISBN 0-391-01000-X). Humanities.

Jespersen, Otto. Philosophy of Grammar. (Illus.). 1965. pap. 7.95 (ISBN 0-393-00307-8, Norton Lib.). Norton.

Johnson, Alexander B. Treatise on Language. Rynin, David, ed. LC 68-25841. 1969. pap. text ed. 4.00 (ISBN 0-486-22019-2). Dover.

Juliard, Pierre. Philosophies of Language in 18th Century France. LC 77-111622. (Janua Linguarum Ser: No. 18). (Orig.). 1970. pap. text ed. 16.25x (ISBN 0-686-22419-1). Mouton.

Kaminsky, Jack. Language & Ontology. LC 69-11516. 330p. 1969. 12.50x (ISBN 0-8093-0367-1). S Ill U Pr.

Kanger, Stig & Ohman, Sven, eds. Philosophy & Grammar. (Synthese Library: No. 143). 168p. 1980. lib. bdg. 28.50 (ISBN 90-277-1091-0, Pub. by Reidel Holland). Kluwer Boston.

Kung, G. Ontology & the Logistic Analysis of Language: An Inquiry into the Contemporary Views on Universals. rev. ed. Mays, E. C., tr. from Ger. (Synthese Library: No. 13). 210p. 1967. lib. bdg. 29.00 (ISBN 90-277-0028-1, Pub. by Reidel Holland); pap. 12.00 (ISBN 90-277-0598-4, Pub. by Reidel Holland). Kluwer Boston.

Kurtz, Paul, ed. Language & Human Nature: A French-American Philosopher's Dialogue. LC 73-108782. 264p. 1971. 17.50 (ISBN 0-87527-022-0). Green.

Lakoff, George & Johnson, Mark. Metaphors We Live By. LC 80-10783. 1980. 13.95 (ISBN 0-226-46800-3). U of Chicago Pr.

Land, Stephen K. From Signs to Propositions: The Concept of Form in 18th-Century Semantic Theory. LC 74-189426. (Linguistics Library). (Illus.). 224p. 1974. text ed. 14.95x (ISBN 0-582-55046-7). Longman.

Landesman, Charles. Discourse & Its Presuppositions. LC 72-75201. 184p. 1972. 15.00x (ISBN 0-300-01526-7). Yale U Pr.

Larkin, Sr. Miriam T. Language in the Philosophy of Aristotle. LC 74-165145. (Janua Linguarum, Ser. Minor: No. 87). 113p. 1971. pap. text ed. 15.75x (ISBN 90-2791-843-0). Mouton.

Lemoine, Roy E. The Anagogic Theory of Wittgenstein's Tractatus. LC 74-80541. (Janua Linguarum Series Minor: No. 214). 215p. (Orig.). 1975. pap. text ed. 36.25x (ISBN 90-2793-393-6). Mouton.

Lewis, David K. Convention: A Philosophical Study. LC 69-12727. (Illus.). 1969. 12.50x (ISBN 0-674-17025-3). Harvard U Pr.

Linsky, Leonard. Referring. 1967. text ed. 9.00x (ISBN 0-7100-3636-1). Humanities.

McCloskey, James. Transformational Syntax & Model Theoretic Semantics. (Synthese Language Library: No. 9). 1979. lib. bdg. 37.00 (ISBN 90-277-1025-2, Pub. by Reidel Holland); pap. 15.00 (ISBN 90-277-1026-0). Kluwer Boston.

McGuinness, Brian, ed. Friedrich Waismann: Philosophical Papers. Kaal, Hans, tr. from Ger. (Vienna Circle Collection Ser.: No. 8). 1976. lib. bdg. 39.50 (ISBN 90-277-0712-X, Pub. by Reidel Holland); pap. 24.00 (ISBN 90-277-0713-8, Pub. by Reidel Holland). Kluwer Boston.

MacKay, Alfred F. & Merrill, Daniel D., eds. Issues in the Philosophy of Language. LC 75-18178. 192p. 1976. 15.00x (ISBN 0-300-01828-2). Yale U Pr.

MacKaye, James. Logic of Language. LC 65-18821. 1965. Repr. of 1939 ed. 8.50 (ISBN 0-8462-0689-7). Russell.
Margalit, A., ed. Meaning & Use. (Syntheses Language Library: No. 3). 1978. lib. bdg. 45.00 (ISBN 90-277-0888-6, Pub. by Reidel Holland). Kluwer Boston.
Martin, R. M. Logic, Language & Metaphysics. LC 74-133025. 1971. 12.50x (ISBN 0-8147-5350-7). NYU Pr.
Merleau-Ponty, Maurice. The Prose of the World. Lefort, Claude, ed. O'Neill, John, tr. from Fr. LC 72-96699. (Studies in Phenomenology & Existential Philosophy). 180p. 1973. text ed. 15.95x (ISBN 0-8101-0412-1); pap. 6.95 (ISBN 0-8101-0615-9). Northwestern U Pr.
Miller, Robert G. Philosophy of Language: The Linguistic Turn. (Orig.). 1968. pap. 0.60x (ISBN 0-87343-011-5). Magi Bks.
Moravcsik, J. M. Understanding Language: A Study of Theories of Language in Linguistics & in Philosophy. (Janua Linguarum, Ser. Minor: No. 169). 95p. 1977. pap. text ed. 20.00x (ISBN 90-279-3111-9). Mouton.
Morgan, George W. Human Predicament: Dissolution & Wholeness. LC 68-23791. 360p. 1971. Repr. of 1968 ed. text ed. 15.00x (ISBN 0-87057-111-7, Pub. by Brown U Pr). U Pr of New Eng.
Mounce, H. O. Wittgenstein's Tractatus: An Introduction. LC 81-40474. 144p. 1981. 19.00 (ISBN 0-226-54318-8). U of Chicago Pr.
--Wittgenstein's Tractatus: An Introduction. 1981. pap. 7.95 (ISBN 0-226-54319-6). U of Chicago Pr.
Mulder, Henk L. & Van De Velde-Schlick, Barbara, eds. Moritz Schlick: Philosophical Papers, Vol. 1, 1909-1922. (Vienna Circle Collection: No. 11). 1978. lib. bdg. 63.00 (ISBN 90-277-0314-0, D. Reidel); pap. 31.50 (ISBN 90-277-0315-9). Kluwer Boston.
Munitz, Milton K. Contemporary Analytic Philosophy. Date not set. pap. text ed. 12.95x (ISBN 0-02-384840-5). Macmillan.
O'Flaherty, James C. Unity & Language: A Study in the Philosophy of Johann Georg Hamann. LC 52-4007. (North Carolina. University. Studies in the Germanic Languages & Literatures: No. 6). Repr. of 1952 ed. 18.50 (ISBN 0-404-50906-1). AMS Pr.
Oller, John W., Jr. Coding Information in Natural Languages. LC 74-182465. (Janua Linguarum, Ser. Minor: No. 123). (Illus.). 120p. (Orig.). 1971. pap. text ed. 11.25x (ISBN 0-686-22496-5). Mouton.
Ong, Walter J. Interfaces of the Word: Studies in the Evolution of Consciousness & Culture. LC 77-3124. 1977. 22.50x (ISBN 0-8014-1105-X). Cornell U Pr.
Papineau, David. Theory & Meaning. 218p. 1979. text ed. 22.50x (ISBN 0-19-824585-8). Oxford U Pr.
Parret, Herman. Language & Discourse. LC 73-170002. (Janua Linguarum, Ser. Minor: No. 119). (Illus.). 292p. (Orig.). 1971. pap. text ed. 30.00x (ISBN 90-2791-854-6). Mouton.
Peterson, Philip L. Concepts & Language: An Essay in Generative Semantics & the Philosophy of Language. 1973. pap. 28.75x (ISBN 90-2792-442-2). Mouton.
Pinxten, Rik, ed. Universalism Versus Relativism in Language & Thought: Proceedings of a Colloquium on the Sapir-Whorf Hypothesis. (Contributions to the Sociology of Language Ser.: No. 11). 1977. text ed. 51.25x (ISBN 90-2797-791-7). Mouton.
Platts, Mark. Ways of Meaning: An Introduction to a Philosophy of Language. 1978. 22.00x (ISBN 0-7100-0000-6); pap. 11.00 (ISBN 0-7100-0001-4). Routledge & Kegan.
Platts, Mark, ed. Reference, Truth & Reality: Essays on the Philosophy of Language. 1980. 27.50x (ISBN 0-7100-0405-2); pap. 13.50 (ISBN 0-7100-0406-0). Routledge & Kegan.
Polakow, Avron. Tense & Performance: An Essay on the Uses of Tensed & Tenseless Language. (Elementa-Schriften Zur Philosophie und Ihrer Probemgeschichte: Vol. 16). 153p. 1981. pap. text ed. 17.25x (ISBN 90-6203-533-7, Pub. by Rodopi Holland). Humanities.
Prazak, Milos. Language & Logic. LC 76-141264. 154p. 1972. Repr. of 1963 ed. lib. bdg. 15.00x (ISBN 0-8371-5860-5, PRLL). Greenwood.
Quine, Willard V. Word & Object. 1960. pap. 8.95 (ISBN 0-262-67001-1). MIT Pr.
Richardson, John T. The Grammar of Justification: An Interpretation of Wittgenstein's Philosophy of Language. LC 75-37303. 160p. 1976. 17.95 (ISBN 0-312-34230-6). St Martin.
Rorty, Richard, ed. Linguistic Turn: Recent Essays in Philosophical Method. LC 67-13811. 1971. pap. 5.95 (ISBN 0-226-72566-9, P421, Phoen). U of Chicago Pr.
Rorty, Richard M., ed. Linguistic Turn: Recent Essays in Philosophic Method. LC 67-13811. 1967. 17.50x (ISBN 0-226-72564-2). U of Chicago Pr.
Rosenberg, Jay F. & Travis, Charles. Readings in the Philosophy of Language. LC 70-132170. 1971. text ed. 20.95 (ISBN 0-13-759332-5). P-H.
--Readings in the Philosophy of Language. LC 70-132170. 1971. text ed. 20.95 (ISBN 0-13-759332-5). P-H.
Rundle, Bede. Grammar in Philosophy. 506p. 1979. text ed. 34.50x (ISBN 0-19-824612-9). Oxford U Pr.
Sanborn, Donald A. The Language Process: Toward a Holistic Schema with Implications for an English Curriculum Theory. LC 70-182464. (Janua Linguarum, Ser. Minor: No. 103). (Illus.). 168p. (Orig.). 1971. pap. text ed. 20.75x (ISBN 90-2791-893-7). Mouton.
Saunders, John T. & Henze, Donald F. Private-Language Problem: A Philosophical Dialogue. (Orig.). 1967. pap. text ed. 3.25 (ISBN 0-685-19755-7). Phila Bk Co.
Schaff, Adam. Language & Cognition. Cohen, Robert S., ed. Wojtasiewicz, Olgierd, tr. from Polish. 192p. (Orig.). 1966. pap. 2.95 (ISBN 0-07-055081-6, SP). McGraw.
Schievella, Pat S. Critical Analysis: Language & Its Functions. LC 68-22331. 1968. text ed. 6.50x (ISBN 0-391-00468-9). Humanities.
Schiffer, Stephen R. Meaning. 184p. 1973. text ed. 32.00x (ISBN 0-19-824367-7). Oxford U Pr.
Searle, J. R., ed. Philosophy of Language. (Oxford Readings in Philosophy Ser). (Orig.). 1971. pap. text ed. 5.95x (ISBN 0-19-875015-3). Oxford U Pr.
Searle, John R. Speech Acts. LC 68-24484. 1970. 29.95 (ISBN 0-521-07184-4); pap. 7.95x (ISBN 0-521-09626-X). Cambridge U Pr.
Sellars, Wilfrid. Pure Pragmatics & Possible Worlds: The Early Essays of Wilfrid Sellars. Sicha, Jeffrey, ed. LC 78-65271. (Orig.). 1980. lib. bdg. 22.00 (ISBN 0-917930-26-6); pap. text ed. 8.50x (ISBN 0-917930-06-1). Ridgeview.
Smerud, Warren B. Can There Be a Private Language: An Examination of Some Principal Arguments. LC 73-126054. (Janua Linguarum, Ser. Minor: No. 100). (Orig.). 1970. pap. text ed. 8.35x (ISBN 0-686-22391-8). Mouton.
Steiner, George. After Babel: Aspects of Language & Translation. LC 74-29207. 519p. 1976. pap. 5.95 (ISBN 0-19-502048-0, 462, GB). Oxford U Pr.
Stevenson, Charles. Ethics & Language. LC 75-41263. Repr. of 1944 ed. 22.50 (ISBN 0-404-14806-9). AMS Pr.
Tartaglia, Philip. Problems in the Construction of a Theory of Natural Language. (Janua Linguarum, Ser. Minor: No. 124). 252p. (Orig.). 1972. pap. text ed. 37.50x (ISBN 90-2792-186-5). Mouton.
Thomas, Lew, ed. & intro. by. Photography & Language. LC 76-43622. (Illus.). pap. 9.95 (ISBN 0-917986-01-6). NFS Pr.
Urban, Wilbur M. Language & Reality: The Philosophy of Language & the Principles of Symbolism. facsimile ed. LC 75-179543. (Select Bibliographies Reprint Ser.). Repr. of 1939 ed. 34.00 (ISBN 0-8369-6672-4). Arno.
Vendler, Zeno. Linguistics in Philosophy. LC 67-18221. 203p. 1967. 18.50x (ISBN 0-8014-0436-3). Cornell U Pr.
The Verb Be & Its Synonyms. Incl. Part 1. Classical Chinese, Athapaskan, Mundari. Verhaar, J. W., ed. 100p. 1967. lib. bdg. 16.00 (ISBN 90-277-0032-X); Part 2. Eskimo, Hindi, Zuni, Modern Greek, Malayalam, Kurukh. Verhaar, J. W., ed. 148p. 1968. lib. bdg. 18.50 (ISBN 90-277-0033-8); Part 3. Japanese, Kashmiri, Armenian, Hungarian, Sumerian, Shona. Verhaar, J. W., ed. 125p. 1968. lib. bdg. 18.50 (ISBN 90-277-0034-6); Part 4. Twi, Modern Chinese, Arabic. Verhaar, J. W., ed. 125p. 1969. lib. bdg. 18.50 (ISBN 90-277-0035-4); Part 5. Urdu, Turkish, Beugali, Amharic, Indonesian, Telegu, Estonian. Verhaar, J. W., ed. LC 79-159659. 233p. 1972. lib. bdg. 31.50 (ISBN 90-277-0217-9); Part 6. Ancient Greek. Kahn, C. H., ed. LC 74-183367. 486p. 1973. lib. bdg. 63.00 (ISBN 90-277-0222-5); pap. 29.00 (ISBN 90-277-0313-2). (Foundations of Language Supplementary Ser., Pub. by Junk Pubs Netherlands). Kluwer Boston.
Verkuyl, H. J. On the Compositional Nature of the Aspects. LC 77-188006. (Foundations of Language Supplementary Ser: No. 15). 185p. 1972. lib. bdg. 28.00 (ISBN 90-277-0227-6, Pub. by Reidel Holland). Kluwer Boston.
Vernon, Thomas S. A Philosophy of Language Primer. LC 80-489. 136p. 1980. text ed. 15.75 (ISBN 0-8191-1023-X); pap. text ed. 7.50 (ISBN 0-8191-1024-8). U Pr of Amer.
Vetterling-Braggin, Mary. Sexist Language: A Modern Philosophical Analysis. (Littlefield, Adams Quality Paperbacks Ser.: No. 353). 1981. pap. 7.95 (ISBN 0-8226-0353-5). Littlefield.
Von Schlegel, Friedrich. Philosophy of Life & Philosophy of Language. Morrison, A. J., tr. LC 70-147991. Repr. of 1847 ed. 27.50 (ISBN 0-404-08249-1). AMS Pr.
Waldrop, Rosemarie. Against Language? Dissatisfaction with Language As Theme & As Impulse Towards Experiments in Twentieth Century Poetry. (De Proprietatibus Litterarum, Ser. Minor: No. 6). 132p. (Orig.). 1971. pap. text ed. 20.00x (ISBN 90-2791-789-2). Mouton.
Weiler, Gershon. Mauthner's Critique of Language. LC 76-114605. 1971. 42.00 (ISBN 0-521-07861-X). Cambridge U Pr.
White, David A. Heidegger & the Language of Poetry. LC 78-5610. 1978. 15.75x (ISBN 0-8032-4703-6). U of Nebr Pr.
Wittgenstein, Ludwig. Prototractatus: An Early Version of Tractatus Logico-Philosophicus. McGuinness, B. F., et al, eds. Pears, D. F. & McGuinness, B. F., trs. LC 79-136737. 1971. 38.50x (ISBN 0-8014-0610-2). Cornell U Pr.
--Remarks on Colour. Anscombe, G. E., ed. McAlister, Linda L. & Schattle, Margarete, trs. from Ger. 1978. 16.50x (ISBN 0-520-03357-4); pap. 3.45 (ISBN 0-520-03727-8, CAL 406). U of Cal Pr.
--Tractatus Logico-Philosophicus: German-English Text. 1963. text ed. 10.75x (ISBN 0-7100-3605-1). Humanities.
Zekowski, Arlene. Image Breaking Images. LC 76-21886. 1976. 15.00 (ISBN 0-8180-1168-8); pap. 4.95 (ISBN 0-8180-1169-6). Horizon.
--Image Breaking Images: A New Mythology of Language. LC 75-36890. (Archives of Post-Modern Literature). 1976. 15.00 (ISBN 0-913844-28-4); pap. 6.00 (ISBN 0-913844-03-9). Am Canadian.

LANGUAGES–POLITICAL ASPECTS

Bosmajian, Haig. Language of Oppression. 1974. pap. 4.50 (ISBN 0-8183-0136-8). Pub Aff Pr.
Corcoran, Paul E. Political Language & Rhetoric. LC 79-63529. 234p. 1979. text ed. 14.95x (ISBN 0-292-76458-8). U of Tex Pr.
Fishman, Joshua A. Language & Nationalism. LC 72-149036. 1973. pap. 11.95 (ISBN 0-912066-15-6). Newbury Hse.
Gopal, Ram. Linguistic Affairs of India. 1967. 8.50x (ISBN 0-210-27158-2). Asia.
Krueger, John R. American Presidents & Their Knowledge of Foreign Languages. 1980. pap. 2.00 (ISBN 0-911706-22-4). Selbstverlag.
Laitin, David D. Politics, Language, & Thought: The Somali Experience. LC 76-22958. (Illus.). 1977. lib. bdg. 19.00x (ISBN 0-226-46791-0). U of Chicago Pr.
Lieberson, Stanley, ed. Explorations in Sociolinguistics. 3rd ed. LC 67-65323. (General Publications Ser: Vol. 44). (Orig.). 1971. pap. text ed. 8.00x (ISBN 0-87750-132-7). Res Ctr Lang Semiotic.
Maranda, Pierre, ed. Soviet Structural Folkloristics: Texts by Meletinsky, Nekludov, Novik, & Segal, with Tests of the Approach by Jilek &Jilek-Aall, Reid, & Layton, Vol. 1. LC 73-79892. (Approaches to Semiotics Ser.: No. 42). 194p. 1974. 38.75x (ISBN 90-2792-683-2). Mouton.
Marx-Nordin, Signe. Studien Zum Stil Deutschsprachiger Parteiprogramme: Ein Beitrag Zu Einer Syntaxorientierten Stillstik. (Goteborg Germanistische Forschungen: No. 17). 1979. pap. text ed. 14.00x (ISBN 91-7346-058-3). Humanities.
O'Barr, William M. & Jean, F. Languages & Politics. (Contributions to the Sociology of Language Ser.: No. 10). 1977. text ed. 46.25x (ISBN 90-279-7761-5). Mouton.

LANGUAGES–PSYCHOANALYSIS

see Psycholinguistics

LANGUAGES–PSYCHOLOGY

see Psycholinguistics

LANGUAGES–RELIGIOUS ASPECTS

see also Aramaic Language; Bible–Language, Style; Bible–Versions; Greek Language, Biblical; Hebrew Language; Latin Language–Church Latin; Religion and Language

Black, M. & Smalley, W. A., eds. On Language, Culture & Religion: In Honor of Eugene A. Nida. (Approaches to Semiotics Ser: No. 56). (Illus.). 386p. 1974. text ed. 45.90x (ISBN 90-2793-236-0). Mouton.
Wild, Laura H. The Romance of the English Bible. 1929. 15.00 (ISBN 0-8274-3303-4). R West.

LANGUAGES–SOCIOLOGICAL ASPECTS

see Sociolinguistics

LANGUAGES–VOCATIONAL GUIDANCE

See Language and Languages–Vocational Guidance

LANGUAGES, ARTIFICIAL

see also Esperanto (Artificial Language); Programming Languages (Electronic Computers)

LANGUAGES, INFINITARY

see Infinitary Languages

LANGUAGES, MIXED

see also Creole Dialects; Pidgin English

Brown, Jason W., ed. Jargonaphasia. LC 80-2328. (Perspectives in Neurolinguistics & Psycholinguistics Ser.). 1981. 29.50 (ISBN 0-12-137580-3). Acad Pr.
Casad, Eugene. Dialect Intelligibility Tests. (Publications in Linguistics & Related Fields Ser.: No. 38). 1974. pap. 8.00x (ISBN 0-88312-040-2); microfiche 2.20 (ISBN 0-88312-440-8). Summer Inst Ling.
Goilo, E. R. Papiamentu Textbook. 4th ed. pap. 10.00 (ISBN 0-685-58559-X). Heinman.
Hall, Robert A., Jr. Pidgin & Creole Languages. (Illus.). 207p. 1966. 17.50x (ISBN 0-8014-0173-9). Cornell U Pr.
Miller, Don. The Book of Jargon: An Essential Guide to the Inside Languages of Today. 384p. 1981. 15.95 (ISBN 0-02-584960-3). Macmillan.
Reinecke, John E., et al. A Bibliography of Pidgin & Creole Languages. LC 73-91459. (Oceanic Linguistics Special Publication Ser.: No. 14). 860p. (Orig.). 1975. pap. 25.00x (ISBN 0-8248-0306-X). U Pr of Hawaii.
Schuchardt, Hugo. The Ethnography of Variation: Selected Writings on Pidgins & Creoles. Markey, T. L., ed. & tr. from Ger. Fr. (Linguistica Extranea: Studia 3). 174p. 1979. lib. bdg. 7.50 (ISBN 0-89720-003-9); pap. 5.50 (ISBN 0-89720-004-7). Karoma.
Valdman, Albert, ed. Pidgin & Creole Linguistics. LC 76-48496. (Illus.). 384p. 1977. 17.50x (ISBN 0-253-34495-6). Ind U Pr.

LANGUAGES, MODERN

Here are entered works dealing with the living literary languages of Europe.

see also Philology

Achtert, Walter S., compiled by. MLA Abstracts of Articles in Scholarly Journals, 1972. 398p. 1974. 25.00x (ISBN 0-87352-225-7). Modern Lang.
Cartier, N. R. Aquila, Vol. 3. (Aquila Chestnut Hill Studies in Modern Languages & Literatures). 1976. pap. 34.00 (ISBN 90-247-1797-3). Kluwer Boston.
Conference on New Methodologies in Modern Language Teaching, University of Northern Iowa, Cedar Falls, October 28 & 29, 1977. Proceedings. Odwarka, Karl, ed. LC 79-10410. 1979. pap. 8.50 (ISBN 0-8357-0401-7, SS-00088). Univ Microfilms.
Dialects & Levels of Language. (Language of Man Ser.). (gr. 10-12). 1972. pap. text ed. 3.96 (ISBN 0-88343-096-7); tchrs'. manual 1.50 (ISBN 0-88343-097-5). McDougal-Littell.
Huffman, Franklin E., et al. Cambodian System of Writing & Beginning Reader. LC 78-104614. 1970. text ed. 30.00x (ISBN 0-300-01199-7). Yale U Pr.
Language of Man. Incl. Book 1. (gr. 7 up). 1972 (ISBN 0-88343-072-X); Book 2. (gr. 8 up). 1972 (ISBN 0-88343-075-4); Book 3. (gr. 9 up). 1971 (ISBN 0-88343-078-9); Book 4. (gr. 10 up). 1971 (ISBN 0-88343-081-9); Book 5. (gr. 11 up). 1971 (ISBN 0-88343-084-3); Book 6. (gr. 12 up). 1971 (ISBN 0-88343-087-8). (Language of Man Ser.). pap. text ed. 4.92 ea.; tchr's. manual 1.50 ea. McDougal-Littell.
Living Language Dictionaries & Manuals. (Living Language Course Ser). pap. 2.00 ea. Crown.
Pei, Mario. The World's Chief Languages. 1960. 16.50x (ISBN 0-913298-07-7). S F Vanni.

LANGUAGES, MODERN–BIBLIOGRAPHY

Johnson, Dora E., et al, eds. A Survey of Materials for the Study of the Uncommonly Taught Languages No. 1: Western Europe-Pidgins & Creoles (European Based) LC 76-44588. 1976. pap. 4.95x (ISBN 0-87281-052-6). Ctr Appl Ling.
Legters, Lyman H. Language & Area Studies. (Occasional Publication). 1967. pap. 2.00 (ISBN 0-89192-143-5). Interbk Inc.
Meserole, Harrison T., compiled by. MLA International Bibliography of Books & Articles on the Modern Languages & Literatures, 1969. 723p. 1970. 150.00x (ISBN 0-87352-409-8). Modern Lang.
--MLA International Bibliography of Books & Articles on the Modern Languages & Literatures, 1974. 884p. 1976. 150.00x (ISBN 0-87352-241-9). Modern Lang.
MLA International Bibliography of Books & Articles on the Modern Languages & Literatures, 1979. LC 64-20773. 1061p. 1980. 150.00x (ISBN 0-87352-418-7). Modern Lang.
MLA International Bibliography of Books & Articles on the Modern Languages & Literatures, 1975. LC 64-20773. 791p. 1977. 150.00x (ISBN 0-87352-245-1). Modern Lang.
Stanford University, Hoover Institution on War, Revolution & Peace. Catalog of the Western Language Collections, First Supplement, 5 vols. 2627p. 1972. Set. lib. bdg. 700.00 (ISBN 0-8161-1019-0). G K Hall.
Wortman, William A. A Guide to Serial Bibliographies for Modern Languages. (Selected Bibliographies in Language & Literature Ser.: No. 3). 60p. 1982. 8.50x (ISBN 0-87352-952-9); pap. 4.85x (ISBN 0-87352-953-7). Modern Lang.

LANGUAGES, MODERN–CONVERSATION AND PHRASE BOOKS

Kettridge, J. O. Travellers' Foreign Phrase Book. 1967. Repr. of 1960 ed. limp 5.00 (ISBN 0-7100-1674-3). Routledge & Kegan.

LANGUAGES, MODERN–EXAMINATIONS, QUESTIONS, ETC.

Gilman, Margaret, ed. Foreign Language Tests & Techniques. 136p. 1956. pap. 7.95x (ISBN 0-915432-56-0). NE Conf Teach Foreign.

Michigan Oral Language Productive Tests. (Michigan Oral Lang Ser.). 1970. pap. 15.00x (ISBN 0-87352-061-0). Modern Lang.

Nute, Grace L. & Ackermann, Gertrudecompiled by. Guide to the Personal Papers in the Manuscripts Collections of the Minnesota Historical Society, Guide No. 1. LC 35-27911. 146p. 1935. pap. 2.00 (ISBN 0-87351-004-6). Minn Hist.

Rudman, Jack. Foreign Languages Chairman - Jr. H.S. (Teachers License Examination Ser.: CH-8). (Cloth bdg. avail. on request). pap. 12.00 (ISBN 0-8373-8158-4). Natl Learning.

--Foreign Languages Chairman - Sr. H.S. (Teachers License Examination Ser.: CH-9). (Cloth bdg. avail. on request). pap. 12.00 (ISBN 0-8373-8159-2). Natl Learning.

Valette, Rebecca M. Directions in Foreign Language Testing. 65p. (Orig.). 1969. pap. 7.50x (ISBN 0-87352-055-6). Modern Lang.

LANGUAGES, MODERN–GLOSSARIES, VOCABULARIES, ETC.

see Polyglot Glossaries, Phrase Books, etc.

LANGUAGES, MODERN–STUDY AND TEACHING

see also Language and Languages–Vocational Guidance; Language Laboratories

American Association of Teachers of French. FLES & Bilingual Education: Getting the Word Out. Kunkle, John F., ed. (Reports of the FLES & Bilingual Education Section). 71p. (Orig.). 1974. pap. 5.00x (ISBN 0-87352-167-6). Modern Lang.

Anthropology & Language Science in Educational Development. LC 73-75746. (Educational Studies & Documents, No. 11). 58p. (Orig.). 1973. pap. 2.50 (ISBN 92-3-101095-6, U32, UNESCO). Unipub.

Bahlsen, Leopold. The Teaching of Modern Languages. Evans, M. Blakemore, tr. from Ger. 97p. 1980. Repr. lib. bdg. 12.50 (ISBN 0-8495-0602-6). Arden Lib.

Baschiera, Karl. Teaching of Modern Languages, in Secondary Vocational & Commercial Schools. LC 72-183343. (Modern Languages in Europe Ser). (Orig.). 1970. pap. 8.75x (ISBN 0-245-50323-4). Intl Pubns Serv.

Bennett, W. A. Aspects of Language & Language Teaching. (Illus., Orig.). 1968. pap. 6.95x (ISBN 0-521-09512-3, 512). Cambridge U Pr.

Bird, Thomas E., ed. Foreign Language Learning: Research & Development. Incl. The Classroom Revisited. Simches, Seymour O; Innovative Foreign Language Programs. Andrews, Oliver, Jr; Liberated Expression. Edgerton, F. Mills. 118p. 1968. pap. 7.95x (ISBN 0-915432-68-4). NE Conf Teach Foreign.

--Foreign Languages: Reading, Literature, Requirements. Incl. The Teaching of Reading. Moulton, William G; The Times & Places for Literature. Paquette, F. Andre; Trends in Foreign Language Requirements & Placement. Gummere, John F. 124p. 1967. pap. 7.95x (ISBN 0-915432-67-6). NE Conf Teach Foreign.

Birkmaier, Emma. Foreign Language Education: An Overview. (ACTFL Review Ser.: Vol. 1). 1972. pap. text ed. 10.00 (ISBN 0-8442-9312-1). Natl Textbk.

Bishop, G. Reginald, Jr., ed. Foreign Language Teaching: Challenges to the Profession. Incl. The Case for Latin. Parker, William R; The Challenge of Bilingualism. Gaarder, A. Bruce; From School to College: The Problem of Continuity. Dufau, Micheline; Study Abroad. Freeman, Stephen A. 158p. 1965. pap. 7.95x (ISBN 0-915432-65-X). NE Conf Teach Foreign.

Bottiglia, William F., ed. The Language Classroom. Incl. The Drop-Out of Students After the Second Year. Fulton, Renee J; The Philosophy of the Language Laboratory. Archer, John B; The Place of Grammar & the Use of English in the Teaching of Foreign Languages. Grew, James H; Spoken Language Tests. Brooks, Nelson; Teaching Aids & Techniques. Pleasants, Jeanne V; Teaching Literature for Admission to College with Advanced Standing. Price, Blanche A. 84p. 1957. pap. 7.95x (ISBN 0-915432-57-9). NE Conf Teach Foreign.

Boyd-Bowman, Peter. Self-Instructional Language Programs: A Handbook for Faculty & Students. (FAMC Occasional Publication Ser.: No. 20). 51p. (Orig.). 1973. pap. text ed. 2.50 (ISBN 0-936876-08-5). Learn Res Intl Stud.

Bree, Germaine, ed. Culture, Literature, & Articulation. Incl. Classical & Modern Foreign Languages: Common Areas & Problems. McCarthy, Barbara P; Foreign Language Instruction in Elementary Schools. Thompson, Mary P; Foreign Language Instruction in the Secondary School. Mead, Robert G., Jr; The Place of Culture & Civilization in Foreign Language Teaching. Wylie, Laurence; The Preparation of Foreign Language Teachers. Grace, Alonzo G; The Role of Foreign Languages in American Life. Starr, Wilmarth H; The Role of Literature in Language Teaching. MacAllister, Archibald T; Teaching Aids & Techniques: Principle Demonstrations. Pleasants, Jeanne V; Tests: All Skills, Speaking Test. Brooks, Nelson. 188p. 1955. pap. 7.95x (ISBN 0-915432-55-2). NE Conf Teach Foreign.

Brod, Richard I. & Fisher, Dexter, eds. Profession Eighty. 60p. (Orig.). 1980. pap. 4.00x (ISBN 0-87352-315-6). Modern Lang.

Centre for Information on Language Teaching & Research, ed. Language Teaching & Linguistics. LC 77-88671. 1978. 11.95 (ISBN 0-521-21926-4). Cambridge U Pr.

Cornfield, Ruth R. Foreign Language Instruction: Dimensions & Horizons. LC 66-24055. 1966. text ed. 12.95x (ISBN 0-89197-167-X); pap. text ed. 6.95x (ISBN 0-89197-168-8). Irvington.

Developing Language Curricula: Programmed Exercises for Teachers. (Michigan Oral Language Ser.). 78p. 1970. pap. 12.00x (ISBN 0-87352-058-0). Modern Lang.

Dodge, James W., ed. Sensitivity in the Foreign Language Classroom. Incl. Individualization of Instruction. Gougher, Ronald L; Interraction in the Foreign Language Class. Moskowitz, Gertrude; Teaching Spanish to the Native Spanish Speaker. LaFontaine, Herman. 142p. 1973. pap. 7.95x (ISBN 0-915432-73-0). NE Conf Teach Foreign.

Dorry, Gertrude N. Games for Second Language Learning. 1966. 1.75 (ISBN 0-07-017653-1, I). McGraw.

Eddy, Frederick D., ed. The Language Learner. Incl. Definition of Language Competences Through Testing. Brooks, Nelson; Elementary & Junior High School Curricula. Peloro, Filomena C; Modern Foreign Language Learning: Assumptions & Implications. Starr, Wilmarth H; A Six-Year Sequence. Silber, Gordon R; Teaching Aids & Techniques: The Secondary School Language Laboratory. Eddy, Frederick D; The Teaching of Classical & Modern Foreign Languages: Common Areas & Problems. Bree, Josephine P. 70p. 1959. pap. 7.95x (ISBN 0-915432-59-5). NE Conf Teach Foreign.

Finocchiaro, Mary. Teaching Children Foreign Languages. 1964. text ed. 13.95 (ISBN 0-07-021067-5, C). McGraw.

Grittner, Frank M. Teaching Foreign Languages. 2nd ed. 1977. text ed. 19.50 scp (ISBN 0-06-042524-5, HarpC); instructor's manual free (ISBN 0-06-362515-6). Har-Row.

Hatch, Evelyn. Second Language Acquisition: A Book of Readings. 1978. pap. 16.95 (ISBN 0-88377-086-5). Newbury Hse.

Huebener, Theodore. How to Teach Foreign Languages Effectively. rev. ed. LC 65-13880. 1965. 14.50x (ISBN 0-8147-0209-0). NYU Pr.

Interdisciplinary Oral Language Guide, Primary 1. 4 Pts. (Michigan Oral Lang. Ser.). 1970. Pt. 1, 214 Pgs. pap. 12.00x (ISBN 0-87352-060-2); Pt. 2, 470 Pgs. pap. 18.00x (ISBN 0-87352-062-9); Pt. 3, 342 Pgs. pap. 15.00x (ISBN 0-87352-063-7); Pt. 4, 360 Pgs. pap. 15.00x (ISBN 0-87352-069-6). Modern Lang.

Jelavich, Charles, ed. Language & Area Studies East Central & Southeastern Europe: A Survey. LC 72-8122. 1969. 17.50x (ISBN 0-226-39615-0). U of Chicago Pr.

Jones, George F., ed. Foreign Language Teaching: Ideals & Practices. Incl. Foreign Languages in Colleges & Universities. Hadlich, Roger L; Foreign Languages in Elementary School. Schmitt, Conrad J; Foreign Languages in the Secondary School. Hahn, Milton R. 62p. 1964. pap. 7.95x (ISBN 0-915432-64-1). NE Conf Teach Foreign.

Kellenberger, Hunter, ed. Foreign Language Teachers & Tests. Incl. Foreign Language Instruction in Elementary Schools. Selvi, Arthur S; Linguistic Aids. Walker, Richard H; The Qualifications of Foreign Language Teachers. Freeman, Stephen A; The Role of Foreign Languages in American Life. Andersson, Theodore; The Teaching of Literature. Torrey, Norman L; Tests: Listening Comprehension, Other Skills. 56p. 1954. pap. 7.95x (ISBN 0-915432-54-4). NE Conf Teach Foreign.

Konnyu, Leslie. Modern Magyar Literature. LC 63-10689. 1964. pap. 3.25 (ISBN 0-911862-04-8). Hungarian Rev.

Lange, Dale L. Foreign Language Education: A Reappraisal. (ACTFL Review Ser.: Vol. 4). 1972. 15.00 (ISBN 0-8442-9333-4); pap. 10.00 (ISBN 0-8442-9347-4). Natl Textbk.

Levy, Harold L., ed. The Language Teacher. Incl. Foreign Language Program: Grades 3-12. Eaton, Margaret E; The Ghosts in the Language Classroom. Walsh, Donald D; Means of Meeting the Shortage of Teachers. Bock, Carolyn E; Patterns As Grammar. Brodin, Dorothy; Single vs. Multiple Languages in Secondary Schools; The Teaching of Writing. Atkins, Jeannette. 84p. 1958. pap. 7.95x (ISBN 0-915432-58-7). NE Conf Teach Foreign.

Maley, A. & Duff, A. Drama Techniques in Language Learning. (English Language Learning Ser.). 1978. limp bdg 7.95x (ISBN 0-521-21877-2). Cambridge U Pr.

Mathieu, G., ed. Advances in the Teaching of Modern Languages, Vol. 2. 1966. 23.00 (ISBN 0-08-011840-2). Pergamon.

Mead, Robert G., Jr., ed. Language Teaching: Broader Contexts. Incl. Coordination of Foreign Language Teaching. Blew, Genevieve S; Research & Language Learning. Sullivan, Edward D; Wider Uses for Foreign Languages. Corrin, Brownlee S. 104p. 1966. pap. 7.95x (ISBN 0-915432-66-8). NE Conf Teach Foreign.

Modern Languages at General Secondary Schools. 1964. pap. 5.50 (ISBN 92-3-100558-8, U387, UNESCO). Unipub.

Modern Languages at General Secondary Schools. 1964. pap. 5.50 (ISBN 92-3-100558-8, U387, UNESCO). Unipub.

Najam, Edward W., ed. Language Learning: The Individual & the Process. LC 66-63007. (General Publications Ser: Vol. 40). (Orig.). 1965. pap. text ed. 5.50x (ISBN 0-87750-128-9). Res Ctr Lang Semiotic.

Nute, Grace L. & Ackermann, Gertrudecompiled by. Guide to the Personal Papers in the Manuscripts Collections of the Minnesota Historical Society, Guide No. 1. LC 35-27911. 146p. 1935. pap. 2.00 (ISBN 0-87351-004-6). Minn Hist.

Pell, Mary & Pell, William. Cumulative Index to the Northeast Conference Reports: 1954-1975. 1975. pap. 5.00x (ISBN 0-915432-00-5). NE Conf Teach Foreign.

Pulgram, E., ed. Applied Linguistics in Language Teaching. 1954. pap. 6.00 (ISBN 0-527-01453-2). Kraus Repr.

Rameh, Clea. Georgetown University Round Table on Languages & Linguistics: Semantics-Theory & Application. LC 58-31607. (Georgetown Univ. Round Table Ser.: 1976). (GURT 1976). 1976. pap. 6.00 (ISBN 0-87840-111-3). Georgetown U Pr.

Rivers, Wilga M. Psychologist & the Foreign-Language Teacher. 1964. 12.00x (ISBN 0-226-72095-0). U of Chicago Pr.

--Teaching Foreign Language Skills. LC 68-26761. 1968. 16.00x (ISBN 0-226-72096-9). U of Chicago Pr.

Roucek, Joseph S., ed. Study of Foreign Languages. LC 68-13396. 1968. 10.00 (ISBN 0-8022-1395-2). Philos Lib.

Spice: A Handbook of Classroom Ideas to Motivate the Teaching of Primary Language Arts. (The Spice Ser). 1973. 6.50 (ISBN 0-89273-101-X). Educ Serv.

Stuart, Hugh. The Training of Modern Foreign Language Teachers for the Secondary Schools in the United States. LC 70-177738. (Columbia University. Teachers College. Contributions to Education: No. 256). Repr. of 1927 ed. 17.50 (ISBN 0-404-55256-0). AMS Pr.

Trim, J. L. Developing a Unit-Credit Scheme of Adult Language Learning. LC 80-40756. (Council of Europe Modern Languages Project). 96p. 1980. pap. 7.95 (ISBN 0-08-024596-X). Pergamon.

Trueba, Henry T. & Barnett-Mizrahi, Carol, eds. Bilingual Multicultural Education & the Professional: From Theory to Practice. 1979. pap. text ed. 15.95 (ISBN 0-88377-138-1). Newbury Hse.

UNESCO. Teaching of Modern Languages. Repr. of 1955 ed. lib. bdg. 15.00x (ISBN 0-8371-2326-7, TEML). Greenwood.

Valdman, Albert. Trends in Language Teaching. 1966. pap. 10.95 (ISBN 0-07-066812-4, C). McGraw.

Valette, Rebecca M. Directions in Foreign Language Testing. 65p. (Orig.). 1969. pap. 7.50x (ISBN 0-87352-055-6). Modern Lang.

Wringe, Colin. Developments in Modern Language Teaching. (Changing Classroom). 1976. pap. text ed. 4.00x (ISBN 0-7291-0090-1). Humanities.

LANGUAGES, MODERN–STUDY AND TEACHING–AUDIO-VISUAL AIDS

Huebener, Theodore. Audio-Visual Techniques in Teaching Foreign Languages: A Practical Handbook. rev. ed. LC 67-10506. 1967. 7.95x (ISBN 0-8147-0208-2). NYU Pr.

LANGUAGES, MODERN–STUDY AND TEACHING–BIBLIOGRAPHY

Language-Teaching Bibliography. 2nd ed. 1971. 34.00x (ISBN 0-521-08183-1). Cambridge U Pr.

LANGUAGES, OCCIDENTAL

see Languages, Modern

LANGUAGES, OFFICIAL

see Languages–Political Aspects

LANGUAGES, ORIENTAL

see Oriental Languages

LANGUAGES, SEMITIC

see Semitic Languages

LANGUAGES, WESTERN

see Languages, Modern

LANGUE D'OC

see Provencal Language

LANGUE D'OIL

see French Language

LANGUEDOC

Bisson, T. N. Assemblies & Representation in Languedoc in the Thirteenth Century. 1964. 24.00 (ISBN 0-691-09201-X). Princeton U Pr.

De Vic, Claude. Histoire Generale de Languedoc, 16 vols. LC 78-63203. (Heresies of the Early Christian & Medieval Era: Second Ser.). Repr. of 1872 ed. 2745.00 set (ISBN 0-404-16380-7); Vols. 1-15. 175.00 ea.; Vol. 16, Pts. 1 & 2. 87.50 ea. AMS Pr.

Ladurie, Emmanuel L. The Peasants of Languedoc. Day, John, tr. from Fr. LC 74-4286. (Illus.). 1977. 18.50 (ISBN 0-252-00411-6); pap. 6.95 (ISBN 0-252-00635-6). U of Ill Pr.

LANGUEDOC–DESCRIPTION AND TRAVEL

Beautes de la France: Auvergne, Languedoc, Rhone-Alpes. (Illus.). 1978. 48.25x (ISBN 0-685-89359-6, 3007). Larousse.

LANIER, SIDNEY, 1842-1881

DeBellis, Jack, ed. Sidney Lanier, Henry Timrod & Paul Hamilton Hayne: A Reference Guide. 1978. lib. bdg. 20.00 (ISBN 0-8161-7967-0). G K Hall.

Gates, Merrill E. Sidney Lanier: A Paper. LC 77-14263. 1977. lib. bdg. 8.50 (ISBN 0-8414-2001-7). Folcroft.

Graham, Philip & Jones, Joseph. A Concordance to the Poems of Sidney Lanier: Including the Poem Outlines & Certain Uncollected Items. (English Literary Reference Ser). 1969. Repr. of 1939 ed. 38.50 (ISBN 0-384-19610-1). Johnson Repr.

Mims, Edwin. Sidney Lanier. LC 68-16281. 1968. Repr. of 1905 ed. 13.50 (ISBN 0-8046-0314-6). Kennikat.

--Sidney Lanier. 59.95 (ISBN 0-8490-1052-7). Gordon Pr.

Wayland, John W. Sidney Lanier at Rockingham Springs. facsmile ed. LC 70-148905. (Select Bibliographies Reprint Ser). Repr. of 1912 ed. 12.00 (ISBN 0-8369-5668-0). Arno.

West, C. A Sketch of the Life & Writings of Sidney Lanier. 59.95 (ISBN 0-8490-1061-6). Gordon Pr.

LANING, EDWARD

Laning, Edward. Mural Paintings of Edward Laning in the New York Public Library. (Illus.). 1963. Repr. of 1951 ed. pap. 2.00 (ISBN 0-87104-123-5). NY Pub Lib.

LANSING, ROBERT, 1864-1928

Beers, Burton F. Vain Endeavor: Robert Lansing's Attempts to End the American-Japanese Rivalry. LC 61-16907. 1962. 12.75 (ISBN 0-8223-0014-1). Duke.

Smith, Daniel M. Robert Lansing & American Neutrality, 1914-1917. LC 79-126610. (American Scene: Comments & Commentators Ser.). (Illus.). 254p. 1972. Repr. of 1958 ed. lib. bdg. 25.00 (ISBN 0-306-70057-3). Da Capo.

LANTERN PROJECTION

see also Moving-Picture Projection; Overhead Projection

LANTERN SLIDES

see Slides (Photography)

LANTHANIDE

Bagnall, K. W. Lanthanides & Actinides. (MTP International Review of Science: Inorganic Chemistry Ser. 2: Vol. 7). (Illus.). 400p. 1975. 37.50 (ISBN 0-8391-0206-2). Univ Park.

Edelstein, Norman, ed. Lanthanide & Actinide Chemistry & Spectroscopy. LC 80-17468. (ACS Symposium Ser.: No. 131). 1980. 40.00 (ISBN 0-8412-0568-X). Am Chemical.

LAO LANGUAGE

Beery, Galen. Basic Spoken Lao in Sixteen Lessons. 1977. pap. 3.00 (ISBN 0-8048-1207-1). C E Tuttle.

Compton, Carol J. Courting Poetry in Laos: A Textual & Linguistic Analysis. (Special Report Ser.: No. 18). (Illus.). 1979. pap. 9.00x (ISBN 0-686-25222-5, Ctr South & Southeast Asian Studies). Cellar.

FSI Reading Lao: A Programmed Introduction. 1974. pap. text ed. 6.50x (ISBN 0-686-10758-6); 40 cassettes 240.00x (ISBN 0-686-10759-4). Intl Learn Syst.

Hoshino, Tatsuo & Marcus, Russell. Lao for Beginners: An Introduction to the Language Through the Written Word. LC 81-50487. 210p. (Orig.). 1981. pap. 13.50 (ISBN 0-8048-1382-5). C E Tuttle.
Kerr, Allen. Lao-English Dictionary, 2 vols. (Publications in the Languages of Asia Ser.: No. 2). 1973. Set. 42.00 (ISBN 0-8132-0526-3). Cath U Pr.
Marcus, Russell. English-Lao, Lao-English Dictionary. LC 77-116487. 1970. 10.50 (ISBN 0-8048-0909-7). C E Tuttle.
Reinhorn, Marc. Dictionnaire Laotien-Francais, 2 vols. 2000p. (Fr.-Lao.). 1970. Set. 85.00 (ISBN 0-686-57204-1, M-6481). French & Eur.
Yates, Warren G. & Sayasithsena, S. Reading Lao: A Programmed Introduction. (Spoken Language Ser.). 483p. 1980. pap. 10.00x (ISBN 0-87950-693-8); cassettes 190.00x (ISBN 0-87950-694-6); book & cassettes 195.00x (ISBN 0-686-66051-X). Spoken Lang Serv.
--Spoken Lao, 2 bks. 1980. pap. 10.00 ea. Bk. I (ISBN 0-87950-691-1). Bk. II (ISBN 0-87950-692-X). Spoken Lang Serv.

LAOCOON

Bieber, Margarete. Laocoon: The Influence of the Group Since Its Rediscovery. 2nd ed. LC 67-16850. (Illus.). 1967. 7.95x (ISBN 0-8143-1323-X). Wayne St U Pr.

LAOS

American National Standards Institute, Standards Committee Z39 on Library Work, Documentation & Related Publishing Practices. American National Standard System for the Romanization of Lao, Khmer, & Pali, Z39.35. 1979. 4.50 (ISBN 0-686-28238-8). ANSI.
Breakey, Gail F. & Voulgaropoulos, Emmanuel. Laos Health Survey: Mekong Valley, 1968-1969. LC 76-14. 140p. 1976. pap. text ed. 6.00x (ISBN 0-8248-0378-7). U Pr of Hawaii.
Lafont, Pierre-Bernard, ed. Bibliographie Du Laos. 2nd ed. Incl. Vol. 1. 1666-1961. 269p; Vol. 2. 1962-1975. 413p. LC 65-53527. (Orig., Fr.). 1978. pap. 55.00x (ISBN 0-686-70204-2). Intl Pubns Serv.
LeBar, Frank M. & Suddard, Adrienne, eds. Laos. LC 60-7381. (Survey of World Cultures Ser). xviii, 294p. (YA) (gr. 10 up). 1967. 15.00x (ISBN 0-87536-915-4). HRAFP.
Lefevre-Pontalis, P. Chansons et fetes du Laos. LC 78-20131. (Collection de contes et de chansons populaires: Vol. 22). Repr. of 1896 ed. 21.50 (ISBN 0-404-60372-6). AMS Pr.
McGilvary, Daniel. A Half Century Among the Siameses & the Lao: An Autobiography. LC 77-87044. Repr. of 1912 ed. 33.00 (ISBN 0-404-16838-8). AMS Pr.
Menger, Matt. Slowly Climbs the Sun. LC 72-96835. 1973. 5.50 (ISBN 0-685-42651-3). Guild Bks.
Menger, Matt J. Slowly Climbs the Sun. LC 72-96835. 1973. 5.50 (ISBN 0-686-18631-1). Oblate.
Viravong, Maha-Sila. History of Laos. 1964. 11.00 (ISBN 0-8188-0091-7). Paragon.
Wyatt, David K., ed. Iron Man of Laos: Prince Phetsarath Ratanavongsa. Murdoch, John B., tr. 1978. 5.00 (ISBN 0-87727-110-0, DP 110). Cornell SE Asia.

LAOS–HISTORY

Bohner, Olive. Demon of Padeng. LC 77-20928. (Nova Ser.). 1977. pap. 5.95 (ISBN 0-8127-0150-X). Review & Herald.
Jumsai, M. L. History of Laos. 2nd rev. & enl. ed. 1971. 12.50x (ISBN 0-685-41963-0). Paragon.
Langer, Paul F. & Zasloff, Joseph J. North Vietnam & the Pathet Lao: Partners in the Struggle for Laos. LC 73-134326. (Rand Corporation Research Studies). 1970. 12.50x (ISBN 0-674-62675-3). Harvard U Pr.
Le Boulanger, Paul. Histoire du Laos francais. LC 77-87070. (Illus.). Repr. of 1931 ed. 27.50 (ISBN 0-404-16831-0). AMS Pr.
Smith, Bardwell L., ed. Religion & Legitimation of Power in Thailand, Laos & Burma. LC 77-7444. 1978. pap. 7.95 (ISBN 0-89012-009-9). Anima Pubns.

LAOS–POLITICS AND GOVERNMENT

Goldstein, Martin E. American Policy Toward Laos. LC 72-416. (Illus.). 347p. 1973. 18.00 (ISBN 0-8386-1131-1). Fairleigh Dickinson.
Sasorith, Katay D. Le Laos: Son Evolution Politique, Sa Place Dans L'Unions Francaise. LC 70-179240. Repr. of 1953 ed. 12.50 (ISBN 0-404-54866-0). AMS Pr.

LAO-TZU

Harris, Iverson L. The Wisdom of Laotse. 36p. 1972. pap. 0.75 (ISBN 0-685-37592-7, 913004-05). Point Loma Pub.
Kwok Yim Weng. Tao Philosophy & Mao Tse Tung's Political Success in New China. Date not set. 10.50 (ISBN 0-533-04179-1). Vantage.
Rump, Ariane & Wing-Tsit Chan, trs. Commentary on the Lao Tzu by Wang Pi. LC 79-11212. (Society for Asian & Comparative Philosophy Monograph: No. 6). 1979. pap. text ed. 5.00x (ISBN 0-8248-0677-8). U Pr of Hawaii.
Welch, Holmes. Taoism: The Parting of the Way. Orig. Title: Parting of the Way. 1966. pap. 4.95 (ISBN 0-8070-5973-0, BP224). Beacon Pr.

LAPAROTOMY

see Abdomen–Surgery

LAPIDAIRE CHRETIEN (MEDIEVAL FRENCH POEM)

Baisier, Leon. Lapidaire Chretien: Its Composition, Its Influence, Its Sources. LC 71-94163. (Catholic University of America Studies in Romance Languages & Literatures Ser: No. 14). 1969. Repr. of 1936 ed. 15.00 (ISBN 0-404-50314-4). AMS Pr.

LAPIDARY ART

see Gem Cutting

LAPLACE, PIERRE SIMON, MARQUIS DE, 1749-1827

Numbers, Ronald L. Creation by Natural Law: Laplace's Nebular Hypothesis in American Thought. LC 76-45810. 196p. 1977. 16.95 (ISBN 0-295-95439-6). U of Wash Pr.

LAPLACE TRANSFORMATION

Beltrami, E. J. & Wohlers, M. R. Distributions & the Boundary Values of Analytic Functions. 1966. 23.50 (ISBN 0-12-085550-X). Acad Pr.
Carslaw, Horatio S. & Jaeger, J. C. Conduction of Heat in Solids. 2nd ed. (Illus.). 1959. 39.50x (ISBN 0-19-853303-9). Oxford U Pr.
Day, William D. Tables of La Place Transforms. 2.50 (ISBN 0-685-20639-4). Transatlantic.
Doetsch, G. Introduction to the Theory & Application of the Laplace Transformation. Nader, W., ed. & tr. LC 73-10661. (Illus.). 340p. 1974. 39.00 (ISBN 0-387-06407-9). Springer-Verlag.
Doetsch, Gustav. Guide to the Application of Laplace & Three-Transforms. 2nd ed. 1971. 18.95x (ISBN 0-442-02163-1). Van Nos Reinhold.
Donaldson, Thomas. A Laplace Transform Calculus for Partial Differential Operators. LC 74-7370. (Memoirs: No. 143). 166p. 1974. pap. 8.80 (ISBN 0-8218-1843-0, MEMO-143). Am Math.
Holbrook, J. G. Laplace Transforms for Electronic Engineers. 2nd ed. 1966. 25.00 (ISBN 0-08-011411-3). Pergamon.
Holl, Dio L., et al. Introduction to the Laplace Transform. LC 59-7720. (Century Mathematics Ser.). (Illus.). 1959. 28.50x (ISBN 0-89197-247-1). Irvington.
Kuhfittig, P. K. Introduction to the Laplace Transform. (Mathematical Concepts & Methods in Science & Engineering Ser.: Vol. 8). (Illus.). 215p. 1978. 19.50 (ISBN 0-306-31060-0, Plenum Pr). Plenum Pub.
LePage, Wilbur R. Complex Variables & the Laplace Transform for Engineers. (Illus.). 1980. pap. text ed. 6.00 (ISBN 0-486-63926-6). Dover.
Muth, Eginhard J. Transform Methods with Applications to Engineering & Operations Research. (Illus.). 1977. ref. ed. 25.95 (ISBN 0-13-928861-9). P-H.
Oberhettinger, F. & Badii, L. Tables of Laplace Transforms. LC 73-81328. vii, 428p. 1973. pap. 34.90 (ISBN 0-387-06350-1). Springer-Verlag.
Smith, Michael G. Laplace Transform Theory. (Illus.). 1966. pap. text ed. 5.50x (ISBN 0-442-07671-1). Van Nos Reinhold.
Spiegel, Murray R. Laplace Transforms. (Orig.). 1965. pap. 6.95 (ISBN 0-07-060231-X, SP). McGraw.
Stroud, K. A. Laplace Transforms: Programmes & Problems. LC 73-6317. 273p. 1973. pap. text ed. 14.95 (ISBN 0-470-83415-3). Halsted Pr.
Widder, D. V. Laplace Transform. (Mathematical Ser.: Vol. 6). 1941. 26.00 (ISBN 0-691-07992-7). Princeton U Pr.
Williams, J. Laplace Transforms. (Problem Solvers). (Illus.). 1973. pap. text ed. 4.95x (ISBN 0-04-512021-8). Allen Unwin.

LAPLACE TRANSFORMATION–PROGRAMMED INSTRUCTION

Strum, Robert D. & Ward, John R. Laplace Transform Solution of Differential Equations. (Orig., Prog. Bk.). 1968. pap. 17.95 ref. ed. (ISBN 0-13-522805-0). P-H.

LAPLACE'S EQUATIONS

see Harmonic Functions

LAPLAND

Crottel, L. & Mendez, M. Lapland. (Illus.). 1968. 17.50x (ISBN 0-686-66879-0, N503). Vanous.
Hagbrink, Bodil. Children of Lapland. Simpson, E., tr. (Illus.). (gr. 2-6). 1979. 12.95 (ISBN 0-88776-114-3). Tundra Bks.
Hietal, Kaija. Lapland. (Panorama Bks.). (Illus.). 1966. 3.95 (ISBN 0-685-11287-X). French & Eur.
Kingman, Lee. The Meeting Post: A Story of Lapland. LC 73-139105. (Stories from Many Lands Ser). (Illus.). (gr. 2-5). 1972. PLB 7.89 (ISBN 0-690-52976-7, TYC-J). Har-Row.
Marsden, Walter. Lapland. (The World's Wild Places Ser.). (Illus.). 1976. 12.95 (ISBN 0-8094-2053-8). Time-Life.
--Lapland. (The World's Wild Places Ser.). (Illus.). 1979. lib. bdg. 11.97 (ISBN 0-686-51021-6). Silver.
Nickul, Karl. The Skolt Lapp Community Suenjelsijd During the Year 1938. LC 77-87728. (Acta Lapponica: 5). Repr. of 1948 ed. 17.00 (ISBN 0-404-16504-4). AMS Pr.
Von Linne, Carl. Lachesis Lapponica: A Tour in Lapland, 2 vols. LC 77-87708. Repr. of 1811 ed. Set. 42.50 (ISBN 0-404-16510-9). AMS Pr.

LAPLANDERS

see Lapps

LA POINTE, WISCONSIN–HISTORY

Thwaites, Reuben G. How George Rogers Clark Won the Northwest, & Other Essays in Western History. facs. ed. LC 68-22949. (Essay Index Reprint Ser). 1903. 19.50 (ISBN 0-8369-0943-7). Arno.

LAPPING

see Grinding and Polishing

LAPPISH FOLK-LORE

see Folk-Lore, Lappish

LAPPISH LANGUAGE

Hasselbrink, Gustav. Alternative Analyses of Phonemic System in Central South-Lappish. LC 65-63390. (Uralic & Altaic Ser: Vol. 49). (Orig., Central South Lappish). 1965. pap. text ed. 5.00x (ISBN 0-87750-015-0). Res Ctr Lang Semiotic.
Nielsen, Konrad & Nesheim, Asbjorn, eds. Lapp Dictionary, 5 vols. 3221p. 1980. 250.00x set (ISBN 82-00-14201-9). Universitet.
Sajnovics, Joannis. Demonstratio Idioma Ungarorum & Lapponum Idem Esse. (Uralic & Altaic Ser: Vol. 91). 1967. pap. text ed. 8.00x (ISBN 0-87750-037-1). Res Ctr Lang Semiotic.
Thomsen, Vilhelm. On the Influence of Germanic Languages on Finnish & Lapp. LC 67-63427. (Uralic & Altaic Ser: Vol. 87). (Ger.). 1967. pap. text ed. 7.00x (ISBN 0-87750-035-5). Res Ctr Lang Semiotic.

LAPPISH MYTHOLOGY

see Mythology, Finno-Ugrian

LAPPLAND

see Lapland

LAPPS

Asbjorn, Nesheim. Introducing the Lapps. 2nd ed. (Norwegian Guides Ser). (Illus., Orig.). 1966. pap. 6.50x (ISBN 0-8002-1585-0). Intl Pubns Serv.
Bosi, Roberto. The Lapps. Cadell, James, tr. LC 75-32455. 1976. Repr. of 1960 ed. lib. bdg. 18.25x (ISBN 0-8371-8545-9, BOTL). Greenwood.
Collinder, Bjorn. Lapps. LC 73-90490. Repr. of 1949 ed. lib. bdg. 15.00x (ISBN 0-8371-2213-9, COL). Greenwood.
Eidheim, Harald. Aspects of the Lappish Minority Situation. 86p. 1971. 10.50x (ISBN 8-200-02328-1, Dist. by Columbia U Pr). Universitet.
Ingold, T. The Skolt Lapps Today. LC 76-8289. (Changing Cultures Ser.). (Illus.). 1977. 27.50 (ISBN 0-521-21299-5); pap. 9.95x (ISBN 0-521-29090-2). Cambridge U Pr.
International Symposium, 3rd, Yellowknife, NWT. Circumpolar Health: Proceedings. Shephard, Roy J. & Itoh, S., eds. LC 76-2608. (Illus.). 1976. 30.00x (ISBN 0-8020-3333-4). U of Toronto Pr.
Irwin, John L. The Finns & the Lapps: How They Live & Work. 171p. 1973. text ed. 8.95 (ISBN 0-03-030206-4, HoltC). HR&W.
Nickul, Karl. The Lappish Nation Citizens of Four Countries. LC 75-39429. (Uralic & Altaic Ser.: No. 122). (Illus.). 1977. pap. text ed. 12.00x (ISBN 0-87750-199-8). Res Ctr Lang Semiotic.
Pelto, Pertti J. The Snowmobile Revolution: Technology & Social Change in the Arctic. LC 72-89138. 210p. 1973. 6.95 (ISBN 0-8465-3755-9). Benjamin-Cummings.
Spencer, Arthur. The Lapps. LC 77-88165. (This Changing World Ser.). 1978. 14.50x (ISBN 0-8448-1263-3). Crane-Russak Co.
Turi, Johan O. Turi's Book of Lappland. (Illus.). 1966. pap. text ed. 8.75x (ISBN 0-391-02064-1). Humanities.

LA RAMEE, PIERRE DE, 1515?-1572

Howell, Wilbur S. Logic & Rhetoric in England, 1500-1700. LC 56-6646. 1961. Repr. of 1956 ed. 19.00 (ISBN 0-8462-0204-2). Russell.
Ong, Walter J. Ramus & Talon Inventory. LC 74-30364. 1958. lib. bdg. 45.00 (ISBN 0-8414-6519-3). Folcroft.
Waddington, Charles. Ramus (Pierre De la Ramee): Sa Vie, Ses Ecrits et Ses Opinions. (Medieval Studies Reprint Ser.). Repr. of 1855 ed. lib. bdg. 29.50x (ISBN 0-697-00020-6). Irvington.

LARAMIE FORMATION

see Geology, Stratigraphic–Cretaceous

LARCENY

see also Art Thefts; Brigands and Robbers; Embezzlement; Pickpockets; Robbery; Shoplifting; Stealing; Thieves

Curtis, Bob. Security Control: External Theft. LC 76-163714. (Security Control Ser.). 1971. 18.95 (ISBN 0-912016-11-6). Lebhar Friedman.
Macdonald, J. M. Burglary & Theft. 292p. 1980. 19.75 (ISBN 0-398-03962-3). C C Thomas.
Walsh, Marilyn E. The Fence: A New Look at the World of Property Theft. LC 76-5266. (Contributions in Sociology Ser.: No. 21). (Illus., Orig.). 1976. lib. bdg. 15.00 (ISBN 0-8371-8910-1, WTF/). Greenwood.

LARCOM, LUCY, 1824-1893

Addison, Daniel D. Lucy Larcom: Life, Letters & Diary. LC 75-99065. (Library of Lives & Letters). 1970. Repr. of 1894 ed. 22.00 (ISBN 0-8103-3611-1). Gale.
--Lucy Larcom: Life, Letters & Diary. facsimile ed. LC 74-154143. (Selected Bibliographies Reprint Ser). Repr. of 1894 ed. 18.00 (ISBN 0-8369-5759-8). Arno.

LARDNER, RINGGOLD WILMER, 1885-1933

Bruccoli, Matthew J. & Layman, Richard. Ring W. Lardner: A Descriptive Bibliography. LC 75-9126. (Pittsburgh Ser. in Bibliography). 1976. 35.00x (ISBN 0-8229-3306-3). U of Pittsburgh Pr.
Evans, Elizabeth. Ring Lardner. LC 79-4829. (Modern Literature Ser.). 1980. 10.95 (ISBN 0-8044-2185-4). Ungar.
Friedrich, Otto. Ring Lardner. (Pamphlets on American Writers Ser: No. 49). (Orig.). 1965. pap. 1.25x (ISBN 0-8166-0364-2, MPAW49). U of Minn Pr.
Geismar, Maxwell. Ring Lardner & the Portrait of Folly. LC 77-175105. (Twentieth-Century American Writers Ser). (gr. 6-9). 1972. 7.95 (ISBN 0-690-70234-5, TYC-J). Har-Row.
Lardner, Ring. Letters from Ring. Caruthers, Clifford M., ed. 1979. 10.95 (ISBN 0-911938-08-7); pap. 6.95 (ISBN 0-911938-09-5). Walden Pr.
--Some Champions: Previously Uncollected Autobiographical Sketches & Fiction. Bruccoli, Matthew J. & Layman, Richard, eds. 208p. 1976. encore ed. o.p. 3.50 (ISBN 0-684-15681-4, ScribT); pap. 3.95 (ISBN 0-684-15065-4, SL729, ScribT). Scribner.
Lardner, Ring W. The Story of a Wonder Man: Being the Autobiography of Ring Lardner. LC 75-26216. 151p. 1975. Repr. of 1927 ed. lib. bdg. 15.00x (ISBN 0-8371-8414-2, LAWOM). Greenwood.
Patrick, Walton R. Ring Lardner. (Twayne's United States Authors Ser). 1963. pap. 3.45 (ISBN 0-8084-0261-7, T32, Twayne). Coll & U Pr.
--Ring Lardner. (U. S. Authors Ser.: No. 32). lib. bdg. 10.95 (ISBN 0-8057-0440-X). Twayne.
Yardley, Jonathan. Ring: A Biography of Ring Lardner. LC 77-1661. (Illus.). 1977. 12.95 (ISBN 0-394-49811-9). Random.

LARGE NUMBERS, LAW OF

see Law of Large Numbers

LARGE PRINT BOOKS

see Large Type Books

LARGE TYPE BOOKS

Ambler, Eric. The Siege of the Villa Lipp. 1977. lib. bdg. 14.95 (ISBN 0-8161-6540-8, Large Print Bks). G K Hall.
Ames, Francis. Callahan Goes South. 1977. lib. bdg. 10.95 (ISBN 0-8161-6457-6, Large Print Bks). G K Hall.
Anderson, Douglas. All About Cribbage. 1977. Repr. lib. bdg. 10.95 (ISBN 0-8161-6464-9, Large Print Bks). G K Hall.
Andress, Lesley. Caper. 1980. lib. bdg. 14.95 (ISBN 0-8161-3117-1, Large Print Bks). G K Hall.
--Caper. 1981. pap. 2.95 (ISBN 0-671-83385-5). PB.
Angus, Sylvia. Dead to Rites. (gr. 7-12). 1979. lib. bdg. 11.95 (ISBN 0-8161-6759-1). G K Hall.
Appelfeld, Aharon. Badenheim Nineteen Thirty-Nine. 1981. lib. bdg. 11.95 (ISBN 0-8161-3205-4, Large Print Bks). G K Hall.
Ashley, Paul P. You & Your Will: The Planning & Management. 1976. Repr. lib. bdg. 11.95 (ISBN 0-8161-6420-7, Large Print Bks). G K Hall.
Ashton, Ann. Concession. large print ed. LC 81-8852. 382p. 1981. Repr. of 1981 ed. 10.95x (ISBN 0-89621-290-4). Thorndike Pr.
Astley, Juliet. Copsi Castle. (gr. 7-12). 1979. lib. bdg. 16.95 (ISBN 0-8161-6669-2). G K Hall.
--The Fall of Midas. 1979. 14.50 (ISBN 0-8161-6727-3, Large Print Bks). G K Hall.
Auchincloss, Louis. The House of the Prophet. (Large Print Bks.). 1980. lib. bdg. 14.95 (ISBN 0-8161-3133-3). G K Hall.
Babson, Marion. The Twelve Deaths of Christmas. 192p. Date not set. pap. 2.25 (ISBN 0-440-19183-1). Dell.
Bach, Richard. Illusions: The Adventures of a Reluctant Messiah. 1977. lib. bdg. 10.95 (ISBN 0-8161-6520-3, Large Print Bks). G K Hall.
Baldwin, Faith. Adam's Eden. 1977. lib. bdg. 11.50 (ISBN 0-8161-6533-5, Large Print Bks). G K Hall.
Ballard, Todhunter. Sheriff of Tombstone. 1977. lib. bdg. 10.95 (ISBN 0-8161-6512-2, Large Print Bks). G K Hall.

Banning, Margaret C. Such Interesting People. 1980. lib. bdg. 15.95 (ISBN 0-8161-3080-9, Large Print Bks). G K Hall.
Bannon, Laura. When the Moon Is New. LC 53-7925. (Illus.). (gr. 3-5). 1953. 5.95g (ISBN 0-8075-8896-2). A Whitman.
Barnard, Robert. Death of a Literary Widow. 1981. lib. bdg. 11.95 (ISBN 0-8161-3249-6, Large Print Bks). G K Hall.
--Death of a Mystery Writer. 1980. lib. bdg. 11.95 (ISBN 0-8161-3081-7, Large Print Bks). G K Hall.
Barr, Jene. Fire Snorkel Number 7. LC 65-15101. (Career-Awareness-Community Helpers Ser.). (Illus.). (gr. k-2). 1965. 5.25g (ISBN 0-8075-2442-5). A Whitman.
--Miss Terry at the Library. rev. ed. LC 62-13170. (Career Awareness-Community Helpers Ser.). (Illus.). (gr. k-2). 1967. 5.25g (ISBN 0-8075-5168-6). A Whitman.
Beaver, Edmund. Word of Life: Scripture Selections. (Illus.). pap. 1.75 (ISBN 0-910208-02-6). Beavers.
Bell, L. J., ed. The Large Print Book & Its User. 1980. pap. 33.00x (ISBN 0-85365-632-0, Pub. by Lib Assn England). Oryx Pr.
Bellow, Saul. To Jerusalem & Back: A Personal Account. 1977. Repr. lib. bdg. 10.95 (ISBN 0-8161-6480-0, Large Print Bks). G K Hall.
Benchley, Nathaniel. Portrait of a Scoundrel. (gr. 7-12). 1979. lib. bdg. 14.95 (ISBN 0-8161-3009-4). G K Hall.
--Sweet Anarchy. (Large Print Bks.). 1980. lib. bdg. 15.50 (ISBN 0-8161-3134-1). G K Hall.
Bergstrom, Louise. Island Lovesong. large print ed. LC 81-5338. 332p. 1981. Repr. of 1980 ed. 9.95x (ISBN 0-89621-282-3). Thorndike Pr.
Berson, Dvera & Roy, Sander. Pain-Free Arthritis. 1979. lib. bdg. 11.95 (ISBN 0-8161-6685-4, Large Print Bks). G K Hall.
Bishop, Adele & Lord, Cile. The Art of Decorative Stenciling. (Large Format Ser). (Illus.). 1978. pap. 12.95 (ISBN 0-14-004842-1). Penguin.
Blackstock, Charity. The Shirt Front. 1978. lib. bdg. 13.50 (ISBN 0-8161-6550-5, Large Print Bks). G K Hall.
Blackwood, Caroline. Great Granny Webster. 1979. lib. bdg. 9.95 (ISBN 0-8161-6713-3, Large Print Bks). G K Hall.
Bombeck, Erma. Aunt Erma's Cope Book: How to Get from Monday to Friday...in Twelve Days. 1980. lib. bdg. 11.25 (ISBN 0-8161-3054-X, Large Print Bks). G K Hall.
--The Grass Is Always Greener Over the Septic Tank. 1977. lib. bdg. 10.95 (ISBN 0-8161-6502-5, Large Print Bks). G K Hall.
--If Life Is a Bowl of Cherries - What Am I Doing in the Pits? 1978. lib. bdg. 10.95 (ISBN 0-8161-6613-7, Large Print Bks). G K Hall.
Boom, Corrie T. In My Father's House. (Inspirational Ser.). 1976. lib. bdg. 10.95 (ISBN 0-8161-6412-6, Large Print Bks). G K Hall.
Boyd, Malcolm. Am I Running with You, God? 1978. lib. bdg. 10.95 (ISBN 0-8161-6577-7, Large Print Bks). G K Hall.
Brand, Max. The Blue Jay. 1981. lib. bdg. 12.95 (ISBN 0-8161-3241-0, Large Print Bks). G K Hall.
--Gunfighter's Return. 1980. lib. bdg. 11.95 (ISBN 0-8161-3055-8, Large Print Bks). G K Hall.
--Rider of the High Hills. 1978. lib. bdg. 11.95 (ISBN 0-8161-6545-9, Large Print Bks). G K Hall.
--Way of the Lawless. (gr. 7-12). 1979. lib. bdg. 12.95 (ISBN 0-8161-6747-8). G K Hall.
Browning, Norma L. & Ogg, Russell. He Saw a Hummingbird. 1979. lib. bdg. 9.95 (ISBN 0-8161-6726-5, Large Print Bks). G K Hall.
Bryant, Anita & Green, Bob. Fishers of Men. 1976. Repr. lib. bdg. 10.95 (ISBN 0-8161-6237-9, Large Print Bks). G K Hall.
--Running the Good Race. 1977. lib. bdg. 10.95 (ISBN 0-8161-6521-1, Large Print Bks). G K Hall.
Cadell, Elizabeth. The Marrying Kind. 1980. lib. bdg. 12.95 (ISBN 0-8161-3083-3, Large Print Bks). G K Hall.
--Parson's House. 1977. lib. bdg. 11.95 (ISBN 0-8161-6528-9, Large Print Bks). G K Hall.
--Return Match. (gr. 7-12). 1979. lib. bdg. 13.95 (ISBN 0-8161-6757-5). G K Hall.
Caine, Jeffrey. Heathcliff. 1978. lib. bdg. 13.50 (ISBN 0-8161-6609-9, Large Print Bks). G K Hall.
Calabrese, Alphonse & Proctor, William. Rx: The Christian Love Treatment. 1977. lib. bdg. 11.95 (ISBN 0-8161-6524-6, Large Print Bks). G K Hall.
Camuti, Louis J., et al. All My Patients Are Under the Bed. 1980. lib. bdg. 14.50 (ISBN 0-8161-3170-8, Large Print Bks). G K Hall.
Capon, Robert F. Bed & Board: Plain Talk About Marriage. pap. 1.95 (ISBN 0-671-07051-7, Fireside). S&S.
Carter, Lillian & Spann, Gloria C. Away from Home: Letters to My Family. (Inspirational Ser.). 1978. lib. bdg. 10.95 (ISBN 0-8161-6572-6, Large Print Bks). G K Hall.
--Away from Home: Letters to My Family. 1978. pap. 1.95 (ISBN 0-446-89892-9). Warner Bks.
Chadsey, Charles P. & Wentworth, Harold, eds. The Grosset Webster Large-Type Dictionary. (Illus.). 1978. pap. 5.95 (ISBN 0-448-14636-3). G&D.
Chandler, Edna W. Five Cent, Five Cent (Liberia) LC 67-17414. (Illus.). (gr. 1-3). 1967. 6.95g (ISBN 0-8075-2463-8). A Whitman.
Chapin, Cynthia. Clean Streets, Clean Water, Clean Air. LC 77-91736. (Career Awareness - Community Helpers Ser.). (Illus.). (gr. k-2). 1970. 5.25g (ISBN 0-8075-1193-5). A Whitman.
--News Travels. LC 66-10786. (Career Awareness - Community Helpers Ser.). (Illus.). (gr. k-2). 1967. 5.25g (ISBN 0-8075-5585-1). A Whitman.
--Squad Car 55. LC 66-16077. (Career Awareness - Community Helpers Ser.). (Illus.). (gr. k-2). 1966. 5.25g (ISBN 0-8075-7593-3). A Whitman.
--What Will the Weather Be. LC 65-23880. (Career Awareness - Community Helpers Ser.). (Illus.). (gr. k-2). 1965. 5.25g (ISBN 0-8075-8862-8). A Whitman.
Christman, Elizabeth. Flesh & Spirit. 1980. pap. 2.25 (ISBN 0-380-52142-3, 52142). Avon.
Clark, Barrett H. European Theories of the Drama. rev. ed. Popkin, Henry, ed. (YA) (gr. 9 up). 1965. 11.95 (ISBN 0-517-50539-8). Crown.
Clark, Eleanor. Eyes, Etc. 1978. lib. bdg. 10.95 (ISBN 0-8161-6554-8, Large Print Bks). G K Hall.
Clark, Glenn. The Soul's Sincere Desire. new ed. (Large-Print Editions Ser). 1977. Repr. 6.95 (ISBN 0-687-39135-0). Abingdon.
Clark, Mary H. The Cradle Will Fall. (Large Print Bks.). 1980. lib. bdg. 13.95 (ISBN 0-8161-3121-X). G K Hall.
Clarke, Anna. The Lady in Black. 1979. lib. bdg. 11.50 (ISBN 0-8161-6712-5, Large Print Bks). G K Hall.
Clarke, Arthur C. Arthur C. Clarke Trilogy, 3 bks. 1980. Set. lib. bdg. 45.00 (ISBN 0-8161-3139-2, Large Print Bks). G K Hall.
--The Fountains of Paradise. 1980. lib. bdg. 15.95 (ISBN 0-8161-3039-6). G K Hall.
--Imperial Earth. 1980. lib. bdg. 16.95 (ISBN 0-8161-3037-X, Large Print Bks). G K Hall.
--Rendezvous with Rama. 1980. lib. bdg. 15.95 (ISBN 0-8161-3038-8). G K Hall.
Clay, George. Family Occasions. 1979. lib. bdg. 13.50 (ISBN 0-8161-6684-6, Large Print Bks). G K Hall.
Coatsworth, Elizabeth. Personal Geography: Almost an Autobiography. 1979. lib. bdg. 9.95 (ISBN 0-8161-6672-2, Large Print Bks). G K Hall.
Coffman, Virginia. The Gaynor Women. 1980. lib. bdg. 16.95 (ISBN 0-8161-3047-7, Large Print Bks). G K Hall.
--Hyde Place. (Large Print Bks.). write for info. (ISBN 0-8161-3256-9). G K Hall.
--Marsanne. 1980. lib. bdg. 14.95 (ISBN 0-8161-3049-3). G K Hall.
--Veronique. 1980. lib. bdg. 17.50 (ISBN 0-8161-3048-5). G K Hall.
--Virginia Coffman Romances, 4 bks. 1980. Set. lib. bdg. 60.00 (ISBN 0-8161-3140-6). G K Hall.
Coffman, Viriginia. Dinah Faire. 1980. lib. bdg. 15.95 (ISBN 0-8161-3046-9, Large Print Bks). G K Hall.
Colwin, Laurie. Happy All the Time. 1979. lib. bdg. 11.95 (ISBN 0-8161-6683-8, Large Print Bks). G K Hall.
Considine, Bob. They Rose Above It. 1977. lib. bdg. 10.95 (ISBN 0-8161-6518-1, Large Print Bks). G K Hall.
Converse, Jane. A Flight for Dreamers. large print ed. LC 81-5661. 248p. 1981. Repr. of 1980 ed. 8.95x (ISBN 0-89621-283-1). Thorndike Pr.
Cook, Robin. Sphinx. (gr. 7-12). 1979. lib. bdg. 13.95 (ISBN 0-8161-3014-0). G K Hall.
Corman, Avery. The Old Neighborhood. 1980. lib. bdg. 12.95 (ISBN 0-8161-3146-5, Large Print Bks). G K Hall.
Corrie Ten Boom. Father Ten Boom. 1979. lib. bdg. 9.95 (ISBN 0-8161-6700-1, Large Print Bks). G K Hall.
Courtney, Caroline. Dangerous Engagement. 1980. lib. bdg. 12.95 (ISBN 0-8161-3094-9, Large Print Bks). G K Hall.
--Duchess in Disguise. (gr. 7-12). 1979. lib. bdg. 12.50 (ISBN 0-8161-3002-7). G K Hall.
--Guardian of the Heart. (Large Print Bks.). 1980. lib. bdg. 11.95 (ISBN 0-8161-3095-7). G K Hall.
--Heart of Honor. (Large Print Bks.). 1981. lib. bdg. 12.95 (ISBN 0-8161-3242-9). G K Hall.
--Love Triumphant. 1981. lib. bdg. 11.95 (ISBN 0-8161-3243-7, Large Print Bks). G K Hall.
--Love Unmasked. 1980. lib. bdg. 11.95 (ISBN 0-8161-3096-5). G K Hall.
--A Wager for Love. (gr. 7-12). 1980. lib. bdg. 13.95 (ISBN 0-8161-3020-5). G K Hall.
Coxe, George H. No Place for Murder. 1976. Repr. lib. bdg. 11.50 (ISBN 0-8161-6380-4, Large Print Bks). G K Hall.
Craig, Alisa. The Grub & Stakers Move a Mountain. large print ed. LC 81-5804. 332p. 1981. Repr. of 1981 ed. 9.95 (ISBN 0-89621-288-2). Thorndike Pr.
Craig, Mary. Were He a Stranger. 1979. lib. bdg. 9.95 (ISBN 0-8161-6668-4, Large Print Bks). G K Hall.
Craven, Margaret. Again Calls the Owl. 1980. lib. bdg. 9.50 (ISBN 0-8161-3115-5, Large Print Bks). G K Hall.
--The Home Front. (Large Print Bks.). 1981. lib. bdg. 17.95 (ISBN 0-686-73367-3). G K Hall.
Crawford, Linda. Something to Make Us Happy. 1978. lib. bdg. 13.50 (ISBN 0-8161-6599-8, Large Print Bks). G K Hall.
Crichton, Michael. Congo. 1981. lib. bdg. 14.95 (ISBN 0-8161-3202-X, Large Print Bks). G K Hall.
--Congo. Date not set. pap. 2.95 (ISBN 0-686-74616-3). Avon.
Crispin, Edmund. The Case of the Gilded Fly. 1980. lib. bdg. 13.95 (ISBN 0-8161-3018-3). G K Hall.
--Holy Disorders. 1980. lib. bdg. 13.95 (ISBN 0-8161-3111-2, Large Print Bks). G K Hall.
Cross, Amanda. Poetic Justice. large print ed. LC 81-8737. 286p. 1981. Repr. 9.95x (ISBN 0-89621-291-2). Thorndike Pr.
Darcy, Clare. Gwendolen. (gr. 7-12). 1979. lib. bdg. 12.95 (ISBN 0-8161-6745-1). G K Hall.
--Gwendolen. 1978. lib. bdg. 11.95 (ISBN 0-8161-6745-1, Large Print Bks). G K Hall.
--Letty. (Large Print Bks.). 1980. lib. bdg. 12.95 (ISBN 0-8161-3127-9). G K Hall.
--Regina. 1977. lib. bdg. 12.50 (ISBN 0-8161-6529-7, Large Print Bks). G K Hall.
--Rolande. 1979. lib. bdg. 10.95 (ISBN 0-8161-6670-6, Large Print Bks). G K Hall.
Deighton, Ken. SS-GB: Nazi-Occupied Britain, 1941. (gr. 7-12). 1979. lib. bdg. 18.95 (ISBN 0-8161-6748-6). G K Hall.
Delderfield, R. F. Charlie, Come Home. 1977. Repr. lib. bdg. 16.95 (ISBN 0-8161-6448-7, Large Print Bks). G K Hall.
Demetz, Hana. The House on Prague Street. 1980. lib. bdg. 12.95 (ISBN 0-8161-3143-0, Large Print Bks). G K Hall.
Di Donato, Georgia. Woman of Justice. (Large Print Bks.). 1980. lib. bdg. 15.95 (ISBN 0-8161-3132-5). G K Hall.
Dillard, Annie. Holy the Firm. 1978. lib. bdg. 10.95 (ISBN 0-8161-6571-8, Large Print Bks). G K Hall.
Downs, Hugh. Thirty Dirty Lies About Old. 1979. lib. bdg. 9.95 (ISBN 0-8161-6758-3). G K Hall.
Dreyfack, Raymond. The Complete Book of Walking. LC 80-26185. (Illus.). 288p. 1981. pap. 5.95 (ISBN 0-668-05167-1, 5167). Arco.
DuMaurier, Daphne. Myself When Young: The Shaping of a Writer. 1978. lib. bdg. 10.95 (ISBN 0-8161-6611-0, Large Print Bks). G K Hall.
Duncan, Jane. My Friends George & Tom. 1977. lib. bdg. 12.50 (ISBN 0-8161-6456-8, Large Print Bks). G K Hall.
Dwyer-Joyce, Alice. The Diamond Cage. 1977. lib. bdg. 10.95 (ISBN 0-8161-6437-1, Large Print Bks). G K Hall.
--The Master of Jethart. 1977. Repr. lib. bdg. 10.95 (ISBN 0-8161-6475-4, Large Print Bks). G K Hall.
Dyer, Ceil. The Eat to Lose Cookbook: How to Be Deliciously Filled - but Not Fattened. (Special Interest Ser.). 1977. lib. bdg. 11.50 (ISBN 0-8161-6511-4, Large Print Bks). G K Hall.
Dyer, Wayne W. Pulling Your Own Strings. 1979. lib. bdg. 16.95 (ISBN 0-8161-6690-0, Large Print Bks). G K Hall.
Earechson, Joni. Joni. (gr. 7-12). 1979. lib. bdg. 12.95 (ISBN 0-8161-6775-3). G K Hall.
Eden, Dorothy. The American Heiress. 1976. Repr. lib. bdg. 13.95 (ISBN 0-8161-3232-1, Large Rint Bks). G K Hall.
--The Salamanca Drum. 1977. lib. bdg. 13.95 (ISBN 0-8161-6501-7, Large Print Bks). G K Hall.
--The Storrington Papers. 1979. lib. bdg. 12.95 (ISBN 0-8161-6714-1, Large Print Bks). G K Hall.
Eisenberg, M. Michael. Ulcers. 1979. lib. bdg. 13.50 (ISBN 0-8161-6687-0, Large Print Bks). G K Hall.
Ellison, Jerome. Life's Second Half: The Pleasures of Aging. 1979. lib. bdg. 13.95 (ISBN 0-8161-6766-4). G K Hall.
Emmons, Helen B. The Mature Heart. new ed. (Large-Print Editions Ser.). 1977. 6.95 (ISBN 0-687-23779-3). Abingdon.
English Language Services. Virginian. (Collier-Macmillan English Readers). pap. 1.60 (ISBN 0-02-971340-4). Macmillan.
Evans, Charles M. New Plants from Old: Pruning & Propagating for the Indoor Gardener. 1977. lib. bdg. 10.95 (ISBN 0-8161-6514-9, Large Print Bks). G K Hall.
Evans, Charles M. & Pliner, Roberta L. Rx for Ailing House Plants. 1978. lib. bdg. 10.95 (ISBN 0-8161-6567-X, Large Print Bks). G K Hall.
Evans, Katherine. Boy Who Cried Wolf. LC 60-8429. (Illus.). (gr. k-2). 1960. 6.50g (ISBN 0-8075-0863-2). A Whitman.
Farm Journal Editors & Larson, Kathryn, eds. Listen to the Land: A Farm Journal Treasury. 1978. lib. bdg. 13.50 (ISBN 0-8161-6574-2, Large Print Bks). G K Hall.
Fast, Howard. The Establishment. (gr. 7-12). 1979. lib. bdg. 16.95 (ISBN 0-8161-3003-5). G K Hall.
--The Immigrants. 1978. lib. bdg. 19.95 (ISBN 0-8161-6546-7, Large Print Bks). G K Hall.
--Second Generation. 1979. lib. bdg. 21.95 (ISBN 0-8161-6715-X, Large Print Bks). G K Hall.
Ferrars, E. X. Witness Before the Fact. (Large Print Bks.). 1980. lib. bdg. 11.95 (ISBN 0-8161-3126-0). G K Hall.
Fitzgerald, Nancy. Chelsea. 1980. lib. bdg. 13.95 (ISBN 0-8161-3059-0, Large Print Bks). G K Hall.
Floren, Lee. Renegade Gambler. 1979. lib. bdg. 10.95 (ISBN 0-8161-6708-7, Large Print Bks). G K Hall.
--Smoky River. (Large Print Bks.). 1980. lib. bdg. 10.95 (ISBN 0-8161-3027-2). G K Hall.
Follett, Ken. Triple. (gr. 7-12). 1979. lib. bdg. 15.95 (ISBN 0-8161-3005-1). G K Hall.
Forbes, Stanton. Buried in So Sweet a Place. 1979. lib. bdg. 9.95 (ISBN 0-8161-6671-4, Large Print Bks). G K Hall.
Francis, Dick. Reflex. (Large Print Bks.). 1981. lib. bdg. 14.95 (ISBN 0-8161-3255-0). G K Hall.
Fraser, Anthea. Home Through the Dark. 1977. lib. bdg. 10.95 (ISBN 0-8161-6442-8, Large Print Bks). G K Hall.
Fraser, James. Heart's Ease in Death. 1978. lib. bdg. 10.95 (ISBN 0-8161-6562-9, Large Print Bks). G K Hall.
Freedman, Nancy. Prima Donna. (Large Print Bks.). 1981. lib. bdg. 16.95 (ISBN 0-8161-3266-6). G K Hall.
Freeman, Cynthia. Come Pour the Wine. 1981. lib. bdg. 15.95 (ISBN 0-8161-3201-1, Large Print Bks). G K Hall.
Galbraith, John K. The Age of Uncertainty, 2 vols. 1977. lib. bdg. 18.95 (ISBN 0-8161-6505-X, Large Print Bks). G K Hall.
Gane, Margaret D. Parade on an Empty Street. 1980. lib. bdg. 12.95 (ISBN 0-8161-3066-3, Large Print Bks). G K Hall.
Gann, Ernest K. The Aviator. (Large Print Bks.). 1981. lib. bdg. 11.95 (ISBN 0-8161-3257-7). G K Hall.
Gardner, Erle S. The Case of the Ice Cold Hands. 1980. lib. bdg. 11.95 (ISBN 0-8161-3174-0, Large Print Bks). G K Hall.
Gardner, John. The Werewolf Trace. 1978. lib. bdg. 12.50 (ISBN 0-8161-6610-2, Large Print Bks). G K Hall.
Garfield, Brian. The Paladin. 1980. lib. bdg. 17.95 (ISBN 0-8161-3116-3). G K Hall.
Gaylin, Willard. Feelings: Our Vital Signs. (gr. 7-12). 1979. lib. bdg. 14.95 (ISBN 0-8161-6767-2). G K Hall.
Geddes, Paul. Hangman. 1978. lib. bdg. 10.95 (ISBN 0-8161-6556-4, Large Print Bks). G K Hall.
Gilbert, Anna. The Leavetaking. 1981. lib. bdg. 13.95 (ISBN 0-8161-3203-8, Large Print Bks). G K Hall.
Giles, Janice H. The Believers. 1980. lib. bdg. 15.95 (ISBN 0-8161-3052-3, Large Print Bks). G K Hall.
--Hannah Fowler. 1980. lib. bdg. 16.95 (ISBN 0-8161-3051-5, Large Print Bks). G K Hall.
--Johnny Osage. 1980. lib. bdg. 15.95 (ISBN 0-8161-3053-1, Large Print Bks). G K Hall.
--The Kentuckians. 1980. lib. bdg. 15.95 (ISBN 0-8161-3050-7, Large Print Bks). G K Hall.
Gilman, Dorothy. A New Kind of Country. 1979. lib. bdg. 9.50 (ISBN 0-8161-6694-3, Large Print Bks). G K Hall.
--The Tightrope Walker. (gr. 7-12). 1980. lib. bdg. 12.95 (ISBN 0-8161-3026-4). G K Hall.
Godden, Jon. Ahmed & the Old Lady. 1977. Repr. lib. bdg. 11.50 (ISBN 0-8161-6483-5, Large Print Bks). G K Hall.
Goldstein, Arthur D. A Person Shouldn't Die Like That. 1976. Repr. lib. bdg. 11.50 (ISBN 0-8161-6376-6, Large Print Bks). G K Hall.
Graham, Billy. Angels: God's Secret Agents. 1976. Repr. lib. bdg. 10.95 (ISBN 0-8161-6367-7, Large Print Bks). G K Hall.
Graham, Winston. The Angry Tide. (gr. 7-12). 1979. lib. bdg. 19.95 (ISBN 0-8161-6682-X). G K Hall.
--The Black Moon, 2 vols. 1979. Set. lib. bdg. 18.95 (ISBN 0-8161-6680-3, Large Print Bks). G K Hall.
--Demelza, 2 vols. 1979. lib. bdg. 17.95 (ISBN 0-8161-6677-3, Large Print Bks). G K Hall.

--The Four Swans. (Large Print Bks.). 1979. lib. bdg. 19.95 (ISBN 0-8161-6681-1). G K Hall.
--Jeremy Poldark, 1 vol. 1979. lib. bdg. 14.95 (ISBN 0-8161-6678-1, Large Print Bks). G K Hall.
--Merciless Ladies. (Large Print Bks.). 1980. lib. bdg. 14.95 (ISBN 0-8161-3119-8). G K Hall.
--Ross Poldark, 2 vols. 1979. lib. bdg. 16.95 (ISBN 0-8161-6676-5, Large Print Bks). G K Hall.
--Warleggan, 2 vols. 1979. Set. lib. bdg. 17.95 (ISBN 0-8161-6679-X, Large Print Bks). G K Hall.
Grandower, Elissa. The Secret Room of Morgate House. 1978. lib. bdg. 12.95 (ISBN 0-8161-6558-0, Large Print Bks). G K Hall.
Green, Henry. Blindness. (Large Print Bks.). 1979. lib. bdg. 12.95 (ISBN 0-8161-6743-5). G K Hall.
Greene, Graham. The Human Factor. 1978. lib. bdg. 13.95 (ISBN 0-8161-6598-X, Large Print Bks). G K Hall.
Gregg, James R. Your Future in New Optometric Careers. (Careers in Depth Ser). (gr. 7 up). 1978. PLB 5.97 (ISBN 0-8239-0449-0). Rosen Pr.
Grey, Zane. Forlorn River. 1977. lib. bdg. 11.95 (ISBN 0-8161-6526-2, Large Print Bks). G K Hall.
--The Other Side of the Canyon. 1981. 15.00x (ISBN 0-86025-182-9, Pub. by Ian Henry Pubns England). State Mutual Bk.
--The Rustlers of Pecos County. 1980. lib. bdg. 12.50 (ISBN 0-8161-3085-X, Large Print Bks). G K Hall.
--The Westerner. (Large Print Bks.). 1980. lib. bdg. 10.95 (ISBN 0-8161-3125-2). G K Hall.
--Wild Horse Mesa. 1981. lib. bdg. 12.95 (ISBN 0-8161-3239-9, Large Print Bks). G K Hall.
Guest, Judith. Ordinary People. 1981. lib. bdg. 12.95 (ISBN 0-8161-3207-0, Large Print Bks). G K Hall.
Hailey, Elizabeth F. A Woman of Independent Means. 1979. lib. bdg. 17.50 (ISBN 0-8161-6716-8, Large Print Bks). G K Hall.
Haldeman, H. R. & Dimona, Joseph. The Ends of Power. 1978. lib. bdg. 16.95 (ISBN 0-8161-6608-0, Large Print Bks). G K Hall.
Haldeman, Linda. Star of the Sea. 176p. 1981. pap. 2.25 (ISBN 0-380-54114-9, 54114). Avon.
Hale, Arlene. Island of Mystery. 1978. lib. bdg. 11.50 (ISBN 0-8161-6552-1, Large Print Bks). G K Hall.
--The Other Side of the World. 1976. Repr. lib. bdg. 11.50 (ISBN 0-8161-6406-1, Large Print Bks). G K Hall.
--The Winds of Summer. 1980. lib. bdg. 13.50 (ISBN 0-8161-3168-6, Large Print Bks). G K Hall.
Haley, Alex. Roots: The Saga of an American Family, 3 vols. 1979. Set. lib. bdg. 29.50 (ISBN 0-8161-6639-0, Large Print Bks). G K Hall.
Hall, Adam. Kobra Manifesto. 1977. lib. bdg. 13.50 (ISBN 0-8161-6454-1, Large Print Bks). G K Hall.
Hall, Donald. String Too Short to Be Saved. 1980. lib. bdg. 11.95 (ISBN 0-8161-3086-8, Large Print Bks). G K Hall.
Hall, Ennen R. Looking Inward, Looking Upward. large type ed. LC 77-83307. 1977. 7.95 (ISBN 0-8499-0042-5). Word Bks.
Hardwick, Michael. Endings & Beginnings. 1980. lib. bdg. 10.95 (ISBN 0-8161-6799-0, Large Print Bks). G K Hall.
--On with the Dance. 1980. lib. bdg. 10.95 (ISBN 0-8161-6798-2, Large Print Bks). G K Hall.
Hardwick, Mollie. Lovers Meeting. 1980. lib. bdg. 16.95 (ISBN 0-8161-3064-7, Large Print Bks). G K Hall.
--The War to End Wars. 1980. lib. bdg. 13.95 (ISBN 0-8161-6797-4, Large Print Bks). G K Hall.
--The Years of Change. 1980. lib. bdg. 14.95 (ISBN 0-8161-6796-6, Large Print Bks). G K Hall.
Hastings, Brooke. Playing for Keeps. (Large Print Bks.). 1981. lib. bdg. 11.95 (ISBN 0-8161-3245-3). G K Hall.
Hawkesworth, John. In My Lady's Chamber. 1980. lib. bdg. 11.95 (ISBN 0-8161-6795-8, Large Print Bks). G K Hall.
--Upstairs Downstairs. 1980. lib. bdg. 13.95 (ISBN 0-8161-6794-X, Large Print Bks). G K Hall.
Hawkinson, John. Old Stump. LC 65-23883. (Self Starter Bks.). (Illus.). (ps-2). 1965. 6.95g (ISBN 0-8075-5969-5). A Whitman.
Haycox, Ernest. Head of the Mountain. 1977. lib. bdg. 10.50 (ISBN 0-8161-6534-3, Large Print Bks). G K Hall.
--Return of a Fighter. 1977. lib. bdg. 7.95 (ISBN 0-8161-6504-1, Large Print Bks). G K Hall.
--Trouble Shooter. (Large Print Bks.). 1981. lib. bdg. 13.95 (ISBN 0-8161-3251-8). G K Hall.
Heaven, Constance. Heir to Kuragin. 1979. lib. bdg. 14.95 (ISBN 0-8161-6703-6, Large Print Bks). G K Hall.
--The Queen & the Gypsy. 1977. lib. bdg. 13.95 (ISBN 0-8161-6497-5, Large Print Bks). G K Hall.
Heller, Joseph. Catch Twenty-Two. 1961. 13.95 (ISBN 0-671-12805-1). S&S.
Hellman, Lillian. Scoundrel Time. 1977. lib. bdg. 8.95 (ISBN 0-8161-6446-0, Large Print Bks). G K Hall.
Herriot, James. All Things Wise & Wonderful. 1977. lib. bdg. 17.95 (ISBN 0-8161-6525-4, Large Print Bks). G K Hall.
--If Only They Could Talk. 1977. lib. bdg. 13.95 (ISBN 0-8161-6415-0, Large Print Bks). G K Hall.
Higgins, Jack. Day of Judgement. (Large Print Bks.). 1979. lib. bdg. 13.95 (ISBN 0-8161-6756-7). G K Hall.
Hill, Fiona. The Stanbroke Girls. (Large Print Bks.). 1981. lib. bdg. 13.95 (ISBN 0-8161-3252-6). G K Hall.
Hoffman, Alice. Angel Landing. large print ed. LC 81-5335. 437p. 1981. Repr. of 1980 ed. 11.95x (ISBN 0-89621-286-6). Thorndike Pr.
Hogan, Ray. The Glory Trail. 1980. lib. bdg. 10.95 (ISBN 0-8161-3107-4, Large Print Bks). G K Hall.
--The Peace Keeper. 1979. lib. bdg. 8.95 (ISBN 0-8161-6660-9, Large Print Bks). G K Hall.
--The Proving Gun. 1980. lib. bdg. 10.95 (ISBN 0-8161-3172-4, Large Print Bks). G K Hall.
Holland, Isabelle. Counterpoint. 256p. 1981. pap. 2.50 (ISBN 0-449-24423-7, Crest). Fawcett.
Holmes, Majorie. Lord, Let Me Love: A Marjorie Holmes Treasury. 1979. lib. bdg. 13.95 (ISBN 0-8161-6701-X, Large Print Bks). G K Hall.
Holmes, Marjorie. Hold Me up a Little Longer, Lord. 1977. lib. bdg. 10.95 (ISBN 0-8161-6530-0, Large Print Bks). G K Hall.
--Love & Laughter. 1978. lib. bdg. 13.50 (ISBN 0-8161-6548-3, Large Print Bks). G K Hall.
Holt, Victoria. The Mask of the Enchantress. 1980. lib. bdg. 16.95 (ISBN 0-8161-3142-2, Large Print Bks). G K Hall.
Holt, Virginia. The Spring of the Tiger. (gr. 7-12). 1979. lib. bdg. 15.95 (ISBN 0-8161-6782-6). G K Hall.
Hough, Henry B. To the Harbor Light. 1976. Repr. lib. bdg. 10.95 (ISBN 0-8161-6435-5, Large Print Bks). G K Hall.
Household, Geoffrey. The Last Two Weeks of Georges Rivac. (Large Print Bks.). (gr. 7-12). 1979. lib. bdg. 12.95 (ISBN 0-8161-6744-3). G K Hall.
Howe, Janet R. The Mystery of the Marmalade Cat. large type ed. LC 69-12908. (Illus.). (gr. 4-9). 1969. 4.25 (ISBN 0-664-32439-8). Westminster.
The Importance of Being Sick: A Christian Reflection. 1977. lib. bdg. 12.50 (ISBN 0-8161-6467-3, Large Print Bks). G K Hall.
Jackson, Eileen. Autumn Lace. 1979. lib. bdg. 12.50 (ISBN 0-8161-6675-7, Large Print Bks). G K Hall.
--Lord Rivington's Lady. 1978. lib. bdg. 11.50 (ISBN 0-8161-6596-3, Large Print Bks). G K Hall.
Jackson, Jesse. Call Me Charley. LC 45-9807. (Illus.). (gr. 5 up). 1945. (HarpJ); PLB 8.79 (ISBN 0-06-022786-9). Har-Row.
James, Margaret. Marionette. 1980. lib. bdg. 11.95 (ISBN 0-8161-3113-9). G K Hall.
--A Voice in the Darkness. (gr. 7-12). 1979. lib. bdg. 10.95 (ISBN 0-8161-6749-4). G K Hall.
James, P. D. Cover Her Face. (gr. 7-12). 1979. lib. bdg. 12.95 (ISBN 0-8161-6793-1). G K Hall.
--Death of an Expert Witness. 1978. lib. bdg. 13.95 (ISBN 0-8161-6600-5, Large Print Bks). G K Hall.
--Innocent Blood. pap. 3.50 (ISBN 0-686-74627-9). Fawcett.
--A Mind to Murder. (gr. 7-12). 1980. lib. bdg. 12.95 (ISBN 0-8161-3057-4, Large Print Bks). G K Hall.
--Unnatural Causes. 1980. lib. bdg. 12.95 (ISBN 0-8161-3106-6). G K Hall.
--An Unsuitable Job for a Woman. 1980. lib. bdg. 13.95 (ISBN 0-8161-6788-5, Large Print Bks). G K Hall.
Jansson, Tove. The Summer Book. 1977. lib. bdg. 10.95 (ISBN 0-8161-6471-1, Large Print Bks.). G K Hall.
Johnson, Annabel & Johnson, Edgar. The Grizzly. LC 64-11831. (Illus.). (gr. 5-9). 1964. PLB 7.89 (ISBN 0-06-022871-7, HarpJ). Har-Row.
Johnson, Pamela H. The Good Husband. (gr. 7-12). 1980. lib. bdg. 13.95 (ISBN 0-8161-3017-5). G K Hall.
Johnston, Jennifer. The Old Jest. 1980. lib. bdg. 10.95 (ISBN 0-8161-3091-4, Large Print Bks). G K Hall.
Johnston, Velda. The Silver Dolphin. 1980. lib. bdg. 13.95 (ISBN 0-8161-3068-X, Large Print Bks). G K Hall.
Jones, Douglas C. Arrest Sitting Bull. 1978. lib. bdg. 13.50 (ISBN 0-8161-6555-6, Large Print Bks). G K Hall.
Kanin, Garson. It Takes a Long Time to Become Young. 1979. pap. 2.50 (ISBN 0-425-05020-3). Berkley Pub.
Kemelman, Harry. Sunday the Rabbi Stayed Home. 1977. lib. bdg. 11.95 (ISBN 0-8161-6499-1, Large Print Bks). G K Hall.
--Thursday the Rabbi Walked Out. 1979. lib. bdg. 13.95 (ISBN 0-8161-6663-3, Large Print Bks). G K Hall.
Kerr, Jean. How I Got to Be Perfect. (gr. 7-12). 1979. lib. bdg. 15.00 (ISBN 0-8161-6704-4, Large Print Bks). G K Hall.
Knebel, Fletcher & Bailey, Charles W., 2nd. Seven Days in May. LC 62-14555. 1962. 10.95 (ISBN 0-06-012435-0, HarpT). Har-Row.
Knight, Alanna. Castle of Foxes. (Large Print Bks.). 1981. lib. bdg. 16.95 (ISBN 0-8161-3258-5). G K Hall.
Knott, Will C. Killer's Canyon. 1978. lib. bdg. 10.95 (ISBN 0-8161-6615-3, Large Print Bks). G K Hall.
Knowles, John. Peace Breaks Out. (Large Print Bks.). 1981. lib. bdg. 12.95 (ISBN 0-8161-3270-4). G K Hall.
Kossoff, David. The Little Book of Sylvanus. 1976. Repr. lib. bdg. 10.95 (ISBN 0-8161-6363-4, Large Print Bks). G K Hall.
Krail, Leo P. Joslin Diabetes Manual. 1979. lib. bdg. 24.95 (ISBN 0-8161-6762-1). G K Hall.
L'Amour, Louis. Bendigo Shafter. 1980. lib. bdg. 15.95 (ISBN 0-8161-3144-9, Large Print Bks). G K Hall.
--Callaghen. 1979. lib. bdg. 10.95 (ISBN 0-8161-6686-2, Large Print Bks). G K Hall.
--Iron Marshall. (gr. 7-12). 1979. lib. bdg. 12.95 (ISBN 0-8161-3015-9). G K Hall.
--Lonely on the Mountain. (Large Print Bks.). 1981. lib. bdg. 11.95 (ISBN 0-8161-3247-X). G K Hall.
--The Proving Trail. 1980. lib. bdg. 12.95 (ISBN 0-8161-3061-2, Large Print Bks). G K Hall.
--To the Far Blue Mountains. 1977. Repr. lib. bdg. 13.50 (ISBN 0-8161-6484-3, Large Print Bks). G K Hall.
--Westward the Tide. (Adult Ser.). 1977. lib. bdg. 11.95 (ISBN 0-8161-6498-3, Large Print Bks). G K Hall.
Large Print Book Catalog. LC 76-48929. 322p. 1976. 8.00 (ISBN 0-913578-13-4). Inglewood Ca.
Large Print Catalog, Boston Public Library. 1976. 7.50 (ISBN 0-685-72171-X). Boston Public Lib.
Large Type Books in Print, 1980. 4th ed. LC 74-102773. 1980. 19.95 (ISBN 0-8352-1296-3). Bowker.
Lathen, Emma. Going for the Gold. 1981. lib. bdg. 12.95 (ISBN 0-8161-3200-3, Large Print Bks). G K Hall.
Lauterbach, William. Es Will Abend Werden. Kujath, Mentor, ed. 1978. pap. 1.95 (ISBN 0-8100-0101-2, 26-0511). Northwest Pub.
Laxalt, Robert. Sweet Promised Land. 1957. 10.00 (ISBN 0-06-012540-3, HarpT). Har-Row.
LaZebnik, Edith. Such a Life. 1979. lib. bdg. 13.95 (ISBN 0-8161-6662-5, Large Print Bks). G K Hall.
Le Carre, John. The Honourable Schoolboy. (Adult Ser.). 1977. lib. bdg. 18.95 (ISBN 0-8161-6539-4, Large Print Bks). G K Hall.
--Smiley's People. 1980. lib. bdg. 16.95 (ISBN 0-8161-3090-6, Large Print Bks). G K Hall.
Levenson, Sam. You Can Say That Again, Sam. (Large Print Bks.). 1979. lib. bdg. 9.95 (ISBN 0-8161-6706-0). G K Hall.
--You Don't Have to Be in Who's Who to Know What's What. 1980. lib. bdg. 11.95 (ISBN 0-8161-3056-6, Large Print Bks). G K Hall.
Lewis, C. S. The Screwtape Letters. (gr. 7-12). 1979. lib. bdg. 11.95 (ISBN 0-8161-6771-0). G K Hall.
--The Screwtape Letters. Bd. with Screwtape Proposes a Toast. 1964-67. 9.95 (ISBN 0-02-571240-3, 57124); large print ed. 9.95 (ISBN 0-02-489410-9, 48941); pap. 1.95 (ISBN 0-685-22912-2, 08686). Macmillan.
Liebman, Joshua L. Peace of Mind. 1965. pap. 2.95 (ISBN 0-671-21347-4, Fireside). S&S.
Lindau, Joan. Mrs. Cooper's Boardinghouse. 1980. lib. bdg. 13.95 (ISBN 0-8161-3150-3, Large Print Bks). G K Hall.
Lindman, Maj. Flicka, Ricka, Dicka & a Little Dog. LC 48-3307. (Illus.). (gr. k-2). 1946. 5.75g (ISBN 0-8075-2486-7). A Whitman.
--Flicka, Ricka, Dicka & the Big Red Hen. LC 60-13634. (Illus.). (gr. k-2). 1960. 5.75g (ISBN 0-8075-2481-6). A Whitman.
--Flicka, Ricka, Dicka & the Girl Next Door. (Illus.). (gr. k-2). 5.75g (ISBN 0-8075-2483-2). A Whitman.
--Flicka, Ricka, Dicka & the New Dotted Dresses. (Illus.). (gr. k-2). 5.75g (ISBN 0-8075-2482-4). A Whitman.
--Flicka, Ricka, Dicka & the Strawberries. (Illus.). (gr. k-2). 1944. 5.75g (ISBN 0-8075-2489-1). A Whitman.
--Flicka, Ricka, Dicka & the Three Kittens. LC 41-17581. (Illus.). (gr. k-2). 1941. 5.75g (ISBN 0-8075-2490-5). A Whitman.
--Flicka, Ricka, Dicka & Their New Friend. (Illus.). (gr. k-2). 1942. 5.75g (ISBN 0-8075-2487-5). A Whitman.
--Flicka, Ricka, Dicka & Their New Skates. (Illus.). (gr. k-2). 1950. 5.75g (ISBN 0-8075-2488-3). A Whitman.
--Flicka, Ricka, Dicka Bake a Cake. LC 55-7571. (Illus.). (gr. k-2). 1955. 5.75g (ISBN 0-8075-2480-8). A Whitman.
--Flicka, Ricka, Dicka Go to Market. LC 58-9950. (Illus.). (gr. k-2). 1958. 5.75g (ISBN 0-8075-2485-9). A Whitman.
--Snipp, Snapp, Snurr & the Big Surprise. LC 37-35180. (Illus.). (gr. k-2). 1937. 5.75g (ISBN 0-8075-7503-8). A Whitman.
--Snipp, Snapp, Snurr & the Buttered Bread. LC 34-37832. (Illus.). (gr. k-2). 1934. 5.75g (ISBN 0-8075-7504-6). A Whitman.
--Snipp, Snapp, Snurr & the Gingerbread. LC 36-32643. (Illus.). (gr. k-2). 1936. 5.75g (ISBN 0-8075-7505-4). A Whitman.
--Snipp, Snapp, Snurr & the Seven Dogs. LC 59-14391. (Illus.). (gr. k-2). 1959. 5.75g (ISBN 0-8075-7512-7). A Whitman.
--Snipp, Snapp, Snurr Learn to Swim. LC 54-9945. (Illus.). (gr. k-2). 1954. 5.75g (ISBN 0-8075-7506-2). A Whitman.
Lockridge, Richard. The Tenth Life. 1979. lib. bdg. 11.95 (ISBN 0-8161-6717-6, Large Print Bks). G K Hall.
Lofts, Norah. The Day of the Butterfly. 1980. lib. bdg. 16.95 (ISBN 0-8161-3097-3, Large Print Bks). G K Hall.
Loring, Emilie. Forever & a Day. 1979. lib. bdg. 13.95 (ISBN 0-8161-6729-X, Large Print Bks). G K Hall.
--I Take This Man. Repr. lib. bdg. 10.85x (ISBN 0-88411-370-1). Amereon Ltd.
--In Times Like These. 1979. lib. bdg. 12.50 (ISBN 0-8161-6731-1, Large Print Bks). G K Hall.
--A Key to Many Doors. 1981. lib. bdg. 12.95 (ISBN 0-8161-3210-0, Large Print Bks). G K Hall.
--Spring Always Comes. 1979. lib. bdg. 13.95 (ISBN 0-8161-6730-3, Large Print Bks). G K Hall.
--Throw Wide the Door. 1979. lib. bdg. 13.95 (ISBN 0-8161-6728-1, Large Print Bks). G K Hall.
McBain, Ed. Ghosts. (Large Print Bks.). 1980. lib. bdg. 12.95 (ISBN 0-8161-3128-7). G K Hall.
McCrady, Lady. Junior's Tune. LC 80-348. (Illus.). 32p. (ps-3). 1980. PLB 8.95 (ISBN 0-8234-0411-0). Holiday.
MacDonald, John B. The Green Ripper. 1980. lib. bdg. 12.95 (ISBN 0-8161-3023-X). G K Hall.
MacDonald, John D. The Empty Copper Sea. 1979. lib. bdg. 13.50 (ISBN 0-8161-6702-8, Large Print Bks). G K Hall.
--The Scarlet Ruse. 1980. lib. bdg. 13.95 (ISBN 0-8161-3118-X). G K Hall.
MacDonald, Ross. The Blue Hammer. 1976. Repr. lib. bdg. 13.50 (ISBN 0-8161-6431-2, Large Print Bks). G K Hall.
MacGil, Gillis. Your Future As a Model. (Careers in Depth Ser). (gr. 7 up). 1971. PLB 5.97 (ISBN 0-8239-0159-9). Rosen Pr.
MacInnes, Helen. Agent in Place. 1976. Repr. lib. bdg. 17.95 (ISBN 0-8161-6401-0, Large Print Bks). G K Hall.
MacLean, Alistair. The Golden Gate. 1977. Repr. lib. bdg. 12.50 (ISBN 0-8161-6477-0, Large Print Bks). G K Hall.
--Goodbye California. 1978. lib. bdg. 13.95 (ISBN 0-8161-6605-6, Large Print Bks). G K Hall.
--Seawitch. (Adult Ser.). 1977. lib. bdg. 11.95 (ISBN 0-8161-6538-6, Large Print Bks). G K Hall.
MacLeod, Charlotte. Rest You Merry. (Large Print Bks.). 1979. lib. bdg. 13.50 (ISBN 0-8161-3000-0). G K Hall.
McMullen, Mary. The Man with Fifty Complaints. 1980. lib. bdg. 12.95 (ISBN 0-8161-3084-1, Large Print Bks.). G K Hall.
Magnuson, James & Petrie, Dorothea G. Orphan Train. 1979. lib. bdg. 14.95 (ISBN 0-8161-6666-8, Large Print Bks). G K Hall.
Mandino, Og & Kaye, Buddy. The Gift of Acabar. 1979. lib. bdg. 8.95 (ISBN 0-8161-6697-8, Large Print Bks). G K Hall.
Marchant, Catherine. Miss Martha Mary Crawford. (Adult Ser.). 1977. lib. bdg. 14.95 (ISBN 0-8161-6493-2, Large Print Bks). G K Hall.
Markus, Julia. A Patron of the Arts: The Tears of San Lorenzo by Barbara Reid. 1978. lib. bdg. 9.95 (ISBN 0-8161-6603-X, Large Print Bks). G K Hall.
Marsh, Ngaio. Grave Mistake. 1979. lib. bdg. 13.95 (ISBN 0-8161-6667-6, Large Print Bks). G K Hall.
--Last Ditch. 1977. lib. bdg. 13.50 (ISBN 0-8161-6537-8, Large Print Bks). G K Hall.
Marshall, Catherine. Adventures in Prayer. 1975. lib. bdg. 10.50 (ISBN 0-8161-6317-0, Large Print Bks). G K Hall.
--Beyond Our Selves. large print ed. 1979. lib. bdg. 14.95 (ISBN 0-8161-6774-5). G K Hall.
--The Helper. 1979. lib. bdg. 12.95 (ISBN 0-8161-6695-1, Large Print Bks). G K Hall.

Marshall, Joanne. The Peacock Bed. 1979. lib. bdg. 11.95 (ISBN 0-8161-6659-5, Large Print Bks). G K Hall.

May, Gerald G. Simply Sane. 1977. lib. bdg. 7.95 (ISBN 0-8161-6516-5, Large Print Bks). G K Hall.

Melville, Jennie. Dragon's Eye. 1977. lib. bdg. 11.50 (ISBN 0-8161-6491-6, Large Print Bks). G K Hall.

The Merriam-Webster Dictionary for Large Print Users. 1977. lib. bdg. 27.50 (ISBN 0-8161-6459-2, Large Print Bks). G K Hall.

Michaels, Barbara. The Walker in Shadows. 1980. lib. bdg. 12.95 (ISBN 0-8161-3060-4, Large Print Bks). G K Hall.

--The Wizard's Daughter. 1981. lib. bdg. 13.95 (ISBN 0-8161-3248-8, Large Print Bks). G K Hall.

Michaels, Fern. Sea Gypsy. 1981. lib. bdg. 10.95 (ISBN 0-8161-3204-6, Large Print Bks). G K Hall.

Mitchell, Margaret. Gone with the Wind. (gr. 9 up). 1936. 12.95 (ISBN 0-02-585390-2); 2 vols. lrg. print ed. o.p. 13.95 (ISBN 0-02-489440-0); anniversary ed. 19.95 (ISBN 0-02-585350-3). Macmillan.

Neville, Emily C. It's Like This, Cat. LC 62-21292. (Illus.). (gr. 7-9). 1963. 8.95 (ISBN 0-06-024390-2, HarpJ); PLB 8.79 (ISBN 0-06-024391-0). Har-Row.

Newman, Sharan. Guinevere. (Large Print Bks.). 1981. text ed. 14.95 (ISBN 0-8161-3254-2). G K Hall.

Oglivie, Elizabeth. An Answer in the Tide. large print ed. 1979. lib. bdg. 15.95 (ISBN 0-8161-6751-6). G K Hall.

Ostrovsky, Erika. Eye of Dawn: The Rise & Fall of Mata Hari. 1978. lib. bdg. 13.50 (ISBN 0-8161-6612-9, Large Print Bks). G K Hall.

Palmer, Lilli. The Red Raven. (gr. 7-12). 1979. lib. bdg. 13.95 (ISBN 0-8161-6750-8). G K Hall.

Patten, Lewis B. Death Rides a Black Horse. (Large Print Bks.). 1979. lib. bdg. 11.95 (ISBN 0-8161-3001-9). G K Hall.

--Man Outgunned. 1979. lib. bdg. 11.50 (ISBN 0-8161-6718-4, Large Print Bks). G K Hall.

--The Trail of the Apache Kid. (Large Print Bks.). 1980. lib. bdg. 10.95 (ISBN 0-8161-3130-9). G K Hall.

Patterson, Harry. To Catch a King. (Lagre Print Bks.). 1979. lib. bdg. 12.95 (ISBN 0-8161-3011-6). G K Hall.

--The Valhalla Exchange. 1977. lib. bdg. 12.50 (ISBN 0-8161-6496-7, Large Print Bks). G K Hall.

Paul, Barbara. Devil's Fire, Love's Revenge. 1977. lib. bdg. 13.50 (ISBN 0-8161-6492-4, Large Print Bks). G K Hall.

--To Love a Stranger. 1980. lib. bdg. 14.95 (ISBN 0-8161-3169-4, Large Print Bks). G K Hall.

Penner, Jonathan. Going Blind. (Adult Ser.). 1977. lib. bdg. 10.95 (ISBN 0-8161-6541-6, Large Print Bks). G K Hall.

Perrin, Noel. Giving up the Gun: Japan's Reversion to the Sword, 1543-1879. (Large Print Bks.). 1979. lib. bdg. 9.95 (ISBN 0-8161-3010-8). G K Hall.

Pinney, John J. Your Future in the Nursery Industry. LC 67-10084. (Careers in Depth Ser). (Illus.). (gr. 7 up). 1978. PLB 5.97 (ISBN 0-8239-0331-1). Rosen Pr.

Pitts, Denis. The Predator. 1977. Repr. lib. bdg. 12.50 (ISBN 0-8161-6485-1, Large Print Bks). G K Hall.

Plain, Belva. Evergreen, 2 vols. 1980. Set. lib. bdg. 23.95 (ISBN 0-8161-3114-7). G K Hall.

Plumb, Barbara. Houses Architects Live in. (Large Format Ser). (Illus.). 1978. pap. 9.95 (ISBN 0-14-004986-X). Penguin.

Portis, Charles. True Grit. 1968. 9.95 (ISBN 0-671-76380-6); large type o.s.i. 6.95 (ISBN 0-671-20301-0). S&S.

Potok, Chaim. Chosen. (gr. 7 up). 1967. 9.95 (ISBN 0-671-13674-7); large type o.s.i. 7.95 (ISBN 0-671-20302-9). S&S.

Priestley, J. B. Found, Lost, Found. 1976. Repr. write for info. (ISBN 0-8161-6436-3, Large Print Bks). G K Hall.

Pym, Barbara. Quartet in Autumn. 1979. lib. bdg. 10.95 (ISBN 0-8161-6661-7, Large Print Bks). G K Hall.

Racham, Arthur. Cinderella. (Large Format Ser). (Illus.). 1978. pap. 4.95 (ISBN 0-14-004907-X). Penguin.

Randall, Rona. The Eagle at the Gate. 1978. lib. bdg. 13.95 (ISBN 0-8161-6601-3, Large Print Bks). G K Hall.

--The Eagle at the Gate. 1978. pap. 2.25 (ISBN 0-380-42846-6, 42846). Avon.

Reed, Barry. The Verdict. 1980. lib. bdg. 14.95 (ISBN 0-8161-3175-9, Large Print Bks). G K Hall.

Rendall, Ruth. A Sleeping Life. 1979. lib. bdg. 11.95 (ISBN 0-8161-6711-7, Large Print Bks). G K Hall.

Rendell, Ruth. A Judgement in Stone. 1978. lib. bdg. 10.95 (ISBN 0-8161-6604-8, Large Print Bks). G K Hall.

--Make Death Love Me. (Large Print Bks.). 1979. lib. bdg. 13.50 (ISBN 0-8161-3012-4). G K Hall.

--The Secret House of Death. Repr. lib. bdg. 12.05x (ISBN 0-88411-144-X). Amereon Ltd.

Reuben, David. Everything You Always Wanted to Know About Nutrition. 1979. lib. bdg. 14.95 (ISBN 0-8161-6673-0, Large Print Bks). G K Hall.

--The Save-Your-Life-Diet. (Special Interest Ser.). 1976. lib. bdg. 9.95 (ISBN 0-8161-6417-7, Large Print Bks). G K Hall.

Rice, Helen S. Everyone Needs Someone. (Large Print Bks.). 1979. lib. bdg. 7.95 (ISBN 0-8161-6772-9). G K Hall.

Richards, Judith. Summer Lightning. 1979. pap. 2.50 (ISBN 0-380-42960-8, 42960). Avon.

Rinehart, Mary R. The After House. 1981. lib. bdg. 11.95 (ISBN 0-8161-3236-4, Large Print Bks). G K Hall.

--Episode of the Wandering Knife. 1981. lib. bdg. 15.95 (ISBN 0-8161-3234-8, Large Print Bks). G K Hall.

--Rinehart Mysteries, Set 2, 4 bks. 1981. Set. lib. bdg. 52.00 (ISBN 0-8161-3228-3, Large Print Bks). G K Hall.

--The State vs. Elinor Norton. 1981. lib. bdg. 13.50 (ISBN 0-8161-3235-6, Large Print Bks). G K Hall.

--The Swimming Pool. 1981. lib. bdg. 16.95 (ISBN 0-8161-3233-X, Large Print Bks). G K Hall.

Roberts, Oral. Daily Blessings: A Guide to Seed-Faith Living. 1979. lib. bdg. 16.95 (ISBN 0-8161-6699-4, Large Print Bks). G K Hall.

Rogers, Dale E. Let Freedom Ring. (Inspirational Ser.). 1976. Repr. lib. bdg. 8.95 (ISBN 0-8161-6427-4, Large Print Bks). G K Hall.

--Trials, Tears & Triumph. (Inspirational Bks). 1977. lib. bdg. 8.95 (ISBN 0-8161-6523-8, Large Print Bks). G K Hall.

Rogers, Harold. A Handful of Quietness. 1979. lib. bdg. 9.95 (ISBN 0-8161-6696-X, Large Print Bks). G K Hall.

Roth, June S. The Troubled Tummy Cookbook. LC 77-630. 1977. lib. bdg. 12.95 (ISBN 0-8161-6462-2, Large Print Bks). G K Hall.

Roth, Oscar. Heart Attack! 1979. lib. bdg. 14.50 (ISBN 0-8161-6688-9, Large Print Bks). G K Hall.

Roth, Philip. The Ghost Writer. (gr. 7-12). 1980. lib. bdg. 10.95 (ISBN 0-8161-3069-8, Large Print Bks). G K Hall.

--The Ghost Writer. 224p. 1980. pap. 2.75 (ISBN 0-449-24322-2, Crest). Fawcett.

Rush, Anna F. McCall's How to Cope with Household Disasters. (Special Interest Ser.). 1977. lib. bdg. 12.95 (ISBN 0-8161-6515-7, Large Print Bks). G K Hall.

Russell, Arthur J., ed. God Calling: A Devotional Diary. 4.95 (ISBN 0-396-02621-4). Dodd.

Sanders, Lawrence. The Tenth Commandment. 1981. lib. bdg. 16.95 (ISBN 0-8161-3208-9, Large Print Bks). G K Hall.

Saroyan, William. Chance Meeting. 1978. lib. bdg. 8.95 (ISBN 0-8161-6614-5, Large Print Bks). G K Hall.

Savage, Elizabeth. The Girls from the Five Great Valleys. LC 77-4512. (Adult Ser.). 1977. Repr. lib. bdg. 10.95 (ISBN 0-8161-6482-7, Large Print Bks). G K Hall.

--Willowwood. 1979. lib. bdg. 11.95 (ISBN 0-8161-6707-9, Large Print Bks). G K Hall.

Savory, Teo. A Childhood. (gr. 7-12). 1980. lib. bdg. 8.95 (ISBN 0-8161-3065-5, Large Print Bks). G K Hall.

Sayers, Dorothy. Hangman's Holiday. (gr. 7-12). 1979. lib. bdg. 12.95 (ISBN 0-8161-6783-4). G K Hall.

Sayers, Dorothy L. Busman's Honeymoon. (Large Print Bks.). 1981. lib. bdg. 16.95 (ISBN 0-8161-3041-8). G K Hall.

--Clouds of Witness. 1979. lib. bdg. 15.95 (ISBN 0-8161-6721-4, Large Print Bks). G K Hall.

--Have His Carcase. (Large Print Bks.). 1980. lib. bdg. 17.95 (ISBN 0-8161-3043-4). G K Hall.

--The Nine Tailors. (Large Print Bks.). 1981. lib. bdg. 15.95 (ISBN 0-8161-3036-1). G K Hall.

--Strong Poison. (Large Print Bks.). 1980. lib. bdg. 15.95 (ISBN 0-8161-3042-6). G K Hall.

--Unnatural Death. 1979. lib. bdg. 15.95 (ISBN 0-8161-6723-0, Large Print Bks). G K Hall.

--The Unpleasantness at the Bellona Club. 1979. lib. bdg. 14.95 (ISBN 0-8161-6724-9, Large Print Bks). G K Hall.

--The Whimsical Christian. 1979. lib. bdg. 14.95 (ISBN 0-8161-6693-5, Large Print Bks). G K Hall.

--Whose Body? 1979. lib. bdg. 12.95 (ISBN 0-8161-6722-2, Large Print Bks). G K Hall.

Scharlemann, Dorothy H. Pearls for a King. 1977. lib. bdg. 10.95 (ISBN 0-8161-6473-8, Large Print Bks.). G K Hall.

Schiff, Harriet S. The Bereaved Parent. 1977. lib. bdg. 8.95 (ISBN 0-8161-6517-3, Large Print Bks). G K Hall.

Schlein, Miriam. Way Mothers Are. LC 63-13332. (Concept Bks.). (Illus.). (ps-2). 1963. 7.50g (ISBN 0-8075-8692-7). A Whitman.

Schneck, Stephen & Norris, Nigel. Complete Home Medical Guide for Cats. (Special Interest Ser.). 1977. Repr. lib. bdg. 10.95 (ISBN 0-8161-6419-3, Large Print Bks). G K Hall.

--Complete Home Medical Guide for Dogs. LC 76-29624. (Special Interest Ser.). 1977. Repr. lib. bdg. 10.95 (ISBN 0-8161-6418-5, Large Print Bks). G K Hall.

Schwed, Peter. Hanging in There! 1979. lib. bdg. 10.95 (ISBN 0-8161-6691-9, Large Print Bks). G K Hall.

Scott, George A. Your Future in Retailing. LC 72-154791. (Careers in Depth Ser). (Illus.). (gr. 7 up). 1978. PLB 5.97 (ISBN 0-8239-0456-3). Rosen Pr.

Segal, Erich. Man, Woman & Child. (Large Print Bks.). 1980. lib. bdg. 10.95 (ISBN 0-8161-3124-4). G K Hall.

--Oliver's Story. (Adult Ser.). 1977. lib. bdg. 10.95 (ISBN 0-8161-6500-9, Large Print Bks). G K Hall.

Seifert, Elizabeth. The Doctors Were Brothers. (Large Print Bks.). 1979. lib. bdg. 12.95 (ISBN 0-8161-6705-2). G K Hall.

Seton, Cynthia P. The Half-Sisters. 224p. 1981. pap. 3.95 (ISBN 0-393-00034-6). Norton.

Settle, Mary Lee. The Scapegoat. large print ed. LC 81-5636. 534p. 1981. Repr. of 1980 ed. 12.95x (ISBN 0-89621-285-8). Thorndike Pr.

Shedd, Charlie W. Grandparents. (Inspirational Bks). 1977. lib. bdg. 7.95 (ISBN 0-8161-6519-X, Large Print Bks). G K Hall.

Shell-Garner, Adeline & Reynolds, Kay. Feel Better After Fifty Food Book. 1979. lib. bdg. 13.95 (ISBN 0-8161-6692-7, Large Print Bks). G K Hall.

Short, Luke. King Colt. (Large Print Bks.). 1980. lib. bdg. 11.95 (ISBN 0-8161-3110-4). G K Hall.

--The Whip. 1980. lib. bdg. 10.95 (ISBN 0-8161-3087-6, Large Print Bks). G K Hall.

Sibley, Celestine. Small Blessings. 1978. lib. bdg. 10.95 (ISBN 0-8161-6570-X, Large Print Bks). G K Hall.

Simon, Norma. What Do I Do. LC 74-79544. (Concept Bks.). (Illus.). (ps-2). 1969. 7.50g (ISBN 0-8075-8822-9). A Whitman.

--What Do I Do: English - Spanish Edition. LC 74-79544. (Concept Bks.). (Illus.). (ps-2). 1969. 7.50g (ISBN 0-8075-8823-7). A Whitman.

Singer, Isaac B. Old Love. 1980. pap. 2.50 (ISBN 0-449-24343-5, Crest). Fawcett.

Smith, Adam. Paper Money. (Large Print Bks.). 1981. lib. bdg. 15.95 (ISBN 0-8161-3259-3). G K Hall.

Smith, Joan. Babe. 1980. lib. bdg. 13.95 (ISBN 0-8161-3112-0, Large Print Bks). G K Hall.

--Imprudent Lady. (Large Print Bks.). 1979. lib. bdg. 13.95 (ISBN 0-8161-6746-X). G K Hall.

--Talk of the Town. (Large Print Bks.). 1979. lib. bdg. 12.50 (ISBN 0-8161-3004-3). G K Hall.

Smith, Robert K. Sadie Shapiro in Miami. 1978. lib. bdg. 9.95 (ISBN 0-8161-6551-3, Large Print Bks). G K Hall.

--Sadie Shapiro, Matchmaker. (Large Print Bks.). 1980. lib. bdg. 10.95 (ISBN 0-8161-3108-2). G K Hall.

Snead, Sam. Golf Begins at Forty. 1979. lib. bdg. 10.95 (ISBN 0-8161-6674-9, Large Print Bks). G K Hall.

Sonnabend, Roger P. Your Future in Hotel Management. LC 64-10199. (Careers in Depth Ser). (gr. 7 up). 1975. PLB 5.97 (ISBN 0-8239-0036-3). Rosen Pr.

Southerland, Ellease. Let the Lion Eat Straw. (gr. 7-12). 1979. lib. bdg. 10.95 (ISBN 0-8161-3006-X). G K Hall.

Stamps, Ellen D. My Years with Corrie. (gr. 7-12). 1979. lib. bdg. 11.95 (ISBN 0-8161-6773-7). G K Hall.

Stanek, Muriel. One, Two, Three for Fun. LC 67-26519. (Concept Bks.). (Illus.). 32p. (ps-2). 1967. 7.50g (ISBN 0-8075-6106-1). A Whitman.

Stapleton, Ruth C. The Experience of Inner Healing. (gr. 7-12). 1979. lib. bdg. 13.95 (ISBN 0-8161-6776-1). G K Hall.

Start Loving: The Miracle of Forgiving. 1977. lib. bdg. 8.95 (ISBN 0-8161-6476-2, Large Print Bks). G K Hall.

Steel, Danielle. Passion's Promise. (Large Print Bks.). 1981. lib. bdg. 16.95 (ISBN 0-8161-3217-8). G K Hall.

--The Ring. (Large Print Bks.). 1981. lib. bdg. 16.95 (ISBN 0-8161-3218-6). G K Hall.

--Summers's End. (Large Print Bks.). 1981. lib. bdg. 15.95 (ISBN 0-686-73368-1). G K Hall.

--To Love Again. (Large Print Bks.). 1981. lib. bdg. 14.95 (ISBN 0-8161-3219-4). G K Hall.

Stegner, Wallace. The Spectator Bird. (Spring Adult Ser.). 1977. lib. bdg. 10.95 (ISBN 0-8161-6443-6, Large Print Bks). G K Hall.

Steinbeck, John. Of Mice & Men. 1937. 12.95 (ISBN 0-670-52071-3); large type ed. 6.50 (ISBN 0-670-52073-X, LT1). Viking Pr.

Stevenson, D. E. Mrs. Tim Carries on. (gr. 7-12). 1980. lib. bdg. 14.95 (ISBN 0-8161-6784-2). G K Hall.

--Mrs. Tim Christle. (gr. 7-12). 1980. lib. bdg. 16.95 (ISBN 0-8161-6786-9). G K Hall.

--Mrs. Tim Flies Home. (gr. 7-12). 1980. lib. bdg. 14.95 (ISBN 0-8161-6785-0). G K Hall.

--Mrs. Tim Gets a Job. (gr. 7-12). 1980. lib. bdg. 13.95 (ISBN 0-8161-6787-7). G K Hall.

Stewart, Mary. Touch Not the Cat. 1976. Repr. lib. bdg. 13.50 (ISBN 0-8161-6403-7, Large Print Bks). G K Hall.

Stolz, Mary. Bully of Barkham Street. LC 63-9090. (Illus.). (gr. 3-6). 1963. PLB 8.79 (ISBN 0-06-025821-7, HarpJ). Har-Row.

Stout, Rex. The Doorbell Rang. 1968. large type ed. 6.50 (ISBN 0-670-28021-6, LT4). Viking Pr.

--A Family Affair. 1978. lib. bdg. 9.95 (ISBN 0-8161-6561-0, Large Print Bks). G K Hall.

--Fer-De-Lance. 1981. lib. bdg. 13.50 (ISBN 0-8161-3222-4, Large Print Bks). G K Hall.

--The League of Frightened Men. 1981. lib. bdg. 14.50 (ISBN 0-8161-3225-9, Large Print Bks). G K Hall.

--The Red Box. 1981. lib. bdg. 13.50 (ISBN 0-8161-3223-2, Large Print Bks). G K Hall.

--Rex Stout Mysteries, 4 bks. 1981. Set. lib. bdg. 48.00 (ISBN 0-8161-3227-5, Large Print Bks). G K Hall.

--The Rubber Band. 1981. lib. bdg. 12.95 (ISBN 0-8161-3224-0, Large Print Bks). G K Hall.

Strober, Gerald S. Graham: A Day in Billy's Life. LC 77-598. (Spring 1977 Inspirational Ser.). 1977. 10.95 (ISBN 0-8161-6468-1, Large Print Books). G K Hall.

Stubbs, Jean. The Golden Crucible. LC 77-5513. (Adult Ser.). 1977. Repr. lib. bdg. 12.95 (ISBN 0-8161-6488-6, Large Print Bks). G K Hall.

Subject Guide to Large Print Book Catalog. LC 76-30595. 110p. 1976. 5.00 (ISBN 0-913578-15-0). Inglewood Ca.

Swarthout, Glendon. The Melodeon. 1978. lib. bdg. 8.95 (ISBN 0-8161-6549-1, Large Print Bks). G K Hall.

Swinnerton, Frank. Some Achieve Greatness. (Spring Adult Ser.). 1977. lib. bdg. 11.95 (ISBN 0-8161-6452-5, Large Print Bks). G K Hall.

Taber, Gladys. Conversations with Amber. 1978. lib. bdg. 9.95 (ISBN 0-8161-6607-2, Large Print Bks). G K Hall.

Tattersall, Jill. Damnation Reef. 288p. 1980. pap. 2.25 (ISBN 0-449-24325-7, Crest). Fawcett.

Thane, Elswyth. Dawn's Earlylight. Repr. lib. bdg. 16.85 (ISBN 0-686-74283-4). Amereon Ltd.

--Ever After. (Williamsburg Ser.: No. 3). 1981. lib. bdg. 17.95 (ISBN 0-8161-3165-1, Large Print Bks). G K Hall.

--Homing. (Williamsburg Ser.: No. 7). 1981. lib. bdg. 15.95 (ISBN 0-8161-3164-3, Large Print Bks). G K Hall.

--Kissing Kin. (Williamsburg Ser.: No. 5). 1981. lib. bdg. 16.95 (ISBN 0-8161-3162-7, Large Print Bks). G K Hall.

--The Light Heart. (Williamsburg Ser.: No. 4). 1981. lib. bdg. 17.95 (ISBN 0-8161-3163-5, Large Print Bks). G K Hall.

Thomas, Lowell. So Long Until Tomorrow. 1978. lib. bdg. 13.95 (ISBN 0-8161-6553-X, Large Print Bks). G K Hall.

Thompson, Joan. Marblehead. 1979. lib. bdg. 11.95 (ISBN 0-8161-6664-1, Large Print Bks). G K Hall.

Truman, Margaret. Murder in the White House. 1980. lib. bdg. 13.95 (ISBN 0-8161-3171-6, Large Print Bks). G K Hall.

Tuchman, Barbara W. Guns of August. (Illus.). (gr. 9 up). 1962. 16.95 (ISBN 0-02-620310-3). Macmillan.

Turnbull, Agnes S. The Two Bishops. 1980. lib. bdg. 14.95 (ISBN 0-8161-3173-2, Large Print Bks). G K Hall.

Tyler, Anne. Earthly Possessions. (Adult Ser.). 1977. lib. bdg. 10.95 (ISBN 0-8161-6532-7, Large Print Bks). G K Hall.

--Morgan's Passing. (Large Print Bks.). 1980. lib. bdg. 16.95 (ISBN 0-8161-3131-7). G K Hall.

Van De Watering, Janwillem. Death of a Hawker. (Adult Ser.). 1977. lib. bdg. 11.95 (ISBN 0-8161-6527-0, Large Print Bks). G K Hall.

Van De Wetering, Janwillem. The Maine Massacre. (Large Print Bks.). 1979. lib. bdg. 13.95 (ISBN 0-8161-6753-2). G K Hall.

--Tumbleweed. (Adult Ser.). 1978. lib. bdg. 10.95 (ISBN 0-8161-6569-6, Large Print Bks). G K Hall.

Von Canon, Claudia. The Moonclock. (Large Print Bks.). 1979. lib. bdg. 10.95 (ISBN 0-8161-3008-6). G K Hall.

Vonnegut, Kurt. Jailbird. (Large Print Bks.). 1980. lib. bdg. 13.95 (ISBN 0-8161-3022-1). G K Hall.

Wallace, Irving. The R Document. (Winter Adult Ser.). 1976. Repr. lib. bdg. 14.95 (ISBN 0-8161-6404-5, Large Print Bks). G K Hall.

Welk, Lawrence. My America, Your America. 1977. lib. bdg. 10.95 (ISBN 0-8161-6466-5, Large Print Bks). G K Hall.

--This I Believe. 1980. lib. bdg. 9.95 (ISBN 0-8161-3062-0, Large Print Bks). G K Hall.

West, Betty M. Diabetic Menus, Meals, & Recipes. 1979. lib. bdg. 12.95 (ISBN 0-8161-6689-7, Large Print Bks). G K Hall.
West, Jessamyn. Double Discovery. 1981. lib. bdg. 15.95 (ISBN 0-8161-3206-2, Large Print Bks). G K Hall.
West, Morris L. The Navigator. LC 77-5651. 1977. Repr. lib. bdg. 17.95 (ISBN 0-8161-6481-9, Large Print Bks). G K Hall.
White, E. B. Charlotte's Web. LC 52-9760. (Illus.). (ps-3). 1952. 6.95 (ISBN 0-06-026385-7, HarpJ); large type ed. 10.00 (ISBN 0-06-026387-3); PLB 7.89 (ISBN 0-06-026386-5). Har-Row.
White, T. H. The Book of Merlyn. 1978. lib. bdg. 9.95 (ISBN 0-8161-6557-2, Large Print Bks). G K Hall.
Whitney, Phyllis. The Golden Unicorn. 1976. Repr. lib. bdg. 13.95 (ISBN 0-8161-6409-6, Large Print Bks). G K Hall.
Whitney, Phyllis A. Domino. (Large Print Bks.). 1979. lib. bdg. 14.95 (ISBN 0-8161-3016-7). G K Hall.
--The Glass Flame. 1979. lib. bdg. 14.95 (ISBN 0-8161-6653-6, Large Print Bks). G K Hall.
--The Glass Flame. 1979. pap. 2.25 (ISBN 0-449-24130-0, Crest). Fawcett.
--The Stone Bull. 1977. lib. bdg. 13.95 (ISBN 0-8161-6535-1, Large Print Bks). G K Hall.
Wister, Owen. Virginian. (Illus.). 1925. 12.95 (ISBN 0-02-630580-1); large print ed. 9.95 (ISBN 0-02-489480-X). Macmillan.
Woman's Day Editors. Cooking for Two. 1976. lib. bdg. 10.95 (ISBN 0-8161-6422-3, Large Print Bks). G K Hall.
Woodward, Bronte. Meet Me at the Melba. 1978. lib. bdg. 12.95 (ISBN 0-8161-6543-2, Large Print Bks). G K Hall.

LARI LANGUAGE
see Congo Language

LARK-HOROVITZ, KARL, 1892-1958
Johnson, V. A. Karl Lark-Horovitz, Pioneer in Solid State Physics. LC 77-91464. (Men of Physics Ser.). 1970. 22.00 (ISBN 0-08-006581-3); pap. 10.75 (ISBN 0-08-006580-5). Pergamon.

LARKIN, JAMES, 1876-1947
Larkin, Emmett. James Larkin, Irish Labor Leader, 1876-1947. (Illus.). 1977. Repr. of 1965 ed. 28.00x (ISBN 0-7100-8606-7). Routledge & Kegan.

LARKIN, PHILIP
Bloomfield, B. C. Philip Larkin: A Bibliography. 192p. 1980. 72.00 (ISBN 0-571-11447-4, Pub. by Faber & Faber). Merrimack Bk Serv.
Kuby, Lolette. An Uncommon Poet for the Common Man: A Study of the Poetry of Philip Larkin. (De Proprietatibus Litterarum, Ser. Practica: No. 60). 190p. 1974. pap. text ed. 26.25x (ISBN 90-2792-720-0). Mouton.
Petch, Simon. Art of Philip Larkin. (Sydney Studies in Literature). 144p. 1981. 21.00 (ISBN 0-424-00090-3, Pub. by Sydney U Pr Australia). Intl Schol Bk Serv.

LARKSPUR
see Delphinium

LA ROCHEFOUCAULD, FRANCOIS, DUC DE, 1613-1680
De Mourgues, Odette. Two French Moralists. LC 77-82506. (Major European Authors Ser.). 1978. 32.50 (ISBN 0-521-21823-3). Cambridge U Pr.
Gosse, Edmund W. Three French Moralists & the Gallantry of France. facs. ed. LC 67-23223. (Essay Index Reprint Ser). 1918. 13.00 (ISBN 0-8369-0489-3). Arno.
Hippeau. Essai sur la morale de La Rochefoucauld. 8.95 (ISBN 0-685-34233-6). French & Eur.
Lewis, Philip E. La Rochefoucauld: The Art of Abstraction. LC 76-28016. 1977. 17.50x (ISBN 0-8014-0848-2). Cornell U Pr.
Zeller, Sr. M. Francine. New Aspects of Style in the Maxims of La Rochefoucauld. LC 77-94186. (Catholic University of America Studies in Romance Languages & Literatures Ser: No. 48). Repr. of 1954 ed. 18.50 (ISBN 0-404-50348-9). AMS Pr.

LARTIGUE, JACQUES-HENRI
Lartigue, J. H. The Autochromes of J. H. Lartigue. Coe, Brian W., tr. LC 81-43020. (Illus.). 78p. 1981. 35.00 (ISBN 0-670-14250-6, Studio). Viking Pr.

LARVAE
see also Caterpillars
Chia, F. & Rice, M. E. Settlement & Metamorphosis of Marine Invertebrate Larvae: Proceedings of a Symposium Held at Toronto, Canada, Dec. 27-28, 1977. 1978. 25.00 (ISBN 0-444-00277-4, North Holland). Elsevier.
Smith, DeBoyd L. A Guide to Marine Coastal Plankton & Marine Invertebrate Larvae. LC 76-62564. (Illus.). 1978. pap. text ed. 8.95 (ISBN 0-8403-1672-0). Kendall-Hunt.

LARVAE-INSECTS
see also Caterpillars; Insects-Development
Chu, H. F. How to Know the Immature Insects. (Pictured Key Nature Ser.). 1949. write for info. wire coil (ISBN 0-697-04807-1); wire coil 5.95x (ISBN 0-697-04806-3). Wm C Brown.
Fracker, Stanley B. The Classification of Lepidopterous Larvae. (Illus.). Repr. of 1915 ed. 12.50 (ISBN 0-384-16670-9). Johnson Repr.
Gage, John H. The Larvae of the Coccinellidae. (Illinois Biological Monographs: Vol. 6, No. 4). pap. 6.00 (ISBN 0-384-17550-3). Johnson Repr.
Hickin, Norman E. Caddis Larvae: Larvae of the British Trichoptera. LC 68-58408. (Illus.). 480p. 1968. 20.00 (ISBN 0-8386-6945-X). Fairleigh Dickinson.
Hinton, H. E. Biology of Insect Eggs, 3 vols. LC 77-30390. (Illus.). 1500p. 1980. Set. 400.00 (ISBN 0-08-021539-4). Pergamon.
Johannsen, Oskar A. Aquatic Diptera. LC 78-7782. (Illus.). 370p. 1969. Repr. of 1937 ed. 17.50 (ISBN 0-911836-01-2). Entomological Repr.
McGinley, Ronald J. Systematics of the Colletidae Based on Mature Larvae with Phenetic Analysis of Apoid Larvae (Hymenoptera, Apoidea) (U. C. Publications in Entomology Ser.: Vol. 91). 332p. 1981. 14.50x (ISBN 0-520-09623-1). U of Cal Pr.
Ritcher, Paul O. White Grubs & Their Allies. LC 66-63008. (Studies in Entomology Ser: No. 4). 1966. 19.95 (ISBN 0-87071-054-0). Oreg St U Pr.
Yuasa, Hachiro. A Classification of the Larvae of the Tenthredinoidea. (Illinois Biological Monographs: Vol. 7, No. 4). 12.50 (ISBN 0-384-70500-6). Johnson Repr.

LARYNGECTOMY
Dabul, Barbara. Laryngectomee: Booklet for Family & Friends. 1973. pap. 0.50x (ISBN 0-8134-1542-X, 1542). Interstate.
Fox, Madeline J. Questions & Answers for the Laryngectomee & the Family. 1979. pap. 0.75x (ISBN 0-8134-2078-4, 2078). Interstate.
Gardner, Warren H. Laryngectomee Speech & Rehabilitation. 2nd ed. (Illus.). 260p. 1978. 22.50 (ISBN 0-398-00643-1). C C Thomas.
Keith, Robert L. A Handbook for the Laryngectomee. 1974 ed. LC 73-93688. pap. text ed. 1.95x (ISBN 0-8134-1638-8, 1638). Interstate.
Keith, Robert L. & Darley, Frederic L., eds. Laryngectomee Rehabilitation. 24.50 (ISBN 0-933014-56-2). College-Hill.
--Laryngectomee Rehabilitation. LC 79-91246. (Illus.). 533p. 1980. text ed. 24.50 (ISBN 0-933014-56-2). College-Hill.
Kelly, Dan H. & Welborn, Peggy. The Cover Up: Neckwear for the Laryngectomee & Other Neck-Breathers. 15.00 (ISBN 0-933014-55-4). College-Hill.
--Neckwear for the Laryngectomee & Other Neck Breathers. LC 80-65470. (Illus.). 98p. 1980. pap. text ed. 15.00 (ISBN 0-933014-55-4). College-Hill.
Salmon, Shirley & Goldstein, Lewis P. The Artificial Larynx Handbook & Cassette Package. 176p. 1978. 33.50 (ISBN 0-8089-1111-2). Grune.
Shedd, Donald P. & Weinberg, Bernd. Surgical-Prosthetic Approaches to Speech Rehabilitation. (Medical Publications Ser.). 1980. lib. bdg. 32.50 (ISBN 0-8161-2186-9). G K Hall.
Weinberg, Bernd, ed. Reading in Speech Following Total Laryngectomy. 587p. pap. text ed. 24.95 (ISBN 0-8391-1570-9). Univ Park.
Wilshaw, John. After the Laryngectomy. 1978. pap. text ed. 0.50x (ISBN 0-8134-1968-9, 1968). Interstate.

LARYNX
see also Trachea; Voice
Archer, Carol R. Computed Tomography of the Larynx. (Illus.). 200p. 1981. 27.50 (ISBN 0-87527-240-1). Green.
Cotton & Seid. Laryngal Disease in Children. 1981. text ed. write for info. (ISBN 0-443-08054-2). Churchill.
DiCarlo, Louis M., et al. Speech After Laryngectomy. (Special Education & Rehabilitation Monograph: No. 1). (Illus.). 1956. 8.95x (ISBN 0-8156-2016-0). Syracuse U Pr.
DuBrul, E. Lloyd. Evolution of the Speech Apparatus. (American Lecture Anatomy). (Illus.). 116p. 1958. ed. spiral bdg. 12.75photocopy (ISBN 0-398-00479-X). C C Thomas.
Fant, G. & Scully, C., eds. The Larynx & Language. (Phonetica: Vol. 34, No. 4). (Illus.). 1977. 14.50 (ISBN 3-8055-2809-4). S Karger.
Fink, B. Raymond. The Human Larynx: A Functional Study. LC 74-80536. 207p. 1975. 19.00 (ISBN 0-911216-86-3). Raven.
Fink, B. Raymond & Demarest, Robert J. Laryngeal Biomechanics. LC 77-26937. (Commonwealth Fund Ser.). 1978. 30.00x (ISBN 0-674-51085-2). Harvard U Pr.
Healy, Gerald B. & McGill, Trevor J. Laryngo-Tracheal Problems in the Pediatric Patient. (Illus.). 144p. 1979. text ed. 13.75 (ISBN 0-398-03910-0). C C Thomas.
International Otoneurological Symposium. Transtemporal Surgery of the Internal Auditory Canal: Proceedings. Pfaltz, C. R. & Fisch, U., eds. (Advances in Oto-Rhino-Laryngology: Vol. 17). 1970. 49.75 (ISBN 3-8055-0237-0). S Karger.
Kleensasser, O. Microlaryngoscopy & Endolaryngeal Microsurgery. 192p. 1979. pap. text ed. 64.50 (ISBN 0-8391-1350-1). Univ Park.
Larrauri, A. Dictionary of Oto-Rhino-Laryngology in Five Languages: English-French-Spanish-German-Italian. LC 71-501781. 1008p. 1971. 60.00x (ISBN 0-8002-0197-3). Intl Pubns Serv.
Lebrun, Yvan, et al. The Artificial Larynx. (Neurolinguistics Ser.: Vol. 1). 90p. 1973. pap. text ed. 15.75 (ISBN 90-265-0173-0, Pub. by Swets Pub Serv Holland). Swets North Am.
Mancuso, Anthony. Computed Tomography of the Larynx & Nasopharynx. (Illus.). 438p. 1981. lib. bdg. 30.00 (ISBN 0-683-05475-9). Williams & Wilkins.
Myerson, Nervin C. The Human Larynx. (Illus.). 408p. 1964. photocopy ed. spiral 39.75 (ISBN 0-398-01377-2). C C Thomas.
Negus, V. E. Comparative Anatomy & Physiology of the Larynx. (Illus.). 1962. Repr. of 1949 ed. 18.50 (ISBN 0-02-849590-X). Hafner.
Salmon, Shirley & Goldstein, Lewis P. The Artificial Larynx Handbook & Cassette Package. 176p. 1978. 33.50 (ISBN 0-8089-1111-2). Grune.
Silver, C. E. Surgery for Cancer of the Larynx. 1981. text ed. write for info. (ISBN 0-443-08064-X). Churchill.
Singh, Roderick P. Anatomy of Hearing & Speech. (Illus.). 176p. 1980. text ed. 13.95x (ISBN 0-19-502665-9); pap. text ed. 7.95x (ISBN 0-19-502666-7). Oxford U Pr.
Snidecor, John C., ed. Speech Rehabilitation of the Laryngectomized. 2nd ed. (Amer. Lec. in Speech & Hearing Ser). (Illus.). 288p. 1978. 16.75 (ISBN 0-398-01803-0). C C Thomas.
Sonninen, Aatto A. Role of the External Laryngeal Muscles in Length-Adjustment of the Vocal Cords in Singing. 1956. pap. 9.00 (ISBN 0-384-56670-7). Johnson Repr.
Tucker. Surgery for Phonatory Disorders. 1981. text ed. write for info. (ISBN 0-443-08058-5). Churchill.
Wright, Jonathan. A History of Laryngology & Rhinology. 2nd rev. enl. ed. LC 75-23771. Repr. of 1914 ed. 30.50 (ISBN 0-404-13397-5). AMS Pr.

LA SALLE, ROBERT CAVELIER, SIEUR DE, 1643-1687
Cox, Isaac J, ed. The Journeys of Rene Robert Cavelier, 2 vols. LC 72-2828. (American Explorers Ser.). (Illus.). Repr. of 1922 ed. Set. 37.50 (ISBN 0-404-54917-9). AMS Pr.
Joutel, Henri. Joutel's Journal of la Salle's Last Voyage. Repr. 21.50 (ISBN 0-8337-3415-6). B Franklin.
Le Clercq, Chretien. First Establishment of the Faith in New France, 2 Vols. LC 77-172312. Repr. of 1881 ed. Set. 55.00 (ISBN 0-404-03914-6); 28.00 ea. Vol. 1 (ISBN 0-404-03915-4). Vol. 2 (ISBN 0-404-03916-2). AMS Pr.
Oncken, Hermann. La Salle. LC 75-25529. 450p. 1904. Repr. 29.50 (ISBN 0-8337-3154-8). B Franklin.
Parkman, Francis. La Salle & the Discovery of the Great West. 560p. 1968. Repr. of 1889 ed. 12.50 (ISBN 0-87928-004-2). Corner Hse.
Weddle, Robert S. Wilderness Manhunt: The Spanish Search for La Salle. LC 72-1579. (Illus.). 307p. 1973. 14.95 (ISBN 0-292-79000-7). U of Tex Pr.

LAS CASAS, BARTOLOME DE, 1474-1566
Brion, M. Bartolome De las Casas. 1976. lib. bdg. 59.95 (ISBN 0-8490-1476-X). Gordon Pr.
Helps, Sir Arthur. The Life of las Casas: The Apostle of the Indies. 1976. lib. bdg. 75.00 (ISBN 0-8490-2165-0). Gordon Pr.
MacNutt, Francis A. Bartholomew De Las Casas: His Life, His Apostolate, & His Writings. LC 70-172712. Repr. of 1909 ed. 32.45 (ISBN 0-404-07146-5). AMS Pr.

LAS VEGAS, NEVADA
Brown, Robert. Psyching Out Vegas. (Illus., Orig.). 1981. pap. text ed. 10.00 (ISBN 0-89746-020-0). Gamblers.
Firestone, Eve & Blackwell, Jim. Las Vegas Guide for New Arrivals: How to Survive in the Fun Capital of the World. (Illus.). 64p. (Orig.). 1980. pap. 2.95 (ISBN 0-89650-790-4). Gamblers.
Gambling Times Complete Guide to Las Vegas. (Gambling Times Complete Guide Ser.). (Illus.). 1983. pap. text ed. 2.95 (ISBN 0-685-44092-3). Gambling Times.
Jones, Florence L. A History of Las Vegas, 2 vols. (Illus.). 1975. 35.00 (ISBN 0-913814-10-5). Nevada Pubns.
Lawlor, Florine. Out from Las Vegas. (Illus.). 1970. wrappers 1.25 (ISBN 0-910856-36-2). La Siesta.
Maggio, Frank. Las Vegas Calling. (Illus.). 1975. 6.50 (ISBN 0-913814-34-2). Nevada Pubns.
Paher, Stanley W. Las Vegas, As It Began, As It Grew. LC 70-175144. (Illus.). 1971. 17.50 (ISBN 0-913814-01-6). Nevada Pubns.
Skolnick, Jerome. House of Cards: Legalization & Control of Casino Gambling. LC 78-16991. 1978. 13.95 (ISBN 0-316-79699-9). Little.

LAS VEGAS, NEVADA-DESCRIPTION
Arthur Frommer's Guide to Las Vegas, 1981-82. 224p. 1981. pap. 2.95 (ISBN 0-671-41432-1). Frommer Pasmantier.
Dollarwise Guide to California & Las Vegas, 1979-80. 312p. pap. 4.95 (ISBN 0-671-24897-9). Frommer-Pasmantier.
Fried, Elliot & Enriquez, Helen. The Weekend Gambler's Guide to Las Vegas. (Weekend Gambler's Ser.). (Illus.). 1980. 10.95 (ISBN 0-935232-01-X); pap. 6.95 (ISBN 0-935232-02-8). Deep River Pr.
Kovell, Hank. Poor Man's Guide to Las Vegas. (Illus.). 128p. 1981. pap. 4.95 (ISBN 0-686-31335-6). Owl Pr NV.
London, Duke. Beautiful Las Vegas. Shangle, Robert D., ed. LC 79-18837. (Illus.). 72p. 1980. 14.95 (ISBN 0-89802-079-4); pap. 7.95 (ISBN 0-89802-078-6). Beautiful Am.
Pearl, Ralph. Las Vegas Is My Beat. 1978. pap. 2.95 (ISBN 0-8065-0618-0). Citadel Pr.
Puzo, Mario. Inside Las Vegas. 352p. 1979. pap. 2.50 (ISBN 0-686-60213-7, Pub. by Charter Bks). Ace Bks.
Roberts, Martin S. & Hardy, John L. Only in Las Vegas. new ed. LC 76-43168. (Illus.). 10.00x (ISBN 0-917844-52-1); lib. bdg. 15.00x (ISBN 0-917844-54-8); pap. 5.00x (ISBN 0-917844-53-X). Hardy Hse.
Venturi, Robert, et al. Learning from Las Vegas. rev. ed. 1977. 20.00x (ISBN 0-262-22020-2); pap. 9.95 (ISBN 0-262-72006-X). MIT Pr.

LASCAUX CAVE, FRANCE
Vanier, Jacques. Basic Theory of Lasers & Masers: A Density Matrix Approach. Montroll, E. W., et al, eds. (Documents on Modern Physics Ser.). (Illus.). 128p. 1971. 29.25x (ISBN 0-677-30340-8). Gordon.

LASER COAGULATION
Skobel'tsyn, D. V., ed. Spectroscopy of Laser Crystals with Ionic Structure. LC 73-83902. (P. N. Lebedev Physics Institute Ser.: Vol. 60). (Illus.). 160p. 1974. 32.50 (ISBN 0-306-10898-4, Consultants). Plenum Pub.

LASER PHOTOGRAPHY
see Holography

LASER SPECTROSCOPY
Balian, R., et al. Frontiers in Laser Spectroscopy, 2 vols. 1977. 136.75 set (ISBN 0-7204-0698-6, North-Holland). Elsevier.
Demtroeder, W. Laser Spectroscopy. 2nd ed. LC 51-5497. (Topics in Current Chemistry: Vol. 17). (Illus.). iii, 106p. 1973. 21.30 (ISBN 0-387-06334-X). Springer-Verlag.
--Laser Spectrosopy: Basic Concepts & Instrumentation. (Springer Series in Chemical Physics: Vol. 5). (Illus.). 700p. 1981. 35.00 (ISBN 0-387-10343-0). Springer-Verlag.
Freeman, Stanley K. Application of Laser Raman Spectroscopy. 350p. 1974. 25.00 (ISBN 0-471-27788-6). Krieger.
Letokhov, V. S. & Chebotayev, V. P. Nonlinear Laser Spectroscopy. (Springer Optical Sciences Ser.: Vol. 4). (Illus.). 1977. 38.20 (ISBN 0-387-08044-9). Springer-Verlag.
Omenetto, N. Analytical Laser Spectroscopy, Vol. 50. (Chemical Analysis Ser.). 550p. 1979. 54.50 (ISBN 0-471-65371-3, 1-075). Wiley.
Shimoda, K., ed. High-Resolution Laser Spectroscopy. (Topics in Applied Physics Ser.: Vol. 13). (Illus.). 1976. 52.90 (ISBN 0-387-07719-7). Springer-Verlag.
Tobin, Marvin C. Laser Raman Spectroscopy. LC 80-11511. 184p. 1981. Repr. of 1971 ed. lib. bdg. write for info. (ISBN 0-89874-159-9). Krieger.
Walther, H., ed. Laser Spectroscopy of Atoms & Molecules. (Topics in Applied Physics Ser.: Vol. 2). (Illus.). 340p. 1976. 52.90 (ISBN 0-387-07324-8). Springer-Verlag.
Walther, H. & Rothe, K. W., eds. Laser Spectroscopy Four. (Springer Ser. in Optical Sciences: Vol. 21). (Illus.). 1980. 46.70 (ISBN 0-387-09766-X). Springer-Verlag.
Yen, W. M. & Selzer, P. M., eds. Laser Spectroscopy of Solids. (Topics in Applied Physics Ser.: Vol. 49). (Illus.). 310p. 1981. 58.80 (ISBN 0-387-10638-3). Springer-Verlag.

LASERS
see also Nonlinear Optics
Akerman, M. Alfred. Demonstration of the First Visible Wave-Length Direct Nuclear Pumped Laser. LC 78-75011. (Outstanding Dissertations on Energy Ser.). 1979. lib. bdg. 11.00 (ISBN 0-8240-3984-X). Garland Pub.
Allen, L. Essentials of Lasers. 1969. text ed. 29.00 (ISBN 0-08-013320-7); pap. text ed. 11.25 (ISBN 0-08-013319-3). Pergamon.
Anderson, John D. Gasdynamic Lasers: An Introduction. (Quantum Electronic Ser.). 1976. 34.00 (ISBN 0-12-056950-7). Acad Pr.

Arecchi, F. T. & Schulz-Dubois, E. D., eds. Laser Handbook, 2 vols. LC 73-146191. 1973. Set. 122.00 (ISBN 0-444-10379-1, North-Holland). Elsevier.
Bachman, Christian G. Laser Radar Systems & Techniques. LC 78-31528. (Artech Radar Library). 1979. 30.00x (ISBN 0-89006-073-8). Artech Hse.
Basov, N. G., ed. High-Power Lasers & Laser Plasmas. (P. N. Lebedev Physics Institute Ser.: Vol. 85). (Illus.). 225p. 1978. 39.50 (ISBN 0-306-10943-3, Consultants). Plenum Pub.
--Lasers & Their Application in Physical Research. (P. N. Lebedev Physics Institute Ser.: Vol. 91). (Illus.). 1979. 42.50 (ISBN 0-306-10949-2, Consultants). Plenum Pub.
--Lasers & Their Applications. (P. N. Lebedev Physics Institute Ser.: Vol. 76). (Illus.). 223p. 1976. 45.00 (ISBN 0-306-10927-1, Consultants). Plenum Pub.
--Pulse Gas Discharge Atomic & Molecular Lasers. (P. N. Lebedev Physics Institute Ser.: Vol. 81). (Illus.). 186p. 1976. 42.50 (ISBN 0-306-10931-X, Consultants). Plenum Pub.
--Research in Molecular Laser Plasmas. (P. N. Lebedev Physics Institute Ser.: Vol. 78). (Illus.). 115p. 1976. 37.50 (ISBN 0-306-10928-X, Consultants). Plenum Pub.
--Temporal Characteristics of Laser Pulses & Interaction of Laser Radiation with Matter. (P. N. Lebedev Physics Institute Ser.: Vol. 84). (Illus.). 208p. 1977. 39.50 (ISBN 0-306-10942-5, Consultants). Plenum Pub.
--Theoretical Problems in Spectroscopy & Gas Dynamics of Lasers. (P. N. Lebedev Physics Institute Ser: Vol. 83). (Illus.). 232p. 1978. 45.00 (ISBN 0-306-10938-7, Consultants). Plenum Pub.
BCC Staff. The Expanding Laser Industry GB-050. 1978. text ed. 750.00 (ISBN 0-89336-172-0). BCC.
Beck, R. & Guers, K. Table of Laser Lines in Gases & Vapors. 2nd rev ed. LC 77-26659. (Springer Series in Optical Sciences: Vol. 2). 1978. 28.40 (ISBN 0-387-08603-X). Springer-Verlag.
Beesley, M. J. Lasers & Their Applications. 2nd ed. 1976. 30.95 (ISBN 0-470-15166-8). Halsted Pr.
Bennett. Atomic Gas Laser Transition Data. 1979. 75.00 (ISBN 0-306-65187-4). IFI Plenum.
Bennett, W. R., ed. The Physics of Gas Lasers. (Documents on Modern Physics Ser.). 1977. 35.75x (ISBN 0-677-03320-6). Gordon.
Ben-Shaul, A., et al. Lasers & Chemical Change. (Springer Ser. in Chemical Physics: Vol. 10). (Illus.). 497p. 1981. 49.90 (ISBN 0-387-10379-1). Springer-Verlag.
Bradley, D. J., et al. Ultra-Short Laser Pulses. (Phil. Strans. Ser. A: Vol. 298). (Illus.). 204p. 1981. text ed. 60.00x (ISBN 0-85403-147-2, Pub. by Royal Soc London). Scholium Intl.
Brewer, Richard G. & Mooradian, Aram, eds. Laser Spectroscopy. LC 74-12090. 671p. 1974. 49.50 (ISBN 0-306-30802-9, Plenum Pr). Plenum Pub.
Burroughs, William. Lasers. LC 77-88173. (Science in Action Ser.). 1977. 9.95x (ISBN 0-8448-1088-6). Crane-Russak Co.
Butler, J. K. Semiconductor Injection Lasers. LC 79-91615. 400p. 1980. 36.95 (ISBN 0-471-08156-6, Pub. by Wiley Interscience); pap. 24.00 (ISBN 0-471-08157-4). Wiley.
Butler, J. K., ed. Semiconductor Injection Lasers. LC 79-91615. 1980. 36.95 (ISBN 0-87942-129-0). Inst Electrical.
Casey, H. C., Jr. & Panish, M. B. Heterostructure Lasers, 2 pts. Incl. Pt. A. Fundamental Principles. 34.00 (ISBN 0-12-163101-X); Pt. B. Materials & Operating Characteristics. 42.00 (ISBN 0-12-163102-8). (Quantum Electronics Ser.). 1978. Acad Pr.
Charschan, S. S. Lasers in Industry. (Western Electric Ser.). 1972. 27.50x (ISBN 0-442-21516-9). Van Nos Reinhold.
Chu, Benjamin. Laser Light Scattering. 1974. 58.00 (ISBN 0-12-174550-3). Acad Pr.
CISM (International Center for Mechanical Sciences) Laser Cinematography of Explosions. Oppenheim, A. K. & Kamel, M. M., eds. (CISM Pubns. Ser.: No. 100). (Illus.). 226p. 1974. pap. 26.60 (ISBN 0-387-81179-6). Springer-Verlag.
Coherent Laser Divison of Coherent, Inc. Lasers: Operation; Equipment; Practical Application; Design. (Illus.). 1980. 21.50 (ISBN 0-07-011593-1). McGraw.
Colloquium on Electronic Transition Lasers, 4th, Munich, June 20-22, 1977. High-Power Lasers & Applications: Proceedings. Kompa, K. L. & Walter, H., eds. (Springer Ser. in Optical Sciences: Vol. 9). (Illus.). 1978. 31.30 (ISBN 0-387-08641-2). Springer-Verlag.
Critser, James R., Jr. Laser Manufacture & Technology 1973. Incl. 150.00 (ISBN 0-914428-18-7). (Ser. 6-73). 1974. Lexington Data.
--Laser Manufacture & Technology 1974. (Ser. 6-74). 1975. 200.00 (ISBN 0-914428-26-8). Lexington Data.
--Lasers: Equipment & Applications. (Ser. 6-78). Date not set. 300.00 (ISBN 0-914428-62-4). Lexington Data.
--Lasers: Equipment & Applications, 2 pts. Incl. No. 6AC-76. Part I-Apparatus & Components. 135.00 (ISBN 0-914428-42-X); No. 6AP-76. Part II-Applications. 125.00 (ISBN 0-914428-43-8). 1977. Set. 225.00 (ISBN 0-914428-53-5). Lexington Data.
--Lasers: Equipment & Applications, 2 pts. Incl. Pt. I. Apparatus & Components. (No. 6AC-77) (ISBN 0-914428-44-6); Pt. II. Applications. (No. 6AP-77) (ISBN 0-914428-45-4). (No. 6-77). 1978. Set. 260.00 (ISBN 0-914428-56-X). Lexington Data.
--Lasers: Equipment & Applications (1975) (Ser. No. 6-75). 1976. 225.00 (ISBN 0-914428-32-2). Lexington Data.
Crosley, David R., ed. Laser Probes for Combustion Chemistry. LC 80-17137. (ACS Symposium Ser.: No. 134). 1980. 44.50 (ISBN 0-8412-0570-1). Am Chemical.
Dainty, J. C., ed. Laser Speckle & Related Phenomena. (Topics in Applied Physics: Vol. 9). (Illus.). 250p. 1976. 51.70 (ISBN 0-387-07498-8). Springer-Verlag.
Dosanjh, Darshan S., ed. Modern Optical Methods in Gas Dynamic Research. LC 75-155352. 295p. 1971. 35.00 (ISBN 0-306-30537-2, Plenum Pr). Plenum Pub.
Drain, L. E. The Laser Doppler Technique. LC 79-40638. 1980. text ed. 55.52 (ISBN 0-471-27627-8, Pub. by Wiley-Interscience). Wiley.
Duley, W. W., ed. Carbon Dioxide Lasers: Effects & Applications. 1976. 58.00 (ISBN 0-12-223350-6). Acad Pr.
Durrani, Tariq S. & Greated, Clive A. Laser Systems in Flow Measurments. LC 76-26093. (Illus.). 289p. 1977. 32.50 (ISBN 0-306-30857-6, Plenum Pr). Plenum Pub.
Educational Research Council of America. Laser Project Engineer. Ferris, Theodore N. & Marchak, John P., eds. (Real People at Work: Series N). (Illus., Orig.). (gr. 5). 1976. pap. text ed. 2.25 (ISBN 0-89247-115-8). Changing Times.
The Expanding Laser Industry GB-050. 1981. 850.00 (ISBN 0-89336-253-0). BCC.
Fabian, M. E. Semiconductor Laser Diodes: A User's Handbook. 1980. 57.00x (ISBN 0-686-71789-9, Pub. by Electrochemical Scotland). State Mutual Bk.
Ferris, S. D., et al, eds. Laser-Solid Interactions & Laser Processing - Nineteen Seventy-Eight: Materials Research Society, Boston. LC 79-51564. (AIP Conference Proceedings Ser.: No. 50). (Illus.). 1979. lib. bdg. 26.00 (ISBN 0-88318-149-5). Am Inst Physics.
Francon, M. Laser Speckle & Application in Optics. LC 79-50215. 1979. 16.00 (ISBN 0-12-265760-8). Acad Pr.
Goldman, Leon. Third Conference on the Lasar, Vol. 267. (Annals of the New York Academy of Sciences). 481p. 1976. 55.00x (ISBN 0-89072-021-5). NY Acad Sci.
Goldman, Leon, Jr. Applications of the Laser. LC 73-89461. (Uniscience Ser.). 325p. 1973. 49.95 (ISBN 0-87819-028-7). CRC Pr.
Goodman, G. & Ross, M., eds. Laser Applications: Video Disc, Vol. 4. 1980. 32.00 (ISBN 0-12-431904-1). Acad Pr.
Gross, R. W. & Bott, J. F. Handbook of Chemical Lasers. 744p. 1976. 65.50 (ISBN 0-471-32804-9, Pub. by Wiley-Interscience). Wiley.
--Handbook of Chemical Lasers. LC 76-6865. 864p. 1976. 57.50 (ISBN 0-471-32804-9, Pub. by Wiley-Interscience). Wiley.
Guinares, W. O., et al, eds. Lasers & Applications: Proceedings. (Springer Series in Optical Sciences: Vol. 26). (Illus.). 337p. 1981. 34.00 (ISBN 0-387-10647-2). Springer-Verlag.
Hallmark, Clayton. Lasers, the Light Fantastic. (Illus.). 1979. 11.95 (ISBN 0-8306-9857-4); pap. 7.95 (ISBN 0-8306-1108-8, 1108). TAB Bks.
Harry, J. E. Industrial Lasers & Their Application. 1974. 29.50 (ISBN 0-07-084443-7, P&RB). McGraw.
Heard, H. G. Laser Parameter Measurements Handbook. 489p. 1968. text ed. 21.00 (ISBN 0-471-36665-X, Pub. by Wiley). Krieger.
Hieftje, Gary, ed. New Applications of Lasers to Chemistry. LC 78-22032. (ACS Symposium Ser.: No. 85). 1978. 23.50 (ISBN 0-8412-0459-4). Am Chemical.
High-Power Gas Lasers Nineteen Seventy-Five: Capri. (Institute of Physics Conference Ser.: No. 29). 1976. 57.50 (ISBN 0-9960030-8-8, Pub. by A Hilger England). Heyden.
Hora, Heinrich. Laser Plasmas & Nuclear Energy. LC 74-32287. 454p. 1975. 35.00 (ISBN 0-306-30785-5, Plenum Pr). Plenum Pub.
--Physics of Laser Driven Plasmas. LC 80-39792. 325p. 1981. 30.00 (ISBN 0-471-07880-8, Pub. by Wiley-Interscience). Wiley.
Houle, M. J., et al. Lasers in Analytical Chemistry. write for info. Pergamon.
House, William C., ed. Laser Beam Information Systems. 1978. text ed. 17.50 (ISBN 0-89433-049-7). Petrocelli.
International Meeting of the Societe de chimie physique, Thiais, 27th, 1975. Lasers in Physical Chemistry & Biophysics: Proceedings. Joussot-Dubien, J., ed. LC 75-29093. 1975. 80.50 (ISBN 0-444-41388-X). Elsevier.
International Symposium on Gas-Flow and Chemical Lasers, 2nd, Rhode-St-Genese, Belgium, Sept. 11-15, 1978. Gas-Flow & Chemical Lasers: Proceedings. new ed. Wendt, John F., ed. LC 79-12779. (Illus.). 608p. 1979. text ed. 49.50 (ISBN 0-89116-147-3). Hemisphere Pub.
Ishii, T. Koryu. Maser & Laser Engineering. LC 78-10694. 412p. 1980. lib. bdg. 22.50 (ISBN 0-88275-776-8). Krieger.
Johnson, Jim. Lasers. LC 80-17871. (A Look Inside Ser.). (Illus.). 48p. (gr. 4-12). 1981. PLB 12.50 (ISBN 0-8172-1400-3). Raintree Child.
Kamal, Ahmad K. Laser Abstracts, Vol. 1. LC 64-20745. 177p. 1964. 45.00 (ISBN 0-306-65106-8). IFI Plenum.
Kaminskii, A. Laser Crystals: Physics & Properties. 2nd,enl ed. Ivey, H. F., tr. (Springer Ser. in Optical Sciences: Vol. 14). (Illus.). 450p. 1980. 67.20 (ISBN 0-387-09576-4). Springer-Verlag.
Kazovsky, L. G. Transmission of Information in the Optical Waveband. LC 77-28102. 1978. 27.95 (ISBN 0-470-26294-X). Halsted Pr.
Kettelkamp, Larry. Lasers, the Miracle Light. LC 79-17486. (Illus.). 128p. (gr. 4-6). 1979. 6.95 (ISBN 0-688-22207-2); PLB 6.67 (ISBN 0-688-32207-7). Morrow.
Klein, H. Arthur. Masers & Lasers. LC 63-18676. (Introducing Modern Science Books Ser). (Illus.). (gr. 7-9). 1963. 7.95 (ISBN 0-397-30696-2, JBL-J). Har-Row.
Kock, Winston E. Engineering Applications of Lasers & Holography. LC 75-17507. (Optical Physics & Engineering Ser.). (Illus.). 400p. 1975. 29.50 (ISBN 0-306-30849-5, Plenum Pr). Plenum Pub.
--Lasers & Holography: An Introduction to Coherent Optics. rev. ed. (Illus.). 128p. 1981. pap. 3.50 (ISBN 0-486-24041-X). Dover.
Koechner, W. Solid-State Laser Engineering. LC 75-40054. (Springer Series in Optical Sciences). 1976. 51.80 (ISBN 0-387-90167-1). Springer-Verlag.
Kompa, K. L. Chemical Lasers. Boschke, F., ed. LC 51-5497. (Topics in Current Chemistry: Vol. 37). (Illus.). 120p. 1973. pap. 26.00 (ISBN 0-387-06099-5). Springer-Verlag.
Kompa, K. L. & Smith, S. D., eds. Laser-Induced Processes in Molecules: Physics & Chemistry. (Springer Series in Chemical Physics: Vol. 6). (Illus.). 1979. 37.00 (ISBN 0-387-09299-4). Springer-Verlag.
Kressel, H. & Butler, J. K. Semiconductor Lasers & LED's. 1977. 60.00 (ISBN 0-12-426250-3). Acad Pr.
Kursunoglu, Behram, et al, eds. Progress in Lasers & Laser Fusion. LC 75-16375. (Studies in the Natural Sciences: Vol. 8). 416p. 1975. 39.50 (ISBN 0-306-36908-7, Plenum Pr). Plenum Pub.
Lapp, Marshall & Penney, C. M., eds. Laser Raman Gas Diagnostics. LC 74-8800. 397p. 1974. 39.50 (ISBN 0-306-30800-2, Plenum Pr). Plenum Pub.
Laser Induced Damage in Optical Materials: 1979. (Special Technical Publications Ser.). 538p. 1980. softcover 9.50 (ISBN 0-686-76054-9, 726, 04-726000-46). ASTM.
Laser Induced Damage in Optical Materials: 1978. (Special Technical Publications Ser.). 329p. 1978. softcover 5.50 (ISBN 0-686-76056-5, 689, 04-689000-46). ASTM.
Laser Spectroscopy II: Proceedings of the Third International Conference,Jackson Lake Lodge, Wyoming, USA, July 4-8, 1977. (Springer Series in Optical Sciences: Vol. 7). (Illus.). 1977. 34.10 (ISBN 0-387-08543-2). Springer-Verlag.
Lengyel, Bela A. Lasers. 2nd ed. LC 77-139279. (Ser. in Pure & Applied Optics). 1971. 39.50 (ISBN 0-471-52620-7, Pub. by Wiley-Interscience). Wiley.
Levine, A. K. & De Maria, A., eds. Lasers: A Series of Advances, Vol. 3. 1971. 49.75 (ISBN 0-8247-1413-X). Dekker.
Levine, Albert K., ed. Lasers: A Series of Advances, Vol. 4. DeMaria, A. 352p. 1976. 39.75 (ISBN 0-8247-1410-5). Dekker.
Lewis, Bruce. What Is a Laser? LC 78-11100. (Skylight Bks.). (Illus.). (gr. 2-5). 1979. 5.95 (ISBN 0-396-07646-7). Dodd.
Losev, S. A. Gasdynamic Laser. (Springer Series in Chemical Physics: Vol. 12). (Illus.). 300p. 1981. 42.00 (ISBN 0-387-10503-4). Springer-Verlag.
Lyubevsky, Yu & Ovchinnikov, V. Solid State Laser Technology. 280p. 1975. 5.40 (ISBN 0-8285-0803-8, Pub. by Mir Pubs Russia). Imported Pubns.
McAleese, Frank G. The Laser Experimenter's Handbook. (Illus.). 1979. 10.95 (ISBN 0-8306-9770-5); pap. 6.95 (ISBN 0-8306-1123-1, 1123). TAB Bks.
Mallow, Alex & Chabot, Leon. Laser Safety Handbook. 1978. text ed. 24.50 (ISBN 0-442-25092-4). Van Nos Reinhold.
Marton, L., ed. Record of the Tenth Symposium on Electron, Ion, & Laser Beam Technology. LC 62-51780. (Illus.). 1969. 20.00 (ISBN 0-911302-08-5). San Francisco Pr.
Metzbower, Edward A., ed. Applications of Lasers in Materials Processing. 1979. 32.00 (ISBN 0-87170-084-0). ASM.
Mooradian, A., et al, eds. Tunable Lasers & Applications. (Optical Sciences Ser: Vol. 3). 1976. 33.10 (ISBN 0-387-07968-8). Springer-Verlag.
Moore, C. Bradley, ed. Chemical & Biochemical Applications of Lasers, Vol. 5. 1980. 23.00 (ISBN 0-12-505405-X). Acad Pr.
Motz, H. The Physics of Laser Fusion. 1979. 51.00 (ISBN 0-12-509350-0). Acad Pr.
Muncheryan, Hrand. Laser Technology. 2nd ed. LC 79-62989. 1979. 14.95 (ISBN 0-672-21588-8). Sams.
National Quantum Electronics Conference, 4th, Heriot-Watt University Edinburgh, 1979. Laser Advances & Applications Proceedings. Wherrett, B. S., ed. LC 80-40119. 278p. 1980. 45.00 (ISBN 0-471-27792-4). Wiley.
O'Shea, Donald C., et al. Introduction to Lasers & Their Applications. (Physics Ser.). 1977. text ed. 20.95 (ISBN 0-201-05509-0). A-W.
Pressley, Robert J. Handbook of Lasers, CRC: With Selected Data on Optical Technology. LC 72-163066. (Handbook Ser.). (Illus.). 631p. 1971. 49.95 (ISBN 0-87819-381-2). CRC Pr.
Raizer, Y. P., ed. Laser Induced Discharge Phenomena. (Illus.). 380p. 1977. 39.50 (ISBN 0-306-10923-9, Consultants). Plenum Pub.
Ratner, A. M. Spectral, Spatial, & Temporal Properties of Lasers. LC 76-167677. (Optical Physics & Engineering Ser). 220p. 1972. 25.00 (ISBN 0-306-30542-9, Plenum Pr). Plenum Pub.
Ready, John, ed. Lasers in Modern Industry. LC 79-66705. (Manufacturing Update Ser.). (Illus.). 1979. 29.00 (ISBN 0-87263-052-8). SME.
Ready, John F. Effects of High-Power Laser Radiation. 1971. 51.00 (ISBN 0-12-583950-2). Acad Pr.
Rhodes, C. K., ed. Excimer Lasers. (Topics in Applied Physics: Vol. 30). (Illus.). 1979. 31.20 (ISBN 0-387-09017-7). Springer-Verlag.
Rieck, Heinrich. Semi-Conductor Lasers. (Illus.). 133p. 1970. 18.95x (ISBN 0-8464-1133-4). Beekman Pubs.
Ross, D. Lasers, Light Amplifiers, & Oscillators. 1969. 108.00 (ISBN 0-12-598150-3). Acad Pr.
Ross, Monte, ed. Laser Applications, 3 vols. Vol. 1, 1971. 50.00 (ISBN 0-12-431901-7); Vol. 2, 1974. 50.00 (ISBN 0-12-431902-5); Vol. 3, 1977. 40.00 (ISBN 0-12-431903-3). Acad Pr.
Rykalin, N., et al. Laser Machinig and Welding. (Illus.). 1979. 48.00 (ISBN 0-08-022724-4). Pergamon.
Sargent, Murray, III, et al. Laser Physics. LC 74-5049. (Illus.). 1974. text ed. 30.50 (ISBN 0-201-06912-1, Adv Bk Prog); pap. text ed. 18.50 (ISBN 0-201-06913-X, Adv Bk Prog). A-W.
Schaefer, F. P., ed. Advances in Laser Chemistry: Proceedings of the Conference on Advances in Laser Chemistry, California Institute of Technology, Pasadena, USA, March 20-22, 1978. (Springer Ser. in Chemical Physics: Vol. 3). (Illus.). 1978. 29.80 (ISBN 0-387-08997-7). Springer-Verlag.
--Dye Lasers. 2nd.rev ed. (Topics in Applied Physics: Vol.1p). (Illus.). 1977. pap. 22.90 (ISBN 0-387-08470-3). Springer-Verlag.
Siegman, A. E. Introduction to Lasers & Masers. 1971. text ed. 29.50 (ISBN 0-07-057362-X, C); solutions manual 2.50 (ISBN 0-07-057368-9). McGraw.
Sixth European Conference on Optical Communication. (IEE Conference Publication Ser.: No. 190). (Illus.). 466p. (Orig.). 1980. soft cover 73.00 (ISBN 0-85296-223-1). Inst Elect Eng.
Skolbel'tsyn, D. V., ed. Physical Processes in Lasers. LC 72-94826. (P. N. Lebedev Physics Institute Ser.: Vol. 56). (Illus.). 181p. 1973. 35.00 (ISBN 0-306-10884-4, Consultants). Plenum Pub.
--Quantum Electronics in Lasers & Masers, Pt. 1. LC 68-13059. (P. N. Lebedev Physics Institute Ser.: Vol. 31). (Illus.). 161p. 1968. 32.50 (ISBN 0-306-10800-3, Consultants). Plenum Pub.
Smith, Kenneth & Thompson, R. M. Computer Modeling of Gas Lasers. (Optical Physics & Engineering Ser.). (Illus.). 432p. 1978. 42.50 (ISBN 0-306-31099-6, Plenum Pr). Plenum Pub.

Smith, William V. Laser Applications. LC 71-119912. (Modern Frontiers in Applied Science). (Illus.). 200p. 1970. 26.00 (ISBN 0-89006-001-0). Artech Hse.

Society of Photo-Optical Instrumentation Engineers, Seminar. Impact of Lasers in Spectroscopy: Proceedings, Vol. 49. 1975. 11.00 (ISBN 0-89252-061-2). Photo-Optical.

Sona. Lasers & Their Applications. 1976. 82.00x (ISBN 0-677-15030-X). Gordon.

Steele, Earl L. Optical Lasers in Electronics. (Pure & Applied Optics Ser). (Illus.). 267p. 1968. text ed. 13.50 (ISBN 0-471-82084-9, Pub. by Wiley). Krieger.

Steinfeld, J. I., ed. Laser & Coherence Spectroscopy. (Illus.). 548p. 1978. 45.00 (ISBN 0-306-31027-9, Plenum Pr). Plenum Pub.

Steinfeld, Jeffrey I., ed. Electronic Transition Lasers. LC 76-4504. 300p. 1976. text ed. 20.00x (ISBN 0-262-19146-6). MIT Pr.

--Laser-Induced Chemical Processes. 255p. 1981. 32.50 (ISBN 0-306-40587-3, Plenum Pr). Plenum Pub.

Stitch, M. L., ed. Laser Handbook. 846p. 1979. 122.00 (ISBN 0-444-85271-9, North Holland). Elsevier.

Strobehn, J. W., ed. Laser Beam Propagation in the Atmosphere. (Topics in Applied Physics: Vol. 25). (Illus.). 1978. 58.40 (ISBN 0-387-08812-1). Springer-Verlag.

Svelto, Orazio. Principles of Lasers. (Illus.). 376p. 1976. 25.00 (ISBN 0-306-30860-6, Plenum Pr). Plenum Pub.

Thompson, H. Doyle & Stevenson, Warren H., eds. Laser Velocimetry & Particle Sizing: Proceedings. new ed. LC 79-59. (Illus.). 1979. text ed. 56.95 (ISBN 0-89116-150-3). Hemisphere Pub.

Thomson, J., et al. Frequency Conversion. (Wykeham Technology Ser.: No. 1). 1969. 9.95x (ISBN 0-8448-1172-6). Crane Russak Co.

Thornley, R. F., ed. Record of the Eleventh Symposium on Electron, Ion, & Laser Beam Technology. LC 62-51780. (Illus.). 1971. 25.00 (ISBN 0-911302-17-4). San Francisco Pr.

Thyagarajan, K. & Ghatak, A. K. Lasers: Theory & Applications. (Optical Physics & Engineering). 424p. 1981. text ed. 39.50 (ISBN 0-306-40598-9, Plenum Pr). Plenum Pub.

Townes, C. H. & Miles, P. A., eds. Quantum Electronics & Coherent Light. (Italian Physical Society: Course 31). 1965. 55.00 (ISBN 0-12-368831-0). Acad Pr.

Unger, H. G. Introduction to Quantum Electronics. LC 76-86534. 1970. 19.50 (ISBN 0-08-006368-3). Pergamon.

Vanier, Jacques. Basic Theory of Lasers & Masers: A Density Matrix Approach. Montroll, E. W., et al, eds. (Documents on Modern Physics Ser.). (Illus.). 128p. 1971. 29.25x (ISBN 0-677-30340-8). Gordon.

Verdeyen, Joseph T. Laser Electronics. (Illus.). 480p. 1981. 32.95 (ISBN 0-13-485201-X). P-H.

Wacker, Charles H. Lasers: How They Work. new ed. (How It Works Ser.). (Illus.). 96p. (gr. 6 up). 1973. PLB 4.79 (ISBN 0-399-60841-9). Putnam.

Watrasiewicz, B. M. & Rudd, M. J. Laser Doppler Measurements. 256p. 1975. 16.95 (ISBN 0-408-70684-8). Butterworth.

Weber, Joseph, ed. Lasers, 2 Vols. (International Science Review Ser). 1968. Vol. 1. 117.25 (ISBN 0-677-00880-5); Vol. 2. 117.25 (ISBN 0-677-00890-2). Gordon.

White, C. W. & Peercy, P. S., eds. Laser & Electron Beam Processing of Materials. 1980. 40.00 (ISBN 0-12-746850-1). Acad Pr.

Willet, C. S. Gas Lasers. 1974. text ed. 90.00 (ISBN 0-08-017803-0). Pergamon.

Wilson, Leroy E., et al, eds. Electronic Transition Lasers II. LC 77-688. 1977. text ed. 25.00x (ISBN 0-262-23084-4). MIT Pr.

Wolbarsht, Myron L., ed. Laser Applications in Medicine & Biology. Incl. Vol. 1. 288p. 1971. 29.50 (ISBN 0-306-37161-8); Vol. 2. 404p. 1974. 37.50 (ISBN 0-306-37162-6); Vol. 3. 348p. 1977. 32.50 (ISBN 0-306-37163-4). LC 77-128514. (Illus., Plenum Pr). Plenum Pub.

Yariv, A. Introduction to Optical Electronics. 2nd ed. LC 76-11773. 1976. text ed. 28.95 (ISBN 0-03-089892-7, HoltC). HR&W.

LASERS–BIBLIOGRAPHY

Ross, D. Lasers, Light Amplifiers, & Oscillators. 1969. 108.00 (ISBN 0-12-598150-3). Acad Pr.

Tomiyasu, Kiyo. Laser Literature: An Annotated Guide. LC 68-21474. 172p. 1968. 27.50 (ISBN 0-306-30335-3, Plenum Pr). Plenum Pub.

LASERS IN MEDICINE

Brown, D. C. High Peak Power Nd: Class Laser Systems. (Springer Series in Optical Sciences: Vol. 25). (Illus.). 276p. 1981. 44.00 (ISBN 0-387-10516-6). Springer-Verlag.

Goldman, L., ed. The Biomedical Laser: Technology & Clinical Applications. (Illus.). 350p. 1981. 39.80 (ISBN 0-387-90571-5). Springer-Verlag.

Goldman, Leon. Laser Cancer Research. (Recent Results in Cancer Research: Vol. 4). (Illus.). 1966. 11.80 (ISBN 0-387-03643-1). Springer-Verlag.

Goldman, Leon & Rockwell, James R., Jr. Lasers in Medicine. LC 77-163181. (Illus.). 394p. 1971. 72.75x (ISBN 0-677-02430-4). Gordon.

Hieftje, Gary M., et al, eds. Lasers in Chemical Analysis. LC 80-84082. (Contemporary Instrumentation & Analysis). (Illus.). 352p. 1981. 39.50 (ISBN 0-89603-027-X). Humana.

Hillenkamp, F., et al, eds. Lasers in Biology & Medicine. (NATO Advanced Study Institute Ser.-Series A-Life Sciences: Vol. 34). 450p. 1981. 49.50 (ISBN 0-306-40470-2, Plenum Pr). Plenum Pub.

Koebner, Hans K. Lasers in Medicine, Vol. 1. LC 79-40525. 274p. 1980. 112.00 (ISBN 0-471-27602-2, Pub. by Wiley-Interscience). Wiley.

McGuff, Paul E. Surgical Applications of Laser. (Illus.). 224p. 1966. photocopy ed. spiral 21.50 (ISBN 0-398-01259-8). C C Thomas.

Pratesi, R. & Sacchi, C. A., eds. Lasers in Photomedicine & Photobiology: Proceedings. (Springer Series in Optical Sciences: Vol. 22). (Illus.). 235p. 1980. 29.50 (ISBN 0-387-10178-0). Springer-Verlag.

Schwartz, Helmut J. & Hora, Heinrich, eds. Laser Interaction & Related Plasma Phenomena. Incl. Vol. 1. 509p. 1970. 45.00 (ISBN 0-306-37141-3); Vol. 2. 385p. 1972. 45.00 (ISBN 0-306-37142-1); Vol. 3A. 396p. 1974. 42.50 (ISBN 0-306-37143-X); Vol. 3B. 551p. 1974. 42.50 (ISBN 0-306-37150-2); Vol. 4A. 602p. 1977. 39.50 (ISBN 0-306-37144-8); Vol. 4B. 559p. 1977. 39.50 (ISBN 0-306-37154-5). LC 79-135851. (Illus., Plenum Pr). Plenum Pub.

Schwarz, H. J., et al, eds. Laser Interaction & Related Plasma Phenomena, Vol. 5. 800p. 1981. 75.00 (ISBN 0-306-40545-8, Plenum Pr). Plenum Pub.

Sliney, David & Wolbarsht, Myron. Safety with Lasers & Other Optical Sources: A Comprehensive Handbook. 1060p. 1980. 49.50 (ISBN 0-306-40434-6, Plenum Pr). Plenum Pub.

Wolbarsht, Myron L., ed. Laser Applications in Medicine & Biology. Incl. Vol. 1. 288p. 1971. 29.50 (ISBN 0-306-37161-8); Vol. 2. 404p. 1974. 37.50 (ISBN 0-306-37162-6); Vol. 3. 348p. 1977. 32.50 (ISBN 0-306-37163-4). LC 77-128514. (Illus., Plenum Pr). Plenum Pub.

LASHIS

see Moso (Tribe)

LASKER, EMANUEL, 1868-1941

Reinfeld, F. & Fine, R. Lasker's Greatest Chess Games 1889-1914. Orig. Title: Doctor Lasker's Chess Career. (Illus.). 4.50 (ISBN 0-8446-2790-9). Peter Smith.

Reinfeld, Fred & Fine, Reuben, eds. Lasker's Greatest Chess Games, 1889-1914. Orig. Title: Dr. (Lasker's Chess Career). 1965. pap. 2.75 (ISBN 0-486-21450-8). Dover.

LASKI, HAROLD JOSEPH, 1893-1950

Deane, Herbert A. The Political Ideas of Harold J. Laski. LC 70-179574. xii, 370p. 1972. Repr. of 1955 ed. 21.50 (ISBN 0-208-01234-6, Archon). Shoe String.

Gupta, Ram C. Harold J. Laski: A Critical Analysis of His Political Ideas. 1966. 5.00x (ISBN 0-8426-1290-4). Verry.

Magid, Henry M. English Political Pluralism: The Problem of Freedom & Organization. LC 41-15264. Repr. of 1941 ed. 12.45 (ISBN 0-404-04149-3). AMS Pr.

Zylstra, Bernard. From Pluralism to Collectivism: The Development of Harold Laski's Political Thought. 1968. pap. text ed. 9.00x (ISBN 0-391-01979-1). Humanities.

LASSALLE, FERDINAND JOHANN GOTTLIEB, 1825-1864

Bernstein, Eduard. Ferdinand Lassalle As a Social Reformer. Aveling, Eleanor M., tr. LC 69-13824. Repr. of 1893 ed. lib. bdg. 15.00x (ISBN 0-8371-0971-X, BEFL). Greenwood.

Bernstein, Edward. Ferdinand Lassalle As a Social Reformer. Aveling, Eleanor Marx, tr. from Ger. LC 74-131631. 1970. Repr. of 1893 ed. 11.00 (ISBN 0-403-00518-3). Scholarly.

Brandes, Georg M. Ferdinand Lassalle. LC 76-97832. Repr. of 1911 ed. lib. bdg. 15.00x (ISBN 0-8371-2800-5, BRFL). Greenwood.

Footman, David. Ferdinand Lassalle, Romantic Revolutionary. LC 70-90145. Repr. of 1947 ed. lib. bdg. 15.00x (ISBN 0-8371-2202-3, FOFL). Greenwood.

LASSEN VOLCANIC NATIONAL PARK

Schaffer, Jeffery P. Lassen Volcanic National Park. Winnett, Thomas, ed. LC 80-53681. (Illus.). 224p. (Orig.). 1981. pap. 9.95 (ISBN 0-89997-004-4). Wilderness.

LASSO

Byers, Chester. Cowboy Roping & Rope Tricks. 1928. pap. 2.00 (ISBN 0-486-21535-0). Dover.

Kramer, William J. Bola Tie: Symbol of the West. LC 78-51854. (Illus., Orig.). pap. 3.95 (ISBN 0-87358-172-5). Northland.

LASSWELL, HAROLD DWIGHT, 1902-

Rogow, Arnold A., ed. Politics, Personality & Social Science in the Twentieth Century: Essays in Honor of Harold D. Lasswell. LC 76-75812. 1969. 21.00x (ISBN 0-226-72399-2). U of Chicago Pr.

LAST JUDGMENT

see Judgment Day

LAST RITES (SACRAMENTS)

see Extreme Unction

LAST SACRAMENTS

see Extreme Unction

LAST SUPPER

Here are entered works on the final meal of Christ with his apostles when the sacrament of the Lord's Supper was instituted.

see also Lord's Supper

Badia, Leonard F. The Dead Sea People's Sacred Meal & Jesus' Last Supper. LC 79-66231. 1979. pap. text ed. 6.50 (ISBN 0-8191-0807-3). U Pr of Amer.

Daughters of St. Paul. Living & Growing Through the Eucharist. 1976. 7.00 (ISBN 0-8198-0432-0); pap. 6.00 (ISBN 0-8198-0433-9). Dghtrs St Paul.

Lussier, Ernest. Christ's Farewell Discourse. LC 79-19798. 90p. (Orig.). 1980. pap. 3.95 (ISBN 0-8189-0394-5). Alba.

Marshall, I. Howard. Last Supper & Lord's Supper. (Orig.). 1981. pap. 6.95 (ISBN 0-8028-1854-4). Eerdmans.

Reumann, John, et al. Holy Communion: The Lord's Supper in Changing Times. LC 79-8901. Date not set. pap. price not set (ISBN 0-8006-1382-1, 1-1382). Fortress.

LAST WORDS

Bega. Last Words of Famous Men (1930) LC 73-405. 1973. lib. bdg. 10.00 (ISBN 0-8414-1378-9). Folcroft.

Brandreth, Gyles. The Last Word. LC 79-65075. 1979. 7.95 (ISBN 0-8069-0172-1); lib. bdg. 7.49 (ISBN 0-8069-0173-X). Sterling.

Coppock, Thomas. The Genuine Dying Speech of the Reverend Parson Coppock, Pretended Bishop of Carlisle: Who Was Drawn, Hanged & Quartered There, Oct. 18, 1746, for High Treason & Rebellion, Etc. LC 80-2477. Repr. of 1746 ed. 23.50 (ISBN 0-404-19109-6). AMS Pr.

Lockyer, Herbert. Last Words of Saints & Sinners. LC 78-85429. 1975. pap. 4.50 (ISBN 0-8254-3111-5). Kregel.

Marvin, F. R. The Last Words of Distinguished Men & Women. 59.95 (ISBN 0-8490-0488-8). Gordon Pr.

Slater, Scott & Solomita, Alec. Exits: Dying Words & Last Moments. 1980. 7.95 (ISBN 0-525-93070-1). Dutton.

LASTS (SHOES)

see Boots and Shoes

LASUEN, FERMIN FRANCISCO, 1736-1803

Guest, Francis F. Fermin Francisco De Lasuen: A Biography. (Monograph Ser.). (Illus.). 1973. 25.00 (ISBN 0-88382-059-5). AAFH.

LATERALITY

see also Left- and Right-Handedness

Dimond, Stuart J. & Blizard, David, eds. Evolution & Lateralization of the Brain, Vol. 299. (Annals of the New York Academy of Sciences). 501p. 1977. 40.00x (ISBN 0-89072-045-2). NY Acad Sci.

Kinsbourne, M., ed. Asymmetrical Function of the Brain. LC 77-8633. (Illus.). 1978. 39.50 (ISBN 0-521-21481-5). Cambridge U Pr.

LATERITE

Evans, D. J., et al, eds. International Laterite Symposium. LC 78-73974. (Illus.). 1979. text ed. 30.00x (ISBN 0-89520-255-7). Soc Mining Eng.

Gidigasu, M. D. Laterite Soil Engineering Pedogenesis & Engineering Principles. (Developments in Geotechnical Engineering: Vol. 9). 1976. 117.00 (ISBN 0-444-41283-2). Elsevier.

McFarlane, J. M. Laterite & Landscape. 1977. 26.50 (ISBN 0-12-484450-2). Acad Pr.

Maignien, R. Review of Research on Laterites. 1966. pap. 7.50 (ISBN 92-3-100623-1, U556, UNESCO). Unipub.

Persons, Benjamin S. Laterite: Genesis, Location, Use. LC 73-107541. (Monographs in Geoscience Ser.). 103p. 1970. 24.50 (ISBN 0-306-30450-3, Plenum Pr). Plenum Pub.

LATHES

see also Turning

Bradley, Ian. The Grinding Machine. (Illus.). 135p. 1973. 7.50x (ISBN 0-85242-324-1). Intl Pubns Serv.

--Myford ML Ten Lathe Manual. (Illus.). 124p. 1972. 7.50x (ISBN 0-85242-545-7). Intl Pubns Serv.

Engineering Industry Training Board, ed. Training for Capstan, Turret, & Sequence Controlled Lathe Setters & Operators, 21 vols. (Illus.). 1973. Set. 39.95x (ISBN 0-89563-023-0). Intl Ideas.

Know Your Lathe. 1977. 10.00x (ISBN 0-85242-557-0). Intl Pubns Serv.

Krar, S. F. & Oswald, J. W. Turning Technology: Engine & Turret Lathes. LC 78-153723. 1971. pap. text ed. 11.60 (ISBN 0-8273-0206-1); instructor's guide 1.60 (ISBN 0-8273-0207-X). Delmar.

Laidlaw-Dickson, D. J. The Book of the Unimat. LC 79-300391. (Illus.). 128p. (Orig.). 1977. pap. 9.50x (ISBN 0-85242-591-0). Intl Pubns Serv.

Mason, L. C. Building a Small Lathe. (Illus.). 82p. 1979. 7.50x (ISBN 0-85242-687-9). Intl Pubns Serv.

Mason, Leonard C. Using the Small Lathe. (Illus.). 112p. 8.50x (ISBN 0-85344-058-1). Intl Pubns Serv.

Milling & Lathe Cutting Tools. (Machinee Tool Ser.: Vol. 5). 1974. pap. text ed. 3.95 (ISBN 0-88462-246-0). Ed Methods.

Tingey, Rex. Making the Most of the Unimat. (Illus., Orig.). 1979. pap. 11.25x (ISBN 0-85242-676-3). Intl Pubns Serv.

Westbury, E. T. Lathe Accessories. 112p. 1964. 7.50x (ISBN 0-85344-100-6). Intl Pubns Serv.

--Metal Turning Lathes: Their Design, Application & Operation. 154p. 1967. 9.50x (ISBN 0-85344-102-2). Intl Pubns Serv.

--Milling in the Lathe. 1967. 6.50x (ISBN 0-85344-101-4). Intl Pubns Serv.

LATHYRUS

Hitchcock, C. Leo. Revision of the North American Species of Lathyrus. LC 53-9615. (Publications in Biology Ser.: No. 15). (Illus.). 104p. 1952. pap. 5.00 (ISBN 0-295-73913-4). U of Wash Pr.

LATIMER, HUGH, BP, OF WORCESTER, 1485-1555

Chester, Allan G. Hugh Latimer, Apostle to the English. 1978. Repr. of 1954 ed. lib. bdg. 15.00x (ISBN 0-374-91492-3). Octagon.

Latimer, Hugh. Selected Sermons of Hugh Latimer. Chester, Allan G., ed. (Documents Ser). 1978. 16.00x (ISBN 0-918016-43-6). Folger Bks.

LATIN AMERICA

see also names of Latin-American countries and geographic areas of Latin America, e.g. Brazil; Caribbean Area; South America; names of cities, towns, and geographic areas in specific countries

Bartley, Russell H., ed. Soviet Historians on Latin America: Recent Scholarly Contributions. LC 77-53648. 364p. 1978. 25.00 (ISBN 0-299-07250-9). U of Wis Pr.

Beaulac, Willard L. The Fractured Continent: Latin America in Close-Up. LC 78-70885. (Publication Ser.: No. 225). (Illus.). 252p. 1980. 11.95 (ISBN 0-8179-7251-X). Hoover Inst Pr.

Brett, Robert & Brett, Patricia. Hispanoamerica One: Al Sur Del Ecuador. LC 78-15378. 1978. pap. 3.75 (ISBN 0-88436-496-8, SP-226051). EMC.

Cline, Howard F., compiled by. Historians of Latin America in the United States, 1965: Bibliographies of 680 Specialists. LC 66-22589. 1966. 9.00 (ISBN 0-8223-0036-2). Duke.

Considine, John J. New Horizons in Latin America. facs. ed. LC 74-93330. (Essay Index Reprint Ser). 1958. 25.00 (ISBN 0-8369-1561-5). Arno.

Cosio Villegas, Daniel. American Extremes. Paredes, Americo, tr. from Span. LC 64-11188. (Texas Pan American Ser.). Orig. Title: Extremos de America. 243p. 1964. pap. 4.95x (ISBN 0-292-70069-5). U of Tex Pr.

Cox, Barbara G., ed. Hispanic American Periodicals Index 1975. LC 75-642408. 1978. lib. bdg. 75.00x (ISBN 0-87903-400-9). UCLA Lat Am Ctr.

Cozean, Jon D. Latin America 1979. 11th ed. (Illus.). 1977. pap. 2.75 (ISBN 0-686-23396-4). Stryker-Post.

Douglas, William O. Holocaust or Hemispheric Co-Op: Crosscurrents in Latin America. 1971. 7.95 (ISBN 0-394-46272-6). Random.

Garcia-Calderon, F. Latin America: Its Rise & Progress. Miall, B., tr. 1977. lib. bdg. 59.95 (ISBN 0-8490-2131-6). Gordon Pr.

Griffin, Charles C., ed. Concerning Latin American Culture. LC 66-27089. 1967. Repr. of 1940 ed. 7.50 (ISBN 0-8462-0841-5). Russell.

Hanke, Lewis. Modern Latin America, Continent in Ferment, Vol. 2, South America. 2nd ed. (Orig.). 1967. pap. 4.95x (ISBN 0-442-04002-4, 46, Anv). Van Nos Reinhold.

Haverstock, Nathan A., ed. Handbook of Latin American Studies: 1957-1958. LC 36-32633. (Latin American Studies Ser.: Vol. 22). 25.00x (ISBN 0-8130-0107-2). U Presses Fla.

Helms, Mary W. Asang: Adaptations to Culture Contact in a Miskito Community. LC 70-630257. (Illus.). 1971. 11.00 (ISBN 0-8130-0298-2). U Presses Fla.

Hirschman, A. O. Latin American Issues: Essays & Comments. (Twentieth Century Fund Ser.). 1961. pap. 4.00 (ISBN 0-527-02821-5). Kraus Repr.

Inman, Samuel G. Latin America: Its Place in World Life. rev. ed. LC 72-5674. (Essay Index Reprint Ser.). 1972. Repr. of 1942 ed. 25.00 (ISBN 0-8369-2993-4). Arno.

Knight, Thomas J. Latin America Comes of Age. LC 79-18702. 335p. 1979. 19.00 (ISBN 0-8108-1243-6). Scarecrow.

Koebel, W. H. Romance of the River Plate, 2 vols. (Latin America Ser.). 1979. Set. lib. bdg. 200.00 (ISBN 0-8490-3002-1). Gordon Pr.

Lamb, Ruth S. America Latina: Contrastes e Confrontos. (Port.). 1973. pap. 4.00 (ISBN 0-912434-05-8). Ocelot Pr.

Lara-Braud, Jorge, ed. Our Claim on the Future: A Controversial Collection from Latin America. (Orig.). 1970. pap. 1.95 (ISBN 0-377-10071-4). Friend Pr.

Latin American Conference on the Conservation of Renewable Natural Resources. 1968. pap. 20.00x (ISBN 2-88032-049-6, IUCN25, IUCN). Unipub.

Martin, Dolores M., ed. Handbook of Latin American Studies: 1977, Social Sciences. LC 36-32633. (Latin American Studies Ser.: Vol. 39). 40.00x (ISBN 0-8130-0600-7). U Presses Fla.

Martin, Dolores M. & Stewart, Donald E., eds. Handbook of Latin Studies: 1976, Humanities. LC 36-32633. (Handbook of Latin American Studies: No. 38). 1976. 40.00x (ISBN 0-8130-0568-X). U Presses Fla.

Miami University - Hispanic American Institute. University of Miami Hispanic-American Studies. facs. ed. McNicoll, R. E. & Owre, J. R., eds. LC 70-117825. (Essay Index Reprint Ser). 1941. 18.00 (ISBN 0-8369-1997-1). Arno.

Mullen, E. Encuentro: Ensayos Sobre Hispanoamerica. LC 73-17222. 1974. pap. text ed. 8.95 (ISBN 0-03-005636-5, HoltC). HR&W.

Owen, J. I., ed. Infantry Weapons of the Armies of Africa, the Orient & Latin America. 196p. 1980. pap. 22.50 (ISBN 0-08-027017-4). Pergamon.

Pacific Coast Council on Latin American Studies. Changing Perspectives on Latin America: Proceedings, Vol. 3. Cunniff, Roger, ed. 1974. pap. 7.00x (ISBN 0-916304-17-5). Campanile.

--New Directions in the Teaching & Research of Latin American Studies: Proceedings, Vol. 2. 1973. pap. 7.00x (ISBN 0-916304-14-0). Campanile.

Paddington Press. Latin America Business Travel Guide. 448p. 1981. 19.95 (ISBN 0-87196-339-6); pap. 11.95 (ISBN 0-87196-345-0). Facts on File.

Remmer, Karen L. & Merkx, Gilbert W., eds. New Perspectives on Latin America: Political Conflict & Social Change. 298p. 1976. pap. text ed. 14.50x (ISBN 0-8422-0533-0). Irvington.

Reyes, Alfonso. Position of America & Other Essays. facs. ed. De Onis, Harriet, tr. LC 77-142690. (Essay Index Reprint Ser). 1950. 15.00 (ISBN 0-8369-2067-8). Arno.

Rippy, James F. Latin America & the Industrial Age. 2nd ed. LC 70-136082. (Illus.). 1971. Repr. of 1947 ed. lib. bdg. 17.50x (ISBN 0-8371-5232-1, RIAM). Greenwood.

Sable, Martin H. A Guide to Nonprint Materials for Latin American Studies. LC 78-24476. 1979. 16.50 (ISBN 0-87917-066-2). Blaine Ethridge.

Schroeder, Richard. Latin America. Woy, Jean, ed. 400p. Date not set. pap. text ed. price not set (ISBN 0-87187-217-X). Congr Quarterly.

Stearman, Allyn M. San Rafael: Camba Town. LC 73-15730. (Latin American Monographs Series Two: No. 12). xvi, 128p. 1973. 7.50 (ISBN 0-8130-0388-1). U Presses Fla.

Stewart, Donald E., ed. Handbook of Latin American Studies: Humanities 1967-1972. LC 36-32633. (Latin American Studies: No. 34). 624p. 1972. 35.00x (ISBN 0-8130-0376-8). U Presses Fla.

--Handbook of Latin American Studies: Social Sciences, 1966-1971. LC 36-32633. (Latin American Studies Ser: Vol. 33). x, 542p. 1971. 35.00x (ISBN 0-8130-0355-5). U Presses Fla.

Szulc, Tad. Latin America. LC 65-27528. (New York Times Byline Books). (Orig.). 1966. pap. 2.95 (ISBN 0-689-10266-6). Atheneum.

Tulchin, Joseph S., ed. Latin America in the Year Two-Thousand. LC 74-19702. 408p. 1975. text ed. 14.95 (ISBN 0-201-07603-9). A-W.

Vasena, Adalbert K. & Pazos, Javier. Latin America: A Broader World Role. 207p. 1973. 15.00x (ISBN 0-87471-424-9). Rowman.

Whitaker, Arthur P., ed. Latin America & the Enlightenment. 2nd ed. 156p. 1961. pap. 3.95 (ISBN 0-8014-9054-5, CP54). Cornell U Pr.

Wilcox, M. Encyclopedia of Latin America, 2 vols. 1976. lib. bdg. 250.00 (ISBN 0-8490-1765-3). Gordon Pr.

Wilgus, A. Curtis, ed. Modern Hispanic America. LC 73-123489. 1971. Repr. of 1933 ed. 25.00x (ISBN 0-8046-1376-1). Kennikat.

Willems, Emilio. Latin American Culture: An Anthropological Synthesis. 384p. 1975. text ed. 22.50 scp (ISBN 0-06-047118-2, HarpC). Har-Row.

Zea, Leopoldo. Latin America & the World. Hendricks, Frances K. & Berler, Beatrice, trs. 1969. 7.95x (ISBN 0-8061-0846-0). U of Okla Pr.

LATIN AMERICA–ANTIQUITIES

Goldschmidt, Walter & Hoijer, Harry, eds. Social Anthropology of Latin America: Essays in Honor of Ralph Leon Beals. LC 70-627663. (Latin American Studies Ser.: Vol. 14). 1970. 12.00 (ISBN 0-87903-014-3). UCLA Lat Am Ctr.

Hardoy, Jorge. Urban Planning in Pre-Columbian America. LC 68-24700. (Planning & Cities Ser). (Illus.). 1968. 7.95 (ISBN 0-8076-0466-6); pap. 3.95 (ISBN 0-8076-0470-4). Braziller.

Kubler, George. The Art and Architecture of Ancient America. 2nd ed. (Pelican History of Art Ser.: No. 21). (Illus.). 1976. 50.00 (ISBN 0-670-13377-9, Pelican). Viking Pr.

LATIN AMERICA–BIBLIOGRAPHY

Adams, Henry E., ed. Handbook of Latin American Studies: Humanities 1965-1966. LC 36-32633. (Latin American Studies Ser: Vol. 30). 1968. 30.00x (ISBN 0-8130-0266-4). U Presses Fla.

--Handbook of Latin American Studies: Social Sciences 1963-1969. LC 36-32633. (Latin American Studies Ser: No. 31). 1969. 35.00x (ISBN 0-8130-0294-X). U Presses Fla.

--Handbook of Latin American Studies: Social Sciences 1962-64. LC 36-32633. (Latin American Studies Ser: Vol. 29). 1967. 30.00x (ISBN 0-8130-0001-7). U Presses Fla.

Aguilera, Francisco, ed. Handbook of Latin American Studies, Vols. 15-20. 1968. lib. bdg. 30.00 ea. Octagon.

--Handbook of Latin American Studies: 1948. LC 36-32633. (Latin American Studies Ser: Vol. 14). 1951. 20.00x (ISBN 0-8130-0003-3). U Presses Fla.

Aguilera, Francisco & Shelby, Charmion, eds. Handbook of Latin American Studies. LC 36-32633. (Latin American Studies Ser: Vols. 12 & 13). 1949. Vol. 12, 1946. 17.50x (ISBN 0-8130-0004-1); Vol. 13, 1947. 20.00x (ISBN 0-8130-0005-X). U Presses Fla.

Bayitch, Stojan A., ed. Latin America & the Caribbean: A Bibliographical Guide to Works in English. LC 67-28900. 1967. 45.00 (ISBN 0-379-00397-X). Oceana.

Bibliografia Selective De Administracion Publica Para la America Latina. (Span.). 1967. pap. 1.00 (ISBN 0-8270-6505-1). OAS.

Bingaman, Joseph W. Latin America: A Survey of Holdings at the Hoover Institution on War, Revolution & Peace. LC 78-142949. (Library Survey Ser.: No. 5). 96p. 1972. pap. 3.00x (ISBN 0-8179-5052-4). Hoover Inst Pr.

Boston Public Library. Catalogue of the Spanish Library, & of the Portuguese Books Bequeathed by George Ticknor to the Boston Public Library. 1970. lib. bdg. 50.00 (ISBN 0-8161-0865-X). G K Hall.

California University Library. Spain & Spanish America in the Libraries of the University of California, 2 vols. LC 68-56591. (Bibliography & Reference Ser.: No. 115). 1968. Repr. of 1928 ed. Set. 80.50 (ISBN 0-8337-4020-2). B Franklin.

Cardona, Francisco J. & Cardona, Maria E. Handbook of Latin American Studies, Author Index to Numbers 1-28. LC 36-32633. 1968. 32.50x (ISBN 0-8130-0265-6). U Presses Fla.

Catalog of the Latin American Collection, University of Florida Libraries, First Supplement, 7 vols. 1980. lib. bdg. 950.00 (ISBN 0-8161-1090-5). G K Hall.

Chaffee, Wilber A., Jr. & Griffin, Honor M. Dissertations on Latin America by U. S. Historians, 1960-1970: A Bibliography. (Ilas Guides & Bibliographies Ser.: No. 7). 74p. 1973. pap. 2.50x (ISBN 0-292-71503-X). U of Tex Pr.

Chilcote, Ronald H. Revolution & Structural Change in Latin America, 2 Vols. LC 68-28100. (Bibliographical Ser.: No. 40). 1970. Set. 40.00 (ISBN 0-8179-2401-9). Hoover Inst Pr.

Columbus Memorial Library - Pan American Union, Washington, D. C. Index to Latin American Periodicals, 2 vols. 55.00 ea. Vol. 1. 1961 (ISBN 0-8161-0502-2). Vol. 2. 1962 (ISBN 0-8161-0236-8). G K Hall.

Delorme, Robert L. Latin America Nineteen Sixty-Seven to Nineteen Seventy-Eight: A Comprehensive Social Science Bibliography & Research Guide. 288p. 1981. text ed. 32.75 (ISBN 0-87436-292-X). ABC-Clio.

Delpar, Helen. Encyclopedia of Latin America. LC 72-11311. (Illus.). 672p. 1974. 36.50 (ISBN 0-07-016263-8, P&RB). McGraw.

Del Toro, Josefina. A Bibliography of the Collective Biography of Spanish America. 1976. lib. bdg. 59.95 (ISBN 0-87968-741-X). Gordon Pr.

Gardner, Mary A. The Press of Latin America: A Tentative & Selected Bibliography in Spanish & Portuguese. (Institute of Latin American Studies Guides & Bibliographies Ser.: No. 4). 44p. 1973. pap. 2.00x (ISBN 0-292-76410-3). U of Tex Pr.

Gordon, Raow, ed. A Guide to the Official Publications of the Latin American Republics, 17 vols. 1976. lib. bdg. 50.00 ea (ISBN 0-8490-1923-0). Gordon Pr.

Graham, Ann H. & Woods, Richard D. Latin America in English-Language Reference Books: A Selected & Annotated Bibliography. LC 80-28880. 49p. 1981. 7.75 (ISBN 0-87111-267-1). SLA.

Hanke, Lewis, ed. Handbook of Latin American Studies: 1935-37. LC 36-32633. (Latin American Studies Ser.: Vol. 1-3). 17.50x ea. Vol. 1, 1935 (ISBN 0-8130-0097-1). Vol. 2, 1936 (ISBN 0-8130-0098-X). Vol. 3, 1937 (ISBN 0-8130-0099-8). U Presses Fla.

Hanke, Lewis & Burgin, Miron, eds. Handbook of Latin American Studies: 1939. LC 36-32633. (Latin American Studies Ser: Vol. 5). 1940. 17.50x (ISBN 0-8130-0101-3). U Presses Fla.

Hanke, Lewis & D'Eca, Raul, eds. Handbook of Latin American Studies: 1938. LC 36-32633. (Latin American Studies Ser: Vol. 4). 1939. 17.50x (ISBN 0-8130-0100-5). U Presses Fla.

Harding, Colin & Roper, Christopher, eds. Latin America Review of Books One. LC 73-17942. (Latin America Review Ser.). 220p. 1974. pap. 3.95 (ISBN 0-87867-048-3). Ramparts.

Haro, Robert P. Latin Americana Research in the United States & Canada: A Guide Directory. 122p. 1971. 7.50 (ISBN 0-8389-0093-3). ALA.

Harvard University Library. Latin American & Latin American Periodicals, 2 vols. Incl. Vol. 1. Classification Schedule, Classified Listing by Call Number. 675p; Vol. 2. Alphabetical Listing by Author or Title, Chronological Listing. 817p. LC 67-1722. (Widener Library Shelflist Ser: No. 5-6). 1966. Set. 65.00x (ISBN 0-674-51247-2). Harvard U Pr.

Haverstock, Nathan A., ed. Handbook of Latin American Studies, Vol. 21. 1968. lib. bdg. 30.00x (ISBN 0-374-93572-6). Octagon.

Haverstock, Nathan A. & Pariseau, Earl J., eds. Handbook of Latin American Studies, Vol. 23. 1968. lib. bdg. 30.00x (ISBN 0-374-93591-2). Octagon.

Hawkins, John N. Teacher's Resource Handbook for Latin American Studies: An Annotated Bibliography of Curriculum Materials. LC 75-620089. (Reference Ser. Vol. 6). 220p. 1975. pap. text ed. 5.00 (ISBN 0-87903-106-9). UCLA Lat Am Ctr.

Hilton, Ronald. A Bibliography of Latin America & the Caribbean: The Hilton Library. LC 79-25777. 679p. 1980. 29.50 (ISBN 0-8108-1275-4). Scarecrow.

Humphreys, Robert A. Latin American History: A Guide to the Literature in English. LC 77-752. 1977. Repr. of 1958 ed. lib. bdg. 15.75x (ISBN 0-8371-9490-3, HULA). Greenwood.

Institute of Latin American Studies. Latin American Research & Publications at the University of Texas at Austin, 1893-1969. (Institute of Latin American Studies Guides & Bibliographies Ser.: No. 3). 197p. 1971. 7.50x (ISBN 0-292-74600-8). U of Tex Pr.

Jones, Cecil K. Bibliography of Latin American Bibliographies. 2nd ed. Repr. of 1942 ed. lib. bdg. 21.00x (ISBN 0-8371-1160-9, JOBL). Greenwood.

Latin America: World List of Specialized Periodicals. (Eng. & Fr.). 1974. pap. text ed. 19.50x (ISBN 0-686-22561-9). Mouton.

Lauerhass, Ludwig. Library Resources on Latin America: Research Guide & Bibliographic Introduction. new ed. LC 78-620045. (Library Guides: Series A, No. 2). (Orig.). 1978. pap. text ed. 5.00 (ISBN 0-87903-302-9). UCLA Lat Am Ctr.

Levine, Robert M. Race & Ethnic Relations in Latin America & the Caribbean: An Historical Dictionary & Bibliography. LC 80-15179. 260p. 1980. 13.50 (ISBN 0-8108-1324-6). Scarecrow.

Library of Congress, Washington, D. C. Index to Latin American Legislation, First Supplement, 1961-1965, 2 vols. 1970. Set. lib bdg. 110.00 (ISBN 0-8161-0875-7). G K Hall.

Martin, Dolores M., ed. Handbook of Latin American Studies: No. 42, Humanities. 720p. 1981. text ed. 55.00x (ISBN 0-292-73016-0). U of Tex Pr.

--Handbook of Latin American Studies, No. 40: 1978 Humanities. LC 36-32633. 47.50x (ISBN 0-8130-0637-6). U Presses Fla.

Martin, Dolores M. & Stewart, Donald E., eds. Handbook of Latin Studies: 1976, Humanities. LC 36-32633. (Handbook of Latin American Studies: No. 38). 1976. 40.00x (ISBN 0-8130-0568-X). U Presses Fla.

Matos, Antonio. Guide to Review of Books from & About Hispanic America, 1975: Guia a las Resenas de Libros de y Sobre Hispanoamerica, 1975. LC 66-96537. 1977. 55.00 (ISBN 0-87917-063-8). Blaine Ethridge.

--Guide to Reviews of Books from & About Hispanic America, 1978: Guia a las Resenas de Libros de y sobre Hispanoamerica, 1978. LC 66-96537. 1980. 80.00 (ISBN 0-87917-073-5). Blaine Ethridge.

Matos, Antonio, ed. Guide to Reviews of Books from & About Hispanic America, 1972: Guia a las Resenas De Libros De y Sobre Hispanoamerica, 1972. LC 66-96537. 924p. (Eng. & Sp.). 1976. 45.00 (ISBN 0-87917-044-1). Blaine Ethridge.

--Guide to Reviews of Books from & About Hispanic America 1973: Guia a las Resenas De Libros De y Sobre Hispanoamerica 1973. LC 66-96537. 980p. 1976. 45.00 (ISBN 0-87917-046-8). Blaine Ethridge.

Nettie Lee Benson Latin American Collection, University of Texas Library, Austin, & the Library of Congress. Bibliographic Guide to Latin American Studies: 1978. (Library Catalogs-Bib. Guides). 1979. lib. bdg. 195.00 (ISBN 0-8161-6857-1). G K Hall.

Okinshevich, Leo & Carlton, Robert G., eds. Latin America in Soviet Writings: A Bibliography. Incl. Vol. 1. 1917-1958. 344p (ISBN 0-8018-0494-9); Vol. 2. 1959-1964. 352p (ISBN 0-8018-0495-7). (Hispanic Foundation Ser). 1967. 25.00x ea. Johns Hopkins.

Pariseau, Earl J., ed. Handbook of Latin American Studies: 1959-61. LC 36-32633. (Latin American Studies Ser: Vol. 24). 1962. 25.00x (ISBN 0-8130-0178-1). U Presses Fla.

Pariseau, Earl J. & Adams, Henry E., eds. Handbook of Latin American Studies: Humanities, 1962-64. LC 36-32633. (Latin American Studies: Vol. 28). 1966. 25.00x (ISBN 0-8130-0181-1). U Presses Fla.

Sable, Martin H. Latin American Studies in the Non-Western World & Eastern Europe: A Bibliography on Latin America in the Languages of Africa, Asia, the Middle East, & Eastern Europe. LC 73-13114. 1970. 21.00 (ISBN 0-8108-0344-5). Scarecrow.

Saulniers, Suzanne S. & Rakowski, Cathy A. Women in the Development Process: A Select Bibliography on Women in Sub-Saharan Africa & Latin America. (Institute of Latin American Studies Special Publications Ser.). 311p. 1978. pap. 6.95x (ISBN 0-292-79010-4). U of Tex Pr.

Spell, Lota M. Research Materials for the Study of Latin-America at the University of Texas. Repr. of 1954 ed. lib. bdg. 14.25x (ISBN 0-8371-5033-7, TLSR). Greenwood.

Texas University Institute of Latin American Studies. Seventy-Five Years of Latin American Research at the University of Texas, Masters Thesis & Doctoral Dissertations, 1893-1958, & Publications of Latin American Interest, 1941-1958. (Latin American Studies: No. 18). 1971. Repr. of 1959 ed. lib. bdg. 15.00x (ISBN 0-8371-6013-8, TLAR). Greenwood.

Thompson, Lawrence S. Essays in Hispanic Bibliography. LC 75-96729. 1970. 15.00 (ISBN 0-208-00978-7, Archon). Shoe String.

Trask, David F., et al, eds. Bibliography of United States - Latin American Relations Since 1810: A Selected List of Eleven Thousand Published References. LC 67-14421. 1968. 23.50x (ISBN 0-8032-0185-0). U of Nebr Pr.

Tulane University, New Orleans. Catalog of the Latin American Library of the Tulane University Library, 9 vols. 1970. Set. lib. bdg. 855.00 (ISBN 0-8161-0894-3). G K Hall.

--Catalog of the Latin American Library of the Tulane University Library, First Supplement, 2 vols. 1973. Set. lib. bdg. 240.00 (ISBN 0-8161-0914-1). G K Hall.

--Catalog of the Latin American Library of the Tulane University Library, Second Supplement. 1975. lib. bdg. 240.00 (ISBN 0-8161-1052-2). G K Hall.

United Nations, Economic Commission for Latin America. Latin American Initialisms & Acronyms-Lista De Siglas Latinoamericanas: Document E-CN, 12-Lib. 3. LC 73-81473. 146p. 1973. Repr. of 1970 ed. 12.50x (ISBN 0-87917-035-2). Blaine Ethridge.

U. S. Library Of Congress. Guide to the Official Publications of Other American Republics: Washington, 1945-48, 2 Vols. Repr. of 1948 ed. Set. 75.00 (ISBN 0-384-63000-6). Johnson Repr.

University of Texas, Austin. Catalog of the Latin American Collection of the University of Texas Library: Second Supplement, 3 vols. 1973. Set. lib. bdg. 325.00 (ISBN 0-8161-0979-6). G K Hall.

--Catalog of the Latin American Collection of the University of Texas Library, Third Supplement, 8 vols. 1975. Set. lib. bdg. 890.00 (ISBN 0-8161-1107-3). G K Hall.

University of Texas Library, Austin. Catalog of the Latin American Collection of the University of Texas Library, First Supplement, 5 vols. 1971. 525.00 (ISBN 0-8161-0889-7). G K Hall.

--Catalog of the Latin American Collection of the University of Texas Library, 31 Vols. 1969. Set. lib. bdg. 2845.00 (ISBN 0-8161-0815-3). G K Hall.

University of Texas Library (Austin) & the Library of Congress. Bibliographic Guide to Latin American Studies: 1979. (Library Catalogs-Bib. Guides). 1980. lib. bdg. 245.00 (ISBN 0-8161-6872-5). G K Hall.

--Bibliographic Guide to Latin American Studies: 1980. (Library Catalogs Bib. Guides). 1981. lib. bdg. 275.00 (ISBN 0-8161-6888-1). G K Hall.

Valk, Barbara G., ed. Hispanic American Periodicals Index Nineteen Seventy-Seven. LC 75-642408. 1980. lib. bdg. 100.00x (ISBN 0-87903-402-5). UCLA Lat Am Ctr.

Wilgus, A. Curtis. Latin America, Spain & Portugal: A Selected & Annotated Bibliographical Guide to Books Published 1954-1974. LC 76-58355. 1977. 40.00 (ISBN 0-8108-1018-2). Scarecrow.

Woods, Richard D. Reference Materials on Latin America in English: The Humanities. LC 80-11412. 651p. 1980. 32.50 (ISBN 0-8108-1294-0). Scarecrow.

Zimmerman, Irene. Current National Bibliographies of Latin America: A State of the Art Study. LC 73-632969. 1971. 7.00 (ISBN 0-8130-0321-0). U Presses Fla.

LATIN AMERICA–BIOGRAPHY

Biogeografia De America Latina. (Serie De Biologia: No. 13). 120p. (Span.). 1973. pap. 1.25 (ISBN 0-8270-6100-5). OAS.

Coker, William S., ed. Hispanic-American Essays in Honor of Max Leon Moorhead. LC 79-11210. (Spanish Borderlands Ser.: Vol. 1). (Illus.). 193p. 1979. 16.95x (ISBN 0-933776-00-4); pap. 9.95 (ISBN 0-933776-01-2). Perdido Bay.

Davis, Harold E. Latin American Leaders. LC 68-56189. Repr. of 1949 ed. 8.50x (ISBN 0-8154-0271-6). Cooper Sq.

--Makers of Democracy in Latin America. LC 68-56190. Repr. of 1945 ed. 8.00x (ISBN 0-8154-0272-4). Cooper Sq.

--Revolutionaries, Traditionalists & Dictators in Latin America. LC 72-77988. 1973. lib. bdg. 11.00x (ISBN 0-8154-0420-4). Cooper Sq.

Del Toro, Josefina. A Bibliography of the Collective Biography of Spanish America. 1976. lib. bdg. 59.95 (ISBN 0-87968-741-X). Gordon Pr.

Dictionary of Latin American & Caribbean Biography. 2nd ed. (Illus.). 459p. 1971. 25.00x (ISBN 0-900332-16-6, Pub by Intl Biog). Biblio Dist.

Foster, David, ed. Latin American Government Leaders. LC 75-15809. 1975. 8.00x (ISBN 0-87918-021-8); pap. 5.50x (ISBN 0-87918-021-8). ASU Lat Am St.

Foster, David W. Augusto Roa Bastos. (World Authors Ser.: No. 507 (Paraguay)). 1978. 12.50 (ISBN 0-8057-6348-1). Twayne.

Henderson, Peter V. Felix Diaz, the Porfirians, & the Mexican Revolution. LC 80-113934. xiv, 239p. 1981. 18.50x (ISBN 0-8032-2312-9). U of Nebr Pr.

Hill, E. Leon. Miguel Angel Asturias, Lo Ancestral En Su Obra Literaria. 1972. 11.95 (ISBN 0-88303-007-1); pap. 9.95 (ISBN 0-685-73211-8). E Torres & Sons.

Hilton, Ronald. Who's Who in Latin America, 2 Vols: Vol. 1, Mexico, Central America, the Caribbean; Vol. 2, South America. 3rd ed. LC 76-165656. (Reprint of original seven vols., 1945-51). 1971. Vol. 1. 20.00x (ISBN 0-87917-019-0); Vol. 2. 30.00x (ISBN 0-87917-020-4); Set. 47.50 (ISBN 0-87917-021-2). Blaine Ethridge.

Robertson, William S. Rise of the Spanish American Republics As Told in the Lives of Their Liberators. 1976. lib. bdg. 59.95 (ISBN 0-8490-2527-3). Gordon Pr.

Robinson, David J. Studying Latin America: Essays in Honor of Preston E. James. LC 80-12413. (Dellplain Latin American Studies: No. 4). 290p. (Orig.). 1980. pap. 19.25 (ISBN 0-8357-0515-3, SS-00135, Pub. by Syracuse U Dept Geog). Univ Microfilms.

Ruple, Joelyn. Antonio Buero Vallejo: The First Fifteen Years. 1971. 12.95 (ISBN 0-88303-006-3); pap. 8.95 (ISBN 0-685-73210-X). E Torres & Sons.

Stewart, Watt & Peterson, Harold I. Builders of Latin America. LC 76-167425. (Essay Index Reprint Ser.). Repr. of 1942 ed. 35.00 (ISBN 0-8369-2724-9). Arno.

Tarry, Ellen. The Other Torussaint. Date not set. price not set. Dghtrs St Paul.

LATIN AMERICA–CIVILIZATION

America Latina En sus Artes. (America Latina En su Cultura Ser.). 237p. 1976. pap. 9.25 (ISBN 0-685-66206-3, U18, UNESCO). Unipub.

Arciniegas, German. Latin America: A Cultural History. (Illus.). (YA) 1967. 15.00 (ISBN 0-394-43257-6). Knopf.

Arrom, Jose. Hispanoamerica: Panorama Contemporaneo De Su Cultura. LC 69-11940. (Illus.). 1969. text ed. 15.50 scp (ISBN 0-06-040348-9, HarpC). Har-Row.

Bailey, Helen M. & Nasatir, Abraham P. Latin America: The Development of Its Civilization. 3rd ed. (Illus.). 896p. 1973. ref. ed. 20.95x (ISBN 0-13-524264-9). P-H.

Balseiro, Jose A. Americans Look at Each Other. Lee, Muna M., tr. LC 69-15925. (Hispanic-American Studies Ser: No. 21). 1969. 12.95x (ISBN 0-87024-110-9). U of Miami Pr.

Brady, Agnes M. Historia De la Cultura Hispanoamericana. 1966. text ed. 9.95 (ISBN 0-02-313370-8). Macmillan.

Conference on Intellectual Trends in Latin America, University of Texas, 1945. Papers. LC 69-19001. Repr. of 1945 ed. lib. bdg. 14.75x (ISBN 0-8371-1037-8, TLIT). Greenwood.

Dealy, Glen C. The Public Man: An Interpretation of Latin American & Other Catholic Countries. LC 77-1423. 1977. 10.00x (ISBN 0-87023-239-8). U of Mass Pr.

Dean, Vera M. Nature of the Non-Western World. (Orig.). pap. 1.50 (ISBN 0-451-61224-8, MW1224, Ment). NAL.

Diffie, Bailey W. Latin-American Civilization: Colonial Period. 1967. lib. bdg. 50.00x (ISBN 0-374-92166-0). Octagon.

Esquenazi-Mayo, R. & Esquenazi-Mayo, C. Esencia De Hispanoamerica. LC 69-11756. (gr. 9-12). 1969. text ed. 15.95 (ISBN 0-03-080027-7, HoltC). HR&W.

Florit, Eugenio & Patt, B. P., eds. Retratos de Hispanoamerica. (Span.). 1962. text ed. 8.95x (ISBN 0-03-017135-0). Irvington.

Fourth Annual Conference on Latin America, April 17-19, 1969 & Taylor, Philip B., Jr., eds. Contemporary Latin America: Proceedings. 113p. 1970. pap. text ed. 2.50 (ISBN 0-915524-05-8). Lat Am Stud.

Henriquez-Urena, Pedro. Literary Currents in Hispanic America. LC 63-11032. 1963. Repr. of 1945 ed. 10.00 (ISBN 0-8462-0345-6). Russell.

Keen, Benjamin, ed. Latin American Civilization, 2 vols. 3rd ed. 1974. Vol. 1. pap. text ed. 11.50 (ISBN 0-395-17582-8); Vol. 2. pap. text ed. 11.50 (ISBN 0-395-17583-6). HM.

Lewald, H. Ernest. Latin America: Sus Culturas y Sociedades. (Illus.). 384p. 1973. text ed. 15.95 (ISBN 0-07-037420-1, C). McGraw.

Loprete, Carlos & McMahon, Dorothy. Iberoamerica: Sintesis De Su Civilization. 2nd ed. 1974. pap. text ed. 10.95x (ISBN 0-684-13801-8, ScribC). Scribner.

McClellan, Grant S., ed. U. S. Policy in Latin America. (Reference Shelf Ser: Vol. 35, No. 1). 1963. 6.25 (ISBN 0-8242-0074-8). Wilson.

Manach, Jorge. Teoria De la Frontera. 3.75 (ISBN 0-8477-2412-3). U of PR Pr.

Moses, Bernard. Spain Overseas. 1929. 7.00 (ISBN 0-527-65410-8). Kraus Repr.

Nunez, Benjamin. Dictionary of Afro-Latin American Civilization. LC 79-7731. (Illus.). xxxv, 525p. 1980. lib. bdg. 45.00 (ISBN 0-313-21138-8, NAL/). Greenwood.

Tannenbaum, Frank. Ten Keys to Latin America. 1966. pap. 2.95 (ISBN 0-394-70312-X, Vin). Random.

Terry, Edward D., ed. Artists & Writers in the Evolution of Latin America. LC 69-16097. 240p. 1969. 12.95x (ISBN 0-8173-5060-8). U of Ala Pr.

Texas University Institute Of Latin-American Studies. Some Educational & Anthropological Aspects of Latin-America. (Illus.). Repr. of 1948 ed. lib. bdg. 15.00x (ISBN 0-8371-1032-7, TLEA). Greenwood.

Urbanski, E. Hispanoamerica y Sus Razas y Civilizaciones. 1973. 15.00 (ISBN 0-88303-014-4); pap. 10.95 (ISBN 0-685-73217-7). E Torres & Sons.

Von Hagen, Victor. The Ancient Sun Kingdoms of the Americas. (Illus.). 1977. pap. 5.95x (ISBN 0-8464-0134-7). Beekman Pubs.

Wagley, Charles. Latin American Tradition: Essays on the Unity & the Diversity of Latin American Culture. LC 67-30968. 1968. 17.50x (ISBN 0-231-03006-1); pap. 6.00x (ISBN 0-231-08333-5). Columbia U Pr.

LATIN AMERICA–CIVILIZATION–STUDY AND TEACHING

Nunez, Benjamin. Dictionary of Afro-Latin American Civilization. LC 79-7731. (Illus.). xxxv, 525p. 1980. lib. bdg. 45.00 (ISBN 0-313-21138-8, NAL/). Greenwood.

Sable, Martin H. A Guide to Nonprint Materials for Latin American Studies. LC 78-24476. 1979. 16.50 (ISBN 0-87917-066-2). Blaine Ethridge.

Wagley, Charles, ed. Social Science Research in Latin America. LC 65-11971. 1965. 22.50x (ISBN 0-231-02772-9). Columbia U Pr.

LATIN AMERICA–COMMERCE

Blough, Roy & Behrman, Jack N. Regional Integration & the Trade of Latin America. LC 68-19545. 184p. 1968. pap. 2.50 (ISBN 0-87186-222-0). Comm Econ Dev.

Business Yearbook of Brazil, Mexico & Venezuela 1980. Date not set. 39.50 (ISBN 0-531-03946-3). Watts.

Carnoy, Martin. Industrialization in a Latin American Common Market. LC 73-161596. 1972. 11.95 (ISBN 0-8157-1294-4). Brookings.

Changing Legal Environment in Latin America Management Implications, Volume III: Brazil, Mexico. 103p. 1980. pap. 10.50 (ISBN 0-917094-14-X, COA 43, CoA). Unipub.

Conference On Some Economic Aspects Of Postwar Inter-American Relations - University Of Texas - 1946. Papers. LC 69-19002. Repr. of 1946 ed. lib. bdg. 15.00x (ISBN 0-8371-1038-6, TLEP). Greenwood.

Estudio Sectorial Sobre Empresas Transacionales En America Latina: La Industria Automotriz. 71p. (Span.). 1977. Repr. of 1974 ed. 5.00 (ISBN 0-8270-3300-1). OAS.

Guide to Latin American Business Information Sources. 29p. 1977. pap. text ed. 1.00 (ISBN 0-8270-3045-2). OAS.

Guisinger, Stephen E., ed. Trade & Investment Policies in the Americas. LC 73-84723. 1973. 5.95 (ISBN 0-87074-136-5). SMU Press.

Haring, Clarence H. Trade & Navigation Between Spain & the Indies. 1964. 9.50 (ISBN 0-8446-1222-7). Peter Smith.

Jones, Chester L. Caribbean Interests of the United States. LC 73-111719. (American Imperialism: Viewpoints of United States Foreign Policy, 1898-1941). 1970. Repr. of 1919 ed. 17.00 (ISBN 0-405-02029-5). Arno.

Krause, Walter. The United States & Latin America: The Alliance for Progress Program. (Studies in Latin American Business: No. 2). pap. 4.00 (ISBN 0-87755-070-0). U of Tex Busn Res.

Major Companies of Brazil, Mexico, & Venezuela 1979. 1979. 114.00x (ISBN 0-685-94071-3). Nichols Pub.

Mathis, F. John. Economic Integration in Latin America. (Studies in Latin American Business: No. 8). pap. 4.00 (ISBN 0-87755-076-X). U of Tex Busn Res.

Methods for Evaluating Latin American Export Operations. 1978. pap. 5.00 (ISBN 0-8270-3185-8). OAS.

Nuclear Energy in Latin America: The Brazilian Case. 20p. 1980. pap. 5.00 (ISBN 92-808-0183-X, TUNU 077, UNU). Unipub.

Orosz, Arpad. The Foreign Trade Turnover of Latin America Until 1970 & Its Prospective Development up to 1980. LC 77-369256. (Studies on Developing Countries). 130p. (Orig.). 1976. pap. 8.50x (ISBN 0-8002-0494-8). Intl Pubns Serv.

Shea, Donald R. & Swacker, Frank W., eds. Business & Legal Aspects of Latin American Trade & Investment. LC 76-44061. 1977. pap. 15.00 (ISBN 0-930450-11-6). Univ of Wis Latin Am.

Wiarda, Howard J. Corporatism & National Development in Latin America. (Westview Replica Edition Ser.). 325p. 1981. PLB 28.25x (ISBN 0-86531-031-9). Westview.

LATIN AMERICA–DESCRIPTION AND TRAVEL

Beddis, R. A. Africa, Latin America & Lands of the South-West Pacific. (New Secondary Geographies Ser.: Pt. 2). 176p. 1968. 4.00 (ISBN 0-340-07413-2). Intl Pubns Serv.

Benton, William. The Voice of Latin America. LC 74-1553. (Illus.). 204p. 1974. Repr. of 1961 ed. lib. bdg. 15.00 (ISBN 0-8371-7393-0, BEVL). Greenwood.

Butterworth, Hezekiah. Traveller Tales of the Pan-American Countries. LC 71-130986. (Illus.). Repr. of 1902 ed. 19.00 (ISBN 0-404-01255-8). AMS Pr.

Christmas in Latin America. (Eng.). 1976. pap. 1.00 (ISBN 0-8270-4365-1). OAS.

De Pons, Francois R. Travels in South America, 2 vols. LC 71-128420. Repr. of 1807 ed. Set. 62.50 (ISBN 0-404-02115-8). AMS Pr.

Epstein, Jack. Along the Gringo Trail: A Budget Travel Guide to Latin America. LC 77-89432. (Illus.). 1977. pap. 9.95 (ISBN 0-915904-25-X). And-or Pr.

Geographic de America Latina. (Coleccion UNESCO programas ymetodos de ensenanza). (Sp.). 1976. pap. 23.75 (ISBN 92-3-301059-7, U262, UNESCO). Unipub.

Gonzalez De Mendoza, Juan. History of the Great & Mighty Kingdom of China & the Situation Thereof, 2 Vols. Staunton, George T., ed. LC 73-141353. (Hakluyt Society First Ser: Nos. 14 & 15). 1971. Repr. of 1854 ed. Set. 58.00 (ISBN 0-8337-2360-X). B Franklin.

Gorden, Raymond L. Living in Latin America. 1974. text ed. 9.00 (ISBN 0-8442-9341-5). Natl Textbk.

Gunther, John. Inside Latin America. LC 74-27666. (Illus.). 498p. 1975. Repr. of 1941 ed. lib. bdg. 25.75x (ISBN 0-8371-7908-4, GULA). Greenwood.

Hewat, Jonathan. Latin American Motoring. (Illus.). 1978. 14.95 (ISBN 0-905064-27-5). Intl Learn Syst.

Lamb, Ruth S. Latin America: Sites & Insights. (gr. 9-12). 1963. pap. 4.00 (ISBN 0-912434-02-3). Ocelot Pr.

Leonard, Irving A. Colonial Travelers in Latin America. (Borzoi Latin American Ser). 1972. pap. text ed. 3.95x (ISBN 0-394-31063-2). Phila Bk Co.

Nakagawa, Tsuyoshi. El Salvador. LC 74-78596. (This Beautiful World Ser.: Vol. 54). (Illus.). 1975. pap. 4.95 (ISBN 0-87011-236-8). Kodansha.

Penfield, Marc. Latin America: An Astrological Portrait of Its Cities & States. 1981. kivar 14.95 (ISBN 0-914350-35-8). Vulcan Bks.

Q A S General Secretariat, Dept. of Echnological & Scientific Affairs. Biogeografia de America Latina. 2nd ed. (Biologia: No. 13). (Illus.). 122p. (Span.). 1980. pap. 2.00 (ISBN 0-8270-1233-0). OAS.

Sandford, Frank W. The Golden Light Upon the Two Americas. (Illus.). 1974. 5.00 (ISBN 0-910840-18-0). Kingdom.

Schmid, Peter. Beggars on Golden Stools: Report on Latin America. Savill, Mervyn, tr. from Ger. LC 74-20278. (Illus.). 327p. 1975. Repr. of 1956 ed. lib. bdg. 19.75x (ISBN 0-8371-7853-3, SCGS). Greenwood.

Wilhelm, R. Dwight. Two Ways to Look South: A Guide to Latin America. (Orig.). 1980. pap. 2.25 (ISBN 0-377-00098-1). Friend Pr.

LATIN AMERICA–DIRECTORIES

Chiefs of State & Cabinet Ministers of the American Republics. 44p. (Semi-annual). pap. 1.00 (ISBN 0-8270-5685-0). OAS.

LATIN AMERICA–DISCOVERY AND EXPLORATION

see America–Discovery and Exploration

LATIN AMERICA–ECONOMIC CONDITIONS

Abu-Lughod, Janet & Hay, Richard, eds. Third World Urbanization. LC 76-53367. (Illus.). 1977. text ed. 14.95x (ISBN 0-685-76992-5); pap. text ed. 7.95x (ISBN 0-88425-005-9). Maaroufa Pr.

Baer, Werner & Samuelson, Larry. Latin America in the Post-Import Substitution Era. 1977. pap. text ed. 21.00 (ISBN 0-08-021822-9). Pergamon.

Baerresen, Donald W., et al. Latin American Trade Patterns. LC 80-479. (Illus.). xix, 329p. 1980. Repr. of 1965 ed. lib. bdg. 28.50x (ISBN 0-313-22288-6, BALT). Greenwood.

Behrman, Jere R. & Hanson, James A., eds. Short-Term Macroeconomic Policy in Latin America: Conference on Planning & Short-Term Marco-Economic Policy in Latin America. LC 78-24053. 1979. reference 25.00 (ISBN 0-88410-489-3, Pub for the National Bureau of Economic Research). Ballinger Pub.

Blakemore, Harold & Smith, Clifford T., eds. Latin America: Geographical Perspectives. (Illus.). 1971. text ed. 39.95x (ISBN 0-416-10820-2); pap. 19.95x (ISBN 0-416-80500-0). Methuen Inc.

Blasier, Cole, ed. Constructive Change in Latin America. LC 68-12724. (Pitt Latin American Ser.). 1968. 11.95 (ISBN 0-8229-3145-1). U of Pittsburgh Pr.

Blough, Roy & Behrman, Jack N. Regional Integration & the Trade of Latin America. LC 68-19545. 184p. 1968. pap. 2.50 (ISBN 0-87186-222-0). Comm Econ Dev.

Boas, Ernest. Latin America's Steel Industry: Present & Future. LC 70-382668. 1968. 17.50x (ISBN 0-8002-0861-7). Intl Pubns Serv.

Bradford, Colin L, Jr. Forces for Change in Latin America: U. S. Policy Implications. LC 70-181831. (Monographs: No. 5). 80p. 1971. 2.00 (ISBN 0-686-28690-1). Overseas Dev Council.

Brundenius, Claes & Lundal, Mats, eds. Development Strategies in Latin America. 200p. 1981. lib. bdg. 17.50 (ISBN 0-86531-261-3). Westview.

Burns, E. Bradford. The Poverty of Progress: Latin America in the Nineteenth Century. LC 80-51236. 224p. 1980. 14.95x (ISBN 0-520-04160-7). U of Cal Pr.

Carnoy, Martin. Industrialization in a Latin American Common Market. LC 73-161596. 1972. 11.95 (ISBN 0-8157-1294-4). Brookings.

Centro Nuclear De Puerto Rico. Simposio Sobre Energia Nuclear y el Desarrollo De Latinoamerica. pap. 3.75 (ISBN 0-8477-2304-6). U of PR Pr.

Chilcote, Ronald H. & Edelstein, Joel C., eds. Latin America: The Struggle with Dependency & Beyond. 800p. 1974. 24.50 (ISBN 0-87073-068-1); pap. 11.50 (ISBN 0-87073-069-X). Schenkman.

Conference On Some Economic Aspects Of Postwar Inter-American Relations - University Of Texas - 1946. Papers. LC 69-19002. Repr. of 1946 ed. lib. bdg. 15.00x (ISBN 0-8371-1038-6, TLEP). Greenwood.

Consideraciones Sobre Politica Gubernamental Hacia las Empresas Transnacionales En America Latina: Un Estudio Preliminar. 31p. (Span.). 1977. pap. 2.50 (ISBN 0-8270-3290-0). OAS.

Considerations on Government Policy Towards Transnational Enterprises in Latin America: A Preliminary Survey. 41p. 1977. Repr. of 1974 ed. 2.50 (ISBN 0-8270-3285-4). OAS.

Consumer Markets in Latin America. (A Euromonitor Publication Ser.). 1978. 124.00 (ISBN 0-89397-065-4). Nichols Pub.

Convencion Interamericana Sobre Arbitraje Comercial Internacional. (Treaty Ser.: No. 42). (Eng. , Span. , Fr. , Port.). 1975. pap. 1.00 (ISBN 0-8270-0520-2). OAS.

Convencion Interamericana Sobre Conflictos De Leyes En Materia De Letras De Cambio, Pagares y Facturas. (Treaty Ser.: No. 40). (Eng. , Span. , Fr. , Port.). 1975. pap. 1.00 (ISBN 0-8270-0510-5). OAS.

Convencion Interamericana Sobre Conflictos De Leyes En Materia De Cheques. (Treaty Ser.: No. 41). (Eng. , Span. , Fr. , Port.). 1975. pap. 1.00 (ISBN 0-8270-0515-6). OAS.

Cornelius, Wayne A. & Trueblood, Felicity M. Urbanization & Inequality: The Political Economy of Urban & Rural Development in Latin America. LC 74-83000. (Latin American Urban Research: Vol. 5). 320p. 1975. 22.50 (ISBN 0-8039-0437-1); pap. 9.95 (ISBN 0-8039-0602-1). Sage.

Cornelius, Wayne A. & Kemper, Robert V., eds. Metropolitan Latin American: The Challenge & the Response. LC 77-79867. (Latin American Urban Research: Vol. 6). (Illus.). 346p. 1978. 22.50 (ISBN 0-8039-0661-7); pap. 9.95 (ISBN 0-8039-0662-5). Sage.

Cortes Conde, Roberto & Stein, Stanley J., eds. Latin America: A Guide to Economic History 1830-1930. LC 74-30534. 1977. 49.50x (ISBN 0-520-02956-9). U of Cal Pr.

Cukor, Gyorgy. Strategies of Industrialisation in the Developing Countries. LC 73-89996. 288p. 1974. 22.50 (ISBN 0-312-76440-5). St Martin.

De Janvry, Alain. The Agrarian Question & Reformism in Latin America. LC 81-4147. (Illus.). 352p. 1982. text ed. 27.50x (ISBN 0-8018-2531-8); pap. text ed. 8.95x (ISBN 0-8018-2532-6). Johns Hopkins.

Descartes, S. L. Credit Institutions for Local Authorities in Latin America. LC 73-75403. 81p. 1973. pap. 1.50 (ISBN 0-913480-16-9). Inter Am U Pr.

Economic Commission for Latin America. Development Problems in Latin America: An Analysis by the United Nations Economic Commission for Latin America. (Institute of Latin American Studies-Special Publication). 366p. 1970. 15.00x (ISBN 0-292-70042-3). U of Tex Pr.

Economic Survey of Latin America 1977. 536p. 1979. pap. 22.00 (ISBN 0-686-68952-6, UN79/2G1, UN). Unipub.

Einaudi, Luigi R., ed. Beyond Cuba: Latin America Takes Charge of Its Future. LC 73-8644. 250p. 1973. pap. 14.00x (ISBN 0-8448-0266-2). Crane-Russak Co.

El Financiamiento Externo Oficial En la Estrategia Del Desarrollo De America Latina: Implicaciones Para los Setenta. (CIES-1856 Corr. 1). 119p. (Span.). 1974. 5.00 (ISBN 0-8270-3695-7). OAS.

Foxley, Alejandro & Whitehead, Laurence, eds. Economic Stabilization in Latin America: Political Dimensions. 120p. 1980. pap. 16.50 (ISBN 0-08-026788-2). Pergamon.

Fraginals, Manuel M. The Sugarmill. Belfrage, Cedric, tr. from Sp. LC 73-90074. (Illus.). 1978. pap. 10.95 (ISBN 0-85345-432-9, PB-432-9). Monthly Rev.

Frank, Andre G. Capitalism & Underdevelopment in Latin America. rev. ed. LC 65-14271. 1969. pap. 6.95 (ISBN 0-85345-093-5, PB0935). Monthly Rev.

--Latin America: Underdevelopment or Revolution. LC 71-81794. 1970. pap. 6.50 (ISBN 0-85345-165-6, PB-1656). Monthly Rev.

--Lumpenbourgeoisie: Lumpendevelopment: Dependence, Class, & Politics in Latin America. Berdicio, Marion D., tr. from Span. LC 72-81764. 160p. 1973. pap. 3.50 (ISBN 0-85345-285-7, PB-2857). Monthly Rev.

Furtado, C. Economic Development of Latin America. 2nd ed. LC 74-121365. (Latin American Studies: No.8). (Illus.). 280p. 1977. 37.50 (ISBN 0-521-21197-2); pap. 9.95x (ISBN 0-521-29070-8). Cambridge U Pr.

--Economic Development of Latin America. 1970. 11.95 (ISBN 0-521-07828-8). Brown Bk.

Galeano, Eduardo. Open Veins of Latin America: Five Centuries of the Pillage of a Continent. Belfrage, Cedric, tr. from Span. LC 72-92036. (Illus.). 320p. 1973. 8.95 (ISBN 0-85345-279-2, CL-2792); pap. 6.95 (ISBN 0-85345-308-X, PB-308X). Monthly Rev.

Gall, Pirie M., et al. Municipal Development Programs in Latin America: An Intercountry Evaluation. LC 76-23401. (Illus.). 1976. 22.95 (ISBN 0-275-23280-8). Praeger.

Garbacz, Christopher. Industrial Polarization Under Economic Integration: Latin America. (Studies in Latin American Business: No. 11). (Orig.). 1971. pap. 4.00 (ISBN 0-87755-138-3). U of Tex Busn Res.

Geithman, David T., ed. Fiscal Policy for Industrialization & Development in Latin America. LC 74-2231. 1974. 12.50 (ISBN 0-8130-0397-0). U Presses Fla.

Gerassi, John. Great Fear in Latin America. 1965. pap. 1.50 (ISBN 0-02-073410-7, Collier). Macmillan.

Gordon, Raoul, ed. Foreign Capital in Latin America. 1976. lib. bdg. 59.95 (ISBN 0-8490-1856-0). Gordon Pr.

--Selected Bibliography on Legal & Related Matters Affecting Business in Latin America. 1976. lib. bdg. 59.95 (ISBN 0-8490-2587-7). Gordon Pr.

Gordon, Wendell C. The Political Economy of Latin America. LC 65-19444. 401p. 1965. 20.00x (ISBN 0-231-02675-7); pap. 10.00x (ISBN 0-231-08572-9). Columbia U Pr.

Greene, David G. Steel & Economic Development: Capital Output Ratios in Three Latin American Steel Plants. LC 67-64602. 1967. 4.50 (ISBN 0-87744-077-8). Mich St U Busn.

Griffin, E. P. Financial Development in Latin America. 280p. 1971. 19.95 (ISBN 0-312-28945-6). St Martin.

Griffin, Keith. Under-Development in Spanish America. 1969. text ed. 16.95x (ISBN 0-04-330150-9). Allen Unwin.

Grunwald, Joseph, ed. Latin America & World Economy: A Changing International Order. LC 77-17031. (Latin American International Affairs Ser.: Vol. 2). 323p. 1978. 22.50x (ISBN 0-8039-0864-4); pap. 9.95 (ISBN 0-8039-0966-7). Sage.

Gudeman, Stephen. The Demise of a Rural Economy: From Subsistence to Capitalism in a Latin American Village. (International Library of Anthropology). 1978. 21.00x (ISBN 0-7100-8835-3); pap. 8.95 (ISBN 0-7100-8836-1). Routledge & Kegan.

Guidelines for Achieving Maximum Employment & Growth in Latin America. 1973. 3.00 (ISBN 0-8270-3540-3). OAS.

Hanson, Simon G., ed. Economic Development in Latin America. LC 73-21100. 531p. 1974. Repr. of 1951 ed. lib. bdg. 25.00x (ISBN 0-8371-6001-4, CEC/). Greenwood.

Harris, Seymour E., ed. Economic Problems of Latin America. LC 79-39069. (Essay Index Reprint Ser.). Repr. of 1944 ed. 25.00 (ISBN 0-8369-2693-5). Arno.

Horowitz, Irving L., ed. Masses in Latin America. LC 73-83045. 1970. pap. 7.95 (ISBN 0-19-500795-6, 297, GB). Oxford U Pr.

Hughlett, Lloyd J., ed. Industrialization of Latin America. Repr. of 1946 ed. lib. bdg. 25.25x (ISBN 0-8371-3954-6, HUIL). Greenwood.

Hunter, John M. & Foley, James W. Economic Problems of Latin America. 1975. text ed. 20.95 (ISBN 0-395-18941-1). HM.

Inter-American Institute of International Legal Studies. Instruments Relating to the Economic Integration of Latin America. LC 67-23682. 1968. 18.00 (ISBN 0-379-00338-4). Oceana.

Kadar, B. Regional Cooperation in Latin America. (Studies in Developing Countries Ser.: No. 84). 46p. 1975. pap. 6.00x (ISBN 0-8002-2194-X). Intl Pubns Serv.

Kadar, Bela. Problems of Economic Growth in Latin America. Felix, Pal, tr. from Hungarian. LC 79-17824. 1979. Repr. of 1977 ed. 27.50x (ISBN 0-312-64758-1). St Martin.

Kahl, Joseph. Modernization, Exploitation & Dependency in Latin America. LC 75-43190. 215p. 1976. pap. text ed. 5.95 (ISBN 0-87855-584-6). Transaction Bks.

Karst, Kenneth L. & Rosen, Keith S. Law & Development in Latin America. LC 74-30525. 750p. 1976. 48.50x (ISBN 0-520-02955-0). U of Cal Pr.

Klochkovski, L., ed. Economia De los Paises Latinoamericanos. 504p. (Span.). 1978. 8.60 (ISBN 0-8285-1418-6, Pub. by Progress Pubs Russia). Imported Pubns.

Krause, Walter & Mathis, F. John. Latin America & Economic Integration: Regional Planning for Development. LC 78-115458. 1970. 5.00x (ISBN 0-87745-003-X). U of Iowa Pr.

Krause, Walter, et al. International Tourism & Latin American Development. LC 73-8378. (Studies in Latin American Business: No. 15). 60p. (Orig.). 1973. pap. 5.00 (ISBN 0-87755-176-6). U of Tex Busn Res.

Lozoya, Jorge & Estevez, Jaime, eds. Latin America & the New International Economic Order. LC 79-27384. (Pergamon Policy Studies in the New International Economic Order). 112p. 1980. 16.50 (ISBN 0-08-025118-8). Pergamon.

Macon, Jorge & Merino Manon, Jose. Financing Urban & Rural Development Through Betterment Levies: The Latin American Experience. LC 76-24359. (Special Studies). 1977. text ed. 24.50 (ISBN 0-275-23970-5). Praeger.

Maritano, Nino. Latin American Economic Community: History, Policies & Problems. LC 68-27581. 1970. 9.95x (ISBN 0-268-00357-2). U of Notre Dame Pr.

Mathis, F. John. Economic Integration in Latin America. (Studies in Latin American Business: No. 8). pap. 4.00 (ISBN 0-87755-076-X). U of Tex Busn Res.

Mauro, Frederic. Des Produits et Des Hommes: Essais Historiques Latino-Americains, XVIe-XXe Siecles. (Civilisations et Societes: No. 34). 1973. pap. 15.50x (ISBN 90-2797-172-2). Mouton.

Ministers of Foreign Affairs of the American Republics-7th-San Jose-Costa Rica-1960. Final Act: Meeting of Consultation. (Sp.). pap. 1.00 (ISBN 0-8270-1700-6). OAS.

Montavon, Remy, et al. The Role of Multinational Companies in Latin America: A Case Study in Mexico. 124p. 1980. 27.50 (ISBN 0-03-057973-2). Praeger.

Morris, Arthur. Latin America: Economic Development & Regional Differentiation. 244p. 1981. text ed. 22.50x (ISBN 0-389-20194-4); pap. text ed. 11.75x (ISBN 0-389-20195-2). B&N.

Musgrove, Philip. Consumer Behavior in Latin America: Income & Spending of Families in Ten Andean Cities. LC 77-1108. 1978. 18.95 (ISBN 0-8157-5914-2). Brookings.

Nehemkis, Peter. Latin America: Myth & Reality. LC 77-2958. 1977. Repr. of 1964 ed. lib. bdg. 20.25x (ISBN 0-8371-9560-8, NELA). Greenwood.

OAS General Secretariat Planning & Statistics. Synthesis Fo Economic Performance in Latin America During 1979. (Statistics Ser.). 40p. 1979. pap. 3.00 (ISBN 0-686-68295-5). OAS.

Odell, Peter R. & Preston, David A. Economies & Societies in Latin America: A Geographical Interpretation. 2nd ed. LC 77-12400. 289p. 1978. text ed. 34.95 (ISBN 0-471-99588-6, Pub. by Wiley-Interscience); pap. text ed. 15.75 (ISBN 0-471-99636-X). Wiley.

Orlove, Benjamin S. & Custred, Glynn, eds. Land & Power in Latin America: Agrarian Economics of Social Process in the Andes. LC 79-26598. 1980. text ed. 35.50x (ISBN 0-8419-0476-6). Holmes & Meier.

Orosz, Arpad. The Foreign Trade Turnover of Latin America Until 1970 & Its Prospective Development up to 1980. LC 77-369256. (Studies on Developing Countries). 130p. (Orig.). 1976. pap. 8.50x (ISBN 0-8002-0494-8). Intl Pubns Serv.

Oxaal, Ivar, et al, eds. Beyond the Sociology of Development. (International Library of Sociology). 1975. 25.00 (ISBN 0-7100-8049-2); pap. 12.00 (ISBN 0-7100-8050-6). Routledge & Kegan.

Pazos, Felipe. Chronic Inflation in Latin America. LC 71-180848. (Special Studies in International Economics & Development). 1972. 24.50x (ISBN 0-275-28282-1). Irvington.

Pollitt, Ernesto. Poverty & Malnutrition in Latin America: Early Childhood Intervention Programs. LC 80-18811. 150p. 1980. 22.95 (ISBN 0-03-058031-5). Praeger.

Randall, Laura. A Comparative Economic History of Latin America: Mexico, Vol. 1. LC 77-81283. (Illus.). 1977. pap. 20.25 (ISBN 0-8357-0261-8, SS-00034). Univ Microfilms.

--A Comparative Economic History of Latin America, 1500-1914. Incl. Vol. 2. Argentina. 18.75 (ISBN 0-8357-0272-3, SS-00043); Vol. 3. Brazil. 18.75 (ISBN 0-8357-0273-1, SS-00044); Vol. 4. Peru. 16.75 (ISBN 0-8357-0274-X, SS-00045). LC 77-81283. 1977. Univ Microfilms.

Ray, Phillip A. South Wind Red. LC 62-17968. 1962. pap. 2.00 (ISBN 0-911956-12-3). Constructive Action.

Regional Employment Programme for Latin America & the Caribbean. Employment in Latin America. (Praeger Special Studies). 1978. 22.95 (ISBN 0-03-042131-4). Praeger.

Register of Development Research Projects in Latin America. 211p. 1979. 13.50x (ISBN 92-64-01956-1). OECD.

Rippy, James F. Latin America & the Industrial Age. 2nd ed. LC 70-136082. (Illus.). 1971. Repr. of 1947 ed. lib. bdg. 17.50x (ISBN 0-8371-5232-1, RIAM). Greenwood.

Ross, Stanley R., ed. Latin America in Transition: Problems in Training & Research. LC 71-112607. 1970. 11.00 (ISBN 0-87395-068-2); microfiche 11.00 (ISBN 0-87395-168-9). State U NY Pr.

Salazar-Carillo, Jorge & Buttari, Juan J. The Structure of Wages in Latin American Manufacturing Industries. (Illus.). 1981. write for info. (ISBN 0-8130-0696-1). U Presses Fla.

Scott, Robert E., ed. Latin American Modernization Problems: Case Studies in the Crises of Change. LC 72-81263. 365p. 1973. 17.50 (ISBN 0-252-00293-8). U of Ill Pr.

Sectoral Study of Transnational Enterprises in Latin America: The Automotive Industry. 41p. 1974. 5.00 (ISBN 0-8270-3295-1). OAS.

Shea, Donald R. & Swacker, Frank W., eds. Business & Legal Aspects of Latin American Trade & Investment. LC 76-44061. 1977. pap. 15.00 (ISBN 0-930450-11-6). Univ of Wis Latin Am.

Social Aspects of Economic Development in Latin America, 2 Vols. 1967. Vol. 1. 9.00 (ISBN 92-3-100512-X, UNESCO); Vol. 2. 6.50 (ISBN 92-3-100510-3). Unipub.

Stein, Stanley J. & Stein, Barbara H. Colonial Heritage of Latin America: Essays on Economic Dependence in Perspective. 1970. pap. text ed. 5.95x (ISBN 0-19-501292-5). Oxford U Pr.

Swansbrough, Robert H. The Embattled Colossus: Economic Nationalism & United States Investors in Latin America. LC 75-43994. (Latin American Monographs: Ser. 2, No. 16). 1976. 12.50 (ISBN 0-8130-0409-8). U Presses Fla.

Swift, Jeannie. Economic Development in Latin America. LC 77-6298. 1978. 14.95x (ISBN 0-312-22880-5); pap. text ed. 6.95x (ISBN 0-312-22881-3). St Martin.

Teichert, Pedro C. Economic Policy Revolution & Industrialization in Latin America. LC 74-2589. 282p. 1975. Repr. of 1959 ed. lib. bdg. 22.75x (ISBN 0-8371-7409-0, TEPR). Greenwood.

Theberge, James D., et al. Latin America: Struggle for Progress, Vol. 14. LC 75-44723. (Critical Choices for Americans Ser.). 1976. 16.95 (ISBN 0-669-00428-6). Lexington Bks.

Thorp, Rosemary & Whitehead, Lawrence, eds. Inflation & Stabilisation in Latin America. LC 79-11887. 1980. text ed. 34.50x (ISBN 0-8419-0512-6). Holmes & Meier.

United Nations. Economic Bulletin for Latin America, Vol. 19, No. 1-2. pap. 5.50 (ISBN 0-685-20775-7, E.75.II.G.2). UN.

--Economic Survey of Latin America 1977. LC 50-3616. 536p. (Orig.). 1978. pap. 22.00x (ISBN 0-8002-1067-0). Intl Pubns Serv.

United Nations Economic Commission for Latin America. Water Management & Environment in Latin America: Analysis & Case Studies of Water Management, Including New Approaches Through Simulation Modelling & the Environmental Consequences of Past & Potential Trends in Water Use. (Environmental Sciences & Applications Ser.: Vol. 12). 1979. 68.00 (ISBN 0-08-023580-8); pap. 23.00 (ISBN 0-08-024457-2). Pergamon.

U.S. Dept. of Commerce, Bureau of Foreign & Domestic Commerce. Investments in Latin America & the British West Indies. Wilkins, Mira, ed. LC 76-29754. (European Business Ser.: Special Agent Ser. 169). (Illus.). 1977. Repr. of 1918 ed. lib. bdg. 33.00x (ISBN 0-405-09770-0). Arno.

Walton, John. Elites & Economic Development: Comparative Studies on the Political Economy of Latin American Cities. LC 75-620108. (Latin American Monographs: No. 41). 269p. 1977. pap. 6.95x (ISBN 0-292-72018-1). U of Tex Pr.

Wilgus, A. Curtis. Historical Atlas of Latin America: Political, Geographic, Economic, Cultural. rev. ed. LC 66-30784. Orig. Title: Latin America in Maps. (Illus.). 1967. Repr. of 1943 ed. 12.00x (ISBN 0-8154-0256-2). Cooper Sq.

Wilkie, James W., ed. Money & Politics in Latin America. LC 77-620008. (Supplements to the Statistical Abstracts of Latin America: Vol. 7). 1977. pap. text ed. 10.95 (ISBN 0-87903-232-4). UCLA Lat Am Ctr.

Williamson, Robert B., et al. Latin American-U. S. Economic Interactions: Conflict, Accommodation & Policies for the Future. 380p. 1975. 16.25 (ISBN 0-8447-2051-8); pap. 8.25 (ISBN 0-8447-2050-X). Am Enterprise.

Winkler, Max. Investments of United States Capital in Latin America. LC 73-123497. 1971. Repr. of 1929 ed. 13.50 (ISBN 0-8046-1384-2). Kennikat.

Wolf, Eric R. & Hansen, Edward C. The Human Condition in Latin America. (Illus.). 392p. 1972. 17.50 (ISBN 0-19-501570-3); pap. 6.95x (ISBN 0-19-501569-X). Oxford U Pr.

Wynia, G. W. The Politics of Latin American Development. LC 77-87395. (Illus.). 1978. 32.95 (ISBN 0-521-21922-1); pap. 9.95x (ISBN 0-521-29310-3). Cambridge U Pr.

Wythe, George. Industry in Latin America. Repr. of 1949 ed. lib. bdg. 19.75x (ISBN 0-8371-1051-3, WYIL). Greenwood.

Yudelman, Montague. Agriculture Development & Economic Integration in Latin America. 1970. 16.95x (ISBN 0-8464-0985-2). Beekman Pubs.

Ziegler, Lawrence F. Monetary Accommodation of Regional Integration in Latin America. (Studies in Latin American Business: No. 92). 1971. pap. 4.00 (ISBN 0-87755-154-5). U of Tex Busn Res.

Zook, Paul D., ed. Foreign Trade & Human Capital. LC 62-13276. 1962. 4.00 (ISBN 0-87074-130-6). SMU Press.

LATIN AMERICA-FOREIGN RELATIONS

Arias, Esther & Arias, Mortimer. El Clamor De Mi Pueblo. Martinez, Ana E., tr. from English. (Illus., Orig., Span.). 1981. pap. 2.95 (ISBN 0-377-00105-8). Friend Pr.

Atkins, G. Pope. Latin America in the International Political System. LC 76-20882. (Illus.). 1977. text ed. 16.95 (ISBN 0-02-901060-8). Free Pr.

Bacon, R. For Better Relations with Our Latin American Neighbors. 1976. lib. bdg. 59.95 (ISBN 0-8490-1855-2). Gordon Pr.

Berle, Adolf A. Latin America: Diplomacy & Reality. LC 81-3818. (Council on Foreign Relations Ser.). xii, 144p. 1981. Repr. of 1962 ed. lib. bdg. 19.75x (ISBN 0-313-22970-8, BELAM). Greenwood.

Blasier, Cole. The Hovering Giant: U. S. Responses to Revolutionary Change in Latin America. LC 75-9130. (Pitt Latin American Ser.). (Illus.). 1976. 15.95 (ISBN 0-8229-3304-7); pap. 7.95x (ISBN 0-8229-5264-5). U of Pittsburgh Pr.

Burr, Robert N. Our Troubled Hemisphere: Perspectives on United States-Latin American Relations. 1967. 9.95 (ISBN 0-8157-1174-3). Brookings.

Callcott, Wilfrid H. Caribbean Policy of the United States, 1890-1920. 1967. lib. bdg. 30.00x (ISBN 0-374-91216-5). Octagon.

Curry, E. R. Hoover's Dominican Diplomacy & the Origins of the Good Neighbor Policy. Freidel, Frank, ed. LC 78-62379. (Modern American History Ser.: Vol. 5). 1979. lib. bdg. 30.00 (ISBN 0-8240-3629-8). Garland Pub.

Davis, Harold E., et al. Latin American Diplomatic History: An Introduction. LC 76-58901. 1977. 22.50x (ISBN 0-8071-0260-1); pap. 7.95x (ISBN 0-8071-0286-5). La State U Pr.

Davis, Harold Eugene, et al. Latin American Foreign Policies: An Analysis. LC 74-24386. (Illus.). 488p. 1975. pap. 6.95x (ISBN 0-8018-1695-5). Johns Hopkins.

DeWitt, R. Peter, Jr. The Inter-American Development Bank & Political Influence: With Special Reference to Costa Rica. LC 77-2929. (Special Studies). 1977. text ed. 24.95 (ISBN 0-275-24460-1). Praeger.

Eister, Allan W. United States & the A. B. C. Powers, 1889-1906. LC 52-4373. (Arnold Foundation Studies: New Ser., No. 1). 1950. pap. 1.50 (ISBN 0-87074-051-2). SMU Press.

Farer, Tom J. The Future of the Inter-American System. LC 78-31153. (Praeger Special Studies). 1979. 24.95 (ISBN 0-03-047391-8). Praeger.

Ferris, Elizabeth G. & Lincoln, Jennie I., eds. Latin American Foreign Policies: Global & Regional Dimensions. (Special Studies on Latin America Ser.). 350p. 1981. lib. bdg. 26.50 (ISBN 0-86531-208-7); pap. text ed. 14.00 (ISBN 0-86531-284-2). Westview.

Finan, John J. & Child, John, eds. Latin America: International Relations: A Guide to Information Sources. LC 73-117508. (International Relations Information Guide Ser.: Vol.11). 250p. 1981. 36.00 (ISBN 0-8103-1325-1). Gale.

Gaspar, Edmund. United States-Latin America: A Special Relationship? 1978. pap. 4.25 (ISBN 0-8447-3287-7). Am Enterprise.

Gil, Federico G. Latin American-United States Relations. 1971. pap. text ed. 10.95 (ISBN 0-15-550195-X, HC). HarBraceJ.

Glauert, Earl T. & Langley, Lester D., eds. The United States & Latin America. LC 79-133376. (History Ser). 1971. pap. 5.95 (ISBN 0-201-02404-7). A-W.

Green, David. Containment of Latin America: A History of the Myths & Realities of the Good Neighbor Policy. LC 76-130384. 320p. 1971. 10.00 (ISBN 0-8129-0160-6). Times Bks.

Grow, Michael. The Good Neighbor Policy & Authoritarianism in Paraguay: United States Economic Expansion & Great Power Rivalry in Latin America During World War II. LC 81-11. (Illus.). xii, 176p. 1981. 20.00x (ISBN 0-7006-0213-5). Regents Pr KS.

Hellman, R. G. & Rosenbaum, H. J. Latin America: The Search for a New International Role. LC 75-692. (Latin American International Affairs Ser: Vol. 1). 1975. 17.50 (ISBN 0-470-36917-5). Halsted Pr.

Hopkins, Jack. Latin America in World Affairs: The Politics of Inequality. Dillon, Mary, ed. LC 76-17616. (Politics of Government Ser.). 1977. pap. 3.50 (ISBN 0-8120-0497-3). Barron.

Inter-American Peace Treaties & Conventions. (Treaty Ser.: No. 16). (Eng. , Span. & Port.). 1961. pap. 1.00 ea. Eng. Ed (ISBN 0-8270-0340-4). Span Ed (ISBN 0-8270-0345-5). Port. Ed (ISBN 0-8270-0350-1). OAS.

Jackson, D. Bruce. Castro, The Kremlin, & Communism in Latin America. LC 68-9696. (Studies in International Affairs: No. 9). 169p. (Orig.). 1969. 12.00x (ISBN 0-8018-0308-X); pap. 3.95x (ISBN 0-8018-0309-8). Johns Hopkins.

Johnson, Cecil. Communist China & Latin America, 1959-1967. LC 76-129054. 324p. 1970. 20.00x (ISBN 0-231-03309-5). Columbia U Pr.

Kane, William Everett. Civil Strife in Latin America: A Legal History of U.S. Involvement. LC 76-184954. (American Society of International Law Ser). (Illus.). 240p. 1972. 16.00x (ISBN 0-8018-1368-9). Johns Hopkins.

Kaufmann, William W. British Policy & the Independence of Latin America, 1804-1828. 1967. Repr. of 1951 ed. 18.50 (ISBN 0-208-00351-7, Archon). Shoe String.

Lockey, Joseph B. Essay in Pan-Americanism. LC 66-25927. Repr. of 1939 ed. 12.00 (ISBN 0-8046-0275-1). Kennikat.

Lowenthal, Abraham F. & Fishlow, Albert. Latin America's Emergence: Toward a U. S. Response. LC 79-51272. (Headline Ser.: No. 243). (Illus.). 1979. pap. 2.00 (ISBN 0-87124-053-X). Foreign Policy.

Lozoya, Jorge & Estevez, Jaime, eds. Latin America & the New International Economic Order. LC 79-27384. (Pergamon Policy Studies in the New International Economic Order). 112p. 1980. 16.50 (ISBN 0-08-025118-8). Pergamon.

Machado, Manuel A., Jr. Aftosa: A Historical Survey of Foot & Mouth Disease & Inter-American Relations. LC 69-11317. 1969. 16.00 (ISBN 0-87395-040-2); microfiche 16.00 (ISBN 0-87395-140-9). State U NY Pr.

Mathis, F. John. Economic Integration in Latin America. (Studies in Latin American Business: No. 8). pap. 4.00 (ISBN 0-87755-076-X). U of Tex Busn Res.

Meeting Of Consultation Of Ministers Of Foreign Affairs Of The American Republics - 8th - Punta Del Este - Uruguay - 1962. Background Memorandum of the Convocation of the Meeting. pap. 1.00 ea. Eng. & Span. eds. OAS.

Ministers of Foreign Affairs of the American Republics-15th Quito, Ecuador. Final Act: Meeting of Consultation. (Eng., Span., Fr.). 1974. pap. 1.00 Eng. ed. (ISBN 0-8270-1745-6); pap. 1.00 Span. ed. (ISBN 0-8270-1750-2); pap. 1.00 French ed. (ISBN 0-8270-1755-3). OAS.

Perkins, Dexter. The Monroe Doctrine, 3 vols. Incl. 1823-1826. 8.00 (ISBN 0-685-22731-6); 1826-1867. 9.50 (ISBN 0-685-22732-4); 1867-1907. 9.50 (ISBN 0-685-22733-2). Set (ISBN 0-8446-1346-0). Peter Smith.

Rippy, J. Fred. Rivalry of the United States & Great Britain Over Latin America, 1808-1830. 1964. lib. bdg. 20.00x (ISBN 0-374-96821-7). Octagon.

Robertson, William S. France & Latin-American Independence. 1967. lib. bdg. 30.00x (ISBN 0-374-96878-0). Octagon.

Slater, Jerome. OAS & United States Foreign Policy. LC 67-10162. 1967. 6.00 (ISBN 0-8142-0111-3). Ohio St U Pr.

Smith, Joseph. Illusions of Conflict: Anglo-American Diplomacy Toward Latin America, 1865-1896. LC 78-53602. (Pitt Latin American Ser.). 1979. 16.95 (ISBN 0-8229-3387-X). U of Pittsburgh Pr.

Tulchin, Joseph S. The Aftermath of War: World War I & U.S. Policy Toward Latin America. LC 71-145515. 1971. 12.00x (ISBN 0-8147-8152-7). NYU Pr.

Wagner, R. Harrison. United States Policy Toward Latin America: A Study in Domestic & International Politics. LC 79-107651. 1970. 15.00x (ISBN 0-8047-0730-8). Stanford U Pr.

Webster, C. K. Britain & the Independence of Latin America, 1812-1830, 2 vols. LC 79-96194. 1969. Repr. Set. lib. bdg. 70.00x (ISBN 0-374-98303-8). Octagon.

Williamson, Rene D. Culture & Policy: The United States & the Hispanic World. 1949. 5.00x (ISBN 0-87049-004-4). U of Tenn Pr.

LATIN AMERICA-HISTORIOGRAPHY

Graham, Richard & Smith, Peter H., eds. New Approaches to Latin American History. LC 74-2017. 289p. 1974. 12.50x (ISBN 0-292-75506-6). U of Tex Pr.

Iglesia, Ramon. Columbus, Cortes, & Other Essays. Simpson, Lesley B., tr. LC 69-13727. 1969. 21.75x (ISBN 0-520-01469-3). U of Cal Pr.

Wilgus, A. Curtis. Historiography of Latin America: A Guide to Historical Writing, 1500-1800. 1975. 18.00 (ISBN 0-8108-0859-5). Scarecrow.

Wilgus, Alva C., ed. Colonial Hispanic America. LC 63-8374. (Illus.). 1963. Repr. of 1936 ed. 13.50 (ISBN 0-8462-0338-3). Russell.

LATIN AMERICA-HISTORY

Aldridge, A. Owen, ed. The Ibero-American Enlightenment: A Collection of Essays. LC 78-126520. 1971. 19.95 (ISBN 0-252-00122-2). U of Ill Pr.

Ashburn, Percy M. The Ranks of Death: A Medical History of the Conquest of America. Ashburn, Frank D., ed. LC 80-24672. (Perspectives in Latin American History Ser.: No. 2). xix, 298p. Repr. of 1947 ed. lib. bdg. 19.50x (ISBN 0-87991-599-4). Porcupine Pr.

Bailey, Helen M. & Nasatir, Abraham P. Latin America: The Development of Its Civilization. 3rd ed. (Illus.). 896p. 1973. ref. ed. 20.95x (ISBN 0-13-524264-9). P-H.

Bannon, John F. & Miller, Robert R. Latin America. 4th ed. 1977. text ed. 14.95 (ISBN 0-02-474350-X). Macmillan.

Barnes, Thomas C., et al. Northern New Spain: A Research Guide. LC 80-24860. 1981. pap. text ed. 9.95x (ISBN 0-8165-0709-0). U of Ariz Pr.

Benzoni, Girolamo. History of the New World. Smyth, William H., ed. & tr. (Hakluyt Soc., First Ser.: No. 21). 1964. 31.50 (ISBN 0-8337-0239-4). B Franklin.

Bernhard, Virginia, ed. Elites, Masses, & Modernization in Latin America, 1850-1930. (Texas Pan American Ser.). 165p. 1979. text ed. 11.00x (ISBN 0-292-76457-X). U of Tex Pr.

Blakemore, Harold. British Nitrates & Chilean Politics, 1886-1896: Balmaceda & North. (Institute of Latin American Studies Monograph Ser: No. 4). (Illus.). 256p. 1974. text ed. 31.25x (ISBN 0-485-17704-8, Athlone Pr). Humanities.

Burgin, Miron, ed. Handbook of Latin American Studies, 1940. LC 36-32633. (Latin American Studies Ser.: No. 6). xiii, 570p. 1963. Repr. 17.50x (ISBN 0-8130-0032-7). U Presses Fla.

--Handbook of Latin American Studies, 1941. LC 36-32633. (Latin American Studies Ser.: No. 7). xv, 649p. 1963. Repr. 17.50x (ISBN 0-8130-0033-5). U Presses Fla.

--Handbook of Latin American Studies, 1942. LC 36-32633. (Latin American Studies: No. 8). xv, 521p. 1963. Repr. 17.50 (ISBN 0-8130-0034-3). U Presses Fla.

--Handbook of Latin American Studies, 1943. LC 36-32633. (Latin American Studies Ser.: No. 9). xvi, 518p. 1963. Repr. 17.50x (ISBN 0-8130-0035-1). U Presses Fla.

--Handbook of Latin American Studies, 1944. LC 36-32633. (Latin American Studies Ser.: No. 10). xvi, 440p. 1963. Repr. 17.50x (ISBN 0-8130-0036-X). U Presses Fla.

--Handbook of Latin American Studies, 1945. LC 36-32633. (Latin American Studies Ser.: No. 11). ix, 404p. 1963. Repr. 17.50x (ISBN 0-8130-0037-8). U Presses Fla.

Burns, E. Bradford. Latin America: A Concise Interpretive History. 3rd ed. (Illus.). 352p. 1982. pap. 12.95 (ISBN 0-13-524322-X). P-H.

--Latin America: A Concise Interpretive History. 2nd ed. LC 76-21677. (Illus.). 1977. pap. text ed. 11.95 (ISBN 0-13-524314-9). P-H.

Cardoso, Fernando E. & Faletto, Enzo. Dependency & Development in Latin America. Urquidi, Marjory M., tr. LC 75-46033. 1979. 25.75x (ISBN 0-520-03193-8); pap. 5.95x (ISBN 0-520-03527-5). U of Cal Pr.

Cespedes, Guillermo. Latin America: History. 1974. 5.95 (ISBN 0-394-31810-2). Knopf.

Charroux, Robert. The Mysteries of the Andes. 1977. pap. 2.25 (ISBN 0-380-01702-4, 33779). Avon.

Costeloe, M. P. Church Wealth in Mexico. (Cambridge Latin American Studies: No. 2). 1968. 17.95 (ISBN 0-521-04729-3). Cambridge U Pr.

Crow, John A. The Epic of Latin America. LC 78-62860. 1000p. 1980. 29.95x (ISBN 0-520-04107-0); pap. 14.95 (ISBN 0-520-03776-6, CAL. NO. 458). U of Cal Pr.

Davies, Nigel. Voyagers to the New World: Fact & Fantasy. LC 79-83937. (Illus.). 1979. 12.95 (ISBN 0-688-03396-2). Morrow.

Debray, Regis. Revolution in the Revolution? Armed Struggle and Political Struggle in Latin America. Ortiz, Bobbye, tr. from Fr., Span. LC 80-19409. 126p. 1980. Repr. of 1967 ed. lib. bdg. 17.50x (ISBN 0-313-22669-5, DERE). Greenwood.

De Imaz, Jose L. Los Que Mandan (Those Who Rule) Astiz, Carlos A., tr. from Span. LC 69-12100. (Orig.). 1970. 21.00 (ISBN 0-87395-044-5); pap. 9.95 (ISBN 0-87395-073-9); microfiche 21.00 (ISBN 0-87395-144-1). State U NY Pr.

Della Cava, Ralph. Miracle at Joaseiro. LC 76-127364. (Institute for Latin American Studies). (Illus.). 324p. 1970. 16.00x (ISBN 0-231-03293-5). Columbia U Pr.

Delpar, Helen. Borzoi Reader in Latin American History. 1972. pap. text ed. 4.25x (ISBN 0-394-31151-5). Phila Bk Co.

Dennis, William J. Documentary History of the Tacna-Arica Dispute. LC 75-130329. (Latin-American History & Culture Ser). 1971. Repr. of 1927 ed. 12.50 (ISBN 0-8046-1391-5). Kennikat.

De Oliveira Lima, Manuel. The Evolution of Brazil Compared with That of Spanish & Anglo-Saxon America. Martin, Percy A., ed. LC 74-12766. (Leland Stanford Jr. Univ. Publications: No. 16). 159p. 1975. Repr. of 1914 ed. lib. bdg. 15.00x (ISBN 0-8371-7740-5, OLEB). Greenwood.

Descola, Jean. Conquistadors. Barnes, Malcolm, tr. LC 72-122060. Repr. of 1957 ed. lib. bdg. 17.50x (ISBN 0-678-03151-7). Kelley.

Dozer, Donald M. Latin America: An Interpretive History. rev. ed. 659p. 1980. text ed. 17.95 (ISBN 0-87918-049-8). ASU Lat Am St.

Duff, Ernest A. & McCamant, John F. Violence & Repression in Latin America: A Quantitative & Historical Analysis. LC 75-16645. (Illus.). 1976. 19.95 (ISBN 0-02-907690-0). Free Pr.

Duncan, W. Raymond & Goodsell, James N., eds. The Quest for Change in Latin America: Sources for a Twentieth Century Analysis. 1970. pap. 6.95x (ISBN 0-19-501254-2). Oxford U Pr.

Ellis, Joseph A. Latin America: Its Peoples & Institutions. 2nd ed. 1975. pap. text ed. 8.25x (ISBN 0-02-474200-7, 47420). Macmillan.

Essays in American History Dedicated to Frederick Jackson Turner. 8.50 (ISBN 0-8446-1451-3). Peter Smith.

Fagg, John E. Latin America: A General History. 3rd ed. (Illus.). 1977. text ed. 18.95x (ISBN 0-02-334770-8, 33478). Macmillan.

Fisher, Lillian E. Champion of Reform: Manuel Abad y Queipo. LC 76-151549. 1971. Repr. of 1955 ed. 15.00 (ISBN 0-8462-1597-7). Russell.

Fitzgibbon, Russell H. The Selected Writings of Russell H. Fitzgibbon. Date not set. text ed. price not set (ISBN 0-87918-039-0). ASU Lat Am St.

Franqui, Carlos. Twelve. Teicher, Albert, tr. LC 68-10011. 1968. 4.50 (ISBN 0-8184-0089-7). Lyle Stuart.

Greater America: Essays in Honor of Herbert Eugene Bolton. facs. ed. LC 68-14905. (Essay Index Reprint Ser). 1945. 27.25 (ISBN 0-8369-0495-8). Arno.

Hanke, Lewis. The Selected Writings of Lewis Hanke. LC 77-5582. 1979. pap. text ed. 14.95 (ISBN 0-87918-036-6). ASU Lat Am St.

Hanke, Lewis, ed. Readings in Latin American History. Incl. Vol. 1. To 1810 (ISBN 0-88295-740-6); Vol. 2. Since 1810 (ISBN 0-88295-741-4). LC 66-17328. 1966. pap. 7.50x ea. Harlan Davidson.

Hanson, Carl A. Dissertations on Iberian & Latin American History. LC 74-97478. 400p. 1975. 20.00 (ISBN 0-87875-073-8). Whitston Pub.

Helps, Arthur. Spanish Conquest in America, & Its Relation to the History of Slavery & to the Government of Colonies, 4 Vols. new ed. Oppenheim, M., ed. LC 72-15297. Repr. of 1904 ed. 85.00 (ISBN 0-404-03270-2). AMS Pr.

Hennessy, Alistair. The Frontier in Latin American History. LC 78-58816. (Histories of the American Frontier Ser). 1978. 14.95x (ISBN 0-8263-0466-4); pap. 8.95x (ISBN 0-8263-0467-2). U of NM Pr.

Herring, Hubert. History of Latin America. 3rd ed. 1968. text ed. 19.95 (ISBN 0-394-30247-8, KnopfC). Knopf.

--History of Latin America. 3rd ed. (YA) 1968. 29.95 (ISBN 0-394-42870-6). Knopf.

Hoskins, H. L. Guide to Latin American History. 59.95 (ISBN 0-8490-0268-0). Gordon Pr.

Humphreys, Robin A. The Evolution of Modern Latin America. LC 72-94054. (Illus.). 196p. 1973. Repr. of 1946 ed. lib. bdg. 11.00x (ISBN 0-8154-0457-3). Cooper Sq.

Introduction a la Cultura Africanа en America Latina. (Sp.). 1979. pap. 12.25 (ISBN 92-3-301585-8, U941, UNESCO). Unipub.

Jamieson, Alfred. Latin America, 4 bks. (Culture Studies Program). (gr. 7-12). 1979. pap. text ed. 6.04 (ISBN 0-201-42669-2, Sch Div); tchr's ed. 2.76 (ISBN 0-201-42670-6). A-W.

Jane, Lionel C. Liberty & Despotism in Spanish America. LC 66-29053. 1966. Repr. of 1929 ed. 11.00x (ISBN 0-8154-0119-1). Cooper Sq.

Keen, Benjamin & Wasserman, Mark. A Short History of Latin America. 1979. pap. text ed. 13.50 (ISBN 0-395-27838-4). HM.

Keen, Benjamin, ed. Latin American Civilization, 2 vols. 3rd ed. 1974. Vol. 1. pap. text ed. 11.50 (ISBN 0-395-17582-8); Vol. 2. pap. text ed. 11.50 (ISBN 0-395-17583-6). HM.

Keith, Robert G., ed. Haciendas & Plantations in Latin American History. LC 77-7587. 1977. text ed. 26.00x (ISBN 0-8419-0319-0). Holmes & Meier.

Keniston, Hayward. List of Works for the Study of Hispanic-American History. LC 20-22697. 1920. 22.00 (ISBN 0-527-48300-1). Kraus Repr.

Kinsbruner, Jay. The Spanish-American Independence Movement. LC 76-15260. (Berkshire Studies Ser.). 158p. 1976. pap. text ed. 5.50 (ISBN 0-88275-428-9). Krieger.

Kirkpatrick, Frederick A. Latin America, a Brief History. LC 75-41166. Repr. of 1939 ed. 28.45 (ISBN 0-685-70792-X). AMS Pr.

Latin America in the Struggle Against Imperialism, for National Independence, Democracy, People's Wlfare, Peace & Socialism. 1975. pap. 0.40 (ISBN 0-87898-117-9). New Outlook.

Latin America: World in Revolution. LC 74-9631. (Illus.). 352p. 1974. Repr. of 1963 ed. lib. bdg. 15.00x (ISBN 0-8371-7598-4, BELAW). Greenwood.

Love, Joseph L. Rio Grande Do Sul & Brazilian Regionalism: 1882-1930. LC 71-130829. (Illus.). 1971. 18.50x (ISBN 0-8047-0759-6). Stanford U Pr.

Loveman, Brian & Davies, Thomas M., Jr., eds. The Politics of Antipolitics: The Military in Latin America. LC 77-25256. 1978. 19.95x (ISBN 0-8032-0954-1); pap. 6.50x (ISBN 0-8032-7900-0, BB 672, Bison). U of Nebr Pr.

McEwen, William J. Changing Rural Society: A Study of Communities in Bolivia. (Illus.). 384p. 1975. text ed. 18.95x (ISBN 0-19-501894-X); pap. text ed. 9.95x (ISBN 0-19-501893-1). Oxford U Pr.

Maguidovich, I. P. Historia Del Descubrimiento y Exploracion De Latinoamerica. 396p. 1979. 6.35 (ISBN 0-8285-1440-2, 001243, Pub. by Progress Pubs Russia). Imported Pubns.

Marban, Edilberto. El Mundo Iberoamericano: Hombres en Su Historia. 390p. (gr. 10-12). 1974. pap. text ed. 6.95 (ISBN 0-88345-066-6, 18084). Regents Pub.

Marti, Jose. Our America: Writings on Latin America & the Cuban Struggle for Independence. Foner, Philip, ed. Randall, Elinor, tr. LC 77-70967. 1978. 16.50 (ISBN 0-85345-414-0, CL4140). Monthly Rev.

--Our America: Writings on Latin America & the Struggle for Cuban Independence. Foner, Philip S., ed. Randall, Elinor, tr. from Sp. LC 77-70967. 1979. pap. 7.50 (ISBN 0-85345-495-7, PB-4957). Monthly Rev.

Martin, Michael R. & Lovett, Gabriel H. Encyclopedia of Latin-American History. rev. ed. Hoffman, Fritz L. & Hughes, Robert L., eds. LC 81-715. vi, 348p. 1981. Repr. of 1968 ed. lib. bdg. 35.00x (ISBN 0-313-22881-7, MAELA). Greenwood.

Mauro, Frederic. Des Produits et Des Hommes: Essais Historiques Latino-Americains, XVIe-XXe Siecles. (Civilisations et Societes: No. 34). 1973. pap. 15.50x (ISBN 90-2797-172-2). Mouton.

Needler, Martin C. The United States & the Latin American Revolution. rev. ed. LC 76-620079. (Latin American Studies: Vol. 38). 1977. pap. text ed. 5.95 (ISBN 0-87903-038-0). UCLA Lat Am Ctr.

Nesheim, Margaret. From the Hinterland of Ecuador to the Shores of Galapagos. (Illus.). 154p. 1981. 10.00 (ISBN 0-682-49673-1). Exposition.

Olien, M. Latin Americans: Contemporary Peoples in Their Cultural Traditions. LC 72-9887. 1973. text ed. 14.95 (ISBN 0-03-086251-5, HoltC). HR&W.

Parkinson, F. Latin America, the Cold War & the World Powers 1945-1973. LC 74-77289. (Sage Library of Social Research: Vol. 9). 288p. 1974. 18.00x (ISBN 0-8039-0413-4); pap. 9.95 (ISBN 0-8039-0412-6). Sage.

Pendle, G. A History of Latin America. 8.00 (ISBN 0-8446-2717-8). Peter Smith.

Pendle, George. History of Latin America. (Orig.). (YA) (gr. 11 up). 1963. pap. 2.95 (ISBN 0-14-020620-5, Pelican). Penguin.

Pierson, W. Hispanic-American History: A Syllabus. 1976. lib. bdg. 59.95 (ISBN 0-8490-1952-4). Gordon Pr.

Randall, Laura. A Comparative Economic History of Latin America: Mexico, Vol. 1. LC 77-81283. (Illus.). 1977. pap. 20.25 (ISBN 0-8357-0261-8, SS-00034). Univ Microfilms.

--A Comparative Economic History of Latin America, 1500-1914. Incl. Vol. 2. Argentina. 18.75 (ISBN 0-8357-0272-3, SS-00043); Vol. 3. Brazil. 18.75 (ISBN 0-8357-0273-1, SS-00044); Vol. 4. Peru. 16.75 (ISBN 0-8357-0274-X, SS-00045). LC 77-81283. 1977. Univ Microfilms.

Reed, John. The Education of John Reed: Selected Writings. Stuart, John, ed. 224p. 1972. pap. 1.45 (ISBN 0-7178-0354-6). Intl Pub Co.

Robertson, William S. Rise of the Spanish-American Republics: As Told in the Lives of Their Liberators. 1965. pap. text ed. 3.50 (ISBN 0-02-926600-9). Free Pr.

Robinson, David J., ed. Social Fabric & Spatial Structure in Colonial Latin America. LC 79-15744. (Illus., Orig.). 1979. pap. 26.50 (ISBN 0-8357-0419-X, SS-00100). Univ Microfilms.

Robinson, H. Latin America. 4th ed. (Illus.). 544p. 1977. pap. text ed. 17.95x (ISBN 0-7121-1235-9, Pub. by Macdonald & Evans England). Intl Ideas.

Ross, Stanley R., ed. Latin America in Transition: Problems in Training & Research. LC 71-112607. 1970. 11.00 (ISBN 0-87395-068-2); microfiche 11.00 (ISBN 0-87395-168-9). State U NY Pr.

Rout, Leslie B., Jr. Politics of the Chaco Peace Conference, 1935-1939. (Latin American Monographs: No. 19). (Illus.). 286p. 1970. 12.50x (ISBN 0-292-70049-0). U of Tex Pr.

Ruiz, Ramon E. Cuba: The Making of a Revolution. 1970. pap. 3.95 (ISBN 0-393-00513-5, N513, Norton Lib). Norton.

Sable, Martin H. Latin American Agriculture: A Bibliography. LC 70-628991. (Center Bibliographic Ser.: No. 1). 1970. pap. 6.00 (ISBN 0-930450-02-7). Univ of Wis Latin Am.

Shafer, Robert J. History of Latin America. 1978. text ed. 17.95x (ISBN 0-669-01283-1). Heath.

Soustelle, Jacques. Daily Life of the Aztecs on the Eve of the Spanish Conquest. 1961. pap. 4.95 (ISBN 0-8047-0721-9, SP114). Stanford U Pr.

Stephens, John. Incidents of Travel in Central America, Chiapas & Yucatan, 2 Vols. (Illus.). 1969. Vol. 1. pap. 5.00 ea. (ISBN 0-486-22404-X); Vol. 2. pap. (ISBN 0-486-22405-8). Dover.

Stewart, Watt & Peterson, Harold I. Builders of Latin America. LC 76-167425. (Essay Index Reprint Ser.). Repr. of 1942 ed. 35.00 (ISBN 0-8369-2724-9). Arno.

TePaske, John J., ed. Research Guide to ANDEAN History: Bolivia, Chile, Ecuador, & Peru. LC 80-29365. 346p. 1981. 18.75 (ISBN 0-8223-0450-3). Duke.

Veliz, Claudio. The Centralist Tradition of Latin America. LC 79-84019. (Illus.). 1980. 22.50 (ISBN 0-691-05280-8); pap. 9.75 (ISBN 0-691-10085-3). Princeton U Pr.

Welsbord. Latin American Actuality. 4.50 (ISBN 0-8065-0321-1). Citadel Pr.

Wiarda, Howard J. Corporatism & National Development in Latin America. (Replica Edition Ser.). 325p. 1981. lib. bdg. 28.25x (ISBN 0-86531-031-9). Westview.

--Critical Elections & Critical Coups: State, Society & the Military in the Processes of Latin American Development. LC 79-4433. (Papers in International Studies: Latin America: No. 5). 1979. pap. 7.00 (ISBN 0-89680-082-2). Ohio U Ctr Intl.

Wilgus, A. Curtis. Historical Atlas of Latin America: Political, Geographic, Economic, Cultural. rev. ed. LC 66-30784. Orig. Title: Latin America in Maps. (Illus.). 1967. Repr. of 1943 ed. 12.00x (ISBN 0-8154-0256-2). Cooper Sq.

--Latin America Fourteen Ninety-Two to Nineteen Forty-Two: A Guide to Historical & Cultural Development Before World War Two. 1973. Repr. of 1941 ed. 27.50 (ISBN 0-8108-0595-2). Scarecrow.

Worcester, Donald E. & Schaeffer, Wendell G. Growth & Culture of Latin America. 1971. Set. 2 vols. in one ed. 25.00 (ISBN 0-19-501421-9). Oxford U Pr.

--Growth & Culture of Latin America. 1971. Set. 2 vols. in one ed. 25.00 (ISBN 0-19-501421-9). Oxford U Pr.

--Growth & Culture of Latin America Vol. 1: From Conquest to Independence. 2nd ed. 1970. pap. 9.95x (ISBN 0-19-501104-X). Oxford U Pr.

--Growth & Culture of Latin America Vol. 2: The Continuing Struggle for Independence. 2nd ed. 1971. pap. 9.95x (ISBN 0-19-501105-8). Oxford U Pr.

Yudelman, Montague. Agriculture Development & Economic Integration in Latin America. 1970. 16.95x (ISBN 0-8464-0985-2). Beekman Pubs.

Zavala, S. Amerique Latine: Philosophie De la Conquete. 1977. 10.50x (ISBN 90-279-7624-4). Mouton.

LATIN AMERICA-HISTORY-INDEXES

DePlatt, Lyman, ed. Genealogical Historical Guide to Latin America. LC 78-75146. (Genealogy & Local History Ser.: Vol. 4). 1978. 36.00 (ISBN 0-8103-1389-8). Gale.

Gibson, Charles & Niemeyer, E. V., eds. Guide to Hispanic American Historical Review: 1946-1955. LC 58-8501. 1976. Repr. of 1958 ed. pap. 12.00 (ISBN 0-527-36705-2). Kraus Repr.

LATIN AMERICA-HISTORY-SOURCES

Duncan, W. Raymond & Goodsell, James N., eds. The Quest for Change in Latin America: Sources for a Twentieth Century Analysis. 1970. pap. 6.95x (ISBN 0-19-501254-2). Oxford U Pr.

LATIN AMERICA-HISTORY-STUDY AND TEACHING

Pacific Coast Council on Latin American Studies. New Directions in the Teaching & Research of Latin American Studies: Proceedings, Vol. 2. 1973. pap. 7.00x (ISBN 0-916304-14-0). Campanile.

LATIN AMERICA-HISTORY-TO 1600

Helms, Mary W. Ancient Panama: Chiefs in Search of Power. (Texas Pan American Ser.). (Illus.). 244p. 1979. text ed. 16.95x (ISBN 0-292-73817-X). U of Tex Pr.

LATIN AMERICA-HISTORY-TO 1830

Belaunde, Victor A. Bolivar & the Political Thought of the Spanish-American Revolution. 1967. lib. bdg. 27.50x (ISBN 0-374-90532-0). Octagon.

Burke, William. Additional Reasons for Our Immediately Emancipating Spanish America. LC 73-128426. Repr. of 1808 ed. 12.50 (ISBN 0-404-01240-X). AMS Pr.

Chew, Benjamin. Sketch of the Politics, Relations & Statistics of the Western World. LC 77-128427. Repr. of 1827 ed. 19.50 (ISBN 0-404-01489-5). AMS Pr.

Diffie, Bailey W. Latin-American Civilization: Colonial Period. 1967. lib. bdg. 50.00x (ISBN 0-374-92166-0). Octagon.

Gibson, Charles, ed. Spanish Tradition in America. LC 68-63011. (Documentary History of the United States Ser). 1968. 14.95x (ISBN 0-87249-112-9). U of SC Pr.

Gongora, M. Studies in the Colonial History of Spanish America. Southern, R., tr. from Span. LC 74-19524. (Latin American Studies: No. 20). 235p. 1975. 32.95 (ISBN 0-521-20686-3). Cambridge U Pr.

Graham, Richard. Independence in Latin America. (Studies in World Civilization). 192p. 1972. pap. text ed. 5.95 (ISBN 0-394-31641-X). Knopf.

Haring, Clarence H. Spanish Empire in America. LC 47-1142. 1963. pap. 4.95 (ISBN 0-15-684701-9, H028, Hbgr). HarBraceJ.

Kaufmann, William W. British Policy & the Independence of Latin America, 1804-1828. 1967. Repr. of 1951 ed. 18.50 (ISBN 0-208-00351-7, Archon). Shoe String.

Lynch, John. The Spanish American Revolutions, 1808-1862. (Revolutions in the Modern World Ser). (Illus.). 352p. 1973. text ed. 15.00x (ISBN 0-393-05388-1); pap. text ed. 6.95x (ISBN 0-393-09411-1). Norton.

Madariaga, Salvador de. The Fall of the Spanish American Empire. LC 75-16849. (Illus.). 443p. 1975. Repr. of 1947 ed. lib. bdg. 24.75x (ISBN 0-8371-8267-0, MAFSE). Greenwood.

--The Rise of the Spanish American Empire. LC 75-16850. (Illus.). 408p. 1975. Repr. of 1947 ed. lib. bdg. 28.50x (ISBN 0-8371-8268-9, MARSE). Greenwood.

Moses, Bernard. Establishment of Spanish Rule in America. LC 65-21909. Repr. of 1898 ed. 12.00x (ISBN 0-8154-0156-6). Cooper Sq.

Parry, John H. Spanish Seaborne Empire. (History of Human Society Ser). (Illus.). 1966. 13.95 (ISBN 0-394-44650-X). Knopf.

Robertson, William S. France & Latin-American Independence. 1967. lib. bdg. 30.00x (ISBN 0-374-96878-0). Octagon.

Rodriguez, O. Jaime. The Emergence of Spanish America: Vincente Rocafuerte & Spanish Americanism, 1808-1832. LC 74-22972. 392p. 1976. 30.00x (ISBN 0-520-02875-9). U of Cal Pr.

Savelle, Max. Empires to Nations: Expansion in America, 1713-1824. Shafer, Boyd C., ed. LC 74-78995. (Europe & the World in the Age of Expansion Ser: Vol. 5). (Illus.). 384p. 1974. 12.50x (ISBN 0-8166-0709-5); pap. 3.45x (ISBN 0-8166-0781-8). U of Minn Pr.

Webster, C. K. Britain & the Independence of Latin America, 1812-1830, 2 vols. LC 79-96194. 1969. Repr. Set. lib. bdg. 70.00x (ISBN 0-374-98303-8). Octagon.

Wilgus, Alva C., ed. Colonial Hispanic America. LC 63-8374. (Illus.). 1963. Repr. of 1936 ed. 13.50 (ISBN 0-8462-0338-3). Russell.

LATIN AMERICA-INTELLECTUAL LIFE

Adams, Henry E., ed. Handbook of Latin American Studies: 1966-1967 Humanities. LC 36-32633. (Latin American Studies: Vol. 32). 1970. 35.00x (ISBN 0-8130-0316-4). U Presses Fla.

Conference on Intellectual Trends in Latin America, University of Texas, 1945. Papers. LC 69-19001. Repr. of 1945 ed. lib. bdg. 14.75x (ISBN 0-8371-1037-8, TLIT). Greenwood.

Jacobini, H. B. A Study of the Philosophy of International Law As Seen in Works of Latin American Writers. LC 78-20471. 1980. Repr. of 1954 ed. 16.50 (ISBN 0-88355-849-1). Hyperion Conn.

LATIN AMERICA-JUVENILE LITERATURE

Hoey, Mary. Journey South: Discovering the Americas. (gr. 4-6). 1980. pap. 3.50 (ISBN 0-377-00099-X). Friend Pr.

Villicana, Eugenio. Viva Morelia. LC 72-159842. (Two Worlds Books Ser). (Illus.). 64p. (gr. 4 up). 1972. 3.95 (ISBN 0-87131-098-8). M Evans.

LATIN AMERICA-LIBRARY RESOURCES

Bartley, Russell H. & Wagner, Stuart L. Latin America in Basic Historical Collections: A Working Guide. LC 77-170204. (Bibliographical Ser.: No. 51). 212p. 1972. 12.95 (ISBN 0-8179-2511-2). Hoover Inst Pr.

Grow, Michael. Scholars' Guide to Washington, D.C., for Latin American & Caribbean Studies. LC 78-21316. (Scholar's Guide to Washington, D.C. Ser.: No. 2). 346p. 1979. text ed. 19.95x (ISBN 0-87474-486-5); pap. text ed. 8.95x (ISBN 0-87474-487-3). Smithsonian.

Planeamiento Nacional De Servicios Bibliotecarios, Vol. 2. (Span.). 1972. pap. 1.00 (ISBN 0-8270-3055-X). OAS.

Seminar on the Acquisitions of Latin American Library Materials, Austin. Final Report. (Illus.). ix, 97p. Repr. of 1958 ed. lib. bdg. 15.00 (ISBN 0-8371-5035-3, TLLR). Greenwood.

Thompson, Lawrence S. Essays in Hispanic Bibliography. LC 75-96729. 1970. 15.00 (ISBN 0-208-00978-7, Archon). Shoe String.

LATIN AMERICA-MAPS

Monteiro, Palmyra V. Catalogue of Latin American Flat Maps, 1926-1964, 2 vols. Incl. Vol. 1. Mexico, Central America, West Indies. 411p. 1967 (ISBN 0-292-78371-X); Vol. 2. South America, Falkland(Malvinas) Islands & the Guianas. 442p. 1969 (ISBN 0-292-78429-5). (Institute of Latin American Studies Guides & Bibliographies Ser.: No. 2). 1967. 10.00x ea.; Set. 15.00x (ISBN 0-292-74612-1). U of Tex Pr.

Wilgus, A. Curtis. Historical Atlas of Latin America: Political, Geographic, Economic, Cultural. rev. ed. LC 66-30784. Orig. Title: Latin America in Maps. (Illus.). 1967. Repr. of 1943 ed. 12.00x (ISBN 0-8154-0256-2). Cooper Sq.

LATIN AMERICA-POLITICS AND GOVERNMENT

see also Inter-American Conferences; Monroe Doctrine

Adie, R. & Poitras, G. Latin America: The Politics of Immobility. 1974. pap. 10.95 (ISBN 0-13-524272-X). P-H.

Aguilar, Luis E., ed. & intro. by. Marxism in Latin America. rev. 2nd ed. LC 77-81331. 1978. pap. 6.95x (ISBN 0-87722-108-1). Temple U Pr.

Alba, Victor. Politics & the Labor Movement in Latin America. 1968. 17.50x (ISBN 0-8047-0193-8). Stanford U Pr.

Bawa, Vasant K. Latin American Integration. 225p. 1980. text ed. 12.50x (ISBN 0-391-01899-X). Humanities.

Belaunde, Victor A. Bolivar & the Political Thought of the Spanish-American Revolution. 1967. lib. bdg. 27.50x (ISBN 0-374-90532-0). Octagon.

Bennett, John M. & Virumbrales, Pablo, eds. El Pensamiento Politico Latinamericano: Selecciones. (Illus.). 192p. 1976. pap. text ed. 3.95x (ISBN 0-19-501962-8). Oxford U Pr.

Benton, William. The Voice of Latin America. LC 74-1553. (Illus.). 204p. 1974. Repr. of 1961 ed. lib. bdg. 15.00 (ISBN 0-8371-7393-0, BEVL). Greenwood.

Blachman, Morris J. & Hellman, Ronald G., eds. Terms of Conflict: Ideology in Latin American Politics. LC 76-54814. (Inter-American Politics Ser.: Vol. 1). 1977. text ed. 8.95x (ISBN 0-915980-05-3). Inst Study Human.

Blakemore, Harold. British Nitrates & Chilean Politics, 1886-1896: Balmaceda & North. (Institute of Latin American Studies Monograph Ser: No. 4). (Illus.). 256p. 1974. text ed. 31.25x (ISBN 0-485-17704-8, Athlone Pr). Humanities.

Booth, John A. & Seligson, Mitchell A., eds. Citizen & State: Vol. 1 of Political Participation in Latin America. LC 77-16666. 260p. 1978. 29.50x (ISBN 0-8419-0334-4); pap. text ed. 11.50x (ISBN 0-8419-0376-X). Holmes & Meier.

Burr, Robert N. Our Troubled Hemisphere: Perspectives on United States-Latin American Relations. 1967. 9.95 (ISBN 0-8157-1174-3). Brookings.

Busey, James L. Latin America: Political Institutions & Processes. (Orig.). 1964. pap. text ed. 3.95 (ISBN 0-685-19741-7). Phila Bk Co.

Chilcote, Ronald H. & Edelstein, Joel C., eds. Latin America: The Struggle with Dependency & Beyond. 800p. 1974. 24.50 (ISBN 0-87073-068-1); pap. 11.50 (ISBN 0-87073-069-X). Schenkman.

Collier, David, ed. The New Authoritarianism in Latin America. LC 79-83982. 1979. 30.00 (ISBN 0-691-07616-2); pap. 6.95 (ISBN 0-691-02194-5). Princeton U Pr.

Conniff, Michael, ed. Latin American Populism in Comparative Perspective. (Illus.). 272p. 1981. 19.95x (ISBN 0-8263-0580-6); pap. 9.95x (ISBN 0-8263-0581-4). U of NM Pr.

Corbett, Charles D. The Latin American Military As a Socio-Political Force: Case Studies of Bolivia & Argentina. new ed. LC 72-86566. (Monographs in International Affairs). 143p. 1972. text ed. 6.95 (ISBN 0-933074-18-2); pap. text ed. 4.95 (ISBN 0-933074-19-0). AISI.

Cornelius, Wayne A. & Kemper, Robert V., eds. Metropolitan Latin American: The Challenge & the Response. LC 77-79867. (Latin American Urban Research: Vol. 6). (Illus.). 346p. 1978. 22.50 (ISBN 0-8039-0661-7); pap. 9.95 (ISBN 0-8039-0662-5). Sage.

Curtis, William E. The Capitals of Spanish America. 1976. lib. bdg. 59.95 (ISBN 0-8490-1570-7). Gordon Pr.

Dahlin, Therrin C., et al. The Catholic Left in Latin America: A Comprehensive Bibliography. (Reference Bks.). 1981. lib. bdg. 35.00 (ISBN 0-8161-8396-1). G K Hall.

Davis, Harold E. Makers of Democracy in Latin America. LC 68-56190. Repr. of 1945 ed. 8.00x (ISBN 0-8154-0272-4). Cooper Sq.

De Armond Marchant, Alexander N. Boundaries of the Latin American Republics: An Annotated List of Documents, 1493-1943. (Latin America Ser.). 1979. lib. bdg. 59.95 (ISBN 0-8490-2876-0). Gordon Pr.

Debray, Regis. Revolution in the Revolution? Ortiz, Bobbye, tr. from Fr. 1967. pap. 1.50 (ISBN 0-394-17121-7, B144, BC). Grove.

--Strategy for Revolution: Essays on Latin America. Blackburn, Robin, ed. LC 78-105315. (Illus.). 1970. 6.50 (ISBN 0-85345-127-3, CL-1273). Monthly Rev.

Dibacco, Thomas V., ed. Presidential Power in Latin American Politics. LC 77-4727. (Special Studies). 1977. text ed. 21.95 (ISBN 0-03-021816-0). Praeger.

Douglas, William O. Holocaust or Hemispheric Coop: Crosscurrents in Latin America. LC 71-140701. 1971. pap. 1.95 (ISBN 0-394-71709-0, Vin). Random.

Duff, Ernest A. & McCamant, John F. Violence & Repression in Latin America: A Quantitative & Historical Analysis. LC 75-16645. (Illus.). 1976. 19.95 (ISBN 0-02-907690-0). Free Pr.

Duncan, W. Raymond & Goodsell, James N., eds. The Quest for Change in Latin America: Sources for a Twentieth Century Analysis. 1970. pap. 6.95x (ISBN 0-19-501254-2). Oxford U Pr.

Einaudi, Luigi R., ed. Beyond Cuba: Latin America Takes Charge of Its Future. LC 73-8644. 250p. 1973. pap. 14.00x (ISBN 0-8448-0266-2). Crane-Russak Co.

Fitzgibbons, R. & Fernandez, J. Latin America: Political Culture & Development. 2nd ed. 1981. pap. 12.95 (ISBN 0-686-64406-9). P-H.

Frei, Eduardo. Latin America: The Hopeful Option. Drury, John, tr. from Sp. LC 78-1358. 1978. pap. 7.95 (ISBN 0-88344-277-9). Orbis Bks.

Garcia Robles, Alfonso. Denuclearization of Latin America. 1967. 6.00 (ISBN 0-87003-018-3); pap. 3.00 (ISBN 0-87003-019-1). Carnegie Endow.

Gerassi, John. Great Fear in Latin America. 1965. pap. 1.50 (ISBN 0-02-073410-7, Collier). Macmillan.

Gomez, Rosendro A. Government & Politics in Latin America. rev. ed. 1963. pap. text ed. 3.10x (ISBN 0-685-19730-1). Phila Bk Co.

Grossman, Jorge, ed. Public Administration in Latin America: A Bibliography. 1976. lib. bdg. 59.95 (ISBN 0-8490-2488-9). Gordon Pr.

Gunther, John. Inside Latin America. LC 74-27666. (Illus.). 498p. 1975. Repr. of 1941 ed. lib. bdg. 25.75x (ISBN 0-8371-7908-4, GULA). Greenwood.

Halper, Stefan A. & Sterling, John R., eds. Latin America: The Dynamics of Social Change. LC 72-88522. 1975. pap. 6.95 (ISBN 0-312-47320-6). St Martin.

Hansen, Joseph. The Leninist Strategy of Party Building: The Debate on Guerrilla Warfare in Latin America. Evans, et al, eds. LC 79-89423. 1979. lib. bdg. 30.00 (ISBN 0-87348-570-X); pap. 7.95 (ISBN 0-87348-571-8). Path Pr NY.

Harris, Louis K. & Alba, Victor. The Political Culture & Behavior of Latin America. LC 74-79151. 250p. 1974. 10.00x (ISBN 0-87338-154-8); pap. text ed. 5.50x (ISBN 0-87338-155-6). Kent St U Pr.

Hilliker, Grant. The Politics of Reform in Peru: The Aprista & Other Mass Parties of Latin America. LC 76-128763. (Illus.). 248p. 1971. 17.00x (ISBN 0-8018-1168-6). Johns Hopkins.

Hodges, Donald C. The Latin American Revolution: Politics & Strategy from Apro-Marxism to Guevarism. LC 74-7085. 1974. 9.95 (ISBN 0-688-00315-X). Morrow.

Holland, Susan S. & Ferrer, Esteban A., eds. Changing Legal Environment in Latin America. LC 74-29066. (Illus.). 370p. 1974. Vol. 2. pap. 16.50 (ISBN 0-685-56605-6, CoA). Unipub.

Honey, John C. Toward Strategies for Public Administration Development in Latin America. LC 68-14963. 1968. 9.95x (ISBN 0-8156-2116-7). Syracuse U Pr.

Index to Latin American Legislation, Third Supplement. 1978. 115.00 (ISBN 0-8161-0094-2). G K Hall.

Jane, Lionel C. Liberty & Despotism in Spanish America. LC 66-29053. 1966. Repr. of 1929 ed. 11.00x (ISBN 0-8154-0119-1). Cooper Sq.

Johnson, Dale. The Sociology of Change & Reaction in Latin America. LC 73-7794. (Studies in Sociology Ser). 1973. pap. text ed. 3.50 (ISBN 0-672-61238-0). Bobbs.

Johnson, John J. Latin America in Caricature. LC 79-19052. (Texas Pan American Ser.). (Illus.). 340p. 1980. text ed. 24.50x (ISBN 0-292-74626-1). U of Tex Pr.

--Political Change in Latin America: The Emergence of the Middle Sectors. 1958. 15.00x (ISBN 0-8047-0528-3). Stanford U Pr.

Johnson, Kenneth F. & Williams, Miles. Democracy, Power, & Intervention in Latin America Political Life: A Study of Scholarly Images. LC 78-10689. (Special Studies: No. 17). 1978. pap. 3.50x (ISBN 0-87918-044-7). ASU Lat Am St.

Karst, Kenneth L. & Rosen, Keith S. Law & Development in Latin America. LC 74-30525. 750p. 1976. 48.50x (ISBN 0-520-02955-0). U of Cal Pr.

Kern, Robert W. & Dolkart, Ronald, eds. The Caciques: Oligarchical Politics & the System of Caciquismo in the Luso-Hispanic World. LC 72-86820. 208p. 1973. 10.00x (ISBN 0-8263-0260-2). U of NM Pr.

Klaren, Peter F. Modernization, Dislocation & Aprismo: Origins of the Peruvian Aprista Party, 1870-1932. LC 73-4915. (Latin American Monographs, No. 32). 213p. 1973. 10.00x (ISBN 0-292-76001-9). U of Tex Pr.

Lambert, Jacques. Latin America: Social Structures & Political Institutions. Katel, Helen, tr. LC 67-29784. 1968. pap. 7.95x (ISBN 0-520-00690-9, CAMPUS5). U of Cal Pr.

Linz, Juan J., ed. The Breakdown of Democratic Regimes: Latin America. LC 78-594. (BDR Ser: No. 3). (Orig.). 1978. pap. text ed. 3.95x (ISBN 0-8018-2023-5). Johns Hopkins.

Lowenthal, Abraham F., ed. Armies & Politics in Latin America. LC 76-17832. 1976. text ed. 24.50x (ISBN 0-8419-0281-X); pap. text ed. 9.50x (ISBN 0-8419-0282-8). Holmes & Meier.

Madariaga, Salvador De. Latin America Between the Eagle & the Bear. LC 75-25494. 192p. 1976. Repr. of 1962 ed. lib. bdg. 15.00 (ISBN 0-8371-8423-1, MALAM). Greenwood.

Martin, Percy A. Latin America & the War. 1925. 7.50 (ISBN 0-8446-1301-0). Peter Smith.

Martz, John D. & Schoultz, Lars. Latin America, the United States, & the Inter-American System. (Westview Special Studies on Latin America & the Caribbean). 272p. 1980. lib. bdg. 27.25x (ISBN 0-89158-874-4). Westview.

Mendes, Candido. Beyond Populism. Cowan, L. Gray, tr. from Fr. LC 76-40257. 1977. 12.00 (ISBN 0-87395-803-9). State U NY Pr.

Moreno, Francisco Jose. Legitimacy & Stability in Latin America: A Study of Chilean Political Culture. LC 76-88137. 1969. 10.00x (ISBN 0-8147-0317-8). NYU Pr.

Moses, Bernard. Establishment of Spanish Rule in America. LC 65-21909. Repr. of 1898 ed. 12.00x (ISBN 0-8154-0156-6). Cooper Sq.

Needler, Martin. Latin American Politics in Perspective. 8.00 (ISBN 0-8446-2639-2). Peter Smith.

Needler, Martin C. An Introduction to Latin American Politics: The Structure of Conflict. LC 77-23222. 1977. text ed. 16.95 (ISBN 0-13-486043-8). P-H.

--Political Development in Latin America: Instability, Violence & Evolutionary Change. 1968. pap. text ed. 3.50x (ISBN 0-685-19751-4). Phila Bk Co.

--Political Systems of Latin America. 2nd ed. (Political Science Ser). 1970. text ed. 12.95x (ISBN 0-442-05962-0). Van Nos Reinhold.

Nehemkis, Peter. Latin America: Myth & Reality. LC 77-2958. 1977. Repr. of 1964 ed. lib. bdg. 20.25x (ISBN 0-8371-9560-8, NELA). Greenwood.

North, Liisa. Civil-Military Relations in Argentina, Chile, & Peru. (Politics of Modernization Ser.: No. 2). 1966. pap. 2.00x (ISBN 0-87725-202-5). U of Cal Intl St.

Palmer, Thomas W., Jr. Search for a Latin American Policy. LC 57-12883. 1957. 6.00 (ISBN 0-8130-0176-5). U Presses Fla.

Petras, James. Politics & Social Structure in Latin America. LC 73-122737. 1970. pap. 5.95 (ISBN 0-85345-195-8, PB-1958). Monthly Rev.

Pierce, Robert N. Keeping the Flame: Media & Government in Latin America. (Humanistic Studies in the Communication Arts). 1979. 16.50 (ISBN 0-8038-3950-2); pap. text ed. 8.95x (ISBN 0-8038-3951-0). Hastings.

Pike, Fredrick B., ed. Freedom & Reform in Latin America. 1967. pap. 3.25x (ISBN 0-268-00107-3). U of Notre Dame Pr.

Plaza, Lasso G. Problems of Democracy in Latin America. LC 81-36. (The Weil Lectures on American Citizenship Ser.). vi, 88p. 1981. Repr. of 1955 ed. lib. bdg. 17.50x (ISBN 0-313-22877-9, PLPD). Greenwood.

Ranis, P. Five Latin American Nations: A Comparative Political Study. 1971. pap. text ed. 6.50x (ISBN 0-02-398200-4). Macmillan.

Rossi, Ernest E. & Plano, Jack C. The Latin American Political Dictionary. 263p. 1980. 25.25 (ISBN 0-87436-302-0). ABC Clio.

Ruddle, Kenneth & Gillette, Philip D., eds. Latin American Political Statistics: A Supplement to the Statistical Abstract of Latin America, Vol. 2. LC 72-9412. 127p. 1972. pap. text ed. 7.50 (ISBN 0-87903-221-9). UCLA Lat Am Ctr.

Schmitter, Philippe, ed. The Military Rule in Latin America. LC 73-77870. (Sage Research Progress Ser. on War, Revolution, & Peacekeeping: Vol. 3). 352p. 1973. 22.50 (ISBN 0-8039-0242-5). Sage.

Seligson, Mitchell A. & Booth, John A., eds. Politics & the Poor. LC 78-9672. (Political Participation in Latin America Ser.: Vol. 2). (Illus.). 1979. text ed. 29.50x (ISBN 0-8419-0405-7); pap. text ed. 11.50x (ISBN 0-8419-0406-5). Holmes & Meier.

Shapiro, Samuel. Invisible Latin America. facsimile ed. LC 70-128331. (Essay Index Reprint Ser). Repr. of 1963 ed. 12.75 (ISBN 0-8369-2521-1). Arno.

Sigmund, Paul E. Multinationals in Latin America: The Politics of Nationalization. 448p. 1980. 22.50 (ISBN 0-299-08260-1); pap. 6.50 (ISBN 0-299-08264-4). U of Wis Pr.

Silvert, Kalman H. Conflict Society: Reaction & Revolution in Latin America. rev. ed. LC 66-20311. 1966. 7.50 (ISBN 0-910116-63-6). Am U Field.

--Essays in Understanding Latin America. LC 77-2340. 256p. 1977. text ed. 14.95x (ISBN 0-915980-02-9); pap. text ed. 6.95x (ISBN 0-915980-82-7). Inst Study Human.

Stavenhagen, Rodolfo. Between Underdevelopment & Revolution: A Latin American Perspective. 1981. 18.00x (ISBN 0-8364-0700-8, Pub. by Abhinav India). South Asia Bks.

Stephansky, Ben S. Latin America: Toward a New Nationalism. LC 72-82610. (Headline Ser.: No. 211). (Illus., Orig.). 1972. pap. 2.00 (ISBN 0-87124-017-3). Foreign Policy.

Szekely, A. Latin America & the Law of the Sea, Release 1. 1980. 32.50 (ISBN 0-379-10180-7). Oceana.

Tambs, Lewis A., ed. Revolution in the Americas: Proceedings. (PCCLAS Ser.: Vol. 6). 1979. pap. 10.00 (ISBN 0-916304-43-4). Campanile.

Taylor, Philip B., Jr., ed. Problems of Law, Politics & Economic Development in Latin American Studies, Conference, University of Houston, Texas, March 1975: Proceedings. 1975. pap. 4.00 (ISBN 0-915524-06-6). Lat Am Stud.

Thorp, Rosemary & Whitehead, Lawrence, eds. Inflation & Stabilisation in Latin America. LC 79-11887. 1980. text ed. 34.50x (ISBN 0-8419-0512-6). Holmes & Meier.

Thurber, Clarence E. & Graham, Lawrence S. Development Administration in Latin America. LC 72-96986. (Comparative Adminstration Group of the American Society for Public Administration Ser.). 550p. 1973. 19.75 (ISBN 0-8223-0292-6). Duke.

Ugarte, Manuel. Destiny of a Continent. Rippey, J. Fred, ed. Philips, Catherine A., tr. from Span. LC 71-111476. Repr. of 1925 ed. 23.00 (ISBN 0-404-06700-X). AMS Pr.

Veliz, Claudio. The Centralist Tradition of Latin America. LC 79-84019. (Illus.). 1980. 22.50 (ISBN 0-691-05280-8); pap. 9.75 (ISBN 0-691-10085-3). Princeton U Pr.

Whitaker, Arthur P. Nationalism in Latin America, Past & Present. LC 76-26167. 1976. Repr. of 1962 ed. lib. bdg. 15.00 (ISBN 0-8371-9027-4, WHNA). Greenwood.

Wiarda, Howard & Kline, Harvey F. Latin American Politics & Development. LC 78-56434. (Illus.). 1979. text ed. 15.50 (ISBN 0-395-27056-1). HM.

Wiarda, Howard J. Critical Elections & Critical Coups: State, Society & the Military in the Processes of Latin American Development. LC 79-4433. (Papers in International Studies: Latin America: No. 5). 1979. pap. 7.00 (ISBN 0-89680-082-2). Ohio U Ctr Intl.

Wiarda, Howard J., ed. The Continuing Struggle for Democracy in Latin America. LC 79-13551. (Westview Special Studies on Latin America). 27.75x (ISBN 0-89158-663-6). Westview.

--Politics & Social Change in Latin America: The Distinct Tradition. 2nd, rev. ed. 346p. 1982. pap. 9.95 (ISBN 0-87023-333-5). U of Mass Pr.

Wilkie, James W., ed. Money & Politics in Latin America. LC 77-620008. (Supplements to the Statistical Abstracts of Latin America: Vol. 7). 1977. pap. text ed. 10.95 (ISBN 0-87903-232-4). UCLA Lat Am Ctr.

Williams, Edward J. Latin American Christian Democratic Parties. LC 67-13159. 1967. 15.00x (ISBN 0-87049-073-7). U of Tenn Pr.

--Latin American Political Thought: A Developmental Perspective. LC 74-77209. (Institute of Government Research Ser). 1974. pap. 1.50x (ISBN 0-8165-0464-4). U of Ariz Pr.

Williams, Edward J. & Wright, Freeman J. Latin American Politics: A Developmental Approach. LC 74-33885. (Illus.). 480p. 1975. 17.95 (ISBN 0-87484-299-9). Mayfield Pub.

Wolf, Eric R. & Hansen, Edward C. The Human Condition in Latin America. (Illus.). 392p. 1972. 17.50 (ISBN 0-19-501570-3); pap. 6.95x (ISBN 0-19-501569-X). Oxford U Pr.

Wynia, G. W. The Politics of Latin American Development. LC 77-87395. (Illus.). 1978. 32.95 (ISBN 0-521-21922-1); pap. 9.95x (ISBN 0-521-29310-3). Cambridge U Pr.

LATIN AMERICA–POPULATION

Arriaga, Eduardo E. Mortality Decline & Its Demographic Effects in Latin America. LC 76-4852. (Population Monograph Ser.: No. 6). (Illus.). 1976. Repr. of 1970 ed. lib. bdg. 34.75x (ISBN 0-8371-8827-X, ARLT). Greenwood.

--New Life Tables for Latin American Populations in the Nineteenth & Twentieth Centuries. LC 76-4841. (Population Monograph Ser.: No. 3). (Illus.). 1976. Repr. of 1968 ed. lib. bdg. 34.75x (ISBN 0-8371-8827-X, ARLT). Greenwood.

Caracteristicas Da Estrutura Demografica Dos Paises Americanos. (Port. & Eng.). 1962-64. pap. 1.00 ea.; Port. ed. (ISBN 0-8270-6585-X). OAS.

Chaplin, David, ed. Population Policies & Growth in Latin America. LC 79-151772. 1971. 24.50x (ISBN 0-89197-896-8). Irvington.

Collver, O. Andrew. Birth Rates in Latin America: New Estimates of Historical Trends & Fluctuations. (Research Ser.: No. 7). 1965. pap. 2.50x (ISBN 0-87725-107-X). U of Cal Intl St.

Committee on Latin American Studies, Conference, University of Houston, Texas, Oct. 1973. Education & Population in Latin America: Proceedings. Harrell, William A., ed. 199p. (Eng.). 1975. pap. text ed. 4.00 (ISBN 0-915524-04-X). Lat Am Stud.

Committee on Latin American Studies, Conference, University of Houston, Texas April 1971. Population & Urbanization Problems of Latin America: Proceedings. Taylor, Philip B., Jr. & Schulman, Sam, eds. 124p. (Eng.). 1971. pap. text ed. 3.00 (ISBN 0-915524-02-3). Lat Am Stud.

De Platt, Lyman. Una Guia genealogico-historica de Latinoamerica. (Illus., Span.). 1978. pap. 6.95 (ISBN 0-916552-14-4). Acoma Bks.

Edmonston, Barry, ed. Population Research in Latin America & the Caribbean: A Reference Bibliography. LC 79-14653. (Orig.). 1979. pap. 17.25 (ISBN 0-8357-0414-9, SS-00091). Univ Microfilms.

FAO Regional Population Workshop for Latin America, Santiago, Chile, 1974. Report. (Illus.). 40p. 1976. pap. 7.50 (ISBN 0-685-66343-4, F1214, FAO). Unipub.

Harris, Marvin. Patterns of Race in the Americas. 144p. 1974. pap. 4.95 (ISBN 0-393-00727-8, Norton Lib). Norton.

McCoy, T. L., ed. Dynamics of Population Policy in Latin America. LC 73-16353. 1974. 20.00 (ISBN 0-88410-350-1). Ballinger Pub.

Sanchez-Albornoz, Nicolas. The Population of Latin America. 1974. 34.50x (ISBN 0-520-01766-8); pap. 7.95x (ISBN 0-520-02745-0). U of Cal Pr.

Smith, T. Lynn. Latin American Population Studies. LC 61-63016. (U of Fla. Social Sciences Monographs: No. 8). (Illus.). 1960. pap. 3.50 (ISBN 0-8130-0210-9). U Presses Fla.

--The Race Between Population & Food Supply in Latin America. LC 75-17375. 194p. 1976. 12.50x (ISBN 0-8263-0366-8). U of NM Pr.

Thomas, Robert N. & Hunter, John M., eds. Internal Migration Systems in the Developing World with Special Reference to Latin America. (University Bks.). 1980. lib. bdg. 19.95 (ISBN 0-8161-8414-3). G K Hall.

Viel, Benjamin V. The Demographic Explosion: The Latin American Experience. Walls, James, tr. LC 75-15837. (Population & Demography Ser.). 1976. 14.95 (ISBN 0-470-90505-0). Halsted Pr.

LATIN AMERICA–RELATIONS (GENERAL) WITH FOREIGN COUNTRIES

Behrman, Jack N. The Role of International Companies in Latin American Integration: Autos & Petrochemicals. LC 79-183711. 185p. 1972. pap. 4.50 (ISBN 0-87186-235-2). Comm Econ Dev.

Chilcote, R. & Edelstein, J., eds. Latin America: The Struggle with Dependency & Beyond. LC 74-8393. (States & Societies of the Third World Ser.). 1974. text ed. 32.95 (ISBN 0-470-15555-8); pap. text ed. 21.50 (ISBN 0-470-15556-6). Halsted Pr.

Goldhamer, Herbert. The Foreign Powers in Latin America. LC 77-173754. (A Rand Corporation Research Study). 296p. 1972. 22.00x (ISBN 0-691-05646-3). Princeton U Pr.

Grunwald, Joseph, ed. Latin America & World Economy: A Changing International Order. LC 77-17031. (Latin American International Affairs Ser.: Vol. 2). 323p. 1978. 22.50x (ISBN 0-8039-0864-4); pap. 9.95 (ISBN 0-8039-0966-7). Sage.

Texas University Institute Of Latin-American Studies. Some Educational & Anthropological Aspects of Latin-America. (Illus.). Repr. of 1948 ed. lib. bdg. 15.00x (ISBN 0-8371-1032-7, TLEA). Greenwood.

LATIN AMERICA–RELATIONS (GENERAL) WITH THE UNITED STATES

Aguilar, Alonso. Pan-Americanism from Monroe to the Present. Zatz, Asa, tr. LC 68-13659. 1969. pap. 4.50 (ISBN 0-85345-098-6, PB-0986). Monthly Rev.

Bernstein, Harry. Making an Inter-American Mind. LC 61-11110. 1961. 7.00 (ISBN 0-8130-0019-X). U Presses Fla.

--Origins of Inter-American Interest, 1700-1812. LC 66-13164. 1965. Repr. of 1945 ed. 7.00 (ISBN 0-8462-0711-7). Russell.

Cabot, John M. Toward Our Common American Destiny. facsimile ed. LC 72-90621. (Essay Index Reprint Ser). 1955. 18.00 (ISBN 0-8369-1553-4). Arno.

Callcott, Wilfrid H. The Western Hemisphere: Its Influence on United States Policies to the End of World War II. 520p. 1968. 27.50x (ISBN 0-292-78390-6). U of Tex Pr.

Child, John. Unequal Alliance: The Inter-American Military System, Nineteen Thirty-Eight to Nineteen Seventy-Nine. (A Westview Replica Edition Ser.). 254p. 1980. 25.25 (ISBN 0-89158-677-6). Westview.

Colter, Julio & Fagen, Richard R., eds. Latin America & the United States: The Changing Political Realities. LC 73-94487. 429p. 1974. 18.75x (ISBN 0-8047-0860-6); pap. 7.50x (ISBN 0-8047-0861-4). Stanford U Pr.

De Onis, Jose. The United States As Seen by Spanish American Writers (1776-1890) LC 74-26684. (Cultural Relations Between the U. S. & the Hispanic World Ser.: Vol. 1). 236p. 1975. Repr. of 1952 ed. 10.00 (ISBN 0-87752-184-0). Gordian.

Dozer, Donald M. Are We Good Neighbors? xi, 456p. 1972. Repr. of 1959 ed. 32.50 (ISBN 0-384-12515-8). Johnson Repr.

Gerassi, John. Great Fear in Latin America. 1965. pap. 1.50 (ISBN 0-02-073410-7, Collier). Macmillan.

Griffin, Charles C., ed. Concerning Latin American Culture. LC 66-27089. 1967. Repr. of 1940 ed. 7.50 (ISBN 0-8462-0841-5). Russell.

Hughes, Charles E. Our Relations to the Nations of the Western Hemisphere. 1971. Repr. of 1928 ed. 11.50 (ISBN 0-384-24860-8). Johnson Repr.

Jones, Chester L. Caribbean Interests of the United States. LC 73-111719. (American Imperialism: Viewpoints of United States Foreign Policy, 1898-1941). 1970. Repr. of 1919 ed. 17.00 (ISBN 0-405-02029-5). Arno.

Lieuwen, Edwin. United States & the Challenge to Security in Latin America. LC 66-63557. (Illus., Orig.). 1966. pap. 1.50 (ISBN 0-8142-0084-2). Ohio St U Pr.

McClellan, Grant S., ed. U. S. Policy in Latin America. (Reference Shelf Ser: Vol. 35, No. 1). 1963. 6.25 (ISBN 0-8242-0074-8). Wilson.

Manach, Jorge. Teoria De la Frontera. 3.75 (ISBN 0-8477-2412-3). U of PR Pr.

Martz, John D. & Schoultz, Lars. Latin America, the United States, & the Inter-American System. (Westview Special Studies on Latin America & the Caribbean). 272p. 1980. lib. bdg. 27.25x (ISBN 0-89158-874-4). Westview.

Meyer, Michael C., ed. Supplement to a Bibliography of United States-Latin American Relations Since 1810. LC 79-1243. xxvi, 193p. 1979. 19.50x (ISBN 0-8032-3051-6). U of Nebr Pr.

Pacific Coast Council on Latin American Studies. Latin America & the United States: Past, Present, & Future: Proceedings, Vol. 1. 1972. pap. 7.00x (ISBN 0-916304-24-8). Campanile.

Reid, John T. Spanish American Images of the United States,1790-1960. LC 77-3621. 1977. 15.00 (ISBN 0-8130-0547-7). U Presses Fla.

Rippy, James F. Globe & Hemisphere: Latin America's Place in the Post-War Foreign Relations of the United States. LC 72-606. 276p. 1972. Repr. of 1958 ed. lib. bdg. 15.00x (ISBN 0-8371-5718-8, RIGH). Greenwood.

Robertson, William S. Hispanic-American Relations with the United States. Kinley, David, ed. LC 23-7693. (Illus.). 1969. Repr. of 1923 ed. 22.00 (ISBN 0-527-75920-1). Kraus Repr.

Rockefeller, Nelson A. Rockefeller Report on the Americas. LC 78-108447. 1972. 5.95 (ISBN 0-8129-0114-2); pap. 2.95 (ISBN 0-8129-6101-3, QP24). Times Bks.

Shapiro, Samuel. Cultural Factors in Inter-American Relations. 1968. 9.95x (ISBN 0-268-00066-2); pap. 3.45x (ISBN 0-268-00309-2). U of Notre Dame Pr.

--Invisible Latin America. facsimile ed. LC 70-128331. (Essay Index Reprint Ser). Repr. of 1963 ed. 12.75 (ISBN 0-8369-2521-1). Arno.

Silvert, Kalman H. Essays in Understanding Latin America. LC 77-2340. 256p. 1977. text ed. 14.95x (ISBN 0-915980-02-9); pap. text ed. 6.95x (ISBN 0-915980-82-7). Inst Study Human.

Tulchin, Joseph S., ed. Hemispheric Perspectives on the United States: Papers from the New World Conference. LC 77-87973. (Contributions in American Studies: No. 36). 1978. lib. bdg. 22.50x (ISBN 0-313-20053-X, TUH/). Greenwood.

Ugarte, Manuel. Destiny of a Continent. Rippey, J. Fred, ed. Philips, Catherine A., tr. from Span. LC 71-111476. Repr. of 1925 ed. 23.00 (ISBN 0-404-06700-X). AMS Pr.

Whitaker, A. P., ed. Inter-American Affairs: An Annual Survey, 5 Vols. 1941-1945. Repr. Set. lib. bdg. 75.50x (ISBN 0-8371-1516-7, IAAS). Greenwood.

LATIN AMERICA–RELIGION

Brown, Lyle C. & Cooper, William F. Religion in Latin American Life & Literature. LC 80-83665. 426p. 1980. 40.00 (ISBN 0-918954-23-1). Baylor Univ Pr.

Costas, O. E. Theology of the Crossroads in Contemporary Latin America: Missiology in Mainline Proestantism 1969-1974. (Orig.). 1976. pap. text ed. 27.50x (ISBN 90-6203-259-1). Humanities.

Dussel, Enrique. The History of the Church in Latin America: Colonialism to Liberation. Neely, Alan, tr. 368p. 1981. 17.95 (ISBN 0-8028-3548-1). Eerdmans.

Latorre Cabal, Hugo. The Revolution of the Latin American Church. Hendricks, Frances K. & Berler, Beatrice, trs. from Span. LC 77-9117. 1978. 10.95 (ISBN 0-8061-1449-5). U of Okla Pr.

Lee, Elizabeth M. He Wears Orchids & Other Latin American Stories. LC 76-117327. (Biography Index Reprint Ser). 1951. 17.00 (ISBN 0-8369-8019-0). Arno.

LATIN AMERICA–RURAL CONDITIONS

Duncan, K. & Rutledge, I., eds. Land & Labour in Latin America. LC 76-11076. (Cambridge Latin American Studies: No. 26). (Illus.). 1978. 49.95 (ISBN 0-521-21206-5). Cambridge U Pr.

Halperin, Rhoda & Dow, James. Peasant Livelihood: Studies in Economic Anthropology & Cultural Ecology. LC 76-28126. 1977. 16.95x (ISBN 0-312-59972-2); pap. text ed. 7.95x (ISBN 0-312-59973-0). St Martin.

Preston, David A. Environment, Society & Rural Change in Latin America: The Past, Present & Future in the Country. LC 79-41481. 256p. 1980. 41.75 (ISBN 0-471-27713-4, Pub. by Wiley-Interscience). Wiley.

Rodriguez, Joaquin P. Reflexiones De un Agricultor. 1978. pap. 9.95 (ISBN 0-89729-203-0). Ediciones.

Singelmann, Peter. Structures of Domination & Peasant Movements in Latin America. LC 79-48030. (Illus.). 240p. 1981. text ed. 20.00 (ISBN 0-8262-0307-8). U of Mo Pr.

Volgyes, Ivan & Lonsdale, Richard E., eds. The Process of Rural Transformation: Eastern Europe, Latin America & Australia. LC 79-10190. (Pergamon Policy Studies). 1980. 39.50 (ISBN 0-08-023110-1). Pergamon.

LATIN AMERICA–SOCIAL CONDITIONS

Arroyo, Anita. Narrativa Hispanoamericana Actual: America y Sus Problemas. LC 79-19468. (Mente y Palabra Ser.). v, 517p. 1980. 20.00 (ISBN 0-8477-0562-5); pap. 15.00 (ISBN 0-8477-0563-3). U of PR Pr.

Bawa, Vasant K. Latin American Integration. 225p. 1980. text ed. 12.50x (ISBN 0-391-01899-X). Humanities.

Benton, William. The Voice of Latin America. LC 74-1553. (Illus.). 204p. 1974. Repr. of 1961 ed. lib. bdg. 15.00 (ISBN 0-8371-7393-0, BEVL). Greenwood.

Bernhard, Virginia, ed. Elites, Masses, & Modernization in Latin America, 1850-1930. (Texas Pan American Ser.). 165p. 1979. text ed. 11.00x (ISBN 0-292-76457-X). U of Tex Pr.

Bernstein, S. P., ed. Labor & Social Welfare in Latin America: A Bibliography. 1976. lib. bdg. 59.95 (ISBN 0-8490-2121-9). Gordon Pr.

Blakemore, Harold & Smith, Clifford T., eds. Latin America: Geographical Perspectives. (Illus.). 1971. text ed. 39.95x (ISBN 0-416-10820-2); pap. 19.95x (ISBN 0-416-80500-0). Methuen Inc.

Blasier, Cole, ed. Constructive Change in Latin America. LC 68-12724. (Pitt Latin American Ser.). 1968. 11.95 (ISBN 0-8229-3145-1). U of Pittsburgh Pr.

Burns, E. Bradford. Latin America: A Concise Interpretive History. 3rd ed. (Illus.). 352p. 1982. pap. 12.95 (ISBN 0-13-524322-X). P-H.

--Latin America: A Concise Interpretive History. 2nd ed. LC 76-21677. (Illus.). 1977. pap. text ed. 11.95 (ISBN 0-13-524314-9). P-H.

--The Poverty of Progress: Latin America in the Nineteenth Century. LC 80-51236. 224p. 1980. 14.95x (ISBN 0-520-04160-7). U of Cal Pr.

Butterworth, Douglas & Chance, John K. Latin American Urbanization. LC 80-18486. (Urbanization in Developing Countries Ser.). (Illus.). 320p. 1981. text ed. 29.95 (ISBN 0-521-23713-0); pap. text ed. 8.95 (ISBN 0-521-28175-X). Cambridge U Pr.

Cornelius, Wayne A. & Kemper, Robert V., eds. Metropolitan Latin American: The Challenge & the Response. LC 77-79867. (Latin American Urban Research: Vol. 6). (Illus.). 346p. 1978. 22.50 (ISBN 0-8039-0661-7); pap. 9.95 (ISBN 0-8039-0662-5). Sage.

De Vries, Egbert & Casanova, P. Gonzales, eds. Social Research & Rural Life in Central America, Mexico & the Caribbean Region. 1966. 7.50 (ISBN 92-3-100617-7, UNESCO). Unipub.

Dixon, Marlene & Jonas, Susanne, eds. Strategies for the Class Struggle in Latin America. (Contemporary Marxism Ser.). (Illus.). 104p. (Orig.). 1980. pap. 5.00 (ISBN 0-89935-010-0). Synthesis Pubns.

Form, William H. & Blum, Albert A., eds. Industrial Relations & Social Change in Latin America. LC 65-18667. 1965. 7.50 (ISBN 0-8130-0079-3). U Presses Fla.

Frank, Andre G. Latin America: Underdevelopment or Revolution. LC 71-81794. 1970. pap. 6.50 (ISBN 0-85345-165-6, PB-1656). Monthly Rev.

--Lumpenbourgeoisie: Lumpendevelopment: Dependence, Class, & Politics in Latin America. Berdicio, Marion D., tr. from Span. LC 72-81764. 160p. 1973. pap. 3.50 (ISBN 0-85345-285-7, PB-2857). Monthly Rev.

Furtado, C. Economic Development of Latin America. 2nd ed. LC 74-121365. (Latin American Studies: No.8). (Illus.). 280p. 1977. 37.50 (ISBN 0-521-21197-2); pap. 9.95x (ISBN 0-521-29070-8). Cambridge U Pr.

Geisse, Guillermo & Hardoy, Jorge E., eds. Regional & Urban Development Policies: A Latin American Perspective. LC 78-103483. (Latin American Urban Research Ser.: Vol. 2). 298p. 1972. 22.50x (ISBN 0-8039-0166-6). Sage.

Green, Dana S., ed. Chasms in the Americas. (Illus., Orig.). 1970. pap. 1.95 (ISBN 0-377-10251-2). Friend Pr.

Halper, Stefan A. & Sterling, John R., eds. Latin America: The Dynamics of Social Change. LC 72-88522. 1975. pap. 6.95 (ISBN 0-312-47320-6). St Martin.

Halperin, Ernst. Terrorism in Latin America. LC 76-4103. (The Washington Papers: No. 33). 90p. 1976. 4.00x (ISBN 0-8039-0648-X). Sage.

Horowitz, Irving L., ed. Masses in Latin America. LC 73-83045. 1970. pap. 7.95 (ISBN 0-19-500795-6, 297, GB). Oxford U Pr.

Johnson, Dale. The Sociology of Change & Reaction in Latin America. LC 73-7794. (Studies in Sociology Ser). 1973. pap. text ed. 3.50 (ISBN 0-672-61238-0). Bobbs.

Johnson, John J. The Military & Society in Latin America. 1964. 15.00x (ISBN 0-8047-0198-9). Stanford U Pr.

--Political Change in Latin America: The Emergence of the Middle Sectors. 1958. 15.00x (ISBN 0-8047-0528-3). Stanford U Pr.

Johnson, John J., ed. Continuity & Change in Latin America. 1964. 12.50x (ISBN 0-8047-0184-9); pap. 3.95 (ISBN 0-8047-0185-7, SP39). Stanford U Pr.

Lagos, Gustavo & Godoy, Horacio H. Revolution of Being: A Latin American View of the Future. LC 77-3848. (Preferred Worlds for the 1990's). 1977. 14.95 (ISBN 0-02-917840-1). Free Pr.

Lambert, Jacques. Latin America: Social Structures & Political Institutions. Katel, Helen, tr. LC 67-29784. 1968. pap. 7.95x (ISBN 0-520-00690-9, CAMPUS5). U of Cal Pr.

Landsberger, Henry A., ed. Church & Social Change in Latin America. LC 77-85355. 1970. 9.50x (ISBN 0-268-00356-4). U of Notre Dame Pr.

Leonard, Olen E. & Loomis, Charles P. Readings in Latin American Social Organizations & Institutions. viii, 320p. 1953. pap. 5.00 (ISBN 0-686-74067-X). Mich St U Pr.

Levine, Robert M. Race & Ethnic Relations in Latin America & the Caribbean: An Historical Dictionary & Bibliography. LC 80-15179. 260p. 1980. 13.50 (ISBN 0-8108-1324-6). Scarecrow.

Lewald, H. Ernest. Latin America: Sus Culturas y Sociedades. (Illus.). 384p. 1973. text ed. 15.95 (ISBN 0-07-037420-1, C). McGraw.

Mesa-Lago, Carmelo. Social Security in Latin America: Pressure Groups, Stratification, & Inequality. LC 77-15732. (Pitt Latin American Ser). 1978. 19.95 (ISBN 0-8229-3368-3). U of Pittsburgh Pr.

Metailie, Anne-Marie, ed. Amerique Latine-Latin America: Catalogues et Inventaires. (Maison Des Sciences De L'homme, Service D'echange D'informations Scientifiques: No. 5). 1974. pap. 19.50x (ISBN 0-686-21808-6). Mouton.

Morner, Magnus. Race Mixture in the History of Latin America. 178p. 1967. pap. 4.95 (ISBN 0-316-58369-3). Little.

Morner, Magnus, ed. Race & Class in Latin America. (Institute for Latin American Studies). 309p. 1970. pap. 5.00x (ISBN 0-231-08661-X). Columbia U Pr.

Nash, June, et al, eds. Ideology & Social Change in Latin America. 1977. 18.75x (ISBN 0-677-04170-5). Gordon.

Needler, Martin C. Political Development in Latin America: Instability, Violence & Evolutionary Change. 1968. pap. text ed. 3.50x (ISBN 0-685-19751-4). Phila Bk Co.

--Political Systems of Latin America. 2nd ed. (Political Science Ser). 1970. text ed. 12.95x (ISBN 0-442-05962-0). Van Nos Reinhold.

Odell, Peter R. & Preston, David A. Economies & Societies in Latin America: A Geographical Interpretation. 2nd ed. LC 77-12400. 289p. 1978. text ed. 34.95 (ISBN 0-471-99588-6, Pub. by Wiley-Interscience); pap. text ed. 15.75 (ISBN 0-471-99636-X). Wiley.

Oxaal, Ivar, et al, eds. Beyond the Sociology of Development. (International Library of Sociology). 1975. 25.00 (ISBN 0-7100-8049-2); pap. 12.00 (ISBN 0-7100-8050-6). Routledge & Kegan.

Pacific Coast Council on Latin American Studies. Latin America: Power & Poverty: Proceedings, Vol. 4. 1975. pap. 7.00x (ISBN 0-916304-27-2). Campanile.

Pescatello, Ann, ed. Female & Male in Latin America: Essays. LC 72-81794. (Pitt Latin American Ser.). (Illus.). 1979. pap. 6.95x (ISBN 0-8229-5306-4). U of Pittsburgh Pr.

Petras, James. Politics & Social Structure in Latin America. LC 73-122737. 1970. pap. 5.95 (ISBN 0-85345-195-8, PB-1958). Monthly Rev.

Pike, Frederick B. Spanish America: Tradition & Social Innovation. (Library of World Civilization Ser.). 1973. 7.95 (ISBN 0-393-05488-8); pap. 4.95x (ISBN 0-393-09340-9). Norton.

Pike, Fredrick B., ed. Freedom & Reform in Latin America. 1967. pap. 3.25x (ISBN 0-268-00107-3). U of Notre Dame Pr.

Pollitt, Ernesto. Poverty & Malnutrition in Latin America: Early Childhood Intervention Programs. LC 80-18811. 150p. 1980. 22.95 (ISBN 0-03-058031-5). Praeger.

Rivera, Julius. Latin America: A Sociocultural Interpretation. rev. ed. LC 77-27271. 268p. 1980. text ed. 20.00x (ISBN 0-8290-0129-8); pap. text ed. 8.95x (ISBN 0-8290-0444-0). Irvington.

Robinson, David J., ed. Studies in Spanish-American Population History, Vol. 8. (Dellplain Latin American Studies). 276p. 1981. lib. bdg. 20.00 (ISBN 0-86531-268-0). Westview.

Schell, Mildred. Look, Listen & Learn: A Primary Class Activity Packet on the Americas. (gr. 1-6). 1973. pap. text ed. 5.95 (ISBN 0-377-58079-1). Friend Pr.

Scott, Robert E., ed. Latin American Modernization Problems: Case Studies in the Crises of Change. LC 72-81263. 365p. 1973. 17.50 (ISBN 0-252-00293-8). U of Ill Pr.

Shapiro, Samuel. Cultural Factors in Inter-American Relations. 1968. 9.95x (ISBN 0-268-00066-2); pap. 3.45x (ISBN 0-268-00309-2). U of Notre Dame Pr.

--Invisible Latin America. facsimile ed. LC 70-128331. (Essay Index Reprint Ser). Repr. of 1963 ed. 12.75 (ISBN 0-8369-2521-1). Arno.

Shapiro, Samuel, ed. Integration of Man & Society in Latin America. (Orig.). 1967. pap. 3.25x (ISBN 0-268-00137-5). U of Notre Dame Pr.

Silvert, Kalman H. Conflict Society: Reaction & Revolution in Latin America. rev. ed. LC 66-20311. 1966. 7.50 (ISBN 0-910116-63-6). Am U Field.

--Essays in Understanding Latin America. LC 77-2340. 256p. 1977. text ed. 14.95x (ISBN 0-915980-02-9); pap. text ed. 6.95x (ISBN 0-915980-82-7). Inst Study Human.

Spalding, Hobart. Organized Labor in Latin America. 1977. pap. 5.95x (ISBN 0-06-131923-6, TB1923, Torch). Har-Row.

Stephansky, Ben S. Latin America: Toward a New Nationalism. LC 72-82610. (Headline Ser.: No. 211). (Illus., Orig.). 1972. pap. 2.00 (ISBN 0-87124-017-3). Foreign Policy.

Strickon, Arnold & Greenfield, Sidney M., eds. Structure & Process in Latin America: Patronage, Clientage, & Power Systems. LC 72-86819. (School of American Research Advanced Seminar Ser.). 256p. 1972. 10.00x (ISBN 0-8263-0259-9). U of NM Pr.

Toplin, Robert B., ed. Slavery & Race Relations in Latin America. LC 74-286. (Contributions in Afro-American & African Studies: No. 17). 450p. (Orig.). 1974. lib. bdg. 29.50x (ISBN 0-8371-7374-4, TSR/); pap. 6.95 (ISBN 0-8371-8929-2). Greenwood.

Wiarda, Howard J. Critical Elections & Critical Coups: State, Society & the Military in the Processes of Latin American Development. LC 79-4433. (Papers in International Studies: Latin America: No. 5). 1979. pap. 7.00 (ISBN 0-89680-082-2). Ohio U Ctr Intl.

Wolf, Eric R. & Hansen, Edward C. The Human Condition in Latin America. (Illus.). 392p. 1972. 17.50 (ISBN 0-19-501570-3); pap. 6.95x (ISBN 0-19-501569-X). Oxford U Pr.

LATIN AMERICA–SOCIAL LIFE AND CUSTOMS

Blouet, Brian W. & Blouet, Olwyn M. Geography of Latin America: An Introductory Survey. 350p. 1981. text ed. 14.95 (ISBN 0-471-08385-2). Wiley.

Burgin, Miron, ed. Handbook of Latin American Studies, 1940. LC 36-32633. (Latin American Studies Ser.: No. 6). xiii, 570p. 1963. Repr. 17.50x (ISBN 0-8130-0032-7). U Presses Fla.

--Handbook of Latin American Studies, 1941. LC 36-32633. (Latin American Studies Ser.: No. 7). xv, 649p. 1963. Repr. 17.50x (ISBN 0-8130-0033-5). U Presses Fla.

--Handbook of Latin American Studies, 1942. LC 36-32633. (Latin American Studies: No. 8). xv, 521p. 1963. Repr. 17.50 (ISBN 0-8130-0034-3). U Presses Fla.

--Handbook of Latin American Studies, 1943. LC 36-32633. (Latin American Studies Ser.: No. 9). xvi, 518p. 1963. Repr. 17.50x (ISBN 0-8130-0035-1). U Presses Fla.

--Handbook of Latin American Studies, 1944. LC 36-32633. (Latin American Studies Ser.: No. 10). xvi, 440p. 1963. Repr. 17.50x (ISBN 0-8130-0036-X). U Presses Fla.

--Handbook of Latin American Studies, 1945. LC 36-32633. (Latin American Studies Ser.: No. 11). ix, 404p. 1963. Repr. 17.50x (ISBN 0-8130-0037-8). U Presses Fla.

Byars, Robert S. & Love, Joseph L., eds. Quantitative Social Science Research on Latin America. LC 72-95001. (Illus.). 275p. 1973. 17.50 (ISBN 0-252-00335-7). U of Ill Pr.

Casanova, Pablo G., ed. La Sociologie Du Developpement Latino-Americain: Tendances Actuelles De la Recherche et Bibliographie. 2 pts. Incl. Pt. 1. Etudes Generales. (No. 18). 1971. pap. 10.00x (ISBN 0-686-22179-6); Pt. 2. Etudes Sectorielles. (No. 19). 1973. pap. 16.75x (ISBN 90-2797-218-4). (La Sociologie Contemporaine). Mouton.

Goldwert, Marvin. History As Neurosis: Paternalism and Machismo in Spanish America. LC 80-5640. 85p. 1980. lib. bdg. 12.50 (ISBN 0-8191-1226-7); pap. text ed. 6.50 (ISBN 0-8191-1227-5). U Pr of Amer.

Liebman, Seymour B. Exploring the Latin American Mind. LC 76-6847. 225p. 1976. 15.95x (ISBN 0-88229-134-3). Nelson-Hall.

Mayers, Marvin K. A Look at Latin America Lifestyles. (Museum of Anthropology Publications Ser.: No. 2). 1976. pap. 3.75x (ISBN 0-88312-151-4); microfiche 1.60 (ISBN 0-88312-238-3). Summer Inst Ling.

Nash, June & Safa, Helen I., eds. Sex & Class in Latin America. new ed. (Illus.). 352p. 1980. lib. bdg. 19.95x (ISBN 0-89789-002-7); pap. text ed. 9.95x (ISBN 0-89789-003-5). J F Bergin.

Picon-Salas, Mariano. A Cultural History of Spanish America: From Conquest to Independence. Leonard, Irving A., tr. 1962. pap. 5.95x (ISBN 0-520-01012-4, CAMPUS15). U of Cal Pr.

Pierce, Robert N. Keeping the Flame: Media & Government in Latin America. (Humanistic Studies in the Communication Arts). 1979. 16.50 (ISBN 0-8038-3950-2); pap. text ed. 8.95x (ISBN 0-8038-3951-0). Hastings.

Robinson, David J., ed. Social Fabric & Spatial Structure in Colonial Latin America. LC 79-15744. (Illus., Orig.). 1979. pap. 26.50 (ISBN 0-8357-0419-X, SS-00100). Univ Microfilms.

Wiarda, Howard J., ed. Politics & Social Change in Latin America: The Distinct Tradition. 2nd, rev. ed. 346p. 1982. pap. 9.95 (ISBN 0-87023-333-5). U of Mass Pr.

Zopf, Paul E., Jr. Cultural Accumulation in Latin America. LC 79-48091. 393p. 1980. text ed. 20.00 (ISBN 0-8191-1012-4); pap. text ed. 12.25 (ISBN 0-8191-1013-2). U Pr of Amer.

LATIN AMERICA–STATISTICS

Arriaga, Eduardo E. Mortality Decline & Its Demographic Effects in Latin America. LC 76-4852. (Population Monograph Ser.: No. 6). (Illus.). 1976. Repr. of 1970 ed. lib. bdg. 34.75x (ISBN 0-8371-8827-X, ARLT). Greenwood.

Graham, Ann. Subject Guide to Statistics in the Presidential Reports of the Brazilian Provinces, 1830-1889. (Institute of Latin American Studies Guides & Bibliographies Ser.: No. 9). 484p. 1977. pap. 9.95x (ISBN 0-292-77536-9). U of Tex Pr.

Reed, Irving B., et al. The Latin American Scene of the Seventies: A Basic Fact Book. LC 72-92185. (Monographs in International Affairs). (Illus.). 220p. 1972. text ed. 6.95 (ISBN 0-933074-16-6); pap. text ed. 4.95 (ISBN 0-933074-17-4). AISI.

Statistical Compendium of the Americas, 1971. (Statistics Ser.). 1971. pap. 1.00 (ISBN 0-8270-6600-7). OAS.

Statistical Yearbook for Latin America 1978. 471p. 1980. pap. 32.00 (ISBN 0-686-68973-9, UN79/2G3, UN). Unipub.

United Nations. Statistical Yearbook for Latin America, 1978. 471p. 1979. pap. 32.00x (ISBN 0-8002-1087-5). Intl Pubns Serv.

Wilkie, James W. Statistics & National Policy. LC 73-620086. (Supplements to the Statistical Abstract of Latin America: Vol. 3). 1974. pap. 20.00 (ISBN 0-87903-224-3). UCLA Lat Am Ctr.

Wilkie, James W., ed. Statistical Abstract of Latin America. LC 56-63569. (Statistical Abstract of Latin America Ser.: Vol. 20). 1980. lib. bdg. 47.50x (ISBN 0-87903-238-3); pap. text ed. 32.50x (ISBN 0-87903-237-5). UCLA Lat Am Ctr.

--Statistical Abstract of Latin America 1981, Vol. 21. LC 56-63569. 1981. lib. bdg. 47.50 (ISBN 0-87903-239-1). UCLA Lat Am Ctr.

Wilkie, James W. & Ruddle, Kenneth, eds. Quantitative Latin American Studies: Methods & Findings. new ed. LC 77-620011. (Supplements to the Statistical Abstract of Latin America: Vol. 6). (Orig.). 1977. pap. text ed. 10.95 (ISBN 0-87903-227-8). UCLA Lat Am Ctr.

Wilkie, James W. & Turovsky, Paul, eds. Statistical Abstract of Latin America, 1976. LC 56-63569. (Statistical Abstracts of Latin America Ser.: Vol. 17). (Illus.). 500p. 1976. pap. text ed. 25.00x (ISBN 0-87903-230-8). UCLA Lat Am Ctr.

LATIN-AMERICAN ARCHITECTURE

see Architecture–Latin-America

LATIN-AMERICAN ART

see Art, Latin-American

LATIN-AMERICAN AUTHORS

see Authors, Latin-American

LATIN-AMERICAN BALLADS AND SONGS

see also Mexican Ballads and Songs

Simmons, Merle E. A Bibliography of the Romance & Related Forms in Spanish America. LC 72-6210. 396p. 1972. Repr. of 1963 ed. lib. bdg. 19.25x (ISBN 0-8371-6478-8, SIBR). Greenwood.

LATIN-AMERICAN COOPERATIVE ACQUISITIONS PROGRAM

Savary, M. J. Latin American Cooperative Program. 1968. 8.75 (ISBN 0-02-851740-7). Hafner.

LATIN-AMERICAN DRAMA (COLLECTIONS)

Colecchia, Francesca & Matas, Julio, trs. Selected Latin American One-Act Plays. LC 72-92696. (Pitt Latin American Ser.). 1974. pap. 4.95x (ISBN 0-8229-5241-6). U of Pittsburgh Pr.

Luzuriaga, Gerardo & Rudder, Robert S., eds. The Orgy: Modern One Act Plays from Latin America. new ed. Luzuriaga, Gerardo & Rudder, Robert S., trs. LC 74-620140. (Latin American Studies Ser.: Vol. 25). (Illus.). 194p. 1974. pap. text ed. 7.50 (ISBN 0-87903-025-9). UCLA Lat Am Ctr.

Lyday, Leon F. & Woodyard, George W., eds. Dramatists in Revolt: The New Latin American Theater. (Texas Pan American Ser.). 291p. 1976. 16.50x (ISBN 0-292-71510-2). U of Tex Pr.

Stanford University Dramatists' Alliance. Plays of the Southern Americas. LC 74-173626. (Play Anthology Reprint Ser). Repr. of 1942 ed. 20.25 (ISBN 0-8369-8231-2). Arno.

LATIN-AMERICAN DRAMA–BIBLIOGRAPHY

Lyday, Leon F. & Woodyard, George W., eds. A Bibliography of Latin American Theater Criticism, 1940-1974. LC 76-4516. (Institute of Latin American Studies, Guides & Bibliographies Ser.: No. 10). 263p. 1976. pap. 5.95x (ISBN 0-292-70717-7). U of Tex Pr.

Thompson, Lawrence S. Bibliography of Spanish Plays on Microcards. 1968. 25.00 (ISBN 0-208-00703-2, Archon). Shoe String.

LATIN-AMERICAN DRAMA–TRANSLATIONS INTO ENGLISH

Jones, Willis K., tr. Men & Angels: Three South American Comedies. LC 72-93883. (Latin American Classics Ser.). 237p. 1970. 8.95x (ISBN 0-8093-0428-7). S Ill U Pr.

LATIN-AMERICAN FICTION

see also Short Stories, Latin American

LATIN-AMERICAN FICTION–HISTORY AND CRITICISM

Bacarisse, Salvador. Contemporary Latin American Fiction. 120p. 1980. 10.00x (ISBN 0-7073-0255-2, Pub. by Scottish Academic Pr Scotland). Columbia U Pr.

Brotherston, Gordon. The Emergence of the Latin American Novel. LC 76-40834. 1977. 27.00 (ISBN 0-521-21478-5); pap. text ed. 8.95 (ISBN 0-521-29565-3). Cambridge U Pr.

Brushwood, John S. The Spanish American Novel: A Twentieth-Century Survey. LC 74-32429. (Texas Pan American Ser.). 404p. 1975. 20.00x (ISBN 0-292-77515-6). U of Tex Pr.

Foster, David W. Twentieth Century Spanish-American Novel: A Bibliographic Guide. LC 75-25787. 1975. 10.00 (ISBN 0-8108-0871-4). Scarecrow.

Fuentes, Carlos, et al. Latin American Fiction Today: A Symposium. Minc, Rose S., ed. LC 79-90483. 198p. (Orig., Eng. & Span.). 1980. 9.95x (ISBN 0-935318-04-6). Edins Hispamerica.

Gonzalez Del Valle, L. & Cabrera, Vicente. La Nueva Ficcion Hispanoamericana A Traves De Miguel Angel Asturias Y Gabriel Garcia Marquez. 1972. 9.95 (ISBN 0-88303-008-X); pap. 6.95 (ISBN 0-685-73212-6). E Torres & Sons.

Janes, Regina. Gabriel Garcia Marquez: Revolutions in Wonderland. LC 80-27286. 136p. 1981. text ed. 8.00x (ISBN 0-8262-0337-X). U of Mo Pr.

MacAdam, Alfred J. Modern Latin American Narratives: The Dreams of Reason. LC 76-8098. 1980. pap. 3.95 (ISBN 0-226-49995-2, 874, Phoen). U of Chicago Pr.

--Modern Latin American Narratives: The Dreams of Reason. LC 76-8098. 1976. lib. bdg. 12.00x (ISBN 0-226-49993-6). U of Chicago Pr.

Menton, Seymour. Prose Fiction of the Cuban Revolution. LC 75-5993. (Latin American Monographs: No. 37). 362p. 1975. 16.50x (ISBN 0-292-76421-9). U of Tex Pr.

Schwartz, Kessel. A New History of Spanish-American Fiction, 2 vols. Incl. Vol. 2. Social Concern, Universalism & the New Novel (ISBN 0-87024-228-8). LC 71-161436. 1972. 14.95x ea. U of Miami Pr.

LATIN-AMERICAN FOLK-LORE

see Folk-Lore, Latin American

LATIN-AMERICAN FOLK SONGS

see Folk-Songs, Latin-American

LATIN-AMERICAN LITERATURE (COLLECTIONS)

see also literature of specific Latin American countries, e.g. Colombian Literature; Mexican Literature, etc.

Adams, M. Ian. Three Authors of Alienation: Bombal, Onetti, Carpentier. LC 74-32397. (Latin American Monographs Ser.: No. 36). 140p. 1975. 10.00x (ISBN 0-292-78009-5). U of Tex Pr.

Adams, Nicholson B., et al, eds. Hispanoamerica En Su Literatura. 1965. 9.95x (ISBN 0-393-09660-2, NortonC). Norton.

Anderson, Imbert E. & Florit, E. Literatura Hispanoamericana, Antologia E Introduccion Historica, 2 Vols. rev ed. LC 70-86101. (Span). 1970. pap. text ed. 18.95 ea. (HoltC); Vol. 1. (ISBN 0-03-083454-6); Vol. 2. (ISBN 0-03-083455-4). HR&W.

Arce De Vazquez, et al. Lecturas Puertorriquenas - Prosa. 1966. 14.95 (ISBN 0-87751-011-3, Pub by Troutman Press). E Torres & Sons.

Englekirk, John E., et al. Outline History of Spanish American Literature. 4th ed. 1981. 24.50x (ISBN 0-89197-874-7); pap. text ed. 12.95x (ISBN 0-89197-326-5). Irvington.

Ferdinandy, Miguel De. Carnaval y Revolucion y Diecinueve Ensayos Mas. De Ferdinandy, Magdalena, et al, trs. from Ger. Port. Hung. (Coleccion Mente y Palabra). (Span.). 1977. 6.25 (ISBN 0-8477-0544-7); pap. 5.00 (ISBN 0-8477-0545-5). U of PR Pr.

Florit, Eugenio & Patt, B. P., eds. Retratos de Hispanoamerica. (Span.). 1962. text ed. 8.95x (ISBN 0-03-017135-0). Irvington.

Lamb, Ruth S. Antologia Del Cuento Guatemalteco. (Span). 1958. pap. 5.00 (ISBN 0-912434-00-7). Ocelot Pr.

Lozano, Anthony G. & Zayas-Bazan, Eduardo, eds. Del Amor a la Revolucion. new ed. 225p. 1975. pap. text ed. 4.95x (ISBN 0-393-09283-6). Norton.

Mancini, Pat M., ed. Contemporary Latin American Short Stories. 480p. 1974. pap. 1.95 (ISBN 0-449-30844-8, Prem). Fawcett.

Pereda, Jose M. Jose Maria Pereda: Selections from Sotileza & Penas Arriba. Talamantes, Florence W., ed. 1978. pap. text ed. 9.00 (ISBN 0-8191-0379-9). U Pr of Amer.

Ramos-Garcia, Luis A., ed. A South American Trilogy: Osman Lins, Felisberto Hernandez & Luis Fernando Vidal. 1981. 5.50 (ISBN 0-934840-04-0). Studia Hispanica.

Stimson, Frederick S. & Navas-Ruiz, Ricardo, eds. Literatura de la America Hispanica, Antologia E Historia, Tomo 2: El Siglo Diecinueve, 1825-1910. (Sp). 1971. pap. text ed. 13.50 scp (ISBN 0-06-046434-8, HarpC). Har-Row.

--Literatura De la America Hispanica, Antologia E Historia Tomo 3: La Epoca Contemporanea (1920 to the Present) LC 72-134323. 528p. (Orig.). 1975. pap. text ed. 13.50 scp (ISBN 0-06-046435-6, HarpC). Har-Row.

Walsh, Donald & Kiddle, L. B., eds. Cuentos Americanos. 3rd ed. (Illus., Span.). 1970. pap. 5.95x (ISBN 0-393-09907-5, NortonC). Norton.

LATIN-AMERICAN LITERATURE–BIBLIOGRAPHY

Bryant, Shasta M. A Selective Bibliography of Bibliographies of Hispanic American Literature. 2nd ed. (Guides & Bibliographies Ser.: No. 8). 110p. 1976. pap. 4.95x (ISBN 0-292-77522-9). U of Tex Pr.

Coll, Edna. Indice Informativo De la Novela Hispano Americana: Centroamerica, Vol. 2. 1977. 9.35 (ISBN 0-8477-2003-9). U of PR Pr.

--Indice Informativo De la Novela Hispano-Americana: Vol. 1, las Antillas. 9.35 (ISBN 0-8477-2001-2). U of PR Pr.

Columbus Memorial Library & Pan American Union. Index to Latin American Periodical Literature 1966-1970. 1980. lib. bdg. 190.00 (ISBN 0-8161-0314-3). G K Hall.

Foster, David W. & Foster, Virginia R. Manual of Hispanic Bibliography. 2nd ed. (Reference Library of the Humanities: Vol. 85). (LC 76-052672). 1977. lib. bdg. 34.00 (ISBN 0-8240-9888-9). Garland Pub.

Foster, David W., ed. Dictionary of Contemporary Latin American Authors. LC 75-17988. 250p. 1975. pap. 6.95x (ISBN 0-686-67186-4). ASU Lat Am St.

Harvard University Library. Latin American Literature: Classification Schedule, Classified Listing by Call Number, Authors and Title Listing. LC 68-31060. (Widener Library Shelflist Ser: No. 21). 1969. 40.00x (ISBN 0-674-51251-0). Harvard U Pr.

Shaw, Bradley A., compiled by. Latin American Literature in English Translation: An Annotated Bibliography. LC 75-7522. 144p. 1976. 17.75x (ISBN 0-8147-7762-7). NYU Pr.

LATIN-AMERICAN LITERATURE–DICTIONARIES

Grismer, Raymond L. Reference Index to Twelve Thousand Spanish American Authors. LC 79-123600. (Bibliography & Reference Ser.: No. 287). 1970. Repr. of 1939 ed. lib. bdg. 19.00 (ISBN 0-8337-1460-0). B Franklin.

Newmark, Maxim. Dictionary of Spanish Literature. (Quality Paperback: No. 149). 1970. pap. 3.50 (ISBN 0-8226-0149-4). Littlefield.

LATIN-AMERICAN LITERATURE–HISTORY AND CRITICISM

Acevedo, Ramon L. La Novela Centroamericana: Desde el Popol-vuh Hasta los Umbrales De la Novela Actual. LC 81-10316. (Coleccion Mente y Palabra). 908p. 1981. price not set (ISBN 0-8477-0584-6); pap. price not set (ISBN 0-8477-0585-4). U of PR Pr.

America Latina En Su Literatura. (America Latina En Su Cultura). 494p. (Orig., Span.). 1974. pap. 9.25 (ISBN 92-3-301025-2, U17, UNESCO). Unipub.

Anderson-Imbert, Enrique. Spanish American Literature: A History, 2 Vols. 2nd rev. & enl. ed. LC 70-75087. (Waynebooks Ser: Vols. 28-29). pap. 5.95x ea; Vol. 1, 1492-1910. pap. (ISBN 0-8143-1386-8); Vol. 2, 1910-1963. pap. (ISBN 0-8143-1388-4). Wayne St U Pr.

Ardura, Ernesto. America En el Horizonte: Una Perspectiva Cultural. LC 79-54965. (Coleccion De Estudios Hispanicos: Hispanic Studies Collection). (Illus.). 161p. (Orig., Span.). 1981. pap. 9.95 (ISBN 0-89729-240-5). Ediciones.

Arias-Larreta, Abraham. From Columbus to Bolivar. 160p. 1965. 5.60 (ISBN 0-685-56791-5); pap. 3.20 (ISBN 0-685-56792-3). Edit Indoamerica.

--Literatura Colonial. 402p. 1970. 10.40 (ISBN 0-685-56796-6); pap. 8.20 (ISBN 0-685-56797-4). Edit Indoamerica.

Arroyo, Anita. America En Su Literatura. 2nd ed. LC 77-3041. (Illus.). 1978. 15.00 (ISBN 0-8477-3175-8); pap. text ed. 12.00 (ISBN 0-8477-3182-0). U of PR Pr.

Avalle-Arce, J. B. Los Narradores Hispanoamericanos de Hoy. (Studies in the Romance Languages & Literatures: No. 157). 1973. pap. 7.00x (ISBN 0-8078-9157-6). U of NC Pr.

Bazik, Martha. The Life & Works of Luis Carlos Lopez. (Studies in the Romance Languages & Literatures Ser: No. 183). 1977. 8.00x (ISBN 0-8078-9183-5). U of NC Pr.
Boldy, Stephen. The Novels of Julio Cortazar. LC 79-41579. (Cambridge Iberian & Latin American Studies). 320p. 1980. 29.50 (ISBN 0-521-23097-7). Cambridge U Pr.
Brown, Lyle C. & Cooper, William F. Religion in Latin American Life & Literature. LC 80-83665. 426p. 1980. 40.00 (ISBN 0-918954-23-1). Baylor Univ Pr.
Committee on Latin American Studies, Conference, University of Houston, Texas March, 1972. Contemporary Latin American Literature: Proceedings. Johnson, Harvey L. & Taylor, Philip B., eds. 122p. 1973. pap. text ed. 4.00 (ISBN 0-915524-03-1). Lat Am Stud.
DeCosta, Miriam, ed. Blacks in Hispanic Literature: A Collection of Critical Essays. (Literary Criticism Ser). 1976. 12.00 (ISBN 0-8046-9140-1, Natl U). Kennikat.
Donoso, Jose. The Boom in Spanish-American Literature: A Personal History. LC 76-53747. (Center for Inter-American Relations). 122p. 1977. pap. 10.00x (ISBN 0-231-04164-0); pap. 5.00x (ISBN 0-231-04165-9). Columbia U Pr.
Engelbert, Jo Anne. Macedonio Fernandez & the Spanish American New Novel. LC 77-76596. 1978. 20.00x (ISBN 0-8147-2153-2). NYU Pr.
Ferdinandy, Georges. L' Oeuvre Hispanoamericaine De Zsigmond Remengik. (De Proprietatibus Litterarum, Series Practica: No. 86). 191p. (Fr.). 1975. pap. text ed. 28.75x (ISBN 90-2793-356-1). Mouton.
Forster, Merlin H., ed. Tradition & Renewal: Essays on Twentieth-Century Latin American Literature & Culture. LC 74-31179. (Office of International Programs & Studies Ser: Vol. 2). 250p. 1975. 14.50 (ISBN 0-252-00440-X). U of Ill Pr.
Foster, David W. Augusto Roa Bastos. (World Authors Ser.: No. 507 (Paraguay)). 1978. 12.50 (ISBN 0-8057-6348-1). Twayne.
Foster, David W. & Foster, Virginia R., eds. Modern Latin American Literature, 2 vols. LC 72-81710. (A Library of Literary Criticism). 1100p. 1975. Set. 75.00 (ISBN 0-8044-3139-6). Ungar.
Franco, Jean. Introduction to Spanish-American Literature. LC 69-12927. 1969. 42.00 (ISBN 0-521-07374-X); pap. 9.95x (ISBN 0-521-09891-2). Cambridge U Pr.
Fremantle, Anne, ed. Latin American Literature Today. (Orig.). 1977. pap. 2.25 (ISBN 0-451-61587-5, ME1587, Ment). NAL.
Gallagher, D. P. Modern Latin American Literature. 210p. 1973. pap. 3.95 (ISBN 0-19-888071-5, 400, GB). Oxford U Pr.
Goldberg, Issac. Studies in Spanish American Literature. LC 67-27600. 1968. Repr. of 1920 ed. 13.50 (ISBN 0-8046-0171-2). Kennikat.
Gomez-Gil, Orlando. Antologia Critica de la Literatura: Hispanoamericana, 2 vols. LC 71-140657. 1971-72. pap. text ed. 20.95 ea. (HoltC); Vol. 1. pap. text ed. (ISBN 0-03-080475-2); Vol. 2. pap. text ed. (ISBN 0-03-080480-9). HR&W.
Graham, R. B. The South American Sketches of R. B. Cunninghame Graham. Walker, John, ed. LC 77-18604. 1978. 16.95 (ISBN 0-8061-1468-1). U of Okla Pr.
Gutierrez De La Solana, A. Maneras De Narrar: Contraste De Lino Novas Calvo y Alfonso Hernandez Cata. 1972. 10.95 (ISBN 0-88303-017-9); pap. 8.95 (ISBN 0-685-73219-3). E Torres & Sons.
Henriquez-Urena, Pedro. Literary Currents in Hispanic America. LC 63-11032. 1963. Repr. of 1945 ed. 10.00 (ISBN 0-8462-0345-6). Russell.
Hiriart, Rosario. Las Alusiones Literarias En la Obra Narrativa De Francisco Ayala. 1972. 10.50 (ISBN 0-88303-016-0); pap. 7.50 (ISBN 0-685-73218-5). E Torres & Sons.
Holmes, H. A. Spanish America in Song & Story. 59.95 (ISBN 0-8490-1099-3). Gordon Pr.
Ibero-American Institute, ed. An Outline History of Spanish American Literature. 1977. lib. bdg. 59.95 (ISBN 0-8490-2394-7). Gordon Pr.
Jackson, Richard L. The Black Image in Latin American Literature. LC 76-21539. 174p. 1976. 10.00x (ISBN 0-8263-0421-4). U of NM Pr.
Jimenez, Francisco, ed. The Identification & Analysis of Chicano Literature. LC 78-67287. (Studies in the Language & Literature of United States Hispanos). 1979. lib. bdg. 17.95x (ISBN 0-916950-12-3); pap. text ed. 11.95x (ISBN 0-916950-11-5). Bilingual Pr.
Jose, Olivio J. Estudios Criticos Sobre la Prosa Modernista Hispanoamericana. 1975. 15.00 (ISBN 0-88303-019-5); pap. 12.00 (ISBN 0-685-73220-7). E Torres & Sons.
Kadir, Djelal, ed. Triple Espera: Novelas Cortas De Hispanoamerica. 235p. (Spanish.). 1976. pap. text ed. 8.95 (ISBN 0-15-592353-6, HC). HarBraceJ.
Leal, Luis. Breve Historia De la Literatura Hispanoamericana. text ed. 6.00x (ISBN 0-685-55627-1, 31015). Phila Bk Co.
McPheeters, D. W., ed. Guia De Nuevos Temas De Literatura Espanola. 415p. 1972. pap. 9.00 (ISBN 0-87535-118-2). Hispanic Soc.
Moreno, Cesar F. & Schulman, Ivan A., eds. Latin America in Its Literature. Berg, Mary G., tr. from Span. LC 79-26626. (Latin America in Its Culture). Orig. Title: America Latina En Su Cultura. 350p. 1980. text ed. 44.50x (ISBN 0-8419-0530-4). Holmes & Meier.
Moses, Bernard. Spanish Colonial Literature in South America. (Illus.). 1922. 22.00 (ISBN 0-527-65420-5). Kraus Repr.
Ortiz Aponte, Sally. La Esoteria En la Narrativa Hispanoamericana. 1976. 9.35 (ISBN 0-8477-3171-5); pap. 7.50 (ISBN 0-8477-3172-3). U of PR Pr.
Quiroga De Cebollero, Carmen. Entrando a "El Tunel" De Ernesto Sabato. enl. ed. LC 77-26126. (Coleccion UPREX: Estudios Literarios, No. 2). 1978. pap. 1.85 (ISBN 0-8477-0053-4). U of PR Pr.
Rabassa, Clementine C. Demetrio Aguilera-Malta & Social Justice: The Tertiary Phase of Epic Tradition in Latin American Literature. LC 78-75193. 304p. 1980. 19.50 (ISBN 0-8386-2079-5). Fairleigh Dickinson.
Spell, Jefferson R. Contemporary Spanish-American Fiction. LC 67-29553. 1968. Repr. of 1944 ed. 12.00x (ISBN 0-8196-0211-6). Biblo.
Stewart, Donald E., ed. Handbook of Latin American Studies: 1974, Humanities. LC 36-32633. (Latin American Studies Ser.: No. 36). 611p. 1974. 35.00x (ISBN 0-8130-0514-0). U Presses Fla.
Suarez-Torres, J. D. Perspectiva Humoristica En la Trilogia De Gironelia. 1975. 12.95 (ISBN 0-88303-021-7); pap. 10.95 (ISBN 0-685-73222-3). E Torres & Sons.
Torres-Rioseco, Arturo. Epic of Latin American Literature. 1957. 6.50 (ISBN 0-8446-3081-0). Peter Smith.
--The Epic of Latin American Literature. 1942. pap. 2.25 (ISBN 0-520-01274-7, CAL27). U of Cal Pr.
White, Thomas. Naval Researches. LC 72-10764. (American Revolutionary Ser.). Repr. of 1830 ed. lib. bdg. 24.00x (ISBN 0-8398-2180-8). Irvington.

LATIN-AMERICAN LITERATURE–STUDY AND TEACHING

Symposium on the Languages, University of Texas, 1956. Literature of Spanish America & Brazil. 1957. lib. bdg. 15.00x (ISBN 0-8371-9253-6, TLLP). Greenwood.
Usigli, Rodolfo. Corona de Fuego: Primer Esquema Para una Tragedia Antihistorica Americana. Ballinger, Rex E., ed. LC 72-167893. (Span.). 1972. pap. text ed. 8.95x (ISBN 0-672-63025-7). Irvington.
Weisinger, Nina L. A Guide to Studies in Spanish American Literature. LC 78-18646. (Illus.). 120p. 1972. Repr. of 1940 ed. lib. bdg. 15.00 (ISBN 0-8371-6010-3, WESA). Greenwood.

LATIN-AMERICAN LITERATURE–TRANSLATIONS INTO ENGLISH

Freudenthal, Juan R., et al. Preliminary Index to Anthologized Contemporary Latin American Literature in Translation. (Reference Publications). 1977. lib. bdg. 15.00 (ISBN 0-8161-7861-5). G K Hall.
Granier, James A. Latin American Belles-Lettres in English Translation. 1976. lib. bdg. 69.95 (ISBN 0-8490-2132-4). Gordon Pr.
Jones, Willis K., ed. Spanish-American Literature in Translation, 2 vols. Incl. Vol. 1. A Selection of Prose, Poetry, & Drama Before 1888. LC 65-28798. xv, 356p. 16.50 (ISBN 0-8044-2435-7); Vol. 2. A Selection of Poetry, Fiction, & Drama Since 1888. LC 63-181511. xxi, 469p. 19.00 (ISBN 0-8044-2436-5); pap. 6.50 (ISBN 0-8044-6319-0). Set (ISBN 0-8044-2434-9). Ungar.
Monegal, Emir R., ed. The Borzoi Anthology of Latin American Literature, 2 vols. 1977. pap. 7.95 ea.; Vol. 1. (ISBN 0-394-73301-0); Vol. 2. (ISBN 0-394-73366-5). Knopf.

LATIN-AMERICAN MUSIC

see Music, Latin-American

LATIN-AMERICAN NEWSPAPERS

Alisky, Marvin. Latin American Media: Guidance & Censorship. (Illus.). 212p. 1981. 16.50 (ISBN 0-8138-1525-8). Iowa St U Pr.

LATIN-AMERICAN NEWSPAPERS–BIBLIOGRAPHY

Gropp, A. E., ed. Latin American Newspapers in Libraries in the United States. 1976. lib. bdg. 59.95 (ISBN 0-8490-2133-2). Gordon Pr.

LATIN-AMERICAN PERIODICALS

Columbus Memorial Library - Pan American Union, Washington, D.C. Index to Latin American Periodical Literature, 1929-1960, 8 Vols. 1962. Set. 420.00 (ISBN 0-8161-0501-4). G K Hall.
Columbus Memorial Libray - Pan American Union, Washington, D.C. Index to Latin American Periodical Literature, 1961-1965, 2 Vols. 1967. Set. 125.00 (ISBN 0-8161-0768-8). G K Hall.
Harvard University Library. Latin American & Latin American Periodicals, 2 vols. Incl. Vol. 1. Classification Schedule, Classified Listing by Call Number. 675p; Vol. 2. Alphabetical Listing by Author or Title, Chronological Listing. 817p. LC 67-1722. (Widener Library Shelflist Ser: No. 5-6). 1966. Set. 65.00x (ISBN 0-674-51247-2). Harvard U Pr.
Zimmerman, Irene. Guide to Current Latin American Periodicals: Humanities & Social Sciences. 1961. 20.00 (ISBN 0-910824-00-2); pap. 7.50 (ISBN 0-910824-01-0). Kallman.

LATIN-AMERICAN PHILOSOPHY

see Philosophy, Latin-American

LATIN-AMERICAN POETRY (COLLECTIONS)

Armand, Octavio, ed. Contemporary Latin American Poetry. 300p. (Orig.). 1981. write for info. (ISBN 0-937406-09-0); pap. write for info. (ISBN 0-937406-08-2); write for info. ltd. ed. (ISBN 0-937406-10-4). Logbridge-Rhodes.
Baciu, Stefan, compiled by. Antologia de la Poesia Latinoamericana, 1950-1970, 2 vols. LC 73-37514. (Port. Fr. Span.). 1974. Set. pap. 15.00 (ISBN 0-87395-077-1); microfiche 42.00 (ISBN 0-87395-177-8). State U NY Pr.
Blackwell, Alice S., tr. Some Spanish-American Poets. LC 68-22694. (Eng. & Span.). 1968. Repr. of 1937 ed. 15.00x (ISBN 0-8196-0217-5). Biblo.
--Some Spanish-American Poets. 2nd ed. LC 68-23276. (Illus.). 1968. Repr. of 1937 ed. lib. bdg. 25.50x (ISBN 0-8371-0022-4, BLSP). Greenwood.
Brotherston, G., ed. Spanish American Modernista Poets. LC 68-31793. 1968. 17.00 (ISBN 0-08-012858-0); pap. 8.00 (ISBN 0-08-012857-2). Pergamon.
Cien Poesias De Cien Autores Hispanoamericanos. pap. 1.95 (ISBN 0-685-11083-4). French & Eur.
Craig, George D. Modernist Trend in Spanish American Poetry. LC 78-131249. 1971. Repr. of 1934 ed. text ed. 10.00 (ISBN 0-87752-129-8). Gordian.
Crow, John A., ed. An Anthology of Spanish Poetry from the Beginnings to the Present Day, Including Both Spain & Spanish America. LC 79-4619. 1979. text ed. 25.00 (ISBN 0-8071-0482-5); pap. text ed. 8.95x (ISBN 0-8071-0483-3). La State U Pr.
Fitts, Dudley, ed. Anthology of Contemporary Latin American Poetry. LC 76-17656. 1976. Repr. of 1947 ed. lib. bdg. 43.00x (ISBN 0-8371-8905-5, FIAC). Greenwood.
Green, Ernest S., ed. & tr. Mexican & South American Poems. 400p. 1974. lib. bdg. 75.00 (ISBN 0-8490-0612-0). Gordon Pr.
Hernandez Aquino, Luis. Antologia Poetica. pap. 3.75 (ISBN 0-8477-3205-3). U of PR Pr.
Lopez Suria, Violeta. Antologia Poetica. 4.35 (ISBN 0-8477-3207-X). U of PR Pr.
Matos Paoli, Francisco. Antologia Poetica. 4.35 (ISBN 0-8477-3208-8). U of PR Pr.
Morales, Jorge L. Poesia Afroantillana y Negrista: Puerto Rico, Republica Dominica, Cuba. LC 80-25893. 480p. write for info. (ISBN 0-8477-3229-0); pap. price not set (ISBN 0-8477-3230-4). U of PR Pr.
Neruda, Pablo, et al. Three Spanish American Poets: Pellicer, Neruda, Andrade. Mallan, Lloyd, ed. Wicker, Mary, tr. 1977. lib. bdg. 59.95 (ISBN 0-8490-2747-0). Gordon Pr.
Poor, Agnes B., ed. Pan American Poems: An Anthology. 1977. lib. bdg. 59.95 (ISBN 0-8490-2400-5). Gordon Pr.
Resnick, Seymour. Spanish-American Poetry: A Bilingual Selection. LC 64-14514. (Mod. For. Lang. Ser). (Illus.). (gr. 5 up). 1964. PLB 5.29 (ISBN 0-8178-3492-3). Harvey.
Simic, Charles & Strand, Mark, eds. Another Republic. Hughes, Ted, et al, trs. LC 75-34558. 1977. pap. 5.95 (ISBN 0-912946-29-6). Ecco Pr.
Tipton, David, ed. Peru - the New Poetry. LC 74-10432. 1977. 10.95 (ISBN 0-87376-024-7). Red Dust.
Townsend, Francis E., ed. Quisqueya: Panoramic Anthology of Dominican Verse. 1976. lib. bdg. 34.95 (ISBN 0-8490-2495-1). Gordon Pr.

LATIN-AMERICAN POETRY–HISTORY AND CRITICISM

Brotherston, G. Latin American Poetry. LC 75-2734. (Illus.). 256p. 1975. 36.00 (ISBN 0-521-20763-0); pap. 9.95x (ISBN 0-521-09944-7). Cambridge U Pr.
Colecchia, Francesca. Garcia Lorca: An Annotated Bibliography of Criticism. LC 78-68301. (Reference Library of Humanities Ser.). 1979. lib. bdg. 34.00 (ISBN 0-8240-9800-5). Garland Pub.
Craig, George D., ed. The Modernist Trend in Spanish American Poetry. 1977. lib. bdg. 59.95 (ISBN 0-8490-2273-8). Gordon Pr.
Garcia-Barron, Carlos. Cancionero De la Hispano-Peruana De 1866. LC 79-51156. (Coleccion De Estudios Hispanicos: Hispanic Studies Collection). (Illus.). 226p. (Span.). 1980. pap. 12.95 (ISBN 0-89729-225-1). Ediciones.
Grossman, Edith. The Antipoetry of Nicanor Parra. LC 74-21609. 201p. 1975. 15.00x (ISBN 0-8147-2958-4); pap. 9.00x (ISBN 0-8147-2969-X). NYU Pr.
Rosenbaum, Sidonia C. Modern Women Poets of Spanish America: The Precursors, Delmira Agustine, Gabriela Mistral, Alfonsina Storni, Juana de Ibarbourou. LC 78-776. 1978. Repr. of 1945 ed. lib. bdg. 31.00x (ISBN 0-313-20289-3, ROMO). Greenwood.
Rossman, Charles & Friedman, Alan W., eds. Mario Vargas Llosa: A Collection of Critical Essays. 194p. 1978. 10.95x (ISBN 0-292-75039-0). U of Tex Pr.

LATIN-AMERICAN POETRY–TRANSLATIONS INTO ENGLISH

Blackwell, Alice S., tr. Some Spanish-American Poets. LC 68-22694. (Eng. & Span.). 1968. Repr. of 1937 ed. 15.00x (ISBN 0-8196-0217-5). Biblo.
--Some Spanish-American Poets. 2nd ed. LC 68-23276. (Illus.). 1968. Repr. of 1937 ed. lib. bdg. 25.50x (ISBN 0-8371-0022-4, BLSP). Greenwood.
Carlisle, Charles R., ed. Beyond the Rivers: An Anthology of Twentieth Century Paraguayan Poetry. LC 77-3497. text ed. 10.00x (ISBN 0-914476-73-4); pap. 5.00x (ISBN 0-914476-64-5). Thorp Springs.
Craig, George D. Modernist Trend in Spanish American Poetry. LC 78-131249. 1971. Repr. of 1934 ed. text ed. 10.00 (ISBN 0-87752-129-8). Gordian.
Fitts, Dudley, ed. Anthology of Contemporary Latin American Poetry. LC 76-17656. 1976. Repr. of 1947 ed. lib. bdg. 43.00x (ISBN 0-8371-8905-5, FIAC). Greenwood.
Gongora, Luis de. Polyphemus & Galatea: A Study in the Interpretation of a Baroque Poem by Alexander A. Parker & Verse Translation by Gilbert F. Cunningham. LC 77-81914. 182p. 1977. 11.00x (ISBN 0-292-72421-7). U of Tex Pr.
Resnick, Seymour. Spanish-American Poetry: A Bilingual Selection. LC 64-14514. (Mod. For. Lang. Ser). (Illus.). (gr. 5 up). 1964. PLB 5.29 (ISBN 0-8178-3492-3). Harvey.
Rodriguez-Nieto, Catherine, tr. Fireflight: Three Latin American Poets. 1976. pap. 2.50 (ISBN 0-685-73658-X, Pub. by Oyez). SBD.
Walsh, Thomas, ed. Hispanic Anthology: Poems Translated from the Spanish by English & North American Poets, 2 vols. 1977. lib. bdg. 200.00 (ISBN 0-8490-1953-2). Gordon Pr.

LATIN AMERICAN STUDIES

Casteel, J. Doyle, et al. Cross-Cultural Models of Teaching: Latin American Examples. LC 76-13369. 1976. pap. 7.50x (ISBN 0-8130-0558-2). U Presses Fla.
Duran, Daniel F. Latino Materials: A Multimedia Guide for Children & Young Adults, No. 1. LC 78-18470. (Selection Guide Ser.). 249p. 1979. text ed. 16.50 (ISBN 0-87436-262-8, Co-Pub. by Neal-Schuman). ABC-Clio.
Esquenazi-Mayo, Roberto & Meyer, Michael C., eds. Latin American Scholarship Since World War II: Trends in History, Political Science, Literature, Geography, & Economics. LC 73-125101. xii, 335p. 1971. 19.95x (ISBN 0-8032-0783-2). U of Nebr Pr.
Ford, Karen C. Las Yerbas de la Gente: A Study of Hispano-American Medicinal Plants. (Anthropological Papers: No. 60). (Illus.). 1975. pap. 5.00x (ISBN 0-932206-58-1). U Mich Mus Anthro.
Knowlton, Robert J. & Price, Joedd. Essays on Teaching in Latin American Studies. LC 75-23825. (Center Higher Education Ser.: No. 2). 1974. pap. 1.50 (ISBN 0-930450-01-9). Univ of Wis Latin Am.
Martin, Dolores M., ed. Handbook of Latin American Studies, Vol. 41: Social Studies. 814p. 1980. 55.00x (ISBN 0-292-73013-6). U of Tex Pr.
Pacific Coast Council on Latin American Studies (PCCLAS), 23rd Annual Meeting. Latin American Frontiers: Proceedings, Vol. 7. Meier, Matt S., ed. (Illus.). 168p. (Orig.). 1981. pap. 10.00 (ISBN 0-916304-50-7). Campanile.
Sable, Martin H. Latin American Studies Directory. LC 81-10256. 1981. write for info. (ISBN 0-87917-079-4). Blaine Ethridge.
Stewart, Donald E., ed. Handbook of Latin American Studies: Social Sciences 1975, No. 37. LC 36-32633. (Latin American Studies Ser.). 1975. 40.00x (ISBN 0-8130-0552-3). U Presses Fla.
--Handbook of Latin American Studies: 1973, Social Sciences. LC 36-32633. (Latin American Studies Ser: Vol. 35). 557p. 1973. 35.00x (ISBN 0-8130-0442-X). U Presses Fla.

Tulane. Catalog of the Latin American Library of the Tulane University Library: Third Supplement, 2 vols. 1978. Set. lib. bdg. 260.00 (ISBN 0-8161-0005-5). G K Hall.

University of Texas at Austin. Catalog of the Latin American Collection of the University of Texas Library, 3 vols, Fourth Suppl. 1977. lib. bdg. 315.00 (ISBN 0-8161-1156-1). G K Hall.

LATIN-AMERICAN TALES

see Tales, Latin-American

LATIN AMERICANS IN THE UNITED STATES

Faugsted, George E., Jr. The Chilenos in the California Gold Rush. LC 73-76008. pap. 7.00 (ISBN 0-88247-210-0). R & E Res Assoc.

Giacobbi, Steve. Chile & Her Argonauts in the Gold Rush, Eighteen Forty-Eight to Eighteen Fifty-Six: Thesis. LC 74-76464. 1974. soft bdg. 8.00 (ISBN 0-88247-252-6). R & E Res Assoc.

Helm, June, ed. Spanish-Speaking People in the United States. LC 69-14209. (American Ethnological Society Proceedings). 224p. 1968. pap. 10.00 (ISBN 0-295-78573-X). U of Wash Pr.

Hendricks, Glenn. The Dominican Diaspora: From the Dominican Republic to New York City, Villagers in Transition. LC 74-4203. 1974. text ed. 10.50x (ISBN 0-8077-2426-2); pap. text ed. 7.95x (ISBN 0-8077-2459-9). Tchrs Coll.

Lopez, Carlos U. Chilenos in California: A Study of the 1850, 1852 & 1860 Censuses. LC 73-85463. 10.00 (ISBN 0-88247-198-8). R & E Res Assoc.

Lucas, Isidro. The Browning of America. LC 81-3172. 1981. pap. 5.95 (ISBN 0-8190-0642-4). Fides Claretian.

Martinez, Rafael V. My House Is Your House. (Illus., Orig.). 1972. pap. 2.50 (ISBN 0-377-04011-8). Friend Pr.

Redden, Charlotte A. A Comparative Study of Colombian & Costa Rican Emigrants to the United States. Cortes, Carlos E., ed. LC 79-6218. (Hispanics in the United States Ser.). (Illus.). 1981. lib. bdg. 18.00x (ISBN 0-405-13166-6). Arno.

Valle, Ramon & Mendoza, Lydia. The Elder Latino. LC 77-83498. (Elder Minority Ser). 1978. 3.50x (ISBN 0-916304-32-9). Campanile.

LATIN AUTHORS

see Authors, Latin

LATIN DRAMA (COLLECTIONS)

Albrecht, Otto E. Four Latin Plays of St. Nicholas from the 12th Century Fleury Playbook. 1935. 17.50 (ISBN 0-8482-7271-4). Norwood Edns.

LATIN DRAMA–HISTORY AND CRITICISM

Baker, David E., et al. Biographia Dramatica, or Companion to the Playhouse, 4 pts. in 3 vols. LC 70-159990. (BCL Ser. I). Repr. of 1812 ed. Set. 110.00 (ISBN 0-404-00530-6); 39.50 ea. Vol. 1 (ISBN 0-404-00531-4). Vol. 2 (ISBN 0-404-00532-2). Vol. 3 (ISBN 0-404-00533-0). AMS Pr.

Beare, W. The Roman Stage. (Illus.). 416p. 1977. Repr. of 1950 ed. 29.50x (ISBN 0-87471-881-3). Rowman.

Charlton, H. B. Shakespeare's Recoil from Romanticism. 1931. lib. bdg. 5.00 (ISBN 0-8414-3493-X). Folcroft.

Harsh, Philip W. A Handbook of Classical Drama. 1944. 18.50x (ISBN 0-8047-0380-9); pap. 5.95 (ISBN 0-8047-0381-7, SP20). Stanford U Pr.

Norwood, Gilbert. Plautus & Terence. LC 63-10276. (Our Debt to Greece & Rome Ser). Repr. of 1930 ed. 7.50x (ISBN 0-8154-0166-3). Cooper Sq.

Sandbach, F. H. The Comic Theatre of Greece & Rome. Finley, M. I., ed. (Ancient Culture & Society Ser.). 1977. 9.95x (ISBN 0-393-04483-1). Norton.

LATIN DRAMA–HISTORY AND CRITICISM–MEDIEVAL AND MODERN

Dronke, Peter. Poetic Individuality in the Middle Ages: New Departures in Poetry 1000-1150. 1970. 22.50x (ISBN 0-19-811693-4). Oxford U Pr.

Hansen, E. C. Rural Catalonia Under the Franco Regime. LC 76-9177. 1977. 19.95 (ISBN 0-521-21457-2). Cambridge U Pr.

LATIN DRAMA–STORIES, PLOTS ETC.

Reinhold, Meyer. Classical Drama, Greek & Roman. (Orig., Summaries, Critiques). (gr. 11 up). 1959. 6.00 (ISBN 0-8120-5018-5); pap. 2.95 (ISBN 0-8120-0042-0). Barron.

LATIN DRAMA–TRANSLATIONS INTO ENGLISH

Copley, Frank O., tr. Roman Drama: Nine Plays of Terence, Plautus & Seneca. LC 64-66074. (YA) (gr. 11 up). 1965. pap. 7.95 (ISBN 0-672-60455-8, LLA209). Bobbs.

Harsh, Philip W., ed. An Anthology of Roman Drama. Incl. Twin Menaechmi. Plautus; Rope. Plautus; Phormio. Terence; Brothers: Adelphoe. Terence; Medea. Seneca; Phaedra. Seneca; Thyestes. Seneca. LC 60-6496. (Orig.). 1960. pap. text ed. 7.50 (ISBN 0-03-008615-9, HoltC). HR&W.

Plautus. Menaechmus Twins & Two Other Plays. Casson, Lionel, ed. 1971. pap. 5.95 (ISBN 0-393-00602-6, Norton Lib). Norton.

LATIN DRAMA, MEDIEVAL AND MODERN

Sticca, Sandro. Latin Passion Play: Its Origins & Development. LC 69-11318. (Illus.). 1970. 15.50 (ISBN 0-87395-045-3); microfiche 15.50 (ISBN 0-87395-145-X). State U NY Pr.

LATIN EMPIRE, 1204-1261

see also Crusades–Fourth, 1202-1204; Latin Orient

De Villehardouin, Geoffroi. De La Conqueste De Constantinoble. Paris, Paulin, ed. 1965. Repr. of 1838 ed. 31.00 (ISBN 0-685-92799-7); pap. 27.00 (ISBN 0-384-64581-X). Johnson Repr.

De Villehardouin, Geoffroy. Conqueste de Constantinoble. White, Julian E., Jr., ed. LC 68-16196. (Medieval French Literature Ser). (Orig., Fr.). 1968. pap. text ed. 3.95x (ISBN 0-89197-102-5). Irvington.

Miller, William. The Latins in the Levant: A History of Frankish Greece. LC 75-41193. Repr. of 1908 ed. 57.50 (ISBN 0-404-14689-9). AMS Pr.

Wolff, Robert L. Studies in the Latin Empire of Constantinople. 412p. 1980. 60.00x (ISBN 0-902089-99-4, Pub. by Variorum England). State Mutual Bk.

LATIN FICTION–HISTORY AND CRITICISM

Haight, Elizabeth H. Essays on Ancient Fiction. facs. ed. LC 67-22097. (Essay Index Reprint Ser). 1936. 12.25 (ISBN 0-8369-0506-7). Arno.

Perry, Ben E. The Ancient Romances: A Literary-Historical Account of Their Origins. (Sather Classical Lectures: No. 37). 1967. 24.50x (ISBN 0-520-01003-5). U of Cal Pr.

Todd, Frederick A. Some Ancient Novels. facs. ed. LC 68-29250. (Essay Index Reprint Ser). 1968. Repr. of 1940 ed. 13.00 (ISBN 0-8369-0947-X). Arno.

LATIN HISTORIANS

Atkinson, J. E. A Commentary on Q. Curtius' Historiae Alexandri Magni. (London Studies in Classical Philology: No. 3). 1980. text ed. 68.50x (ISBN 90-70265-61-3). Humanities.

Bott, D. H. A Nepos Selection. 1970. text ed. 4.50 (ISBN 0-312-56420-1). St Martin.

Robinson, Charles A., ed. Selections from Greek & Roman Historians. LC 57-7740. (Rinehart Editions). 1957. pap. text ed. 8.50 (ISBN 0-03-009425-9, HoltC). HR&W.

Usher, Stephen. Historians of Greece & Rome. LC 72-97192. 1970. 6.50 (ISBN 0-8008-3845-9). Taplinger.

LATIN HYMNS

see Hymns, Latin

LATIN INSCRIPTIONS

see Inscriptions, Latin

LATIN KINGDOM OF JERUSALEM

see Jerusalem–History–Latin Kingdom, 1099-1244

LATIN LANGUAGE

see also Classical Philology; Inscriptions, Latin; Italic Languages and Dialects; Latin Philology; Romance Languages

Assimil. Assimil Language Course: For French Speaking People Who Want to Learn Latin - le Latin Sans Peine. 11.95 (ISBN 0-686-56090-6); accompanying records & tapes 75.00 (ISBN 0-686-56091-4). French & Eur.

Barbarino, Joseph. The Evolution of the Latin -B-U- Merger: A Quantitative & Comparative Analysis of the B-V Alteration in Latin Inscriptions. LC 78-20445. (Studies in the Romance Languages & Literatures: No. 203). 1979. 12.50x (ISBN 0-8078-9203-3). U of NC Pr.

Boyd-Bowman, Peter. From Latin to Romance in Sound Charts. 134p. 1980. pap. text ed. 7.95 (ISBN 0-87840-077-X). Georgetown U Pr.

Buehner, William J. & Colby, John K. Comprehensive Second Year Latin. (Orig.). (gr. 9-10). 1977. pap. text ed. 5.50x (ISBN 0-88334-034-8). Ind Sch Pr.

Burns, M. A., et al. Lingua Latina: Liber Alter. 1965. 7.45 (ISBN 0-02-812760-9); manual & key o. p. (ISBN 0-02-812780-3); classical tapes 60.00 (ISBN 0-685-38291-5, 81282). Glencoe.

--Lingua Latina: Liber Primus. 1964. 7.45 (ISBN 0-02-812720-X); manual & key o. p. (ISBN 0-02-812740-4); classical tapes 138.00 (ISBN 0-685-38293-1, 81286). Glencoe.

Cappellanus, George. Latin Can Be Fun. Needham, Peter, tr. (Lat.). 1977. 7.95 (ISBN 0-285-62161-0, Pub. by Souvenir Pr). Intl Schol Bk Serv.

Catholicon Anglicum. An English Latin Wordbook. (EETS, OS Ser.: No. 75). Repr. of 1881 ed. 25.00 (ISBN 0-527-00074-4). Kraus Repr.

Deferrari, Roy. First Year Latin. 1st ed. 1958. 3.96 (ISBN 0-02-814220-9). Glencoe.

Devine, Andrew M. & Stephens, Laurence D. Two Studies in Latin Phonology. (Studia Linguistica et Philologica: No. 3). 1978. pap. 20.00 (ISBN 0-915838-42-7). Anma Libri.

Erasmus, Desiderius. Ciceronianus: Or a Dialogue on the Best Style of Speaking. Scott, Izora, tr. LC 73-176755. (Columbia University. Teachers College. Contributions to Education: No. 21). Repr. of 1908 ed. 17.50 (ISBN 0-404-55021-5). AMS Pr.

Faral, Edmond. Recherches Sur les Sources Latines Des Contes et Romans Courtois Du Moyen Age. LC 72-178580. Repr. of 1913 ed. 27.50 (ISBN 0-404-56600-6). AMS Pr.

Freundlich, Charles I. Review Text in Latin First Year. 2nd ed. (Illus., Orig.). (gr. 7-12). 1966. pap. text ed. 5.33 (ISBN 0-87720-551-5). AMSCO Sch.

--Review Text in Latin Three & Four Years. (Orig.). (gr. 7-12). 1967. pap. text ed. 6.42 (ISBN 0-87720-558-2). AMSCO Sch.

--Workbook in Latin First Year. (Illus., Orig.). (gr. 8-11). 1963. wkbk 6.75 (ISBN 0-87720-553-1). AMSCO Sch.

--Workbook in Latin Two Years. (Illus., Orig.). (gr. 9-12). 1965. wkbk 6.75 (ISBN 0-87720-556-6). AMSCO Sch.

Fridh, Ake. L' Emploi Casual De la Conjonction Ut En Latin Tardif. (Studia Graeca et Latina Gothoburgensia Ser.: 35). 1977. pap. text ed. 9.50x (ISBN 9-17346-029-X). Humanities.

Gordon, Arthur E. The Letter Names of the Latin Alphabet. (U. C. Publ. in Classical Studies: Vol. 9). 1973. pap. 9.00x (ISBN 0-520-09422-0). U of Cal Pr.

Humez, Alexander & Humez, Nicholas. Latin for People: Latina Pro Populo. 1976. pap. 6.95 (ISBN 0-316-38149-7). Little.

--Latin for People: Latina Pro Populo. 1976. 7.95 (ISBN 0-316-38150-0). Little.

Jenney, Charles, Jr. & Scudder, Rogers V. First Year Latin. rev. ed. 1979. text ed. 14.40 (ISBN 0-205-06177-X, 396177X); wkbk. 5.40 (ISBN 0-205-06178-8, 3961796); tchrs.' guide 3.60 (ISBN 0-686-77125-7, 3961788). Allyn.

Jenney, Charles, Jr., et al. Second Year Latin. rev. ed. (gr. 7-12). 1979. text ed. 14.80 (ISBN 0-205-06182-6, 3961826); 4.96 (ISBN 0-205-02488-2, 3924882); tchrs'. guide 3.60 (ISBN 0-205-02489-0, 3924890); tests 3.60 (ISBN 0-205-02490-4, 3924904); tchrs'. ed. 3.60 (ISBN 0-205-02491-2, 3924912). Allyn.

Kent, Roland G. Sounds of Latin. 1932. pap. 12.00 (ISBN 0-527-00816-8). Kraus Repr.

Latin in Three Months. (Hugo's Language Courses Ser.: No. 526). 1939. pap. 3.50 (ISBN 0-8226-0526-0). Littlefield.

Leinieks, Valdis, ed. The Structure of Latin: An Introductory Text Based on Caesar & Cicero. 423p. 1975. text ed. 34.00x (ISBN 0-8422-5236-3); pap. text ed. 14.95x (ISBN 0-8422-0530-6). Irvington.

Matthews, P. H. Inflectional Morphology: A Theoretical Study Based on Aspects of Latin Verb Conjugation. LC 76-171678. (Studies in Linguistics Ser., No. 6). (Illus.). 500p. 1972. pap. 14.95x (ISBN 0-521-29065-1). Cambridge U Pr.

Moreland, Floyd L & Fleischer, Rita M. Latin: An Intensive Course. LC 75-36500. (Campus Ser.: No. 186). (gr. 10 up). 1977. 14.95x (ISBN 0-520-03183-0). U of Cal Pr.

O'Brien, Richard J. & Twombly, Neil J. Intermediate Course in Latin: Drills. (gr. 9-12). 1964. 3.00 (ISBN 0-8294-0121-0). Loyola.

--An Intermediate Course in Latin: Readings. (gr. 9-12). 1967. pap. 3.80 (ISBN 0-8294-0119-9). Loyola.

Palmer, L. R. The Latin Language. (Great Languages Ser). 1961. text ed. 19.50x (ISBN 0-571-06813-8). Humanities.

Scanlon, Cora C. & Scanlon, Charles L. Second Latin. LC 48-748. 1976. pap. 6.00 (ISBN 0-89555-003-2). TAN Bks Pubs.

Schofield, H. Latin by Stave Analysis. 1969. 4.95 (ISBN 0-85225-490-3). Ed Solutions.

Scott, Izora. Controversies Over the Imitation of Cicero As a Model for Style & Some Phrases of Their Influence on the Schools of the Renaissance. LC 71-177801. (Columbia University. Teachers College. Contributions to Education: No. 35). Repr. of 1910 ed. 17.50 (ISBN 0-404-55035-5). AMS Pr.

Scottish Classics Group. Ecce Romani. (Illus.). 1971. write for info. (ISBN 0-686-19165-X). Longman.

Strodach, George K. Latin Diminutives in -Ello-a & -Illo-a: A Study in Diminutive Formation. 1933. pap. 6.00 (ISBN 0-527-00760-9). Kraus Repr.

Taylor, B. C. Latin Is Alive & Well. 1973. pap. text ed. 2.25x (ISBN 0-8077-8017-0). Tchrs Coll.

Varro, Marcus T. De Lingua Latina, 2 Vols. (Loeb Classical Library: No. 333-334). 11.00x ea. Vol. 1 (ISBN 0-674-99367-5). Vol. 2 (ISBN 0-674-99368-3). Harvard U Pr.

Woodring, Maxie N. A Study of the Quality of English in Latin Translations. LC 78-177626. (Columbia University. Teachers College. Contributions to Education: No. 187). Repr. of 1925 ed. 17.50 (ISBN 0-404-55187-4). AMS Pr.

LATIN LANGUAGE–ABBREVIATIONS

see Abbreviations

LATIN LANGUAGE–CHURCH LATIN

Galfridus Anglicus. Promptorium Parvulorum Sive Clericorum, Dictionarius Anglolatinus Princeps, 3 Pts. Repr. of 1865 ed. 31.00 ea. Johnson Repr.

O'Brien, Richard J. A Descriptive Grammar of Ecclesiastical Latin Based on Modern Structural Analysis. LC 65-25149. (Orig.). 1965. pap. 2.95 (ISBN 0-8294-0061-3). Loyola.

Rosenstock-Huessy, Eugen & Battles, Ford L. Magna Carta Latina: The Privilege of Singing, Articulating & Reading a Language & Keeping It Alive. 2nd ed. LC 75-23378. (Pittsburgh Reprint Ser.: No. 1). 1975. pap. text ed. 6.75 (ISBN 0-915138-07-7). Pickwick.

LATIN LANGUAGE–COMPOSITION AND EXERCISES

Baker, Charles M. & Inglis, Alexander J. High School Course in Latin Composition. (gr. 9-12). 1969. text ed. 7.04 (ISBN 0-02-102420-0). Macmillan.

Balme, M. G. & Greenstock, M. C. Scrutanda. 1973. pap. 7.95x (ISBN 0-19-831777-8). Oxford U Pr.

Catholicon Anglicum, an English-Latin Workbook Dated 1483. Repr. of 1882 ed. 22.50 (ISBN 0-384-07890-7). Johnson Repr.

Comeau, Paul T. Workbook for Wheelock's Latin: An Introductory Course. 112p. (Orig.). 1980. pap. 4.95 (ISBN 0-06-460192-7). Har-Row.

Hayes, Walter M. An Introductory Latin Program, 5 Bks., with Panels, Post-Tests, Key, Text Aids. (Orig.). 1966. Set. pap. text ed. 14.00 (ISBN 0-8294-0129-6); 17 tapes 120.00 (ISBN 0-685-14282-5). Loyola.

Jenney, Charles, Jr. & Scudder, Robers V. Third Year Latin. (Latin Program Ser.). (gr. 9-12). 1980. text ed. 15.24 (ISBN 0-205-06811-1, 3968111); tchrs.' guide 2.40 (ISBN 0-205-00541-1, 3905411). Allyn.

Mountford, J. F. Bradley's Arnold Latin Prose Composition. (College Classical Ser.). (gr. 11-12). Date not set. 22.50x (ISBN 0-89241-344-1); pap. text ed. 12.50x (ISBN 0-89241-119-8). Caratzas Bros.

North, M. A. & Hillard, A. E. Latin Prose Composition. 320p. (gr. 8-12). 1979. 20.00x (ISBN 0-7156-1321-9, Pub. by Duckworth England); pap. 10.95x (ISBN 0-7156-1322-7, Pub. by Duckworth England). Biblio Dist.

Welch, W. & Duffield, C. G., eds. Exercises in Unseen Translation in Latin. 1969. 3.50 (ISBN 0-312-27475-0). St Martin.

LATIN LANGUAGE–DICTIONARIES

Blanquez. Diccionario Latino-Espanol, Espanol-Latino, 3 vols. 2703p. (Lat. -Espn.). Set. leatherette 75.00 (ISBN 84-303-0151-8, S-50419). French & Eur.

Cassells. Latin Concise Dictionary. 1977. 8.95 (ISBN 0-02-052263-0). Macmillan.

Colby, John K. Latin Word Lists. 1978. pap. text ed. 1.50x (ISBN 0-88334-097-6). Ind Sch Pr.

Estienne, Robert. Dictionariolum Puerorum Tribus Linguis: Lat., Ang. & Gall. Conscriptum. LC 72-194. (English Experience Ser.: No. 351). 616p. 1971. Repr. of 1552 ed. 76.00 (ISBN 90-221-0351-X). Walter J Johnson.

Freytag, George W. Lexicon Arabico-Latimun. 70.00x (ISBN 0-86685-124-0). Intl Bk Ctr.

Glare, G. P., ed. Oxford Latin Dictionary, Fascicle IV: Gorgonia-Libero. 260p. 1973. pap. 49.50x (ISBN 0-19-864217-2). Oxford U Pr.

Glare, P. G., ed. Oxford Latin Dictionary, Fascicle 3: Demiurgus-Gorgoneus. 264p. 1971. pap. 49.50x (ISBN 0-19-864216-4). Oxford U Pr.

Graesse, Johann G. Orbis Latinus: Lexikon lateinischer geographischer Namen des Mittelalters und der Neuzeit, 3 vols. new ed. Plechl, Helmut, ed. 1800p. (Latin & Ger.). 1970. 275.00x (ISBN 3-7814-0087-5). Intl Pubns Serv.

Latham, R. E., compiled by. Dictionary of Medieval Latin from British Sources: Fascicule I, A-B. 280p. 1975. pap. 49.00x (ISBN 0-19-725948-0). Oxford U Pr.

MacDonald, Gerald, ed. Antonio De Nebrija: Vocabulario De Romance En Latin. LC 72-96003. 214p. (Lat. & Sp.). 1973. 12.00x (ISBN 0-87722-018-2). Temple U Pr.

Spes--Diccionario Abreviado Latino-Espanol, Espanol-Latino. 9th ed. 316p. (Lat. -Espn.). 1978. leatherette 7.25 (ISBN 84-7153-221-2, S-12409). French & Eur.

Tucker, T. G. Etymological Dictionary of Latin. 1976. 20.00 (ISBN 0-89005-172-0). Ares.

LATIN LANGUAGE–DICTIONARIES–BIBLIOGRAPHY

Faider, Paul. Repertoire Des Index et Lexiques D'Auteurs Latins. LC 77-150150. (Fr). 1971. Repr. of 1926 ed. lib. bdg. 16.50 (ISBN 0-8337-1097-4). B Franklin.

LATIN LANGUAGE–DICTIONARIES–ENGLISH

Cassells. Latin-English Dictionary. 1977. standard 14.95 (ISBN 0-686-63973-1); index 16.95 (ISBN 0-02-052258-4). Macmillan.

Cassell's New Compact Latin Dictionary. 1981. pap. price not set (ISBN 0-440-31101-2, LE). Dell.

Galfridus Anglicus. Promptorium Parvulorum Sive Clericorum, Dictionarius Anglolatinus Princeps, 3 Pts. Repr. of 1865 ed. 31.00 ea. Johnson Repr.

Glare, P. G., ed. Oxford Latin Dictionary, Fascicle 5. 260p. 1975. pap. 49.50x (ISBN 0-19-864218-0). Oxford U Pr.

--Oxford Latin Dictionary: Fascicle VII. 256p. (Orig.). 1980. pap. 49.50x (ISBN 0-19-864220-2). Oxford U Pr.

--Oxford Latin Dictionary: Fascicle 1, a-Calcitro. 1968. pap. 49.50x (ISBN 0-19-864209-1). Oxford U Pr.

--Oxford Latin Dictionary: Fascicle 2, Calcitro-Demitto. 1969. pap. 49.50x (ISBN 0-19-864215-6). Oxford U Pr.

Glare, P. G. W., ed. Oxford Latin Dictionary: Fascicle VI-a-Calcitro. 1978. pap. 49.50x (ISBN 0-19-864219-9). Oxford U Pr.

Kidd, D. A. Latin-English, English-Latin Dictionary. 19.50 (ISBN 0-87557-050-X, 052-6). Saphrograph.

Latin-English & English-Latin Dictionary. pap. 1.35 (ISBN 0-686-00473-6). Dennison.

Lewis, Charlton T. Elementary Latin Dictionary. 1891. 22.00x (ISBN 0-19-910205-8). Oxford U Pr.

Lewis, Charlton T. & Short, Charles. Latin Dictionary: Founded on Andrews Edition of Freund's Latin Dictionary. 1879. 69.00x (ISBN 0-19-864201-6). Oxford U Pr.

Simpson, D. P., compiled by. Cassell's Concise Latin-English, English-Latin Dictionary. abr. ed. LC 77-7660. 1977. 6.95 (ISBN 0-02-522630-4). Macmillan.

Simpson, D. P., ed. Cassell's Latin Dictionary: Latin-English, English-Latin. 1977. indexed 13.95 (ISBN 0-02-522580-4); plain 12.50 (ISBN 0-02-522570-7). Macmillan.

Smith, William & Lockwood, J. F., eds. Chambers Murray Latin-English Dictionary. 3rd ed. (Totally recast version). 1976. Repr. of 1934 ed. 15.75x (ISBN 0-06-496367-5). B&N.

Traupman, John C. New College Latin & English Dictionary. (gr. 7-12). 1966. pap. text ed. 6.25 (ISBN 0-87720-560-4). AMSCO Sch.

Traupman, John C., ed. New College Latin & English Dictionary. (Language Library). (Orig.). 1970. pap. 2.95 (ISBN 0-553-20255-3). Bantam.

LATIN LANGUAGE–DICTIONARIES–FRENCH

Bornecque, Henri & Cauet, Fernand. Dictionnaire Latin-Francais. 560p. (Fr.-Lat.). 1953. 25.00 (ISBN 0-686-56926-1, M-6044). French & Eur.

Edon, Georges. Dictionnaire Francais-Latin. (Fr.-Lat.). 37.50 (ISBN 0-686-57201-7, M-6703). French & Eur.

Gaffiot, Felix. Dictionnaire Abrege Latin-Francais. 1720p. (Lat.-Fr.). 1970. pap. 15.95 (ISBN 0-686-57186-X, M-6258). French & Eur.

--Dictionnaire Latin-Francais. (Lat.-Fr.). 1967. pap. 32.50 (ISBN 0-686-57187-8, M-6259). French & Eur.

Lebaigue, Charles. Dictionnaire Latin-Francais. 1382p. (Fr. & Lat.). 33.50 (ISBN 0-686-56999-7, M-6340). French & Eur.

Quicherat, Louis. Dictionnaire Francais-Latin. (Fr.-Lat.). 1967. pap. 35.00 (ISBN 0-686-57202-5, M-6472). French & Eur.

LATIN LANGUAGE–EXAMINATIONS, QUESTIONS, ETC.

Gerwig, Anne M. Barron's How to Prepare for the College Board Achievement Tests - Latin. LC 64-23527. (gr. 11-12). 1965. pap. 3.95 (ISBN 0-8120-0125-7). Barron.

Rudman, Jack. Latin. (National Teachers Examination Ser.: NT-18). (Cloth bdg. avail. on request). pap. 9.95 (ISBN 0-8373-8408-7). Natl Learning.

--Latin Sr. H. S. (Teachers License Examination Ser.: T-37). (Cloth bng. avail. on request). pap. 10.00 (ISBN 0-8373-8037-5). Natl Learning.

LATIN LANGUAGE–GLOSSARIES, VOCABULARIES, ETC.

Latin Word List. 1969. pap. 3.25 (ISBN 0-934338-20-5). NAIS.

Lodge, Gonzalez. The Vocabulary of High School Latin. LC 73-177003. (Columbia University. Teachers College. Contributions to Education: No. 9). Repr. of 1912 ed. 17.50 (ISBN 0-404-55009-6). AMS Pr.

McCulloch, James A. Medical Greek & Latin Workbook. 174p. 1977. pap. 8.50 (ISBN 0-398-01249-0). C C Thomas.

Oliphant, Robert. Harley Latin-Old English Glossary. (Janua Linguarum, Ser. Practica: No. 20). 1966. pap. text ed. 45.00x (ISBN 90-2790-639-4). Mouton.

Paschall, Dorothy M. Vocabulary of Mental Aberration in Roman Comedy & Petronius. (Language Dissertations: No. 27). 1939. pap. 6.00 (ISBN 0-527-00773-0). Kraus Repr.

Wilson, John & Parsons, C. Basic Latin Vocabulary. 1960. text ed. 5.95 (ISBN 0-312-06825-5). St Martin.

LATIN LANGUAGE–GRAMMAR

see also Latin Language–Syntax

Barwick, Karl. Remmius Palaemon und Die Romische Ars Grammatica. Repr. of 1922 ed. pap. 14.00 (ISBN 0-384-03505-1). Johnson Repr.

Bibby, W. & Clare, E. N. Introduction to Latin Comprehension. 1971. pap. text ed. 3.00x (ISBN 0-435-36036-1). Heinemann Ed.

--New Latin Comprehension. 1970. pap. text ed. 3.00x (ISBN 0-435-36035-3). Heinemann Ed.

Cherel, Albert O. Latin Sans Peine. 9.95 (ISBN 0-685-11288-8). French & Eur.

Dewitt, Norman J., et al. College Latin. 1954. text ed. 16.95x (ISBN 0-673-05105-6). Scott F.

Elmer, Herbert C. Studies in Latin Moods & Tenses. 1898. 20.00 (ISBN 0-384-14275-3). Johnson Repr.

Fantham, Elaine. Comparative Studies in Republican Latin Imagery. LC 77-185710. (Phoenix Supplementary Volumes Ser.). 224p. 1972. 17.50x (ISBN 0-8020-5262-2). U of Toronto Pr.

Freundlich, Charles I. Latin for the Grades, 3 Bks. (gr. 4-6). 1970. Bk. 1. pap. text ed. 3.75 (ISBN 0-87720-562-0); Bk. 2. pap. text ed. 3.75 (ISBN 0-87720-564-7); Bk. 3. pap. text ed. 3.75 (ISBN 0-87720-566-3). AMSCO Sch.

Gildersleeve, Basil L. & Lodge, G. Latin Grammar. 3rd ed. 1895. 14.95 (ISBN 0-312-47355-9). St Martin.

Glenn, Jessie M. Neuter Plural in Latin Iambic & Trochaic Verse. 1939. pap. 6.00 (ISBN 0-527-00776-5). Kraus Repr.

Green, John C., Jr. Ritchie's First Steps in Latin. 3rd ed. 1978. text ed. 4.95x (ISBN 0-582-28085-0). Longman.

--Ritchie's Second Steps in Latin. 3rd ed. 1924. text ed. 5.95x (ISBN 0-582-28086-9). Longman.

Gummere, John F. Neuter Plural in Vergil. 1934. pap. 6.00 (ISBN 0-527-00763-3). Kraus Repr.

Hale, William G. The Cum-Constructions: Their History & Functions, 2 Vols in One. 1887-89. 23.00 (ISBN 0-384-20930-0). Johnson Repr.

Hale, William G. & Buck, Carl D. A Latin Grammar. LC 65-19660. (Alabama Linguistic & Philological Ser: Vol. 8). 400p. 1966. pap. 6.95 (ISBN 0-8173-0350-2). U of Ala Pr.

Hammond, Mason. Latin: A Historical & Linguistic Handbook. 272p. 1976. 16.50x (ISBN 0-674-51290-1); pap. text ed. 7.95x (ISBN 0-674-51289-8). Harvard U Pr.

Hayes, Walter M. An Introductory Latin Program, 5 Bks., with Panels, Post-Tests, Key, Text Aids. (Orig.). 1966. Set. pap. text ed. 14.00 (ISBN 0-8294-0129-6); 17 tapes 120.00 (ISBN 0-685-14282-5). Loyola.

Hendricks, Rhoda A. Latin Made Simple. LC 62-12101. pap. 3.50 (ISBN 0-385-01756-1, Made). Doubleday.

Jenney, Charles, Jr. & Scudder, Robers V. Third Year Latin. (Latin Program Ser.). (gr. 9-12). 1980. text ed. 15.24 (ISBN 0-205-06811-1, 3968111); tchrs.' guide 2.40 (ISBN 0-205-00541-1, 3905411). Allyn.

Lane, George M. Latin Grammar for Schools & Colleges. rev. ed. LC 78-107458. Repr. of 1903 ed. 19.50 (ISBN 0-404-00634-5). AMS Pr.

--Latin Grammar for Schools & Colleges. Morgan, Morris H., ed. Repr. of 1903 ed. lib. bdg. 22.25x (ISBN 0-8371-0523-4, LALG). Greenwood.

--Latin Grammar for Schools & Colleges. LC 74-107177. 1970. Repr. of 1903 ed. 25.00 (ISBN 0-403-00213-3). Scholarly.

La Ramee, Pierre De. The Latine Grammar of P. Ramus. LC 78-26236. (English Experience Ser.: No. 289). 1971. Repr. of 1585 ed. 16.00 (ISBN 90-221-0289-0). Walter J Johnson.

Lewis, Carolyn D. Medical Latin. (YA) (gr. 12). 2.50x (ISBN 0-8338-0040-X). M Jones.

McGill, Thornton A., Jr. Barron's Card Guide to Latin Grammar. 1966. pap. text ed. 1.75 (ISBN 0-8120-5056-8). Barron.

Most, William G. Fifty Units of Basic Latin Grammar. 1965. pap. text ed. 2.00 (ISBN 0-685-14104-7). Lawrence.

O'Brien, Richard J. & Twombly, Neil J. A Basic Course in Latin. (Orig.). (gr. 9-12). 1967. pap. text ed. 5.00 (ISBN 0-8294-0117-2); study guide 0.60 (ISBN 0-8294-0118-0). Loyola.

Pinkster, H. On Latin Adverbs, Vol. 6. (North-Holland Linguistics Ser.). 1973. pap. 22.00 (ISBN 0-444-10511-5, North-Holland). Elsevier.

Scanlon, Cora C. & Scanlon, Charles L. Latin Grammar: Grammar Vocabularies & Exercises in Preparation for the Reading of the Missal & Breviary. Thompson, Newton, ed. LC 79-112494. 1976. pap. text ed. 6.00 (ISBN 0-89555-002-4, 168). TAN Bks Pubs.

Smith, F. K. Teach Yourself Latin. (Teach Yourself Ser.). pap. 4.95 (ISBN 0-679-10186-1). McKay.

Solodow, Joseph B. The Latin Particle Quidem. (American Philological Association, American Classical Studies). 1978. pap. 6.00 (ISBN 0-89130-252-2, 400404). Scholars Pr Ca.

Sweet, Waldo E., et al. Latin: A Structural Approach. rev. ed. LC 66-17030. (gr. 9-12). 1966. text ed. 9.50x (ISBN 0-472-08803-3); tapes avail. U of Mich Pr.

Ullman, B. L., et al. Latin for Americans, 3 bks. Incl. Bk. 1. 5th ed. 1968. text ed. 7.04 (ISBN 0-685-39252-X, 23366); tchrs' manual 1.44 (ISBN 0-685-39253-8); tchrs' key 1.00 (ISBN 0-685-39254-6); progress tests 2.60 (ISBN 0-685-39255-4); key 3.24 (ISBN 0-685-39256-2); 14 tapes with manual & script 105.00 (ISBN 0-685-39257-0); tchrs' manual & script 1.20 (ISBN 0-685-39258-9); Bk. 2. 5th ed. 1969. text ed. 7.28 (ISBN 0-685-39259-7); tchrs' manual & key 2.36 (ISBN 0-685-39260-0); progress tests 2.60 (ISBN 0-685-39261-9); key 3.24 (ISBN 0-685-39262-7); 8 tapes with manual & script 69.95 (ISBN 0-685-39263-5); manual & script 1.16 (ISBN 0-685-39264-3); Bk. 3. Ullman, B. L. & Suskin, Albert I. text ed. 7.36 (ISBN 0-685-39265-1); tchrs' key 2.36 (ISBN 0-685-39266-X). (gr. 9-12). Macmillan.

Vaughan, Alden G. Latin Adjectives with Partitive Meaning in Republican Literature. 1942. pap. 6.00 (ISBN 0-527-00782-X). Kraus Repr.

Wingo, E. Otha. Latin Punctuation in the Classical Age. (Janua Linguarum, Ser. Practica: No. 133). 166p. 1972. pap. text ed. 45.00x (ISBN 0-686-22548-1). Mouton.

Yoder, Edward. Position of Possessive & Demonstrative Adjectives in the Noctes Atticae of Aulus Gellius. 1928. pap. 6.00 (ISBN 0-527-00748-X). Kraus Repr.

Zenn, Elizabeth G. Neuter Plural in Latin Lyric Verse. 1948. pap. 6.00 (ISBN 0-527-00788-9). Kraus Repr.

LATIN LANGUAGE–GRAMMAR, COMPARATIVE

Buck, Carl D. Comparative Grammar of Greek & Latin. LC 33-11254. 1933. 22.00x (ISBN 0-226-07931-7). U of Chicago Pr.

LATIN LANGUAGE–HISTORY

Cole, A. T. & Ross, D. O., eds. Studies in Latin Language & Literature. LC 72-80595. (Yale Classical Studies: No. 23). 1972. 36.00 (ISBN 0-521-08683-3). Cambridge U Pr.

Hammond, Mason. Latin: A Historical & Linguistic Handbook. 272p. 1976. 16.50x (ISBN 0-674-51290-1); pap. text ed. 7.95x (ISBN 0-674-51289-8). Harvard U Pr.

Pei, Mario. The Story of Latin & the Romance Languages. LC 75-6352. (Illus.). 384p. (YA) 1976. 17.50 (ISBN 0-06-013312-0, HarpT). Har-Row.

Postel, G. De Originibus seu de Hebraicae Linguae et Gentis Antiquitate, Atque Variarum Linguarum Affinitate. (Linguistics 13th-18th Centuries). 60p. (Fr.). 1974. Repr. of 1538 ed. lib. bdg. 26.00 (ISBN 0-8287-0698-0, 71-5010). Clearwater Pub.

--Linguarum Douze Characteribus Differentium Introductio ac Legendi Methodus. (Linguistics 13th-18th Centuries). 180p. (Fr.). 1974. Repr. of 1538 ed. lib. bdg. 53.00x (ISBN 0-8287-0699-9, 71-5009). Clearwater Pub.

Pulgram, Ernst. Tongues of Italy, Prehistory & History. Repr. of 1958 ed. lib. bdg. 24.75x (ISBN 0-8371-2438-7, PUTI). Greenwood.

Sanchez de Las Brozas, F. Minerva, Sive de Causis Linguae Latinae. (Linguistics 13th-18th Centuries). 588p. (Fr.). 1974. Repr. of 1587 ed. lib. bdg. 144.00x (ISBN 0-8287-0758-8, 71-5011). Clearwater Pub.

Scaliger, Julius C. De Causis Linguae Latinae. (Linguistics 13th-18th Centuries). 474p. (Fr.). 1974. Repr. of 1598 ed. lib. bdg. 118.00 (ISBN 0-8287-0765-0, 71-5012). Clearwater Pub.

Warmington, E. H., ed. Remains of Old Latin, 4 vols. Incl. Vol. 1. Ennius. Caecilius (ISBN 0-674-99324-1); Vol. 2. Livius Andronicus, Naevius, Pacuvius, Accius (ISBN 0-674-99347-0); Vol. 3. Lucilius. Laws of the XII Tables (ISBN 0-674-99363-2); Vol. 4. Archaic Inscriptions (ISBN 0-674-99396-9). (Loeb Classical Library: No. 294, 314, 329, 359). (Lat. & Eng.). 10.00x ea. Harvard U Pr.

LATIN LANGUAGE–METRICS AND RHYTHMICS

Allen, W. Sidney. Accent & Rhythm: Prosodic Features of Latin & Greek. LC 72-91361. (Studies in Linguistics). 432p. 1973. 57.50 (ISBN 0-521-20098-9). Cambridge U Pr.

Ewbank, William W. The Poems of Cicero. Commager, Steele, ed. LC 77-70814. (Latin Poetry Ser.). 1978. lib. bdg. 28.00 (ISBN 0-8240-2955-0). Garland Pub.

Harsh, Philip W. Iambic Words & Regard for Accent in Plautus. LC 49-11495. (Stanford University. Stanford Studies in Language & Literature: Vol. 7, Pt. 2). Repr. of 1949 ed. 15.00 (ISBN 0-404-51814-1). AMS Pr.

Platnauer, Maurice. Latin Elegiac Verse: A Study of the Metrical Usages of Tibullus, Propertius, & Ovid. LC 79-143886. 1971. Repr. of 1951 ed. 13.50 (ISBN 0-208-01116-1, Archon). Shoe String.

Rosenmeyer, Thomas W., et al. Meters of Greek & Latin Poetry. LC 62-21264. (Orig.). 1973. pap. text ed. 4.95x (ISBN 0-672-60328-4). Irvington.

Wilkinson, L. P. Golden Latin Artistry. 1963. 42.00 (ISBN 0-521-06807-X). Cambridge U Pr.

Winbolt, Samuel E. Latin Hexametre Verse. Commager, Steele, ed. LC 77-70818. (Latin Poetry Ser.). 1978. lib. bdg. 27.50 (ISBN 0-8240-2982-8). Garland Pub.

Zenn, Elizabeth G. Neuter Plural in Latin Lyric Verse. 1948. pap. 6.00 (ISBN 0-527-00788-9). Kraus Repr.

LATIN LANGUAGE–PRONUNCIATION

Allen, W. S. Vox Latina. 2nd ed. LC 78-1153. (Illus.). 1978. 15.95 (ISBN 0-521-22049-1). Cambridge U Pr.

Hines, Robert S. Singers Manual of Latin Diction & Phonetics. LC 74-34130. 1975. 8.95 (ISBN 0-02-870800-8). Schirmer Bks.

Holland, Louise A. Lucretius & the Transpadanes. LC 79-1415. 1979. 15.00 (ISBN 0-691-06401-6). Princeton U Pr.

Sturtevant, E. H. The Pronunciation of Greek & Latin. pap. 6.00 (ISBN 0-89005-087-2). Ares.

Sturtevant, Edgar H. The Pronunciation of Greek & Latin. 2d ed. LC 77-1194. (William Dwight Whitney Linguistic Ser.). 1977. Repr. of 1940 ed. lib. bdg. 14.25x (ISBN 0-8371-9516-0, STPRO). Greenwood.

LATIN LANGUAGE–READERS

Balme, M. G. Intellegenda: Comprehension Exercises in Latin Prose & Verse. 1970. pap. 6.95x (ISBN 0-19-831775-1). Oxford U Pr.

Balme, M. G. & Warman, M. S. Aestimanda: Practical Criticism of Latin & Greek Poetry & Prose. 1965. pap. 6.95 (ISBN 0-19-831766-2). Oxford U Pr.

Comenius, John A. Orbis Pictus of John Amos Comenius. Bardeen, Charles W., ed. LC 67-23933. (Illus., Eng. & Lat.). 1968. Repr. of 1887 ed. 22.00 (ISBN 0-8103-3476-3). Gale.

Corcoran, Thomas H. Latin Prose & Poetry: Selections for the Classroom, Book One. LC 76-26771. 1976. 18.00 (ISBN 0-8357-0183-2, SS-00016). Univ Microfilms.

--Latin Prose & Poetry: Selections for the Classroom, Book Two. LC 76-26771. 1977. 18.50 (ISBN 0-8357-0196-4, SS-00024). Univ Microfilms.

Daimon: An Adventure Story for First Year Latin Students. (Illus.). (gr. 7-10). 1977. pap. text ed. 2.25x (ISBN 0-88334-095-X). Ind Sch Pr.

Dewitt, Norman J., et al. College Latin. 1954. text ed. 16.95x (ISBN 0-673-05105-6). Scott F.

Echols, Edvardus C. Freddus Elephantus et Horatius Porcus Saltans Cincinnatis. 129p. (Orig., Latin.). (gr. 10-11). 1980. pap. text ed. 3.50x (ISBN 0-88334-139-5). Ind Sch Pr.

Flewett, H. W. & Pantin, William E. First Book of Latin Poetry. (Illus., Lat.). 1977. pap. text ed. 5.95 (ISBN 0-312-29226-0). St Martin.

Fratter, David G. Aere Perennius. (Lat. & Eng.). 1969. 4.95 (ISBN 0-312-00735-3). St Martin.

Goldman, Norma & Nyenhuis, Jacob E. Latin Via Ovid: A First Course. LC 77-22501. (Illus.). 1977. 15.95x (ISBN 0-8143-1573-9). Wayne St U Pr.

Gould, Howard E. & Whiteley, Joseph L., eds. Selections from Five Roman Authors: Nepos, Caesar, Sallust, Livy, Cicero. (Illus., Lat.). 1942. 6.95 (ISBN 0-312-71190-5). St Martin.

--Selections from Five Roman Poets: Catullus, Virgil, Horace, Tibullus, Ovid. (Illus., Lat.). 1941. 6.95 (ISBN 0-312-71225-1). St Martin.

Hammond, Mason & Amory, Anne R. Aeneas to Augustus: A Beginning Latin Reader for College Students. 2nd ed. LC 67-12104. (Orig.). 1967. pap. text ed. 10.00x (ISBN 0-674-00600-3). Harvard U Pr.

Hawthorn, J. R. Rome & Jugurtha: Selections from Sallust's Jugurtha. (Illus.). (gr. 10-12). 1970. text ed. 6.95 (ISBN 0-312-69195-5). St Martin.

Hornsby, Roger A. Reading Latin Poetry. 1969. Repr. of 1967 ed. 9.95x (ISBN 0-8061-0741-3). U of Okla Pr.

Kennedy, Eberhard C., ed. Four Latin Authors. 1940. text ed. 7.50x (ISBN 0-521-05881-3). Cambridge U Pr.

--Latin Unseens from Roman History. 1951. 4.50 (ISBN 0-312-47460-1). St Martin.

Kennedy, Eberhard C. & Davis, A. R., eds. Two Centuries of Roman Poetry. (Illus.). 1964. 7.95 (ISBN 0-312-82565-X). St Martin.
Levy, Harry L. Latin Reader for Colleges. LC 62-18119. 1962. pap. 6.00x (ISBN 0-226-47602-2). U of Chicago Pr.
Livy. Ab Urbe Condita, Bk. 1. Gould, Howard E. & Whiteley, Joseph L., eds. (Modern School Classics Ser). (Lat). 1952. 7.95 (ISBN 0-312-49280-4). St Martin.
--Ab Urbe Condita, Bk. 30. Whiteley, Joseph L., ed. (Modern School Classics Ser.). (Lat). 5.95 (ISBN 0-312-49315-0). St Martin.
Lockwood, Dean P. Survey of Classical Roman Literature, 2 Vols. LC 34-40316. 1962. Vol. 1. pap. 7.50x (ISBN 0-226-48962-0); Vol. 2. pap. 9.50x (ISBN 0-226-48963-9, Midway Reprint). U of Chicago Pr.
Macdonald, C., ed. Cicero: Pro Murena. (Modern School Classics Ser). (Illus.). (gr. 10-12). 1969. text ed. 5.95 (ISBN 0-312-13755-9). St Martin.
O'Brien, Richard J. & Twombly, Neil J. The Men on the Tiber. (Eng., Translation of intermediate latin readings). (gr. 9-12). 1965. pap. text ed. 2.00 (ISBN 0-8294-0120-2). Loyola.
Potter, Beatrix. Fabula Petro Cuniculo: Peter Rabbit. (Latin). (gr. 3-7). Date not set. bds. 4.50 (ISBN 0-7232-0648-1). Warne.
Sallust. Cataline. Merivale, C., ed. (Classical Ser). (Lat). 1870. pap. text ed. 7.95 (ISBN 0-312-12460-0). St Martin.
Tennick, M. Libellus: Handbook. LC 77-28241. (Latin Texts Ser.). 1979. 9.95x (ISBN 0-521-21911-6). Cambridge U Pr.
Wormald, R. D. & Lyne, G. M. Rogues' Gallery. (Lat). 1939. text ed. 7.95x (ISBN 0-521-06869-X). Cambridge U Pr.

LATIN LANGUAGE–SEMANTICS

Odgers, Merle M. Latin Parens, Its Meanings & Uses. (Language Dissertations: No. 3). 1928. pap. 6.00 (ISBN 0-527-00749-8). Kraus Repr.
Teeuwen, S. W. Sprachlicher Bedeutungswandel Bei Tertullian. Repr. of 1926 ed. pap. 9.50 (ISBN 0-384-59790-4). Johnson Repr.

LATIN LANGUAGE–STUDY AND TEACHING

Allen, J. H. & Greenough, J. B. New Latin Grammar. Kittredge, G. L., et al, eds. (College Classical Ser.). 490p. 1975. lib. bdg. 22.50x (ISBN 0-89241-001-9); pap. 12.50x (ISBN 0-89241-331-X). Caratzas Bros.
Allen, William S. A Study in Latin Prognosis. LC 70-176513. (Columbia University. Teachers College. Contributions to Education: No. 135). Repr. of 1923 ed. 17.50 (ISBN 0-404-55135-1). AMS Pr.
Ascham, Roger. Scholemaster. Mayor, J. E., ed. LC 75-161717. Repr. of 1863 ed. 14.00 (ISBN 0-404-00409-1). AMS Pr.
--The Scholemaster. Arber, Edward, ed. LC 76-13152. Repr. of 1870 ed. lib. bdg. 15.00 (ISBN 0-8414-2976-6). Folcroft.
--The Scholemaster: Or, Plaine & Perfite Way of Teachyng Children the Latin Tong. LC 68-54609. (English Experience Ser.: No. 15). 134p. 1968. Repr. of 1570 ed. 14.00 (ISBN 90-221-0015-4). Walter J Johnson.
Association of Assistant Masters in Secondary Schools: Teaching of Classics. rev. ed. 1962. 13.95 (ISBN 0-521-05363-3). Cambridge U Pr.
Bennett, Charles E. & Bristol, George P. The Teaching of Latin & Greek in the Secondary School. 1901. Repr. 35.00 (ISBN 0-685-43062-6). Norwood Edns.
Cambridge School Classics Project. Cambridge Latin Course, 3 bklts, Unit 5, Pupils Books. Incl. Dido et Aeneas; Nero et Agrippina; Words & Phrases. (Illus.). 1974. pap. text ed. 4.50x (ISBN 0-521-08545-4). Cambridge U Pr.
--Latin Course: Information About the Language, Units 4 & 5. 80p. (gr. 7-12). 1975. pap. 2.95x (ISBN 0-521-20822-X). Cambridge U Pr.
Clem, Orlie M. Detailed Factors in Latin Prognosis. LC 78-176653. (Columbia University. Teachers College. Contributions to Education: No. 144). Repr. of 1924 ed. 17.50 (ISBN 0-404-55144-0). AMS Pr.
Cook, A. M. Macmillan's Shorter Latin Course, Part I. 1969. pap. text ed. 2.50 (ISBN 0-312-50295-8). St Martin.
Dorey, T. A., ed. Empire & Aftermath. (Greek & Latin Studies). 1975. 19.50x (ISBN 0-7100-8087-5). Routledge & Kegan.
Freundlich, Charles I. Review Text in Latin Two Years. (gr. 7-12). 1966. pap. text ed. 5.75 (ISBN 0-87720-555-8). AMSCO Sch.
Griffiths, Anna H. Latin. (Blue Book Ser). pap. 1.25 (ISBN 0-671-18122-X). Monarch Pr.
Jenney, Charles & Scudder, Rogers. First Year Latin. (New Jenney Latin Series). (gr. 10). 1975. text ed. 14.40 (ISBN 0-205-04595-2, 3945952); tchr's. guide 3.60 (ISBN 0-205-04596-0, 3945960); wkbk 5.40 (ISBN 0-205-02482-3, 3924823); tchrs'. guide to wkbk. 3.60 (ISBN 0-205-02483-1, 3924831); tests 4.12 (ISBN 0-205-02484-X, 392484X); tchrs'. ed. 4.12 (ISBN 0-205-02485-8, 3924858). Allyn.
Kennedy, Benjamin H. Kennedy's Revised Latin Primer. 1962. pap. text ed. 5.50x (ISBN 0-582-36240-7). Longman.
Learn Latin for English Speakers. pap. 7.00 (ISBN 0-87557-051-8, 051-8). Saphrograph.
MacNaughton, E. G. & McDougall, T. W. A New Approach to Latin: 1. (Illus.). 1973. pap. text ed. 5.50x (ISBN 0-05-002185-0). Longman.
--A New Approach to Latin: 2. (Illus.). 1974. pap. text ed. 5.50x (ISBN 0-05-002365-9). Longman.
Most, William G. Latin by the Natural Method, Bks. 1 & 3. Bk. 1. 3.67 (ISBN 0-685-36882-3); Bk. 3. 2.67 (ISBN 0-685-36883-1); tape script 0.67 (ISBN 0-685-36884-X). Lawrence.
Paterson, James & Macnaughton, Edwin. The Approach to Latin. (Illus.). Pt. 1, 1938. text ed. 5.50x (ISBN 0-05-000292-9); Pt. 2, 1969. text ed. 5.50x (ISBN 0-05-000293-7). Longman.
Sadler, J. D. Modern Latin, Bk. II. LC 73-19382. 330p. 1974. text ed. 10.95x (ISBN 0-8061-1183-6); pap. text ed. 5.95x (ISBN 0-8061-1189-5). U of Okla Pr.
Wheelock, Frederic M. Latin: An Introductory Course Based on Ancient Authors, Including Readings. 3rd ed. LC 63-8289. 1963. 12.50x (ISBN 0-06-480944-7). B&N.

LATIN LANGUAGE–SUFFIXES AND PREFIXES

Hendrickson, J. R. Old English Prepositional Compounds in Relationship to Their Latin Originals. 1948. pap. 6.00 (ISBN 0-527-00789-7). Kraus Repr.
Rosen, Harold. Old High German Preposition Compounds in Relation to Their Latin Originals. 1934. pap. 6.00 (ISBN 0-527-00762-5). Kraus Repr.

LATIN LANGUAGE–SYNTAX

Bennett, Charles E. Syntax of Early Latin, 2 Vols. Repr. of 1910 ed. Set. 100.00 (ISBN 0-685-05294-X). Adler.
Dahlen, Eric M. V. Remarques Syntaxiques Sur Certains Verbes Pronominaux En Latin et En Langues Romanes. (Studia Graeca et Latina Gothorburgensia). 1977. pap. text ed. 9.25x (ISBN 91-7346-037-0). Humanities.
Gavigan, John J. Syntax of the Gesta Francorum. 1943. pap. 6.00 (ISBN 0-527-00783-8). Kraus Repr.
Nutting, Herbert C. Studies in Latin Syntax, 2 Vols. pap. 31.00 ea. Johnson Repr.
Yoder, Edward. Position of Possessive & Demonstrative Adjectives in the Noctes Atticae of Aulus Gellius. 1928. pap. 6.00 (ISBN 0-527-00748-X). Kraus Repr.

LATIN LANGUAGE–VERB

Bauer, C. F. Latin Perfect Endings -ere & -erunt. 1933. pap. 6.00 (ISBN 0-527-00759-5). Kraus Repr.
Bolkestein, A. M. Problems in the Description of Modal Verbs: An Investigation of Latin. (Studies in Greek & Latin Linguistics). 180p. 1980. pap. text ed. 21.00x (ISBN 90-232-1764-0). Humanities.
Dahlen, Eric M. V. Remarques Syntaxiques Sur Certains Verbes Pronominaux En Latin et En Langues Romanes. (Studia Graeca et Latina Gothorburgensia). 1977. pap. text ed. 9.25x (ISBN 91-7346-037-0). Humanities.
Hendrickson, J. R. Old English Prepositional Compounds in Relationship to Their Latin Originals. 1948. pap. 6.00 (ISBN 0-527-00789-7). Kraus Repr.
Rosen, Harold. Old High German Preposition Compounds in Relation to Their Latin Originals. 1934. pap. 6.00 (ISBN 0-527-00762-5). Kraus Repr.
Wohlberg, Joseph. Two Hundred & One Latin Verbs Fully Conjugated in All the Tenses. LC 63-23374. (Orig.). 1964. text ed. 7.00 (ISBN 0-8120-6051-2); pap. text ed. 2.95 (ISBN 0-8120-0211-3). Barron.

LATIN LANGUAGE–WORD FORMATION

Burriss, Eli E. & Casson, Lionel. Latin & Greek in Current Use. 2nd ed. 1949. text ed. 13.95 (ISBN 0-13-524991-0). P-H.

LATIN LANGUAGE, COLLOQUIAL

see also Latin Language, Vulgar

LATIN LANGUAGE, MEDIEVAL AND MODERN

see also Christian Literature, Early

Benner, Margareta & Tengstrom, Emin. On the Interpretation of Learned Neo-Latin: An Explorative Study Based on Some Texts from Sweden 1611-1716. (Studia Graeca et Latina Goteborg: No. 39). 1977. 16.25x (ISBN 91-7346-044-3). Humanities.
Harrington, Karl P. Medieval Latin. LC 62-18114. 1962. pap. 12.00x (ISBN 0-226-31711-0). U of Chicago Pr.
Sadler, J. D. Modern Latin, Bk. I. 1978. pap. 7.95x (ISBN 0-8061-1046-5). U of Okla Pr.

LATIN LANGUAGE, MEDIEVAL AND MODERN–DICTIONARIES

Latham, Ronald E., ed. Revised Medieval Latin Word-List from British & Irish Sources. (British Academy Ser.). 1965. 49.00x (ISBN 0-19-725891-3). Oxford U Pr.

LATIN LANGUAGE, MEDIEVAL AND MODERN–GLOSSARIES, VOCABULARIES, ETC.

Galfridus Anglicus. Promptorium Parvulorum Sive Clericorum, Dictionarius Anglolatinus Princeps, 3 Pts. Repr. of 1865 ed. 31.00 ea. Johnson Repr.
Galfridus Anglicus. Promptorium Parvulorum Sive Clericorum, Lexicon Anglo-Latinum Princeps, 3 Vols. LC 70-168091. (Camden Society, London. Publications, First Ser.: Nos. 25, 54, 89). Repr. of 1865 ed. Set. 84.00 (ISBN 0-404-50209-1); 28.00 ea. AMS Pr.
Meritt, H. D. Old English Glosses: A Collection. 1945. 9.00 (ISBN 0-527-63350-X). Kraus Repr.

LATIN LANGUAGE, MEDIEVAL AND MODERN–GRAMMAR

Gooder, Eileen A. Latin for Local History: An Introduction. 2nd ed. (Illus.). 1978. pap. text ed. 11.95x (ISBN 0-582-48728-5). Longman.

LATIN LANGUAGE, MEDIEVAL AND MODERN–READERS

Waddell, Helen, ed. Book of Medieval Latin for Schools. 3rd ed. 1979. pap. 7.50x (ISBN 0-06-497276-3). B&N.

LATIN LANGUAGE, MEDIEVAL AND MODERN–SYNTAX

Friebel, Otto. Fulgentius, der Mythograph und Bischof. pap. 12.50 (ISBN 0-384-16880-9). Johnson Repr.

LATIN LANGUAGE, POPULAR

see Latin Language, Vulgar

LATIN LANGUAGE, POSTCLASSICAL

Allen, W. S. Vox Latina. 2nd ed. LC 78-1153. (Illus.). 1978. 15.95 (ISBN 0-521-22049-1). Cambridge U Pr.
Garey, H. B. Historical Development of Tenses from Late Latin to Old French. 1955. pap. 6.00 (ISBN 0-527-00797-8). Kraus Repr.
Teeuwen, S. W. Sprachlicher Bedeutungswandel Bei Tertullian. Repr. of 1926 ed. pap. 9.50 (ISBN 0-384-59790-4). Johnson Repr.

LATIN LANGUAGE, PRECLASSICAL TO ca. 100 B.C.

Bennett, Charles E. Syntax of Early Latin, 2 Vols. Repr. of 1910 ed. Set. 100.00 (ISBN 0-685-05294-X). Adler.

LATIN LANGUAGE, VULGAR

Adams, J. N. The Vulgar Latin of the Letters of Claudius Terentianus (P. Mich. VIII, 467-75) 100p. 1977. 22.75x (ISBN 0-8476-1428-X). Rowman.
Duran, Richard P., ed. Latino Language & Communicative Behavior, Vol. 6. 384p. 1981. 29.50 (ISBN 0-89391-038-4). Ablex Pub.
Gaeng, Paul A. An Inquiry into the Local Variations in Vulgar Latin As Reflected in the Vocalism of Christian Inscriptions. (Studies in the Romance Languages & Literatures: No. 77). 1968. pap. 16.50x (ISBN 0-8078-9077-4). U of NC Pr.
Mazzola, Michael L. Proto-Romance & Sicilian. 1977. pap. text ed. 11.00x (ISBN 90-316-0088-1). Humanities.

LATIN LETTERS

Alan Of Tewkesbury. Alani Priors Cantuariensis Postea Abbatis Tewkesberiensis Scripta Quae Extant. Giles, J. A., ed. 1966. Repr. of 1848 ed. 24.00 (ISBN 0-8337-1340-X). B Franklin.
Cicero. Letters to His Brother Quintus. Bd. with Letters to Brutus; Handbook of Electioneering; Letter to Octavian. (Loeb Classical Library: No. 462). 11.00x (ISBN 0-674-99509-0). Harvard U Pr.
Levens, R. G. A Book of Latin Letters, Chosen & Annotated. 1979. Repr. of 1930 ed. lib. bdg. 30.00 (ISBN 0-8495-3312-0). Arden Lib.

LATIN LITERATURE (COLLECTIONS)

see also Classical Literature (Collections); Classical Philology; Latin Philology

Brooks, Charles, ed. Best Editorial Cartoons of the Year: 1975 Edition. LC 74-29707. (Best Editorial Cartoon Ser.). (Illus.). 160p. 1975. 11.95 (ISBN 0-88289-077-8). Pelican.
Cicero. De Natura Deorum. Bd. with Academica 1-2. (Loeb Classical Library: No. 268). 11.00x (ISBN 0-674-99296-2). Harvard U Pr.
--Offices. Cockman, Thomas, tr. Incl. Laelius, on Friendship; & Cato, on Old Age & Selected Letters. Melmouth, W., tr. 1953. 9.95x (ISBN 0-460-00345-3, Evman). Dutton.
Cook, A. M. A Latin Anthology. 187p. 1981. Repr. of 1912 ed. lib. bdg. 30.00 (ISBN 0-89987-126-7). Darby Bks.
--A Latin Anthology. 1912. 25.00 (ISBN 0-8274-3942-3). R West.
Cook, A. M., ed. A Latin Anthology. 1978. Repr. of 1912 ed. lib. bdg. 20.00 (ISBN 0-89760-104-1, Telegraph). Dynamic Learn Corp.
Cutt, Thomas & Nyenhuis, Jacob E., eds. Petronius: Cena Trimalchionis. rev. ed. LC 73-105090. (Classical Text Ser). (Latin). 1970. pap. text ed. 4.95x (ISBN 0-8143-1410-4). Wayne St U Pr.
--Plautus: Amphitruo. rev. ed. (Classical Text Ser). (Lat). 1970. pap. text ed. 4.95x (ISBN 0-8143-1411-2). Wayne St U Pr.
Dudley, D. R., ed. Neronians & Flavians: Silver Latin I. (Greek & Latin Studies Ser). 1972. 21.00x (ISBN 0-7100-7273-2). Routledge & Kegan.
Grant, Michael, ed. Latin Literature: An Anthology. (Penguin Classics Ser.). 1979. pap. 3.95 (ISBN 0-14-044389-4). Penguin.
Laing, Gordon J. Masterpieces of Latin Literature. 1902. 30.00 (ISBN 0-8274-3959-8). R West.
Leabhar Breac. LC 78-72638. (Celtic Language & Literature: Goidelic & Brythonic). Repr. of 1876 ed. 145.00 (ISBN 0-404-17565-1). AMS Pr.
McArdle, H. & Suggitt, G. Per Saecula. 1974. Pt. 1. pap. text ed. 3.50x (ISBN 0-05-002171-0); Pt. 2. pap. text ed. 3.50x (ISBN 0-05-002684-4); Pt. 3. pap. text ed. 3.50x (ISBN 0-05-002685-2). Longman.
Quintilian. Institutionis Oratoriae, 2 vols. Winterbottom, M., ed. (Oxford Classical Texts Ser). (Latin). Vol. 1. 22.50x (ISBN 0-19-814654-X); Vol. 2. 22.50x (ISBN 0-19-814655-8). Oxford U Pr.
Ragman Rolls. Instrumenta Publica Sive Processus Super Fidelitatibus et Homagiis Scotorum Domino Regi Angliae Factis A.D. MCCXCI MCCXCVI. Thomson, Thomas, ed. LC 76-174294. (Bannatyne Club, Edinburgh. Publications: No. 47). Repr. of 1834 ed. 27.50 (ISBN 0-404-52757-4). AMS Pr.
Soulsby, D., ed. Selections from Tacitus: Agricola. (Latin Texts Ser.). (Illus.). 64p. 1973. 2.95 (ISBN 0-521-20308-2). Cambridge U Pr.
Warmington, E. H., ed. Minor Latin Poets. (Loeb Classical Library: No. 284). (Lat. & Eng.). 11.00x (ISBN 0-674-99314-4). Harvard U Pr.
Wilkins, A. S. Roman Literature. 1890. 20.00 (ISBN 0-8274-3988-1). R West.

LATIN LITERATURE (SELECTIONS: EXTRACTS, ETC.)

Bloomfield, Morton W., et al. Incipits of Latin Works on the Virtues & Vices, 1100-1500 A. D. 1979. 75.00 (ISBN 0-910956-65-0). Medieval Acad.
Cree, A. Cree's Dictionary of Latin Quotations. LC 78-51482. 1979. 15.00 (ISBN 0-912728-12-4). Newbury Bks.
Gould, Howard E. & Whiteley, Joseph L., eds. Selections from Five Roman Authors: Nepos, Caesar, Sallust, Livy, Cicero. (Illus., Lat.). 1942. 6.95 (ISBN 0-312-71190-5). St Martin.
Herbert, Peter E. Selections from the Latin Fathers with Commentary & Notes. 186p. 1981. Repr. of 1924 ed. lib. bdg. 25.00 (ISBN 0-89760-343-5). Telegraph Bks.
Kennedy, Eberhard C. Roman Poetry & Prose. 1957. text ed. 7.50x (ISBN 0-521-05880-5). Cambridge U Pr.
Levy, Harry L. Latin Reader for Colleges. LC 62-18119. 1962. pap. 6.00x (ISBN 0-226-47602-2). U of Chicago Pr.
Lockwood, Dean P. Survey of Classical Roman Literature, 2 Vols. LC 34-40316. 1962. Vol. 1. pap. 7.50x (ISBN 0-226-48962-0); Vol. 2. pap. 9.50x (ISBN 0-226-48963-9, Midway Reprint). U of Chicago Pr.
Luarens, Henry, ed. The Papers of Henry Laurens, Vol. 9: April 19, 1773-Dec. 12, 1774. LC 67-29381. (Laurens Papers). (Illus.). 770p. 1981. text ed. 27.50 (ISBN 0-87249-399-7). U of SC Pr.
Pym, Dora. Readings from the Literature of Ancient Rome. 1975. Repr. of 1922 ed. 25.00 (ISBN 0-8274-4053-7). R West.

LATIN LITERATURE–BIBLIOGRAPHY

Bibliografia General de la Literatura Latinoamericana. (Orig., Sp.). 1973. pap. 6.75 (ISBN 0-685-39009-8, U46, UNESCO). Unipub.
Donlan, Walter, intro. by. The Classical World Bibliography of Roman Drama & Poetry & Ancient Fiction. LC 76-52516. (Library of Humanities Reference Bks.: No. 97). lib. bdg. 41.00 (ISBN 0-8240-9876-5). Garland Pub.
Esposito, Mario. Bibliography of the Latin Writers of Mediaeval Ireland. 1979. pap. 5.00 (ISBN 0-686-25173-3). British Am Bks.
Faider, Paul. Repertoire Des Index et Lexiques D'Auteurs Latins. LC 77-150150. (Fr). 1971. Repr. of 1926 ed. lib. bdg. 16.50 (ISBN 0-8337-1097-4). B Franklin.
Valk, Barbara G., ed. Hispanic American Periodicals Index 1978. LC 75-642408. 1981. lib. bdg. 100.00 (ISBN 0-87903-404-1). UCLA Lat Am Ctr.

LATIN LITERATURE–DICTIONARIES

Faider, Paul. Repertoire Des Index et Lexiques D'Auteurs Latins. LC 77-150150. (Fr). 1971. Repr. of 1926 ed. lib. bdg. 16.50 (ISBN 0-8337-1097-4). B Franklin.
Mantinband, James H. Dictionary of Latin Literature. (Quality Paperback: No. 152). 1964. pap. 3.50 (ISBN 0-8226-0152-4). Littlefield.
Mic, Rose S., ed. The Contemporary Latin American Short Story. LC 78-73619. (Senda De Estudios y Ensayos Ser.). (Orig., Span.). 1979. pap. 8.95 (ISBN 0-918454-10-7). Senda Nueva.

LATIN LITERATURE–HISTORY AND CRITICISM

Binns, J. W., ed. Latin Literature of the Fourth Century. (Greek & Latin Studies). 1974. 14.95 (ISBN 0-7100-7796-3). Routledge & Kegan.

Block, Elizabeth. The Effects of Divine Manifestations on the Reader's Perspective in Virgil's "Aneid". rev. ed. Connor, W. R., ed. LC 80-2640. (Monographs in Classical Studies). 1981. lib. bdg. 39.00 (ISBN 0-405-14028-2). Arno.

Clinton, Henry F. Fasti Hellenici: The Civil & Literary Chronology of Greece Through the Death of Augustus, 3 Vols. 1965. Repr. of 1834 ed. Set. 137.00 (ISBN 0-8337-0599-7). B Franklin.

--Fasti Romani: The Civil & Literary Chronology of Rome & Constantinople from the Death of Augustus to the Death of Justin the 2nd, 2 Vols. 1965. Repr. of 1850 ed. Set. 105.50 (ISBN 0-8337-0602-0). B Franklin.

Cole, A. T. & Ross, D. O., eds. Studies in Latin Language & Literature. LC 72-80595. (Yale Classical Studies: No. 23). 1972. 36.00 (ISBN 0-521-08683-3). Cambridge U Pr.

Conway, Robert S. Harvard Lectures on the Vergilian Age. LC 67-13861. 1928. 9.50x (ISBN 0-8196-0182-9). Biblo.

Copley, Frank O. Latin Literature: From the Beginnings to the Close of the Second Century A.D. LC 76-90760. 1969. 12.50x (ISBN 0-472-08240-X). U of Mich Pr.

Cruttwell, Charles T. A History of Roman Literature: From the Earliest Period to the Death of Marcus Aurelius. 1898. 25.00 (ISBN 0-8274-3943-1). R West.

D'Alton, John F. Roman Literary Theory & Criticism. LC 62-10683. 1962. Repr. of 1931 ed. 12.50 (ISBN 0-8462-0162-3). Russell.

Dimsdale, Marcus S. A History of Latin Literature. (Select Bibliographies Reprint Ser.). Repr. of 1915 ed. 25.00 (ISBN 0-8369-6684-8). Arno.

Dudley, D. R., ed. Virgil. (Studies in Latin Literature). 1969. 14.50x (ISBN 0-7100-6212-5). Routledge & Kegan.

Duff, John W. A Literary History of Rome in the Silver Age: From Tiberius to Hadrian. 3rd ed. Duff, A. M., ed. LC 79-9906. 1979. Repr. of 1964 ed. lib. bdg. 35.00x (ISBN 0-313-20939-1, DULH). Greenwood.

Fairclough, Henry R. Love of Nature Among the Greeks & Romans. LC 63-10298. (Our Debt to Greece & Rome Ser). (Illus.). Repr. of 1930 ed. 7.50x (ISBN 0-8154-0063-2). Cooper Sq.

Fantham, Elaine. Comparative Studies in Republican Latin Imagery. LC 77-185710. (Phoenix Supplementary Volumes Ser.). 224p. 1972. 17.50x (ISBN 0-8020-5262-2). U of Toronto Pr.

Frank, Tenney. Life & Literature in the Roman Republic. (Sather Classical Lectures: No. 7). (YA) (gr. 9-12). 1930. pap. 2.65x (ISBN 0-520-00428-0, CAMPUS73). U of Cal Pr.

Glover, Terrot R. Life & Letters in the Fourth Century. LC 68-10923. 1968. Repr. of 1901 ed. 11.00 (ISBN 0-8462-1065-7). Russell.

Grenier, Albert. Roman Spirit in Religion, Thought & Art. Dobie, M. R., tr. LC 76-118639. (Illus.). 423p. 1970. Repr. of 1926 ed. lib. bdg. 29.50x (ISBN 0-8154-0330-5). Cooper Sq.

Gwynn, Aubrey. Roman Education from Cicero to Quintilian. LC 66-13555. (Orig.). 1966. text ed. 9.75 (ISBN 0-8077-1479-8); pap. text ed. 5.25 (ISBN 0-8077-1476-3). Tchrs Coll.

Hadas, Moses. History of Latin Literature. LC 52-7637. 1952. 27.50x (ISBN 0-231-01848-7, 56). Columbia U Pr.

Hamilton, Edith. Roman Way. (gr. 7 up). 1932. 9.25 (ISBN 0-393-04173-5). Norton.

Harvard University Library. Latin Literature. (Widener Library Shelflist Ser.: No. 59). 1977. 55.00x (ISBN 0-674-51295-2). Harvard U Pr.

Hawes, Adeline B. Citizens of Long Ago: Essays on Life & Letters in the Roman Empire. facs. ed. LC 67-23228. (Essay Index Reprint Ser). 1967. Repr. of 1934 ed. 13.00 (ISBN 0-8369-0520-2). Arno.

Hervieux, A. Leopold. Les Fabulistes Latins Depuis le Siecle d'Auguste Jusqu'a la Fin Du Moyen Age, 5 Vols. 1964. Set. 210.00 (ISBN 0-8337-1685-9). B Franklin.

Hocking, G. D. Study of the Tragoediae Sacrae of Father Caussin, 1583-1651. 1973. Repr. of 1943 ed. 11.50 (ISBN 0-384-23783-5). Johnson Repr.

Horace. Sermons & Epistles. Rolfe, John C., ed. (College Classical Ser). 1977. text ed. 12.00x (ISBN 0-89241-026-4). Caratzas Bros.

Jenkinson, J. R. Persius - The Satires. 131p. 1981. text ed. 18.75x (ISBN 0-85668-159-8, Pub. by Aris & Phillips England); pap. text ed. 10.74x (ISBN 0-85668-173-3, Pub. by Aris & Phillips England). Humanities.

Joachim, Hermann. A Brief History of Roman Literature. Barnett, L. D., tr. 1977. Repr. of 1904 ed. lib. bdg. 10.00 (ISBN 0-8495-2705-8). Arden Lib.

Keeler, Laura. Geoffrey of Monmouth & the Late Latin Chroniclers, 1300-1500. 151p. 1980. Repr. of 1946 ed. lib. bdg. 30.00 (ISBN 0-8495-3040-7). Arden Lib.

Kenney, E. J. & Clausen, W. V., eds. The Cambridge History of Classical Literature Vol. 2, Latin Literature. LC 79-121. (Illus.). 960p. Date not set. price not set (ISBN 0-521-21043-7). Cambridge U Pr.

Kroll, Wilhelm. Studien zum Verstaendnis der Romischen Literatur. Commager, Steele, ed. LC 77-70839. (Latin Poetry Ser.: Vol. 23). 1978. lib. bdg. 41.00 (ISBN 0-8240-2972-0). Garland Pub.

Lawton, William C. Introduction to Classical Latin Literature. 1973. Repr. of 1904 ed. 25.00 (ISBN 0-8274-1578-8). R West.

Lewis, Clive S. Discarded Image. LC 64-21555. (Orig.). 1968. 29.95 (ISBN 0-521-05551-2); pap. 7.50 (ISBN 0-521-09450-X). Cambridge U Pr.

Lindsay, Jack. Song of a Falling World: Culture During the Break-up of the Roman Empire (A.D. 350-600) LC 78-59028. 1979. Repr. of 1948 ed. 22.00 (ISBN 0-88355-701-0). Hyperion Conn.

Lipphardt, Walther, ed. Die Lateinische Osterf und Osterspiele. LC 74-80629. (Ausgaben Deutscher Literaturdes Xv.bis Xviii. Jahrhunderts, Reihe Drama: Vol. 5). 1452p. (Ger.). 1975. 98.00x (ISBN 3-11-006742-0). De Gruyter.

Livy. Livy, Books I & II. Greenough, J. B., ed. (College Classical Ser). 1977. text ed. 10.00 (ISBN 0-89241-026-4). Caratzas Bros.

Lofstedt, Einar. Roman Literary Portraits. Fraser, P. M., tr. LC 78-5638. 1978. Repr. of 1958 ed. lib. bdg. 17.25x (ISBN 0-313-20455-1, LORL). Greenwood.

Mackail, J. W. Latin Literature. Repr. of 1895 ed. 7.50 (ISBN 0-686-20104-3). Quality Lib.

Mackail, John W. Latin Literature. LC 66-16865. 1966. 10.50 (ISBN 0-8044-2570-1). Ungar.

Marcovich, Miroslav, ed. Illinois Classical Studies, Vol. IV. 1979. 20.00 (ISBN 0-252-00694-1). U of Ill Pr.

Minta, Erik. Miscellanea Propertiana. (Studia Graeca et Latina Gothoburgensia: No. 38). 1977. pap. text ed. 13.50x (ISBN 91-7346-041-9). Humanities.

More, Brookes, tr. Ovid's Metamorphoses in European Culture Combined with Ovid's Metamorposes (Translation in Blank Verse, 2 vols. Incl. Vol. I, Bks. I-VIII. (ISBN 0-685-89247-6); Vol. II, Bks IX-XV. (ISBN 0-685-89248-4). (Illus.). 10.00 set (ISBN 0-685-89246-8). M Jones.

Nairn, John A. Authors of Rome. LC 70-101050. 1969. Repr. of 1924 ed. 14.00 (ISBN 0-8046-0715-X). Kennikat.

Naylor, Henry D. Horace, Odes & Epodes: A Study in Poetic Word-Order. (Latin Poetry Ser.: Vol. 9). (LC 77-070832). 1977. Repr. of 1922 ed. lib. bdg. 33.00 (ISBN 0-8240-2958-5). Garland Pub.

Ogilvie, R. M. Roman Literature & Society. 303p. 1980. 23.50x (ISBN 0-389-20069-7). B&N.

--Roman Literature & Society. 1980. text ed. 19.50x (ISBN 0-391-01679-2). Humanities.

Ovid. Ars Amatoris Book I. Hollis, A. S., ed. (Illus.). 1977. 18.50x (ISBN 0-19-814441-5). Oxford U Pr.

Paschall, Dorothy M. Vocabulary of Mental Aberration in Roman Comedy & Petronius. (Language Dissertations: No. 27). 1939. pap. 6.00 (ISBN 0-527-00773-0). Kraus Repr.

Patch, Howard R. The Tradition of the Goddess Fortuna in Roman Literature & in the Transitional Period. LC 76-41188. 1976. Repr. of 1922 ed. lib. bdg. 10.00 (ISBN 0-8414-6753-6). Folcroft.

Percival, Keith W. On Plagiarisms in the "Minerva" of Franciscus Sanctius. 1977. pap. text ed. 1.00x (ISBN 90-316-0024-5). Humanities.

Quinn, Kenneth. Texts & Contexts: The Roman Writers & Their Audience. 1979. 27.50x (ISBN 0-7100-0279-3). Routledge & Kegan.

Rand, Edward K. The Building of Eternal Rome. LC 72-87173. xi, 318p. 1973. Repr. of 1943 ed. lib. bdg. 14.50x (ISBN 0-8154-0437-9). Cooper Sq.

Reinhold, Meyer. Classics, Greek & Roman. LC 72-140633. (Orig.). (gr. 10 up). 1971. 6.95 (ISBN 0-8120-5020-7); pap. 2.95 (ISBN 0-8120-0044-7). Barron.

Reynolds, L. D. & Wilson, N. G. Scribes & Scholars: A Guide to the Transmission of Greek & Latin Literature. 2nd ed. (Illus.). 266p. 1974. pap. text ed. 11.50x (ISBN 0-19-814372-9). Oxford U Pr.

Rudd, N. Lines of Inquiry. LC 75-12467. 280p. 1976. 36.00 (ISBN 0-521-20993-5). Cambridge U Pr.

Schmugge, Ludwig, ed. Radulfus Niger "De Re Militari et Triplici Via Peregrinationis Ierosolimitane" (1187 88) (Beitrage Zur Geschichte und Quellenkunde des Mittelalters: Vol. 6). 1976. 72.25x (ISBN 3-11-006827-3). De Gruyter.

Scottish Classics Group, ed. Cicero: Pro Lege Manilia. (Ecce Romani Ser.). (Illus.). 64p. (Lat.). 1980. pap. text ed. 2.95x (ISBN 0-05-003259-3). Longman.

Simcox, George A. History of Latin Literature, 2 vols. LC 78-113307. Repr. of 1883 ed. lib. bdg. 55.00x set (ISBN 0-8046-1204-8). Irvington.

Stuart, Duane R. Epochs of Greek & Roman Biography. LC 67-19532. 1928. 12.00x (ISBN 0-8196-0193-4). Biblo.

Tavenner, Eugene. Studies in Magic from Latin Literature. LC 16-25151. Repr. of 1916 ed. 16.50 (ISBN 0-404-06350-0). AMS Pr.

Teuffel, Wilhelm S. Teuffel's History of Roman Literature, 2 Vols. Schwabe, Ludwig, ed. Warr, George C., tr. (Research & Source Works Ser.: No. 168). 1968. Set. 55.50 (ISBN 0-8337-3494-6). B Franklin.

West, D. & Woodman, T., eds. Creative Imitation & Latin Literature. LC 79-1181. 1980. 36.00 (ISBN 0-521-22668-6). Cambridge U Pr.

Wilkins, A. S. Roman Literature. Repr. of 1890 ed. 10.00 (ISBN 0-686-20109-4). Quality Lib.

Wilkinson, L. P. Golden Latin Artistry. 1963. 42.00 (ISBN 0-521-06807-X). Cambridge U Pr.

Williams, Gordon. Change & Decline: Roman Literature in the Early Empire. LC 76-24598. (Sather Classical Lectures: No. 45). 1978. 21.50x (ISBN 0-520-03333-7). U of Cal Pr.

Willis, James. Latin Textual Criticism. LC 71-106601. (Studies in Language & Literature Ser: Vol. 61). 1972. 12.50 (ISBN 0-252-00101-X). U of Ill Pr.

Wistrand, Erik. The So-Called Laudatio Turiae. (Studia Graeca et Latina Gothoburgensia: No. 34). (Illus.). 1976. pap. text ed. 16.25x (ISBN 91-7346-009-5). Humanities.

LATIN LITERATURE–OUTLINES, SYLLABI, ETC.

Grey, Henry. The Classics for the Million: Being an Epitome in English of the Works of the Principal Greek & Latin Authors. 1898. 30.00 (ISBN 0-89984-221-6). Century Bookbindery.

Muir, J. V., ed. Virgil: Selection from Aeneid Four Handbook. LC 76-52324. (Cambridge Latin Texts Ser.). 1977. 6.95x (ISBN 0-521-21645-1). Cambridge U Pr.

LATIN LITERATURE–TRANSLATIONS INTO ENGLISH

Bidermann, Jacob. Cenodoxus. Dyer, D. G. & Longrigg, Cecily, trs. from Latin. LC 74-15527. (Edinburgh Bilingual Library: No. 9). 211p. 1975. 9.50x (ISBN 0-292-71027-5); pap. 4.95x (ISBN 0-292-71028-3). U of Tex Pr.

Boncompagno da Signa. Rota Veneris. Purkart, Josef, ed. LC 74-18250. 128p. 1975. Repr. of 1474 ed. lib. bdg. 20.00x (ISBN 0-8201-1137-6). Schol Facsimiles.

Cranz, Edward & Kristeller, Paul O., eds. Catalogus Translationum et Commentariorum: Mediaeval & Renaissance Latin Translations & Commentaries, Annotated Lists & Guides, Vol. 4. LC 60-4006. 1980. 59.95 (ISBN 0-8132-0547-6). Cath U Pr.

Dickinson, G. Lowes & Meredith, H. O., eds. Temple Greek & Latin Classics, 5 Vols. Repr. of 1907 ed. Set. 120.00 (ISBN 0-404-07900-8). AMS Pr.

Gesta Romanorum (1595). LC 73-7769. 400p. 1973. lib. bdg. 35.00x (ISBN 0-8201-1118-X). Schol Facsimiles.

Howe, George & Harrer, Gustave A., eds. Roman Literature in Translation. 1979. Repr. of 1924 ed. lib. bdg. 35.00 (ISBN 0-8495-2256-0). Arden Lib.

Ito, Shuntaro. The Medieval Latin Translation of the Data of Euclid. (Illus.). 246p. 1980. 34.00 (ISBN 3-7643-3005-8). Birkhauser.

Johannes De Alta Silva. Dolopathos: Or, the King & the Seven Wise Men. Gilleland, Brady B., tr. from Latin. (Medieval & Renaissance Texts & Studies: 2). (Illus.). 140p. (Orig.). 1981. 10.95 (ISBN 0-86698-001-6); pap. 5.95 (ISBN 0-86698-006-7). Medieval.

Kalechofsky, Roberta, ed. Echad: An Anthology of Latin American Jewish Writings. LC 79-88853. 1980. pap. 9.00x (ISBN 0-916288-06-4). Micah Pubns.

Kratz, Dennis, ed. Waltharius & Ruodlieb. (The Garland Library of Medieval Literature Ser.). 1981. lib. bdg. 35.00 (ISBN 0-8240-9444-1). Garland Pub.

Laing, Gordon J. Masterpiece of Latin Literature. Repr. of 1903 ed. lib. bdg. 30.00 (ISBN 0-8482-1613-X). Norwood Edns.

MacKendrick, Paul L & Howe, Herbert M, eds. Classics in Translation, 2 vols. Incl. Vol. 1. Greek Literature. 444p (ISBN 0-299-80895-5); Vol. 2. Latin Literature. 452p (ISBN 0-299-80896-3). 1952. text ed. 7.95 ea. U of Wis Pr.

Nivardus, Magister. Ysengrimus. Sypher, F. J. & Sypher, Eleanor, trs. from Lat. (Illus.). 280p. 1980. 95.00x (ISBN 0-8386-3005-7). F Sypher.

Ovid. Ars Amatoris Book I. Hollis, A. S., ed. (Illus.). 1977. 18.50x (ISBN 0-19-814441-5). Oxford U Pr.

Robertson, D. W., Jr. Literature of Medieval England. LC 75-95827. 1970. text ed. 17.50 (ISBN 0-07-053158-7, C). McGraw.

Schevill, Ferdinand. First Century of Italian Humanism. (World History Ser., No. 48). 1970. pap. 12.95 (ISBN 0-8383-0100-2). Haskell.

--First Century of Italian Humanism. LC 66-27145. 1967. Repr. of 1928 ed. 5.00 (ISBN 0-8462-1029-0). Russell.

Seneca. Dialogues. Reynolds, Leighton D., ed. (Oxford Classical Texts). 1977. text ed. 22.50x (ISBN 0-19-814659-0). Oxford U Pr.

Wedeck, Harry E., ed. Classics of Roman Literature. (Quality Paperback: No. 155). 1964. pap. 4.95 (ISBN 0-8226-0155-9). Littlefield.

--Classics of Roman Literature. LC 63-13350. 10.00 (ISBN 0-8022-1827-X). Philos Lib.

Wills, Garry, ed. Roman Culture. LC 66-15757. (Cultures of Mankind Ser). (Illus.). 1966. 6.95 (ISBN 0-8076-0367-8). Braziller.

LATIN LITERATURE, MEDIEVAL AND MODERN

Here are entered collections in Latin. English translations are listed under the subdivision Translations into English.

see also Christian Literature, Early

Aconcio, Giacomo. Darkness Discovered (Satans Stratagems) LC 78-9490. 1978. Repr. of 1651 ed. 22.00x (ISBN 0-8201-1313-1). Schol Facsimiles.

Cranz, Edward & Kristeller, Paul O., eds. Catalogus Translationum et Commentariorum: Mediaeval & Renaissance Latin Translations & Commentaries, Annotated Lists & Guides, Vol. 4. LC 60-4006. 1980. 59.95 (ISBN 0-8132-0547-6). Cath U Pr.

Ijsewijn, J., ed. Companion to Neo-Latin Studies. 1977. 46.50 (ISBN 0-7204-0510-6, North-Holland). Elsevier.

Potter, K. R., ed. Gesta Stephani. (Oxford Medieval Texts). 1976. 67.50x (ISBN 0-19-822234-3). Oxford U Pr.

LATIN LITERATURE, MEDIEVAL AND MODERN–BIBLIOGRAPHY

Cranz, F. Edward & Kristeller, Paul O., eds. Catalogus Translationum et Commentariorum: Mediaeval & Renaissance Latin Translations & Commentaries, Annotated Lists & Guides, Vol. 3. 1976. pap. 35.00 (ISBN 0-8132-0540-9). Intl Schol Bk Serv.

Ijsewijn, J., ed. Companion to Neo-Latin Studies. 1977. 46.50 (ISBN 0-7204-0510-6, North-Holland). Elsevier.

Kristeller, Paul O. & Cranz, F. Edward, eds. Catalogus Translationum et Commentariorum: Mediaeval & Renaissance Latin Translations & Commentaries, Annotated Lists & Guides, Vol. 2. 1971. pap. 16.95 (ISBN 0-8132-0400-3). Cath U Pr.

Little, Andrew G. Initia Operum Latinorum, Quae Saeculis Treizieme Quatorzieme Quinzieme Attribuuntur, Secundum Ordinem Alphabeti Disposita. (Victoria Univ. of Manchester). 1904. 26.50 (ISBN 0-8337-2118-6). B Franklin.

Wingate, S. D. The Mediaeval Latin Versions of the Aristotelian Scientific Corpus: With Special Reference to the Biological Works. (Medieval Studies Reprint Ser.). Repr. of 1931 ed. lib. bdg. 21.00x (ISBN 0-697-00023-0). Irvington.

LATIN LITERATURE, MEDIEVAL AND MODERN–HISTORY AND CRITICISM

Baron, Hans. From Petrarch to Leonardo Bruni: Studies in Humanistic & Political Literature. LC 68-16686. 1968. 12.00x (ISBN 0-226-03801-7); pap. 3.25 (ISBN 0-226-03802-5). U of Chicago Pr.

Cranz, Edward & Kristeller, Paul O., eds. Catalogus Translationum et Commentariorum: Mediaeval & Renaissance Latin Translations & Commentaries, Annotated Lists & Guides, Vol. 4. LC 60-4006. 1980. 59.95 (ISBN 0-8132-0547-6). Cath U Pr.

Curtius, E. R. European Literature & the Latin Middle Ages. Trask, Willard R., tr. LC 52-10619. (Bollingen Ser., Vol. 36). 682p. 1953. 36.00 (ISBN 0-691-09739-9); pap. 8.50 (ISBN 0-691-01793-X). Princeton U Pr.

Helin, Maurice. A History of Medieval Latin Literature. rev. ed. Snow, Jean C., tr. v, 130p. Repr. of 1949 ed. lib. bdg. 15.00x (ISBN 0-87991-089-5). Porcupine Pr.

Hutton, James. Greek Anthology in France & in the Latin Writers of the Netherlands to the Year 1800. 1946. 58.00 (ISBN 0-384-25150-1). Johnson Repr.

Vollert, Konrad. Zur Geschichte der Lateinischen Facetiensammlunge Des Xv & Xvi Jahrhunderts. (Ger). 14.00 (ISBN 0-384-64870-3); pap. 11.00 (ISBN 0-685-02161-0). Johnson Repr.

LATIN MONETARY UNION

Willis, Henry P. History of the Latin Monetary Union. LC 75-137307. Repr. of 1901 ed. 14.50 (ISBN 0-404-06988-6). AMS Pr.

--History of the Latin Monetary Union: A Study of International Monetary Action. LC 68-54443. (Illus.). 1968. Repr. of 1901 ed. lib. bdg. 18.00x (ISBN 0-8371-0271-5, WILM). Greenwood.

LATIN ORATIONS

Cicero. Pro Milone. Bd. with In Prisonen; Pro Sauro; Pro Fonteio; Pro Rabirio Postumo; Pro Marcello; Pro Ligario; Pro Rege Deiotaro. (Loeb Classical Library: No. 252). 11.00x (ISBN 0-674-99278-4). Harvard U Pr.

LATIN ORIENT

see also Crusades; Crusades–Fourth, 1202-1204; Jerusalem–History–Latin Kingdom, 1099-1244; Latin Empire, 1204-1261; Templars

Hirth, F. China & the Roman Orient. pap. 6.00 (ISBN 0-89005-093-7). Ares.

Miller, William. The Latins in the Levant: A History of Frankish Greece. LC 75-41193. Repr. of 1908 ed. 57.50 (ISBN 0-404-14689-9). AMS Pr.

LATIN PEOPLES

see also Mediterranean Race

LATIN PHILOLOGY

see also Classical Philology; Inscriptions, Latin; Latin Language; Latin Literature (Collections)

McGuire, Martin R. & Dressler, Hermigild. Introduction to Medieval Latin Studies: A Syllabus & Bibliographical Guide. 2nd ed. LC 77-23238. 1977. pap. 16.95 (ISBN 0-8132-0542-5). Cath U Pr.

Meader, Clarence L., ed. Latin Philology. 1910. pap. 31.00 (ISBN 0-384-38803-5). Johnson Repr.

Wagenvoort, Hendrik. Studies in Roman Literature, Culture & Religion. Commager, Steele, ed. LC 77-70817. (Latin Poetry Ser.: Vol. 31). 1978. lib. bdg. 33.00 (ISBN 0-8240-2981-X). Garland Pub.

LATIN PHILOLOGY–BIBLIOGRAPHY

McGuire, Martin R. & Dressler, Hermigild. Introduction to Medieval Latin Studies: A Syllabus & Bibliographical Guide. 2nd ed. LC 77-23238. 1977. pap. 16.95 (ISBN 0-8132-0542-5). Cath U Pr.

LATIN POETRY (COLLECTIONS)

Bae Hrens, Aemilius. Poetae Latini Minores, Leipzig, 1879-1883, 5 vols. Commager, Steele, ed. LC 77-70775. (Latin Poetry Ser.). 1979. Set. lib. bdg. 170.00 (ISBN 0-8240-2950-X). Garland Pub.

Ball, Allan P. Seneca's Apocolocyntosis, New York, Nineteen Hundred & Two. Commager, Steele, ed. LC 77-70769. (Latin Poetry Ser.). 1979. lib. bdg. 27.50 (ISBN 0-8240-2951-8). Garland Pub.

Butler, H. E. Post-Augustan Poetry from Seneca to Juvenal. 1909. 25.00 (ISBN 0-89984-036-1). Century Bookbindery.

Davie, Donald, ed. Augustan Lyric. (The Poetry Bookshelf). 1974. pap. text ed. 5.00x (ISBN 0-435-15701-9). Heinemann Ed.

Flewett, H. W. & Pantin, William E. First Book of Latin Poetry. (Illus., Lat.). 1977. pap. text ed. 5.95 (ISBN 0-312-29226-0). St Martin.

Garrod, Heathcote W., ed. Oxford Book of Latin Verse from the Earliest Fragments to the End of the 5th Century A. D. (Lat). 1912. 16.95x (ISBN 0-19-812117-2). Oxford U Pr.

Gould, Howard E. & Whiteley, Joseph L., eds. Selections from Five Roman Poets: Catullus, Virgil, Horace, Tibullus, Ovid. (Illus., Lat.). 1941. 6.95 (ISBN 0-312-71225-1). St Martin.

Harrington, Karl P., ed. Roman Elegiac Poets. 1969. Repr. of 1968 ed. 9.95x (ISBN 0-8061-0783-9). U of Okla Pr.

Hornsby, Roger A. Reading Latin Poetry. 1969. Repr. of 1967 ed. 9.95x (ISBN 0-8061-0741-3). U of Okla Pr.

Kennedy, Eberhard C. & Davis, A. R., eds. Two Centuries of Roman Poetry. (Illus.). 1964. 7.95 (ISBN 0-312-82565-X). St Martin.

Lembke, Janet. Bronze & Iron: Old Latin Poetry from Its Beginning to 100 B. C. 1973. 19.00x (ISBN 0-520-02164-9). U of Cal Pr.

Lier, Bruno, et al. Bruno Lier: Ad Topica Carminum Amatorium Symbolae, Repr. Of 1914 Ed. Commager, Steele, ed. Bd. with Keith Preston: Studies in the Diction of the Sermo Amatorius in Roman Comedy. Repr. of 1916 ed; Alfons Spies: Militat Omnis Amons. Repr. of 1930 ed. LC 77-70837. (Latin Poetry Ser.). 1979. lib. bdg. 25.00 (ISBN 0-8240-2973-9). Garland Pub.

Perosa, Alessandro & Sparrow, John, eds. Rennaissance Latin Verse: An Anthology. LC 78-10969. 1979. 24.00x (ISBN 0-8078-1350-8). U of NC Pr.

Roberts, G. D. An Anthology of Latin & English Verse. 1979. Repr. of 1934 ed. lib. bdg. 30.00 (ISBN 0-8495-4622-2). Arden Lib.

--An Anthology of Latin & English Verse. 1977. Repr. of 1925 ed. 10.00 (ISBN 0-89984-102-3). Century Bookbindery.

Salustri, Carlo A. Roman Satirical Poems & Their Translation. Showerman, Grant, tr. from Ital. LC 78-21559. 1979. Repr. of 1945 ed. lib. bdg. 15.25x (ISBN 0-313-20745-3, SARS). Greenwood.

Salway, Peter. Frontier People of Roman Britain. (Cambridge Classical Studies). 1965. 34.00 (ISBN 0-521-06187-3). Cambridge U Pr.

Stebbing, William. Some Masterpieces of Latin Poetry. 1920. 25.00 (ISBN 0-8274-3980-6). R West.

Venables, Francis, ed. The Early Augustans. (The Poetry Bookshelf). 1972. pap. text ed. 5.00x (ISBN 0-435-15068-5). Heinemann Ed.

Walker, Gulielmus S. Corpus Poetarum Latinorum. Repr. of 1854 ed. 200.00 (ISBN 0-8492-9976-4). R West.

Wyke, Barry, ed. Vetilatory & Phonatory Control Systems: An International Symposium. (Illus.). 550p. 1974. text ed. 45.00x (ISBN 0-19-264158-1). Oxford U Pr.

LATIN POETRY–DICTIONARIES

Swanson, Donald C. Names in Roman Verse: A Lexicon & Reverse Index of All Proper Names of History, Mythology & Geography Found in the Classical Roman Poets. 446p. 1967. 30.00x (ISBN 0-299-04560-9). U of Wis Pr.

LATIN POETRY–GENERAL–TRANSLATIONS INTO ENGLISH

Bradner, Leicester. Musae Anglicanae: A History of Anglo-Latin Poetry, 1500-1925. (MLA Mono. General Ser.). 1940. pap. 22.00 (ISBN 0-527-10650-X). Kraus Repr.

Brittain, Fred. Medieval Latin & Romance Lyric to A. D. 1300. 2nd ed. LC 38-9391. 1969. Repr. of 1951 ed. 14.00 (ISBN 0-527-11300-X). Kraus Repr.

Dronke, Peter. Medieval Latin & the Rise of the European Love Lyric, 2 Vols. 2nd ed. (Latin). 1969. Set. 59.00x (ISBN 0-19-814346-X). Oxford U Pr.

Fitzgerald, Robert. Spring Shade: Poems 1931-1970. LC 74-145931. 1971. 6.50 (ISBN 0-8112-0280-1); pap. 2.75 (ISBN 0-8112-0052-3, NDP311). New Directions.

Waddell, Helen. Wandering Scholars. 7th, rev. ed. 1968. Repr. of 1934 ed. 21.50x (ISBN 0-06-497280-1). B&N.

LATIN POETRY–HISTORY AND CRITICISM

Bentley, Richard. Q. Horatius Flaccus, 2 vols. 3rd ed. Commager, Steele, ed. LC 77-24817. (Latin Poetry Ser.: Vol. 3). 1979. Repr. of 1869 ed. Set. lib. bdg. 73.00 (ISBN 0-8240-2952-6). Garland Pub.

Butler, Harold E. Post-Augustan Poetry. (Latin Poetry Ser.: Vol. 15). (LC 77-070766). 1977. Repr. of 1909 ed. lib. bdg. 33.00 (ISBN 0-8240-2964-X). Garland Pub.

--Post-Augustan Poetry from Seneca to Juvenal. facsimile ed. LC 70-99656. (Select Bibliographies Reprint Ser). 1909. 25.00 (ISBN 0-8369-5085-2). Arno.

Cairns, F. Genetic Composition in Greek & Roman Poetry. 1973. 18.50x (ISBN 0-85224-224-7, Pub. by Edinburgh U Pr Scotland). Columbia U Pr.

Coleman, Dorothy. The Gallo-Roman Muse. LC 79-71. 1979. 32.50 (ISBN 0-521-22254-0). Cambridge U Pr.

Cousin, Jean. Etudes sur la Poesie Latine: Nature et Mission du Poete. Commager, Steele, ed. LC 77-70760. (Latin Poetry Ser.). 1979. Repr. of 1945 ed. lib. bdg. 28.00 (ISBN 0-8240-2965-8). Garland Pub.

Crump, Mary M. The Epyllion from Theocritus to Ovid. Commager, Steele, ed. LC 77-70761. (Latin Poetry Ser.). 1978. lib. bdg. 32.00 (ISBN 0-8240-2966-6). Garland Pub.

Dawson, M. & Cole, A. T., eds. Studies in Latin Poetry. (Yale Classical Studies: Vol. 21). 1969. 36.00 (ISBN 0-521-07395-2). Cambridge U Pr.

Enk, P. J. Ad Propertii Carmina Commentarius Criticus, Zutpen. Commager, Steele, ed. LC 77-70813. (Latin Poetry Ser.). 1978. Repr. of 1911 ed. lib. bdg. 48.50 (ISBN 0-8240-2954-2). Garland Pub.

Halporn, James, et al. The Meters of Greek & Latin Poetry. rev. ed. LC 79-6718. 138p. 1980. pap. 4.95x (ISBN 0-8061-1558-0). U of Okla Pr.

Highet, Gilbert. Poets in a Landscape. LC 78-12220. 1979. Repr. of 1962 ed. lib. bdg. 25.00x (ISBN 0-313-21208-2, HIPL). Greenwood.

Horace. Horace Odes & Epodes. Bennett, Charles E., ed. (College Classical Ser). 1977. text ed. 12.50x (ISBN 0-89241-024-8). Caratzas Bros.

Lembke, Janet. Bronze & Iron: Old Latin Poetry from Its Beginning to 100 B. C. 1973. 19.00x (ISBN 0-520-02164-9). U of Cal Pr.

Lilja, Saara. The Roman Elegists' Attitude Towards Women. Commager, Steele, ed. LC 77-70836. (Latin Poetry Ser.: Vol. 25). 1979. Repr. of 1965 ed. lib. bdg. 31.00 (ISBN 0-8240-2974-7). Garland Pub.

McFarlane, I. D., ed. Renaissance Latin Poetry. LC 79-55022. (Literature in Context Ser.). 1980. text ed. 21.50x (ISBN 0-06-494702-5). B&N.

Mendell, Clarence W. Latin Poetry: Before & After. LC 70-96730. 1970. 14.00 (ISBN 0-208-00844-6, Archon). Shoe String.

--Latin Poetry: The Age of Rhetoric & Satire. 1967. 17.50 (ISBN 0-208-00474-2, Archon). Shoe String.

Osiek, Betty T. Jose Asuncion Silva. (World Authors Ser.: No. 505 (Colombia)). 1978. 13.50 (ISBN 0-8057-6346-5). Twayne.

Piwonka, Mario P. Lucilius und Kallimachos. Commager, Steele, ed. LC 77-70830. (Latin Poetry Ser.). 1978. lib. bdg. 41.00 (ISBN 0-8240-2976-3). Garland Pub.

Richardson, L., Jr., ed. Propertius: Elegies I-IV. LC 76-26153. (American Philological Association Ser.: Vol. 5). 1977. 13.95x (ISBN 0-8061-1371-5). U of Okla Pr.

Richardson, Lawrence. Poetical Theory in Republican Rome. Commager, Steele, ed. LC 77-70825. (Latin Poetry Ser.). 1978. lib. bdg. 22.00 (ISBN 0-8240-2977-1). Garland Pub.

Richardson, Lawrence, Jr. Poetical Theory in Republican Rome: An Analytical Discussion of the Shorter Narrative Hexameter Poems Written in Latin. 1944. lib. bdg. 20.00 (ISBN 0-8414-9117-8). Folcroft.

Robinson, Ellis. A Commentary on Catulus, Oxford, Eighteen Eighty-Nine. 2nd ed. Commager, Steele, ed. LC 77-70812. (Latin Poetry-Editions, Commentations Critical Works). 1979. lib. bdg. 55.00 (ISBN 0-8240-2953-4). Garland Pub.

Ross, D. O. Backgrounds to Augustan Poetry, Gallus, Elegy & Rome. LC 74-31782. 260p. 1975. 32.00 (ISBN 0-521-20704-5). Cambridge U Pr.

Sellar, W. Y. Roman Poets of the Augustan Age: Virgil. 1877. Repr. 35.00 (ISBN 0-8274-3299-2). R West.

Sellar, William Y. Roman Poets of the Augustan Age. Incl. Bk. 1. Horace & the Elegiac Poets. Lang, Andrew, memoir by. LC 65-23488. (Illus.). xviii, 362p. Repr. of 1892 ed; Bk. 2. Virgil. 3rd ed. LC 65-23489. xiv, 423p. Repr. of 1908 ed. 15.00x (ISBN 0-8196-0162-4). Biblo.

Siefert, G. J. Meter & Case in Latin Elegiac Pentameter. (Language Dissertations: No. 49). 1952. pap. 8.00 (ISBN 0-527-00795-1). Kraus Repr.

Sikes, Edward E. Roman Poetry. LC 78-20495. 1980. Repr. of 1923 ed. 22.00 (ISBN 0-88355-871-8). Hyperion Conn.

Tyrell, R. Y. Latin Poetry. LC 68-26294. 1969. Repr. of 1895 ed. 13.50 (ISBN 0-8046-0468-1). Kennikat.

Virgil. Virgil Eclogues & a Special Vocabulary to Virgil. Greenough, J. B. & Kittredge, G. L., eds. (College Classical Ser). 1977. text ed. 15.00x (ISBN 0-89241-027-2). Caratzas Bros.

Warmington, E. H., ed. Minor Latin Poets. (Loeb Classical Library: No. 284). (Lat. & Eng.). 11.00x (ISBN 0-674-99314-4). Harvard U Pr.

Williams, Gordon. Figures of Thought in Roman Poetry. LC 79-23725. 1980. 25.00x (ISBN 0-300-02456-8). Yale U Pr.

--Tradition & Originality in Roman Poetry. 1968. 59.00x (ISBN 0-19-814347-8). Oxford U Pr.

Woodman, A. J. & West, D., eds. Quality & Pleasure in Latin Poetry. 184p. 1975. 28.50 (ISBN 0-521-20532-8). Cambridge U Pr.

Wright, F. A. Three Roman Poets: Plautus, Catullus, Ovid. Their Lives, Times & Works. 1928. 40.00 (ISBN 0-8274-3991-1). R West.

LATIN POETRY–HISTORY AND CRITICISM–MEDIEVAL AND MODERN

Binns, J. W., ed. The Latin Poetry of English Poets. 1974. 18.00x (ISBN 0-7100-7845-5). Routledge & Kegan.

Dronke, Peter. Poetic Individuality in the Middle Ages: New Departures in Poetry 1000-1150. 1970. 22.50x (ISBN 0-19-811693-4). Oxford U Pr.

Gourmont, Remy De. Le Latin mystique: Les Poetes de l'antiphonaire et la symbolique au moyen age. LC 77-10268. 400p. Repr. of 1895 ed. 37.50 (ISBN 0-404-16320-3). AMS Pr.

Lewis, Robert E., ed. De Miseria Condicionis Humane. LC 75-26119. 310p. 1978. 25.00 (ISBN 0-8203-0395-X). U of Ga Pr.

Vessey, D. W. Statius & the Thebaid. LC 72-83578. 300p. 1973. 49.50 (ISBN 0-521-20052-0). Cambridge U Pr.

LATIN POETRY–TRANSLATIONS INTO ENGLISH

Aldington, Richard, ed. The Poet's Translation Series, 2 vols. Incl. Series One. LC 78-64005 (ISBN 0-404-17101-X); Second Series. LC 78-64016 (ISBN 0-404-17102-8). (Des Imagistes: Literature of the Imagist Movement). Repr. of 1920 ed. Set. 49.00 (ISBN 0-404-17100-1); 25.00 ea. AMS Pr.

Cambridge School Classics Project Foundation Course. Two Journeys. (Roman World Ser.). (Illus.). 1978. 1.50x (ISBN 0-521-21603-6). Cambridge U Pr.

Corrigan, Felicitas, ed. More Latin Lyrics. Waddell, Helen, tr. 1977. 12.95x (ISBN 0-393-04469-6). Norton.

Lind, Levi R., ed. Latin Poetry in Verse Translation. LC 57-59176. (YA) (gr. 9 up). 1957. pap. 3.95 (ISBN 0-395-05118-5, 3-47654, RivEd, C20). HM.

Martialis, Marcus V. One Hundred Epigrams of Martial. O'Connell, Richard, ed. LC 76-3066. (Translation Ser.: No.3). 1976. pap. 3.75 (ISBN 0-912288-07-8). Perivale Pr.

Ovidius Naso, Publius. The XV Bookes Entytuled Metamorphosis. Golding, Arthur, tr. LC 77-7418. (English Experience Ser.: No. 881). 1977. Repr. of 1567 ed. lib. bdg. 40.00 (ISBN 90-221-0881-3). Walter J Johnson.

Trilussa, pseud. Trilussa: Roman Satirical Poems & Their Translation. Showerman, Grant, tr. & intro. by. 185p. (It. & Eng.). 1945. 6.50x (ISBN 0-913298-47-6). S F Vanni.

Wender, Dorothea, tr. from Latin. Roman Poetry from the Republic to the Silver Age. LC 79-28219. 160p. 1980. 9.95x (ISBN 0-8093-0963-7). S Ill U Pr.

LATIN POETRY, MEDIEVAL AND MODERN

Here are entered collections in Latin. For English translations see subdivision Translations into English.

Brittain, Fred. Medieval Latin & Romance Lyric to A. D. 1300. 2nd ed. LC 38-9391. 1969. Repr. of 1951 ed. 14.00 (ISBN 0-527-11300-X). Kraus Repr.

Florit, Eugenio. Poesia En Jose Marti, Juan Ramon Jimenez, Alfonso Reyes, Federico Garcia Lorca y Pablo Neruda. LC 78-55266. 1978. pap. 6.95 (ISBN 0-89729-207-3). Ediciones.

Nichols, Fred J. Anthology of Neo-Latin Poetry. LC 78-994. 1979. text ed. 60.00 (ISBN 0-300-02017-1); pap. 22.00x (ISBN 0-300-02365-0). Yale U Pr.

Stock, Brian, ed. Medieval Latin Lyrics. LC 79-104913. (Illus., Orig.). 1971. 15.00x (ISBN 0-87923-027-4); ltd. ed. 25.00 (ISBN 0-87923-026-6). Godine.

Waddell, Helen, tr. Medieval Latin Lyrics. 1977. pap. 12.95x (ISBN 0-393-04493-9, N873, Norton Lib); pap. 4.95x (ISBN 0-393-00873-8). Norton.

LATIN POETRY, MEDIEVAL AND MODERN–TRANSLATIONS INTO ENGLISH

Carney, James. Medieval Irish Lyrics. 1967. 16.50x (ISBN 0-520-00210-5). U of Cal Pr.

Joachim Of Fiore. Two Poems Attributed to Joachim of Fiore. Fleming, John V. & Reeves, Marjorie, eds. 1978. boards 12.00 (ISBN 0-933476-05-1); pap. 7.50 (ISBN 0-933476-04-3). Pilgrim Pr.

Nichols, Fred J. Anthology of Neo-Latin Poetry. LC 78-994. 1979. text ed. 60.00 (ISBN 0-300-02017-1); pap. 22.00x (ISBN 0-300-02365-0). Yale U Pr.

Waddell, Helen, tr. Medieval Latin Lyrics. 1977. pap. 12.95x (ISBN 0-393-04493-9, N873, Norton Lib); pap. 4.95x (ISBN 0-393-00873-8). Norton.

LATIN RHETORIC

see Rhetoric, Ancient

LATIN SATIRE

see Satire, Latin

LATITUDE VARIATION

Klein, Felix. Ueber Die Theorie Des Kreisels. 1965. 46.00 (ISBN 0-384-29720-X). Johnson Repr.

LA TOUCHE, ROSE

LaTouche, Rose. John Ruskin & Rose la Touche: New Unpublished Diaries of 1861 & 1867. Burd, Van Akin, ed. (Illus.). 212p. 1979. text ed. 19.95x (ISBN 0-19-812633-6). Oxford U Pr.

Ruskin, John. Letters of John Ruskin to Lord & Lady Mount-Temple. Bradley, John L., ed. LC 64-20414. 1964. 6.25 (ISBN 0-8142-0026-5). Ohio St U Pr.

LATRINES

see Water-Closets

LATROBE, BENJAMIN HENRY, 1764-1820

Benson, Barbara, ed. Benjamin Henry Latrobe & Moncure Robinson: The Engineer As Agent of Technological Transfer. (Illus.). 72p. 1975. pap. 1.25 (ISBN 0-914650-07-6). Eleutherian Mills-Hagley.

Latrobe, Benjamin H. Journal of Latrobe: Being the Notes & Sketches of an Architect, Naturalist & Traveler in the U.S. from 1796-1820. LC 78-170187. (Research & Source Works Ser.: No. 888). (Illus.). 362p. (American Classics in History & Social Science ser., No. 224). 1972. Repr. of 1905 ed. lib. bdg. 23.50 (ISBN 0-8337-2018-X). B Franklin.

Latrobe, Benjamin H., et al, eds. The Journals of Benjamin Henry Latrobe, 1799-1820: From Philadelphia to New Orleans. LC 79-19001. (Papers of Benjamin Henry Latrobe Ser. 1: Vol. 3). (Illus.). 432p. 1981. text ed. 65.00x (ISBN 0-300-02383-9). Yale U Pr.

Norton, Paul F. Latrobe, Jefferson, & the National Capitol. LC 76-23662. (Outstanding Dissertations in the Fine Arts Ser.). 1977. lib. bdg. 56.00x (ISBN 0-8240-2716-7). Garland Pub.

LA TROBE, CHARLES JOSEPH
Gross, Alan. Charles Joseph La Trobe. 167p. 1980. pap. 9.95x (ISBN 0-522-84210-0, Pub. by Melbourne Univ Pr Australia). Intl Schol Bk Serv.
--Charles Joseph La Trobe. 1956. 9.95x (ISBN 0-522-83621-6, Pub. by Melbourne U Pr). Intl Schol Bk Serv.
LATTER-DAY SAINTS
see Mormons and Mormonism
LATTER RAIN MOVEMENT
see Pentecostal Churches
LATTICE THEORY
see also Crystal Lattices; Crystallography, Mathematical
Advanced Structural Analysis: Worked Examples. 260p. 1978. pap. text ed. 42.00x (ISBN 0-258-97030-8, Pub. by Granada England). Renouf.
Balbes, Raymond & Dwinger, Philip. Distributive Lattices. LC 73-94309. 320p. 1975. 25.00x (ISBN 0-8262-0163-6). U of Mo Pr.
Bilz, H. & Kress, W. Phonon Dispersion Relations in Insulators. (Springer Ser. in Solid-State Sciences: Vol. 10). (Illus.). 1979. 41.50 (ISBN 0-387-09399-0). Springer-Verlag.
Birkhoff, Garrett D. Lattice Theory. rev. ed. LC 66-23707. (Colloquium Pubns. Ser.: Vol. 25). 1979. Repr. of 1967 ed. 22.00 (ISBN 0-8218-1025-1, COLL-25). Am Math.
Blumenthal, Leonard M. & Menger, Karl. Studies in Geometry. LC 74-75624. (Illus.). 1970. text ed. 25.95x (ISBN 0-7167-0437-4). W H Freeman.
Born, Max. Problems of Atomic Dynamics. 1970. pap. 4.95 (ISBN 0-262-52019-2). MIT Pr.
--Problems of Atomic Dynamics: The Structure of the Atom; the Lattice Theory of Rigid Bodies. Allis, W. P., et al, trs. LC 60-53099. 1960. 9.50 (ISBN 0-8044-4110-3). Ungar.
Cartwright, Donald. Extensions of Positive Operators Between Banach Lattices. LC 75-19496. (Memoirs: No. 164). 1975. pap. 9.60 (ISBN 0-8218-1864-3, MEMO-164). Am Math.
Cheung, Y. K. Finite Strip Method in Structural Analysis. Neal, B. G., ed. 130p. 1976. text ed. 32.00 (ISBN 0-08-018308-5). Pergamon.
Cruse, Thomas A. & Griffin, Donald S., eds. Three-Dimensional Continuum Computer Programs for Structural Analysis. 1972. pap. text ed. 6.00 (ISBN 0-685-30781-6, I00021). ASME.
Donnellan, T. Lattice Theory. LC 67-28661. 1968. 35.00 (ISBN 0-08-012563-8); pap. 9.75 (ISBN 0-08-012562-X). Pergamon.
Elms, D. An Introduction to Modern Structural Analysis. 230p. 1971. 54.50x (ISBN 0-677-62030-6). Gordon.
Fateley, William G. Infrared & Raman Selection Rules for Molecular & Lattice Vibrations. 222p. 1972. 18.50 (ISBN 0-471-25620-X, Pub. by W & W). Krieger.
Freese, R. S. The Structure of Modular Lattices of Width Four with Applications to Varieties of Lattices. LC 76-49468. (Memoirs: No. 181). 1977. 10.80 (ISBN 0-8218-2181-4, MEMO-181). Am Math.
Gericke, Helmuth. Lattice Theory. LC 66-26204. 8.50 (ISBN 0-8044-4266-5). Ungar.
Gierz, G., et al. A Compendium of Continuous Lattices. 380p. 1980. 19.80 (ISBN 0-387-10111-X). Springer-Verlag.
Gratzer, G. H. Lattice Theory: First Concepts & Distributive Lattices. LC 75-151136. (Mathematics Ser). (Illus.). 1971. text ed. 25.95x (ISBN 0-7167-0442-0). W H Freeman.
Gruber, C., et al. Group Analysis of Classical Lattice Systems. LC 77-2821. (Lecture Notes in Physics: Vol. 60). 1977. pap. 17.40 (ISBN 0-387-08137-2). Springer-Verlag.
Gutkowski, Richard M. Structures: Fundamental Theory & Behavior. 592p. 1980. text ed. 34.50 (ISBN 0-442-22983-6). Van Nos Reinhold.
Hammer, Joseph. Unsolved Problems Concerning Lattice Points. LC 72-95013. (Research Notes in Mathematics Ser.: No. 15). 1978. pap. cancelled (ISBN 0-8224-1717-0, 1717). Pitman Learning.
Hardy & Karo. The Lattice Dynamics & Statistics of Alkali Halide Crystals. 1979. 32.50 (ISBN 0-306-40221-1, Plenum Pr). Plenum Pub.
Hermann, Robert. Toda Lattices, Cosymplectic Manifolds, Baecklund Transformations & Kinks, Pt. B. (Interdisciplinary Mathematics Ser.: No. 18). 1979. 15.00 (ISBN 0-915692-24-4). Math Sci Pr.
Hossdorf, Heinz. Model Analysis of Structures. 1974. 21.95x (ISBN 0-442-30018-2). Van Nos Reinhold.
Huhn, A. P. & Schmidt, E. T. Lattice Theory. (Colloquia Mathematic Societatis Ser.: Vol.14). 1977. 61.00 (ISBN 0-7204-0498-3, North-Holland). Elsevier.
Hult, J. & Lemaitre, J., eds. Physical Non-Linearities in Structural Analysis Symposium. (IUTAM Ser.). (Illus.). 287p. 1981. 34.50 (ISBN 0-387-10544-1). Springer-Verlag.
International Conference on Low Lying Lattice Vibrational Modes & Their Relationship to Superconductivity & Ferroelectricity, Puerto Rico, 1975 & Lefkowitz, I. Proceedings, 2 vols. 477p. 1977. pap. 252.50 (ISBN 0-677-15535-2). Gordon.
Israel, Robert B. Convexity in the Theory of Lattice Gasses. LC 78-51171. (Physic Ser). 1979. 18.00 (ISBN 0-691-08209-X); pap. 8.50 (ISBN 0-691-08216-2). Princeton U Pr.
Kapp, Kenneth M. & Schneider, Hans. Completely O-Simple Semigroups: An Abstract Treatment of the Lattice of Congruences. (Math Lecture Notes Ser.: No. 34). 1969. pap. 8.50 (ISBN 0-8053-5213-9, Adv Bk Prog). Benjamin-Cummings.
Keimel, K. & Hofmann, K. H. General Character Theory for Partially Ordered Sets & Lattices. LC 52-42839. (Memoirs: No. 122). 1972. pap. 6.40 (ISBN 0-8218-1822-8, MEMO-122). Am Math.
Lax, Melvin. Symmetry Principles in Solid State & Molecular Physics. LC 74-1215. 499p. 1974. (Pub. by Wiley-Interscience); pap. 23.95x (ISBN 0-471-51904-9). Wiley.
Light Water Lattices. (Technical Reports Ser.: No. 12). 1962. pap. 17.50 (ISBN 92-0-055062-2, IDC12, IAEA). Unipub.
Livesley, R. K. Matrix Methods of Structural Analysis. 2nd ed. 208p. 1975. text ed. 28.00 (ISBN 0-08-018888-5); pap. text ed. 15.00 (ISBN 0-08-018887-7). Pergamon.
Loomis, Lynn H. Lattice Theoretic Background of the Dimension Theory of Operator Algebras. LC 52-42839. (Memoirs: No. 18). 1972. pap. 8.40 (ISBN 0-8218-1218-1, MEMO-18). Am Math.
Ludwig, W. Recent Developments in Lattice Theory. (Springer Tracts in Modern Physics: Vol. 43). (Illus.). 1967. 69.70 (ISBN 0-387-03982-1). Springer-Verlag.
Maeda, F. & Maeda, S. Theory of Symmetric Lattices. LC 73-128138. (Grundlehren der Mathematischen Wissenschaften: Vol. 173). (Illus.). 1970. 31.20 (ISBN 0-387-05118-X). Springer-Verlag.
Messing, W. The Crystals Associated to Barsotti-Tate Groups: With Applications to Abelian Schemes. LC 72-79007. (Lecture Notes in Mathematics: Vol. 264). 193p. 1972. pap. 7.00 (ISBN 0-387-05840-0). Springer-Verlag.
Mohanty, Gopal. Lattice Path Counting & Applications. LC 79-23524. (Probability & Mathematical Ser.). 1979. 27.50 (ISBN 0-12-504050-4). Acad Pr.
Nakano, Hidegoro. Linear Lattices. abr. ed. LC 66-24169. (Orig.). 1966. 4.95x (ISBN 0-8143-1293-4). Wayne St U Pr.
Narayana, T. V. Lattice Path Combinatorics with Statistical Applications. LC 78-6710. (Mathematical Expositions Ser.). 1979. 17.50x (ISBN 0-8020-5405-6). U of Toronto Pr.
Nikodym, Otton M. Mathematical Apparatus for Quantum-Theories. (Grundlehren der Mathematischen Wissenschaften: Vol. 129). 1966. 85.50 (ISBN 0-387-03523-0). Springer-Verlag.
Ordres Totaux Finis: Travaux Du Seminaire Sur les Ordres Totaux Finis, Aix-En-Provence, Juillet 1967. (Mathematiques et Sciences De L'homme: No. 12). 1971. pap. 25.00x (ISBN 90-2796-881-0). Mouton.
Pierce, Richard S. Translation Lattices. LC 52-42839. (Memoirs: No. 32). 1978. pap. 12.00 (ISBN 0-8218-1232-7, MEMO-32). Am Math.
Roggenkamp, K. W. Lattices Over Orders 2. new ed. LC 71-108334. (Lecture Notes in Mathematics: Vol. 142). 1970. pap. 18.30 (ISBN 0-387-04931-2). Springer-Verlag.
Roggenkamp, K. W. & Huber-Dyson, V. Lattices Over Orders 1. (Lecture Notes in Mathematics: Vol. 115). 1970. pap. 18.30 (ISBN 0-387-04904-5). Springer-Verlag.
Rutherford, Daniel E. Introduction to Lattice Theory. 1964. 8.75 (ISBN 0-02-851210-3). Hafner.
Schaefer, H. H. Branach Lattices & Positive Operators. (Die Grundlehren der Mathematischen Wissenschaften Ser.: Vol. 215). xi, 376p. 1975. 51.00 (ISBN 0-387-06936-4). Springer-Verlag.
Skala, H. Trellis Theory. LC 52-42839. (Memoirs: No. 121). 41p. 1972. pap. 7.20 (ISBN 0-8218-1821-X, MEMO-121). Am Math.
Skonjakov, L. A. Elements of Lattice Theorgy. 1978. 49.50 (ISBN 0-9960018-6-7, Pub. by A Hilger England). Heyden.
Spillers, W. R. Automated Structural Analysis: An Introduction. 1972. 21.00 (ISBN 0-08-016782-9). Pergamon.
Stone, Harold S. Discrete Mathematical Structures & Their Applications. LC 72-96797. 401p. 1973. text ed. 21.95 (ISBN 0-574-17982-8, 13-0982). SRA.
Symposium in Pure Mathematics - Monterey Calif - 1959. Lattice Theory: Proceedings, Vol. 2. Dilworth, R. P., ed. LC 50-1183. 1961. 21.20 (ISBN 0-8218-1402-8, PSPUM-2). Am Math.
Thelliez, S. Introduction a l'Etude des Structures Ternaires de Commutation. (Theorie des Systemes Ser.). 1973. 50.75x (ISBN 0-677-50330-X). Gordon.
Thompson, Richard L. Equilibrium States on Thin Energy Shells. LC 74-14723. (Memoirs: No. 150). 110p. 1974. pap. 8.80 (ISBN 0-8218-1850-3, MEMO-150). Am Math.
Toda, M. Theory of Nonlinear Lattices. (Springer Series in Solid-State Sciences: Vol. 20). (Illus.). 220p. 1981. 35.00 (ISBN 0-387-10224-8). Springer-Verlag.
Tuma, J. J. Advanced Structural Analysis. (Schaum's Outline Ser). pap. 6.95 (ISBN 0-07-065426-3, SP). McGraw.
Vulikh, B. Z. Introduction to the Theory of Partially Ordered Spaces. 1967. 76.00x (ISBN 0-677-61330-X). Gordon.
White, J. W. Structural Analysis Learnt by Example. 1972. 8.85x (ISBN 0-258-96810-9, Pub. by Granada England). State Mutual Bk.
LATVIA
Berzins, Alfred. Unpunished Crime. 8.95 (ISBN 0-8315-0021-2). Speller.
Bilmanis, Alfred. History of Latvia. LC 69-13827. Repr. of 1951 ed. lib. bdg. 27.00x (ISBN 0-8371-1446-2, BIHL). Greenwood.
Blodnieks, Adolfs. Undefeated Nation. 1959. 6.00 (ISBN 0-8315-0019-0). Speller.
Ezergailis, Andrew. The Nineteen Hundred Seventeen Revolution in Latvia. (East European Monographs: No. 8). 260p. 1974. 13.50x (ISBN 0-914710-01-X). East Eur Quarterly.
Fennel, T. G. & Gelsen, H. A Grammar of Modern Latvian, 3 vols. (Slavistic Printings & Reprintings: No. 303). 1980. text ed. 176.50x (ISBN 0-686-26963-2). Mouton.
Karklis, Maruta, et al. The Latvians in America. LC 74-13105. (Ethnic Chronology Ser). 160p. (gr. 9 up). 1974. text ed. 8.50 (ISBN 0-379-00508-5). Oceana.
Smith, Graham E. The Latvian Nation. (Studies in Russian & East European History). (Illus.). 1981. 29.00x (ISBN 0-389-20025-5). B&N.
LATVIAN FICTION
Bels, Albert. The Inspector. Cedrins, Inara, tr. from Latvian. 125p. 1981. 13.50 (ISBN 0-931556-08-2); pap. 4.50 (ISBN 0-931556-09-0). Translation Pr.
Ekmanis, Rolfs. Latvian Literature Under the Soviets: 1940-1975. LC 77-95206. 1977. 47.50 (ISBN 0-913124-26-5). Nordland Pub.
LATVIAN LANGUAGE
Fennel, T. G. & Gelsen, H. A Grammar of Modern Latvian, 3 vols. (Slavistic Printings & Reprintings: No. 303). 1980. text ed. 176.50x (ISBN 0-686-26963-2). Mouton.
Millers, Antonia. Grammar, Vocabulary, Exercises of the Latvian Language for the Use of Students. LC 79-89077. 10.00 (ISBN 0-912852-26-7). Echo Pubs.
Turkina, Phil E. Latvian-English Dictionary. 17.50 (ISBN 0-87557-052-6, 052-6). Saphrograph.
LATVIAN TALES
see Tales, Latvian
LAUD, WILLIAM ABP. OF CANTERBURY, 1573-1645
Collins, William E., ed. Archbishop Laud Commemoration, 1895. (Bibliography & Reference Ser: No. 257). 1969. Repr. of 1895 ed. 23.50 (ISBN 0-8337-0628-4). B Franklin.
Laud, William. Articles Exhibited in Parliament Against William, Archbishop of Canterbury. LC 72-212. (English Experience Ser.: No. 333). 16p. 1971. Repr. of 1640 ed. 7.00 (ISBN 90-221-0333-1). Walter J Johnson.
LAUDER, WILLIAM, d. 1771
Douglas, John. Milton No Plagiary; or a Detection of the Forgeries. LC 72-187954. Repr. of 1756 ed. lib. bdg. 10.00 (ISBN 0-8414-0508-5). Folcroft.
LAUDERDALE, JAMES MAITLAND, 8TH EARL OF, 1759-1839
Paglin, Morton. Malthus & Lauderdale: The Anti-Ricardian Tradition. LC 62-409. Repr. of 1961 ed. 13.50x (ISBN 0-678-00859-0). Kelley.
LAUDERDALE, JOHN MAITLAND, 1ST DUKE OF, 1616-1682
Argyll, Archibald C. Letters from Archibald, Earl of Argyll, to John, Duke of Lauderdale. Sinclair, George & Sharpe, C. K., eds. LC 75-38489. Repr. of 1829 ed. 17.50 (ISBN 0-404-52739-6). AMS Pr.
LAUGHING GAS
see Nitrous Oxide
LAUGHLIN, CLARENCE JOHN
Laughlin, Clarence J. The Transforming Eye: Photographs by Clarence John Laughlin. Gruber, Fritz, frwd. by. (Illus.). 1976. pap. 0.50 (ISBN 0-88397-068-6). Intl Exhibit Foun.
LAUGHTER
Bergler, Edmund. Laughter & the Sense of Humor. LC 56-7937. 297p. 1967. Repr. text ed. 11.75 (ISBN 0-685-62017-4). Thieme-Stratton.
Bergson, Henri. Risa. pap. 2.95 (ISBN 0-685-11531-3). French & Eur.
Chapman, Anthony J. & Foot, Hugh C., eds. Humor & Laughter: Theory, Research & Applications. LC 73-14378. 348p. 1976. 47.25 (ISBN 0-471-14612-9, Pub. by Wiley-Interscience). Wiley.
Cox, Samuel S. Why We Laugh. 1876. 25.00 (ISBN 0-8274-3702-1). R West.
Gardner, Judith & Gardner, Howard. Monographs on Infancy: An Original Anthology. LC 74-21702. 316p. 1975. Repr. 19.00x (ISBN 0-405-06472-1). Arno.
Greig, John Y. Psychology of Laughter & Comedy. LC 72-79198. 1969. Repr. of 1923 ed. 11.50x (ISBN 0-8154-0295-3). Cooper Sq.
Joubert, Laurent. Treatise on Laughter. Rocher, Gregory D. de, tr. from Fr. LC 79-16796. 224p. 1980. 16.75x (ISBN 0-8173-0026-0). U of Ala Pr.
Kahn, Samuel. Why & How We Laugh. LC 74-29536. 96p. 1975. 10.00 (ISBN 0-8022-2160-2). Philos Lib.
Kallen, Horace M. Liberty, Laughter & Tears: Reflections on the Relation of Comedy & Tragedy to Human Freedom. LC 68-26268. 380p. 1968. 8.50 (ISBN 0-87580-006-8). N Ill U Pr.
Ludovici, A. M. The Secret of Laughter. 35.00 (ISBN 0-8490-1011-X). Gordon Pr.
Ludovici, Anthony M. The Secret of Laughter. LC 74-8681. 1932. lib. bdg. 25.00 (ISBN 0-8414-5727-1). Folcroft.
--The Secret of Laughter. 1979. Repr. of 1932 ed. lib. bdg. 20.00 (ISBN 0-8492-1613-3). R West.
MacKenzie, Harriet M. Byron's Laughter. LC 73-1778. 1939. lib. bdg. 22.50 (ISBN 0-8414-2309-1). Folcroft.
Menon, V. K. A Theory of Laughter. LC 78-21711. 1972. Repr. of 1931 ed. lib. bdg. 20.00 (ISBN 0-8414-6329-8). Folcroft.
Piddington, Ralph. The Psychology of Laughter. 6.00 (ISBN 0-8008-6558-8); pap. 1.95 (ISBN 0-685-45969-1). Taplinger.
Rocher, Gregory De, ed. Rabelais's Laughers & Joubert's Traite du Ris. LC 78-15341. (Illus.). 1979. 12.50x (ISBN 0-8173-7610-0). U of Ala Pr.
Schaeffer, Neil. The Art of Laughter. LC 81-3807. 192p. 1981. 18.50x (ISBN 0-231-05224-3). Columbia U Pr.
Smith, Willard. Nature of Comedy. 1930. lib. bdg. 20.00 (ISBN 0-8414-1593-5). Folcroft.
Stearns, Frederick R. Laughing: Physiology, Pathophysiology, Psychology, Pathopsychology & Development. 84p. 1972. photocopy ed. spiral 8.75 (ISBN 0-398-02420-0). C C Thomas.
Stern, Alfred. Filosofía De la Risa y el Llanto. LC 76-1912. 6.25 (ISBN 0-8477-0520-X); pap. 5.00 (ISBN 0-8477-0521-8). U of PR Pr.
Sully, James. An Essay on Laughter: Its Forms, Its Causes, Its Development, & Its Values. Repr. of 1907 ed. 45.00 (ISBN 0-8274-4177-0). R West.
Swabey, Marie C. Comic Laughter: A Philosophical Essay. 1970. Repr. of 1961 ed. 18.50 (ISBN 0-208-00825-X, Archon). Shoe String.
Vassey, George. The Philosophy of Laughter & Smiling. Repr. of 1875 ed. 30.00 (ISBN 0-8274-4178-9). R West.
LAUNDRY
Cox, M. E. Practical Laundrywork. 147p. 1961. 11.50x (ISBN 0-85264-080-3, Pub. by Griffin England). State Mutual Bk.
Lyle, Dorothy S. Performance of Textiles. LC 76-54110. 1977. 29.95x (ISBN 0-471-01418-4). Wiley.
Rudman, Jack. Superintendent of Laundries. (Career Examination Ser.: C-1882). (Cloth bdg. avail. on request). pap. 10.00 (ISBN 0-8373-1882-3). Natl Learning.
Wyland, Johanna L. Housewives' Guide in Laundering. new ed. 25p. 1977. pap. 3.50 (ISBN 0-932044-01-8). M O Pub Co.
LAUNDRY AND LAUNDRY INDUSTRY
Arco Editorial Board. Laundry Worker. LC 68-55394. 1970. pap. 4.00 (ISBN 0-668-01834-8). Arco.
Rudman, Jack. Head Laundry Supervisor. (Career Examination Ser.: C-2426). (Cloth bdg. avail. on request). pap. 10.00 (ISBN 0-8373-2426-2). Natl Learning.
--Laundry Foreman. (Career Examination Ser.: C-2244). (Cloth bdg. avail. on request). pap. 8.00 (ISBN 0-8373-2244-8). Natl Learning.
--Laundry Manager. (Career Examination Ser.: C-2427). (Cloth bdg. avail. on request). pap. 10.00 (ISBN 0-686-53359-3). Natl Learning.
--Laundry Supervisor. (Career Examination Ser.: C-1339). (Cloth ndg. avail. on request). pap. 8.00 (ISBN 0-8373-1339-2). Natl Learning.
--Laundry Washman. (Career Examination Ser.: C-1340). (Cloth bdg. avail. on request). pap. 6.00 (ISBN 0-8373-1340-6). Natl Learning.
--Laundry Worker. (Career Examination Ser.: C-435). (Cloth bdg. avail. on request). pap. 12.00 (ISBN 0-8373-0435-0). Natl Learning.

--Senior Laundry Supervisor. (Career Examination Ser.: C-2220). (Cloth bdg. avail. on request). pap. 10.00 (ISBN 0-8373-2220-0). Natl Learning.
--Senior Laundry Worker. (Career Examination Ser.: C-719). (Cloth bdg. avail. on request). pap. 8.00 (ISBN 0-8373-0719-8). Natl Learning.
--Supervising Laundry Worker. (Career Examination Ser.: C-2200). (Cloth bdg. avail. on request). pap. 10.00 (ISBN 0-8373-2200-6). Natl Learning.

LAURACEAE

Mez, Carl. Lauraceae Americaneae Monographice Descrips. 1963. Repr. of 1889 ed. 32.00 (ISBN 3-7682-0171-6). Lubrecht & Cramer.

LAUREATES

see Poets Laureate

LAUREL

Jaynes, Richard A. The Laurel Book. LC 75-20015. (Illus.). 196p. 1975. 13.00 (ISBN 0-02-847180-6). Hafner.

LAUREL, STANLEY

Barr, Charles. Laurel & Hardy. movie ed. LC 68-31074. (Illus.). 1968. pap. 2.95 (ISBN 0-520-00085-4, CAL170). U of Cal Pr.
Everson, Bill. Films of Laurel & Hardy. 1969. 12.00 (ISBN 0-685-08133-8); pap. 6.95 (ISBN 0-8065-0146-4). Citadel Pr.
Guiles, Fred L. Stan: The Life of Stan Laurel. LC 80-5806. (Illus.). 272p. 1980. 12.95 (ISBN 0-8128-2762-7). Stein & Day.
McCabe, John. Mr. Laurel & Mr. Hardy. (RL 9). pap. 1.50 (ISBN 0-451-07313-4, W7313, Sig). NAL.
Scagnetti, Jack. The Laurel & Hardy Scrapbook. LC 76-6566. (Illus.). 160p. 1976. 12.95 (ISBN 0-8246-0207-2). Jonathan David.

LAURENS, HENRY 1724-1792

Laurens, Henry. The Papers of Henry Laurens: Vol. 5, September 1, 1765 - July 31, 1768. Rogers, George C., Jr. & Chesnutt, David R., eds. LC 67-29381. 1976. 27.50x (ISBN 0-87249-331-8). U of SC Pr.
--Papers of Henry Laurens: Vol. 7, Aug. 1, 1769 to Oct. 9, 1771. Rogers, George C., Jr. & Chesnutt, David R., eds. LC 67-29381. 1979. lib. bdg. 27.50 (ISBN 0-87249-372-5). U of SC Pr.
--The Papers of Henry Laurens: Vol. 8, Oct 10, 1771 to April 19, 1773. Rogers, George C., Jr., ed. LC 67-29381. 1980. lib. bdg. 27.50 (ISBN 0-87249-385-7). U of SC Pr.
Wallace, David D. Life of Henry Laurens. LC 66-27173. (Illus.). 1967. Repr. of 1915 ed. 12.50 (ISBN 0-8462-1015-0). Russell.

LAURENS, HENRI, 1885-1954

Laurens, Henry. The Papers of Henry Laurens: Vol. 3, January 1, 1759-August 31, 1763. Hamer, Philip M. & Rogers, George C., Jr., eds. LC 67-29381. (Papers of Henry Laurens Ser). 1972. lib. bdg. 27.50x (ISBN 0-87249-228-1). U of SC Pr.
Waldberg, Patrick. Henri Laurens Ou la Femme Placee En Abime. (Illus.). 201p. (Fr.). 1980. lib. bdg. 39.95 (ISBN 2-902780-06-0, Pub. by Edition Du Sphinx France). Humanities.

LAURENS, JOHN, 1754-1782

Wallace, David D. Life of Henry Laurens. LC 66-27173. (Illus.). 1967. Repr. of 1915 ed. 12.50 (ISBN 0-8462-1015-0). Russell.

LAURIE, ROCCO, 1948-1972

Silverman, Al. Foster & Laurie. 1974. 7.95 (ISBN 0-316-79116-4). Little.

LAURIER, WILFRID, SIR, 1841-1919

Berger, Carl, ed. Imperial Relations in the Age of Laurier. LC 23-16213. (Canadian Historical Readings Ser.: No. 6). 1969. pap. 2.00x (ISBN 0-8020-1616-2). U of Toronto Pr.

LAUTREC MONFA, HENRI MARIE RAYMOND DE TOULOUSE

see Toulouse-Lautrec Monfa, Henri Marie Raymond De, 1864-1901

LAVAGE, PERITONEAL

see Peritoneal Dialysis

LAVAL, PIERRE, 1883-1945

Baillargeon, Noel. Le Seminaire De Quebec Sous l'Episcopat De M G R Laval. (Fr.). 1972. 14.50x (ISBN 2-7637-6479-7, Pub by Laval). Intl Schol Bk Serv.
Laval, Pierre. The Diary of Pierre Laval. LC 72-6725. Repr. of 1948 ed. 18.75 (ISBN 0-404-10644-7). AMS Pr.
Thomson, David. Two Frenchmen. LC 75-8806. 255p. 1975. Repr. of 1951 ed. lib. bdg. 14.50x (ISBN 0-8371-8115-1, THTWF). Greenwood.

LAVER, RODNEY GEORGE

Laver, Rod. The Education of a Tennis Player. (Illus.). 1973. pap. 2.95 (ISBN 0-671-21533-7, Fireside). S&S.

LA VERENDRYE, PIERRE GAULTIER DE VARENNES, SIEUR DE, 1685-1749

Laut, Agnes C. Pathfinders of the West. LC 74-90651. (Essay Index Reprint Ser). 1904. 25.00 (ISBN 0-8369-1220-9). Arno.
Smith, G. Hubert. The Explorations of the La Verendryes in the Northern Plains, 1738-43. Wood, W. Raymond, ed. LC 79-26518. (Illus.). xx, 160p. 1980. 13.95x (ISBN 0-8032-4712-5). U of Nebr Pr.

LAVIGERIE, CHARLES MARTIAL ALLEMAND, CARDINAL, 1825-1892

Clarke, Richard F., ed. Cardinal Lavigerie & the African Slave Trade. LC 74-77199. Repr. of 1889 ed. 17.75x (ISBN 0-8371-1283-4, Pub. by Negro U Pr). Greenwood.

LAVIN, MARY, 1912-

Bowen, Zack. Mary Lavin. LC 73-126002. (Irish Writers Ser.). 77p. 1975. 4.50 (ISBN 0-8387-7762-7); pap. 1.95 (ISBN 0-8387-7701-5). Bucknell U Pr.
Kelly, A. A. Mary Lavin: Quiet Rebel; a Study of Her Short Stories. LC 79-55699. (Illus.). 1980. text ed. 22.50x (ISBN 0-06-493617-1). B&N.

LAVOISIER, ANTOINE LAURENT, 1743-1794

Aykroyd, Wallace R. Three Philosophers: Lavoisier, Priestley & Cavendish. LC 77-98808. Repr. of 1935 ed. lib. bdg. 15.00 (ISBN 0-8371-2890-0, AYTB). Greenwood.
Duveen, Dennis I. Supplementary Volume to a Bibliography of the Works of Antoine Lavoisier: 1753-1794. 173p. 1965. 26.50x (ISBN 0-8464-0900-3). Beekman Pubs.
Duveen, Dennis I. & Klickstein, H. S. Bibliography of the Works of Antoine Lavoisier: Bibliography of the Works of Antoine Lavoisier: Seventeen Forty-Three to Seventeen Ninety-Four. (Illus.). 491p. 1954. 37.50x (ISBN 0-8464-0192-4). Beekman Pubs.
Grimaux, Edouard. Lavoisier: 1743-1794. Cohen, I. Bernard, ed. LC 80-2124. (Development of Science Ser.). (Illus.). 1981. lib. bdg. 35.00x (ISBN 0-405-13963-2). Arno.
Guerlac, Henry. Antoine-Laurent Lavoisier: Chemist & Revolutionary. 1975. pap. 2.95 (ISBN 0-684-14222-8, SL583, ScribT). Scribner.
Lavoisier, A. L. & Laplace, P. S. Memoirs on Heat. Guerlac, Henry, ed. 1981. write for info. (ISBN 0-88202-195-8). N Watson.

LAW, JOHN, 1671-1729

Green, Frederick C. Eighteenth-Century France: Six Essays. LC 64-21609. 9.00 (ISBN 0-8044-1315-0); pap. 4.95 (ISBN 0-8044-6221-6). Ungar.
Levasseur, Emile. Recherches Historiques Sur le Systeme De (John) Law. LC 74-133549. 1970. Repr. of 1854 ed. lib. bdg. 29.00 (ISBN 0-8337-2091-0). B Franklin.
Thiers, Adolphe. The Mississippi Bubble: A Memoir of John Law. Fisk, Frank S., ed. Fiske, Frank S., tr. LC 69-19685. xii, 338p. Repr. of 1859 ed. lib. bdg. 18.50x (ISBN 0-8371-0681-8, THMB). Greenwood.

LAW, WILLIAM, 1686-1761

Law, William. William Law & Eighteenth-Century Quakerism. Hobhouse, Stephen, ed. LC 77-175870. (Illus.). Repr. of 1927 ed. 18.00 (ISBN 0-405-08736-5). Arno.
Randolph, Erwin P. William Law. (English Authors Ser.: No. 282). 1980. lib. bdg. 11.95 (ISBN 0-8057-6765-7). Twayne.
Stanwood, Paul & Warren, Austin, eds. William Law: A Serious Call to a Devout & Holy Life & the Spirit of Love. LC 78-61418. (Classics of Western Spirituality). 542p. 1978. 11.95 (ISBN 0-8091-0265-X); pap. 7.95 (ISBN 0-8091-2144-1). Paulist Pr.

LAW

see also Courts; Illegality; Jurisdiction; Jurisprudence; Justice; Justice, Administration Of; Lawyers; Legal Ethics; Legislation; Natural Law; Statutes;
also names of legal systems, e.g. Canon Law, Common Law, Roman Law; special branches of law, e.g. Constitutional Law, Criminal Law, Maritime Law; specific legal topics, e.g. Contracts, Mortgages, Sanctions (Law); subdivision Laws and Legislation under subjects, e.g. Postal Service–Law

Abel-Smith, Brian, et al. Legal Problems & the Citizen. 1973. text ed. 26.00x (ISBN 0-435-82865-7). Heinemann Ed.
Ajisafa, Ajawi K. The Laws & Customs of the Yoruba People. 1976. lib. bdg. 59.95 (ISBN 0-8490-2135-9). Gordon Pr.
Akzin, Benjamin, ed. Studies in Law, Vol. V. 259p. 1958. pap. 17.25x (ISBN 0-686-74321-0, Pub. by Magnes Israel). Humanities.
Allen, Carleton K. Law in the Making. 7th ed. 1964. pap. 16.95x (ISBN 0-19-881029-6, OPB29). Oxford U Pr.
Allen, Francis A. Law, Intellect, & Education. (Michigan Faculty Ser.). 1979. lib. bdg. 12.00x (ISBN 0-472-09309-6, 09309); pap. 5.95 (ISBN 0-472-06309-X, 06309). U of Mich Pr.
American Bar Foundation, Corporate Debt Financing Project. Commentaries on Model Debenture Indenture Provisiions, 1965. Bd. with Model Debenture Indenture Provisions, All Registered Issues, 1967; Certain Negotiable Provisions Which May Be Included in a Particular Incorporating Indenture. LC 79-127110. 591p. 1971. 100.00 (ISBN 0-910058-00-8). Am Bar Foun.
Anderson, Ronald A. Social Forces & the Law. LC 69-20122. 1969. pap. 7.25 (ISBN 0-538-12200-5). SW Pub.
Andrews, Burton. The Law-Analysis & Synthesis. rev., 2nd ed. (Introduction to Law). 354p. 1980. 19.00x (ISBN 0-686-31006-3). Liberty Bk.
Atiyah, P. S. Promises, Morals, & Law. 216p. 1981. 29.95x (ISBN 0-19-825377-X). Oxford U Pr.
Bander, E. J., ed. Mr. Dooley on the Choice of Law. 1963. 9.95 (ISBN 0-87215-004-6). Michie-Bobbs.
Bechtler, Thomas W., ed. Law in a Social Context. 1978. lib. bdg. 34.00 (ISBN 90-2680-973-5, Pub. by Kluwer Law Netherlands). Kluwer Boston.
Beck, James M. May It Please the Court. 1979. Repr. of 1930 ed. lib. bdg. 30.00 (ISBN 0-8495-0399-X). Arden Lib.
Birrell, Augustine. Seven Lectures on the Law & History of Copyright in Books. LC 74-112404. Repr. of 1899 ed. 15.00x (ISBN 0-678-04538-0). Kelley.
Bishop, Joel P. The First Book of the Law: Explaining the Nature, Sources, Books & Practical Applications of Legal Science & Methods of Study & Practice. 1976. Repr. of 1868 ed. 59.00 (ISBN 0-685-71302-4, Regency). Scholarly.
Black, Donald. The Behavior of Law. 1980. pap. 6.50 (ISBN 0-12-102652-3). Acad Pr.
--The Behavior of Law. 1976. 18.50 (ISBN 0-12-102650-7). Acad Pr.
Blumer, Dennis H., ed. Briefing Papers II: Legal Issues for Postsecondary Education. 1976. pap. 5.00 (ISBN 0-87117-063-9). Am Assn Comm Jr Coll.
Bonsignore, John J., et al. Before the Law: An Introduction to the Legal Process. 2nd ed. LC 78-69606. (Illus.). 1979. pap. text ed. 12.50 (ISBN 0-395-27514-8). HM.
Boy Scouts of America. Law. LC 19-600. (Illus.). 64p. (gr. 6-12). 1975. pap. 0.70x (ISBN 0-8395-3389-6, 3389). BSA.
Boynton, G. R. & Chong Lim Kim. Legislative Systems in Developing Countries. LC 75-13342. 1975. 14.75 (ISBN 0-8223-0344-2). Duke.
Bradway, John S. Progress in Family Law. Lambert, Richard D., ed. LC 71-81088. (Annals Ser.: No. 383). 1969. 7.50 (ISBN 0-87761-116-5); pap. 6.00 (ISBN 0-87761-115-7). Am Acad Pol Soc Sci.
Brandis, Henry. Stansbury's North Carolina Evidence: Brandis Revision, 2 vols. rev. ed. LC 72-97320. 1038p. 1973. with 1979 suppl 75.00 (ISBN 0-87215-159-X); 1979 suppl. separately 25.00 (ISBN 0-87215-278-2). Michie-Bobbs.
Cain, Maureen & Hunt, Alan. Marx & Engels on Law. (Law, State & Society Ser.). 1979. 29.00 (ISBN 0-12-154850-3); pap. 15.00 (ISBN 0-12-154852-X). Acad Pr.
Cairns, Huntington. Law & the Social Sciences. LC 69-18855. Repr. of 1935 ed. lib. bdg. 12.00x (ISBN 0-678-04536-4). Kelley.
--Law & the Social Sciences. LC 70-100121. xiv, 279p. 1970. Repr. of 1935 ed. text ed. 12.00x (ISBN 0-8377-2001-X). Rothman.
Cappelletti, Mauro & Tallon, Denis, eds. Fundamental Guarantees of Parties in Civil Litigation: Studies in National & Comparative Law. LC 73-762. 846p. (Eng. & Fr.). 1973. lib. bdg. 35.00 (ISBN 0-379-00007-5). Oceana.
Carlsen, Martin, et al. Student Workbook for Introduction to the Administration of Justice. 1978. pap. text ed. 9.95 (ISBN 0-8403-1921-5). Kendall-Hunt.
Carlston, Kenneth S. Law & Structures of Social Action. LC 80-19159. (The Library of World Affairs Ser.: No. 30). xii, 288p. 1980. Repr. of 1956 ed. lib. bdg. 27.50x (ISBN 0-313-20837-9, CALW). Greenwood.
Carter, Lief H. Reason in Law. 1979. pap. text ed. 8.95 (ISBN 0-316-13045-1). Little.
Casese, Antonio. The New Human Law of Armed Conflict. 1979. lib. bdg. 44.00 (ISBN 0-379-20458-4). Oceana.
Cataldo, Bernard F., et al. Introduction to Law & the Legal Process. 3rd ed. LC 79-13193. 1980. 28.95 (ISBN 0-471-14082-1); tchr's manual avail. (ISBN 0-471-02267-5). Wiley.
Chambliss, William J. & Mankoff, Milton. Whose Law? What Order? A Conflict Approach to Criminology. LC 75-23220. 256p. 1976. pap. text ed. 13.50x (ISBN 0-471-14476-2). Wiley.
Chayet, Neil. Looking at the Law. 448p. 1981. 14.95 (ISBN 0-8317-5623-3, Rutledge Pr). Smith Pubs.
Clarkson, Kenneth W. & Martin, Donald L. Economics of Nonproprietary Organizations, No. 1. Zerbe, Richard O., Jr., ed. (Research in Law & Economics Supplement Ser.: N. 1). 288p. 34.50 (ISBN 0-89232-132-6). Jai Pr.
Cohen, Julius H. The Law: Business or Profession? 1980. lib. bdg. 79.95 (ISBN 0-8490-3133-8). Gordon Pr.
Constitution & Laws of the Chickasaw Nation Together with the Treaties of 1832, 1833, 1834, 1837, 1852, 1855, & 1866 Compiled by Davis A. Homer. LC 73-88755. (Constitution & Laws of the American Indian Tribes Ser. 1: Vol. 2). 1973. Repr. of 1899 ed. 45.00 (ISBN 0-8420-1719-4). Scholarly Res Inc.
Crowley, Aleister. Book of the Law: Technically Called Liber AL vel Legis - Sub Figura CCXX As Delivered by XCIII 418 to DCLXVI. LC 72-96601. 1976. 8.50x (ISBN 0-913576-12-3); deluxe ed. 30.00x leather (ISBN 0-913576-11-5). Thelema Pubns.
Dais, E. E. Law & the Ecological Challenge: Amintaphil, IVR-Northam, Vol. 2. LC 78-61842. 1979. lib. bdg. 32.50 (ISBN 0-930342-66-6). W S Hein.
Davitt, Thomas E. The Elements of Law. LC 59-10419. 1959. pap. 8.95 (ISBN 0-87462-475-4). Marquette.
Dell, Susanne. Silent in Court. 64p. 1971. pap. text ed. 5.00x (ISBN 0-7135-1576-7, Pub. by Bedford England). Renouf.
Dinnerstein, L. The Leo Frank Case. LC 68-199750. 248p. 1968. 16.00x (ISBN 0-231-03067-3). Columbia U Pr.
Edelman, Bernard. Ownership of the Image. Kingdom, Elizabeth, tr. from Fr. 1979. 20.00x (ISBN 0-7100-0103-7). Routledge & Kegan.
Edmunds, Palmer D. Law & Civilization. 1959. 8.00 (ISBN 0-8183-0177-5). Pub Aff Pr.
Eggleston, Richard. Evidence, Proof & Probability. (Law in Context Ser.). xiv, 226p. 1978. 17.50x (ISBN 0-297-77404-2, Pub by Weidenfeld & Nicolson). Rothman.
Ehrmann, Henry W. Comparative Legal Cultures. 176p. 1976. pap. text ed. 7.95 (ISBN 0-13-153858-6). P-H.
Elles, Neil. Community Law Through the Cases. 1973. 18.50 (ISBN 0-685-32576-8). Bender.
Faber, Stuart J. Handbook of Construction Law. 350p. (Orig.). 1980. pap. text ed. 23.50 (ISBN 0-89074-078-X). Lega Bks.
--Handbook of Criminal Procedure. 3rd ed. 360p. (Orig.). 1980. pap. text ed. 24.50 (ISBN 0-89074-076-3). Lega Bks.
--Handbook of Family Law. 3rd ed. 350p. (Orig.). 1980. pap. text ed. 24.50 (ISBN 0-89074-075-5). Lega Bks.
Fallers, Lloyd A. Law Without Precedent: Legal Ideas in Action in the Courts of Colonial Busoga. LC 65-10270. 1969. 14.50x (ISBN 0-226-23681-1). U of Chicago Pr.
Feenstra, Robert. Catalogue des Imprimes de la Collection Meijers, de la Bibliotheque de l'Universite de Leyde. 479p. (Fr.). 1980. lib. bdg. 45.00 (ISBN 90-271-1654-7). Kluwer Boston.
Fenwick, C. Foreign Policy & International Law. LC 68-57015. 1968. 8.50 (ISBN 0-379-00366-X). Oceana.
Finnis, J. M. Annual Survey of Commonwealth Law Nineteen Seventy-Seven. 1979. 98.00x (ISBN 0-19-825352-4). Oxford U Pr.
Fisher, Mary L., ed. Guide to State Legislative Materials. LC 79-21870. (AALL Publications Ser.: Vol. 15). 1979. loose-leaf 28.50x (ISBN 0-8377-0113-9). Rothman.
Gareis, Karl. Introduction to the Science of Law: A Systematic Survey of the Law & Principles of Legal Study. Kocurek, A. & Pound, Roscoe, trs. 1977. lib. bdg. 59.95 (ISBN 0-8490-2072-7). Gordon Pr.
--Introduction to the Science of Law: Systematic Survey of the Law & Principles of Legal Study. (Modern Legal Philosophy Ser: Vol. 1). xxx, 376p. 1968. Repr. of 1911 ed. 18.00x (ISBN 0-8377-2200-4). Rothman.
Garlan, Edwin N. Legal Realism & Justice. xii, 161p. 1981. Repr. of 1941 ed. lib. bdg. 20.00x (ISBN 0-8377-0614-9). Rothman.
Gaynor, James K. Profile of the Law. 4th ed. 160p. 1978. 3.95 (ISBN 0-87179-284-2). BNA.
Geis, Gilbert & Stotland, Ezra, eds. White-Collar Crime: Theory & Research. LC 79-26672. (Sage Criminal Justice System Annuals: Vol. 13). (Illus.). 320p. 1980. 22.50x (ISBN 0-8039-1404-0); pap. 9.95 (ISBN 0-8039-1405-9). Sage.
Glos, George E. Comparative Law. xxxv, 787p. 1979. 35.00x (ISBN 0-8377-0610-6). Rothman.
Gray, John C. Nature & Sources of the Law. 2nd ed. 8.50 (ISBN 0-8446-2156-0). Peter Smith.
Green, Mark J. & Wasserstein, Bruce, eds. With Justice for Some: An Indictment of the Law by Young Advocates. 416p. 1972. pap. 3.95x (ISBN 0-8070-0541-X, BP429). Beacon Pr.
Greenman, Russell L. & Schmertz, Eric J. Personnel Administration & the Law. 2nd ed. 486p. 1979. 19.50 (ISBN 0-87179-234-6). BNA.
Grossman, Bernard A., ed. Letters Rogatory. 97p. 1956. 8.00 (ISBN 0-87945-015-0). Fed Legal Pubn.
Hamburger, Max. Equitable Law: New Reflections on Old Conceptions. 1976. pap. 1.50 (ISBN 0-918230-03-9). Barnstable.

Hanna, Donald G. & Kleberg, John R. Law Handbook for Ohio Law Enforcement Officers. 1979. pap. text ed. 3.40 (ISBN 0-87563-170-3). Stipes.
Harding, Arthur L., ed. Religion, Morality & Law. LC 56-8945. (Studies in Jurisprudence: No. 3). 1956. 4.00 (ISBN 0-87074-069-5). SMU Press.
Hargrove, John L., ed. Law, Institutions & the Global Environment. LC 72-1153. 500p. 1972. lib. bdg. 30.00 (ISBN 0-379-00024-5). Oceana.
Harris, J. W. Law & Legal Science: An Inquiry into the Concepts Legal Rule & Legal System. 1979. 22.00x (ISBN 0-19-825353-2). Oxford U Pr.
Harris, Phil. An Introduction to Law. (Law in Context Ser.). xvi, 320p. 1980. 31.00x (ISBN 0-297-77826-9, Pub. by Weidenfeld & Nicolson England). Rothman.
Hart, Herbert L. The Concept of Law. 1976. pap. text ed. 7.95x (ISBN 0-19-876072-8). Oxford U Pr.
Hayek, F. A. Law, Legislation, & Liberty: Vol. 1: Rules & Order. 15.00 (ISBN 0-226-32080-4). U of Chicago Pr.
--Law, Legislation, & Liberty: Vol. 3: the Political Order of a Free People. pap. 7.50 (ISBN 0-226-32090-1). U of Chicago Pr.
Hayek, Friedrich A. Law, Legislation & Liberty: Rules & Order, Vol. 1. LC 73-82488. 1978. pap. 4.45 (ISBN 0-226-32086-3, P763, Phoen). U of Chicago Pr.
Hazard, Geoffrey C., Jr., ed. Law in a Changing Society. LC 68-27498. 1968. 5.95 (ISBN 0-936904-02-X); pap. 2.95 (ISBN 0-936904-27-5). Am Assembly.
Hegland, Kenney F. Trial & Practice Skills in a Nutshell. LC 78-2731. (Nutshell Ser.). 346p. 1978. pap. text ed. 6.95 (ISBN 0-8299-2001-3). West Pub.
Henszey, Benjamin N., et al. Introduction to Basic Legal Principles. 2nd ed. LC 64-14432. 1977. pap. text ed. 11.95 (ISBN 0-8403-0684-9). Kendall-Hunt.
Hermann, Philip J. Do You Need a Lawyer? (Illus.). 160p. 1980. 12.95 (ISBN 0-13-216721-2, Spec); pap. 5.95 (ISBN 0-13-216713-1). P-H.
Hobbes, Thomas. Elements of Law, Natural & Politic. 2nd rev. ed. Tonnies, Ferdinand, ed. 236p. 1969. 27.50x (ISBN 0-7146-2540-X, F Cass Co). Biblio Dist.
Hooker, M. B. Legal Pluralism: An Introduction to Colonial & Neo - Colonial Laws. 500p. 1975. 49.50x (ISBN 0-19-825329-X). Oxford U Pr.
Institute of Advanced Legal Studies, University of London. Catalogue of the Library of the Institute of Advanced Legal Studies, 6 vols. 1978. lib. bdg. 480.00 (ISBN 0-8161-0099-3). G K Hall.
International Institute for the Unification of Private Law. Uniform Law Cases, 1959-1970. 162.50 (ISBN 0-685-47349-X). Oceana.
Ivener, Mark & Blalock, Steven. Immigration Law Handbook, 2 vols. 650p. (Orig.). 1980. Set. pap. text ed. 59.50 (ISBN 0-89074-080-1). Lega Bks.
Jackson, Percival E., ed. The Wisdom of the Supreme Court. LC 73-8565. 524p. 1973. Repr. of 1962 ed. lib. bdg. 24.75x (ISBN 0-8371-6960-7, JASC). Greenwood.
Johns, C. H. The Oldest Code of Laws in the World. 1977. lib. bdg. 59.95 (ISBN 0-8490-2374-2). Gordon Pr.
Jones, F. C. Extraterritoriality in Japan. LC 77-114048. Repr. of 1931 ed. 19.50 (ISBN 0-404-03598-1). AMS Pr.
Jones, Gareth. Anglo-American Trends in Restitution. 1978. pap. 4.00 (ISBN 9-0268-0981-6, Pub. by Kluwer Law Netherlands). Kluwer Boston.
Kantrowitz, Walter & Eisenberg, Howard. How to Be Your Own Lawyer (Sometimes) LC 78-5053. 1979. 12.95 (ISBN 0-399-11985-X). Putnam.
Kavass, Igor I. & Michael, Mark A., eds. UST Cumulative Index: 1776-1949, 4 vols. LC 74-29385. 1975. Set. lib. bdg. 295.00 (ISBN 0-930342-02-X). W S Hein.
Kavass, Igor I. & Sprudzs, Adolf, eds. UST Cumulative Index: 1950-1970, 4 vols. LC 72-92824. 1973. Set. lib. bdg. 300.00 (ISBN 0-930342-01-1). W S Hein.
Kimbrough, Robert A. Summary of American Law. LC 73-88586. 1974. 18.50 (ISBN 0-686-14541-0). Lawyers Co-Op.
Kocourek, Albert & Wigmore, John H., eds. Formative Influences of Legal Development. (Evolution of Law: Select Readings on the Origin & Development of Legal Institutions Ser.: Vol. 3). xxiv, 705p. 1979. Repr. of 1918 ed. lib. bdg. 38.50x (ISBN 0-8377-2330-2). Rothman.
--Sources of Ancient & Primitive Law. (Evolution of Law: Select Readings on the Origin & Development of Legal Institutions Ser.: Vol. 1). xvii, 702p. 1979. Repr. of 1915 ed. lib. bdg. 38.50x (ISBN 0-8377-2328-0). Rothman.
Korkunov, Nikolai. General Theory of Law. Hastings, W. G., tr. (Modern Legal Philosophy Ser: Vol. 4). xxviii, 524p. 1969. Repr. of 1922 ed. 18.00x (ISBN 0-8377-2327-2). Rothman.
Krislov, Samuel, et al, eds. Compliance & the Law: A Multi-Disciplinary Approach. LC 73-151670. 391p. 1972. 20.00 (ISBN 0-8039-0119-4). Sage.
Law & Government. (Franciscan Educational Conferences Ser). 1950. pap. 3.50 (ISBN 0-685-77544-5). Franciscan Herald.
Legal First Aid. (Illus.). 9.95 (ISBN 0-686-09002-0). Legal First Aid.
Lieberman, Jethro K. Privacy & the Law. (gr. 7 up). 1978. 7.95 (ISBN 0-688-41866-X); lib. bdg. 7.63 (ISBN 0-688-51866-4). Lothrop.
London, Ephraim, ed. World of Law, 2 Vols. 1960. Set. 25.00 (ISBN 0-671-82936-X). S&S.
Lovett, Steven R. Search & Seizure Courtroombook. 500p. (Orig.). 1980. pap. text ed. 49.50 (ISBN 0-89074-077-1). Lega Bks.
MacCormick, Neil. Legal Reasoning & Legal Theory. (Clarendon Law Ser.). 1979. 14.95x (ISBN 0-19-876080-9). Oxford U Pr.
Mack, Stan. Runaway Road. LC 79-5265. (Illus.). 48p. (ps-3). 1980. 4.95 (ISBN 0-8193-1017-4); PLB 5.95 (ISBN 0-8193-1018-2). Parents.
McNair, Arnold D., ed. Selected Papers & Bibliography. LC 73-85761. 396p. 1974. lib. bdg. 27.50 (ISBN 0-379-00228-0). Oceana.
Manne, Henry G. The Economics of Legal Relationships. LC 75-4884. (Illus.). 660p. 1975. text ed. 25.95 (ISBN 0-8299-0048-9). West Pub.
Martin, James A. Perspectives on Conflict of Laws: Choice of Law. 1980. pap. text ed. 6.95 (ISBN 0-316-54853-7). Little.
Mason, L. Ryder. California Family Law Handbook. LC 79-90704. 1981. 36.00 (ISBN 0-911110-31-3); 1980 suppl. incl. Parker & Son.
Matthews, Douglas. Sue the B-St-Rds: The Victim's Handbook. LC 72-97686. 1973. 6.95 (ISBN 0-87795-059-8); pap. 2.95 (ISBN 0-87795-125-X). Arbor Hse.
Meador, Daniel J. Preludes to Gideon. 1967. 10.00 (ISBN 0-87215-009-7). Michie-Bobbs.
Menendez Menendez, Emilio. Lecciones de teoria general del derecho. LC 79-16559. 262p. (Sp.). 1981. pap. text ed. 9.00 (ISBN 0-8477-3017-4). U of PR Pr.
Millington, William G. Law & the College Student: Justice in Evolution. LC 79-14211. 629p. 1979. text ed. 18.95 (ISBN 0-8299-2047-1). West Pub.
Morris, Clarence & Morris, C. Robert. Morris on Torts. 2nd ed. LC 80-170. (University Textbook Ser.). 457p. 1980. write for info. (ISBN 0-88277-002-0). Foundation Pr.
Murphy, Thomas P. & Kline, Robert D., eds. Urban Law: A Guide to Information Sources. (Urban Studies Information Guide Ser.: Vol. 11). 1980. 36.00 (ISBN 0-8103-1409-6). Gale.
Mylonas, Anastassios D. Prisoners' Attitudes Toward Law & Legal Institutions. LC 74-29570. 1975. soft bdg. 8.00 (ISBN 0-88247-314-X). R & E Res Assoc.
National Association of Legal Assistants Inc. Manual for Legal Assistants. Park, William R., ed. LC 79-18552. 529p. 1979. text ed. 19.95 (ISBN 0-8299-2059-5). West Pub.
National Center for State Courts. Pretrial Delay: A Review & Bibliography. 1978. pap. 2.00 (ISBN 0-89656-024-4, R0036). Natl Ctr St Courts.
Nekam, Alexander. Personality Conception of the Legal Entity. 1938. 24.50x (ISBN 0-686-51287-1). Elliots Bks.
New York University Contemporary Law Pamphlets, 58 nos. in 5 vols. 1963. Repr. of 1941 ed. Set. 350.00 (ISBN 0-379-00179-9). Oceana.
Newberg, Herbert B., ed. Public Interest Practice & Fee Awards. LC 80-80441. 567p. 1980. text ed. 30.00 (ISBN 0-686-61029-6, H1-2953). PLI.
Nice, Richard W. Treasury of the Rule of Law. (Quality Paperback: No. 168). Orig. Title: Treasury of Law. 1965. pap. 4.95 (ISBN 0-8226-0168-0). Littlefield.
Ohler, K. J. Le Notariat De Demain. 1977. lib. bdg. 39.00 (ISBN 90-268-0840-2, Pub. by Kluwer Law Netherlands). Kluwer Boston.
Osuagwu, Harold G. Cases in Business Law 1: With Learning Objectives. 1979. pap. text ed. 7.95 (ISBN 0-89669-019-9). Collegium Bk Pubs.
Paget, John. Judicial Puzzles, Gathered from the State Trials. (Legal Recreations Ser.: Vol. 3). 155p. 1979. Repr. of 1876 ed. lib. bdg. 15.00x (ISBN 0-8377-1003-0). Rothman.
Parkinson, C. Northcote. Parkinson: The Law. (Illus.). 1980. 8.95 (ISBN 0-395-29131-3). HM.
Parsons, Theophilus. Memoir of Theophilus Parsons. LC 71-118032. (American Constitutional & Legal History Ser). 1970. Repr. of 1859 ed. lib. bdg. 45.00 (ISBN 0-306-71939-8). Da Capo.
Patterson, E. Law in a Scientific Age. LC 63-9872. 87p. 1963. 12.50x (ISBN 0-231-02617-X). Columbia U Pr.
Payler, Frederick. Law Courts, Lawyers & Litigants. xiv, 242p. 1980. Repr. of 1926 ed. lib. bdg. 24.00x (ISBN 0-8377-1006-5). Rothman.
Pelton, Robert W. Loony Laws: You Never Knew You Were Breaking. LC 80-54814. (Illus.). 160p. 1981. 9.95 (ISBN 0-8027-0687-8); pap. 4.95 (ISBN 0-8027-7174-2). Walker & Co.
Pennock, J. Roland & Chapman, John W., eds. The Limits of Law. (Nomos Ser.: No. 15). 325p. 1973. text ed. 15.00x (ISBN 0-88311-008-3). Lieber-Atherton.
Phillipps, S. M., intro. by. Famous Cases of Circumstantial Evidence, 2 vols. in 1. 1979. Repr. of 1878 ed. lib. bdg. 42.50x (ISBN 0-8377-1002-2). Rothman.
Polyviou, Polyvios G. The Equal Protection of the Laws. 774p. 1980. 65.00x (ISBN 0-7156-1399-5, Pub. by Duckworth England). Biblio Dist.
Posner, Richard A. Economic Analysis of Law. 2nd ed. 1977. 18.00 (ISBN 0-316-71432-1). Little.
Pospisil, Leopold J. The Ethnology of Law. 2nd ed. LC 77-75811. 1978. pap. text ed. 6.95 (ISBN 0-8465-5825-4). Benjamin-Cummings.
Radin, Max. Law As Logic & Experience. LC 70-122408. 1971. Repr. of 1940 ed. 16.50 (ISBN 0-208-01048-3, Archon). Shoe String.
Raz, Joseph. The Concept of a Legal System: An Introduction to the Theory of a Legal System. 2nd ed. 244p. 1980. 24.95x (ISBN 0-19-825362-1); pap. 11.95x (ISBN 0-19-825363-X). Oxford U Pr.
Redden, Kenneth. Introductory Survey of the Place of Law in Our Civilization. 1946. 7.50 (ISBN 0-87215-071-2). Michie-Bobbs.
Redish, Martin H. Federal Jurisdiction: Tensions in the Allocation of Judicial Power. 370p. 1980. 25.00 (ISBN 0-672-84196-7). Michie-Bobbs.
Reuschlein, Harold G. & Gregory, William A. Handbook on the Law of Agency & Partnership. LC 78-12853. (Hornbook Ser.). 625p. 1978. text ed. 17.95 (ISBN 0-8299-2016-1). West Pub.
Roberts, William. A Treatise on the Construction of the Statutes, 13 Eliz. C.5. & 27 Eliz. C.4. Relating to Voluntary & Fraudulent Conveyances, & on the Nature & Force of Different Considerations to Support Deeds & Other Legal Instruments, in the Courts of Law & Equity. 2nd ed. xv, 667p. 1979. Repr. of 1825 ed. lib. bdg. 35.00x (ISBN 0-8377-1028-6). Rothman.
Robson, William A. Civilization & the Growth of Law: Study of Relations Between Men's Ideas About the Universe & the Institutions of Law & Government. LC 74-25779. (European Sociology Ser.). 374p. 1975. Repr. 21.00x (ISBN 0-405-06532-9). Arno.
Roets, Perry J. The Economic Order. 1969. pap. 7.95 (ISBN 0-87462-457-6). Marquette.
Rombauer, Marjorie D. Legal Problem Solving: Analysis Research & Writing. 3rd ed. LC 78-3468. (American Casebook Ser). 352p. 1978. text ed. 13.95 (ISBN 0-8299-2002-1). West Pub.
St. Clair, Sheldon. Worker's Compensation Law. 350p. (Orig.). 1980. pap. text ed. 23.50 (ISBN 0-89074-079-8). Lega Bks.
Samek, Robert A. The Legal Point of View. new ed. LC 73-82165. 1973. 15.00 (ISBN 0-8022-2127-0). Philos Lib.
Schwartz, Murray. Law & the American Future: An American Assembly Book. 1976. 9.95 (ISBN 0-13-526061-2, Spec); pap. 4.95 (ISBN 0-13-526053-1, Spec). P-H.
Scioletti, Daniel C. Legal Decisions for CPA's & Business People. 1979. text ed. 16.95 (ISBN 0-8403-1922-3). Kendall-Hunt.
Silving, Helen. Sources of Law. LC 68-54166. 1968. lib. bdg. 30.00 (ISBN 0-930342-22-4). W S Hein.
Simon, Rita J., ed. Research in Law & Sociology: An Annual Compilation of Research, Vol. 1. 1978. lib. bdg. 34.50 (ISBN 0-89232-024-9). Jai Pr.
Sirkin, Gerald, ed. Lexeconics: The Interaction of Law & Economics. (Social Dimensions of Economics, CCNY Ser.: Vol. 2). 272p. 1981. lib. bdg. 17.50 (ISBN 0-89838-053-7, Pub. by Martinus Nijhoff). Kluwer Boston.
Sommerich, Otto C. & Busch, Benjamin. Foreign Law: A Guide to Pleading & Proof. LC 59-8604. 1959. 10.00 (ISBN 0-379-00109-8). Oceana.
Spiro, George W. & Houghteling, James L., Jr. The Dynamics of Law. 2nd ed. 229p. 1981. pap. text ed. 9.95 (ISBN 0-15-518513-6). HarBraceJ.
Spitzer, Steven, ed. Research in Law & Sociology, Vol. 3. 368p. 1980. 34.50 (ISBN 0-89232-186-5). Jai Pr.
Status of Legal Instruments. 1972. 45.00 (ISBN 0-685-24998-0, GATT). Unipub.
Stern, Arlene L. Legal Looseleafs in Print 1981. LC 81-4873. 192p. 1981. pap. 20.00 (ISBN 0-939486-00-8). Infosources.
Steuer, Aron. Aesop in the Courts. LC 77-144790. 388p. 1971. 9.95 (ISBN 0-88238-075-3). Law-Arts.
Stone, Julius. Of Law & Nations: Between Power Politics & Human Hopes. LC 73-93977. 1974. lib. bdg. 37.50 (ISBN 0-930342-03-8). W S Hein.
Strachey, William. For the Colony of Virginia Britannia. LC 70-38225. (English Experience Ser.: No. 488). 108p. 1972. Repr. of 1612 ed. 9.50 (ISBN 90-221-0488-5). Walter J Johnson.
Straits Settlements Law Reports: 1893-1923, 15 vols. Repr. 30.00 ea. Oceana.
Striker, John M. & Shapiro, Andrew. Power Plays. 1981. pap. 2.95 (ISBN 0-440-17203-9). Dell.
Swiger, Elinor P. Law in Everyday Life. Clark, James I., ed. (Law Education Ser.). 1977. pap. text ed. 5.20 (ISBN 0-88343-697-3); tchrs'. manual 1.50 (ISBN 0-686-67152-X). McDougal-Littell.
Traynor, Roger J. Riddle of Harmless Error. LC 77-123108. (Law Forum Ser.: No. 7). 1970. 6.00 (ISBN 0-8142-0147-4). Ohio St U Pr.
Tullock, Gordon. Logic of the Law. LC 74-147010. 1971. text ed. 10.95x (ISBN 0-465-04165-5). Basic.
Vanderbilt, Arthur T. Men & Measures in the Law. xxii, 156p. 1981. Repr. of 1949 ed. lib. bdg. 22.50x (ISBN 0-8377-1230-0). Rothman.
Vinogradoff, Paul. Common-Sense in Law. LC 74-25793. (European Sociology Ser.). 260p. 1975. Repr. 14.00x (ISBN 0-405-06545-0). Arno.
Walker, David M., ed. Oxford Companion to Law. 1376p. 1980. 49.95 (ISBN 0-19-866110-X). Oxford U Pr.
Wasserman, Paul & Kaszubski, Marek, eds. Law & Legal Information Directory: A Guide to National & International Organizations, Bar Associations, Federal Court System, Federal Regulatory Agencies, Law Schools, Continuing Legal Education, Scholarships & Grants, Awards & Prizes, Special Libraries, Information Systems & Services, Research Centers, Etc. 800p. 1980. 110.00 (ISBN 0-8103-0169-5). Gale.
Weintraub, Russell J. Commentary on the Conflict of Laws. 2nd ed. LC 80-10480. (University Textbook Ser.). 655p. 1980. write for info. (ISBN 0-88277-000-4). Foundation Pr.
Weisberg, D. Kelly, ed. Women & the Law: The Social Historical Perspective. 600p. 1982. text ed. 28.95x (ISBN 0-87073-586-1); pap. text ed. 14.95x (ISBN 0-87073-587-X). Schenkman.
Wilcox, Henry S. Foibles of the Bench. 144p. 1980. Repr. of 1906 ed. lib. bdg. 18.50x (ISBN 0-8377-1304-8). Rothman.
Wolff, Robert P., ed. Rule of Law. LC 72-139669. 1971. pap. 3.95 (ISBN 0-671-20891-8, Touchstone Bks). S&S.
Woodbine, George E., ed. Four Thirteenth Century Law Tracts. 1910. 24.50x (ISBN 0-685-69888-2). Elliots Bks.
York, Kenneth H. & Bauman, John A. Cases & Materials on Remedies. 3rd ed. LC 78-23510. (American Casebook Ser.). 1250p. 1979. text ed. 23.95 (ISBN 0-8299-2021-8). West Pub.
Zander, Michael. The Law-Making Process. (Law in Context Ser.). xxiii, 309p. 1980. 40.00x (ISBN 0-297-77750-5, Pub. by Weidenfeld & Nicolson England). Rothman.
Zander, Michael, ed. What's Wrong with the Law? 136p. 1970. 5.00 (ISBN 0-7735-0086-3). McGill-Queens U Pr.
Zerbe, Richard O., ed. Research in Law & Economics, Vol. 3. 275p. 1981. 32.50 (ISBN 0-89232-231-4). Jai Pr.

LAW-ABBREVIATIONS

Bryson, William H. A Dictionary of Sigla & Abbreviations to & in Law Books Before 1607. LC 75-5675. (Virginia Legal Studies). 224p. 1975. 20.00x (ISBN 0-8139-0615-6). U Pr of Va.
Leistner, Georg. Abbreviations Guide to French Forms in Justice & Administration. 191p. 1975. 17.25 (ISBN 3-7940-3016-8, Pub. by K G Saur). Shoe String.
Rich, Vernon. Law & the Administration of Justice. 2nd ed. LC 78-31516. 1979. text ed. 19.95 (ISBN 0-471-04961-1). Wiley.
Rogers, Walter T. Dictionary of Abbreviations. LC 68-30662. 1969. Repr. of 1913 ed. 24.00 (ISBN 0-8103-3338-4). Gale.
Sprudzs, Adolph. Benelux Abbreviations & Symbols: Law & Related Subjects. LC 74-140620. 1971. lib. bdg. 20.00 (ISBN 0-379-00120-9). Oceana.
--Benelux Abbreviations & Symbols: Law & Related Subjects. LC 74-140620. 1971. lib. bdg. 20.00 (ISBN 0-379-00120-9). Oceana.

LAW-ADDRESSES, ESSAYS, LECTURES

see also Forensic Orations

Beck, Carl, ed. Law & Justice: Essays in Honor of Robert S. Rankin. LC 74-86476. 1970. 16.75 (ISBN 0-8223-0213-6). Duke.

Beck, James M. May It Please the Court. facs. ed. McGuire, O. R., ed. LC 75-121447. (Essay Index Reprint Ser). 1930. 25.00 (ISBN 0-8369-1694-8). Arno.

Beirne, Piers & Sharlet, Robert, eds. Pashukanis: Selected Writings on Maxism & Law. LC 79-40895. (Law, State & Society Ser.). 1980. 48.00 (ISBN 0-12-086350-2). Acad Pr.

Birkenhead, Frederick E. Points of View, 2 Vols. facsimile ed. LC 77-111815. (Essay Index Reprint Ser.). 1923. 33.00 (ISBN 0-8369-1594-1). Arno.

Birrell, Augustine. Obiter Dicta. LC 17-21084. (First & Second Ser). 1969. Repr. of 1887 ed. 8.00 (ISBN 0-403-00131-5). Scholarly.

Black, Charles L., Jr. Decision According to Law: The 1979 Holmes Lectures. 1981. 12.95 (ISBN 0-393-01452-5). Norton.

Black, Henry C. An Essay on the Constitutional Prohibitions Against Legislation Impairing the Obligation of Contracts, & Against Retroactive & Ex Post Facto Laws. xxvi, 355p. 1980. Repr. of 1887 ed. lib. bdg. 32.50x (ISBN 0-8377-0312-3). Rothman.

Blankenburg, Erhard, ed. Innovations in the Legal Services. LC 79-24923. (Research on Service Delivery, Vol. 1). 336p. 1980. text ed. 27.50 (ISBN 0-89946-010-0). Oelgeschlager.

Brown, Cynthia S. Alexander Meiklejohn: Teacher of Freedom. Ginger, Ann F., ed. LC 81-81355. (Studies in Law & Social Change: No. 2). (Illus.). 304p. (Orig.). 1981. 13.95x (ISBN 0-913876-16-X, 176); pap. 7.95x (ISBN 0-913876-17-8, 177). Meiklejohn Civ Lib.

California Law Review, ed. Essays in Honor of Hans Kelsen Celebrating the 90th Anniversary of His Birth. LC 70-178735. (Illus.). 1971. text ed. 17.50x (ISBN 0-8377-0528-2). Rothman.

Catholic University Of America - School Of Law. Jubilee Law Lectures. facs. ed. LC 71-134067. (Essay Index Reprint Ser). 1939. 15.00 (ISBN 0-8369-1907-6). Arno.

Celebration Legal Essays by Various Authors to Mark the Twenty-Fifth Year of Service of John H. Wigmore As Professor of Law in Northwestern University. xi, 602p. 1981. Repr. of 1918 ed. lib. bdg. 42.50x (ISBN 0-8377-0432-4). Rothman.

Cohen, Morris R. Law & the Social Order: Essays in Legal Philosophy. 1967. Repr. of 1933 ed. 22.50 (ISBN 0-208-00484-X, Archon). Shoe String.

Del Vecchio, Giorgio. Man & Nature: Selected Essays. Newman, Ralph A., ed. Campbell, A. H., tr. LC 72-75156. 1969. 9.00x (ISBN 0-268-00316-5). U of Notre Dame Pr.

Enchiridion Legum: A Discourse. Bd. with John Brydall: Speculum Juris Anglicani: or, a View of the Laws of England, As They Are Divided into Statute, Common-Law & Customs. Brydall, John. LC 77-86567. (Classics of English Legal History in the Modern Era: Vol. 69). 1978. Repr. of 1673 ed. lib. bdg. 55.00 (ISBN 0-8240-3056-7). Garland Pub.

Fortescue, John. De Laudibus Legum Anglie. Chrimes, S. B., intro. by. LC 78-62331. 1979. Repr. of 1942 ed. 26.50 (ISBN 0-88355-793-2). Hyperion Conn.

Frankfurter, Felix. Of Law & Life & Other Things That Matter: Papers & Addresses of Felix Frankfurter, 1956-1963. Kurland, Philip B., ed. LC 65-7916. 1969. pap. 2.95 (ISBN 0-689-70076-8, 138). Atheneum.

--Of Law & Men: Papers & Addresses, 1939-1956. Elman, Philip, ed. 1965. Repr. of 1956 ed. 19.50 (ISBN 0-208-00319-3, Archon). Shoe String.

Fuller, Lon L. The Law in Quest of Itself. LC 75-41105. Repr. of 1940 ed. 15.75 (ISBN 0-404-14665-1). AMS Pr.

Graveson, R. H. Comparative Conflict of Laws, Vol. 1: Selected Essays. new ed. (European Studies in Law). 1977. 42.75 (ISBN 0-7204-0486-X, North-Holland). Elsevier.

Harvard Legal Essays, Written in Honor of & Presented to John Henry Beale & Samuel Williston. facs. ed. LC 67-22062. (Essay Index Reprint Ser). 1934. 18.75 (ISBN 0-8369-0516-4). Arno.

Harvard University Law School. Path of Law from 1967: Proceedings & Papers at the Harvard Law School Convocation Held on the 150th Anniversary of Its Founding. Sutherland, Arthur E., ed. LC 69-71044. 1968. 7.50x (ISBN 0-674-65785-3). Harvard U Pr.

Hohfeld, Wesley N. Fundamental Legal Conceptions, As Applied in Judicial Reasoning. Wheeler, Walter C., ed. LC 75-31367. 1978. Repr. of 1964 ed. lib. bdg. 14.00x (ISBN 0-8371-8525-4, HOLC). Greenwood.

Holmes, Oliver W., Jr. Collected Legal Papers. 8.50 (ISBN 0-8446-1241-3). Peter Smith.

Iyer, V. Krishna. Of Law & Life. 1980. text ed. 15.00x (ISBN 0-686-59475-4, Pub. by Vikas India). Advent NY.

Laski, Harold J. Studies in Law & Politics. facs. ed. LC 68-22106. (Essay Index Reprint Ser). 1932. 16.00 (ISBN 0-8369-0608-X). Arno.

--Studies in Law & Politics. LC 68-57616. (Illus.). 1969. Repr. of 1932 ed. lib. bdg. 14.00x (ISBN 0-8371-0528-5, LALP). Greenwood.

--Studies in Law & Politics. 1969. Repr. of 1932 ed. 19.50 (ISBN 0-208-00731-8, Archon). Shoe String.

Llewellyn, Karl N. Bramble Bush. LC 51-1727. 1960. 8.00 (ISBN 0-379-00073-3). Oceana.

Macmillan, Hugh P. Law & Other Things. facs. ed. LC 76-152195. (Essay Index Reprint Ser). 1937. 16.00 (ISBN 0-8369-2196-8). Arno.

Marke, Julius J., ed. Holmes Reader. rev. ed. LC 55-5961. 1964. pap. 2.50 (ISBN 0-379-11301-5). Oceana.

Merryman, John H., ed. Stanford Legal Essays. LC 75-182. 480p. 1975. 18.50x (ISBN 0-8047-0884-3). Stanford U Pr.

Mersky, Roy M., ed. Conference on Transnational Economic Boycotts & Coercion, 2 vols. LC 78-7049. 1978. 85.00 set (ISBN 0-379-20335-9). Oceana.

New York University School of Law. Annual Survey of American Law 1977. LC 46-30513. (Annual Survey of American Law Ser.). 1978. 25.00 (ISBN 0-379-12236-7). Oceana.

Paulsen, Monrad G., ed. Legal Institutions Today & Tomorrow: The Centennial Conference Volume of the Columbia Law School. LC 80-11632. xiv, 346p. 1980. Repr. of 1959 ed. lib. bdg. 31.50x (ISBN 0-313-22322-X, CMLI). Greenwood.

Pollock, Frederick. Essays in the Law. LC 69-19230. 1969. Repr. of 1922 ed. 19.50 (ISBN 0-208-00807-1, Archon). Shoe String.

--Genius of the Common Law. LC 12-6106. Repr. of 1912 ed. 16.00 (ISBN 0-404-05075-1). AMS Pr.

--Oxford Lecture: And Other Discourses. LC 76-39718. (Essay Index Reprint Ser.). Repr. of 1890 ed. 18.00 (ISBN 0-8369-2780-X). Arno.

Pound, Roscoe. Formative Era of American Law. 7.00 (ISBN 0-8446-1359-2). Peter Smith.

Reisman, W. Michael & Weston, Burns H., eds. Toward World Order & Human Dignity: Essays in Honor of Myres S. McDougal. LC 75-36109. (Illus.). 1976. 25.00 (ISBN 0-02-926290-9). Free Pr.

Root, Elihu. Men & Policies: Addresses. facs. ed. Bacon, Robert & Scott, J. B., eds. LC 68-22942. (Essay Index Reprint Ser). 1968. Repr. of 1924 ed. 19.50 (ISBN 0-8369-0832-5). Arno.

Samuels, Warren J. & Schmid, A. Allan. Law & Economics: An Institutionalist Perspective. 272p. 1980. lib. bdg. 18.50 (ISBN 0-89838-049-9). Kluwer Boston.

Sayre, Paul, ed. Interpretations of Modern Legal Philosophies: Essays in Honor of Roscoe Pound. ix, 807p. 1981. Repr. of 1947 ed. lib. bdg. 48.50x (ISBN 0-8377-1122-3). Rothman.

Seebohm, Frederic. Tribal Custom in Anglo-Saxon Law Being an Essay Supplemental to 'The English Village Community' & 'The Tribal System in Wales' LC 79-190292. xvi, 538p. 1972. Repr. of 1911 ed. lib. bdg. 25.00x (ISBN 0-8377-2605-0). Rothman.

Shriver, H. C., ed. Justice Oliver Wendell Holmes: His Book Notices & Uncollected Letters & Papers. LC 72-10336. (American Constitutional & Legal History Ser). 300p. 1973. Repr. of 1936 ed. lib. bdg. 29.50 (ISBN 0-306-70557-5). Da Capo.

Smith, Munroe. General View of European Legal History & Other Papers. LC 28-701. Repr. of 1927 ed. 16.50 (ISBN 0-404-06127-3). AMS Pr.

Snyder, William L. Great Speeches by Great Lawyers: A Collection of Arguments & Speeches Before Courts & Juries by Eminent Lawyers, with Introductory Notes, Analyses, Etc. xvi, 748p. 1981. Repr. of 1881 ed. lib. bdg. 47.50x (ISBN 0-8377-1118-5). Rothman.

Stone, Harlan F. Law & Its Administration. LC 33-17836. Repr. of 1924 ed. 20.00 (ISBN 0-404-06284-9). AMS Pr.

Thomas, John L. The Law of Constructive Contempt: The Shepherd Case Reviewed. 270p. 1980. Repr. of 1904 ed. lib. bdg. 24.00x (ISBN 0-8377-1203-3). Rothman.

Timberg, Sigmund & Zaidins, Earle W., eds. Proceedings. Incl. Symposium on Twenty Years of Robinson-Putman, the Record & the Issues; Symposium on the House Counsel; Attorney General's Committee Report. 210p. 1956. 10.00 (ISBN 0-87956-003-7). Fed Legal Pubn.

Welzel, Hans. Abhandlungen zum Strafrecht zur Rechtsphilosophie. viii, 366p. (Ger.). 1975. 79.50x (ISBN 3-11-004792-6). De Gruyter.

Windolph, F. Lyman. Selected Essays. LC 72-186116. 1972. 7.50 (ISBN 0-685-36105-5). Franklin & Marsh.

Wormuth, Francis D. Essays in Law & Politics. Nelson, Dalmas H. & Sklar, Richard L., eds. (National University Pubns. Multi-Disciplinary Studies in the Law). 1978. 16.50 (ISBN 0-8046-9211-4). Kennikat.

Yntema, Hessel E., ed. American Journal of Comparative Law Reader. LC 66-11925. 520p. (Orig.). 1966. 12.50 (ISBN 0-379-11702-9); pap. 6.00 (ISBN 0-379-11702-9). Oceana.

LAW-BIBLIOGRAPHY

see also Information Storage and Retrieval Systems-Law; Legal Literature

Andrews, Joseph L., et al, eds. The Law in the United States of America: A Selective Bibliographical Guide. LC 64-22264. 100p. 1966. 8.50x (ISBN 0-8147-0009-8). NYU Pr.

Association Of American Law School. Law Books Recommended for Libraries. (Compilation of 46 subject lists complete in ten binders). 1967-70. loose leaf 475.00x, with 1974-1976 suppl. (ISBN 0-8377-0201-1). Rothman.

Bibliographic Guide to Law: 1976. (Bibliographic Guides Ser.). 1976. lib. bdg. 75.00 (ISBN 0-8161-6828-8). G K Hall.

Bryson, William H. Census of Law Books in Colonial Virginia. LC 77-22067. 1978. 12.00x (ISBN 0-8139-0746-2). U Pr of Va.

Carbone, Salvatore & Gueze, Raoul. Draft Model Law on Archives: Descriptions & Text. LC 72-82782. (Documentation, Libraries, Archives Studies & Research, No. 1). 225p. (Orig.). 1972. pap. 8.75 (ISBN 92-3-100962-1, U171, UNESCO). Unipub.

Clagett, Helen L. A Guide to the Law & Legal Literature of Bolivia. 1977. lib. bdg. 75.00 (ISBN 0-8490-1918-4). Gordon Pr.

--A Guide to the Law & Legal Literature of Paraguay. 1977. 75.00 (ISBN 0-8490-1919-2). Gordon Pr.

--A Guide to the Law & Legal Literature of Urug. 1977. lib. bdg. 75.00 (ISBN 0-8490-1920-6). Gordon Pr.

--A Guide to the Law & Legal Literature of Argentina. 1977. lib. bdg. 75.00 (ISBN 0-8490-1921-4). Gordon Pr.

--A Guide to the Law & Legal Literature of the Mexican States. 1977. 75.00 (ISBN 0-8490-1922-2). Gordon Pr.

Davies, Bernita J. & Rooney, Francis J. Research in Illinois Law. LC 54-12404. 1954. 7.50 (ISBN 0-379-11652-9). Oceana.

De Vergie, Adrienne & Kell, Mary K. Location Guide to the Manuscripts of Supreme Court Justices. rev. ed. (Tarlton Law Library Legal Bibliography Ser.: No. 24). 146p. 1981. 15.00 (ISBN 0-935630-07-4). U of Tex Tarlton Law Lib.

Dooley, Dennis A., ed. Index to State Bar Association Reports & Proceedings. LC 76-48816. 1976. Repr. lib. bdg. 30.00 (ISBN 0-930342-30-5). W S Hein.

Eder, Phanor J. Law Books in Spanish Translation. LC 66-64733. 1966. 10.00 (ISBN 0-8130-0071-8). U Presses Fla.

French, Harriet L. Research in Florida Law. 2nd ed. LC 65-27630. 1965. 7.50 (ISBN 0-379-11653-7). Oceana.

Friend, W. L. Anglo-American Legal Bibliographies. xii, 166p. 1966. Repr. of 1944 ed. 15.00x (ISBN 0-8377-2128-8). Rothman.

Friend, William L. Anglo-American Legal Bibliographies: An Annotated Guide. LC 78-168085. Repr. of 1944 ed. 10.00 (ISBN 0-404-02599-4). AMS Pr.

Griswold, H. E. Catalog of Law Books: Reference Catalogue of Law Books Published Prior to 1894. LC 76-52290. 1977. Repr. lib. bdg. 27.50 (ISBN 0-930342-31-3). W S Hein.

Hicks, Frederick C. Men & Books Famous in the Law. LC 72-81454. (Illus.). vi, 259p. 1972. Repr. of 1921 ed. 20.00x (ISBN 0-8377-2230-6). Rothman.

Hoffman, David. A Course of Legal Study, Addressed to Students & the Profession Generally, 2 vols. in 1. LC 72-37980. (American Law Ser.: The Formative Years). 888p. 1972. Repr. of 1836 ed. 38.00 (ISBN 0-405-04023-7). Arno.

International Directory of Bar Associations. 3rd ed. LC 73-78886. ix, 45p. 1973. pap. 2.00 (ISBN 0-910058-57-1). Am Bar Foun.

Jacobstein, J. Myron & Pimsleur, Meira. Law Books in Print: Through 1969, 4 vols. LC 76-12173. 1976. Set. lib. bdg. 300.00 (ISBN 0-87802-010-1). Glanville.

Jacobstein, J. Myron & Pimsleur, Meira G., eds. Law Books in Print Through 1969, 3 vols. LC 74-160114. 1971. Set. 75.00x (ISBN 0-87802-002-0). Glanville.

--Law Books in Print, 1965: Through 1965, 2 vols. 1966. Set. 50.00 (ISBN 0-87802-000-4). Glanville.

Johnson, Herbert A. Imported Eighteenth-Century Law Treatises in American Libraries, 1700-1799. LC 78-7368. (Illus.). 1978. 16.50x (ISBN 0-87049-220-9). U of Tenn Pr.

Keitt, Lawrence. Annotated Bibliography of Bibliographies of Statutory Materials of the United States. xvii, 191p. 1934. 6.50x (ISBN 0-8377-2325-6). Rothman.

Law Books 1876-1981, 4 vols. 4628p. until sept. 30th 325.00 (ISBN 0-8352-1397-8); thereafter 375.00 (ISBN 0-686-73341-X). Bowker.

Leideritz, Paula M. Key to the Study of East European Law. 1978. pap. 16.00 (ISBN 90-268-0980-8, Pub. by Kluwer Law Netherlands). Kluwer Boston.

Library of Congress. Bibliographic Guide to Law. 1979. lib. bdg. 99.50 (ISBN 0-8161-6873-3). G K Hall.

--Bibliographic Guide to Law: Nineteen Seventy-Eight. (Library Catalogs-Bib. Guides). 1979. lib. bdg. 95.00 (ISBN 0-8161-6856-3). G K Hall.

--Bibliographic Guide to Law: 1977. 1977. lib. bdg. 75.00 (ISBN 0-8161-6841-5). G K Hall.

Pederson, Virgil L. A Checklist of the American Bar Association Materials in the William Nelson Cromwell Library of the American Bar Foundation As of December 31, 1975. Lachmann, Dorothy H., ed. 1977. 20.00 (ISBN 0-910058-80-6). Am Bar Foun.

Pimsleur, M. G., ed. Checklists of Basic American Legal Publications, 5 pts. Incl. Pt. 1. Statutes; Pt. 2. Session Laws; Pt. 3. Attorneys General Opinions & Reports; Pt. 4. Judicial Councils; Pt. 5. Restatements. (AALL Publications Ser: No. 4). (5 sections with 1978 supplement). looseleaf bdg., 1978 supplement incl. 140.00x (ISBN 0-8377-0104-X). Rothman.

Readers' Guide to the Tarlton Law Library. rev. & updated ed. (Illus.). 27p. 1981. 2.00 (ISBN 0-686-75485-9). U of Tex Tarlton Law Lib.

Research Libraries of the New York Public Library & the Library of Congress. Bibliographic Guide to Law: 1980. (Library Catalogs Bib. Guides Ser.). 1981. lib. bdg. 125.00 (ISBN 0-8161-6889-X). G K Hall.

Schultz, J. S. Comparative Statutory Sources. 2nd ed. LC 78-60176. 1978. 19.50 (ISBN 0-930342-62-3). W S Hein.

Soule, Charles C. Lawyer's Manual of Lawbooks & Citations. 507p. 1973. Repr. of 1883 ed. lib. bdg. 25.00 (ISBN 0-87821-189-6). Milford Hse.

Surrency, Erwin C. Research in Pennsylvania Law. 2nd ed. LC 65-27629. 1965. 11.00 (ISBN 0-379-11651-0). Oceana.

Surrency, Erwin C., et al. Guide to Legal Research with 1966 Supplement. LC 59-14272. (Orig.). 1959. pap. 6.00 (ISBN 0-379-00111-X). Oceana.

Szladits, Charles. Guide to Foreign Legal Materials: French, German, Swiss. LC 59-8608. 1959. 25.00 (ISBN 0-379-11751-7). Oceana.

Szladits, Charles, ed. A Bibliography of Foreign & Comparative Law: Books & Articles in English, 1955-77, Supplements 1972, 73, 74, 5 vols., 4 supplements. 1978. lib. bdg. 40.00 ea. pap. 15.00 ea. supplements; pap. 17.50 1975 supplement (ISBN 0-685-94149-3). Oceana.

Tseng, Henry P. Complete Guide to Legal Materials in Microform. 1976. 44.00 (ISBN 0-89093-099-6). U Pubns Amer.

--Complete Guide to Legal Materials in Microforms: 1980 Supplement. 1980. perfect bdg. 25.00 (ISBN 0-9602406-2-4). AMCO Intl.

--Complete Guide to Legal Materials in Microform: 1976 Supplement. 1977. pap. 17.00 (ISBN 0-89093-102-X). U Pubns Amer.

University of Cambridge Squire Law Library. Law Catalogue, 14 vols. 1974. Set. 700.00 (ISBN 0-379-20176-3). Oceana.

LAW-BIOGRAPHY

see also Judges; Lawyers

Binney, Charles C. Life of Horace Binney. LC 72-2577. (Select Bibliographies Reprint Ser). 1972. Repr. of 1903 ed. 24.00 (ISBN 0-8369-6849-2). Arno.

Burnett, Gilbert. The Life & Death of Sir Matthew Hale, Kt: Sometime Lord Chief Justice of His Majesties Court of Kings Bench. LC 70-181890. 128p. 1972. Repr. of 1682 ed. text ed. 12.50x (ISBN 0-8377-1934-8). Rothman.

Cosgrove, Richard A. The Rule of Law: Albert Venn Dicey, Victorian Jurist. LC 79-18027. (Studies in Legal History Ser.). xv, 319p. 1980. 19.50x (ISBN 0-8078-1410-5). U of NC Pr.

Davis, Deane C. Justice in the Mountains: Stories & Tales by a Vermont Country Lawyer. LC 80-82866. (Illus.). 192p. 1980. 9.95 (ISBN 0-933050-05-4); pap. 6.95 (ISBN 0-933050-06-2). New Eng Pr VT.

Turow, Scott. One "L". LC 76-57246. 1977. 8.95 (ISBN 0-399-11932-9). Putnam.

Vanderbilt, Arthur T., 2nd. Changing Law: A Biography of Arthur T. Vanderbilt. (Illus.). 1976. 17.50 (ISBN 0-8135-0811-8). Rutgers U Pr.

Woolrych, Humphrey W. The Life of the Right Honourable Sir Edward Coke, Knt. Lord Chief of the King's Bench. LC 76-181857. 243p. 1972. Repr. of 1826 ed. text ed. 17.50x (ISBN 0-8377-2727-8). Rothman.

LAW-CODIFICATION

De Le, Vergne. Orleans Digest of Laws (with Moreau Lislet Notes) 1972. 25.00 (ISBN 0-685-42975-X). Claitors.

Dhokalia, R. P. The Codification of Public International Law. LC 66-11927. 1971. 22.50 (ISBN 0-379-00264-7). Oceana.
Graveson, R. H. One Law: On Jurisprudence & the Unification of Law - Selected Essays, Vol. 2. 1977. 40.25 (ISBN 0-7204-0487-8, North-Holland). Elsevier.
International Institute for the Unification of Private Law. Digest of Legal Activities of International Organizations & Other Institutions. 4th ed. LC 74-19327. 1980. 85.00 (ISBN 0-379-00525-5); suppplement 1977 15.00 (ISBN 0-379-00525-5). Oceana.
International Institute for the Unification of Private Law: Yearbook. Set Vols. 1926-55 4 vols. 48.00 (ISBN 0-685-01638-2); Set Vols. 1956-71 fifteen vols. 160.00 (ISBN 0-685-01639-0). Oceana.
Schwartz, Bernard, ed. The Code Napoleon & the Common-Law World. LC 73-16951. 438p. 1975. Repr. of 1956 ed. lib. bdg. 28.75 (ISBN 0-8371-7250-0, SCCN). Greenwood.
Science of Legal Method. LC 68-54756. (Modern Legal Philosophy Ser.: Vol. 9). Repr. of 1917 ed. 20.00x (ISBN 0-678-04520-8). Kelley.

LAW–CONSTRUCTION
see Law–Interpretation and Construction

LAW–DATA PROCESSING
National Center for State Courts. Computer-Aided Transcription in the Courts: Executive Summary. (Illus., Orig.). 1981. pap. write for info. (ISBN 0-89656-052-X, R0058). Natl Ctr St Courts.
--Computer-Aided Transcription in the Courts. (Illus., Orig.). 1981. pap. 12.50 (ISBN 0-89656-051-1, R0057). Natl Ctr St Courts.

LAW–DICTIONARIES
see also Law–Terms and Phrases
Anderson, R. Anglo-Scandinavian Law Dictionary. 1977. pap. 15.00x (ISBN 82-00-02365-6, Dist. by Columbia U Pr). Universitet.
Antolinez, Crescencio. Fachwoerterbuch Fur Recht und Verwaltung. (Span. & Ger.). 1970. leatherette 25.00 (ISBN 3-452-17065-9, M-7398, Pub. by Carl Heymanns Verlag KG). French & Eur.
Backe, Torild, et al. Concise Swedish-English Glossary of Legal Terms. 164p. 1973. text ed. 13.50x (ISBN 0-8377-0305-0). Rothman.
Barraine, Raymond. Nouveau Dictionnaire de Droit et de Sciences Economiques. 540p. (Fr.). 1974. 22.50 (ISBN 0-686-56779-X, M-6023). French & Eur.
Becher, H. Woerterbuch der Deutschen und Spanischen Rects und Wirtschaftssprache, Vol. 2. (Ger. -Span.). 1972. 70.00 (ISBN 3-406-00470-9, M-7022). French & Eur.
--Woerterbuch der Spanischen und Deutschen Rechts und Wirtschaftssprache, Vol. 1. (Span. -Ger.). 1971. 76.00 (ISBN 3-406-00469-5, M-6956). French & Eur.
Beseler, D. & Jacobs, B. Technical Dictionary of Anglo-American Legal Terminology. 3rd ed. 385p. (Ger. & Eng.). 1971. 57.50 (ISBN 3-11-002187-0, M-7636, Pub. by de Gruyter). French & Eur.
Beseler, D. v. & Jacobs, B., eds. Law Dictionary: Technical Dictionary of Anglo-American Legal Terminology, German-English. 3rd rev. ed. 385p. 1971. 56.00x (ISBN 3-11-006775-7); pap. 45.00x (ISBN 3-11-002187-0). De Gruyter.
Beseler, Dora Von & Jacobs, Barbara. Law Dictionary: Fachwoerterbuch der anglo-Amerikanischen Rechtssprache, English-Deutsch. 3rd. rev. ed. (Ger.). 1976. 123.25x (ISBN 3-11-006774-9); pap. 111.00x (ISBN 3-11-001698-2). De Gruyter.
Black, Henry C. Black's Law Dictionary. 5th ed. Nolan, Joseph R. & Connolly, Michael J., eds. LC 79-12547. 1511p. 1979. text ed. 17.95 (ISBN 0-8299-2041-2); deluxe ed. 37.50 (ISBN 0-8299-2045-5). West Pub.
Bonnefoi, Alexandre. Woerterbuch des Arbeits und Sozialrechtd. (Ger. -Fr.). 1975. 36.00 (ISBN 3-19-006293-5, M-6938). French & Eur.
Columbia University Law Library, New York. Dictionary Catalog of the Columbia University Law Library, 28 Vols. 1969. Set. lib. bdg. 2750.00 (ISBN 0-8161-0800-5). G K Hall.
The Complete Encyclopedia of Legal Knowledge for Small Business Survival. LC 80-65101. 1980. write for info. (ISBN 0-89648-083-6); pap. write for info. (ISBN 0-89648-082-8). Citizens Law.
Conte, Giuseppe. Woerterbuch der Deutschen und Italienischen Wirtschafts und Rechtssprache, Vol. 1. 2nd ed. (It. -Ger.). 1971. 30.00 (ISBN 3-406-01195-0, M-7028). French & Eur.
--Woerterbuch der Deutschen und Italienischen Wirtschafts und Rechtssprache, Vol. 2. 2nd ed. (Ger. -It.). 1969. 30.00 (ISBN 3-406-00887-9, M-7027). French & Eur.
Coughlin, George C. Law for the Layman. LC 75-547. 320p. 1976. pap. 2.95 (ISBN 0-06-465020-0, PBN 5000, BN). Har-Row.
Cowell, John. The Interpreter: Or, Book Containing the Signification of Words. LC 76-25757. (English Experience Ser.: No. 231). 584p. 1970. Repr. of 1607 ed. 69.00 (ISBN 90-221-0231-9). Walter J Johnson.
Curzon, L. B. A Dictionary of Law. 384p. 1979. pap. 14.95x (ISBN 0-7121-0380-5, Pub. by Macdonald & Evans England). Intl Ideas.
Dictionnaire de Droit, 2 vols. 2nd ed. (Fr.). 1966. Set. 17.50 (ISBN 0-686-57096-0, M-6120). French & Eur.
Dietl, C. Woerterbuch des Wirtschafts, Rechts und Handelssprache. (Eng. & Ger., Dictionary of Economic, Legal & Commercial Terms). 1970. 33.00 (ISBN 3-87527-003-7, M-6939). French & Eur.
Doucet, Michel. Woerterbuch der Deutschen und Franzoesischen Rechtssprache, Vol. 1. 2nd ed. (Ger. -Fr.). 1966. 28.00 (ISBN 3-406-00969-7, M-7030). French & Eur.
--Woerterbuch der Deutschen und Franzoesischen Rechtssprache, Vol. 2. 2nd ed. (Ger. -Fr.). 1977. 54.00 (ISBN 3-406-01196-9, M-7029). French & Eur.
Douret, Michel. Dictionnaire Juridique et Economique, 1: Francais-Allemand. 2nd ed. (Fr.-Ger.). 1967. 39.95 (ISBN 0-686-57122-3, M-6170). French & Eur.
Egbert, Lawrence D. Multilingual Law Dictionary: English, French, Spanish, German. LC 77-25072. 1978. lib. bdg. 50.00 (ISBN 0-379-00589-1); pap. 37.00 (ISBN 0-379-00598-0). Oceana.
ESQ. a Lawyers Desk Treasure, Release No. 2. rev ed. LC 76-8795. 1981. 27.50 (ISBN 0-915362-18-X). M K Heller.
Faruqi, Harith. Law Dictionary (English-Arabic) rev. ed. 1972. 35.00x (ISBN 0-86685-065-1). Intl Bk Ctr.
Finnegan, Edward G., ed. New Webster's Law for Everyone: Vest Pocket Edition. 1980. pap. 1.75 (ISBN 0-8326-0049-0, 6452). Delair.
Gifis, Steven H. Dictionary of Legal Terms. Date not set. pap. 2.95 (ISBN 0-8120-2013-8). Barron.
Gilmer, Wesley. The Law Dictionary. 1981. pap. 6.00 (ISBN 0-684-17329-8, ScribT). Scribner.
--The Law Dictionary. LC 72-95860. 1973. pap. text ed. 6.00 (ISBN 0-87084-149-1). Anderson Pub Co.
Goehler, Erich. Lexikon des Nebenstrafrechts. 2nd ed. (Ger.). 1977. pap. 44.00 (ISBN 3-406-01806-8, M-7245). French & Eur.
Gordon, Frank S. & Hemnes, Thomas. The Legal Word Book. 1978. 7.95 (ISBN 0-395-26662-9). HM.
Gritschneder, Otto. Ullstein Lexikon des Rechts. (Ger.). 1971. 20.00 (ISBN 3-550-06018-1, M-7677, Pub. by Ullstein Verlag/VVA). French & Eur.
Hamilton, Harper. Harper Hamilton's Law Dictionary for Laymen. 1978. pap. 6.95 (ISBN 0-685-86645-9). Stein & Day.
Harugi, Harith. Law Dictionary (Arabic-English) 1972. 30.00x (ISBN 0-86685-085-6). Intl Bk Ctr.
Hemphill, Charles F., Jr. & Hemphill, Phyllis. Dictionary of Practical Law. 1979. text ed. 12.95 (ISBN 0-13-210567-5, Spec); pap. text ed. 4.95 (ISBN 0-13-210559-4). P-H.
Herbst, R. Dictionary of Commercial, Financial & Legal Terms, 3 Vols. (Eng, Fr. & Ger.). 98.60 ea.; Vol. I. (ISBN 3-85942-000-3); Vol. II. (ISBN 3-85942-006-2); Vol. III. Adler.
--Dictionary of Commerical, Financial & Legal Terms, 3 Vols. 2nd ed. (Eng, Fr, & Ger.). Set. 330.00 (ISBN 0-686-76877-9); Vol. 1. 125.00 ea. (ISBN 3-8594-2000-3). Vol. 2 (ISBN 3-8594-2006-2). Vol. 3 (ISBN 3-8594-2002-X). Heinman.
Herbst, Robert. Dictionary of Commerce, Finance & Law. (Eng. -Ger.). 1975. 92.00 (ISBN 3-85942-003-8, M-7118). French & Eur.
--Woerterbuch der Handels, Finanz und Rechtssprache. 2nd ed. (Ger., Eng. & Fr., Dictionary of Commercial, Fininancial & Legal Terms). 1975. 92.00 (ISBN 3-85942-001-1, M-7002). French & Eur.
Howell, John C. The Family Encyclopedia of Practical Legal Knowledge. LC 80-65102. 1980. write for info. (ISBN 0-89648-085-2); pap. write for info. Citizens Law.
Jordana de Pozas, Luis & Merlin, Olivier. Dictionnaire Juridique, Francais-Espagnol, Espagnol-Francais. 608p. (Fr.-Span.). 1968. 45.00 (ISBN 0-686-57112-6, M-6148). French & Eur.
Karcsay, Sandor. Woerterbuch der Ungarischen Rechts und Verwaltungssprache, Vol. 1. 2nd ed. (Ger. & Hung.). 1969. 38.00 (ISBN 3-406-03325-3, M-6947). French & Eur.
Keyes, W. Noel. Keyes Encyclopedic Dictionary of Procurement Law: Definitions of Legal Terms & Concepts in Private Procurement & Public Procurement of Federal, State & Local Governments, Their Contractors & Subcontractors. LC 75-9984. 500p. 1976. text ed. 100.00x looseleaf (ISBN 0-379-00311-2); supplements 1 & 2 20.00 ea. Oceana.
Kniepkamp, H. P. Legal Dictionary. (Eng-Ger. & Ger-Eng.). 26.00 (ISBN 3-7678-0013-6). Adler.
Langendorf, Hans. Woerterbuch der Deutschen und Nierderlaendischen Rechtssprache, Vol. 1. (Dutch-Ger.). 1976. 44.00 (ISBN 3-406-06672-0, M-7025). French & Eur.
--Woerterbuch der Deutschen und Nierderlaendischen Rechtssprache, Vol. 2. (Dutch-Ger.). 1976. 44.00 (ISBN 3-406-06673-9, M-7026). French & Eur.
Law Dictionary for Laymen. LC 80-65097. 1980. write for info. (ISBN 0-89648-074-7); pap. write for info. (ISBN 0-89648-075-5). Citizens Law.
Le Docte, E. Dictionnaire des Termes Juridique en Quartre Langues: Francais, Neerlandais, Anglais, Allemand. (Fr., Dutch, Eng. & Ger.). 1978. 95.00 (ISBN 0-686-57008-1, M-6349). French & Eur.
Le Docte, E., ed. Legal Dictionary in Four Languages. 2nd ed. 696p. 1978. 75.00x (ISBN 0-8377-0808-7). Oyez.
Matteucci, M. Dictionnaire Juridique. (Fr.-It.). 39.95 (ISBN 0-686-57042-1, M-6402). French & Eur.
Merriam-Webster Editorial Staff. Webster's Legal Speller. 1978. 3.95 (ISBN 0-87779-038-8). Merriam.
Murray, John. The Media Law Dictionary. LC 78-63257. 1978. pap. text ed. 7.50 (ISBN 0-8191-0616-X). U Pr of Amer.
Neumann, Hugo. Dictionnaire Juridique Francais-Allemand, Allemand-Francais. Quemner, Thomas A., ed. 592p. (Fr.-Ger.). 1964. 59.95 (ISBN 0-686-57058-8, M-6425). French & Eur.
Norton-Kyshe, J. W. Dictionary of Legal Quotations. 75.00 (ISBN 0-8490-0037-8). Gordon Pr.
Norton-Kyshe, James W. Dictionary of Legal Quotations. LC 68-30648. 1968. Repr. of 1904 ed. 36.00 (ISBN 0-8103-3189-6). Gale.
Oran, Daniel. Law Dictionary for Non-Lawyers. 333p. 1980. pap. text ed. 6.95 (ISBN 0-8299-2062-5). West Pub.
Pallares, Eduardo. Diccionario Teorico y Practico del Juicio de Amparo. 321p. (Span.). 17.50 (ISBN 0-686-56705-6, S-21916). French & Eur.
Parsenow, Gunther. Fachwoerterbuch Fur Recht und Wirtschaft. 504p. (Swed. & Ger.). 1975. 68.00 (ISBN 3-452-18010-7, M-7399, Pub. by Carl Heymanns Verlag KG). French & Eur.
Philo, Harry, et al. Lawyers Desk Reference, 2 vols. 6th ed. 1979. 85.00 (ISBN 0-686-27087-8). Lawyers Co-Op.
Pina, Rafael de. Diccionario de Derecho. 355p. (Span.). 25.95 (ISBN 0-686-56688-2, S-12345). French & Eur.
Potonnier, Georges. Woerterbuch fuer Wirtschaft: Recht und Handel, Vol. 1. (Ger. -Fr.). 1970. 56.00 (ISBN 3-87097-030-8, M-6919). French & Eur.
--Woerterbuch fuer Wirtschaft: Recht und Handel, Vol. 2. (Fr. -Ger.). 1970. 80.00 (ISBN 3-87097-031-6, M-6918). French & Eur.
Quemner. Dictionaire Juridique Francais-Anglais, Anglais-Francais, 2 vols. in 1. 75.00 (ISBN 0-685-36688-X). French & Eur.
Quemner, T. A. French-English, English-French Legal Dictionary. new ed. Baleyte, Jean & Kurgansky, Alexander, eds. 75.00 (ISBN 0-685-01106-2). Heinman.
Radin, Max & Greene, Lawrence G., eds. Law Dictionary. rev. ed. LC 74-123997. (Illus.). 1970. 17.50 (ISBN 0-379-00465-8). Oceana.
Redden, Kenneth R. & Veron, Enid L. Modern Legal Glossary. 576p. 1980. 19.00 (ISBN 0-87215-237-5). Michie-Bobbs.
Renner, R. & Tooth, J. Rechtssprache Englisch-Deutsch. 526p. (Ger.). 1971. 35.00 (ISBN 3-19-006280-3, M-7597, Pub. by M. Hueber). French & Eur.
Robb, Louis A. Diccionario de Terminos Legales Espanol-Ingles e Ingles-Espanol: Spanish-English, English-Spanish Dictionary of Legal Terms. pap. 13.95 (ISBN 0-88332-134-3). Larousse.
--Dictionary of Legal Terms: Spanish-English,English-Spanish. 1976. pap. 10.95x (ISBN 0-686-19954-5). Intl Learn Syst.
Romain, Alfred. Dictionary of German & English Legal & Economic Terminology, Vol. 1. (Eng. -Ger.). 1976. 78.00 (ISBN 3-406-03370-9, M-7101). French & Eur.
--Dictionary of German & English Legal & Economic Terminology, Vol. 2. (Ger. -Fr.). 1975. 78.00 (ISBN 3-406-03371-7, M-7100). French & Eur.
Roshton, M. Legal Secretary's Concise Dictionary. 1974. 5.50 (ISBN 0-685-42669-6). Claitors.
Rothenberg, Robert. The Plain-Language Law Dictionary. (Reference Ser.). 1981. pap. 7.95 (ISBN 0-14-051109-1). Penguin.
Sprudzs, Adolph. Italian Abbreviations & Symbols: Law & Related Subjects. LC 70-95307. 1969. 20.00 (ISBN 0-379-00451-8). Oceana.
Sturgess, H. & Hewitt, A. A Dictionary of Legal Terms & Citations. 75.00 (ISBN 0-87968-408-9). Gordon Pr.
Touati, Maurice A. Lexique Francais De la Reparation Juridique Du Dommage Corporel. 268p. (Fr.). 1976. 32.50 (ISBN 0-686-57233-5, M-6534). French & Eur.
Wahab, Ibrahim. Law Dictionary (English-Arabic) 1972. 20.00x (ISBN 0-86685-082-1). Intl Bk Ctr.
Woerterbuch der Ungarischen Rechts und Verwaltungssprache, Vol. 2. 2nd ed. (Ger. & Hung.). 1972. 38.00 (ISBN 3-406-03326-1, M-6946). French & Eur.

LAW–DIRECTORIES
see Lawyers–Directories

LAW–EXAMINATIONS
see Law Examinations

LAW–HISTORY AND CRITICISM
see also Comparative Law
Alvarez, A., et al. Progress of Continental Law in the Nineteenth Century. Register, L. B., tr. (Continental Legal History Ser.: Vol. 11). (Illus.). xlix, 558p. 1969. Repr. of 1918 ed. 22.50x (ISBN 0-8377-1900-3). Rothman.
Ames, James B. Lectures on Legal History & Miscellaneous Legal Essays. 1976. lib. bdg. 59.95 (ISBN 0-8490-2137-5). Gordon Pr.
The Boke of Iustices of Peas, the Charge with All the Processe of the Cessions. LC 76-57391. (English Experience Ser.: No. 808). 1977. Repr. of 1506 ed. lib. bdg. 11.50 (ISBN 90-221-0808-2). Walter J Johnson.
Bott, Edmund. A Collection of Decisions of the Court of the King Bench Upon the Poor Laws. Berkowitz, David S. & Thorne, Samuel E., eds. LC 77-89222. (Classics of English Legal History in the Modern Era: Vol. 67). 399p. 1979. lib. bdg. 40.00 (ISBN 0-8240-3166-0). Garland Pub.
Bryce, James B. Studies in History & Jurisprudence, 2 Vols. facs. ed. LC 68-8444. (Essay Index Reprint Ser). 1968. Repr. of 1901 ed. Set. 40.00 (ISBN 0-8369-0261-0). Arno.
Carpenter, William S. Foundations of Modern Jurisprudence. LC 58-5314. 1958. 24.00x (ISBN 0-89197-174-2); pap. text ed. 12.95x (ISBN 0-89197-175-0). Irvington.
Catholic University Of America - School Of Law. Jubilee Law Lectures. facs. ed. LC 71-134067. (Essay Index Reprint Ser). 1939. 15.00 (ISBN 0-8369-1907-6). Arno.
Cheyney, E. P. Law in History, & Other Essays. 1977. lib. bdg. 59.95 (ISBN 0-8490-2134-0). Gordon Pr.
Chitty, Joseph. A Treatise on the Game Laws & on Fisheries, 2 vols. Berkowitz, David S. & Thorne, Samuel E., eds. LC 77-86657. (Classics of English Legal History in the Modern Era Ser.: Vol. 41). 1662p. 1979. lib. bdg. 80.00 (ISBN 0-8240-3090-7). Garland Pub.
Cohen, Jerome A., et al, eds. Essays on China's Legal Tradition. LC 79-3197. (Studies in East Asian Law, Harvard U). 1980. 30.00x (ISBN 0-691-09238-9). Princeton U Pr.
Continental Legal History Series, 10 Vols. 1969. Repr. 225.00x (ISBN 0-8377-2003-6). Rothman.
Curzon, L. B. English Legal History. 2nd ed. 352p. 1979. pap. 12.95x (ISBN 0-7121-0578-6, Pub. by Macdonald & Evans England). Intl Ideas.
Diamond, Arthur S. The Evolution of Law & Order. LC 72-9372. 342p. 1973. Repr. of 1951 ed. lib. bdg. 19.00x (ISBN 0-8371-6580-6, DIEL). Greenwood.
Folsom, Gwendolyn B. Legislative History: Research for the Interpretation of Laws. viii, 136p. 1979. Repr. of 1972 ed. lib. bdg. 17.50x (ISBN 0-8377-0532-0). Rothman.
Forkosch, Morris D. Essays in Legal History in Honor of Felix Frankfurter. 1966. 17.50 (ISBN 0-672-80026-8, Bobbs-Merrill Law). Michie-Bobbs.
Forsyth, William. The History of Lawyers, Ancient & Modern. 1977. lib. bdg. 59.95 (ISBN 0-8490-1976-1). Gordon Pr.
Fowler, William C. Local Law in Massachusetts & Connecticut. facsimile ed. LC 70-161259. (Black Heritage Library Collection). Repr. of 1875 ed. 14.00 (ISBN 0-8369-8818-3). Arno.
Friedmann, Wolfgang G. Law in a Changing Society. 2nd ed. LC 77-186229. 580p. 1970. 27.50x (ISBN 0-231-03653-1). Columbia U Pr.
Fuller, Lon L. Anatomy of the Law. LC 75-36095. 1976. Repr. of 1968 ed. lib. bdg. 15.00x (ISBN 0-8371-8622-6, FUAL). Greenwood.
Gagarin, Michael. Drakon & Early Athenian Homicide Law. LC 81-2370. (Classical Monographs). 208p. 1981. text ed. 20.00x (ISBN 0-300-02627-7). Yale U Pr.
Giraldus Cambrensis. Speculum Duorum: Or, a Mirror of Two Men. (University of Wales, History & Law Ser.: No. 27). 1974. 25.00 (ISBN 0-7083-0544-X). Verry.

Goguet, Antoine Y. & Fugere, A. C. The Origin of Laws, Arts, & Sciences & Their Progress Among the Most Ancient Nations, 3 vols. LC 72-1630. (Illus.). Repr. of 1761 ed. 87.50 set (ISBN 0-404-08230-0). AMS Pr.

Goitein, H. Primitive Ordeal & Modern Law. xvii, 302p. 1980. Repr. of 1923 ed. lib. bdg. 32.50x (ISBN 0-8377-0612-2). Rothman.

Hilkey, Charles J. Legal Development in Colonial Massachusetts, 1630-1686. LC 10-15387. (Columbia University. Studies in the Social Sciences: No. 98). Repr. of 1910 ed. 15.00 (ISBN 0-404-51098-1). AMS Pr.

Holt, Wythe. Essays in Nineteenth-Century American Legal History. LC 76-27129. (Contributions in American History: No. 60). 800p. 1976. lib. bdg. 25.00 (ISBN 0-8371-9285-4, HEN/). Greenwood.

Jacob, Giles, et al. Laws of Liberty & Property. Berkowitz, David. S. & Thorne, Samuel E., eds. LC 77-89197. (Classics of English Legal History in the Modern Era Ser.: Vol. 56). 325p. 1979. lib. bdg. 40.00 (ISBN 0-8240-3156-3). Garland Pub.

Jenkins, Dafydd, ed. Legal History Studies, 1972. 155p. 1975. pap. text ed. 12.50x (ISBN 0-7083-0588-1). Verry.

Johnson, Herbert A., ed. South Carolina Legal History. LC 79-24275. 1980. 16.50 (ISBN 0-87152-312-4). Reprint.

Jones, John W. Historical Introduction to the Theory of Law. Repr. of 1940 ed. lib. bdg. 17.50x (ISBN 0-8371-2810-2, JOTL). Greenwood.

--Historical Introduction to the Theory of Law. LC 72-96337. Repr. of 1940 ed. 11.50x (ISBN 0-678-04534-8). Kelley.

Kames, Henry H. Historical Law-Tracts. 3rd, rev. & enl. ed. LC 78-67530. Repr. of 1776 ed. 44.00 (ISBN 0-404-17659-3, KD600). AMS Pr.

Kocourek, Albert & Wigmore, John H., eds. Primitive & Ancient Legal Institutions. (Evolution of Law: Select Readings on the Origin & Development of Legal Institutions Ser.: Vol. 2). xii, 704p. 1979. Repr. of 1915 ed. lib. bdg. 38.50x (ISBN 0-8377-2329-9). Rothman.

Lodowick, Lloyd. A Briefe Conference of Divers Laws: Divided into Certain Regiments. Berkowitz, David & Thorne, Samuel, eds. LC 77-86562. (Classics of English Legal History in the Modern Era Ser.: Vol. 64). 1979. Repr. of 1602 ed. lib. bdg. 55.00 (ISBN 0-8240-3051-6). Garland Pub.

Maine, Henry. Ancient Law. 1954. 10.95x (ISBN 0-460-00734-3, Evman). Biblio Dist.

Maine, Henry S. Dissertations on Early Law & Custom Chiefly Selected from Lectures Delivered at Oxford. LC 74-25768. (European Sociology Ser.). 414p. 1975. Repr. 23.00x (ISBN 0-405-06522-1). Arno.

--Lectures on the Early History of Institutions. LC 66-21392. Repr. of 1914 ed. 15.00 (ISBN 0-8046-0296-4). Kennikat.

Marke, Julius J. Vignettes of Legal History. LC 65-22980. (Illus.). xv, 337p. 1977. Repr. of 1965 ed. lib. bdg. 15.00x (ISBN 0-8377-0832-X). Rothman.

--Vignettes of Legal History: Second Series. LC 77-23648. (Illus.). xiv, 274p. 1977. lib. bdg. 15.00x (ISBN 0-8377-0833-8). Rothman.

Mill, James. Essays on Jurisprudence Government, Liberty of the Press, Law of Nations, Education, Colony & Prison Discipline. LC 66-21685. Repr. of 1825 ed. 17.50x (ISBN 0-678-00297-5). Kelley.

Miller, Arthur R. Miller's Court. 288p. 1982. 12.95 (ISBN 0-395-31323-6). HM.

Mitchell, William. Essay on Early History of the Law Merchant: Being the Yorke Prize Essay for the Year 1903. 1969. Repr. of 1904 ed. 22.50 (ISBN 0-8337-2409-6). B Franklin.

Paul, Arnold M. Conservative Crisis & the Rule of Law: Attitudes of Bar & Bench 1887-1895. 7.50 (ISBN 0-8446-0839-4). Peter Smith.

Pollock, Frederick. First Book of Jurisprudence. 1967. 23.50 (ISBN 0-8337-2803-2). B Franklin.

Pospisil, Leopold. Anthropology of Law: A Comparative Theory. LC 70-154880. (Behavior Science Reprint Ser.). xiv, 386p. 1974. Repr. 20.00x (ISBN 0-87536-813-1). HRAFP.

Post, Gaines. Studies in Medieval Legal Thought: Public Law & the State 1100-1322. xv, 633p. Repr. of 1964 ed. lib. bdg. 30.00x (ISBN 0-87991-053-4). Porcupine Pr.

Pound, Roscoe. Interpretations of Legal History. 7.50 (ISBN 0-8446-1360-6). Peter Smith.

--Spirit of the Common Law. (gr. 11-12). text ed. 5.00x (ISBN 0-8338-0056-6). M Jones.

Read, James & Yapp, Malcolm. Law. Killingray, Margaret & O'Connor, Edmund, eds. (World History Ser.). (Illus.). (gr. 10). 1980. Repr. of 1977 ed. lib. bdg. 5.95 (ISBN 0-89908-144-4); pap. text ed. 1.95 (ISBN 0-89908-119-3). Greenhaven.

Samaha, Joel B. Law & Order in Historical Perspective: The Case of Elizabethan Essex. LC 73-812. 1974. 23.00 (ISBN 0-12-785756-7). Acad Pr.

Savigny, Friedrich K. The History of the Roman Law During the Middle Ages, Vol. 1. Cathcart, E., tr. LC 78-72146. 1979. Repr. of 1829 ed. 35.00 (ISBN 0-88355-815-7). Hyperion Conn.

Scott, James B. Law, the State & the International Community. Repr. of 1939 ed. lib. bdg. 38.00x (ISBN 0-8371-2809-9, SCLI). Greenwood.

Smith, Munroe. General View of European Legal History & Other Papers. LC 28-701. Repr. of 1927 ed. 16.50 (ISBN 0-404-06127-3). AMS Pr.

Stubbs, W. Historical Introductions to the Rolls Series. LC 68-25267. (British History Ser., No. 30). 1969. Repr. of 1902 ed. lib. bdg. 45.95 (ISBN 0-8383-0243-2). Haskell.

Ullmann, Walter. Law & Politics in the Middle Ages: An Introduction to the Sources of Medieval Political Ideas. LC 74-19415. (Sources of History Ser.). 1975. 22.50x (ISBN 0-8014-0940-3). Cornell U Pr.

Von Bar, Carl L., et al. History of Continental Criminal Law. Bell, Thomas S., et al, trs. LC 68-54743. (Continental Legal History Ser.: No. 6). Repr. of 1916 ed. 22.50x (ISBN 0-678-04507-0). Kelley.

Watson, Alan. Daube Noster: Essays in Legal History for David Daube. xvii, 374p. 1974. text ed. 22.50x (ISBN 0-686-77043-9). Rothman.

--Legal Transplants. LC 73-94276. 250p. 1974. 10.00x (ISBN 0-8139-0576-1). U Pr of Va.

Weisbrod, Carol. The Boundaries of Utopia. LC 79-1898. 1980. 15.95 (ISBN 0-394-50781-9). Pantheon.

Williams, Sam P., ed. Law Books in Review: 1974-1980. 1981. Set. 185.00 (ISBN 0-686-74113-7); Each Year. 35.00 (ISBN 0-686-74114-5). Glanville.

Wormser, Rene A. The Story of the Law. 1972. pap. 6.95 (ISBN 0-671-21333-4, Touchstone Bks). S&S.

LAW-INTERPRETATION AND CONSTRUCTION

see also Judge-Made Law; Judicial Process; Stare Decisis; Statutes

Brigham, John. Constitutional Language: An Interpretation of Judicial Decision. LC 78-4020. (Contribution in Political Science: No. 17). 1978. lib. bdg. 17.50 (ISBN 0-313-20420-9, BCO/). Greenwood.

Grace, Clive & Wilkinson, Philip. Sociological Inquiry & Legal Reasoning. LC 78-55401. 1978. 14.95x (ISBN 0-312-73972-9). St Martin.

Horovitz, J. Law & Logic: A Critical Account of Legal Argument. LC 72-76386. (Library of Exact Philosophy: Vol. 8). 240p. 1972. 24.20 (ISBN 0-387-81066-8). Springer-Verlag.

Levi, Edward H. Introduction to Legal Reasoning. rev. ed. LC 49-11213. 1962. pap. 2.25 (ISBN 0-226-47408-9, P84, Phoen). U of Chicago Pr.

Mellinkoff, David. The Language of the Law. 526p. 1963. pap. 10.95 (ISBN 0-316-56627-6). Little.

Pennock, J. Roland & Chapman, John W., eds. The Limits of Law. (Nomos Ser.: No. 15). 325p. 1973. text ed. 15.00x (ISBN 0-88311-008-3). Lieber-Atherton.

Science of Legal Method. LC 68-54756. (Modern Legal Philosophy Ser.: Vol. 9). Repr. of 1917 ed. 20.00x (ISBN 0-678-04520-8). Kelley.

Tullock, Gordon. Trials on Trial: The Pure Theory of Legal Procedure. LC 80-13113. 264p. 1980. 20.00x (ISBN 0-231-04952-8). Columbia U Pr.

LAW-JEWS

see Jewish Law

LAW-LANGUAGE

see also Bill Drafting

Bach, Heinrich. Die Thuringisch-Sachsische Kanzleisprache Bis 1325, Miteiner Neven Einleitung Von Richard K. Seymour, 2 Vols. 31.00 (ISBN 0-384-02945-0). Johnson Repr.

Bander, Edward J. Dictionary of Legal Terms & Maxims, Vol. 58. 2nd ed. 1979. 5.95 (ISBN 0-379-11119-5). Oceana.

Biskind, Elliott L. Simplify Legal Writing. LC 72-163721. 1975. lib. bdg. 8.95 (ISBN 0-668-03800-4); pap. 5.00 (ISBN 0-668-03801-2). Arco.

Brand, Norman & White, John O. Legal Writing: The Strategy of Persuasion. LC 75-38015. 300p. 1976. text ed. 9.95 (ISBN 0-312-47810-0). St Martin.

Educational Research Associates, ed. Legal Terms for Secretaries. (gr. 11-12). 1974. 3.35 (ISBN 0-89420-096-8, 299900). Natl Book.

Flesch, Rudolf. How to Write Plain English: A Book for Lawyers & Consumers. LC 76-26225. (Illus.). 144p. 1981. pap. 4.25 (ISBN 0-06-463536-8, EH 536, BN). Har-Row.

--How to Write Plain English: A Book for Lawyers & Consumers. LC 76-26225. 1979. 8.95 (ISBN 0-06-011278-6, HarpT). Har-Row.

Gilmer, Wesley. Cochran's Law Lexicon. 5th ed. LC 72-95860. 1973. Repr. text ed. 8.00 (ISBN 0-87084-148-3). Anderson Pub Co.

Mellinkoff, David. The Language of the Law. 526p. 1963. pap. 10.95 (ISBN 0-316-56627-6). Little.

Probert, Walter. Law, Language & Communication. (Amer. Lec. Behavioral Science & Law Ser.). 408p. 1972. 19.50 (ISBN 0-398-02477-4). C C Thomas.

Taylor, Richard W., ed. Life, Language, Law: Essays in Honor of Arthur F. Bentley. LC 56-8248. (Illus.). 1957. 6.00x (ISBN 0-87338-074-6). Kent St U Pr.

Till, Paul & Gargiulo, Albert. Plain Language Acts. 1979. pap. 7.50 (ISBN 0-8144-2241-1). Am Mgmt.

Weihofen, Henry. Legal Writing Style. 2nd ed. LC 79-23662. 332p. 1980. text ed. 11.95 (ISBN 0-8299-2066-8). West Pub.

Wydick, Richard C. Plain English for Lawyers. LC 79-53956. 91p. 1979. lib. bdg. 8.95 (ISBN 0-89089-175-3); pap. text ed. 3.95 (ISBN 0-89089-176-1). Carolina Acad Pr.

LAW-LITERARY HISTORY

see Jurisprudence-History

LAW-METHODOLOGY

Alchourron, C. E. & Bulygin, E. Normative Systems. LC 75-170895. (Library of Exact Philosophy: Vol. 5). (Illus.). 1971. 26.40 (ISBN 0-387-81019-6). Springer-Verlag.

Beutel, Frederick K. Democracy of the Scientific Method in Law & Policy Making. 6.25 (ISBN 0-8477-3000-X). U of PR Pr.

Bruncken, Ernest & Register, Layton B., trs. Science of Legal Method: Select Essays. (Modern Legal Philosophy Ser: Vol. 9). lxxxvi, 593p. 1969. Repr. of 1917 ed. 20.00x (ISBN 0-8377-2600-X). Rothman.

Brunsken, E. & Register, L. B., eds. The Science of Legal Method. 1977. lib. bdg. 59.95 (ISBN 0-8490-2571-0). Gordon Pr.

Dernbach, John C. & Singleton, Richard V., II. A Practical Guide to Legal Writing & Legal Method. xviii, 246p. 1981. pap. text ed. 14.95x (ISBN 0-8377-0513-4). Rothman.

Franklin, Julian H. Jean Bodin & the Sixteenth-Century Revolution in the Methodology of Law & History. LC 77-1187. 1977. Repr. of 1963 ed. lib. bdg. 15.00x (ISBN 0-8371-9525-X, FRJEB). Greenwood.

Garner, J. F. Practical Planning Law. 192p. 1981. 29.50x (ISBN 0-7099-1106-8, Pub. by Croom Helm Ltd England). Biblio Dist.

Hohfeld, Wesley N. Fundamental Legal Conceptions, As Applied in Judicial Reasoning. Wheeler, Walter C., ed. LC 75-31367. 1978. Repr. of 1964 ed. lib. bdg. 14.00x (ISBN 0-8371-8525-4, HOLC). Greenwood.

Horovitz, J. Law & Logic: A Critical Account of Legal Argument. LC 72-76386. (Library of Exact Philosophy: Vol. 8). 240p. 1972. 24.20 (ISBN 0-387-81066-8). Springer-Verlag.

Jones, Harry W., et al. Cases & Text Materials on Legal Method: Successor Edition. LC 80-13230. (University Casebook Ser.). Orig. Title: Materials for Legal Method. 817p. 1980. text ed. write for info. (ISBN 0-88277-004-7). Foundation Pr.

Nagel, Stuart S. & Neef, Marian. Legal Policy Analysis. LC 76-14046. 1977. 23.95 (ISBN 0-669-00731-5). Lexington Bks.

Stone, Julius. Legal System & Lawyers' Reasonings. 1964. 18.75x (ISBN 0-8047-0214-4). Stanford U Pr.

Tammelo, I. Modern Logic in the Service of Law. 1978. pap. 16.70 (ISBN 0-387-81486-8). Springer-Verlag.

Thibaut, J. & Walker, L. Procedural Justice: A Psychological Analysis. LC 75-15944. 1975. pap. 4.95 (ISBN 0-470-85869-9). Halsted Pr.

Waddell, Ward, Jr. Structure of Laws As Represented by Symbolic Methods. 1961. pap. 2.75 (ISBN 0-9600130-0-8). Waddell.

Wasserstrom, Richard A. The Judicial Decision: Toward a Theory of Legal Justification. LC 61-6535. 1961. 10.00x (ISBN 0-8047-0036-2); pap. 3.25 (ISBN 0-8047-0037-0, SP104). Stanford U Pr.

LAW-PERIODICALS

Blaustein, Albert P., ed. Manual on Foreign Legal Periodicals & Their Index. LC 62-11757. 1962. 17.50 (ISBN 0-379-00119-5). Oceana.

Broder, Aaron J., ed. Trial Lawyer's Quarterly & Plaintiff's Advocate, 6 vols. LC 67-27791. 1967. Set. 75.00 (ISBN 0-88238-030-3). Law-Arts.

China Law Review, 10 vols, Vols. 1-10. LC 74-28774. 1975. Repr. of 1922 ed. lib. bdg. 45.00 ea. (ISBN 0-379-20201-8); 400.00 set (ISBN 0-685-52943-6). Oceana.

Index to Legal Periodicals. 1952-70. Vols. 10-15. 85.00 ea. (ISBN 0-685-22250-0); Vols. 16 To Date. 170.00 ea. (ISBN 0-686-66572-4). Wilson.

Jones, Leonard A., ed. Index to Legal Periodical Literature, 1888-1899, 2 Vols. 1963. 40.00 (ISBN 0-379-20008-2). Oceana.

Juridical Review, First Series, Vols. 1-67, 1899-1955. Set. 250.00 (ISBN 0-685-18996-1). Oceana.

Katz, Richard N., et al, eds. An Inventory of the Records of the National Lawyers Guild, 1936-1976, & an Index to NLG Periodica, 1936-1979. LC 80-81943. (Meiklejohn Institute Inventory: No. 2). 1980. pap. 10.00 (ISBN 0-913876-12-7). Meiklejohn Civil Lib.

Mersky, Roy, et al, eds. Author's Guide to Journals in Law, Criminal Justice & Criminology. LC 78-18805. (Author's Guide to Journals Ser.). 1979. 16.95 (ISBN 0-917724-06-2). Haworth Pr.

Mersky, Roy M. & Jacobstein, J. Myron, eds. Ten Year Index to Periodical Articles Related to Law (1958-1968) LC 65-29677. 1970. 35.00 (ISBN 0-87802-050-0). Glanville.

Mersky, Roy M., et al, eds. Index to Periodical Articles Related to Law: Five Year Cumulation,(1969-1973) LC 65-29677. 428p. 1974. lib. bdg. 35.00 (ISBN 0-87802-051-9). Glanville.

Oklahoma Decisions. write for info (ISBN 0-685-37676-1). West Pub.

Oxbridge Communications, Inc., compiled by. Legal & Law Enforcement Periodicals: A Directory. LC 80-39754. 238p. 1981. 35.00 (ISBN 0-87196-335-3). Facts on File.

Oxford Lawyer, 1958-1965, 8 Vols. in 3. 1968. Set. 75.00 (ISBN 0-379-20850-4). Oceana.

South Pacific Law Review. 17.50 (ISBN 0-379-00181-0). Oceana.

Wypyski, Eugene M. Legal Periodicals in English, 4 bks. 500p. 1976. text ed. 75.00 ea. loose leaf (ISBN 0-87802-054-3). Glanville.

LAW-PHILOSOPHY

see also Free Will and Determinism; Jurisprudence; Law and Ethics; Law and Socialism

Austin, John. The Austinian Theory of Law. 1976. Repr. of 1906 ed. 45.00 (ISBN 0-403-00155-6, Regency). Scholarly.

--Lectures on Jurisprudence, or the Philosophy of Positive Law. 1976. Repr. of 1879 ed. 69.00 (ISBN 0-403-06116-4, Regency). Scholarly.

Barth, H. The Idea of Order: Contributions to a Philosophy of Politics. Hankamer, Ernest W. & Newell, William M., trs. from Ger. 209p. 1960. 24.00 (ISBN 90-277-0001-X, Pub. by Reidel Holland). Kluwer Boston.

Bastiat, Frederic. Law. 76p. 1961. 2.50 (ISBN 0-910614-30-X); pap. 1.00 (ISBN 0-910614-01-6). Foun Econ Ed.

Belaief, Gail. Spinoza's Philosophy of Law. LC 78-118275. (Studies in Philosophy: No. 24). (Illus.). 151p. (Orig.). 1971. pap. text ed. 17.65x (ISBN 90-2791-851-1). Mouton.

Benditt, Theodore M. Law As Rule & Principle: Problems of Legal Philosophy. LC 77-89180. 1978. 12.50x (ISBN 0-8047-0963-7). Stanford U Pr.

Bentham, Jeremy & Mill, John S. The Utilitarians. Incl. Principles of Morals & Legislation. Bentham; Utilitarianism & on Liberty. Mill, John S. LC 62-2159. pap. 3.50 (ISBN 0-385-08256-8, C265, Anch). Doubleday.

Berolzheimer, Fritz. World's Legal Philosophies. Jastrow, Rachel, tr. LC 68-54750. (Modern Legal Philosophy Ser: Vol. 2). 1912. 18.00x (ISBN 0-678-04514-3). Kelley.

Bigelow, Melville M., intro. by. Centralization & the Law: Scientific Legal Education, an Illustration. LC 72-181856. xviii, 296p. 1972. Repr. of 1906 ed. text ed. 16.50x (ISBN 0-8377-2004-4). Rothman.

Bodenheimer, Edgar. Power, Law & Society. LC 73-81049. 211p. 1973. 19.50x (ISBN 0-8448-0215-8). Crane-Russak Co.

Boorstin, Daniel J. Mysterious Science of the Law. 7.50 (ISBN 0-8446-1702-4). Peter Smith.

Bronaugh, Richard, ed. Philosophical Law: Authority, Equality, Adjudication, Privacy. (Contributions in Legal Studies: No. 2). 1978. lib. bdg. 19.95 (ISBN 0-8371-9809-7, BPL/). Greenwood.

Broom, Herbert. The Philosophy of Law: Being Notes of Lectures Delivered During Twenty-Three Years (1852 to 1875) in the Inner Temple Hall Adapted for Students & the Public. xi, 338p. 1980. Repr. of 1878 ed. lib. bdg. 27.50x (ISBN 0-8377-0310-7). Rothman.

Bruening, William H. Introduction to the Philosophy of Law. LC 78-62249. 1978. pap. text ed. 9.00 (ISBN 0-8191-0570-8). U Pr of Amer.

Buckland, W. W. Some Reflections on Jurisprudence. viii, 118p. 1974. Repr. of 1945 ed. 13.50 (ISBN 0-208-01407-1, Archon). Shoe String.

Cahn, Edmond. Sense of Injustice. 7.50 (ISBN 0-8446-1795-4). Peter Smith.

--The Sense of Injustice. (Midland Bks.: No. 55). (Illus.). 200p. 1964. pap. 2.95x (ISBN 0-253-20055-5). Ind U Pr.

Cairns, Huntington. Legal Philosophy from Plato to Hegel. LC 79-12703. 1980. Repr. of 1949 ed. lib. bdg. 43.75x (ISBN 0-313-21499-9, CALP). Greenwood.

Cardozo, Benjamin N. The Growth of the Law. LC 73-8154. xvi, 145p. 1973. Repr. of 1963 ed. lib. bdg. 15.75x (ISBN 0-8371-6953-4, CAGL). Greenwood.
Chambliss, William J. & Seidman, Robert B. Law, Order & Power. 1971. text ed. 18.95 (ISBN 0-201-00957-9). A-W.
Cohen, Felix. Ethical Systems & Legal Ideals. LC 75-40440. 303p. 1976. Repr. of 1933 ed. lib. bdg. 19.75x (ISBN 0-8371-8643-9, COETS). Greenwood.
Cohen, L. Jonathan. The Probable & the Provable. (Clarendon Library of Logic & Philosophy). 1977. 45.00x (ISBN 0-19-824412-6). Oxford U Pr.
Cohen, Morris R. Law & the Social Order: Essays in Legal Philosophy. 1967. Repr. of 1933 ed. 22.50 (ISBN 0-208-00484-X, Archon). Shoe String.
--Law & the Social Order: Essays in Legal Philosophy. Supplemented by Cohen's "Moral Aspects of Criminal Law". (Social & Moral Thought Ser.). 520p. (Orig.). 1982. pap. 14.95 (ISBN 0-87855-876-4). Transaction Bks.
Del Vecchio, Giorgio. Formal Bases of Law. Lisle, John, tr. LC 68-54757. (Modern Legal Philosophy Ser.: Vol. 10). Repr. of 1914 ed. 20.00x (ISBN 0-678-04521-6). Kelley.
--Formal Basis of Law. (Modern Legal Philosophy Ser.: Vol. 10). lvii, 412p. 1969. Repr. of 1914 ed. 20.00x (ISBN 0-8377-2700-6). Rothman.
De Montesquieu, Charles. Esprit des lois, 2 Vols. (Fr). pap. 2.95 ea. Larousse.
De Tourtoulon, Pierre. Philosophy in the Development of Law. Reed, Martha, tr. LC 68-54759. (Modern Legal Philosophy Ser.: Vol. 13). Repr. of 1922 ed. 25.00x (ISBN 0-678-04523-2). Kelley.
--Philosophy in the Development of Law. Cohen, Morris R., ed. Read, M. M., tr. 1977. lib. bdg. 59.95 (ISBN 0-8490-2428-5). Gordon Pr.
Dworkin, Ronald M., ed. The Philosophy of Law. (Oxford Readings in Philosophy). 1977. pap. 4.95x (ISBN 0-19-875022-6). Oxford U Pr.
Ebenstein, William. Pure Theory of Law. LC 79-96336. Repr. of 1945 ed. 9.50x (ISBN 0-678-04535-6). Kelley.
--Pure Theory of Law. LC 79-96336. xii, 211p. 1970. Repr. of 1945 ed. text ed. 9.50x (ISBN 0-8377-2100-8). Rothman.
Engel, Salo & Metall, R. A., eds. Law, State & International Legal Order: Essays in Honor of Hans Kelsen. LC 64-16881. 1964. 19.50x (ISBN 0-87049-052-4). U of Tenn Pr.
Feinberg, Joel & Gross, Hyman. Philosophy of Law. 2nd ed. 656p. 1980. text ed. 25.95x (ISBN 0-534-00835-6). Wadsworth Pub.
Finnis, John. Natural Law & Natural. (Clarendon Law Ser.). 442p. text ed. 39.50x (ISBN 0-19-876098-1); pap. text ed. 19.50x (ISBN 0-19-876110-4). Oxford U Pr.
Fouillee, A., et al. Modern French Legal Philosophy. Scott, Mrs. Franklin W. & Chamberlin, Joseph P., trs. LC 68-54754. (Modern Legal Philosophy Ser.: Vol. 7). Repr. of 1916 ed. 20.00x (ISBN 0-678-04518-6). Kelley.
--Modern French Legal Philosophy. (Modern Legal Philosophy Ser: Vol. 7). lxvi, 578p. 1969. Repr. of 1916 ed. 20.00x (ISBN 0-8377-2126-1). Rothman.
Friedmann, Wolfgang G. Legal Theory. 5th ed. LC 67-26509. 607p. 1967. 27.50x (ISBN 0-231-03100-9). Columbia U Pr.
Friedrich, Carl J. Philosophy of Law in Historical Perspective. 2nd ed. LC 57-9546. 1963. pap. 5.50 (ISBN 0-226-26466-1, P135, Phoen). U of Chicago Pr.
Friedrich, Carl J., ed. Community. (Nomos Ser: No. 2). 304p. 1959. 15.00x (ISBN 0-88311-032-6). Lieber-Atherton.
Golding, Martin P. Philosophy of Law. (Foundation of Philosophy Ser.). 176p. 1975. pap. text ed. 7.95x (ISBN 0-13-664128-8). P-H.
Golding, Martin P., ed. Nature of Law. 1966. 14.95 (ISBN 0-394-30213-3). Random.
Hall, Jerome. Readings in Jurisprudence. 1938. 15.00 (ISBN 0-672-81013-1, Bobbs-Merrill Law). Michie-Bobbs.
Hamburger, Max. Awakening of Western Legal Thought. LC 76-79515. 1969. Repr. of 1942 ed. 12.00x (ISBN 0-8196-0246-9). Biblo.
--Awakening of Western Legal Thought. Miall, Bernard, tr. Repr. of 1942 ed. lib. bdg. 15.00x (ISBN 0-8371-3103-0, HALT). Greenwood.
--Morals & Law. LC 65-15244. 1965. 12.00x (ISBN 0-8196-0151-9). Biblo.
Hegel, G. W. Philosophy of Right. Knox, T. M., tr. 1942. 42.00x (ISBN 0-19-824128-3); pap. 6.95x (ISBN 0-19-500276-8). Oxford U Pr.
Hobbes, Thomas. Dialogue Between a Philosopher & a Student of the Common Laws of England. Cropsey, Joseph, ed. LC 76-120008. 1971. lib. bdg. 11.00x (ISBN 0-226-34540-8). U of Chicago Pr.
Holmes, Oliver W., Jr., et alintro. by. Rational Basis of Legal Institutions. (Modern Legal Philosophy Ser: Vol. 14). xxxii, 603p. 1969. Repr. of 1923 ed. 20.00x (ISBN 0-8377-2525-9). Rothman.
Hughes, Graham, ed. Law, Reason, & Justice: Essays in Legal Philosophy. LC 69-19264. (Studies in Peaceful Change: Vol. 3). 269p. 1969. 15.00x (ISBN 0-8147-0212-0). NYU Pr.
Jenkins, Iredell. Social Order & the Limits of Law: A Theoretical Essay. LC 79-3216. 1980. 25.00x (ISBN 0-691-07241-8); pap. 6.95 (ISBN 0-691-02007-8). Princeton U Pr.
Jones, John W. Historical Introduction to the Theory of Law. LC 72-96337. xi, 304p. 1970. Repr. of 1940 ed. text ed. 11.50x (ISBN 0-8377-2300-0). Rothman.
Kamenka, Eugene, et al, eds. Law & Society: The Crisis in Legal Ideals. LC 78-7421. (Ideas & Ideologies Ser.). 1978. 17.50x (ISBN 0-312-47545-4). St Martin.
Kant, Immanuel. Philosophy of Law. Hastie, W., tr. LC 77-146882. 265p. Repr. of 1887 ed. lib. bdg. 15.00x (ISBN 0-678-01152-4). Kelley.
Kantorowicz, Hermann. The Definition of Law. Campbell, A. H., ed. 113p. 1980. Repr. of 1958 ed. lib. bdg. 13.50x (ISBN 0-374-94521-7). Octagon.
Kelsen, Hans. General Theory of Law & State. Wedberg, Anders, tr. LC 61-12122. 1961. Repr. of 1945 ed. 25.00 (ISBN 0-8462-0215-8). Russell.
--Pure Theory of Law. Knight, Max, tr. from Ger. LC 67-10234. (Library Reprint Ser.: Vol. 94). 1978. pap. text ed. 29.75x (ISBN 0-520-03692-1). U of Cal Pr.
Kent, Edward A., ed. Law & Philosophy: Readings in Legal Philosophy. 1970. text ed. 19.95 (ISBN 0-13-526459-6). P-H.
Kim, Hyung I. Fundamental Legal Concepts of China & the West: A Comparative Study. (National University Publications, Multidisciplinary Studies in the Law). 1981. 17.50 (ISBN 0-8046-9275-0). Kennikat.
Kipnis, Kenneth. Philosophical Issues in Law: Cases & Materials. 1977. pap. text ed. 13.50 (ISBN 0-13-662296-8). P-H.
Kisch, Guido. Studien zur humanistischen Jurisprudenz. 1972. 61.00x (ISBN 3-11-003600-2). De Gruyter.
Kohler, Josef. Philosophy of Law. Albrecht, Adalbert, tr. LC 68-54758. (Modern Legal Philosophy Ser.: Vol. 12). Repr. of 1914 ed. 18.00x (ISBN 0-678-04522-4). Kelley.
--Philosophy of Law. (Modern Legal Philosophy Ser: Vol. 12). xliv, 390p. 1969. Repr. of 1914 ed. 18.00x (ISBN 0-8377-2326-4). Rothman.
Kraines, Oscar. The World & Ideas of Ernst Freund: The Search for General Principles of Legistlation & Administrative Law. LC 73-22719. 224p. 1974. 15.95x (ISBN 0-8173-4819-0); pap. 3.50 (ISBN 0-8173-4822-0). U of Ala Pr.
Kunz, Josef L. Latin-American Philosophy of Law in the Twentieth Century. LC 50-14476. 1950. 12.50 (ISBN 0-379-00149-7). Oceana.
Lenin, V. I., et al. Soviet Legal Philosophy. Babb, Hugh W., tr. 1951. 31.00 (ISBN 0-384-56790-8). Johnson Repr.
Levy, Beryl H. Cardozo & Frontiers of Legal Thinking. LC 65-14787. Repr. of 1938 ed. 12.25 (ISBN 0-8046-0270-0). Kennikat.
Lindahl, Lars. Position & Change. Needham, Paul, tr. from Swedish. (Synthese Library: No. 112). 1977. lib. bdg. 45.00 (ISBN 90-277-0787-1, Pub. by Reidel Holland). Kluwer Boston.
MacCormick, Neil. H. L. A. Hart. Twining, William, ed. LC 81-50790. (Jurists: Profiles in Legal Theory Ser.). 192p. 1981. 18.50x (ISBN 0-8047-1107-0). Stanford U Pr.
McLean, George F., ed. Philosophy & Civil Law. LC 76-150281. (Proceedings of the American Catholic Philosophical Association: Vol. 49). 1975. pap. 8.00 (ISBN 0-918090-09-1). Am Cath Philo.
Miller, William G. Lectures on the Philosophy of Law, Designed Mainly As an Introduction to the Study of International Law. xv, 432p. 1979. Repr. of 1884 ed. lib. bdg. 35.00x (ISBN 0-8377-0834-6). Rothman.
Miraglia, Luigi. Comparative Legal Philosophies Applied to Legal Institutions. 1977. lib. bdg. 59.95 (ISBN 0-8490-1653-3). Gordon Pr.
--Comparative Legal Philosophy Applied to Legal Institutions. (Modern Legal Philosophy Ser: Vol. 3). 793p. 1969. Repr. of 1912 ed. 25.00x (ISBN 0-8377-2427-9). Rothman.
Montesquieu. The Spirit of Laws: A Compendium of the First English Editon with an English Translation of "an Essay on Causes Affecting Mind & Characters", 1737-1743. Carrithers, David W., ed. (No. 192). 1978. 34.50x (ISBN 0-520-02566-0); pap. 6.95x (ISBN 0-520-03455-4, CAMPUS SER., NO. 192). U of Cal Pr.
Montesquieu, C. de. Spirit of the Laws. (Library of Classic: No. 9). pap. text ed. 5.25 (ISBN 0-02-849270-6). Hafner.
--Spirit of the Laws. (Library of Classic: No. 9). pap. text ed. 5.25 (ISBN 0-02-849270-6). Hafner.
Montesquieu, Charles de. De l'Espirit des Lois: Les Grands Themes. 1970. 4.95 (ISBN 0-686-54781-0). French & Eur.
Moore, Ronald. Legal Norms & Legal Science: A Critical Study of Kelsen's Pure Theory of Law. LC 77-12392. 1978. text ed. 12.00x (ISBN 0-8248-0516-X). U Pr of Hawaii.
Morawetz, Thomas A. The Philosophy of Law: An Introduction. 1980. pap. text ed. 10.95 (ISBN 0-02-383340-8). Macmillan.
Morris, Clarence. Justification of the Law. LC 77-153424. 1971-72. 15.00x (ISBN 0-8122-7639-6); pap. 5.95x (ISBN 0-8122-1030-1, Pa Paperbacks). U of Pa Pr.
Morris, Clarence, ed. Great Legal Philosophers: Selected Readings in Jurisprudence. LC 57-11955. 1971. pap. 8.95x (ISBN 0-8122-1008-5, Pa Paperbks). U of Pa Pr.
Murphy, Cornelius F. Modern Legal Philosophy. 1978. text ed. 15.00x (ISBN 0-391-00859-5). Duquesne.
Murphy, Jefferie G. Kant: The Philosophy of Right. (Philosophers in Perspective Ser). 1970. pap. 5.50 (ISBN 0-312-44975-5). St Martin.
Murphy, Jeffrie G. The Philosophy of Law. (Philosophy & Society Ser.). 1981. 18.50x (ISBN 0-8476-6277-2); pap. 9.95x (ISBN 0-8476-6278-0). Rowman.
--Retribution, Justice & Therapy. 1979. lib. bdg. 31.50 (ISBN 90-277-0998-X, Pub. by Reidel Holland); pap. 11.85 (ISBN 90-277-0999-8). Kluwer Boston.
Newman, Jeremiah. Conscience Versus Law. 260p. 1972. 5.95 (ISBN 0-8199-0433-3). Franciscan Herald.
Northrop, Filmer S. The Complexity of Legal & Ethical Experience: Studies in the Method of Normative Subjects. LC 78-790. 1978. Repr. of 1959 ed. lib. bdg. 27.75x (ISBN 0-313-20286-9, NOCL). Greenwood.
Pashukanis, Evgeny B. Law & Marxism: A General Theory. Einhorn, Barbara, tr. from Ger. 196p. 1980. text ed. 13.00x (ISBN 0-906133-04-1). Humanities.
Pound, Roscoe. Introduction to the Philosophy of Law. rev. ed. (Storrs Lectures Ser.). 1954. 17.50x (ISBN 0-300-00839-2); pap. 4.95 1959 (ISBN 0-300-00188-6, Y10). Yale U Pr.
Progress Publishers, Moscow, ed. Contemporary Bourgeois Legal Thought: A Marxist Analysis. 311p. 1975. 16.00x (ISBN 0-8464-0277-7). Beekman Pubs.
Pulszky, Agost. The Theory of Law & Civil Society. LC 79-1616. 1980. Repr. of 1888 ed. 31.50 (ISBN 0-88355-919-6). Hyperion Conn.
Rational Basis of Legal Institutions. LC 68-57095. (Modern Legal Philosphy Ser.: Vol. 14). Repr. of 1923 ed. 20.00x (ISBN 0-678-04524-0). Kelley.
Raz, Joseph. The Authority of Law: Essays on Law & Morality. 304p. 1979. text ed. 29.00x (ISBN 0-19-825345-1). Oxford U Pr.
Reichenbach, Hans. Laws, Modalities, & Counterfactuals. LC 74-29798. Orig. Title: Nomological Statements & Admissible Operations. 1977. 21.50x (ISBN 0-520-02966-6). U of Cal Pr.
Sayre, Paul. Philosophy of Law. vi, 148p. 1981. Repr. of 1954 ed. lib. bdg. 22.50x (ISBN 0-8377-1121-5). Rothman.
Sayre, Paul, ed. Interpretations of Modern Legal Philosophies: Essays in Honor of Roscoe Pound. ix, 807p. 1981. Repr. of 1947 ed. lib. bdg. 48.50x (ISBN 0-8377-1122-3). Rothman.
Schafer, Stephen. The Political Criminal. LC 73-10700. 1974. 8.95 (ISBN 0-02-927820-1). Free Pr.
Schwarz-Liebermann Von Wahlendorf, H. A. Fondements et Principes D'un Ordre Juridique Naissant: Essai De Philosophie Empirique Du Droit. 1972. 47.50x (ISBN 90-2796-957-4). Mouton.
--Relexions Sur la Nature Des Choses et la Logique Du Droit: Contribution a L'ontologie & a L'epistemologie Juridiques. 1973. 32.50x (ISBN 90-2797-168-4). Mouton.
Science of Legal Method. LC 68-54756. (Modern Legal Philosophy Ser.: Vol. 9). Repr. of 1917 ed. 20.00x (ISBN 0-678-04520-8). Kelley.
Shimanoff, Susan B. Communication Rules: Theory & Research. LC 79-25077. (Sage Library of Social Research: Vol. 97). (Illus.). 309p. 1980. 20.00 (ISBN 0-8039-1392-3); pap. 9.95x (ISBN 0-8039-1393-1). Sage.
Shuchman, Philip. Cohen & Cohen's Readings in Jurisprudence & Legal Philosophy. 2nd ed. 1099p. 1979. text ed. 25.00 (ISBN 0-316-78877-5). Little.
Shuman, Samuel I. Legal Positivism: Its Scope & Limitations. LC 62-14874. 1963. 11.95x (ISBN 0-8143-1213-6). Wayne St U Pr.
Stammler, Rudolf. Theory of Justice. Husik, Issac, tr. LC 68-54755. (Modern Legal Philosophy Ser.: Vol. 8). Repr. of 1925 ed. 20.00x (ISBN 0-678-04519-4). Kelley.
Stein, Peter S. & Shand, J. Legal Values in Western Society. 1974. 10.00x (ISBN 0-85224-257-3, Pub. by Edinburgh U Pr Scotland). Columbia U Pr.
Steintrager, James. Bentham. LC 76-55852. 1977. 19.50x (ISBN 0-8014-1096-7). Cornell U Pr.
Sterba, James P. Justice: Alternative Political Perspectives. 272p. 1979. pap. text ed. 8.95x (ISBN 0-534-00762-7). Wadsworth Pub.
Stone, Julius. Human Law & Human Justice. 1965. 18.75x (ISBN 0-8047-0215-2). Stanford U Pr.
Summers, Robert S., ed. Essays in Legal Philosophy. (Library Reprint Ser.). 1976. 22.75x (ISBN 0-520-03213-6). U of Cal Pr.
--More Essays in Legal Philosophy: General Assessment of Legal Philosophies. 1971. 17.50x (ISBN 0-520-01971-7). U of Cal Pr.
Tammelo, I. Modern Logic in the Service of Law. 1978. pap. 16.70 (ISBN 0-387-81486-8). Springer-Verlag.
Thomas Aquinas, Saint Political Ideas of St. Thomas Aquinas. Bigongiari, Dino, ed. (Library of Classics Ser.: No. 15). 1973. pap. text ed. 4.95 (ISBN 0-02-840380-0). Hafner.
--Treatise on Law. 1963. pap. 2.45 (ISBN 0-89526-918-X). Regnery-Gateway.
Tourtoulon, Pierre De. Philosophy in the Development of Law. (Modern Legal Philosophy Ser: Vol. 13). lxii, 654p. 1969. Repr. of 1922 ed. 25.00x (ISBN 0-8377-2626-3). Rothman.
Twentieth Century Legal Philosophy Series, Vols. 2-7. 1948-1955. Set. 125.00 (ISBN 0-384-62115-5). Johnson Repr.
Unger, Roberto M. Law in Modern Society. LC 74-27853. 1977. pap. text ed. 7.95 (ISBN 0-02-932880-2). Free Pr.
Van Eikema Hommes, H. J. Major Trends in the History of Legal Philosophy. LC 78-26072. 1979. 46.50 (ISBN 0-444-85263-8, North Holland). Elsevier.
Von Jhering, Rudolf. Law As a Means to an End. Husik, Isaac, tr. LC 68-54753. (Modern Legal Philosophy Ser.: Vol. 5). Repr. of 1913 ed. 18.00x (ISBN 0-678-04517-8). Kelley.
--The Struggle for Law. Labor, John, tr. from Ger. LC 79-1610. 1980. Repr. of 1915 ed. 18.50 (ISBN 0-88355-913-7). Hyperion Conn.
Watson, Alan. The Nature of Law. 1978. 8.50x (ISBN 0-85224-318-9, Pub. by Edinburg U Pr). Columbia U Pr.
Weber, Max. Critique of Stammler. Oakes, Guy, tr. LC 77-72682. 1977. 12.95 (ISBN 0-02-934100-0). Free Pr.
West, Ranyard. Conscience & Society: A Study of the Psychological Prerequisites of Law & Order. LC 77-138192. 261p. 1972. Repr. of 1945 ed. lib. bdg. 15.00 (ISBN 0-8371-5649-1, WESO). Greenwood.
--International Law & Psychology. LC 73-17217. 380p. 1974. lib. bdg. 25.00 (ISBN 0-379-00022-9). Oceana.
White, James B. The Legal Imagination: Studies in the Nature of Legal Thought & Expression. 1973. 24.50 (ISBN 0-316-93602-2). Little.
Wilkin, Robert N. The Spirit of the Legal Profession. viii, 178p. 1981. Repr. of 1938 ed. lib. bdg. 18.50x (ISBN 0-8377-1308-0). Rothman.
Woozley, A. D. Law & Obedience: The Arguments of Plato's Crito. LC 79-456. 1979. 14.00x (ISBN 0-8078-1366-4). U of NC Pr.

LAW-POPULAR WORKS

Anosike, Benji O. How to Draw Up Your Legal Separation, Cohabitation, or Property Settlement Agreement Without a Lawyer. LC 80-66443. 120p. (Orig.). 1981. pap. text ed. 7.95x (ISBN 0-932704-04-2). Do-It-Yourself Pubs.
Arbetman, Lee, et al. Street Law: A Course in Practical Law. 2nd ed. 383p. 1980. pap. text ed. 8.75 (ISBN 0-8299-1031-X). West Pub.
Blackstone, William, Jr. Be Your Own Lawyer: How to Judge, Deal & Win in & Out of Court. LC 81-6076. 192p. 1981. 10.95 (ISBN 0-8253-0071-1). Beaufort Bks NY.
Caudill, Harry M. The Mountain, the Miner & the Lord, & Other Tales from a Country Law Office. LC 80-51012. 192p. 1980. 12.50 (ISBN 0-8131-1403-9). U Pr of Ky.
Cohn, Roy. How to Stand up for Your Rights - and Win! 1981. 13.95 (ISBN 0-671-25341-7). S&S.
Colby, Edward E. Everything You've Always Wanted to Know About the Law. LC 75-36079. 432p. pap. 2.50 (ISBN 0-89041-207-3, 3207). Major Bks.
Freifeld, Wilbur & Taddeo, Frank. The Legal Facts of Life: How the Courts Have Ruled in Hundreds of Everyday Situations. 224p. 1982. 13.50 (ISBN 0-525-93212-7); pap. 8.25 (ISBN 0-525-93211-9). Dutton.
Furcolo, Foster. Practical Law for the Layman. 1980. pap. 6.95 (ISBN 0-87491-612-7). Acropolis.
Goldstein, Lee. Communes, Law & Commonsense: A Legal Manual for Communities. LC 74-77447. (Illus.). 1974. pap. 3.35 (ISBN 0-9603468-0-5). New Community.

Hamilton, Harper. Harper Hamilton's Law Dictionary for Laymen. 1978. pap. 6.95 (ISBN 0-685-86645-9). Stein & Day.
--Harper Hamilton's Legal Guide for Laymen. 1978. pap. 6.95 (ISBN 0-685-86646-7). Stein & Day.
--How to Be Your Own Lawyer in Court. 1978. pap. 6.95 (ISBN 0-685-86647-5). Stein & Day.
Hanna, John P. Complete Layman's Guide to the Law. (Illus.). 544p. pap. 8.95 (ISBN 0-13-161224-7, Spec). P-H.
Helm, Alice K., et al, eds. The Family Legal Advisor. (Illus.). 480p. 1974. 12.95 (ISBN 0-517-51547-4). Crown.
Helm, Mike. How I Did My Own Legal Work for Our Adoption Book. 1978. 4.00 (ISBN 0-931742-00-5). Rainy Day Oreg.
Howell, John C. The Citizens Do-It-Yourself Legal Guide. (Howell Legal Guide Ser.). 256p. 1981. pap. 9.95 (ISBN 0-89648-088-7). Hamilton Pr.
Kahan, Stuart & Cavallo, Robert M. Do I Really Need a Lawyer? LC 78-14636. 1979. 9.95 (ISBN 0-8019-6775-9). Chilton.
Kantrowitz, Walter & Eisenberg, Howard. How to Be Your Own Lawyer (Sometimes) 1980. pap. 5.95 (ISBN 0-399-50457-5, Perigee). Putnam.
Kling, Samuel G. The Complete Guide to Everyday Law. 1975. pap. 3.95 (ISBN 0-515-05824-6, Y3703). Jove Pubns.
Last, Jack, et al. Everyday Law Made Simple. LC 77-15164. 1978. softbound 3.50 (ISBN 0-385-12921-1, Made). Doubleday.
Legal Guide for Laymen. LC 80-65091. 1980. write for info. (ISBN 0-89648-062-3); pap. write for info. (ISBN 0-89648-063-1). Citizens Law.
Marks, Burton & Golfarb, Gerald. Winning with Your Lawyer. (McGraw-Hill Paperbacks Ser.). 224p. (Orig.). 1980. pap. 6.95 (ISBN 0-07-040390-2, SB). McGraw.
Matthews, Douglas. Sue the B-st-rds: The Victim's Handbook. rev. ed. LC 80-52011. 1981. pap. 7.95 (ISBN 0-87795-288-4). Arbor Hse.
Oleck, Howard. Law for Living. 1967. 7.50 (ISBN 0-685-92669-9); pap. 4.25 (ISBN 0-685-92670-2). Prof Bks Serv.
Rice, Jerome S. How to Handle Your Own Lawsuit. LC 79-50989. 1979. 9.95 (ISBN 0-8092-7331-4); pap. 5.95 o. p. (ISBN 0-8092-7330-6). Contemp Bks.
Ross, Martin J. Handbook of Everyday Law. 1977. pap. 2.95 (ISBN 0-449-23126-7, Crest). Fawcett.
Sarshik, Steve & Szykitka, Walter. Without a Lawyer. (Orig.). 1980. pap. 5.95 (ISBN 0-452-25226-1, Z5226, Plume). NAL.
Smedley, Robert W. So You're Going to Court: The Law and You. 302p. 6.00 (ISBN 0-685-41739-5). Fountainhead.
Stern, Philip M. Lawyers on Trial: A Book for People Who Are Fed up with Lawyers. 288p. 1980. 12.50 (ISBN 0-8129-0904-6). Times Bks.
Striker, John & Shapiro, Andrew O. Power Plays: How to Deal Like a Lawyer in Person-to-Person Confrontations & Get Your Rights. LC 78-64811. 1979. 9.95 (ISBN 0-89256-094-0). Rawson Wade.
Swiger, E. Law in Your Everyday Life. 1978. 8.95 (ISBN 0-13-526202-X). P-H.
Taylor, Steven J. & Biklen, Douglas. Understanding the Law: An Advocates Guide to the Law & Developmental Disabilities. 67p. 1980. pap. 3.25 (ISBN 0-937540-10-2, HPP-13). Human Policy Pr.
Weber, Robert. Before You See a Lawyer. 320p. 1981. 14.95 (ISBN 0-8329-0101-6). New Century.
Weinerman, Chester S. Practical Law: A Layperson's Handbook. LC 77-26164. 1978. 13.95 (ISBN 0-13-691113-7, Spec); pap. 4.95 (ISBN 0-13-691105-6, Spec). P-H.
Zepke, Brent E. Law for Non-Lawyers. (Littlefield, Adams Quality Paperbacks: No. 355). 224p. (Orig.). 1981. pap. 4.95 (ISBN 0-8226-0355-1). Littlefield.

LAW-PRACTICE
see Procedure (Law)

LAW-PSYCHOLOGY
see also Criminal Psychology; Judicial Process; Psychology, Forensic

Abt, Lawrence E. & Stuart, Irving R. Social Psychology & Discretionary Law. 1979. text ed. 19.50 (ISBN 0-442-27907-8). Van Nos Reinhold.
Amneus, Nils. Does Chance or Justice Rule Our Lives? 97p. 1972. pap. 2.00 (ISBN 0-685-28752-1, 913004-08). Point Loma Pub.
Ellison, Katherine W. & Buckhout, Robert. Psychology & Criminal Justice: Common Grounds. 432p. 1981. text ed. 19.50 scp (ISBN 0-686-72761-4, HarpC). Har-Row.
Farrington, David P., et al, eds. Psychology, Law & Legal Processes. (Oxford Sociolegal Studies). 1979. text ed. 27.50x (ISBN 0-391-01026-3). Humanities.
Fersch, Ellsworth A. Psychology & Psychiatry in Courts & Corrections: Controversy & Change. LC 80-11726. (Wiley Series on Personality Processes). 370p. 1980. 27.50 (ISBN 0-471-05604-9, Pub. by Wiley-Interscience). Wiley.
Finkel, Norman J. Therapy & Ethics: The Courtship of Law & Psychology. (Current Issues in Behavioral Psychology Ser.). 208p. 1980. 21.00 (ISBN 0-8089-1222-4). Grune.
Frank, Jerome. Courts on Trial: Myth & Reality in American Justice. LC 72-11942. 454p. 1949. 30.00 (ISBN 0-691-09205-2); pap. 6.95 (ISBN 0-691-02755-2). Princeton U Pr.
--Law & the Modern Mind. 8.50 (ISBN 0-8446-0629-4). Peter Smith.
Herbert, David L. & Barrett, Roger K. Attorney's Master Guide to Courtroom Psychology: How to Apply Behavioral Science Techniques for New Trial Success. 1980. 69.50 (ISBN 0-13-050443-2). Exec Reports.
Lipsitt, Paul D. & Sales, Bruce D., eds. New Directions in Psycholegal Research. 352p. 1980. text ed. 18.95 (ISBN 0-442-26267-1). Van Nos Reinhold.
Marshall, James. Law & Psychology in Conflict. 1979. 14.50 (ISBN 0-672-83700-5). Bobbs.
Robinson, Daniel N., ed. Seminal Cases & Contemporary Commentaries: England. (Contributions to the History of Psychology Ser.: Insanity & Jurisprudence). 1980. 30.00 (ISBN 0-89093-331-6). U Pubns Amer.
--Seminal Cases & Contemporary Commentaries: The United States. (Insanity & Jurisprudence). 1980. 30.00 (ISBN 0-89093-330-8). U Pubns Amer.
Rosner, Richard. Critical Issues in American Psychiatry & the Law. 352p. 1982. price not set (ISBN 0-398-04578-X). C C Thomas.
Schoenfeld, C. G. Psychoanalysis & the Law. (Amer. Lec. Behavioral Science & Law). 296p. 1973. 17.50 (ISBN 0-398-02656-4). C C Thomas.
Schwitzgebel, Robert L. & Schwitzgebel, R. Kirkland. Law & Psychological Practice. LC 79-20112. 1980. text ed. 15.95 (ISBN 0-471-76694-1). Wiley.
Slovenko, Ralph. Psychiatry & Law. 1973. 37.50 (ISBN 0-316-79868-1). Little.
Tapp, June L. & Levine, Felice. Law, Justice, & the Individual in Society. LC 77-24022. 1977. 18.95 (ISBN 0-03-012156-6, HoltC). HR&W.
Thibaut, J. & Walker, L. Procedural Justice: A Psychological Analysis. LC 75-15944. 1975. pap. 4.95 (ISBN 0-470-85869-9). Halsted Pr.

LAW-RELIGIOUS ASPECTS
see Religion and Law

LAW-SANCTION
see Sanctions (Law)

LAW-SOCIOLOGY
see Sociological Jurisprudence

LAW-STATISTICS
see Judicial Statistics

LAW-STUDY AND TEACHING
see also Law Examinations

Allen, Francis A. The Causes of Popular Dissatisfaction with Legal Education. 1977. pap. 0.95x (ISBN 0-916054-43-8, Caroline Hse Inc). Green Hill.
Bainbridge, John S. & Wood, Terry. The Study & Teaching of Law in Africa with a Survey of Institutions of Legal Education in Africa. LC 72-84328. x, 342p. 1972. text ed. 12.50x (ISBN 0-8377-0304-2). Rothman.
Boyer, Barry B. & Cramton, Roger C. American Legal Education: An Agenda for Research & Reform. (Research Contribution Ser.: No. 1). 1974. pap. 2.00 (ISBN 0-685-48016-X). Am Bar Foun.
Broun, Kenneth S. & Meisenholder, Robert. Teacher's Manual to Accompany Problems in Evidence. 2nd ed. (American Casebook Ser.). 180p. 1981. tchrs. manual avail. West Pub.
Brown, Esther L. Lawyers & the Promotion of Justice. (Russell Sage Foundation Reprint Ser). Repr. of 1938 ed. lib. bdg. 26.00x (ISBN 0-697-00201-2). Irvington.
Daly, Joseph L. The Student Lawyer: High School Handbook of Minnesota Law. 3rd ed. (Illus.). 200p. 1981. pap. text ed. 5.95 (ISBN 0-314-63145-3). West Pub.
Djonovich, Dusan J., ed. Legal Education, a Selective Bibliography. LC 73-21942. (Annual Survey of American Law Ser). 1970. 26.00 (ISBN 0-379-12229-4). Oceana.
Dupry, Renee J. The University Teaching of Social Sciences: International Law. 1967. pap. 6.00 (ISBN 92-3-100653-3, U707, UNESCO). Unipub.
Dutile, Fernand N., ed. Legal Education & Lawyer Competency: Curricula for Change. LC 81-50458. 160p. 1981. 15.00 (ISBN 0-268-01264-4). U of Notre Dame Pr.
Eisenmann, Charles. The University Teaching of Social Sciences: Law. LC 72-95476. (Teaching in the Social Sciences Ser.). 182p. (Orig.). 1973. pap. 7.50 (ISBN 92-3-101035-2, UNESCO). Unipub.
Fischer, Louis, et al. Teachers & the Law: A Guide for Educators. LC 80-23394. 448p. 1981. text ed. 25.00x (ISBN 0-582-28135-0). Longman.
Franks, Betty B. & Howard, Mary K. People, Law & the Futures Perspective. 56p. 1979. pap. 2.50 (ISBN 0-686-63718-6, 1676-9-06). NEA.
Gallagher, Arlene F. The Methods Book: Stategies for Law-Focused Education. LC 77-80622. 1977. pap. 8.95 (ISBN 0-89994-226-1). Soc Sci Ed.
Gaubatz, John. The Moot Court Book. 110p. (Orig.). 1979. pap. text ed. 8.00 (ISBN 0-672-83854-0). Bobbs.
Gerlach, Ronald & Lamprecht, Lynn. Teaching About the Law. 1975. 10.95 (ISBN 0-87084-834-8). Anderson Pub Co.
Gillers, Stephen, ed. Looking at Law School: A Student Guide from the Society of American Law Teachers. LC 76-53301. 1977. 9.95 (ISBN 0-8008-4966-3). Taplinger.
Graveson, R. H., ed. Law: An Outline for the Intending Student. (Outlines Ser). 1967. cased 15.00x (ISBN 0-7100-2999-3); pap. 8.95 (ISBN 0-7100-6028-9). Routledge & Kegan.
Harno, Albert J. Legal Education in the United States: A Report Prepared for the Survey of the Legal Profession. LC 80-23717. v, 211p. 1980. Repr. of 1953 ed. lib. bdg. 19.75x (ISBN 0-313-22425-0, HALG). Greenwood.
Hoffman, David. A Course of Legal Study, Addressed to Students & the Profession Generally, 2 vols. in 1. LC 72-37980. (American Law Ser.: The Formative Years). 888p. 1972. Repr. of 1836 ed. 38.00 (ISBN 0-405-04023-7). Arno.
Jacobs, Clyde E. Law Writers & the Courts. LC 73-251. (American Constitutional & Legal History Ser.). 234p. 1973. Repr. of 1954 ed. lib. bdg. 25.00 (ISBN 0-306-70570-2). Da Capo.
Kelso, Charles D. Programmed Introduction to the Study of Law, Pt. 1. Case Skills. 1965. 23.00 (ISBN 0-672-81012-3, Bobbs-Merrill Law). Michie-Bobbs.
Lammers, Bernard. The Teaching of Legislative Drafting & Process in U.S. Law Schools. 1977. pap. 5.00 (ISBN 0-910058-87-3). Am Bar Foun.
Leonard, Walter J. Black Lawyers: Training & Results Then & Now. LC 77-7969. (Illus.). 1977. 15.00 (ISBN 0-89460-000-1). Senna & Shih.
Llewellyn, Karl N. Bramble Bush. LC 51-1727. 1960. 8.00 (ISBN 0-379-00073-3). Oceana.
Newman, Jason & O'Brien, Edward. Street Law the D.C. Project: Community Legal Assistance & Street Law. (Illus.). (gr. 9-12). 1976. pap. text ed. 4.00 (ISBN 0-8299-1012-3). West Pub.
Reed, Alfred Z. Present-Day Law Schools in the United States & Canada. LC 75-22836. (America in Two Centuries Ser). 1976. Repr. of 1928 ed. 35.00x (ISBN 0-405-07707-6). Arno.
--Training for the Public Profession of the Law. LC 75-22837. (America in Two Centuries Ser). 1976. Repr. of 1921 ed. 29.00x (ISBN 0-405-07708-4). Arno.
Roth, George J. Slaying the Law School Dragon. LC 80-16974. 284p. 1980. 10.95 (ISBN 0-396-07880-X); pap. 7.95 (ISBN 0-396-07879-6). Dodd.
Schwarzrock, Shirley & Wrenn, C. Gilbert. Understanding the Law of Our Land. (Coping with Ser.). (Illus.). 51p. (gr. 7-12). 1973. pap. text ed. 1.30 (ISBN 0-913476-21-8). Am Guidance.
Shuchman, Philip. Problems of Knowledge in Legal Scholarship. LC 79-80252. 136p. 1979. pap. text ed. 8.95 (ISBN 0-939328-00-3). U Conn Sch Law.
Siegel, Brian. How to Succeed in Law School. LC 75-17848. 96p. 1975. pap. text ed. 4.95 (ISBN 0-8120-0609-7). Barron.
Stone, Ferdinand F. Handbook of Law Study. 164p. 1952. pap. 6.95 (ISBN 0-316-81754-6). Little.
Swann, Ruth. Financial Aid for Minorities in Law. 37p. 1980. pap. 3.00 (ISBN 0-912048-01-8). Garrett Pk.
Swords, Peter D. & Walwer, Frank K. Costs & Resorces of Legal Education: A Study in the Management of Educational Resources. new ed. LC 74-22459. 345p. 1975. 17.50x (ISBN 0-915120-00-3). Columbia U Pr.
Turner, Mary Jane. Law in the Classroom: Activities & Resources. LC 79-22527. (Illus.). 1980. pap. 17.00 (ISBN 0-89994-239-3). Soc Sci Ed.
Vanderbilt, Arthur T., II. Law School: Briefing for a Legal Education. 224p. 1981. pap. 3.95 (ISBN 0-14-005916-4). Penguin.
Volkell, Randolph. LSAT: Law School Admission Test. (Wiley Self-Teaching Guides Ser.). 288p. 1981. pap. text ed. 7.95 (ISBN 0-471-09647-4). Wiley.
Wambaugh, Eugene. The Study of Cases: A Course of Instruction in Reading & Stating Reported Cases, Composing Head-notes & Briefs, Criticising & Comparing Authorities, & Compiling Digests. xi, 306p. 1981. Repr. of 1892 ed. lib. bdg. 28.50x (ISBN 0-8377-1310-2). Rothman.

LAW-STUDY AND TEACHING-CANADA

Hoffman, David. A Course of Legal Study, Addressed to Students & the Profession Generally, 2 vols. in 1. LC 72-37980. (American Law Ser.: The Formative Years). 888p. 1972. Repr. of 1836 ed. 38.00 (ISBN 0-405-04023-7). Arno.

LAW-TERMS AND PHRASES

Beseler, D. & Jacobs, B. Technical Dictionary of Anglo-American Legal Terminology. 3rd ed. 385p. (Ger. & Eng.). 1971. 57.50 (ISBN 3-11-002187-0, M-7636, Pub. by de Gruyter). French & Eur.
Bieber, Doris M. Dictionary of Legal Abbreviations Used in American Law Books. LC 78-60173. 1979. lib. bdg. 19.50 (ISBN 0-930342-61-5); pap. text ed. 7.50 (ISBN 0-930342-96-8). W S Hein.
Burton, William C. & DeCosta, Steven E. The Legal Thesaurus. LC 80-83803. 1980. 35.00 (ISBN 0-02-691000-4). Free Pr.
D'Auria, Michael & Ryan, Herbert F. Legal Terms & Concepts in Criminal Justice. 1982. pap. 6.95 (ISBN 0-89529-153-3). Avery Pub.
Dictionary of Law. rev. ed. LC 75-40443. 144p. 1976. lib. bdg. 12.90 (ISBN 0-914294-44-X); pap. 2.95 (ISBN 0-914294-43-1). Running Pr.
Dictionary of Legal Words & Phrases. 1981 ed. 1981. 10.00 (ISBN 0-87526-205-8). Gould.
Dietl, C. Woerterbuch des Wirtschafts, Rechts und Handelssprache. (Eng. & Ger., Dictionary of Economic, Legal & Commercial Terms). 1970. 33.00 (ISBN 3-87527-003-7, M-6939). French & Eur.
Educational Research Associates, ed. Legal Terms for Secretaries. (gr. 11-12). 1974. 3.35 (ISBN 0-89420-096-8, 299900). Natl Book.
ESQ. a Lawyers Desk Treasure, Release No. 2. rev ed. LC 76-8795. 1981. 27.50 (ISBN 0-915362-18-X). M K Heller.
Guillien, Raymond & Vincent, Jean. Lexique des Termes Juridiques. 3rd ed. 354p. (Fr.). 1978. pap. 14.95 (ISBN 0-686-57321-8, M-6304). French & Eur.
Heimanson, Rudolph. Dictionary of Political Science & Law. LC 67-14401. 1967. 12.00 (ISBN 0-379-00325-2). Oceana.
Herbst, R. Dictionary of Commericial, Financial & Legal Terms in 2 Languages. 86.00 ea. Vol. A Eng. & Ger. Vol. B Ger. & Eng (ISBN 3-85942-004-6). Adler.
Herbst, Robert. Woerterbuch der Handels, Finanz und Rechtssprache. 2nd ed. (Ger., Eng. & Fr., Dictionary of Commercial, Fininancial & Legal Terms). 1975. 92.00 (ISBN 3-85942-001-1, M-7002). French & Eur.
Hexner, Erwin. Studies in Legal Terminology. vi, 150p. 1981. Repr. of 1941 ed. lib. bdg. 20.00x (ISBN 0-8377-0635-1). Rothman.
Keeton, Robert E. Basic Expressions for Trial Lawyers Nineteen Seventy Nine: Supplement to "Trial Tactics". 3.95 (ISBN 0-316-48581-0). Little.
Kniepkamp, H. Rechtswoerterbuch. 216p. (Ger. & Eng., Dictionary of Legal Terms). 1954. 27.50 (ISBN 3-7678-0013-6, M-7598, Pub. by Colloquium Vlg.). French & Eur.
Lane, A. & Catrice, R. Formulaire International: Modeles D'actes, Formules et Locutions Pour la Pratique Jurisdiques. 724p. (Ger. & Fr.). 1969. 49.95 (ISBN 0-686-56990-3, M-6330). French & Eur.
Merriam-Webster Editorial Staff. Webster's Legal Speller. 1978. 3.95 (ISBN 0-87779-038-8). Merriam.
Reilly, Theresa M. Legal Secretary's Word Finder & Desk Book. 1974. 12.95 (ISBN 0-13-528588-7, Parker). P-H.
Renner, Ruediger & Tooth, Jeffery. Legal Terminology English & German. 1971. 35.75 (ISBN 3-1900-6280-3). Adler.
--Legal Terminology English-German. 526p. 1971. 22.50x (ISBN 3-19-006280-3). Intl Pubns Serv.
Robb, Louis A. Dictionary of Legal Terms, Spanish-English & English-Spanish. 1955. 20.50 (ISBN 0-471-72534-X, Pub. by Wiley-Interscience). Wiley.
Romain, Alfred. Dictionary of German & English Legal & Economic Terminology, Vol. 1. (Eng. -Ger.). 1976. 78.00 (ISBN 3-406-03370-9, M-7101). French & Eur.
--Dictionary of German & English Legal & Economic Terminology, Vol. 2. (Ger. -Fr.). 1975. 78.00 (ISBN 3-406-03371-7, M-7100). French & Eur.
Shorthand Guide to Legal Terminology. 1982 ed. 700p. 1978. 7.00 (ISBN 0-87526-211-2). Gould.

LAW-VOCATIONAL GUIDANCE

Brakel, Samuel J. & Loh, Wallace D. Regulating the Multistate Practice of Law. (Research Contributions Ser: No. 5). 1975. pap. 2.00 (ISBN 0-685-64480-4). Am Bar Foun.

Cohen, Charles Z. Your Future As a Lawyer. (Careers in Depth Ser). (YA) 1977. PLB 5.97 (ISBN 0-8239-0382-6). Rosen Pr.

Coughlin, George C. Here Is Your Career: The Law. LC 78-14176. (Here Is Your Career Ser.). (Illus.). (gr. 6-12). 1979. 7.95 (ISBN 0-399-20655-8). Putnam.

Donnell, John D. Corporate Counsel: A Role Study. LC 78-633785. (Business Study Ser: No. 40). 1971. 15.00 (ISBN 0-685-03851-3, IBS40). Ind U Busn Res.

Educational Research Council of America. Corporate Lawyer. Ferris, Theodore N. & Marchak, John P., eds. (Real People at Work Ser: I). (Illus.). 1975. pap. text ed. 2.25 (ISBN 0-89247-068-2). Changing Times.

Ehrlich, Thomas & Hazard, Geoffrey C., Jr. Going to Law School? Readings on a Legal Career. 252p. 1975. 8.95 (ISBN 0-316-22287-9); pap. 7.95 (ISBN 0-316-22288-7). Little.

Elliott, Shelden D. Opportunities in a Law Career. LC 70-76321. (gr. 8 up). 1969. pap. 1.25 (ISBN 0-8442-6486-5). Natl Textbk.

Grossblat, Martha & Sikes, Bette H., eds. Women Lawyers: Supplementary Data to the 1971 Lawyer Statistical Report. LC 52-1123. (Illus.). 92p. (Orig.). 1973. pap. 5.00 (ISBN 0-910058-52-0). Am Bar Foun.

Heath, Charles D. Your Future As a Legal Assistant. (Careers in Depth Ser.). (gr. 7-12). 1979. PLB 5.97 (ISBN 0-8239-0477-6). Rosen Pr.

Law Careers. 1981. text ed. 7.95 (ISBN 0-686-65129-4, 65489); pap. text ed. 5.95 (ISBN 0-686-65130-8, 65462). Natl Textbk.

Maru, Olavi. Research on the Legal Profession: A Review of Work Done. LC 72-95563. (Orig.). 1972. pap. 2.00 (ISBN 0-910058-55-5). Am Bar Foun.

Mayes, Joseph R., ed. Virginia Lawyer: A Basic Practice Handbook. 1979. 40.00 (ISBN 0-87215-125-5). Michie-Bobbs.

Miller, Saul. After Law School: Finding a Job in a Tight Market. 1978. pap. 6.95 (ISBN 0-316-57362-0). Little.

Schneider, Hans J. Masters of Legalized Confusion & Their Puppets. LC 78-12609. 32p. 1979. 1.45 (ISBN 0-930294-11-4). World Wide OR.

Singer, Gerald M. How to Go Directly into Solo Law Practice: Without Missing a Meal. LC 76-3083. (Student Books). 1976. 19.00 (ISBN 0-686-20649-5). Lawyers Co-Op.

Stern, Duke N. & Sampson, Karen G., eds. West Virginia Practice Handbook. 1977. 60.00 (ISBN 0-87215-195-6). Michie-Bobbs.

Would You Like to Be a Lawyer? 48p. (gr. 4-6). 1980. 2.95 (ISBN 0-686-31330-5). Unica Inc.

LAW-AFRICA

Allott, Antony N. Essays in African Law, with Special Reference to the Law of Ghana. LC 74-30925. 323p. 1975. Repr. of 1960 ed. lib. bdg. 17.25x (ISBN 0-8371-7885-1, ALAL). Greenwood.

Baade, Hans W. & Everett, Robinson O., eds. African Law, New Law for New Nations. LC 63-17558. 1963. 10.00 (ISBN 0-379-11503-4). Oceana.

Comaroff, John L. & Roberts, Simon. Rules & Processes: The Cultural Logic of Dispute in an African Context. LC 80-26640. (Illus.). 1981. lib. bdg. 27.50x (ISBN 0-226-11424-4). U of Chicago Pr.

Crabb, John H. Legal System of Congo-Kinshasa. (Legal Systems of Africa Ser). 1970. 25.00 (ISBN 0-87215-066-6). Michie-Bobbs.

Gower, Laurence C. Independent Africa, the Challenge to the Legal Profession. LC 67-20877. (Oliver Wendell Holmes Lecture Ser: 1966). 1967. 8.95x (ISBN 0-674-44800-6). Harvard U Pr.

Hamnett, Ian. Chieftainship & Legitimacy. (International Library of Anthropology). 1975. 15.00x (ISBN 0-7100-8177-4). Routledge & Kegan.

Holleman, J. E. Issues in African Law. (Change & Continuity in Africa Ser). 179p. 1974. text ed. 17.25x (ISBN 90-2797-571-X). Mouton.

Hutchison, Thomas W., et al, eds. Africa & Law: Developing Legal Systems in African Commonwealth Nations. 1967. 15.00x (ISBN 0-299-04610-9). U of Wis Pr.

Introduction to Law in Contemporary Africa. 100p. 1976. pap. 10.00 (ISBN 0-914970-18-6, CM 002, Conch Mag). Unipub.

Kerr, Robert J. A Handbook of Mexican Law. 1976. lib. bdg. 59.95 (ISBN 0-8490-0280-X). Gordon Pr.

Levasseur, Alain A. & Jouvel, Francois. The Civil Code of the Ivory Coast. new ed. LC 75-42963. 1976. 25.00 (ISBN 0-87215-185-9). Michie-Bobbs.

Mensah-Brown, A. Kodwo. Introduction to Law in Contemporary Africa. LC 75-18488. (Law in Contemporary Africa Ser.). 1976. lib. bdg. 29.95 (ISBN 0-914970-17-8); pap. 15.00 (ISBN 0-914970-18-6). Conch Mag.

Milner, Alan, ed. African Law Reports: Commercial Series, 1964-1969, 14 vols. LC 67-26375. (African Law Reports Ser). 1973. lib. bdg. 45.00x ea. (ISBN 0-379-13700-3). Oceana.

Palmer, Vernon V. & Poulter, Sebastian M. Legal System of Lesotho. (Legal Systems of Africa Ser). 1972. 25.00 (ISBN 0-87215-147-6). Michie-Bobbs.

Redden, Kenneth. Legal System of Ethiopia. (Legal Systems of Africa Ser). 1968. 25.00 (ISBN 0-87215-064-X). Michie-Bobbs.

Rubin, N. N. & Cotran, E., eds. Readings in African Law, 2 vols. 351p. 1970. 65.00x set (ISBN 0-7146-2480-2, F Cass Co). Biblio Dist.

Rubin, Neville & Cotran, Eugene, eds. Annual Survey of African Law, 1971, Vol. 5. 339p. 1975. 45.00x (ISBN 0-87471-765-5). Rowman.

--Annual Survey of African Law, 1972, Vol. 6. 358p. 1975. 45.00x (ISBN 0-87471-790-6). Rowman.

--Annual Survey of African Law, 1973, Vol. 7. 384p. 1977. 47.50x (ISBN 0-87471-923-2). Rowman.

Rubin, Neville N. & Cotran, Eugene, eds. Annual Survey of African Law, Vol. 4: 1970. 375p. 1974. 37.50x (ISBN 0-87471-503-2). Rowman.

Salacuse, Jeswald. Introduction to Law in French Speaking Africa, Vol. 2. LC 75-24517. 542p. 1975. 25.00 (ISBN 0-87215-178-6). Michie-Bobbs.

Salacuse, Jeswald W. Introduction to Law in French Speaking Africa: Africa South of the Sahara, Vol. 1. (Legal Systems of Africa Ser). 1969. 25.00 (ISBN 0-87215-065-8). Michie-Bobbs.

Seidman, Robert B. The State, Law & Development. LC 78-18769. 1978. 29.95 (ISBN 0-312-75613-5). St Martin.

Sudan Law Reports: Civil Cases, 1900-1940, 2 vols. LC 69-15390. 1969. Repr. Set. 90.00 (ISBN 0-379-12751-2); 40.00 ea. Oceana.

University of Ife, Institute of African Studies. Integration of Customary & Modern Legal Systems in Africa. LC 71-151214. 461p. 1972. text ed. 45.00x (ISBN 0-8419-0068-X, Africana). Holmes & Meier.

Vance, John T. & Clagett, Helen L. A Guide to the Law & Legal Literature of Mexico. 1976. lib. bdg. 75.00 (ISBN 0-8490-0271-0). Gordon Pr.

LAW-AMERICA

De Cervera, Alejo. The Statute of Limitations in American Conflicts of Law. 5.00 (ISBN 0-8477-3001-8). U of PR Pr.

Nader, Laura, ed. No Access to Law: Alternatives to the American Judicial System. LC 80-526. 1980. 27.50 (ISBN 0-12-513560-2); pap. 12.95 (ISBN 0-12-513562-9). Acad Pr.

New York University School of Law. Annual Survey of American Law 1977. LC 46-30513. (Annual Survey of American Law Ser.). 1978. 25.00 (ISBN 0-379-12236-7). Oceana.

Pomeroy, John N. An Introduction to the Constitutional Law of the United States, 3 vols. 1980. Set. lib. bdg. 250.00 (ISBN 0-8490-3169-9). Gordon Pr.

Schwartz, Bernard & Jensen, Oliver, eds. American Heritage History of the Law in America. Incl. 25.00 (ISBN 0-8281-0290-2, B059R). (Illus.). 379p. 1974 (ISBN 0-07-079385-9). Am Heritage.

LAW-ASIA

Hoadley, M. C. & Hooker, M. B. Introduction to Javanese Law. LC 80-26636. (Monographs of the Association for Asian Studies: No. XXXVII). 1981. text ed. 9.95x (ISBN 0-8165-0727-9). U of Ariz Pr.

Hooker, M. B. A Concise Legal History of South-East Asia. 1978. lib. bdg. 48.00x (ISBN 0-19-825344-3). Oxford U Pr.

LAW-ASSYRIA

Johns, C. H. Babylonian & Assyrian Laws, Contracts, & Letters. 1977. lib. bdg. 59.95 (ISBN 0-8490-1467-0). Gordon Pr.

Postgate, J. N. Fifty Neo-Assyrian Legal Documents. (Illus.). 1976. 22.00x (ISBN 0-85668-054-0, Pub. by Aris & Phillips); pap. 11.50x (ISBN 0-85668-042-7, Pub. by Aris & Phillips). Intl Schol Bk Serv.

Postgate, J. N., ed. Fifty-Neo-Assyrian Legal Documents. 221p. 1976. text ed. 22.00x (ISBN 0-85668-054-0, Pub. by Aris & Phillips England). Humanities.

LAW-AUSTRALIA

Golding, J., et al, eds. Access to Law: The Second Seminar on Australian Lawyers & Social Change. 336p. (Orig.). 1980. pap. text ed. 16.95 (ISBN 0-7081-1305-2, 0581). Bks Australia.

Palmer, Geoffrey. Compensation for Incapacity: A Study of Law & Social Change in New Zealand & Australia. 460p. 1980. 49.50x (ISBN 0-19-558045-1). Oxford U Pr.

Russell, Enid. A History of the Law in Western Australia. 413p. 1980. 30.00 (ISBN 0-85564-171-1, Pub. by U of West Australia). Intl Schol Bk Serv.

Sawer, Geoffrey. Guide to Australian Law for Journalists, Authors, Printers & Publishers. 2nd ed. 1968. pap. 9.00x (ISBN 0-522-83925-8, Pub. by Melbourne U Pr). Intl Schol Bk Serv.

LAW-BABYLONIA

Clay, Albert T. Legal Documents from Erech, Dated in the Seleucid Era (312-65 B.C.) LC 78-63517. (Babylonian Records in the Library of J. Pierpont Morgan: 2). Repr. of 1913 ed. 34.50 (ISBN 0-404-60122-7). AMS Pr.

Feigen, Samuel I. Legal & Administrative Texts in the Reign of Samsu-Iluna. LC 78-4032. (Yale Oriental Series-Babylonian Text: No. 12). (Illus.). 1979. text ed. 30.00 (ISBN 0-300-01963-7). Yale U Pr.

Johns, C. H. Babylonian & Assyrian Laws, Contracts, & Letters. 1977. lib. bdg. 59.95 (ISBN 0-8490-1467-0). Gordon Pr.

Postgate, J. N. Fifty Neo-Assyrian Legal Documents. (Illus.). 1976. 22.00x (ISBN 0-85668-054-0, Pub. by Aris & Phillips); pap. 11.50x (ISBN 0-85668-042-7, Pub. by Aris & Phillips). Intl Schol Bk Serv.

LAW-BELGIUM

Belgium. Parliament. Library. Catalogue systematique de la Bibliotheque de la Chambre des representants, 2 vols. in 1. LC 68-57256. (Bibliography & Reference Ser.: No. 223). (Fr). 1968. Repr. of 1847 ed. 43.00 (ISBN 0-8337-0218-1). B Franklin.

Didier, J. M., et al. Law & Practice Relating to Pollution Control in Belgium & Luxembourg. 1976. 20.00x (ISBN 0-86010-038-3, Graham & Trotman). Nichols Pub.

Sprudzs, Adolph. Benelux Abbreviations & Symbols: Law & Related Subjects. LC 74-140620. 1971. lib. bdg. 20.00 (ISBN 0-379-00120-9). Oceana.

LAW-CANADA

Flaherty, David H., ed. Essays in the History of Canadian Law. (Publications of the Osgood Society Ser.: No. 1). 432p. 1981. 25.00x (ISBN 0-8020-3382-2). U of Toronto Pr.

Howard, John H. Laws of the British Colonies in the West Indies, & Other Parts of America, 2 Vols. in 1. LC 77-110006. Repr. of 1827 ed. 44.00x (ISBN 0-8371-4165-6, Pub. by Negro U Pr). Greenwood.

Livermore, Sarah, et al, eds. The American Bar - The Canadian Bar - The International Bar: 1981. 63rd ed. LC 18-21110. 3062p. 1981. 130.00 (ISBN 0-931398-06-1). R B Forster.

MacKenzie, N. A. Canada & the Law of Nations. Repr. of 1938 ed. 26.00 (ISBN 0-527-59750-3). Kraus Repr.

Macleod, R. C. The NWMP & Law Enforcement, 1873-1905. LC 76-3709. 200p. 1976. 20.00x (ISBN 0-8020-5333-5). U of Toronto Pr.

Millar, Perry S. & Baar, Carl. Judicial Administration in Canada. (Institute of Public Administration of Canada, Ipac Ser.). (Illus.). 550p. 1981. text ed. 37.95x (ISBN 0-7735-0339-0); pap. 18.95x (ISBN 0-7735-0368-4). McGill-Queens U Pr.

Tancelin, Maurice A. Jurisprudence sur les Obligations. 655p. (Fr.). 1974. pap. 18.00x (ISBN 2-7637-6682-X, Pub. by Laval). Intl Schol Bk Serv.

Wife Battering in Canada: The Vicious Circle. 72p. 1980. pap. 5.50 (ISBN 0-660-10483-0, SSC162, SSC). Unipub.

LAW-CANAL ZONE

Bray, Wayne D. Common Law Zone in Panama: A Case Study in Reception. Zebrowski, John, ed. LC 76-23354. (Illus.). 150p. 1976. 20.00 (ISBN 0-913480-35-5). Inter Am U Pr.

LAW-CHINA

Ch'u Tung-Tsu. Law & Society in Traditional China. LC 79-1602. 1981. Repr. of 1961 ed. 22.50 (ISBN 0-88355-905-6). Hyperion Conn.

Cohen, Jerome A., et al, eds. Contemporary Chinese Law: Research Problems & Perspectives. LC 74-106957. (Studies in East Asian Law: No. 4). 1970. 18.50x (ISBN 0-674-16675-2). Harvard U Pr.

Harvard University Law School Library. Preliminary Union List of Materials on Chinese Law: With a List of Chinese Studies & Translations of Foreign Law. (Studies in Chinese Law: No. 6). 1967. 35.00x (ISBN 0-674-70070-8). Harvard U Pr.

Johnson, Wallace, tr. from Chinese. The T'ang Code: General Principles, Vol. I. LC 78-51172. (Studies in East Asia Law Ser.). 1979. 25.00x (ISBN 0-691-09239-7). Princeton U Pr.

Republic of China. Laws, Ordinances, Regulations, & Rules Relating to the Judicial Administration of the Republic of China. (Studies in Chinese Government & Law). 364p. 1977. Repr. of 1923 ed. 24.00 (ISBN 0-89093-062-7). U Pubns Amer.

Tyan, Min-Ch' ien T. Legal Obligations Arising Out of Treaty Relations Between China & Other States. Kavass, Igor I. & Sprudz, Adolf, eds. LC 72-76347. (International Military Law & History Ser.: Vol. 3). 1972. Repr. of 1917 ed. lib. bdg. 20.50 (ISBN 0-930342-40-2). W S Hein.

Van Der Sprenkel, Sybille. Legal Institutions in Manchu China: A Socialogical Analysis. (Monographs on Social Anthropology: No. 24). 1962. pap. text ed. 6.25x (ISBN 0-391-00755-6, Athlone Pr). Humanities.

Van Gulik, Robert H., tr. T'ang-Yin-Pi-Shis: Parallel Cases from Under the Pear Tree. LC 79-1605. 1980. Repr. of 1956 ed. 18.00 (ISBN 0-88355-908-0). Hyperion Conn.

Wang, Joseph E., ed. Selected Legal Documents of the People's Republic of China. LC 76-5167. (Studies in Chinese Government & Law). 564p. 1979. 32.50 (ISBN 0-89093-067-8). U Pubns Amer.

--Selected Legal Documents of the People's Republic of China: Volume II. LC 76-5167. (Studies in Chinese Government & Law). 564p. 1979. 32.50 (ISBN 0-89093-241-7). U Pubns Amer.

LAW-COMMONWEALTH OF NATIONS

Phillips, Fred. The Evolving Legal Profession in the Commonwealth. LC 78-14903. 1978. lib. bdg. 32.50 (ISBN 0-379-20331-6). Oceana.

LAW-EGYPT

Maunier, Rene. Bibliographie Economique, Juridique et Sociale de l'Egypte Moderne (1798-1916) 1971. Repr. of 1918 ed. 25.50 (ISBN 0-8337-2305-7). B Franklin.

Ziadeh, Farhat J. Lawyers, the Rule of Law & Liberalism in Modern Egypt. LC 68-9503. (Publications Ser.: No. 75). 177p. 1968. 10.95 (ISBN 0-8179-1751-9); pap. 5.95 (ISBN 0-8179-1752-7). Hoover Inst Pr.

LAW-EUROPE

Alvarez, A., et al. Progress of Continental Law in the Nineteenth Century. Register, Layton B., tr. LC 68-54747. (Continental Legal History Ser.: Vol. 11). 1918. 22.50x (ISBN 0-678-04511-9). Kelley.

Audretsch, H. Supervision in European Community Law: Observance by the Member States of Their Treaty Obligations - a Treatise on International & Supranational Supervision. 1978. 63.50 (ISBN 0-444-85037-6, North-Holland). Elsevier.

Blegvad, B. M., ed. European Yearbook in Law & Sociology. (European Studies in Law & Sociology). 1979. lib. bdg. 39.00 (ISBN 90-247-2158-X, Pub. by Martinus Nijhoff Netherlands). Kluwer Boston.

Bredimas, A. E. Methods of Interpretation & Community Law. (European Studies in Law Ser: Vol. 6). 1978. 36.75 (ISBN 0-444-85081-3, North-Holland). Elsevier.

Brinkhorst, L. J. & Schermers, H. G. Judicial Remedies in the European Communities: A Case Book, Supplement. 1972. pap. 29.00 (ISBN 9-0268-0951-4, Pub. by Kluwer Law Netherlands). Kluwer Boston.

--Supplement to Judicial Remedies in the Eupopean Communities. LC 71-92205. xii, 183p. 1972. pap. text ed. 10.00x (ISBN 90-268-0641-8). Rothman.

Chloros, A. G. European Family Law. 1978. pap. 53.00 (ISBN 90-268-0899-2, Pub. by Kluwer Law Netherlands). Kluwer Boston.

Continental Legal History Series, 1912-1928, 10 Vols. Repr. of 1912 ed. Set. 225.00x (ISBN 0-678-04501-1). Kelley.

Council of Europe, ed. Monument Protection in Europe. 1980. lib. bdg. 31.50 (ISBN 90-268-1107-1, Pub. by Kluwer Law Netherlands). Kluwer Boston.

Esmein, Adhemar. History of Continental Criminal Procedure with Special Reference to France. (Continental Legal History Ser: Vol. 5). xlv, 640p. 1969. Repr. of 1913 ed. 22.50x (ISBN 0-8377-2102-4). Rothman.

Eversen, H. J., et al. Compendium of Case Law Relating to the European Communities, 1973. LC 74-23454. 304p. 1975. 75.75 (ISBN 0-444-10794-0, North-Holland). Elsevier.

--Compendium of Case Law Relating to the European Communities, 1974. 1976. 58.75 (ISBN 0-444-11047-X, North-Holland). Elsevier.

Everson, H. J., et al, eds. Compendium of Case Law Relating to the European Communities, 1975. 1977. 78.00 (ISBN 0-7204-0579-3, North-Holland). Elsevier.

General Survey of Events, Sources, Persons & Movements in Continental Legal History. LC 68-54738. (Continental Legal History Ser.: Vol. 1). (Illus.). Repr. of 1912 ed. 22.50x (ISBN 0-678-04502-X). Kelley.

General Survey of Events, Sources, Persons & Movements in Continental Legal History. (Continental Legal History Ser: Vol. 1). (Illus.). liii, 754p. 1968. Repr. of 1912 ed. 22.50x (ISBN 0-8377-2201-2). Rothman.

Gijlstra, D. J., ed. Legal Issues of European Integration. (Law Review of the Europa Institute of the University of Amsterdam: Vol. 1977). 1978. pap. 10.00 (ISBN 90-268-0964-6, Pub. by Kluwer Law Netherlands). Kluwer Boston.

Gijlstra, D. J., et al. Leading Cases & Materials on the Law of the European Communities. 3rd., rev. & expanded ed. 1979. pap. 26.00 (ISBN 90-268-1095-4, Pub. by Kluwer Law Netherlands). Kluwer Boston.

Gijlstra, D. J., et al, eds. Leading Cases & Materials on the Law of the European Communities. 1975. pap. 17.00 (ISBN 90-268-0806-2, Pub. by Kluwer Law Netherlands). Kluwer Boston.

Giljlstra, D. J., et al, eds. Legal Isssues of European Integration 1979. 2nd ed. 130p. 1980. pap. 21.50 (ISBN 90-2681-178-0, Pub. by Kluwer Law & Taxation). Kluwer Boston.

Hartley, T. C. The Foundations of European Community Law: An Introduction to the Constitutional & Administrative Law of the European Community. (Clarendon Law Ser.). (Illus.). 640p. 1981. 52.00 (ISBN 0-19-876081-7); pap. 36.50 (ISBN 0-19-876082-5). Oxford U Pr.

International Association of Law Libraries. European Law Libraries Guide. LC 70-873776. 678p. 1971. 30.00x (ISBN 0-900865-75-X). Intl Pubns Serv.

Jacobs, G. F. European Law & the Individual. 1976. 27.00 (ISBN 0-444-11115-8, North-Holland). Elsevier.

Keeton, G. W. & Frommel, S. N., eds. British Industry & European Law. xiv, 191p. 1974. text ed. 17.50x (ISBN 0-8377-0727-7). Rothman.

Lawson, F. H. The Comparison: Selected Essays, Vol. 2. (European Studies in Law: Vol. 5). 1978. 58.75 (ISBN 0-7204-0760-5, North-Holland). Elsevier.

Lawson, P. H. Many Laws: Selected Essays. (European Studies in Law: Vol. 4). 1978. 51.25 (ISBN 0-7204-0759-1, North-Holland). Elsevier.

Leideritz, Paula M. Key to the Study of East European Law. 1978. pap. 16.00 (ISBN 90-268-0980-8, Pub. by Kluwer Law Netherlands). Kluwer Boston.

McLoughlin, J. Law & Practice Relating to Pollution Control in the Member States of the European Communities: A Comparative Survey. 1976. 20.00x (ISBN 0-86010-040-5, Graham & Trotman). Nichols Pub.

Merryman, J. H. Law & Social Change in Mediterranean Europe & Latin America: A Handbook of Legal & Social Indicators for Comparative Study. 1980. 47.50 (ISBN 0-379-20700-1). Oceana.

Merryman, John H. & Clark, David S. Comparative Law: Western European & Latin American Legal Systems. (Contemporary Legal Education Ser.). 1978. 25.00 (ISBN 0-672-83379-4, Bobbs-Merrill Law). Michie-Bobbs.

Merryman, John H, et al. Law & Social Change in Mediterranean Europe & Latin America: A Handbook of Legal & Social Indicators of Comparative Study. 618p. 1980. lib. bdg. 47.50 (ISBN 0-379-20700-1). Oceana.

Offner, Eric D. International Trademark Service, 3 vols. LC 79-89849. 1970. 96.00 (ISBN 0-912166-04-5). Fieldston.

--International Trademark Service: Supplement, 1971, 1972, 1973. 1973. 35.00 (ISBN 0-685-22596-8). Fieldston.

Plender, Richard & Usher, J., eds. A Casebook of European Community Law. (Illus.). 1979. text ed. 62.50x (ISBN 0-333-23144-9). Humanities.

Rudden, Bernard & Wyatt, Derrick, eds. Basic Community Laws. 318p. 1980. 37.40x (ISBN 0-19-876119-8). Oxford U Pr.

Savigny, Friedrich K. The History of the Roman Law During the Middle Ages, Vol. 1. Cathcart, E., tr. LC 78-72146. 1979. Repr. of 1829 ed. 35.00 (ISBN 0-88355-815-7). Hyperion Conn.

Schermers, Henry G. Judicial Protection in the European Communities. 1979. pap. 37.00 (ISBN 90-268-1096-2, Pub. by Kluwer Law Netherlands). Kluwer Boston.

Smith, Hans & Herzog, Peter E. The Law of the European Economic Community. 1976. 500.000 set (ISBN 0-685-32577-6). Bender.

Smith, Munroe. The Development of European Law. LC 79-1621. 1980. Repr. of 1928 ed. 23.50 (ISBN 0-88355-925-0). Hyperion Conn.

Stein, et al. European Community Law. (Contemporary Legal Education Ser.). 1976. 25.00 (ISBN 0-672-82398-5, Bobb-Merrill Law); documents 11.50 (ISBN 0-672-82526-0); combined 33.00 (ISBN 0-672-82834-0). Michie-Bobbs.

Tigar, Michael & Levy, Madeleine. Law & the Rise of Capitalism. LC 77-70968. 1978. pap. 6.95 (ISBN 0-85345-477-9, PB4779). Monthly Rev.

Toth, A. G. Legal Protection of Individuals in the European Communities, Vols. 1 & 2. 1978. Vol. 1. pap. 27.00 (ISBN 0-444-85044-9, North-Holland); Vol. 2. pap. 58.75 (ISBN 0-444-85045-7); 2 vol. set 77.00 (ISBN 0-444-85046-5). Elsevier.

Von Bar, Carl L. History of Continental Criminal Law. (Continental Legal History Ser: Vol. 6). lvi, 561p. 1969. Repr. of 1916 ed. 22.50x (ISBN 0-8377-1925-9). Rothman.

Watson, Philippa, ed. Social Security Law of the European Communities. (Studies in Labour & Social Law). 292p. 1981. text ed. 38.50 (ISBN 0-7201-0926-4, Pub. by Mansell England). Merrimack Bk Serv.

Wheaton, Henry. History of the Law of Nations in Europe & America Since the Treaty of Westphalia; from the Earliest Times to the Peace of Washington, 3 vols. in 1. Incl. Law of Nations. LC 70-147604. (Library of War & Peace; International Law). lib. bdg. 38.00 ea. (ISBN 0-8240-0456-6). Garland Pub.

Zigel, Feodor F. Lectures on Slavonic Law. LC 72-97042. (Central & East European Ser.: No. 4). 1974. Repr. of 1902 ed. 12.50 (ISBN 0-87569-055-6). Academic Intl.

LAW–FRANCE

Baker, J. H. Manual of Law French. 1979. 45.00x (ISBN 0-86127-401-6, Pub. by Avebury Pub England). State Mutual Bk.

Brissaud, J. B. History of French Private Law. (Continental Legal History Ser: Vol. 3). (Illus.). xlviii, 922p. 1969. Repr. of 1912 ed. 27.50x (ISBN 0-8377-1931-3). Rothman.

--History of French Public Law. (Continental Legal History Ser: Vol. 9). lviii, 581p. 1969. Repr. of 1915 ed. 22.50x (ISBN 0-8377-1932-1). Rothman.

Brissaud, Jean B. History of French Private Law. Howell, Rapelje, tr. LC 68-54740. (Continental Legal History Ser., No. 3). Repr. of 1912 ed. 27.50x (ISBN 0-678-04504-6). Kelley.

--History of French Public Law. Garner, James W., tr. LC 68-54746. (Continental Legal History Ser., No. 9). Repr. of 1915 ed. 22.50x (ISBN 0-678-04510-0). Kelley.

Colliard, C. A. Law & Practice Relating to Pollution Control in France. 1976. 20.00x (ISBN 0-86010-033-2, Graham & Trotman). Nichols Pub.

Crabb, John H., tr. from Fr. French Business Enterprises: Basic Legislative Texts. LC 79-19925. viii, 355p. 1979. 45.00x (ISBN 0-8377-0425-1). Rothman.

David, R. & De Vries, H. French Legal System. LC 58-9194. 1958. 10.50 (ISBN 0-379-00043-1). Oceana.

David, Rene. French Law: Its Structure, Sources, & Methodology. Kindred, Michael, tr. from Fr. LC 74-181563. 216p. 1972. 17.50x (ISBN 0-8071-0248-2). La State U Pr.

De Vries, Henry. Civil Law & the Anglo-American Lawyer. LC 75-11645. 544p. 1975. text ed. 27.50 (ISBN 0-379-00222-1). Oceana.

Favre, Jules. Plaidoyers et Discours du Batonnat, 2 vols. (Fr.). 1981. Repr. of 1893 ed. Set. lib. bdg. 495.00 (ISBN 0-8287-1495-9). Vol. 1, 665 Pgs (ISBN 0-8287-1496-7). Vol. 2, 664 Pgs (ISBN 0-8287-1497-5). Clearwater Pub.

Kahn-Freund, Otto, et al. A Source-Book on French Law: System, Methods, Outlines of Contract. 2nd ed. 1979. pap. 27.00 (ISBN 0-19-825349-4). Oxford U Pr.

New Code of Civil Procedure in France, Bk. 1. 1978. 32.50 (ISBN 0-379-20266-2). Oceana.

Packard, Sidney R. Europe & the Church Under Innocent Third. enl. ed. LC 67-18294. 1968. Repr. of 1927 ed. 7.00 (ISBN 0-8462-1082-7). Russell.

Seruzier, Charles. Historical Summary of the French Codes with French & Foreign Bibliographical Annotations Concerning the General Principles of the Codes Followed by a Dissertation on Codification. Combe, David A. & Gruning, Martha S., trs. from Fr. LC 79-18107. v, 203p. 1979. lib. bdg. 32.50x (ISBN 0-8377-0424-3). Rothman.

LAW–GERMANY

Cohn, E. J. Manual of German Law, 2 Vols. LC 67-28195. 1968-71. Set. 40.00 (ISBN 0-379-00296-5); Vol. 1. 23.00 (ISBN 0-379-00296-5); Vol. 2. 23.00 (ISBN 0-379-00297-3). Oceana.

Forrester, Ian S. & Ilgen, Hans-Michael. The German Legal System. v, 25p. 1972. pap. 2.95x (ISBN 0-8377-0529-0). Rothman.

Forrester, Ian S., et al, trs. from Ger. German Civil Code of August 18, 1896. LC 75-7935. xxxvii, 434p. (Amended as of january 1, 1975). 1975. text ed. 60.00x (ISBN 0-8377-0601-7). Rothman.

German Law on Standing to Sue: (EPLP 3) 1972. pap. 7.50x (ISBN 2-88032-073-9, IUCN51, IUCN). Unipub.

Hatschek, Julius. Das Parlamentsrecht Des Deutschen Reiches: Im Auftrage des Deutschen Reichstages dargestellt, Pt. 1. xiii, 628p. (Ger.). 1973. Repr. of 1915 ed. 99.75x (ISBN 3-11-002157-9). De Gruyter.

Hoffmann, Dietrich, tr. from Ger. The German Co-Determination Act 1976 (Mitbestimmungsgesetz 1976) 96p. (Orig.). 1976. pap. text ed. 14.50x (ISBN 3-7875-5259-6). Rothman.

Huebner, Rudolf. History of Germanic Private Laws. Philbrick, Francis S., tr. LC 68-54741. (Continental Legal History Ser.: No. 4). Repr. of 1918 ed. 27.50x (ISBN 0-678-04505-4). Kelley.

Kisch, Guido. Studien zur humanistischen Jurisprudenz. 1972. 61.00x (ISBN 3-11-003600-2). De Gruyter.

Lackner, Karl, et al, eds. Festschrift fuer Wilhelm Gallas zum 70. Geburtstag. 457p. 1973. 72.75x (ISBN 3-11-004062-X). De Gruyter.

Munske, Horst H. Der Germanische Rechtswortschatz im Bereich der Missetaten, Philologische und sprachgeographische Untersuchungen Vol. 1: Die Terminologie der aelteren westgermanischen Rechtsquellen. LC 72-76055. (Studia Linguista Germanica, Vol. 8, 1). 335p. 1973. 48.75x (ISBN 3-11-003578-2). De Gruyter.

Piirainen, Ilpo T. Das Stadtrechtsbuch von Sillein: Einleitung Edition und Glossar. (Quellen und Forschungen Zur Sprach und Kulturgeschichte der Germanischen Voelker 46). 1972. 42.25x (ISBN 3-11-003543-X). De Gruyter.

Staatsbibliothek Prevssischer Kulturbesitz. Union List of Legal Journals & Serials in West Germany. 350p. 1978. 52.75 (ISBN 3-5980-7079-9). K G Saur.

Steiger, H. Law & Practice Relating to Pollution Control in the Federal Republic of Germany. 1976. 20.00x (ISBN 0-86010-032-4, Graham & Trotman). Nichols Pub.

Stratenwerth, Guenter, et al, eds. Festschrift fuer Hans Welzel zum 70.Geburtstag am 25.3.1974. viii, 956p. 1974. 135.50x (ISBN 3-11-004345-9). De Gruyter.

Von Amira, Karl. Germanisches Recht Vol. 1: Rechtsdenkmael Vol. 2: Rechtsaltertuemer. 4th ed. Eckhart, Karl A., ed. (Ger). 1960-67. Vol 1. 17.75x (ISBN 3-11-000160-8); Vol 2. 30.00x (ISBN 3-11-000173-X). De Gruyter.

--Nordgermanisches Obligationenrecht, 2 vols. Incl. Vol. 1. Altschwedisches Obligationenrecht. xiii, 788p. Repr. of 1882 ed; Vol. 2. Westnordisches Obligationenrecht. xvi, 964p. Repr. of 1895 ed. 1973. Set. 324.50x (ISBN 3-11-002183-8). De Gruyter.

LAW–GHANA

Harvey, William B. Law & Social Change in Ghana. 1966. 26.00 (ISBN 0-691-03033-2). Princeton U Pr.

LAW–GREAT BRITAIN

Allen, Carleton K. Law in the Making. 7th ed. 1964. pap. 16.95x (ISBN 0-19-881029-6, OPB29). Oxford U Pr.

Allott, Antony N. Essays in African Law, with Special Reference to the Law of Ghana. LC 74-30925. 323p. 1975. Repr. of 1960 ed. lib. bdg. 17.25x (ISBN 0-8371-7885-1, ALAL). Greenwood.

Anson, William. Anson's Law of Contract. 25th ed. Guest, A. G., ed. 1980. 39.00 (ISBN 0-19-876068-X). Oxford U Pr.

Austin, John. The Austinian Theory of Law. 1976. Repr. of 1906 ed. 45.00 (ISBN 0-403-06115-6, Regency). Scholarly.

Bacon, Francis. The Elements of the Common Lawes of England. LC 77-26477. (English Experience Ser.: No. 164). 104p. 1969. Repr. of 1630 ed. 25.00 (ISBN 90-221-0164-9). Walter J Johnson.

Bentham, Jeremy. Bentham's Theory of Fictions. LC 75-41026. Repr. of 1932 ed. 22.50 (ISBN 0-404-14508-6). AMS Pr.

--Rationale of Judicial Evidence, Specially Applied to English Practice, 5 vols. Berkowitz, David & Thorne, Samuel, eds. LC 77-86645. (Classics of English Legal History in the Modern Era Ser.: Vol. 98). 1979. Set. lib. bdg. 200.00 (ISBN 0-8240-3085-0); lib. bdg. 55.00 ea. Garland Pub.

Berkowitz, David S. & Thorne, Samuel E., eds. George Meriton. Sir Henry Spelman. Anon. Charles Fearne. (English Legal History Ser.: Vol. 137). 370p. 1979. lib. bdg. 55.00 (ISBN 0-8240-3174-1). Garland Pub.

--Sir Edward Coke, 4 vols. (English Legal History Ser.). 1468p. 1979. lib. bdg. 55.00 (ISBN 0-8240-3053-2). Garland Pub.

--Sir Henry Finch. Edmund Wingate. William Phillips. (English Legal History Ser.: Vol. 68). 462p. 1979. lib. bdg. 55.00 (ISBN 0-8240-3055-9). Garland Pub.

--Sir William Staunford. William Dickinson. Roger Maynwaring. Robert Sibthorpe. Sir Walter Raleigh. (English Legal History Ser.: Vol. 131). 426p. 1979. lib. bdg. 55.00 (ISBN 0-8240-3168-7). Garland Pub.

Blackstone, W. Commentaries on the Law of England: First English Edition, Oxford, 1765-1769, 4 Vols. 1966. 150.00 (ISBN 0-379-00414-3). Oceana.

--Commentaries on the Laws of England: First American Edition, Philadelphia, 1771-1772, 5 Vols. 1966. 150.00 (ISBN 0-379-00418-6). Oceana.

Blackstone, William. Blackstone's Commentaries with Notes of Reference to the Constitution & Laws of the Federal Government of the United States & of the Commonwealth of Virginia, 5 Vols. Tucker, St. George, ed. LC 68-57388. 1969. Repr. of 1802 ed. 135.00x (ISBN 0-8377-1930-5). Rothman.

--Commentaries on the Laws of England: A Facsimile of the First Edition of 1765-1769, 4 vols. LC 79-11753. 1979. Set. lib. bdg. 90.00x (ISBN 0-226-05536-1); pap. 8.95x ea. Vol. I (ISBN 0-226-05538-8). Vol. II (ISBN 0-226-05541-8). Vol. III (ISBN 0-226-05543-4). Vol. IV (ISBN 0-226-05545-0). U of Chicago Pr.

--Ehrlich's Blackstone. Ehrlich, J. W., ed. LC 72-5652. 987p. 1973. Repr. of 1959 ed. lib. bdg. 39.75x (ISBN 0-8371-6446-X, BLER). Greenwood.

Blackstone, Sir William. Blackstone's Commentaries, 5 Vols. Tucker, St. George, ed. LC 68-57388. 1803. 135.00x (ISBN 0-678-04530-5). Kelley.

Boorstin, Daniel J. Mysterious Science of the Law. 7.50 (ISBN 0-8446-1702-4). Peter Smith.

Booth, V. Hartley. British Extradition Law & Procedure, Vol. II. 604p. 1981. 35.00 (ISBN 90-286-0079-5). Sijthoff & Noordhoff.

Brackenridge, Hugh H. Law Miscellanies: Containing an Introduction to the Study of the Law. LC 73-37967. (American Law: The Formative Years). 600p. 1972. Repr. of 1814 ed. 26.00 (ISBN 0-405-03994-8). Arno.

Bracton, Henry de. Bracton on the Laws & Customs of England, Vols. 1-4. Thorne, Samuel E., ed. LC 68-28697. Orig. Title: Legibus et Consuetudinibus Angliae. 1400p. 1968. Vols. 1 & 2. 65.00x (ISBN 0-674-08035-1, Belknap Pr); Vols. 3 & 4. 85.00x (ISBN 0-674-08038-6, Belknap Pr). Harvard U Pr.

--De Legibus et Consuetudinibus Angliae. Woodbine, G. E., ed. 1942. Vol. 4. 75.00x (ISBN 0-686-51370-3). Elliots Bks.

Brydall, John & Highmore, Anthony. Non Compos Mentis. Berkowitz, David S. & Thorne, Samuel E., eds. LC 77-86669. (Classics of English Legal History in the Modern Era Ser.: Vol. 46). 471p. 1979. lib. bdg. 40.00 (ISBN 0-8240-3095-8). Garland Pub.

Chester, Samuel B. Anomalies of the English Law. 287p. 1980. Repr. of 1911 ed. lib. bdg. 22.50x (ISBN 0-8377-0426-X). Rothman.

Chitty, Joseph, Jr. A Practical Treatise on the Law of Contracts. Berkowitz, David S. & Thorne, Samuel E., eds. LC 77-86636. (Classics of English Legal History in the Modern Era Ser.: Vol. 25). 807p. 1979. lib. bdg. 40.00 (ISBN 0-8240-3074-5). Garland Pub.

Coke, Edward. Lord Coke, His Speech & Charge. LC 79-38167. (English Experience Ser.: No. 444). 64p. 1972. Repr. of 1607 ed. 9.50 (ISBN 90-221-0444-3). Walter J Johnson.

Cowell, John. The Interpreter: Or, Book Containing the Signification of Words. LC 76-25757. (English Experience Ser.: No. 231). 584p. 1970. Repr. of 1607 ed. 69.00 (ISBN 90-221-0231-9). Walter J Johnson.

Crime & Punishment, 6 pts. Incl. Pt. 1. Civil Disorder, 8 vols. Set. 612.00x (ISBN 0-686-01180-5); Pt. 2. Juvenile Offenders, 6 vols. Set. 495.00x (ISBN 0-686-01181-3); Pt. 3. Penal Servitude, 2 vols. Set. 153.00x (ISBN 0-686-01182-1); Pt. 4. Police, 10 vols. Set. 621.00x (ISBN 0-686-01183-X); Pt. 5. Prisons, 21 vols. Set. 1837.00x (ISBN 0-686-01184-8); Pt. 6. Transportation, 16 vols. Set. 1296.00x (ISBN 0-686-01185-6). (British Parliamentary Papers Ser.). 1971 (Pub. by Irish Academic Pr Ireland). Biblio Dist.

Cross, Rupert. The Precedent in English Law. 3rd ed. 252p. 1977. pap. 11.95x (ISBN 0-19-876073-6). Oxford U Pr.

Dalrymple, John. An Essay Towards a General History of Feudal Property in Great Britain. vii, 332p. 1979. Repr. of 1757 ed. lib. bdg. 35.00x (ISBN 0-8377-0508-8). Rothman.

Delany, Vincent T., ed. Frederic William Maitland Reader. LC 57-10624. 1957. 7.50 (ISBN 0-379-11310-4); pap. 2.50 (ISBN 0-685-18990-2). Oceana.

De Lolme, Jean L. The Rise & Progress of the English Constitution, Vol. 82. Berkowitz, David & Thorne, Samuel, eds. LC 77-86589. (Classics of English Legal History in the Modern Era). 1979. Repr. of 1838 ed. lib. bdg. 55.00 (ISBN 0-686-77117-6). Garland Pub.

Devlin, Patrick. The Judge. 1979. 22.00x (ISBN 0-19-215949-6). Oxford U Pr.

Dillon, J. F. The Law & Jurisprudence of England & America. LC 75-99475. (American Constitutional & Legal History Ser). 1970. Repr. of 1894 ed. lib. bdg. 42.50 (ISBN 0-306-71854-5). Da Capo.

Doddridge, John. The English Lawyer, Describing a Method for the Managing of the Lawes of This Land. LC 72-5973. (English Experience Ser.: No. 503). 280p. 1973. Repr. of 1631 ed. 30.00 (ISBN 90-221-0503-2). Walter J Johnson.

Finch, Henry. Law, or a Discourse Thereof. LC 68-57385. Repr. of 1759 ed. 22.50x (ISBN 0-678-04526-7). Kelley.

--Law, Or, a Discourse Thereof: In Four Books. LC 68-57385. 528p. 1969. Repr. of 1759 ed. 22.50x (ISBN 0-8377-2125-3). Rothman.

Finch, Sir Henry. Law, or a Discourse Thereof Done into English. Berkowitz, David & Thorne, Samuel, eds. LC 77-86560. (Classics of English Legal History in the Modern Era Ser.: Vol. 65). 1979. Repr. of 1759 ed. lib. bdg. 55.00 (ISBN 0-8240-3052-4). Garland Pub.

Finlason, W. F. Commentaries Upon Martial Law, with Special Reference to Its Regulation & Restraint: With an Introduction, Containing Comments Upon the Charge of the Lord Chief Justice in the Jamaica Case. 287p. 1980. Repr. of 1867 ed. lib. bdg. 28.50x (ISBN 0-8377-0536-3). Rothman.

Fonblanque, John. A Treatise of Equity. Ballow, Henry, et al, eds. LC 77-86649. (Classics of English Legal History in the Modern Era Ser.: Vol. 34). 775p. 1979. lib. bdg. 40.00 (ISBN 0-8240-3083-4). Garland Pub.

Fowle, T. W. The Poor Law: The English Citizen: His Rights & Responsibilities. vi, 175p. 1979. Repr. of 1893 ed. lib. bdg. 17.50x (ISBN 0-8377-0534-7). Rothman.

Geldart, William. Elements of English Law. 8th ed. Yardley, D. C., ed. (Oxford Paperbacks University Ser: No. 6). 196p. 1975. pap. 7.95x (ISBN 0-19-289071-9, OPUS6). Oxford U Pr.

Gomme, George L. Primitive Folk-Moots: Or, Open-Air Assemblies in Britain. LC 67-23899. 1968. Repr. of 1880 ed. 14.00 (ISBN 0-8103-3433-X). Gale.

Hale, Sir Matthew. Sir Matthew Hale: The Analysis of the Law: Being a Scheme or Abstract of the Several Titles & Portions of the Law of England, Digested into Method, Repr. Of 1713 Ed. Berkowitz, David & Thorne, Samuel, eds. Bd. with Giles Jacob: The Student's Companion: or, the Reason of the Laws of England, Shewing the Principal Reasons & Motives Wherein Our Laws & Statutes Are Criminal Cases; Together with the Law Itself. Jacob, Giles. Repr. of 1725 ed. LC 77-86566. (Classics of English Legal History in the Modern Era Ser.: Vol. 70). 1979. lib. bdg. 55.00 (ISBN 0-8240-3057-5). Garland Pub.

Hanbury, H. G. & Yardley, D. C. English Courts of Law. 5th ed. 1979. 14.50x (ISBN 0-19-219139-X). Oxford U Pr.

Hargrave, Francis. Collectanea Juridica: Consisting of Tracts Relative to the Law & Constitution of England, 2 vols. 1981. Repr. of 1791 ed. lib. bdg. 75.00x (ISBN 0-8377-0632-7). Rothman.

Hawkins, William. A Treatise of the Pleas of the Crown: Or a System of the Principal... LC 70-37977. (American Law Ser.: The Formative Years). 876p. 1972. Repr. of 1726 ed. 44.00 (ISBN 0-405-04020-2). Arno.

--A Treatise on the Pleas of the Crown, 2 vols. Berkowitz, David S. & Thorne, Samuel E., eds. LC 77-86643. (Classics of English Legal History in the Modern Era Ser.: Vol. 30). 874p. 1979. lib. bdg. 80.00 (ISBN 0-8240-3079-6). Garland Pub.

Henderson, Edith G. Foundations of English Administrative Law. 204p. 1963. 6.50x (ISBN 0-8377-2226-8). Rothman.

Horn, Andrew. Mirrour of Justices. LC 68-54748. Repr. of 1903 ed. 13.50x (ISBN 0-678-04527-5). Kelley.

Keeton, George W. English Law: The Judicial Contribution. 384p. 1974. 8.95 (ISBN 0-7153-6410-3). David & Charles.

Knafla, L. A. Law & Politics in Jacobean England. LC 76-4757. (Cambridge Studies in English Legal History). (Illus.). 1977. 59.00 (ISBN 0-521-21191-3). Cambridge U Pr.

Legal Administration, 3 pts. Incl. Pt. 1. General, 16 vols. Set. 1378.00x (ISBN 0-686-01177-5); Pt. 2. Criminal Law, 6 vols. Set. 423.00x (ISBN 0-686-01178-3); Pt. 3. Marriage - Divorce, 3 vols. Set. 198.00x (ISBN 0-686-01179-1). (British Parliamentary Papers Ser.). 1971 (Pub. by Irish Academic Pr Ireland). Biblio Dist.

Lester, Anthony & Bindman, Geoffrey. Race & Law in Great Britain. LC 73-189159. 1972. 22.50x (ISBN 0-674-74570-1). Harvard U Pr.

Lewis, J. R. Cases for Discussion. 1966. 13.75 (ISBN 0-08-011352-4); pap. 6.25 (ISBN 0-08-011351-6). Pergamon.

Lunt, Dudley C. Road to the Law. 1962. pap. 1.65x (ISBN 0-393-00183-0, Norton Lib). Norton.

McLoughlin, J. Law & Practice Relating to Pollution Control in the United Kingdom. 1976. 20.00x (ISBN 0-86010-037-5, Graham & Trotman). Nichols Pub.

Maitland, Frederic W. Selected Essays. facs. ed. Hazeltine, H. D., et al, eds. LC 68-20316. (Essay Index Reprint Ser). 1936. 15.50 (ISBN 0-8369-0670-5). Arno.

Mantell, Walter, et al. Short Treatise of the Laws of England. Berkowitz, David S. & Thorne, Samuel E., eds. LC 77-86578. (Classics of English Legal History in the Modern Era Ser.: Vol. 17). 351p. 1979. lib. bdg. 40.00 (ISBN 0-8240-3066-4). Garland Pub.

Manwood, John. A Brefe Collection of the Lawes of the Forest. Berkowitz, David & Thorne, Samuel, eds. LC 77-86654. (Classics of English Legal History in the Modern Era Ser.: Vol. 100). 1979. Repr. of 1598 ed. lib. bdg. 40.00 (ISBN 0-8240-3087-7). Garland Pub.

Marston, Geoffrey. The Marginal Seabed in United Kingdom Legal Practice. 260p. 1981. 55.00 (ISBN 0-19-825369-9). Oxford U Pr.

Meek, Charles K. Colonial Law, a Bibliography with Special Reference to Native African Systems of Law & Land Tenure. LC 78-14383. 1978. lib. bdg. 15.00 (ISBN 0-313-21011-X, MECL). Greenwood.

Nasmith, David. Institutes of English Adjective Law (Procedure in Court) Embracing an Outline of the Law of Evidence & Measure of Damages. xxii, 355p. 1980. Repr. of 1878 ed. lib. bdg. 30.00x (ISBN 0-8377-0904-0). Rothman.

--Institutes of English Private Law: Embracing an Outline of the Substantive Branch of the Law of Persons & Things, 2 vols. 720p. 1980. Repr. of 1875 ed. Set. lib. bdg. 57.50x (ISBN 0-8377-0903-2). Rothman.

Nelson, William. Lex Testamentaria. Berkowits, David S. & Thorne, Samuel E., eds. LC 77-89254. (Classics of English Legal History in the Modern Era Ser.: Vol. 81). 552p. 1979. lib. bdg. 40.00 (ISBN 0-8240-3180-6). Garland Pub.

Noy, William. The Principal Grounds & Maxims with an Analysis of the Laws of England. 3rd ed. xxviii, 219p. 1980. Repr. of 1845 ed. lib. bdg. 25.00x (ISBN 0-8377-0906-7). Rothman.

Palmer, Sir Francis B. Peerage Law in England: A Practical Treatise for Lawyers & Laymen. with an Appendix of Peerage Charters & Letters Patent (in English) Berkowitz, David & Thorne, Samuel, eds. LC 77-89217. (Classics of English Legal History in the Modern Era Ser.: Vol. 128). 1979. Repr. of 1907 ed. lib. bdg. 40.00 (ISBN 0-8240-3165-2). Garland Pub.

Paterson, James. Commentaries on the Liberty of the Subject & the Laws of England Relating to the Security of the Person, 2 vols 1010p. 1980. Repr. of 1877 ed. Set. lib. bdg. 75.00x (ISBN 0-8377-1005-7). Rothman.

Paulus, Ingeborg. Search for Pure Food: A Sociology of Legislation in Britain. (Law in Society Ser.). 144p. 1974. text ed. 8.50x (ISBN 0-85520-076-6). Rothman.

Perkins, John. A Profitable Book...Treating of the Lawes of England. And Now Translated Out of French into English, Vol. 63. Berkowitz, David S. & Thorne, Samuel E., eds. LC 77-86556. (Classics of English Legal History in the Modern Era Ser.). 1979. Repr. of 1827 ed. lib. bdg. 55.00 (ISBN 0-8240-3050-8). Garland Pub.

Pollock, Frederick. The Land Laws. x, 233p. 1979. Repr. of 1896 ed. lib. bdg. 20.00x (ISBN 0-8377-1001-4). Rothman.

Powell, John J. Essays Upon the Law of Contracts & Agreements, 2 vols. in 1. Berkowitz, David & Thorne, Samuel, eds. LC 77-86628. (Classics of English Legal History in the Modern Era Ser.: Vol. 86). 1979. Repr. of 1970 ed. lib. bdg. 80.00 (ISBN 0-8240-3073-7). Garland Pub.

Pritt, D. N. Law, Class & Society, 4 vols. 174p. 1970. 44.00x set (ISBN 0-8464-0547-4). Beekman Pubs.

Pulton, Ferdinand. De Pace Regis et Regni. Berkowitz, David S. & Thorne, Samuel E., eds. LC 77-86638. (Classics of English Legal History in the Modern Era Ser.: Vol.29). 574p. 1979. lib. bdg. 40.00 (ISBN 0-8240-3078-8). Garland Pub.

Rastell, John. An Exposition of Certaine Difficult & Obscure Wordes & Termes of the Lawes of This Realme. LC 72-226. (English Experience Ser.: No. 210). 392p. 1969. Repr. of 1579 ed. 35.00 (ISBN 90-221-0210-6). Walter J Johnson.

Rosenbach, A. S. American Jewish Bibliography. 1977. Set. write for info. (ISBN 0-939084-12-0, BRCB, Pub. by Rosenbach Mus & Lib). U Pr of Va.

Rushton, William L. Shakespeare a Lawyer. LC 72-174790. Repr. of 1858 ed. 16.50 (ISBN 0-404-05452-8). AMS Pr.

Sachs, Albie & Wilson, Joan H. Sexism & the Law: Male Beliefs & Legal Bias in Britain & the United States. LC 78-63402. 1979. 15.95 (ISBN 0-02-927640-3). Free Pr.

Saint German, Christopher. Hereafter Foloweth a Dyaloge in Englysshe Betwyxt a Doctoure of Dyvynyte & a Student in the Lawes of Englande. LC 72-6026. (English Experience Ser.: No. 552). 456p. 1973. Repr. of 1530 ed. 39.00 (ISBN 90-221-0552-0). Walter J Johnson.

Schwartz, Mortimer D. & Henke, Dan F., eds. Combined Catalog Anglo-American Law Collections University of California Law Libraries Berkeley & Davis with Library of Congress Class K Added, 9 vols. (Supplement). 1979. text ed. 750.00x (ISBN 0-8377-0423-5). Rothman.

Schwarzenberger, Georg, ed. Law, Justice & Equity. LC 67-20413. 1967. 14.00 (ISBN 0-379-00344-9). Oceana.

Sheridan, Thomas. Some Revelations on Irish History. Bannister, Saxe, ed. LC 73-102592. (Irish Culture & History Ser). Repr. of 1870 ed. 14.50 (ISBN 0-8046-0769-9). Kennikat.

Slavin, Arthur J., ed. Tudor Men & Institutions: Studies in English Law & Government. LC 72-79337. 304p. 1972. 20.00x (ISBN 0-8071-0227-X). La State U Pr.

Smith, T. E. Elections in Developing Countries. LC 73-9130. 278p. 1973. Repr. of 1960 ed. lib. bdg. 14.00x (ISBN 0-8371-6987-9, SMED). Greenwood.

Smith, Thomas B. Studies Critical & Comparative. LC 62-20563. 1962. 17.50 (ISBN 0-379-00118-7). Oceana.

Staunford, William & Romilly, Samuel. Les Plees Del Coron. Berkowitz, David S. & Thorne, Samuel E., eds. LC 77-86634. (Classics of English Legal History in the Modern Era Ser.: Vol. 28). 484p. 1979. lib. bdg. 40.00 (ISBN 0-8240-3077-X). Garland Pub.

Stephen, Henry J. New Commentaries on the Law of England, 4 vols. Berkowitz, David S. & Thorne, Samuel E., eds. LC 77-86571. (Classics of English Legal History in the Modern Era Ser.: Vol. 73). 1979. lib. bdg. 55.00 ea. (ISBN 0-8240-3060-5). Garland Pub.

Surridge, B. J. & Digby, Margaret. A Manual of Co-Operative Law & Practice. Plunkett Foundation for Co-Operative Studies, ed. 274p. 1978. 25.00x (ISBN 0-686-75621-5, Pub. by Plunkett Found England). State Mutual Bk.

Sutherland, Donald W. The Assize of Novel Disseisin. 1973. 29.95x (ISBN 0-19-822410-9). Oxford U Pr.

Thayer, James B. Legal Essays. LC 72-81340. (Illus.). xvi, 402p. 1972. Repr. of 1908 ed. lib. bdg. 19.50x (ISBN 0-8377-2627-1). Rothman.

Twining, William & Miers, David. How to Do Things with Rules: A Primer of Interpretation. (Law in Context Ser). xiv, 322p. 1975. text ed. 16.00x (ISBN 0-297-77132-9). Rothman.

Watt, Francis. The Law's Lumber Room. LC 72-96203. 166p. 1973. Repr. of 1896 ed. 18.50x (ISBN 0-912004-08-8). W W Gaunt.

--The Law's Lumber Room, Second Series. LC 72-96204. viii, 202p. 1973. Repr. of 1898 ed. 18.75x (ISBN 0-912004-09-6). W W Gaunt.

Webb, Philip C. & Grove, Joseph. The Question Whether a Jew, Born Within the British Dominions, Was, Before the Making of the Late Act of Parliament, a Person Capable by Law, to Purchase & Hold Lands to Him and His Heirs. Berkowitz, David S. & Thorne, Samuel E., eds. LC 77-86671. (Classics of English Legal History in the Modern Era Ser.: Vol. 48). 169p. 1979. lib. bdg. 40.00 (ISBN 0-8240-3097-4). Garland Pub.

West, William. Symbolaeographia, Which May Be Termed the Art, Description, or Image of Instruments Covenants, Contracts, 2 vols. Berkowitz, David S. & Thorne, Samuel E., eds. LC 77-86629. (Classics of English Legal History in the Modern Era Ser.: Vol. 85). 1979. Set. lib. bdg. 110.00 (ISBN 0-8240-3072-9); lib. bdg. 55.00 ea. Garland Pub.

--Symbolaeographia Which Termed the Art, Description of Instruments, Covenants, Contracts, Etc. LC 74-28892. (English Experience Ser.: No. 768). 1975. Repr. of 1590 ed. 43.00 (ISBN 90-221-0768-X). Walter J Johnson.

Wood, Thomas. An Institute of the Laws of England: Or Laws of England in Their Natural Order According to Common Use. Berkowitz, David S. & Thorne, Samuel E., eds. LC 77-86569. (Classics of English Legal History in the Modern Era Ser.: Vol. 71). 1979. lib. bdg. 55.00 (ISBN 0-8240-3058-3). Garland Pub.

Wooddeson, Richard. Elements of Jurisprudence, Treated of in the Preliminary Part of a Course of Lectures on the Laws of England. 118p. 1979. Repr. of 1783 ed. lib. bdg. 35.00x (ISBN 0-8377-0533-9). Rothman.

Zander, Michael. Cases & Materials on the English Legal System. 3rd ed. (Law in Context Ser.). xxvii, 476p. 1980. 47.95x (ISBN 0-297-77822-6, Pub. by Weidenfeld & Nicholson England). Rothman.

LAW-GREAT BRITAIN-BIBLIOGRAPHY

Cowley, John D. Bibliography of Abridgments, Digests, Dictionaries & Indexes of English Law to the Year Eighteen Hundred. LC 79-54199. (Illus.). 1979. Repr. of 1932 ed. lib. bdg. 85.00 (ISBN 0-912004-15-0). W W Gaunt.

Friend, William L. Anglo-American Legal Bibliographies: An Annotated Guide. LC 78-168085. Repr. of 1944 ed. 10.00 (ISBN 0-404-02599-4). AMS Pr.

LAW-GREAT BRITAIN-HISTORY AND CRITICISM

Adams, George B. Council & Courts in Anglo-Norman England. LC 64-66387. 1965. Repr. of 1926 ed. 10.00 (ISBN 0-8462-0552-1). Russell.

Arnold, Morris S., et al, eds. On the Laws & Customs of England: Essays in Honor of Samuel E. Thorne. LC 80-11909. (Studies in Legal History). xx, 426p. 1981. 25.00x (ISBN 0-8078-1434-2). U of NC Pr.

Association of American Law Schools. Selected Essays in Anglo-American Legal History 1907-09, 3 Vols. 1969. Set. 120.00 (ISBN 0-379-00426-7). Oceana.

Best, William M. William Mawdesley Best: Treatise on the Principles of Evidence & Practice As to Proofs in Courts of Common Law, Repr. Of 1849 Ed. Berkowitz, David & Thorne, Samuel, eds. Bd. with Sir James Fitzjames Stephen: Digest of the Law of Evidence. Stephen, Sir James F. Repr. of 1876 ed. LC 77-86653. (Classics of English Legal History in the Modern Era Ser.). 1979. lib. bdg. 55.00 (ISBN 0-8240-3086-9). Garland Pub.

Bigelow, Melville M. Placita Anglo-Normannica: Law Cases from William One to Richard One. LC 78-112405. Repr. of 1881 ed. lib. bdg. 15.00x (ISBN 0-678-04539-9). Kelley.

Brewer, John & Styles, John, eds. An Ungovernable People: The English & Their Law in the Seventeenth & Eighteenth Centuries. 1980. 24.00 (ISBN 0-8135-0891-6). Rutgers U Pr.

Bryan, J. W. Development of the English Law of Conspiracy. LC 72-77737. (Law, Politics, & History Ser). 1970. Repr. of 1909 ed. lib. bdg. 20.00 (ISBN 0-306-71375-6). Da Capo.

Bryce, James B. Studies in History & Jurisprudence, 2 Vols. facs. ed. LC 68-8444. (Essay Index Reprint Ser). 1968. Repr. of 1901 ed. Set. 40.00 (ISBN 0-8369-0261-0). Arno.

Buller, Francis. An Introduction to the Law Relative to Trials at Nisi Prius. Berkowitz, David S. & Thorne, Samuel E., eds. LC 77-89211. (Classics of English Legal History in the Modern Era Ser.: Vol. 60). 670p. 1979. lib. bdg. 40.00 (ISBN 0-8240-3159-8). Garland Pub.

Cam, Helen. Law-Finders & Law Makers in Medieval England: Collected Studies in Legal & Constitutional History. LC 79-13344. 1962. lib. bdg. 15.00x (ISBN 0-678-08062-3). Kelley.

Cameron, James R. Frederick William Maitland & the History of English Law. LC 77-677. 1977. Repr. of 1961 ed. lib. bdg. 17.75x (ISBN 0-8371-9499-7, CAFWM). Greenwood.

A Century of Law Reform: 1971-1978. LC 71-181888. xi, 431p. 1972. Repr. of 1901 ed. text ed. 22.50x (ISBN 0-8377-2005-2). Rothman.

Clerk, William. An Epitome of Certaine Late Aspersions Cast at Civilians. LC 79-84095. (English Experience Ser.: No.915). 56p. 1979. Repr. of 1631 ed. lib. bdg. 7.00 (ISBN 90-221-0915-1). Walter J Johnson.

Cohen, Herman J. A History of the English Bar & "Attornatus" to 1450. x, 622p. 1980. Repr. of 1929 ed. lib. bdg. 37.50x (ISBN 0-87991-093-3). Porcupine Pr.

Cosgrove, Richard A. The Rule of Law: Albert Venn Dicey, Victorian Jurist. LC 79-18027. (Studies in Legal History Ser.). xv, 319p. 1980. 19.50x (ISBN 0-8078-1410-5). U of NC Pr.

Cowley, John D. Bibliography of Abridgments, Digests, Dictionaries & Indexes of English Law to the Year Eighteen Hundred. LC 79-54199. (Illus.). 1979. Repr. of 1932 ed. lib. bdg. 85.00 (ISBN 0-912004-15-0). W W Gaunt.

Curzon, L. B. English Legal History. 352p. 1980. 12.00x (ISBN 0-7121-0578-6, Pub. by Macdonald & Evans). State Mutual Bk.

Dicey, Albert V. Lectures on the Relation Between Law & Public Opinion in England, During the Nineteenth Century. 2nd ed. LC 75-41074. Repr. of 1914 ed. 34.50 (ISBN 0-404-14532-9). AMS Pr.

Fortescue, John. De Laudibus Legum Anglie. Chrimes, S. B., intro. by. LC 78-62331. 1979. Repr. of 1942 ed. 26.50 (ISBN 0-88355-793-2). Hyperion Conn.

Gilbert, Sir Gefrey & Peake, Thomas. The Law of Evidence: A Compendium of the Law of Evidence, Vol. 35A & B. Berkowitz, David S. & Thorne, Samuel E., eds. LC 77-86648. (Classics of English Legal History in the Modern Era Ser.: Vol. 97). 1979. lib. bdg. 55.00 (ISBN 0-8240-3084-2). Garland Pub.
Ginsberg, Morris, ed. Law & Opinion in England in the Twentieth Century. LC 74-7537. 407p. 1974. Repr. of 1959 ed. lib. bdg. 35.00x (ISBN 0-8371-7576-3, GILO). Greenwood.
Glanville, Ranulph de. Translation of Glanville: (A Treatise on the Laws & Customs of the Kingdom of England) Beames, John, tr. from Latin. xl, 362p. 1980. Repr. of 1812 ed. lib. bdg. 30.00x (ISBN 0-8377-0313-1). Rothman.
Hale, Matthew. History of the Common Law of England. Gray, Charles M., ed. LC 70-155856. (Classics of British Historical Literature Ser). 1971. 9.00x (ISBN 0-226-31304-2). U of Chicago Pr.
Hammond, Henry. The Lawfull Magistrate Upon Colour of Religion. Berkowitz, David S. & Thorne, Samuel E., eds. LC 77-89203. (Classics of English Legal History in the Modern Era Ser.: Vol. 58). 1979. lib. bdg. 40.00 (ISBN 0-8240-3157-1). Garland Pub.
Harding, A. Social History of English Law. 8.75 (ISBN 0-8446-2204-4). Peter Smith.
Heath, James. Torture & English Law: An Administrative & Legal History from the Plantagenets to the Stuarts. LC 80-24552. (Contributions in Legal Studies: No. 18). 272p. 1981. lib. bdg. 35.00 (ISBN 0-313-22598-2, HTE/). Greenwood.
Holdsworth, William S. Historians of Anglo-American Law. 1966. Repr. of 1928 ed. 16.50 (ISBN 0-208-00347-9, Archon). Shoe String.
Jenks, Edward. Edward Plantagenet: The English Justinian or the Making of Common Law. (Select Bibliographies Reprint Ser). 1901. 15.00 (ISBN 0-8369-5070-4). Arno.
Knappen, Marshall M. Constitutional & Legal History of England. 607p. 1964. Repr. of 1942 ed. 17.50 (ISBN 0-208-01439-X, Archon). Shoe String.
Lambert, Sheila. Bills & Acts: Legislative Procedure in Eighteenth Century England. 1971. 39.00 (ISBN 0-521-08119-X). Cambridge U Pr.
Maitland, Frederic W. Frederic William Maitland, Historian: Selections from His Writings. Schuyler, Robert L., ed. & intro. by. 1960. pap. 1.50 (ISBN 0-520-00796-4, CAL33). U of Cal Pr.
--Selected Historical Essays. Cam, H. M., ed. 1957. 41.50 (ISBN 0-521-05659-4). Cambridge U Pr.
--A Sketch of English Legal History. LC 75-41185. 1976. Repr. of 1915 ed. 17.45 (ISBN 0-404-14684-8). AMS Pr.
Nasmith, David. Institutes of English Public Law: Embracing an Outline of General Jurisprudence, the Development of the British Constitution, Public International Law, & the Public Municipal Law of England. vi, 455p. 1980. Repr. of 1873 ed. lib. bdg. 35.00x (ISBN 0-8377-0905-9). Rothman.
New York University. Anglo-American Legal History Series, Nos. 2-9 In 1 Vol. 1939-1944. 25.00 (ISBN 0-379-00178-0). Oceana.
Pollock, Edward & Maitland, Frederic W. History of English Law Before the Time of Edward First, 2 vols. Vol. 2. 59.00 (ISBN 0-521-07062-7); Vol. 1. pap. 24.95x (ISBN 0-521-09515-8); Vol. 2. pap. 24.95x (ISBN 0-521-09516-6). Cambridge U Pr.
Pratt, John T. The Law Relating to Friendly Societies. Berkowitz, David S. & Thorne, Samuel E., eds. LC 77-86656. (Classics of English Legal History in the Modern Era Ser.: Vol. 40). 160p. 1979. lib. bdg. 40.00 (ISBN 0-8240-3089-3). Garland Pub.
Reeves, John. History of the English Law, from the Time of the Saxons, to the End of the Reign of Philip & Mary, 4 Vols. 2nd ed. LC 68-57387. 1969. Repr. of 1787 ed. 75.00x (ISBN 0-8377-2526-7). Rothman.
Riess, Ludwig. The History of English Electoral Law in the Middle Ages. LC 73-18151. 107p. 1973. Repr. of 1940 ed. lib. bdg. 13.00x (ISBN 0-374-96804-7). Octagon.
Robertson, A. J., ed. The Laws of the Kings of England from Edmund to Henry I. LC 80-2210. Repr. of 1925 ed. 52.50 (ISBN 0-404-18784-6). AMS Pr.
Roscoe, Edward S. The Growth of English Law. Being Studies in the Evolution of Law & Procedure in England. viii, 260p. 1980. Repr. of 1911 ed. lib. bdg. 26.00x (ISBN 0-8377-1029-4). Rothman.
Russell, Sir William O. A Treatise on Crimes & Misdemeanors, 6 vols. Berkowitz, David S. & Thorne, Samuel E., eds. LC 77-86641. (Classics of English Legal History in the Modern Era Ser.: Vol. 94). 1979. Set. lib. bdg. 55.00 ea. (ISBN 0-8240-3081-8). Garland Pub.
Schuyler, R. L. Editor: Writings of Frederic William Maitland, Historian. 5.50 (ISBN 0-8446-2890-5). Peter Smith.
Seebohm, Frederic. Tribal Custom in Anglo-Saxon Law Being an Essay Supplemental to 'The English Village Community' & 'The Tribal System in Wales' LC 79-190292. xvi, 538p. 1972. Repr. of 1911 ed. lib. bdg. 25.00x (ISBN 0-8377-2605-0). Rothman.
Somers, John & Jacob, Giles. Judgment of Whole Kingdoms & Nations. Berkowitz, David S. & Thorne, Samuel E., eds. LC 77-86589. (Classics of English Legal History in the Modern Era Ser.: Vol. 19). 467p. 1979. lib. bdg. 40.00 (ISBN 0-8240-3069-9). Garland Pub.
Stenton, Doris M. English Justice Between the Norman Conquest & the Great Charter 1066-1215. LC 64-14094. (Memoirs Ser.: Vol. 60). (Illus.). 1964. 4.00 (ISBN 0-87169-060-8). Am Philos.
Stubbs, William. Lectures on Early English History. Hassall, Arthur, ed. vi, 391p. 1980. Repr. of 1906 ed. lib. bdg. 35.00x (ISBN 0-8377-1109-6). Rothman.
Theloall, Simon. Le Digest Des Briefes Originals, et Des Choses Concernant Eux. Berkowitz, David S. & Thorne, Samuel E., eds. LC 77-89257. (Classics of English Legal History in the Modern Era: Vol. 145). 1979. lib. bdg. 55.00 (ISBN 0-8240-3182-2). Garland Pub.
Thompson, E. P. Whigs & Hunters. LC 75-23168. 1976. 15.00 (ISBN 0-394-40011-9); pap. 5.95 (ISBN 0-394-73086-0). Pantheon.
Vinogradoff, Paul, ed. Oxford Studies in Social & Legal History, 9 vols. 1974. lib. bdg. 160.00x (ISBN 0-374-96157-3). Octagon.
White, Stephen D. Sir Edward Coke & "The Grievances of the Commonwealth," 1621-1628. LC 78-16418. (Studies in Legal History). 22.50x (ISBN 0-8078-1335-4). U of NC Pr.
Williams, Thomas & Somers, John. Excellency & Praeheminence of the Law of England. Berkowitz, David S. & Thorne, Samuel E., eds. LC 77-86674. (Classics of English Legal History in the Modern Era Ser.: Vol. 50). 357p. 1979. lib. bdg. 40.00 (ISBN 0-8240-3099-0). Garland Pub.
Winfield, Percy H. The Chief Sources of English Legal History. LC 74-187697. (Bibliography & Reference Ser.). 402p. 1972. Repr. of 1925 ed. lib. bdg. 24.50 (ISBN 0-8337-3815-1). B Franklin.

LAW–GREECE (ANCIENT)

see Law, Greek

LAW–GREECE, MODERN

Greek Penal Code. (American Series of Foreign Penal Codes: Vol. 18). xii, 205p. 1973. 17.50x (ISBN 0-8377-0038-8). Rothman.

LAW–HITTITE

see Law, Hittite

LAW–HUNGARY

International Congress of Comparative Law, 8th, Budapest. Hungarian Law - Comparative Law. Peteri, Zoltan, ed. 357p. 1970. 20.00x (ISBN 0-8002-1519-2). Intl Pubns Serv.
Szabo, Imre & Peteri, Zoltan, eds. Comparative Law-Droit Compare 1978: Selected Essays for the 10th International Congress of Comparative Law. 1978. 38.00x (ISBN 963-05-1650-0). Intl Pubns Serv.

LAW–ICELAND

Conybeare, Charles A. Place of Iceland in the History of European Institutions, Being the Lothian Prize Essay, 1877. Repr. of 1877 ed. 15.00 (ISBN 0-404-01696-0). AMS Pr.

LAW–ICELAND–BIBLIOGRAPHY

Hermannsson, Halldor. Ancient Laws of Norway & Iceland. LC 11-20654. (Islandica Ser.: Vol. 4). 1911. pap. 6.00 (ISBN 0-527-00334-4). Kraus Repr.

LAW–INDIA

Agawala, B. R. Practice & Procedure of the Supreme Court. 376p. 1973. 9.50x (ISBN 0-8002-1826-4). Intl Pubns Serv.
Baxi, Upendra. Alternatives in Development Law: The Crisis of the Indian Legal System. 200p. 1981. text ed. 20.00 (ISBN 0-7069-1369-8, Pub. by Vikas India). Advent NY.
Gledhill, Alan. Republic of India, Development of Its Laws & Constitution. LC 77-98761. Repr. of 1951 ed. lib. bdg. 14.25x (ISBN 0-8371-2813-7, GLRI). Greenwood.
Hegde, K. S. Crisis in Indian Judiciary. 1973. 6.00x (ISBN 0-88386-546-7). South Asia Bks.
Indian Law Institute. Indian Legal System. 1979. 28.00 (ISBN 0-379-20368-5). Oceana.
Jain, H. C. Indian Legal Materials, a Bibliographical Guide. 1970. 8.50 (ISBN 0-379-00466-6). Oceana.
Kagzi, Mangal C. Estate Duty Law & Cases. 438p. 1972. 11.25x (ISBN 0-8002-1404-8). Intl Pubns Serv.
Krishna Iyer, V. R. Social Mission of Law in India. 1976. lib. bdg. 10.00 (ISBN 0-88386-733-8); pap. 5.00 (ISBN 0-685-63870-7). South Asia Bks.
McKinstry, Sam W. The Brokerage Role of Rajasthani Lawyers in Three Districts of Rajasthan, India: As Evidenced Through Lawyer-Client Relations-Fact or Fiction? LC 80-5232. 90p. 1980. pap. text ed. 6.75 (ISBN 0-8191-1062-0). U Pr of Amer.
National Convention on Union-State Relations, Indian Institute, 1970. The Union & the States. Jain, S. N., ed. 522p. 1974. 25.00x (ISBN 0-8002-2120-6). Intl Pubns Serv.
Pachauri, P. S. Law of Parliamentary Privileges in U. K. & in India. LC 77-28463. 1971. 15.00 (ISBN 0-379-00326-0). Oceana.
Rudolph, Lloyd I. & Rudolph, Susanne H. Modernity of Tradition: Political Development in India. LC 67-25527. 1967. 12.50x (ISBN 0-226-73134-0). U of Chicago Pr.
Seervai, H. M. Constitutional Law of India, 2 vols. 2nd rev. ed. LC 75-908865. 1975. Set. 40.00x (ISBN 0-8002-0235-X). Intl Pubns Serv.
Setalvad, M. C. Common Law in India. 1970. 5.00x (ISBN 0-8002-0965-6). Intl Pubns Serv.
Sternbach, L. Juridical Studies in Ancient Indian Law, 2 Vols. 1965. Set. 27.50x (ISBN 0-8426-1553-9). Verry.
Subba Rao, K. Social Justice & Law. LC 74-903851. 1975. 9.00x (ISBN 0-8002-1986-4). Intl Pubns Serv.
Wilson, H. H., ed. Glossary of Judicial & Revenue Terms & of Useful Words Occuring in Official Documents Relating to the Administration of the Government of British India, Etc. 1968. Repr. of 1885 ed. 35.00x (ISBN 0-8426-1596-2). Verry.

LAW–IRELAND

Bartholomew, Paul C. The Irish Judiciary. LC 70-175024. 112p. (Orig.). 1972. pap. 3.95x (ISBN 0-268-00457-9). U of Notre Dame Pr.
Donaldson, Alfred G. Some Comparative Aspects of Irish Law. LC 57-8815. (Commonwealth Studies Center: No. 3). 1957. 14.75 (ISBN 0-8223-0047-8). Duke.
Mountmorres. History of the Principal Transactions of the Irish Parliament from 1634-1666, 2 Vols. (Parliamentary & Congressional Ser). 1971. Repr. of 1792 ed. Set. text ed. 36.00x (ISBN 0-7165-2010-9). Irish Academic Pr.
Northern Ireland Law Reports, 25 Vols. 1925-1949. 1966. Set. 500.00 (ISBN 0-379-00218-3); 20.00 ea. Oceana.
Reid, John P. In a Defiant Stance: The Conditions of Law in Massachusetts Bay, the Irish Comparison, & the Coming of the American Revolution. LC 76-42453. 1977. 16.75x (ISBN 0-271-01240-4). Pa St U Pr.
Scannell, Y. Law & Practice Relating to Pollution Control in Ireland. 1976. 20.00x (ISBN 0-86010-031-6, Graham & Trotman). Nichols Pub.

LAW–ISRAEL

Badi, Joeph. Fundamental Laws of the State of Israel. 19.00 (ISBN 0-685-60127-7, Pub by Twayne). Cyrco Pr.
Kent, Charles F. Israel's Laws & Legal Precedents: From the Days of Moses to the Closing of the Legal Cahon. 1977. lib. bdg. 59.95 (ISBN 0-8490-2083-2). Gordon Pr.
Tedeschi, G. Studies in Israel Law. (Hebrew University Legal Studies: No. 7). vi, 302p. 1960. 10.00x (ISBN 0-8377-1200-9). Rothman.
Zemach, Yaacov S. Political Questions in the Courts: A Judicial Function in Democracies - Israel & the United States. LC 76-14392. 1976. 13.95 (ISBN 0-8143-1566-6). Wayne St U Pr.

LAW–ITALY

Beltramo, Mario & Longo, Giovanni E. The Italian Civil Code, Supplement. 1979. lib. bdg. 25.00 (ISBN 0-379-20292-1). Oceana.
Calisse, Carlo. History of Italian Law. Register, Layton B., tr. LC 68-54745. (Continental Legal History Ser.: Vol. 8). Repr. of 1928 ed. 27.50x (ISBN 0-678-04509-7). Kelley.
--History of Italian Law. (Continental Legal History Ser: Vol. 8). lix, 822p. 1969. Repr. of 1928 ed. 27.50x (ISBN 0-8377-2002-8). Rothman.
Cappelletti, Mauro, et al. The Italian Legal System: An Introduction. 1967. 18.75x (ISBN 0-8047-0285-3). Stanford U Pr.
Dell'Anno, P. Law & Practice Relating to Pollution Control in Italy. 1976. 20.00x (ISBN 0-685-74547-3, Graham & Trotman). Nichols Pub.
Grisoli, Angelo. Guide to Foreign Legal Materials, Italian. LC 59-8608. 1965. 17.50 (ISBN 0-379-11752-5). Oceana.
Karsten, C. Die Lehre vom Vertrage Bei Den Italienischen Juristen des Mittelalters. (Ger.). 1882. text ed. 23.50x (ISBN 90-6090-041-3). Humanities.

LAW–JAMAICA

Barnett, Lloyd G. The Constitutional Law of Jamaica. 1977. text ed. 39.95x (ISBN 0-19-920077-7). Oxford U Pr.

LAW–JAPAN

Coleman, Rex & Haley, John O., eds. An Index to Japanese Law: A Bibliography of Western Language Materials, 1867-1973. 182p. 1976. pap. 8.00x (ISBN 0-86008-141-9, Pub. by U of Tokyo Pr). Intl Schol Bk Serv.
Doi, T., ed. The Intellectual Property Law of Japan. 352p. 1980. 65.00x (ISBN 90-286-0649-1). Sijthoff & Noordhoff.
Itoh, Hiroshi & Beer, Lawrence W. The Constitutional Case Law of Japan: Selected Supreme Court Decisions, 1961-70. LC 77-24669. (Asian Law Ser.: No. 6). 288p. 1978. 32.50 (ISBN 0-295-95571-6). U of Wash Pr.
Jones, F. C. Extraterritoriality in Japan. LC 77-114048. Repr. of 1931 ed. 19.50 (ISBN 0-404-03598-1). AMS Pr.
Koshi, George M. Japanese Legal Advisor: Crimes & Punishments. LC 70-83079. 1970. 15.00 (ISBN 0-8048-0306-4). C E Tuttle.
Maki, John M. Court & Constitution in Japan: Selected Supreme Court Decisions, 1948-60. LC 78-23431. (University of Washington Publications on Asia). 1978. pap. 40.00 (ISBN 0-8357-0335-5, ST-00017, Pub. by U of Wash Pr). Univ Microfilms.
Ministry of Labor, Japan. Japan Labor Code, 2 vols. (Studies in Japanese Law & Government). 1979. Repr. of 1953 ed. Set. 56.00 (ISBN 0-89093-217-4). U Pubns Amer.
Noda, Yoshiyuki. Introduction to Japanese Law. Angelo, Anthony H., tr. from Japanese. 1976. 15.00x (ISBN 0-86008-160-5, Pub. by U of Tokyo Pr). Intl Schol Bk Serv.
Tanaka, Hideo & Smith, Malcolm, eds. Japanese Legal System: Introductory Cases & Materials. 1976. 40.00x (ISBN 0-86008-161-3, Pub by U of Tokyo Pr). Intl Schol Bk Serv.
Von Mehren, Arthur T., ed. Law in Japan: The Legal Order in a Changing Society. LC 62-19226. 1963. 35.00x (ISBN 0-674-51600-1). Harvard U Pr.
Ward, Robert E., ed. Five Studies in Japanese Politics. facs. ed. LC 68-58816. (Essay Index Reprint Ser). 1957. 18.00 (ISBN 0-8369-0130-4). Arno.
Wigmore, John H. Law & Justice in Tokugawa Japan: Legal Precedents, Pt. VI-g. 300p. 1981. 25.00x (ISBN 0-86008-286-5, Pub. by U of Tokyo Japan). Columbia U Pr.
Wigmore, John H., ed. Law & Justice in Tokugawa Japan: Part III-B Contract: Legal Precedents. (Law & Justice in Tokugawa Japan). 1976. 19.50x (ISBN 0-86008-166-4, Pub. by U of Tokyo Pr). Intl Schol Bk Serv.
--Law & Justice in Tokugawa Japan: Part VI-B Property: Legal Precedents. 1978. 23.50x (ISBN 0-86008-232-6, Pub. by U of Tokyo Pr). Intl Schol Bk Serv.
--Law & Justice in Tokugawa Japan: Part VI-C Property: Legal Precedents. 1978. 23.50x (ISBN 0-86008-233-4, Pub. by U of Tokyo Pr). Intl Schol Bk Serv.
--Law & Justice in Tokugawa Japan: Part VI-D Property: Legal Precedents. 1978. 23.50x (ISBN 0-86008-234-2, Pub. by U of Tokyo Pr). Intl Schol Bk Serv.
--Law & Justice in Tokugawa Japan Pt. VI-E Property: Legal Precedents. 1979. 23.50x (ISBN 0-86008-257-1, Pub. by U of Tokyo Pr). Intl Schol Bk Serv.
--Law & Justice in Tokugawa Japan, Pt. 3-C Contract: Legal Precedents. 1977. 19.50x (ISBN 0-86008-186-9, Pub. by U of Tokyo Pr). Intl Schol Bk Serv.
--Law & Justice in Tokugawa Japan, Pt. 6-A Property: Legal Precedents. 1977. 19.50x (ISBN 0-86008-187-7, Pub. by U of Tokyo Pr). Intl Schol Bk Serv.

LAW–KENYA

Kenya Law Reports, Vols. 1-29, 1897-1956. LC 67-25059. 1967. Set. 362.50 (ISBN 0-379-20575-0); 15.00 ea. Oceana.
Laws of Kenya, 11 vols & 4 suppls. 1963-68. Set. 404.00 (ISBN 0-379-16100-1). Oceana.

LAW–KOREA

Chun, Bong D., et al. Traditional Korean Legal Attitudes. (Korean Research Monographs: No. 2). 101p. 1980. pap. 8.00 (ISBN 0-912966-30-0). IEAS Ctr Chinese Stud.
Kwun Sup Chung, et al. Modernization & Its Impact Upon Korean Law. (Korea Research Monographs: No. 3). 150p. 1981. pap. 12.50 (ISBN 0-686-69422-8). IEAS Ctr Chinese Stud.
Shaw, William. Legal Norms in a Confucian State. (Korea Research Monographs: No. 5). 235p. 1981. 10.00 (ISBN 0-912966-32-7). IEAS Ctr Chinese Stud.
Tax Laws of Korea, 3 vols. Incl. Vol. 1. Income Tax Law & Enforcement Decree; Vol. 2. Value Added Tax Law, Tax Exemption & Reduction Control Law, & Asset Revaluation Law & Enforcement Decrees; Vol. 3. Corporate Tax Law & Enforcement Decree. 1979. Set. 30.00 (ISBN 0-686-17655-3). A M Newman.

LAW–LATIN-AMERICA

Aguilar, Juan & Gonzalez, Armando E., eds. Basic Latin American Legal Materials 1970-1975. LC 77-78814. (American Association of Law Libraries Publication Ser: No. 13). vi, 106p. 1977. pap. 12.50x (ISBN 0-8377-0111-2). Rothman.

Anuario Juridico Interamericano, 1949; 1952-1954; 1955-1957, 3 vols. (Span. , Eng. , Port. & Fr.). 3.00 ea. (ISBN 0-8270-5205-7). OAS.

Bejarano, Manuel. Obligaciones Civiles. (Span.). 1980. pap. text ed. 13.80 (ISBN 0-06-310063-0, Pub. by HarLA Mexico). Har-Row.

Beutel, Frederick K. The Operation of the Bad Check Laws of Puerto Rico. 3.75 (ISBN 0-8477-2200-7); pap. 3.10 (ISBN 0-8477-2201-5). U of PR Pr.

Blanco, Alberto. Curso De Obligaciones y Contratos: Doctrina General De los Contratos, Vol. II. 3rd, enl. ed. LC 77-4251. (Span.). 1979. 12.00 (ISBN 0-8477-3008-5); pap. 9.00 (ISBN 0-8477-3009-3). U of PR Pr.

Borchard, Edwin M. Guide to the Law & Legal Literature of Argentina, Brazil, & Chile. (Latin America Ser.). 1979. lib. bdg. 75.00 (ISBN 0-8490-2931-7). Gordon Pr.

Changing Legal Environment in Costa Rica, Guatemala & Panama: Management Implications. 25p. 1980. pap. 5.50 (ISBN 0-686-61368-6, COA 41, COA). Unipub.

Changing Legal Environment in Latin America: Management Implications, Vol. V. 243p. 1980. pap. 22.00 (ISBN 0-917094-15-8, COA 42, COA). Unipub.

Convencion Interamericana Sobre Conflictos De Leyes En Materia De Letras De Cambio, Pagares y Facturas. (Treaty Ser.: No. 40). (Eng. , Span. , Fr. , Port.). 1975. pap. 1.00 (ISBN 0-8270-0510-5). OAS.

Convencion Interamericana Sobre Conflictos De Leyes En Materia De Cheques. (Treaty Ser.: No. 41). (Eng. , Span. , Fr. , Port.). 1975. pap. 1.00 (ISBN 0-8270-0515-6). OAS.

Convencion Interamericana Sobre Exhortos O Cartas Rogatorias. (Treaty Ser.: No. 43). (Eng. , Span. , Fr. , Port.). 1975. pap. 1.00 (ISBN 0-8270-0525-3). OAS.

Convencion Interamericana Sobre Recepcion De Pruebas En el Extranjero. (Treaty Ser.: No. 44). (Eng. , Span. , Fr. , Port.). 1975. pap. 1.00 (ISBN 0-8270-0530-X). OAS.

Convencion Interamericana Sobre Regimen Legal De Poderes Para Ser Utitizados En el Extranjero. (Treaty Ser.: No. 45). (Eng. , Span. , Fr. , Port.). 1975. pap. 1.00 (ISBN 0-8270-0535-0). OAS.

De Vries, H. P. & Rodriguez-Novas, J. The Law of the Americas. LC 66-27792. 1965. 20.00 (ISBN 0-379-00268-X). Oceana.

Documentos De la Organizacion De los Estados Americanos Sobra Derecho Internacional Privado. (Span.). 1973. 5.00 (ISBN 0-8270-5230-8). OAS.

Estudio Comparativo De las Legislaciones Latino Americanas Sobre Regulacion y Control de la Inversin Privada Extranqera. (Span.). 1975. 10.00 (ISBN 0-8270-5235-9). OAS.

Garcia-Amador, F. V. The Andean Legal Order: A New Community Law. LC 78-11916. 1978. lib. bdg. 32.50 (ISBN 0-379-20285-9). Oceana.

Henriques, Maria H. Unioes Legais e Consensuais: Incidencia e Fecundidade na America Latina. LC 80-20703. (Scientific Report Ser.: No. 32). (Port.). 1980. pap. text ed. 2.00 (ISBN 0-89383-069-0). Intl Program Labs.

Herget, James E. & Camil, Jorge. An Introduction to the Mexican Legal System. LC 78-58550. 1978. lib. bdg. 19.50 (ISBN 0-930342-60-7). W S Hein.

Holland, Susan S. & Ferrer, Esteban A., eds. Changing Legal Environment in Latin America. LC 74-29066. (Illus.). 370p. 1974. Vol. 2. pap. 16.50 (ISBN 0-685-56605-6, CoA). Unipub.

Index to Latin American Legislation, Third Supplement. 1978. 115.00 (ISBN 0-8161-0094-2). G K Hall.

Kunz, Josef L. Latin-American Philosophy of Law in the Twentieth Century. viii, 120p. 1981. Repr. of 1950 ed. lib. bdg. 20.00x (ISBN 0-8377-0736-6). Rothman.

Legal Codes of the Latin American Republics. 1980. lib. bdg. 49.95 (ISBN 0-8490-3104-4). Gordon Pr.

Library of Congress, Washington, D. C. Index to Latin American Legislation, Second Supplement, 2 vols. 1973. Set. lib. bdg. 115.00 (ISBN 0-8161-1020-4). G K Hall.

--Index to Latin American Legislation, 1950-1960, 2 Vols. 1961. Set. 185.00 (ISBN 0-8161-0594-4). G K Hall.

Merryman, J. H. Law & Social Change in Mediterranean Europe & Latin America: A Handbook of Legal & Social Indicators for Comparative Study. 1980. 47.50 (ISBN 0-379-20700-1). Oceana.

Merryman, John H. & Clark, David S. Comparative Law: Western European & Latin American Legal Systems. (Contemporary Legal Education Ser.). 1978. 25.00 (ISBN 0-672-83379-4, Bobbs-Merrill Law). Michie-Bobbs.

Merryman, John H, et al. Law & Social Change in Mediterranean Europe & Latin America: A Handbook of Legal & Social Indicators of Comparative Study. 618p. 1980. lib. bdg. 47.50 (ISBN 0-379-20700-1). Oceana.

Ovalle, Jose. Derecho Procesal Civil. (Span.). 1980. pap. text ed. 10.80 (ISBN 0-06-316653-4, Pub. by HarLA Mexico). Har-Row.

Pereznieto, Leonel. Derecho Internacional Privado. (Span.). 1980. pap. text ed. 9.80 (ISBN 0-06-316701-8, Pub. by HarLA Mexico). Har-Row.

Szekely, Alberto, ed. Latin America & the Development of the Law of the Sea: Regional Documents, National Legislation, 2 vols. LC 76-40510. 1977. lib. bdg. 75.00 ea. looseleaf. Oceana.

Trabajos Realizados Por el Comite Juridico Interamericano Durante el Periodo Ordinario De Sesiones. Incl. Celebrado Del 21 De Julio Al 15 De Agosto De 1975. 1975. pap. 5.00 (ISBN 0-8270-2305-7); Celebrado Del 14 De Enero Al 20 De Febrero De 1974. (Span. & Eng.). pap. 1.00 (ISBN 0-685-00014-1); Celebrado Del 16 De Agosto Al 13 De Septiembre De 1971. 1971. pap. 1.00 (ISBN 0-685-00015-X); Celebrado Del 17 De Enero Al 11 De Febrero De 1972. 1972. pap. 1.00 (ISBN 0-685-00016-8); Celebrado Del 25 De Julio Al 23 De Agosto De 1972. 1972. pap. 1.00 (ISBN 0-685-00017-6); Celebrado Del 15 De Enero Al 16 De Febrero De 1973. 1973. pap. 1.00 (ISBN 0-685-00018-4); Celebrado Del 30 De Septiembre Al 28 De Octubre De 1974. 1974. pap. 3.00 (ISBN 0-685-00019-2); Celebrado Del 26 De Julio Al 27 De Agosto De 1973. 1973. pap. 1.00 (ISBN 0-685-00020-6). (Eng. , Span, & Port.). OAS.

LAW–LIBERIA

Liberian Law Reports, Vol. 26. 1981. 35.00x (ISBN 0-8014-1314-1). Cornell U Pr.

Liberian Law Reports, Vol. 27. 1981. 35.00x (ISBN 0-8014-1380-X). Cornell U Pr.

LAW–MALAYSIA

Wu Min Aun. An Introduction to the Malaysian Legal System. LC 79-118821. 1979. pap. text ed. 7.95x (ISBN 0-686-60441-5, 00112). Heinemann Ed.

LAW–MEXICO

Mayagoitia, Alberto. A Layman's Guide to Mexican Law. LC 76-57534. 1977. pap. 4.95 (ISBN 0-8263-0444-3). U of NM Pr.

Workshop on Mexico: Management Implications of the Changing Investment Environment. 75p. 1980. pap. 5.50 (ISBN 0-686-61371-6, COA 38, COA). Unipub.

LAW–NEAR EAST

Glover, J. N. Laws of the Turks & Caicos, Vol. 7. 1980. 47.50 (ISBN 0-379-12707-5). Oceana.

Khadduri, Majid & Liebesny, Herbert J., eds. Law in the Middle East: Origin & Development of Islamic Law, Vol. 1. LC 80-1921. Repr. of 1955 ed. 41.50 (ISBN 0-404-18974-1). AMS Pr.

Liebesny, Herbert J. The Law of the Near & Middle East: Readings, Cases & Materials. LC 74-22046. 1975. 27.50 (ISBN 0-87395-256-1); microfiche 27.50 (ISBN 0-87395-257-X). State U NY Pr.

Ziadeh, F. Property Law in the Arab World. 112p. 1979. 55.00x (ISBN 0-86010-112-6, Pub. by Graham & Trotman England). State Mutual Bk.

LAW–NIGERIA

Adesanya, M. O. & Oloyede, E. O. Business Law in Nigeria. LC 77-188223. 320p. 1972. 35.00x (ISBN 0-8419-0115-5, Africana). Holmes & Meier.

Elias, T. O. Groundwork of Nigerian Law. 1976. lib. bdg. 59.95 (ISBN 0-8490-1908-7). Gordon Pr.

--Nigerian Land Law & Custom. 1976. lib. bdg. 59.95 (ISBN 0-8490-2346-7). Gordon Pr.

Elias, T. O., ed. Nigerian Press Law. 156p. 1969. 10.50x (ISBN 0-237-28989-X). Intl Pubns Serv.

Nwogugu, E. I. Family Law in Nigeria. 1977. pap. text ed. 50.00x (ISBN 0-435-89601-6). Heinemann Ed.

Ola, C. S. Income Tax Law & Practice in Nigeria. 1977. pap. text ed. 50.00x (ISBN 0-435-89671-7). Heinemann Ed.

LAW–NORWAY

Hermannsson, Halldor. Ancient Laws of Norway & Iceland. LC 11-20654. (Islandica Ser.: Vol. 4). 1911. pap. 6.00 (ISBN 0-527-00334-4). Kraus Repr.

Royal Norwegian Ministry of Justice. Administration of Justice in Norway: A Brief Survey. 96p. 1981. pap. 12.00x (ISBN 82-00-05501-9). Universitet.

LAW–PAKISTAN

Farani, M. The Arbitration Laws. LC 76-932714. 408p. 1971. 10.00x (ISBN 0-8002-0434-4). Intl Pubns Serv.

Mirza, Mukarram. The Municipal Administration Laws. 326p. 1971. 6.50x (ISBN 0-8002-1734-9). Intl Pubns Serv.

Sabri, Masud-Ul-Hasan K. The Law of Cross Examination: Pakistan & International. 2nd ed. 478p. 1971. 11.25x (ISBN 0-8002-1643-1). Intl Pubns Serv.

LAW–PHILIPPINE ISLANDS

Barton, Roy F. Kalingas, Their Institutions & Custom Law. LC 72-161778. Repr. of 1949 ed. 18.00 (ISBN 0-404-09015-X). AMS Pr.

Philippine Supreme Court Reports Annotated, 1961-1975, 66 vols. 3 vol. set quick index digest 75.00 (ISBN 0-379-12500-5). Oceana.

University Of The Philippines Law Center Editors. Philippine Permanent & General Statutes, 4 vols. (Illus.). 1971-73. Set. lib. bdg. 160.00 (ISBN 0-379-20125-9); lib. bdg. 40.00 ea. Oceana.

LAW–POLAND

Penal Code of the Polish People's Republic. (American Series of Foreign Penal Codes: Vol. 19). xiii, 139p. 1973. 17.50x (ISBN 0-8377-0039-6). Rothman.

Wagner, W. J., ed. Polish Law Throughout the Ages. LC 76-115759. (Publications Ser.: No. 91). 1970. 16.95 (ISBN 0-8179-1911-2). Hoover Inst Pr.

LAW–POLYNESIA

Hogbin, H. Ian. Law & Order in Polynesia. LC 72-85663. (Illus.). lxxii, 296p. 1973. Repr. of 1934 ed. lib. bdg. 12.50x (ISBN 0-8154-0435-2). Cooper Sq.

LAW–RUSSIA

Berman, Harold B. & Maggs, Peter B. Disarmament Inspection Under Soviet Law. LC 66-13368. 1967. 10.00 (ISBN 0-379-00293-0). Oceana.

Berman, Harold J. Justice in the U. S. S. R: An Interpretation of the Soviet Law. rev. ed. LC 63-15045. (Russian Research Center Studies: No. 3). 1963. pap. text ed. 9.00x (ISBN 0-674-49151-3). Harvard U Pr.

Butler, W. E. The Soviet Legal System: Selected Contemporary Legislation & Documents. 1978. 45.00 (ISBN 0-379-00791-6). Oceana.

Dewey, H. W. & Kleimola, A. M., trs. Zakon Sudnyj Ljudem: Court Law for the People. (Michigan Slavic Materials: No. 14). 1977. pap. 4.50 (ISBN 0-930042-07-7). Mich Slavic Pubns.

Eorsi, Gyula. Fundamental Problems of Socialist Civil Law. LC 71-235359. 135p. 1970. 5.50x (ISBN 0-8002-1437-4). Intl Pubns Serv.

Feldbrugge, F. J. Encyclopedia of Soviet Law, 2 vols. LC 73-85236. 900p. 1974. lib. bdg. 120.00 (ISBN 0-379-00481-X). Oceana.

Guins, George C. Soviet Law & Soviet Society. LC 79-1604. 1980. Repr. of 1954 ed. 32.50 (ISBN 0-88355-907-2). Hyperion Conn.

Harvard University Law School Library. Soviet Legal Bibliography: A Classified & Annotated Listing of Books & Serials Published in the Soviet Union Since 1917 As Represented in the Collection of the Harvard Law School Library As of January 1, 1965. xii, 288p. 1965. 22.50x (ISBN 0-674-82745-7). Harvard U Pr.

--Writings on Soviet Law & Soviet Internatioal Law: A Bibliography of Books & Articles Published Since 1917 in Languages Other Than East European. xii, 165p. 1966. 17.50x (ISBN 0-674-96250-8). Harvard U Pr.

Hazard, J. N. Soviet Legal System. 3rd ed. 1977. 20.00 (ISBN 0-686-70252-2). Oceana.

Heisler, Francis. The Moscow Trials. 1976. lib. bdg. 59.95 (ISBN 0-8490-2284-3). Gordon Pr.

Kaiser, D. H. The Growth of the Law in Medieval Russia. 1980. 25.00 (ISBN 0-691-05311-1). Princeton U Pr.

Kovalevskii, Maxime. Modern Customs & Ancient Laws of Russia: Being the Ilchester Lectures 1889-90. LC 78-130599. (Research & Source Works Ser: No. 542). 1970. Repr. of 1891 ed. 22.50 (ISBN 0-8337-1952-1). B Franklin.

LaFave, Wayne R., ed. Law in the Soviet Society. LC 65-19109. 297p. 1965. pap. 5.95 (ISBN 0-252-72524-7). U of Ill Pr.

Lenin, V. I., et al. Soviet Legal Philosophy. Babb, Hugh W., tr. 1951. 31.00 (ISBN 0-384-56790-8). Johnson Repr.

Luryi, Yuri I. Soviet Family Law. LC 80-83797. 93p. 1980. lib. bdg. 19.50 (ISBN 0-89941-062-6). W S Hein.

Makepeace, R. W. Marxist Ideology & Soviet Criminal Law. 319p. 1980. 26.50x (ISBN 0-389-20099-9). B&N.

Shafirov, P. P. A Discourse Concerning the Just Causes of the War Between Sweden & Russia, 1700-1721. LC 73-3738. (Illus.). 325p. 1973. Repr. of 1717 ed. lib. bdg. 38.00 (ISBN 0-379-00162-4). Oceana.

Vernadsky, George. Medieval Russian Laws. 1965. lib. bdg. 14.00x (ISBN 0-374-98075-6). Octagon.

LAW–SCANDINAVIA

Ginsburg, Ruth B. Selective Survey of English Language Studies on Scandinavian Law. vi, 53p. (Orig.). 1970. pap. text ed. 4.50x (ISBN 0-8377-0600-9). Rothman.

Panhuys, H. F. Van. International Law in the Netherlands, 3 vols, Vol. 1. Ea. lib. bdg. 50.00 (ISBN 0-379-20392-8); vol. I, 1978; vol. II, 1979. Oceana.

LAW–SCOTLAND

Stair, James V. The Institutions of the Law of Scotland. Walker, David M., ed. LC 81-1505. 1200p. 1981. text ed. 74.50x (ISBN 0-300-02719-2). Yale U Pr.

LAW–SIERRA LEONE

Milner, A., ed. African Law Reports, Sierra Leone Ser, 1950-1969, 5 vols. LC 67-26375. 1970-72. 45.00 ea. (ISBN 0-379-16000-5). Oceana.

Sharp, Granville. Short Sketch of Temporary Regulations for the Intended Settlement on the Grain Coast of Africa, Near Sierra Leone. LC 71-109366. Repr. of 1788 ed. 13.50x (ISBN 0-8371-3715-2). Greenwood.

Sierra Leone Law Reports: 1960, 1961, 1962, 2 vols. LC 67-26375. 1966. Set. 90.00 (ISBN 0-379-16001-3). Oceana.

LAW–SPAIN

Palmer, Thomas W. Guide to the Law & Legal Literature of Spain. LC 79-1615. 1980. Repr. of 1915 ed. 16.00 (ISBN 0-88355-918-8). Hyperion Conn.

Vance, John T. The Background of Hispanic-American Law: Legal Sources & Juridical Literature of Spain. LC 79-1622. 1980. Repr. of 1937 ed. 21.50 (ISBN 0-88355-926-9). Hyperion Conn.

LAW–SWEDEN

Bruzelius, Anders & Thelin, Krister, eds. The Swedish Code of Judicial Procedure. rev ed. (The American Ser. of Foreign Penal Codes: No. 24). xvii, 253p. 1979. 28.50x (ISBN 0-8377-0044-2). Rothman.

Nelson, Alvar. Responses to Crime: An Introduction to Swedish Criminal Law & Administration. Getz, Jerome L., tr. from Swedish. (New York University Criminal Law Education & Research Center Monograph: No. 6). vi, 90p. 1972. pap. text ed. 8.50x (ISBN 0-8377-0900-8). Rothman.

Schmidt, Folke. Law & Industrial Relations in Sweden. 255p. 1977. text ed. 21.00x (ISBN 0-8377-1107-X). Rothman.

LAW–SWITZERLAND

Huber, Eugen. The Swiss Civil Code. LC 79-1609. 1980. Repr. of 1925 ed. 23.50 (ISBN 0-88355-912-9). Hyperion Conn.

LAW–TURKEY

Ansay, Tugrue. Introduction to Turkish Law. 2nd ed. 1978. 22.00 (ISBN 0-379-20332-4). Oceana.

Glover, J. N. Laws of the Turks & Caicos, Vol. 7. 1980. 47.50 (ISBN 0-379-12707-5). Oceana.

--Laws of the Turks & Caicos Islands, 7 vols. rev. ed. 1970-80. 327.50 set (ISBN 0-379-12700-8). Oceana.

Ostrorog, Leon. The Angora Reform. LC 79-1614. 1980. Repr. of 1927 ed. 11.00 (ISBN 0-88355-917-X). Hyperion Conn.

LAW–UNITED STATES

Abbott, Earl L. & Solomon, Erwin S., eds. Instructions for Virginia & West Virginia, 3 vols. 2nd ed. 1962. with 1980 suppl. 75.00 (ISBN 0-87215-077-1); 1980 suppl. 25.00 (ISBN 0-87215-343-6). Michie-Bobbs.

Allen, James L. The Reign of Law: A Tale of the Kentucky Hemp Fields. facsimile ed. LC 77-164556. (American Fiction Reprint Ser). Repr. of 1900 ed. 28.00 (ISBN 0-8369-7032-2). Arno.

American Legal System. (gr. 4 up). 1980. PLB 6.90 (ISBN 0-531-04100-X). Watts.

Andrews, Joseph L., et al, eds. The Law in the United States of America: A Selective Bibliographical Guide. LC 64-22264. 100p. 1966. 8.50x (ISBN 0-8147-0009-8). NYU Pr.

Annual Survey of American Law, 1979. 1980. 26.00 (ISBN 0-379-12238-3). Oceana.

Appeals to the Second Circuit: With 1975 Supplement. 117p. 1980. pap. 7.95 (ISBN 0-87945-019-3). Fed Legal Pubn.

Appenzeller, Herb. Physical Education & the Law. 1978. 15.00 (ISBN 0-87215-210-3). Michie-Bobbs.

Baker, J. Newton. Law of Disputed & Forged Documents. (Illus.). 1955. 35.00 (ISBN 0-87215-079-8). Michie-Bobbs.

Ball, Milner S. The Promise of American Law: A Theological, Humanistic View of Legal Process. LC 81-4325. 208p. 1981. text ed. 15.00 (ISBN 0-686-76232-0). U of Ga Pr.

Beck, Carl, ed. Law & Justice: Essays in Honor of Robert S. Rankin. LC 74-86476. 1970. 16.75 (ISBN 0-8223-0213-6). Duke.

Blackstone, William. Blackstone's Commentaries with Notes of Reference to the Constitution & Laws of the Federal Government of the United States & of the Commonwealth of Virginia, 5 Vols. Tucker, St. George, ed. LC 68-57388. 1969. Repr. of 1802 ed. 135.00x (ISBN 0-8377-1930-5). Rothman.

Blackstone, Sir William. Blackstone's Commentaries, 5 Vols. Tucker, St. George, ed. LC 68-57388. 1803. 135.00x (ISBN 0-678-04530-5). Kelley.

Blumberg, Abraham S., ed. The Scales of Justice. rev. 2nd. ed. LC 72-87667. 325p. 1973. pap. text ed. 4.95 (ISBN 0-87855-543-9). Transaction Bks.

Bodenheimer, Edgar, et al. An Introduction to the Anglo-American Legal System, Readings & Cases. LC 80-18757. (American Casebook Ser.). 185p. 1980. pap. text ed. 6.95 (ISBN 0-8299-2103-6). West Pub.

Brackenridge, Hugh H. Law Miscellanies: Containing an Introduction to the Study of the Law. LC 73-37967. (American Law: The Formative Years). 600p. 1972. Repr. of 1814 ed. 26.00 (ISBN 0-405-03994-8). Arno.

Brenner, Saul, ed. American Judicial Behavior. LC 73-10235. 250p. 1974. text ed. 28.50x (ISBN 0-8422-5116-2); pap. text ed. 12.50x (ISBN 0-8422-0307-9). Irvington.

Brody, David E. The American Legal System. 1978. text ed. 17.95x (ISBN 0-669-01439-7); instr's manual 1.95 (ISBN 0-669-01840-6). Heath.

Brown, Wilmore. Ohio Domestic Authorities. 1978. 40.00 (ISBN 0-672-83380-8, Bobbs-Merrill Law). Michie-Bobbs.

Brownell, Emery A. Legal Aid in the United States: A Study of the Availability of Lawyers Services for Persons Unable to Pay Fees. LC 77-141417. (Illus.). 1971. Repr. of 1951 ed. lib. bdg. 26.50x (ISBN 0-8371-4689-5, BRLE). Greenwood.

Bryson, William H. Discovery in Virginia. 1978. 25.00 (ISBN 0-87215-213-8). Michie-Bobbs.

Burns Indiana Statutes Annotated, 39 vols. write for info. (ISBN 0-672-83879-6, Bobbs-Merrill Law); write for info 1980 supplement (ISBN 0-672-84244-0). Michie-Bobbs.

California Penal Code: 1980-81 Annual. 1981. 14.00 (ISBN 0-910874-52-2). Legal Bk Corp.

Campbell, E. L. The Science of Law According to the American Theory of Government. viii, 375p. 1981. Repr. of 1887 ed. lib. bdg. 32.50x (ISBN 0-8377-0433-2). Rothman.

Carter, James. Law: Law: Its Origin, Growth & Function. LC 74-6413. (American Constitutional & Legal History Ser.). 1974. Repr. of 1907 ed. lib. bdg. 35.00 (ISBN 0-306-70631-8). Da Capo.

Chambliss, William J. & Seidman, Robert B. Law, Order & Power. 1971. text ed. 18.95 (ISBN 0-201-00957-9). A-W.

Chanin, Leah F. Reference Guide to Georgia Legal History & Legal Research. 175p. 1980. 20.00 (ISBN 0-87215-315-0). Michie-Bobbs.

Chommie, J. G. El Derecho De los Estados Unidos: 3 Vols. (Orig., Span.). 1963. Set. pap. 24.50 (ISBN 0-379-00411-9). Oceana.

City of Los Angeles, City Attorney's Office. Los Angeles Municipal Code, 5 vols. 4th rev. ed. City Clerk's Office, ed. 3300p. 1972. looseleaf 325.00 (ISBN 0-911110-33-X); with current 1981 changes avail. (ISBN 0-685-26720-2). Parker & Son.

Cleary, Edward W. & Graham, Michael H. Handbook of Illinois Evidence. 1979. text ed. 50.00 (ISBN 0-316-14720-6). Little.

Cleckley, Franklin D. Handbook on Evidence for West Virginia Lawyers. 1978. 40.00, with 1979 suppl (ISBN 0-87215-202-2); 1979 suppl 15.00 (ISBN 0-87215-285-5). Michie-Bobbs.

Conner, Ross F. & Huff, C. Ronald. Attorneys As Activists: Evaluating the American Bar Association's BASICS Program. LC 79-19830. (Contemporary Evaluation Research: Vol. 1). (Illus.). 263p. 1979. 20.00 (ISBN 0-8039-1363-X); pap. 9.95 (ISBN 0-8039-1364-8). Sage.

Countryman, Vern, et al. Law in Contemporary Society: The Orgain Lectures. 115p. 1973. 7.50x (ISBN 0-292-74606-7). U of Tex Pr.

Cowan, Z. Individual Liberty & the Law. 1977. 10.00 (ISBN 0-379-00597-2). Oceana.

Danzig, Richard. Hadly v Baxendale: A Study in the Industrialization of Law. (Research Contributions Ser: No. 6). 1975. pap. 2.00 (ISBN 0-685-64481-2). Am Bar Foun.

Davidson, Marion & Blue, Martha. Making It Legal: A Law Primer for the Craftmaker, Visual Artist, & Writer. (Illus.). 1979. pap. 8.95 (ISBN 0-07-015431-7, SP). McGraw.

Dillon, J. F. The Law & Jurisprudence of England & America. LC 75-99475. (American Constitutional & Legal History Ser). 1970. Repr. of 1894 ed. lib. bdg. 42.50 (ISBN 0-306-71854-5). Da Capo.

Donley, R. Tucker. Law of Coal, Oil & Gas in Virginia & West Virginia. 1951. with 1972 suppl. 25.00 (ISBN 0-87215-084-4). Michie-Bobbs.

Douglas, Robert D. Douglas' Forms, 4 Vols. 2nd ed. Ussery, Robert D., ed. 1953. 75.00 (ISBN 0-87215-086-0). Michie-Bobbs.

Douglas, William D. An Almanac of Liberty. LC 73-10752. 409p. 1973. Repr. of 1954 ed. lib. bdg. 19.75x (ISBN 0-8371-7019-2, DOAL). Greenwood.

Douthewaite, Graham. Attorney's Guide to Restitution: 1980 Supplement. 1980. 8.50 (ISBN 0-686-66060-9). A Smith Co.

Drayton, William H. The Letters of Freeman, Etc. LC 75-31089. Repr. of 1771 ed. 19.50 (ISBN 0-404-13507-2). AMS Pr.

Edwards, Harry T. & Nordin, Virginia D. An Introduction to the American Legal System: A Supplement to Higher Education & the Law. LC 80-82033. 76p. (Orig.). 1980. pap. text ed. 5.95x (ISBN 0-934222-02-9). Inst Ed Manage.

--Nineteen Eighty Cumulative Supplement Higher Education & the Law. LC 80-82432. 136p. (Orig.). 1980. pap. text ed. 5.95x (ISBN 0-934222-03-7). Inst Ed Manage.

Elliot, Jonathan. Elliot's Debates, 5 vols. in two binders. 2nd ed. 1937. Repr. Set. 75.00 (ISBN 0-87215-019-4). Michie-Bobbs.

Fabris, Alfred C. A Prosecutor's Guide for California Peace Officers. LC 76-45963. 1977. text ed. 9.95 (ISBN 0-8465-1519-9); pap. text ed. 7.50 (ISBN 0-8465-1520-2). Benjamin-Cummings.

Fehrenbacher, Don E. The Dred Scott Case: Its Significance in American Law & Politics. LC 78-4665. (Illus.). 1978. 27.50x (ISBN 0-19-502403-6). Oxford U Pr.

Fein, Bruce E. Significant Decisions of the Supreme Court: 1978-1979 Term. 1980. pap. 6.25 (ISBN 0-8447-3387-3). Am Enterprise.

Ferguson, William D. Statutes of Limitation Saving Statutes. 1978. 35.00 (ISBN 0-87215-214-6). Michie-Bobbs.

Fiedler, George. The Illinois Law Courts in Three Centuries. 1973. 12.75 (ISBN 0-917036-05-0). Physicians Rec.

Fitzgerald, P. This Law of Ours. 1977. 9.95 (ISBN 0-13-919274-3); pap. 4.95 study guide (ISBN 0-13-919266-2); pap. 7.50 tchr's guide (ISBN 0-13-919282-4). P-H.

Fortman, Marvin & Goodson, John. The Legal Aspects of Doing Business in Arizona. LC 79-113255. 190p. 1970. 6.50x (ISBN 0-8165-0255-2). U of Ariz Pr.

Fox, Ivan & Raphael, Jesse. College Law Guide. 1966. 5.85 (ISBN 0-914770-05-5). Littoral Develop.

Francis, Philip. Protection Through the Law. 2nd ed. (Legal Almanac Ser.). 1978. 5.95 (ISBN 0-379-11116-0). Oceana.

Frank, J. American Law: The Case for Radical Reform. 1969. 5.95 (ISBN 0-02-896020-3). Macmillan.

Frankfurter, Felix. Law & Politics. Prichard, E. F., Jr. & Macleish, A., eds. 6.50 (ISBN 0-8446-0097-0). Peter Smith.

--Of Law & Life & Other Things That Matter: Papers & Addresses of Felix Frankfurter, 1956-1963. Kurland, Philip B., ed. LC 65-13221. (Illus.). 1965. 15.00x (ISBN 0-674-63100-5, Belknap Pr). Harvard U Pr.

Friedman, Lawrence M. Law & Society: An Introduction. 192p. 1977. text ed. 11.95 (ISBN 0-13-526616-5); pap. text ed. 7.85 (ISBN 0-13-526608-4). P-H.

Friedman, Leon, ed. Oral Arguments Before the Supreme Court, 2 vols. 975p. 1981. Set. pap. 20.00 (ISBN 0-87754-147-7). Chelsea Hse.

Friendly, Henry J. Benchmarks. LC 67-12149. 1967. 15.00x (ISBN 0-226-26530-7). U of Chicago Pr.

Gething, Judith. Sex Discrimination & the Law in Hawaii: A Guide to Your Legal Rights. LC 78-10636. 1979. pap. 3.95 (ISBN 0-8248-0620-4). U Pr of Hawaii.

Gordon, Gary J. Product Liability Litigation. 206p. 1980. pap. 24.50 (ISBN 0-917126-20-3). Mason Pub.

Gould, David J. Law & the Administrative Process: Analytic Frameworks for Understanding Public Policy Making. LC 79-63850. 1979. pap. text ed. 11.25 (ISBN 0-8191-0746-8). U Pr of Amer.

Gould Editorial Staff. Agency Law of U. S., 1981. 1981. pap. text ed. 5.75x (ISBN 0-87526-191-4). Gould.

--Criminal Justice Code of New Jersey. 150p. looseleaf 10.50 (ISBN 0-87526-024-1). Gould.

Griffith, William. Annual Law Register of the United States, Vols. 3 & 4. LC 77-37976. (American Law Ser.: The Formative Years). 1468p. 1972. Repr. of 1822 ed. 62.00 (ISBN 0-405-04019-9). Arno.

Grilliot, Harold J. Introduction to Law & the Legal System. 2nd ed. LC 78-69579. (Illus.). 1979. text ed. 18.50 (ISBN 0-395-26866-4); inst. manual 0.80 (ISBN 0-395-26865-6). HM.

Gugdger, Charles M. & Bailes, Jack C. The Economic Impact of Oregon's Bottle Bill. 1974. pap. 3.95 (ISBN 0-87071-037-0). Oreg St U Pr.

Guice, John D. The Rocky Mountain Bench: The Territorial Supreme Courts of Colorado, Montana, & Wyoming 1861-1890. LC 72-75195. (Western Americana Ser.: No. 23). 232p. 1972. 20.00x (ISBN 0-300-01479-1). Yale U Pr.

Hay, P. An Introduction to United States Law. 1976. text ed. 19.50 (ISBN 0-444-11059-3, North-Holland); pap. text ed. 20.00 (ISBN 0-444-11091-7). Elsevier.

Hening, William W., ed. Statutes at Large, Being a Collection of All the Laws of Virginia from the First Session of the Legislature in the Year 1619, 13 Vols. fascim. ed. LC 69-18889. (Jamestown Foundation of the Commonwealth of Va). 1969. 175.00x set (ISBN 0-8139-0254-1); 15.00x ea. U Pr of Va.

Henke, Dan. California Law Guide. LC 76-19950. 1976. 50.00 (ISBN 0-911110-21-6); 1980 suppl. incl. Parker & Son.

Hilliard, Francis. The Elements of Law: Being a Comprehensive Summary of American Civil Jurisprudence. LC 78-37979. (American Law Ser.: The Formative Years). 372p. 1972. Repr. of 1835 ed. 16.00 (ISBN 0-405-04022-9). Arno.

Hineline, Harris D. Forms & Their Use in Patent & Trade Mark Practice in the United States & Canada. 1951. 25.00 (ISBN 0-87215-023-2). Michie-Bobbs.

Holt, George C. The Concurrent Jurisdiction of the Federal & State Courts. xxvi, 237p. 1980. Repr. of 1888 ed. lib. bdg. 24.00x (ISBN 0-8377-0630-0). Rothman.

Horn, Robert A. Groups & the Constitution. LC 78-156942. (Stanford University. Stanford Studies in History, Economics, & Political Science: No. 12). Repr. of 1956 ed. 18.50 (ISBN 0-404-50975-4). AMS Pr.

Horwitz, Morton J. The Transformation of American Law, Seventeen Eighty to Eighteen Sixty. LC 76-26500. 1979. text ed. 18.50x (ISBN 0-674-90370-6); pap. text ed. 6.95x (ISBN 0-674-90371-4). Harvard U Pr.

Idaho State Department of Education & Northwest Regional Educational Laboratory. Understanding Contracts & Legal Documents & Understanding Criminal Law. (Lifeworks Ser.). (Illus.). 1980. pap. text ed. 4.00 (ISBN 0-07-060913-6). McGraw.

Information Handling Services. Index to the Code of Federal Regulations, 1977. LC 78-379. (Orig.). 1980. pap. text ed. write for info. (ISBN 0-89847-007-2). IHS-PDS.

Jessup, L. F. New Life Style & the Changing Law. LC 73-165997. 128p. 1971. 5.95 (ISBN 0-379-11079-2). Oceana.

Johnson, Bradley T. Reports of Cases Decided by Chief Justice Chase in the Circuit Court of the United States for the Fourth Circuit: 1865-1869. facsimile ed. LC 75-75292. (American Constitutional & Legal History Ser.). 1972. Repr. of 1876 ed. lib. bdg. 59.50 (ISBN 0-306-71291-1). Da Capo.

Johnson, Elmer C. Survey of American Law. LC 78-98957. 1970. text ed. 9.95 (ISBN 0-682-47032-5, University). Exposition.

Johnston, Norman & Savitz, Leonard D. American Legal Process & Corrections. 400p. 1982. pap. text ed. 12.95 (ISBN 0-471-08337-2). Wiley.

Kavass, Igor I. & Blake, Michael J., eds. United States Legislation on Foreign Relations & International Commerce: 1789-1949, 4 vols. LC 76-51898. 1977. Set. lib. bdg. 295.00 (ISBN 0-930342-00-3). W S Hein.

Kent, J. Commentaries on American Law, 4 Vols. LC 78-75290. (American Constitutional & Legal History Ser). 1971. Repr. of 1826 ed. Set. lib. bdg. 195.00 (ISBN 0-306-71293-8). Da Capo.

Kipnis, Kenneth. Philosophical Issues in Law: Cases & Materials. 1977. pap. text ed. 13.50 (ISBN 0-13-662296-8). P-H.

Klein, F. J. & Lee, J. S., eds. Selected Writings of A. T. Vanderbilt, 2 Vols. LC 65-14216. 1966. 15.00 ea. (ISBN 0-379-00226-4). Oceana.

Knepper, William E. & Frye, Richard. Ohio Eminent Domain Practice: 1979 Supplement. 1979. 5.50 (ISBN 0-686-60286-2). A Smith Co.

Koch, Harry W. A Guide to California Law. 1978. pap. 6.00 (ISBN 0-913164-76-3). Ken-Bks.

Lamb, Brockenbrough. Virginia Probate Practice. 1957. Repr. of 1969 ed. 25.00 (ISBN 0-87215-095-X). Michie-Bobbs.

Landsman, Stephen, et al. What to Do Until the Lawyer Comes. LC 76-2802. 1977. pap. 2.95 (ISBN 0-385-11163-0, Anch). Doubleday.

The Legal Profession in the United States. 2nd ed. 37p. (Span.). 1971. pap. 0.50 (ISBN 0-910058-21-0). Am Bar Foun.

The Legal Profession in the United States. 2nd ed. 41p. 1970. pap. 0.50 (ISBN 0-910058-18-0). Am Bar Foun.

The Legal Profession in the United States. 37p. (Fr.). 1971. pap. 0.50 (ISBN 0-910058-19-9). Am Bar Foun.

The Legal Profession in the United States. 40p. (Rus.). 1971. pap. 0.50 (ISBN 0-910058-20-2). Am Bar Foun.

Lieberman, Jethro. The Litigious Society. LC 80-68181. 212p. 1981. 13.95 (ISBN 0-465-04134-5). Basic.

Livermore, Sarah, et al, eds. The American Bar - The Canadian Bar - The International Bar: 1981. 63rd ed. LC 18-21110. 3062p. 1981. 130.00 (ISBN 0-931398-06-1). R B Forster.

Llewellyn, Karl N. Jurisprudence: Realism in Theory & Practice. LC 62-12634. 1962. 17.50x (ISBN 0-226-48787-3). U of Chicago Pr.

Loiseaux, Pierre R. & Hawkland, William. Cases & Materials on Debtor-Creditor Relations. (Contemporary Legal Education Ser.). 1979. 23.50 (ISBN 0-672-82028-5, Bobbs-Merrill Law); statutory appendix 4.50 (ISBN 0-672-83731-5). Michie-Bobbs.

Lunt, Dudley C. Road to the Law. 1962. pap. 1.65x (ISBN 0-393-00183-0, Norton Lib). Norton.

Maloy, Richard H. Your Questions Answered About Florida Divorce Law. LC 77-81168. (Your Questions Answered on Florida Law Ser.). 1977. pap. 1.95 (ISBN 0-89317-023-2). Windward Pub.

--Your Questions Answered About Florida Law & Family Relationships in Life & Death. LC 77-93147. (Your Questions Answered on Florida Law Ser.). 1978. pap. 1.95 (ISBN 0-89317-026-7). Windward Pub.

--Your Questions Answered About Florida Law & Your Continuing Obligations After Divorce. LC 77-93148. (Your Questions Answered on Florida Law Ser.). 1978. pap. 1.95 (ISBN 0-89317-025-9). Windward Pub.

Marvell, Thomas B. Appellate Courts & Lawyers: Information Gathering in the Adversary System. LC 77-94743. (Contributions in Legal Studies: No. 4). 1978. lib. bdg. 22.50x (ISBN 0-313-20312-1, MAA/). Greenwood.

Marwick, Christine M. Litigation Under the Federal Freedom of Information Act & Privacy Act: 1981 Edition. LC 80-683. 400p. 1980. pap. 25.00 (ISBN 0-86566-019-0). Ctr Natl Security.

Maryland Appellate Reports-Bound Volumes. cancelled. Michie-Bobbs.

Maryland Reports. write for info. (ISBN 0-685-02789-9). Michie-Bobbs.

Mermin, Samuel. Law & the Legal System: An Introduction. 1973. pap. 7.95 (ISBN 0-316-56730-2). Little.

Michie Editorial. Delaware Code: Annotated, Revised 1974, 20 vols. write for info (ISBN 0-87215-247-2); write for info. 1979 suppl. (ISBN 0-87215-319-3). Michie-Bobbs.

Michie Editorial Staff. Harmer's Magistrates Manual for West Virginia, with 1965 Supplement. rev. 7th ed. 1961. 25.00 (ISBN 0-87215-102-6). Michie-Bobbs.

--Maryland Code of 1957, 32 vols., with 1980 cum. suppl. 1957. Set. write for info (ISBN 0-87215-129-8). Michie-Bobbs.

--Michie's Jurisprudence of Virginia & West Virginia, 40 vols., with 1979 cum. suppl. rev. ed. 1948. 975.00 set (ISBN 0-87215-128-X); 1979 cum. suppl. only 145.00 (ISBN 0-87215-350-9). Michie-Bobbs.

Michie, Thomas J., ed. Virginia Reports Annotated, Jefferson to 33 Grattan, 26 Vols. 1900. Repr. 300.00 (ISBN 0-87215-142-5). Michie-Bobbs.

Michie's Digest of Tennessee Reports, 18 vols. 1973. with 1977 cum. suppl. 300.00 (ISBN 0-87215-136-0); 1977 cum. suppl. 25.00 (ISBN 0-87215-265-0). Michie-Bobbs.

Mietus, Norbert J. & West, Bill W. Personal Law. 2nd ed. 512p. 1981. text ed. 19.95 (ISBN 0-574-19505-X, 13-2505); instr's. guide avail. (ISBN 0-574-19506-8, 13-2506). Sci Res Assoc Coll.

Miles, John G., Jr., et al. The Law Officer's Pocket Manual: 1980-81 Edition. 128p. 1980. 5.00 (ISBN 0-87179-341-5). BNA.

Miller, Perry, ed. Legal Mind in America: From Independence to the Civil War. LC 63-13082. 1970. pap. 5.95 (ISBN 0-8014-9097-9, CP97). Cornell U Pr.

Moore, Russell F., ed. Law for Executives. LC 68-57686. 1968. 12.75 (ISBN 0-8144-5154-3). Am Mgmt.

New York University School of Law. Annual Survey of American Law 1977. LC 46-30513. (Annual Survey of American Law Ser.). 1978. 25.00 (ISBN 0-379-12236-7). Oceana.

Newman, Jason & O'Brien, Edward. Street Law the D.C. Project: Community Legal Assistance & Street Law. (Illus.). (gr. 9-12). 1976. pap. text ed. 4.00 (ISBN 0-8299-1012-3). West Pub.

Noonan, John T., Jr. Persons & Masks of the Law: Cardoza, Holmes, Jefferson & Wythe As Makers of the Masks. LC 75-30991. 1976. 10.00 (ISBN 0-374-23076-5); pap. 3.95 (ISBN 0-374-51396-1). FS&G.

Oliver, Benjamin L. The Rights of an American Citizen. facsimile ed. LC 76-119940. (Select Bibliographies Reprint Ser). Repr. of 1832 ed. 21.00 (ISBN 0-8369-5383-5). Arno.

Parham, Sidney F., Jr. Title Examination in Virginia. 1965. pap. 10.00 (ISBN 0-87215-107-7). Michie-Bobbs.

Piper, Patricia L., et al. Manual on K F: The Library of Congress Classification Schedule for Law of the United States. LC 72-86471. (AALL Publications Ser.: No. 11). viii, 135p. 1972. text ed. 22.50x (ISBN 0-8377-0109-0). Rothman.

Police, Crimes & Offenses & Motor Vehicle Laws of Virginia, 2 vols., with 1979 cum. suppl. 1976. 35.00 (ISBN 0-87215-134-4); 1979 cum. suppl. 15.00 (ISBN 0-87215-306-1). Michie-Bobbs.

Potter, J. Reid. North Carolina Appellate Handbook. 1978. 28.50 (ISBN 0-87215-211-1, Bobbs-Merrill Law). Michie-Bobbs.

Potts, James L., et al. Prisoner's Self Help Litigation Manual. LC 77-6191. 1977. 15.95 (ISBN 0-669-01640-3). Lexington Bks.

Redden, Kenneth R. Punitive Damages. 1000p. 1980. 40.00 (ISBN 0-87215-303-7). Michie-Bobbs.

Reppy, Alison, ed. David Dudley Field: Centenary Essays Celebrating 100 Years of Legal Reform. 1949. 25.00 (ISBN 0-379-00145-4). Oceana.

Reuschlein, Harold G. Jurisprudence: Its American Prophets; a Survey of Taught Jurisprudence. LC 70-158741. 1971. Repr. of 1951 ed. lib. bdg. 25.75x (ISBN 0-8371-6180-0). Greenwood.

Riekes, Linda & Ackerly, Salley M. Lawmaking. 2nd ed. (Law in Action Ser.). (Illus.). (gr. 5-9). 1980. pap. 4.95 (ISBN 0-8299-1023-9); tchrs.' ed. 4.95 (ISBN 0-8299-1024-7). West Pub.

Riekes, Linda & Ackerly, Sally M. Lawmaking. (Law in Action Ser.). (Illus.). (gr. 7-8). 1975. pap. text ed. 4.95 (ISBN 0-8299-1000-X); tchr's manual 4.95 (ISBN 0-8299-1001-8). West Pub.

Rivise, Charles W. & Caesar, A. D. Interference Law & Practice with Forms, 4 Vols. 1940. 75.00 (ISBN 0-87215-111-5). Michie-Bobbs.

Rose, Gerald, ed. Intellectual Property Law Review: Annual. Incl. 1976 (ISBN 0-87632-142-2); 1977 (ISBN 0-87632-143-0); 1978 (ISBN 0-87632-144-9); 1979 (ISBN 0-87632-145-7). LC 79-88703. 42.50 ea. Boardman.

Ross, Alf. On Law & Justice. (California Library Repr). 1975. Repr. of 1959 ed. 27.50x (ISBN 0-520-02851-1). U. of Cal Pr.

Rostow, Eugene V. The Ideal in Law. LC 77-81733. 1978. 20.00 (ISBN 0-226-72818-8). U of Chicago Pr.

Rothman, Daniel A. & Rothman, Nancy L. The Professional Nurse & the Law. 1977. 8.95 (ISBN 0-316-75768-3). Little.

Sachs, Albie & Wilson, Joan H. Sexism & the Law: Male Beliefs & Legal Bias in Britain & the United States. LC 78-63402. 1979. 15.95 (ISBN 0-02-927640-3). Free Pr.

Salser, Carl W. U.S. Government: How Our Laws Are Made: Syllabus. 1973. pap. text ed. 4.55 (ISBN 0-89420-091-7, 196033); cassette recordings 36.05 (ISBN 0-89420-191-3, 196000). Natl Book.

Sato, Sho. State & Local Government Law: 1981 Supplement. 1981. 26.00 (ISBN 0-316-77117-1). Little.

Scheingold, Stuart A. The Politics of Rights: Lawyers, Public Policy & Political Change. LC 74-79972. 240p. 1974. 17.50x (ISBN 0-300-01783-9); pap. 4.95x (ISBN 0-300-01811-8). Yale U Pr.

Schwartz, Bernard. The American Heritage History of the Law in America. LC 74-8264. (Illus.). 379p. 1981. pap. 12.95 (ISBN 0-8281-0426-3, Dist. by Scribner). Am Heritage.

Schwartz, Bernard, ed. American Law: The Third Century: the Law Bicentennial Volume. LC 76-50507. iv, 454p. 1976. text ed. 22.50x (ISBN 0-8377-0204-6); text ed. 37.50x signed, boxed ed. (ISBN 0-8377-0205-4). Rothman.

Schwartz, Bernard & Jensen, Oliver, eds. American Heritage History of the Law in America. Incl. 25.00 (ISBN 0-8281-0290-2, B059R). (Illus.). 379p. 1974 (ISBN 0-07-079385-9). Am Heritage.

Schwartz, Mortimer D. & Henke, Dan F., eds. Combined Catalog Anglo-American Law Collections University of California Law Libraries Berkeley & Davis with Library of Congress Class K Added, 9 vols. (Supplement). 1979. text ed. 750.00x (ISBN 0-8377-0423-5). Rothman.

Schwartz, Murray L., ed. Law & the American Future. 1975. 9.95 (ISBN 0-13-526061-2); pap. 4.95 (ISBN 0-13-526053-1). Am Assembly.

Seuling, Barbara. You Can't Eat Peanuts in Church & Other Little-Known Laws. LC 74-19384. 64p. (gr. 4-7). 1975. 4.95a (ISBN 0-385-01393-0); PLB (ISBN 0-385-01435-X); pap. 1.75 (ISBN 0-385-12137-7). Doubleday.

Shartel, Burke. Our Legal System & How It Operates. LC 73-173666. (American Constitutional & Legal History Ser.). 628p. 1972. Repr. of 1951 ed. lib. bdg. 59.50 (ISBN 0-306-70411-0). Da Capo.

Shepherd, Samuel, ed. Statutes at Large of Virginia from October Session 1792, to December Session 1806, 3 Vols. LC 79-119153. Repr. of 1835 ed. Set. lib. bdg. 75.00 (ISBN 0-404-06010-2); lib. bdg. 25.00 ea. Vol. 1 (ISBN 0-404-06011-0). Vol. 2 (ISBN 0-404-06012-9). Vol. 3 (ISBN 0-404-06013-7). AMS Pr.

Shuman, Samuel I. & West, Norbert D. American Law: An Introductory Survey of Some Principles, Cases & Text. LC 71-13042. 1971. text ed. 19.95x (ISBN 0-8143-1434-1). Wayne St U Pr.

Simpson, William. The Practical Justice of the Peace & Parish-Officer, of His Majesty's Province of South Carolina. LC 70-37985. (American Law Ser.: The Formative Years). 288p. 1972. Repr. of 1761 ed. 15.00 (ISBN 0-405-04028-8). Arno.

Sinclair, Kent, Jr. Federal Civil Practice. LC 80-81332. 1119p. 1980. text ed. 60.00 (ISBN 0-686-62634-6, H1-2957). PLI.

Smith, George P., ed. Wills & Administration for Virginia & West Virginia, 3 vols. 2nd ed. 1960. with 1975 Cum. Suppl. 75.00 (ISBN 0-87215-114-X); 1975 Cum. Suppl. only 15.00 (ISBN 0-87215-296-0). Michie-Bobbs.

Smith, Robert S. Alabama Law for the Layman. LC 74-15508. 1975. 7.95 (ISBN 0-87397-058-6). Strode.

Smith, W. J. Annotated Instructions to Juries in Civil & Criminal Cases, 2 vols. 1963. with 1970 suppl. to Civil vol. 40.00 (ISBN 0-87215-048-8); 1970 suppl. (to Civil vol) 7.50 (ISBN 0-87215-279-0). Michie-Bobbs.

Sokol, Ronald P. Brief of Amicus Curiae in the Escobedo Cases. 1966. 12.50 (ISBN 0-87215-051-8). Michie-Bobbs.

--Language & Litigation. 1967. 10.00 (ISBN 0-87215-053-4). Michie-Bobbs.

--Puzzle of Equality. 1967. 8.95 (ISBN 0-87215-055-0). Michie-Bobbs.

Stephenson, G. T. Race Distinctions in American Law. 1977. lib. bdg. 69.95 (ISBN 0-8490-2496-X). Gordon Pr.

Stone, Christopher D. Should Trees Have Standing? Toward Legal Rights for Natural Objects. LC 73-19535. 121p. 1974. 8.95 (ISBN 0-913232-09-2); pap. 4.50 (ISBN 0-913232-08-4). W Kaufmann.

Story, Joseph. The Miscellaneous Writings of Joseph Story. Story, William W., ed. LC 79-75269. (American Constitutional & Legal History Ser). 828p. 1972. Repr. of 1852 ed. lib. bdg. 75.00 (ISBN 0-306-71314-4). Da Capo.

Strom, Frederic A. Land Use & Environment Law Review: Annual. Incl. 1975 (ISBN 0-87632-116-3); 1976 (ISBN 0-87632-117-1); 1977 (ISBN 0-87632-118-X); 1978 (ISBN 0-87632-119-8); 1979 (ISBN 0-87632-120-1). 1980 45.00, (ISBN 0-87632-121-X). LC 70-127585. 42.50 ea. Boardman.

Summers, Robert S. & Howard, C. Law, Its Nature, Functions & Limits. 2nd ed. (Illus.). 1024p. 1972. text ed. 22.95 (ISBN 0-13-526400-6). P-H.

Swancara, Frank. Obstruction of Justice by Religion: A Treatise on Religious Barbarities of the Common Law, & a Review of Judicial Oppressions of the Non-Religious in the U.S. LC 70-139581. (Civil Liberties in American History Ser). (Illus.). 1970. Repr. of 1936 ed. lib. bdg. 29.50 (ISBN 0-306-71964-9). Da Capo.

Swift, Zephaniah. A System of the Laws of the State of Connecticut, 2 vols. LC 73-37991. (American Law Ser.: The Formative Law). 962p. 1972. Repr. of 1795 ed. Set. 41.00 (ISBN 0-405-04036-9); 20.50 ea. Vol. 1 (ISBN 0-405-04037-7). Vol. 2 (ISBN 0-405-04038-5). Arno.

Texas Young Lawyers Association. A Survey of Idea Law for the Texas General Practitioner. Hewitt, Lester L., ed. LC 75-58705. 285p. 1978. 20.00 (ISBN 0-938160-19-2, 6314). State Bar TX.

Thayer, James B. Legal Essays. LC 72-81340. (Illus.). xvi, 402p. 1972. Repr. of 1908 ed. lib. bdg. 19.50x (ISBN 0-8377-2627-1). Rothman.

Underwood, James L. A Guide to Federal Discovery Rules. 286p. 45.00 (ISBN 0-686-61149-7, B114-B115). Am Law Inst.

Update Nineteen Seventy-Nine. (The Great Contemporary Issues Ser.). 1979. lib. bdg. 35.00x (ISBN 0-686-59848-2). Arno.

Virginia Decisions, 2 Vols. 1902. 25.00 (ISBN 0-87215-141-7). Michie-Bobbs.

Von Mehren, Arthur T. & Trautman, Donald T. The Law of Multistate Problems: Cases & Materials on Conflict of Laws. 1646p. 1965. 20.00 (ISBN 0-316-90756-1). Little.

Watkins, Robert D. The State As a Major Party Litigant. LC 78-64122. (Johns Hopkins University. Studies in the Social Sciences. Fourty-Fifth Ser. 1927: 1). Repr. of 1927 ed. 18.00 (ISBN 0-404-61236-9). AMS Pr.

Weber, Robert. Before You See a Lawyer. 320p. 1981. 14.95 (ISBN 0-8329-0101-6). New Century.

Weistart, John C. & Lowell, Cym H. The Law of Sports. 1979. 40.00 (ISBN 0-672-82337-3, Bobbs-Merrill Law). Michie-Bobbs.

West Virginia Code Annotated, 20 vols. write for info. incl. 1980 suppl. & index (ISBN 0-87215-138-7); write for info. 1980 suppl. (ISBN 0-87215-346-0). Michie-Bobbs.

West's Review Covering Multistate Subjects. LC 79-24976. 448p. 1979. pap. text ed. 23.95 (ISBN 0-8299-2081-1). West Pub.

White, Edward. Patterns of American Legal Thought. 1978. 17.00 (ISBN 0-672-83417-0, Bobbs-Merrill Law). Michie-Bobbs.

Whitinger, Robert G. Indiana Small Claims. 180p. 1980. 20.00 (ISBN 0-87215-326-6). Michie-Bobbs.

Who's Who in American Law 1977-78. 1st ed. LC 77-79896. 1977. 52.50 (ISBN 0-8379-3501-6). Marquis.

Wyoming Statutes, Annotated, 11 vols. with indexes & rules. 1979. write for info. (ISBN 0-87215-139-5); 1980 suppl. avail. (ISBN 0-87215-348-7). Michie-Bobbs.

Yokley, E. C. The Law of Subdivisions. 1963. with 1980 suppl. 50.00 (ISBN 0-87215-061-5); 1980 suppl 25.00 (ISBN 0-87215-344-4). Michie-Bobbs.

LAW-UNITED STATES-ADDRESSES, ESSAYS, LECTURES

Bigelow, Melville M., intro. by. Centralization & the Law: Scientific Legal Education, an Illustration. LC 72-181856. xviii, 296p. 1972. Repr. of 1906 ed. text ed. 16.50x (ISBN 0-8377-2004-4). Rothman.

Burris, Russel W., et al. Teaching Law with Computers. (EDUCOM Series in Computing & Telecommunications in Higher Education). 1979. lib. bdg. 19.50x (ISBN 0-89158-193-6). Westview.

Crowin, Stanley. Plaintiff's Proof of a Prima Facie Case. 35.00 (ISBN 0-685-22646-8). Acme Law.

Frank, Jerome. A Man's Reach: The Philosophy of Judge Jerome Frank. Kristein, Barbara F., ed. LC 77-7288. 1977. Repr. of 1965 ed. lib. bdg. 27.75x (ISBN 0-8371-9669-8, FRMR). Greenwood.

Frankfurter, Felix. Felix Frankfurter on the Supreme Court: Extrajudicial Essays on the Court & the Constitution. Kurland, Philip B., ed. LC 70-99518. (Illus.). 1970. 25.00x (ISBN 0-674-29835-7, Belknap Pr). Harvard U Pr.

Frankfurter, Felix & Landis, James M. Business of the Supreme Court: A Study in the Federal Judicial System. LC 26-24024. 1971. Repr. of 1928 ed. 25.50 (ISBN 0-384-16730-6). Johnson Repr.

Frankfurter, Felix, ed. Mr. Justice Brandeis. LC 73-37766. (American Constitutional & Legal History Ser). (Illus.). 232p. 1972. Repr. of 1932 ed. lib. bdg. 22.50 (ISBN 0-306-70430-7). Da Capo.

Gilmore, Grant. The Ages of American Law. LC 76-49988. (Storrs Lectures). 1977. 15.00x (ISBN 0-300-01951-3). Yale U Pr.

Hurst, James W. Law & Social Process in United States History. LC 74-173669. (American Constitutional & Legal History Ser.). 359p. 1971. Repr. of 1960 ed. lib. bdg. 35.00 (ISBN 0-306-70409-9). Da Capo.

Morrison Foundation Lectures. facsimile ed. LC 71-156698. (Essay Index Reprint Ser). Repr. of 1940 ed. 14.75 (ISBN 0-8369-2419-3). Arno.

Rutledge, Wiley. Declaration of Legal Faith. LC 74-114563. (American Constitutional & Legal History Ser). 1970. Repr. of 1947 ed. lib. bdg. 14.95 (ISBN 0-306-71921-5). Da Capo.

Shartel, Burke. Our Legal System & How It Operates. LC 73-173666. (American Constitutional & Legal History Ser.). 628p. 1972. Repr. of 1951 ed. lib. bdg. 59.50 (ISBN 0-306-70411-0). Da Capo.

Shriver, Harry C. The Government Lawyer: Essays on Men, Books, & the Law. LC 74-83402. (Illus.). 1975. 6.95 (ISBN 0-914932-01-2). Fox Hills.

Taubman, Joseph. Forms Book 7: Actions, Proceedings & Arbitration. 1980. 50.00 (ISBN 0-88238-088-5). Law-Arts.

Windolph, Francis L. Country Lawyer. LC 77-107743. (Essay Index Reprint Ser). 1938. 15.00 (ISBN 0-8369-1638-7). Arno.

Wyzanski, Charles E. Whereas....a Judge's Premises: Essays in Judgement, Ethics, & the Law. LC 76-43310. 1976. Repr. of 1965 ed. lib. bdg. 18.00x (ISBN 0-8371-9298-6, WYWH). Greenwood.

LAW-UNITED STATES-BIBLIOGRAPHY

Bryson, William H. Bibliography of Virginia Legal History Before Nineteen Hundred. LC 78-26684. 1979. 14.95x (ISBN 0-8139-0773-X). U Pr of Va.

Foster, Lynn & Boast, Carol. Subject Compilations of State Laws: Research Guide & Annotated Bibliography. LC 80-1788. 473p. 1981. lib. bdg. 45.00 (ISBN 0-313-21255-4, FOS). Greenwood.

Gifis, Steven H. Law Dictionary. LC 74-18126. 240p. 1975. pap. 3.95 (ISBN 0-8120-0543-0). Barron.

Keitt, Lawrence. Annotated Bibliography of Bibliographies of Statutory Materials of the United States. 1934. 6.50x (ISBN 0-678-08035-6). Kelley.

Schultz, J. S. Comparative Statutory Sources. LC 73-86848. 1973. lib. bdg. 18.00 (ISBN 0-930342-18-6). W S Hein.

Schwartz, Mortimer D. & Henke, Dan F., eds. Combined Catalog Anglo-American Law Collections University of California Law Libraries Berkeley & Davis with Library of Congress Class K Added, 9 vols. (Supplement). 1979. text ed. 750.00x (ISBN 0-8377-0423-5). Rothman.

Who's Who in American Law. 2nd ed. LC 77-79896. 1007p. 1979. 57.50 (ISBN 0-8379-3502-4, 030226). Marquis.

LAW-UNITED STATES-COMPENDS

Annual Survey of American Law, 1942-78, 37 vols. Set. 1050.00 (ISBN 0-379-12200-6). Oceana.

Johnson, Bradley T. Reports of Cases Decided by Chief Justice Chase in the Circuit Court of the United States for the Fourth Circuit: 1865-1869. facsimile ed. LC 75-75292. (American Constitutional & Legal History Ser.). 1972. Repr. of 1876 ed. lib. bdg. 59.50 (ISBN 0-306-71291-1). Da Capo.

Johnson, Elmer C. Survey of American Law. LC 78-98957. 1970. text ed. 9.95 (ISBN 0-682-47032-5, University). Exposition.

Lane, Marc J. The Doctor's Lawyer: A Legal Handbook for Doctors. (Illus.). 112p. 1974. text ed. 17.50 (ISBN 0-398-02988-1). C C Thomas.

Linn, Jo W. Abstracts of the Minutes of the Court of Pleas & Quarter Sessions Rowan Co., N. C., 1753-1762. 1978. 25.00 (ISBN 0-918470-02-1). J W Linn.

Robinson, Joan. An American Legal Almanac: Law in All States Summary & Update. LC 78-58299. (The Legal Almanac Ser.). 1978. lib. bdg. 20.00 (ISBN 0-379-11125-X). Oceana.

Walker, Timothy. Introduction to American Law. LC 79-172176. (American Constitutional & Legal History Ser). 672p. 1972. Repr. of 1837 ed. lib. bdg. 59.50 (ISBN 0-306-70224-X). Da Capo.

LAW-UNITED STATES-EXAMINATIONS, QUESTIONS, ETC.

Arco Editorial Board. Attorney-Assistant Trainee. 3rd. ed. (Orig.). 1975. pap. 8.00 (ISBN 0-668-01084-3); PLB 7.50 (ISBN 0-668-01707-4). Arco.

--Law & Court Stenographer. 3rd ed. LC 67-20835. 1971. pap. 8.00 (ISBN 0-668-00783-4). Arco.

Brown, Esther L. Lawyers & the Promotion of Justice. (Russell Sage Foundation Reprint Ser). Repr. of 1938 ed. lib. bdg. 26.00x (ISBN 0-697-00201-2). Irvington.

Multistate Bar Exam V. 1980. write for info. (ISBN 0-87543-162-3). Lucas.

Rudman, Jack. Junior Attorney. (Career Examination Ser.: C-391). (Cloth bdg. avail. on request). pap. 10.00 (ISBN 0-8373-0391-5). Natl Learning.

--New York State Bar Examination (NYBE) (Admission Test Ser.: ATS-25). (Cloth bdg. avail. on request). pap. 13.95 (ISBN 0-8373-5125-1); pap. 13.95 (ISBN 0-8373-5025-5). Natl Learning.

LAW-UNITED STATES-HISTORY AND CRITICISM

Association of American Law Schools. Selected Essays in Anglo-American Legal History 1907-09, 3 Vols. 1969. Set. 120.00 (ISBN 0-379-00426-7). Oceana.

Aumann, Francis R. Changing American Legal System: Some Selected Phases. LC 79-92625. (Law, Politics, & History Ser). 1969. Repr. of 1940 ed. 29.50 (ISBN 0-306-71762-X). Da Capo.

Bennett, W. Lance & Feldman, Martha S. Reconstructing Reality in the Courtroom: Justice & Judgment in American Culture. (Crime, Law, & Deviance Ser.). 208p. 1981. 14.50 (ISBN 0-8135-0922-X). Rutgers U Pr.

Bloomfield, Maxwell. American Lawyers in a Changing Society, 1776-1876: American Lawyers & Social Change, 1776-1876. (Studies in Legal History). 416p. 1976. 18.50x (ISBN 0-674-02910-0). Harvard U Pr.

Boner, Marian. A Reference Guide to Texas Law & Legal History: Sources & Documentation. LC 75-19408. 118p. 1976. 10.00x (ISBN 0-292-77007-3). U of Tex Pr.

Brown, Elizabeth G. British Statutes in American Law. LC 73-21605. (American Constitutional & Legal History Ser). 1974. Repr. of 1964 ed. lib. bdg. 35.00 (ISBN 0-306-70610-5). Da Capo.

Cushing, John D., compiled by. The First Laws of the Commonwealth of Massachusetts. (Earliest Laws of the Original Thirteen States Ser.). 1981. 48.00 (ISBN 0-89453-212-X). M Glazier.

--The First Laws of the State of Georgia, 2 vols. (Earliest Laws of the Original Thirteen States Ser.). 1981. 49.00 ea. Set (ISBN 0-89453-218-9). M Glazier.

--The First Laws of the State of Maryland. (Earliest Laws of the Original Thirteen States Ser.). 1981. 49.00 (ISBN 0-89453-213-8). M Glazier.

--The First Laws of the State of New Jersey. (Earliest Laws of the Original Thirteen States Ser.). 1981. 49.00 (ISBN 0-89453-217-0). M Glazier.

--The First Laws of the State of South Carolina, 2 vols. (Earliest Laws of the Original Thirteen States Ser.). 1981. write for info. (ISBN 0-89453-214-6). M Glazier.

--The First Laws of the State of New Hampshire. (Law Ser.). 1981. 35.00 (ISBN 0-89453-215-4). M Glazier.

Davis, William. History of the Judiciary of Massachusetts. LC 74-8535. (American Constitutional & Legal History Ser). xxiv, 446p. 1974. Repr. of 1900 ed. lib. bdg. 45.00 (ISBN 0-306-70613-X). Da Capo.

Dillon, J. F. The Law & Jurisprudence of England & America. LC 75-99475. (American Constitutional & Legal History Ser). 1970. Repr. of 1894 ed. lib. bdg. 42.50 (ISBN 0-306-71854-5). Da Capo.

Dillon, John F. Removal of Causes from State Courts to Federal Courts, with Forms Adapted to the Several Acts of Congress on the Subject. 3rd ed. xxiii, 168p. 1981. Repr. of 1881 ed. lib. bdg. 22.00x (ISBN 0-8377-0514-2). Rothman.

Eades, Ronald W. Watson V. Jones: The Walnut Street Presbyterian Church & the First Amendment. 132p. 1981. 18.50 (ISBN 0-89097-023-8). Archer Edns.

Ernst, M. L. The First Freedom. LC 73-166324. (Civil Liberties in American History Ser.). 316p. 1971. Repr. of 1946 ed. lib. bdg. 29.50 (ISBN 0-306-70242-8). Da Capo.

Friedman, Lawrence M. A History of American Law. 1974. pap. 7.95 (ISBN 0-671-21742-9, Touchstone Bks). S&S.

Friedman, Lawrence M. & Scheiber, Harry N., eds. American Law & the Constitutional Order: Historical Perspectives. LC 77-16640. 1978. 25.00x (ISBN 0-674-02525-3). Harvard U Pr.

Gilmore, Grant. The Ages of American Law. LC 76-49988. (Storrs Lectures). 1977. 15.00x (ISBN 0-300-01951-3). Yale U Pr.

Goebel, Julius, Jr. & Smith, Joseph H., eds. The Law Practice of Alexander Hamilton, Vol. 3. 1980. 50.00x (ISBN 0-231-08946-5). Columbia U Pr.

--The Law Practice of Alexander Hamilton, Vol. 4. 1980. 50.00x (ISBN 0-231-08930-9). Columbia U Pr.

Haar, Charles, ed. The Golden Age of American Law. LC 65-14603. (Golden Age Ser). 1965. 8.50 (ISBN 0-8076-0297-3). Braziller.

Haines, Charles G. The Role of the Supreme Court in American Government & Politics 1835-1864. LC 73-604. (American Constitutional & Legal History Ser.). 544p. 1973. Repr. of 1957 ed. lib. bdg. 49.50 (ISBN 0-306-70566-4). Da Capo.

Hartog, Hendrik A., ed. Law in the American Revolution & the Revolution in the Law. (New York University School of Law Ser. in Anglo-American Legal History). 272p. 1981. text ed. 22.50x (ISBN 0-8147-3413-8). NYU Pr.

Haskins, George L. Law & Authority in Early Massachusetts: A Study in Tradition & Design. 1968. Repr. of 1960 ed. 18.50 (ISBN 0-208-00685-0, Archon). Shoe String.

Holdsworth, William S. Historians of Anglo-American Law. 1966. Repr. of 1928 ed. 16.50 (ISBN 0-208-00347-9, Archon). Shoe String.

Horwitz, Morton J., et al, eds. American Law: The Formative Years, 28 bks. 1972. Repr. 845.00 (ISBN 0-405-03990-5). Arno.

Howe, M., ed. Readings in American Legal History. LC 70-155924. (American Constitutional & Legal History Ser). 1971. Repr. of 1949 ed. lib. bdg. 49.50 (ISBN 0-306-70159-6). Da Capo.

Howland, Henry E. The Practice of Law in the United States at the Beginning of the Century. (Illus.). 1979. Repr. of 1901 ed. 29.75 (ISBN 0-89266-195-X). Am Classical Coll Pr.

Hurst, J. Willard. Law & the Conditions of Freedom in the Nineteenth-Century United States. 150p. 1956. pap. 5.45 (ISBN 0-299-01363-4). U of Wis Pr.

Hurst, James B. Law & Social Order in the United States. LC 76-28015. 1977. 22.50x (ISBN 0-8014-1063-0). Cornell U Pr.

Hurst, James W. Dealing with Statutes. (Carpenter Lecture Ser.). 144p. 1981. text ed. 15.00x (ISBN 0-231-05390-8). Columbia U Pr.

--The Growth of American Law: The Law Makers. 1950. 15.00 (ISBN 0-316-38357-0). Little.

--Law & Social Process in United States History. LC 74-173669. (American Constitutional & Legal History Ser.). 359p. 1971. Repr. of 1960 ed. lib. bdg. 35.00 (ISBN 0-306-70409-9). Da Capo.

Johnson, John W. American Legal Culture, 1908-1940. LC 80-1027. (Contributions in Legal Studies: No. 16). x, 185p. 1981. lib. bdg. 23.95 (ISBN 0-313-22337-8, JAM/). Greenwood.

Konig, David T. Law & Society in Puritan Massachusetts: Essex County, 1629-1692. LC 78-26685. 1979. 21.00x (ISBN 0-8078-1336-2); pap. 9.95x (ISBN 0-8078-4081-5). U of NC Pr.

Land, Aubrey G., et al, eds. Law, Society, & Politics in Early Maryland. LC 76-47374. (Illus.). 400p. 1977. 22.50x (ISBN 0-8018-1872-9). Johns Hopkins.

Law in America, 2 vols. Incl. Vol. 1. Stories of Great Crimes & Trials from American Heritage Magazine. American Heritage Editors. LC 74-4031. 382p; Vol. 2. The American Heritage History of Law in America. Schwartz, Bernard. LC 74-8264. (Illus.). 379p. 1974. Boxed Set. deluxe ed. 45.00 (ISBN 0-8281-0292-9, Dist. by Scribner). Am Heritage.

Levy, Leonard W. Law of the Commonwealth & Chief Justice Shaw. LC 57-6350. 1957. 7.50x (ISBN 0-678-08037-2). Kelley.

Luce, Robert. Legislative Principles. LC 77-148083. (American Constitutional & Legal History Ser). 1971. Repr. of 1930 ed. lib. bdg. 59.50 (ISBN 0-306-70144-8). Da Capo.

Meyer, Balthasar Henry. A History of the Northern Securities Case. LC 70-124898. (American Constitutional & Legal History Ser). 136p. 1972. Repr. of 1906 ed. lib. bdg. 19.50 (ISBN 0-306-71989-4). Da Capo.

Moore, Philip S. Century of Law at Notre Dame. LC 74-105724. 1970. pap. 2.95x (ISBN 0-268-00416-1, 114). U of Notre Dame Pr.

Morris, Richard B. Studies in the History of American Law. 2nd ed. 1964. lib. bdg. 18.50x (ISBN 0-374-95909-9). Octagon.

Muir, Edward. The Social Studies Student Investigates American Law. (Social Studies Student Ser.). (Illus.). (YA) 1977. lib. bdg. 7.97 (ISBN 0-8239-0396-6). Rosen Pr.

Murphy, James M. Laws, Courts, & Lawyers: Through the Years in Arizona. LC 79-89656. (Illus.). 256p. 1970. 2.00 (ISBN 0-8165-0197-1). U of Ariz Pr.

Nelson, William E. The Americanization of the Common Law: The Impact of Legal Change of Massachusetts Society 1760-1830. LC 74-21231. (Studies in Legal History). 288p. 1975. pap. 5.95x (ISBN 0-674-02972-0). Harvard U Pr.

New York University. Anglo-American Legal History Series, Nos. 2-9 In 1 Vol. 1939-1944. 25.00 (ISBN 0-379-00178-0). Oceana.

Nolan, Dennis R., ed. Readings in the History of the American Legal Profession. 320p. (Orig.). 1980. pap. text ed. 15.00 (ISBN 0-672-84197-5). Bobbs.

Pound, Roscoe. Formative Era of American Law. 7.00 (ISBN 0-8446-1359-2). Peter Smith.

--Spirit of the Common Law. (gr. 11-12). text ed. 5.00x (ISBN 0-8338-0056-6). M Jones.

Powell, Richard R. Compromises of Conflicting Claims: A History of California Law in the Period 1760-1860. LC 77-54938. (Orig.). 1977. lib. bdg. 22.50 (ISBN 0-379-00655-3). Oceana.

Presser, Stephen B. & Zainaldin, Jamil S. Law & American History: Cases & Materials. LC 80-15905. (American Casebook Ser.). 897p. 1980. text ed. 19.95 (ISBN 0-8299-2094-3). West Pub.

Ratcliffe, Robert H., ed. Law in a New Land. LC 72-406. (Trailmarks of Liberty Ser.). (Illus.). 102p. (gr. 4-5). 1975. pap. text ed. 4.41 (ISBN 0-395-13817-5, 2-32290); teacher's guide 3.63 (ISBN 0-395-13818-3). HM.

Reid, John P. In a Defiant Stance: The Conditions of Law in Massachusetts Bay, the Irish Comparison, & the Coming of the American Revolution. LC 76-42453. 1977. 16.75x (ISBN 0-271-01240-4). Pa St U Pr.

--In a Rebellious Spirit: The Argument of Facts, the Liberty Riot, & the Coming of the American Revolution. LC 78-50065. 1979. 15.95x (ISBN 0-271-00202-6). Pa St U Pr.

--Law for the Elephant: Property & Social Behavior on the Overland Trail. LC 79-26989. (Illus.). 1980. 18.50 (ISBN 0-87328-104-7). Huntington Lib.

Reinsch, Paul S. English Common Law in the Early American Colonies. LC 75-110969. (American Constitutional & Legal History Ser). 1970. Repr. of 1899 ed. lib. bdg. 14.95 (ISBN 0-306-71910-X). Da Capo.

Reinsch, Paul Si. English Common Law in the Early American Colonies. 1976. lib. bdg. 69.95 (ISBN 0-8490-1373-9). Gordon Pr.

Rembar, Charles. The Law of the Land. 1980. 15.00 (ISBN 0-671-24322-5). S&S.

--The Law of the Land: The Evolution of Our Legal System. 1981. pap. 7.95 (ISBN 0-671-43828-X, Touchstone Bks). S&S.

Stephenson, Gilbert T. Race Distinctions in American Law. LC 10-21327. (Basic Afro-American Reprint Library). 18.50 (ISBN 0-384-58030-0). Johnson Repr.

Valente, William D. Local Government Law, Cases & Materials. 2nd ed. LC 80-10272. (American Casebook Ser.). 1048p. 1980. text ed. 21.95 (ISBN 0-8299-2087-0). West Pub.

Warren, Charles. History of the Harvard Law School & of Early Legal Conditions in America. LC 72-112311. (American Constitutional & Legal History Ser). 1970. Repr. of 1908 ed. lib. bdg. 75.00 (ISBN 0-306-71913-4). Da Capo.

Worrell, Anne L. Over the Mountain Men: Their Early Court Records in Southwest Virginia. LC 63-495. 1979. Repr. of 1934 ed. 5.00 (ISBN 0-8063-0671-8). Genealog Pub.

LAW–UNITED STATES–POPULAR WORKS

Coughlin, George G. Your Introduction to Law. 3rd ed. LC 74-29435. 320p. 1979. pap. 4.50 (ISBN 0-06-463472-8, EH 472, BN). Har-Row.

Greenburg, Joanne. Jack in the Beanstalk. (Illus.). 48p. (gr. 3 up). 1980. write for info. (ISBN 0-8299-1033-6). West Pub.

How to Be Your Own Lawyer in Court. 1980. write for info. (ISBN 0-89648-068-2); pap. write for info. (ISBN 0-89648-069-0). Citizens Law.

Koch, Harry W. California Paralegal Guide. 1978. pap. 7.00 (ISBN 0-913164-74-7). Ken-Bks.

--Your Everyday Legal Problems Under California Law. 1979. pap. 6.00 (ISBN 0-913164-80-1). Ken-Bks.

Kutner, Luis. Intelligent Woman's Guide to Future Security. LC 74-99184. Orig. Title: How to Be a Wise Widow. 1970. 4.95 (ISBN 0-396-06059-5). Dodd.

Lefcourt, Robert, ed. Law Against the People: Essays to Demystify Law, Order & the Courts. LC 79-143827. 1971. pap. 3.45 (ISBN 0-394-71038-X, Vin). Random.

Post, C. Gordon. Introduction to the Law. (Orig.). 1963. pap. 3.45 (ISBN 0-13-499780-8). P-H.

Ross, Martin J. & Ross, Jeffrey S. Handbook of Everyday Law. 4th, rev. ed. LC 80-8216. (Illus.). 384p. 1981. 14.95 (ISBN 0-06-013659-6, HarpT). Har-Row.

Seuling, Barbara. You Can't Eat Peanuts in Church & Other Little Known Laws. (Illus.). 120p. 1976. pap. 1.75 (ISBN 0-385-12137-7, Dolp). Doubleday.

Speiser, Stuart M. Lawsuit. 600p. 1980. 40.00 (ISBN 0-8180-2200-0); pap. 12.50 (ISBN 0-8180-2201-9). Horizon.

LAW–WALES

Andrews, J. A., ed. Welsh Studies in Public Law. 1970. 15.00x (ISBN 0-8426-0152-X). Verry.

Rhys, John & Jones, David B. Welsh People. LC 68-25263. (British History Ser., No. 30). 1969. Repr. of 1906 ed. lib. bdg. 62.95 (ISBN 0-8383-0233-5). Haskell.

LAW (THEOLOGY)

see also Antinomianism; Law and Gospel

Feldman, E. Biblical & Post-Biblical Defilement & Mourning: Law As Theology. (The Library of Jewish Law & Ethics: Vol. 3). 20.00x (ISBN 0-87068-287-3). Ktav.

Kaye, Bruce & Wenham, Gordon, eds. Law, Morality & the Bible. LC 78-18549. 1978. pap. 5.95 (ISBN 0-87784-795-9). Inter-Varsity.

Suggs, M. Jack. Wisdom, Christology, & Law in Matthew's Gospel. LC 75-95930. 1970. text ed. 7.95x (ISBN 0-674-95375-4). Harvard U Pr.

LAW, ACCIDENT

see Accident Law

LAW, ADMINISTRATIVE

see Administrative Law

LAW, ADVERTISING

see Advertising Laws

LAW, AGRICULTURAL

see Agricultural Laws and Legislation

LAW, ANCIENT

see Law, Greek; Law, Hittite

LAW, ANGLO-AMERICAN

see Common Law; Law–Great Britain; Law–United States

LAW, ANGLO-SAXON

Bigelow, Melville M. Placita Anglo-Normannica: Law Cases from William One to Richard One. LC 78-112405. Repr. of 1881 ed. lib. bdg. 15.00x (ISBN 0-678-04539-9). Kelley.

Essays in Anglo-Saxon Law. LC 79-181855. xiv, 392p. 1972. Repr. of 1905 ed. text ed. 20.00x (ISBN 0-8377-2103-2). Rothman.

LAW, ARAB

see Islamic Law

LAW, ARUSHA

Gulliver, P. H. Social Control in an African Society: A Study of the Arusha: Agricultural Masai of Northern Tanganyika. LC 63-7547. 306p. 1963. u. s. a. 12.00x (ISBN 0-8147-0176-0). NYU Pr.

LAW, AUTOMOBILE

see Automobiles–Law and Legislation

LAW, BANKING

see Banking Law

LAW, BUILDING

see Building Laws

LAW, BURIAL

see Burial Laws

LAW, BUSINESS

see Business Law

LAW, CHARITY

see Charity Laws and Legislation

LAW, CIVIL

see Civil Law

LAW, COMMERCIAL

see Commercial Law

LAW, COMPARATIVE

see Comparative Law

LAW, CONSTITUTIONAL

see Constitutional Law

LAW, CONSULAR

see Consular Law

LAW, CORPORATION

see Corporation Law

LAW, CRIMINAL

see Criminal Law

LAW, DAIRY

see also Dairy Laws

LAW, DENTAL

see Dental Laws and Legislation

LAW, ECCLESIASTICAL

see Ecclesiastical Law

LAW, EDUCATIONAL

see Educational Law and Legislation

LAW, ELECTION

see Election Law

LAW, EMIGRATION

see Emigration and Immigration Law

LAW, ENGINEERING

see Engineering Law

LAW, FACTORY

see Factory Laws and Legislation

LAW, FANTI

Sarbah, John M. Fanti Customary Laws. 3rd ed. 317p. 1968. 27.50x (ISBN 0-7146-1768-7, F Cass Co). Biblio Dist.

--Fanti National Constitution. 2nd ed. 273p. 1968. 27.50x (ISBN 0-7146-1767-9, F Cass Co). Biblio Dist.

LAW, FARM

see Farm Law

LAW, FEUDAL

see Feudal Law

LAW, FISHERY

see Fishery Law and Legislation

LAW, FOOD

see Food Law and Legislation

LAW, FORESTRY

see Forestry Law and Legislation

LAW, GERMANIC

see also Law, Anglo-Saxon

Bach, Heinrich. Die Thuringisch-Sachsische Kanzleisprache Bis 1325, Miteiner Neven Einleitung Von Richard K. Seymour, 2 Vols. 31.00 (ISBN 0-384-02945-0). Johnson Repr.

Homan, Theo, ed. Skidarima: An Inquiry into the Written & Printed Texts, References & Commentaries. (Amsterdamer Publikationen Zur Sprache und Literatur: No. 20). 430p. (Orig.). 1975. pap. text ed. 85.50x (ISBN 90-6203-079-3). Humanities.

Huebner, Rudolf. History of Germanic Private Laws. Philbrick, Francis S., tr. LC 68-54741. (Continental Legal History Ser.: No. 4). Repr. of 1918 ed. 27.50x (ISBN 0-678-04505-4). Kelley.

Huebner, Rudolph. History of Germanic Private Law. (Continental Legal History Ser: Vol. 4). lix, 785p. 1969. Repr. of 1918 ed. 27.50x (ISBN 0-8377-2228-4). Rothman.

Jenks, Edward. Law & Politics in the Middle Ages with a Synoptic Table of Sources. LC 76-114814. (Research & Source Works: No. 429). 1970. Repr. of 1913 ed. text ed. 22.50 (ISBN 0-8337-1839-8). B Franklin.

Rivers, Theodore J. Laws of the Alamans & Bavarians. LC 77-81449. (Middle Ages Ser). 1977. 17.50x (ISBN 0-8122-7731-7). U of Pa Pr.

LAW, GREEK

Here are entered works on Ancient Greek law. Works on modern Greek Law would be entered under the heading Law–Greece, Modern.

Bonner, Robert J. Lawyers & Litigants in Ancient Athens: The Genesis of the Legal Profession. LC 68-57185. Repr. of 1927 ed. 15.00 (ISBN 0-405-08289-4, Blom Pubns). Arno.

Bonner, Robert J. & Harrell, Hansen C. Evidence in Athenian Courts & Public Arbitration in Athenian Law: Public Arbitration in Athenian Law, 2 vols. in one. Vlastos, Gregory, ed. LC 78-14610. (Morals & Law in Ancient Greece Ser.). (Eng. & Gr.). 1979. Repr. of 1936 ed. lib. bdg. 12.00x (ISBN 0-405-11586-5). Arno.

Bonner, Robert J. & Smith, Gertrude E. Administration of Justice from Homer to Aristotle, 2 Vols. LC 69-13832. (Illus.). 1969. Repr. of 1938 ed. Set. lib. bdg. 55.00x (ISBN 0-8371-0320-7, BOAJ). Greenwood.

Etudes sur les Antiquites Juridiques D'athenes, 10 pts. in one. Caillemer, Exupere. LC 78-15859. (Morals & Law in Ancient Greece Ser.). (Fr.). 1979. Repr. of 1872 ed. lib. bdg. 22.00x (ISBN 0-405-11532-6). Arno.

Garnet, Louis. Droit et Societe dans la Grece Ancienne. Vlastos, Gregory, ed. LC 78-19346. (Morals & Law in Ancient Greece Ser.). (Fr. & Gr.). 1979. Repr. of 1955 ed. lib. bdg. 16.00x (ISBN 0-405-11543-1). Arno.

Guiraud, Paul. La Propriete Fonciere En Grece Jusqua la Conquete Romaine. Vlastos, Gregory, ed. LC 78-19357. (Morals & Law in Ancient Greece Ser.). 1979. Repr. of 1893 ed. lib. bdg. 40.00x (ISBN 0-405-11549-0). Arno.

Hruza, Ernst. Die Ehebegrundung Nach Attischem Recute & Polygami und Pellikat Nach Griechischem Rechte, 2 vols. in one. Vlastos, Gregory, ed. LC 78-19367. (Morals & Law in Ancient Greece Ser.). (Ger. & Gr.). 1979. Repr. of 1892 ed. lib. bdg. 22.00x (ISBN 0-405-11554-7). Arno.

Leisi, Ernst & Schlesinger, Eilhard. Der Zeuge Im Attischen Recht & Die Griechische Asylie, 2 vols. in one. Vlastos, Gregory, ed. LC 78-14608. (Morals & Law in Ancient Greece Ser.). 1979. Repr. of 1933 ed. lib. bdg. 18.00x (ISBN 0-405-11584-9). Arno.

MacDowell, Douglas M. The Law in Classical Athens. LC 78-54141. (Aspects of Greek & Roman Life Ser.). 1978. 27.50x (ISBN 0-8014-1198-X). Cornell U Pr.

Maine, Henry S. Ancient Law: The Connection with the Early History of Society & Its Relation to Modern Ideas. 9.00 (ISBN 0-8446-0784-3). Peter Smith.

Maschko, Richard. Die Villdemslekre Im Griechischen Recht. Vlastos, Gregory, ed. LC 78-19369. (Morals & Law in Ancient Greece Ser.). 1979. Repr. of 1926 ed. lib. bdg. 14.00x (ISBN 0-405-11560-1). Arno.

Morrow, Glenn R. Plato's Law of Slavery in Its Relation to Greek Law. facsimile ed. LC 75-13283. (History of Ideas in Ancient Greece Ser.). 1976. Repr. of 1939 ed. 10.00x (ISBN 0-405-07325-9). Arno.

Phillipson, Coleman. The International Law & Custom of Ancient Greece & Rome, Vol. 1. Vlastos, Gregory, ed. LC 78-19383. (Morals & Law in Ancient Greece Ser.). 1979. Repr. of 1911 ed. lib. bdg. 26.00x (ISBN 0-405-11565-2). Arno.

Plescia, Joseph. The Oath & Perjury in Ancient Greece. LC 79-94804. viii, 116p. 1970. 5.00 (ISBN 0-8130-0432-2). U Presses Fla.

Schodorf, Konrad & Demisch, Edwin. Beitrage zue Genaueren Kenntnis der Attischen Gerichtssprache aus den Zehn Rednern & Die Schuldenerbfoige im Attischen Recht, 2 vols. in one. Vlastos, Gregory, ed. LC 78-14617. (Morals & Law in Ancient Greece Ser.). (Ger. & Greek.). 1979. Repr. of 1910 ed. lib. bdg. 14.00x (ISBN 0-405-11592-X). Arno.

Schulthess, Otto. Vormundschaft Mach Attischem Recht. Vlastos, Gregory, ed. LC 78-19379. (Morals & Law in Ancient Greece Ser.). 1979. Repr. of 1886 ed. lib. bdg. 18.00x (ISBN 0-405-11573-3). Arno.

Szanto, Emil. Das Griechische Burgerrecht. Vlastos, Gregory, ed. LC 78-14595. (Morals & Law in Ancient Greece Ser.). (Ger. & Gr.). 1979. Repr. of 1892 ed. lib. bdg. 12.00x (ISBN 0-405-11577-6). Arno.

Szegedy-Maszak, Andrew. The "Nomoi" of Theophrastus. rev. ed. Connor, W. R., ed. LC 80-2670. (Monographs in Classical Studies). 1981. lib. bdg. 19.00 (ISBN 0-405-14053-3). Arno.

Vinogradoff, Paul. Outlines of Historical Jurisprudence, 2 vols. LC 74-177869. Repr. of 1922 ed. Set. 34.50 (ISBN 0-404-06784-0). AMS Pr.

Vlastos, Gregory, ed. Morals & Law in Ancient Greece Series, 57 bks. 1979. Set. lib. bdg. 1165.00x (ISBN 0-405-11529-6). Arno.

LAW, HEBREW
see Jewish Law
LAW, HINDU
see Hindu Law
LAW, HITTITE

Garstang, John. The Land of the Hittites. 1976. lib. bdg. 59.95 (ISBN 0-8490-2124-3). Gordon Pr.

Maine, Henry S. Ancient Law: The Connection with the Early History of Society & Its Relation to Modern Ideas. 9.00 (ISBN 0-8446-0784-3). Peter Smith.

LAW, HOMESTEAD
see Homestead Law
LAW, IMMIGRATION
see Emigration and Immigration Law
LAW, INCA

Moore, Sally F. Power & Property in Inca Peru. LC 72-5456. 190p. 1973. Repr. of 1958 ed. lib. bdg. 14.50x (ISBN 0-8371-6441-9, MOPO). Greenwood.

Sternbach, L. Juridical Studies in Ancient Indian Law, 2 vols. 1967. 24.00 set (ISBN 0-89684-232-0). Orient Bk Dist.

LAW, INDUSTRIAL
see Factory Laws and Legislation; Industrial Laws and Legislation; Industry and State; Labor Laws and Legislation
LAW, INSURANCE
see Insurance Law
LAW, INTERNAL REVENUE
see Internal Revenue Law
LAW, INTERNATIONAL
see International Law
LAW, ISLAMIC
see Islamic Law
LAW, JEWISH
see Jewish Law
LAW, JUDGE-MADE
see Judge-Made Law
LAW, KAPAUKU

Pospisil, Leopold. Kapauku Papuans & Their Law. LC 64-20560. (Yale University Publications in Anthropology Reprints Ser: No. 54). 296p. 1964. pap. 10.00x (ISBN 0-87536-502-7). HRAFP.

LAW, LABOR
see Labor Laws and Legislation
LAW, LIBRARY
see Library Legislation
LAW, LIQUOR
see Liquor Laws
LAW, LOZI

Gluckman, Max. The Ideas in Barotse Jurisprudence. (Institute for African Studies). (Illus.). 299p. (Orig.). text ed. 17.50x (ISBN 0-7190-1030-6); pap. text ed. 16.75x (ISBN 0-7190-1031-4). Humanities.

--Judicial Process Among the Barotse of Northern Rhodesia. (Rhodes Livingston Institute Bks). 1955. pap. text ed. 15.00x (ISBN 0-7190-1040-3). Humanities.

LAW, MAORI
see also Land Tenure (Maori Law)
LAW, MARTIAL
see Martial Law
LAW, MARITIME
see Maritime Law
LAW, MARRIAGE
see Marriage Law
LAW, MEDICAL
see Medical Laws and Legislation
LAW, MERCHANT
see Commercial Law
LAW, MILITARY
see Military Law
LAW, MINING
see Mining Law
LAW, MOSAIC
see Jewish Law
LAW, NATURAL
see Natural Law
LAW, ORIENTAL
see also Islamic Law; Jewish Law
LAW, PATENT
see Patent Laws and Legislation
LAW, PLUMBING
see Plumbing–Laws and Regulations
LAW, PRACTICE OF
see Practice of Law
LAW, PRESS
see Press Law
LAW, PRIMITIVE
see also Ethnological Jurisprudence

Barton, Roy F. Ifugao Law. LC 78-76334. (Illus.). 1969. Repr. of 1919 ed. 16.75x (ISBN 0-520-01427-8). U of Cal Pr.

Bohannan, Paul, ed. Law & Warfare: Studies in the Anthropology of Conflict. (Texas Press Sourcebooks: No. 1). 455p. 1976. pap. 7.95x (ISBN 0-292-74617-2). U of Tex Pr.

Diamond, Arthur S. The Evolution of Law & Order. LC 72-9372. 342p. 1973. Repr. of 1951 ed. lib. bdg. 19.00x (ISBN 0-8371-6580-6, DIEL). Greenwood.

Gluckman, Max. Politics, Law & Ritual in Tribal Society. (Illus.). 339p. 1977. pap. 15.95x (ISBN 0-631-08750-8, Pub. by Basil Blackwell). Biblio Dist.

Goitein, H. Primitive Ordeal & Modern Law. xvii, 302p. 1980. Repr. of 1923 ed. lib. bdg. 32.50x (ISBN 0-8377-0612-2). Rothman.

Goldschmidt, Walter. Sebei Law. LC 67-15561. 1967. 23.75x (ISBN 0-520-00489-2). U of Cal Pr.

Hartland, E. Sidney. Primitive Law. LC 79-115320. 1971. Repr. of 1924 ed. 12.00 (ISBN 0-8046-1111-4). Kennikat.

Hoebel, E. Adamson. Law of Primitive Man: A Study in Comparative Legal Dynamics. LC 54-9331. 1968. pap. text ed. 4.95x (ISBN 0-689-70096-2, 119). Atheneum.

Maine, Henry S. Lectures on the Early History of Institutions. LC 66-21392. Repr. of 1914 ed. 15.00 (ISBN 0-8046-0296-4). Kennikat.

Malinowski, Bronislaw. Crime & Custom in Savage Society. (International Library of Psychological Philosophy & Scientific Mathematics). 1970. text ed. 12.00x (ISBN 0-7100-3043-6). Humanities.

Meek, Charles K. Colonial Law, a Bibliography with Special Reference to Native African Systems of Law & Land Tenure. LC 78-14383. 1978. lib. bdg. 15.00 (ISBN 0-313-21011-X, MECL). Greenwood.

--Law & Authority in a Nigerian Tribe. LC 76-44756. Repr. of 1937 ed. 28.50 (ISBN 0-404-15951-6). AMS Pr.

Schlegel, Stuart A. Tiruray Justice: Traditional Tiruray Law & Morality. LC 72-107660. 1970. 21.75x (ISBN 0-520-01686-6). U of Cal Pr.

Smith, W. & Roberts, J. Zuni Law: A Field of Values, with an Appendix. Incl. A Practical Zuni Orthography. Newman, Stanley. 1954. pap. 20.00 (ISBN 0-527-01312-9). Kraus Repr.

Vinogradoff, Paul. Outlines of Historical Jurisprudence, 2 vols. LC 74-177869. Repr. of 1922 ed. Set. 34.50 (ISBN 0-404-06784-0). AMS Pr.

LAW, PROBATE
see Probate Law and Practice
LAW, PUBLIC
see Public Law
LAW, RAILROAD
see Railroad Law
LAW, ROMAN
see Roman Law
LAW, SCROLL OF THE
see Torah Scrolls
LAW, SEMITIC
see Islamic Law; Jewish Law
LAW, SUMPTUARY
see Sumptuary Laws
LAW, SUNDAY
see Sunday Legislation
LAW, TSWANA

Schapera, I. Handbook of Tswana Law & Custom. 328p. 1970. 50.00x (ISBN 0-7146-2481-0). Intl Pubns Serv.

Schapera, Isaac. Handbook of Tswana Law & Custom. 328p. 1970. Repr. 28.50x (ISBN 0-7146-2481-0, F Cass Co). Biblio Dist.

LAW, WATER
see Water–Laws and Legislation
LAW AND ART

Barton, J. E. Purpose & Admiration: A Law Study of the Visual Arts. 1978. Repr. of 1933 ed. lib. bdg. 30.00 (ISBN 0-8492-3562-6). R West.

Beverly Hills Bar Association. Barristers Committee for the Arts. The Actor's Manual: A Practical Legal Guide. Beil, Norman, et al, eds. 288p. 1981. o. p. 13.95 (ISBN 0-8015-0040-0, Hawthorn); pap. 9.95 (ISBN 0-8015-0041-9, Hawthorn). Dutton.

DuBoff, Leonard D., ed. Art Law, Domestic & International. LC 75-7668. (Illus.). x, 627p. 1975. text ed. 27.50x (ISBN 0-8377-0503-7). Rothman.

Duffy, Robert E. Art Law: Representing Artists, Dealers & Collectors. LC 77-86511. 1977. text ed. 25.00 (ISBN 0-685-86794-3, G1-0647). PLI.

Hodes, Scott. Law of Art & Antiques. LC 65-16840. (Legal Almanac Ser.: No. 56). 1966. 5.95 (ISBN 0-379-11056-3). Oceana.

Horwitz, T. Law & the Arts: Arts & the Law. LC 79-54026. 1979. pap. 6.95 (ISBN 0-914090-71-2). Chicago Review.

Horwitz, Tem, ed. Law & the Arts: Arts & the Law. 264p. (Orig.). 1979. pap. 6.95 (ISBN 0-936122-00-5). Lawyers Creative Arts.

LAW AND CHRISTIANITY
see Religion and Law
LAW AND COMMUNISM
see Law and Socialism
LAW AND ETHICS
see also Legal Ethics

Abrahams, Gerald. Morality & the Law. LC 71-580486. 256p. 1980. 15.00 (ISBN 0-7145-0662-1, Pub. by M Boyars); pap. 7.95 (ISBN 0-7145-0663-X). Merrimack Bk Serv.

Ball, Milner S. The Promise of American Law: A Theological, Humanistic View of Legal Process. LC 81-4325. 208p. 1981. text ed. 15.00 (ISBN 0-686-76232-0). U of Ga Pr.

Bayne, David C. Conscience, Obligation & the Law: The Moral Binding Power of the Civil Law. LC 66-12757. (Jesuit Studies). 1966. 3.45 (ISBN 0-8294-0001-X). Loyola.

Bentham, Jeremy. An Introduction to the Principles of Morals & Legislation. Burns, J. H. & Hart, H. L., eds. (Collected Works of Jeremy Bentham Ser.). 1970. text ed. 47.00x (ISBN 0-485-13211-7, Athlone Pr). Humanities.

--Of Laws in General. Hart, H. L., ed. (Collected Works of Jeremy Bentham Ser.). 1970. text ed. 27.00x (ISBN 0-485-13210-9, Athlone Pr). Humanities.

Blom-Cooper, L. & Dreway, Gavin, eds. Law & Morality: A Reader. 265p. 1976. 40.50x (ISBN 0-7156-0805-3, Pub. by Duckworth England); pap. 13.50x (ISBN 0-7156-0804-5). Biblio Dist.

Cahn, Edmond. The Moral Decision: Right & Wrong in the Light of American Law. LC 81-47586. (Midland Bks.: No. 273). 352p. 1981. 17.50x (ISBN 0-253-33875-1); pap. 6.95x (ISBN 0-253-20273-6). Ind U Pr.

Davis, Philip E., ed. Moral Duty & Legal Responsibility: A Philosophical-Legal Casebook. 2nd ed. (Orig.). 1981. 18.50x (ISBN 0-8290-0681-8). Irvington.

Duster, Troy. The Legislation of Morality: Laws, Drugs & Moral Judgement. LC 72-80469. (Illus.). 1972. pap. text ed. 7.95 (ISBN 0-02-908680-9). Free Pr.

Fuller, Lon L. Morality of Law. rev. ed. (Storr Lectures Ser.). 1965. pap. 4.95x (ISBN 0-300-01070-2, Y152). Yale U Pr.

Gerson, Allan, ed. Lawyers' Ethics. LC 78-62895. 280p. 1980. text ed. 17.95 (ISBN 0-87855-293-6). Transaction Bks.

Hagen, John D., Jr. What's Wrong with America. LC 79-88085. 1979. pap. 4.95 (ISBN 0-87973-522-8). Our Sunday Visitor.

Hamburger, Max. Morals & Law. LC 65-15244. 1965. 12.00x (ISBN 0-8196-0151-9). Biblo.

Hart, H. L. Law, Liberty & Morality. LC 62-18743. 1963. 7.50x (ISBN 0-8047-0153-9); pap. 1.85 (ISBN 0-8047-0154-7, SP119). Stanford U Pr.

Hazard, Geoffrey C., Jr. Ethics in the Practice of Law. LC 77-16357. 177p. 1980. 15.00x (ISBN 0-300-02206-9); pap. 5.95 (ISBN 0-300-02601-3). Yale U Pr.

Horwitz, Robert H. Moral Foundations of the American Republic. 2nd ed. LC 79-20387. 1980. 15.00x (ISBN 0-8139-0853-1); pap. 3.95x (ISBN 0-8139-0854-X). U Pr of Va.

Kadish, Mortimer R. & Kadish, Sanford H. Discretion to Disobey: A Study of Lawful Departures from Legal Rules. LC 72-97201. 256p. 1973. 12.50x (ISBN 0-8047-0832-0); pap. 4.95 (ISBN 0-8047-1010-4, SP148). Stanford U Pr.

Kindregan, Charles P. Quality of Life: Reflections on the Moral Values of American Law. LC 69-17321. 1969. 6.50 (ISBN 0-02-803590-9). Macmillan.

Lamont, W. D. Law & the Moral Order. 150p. 13.50 (ISBN 0-08-025726-7). Pergamon.

--Law & the Moral Order: A Study in Ethics & Jurisprudence. 128p. 1981. 22.00 (ISBN 0-08-025742-9); pap. 12.00 (ISBN 0-08-025746-1). Pergamon.

Leoni, Bruno. Freedom & the Law. (Humane Studies). 204p. 1980. text ed. 7.50x (ISBN 0-8402-1215-1); pap. text ed. 4.95x (ISBN 0-8402-1215-1). Humanities.

Mitchell, Basil. Law, Morality & Religion in a Secular Society. (Oxford Paperbacks Ser). 1970. pap. 4.95x (ISBN 0-19-283010-4). Oxford U Pr.

Northrop, Filmer S. The Complexity of Legal & Ethical Experience: Studies in the Method of Normative Subjects. LC 78-790. 1978. Repr. of 1959 ed. lib. bdg. 27.75x (ISBN 0-313-20286-9, NOCL). Greenwood.

Ossowska, Maria. Social Determinants of Moral Ideas. LC 69-16540. (Haney Foundation Publication Ser.). 1970. 9.95x (ISBN 0-8122-7598-5); pap. 4.95x (ISBN 0-8122-1031-X, Pa Paperbacks). U of Pa Pr.

Petrazhitskii, Lev I. Law & Morality. Babb, Hugh W., tr. xlvi, 335p. Repr. of 1955 ed. 31.00 (ISBN 0-384-45970-6). Johnson Repr.

Pound, Roscoe. Law & Morals. LC 70-96339. ix, 144p. 1970. Repr. of 1924 ed. text ed. 17.50x (ISBN 0-8377-2501-1). Rothman.

Ratcliffe, James M. Good Samaritan & the Law. 8.75 (ISBN 0-8446-2783-6). Peter Smith.

Rostow, Eugene V. The Ideal in Law. LC 77-81733. 1978. 20.00 (ISBN 0-226-72818-8). U of Chicago Pr.

St. John-Stevas, Norman. Life, Death & the Law: A Study of the Relationship Between Law & Christian Morals in the English & American Legal Systems. 375p. 1981. Repr. of 1961 ed. lib. bdg. 32.50x (ISBN 0-8377-1119-3). Rothman.

Shaffer, Thomas L. On Being a Christian and a Lawyer: Law for the Innocent. LC 80-25215. 288p. 1980. 19.95x (ISBN 0-8425-1833-9). Brigham.

Shuman, Samuel I. Legal Positivism: Its Scope & Limitations. LC 62-14874. 1963. 11.95x (ISBN 0-8143-1213-6). Wayne St U Pr.

Texas Young Lawyers Association, ed. Texas Lawyer's Professional Ethics. LC 78-620070. 285p. 1979. 25.00 (ISBN 0-938160-22-2, 6333). State Bar TX.

Vinet, Alexandre R. Moralistes Des Seizieme et Dix-Septieme Siecles. Mayer, J. P., ed. LC 78-67394. (European Political Thought Ser.). (Fr.). 1979. Repr. of 1904 ed. lib. bdg. 26.00x (ISBN 0-405-11747-7). Arno.

Wasserstrom, Richard A. Morality & the Law. 1970. pap. 8.95x (ISBN 0-534-00167-X). Wadsworth Pub.

LAW AND GOSPEL

see also Freedom (Theology); Law (Theology)

Casebolt, Don E. Saturday or Sunday? Letter to a Sunday-Keeping Minister. LC 78-8672. (Flame Ser.). 1978. pap. 0.95 (ISBN 0-8127-0182-8). Review & Herald.

Elert, Werner. Law & Gospel. Sherman, Franklin, ed. Schroeder, Edward H., tr. from Ger. LC 66-25263. (Facet Bks). 64p. (Orig.). 1967. pap. 1.50 (ISBN 0-8006-3035-1, 1-3035). Fortress.

Feldman, E. Biblical & Post-Biblical Defilement & Mourning: Law As Theology. (The Library of Jewish Law & Ethics: Vol. 3). 20.00x (ISBN 0-87068-287-3). Ktav.

Walther, Carl F. Proper Distinction Between Law & Gospel. Dau, W. H., tr. 1929. 9.95 (ISBN 0-570-03248-2, 15-1601). Concordia.

LAW AND LITERATURE

Bloch, R. Howard. Medieval French Literature & Law. LC 76-7754. 1977. 22.75x (ISBN 0-520-03230-6). U of Cal Pr.

Crawford, Ted. The Writer's Legal Guide. LC 76-56516. 1978. (Hawthorn); pap. 5.95 (ISBN 0-8015-8938-X, Hawthorn). Dutton.

London, Ephraim, ed. Law As Literature. 1965. pap. 8.95 (ISBN 0-671-41060-1, Touchstone Bks). S&S.

Wydick, Richard C. Plain English for Lawyers. LC 79-53956. 91p. 1979. lib. bdg. 8.95 (ISBN 0-89089-175-3); pap. text ed. 3.95 (ISBN 0-89089-176-1). Carolina Acad Pr.

LAW AND MENTAL ILLNESS

see Insanity-Jurisprudence; Mental Health Laws

LAW AND MORALS

see Law and Ethics

LAW AND POLITICS

Bardach, Eugene. The Skill Factor in Politics: Repealing the Mental Commitment Laws in California. LC 79-157820. 300p. 1972. 20.00x (ISBN 0-520-02042-1). U of Cal Pr.

Bickel, Alexander M. Politics & the Warren Court. LC 73-398. (American Constitutional & Legal History Ser.). 314p. 1973. Repr. of 1955 ed. lib. bdg. 27.50 (ISBN 0-306-70573-7). Da Capo.

Dolbeare, Kenneth M. Trial Courts in Urban Politics: State Court Policy Impact & Functions in a Local Political System. LC 75-32506. 156p. 1976. Repr. of 1967 ed. 7.95 (ISBN 0-88275-360-6). Krieger.

Drewry, G. Law, Justice & Politics. (Political Realities). 140p. 1976. text ed. 9.95x (ISBN 0-582-36612-7); pap. text ed. 5.50x (ISBN 0-582-36623-2). Longman.

Eisenstein, James. Politics & the Legal Process. (Danelski Ser.). 356p. 1973. pap. text ed. 10.95 scp (ISBN 0-06-041883-4, HarpC). Har-Row.

Ely, John H. Democracy & Distrust: A Theory of Judicial Review. LC 79-19859. (Harvard Paperbacks Ser.). 280p. 1981. pap. 6.95 (ISBN 0-674-19637-6). Harvard U Pr.

Gaikwad, V. R. Anglo-Indians. 1968. 10.00x (ISBN 0-210-27090-X). Asia.

Garber, Lyman A. Of Men & Not of Law. 1966. 5.95 (ISBN 0-8159-6400-5). Devin.

Georgetown Law Journal Editors. Georgetown Law Journal: Media & the First Amendment in a Free Society. LC 73-81557. 1973. 12.00x (ISBN 0-87023-150-2); pap. 5.00x (ISBN 0-87023-151-0). U of Mass Pr.

Goldman, Sheldon & Jahnige, Thomas P. The Federal Courts As a Political System. 2nd ed. (American Political Ser.). 305p. 1976. pap. text ed. 9.95 scp (ISBN 0-06-042382-X, HarpC). Har-Row.

Hibbs, Douglas A. Mass Political Violence: A Cross-National Causal Analysis. 270p. 1973. 17.75 (ISBN 0-471-38600-6, Pub. by Wiley). Krieger.

Hochschild, Jennifer. What's Fair? LC 81-6272. (Illus.). 384p. 1981. text ed. 22.50 (ISBN 0-674-95086-0). Harvard U Pr.

Jacob, Herbert. Justice in America: Courts, Lawyers, & the Judicial Process. 3rd ed. 237p. 1978. pap. text ed. 6.95 (ISBN 0-316-45524-5). Little.

Kirchheimer, Otto. Political Justice: The Use of Legal Procedure for Political Ends. LC 80-14279. xiv, 452p. 1980. Repr. of 1961 ed. lib. bdg. 34.50x (ISBN 0-313-22509-5, KIPJ). Greenwood.

--Political Justice: The Use of Legal Procedure for Political Ends. 1961. pap. 8.95 (ISBN 0-691-02750-1). Princeton U Pr.

Moley, Raymond. Politics & Criminal Prosecution. LC 73-19161. (Politics & People Ser.). 256p. 1974. Repr. 13.00x (ISBN 0-405-05883-7). Arno.

Murphy, Walter F. & Pritchett, Herman C., eds. Courts, Judges & Politics: An Introduction to the Judicial Process. 3rd ed. LC 78-24033. 1979. text ed. 19.95x (ISBN 0-394-32117-0). Random.

Negley, Glenn R. Political Authority & Moral Judgment. LC 65-13654. 1965. 9.75 (ISBN 0-8223-0120-2). Duke.

Rembar, Charles. Perspective. LC 73-90111. 1974. 8.95 (ISBN 0-87795-105-5). Arbor Hse.

Scheingold, Stuart A. The Politics of Rights: Lawyers, Public Policy & Political Change. LC 74-79972. 240p. 1974. 17.50x (ISBN 0-300-01783-9); pap. 4.95x (ISBN 0-300-01811-8). Yale U Pr.

Scindler, D. & Toman, J. The Laws of Armed Conflicts. rev. ed. 904p. 1980. 105.00x (ISBN 90-286-0199-6). Sijthoff & Noordhoff.

Shapiro, Martin & Hobbs, Douglas. The Politics of Constitutional Law. 554p. 1974. text ed. 16.95 (ISBN 0-87626-682-0). Winthrop.

United States Senate Committee On The Judiciary - 89th Congress - 1st Session. Internal Security & Subversion: Principal State Laws & Cases. LC 70-167844. (Civil Liberties in American History Ser.). 1971. Repr. of 1965 ed. lib. bdg. 69.50 (ISBN 0-306-70121-9). Da Capo.

LAW AND RELIGION

see Religion and Law

LAW AND SCIENCE

see Science and Law

LAW AND SEX

see Sex and Law

LAW AND SOCIALISM

Bankowski, Zenon & Mungham, Geoff. Images of Law. (Direct Edition Ser.). (Orig.). 1976. pap. 9.95 (ISBN 0-7100-8339-4). Routledge & Kegan.

Beirne, Piers & Quinney, Richard. Marxism & Law. 550p. 1982. text ed. 15.95 (ISBN 0-471-08758-0). Wiley.

Hazard, John N. Communists & Their Law: A Search for the Common Core of the Legal Systems of the Marxian Socialist States. LC 75-92770. 1969. 17.50x (ISBN 0-226-32189-4). U of Chicago Pr.

Pashukanis, Evgeny B. Law & Marxism: A General Theory. Arthur, Chris, ed. Einhorn, Barbara, tr. from Ger. 1978. lib. bdg. 15.00 (ISBN 0-906133-04-1, Pub. by Inks Links England). Path Pr NY.

Phillips, Paul. Marx & Engels on Law & Laws. 238p. 1980. 27.50x (ISBN 0-389-20120-0). B&N.

Sumner, Colin. Reading Ideologies: An Investigation into the Marxist Theory of Ideology & Law. (Law, State & Society Ser.). 1979. 39.50 (ISBN 0-12-676650-9); pap. 12.00 (ISBN 0-12-676652-5). Acad Pr.

Terez, Szabo. The Unification & Differentiation in Socialist Criminal Justice. 1978. 27.50x (ISBN 963-05-1685-3). Intl Pubns Serv.

LAW AND SOCIETY

see Sociological Jurisprudence

LAW AND TECHNOLOGY

see Technology and Law

LAW AND THE BIBLE

see Bible and Law

LAW BOOKS

see Law-Bibliography; Legal Literature

LAW ENFORCEMENT

see also Peace Officers

Armstrong, Terry R. & Cinnamon, Kenneth M. Power & Authority in Law Enforcement. 208p. 1976. 17.25 (ISBN 0-398-03571-7). C C Thomas.

Baker, Ralph & Meyer, Fred, eds. Evaluating Alternative Law-Enforcement Policies. LC 79-1541. (Policy Studies Organization Bk.). (Illus.). 240p. 1979. 19.95 (ISBN 0-669-02898-3). Lexington Bks.

Beckman, Erik. Law Enforcement in a Democratic Society: An Introduction. LC 79-16306. (Nelson-Hall Law Enforcement Ser.). 1980. 22.95x (ISBN 0-88229-151-3); pap. 13.95x (ISBN 0-88229-753-8). Nelson-Hall.

Berney, Donald W. American Government for Law Enforcement Training. LC 75-8915. (Nelson Hall Law Enforcement Ser.). 1976. 22.95x (ISBN 0-88229-152-1). Nelson-Hall.

Brekke, Jerald. An Assessment of the Bloc Grant Provisions of the Omnibus Crime Control & Safe Streets Act of 1968: The Missouri Experience. 1977. pap. text ed. 6.75 (ISBN 0-8191-0254-7). U Pr of Amer.

Brounstein, Sidney H. & Kamrass, Murray, eds. Operations Research in Law Enforcement & Societal Security. (Illus.). 1976. 21.95 (ISBN 0-669-00732-3). Lexington Bks.

Caldwell, Robert G. Foundations of Law Enforcement & Criminal Justice. Nardini, William, ed. LC 76-46478. 1977. 16.95 (ISBN 0-672-61412-X). Bobbs.

Chambliss, William J. Criminal Law in Action. LC 74-32149. 480p. 1975. text ed. 19.95 (ISBN 0-471-14474-6). Wiley.

Chibnall, Steve. Law & Order News. 1977. pap. 10.95x (ISBN 0-422-74970-2, Pub. by Tavistock). Metheun Inc.

Clifford, William. Crime Control in Japan. LC 75-22883. 224p. 1976. 19.95 (ISBN 0-669-00184-8). Lexington Bks.

Coffey, Alan, et al. Human Relations: Law Enforcement in a Changing Community. (Illus.). 304p. 1982. reference 18.95 (ISBN 0-13-445700-5). P-H.

Coleman, Joseph. Your Career in Law Enforcement. LC 79-14314. (Arco's Career Guidence Ser.). 1979. pap. 3.95 (ISBN 0-668-04740-2, 4740); pap. 3.50 (ISBN 0-668-04751-8, 4751). Arco.

Cope, Jeff & Goddard, Kenneth. Weaponless Control: For Law Enforcement & Security Personnel. (Illus.). 302p. 1979. text ed. 19.50 (ISBN 0-398-03902-X). C C Thomas.

Edelhertz, Herbert & Rogovin, Charles, eds. A National Strategy for Continuing White-Collar Crime. LC 79-2373. (Human Affairs Research Center Ser.). 160p. 1980. 15.95x (ISBN 0-669-03166-6). Lexington Bks.

Eldefonso, Edward. Law Enforcement & the Youthful Offender. 3rd ed. LC 77-13331. 363p. 1978. 18.95 (ISBN 0-471-03234-4); tchrs. manual avail. (ISBN 0-471-03769-9). Wiley.

Eldefonso, Edward, et al. Principles of Law Enforcement: Overview of the Justice System. 400p. 1982. text ed. 19.95 (ISBN 0-471-05509-3). Wiley.

Farmer, Richard & Kowalewski, Victor. Law Enforcement & Community Relations. 160p. 1976. 11.50 (ISBN 0-87909-434-6); instrs'. manual avail. Reston.

Felkenes, George T. & Becker, Harold K. Law Enforcement: A Selected Bibliography. 2nd ed. LC 76-50010. 1977. 15.00 (ISBN 0-8108-0995-8). Scarecrow.

Ferdico, John M. Criminal Procedure for the Law Enforcement Officer. 2nd ed. (Criminal Justice Ser.). (Illus.). 1979. text ed. 18.95 (ISBN 0-8299-0188-4). West Pub.

Folley. American Law Enforcement: Police, Courts, & Corrections. 3rd ed. 512p. 1980. text ed. 18.95 (ISBN 0-205-06651-8, 8266514). Allyn.

Galaway, Burton & Hudson, Hamilton C. Perspectives on Crime Victims. LC 80-19922. (Illus.). 435p. 1980. pap. 16.95 (ISBN 0-8016-1733-2). Mosby.

Greenberg, Douglas. Crime & Law Enforcement in the Colony of New York, 1691-1776. LC 76-13658. (Illus.). 1976. 19.50x (ISBN 0-8014-1020-7). Cornell U Pr.

Hall, James P. Peacekeeping in America: A Developmental Study of American Law Enforcement: Philosophy & Systems. 1978. pap. text ed. 11.95 (ISBN 0-8403-1143-5). Kendall-Hunt.

Hess, Karen M. & Wrobleski, Henry M. For the Record: Report Writing in Law Enforcement. LC 77-20238. (Wiley Self-Teaching Guides). 1978. pap. text ed. 6.95 (ISBN 0-471-03006-6). Wiley.

Johnson, David. American Law Enforcement: A History. LC 80-68814. (Orig.). 1981. text ed. 15.95x (ISBN 0-88273-271-4). Forum Pr MO.

Kinton, J., ed. Criminology, Law Enforcement & Offender Treatment: A Sourcebook. rev. ed. 1981. write for info. (ISBN 0-685-96247-4). Soc Sci & Soc Res.

Kirkham, George L. & Wollan, Laurin A., Jr. Introduction to Law Enforcement. (Illus.). 1980. text ed. 18.95 scp (ISBN 0-06-043666-2, HarpC); instrs'. manual free (ISBN 0-06-363650-6). Har-Row.

Klotter, John C. & Kanovitz, Jacqueline R. Constitutional Law. 4th ed. (Justice Administration Legal Ser.). 900p. 1981. 19.95 (ISBN 0-87084-492-X). Anderson Pub Co.

Lee, Dick & Pratt, Colin. Operation Julie. 1980. 10.95 (ISBN 0-312-58681-7). St Martin.

Leonard, V. A. Fundamentals of Law Enforcement: Problems & Issues. (Criminal Jusice Ser.). (Illus.). 350p. 1980. text ed. 16.50 (ISBN 0-8299-0222-8); instrs.' manual avail. (ISBN 0-8299-0596-0). West Pub.

Lewis, Jack. Law Enforcement Handgun Digest. 3rd ed. (Illus.). 288p. 1980. pap. 8.95 (ISBN 0-695-81413-3). DBI.

McDonald, Phyllis. Law Enforcement Education in the Middle Grades: Police-Student Relations. 96p. 1978. pap. 4.50 (ISBN 0-686-63712-7, 1710-2-06). NEA.

Meyer, Fred & Baker, Ralph, eds. Determinants of Law Enforcement Policies. LC 79-1540. (Policy Studies Organization Bk.). 240p. 1979. 19.95 (ISBN 0-669-02900-9). Lexington Bks.

--Law Enforcement & Police Policy. 1979. pap. 5.00 (ISBN 0-918592-31-3). Policy Studies.

More, Harry, ed. Critical Issues in Law Enforcement. 3d ed. LC 79-55205. 352p. 1981. pap. text ed. 14.95 (ISBN 0-87084-582-9). Anderson Pub Co.

More, Harry W., Jr. Critical Issues in Law Enforcement. 2nd ed. 1975. text ed. 8.95 (ISBN 0-87084-581-0). Anderson Pub Co.

Olson, Bruce T. Pattern of American Law Enforcement: Research by Questionnaire. 1968. 2.50 (ISBN 0-686-16215-3). MSU-Inst Comm Devel.

Oxbridge Communications, Inc., compiled by. Legal & Law Enforcement Periodicals: A Directory. LC 80-39754. 238p. 1981. 35.00 (ISBN 0-87196-335-3). Facts on File.

Pace, Denny F. & Styles, Jimmie C. Organized Crime: Concepts & Control. (Law Enforcement Ser.). (Illus.). 352p. 1974. ref. ed. 16.95 (ISBN 0-13-640961-X). P-H.

Palmquist, Al & Hovelsrud, Joyce. The Real Centurions. 2nd ed. Orig. Title: Holy Smokies. 173p. 1979. pap. 2.25 (ISBN 0-934400-13-X). Landmark Bks.

Petersen, David M., ed. Police Work: Strategies & Outcomes in Law Enforcement. LC 79-9530. (Sage Research Progress Ser. in Criminology: Vol. 12). (Illus.). 128p. 1979. 15.00 (ISBN 0-8039-1325-7); pap. 7.50 (ISBN 0-8039-1326-5). Sage.

Powis, David. The Signs of Crime: A Field of Manual for Police. LC 77-30173. (Illus.). 1978. pap. text ed. 5.95 (ISBN 0-89444-007-1). John Jay Pr.

Punch, Maurice. Policing the Inner City: A Study of Amsterdam's Warmoesstraat. 231p. 1979. 17.50 (ISBN 0-208-01819-0, Archon). Shoe String.

Radzinowicz, Sir Leon & King, Joan. The Growth of Crime: The International Experience. LC 76-9342. 1977. 11.95x (ISBN 0-465-02767-9). Basic.

Reith, Charles. The Blind Eye of History: A Study of the Origins of the Present Police Era. LC 74-26636. (Criminology, Law Enforcement, & Social Problems Ser.: No. 203). 1975. Repr. of 1952 ed. 14.00 (ISBN 0-87585-203-3). Patterson Smith.

San Diego Police Dept. Police Tactics in Hazardous Situations. (Criminal Justice Ser.). 1976. pap. text ed. 9.50 (ISBN 0-8299-0628-2). West Pub.

Scanlon, Robert A., ed. Law Enforcement Bible, No. 2. 408p. 1981. pap. 11.95 (ISBN 0-88317-106-6). Stoeger Pub Co.

Skolnick, Jerome H. Justice Without Trial: Law Enforcement in Democratic Society. 2nd ed. LC 74-34145. 320p. 1975. pap. text ed. 10.50x (ISBN 0-471-79542-9). Wiley.

Stinchcomb, James. Opportunities in Law Enforcement & Related Careers. rev. ed. LC 75-32614. (Illus.). (gr. 8 up). 1976. PLB 6.60 (ISBN 0-8442-6420-2); pap. text ed. 4.95 (ISBN 0-685-61135-3). Natl Textbk.

Tegner, Bruce. Defense Tactics for Law Enforcement: Weaponless Defense & Control & Baton Techniques. rev. ed. LC 77-28136. (Illus.). 1978. pap. 4.95 (ISBN 0-87407-028-7, T-28). Thor.

Tobias, Marc W. Locks, Safes, & Security: A Handbook for Law Enforcement Personnel. (Illus.). 352p. 1971. photocopy ed. spiral 34.50 (ISBN 0-398-02155-4). C C Thomas.

Wadman, Robert C. & Svet, Don. Rules & Regulations for State and Local Law Enforcement Agencies. 108p. 1975. pap. 7.75 (ISBN 0-398-03366-8). C C Thomas.

Wadman, Robert C., et al. Law Enforcement Supervision: A Case Study Approach. (Criminal Justice Ser.). 1975. pap. text ed. 10.50 (ISBN 0-8299-0631-2). West Pub.

Weinreb, Lloyd L. Denial of Justice: Criminal Process in the United States. LC 76-27222. 1977. 12.95 (ISBN 0-02-934900-1). Free Pr.

Woodson, Robert. A Summons to Life: Mediating Structures & the Prevention of Youth Crime. 150p. 1981. 17.50 (ISBN 0-88410-826-0). Ballinger Pub.

Worton, Stanley N. Law Enforcement & Justice. (American Issues in Perspective Ser.). (gr. 10 up). 1977. pap. text ed. 4.50x (ISBN 0-8104-6011-4). Hayden.

Wrobleski, Henry M. & Hess, Karen M. Introduction to Law Enforcement & Criminal Justice. (Criminal Justice Ser.). (Illus.). 1979. text ed. 18.95 (ISBN 0-8299-0250-3); instrs.' manual avail. (ISBN 0-8299-0602-9). West Pub.

Zeichner, Irving B., ed. Law Enforcement Reference Manual: 1981 Edition. 1980. 19.50 (ISBN 0-686-63078-5). Law Enforce Ref.

LAW ENFORCEMENT OFFICERS

see also Peace Officers

Adams, Ramon F., compiled by. The Adams One-Fifty. LC 76-8959. (Illus.). 100p. 1976. 30.00 (ISBN 0-8363-0143-9). Jenkins.

Ahern, James F. Police in Trouble: Our Frightening Crisis in Law Enforcement. 256p. 1971. 9.95 (ISBN 0-8015-5928-6, Hawthorn). Dutton.

Bopp, William J. & Schultz, Donald O. Principles of American Law Enforcement & Criminal Justice. (Illus.). 596p. 1975. 15.25 (ISBN 0-398-02236-4). C C Thomas.

--A Short History of American Law Enforcement. (Illus.). 192p. 1977. pap. 8.75 (ISBN 0-398-02479-0). C C Thomas.

Chambliss, William J. Crime & the Legal Process. (Sociology Ser.). 1968. text ed. 11.50 (ISBN 0-07-010460-3, C); pap. text ed. 10.95 (ISBN 0-07-010461-1). McGraw.

Cohen, Stanley. Law Enforcement Guide to United States Supreme Court Decisions. (Illus.). 232p. 1972. text ed. 19.75 (ISBN 0-398-02261-5). C C Thomas.

Cronkhite, C. L. Automation & Law Enforcement. (Illus.). 160p. 1974. 13.50 (ISBN 0-398-03200-9); pap. 8.75 (ISBN 0-398-03201-7). C C Thomas.
Curran, James T., et al, eds. Police & Law Enforcement, Nineteen Seventy-Three to Nineteen Seventy-Five, 2 vols. LC 73-7210. (Orig.). 1973. Set. lib. bdg. 60.00 (ISBN 0-404-11199-8); Vol. 1. lib. bdg. 30.00 (ISBN 0-404-11200-5); Vol. 2. lib. bdg. 30.00 (ISBN 0-404-11205-6); Vol. 1. pap. 8.95 (ISBN 0-404-11204-8); Vol. 2. pap. 8.95 (ISBN 0-404-11206-4). AMS Pr.
Didactic System Staff. Handling Conflict in Law Enforcement Management: Conflict Among Peers. (Simulation Game Ser.). 1978. pap. 24.90 (ISBN 0-89401-144-8); pap. 21.50 two or more (ISBN 0-685-89725-7); leader's guide 0.50 (ISBN 0-685-89726-5). Didactic Syst.
--Handling Conflict in Law Enforcement Management: Superior Subordinate Conflict. (Simulation Game Ser.). 1978. pap. 24.90 (ISBN 0-685-89727-3); pap. 21.50 two or more (ISBN 0-685-89728-1); leader's guide 0.50 (ISBN 0-685-89729-X). Didactic Syst.
Eisenhower, Milton S. Rule of Law: An Alternative to Violence. (Illus.). 7.95 (ISBN 0-87695-025-X); pap. 3.95 (ISBN 0-87695-138-8). Aurora Pubs.
Eldefonso, Edward, et al. Principles of Law Enforcement. 2nd ed. LC 74-1275. 455p. 1974. text ed. 18.95x (ISBN 0-471-23501-6). Wiley.
Felkenes, George T. Criminal Justice System: Its Function & Personnel. (Illus.). 336p. 1974. text ed. 16.95 (ISBN 0-13-193052-4). P-H.
Fraenkel, Jack R. Crime & Criminals: What Should We Do About Them. (gr. 10-12). 1977. text ed. 8.84 (ISBN 0-13-192872-4); pap. text ed. 5.28 (ISBN 0-13-192880-5). P-H.
Gammage, Allen Z. Your Future in Law Enforcement. LC 70-88828. (Careers in Depth Ser). (gr. 7 up). 1974. PLB 5.97 (ISBN 0-8239-0044-4). Rosen Pr.
Germann, A. C., et al. Introduction to Law Enforcement & Criminal Justice. rev. ed. (Illus.). 400p. 1980. 11.75 (ISBN 0-398-03799-X). C C Thomas.
Hanna, Donald G. & Kleberg, John R. Law Handbook for Ohio Law Enforcement Officers. 1979. pap. text ed. 3.40 (ISBN 0-87563-170-3). Stipes.
Hardy, Richard E. & Cull, John G., eds. Applied Psychology in Law Enforcement & Corrections. (American Lectures in Social & Rehabilitation Psychology Ser.). (Illus.). 248p. 1973. 14.50 (ISBN 0-398-02862-1). C C Thomas.
Iannone, N. F. Principles of Police Patrol. 1974. 13.95 (ISBN 0-07-031667-8, G); instructor's manual 3.00 (ISBN 0-07-031669-4). McGraw.
Jordan, Philip D. Frontier Law & Order: Ten Essays. LC 70-88086. (Illus.). 1970. 13.50 (ISBN 0-8032-0709-3). U of Nebr Pr.
Journal Of Urban Law Editors. Riot in the Cities. Moran, Michael C. & Chikota, Richard A., eds. LC 74-76132. 411p. 1970. 20.00 (ISBN 0-8386-7443-7). Fairleigh Dickinson.
Leonard, V. A. The Police, the Judiciary, & the Criminal. 2nd ed. (Illus.). 320p. 1975. 18.75 (ISBN 0-398-03332-3). C C Thomas.
Lewin, Stephen, ed. Crime & Its Prevention. LC 68-17131. (Reference Shelf Ser: Vol. 40, No. 4). 1968. 6.25 (ISBN 0-8242-0103-5). Wilson.
Martin, Julian A. Law Enforcement Vocabulary. 262p. 1973. 13.75 (ISBN 0-398-02599-1). C C Thomas.
Millspaugh, Arthur Chester. Crime Control by the National Government. LC 70-168678. (American Constitutional Legal History Ser). 306p. 1972. Repr. of 1937 ed. lib. bdg. 29.50 (ISBN 0-306-70418-8). Da Capo.
Milner, Neal A. Court & Local Law Enforcement: The Impact of Miranda. LC 76-127991. 272p. 1971. 20.00 (ISBN 0-8039-0075-9). Sage.
Morris, Jack. Th Deadly Routine. (Illus.). 175p. 1981. pap. 11.95 (ISBN 0-87364-241-4). Paladin Ent.
Osborn, Albert S. Questioned Documents. rev. 2nd ed. LC 73-9875. (Criminology, Law Enforcement, & Social Problems Ser.: No. 207). (Illus.). 760p. 1973. lib. bdg. 27.50 (ISBN 0-87585-207-6). Patterson Smith.
Prassel, Frank R. The Western Peace Officer: The Legacy of Law & Order. LC 71-39627. 304p. 1972. 14.95 (ISBN 0-8061-1010-4). U of Okla Pr.
Rieder, Robert J. Law Enforcement Information Systems. (Illus.). 272p. 1972. text ed. 14.25 (ISBN 0-398-02391-3). C C Thomas.
Seitzinger, Jack M. & Kelley, Thomas M. Police Terminology: Programmed Manual for Criminal Justice Personnel. (Illus.). 152p. 1974. pap. 11.75 (ISBN 0-398-02947-4). C C Thomas.
South Carolina General Assembly Joint Committee to Investigate Law Enforcement. Report. facsimile ed. LC 74-3855. (Criminal Justice in America Ser.). 1974. Repr. of 1937 ed. 47.00x (ISBN 0-405-06168-4). Arno.
Spackman, Robert R., Jr. & Vincent, William F. Physical Fitness in Law Enforcement: A Guide to More Efficient Service. LC 70-83663. (Illus.). 123p. 1969. pap. 3.95 (ISBN 0-8093-0406-6). S Ill U Pr.
Swisher, Carl B., ed. Selected Papers of Homer Cummings. LC 79-168392. (FDR & the Era of the New Deal Ser.). (Illus.). 1972. Repr. of 1939 ed. lib. bdg. 32.50 (ISBN 0-306-70329-7). Da Capo.
Trojanowicz, Robert & Dixon, Samuel. Criminal Justice & the Community. (Illus.). 464p. 1974. ref. ed. 17.95x (ISBN 0-13-193557-7). P-H.
Wickersham Commission - National Commission On Law Observance And Enforcement. Wickersham Commission, National Commission on Law Observance & Enforcement: Complete Reports, Including the Mooney-Billings Report, 14 Vols. LC 68-55277. (Criminology, Law Enforcement, & Social Problems Ser.: No. 6). (Illus.). 1968. Repr. of 1931 ed. 250.00 (ISBN 0-87585-006-5). Patterson Smith.

LAW EXAMINATIONS
see also Law Schools–Entrance Examinations
Gruber, et al. The Multistate Bar Examination. rev. ed. (Exam Prep. Ser.). 256p. 1981. pap. text ed. 7.95 (ISBN 0-671-18965-4). Monarch Pr.
National Conference Bar Exam. Multistate Bar Exam IV. 1978. text ed. 2.50x (ISBN 0-87543-144-5). Lucas.
Reburn, Rockne. How to Pass the California Bar Exam. (Illus.). 141p. (Orig.). 1980. 14.00 (ISBN 0-9605672-0-8). Bar-None.
Rudman, Jack. Assistant Departmental Attorney. (Career Examination Ser.: C-2233). (Cloth bdg. avail. on request). pap. 10.00 (ISBN 0-8373-2234-0). Natl Learning.
--Assistant District Attorney. (Career Examination Ser.: C-1103). (Cloth bdg. avail. on request). pap. 10.00 (ISBN 0-8373-1103-9). Natl Learning.
--Attorney. (Career Examination Ser.: C-56). (Cloth bdg. avail. on request). pap. 10.00 (ISBN 0-8373-0056-8). Natl Learning.
--Attorney-Departmental. (Career Examination Ser.: C-2234). (Cloth bdg. avail. on request). pap. 10.00 (ISBN 0-8373-2234-0). Natl Learning.
--Attorney Trainee. (Career Examination Ser.: C-57). (Cloth bdg. avail. on request). pap. 8.00 (ISBN 0-8373-0057-6). Natl Learning.
--Chief Deputy County Attorney. (Career Examination Ser.: C-1172). (Cloth bdg. avail. on request). pap. 10.00 (ISBN 0-8373-1172-1). Natl Learning.
--Chief Law Assistant. (Career Examination Ser.: C-177). (Cloth bdg. avail. on request). pap. 10.00 (ISBN 0-8373-1177-2). Natl Learning.
--Commissioner of Jurors. (Career Examination Ser.: C-1204). (Cloth bdg. avail. on request). pap. 10.00 (ISBN 0-8373-1204-3). Natl Learning.
--County Attorney. (Career Examination Ser.: C-1220). (Cloth bdg. avail on request). pap. 10.00 (ISBN 0-8373-1220-5). Natl Learning.
--Deputy County Attorney. (Career Examination Ser.: C-1244). (Cloth bdg. avail. on request). pap. 10.00 (ISBN 0-8373-1244-2). Natl Learning.
--District Attorney. (Career Examination Ser.: C-1257). (Cloth bdg. avail. on request). pap. 10.00 (ISBN 0-8373-1257-4). Natl Learning.
--Law Assistant. (Career Examination Ser.: C-1341). (Cloth bdg. avail. on request-). pap. 10.00 (ISBN 0-8373-1341-4). Natl Learning.
--Law Clerk. (Career Examination Ser.: C-448). (Cloth bdg. avail. on request). pap. 10.00 (ISBN 0-8373-0448-2). Natl Learning.
--Multistate Bar Examination (MBE) (Admission Test Ser.: ATS-8). 300p. 10.95 (ISBN 0-8373-5108-1); pap. 6.95 (ISBN 0-8373-5008-5). Natl Learning.
--Paralegal Aide. (Career Examination Ser.: C-2245). (Cloth bdg. avail. on request). pap. 8.00 (ISBN 0-8373-2245-6). Natl Learning.
--Pre-Law Equivalency Examination. (Admission Test Ser.: ATS-40). (Cloth bdg. avail. on request). pap. 9.95 (ISBN 0-8373-5040-9). Natl Learning.
--Senior Attorney. (Career Examination Ser.: C-996). (Cloth bdg. avail. on request). pap. 10.00 (ISBN 0-8373-0996-4). Natl Learning.
Schwartz, Victor E. Bar Examination: How to Prepare for the Multi-State. LC 77-80605. 1977. pap. 5.95 (ISBN 0-8120-0548-1). Barron.
Spaulding, R. M. Imperial Japan's Higher Civil Service Examinations. 1967. 26.50x (ISBN 0-691-03024-3). Princeton U Pr.
Turner, David R. Claim Examiner -- Investigator. 4th ed. LC 72-92669. (Orig.). 1971. pap. 8.00 (ISBN 0-668-00149-6). Arco.
Volkell, Randolph. LSAT: Law School Admission Test. (Wiley Self-Teaching Guides Ser.). 288p. 1981. pap. text ed. 7.95 (ISBN 0-471-09647-4). Wiley.
Whitman, Robert. Preparation for the Bar Examination. rev. ed. 1978. pap. 7.95 (ISBN 0-671-18997-2). Monarch Pr.

LAW IN ART
Daumier, Honore. Lawyers & Law Courts. portfolio of loose prints ed. (Illus.). 10.00 (ISBN 0-685-07363-7). Borden.

LAW IN LITERATURE
Gest, John M. The Lawyer in Literature (Dickens, Scott, Balzac) 1913. 35.00 (ISBN 0-89984-231-3). Century Bookbindery.
London, Ephraim, ed. World of Law, 2 Vols. 1960. Set. 25.00 (ISBN 0-671-82936-X). S&S.
Siegchrist, Mark. Rough in Brutal Print: The Legal Sources of Browning's "Red Cotton Night-Cap Country". 200p. 1981. 15.00 (ISBN 0-8142-0327-2). Ohio St U Pr.
Windolph, F. Lyman. Selected Essays. LC 72-186116. 1972. 7.50 (ISBN 0-685-36105-5). Franklin & Marsh.
Windolph, Francis L. Reflections of the Law in Literature. LC 71-117863. (Essay Index Reprint Ser). 1956. 11.00 (ISBN 0-8369-1739-1). Arno.

LAW IN THE BIBLE
see Jewish Law

LAW IN THE KORAN
see Islamic Law

LAW LIBRARIES
see also Information Storage and Retrieval Systems–Law
Altman, Devra L. A Manual for Small & Medium-Sized Law Libraries. (Illus.). 1976. pap. 3.50 (ISBN 0-910058-75-X). Am Bar Foun.
Bird, Viola, et al. Order Procedures. (AALL Publications Ser.: No. 2). v, 66p. (Orig.). 1960. pap. 8.50x (ISBN 0-8377-0102-3). Rothman.
Columbia University Law Library, New York. Dictionary Catalog of the Columbia University Law Library, First Supplement, 7 vols. 1973. Set. lib. bdg. 900.00 (ISBN 0-8161-0802-1). G K Hall.
Finley, Elizabeth. Manual of Procedures for Private Law Libraries. rev. ed. (A.A.L.L. Publications Ser.: No. 8). xi, 176p. 1966. 12.50x (ISBN 0-8377-0106-6). Rothman.
Institute For Law Librarians - 6th Biennial - 1963. Law Library - a Living Trust. (AALL Publications Ser: No. 7). vi, 58p. (Orig.). 1964. pap. text ed. 8.50x (ISBN 0-8377-0105-8). Rothman.
Jain, H. C. Law Library Administration & Reference. LC 72-902857. (Illus.). 172p. 1972. 9.50x (ISBN 0-8002-1642-3). Intl Pubns Serv.
Johnson, Herbert A. Imported Eighteenth-Century Law Treatises in American Libraries, 1700-1799. LC 78-7368. (Illus.). 1978. 16.50x (ISBN 0-87049-220-9). U of Tenn Pr.
Reams, Bernard D., Jr., ed. Reader in Law Librarianship. LC 76-10125. (Reader in Librarianship & Information Science Ser.: Vol. 22). 1976. 21.00 (ISBN 0-910972-58-3). IHS-PDS.
Sloane, Richard & Wallace, Marie. Private Law Library: Nineteen Eighties & Beyond. LC 79-87893. (Patents, Copyrights, Trademarks, & Literary Property Course Handbook Ser.: 1978-1979). 1979. pap. text ed. 20.00 (ISBN 0-686-59557-2, G4-3653). PLI.
Steiner, W. A. Classification Scheme & List of Subject Headings for the Squire Law Library of the University of Cambridge. LC 73-19917. 160p. 1974. lib. bdg. 15.00 (ISBN 0-379-20060-0). Oceana.
Steiner, W. A. & Lekner, M. A., eds. University of Cambridge, The Squire Law Library Catalogue, 14 vols. LC 73-17137. 1974. Set. 700.00 (ISBN 0-379-20175-5). Oceana.
Taylor, Raymond M. Federal Court Libraries, 2 vols. LC 81-81758. 2089p. 1980. lib. bdg. 90.00 (ISBN 0-89941-100-2). W S Hein.
Werner, O. James. Manual for Prison Law Libraries. (A. A. L. L. Publication Ser.: No. 12). viii, 117p. 1976. text ed. 12.50x (ISBN 0-8377-0110-4). Rothman.

LAW LISTS
see Lawyers–Directories

LAW MERCHANT
see also Commercial Law
Mitchell, William. Essay on Early History of the Law Merchant: Being the Yorke Prize Essay for the Year 1903. 1969. Repr. of 1904 ed. 22.50 (ISBN 0-8337-2409-6). B Franklin.

LAW OF LARGE NUMBERS
Davis, P. J. The Lore of Large Numbers. (New Mathematical Library: No. 6). 1975. pap. 6.50 (ISBN 0-88385-606-9). Math Assn.
Padgett, W. J. & Taylor, R. L. Laws of Large Numbers for Normed Linear Spaces & Certain Frechet Spaces. (Lecture Notes in Mathematics: Vol. 360). 111p. 1974. pap. 9.10 (ISBN 0-387-06585-7). Springer-Verlag.

LAW OF NATIONS
see International Law

LAW OF NATURE
see Natural Law

LAW OF SUCCESSION
see Inheritance and Succession

LAW OF SUPPLY AND DEMAND
see Supply and Demand

LAW OF THE SEA
see Maritime Law

LAW OFFICES
see also Legal Secretaries
Adams, Harold W. & Stringham, Ray. Lawyer's Management Principles: A Course for Assistants, Student Syllabus. (gr. 11-12). 1975. pap. text ed. 6.65 (ISBN 0-89420-079-8, 101028); cassette recordings 86.90 (ISBN 0-89420-200-6, 101000). Natl Book.
Altman & Weil. How to Manage Your Law Office. 1973. 38.50 (ISBN 0-685-40615-6). Bender.
Bate, Marjorie & Casey, Mary. Legal Office Procedures. (Illus.). 448p. 1975. pap. text ed. 13.95 (ISBN 0-07-004056-7, G); instructor's manual & key 6.00 (ISBN 0-07-004057-5). McGraw.
Bate, Marjorie D. & Casey, Mary C. Legal Office Procedures. 2nd ed. (Illus.). 544p. 1980. pap. text ed. 15.25 (ISBN 0-07-004058-3, G); instructor's manual & key avail. (ISBN 0-07-004059-1). McGraw.
Gilson, Christopher, et al. How to Market Your Law Practice. LC 79-15572. 290p. 1979. text ed. 24.95 (ISBN 0-89443-155-2). Aspen Systems.
Guide & Compendium for the Lawyer's Secretary, No. 5. rev. ed. LC 75-1667. 1981. 26.50 (ISBN 0-915362-17-1). M K Heller.
Karcher, Joseph T. New Guide to Building a One Hundred Thousand Dollar Law Practice. 300p. 1981. 29.95 (ISBN 0-87624-402-9). Inst Busn Plan.
Law Office Portfolio. 2nd ed. 1976. 5.00 (ISBN 0-915362-05-8). M K Heller.
Shayne, Neil T. The Paralegal Profession: A Career Guide. LC 77-4914. 1977. 15.00 (ISBN 0-379-00684-7). Oceana.
Smigel, Erwin O. The Wall Street Lawyer. rev. ed. LC 64-16968. (Midland Bks.: No. 130). 400p. 1970. pap. 2.95x (ISBN 0-253-20130-6). Ind U Pr.
Working Papers in the Matter of Training the Legal Secretary. rev. ed. LC 79-90998. 1979. 15.00 (ISBN 0-915362-16-3). M K Heller.

LAW REFORM
Belli, M. M. The Law Revolt, 2 vols. 1126p. 1968. Set. 30.00 (ISBN 0-913338-03-6). Trans-Media Pub.
Dillon, J. F. The Law & Jurisprudence of England & America. LC 75-99475. (American Constitutional & Legal History Ser). 1970. Repr. of 1894 ed. lib. bdg. 42.50 (ISBN 0-306-71854-5). Da Capo.
Friedmann, Wolfgang G. Law in a Changing Society. 2nd ed. LC 77-186229. 580p. 1970. 27.50x (ISBN 0-231-03653-1). Columbia U Pr.
Hazard, Geoffrey C., Jr. Law Reforming in the Anti-Poverty Effort. (Legal Services for the Poor Ser). 1970. pap. 2.00 (ISBN 0-685-48020-8). Am Bar Foun.
Kamenka, Eugene & Erh-Soon Tay, Alice, trs. Law & Social Control. 1980. 22.50 (ISBN 0-312-47546-2). St Martin.
Keeton, Robert E. Venturing to Do Justice: Reforming Private Law. LC 69-18035. 1969. text ed. 10.00x (ISBN 0-674-93355-9). Harvard U Pr.
Science of Legal Method. LC 68-54756. (Modern Legal Philosophy Ser.: Vol. 9). Repr. of 1917 ed. 20.00x (ISBN 0-678-04520-8). Kelley.
Tullock, Gordon. Logic of the Law. LC 74-147010. 1971. text ed. 10.95x (ISBN 0-465-04165-5). Basic.
Vanderbilt, Arthur T. The Challenge of Law Reform. LC 76-3784. 194p. 1976. Repr. of 1955 ed. lib. bdg. 16.75 (ISBN 0-8371-8809-1, VALR). Greenwood.

LAW REFORM–GREAT BRITAIN
A Century of Law Reform: 1971-1978. LC 71-181888. xi, 431p. 1972. Repr. of 1901 ed. text ed. 22.50x (ISBN 0-8377-2005-2). Rothman.
Hall, Richard J. British Labour Costs 1975-1980. LC 76-35345. 1975. pap. 90.00x (ISBN 0-8002-0736-X). Intl Pubns Serv.

LAW REPORTING
Bryson, William H., ed. The Virginia Law Reporters Before 1880. LC 77-21451. 1978. 9.75x (ISBN 0-8139-0747-0). U Pr of Va.
Denniston, Lyle W. The Reporter & the Law: Techniques of Covering the Courts. 1980. 17.50 (ISBN 0-8038-6341-1); pap. text ed. 9.95 (ISBN 0-8038-6343-8). Hastings.
Greenwood, Michael & Tollar, Jerry R., eds. Evaluation Guidebook to Computer-Aided Transcription. 1975. pap. 3.00 (ISBN 0-89656-001-5, R0019). Natl Ctr St Courts.
Rudman, Jack. Chief Law Stenographer. (Career Examination Ser.: C-941). (Cloth bdg. avail. on request). pap. 10.00 (ISBN 0-8373-0941-7). Natl Learning.
--Court Hearing Reporter. (Career Examination Ser.: C-172). (Cloth bdg. avail. on request). pap. 8.00 (ISBN 0-8373-0172-6). Natl Learning.

--Court Reporter. (Career Examination Ser.: C-174). (Cloth bdg. avail on request). pap. 8.00 (ISBN 0-8373-0174-2). Natl Learning.

--Court Reporter One. (Career Examination Ser.: C-967). (Cloth bdg. avail on request). pap. 8.00 (ISBN 0-686-66499-X). Natl Learning.

--Court Reporter Two. (Career Examination Ser.: C-968). (Cloth bdg. avail on request). pap. 8.00 (ISBN 0-8373-0968-9). Natl Learning.

Tridico, Russell T. National Directory of Court Reporters. 1965. 9.50x (ISBN 0-685-37727-X). Claitors.

LAW REPORTS, DIGESTS, ETC.

see also Advisory Opinions; Judicial Opinions

also subdivision Cases under legal subjects

Anderman, Nancy. United States Supreme Court Decisions: An Index to Their Locations. LC 76-8479. 323p. 1976. 14.50 (ISBN 0-8108-0932-X). Scarecrow.

Bigelow, Melville M. Placita Anglo - Normannica: Law Cases from William First to Richard First. lxiv, 328p. 1970. Repr. of 1881 ed. text ed. 15.00x (ISBN 0-8377-1928-3). Rothman.

Columbia Law Review: Essays on Jurisprudence from the Columbia Law Review. 414p. 1963. 20.00 (ISBN 0-379-00159-4); pap. 8.50 (ISBN 0-379-00160-8). Oceana.

Everson, H. J., et al. Compendium of Case Law Relating to the European Communities, 1976. 1978. 63.50 (ISBN 0-444-85206-9, North Holland). Elsevier.

Goldberg, Louis P. Lawless Judges. LC 74-97451. Repr. of 1935 ed. 17.50x (ISBN 0-8371-2696-7, Pub. by Negro U Pr). Greenwood.

Goldberg, Louis P. & Levenson, Eleanore. Lawless Judges. LC 73-138498. (Civil Liberties in American History Ser). 1970. Repr. of 1935 ed. lib. bdg. 29.50 (ISBN 0-306-70070-0). Da Capo.

Great Britain Court Of The Star Chamber. Reports of Cases in Courts of Star Chamber & High Commission. Gardiner, Samuel R., ed. 1886. 22.50 (ISBN 0-384-19760-4). Johnson Repr.

Guild, June. Black Laws of Virginia. LC 78-98721. Repr. of 1936 ed. 12.25x (ISBN 0-8371-2777-7, Pub. by Negro U Pr). Greenwood.

Israel - State Of - Ministry Of Justice. Selected Judgments of the Supreme Court of Israel, 5 vols. 1976. 30.00 ea. Vol. 1 (ISBN 0-379-13901-4). Vol. 2 (ISBN 0-379-13902-2). Vol. 3 (ISBN 0-379-13903-0). Vol. 4 (ISBN 0-379-13904-9). Vol. 5 (ISBN 0-379-13905-7). Oceana.

Jones, T. Jeffreys, ed. Exchequer Proceedings Concerning Wales in Tempore James First. (History & Law Ser.). 1955. 8.25x (ISBN 0-7083-0110-X). Verry.

Kurland, Philip B., ed. The Supreme Court Review, 1974. LC 60-14353. 1975. 25.00x (ISBN 0-226-46425-3). U of Chicago Pr.

Lawyers Co-Operative Publishing Company Staff. Decisions of the United States Supreme Court: 1963-64, 1964-65, 1965-66, 1966-67, 1967-68, 1968-69, 1969-70, 1970-71, 1971-72, 1972-73, 1973-74, 1974-75, 1975-76, 1976-77, 1977-78, 1978-79, 1979-80, 1980-81, 18 vols. 25.00 ea.; 425.00 set (ISBN 0-686-28514-X). Lawyers Co-Op.

Levy, Beryl H. Cardozo & Frontiers of Legal Thinking. LC 65-14787. Repr. of 1938 ed. 12.25 (ISBN 0-8046-0270-0). Kennikat.

Liberia, Republic of. Liberia Supreme Court Reports, 23 vols. Incl. Vol. 1. January Term, 1861-January Term 1907. 556p (ISBN 0-8014-0466-5); Vol. 2. January Term, 1908-November Term, 1926. (Illus.). xvi, 687p. Repr (ISBN 0-8014-0261-1); Vol. 3. November Term, 1927-November Term, 1932. xii, 479p (ISBN 0-8014-0262-X); Vol. 4. November Term, 1933-April Term, 1935. ix, 444p (ISBN 0-8014-0263-8); Vol. 5. November Term, 1935-November Term, 1936. rev ed. ix, 474p (ISBN 0-8014-0264-6); Vol. 6. April Term, 1937-November Term, 1938. viii, 345p (ISBN 0-8014-0265-4); Vol. 7. April Term, 1939-November Term, 1941. ix, 423p (ISBN 0-8014-0266-2); Vol. 8. April Term, 1942-October Term, 1944. x, 500p (ISBN 0-8014-0267-0); Vol. 9. March Term, 1945-October Term, 1947. ix, 476p (ISBN 0-8014-0268-9); Vol. 10. April Term, 1948-October Term, 1950. ix, 478p (ISBN 0-8014-0269-7); Vol. 11. March Term, 1951-October Term, 1953. ix, 509p (ISBN 0-8014-0270-0); Vol. 12. March Term, 1954-October Term, 1956. x, 491p (ISBN 0-8014-0271-9); Vol. 13. March Term, 1957-October Term, 1959. xii, 730p (ISBN 0-8014-0272-7); Vol. 14. March Term, 1960-October Term, 1961. x, 642p (ISBN 0-8014-0273-5); Vol. 15. March Term, 1962-October Term, 1963. 732p (ISBN 0-8014-0274-3); Vol. 16. March Term, 1964-October Term, 1964. 413p (ISBN 0-8014-0275-1); Vol. 17. March Term, 1965-October Term, 1966. 776p (ISBN 0-8014-0646-3); Vol. 18. March Term, 1967 - October Term, 1967. 384p (ISBN 0-8014-0755-9); Vol. 19. March Term, 1968 - October Term, 1969. 571p (ISBN 0-8014-0781-8); Cumulative Index & Table of Cases. 163p (ISBN 0-8014-0503-3). 1959-66. 40.00x ea.; index 30.00x (ISBN 0-686-66590-2). Cornell U Pr.

Lunt, Dudley C. Road to the Law. 1962. pap. 1.65x (ISBN 0-393-00183-0, Norton Lib). Norton.

Milner, A., ed. African Law Reports, Sierra Leone Ser, 1950-1969, 5 vols. LC 67-26375. 1970-72. 45.00 ea. (ISBN 0-379-16000-5). Oceana.

Philippine Supreme Court Reports Annotated, 1961-1975, 66 vols. 3 vol. set quick index digest 75.00 (ISBN 0-379-12500-5). Oceana.

Trevelyan, E. East African Court of Appeals, Civil Appeals Digest, 1868-1956. LC 68-1549. 1967. 27.50 (ISBN 0-379-00350-3). Oceana.

UN Law Reports, Vol. 15: Sept. 1980 to Aug. 1981. 1981. 50.00 (ISBN 0-8027-2985-1). Walker & Co.

LAW SCHOOLS

Brown, Esther L. Lawyers & the Promotion of Justice. (Russell Sage Foundation Reprint Ser). Repr. of 1938 ed. lib. bdg. 26.00x (ISBN 0-697-00201-2). Irvington.

--Lawyers, Law Schools & the Public Service. (Russell Sage Foundation Reprint Ser). Repr. of 1948 ed. lib. bdg. 24.50x (ISBN 0-697-00200-4). Irvington.

Canada, et al. Surviving the First Year of Law School. 1979. pap. 7.95 (ISBN 0-930204-03-4). Lord Pub.

Ellsworth, Frank L. Law on the Midway: The Founding of the University of Chicago Law School. LC 77-78777. 1977. lib. bdg. 8.95x (ISBN 0-226-20608-4). U of Chicago Pr.

Epstein & Troy. Barron's Guide to Law Schools. 1980. pap. 5.50 (ISBN 0-8120-2067-7). Barron.

Gillers, Stephen. Looking at Law School: A Student Guide from the Society of American Law Teachers. (Orig.). 1977. pap. 4.95 (ISBN 0-452-00477-2, F477, Mer). NAL.

Gillers, Stephen, ed. Looking at Law School: A Student Guide from the Society of American Law Teachers. LC 76-53301. 1977. 9.95 (ISBN 0-8008-4966-3). Taplinger.

Glotzer, Arline. Monarch's Complete Guide to Law Schools. (Illus.). 192p. (Orig.). 1981. pap. 5.95 (ISBN 0-671-09192-1). Monarch Pr.

Goldfarb, Sally. Inside the Law Schools. 1980. pap. 8.95 (ISBN 0-525-47638-5). Dutton.

Johnson, William R. Schooled Lawyers: A Study in the Clash of Professional Cultures. LC 77-82753. 1978. 19.95x (ISBN 0-8147-4159-2). NYU Pr.

Knott, A. E., et al. Australian Schools & the Law. 2nd ed. (Educational Organization & Administration Ser.). 180p. (Orig.). 1981. pap. text ed. 10.25 (ISBN 0-7022-1549-X). U of Queensland Pr.

Nelson, Murry. Law in the Curriculum. LC 78-50367. (Fastback Ser.: No. 106). 1978. pap. 0.75 (ISBN 0-87367-106-6). Phi Delta Kappa.

Neubert, Christopher & Withiam, Jack, Jr. The Law School Game. 1979. pap. 6.95 (ISBN 0-8069-8872-X). Sterling.

Reed, Alfred Z. Present-Day Law Schools in the United States & Canada. LC 75-22836. (America in Two Centuries Ser). 1976. Repr. of 1928 ed. 35.00x (ISBN 0-405-07707-6). Arno.

Ritchie, John. The First Hundred Years: A Short History of the School of Law of the University of Virginia for the Period 1826-1926. LC 77-26281. (Illus.). 1978. 9.95x (ISBN 0-8139-0755-1). U Pr of Va.

Roth, George J. Slaying the Law School Dragon. LC 80-16974. 284p. 1980. 10.95 (ISBN 0-396-07880-X); pap. 7.95 (ISBN 0-396-07879-6). Dodd.

Silver, Theodore & Sacks, Howard R. Your Key to Success in Law School. (Orig.). 1981. pap. 6.95 (ISBN 0-671-09256-1). Monarch Pr.

Smith, Alfred G. Cognitive Styles in Law Schools. 190p. 1979. 11.00x (ISBN 0-292-71054-2). U of Tex Pr.

Squibb, G. D. Doctors' Commons: A History of the College of Advocates & Doctors of Law. (Illus.). 1977. 24.95x (ISBN 0-19-825339-7). Oxford U Pr.

Stein, Robert A. In Pursuit of Excellence. (Illus.). 545p. 1980. 24.50 (ISBN 0-917126-13-0). Mason Pub.

Strickland, Rennard. How to Get into Law School. rev. ed. LC 73-10885. 1977. pap. 4.95 (ISBN 0-8015-3767-3, Hawthorn). Dutton.

Tseng, Henry P. Law Schools of the World. LC 77-85344. 1977. lib. bdg. 47.50 (ISBN 0-930342-09-7). W S Hein.

Wasserman, Paul & Kaszubski, Marek, eds. Law & Legal Information Directory: A Guide to National & International Organizations, Bar Associations, Federal Court System, Federal Regulatory Agencies, Law Schools, Continuing Legal Education, Scholarships & Grants, Awards & Prizes, Special Libraries, Information Systems & Services, Research Centers, Etc. 800p. 1980. 110.00 (ISBN 0-8103-0169-5). Gale.

Willis, John. A History of Dalhousie Law School. 1979. 20.00x (ISBN 0-8020-2337-1). U of Toronto Pr.

LAW SCHOOLS–ENTRANCE EXAMINATIONS

Bobrow, Jerry. Barron's How to Prepare for the Law School Admission Test (LSAT) LC 79-12930. 1979. pap. 6.95 (ISBN 0-8120-2035-9). Barron.

Candrilli, Alfred J., et al. Law School Admission Test. rev. ed. LC 80-22181. 448p. 1981. lib. bdg. 14.00 (ISBN 0-668-05146-9); pap. 6.95 (ISBN 0-668-05153-1). Arco.

Gruber, Edward C. & Wildorf, Barry L. Law School Admission Test. (Exam Prep. Ser.). pap. 6.95 (ISBN 0-671-18984-0). Monarch Pr.

Klein, Fannie J. & Leleiko, Steven H. Bar Admission Rules & Student Practice Rules. LC 77-17177. 1978. 95.00 (ISBN 0-88410-791-4). Ballinger Pub.

Rudman, Jack. Law School Admission Test (LSAT) (Admission Test Ser.: ATS-13). 300p. (Cloth bdg. avail. on request). pap. 9.95 (ISBN 0-8373-5013-1). Natl Learning.

Shostak, et al. Barron's How to Prepare for the LSAT: Canadian Edition. LC 77-80603. 1977. pap. text ed. 6.95 (ISBN 0-8120-0864-2). Barron.

Strickland, Rennard. How to Get into Law School. rev. ed. LC 73-10885. 1977. pap. 4.95 (ISBN 0-8015-3767-3, Hawthorn). Dutton.

Theofan, Charles T. How to Prepare for the Law School Admission Test (LSAT) (Orig.). 1980. pap. 6.95 (ISBN 0-07-063785-7). McGraw.

Volkell, R. Z. LSAT Law School Admission Test: A Practical Guide. 1977. 6.95 (ISBN 0-471-02138-5). Wiley.

LAWBOOKS

see Law–Bibliography; Legal Literature

LAWES, HENRY, 1595-1662

Evans, Willa M. Henry Lawes, Musician & Friend of Poets. 1941. pap. 15.00 (ISBN 0-527-27900-5). Kraus Repr.

LAWN BOWLS

see Bowling on the Green

LAWN FURNITURE

see Garden Ornaments and Furniture

LAWN TENNIS

see Tennis

LAWNS

see also Grasses; Ground Cover Plants

Beard, James B., et al, eds. Turfgrass Bibliography from 1672-1972. 730p. 1977. 35.00x (ISBN 0-87013-195-8). Mich St U Pr.

Crockett, James U. Lawns & Ground Covers. (Encyclopedia of Gardening Ser). (Illus.). 1971. 12.95 (ISBN 0-8094-1093-1); lib. bdg. avail. (ISBN 0-685-00194-6). Time-Life.

Crockett, James V. Lawns & Ground Covers. LC 78-140420. (Time-Life Encyclopedia of Gardening). (Illus.). (gr. 6 up). 1971. lib. bdg. 11.97 (ISBN 0-8094-1094-X, Pub. by Time-Life). Silver.

Duble, Richard & Kell, J. Carroll. Southern Lawns & Groundcovers. LC 77-73533. (Illus.). 96p. 1977. pap. 3.95 (ISBN 0-88415-426-2). Pacesetter Pr.

Fichter, Harold. The Master Lawnmower Repair Book. (Illus.). 1978. pap. 10.95 (ISBN 0-8306-1067-7, 1067). TAB Bks.

Guide to Landscape & Lawn Care. (McGraw-Hill Paperbacks Home Improvement Ser.). (Illus.). 112p. 1980. pap. 3.95 (ISBN 0-07-045972-X). McGraw.

Hawthorne, R. Dawson's Practical Lawncraft. (Illus.). 313p. 1977. 24.95x (ISBN 0-8464-1085-0). Beekman Pubs.

Hellyer, Arthur. Your Lawn. (Leisure Plan Books in Color). pap. 2.95 (ISBN 0-600-44325-6). Transatlantic.

The Home Lawn Handbook. 1.95 (ISBN 0-686-21163-4). Bklyn Botanic.

MacCaskey, Michael R. All About Lawns. Ortho Books Editorial Staff, ed. LC 79-52995. (Illus.). 96p. 1980. pap. 4.95 ea. Midwest-Northeast Ed (ISBN 0-917102-83-5). Southern Ed (ISBN 0-917102-84-3). Western Ed (ISBN 0-917102-77-0). Ortho.

Perry, Mac. Florida Lawn & Garden Care. (Illus.). 1977. cancelled (ISBN 0-912458-98-4). E A Seemann.

--Mac Perry's Florida Lawn & Garden Care. 1980. pap. 7.95 (ISBN 0-916224-57-0). Banyan Bks.

Schery, Robert W. Lawn Keeping. 1976. 12.95 (ISBN 0-13-526889-3, Spec); pap. 5.95 (ISBN 0-13-526863-X). P-H.

--A Perfect Lawn: The Easy Way. LC 72-88150. 320p. 1973. 8.95 (ISBN 0-02-606980-6). Macmillan.

Sprague, Howard B. Turf Management Handbook. 2nd ed. LC 74-19656. 1976. 14.65 (ISBN 0-8134-1692-2). Interstate.

Sunset Editors. Lawns & Ground Covers. LC 78-70267. (Illus.). 96p. 1979. pap. 3.95 (ISBN 0-376-03506-4, Sunset Bks.). Sunset-Lane.

Thompson, H. C. & Bonnie, Fred. Growing Lawns & Ground Covers. LC 75-12125. (Family Guidebooks Ser.). (Illus.). 96p. 1975. pap. 1.95 (ISBN 0-8487-0383-9). Oxmoor Hse.

Voykin, Paul N. Ask the Lawn Expert. LC 75-24232. 288p. 1976. 9.95 (ISBN 0-02-622170-5, 62217). Macmillan.

LAWRENCE, DAVID HENRY

Fabes, Gilbert H. D. H. Lawrence: His First Editions. 104p. 1980. Repr. of 1933 ed. lib. bdg. 15.00 (ISBN 0-89987-275-1). Darby Bks.

Hamalian, Leo. D. H. Lawrence in Italy. 224p. 1982. 10.95 (ISBN 0-8008-4572-2). Taplinger.

Harmon, Robert, compiled by. First Editions of D. H. Lawrence. (First Edition Pocket Guides Ser.). 30p. softcover 3.95 (ISBN 0-910720-18-5). Hermes.

Kiernan, Reginald H. Lawrence of Arabia. 1980. Repr. of 1935 ed. lib. bdg. 25.00 (ISBN 0-8492-1493-9). R West.

LAWRENCE, DAVID HERBERT, 1885-1930

Albright, Daniel. Personality & Impersonality: Lawrence, Wolf & Mann. LC 77-23873. 1978. lib. bdg. 19.50x (ISBN 0-226-01249-2). U of Chicago Pr.

Alcorn, John. The Nature Novel from Hardy to Lawrence. LC 76-17552. 139p. 1977. 16.00x (ISBN 0-231-04122-5). Columbia U Pr.

Aldington, Richard. D. H. Lawrence. 1978. Repr. of 1935 ed. lib. bdg. 7.50 (ISBN 0-8495-0045-1). Arden Lib.

--D. H. Lawrence: An Appreciation. LC 76-462799. 1978. Repr. of 1930 ed. lib. bdg. 7.50 (ISBN 0-8492-0007-5). R West.

--D. H. Lawrence: An Indiscretion. LC 74-13379. Repr. of 1927 ed. lib. bdg. 6.50 (ISBN 0-8414-2995-2). Folcroft.

--D. H. Lawrence: Portrait of a Genius But-- 1961. pap. 1.50 (ISBN 0-02-001070-2, Collier). Macmillan.

Andrews, W. T., ed. Critics on D. H. Lawrence. LC 77-159294. (Readings in Literary Criticism Ser: No. 9). 1979. pap. 5.95x (ISBN 0-87024-207-5). U of Miami Pr.

Arrow, John. J. C. Squire & D. H. Lawrence. 1973. 5.00 (ISBN 0-8274-1547-8). R West.

Becker, George J. D. H. Lawrence. LC 79-48075. (Modern Literature Ser.). 160p. 1980. 10.95 (ISBN 0-8044-2029-7); pap. 4.95 (ISBN 0-8044-6033-7). Ungar.

Ben-Ephraim, Gavriel. The Moon's Dominion: Narrative Dichotomy & Female Dominance in the First Five Novels of D. H. Lawrence. LC 78-75172. 256p. 1981. 21.50 (ISBN 0-8386-2266-6). Fairleigh Dickinson.

Boadella, David. The Spiral Flame: A Study in the Meaning of D. H. Lawrence. Efron, Arthur & Hoerner, Dennis, eds. 1977. pap. 3.00 (ISBN 0-9602478-2-3). Paunch.

Boulton, J. T., ed. The Letters of D. H. Lawrence, Vol. 1. LC 78-7531. (Illus.). 1979. 39.50 (ISBN 0-521-22147-1). Cambridge U Pr.

Burns, Aidan. Nature & Culture in D. H. Lawrence. 137p. 1980. 19.50x (ISBN 0-389-20091-3). B&N.

Bynner, Witter. Journey with Genius: Recollections & Reflections Concerning D. H. Lawrence. 361p. 1974. Repr. of 1951 ed. lib. bdg. 23.00x (ISBN 0-374-91137-1). Octagon.

Callow, Philip. Son & Lover: The Young D. H. Lawrence. LC 75-9615. 300p. 1975. 25.00 (ISBN 0-8128-1819-9). Stein & Day.

Carswell, Catherine. The Savage Pilgrimage: A Narrative of D. H. Lawrence. LC 81-3891. 330p. Date not set. price not set (ISBN 0-521-23975-3); pap. price not set (ISBN 0-521-28386-8). Cambridge U Pr.
Carswell, Catherine M. The Savage Pilgrimage: A Narrative by D. H. Lawrence. LC 75-144937. 307p. 1972. Repr. of 1932 ed. 29.00 (ISBN 0-403-01760-2). Scholarly.
Carter, Frederick. D. H. Lawrence & the Body Mystical. LC 68-910. (Studies in D. H. Lawrence, No. 20). 1969. Repr. of 1932 ed. lib. bdg. 22.95 (ISBN 0-8383-0653-5). Haskell.
--D. H. Lawrence & the Body Mystical. 1978. Repr. lib. bdg. 10.00 (ISBN 0-8495-0823-1). Arden Lib.
Carter, Frederick D. D. H. Lawrence - the Body Mystical. 1932. lib. bdg. 12.50 (ISBN 0-8414-3356-9). Folcroft.
Cavitch, David. D. H. Lawrence & the New World. 1969. pap. 4.95 (ISBN 0-19-501486-3, 364, GB). Oxford U Pr.
Chambers, Jessie. D. H. Lawrence: A Personal Record, by E. T. LC 80-40254. 223p. 1980. pap. 8.95 (ISBN 0-521-29919-5). Cambridge U Pr.
--D. H. Lawrence Personal Record. 2nd ed. 242p. 1965. 22.50x (ISBN 0-7146-2059-9, F Cass Co). Biblio Dist.
Corke, Helen. D. H. Lawrence's Princess. LC 73-18344. 1899. lib. bdg. 10.00 (ISBN 0-8414-3528-6). Folcroft.
--In Our Infancy: An Autobiography, Pt. 1, 1882-1912. LC 74-31799. (Illus.). 250p. 1975. 32.50 (ISBN 0-521-20797-5). Cambridge U Pr.
Cushman, Keith. D. H. Lawrence at Work: The Emergence of the Prussian Officer Stories. LC 77-22149. 1978. 12.50x (ISBN 0-8139-0728-4). U Pr of Va.
Daiches, David. D. H. Lawrence. 240p. 1980. Repr. of 1963 ed. lib. bdg. 7.50 (ISBN 0-8492-4210-X). R West.
--D. H. Lawrence. LC 77-1281. 1977. lib. bdg. 6.50 (ISBN 0-8414-3821-8). Folcroft.
Delany, Paul. D. H. Lawrence's Nightmare: The Writer & His Circle in the Years of the Great War. LC 78-54998. 1978. 16.95 (ISBN 0-465-01641-3). Basic.
De Sola Pinto, Vivian. D. H. Lawrence Prophet of the Midlands: A Lecture. LC 75-17879. Repr. of 1951 ed. lib. bdg. 6.50 (ISBN 0-8414-3677-0). Folcroft.
Dix, Carol. D. H. Lawrence & Women. 126p. 1980. 18.75x (ISBN 0-8476-6196-2). Rowman.
Douglas, Norman. D. H. Lawrence & Maurice Magnus. LC 72-8663. (Studies in D. H. Lawrence, No. 20). 1973. Repr. of 1924 ed. lib. bdg. 22.95 (ISBN 0-8383-1673-5). Haskell.
Draper, R. P., ed. D. H. Lawrence: The Critical Heritage. (Critical Heritage Ser.). 1970. 35.00x (ISBN 0-7100-6591-4). Routledge & Kegan.
Draper, Ronald P. D. H. Lawrence. (English Authors Ser.: No. 7). 1964. lib. bdg. 9.95 (ISBN 0-8057-1320-4). Twayne.
--D. H. Lawrence. LC 74-80241. (Griffin Authors Ser). 200p. 1975. pap. 4.95 (ISBN 0-312-18095-0). St Martin.
Eisenstein, Samuel A., ed. Boarding the Ship of Death: D. H. Lawrence's Quester Heroes. (De Proprietatibus Litterarum, Ser. Practica: No. 42). 171p. 1974. pap. text ed. 23.75x (ISBN 90-2792-719-7). Mouton.
Fabes, G. D. H. Lawrence: His First Editions. 59.95 (ISBN 0-87968-989-7). Gordon Pr.
Fabes, Gilbert H. D. H. Lawrence-His First Editions: Points & Values. LC 76-49819. 1933. lib. bdg. 12.50 (ISBN 0-8414-4157-X). Folcroft.
Fay, Eliot G. Lorenzo in Search of the Sun. 1955. Repr. 7.95 (ISBN 0-8274-2992-4). R West.
--Lorenzo in Search of the Sun: D. H. Lawrence in Italy, Mexico & the American Southwest. LC 76-168012. Repr. of 1953 ed. 11.50 (ISBN 0-404-02373-8). AMS Pr.
Garcia, Reloy & Karabatsos, James, eds. A Concordance to the Poetry of D. H. Lawrence. LC 70-120277. 1970. 26.50x (ISBN 0-8032-0768-9). U of Nebr Pr.
--A Concordance to the Short Fiction of D H Lawrence. LC 72-77195. xx, 474p. 1972. 25.00x (ISBN 0-8032-0807-3). U of Nebr Pr.
Gilbert, Sandra. Monarch Notes on Lawrence's Sons & Lovers & Other Works. (Orig.). pap. 1.95 (ISBN 0-671-00716-5). Monarch Pr.
Gilbert, Sandra M. Acts of Attention: The Poems of D. H. Lawrence. 341p. 1972. 19.50x (ISBN 0-8014-0731-1). Cornell U Pr.
Gloversmith, F. Lawrence: The Rainbow. (Studies in English Literature Ser.). 1971. pap. text ed. 3.95x (ISBN 0-7131-5592-2). Dynamic Learn Corp.
Gomme, A. H., ed. D. H. Lawrence: Critical Studies on the Major Novels & Other Writings. 1979. Repr. of 1978 ed. text ed. 23.50x (ISBN 0-06-492480-7). B&N.
Goodheart, Eugene. Utopian Vision of D. H. Lawrence. LC 63-22817. 1963. 12.00x (ISBN 0-226-30288-1). U of Chicago Pr.
Goodman, Richard. Footnote to Lawrence. LC 77-7129. 1932. lib. bdg. 5.00 (ISBN 0-8414-4593-1). Folcroft.
Gregory, Horace. D. H. Lawrence: Pilgrim of the Apocalypse. facs. ed. LC 70-140355. (Select Bibliographies Reprint Ser). 1933. 15.00 (ISBN 0-8369-5598-6). Arno.
Gutierrez, Donald. Lapsing Out: Embodiments of Death & Rebirth in the Last Writings of D. H. Lawrence. LC 78-75177. 184p. 1980. 14.50 (ISBN 0-8386-2293-3). Fairleigh Dickinson.
Hamalian, Leo, ed. D. H. Lawrence. 160p. (Orig.). 1973. pap. 1.95 (ISBN 0-07-025690-X, SP). McGraw.
Hess, Elisabeth. Die Naturebetrachtung Im Prosawerk Von D. H. Lawrence. 1977. Repr. of 1957 ed. lib. bdg. 30.00 (ISBN 0-8492-1144-1). R West.
Hochman, Baruch. Another Ego: The Changing View of Self & Society in the Work of D. H. Lawrence. LC 70-86192. 1970. 14.95x (ISBN 0-87249-168-4). U of SC Pr.
Holderness, Graham. Who's Who in D. H. Lawrence. LC 75-34782. (Who's Who in Literature Ser.). 128p. 1976. 8.95 (ISBN 0-8008-8272-5). Taplinger.
Hough, Graham. The Dark Sun: A Study of D. H. Lawrence. LC 73-314. ix, 265p. 1972. Repr. lib. bdg. 17.50x (ISBN 0-374-93980-2). Octagon.
--Two Exiles: Lord Byron & D. H. Lawrence. LC 76-23314. 1956. lib. bdg. 5.00 (ISBN 0-8414-4741-1). Folcroft.
Howe, Marguerite B. The Art of the Self in D. H. Lawrence. LC 75-39864. 164p. 1977. 12.00x (ISBN 0-8214-0234-X). Ohio U Pr.
Hyde, G. M. D. H. Lawrence & the Art of Translation. 128p. 1981. 24.50x (ISBN 0-389-20077-8). B&N.
Inniss, Kenneth. D. H. Lawrence's Bestiary: A Study of His Animal Trope & Symbol. LC 70-165144. (De Proprietatibus Litterarum, Ser. Practica: No. 30). 207p. (Orig.). 1971. pap. text ed. 30.00x (ISBN 0-686-22499-X). Mouton.
Jarrett-Kerr, Martin. D. H. Lawrence & Human Existence. 2nd ed. 160p. 1971. 18.75 (ISBN 0-912378-03-4). Chips.
John, Brian. Supreme Fictions: Studies in the Work of William Blake, Thomas Carlyle, W. B. Yeats & D. H. Lawrence. 336p. 1974. 13.50x (ISBN 0-7735-0213-0). McGill-Queens U Pr.
Kenmare, Dallas. Fire-Bird: A Study of D. H. Lawrence. LC 77-2140. 1951. lib. bdg. 12.50 (ISBN 0-8414-5539-2). Folcroft.
--Fire Bird: A Study of D. H. Lawrence. 1978. 22.50 (ISBN 0-685-86101-5). Porter.
Kermode, Frank. D. H. Lawrence. LC 72-76430. (Modern Masters Ser.). 192p. 1973. 6.95 (ISBN 0-670-27130-6). Viking Pr.
Kiely, Robert. Beyond Egotism: The Fiction of James Joyce, Virginia Woolf & D. H. Lawrence. LC 80-14231. 1980. text ed. 14.00x (ISBN 0-674-06896-3). Harvard U Pr.
Lawrence, Ada & Gelder, George S. Young Lorenzo: The Early Life of D. H. Lawrence. LC 66-11880. (Illus.). 1966. Repr. of 1931 ed. 8.50 (ISBN 0-8462-0704-4). Russell.
Lawrence, D. H. The Centaur Letters. Roberts, F. W., ed. LC 75-110977. 1970. 15.00 (ISBN 0-87959-060-2). U of Tex Hum Res.
--Letters to Thomas & Adele Seltzer. Lacy, Gerald M., ed. (Illus.). 290p. (Orig.). 1976. 14.00 (ISBN 0-87685-225-8); pap. 6.00 (ISBN 0-87685-224-X). Black Sparrow.
--Selected Letters. 1978. pap. 2.50 (ISBN 0-14-000759-8). Penguin.
--Ten Paintings. (Illus.). 64p. 1981. 20.00x (ISBN 0-933806-13-2). Black Swan CT.
Leavis, F. R. D. H. Lawrence. LC 72-3172. (Studies in D. H. Lawrence, No. 20). 1972. Repr. of 1930 ed. lib. bdg. 22.95 (ISBN 0-8383-1541-0). Haskell.
--D. H. Lawrence: Novelist. 1979. pap. 6.95 (ISBN 0-226-46971-9, P805, Phoen). U of Chicago Pr.
--Thought, Words & Creativity: Art & Thought in Lawrence. 1976. 12.95 (ISBN 0-19-519884-0). Oxford U Pr.
Leavis, Frank R. D. H. Lawrence. LC 73-4761. 1930. lib. bdg. 12.50 (ISBN 0-8414-2275-3). Folcroft.
Luhan, Mabel G. Lorenzo in Taos. LC 32-26208. 1969. Repr. of 1932 ed. 18.00 (ISBN 0-527-58810-5). Kraus Repr.
Miko, Stephen J. Toward Women in Love: The Emergence of a Lawrentian Aesthetic. LC 73-151583. (Studies in English: No. 117). 393p. 1972. 25.00x (ISBN 0-300-01470-8). Yale U Pr.
Miller, Henry. Notes on "Aaron's Rod" & Other Notes on Lawrence from the Paris Notebooks of Henry Miller. Cooney, Seamus, ed. 65p. 1980. 14.00 (ISBN 0-87685-474-9). Black Sparrow.
--The World of Lawrence: A Passionate Appreciation. Hinz, Evelyn & Teunissen, John J., eds. 1980. 15.00 (ISBN 0-88496-147-8). Capra Pr.
Moore, Harry T. D. H. Lawrence: His Life & Works. (Illus.). 330p. 1964. 24.50x (ISBN 0-8290-0164-6). Irvington.
--D. H. Lawrence: His Life & Works. 9.95 (ISBN 0-685-60120-X, Pub by Twayne). Cyrco Pr.
--The Priest of Love: A Life of D. H. Lawrence. rev. ed. Orig. Title: The Intelligent Heart. (Illus.). 1974. 15.00 (ISBN 0-374-23718-2). FS&G.
--The Priest of Love: A Life of D. H. Lawrence. rev ed. LC 77-5714. (Illus.). 560p. 1977. pap. 12.95 (ISBN 0-8093-0839-8). S Ill U Pr.
Moynahan, Julian. Deed of Life: The Novels & Tales of D. H. Lawrence. 1963. 17.50 (ISBN 0-691-06023-1); pap. 4.95 (ISBN 0-691-01257-1). Princeton U Pr.
Murry, John M. D. H. Lawrence: Son of Woman. Repr. of 1954 ed. 35.00 (ISBN 0-527-65950-9). Kraus Repr.
--D. H. Lawrence: Two Essays. LC 73-5880. 1930. Repr. lib. bdg. 4.50 (ISBN 0-8414-5925-8). Folcroft.
--Reminiscences of D. H. Lawrence. facsimile ed. LC 75-157349. (Select Bibliographies Reprint Ser). Repr. of 1933 ed. 17.00 (ISBN 0-8369-5810-1). Arno.
Nath, Suresh. D. H. Lawrence the Dramatist. 183p. 1979. text ed. 12.00x (ISBN 0-391-02254-7, Pub. by UBS India). Humanities.
Nehls, Edward H., ed. D. H. Lawrence: A Composite Biography, 3 vols. 1957-59. 30.00 ea.; Vol. 1. (ISBN 0-299-81501-3); Vol. 2. (ISBN 0-299-81502-1); Vol. 3. (ISBN 0-299-81503-X). U of Wis Pr.
Nin, Anais. D. H. Lawrence: An Unprofessional Study. LC 64-16109. 110p. (Orig.). 1964. pap. 4.95x (ISBN 0-8040-0067-0). Swallow.
Niven, A. D. H. Lawrence: The Novels. LC 77-8475. (British Authors Ser.). 1978. 26.50 (ISBN 0-521-21744-X); pap. 7.95 (ISBN 0-521-29272-7). Cambridge U Pr.
Niven, Alistair. D. H. Lawrence: The Writer & His Work. 1980. 10.95 (ISBN 0-684-16666-6, ScribT). Scribner.
Page, Norman, ed. D. H. Lawrence: Interviews & Recollections, 2 vols. (Interviews & Recollections Ser). 1981. Vol. 1, 160p. 26.50x (ISBN 0-389-20031-X); Vol. 2, 160p. 26.50x (ISBN 0-389-20070-0). B&N.
Pinion, F. B. A D. H. Lawrence Companion: Life, Thought & Works. LC 78-12348. (Illus.). 1979. text ed. 25.00x (ISBN 0-06-495574-5). B&N.
Potter, Stephen. D. H. Lawrence. LC 78-64051. (Des Imagistes: Literature of the Imagist Movement). Repr. of 1930 ed. 17.50 (ISBN 0-404-17091-9). AMS Pr.
Powell, Lawrence C. Manuscripts of D. H. Lawrence. (Studies in D. H. Lawrence, No. 20). 1970. pap. 12.95 (ISBN 0-8383-0099-5). Haskell.
Pritchard, R. E. D. H. Lawrence: Body of Darkness. LC 71-181399. (Critical Essays in Modern Literature Ser). 1972. pap. 4.95 (ISBN 0-8229-5227-0). U of Pittsburgh Pr.
Robinson, Edward. Lawrence: The Rebel. 228p. 1980. Repr. of 1946 ed. lib. bdg. 25.00 (ISBN 0-8495-4641-9). Arden Lib.
--Lawrence, the Story of His Life. 250p. 1980. Repr. of 1935 ed. lib. bdg. 25.00 (ISBN 0-8482-5877-0). Norwood Edns.
Ross, Charles L. The Composition of The Rainbow & Women in Love: A History. LC 79-1422. 1980. 13.50x (ISBN 0-8139-0704-7). U Pr of Va.
Sagar, K. The Art of D. H. Lawrence. 279p. 1976. 42.00 (ISBN 0-521-06181-4); pap. 10.95 (ISBN 0-521-09387-2). Cambridge U Pr.
Sagar, Keith. D. H. Lawrence: A Calendar of His Works. 304p. 1979. text ed. 19.95x (ISBN 0-292-71519-6). U of Tex Pr.
Sagar, Keith M. The Life of D. H. Lawrence. (Illus.). 1980. 17.95 (ISBN 0-394-50953-6). Pantheon.
Sale, Roger. Modern Heroism: Essays on D. H. Lawrence, William Empson, & J. R. R. Tolkien. LC 73-186106. 1973. 25.00x (ISBN 0-520-02208-4). U of Cal Pr.
Salgado, Gamini. D. H. Lawrence: Sons & Lovers. (Studies in English Literature). 1974. pap. text ed. 3.95x (ISBN 0-7131-5107-2). Dynamic Learn Corp.
Seligmann, Herbert J. D. H. Lawrence: An American Interpretation. LC 73-163113. (Studies in D. H. Lawrence, No. 20). 1971. Repr. of 1924 ed. lib. bdg. 32.95 (ISBN 0-8383-1306-X). Haskell.
Shaw, Rita G. Sons & Lovers Notes. (Orig.). pap. 1.95 (ISBN 0-8220-1210-3). Cliffs.
Sitesh, Aruna. D. H. Lawrence: The Crusader As Critic. LC 75-904385. 1975. 10.50x (ISBN 0-333-90066-9). South Asia Bks.
Smith, Anne, ed. Lawrence & Women. LC 78-62592. (Critical Studies Ser.). 1978. o. p. 23.50x (ISBN 0-06-496377-2); pap. text ed. 8.95x (ISBN 0-389-20055-7). B&N.
Spilka, M., ed. D. H. Lawrence: A Collection of Critical Essays. 1963. 10.95 (ISBN 0-13-526855-9, Spec); pap. 2.45 (ISBN 0-13-526848-6). P-H.
Spilka, Mark. Love Ethic of D. H. Lawrence. 8.50 (ISBN 0-8446-2985-5). Peter Smith.
--Love Ethic of O. H. Lawrence. LC 55-8447. (Midland Bks.: No. 3). 256p. 1955. pap. 2.95x (ISBN 0-253-20003-2). Ind U Pr.
Stoll, John E. Novels of D. H. Lawrence: A Search for Integration. LC 76-158077. 1971. 13.50x (ISBN 0-8262-0110-5). U of Mo Pr.
Tedlock, E. W., Jr., ed. D. H. Lawrence & "Sons & Lovers". Sources & Criticism. LC 65-22471. (Gotham Library). (Orig.). 1965. 12.00x (ISBN 0-8147-0412-3); pap. 4.95 (ISBN 0-8147-0413-1). NYU Pr.
Tindall, William Y. D. H. Lawrence & Susan His Cow. LC 72-85664. xiv, 231p. 1973. Repr. of 1939 ed. 11.00x (ISBN 0-8154-0436-0). Cooper Sq.
Weiss, Daniel. Oedipus in Nottingham: D. H. Lawrence. LC 62-17149. (Illus.). 142p. 1962. 10.50 (ISBN 0-295-73858-8). U of Wash Pr.
West, Anthony. D. H. Lawrence. LC 73-477. 1973. lib. bdg. 12.50 (ISBN 0-8414-1422-X). Folcroft.
Wilt, Judith. Ghosts of the Gothic: Austen, Eliot, & Lawrence. LC 80-7559. 1980. 18.50 (ISBN 0-691-06439-3). Princeton U Pr.
Wolfe, Humbert. D. H. Lawrence. LC 73-13840. (The Augustan Bks. of Poetry). lib. bdg. 8.50 (ISBN 0-685-45261-1). Folcroft.
Worthen, J., ed. D. H. Lawrence: The Lost Girl. LC 80-40457. (The Cambridge Edition of the Letters & Works of D. H. Lawrence Ser.). (Illus.). Date not set. price not set (ISBN 0-521-22263-X); pap. price not set (ISBN 0-521-29423-1). Cambridge U Pr.
Worthen, John. D. H. Lawrence & the Idea of the Novel. 198p. 1979. 22.50x (ISBN 0-8476-6175-X). Rowman.
Zytaruk, George J. & Boulton, James T., eds. D. H. Lawrence: The Letters of D. H. Lawrence, Vol. 2: June 1913-October 1916. LC 80-42111. (The Cambridge Editions of the Letters & Works of D. H. Lawrence Ser.). (Illus.). 700p. Date not set. price not set (ISBN 0-521-23111-6). Cambridge U Pr.

LAWRENCE, DAVID HERBERT, 1885-1930-BIBLIOGRAPHY

Aldington, Richard. D. H. Lawrence: A Complete List of His Works, Together with a Critical Appreciation. LC 73-1263. lib. bdg. 6.00 (ISBN 0-8414-1700-8). Folcroft.
Fabes, Gilbert H. D. H. Lawrence: His First Editions. 1978. Repr. of 1933 ed. lib. bdg. 15.00 (ISBN 0-8495-1626-9). Arden Lib.
MacDonald, Edward D. A Bibliography of the Writings of D. H. Lawrence. LC 74-19301. 1974. Repr. of 1925 ed. lib. bdg. 10.00 (ISBN 0-8414-5907-X). Folcroft.
Partlow, Robert B., Jr. & Moore, Harry T., eds. D. H. Lawrence, the Man Who Lived: Papers. LC 80-15262. 320p. 1980. 18.95 (ISBN 0-8093-0981-5). S Ill U Pr.
Powell, L. C. Manuscripts of D. H. Lawrence. 69.95 (ISBN 0-87968-020-2). Gordon Pr.

LAWRENCE, FRIEDA (VON RICHTHOFEN), 1879-1956

Moore, Harry T. & Montague, Dale B., eds. Frieda Lawrence & Her Circle: Letters from, to, & About Frieda Lawrence. 1981. 27.50 (ISBN 0-208-01886-7, Archon). Shoe String.

LAWRENCE, GERTRUDE

Aldrich, Richard S. Gertrude Lawrence As Mrs. A: An Intimate Biography of the Great Star. LC 78-94600. Repr. of 1954 ed. lib. bdg. 21.75 (ISBN 0-8371-2469-7, ALGL). Greenwood.
Morley, Sheridan. Gertrude Lawrence. (Illus.). 208p. Date not set. 10.95 (ISBN 0-07-043149-3, GB). McGraw.

LAWRENCE, HENRY MONTGOMERY, SIR, 1806-1857

Abdullah, Achmed & Pakenham, Thomas C. Dreamers of Empire. facs. ed. LC 68-57300. (Essay Index Reprint Ser). 1929. 16.00 (ISBN 0-8369-0099-5). Arno.

LAWRENCE, THOMAS, SIR, 1769-1830

Armstrong, Walter. Lawrence. LC 70-100531. (Illus.). Repr. of 1913 ed. 18.50 (ISBN 0-404-00385-0). AMS Pr.
Levey, Michael. Sir Thomas Lawrence. (Illus.). 116p. 1980. lib. bdg. cancelled (ISBN 0-904017-31-1, 56677-3, Pub. by Natl Portrait Gallery England); pap. cancelled (ISBN 0-904017-32-X, 56678-1). U of Chicago Pr.

LAWRENCE, THOMAS EDWARD, 1888-1935

Aldington, Richard. Lawrence of Arabia: A Biographical Inquiry. LC 75-36506. (Illus.). 448p. 1976. Repr. of 1955 ed. lib. bdg. 31.50 (ISBN 0-8371-8634-X, ALLA). Greenwood.
Clements, Frank. T. E. Lawrence: A Reader's Guide. 208p. 1973. 17.50 (ISBN 0-208-01313-X, Archon). Shoe String.
Duval, Elizabeth W. T. E. Lawrence: A Bibliography. LC 74-185877. (Reference Ser., No. 44). 1972. Repr. of 1938 ed. lib. bdg. 49.95 (ISBN 0-8383-1385-X). Haskell.
Edmonds, Charles. T. E. Lawrence. LC 76-52954. (English Biography Ser, No. 31). 1977. lib. bdg. 32.95 (ISBN 0-8383-2177-1). Haskell.
--T. E. Lawrence (of Arabia) 1936. Repr. 20.00 (ISBN 0-8274-3576-2). R West.

German-Reed, T. Bibliographical Notes on T. E. Lawrence's Seven Pillars of Wisdom & Revolt in the Desert. LC 76-57939. 1977. Repr. of 1928 ed. lib. bdg. 8.50 (ISBN 0-8414-4413-7). Folcroft.
Graves, Richard P. Lawrence of Arabia & His World. LC 76-7183. (Encore Edition). (Illus.). 128p. 1976. 3.95 (ISBN 0-684-16543-0, ScribT). Scribner.
Hyde, H. Montgomery. A Solitary in the Ranks: Lawrence of Arabia As Airman & Private Soldier. LC 77-88903. 1978. 11.95 (ISBN 0-689-10848-6). Atheneum.
Kiernan, Reginald H. Lawrence of Arabia. LC 77-17428. 1977. Repr. of 1935 ed. lib. bdg. 25.00 (ISBN 0-8414-5451-5). Folcroft.
Lawrence, A. W. T. E. Lawrence by His Friends. 1937. Repr. 35.00 (ISBN 0-8274-3575-4). R West.
Lawrence, A. W., ed. T. E. Lawrence by His Friends. 576p. 1980. Repr. of 1937 ed. text ed. 19.50 (ISBN 0-87752-196-4). Gordian.
Lawrence, Thomas E. Selected Letters. Garnett, David, ed. LC 78-20478. 1980. Repr. of 1952 ed. 26.50 (ISBN 0-88355-856-4). Hyperion Conn.
--T. E. Lawrence to His Biographers, Robert Graves & Liddell Hart. LC 76-25030. 260p. 1976. Repr. of 1963 ed. lib. bdg. 27.25x (ISBN 0-8371-9006-1, GRLB). Greenwood.
Liddell Hart, Basil H. T. E. Lawrence: In Arabia & After. LC 71-109768. (Illus.). 1979. Repr. of 1936 ed. lib. bdg. 29.25x (ISBN 0-8371-4258-X, LITL). Greenwood.
Meyers, Jeffrey. T. E. Lawrence: A Bibliography. LC 74-11361. (Reference Library of the Humanities: No. 5). 50p. 1974. lib. bdg. 15.00 (ISBN 0-8240-1052-3). Garland Pub.
O'Donnell, Thomas J. The Confessions of T. E. Lawrence: The Romantic Hero's Presentation of Self. LC 77-92257. x, 196p. 1979. 15.00 (ISBN 0-8214-0370-2). Ohio U Pr.
Phillips, Jill M. T. E. Lawrence: A Portrait in Paradox Controversy & Caricature in the Biographies of T. E. Lawrence. 600p. 1975. 75.00 (ISBN 0-8490-1172-8). Gordon Pr.
Richards, Vyvyan. Portrait of T. E. Lawrence. LC 75-22043. (English Biography Ser., No. 31). 1975. lib. bdg. 31.95 (ISBN 0-8383-2093-7). Haskell.
Robinson, Edward. Lawrence - the Story of His Life. 1935. Repr. 20.00 (ISBN 0-8274-2810-3). R West.
--Lawrence: The Rebel. 1946. Repr. 20.00 (ISBN 0-8274-2809-X). R West.
--Lawrence: The Story of His Life. 1979. Repr. of 1935 ed. lib. bdg. 25.00 (ISBN 0-8414-7442-7). Folcroft.
Tabachnick, Stephen E. T. E. Lawrence. (English Authors Ser.: No. 233). 1978. lib. bdg. 10.95 (ISBN 0-8057-6704-5). Twayne.
Weintraub, Stanley & Weintraub, Rodelle. Lawrence of Arabia - the Literary Impulse. LC 74-27195. 184p. 1975. 12.50x (ISBN 0-8071-0152-4). La State U Pr.

LAWRENCE, THOMAS EDWARD, 1888-1935–JUVENILE LITERATURE

Ebert, Richard. Lawrence of Arabia. LC 78-31450. (Raintree Great Adventures). (Illus.). (gr. 3-6). 1979. PLB 10.25 (ISBN 0-8393-0150-2). Raintree Child.
Knightley, Phillip. Lawrence of Arabia. LC 76-42226. (Illus.). (gr. 6-12). 1976. 6.95 (ISBN 0-525-66507-2). Elsevier-Nelson.
MacLean, Alistair. Lawrence of Arabia. (World Landmark Ser: No. 52). (Illus.). (gr. 7-9). 1962. PLB 5.99 (ISBN 0-394-90552-0, BYR). Random.

LAWRENCE, MASSACHUSETTS–FOREIGN POPULATION

Cole, Donald B. Immigrant City: Lawrence, Massachusetts 1845-1921. LC 63-39156. ix, 248p. 1980. Repr. of 1963 ed. 13.50x (ISBN 0-8078-0876-8). U of NC Pr.

LAWSON, HENRY ARCHIBALD HERTZBERG, 1867-1922

Matthews, Brian. The Receding Wave: Henry Lawson's Prose. 214p. 1972. 16.00x (ISBN 0-522-84039-6, Pub. by Melbourne U Pr). Intl Schol Bk Serv.
Smith, Stephen M. Henry Lawson. Date not set. pap. 3.50x (ISBN 0-392-09480-0, ABC). Sportshelf.

LAWSON, VICTOR FREMONT, 1850-1925

Dennis, Charles H. Victor Lawson: His Time & His Work. LC 68-57598. (Illus.). 1968. Repr. of 1935 ed. lib. bdg. 20.25x (ISBN 0-8371-0376-2, DEVL). Greenwood.

LAWYERS

see also Attorney and Client; Bar Associations; Government Attorneys; Judges; Law Offices; Legal Ethics; Practice of Law; Right to Counsel; Tax Consultants; Women Lawyers

Abbott, Othman A. & Sheldon, Addison E. Recollections of a Pioneer Lawyer: A Special Publication of the Nebraska State Historical Society. (Illus.). 1929. write for info. Nebraska Hist.
American Law Institute-American Bar Association Committee on Continuing Professional Education. A Model Peer Review System. 1980. 25.00 (ISBN 0-686-77589-9, B218). Am Law Inst.
Archer, Fred. Sir Lionel. (Illus.). 339p. 1980. 12.95 (ISBN 0-86595-005-9). Gift Pubns.
Association of the Bar of the City of New York, ed. Professional Responsibility of the Lawyer: The Murky Divide Between Right and Wrong. LC 77-86339. 1977. lib. bdg. 38.00 (ISBN 0-379-00775-4); pap. 8.50 (ISBN 0-379-00776-2). Oceana.
Auchincloss, Louis. Life, Law, & Letters: Essays & Sketches. 1979. 8.95 (ISBN 0-395-28151-2). HM.
Auerbach, Jerold S. Unequal Justice: Lawyers & Social Change in Modern America. LC 75-7364. 1977. pap. 6.95 (ISBN 0-19-502170-3, 490, GB). Oxford U Pr.
Beagle, Legal. The Legal Beagle. LC 79-56874. 1980. 8.95 (ISBN 0-533-04538-X). Vantage.
Bellow, Gary & Moulton, Bea. The Lawyering Process: Ethics & Professional Responsibility. LC 81-67777. (University Casebook Ser.). 479p. 1981. pap. text ed. write for info. (ISBN 0-88277-038-1). Foundation Pr.
--The Lawyering Process: Negotiation. LC 81-67776. (University Casebook Ser.). 299p. 1981. pap. text ed. write for info. (ISBN 0-88277-039-X). Foundation Pr.
--The Lawyering Process: Preparing & Presenting the Case. LC 81-67655. (University Casebook Ser.). 516p. 1981. pap. text ed. write for info. (ISBN 0-88277-040-3). Foundation Pr.
Bigelow, Lafayette J. Bench & Bar: A Complete Digest of the Wit, Humor, Asperities & Amenities of the Law. Repr. of 1871 ed. 38.50 (ISBN 0-384-04260-0). Johnson Repr.
Blackwell, Victor V. O'er the Ramparts They Watched. (Illus.). 1978. 8.95 (ISBN 0-89200-027-9). Atlantis-by-the-Sea.
Blaustein, Albert P. & Porter, Charles O. The American Lawyer: A Summary of the Survey of the Legal Profession. LC 72-5452. 360p. 1972. Repr. of 1954 ed. lib. bdg. 19.50x (ISBN 0-8371-6438-9, BLAL). Greenwood.
Bloomfield, Maxwell. American Lawyers in a Changing Society, 1776-1876: American Lawyers & Social Change, 1776-1876. (Studies in Legal History). 416p. 1976. 18.50x (ISBN 0-674-02910-0). Harvard U Pr.
Bradford, Clyde M., ed. Lawyer Humor: A Collection of Humorous Stories, Definitions & Comments Relating to Lawyers & Their Work. 1981. pap. 4.95 (ISBN 0-932364-02-0). Ann Arbor Bk.
Brown, Esther L. Lawyers & the Promotion of Justice. (Russell Sage Foundation Reprint Ser). Repr. of 1938 ed. lib. bdg. 26.00x (ISBN 0-697-00201-2). Irvington.
--Lawyers, Law Schools & the Public Service. (Russell Sage Foundation Reprint Ser). Repr. of 1948 ed. lib. bdg. 24.50x (ISBN 0-697-00200-4). Irvington.
Brugger, Robert J. Beverley Tucker: Heart Over Head in the Old South. 1978. text ed. 16.50 (ISBN 0-8018-1982-2). Johns Hopkins.
Bryson, Thomas A. Walter George Smith. LC 77-9967. 1978. 13.95 (ISBN 0-8132-0539-5). Cath U Pr.
Carlin, Jerome E. Lawyers on Their Own: A Study of Individual Practitioners in Chicago. 1962. 15.00 (ISBN 0-8135-0412-0). Rutgers U Pr.
Chroust, Anton-Hermann. The Rise of the Legal Profession in America, 2 Vols. 1965. boxed set 37.50x (ISBN 0-8061-0654-9). U of Okla Pr.
Claerbaut, David. The Reluctant Defender. 1978. pap. 4.95 (ISBN 0-8423-5425-5). Tyndale.
Cohen, Morris R. Law & the Social Order: Essays in Legal Philosophy. 1967. Repr. of 1933 ed. 22.50 (ISBN 0-208-00484-X, Archon). Shoe String.
Countryman, Vern, et al. The Lawyer in Modern Society. 2nd ed. 1976. 24.00 (ISBN 0-316-15800-3). Little.
Danielle, T. The Lawyers. 1976. 17.50 (ISBN 0-379-00593-X). Oceana.
Davis, William. Bench & Bar of the Commonwealth of Massachusetts, 2 vols. (American Constitutional & Legal History Ser). 1299p. 1974. Repr. of 1895 ed. Set. lib. bdg. 115.00 (ISBN 0-306-70612-1). Da Capo.
Dean, John. Blind Ambition: The White House Years. 1976. 13.95 (ISBN 0-671-22438-7). S&S.
Digby, K. H. Lawyer in the Wilderness, Data Paper No. 114. 150p. 1980. 5.75 (ISBN 0-87727-114-3). Cornell SE Asia.
Divided on the Issue: A Directory of Advocacy Groups, Publications, & Information Services. 200p. 1981. pap. 14.95 (ISBN 0-918212-57-X). Neal Schuman.
Douglas, C. H. The Brief for the Prosecution. 59.95 (ISBN 0-87968-787-8). Gordon Pr.
Douglas, D. Biographical History of Sir William Blackstone. 1971. Repr. of 1782 ed. 22.50x (ISBN 0-8377-2025-7). Rothman.
Dumbauld, Edward. Thomas Jefferson & the Law. LC 78-5742. (Illus.). 1978. 25.00 (ISBN 0-8061-1441-X). U of Okla Pr.
Dutile, Fernand N., ed. Legal Education & Lawyer Competency: Curricula for Change. LC 81-50458. 160p. 1981. 15.00 (ISBN 0-268-01264-4). U of Notre Dame Pr.
Dvorkin, Elizabeth, et al. Becoming a Lawyer: A Humanistic Perspective on Legal Education, Professionalism. LC 80-6225. 224p. 1980. pap. text ed. 17.95 (ISBN 0-8299-2126-5). West Pub.
Edwards, George. Pioneer-at-Law: A Legacy in the Pursuit of Justice. 256p. 1974. 7.95 (ISBN 0-393-07483-8). Norton.
Fisch, Edith L., et al. Lawyers in Industry. LC 55-11077. 1956. 8.50 (ISBN 0-379-00052-0). Oceana.
Frankel, Marvin. Partisan Justice. 142p. 1980. 9.95 (ISBN 0-8090-6478-2). Hill & Wang.
Gawalt, Gerald W. The Promise of Power: The Emergence of the Legal Profession in Massachusetts, 1760-1840. LC 78-57765. (Contributions in Legal Studies: No. 6). 1979. lib. bdg. 19.95x (ISBN 0-313-20612-0, GPP/). Greenwood.
Gaynor, James K. Lawyers in Heaven. 96p. 1979. 5.95 (ISBN 0-8059-2609-7). Dorrance.
Gest, J. M. The Lawyer in Literature. 59.95 (ISBN 0-8490-0490-X). Gordon Pr.
Goodhart, Arthur L. Five Jewish Lawyers of the Common Law. facs. ed. LC 79-148212. (Biography Index Reprint Ser.). 1949. 12.00 (ISBN 0-8369-8059-X). Arno.
Goulden, Joseph C. The Million Dollar Lawyer's. 336p. 1981. pap. 2.75 (ISBN 0-425-05149-8). Berkley Pub.
--The Million Dollar Lawyers. LC 78-4680. 1978. 10.95 (ISBN 0-399-12239-7). Putnam.
Green, Mark J. The Other Government: The Unseen Power of Washington Lawyers. new ed. 1978. pap. 3.45 (ISBN 0-393-00865-7, N865, Norton Lib). Norton.
Handler, Joel F., et al. Lawyers & the Pursuit of Legal Right. (Poverty Policy Analysis Ser.). 1978. 14.50 (ISBN 0-12-322860-3); pap. 5.95 (ISBN 0-12-322866-2). Acad Pr.
Harbaugh, William H. Lawyer's Lawyer: The Life of John W. Davis. 550p. 1973. 25.00 (ISBN 0-19-501699-8). Oxford U Pr.
Hicks, Frederick C. Men & Books Famous in the Law. LC 72-81454. (Illus.). vi, 259p. 1972. Repr. of 1921 ed. 20.00x (ISBN 0-8377-2230-6). Rothman.
Holdsworth, William S. Charles Dickens As a Legal Historian. LC 72-181001. (Studies in Dickens, No. 52). 157p. 1972. Repr. of 1928 ed. lib. bdg. 32.95 (ISBN 0-8383-1375-2). Haskell.
--Historians of Anglo-American Law. 1966. Repr. of 1928 ed. 16.50 (ISBN 0-208-00347-9, Archon). Shoe String.
Horsky, Charles A. The Washington Lawyer: A Series of Lectures Delivered Under the Auspices of the Julius Rosenthal Foundation at Northwestern University School of Law in April, 1952. LC 81-646. viii, 179p. 1981. Repr. of 1952 ed. lib. bdg. 18.50x (ISBN 0-313-22736-5, HOWL). Greenwood.
Howard, Elizabeth S. The Vagabond Dreamer. LC 76-54447. (Illus.). 1976. 10.00 (ISBN 0-87397-111-6). Strode.
Hulse, J. F. Texas Lawyer: The Cases of W. H. Burges. 1981. 30.00x (ISBN 0-930208-12-9). Mangan Bks.
IBP Research & Editorial Staff. Lawyer's Desk Book. 6th ed. 1979. 39.50 (ISBN 0-87624-323-5). Inst Busn Plan.
Kerschner, Paul A., ed. Advocacy & Age: Issues, Experiences, Strategies. LC 76-22321. 1976. 4.50 (ISBN 0-88474-035-8). USC Andrus Geron.
Knight, Gary, ed. Advertising Sourcebook for Lawyers. LC 81-82089. (Illus.). 211p. (Orig.). 1981. pap. 40.00 (ISBN 0-940718-00-6). Jonathan LA.
Leibowitz, Robert. The Defender. (Illus.). 320p. 1981. 15.00 (ISBN 0-13-197798-9). P-H.
Levy, Elizabeth. Lawyers for the People: A New Breed of Defenders & Their Work. LC 74-156. (Illus.). 160p. (gr. 7 up). 1974. PLB 5.99 (ISBN 0-394-92659-5). Knopf.
Lewis, John F. Thomas Spry: Lawyer & Physician. Repr. of 1932 ed. lib. bdg. 25.00 (ISBN 0-8495-3428-3). Arden Lib.
Lewis, William D., ed. Great American Lawyers, 8 Vols. LC 75-157105. (Illus.). 1971. Repr. of 1909 ed. Set. text ed. 250.00x (ISBN 0-8377-2402-3). Rothman.
Lynn, Conrad & Hoffman, William. There Is a Fountain: The Autobiography of a Civil Rights Lawyer. LC 78-19854. 288p. 1979. 12.00 (ISBN 0-88208-098-9). Lawrence Hill.
MacDonnell, John & Manson, Edward, eds. Great Jurists of the World. LC 68-54739. (Continental Legal History Ser.: Vol. 2). (Illus.). Repr. of 1914 ed. 22.50x (ISBN 0-678-04503-8). Kelley.
--Great Jurists of the World, from Gaius to Von Ihering. (Continental Legal History Ser: Vol. 2). (Illus.). xxxii, 608p. 1968. Repr. of 1914 ed. 22.50x (ISBN 0-8377-2425-2). Rothman.
Maestro, Marcello. Gaetano Filangieri & His Science of Legislation. LC 76-24256. (Transactions Ser.: Vol. 66, Pt. 6). (Illus.). 1976. pap. 6.00 (ISBN 0-87169-666-5). Am Philos.
Mayer, Martin. The Lawyers. LC 79-26324. 1980. Repr. of 1967 ed. lib. bdg. 35.00x (ISBN 0-313-22222-3, MALY). Greenwood.
Melone, Albert P. Lawyers, Public Policy & Interest Group Politics. 265p. 1977. pap. text ed. 9.75 (ISBN 0-8191-0297-0). U Pr of Amer.
Melone, Albert P., et al. North Dakota Lawyers: Mapping the Socio-Political Dimensions. LC 74-4047. (Publisher's Social Science Report Ser.: No. 1). (Illus.). 1975. pap. 1.75 (ISBN 0-911042-20-2). N Dak Inst.
Merillat, Herbert C., ed. Legal Advisers & Foreign Affairs. LC 64-19355. 1964. 8.50 (ISBN 0-379-00223-X). Oceana.
Morgan, Charles. One Man, One Voice. LC 78-12590. 1979. 12.95 (ISBN 0-03-013961-9). HR&W.
--A Time to Speak. LC 78-14177. 1979. 9.95 (ISBN 0-03-050576-3); pap. 4.95 (ISBN 0-03-013956-2). HR&W.
Nader, Ralph & Green, Mark. Verdicts on Lawyers. LC 75-23292. 1977. pap. 4.95 (ISBN 0-690-01667-0, TYC-T). T Y Crowell.
Nizer, Louis. Reflections Without Mirrors. 1979. pap. 2.95 (ISBN 0-425-04637-0). Berkley Pub.
Noonan, John T., Jr. Persons & Masks of the Law: Cardoza, Holmes, Jefferson & Wythe As Makers of the Masks. LC 75-30991. 1976. 10.00 (ISBN 0-374-23076-5); pap. 3.95 (ISBN 0-374-51396-1). FS&G.
O'Connor, John E. William Paterson: Lawyer & Statesman, 1745-1806. 1979. 25.00 (ISBN 0-8135-0880-0). Rutgers U Pr.
Parry, Edward A. Seven Lamps of Advocacy. facs. ed. LC 68-16965. (Essay Index Reprint Ser). 1968. Repr. of 1923 ed. 12.00 (ISBN 0-8369-0773-6). Arno.
Partridge, Bellamy. Country Lawyer. (Illus.). 330p. 1979. pap. 6.95 (ISBN 0-89062-070-9, Pub. by Hughes Press). Pub Ctr Cult Res.
Prest, Wilfrid, ed. Lawyers in Early Modern Europe & America. LC 80-22574. 224p. 1981. text ed. 29.50x (ISBN 0-8419-0679-3). Holmes & Meier.
Rabin, Robert L. Lawyer for Social Change: Perspectives on Public Interest Law. ABF Staff, ed. 1976. pap. 2.00 (ISBN 0-685-70894-2). Am Bar Foun.
Ream, Davidson, ed. Professional Responsibility: A Guide for Attorneys. LC 77-94791. (Professional Education Publications). 1978. pap. text ed. 9.00 (ISBN 0-89707-004-6). Amer Bar Assn.
Reuschlein, Harold G. Jurisprudence: Its American Prophets; a Survey of Taught Jurisprudence. LC 70-158741. 1971. Repr. of 1951 ed. lib. bdg. 25.75x (ISBN 0-8371-6180-0). Greenwood.
Roalfe, Willima R. John Henry Wigmore. LC 77-73200. (Illus.). 1977. 21.95 (ISBN 0-8101-0465-2). Northwestern U Pr.
Rogers, R. Vashon, Jr. The Law & Medical Men. xiii, 214p. 1981. Repr. of 1884 ed. lib. bdg. 22.00x (ISBN 0-8377-1032-4). Rothman.
Rudman, Jack. Assistant Attorney. (Career Examination Ser.: C-24). (Cloth bdg. avail. on request). pap. 10.00 (ISBN 0-8373-0024-X). Natl Learning.
--Associate Attorney. (Career Examination Ser.: C-2269). (Cloth bdg. avail. on request). 1977. pap. 10.00 (ISBN 0-8373-2269-3). Natl Learning.
Rueschemeyer, Dietrich. Lawyers & Their Society: A Comparative Study of the Legal Profession in Germany & the United States. LC 72-93953. 320p. 1973. 16.50x (ISBN 0-674-51826-8). Harvard U Pr.
Sabin, Arthur J. All About Suing & Being Sued. LC 80-23991. (Illus.). 91p. (Orig.). 1981. pap. 12.95 (ISBN 0-89037-185-7); handbk. 15.00 (ISBN 0-89037-188-1). Anderson World.
Schwartz, Murray L. Lawyers & the Legal Profession. (Contemporary Legal Education Ser). 1979. text ed. 21.00 (ISBN 0-672-82802-2). Bobbs.
Sevaried, Paul. People's Lawyer. 5.75 (ISBN 0-87018-056-8). Ross.
Shientag, Bernard L. Moulders of Legal Thought. LC 67-27648. 1968. Repr. of 1943 ed. 11.50 (ISBN 0-8046-0419-3). Kennikat.
Siegel, Edward. How to Avoid Lawyers. 1979. pap. 2.50 (ISBN 0-449-24120-3, Crest). Fawcett.
Silver, Bertram S. How to Make a Better Profit in the Law Office - Year After Year. 1978. 15.00 (ISBN 0-9601938-1-2). Three L Pr.
Simons, Blaine N. Games Lawyers Play with Your Money. LC 77-88488. 1978. pap. 2.25 (ISBN 0-89516-018-8). Condor Pub Co.

Smigel, Erwin O. The Wall Street Lawyer. rev. ed. LC 64-16968. (Midland Bks.: No. 130). 400p. 1970. pap. 2.95x (ISBN 0-253-20130-6). Ind U Pr.
Smith, Talbot. Lawyer: Opportunities for Careers in the Legal Profession. (gr. 9 up). 1961. 3.50 (ISBN 0-02-612130-1). Macmillan.
Stryker, Lloyd P. The Art of Advocacy. 284p. 1979. pap. 5.95 (ISBN 0-89062-069-5, Pub. by Hughes Press). Pub Ctr Cult Res.
Vadney, Thomas E. The Wayward Liberal: A Political Biography of Donald Richberg. LC 75-132832. 242p. 1970. 12.50x (ISBN 0-8131-1243-5). U Pr of Ky.
Ward, Robert E. & Ward, Catherine C. The Letters of Charles O'connor of Belanagare, Seventeen Seventy-Two to Seventeen Ninety, Vol. II. LC 80-11602. (Sponsor Ser.). 341p. 1980. 24.75 (ISBN 0-8357-0535-8, SS-00145). Univ Microfilms.
Warkov, Seymour. Lawyers in the Making. LC 79-26229. (National Opinion Research Center Monographs in Social Research: No. 7). (Illus.). 1980. Repr. of 1965 ed. lib. bdg. 18.00x (ISBN 0-313-22215-0, WALM). Greenwood.
Warren, Charles. History of the Harvard Law School & of Early Legal Conditions in America. LC 72-112311. (American Constitutional & Legal History Ser). 1970. Repr. of 1908 ed. lib. bdg. 75.00 (ISBN 0-306-71913-4). Da Capo.
Washburn, Edwin C. John Read: American. 1978. Repr. of 1928 ed. lib. bdg. 25.00 (ISBN 0-8492-2952-9). R West.
Weckstein, Donald T., ed. Education in the Professional Responsibilities of the Lawyer. LC 75-119491. (Virginia Legal Studies Ser). 275p. 1970. 20.00x (ISBN 0-8139-0300-9). U Pr of Va.
Wellman, Francis L. Gentlemen of the Jury. 298p. 1981. Repr. of 1924 ed. lib. bdg. 25.00 (ISBN 0-8495-5661-9). Arden Lib.
Wice, Paul B. Criminal Lawyers: An Endangered Species. LC 78-14478. (Sage Library of Social Research: Vol. 67). 233p. 1978. 20.00 (ISBN 0-8039-1097-5); pap. 9.95 (ISBN 0-8039-1098-3). Sage.
Wishman, Seymour. Confessions of a Criminal Lawyer. Chase, Edward T., ed. LC 81-50096. 224p. 1981. 12.95 (ISBN 0-8129-1005-2). Times Bks.
Wood, Arthur L. Criminal Lawyer. 1967. 6.50x (ISBN 0-8084-0095-9). Coll & U Pr.
Yale Law Journal Staff. The New Public Interest Lawyers. (Law Review Research Project Ser). 1971. pap. 2.00 (ISBN 0-685-48021-6). Am Bar Foun.

LAWYERS–ACCOUNTING

Lawyers & CPAs. 1977. pap. 2.75 (ISBN 0-685-58513-1). Am Inst CPA.

LAWYERS–CORRESPONDENCE, REMINISCENCES, ETC.

Bailey, F. Lee. The Defense Never Rests. pap. 2.50 (ISBN 0-451-08236-2, E9236, Sig). NAL.
--For the Defense. 1976. pap. 2.50 (ISBN 0-451-09050-0, E9050, Sig). NAL.
Baldwin, Simeon E. Life & Letters of Simeon Baldwin. 1919. 47.50x (ISBN 0-685-89762-1). Elliots Bks.
Belli, Melvin & Kaiser, Robert. My Life on Trial. 1977. pap. 1.95 (ISBN 0-445-04025-4). Popular Lib.
Biddle, Francis. In Brief Authority. LC 76-5432. (Illus.). 494p. 1976. Repr. of 1962 ed. lib. bdg. 19.75x (ISBN 0-8371-8807-5, BIIB). Greenwood.
Burgess, Harold D. Sixty Years at the Bar: Anecdotes of a Corporation Lawyer. 160p. 1981. 10.00 (ISBN 0-682-49781-9). Exposition.
Cohen, Julius H. They Builded Better Than They Knew. facsimile ed. LC 70-156633. (Essay Index Reprint Ser). Repr. of 1946 ed. 19.50 (ISBN 0-8369-2350-2). Arno.
Depew, Chauncey M. My Memories of Eighty Years: Mark Twain. 1924. 25.00 (ISBN 0-8274-2781-6). R West.
Fleishman, Neil. Counsel for the Damned. 10.50 (ISBN 0-88894-022-X, Pub. by Douglas & McIntyre). Intl Schol Bk Serv.
Gould, Milton S. The Witness Who Spoke with God: And Other Tales from the Courthouse. 1979. 12.95 (ISBN 0-670-69158-5). Viking Pr.
Harrison, Frederic. Autobiographic Memoirs, 2 vols. LC 75-30025. Repr. of 1911 ed. Set. 42.50 (ISBN 0-404-13990-6). AMS Pr.
Hazard, Leland. Attorney for the Situation. LC 74-83549. 314p. 1975. 12.50x (ISBN 0-231-03898-4). Columbia U Pr.
Hopkins, William F. Murder Is My Business. 350p. 1974. pap. 4.50 (ISBN 0-913428-16-7). Landfall Pr.
House, Victor. Such Sometimes Is the Law. 1980. 6.95 (ISBN 0-533-04651-3). Vantage.
Howe, Frederic C. Confessions of a Reformer. 6.00 (ISBN 0-8446-2276-1). Peter Smith.
Hughes, Charles E. The Autobiographical Notes of Charles Evans Hughes. Danelski, David J. & Tulchin, Joseph S., eds. LC 72-88130. (Studies in Legal History). 1973. 17.50x (ISBN 0-674-05325-7). Harvard U Pr.
Jaworski, Leon & Herskowitz, Mickey. Confession & Avoidance: A Memoir. LC 77-16926. 1979. 10.95 (ISBN 0-385-13440-1, Anchor Pr). Doubleday.
Kelly, James Y. The Emmaline Letters. Kelly, Emma C. & Tolle, Alice E., eds. LC 81-65042. 440p. 1981. 10.00 (ISBN 0-8059-2787-5). Dorrance.
Kuhn, Arthur K. Pathways in International Law, a Personal Narrative. Repr. of 1953 ed. lib. bdg. 15.00x (ISBN 0-8371-2211-2, KUPI). Greenwood.
Lechford, Thomas. Note-Book. Repr. of 1885 ed. pap. 31.00 (ISBN 0-384-31988-2). Johnson Repr.
Pendleton, Charles E. At the Home Front in War & Life: Confessions of a Lawyer. 1978. 15.00 (ISBN 0-682-48982-4). Exposition.
Reich, Charles A. The Sorcerer of Bolinas Reef. 1976. 8.95 (ISBN 0-394-49192-0). Random.
Tomkins, D. Michael. Trial & Error. LC 80-39757. 1981. 9.95 (ISBN 0-396-07944-X). Dodd.
Weinberg. Attorney for the Damned. pap. 6.95 (ISBN 0-671-06181-X, Touchstone Bks). S&S.
Williams, Edward B. One Man's Freedom. LC 62-11689. 1977. pap. 4.95 (ISBN 0-689-70544-1, 227). Atheneum.

LAWYERS–DIRECTORIES

Blunt, Adrian. Law Librarianship. (Outlines of Modern Librarianship Ser.). 1979. text ed. 12.00 (ISBN 0-89664-434-0). K G Saur.
Christensen, Carol W., compiled by. Guide to Religion-Based Organizations of Attorneys. (Tarlton Law Library Legal Bibliography Ser.: No. 19). 33p. 1979. 15.00 (ISBN 0-935630-01-5). U of Tex Tarlton Law Lib.
Katz, Richard N., et al, eds. An Inventory of the Records of the National Lawyers Guild, 1936-1976, & an Index to NLG Periodica, 1936-1979. LC 80-81943. (Meiklejohn Institute Inventory: No. 2). 1980. pap. 10.00 (ISBN 0-913876-12-7). Meiklejohn Civil Lib.
Lipscher, Betty S. Forensic Services Directory: A National Register of Forensic Experts, Litigation Consultants & Legal Support Specialists. 1980. 47.50 (ISBN 0-686-27688-4). Natl Forensic.
Parker & Son Staff. Parker Directory of Attorneys. LC 75-41995. 1981. 11.50 (ISBN 0-911110-18-6). Parker & Son.
Quemner, Thomas A. Legal Dictionary: French-English & English French. 1969. 62.50x (ISBN 0-8002-1647-4). Intl Pubns Serv.
Roessler, Rudolf. Woerterbuch des Steuerrechts. (Ger.). 1971. 54.00 (ISBN 3-448-00204-6, M-6934). French & Eur.
Wasserman, Paul & Kaszubski, Marek, eds. Law & Legal Information Directory: A Guide to National & International Organizations, Bar Associations, Federal Court System, Federal Regulatory Agencies, Law Schools, Continuing Legal Education, Scholarships & Grants, Awards & Prizes, Special Libraries, Information Systems & Services, Research Centers, Etc. 800p. 1980. 110.00 (ISBN 0-8103-0169-5). Gale.

LAWYERS–FEES

Langer, Steven, ed. Compensation of Attorneys, Pt. I: Non-Law Firms. 2nd ed. 1980. pap. 50.00 (ISBN 0-916506-51-7). Abbott Langer Assocs.
--Compensation of Attorneys Pt. II: Law Firms. 1978. pap. 50.00 (ISBN 0-916506-26-6). Abbott Langer Assocs.
Pfennigstorf, Werner. Legal Expense Insurance: The European Experience in Financing Legal Services. LC 75-996. 1975. 5.00 (ISBN 0-910058-69-5). Am Bar Foun.
Speiser, Stuart M. Attorney's Fees, 2 vols. LC 72-91431. 1973. 100.00 (ISBN 0-686-05453-9). Lawyers Co-Op.

LAWYERS–AFRICA

Blackwell, Leslie. African Occasions: Reminiscences of Thirty Years of Bar, Bench, & Politics in South Africa. LC 76-109319. (Illus.). Repr. of 1938 ed. 14.50x (ISBN 0-8371-3574-5, Pub. by Negro U Pr). Greenwood.
Gower, Laurence C. Independent Africa, the Challenge to the Legal Profession. LC 67-20877. (Oliver Wendell Holmes Lecture Ser: 1966). 1967. 8.95x (ISBN 0-674-44800-6). Harvard U Pr.

LAWYERS–AUSTRALIA

Tomasic, Roman, ed. Lawyers & the Community. LC 78-52240. (Law in Society Ser.). 1978. text ed. 21.00x (ISBN 0-86861-168-9); pap. text ed. 9.50x (ISBN 0-86861-240-5). Allen Unwin.
--Understanding Lawyers. LC 78-52239. (Law in Society Ser.). 1978. text ed. 25.00x (ISBN 0-86861-160-3); pap. text ed. 11.50x (ISBN 0-86861-248-0). Allen Unwin.

LAWYERS–ATHENS

Bonner, Robert J. Lawyers & Litigants in Ancient Athens: The Genesis of the Legal Profession. LC 68-57185. Repr. of 1927 ed. 15.00 (ISBN 0-405-08289-4, Blom Pubns). Arno.

LAWYERS–FRANCE

Berlanstein, Lenard R. The Barristers of Toulouse in the Eighteenth Century, 1740-1793. LC 75-9784. (J. H. Studies in Historical & Political Science Ser: Ninety-Third Series (1975)). (Illus.). 224p. 1975. 14.50x (ISBN 0-8018-1582-7). Johns Hopkins.

LAWYERS–GERMANY (FEDERAL REPUBLIC, 1949-)

Rueschemeyer, Dietrich. Lawyers & Their Society: A Comparative Study of the Legal Profession in Germany & the United States. LC 72-93953. 320p. 1973. 16.50x (ISBN 0-674-51826-8). Harvard U Pr.

LAWYERS–GREAT BRITAIN

Douglas, D. Biographical History of Sir William Blackstone. LC 70-112403. Repr. of 1782 ed. lib. bdg. 22.50x (ISBN 0-678-04537-2). Kelley.
Eusden, John D. Puritans, Lawyers & Politics in Early Seventeenth Century England. LC 68-12524. 1968. Repr. of 1958 ed. 17.50 (ISBN 0-208-00186-7, Archon). Shoe String.
Hicks, Frederick C. Men & Books Famous in the Law. LC 72-81454. (Illus.). vi, 259p. 1972. Repr. of 1921 ed. 20.00x (ISBN 0-8377-2230-6). Rothman.
Holdsworth, William S. Historians of Anglo-American Law. 1966. Repr. of 1928 ed. 16.50 (ISBN 0-208-00347-9, Archon). Shoe String.
Majoribanks, Edward. For the Defense: The Life of Sir Edward Marshall Hall. 1979. Repr. of 1929 ed. lib. bdg. 15.00 (ISBN 0-8495-3786-X). Arden Lib.
Manningham, John. The Diary of John Manningham of the Middle Temple, 1602-1603. Sorlien, Robert P., ed. LC 74-22553. 481p. 1976. text ed. 27.50x (ISBN 0-87451-113-5). U Pr of New Eng.
Podmore, David. Solicitors & the Wider Community. 1980. text ed. 43.95x (ISBN 0-435-82696-4). Heinemann Ed.
Vick, R. W. & Schoolbred, C. F. The Administration of Civil Justice in England & Wales. LC 67-31508. 1968. 23.00 (ISBN 0-08-013299-5). Pergamon.

LAWYERS–HUNGARY

Kalman, Lajos. Lawyer in Communism. (Illus.). 1960. 3.00 (ISBN 0-8198-0073-2); pap. 2.00 (ISBN 0-8198-0074-0). Dghtrs St Paul.

LAWYERS–RUSSIA

Cameron, George D., III: The Soviet Lawyer & His System: A Historical & Bibliographical Study. (Michigan International Business Studies: No. 14). 1978. pap. 9.00 (ISBN 0-87712-185-0). U Mich Busn Div Res.
Gruzenberg, O. O. Yesterday: Memoirs of a Russian-Jewish Lawyer. Rawson, Don C., ed. & tr. from Rus. LC 80-39850. 288p. 1981. 27.50x (ISBN 0-520-04264-6). U of Cal Pr.
Hazard, John N. Settling Disputes in Soviet Society: The Formative Years of Legal Institutions. 1978. Repr. of 1960 ed. lib. bdg. 32.50x (ISBN 0-374-93758-3). Octagon.
Wortman, Richard S. The Development of a Russian Legal Consciousness. LC 76-600. (Illus.). 1976. lib. bdg. 20.00x (ISBN 0-226-90776-7). U of Chicago Pr.

LAWYERS, AFRO-AMERICAN

see Afro-American Lawyers

LAXALT, DOMINIQUE

Laxalt, Robert. Sweet Promised Land. 1957. 10.00 (ISBN 0-06-012540-3, HarpT). Har-Row.

LAXALT, ROBERT, 1921-

Laxalt, Robert. In a Hundred Graves: A Basque Portrait. LC 72-86404. (Basque Bk. Ser.). (Illus.). 146p. 1972. 8.00 (ISBN 0-87417-035-4). U of Nev Pr.

LAXNESS, HALLDOR KILJAN, 1902-

Hallberg, Peter. Halldor Laxness. (World Authors Ser.: No. 89). 12.50 (ISBN 0-8057-2516-4). Twayne.
--Halldor Laxness. McTurk, Rory, tr. LC 75-79208. (World Authors Ser.). 1971. lib. bdg. 12.95x (ISBN 0-8057-2516-4). Irvington.

LAY APOSTOLATE

see Catholic Action

LAY LEADERSHIP

see Christian Leadership

LAY READERS

Allen, Horace T., ed. The Reader As Minister. 1980. pap. 6.95 (ISBN 0-686-57954-2). Liturgical Conf.
Lamar, Nedra N. How to Speak the Written Word: A Guide to Effective Public Reading. rev. ed. 8.95 (ISBN 0-8007-0143-7). Revell.
Partridge, Edmund. Church in Perspective: Standard Course for Layreaders. rev. ed. 1976. 3.95 (ISBN 0-8192-1210-5). Morehouse.
Sleeth, Ronald E. Look Who's Talking: A Guide for Lay Speakers in the Church. LC 77-1171. 1977. pap. 3.95 (ISBN 0-687-22630-9). Abingdon.
Staudacher, Joseph M. Laymen Proclaim the Word. LC 73-630. 1973. pap. 2.25 (ISBN 0-8199-0451-1). Franciscan Herald.
Tate, Judith. Manual for Lectors. (Orig.). 1975. 2.25 (ISBN 0-8278-0030-4). Pflaum Pr.
Widdowson, Gregory C. An Outline of Lay Sanctity. LC 79-84532. 1979. pap. 2.95 (ISBN 0-87973-737-9). Our Sunday Visitor.

LAYAMON, fl. 1200

Blenner-Hassett, Roland. Study of the Place-Names in Lawman's Brut. LC 50-4808. (Stanford University. Stanford Studies in Language & Literature: No. 1). Repr. of 1950 ed. 14.50 (ISBN 0-404-51817-6). AMS Pr.

LAYAWAY PLAN

see also Instalment Plan

LAYING OF CARPETS

see Carpet Laying

LAYMEN

see Laity

LAY-OFF COMPENSATION

see Wages–Dismissal Wage

LAYOUT

see Printing–Layout and Typography

LAYOUT, FACTORY

see Factories–Design and Construction

LAYOUT AND TYPOGRAPHY, ADVERTISING

see Advertising Layout and Typography

LAYOUT AND TYPOGRAPHY, NEWSPAPER

see Newspaper Layout and Typography

LAYS

Donovan, Mortimer J. Breton Lay: A Guide to Varieties. 1968. 9.95x (ISBN 0-268-00024-7). U of Notre Dame Pr.

LAZARUS, EMMA, 1849-1889

Angoff, Charles. Emma Lazarus: Poet, Jewish Activist, Pioneer Zionist. LC 79-11570. (Illus.). 1929. pap. 2.00 (ISBN 0-916790-01-0). Jewish Hist.
Gerber, Irving. Emma Lazarus: Poet of Liberty. 1979. of 10 6.75 set (ISBN 0-87594-183-4). Book Lab.
Vogel, Dan. Emma Lazarus. (United States Authors Ser.: No. 353). 1980. lib. bdg. 11.95 (ISBN 0-8057-7233-2). Twayne.

LAZARUS, SAINT

Cornish, John. The Raising of Lazarus. 1979. pap. 2.50 (ISBN 0-916786-36-6). St George Bk Serv.
Kastenbaum, Robert, ed. Return to Life: Two Imaginings of the Lazarus Theme. an original anthology ed. LC 76-19587. (Death & Dying Ser.). 1977. Repr. of 1976 ed. lib. bdg. 14.00x (ISBN 0-405-09582-1). Arno.
North, Brownlow. The Rich Man & Lazarus. 1979. pap. 2.45 (ISBN 0-85151-121-X). Banner of Truth.

LAZINESS

see also Procrastination

LEA, HENRY CHARLES, 1843-1880

Bradley, E. S. Henry Charles Lea. 59.95 (ISBN 0-8490-0293-1). Gordon Pr.

LEACH, BERNARD

Bernard Leach: A Potter's Work. LC 73-92991. 305p. 1967. 14.95 (ISBN 0-87011-226-0). Kodansha.

LEACOCK, STEPHEN BUTLER, 1869-1944

Lomer, Gerhard R. Stephen Leacock. 1954. Repr. lib. bdg. 20.00 (ISBN 0-8414-5881-2). Folcroft.
--Stephen Leacock: A Check-List & Index of His Writings. 1978. Repr. of 1954 ed. lib. bdg. 25.00 (ISBN 0-8492-1596-X). R West.
McArthur, Peter. Stephen Leacock. LC 74-19412. 1974. Repr. of 1923 ed. lib. bdg. 10.00 (ISBN 0-8414-5926-6). Folcroft.

LEAD

Boggess, W. R. & Wixson, B. G., eds. Lead in the Environment. (Illus.). 272p. 1979. text ed. 48.00 (ISBN 0-7194-0024-4, Pub. by Castle Hse England). J K Burgess.
Boggess, William R., ed. Lead in the Environment. (Illus.). 272p. 1979. 45.00x (ISBN 0-7194-0024-4). Intl Pubns Serv.
Dasoyan, K. A. & Aguf, I. A. Lead Accumulator. 1968. 5.95x (ISBN 0-210-27168-X). Asia.
Doe, Bruce R. Lead Isotopes. LC 70-124067. (Minerals, Rocks & Inorganic Materials: Vol. 3). (Illus.). 1970. 22.20 (ISBN 0-387-05205-4). Springer-Verlag.
Harrison, R. M. & Laxen, D. P. Lead Pollution: Causes & Control. 1981. 19.95x (ISBN 0-412-16360-8, Pub. by Chapman & Hall). Methuen Inc.
Hehner, Nels E. & Ritchie, Everett J. Lead Oxides: Chemistry, Technology, Battery Manufacturing Uses, History. 1974. 15.00 (ISBN 0-685-56653-6). IBMA Pubns.
Hepple, P., ed. Lead in the Environment. 1972. 16.20x (ISBN 0-85334-485-X). Intl Ideas.
Hofmann, W. Lead & Lead Alloys: Properties & Technology. Lead Development Association, tr. (Illus.). 1970. 65.20 (ISBN 0-387-04880-4). Springer-Verlag.
Hughes, A. I., ed. Lead Nineteen Sixty-Eight: Proceedings, International Conference on Lead - 3rd - Venice - 1968. LC 66-18688. 1970. 69.00 (ISBN 0-08-015644-4). Pergamon.

International Experts Discussion on Lead Occurrence, Fate & Pollution in the Marine Environment, Rovinj, Yugoslavia, 18-22 October 1977. Lead in the Marine Environment: Proceedings. Konrad, Z. & Branica, M., eds. LC 80-40023. (Illus.). 364p. 1980. pap. 69.00 (ISBN 0-08-022960-3). Pergamon.
Kolisko, E. Lead & the Human Organism. 1980. pap. 3.95x (ISBN 0-906492-31-9, Pub. by Kolisko Archives). St George Bk Serv.
Kuhn, A. T., ed. The Electrochemistry of Leads. 1978. 78.50 (ISBN 0-12-428350-0). Acad Pr.
Lynam, Donald R. & Piantanida, Lillian, eds. Environmental Lead. (Ecotoxicology & Environmental Quality Ser.). 1981. write for info. (ISBN 0-12-460520-6). Acad Pr.
Measurement to Lead in the Atmosphere: Sampling Stacks for Particulates; & Determination of Oxides of Nitrogen in Combustion Products. 1975. pap. 18.00 (ISBN 0-686-51985-X, 05-055099-17). ASTM.
Needleman, Herbert L., ed. Low Level Lead Exposure: The Clinical Implications of Current Research. 336p. 1980. text ed. 36.50 (ISBN 0-89004-455-4). Raven.
Nriagu, J. O., ed. The Biogeochemistry of Lead in the Environment. (Topics in Environmental Health Ser.: Vol. 1A). 1978. 80.50 (ISBN 0-444-41599-8, TEH 1:A, Biomedical Pr). Elsevier.
Singhal, Radhey L. & Thomas, John A., eds. Lead Toxicity. LC 79-16784. (Illus.). 524p. 1980. text ed. 39.50 (ISBN 0-8067-1801-3). Urban & S.
Weaver, Lawrence. English Leadwork: Its Art & History. LC 68-57195. (Illus.). 1969. Repr. of 1909 ed. lib. bdg. 26.00 (ISBN 0-405-09057-9, Pub. by Blom). Arno.
Wemyss, Francis C. Wemyss Chronology of the American Stage from 1752-1852. LC 67-31455. 1968. Repr. of 1852 ed. 15.00 (ISBN 0-405-09058-7, Pub. by Blom). Arno.

LEAD MINES AND MINING

AIME International Symposium: Mining & Metallurgy of Lead & Zinc. LC 78-132404. 1970. 50.00x (ISBN 0-89520-040-6). Soc Mining Eng.
Clark, James I. Life on Wisconsin's Lead-Mining Frontier. (Illus.). 1976. pap. 1.00 (ISBN 0-87020-166-2). State Hist Soc Wis.
Gibson, Arrell M. Wilderness Bonanza: The Tri-State Mining District of Missouri, Kansas & Oklahoma. LC 77-177335. (Illus.). 350p. 1972. 16.95 (ISBN 0-8061-0990-4); pap. 8.95 (ISBN 0-8061-1033-3). U of Okla Pr.
Hunt, Christopher J. Lead Miners of the Northern Pennines in the 18th & 19th Centuries. LC 77-103011. (Illus.). 1970. lib. bdg. 15.00x (ISBN 0-678-06779-1). Kelley.
Rausch, D. O., et al, eds. Lead-Zinc Update. LC 77-83619. (Illus.). 1977. text ed. 22.00x (ISBN 0-89520-250-6). Soc Mining Eng.
Schoolcraft, Henry R. A View of the Lead Mines of Missouri: Including Some Observations on the Mineralogy, Geology, Geography, Antiquities, Soil, Climate, Population & Productions of Missouri & Arkansas, & Other Sections of the Western Country. LC 72-2867. (Use & Abuse of America's Natural Resources Ser). (Illus.). 302p. 1972. Repr. of 1819 ed. 16.00 (ISBN 0-405-04534-4). Arno.

LEAD ORGANIC COMPOUNDS

see Organolead Compounds

LEAD-POISONING

Chisolm, J. J. & O'Hara, D. M. Lead Absorption in Children: Management, Clinical & Environmental Aspects. 1981. 32.50 (ISBN 0-8067-0331-8). Urban & S.
Chisolm, J. J., Jr., et al, eds. Diagnosis & Treatment of Lead Poisoning. 213p. 1976. text ed. 32.50x (ISBN 0-8422-7262-3). Irvington.
Committee on Biological Effects of Atmospheric Pollutants. Lead: Airborne Lead in Perspective. LC 71-186214. (Biological Effects of Atmospheric Pollutants Ser.). (Illus.). 1972. pap. 9.50 (ISBN 0-309-01941-9). Natl Acad Pr.
--Lead: Airborne Lead in Perspective. LC 71-186214. (Biological Effects of Atmospheric Pollutants Ser.). (Illus.). 1972. pap. 9.50 (ISBN 0-309-01941-9). Natl Acad Pr.
Doss, M., ed. Diagnosis & Therapy of Porphyrias & Lead Toxication. (International Symposium Clinical Biochemistry). (Illus.). 1978. pap. 39.30 (ISBN 0-387-08863-6). Springer-Verlag.
Elbert, Lisa. Lead Poisoning in Man. (Illus.). 1978. 20.00 (ISBN 0-916750-31-0). Dayton Labs.
Hardy, H. L., et al, eds. Epidemiology & Detection of Lead Toxicity. LC 74-26934. (Lead Toxicity Ser.: Vol. 3). 147p. 1976. text ed. 29.50x (ISBN 0-8422-7261-5). Irvington.
Kolisko, E. Lead & the Human Organism. 1980. pap. 3.95x (ISBN 0-906492-31-9, Pub. by Kolisko Archives). St George Bk Serv.
Lead in the Human Environment. 1980. 13.50 (ISBN 0-309-03021-8). Natl Acad Pr.
Needleman, Herbert L., ed. Low Level Lead Exposure: The Clinical Implications of Current Research. 336p. 1980. text ed. 36.50 (ISBN 0-89004-455-4). Raven.
Simpson, C. F., et al. Lead Poisoning in Animal Models. 160p. 1976. text ed. 29.50x (ISBN 0-8422-7268-2). Irvington.
Stofen, D. & Walsren, H. A. Sub-Clinical Lead Poisoning. 1974. 37.00 (ISBN 0-12-671650-1). Acad Pr.

LEADERSHIP

see also Christian Leadership; Community Leadership; Discussion; Elite (Social Sciences); Meetings; Recreation Leadership; Small Groups

Adair, John. Action Centered Leadership. 1979. text ed. 31.00x (ISBN 0-566-02143-9, Pub. by Gower Pub Co England). Renouf.
Akens, David S. World's Greatest Leaders: The Akens Book of Supernatural Records. 1980. pap. 4.95 (ISBN 0-87397-181-7). Strode.
Arbous, A. Selection for Industrial Leadership. LC 77-110266. 1971. Repr. of 1953 ed. lib. bdg. 15.00 (ISBN 0-8371-4492-2, ARIL). Greenwood.
Argyris, Chris. Increasing Leadership Effectiveness. LC 76-12784. (Wiley Ser. in Behavior). 286p. 1976. 23.50 (ISBN 0-471-01668-3, Pub. by Wiley-Interscience). Wiley.
Argyris, Chris & Cyert, Richard M. Leadership in the Eighties: Essays on Higher Education. LC 80-80425. 100p. 1980. pap. text ed. 5.95x (ISBN 0-934222-01-0). Inst Ed Manage.
Armerding, Hudson T. Leadership. 1978. 6.95 (ISBN 0-8423-2126-8); pap. 3.95 (ISBN 0-8423-2125-X). Tyndale.
Axelrod, Nathan. Executive Leadership. 1969. pap. text ed. 9.10 (ISBN 0-672-96054-0); tchr's manual 5.00 (ISBN 0-672-96055-9). Bobbs.
Babbitt, Irving. Democracy & Leadership. LC 78-11418. 1979. 9.00 (ISBN 0-913966-54-1, Liberty Classics); pap. 4.00 (ISBN 0-913966-55-X). Liberty Fund.
Bailey, F. G. Stratagems & Spoils: A Social Anthropology of Politics. LC 70-75221. (Pavilion Social Anthropology Ser.). 1973. 10.00x (ISBN 0-8052-3254-0). Schocken.
Ballard, Jim. Circlebook: A Leader Handbook for Conducting Circletime - a Curriculum of Affect. LC 75-25396. (Mandala Ser. in Education). (Illus.). 60p. (Orig.). 1975. pap. 4.25 (ISBN 0-916250-00-8). Irvington.
Barber, Cyril J. Nehemiah & the Dynamics of Effective Leadership. LC 76-22567. 1976. pap. 3.00 (ISBN 0-87213-021-5). Loizeaux.
Basil, Douglas C. Leadership Skills for Executive Action. LC 79-138565. 1971. 12.95 (ISBN 0-8144-5247-7). Am Mgmt.
Bass, Bernard M. Leadership, Psychology, & Organizational Behavior. LC 72-10715. (Illus.). 548p. 1973. Repr. of 1960 ed. lib. bdg. 37.00 (ISBN 0-8371-6631-4, BALP); pap. 7.95 (ISBN 0-8371-8960-8, BAL). Greenwood.
Beal, George M., et al. Leadership & Dynamic Group Action. (Illus.). 365p. 1962. pap. text ed. 7.95x (ISBN 0-8138-0981-9). Iowa St U Pr.
Bellingrath, George C. Qualities Associated with Leadership in the Extra-Curricular Activities of the High School. LC 74-176549. (Columbia University. Teachers College. Contributions: No. 399). Repr. of 1930 ed. 17.50 (ISBN 0-404-55399-0). AMS Pr.
Bennis, Warren. The Unconscious Conspiracy: Why Leaders Can't Lead. LC 75-37851. 190p. 1976. 10.95 (ISBN 0-8144-5406-2). Am Mgmt.
Bennis, Warren G., et al, eds. Leadership & Motivation: Essays of Douglas McGregor. 1966. pap. 5.95x (ISBN 0-262-63015-X). MIT Pr.
Berman, Louise M. Supervision, Staff Development & Leadership. LC 76-141938. 1971. pap. text ed. 5.95x (ISBN 0-675-09242-6). Merrill.
Bernhard, Linda A. & Walsh, Michelle. Leadership: The Key to Professionalization of Nursing. (Illus.). 256p. 1981. pap. text ed. 8.95 (ISBN 0-07-004936-X, HP). McGraw.
Betz, Don. Cultivating Leadership: An Approach. LC 80-69039. 120p. (Orig.). 1981. pap. text ed. 4.95 (ISBN 0-8191-1441-3). U Pr of Amer.
Boles, Harold W. Leaders, Leading, & Leadership. LC 80-65616. 170p. 1981. cancelled (ISBN 0-86548-023-0). Century Twenty One.
Bradford, Leland P. Making Meetings Work: A Guide for Leaders & Group Members. LC 76-16886. 122p. 1976. pap. 12.50 (ISBN 0-88390-122-6). Univ Assocs.
Breen, T. H. The Character of the Good Ruler: Puritan Political Ideas in New England, 1630-1730. 320p. 1974. pap. 3.95 (ISBN 0-393-00747-2, Norton Lib.). Norton.
Brooten, Dorothy A., et al. Leadership for Change: A Guide for the Frustrated Nurse. LC 78-8661. pap. 8.25 (ISBN 0-397-54218-6). Har-Row.
Brown, David G. Leadership Vitality: A Workbook for Academic Administrators. 5.00 (ISBN 0-8268-1331-3). ACE.
Brown, J. Douglas. The Human Nature of Organizations. LC 73-85862. 168p. 1973. 9.95 (ISBN 0-8144-5350-3). Am Mgmt.
Brown, Marion. Leadership Among High School Pupils. LC 77-176598. (Columbia University. Teachers College. Contributions to Education: No. 559). Repr. of 1933 ed. 17.50 (ISBN 0-404-55559-4). AMS Pr.
Burby, Raymond J. Fundamentals of Leadership: A Guide for the Supervisor. LC 72-2644. (Illus.). 128p. (Prog. Bk.). 1972. pap. text ed. 8.95 (ISBN 0-201-00744-4). A-W.
Burgess, M. Elaine. Negro Leadership in a Southern City. 1962. pap. 2.25 (ISBN 0-8084-0231-5, B22). Coll & U Pr.
Burns, James M. Leadership. LC 76-5117. 1979. pap. 8.95 (ISBN 0-06-090697-9, CN 697, CN). Har-Row.
--Leadership. LC 76-5117. 1978. 19.95 (ISBN 0-06-010588-7, HarpT). Har-Row.
Cartwright, Dorwin & Zander, Alvin, eds. Group Dynamics: Research & Theory. 3rd ed. 1968. text ed. 24.95 scp (ISBN 0-06-041201-1, HarpC). Har-Row.
Cassel, Russell N. & Heichberger, Robert L., eds. Leadership Development: Theory & Practice. 352p. 1975. 9.75 (ISBN 0-8158-0319-2). Chris Mass.
Cope, Harley F. Command at Sea. 3rd ed. Bucknell, Howard, 3rd, ed. LC 66-28158. 1966. 9.50x (ISBN 0-87021-124-2). Naval Inst Pr.
Corbett, Jan. Creative Youth Leadership. LC 77-778950. 1977. pap. 4.95 (ISBN 0-8170-0761-X). Judson.
Cribbin, James J. Effective Managerial Leadership. LC 71-166554. 264p. 1972. 13.95 (ISBN 0-8144-5277-9). Am Mgmt.
Cunningham, Luvern L. & Gephart, William J., eds. Leadership: The Science & the Art Today. LC 60-2874. 1973. text ed. 12.50 (ISBN 0-87581-155-8). Peacock Pubs.
Dale, Edgar. The Humane Leader. LC 73-93698. (Fastback Ser.: No. 38). (Illus., Orig.). 1974. pap. 0.75 (ISBN 0-87367-038-8). Phi Delta Kappa.
Damazio, Franky. The Making of a Leader. 246p. 1979. pap. 10.95 (ISBN 0-914936-37-9). Bible Pr.
De Gaulle, Charles. The Edge of the Sword. LC 75-26731. 128p. 1975. Repr. of 1960 ed. lib. bdg. 15.00x (ISBN 0-8371-8366-9, GAES). Greenwood.
Dobbins, Gaines S. Learning to Lead. LC 68-12342. (Orig.). 1968. pap. 3.50 (ISBN 0-8054-3208-6). Broadman.
Downton, James V., Jr. Rebel Leadership: Commitment & Charisma in the Revolutionary Process. LC 72-77283. 1973. 19.95 (ISBN 0-02-907560-2). Free Pr.
Dyer, Frederick C. & Dyer, John M. Bureaucracy Vs Creativity: The Dilemna of Modern Leadership. LC 65-25638. (Business & Economic Ser: No. 9). 1965. 7.95x (ISBN 0-87024-134-6). U of Miami Pr.
Fallon, Berlie J. The Art of Followership (What Happened to the Indians?) LC 73-90397. (Fastback Ser.: No. 33). (Illus., Orig.). 1974. pap. 0.75 (ISBN 0-87367-033-7). Phi Delta Kappa.
Fallon, William K. Leadership on the Job: Guides to Good Supervision. 320p. 1982. 17.95 (ISBN 0-8144-5727-4). Am Mgmt.
Fessler, Donald R. Facilitating Community Change: A Basic Guide. LC 76-12768. 146p. 1976. pap. 11.50 (ISBN 0-88390-121-8). Univ Assocs.
Fiedler, F. Theory of Leadership Effectiveness. 1967. text ed. 22.50 (ISBN 0-07-020675-9, C). McGraw.
Fiedler, Fred E. Leader Attitudes & Group Effectiveness. LC 81-1151. (Illus.). 69p. 1981. Repr. of 1958 ed. lib. bdg. 21.75x (ISBN 0-313-22967-8, FILA). Greenwood.
Fiedler, Fred E., et al. Improving Leadership Effectiveness: The Leader Match Concept. LC 76-20632. (Self-Teaching Guides). 1976. pap. text ed. 8.95 (ISBN 0-471-25811-3). Wiley.
Fiore, M. V. & Strauss, P. S. How to Develop Dynamic Leadership: A Short Course for Professionals. (Wiley Professional Development Programs). 1977. 24.95 (ISBN 0-471-02314-0). Wiley.
Flores, Ernest Y. The Mini-Guide to Leadership. LC 80-83627. 90p. 1981. perfect bdg. 5.50 (ISBN 0-86548-037-0). Century Twenty One.
--The Nature of Leadership for Hispanics & Other Minorities. LC 80-69239. 140p. 1981. perfect bdg. 10.95 (ISBN 0-86548-036-2). Century Twenty One.
--Teaching Your Child to Lead: A Parents Guide. LC 81-51217. (Illus.). 60p. 1981. perfect bound 4.95 (ISBN 0-88247-592-4). R & E Res Assocs.
Fort, J. V. & Anderson, George B. Dynamic Sales Leadership. 1974. 65.50 (ISBN 0-85013-054-9). Dartnell Corp.
Francis, Michael J. The Limits of Hegemony: United States Relations with Argentina & Chile During World War II. LC 77-89754. (International Studies Ser). 1977. text ed. 15.95x (ISBN 0-268-01260-1). U of Notre Dame Pr.
Gardner, Jane. Leadership & the Cult of Personality. LC 74-80346. (The Ancient World: Source Books: Vol. 2). 1974. 8.00 (ISBN 0-88866-549-0); pap. 3.95 (ISBN 0-88866-550-4). Samuel Stevens.
Glass, Sheldon. Life Control: How to Assert Leadership in Any Situation. LC 75-44292. 252p. 1976. 7.95 (ISBN 0-87131-205-0). M Evans.
Goble, Frank. Excellence in Leadership. LC 72-79880. (Illus.). 1978. pap. 5.95 (ISBN 0-916054-84-5). Caroline Hse.
Gordon, Thomas. Leader Effectiveness Training. 1980. pap. 6.95 (ISBN 0-553-01318-1). Bantam.
--Leadership Effectiveness Training (L.E.T.) The No-Lose Way to Release the Productive Potential of People. LC 77-14004. (Illus.). 1978. 10.95 (ISBN 0-671-22960-5, Dist. by Har-Row). Wyden.
Gouldner, Alvin W., ed. Studies in Leadership: Leadership & Democratic Action. LC 64-66395. (Illus.). 1965. Repr. of 1950 ed. 20.00 (ISBN 0-8462-0560-2). Russell.
Graubard, Stephen R. & Holton, Gerald, eds. Excellence & Leadership in a Democracy. LC 62-20743. 222p. 1962. text ed. 20.00x (ISBN 0-231-02567-X). Columbia U Pr.
Greenauer, Felix. The Major Forces Which Dominate the World & the Destinies of Mankind. (Illus.). 1978. deluxe bdg. 49.85 (ISBN 0-930008-02-2). Inst Econ Pol.
Greenleaf, Robert K. Servant Leadership: A Journey into the Nature of Legitimate Power & Greatness. LC 76-45678. 352p. 1977. 12.95 (ISBN 0-8091-0220-X). Paulist Pr.
Guide to Money, Power, & Politics. 1981. 8.00 (ISBN 0-686-31341-0). Common Cause.
Hagen, Elizabeth & Wolff, Luverne. Nursing Leadership Behavior in General Hospitals. LC 61-18762. 1961. pap. text ed. 4.75x (ISBN 0-8077-1482-8). Tchrs Coll.
Hart, Lois B. Moving up: Women & Leadership. (Illus.). 1980. 13.95 (ISBN 0-8144-5570-0). Am Mgmt.
Heatherly, Charles L., ed. Mandate for Leadership. 1981. pap. 12.95 (ISBN 0-686-29633-8). Caroline Hse.
Heller, Melvin. Preparing Educational Leaders: New Challenges & New Perspectives. LC 73-90398. (Fastback Ser: No. 36). 1974. pap. 0.75 (ISBN 0-87367-036-1). Phi Delta Kappa.
Heller, Trudy. Women & Men As Leaders: Contemporary Images. 168p. 1981. 23.95 (ISBN 0-03-058948-7). Praeger.
--Women & Men As Leaders: Contemporary Images. 200p. 1981. 22.95x (ISBN 0-686-76472-2). J F Bergin.
Hermann, Margaret G. & Milburn, Thomas W., eds. A Psychological Examination of Political Leaders. LC 75-32366. 1977. 19.95 (ISBN 0-02-914590-2). Free Pr.
Hersey, Paul & Stinson, John E., eds. Perspectives in Leader Effectiveness. LC 79-14646. (Illus.). vii, 175p. 1980. 11.95x (ISBN 0-8214-0411-3). Ohio U Pr.
Hodges, Melvin, tr. Desarrollo Del Varon De Dios. (Spanish Bks.). (Span.). 1978. 0.80 (ISBN 0-8297-0528-7). Life Pubs Intl.
Hollander, Edwin P. Leadership Dynamics: A Practical Guide to Effective Relationships. LC 77-15884. 1978. 15.95 (ISBN 0-02-914820-0). Free Pr.
Horne, Herman H. Essentials of Leadership & Other Papers in Moral & Religious Education. LC 76-117808. (Essay Index Reprint Ser). 1931. 12.00 (ISBN 0-8369-1660-3). Arno.
Horsfield, John. The Art of Leadership in War: The Royal Navy from the Age of Nelson to the End of World War II. LC 79-54059. (Contributions in Military History: No. 21). (Illus.). xiv, 240p. 1980. lib. bdg. 25.00 (ISBN 0-313-20919-7, HLE/). Greenwood.
Hunt, James G. & Larson, Lars L. Leadership Frontiers. LC 75-17489. 1976. 12.50x (ISBN 0-87338-181-5, Pub. by Comp. Adm. Research Inst.). Kent St U Pr.
Hunt, James G. & Larson, Lars L., eds. Crosscurrents in Leadership. LC 79-13576. (Southern Illinois Leadership Symposium Ser.). 316p. 1979. 18.95x (ISBN 0-8093-0932-7). S Ill U Pr.
Hunt, James G., et al, eds. Leadership: Beyond Establishment Views. 288p. 1981. price not set (ISBN 0-8093-1026-0). S Ill U Pr.
Hyde, Douglas. Dedication & Leadership. 1966. pap. 3.45 (ISBN 0-268-00073-5). U of Notre Dame Pr.
Isaak, Robert A. Individuals & World Politics. 1975. pap. 7.95 (ISBN 0-87872-094-4). Duxbury Pr.

Janowitz, Morris. Professional Soldier: A Social & Political Portrait. LC 60-7090. 1960. 12.95 (ISBN 0-02-916170-3); pap. 8.95 (ISBN 0-02-916180-0). Free Pr.

Jennings, Eugene E. An Anatomy of Leadership: Princes, Heroes & Supermen. 1972. pap. 3.95 (ISBN 0-07-032449-2, SP). McGraw.

Jentz, Barry C. & Wofford, Joan W. Leadership & Learning: Personal Change in a Professional Setting. 1979. text ed. 10.95 (ISBN 0-07-032497-2, P&RB). McGraw.

Johnson, David W. & Johnson, Frank P. Joining Together: Group Theory & Group Skills. LC 74-23698. (Illus.). 480p. 1975. pap. 13.95 (ISBN 0-13-510370-3). P-H.

Kasschau, Patricia L. Aging & Social Policy: Leadership Planning. LC 78-15481. 1978. 29.95 (ISBN 0-03-046411-0). Praeger.

Kauss, Theodore. Leaders Live with Crises. LC 73-90396. (Fastback Ser.: No. 34). (Illus., Orig.). 1974. pap. 0.75 (ISBN 0-87367-034-5). Phi Delta Kappa.

Kemp, C. Gratton. Perspectives on the Group Process: A Foundation for Counseling with Groups. 2nd ed. LC 64-346. 1970. text ed. 18.50 (ISBN 0-395-04723-4, 3-29410). HM.

King, Bert, et al, eds. Managerial Control & Organizational Democracy. LC 77-13200. (Scripta Ser. in Personality & Social Psychology). 1978. 22.95 (ISBN 0-470-99323-5). Halsted Pr.

Klapp, Orrin E. Symbolic Leaders: Public Dramas & Public Men. LC 64-23369. 1964. 24.00x (ISBN 0-202-30024-2); pap. text ed. 2.95 (ISBN 0-8290-0688-5). Irvington.

Kracke, Waud H. Force & Persuasion: Leadership in an Amazonian Society. LC 78-3179. 1979. lib. bdg. 21.00x (ISBN 0-226-45210-7). U of Chicago Pr.

Kuzmits, Frank E. Leadership in a Dynamic Society. (Key Issues Lecture Ser.). 1979. 9.95 (ISBN 0-672-97329-4); pap. 4.95 (ISBN 0-672-97330-8). Bobbs.

Laird, Donald & Laird, Eleanor. The New Psychology for Leadership, Based on Researches in Group Dynamics & Human Relations. LC 75-26763. (Illus.). 226p. 1975. Repr. of 1956 ed. lib. bdg. 14.25x (ISBN 0-8371-8370-7, LANP). Greenwood.

Lassey, William R. & Fernandez, Richard R., eds. Leadership & Social Change. 2nd, rev. & enl. ed. LC 75-41687. 368p. 1976. pap. 13.50 (ISBN 0-88390-114-5). Univ Assocs.

Lawson, John D., et al. Leadership Is Everybody's Business: A Practical Guide for Volunteer Membership Groups. LC 76-26303. (Illus.). 1976. 8.95 (ISBN 0-915166-26-7); pap. 5.95 (ISBN 0-915166-25-9). Impact Pubs Cal.

Leadership: A Process-Not a Position. 93p. 1977. pap. 4.00 (ISBN 0-686-63690-2, A501-00070). NEA.

Lilienthal, David E. Management: A Humanist Art. LC 67-20667. (Benjamin Fairless Memorial Lectures Ser.). 67p. 1967. 9.00x (ISBN 0-231-03064-9). Columbia U Pr.

Lindgren, Henry C. Authority & Leadership. Date not set. price not set (ISBN 0-89874-251-X). Krieger.

Liu, Shao. Study of Human Abilities. 1937. pap. 12.00 (ISBN 0-527-02685-9). Kraus Repr.

Loye, David. The Leadership Passion: A Psychology of Ideology. LC 76-45481. (Social & Behavioral Science Ser.). (Illus.). 1977. 16.95x (ISBN 0-87589-302-3). Jossey-Bass.

McCall, Morgan W., Jr. Leadership: Where Else Can We Go? Lombardo, Michael M., ed. LC 77-85524. 1978. 12.75 (ISBN 0-8223-0397-3). Duke.

MacDonald, Lois, et al. Leadership Dynamics & the Trade-Union Leader. LC 60-6045. 156p. 1959. 7.95x (ISBN 0-8147-0272-4). NYU Pr.

McFarland, Andrew S. Power & Leadership in Pluralist Systems. LC 68-26781. 1969. 12.50x (ISBN 0-8047-0677-8). Stanford U Pr.

McKenna, Eugene F. The Management Style of the Chief Accountant: A Situational Perspective. 1978. 24.95 (ISBN 0-566-00216-7, 02176-8, Pub. by Saxon Hse England). Lexington Bks.

MacMunn, George F. Leadership Through the Ages. facs. ed. LC 68-16951. (Essay Index Reprint Ser). 1935. 17.00 (ISBN 0-8369-0657-8). Arno.

McWilliams, Wilson C. & Bathorey, Dennis. Leadership in America: The Inner Frontier & National Community. (Special Studies). 1977. pap. 2.00 (ISBN 0-87641-216-9). Coun Rel & Intl.

Madsen, Paul O. The Person Who Chairs the Meeting. (Illus.). 96p. (Orig.). 1973. tanalin 2.95 (ISBN 0-8170-0582-X). Judson.

Maier, Norman R. Problem-Solving Discussions & Conferences: Leadership Methods & Skills. 1963. text ed. 15.95 (ISBN 0-07-039715-5, C). McGraw.

Martin, George E. Ethnic Political Leadership: The Case of Puerto Ricans. LC 77-75490. 1977. 12.00 (ISBN 0-88247-461-8). R & E Res Assoc.

Marvell, Charles. In Defense of Nixon: A Study in Political Psychology & Political Pathology. LC 76-25960. 1977. 39.65 (ISBN 0-913314-74-9). Am Classical Coll Pr.

Maude, Barry. Leadership in Management. 240p. 1978. text ed. 29.50x (ISBN 0-220-66361-0, Pub. by Busn Bks England). Renouf.

Mwaipaya, Paul A. The Importance of Quality Leadership in National Development, with Special Reference to Africa. 1980. 4.95 (ISBN 0-533-04409-X). Vantage.

National Association of Women Deans, Administrators & Counselors. A Program for Optimizing Women's Leadership Skills (Owls) 1977. pap. 7.00 (ISBN 0-686-23290-9). Natl Assn Women.

Nelson, C. A. Developing Responsible Public Leaders. LC 62-20880. 1963. 10.00 (ISBN 0-379-00116-0). Oceana.

O'Connell, Brian. Effective Leadership in Voluntary Organizations. 1976. 8.95 (ISBN 0-8096-1906-7, Assn Pr). New Century.

Office of Military Leadership, United States Military Academy Associates, ed. A Study of Organizational Leadership. LC 76-25242. 600p. 1976. pap. 12.95 (ISBN 0-8117-2059-4). Stackpole.

Paige, Glenn D. The Scientific Study of Political Leadership. LC 76-50464. (Illus.). 1977. 19.95 (ISBN 0-02-923630-4). Free Pr.

Partridge, Ernest D. Leadership Among Adolescent Boys. LC 74-177144. (Columbia University. Teachers College. Contributions to Education: No. 608). Repr. of 1934 ed. 17.50 (ISBN 0-404-55608-6). AMS Pr.

Phillips, Gerald M., et al. Group Discussion: A Practical Guide to Participation & Leadership. LC 78-56441. (Illus.). 1978. text ed. 13.95 (ISBN 0-395-25415-9); inst. manual 0.65 (ISBN 0-395-25416-7). HM.

Prior, Peter J. Leadership Is Not a Bowler Hat. (Illus.). 1977. 7.50 (ISBN 0-7153-7487-7). David & Charles.

Robinson, Russell D. An Introduction to Dynamics of Group Leadership. 1979. pap. 5.95 (ISBN 0-9600154-7-7). Bible Study Pr.

Rustow, Dankwart A., ed. Philosophers & Kings: Studies in Leadership. LC 77-7778. (Daedalus Library Ser). 1970. pap. 3.75 (ISBN 0-8076-0539-5). Braziller.

Sarthory, Joseph A., ed. Educational Leadership, Renewal & Planning. 158p. 1974. pap. text ed. 9.95x (ISBN 0-8422-0398-2). Irvington.

Sayles, Leonard R. Leadership, What Effective Managers Really Do & How They Do It: Effective Behavioral Skills. (Management Ser.). (Illus.). 1979. text ed. 12.95 (ISBN 0-07-055012-3, C); pap. text ed. 7.95 (ISBN 0-07-055011-5). McGraw.

Scannell, E. E. Communications for Leadership. 1970. 7.95 (ISBN 0-07-055037-9, G); tchr's manual 3.00 (ISBN 0-07-055038-7). McGraw.

Schaller, Lyle E. The Change Agent: The Strategy of Innovative Leadership. LC 77-185544. 208p. (Orig.). 1972. pap. 3.95 (ISBN 0-687-06042-7). Abingdon.

Schiffer, Irvine. Charisma: A Psychoanalytic Look at Mass Society. LC 72-95816. 1973. pap. 5.00 (ISBN 0-8020-6221-0). U of Toronto Pr.

Schul, Bill D. How to Be an Effective Group Leader. LC 74-31420. 208p. 1975. 14.95x (ISBN 0-911012-61-3); pap. 8.95 (ISBN 0-88229-497-0). Nelson-Hall.

Schutz, Will. Leaders of Schools: FIRO Theory Applied to Administrators. LC 76-41489. 216p. 1977. pap. 12.50 (ISBN 0-88390-053-X). Univ Assocs.

Scott, Ellis L. Leadership & Perceptions of Organizations. (Illus.). 1956. pap. 2.00x (ISBN 0-87776-082-9, R82). Ohio St U Admin Sci.

Selznick, Philip. Leadership in Administration: A Sociological Interpretation. 1957. text ed. 11.95 scp (ISBN 0-06-045900-X, HarpC). Har-Row.

Shryock, John K., tr. Study of Human Abilities: The Jen Wu Chin of Li Shao. 1966. Repr. of 1937 ed. 10.00 (ISBN 0-8188-0080-1). Paragon.

Sinha, Jai B. The Nurturant Task Leader: A Model of the Effective Executive. 1980. text ed. 11.25x (ISBN 0-391-01823-X). Humanities.

Solomon, Ben & Bowers, Ethel M. You Can Be a Leader. LC 81-80515. 160p. (Orig.). 1981. pap. 5.90 (ISBN 0-936626-03-8). Leadership Pr.

Stewart, Robert. Leadership for Agricultural Industry. Amberson, Max L., ed. (Career Preparation for Agricultural-Agribusiness). (Illus.). (gr. 9-10). 1978. pap. text ed. 5.32 (ISBN 0-07-000847-7, G); activity guide 3.00 (ISBN 0-07-000848-5); tchrs. manual & key 2.75 (ISBN 0-07-000849-3); transparency masters 5.80 (ISBN 0-07-000850-7); box 72.00 set (ISBN 0-07-079315-8). McGraw.

Stogdill, Ralph M. Handbook of Leadership: A Survey of Theory & Research. LC 73-6494. (Illus.). 1974. 25.00 (ISBN 0-02-931660-X). Free Pr.

Stogdill, Ralph M. & Shartle, Carroll L. Methods in the Study of Administrative Leadership. (Illus.). 1955. pap. 2.00x (ISBN 0-87776-080-2, R80). Ohio St U Admin Sci.

Stogdill, Ralph M. & Coons, Alvin E., eds. Leader Behavior: Its Description & Measurement. 1957. pap. 4.00x (ISBN 0-87776-088-8, R88). Ohio St U Admin Sci.

Stogdill, Ralph M., et al. Leadership & Role Expectations. (Illus.). 1956. pap. 2.00x (ISBN 0-87776-086-1, R86). Ohio St U Admin Sci.

Tannenbaum, R., et al. Leadership & Organization: A Behavioral Science Approach. (Management Ser.). 1961. text ed. 15.95 (ISBN 0-07-062845-9, C). McGraw.

Teitler, G. The Genesis of the Professional Officers' Corps. LC 77-23307. (Sage Series on Armed Forces & Society: Vol. 11). 246p. 1977. 20.00 (ISBN 0-8039-0841-5). Sage.

Tralle, Henry F. Psychology of Leadership. 234p. 1981. Repr. of 1925 ed. lib. bdg. 30.00 (ISBN 0-89760-887-9). Telegraph Bks.

Tramel, Mary E. & Reynolds, Helen. Executive Leadership: How to Get It - & Make It Work. (Illus.). 272p. 1981. 13.95 (ISBN 0-13-294132-5, Spec); pap. 6.95 (ISBN 0-686-69280-2). P-H.

Tucker, Robert C. Politics As Leadership. LC 81-1982. (The Paul Anthony Brick Lectures, Eleventh Ser.). 192p. 1981. text ed. 15.00x (ISBN 0-8262-0341-8). U of Mo Pr.

Turner, Nathan W. Effective Leadership in Small Groups. LC 77-8411. 1977. pap. 2.95 (ISBN 0-8170-0737-7). Judson.

Uris, Auren. Techniques of Leadership. 1957. pap. 4.95 (ISBN 0-07-066104-9, SP). McGraw.

Verba, Sidney. Small Groups & Political Behavior: A Study of Leadership. (Center of International Studies Ser.). 1961. 17.50 (ISBN 0-691-09333-4). Princeton U Pr.

Weber, Clarence A. Leadership in Personnel Management in Public Schools. LC 74-96994. 274p. 1970. 12.50 (ISBN 0-87527-084-0). Fireside Bks.

Wicks, Robert J. & Josephs, Ernest H., Jr. Practical Psychology of Leadership for Criminal Justice Officers: A Basic Programmed Text. 128p. 1973. pap. 8.75 (ISBN 0-398-02783-8). C C Thomas.

Wilson, Bryan. The Noble Savages: An Essay on Charisma-the Rehabilitation of a Concept. LC 74-81444. (Quantum Bk Ser.). 1975. 14.95x (ISBN 0-520-02815-5). U of Cal Pr.

Woods, Frances J. Mexican Ethnic Leadership in San Antonio, Texas. Cortes, Carlos E., ed. LC 76-1623. (Chicano Heritage Ser.). 1976. Repr. of 1949 ed. 10.00x (ISBN 0-405-09533-3). Arno.

Young, Sandy. Developing a Student Leadership Class. 1977. pap. text ed. 3.00 (ISBN 0-88210-084-X). Natl Assn Principals.

Yukl, Gary. Leadership in Organizations. (Illus.). 336p. 1981. text ed. 18.95 (ISBN 0-13-527176-2). P-H.

LEADVILLE, COLORADO–HISTORY

Blair, Edward. Leadville: Colorado's Magic City. (Illus.). 1980. 27.95 (ISBN 0-87108-544-5). Pruett.

LEAFLETS

see Pamphlets

LEAGUE FOR INDUSTRIAL RIGHTS

Merrit, Walter. History for the League for Industrial Rights. LC 76-120852. (Civil Liberties in Americana History Ser.). 1970. Repr. of 1925 ed. lib. bdg. 17.50 (ISBN 0-306-71961-4). Da Capo.

LEAGUE OF ARAB STATES

Hassouna, Hussein. The League of Arab States & Regional Disputes: A Study of Middle East Conflicts. LC 75-33041. 530p. 1975. text ed. 30.00 (ISBN 0-379-00291-4). Oceana.

Macdonald, Robert W. League of Arab States: A Study in the Dynamics of Regional Organization. 1965. 22.50x (ISBN 0-691-03034-0); pap. 8.95 (ISBN 0-691-00003-4). Princeton U Pr.

Rappard, William E. International Relations As Viewed from Geneva. LC 72-4290. (World Affairs Ser.: National & International Viewpoints). 238p. 1972. Repr. of 1925 ed. 15.00 (ISBN 0-405-04582-4). Arno.

LEAGUE OF NATIONS

see also European War, 1914-1918–Peace

Aufricht, Hans. Guide to League of Nations Publications. LC 73-161711. Repr. of 1951 ed. 32.50 (ISBN 0-404-00418-0). AMS Pr.

Baer, George W. Test Case: Italy, Ethiopia & the League of Nations. new ed. LC 76-20293. (Publications Ser.: No. 159). 384p. 1977. 15.95 (ISBN 0-8179-6591-2). Hoover Inst Pr.

Barros, James. Betrayal from Within: Joseph Avenol, Secretary-General of the League of Nations, 1933-1940. LC 75-81413. 1969. 23.00x (ISBN 0-300-01112-1). Yale U Pr.

--Corfu Incident of Nineteen Twenty-Three: Mussolini & the League of Nations. 1965. 23.00 (ISBN 0-691-05113-5). Princeton U Pr.

Bhuinya, Niranjan. International Organizations. 159p. 1970. 10.00x (ISBN 0-8002-1576-1). Intl Pubns Serv.

Birchfield, Mary E. Consolidated Catalog of League of Nations Publications Offered for Sale. LC 75-17970. 400p. 1976. 55.00x (ISBN 0-379-00328-7). Oceana.

Birn, Donald S. The League of Nations Unions, Nineteen Eighteen to Nineteen Forty-Five. 336p. 1981. 55.00 (ISBN 0-19-822650-0). Oxford U Pr.

Brailsford, Henry N. A League of Nations. 1917. 10.00 (ISBN 0-8482-7393-1). Norwood Edns.

Carnegie Endowment for International Peace. A Repertoire of League of Nations Documents, 1919-1947, 2 vols. Ghebali, Victor-Yves, ed. LC 73-7839. 650p. 1973. lib. bdg. 85.00 (ISBN 0-379-00371-6). Oceana.

Carr, Edward H. International Relations Between the Two World Wars: 1919-1939. (Illus.). 1947. 15.95 (ISBN 0-312-42315-2). St Martin.

Childs, James B., ed. Government Document Bibliography in the United States & Elsewhere. 3rd ed. 1942. 8.00 (ISBN 0-384-08785-X). Johnson Repr.

Davies, Kathryn. The Soviets at Geneva: The USSR & the League of Nations, 1919-1939. LC 75-39051. (Russian Studies: Perspectives on the Revolution Ser). 315p. 1977. Repr. of 1934 ed. 25.00 (ISBN 0-88355-430-5). Hyperion Conn.

Davis, Harriet E., ed. Pioneers in World Order. facs. ed. LC 70-128232. (Essay Index Reprint Ser). 1944. 17.00 (ISBN 0-8369-1913-0). Arno.

De Azcarate, P. League of Nations & National Minorities: An Experiment. (Studies in the Administration of International Law & Organization). Repr. of 1945 ed. pap. 14.00 (ISBN 0-527-00883-4). Kraus Repr.

De Madariaga, Salvador. Americans. facs. ed. LC 68-29229. (Essay Index Reprint Ser). 1968. Repr. of 1930 ed. 11.75 (ISBN 0-8369-0661-6). Arno.

Dexter, Byron. The Years of Opportunity: The League of Nations, 1920-1926. 1967. 8.50 (ISBN 0-670-79376-0). Viking Pr.

Egerton, George W. Great Britain & the Creation of the League of Nations: Strategy, Politics, & International Organization, 1914-1919. LC 77-17897. (Supplementary Volume to The Papers of Woodrow Wilson). 1978. 19.00x (ISBN 0-8078-1320-6). U of NC Pr.

Fleming, Denna F. United States & World Organization, 1920-1933. LC 70-168040. Repr. of 1938 ed. 41.50 (ISBN 0-404-02435-1). AMS Pr.

Fosdick, Raymond B. Letters on the League of Nations. (The Papers of Woodrow Wilson). 1966. 14.00x (ISBN 0-691-04523-2). Princeton U Pr.

Geneva Institute Of International Relations. Problems of Peace, Fifth Series. facs. ed. LC 71-121470. (Essay Index Reprint Ser). 1930. 19.00 (ISBN 0-8369-1808-8). Arno.

--Problems of Peace, First Ser. LC 73-105015. (Essay Index Reprint Ser). 1927. 22.00 (ISBN 0-8369-1468-6). Arno.

--Problems of Peace: Lectures. Eighth Series. facs. ed. LC 68-22914. (Essay Index Reprint Ser). 1968. Repr. of 1934 ed. 16.00 (ISBN 0-8369-0470-2). Arno.

--Problems of Peace: Lectures. Second Series. facs. ed. LC 70-76899. (Essay Index Reprint Ser). 1928. 17.00 (ISBN 0-8369-0014-6). Arno.

--Problems of Peace: Lectures. Third Series. facs. ed. LC 68-57317. (Essay Index Reprint Ser). 1929. 16.00 (ISBN 0-8369-0115-0). Arno.

--Problems of Peace, Thirteenth Ser. facs. ed. LC 68-57317. (Essay Index Reprint Ser). 1939. 16.00 (ISBN 0-8369-0042-1). Arno.

Graduate Institute Of International Studies - Geneva. World Crisis by the Professors of the Institute. facs. ed. LC 73-86753. (Essay Index Reprint Ser). 1938. 17.00 (ISBN 0-8369-1133-4). Arno.

Greaves, Harold R. The League Committees & World Order. LC 76-29430. Repr. of 1931 ed. 23.00 (ISBN 0-404-15336-4). AMS Pr.

Hardie, Frank. The Abyssinian Crisis. 320p. 1974. 18.50 (ISBN 0-208-01435-7, Archon). Shoe String.

Harris, H. Wilson. The League of Nations. 1929. 12.50 (ISBN 0-686-17734-7). Quest Edns.

Hill, M. The Economic & Financial Organization of the League of Nations: A Survey of Twenty-Five Years' Experience. (Studies in the Administration of International Law & Organization). 1947. Repr. of 1946 ed. pap. 14.00 (ISBN 0-527-00884-2). Kraus Repr.

Hindmarsh, Albert E. Force in Peace: Force Short of War in International Relations. LC 72-89264. 264p. 1973. Repr. of 1933 ed. 15.00 (ISBN 0-8046-1757-0). Kennikat.

House, Edward M. Intimate Papers of Colonel House, 4 vols. Seymour, Charles, ed. LC 71-145093. (Illus.). 1971. Repr. of 1928 ed. Set. 89.00 (ISBN 0-403-01031-4). Scholarly.

Jacobs, David. An American Conscience: Woodrow Wilson's Search for World Peace. LC 71-135770. (Illus.). (gr. 5-9). 8.95 (ISBN 0-06-022794-X, HarpJ). Har-Row.

Jones, Samuel S. Scandinavian States & the League of Nations. Repr. of 1939 ed. lib. bdg. 15.25x (ISBN 0-8371-0974-4, JOSS). Greenwood.

Joyce, James A. Broken Star: The Story of the League of Nations 1919-39. 1978. text ed. 12.50x (ISBN 0-7154-0419-9). Humanities.

Kimmich, Christoph M. Germany & the League of Nations. LC 75-36400. 1976. lib. bdg. 17.50x (ISBN 0-226-43534-2). U of Chicago Pr.

Lansing, Robert. Peace Negotiations. LC 71-86033. 1969. Repr. of 1921 ed. 14.00 (ISBN 0-8046-0621-8). Kennikat.

--Peace Negotiations: A Personal Narrative. LC 74-110852. (Illus.). 1971. Repr. of 1921 ed. lib. bdg. 14.50x (ISBN 0-8371-4519-8, LAPN). Greenwood.

League of Nations Documents, 1919-1946: A Descriptive Guide & Key to the Microfilm Collection, New Haven, 1973-1975, 3 vols. LC 73-3061. 500.00 (ISBN 0-89235-008-3). Res Pubns Conn.

Macartney, Carlile A. National States & National Minorities. 2nd ed. LC 68-15136. (With a new intro. & epilogue). 1968. Repr. of 1934 ed. 18.50 (ISBN 0-8462-1266-8). Russell.

Madariaga, Salvador De. Disarmament. LC 66-25928. 1967. Repr. of 1929 ed. 13.50 (ISBN 0-8046-0287-5). Kennikat.

Marks, Sally. The Illusion of Peace: International Relations 1918-1933. LC 76-11281. (The Making of the Twentieth Century Ser.). (Illus.). 1976. 16.95x (ISBN 0-312-40600-2); pap. text ed. 6.95x (ISBN 0-312-40635-5). St Martin.

Marvin, Francis S., ed. Evolution of World-Peace: Essays. Unity Ser. 4. facs. ed. LC 68-20318. (Essay Index Reprint Ser). 1921. 12.25 (ISBN 0-8369-0682-9). Arno.

--Western Races & the World. Unity Ser. 5. facs. ed. LC 68-22929. (Essay Index Reprint Ser). 1968. Repr. of 1922 ed. 15.00 (ISBN 0-8369-0684-5). Arno.

Matsushita, Masatoshi. Japan in the League of Nations. LC 68-58606. (Columbia University. Studies in the Social Sciences: No. 314). Repr. of 1929 ed. 16.50 (ISBN 0-404-51314-X). AMS Pr.

Miller, David H. Drafting of the Covenant, 2 Vols. 1969. Repr. of 1928 ed. Set. 69.50 (ISBN 0-384-38920-1). Johnson Repr.

Ostrower, Gary B. Collective Insecurity: The United States and the League of Nations During the Early Thirties. LC 76-754. 287p. 1979. 19.50 (ISBN 0-8387-1799-3). Bucknell U Pr.

Riches, Cromwell A. Unanimity Role & the League of Nations. LC 70-174318. Repr. of 1933 ed. 15.00 (ISBN 0-404-05330-0). AMS Pr.

Rosenne, Shabtai, ed. League of Nations Committee of Experts for the Progressive Codification of International Law. LC 77-165998. 1972. Set. lib. bdg. 75.00 (ISBN 0-379-00147-0). Oceana.

Schiffer, Walter. The Legal Community of Mankind. LC 74-152603. 367p. 1972. Repr. of 1954 ed. lib. bdg. 21.00x (ISBN 0-8371-6038-3, SCLC). Greenwood.

Schwartzenberger, Georg & Keeton, George W. Making International Law Work. LC 70-147758. (Library of War & Peace; International Law). lib. bdg. 38.00 (ISBN 0-8240-0491-4). Garland Pub.

Schwarzenberger, Georg. The League of Nations & World Order: A Treatise on the Principal of Universality in the Theory & Practice of the League of Nations. LC 79-1642. 1980. Repr. of 1936 ed. 18.50 (ISBN 0-88355-945-5). Hyperion Conn.

Short, Frederick W. The Man Behind the League of Nations. 1979. pap. 2.50 (ISBN 0-532-25102-4). Woodhill.

Shotwell, James T. On the Rim of the Abyss. LC 73-147590. (Library of War & Peace; Int'l. Organization, Arbitration & Law). lib. bdg. 38.00 (ISBN 0-8240-0351-9). Garland Pub.

Shotwell, James T. & Salvin, Marina. Lessons on Security & Disarmament from the History of the League of Nations. LC 74-15557. 149p. 1974. Repr. of 1949 ed. lib. bdg. 15.00 (ISBN 0-8371-7824-X, SHSD). Greenwood.

Slocombe, George E. Mirror to Geneva. LC 70-121506. (Essay Index Reprint Ser). 1938. 19.50 (ISBN 0-8369-1852-5). Arno.

Smith, Sara R. Manchurian Crisis Nineteen Thirty One to Nineteen Thirty Two: A Tragedy in International Relations. Repr. of 1948 ed. lib. bdg. 14.50x (ISBN 0-8371-3344-0, SMMC). Greenwood.

Stone, Ralph. The Irreconcilables: The Fight Against the League of Nations. 224p. 1973. pap. 2.75x (ISBN 0-393-00671-9). Norton.

Stone, Ralph A., ed. Wilson & the League of Nations: Why America's Rejection? LC 78-8323. 128p. 1978. Repr. of 1967 ed. lib. bdg. 5.50 (ISBN 0-88275-679-6). Krieger.

Taft, William H. Taft Papers on the League of Nations. Marburg, T. & Flack, H., eds. Repr. of 1920 ed. 15.00 (ISBN 0-527-88618-1). Kraus Repr.

Williams, Bruce S. State Security & the League of Nations. LC 75-177845. Repr. of 1927 ed. 26.00 (ISBN 0-404-06959-2). AMS Pr.

Willoughby, Westel W. Sino-Japanese Controversy & the League of Nations. LC 68-54995. (Illus.). 1968. Repr. of 1935 ed. lib. bdg. 26.25x (ISBN 0-8371-0755-5, WISJ). Greenwood.

Wilson, Woodrow. Case for the League of Nations. Foley, H., ed. LC 67-27666. 1967. Repr. of 1923 ed. 10.50 (ISBN 0-8046-0506-8). Kennikat.

--Woodrow Wilson's Case for the League of Nations. Foley, Hamilton, ed. LC 23-17370. (Illus.). 1969. Repr. of 1923 ed. 12.00 (ISBN 0-527-97180-4). Kraus Repr.

Woolf, Leonard, ed. Intelligent Man's Way to Prevent War. LC 70-148372. (Library of War & Peace; the Character & Causes of War). lib. bdg. 38.00 (ISBN 0-8240-0464-7). Garland Pub.

Wright, Quincy. Mandates Under the League of Nations. LC 68-57649. (Illus.). 1968. Repr. of 1930 ed. lib. bdg. 27.75x (ISBN 0-8371-0765-2, WRLN). Greenwood.

Zimmern, Alfred E. League of Nations & the Rule of Law, 1918-1935. 2nd ed. LC 69-17852. 1969. Repr. of 1939 ed. 16.00 (ISBN 0-8462-1330-3). Russell.

--Prospects of Democracy & Other Essays. facs. ed. LC 68-8506. (Essay Index Reprint Ser). 1929. 17.00 (ISBN 0-8369-1017-6). Arno.

LEAGUE OF NATIONS–MANDATORY SYSTEM

see Mandates

LEAGUE TO ENFORCE PEACE

Taft, William H. World Peace: A Written Debate Between William Howard Taft & William Jennings Bryan. LC 73-137553. (Peace Movement in America Ser). 156p. 1972. Repr. of 1917 ed. lib. bdg. 9.95x (ISBN 0-89198-083-0). Ozer.

LEAKEY, LOUIS SEYMOUR BAZETT, 1903-

Cole, Sonia. Leakey's Luck: The Life of Louis Seymour Bazett Leakey. 448p. 1975. 15.95 (ISBN 0-15-149456-8). HarBraceJ.

Leakey, L. S. By the Evidence: Memoirs, Nineteen Thirty-Two to Nineteen Fifty-One: Memoirs, 1932-1951. LC 76-14846. (Illus.). 1976. pap. 3.95 (ISBN 0-15-615000-X, Harv). HarBraceJ.

Malatesta, Anne & Friedland, Ronald. The White Kikuyu. LC 77-78765. (gr. 6 up). 1978. PLB 7.95 (ISBN 0-07-039750-3, GB). McGraw.

LEAN, DAVID, 1908-

Castelli, Louis & Cleeland, Caryn L. David Lean: A Guide to References & Resources. 1980. lib. bdg. 18.50 (ISBN 0-8161-7933-6). G K Hall.

LEAR, EDWARD, 1812-1888

Hofer, Philip. Edward Lear As a Landscape Draughtsman. LC 67-22865. (Illus.). 1967. 10.00x (ISBN 0-674-23950-4, Belknap Pr). Harvard U Pr.

Hyman, Susan. Edward Lear's Birds. LC 80-80860. (Illus.). 96p. 1980. 37.95 (ISBN 0-688-03671-6). Morrow.

Lear, Edward. Letters of Edward Lear, 2 vols. 1976. lib. bdg. 200.00 (ISBN 0-8490-2151-0). Gordon Pr.

Lehmann, John. Edward Lear & His World. LC 77-73133. (Encore Edition). (Illus.). 1977. 3.95 (ISBN 0-684-16548-1, ScribT). Scribner.

LEARNED INSTITUTIONS AND SOCIETIES

see also Societies

A. A. U. P. Ohio Conference. History - 1949-1974. LC 74-620076. 1974. 3.50 (ISBN 0-88215-038-3). Ohio St U Lib.

Alembert, Jean Le Rond. Histoire De L'academie De Berlin, Excerpts. Repr. of 1746 ed. 52.00 (ISBN 0-8287-0011-7). Clearwater Pub.

Anderson, I. G., ed. Directory of European Associations: National Industrial Trade & Professional Associations, Pt. 1. 2nd ed. 557p. 1976. 125.00 (ISBN 0-686-74474-8). Gale.

--Directory of European Associations: National Learned, Scientific & Technical Societies, Pt. 2. 2nd ed. 349p. 1979. 130.00 (ISBN 0-686-74475-6). Gale.

Australian Academy of the Humanities, 1971. Proceedings. 72p. 1971. 10.00x (ISBN 0-424-06330-1, Pub. by Sydney U Pr). Intl Schol Bk Serv.

Boland, Bill, ed. Annals Index, Vol. 289. (Annals of the New York Academy of Sciences). 581p. 1977. 45.00x (ISBN 0-89072-035-5). NY Acad Sci.

Brown, Harcourt. Scientific Organizations in Seventeenth Century France, 1620-1680. LC 66-27046. 1967. Repr. of 1934 ed. 8.50 (ISBN 0-8462-0974-8). Russell.

Carnegie Commission on Higher Education. American Learned Societies in Transition: The Impact of Dissent & Disruption. Boland, H. & Boland, S., eds. 1974. 8.95 (ISBN 0-07-010107-8, P&RB). McGraw.

Cochrane, Eric W. Tradition & Enlightenment in the Tuscan Academies, 1690-1800. LC 60-14232. 1962. 16.00x (ISBN 0-226-11145-8). U of Chicago Pr.

Crump, Ian A. Australian Scientific Societies & Professional Associations. 2nd ed. 1979. pap. 10.00x (ISBN 0-643-00282-0, Pub. by CSIRO). Intl Schol Bk Serv.

Graves, Algernon. British Institution: Contribution & Works 1806-1969. 28.00 (ISBN 0-87556-110-1). Saifer.

Groeg, Otto J., ed. Who's Who in Literature: Edition Austria-Germany-Switzerland, 2 vols. (Who's Who Ser.). 1978. Set. 123.00x (ISBN 3-921220-20-3). Standing Orders.

Hill, Charles C. Royal Canadian Academy, Eighteen Hundred to Nineteen Thirteen. (Illus.). 225p. 1980. write for info. (ISBN 0-88884-429-8, 56496-7, Pub. by Natl Mus Canada). U of Chicago Pr.

Hole, James. Essay on the History & Management of Literary, Scientific & Mechanics' Institutes. 186p. 1970. Repr. of 1853 ed. 24.00x (ISBN 0-7146-2410-1, F Cass Co). Biblio Dist.

Hope, A. D. Literary Influence Academies. 12p. 1970. 2.00x (ISBN 0-424-06150-3, Pub. by Sydney U Pr). Intl Schol Bk Serv.

Hume, Abraham. Learned Societies & Printing Clubs of the United Kingdom. LC 66-16418. 1966. Repr. of 1853 ed. 22.00 (ISBN 0-8103-3081-4). Gale.

Kiger, Joseph C. American Learned Societies. 1963. 10.00 (ISBN 0-8183-0150-3). Pub Aff Pr.

Office Of The Foreign Secretary. Eastern European Academies of Sciences: A Directory. 1963. pap. 3.50 (ISBN 0-309-01090-X). Natl Acad Pr.

Oleson, Alexandra & Brown, Sanborn C., eds. The Pursuit of Knowledge in the Early American Republic: American Scientific & Learned Societies from Colonial Times to the Civil War. LC 75-36941. (Illus.). 398p. 1976. 22.50x (ISBN 0-8018-1679-3). Johns Hopkins.

Osterweis, Rollin G. Sesquicentennial History of the Connecticut Academy of Arts & Sciences. (Connecticut Academy of Arts & Sciences Transaction: Vol. 38). 1949. pap. 7.50 (ISBN 0-208-01095-5). Shoe String.

Reuss, Jeremias D. Repertorium Commentationuma Societatibus Litterariis Editarum Secundum Disciplinarum Ordinem, 16 vols. 1962. 550.00 (ISBN 0-8337-2966-7). B Franklin.

Silverman, Hirsch L., ed. Annals of the Jewish Academy of Arts & Sciences. 213p. 1974. pap. text ed. 12.50x (ISBN 0-8422-0406-7). Irvington.

Societe Philomatique De Paris: 1791-1804, Vols. 1-11. 324.00 (ISBN 0-8287-0782-0). Clearwater Pub.

Steeves, Harrison R. Learned Societies & English Literary Scholarship in Great Britain & the United States. LC 70-112943. 1970. Repr. of 1913 ed. 8.00 (ISBN 0-404-06238-5). AMS Pr.

Thomas, R. Hinton. Liberalism, Nationalism & the German Intellectuals, 1822-1847. LC 75-11803. 148p. 1975. Repr. of 1951 ed. lib. bdg. 15.00x (ISBN 0-8371-8140-2, THLI). Greenwood.

Vlangas, Alex W. & Williams, Richard J. Learning Centers & Individualized Reading in Behavioral Terms. (Illus.). 1973. pap. text ed. 6.95x (ISBN 0-8422-0292-7). Irvington.

Voss, John & Ward, Paul L., eds. Confrontation & Learned Societies. LC 78-133026. 1970. 6.95x (ISBN 0-8147-8750-9). NYU Pr.

Walden, John W. Universities of Ancient Greece. facsimile ed. LC 70-109635. (Select Bibliographies Reprint Ser). 1909. 22.00 (ISBN 0-8369-5244-8). Arno.

World Guide to Scientific Associations & Learned Societies. 2nd ed. LC 74-3676. 1978. 62.50 (ISBN 3-7940-1213-5, Pub. by Verlag Dokumentation). Bowker.

Young, Robert F. Comenius in England: The Visit of Jan Amos Komensky Comenius, Czech Philosopher & Educationalist, to London in 1641-1642. LC 70-135838. (Eastern Europe Collection Ser). 1970. Repr. of 1932 ed. 8.00 (ISBN 0-405-02780-X). Arno.

Zils, Michael, ed. World Guide to Scientific Associations & Learned Societies. 3rd ed. (Handbook of International Documentation & Information Ser.: Vol. 13). 400p. 1981. 145.00 (ISBN 3-598-20517-1, Dist. by Gale Research). K G Saur.

LEARNING, ART OF

see Study, Method of

LEARNING, PSYCHOLOGY OF

see also Comprehension; Conditioned Response; Learning Ability; Learning Disabilities; Learning by Discovery; Maze Tests; Paired-Association Learning; Perceptual-Motor Learning; Praise; Programmed Instruction; Sleep Learning; Transfer of Training; Verbal Learning

Ackerman, J. Mark. Operant Conditioning Techniques for the Classroom Teacher. 143p. 1972. pap. 5.95x (ISBN 0-673-07664-4). Scott F.

Ameican Psychological Association. Social Influences on Behavior: Teachers Handbook. (Human Behavior Curriculum Project Ser.). 48p. (Orig.). (gr. 9-12). 1981. pap. 9.95 (ISBN 0-8077-2620-6). Tchrs Coll.

American Psychological Association. Conditioning & Learning: Student Booklet. (Human Behavior Curriculum Project Ser.). 64p. (gr. 9-12). 1981. pap. text ed. 3.95x (ISBN 0-8077-2623-0). Tchrs Coll.

--Conditioning & Learning: Teachers Handbook & Duplication Masters. (Human Behavior Curriculum Project Ser.). 48p. (gr. 9-12). 1981. 9.95x (ISBN 0-8077-2624-9). Tchrs Coll.

--Social Influences on Behavior: Student Booklet. (Human Behavior Curriculum Project Ser.). 64p. (Orig.). (gr. 9-12). 1981. pap. text ed. 3.95x (ISBN 0-8077-2619-2). Tchrs Coll.

Ashlock, Robert B. Error Patterns in Computation. 2nd ed. (Elementary Education Ser.). 128p. 1976. pap. text ed. 9.95x (ISBN 0-675-08654-X). Merrill.

Bandura, A. Social Learning Theory. 1977. text ed. 15.95 (ISBN 0-13-816751-6); pap. text ed. 9.95 (ISBN 0-13-816744-3). P-H.

Bandura, Albert, ed. Psychological Modeling: Conflicting Theories. (Controversy Ser). 1971. 9.95x (ISBN 0-88311-403-8); pap. 3.95 (ISBN 0-88311-404-6). Lieber-Atherton.

Belton, Sandra & Terbough, Christine. Sparks: Activities to Help Children Learn at Home. LC 74-11878. 120p. pap. text ed. 9.95 (ISBN 0-87705-710-9). Human Sci Pr.

Benne, Kenneth D., et al, eds. Laboratory Method of Changing & Learning: Theory & Application. LC 74-32598. 1975. 15.95 (ISBN 0-685-59371-1). Sci & Behavior.

Bergen, C. M. Some Sources of Childrens Science Information: An Investigation of Sources of Information & Attitudes Toward Such Sources As Used or Expressed by Children. LC 71-176689. (Columbia University. Teachers College. Contributions to Education: No. 881). Repr. of 1943 ed. 17.50 (ISBN 0-404-55881-X). AMS Pr.

Berman, Louise M. & Roderick, Jessie A., eds. Feeling, Valuing & the Art of Growing: Insights into the Affective. LC 76-54454. (ASCD Yearbook, 1977). 1977. 9.75 (ISBN 0-87120-082-1, 610-77104). Assn Supervision.

Berman, Mark L., ed. Motivation & Learning: Applying Contingency Management Techniques. LC 70-160894. 222p. 1972. pap. 10.95 (ISBN 0-87778-023-4). Educ Tech Pubns.

Bigge, Morris L. Learning Theories for Teachers. 3rd ed. 386p. 1976. pap. text ed. 12.50 scp (ISBN 0-06-040672-0, HarpC). Har-Row.

Biggs, J. B. Information & Human Learning. Lyman, John, adapted by. 152p. 1971. pap. 4.95x (ISBN 0-673-07555-9). Scott F.

Bilodeau, Edward A., ed. Acquisition of Skill. 1966. 42.50 (ISBN 0-12-099150-0). Acad Pr.

Block, J. H. Mastery Learning: Theory & Practice. LC 70-147025. 1971. pap. text ed. 6.95 (ISBN 0-03-086073-3, HoltC). HR&W.

--Mastery Learning: Theory & Practice. LC 70-147025. 1971. pap. text ed. 6.95 (ISBN 0-03-086073-3, HoltC). HR&W.

Bode, Boyd H. Conflicting Psychologies of Learning. 1978. Repr. of 1929 ed. lib. bdg. 20.00 (ISBN 0-89760-036-3, Telegraph). Dynamic Learn Corp.

--How We Learn. LC 77-138204. 308p. 1972. Repr. of 1940 ed. lib. bdg. 20.00x (ISBN 0-8371-5562-2, BOWL). Greenwood.

Bolles, Robert. Learning Theory. 2nd ed. LC 78-2768. 1979. text ed. 16.95 (ISBN 0-03-019306-0, HoltC). HR&W.

Borger, R. & Seaborne, A. Psychology of Learning. 1981. pap. 4.95 (ISBN 0-14-080443-9). Penguin.

Bower, Gordon, ed. The Psychology of Learning & Motivation: Advances in Research & Motivation, Vol. 13. LC 66-30104. (Serial Publication). 1979. 43.50 (ISBN 0-12-543313-1). Acad Pr.

Bower, Gordon & Lang, Albert R., eds. The Psychology of Learning & Motivation, Vol. 15. (Serial Publication). 1981. price not set (ISBN 0-12-543315-8). Acad Pr.

Bower, Gordon H. & Hilgard, Ernest J. Theories of Learning. 5th ed. (Illus.). 640p. 1981. text ed. 22.95 (ISBN 0-13-914432-3). P-H.

Brandon, William. Manual of Concealed Image Response Techniques. 1978. 5.95 (ISBN 0-915474-02-6). Effective Learn.

Bransford, John D. Human Cognition: Learning, Understanding & Remembering. 1979. pap. text ed. 12.95x (ISBN 0-534-00699-X). Wadsworth Pub.

Brearley, Molly, ed. The Teaching of Young Children: Some Applications of Piaget's Learning Theory. LC 70-98939. (Illus.). 1978. pap. 5.50 (ISBN 0-8052-0597-7). Schocken.

Breslin, Frederick. The Adolescent & Learning. 1978. pap. text ed. 9.95 (ISBN 0-686-62265-0). Collegium Bk Pubs.
Bridgeman, Bruce, et al, eds. Readings on Fundamental Issues on Learning & Memory. 1977. pap. text ed. 12.50x (ISBN 0-685-81867-5). Whitehall Co.
Briere, Eugene J. Psycholinguistic Study of Phonological Interference. LC 68-13339. (Janua Linguarum, Ser. Minor: No. 66). 1968. pap. text ed. 15.00x (ISBN 90-2790-594-0). Mouton.
Bruner, Jerome S. On Knowing: Essays for the Left Hand. expanded ed. LC 62-13264. (Paperback Ser.: No. 143). (Illus.). 1979. 10.00x (ISBN 0-674-63475-6, Belknap Pr); pap. 3.95 (ISBN 0-674-63525-6, Belknap Pr). Harvard U Pr.
--Toward a Theory of Instruction. LC 66-13179. (Illus.). 1966. 8.95x (ISBN 0-674-89700-5, Belknap Pr); pap. 4.50 (ISBN 0-674-89701-3). Harvard U Pr.
Brush, F. Robert, ed. Aversive Conditioning & Learning. LC 70-127680. 1971. 57.00 (ISBN 0-12-137950-7). Acad Pr.
Bugelski, B. R. The Psychology of Learning Applied to Teaching. 2nd ed. LC 79-149402. (Illus.). 1971. text ed. 13.95 (ISBN 0-672-60785-9). Bobbs.
--Some Practical Laws of Learning. LC 77-84042. (Fastback Ser.: No. 96). 1977. pap. 0.75 (ISBN 0-87367-096-5). Phi Delta Kappa.
Bugelski, B. R., ed. Empirical Studies in the Psychology of Learning. LC 74-22867. (Illus.). 1975. lib. bdg. 17.50x (ISBN 0-915144-01-8); pap. text ed. 4.95x (ISBN 0-915144-02-6). Hackett Pub.
Burkowsky, Mitchell R. An Orientation to Learning & Language Disorders in Children. LC 75-176182. 304p. 1973. 16.50 (ISBN 0-87527-098-0). Green.
Bush, Robert R. & Estes, William K., eds. Studies in Mathematical Learning Theory. 1959. 20.00x (ISBN 0-8047-0563-1). Stanford U Pr.
Butler, Frank A. Improvement of Teaching in Secondary Schools. 3rd ed. LC 54-10718. 1954. 15.00x (ISBN 0-226-08513-9). U of Chicago Pr.
Cantor, Nathaniel. Dynamics of Learning. LC 71-166546. 1950. 10.00x (ISBN 0-87586-026-5). Agathon.
Carlson, Robert A. Conceptual Learning: From Mollusks to Adult Education. LC 73-72. (Ocassional Paper Ser.: No. 35). 1973. pap. 2.00 (ISBN 0-87060-058-3). Syracuse U Cont Ed.
Catania, A. Charles. Learning. (Century Psychology Ser.). (Illus.). 1979. text ed. 18.95 (ISBN 0-13-527432-X). P-H.
Cattell, Raymond B. Personality & Learning Theory: A Systems Theory of Maturation & Structures Learning, Vol. 2. LC 79-594. 1980. text ed. 44.50 (ISBN 0-8261-2124-1). Springer Pub.
Champion, R. A. Learning & Activiation. LC 70-75658. (Basic Topics in Psychology Ser). 1969. pap. 7.50 (ISBN 0-471-14395-2, Pub. by Wiley-Interscience). Wiley.
Chappel, Bernice M. Listening & Learning: Practical Activities for Developing Listening Skills. (gr. k-3). 1973. pap. 6.50 (ISBN 0-8224-4306-6). Pitman Learning.
Chicorel, Marietta. Chicorel Abstracts to Reading & Learning Disabilities, 1976 Annual. annual ed. (Chicorel Index Ser.). 1000p. 1976. text ed. 85.00 ca. (ISBN 0-934598-15-0); Vol. 19. text ed. (ISBN 0-934598-15-0). Am Lib Pub Co.
Chicorel, Marietta, ed. Chicorel Index to Learning Disorders: Books, Vols. 18 & 18A. LC 75-9713. (Index Ser.). 1000p. 1975. Set. 170.00 (ISBN 0-934598-32-0). Am Lib Pub Co.
Christ, F. & Adams, R. You Can Learn to Learn. 750.00 (ISBN 0-13-976704-5). P-H.
Clifford, Margaret M. & Grandgenett, Myrna. Activities & Readings in Learning & Development. LC 80-84892. (Illus.). 256p. 1981. pap. text ed. 7.95 (ISBN 0-395-29924-1). HM.
Conference on Learning, Remembering & Forgetting, 3rd. Proceedings: Readiness to Remember, 2 pts. Kimble, D. P., ed. Incl. Vol. 1. 354p. 63.25x (ISBN 0-677-14420-2); Vol. 2. 310p. 63.25x (ISBN 0-677-14430-X). 762p. 1969. Set. 111.75x (ISBN 0-677-13420-7). Gordon.
Craig, Robert C. Psychology of Learning in the Classroom. (Orig.). 1966. pap. text ed. 3.25x (ISBN 0-02-325450-5, 32545). Macmillan.
Crow, Lester D. & Crow, Alice. Human Development & Learning. 2nd ed. LC 74-26685. 590p. 1975. Repr. of 1965 ed. 21.50 (ISBN 0-88275-252-9). Krieger.
Dahlgren, Lars O. Qualitative Differences in Learning As a Function of Content-Oriented Guidance. (Goteburg Studies in Educational Sciences Ser.: No. 15). 172p. 1975. pap. text ed. 8.25x (ISBN 91-7346-013-3). Humanities.
Davis, Robert A. Psychology of Learning. (Educational Ser.). 1935. Repr. 20.00 (ISBN 0-685-43011-1). Norwood Edns.
Davis, Robert H., et al. Learning System Design. (Illus.). 320p. 1974. text ed. 16.95 (ISBN 0-07-074334-7, C). McGraw.
Dembo, Myron H. Teaching for Learning: Applying Educational Psychology in the Classroom. LC 76-29390. (Illus.). 1977. pap. text ed. 13.50 (ISBN 0-87620-885-5); test items free (ISBN 0-87620-886-3). Goodyear.
Deutsch, Martin, et al. Disadvantaged Child: Studies of the Social Environment & the Learning Process. LC 67-28504. 1968. 15.00x (ISBN 0-465-01644-8). Basic.
Donahoe, John W. & Wessells, Michael G. Learning, Language, & Memory. (Illus.). 1979. text ed. 19.50 scp (ISBN 0-06-041685-8, HarpC); instructor's manual avail. (ISBN 0-06-361699-8). Har-Row.
Drumheller, Sidney J. Teacher's Handbook for a Functional Behavior-Based Curriculum: Communicable Models & Guides for Classroom Use. LC 72-933. 138p. 1972. pap. 9.95 (ISBN 0-87778-036-6). Educ Tech Pubns.
Dunham, Philip J. Experimental Psychology: Theory & Practice. LC 77-5688. (Harper's Experimental Psychology Ser.). (Illus.). 1977. text ed. 20.50 scp (ISBN 0-06-041805-2, HarpC); tchrs' manual avail. (ISBN 0-06-361783-8). Har-Row.
Dunlap, Knight. Habits: Their Making & Unmaking. LC 77-184102. 336p. 1949. pap. 3.95 (ISBN 0-87140-072-3). Liveright.
Edson, Lee. How We Learn. (Human Behavior Ser). 176p. 1975. 9.95 (ISBN 0-8094-1916-5); lib. bdg. avail. (ISBN 0-685-52491-4). Time-Life.
Ellis, Henry C. Fundamentals of Human Learning, Memory & Cognition. 2nd ed. (Fundamentals of Psychology Ser.). 240p. 1978. pap. text ed. write for info. (ISBN 0-697-06623-1); tchrs.' manual avail. (ISBN 0-686-67920-2). Wm C Brown.
Ellis, Henry C., et al. Psychology of Learning & Memory. LC 78-16292. (Illus.). 1979. text ed. 18.95 (ISBN 0-8185-0267-3). Brooks-Cole.
Epstein, Bertram. Immediate & Retention Effects of Interpolated Rest Periods on Learning Performance. LC 70-176754. (Columbia University. Teachers College. Contributions to Education: No. 949). Repr. of 1949 ed. 17.50 (ISBN 0-404-55949-2). AMS Pr.
Estes, W. K., ed. Handbook of Learning & Cognitive Processes, 6 vols. Incl. Vol. 1. Introduction to Concepts & Issues. LC 75-20113. 303p. 1975; Vol. 2. Conditioning & Behavior Therapy. LC 75-20113. 350p. 1975. 18.50 (ISBN 0-470-24586-7); Vol. 3. Approaches to Human Learning & Motivation. LC 76-15010. 1976. 18.50 (ISBN 0-470-15121-8); Vol. 4. Attention & Memory. LC 76-26002. 1976; Vol. 5. Human Information Processing. LC 78-3847. 1978. 26.50 (ISBN 0-470-26310-5); Vol. 6. Linguistic Functions in Cognitive Theory. 1978. 18.00 (ISBN 0-470-26311-3). Halsted Pr.
Estes, William K. Learning Theory & Mental Development. 1970. 28.00 (ISBN 0-12-243550-8). Acad Pr.
Faas, Larry A. Learning Disabilities: A Competency Based Approach. LC 75-31010. (Illus.). 512p. 1976. pap. text ed. 15.25 (ISBN 0-395-20586-7); inst. resource guide 1.25 (ISBN 0-395-20585-9). HM.
Faust, Verne. Self Esteem in the Classroom. LC 79-65212. 1980. 13.95 (ISBN 0-934162-02-6). Thomas Paine Pr.
Felker, Donald W. Building Positive Self-Concepts. LC 74-76647. 1974. pap. text ed. 8.95x (ISBN 0-8087-0620-9). Burgess.
Fink, Harold K. Mind & Performance: A Comparative Study of Learning in Mammals, Birds, & Reptiles. LC 70-138229. (Illus.). 113p. 1972. Repr. of 1954 ed. lib. bdg. 15.00x (ISBN 0-8371-5586-X, FIMI). Greenwood.
Fishbein, Harold. Evolution, Development & Children's Learning. Siegal, Alex, ed. LC 75-13478. (Goodyear Development Psychology Ser.). 320p. 1976. text ed. 14.95 (ISBN 0-87620-282-2). Goodyear.
Friedman, Morton P., et al, eds. Intelligence & Learning. (NATO Conference Series III-Human Factors: Vol. 14). 605p. 1981. 42.50 (ISBN 0-306-40643-8, Plenum Pr). Plenum Pub.
Frymier, Jack. Motivation & Learning in School. LC 74-83881. (Fastback Ser.: No. 43). (Orig.). 1974. pap. 0.75 (ISBN 0-87367-043-4). Phi Delta Kappa.
Gagne, Robert M. The Conditions of Learning. 3rd ed. LC 76-45797. (Illus.). 1977. text ed. 18.95 (ISBN 0-03-089965-6, HoltC). HR&W.
Gagne, Robert M. & Briggs, Leslie J. Principles of Instructional Design. 2nd ed. LC 78-27628. 1979. text ed. 17.95 (ISBN 0-03-040806-7, HoltC). HR&W.
Gallagher, Jeanette & Reid, D. Kim. The Learning Theory of Piaget & Inhelder. LC 80-24410. (Orig.). 1981. pap. text ed. 9.95 (ISBN 0-8185-0343-2). Brooks-Cole.
Gallahue, David L. Motor Development & Movement Experiences for Young Children. LC 75-37676. 1976. text ed. 20.95 (ISBN 0-471-29042-4). Wiley.
Gallahue, David L., et al. A Conceptual Approach to Moving & Learning. LC 75-2369. 423p. 1975. text ed. 21.95 (ISBN 0-471-29043-2); tchrs' resource bk. avail. (ISBN 0-471-29039-4). Wiley.
Gazda, George M. & Corsini, Raymond J. Theories of Learning: A Comparative Approach. LC 79-91101. 483p. 1980. text ed. 15.95 (ISBN 0-87581-253-8). Peacock Pubs.
Gentry, John R. Immediate Effects of Interpolated Rest Periods on Learning & Performance. LC 78-176803. (Columbia University. Teachers College. Contributions to Education: No. 799). Repr. of 1940 ed. 17.50 (ISBN 0-404-55799-6). AMS Pr.
Gerhard, Muriel. The Behavioral Outcomes Handbook: A Practical Guide for Teachers & Administrators. 1977. 11.95 (ISBN 0-13-074542-1, Parker). P-H.
Gholson, Barry. The Cognitive-Developmental Basis of Human Learning: Studies in Hypothesis Testing. LC 80-307. (Developmental Psychology Ser.). 1980. 19.50 (ISBN 0-12-282350-8). Acad Pr.
Gilbert, R. M. & Sutherland, N. S., eds. Animal Discrimination Learning. 1969. 79.50 (ISBN 0-12-283250-7). Acad Pr.
Glidewell, John C., ed. The Social Context of Learning & Development. LC 76-8867. 239p. 1976. 18.95 (ISBN 0-470-15078-5). Halsted Pr.
Goldstein, A. P. Structured Learning Therapy: Toward a Psychotherapy for the Poor. 1973. 36.00 (ISBN 0-12-288750-6). Acad Pr.
Goss, Albert E. & Nodine, Calvin F. Paired-Associates Learning: The Role of Meaningfulness, Similarity & Familiarization. 1965. 44.50 (ISBN 0-12-292350-2). Acad Pr.
Gray, J. A. Elements of a Two-Process Theory of Learning. 1975. 40.00 (ISBN 0-12-296850-6). Acad Pr.
Greeno, James G., et al. Associative Learning: A Cognitive Analysis. LC 77-17096. (Century Psychology Ser.). (Illus.). 1978. 18.95 (ISBN 0-13-049650-2). P-H.
Gregory, Hugo H., ed. Learning Theory & Stuttering Therapy. LC 68-15332. 1968. 11.95x (ISBN 0-8101-0107-6). Northwestern U Pr.
Griffith, Coleman R. Psychology Applied to Teaching & Learning. 650p. 1981. Repr. of 1939 ed. lib. bdg. 40.00 (ISBN 0-89984-247-X). Century Bookbindery.
Guilford, J. P. Intelligence, Creativity & Their Educational Implications. LC 68-26627. 1968. pap. text ed. 8.95 (ISBN 0-912736-09-7). EDITS Pubs.
Guillaume, Paul. Imitation in Children. Halperin, Elaine P., tr. from Fr. LC 77-135742. xviii, 214p. 1973. pap. 2.95 (ISBN 0-226-31046-9, P423, Phoen). U of Chicago Pr.
Guthrie, Edwin. The Psychology of Learning. rev. ed. 1952. 8.00 (ISBN 0-8446-1213-8). Peter Smith.
Hallahan, D. & Kauffman, J. Introduction to Learning Disabilities: The Psycho-Behavioral Approach. 1976. 18.95 (ISBN 0-13-485524-8). P-H.
Hanzen, Judith F. Sociocultural Perspectives on Human Learning: An Introduction to Educational Anthropology. 1979. pap. 10.95 (ISBN 0-13-821041-1). P-H.
Harcum, E. Rae. Serial Learning & Paralearning. 464p. 1975. 16.50 (ISBN 0-471-35137-7, Pub. by Wiley). Krieger.
Harrell, Ruth F. Effect of Added Thiamine on Learning. LC 70-176841. (Columbia University. Teachers College. Contributions to Education: No. 877). Repr. of 1943 ed. 17.50 (ISBN 0-404-55877-1). AMS Pr.
--Further Effects of Added Thiamin on Learning & Other Processes. LC 73-176842. (Columbia University. Teachers College. Contributions to Education: No. 928). Repr. of 1947 ed. 17.50 (ISBN 0-404-55928-X). AMS Pr.
Henry, George H. Teaching Reading As Concept Development: Emphasis on Affective Thinking. LC 73-85480. 120p. 1974. pap. 5.00 (ISBN 0-87207-852-3). Intl Reading.
Hergenhahn, B. R. An Introduction to Theories of Learning. 2nd ed. 512p. 1982. 18.95 (ISBN 0-686-76576-1). P-H.
--An Introduction to Theories of Learning. (Illus.). 352p. 1976. 19.95 (ISBN 0-13-498733-0). P-H.
Hilgard, Ernest R., ed. Theories of Learning & Instruction. LC 64-3324. (National Society for the Study of Education Yearbooks Ser: No. 63, Pt. 1). 1964. lib. bdg. 6.00x (ISBN 0-226-60073-4); pap. 4.50x (ISBN 0-226-60074-2). U of Chicago Pr.
Hill, W. F. Learning: A Survey of Psychological Interpretations. 3rd ed. 1977. pap. text ed. 10.50 scp (ISBN 0-690-00881-3, HarpC). Har-Row.
Hills, Phillip J. Teaching & Learning As a Communication Process. LC 79-1060. 1979. 21.95 (ISBN 0-470-26700-3). Halsted Pr.
Hintzman, Douglas L. The Psychology of Learning & Memory. LC 77-16295. (Psychology Ser.). (Illus.). 1978. text ed. 19.95x (ISBN 0-7167-0035-2). W H Freeman.
Holt, John. How Children Learn. 1970. pap. text ed. 1.95 (ISBN 0-440-33871-9). Dell.
Horton, David L. & Turnage, Thomas W. Human Learning. (P-H Series in Experimental Psychology). (Illus.). 464p. 1976. Ref. Ed. 20.95 (ISBN 0-13-445312-3). P-H.
Houston, John P. Fundamentals of Learning. 1976. text ed. 16.95 (ISBN 0-12-356850-1); instrs' manual 3.00 (ISBN 0-12-356852-8). Acad Pr.
--Fundamentals of Learning & Memory. 2nd ed. 500p. 1981. 18.95 (ISBN 0-12-356840-4). Acad Pr.
How We Learn. (Human Behavior Ser.). 1975. pap. 4.95 (ISBN 0-316-84656-2). Little.
Howe, Michael. Learning in Infants & Young Children. LC 75-44902. 1976. 10.00x (ISBN 0-8047-0913-0); pap. 4.95 (ISBN 0-8047-0973-4, SP145). Stanford U Pr.
Howe, Michael J. The Psychology of Human Learning. (Illus.). 1980. text ed. 20.95 scp (ISBN 0-06-042938-0, HarpC). Har-Row.
--Understanding School Learning: A New Look at Educational Psychology. 1972. pap. text ed. 10.50 scp (ISBN 0-06-042924-0, HarpC). Har-Row.
Howe, Michael J. A. Adult Learning: Psychological Research & Applications. LC 76-44226. 256p. 1977. 39.50 (ISBN 0-471-99458-8, Pub. by Wiley-Interscience). Wiley.
Hull, Clark L., et al. Mathematico-Deductive Theory of Rote Learning: A Study in Scientific Methodology. Repr. of 1940 ed. lib. bdg. 17.75x (ISBN 0-8371-3126-X, HURL). Greenwood.
Ibuka, Masaru. Kindergarten Is Too Late! 1980. 4.95 (ISBN 0-686-62839-X, 25363, Fireside). S&S.
Jackins, Harvey. Nature of the Learning Process. 1966. pap. 0.50 (ISBN 0-911214-14-3). Rational Isl.
James, D. G. The Dream of Learning. LC 76-29035. 1951. Repr. lib. bdg. 25.00 (ISBN 0-8414-5328-4). Folcroft.
Johnson, G. Orville & Blake, Kathryn A. Learning Performance of Retarded & Normal Children. LC 77-22852. (Syracuse University Special Education & Rehabilitation Monograph Ser.: No. 5). (Illus.). 1977. Repr. of 1960 ed. lib. bdg. 21.00x (ISBN 0-8371-9725-2, JOLE). Greenwood.
Jonas, Gerald. Visceral Learning. 1974. pap. 1.25 (ISBN 0-671-78398-X). PB.
Kausler, Donald H. Psychology of Verbal Learning & Memory. 1974. 20.95 (ISBN 0-12-402650-8). Acad Pr.
Keller, Fred S. Learning: Reinforcement Theory. 2nd ed. (Psychology Studies). 1969. pap. text ed. 4.50x (ISBN 0-394-30898-0, RanC). Random.
Kevles, Bettyann. Thinking Gorillas: Testing & Teaching the Greatest Ape. LC 79-12782. (gr. 7 up). 1980. 10.95 (ISBN 0-525-41074-0). Dutton.
Kimble, Daniel P., ed. Anatomy of Memory: Proceedings. LC 64-8098. (Orig.). 1965. pap. 4.35x (ISBN 0-8314-0004-8). Sci & Behavior.
Kimble, Gregory A., ed. Foundations of Conditioning & Learning. LC 67-10442. (Century Psychology Ser.). (Illus.). 1967. 38.50x (ISBN 0-89197-172-6); pap. text ed. 18.50x o. p. (ISBN 0-89197-762-7). Irvington.
--Hilgard & Marquis' Conditioning & Learning. 2nd ed. 1961. 24.95 (ISBN 0-13-388876-2). P-H.
Kirby, John R. & Biggs, J. B., eds. Cognition, Development & Instruction. LC 80-523. (Educational Psychology Ser.). 1980. 19.00 (ISBN 0-12-409550-X). Acad Pr.
Klahr, David, ed. Cognition & Instruction. LC 75-42102. (Carnegie Mellon U. Cognition Ser.). 361p. 1976. 19.95 (ISBN 0-470-15226-5). Halsted Pr.
Klausmeier, Herbert J. Learning & Teaching Concepts: A Strategy for Testing Applications Theory. Sipple, Thomas S., ed. LC 80-758. (Educational Psychology Ser.). 1980. 22.50 (ISBN 0-12-411450-4). Acad Pr.
Koffka, Kurt. Growth of the Mind. LC 80-50103. (Social Science Classics Ser.). 383p. 1980. text ed. 19.95 (ISBN 0-87855-360-6); pap. text ed. 7.95 (ISBN 0-87855-784-9). Transaction Bks.
Kolesnik, Walter B. Learning: Educational Applications. 240p. 1976. pap. text ed. 11.95 (ISBN 0-205-05443-9). Allyn.
Lapp, Diane, et al. Teaching & Learning: Philosophical, Psychological, Curricular Applications. (Illus.). 320p. 1975. text ed. 13.50 (ISBN 0-685-51924-4). Macmillan.

Lawrence, Douglas H. & Festinger, Leon. Deterrents & Reinforcement: The Psychology of Insufficient Reward. 1962. 10.00x (ISBN 0-8047-0117-2). Stanford U Pr.

Lefrancois, Guy R. Human Learning. 2nd ed. (Psychology Ser.). 483p. 1982. text ed. 17.95 (ISBN 0-8185-0501-X). Brooks-Cole.

--Psychological Theories & Human Learning: Kongor's Report. LC 76-164998. (Core Bks. in Psychology Ser.). 384p. 1971. text ed. 15.95 (ISBN 0-8185-0014-X); test items avail. (ISBN 0-685-23472-X). Brooks-Cole.

Lembo, John M. When Learning Happens. LC 70-185317. 1972. 6.95x (ISBN 0-8052-3444-6). Schocken.

Lesgold, A. M., et al, eds. Cognitive Psychology & Instruction. LC 77-27133. (NATO Conference Ser., Series III: Human Factors, Vol. 5). 539p. 1978. 27.50 (ISBN 0-306-32886-0, Plenum Pr). Plenum Pub.

Levin, Joel R. Learner Differences: Diagnosis & Prescription. LC 76-46364. 1977. pap. text ed. 5.95 (ISBN 0-03-015296-8, HoltC). HR&W.

Levine, Martin. A Cognitive Theory of Learning: Research on Hypotheses Testing. (Experimental Psychology Ser.). 1975. text ed. 16.50 (ISBN 0-470-53126-6). Halsted Pr.

Levine, Marvin. A Cognitive Theory of Learning: Research on Hypothesis Testing. LC 75-5561. 313p. 1975. 16.50 (ISBN 0-470-53126-6, Pub. by Wiley). Krieger.

Ling, Bing-Chung. Form Discrimination As a Learning Cue in Infants. LC 41-14185. 1941. pap. 5.00 (ISBN 0-527-24852-5). Kraus Repr.

Lochhead, Jack & Clement, John, eds. Cognitive Process Instruction. LC 78-22122. (Illus.). 1979. pap. 16.00 (ISBN 0-89168-014-4). Franklin Inst Pr.

Logan, Frank A. & Ferraro, Douglas P. Systematic Analyses of Learning & Motivation. LC 78-6870. 1978. text ed. 22.50x (ISBN 0-471-04130-0). Wiley.

Logan, Frank A. & Gordon, William C. Fundamentals of Learning & Motivation. 3rd ed. 239p. 1981. pap. text ed. write for info. (ISBN 0-697-06634-7); instrs. manual avail. (ISBN 0-697-06639-8). Wm C Brown.

Lumsden, D. B. & Sherron, R. H., eds. Experimental Studies in Adult Learning & Memory. LC 74-31210. 1975. 14.95 (ISBN 0-470-55370-7). Halsted Pr.

McConnell, Thomas R. Psychology of Learning. (National Society for the Study of Education Yearbooks Ser: No 41, Pt. 2). 1942. 7.00x (ISBN 0-226-59976-0). U of Chicago Pr.

McFarland, H. S. Psychological Theory & Educational Practice: Human Development, Learning & Assessment. 1971. 20.00x (ISBN 0-7100-7009-8); pap. 8.95 (ISBN 0-7100-7010-1). Routledge & Kegan.

McFarland, Robert & Burton, John. Learning for Loving. 160p. 1969. pap. text ed. 3.95x (ISBN 0-8134-1481-4, 1481). Interstate.

McGaugh, James L. Learning & Memory. (Illus.). pap. 3.95 (ISBN 0-87843-608-1). Albion.

McGuigan, F. J. & Lumsden, D. B., eds. Contemporary Approaches to Conditioning & Learning. LC 73-4663. (Experimental Psychology Ser.). 317p. 1973. 12.95 (ISBN 0-470-58428-9). Halsted Pr.

McIntosh, John R. Learning by Exposure to Wrong Forms in Grammer & Spelling: An Experimental Study of the Effect of Correcting Wrong Forms As a Practice Method. LC 70-177029. (Columbia University. Teachers College. Contributions to Education: No. 892). Repr. of 1944 ed. 17.50 (ISBN 0-404-55892-5). AMS Pr.

McLaughlin, Barry. Learning & Social Behavior. LC 74-143176. 1971. 12.95 (ISBN 0-02-920570-0). Free Pr.

McLeish, John, et al. The Psychology of the Learning Group. 1973. text ed. 9.00x (ISBN 0-09-114010-2, Hutchinson U Lib). Humanities.

McMillan, James H., ed. The Social Psychology of School Learning. LC 79-6797. (Educational Psychology Ser.). 1980. 21.00 (ISBN 0-12-485750-7). Acad Pr.

Maehr, Martin L. & Stallings, William M. Culture, Child & School: Sociocultural Influences on Learning. LC 75-10058. 1975. pap. text ed. 9.95 (ISBN 0-8185-0169-3). Brooks-Cole.

Mager, Robert F. Developing Attitude Toward Learning. LC 68-54250. 1968. pap. 5.50 (ISBN 0-8224-2000-7). Pitman Learning.

Maggio, Elio. Psychophysiology of Learning & Memory. 196p. 1971. photocopy ed. spiral 19.75 (ISBN 0-398-01198-2). C C Thomas.

Magnusson, David, ed. Toward a Psychology of Situations: An International Perspective. 488p. 1981. text ed. 29.95 (ISBN 0-89859-061-2). L Erlbaum Assocs.

Marshall, Wallace. Immunologic Psychology & Psychiatry. LC 75-8713. 240p. 1977. 16.75x (ISBN 0-8173-2703-7). U of Ala Pr.

Marx, Melvin H. Effects of Cumulative Training Upon Retroactive Inhibition & Transfer. (Comparitive Psychology Monographs: No. 94). Repr. of 1944 ed. pap. 5.00 (ISBN 0-527-24929-7). Kraus Repr.

--Learning: Interactions. (Illus.). 1970. text ed. 19.95 (ISBN 0-02-376810-X). Macmillan.

--Learning: Processes. (Illus.). 1969. text ed. 17.50x (ISBN 0-02-376820-7). Macmillan.

Meenes, Max. Studying & Learning. (Orig.). 1954. pap. text ed. 2.25 (ISBN 0-685-19774-3). Phila Bk Co.

Meier, J. H. Developmental & Learning Disabilities: Evaluation, Management & Prevention in Children. (Illus.). 300p. 1976. 16.50 (ISBN 0-8391-0762-5). Univ Park.

Meihofer, Susan S., ed. Student & the Learning Environment. 1974. pap. 4.00 (ISBN 0-8106-0627-5). NEA.

Melton, Arthur W. & Martin, Edwin, eds. Coding Processes in Human Memory. LC 72-5431. 448p. 1972. text ed. 12.95x (ISBN 0-470-59335-0). Halsted Pr.

Mikulas, William L., ed. Psychology of Learning: Readings. LC 77-8234. 1977. text ed. 25.95x (ISBN 0-88229-226-9); pap. 12.95x (ISBN 0-88229-519-5). Nelson-Hall.

Miller, Neal E. & Dollard, John. Social Learning & Imitation. LC 78-23728. (Illus.). 1979. Repr. of 1962 ed. lib. bdg. 21.50x (ISBN 0-313-20714-3, MISL). Greenwood.

Minnesota Symposia on Child Psychology. Incl. Vol. 1; Vol. 2. 7.50x (ISBN 0-8166-0506-8); Vol. 3. 7.50x (ISBN 0-8166-0540-8); Vol. 4. 7.50x (ISBN 0-8166-0568-8); Vol. 5. 7.50x (ISBN 0-8166-0614-5); Vol. 6. 1972. 7.50x (ISBN 0-8166-0641-2); Vol. 7. 1973. 8.75x (ISBN 0-8166-0699-4); Vol. 8. 1975. 9.50x (ISBN 0-8166-0722-2); Vol. 9. LC 76-30520. 1975. 12.50x (ISBN 0-8166-0753-2); Vol. 10. LC 67-30520. 1976. 14.50x (ISBN 0-8166-0791-5). LC 67-30520. (Illus.). Vols. 2-5. Ed. by John P. Hill (ISBN 0-685-73225-8); Vols. 6-10. Ed. by Anne D. Pick (ISBN 0-685-73226-6). U of Minn Pr.

Morris, Joseph. Psychology & Teaching: A Humanistic View. 1978. pap. text ed. 13.95 (ISBN 0-394-31797-1). Random.

Morris T. Keeton & Associates. Experiential Learning: Rationale, Characteristics, & Assessment. LC 75-44884. (Higher Education Ser). (Illus.). 296p. 1976. 15.95x (ISBN 0-87589-277-9). Jossey-Bass.

Morse, William C. & Wingo, G. Max. Psychology & Teaching. 3rd ed. 1969. text ed. 12.95x (ISBN 0-673-05854-9). Scott F.

Moursund, Janet P. Learning & the Learner. LC 76-7717. 1976. pap. text ed. 11.95 (ISBN 0-8185-0197-9). Brooks-Cole.

Mowrer, O. Hobart. Learning Theory & Behavior. LC 59-15671. 576p. 1973. Repr. of 1960 ed. 21.50 (ISBN 0-88275-127-1). Krieger.

--Learning Theory & Personality Dynamics: Selected Papers. 776p. 1950. 22.50 (ISBN 0-471-06920-5, Pub. by Wiley). Krieger.

--Psychology of Language & Learning. (Cognition & Language Ser.). (Illus.). 275p. 1980. 27.50 (ISBN 0-306-40371-4, Plenum Pr). Plenum Pub.

Murphy, Gardner. Freeing Intelligence Through Teaching: A Dialectic of the Rational & the Personal. LC 77-4217. 1977. Repr. of 1961 ed. lib. bdg. 15.00 (ISBN 0-8371-9593-4, MUFI). Greenwood.

Murphy, Lois. Emotional Factors in Learning. Repr. of 1944 ed. lib. bdg. 17.25x (ISBN 0-8371-3429-3, MUEF). Greenwood.

Nakao, H. Brain Stimulation & Learning: Switch-off Behaviour. (Illus.). 1971. pap. 23.80 (ISBN 0-685-39791-2). Adler.

Nash, Roy. Teacher Expectations & Pupil Learning. (Student's Library of Education). 1967. 9.95 (ISBN 0-7100-8338-6). Routledge & Kegan.

National Association of Secondary School Principals. Student Learning Styles: Diagnosing & Prescribing Programs. Koerner, Thomas F., ed. (Orig.). 1979. pap. text ed. 5.00 (ISBN 0-88210-103-X). Natl Assn Principals.

National Education Association & Trow, William C. Learning Process. (What Research Says to the Teacher Ser.). 1963. pap. 1.00 (ISBN 0-8106-1011-6); 4-color filmstrips plus elements of the learning process filmstrip with cassette narration 86.70 (ISBN 0-8106-0626-7). NEA.

Norman, Donald A. Learning & Memory. (Illus.). 1982. text ed. price not set (ISBN 0-7167-1299-7); pap. text ed. price not set (ISBN 0-7167-1300-4). W H Freeman.

O'Connor, Kathleen & Elkind, David. Learning: An Introduction for Students of Education. 1971. pap. 4.95x (ISBN 0-673-07584-2). Scott F.

O'Neil, Harold F., Jr., ed. Learning Strategies. (The Educational Technology Ser.). 1978. 16.00 (ISBN 0-12-526650-2). Acad Pr.

Pai, Young. Teaching, Learning, & the Mind. LC 72-3512. 250p. (Orig.). 1973. pap. text ed. 10.95 (ISBN 0-395-12663-0, 3-42835). HM.

Parente, Frederick J., et al. Ellis, Bennett, Daniel, & Rickert's Psychology of Learning & Memory: Study Guide. (Orig.). 1979. pap. text ed. 5.95 (ISBN 0-8185-0369-6). Brooks-Cole.

Pask, G. Conversation Theory. new ed. 1976. 47.00 (ISBN 0-444-41424-X). Elsevier.

Perkins, Hugh V. Human Development & Learning. 2nd ed. 1974. 19.95x (ISBN 0-534-00345-1). Wadsworth Pub.

Peterson, Lloyd R. Learning. 134p. 1975. pap. 5.95x (ISBN 0-673-05050-5). Scott F.

Piaget, Jean. Construction of Reality in the Child. LC 54-8278. 1954. 13.95x (ISBN 0-465-01407-0). Basic.

--Success & Understanding. LC 78-16435. (Illus.). 1978. 15.00x (ISBN 0-674-85387-3). Harvard U Pr.

Piaget, Jean, et al. Epistemology & Psychology of Functions. Castellanos, Javier & Anderson, Vivian, trs. (Synthese Library: No. 83). 1977. lib. bdg. 45.00 (ISBN 90-277-0804-5, Pub. by Reidel Holland). Kluwer Boston.

Piltch, Benjamin. Eddie in School. (Illus.). (gr. 7-12,RL 2.2). 1967. pap. 3.20 (ISBN 0-8224-2590-4); tchrs' manual free (ISBN 0-8224-2591-2). Pitman Learning.

Pintner, Rudolf, et al. Educational Psychology. 6th ed. (Orig.). 1970. pap. 4.95 (ISBN 0-06-460023-8, CO 23, COS). Har-Row.

Pope, Lillie. Psycho-Educational Battery. 1976. 6.75 (ISBN 0-87594-155-9, 2812). Book-Lab.

Powers, Melvin. Practical Guide to Better Concentration. (Orig.). pap. 2.00 (ISBN 0-87980-120-4). Wilshire.

Race, Henrietta V. Improvability: Its Intercorrelations & Its Relations to Initial Ability. LC 73-177176. (Columbia University. Teachers College. Contributions to Education: No. 124). Repr. of 1922 ed. 17.50 (ISBN 0-404-55124-6). AMS Pr.

Research on Mathematical Thinking of Young Children. LC 75-22461. 1975. pap. 6.00 (ISBN 0-87353-088-8). NCTM.

Restle, Frank. Learning: Animal Behavior & Human Cognition. (Psychology Ser.). (Illus.). 330p. 1975. text ed. 15.95 (ISBN 0-07-051910-2, C). McGraw.

Reynierse, James H., ed. Current Issues in Animal Learning: A Colloquium. LC 78-98389. 1970. 21.50x (ISBN 0-8032-0744-1). U of Nebr Pr.

Riegel, K. F., ed. The Development of Dialectal Operations. (Human Development: Vol. 18, Nos. 1-2). (Illus.). vii, 241p. 1975. 22.75 (ISBN 3-8055-2225-8). S Karger.

Ringness, Thomas A. The Affective Domain in Education. 184p. 1975. pap. text ed. 6.95 (ISBN 0-316-74660-6). Little.

Rivers, Wilga M. The Psychologist & the Foreign Language Teacher. LC 64-15809. 1977. pap. 4.95 (ISBN 0-226-72094-2, P741, Phoen). U of Chicago Pr.

Robeck, Mildred C. Infants & Children. (Illus.). 1978. text ed. 18.95 (ISBN 0-07-053108-0, C); instructor's manual 4.95 (ISBN 0-07-053109-9). McGraw.

Robinson, Russell D. An Intoduction to Helping Adults Learn & Change. 1979. pap. 8.95 (ISBN 0-9600154-9-3). Bible Study Pr.

Rock, Robert T. The Influence Upon Learning of the Quantitative Variation of After-Effects. LC 79-177199. (Columbia University. Teachers College. Contributions to Education: No. 650). Repr. of 1935 ed. 17.50 (ISBN 0-404-55650-7). AMS Pr.

Rogers, Carl. Freedom to Learn: A View of What Education Might Become. LC 72-75629. 1969. text ed. 11.95 o. p. (ISBN 0-675-09519-0); pap. text ed. 6.95x (ISBN 0-675-09579-4). Merrill.

Rosenberg, Marshall B. Diagnostic Teaching. LC 68-57927. (Orig.). 1968. pap. 7.00x (ISBN 0-87562-013-2). Spec Child.

Rouanet, Henry. Les Modeles Stochastiques D'apprentissage: Recherches & Perspectives. (Mathematiques & Sciences De L'homme: No. 4). 1967. pap. 14.00x (ISBN 90-2796-314-2). Mouton.

Royer, James M. & Allan, Richard G. Psychology of Learning: Educational Applications. LC 77-12390. (Self-Teaching Guide Ser.). 1978. pap. text ed. 4.95 (ISBN 0-471-02270-5). Wiley.

Saljo, Roger. Qualitative Differences in Learning As a Function of the Learner's Conception of the Task. (Gotenburg Studies in Educational Sciences: No. 14). 170p. 1976. pap. text ed. 8.25x (ISBN 91-7346-012-5). Humanities.

Salmon, Phillida, ed. Coming to Know. 180p. 1980. pap. 17.50 (ISBN 0-686-65610-5). Routledge & Kegan.

Salomon, Gavriel. Interaction of Media, Cognition, & Learning: An Exploration of How Symbolic Forms Cultivate Mental Skills & Affect Knowledge Acquisition. LC 79-83578. (Social & Behavioral Science Ser.). (Illus.). 1979. text ed. 16.95x (ISBN 0-87589-403-8). Jossey-Bass.

Saltz, Eli. The Cognitive Bases of Human Learning: From Association to Concepts. 525p. 1971. text ed. 18.95x (ISBN 0-256-01180-X). Dorsey.

Scandura, Joseph M. Structural Learning, Vol. 1: Theory & Research. LC 73-76710. 378p. 1973. 41.75 (ISBN 0-677-04720-7). Gordon.

--Structural Learning, Vol. 2: Issues & Approaches. 1976. 39.75x (ISBN 0-677-15110-1). Gordon.

Schoonover, Robert J. Handbook for Parents of Children with Learning Disabilities. LC 76-1754. 1976. pap. text ed. 1.95x (ISBN 0-8134-1795-3, 1795). Interstate.

Schwartz, Barry. Psychology of Learning & Behavior. (Illus.). 1978. 17.95x (ISBN 0-393-09070-1). Norton.

Schwartz, Fred & Schiller, Peter H. Psychoanalytic Model of Attention & Learning. LC 79-105070. (Psychological Issues Monograph: No. 23, Vol. 6, No. 3). (Orig.). 1970. text ed. 11.00 (ISBN 0-8236-4450-2). Intl Univs Pr.

Sieber, J. E., et al. Anxiety, Learning, & Instruction. LC 77-11028. 1977. 16.50 (ISBN 0-470-99299-9). Halsted Pr.

Silberman, Melvin L., et al, eds. The Psychology of Open Teaching & Learning: An Inquiry Approach. 307p. 1972. pap. text ed. 8.95 (ISBN 0-316-79100-8). Little.

Simmons, Vickie & Williams, Irene. Attending: Steps up to Language for the Learning Impaired. 1976. 6.00 (ISBN 0-88450-755-6, 4015-B). Communication Skill.

Slamecka, Norman J., ed. Human Learning & Memory: Selected Readings. (Orig.). 1967. pap. 8.95x (ISBN 0-19-501054-X). Oxford U Pr.

Smith, Frank. Comprehension & Learning: A Conceptual Framework for Teachers. LC 75-2041. 1975. pap. text ed. 11.95 (ISBN 0-03-011011-4, HoltC). HR&W.

Smith, Wendell & Rohrman, N. Human Learning. text ed. 10.95 (ISBN 0-07-058695-0, C); pap. text ed. 6.95 (ISBN 0-07-058694-2). McGraw.

Snelbecker, Glenn E. Learning Theory: Instructional Theory & Psychoeducational Design. (Illus.). 544p. 1974. text ed. 17.50 (ISBN 0-07-059450-3, C). McGraw.

Solan, Harold. Psychology of Reading & Learning Difficulties. pap. 7.95 (ISBN 0-671-18713-9). Monarch Pr.

Spear, Norman E. & Campbell, Byron A., eds. Ontogeny of Learning & Memory. LC 79-19045. 321p. 1979. 19.95x (ISBN 0-470-26849-2). Halsted Pr.

Spence, Kenneth W., et al, eds. The Psychology of Learning & Motivation: Advances in Research & Theory, 14 vols. Incl. Vol. 1. Spence, Kenneth W. & Spence, Janet T., eds. 1967. 43.00 (ISBN 0-12-543301-8); Vol. 2. 1968. 43.00 (ISBN 0-12-543302-6); Vol. 3. Bower, G. H. & Spence, J. T., eds. 1970. 43.00 (ISBN 0-12-543303-4); Vol. 4. Bower, G. H., ed. 1970. 43.00 (ISBN 0-12-543304-2); Vol. 5. 1972. 43.00 (ISBN 0-12-543305-0); Vol. 6. 1972. 43.00 (ISBN 0-12-543306-9); Vol. 7. 1973. 43.00 (ISBN 0-12-543307-7); Vol. 8. 1974. 43.00 (ISBN 0-12-543308-5); Vol. 9. 1975. 43.00 (ISBN 0-12-543309-3); Vol. 10. 1976. 37.50 (ISBN 0-12-543310-7); Vol. 12. Spence, Kenneth W., ed. 1977. 33.50 (ISBN 0-12-543312-3); Vol. 13. 1979. 43.50 (ISBN 0-12-543311-5); Vol. 14. 1980. 36.00 (ISBN 0-12-543314-X). Acad Pr.

Sprott, Richard L., ed. Age, Learning Ability & Intelligence. 176p. 1980. text ed. 15.00 (ISBN 0-442-27895-0). Van Nos Reinhold.

Staats, Arthur W. Learning, Language, & Cognition: Theory, Research, & Method for the Study of Human Behavior & Its Development. 1968. 39.50x (ISBN 0-03-066565-5); pap. text ed. 18.50x (ISBN 0-8290-0687-7). Irvington.

Stephens, John M. Influence of Different Stimuli Upon Preceding Bonds: An Examination of the Law of Effect. LC 73-177823. (Columbia University. Teachers College. Contributions to Education: No. 493). Repr. of 1931 ed. 17.50 (ISBN 0-404-55493-8). AMS Pr.

Stern, William. Psychology of Early Childhood up to the Sixth Year of Age. LC 74-21428. (Classics in Child Development Ser). (Illus.). 566p. 1975. Repr. 38.00x (ISBN 0-405-06477-2). Arno.

Stevens, John O. Awareness: Exploring, Experimenting, Experiencing. LC 76-160226. 270p. 1971. 9.00 (ISBN 0-911226-10-9); pap. 5.50 (ISBN 0-911226-11-7). Real People.

Stevenson, Harold W. Children's Learning. (Illus.). 425p. 1972. 16.95 (ISBN 0-13-132472-1). P-H.

Storey, Arthur. The Measurement of Classroom Learning: Teacher Directed Assessment. LC 72-130584. (Illus.). 1970. pap. text ed. 6.95 (ISBN 0-574-17392-7, 13-0392); test set 1.20 (ISBN 0-574-17393-5, 13-0393). SRA.

Stuart, Marion F. Neurophysiological Insights into Teaching. LC 62-21040. (Illus., Orig.). 1963. pap. text ed. 6.95x (ISBN 0-87015-114-2). Pacific Bks.

Suppes, Patrick & Atkinson, Richard C. Markov Learning Models for Multiperson Interactions. 1960. 15.00x (ISBN 0-8047-0038-9). Stanford U Pr.

Swenson, Leland C. Theories of Learning: Traditional Perspectives - Contemporary Development. 1979. text ed. 20.95x (ISBN 0-534-00698-1). Wadsworth Pub.

Szurek, S. A. & Berlin, I. N., eds. Learning & Its Disorders. LC 66-18126. (Langley Porter Child Psychiatry Ser: Vol. 1). (Orig.). 1966. pap. 6.95x (ISBN 0-8314-0007-2). Sci & Behavior.

Tarpy, Roger M. Basic Principles of Learning. 261p. 1975. pap. 8.95x (ISBN 0-673-07905-8). Scott F.

Tarpy, Roger M. & Mayer, Richard E. Foundations of Learning & Memory. 1978. text ed. 15.95x (ISBN 0-673-15074-7). Scott F.

Teyler, Timothy J. The Brain & Learning. LC 77-17744. 1978. 9.95 (ISBN 0-89223-008-8). Greylock Pubs.

Thorndike, E. L. Human Learning. Repr. of 1931 ed. 11.50 (ISBN 0-384-60360-2). Johnson Repr.

Thorndike, Edward. Human Learning. pap. 5.95x (ISBN 0-262-70001-8). MIT Pr.

Thorndike, Edward L. Education: A First Book. LC 73-2992. (Classics in Psychology Ser). Repr. of 1912 ed. 15.00 (ISBN 0-405-05164-6). Arno.

--Human Learning. 1931. lib. bdg. 27.50 (ISBN 0-8482-9978-7). Norwood Edns.

--The Psychology of Wants, Interests & Attitudes. LC 35-1773. (Psychology Ser). Repr. of 1935 ed. 18.50 (ISBN 0-384-60370-X). Johnson Repr.

Torbert, William R. Learning from Experience: Towards Consciousness. LC 72-8337. 320p. 1973. 17.50x (ISBN 0-231-03672-8). Columbia U Pr.

Travers, Robert M. Essentials of Learning. 4th ed. (Illus.). 560p. 1977. text ed. 19.95 (ISBN 0-02-421350-0). Macmillan.

Turner, Johanna. Psychology for the Classroom. 1977. pap. text ed. 14.95x (ISBN 0-416-76800-8). Methuen Inc.

Ungar, G. Molecular Mechanisms in Memory & Learning. LC 70-107543. 296p. 1970. 29.50 (ISBN 0-306-30452-X, Plenum Pr). Plenum Pub.

Urban, John. Behavior Changes Resulting from a Study of Communicable Diseases: An Evaluation of the Effects of Learning on Certain Actions of High School Pupils. LC 75-177687. (Columbia University. Teachers College. Contributions to Education: No. 896). Repr. of 1943 ed. 17.50 (ISBN 0-404-55896-8). AMS Pr.

Van Meel-Jansen, Annelies. Kreativiteit En Kognitieve Stijl. 1974. 19.00x (ISBN 90-2797-321-0). Mouton.

Vargas, Julie S. Writing Worthwhile Behavioral Objectives. 1972. pap. text ed. 11.50 scp (ISBN 0-06-046812-2, HarpC). Har-Row.

Vlangas, Alex W. & Williams, Richard J. Learning Centers & Individualized Reading in Behavioral Terms. (Illus.). 1973. pap. text ed. 6.95x (ISBN 0-8422-0292-7). Irvington.

Walker, Edward L. Conditioning & Instrumental Learning. LC 67-17555. (Basic Concepts in Psychology Ser). (Orig.). 1967. pap. text ed. 6.95 (ISBN 0-8185-0299-1). Brooks-Cole.

Walker, Stephen. Learning & Reinforcement. (Essential Psychology Ser.). 1976. pap. 4.50x (ISBN 0-416-82790-X). Methuen Inc.

Wallace, S. Concomitant Learnings: Hidden Influences in the Classroom. LC 78-68027. 1978. pap. 3.00 (ISBN 0-686-26202-6, 261-08432). Home Econ Educ.

Weigand, James E., ed. Developing Teacher Competencies. LC 70-149972. (Illus.). 1971. pap. text ed. 12.95 (ISBN 0-13-205278-4). P-H.

Welles, E. R. The Learning Incorporated Dictionary of Learning Handicaps. 3rd ed. 1970. prepaid 1.00 ea. (ISBN 0-913692-01-8). Learning Inc.

Weltner, K. The Measurement of Verbal Information in Psychology & Education. Crook, B. M., tr. from Ger. LC 73-80874. (Communications & Cybernetics Ser.: Vol. 7). (Illus.). 185p. 1974. 37.00 (ISBN 0-387-06335-8). Springer-Verlag.

Whitney, George & Hughes, Donna. Individualized Instruction: Together Not Alone. LC 73-81098. (Illus.). 117p. (Orig.). 1973. pap. 5.50x (ISBN 0-87562-046-9). Spec Child.

Wickelgren, Wayne A. Learning & Memory. (Experimental Psychology Ser.). 1977. 19.95 (ISBN 0-13-527663-2). P-H.

Wilson, John A., et al. Psychological Foundations of Learning & Teaching. 2nd ed. (Illus.). 608p. 1974. pap. text ed. 14.95 (ISBN 0-07-070856-8, C); instr's. manual 3.95 (ISBN 0-07-070844-4). McGraw.

Wingfield, Arthur. Human Learning & Memory: An Introduction. LC 78-18197. 1978. text ed. 17.50 scp (ISBN 0-06-047149-2, HarpC). Har-Row.

Wolff, Peter, ed. Planning for Better Learning. (Clinics in Developmental Medicine Ser. No. 33). 159p. 1969. 15.50 (ISBN 0-685-24741-4). Lippincott.

Yarbrough, V. Eugene, et al, eds. Readings in Curriculum & Supervision. 250p. 1974. 29.00x (ISBN 0-8422-5203-7); pap. text ed. 7.25x (ISBN 0-8422-0448-2). Irvington.

Young, Betty M. Learning Together: One School Reports. 107p. 1969. pap. 2.75 (ISBN 0-85225-537-3). Ed Solutions.

Young, D. R., ed. Academic Underachiever. 2nd ed. LC 67-18845. (Handbook Ser). (Illus.). 1970. 5.95 (ISBN 0-87558-052-1). Porter Sargent.

Young, Michael & McGeeney, Patrick. Learning Begins at Home: A Study of a Junior School & Its Parents. 1968. text ed. 10.00x (ISBN 0-7100-6529-9). Humanities.

Zamble, Edward, ed. Basic Source Readings in the Psychology of Learning. LC 72-6357. 296p. 1972. pap. text ed. 16.95x (ISBN 0-8290-0652-4). Irvington.

Zippel, H. P., ed. Memory & Transfer of Information. LC 73-80325. 582p. 1973. 42.50 (ISBN 0-306-30743-X, Plenum Pr). Plenum Pub.

LEARNING, PSYCHOLOGY OF-MATHEMATICAL MODELS

Iosifescu, Marius & Theodorescu, Radu. Random Processes & Learning. LC 68-54828. (Grundlehren der Mathematischen Wissenschaften: Vol. 150). 1969. 42.50 (ISBN 0-387-04504-X). Springer-Verlag.

Levine, Gustav & Burke, C. Mathematical Model Techniques for Learning Theories. 1972. text ed. 17.95 (ISBN 0-12-445250-7). Acad Pr.

Norman, M. Frank. Markov Processes & Learning Models. (Mathematics in Science & Engineering Ser.: Vol. 84). 1972. 37.50 (ISBN 0-12-521450-2). Acad Pr.

Snyder, Helen I. Contemporary Educational Psychology: Some Models Applied to the School Setting. 236p. 1968. 10.75 (ISBN 0-471-81020-7, Pub. by Wiley). Krieger.

Tsypkin, Ya Z. Foundations of the Theory of Learning Systems. (Mathematics in Science & Engineeringser.). 1973. 37.50 (ISBN 0-12-702060-8). Acad Pr.

LEARNING, VERBAL

see also Verbal Learning

Blank, Marion, et al. The Language of Learning: The Preschool Years. 208p. 1978. pap. 21.00 (ISBN 0-8089-1058-2). Grune.

Karpova, S. The Realization of the Verbal Composition of Speech by Preschool Children. (Janua Linguarum, Ser. Major: No. 56). 1977. 44.50x (ISBN 90-279-3186-0). Mouton.

Shands, H. Speech As Instruction. 1977. 45.75x (ISBN 90-279-7725-9). Mouton.

LEARNING ABILITY

see also Learning, Psychology Of; Learning Disabilities; Self-Organizing Systems

Adams, A. W. Threshhold Learning Abilities. 1972. loose-leaf 9.95 (ISBN 0-02-958580-5). Macmillan.

Ayres, A. Jean. Sensory Integration & Learning Disorders. LC 72-91446. 294p. 1973. 22.80x (ISBN 0-87424-303-3). Western Psych.

Banas, Norma & Wills, I. H. Identifying Early Learning Gaps: A Guide to the Assessment of Academic Readiness. 4.95 (ISBN 0-89269-013-5, 401). Humanics Ltd.

Blake, James N. Speech, Language & Learning Disorders: Education & Therapy. (Illus.). 172p. 1971. 12.75 (ISBN 0-398-00166-9). C C Thomas.

Boakes, R. A. & Halliday, M. S. Inhibition & Learning. 1972. 87.00 (ISBN 0-12-108050-1). Acad Pr.

Bridgeman, Bruce, et al, eds. Readings on Fundamental Issues on Learning & Memory. 1977. pap. text ed. 12.50x (ISBN 0-685-81867-5). Whitehall Co.

Bugelski, B. R. Some Practical Laws of Learning. LC 77-84042. (Fastback Ser.: No. 96). 1977. pap. 0.75 (ISBN 0-87367-096-5). Phi Delta Kappa.

Cihak, Mary K. & Heron, Barbara J. Games Children Should Play: Sequential Lessons for Teaching Communication Skills in Grades K-6. 1980. pap. text ed. 10.95 (ISBN 0-8302-8494-X). Goodyear.

Colman, Raphael. How to Develop the Learning Powers of the Child & of the Teenager. (Illus.). 1977. 39.50 (ISBN 0-89266-086-4). Am Classical Coll Pr.

Estes, William K. Learning Theory & Mental Development. 1970. 28.00 (ISBN 0-12-243550-8). Acad Pr.

Gazda, George M. & Corsini, Raymond J. Theories of Learning: A Comparative Approach. LC 79-91101. 483p. 1980. text ed. 15.95 (ISBN 0-87581-253-8). Peacock Pubs.

Gearheart, Bill R. Learning Disabilities: Educational Strategies. 2nd ed. LC 76-28435. (Illus.). 1977. text ed. 15.50 (ISBN 0-8016-1767-7). Mosby.

Goldsmith, Robert H. Nutrition & Learning. LC 80-82680. (Fastback Ser.: No. 147). 1980. pap. 0.75 (ISBN 0-87367-147-3). Phi Delta Kappa.

Golick, M. A Parents Guide to Learning Problems. 1970. pap. 1.95x (ISBN 0-88432-009-X). J Norton Pubs.

--She Thought I Was Dumb but I Told Her I Had a Learning Disability. 1969. pap. 1.95x (ISBN 0-88432-010-3). J Norton Pubs.

Guevara, Carlos I. & Sesman, Myrna. La Madre y el Aprendizaje Del Nino: La Experiencia Urbana Puertorriquena. LC 77-9261. 1978. pap. 5.50 (ISBN 0-8477-2739-4). U of PR Pr.

Hegarty, Seamus & Lucas, Dorothy. Able to Learn? the Pursuit of Culture-Fair Assessment. (General Ser.). 1979. pap. text ed. 11.00x (ISBN 0-85633-173-2, NFER). Humanities.

Hill, Wm. F. Learning Thru Discussion. rev., 2nd ed. LC 78-87064. 58p. 1977. 2.95 (ISBN 0-8039-0711-7). Sage.

Hinde, R. A. & Stevenson-Hinde, J., eds. Constraints on Learning: Limitations & Predispositions. 1973. 57.50 (ISBN 0-12-349150-9). Acad Pr.

Hobbs, Nicholas, et al. Exceptional Teaching for Exceptional Learning: A Report to the Ford Foundation Papers on Research About Learning. LC 79-65207. 1979. pap. 3.95 (ISBN 0-916584-11-9). Ford Found.

Holt, John. Never Too Late. 1978. 10.00 (ISBN 0-440-06641-7, Sey Lawr). Delacorte.

Howe, Michael. Learning in Infants & Young Children. LC 75-44902. 1976. 10.00x (ISBN 0-8047-0913-0); pap. 4.95 (ISBN 0-8047-0973-4, SP145). Stanford U Pr.

Humphrey, James H. Improving Learning Ability Through Compensatory Physical Education. (Illus.). 160p. 1976. 14.75 (ISBN 0-398-03561-X). C C Thomas.

Konsler, Runelle & Mirabella, Lauren. Math Activities with a Porpoise. 1980. pap. text ed. 7.95 (ISBN 0-8302-5631-8). Goodyear.

Lien, Arnold J. & Lien, Harriet S. Measurement & Evaluation of Learning. 4th ed. 440p. 1980. text ed. write for info. (ISBN 0-697-06128-0) (ISBN 0-697-06124-8). instructor's manual available. Wm C Brown.

Martinez, J. L., et al, eds. Endogenous Peptides & Learning & Memory Processes. (Behavioral Biology Ser.). 1981. price not set (ISBN 0-12-474980-1). Acad Pr.

Mumford, Alan. Making Experience Pay: Management Success Through Effective Learning. 184p. 1981. 19.95 (ISBN 0-07-084536-0, P&RB). McGraw.

Oliverio, A., ed. Genetics, Environment & Intelligence. 1977. 91.25 (ISBN 0-7204-0644-7, North-Holland). Elsevier.

Osherson, Daniel N. Logical Abilities in Children, 4 vols. Incl. Vol. 1. Organization of Length & Class: Empirical Consequences of a Piagetion Formulism. 11.95 (ISBN 0-470-65723-5); Vol. 2. Logical Inference. 11.95 (ISBN 0-470-65724-3); Vol. 3. Reasoning in Adolescence-Deductive Inference. LC 75-25623. 1975. 14.95 (ISBN 0-470-65730-8); Vol. 4. Reasoning & Concepts. 14.95 (ISBN 0-470-99009-0). LC 74-2298. 1974-77. Halsted Pr.

Postal, Paul, et al. Language & Learning: Investigations & Interpretations. (Reprint Ser.: No. 7). 4.50 (ISBN 0-916690-07-5). Harvard Educ Rev.

Raskin, Bruce, ed. The Whole Learning Catalog. LC 76-29238. (Learning Ideabooks Ser.). 1976. pap. 10.95 (ISBN 0-8224-1913-0). Pitman Learning.

Reese, H. W. Basic Learning Processes in Childhood. LC 74-25530. 1976. pap. text ed. 5.95 (ISBN 0-03-013216-9, HoltC). HR&W.

Riegel, K. F., ed. Intelligence: Alternative Views of a Paradigm. (Human Development: Vol. 16, No. 1-2). 132p. 1974. pap. 9.75 (ISBN 3-8055-1710-6). S Karger.

Ross, Alan O. Psychological Aspects of Learning Disorders of Children. (Special Education Ser.). (Illus.). 320p. 1976. text ed. 12.95 (ISBN 0-07-053845-X, C). McGraw.

Rudman, Jack. Learning Ability Test (LAT) (Career Examination Ser.: C-1062). (Cloth bdg. avail. on request). pap. 8.00 (ISBN 0-8373-1062-8). Natl Learning.

Salomon, Gavriel. Interaction of Media, Cognition, & Learning: An Exploration of How Symbolic Forms Cultivate Mental Skills & Affect Knowledge Acquisition. LC 79-83578. (Social & Behavioral Science Ser.). (Illus.). 1979. text ed. 16.95x (ISBN 0-87589-403-8). Jossey-Bass.

Tarpy, Roger & Mayer, Richard. Readings in Learning & Memory. 1979. pap. text ed. 7.95x (ISBN 0-673-15110-7). Scott F.

Thornley, Margo L. Every Child Can Learn-Something. LC 73-81605. (Illus.). 1973. pap. 6.50x (ISBN 0-87562-043-4). Spec Child.

Wagoner, Louisa C. The Development of Learning in Young Children. (Educational Ser.). 1933. Repr. 10.00 (ISBN 0-685-43641-1). Norwood Edns.

Wilson, Frank T. Learning of Bright & Dull Children. LC 77-177631. (Columbia University. Teachers College. Contributions to Education: No. 292). Repr. of 1928 ed. 17.50 (ISBN 0-404-55292-7). AMS Pr.

Wold, Robert M., ed. Vision: Its Impact on Learning. LC 74-84847. (Illus.). 1978. pap. 12.50x (ISBN 0-87562-055-8). Spec Child.

--Visual & Perceptual Aspects for the Achieving & Underachieving Child. LC 69-20314. (Illus., Orig.). 1969. pap. 10.00x (ISBN 0-87562-016-7). Spec Child.

Wolfe, W. Dean & Goulding, Daniel J., eds. Articulation & Learning: New Dimensions in Research, Diagnostics, & Therapy. 2nd ed. (Illus.). 350p. 1980. text ed. 23.75 (ISBN 0-398-04007-9). C C Thomas.

LEARNING AND SCHOLARSHIP

see also Culture; Education; Humanism; Learned Institutions and Societies; Professional Education; Research; Wisdom

Adams, Eleanor N. Old English Scholarship in England from 1556-1800. LC 70-91177. (Yale Studies in English Ser.: No. 55). 1970. Repr. of 1917 ed. 16.50 (ISBN 0-208-00913-2, Archon). Shoe String.

Adler, Franx, et al. The Home of the Learned Man: A Symposium on the Immigrant Scholar in America. Kosa, John, ed. LC 68-22380. 1968. 4.50 (ISBN 0-8084-0160-2). Coll & U Pr.

Baldwin, John W. The Scholastic Culture of the Middle Ages: 1000-1300. LC 70-120060. (Civilization & Society Ser). 192p. 1971. pap. 5.95x (ISBN 0-669-62059-9). Heath.

Biggs, E. & MacLean, J. Freedom to Learn: An Active Learning Approach to Mathematics. 1969. text ed. 14.00 (ISBN 0-201-00572-7). A-W.

Binyon, Gilbert C. The Christian Socialist Movement in England: An Introduction to the Study of Its History. Repr. of 1931 ed. lib. bdg. 15.00x (ISBN 0-87991-628-1). Porcupine Pr.

Boy Scouts Of America. Scholarship. LC 19-600. (Illus.). 64p. (gr. 6-12). 1970. pap. 0.70x (ISBN 0-8395-3384-5, 3384). BSA.

Butler, Nicholas M. Scholarship & Service: The Policies & Ideals of a National University in a Modern Democracy. facsimile ed. LC 78-134066. (Essay Index Reprint Ser). Repr. of 1921 ed. 19.50 (ISBN 0-8369-2220-4). Arno.

Columbia University. Quarter Century of Learning, 1904-1929. facs. ed. LC 68-58780. (Essay Index Reprint Ser). 1931. 19.50 (ISBN 0-8369-1028-1). Arno.

Comenius, John A. The Great Didactic of John Amos Comenius, 2 pts. in 1 vol. Keatinge, M. W., ed. & tr. LC 66-24715. (1967. Repr. of 1896, 1910 eds). 17.50 (ISBN 0-8462-0818-0). Russell.

Curti, Merle E., ed. American Scholarship in the Twentieth Century. LC 66-27057. 1967. Repr. of 1953 ed. 8.50 (ISBN 0-8462-0919-5). Russell.

Davenport, W. H. The One Culture. LC 70-106054. 1970. 12.75 (ISBN 0-08-016322-X). Pergamon.

Douglas, David. English Scholars, Sixteen Sixty to Seventeen Thirty. LC 75-3865. (Illus.). 291p. 1975. Repr. of 1951 ed. lib. bdg. 16.25x (ISBN 0-8371-8093-7, DOES). Greenwood.

Duckworth, Eleanor. Learning with Breadth & Depth. 1979. pap. 2.50 (ISBN 0-918374-09-X). Workshop Ctr.

Erdey-Gruz, Tibor & Kulcsar, Kalman, eds. Science & Scholarship in Hungary. 2nd ed. 1975. 16.95x (ISBN 0-8464-0816-3). Beekman Pubs.

Foerster, Norman. American Scholar. LC 65-18604. 1965. Repr. of 1929 ed. 8.50 (ISBN 0-8046-0155-0). Kennikat.

Foucault, Michel. Archaeology of Knowledge: Includes the Discourse on Language. Sheridan-Smith, A. M., tr. LC 72-1135. 1972. 29.50x (ISBN 0-394-47118-0). Irvington.

--Order of Things: An Archaeology of the Human Sciences. 1973. pap. 3.95 (ISBN 0-394-71935-2, V935, Vin). Random.

Frye, Northrop, et al. Morality of Scholarship. Black, Max, ed. (Studies in Humanities Ser.). 101p. 1967. 12.50 (ISBN 0-8014-0042-2). Cornell U Pr.

Fukuzawa, Yukichi. An Encouragement of Learning. LC 70-97722. 143p. 1970. pap. 10.00x (ISBN 0-8002-1393-9). Intl Pubns Serv.

Geanakoplos, Deno J. Byzantium & the Renaissance: Greek Scholars in Venice: Studies in the Dissemination of Greek Learning from Byzantium to Western Europe. (Illus.). xiii, 348p. 1973. Repr. of 1962 ed. 17.50 (ISBN 0-208-01311-3, Archon). Shoe String.

Guitton, Jean. Student's Guide to Intellectual Work. Foulke, Adrienne, tr. 1964. pap. 1.75x (ISBN 0-268-00266-5). U of Notre Dame Pr.

Harbison, E. Harris. The Christian Scholar in the Age of the Reformation. LC 80-20805. Repr. of 1956 ed. lib. bdg. 15.00x (ISBN 0-87991-954-X). Porcupine Pr.

Herbst, Jurgen. German Historical School in American Scholarship. LC 79-159072. 1971. Repr. of 1965 ed. 13.50 (ISBN 0-8046-1666-3). Kennikat.

Hyman, Herbert H., et al. The Enduring Effects of Education. LC 75-9860. x, 314p. 1975. 12.50x (ISBN 0-226-36549-2); pap. 5.95 (ISBN 0-226-36550-6, P792, Phoen). U of Chicago Pr.

Laistner, Max L. & King, H. H. Thought & Letters in Western Europe, A.D. 500 to 900. 2nd ed. 416p. 1966. 20.00x (ISBN 0-8014-0243-3); pap. 7.95 (ISBN 0-8014-9037-5, CP37). Cornell U Pr.

Langridge, Derek & Herman, Esther, eds. Universe of Knowledge. LC 68-66990. (Student Contribution Ser.: No. 2). 1969. pap. 3.50 (ISBN 0-911808-04-3). U of Md Lib Serv.

Learning Resource Guide: Educational Motion Pictures. 198p. 1980. pap. 2.50 (ISBN 0-930214-05-6). U TX Austin Gen Libs.

Lloyd, Roger B. Golden Middle Age. LC 75-90654. (Essay Index Reprint Ser). 1939. 16.00 (ISBN 0-8369-1208-X). Arno.

Lyman, Thomas G. New, Tested Techniques for Independent Learning. (Human Development Library Bk). (Illus.). 131p. 1981. 37.85 (ISBN 0-89266-291-3). Am Classical Coll Pr.

Machlup, Fritz, et al. The Production & Distribution of Knowledge in the United States. 415p. 1972. pap. 6.95 (ISBN 0-686-76943-0) (ISBN 0-691-00356-4). Princeton U Pr.

Nock, Albert J. Theory of Education in the United States. LC 72-89212. (American Education: Its Men, Institutions & Ideas, Ser. 1). 1969. Repr. of 1932 ed. 13.00 (ISBN 0-405-01451-1). Arno.

Pennsylvania University Library. Changing Patterns of Scholarship & the Future of Research Libraries. facs. ed. LC 68-14910. (Essay Index Reprint Ser). 1951. 15.00 (ISBN 0-8369-0782-5). Arno.

Petrie, Hugh G. The Dilemma of Enquiry & Learning. LC 81-3381. 1981. price not set (ISBN 0-226-66349-3, Phoen). U of Chicago Pr.

Pfeiffer, Rudolph. History of Classical Scholarship: From the Beginning to the End of the Hellenistic Age. 1968. 37.50x (ISBN 0-19-814342-7). Oxford U Pr.

Potter, Henry C. The Scholar & the State: And Other Orations & Addresses. LC 72-4509. (Essay Index Reprint Ser.). Repr. of 1897 ed. 19.00 (ISBN 0-8369-2969-1). Arno.

Robbins, J. Albert, ed. American Literary Scholarship: An Annual, 1970. LC 65-19450. xiv, 360p. 1972. 14.75 (ISBN 0-8223-0270-5). Duke.

Robinson, James H. Humanizing of Knowledge. LC 72-165742. (American Education Ser, No. 2). 1971. Repr. of 1924 ed. 9.00 (ISBN 0-405-03613-2). Arno.

Sandys, John E. History of Classical Scholarship, 3 Vols. 2nd ed. (Illus.). 1967. Repr. of 1920 ed. Set. 52.75 (ISBN 0-02-851610-9). Hafner.

Sanford, N. R. & Adkins, M. M. Physique Personality & Scholarship. (Society for Research in Child Development Monographs Ser). Repr. of 1943 ed. pap. 31.00 (ISBN 0-527-01526-1). Kraus Repr.

Scholarly Communication: The Report of the National Enquiry. LC 79-51420. 1979. 12.95x (ISBN 0-8018-2267-X); pap. 4.95 (ISBN 0-8018-2268-8). Johns Hopkins.

Sibley, Elbridge. Support for Independent Scholarship & Research. LC 51-5070. (Social Science Research Council Bulletin). 1951. pap. 2.50 (ISBN 0-527-03310-3). Kraus Repr.

Simonini, R. C., Jr. Italian Scholarship in Renaissance England. (University of North Carolina Studies in Comparative Literature: No. 3). 1969. Repr. of 1952 ed. 19.50 (ISBN 0-384-55520-9). Johnson Repr.

Smith, Goldwin, ed. The Professor & the Public: The Role of the Scholar in the Modern World. LC 72-2088. (Leo M. Franklin Memorial Lectures in Human Relations Ser: Vol. 20). 128p. 1972. 5.95x (ISBN 0-8143-1477-5). Wayne St U Pr.

Steffen, Jerome O., ed. The American West: New Perspectives, New Dimensions. LC 78-58097. 238p. 1981. pap. 6.95 (ISBN 0-8061-1744-3). U of Okla Pr.

Steinberg, Stephen. Academic Melting Pot. LC 73-9656. (Illus.). 1977. pap. text ed. 4.95 (ISBN 0-87855-635-4). Transaction Bks.

Taylor, Henry O. Freedom of the Mind in History. Repr. of 1923 ed. lib. bdg. 14.00x (ISBN 0-8371-4352-7, TAMH). Greenwood.

Thorndike, Lynn. Science & Thought in the Fifteenth Century. (Illus.). 1967. Repr. of 1929 ed. 14.95 (ISBN 0-02-853480-8). Hafner.

Warton, Thomas. History of English Poetry, 4 Vols in 3. (Classics in Art & Literary Criticism). Repr. of 1774 ed. Set. 69.50 (ISBN 0-384-65930-6). Johnson Repr.

Weiss, John, ed. The Origins of Modern Consciousness. LC 65-10145. (Waynebooks Ser: No. 18). (Orig.). 1965. 6.95x (ISBN 0-8143-1260-8); pap. 4.95x (ISBN 0-8143-1261-6). Wayne St U Pr.

World of Learning: 1981-82, 2 vols. 32nd ed. LC 47-30172. 2110p. 1982. Set. 140.00x (ISBN 0-905118-70-7). Intl Pubns Serv.

Znaniecki, Florian. Social Role of the Man of Knowledge. 1965. lib. bdg. 14.00 (ISBN 0-374-98892-7). Octagon.

LEARNING AND SCHOLARSHIP–CATHOLICS

see Catholic Learning and Scholarship

LEARNING AND SCHOLARSHIP–JEWS

see Jewish Learning and Scholarship

LEARNING AND SCHOLARSHIP–MUSLIMS

see Islamic Learning and Scholarship

LEARNING BY DISCOVERY

Foster, John. Discovery Learning in the Primary School. (Students Library of Education). 160p. 1972. 12.50x (ISBN 0-7100-7356-9); pap. 6.25 (ISBN 0-7100-7357-7). Routledge & Kegan.

Nagel, Charles. Children Learning by Doing. (Illus.). (gr. k-3). 1973. 3.25x (ISBN 0-933892-01-2). Child Focus Co.

Rosner, Jerome. Helping Children Overcome Learning Difficulties: A Step-by-Step Guide for Parents & Teachers. 2nd, rev. & exp. ed. (Illus.). 1979. 15.95 (ISBN 0-8027-0609-6). Walker & Co.

Sava, Samuel G. Learning Through Discovery for Young Children. 1975. 9.95 (ISBN 0-07-054963-X, P&RB). McGraw.

Schmidt, Victor E. & Rockcastle, Verne N. Teaching Science with Everyday Things. 1968. pap. text ed. 8.95 (ISBN 0-07-055351-3, C). McGraw.

Themal, Joachim. A Contemporary Approach to Art Teaching. (Illus.). 1977. pap. 5.95 (ISBN 0-442-28450-0). Van Nos Reinhold.

Wedemeyer, Charles A. Learning at the Back Door: Reflections on Non-Traditional Learning in the Lifespan. LC 80-52301. 286p. 1981. 19.50x (ISBN 0-299-08560-0). U of Wis Pr.

LEARNING CENTER APPROACH TO TEACHING

see Open Plan Schools

LEARNING DISABILITIES

see also Reading Disability

Adamson, William C. & Adamson, Katherine K., eds. A Handbook for Specific Learning Disabilities. LC 78-43. 512p. 1979. 27.50 (ISBN 0-470-26308-3). Halsted Pr.

Ainscow, Mel & Tweddle, David A. Preventing Classroom Failure: An Objectives Approach. LC 78-31618. 205p. 1979. 26.50 (ISBN 0-471-27564-6, Pub. by Wiley-Interscience). Wiley.

Anderson, Robert P. & Halcomb, Charles G. Learning Disability-Minimal Brain Dysfunction Syndrome: Research Perspectives & Applications. (Illus.). 296p. 1976. 24.50 (ISBN 0-398-03395-1). C C Thomas.

Ashlock, Patrick & Stephen, Alberta. Educational Therapy in the Elementary School: An Educational Approach to the Learning Problems of Children. (Illus.). 120p. 1970. ed. spiral bdg. 14.75photocopy (ISBN 0-398-00060-3). C C Thomas.

Bangs, Tina E. Language & Learning Disorders of the Pre-Academic Child: With Curriculum Guide. 2nd ed. (Illus.). 304p. 1982. 19.95 (ISBN 0-13-523001-2). P-H.

Baren, Martin, et al. Overcoming Learning Disabilities: A Team Approach (Parent-Teacher-Physician-Child) 1978. text ed. 16.95 (ISBN 0-8359-5365-3). Reston.

Behr, Marcia W., et al. Drama Integrates Basic Skills: Lesson Plans for the Learning Disabled. (Illus.). 144p. 1979. vinyl spiral bdg. 12.75 (ISBN 0-398-03881-3). C C Thomas.

Bell, Peter. Basic Teaching for Slow Learners. 248p. 30.00x (ISBN 0-584-10361-1, Pub. by Muller Ltd). State Mutual Bk.

Berger, Gilda. Learning Disabilities & Handicaps. (Impact Bks.). (Illus.). (gr. 7 up). 1978. PLB 7.45 s&l (ISBN 0-531-01457-6). Watts.

Blackwell, Robert B. & Joynt, Robert R., eds. Learning Disabilities Handbook for Teachers. 208p. 1976. text ed. 16.50 (ISBN 0-398-02234-8). C C Thomas.

Blanco, Ralph F. Prescriptions for Children with Learning & Adjustment Problems. 320p. 1980. 13.75 (ISBN 0-685-02633-7). C C Thomas.

Bley, Nancy S. & Thornton, Carol A. Teaching Mathematics to the Learning Disabled. 350p. 1981. text ed. write for info. (ISBN 0-89443-357-1). Aspen Systems.

Brutten, et al. Something's Wrong with My Child: A Parent's Handbook About Children with Learning Disabilities. LC 79-10285. 1979. pap. 3.95 (ISBN 0-15-683805-2, Harv). HarBraceJ.

Bryan, Tanis & Bryan, James. Understanding Learning Disabilities. 2nd ed. LC 77-25987. 382p. 1978. text ed. 15.95x (ISBN 0-88284-056-8). Alfred Pub.

Bush, Clifford L. & Andrews, Robert C. Dictionary of Reading & Learning Disability. LC 79-57293. 179p. 1978. pap. 13.40x (ISBN 0-87424-153-7). Western Psych.

Button, James E. Communications Research in Learning Disabilities & Mental Retardation. 356p. 1979. pap. text ed. 22.50 (ISBN 0-8391-1262-9). Univ Park.

Carlson, Luis. The Nexus: Test Results to Insights for Remediation. 1978. pap. text ed. 15.00x binder with 2nd addenda (ISBN 0-87879-147-7). Acad Therapy.

Chapman, James W. & Boersma, Frederic J. Affective Correlates of Learning Disabilities. (Modern Approaches to the Diagnosis & Instruction of Multihandicapped Children Ser.: Vol. 15). 108p. 1980. text ed. 22.50 (ISBN 90-265-0341-5, Pub. by Swets Pub Serv Holland). Swets North Am.

Chicoral Index to Reading & Learning Disabilities: Books, 1978 Annual, Vol. 14A. 400p. 1980. 85.00 (ISBN 0-934598-09-6). Am Lib Pub Co.

Chicorel Abstracts to Reading & Learning Disabilities: Periodicals, 1978 Annual, Vol. 19. 400p. 1979. 85.00 (ISBN 0-934598-16-9). Am Lib Pub Co.

Chicorel Abstracts to Reading & Learning Disabilities: Periodicals, 1979 Annual, Vol. 19. 400p. 1980. 85.00 (ISBN 0-934598-10-X). Am Lib Pub Co.

Chicorel, Marietta. Chicorel Abstracts to Reading & Learning Disabilities, 1976 Annual. annual ed. (Chicorel Index Ser.). 1000p. 1976. text ed. 85.00 ca. (ISBN 0-934598-15-0); Vol. 19. text ed. (ISBN 0-934598-15-0). Am Lib Pub Co.

Chicorel, Marietta, ed. Chicorel Abstracts to Reading and Learning Disabilities: 1977 Annual, Vol. 19. annual ed. (Index Ser). 1977. text ed. 85.00 (ISBN 0-934598-17-7). Am Lib Pub Co.

--Chicorel Index to Reading & Learning Disabilities: Books, 1977 Annual, Vol. 14A. LC 76-14381. (Index Ser). 1977. text ed. 85.00x (ISBN 0-934598-50-9). Am Lib Pub Co.

Clarke, Cynthia A., et al. A Teacher's Notebook: Alternatives for Children with Learning Problems. 1975. pap. 5.75 (ISBN 0-934338-09-4). NAIS.

Cole, Martha L. & Cole, Jack T. Effective Intervention with the Language Impaired Child. LC 80-28037. 291p. 1981. text ed. 26.95 (ISBN 0-89443-344-X). Aspen Systems.

Cott, Allan. The Orthomolecular Approach to Learning Disabilities. LC 77-22609. 1977. pap. text ed. 3.50x (ISBN 0-87879-174-4). Acad Therapy.

Crowther, Jean D. What Do I Do Now, Mom? LC 80-82257. (Illus.). 86p. (gr. 9-12). 1980. 6.95 (ISBN 0-88290-134-6). Horizon Utah.

Cruickshank, William M. Concepts in Learning Disabilities: Selected Writings, Vol. 2. LC 80-29024. 296p. 1981. text ed. 20.00x (ISBN 0-8156-2239-2). Syracuse U Pr.

Cruickshank, William M., ed. Approaches to Learning: The Best of ACLD, Vol. 1. (Illus.). 240p. 1980. pap. 11.95x (ISBN 0-8156-2203-1). Syracuse U Pr.

--Learning Disabilities in Home, School, & Community. 1979. pap. 8.95x (ISBN 0-8156-2208-2). Syracuse U Pr.

Cruickshank, William M. & Hallahan, Daniel P., eds. Perceptual & Learning Disabilities in Children. Incl. Vol. 1. Psychoeducational Practices. LC 74-24303. 496p. 23.00x (ISBN 0-8156-2165-5); Vol. 2. Research & Theory. LC 74-24303. 498p. 27.00x (ISBN 0-8156-2166-3). (Illus.). 1975. Set. 45.00x (ISBN 0-685-51977-5). Syracuse U Pr.

Cruickshank, William M. & Silver, Archie A., eds. Bridges to Tomorrow: The Best of ACLD, Vol. 2. 1981. pap. 11.95x (ISBN 0-8156-2237-6). Syracuse U Pr.

Cruickshank, William M., et al. Learning Disabilities: The Struggle from Adolescence Toward Adulthood. (Illus.). 304p. 1980. 22.95x (ISBN 0-8156-2220-1); pap. 9.95x (ISBN 0-8156-2221-X). Syracuse U Pr.

Darrow, Frank M. Girls, & Boys, & Women. (Illus.). 1977. pap. 3.50 (ISBN 0-685-86446-4). Darrow.

De Quiros, J. & Schrager, O. Neuropsychological Fundamentals. 2nd ed. (Illus.). 292p. 1980. 20.00 (ISBN 0-87879-184-1). Acad Therapy.

DeWitt, Frances B. Our Educational Challenge: Specific Learning Disabled Adolescents. 1977. pap. 5.00x (ISBN 0-87879-163-9). Acad Therapy.

Ellingson, Careth. Speaking of Children, Their Learning Abilities-Disabilities. LC 73-14256. (Illus.). 300p. 1975. 10.95 (ISBN 0-06-011178-X, HarpT). Har-Row.

Faas, Larry A. Children with Learning Problems: A Handbook for Teachers. LC 79-89741. (Illus.). 1980. text ed. 14.95 (ISBN 0-395-28352-3); inst. manual 0.65 (ISBN 0-395-28353-1). HM.

--Learning Disabilities: A Competency-Based Approach. 2nd ed. (Illus.). 480p. 1981. pap. text ed. 15.95 (ISBN 0-686-77600-3); instr's. manual 0.75 (ISBN 0-395-29700-1). HM.

Faas, Larry A., ed. Learning Disabilities: A Book of Readings. (Illus.). 272p. 1972. 13.75 (ISBN 0-398-02276-3). C C Thomas.

Farnham-Diggory, Sylvia. Learning Disabilities: A Psychological Perspective. LC 78-5514. (Developing Child Ser.). 1978. 8.95x (ISBN 0-674-51921-3); pap. 3.95 (ISBN 0-674-51922-1). Harvard U Pr.

Fremont, Theodore S., et al. Informal Diagnostic Assessment of Children. (Illus.). 176p. 1977. 16.75 (ISBN 0-398-03646-2). C C Thomas.

Gaddes, W. H. Learning Disabilities & Brain Function: A Neuropsychological Approach. (Illus.). 350p. 1980. 26.90 (ISBN 0-387-90486-7). Springer-Verlag.

Gadow, Kenneth D. & Bialer, Irv., eds. Advances in Learning & Behavioral Disabilities, Vol. 1. 450p. 1981. 37.50 (ISBN 0-89232-209-8). Jai Pr.

Gearheart, Bill. Learning Disabilities: Educational Strategies. 3rd ed. LC 80-39700. (Illus.). 302p. 1981. text ed. 17.95 (ISBN 0-8016-1768-5). Mosby.

Gerber, Adele & Bryen, Diane N. Language & Learning Disabilities. 360p. 1981. pap. text ed. 19.95 (ISBN 0-686-75110-8). Univ Park.

Gillett, Pamela. Career Education for Children with Learning Disabilities. 1978. pap. text ed. 15.00x binder (ISBN 0-87879-192-2). Acad Therapy.

Glaser, Kurt. Learning Difficulties: Causes & Psychological Implications - A Guide for Professionals. (Illus.). 112p. 1974. 11.25 (ISBN 0-398-03157-6). C C Thomas.

Glazzard, Margaret H. Meet Scott: Learning Disabled. 1978. 8.95 (ISBN 0-89079-036-1). H & H Ent.

Golden, Charles J. & Anderson, Sandra. Learning Disabilities & Brain Dysfunction: An Introduction for Educators & Parents. (Illus.). 176p. 1979. text ed. 14.00 (ISBN 0-398-03861-9). C C Thomas.

Goleta, Calif. Union School District. Sensorimotor Activities for the Remediation of Learning Disabilities. 1977. pap. 2.50x (ISBN 0-87879-182-5). Acad Therapy.

Goodman, Libby & Mann, Lester. Learning Disabilities in the Secondary School: Issues & Practices. LC 76-19050. 288p. 1976. 26.75 (ISBN 0-8089-0949-5). Grune.

Gottlieb, Jay & Strichart, Stephen S., eds. Developmental Theory & Research in Learning Disabilities. 352p. 1981. text ed. 22.95 (ISBN 0-8391-1624-1). Univ Park.

Gottlieb, Marvin I., et al, eds. The Learning-Disabled Child. (Current Issues in Developmental Pediatrics). 448p. 1979. 28.25 (ISBN 0-8089-1179-1). Grune.

Greene, Roberta M. & Heavenrich, Elaine. A Question in Search of an Answer: Understanding Learning Disability in Jewish Education. LC 8-18059. (Illus.). 262p. 1981. pap. 5.00 (ISBN 0-8074-0029-7). UAHC.

Grzynkowicz, Wineva. Basic Education for Children with Learning Disabilities. (Illus.). 296p. 1979. text ed. 15.50 (ISBN 0-398-03875-9). C C Thomas.

--Meeting the Needs of Learning Disabled Children in the Regular Class. 208p. 1975. photocopy ed. spiral 16.50 (ISBN 0-398-03159-2). C C Thomas.

Hagin, Rosa A., et al. Teach Manual with Task Cards. LC 76-3338. 186p. 1975. pap. text ed. 47.50 (ISBN 0-8027-9036-4). Walker Educ.

Hallahan, D. & Cruickshank, W. Psychoeducational Foundations of Learning Disabilities. 1979. 18.95 (ISBN 0-13-734285-3). P-H.

Hannah, Marta, et al. SCIL: Systematic Curriculum for Independent Living, 4 vols. 1977. Set. binders 165.00x (ISBN 0-87879-187-6). Acad Therapy.

Hart, Jane & Jones, Beverly. Where's Hannah? An Inspiring Story for Teachers & Parents of Learning Disabled Children. 1980. pap. 4.95 (ISBN 0-14-005454-5). Penguin.

Hayes, Marnell. Tuned-in, Turned-on Book About Learning Problems. LC 74-80091. 1974. pap. 2.50x (ISBN 0-87879-090-X); optional 90-minute cassette tape 7.95 (ISBN 0-87879-090-X). Acad Therapy.

Hayes, Rosa & Stevenson, Merce G. Teaching the Emotionally Disturbed-Learning Disabled Child: A Practical Guide, 4 vols. 1980. Set. pap. 36.00 (ISBN 0-87491-614-3); 9.95 ea. Vol. 1. Vol. 2 (ISBN 0-87491-405-1). Vol. 3 (ISBN 0-87491-406-X). Vol. 4 (ISBN 0-87491-407-8). Acropolis.

Hollingworth, Leta. Psychology of Special Disability in Spelling. LC 79-176873. (Columbia University. Teachers College. Contributions to Education: No. 88). Repr. of 1918 ed. 17.50 (ISBN 0-404-55088-6). AMS Pr.

Jacobs, Wilma J. Any Love Notes Today? LC 76-48409. 143p. (Orig.). 1976. pap. 4.95 (ISBN 0-89146-002-0). J & J Dist.

Jarman, Ronald F. & Das, J. P. Issues in Developmental Disabilities. LC 80-12931. 136p. (Orig.). 1980. pap. 11.50 (ISBN 0-8357-0524-2, SS-00136). Univ Microfilms.

Jenkins, Joseph R. & Jenkins, Linda M. Cross Age & Peer Tutoring: Help for Children with Learning Problems. LC 80-68283. 104p. 1981. pap. 7.25 (ISBN 0-86586-110-2). Coun Exc Child.

Johnson & Morasky. Learning Disabilities. 2nd ed. 450p. text ed. 19.95 (ISBN 0-205-06898-7, 2468980). Allyn.

Johnson, Clark. The Diagnosis of Learning Disabilities. 400p. 1981. text ed. 22.50x (ISBN 0-87108-236-5). Pruett.

Kaluger, George & Kolson, Clifford. Reading & Learning Disabilities. 2nd ed. (Special Education Ser.). 1978. text ed. 19.95 (ISBN 0-675-08524-1). Merrill.

Kaplan-Fitzgerald, Karen. Reach Me, Teach Me. 1977. pap. text ed. 5.00x (ISBN 0-87879-171-X). Acad Therapy.

Kauffman, James & Hallahan, Daniel, eds. Handbook of Special Education. (Illus.). 992p. 1981. text ed. 59.95 (ISBN 0-13-381756-3). P-H.

Kaufman, Alan S. & Kaufman, Nadeen L., eds. Clinical Evaluation of Young Children with the McCarthy Scales. LC 77-8969. 320p. 1977. 22.75 (ISBN 0-8089-1013-2). Grune.

Keith, Robert L. Graduated Language Training: For Patients with Aphasia & Children with Language Deficiencies. LC 79-91245. (Illus.). 308p. 1980. clinical test 30.00 (ISBN 0-933014-57-0). College-Hill.

Kinsbourne, Marcel & Caplan, Paula. Children's Learning & Attention Problems. 1979. 19.95 (ISBN 0-316-49395-3). Little.

Knickbocker, Barbara. Holistic Approach to Treatment of Learning Disorders. LC 79-65453. 1980. pap. 21.50 (ISBN 0-913590-58-4). C B Slack.

Knights, R. Treatment of Hyperactivity & Learning Disorders. 1979. 24.50 (ISBN 0-8391-1515-6). Univ Park.

Knights, Robert M. & Bakker, Dirk J., eds. The Neuropsychology of Learning Disorders: Theoretical Approaches. (Illus.). 1976. 24.50 (ISBN 0-8391-0951-2). Univ Park.

Kozloff, Martin A. A Program for Families of Children with Learning & Behavior Problems. LC 78-26578. 450p. 1979. 31.95 (ISBN 0-471-04434-2, Pub. by Wiley-Interscience). Wiley.

Kronick, Doreen. Social Development of Learning Disabled Persons: Examining the Effects & Treatments of Inadequate Interpersonal Skills. LC 81-81960. (Social & Behavioral Science Ser.). Date not set. text ed. price not set (ISBN 0-87589-499-2). Jossey-Bass.

La Brie, Vicki G. A Learning Disabilities Activity Guide for the Elementary Classroom. 50p. (Orig.). 1975. pap. 3.50 (ISBN 0-89080-029-4). Mercer Hse.

Lahey, Benjamin B., ed. Behavior Therapy with Hyperactive & Learning Disabled Children. (Illus.). 1979. text ed. 16.95x (ISBN 0-19-502478-8); pap. text ed. 8.95x (ISBN 0-19-502479-6). Oxford U Pr.

Lerner, Janet, et al. Cases in Learning & Behavior Problems: A Guide to Individualized Education Programs. LC 79-88101. 1979. pap. text ed. 9.50 (ISBN 0-395-28493-7); instructor's manual 0.25 (ISBN 0-395-28494-5). HM.

Lerner, Janet W. Learning Disabilities: Theories, Diagnosis, & Teaching Strategies. 3rd ed. LC 80-82975. (Illus.). 560p. 1981. text ed. 18.50 (ISBN 0-395-29710-9); write for info. set study guide (ISBN 0-395-30371-0); instr's manual 1.00 (ISBN 0-395-29711-7). HM.

Levine, Melvin D., et al. Pediatric Approach to Learning Disorders. LC 79-21839. 1980. 22.50 (ISBN 0-471-04736-8, Pub. by Wiley-Medical). Wiley.

Lewis, Richard S. The Other Child Grows up. LC 77-79032. 1977. 12.95 (ISBN 0-8129-0700-0). Times Bks.

Lovinger, Sophie L. Learning Disabilities & Games. LC 78-24619. (Illus.). 1979. text ed. 15.95x (ISBN 0-88229-353-2); pap. 8.95x (ISBN 0-88229-652-3). Nelson-Hall.

Lynn, Roa, et al. Learning Disabilities: An Overflow of Theories, Approaches & Politics. LC 79-7477. (Illus.). 1979. text ed. 15.95 (ISBN 0-02-919490-3). Free Pr.

McWhirter, J. Jeffries. The Learning Disabled Child: A School & Family Concern. LC 77-81300. (Illus.). 1977. text ed. 8.95 (ISBN 0-87822-147-6); pap. text ed. 8.95 (ISBN 0-87822-142-5). Res Press.

Major, Suzanne & Walsh, Mary Ann. Learning Activities for the Learning Disabled. LC 77-80656. (gr. 1-6). 1977. pap. 5.50 (ISBN 0-8224-4249-3). Pitman Learning.

Mann, Lester, et al. Teaching the Learning-Disabled Adolescent. LC 77-74377. (Illus.). 1977. pap. text ed. 16.75 (ISBN 0-395-25434-5). HM.

Marsh, George E., et al. The Learning Disabled Adolescent: Program Alternatives in the Secondary School. new ed. LC 77-18050. (Illus.). 1978. text ed. 16.95 (ISBN 0-8016-3118-1). Mosby.

Mauser, August J. Assessing the Learning Disabled: Selected Instruments. 3rd ed. LC 77-5099. 1977. pap. text ed. 12.50 (ISBN 0-87879-167-1). Acad Therapy.

Mercer, Cecil & Mercer, Ann. Teaching Students with Learning Problems. (Orig.). 1981. pap. text ed. 14.95 (ISBN 0-675-08040-1). Merrill.

Mercer, Cecil D. Children & Adolescents with Learning Disabilities. (Special Education Ser.). 1979. text ed. 19.95 (ISBN 0-675-08272-2). Merrill.

Migdail, Sherry R. & Vail, Priscilla L. Supplement to a Teacher's Notebook: Alternatives for Children with Learning Problems. 1978. pap. 4.25 (ISBN 0-934338-10-8). NAIS.

Millicap, J. Gordon. Learning Disabilities & Related Disorders: Facts & Current Issues. 1977. pap. 19.95 (ISBN 0-8151-5913-7). Year Bk Med.

Myklebust, Helmer R., ed. Progress in Learning Disabilities, Vol. 2. LC 67-24545. 416p. 1971. 34.00 (ISBN 0-8089-0711-5). Grune.

--Progress in Learning Disabilities, Vol. 3. 224p. 1975. 28.25 (ISBN 0-8089-0911-8). Grune.

--Progress in Learning Disabilities, Vol. 4. 272p. 1978. 24.00 (ISBN 0-8089-1128-7). Grune.

Myklebust, Helmer R. & Johnson, Doris, eds. Learning Disabilities-Educational Principles & Practices. (Illus.). 352p. 1967. 15.00 (ISBN 0-8089-0219-9). Grune.

Oettinger, Leon, Jr., ed. The Psychologist, The School & The Child with MBD-LD. 224p. 1978. 20.25 (ISBN 0-8089-1063-9). Grune.

Ohlson, E. LaMonte. Identification of Specific Learning Disabilities. LC 78-50726. 1978. pap. text ed. 8.95 (ISBN 0-87822-183-2). Res Press.

Osman, Betty. Learning Disabilities: A Family Affair. 1979. 10.00 (ISBN 0-394-42127-2). Random.

Osman, Betty B. Learning Disabilities: A Family Affair. 1980. pap. 5.95 (ISBN 0-446-97732-2). Warner Bks.

Parrill-Burnstein, Melinda. Problem-Solving & Learning Disabilities: An Information Processing Approach. (Illus.). 240p. 1981. 19.50 (ISBN 0-8089-1340-9, 793247). Grune.

Pavy, Robert N. & Metcalfe, Jean V. The Teacher's & Doctor's Guide to a Practical Approach to Learning Problems. 84p. 1974. text ed. 8.75 (ISBN 0-398-02991-1); pap. text ed. 5.50 (ISBN 0-398-02993-8). C C Thomas.

Piazza, Robert, ed. Learning Disabilities: Revision. (Special Education Ser.). (Illus., Orig.). 1980. pap. text ed. 10.95 (ISBN 0-89568-119-6). Spec Learn Corp.

--Readings in Language & Writing Disorders. (Special Education Ser.). (Illus., Orig.). 1978. pap. text ed. 10.95 (ISBN 0-89568-087-4). Spec Learn Corp.

--Three Models of Learning Disabilities. (Special Education Ser.). (Illus., Orig.). 1978. pap. text ed. 10.95 (ISBN 0-89568-089-0). Spec Learn Corp.

Ramos, Nancy P., ed. Delinquent Youth & Learning Disabilities. 1978. pap. text ed. 4.00x (ISBN 0-87879-190-6). Acad Therapy.

Rampp, Donald L. Auditory Processing & Learning Disabilities. LC 79-55973. (Cliffs Speech & Hearing Ser.). (Illus., Orig.). 1980. pap. text ed. 3.95 (ISBN 0-8220-1830-6). Cliffs.

Readings in Learning Disabilities. (Special Education Ser.). 1978. pap. text ed. 10.95 (ISBN 0-89568-001-7). Spec Learn Corp.

Reid, D. K. & Hresko, W. P. A Cognitive Approach to Learning Disabilities. 1981. 18.95 (ISBN 0-07-051768-1). McGraw.

Reid, Kim & Hresko, Wayne. Introduction to Learning Disabilities. (Illus.). 432p. 1981. text ed. 18.95x (ISBN 0-07-051768-1, C). McGraw.

Rosner, Jerome. Helping Children Overcome Learning Difficulties: A Step-by-Step Guide for Parents & Teachers. 2nd, rev. ed. (Illus.). 377p. pap. 8.95 (ISBN 0-8027-7178-5). Walker & Co.

Ross, Alan O. Learning Disability: The Unrealized Potential. (McGraw-Hill Paperbacks). 228p. 1980. pap. 4.95 (ISBN 0-07-053878-6, P&RB). McGraw.

--Learning Disability: The Unrealized Potential. 1977. 12.95 (ISBN 0-07-053875-1, P&RB). McGraw.

Roueche, John E. & Snow, Jerry J. Overcoming Learning Problems: A Guide to Developmental Education in College. LC 76-50724. (Higher Education Ser.). 1977. text ed. 13.95x (ISBN 0-87589-340-6). Jossey-Bass.

Rowan, Ruth D. Helping Children with Learning Disabilities: In the Home, School, Church & Community. LC 76-50001. 1977. 5.95 (ISBN 0-687-16832-5). Abingdon.

Rutledge, M. Suzanne. Stand on My Mountain. 1980. 5.50 (ISBN 0-8062-1489-9). Carlton.

Sabatino, David, et al. Learning Disabilities: Systemizing Teaching & Service Delivery. 350p. 1981. text ed. write for info. (ISBN 0-89443-361-X). Aspen Systems.

Sabatino, David A. & Mauser, August J. Intervention Strategies for Specialized Secondary Education. new ed. 1978. text ed. 22.95 (ISBN 0-686-52747-X). Allyn.

Sabatino, David A., ed. Learning Disabilities Handbook: A Technical Guide to Program Development. LC 75-26474. 549p. 1976. pap. 8.50 (ISBN 0-87580-521-3). N Ill U Pr.

Sanders, Marion. Clinical Assessment of Learning Problems: Model, Process & Remedial Planning. new ed. 1978. text ed. 21.95 (ISBN 0-205-06149-4, 2461498). Allyn.

Sapir, Selma & Wilson, Bernice. A Professional's Guide to Working with the Learning-Disabled Child. LC 77-94737. 1978. 15.00 (ISBN 0-87630-169-3). Brunner-Mazel.

Sasse, Margaret. Learning Difficulties, 'If Only We'd Known...' 2nd ed. (Illus.). 63p. 1980. pap. 4.95x (ISBN 0-9595417-1-3). Johnny Reads.

Schain, Richard J. Neurology of Childhood Learning Disorders. 2nd ed. (Illus.). 178p. 1977. 16.95 (ISBN 0-683-07566-7). Williams & Wilkins.

Scheiner, Albert P. & Abroms. The Practical Management of the Developmentally Disabled Child. LC 80-13725. (Illus.). 1980. text ed. 38.50 (ISBN 0-8016-0061-8). Mosby.

Shea, Thomas M. Teaching Children & Youth with Behavior Disorders. LC 77-22407. (Illus.). 1978. text ed. 18.95 (ISBN 0-8016-4565-4). Mosby.

Shelby, Madge E. Teaching the Learning Disabled & Emotionally Disturbed Child. 120p. (Orig.). 1979. pap. text ed. 4.50 (ISBN 0-935648-00-3). Halldin Pub.

Simonson, L. A. A Curriculum Model for Individuals with Severe Learning & Behavior Disorders. 1979. 17.95 (ISBN 0-8391-1322-6). Univ Park.

Smith, Deboral D. Teaching the Learning Disabled. (Illus.). 284p. 1981. text ed. 18.95 (ISBN 0-13-893511-4). P-H.

Smith, Sally L. No Easy Answers: Teaching the Learning Disabled Child. 1979. text ed. 12.95 (ISBN 0-87626-616-2); pap. text ed. 7.95 (ISBN 0-87626-615-4). Winthrop.

--No Easy Answers: The Learning Disabled Child. 352p. 1981. pap. 3.95 (ISBN 0-553-14138-4). Bantam.

Sobotowicz, William S. & Evans, James R. Cortical Dysfunctioning in Children with Specific Learning Disabilities. 104p. Date not set. price not set (ISBN 0-398-04593-3). C C Thomas.

Spadafore, Gerald J. & Spadafore, Sharon J. Learning Disability Rating Procedure. 32p. (Orig.). 1981. pap. 7.50 (ISBN 0-87879-265-1); pap. text ed. 6.00 set of 25 rating forms (ISBN 0-87879-266-X). Acad Therapy.

Special Learning Corp., ed. Learning Disabilities: Reference Book. (Special Education Ser.). (Illus., Orig.). 1980. text ed. 64.00 (ISBN 0-89568-116-1). Spec Learn Corp.

Sperry, Victoria B. A Language Approach to Learning Disabilities. (Orig.). 1972. pap. 3.00 (ISBN 0-89106-012-X, 0786). Consulting Psychol.

Stephens, Thomas M. Teaching Skills to Children with Learning & Behavioral Disorders. 1977. text ed. 19.95 (ISBN 0-675-08533-0). Merrill.

Stevens, Suzanne H. The Learning Disabled Child: Ways That Parents Can Help. 1980. 8.95 (ISBN 0-89587-013-4); pap. 4.95 (ISBN 0-89587-014-2). Blair.

Tarnopol, Lester. Learning Disabilities: Introduction to Educational & Medical Management. (Illus.). 412p. 1974. 18.75 (ISBN 0-398-01897-9); pap. 13.50 (ISBN 0-398-02894-X). C C Thomas.

Tarnopol, Lester, ed. Comparative Reading & Learning Difficulties. Tarnopol, Muriel. 1981. write for info. (ISBN 0-669-04107-6). Lexington Bks.

Valett, Robert. Developing Cognitive Abilities: Teaching Children to Think. LC 77-9912. (Illus.). 1978. pap. text ed. 11.45 (ISBN 0-8016-5213-8). Mosby.

Valett, Robert E. Remediation of Learning Disabilities: A Handbook of Psychoeducational Resource Programs. 2nd ed. LC 67-26847. 1974. 3-ring bdg. 22.50 (ISBN 0-8224-5850-0); pap. 18.95 (ISBN 0-8224-5851-9). Pitman Learning.

Van Dusen Pysh, Margaret & Chalfant, James C. The Learning Disabilities Manual: Recommended Procedures & Practices. rev. ed. LC 79-90979. (Illus.). 100p. 1980. pap. 5.95 (ISBN 0-933922-00-0, P500). PEM Pr.

Velten, Emmett C., Jr. & Sampson, Carlene. Rx for Learning Disability. LC 77-8595. 1978. 15.95x (ISBN 0-88229-330-3); pap. 8.95x (ISBN 0-88229-559-4). Nelson-Hall.

Wallace, Gerald & Larsen, Stephen C. Educational Assessment of Learning Problems: Testing for Teaching. new ed. 1978. text ed. 22.95 (ISBN 0-205-06090-0). Allyn.

--Educational Assessment of Learning Problems: Testing for Teaching. 1978. pap. text ed. 13.95 (ISBN 0-205-06089-7). Allyn.

Wallace, Gerald M. & Kauffman, James M. Teaching Children with Learning Problems. 2nd ed. (Special Education Ser.). 1978. text ed. 19.95 (ISBN 0-675-08425-3). Merrill.

Wallbrown, Jane D. & Wallbrown, Fred H. So Your Child Has a Learning Problem: Now What? 144p. (Orig.). 1981. pap. 9.95x (ISBN 0-88422-015-X). Clinical Psych.

Warner, Joan M. Learning Disabilities: Activities for Remediation. 2nd ed. 84p. 1980. pap. text ed. 3.95x (ISBN 0-8134-2118-7). Interstate.

Webber, Margaret S. Communication Skills for Exceptional Learners. LC 80-28094. 275p. 1981. text ed. 24.95 (ISBN 0-89443-343-1). Aspen Systems.

Weiss, Helen G. & Weiss, Martin S. Home Is a Learning Place: A Parents Guide to Learning Disabilities. 1976. pap. 5.95 (ISBN 0-316-92887-9). Little.

Weller, Carol & Strawser, Sherri. Weller-Strawser Scales of Adaptive Behavior for the Learning Disabled. 112p. (Orig.). 1981. pap. 15.00 (ISBN 0-87879-258-9). Acad Therapy.

Welton, Marion C. Something Is Right with This Child: A Positive Approach to Learning Disabilities. 1978. 6.50 (ISBN 0-533-02961-9). Vantage.

Wiig, Elisabeth H. & Semel, Eleanor M. Language Assessment & Intervention for the Learning Disabled. (Special Education Ser.). 464p. 1980. text ed. 19.95 (ISBN 0-675-08180-7). Merrill.

Wold, Robert M., ed. Vision: Its Impact on Learning. LC 74-84847. (Illus.). 1978. pap. 12.50x (ISBN 0-87562-055-8). Spec Child.

LEARNING DISORDERS

see Learning Disabilities

LEARY, TIMOTHY

Kleps, Art. Millbrook: The True Story of the Early Years of the Psychedelic Revolution. LC 76-54660. (Illus.). 1977. 10.00 (ISBN 0-916534-05-7); pap. 4.95 (ISBN 0-916534-06-5). Bench Pr.

LEASE AND RENTAL SERVICES

see also Automobiles, Rental; Industrial Equipment Leases

Davey, Patrick J. Leasing: Experiences & Expectations, Report No. 791. (Illus.). v, 58p. (Orig.). 1980. pap. 30.00 (ISBN 0-8237-0222-7). Conference Bd.

Green, Jack L. Leasing: Principles & Methods. 49.95 (ISBN 0-686-23598-3). Sound Pub.

LEASE SYSTEM

see Convict Labor

LEASES

see also Landlord and Tenant

Baker, C. R. & Hayes, R. S. Lease Financing: Alternative to Buying. LC 8-1576. 200p. 1981. 19.95 (ISBN 0-471-06040-2, Pub. by Wiley Interscience). Wiley.

Brue, Nordahl L. Retailer's Guide to Understanding Leases. 200p. 1980. 26.00 (ISBN 0-686-77799-9, C6580). Natl Ret Merch.

Collins, Robert L. Commericial Leasing. 1977. looseleaf 25.00 (ISBN 0-915260-03-4). Atcom.

Friedman, Milton R. Friedman on Leases, Vol. 3. 1978. 40.00 (ISBN 0-685-31251-8, N1-1312). PLI.

--Friedman on Leases: Nineteen Eighty Cumulative Supplement. LC 73-80968. 551p. 1980. pap. 30.00 (ISBN 0-686-61934-X, N5-1327); text ed. 140.00 three vol. set plus 1980 supplement (ISBN 0-686-61935-8, N6-1326). PLI.

Illustrations of Accounting for Leases. (Financial Report Survey: No. 16). 1978. pap. 8.00 (ISBN 0-685-92036-4). Am Inst CPA.

Kass, Louis A. Landlord - Tenant (N.Y.) 1964. pap. 2.00x (ISBN 0-87526-043-8). Gould.

Kaster, Lewis R., ed. Sale-Leasebacks: Economics, Tax Aspects, & Lease Terms. LC 79-87444. 1979. text ed. 35.00 (ISBN 0-685-95818-3, N2-1314). PLI.

McMichael, Stanley L. & O'Keepe, P. Leases: Percentage, Short & Long Term. 6th ed. 1974. 24.95 (ISBN 0-13-527309-9). P-H.

National Association of Home Builders. Sample Office Building Lease Form. 5p. 1978. 8.00 (ISBN 0-86718-042-0). Natl Assn Home Builders.

--Sample Shopping Center Lease Form. 10p. 1978. pap. 7.50 (ISBN 0-86718-034-X). Natl Assn Home Builders.

Pritchard, Robert E. & Hindelang, Thomas. The Lease-Buy Decision. (Illus.). 1980. 24.95 (ISBN 0-8144-5557-3). Am Mgmt.
Rudman, Jack. Senior Leasing Agent. (Career Examination Ser.: C-2494). (Cloth bdg. avail. on request). pap. 10.00 (ISBN 0-8373-2494-7). Natl Learning.
Thypin, Marilyn & Glasner, Lynne. Leases & Landlords. LC 79-9391. (Consumer Education Ser.: No. 2). (Orig.). (gr. 9-12). 1980. pap. text ed. 3.50 (ISBN 0-88436-515-8). EMC.

LEASES, INDUSTRIAL EQUIPMENT
see Industrial Equipment Leases

LEAST SQUARES
see also Correlation (Statistics); Estimation Theory; Graphic Methods; Probabilities
Anderssen, R. S. & Osborne, M. R. Least Squares Method in Data Analysis. (Series on Computing). 1969. pap. 9.95x (ISBN 0-7022-0903-1). U of Queensland Pr.
Bernstein, Serge & Poussin, Charles D. Approximation, 2 Vols. in 1. LC 69-16996. (Fr). 13.95 (ISBN 0-8284-0198-5). Chelsea Pub.
Bevington, Philip R. Data Reduction & Error Analysis for the Physical Sciences. LC 69-16942. 1969. pap. text ed. 12.95 (ISBN 0-07-005135-6, C). McGraw.
Chauvenet, William. Manual of Spherical & Practical Astronomy, 2 Vols. 5th & rev. ed. Set. 16.00 (ISBN 0-8446-1845-4). Peter Smith.
Hirvonen, R. A. Adjustment by Least Squares in Geodesy & Photogrammetry. LC 71-158408. 261p. 15.50 (ISBN 0-8044-4397-1). Ungar.
Mikhail, Edward M. Observations & Least Squares. 1976. text ed. 45.95 scp (ISBN 0-7002-2481-5, HarpC). Har-Row.
Slater, P., ed. The Measurement of Intrapersonal Space by Grid Techniques: Explorations of Intrapersonal Space, Vol. 1. LC 76-8908. 1976. 45.00 (ISBN 0-471-01360-9, Pub. by Wiley-Interscience). Wiley.
Taylor, B. N., et al. Fundamental Constants & Quantum Electrodynamics. (Reviews of Modern Physics Monographs). 1969. 22.50 (ISBN 0-12-684050-4). Acad Pr.

LEATHER
see also Tanning
Information Sources on Leather & Leather Products Industries. (UNIDO Guides to Information Sources Ser.: No. 3). 85p. 1980. pap. 4.00 (ISBN 0-686-70130-5, UNID 226, UN). Unipub.
Leather Accessories & Travelware. (BTA Studies). 1980. 335.00 (ISBN 0-686-31559-6). Busn Trend.
Middleton, Bernard C. Restoration of Leather Bindings. LC 72-184464. (Illus.). 220p. 1972. pap. 10.00 (ISBN 0-8389-3133-2). ALA.
Thomas, Bill & Stebel, Sid. Shoe Leather Treatment... LC 79-56300. (Illus.). 1979. 11.95 (ISBN 0-312-90861-X). J P Tarcher.
Thorstensen, Thomas C. Practical Leather Technology. rev ed. LC 75-12615. 304p. 1976. Repr. of 1969 ed. 22.50 (ISBN 0-88275-284-7). Krieger.

LEATHER, CORDOVAN
see Leather Work

LEATHER GARMENTS
The Leather Jacket Soldier. 10.00 (ISBN 0-686-74361-X). Westernlore.
Schwebke, Phyllis W. & Krohn, Margaret B. How to Sew Leather, Suede & Fur. (Illus.). 160p. 1974. pap. 3.95 (ISBN 0-02-011930-5, Collier). Macmillan.

LEATHER INDUSTRY AND TRADE
see also Bookbinding; Boots and Shoes; Handbags; Harness Making and Trade
A Discourse, Tendered to the High Court of Parliament. LC 74-28870. (English Experience Ser.: No. 749). 1975. Repr. of 1629 ed. 3.50 (ISBN 90-221-0749-3). Walter J Johnson.
Educational Research Council of America. Luggage Maker. Ferris, Theodore N. & Marchak, John P., eds. (Real People at Work Ser.: R). (Illus.). 36p. 1977. 2.25 (ISBN 0-89247-139-5). Changing Times.
Ellsworth, Lucius F. Craft to National Industry in the Nineteenth Century: A Case Study of the Transformation of the New York State Tanning Industry. new ed. LC 75-2578. (Dissertations in American Economic History). 1975. 23.00x (ISBN 0-405-07259-7). Arno.
European Leather Guide & Tanners of the World. 1980. 75.00x (ISBN 0-685-79495-4). State Mutual Bk.
The Footwear, Raw Hides & Skins & Leather Industry in OECD Countries, 1976-1977. 1979. 5.00x (ISBN 92-64-01874-3). OECD.
The Footwear, Raw Hides & Skins & Leather Industry in OECD Countries 1977-1978. 1979. 5.00x (ISBN 92-64-01927-8). OECD.
Information Sources on Leather & Leather Products Industries. (UNIDO Guides to Information Sources Ser.: No. 3). 85p. 1980. pap. 4.00 (ISBN 0-686-70130-5, UNID 226, UN). Unipub.
Leather Guide 1979-80. (Benn Directories Ser). 1979. 52.50 (ISBN 0-686-60658-2, Pub by Benn Pubns). Nichols Pub.
Lingwood, Rex. Leather in Three Dimensions. 144p. 1980. pap. 12.95 (ISBN 0-442-29733-5). Van Nos Reinhold.
O'Flaherty, Fred, et al, eds. The Chemistry & Technology of Leather, 4 vols. LC 76-50622. (ACS Monographs Ser.). 1978. Repr. of 1956 ed. Vol. 1 510p. 27.50 (ISBN 0-88275-474-2); Vol. 2 568p. 31.00 (ISBN 0-88275-886-1); Vol. 3 528p. 28.50 (ISBN 0-88275-887-X); Vol. 4 448. 25.50 (ISBN 0-88275-888-8). Krieger.
Proper, Churchill. Leathercraft: Bags, Cases, Purses. LC 72-185670. (Handicraft Ser.: No. 2). (Illus.). 32p. (Orig.). (gr. 7-12). 1971. lib. bdg. 2.45 incl. catalog cards (ISBN 0-87157-902-2); pap. 1.25 vinyl laminated covers (ISBN 0-87157-402-0). SamHar Pr.
World Hides, Skins, Leather & Footwear Economy. (Commodity Bulletin Ser.: No. 48). (Orig.). 1971. pap. 6.00 (ISBN 0-685-02927-1, F524, FAO). Unipub.

LEATHER WORK
see also Saddlery
Anderson, Lorraine. Leathercraft. LC 74-33529. (Early Craft Bks). (Illus.). 32p. (gr. 1-4). 1975. PLB 3.95 (ISBN 0-8225-0872-9). Lerner Pubns.
Boy Scouts Of America. Leatherwork. LC 19-600. (Illus.). 48p. (gr. 6-12). 1970. pap. 0.70x (ISBN 0-8395-3310-1, 3310). BSA.
Cherry, Raymond. Leathercrafting: Procedures & Projects. LC 79-83885. (Illus.). 1979. pap. 5.00 (ISBN 0-87345-153-8, B81925). McKnight.
Csiba, E. Leathercraft. (Illus.). 8.50 (ISBN 963-13-4641-2). Newbury Bks Inc.
Dorne, David. Easy-to-Do Leathercraft Projects with Full Size Templates. 1976. pap. 2.75 (ISBN 0-486-23319-7). Dover.
Educational Research Council of America. Leather Worker. Ferris, Theodore & Marchak, John P., eds. (Real People at Work Ser: B). (Illus.). 1974. pap. text ed. 2.25 (ISBN 0-89247-010-0). Changing Times.
Ericson, Lois & Ericson, Diane. The Bag Book. 1976. pap. 6.95 (ISBN 0-442-22327-7). Van Nos Reinhold.
Farnham, Albert S. Home Manufacture of Furs & Skins. (Illus.). 283p. pap. 3.00 (ISBN 0-936622-10-5). A R Harding Pub.
--Home Tanning & Leather Making Guide. (Illus.). 176p. pap. 3.00 (ISBN 0-936622-11-3). A R Harding Pub.
Ford, Thomas K. Leatherworker in Eighteenth-Century Williamsburg. (Williamsburg Craft Ser). (Illus., Orig.). 1967. pap. 1.25 (ISBN 0-910412-18-9). Williamsburg.
Goldsworthy, Maureen. Dressmaking with Leather. 1977. 17.95 (ISBN 0-7134-3240-3, Pub. by Batsford England). David & Charles.
Grainger, Sylvia. Leatherwork. LC 76-21871. (Illus.). (gr. 5-12). 1976. 7.95 (ISBN 0-397-31692-5, JBL-J). Har-Row.
Grant, Bruce. Encyclopedia of Rawhide & Leather Braiding. LC 72-10407. (Illus.). 1972. 15.00 (ISBN 0-87033-161-2). Cornell Maritime.
--Leather Braiding. (Illus.). 1950. 6.00 (ISBN 0-87033-039-X). Cornell Maritime.
Groneman, Chris. Leathercraft. (gr. 9-12). 1963. pap. 9.24 (ISBN 0-87002-204-0). Bennett IL.
Groneman, Chris H. Leather Tooling & Carving. LC 74-75258. (Illus.). 128p. 1974. pap. 3.00 (ISBN 0-486-23061-9). Dover.
--Leather Tooling & Carving. (Illus.). 7.50 (ISBN 0-8446-5042-0). Peter Smith.
Hamilton-Head, Ian. Leatherwork. (Illus.). 1979. 14.95 (ISBN 0-7137-0928-6, Pub by Blandford Pr England). Sterling.
Hanauer, Elsie. Creating With Leather. LC 73-107115. (Illus.). 1970. 7.95 (ISBN 0-498-07620-2). A S Barnes.
Hayden, Nicky. Leather. (Illus.). 1979. 8.95 (ISBN 0-684-16125-7, ScribT); encore ed. 3.95 (ISBN 0-686-77143-5). Scribner.
Hemard, Larry. Leathercraft: Creative Technique & Design. (Illus.). 7.00 (ISBN 0-8446-4424-2). Peter Smith.
Hobson, Phyllis. Tan Your Hide: Home Tanning Furs and Leathers. (Illus.). 1977. pap. 4.95 (ISBN 0-88266-101-9). Garden Way Pub.
Latham, Sid. Leathercraft. (Illus.). 1977. 13.95 (ISBN 0-87691-227-7). Winchester Pr.
Maleson, Benjamin. Leatherwork: A Basic Manual. (The Crafts Ser). (Illus.). 1974. pap. 3.95 (ISBN 0-316-54450-7). Little.
Mills, Brenda. Made in Suede: The Art of Tailoring in Soft Leather. (Illus.). 96p. 1976. 10.00 (ISBN 0-7135-1765-4). Transatlantic.
Morris, Ben & Morris, Elizabeth. Making Clothes in Leather. LC 75-21619. (Illus.). 95p. 1976. 10.95 (ISBN 0-8008-5063-7). Taplinger.
Newman, Thelma R. Leather As Art & Craft. (Arts & Crafts Ser.). (Illus.). 224p. 1973. 9.95 (ISBN 0-517-50574-6); pap. 7.95 (ISBN 0-517-50575-4). Crown.
Patton, Mary A. Designing with Leather & Fur (Real & Fake) 1972. 8.95 (ISBN 0-8208-0346-4). Hearthside.
Petersen, Grete. Leathercrafting. LC 80-95205. (Illus.). 96p. 1980. pap. 4.95 (ISBN 0-8069-8942-4). Sterling.
Pownall, Glen. Leathercraft. (Creative Leisure Ser.). (Illus.). 76p. 1974. 7.50x (ISBN 0-85467-019-X). Intl Pubns Serv.
--Leathercraft. (New Crafts Books Ser.). 76p. 1980. 7.50 (ISBN 0-85467-019-X, Pub. by Viking Sevenseas New Zealand). Intl Schol Bk Serv.
Shaw, Gladys J. Leather Craft. (Illus.). 62p. 1971. pap. 2.95 (ISBN 0-915462-08-7). Paragraph Pr.
Smith, Brendan. Brendan's Leather Book. (Illus.). 168p. (Orig.). 1972. pap. 4.50 (ISBN 0-686-02406-0). Outer Straubville.
Wilder, Edna. Secrets of Eskimo Skin Sewing. LC 76-3783. (Illus., Orig.). 1976. pap. 6.95 (ISBN 0-88240-026-6). Alaska Northwest.
Willcox, Donald. Modern Leather Design. (Illus.). 160p. 1981. pap. 10.95 (ISBN 0-8230-3101-2). Watson-Guptill.
--Modern Leather Design. (Illus.). 1969. 16.50 (ISBN 0-8230-3100-4). Watson-Guptill.
Working with Leather. pap. 1.50 (ISBN 0-8277-5713-1). British Bk Ctr.
Yount, John T. Leathercraft Handbook. LC 78-180260. 1971. 6.95 (ISBN 0-912092-43-2). Educator Bks.
Zimmerman, Fred W. Leathercraft. LC 77-8007. (Illus.). 120p. 1977. text ed. 5.20 (ISBN 0-87006-234-4). Goodheart.

LEATON, BEN
Corning, Leavitt, Jr. Baronial Forts of the Big Bend. (Illus.). 1969. 4.00 (ISBN 0-911536-08-6). Trinity U Pr.

LEAVE OF ABSENCE
see Teachers–Leaves of Absence

LEAVENWORTH, FORT
Hunt, Elvid. History of Fort Leavenworth, Eighteen Twenty-Seven to Nineteen Twenty-Seven. Kohn, Richard H., ed. LC 78-22418. (American Military Experience Ser.). (Illus.). 1979. Repr. of 1926 ed. lib. bdg. 22.00x (ISBN 0-405-11892-9). Arno.

LEAVES
Bancroft, Henrietta. Down Come the Leaves. LC 61-10496. (A Let's-Read-&-Find-Out Science Bk). (Illus.). (gr. k-3). 1961. PLB 8.79 (ISBN 0-690-24313-8, TYC-J). Har-Row.
Control of Bitter Pit & Breakdown by Calcium in the Apples Cox's Orange Pippin & Jonathan. (Agricultural Research Reports Ser.: No. 711). 43p. 1968. pap. 4.00 (ISBN 0-686-71855-0, PDC 173, Pudoc). Unipub.
Cyphers, Emma. New Book of Foliage Arrangements. rev. ed. LC 64-21085. (Illus.). 1965. 4.95 (ISBN 0-8208-0018-X). Hearthside.
Gates, D. M. & Papian, U. N. Atlas of Energy Budgets of Plant Leaves. 1971. 44.00 (ISBN 0-12-277250-4). Acad Pr.
Helmer, M. Jane. Foliage Plants for Modern Living. 2nd rev. ed. (Modern Living Ser.). (Illus.). 80p. 1977. pap. 2.95 (ISBN 0-89484-009-6, 10101). Merchants Pub Co.
Lerner, Sharon. I Found a Leaf. LC 64-25679. (Nature Bks for Young Readers). (Illus.). (gr. k-5). 1967. PLB 4.95 (ISBN 0-8225-0251-8). Lerner Pubns.
Montgomery, G. Gene, ed. The Ecology of Arboreal Folivores. LC 78-3103. (Symposia of the National Zoological Park Ser.: No. 3). (Illus.). 574p. 1978. 35.00x (ISBN 0-87474-646-9); pap. 15.00x (ISBN 0-87474-647-7). Smithsonian.
Williams, R. F. The Shoot Apex & Leaf Growth. (Illus.). 280p. 1975. 35.50 (ISBN 0-521-20453-4). Cambridge U Pr.

LEAVES–ANATOMY
see also Stomata
Maksymowych, R. Analysis of Leaf Development. LC 72-83585. (Developmental & Cell Biology Monographs: No. 1). (Illus.). 112p. 1973. 35.50 (ISBN 0-521-20017-2). Cambridge U Pr.
Preece, T. P. & Dickinson, C. H., eds. Ecology of Leaf Surface Micro-Organisms: Proceedings. 1971. 98.00 (ISBN 0-12-563950-3). Acad Pr.

LEAVES–JUVENILE LITERATURE
Kirkpatrick, Rena K. Look at Leaves. LC 77-26662. (Look at Science Ser.). (Illus.). (gr. k-3). 1978. PLB 11.15 (ISBN 0-8393-0060-3). Raintree Child.
Selsam & Hunt. A First Look at Leaves. (gr. k-3). 1976. pap. 1.50 (ISBN 0-590-10290-7). Schol Bk Serv.
Selsam, Millicent E. A First Look at Leaves. Selsam, Millicent E. & Hunt, Joyce, eds. LC 72-81376. (First Look at Ser). (Illus.). 32p. (gr. 2-4). 1972. PLB 5.39 (ISBN 0-8027-6118-6). Walker & Co.
Wohlrabe, Raymond A. Exploring the World of Leaves. LC 75-15865. (Illus.). 160p. (gr. 7 up). 1976. 12.95 (ISBN 0-690-00511-3, TYC-J). Har-Row.

LEAVIS, FRANK RAYMOND, 1895-
Bilan, R. P. The Literary Criticism of F. R. Leavis. LC 78-18089. 1979. 32.50 (ISBN 0-521-22324-5). Cambridge U Pr.
French, Philip, ed. Three Honest Men: Edmund Wilson, F. R. Leavis, Lionel Trilling, a Critical Mosaic. 192p. 1981. 18.95 (ISBN 0-85635-299-3, Pub. by Carcanet New Pr England). Persea Bks.
Hayman, Ronald. Leavis. 161p. 1977. 11.50x (ISBN 0-87471-917-8). Rowman.
Mulhern, Francis. The Moment of Scrutiny. 1979. 24.00 (ISBN 0-86091-007-5, Pub. by NLB). Schocken.
Robertson, P. J. The Leavies on Fiction: An Historic Partnership. LC 80-5099. 172p. 1980. 16.95x (ISBN 0-312-47731-7). St Martin.
Walsh, William. F. R. Leavis. LC 80-7971. 192p. 1980. 15.00x (ISBN 0-253-19426-1). Ind U Pr.

LEBANON
Eid, Nimr. Legal Aspects of Marketing Behavior in Lebanon & Kuwait. 8.00x (ISBN 0-86685-013-9). Intl Bk Ctr.
Fei, Edward & Klat, Paul. Balance of Payments of Lebanon, 1951 & 1952. 1954. pap. 11.95x (ISBN 0-8156-6024-3, Am U Beirut). Syracuse U Pr.
Freyha, Anis. Dictionary of Modern Lebanese Proverbs. (Arabic-Eng.). 1974. 25.00x (ISBN 0-86685-086-4). Intl Bk Ctr.
Ghattas, Emile. Inventory Management in Lebanon. 1977. 15.00x (ISBN 0-8156-6047-2, Am U Beirut). Syracuse U Pr.
Gordon, David C. Lebanon: The Fragmented Nation. LC 79-3174. (Publication Ser.: No. 227). 304p. 1980. 17.95 (ISBN 0-8179-7271-4). Hoover Inst Pr.
Khairallah, Shereen. Lebanon. (World Bibliographical Ser.: No. 2). 154p. 1979. 25.25 (ISBN 0-903450-10-0). ABC-Clio.
Lebanese Industrial & Commercial Directory 1980-81. 682p. 1980. 25.00 (ISBN 2-903188-05-X, PUB8, Publitec). Unipub.
Makdisi, Samir A. Financial Policy & Economic Growth: The Labanese Experience. LC 78-31561. (Modern Middle East Ser.). 1979. 20.00x (ISBN 0-231-04614-6). Columbia U Pr.
Middle East Commercial Information Centre. Yearbook of the Lebanese Joint-Stock Companies, 1977. 12th ed. 1977. 87.50x (ISBN 0-8002-0408-5). Intl Pubns Serv.
Salem, Elie A. Modernization Without Revolution: Lebanon's Experience. LC 72-85854. (International Development Research Center, Studies in Development: No. 6). 192p. 1973. 7.95x (ISBN 0-253-33870-0). Ind U Pr.
Salibi, Kemal S. Crossroads to Civil War: Lebanon, 1958-1976. LC 75-45397. (Illus.). 1976. 18.00x (ISBN 0-88206-010-4). Caravan Bks.
Who's Who in Lebanon, Nineteen Seventy-Seven to Nineteen Seventy Eight. 1978. 40.00 (ISBN 0-685-89831-8, PUB 2, Publitec). Unipub.
Who's Who in Lebanon 1980-1981. 821p. 1980. 60.00 (ISBN 2-903188-01-7, PUB5, Publitec). Unipub.
Yaukey, David. Fertility Differences in a Modernizing Country. LC 71-159109. 1971. Repr. of 1961 ed. 12.50 (ISBN 0-8046-1652-3). Kennikat.
Year-Book of the Lebanese Joint-Stock Companies 1980-81. 1187p. 1980. 60.00 (ISBN 2-903188-03-3, PUB7). Unipub.
Yearbook of the Lebanese Limited Liability Companies. 4th ed. 1405p. 1981. 60.00 (ISBN 2-903188-04-1, PUB9, Publitec). Unipub.
Ziadeh, Nicola. Syria & Lebanon. (Arab Background Ser.). 1968. 16.00x (ISBN 0-86685-034-1). Intl Bk Ctr.

LEBANON–DESCRIPTION AND TRAVEL
Brown, John P. Lebanon & Phoenicia: Ancient Texts Illustrating Their Physical Geography & Native Industries, Vol.1. The Physical Setting & The Forest. 1969. 20.00x (ISBN 0-8156-6014-6, Am U Beirut). Syracuse U Pr.
Buheiry, Marwan R. & Buheiry, Leila G., eds. The Splendor of Lebanon. LC 77-13169. 1977. deluxe ed. 350.00x (ISBN 0-88206-018-X). Caravan Bks.
Churchill, Charles H. Mount Lebanon: A Ten Years' Residence, from 1842 to 1852, 3 vols. LC 77-87615. Repr. of 1853 ed. Set. 87.50 (ISBN 0-404-16440-4). AMS Pr.
Cultural Resources in Lebanon. 384p. 1972. 6.00x (ISBN 0-8426-1222-X). Verry.
Freyha, Annis. Arabic-Arabic Dictionary of the Names of Towns & Villages in Lebanon. 1974. 16.00x (ISBN 0-86685-099-6). Intl Bk Ctr.
Khairallah. This Is Lebanon. 5.95 (ISBN 0-86685-017-1). Intl Bk Ctr.
Khayat, Marie. Lebanon, Land of the Cedars. 8.95x (ISBN 0-86685-018-X). Intl Bk Ctr.
Penwarden, Thelma. Colourful Lady Lebanon. 1978. 4.00 (ISBN 0-682-49242-6). Exposition.
Sterling Publishing Company Editors. Lebanon in Pictures. rev. ed. LC 73-90809. (Visual Geography Ser). (Illus., Orig.). (gr. 7 up). 1978. PLB 4.99 (ISBN 0-8069-1123-9); pap. 2.95 (ISBN 0-8069-1122-0). Sterling.
Ward, Philip. Touring Lebanon. (Illus.). 1971. 9.50 (ISBN 0-571-09433-3). Transatlantic.

LEBANON–DESCRIPTION AND TRAVEL–GUIDEBOOKS
Taylor, George. The Roman Temples of Lebanon: A Pictorial Guide. 2nd ed. (Illus.). 133p. 1971. 27.50x (ISBN 0-8002-1932-5). Intl Pubns Serv.

LEBANON–HISTORIOGRAPHY

Salibi, Kamal S. Maronite Historians of Medieval Lebanon. LC 78-63369. (The Crusades & Military Orders: Second Ser.). Repr. of 1959 ed. 31.50 (ISBN 0-404-17035-8). AMS Pr.

LEBANON–HISTORY

Abraham, A. J. Lebanon at Mid-Century: Maronite-Druze Relations in Lebanon 1840-1860; a Prelude to Arab Nationalism. LC 80-6253. 156p. 1981. lib. bdg. 17.50 (ISBN 0-8191-1536-3); pap. text ed. 8.50 (ISBN 0-8191-1537-1). U Pr of Amer.

Barakat, Halim. Lebanon in Strife: Student Preludes to the Civil War. (Modern Middle East Ser.: No. 2). 2656p. 1977. text ed. 15.00x (ISBN 0-292-70322-8). U of Tex Pr.

Browne, Walter E., ed. Documents on the French Mandate & World War II, 1936-1943. (The Political History of Lebanon, 1920-1950: Vol. 2). 1977. lib. bdg. 24.95 (ISBN 0-89712-023-X). Documentary Pubns.

Browne, Walter L. Lebanon's Struggle for Independence: Nineteen Forty-Three to Nineteen Fory-Seven, 2 vols. new ed. 1980. lib. bdg. 24.95 set (ISBN 0-89712-024-8). Vol. 1, Viii, 262 P. Vol. 2, V, 286 P. Documentary Pubns.

Browne, Walter L., ed. Documents on Politics & Political Parties Under the French Mandate, 1920-1936. (The Political History of Lebanon: Vol. 1). 1976. 24.95 (ISBN 0-89712-022-1). Documentary Pubns.

--Lebanon's Struggle for Independence, 2 vols. 1980. Set. 40.00 (ISBN 0-89712-025-6). Documentary Pubns.

Churchill, Charles H. The Druzes & the Maronites Under the Turkish Rule from 1840 to 1860. LC 73-6273. (The Middle East Ser.). Repr. of 1862 ed. 15.00 (ISBN 0-405-05329-0). Arno.

Deeb, Marius. The Lebanese Civil War. LC 79-19833. (Praeger Special Studies). 176p. 1980. 25.95 (ISBN 0-03-039701-4). Praeger.

Fedden, Robin. Phoenix Land. LC 66-20190. (Illus.). 1966. 6.50 (ISBN 0-8076-0380-5). Braziller.

Gabriel, Philip L. In the Ashes: The Story of Lebanon. LC 78-57513. 1978. 7.95 (ISBN 0-87426-046-9). Whitmore.

Jabbra, Joseph G. Political Socialization & Political Development: A Case Study. 31p. 1972. pap. 3.00 (ISBN 0-934484-02-3). Inst Mid East & North Africa.

Khalaf, Samir. Persistence & Change in Nineteenth Century Lebanon: A Sociological Essay. 1979. 20.00x (ISBN 0-8156-6053-7, Am U Beirut). Syracuse U Pr.

Khalidi, Walid. Conflict & Violence in Lebanon: Confrontation in the Middle East. LC 77-89806. (Harvard Studies in International Affairs: No. 38). (gr. 10 up). 1980. text ed. 12.95x (ISBN 0-87674-037-9); pap. 6.95x (ISBN 0-87674-038-7). Harvard U Intl Aff.

Longrigg, Stephen. Syria & Lebanon Under French Mandate, 1968. (Arab Background Ser.). 16.00x (ISBN 0-86685-021-X). Intl Bk Ctr.

Longrigg, Stephen H. Syria & Lebanon Under French Mandate. 1972. lib. bdg. 20.00x (ISBN 0-374-95088-1). Octagon.

Mahfoud, Peter. Lebanon & the Turmoil of the Middle East. 1979. 5.95 (ISBN 0-533-04253-4). Vantage.

Pritchard, James B. Recovering Sarepta, a Phoenician City. LC 77-28304. (Illus.). 1978. 21.00 (ISBN 0-691-09378-4). Princeton U Pr.

Salibi, Kamal S. Maronite Historians of Medieval Lebanon. LC 78-63369. (The Crusades & Military Orders: Second Ser.). Repr. of 1959 ed. 31.50 (ISBN 0-404-17035-8). AMS Pr.

--The Modern History of Lebanon. LC 75-14703. (Illus.). 1976. Repr. of 1965 ed. lib. bdg. 17.25x (ISBN 0-8371-8230-1, SAHL). Greenwood.

Scheltema, J. F., tr. Lebanon in Turmoil: Syria & the Powers in 1860. (Yale Oriental Researches Ser.: No. VII). 1920. 29.50x (ISBN 0-685-69861-0). Elliots Bks.

Scheltema, J. F. & Iskandar, Abkariyus, trs. The Lebanon in Turmoil: Syria & the Powers in 1860. LC 78-63551. (Yale Oriental Ser. Researches: 7). 1979. Repr. of 1920 ed. 30.00 (ISBN 0-404-60277-0). AMS Pr.

Vocke, Harold. The Lebanese Civil War. LC 78-50674. (Illus.). 1978. 12.95 (ISBN 0-312-47733-3). St Martin.

LEBANON–JUVENILE LITERATURE

Abood, Doris M. Lebanon: Bridge Between East & West. LC 73-84565. (Illus.). 40p. (gr. 5-10). 1973. 3.50 (ISBN 0-913228-07-9). Dillon-Liederbach.

Newman, Gerald. Lebanon. (First Bks). (Illus.). (gr. 4-6). 1978. PLB 6.90 s&l (ISBN 0-531-02237-4). Watts.

Winder, Viola H. The Land & People of Lebanon. rev. ed. LC 72-13164. (Portraits of the Nations Series). (Illus.). 1973. 8.95 (ISBN 0-397-31407-8). Lippincott.

LEBANON–POLITICS AND GOVERNMENT

Baaklini, Abdo I. Legislature & Political Development: Lebanon 1842-1972. LC 75-18369. 1976. 14.75 (ISBN 0-8223-0335-3). Duke.

Barakat, Halim. Lebanon in Strife: Student Preludes to the Civil War. (Modern Middle East Ser.: No. 2). 2656p. 1977. text ed. 15.00x (ISBN 0-292-70322-8). U of Tex Pr.

Bashir, Iskandar. Civil Service Reform in Lebanon. 1977. 17.95x (ISBN 0-8156-6050-2, Am U Beirut). Syracuse U Pr.

Browne, Walter L., ed. The Political History of Lebanon, 1920-1950, 2 vols. Incl. Vol. I. Documents on Politics & Political Parties Under the French Mandate, 1920-1936. 1976 (ISBN 0-89712-022-1); Documents on the French Mandate & World War II, 1936-1943. 1977 (ISBN 0-89712-023-X). lib. bdg. 24.95 ea. Documentary Pubns.

Grassmuck, George & Salibi, Kamal. Reformed Administration in Lebanon. LC 66-3550. 1964. pap. text ed. 1.00 (ISBN 0-932098-00-2). Ctr for NE & North African Stud.

Haley, P. Edward & Snider, Lewis W., eds. Lebanon in Crisis: Participants & Issues. 1979. text ed. 18.00x (ISBN 0-8156-2210-4); pap. text ed. 7.95x (ISBN 0-8156-2213-9). Syracuse U Pr.

Hourani, A. H. Syria & Lebanon: a Political Essay. 1977. lib. bdg. 59.95 (ISBN 0-8490-2714-4). Gordon Pr.

Jabbra, Joseph G. Political Socialization & Political Development: A Case Study. 31p. 1972. pap. 3.00 (ISBN 0-934484-02-3). Inst Mid East & North Africa.

Khalidi, Walid. Conflict & Violence in Lebanon: Confrontation in the Middle East. LC 77-89806. (Harvard Studies in International Affairs: No. 38). (gr. 10 up). 1980. text ed. 12.95x (ISBN 0-87674-037-9); pap. 6.95x (ISBN 0-87674-038-7). Harvard U Intl Aff.

Kisirwani, Marum. Patron-Client Politics & Bureaucratic Corruption: The Case of Lebanon. 42p. 1975. pap. text ed. 1.00 (ISBN 0-89249-006-3). Intl Development.

Koury, Enver M. The Crisis in the Lebanese System. LC 76-23477. 1976. pap. 4.25 (ISBN 0-8447-3216-8). Am Enterprise.

--The Operational Capability of the Lebanese Political System. LC 75-131973. 455p. 1972. pap. 7.00 (ISBN 0-934484-00-7). Inst Mid East & North Africa.

Meo, Leila. Lebanon, Improbable Nation: A Study in Political Development. LC 75-46621. 246p. 1976. Repr. of 1965 ed. lib. bdg. 20.25x (ISBN 0-8371-8727-3, MELE). Greenwood.

Qubain, Fahim I. Crisis in Lebanon. LC 61-19686. 1961. 5.00 (ISBN 0-916808-01-7). Mid East Inst.

Salem, Elie A. Modernization Without Revolution: Lebanon's Experience. LC 72-85854. (International Development Research Center, Studies in Development: No. 6). 192p. 1973. 7.95x (ISBN 0-253-33870-0). Ind U Pr.

Salem, Sema'An. Khalil & All of Lebanon. (Illus.). 135p. 1981. pap. 5.95 (ISBN 0-89260-205-8). Hwong Pub.

Smock, David R. & Smock, Audrey C. The Politics of Pluralism: A Comparative Study of Lebanon and Ghana. LC 75-8278. 356p. 1975. 14.95 (ISBN 0-444-99008-9). Elsevier.

Suleiman, Michael W. Political Parties in Lebanon: The Challenge of a Fragmented Political Culture. LC 67-14604. (Illus.). 1967. 22.50x (ISBN 0-8014-0422-3). Cornell U Pr.

LEBANON–SOCIAL CONDITIONS

Barakat, Halim. Lebanon in Strife: Student Preludes to the Civil War. (Modern Middle East Ser.: No. 2). 2656p. 1977. text ed. 15.00x (ISBN 0-292-70322-8). U of Tex Pr.

Fuller, Anne H. Buarij: Portrait of a Lebanese Muslim Village. LC 61-14633. (Middle Eastern Monographs Ser: No. 6). 1961. pap. 4.50x (ISBN 0-674-08550-7). Harvard U Pr.

Gulick, John. Social Structure & Culture Changes in a Lebanese Village. pap. 15.50 (ISBN 0-384-20440-6). Johnson Repr.

Haley, P. Edward & Snider, Lewis W., eds. Lebanon in Crisis: Participants & Issues. 1979. text ed. 18.00x (ISBN 0-8156-2210-4); pap. text ed. 7.95x (ISBN 0-8156-2213-9). Syracuse U Pr.

Williams, Judith R. Youth of Haouch el Harimi, a Lebanese Village. LC 68-23032. (Middle Eastern Monographs Ser: No. 20). 1968. pap. 4.50x (ISBN 0-674-96675-9). Harvard U Pr.

Witty, Cathie J. Mediation & Society: Conflict Management in Lebanon. LC 79-8863. (Studies on Law & Social Control Ser.). 1980. 14.50 (ISBN 0-12-760850-8). Acad Pr.

LEBANON–SOCIAL LIFE AND CUSTOMS

Evans, Louella M. Lebanon, Portrait of a People. (Illus.). 148p. 1967. 22.50x (ISBN 0-8002-1645-8). Intl Pubns Serv.

LEBESGUE MEASURE

see Measure Theory

LEBLANC, DUDLEY J.

Clay, Floyd M. Coozan Dudley LeBlanc: From Huey Long to Hadacol. LC 73-14609. (Illus.). 1974. 10.00 (ISBN 0-911116-69-9). Pelican.

LEBOU (AFRICAN PEOPLE)

Gamble, David. Wolof of Senegambia. LC 59-1106. 1967. 10.00x (ISBN 0-85302-008-6). Intl Pubns Serv.

LECHAUSSEE, PIERRE CLAUDE NIVELLE DE, 1692-1754

Lanson, Gustave. Nivelle De la Chaussee et la Comedie Larmoyante. 2nd ed. LC 74-170955. (Essays in Literature & Criticism Ser.: No. 155). 22.50 (ISBN 0-8337-4214-0). B Franklin.

LECIDEA

Hertel, Hannes. Revision Einiger Calciphiler Formenkreise der Flechtengattung Lecidea. (Illus.). 1967. pap. 30.00 (ISBN 3-7682-5424-0). Lubrecht & Cramer.

LECITHIN

Barbeau, Andre, et al, eds. Choline & Lecithin in Brain Disorders. LC 78-68608. (Nutrition & the Brain Ser.: Vol. 5). 1979. text ed. 47.50 (ISBN 0-89004-366-3). Raven.

Wade, Carlson. Lecithin Book. LC 80-82319. 128p. (Orig.). 1980. pap. 2.25 (ISBN 0-87983-226-6). Keats.

LECKIE, WILLIAM EDWARD HARTPOLE, 1838-1903

Lippincott, Benjamin E. Victorian Critics of Democracy. 1964. lib. bdg. 15.50x (ISBN 0-374-95035-0). Octagon.

LE CLERC DU TREMBLAY, FRANCOIS, 1577-1638

Huxley, Aldous. Grey Eminence. LC 74-5555. 342p. 1975. Repr. of 1941 ed. lib. bdg. 22.00x (ISBN 0-8371-7508-9, HUGE). Greenwood.

LECLERCQ, JEAN, 1911-

Bernard of Clairvaux: Studies Presented to Dom Jean Leclercq. LC 73-8099. (Cistercian Studies: No. 23). 1973. 5.50 (ISBN 0-87907-823-5). Cistercian Pubns.

LECOMTE DU NOUY, PIERRE, 1883-1947

Shuster, George N. & Thorson, Ralph E., eds. Evolution in Perspective: Commentaries in Honor of Pierre Lecomte Du Nouy. LC 78-105725. 1970. 10.00x (ISBN 0-268-00418-8). U of Notre Dame Pr.

LE CONTE DE LISLE, CHARLES MARIE RENE, 1818-1894

Brown, Irving H. Leconte De Lisle: A Study of the Man & His Poetry. LC 24-19430. (Columbia University. Studies in Romance Philology & Literature: No. 37). Repr. of 1924 ed. 22.50 (ISBN 0-404-50637-2). AMS Pr.

Denomme, Robert T. Leconte de Lisle. (World Authors Ser.: France: No. 278). 1973. lib. bdg. 10.95 (ISBN 0-8057-2518-0). Twayne.

LE CORBUSIER

see Jeanneret-Gris, Charles Edouard, 1887-1965

LECTIONARIES

Allen, Horace T., Jr. A Handbook for the Lectionary. LC 80-19735. pap. 8.95 (ISBN 0-686-70344-8). Geneva Pr.

Brokhoff, John R. Lectionary Preaching Workbook-C. 1979. pap. 16.35 (ISBN 0-89536-390-9). CSS Pub.

Catholic Church, Sacred Congregation for Divine Worship. The Study Edition (Lectors' Guide) of the Lectionary for Mass, Cycle a Sundays & Solemnities. International Committee on English in the Liturgy, tr. (The Study Edition (Lector's Guide) of the Lectionary for Mass Ser.: Texts from the New American Bible). 1977. pap. 5.95 (ISBN 0-916134-04-0). Pueblo Pub Co.

--The Study Edition (Lectors' Guide) of the Lectionary for Mass, Cycle B Sundays & Solemnities. 1978. pap. 5.95 (ISBN 0-916134-05-9). Pueblo Pub Co.

Corl, Heth H. Lectionary Worship Aids "B". 1978. pap. 5.20 (ISBN 0-89536-319-4). CSS Pub.

--Lectionary Worship Aids: Series A. 1977. pap. 5.20 (ISBN 0-89536-147-7). CSS Pub.

--Lectionary Worship Aids-Series C. rev. ed. 1976. pap. 5.20 (ISBN 0-89536-142-6). CSS Pub.

Crotty, Robert & Manley, Gregory. Commentaries on the Readings of the Lectionary: Cycles A, B, C. 1975. pap. 10.95 (ISBN 0-916134-20-2). Pueblo Pub Co.

Harrison, G. B. & McCabe, John. Proclaiming the Word. 2nd ed. 1976. pap. 4.95 (ISBN 0-916134-00-8). Pueblo Pub Co.

International Committee on English in the Liturgy Confraternity of Christian Doctrine for the New American Bible. Lectionary for Childrens Mass, Cycle a. Tos, Aldo J., intro. by. (Illus.). (gr. 6-8). 1974. 12.50 (ISBN 0-916134-10-5). Pueblo Pub Co.

--Lectionary for Children's Mass, Cycle C. Tos, Aldo J., intro. by. (gr. 6-8). 1976. 12.50 (ISBN 0-916134-12-1). Pueblo Pub Co.

Lectionary. 1970. 34.95 (ISBN 0-02-640400-1, 64040). Benziger Pub Co.

Lectionary from the Living Bible: Series A, B & C. 1974. Ser. A. 5.25 ea. (ISBN 0-89536-121-3). Ser. B (ISBN 0-89536-122-1). Ser.C (0-89536-123-X). CSS Pub.

Lectionary: New American Bible Version. small size ed. 15.00 (ISBN 0-686-14281-0, 25/22). Catholic Bk Pub.

Lectionary: New American Bible Version. large size ed. (Large Red & Black type, Ribbon Markers). red simulated leather 40.00 (ISBN 0-686-14282-9, 35/02); protective jacket 1.35 (ISBN 0-686-14283-7). Catholic Bk Pub.

Sloyan, Gerard S. Commentary on the New Lectionary. LC 75-22781. 444p. 1975. pap. 10.00 (ISBN 0-8091-1895-5). Paulist Pr.

The Study Edition (Lectors' Guide) of the Lectionary for Mass, Cycle C, Sunday & Solemnities. International Committee on English in the Liturgy, tr. from Latin. (The Study Edition (Lectors' Guide) of the Lectionary for Mass Ser.: Texts from the New American Bible). 1976. pap. 5.95 (ISBN 0-916134-06-7). Pueblo Pub Co.

Ullery, David. Keys to the Lectionary: Series C. 1973. 3.70 (ISBN 0-89536-118-3). CSS Pub.

LECTORS

see Lay Readers

LECTURE METHOD IN TEACHING

Ford, LeRoy. Using the Lecture in Teaching & Training. LC 68-20673. (Multi-Media Teaching & Training Ser.). (Orig.). 1968. pap. 3.95 (ISBN 0-8054-3412-7). Broadman.

Quiller-Couch, Arthur. A Lecture on Lectures. LC 74-7042. (English Literature Ser., No. 33). 1974. lib. bdg. 40.95 (ISBN 0-8383-1994-7). Haskell.

LECTURES AND LECTURING

see also Chautauquas; Lecture Method in Teaching; Lyceums; Oratory; Public Speaking also subdivision Addresses, Essays, Lectures, under specific subjects, e.g. Art-Addresses, Essays, Lectures

Brown, George. Lecturing & Explaining. 1978. 19.95x (ISBN 0-416-70910-9); pap. 10.95 (ISBN 0-416-70920-6). Methuen Inc.

Cairns, William B. The Forms of Discourse. 356p. 1980. Repr. of 1898 ed. lib. bdg. 20.00 (ISBN 0-89987-106-2). Darby Bks.

Friant, Ray J., Jr. Preparing Effective Presentations. rev. ed. LC 74-133853. 1980. pap. 3.50 (ISBN 0-87576-033-3). Pilot Bks.

Grimes, Joseph E. Papers on Discourse. (Publications in Linguistics & Related Fields Ser: No. 51). 1976. pap. 10.50 (ISBN 0-88312-061-5); microfiche 3.40 (ISBN 0-88312-461-0). Summer Inst Ling.

Hubbard, L. Ron. The Phoenix Lectures. 325p. 1968. 32.00 (ISBN 0-88404-006-2). Pubns Organization.

Joshi, Aravind, et al. Elements of Discourse Understanding. LC 80-29393. (Illus.). 352p. Date not set. 32.50 (ISBN 0-521-23327-5). Cambridge U Pr.

Labanna, Wallace D. Groupwork Guide for Discussion Leaders to the Cure Is in the Cause. 1972. 1.00x (ISBN 0-89039-003-7). Ann Arbor Pubs.

Long, George, tr. The Discourses of Epictetus; with the Encheiridion & Fragments. 25.00 (ISBN 0-8274-2188-5). R West.

Machiavelli. Discourses. Crick, Bernard, ed. (Classics Ser.). 1971. pap. 3.95 (ISBN 0-14-040014-1, Pelican). Penguin.

Markley, Kenneth A. Our Speaker This Evening: A Helpful Book on Effective Planning for a Special Speaker. 64p. 1974. pap. 1.95 (ISBN 0-310-28641-7). Zondervan.

Mead, Carl D. Yankee Eloquence in the Middle West: The Ohio Lyceum, 1850-1870. LC 77-5130. 1977. Repr. of 1951 ed. lib. bdg. 19.50x (ISBN 0-8371-9323-0, MEYE). Greenwood.

Morgan, Charles. Liberties of the Mind. 252p. 1979. Repr. of 1951 ed. lib. bdg. 25.00 (ISBN 0-89984-325-5). Century Bookbindery.

Nelson, Florence. How to Teach a Lecture-Type Subject. 1980. pap. 3.50 (ISBN 0-918328-06-3). Carma.

Petofi, J. S. & Rieser, H., eds. Studies in Text Grammar. LC 73-75766. (Foundations of Language Supplementary Ser.: No. 19). 370p. 1973. lib. bdg. 53.00 (ISBN 90-277-0368-X, Pub. by Reidel Holland). Kluwer Boston.

Pike, Kenneth L. Tagmemics, Discourse & Verbal Art. (Michigan Studies in the Humanities: No. 3). 1981. pap. 4.00 (ISBN 0-936534-02-8). Mich Slavic Pubns.

Reiss, Timothy J. Tragedy & Truth: Studies in the Development of a Neoclassical Discourse. LC 80-10413. 320p. 1980. 27.50x (ISBN 0-300-02461-4). Yale U Pr.

Scott, A. Boyd. Lectures for Club & Cloister. 1978. Repr. of 1907 ed. lib. bdg. 25.00 (ISBN 0-8492-8014-1). R West.

Sheehan, Cannon. Early Essays & Lectures: Emerson, Matthew Arnold, Aubrey De Vere. 1906. Repr. 17.50 (ISBN 0-8274-2209-1). R West.

Singer, Isaac B. Nobel Lecture. bilingual ed. 32p. 1979. 9.95 (ISBN 0-374-22302-5); pap. 3.25 (ISBN 0-374-51518-2). FS&G.

Smith, Peter H. Upgrading Lecture Rooms. (Illus.). 1979. 38.90x (ISBN 0-85334-849-9, Pub. by Applied Science). Burgess-Intl Ideas.

Van Dijk, T. A. & Petoefi, J., eds. Grammars & Description: Studies in Text Theory & Text Analysis. (Research in Text Theory: Vol. 1). (Illus.). 1977. 91.75x (ISBN 3-11-005741-7). De Gruyter.

Van Dijk, Teun A. Some Aspects of Text Grammers: A Study in Theoretical Linguistics & Poetics. (Janua Linguarum, Ser. Major: No. 63). 375p. 1972. text ed. 64.00x (ISBN 0-686-22546-5). Mouton.

--Text & Context: Some Explorations in the Semantics & Pragmatics of Discourse. (Longman Linguistics Library). (Illus.). 1977. text ed. 19.95x (ISBN 0-582-55085-8); pap. text ed. 11.95x (ISBN 0-582-29105-4). Longman.

LECYTHI

Prance, Ghillean T. & Mori, Scott A. Lecythidaceae - Part One the Actinomonophic-Flowered New World Lecythidaceae: Asteranthos, Gustavia, Grias, Allantoma & Cariniana. LC 79-4659. (Flora Neotropica Ser.: Vol. 21). 1979. pap. 28.00 (ISBN 0-89327-193-4). NY Botanical.

LEDERER, WILLIAM JOHN, 1912-

White, John S. Monarch Notes on Burdick & Lederer's the Ugly American. (Orig.). pap. 1.50 (ISBN 0-671-00812-9). Monarch Pr.

LEDOUX, CLAUDE NICHOLAS, 1736-1806

Lemagny, J. C. & De Menil, Dominiqueintro. by. Visionary Architects: Boullee, Ledoux, Lequeu. (Illus.). 1968. pap. 8.00 (ISBN 0-914412-21-3). Inst for the Arts.

LEE, ARTHUR, 1740-1792

Lee, Richard H. Life of Arthur Lee, 2 vols. facs. ed. LC 69-18528. (Select Bibliographies Reprint Ser). 1829. Set. 45.00 (ISBN 0-8369-5010-0). Arno.

Potts, Louis W. Arthur Lee: A Virtuous Revolutionary. LC 80-21831. (Southern Biography Ser.). 320p. 1981. 25.00x (ISBN 0-8071-0785-9). La State U Pr.

LEE, CHARLES, 1731-1782

The Lee Papers: Collections 1871-1874, 4 vols. LC 1-13394. 25.00x (ISBN 0-685-73906-6, New York Historical Society). U Pr of Va.

Moore, George H. Treason of Charles Lee. LC 79-120885. (American Bicentennial Ser). 1970. Repr. of 1860 ed. 12.00 (ISBN 0-8046-1278-1). Kennikat.

Thayer, Theodore. Washington & Lee at Monmouth: The Making of a Scapegoat. 1976. 9.95 (ISBN 0-8046-9139-8, Natl U). Kennikat.

LEE, HARPER, 1926-

Fitzwater, Eva. To Kill a Mockingbird Notes. (Orig.). pap. 2.25 (ISBN 0-8220-1282-0). Cliffs.

Monarch Notes on Lee's to Kill a Mockingbird. (Orig.). pap. 1.75 (ISBN 0-671-00681-9). Monarch Pr.

LEE, HENRY, 1756-1818

Chitwood, Oliver P. Richard Henry Lee: Statesman of the Revolution. (Illus.). 1967. 7.00 (ISBN 0-685-30817-0). McClain.

Royster, Charles. Light-Horse Harry Lee: The Legacy of the American Revolution. LC 80-2706. (Illus.). 320p. 1981. 15.00 (ISBN 0-394-51337-1). Knopf.

LEE, JAMES PRINCE, BP. OF MANCHESTER, 1804-1869

Newsome, David. Godliness & Good Learning: Four Studies on a Victorian Ideal. (Illus.). 1961. 16.00 (ISBN 0-7195-1015-5). Transatlantic.

LEE, JESSE, 1758-1816

Lee, Jesse & Thrift, Minton. Memoir of the Reverend Jesse Lee, with Extracts from His Journals. LC 72-83428. (Religion in America, Ser. 1). 1969. Repr. of 1823 ed. 14.00 (ISBN 0-405-00253-X). Arno.

LEE, JOHN DOYLE

Brooks, Juanita. John Doyle Lee. (Illus.). 1972. 12.50 (ISBN 0-87062-007-X). A H Clark.

Measeles, Evelyn B. Lee's Ferry: A Crossing on the Colorado. (Illus.). 150p. 1981. 12.95 (ISBN 0-87108-576-3). Pruett.

LEE, JOSEPH BRACKEN, 1899-

Russell, George B. J. Bracken Lee: The Taxpayer's Champion. 4.95 (ISBN 0-8315-0037-9). Speller.

LEE, NATHANIEL, 1635?-1692

Armistead, J. M. Nathaniel Lee. (English Authors Ser.: No. 270). 1979. 14.50 (ISBN 0-8057-6748-7). Twayne.

LEE, ROBERT EDWARD, 1807-1870

Adams, Charles F. Lee at Appomattox, & Other Papers. 2nd facs. ed. LC 77-134047. (Essay Index Reprint Ser). 1902. 23.00 (ISBN 0-8369-1901-7). Arno.

Alexander, Holmes. Washington & Lee. LC 65-28197. 1966. 3.00 (ISBN 0-88279-210-5). Western Islands.

Brooks, William E. Lee of Virginia: A Biography. LC 75-16842. (Illus.). 361p. 1975. Repr. of 1932 ed. lib. bdg. 20.00x (ISBN 0-8371-8270-0, BRLV). Greenwood.

Connelly, Thomas L. The Marble Man: Robert E. Lee & His Image in American Society. LC 76-41778. 1978. pap. 7.95 (ISBN 0-8071-0474-4). La State U Pr.

--The Marble Man: Robert E Lee & His Image in American Society. 1977. 12.50 (ISBN 0-394-47179-2). Knopf.

Dodd, William E. Lincoln or Lee. 1964. 5.00 (ISBN 0-8446-1155-7). Peter Smith.

Fishwick, Marshall W. Lee After the War. LC 73-7102. (Illus.). 242p. 1973. Repr. of 1963 ed. lib. bdg. 14.75x (ISBN 0-8371-6911-9, FILW). Greenwood.

Flood, Charles B. Lee - the Last Years. (Illus.). 352p. 1981. 14.95 (ISBN 0-395-31292-2). HM.

Freeman, Douglas. R. E. Lee, 4 vols. (Illus.). 1935. Set. lib. rep. ed. 100.00 (ISBN 0-684-15629-6, ScribT). Scribner.

Freeman, Douglas S. Lee's Lieutenants, 3 vols. 1942-1944. Set. lib. rep. ed. 90.00x (ISBN 0-684-15630-X, ScribT). Scribner.

--R. E. Lee: An Abridgement. (Illus.). 1961. lib. rep. ed. 30.00x (ISBN 0-684-15489-7, ScribT). Scribner.

Fuller, John F. Grant & Lee: A Study in Personality & Generalship. LC 57-10723. (Civil War Centennial Ser). (Illus.). 336p. 1957. 10.50x (ISBN 0-253-13400-5). Ind U Pr.

Griggs, Edward H. American Statesmen: An Interpretation of Our History & Heritage. LC 76-121474. (Essay Index Reprint Ser). 1927. 19.50 (ISBN 0-8369-1810-X). Arno.

Horn, Stanley F. Boy's Life of Robert E Lee. 59.95 (ISBN 0-87968-779-7). Gordon Pr.

Johnson, William J. Robert E. Lee the Christian. (Great American Christian Ser.). (Illus.). 1976. pap. 4.25 (ISBN 0-915134-14-4). Mott Media.

Riley, Franklin L., ed. General Robert E. Lee After Appomattox. facsimile ed. LC 72-37353. (Select Bibliographies Reprint Ser). Repr. of 1922 ed. 19.00 (ISBN 0-8369-6700-3). Arno.

Taylor, Walter H. General Lee, His Campaigns in Virginia. (Illus.). 1975. Repr. 22.50 (ISBN 0-685-69610-3). Pr of Morningside.

Trent, William P. Robert E. Lee. 34.95 (ISBN 0-8490-0962-6). Gordon Pr.

White, Henry A. Robert E. Lee. Repr. of 1902 ed. lib. bdg. 22.75 (ISBN 0-8371-1864-6, WHRL). Greenwood.

--Robert E. Lee & the Southern Confederacy, 1807-1870. LC 72-108554. 1971. Repr. of 1898 ed. 22.00 (ISBN 0-403-00258-3). Scholarly.

Zinn, Jack. R. E. Lee's Cheat Mountain Campaign. 1974. 10.00 (ISBN 0-87012-151-0). McClain.

LEE, ROBERT EDWARD, 1807-1870–JUVENILE LITERATURE

Commager, Henry S. & Ward, Lynd. America's Robert E. Lee. (Illus.). (gr. 7-9). 10.95 (ISBN 0-395-06707-3). HM.

Grant, Matthew G. Robert E. Lee. LC 73-18078. 1974. PLB 5.95 (ISBN 0-87191-302-X). Creative Ed.

Roddy, Lee. Robert E. Lee: Christian General & Gentleman. LC 77-7520. (Sowers Ser.). (Illus.). (gr. 3-6). 1977. pap. 4.25 (ISBN 0-915134-40-3). Mott Media.

LEE, ROBERT GREENE, 1886-

Lee, Robert G. Payday Everyday. LC 74-80721. 1975. 4.95 (ISBN 0-8054-5548-5). Broadman.

LEE FAMILY

Templeman, Eleanor L. Virginia Homes of the Lees. rev. ed. LC 73-81139. 1975. 1.90x (ISBN 0-911044-03-5). Templeman.

LEECH, JOHN, 1817-1864

Frith, William P. John Leech: His Life & Work, 2 Vols. LC 69-17491. 1969. Repr. of 1891 ed. Set. 39.00 (ISBN 0-8103-3831-9). Gale.

LEECHES

Bennike, S. Boisen. Contributions to the Ecology & Biology of the Danish Fresh-Water Leeches. Repr. of 1943 ed. pap. 17.00 (ISBN 0-384-03905-7). Johnson Repr.

Elliott, J. M. & Mann, K. H. A Key to the British Freshwater Leeches. 1979. 25.00x (ISBN 0-900386-38-X, Pub. by Freshwater Bio). State Mutual Bk.

LEEDS, ENGLAND

Thompson, Brian. Portrait of Leeds: History & Guide of the City of Leeds, England. LC 76-31673. (Illus.). 191p. 1971. 10.50x (ISBN 0-7091-2773-1). Intl Pubns Serv.

Wiseman, Herbert V. Local Government at Work: A Case Study of a County Borough. (Library of Political Science). 1967. text ed. 5.75x (ISBN 0-7100-5128-X); pap. 2.75x (ISBN 0-7100-5117-4). Humanities.

LEE'S 1ST NORTHERN INVASION

see Maryland Campaign, 1862

LEE'S 2ND NORTHERN INVASION

see Gettysburg Campaign, 1863

LEETER PICTURES

see also Concrete Poetry

LEETH, JOHN, 1755-1832

Jeffries, Ewel. A Short Biography of John Leeth, with an Account of His Life Among the Indians. Thwaites, Reuben G., ed. LC 74-180034. 12.00 (ISBN 0-405-08669-5, Pub. by Blom). Arno.

LEEUWENHOEK, ANTHONY VAN, 1632-1723

Leeuwenhoek, Anthony Van. Anthony Van Leeuwenhoek & His Little Animals. pap. 5.00 (ISBN 0-486-60594-9). Dover.

LEEWARD ISLANDS

Gurney, Joseph J. Winter in the West Indies, Described in Familiar Letters to Henry Clay, of Kentucky. 2nd ed. LC 69-19356. (Illus.). Repr. of 1840 ed. 13.75x (ISBN 0-8371-1022-X). Greenwood.

LE FANU, JOSEPH SHERIDAN, 1814-1873

Begnal, Michael. Joseph Sheridan Lefanu. LC 71-126032. (Irish Writers Ser.). 87p. 4.50 (ISBN 0-8387-7766-X); pap. 1.95 (ISBN 0-8387-7735-X). Bucknell U Pr.

Ellis, Stewart M. Wilkie Collins, Le Fanu, & Others. facs. ed. LC 68-29203. (Essay Index Reprint Ser). 1968. Repr. of 1931 ed. 17.00 (ISBN 0-8369-0413-3). Arno.

McCormack, W. J. Sheridan le Fanu & Victorian Ireland. (Illus.). 334p. 1980. text ed. 42.00x (ISBN 0-19-812629-8). Oxford U Pr.

LEFT- AND RIGHT-HANDEDNESS

Barsley, Michael. Left-Handed People. pap. 4.00 (ISBN 0-87980-087-9). Wilshire.

Beeley, Arthur L. An Experimental Study in Left-Handedness, with Practical Suggestions for Schoolroom Tests. LC 78-72787. (Brainedness, Handedness, & Mental Ability Ser.). Repr. of 1918 ed. 22.50 (ISBN 0-404-60852-3). AMS Pr.

Blau, Abram. The Master Hand: A Study of the Origin & Meaning of Right & Left Sidedness & Its Relation to Personality & Language. LC 78-72790. (Brainedness, Handedness, & Mental Ability Ser.). Repr. of 1946 ed. 21.50 (ISBN 0-404-60854-X). AMS Pr.

Bliss, James & Morella, Joseph. The Left Hander's Handbook: A Catalog, Guide & Informal History of Living Left in a Right-Handed World. LC 78-71038. 1980. 12.95 (ISBN 0-89104-134-6); pap. 6.95 (ISBN 0-89104-133-8). A & W Pubs.

Brainedness, Handedness, & Mental Abilities: The Foundations of Neuropsychology, 40 titles in 44 vols. write for info. (ISBN 0-404-60850-7). AMS Pr.

Brown, Mark. Left Handed: Right Handed. LC 80-66094. (Illus.). 160p. 1980. 14.95 (ISBN 0-7153-7510-5). David & Charles.

De Kay, James T. Left-Handed Book. LC 66-23271. (Illus.). 64p. 1966. pap. 2.95 (ISBN 0-87131-156-9). M Evans.

--The Natural Superiority of the Left-Hander. LC 79-15824. (Illus.). 128p. 1979. pap. 3.95 (ISBN 0-87131-307-3). M Evans.

Fadely, Jack L. & Hosler, Virginia N. Understanding the Alpha Child at Home & School: Left & Right Hemispheric Function in Relation to Personality & Learning. (Illus.). 256p. 1979. text ed. 17.25 (ISBN 0-398-03862-7). C C Thomas.

Fincher, Jack. Lefties: The Origins & Consequences of Being Left-Handed. 1980. pap. 4.95 (ISBN 0-399-50460-5, Perigee). Putnam.

Gardner, Warren H. Left Handed Writing Instruction Manual. (Illus.). 1958. pap. text ed. 1.25x (ISBN 0-8134-0058-9, 58). Interstate.

Giesecke, Minnie. The Genesis of Hand Preference. LC 78-72795. Repr. of 1936 ed. 18.00 (ISBN 0-686-63637-6). AMS Pr.

--Genesis of Hand Preference. 1936. pap. 7.00 (ISBN 0-527-01490-7). Kraus Repr.

Gould, George M. Righthandedness & Lefthandedness: With Chapters Treating of the Writing Posture, the Rule of the Road, Etc. LC 78-72794. Repr. of 1908 ed. 26.50 (ISBN 0-404-60859-0). AMS Pr.

Haefner, Ralph. Educational Significance of Left-Handedness. LC 73-178804. (Columbia University. Teachers College. Contributions to Education: No. 360). Repr. of 1929 ed. 17.50 (ISBN 0-404-55360-5). AMS Pr.

Haislet, Barbara. Why Are Some People Left-Handed? (Creative's Questions & Answers Ser.). (Illus.). 32p. (gr. 3-4). Date not set. PLB 5.65 (ISBN 0-87191-753-X); pap. 2.75 (ISBN 0-89812-222-8). Creative Ed.

Herron, Jeannine, ed. Neuropsychology of Left-Handedness. LC 79-23854. (Perspectives in Neurolinguistics & Psycholinguistics Ser.). 1980. 24.50 (ISBN 0-12-343150-6). Acad Pr.

Johnston, Philip W. Relation of Certain Anomalies of Vision & Lateral Dominance to Reading Disability. 1942. pap. 8.00 (ISBN 0-527-01523-7). Kraus Repr.

Jones, Wallace F. A Study of Handedness. LC 78-72804. (Brainedness, Handedness, & Mental Abilities Ser.). Repr. of 1918 ed. 21.50 (ISBN 0-404-60867-1). AMS Pr.

Lerner, Marguerite R. Lefty: The Story of Left-Handedness. LC 60-14007. (Medical Bks for Children). (Illus.). (gr. k-5). 1960. PLB 3.95 (ISBN 0-8225-0005-1). Lerner Pubns.

Lindsay, Rae. The Left-Handed Book. (gr. 4 up). 1980. PLB 6.90 (ISBN 0-531-02258-7). Watts.

Miller, Elizabeth & Cohen, Jane. Cat & Dog Have a Parade. (Cat & Dog Ser.). (Illus.). 48p. (ps-3). 1981. PLB 5.90 (ISBN 0-531-04295-2). Watts.

Neiman, Peter. The Lefty's Survival Manual. 1980. pap. 2.95 (ISBN 0-553-01225-8). Bantam.

Teaching Left-Handed Children. 1974. pap. 3.00 (ISBN 0-340-18199-0). Verry.

Wilson, David. The Right Hand: Left-Handedness. LC 78-72830. (Brainedness, Handedness, & Mental Ability Ser.). Repr. of 1891 ed. 22.50 (ISBN 0-404-60898-1). AMS Pr.

LEG

see also Femur

American Academy of Orthopaedic Surgeons. Symposium on Trauma to the Leg & Its Sequelae. LC 81-11104. (Illus.). 448p. 1981. text ed. 47.50 (ISBN 0-8016-0081-2). Mosby.

Gerrick, David J. Surface Anatomy: The Leg. 1979. 20.00 (ISBN 0-916750-61-2). Dayton Labs.

Johnson, Daintree & Pflug, Joseph. The Swollen Leg - Causes & Treatment. 1975. 20.00 (ISBN 0-397-58155-6, JBL-Med-Nursing). Har-Row.

Kabat, Herman. Low Back & Leg Pain from Herniated Cervical Disk. 164p. 1980. 14.50 (ISBN 0-87527-246-0). Green.

Kessler, Ethel & Kessler, Leonard. Two, Four, Six, Eight: A Book About Legs. LC 80-12574. (Illus.). 48p. (ps-3). 1980. PLB 7.95 (ISBN 0-396-07842-7). Dodd.

Roenigk, Henry H., Jr. & Young, Jess R. Leg Ulcers: Medical & Surgical Management. (Illus.). 1975. 34.50x (ISBN 0-06-142278-9, Harper Medical). Har-Row.

Rutt. Surgery of the Leg & Foot. (Hackenbroch Ser.). 1980. text ed. write for info. (ISBN 0-7216-4446-5). Saunders.

Stuart, Harold C. Growth of Bone, Muscle & Overlying Tissues. 1940. pap. 13.00 (ISBN 0-527-01515-6). Kraus Repr.

LEGACIES

see also Wills

Behee, John R. Fielding Yost's Legacy. LC 77-173360. (Illus.). 210p. 1971. 6.95 (ISBN 0-914464-00-0). J & J Bks.

LEGACIES, TAXATION OF

see Inheritance and Transfer Tax

LEGAL ABBREVIATIONS

see Law–Abbreviations

LEGAL AID

see also In Forma Pauperis; Legal Assistance to the Poor; Public Defenders

Brakel, Samuel J. Judicare: Public Funds, Private Lawyers, and Poor People. LC 74-75748. 1974. 10.00 (ISBN 0-910058-62-8); pap. 5.00 (ISBN 0-910058-60-1). Am Bar Foun.

Brown, Esther L. Lawyers & the Promotion of Justice. (Russell Sage Foundation Reprint Ser). Repr. of 1938 ed. lib. bdg. 26.00x (ISBN 0-697-00201-2). Irvington.

Brownell, Emery A. Legal Aid in the United States: A Study of the Availability of Lawyers Services for Persons Unable to Pay Fees. LC 77-141417. (Illus.). 1971. Repr. of 1951 ed. lib. bdg. 26.50x (ISBN 0-8371-4689-5, BRLE). Greenwood.

Conference of the Institute of Industrial Relations. The Development of Prepaid Legal Services: Proceedings. 1972. 2.50 (ISBN 0-89215-039-4). U Cal LA Indus Rel.

Deitch, Lillian & Weinstein, David. Prepaid Legal Services: Socio-Economic Impacts. LC 76-5582. 1976. 19.50 (ISBN 0-669-00659-9). Lexington Bks.

Denver Law Journal Staff. Rural Poverty & the Law in Southern Colorado. (Legal Services for the Poor Ser). 85p. 1971. pap. 2.00 (ISBN 0-685-32708-6). Am Bar Foun.

Ellis, Robert L., ed. Taking Ideals Seriously: The Case for a Lawyers' Public Interest Movement. LC 80-26380. (Orig.). 1981. pap. 6.95 (ISBN 0-938848-00-3). Equal Justice Foun.

Fisher, Kenneth P. & Ivie, Charles C. Franchising Justice: The Office of Economic Opportunity Legal Services Program & Traditional Legal Aid. (Legal Services for the Poor Ser). 18p. (Orig.). 1971. pap. 2.00 (ISBN 0-910058-06-7). Am Bar Foun.

Garth, Bryant. Neighborhood Law Firms for the Poor: A Comparative Study of Recent Developments in Legal Aid & in the Legal Profession. LC 80-51739. 282p. 1980. 40.00x (ISBN 90-286-0180-5). Sijthoff & Noordhoff.

Krantz, Sheldon, et al. Right to Counsel in Criminal Cases: The Mandate of Argersinger V Hamlin. LC 75-14111. 1976. 35.00 (ISBN 0-88410-213-0). Ballinger Pub.

Marks, F. Raymond, et al. The Shreveport Plan: An Experiment in the Delivery of Legal Services. LC 74-77636. 1974. pap. 5.00 (ISBN 0-910058-61-X). Am Bar Foun.

Pfennigstorf, Werner & Kimball, Spencer L., eds. Legal Service Plans: Approaches to Regulation. 1977. 16.00 (ISBN 0-910058-86-5). Am Bar Foun.

Silverstein, Lee. Defense of the Poor in Criminal Cases in American State Courts, 3 Vols. LC 65-23152. 1965. Set. 15.00 (ISBN 0-910058-51-2); Vol. 2. 5.00 (ISBN 0-910058-03-2); Vol. 3. 5.00 (ISBN 0-910058-04-0). Am Bar Foun.
--Waiver of Court Costs & Appointment of Counsel for Poor Persons in Civil Cases. (Legal Services for the Poor Ser). 36p. 1968. Repr. 2.00 (ISBN 0-685-22684-0). Am Bar Foun.
Smith, Reginald H. Justice & the Poor: A Study of the Present Denial of Justice to the Poor. LC 70-137188. (Poverty U.S.A. Historical Record Ser). 1971. Repr. of 1919 ed. 17.00 (ISBN 0-405-03126-2). Arno.
Wilkins, James L. Legal Aid in the Criminal Courts. LC 75-16176. 1975. 15.00x (ISBN 0-8020-2191-3). U of Toronto Pr.
Zander, Michael. Legal Services for the Community. (Illus.). 1978. 35.00x (ISBN 0-85117-155-9). Intl Pubns Serv.
Zemans, Fredrick H., ed. Perspectives on Legal Aid: An International Survey. LC 79-833. 1979. lib. bdg. 27.50 (ISBN 0-313-20986-3, ZLA/). Greenwood.

LEGAL AID-GREAT BRITAIN

Byles, Anthea & Morris, Pauline. Unmet Need: The Case of the Neighborhood Law Center. (Direct Editions Ser). 1978. pap. 9.95 (ISBN 0-7100-8649-0). Routledge & Kegan.

LEGAL AID SOCIETIES

Johnson, Earl, Jr. Justice & Reform: The Formative Years of the American Legal Service Program. rev ed. LC 75-44823. 1978. pap. text ed. 6.95 (ISBN 0-87855-612-5). Transaction Bks.
Smith, Reginald H. Justice & the Poor: A Study of Present Day Denial of Justice to the Poor. 3rd ed. (Criminology, Law Enforcement, & Social Problems Ser.: No. 139). (With introductory essay added). 1972. Repr. of 1924 ed. 10.00 (ISBN 0-87585-139-8). Patterson Smith.

LEGAL ARGUMENTS

see Forensic Orations

LEGAL ASSISTANCE TO THE POOR

Berney, Arthur L., et al. Legal Problems of the Poor: Cases & Materials. 1440p. 1975. 25.50 (ISBN 0-316-09189-8). Little.
Brakel, Samuel J. Free Legal Services for the Poor: Staffed Office Vs. Judicare: the Client's Evaluation. (Research Contribution Ser.: No. 3). 1973. pap. 2.00 (ISBN 0-685-39800-5). Am Bar Foun.
Carpenter, J. Estlin. The Life and Work of Mary Carpenter. 2nd ed. LC 77-172564. (Criminology, Law Enforcement, & Social Problems Ser.: No. 145). (Illus.). 420p. (Index added). 1974. Repr. of 1881 ed. lib. bdg. 20.00 (ISBN 0-87585-145-2). Patterson Smith.
Hermann, Robert, et al. Counsel for the Poor: Criminal Defense in Urban America. LC 77-9151. 1977. 17.95 (ISBN 0-669-01810-4). Lexington Bks.
Smith, Chris & Hoath, David C. Law & the Underprivileged. 280p. 1975. 20.00x (ISBN 0-7100-8259-2). Routledge & Kegan.

LEGAL ASSISTANTS

Adams, Harold W. & Stringham, Ray. Lawyer's Management Principles: A Course for Assistants, Student Syllabus. (gr. 11-12). 1975. pap. text ed. 6.65 (ISBN 0-89420-079-8, 101028); cassette recordings 86.90 (ISBN 0-89420-200-6, 101000). Natl Book.
Arco Editorial Board. Attorney-Assistant Trainee. 3rd. ed. (Orig.). 1975. pap. 8.00 (ISBN 0-668-01084-3); PLB 7.50 (ISBN 0-668-01707-4). Arco.
Blackstone Associates. Paralegals & Administrative Assistants. 5.00 (ISBN 0-686-22354-3). Natl Dist Atty.
Bruno, Carole. Paralegal's Litigation Handbook. 1979. 27.50 (ISBN 0-87624-425-8). Inst Busn Plan.
Deming, Richard. The Paralegal: A New Career. LC 79-27172. 1979. 7.95 (ISBN 0-525-66655-9). Elsevier-Nelson.
Eimermann, Thomas E. Fundamentals of Paralegalism. (Illus.). 420p. 1980. pap. text ed. 18.95 (ISBN 0-316-23120-7); instructor's manual free (ISBN 0-316-23121-5). Little.
Larbalestrier, D. Paralegal Practice & Procedure: A Practical Guide for the Legal Assistant. 1979. pap. 9.95 (ISBN 0-13-648691-6). P-H.
National Association of Legal Assistants Inc. Manual for Legal Assistants. Park, William R., ed. LC 79-18552. 529p. 1979. text ed. 19.95 (ISBN 0-8299-2059-5). West Pub.
Paralegal Practice Handbook, No. 2. rev. ed. LC 77-85386. 1981. 27.50 (ISBN 0-915362-19-8). M K Heller.
Ulrich, Paul G. & Mucklestone, Robert S., eds. Working with Legal Assistants: A Team Approach for Lawyers & Legal Assistants--I. LC 80-69532. 278p. (Orig.). 1980. pap. text ed. 25.00x (ISBN 0-89707-030-5, 5110060). Amer Bar Assn.

LEGAL AUTHORITIES

see also Citation of Legal Authorities

LEGAL BIBLIOGRAPHY

see Law-Bibliography; Legal Research

LEGAL CERTAINTY

see Law-Interpretation and Construction; Stare Decisis

LEGAL CHARITIES

see Legal Aid

LEGAL CHEMISTRY

see Chemistry, Forensic

LEGAL CITATION

see Citation of Legal Authorities

LEGAL COMPOSITION

see also Briefs; Conveyancing; Forms (Law)

Block, Gertrude. Effective Legal Writing: A Style Book for Students & Lawyers. 150p. 1981. pap. text ed. 5.95 (ISBN 0-88277-033-0). Foundation Pr.
Cooper, Frank E. Writing in Law Practice. 1963. text ed. 17.00 (ISBN 0-672-81021-2, Bobbs-Merrill Law). Michie-Bobbs.
Dickerson, F. Reed. The Fundamentals of Legal Drafting. 1965. 13.00 (ISBN 0-316-18394-6). Little.
--Materials on Legal Drafting. LC 81-1359. (American Casebook Ser.). 407p. 1981. text ed. 14.95 (ISBN 0-686-69769-3). West Pub.
Mellinkoff, David. Legal Writing: Sense & Nonsense. 320p. 1982. 14.95 (ISBN 0-684-17293-3, ScribT). Scribner.
Rossman, George, ed. Advocacy & the King's English. 1960. 17.50 (ISBN 0-672-80002-0, Bobbs-Merrill Law). Michie-Bobbs.
Wincor, Richard. Contracts in Plain English. 128p. 1975. 16.50 (ISBN 0-07-070966-1, P&RB). McGraw.

LEGAL DIRECTORIES

see Lawyers-Directories

LEGAL DOCUMENTS

see also Evidence, Documentary; Writing-Identification

Dickerson, F. Reed. Materials on Legal Drafting. LC 81-1359. (American Casebook Ser.). 407p. 1981. text ed. 14.95 (ISBN 0-686-69769-3). West Pub.
Harrison, Wilson R. Suspect Documents: Their Scientific Examination. (Illus.). 594p. 1981. text ed. 41.95 (ISBN 0-88229-759-7). Nelson-Hall.
Osborn, Albert S. Questioned Documents. 2nd ed. LC 74-78841. (Illus.). 1072p. 1974. Repr. of 1926 ed. 27.95x (ISBN 0-88229-190-4). Nelson-Hall.
Taubenschlag, Rafael, ed. The Journal of Juristic Papyrology, Vol. 1, No. 1. 155p. 1946. pap. 5.00 (ISBN 0-686-09127-2). Polish Inst Arts.

LEGAL EDUCATION

see Law-Study and Teaching

LEGAL ESSAYS

see Law-Addresses, Essays, Lectures

LEGAL ETHICS

see also Attorney and Client

Archer, Gleason L. Ethical Obligations of the Lawyer. 367p. 1981. Repr. of 1910 ed. lib. bdg. 27.50x (ISBN 0-8377-0207-0). Rothman.
Aronson, Robert H. & Weckstein, Donald T. Professional Responsibility in a Nutshell. LC 80-15007. (Nutshell Ser.). 448p. 1980. pap. text ed. 6.95 (ISBN 0-8299-2095-1). West Pub.
Association Of The Bar Of The City Of New York. Opinions of the Committees on Professional Ethics of the Association of the Bar of the City of New York & the New York County Lawyer's Association. LC 73-20262. 905p. 1973. 25.00x (ISBN 0-231-02144-5). Columbia U Pr.
Bellow, Gary & Moulton, Bea. The Lawyering Process: Ethics & Professional Responsibility. LC 81-67777. (University Casebook Ser.). 479p. 1981. pap. text ed. write for info. (ISBN 0-88277-038-1). Foundation Pr.
Cohen, Felix. Ethical Systems & Legal Ideals. LC 75-40440. 303p. 1976. Repr. of 1933 ed. lib. bdg. 19.75x (ISBN 0-8371-8643-9, COETS). Greenwood.
Davitt, Thomas E. The Basic Values in Law: A Study of the Ethico-Legal Implications of Psychology & Anthropology, Vol. 58, Pt 5. LC 78-7986. 1978. pap. 15.00 (ISBN 0-8357-0313-4, ST-00005, Pub. by Amer. Philosophical Soc.). Univ Microfilms.
Drinker, Henry S. Legal Ethics. LC 80-11445. (Legal Studies of the William Nelson Cromwell Foundation). xxii, 448p. 1980. Repr. of 1953 ed. lib. bdg. 38.00x (ISBN 0-313-22321-1, DRLG). Greenwood.
Finnis, John. Natural Law & Natural. (Clarendon Law Ser.). 442p. text ed. 39.50x (ISBN 0-19-876098-1); pap. text ed. 19.50x (ISBN 0-19-876110-4). Oxford U Pr.
Freedman, Monroe. Lawyers' Ethics in an Adversary System. 1975. 15.00 (ISBN 0-672-82065-X, Bobbs-Merrill Law). Michie-Bobbs.
Hazard, Geoffrey C., Jr. Ethics in the Practice of Law. LC 77-16357. 177p. 1980. 15.00x (ISBN 0-300-02206-9); pap. 5.95 (ISBN 0-300-02601-3). Yale U Pr.
Kelly, Michael J. Legal Ethics & Legal Education. LC 80-10825. (The Teaching of Ethics Ser.). 69p. 1980. pap. 4.00 (ISBN 0-916558-06-1). Hastings Ctr Inst Soc.
Legal Profession. (Co-Op East Law Outline Ser.). 1974. pap. text ed. 6.00 (ISBN 0-88408-061-7). Sterling Swift.
Lieberman, Jethro K. Crisis at the Bar: The Unethical Ethics of Lawyers (and What to Do About It) 1978. 14.95x (ISBN 0-393-05644-9). Norton.
Marks, F. Raymond & Cathcart, Darlene. Discipline Within the Legal Profession: Is It Self-Regulation? (Research Contributions Ser: No. 5). 1974. pap. 2.00 (ISBN 0-685-64478-2). Am Bar Foun.
Maru, Olavi. Digest of Bar Association Ethic Opinion: 1975 Supplement. Sikes, Bette, ed. 1977. lib. bdg. 20.00 (ISBN 0-910058-84-9). Am Bar Foun.
--Digest of Bar Association Ethics Opinions. LC 74-127109. vi, 633p. 1970. 20.00 (ISBN 0-910058-05-9). Am Bar Foun.
--Digest of Bar Association Ethics Opinions, 1970 Supplement. LC 74-127109. 1973. 15.00 (ISBN 0-910058-54-7). Am Bar Foun.
Morgan, Thomas D. & Rotunda, Ronald D. Problems & Materials on Professional Responsibility. 2nd ed. LC 81-3205. (University Casebook Ser.). 489p. 1981. text ed. write for info. (ISBN 0-88277-031-4). Foundation Pr.
Parry, Edward A. Seven Lamps of Advocacy. facs. ed. LC 68-16965. (Essay Index Reprint Ser). 1968. Repr. of 1923 ed. 12.00 (ISBN 0-8369-0773-6). Arno.
Pike, James A. Beyond the Law. LC 73-10754. 102p. 1974. Repr. of 1963 ed. lib. bdg. 15.00x (ISBN 0-8371-7021-4, PIBL). Greenwood.
Pimsleur, Meira G. Opinions: Committees on Professional Ethics: the Association of the Bar of the City of New York, the New York County Lawyer's Association, New York State Bar Association. LC 80-14204. 1000p. 1980. Set. looseleaf bdg. 150.00 (ISBN 0-379-20670-6). Oceana.
Simons, Blaine N. Games Lawyers Play with Your Money. LC 77-88488. 1978. pap. 2.25 (ISBN 0-89516-018-8). Condor Pub Co.
Smith, J. C. Legal Obligation. 1976. 25.00x (ISBN 0-8020-2240-5). U of Toronto Pr.
Taft, William H. Ethics in Service. LC 77-76064. 1969. Repr. of 1915 ed. 10.00 (ISBN 0-8046-0640-4). Kennikat.
Warvelle, Geo W. Essays in Legal Ethics. xiii, 234p. 1980. Repr. of 1902 ed. lib. bdg. 22.50x (ISBN 0-8377-1305-6). Rothman.

LEGAL FEES

see Costs (Law); Lawyers-Fees

LEGAL FICTION

see Fictions (Law)

LEGAL FORMS

see Forms (Law)

LEGAL HISTORY

see Law-History and Criticism

LEGAL HOLIDAYS

see Holidays

LEGAL INSTRUMENTS

see also Legal Documents; Negotiable Instruments

LEGAL LANGUAGE

see Law-Language

LEGAL LITERATURE

see also Law-Bibliography

Bryson, William H. Census of Law Books in Colonial Virginia. LC 77-22067. 1978. 12.00x (ISBN 0-8139-0746-2). U Pr of Va.
Gopen, George D. Writing from a Legal Perspective. 250p. 1981. text ed. 11.95 (ISBN 0-8299-2123-0). West Pub.
Hein, William S., Jr., et al, eds. Hein's Legal Periodical Checklist. LC 77-80652. 1977. Set. lib. bdg. 135.00 (ISBN 0-930342-05-4). Vol. 1 (ISBN 0-930342-51-8). Vol. 2 (ISBN 0-930342-52-6). W S Hein.
Institute For Law Librarians - 6th Biennial - 1963. Law Library - a Living Trust. (AALL Publications Ser: No. 7). vi, 58p. (Orig.). 1964. pap. text ed. 8.50x (ISBN 0-8377-0105-8). Rothman.
Leavell, Robert N., et al. Cases & Materials on Equitable Remedies & Restitution. 3rd ed. LC 79-27903. (American Casebook Ser.). 736p. 1980. text ed. 19.95 (ISBN 0-8299-2084-6). West Pub.
Lewis, Alfred J. Using Law Books. LC 75-35385. 1977. perfect bdg. 4.95 (ISBN 0-685-71354-7). Kendall-Hunt.
Mack, Zella. California Paralegal's Handbook. LC 77-71561. 1977. incl. 1981 suppl. 38.00 (ISBN 0-911110-23-2). Parker & Son.
Parham, Sidney F., Jr. Fundamentals of Legal Writing. 1967. 10.00 (ISBN 0-87215-039-9). Michie-Bobbs.
Surles, Richard H., Jr. & Mukerji, Jatin M., eds. Legal Periodical Management Data. LC 77-81317. 1977. lib. bdg. 20.00 (ISBN 0-930342-06-2). W S Hein.
Tseng, Henry P. Complete Guide to Legal Materials in Microform: 1976 Supplement. 1977. pap. 17.00 (ISBN 0-89093-102-X). U Pubns Amer.

LEGAL LITERATURE SEARCHING

see Information Storage and Retrieval Systems-Law

LEGAL MEDICINE

see Medical Jurisprudence

LEGAL OFFICES

see Law Offices

LEGAL PHOTOGRAPHY

see Photography, Legal

LEGAL PROCEDURE

see Procedure (Law)

LEGAL PROFESSION

see Lawyers

LEGAL PSYCHOLOGY

see Law-Psychology; Psychology, Forensic

LEGAL RESEARCH

see also Citation of Legal Authorities

Bander, Edward & Bander, David F. Legal Research & Education Abridgment: A Manual for Law Students, Paralegals & Researchers. LC 78-2408. 1978. 20.00 (ISBN 0-88410-794-9). Ballinger Pub.
Conference on Aims & Methods of Legal Research, University of Michigan Law School, Nov. 4-5, 1955. Proceedings. Conrad, Alfred F., ed. LC 72-94612. 1955. lib. bdg. 15.00x (ISBN 0-8371-2460-3, COLR). Greenwood.
Davies, Bernita J. & Rooney, Francis J. Research in Illinois Law. LC 54-12404. 1954. 7.50 (ISBN 0-379-11652-9). Oceana.
Elias, Stephen. Legal Research. (Orig.). 1981. pap. 10.00 (ISBN 0-917316-39-8). Nolo Pr.
Foster, Lynn & Boast, Carol. Subject Compilations of State Laws: Research Guide & Annotated Bibliography. LC 80-1788. 473p. 1981. lib. bdg. 45.00 (ISBN 0-313-21255-4, FOS). Greenwood.
French, Harriet L. Research in Florida Law. 2nd ed. LC 65-27630. 1965. 7.50 (ISBN 0-379-11653-7). Oceana.
Goehlert, Robert. Congress & Law-Making: Researching the Legislative Process. LC 79-11554. (Illus.). 168p. 1979. text ed. 19.25 (ISBN 0-87436-294-6). ABC-Clio.
Golec, Anthony M. Techniques of Legal Investigation. (Illus.). 280p. 1976. 19.75 (ISBN 0-398-03522-9). C C Thomas.
Graulich, Paul. Guide to Foreign Legal Materials: Belgium, Luxembourg, Netherlands. LC 68-7723. 1968. 17.50 (ISBN 0-379-11753-3). Oceana.
Jacobstein, J. Myron & Mersky, Roy M. Fundamentals of Legal Research. 2nd ed. (University Textbook Ser.). 567p. 1981. text ed. write for info. (ISBN 0-88277-034-9). Foundation Pr.
Jacobstein, Myron J. & Mersky, Roy M. Legal Research Illustrated: University Casebook Ser. 2nd ed. 1981. pap. text ed. write for info. (ISBN 0-88277-048-9). Foundation Pr.
Kavass, Igor I. & Christensen, Bruce A. Guide to North Carolina Legal Research. LC 73-90479. 1973. lib. bdg. 15.00 (ISBN 0-930342-23-2); pap. text ed. 5.00 (ISBN 0-930342-24-0). W S Hein.
Laska, Lewis L. Tennessee Legal Research Handbook. LC 77-71305. 1977. lib. bdg. 17.50 (ISBN 0-930342-04-6). W S Hein.
Lloyd, David. Finding the Law: A Guide to Legal Research. LC 74-10762. (Legal Almanac Ser.: No. 74). 128p. 1974. text ed. 5.95 (ISBN 0-379-11090-3). Oceana.
Mills, Robin K. & Schultz, Jon S. South Carolina Legal Research Handbook. LC 75-21933. 1976. lib. bdg. 15.00 (ISBN 0-930342-16-X). W S Hein.
Powell, Thomas. Direction for Search of Records. LC 74-80208. (English Experience Ser.: No. 685). 1974. Repr. of 1622 ed. 9.50 (ISBN 90-221-0685-3). Walter J Johnson.
Price, Miles O. & Bitner, Harry. Effective Legal Research. LC 53-11286. xii, 633p. 1969. Repr. of 1953 ed. lib. bdg. 32.50x (ISBN 0-8377-2502-X). Rothman.
Price, Miles O., et al. Effective Legal Research. 4th ed. 501p. 1979. 18.50 (ISBN 0-316-71832-7); problems wkbk., 1979 6.95 (ISBN 0-316-71855-6). Little.
Sprowl, James A. Manual for Computer-Assisted Legal Research. new ed. Sikes, Bette, ed. 1976. pap. 5.00 (ISBN 0-910058-76-8). Am Bar Foun.
Surrency, Erwin C. Research in Pennsylvania Law. 2nd ed. LC 65-27629. 1965. 11.00 (ISBN 0-379-11651-0). Oceana.
Surrency, Erwin C., et al. Guide to Legal Research with 1966 Supplement. LC 59-14272. (Orig.). 1959. pap. 6.00 (ISBN 0-379-00111-X). Oceana.
Zerbe, Richard, Jr., ed. Research in Law & Economics: Annual, Vol. 2. (Orig.). 1980. lib. bdg. 32.50 (ISBN 0-89232-131-8). Jai Pr.

LEGAL RESEARCH-DATA PROCESSING
Schubert, Wolfram & Steinmueller, Wilhelm. JUDAC - Jurisprudence-Data Processing-Cybernetics: International Bibliography, English-French-German-Russian. LC 76-864294. 314p. 1971. 45.00x (ISBN 3-406-03084-X). Intl Pubns Serv.

LEGAL RESPONSIBILITY
see Liability (Law)

LEGAL SECRETARIES
see also Law Offices
Adams, Dorothy & Kurtz, Margaret. The Legal Secretary: Terminology & Transcription. (Illus.). 1980. text ed. 10.95t (ISBN 0-07-000330-0, G); legal typing practice avail. (ISBN 0-07-000336-X); student transcript avail. (ISBN 0-07-000337-8). McGraw.
Bate, Marjorie D. & Casey, Mary C. Legal Office Procedures. 2nd ed. (Illus.). 544p. 1980. pap. text ed. 15.25 (ISBN 0-07-004058-3, G); instructor's manual & key avail. (ISBN 0-07-004059-1). McGraw.
Blackburn, Norma D. Legal Secretaryship. 2nd ed. (Illus.). 400p. 1981. text ed. 15.95 (ISBN 0-13-528927-0). P-H.
A Bridge to the World of the Legal Secretary. pap. text ed. 2.00 (ISBN 0-915362-11-2). M K Heller.
Craft, Berniece, et al. Speedwriting for the Legal Secretary. LC 78-10833. 1979. pap. 11.95 (ISBN 0-672-97013-9); tchr's. manual 3.33 (ISBN 0-672-97014-7). Bobbs.
Freeman, Marian, ed. Legal Secretary's Handbook. 11th ed. LC 76-52065. 1980. incl. 1981 suppl. 60.00 (ISBN 0-911110-22-4). Parker & Son.
Grahm, Milton, et al. Legal Typewriting. 1968. text ed. 9.95 (ISBN 0-07-024045-0, G). McGraw.
Guide & Compendium for the Lawyer's Secretary, No. 5. rev. ed. LC 75-1667. 1981. 26.50 (ISBN 0-915362-17-1). M K Heller.
Heller, Marjorie K. Enter the Working World of the Legal Secretary. 1978. pap. text ed. 2.00 (ISBN 0-915362-12-0). M K Heller.
Heller, Marjorie K. & Cohen, Betty. A Complete Course in Legal Secretarial Practice. 1977. pap. 9.95 (ISBN 0-671-18760-0). Monarch Pr.
Larbalestrier, Deborah. Paralegal Practice & Procedure: A Practical Guide for the Legal Assistant. (Illus.). 1977. 19.95 (ISBN 0-13-648683-5, Busn). P-H.
Lawyer's Assistant: Paraprofessional & Secretary 1978, 3 vols. (Commercial Law & Practice Course Handbook Ser. 1977-78: Vols. 190, 191 & 192). 1978. pap. 20.00 (ISBN 0-685-63700-X, A6-3017). PLI.
Leslie, Louis A. & Coffin, Kenneth B. Handbook for the Legal Secretary: Diamond Jubilee Series. 1968. 15.25 (ISBN 0-07-037277-2, G); pap. 3.95 (ISBN 0-07-037279-9). McGraw.
Miller. Legal Secretary's Complete Handbook. 3rd ed. (Illus.). 1980. 19.95 (ISBN 0-13-528562-3, Busn). P-H.
Morton, Joyce. Legal Secretarial Procedures. LC 78-23892. 1979. pap. text ed. 13.95 (ISBN 0-13-528489-9). P-H.
Paralegal Practice Handbook, No. 2. rev. ed. LC 77-85386. 1981. 27.50 (ISBN 0-915362-19-8). M K Heller.
Prentice-Hall Editorial Staff. Legal Secretary's Encyclopedic Dictionary. 2nd ed. (Illus.). 1977. 14.95 (ISBN 0-13-528943-2). P-H.
Rudman, Jack. Legal Secretary. (Career Examination Ser.: C-1343). (Cloth bdg. avail. on request). 14.00 (ISBN 0-8373-1343-0). Natl Learning.
Schoepfer, Virginia B. Legal Secretarial; Typewriting & Dictation: Syllabus. 1974. pap. text ed. 6.75 (ISBN 0-89420-014-3, 290055); cassette recordings 102.55 (ISBN 0-89420-159-X, 290000). Natl Book.
Sletwold, Evangeline. Sletwold's Manual of Documents Forms for the Legal Secretary. 19.95 (ISBN 0-13-812909-6). P-H.
Virginia Association of Legal Secretaries. Handbook for Legal Secretaries in Virginia. 2nd ed. 364p. 1975. with 1977 suppl. 30.00 (ISBN 0-87215-174-3); suppl seperately 12.50 (ISBN 0-87215-267-7). Michie-Bobbs.
Working Papers in the Matter of Training the Legal Secretary. rev. ed. LC 79-90998. 1979. 15.00 (ISBN 0-915362-16-3). M K Heller.

LEGAL STATISTICS
see Judicial Statistics

LEGAL STATUS OF WOMEN
see Women-Legal Status, Laws, etc.

LEGAL STYLE
see Law-Language

LEGAL TENDER
see also Currency Question; Greenbacks; Money; Paper Money

LE GALLIENNE, EVA, 1899-
LeGallienne, Eva. With a Quiet Heart: An Autobiography. LC 74-3745. (Illus.). 311p. 1974. Repr. of 1953 ed. lib. bdg. 17.25x (ISBN 0-8371-7470-8, LEQH). Greenwood.

LE GALLIENE, RICHARD, 1866-1947
Whittington-Egan, Richard & Smerdon, Geoffrey. The Quest of the Golden Boy: The Life & Letters of Richard Le Gallienne. LC 79-8087. Repr. of 1962 ed. 49.50 (ISBN 0-404-18395-6). AMS Pr.

LEGATES (ROME)
Sherk, Robert K. The Legates of Galatia from Augustus to Diocletian. LC 78-64216. (Johns Hopkins University. Studies in the Social Sciences. Sixty-Ninth Ser. 1951: 2). Repr. of 1951 ed. 15.50 (ISBN 0-404-61320-9). AMS Pr.

LEGATES, PAPAL
Oliveri, Mario. The Representatives: The Real Nature & Function of Papal Legates. LC 81-108171. 192p. (Orig.). 1981. pap. 4.95 (ISBN 0-686-72636-7). Wanderer Bks.

LEGATIONS
see Diplomatic and Consular Service

LEGEND OF THE FIFTEEN SIGNS
see Quindecim Signa Anti Indicium

LEGENDS
see also Chansons De Geste; Fables; Fairy Tales; Folk-Lore; Heldensage; Mythology; Romances; Saints;
also subdivisions Legends under special subjects, e.g. Mary, Virgin-Legends
Adams, Henry C. Wonder Book of Travellers' Tales. (Black & Gold Lib). (Illus.). 6.95 (ISBN 0-87140-998-4). Liveright.
Blair, Walter & Meine, Franklin J., eds. Half Horse Half Alligator: The Growth of the Mike Fink Legend. LC 81-3358. (Illus.). x, 289p. 1981. Repr. of 1956 ed. price not set (ISBN 0-8032-6060-1, BB 772). U of Nebr Pr.
Bokenham, O. Legendys of Hooly Wummen. (EETS, OS Ser.: No. 206). Repr. of 1938 ed. 16.00 (ISBN 0-527-00206-2). Kraus Repr.
Davis, Hubert J. Myths & Legends of the Great Dismal Swamp. (Illus.). 112p. 1981. 7.50 (ISBN 0-930230-42-6). Johnson NC.
Dobie, J. Frank, et al, eds. In the Shadow of History. (Texas Folklore Society Publication Ser.: No. 25). 192p. 1980. Repr. of 1939 ed. 6.95 (ISBN 0-87074-173-X). SMU Press.
Fierabras. Firumbras & Otuel & Roland. (EETS, OS Ser.: No. 198). Repr. of 1935 ed. 14.00 (ISBN 0-527-00198-8). Kraus Repr.
Higginson, Thomas W. Tales of the Enchanted Islands of the Atlantic. LC 76-9894. (Children's Literature Reprint Ser). (Illus.). (gr. 6-7). 1976. Repr. of 1898 ed. 17.50x (ISBN 0-8486-0203-X). Core Collection.
Irving, Washington. Rip Van Winkle & the Legend of Sleepy Hollow. 2nd ed. (Illus.). 128p. (gr. 4-12). 1980. 13.95 (ISBN 0-912882-42-5). Sleepy Hollow.
Lathrop, Thomas A., ed. The Legend of the "Siete Infantes de Lara". A Study & Critical Edition. (Studies in the Romance Languages & Literatures: No. 122). 1972. pap. 9.00x (ISBN 0-8078-9122-3). U of NC Pr.
Lethbridge, T. C. The Legend of the Sons of God: A Fantasy? (Illus.). 1972. 12.00 (ISBN 0-7100-7159-0). Routledge & Kegan.
Mabie, Hamilton W. World-Famed Stories & Legends. Repr. of 1908 ed. 20.00 (ISBN 0-89987-125-9). Darby Bks.
McElhanon, K. A., ed. Legends of Papua, New Guinea. 237p. 1974. pap. 7.00x (ISBN 0-7263-0274-0). Summer Inst Ling.
Morris, Ernest. Legends O' the Bells: Being a Collection of Legends; Traditions; Folktales, Myths, Etc. Centred Around the Bells of All Lands. LC 74-9742. lib. bdg. 30.00 (ISBN 0-8414-6144-9). Folcroft.
Parry-Jones, Daniel. Welsh Legends & Fairy Lore. LC 76-10823. 1976. Repr. of 1963 ed. lib. bdg. 17.50 (ISBN 0-8414-6724-2). Folcroft.
Pettazzoni, Raffaele & Bolle, Kees W., eds. Miti E Leggende: Myths & Legends, 4 vols. in 1. LC 77-79151. (Mythology Ser.). (Italian.). 1978. Repr. of 1959 ed. lib. bdg. 146.00x (ISBN 0-405-10560-6). Arno.
Schlauch, Margaret. Medieval Narrative: A Book of Translations. LC 75-93254. 1970. Repr. of 1928 ed. 12.50 (ISBN 0-87752-098-4). Gordian.
Shackford, M. H. Legends & Satires from Medieval Literature. 59.95 (ISBN 0-8490-0503-5). Gordon Pr.
Shackford, Martha H. Legends & Satires from Medieval Literature. LC 77-7379. 1913. lib. bdg. 20.00 (ISBN 0-8414-7588-1). Folcroft.

LEGENDS-HISTORY AND CRITICISM
Baring-Gould, Sabine. Curious Myths of the Middle Ages. Hardy, Edward, ed. (Illus.). 1978. 8.95 (ISBN 0-19-520078-0). Oxford U Pr.
Bedier, Joseph. Les Legendes epiques: Recherches sur la formation des chansons de geste, 4 vols. LC 78-63487. Repr. of 1913 ed. Set. 159.00 (ISBN 0-404-17130-3). AMS Pr.
Bergsten, Staffan. Mary Poppins & Myth. (Illus.). 1978. text ed. 14.25x (ISBN 91-22-00127-1). Humanities.
Gripkey, Sr. M. Vincentine. Blessed Virgin Mary As Mediatrix in the Latin & Old French Legend Prior to the Fourteenth Century. LC 72-94166. (Catholic University of America Studies in Romance Languages & Literatures Ser: No. 17). 1969. Repr. of 1938 ed. 20.50 (ISBN 0-404-50317-9). Ams Pr.
Guerber, H. A. Legends of the Middle Ages: Narrated with Special Reference to Literature & Art. 59.95 (ISBN 0-8490-0506-X). Gordon Pr.
Harper, G. M. The Legend of the Holy Grail. 59.95 (ISBN 0-8490-0502-7). Gordon Pr.
Jolicoeur, Catherine. Le Vasseau Fantome-Legende Etiologique (The Phantom Ship-A Phenomenological Legend) 337p. 1970. pap. 12.00x (ISBN 2-7637-6382-0, Pub. by Laval). Intl. Schol Bk Serv.
Kris, Ernst & Kurz, Otto. Legend, Myth, & Magic in the Image of the Artist: A Historical Experiment. LC 78-24024. (Illus.). 175p. 1981. pap. 5.95 (ISBN 0-300-02669-2, Y-386). Yale U Pr.
Leach, ed. Funk & Wagnalls Standard Dictionary of Folklore, Mythology & Legend. LC 72-78268. (Funk & W Bk.). 22.95 (ISBN 0-308-40090-9). T Y Crowell.
Sturdevant, Winifred. The Misterio De los Reyes Magos, Its Position in the Development of the Mediaeval Legend of the Three Kings. Repr. of 1927 ed. 15.50 (ISBN 0-384-58735-6). Johnson Repr.
West, John F. The Ballad of Tom Dula. 212p. 9.95 (ISBN 0-87716-019-8, Pub. by Moore Pub Co); pap. 4.50 (ISBN 0-686-66593-7). F Apple.
Wilson, H. Schutz. Studies in History, Legend & Literature. 1977. Repr. of 1884 ed. lib. bdg. 35.00 (ISBN 0-8492-2884-0). R West.
Young, K. The Origin & Development of the Story of Troilus & Criseyde. 59.95 (ISBN 0-8490-0773-9). Gordon Pr.

LEGENDS-JUVENILE LITERATURE
see also Legends, American, French, etc. for other juvenile works
Briggs, Katharine M. The Vanishing People: Fairy Lore & Legends. LC 78-53523. (Illus.). 1978. 8.95 (ISBN 0-394-50248-5). Pantheon.
De Coster, Charles T. Flemish Legends. Taylor, Harold, tr. LC 78-74513. (Children's Literature Reprint Ser.). (Illus.). (gr. 7 up). 1979. Repr. of 1920 ed. 18.75x (ISBN 0-8486-0217-X). Core Collection.
Guard, David. Deirdre: A Celtic Legend. LC 80-69774. (Illus.). 118p. (gr. 6). 1981. Repr. of 1977 ed. 9.95 (ISBN 0-89742-047-0, Dawne-Leigh). Celestial Arts.
--Hale-Mano: A Legend of Hawaii. LC 80-69773. (Illus.). 118p. (gr. 6). 1981. 9.95 (ISBN 0-89742-048-9, Dawne-Leigh). Celestial Arts.
Haviland, Virginia, ed. North American Legends. (gr. 4 up). 1979. 8.95 (ISBN 0-529-05457-4). Philomel.
Mabie, Hamilton W. Legends That Every Child Should Know. Repr. of 1907 ed. 20.00 (ISBN 0-89987-164-X). Darby Bks.
Ross, Harriet, compiled by. Heroes & Heroines of Many Lands. (Illus.). 160p. 1981. PLB 7.95 (ISBN 0-87460-214-9). Lion Bks.
Untermeyer, Louis. Firebringer & Other Great Stories: Fifty-Five Legends That Live Forever. (Illus.). (gr. 2-7). 1968. 5.95 (ISBN 0-87131-047-3). M Evans.
--World's Great Stories: Fifty-Five Legends That Live Forever. (Illus.). (gr. 2-7). 1964. 5.95 (ISBN 0-87131-109-7). M Evans.

LEGENDS, AFRICAN
Ogumefu, M. I. Yoruba Legends. LC 78-63217. (The Folktale). Repr. of 1929 ed. 14.50 (ISBN 0-404-16153-7). AMS Pr.

LEGENDS, AMERICAN
Ainsworth, Catherine H. Legends of New York State. LC 78-54873. (Folklore Bks.). vi, 96p. 1980. 4.00 (ISBN 0-933190-05-0). Clyde Pr.
Alaska Native Language Workshop, tr. Stories of Native Alaskans. (Alaska Library Association). 1977. 12.95 (ISBN 0-912006-03-X, Pub by U of Alaska Pr). Intl Schol Bk Serv.
Blair, Walter. Tall Tale America. (Illus.). (gr. 4-9). 1944. PLB 6.59 (ISBN 0-698-30350-4). Coward.
Brunvand, Jan H. The Vanishing Hitchhiker: American Urban Legends & Their Meanings. 1981. 14.95 (ISBN 0-393-01473-8). Norton.
Clark, Ella E. Indian Legends of the Pacific Northwest. (Illus.). (YA) (gr. 9-12). 1953. pap. 3.95 (ISBN 0-520-00243-1, CAL18). U of Cal Pr.
Dobie, J. Frank. Apache Gold & Yaqui Silver. (Illus.). 1939. 9.95 (ISBN 0-316-18791-7). Little.
Dobie, J. Frank, ed. Man, Bird, & Beast. LC 33-1132. (Texas Folklore Society Publications: No. 8). (Illus.). 1965. Repr. of 1930 ed. 5.95 (ISBN 0-87074-131-4). SMU Press.
--Southwestern Lore. LC 33-1134. (Texas Folklore Society Publications: No. 9). 1965. Repr. of 1931 ed. 6.95 (ISBN 0-87074-042-3). SMU Press.
--Spur-Of-The-Cock. LC 34-1434. (Texas Folklore Society Publications: No. 11). 1965. Repr. of 1933 ed. 4.95 (ISBN 0-87074-043-1). SMU Press.
--Tone the Bell Easy. LC 33-1135. (Texas Folklore Society Publications: No. 10). (Illus.). 1965. Repr. of 1932 ed. 5.95 (ISBN 0-87074-045-8). SMU Press.
Drake, Samuel A. Book of New England Legends & Folk Lore. LC 69-19881. 1969. Repr. of 1901 ed. 24.00 (ISBN 0-8103-3829-7). Gale.
Eberhart, Perry. Treasure Tales of the Rockies. 3rd ed. LC 61-14373. (Illus.). 315p. 1969. 14.95 (ISBN 0-8040-0295-9, SB). Swallow.
Helm, Mike. Ghosts, Monsters, & Wild Men: Legends of the Oregon Country. (Illus.). 1981. write for info. (ISBN 0-931742-03-X). Rainy Day Oreg.
Hiser, Berniece T. Quare Do's in Appalachia: Thirty Legends & Memorats of Eastern Kentucky. LC 78-56593. 1978. pap. 6.00 (ISBN 0-933302-07-X). Pikeville Coll.
Increase, Mather. Remarkable Providences Illustrative of the Earlier Days of American Colonisation. Dorsen, Richard M., ed. LC 77-70610. (International Folklore Ser.). 1977. Repr. of 1856 ed. lib. bdg. 18.00x (ISBN 0-405-10107-4). Arno.
Judson, Katherine. Myths & Legends of the Pacific Northwest. Repr. of 1910 ed. pap. 16.00 (ISBN 0-8466-0147-8, SJS147). Shorey.
Kane, Grace F. Myths & Legends of the Mackinacs & the Lake Region. 2nd ed. (Illus.). 164p. 1972. pap. 4.50 (ISBN 0-912382-09-0). Black Letter.
Martin, Margaret R. Charleston Ghosts. LC 63-22508. (Illus.). 1963. 5.95 (ISBN 0-87249-091-2); pap. 2.25x (ISBN 0-87249-286-9). U of SC Pr.
Mitchell, John D. Lost Mines of the Great Southwest. (Illus.). lib. bdg. 10.00 (ISBN 0-87380-013-3). Rio Grande.
Rip Van Winkle. (Classics Illus. Ser.). (Illus.). pap. 0.59 (ISBN 0-685-74110-9, 12). Guild Bks.
Sauvageau, Juan. Stories That Must Not Die, Vol. 1. LC 75-36692. (Illus., Eng. & Span.). 1975. pap. 3.00 (ISBN 0-916378-00-4). PSI Res.
Shay, Frank. Here's Audacity! American Legendary Heroes. facs. ed. LC 67-28765. (Essay Index Reprint Ser). 1930. 16.00 (ISBN 0-8369-0872-4). Arno.
Welles, E. R., 3rd & Evans, J. P. The Forgotten Legend of Sleepy Hollow. LC 73-77815. 1973. prepaid 7.00x (ISBN 0-913692-03-4); pap. 2.00x prepaid (ISBN 0-913692-02-6). Learning Inc.
Williams, Brad & Pepper, Choral. Lost Legends of the West. LC 70-80368. 1970. 7.95 (ISBN 0-03-081867-2). HR&W.

LEGENDS, AUSTRALIAN
Berndt, Ronald M. & Berndt, Catherine H. Man, Land & Myth in North Australia: The Gunwinggu People. (Illus.). 262p. 1970. text ed. 10.00x (ISBN 0-87013-165-6). Mich St U Pr.
Lawrie, Margaret, ed. Myths & Legends of the Torres Strait. LC 73-163219. (Illus.). 1972. 25.00 (ISBN 0-8008-5464-0). Taplinger.
Massola, Aldo. Bunjil's Cave: Myths, Legends & Superstitions of the Aborigines of South-East Australia. (Illus.). 1968. text ed. 14.25x (ISBN 0-391-01962-7). Humanities.
Reed, A. W. Aboriginal Legends: Animal Tales. 1979. pap. 5.95 (ISBN 0-589-50018-X, Pub. by Reed Books Australia). C E Tuttle.
Smith, William R. Myths & Legends of the Australian Aboriginals. LC 77-135919. 1971. Repr. of 1932 ed. 28.50 (ISBN 0-384-56205-1). Johnson Repr.
Van Gennep, Arnold. Mythes et legendes d'Australie. LC 78-63231. (The Folktale). Repr. of 1906 ed. 28.00 (ISBN 0-404-16174-X). AMS Pr.

LEGENDS, BRITISH
Aurner, Nellie S. Hengest: A Study in Early English Hero Legend. 1978. lib. bdg. 25.00 (ISBN 0-8495-0044-3). Arden Lib.
Close, J. Tales & Legends of Westmorland. (Folklore Ser). 12.50 (ISBN 0-685-36442-9). Norwood Edns.
Courtney, Margaret A. Cornish Feasts & Folk-Lore. LC 77-8082. 1977. lib. bdg. 25.00 (ISBN 0-8414-1829-2). Folcroft.
Dalesman, compiled by. Yorkshire Legends. 2nd ed. (Illus.). 71p. (Orig.). 1976. pap. 3.00 (ISBN 0-686-64123-X). Legacy Bks.
EP Books, ed. Folk Lore & Legends of England. 1972. Repr. of 1890 ed. 14.95x (ISBN 0-8464-0418-4). Beekman Pubs.
Folklore, Myths & Legends of Britain. (Automobile Association of England Ser.). 1979. 22.95 (ISBN 0-393-01231-X). Norton.
Ghosts Legends of Wiltshire. 12.00 (ISBN 0-8277-7262-9). British Bk Ctr.
Hazlitt, William C. Tales & Legends of National Origin: Or Widely Current in England from Early Times. LC 72-80500. Repr. of 1891 ed. 24.00 (ISBN 0-405-08607-5, Blom Pubns). Arno.

Horstmann, Carl, ed. South English Legendary. (EETS, OS Ser.: No. 87). Repr. of 1887 ed. 29.00 (ISBN 0-527-00084-1). Kraus Repr.
Hunt, Robert, ed. Popular Romances of the West of England. LC 68-56495. 1968. Repr. of 1916 ed. 20.00 (ISBN 0-405-08643-1, Blom Pubns). Arno.
Lawrence, Berta. Somerset Legends. 5.95 (ISBN 0-7153-6185-6). David & Charles.
Long, George. Folklore Calendar. LC 76-78191. 1970. Repr. of 1930 ed. 21.00 (ISBN 0-8103-3367-8). Gale.
Merrill, John N. Legends of Derbyshire. 2nd ed. (Illus.). 71p. (Orig.). (gr. 6 up). 1975. pap. 3.00 (ISBN 0-913714-15-1). Legacy Bks.
Parkinson, Thomas. Yorkshire Legends & Traditions. Dorson, Richard M., ed. LC 77-70615. (International Folklore Ser.). 1977. Repr. of 1888 ed. lib. bdg. 14.00x (ISBN 0-405-10117-1). Arno.
Pyle, Howard. The Story of King Arthur & His Knights. (Illus.). 1978. Repr. of 1903 ed. lib. bdg. 9.95 luxury ed. (ISBN 0-932106-01-3, Pub by Marathon Pr). S J Durst.
Weston, Jessie L. The Legend of Sir Gawain. 59.95 (ISBN 0-8490-0500-0). Gordon Pr.
--The Legend of Sir Launcelot Du Lake. 59.95 (ISBN 0-8490-0501-9). Gordon Pr.
--The Quest of the Holy Grail. 59.95 (ISBN 0-87968-094-6). Gordon Pr.

LEGENDS, BUDDHIST

Budge, Ernest A., ed. Baralam & Yewasef - Baralaam & Joaseph, 3 pts. in 2 vols. LC 73-18832. (Illus.). Repr. of 1923 ed. Set. 55.00 (ISBN 0-404-11300-1). AMS Pr.
Burlingame, E. W. Buddhist Parables. lib. bdg. 59.95 (ISBN 0-87968-494-1). Krishna Pr.
Cranmer-Byng, L. & Kapadia, S. A., eds. Legends of Indian Buddhism. LC 78-670089. 1976. Repr. of 1903 ed. 8.50x (ISBN 0-8002-0252-X). Intl Pubns Serv.
Dhammapadatthakatha. Buddhist Legends, 3 vols. Burlingame, Eugene W., tr. from Pali. LC 78-72421. Repr. of 1929 ed. Set. 105.00 (ISBN 0-404-17610-0). Vol. 1 (ISBN 0-404-17611-9). Vol. 2 (ISBN 0-404-17612-7). Vol. 3 (ISBN 0-404-17613-5). AMS Pr.
Somadeva, Bhatta. The Buddhist Legend of Jimutavahana. LC 78-70116. Repr. of 1911 ed. 20.50 (ISBN 0-404-17373-X). AMS Pr.

LEGENDS, BURMESE

Cocks, S. W. Tales & Legends of Ancient Burma. new ed. LC 78-67697. (The Folktale). Repr. of 1916 ed. 17.00 (ISBN 0-404-16068-9). AMS Pr.

LEGENDS, CANADIAN

Bemister, Margaret. Thirty Indian Legends of Canada. pap. 6.50 (ISBN 0-88894-025-4, Pub. by Douglas & McIntyre). Intl Schol Bk Serv.
Wilson, Marie, ed. We-Gyet Wanders on. (Illus.). 1977. 9.95 (ISBN 0-919654-99-1, Pub. by Hancock Hse). Universe.
Woodley, Edward C. Legends of French Canada. LC 75-174354. (Illus.). Repr. of 1938 ed. 13.00 (ISBN 0-405-09102-8). Arno.

LEGENDS, CELTIC

Geoffrey of Monmouth. History of the Kings of Britain. Dunn, Charles W., ed. Evans, Sebastian, tr. 1958. pap. 3.95 (ISBN 0-525-47014-X). Dutton.
--Galfredi Monumentensis Historia Britonum. Giles, John A., ed. 1966. 24.00 (ISBN 0-8337-1344-2). B Franklin.
Parry, John J., ed. Brut Y Brenhinedd, Cotton Cleopatra Version. 1937. 12.00 (ISBN 0-910956-10-3). Medieval Acad.
Squire, Charles. Celtic Myth & Legend, Poetry & Romance. LC 80-53343. (Newcastle Mythology Library: Vol. 1). 450p. 1980. Repr. of 1975 ed. lib. bdg. 12.95x (ISBN 0-89370-630-2). Borgo Pr.
--Celtic Myth & Legend, Poetry and Romance. LC 77-6985. 1977. Repr. of 1910 ed. lib. bdg. 45.00 (ISBN 0-89341-164-7). Longwood Pr.

LEGENDS, CHINESE

Brown, Brian. Chinese Nights Entertainment: Stories of Old China. lib. bdg. 59.95 (ISBN 0-87968-491-7). Krishna Pr.
Chih-Nung. Legends & Riddles of Fu-Chien. (National Peking University & Chinese Assn. for Folklore, Folklore & Folkliterature Ser.: No. 138). (Chinese.). 6.00 (ISBN 0-89986-212-8). E Langstaff.
Chung Ching-Wen. Legends About Relics & Living Things. Lin Lan, ed. (Tales from the Orient Ser.: No. 5). (Chinese.). 5.00 (ISBN 0-89986-229-2). E Langstaff.
--Myths & Legends in the Ch'u Tz'u. (Folklore Series of National Sun Yat-Sen University: No. 11). (Chinese.). 5.50 (ISBN 0-89986-081-8). E Langstaff.
Jung Chao-Tsu. Superstitions & Legends. (Folklore Series of National Sun Yat-Sen University: No. 2). (Chinese.). 6.00 (ISBN 0-89986-072-9). E Langstaff.
Karlgren, Bernard. Legends & Cults in Ancient China. (Perspectives in Asian History Ser.: No. 7). 167p. Repr. of 1946 ed. lib. bdg. 17.50x (ISBN 0-87991-478-5). Porcupine Pr.
Lin Lan & Yi Ping, eds. Legends About Chu Yuan-Chang & Others. (Tales from the Orient Ser.: No. 1). (Chinese.). 5.00 (ISBN 0-89986-225-X). E Langstaff.
Lin P'ei-Lu. Personal Legends from Eastern Canton. (National Peking University & Chinese Assn. for Folklore, Folklore & Folkliterature Ser.: No. 25). (Chinese.). 6.50 (ISBN 0-89986-121-0). E Langstaff.
Lou Tsu-K'uang. Legends of Formosa, No. 10. (Asian Folklore & Social Life Monograph). (Chinese.). 1970. 5.90 (ISBN 0-89986-013-3). E Langstaff.
Lou Tsu-Kuang. Myths & Legends. (National Peking University & Chinese Assn. for Folklore, Folklore & Folkliterature Ser.: No. 13). (Chinese.). 6.00 (ISBN 0-89986-113-X). E Langstaff.
Mui, Shan. The Seven Magic Orders. Tabrah, Ruth, ed. LC 72-86743. (Illus.). (gr. 1-7). 1973. 5.95 (ISBN 0-89610-011-1). Island Her.
Werner, E. T. Myths & Legends of China. LC 71-172541. (Illus.). Repr. of 1922 ed. 25.00 (ISBN 0-405-09059-5, Pub. by Blom). Arno.
Wong Kuo-Liang. Legends from Changchou Fu-Chien. (National Pekinguniversity & Chinese Assn. for Folklore, Folklore & Folkliterature Ser.: No. 115). (Chinese.). 6.00 (ISBN 0-89986-192-X). E Langstaff.
Wu Tsao-Ting. Legends from Southern Fu-Chien. (Folklore Series of National Sun Yat-Sen University: No. 5). (Chinese.). 5.50 (ISBN 0-89986-075-3). E Langstaff.
Wu Yen-Jen. Legends About Lu Tung-Pin & Other Fairies. Lin Lan, ed. (Tales from the Orient Ser.: No. 2). (Chinese.). 5.00 (ISBN 0-89986-226-8). E Langstaff.

LEGENDS, CHRISTIAN

Bousset, Wilhelm. The Antichrist Legend: A Chapter in Christian & Jewish Folklore. 1977. lib. bdg. 59.95 (ISBN 0-8490-1439-5). Gordon Pr.
Douhet, J. Dictionnaire des Legendes du Christianisme. Migne, J. P., ed. (Troisieme et Derniere Encyclopedie Theologique Ser.: Vol. 14). 764p. (Fr.). Date not set. Repr. of 1855 ed. lib. bdg. 97.50x (ISBN 0-89241-297-6). Caratzas Bros.

LEGENDS, DANISH

Olrik, A. Heroic Legends of Denmark. Hollander, L. M., tr. (Scandinavian Monographs: Vol. 4). Repr. of 1919 ed. 25.00 (ISBN 0-527-68400-7). Kraus Repr.

LEGENDS, EGYPTIAN

King, L. W. Legends of Babylon & Egypt in Relation to Hebrew Tradition. 59.95 (ISBN 0-8490-0504-3). Gordon Pr.
King, Leonard W. Legends of Babylonia & Egypt in Relation to the Hebrew Tradition. LC 77-94593. 1979. Repr. of 1918 ed. lib. bdg. 20.00 (ISBN 0-89341-310-0). Longwood Pr.

LEGENDS, FRENCH

Barth, Bruno. Liebe und Ehe Im Altfranzosischen Fabel und in der Mittelhochdeutschen Novelle. Repr. of 1910 ed. 21.50 (ISBN 0-384-03465-9); pap. 18.50 (ISBN 0-685-02215-3). Johnson Repr.

LEGENDS, GERMANIC

Gauch, Patricia L. Once Upon a Dinkelsbuhl. LC 76-29356. (Illus.). (gr. k-4). 1977. 6.95 (ISBN 0-399-20560-8). Putnam.
Moser, Dietz-Ruediger. Die Tannhaeuser Legende. (Fabula Supplement Ser: Vol. 4). 1977. 42.25x (ISBN 3-11-005957-6). De Gruyter.
Spector, Norman B., tr. The Romance of Tristan & Isolt. (Medieval French Texts). 91p. 1973. text ed. 11.95x (ISBN 0-8101-0405-9). Northwestern U Pr.
Ward, Donald, ed. & tr. from Ger. The German Legends of the Brothers Grimm, 2 vols. LC 80-24596. (Translations in Folklore Studies Ser.). (Illus.). 1981. Set. 42.00x (ISBN 0-915980-79-7, AACR1). Inst Study Human.
Weston, Jessie L. The Legends of the Wagner Drama. LC 74-24255. Repr. of 1896 ed. 24.00 (ISBN 0-404-13132-8). AMS Pr.
--The Legends of the Wagner Drama: Studies in Mythology & Romance. LC 76-22354. 1976. Repr. of 1903 ed. lib. bdg. 35.00 (ISBN 0-89341-003-9). Longwood Pr.
Williams, Charles A. The German Legends of the Hairy Anchorite. 1935. Repr. 20.00 (ISBN 0-8274-2404-3). R West.

LEGENDS, HAWAIIAN

Ashdown, Inez. Stories of Old Lahaina. soft bdg. 1.50 (ISBN 0-930492-12-9). Hawaiian Serv.
Colum, Padriac. Legends of Hawaii. (Illus.). 1937. 20.00 (ISBN 0-300-00376-5). Yale U Pr.
Hoffa, Helynn. UA. (Illus.). 48p. 1981. 24.00 (ISBN 0-686-74851-4). Mosaic Pr.
Kalakaua. The Legends & Myths of Hawaii: The Fables & Folk-Lore of a Strange People. Daggett, R. M., ed. & illus. LC 72-77519. (Illus.). (gr. 9 up). 1972. pap. 7.75 (ISBN 0-8048-1032-X). C E Tuttle.
Maguire, Eliza D. Kona Legends. (Illus.). 1966. pap. 2.75 (ISBN 0-912180-05-6). Petroglyph.
Pratt, Helen G. Hawaiians: An Island People. LC 63-22620. (Illus.). (YA) (gr. 7-9). 1963. 8.95 (ISBN 0-8048-0242-4). C E Tuttle.
Rice, W. H. Hawaiian Legends. Repr. of 1923 ed. pap. 14.00 (ISBN 0-527-02106-7). Kraus Repr.
Rice, William Hyde. Hawaiian Legends. LC 77-83648. (Special Publications Ser: No. 63). (Illus.). 1977. pap. 23.50 (ISBN 0-910240-21-3). Bishop Mus.
Springer, Philipo. Makaha: The Legend of the Broken Promise. Tabrah, Ruth, ed. LC 74-80511. (Illus.). (gr. 1-7). 1974. 5.95 (ISBN 0-89610-008-1). Island Her.
Stimson, J. F. Legends of Maui & Tahaki. Repr. of 1934 ed. pap. 9.00 (ISBN 0-527-02233-0). Kraus Repr.
--Tuamotuan Legends (Island of Anaa), Pt. 1: The Demigods. Repr. of 1937 ed. 14.00 (ISBN 0-527-02256-X). Kraus Repr.
Thompson, Vivian L. Hawaiian Legends of Tricksters & Riddlers. (Illus.). (gr. 4-6). 1969. reinforced bdg. 7.95 (ISBN 0-8234-0041-7). Holiday.
Westervelt, William D. Hawaiian Historical Legends. LC 76-434060. 1976. pap. 4.50 (ISBN 0-8048-1216-0). C E Tuttle.
Westervelt, William D., ed. Hawaiian Legends of Ghosts & Ghost-Gods. LC 63-22543. (Illus.). 1963. 7.25 (ISBN 0-8048-0238-6). C E Tuttle.
--Hawaiian Legends of Old Honolulu. LC 63-22541. (Illus.). 1963. 6.75 (ISBN 0-8048-0239-4). C E Tuttle.
--Hawaiian Legends of Volcanoes. LC 63-22542. (Illus.). 1963. 6.75 (ISBN 0-8048-0240-8). C E Tuttle.

LEGENDS, HINDU

Frere, M. Hindoo Fairy Legends: (Old Deccan Days) 7.50 (ISBN 0-8446-2095-5). Peter Smith.

LEGENDS, HUNGARIAN

Seredy, Kate. White Stag. (Illus.). (gr. 7 up). 1937. 8.95 (ISBN 0-670-76375-6). Viking Pr.

LEGENDS, INDIAN

see Indians–Legends; Indians of Mexico–Legends; Indians of North America–Legends

LEGENDS, INDIC

Ghosh, A. Legends from Indian History. (Illus.). (gr. 1-8). 1979. pap. 3.00 (ISBN 0-89744-157-5). Auromere.
Hemalata. Dhruva. (Illus.). (gr. 1-8). 1979. pap. 1.50 (ISBN 0-89744-153-2). Auromere.
Hopkins, Washburn. Legends of India. 1928. 22.50x (ISBN 0-686-51410-6). Elliots Bks.
Jha, Akhileshwar. Sexual Designs in Indian Culture. 1979. text ed. 12.50x (ISBN 0-7069-0744-2). Humanities.
Oppert, Gustav. On the Original Inhabitants of Bharatavarsa or India. Bolle, Kees W., ed. (Mythology Ser.). 1978. Repr. of 1893 ed. lib. bdg. 42.00x (ISBN 0-405-10557-6). Arno.
Reed, Gwendolyn. Talkative Beasts: Myths, Fables, & Poems of India. LC 69-16817. (Illus.). (gr. 4-6). 1969. PLB 7.92 (ISBN 0-688-50053-6). Lothrop.
Savitri. Savitri & Satyavan. (Illus.). (gr. 1-9). 1979. pap. 1.75 (ISBN 0-89744-160-5). Auromere.
Savitri & Dutta, S. Shakuntala. (Illus.). (gr. 1-9). 1979. pap. 1.75 (ISBN 0-89744-161-3). Auromere.
Temple, Richard C. The Legends of the Panjab, 3 vols. Dorson, Richard M., ed. LC 77-70627. (International Folklore). 1977. Repr. of 1903 ed. Set. 96.00x (ISBN 0-405-10128-7); lib. bdg. 32.00x ea. Vol. 1 (ISBN 0-405-10129-5). Vol. 2 (ISBN 0-405-10130-9). Vol. 3 (ISBN 0-405-10131-7). Arno.
Wasi, Muriel. Legends of India. 2nd. ed. (Illus.). 1973. pap. 2.25 (ISBN 0-88253-326-6). Ind-US Inc.

LEGENDS, IRISH

Croker, Thomas C. Fairy Legends & Traditions of the South of Ireland, 1825-1828. 1971. text ed. 27.50x (ISBN 0-87696-012-3). Humanities.
Kennedy, Patrick. The Bardic Stories of Ireland. LC 76-53557. 1976. Repr. of 1871 ed. lib. bdg. 30.00 (ISBN 0-8414-5535-X). Folcroft.
Lover, Samuel. Legends & Stories of Ireland. LC 78-15789. 1978. Repr. of 1902 ed. lib. bdg. 25.00 (ISBN 0-8414-5840-5). Folcroft.
O'Hanlon, John. Irish Local Legends. LC 73-9868. (Folklore Ser). 10.00 (ISBN 0-88305-489-2). Norwood Edns.
O'Sullivan, Sean. Legends from Ireland. (Folklore of the British Isles Ser.). (Illus.). 176p. 1978. Repr. of 1977 ed. 11.00x (ISBN 0-87471-986-0). Rowman.

LEGENDS, ISLAMIC

Vilnay, Zev. Legends of Galilee, Jordan & Sinai. LC 73-168156. (Sacred Land Ser.: Vol. 3). (Illus.). 1978. 10.95 (ISBN 0-8276-0106-9, 419). Jewish Pubn.

LEGENDS, JAPANESE

Chiba, Reiko. Seven Lucky Gods of Japan. LC 65-25467. (Illus.). 1966. 7.95 (ISBN 0-8048-0521-0). C E Tuttle.
Davis, F. Hadland. Myths and Legends of Japan. 1978. Repr. of 1912 ed. lib. bdg. 45.00 (ISBN 0-8495-1008-2). Arden Lib.
Joly, Henri L. Legends in Japanese Art: A Description of Historical Episodes, Legendary Characters, Folklore Myths, Religious Symbolism. LC 67-16411. (Illus.). 1967. 60.00 (ISBN 0-8048-0358-7). C E Tuttle.
McAlpine, Helen & McAlpine, William. Japanese Tales & Legends. (Oxford Myths & Legends Ser.). (Illus.). (gr. 3-12). 1980. 10.95 (ISBN 0-19-274125-X). Oxford U Pr.
Matisoff, Susan. The Legend of Semimaru: Blind Musician of Japan. LC 77-24601. (Studies in Oriental Cultures Ser.: No. 14). 290p. 1978. 17.50x (ISBN 0-231-03947-6). Columbia U Pr.
Tompkins, John B. & Tompkins, Dorothy C., eds. People, Places & Things in Henri Joly's Legend in Japanese Art: An Analytical Index. LC 78-61162. 218p. 1978. 12.50 (ISBN 0-935034-00-5). Kirin Bks & Art.

LEGENDS, JEWISH

Agnon, Shmuel Y. Days of Awe: A Treasury of Tradition, Legends & Learned Commentaries Concerning Rosh Hashanah, Yom Kippur & the Days Between. LC 48-8316. 1965. 7.50x (ISBN 0-8052-3049-1); pap. 5.95 (ISBN 0-8052-0100-9). Schocken.
Bousset, Wilhelm. The Antichrist Legend: A Chapter in Christian & Jewish Folklore. 1977. lib. bdg. 59.95 (ISBN 0-8490-1439-5). Gordon Pr.
Field, Claud H. Jewish Legends of the Middle Ages. LC 76-48141. 1976. Repr. of 1930 ed. lib. bdg. 10.00 (ISBN 0-8414-6771-4). Folcroft.
Gaster, Moses. The Chronicles of Jerahmeel. rev. ed. 1971. 29.50x (ISBN 0-87068-162-1). Ktav.
Gaster, Moses, tr. from Judeo-German. Ma'aseh Book: Book of Jewish Tales & Legends. LC 81-80356. 694p. 1981. pap. 10.95 (ISBN 0-8276-0189-1, 471). Jewish Pubn.
Ginzberg, Louis. Legends of the Jews, 7 Vols. LC 76-58650. 1956. Set. 60.00 (ISBN 0-8276-0148-4); 8.95 ea. Vol. 1 (172). Vol. 2 (173). Vol. 3 (174). Vol. 4 (174). Vol. 5 (175). Vol. 6 (177). Vol. 7 (178). Jewish Pubn.
Kahana, S. Z. Legends of Israel. 8.00 (ISBN 0-686-21761-6). Res Ctr Kabbalah.
King, Leonard W. Legends of Babylonia & Egypt in Relation to the Hebrew Tradition. LC 77-94593. 1979. Repr. of 1918 ed. lib. bdg. 20.00 (ISBN 0-89341-310-0). Longwood Pr.
Mendelssohn, S. Judaic or Semitic Legends & Customs Amongst South African Natives. 1976. lib. bdg. 59.95 (ISBN 0-8490-2111-1). Gordon Pr.
Patai, Raphael. Gates to the Old City: A Book of Jewish Legends. 858p. 1981. 27.50 (ISBN 0-8143-1679-4). Wayne St U Pr.
Rappoport, Angelo S. Myth & Legend of Ancient Israel, 3 Vols. rev. ed. 1966. 39.50x (ISBN 0-87068-099-4). Ktav.
Vilnay, Zev. Legends of Galilee, Jordan & Sinai. LC 73-168156. (Sacred Land Ser.: Vol. 3). (Illus.). 1978. 10.95 (ISBN 0-8276-0106-9, 419). Jewish Pubn.
--Legends of Jerusalem. (The Sacred Land Ser.: Vol. 1). (Illus.). 1973. 7.95 (ISBN 0-8276-0004-6, 323). Jewish Pubn.

LEGENDS, MAORI

see Legends, Polynesian

LEGENDS, MEXICAN

Davis, E. Adams. Of the Night Wind's Telling: Legends from the Valley of Mexico. (Illus.). 270p. 1976. pap. 5.95 (ISBN 0-8061-1304-9). U of Okla Pr.
Diehl, Richard, et al, eds. Tzeltal Tales of Demons & Monsters. Stross, Brian, tr. LC 78-622530. (Museum Briefs Ser.: No. 24). 1978. pap. 2.00 (ISBN 0-913134-24-4). Mus Anthro Mo.
Robe, Stanley L., ed. Hispanic Legends from New Mexico: Narratives from the R. D. Jameson Collection. (U. C. Publications in Folkore & Mythology Studies: Vol. 31). pap. 27.50 (ISBN 0-520-09614-2). U of Cal Pr.

LEGENDS, MICRONESIAN

Johnson, Margaret & Johnson, Roy. Life & Legends of Micronesia. (Illus.). 104p. 1980. 7.50 (ISBN 0-930230-40-X). Johnson NC.

LEGENDS, MOROCCAN

Chimenti, Elisa. Tales & Legends of Morocco. Benamy, Arnon, tr. (Illus.). (gr. 5 up). 1965. 4.95 (ISBN 0-8392-3049-4). Astor-Honor.

LEGENDS, MUSLIMS

see Legends, Islamic

LEGENDS, NEW ZEALAND

Henderson, Jim. Swagger Country. LC 77-373798. (Illus.). 1977. Repr. of 1976 ed. 11.25x (ISBN 0-340-20927-5). Intl Pubns Serv.

LEGENDS, NORSE

Andersson, Theodore M. The Legend of Brynhild. (Islandica Ser.: Vol. XLII). 288p. 1980. 22.50x (ISBN 0-8014-1302-8). Cornell U Pr.
Colum, Padraic. The Children of Odin. Repr. of 1920 ed. 35.00 (ISBN 0-89987-140-2). Darby Bks.
Jones, Gwyn, ed. Eirik the Red & Other Icelandic Sagas. (World's Classics Paperback Ser.). 336p. 1981. pap. 3.95 (ISBN 0-19-281528-8). Oxford U Pr.

Mabie, Hamilton W. Norse Stories. Repr. of 1882 ed. 25.00 (ISBN 0-89987-177-1). Darby Bks.
--Norse Stories (Retold from the Eddas) 1978. Repr. of 1882 ed. lib. bdg. 20.00 (ISBN 0-8482-4993-3). Norwood Edns.
Major, Albany F. Sagas & Songs of Norseman. LC 73-15520. 1904. Repr. lib. bdg. 15.00 (ISBN 0-8414-6046-9). Folcroft.
Munch, Peter A. & Olsen, Magnus, eds. Norse Mythology: Legends of Gods & Heroes. rev. ed. Hustuedt, Sigurd B., tr. LC 68-31092. (Illus.). 1968. Repr. of 1926 ed. 22.00 (ISBN 0-8103-3454-2). Gale.
Nielsen, Kay. East of the Sun & West of the Moon. (gr. 1 up). 1977. 8.95a (ISBN 0-385-13213-1); PLB (ISBN 0-385-13214-X). Doubleday.
Snorri. Heimskringla: From the Sagas of the Norse Kings. Monsen, Erling, tr. (Illus.). 398p. 1980. 35.00 (ISBN 0-906191-39-4, Pub. by Thule Pr England). Intl Schol Bk Serv.

LEGENDS, ORIENTAL
Courlander, Harold. Tiger's Whisker & Other Tales & Legends from Asia & the Pacific. LC 59-10172. (Illus.). (gr. 4-6). 1959. 5.25 (ISBN 0-15-287652-9, HJ). HarBraceJ.
David-Neel, Alexandra & Yongden, Lama. The Superhuman Life of Gesar of Ling. 400p. (Orig.). 1981. pap. 8.95 (ISBN 0-87773-753-3). Great Eastern.

LEGENDS, PERUVIAN
Francis, P., ed. Ricardo Palma: Tradiciones Peruanas. LC 72-92110. 1970. 5.40 (ISBN 0-08-006665-8); pap. 4.30 (ISBN 0-08-006666-6). Pergamon.

LEGENDS, POLYNESIAN
Andersen, Johannes C. Maori Life in Ao-tea. LC 75-35221. Repr. of 1907 ed. 56.00 (ISBN 0-404-14400-4). AMS Pr.
--Myths & Legends of the Polynesians. LC 75-35170. (Illus.). Repr. of 1931 ed. 43.50 (ISBN 0-404-14200-1). AMS Pr.
Anderson, Johannes E. Myths & Legends of the Polynesians. LC 69-13509. (Illus.). (gr. 9 up). 1969. Repr. of 1928 ed. 15.00 (ISBN 0-8048-0414-1). C E Tuttle.
Campbell, Alistair. Maori Legends. 60p. 1969. pap. 2.50x (ISBN 0-85467-017-3, Pub. by Viking New Zealand). Intl Schol Bk Serv.
Handy, E. S. Marquesan Legends. Repr. of 1930 ed. pap. 14.00 (ISBN 0-527-02175-X). Kraus Repr.
Reed, A. W. Myths & Legends of Maoriland. (Illus.). 1946. 8.25 (ISBN 0-589-00232-5, Pub. by Reed Books Australia). C E Tuttle.
Shortland, Edward. Traditions & Superstitions of the New Zealanders. 2nd ed. LC 75-35270. Repr. of 1856 ed. 32.50 (ISBN 0-404-14439-X). AMS Pr.
Sperry, Armstrong. Call It Courage. (gr. 4-6). 1940. 8.95 (ISBN 0-02-786030-2). Macmillan.
Stirling, Eruera. Eruera: The Teachings of a Maori Elder. Salmond, Anne, ed. (Illus.). 200p. 1981. 45.00 (ISBN 0-19-558069-9). Oxford U Pr.
Westervelt, William D. Legends of Maui, a Demi God of Polynesia, & of His Mother Hina. LC 75-35217. Repr. of 1910 ed. 22.50 (ISBN 0-404-14240-0). AMS Pr.

LEGENDS, RUSSIAN
Hodgetts, E. M. Tales & Legends from the Land of the Tzar. Repr. of 1891 ed. 19.00 (ISBN 0-527-41400-X). Kraus Repr.
Magnus, Leonard A. Heroic Ballads of Russia. LC 67-27623. 1967. Repr. of 1921 ed. 12.50 (ISBN 0-8046-0293-X). Kennikat.

LEGENDS, SCANDINAVIAN
Lindow, John. Swedish Legends & Folktales. LC 77-7830. 1978. 10.95 (ISBN 0-520-03520-8). U of Cal Pr.

LEGENDS, SCOTTISH
Bradley, Edward. The White Wife, with Other Stories Supernatural, Romantic, & Legendary. LC 76-49836. 1976. Repr. of 1865 ed. lib. bdg. 20.00 (ISBN 0-8414-1757-1). Folcroft.
Hogg, James. The Jacobite Relics of Scotland: Being the Songs, Airs, & Legends of the Adherents to the House of Stuart. 1979. Repr. of 1874 ed. lib. bdg. 45.00 (ISBN 0-8495-2276-5). Arden Lib.
Miller, Hugh. Scenes & Legends of the North of Scotland: Traditional History of Cromarty. 2nd rev. ed. Dorson, Richard M., ed. (International Folklore Ser.). 1977. Repr. of 1869 ed. lib. bdg. 28.00x (ISBN 0-405-10110-4). Arno.
Snyder, Gerald S. Is There a Loch Ness Monster? The Search for a Legend. LC 77-22700. (Illus.). 192p. (gr. 7 up). 1977. PLB 7.79 (ISBN 0-671-32853-0). Messner.

LEGENDS, SERBIAN
Petrovic, V. M. Hero Tales & Legends of the Serbians. Repr. of 1914 ed. 29.00 (ISBN 0-527-70800-3). Kraus Repr.

LEGENDS, SPANISH
Webster, Wentworth. Basque Legends. LC 78-63236. (The Folktale). Repr. of 1877 ed. 22.50 (ISBN 0-404-16175-8). AMS Pr.

LEGENDS, SUMATRAN
Schnitger, F. M. Forgotten Kingdoms in Sumatra. 1964. text ed. 23.25x (ISBN 90-040-1971-5). Humanities.

LEGENDS, SWISS
Guerber, H. A. Legends of Switzerland. Repr. of 1899 ed. lib. bdg. 15.00 (ISBN 0-8414-4698-9). Folcroft.

LEGENDS, WEST INDIAN
Aspinall, Algernon E. West Indian Tales of Old. LC 69-18650. (Illus.). Repr. of 1915 ed. 16.50x (ISBN 0-8371-4977-0). Greenwood.

LEGENDS AND STORIES OF ANIMALS
see Animals, Legends and Stories Of

LEGER, ALEXIS SAINT-LEGER, 1889-
Galand, Rene. Saint-John Perse. (World Authors Ser.: France: No. 244). lib. bdg. 10.95 (ISBN 0-8057-2690-X). Twayne.

LEGER, FERNAND, 1881-1955
Beyeler, Ernst. Picasso, Braque, Leger: Masterpieces from Swiss Collections. LC 75-34717. (Illus.). 1975. 6.00 (ISBN 0-912964-09-X). Minneapolis Inst Arts.
Di San Lazzaro, G., ed. Homage to Fernand Leger. (Twentieth Century Art Ser.). (Illus.). 1972. 19.95 (ISBN 0-8148-0501-9). L Amiel Pub.
Golding, John. Fernand Leger: The Mechanic. (Masterpieces in the National Gallery of Canada Ser.). 1976. pap. 2.95 (ISBN 0-88884-308-9, 56344-8, Pub. by Natl Gallery Canada). U of Chicago Pr.
Golding, John & Green, Christopher. Leger & Purist Paris. (Tate Gallery Art Ser.). (Illus.). 1977. pap. 4.50 (ISBN 0-8120-0845-6). Barron.
Institute for the Arts, ed. Leger, Our Contemporary. (Illus.). 1978. pap. 3.00 (ISBN 0-914412-13-2). Inst for the Arts.
Lewis, Barbara. Fernand Leger: The Paintings. LC 79-91826. (Illus.). 40p. 1981. lib. bdg. 200.00 (ISBN 0-87817-256-4). Hacker.
Schmalenbach, Werner. Leger. LC 75-5520. (Library of Great Painters). (Illus.). 1976. 40.00 (ISBN 0-8109-0252-4). Abrams.

LEGERDEMAIN
see Conjuring; Jugglers and Juggling; Magic

LEGIBILITY (PRINTING)
McNally, Harold J. The Readability of Certain Type Sizes & Forms in Sight-Saving Classes. LC 71-177040. (Columbia University. Teachers College. Contributions to Education: No. 883). Repr. of 1943 ed. 17.50 (ISBN 0-404-55883-6). AMS Pr.

LEGION ETRANGERE
see France–Army–Foreign Legion

LEGION OF MARY
Duff, Frank. Miracles on Tap. 5.00 (ISBN 0-910984-14-X); pap. 3.50 (ISBN 0-910984-15-8). Montfort Pubns.

LEGISLATION
see also Bill Drafting; Bills, Legislative; Governmental Investigations; Judge-Made Law; Judicial Review; Law; Legislative Bodies; Legislative Power; Parliamentary Practice; also legislation on particular subjects; e.g. Factory Laws and Legislation
Bayles, Michael D. Principles of Legislation: The Uses of Political Authority. 1978. 17.95 (ISBN 0-8143-1599-2). Wayne St U Pr.
Bernick, E. Lee. Legislative Decision-Making & the Politics of Tax Reform: The Oklahoma Senate. (Legislative Research Ser: No. 9). 35p. 1973. pap. 2.50 (ISBN 0-686-20786-6). Univ OK Gov Res.
--Legislative Voting Patterns & Partisan Cohesion in a One-Party Dominant Legislature. (Legislative Research Ser: No. 3). 26p. 1973. pap. 1.00 (ISBN 0-686-20788-2). Univ OK Gov Res.
Black, Henry C. The Relation of the Executive Power to Legislation. LC 73-19130. (Politics & People Ser.). 192p. 1974. Repr. 10.00x (ISBN 0-405-05855-1). Arno.
Boudin, Louis B. Government by Judiciary, 2 Vols. LC 66-27042. 1968. Repr. of 1932 ed. Set. 25.00 (ISBN 0-8462-0997-7). Russell.
Brown, Richard E., ed. The Effectiveness of Legislative Program Review. LC 78-66237. 150p. 1979. pap. text ed. 4.95 (ISBN 0-87855-712-1). Transaction Bks.
Chamberlain, Joseph P. Legislative Processes: National & State. LC 73-95087. Repr. of 1936 ed. lib. bdg. 19.75x (ISBN 0-8371-2580-4, CHLP). Greenwood.
Chamberlain, Lawrence H. President, Congress & Legislation. LC 72-181927. (Columbia University Studies in the Social Sciences: No. 523). Repr. of 1946 ed. 24.50 (ISBN 0-404-51523-1). AMS Pr.
Chronological Index of Legislation, 1919-1978. 238p. 1980. pap. 11.40 (ISBN 92-2-102288-9). Intl Labour Office.
Congressional Quarterly. Congressional Roll Call, 1980: A Chronology & Analysis of Votes in the House & Senate. Date not set. 12.95 (ISBN 0-87187-168-8). Congr Quarterly.
Cummings, Frank. Capitol Hill Manual. LC 76-608060. 342p. 1976. 17.50 (ISBN 0-87179-226-5). BNA.
Freund, Ernst. Standards of American Legislation. 2nd ed. LC 65-17289. 1965. 12.50x (ISBN 0-226-26270-7). U of Chicago Pr.
--Standards of American Legislation. rev. ed. LC 65-17289. 1965. pap. 2.45 (ISBN 0-226-26271-5, P182, Phoen). U of Chicago Pr.
Goehlert, Robert. Congress & Law-Making: Researching the Legislative Process. LC 79-11554. (Illus.). 168p. 1979. text ed. 19.25 (ISBN 0-87436-294-6). ABC-Clio.
Gross, Bertram M. The Legislative Struggle: A Study in Social Combat. LC 77-18784. 1978. Repr. of 1953 ed. lib. bdg. 36.75x (ISBN 0-313-20205-2, GRLS). Greenwood.
Hurst, James W. Dealing with Statutes. (Carpenter Lecture Ser.). 144p. 1981. text ed. 15.00x (ISBN 0-231-05390-8). Columbia U Pr.
Keefe, William J. & Ogul, Morris. The American Legislative Process: Congress & the States. 4th ed. (Illus.). 1977. text ed. 17.95 (ISBN 0-13-028100-X). P-H.
Kernochan, John M. The Legislative Process. abr. ed. LC 78-70768. 71p. 1980. pap. text ed. write for info. (ISBN 0-88277-023-3). Foundation Pr.
Luce, Robert. Legislative Principles. LC 77-148083. (American Constitutional & Legal History Ser). 1971. Repr. of 1930 ed. lib. bdg. 59.50 (ISBN 0-306-70144-8). Da Capo.
--Legislative Problems. LC 76-152834. (American Constitutional & Legal History Ser). 1971. Repr. of 1935 ed. lib. bdg. 59.50 (ISBN 0-306-70153-7). Da Capo.
McDonnell, Timothy L. The Wagner Housing Act. LC 57-12416. (Jesuit Studies). 1957. 2.95 (ISBN 0-8294-0051-6). Loyola.
Neilson, W. A. & MacPherson, J. C. The Legislative Process in Canada: The Need for Reform. 328p. 1978. pap. text ed. 12.95x (ISBN 0-920380-11-5, Pub. by Inst Res Pub Canada). Renouf.
Price, David E. Who Makes the Laws? Creativity & Power in Senate Committees. 380p. 1972. pap. text ed. 8.95x (ISBN 0-87073-299-4). Schenkman.
Redman, Eric. The Dance of Legislation. 320p. 1973. 9.95 (ISBN 0-671-21494-2). S&S.
--The Dance of Legislation. 1974. pap. 4.95 (ISBN 0-671-21746-1, Touchstone Bks). S&S.
Reid, John. The Magnificent Society & the Democracy Amendments: How to Free Your Congressmen from the Control of the Special Interests. LC 80-85474. 220p. 1981. 11.95 (ISBN 0-939428-00-8); pap. 8.95 (ISBN 0-939428-01-6). Pony X Pr.
Review-1974 Session of the Congress & Index of AEI Publications. 1975. pap. 3.75 (ISBN 0-8447-0167-X). Am Enterprise.
Review-1977 Session of the Congress & Index of AEI Publications. 1978. pap. 3.75 (ISBN 0-8447-0206-4). Am Enterprise.
Ruthnaswamy, M. Legislation: Principles & Practice. 262p. 1974. 17.50x (ISBN 0-8002-0974-5). Intl Pubns Serv.
Shannon, W. Wayne. Party, Constituency & Congressional Voting: A Study of Legislative Behavior in the United States House of Representatives. LC 80-25798. (Louisiana State University Studies, Social Science Ser.: No. 14). (Illus.). xii, 202p. 1981. Repr. of 1968 ed. lib. bdg. 23.50x (ISBN 0-313-22771-3, SHPV). Greenwood.
Sietzer. How Laws Are Really Made. (Contemporary Concerns Ser.). (gr. 10-12). 1974. pap. text ed. 4.92 (ISBN 0-88343-622-1); tchrs'. manual 1.50 (ISBN 0-88343-623-X). McDougal-Littell.
Wayne, Stephen J. The Legislative Presidency. 1978. pap. text ed. 10.50 scp (ISBN 0-06-046964-1, HarpC). Har-Row.

LEGISLATION–GREAT BRITAIN
Carr, Cecil T. Concerning English Administrative Law. LC 70-38958. Repr. of 1941 ed. 17.50 (ISBN 0-404-01395-3). AMS Pr.
Chen Chih-Mai. Parliamentary Opinion of Delegated Legislation. LC 70-76628. (Columbia University Studies in the Social Sciences: No. 394). Repr. of 1933 ed. 15.00 (ISBN 0-404-51394-8). AMS Pr.
Paulus, Ingeborg. Search for Pure Food: A Sociology of Legislation in Britain. (Law in Society Ser.). 144p. 1974. text ed. 8.50x (ISBN 0-85520-076-6). Rothman.

LEGISLATION–ROME
Daube, David. Forms of Roman Legislation. LC 78-12308. 1979. Repr. of 1956 ed. lib. bdg. 15.50x (ISBN 0-313-21146-9, DAFR). Greenwood.

LEGISLATION, COMPARATIVE
see Comparative Law

LEGISLATION, DRAFTING
see Bill Drafting

LEGISLATIVE, EXECUTIVE AND JUDICIAL APPROPRIATION BILLS
see United States–Appropriations and Expenditures

LEGISLATIVE BILLS
see Bills, Legislative

LEGISLATIVE BODIES
see also Gerrymander; Legislative Power; Legislators; Ministerial Responsibility; Parliamentary Practice; Right and Left (Political Science)
Aldon, Edmund K. The World's Representative Assemblies of Today: A Study in Comparative Legislation. Repr. of 1893 ed. pap. 7.00 (ISBN 0-384-00640-X). Johnson Repr.
American Political Science Association, & Committee on American Legislatures. American State Legislatures. Zeller, Belle, ed. LC 73-92294. Repr. of 1954 ed. lib. bdg. 15.00 (ISBN 0-8371-2434-4, AMSL). Greenwood.
Aydelotte, William O. History of Parliamentary Behavior. LC 76-24290. (Quantative Studies in History). 1977. text ed. 30.00x (ISBN 0-691-05242-5); pap. 11.50 (ISBN 0-691-10046-2). Princeton U Pr.
Baaklini, Abdo I. & Heaphy, James J., eds. Comparative Legislative Reforms & Innovations. LC 77-4249. 1977. 15.00 (ISBN 0-87395-805-5). State U NY Pr.
Bell, Charles & Price, Charles. The First Term: A Study of Legislative Socialization. LC 75-11130. (Sage Library of Social Research: Vol. 18). 1975. 20.00x (ISBN 0-8039-0500-9); pap. 8.95 (ISBN 0-8039-0501-7). Sage.
Bentham, Jeremy. Bentham's Handbook of Political Fallacies. Larrabee, Harold A., ed. xxxii, 269p. 1980. Repr. of 1952 ed. lib. bdg. 17.50x (ISBN 0-374-90580-0). Octagon.
Bernick, E. Lee. Legislative Voting Patterns & Partisan Cohesion in a One-Party Dominant Legislature. (Legislative Research Ser: No. 3). 26p. 1973. pap. 1.00 (ISBN 0-686-20788-2). Univ OK Gov Res.
Blondel, Jean. Comparative Legislatures. (Contemporary Comparative Politics Ser.). (Illus.). 176p. 1973. ref. ed. 7.95 (ISBN 0-13-153874-8); pap. text ed. 7.95 (ISBN 0-13-153866-7). P-H.
Campbell, Ballard C. Representative Democracy: Public Policy & Midwestern Legislatures in the Late Nineteenth Century. 267p. 1980. text ed. 20.00x (ISBN 0-674-76275-4). Harvard U Pr.
Chamberlain, Joseph P. Legislative Processes: National & State. LC 73-95087. Repr. of 1936 ed. lib. bdg. 19.75x (ISBN 0-8371-2580-4, CHLP). Greenwood.
Comer, John C. & Johnson, James B., eds. Nonpartisanship in the Legislative Process: Essays on the Nebraska Legislature. LC 78-69835. 1978. pap. text ed. 7.50 (ISBN 0-8191-0579-1). U Pr of Amer.
Committee for Economic Development. Making Congress More Effective. LC 70-136764. 84p. 1970. lib. bdg. 2.00 (ISBN 0-87186-739-7); pap. 1.00 (ISBN 0-87186-039-2). Comm Econ Dev.
Compendium of Legislative Authority: Vol. 1, Suppl. 1, 1978. 66p. 1979. pap. 7.50 (ISBN 0-686-70667-6, UNEP 39, UNEP). Unipub.
Congressional Quarterly Inc. Congressional Roll Call, Nineteen Eighty. 320p. (Orig.). 1981. pap. 12.95 (ISBN 0-87187-168-8). Congr Quarterly.
Congressional Quarterly Inc., ed. Congress & the Nation. vol. 5 ed. 12000p. 1981. 85.00 (ISBN 0-87187-216-1). Congr Quarterly.
--Congressional Quarterly Nineteen Eighty Almanac. 1000p. 1981. 96.00 (ISBN 0-87187-170-X). Congr Quarterly.
Congressional Quarterly Staff. Congressional Roll Call, 1977. LC 72-77849. 1977. pap. text ed. 12.00 (ISBN 0-87187-121-1). Congr Quarterly.
Cooper, Joseph & MacKenzie, G. Calvin, eds. The House at Work. (Illus.). 320p. 1981. text ed. 25.00x (ISBN 0-292-73017-9). U of Tex Pr.
Davidson, Roger & Oleszek, Walter. Congress & Its Members. Way, Jean, ed. 425p. (Orig.). 1981. pap. 8.75 (ISBN 0-87187-202-1). Congr Quarterly.
Decisions & Decision-Makers in the Modern State. 1967. pap. 11.50 (ISBN 92-3-100679-7, U151, UNESCO). Unipub.
Eldridge, Albert F., ed. Legislatures in Plural Societies: The Search for Cohesion in National Development. LC 76-28916. 1977. 14.75 (ISBN 0-8223-0373-6). Duke.
Eulau, Heinz, et al. The Politics of Representation. LC 78-17128. 312p. 1978. 22.50 (ISBN 0-8039-1013-4); pap. 9.95 (ISBN 0-8039-1014-2). Sage.
Harder, Marvin A. & Davis, Raymond G. The Legislature As an Organization: A Study of the Kansas Legislature. (Illus.). 1979. pap. 11.50x (ISBN 0-7006-0187-2). Regents Pr KS.
Hebert, F. Ted. Oklahoma Legislative Voting: A Roll Call Analysis for 1970-1974. (Legislative Research Ser.: No. 12). 29p. 1978. 2.00 (ISBN 0-686-04909-8). Univ OK Gov Res.
Hinckley, Barbara. Congressional Elections. (CQ Politics & Public Policy). 187p. 1981. pap. 7.50 (ISBN 0-87187-171-8). Congr Quarterly.
Hirsch, H. & Hancock, M. Comparative Legislative Systems. LC 78-136612. 1971. 14.95 (ISBN 0-02-914720-4). Free Pr.

Kirkpatrick, Samuel A. & Pettit, Lawrence K. Legislative Role Structures, Power Bases & Behavior Patterns: An Empirical Examination of the U. S. Senate. (Legislative Research Ser.: No. 6). 1973. pap. 2.50 (ISBN 0-686-18646-X). Univ OK Gov Res.
Kornberg, Allan & Musolf, Lloyd A., eds. Legislatures in Developmental Perspectives. LC 78-111416. 1970. 22.50 (ISBN 0-8223-0231-4). Duke.
Lacy, Alex B., Jr., ed. Power in American State Legislatures, Vol. 11. 1967. 5.00 (ISBN 0-930598-10-5). Tulane Stud Pol.
Lewak, Ben. The Social Studies Student Investigates the Legislative Process. (Illus.). 128p. (gr. 7-12). 1976. PLB 7.97 (ISBN 0-8239-0368-0). Rosen Pr.
Loewenberg, Gerhard, ed. Modern Parliaments: Change or Decline. (Controversy Ser). 1971. 9.95x (ISBN 0-202-24075-4); pap. 3.95 (ISBN 0-202-24103-3). Lieber-Atherton.
Lowi, Theodore J. & Ripley, Randall B. Legislative Politics U. S. A. 3rd ed. 1973. pap. text ed. 7.95 (ISBN 0-316-53389-0). Little.
Luce, Robert. Legislative Assemblies. LC 73-5617. (American Constitutional & Legal History Ser.). 692p. 1974. Repr. of 1924 ed. lib. bdg. 59.50 (ISBN 0-306-70583-4). Da Capo.
--Legislative Problems. LC 76-152834. (American Constitutional & Legal History Ser). 1971. Repr. of 1935 ed. lib. bdg. 59.50 (ISBN 0-306-70153-7). Da Capo.
McIlwain, Charles H. The High Court of Parliament. Mayer, J. P., ed. LC 78-67368. (European Political Thought Ser.). 1979. Repr. of 1910 ed. lib. bdg. 26.00x (ISBN 0-405-11719-1). Arno.
Main, Jackson T. Political Parties Before the Constitution. LC 71-184228. (Institute of Early American History & Culture Ser.). (Illus.). 460p. 1973. 24.00x (ISBN 0-8078-1194-7). U of NC Pr.
--Political Parties Before the Constitution. (Illus.). 512p. 1974. pap. 4.95x (ISBN 0-393-00718-9). Norton.
Markesinis, B. S. The Theory & Practice of Dissolution of Parliament. LC 70-189592. (Studies in International & Comparative Law). (Illus.). 300p. 1972. 37.50 (ISBN 0-521-08524-1). Cambridge U Pr.
Mezey, Michael L. Comparative Literatures. LC 77-91086. (Publications of the Consortium for Comparative Legislative Studies). (Illus.). 1979. 17.75 (ISBN 0-8223-0411-2). Duke.
Moran, T. F. The Rise & Development of the Bicameral System in America. 1973. pap. 7.00 (ISBN 0-384-40025-6). Johnson Repr.
Moran, Thomas F. The Rise & Development of the Bicameral System in America. LC 78-63839. (Johns Hopkins University. Studies in the Social Sciences. Thirteenth Ser. 1895: 5). Repr. of 1895 ed. 11.50 (ISBN 0-404-61097-8). AMS Pr.
Olson, David M. The Legislative Process: A Comparative Approach. (Illus.). 1980. text ed. 18.95 scp (ISBN 0-06-044919-5, HarpC). Har-Row.
Rieselbach, Leroy, ed. Legislative Reform. new ed. 1977. pap. 5.00 (ISBN 0-918592-21-6). Policy Studies.
Riley, Franklin L. Colonial Origins of New England Senates. 1973. Repr. of 1896 ed. pap. 7.00 (ISBN 0-384-50860-X). Johnson Repr.
Sawer, Geoffrey. Australian Federal Politics & Law, 2 vols. Incl. Vol. 1. 1901-1929. 350p. 1972. 18.50x (ISBN 0-522-84033-7); Vol. 2. 1929-1949. 244p. 1974. 16.00x (ISBN 0-522-83732-8). Repr (Pub. by Melbourne U Pr). Intl Schol Bk Serv.
Sayles, George O. The King's Parliament of England. (Historical Controversies). 164p. 1974. 7.95 (ISBN 0-393-05508-6); pap. text ed. 4.95x (ISBN 0-393-09322-0). Norton.
Smith, Joel & Musolf, Lloyd D., eds. Legislatures in Development: Dynamics of Change in New & Old States. LC 77-92912. (Publications of the Consortium for Comparative Legislative Studies). (Illus.). 1979. 19.75 (ISBN 0-8223-0405-8). Duke.
U. S. Library of Congress. Science Policy Reseach Division, 95th Congress, 1st Session 1977, et al. State Legislature Use of Information Technology. LC 78-18915. (House Document Ser.: No. 271). 1978. Repr. of 1977 ed. lib. bdg. 17.00x (ISBN 0-313-20519-1, CHSL). Greenwood.
Uslaner, Eric M. & Weber, Ronald E. Patterns of Decision Making in State Legislatures. LC 76-12884. (Special Studies). 1977. text ed. 23.95 (ISBN 0-275-23230-1). Praeger.
Winslow, Clinton I. State Legislative Committees: A Study in Procedure. LC 74-2797. 1974. Repr. of 1931 ed. lib. bdg. 15.00x (ISBN 0-8371-7435-X, WISL). Greenwood.
Worthley, John A. Public Administration & Legislatures: Experimentation & Exploration. LC 75-23150. 256p. 1976. 18.95x (ISBN 0-88229-233-1). Nelson-Hall.

LEGISLATIVE BODIES-COMMITTEES
see also Governmental Investigations; Legislative Hearings; United States-Congress-Committees
Lees, John D. & Shaw, Malcolm. Committees in Legislatures: A Comparative Analysis. LC 77-91077. 1979. 19.75 (ISBN 0-8223-0399-X). Duke.
Luce, Robert. Legislative Procedure. LC 72-6113. (American Constitutional & Legal History Ser). 640p. 1972. Repr. of 1922 ed. lib. bdg. 59.50 (ISBN 0-306-70522-2). Da Capo.
Winslow, Clinton I. State Legislative Committees: A Study in Procedure. LC 74-2797. 1974. Repr. of 1931 ed. lib. bdg. 15.00x (ISBN 0-8371-7435-X, WISL). Greenwood.
--State Legislative Committees, a Study in Procedure. LC 78-64140. (Johns Hopkins University. Studies in the Social Sciences. Forty-Ninth Ser. 1931: 2). Repr. of 1931 ed. 11.50 (ISBN 0-404-61252-0). AMS Pr.

LEGISLATIVE BODIES-RULES AND PRACTICE
see Parliamentary Practice

LEGISLATIVE BODIES-EUROPE
Cassese, A. Parliamentary Control Over Foreign Policy. 216p. 1980. 32.50x (ISBN 90-286-0019-1). Sijthoff & Noordhoff.
Coombes, D. & Walkland, S. A., eds. Parliaments & Economic Affairs. (Policy Studies Institute Ser.). 1981. text ed. 42.00x (ISBN 0-435-83804-0). Heinemann Ed.
Coombes, David, ed. The Power of the Purse: A Symposium on the Role of European Parliaments in Budgetary Decisions. LC 75-23959. (Illus.). 380p. 1976. text ed. 28.95 (ISBN 0-275-05790-9). Praeger.
Herman, Valentine & Hagger, Mark. The Legislation of Direct Elections to the European Parliament. 1979. text ed. 36.00 (ISBN 0-566-00247-7, Pub. by Gower Pub Co England). Renouf.

LEGISLATIVE BODIES-GREAT BRITAIN
Furio Ceriol, Fadrique. Of Councils & Counselors, 1570: An English Reworking by Thomas Blundeville of el Consejo I Consejeros Del Principe, 1559. LC 63-7083. 1963. 20.00x (ISBN 0-8201-1018-3). Schol Facsimiles.
Marriott, John A. Second Chambers. LC 78-102250. (Select Bibliographies Reprint Ser). 1910. 24.00 (ISBN 0-8369-5135-2). Arno.
Morris, R. J. Parliament & the Public Libraries: A Survey of Legislative Activity Promoting the Municipal Library Service in England & Wales 1850-1976. 1977. 44.00 (ISBN 0-7201-0554-4, Pub. by Mansell England). Merrimack Bk Serv.
Vallance, Elizabeth. Woman in the House: A Study of Women Members of Parliament. 1979. text ed. 23.75x (ISBN 0-485-11186-1, Athlone Pr). Humanities.

LEGISLATIVE BODIES AS COURTS
see also Impeachments

LEGISLATIVE DISTRICTS
see Election Districts

LEGISLATIVE DOCUMENTS
see Legislative Hearings

LEGISLATIVE HEARINGS
Burt, Richard & Kemp, Geoffrey, eds. Congressional Hearings on American Defense Policy, Nineteen Forty-Seven to Nineteen Seventy-One: An Annotated Bibliography. LC 73-11321. (The National Security Studies Ser.). 360p. (Orig.). 1974. pap. 5.95x (ISBN 0-7006-0109-0). Regents Pr KS.
Thomen, Harold O., compiled by. Supplement to the Index of Congressional Committee Hearings Prior to January 3, 1935. LC 73-7481. 1973. lib. bdg. 25.00x (ISBN 0-8371-5909-1, CHI/). Greenwood.
U. S. Congress-Senate Library. Cumulative Index of Congressional Committee Hearings (Not Confidential in Character) from Seventy-Fourth Congress (January 3, 1935) Through Eighty-Fifth Congress (January 3, 1959) in the United States Senate Library. LC 71-179952. 823p. 1959. Repr. lib. bdg. 35.00x (ISBN 0-8371-6320-X, CHG/). Greenwood.
U. S. Congress - Senate Library. Shelflist of Congressional Hearings (Not Confidential in Character) Prior to January 3, 1935 in the United States Senate Library. LC 78-159498. 716p. 1971. Repr. lib. bdg. 35.00x (ISBN 0-8371-6187-8, CHF/). Greenwood.

LEGISLATIVE HISTORIES
Goehlert, Robert. Congress & Law-Making: Researching the Legislative Process. LC 79-11554. (Illus.). 168p. 1979. text ed. 19.25 (ISBN 0-87436-294-6). ABC-Clio.

LEGISLATIVE HISTORY
see also Bills, Legislative
Ferejohn, John A. Pork Barrel Politics: Rivers & Harbors Legislation, 1947-1968. LC 73-89859. 304p. 1974. 12.50x (ISBN 0-8047-0854-1). Stanford U Pr.
Reams, Bernard D., Jr. & Haworth, Charles R., eds. Congress & the Courts: A Legislative History, Seventeen Eighty-Seven to Nineteen Seventy-Seven, 5 vols. in 30. LC 78-50643. 1978. lib. bdg. 975.00 (ISBN 0-930342-56-9). W S Hein.

LEGISLATIVE INVESTIGATIONS
see Governmental Investigations

LEGISLATIVE POWER
see also Civil Supremacy over the Military; Delegation of Powers; Federal Government; Judge-Made Law; Judicial Review; Legislative Bodies; Legislation; Separation of Powers; State Governments; Treaty-Making Power; War and Emergency Powers
Bokor-Szego, H. The Role of the United States in International Legislation. 1979. 29.50 (ISBN 0-444-85041-4, North Holland). Elsevier.
Bolton, John R. Legislative Veto: Unseparating the Powers. 1977. pap. 4.25 (ISBN 0-8447-3245-1). Am Enterprise.
Boyle, James A., Jr. Return to Runnymede. LC 77-319. (Orig.). 1977. pap. 1.25 (ISBN 0-915144-31-X). Hackett Pub.
Cooley, Thomas M. A Treatise on the Constitutional Limitations. LC 78-87510. (American Constitutional & Legal History Ser). 720p. 1972. Repr. of 1868 ed. lib. bdg. 59.50 (ISBN 0-306-71403-5). Da Capo.
Fisher, Louis. President & Congress. LC 78-142362. 1972. 14.95 (ISBN 0-02-910320-7); pap. text ed. 4.95 (ISBN 0-02-910340-1). Free Pr.
Haines, Charles G. Revival of Natural Law Concepts. LC 65-13943. 1965. Repr. of 1930 ed. 9.50 (ISBN 0-8462-0535-1). Russell.
Kingdon, John W. Congressmen's Voting Decisions. 2nd ed. 246p. (Orig.). 1980. pap. text ed. 12.50 scp (ISBN 0-06-043657-3, HarpC). Har-Row.
Muchow, David J. The Vanishing Congress: Where Has All the Power Gone? 230p. 1976. 10.00 (ISBN 0-88265-005-X). North Am Intl.
Orfield, Gary. Congressional Power: Congress & Social Change. 339p. (Orig.). 1974. pap. text ed. 10.95 (ISBN 0-15-513081-1, HC). HarBraceJ.
Pritchett, C. Herman. Congress Versus the Supreme Court, Nineteen Fifty-Seven O Nineteen Sixty. LC 73-249. (American Constitutional & Legal History Ser.). 182p. 1973. Repr. of 1961 ed. lib. bdg. 19.50 (ISBN 0-306-70568-0). Da Capo.
Rosenthal, Alan. Legislative Life: Process, & Performance in the States. 354p. 1981. pap. text ed. 10.95 scp (ISBN 0-06-045585-3, HarpC). Har-Row.
Sloan, Irving J. American Landmark Legislation: Primary Materials, 10 vols. LC 75-42876. 1978. 50.00 ea. (ISBN 0-379-10126-2). Oceana.
Smith, T. V. The Legislative Way of Life. (Midway Reprints Ser.). x, 102p. 1975. pap. 4.50x (ISBN 0-226-76369-2). U of Chicago Pr.
Vreeland, Hamilton, Jr. Twilight of Individual Liberty. LC 75-172238. (Right Wing Individualist Tradition in America Ser). 1972. Repr. of 1944 ed. 11.00 (ISBN 0-405-00446-X). Arno.
Wahlke, John & Eulau, Heinz. Legislative Behavior Study, Nineteen Fifty-Nine. 1974. codebk. 10.00 (ISBN 0-89138-120-1). ICPSR.

LEGISLATORS
see also Afro-American Legislators
Adams, Henry. John Randolph. 7.50 (ISBN 0-8446-0451-8). Peter Smith.
Alexander, Thomas B. & Beringer, Richard E. Anatomy of the Confederate Congress: A Study of the Influences of Member Characteristics on Legislative Voting Behavior, 1861-1865. LC 76-138985. (Illus.). 1972. 12.95 (ISBN 0-8265-1175-9). Vanderbilt U Pr.
Anderson, Lee F., et al. Legislative Roll-Call Analysis. (Handbooks for Research in Political Behavior). 1966. 8.95x (ISBN 0-8101-0052-5). Northwestern U Pr.
Aydelotte, William O. History of Parliamentary Behavior. LC 76-24290. (Quantative Studies in History). 1977. text ed. 30.00x (ISBN 0-691-05242-5); pap. 11.50 (ISBN 0-691-10046-2). Princeton U Pr.
Barber, James D. The Lawmakers: Recruitment & Adaptation to Legislative Life. xii, 314p. 1980. Repr. of 1965 ed. lib. bdg. 27.25x (ISBN 0-313-22200-2, BALA). Greenwood.
Barker, A. & Rush, M. The Member of Parliament & His Information. (Political & Economic Planning Ser.). 1970. text ed. 27.50x (ISBN 0-04-329012-4). Allen Unwin.
Beyle, Herman C. Identification & Analysis of Attribute-Cluster-Blocs: A Technique for Use in the Investigation of Behavior in Governance. LC 77-108602. 1970. 19.50 (ISBN 0-384-04085-3). Johnson Repr.
Brownson, Charles B., ed. Congressional Staff Directory. 22nd ed. 1096p. 1980. 24.00 (ISBN 0-686-65229-0). Congr Staff.
Bryant, Lawrence C. South Carolina Negro Legislators: A Glorious Success. 1974. 15.00 (ISBN 0-686-05553-5); pap. 10.00 (ISBN 0-686-05554-3). L C Bryant.
Christopher, Maurine. Black Americans in Congress. rev. ed. LC 76-8943. (Illus.). 1976. 12.95 (ISBN 0-690-01102-4). T Y Crowell.
Clausen, Aage R. How Congressmen Decide: A Policy Focus. 192p. 1973. text ed. 15.95 (ISBN 0-312-39480-2); pap. text ed. 5.95 (ISBN 0-312-39445-4). St Martin.
Cohen, Dan. Undefeated: The Life of Hubert H. Humphrey. LC 78-53933. (Adult & Young Adult Bks.). (Illus.). 1978. 25.00 (ISBN 0-8225-9953-8). Lerner Pubns.
Cohen, William. Roll Call. 1981. 14.95 (ISBN 0-671-25142-2). S&S.
Cole, Wayne S. Senator Gerald P. Nye & American Foreign Relations. LC 80-17370. (Illus.). 293p. 1980. Repr. of 1962 ed. lib. bdg. 25.00x (ISBN 0-313-22660-1, COSN). Greenwood.
Congressional Quarterly Staff. Members of Congress Since 1789. LC 76-57729. 1977. pap. 6.95 (ISBN 0-87187-105-X). Congr Quarterly.
Crater, Flora, et al. The Almanac of Virginia Politics. LC 76-24321. (Illus.). 1977. pap. 3.95 (ISBN 0-917560-07-8). Woman Activist.
Crosby, Donald F. God, Church, & Flag: Senator Joseph R. McCarthy & the Catholic Church, 1950-1957. LC 77-14064. 1978. 19.50x (ISBN 0-8078-1312-5). U of NC Pr.
Davidson, Roger H. The Role of the Congressman. LC 68-27986. 1969. 18.50x (ISBN 0-672-53587-4). Irvington.
Diamond, Irene. Sex Roles in the State House. LC 76-49708. 1977. 17.50x (ISBN 0-300-02115-1). Yale U Pr.
Elliot, Jeffrey M. & Reginald, R. The Analytical Congressional Directory. (Borgo Reference Library: Vol. 12). 256p. (Orig.). 1981. lib. bdg. 19.95 (ISBN 0-89370-141-6); pap. text ed. 9.95 (ISBN 0-89370-241-2). Borgo Pr.
Fenno, Richard F., Jr. Home Style: House Members in Their Districts. 1978. pap. text ed. 7.95 (ISBN 0-316-27809-2). Little.
Flexner, James T. The Young Hamilton: A Biography. LC 77-13877. 1978. 15.00 (ISBN 0-316-28594-3). Little.
Goehlert, Robert. Congress & Law-Making: Researching the Legislative Process. LC 79-11554. (Illus.). 168p. 1979. text ed. 19.25 (ISBN 0-87436-294-6). ABC-Clio.
Goodsell, Jane. Daniel Inouye. LC 77-1405. (Biography Ser.). (Illus.). (gr. 1-4). 1977. PLB 8.79 (ISBN 0-690-01358-2, TYC-J). Har-Row.
Harris, Fred R. Potomac Fever. 1977. 8.95 (ISBN 0-393-05610-4). Norton.
Haskins, James. Barbara Jordan. LC 77-71522. (Illus.). (gr. 7up). 1977. 8.95 (ISBN 0-8037-0452-6). Dial.
Hayes, Michael J. Lobbyists & Legislators: A Theory of Political Markets. 208p. 1981. 16.00 (ISBN 0-8135-0910-6). Rutgers U Pr.
Heck, Frank H. Proud Kentuckian: John C. Breckinridge, 1821-1875. LC 76-9502. (Kentucky Bicentennial Bookshelf Ser.). 184p. 1976. 6.95 (ISBN 0-8131-0217-0). U Pr of Ky.
Holmes, James. Dr. Bullie's Notes: Reminiscences of Early Georgia & of Philadelphia & New Haven in the 1800s. Presley, Delma E., ed. LC 76-14370. (Illus.). 10.00 (ISBN 0-87797-038-6). Cherokee.
Jackson, John. Constituencies & Leaders in Congress: Their Effects on Senate Voting Behavior. LC 73-93372. (Political Studies). 224p. 1974. text ed. 10.00x (ISBN 0-674-16540-3). Harvard U Pr.
Javits, Jacob K. & Steinberg, Rafael. Javits: The Autobiography of a Public Man. (Illus.). 1981. 16.95 (ISBN 0-395-29912-8). HM.
Kehl, James A. Boss Rule in the Gilded Age: Matt Quay of Pennsylvania. LC 80-5254. (Illus.). 315p. 1980. 24.95 (ISBN 0-8229-3426-4). U of Pittsburgh Pr.
Kirkpatrick, Samuel A. & Pettit, Lawrence K. Legislative Role Structures, Power Bases & Behavior Patterns: An Empirical Examination of the U. S. Senate. (Legislative Research Ser.: No. 6). 1973. pap. 2.50 (ISBN 0-686-18646-X). Univ OK Gov Res.
Kornberg, Allan & Mishler, William. Influence in Parliament: Canada. LC 76-5322. 1976. 19.75 (ISBN 0-8223-0364-7). Duke.
Lyons, Kathleen. Dear Congressman Howard. LC 74-183052. (Congressional Leadership Ser: VOl. 5). (Illus.). 1972. 4.95 (ISBN 0-87491-321-7); pap. 2.95 (ISBN 0-87491-322-5). Acropolis.
Mellors, Colin. The British MP: A Socio-Economic Study of the House of Commons. (Illus.). 1978. 18.95 (ISBN 0-566-00138-1, 00708-0, Pub. by Saxon Hse England). Lexington Bks.
Miller, William. Fishbait: The Memoirs of the Congressional Doorkeeper. (Illus.). 1978. pap. 2.50 (ISBN 0-446-81637-X). Warner Bks.
Moffett, Toby. Nobody's Business: The Political Intruder's Guide to Everyone's State Legislature. LC 73-83355. 196p. 1973. 6.50 (ISBN 0-85699-080-9); pap. 3.95 (ISBN 0-85699-081-7). Chatham Pr.
Morgan, Anne H. Robert S. Kerr: The Senate Years. LC 76-62514. (Illus.). 1977. 16.95 (ISBN 0-8061-1402-9). U of Okla Pr.

Papenfuse, Edward C., et al, eds. A Biographical Dictionary of the Maryland Legislature, 1635-1789, Vol. 1, A-H. 1979. text ed. 19.50 (ISBN 0-8018-1995-4). Johns Hopkins.
Parks, Joseph H. Joseph E. Brown of Georgia. LC 74-27192. 1976. 40.00x (ISBN 0-8071-0189-3). La State U Pr.
Paul, Justus F. Senator Hugh Butler & Nebraska Republicanism. LC 76-42167. (Nebraska State Historical Society Miscellaneous Ser.: No. 1). 1976. 15.50 (ISBN 0-8357-0185-9, IS-00014, Pub. by Nebraska State Historical Society). Univ Microfilms.
Perry, Robert T. Black Legislators. LC 75-5333. 1976. perfect bdg. softcover 9.00 (ISBN 0-88247-389-1). R & E Res Assoc.
Pierce, Lawrence. Freshman Legislator. 2nd ed. (Illus.). 112p. 1973. pap. 2.00 (ISBN 0-8323-0210-4). Binford.
Pierce, Walter M. Oregon Cattleman, Governor, Congressman: Memoirs & Times of Walter M. Pierce. Bone, Arthur H., ed. LC 80-81718. (Illus.). 528p. 1981. pap. 14.95 (ISBN 0-87595-098-1). Oreg Hist Soc.
Ruchelman, Leonard I. Political Careers: Recruitment Through the Legislature. LC 70-99325. 216p. 1970. 11.50 (ISBN 0-8386-7613-8). Fairleigh Dickinson.
Sills, Louise J. Sills Family & Related Lines. 1969. pap. 8.00 (ISBN 0-686-05558-6). L C Bryant.
--Sketch of Sills Family. 1969. pap. 8.00 (ISBN 0-686-05559-4). L C Bryant.
Smallwood, Frank. Free & Independent. LC 75-41878. 1977 (ISBN 0-8289-0272-0). pap. 7.95 (ISBN 0-8289-0279-8). Greene.
Smith, Glenn H. Langer of North Dakota. Freidel, Frank, ed. LC 78-62502. (Modern American History Ser.: Vol. 16). 1979. lib. bdg. 25.00 (ISBN 0-8240-3639-5). Garland Pub.
Tacheron, Donald G. & Udall, Morris K., eds. Job of the Congressman: An Introduction to Service in the U. S. House of Representatives. 2nd ed. LC 77-140113. (Orig.). 1970. pap. 9.50 (ISBN 0-672-51416-8). Bobbs.
They Represent You, 1980. 1981. pap. 1.75 (ISBN 0-686-64779-3). LWV NYC.
Uslaner, Eric M. & Weber, Ronald E. Patterns of Decision Making in State Legislatures. LC 76-12884. (Special Studies). 1977. text ed. 23.95 (ISBN 0-275-23230-1). Praeger.
Voorhis, Jerry. Confession of Faith. 1978. 5.95 (ISBN 0-533-03284-9). Vantage.
Waller, Robert A. Rainey of Illinois: A Political Biography, 1903-34. LC 77-23859. (Illnois Studies in Social Sciences: No. 60). 1977. 12.50 (ISBN 0-252-00647-X). U of Ill Pr.
Woshinsky, Oliver H. The French Deputy. LC 73-7960. 233p. 1980. Repr. of 1973 ed. text ed. 9.95x (ISBN 0-686-64208-2). Lytton Pub.

LEGISLATORS, AFRO-AMERICAN
see Afro-American Legislators

LEGITIMACY (LAW)
see Illegitimacy

LEGITIME
A Breefe Discourse Declaring & Approving the Necessarie Maintenance of the Laudable Customes of London. LC 72-6012. (English Experience Ser.: No. 538). 48p. Repr. of 1584 ed. 6.00 (ISBN 9-0221-0538-5). Walter J Johnson.

LEGUMES
Here are entered works on those plants belonging to the family Leguminosae, the pods or seeds of which are edible for man or domestic animals, e.g. peas, beans, lentils, etc., treated collectively.
see also names of luguminous plants
Allen, O. N. & Allen, Ethel K. The Leguminosae: A Source Book of Characteristics, Uses & Nodulation. LC 80-5104. (Illus.). 806p. 1981. 60.00 (ISBN 0-299-08400-0). U of Wis Pr.
Andrew, C. S. & Kamprath, E. J., eds. Mineral Nutrition of Legumes in Tropical & Subtropical Soils. 1979. 22.50x (ISBN 0-643-00311-8, Pub. by CSIRO). Intl Schol Bk Serv.
Andrews, C. S. & Kamprath, E. J. Mineral Nutrition of Legumes in Tropical & Subtropical Soils. 415p. 1981. 79.50x (ISBN 0-643-00311-8, Pub. by CSIRO Australia). State Mutual Bk.
Bird, Julio & Maramorosch, Karl, eds. Tropical Diseases of Legumes: Papers Presented at the Rio Piedras Agricultural Experiment Station of the University of Puerto Rico, Mayaguez Campus, June, 1974. 1975. 25.00 (ISBN 0-12-099950-1). Acad Pr.
Bland, Brian F. Crop Production: Cereals & Legumes. 1971. 73.50 (ISBN 0-12-104050-X). Acad Pr.
Bond, D. A., ed. Vicia Faba: Feeding Value, Processing & Viruses. (World Crops: Production, Utilization, & Description: Vol. 3). x, 424p. 1980. lib. bdg. 50.00 (ISBN 9-0247-2362-0, Pub. by Martinus Nijhoff Netherlands). Kluwer Boston.
Candolle, A. De. Memoires Sur la Famille Des Legumineuses. (Illus.). 1966. Repr. of 1825 ed. 112.00 (ISBN 3-7682-0299-2). Lubrecht & Cramer.
Courter, Gay. The Beansprout Book. (Illus.). 1977. pap. 1.95 (ISBN 0-671-22947-8, Fireside): S&S.
Cummins, George B. Rust Fungi on Legumes & Composites in North America. LC 78-60541. 1978. pap. 8.95x (ISBN 0-8165-0653-1). U of Ariz Pr.
Duke, James A. Handbook of Legumes of World Economic Importance. (Illus.). 350p. 1981. 45.00 (ISBN 0-306-40406-0, Plenum Pr). Plenum Pub.
Elementary Science Study. Life of Beans & Peas. 2nd ed. 1975. 5.40 (ISBN 0-07-018581-6, W). McGraw.
Farwagi, Peta L. Full of Beans: An International Bean Cookbook. 1978. pap. 4.95 (ISBN 0-06-090601-4, CN 601, CN). Har-Row.
Fassett, Norman C. Leguminous Plants of Wisconsin. 174p. 1939. 17.00x (ISBN 0-299-00080-X). U of Wis Pr.
First FAO-DANIDA Training Course on Improvement & Production of Food Legumes for Africa & the Near East. (Danish Funds-in-Trust). 1976. pap. 4.00 (ISBN 0-685-65006-5, FAO). Unipub.
Food Legume Crops: Improvement & Production. (FAO Plant Production & Protection Paper Ser.: No. 9). 1978. pap. 16.50 (ISBN 92-5-100404-8, F1377, FAO). Unipub.
Food Legume Improvement & Development. 1979. pap. 12.00 (ISBN 0-88936-202-5, IDRC126, IDRC). Unipub.
Grear, John W. A Revision of the New World Species of Rhynchosia(Leguminosae-Faboideae) LC 78-17663. (Memoirs Ser.: Vol. 31, No. 1). 1978. pap. 15.00 (ISBN 0-89327-208-6). NY Botanical.
Harbourne, J. B., et al, eds. Chemotaxonomy of Leguminosae. 1971. 96.00 (ISBN 0-12-324652-0). Acad Pr.
Heywood, V. H., ed. Botanical Systematics, Vol. 1. 1976. 70.50 (ISBN 0-12-346901-5). Acad Pr.
Isely, Duane. Leguminosae of the United States Pt. III: Subfamily Papilionoideae - Tribes Sophoreae, Podalyreae, Loteae. (Memoirs of the New York Botanical Garden Ser.: Vol. 23, No. 3). (Illus.). 1981. pap. write for info. (ISBN 0-89327-232-9). NY Botanical.
--Leguminosae of the United States: Subfamily Caesalpinioideae. LC 66-6394. (Memoirs of the New York Botanical Garden: Vol. 25, No. 2). (Illus.). 1975. pap. 16.00 (ISBN 0-89327-054-7). NY Botanical.
--Leguminosae of the United States: Subfamily Mimosoideae. LC 66-6394. (Memoirs of the New York Botanical Carden: Vol. 25, No. 1). (Illus.). 1975. pap. 8.00 (ISBN 0-89327-053-9). NY Botanical.
Mineral Nutrition of Legumes in Tropical & Subtropical Soils. 415p. 1978. 29.00 (ISBN 0-643-00311-8, CO14, CSIRO). Unipub.
Plant Relations in Pastures. 475p. 1980. pap. 45.00 (ISBN 0-643-00264-2, CO05, CSIRO). Unipub.
Protein Advisory Group of the United Nations System. Nutritional Improvement of Food Legumes by Breeding. Milner, Max, ed. LC 7-28198. 416p. 1975. 47.00 (ISBN 0-471-70112-2, Pub. by Wiley-Interscience). Wiley.
Rahn, Joan E. Alfalfa, Beans & Clover. LC 76-67. (Illus.). 128p. (gr. 4-6). 1976. 6.50 (ISBN 0-689-30528-1). Atheneum.
Report of the First FAO-DANIDA Training Course on Improvement & Production of Food Legumes for Africa & the Near East, University of Teheran, May 3-August 30, 1975. (Danish Funds-in-Trust: TP REM Den). 24p. 1976. pap. 7.50 (ISBN 0-685-66333-7, F1095, FAO). Unipub.
Seed Protein Improvement in Cereals & Grain Legumes, 2 vols. 1979. pap. 53.75 (ISBN 92-0-010079-1, ISP496-1, IAEA); pap. 59.50 (ISBN 92-0-010179-8, ISP496-2, IAEA). Unipub.
Smartt, J. Tropical Pulses. (Tropical Agriculture Ser.). (Illus.). 1976. text ed. 36.00x (ISBN 0-582-46679-2). Longman.
Summerfield, R. J. & Bunting, A. H., eds. Advances in Legume Science. (Vol. 1). (Illus.). xvi, 667p. 1980. pap. 40.00x (ISBN 0-85521-223-3, Pub by Brit Mus Nat Hist England). Sabbot-Natural Hist Bks.
Turner, B. L. The Legumes of Texas. LC 59-12857. (Illus.). 298p. 1977. pap. text ed. 12.50x (ISBN 0-292-74618-0). U of Tex Pr.
Turvey, Valerie. Bean Feast: An International Legumes Cookbook. LC 79-5447. (Illus.). 160p. 1979. pap. 5.95 (ISBN 0-89286-158-4). One Hund One Prods.
Whistler, Roy L. & Hymowitz, Theodore. Guar: Agronomy, Production, Industrial Use, & Nutrition. LC 78-58137. (Illus.). 1979. 9.95 (ISBN 0-911198-51-2). Purdue.
Whyte, R. O., et al. Legumes in Agriculture. (FAO Agricultural Studies: No. 21). (Orig.). 1973. pap. 13.25 (ISBN 0-685-02453-9, F255, FAO). Unipub.
Withee, John. Growing & Cooking Beans. Orcutt, Georgia, ed. LC 79-57179. 144p. (Orig.). 1980. pap. 7.95 (ISBN 0-911658-05-X, 3070). Yankee Bks.

LEHMAN, HERBERT HENRY, 1878-1963
Ingalls, Robert P. Herbert H. Lehman & New York's Little New Deal. LC 75-13744. 287p. 1975. 16.00x (ISBN 0-8147-3750-1). NYU Pr.

LEHMANN, LILLI, 1848-1929
Lehman, Lilli. My Path Through Life. Farkas, Andrew, ed. Seligman, Alice B., tr. LC 76-29947. (Opera Biographies). (Illus.). 1977. Repr. of 1914 ed. lib. bdg. 37.00x (ISBN 0-405-09689-5). Arno.
Lissfelt, J. Fred. Basic Principles of Artistic Singing. 1938. pap. 2.50 (ISBN 0-911318-00-3). E C Schirmer.

LEHMBRUCK, WILHELM, 1881-1919
Heller, Reinhold. The Art of Wilhelm Lehmbruck. (Illus.). 1972. pap. 7.75 (ISBN 0-87846-158-2). Mus Fine Arts Boston.
Petermann, Erwin, ed. Lehmbruck: Die Druckgraphik Von Wilhelm Lehmbruck. (Illus., Ger). 1964. 45.00x (ISBN 0-8150-0071-5). Wittenborn.

LEIBNIZ, GOTTFRIED WILHELM, FREIHERR VON, 1646-1716
Adams, Robert M., et al. Essays on the Philosophy of Leibniz. Kulstad, Mark, ed. (Rice University Studies: Vol. 63, No. 4). 143p. 1978. pap. 4.25x (ISBN 0-89263-234-8). Rice Univ.
Axelos, Christos. Die Ontologischen Grundlagen der Freiheitstheorie von Leibniz. LC 72-81544. 385p. 1973. 36.00x (ISBN 3-11-002221-4). De Gruyter.
Broad, C. D. & Lewy, C. Leibniz: An Introduction. LC 74-31784. 192p. 1975. 26.95 (ISBN 0-521-20691-X); pap. 7.95x (ISBN 0-521-09925-0). Cambridge U Pr.
Calinger, Ronald. Gottfried Wilhelm Leibniz. 1976. pap. 5.00 (ISBN 0-685-83795-5, Sci Hist). N Watson.
Collins, James. Continental Rationalists: Descartes, Spinoza, Leibniz. (Orig.). 1967. pap. 3.50 (ISBN 0-02-813480-X). Glencoe.
Costabel, Pierre. Leibniz & Dynamics. Maddison, R. E., tr. from Fr. (Illus.). 141p. 1973. 22.50x (ISBN 0-8014-0775-3). Cornell U Pr.
Danek, Jaromir. Les Projets de Leibniz et de Bolzano: Deux Sources de la Logique Contemporaine. 276p. (Fr.). 1975. pap. 10.50x (ISBN 2-7637-6688-9, Pub. by Laval). Intl Schol Bk Serv.
Dewey, John. Leibniz's New Essays Concerning the Human Understanding: A Critical Exposition. 1977. lib. bdg. 59.95 (ISBN 0-8490-2148-0). Gordon Pr.
Eliot, T. S. Knowledge & Experience in the Philosophy of F. H. Bradley. 1964. 4.50 (ISBN 0-374-18176-4). FS&G.
Frankfurt, Harry G., ed. Leibniz: A Collection of Critical Essays. LC 76-41843. (Modern Studies in Philosophy). 1976. text ed. 16.95x (ISBN 0-268-01258-X); pap. text ed. 5.95x (ISBN 0-268-01259-8). U of Notre Dame Pr.
Gurwitsch, Aron. Leibniz: Philosophie des Panlogismus. LC 73-88298. (Ger.). 1974. 69.50x (ISBN 3-11-004358-0). De Gruyter.
Hofmann, J. E. Leibniz in Paris, 1672-1676. LC 73-80469. (Illus.). 230p. 1974. 65.00 (ISBN 0-521-20258-2). Cambridge U Pr.
Ishiguro, Hide. Leibniz's Philosophy of Logic & Language. LC 72-2357. 165p. 1972. 19.50x (ISBN 0-8014-0737-0). Cornell U Pr.
Joseph, Horace W. Lectures on the Philosophy of Leibniz. LC 73-9264. 190p. 1974. Repr. of 1949 ed. lib. bdg. 15.00x (ISBN 0-8371-7002-8, JOPL). Greenwood.
Leclerc, Ivor, ed. The Philosophy of Leibniz & the Modern World. LC 72-1346. 365p. 1973. 15.00 (ISBN 0-8265-1181-3). Vanderbilt U Pr.
Leibniz. The Leibniz-Clarke Correspondence. Alexander, H. G., ed. 200p. 1977. 15.00x (ISBN 0-7190-0669-4, Pub. by Manchester U Pr England). State Mutual Bk.
Leibniz, Gottfried W. La Monadologie. 245p. 1981. Repr. of 1881 ed. lib. bdg. 100.00 (ISBN 0-8287-1478-9). Clearwater Pub.
Loemker, Leroy E. Struggle for Synthesis: The Seventeenth Century Background of Leibniz's Synthesis of Order & Freedom. LC 72-79308. 529p. 1972. 16.50x (ISBN 0-674-84545-5). Harvard U Pr.
Loemker, Leroy E., ed. Gottfried Wilhelm Leibniz: Philosophical Papers & Letters. (Synthese Historical Library: No. 2). 1976. lib. bdg. 55.00 (ISBN 90-277-0008-7, Pub. by Reidel Holland); pap. 26.00 (ISBN 90-277-0693-X, Pub. by Reidel Holland). Kluwer Boston.
Martin, Gottfried. Leibniz: Logik und Metaphysik. 2nd ed. (Ger). 1967. 24.00x (ISBN 3-11-005160-5). De Gruyter.
Merz, John T. Leibniz. 1978. Repr. of 1901 ed. lib. bdg. 35.00 (ISBN 0-8495-3823-8). Arden Lib.
Meyer, R. W. Leibniz & the Seventeenth Century Revolution. Stern, J. P., tr. 1952. text ed. 6.75x (ISBN 0-391-02000-5). Humanities.
Mungello, David E. Leibniz & Confucianism: The Search for Accord. LC 77-4053. 1977. text ed. 12.00x (ISBN 0-8248-0545-3). U Pr of Hawaii.
Nölen, Desire. La Critique De Kant et la Metaphysique De Leibniz: histoire et theorie De leurs rapports... 476p. 1981. Repr. of 1875 ed. lib. bdg. 185.00 (ISBN 0-8287-1485-1). Clearwater Pub.
Ortega Y Gasset, Jose. Idea of Principle in Leibnitz & the Evolution of Deductive Theory. LC 66-18068. 1971. 10.00x (ISBN 0-393-01086-4). Norton.
Rescher, Nicholas. Leibniz: An Introduction to His Philosophy. (American Philosophical Quarterly Library of Philosophy). (Illus.). 167p. 1979. 18.00x (ISBN 0-8476-6110-5). Rowman.
Russell, B. La Philosophie De Leibniz. (Reimpressions G & B Ser.). 1971. 29.25x (ISBN 0-685-33031-1). Gordon.
Waterman, John T. Leibniz & Ludolf on Things Linguistic: Excerpts from Their Correspondence, (1688-1703) (Publications in Linguistics: No. 88). 1978. pap. 11.00x (ISBN 0-520-09586-3). U of Cal Pr.
Wiener, Philip, ed. Leibniz: Selections. 1971. pap. text ed. 7.95x (ISBN 0-684-14680-0, ScribC). Scribner.

LEIBOWITZ, SAMUEL SIMON, 1893-
Reynolds, Quentin. Courtroom. facs. ed. LC 77-119943. (Select Bibliographies Reprint Ser). 1950. 25.00 (ISBN 0-8369-5386-X). Arno.

LEICA CAMERAS
see Cameras–Types–Leica

LEICESTER, ROBERT DUDLEY, EARL OF, 1532-1588
Rosenberg, Eleanor. Leicester, Patron of Letters. 395p. 1976. Repr. of 1958 ed. lib. bdg. 22.50x (ISBN 0-374-96915-9). Octagon.

LEICESTER, ENGLAND
Aston, Norman. Leicestershire Watermills. 1981. 20.00x (ISBN 0-905837-02-9, Pub. by Sycamore Pr England). State Mutual Bk.
Graham, Rigby. Leicestershire. 1981. 200.00x (ISBN 0-905837-07-X, Pub. by Sycamore Pr England). State Mutual Bk.
Pritchard, R. M. Housing & the Spatial Structure of the City. LC 75-3859. (Cambridge Geographical Studies). (Illus.). 403p. 1976. 41.50 (ISBN 0-521-20882-3). Cambridge U Pr.
Watts. A Walk Through Leicester. 1967. Repr. of 1804 ed. text ed. 5.00x (ISBN 0-7185-1073-9, Leicester). Humanities.

LEICESTER, ENGLAND–HISTORY
Knight, William. Memorials of Coleorton, 2 vols. limited ed. LC 74-6115. 1887. Repr. lib. bdg. 75.00 (ISBN 0-8414-5491-4). Folcroft.
Leicester Old & New. 1975. pap. text ed. 8.50x (ISBN 0-8277-4161-8). British Bk Ctr.
Stevens, Philip A. The Leicester Line: A History of the Old Union & Grand Union Canals. (Inland Waterways Histories Ser.). (Illus.). 200p. 1972. 6.50 (ISBN 0-7153-5536-8). David & Charles.

LEICESTERSHIRE, ENGLAND
Gaudeamus. A Leicestershire Garland for Europa Cantat 6. 1976. 4.75 (ISBN 0-19-343615-9). Oxford U Pr.
Hoskins, W. G. Leicestershire: A Shell Guide. 123p. 1970. 9.95 (ISBN 0-571-09467-8, Pub. by Faber & Faber). Merrimack Bk Serv.
Morgan, Philip, ed. Leicestershire. (Domesday Book Ser.). (Illus.). 146p. 1979. 18.00x (ISBN 0-8476-2437-4). Rowman.

LEICHHARDT, LUDWIG, 1813-1848–JUVENILE LITERATURE
Webster, E. M. Whirlwinds in the Plain: Ludwig Leichardt - Friends, Foes & History. 484p. 1980. 40.00x (ISBN 0-522-84181-3, Pub. by Melbourne U Pr Australia). Intl Schol Bk Serv.

LEIGH, AUGUSTA, 1784-1851
Milbanke, Ralph G. Astarte: A Fragment of Truth Concerning George Gordon Byron, Sixth Lord Byron. LC 75-29380. 1975. Repr. of 1921 ed. lib. bdg. 65.00 (ISBN 0-8414-6041-8). Folcroft.

LEIGHTON, FREDERICK LEIGHTON, BARON, 1830-1896
Barrington, Emilie I. Life, Letters & Work of Frederic Baron Leighton, 2 Vols. LC 70-140032. (Illus.). Repr. of 1906 ed. Set. 95.00 (ISBN 0-404-00659-0); 47.50 ea. AMS Pr.
Ormond, Leonee & Ormond, Richard. Lord Leighton. LC 75-2773. (Studies in British Art Ser.). 192p. 1976. 70.00x (ISBN 0-300-01896-7). Yale U Pr.

LEISERSON, WILLIAM MORRIS, 1883-1957
Eisner, J. Michael. William Morris Leiserson: A Biography. (Illus.). 154p. 1967. 11.50x (ISBN 0-299-04360-6). U of Wis Pr.

LEISLER, JACOB, d. 1691
Andrews, Charles M., ed. Narratives of the Insurrections, Sixteen Seventy-Five to Sixteen Ninety. (Original Narratives). 1967. Repr. of 1915 ed. 18.50x (ISBN 0-06-480028-8). B&N.

LEISURE
see also Hobbies; Recreation; Retirement; Time Allocation

Allard, Lucile E. A Study of the Leisure Activities of Certain Elementary School Teachers of Long Island. LC 70-176510. (Columbia University. Teachers College. Contributions to Education: No. 779). Repr. of 1939 ed. 17.50 (ISBN 0-404-55779-1). AMS Pr.

American Alliance for Health, Physical Education, & Recreation. Leisure Today: Selected Readings. 1975. 8.00x (ISBN 0-685-57475-X). AAHPERD.

Appleton, I., ed. Leisure, Research & Policy. 1974. 15.00x (ISBN 0-7073-0193-9, Pub. by Scottish Academic Pr Scotland). Columbia U Pr.

Bailey, Lorraine H. Time to Spare. (Gregg-McGraw-Hill Series for Independent Living). 1978. pap. text ed. 5.32 (ISBN 0-07-003223-8, G); tchr's. manual 3.30 (ISBN 0-07-003225-4); wkbk 2.52 (ISBN 0-07-003224-6). McGraw.

Ball, Edith L. & Cipriano, Robert E. Leisure Services Preparation: A Competency Based Approach. (Illus.). 1978. ref. ed. 17.95 (ISBN 0-13-528273-X). P-H.

Bammel, Lei G. & Bammel, Lane B. Leisure & Human Behavior. 352p. 1982. text ed. price not set (ISBN 0-697-07183-9). Wm C Brown.

Brightbill, Charles K. Challenge of Leisure. (Orig.). 1963. pap. 2.45 (ISBN 0-13-124859-6, S67, Spec). P-H.

--Man & Leisure: A Philosophy of Recreation. LC 73-3009. 292p. 1973. Repr. of 1961 ed. lib. bdg. 19.50x (ISBN 0-8371-6836-8); pap. 5.95 (ISBN 0-8371-8956-X, BRML). Greenwood.

Brightbill, Charles K. & Mobley, Tony A. Educating for Leisure-Centered Living. 2nd ed. LC 76-47010. 1977. pap. text ed. 11.95 (ISBN 0-471-94914-0). Wiley.

Bucher, Charles A. & Bucher, Richard D. Recreation for Today's Society. (Illus.). 224p. 1974. 13.50 (ISBN 0-13-768721-4). P-H.

Burby, Raymond J., 3rd. Recreation & Leisure in New Communities. LC 76-17871. (New Communities Research Ser.). 1976. 19.50 (ISBN 0-88410-448-6). Ballinger Pub.

Carlson, Reynolds E., et al. Recreation & Leisure: The Changing Scene. 3rd ed. 1979. text ed. 17.95x (ISBN 0-534-00585-3). Wadsworth Pub.

Cheek, N. H., et al. Leisure & Recreation Places. LC 74-83856. (Man, the Community & Natural Resources: No. 3). (Illus.). 1978. pap. text ed. 12.50 (ISBN 0-250-40259-9). Ann Arbor Science.

Cheek, Neil H., Jr. & Burch, William R., Jr. The Social Organization of Leisure in Human Society. (Illus.). 1976. text ed. 18.95 scp (ISBN 0-06-041037-X, HarpC). Har-Row.

Crandall, R. & Ibrahim, Hilmi, eds. Leisure Behavior: A Psychological Approach. LC 78-66381. 1979. 8.95x (ISBN 0-89260-138-8). Hwong Pub.

Dahl, Gordon. Work, Play, & Worship in a Leisure-Oriented Society. LC 72-78566. 128p. 1972. pap. 3.50 (ISBN 0-8066-1233-9, 10-7290). Augsburg.

Dahlberg, Arthur A. Jobs, Machines & Capitalism. LC 70-91296. (BCL Ser. I). Repr. of 1932 ed. 16.50 (ISBN 0-404-01917-X). AMS Pr.

Dana, Richard H. The Idle Man. 59.95 (ISBN 0-87968-271-X). Gordon Pr.

De Grazia, Sebastian. Of Time, Work & Leisure. LC 73-12379. 572p. 1973. lib. bdg. cancelled (ISBN 0-527-22100-7); pap. 18.00 (ISBN 0-527-22101-5). Kraus Repr.

Downes, D. M., et al. Gambling, Work & Leisure: A Study Across Three Areas. (International Library of Sociology). 1976. 25.00 (ISBN 0-7100-7708-4). Routledge & Kegan.

Dumazedier, Joffre. Sociology of Leisure. McKenzie, Marea A., tr. from Fr. LC 74-77580. 231p. 1974. 11.95 (ISBN 0-444-41226-3). Elsevier.

Dumazedier, Joffre & Guinchat, Claire. La Sociologie Du Loisir: Tendances Actuelles De la Recherche & Bibliographie (1945-65) (Current Sociology-la Sociologie Contemporaine: No. 16-1). 1969. pap. 13.50x (ISBN 90-2796-576-5). Mouton.

Edginton, C. R. & Williams, J. G. Productive Management of Leisure Service Organizations: A Behavioral Approach. 530p. 1978. 20.95 (ISBN 0-471-01574-1). Wiley.

Ellis, Michael J. Why People Play. (Illus.). 192p. 1973. 12.95 (ISBN 0-13-958991-0). P-H.

Encyclopedie du Bricolage et des Loisirs Manuels, 1, 6 vols. 195p. (Fr.). 1976. 225.00 (ISBN 0-686-56772-2, M-6206). French & Eur.

Epperson, Arlin, et al. Leisure Counseling: An Aspect of Leisure Education. (Illus.). 392p. 1977. 22.75 (ISBN 0-398-03619-5). C C Thomas.

Fodor. Fodor's Sunbelt Leisure Guide. 1979. 12.95 (ISBN 0-679-00431-9); pap. 9.95 (ISBN 0-679-00432-7). McKay.

Godbey, Geoffrey & Parker, Stanley. Leisure Studies & Services: An Overview. LC 75-5048. 194p. 1976. text ed. 9.95 (ISBN 0-7216-4141-5). HR&W.

Godbey, Geoffrey C. Leisure in Your Life: An Exploration. 1981. pap. text ed. 14.95 (ISBN 0-03-057673-3, HoltC); instr's manual 9.95 (ISBN 0-03-058258-X). HR&W.

Gordon, L. & Klopov, E. Man After Work. 306p. 1975. 2.10 (ISBN 0-8285-0274-9, Pub. by Progress Pubs Russia). Imported Pubns.

Gower Economic Publications. Leisure Industries Review, 1974. 1973. 60.00x (ISBN 0-8464-0552-0). Beekman Pubs.

Graham, Peter J. & Klar, Lawrence R. Planning & Delivering Leisure Services. Orig. Title: Leisure Service Planning & Community Programming. 350p. 1979. text ed. write for info. (ISBN 0-697-07384-X). Wm C Brown.

Hansel, Tim. When I Relax I Feel Guilty. LC 78-73460. 1979. pap. 3.95 (ISBN 0-89191-137-5). Cook.

Haworth, J. T. Community Involvement & Leisure. 216p. 1980. 18.00x (ISBN 0-86019-018-8, Pub. by Kimpton). State Mutual Bk.

Haworth, J. T., ed. Work & Leisure. 204p. 1980. 15.00x (ISBN 0-86019-009-9, Pub. by Kimpton). State Mutual Bk.

Hellman, Geoffrey T. How to Disappear for an Hour. LC 71-179727. (Biography Index Reprint Ser). Repr. of 1947 ed. 16.75 (ISBN 0-8369-8095-6). Arno.

Ibrahim, Hilmi & Shivers, Jay, eds. Leisure: Emergence & Expansion. LC 78-66379. 1979. pap. text ed. 8.95 (ISBN 0-89260-137-X). Hwong Pub.

Ibrahim, Hilmi M. & Martin, Fred, eds. Leisure: An Introduction. 2nd ed. LC 77-89694. 1978. pap. text ed. 8.95x (ISBN 0-89260-085-3). Hwong Pub.

Iso-Ahola, Seppo E. Social Psychological Perspectives on Leisure & Recreation. (Illus.). 448p. 1980. 19.75 (ISBN 0-398-03968-2). C C Thomas.

--The Social Psychology of Leisure & Recreation. 350p. 1980. text ed. write for info. (ISBN 0-697-07167-7). Wm C Brown.

Jensen, Clayne R. Leisure & Recreation: Introduction & Overview. LC 77-22992. 295p. 1977. pap. 13.50 (ISBN 0-8121-0595-8). Lea & Febiger.

Johannis, Theodore B., Jr. & Bull, Neil, eds. Sociology of Leisure. LC 73-87853. (Sage Contemporary Social Science Issues: No. 1). 135p. 1974. 5.95x (ISBN 0-8039-0318-9). Sage.

Kando, Thomas M. Leisure & Popular Culture in Transition. 2nd ed. LC 79-26032. (Illus.). 1980. text ed. 15.95 (ISBN 0-8016-2618-8). Mosby.

Kaplan, M. Leisure. 2nd ed. 1981. 24.75 (ISBN 0-398-04551-8). C C Thomas.

Kaplan, Max. Leisure: Perspectives on Education Policy. 128p. 1978. pap. 5.75 (ISBN 0-686-63673-2, 1494-14-06). NEA.

Kelly, John R. Leisure: An Introduction. (Illus.). 450p. 1982. 16.95 (ISBN 0-13-530055-X). P-H.

Kleindienst, V. K. & Weston, A. Recreational Sports Program: Schools...Colleges...Communities. LC 77-16808. 1978. 17.95 (ISBN 0-13-767905-X). P-H.

Koenig, Norma E. Ventures in Leisure-Time Christian Education. (Orig.). 1979. pap. 2.95 (ISBN 0-687-43670-2). Abingdon.

Kraus, Richard. Recreation & Leisure in Modern Society. 2nd ed. LC 77-20705. 1978. text ed. 17.95 (ISBN 0-87620-811-1). Goodyear.

Lafargue, Paul. The Right to Be Lazy. Kerr, Charles H., tr. from Fr. LC 73-77549. Orig. Title: Le Droit a la Paresse. 82p. 1975. 5.00 (ISBN 0-88286-040-2); pap. 1.25 (ISBN 0-88286-026-7). C H Kerr.

Lehman, Harold D. In Praise of Leisure. 200p. 1974. 5.95 (ISBN 0-8361-1752-2); pap. 3.95 (ISBN 0-8361-1749-2); leader's guide 1.75 (ISBN 0-8361-1750-6). Herald Pr.

Leisure in the Twentieth Century: Second Conference on Twentieth Century Design Histor. 1977. 20.00 (ISBN 0-435-86500-5). Nichols Pub.

Linder, Staffan B. The Harried Leisure Class. LC 73-92909. 182p. 1970. 17.50x (ISBN 0-231-03302-8); pap. 6.00x (ISBN 0-231-08649-0). Columbia U Pr.

Lundberg, George, et al. Leisure: A Suburban Study. LC 70-76845. 1969. Repr. 15.00x (ISBN 0-87586-016-8). Agathon.

Madow, Pauline, ed. Recreation in America. (Reference Shelf Ser: Vol. 37, No. 2). 1965. 6.25 (ISBN 0-8242-0085-3). Wilson.

Mankin, Don. Toward a Post-Industrial Psychology: Emerging Perspectives on Technology, Work, Education & Leisure. LC 78-5302. 1978. pap. text ed. 14.95x (ISBN 0-471-02086-9). Wiley.

Mundy, Jean & Odum, Linda. Leisure Education: Theory & Practice. LC 78-12434. 1979. text ed. 19.50 (ISBN 0-471-01347-1). Wiley.

Murphy, James F. Concepts of Leisure. 2nd ed. (Illus.). 192p. 1981. text ed. 13.95 (ISBN 0-13-166512-X). P-H.

Nestrick, William V. Constructional Activities of Adult Males. LC 76-177115. (Columbia University. Teachers College. Contributions to Education: No. 780). Repr. of 1939 ed. 17.50 (ISBN 0-404-55780-5). AMS Pr.

Neulinger, John. The Psychology of Leisure. 2nd ed. (Illus.). 384p. 1981. 28.75 (ISBN 0-398-04492-9). C C Thomas.

--The Psychology of Leisure: Research Approaches to the Study of Leisure. (Illus.). 240p. 1978. text ed. 13.50 (ISBN 0-398-03106-1). C C Thomas.

--To Leisure: An Introduction. 276p. 1980. text ed. 18.95 (ISBN 0-205-06936-3, 8469369). Allyn.

Oates, Wayne E. Workaholics, Make Laziness Work for You. (Festival Books Ser.). 1979. pap. 1.50 (ISBN 0-687-46270-3). Abingdon.

O'Loughlin, Michael. The Garlands of Repose: The Literary Celebration of Civic & Retired Leisure,the Tradition of Homer & Vergil, Horace & Montaigne. LC 77-2206. 1978. lib. bdg. 23.00x (ISBN 0-226-62657-1). U of Chicago Pr.

Overstreet, Harry A. Guide to Civilized Leisure. facs. ed. LC 73-84357. (Essay Index Reprint Ser.). 1934. 16.00 (ISBN 0-8369-1151-2). Arno.

Owen, John D. The Price of Leisure. 1970. 10.00x (ISBN 0-7735-0094-4). McGill-Queens U Pr.

--Price of Leisure: An Economic Analysis of the Demand for Leisure Time. LC 78-123194. (Illus.). 1969. 12.50x (ISBN 90-237-2216-7). Intl Pubns Serv.

Parker, Stanley. The Sociology of Leisure. (Studies in Sociology Ser.). 1976. pap. text ed. 8.95x (ISBN 0-04-301075-X). Allen Unwin.

--Sociology of Leisure. LC 75-31565. (Studies in Sociology Ser.: No. 9). 184p. 1976. 23.50x (ISBN 0-8002-0163-9). Intl Pubns Serv.

Pelegrino, Donald A. Research Methods for Recreation & Leisure: A Theoretical & Practical Guide. 200p. 1979. pap. text ed. write for info. (ISBN 0-697-07381-5). Wm C Brown.

Perspectives of Leisure Counseling. 5.95 (ISBN 0-686-16188-2). Natl Rec & Pk Assn.

Pieper, Josef. Leisure: The Basis of Culture. 1964. pap. 1.50 (ISBN 0-451-61723-1, MW1723, Ment). NAL.

Pruette, Lorine. Women & Leisure: A Study of Social Waste. LC 72-2620. (American Women Ser: Images & Realities). 230p. 1972. Repr. of 1924 ed. 12.00 (ISBN 0-405-04473-9). Arno.

Putterill, Martin & Bloch, Cheree. Providing for Leisure for the City Dweller: A Review of Needs & Processes with Guidelines for Change. (Illus.). 141p. 1978. pap. 16.00x (ISBN 0-8476-3113-3). Rowman.

Rapoport, Rhona & Rapoport, Robert N. Leisure & the Family Life Cycle. 1975. 32.00x (ISBN 0-7100-8134-0). Routledge & Kegan.

--Leisure & the Family Life Cycle. 1978. pap. 12.50 (ISBN 0-7100-8825-6). Routledge & Kegan.

Roberts, Kenneth. Contemporary Society & Growth of Leisure. 1979. pap. text ed. 12.95x (ISBN 0-582-48990-3). Longman.

Ross, Marilyn H. Creative Loafing: A Shoestring Guide to New Leisure Fun. LC 78-59410. 1978. 9.95 (ISBN 0-918880-01-7). Comm Creat.

Shivers, Jay S. Essentials of Recreational Services. LC 78-9052. 348p. 1978. text ed. 15.75 (ISBN 0-8121-0638-5). Lea & Febiger.

Smigel, Edwin O., ed. Work & Leisure: A Contemporary Social Problem. (Orig.). 1963. 6.00 (ISBN 0-8084-0334-6). Coll & U Pr.

Stebbins, Robert A. Amateurs: On the Margin Between Work & Leisure. LC 79-10769. (Sociological Observations: Vol. 6). 280p. 1979. pap. 20.00 (ISBN 0-8039-1200-5); 9.95 (ISBN 0-8039-1201-3). Sage.

Walvin, James. Leisure & Society: 1830-1950. (Themes in British Social History). 1979. text ed. 18.00x (ISBN 0-582-48681-5); pap. text ed. 9.50x (ISBN 0-582-48682-3). Longman.

Wrenn, C. Gilbert & Harley, D. L. Time on Their Hands: A Report on Leisure, Recreation, & Young People. LC 74-1718. (Children & Youth Ser.: Vol. 11). (Illus.). 1974. Repr. of 1941 ed. 19.00x (ISBN 0-405-05993-0). Arno.

LEISURE CLASS

see also Luxury

Ackerman, Martin S. & Ackerman, Diane L. Money, Ego, Power. 1978. pap. 1.95 (ISBN 0-87216-460-8, E16460). Playboy Pbks.

Camplin, Jamie. The Rise of the Rich. LC 79-4841. 1979. 11.95 (ISBN 0-312-68435-5). St Martin.

Coles, Robert. Privileged Ones: The Well-off & the Rich in America. (Children of Crises Ser.: Vol. 5). 1978. 15.00 (ISBN 0-316-15149-1, Atlantic-Little, Brown). Little.

Gunther, Max. The Very, Very Rich & How They Got That Way. LC 74-187402. 1979. pap. 2.50 (ISBN 0-87216-645-7). Playboy Pbks.

LeBlanc, Jerry & LeBlanc, Rena. Suddenly Rich. LC 78-3491. 1978. 8.95 (ISBN 0-13-875609-0). P-H.

McAllister, Samuel W. Society As I Have Found It. facsimile ed. LC 75-1855. (Leisure Class in America Ser.). 1975. Repr. of 1890 ed. 28.00x (ISBN 0-405-06921-9). Arno.

Martin, Frederick T. Things I Remember. facsimile ed. LC 75-1859. (Leisure Class in America Ser.). (Illus.). 1975. Repr. of 1913 ed. 17.00x (ISBN 0-405-06925-1). Arno.

Nichols, Charle W. De Lyon. The Ultra-Fashionable Peerage of America. facsimile ed. LC 75-1864. (Leisure Class in America Ser.). 1975. Repr. of 1904 ed. 11.00x (ISBN 0-405-06930-8). Arno.

Ross, Ishbel. Silhouette in Diamonds: The Life of Mrs. Potter Palmer. facsimile ed. LC 75-1868. (Leisure Class in America Ser.). (Illus.). 1975. Repr. of 1960 ed. 21.00x (ISBN 0-405-06934-0). Arno.

Rubinstein, W. D. Men of Property: The Very Wealthy in Britain Since the Industrial Revolution. 256p. 1981. 22.00 (ISBN 0-8135-0927-0). Rutgers U Pr.

Stein, Leon, ed. The Sporting Set: An Original Anthology. LC 75-1877. (Leisure Class in America Ser.). (Illus.). 1975. 18.00x (ISBN 0-405-06941-3). Arno.

Van Rensselaer, May K. Newport: Our Social Capital. facsimile ed. LC 75-910. (Leisure Class in America Ser.). (Illus.). 1975. Repr. of 1905 ed. 30.00x (ISBN 0-405-06936-7). Arno.

Veblen, Thorstein. The Theory of the Leisure Class. 1979. pap. 3.95 (ISBN 0-14-005363-8). Penguin.

--Theory of the Leisure Class. 1954. pap. 2.95 (ISBN 0-451-61999-4, ME1999, Ment). NAL.

Veblen, Thorstein B. Theory of the Leisure Class. LC 65-15958. Repr. of 1899 ed. 19.50x (ISBN 0-678-00057-3). Kelley.

LEJEUNEACEAE

Schuster, R. M. An Annotated Synopsis of the Genera & Subgenera of Lejeuneacea, 1: Introduction, Annotated Keys to Subfamilies & Genera. 1963. 30.00 (ISBN 3-7682-5409-7). Lubrecht & Cramer.

LELAND, HENRY M., b. 1843

Leland, Ottilie & Millbrook, Minie D. Master of Precision: Henry M. Leland. LC 73-15315. (Illus.). 296p. 1975. Repr. of 1966 ed. lib. bdg. 20.50x (ISBN 0-8371-7192-X, LEMP). Greenwood.

LELAND STANFORD UNIVERSITY

see Stanford University

LELY, PETER, SIR, 1618-1680

Millar, Oliver. Sir Peter Lely: A Catalogue. (Illus.). 88p. 1980. 18.50 (ISBN 0-8390-0249-1, Pub. by Natl Portrait Gallery England). Allanheld & Schram.

LE MANS-CHURCH HISTORY-SOURCES-HISTORY AND CRITICISM

Goffart, Walter A. Le Mans Forgeries: A Chapter from the History of Church Property in the Ninth Century. LC 66-18246. (Historical Studies: No. 76). 1966. 18.50x (ISBN 0-674-51875-6). Harvard U Pr.

LE MANS ENDURANCE RACE

Clavel, Bernard. Victory at Le Mans. Fielding, Ian, tr. LC 72-101998. (Illus.). (gr. 7 up). 1971. 5.95 (ISBN 0-440-09417-8, Sey Lawr); PLB 5.47 (ISBN 0-440-09421-6). Delacorte.

LEMHI COUNTY, IDAHO-HISTORY

Crowder, David L. Tendoy, Chief of the Lemhis. LC 75-76336. (Illus., Orig.). (gr. 5-9). 1969. pap. 2.75 (ISBN 0-87004-129-0). Caxton.

LEMMINGS

Elton, Charles. Voles, Mice & Lemmings. 1971. Repr. of 1942 ed. 42.00 (ISBN 3-7682-0275-5). Lubrecht & Cramer.

Krebs, Charles J. The Lemming Cycle at Baker Lake: Northwest Territories During 1959-1962. Repr. of 1964 ed. 9.50 (ISBN 0-384-30423-0). Johnson Repr.

Newton, James R. The March of the Lemmings. LC 75-42491. (A Lets-Read-&-Find-Out Bk). (Illus.). 40p. (gr. k-3). 1976. PLB 8.79 (ISBN 0-690-01085-0, TYC-J). Har-Row.

LEMON

Casson, Chris & Lee, Susan. The Compleat Lemon. LC 78-18261. (Illus.). 1979. 6.95 (ISBN 0-03-041881-X). HR&W.

Tobias, Doris & Merris, Mary. The Golden Lemon: A Collection of Special Recipes. LC 77-88908. viii, 210p. 1981. pap. 6.95 (ISBN 0-689-70609-X, 268). Atheneum.

LE MOYNE DE BIENVILLE, JEAN BAPTISTE, 1680-1768

King, Grace E. Jean Baptiste Le Moyne: Sieur De Bienville. LC 72-78764. 1892. Repr. 19.00 (ISBN 0-403-02087-5). Somerset Pub.

LEMURS

see also Monkeys

Jolly, Alison. Lemur Behavior: A Madagascar Field Study. LC 66-23690. (Illus.). xiv, 187p. 1967. 12.50x (ISBN 0-226-40552-4). U of Chicago Pr.

Lamberton, Charles. Selected Papers on the Subfossil Lemurs of Madagascar: 1934-1956. LC 78-72726. 67.50 (ISBN 0-404-18297-6). AMS Pr.

Tattersall, Ian T. & Sussman, Robert W., eds. Lemur Biology. LC 74-28112. (Illus.). 366p. 1975. 29.50 (ISBN 0-306-30817-7, Plenum Pr). Plenum Pub.

LENAPE LANGUAGE

see Delaware Language

LENAU, NICOLAUS, 1802-1850

Braun, Wilhelm A. Types of Weltschmerz in German Poetry. LC 5-33195. (Columbia University. Germanic Studies, Old Ser.: No. 6). Repr. of 1905 ed. 14.50 (ISBN 0-404-50406-X). AMS Pr.

Schmidt, Hugo. Nikolaus Lenau. LC 68-17227. (World Authors Ser.). 1971. lib. bdg. 12.95x (ISBN 0-8057-2520-2). Irvington.

LEND-LEASE OPERATIONS (1941-1945)

Herring, George C., Jr. Aid to Russia, Nineteen Forty-One to Nineteen Forty-Six: Strategy, Diplomacy, the Origins of the Cold War. 364p. 1973. 22.50x (ISBN 0-231-03336-2); pap. 9.00x (ISBN 0-686-76956-2). Columbia U Pr.

Jones, Robert H. The Roads to Russia: United States Lend-Lease to the Soviet Union. LC 68-15679. (Illus.). 1969. 16.95x (ISBN 0-8061-0823-1). U of Okla Pr.

Kimball, Warren F. The Most Unsordid Act: Lend-Lease, 1939-1941. LC 69-14712. 381p. 1969. 24.00x (ISBN 0-8018-1017-5). Johns Hopkins.

LENDING

see Loans

LENGTH MEASUREMENT

see also Area Measurement

LENIN, VLADIMIR ILICH, 1870-1924

Appignanesi, Richard. Lenin for Beginners. LC 78-20408. (Illus.). 1979. pap. 2.95 (ISBN 0-394-73715-6). Pantheon.

Baker, Nina B. Lenin. (Illus.). (gr. 7-9). 1945. 7.95 (ISBN 0-8149-0265-0). Vanguard.

Baranov, I. The Ulyanov Family: Lenin's Domestic Environment. pap. 4.00x (ISBN 0-8464-0943-7). Beekman Pubs.

Bonch-Bruyevich. Lenin's Boyhood & Adolescence. (Illus.). 16p. 1979. pap. 0.50 (ISBN 0-8285-1580-8, Pub. by Progress Pubs Russia). Imported Pubns.

Box, Pelham H. Three Master Builders, & Another: Studies in Modern Revolutionary & Liberal Statesmanship. facs. ed. LC 68-22904. (Essay Index Reprint Ser). 1925. 18.00 (ISBN 0-8369-0234-3). Arno.

Bradford, Gamaliel. Quick & the Dead. LC 70-85991. (Essay & General Literature Index Reprint Ser). 1969. Repr. of 1931 ed. 13.50 (ISBN 0-8046-0544-0). Kennikat.

Cash, Anthony. Lenin. (Jackdaw Ser: No. 113). (Illus.). 1972. 6.95 (ISBN 0-670-42343-2, Grossman). Viking Pr.

Claudin-Urondo, Carmen. Lenin & the Cultural Revolution. Pearce, Brian, tr. from Fr. (Marxist Theory & Contemporary Capitalism Ser.). 1977. text ed. 13.00x (ISBN 0-391-00739-4). Humanities.

--Lenine & la Revolution Culturelle. (Archontes Ser: No. 4). 119p. (Fr.). 1975. pap. text ed. 22.00x (ISBN 90-2797-625-2). Mouton.

Cliff, Tony. Lenin: All Power to the Soviets, Vol. 2. 416p. 1980. text ed. 17.00 (ISBN 0-904383-07-5); pap. 7.95 (ISBN 0-904383-06-7). Pluto Pr.

--Lenin: Building the Party, Vol. 1. 416p. 1980. text ed. 17.00 (ISBN 0-902818-58-9); pap. 7.95 (ISBN 0-902818-57-0). Pluto Pr.

--Lenin: Revolution Beseiged, Vol. 3. 256p. 1980. text ed. 17.00 (ISBN 0-904383-10-5); pap. 7.95 (ISBN 0-904383-09-1). Pluto Pr.

--Lenin Volume Four: Bolsheviks & World Revolution. 240p. 1981. text ed. 17.00 (ISBN 0-86104-023-6); pap. 7.95 (ISBN 0-86104-022-8). Pluto Pr.

Derzhavina, M. Central V. I. Lenin Museum. 3.50 (ISBN 0-8285-1790-8, Pub by Progress Pubs Russia). Imported Pubns.

Deutscher, Isaac. Lenin's Childhood. 1970. 9.95 (ISBN 0-19-211704-1). Oxford U Pr.

Deutscher, Tamara. Not by Politics Alone - the Other Lenin. LC 73-180508. 256p. 1973. 13.75x (ISBN 0-04-923062-X). Intl Pubns Serv.

Deutscher, Tamara, ed. Not by Politics Alone: The Other Lenin. LC 75-35301. 256p. 1976. pap. 4.95 (ISBN 0-88208-063-6). Lawrence Hill.

Eastman, Max F. Marx, Lenin & the Science of Revolution. LC 73-838. (Russian Studies: Perspectives on the Revolution Ser). 267p. 1973. Repr. of 1926 ed. 19.75 (ISBN 0-88355-034-2). Hyperion Conn.

Eastman, Max. F. Since Lenin Died. LC 73-839. (Russian Studies: Perspectives on the Revolution Ser.). 158p. 1973. Repr. of 1925 ed. 16.00 (ISBN 0-88355-035-0). Hyperion Conn.

Eissenstat, Bernard W. Lenin & Leninism: State, Law & Society. LC 71-145909. 1971. 29.50x (ISBN 0-89197-983-2). Irvington.

Fedoseyev, P. N. Leninism & the National Question. 504p. 1977. 4.80 (ISBN 0-8285-0400-8, Pub. by Progress Pubs Russia). Imported Pubns.

Filatov, V. P., et al. Lenin the Revolutionary. 1980. 4.00 (ISBN 0-8285-1849-1, Pub. by Progress Pubs Russia). Imported Pubns.

Fischer, Ernst & Marek, Franz, eds. The Essential Lenin. LC 73-127871. 1972. 5.95 (ISBN 0-8164-9114-3); pap. 3.95 (ISBN 0-8164-9115-1, Continuum). Continuum.

Fulop-Miller, Rene. Lenin & Gandhi. Flint, F. S. & Tait, D. F., trs. from Ger. LC 72-7057. (Select Bibliographies Reprint Ser.). 1972. Repr. of 1927 ed. 21.00 (ISBN 0-8369-6932-4). Arno.

--Lenin & Ghandi. LC 79-147617. (Library of War & Peace: Non-Resistance & Non-Violence). lib. bdg. 38.00 (ISBN 0-8240-0374-8). Garland Pub.

Gafurov, G. & Kim, G. F., eds. Lenin & National Liberation in the East. 468p. 1978. 7.50 (ISBN 0-8285-0399-0, Pub. by Progress Pubs Russia). Imported Pubns.

Gorky, M. Lenin in Profile, 2 vols. 1975. 7.25 (ISBN 0-8285-0182-3, Pub. by Progress Pubs Russia). Imported Pubns.

Gorky, M., et al. About Lenin. 1980. 9.00 (ISBN 0-8285-1835-1, Pub. by Progress Pubs Russia). Imported Pubns.

Gourfinkel, Nina. Lenin. Thornton, Maurice, tr. LC 75-11424. (Illus.). 189p. 1975. Repr. of 1961 ed. lib. bdg. 17.25x (ISBN 0-8371-8191-7, GOLE). Greenwood.

Gurley, John G. Challengers to Capitalism. LC 75-29749. (Portable Stanford Ser.). (Illus.). 1976. 8.95 (ISBN 0-913374-34-2); pap. 4.95 (ISBN 0-913374-35-0). SF Bk Co.

--Challengers to Capitalism, Marx, Lenin, Stalin & Mao. (Illus.). 224p. 1980. 12.95 (ISBN 0-393-01224-7); Portable Stanford Ser. pap. 4.95x (ISBN 0-393-95005-0). Norton.

Hammond, Thomas T. Lenin on Trade Unions & Revolution, 1893-1917. LC 74-12882. 155p. 1974. Repr. of 1957 ed. lib. bdg. 15.00x (ISBN 0-8371-7768-5, HATU). Greenwood.

Harding, Neil. Lenin's Political Thought, Vol. 2. LC 78-423. 1980. 32.50 (ISBN 0-686-63200-1). St Martin.

--Lenin's Political Thought: Theory & Practice in the Democratic Revolution, Vol. 1. LC 78-423. (Illus.). Date not set. 25.00x (ISBN 0-312-47958-1). St Martin.

Hill, Christopher. Lenin & the Russian Revolution. (Pelican Ser.). 1978. pap. 2.95 (ISBN 0-14-021297-3). Penguin.

Jenness, Doug. Lenin As Election Campaign Manager. pap. 0.25 (ISBN 0-87348-201-8). Path Pr NY.

Kaushik, D. & Mitrokhin, L., eds. Lenin: His Image in India. 1970. 6.75x (ISBN 0-8426-0064-7). Verry.

Kiernan, T., ed. Selected Essays of Lenin. LC 77-115404. 1971. 2.75 (ISBN 0-8022-2027-4). Philos Lib.

Krupskaya, N. K. Reminiscences of Lenin. LC 67-27253. (Illus.). 1970. 7.50 (ISBN 0-7178-0253-1); pap. 4.95 (ISBN 0-7178-0254-X). Intl Pub Co.

Kudryavtsev, A., et al, eds. Lenin's Geneva Addresses. 10.95x (ISBN 0-8464-0559-8). Beekman Pubs.

Lane, David. Leninism: A Sociological Interpretation. (Themes in the Social Sciences Ser.). (Illus.). 176p. 1981. 29.95 (ISBN 0-521-23855-2); pap. 9.95 (ISBN 0-521-28259-4). Cambridge U Pr.

Lazitch, Branko & Drachkovitch, Milorad. Lenin & the Comintern, Vol. 1. LC 74-157886. (Publications Ser.: No. 106). 683p. 1972. 17.50 (ISBN 0-8179-6061-9). Hoover Inst Pr.

Lenin. Lenin: Against Liquidationism. 1978. 16.00x (ISBN 0-8464-0553-9). Beekman Pubs.

Lenin on Marx & Engels. 1975. pap. 1.50 (ISBN 0-8351-0183-5). China Bks.

Lenin, V. I. & Trotsky, Leon. Lenin's Fight Against Stalinism. LC 74-14167. 160p. 1975. 12.00 (ISBN 0-87348-414-2); pap. 3.45 (ISBN 0-87348-415-0). Path Pr NY.

Lenin, Vladimir I. Letters of Lenin. Hill, Elizabeth & Mudie, Doris, eds. Hill, Elizabeth & Mudie, Doris, trs. from Rus. LC 73-848. (Russian Studies: Perspectives on the Revolution Ser). (Illus.). 499p. 1973. Repr. of 1937 ed. 29.50 (ISBN 0-88355-045-8). Hyperion Conn.

Lenin, Vladimir I. & Gorky, M. Letters, Reminiscences, Articles. 429p. 1973. 4.10 (ISBN 0-8285-0184-X, Pub. by Progress Pubs Russia). Imported Pubns.

Lewin, Moshe. Lenin's Last Struggle. 1978. pap. 5.95 (ISBN 0-85345-473-6, PB-4736). Monthly Rev.

Lukacs, Georg. Lenin: A Study on the Unity of His Thought. Jacobs, Nicholas, tr. from Ger. 1971. pap. 4.95 (ISBN 0-262-62024-3). MIT Pr.

McNeal, Robert H. The Bolshevik Tradition: Lenin, Stalin, Khrushchev, Brezhnev. rev. ed. 224p. 1975. (Spec); pap. 3.95 (ISBN 0-13-079764-2, Spec). P-H.

Maxton, James. Lenin. 152p. 1979. Repr. lib. bdg. 20.00 (ISBN 0-89987-554-8). Darby Bks.

Menon, P. Sivasankara. Lenin Through Indian Eyes. LC 79-915435. (Illus.). 79p. 1970. 4.50x (ISBN 0-8002-0918-4). Intl Pubns Serv.

MIR Publishers, ed. Lenin & Gorky: Letters, Reminiscences, Articles. (Illus.). 429p. 1973. 19.95x (ISBN 0-8464-0555-5). Beekman Pubs.

Morgan, Michael. Lenin. 1972. 12.95 (ISBN 0-8214-0094-0). Lib Soc Sci.

Omelyanovsky, M. E. Lenin & Modern Natural Science. 422p. 1978. 5.75 (ISBN 0-8285-0198-X, Pub. by Progress Pubs Russia). Imported Pubns.

Page, S. W. Lenin & World Revolution. 7.00 (ISBN 0-8446-1338-X). Peter Smith.

Page, Stanley W. Lenin: Dedicated Marxist or Revolutionary Pragmatist. LC 77-76608. (Problems in Civilization). 1977. pap. text ed. 3.95x (ISBN 0-88273-402-4). Forum Pr MO.

Ponomarev, B. Lenin & the World Revolutionary Processes. 525p. 1980. 11.00 (ISBN 0-8285-1661-8, Pub. by Progress Pubs Russia). Imported Pubns.

Prilezhaeva, M. V. I. Lenin: The Story of His Life. 175p. 1973. 3.00 (ISBN 0-8285-0187-4, Pub. by Progress Pubs Russia). Imported Pubns.

Prilezhaeva, Maria. La Vida De Lenin. 190p. (Span.). 1974. 3.25 (ISBN 0-8285-1411-9, Pub. by Progress Pubs Russia). Imported Pubns.

Progress Publishers, Moscow. Lenin: Collected Works, 45 vols. 1975. 299.00x set (ISBN 0-8464-0557-1). Beekman Pubs.

Sheherbina, Vladimir. Lenin & the Problems of Literature: Twentieth Century Progress in the Arts & Aesthetic Ideas & Literary Phenomena. 396p. 1975. 16.00x (ISBN 0-8464-0556-3). Beekman Pubs.

Simsova, S., ed. Lenin, Krupskaia & Libraries. Peacock, G. & Prescott, Lucy, trs. (World Classics of Librarianship Ser). 1968. 10.50 (ISBN 0-208-00615-X, Archon). Shoe String.

Sollers, Philippe. Sur le Materialisme: De l'Atomisme a la Dialectique Revolutionnaire. 192p. 1974. 11.95 (ISBN 0-686-55017-X). French & Eur.

Stalin, J. V. Problems of Leninism. 1976. 6.95 (ISBN 0-8351-0270-X); pap. 4.95 (ISBN 0-8351-0271-8). China Bks.

Stalin, Joseph. Foundations of Leninism. 1965. 3.50 (ISBN 0-8351-0563-6); pap. 1.95 (ISBN 0-8351-0089-8). China Bks.

--Foundations of Leninism. (Orig.). 1939. pap. 1.25 (ISBN 0-7178-0070-9). Intl Pub Co.

Theen, Rolf H. Lenin: Genesis & Development of a Revolutionary. LC 79-87768. 1980. 13.50x (ISBN 0-691-05289-1); pap. 4.95 (ISBN 0-691-00777-2). Princeton U Pr.

Tomashevsky, D. Lenin's Ideas & Modern International Relations. 288p. 1974. 3.85 (ISBN 0-8285-0307-9, Pub. by Progress Pubs Russia). Imported Pubns.

Treadgold, Donald W. Lenin & His Rivals: The Struggle for Russia's Future 1898-1906. LC 76-28338. 1976. Repr. of 1955 ed. lib. bdg. 22.00x (ISBN 0-8371-9045-2, TRLR). Greenwood.

Tucker, Robert C., ed. The Lenin Anthology. 1975. pap. text ed. 11.95x (ISBN 0-393-09236-4). Norton.

Ulyanova, A. I. Lenin's Boyhood Adolescence. 31p. 1972. pap. 0.50 (ISBN 0-8285-1177-2, Pub. by Progress Pubs Russia). Imported Pubns.

Valentinov, Nikolay. The Early Years of Lenin. Theen, Rolf H., tr. from Rus. 1980. cancelled (ISBN 0-915042-05-3). Lib Soc Sci.

--Encounters with Lenin. Rosta, Paul & Pearce, Brian, trs. from Rus. 1980. cancelled (ISBN 0-915042-04-5). Lib Soc Sci.

Vernadskii, Georgii. Lenin, Red Dictator. Malcolm, Davis W., tr. LC 76-119660. Repr. of 1931 ed. 18.50 (ISBN 0-404-06758-1). AMS Pr.

Weber, Gerda & Weber, Herman. Lenin: Life & Works. (Chronology Ser.). 226p. 1981. lib. bdg. 22.50 (ISBN 0-87196-515-1). Facts on File.

Wolfe, Bertram D. Three Who Made a Revolution. 1964. pap. 4.95 (ISBN 0-440-58869-3, Delta). Dell.

Wolfenstein, E. Victor. Revolutionary Personality: Lenin, Trotsky, Gandhi. (Center of International Studies Ser.). 1971. 24.00 (ISBN 0-691-08611-7); pap. 8.95 (ISBN 0-691-02450-2, 251). Princeton U Pr.

LENIN, VLADIMIR ILICH, 1870-1924–POETRY

Mayahovsky, V. Vladimir Ilyich Lenin (Poem) 209p. 1970. 2.10 (ISBN 0-8285-1014-8, 180399, Pub. by Progress Pubs Russia). Imported Pubns.

LENINGRAD

Andrews, David & Andrews, Judith, trs. St. Isaac's Cathedral, Leningrad. (Illus.). 164p. 1981. 14.95 (ISBN 0-686-31507-3). CDP.

Berlitz Travel Guide to Leningrad. 1976. pap. 2.95 (ISBN 0-02-969300-4, 0-02-96930, Berlitz). Macmillan.

Blue Guide - Moscow & Leningrad. 1980. 39.95 (ISBN 0-528-84611-6); pap. 24.95 (ISBN 0-528-84607-8). Rand.

Bortoli, Georges. Moscow & Leningrad Observed. Thomson, Amanda & Thomson, Edward, trs. from Fr. (Realites Ser). (Illus.). 166p. 1975. 24.95 (ISBN 0-19-519809-3). Oxford U Pr.

Butikov, Georgy, compiled by. St. Isacc's Cathedral, Leningrad. Andrews, Daniel & Andrews, Judith, trs. 1981. 14.95 (ISBN 0-89893-078-2). CDP.

Doroshinskaya, Y. & Kruchina-Bogdanov, V. Leningrad & Its Environs: A Guide. 1979. 7.00 (ISBN 0-8285-1781-9, Pub. by Progress Pubs Russia). Imported Pubns.

Kann, P. A. Leningrad in Three Days. 255p. 1978. 7.50 (ISBN 0-8285-1584-0, Pub. by Progress Pubs Russia). Imported Pubns.

Merian, Maria S. Leningrad Water Colors, 2 vols. LC 76-4690. (A Hellen & Kurt Wolff Bk). (Illus.). 1976. Set. 900.00x (ISBN 0-15-149837-7). HarBraceJ.

Sevruk, V., ed. Moscow-Stalingrad. 279p. 1974. 4.80 (ISBN 0-8285-0485-7, Pub. by Progress Pubs Russia). Imported Pubns.

Ward, Charles A. Cultural Historic Places. (Moscow & Leningrad: Cultural History & Architecture Ser.). Date not set. price not set. K G Saur.

--An Index to Buildings, Vol. 1. (Moscow & Leningrad: Cultural History & Architecture Ser.). 1980. text ed. write for info. (ISBN 0-89664-260-7). K G Saur.

--Their Development As Cultural Centers, Vol. 3. (Moscow & Leningrad: Cultural & History Architecture Ser.). 1980. write for info. K G Saur.

Wechsberg, Joseph. In Leningrad. LC 76-18372. 1977. 12.50 (ISBN 0-385-01563-1). Doubleday.

Yevangulova, O., intro. by. Leningrad in Works of Graphic Art & Painting. Date not set. 27.50 (ISBN 0-89893-009-X). CDP.

LENINGRAD–HERMITAGE MUSEUM

Barskaya, Anna & Izerghina, Antonina. French Painting from the Hermitage Museum. (Illus.). 1977. 60.00 (ISBN 0-8109-0908-1). Abrams.

Descarques, Pierre. Art Treasures of the Hermitage. LC 72-142741. (Illus.). 1976. 40.00 (ISBN 0-8109-0023-8). Abrams.

Kozhina, Elena, intro. by. The Hermitage: Western European Painting of the 13th to 18th Centuries. Date not set. 19.95 (ISBN 0-89893-002-2). CDP.

Linnik, I., compiled by. The Hermitage: Western European Painting. Pamfilov, Yu. & Nemetsky, Yu., trs. Date not set. 24.95 (ISBN 0-89893-001-4). CDP.

Piotrovsky, B. Western European Painting in the Hermitage. (Illus.). 1979. 40.00 (ISBN 0-8109-1751-3). Abrams.

Piotrovsky, Boris, intro. by. The Hermitage Picture Gallery. Date not set. 24.95 (ISBN 0-686-31466-2). CDP.

Suslov, Vitaly. Treasures of the Hermitage. LC 80-81382. (Illus.). 1980. 19.95 (ISBN 0-88225-301-8). Newsweek.

LENINGRAD–SIEGE, 1941-1944

Fadeev, Aleksandr A. Leningrad in the Days of the Blockade. Charques, R. D., tr. from Rus. LC 77-156189. 1971. Repr. of 1946 ed. lib. bdg. 15.00x (ISBN 0-8371-6137-1, FALE). Greenwood.

--Leningrad in the Days of the Blockade. Charques, R. D., tr. from Rus. LC 77-156189. 1971. Repr. of 1946 ed. lib. bdg. 15.00x (ISBN 0-8371-6137-1, FALE). Greenwood.

Goure, Leon. The Siege of Leningrad. LC 62-8662. 1962. 22.50x (ISBN 0-8047-0115-6). Stanford U Pr.

Pavlov, D. V. Leningrad, Nineteen Hundred Forty One: The Blockade. Adams, John C., tr. LC 65-24979. (Illus.). 1965. 7.50x (ISBN 0-226-65076-6). U of Chicago Pr.

Salisbury, Harrison. Nine Hundred Days: The Siege of Leningrad. 1970. pap. 2.50 (ISBN 0-380-01634-6, 35899). Avon.

Skrjabina, Elena. Siege & Survival. 1979. pap. 1.95 (ISBN 0-523-40479-4). Pinnacle Bks.

--Siege & Survival: The Odyssey of a Leningrader. Luxenburg, Norman, ed. LC 70-156790. 186p. 1971. 6.95x (ISBN 0-8093-0511-9). S Ill U Pr.

LENNI LENAPE LANGUAGE

see Delaware Language

LENNOX, CHARLOTTE (RAMSAY), 1720-1804

Small, Miriam R. Charlotte Ramsay Lennox: An Eighteenth Century Lady of Letters. 1978. Repr. of 1935 ed. lib. bdg. 30.00 (ISBN 0-8495-4841-1). Arden Lib.

--Charlotte Ramsay Lennox: An Eighteenth Century Lady of Letters. (Yale Studies in English Ser.: No. 85). (Illus.). vii, 268p. 1969. Repr. of 1935 ed. 17.50 (ISBN 0-208-00770-9, Archon). Shoe String.
--Charlotte Ramsay Lennox: An Eighteenth Century Lady of Letters. 1977. Repr. of 1935 ed. 30.00 (ISBN 0-8274-4281-5). R West.

LENOX, JAMES, 1800-1880

Stevens, Henry. Recollections of James Lenox & the Formation of His Library. rev. ed. Paltsits, Victor H., ed. 1951. 6.00 (ISBN 0-87104-155-3). NY Pub Lib.

LENOX LIBRARY, NEW YORK

Stevens, Henry. Recollections of James Lenox & the Formation of His Library. rev. ed. Paltsits, Victor H., ed. 1951. 6.00 (ISBN 0-87104-155-3). NY Pub Lib.

LENS, CRYSTALLINE

see Crystalline Lens

LENSES

see also Contact Lenses

Brindze, Ruth. Look How Many People Wear Glasses: The Magic of Lenses. LC 75-8947. (gr. 5-9). 1975. 7.95 (ISBN 0-689-50028-9, McElderry Bk). Atheneum.
Harting, E. & Read, F. H. Electrostatic Lenses. 1976. 68.50 (ISBN 0-444-41319-7). Elsevier.
Horne, D. F. Lens Mechanism Technology. LC 75-21733. (Illus.). 266p. 1975. 79.50x (ISBN 0-8448-0770-2). Crane-Russak Co.
--Spectacle Lens Technology. LC 77-90820. 1978. 62.50x (ISBN 0-8448-1265-X). Crane-Russak Co.
Jalie, M. & Wray, L. Practical Opthalmic Lenses. 1974. 21.95 (ISBN 0-407-50004-9). Butterworth.
Jamieson, T. H. Optimization of Techniques in Lens Design. (Applied Optics Monographs: No. 5). 1971. 25.00 (ISBN 0-444-19590-4). Elsevier.
Ogle, Kenneth N. Optics: An Introduction for Ophthalmologists. 2nd ed. (Illus.). 288p. 1979. 13.75 (ISBN 0-398-01417-5). C C Thomas.
Olmos, Edwin, et al. Intraocular Lenses. 270p. 1981. 34.50 (ISBN 0-03-058033-1). Praeger.
Schacher, Ronald A. Intraocular Lenses. (Illus.). 144p. 1979. 18.50 (ISBN 0-398-03800-7). C C Thomas.
Shepard, Dennis D., ed. Intraocular Lens Manual. rev. 3rd ed. LC 80-51743. 464p. 1980. 40.00 (ISBN 0-9601234-2-3). D D Shepard.

LENSES, PHOTOGRAPHIC

Eastman Kodak Company. Filters & Lens Attachments for Black-&-White & Color Pictures. 1975. pap. 2.95 (ISBN 0-87985-254-2, AB-1). Eastman Kodak.
Gaunt, Leonard. Focalguide to Lenses. (Focalguide Ser.). (Illus.). 1977. pap. 7.95 (ISBN 0-240-50959-5). Focal Pr.
--Los Objectivos: Una Guia Para Aficionados. Larrea, Gabriel P., tr. from Eng. (Focalguide Ser.). 263p. (Span.). 1978. pap. 8.95 (ISBN 0-240-51096-8, Pub. by Ediciones Spain). Focal Pr.
--Zoom & Special Lenses. LC 80-41245. (Illus.). 128p. 1981. pap. 9.95 (ISBN 0-240-51069-0). Focal Pr.
Hawken, William. Zoom Lens Photography. (Illus.). 180p. (Orig.). 1981. pap. 10.95 (ISBN 0-930764-29-3). Curtin & London.
Hawken, William R. You & Your Lenses. (Illus.). 144p. 1975. pap. 6.95 (ISBN 0-8174-0592-5). Amphoto.
How to Use Interchangeable Lenses. 1981. 2.50 (ISBN 0-88284-141-6). Alfred Pub.
Lahue, Kalton C. Photo Filters & Lens Attachments. (Petersen's Photographic Library: Vol. 5). (Illus.). 160p. 1981. pap. 8.95 (ISBN 0-8227-4044-3). Petersen Pub.
--Wide Angle Photography. LC 77-74100. (Photography How-to Ser.). (Illus.). 1977. pap. 3.95 (ISBN 0-8227-4014-1). Petersen Pub.
Neblette, C. B. & Murray, Allen E. Photographic Lenses. LC 72-86799. 1973. 8.95 (ISBN 0-87100-070-9). Morgan.
Ray, Sidney. The Lens in Action. (Media Manuals Ser). (Illus.). 160p. 1976. pap. 8.95 (ISBN 0-240-50879-3). Focal Pr.
Ray, Sidney F. The Lens & All Its Jobs. (Media Manuals Ser.). 1979. pap. 9.95 (ISBN 0-8038-4299-6). Hastings.
--The Lens & All Its Jobs. (Media Manuals Ser.). (Illus.). 1978. pap. 9.95 (ISBN 0-240-50951-X). Focal Pr.
--Lens in Action. (Media Manuals Ser.). 1976. pap. 8.95 (ISBN 0-8038-4296-1). Hastings.
--The Photographic Lens. (Illus.). 1979. 24.95 (ISBN 0-240-51032-1). Focal Pr.
Smith, Robb. The Complete Guide to Camera Accessories: & How to Use Them. (Illus.). 1979. 14.95 (ISBN 0-87165-074-6). Ziff-Davis Pub.
Voogel, Emile & Keyzer, Peter. Two Hundred Filter & Lens Tips. (Illus.). 1978. pap. 6.50x (ISBN 0-85242-612-7). Intl Pubns Serv.
Werner, Donald L., ed. Light & Lens: Methods of Photography. LC 73-84659. (Illus.). 80p. 1973. pap. 8.00 (ISBN 0-87100-043-1, Pub. by Hudson River Mus). Pub Ctr Cult Res.

LENSLESS PHOTOGRAPHY

see Holography

LENT

see also Easter; Good Friday; Holy Week

Alessi, Vincie, ed. Programs for Lent & Easter. 1979. pap. 2.95 (ISBN 0-8170-0861-6). Judson.
Becker, Ralph. Lent, Good Friday & Easter. pap. 0.50 (ISBN 0-685-41825-1). Reiner.
Bishop, Irene S. The Lenten Tree. 12p. 1976. pap. 2.15 (ISBN 0-89536-119-1). CSS Pub.
Bosch, Paul. The Paschal Cycle. 1979. pap. 6.75 (ISBN 0-570-03796-4, 12-2778). Concordia.
Collins, John P. These Forty Days: A Lenten Journey for Young People & Their Families. 1980. pap. 3.95 (ISBN 0-529-05778-6, FT 5778). Collins Pubs.
Darian, Mujana. Thoughts to Take Home - for Lent. 1976. pap. 2.75 (ISBN 0-8199-0452-X). Franciscan Herald.
Dessem, Ralph E., ed. A Season to Return. 119p. 1976. pap. 4.30 (ISBN 0-89536-205-8). CSS Pub.
Ehlen-Miller, Margaret, et al. A Time of Hope: Family Celebrations & Activities for Lent & Easter. (Illus., Orig.). 1979. pap. 3.50 (ISBN 0-8192-1247-4). Morehouse.
Griggs, Patricia & Griggs, Donald. Teaching & Celebrating Lent-Easter. (Griggs Educational Resources Ser.). 1980. pap. 4.95 (ISBN 0-687-41081-9). Abingdon.
Gunning, Peter. Paschal or Lent Fast. LC 70-168214. (Library of Anglo-Catholic Theology: No. 7). Repr. of 1845 ed. 27.50 (ISBN 0-404-52088-X). AMS Pr.
Hickman, Hoyt, ed. From Ashes to Fire: Services of Worship for the Seasons of Lent & Easter, with Introduction & Commentary. 1979. pap. 7.95 (ISBN 0-687-13634-2). Abingdon.
Hordern, William & Otwell, John. Lent. LC 74-24901. (Proclamation 1: Aids for Interpreting the Lessons of the Church Year Ser. B). 64p. 1974. pap. 1.95 (ISBN 0-8006-4073-X, 1-4073). Fortress.
Kingsbury, Jack D. & Pennington, Chester. Lent. Achtemeier, Elizabeth, et al, eds. LC 79-7377. (Proclamation 2: Aids for Interpreting the Lessons of the Church Year, Ser. A). 64p. (Orig.). 1980. pap. 2.50 (ISBN 0-8006-4093-4, 1-4093). Fortress.
Mary, Mother & Ware, Archimandrite K., trs. The Lenten Triodion. 700p. 1979. 28.00 (ISBN 0-571-11253-6, Pub. by Faber & Faber). Merrimack Bk Serv.
Micks, Marianne H. & Ridenhour, Thomas E. Lent. Achtemeier, Elizabeth, et al, eds. LC 79-7377. (Proclamation 2: Aids for Interpreting the Lessons of the Church Year Ser. C). 64p. 1979. pap. 2.50 (ISBN 0-8006-4082-9, 1-4082). Fortress.
Miles, Cassian. The Masses of Lent. 48p. (Orig.). 1980. pap. 0.95 (ISBN 0-912228-67-9). St Anthony Mess Pr.
Montgomery, Herb & Montgomery, Mary. Easter Is Coming. 96p. (Orig.). (gr. 3 up). 1981. pap. 6.95 (ISBN 0-86683-609-8). Winston Pr.
Mueller, Jeanne C. Welcome To the Lenten Fair. (Orig.). 1977. pap. 3.00 (ISBN 0-89536-266-X). CSS Pub.
Palassis, Neketas S., ed. A Lenten Cookbook for Orthodox Christians. 260p. 1981. pap. 7.00 (ISBN 0-913026-13-1). St Nectarios.
Poovey, W. A. The Days Before Easter. LC 76-27074. 1977. pap. 3.50 (ISBN 0-8066-1557-5, 10-1835). Augsburg.
Poovey, William A. Lenten Chancel Dramas. LC 68-13421. 1968. pap. 1.50 (ISBN 0-8066-0801-3, 10-3816). Augsburg.
--Six Faces of Lent: Dramas. LC 73-88599. 96p. (Orig.). 1974. pap. 2.50 (ISBN 0-8066-1403-X, 10-5805). Augsburg.
Recker, Colane. All the Days of Lent. LC 78-73825. (Illus.). 64p. 1978. pap. 2.45 (ISBN 0-87793-168-2). Ave Maria.
Reilly, Barbara & Reilly, Don. Children's Bulletin: Ash Wednesday to Easter Sunday. 1978. pap. 7.55 (ISBN 0-88479-010-X). Arena Lettres.
Ryan, Pat & Ryan, Rosemary. Lent Begins at Home. 1979. pap. 1.50 (ISBN 0-89243-101-6). Liguori Pubns.
Smith, Charles W. & Koester, Helmut. Lent. LC 74-76925. (Proclamation 1: Aids for Interpreting the Lessons of the Church Year, Ser. A). 64p. 1974. pap. 1.95 (ISBN 0-8006-4063-2, 1-4063). Fortress.
Sullivan, Barbara. A Page a Day for Lent Nineteen Eighty-One. LC 80-82807. 100p. 1981. pap. 2.50 (ISBN 0-8091-2340-1). Paulist Pr.
Wallis, Charles L., ed. Lenten-Easter Sourcebook. (Source Bks for Ministers). 1978. pap. 3.95 (ISBN 0-8010-9613-8). Baker Bk.

LENT–PRAYER BOOKS AND DEVOTIONS

Adams, John. The Lenten Psalms. (Short Course Ser.). 124p. Repr. of 1912 ed. text ed. 3.95 (ISBN 0-567-08304-7). Attic Pr.
Dessem, Ralph E., ed. Contemporary Worship Resources for Lent. 1973. 3.25 (ISBN 0-89536-031-4). CSS Pub.
Dunnam, Maxie D. Sanctuary for Lent, Nineteen Eighty-One. (Orig.). 1981. pap. 20.00 per 100 (ISBN 0-687-36843-X). Abingdon.
Elberfeld, Katie. Jordan to Jerusalem: A Lenten Pilgrimage. 1979. 1.20 (ISBN 0-686-28783-5). Forward Movement.
Fillmore, Charles. Keep a True Lent. 1953. 2.95 (ISBN 0-87159-076-X). Unity Bks.
Girod, Gordon H. Words & Wonders of the Cross. (Pocket Pulpit Library). 1979. pap. 2.95 (ISBN 0-8010-3741-7). Baker Bk.
Griffin, James A. Sackcloth & Ashes: Liturgical Reflections for Lenten Weekdays. LC 74-44463. 1976. pap. 2.50 (ISBN 0-8189-0336-8). Alba.
Kretzmann, O. P. & Oldsen, A. C. Voices of the Passion: Meditations for Lent & Easter. rev. ed. LC 77-84080. 1977. pap. 3.50 (ISBN 0-8066-1605-9, 10-6860). Augsburg.
Lane, Ellery. Youth Vespers for Lent. 1972. 2.70 (ISBN 0-89536-275-9). CSS Pub.
McCarthy, Joe. Papal Bulls & English Muffins: Meditations for Everyday in Lent. LC 73-91372. 128p. 1974. pap. 2.45 (ISBN 0-8091-1812-2). Paulist Pr.
McClain, W. Blair. Easterglow. LC 77-17047. 1978. pap. 4.50 (ISBN 0-8309-0197-3). Herald Hse.
McCoy, Charles S. & McCoy, Marjorie C. The Transforming Cross. LC 77-10884. 1978. pap. 2.95 (ISBN 0-687-42507-7). Abingdon.
Manning, Michael. Pardon My Lenten Smile: Daily Homily-Meditation Themes for the Weekdays of Lent. 90p. 1976. pap. 3.95 (ISBN 0-8189-0325-2). Alba.
Newhouse, Flower A. Through Lent to Resurrection. Bengtson, Melodie N., ed. LC 77-77088. (Illus.). 1977. pap. 4.00 (ISBN 0-910378-13-4). Christward.
Patrick, John, tr. Lenten Readings from the Writings of the Fathers of the Church. pap. 1.50 (ISBN 0-686-05647-7). Eastern Orthodox.
Poovey, W. A. The Days Before Easter. LC 76-27074. 1977. pap. 3.50 (ISBN 0-8066-1557-5, 10-1835). Augsburg.
Poovey, William A. What Did Jesus Do. LC 69-14180. 1969. pap. 3.50 (ISBN 0-8066-0901-X, 10-7042). Augsburg.
Powers, Isaias. Daily Scripture Meditations for Lent. 48p. 1982. pap. 0.50 (ISBN 0-89622-150-4). Twenty-Third.
Rosage, David E. A Lenten Pilgrimage: Scriptural Meditations in the Holy Land. (Orig.). 1980. pap. 2.50 (ISBN 0-89283-081-6). Servant.
Schmemann, Alexander. Great Lent: Journey to Pascha. 1974. pap. 4.95 (ISBN 0-913836-04-4). St Vladimirs.
Stuhlmueller, Carroll. Biblical Meditations for Lent. rev. ed. LC 77-91366. 190p. 1978. pap. 2.95 (ISBN 0-8091-2089-5). Paulist Pr.
Sullivan, Barbara. A Page a Day for Lent 1982. 100p. (Orig.). 1982. pap. 2.50 (ISBN 0-8091-2409-2). Paulist Pr.

LENTEN MUSIC

see Passion-Music

LENTEN SERMONS

Here are entered sermons preached during the season of Lent. If they are limited in their scope to the passion of Jesus Christ, entry is made under Jesus Christ–Passion–Sermons.

see also Jesus Christ–Passion–Sermons

Andersen, R. & Barlag, R. They Were There. 1977. pap. 4.50 (ISBN 0-570-03769-7, 12-2704). Concordia.
Bjorge, James R. Lord of the Mountain: Messages for Lent & Easter. LC 78-66941. 1979. pap. 3.50 (ISBN 0-8066-1687-3, 10-4110). Augsburg.
Burrell, D. J. In the Upper Room. (Short Course Ser.). 146p. 1913. text ed. 3.95 (ISBN 0-567-08317-9). Attic Pr.
Fetty, Maurice A. Putting Your Life on the Line: Seven Sermons for the Lenten-Easter Season. LC 76-43351. 1977. pap. 2.95 (ISBN 0-687-34945-1). Abingdon.
Hoenecke, Adolf. Glorified in His Passion. Franzmann, Werner, tr. 1957. 0.95 (ISBN 0-8100-0040-7, 05N0317). Northwest Pub.
Jarrett, Bede. No Abiding City. 1.95 (ISBN 0-87243-012-X). Templegate.
Kretzmann, Paul E. Jesus Only. 1956. 1.25 (ISBN 0-8100-0037-7, 05N0314). Northwest Pub.
Loughhead, LaRue A. Eyewitnesses at the Cross. LC 73-16692. 128p. 1974. 4.95 (ISBN 0-8170-0626-5). Judson.
Schreiber, Vernon R. Wrestling with God: Messages for Lent & Easter on the Life of Jacob. LC 78-66939. 1979. pap. 3.50 (ISBN 0-8066-1696-2, 10-7360). Augsburg.
Shiley, Harry. Solemn Hours of Lent. 1956. pap. 0.50 (ISBN 0-8100-0041-5, 15-0318). Northwest Pub.

LEO 10TH, POPE, 1475-1521

Gobineau, Joseph A. Golden Flower. facsimile ed. Redman, B. R., tr. LC 68-54347. (Essay Index Reprint Ser). 1924. 13.00 (ISBN 0-8369-0477-X). Arno.
Roscoe, William. Life & Pontificate of Pope Leo the Tenth, 2 vols. rev. ed. 6th ed. Roscoe, Thomas, ed. LC 75-174965. Repr. of 1853 ed. 64.00 (ISBN 0-404-05430-7). AMS Pr.

LEO 13TH, POPE, 1810-1903

Keller, Joseph. The Life & Acts of Pope Leo Thirteenth. 1882. 10.00 (ISBN 0-8414-5553-8). Folcroft.

LEON COUNTY, FLORIDA

Paisley, Clifton. From Cotton to Quail: An Agricultural Chronicle of Leon County, Florida, 1860-1967. LC 68-9708. (Illus.). 192p. 1981. Repr. 10.00 (ISBN 0-8130-0718-6). U Presses Fla.

LEONARD, GLADYS OSBORNE

Smith, Susy. Mediumship of Mrs. Leonard. (Illus.). 1964. 7.50 (ISBN 0-8216-0116-4). Univ Bks.
Stopplewoth, L. J., ed. Everything Is Fine Now That Leonard Isn't Here... 1973. 19.00x (ISBN 0-8422-5103-0). Irvington.

LEONARDO DA PISA B.C. 1170-1240

Gies, Frances & Gies, Joseph. Leonard of Pisa & the New Mathematics of the Middle Ages. LC 71-81952. (Illus.). (gr. 7 up). 1969. 7.95 (ISBN 0-690-48809-2, TYC-J). Har-Row.

LEONARDO DA VINCI, 1452-1519

Amey, Peter, et al. Leonardo Da Vinci. Yapp, Malcolm, et al, eds. (World History Ser.). (Illus.). (gr. 10). 1980. lib. bdg. 5.95 (ISBN 0-89908-041-3); pap. text ed. 1.95 (ISBN 0-89908-016-2). Greenhaven.
Bax, Clifford. Leonardo Da Vinci. 160p. 1980. Repr. of 1932 ed. lib. bdg. 27.50 (ISBN 0-8495-0464-3). Arden Lib.
Beck, James. Leonardo's Rules of Painting: An Unconventional Approach to Modern Art. (Illus.). 1979. 10.95 (ISBN 0-670-42427-7, Studio). Viking Pr.
Brizio & Chastel. Leonardo the Artist. Date not set. 9.95 (ISBN 0-07-007931-5). McGraw.
Clark, Kenneth. Leonardo Da Vinci. 256p. 1976. pap. 4.95 (ISBN 0-14-020430-X, Pelican). Penguin.
--Leonardo Da Vinci: An Account of His Development As an Artist. lib. bdg. 10.50x (ISBN 0-88307-056-1). Gannon.
Cooper, Margaret. Inventions of Leonardo Da Vinci. (Illus.). (gr. 7 up). 1968. 9.95 (ISBN 0-02-724490-3). Macmillan.
Da Vinci, Leonardo. Drawings of Da Vinci. Belt, Elmer, ed. (Master Draughtsman Ser). (Illus., Orig.). treasure trove bdg. 6.47x (ISBN 0-685-07241-X); pap. 2.95 (ISBN 0-685-07242-8). Borden.
--Leonardo Drawings: Sixty Works. (Dover Art Library Ser.). (Illus.). 64p. (Orig.). 1980. pap. 2.00 (ISBN 0-486-23951-9). Dover.
Dibner, Bern, et al. Leonardo the Inventor. LC 80-18713. (Illus.). 192p. 1980. 9.95 (ISBN 0-07-016765-6). McGraw.
Eissler, Kurt R. Leonardo Da Vinci: Psychoanalytic Notes on the Enigma. LC 61-11610. (Illus.). 1961. text ed. 25.00 (ISBN 0-8236-3000-5). Intl Univs Pr.
Freud, Sigmund. Leonardo Da Vinci: A Study in Psychosexuality. 1966. pap. 2.45 (ISBN 0-394-70132-1, V132, Vin). Random.
--Leonardo Da Vinci & a Memory of His Childhood. Strachey, James, ed. Tyson, Alan, tr. 1965. pap. 2.95 (ISBN 0-393-00149-0, Norton Lib). Norton.
Glasser, Hannelore. Artist's Contracts of the Early Renaissance. LC 76-23624. (Outstanding Dissertations in the Fine Arts - 2nd Series - 15th Century). (Illus.). 1977. Repr. of 1965 ed. lib. bdg. 56.00 (ISBN 0-8240-2694-2). Garland Pub.
Hart, Ivor B. World of Leonardo Da Vinci. LC 74-122058. (Illus.). Repr. of 1962 ed. 25.00x (ISBN 0-678-03162-2). Kelley.
Heydenreich, Ludwig H. Leonardo: The Last Supper. Fleming, John & Honour, Hugh, eds. LC 73-3233. (Art in Context Ser.). (Illus.). 128p. 1974. 8.95 (ISBN 0-670-42387-4). Viking Pr.
Kemp, Martin. Leonardo da Vinci: The Marvellous Works of Nature & Man. LC 81-279. (Illus.). 384p. 1981. 30.00 (ISBN 0-674-52460-8). Harvard U Pr.
MacCurdy, Edward, tr. The Notebooks of Leonardo Da Vinci, 2 vols. 1978. 39.95 (ISBN 0-224-01279-7, Pub. by Chatto Bodley Jonathan). Merrimack Bk Serv.
McMullen, Roy. Mona Lisa: The Picture & the Myth. LC 77-23574. 1977. pap. 7.95 (ISBN 0-306-80067-5). Da Capo.
O'Malley, C. D., ed. Leonardo's Legacy: An International Symposium. LC 68-14976. (UCLA Center for Medieval & Renaissance Studies). (Illus.). 1968. 40.00x (ISBN 0-520-00956-8). U of Cal Pr.
Ost, Hans. Leonardo-Studien. (Beitraege Zur Kunstgeschichte: Vol. 11). (Illus.). xii, 750p. (Ger.). 1975. 78.50x (ISBN 3-11-005727-1). De Gruyter.
Panofsky, Erwin. Codex Huygens & Leonardo Da Vinci's Art Theory. LC 79-109814. (Illus.). 1971. Repr. of 1940 ed. lib. bdg. 16.75 (ISBN 0-8371-4306-3, PACH). Greenwood.

Pedretti, Carlo. Catalogue of the Newly Restored Sheets of the Leonardo Da Vinci Codex Atlanticus. 1978. leather bdg. 100.00 (ISBN 0-685-81981-7); cloth bdg. 60.00 (ISBN 0-685-81982-5). Johnson Repr.

--Leonardo Da Vinci Nature Studies from the Royal Library at Windsor Castle. (Illus.). 95p. (Orig.). 1980. pap. 10.00 (ISBN 0-384-32298-0). J P Getty Mus.

--Leonardo Da Vinci: The Royal Palace at Romorantin. LC 76-102673. 1972. 40.00x (ISBN 0-674-52455-1, Belknap Pr). Harvard U Pr.

--Literary Works of Leonardo Da Vinci: A Commentary of Jean Paul Richter's Edition, 2 vols. LC 76-24595. 1977. Set. 100.00x (ISBN 0-520-03329-9). U of Cal Pr.

Podwal, Mark. Freud's Da Vinci. 1977. 9.95 (ISBN 0-89545-002-X); pap. 4.95 (ISBN 0-89545-003-8). Images Graphiques.

Ponting, Kenneth G. & Litt, M. Leonardo da Vinci: Drawings of Textile Machines. (Illus.). 1979. text ed. 26.00x (ISBN 0-239-00193-1). Humanities.

Popham, A. E. The Drawings of Leonardo da Vinci. (Illus.). 320p. 1981. 15.95 (ISBN 0-224-00909-5, Pub. by Chatto-Bodley-Jonathan); pap. 8.95 (ISBN 0-224-60462-7, Pub. by Chatto-Bodley-Jonathan). Merrimack Bk Serv.

Reti, Ladislao, tr. from Italian. The Madrid Codices of Leonardo Da Vinci. LC 73-23091. 1974. 400.00 (ISBN 0-07-037194-6, GB). McGraw.

Richter, Irma, ed. Selections from the Notebooks of Leonardo Da Vinci. (Illus.). 1977. pap. 3.95 (ISBN 0-19-281214-9, GB504, GB). Oxford U Pr.

Stites, Raymond S. The Sublimations of Leonardo da Vinci. LC 70-104774. (Illus.). 422p. 1970. text ed. 25.00x (ISBN 0-87474-101-7). Smithsonian.

Storey, Mary R. Mona Lisas. (Illus.). 1980. pap. 6.95 (ISBN 0-8109-2194-4). Abrams.

Strong, Donald S. Leonardo on the Eye: An English Translation & Critical Commentary of MS.D in the Bibliotheque Nationale, Paris, with Studies on Leonardo's Methodology & Theories on Optics. LC 78-74382. (Fine Arts Dissertations, Fourth Ser.). (Illus.). 1980. lib. bdg. 44.00 (ISBN 0-8240-3968-8). Garland Pub.

Taylor, Pamela, ed. Notebooks of Leonardo Da Vinci. pap. 3.95 (ISBN 0-452-25033-1, Z5033, Plume). NAL.

Taylor, Rachel A. Leonardo the Florentine. 1973. Repr. of 1928 ed. 40.00 (ISBN 0-8274-1615-6). R West.

Valery, Paul. Introduction a la Methode de Leonardo de Vinci. (Coll. Idees). pap. 3.95 (ISBN 0-685-36615-4). French & Eur.

Wallace, Robert. World of Leonardo. (Library of Art). (Illus.). 1966. 15.95 (ISBN 0-8094-0234-3). Time-Life.

Wasserman, Jack. Leonardo. LC 80-645. (Illus.). 160p. 1980. 14.95 (ISBN 0-385-17167-6). Doubleday.

--Leonardo Da Vinci. LC 74-13112. (Library of Great Painters). (Illus.). 160p. 1975. 40.00 (ISBN 0-8109-0262-1). Abrams.

Wohl, Hellmut. Leonardo Da Vinci. 1967. 17.95 (ISBN 0-07-071272-7, P&RB). McGraw.

Zammattio, Carlo, et al. Leonardo the Scientist. LC 80-18436. (Illus.). 192p. 1980. 9.95 (ISBN 0-07-007933-1). McGraw.

Zubov, V. P. Leonardo Da Vinci. Kraus, David, tr. LC 67-27096. (Illus.). 1968. 16.50x (ISBN 0-674-52450-0). Harvard U Pr.

LEONARDO DA VINCI, 1452-1519–BIBLIOGRAPHY

Verga, Ettore. Bibliografia Vinciana 1493-1930, 2 Vols. 1967. Repr. of 1931 ed. 50.50 (ISBN 0-8337-3634-5). B Franklin.

LEONARDO DA VINCI, 1452-1519–JUVENILE LITERATURE

Leonardo Da Vinci. (MacDonald Educational Ser.). (Illus., Arabic.). 3.50 (ISBN 0-86685-202-6). Intl Bk Ctr.

Thomas, John. Leonardo Da Vinci. LC 57-6244. (Illus.). (gr. 6-10). 1957. 9.95 (ISBN 0-87599-112-2). S G Phillips.

Tynan, D. M. Leonardo Da Vinci. (History First Ser.). (gr. 3-4). 1977. pap. text ed. 7.95x (ISBN 0-521-21209-X). Cambridge U Pr.

Wallace, Robert. World of Leonardo. LC 66-24104. (Library of Art Ser.). (Illus.). (gr. 6 up). 1966. 12.96 (ISBN 0-8094-0263-7, Pub. by Time-Life). Silver.

Williams, Jay. Leonardo Da Vinci. LC 65-20599. (Horizon Caravel Bks.). 154p. (YA) (gr. 7 up). 1965. 9.95 (ISBN 0-06-026535-3, HarpJ); PLB 12.89 (ISBN 0-06-026536-1). Har-Row.

LEONI, POMPEO, d. 1610

Proske, B. G. Pompeo Leoni: Work in Marble & Alabaster in Relation to Spanish Sculpture. (Illus.). 1956. 1.50 (ISBN 0-87535-088-7). Hispanic Soc.

LEONOWENS, ANNA HARRIETTE (CRAWFORD) 1834-1914

Landon, Margaret. Anna & the King of Siam. (Illus.). 1944. 12.95 (ISBN 0-381-98136-3, A05201, JD-J). Har-Row.

LEONTEV, KONSTANTIN, 1831-1891

Berdiaev, Nicolas. Leontiev. (Russian Ser.: Vol. 15). 1968. pap. 8.00x (ISBN 0-87569-004-1). Academic Intl.

Berdiaev, Nikolai A. Leontiev. 1978. Repr. of 1940 ed. lib. bdg. 25.00 (ISBN 0-8495-0405-8). Arden Lib.

Berdyaev, Nicholas. Leontiev. LC 73-9622. 1914. lib. bdg. 20.00 (ISBN 0-8414-3152-3). Folcroft.

LEOPARD MEN

Beatty, Kenneth J. Human Leopards: Account of the Trials of Human Leopards Before the Special Commisson Court. LC 74-15011. (Illus.). Repr. of 1915 ed. 18.50 (ISBN 0-404-12006-7). AMS Pr.

LEOPARDI, GIACOMO, CONTE, 1798-1837

Bickersteth, Geoffrey L. Leopardi & Wordsworth: A Lecture. LC 73-9786. lib. bdg. 5.50 (ISBN 0-8414-3175-2). Folcroft.

Carsaniga, Giovanni. Leopardi. 1977. 10.00x (ISBN 0-85224-297-2, Pub. by Edinburgh U Pr Scotland). Columbia U Pr.

Caserta, Ernesto. Giacomo Leopardi: The War of the Mice & the Crabs. (Studies in the Romance Languages & Literatures Ser: No. 164). 1976. 8.00x (ISBN 0-8078-9164-9). U of NC Pr.

Robb, Nesca A. Four in Exile: Critical Essays on Leopardi, Hans Christian Anderson, Christina Rossetti & A. E. Housman. LC 68-26275. 1968. Repr. of 1948 ed. 10.00 (ISBN 0-8046-0384-7). Kennikat.

LEOPARDS

Adamson, Joy. Queen of Shaba: The Story of an African Leopard. LC 80-7931. (Helen & Kurt Wolff Bk). (Illus.). 256p. 1980. 14.95 (ISBN 0-15-175651-1). HarBraceJ.

Corbett, Jim. Jim Corbett's India: Stories Selected by R. E. Hawkins. Hawkins, R. E., ed. (Illus.). 1979. 14.95 (ISBN 0-19-212968-6). Oxford U Pr.

The Leopard Panthera pardus in Africa. (Illus.). 1975. pap. 9.50x (ISBN 2-88032-017-8, IUCN24, IUCN). Unipub.

Schick, Alice. Serengeti Cats. LC 77-812. (gr. 4 up). 1977. 6.95 (ISBN 0-397-31757-3, JBL-J). Har-Row.

LEOPOLD 2ND, EMPEROR OF GERMANY, 1747-1792

Kerner, Robert J. Bohemia in the Eighteenth Century. LC 79-94315. Repr. of 1932 ed. 14.00 (ISBN 0-404-01948-X). AMS Pr.

LEOPOLD 2ND, KING OF BELGIUM, 1835-1901

Emerson, Barbara. Leopold II of the Belgians: King of Colonialism. 1979. 25.00x (ISBN 0-312-48012-1). St Martin.

MacDonnell, John D. King Leopold Second: His Rule in Belgium & the Congo. (Illus.). 1970. Repr. of 1905 ed. 17.50 (ISBN 0-87266-041-9). Argosy.

Twain, Mark. King Leopold's Soliloquy. Heym, Stefan, ed. (Illus.). 1970. pap. 1.25 (ISBN 0-7178-0114-4). Intl Pub Co.

LEOPOLD 3RD, KING OF THE BELGIANS, 1901-

MacDonnell, John D. King Leopold, Second: His Rule in Belgium & the Congo. LC 70-97407. (Illus.). Repr. of 1905 ed. 23.00x (ISBN 0-8371-2657-6, Pub. by Negro U Pr). Greenwood.

Remy. The Eighteenth Day. LC 78-74577. 1979. 10.00 (ISBN 0-89696-042-0). Everest Hse.

LEOPOLD, ALDO, 1886-1948

Flader, Susan L. Thinking Like a Mountain: Aldo Leopold & the Evolution of an Ecological Attitude Toward Deer, Wolves, & Forests. LC 74-80389. 280p. 1974. 15.00x (ISBN 0-8262-0167-9). U of Mo Pr.

LEOPOLD, NATHAN FREUDENTHAL, 1904?-

Leopold, Nathan F., Jr. Life Plus Ninety-Nine Years. LC 73-16644. 381p. 1974. Repr. of 1958 ed. lib. bdg. 22.25x (ISBN 0-8371-7207-1, LELP). Greenwood.

LEOPOLDVILLE

La Fontaine, J. S. City Politics: A Study of Leopoldville, 1962-63. (African Studies). (Illus.). 1970. 26.95 (ISBN 0-521-07627-7). Cambridge U Pr.

LEPADIDAE

Darwin, Charles. The Fossil Lepadidae. 1851. pap. 11.50 (ISBN 0-384-10860-1). Johnson Repr.

LEPANTO, BATTLE OF, 1571

Manfroni, Camillo. Storia Della Marina Italiana: Dalle Invasioni Barbariche Alla Battaglia Di Lepanto, Livorno, Roma, 1899-1902, 3 Vols. Repr. of 1897 ed. 74.00 (ISBN 0-384-35145-X). Johnson Repr.

LE PAUTRE, ANTOINE

Berger, Robert W. Antoine Le Pautre: A French Architect of the Era of Louis XIV. LC 69-18276. (College Art Ass. Monograph Ser). (Illus.). 1969. 18.50x (ISBN 0-8147-0039-X). NYU Pr.

LEPCHAS

Siiger, Halfdan. The Lepchas: Culture & Religion of a Himalayan People, 2 pts. (Ethnographical Ser.: No. 2). (Illus.). 1967. pap. 19.50x ea. Humanities.

LEPIDOPTERA

Application of Induced Sterility for Control of Lepidopterous Populations. (Orig.). 1971. pap. 13.00 (ISBN 92-0-111271-8, ISP281, IAEA). Unipub.

Burns, Alexander. Australian Butterflies in Colour. (Illus.). 112p. 1969. 11.50 (ISBN 0-589-07007-X, Pub. by Reed Books Australia). C E Tuttle.

Dickson, R. A Lepidopterist's Handbook. 136p. 1976. 24.00x (ISBN 0-686-75579-0, Pub. by Amateur Entomol Soc). State Mutual Bk.

Fletcher, D. S. A Revision of the Old World Genus Zamarada: (Lepidoptera: Geometridae) (Bulletin of the British Museum Natural History Ser.: Supplement No. 2). (Illus.). 1974. pap. text ed. 90.00x (ISBN 0-8277-4358-0, Pub. by Brit Mus Nat Hist). Sabbot-Natural Hist Bks.

Fox, R. M. & Real, H. G. A Monograph of the Ithomiidae: Napeogenini, Pt. 4. (Memoirs Ser: No. 15). (Illus.). 368p. 1971. 25.00 (ISBN 0-686-01270-4). Am Entom Inst.

Fracker, Stanley B. The Classification of Lepidopterous Larvae. (Illus.). Repr. of 1915 ed. 12.50 (ISBN 0-384-16670-9). Johnson Repr.

Holloway, J. D. The Lepidoptera of Norfolk Island. (Series Entomologica: No. 13). (Illus.). 1977. lib. bdg. 45.00 (ISBN 90-6193-123-1, Pub. by Junk Pubs Netherlands). Kluwer Boston.

Morris, Dean. Butterflies & Moths. LC 77-7912. (Read About Animals Ser.). (Illus.). (gr. k-3). 1977. PLB 11.15 (ISBN 0-8393-0010-7). Raintree Child.

Schmid, Michael & Endicott, Bradford M. Mariposas De Venezuela. (Illus.). xi, 67p. (Orig., Span & Eng.). 1968. 9.95x (ISBN 0-685-09292-5). Entomological Repr.

Schreiber, Harold. Disperal Centres of Sphingidae (Lepidoptera) in the Neotropical Region. (Biogeographica Ser.: No. 10). (Illus.). 1978. lib. bdg. 34.00 (ISBN 90-6193-211-4, Pub. by Junk Pubs. Netherlands). Kluwer Boston.

Selman, Charles L. A Pictorial Key to the Hawkmoths (Lepidotera: Sphingidae) of Eastern United States (Except Florida) 1975. 1.50 (ISBN 0-686-30340-7). Ohio Bio Survey.

Sokoloff, P. A. Practical Hints for Collecting & Studying the Microlepidoptera. 40p. 21.00x (ISBN 0-686-75581-2, Pub. by Amateur Entomol Soc). State Mutual Bk.

Tietz, Harrison M. An Index to the Described Life Histories, Early Stages & Hosts of the Macrolepidoptera of the Continental United States & Canada, 2 vols. iv, 1041p. 1972. text ed. 25.00x (ISBN 0-913492-01-9). Entomological Repr.

Weismann, August. Studies in the Theory of Descent, 2 vols. in 1. LC 72-1661. Repr. of 1882 ed. 57.50 (ISBN 0-404-08192-4). AMS Pr.

LEPROSY

see also Missions to Lepers

Arnold, Harry L., Jr. & Fasal, Paul. Leprosy: Diagnosis & Management. 2nd ed. (American Lecture Dermatology Ser.). (Illus.). 108p. 1973. 18.75 (ISBN 0-398-02681-5). C C Thomas.

Brody, Saul N. The Disease of the Soul: Leprosy in Medieval Literature. LC 73-8407. (Illus.). 233p. 1974. 17.50x (ISBN 0-8014-0804-0). Cornell U Pr.

Bryceson & Pfaltzgraff. Leprosy. 2nd ed. (Medicine in the Tropics Ser.). (Illus.). 208p. 1978. pap. text ed. 12.00 (ISBN 0-443-01588-0). Churchill.

Davidson, W. S. Havens of Refuge: A History of Leprosy in Western Australia. 1979. 24.00x (ISBN 0-85564-141-X, Pub. by U of W Austral Pr). Intl Schol Bk Serv.

Farrow, John. Damien the Leper. 1954. pap. 2.95 (ISBN 0-385-02918-7, D3, Im). Doubleday.

Freeman, James A., et al. Pathology of Leprosy. LC 80-720434. 1980. softbound incl. slides 50.00 (ISBN 0-89189-101-3, 15-7-011-00). Am Soc Clinical.

Gill, I. K. Friends, Not Outcasts. LC 79-184944. (Illus.). 1972. 4.50 (ISBN 0-685-25499-2). Helios.

Gokhale, S. D. Valley of Shadows: Problem of Leprosy in India. 132p. text ed. 12.00 (ISBN 0-8426-1641-1). Verry.

Hill, George J. Leprosy in Five Young Men. LC 79-125621. (Illus.). 1971. 10.00x (ISBN 0-87081-003-0). Colo Assoc.

Jopling, W. H. Handbook of Leprosy. 2nd ed. (Illus.). 1978. pap. 14.95x (ISBN 0-433-17566-4). Intl Ideas.

McDowell, Frank, et al. Surgical Rehabilitation in Leprosy. 448p. 1974. 40.00 (ISBN 0-683-05853-3). Krieger.

Noussitou, F. M., et al. Leprosy in Children. (Also avail. in French). 1976. pap. 3.60 (ISBN 92-4-154053-2). World Health.

Richards, Peter. The Medieval Leper: And His Northern Heirs. (Illus.). 178p. 1977. 18.50x (ISBN 0-87471-960-7). Rowman.

Sehgal, V. N. Clinical Leprosy. (Illus.). 1980. text ed. 13.50x (ISBN 0-7069-0785-X, Pub. by Vikas India). Advent NY.

Weymouth, Anthony. Through the Leper-Squint. LC 75-23769. (Illus.). Repr. of 1938 ed. 25.00 (ISBN 0-404-13395-9). AMS Pr.

WHO Expert Committee. Geneva, 1970, 4th. WHO Expert Committee on Leprosy: Report. (Technical Report Ser.: No. 459). (Also avail. in French & Spanish). 1970. pap. 2.00 (ISBN 92-4-120459-1). World Health.

LEPROSY–PERSONAL NARRATIVES

Graves, Peter. The Seventh Gate. 1978. 9.75 (ISBN 0-85117-078-1). Transatlantic.

LEPTOME

see Phloem

LEPTOMENINGITIS

see Meningitis

LEPTONS (NUCLEAR PHYSICS)

see also Electrons; Fermions; Muons; Neutrinos; Positrons

Levy, Maurice, et al, eds. Quarks & Leptons: Cargese Nineteen Seventy-Nine. (NATO Advanced Study Institutes Ser. (Series B--Physics): Vol. 61). 760p. 1981. 75.00 (ISBN 0-306-40560-1, Plenum Pr). Plenum Pub.

Preparata, G. & Aubert, J. J., eds. Probing Hadrons with Leptons. (Ettore Majorana International Science Ser., Physical Sciences: Vol. 5). 502p. 1980. 59.50 (ISBN 0-306-40438-9, Plenum Pr). Plenum Pub.

Roy, Probir. Theory of Lepton-Hadron Processes at High Energies: Partons, Scale Invariance & Light-Cone Physics. (Oxford Studies in Physics). (Illus.). 188p. 1975. 33.50x (ISBN 0-19-851452-2). Oxford U Pr.

Roy, R. R. & Reed, R. D. Interactions of Photons & Leptons with Matter. LC 68-23487. 1969. 44.00 (ISBN 0-12-601350-0). Acad Pr.

Urban, P., ed. Quarks & Leptoms As Fundamental Particles. (Acta Physica Austriaca Supplemetum: No. 21). (Illus.). 720p. 1980. 88.00 (ISBN 0-387-81564-3). Springer-Verlag.

LEQUEU, JEAN JACQUES, 1757-1825?

Lemagny, J. C. & De Menil, Dominiqueintro. by. Visionary Architects: Boullee, Ledoux, Lequeu. (Illus.). 1968. pap. 8.00 (ISBN 0-914412-21-3). Inst for the Arts.

LE RAMEE, PIERRE DE, 1515?-1572

Ong, Walter J. Ramus: Method, & the Decay of Dialogue. LC 73-19771. 408p. 1974. Repr. of 1958 ed. lib. bdg. 21.50x (ISBN 0-374-96148-4). Octagon.

LERDO DE TEJADA, SEBASTIAN, PRES. MEXICO, 1820-1889

Knapp, Frank A. Life of Sebastian Lerdo De Tejada, 1823-1889: A Study of Influence & Obscurity. LC 68-23305. 1968. Repr. of 1951 ed. lib. bdg. 17.75x (ISBN 0-8371-0132-8, KNLT). Greenwood.

LERMONTOV, MIKHAIL IUREVICH, 1814-1841

Eikhenbaum, Boris. Lermontov: An Essay in Literary Historical Evaluation. Parrott, Ray & Weber, Harry, trs. 1981. 16.50 (ISBN 0-686-70084-8). Ardis Pubs.

Lavrin, Janko. Lermontov. 1959. pap. text ed. 3.25x (ISBN 0-391-02003-X). Humanities.

Mersereau, John, Jr. Mikhail Lermontov. LC 62-7722. (Crosscurrents-Modern Critiques Ser.). 183p. 1962. 7.95 (ISBN 0-8093-0059-1). S Ill U Pr.

Michailoff, Helen. Mikhail Lermontov: Magic & Mystery. 1981. 20.00 (ISBN 0-686-70085-6). Ardis Pubs.

LESBIANISM

Abbott & Love, eds. Sappho Was a Right-on Woman. 1978. pap. 1.95 (ISBN 0-8128-7006-9). Stein & Day.

Abbott, Sidney & Love, Barbara. Sappho Was a Right-on Woman: A Liberated View of Lesbianism. LC 77-160348. 1973. pap. 3.95 (ISBN 0-8128-1590-4). Stein & Day.

Baetz, Ruth. Lesbian Crossroads: Personal Stories of Lesbian Struggles & Triumphs. LC 80-12440. 288p. 1980. 10.95 (ISBN 0-688-03712-7). Morrow.

Bethel, Lorraine & Smith, Barbara, eds. Conditions: Five-the Black Women's Issue. 4.50 (ISBN 0-686-31642-8). Conditions.

Biren, Joan E. Eye to Eye: Portraits of Lesbians. 90p. pap. 8.95 (ISBN 0-9603176-0-0). Crossing Pr.

Birkby, Phyllis, et al, eds. Amazon Expedition. 96p. pap. 3.00 (ISBN 0-87810-026-1). Crossing Pr.

--Amazon Expedition: A Lesbian-Feminist Anthology. LC 73-79902. (Illus.). 96p. (Orig.). 1973. 6.50 (ISBN 0-87810-526-3); pap. 3.00 (ISBN 0-87810-026-1). Times Change.
Brooks, Virginia R. Minority Stress & Lesbian Women. LC 80-8116. 240p. 1981. 22.95x (ISBN 0-669-03953-5). Lexington Bks.
Bulkin, Elly & Larkin, Joan, eds. Lesbian Poetry: An Anthology. 336p. (Orig.). 1981. pap. 10.95 (ISBN 0-930436-08-3). Persephone.
Califia, Pat. Sapphistry: The Book of Lesbian Sexuality. LC 80-80379. (Illus.). 200p. 1980. pap. 6.95 (ISBN 0-930044-14-2). Naiad Pr.
Caprio, Frank S. Female Homosexuality: A Psychodynamic Study of Lesbianism. 1967. pap. 2.25 (ISBN 0-8065-0151-0, 258). Citadel Pr.
Cheseboro, James W., ed. Gayspeak: Gay Male & Lesbian Communication. 448p. 1981. 17.95 (ISBN 0-8298-0472-2); pap. 9.95 (ISBN 0-8298-0456-0). Pilgrim NY.
Covina, Gina & Galana, Laurel, eds. Lesbian Reader. 1975. pap. 5.95 (ISBN 0-686-22379-9). Amazon Pr.
--The New Lesbians. 220p. pap. 4.95 (ISBN 0-394-73479-3). Crossing Pr.
Craigin, Elisabeth. Either Is Love. LC 75-12311. (Homosexuality). 1975. Repr. of 1937 ed. 9.00x (ISBN 0-405-07379-8). Arno.
Cruikshank, Margaret. The Lesbian Path. 1980. pap. 6.95 (ISBN 0-912216-20-4). Angel Pr.
Damon, Gene, pseud. Lesbiana. LC 76-45683. 1976. 5.00 (ISBN 0-930044-05-3). Naiad Pr.
Davis, Katharine B. Factors in the Sex Life of Twenty-Two Hundred Women. LC 70-169379. (Family in America). 456p. 1972. Repr. of 1929 ed. 22.00 (ISBN 0-405-03856-9). Arno.
Diamond, Liz. The Lesbian Primer. 82p. pap. 3.95 (ISBN 0-686-74692-9). Crossing Pr.
Dobkin, Alix. Alix Dobkin's Adventures in Womens Music. (Illus., Orig.). 1979. pap. text ed. 8.50 (ISBN 0-934166-00-5). Tomato Pubns.
Ettorre, E. M. Lesbians, Women & Society. 1980. 18.95x (ISBN 0-7100-0546-6); pap. 7.95 (ISBN 0-7100-0330-7). Routledge & Kegan.
Faderman, Lillian. Surpassing the Love of Men: Love Between Women from the Renaissance to the Present. Guarnaschelli, Maria, ed. LC 80-24482. (Illus.). 488p. 1981. 18.95 (ISBN 0-688-03733-X); pap. 10.95 (ISBN 0-688-00396-6, Quill). Morrow.
Fredericks, Diana. Diana: A Strange Autobiography. LC 75-12315. (Homosexuality). 1976. Repr. of 1939 ed. 15.00x (ISBN 0-405-07359-3). Arno.
Galana, Laurel & Covina, Gina. The New Lesbians. 1977. pap. 4.95 (ISBN 0-685-80311-2). Moon Bks.
Gidlow, Elsa. Ask No Man Pardon: The Philosophical Significanco of Being Lesbian. 1976. 2.00 (ISBN 0-9606568-1-2). Druid Heights.
Goodman, Bernice. The Lesbian: A Celebration of Difference. 1977. pap. 3.50 (ISBN 0-918314-04-6). Out & Out.
Gordon, Mary. Chase of the Wild Goose: The Story of Lady Eleanor Butler & Miss Sarah Ponsonby. LC 75-12319. (Homosexuality). 1975. Repr. of 1936 ed. 15.00x (ISBN 0-405-07354-2). Arno.
Grahn, Judy, ed. Lesbians Speak Out. (Illus.). 1974. pap. 5.00 (ISBN 0-88447-028-8). Diana Pr.
Grier, Barbara, et al. The Lesbian in Literature: A Bibliography. 3rd ed. 200p. (Orig.). 1981. pap. 10.00 (ISBN 0-930044-23-1). Naiad Pr.
Johnston, Jill. The Lesbian Nation. LC 72-83934. 1973. 7.95 (ISBN 0-671-21433-0). S&S.
--Lesbian Nation: The Feminist Solution. 1974. pap. 5.95 (ISBN 0-671-21729-1, Touchstone Bks). S&S.
Katz, Jonathan. Gay American History: Lesbians & Gay Men in the U.S.A., a Documentary. LC 76-2039. (Illus.). 1976. pap. 9.95 (ISBN 0-690-01165-2, TYC-T). T Y Crowell.
Katz, Jonathan, ed. Miss Marianne Woods & Miss Jane Pirie Against Dame Helen Cumming Gordon. LC 75-13707. (Homosexuality: Lesbians & Gay Men in Society, History & Literature Ser.). 1975. Repr. 36.00x (ISBN 0-405-07403-4). Arno.
Klaich, Dolores. Woman Plus Woman. LC 74-31202. 288p. 1975. pap. 5.95 (ISBN 0-688-07918-0). Morrow.
Lesbians Speak Out. 150p. pap. 5.00 (ISBN 0-686-74712-7). Crossing Pr.
Lewis, Sasha G. Sunday's Women: A Report on Lesbian Life Today. LC 78-53655. 1979. 10.95 (ISBN 0-8070-3794-X). Beacon Pr.
--Sunday's Women: Lesbian Life Today. LC 78-53655. 232p. 1981. pap. 5.95 (ISBN 0-8070-3795-8, BP622). Beacon Pr.
Martin, Del & Lyon, Phyllis. Lesbian-Woman. LC 72-76532. 300p. 1972. 7.95 (ISBN 0-912078-20-0). New Glide.
Millett, Kate. Sita. 1978. pap. 2.25 (ISBN 0-345-27362-1). Ballantine.
Moses, Alice E. Identity Management in Lesbian Women. (Praeger Special Studies). 1978. 21.95 (ISBN 0-03-047641-0). Praeger.
Myron, Nancy & Bunch, Charlotte, eds. Lesbianism & the Women's Movement. (Illus.). 1976. pap. 3.50 (ISBN 0-88447-006-7). Diana Pr.
Odette. Pleasures: The Secret Garden of Sexual Love Between Women. 1978. pap. 2.25 (ISBN 0-446-82263-9). Warner Bks.
Perrin, Elula. So Long As There Are Women. Salemson, Harold J., tr. from Fr. LC 79-26502. 1980. 10.95 (ISBN 0-688-03596-5). Morrow.
--Women Prefer Women. Salemson, Harold J., tr. from Fr. LC 78-13330. 1979. 8.95 (ISBN 0-688-03407-1). Morrow.
Ponse, Barbara. Identities in the Lesbian World: The Social Construction of Self. LC 77-84763. (Contributions in Sociology: No. 28). 1978. lib. bdg. 18.95x (ISBN 0-8371-9889-5, PLW/). Greenwood.
Propper, Alice M. Prison Homosexuality: Myth & Reality. LC 79-48003. 256p. 1981. 23.95x (ISBN 0-669-03628-5). Lexington Bks.
Roberta. Gay Liberation. 1.49 (ISBN 0-915420-01-5). PTL Pubns.
Roberts, J. R., compiled by. Black Lesbians: An Annotated Bibliography. LC 81-80662. (Illus.). 93p. 1981. 5.95 (ISBN 0-930044-21-5). Naiad Pr.
Rosen, David H. Lesbianism: A Study of Female Homosexuality. (Illus.). 140p. 1974. 11.75 (ISBN 0-398-02924-5); pap. 7.50 (ISBN 0-398-03116-9). C C Thomas.
Rule, Jane. Outlander. LC 80-84221. 220p. (Orig.). 1981. pap. 6.95 (ISBN 0-930044-17-7). Naiad Pr.
Scott, Jane. Wives Who Love Women. LC 77-91905. 1978. 8.95 (ISBN 0-8027-0597-9). Walker & Co.
Simpson, Ruth. From the Closet to the Courts: The Lesbian Transition. 1977. pap. 2.25 (ISBN 0-14-004353-5). Penguin.
Sisley, Emily L. & Harris, Bertha. The Joy of Lesbian Sex. 1978. pap. 7.95 (ISBN 0-671-24080-3, Fireside). S&S.
Stearn, Jess. The Grapevine. (Illus.). 320p. 1973. pap. 1.25 (ISBN 0-532-12151-1). Woodhill.
Stewart-Park, Angela & Cassidy, Jules. We're Here: Conversations with Lesbian Women. 3.95 (ISBN 0-7043-3117-9, Pub. by Quartet England). Charles River Bks.
Tanner, Donna M. The Lesbian Couple. LC 77-16720. 1978. 15.95x (ISBN 0-669-02078-8). Lexington Bks.
Tobin, Kay & Wicker, Randy. The Gay Crusaders. LC 75-12349. (Homosexuality). (Illus.). 1975. Repr. 12.00x (ISBN 0-405-07374-7). Arno.
Toder, Nancy. Choices. LC 80-20836. 320p. (Orig.). 1980. pap. 6.00 (ISBN 0-930436-05-9). Persephone.
Trump, Barbara. Forgiven Love. LC 79-84793. (Orig.). 1979. pap. 2.25 (ISBN 0-89877-010-6). Jeremy Bks.
Vida, Ginny, ed. Our Right to Love: A Lesbian Resource Book. LC 77-20184. 1978. 12.95 (ISBN 0-13-644401-6); pap. 9.95 (ISBN 0-13-644393-1). P-H.
Wolf, Deborah G. The Lesbian Community. LC 77-93478. 1979. 12.95 (ISBN 0-520-03657-3); pap. 4.95 (ISBN 0-520-04248-4, CAL 484). U of Cal Pr.

LESCHETITZKI, THEODOR, 1830-1915

Bree, Malwine. The Groundwork of Leschetizky Method. Baker, Th., tr. from Ger. LC 74-144898. (Illus.). 1972. Repr. of 1920 ed. 25.00 (ISBN 0-403-00837-9). Scholarly.
--Groundwork of the Leschetizky Method. LC 68-25284. (Studies in Music, No. 42). (Illus.). 1969. Repr. of 1902 ed. lib. bdg. 36.95 (ISBN 0-8383-0290-4). Haskell.

LESEUR, ELIZABETH (ARRIGHI), 1866-1914

Eustace, Cecil J. Infinity of Questions. facs. ed. LC 70-84356. (Essay Index Reprint Ser). 1946. 14.50 (ISBN 0-8369-1080-X). Arno.

LESLIE, MIRIAM FLORENCE (FOLLINE) SQUIER, d. 1914

Stern, Madeleine B. Purple Passage: The/Life of Mrs Frank Leslie. (Illus.). 1970. Repr. of 1953 ed. 12.95 (ISBN 0-8061-0271-3); pap. 6.95 (ISBN 0-8061-0939-4). U of Okla Pr.

LESOTHO

Burman, Sandra. Chiefdom Politics & Alien Law. LC 79-25600. 1981. text ed. 38.00x (ISBN 0-8419-0591-6, Africana). Holmes & Meier.
Haliburton, Gordon. Historical Dictionary of Lesotho. LC 76-49550. (African Historical Dictionaries Ser.: No. 10). (Illus.). 1977. 12.00 (ISBN 0-8108-0993-1). Scarecrow.
Lagden, Godfrey Y. Basutos: The Mountaineers & Their Country, 2 vols. LC 73-89006. (Illus.). Repr. of 1909 ed. 42.00x (ISBN 0-8371-2483-2, Pub. by Negro U Pr). Greenwood.
Sanders, Peter. Moshweshwe of Lesotho. pap. text ed. 2.75x (ISBN 0-435-94468-1). Heinemann Ed.
Thompson, Leonard. Survival in Two Worlds: Moshoeshoe of Lesotho, 1786-1870. (Illus.). 366p. 1975. text ed. 36.00x (ISBN 0-19-821693-9). Oxford U Pr.
--Survival in Two Worlds: Moshoeshoe of Lesotho 1786-1870. (Illus.). 1975. pap. 12.50x (ISBN 0-19-822702-7). Oxford U Pr.
Weisfelder, Richard F. Defining National Purpose in Lesotho. LC 72-630647. (Papers in International Studies: Africa: No. 3). (Illus.). 1969. pap. 3.25 (ISBN 0-89680-037-7). Ohio U Ctr Intl.
Willet, Shelagh M. & Ambrose, David. Lesotho. (World Bibliographical Ser.: No. 3). 496p. 1980. 54.25 (ISBN 0-903450-11-9). Abc-Clio.
World Bank. Lesotho: A Development Challenge. LC 75-30508. (A World Bank Country Economic Report Ser). (Illus.). 118p. 1975. pap. 4.75x (ISBN 0-8018-1833-8). Johns Hopkins.

LESS DEVELOPED COUNTRIES

see Underdeveloped Areas

LESSEPS, FERDINAND MARIE, COMTE DE, 1805-1894

Fitzgerald, Percy H. The Great Canal at Suez: Its Political, Engineering & Financial History, 2 vols. LC 74-15037. Repr. of 1876 ed. Set. 52.50 (ISBN 0-404-12042-3). AMS Pr.

LESSING, DORIS MAY, 1919-

Burkom, Selma R. Doris Lessing: A Checklist of Primary & Secondary Sources. LC 72-87109. iv, 88p. 1973. 7.50x (ISBN 0-87875-039-8). Whitston Pub.
Carlson, Edgar M. The Church & the Public Conscience. LC 79-8710. xii, 104p. 1981. Repr. of 1956 ed. lib. bdg. 17.50x (ISBN 0-313-22195-2, CACH). Greenwood.
Holmquist, Ingrid. From Society to Nature: A Study of Doris Lessing's "Children of Violence". (Gothenburg Studies in English: No. 46). 1980. pap. 19.75x (ISBN 91-7346-083-4). Humanities.
Lessing, Doris. A Small Personal Voice: Essays, Reviews, Interviews. 1975. pap. 2.45 (ISBN 0-394-71685-X, Vin). Random.
Monarch Notes on Lessing's the Golden Notebook. pap. 1.50 (ISBN 0-671-00934-6). Monarch Pr.
Rose, Ellen C. The Tree Outside the Window. LC 76-44671. 1976. 16.00 (ISBN 0-8357-0189-1, IS-00018, Pub. by U Press of New England). Univ Microfilms.
--The Tree Outside the Window: Doris Lessing's "Children of Violence". LC 76-44671. 94p. 1976. text ed. 11.00x (ISBN 0-8357-0189-1, Pub. by Univ. Microfilms Intl.). U Pr of New Eng.
Rubenstein, Roberta. The Novelistic Vision of Doris Lessing: Breaking the Forms of Consciousness. LC 78-25916. 1979. 14.00 (ISBN 0-252-00706-9). U of Ill Pr.
Schlueter, Paul. The Novels of Doris Lessing. LC 72-10281. (Crosscurrents-Modern Critiques Ser.). 155p. 1973. 6.95 (ISBN 0-8093-0612-3). S Ill U Pr.
Thorpe, Michael. Doris Lessing's Africa. LC 79-15676. 1979. text ed. 17.50x (ISBN 0-8419-6000-3); pap. text ed. 8.50x (ISBN 0-8419-6001-1). Holmes & Meier.

LESSING, GOTTHOLD EPHRAIM, 1729-1781

Coleridge, Samuel T. Confessions of an Inquiring Spirit. Hart, H. S., ed. 1957. pap. 1.85 (ISBN 0-8047-0331-0, SP48). Stanford U Pr.
Fittbogen, Gottfried. Die Religion Lessings. 1967. 29.00 (ISBN 0-685-13574-8); pap. 26.00 (ISBN 0-685-13575-6). Johnson Repr.
Garland, Henry B. Lessing: The Founder of Modern German Literature. LC 73-95. 1973. lib. bdg. 15.00 (ISBN 0-685-33789-8). Folcroft.
Haney, John D. Lessing's Education of the Human Race. LC 77-176835. (Columbia University. Teachers College. Contributions to Education: No. 20). Repr. of 1908 ed. 17.50 (ISBN 0-404-55020-7). AMS Pr.
Heller, Peter. Dialectics & Nihilism: Essays on Lessing, Nietzsche, Mann & Kafka. LC 65-26240. 1969. Repr. of 1966 ed. 15.00x (ISBN 0-87023-019-0). U of Mass Pr.
Lessing, Gotthold E. Lessings Saemtliche Schriften, 23 vols. 3rd ed. Lachmann, Karl, ed. (Ger). 1968. Repr. of 1886 ed. Set. 870.75x (ISBN 3-11-005161-3). De Gruyter.
Lowell, James R. English Poets: Lessing, Rousseau. LC 74-105783. 1970. Repr. of 1888 ed. 13.50 (ISBN 0-8046-1047-9). Kennikat.
--English Poets: Lessing, Rousseau. 1973. Repr. of 1888 ed. 20.00 (ISBN 0-8274-0101-9). R West.
Robertson, John G., ed. Lessing's Dramatic Theory. LC 63-14713. (Illus.). 1939. 25.00 (ISBN 0-405-08894-9). Arno.
Rolleston, T. W. Life of Gotthold Ephraim Lessing. 1889. Repr. 11.50 (ISBN 0-8274-2930-4). R West.
Rolleston, Thomas W. Life of Gotthold Ephraim Lessing. LC 78-160777. 1971. Repr. of 1889 ed. 12.00 (ISBN 0-8046-1609-4). Kennikat.
Rudowski, Victor A. Lessing's "Aesthetica in Nuce". An Analysis of the May 26, 1769, Letter to Nicolai. (Studies in the Germanic Languages & Literatures Ser.: No. 69). 144p. 1971. 9.50x (ISBN 0-8078-8069-8). U of NC Pr.
Vail, Curtis C. Lessing's Relation to the English Language & Literature. LC 36-30041. (Columbia University. Germanic Studies, New Series: No. 3). Repr. of 1936 ed. 27.00 (ISBN 0-404-50453-1). AMS Pr.
Wessell, Leonard P. G.E Lessing's Theology: A Reinterpretation, a Study in the Problematic Nature of the Enlightenment. 1977. 26.75x (ISBN 90-279-7801-8). Mouton.

LESSON PLANNING

Briggs, Leslie J., et al. Instructional Design: Principles & Applications. LC 77-23216. 562p. 1977. 19.95 (ISBN 0-87778-098-6). Educ Tech Pubns.
Coger, Rick. Developing Effective Instructional Systems. 144p. 1975. pap. 4.95 (ISBN 0-8158-0327-3). Chris Mass.
Davis, Robert H., et al. Learning System Design. (Illus.). 320p. 1974. text ed. 16.95 (ISBN 0-07-074334-7, C). McGraw.
Edwards, Clifford H., et al. Planning, Teaching & Evaluating: A Competency Approach. LC 76-41903. 1977. 19.95x (ISBN 0-88229-204-8). Nelson-Hall.
Emmers, Amy P. After the Lesson Plan: Realities of High School Teaching. 1981. 19.95 (ISBN 0-8077-2654-0); pap. 10.95x (ISBN 0-8077-2605-2). Tchrs Coll.
Gagne, Robert M. & Briggs, Leslie J. Principles of Instructional Design. 2nd ed. LC 78-27628. 1979. text ed. 17.95 (ISBN 0-03-040806-7, HoltC). HR&W.
Henak, Richard M. Lesson Planning for Meaningful Variety in Teaching. 110p. 1980. 6.25 (ISBN 0-8106-1515-0). NEA.
Jarolimek, John & Foster, Clifford D. Teaching & Learning in the Elementary School. (Illus.). 416p. 1976. text ed. 15.95 (ISBN 0-02-360390-9). Macmillan.
Johnson, David W. & Johnson, Roger T. Learning Together & Alone: Cooperation, Competition, & Individualization. (Illus.). 224p. 1975. pap. text ed. 11.95 (ISBN 0-13-527945-3). P-H.
Langdon, Danny G. Interactive Instructional Designs for Individualized Learning. LC 72-89577. 176p. 1973. pap. 9.95 (ISBN 0-87778-041-2). Educ Tech Pubns.
McAshan, H. H. The Goals Approach to Performance Objectives. LC 74-4577. 305p. 1974. pap. text ed. 7.95 (ISBN 0-7216-5860-1). HR&W.
Massialas, Byron, et al. Social Issues Through Inquiry: Coping in an Age of Crisis. (Illus.). 288p. 1975. pap. text ed. 11.95 (ISBN 0-13-815852-5). P-H.
Mehan, Hugh. Learning Lessons: Social Organization in the Classroom. LC 78-24298. (Illus.). 1979. text ed. 15.00 (ISBN 0-674-52015-7). Harvard U Pr.
Mossman, Lois Coffey. Changing Conception Relative to the Planning of Lessons. LC 72-177094. (Columbia University. Teachers College. Contributions to Education: No. 147). Repr. of 1924 ed. 17.50 (ISBN 0-404-55147-5). AMS Pr.
Siegel, Ernest & Siegel, Rita. Creating Instructional Sequences. LC 77-11107. 1977. text ed. 12.50 (ISBN 0-87879-175-2); pap. text ed. 6.50 (ISBN 0-87879-176-0). Acad Therapy.
Weaver, Horace R., ed. The International Lesson Annual 1981-1982. 448p. (Orig.). 1981. pap. 4.50 (ISBN 0-687-19145-9). Abingdon.
Weil, Marsha & Joyce, Bruce. Information Processing Models of Teaching: Expanding Your Teaching Repertoire. LC 77-5414. (Illus.). 1978. ref. ed. 15.95 (ISBN 0-13-464552-9); pap. text ed. 11.95 (ISBN 0-13-464545-6). P-H.

L'ESTOILE, CLAUDE DE, 1597-1652

Parker, R. A. Claude De l' Estoille, Poet & Dramatist, 1597-1652. 1973. Repr. of 1930 ed. pap. 11.50 (ISBN 0-384-44862-3). Johnson Repr.

L'ESTRANGE, SIR ROGER, 1616-1704

Kitchin, George. Sir Roger L'Estrange: A Contribution to the History of the Press in the 17th Century. LC 74-120325. (English Book Trade). Repr. of 1913 ed. 17.50x (ISBN 0-678-00703-9). Kelley.

LETCHER, JOHN, 1813-1884

Boney, F. N. John Letcher of Virginia: The Story of Virginia's Civil War Governor. LC 66-25023. (Southern Historical Ser: Vol. 11). 1967. 19.95x (ISBN 0-8173-5216-3). U of Ala Pr.

LETHORONET, FRANCE (CISTERCIAN ABBEY)

Pouillon, Fernand. Stones of the Abbey. Gillott, Edward, tr. LC 70-95858. (Helen & Kurt Wolff Bk). 1970. 5.95 (ISBN 0-15-185075-5). HarBraceJ.

LE TOURNEAU, ROBERT GILMOUR, 1888-

LeTourneau, R. G. Mover of Men & Mountains: The Autobiography of R. G. LeTourneau. 1967. pap. 2.95 (ISBN 0-8024-3818-0). Moody.

LE TOURNEUR, PIERRE PRIME FELICIEN, 1732-1788

Cushing, Mary G. Pierre Le Tourneur. LC 8-30946. (Columbia University. Studies in Romance Philology & Literature: No. 8). Repr. of 1908 ed. 22.50 (ISBN 0-404-50608-9). AMS Pr.

LE TROSNE, GUILLAUME FRANCOIS, 1728-1780

Mille, Jerome. G.F. le Trosne (1728-1780) Physiocrate Oublie: Etude Economique, Fiscale et Politique. LC 70-140990. 1971. Repr. of 1905 ed. 20.50 (ISBN 0-8337-2390-1). B Franklin.

LETTER PICTURES

Butterworth, Emma M. The Complete Book of Calligraphy. LC 79-7642. (Illus.). 164p. 1980. 14.95 (ISBN 0-690-01852-5). Har-Row.

Yasek, Elizabeth. The Visual Gourmet: A Calligraphic Treasury of International Vegetarian Recipes. (Illus.). 160p. (Orig.). 1981. pap. 12.95 (ISBN 0-939212-00-5). Katahdin.

LETTER-WRITING

see also Commercial Correspondence; Form Letters; Forms of Address; Love Letters

Altman, Janet. Epistolarity: Approaches to a Form. 1981. 20.00x (ISBN 0-8142-0313-2). Ohio St U Pr.

Atkinson, Caroline P., ed. Letters of Susan Hale. 472p. 1981. lib. bdg. 40.00 (ISBN 0-89760-339-7). Telegraph Bks.

Avett, Elizabeth M. Today's Business Letter Writing. (Illus.). 1977. pap. 10.95 (ISBN 0-13-924027-6). P-H.

Baker, Rance G. & Phillips, Billie R. The Sampler: Patterns for Composition. 1979. pap. text ed. 5.95x (ISBN 0-669-02267-5). Heath.

Beach, Mark. Editing Your Own Newsletter: A Guide to Writing, Design & Production. LC 79-55630. (Illus.). 1980. pap. 6.95 (ISBN 0-9602664-2-9). Coast to Coast.

Day, Angell. English Secretary. LC 67-10122. 1967. Repr. of 1599 ed. 35.00 (ISBN 0-8201-1012-4). Schol Facsimiles.

English Language Services. Key to English Letter Writing. (Key to English Ser.). pap. 1.60 (ISBN 0-02-971790-6). Macmillan.

Fruehling, Rosemary T. & Bouchard, Sharon. Art of Writing Effective Letters. 1972. 8.95 (ISBN 0-07-022345-9, GB). McGraw.

Gainsford, Thomas. The Secretaries Study: Directions for the Inditing of Letters. LC 74-80177. (English Experience Ser.: No. 658). 1974. Repr. of 1616 ed. 14.00 (ISBN 90-221-0658-6). Walter J Johnson.

Gilbert, Marilyn B. Communicating by Letter. LC 72-11879. (Self-Teaching Guides Ser.). 256p. 1973. 6.95 (ISBN 0-471-29897-2). Wiley.

Gonshack, Sal & McKenzie, Joanna. Send Me a Letter: A Basic Guide to Letter Writing. (Illus.). 224p. 1982. pap. text ed. 6.95 (ISBN 0-13-806604-3). P-H.

Gordon, Ian. Practical Letter Writing. 1967. pap. text ed. 3.50x (ISBN 0-435-28359-6). Heinemann Ed.

Howard, Godfrey. Getting Through: How to Make Words Work for You. LC 80-66087. 176p. 1980. 11.95 (ISBN 0-7153-7821-X). David & Charles.

Humphreys, G. S. Letter Writer. (Teach Yourself Ser.). 1975. pap. 4.95 (ISBN 0-679-10475-5). McKay.

Ingalls, Edna & Sheff, Alexander L. How to Write Letters for All Occasions. LC 61-10015. 6.95 (ISBN 0-385-08924-4). Doubleday.

Irvine, Lyn. Ten Letter-Writers. 1932. Repr. 30.00 (ISBN 0-8274-2856-1). R West.

Irvine, Lyn L. Ten Letter-Writers. facs. ed. LC 68-16942. (Essay Index Reprint Ser). 1932. 15.00 (ISBN 0-8369-0560-1). Arno.

Johnson, Samuel. New London Letter Writer. LC 73-19893. 1948. lib. bdg. 12.50 (ISBN 0-8414-5281-4). Folcroft.

Kindersley, David. Optical Letterspacing. (Illus.). pap. 11.50 (ISBN 0-913720-05-4). Sandstone.

L'Heureux, Marc. How to Write a Love Letter. 1966. pap. 2.00 (ISBN 0-8065-0119-7). Citadel Pr.

Liles, Parker, et al. Typing Mailable Letters. 3rd ed. Rubin, Audrey, ed. (Illus.). (gr. 9-12). 1978. pap. 4.96 (ISBN 0-07-037855-X, G); solutions manual 3.00 (ISBN 0-07-037856-8). McGraw.

Lyon, Greg & O'Neil, Peggy. I Hate to Write Book. 1980. 2.95 (ISBN 0-8431-0163-6). Price Stern.

McMahan, Elizabeth & Day, Susan. The Writer's Rhetoric & Handbook. (Illus.). 1980. text ed. 9.95x (ISBN 0-07-045421-3); instructor's manual 4.95 (ISBN 0-07-045422-1); wkbk. avail. McGraw.

Martin, George W. Let's Communicate: A Self-Help Program on Writing Letters & Memos. LC 71-109516. (Supervisory Management Ser). 1970. pap. text ed. 8.95 (ISBN 0-201-04500-1). A-W.

Minnick, Sally. Dear World.., 2 vols. LC 80-81165. 212p. (Orig.). 1980. pap. 9.95 (ISBN 0-9604180-0-8, 101). Hard Press'd.

Myers, Alfred S. Letters for All Occasions. (Orig.). 1952. pap. 3.50 (ISBN 0-06-463237-7, EH 237, EH). Har-Row.

Reid, James M. & Wendlinger, Robert M. Effective Letters: A Program for Self-Instruction. 3rd ed. (Illus.). 1978. pap. text ed. 9.95 (ISBN 0-07-051817-3, C); instructor's manual 4.95 (ISBN 0-07-051818-1). McGraw.

Revelis, B. G. Greek-English Letterwriting. 5.00 (ISBN 0-685-09036-1). Divry.

Riebel, John P. How to Write Reports, Papers, Theses Articles. 128p. 1972. lib. bdg. 8.00 (ISBN 0-668-02392-9); pap. 6.00 (ISBN 0-668-02391-0). Arco.

Robertson, Jean. The Art of Letter Writing. LC 74-543. 1942. Repr. lib. bdg. 12.50 (ISBN 0-8414-7289-0). Folcroft.

Russell & Eschenburg. Contemporary Letter Writing. (Illus.). 5.95 (ISBN 0-8208-0336-7). Hearthside.

Saintsbury, George. A Letter Book: Selected with an Introduction on the History & Art of Letter-Writing. 1979. Repr. of 1922 ed. lib. bdg. 25.00 (ISBN 0-8495-5031-9). Arden Lib.

Saville, Tim & Saville, Jenny. The Complete Letter-Writer. (Illus.). text ed. 9.95x (ISBN 0-8464-0267-X); pap. 4.95 (ISBN 0-8464-0272-6). Beekman Pubs.

Seton, George. Gossip About Letters & Letter-Writers. 1979. Repr. of 1870 ed. lib. bdg. 45.00 (ISBN 0-89760-812-7). Dynamic Learn Corp.

Shew-Pincar. Writing Skills. Raygor, Alton L., ed. (Basic Skills Ser.). (Illus.). 1980. pap. 7.95x (ISBN 0-07-056690-9). McGraw.

Shidle, Norman G. Art of Successful Communication: Business & Personal Achievement Through Written Communication. 1965. 17.00 (ISBN 0-07-056798-0, P&RB). McGraw.

Smith, Robert S. Lawyer's Model Letter Book. 1978. 34.95 (ISBN 0-13-526897-4, Busn). P-H.

Valois, Noel. Arte Scribendi Epistolas Apud Gallicos Medii Avei Scriptores Rhetoresve. 1880. 20.50 (ISBN 0-8337-3612-4). B Franklin.

Venolia, Jan. Better Letters: A Handbook of Business & Personal Correspondence. LC 80-82634. (Illus.). 148p. (Orig.). 1981. 9.95 (ISBN 0-9602584-3-4); pap. 5.95 (ISBN 0-9602584-2-6); plastic spiral bdg. 6.95 (ISBN 0-9602584-5-0). Periwinkle Pr.

Villiers, Arnold. Routledge's Complete Letter Writer: For Ladies & Gentlemen in Society, in Love & in Business. rev. ed. 1965. pap. 3.00 (ISBN 0-7100-2238-7). Routledge & Kegan.

Vogel, Erwin. How to Write Collection Letters That Click & Collect (Without Really Crying) (Business Reference Ser.). (Illus.). 22p. (Microfiche avail., ISBN 0-912392-06-1). (gr. 9 up). 1970. pap. 2.40 (ISBN 0-912392-03-7, CL2). Copy-Write.

Watson, Lillian E. The Bantam Book of Correct Letter Writing. abr ed. (gr. 7 up). 1962. pap. 2.75 (ISBN 0-553-14047-7, 12419-6). Bantam.

--Standard Book of Letter Writing & Correct Social Forms. rev. ed. 1958. 10.95 (ISBN 0-13-841627-3). P-H.

LETTERHEADS

Carter, David E., ed. Letterheads-One: The International Annual of Letterhead Design. LC 78-58439. (Illus.). 1977. 30.00 (ISBN 0-910158-42-8). Art Dir.

--Letterheads Two: The Second International Annual of Letterhead Design. LC 78-58439. (Letterheads Ser.). (Illus.). 1979. 30.00 (ISBN 0-910158-57-6). Art Dir.

LETTERING

see also Alphabets; Architectural Inscriptions; Illumination of Books and Manuscripts; Initials; Monograms; Sign Painting

Art of Hebrew Lettering. Date not set. pap. 5.50 (ISBN 0-686-76480-3). Feldheim.

Ballinger, Raymond A. Lettering Art in Modern Use: Student Edition. 1979. pap. 5.95 (ISBN 0-442-26158-6). Van Nos Reinhold.

Bartram, Alan. Fascia Lettering in the British Isles. (Lettering in the British Isles Ser.). (Illus.). 1978. pap. 8.95 (ISBN 0-8230-1640-4). Watson-Guptill.

--Street Name Lettering in the British Isles. (Lettering in the British Isles Ser.). (Illus.). 1978. pap. 8.95 (ISBN 0-8230-4930-2). Watson-Guptill.

Benson, John H. & Carey, A. G. Elements of Lettering. 2nd ed. 1962. text ed. 10.95 (ISBN 0-07-004775-8, G). McGraw.

Benson, John H., tr. First Writing Book: An English Translation & Facsimile Text of Arrighi's Operina. (Illus.). 1966. pap. 3.95 (ISBN 0-300-00020-0, Y178). Yale U Pr.

Bergling, J. M. Art Alphabets & Lettering. 9th ed. Bergling, V. C., ed. LC 67-29582. 1967. 17.95 (ISBN 0-910222-01-0). Gem City Coll.

--Art Monograms & Lettering. 20th ed. Bergling, V. C., ed. LC 63-22577. 1964. 17.95 (ISBN 0-910222-02-9). Gem City Coll.

Biegeleisen, J. I. Design & Print Your Own Posters. (Illus.). 168p. 1976. 15.95 (ISBN 0-8230-1309-X). Watson-Guptill.

Biegeleison, J. I. The ABC of Lettering. 5th, rev., enl. ed. LC 76-5165. (Illus.). 296p. 1976. pap. text ed. 18.50 (ISBN 0-06-010329-9, HarpT). Har-Row.

Biggs, John R. Letter Forms & Lettering. 1977. 6.95 (ISBN 0-8008-4724-5, Pentalic). Taplinger.

Book of Alphabets. 1946. 1.50 (ISBN 0-685-19467-1). Powner.

Camp, Ann. Pen Lettering. pap. 3.95 (ISBN 0-8008-6272-4, Pentalic). Taplinger.

Cataldo, John W. Lettering: A Guide for Teachers. new ed. LC 58-13613. (Illus.). 111p. 1974. 12.95 (ISBN 0-87192-015-8). Davis Mass.

Cavanaugh, J. Albert. Lettering & Alphabets. 1946. pap. 3.00 (ISBN 0-486-20053-1). Dover.

--Lettering & Alphabets. (Illus.). 8.50 (ISBN 0-8446-0541-7). Peter Smith.

Cirillo, Bob & Ahearn, Kevin. Dry Faces. (Illus.). 1978. pap. 7.50 (ISBN 0-910158-37-1). Art Dir.

Claus, James, et al. Psychological Considerations of Lettering for Identification. 47p. 1972. pap. 5.00 (ISBN 0-911380-05-1). Signs of Times.

Degering, Hermann. Lettering: Modes of Writing in Western Europe. 1978. pap. 8.95 (ISBN 0-8008-4727-X, Pentalic). Taplinger.

Douglass, Ralph. Calligraphic Lettering. 3rd ed. 1975. 10.95 (ISBN 0-8230-0551-8); sheet stock avail. Watson-Guptill.

Durer, A. Of the Just Shaping of Letters from the Applied Geometry, Bk. 3. LC 23-671. 1917. 42.00 (ISBN 0-527-25400-2). Kraus Repr.

Durer, Albrecht. Of the Just Shaping of Letters. Nichol, tr. 7.50 (ISBN 0-8446-2016-5). Peter Smith.

--Of the Just Shaping of Letters: From the Applied Geometry of Albrecht Durer, Book 3. Nichol, R. T., tr. (Illus.). 1917. pap. 3.00 (ISBN 0-486-21306-4). Dover.

Evetts, L. C. Roman Lettering. LC 78-72593. 1979. pap. 6.95 (ISBN 0-8008-6822-6, Pentalic). Taplinger.

Gillon, Edmund V., Jr. Pictorial Calligraphy & Ornamentation. (Illus.). 96p. (Orig.). 1972. pap. 3.50 (ISBN 0-486-22788-X). Dover.

Goudy, Frederic W. Alphabet & Elements of Lettering. rev. ed. 8.50 (ISBN 0-8446-2145-5). Peter Smith.

Goudy, Frederick W. Alphabet & Elements of Lettering. (Illus.). 1922. pap. 3.50 (ISBN 0-486-20792-7). Dover.

Gourdie, Tom. Puffin Book of Lettering. (Picture Bks.). 32p. (ps-3). 1962. pap. 1.95 (ISBN 0-14-049117-1, Puffin). Penguin.

Greer, Alan & Greer, Rita. An Introduction to Lettering. (Handbooks Ser). 1978. pap. 3.50 (ISBN 0-14-046329-1). Penguin.

Harvey, A. Lettering Design: Form & Skill in the Design & Use of Letters. 5.98 (ISBN 0-517-31849-0). Bonanza.

Harvey, Michael. Lettering Design. (Illus.). 1976. 10.95 (ISBN 0-517-52744-8). Barre.

Hess, Stanley. The Modification of Letter-Forms. LC 72-85237. (Illus.). 1972. 7.95 (ISBN 0-910158-03-7). Art Dir.

Hewitt, Graily. Lettering. LC 76-26844. (Illus.). 336p. 1981. pap. 9.95 (ISBN 0-8008-4728-8, Pentalic). Taplinger.

Johnson, Robert W. The Letter of the Law & the Lore of the Letter. Hesselton, Catherine A., ed. LC 81-67792. (Illus.). 72p. (Orig.). 1981. pap. 5.95 (ISBN 0-940332-01-9). Alpha Centauri.

Johnston, Edward. Writing & Illuminating & Lettering. 1977. pap. 10.95 (ISBN 0-8008-8731-X, Pentalic). Taplinger.

Klager, Max. Letters, Types & Pictures. (Illus.). 1975. 10.95 (ISBN 0-442-24482-7); pap. 6.95 (ISBN 0-442-24481-9). Van Nos Reinhold.

Krimm, Gerald. A Copperplate Manual: An Introduction to Writing with the Pointed Pen. LC 78-20703. (Illus.). 1979. pap. 3.95 (ISBN 0-8008-1865-2, Pentalic). Taplinger.

Lambert, Frederick. Letter Forms: 110 Complete Alphabets. Menten, Theodore, ed. (Illus.). 8.00 (ISBN 0-8446-4567-2). Peter Smith.

Lesiak, Michaeline. Art of Fine Lettering: Basic Skills & Techniques. 1965. 11.95x (ISBN 0-268-00014-X). U of Notre Dame Pr.

Lettering Techniques. (Bridges for Ideas Handbook Ser.). pap. text ed. 2.50 (ISBN 0-913648-06-X). U Tex Austin Film Lib.

Loewy, E. M. Inschriften Griechischer Bildhauer. 1976. 25.00 (ISBN 0-89005-112-7). Ares.

Mann, William. Lettering & Lettering Display. (Illus.). 96p. 1974. 11.95 (ISBN 0-442-30040-9). Van Nos Reinhold.

Mitchell, Frederick. Practical Lettering & Layout. 2nd ed. (Illus.). 1960. 7.50 (ISBN 0-7136-0569-3). Dufour.

Modern Scribes & Lettering Artists. LC 80-50362. (Illus.). 112p. 1980. 20.00 (ISBN 0-8008-5297-4, Pentalic). Taplinger.

Morison, S. Fra Luca De Pacioli of Borgo S. Sepolcro. 1933. 70.00 (ISBN 0-527-65150-8). Kraus Repr.

Morison, Stanley. Politics & Script: Aspects of Athority & Freedom in the Development of Graeco-Latin Script from the Sixth Century B.C. to the Twentieth Century A.D. Barker, Nicolas, ed. (Lyell Lecture Ser). (Illus.). 1972. 45.00x (ISBN 0-19-818146-9). Oxford U Pr.

Nesbitt, Alexander. The History & Technique of Lettering. Orig. Title: Lettering: The History & Technique of Lettering As Design. 1950. pap. 5.00 (ISBN 0-486-20427-8). Dover.

Neugebauer, Friedrich. The Mystic Art of Written Forms: An Illustrated Handbook for Lettering. Kennett, Bruce, tr. from Ger. (Illus.). 144p. 1980. 23.00 (ISBN 0-907234-00-3, Pub. by Neugebauer Austria). Alphabet Quincy.

Ogg, Oscar, ed. Three Classics of Italian Calligraphy. 1953. pap. 4.50 (ISBN 0-486-20212-7). Dover.

Osley, A. S., ed. Scribes & Sources. LC 79-88418. (Illus.). 1980. 25.00 (ISBN 0-87923-297-8). Godine.

Pen & Brush Lettering & Alphabets. 1960. soft cover 2.95 (ISBN 0-7137-0187-0, Pub by Blandford Pr England). Sterling.

Reynolds, Linda & Barrett, Stephen. Library Signs & Guiding: A Practical Guide to Design & Production. 120p. 1981. 32.50 (ISBN 0-208-01927-8, Linnet). Shoe String.

Ross, George F. Speedball Textbook for Pen & Brush Lettering. 20th ed. 96p. 1973. pap. 2.15 (ISBN 0-685-56768-0). Landau.

Saintsbury, George. A Letter Book. 1977. Repr. of 1922 ed. 25.00 (ISBN 0-89984-107-4). Century Bookbindery.

Schwandner, George. Calligraphy. Orig. Title: Calligraphia Latina. 1958. pap. 6.00 (ISBN 0-486-20475-8). Dover.

Semere, Mario G. A Guide to Hand Lettering. 2nd ed. (Illus.). 1977. pap. text ed. 9.95 (ISBN 0-8403-1780-8). Kendall-Hunt.

Shaw, Paul. Black Letter Primer: An Introduction to Gothic Alphabets. LC 78-20699. (Illus.). 1981. pap. 4.95 (ISBN 0-8008-0808-8, Pentalic). Taplinger.

Switkin, Abraham. Hand Lettering Today. LC 75-25067. (Illus.). 192p. (YA) 1976. 14.95x (ISBN 0-06-014204-9, HarpT). Har-Row.

Thompson, Tommy. Script Letter: Its Form, Construction & Application. 8.00 (ISBN 0-8446-3068-3). Peter Smith.

--Script Lettering for Artists. rev. ed. (Illus.). 1955. pap. 2.75 (ISBN 0-486-21311-0). Dover.

Tory, G., ed. Champ Fleury. Ives, George B., tr. 1927. 70.00 (ISBN 0-527-90600-X). Kraus Repr.

Wotzkow, H. Art of Hand-Lettering: Its Mastery & Practice. (Illus.). 8.00 (ISBN 0-8446-3213-9). Peter Smith.

Wotzkow, Helm. Art of Hand-Lettering: Its Mastery & Practice. (Illus.). (YA) (gr. 9-12). pap. 4.00 (ISBN 0-486-21797-3). Dover.

Wright. Lettering. (Grosset Art Introduction Ser.: Vol. 21). pap. 2.95 (ISBN 0-448-00530-1). G&D.

LETTERS

see also English Letters; French Letters; Love Letters

Adkins, Jan. Letterbox: The Art & History of Letters. (Illus.). (gr. 3-up). 1981. 10.95 (ISBN 0-8027-6385-5); PLB 11.85 (ISBN 0-8027-6386-3). Walker & Co.

Alciphron, et al. Letters: Alciphron, Aelian, Philostratus. Warmington, E. H., ed. (Loeb Classical Library: No. 383). (Gr. & Eng.). 11.00x (ISBN 0-674-99421-3). Harvard U Pr.

Ambrose, St. Complete Letters. (Fathers of the Church Ser.: Vol. 26). 26.00 (ISBN 0-8132-0026-1). Cath U Pr.

Augustine, St. Letters, Nos. 1-82. (Fathers of the Church Ser.: Vol. 12). 22.00 (ISBN 0-8132-0012-1). Cath U Pr.

--Letters, Nos. 131-164. (Fathers of the Church Ser.: Vol. 20). 20.00 (ISBN 0-8132-0020-2). Cath U Pr.

--Letters, Nos. 83-130. (Fathers of the Church Ser.: Vol. 18). 20.00 (ISBN 0-8132-0018-0). Cath U Pr.

Bailey, J. C. Studies in Some Famous Letters. 1972. Repr. of 1899 ed. lib. bdg. 27.50 (ISBN 0-685-28148-5). Folcroft.

Baillie, Robert. Letters & Journals, 3 vols. Laing, David, ed. LC 70-161745. (Bannatyne Club, Edinburgh. Publications: No. 73). Repr. of 1842 ed. Set. 195.00 (ISBN 0-404-52800-7). AMS Pr.

Baring, Maurice. Dead Letters. 1925. 25.00 (ISBN 0-8274-2157-5). R West.

Barker, A. Trevor, compiled by. The Letters of H. P. Blavatsky to A. P. Sinnett. facsimile of 1925 ed. LC 73-84138. 1973. 10.00 (ISBN 0-911500-23-5). Theos U Pr.

--The Mahatma Letters to A. P. Sinnett. facsimile of 1926, 2nd ed. LC 75-10574. 1975. 10.00 (ISBN 0-911500-20-0); pap. 5.95 (ISBN 0-911500-21-9). Theos U Pr.
Barnes, Gilbert H. & Dumond, Dwight L., eds. Letters of Theodore Dwight Weld, Angelina Grimke Weld, & Sarah Grimke. LC 77-121103. (American Public Figures Ser). 1970. Repr. of 1934 ed. lib. bdg. 75.00 (ISBN 0-306-71981-9). Da Capo.
Basil, St. Letters, Nos. 1-185. (Fathers of the Church Ser.: Vol. 13). 18.00 (ISBN 0-8132-0013-X). Cath U Pr.
--Letters, Nos. 186-368. (Fathers of the Church Ser.: Vol. 28). 19.00 (ISBN 0-8132-0028-8). Cath U Pr.
Beaconsfield, B. D. Home Letters. LC 78-137427. Repr. of 1885 ed. 10.00 (ISBN 0-527-06200-6). Kraus Repr.
Bickerstaffe-Drew, Frank. John Ayscough's Letters to His Mother, During 1914, 1915, & 1916. 1919. 15.00 (ISBN 0-932062-07-5). Sharon Hill.
Billington, Ray A. & Whitehill, Walter M., eds. Dear Lady: The Letters of Frederick Jackson Turner & Alice Forbes Perkins Hooper, 1910-1932. LC 76-134261. (Illus.). 1970. 15.00 (ISBN 0-87328-046-6). Huntington Lib.
Block, Michael, compiled by. Letters to Michael: How Women in the Seventies Really Feel, As Revealed in Their Letters to the Man Who Advertised for Wife. LC 78-11128. 1979. 8.95 (ISBN 0-698-10932-5). Coward.
Bode, Carl. The New Mencken Letters. 1977. 19.95 (ISBN 0-8037-1379-7). Dial.
Cannon, James P. Speeches to the Party. LC 73-86189. 352p. 1973. 19.00 (ISBN 0-87348-320-0); pap. 4.95 (ISBN 0-87348-321-9). Path Pr NY.
Carlyle, Thomas. New Letters, 2 Vols. Carlyle, A., ed. (Illus.). 1969. Repr. of 1904 ed. Set. 62.00 (ISBN 3-4870-2525-6). Adler.
Carrol, Donald, ed. Dear, Drop Dead! Hate Mail Through the Ages. 1979. pap. 4.95 (ISBN 0-02-040360-7, Collier). Macmillan.
Carter, Jimmy. Letters to Hon. William Prescott. 1977. lib. bdg. 59.95 (ISBN 0-8490-2156-1). Gordon Pr.
Chapdelaine, Perry A., Sr. & Hay, George, eds. John W. Campbell & L. Ron Hubbard, 3 vols. Incl. Vol. 1. write for info. (ISBN 0-931150-05-1); pap. write for info (ISBN 0-931150-06-X); lib. bdg. write for info. (ISBN 0-931150-07-8); Vol 2. Chapdelaine, Perry A., Sr. & Hay, George, eds. write for info; pap. write for info; lib. bdg. write for info; Vol. 3. Vogt, A. E., ed. write for info (ISBN 0-931150-08-6); pap. write for info (ISBN 0-931150-09-4); lib. bdg. write for info (ISBN 0-931150-10-8). 1981. Authors Co Op.
Cohen, Randy. Modest Proposals: The Official Correspondence of Randy Cohen. 128p. 1981. pap. 3.95 (ISBN 0-312-54365-4). St Martin.
Cresci, Giovan F. Essemplaire Di Piu Sorti Lettere, 1578. Osley, A. S., tr. 1978. 19.95 (ISBN 0-370-00170-2, Pub. by Chatto Bodley Jonathan). Merrimack Bk Serv.
Curtiss, Mina. Other People's Letters: A Memoir. 1978. 9.95 (ISBN 0-395-26291-7). HM.
Cyprian, St. Complete Letters. (Fathers of the Church Ser.: Vol. 51). 19.00 (ISBN 0-8132-0051-2). Cath U Pr.
Deffand, Madame du. Letters to & from Madame Du Deffand & Julie De Lespinasse. limited ed. Smith, W. H., ed. 1938. 24.50x (ISBN 0-685-69810-6). Elliots Bks.
Degas, Edgar G. Degas Letters. Guerin, Marcel, ed. Kay, Marguerite, tr. (Illus.). 12.50 (ISBN 0-912158-53-0). Hennessey.
De Salvatierra, Juan M. Selected Letters. Burrus, Ernest, ed. (Baja California Travels Ser.: No. 25). 1972. 20.00 (ISBN 0-87093-225-X). Dawsons.
D'Holbach, Paul H. A Letter from Thrasybus to Leucippe. 59.95 (ISBN 0-8490-0508-6). Gordon Pr.
--Letters to Eugenia. 59.95 (ISBN 0-8490-0514-0). Gordon Pr.
Dods, Marcus. Later Letters of Marcus Dods,D. D. 1895-1909. 1911. 25.00 (ISBN 0-932062-46-6). Sharon Hill.
Doty, William G. Letters in Primitive Christianity. Via, Dan O., Jr., ed. LC 72-87058. (Guides to Biblical Scholarship: New Testament Ser.). 96p. 1973. pap. 3.25 (ISBN 0-8006-0170-X, 1-170). Fortress.
Doucet, Jacques. Cataloguede Fonds Speciauxde la Bibliotheque Litteraire Jacques Doucet (Paris, France) (Lettres a Andre Gide). 1972. 90.00 (ISBN 0-8161-0951-6). G K Hall.
Duncan, Jane. Letter from Reachfar. LC 75-13787. (Illus.). 164p. 1976. 7.95 (ISBN 0-312-48230-2). St Martin.
Emmons, Andrea L. Letters I Wish I'd Mailed to the Man Who Divorced Me to Marry a Waitress. 1978. pap. 1.50 (ISBN 0-8439-0537-9, Leisure Bks). Nordon Pubns.
Erikson, Alvar, ed. Letters from Erik Benzelius the Younger from Learned Foreigners, 2 vols. Orig. Title: Acta Regiae Societatis Scientarium et Literarum. (Orig.). 1980. 31.00 (ISBN 0-686-77483-3). Vol. 1, 1697-1722. Vol. 2, 1723-1743 (ISBN 91-85252-22-0). Humanities.
Fedorovna, Alexandra. The Letters of the Tsaritsa to the Tsar (1914-1916) (Special Project). 1973. Repr. 10.95 (ISBN 0-8179-9992-2). Hoover Inst Pr.
Flaubert, Gustave. Selected Letters. facsimile ed. Steegmuller, Francis, tr. LC 78-160919. (Biography Index Reprint Ser.). Repr. of 1953 ed. 17.50 (ISBN 0-8369-8082-4). Arno.
Garab, Arra M. Beyond Byzantium: The Last Phase of Yeats's Career. LC 74-85148. 1969. 8.50 (ISBN 0-87580-012-2). N Ill U Pr.
Garner, William R. Letters from California, 1846-1847. Craig, Donald M., ed. LC 71-124736. (Illus.). 1970. 19.95 (ISBN 0-520-01565-7). U of Cal Pr.
Geiger, Maynard, tr. Letters of Alfred Robinson to the De la Guerra Family of Santa Barbara 1834-1873. 1972. 10.00 (ISBN 0-87093-162-8). Dawsons.
Gippius, Zinaida. Pis'ma K Berberovoi I Khodasevichu. Sheikholeslami, Erika F., ed. (Rus.). 1978. pap. 3.00 (ISBN 0-88233-298-8). Ardis Pubs.
Gissing, George. Letters of George Gissing to Gabrielle Fleury. Coustillas, Pierre, ed. LC 64-8185. 1965. 11.000 (ISBN 0-87104-106-5); pap. 8.50 (ISBN 0-87104-105-7). NY Pub Lib.
Goodall, Blake. The Homilies of St. John Chrysostom on the Letters of St. Paul to Titus & Philemon. (Univ. of California Publications in Classical Studies: Vol. 20). 1979. 12.00x (ISBN 0-520-09596-0). U of Cal Pr.
Gottlieb, Nora & Chapman, Raymond, eds. Letters to an Actress: The Story of Turgenev & Savina. LC 73-92898. 155p. 1973. 8.95 (ISBN 0-8214-0146-7). Ohio U Pr.
Grant, U. S. Letters of Ulysses S. Grant to His Father & His Youngest Sister. LC 12-24177. Repr. of 1912 ed. 10.00 (ISBN 0-527-35350-7). Kraus Repr.
Graziano, Robert. Telling It Like It Is. 1981. 6.95 (ISBN 0-533-04858-3). Vantage.
Haab, Armin, et al. Lettera, 4 vols. Date not set. pap. 25.00 ea. Vol. 1 (ISBN 0-8038-4233-3). Vol. 2 (ISBN 0-8038-4232-5). Vol. 3 (ISBN 0-8038-4231-7). Vol. 4 (ISBN 0-8038-4331-3). Set. pap. 82.50 (ISBN 0-8038-4331-3). Hastings.
Haines, Gregory, et al. The Eye of Faith: The Pastoral Letters of John Bede Polding. new ed. text ed. 45.00 (ISBN 0-909706-62-X, Lowden Pub). Bks Australia.
Hall, Rupert A. & Hall, Marie B., trs. Correspondence of Henry Oldenburg, 9 vols. Incl. Vol 1. 1641-1662. 1965 (ISBN 0-299-03760-6); Vol 2. 1663-1665. 1966 (ISBN 0-299-03770-3); Vol. 3. 1666-1667. 1966 (ISBN 0-299-03780-0); Vol. 4. 1667-1668. 1967 (ISBN 0-299-04650-8); Vol. 5. 1668-1669. 1968 (ISBN 0-299-04890-X); Vol. 6. 1669-1670. 1969 (ISBN 0-299-05280-X); Vol. 7. 1670-1671. 1970 (ISBN 0-299-05630-9); Vol. 8. 1671-1672. 1971 (ISBN 0-299-05950-2); Vol. 9. 1672-1673. 1973. 30.00 (ISBN 0-299-06390-9). (Illus.). 30.00x ea. U of Wis Pr.
Harding, Rachel & Dyson, Mary. A Book of Condolenses from the Private Letters of Illustrious People. 192p. 1981. price not set (ISBN 0-8264-0053-1). Continuum.
Harelson, Randy. SWAK: The Complete Book of Mail Fun for Kids. LC 80-54624. (Illus.). 160p. (gr. 3-7). 1981. pap. 3.95 (ISBN 0-89480-150-3). Workman Pub.
Hayes, R. B. Diary & Letters of Rutherford Birchard Hayes, Nineteenth President of the United States, 5 vols. Repr. of 1922 ed. Set. 155.00 (ISBN 0-527-38920-X). Kraus Repr.
Hoge, James O. & Olney, Clarke, eds. The Letters of Caroline Norton to Lord Melbourne. LC 74-12344. (Illus.). 1974. 10.75 (ISBN 0-8142-0208-X). Ohio St U Pr.
Hoover, Paul. Letter to Einstein Beginning Dear Albert. LC 79-12329. 1979. 3.00 (ISBN 0-916328-12-0, Pub. by Yellow Pr). SBD.
Ingpen, Ada M., ed. Women As Letter Writers. 444p. 1981. Repr. of 1909 ed. lib. bdg. 40.00 (ISBN 0-89760-376-1). Telegraph Bks.
Jordan, De Esta, ed. Letters. 1979. 7.95 (ISBN 0-533-03928-2). Vantage.
Judd, Jacob, ed. Correspondence of the Van Cortlandt Family of Cortlandt Manor 1814-1848. LC 80-22763. (The Van Cortlandt Family Papers: Vol. IV). 653p. 1981. 27.00 (ISBN 0-912882-41-7). Sleepy Hollow.
Keane, John B. Letters of a Successful T. D. 87p. 1967. pap. 3.95 (ISBN 0-85342-094-7). Irish Bk Ctr.
--Letters of an Irish Publican. 88p. 1974. pap. 3.95 (ISBN 0-85342-390-3). Irish Bk Ctr.
Kneass, Jack & Myers, Marv. Ask Aunt Gabby. LC 70-154316. (Illus., Orig.). 1971. pap. 2.95 (ISBN 0-87593-082-4). Trail-R.
Kraske, Robert. The Twelve Million Dollar Note: Strange but True Stories of Notes Found in Seagoing Bottles. LC 77-24164. (gr. 5-8). 1977. 6.95 (ISBN 0-525-66575-7). Elsevier-Nelson.
Kriloff, Lou. Letterpower in Action, 12 vols. pap. 16.80 boxed (ISBN 0-911744-53-3). Career Inst.
Lane, Anne W. & Wall, Louise H., eds. The Letters of Franklin K. Lane: Personal & Political. 473p. 1980. Repr. of 1922 ed. lib. bdg. 25.00 (ISBN 0-89984-320-4). Century Bookbindery.
Lang, Andrew. Letters to Dead Authors. 1973. lib. bdg. 15.00 (ISBN 0-8414-5773-5). Folcroft.
Lehman, John. The Craft of Letters in England. 1973. lib. bdg. 20.00 (ISBN 0-8414-5850-2). Folcroft.
Leo The Great, St. Selected Letters. (Fathers of the Church Ser: Vol. 34). 15.00 (ISBN 0-8132-0034-2). Cath U Pr.
Lindeboom, G. A. The Letters of Jan Swammerdam to Melchisedec Thevenot, with English Translation & a Biographical Sketch. 202p. 1975. text ed. 47.50 (ISBN 90-265-0222-2, Pub. by Swets Pub Serv Holland). Swets North Am.
Lucas, E. V. The Gentlest Art. 422p. 1981. Repr. of 1913 ed. lib. bdg. 25.00 (ISBN 0-89987-509-2). Darby Bks.
Mabbott, Thomas O. The Letters from George W. Eveleth to Edgar Allan Poe. LC 73-4872. 1973. lib. bdg. 10.00 (ISBN 0-8414-5915-0). Folcroft.
Miller, Henry & Childs, J. Rives. Collector's Quest: The Correspondence of Henry Miller & J. Rives Childs, 1947-1965. Wood, Richard C., ed. LC 67-28795. 1968. 6.00x (ISBN 0-8139-0180-4). U Pr of Va.
Mitchell, Donald G. American Lands & Letters, 2 vols. 1973. Set. lib. bdg. 40.00 (ISBN 0-8414-6625-4). Folcroft.
Monroe, James. Calender of the Correspondence of James Monroe. new ed. Repr. of 1902 ed. 18.00 (ISBN 0-527-64500-1). Kraus Repr.
Nachalo, Sophia & Vochek, Yarostan. Letters of Insurgents. 1976. 6.75 (ISBN 0-934868-13-1). Black & Red.
Netanyahu, Benjamin & Netanyahu, Iddo, eds. Self-Portrait of a Hero: The Letters of Jonathan Netanyahu (1963-1976) 1981. 12.95 (ISBN 0-394-51376-2). Random.
Pacific Northwest Letters of Geo Gibbs, 1850-53. 54p. 2.95 (ISBN 0-87595-018-3); pap. 1.95 (ISBN 0-686-75144-2). Oreg Hist Soc.
Petrus De Hallis. Summa De Literis Missilibus. Repr. of 1853 ed. pap. 19.00 (ISBN 0-384-46030-5). Johnson Repr.
Philpot, Joseph C. Letters & Memoir of Joseph Charles Philpot. (Giant Summit Ser.). 568p. 1981. pap. 9.95 (ISBN 0-8010-7060-0). Baker Bk.
Potter, Stephen, ed. Minnow Among Tritons: Mrs. S. T. Coleridge's Letters to Thomas Poole, 1799-1834. LC 73-21992. 1934. lib. bdg. 13.75 (ISBN 0-685-01316-2). Folcroft.
Powell, Maude & Powell, Ralph. Eternally Yours: A Legacy of Letters. Lewis, Rose, ed. LC 79-56761. (Illus.). 320p. 1979. 10.00 (ISBN 0-914064-14-2); pap. 10.00 (ISBN 0-914064-15-0). Celo Pr.
Prophet, Elizabeth C., ed. Pearls of Wisdom 1968, Vol. 11. LC 78-64502. 9.95 (ISBN 0-916766-33-0). Summit Univ.
Prophet, Mark & Prophet, Elizabeth C., eds. Pearls of Wisdom 1970, Vol. 13. LC 78-60615. 9.95 (ISBN 0-916766-32-2). Summit Univ.
Richardson, Samuel. Familiar Letters on Important Occasions. LC 73-14753. 1938. Repr. lib. bdg. 30.00 (ISBN 0-8414-7246-7). Folcroft.
Rickwood, Edgell. Calendar of Modern Letters, 3 vols. Garman, D., ed. 1966. Repr. 175.00x set (ISBN 0-7146-2104-8, F Cass Co). Biblio Dist.
Rilke, Rainer M. Letters of Rainer Maria Rilke, 2 vols. Greene, Jane B. & Norton, M. D., trs. Incl. Vol. 1. 1892-1910; Vol. 2. 1910-1926. (Illus.). Set. 22.50 (ISBN 0-8446-2809-3). Peter Smith.
Robinson, Edwin A. Untriangulated Stars: Letters of Edwin Arlington Robinson to Harry de Forest Smith, 1890-1905. Sutcliffe, Denham, ed. LC 76-113064. (Illus.). xxvii, 348p. Repr. of 1947 ed. lib. bdg. 18.75x (ISBN 0-8371-4704-2, ROUS). Greenwood.
Rolfe, Frederick. Letters to Harry Bainbridge. Corvo, Baron, ed. 1977. 10.00 (ISBN 0-685-85029-3, Pub. by Enitharmon Pr). SBD.
Schuster, M. Lincoln, ed. Treasury of the World's Great Letters: From Ancient Days to Our Own Time. 1960. pap. 3.45 (ISBN 0-671-76001-7, Fireside). S&S.
Selections from the Letters of Abdu'l-Baha. 309p. (Persian.). 1980. 12.95 (ISBN 0-87743-157-4, 406-046-89); pap. 6.95 (ISBN 0-87743-158-2, 406-047-89). Baha'i.
Shelley, Percy B. Lost Letters to Harriet. LC 72-2571. (Select Bibliographies Reprint Ser). 1972. Repr. of 1929 ed. 12.00 (ISBN 0-8369-6864-6). Arno.
Silver, Rollo G. Letters Written by Walt Whitman to His Mother. LC 77-7610. 1936. lib. bdg. 12.50 (ISBN 0-8414-7571-7). Folcroft.
Smith, Audley L. Richard Hurd's Letters on Chivalry & Romance. 1939. lib. bdg. 8.50 (ISBN 0-8414-7540-7). Folcroft.
Smith, Sydney. Letters of Peter Plymley. LC 72-11. (Select Bibliographies Reprint Ser). 1972. Repr. of 1929 ed. 15.25 (ISBN 0-8369-9972-X). Arno.
Snow, Horace. Dear Charlie. (Illus.). 1979. softcover 3.95 (ISBN 0-914330-22-5). Pioneer Pub Co.
Springer, Edward, ed. The Penthouse Letters. 1977. pap. 2.95 (ISBN 0-446-33025-6). Warner Bks.
Stephens, Fran C., compiled by. The Hartley Coleridge Letters: A Calendar & Index. LC 76-620064. (Tower Bibliographical Ser: No. 15). 1979. 18.50 (ISBN 0-87959-078-5). U of Tex Hum Res.
Swisshelm, Jane G. Crusader & Feminist: Letters of Jane Grey Swisshelm, 1858-1865. LC 74-33957. (Pioneers of the Woman's Movement: an International Perspective Ser.). ix, 327p. 1976. Repr. of 1934 ed. 25.00 (ISBN 0-88355-276-0). Hyperion Conn.
Teresa, Saint The Letters of St. Teresa, 4 vols. Gasquet, Cardinal, ed. 1977. Set. lib. bdg. 400.00 (ISBN 0-8490-2154-5). Gordon Pr.
The Three Literary Letters. LC 76-115235. 1976. Repr. of 1901 ed. lib. bdg. 17.00 (ISBN 0-403-00422-5). Scholarly.
Tracy, James D., ed. True Ocean Found: Paludanus's Letters on Dutch Voyages to the Kara Sea, 1595-1596. LC 80-13962. (A Publication from the James Ford Bell Library at the University of Minnesota). (Illus.). 1980. 10.00x (ISBN 0-8166-0961-6). U of Minn Pr.
Twitchell, Paul. Letters to Gail, 2 vols. 1977. Vol. 1 1973. 9.95 ea. (ISBN 0-914766-12-0); Vol. 2 1977. (ISBN 0-914766-33-3). IWP Pub.
Valentine, Alan C., ed. Fathers to Sons: Advice Without Consent. 1963. 12.95x (ISBN 0-8061-0586-0). U of Okla Pr.
Vaughan Williams, Ralph & Holst, Gustav. Heirs & Rebels: Letters Written to Each Other & Occasional Writings on Music. Vaughan Williams, Ursula & Holst, Imogen, eds. LC 80-12245. (Illus.). xiii, 111p. 1980. Repr. of 1959 ed. lib. bdg. 16.50x (ISBN 0-313-22384-X, VWHR). Greenwood.
Walpole, Horace. Selected Letters. Hadley, W., ed. 1959. 8.95x (ISBN 0-460-00775-0, Evman). Biblio Dist.
Ward, Catherine C. & Ward, Robert E., eds. The Letters of Charles O'Conor of Belanagare: Vol. 1, 1731-1771. LC 80-11602. 346p. 1980. 25.00 (ISBN 0-8357-0508-0, SS-00128). Univ Microfilms.
Weir, Robert M. The Letters of Freeman, Etc. (Tricentennial Edition Ser.: No. 6). 1977. 14.95x (ISBN 0-87249-260-5). U of SC Pr.
Witte, John, ed. Pioneer Letters: The Letter As Literature. LC 81-1903. (Illus.). 1981. pap. 6.95 (ISBN 0-918402-05-0). NW Review Bks.
Wright, James & Wright, Ann. The Summers of James & Annie Wright. 100p. (Orig.). 1980. 10.95 (ISBN 0-935296-17-4); pap. 5.95 (ISBN 0-935296-18-2). Sheep Meadow.
Zytaruk, George J., ed. The Quest for Rananim: D.H. Lawrence's Letters to S.S. Koteliansky, 1914-1930. 1970. 14.00 (ISBN 0-7735-0054-5). McGill-Queens U Pr.

LETTERS, PAPAL

Epistulae Imperatorum Pontificum Aliorum Inde Ab Anno. 367 Usque Ad Annum 553 Datae Avellana Quae Dicitur Collectio, 2 Pts. 1895-1898. 41.50 ea. (ISBN 0-384-14515-9). Johnson Repr.

LETTERS IN MANUSCRIPT

see Autographs

LETTERS OF CREDIT

Harffeld, Henry. Bank Credits & Acceptances. 5th ed. (Illus.). 363p. 1974. 27.50 (ISBN 0-471-06564-1). Ronald Pr.
Policano, Dominick J. Letter of Credit Guidebook. LC 81-66568. (Illus., Orig.). 1981. pap. 4.00 (ISBN 0-9606022-0-8). Exec Ed Pr.

LETTERS OF MARQUE

see Privateering

LETTERS OF THE ALPHABET

see Alphabet

LEUCEMIA

see Leukemia

LEUCOCYTES

see also Eosinophiles; Granulocytes; Lymphocytes; Mast Cells

Boggs, Dane R. & Winkelstein, Alan. White Cell Manual. 3rd ed. 78p. 1975. pap. text ed. 3.00 (ISBN 0-8036-0960-4). Davis Co.
Cline, Martin, ed. Leukocyte Function, Vol. 3. (Methods in Hematology). (Illus.). 224p. 1981. lib. bdg. write for info. (ISBN 0-686-28872-6). Churchill.

Cline, Martin J. The White Cell. LC 74-25998. (Commonwealth Fund Publications Ser). (Illus.). 608p. 1975. text ed. 35.00x (ISBN 0-674-95142-5). Harvard U Pr.
Eijsvoogel, Vincent P., et al, eds. Leukocyte Membrane Determinants Regulating Immune Reactivity. 1976. 51.00 (ISBN 0-12-233750-6). Acad Pr.
Fulop. Alloantigen Systems of Human Leucocytes & Platelets. 1979. 32.00 (ISBN 0-9960015-2-2, Pub. by Kaido Hungary). Heyden.
Fulop-Aszodi, Lili. Alloantigen Systems of Human Leucocytes & Platelets. Farkas, E., tr. from Hungarian. (Illus.). 336p. 1979. 32.50x (ISBN 963-05-1721-3). Intl Pubns Serv.
Gallin, John I. & Quie, Paul G., eds. Leukocyte Chemotaxis: Methods, Physiology, & Clinical Implications. LC 76-58053. 442p. 1978. 42.50 (ISBN 0-89004-198-9). Raven.
Goldman, J. M. & Lowenthal, R. M., eds. Leucocytes: Separation Collection & Transfusion. 1976. 79.50 (ISBN 0-12-288550-3). Acad Pr.
Klebanoff, S. & Clark, R. A. The Neutrophil: Function & Clinical Disorders. 1978. 162.50 (ISBN 0-444-80020-4, Biomedical Pr). Elsevier.
Leucocyte Culture Conference, Fourth, Hanover, New Hampshire, June 1969. Proceeedings. Mc Intyre, O. Ross, ed. LC 69-19545. 581p. 1971. 49.50 (ISBN 0-306-50084-1, Plenum Pr). Plenum Pub.
Leucocyte Culture Conference, Seventh, Universite Laval, June, 1972. Proceedings. Daguillard, Fritz, ed. 1973. 55.00 (ISBN 0-12-200450-7). Acad Pr.
Leukocyte Culture Conference, 5th. Proceedings. Harris, Jules, ed. 1971. 54.00 (ISBN 0-12-327050-2). Acad Pr.
Leukocyte Culture Conference, 6th. Proceedings. Schwarz, M. Roy, ed. 1972. 58.50 (ISBN 0-12-633150-2). Acad Pr.
Lindahl & Osaba, David, eds. Lymphocyte Recognition & Effector Mechanisms. 1974. 51.50 (ISBN 0-12-450250-4). Acad Pr.
Murphy, Patrick. The Neutrophil. LC 76-29007. (Illus.). 217p. 1976. 24.50 (ISBN 0-306-30951-3, Plenum Pr). Plenum Pub.
Parwaresch, M. R. The Human Blood Basophil. 1976. 41.80 (ISBN 0-387-07649-2). Springer-Verlag.
Polliack, A. Normal, Transformed & Leukemic Leukocytes: A Scanning Electron Microscopy Atlas. (Illus.). 1977. 50.40 (ISBN 0-387-08376-6). Springer-Verlag.
Quastel, Michael R., ed. Cell Biology & Immunology of Leukocyte Function. LC 79-11926. 1979. 55.00 (ISBN 0-12-569650-7). Acad Pr.
Van Arman, C. Gordon, ed. White Cells in Inflammation. (Illus.). 160p. 1974. text ed. 19.00 (ISBN 0-398-03120-7). C C Thomas.

LEUCODYSTROPHY

Kretschmer, V. Leukozytenseparation und Transfusion. (Beitraege Zu Infusionstherapie und Klinische Ernaehrung Ser.: Vol. 6). (Illus.). viii, 188p. 1981. 36.00 (ISBN 3-8055-1946-X). S Karger.

LEUKEMIA

Bachmann, Peter A., ed. Leukaemias, Lymphomas & Papillomas: Comparative Aspects. (Munich Symposia on Microbiology). (Illus.). 273p. (Orig.). 1980. pap. text ed. 26.00 (ISBN 0-85066-213-3, Pub. by Taylor & Francis England). J K Burgess.
Baker, Lynn S. You & Leukemia: A Day at a Time. LC 77-27744. 1978. pap. text ed. 7.95 (ISBN 0-7216-1495-7). Saunders.
Bentvelzen, P. & Hilgers, J., eds. Advances in Comparative Leukemia Research 1977. 1978. 68.50 (ISBN 0-444-80042-5, North-Holland). Elsevier.
Bessis, M., ed. Unclassifiable Leukemias. (Illus.). 270p. 1975. pap. 25.00 (ISBN 0-387-07242-X). Springer-Verlag.
Bluefarb, Samuel M. Leukemia Cutis. (American Lecture Dermatology). (Illus.). 536p. 1960. pap. 44.50 (ISBN 0-398-00176-6). C C Thomas.
Broder, L. E. & Carter, S. K. Meningeal Leukemia. LC 74-190394. 132p. 1972. 25.00 (ISBN 0-306-30594-1, Plenum Pr). Plenum Pub.
Catovsky, Daniel. The Leukemic Cell, Vol. 2. (Methods in Haematology). (Illus.). 230p. 1981. lib. bdg. 35.00 (ISBN 0-443-01911-8). Churchill.
Cawley, J. C., et al, eds. Hairy Cell Leukaemia. (Recent Results in Cancer Research Ser.: Vol. 72). (Illus.). 180p. 1980. 33.00 (ISBN 0-387-09920-4). Springer-Verlag.
Dameshek, William & Dutcher, Raymond M., eds. Perspectives in Leukemia. LC 67-26211. (A Leukemia Society Symposium). (Illus.). 312p. 1968. 54.75 (ISBN 0-8089-0108-7). Grune.
Durant, John R. & Smalley, Richard V. The Chronic Leukemias: Chemistry, Pathophysiology & Treatment. (Amer. Lec. Living Chemistry Ser). (Illus.). 240p. 1972. 19.75 (ISBN 0-398-02275-5). C C Thomas.
European Organization for Research on Treatment of Cancer, Plenary Session, Paris, 1969. Advances in the Treatment of Acute (Blastic) Leukemias: Proceedings. Mathe, G., ed. LC 71-117717. (Recent Results in Cancer Research: Vol. 30). (Illus.). xi, 177p. 1970. 24.90 (ISBN 0-387-04995-9). Springer-Verlag.
Fairley, G. Hamilton, et al. Leukemia & Lymphoma. LC 74-26642. 238p. 1974. Repr. 36.00 (ISBN 0-8089-0858-8). Grune.
Felix, H., et al. Dynamic Morphology of Leukemia Cells: A Comparative Study by Scanning Electron Microscopy & Microcinematography. (Illus.). 1978. 56.70 (ISBN 0-387-08495-9). Springer-Verlag.
Freireich, Emil J., et al, eds. Leukemia & Lymphoma. 368p. 1978. 36.00 (ISBN 0-8089-1166-X). Grune.
Goldstone, A. H., et al. Leukaemias, Lymphomas & Allied Disorders. LC 75-44603. (Illus.). 1976. text ed. 18.50 (ISBN 0-7216-4149-0). Saunders.
Gunz, Frederick W. & Baikie, A. G., eds. Leukemia. rev. 3rd ed. LC 74-13366. 864p. 1974. 79.50 (ISBN 0-8089-0843-X). Grune.
Huggins, Charles B. Experimental Leukemia & Mammary Cancer: Induction, Prevention, Cure. LC 78-25790. (Illus.). 1979. lib. bdg. 20.00x (ISBN 0-226-35860-7). U of Chicago Pr.
International Symposium on Comparative Leukemia Research, 4th, Cherry Hill, N.J., 1969. Comparative Leukemia Research, 1969: Proceedings. Dutcher, R. M., ed. (Bibliotheca Haematologica: No. 36). 1970. 93.50 (ISBN 3-8055-1160-4). S Karger.
International Symposium on Comparative Leukemia Research, 5th, Padova-Venice, 1971. Unifying Concepts of Leukemia: Proceedings. Dutcher, R. M., ed. (Bibliotheca Haematologica: No. 39). 1973. 135.50 (ISBN 3-8055-1383-6). S Karger.
International Symposium on Radiation-Induced Leukemogenesis & Related Viruses, Bordeaux, Dec. 1976. Radiation-Induced Leukemogenesis & Related Viruses: Proceedings. Duplan, J. F., ed. (INSERM Symposia: Vol. 4). 1977. 35.75 (ISBN 0-7204-0634-X, North-Holland). Elsevier.
Kass, Lawrence. Leukemia: Cytology & Cytochemistry. (Illus.). 272p. 1981. text ed. price not set (ISBN 0-397-50463-2, JBL-Med-Nursing). Har-Row.
--Preleukemic Disorders. (Illus.). 200p. 1979. 21.75 (ISBN 0-398-03796-5). C C Thomas.
Kass, Lawrence & Schnitzer, Bertram. Monocytes, Monocytosis & Monocytic Leukemia. (Illus.). 120p. 1973. 23.75 (ISBN 0-398-02883-4). C C Thomas.
Knapp, W., ed. Leukemia Markers. 1981. write for info. (ISBN 0-12-416750-0). Acad Pr.
Lascari, Andre D. Leukemia in Childhood. (Illus.). 504p. 1973. 22.75 (ISBN 0-398-02810-9). C C Thomas.
Leukaemia & Aleukaemia: Mortality Statistics, 1950-1966. (World Health Statistics Ser: Vol. 22, No. 10). 51p. 1969. pap. 5.60 (ISBN 0-686-09010-1, 1073). World Health.
Liss, Robert E. Fading Rainbow. LC 79-25812. (Illus.). 1980. 9.95 (ISBN 0-416-00631-0). Methuen Inc.
McCredie, Kenneth B., ed. Diagnosis & the Management of the Leukemias. (M. D. Anderson Ser. on the Diagnosis & Management of Cancer). 1981. write for info. (ISBN 0-89004-323-X, 472). Raven.
Mathe, G., ed. Nomenclature, Methodology & Results of Clinical Trials in Acute Leukemias. (Recent Results in Cancer Research: Vol. 43). (Illus.). 168p. 1974. 39.30 (ISBN 0-387-06401-X). Springer-Verlag.
Neth, R., ed. Modern Trends in Human Leukemia IV: Latest Results. (Haematology & Blood Transfusion Supplement Ser.: No. 26). (Illus.). 650p. 1981. pap. 80.00 (ISBN 0-387-10622-7). Springer-Verlag.
Neth, R., et al, eds. Modern Trends in Human Leukemia Three. (Illus.). 1979. 73.20 (ISBN 0-387-08999-3). Springer-Verlag.
Neth, Rolf, et al, eds. Modern Trends in Human Leukemia. (Illus.). 372p. 1971. 65.00 (ISBN 0-8089-0852-9). Grune.
O'Kunewick, James P. & Meredith, Ruby F., eds. Graft vs. Leukemia in Man & Animal Models. 304p. 1981. 74.95 (ISBN 0-8493-5745-4). CRC Pr.
Olsen, Richard G., ed. Feline Leukemia. 176p. 1981. 54.95 (ISBN 0-8493-6070-6). CRC Pr.
Pochedly, C, ed. Acute Childhood Leukemia. (Modern Problems in Paediatrics: Vol. 16). (Illus.). viii, 214p. 1975. 56.50 (ISBN 3-8055-2065-4). S Karger.
Pochedly, Carl. The Child with Leukemia. (Illus.). 312p. 1973. text ed. 15.25 (ISBN 0-398-02735-8). C C Thomas.
--Leukemia & Lymphoma in the Nervous System. (Illus.). 248p. 1977. 30.00 (ISBN 0-685-73596-6). C C Thomas.
Polliack, A. Normal, Transformed & Leukemic Leukocytes: A Scanning Electron Microscopy Atlas. (Illus.). 1977. 50.40 (ISBN 0-387-08376-6). Springer-Verlag.
Rosenfield, Nancy S. The Radiology of Childhood Leukemia & Its Therapy. (Illus.). 164p. 1981. 17.50 (ISBN 0-87527-173-1). Green.
Rubin, Arnold & Waxman, Samuel. The Leukemia Cell. (Uniscience Ser.). 192p. 1979. 59.95 (ISBN 0-8493-5009-3). CRC Pr.
Sanberg, A. A. The Chromosomes in Human Cancer & Leukemia. LC 79-22474. 776p. 1979. 97.50 (ISBN 0-444-00289-8, North Holland). Elsevier.
Schmalzl, F., ed. Preleukemia International Workshop. (Illus.). 200p. 1980. pap. 26.40 (ISBN 0-387-09698-1). Springer-Verlag.
Symposium on Comparative Leukemia Research, 7th International, Copenhagen, October, 1975. Comparative Leukemia Research 1975: Proceedings. Clemmesen, J., et al, eds. (Bibliotheca Haemalologica: No. 43). (Illus.). 600p. 1976. 127.75 (ISBN 0-8055-2316-2). S Karger.
Thierfelder, S., et al, eds. Immunological Diagnosis of Leukemias & Lymphomas. (Haematologie und Bluttransfusion: Vol. 20). 1977. soft cover 43.80 (ISBN 0-387-08216-6). Springer-Verlag.
Ultmann, J. E., et al, eds. Current Concepts in the Management of Lymphoma & Leukemia. LC 71-146232. (Recent Results in Cancer Research: Vol. 36). (Illus.). 1971. 28.60 (ISBN 0-387-05309-3). Springer-Verlag.
Yamamoto & Sugano, eds. Experimental Leukemogenesis. (Gann Monograph on Cancer Research Ser.: No. 12). 1972. 49.50 (ISBN 0-8391-0650-5). Univ Park.

LEUKEMIA-PERSONAL NARRATIVES

Alsop, Stewart. Stay of Execution: A Sort of Memoir. LC 73-13691. 1973. 9.95 (ISBN 0-397-00897-X). Har-Row.
Bloch, Alice. Lifetime Guarantee. (Orig.). 1981. pap. 6.95 (ISBN 0-930436-09-1). Persephone.
Fox, Ray E. Angela Ambrosia. LC 78-20386. 1979. 7.95 (ISBN 0-394-50096-2). Knopf.
Liss, Robert E. Fading Rainbow. LC 79-25812. (Illus.). 1980. 9.95 (ISBN 0-416-00631-0). Methuen Inc.
Lund, Doris. Eric. LC 74-7061. 1974. 11.95 (ISBN 0-397-01046-X). Har-Row.
Sanderlin, Owenita. Johnny. LC 68-27234. (YA) 1968. 7.95 (ISBN 0-498-06766-1); pap. 3.95 (ISBN 0-498-02400-8). A S Barnes.

LEUKOPLAKIA

Welsh, Ashton L. Differential Diagnosis of Leukoplakia, Leukokeratosis & Cancer in the Mouth. (American Lecture Dermatology). 80p. 1955. pap. 9.75 (ISBN 0-398-04426-0). C C Thomas.

LEUKOTOMY

see Frontal Lobotomy

LEVANT

Here are entered works which treat of the Mediterranean countries east of the Adriatic, Greece, Asia Minor, Armenia, Syria, Palestine, Egypt, Cyprus, Rhodes.
see also Latin Orient; Near East

Charriere, Ernest, compiled by. Negociations de la France dans le Levant, 4 Vols. 1965. Repr. of 1848 ed. Set. 261.00 (ISBN 0-8337-0544-X). B Franklin.
Kohn, Hans. Western Civilization in the Near East. Dickes, E. W., tr. LC 37-23489. Repr. of 1936 ed. 10.00 (ISBN 0-404-03739-9). AMS Pr.
Montagu, Mary W. Letters from the Levant: During the Embassy to Constantinople 1716-18. LC 71-135825. (Eastern Europe Collection Ser). 1970. Repr. of 1838 ed. 16.00 (ISBN 0-405-02767-2). Arno.
Patai, Raphael. Jordan, Lebanon, & Syria: An Annotated Bibliography. LC 73-6215. 289p. 1973. Repr. of 1957 ed. lib. bdg. 14.25x (ISBN 0-8371-6894-5, PAJL). Greenwood.
Stern, Bernhard J. The Scented Garden: Anthropology of the Sex Life in the Levant. Berger, David, tr. from Ger. LC 72-9680. Repr. of 1934 ed. 22.50 (ISBN 0-404-57497-1). AMS Pr.
Thomas, George M., ed. Diplomatarium Veneto-Levantinum. 1969. Repr. of 1889 ed. 83.00 (ISBN 0-8337-3509-8). B Franklin.

LEVANT-ANTIQUITIES

Parr, Peter. Archaeology in the Levant: Essays for Kathleen Kenyon. Moorey, Roger, ed. (Illus.). 1978. 51.00x (ISBN 0-85668-084-2, Pub. by Aris & Phillips). Intl Schol Bk Serv.

LEVANT-COMMERCE

Depping, George B. Histoire du Commerce entre la Levant et l'Europe, depuis les Croisades Jusqu'a la Foundation des Colonies d'Amerique. LC 77-115814. (Research & Source Works Ser.: No. 425). (Fr). 1970. Repr. of 1830 ed. Set. text ed. 49.50 (ISBN 0-8337-0836-8). B Franklin.
Masson, Paul. Histoire Du Commerce Francais Dans Le Levant Au Dix-Huitieme Siecle. LC 12-23170. 1967. Repr. of 1911 ed. 62.50 (ISBN 0-8337-2287-5). B Franklin.
Puryear, Vernon J. France & the Levant: From the Bourbon Restoration to the Peace of Kutiah. 1968. Repr. of 1941 ed. 18.50 (ISBN 0-208-00721-0, Archon). Shoe String.
--International Economics & Diplomacy in the Near East: A Study of British Commercial Policy in the Levant, 1834-1853. (Illus.). 1969. Repr. of 1935 ed. 18.50 (ISBN 0-208-00699-0, Archon). Shoe String.

LEVANT-DESCRIPTION AND TRAVEL

Addison, Charles G. Damascus & Palmyra, 2 vols. in 1. LC 73-6265. (The Middle East Ser.). Repr. of 1838 ed. 26.00 (ISBN 0-405-05319-3). Arno.
Bent, J. Theodore. Early Voyages & Travels in the Levant. 1917. 30.00 (ISBN 0-8482-7357-5). Norwood Edns.
--Early Voyages in The Levant: With Some Account of The Levant Company of Turkey Merchants. 1979. Repr. of 1893 ed. lib. bdg. 45.00 (ISBN 0-8495-0516-X). Arden Lib.
Bent, James T., ed. Early Voyages & Travels in the Levant: The Diary of Thomas Dallam, 1599-1600 & Extracts from the Diaries of Dr. John Covel 1670-1679. 1670-79. 29.50 (ISBN 0-8337-0233-5). B Franklin.
Biddulph, William & Biddulph, Peter. Travels of Certaine Englishmen into Africa, Asia & to the Blacke Sea, Finished 1608. LC 72-6344. (English Experience Ser.: No. 22). 144p. 1968. Repr. of 1609 ed. 25.00 (ISBN 90-221-0022-7). Walter J Johnson.
Chateaubriand, Rene de & Mourot, Jean. Itineraire De Paris a Jerusalem. 448p. 1968. 3.50 (ISBN 0-686-54365-3). French & Eur.
Dannenfeldt, Karl H. Leonhard Rauwolf: Sixteenth-Century Physician, Botanist, & Traveler. LC 68-15634. (Monographs in the History of Science Ser). (Illus.). 1968. 16.50x (ISBN 0-674-52500-0). Harvard U Pr.
Denham, H. M. Southern Turkey, the Levant & Cyprus: A Sea-Guide to the Coasts & Islands. (Illus.). 1976. 19.95 (ISBN 0-393-03198-5). Norton.
Kinglake, A. W. Eothen. LC 71-93107. xxvi, 371p. 1970. pap. 4.50x (ISBN 0-8032-5711-2, BB 509, Bison). U of Nebr Pr.
Melville, Herman. Journal up the Straits: Oct. 11, 1856-May 5, 1857. Weaver, Raymond, ed. LC 74-143858. (Illus.). 1971. Repr. of 1935 ed. lib. bdg. 10.00x (ISBN 0-8154-0383-6). Cooper Sq.
Melville, Hermann. Journal of a Visit to Europe & the Levant, 1856-57. Horsford, Howard C., ed. LC 75-27655. (Princeton Studies in English Ser.: No.35). (Illus.). 1976. Repr. of 1955 ed. lib. bdg. 19.50x (ISBN 0-8371-8448-7, MEJV). Greenwood.
Sandys, George. A Relation of a Journey Begun Anno Domini 1610, 4 bks. LC 72-6028. (English Experience Ser.: No. 554). (Illus.). 316p. 1973. Repr. of 1615 ed. 53.00 (ISBN 90-221-0554-7). Walter J Johnson.
Seddon, Thomas. Memoir & Letters. Seddon, John P., ed. LC 72-148300. Repr. of 1858 ed. 18.00 (ISBN 0-404-05668-7). AMS Pr.
Stark, Freya. East Is West. (Illus.). 19.50 (ISBN 0-7195-1324-3). Transatlantic.
Twain, Mark. Innocents Abroad. pap. 2.50 (ISBN 0-451-51142-5, CE1379, Sig Classics). NAL.
Webbe, Edward. The Rare & Most Wonderfull Things Whiche. Webbe Hath Seene, Newly Enlarged. LC 72-6038. (English Experience Ser.: No. 564). (Illus.). 33p. 1973. Repr. of 1590 ed. 6.00 (ISBN 90-221-0564-4). Walter J Johnson.
Wright, Thomas. Early Travels in Palestine. 1848. 25.00x (ISBN 0-87068-118-4). Ktav.
Wright, Thomas, ed. Early Travels in Palestine. LC 77-84863. (Bohn's Antiquarian Library). Repr. of 1848 ed. 12.50 (ISBN 0-404-50026-9). AMS Pr.
Zouche, Robert C. Visits to Monasteries in the Levant. LC 80-2200. Repr. of 1916 ed. 45.00 (ISBN 0-404-18989-X). AMS Pr.

LEVANT-DESCRIPTION AND TRAVEL-BIBLIOGRAPHY

Nicolay, Nicolas de. The Nauigations into Turkie. Washington, T., tr. LC 68-54638. (English Experience Ser.: No. 48). 322p. 1968. Repr. of 1585 ed. 35.00 (ISBN 90-221-0048-0). Walter J Johnson.

LEVEES

see also Flood Dams and Reservoirs; Sea-Walls

LEVEL OF ASPIRATION

Escalona, Sibylle K. Application of the Level of Aspiration Experiment to the Study of Personality. LC 77-176756. (Columbia University. Teachers College. Contributions to Education: No. 937). Repr. of 1948 ed. 17.50 (ISBN 0-404-55937-9). AMS Pr.
Zaleznik, Abraham, et al. Orientation and Conflict in Career. LC 70-117971. (Illus.). 1970. 25.00x (ISBN 0-87584-085-X). Harvard Busn.

LEVELING
see also Surveying
LEVELLERS
Aylmer, G. E., ed. The Levellers in the English Revolution. LC 74-25313. (Documents of Revolution Ser). (Illus.). 178p. 1975. 18.50x (ISBN 0-8014-0957-8); pap. 3.95 (ISBN 0-8014-9153-3). Cornell U Pr.
Brailsford, H. N. The Levellers & the English Revolution. Hill, Christopher, ed. 1961. 22.50x (ISBN 0-8047-0095-8). Stanford U Pr.
Frank, Joseph. Levellers: John Lilburne, Richard Overton, William Walwyn. LC 68-27058. 1969. Repr. of 1955 ed. 12.00 (ISBN 0-8462-1278-1). Russell.
Haller, William & Davies, Godfrey, eds. The Leveller Tracts 1647-1653: 1647-1653. 1964. 8.50 (ISBN 0-8446-1218-9). Peter Smith.
Hayes, T. Wilson. Winstanley the Digger: A Literary Analysis of Radical Ideas in the English Revolution. LC 79-695. 1979. text ed. 16.50x (ISBN 0-674-95368-1). Harvard U Pr.
Holorenshaw, Henry. Levellers & the English Revolution. LC 73-80559. 1971. Repr. 17.50 (ISBN 0-86527-116-X). Fertig.
Morton, A. L., ed. Freedom in Arms: A Selection of Leveller Writings. LC 74-30435. 1976. pap. 2.25 (ISBN 0-7178-0425-9). Intl Pub Co.
Pease, T. C. The Leveller Movement. 8.00 (ISBN 0-8446-1345-2). Peter Smith.
Winstanley, Gerrard. Works of Gerrard Winstanley. Sabine, George H., ed. LC 64-66399. 1965. Repr. of 1941 ed. 20.00 (ISBN 0-8462-0572-6). Russell.
Wolfe, Don M., ed. Leveller Manifestoes of the Puritan Revolution. 1968. text ed. 15.00x (ISBN 0-391-00476-X). Humanities.
LEVER, CHARLES JAMES, 1806-1872
Stevenson, Lionel. Dr. Quicksilver: The Life of Charles Lever. LC 68-27089. (Illus.). 1969. Repr. of 1939 ed. 11.00 (ISBN 0-8462-1216-1). Russell.
LEVERS
Hellman, Hal. The Lever & the Pulley. LC 74-161363. (Illus.). 48p. (gr. 2-5). 1971. 4.95 (ISBN 0-87131-072-4). M Evans.
Wade, Harlan. Le Levier. Potvin, Claude & Potvin, Rose-Ella, trs. from Eng. (A Book About Ser.). Orig. Title: The Lever. (Illus., Fr.). (gr. k-3). 1979. PLB 7.95 (ISBN 0-8172-1464-X). Raintree Pubs.
--La Palanca. Contreras, Mamie M., tr. from Eng. LC 78-26992. (A Book About Ser.). Orig. Title: The Lever. (Illus., Sp.). (gr. k-3). 1979. PLB 7.95 (ISBN 0-8172-1489-5). Raintree Pubs.
LEVERSON, ADA, 1862-1933
Wyndham, Violet. The Sphinx & Her Circle: A Biographical Sketch of Ada Leverson, 1862-1933. LC 79-8089. Repr. of 1963 ed. 19.50 (ISBN 0-404-18397-2). AMS Pr.
LEVERTOV, DENISE
Atchity, John K. Denise Lervertov: An Interview. (New London Interviews). 1980. signed ltd. ed 10.00 (ISBN 0-89683-031-4); pap. 3.95 (ISBN 0-89683-030-6). New London Pr.
Wagner, Linda W. Denise Levertov. (Twayne's United States Authors Ser). 1967. pap. 3.45 (ISBN 0-8084-0103-3, T113, Twayne). Coll & U Pr.
LEVIBEN GERSHON, d. 1344
Adlerblum, Nima H. Study of Gersonides in His Proper Perspective. LC 73-158229. Repr. of 1926 ed. 14.50 (ISBN 0-404-00296-X). AMS Pr.
LEVI-STRAUSS, CLAUDE
Badcock, C. R. Levi-Strauss: Structuralism & Sociological Theory. LC 75-45308. 121p. 1976. text ed. 12.75x (ISBN 0-8419-0258-5). Holmes & Meier.
Barksdale, E. C. The Dacha & the Duchess. LC 74-75086. 203p. 1975. 7.50 (ISBN 0-8022-2143-2). Philos Lib.
Clarke, Simon. Foundations of Structuralism: A Critique of Levi-Strauss & the Structuralist Movement. 272p. 1981. 26.50x (ISBN 0-389-20115-4). B&N.
Jenkins, Alan. The Social Theory of Levi-Strauss. 1979. 22.50x (ISBN 0-312-73549-9). St Martin.
Korn, Francis. Elementary Structures Reconsidered: Levi-Strauss on Kinship. LC 73-78212. 1973. 20.00x (ISBN 0-520-02476-1). U of Cal Pr.
Lapointe, Francois H. & Lapointe, Claire C. Claude Levi-Strauss & His Critics: An International Bibliography (1950-1976) LC 76-24752. (Reference Library of the Humanities Ser.: Vol. 72). 1977. lib. bdg. 27.00 (ISBN 0-8240-9925-7). Garland Pub.
Leach, Edmund. Claude Levi-Strauss. rev. ed. LC 74-6853. (Modern Masters Ser). 160p. (Orig.). 1974. 7.50 (ISBN 0-670-22515-0). Viking Pr.
--Claude Levi-Strauss. rev. ed. (Modern Masters Ser.). 1976. pap. 3.50 (ISBN 0-14-004300-4). Penguin.
Leach, Edmund, ed. Structural Study of Myth & Totemism. (Orig.). 1968. pap. 8.95x (ISBN 0-422-72530-7, 44). Methuen Inc.
Needham, Rodney. Structure & Sentiment: A Test Case in Social Anthropology. LC 62-9738. 1962. 6.50x (ISBN 0-226-56991-8); pap. 1.95 (ISBN 0-226-56992-6). U of Chicago Pr.
Paz, Octavio. Claude Levi-Strauss. 176p. 1974. pap. 2.95 (ISBN 0-440-52091-6, Delta). Dell.
Pouillon, Jean & Maranda, Pierre, eds. Echanges & Communications, Melanges Offerts a Claude Levi-Strauss, a L'occasion De Son 60'eme Anniversaire: 2 Vols. LC 78-91207. (Studies in General Anthropology: No. 5). 1970. Set. 205.50x (ISBN 90-2790-540-1). Mouton.
LEVITTOWN, NEW JERSEY
Gans, Herbert J. Levittowners: Ways of Life & Politics in a New Suburban Community. 1969. pap. 4.95 (ISBN 0-394-70491-6, V491, Vin). Random.
LEVY, AARON, 1742-1815
Fish, S. M. Aaron Levy Founder of Aaronsburg. LC 51-2554. (Studies in American Jewish History: No. 1). 10.00 (ISBN 0-527-02382-5); pap. 5.00 (ISBN 0-527-02383-3). Kraus Repr.
Fish, Sidney M. Aaron Levy, Founder of Aaronsburg. 1951. pap. 2.50 (ISBN 0-911934-00-6). Am Jewish Hist Soc.
LEVY, URIAH PHILLIPS, 1795-1862
Felton, Harold W. Uriah Phillips Levy. LC 78-7726. (Illus.). (gr. 5 up). 1979. 5.95 (ISBN 0-396-07604-1). Dodd.
LEVY ON CAPITAL
see Capital Levy
LEWES, GEORGE HENRY, 1817-1878
Hirshberg, Edgar W. George Henry Lewes. (English Authors Ser.: No. 100). lib. bdg. 10.95 (ISBN 0-8057-1332-8). Twayne.
Kaminsky, Alice R. George Henry Lewes As Literary Critic. LC 68-54067. 1968. 11.95x (ISBN 0-8156-2125-6). Syracuse U Pr.
Tjoa, Hock G. George Henry Lewes: A Victorian Mind. (Harvard Historical Monographs: No. 70). 1977. 10.00x (ISBN 0-674-34874-5). Harvard U Pr.
LEWIN, KURT, 1890-1947
De Rivera, Joseph. Field Theory As Human-Science: Contributions of Lewin's Berlin Group. LC 75-35530. 1976. 24.50x (ISBN 0-470-20368-4). Halsted Pr.
Marrow, Alfred J. Practical Theorist: The Life & Work of Kurt Lewin. LC 77-1400, 1977. pap. text ed. 7.50x (ISBN 0-8077-2525-0). Tchrs Coll.
Schellenberg, James A. Masters of Social Psychology: Freud, Mead, Lewin, & Skinner. 1979. pap. 3.95 (ISBN 0-19-502622-5, GB 590, GB). Oxford U Pr.
LEWIS, CLARENCE IRVING, 1883-1964
Luizzi, Vincent. A Naturalist Theory of Justice: Critical Commentary on, & Selected Readings from, C. I. Lewis' Ethics. LC 80-69055. 120p. (Orig.). 1981. lib. bdg. 18.25 (ISBN 0-8191-1732-3); pap. text ed. 8.50 (ISBN 0-8191-1733-1). U Pr of Amer.
Schilpp, Paul A., ed. & intro. by. The Philosophy of C. I. Lewis. LC 67-10007. (Library of Living Philosophers: Vol. Xiii). 709p. 1968. 25.00 (ISBN 0-87548-135-3). Open Court.
Washington, Gregory. C. I. Lewis' Theory of Meaning & Theory of Value. 1978. pap. text ed. 6.50 (ISBN 0-8191-0388-8). U Pr of Amer.
LEWIS, CLIVE STAPLES, 1898-1963
Carpenter, Humphrey. Inklings: C. S. Lewis & His Friends. 1979. 10.95 (ISBN 0-395-27628-4). HM.
Christensen, Michael J. C. S. Lewis on Scripture: His Thoughts on the Nature of Biblical Inspiration, the Role of Revelation, & the Question of Inerrancy. 1979. 6.95 (ISBN 0-8499-0115-4). Word Bks.
Christopher, J. R. & Ostling, Joan K. C. S. Lewis: An Annotated Checklist. LC 73-76556. (Serif Ser.: No. 30). 1974. 17.50x (ISBN 0-87338-138-6). Kent St U Pr.
Como, James T., ed. C. S. Lewis at the Breakfast Table & Other Reminiscences. 1979. 9.95 (ISBN 0-02-570620-9). Macmillan.
Derrick, Christopher. C.S. Lewis & the Church of Rome. LC 80-83049. (Orig.). 1981. pap. 6.50 (ISBN 0-89870-009-4). Ignatius Pr.
Ford, Paul. Companion to Narnia, a Complete Illustrated Guide to the Themes, Characters & Events of C. S. Lewis Imaginary World. LC 80-7734. (Illus.). 304p. 1980. 12.95 (ISBN 0-06-250340-5, HarpR). Har-Row.
Gibson, Evan K. C. S. Lewis: Spinner of Tales. (Orig.). 1980. pap. 8.95 (ISBN 0-8028-1826-9). Eerdmans.
Glover, Donald E. C. S. Lewis: The Art of Enchantment. LC 80-21421. xii, 235p. 1981. 15.95x (ISBN 0-8214-0566-7); pap. 6.95x-(ISBN 0-8214-0609-4). Ohio U Pr.
Green, Roger L. & Hooper, Walter. C. S. Lewis: A Biography. LC 75-29425. 320p. 1976. pap. 4.75 (ISBN 0-15-623205-7, HB331, Harv). HarBraceJ.
Hannay, Margaret P. C. S. Lewis. LC 80-53700. (Modern Literature Ser.). 350p. 1981. 13.50 (ISBN 0-8044-2341-5). Ungar.
Hillegas, Mark R., ed. Shadows of Imagination: The Fantasies of C. S. Lewis, J. R. R. Tolkien, & Charles Williams. 2nd ed. LC 78-13983. (Crosscurrents Modern Critiques Ser.). 210p. 1979. 12.95 (ISBN 0-8093-0897-5). S Ill U Pr.
Hooper, Walter. Past Watchful Dragons: The Narnian Chronicles of C. S. Lewis. (Illus.). 1979. pap. 2.95 (ISBN 0-02-051970-2, Collier). Macmillan.
Hooper, Walter, ed. They Stand Together: The Letters of C. S. Lewis to Arthur Greeves (1914-1963) 1979. 13.95 (ISBN 0-02-553660-5). Macmillan.
Howard, Thomas. The Achievement of C. S. Lewis: A Reading of His Fiction. LC 80-14188. (Wheaton Literary Ser.). 200p. 1980. pap. 5.95 (ISBN 0-87788-004-2). Shaw Pubs.
Keefe, Carolyn. C. S. Lewis: Speaker & Teacher. 144p. 1974. pap. 4.95 (ISBN 0-310-26781-1). Zondervan.
Kilby, Clyde. Images of Salvation in the Fiction of C. S. Lewis. LC 78-53011. 1978. 5.95 (ISBN 0-87788-391-2). Shaw Pubs.
Kilby, Clyde & Mead, Marj, eds. Brothers & Friends: An Intimate Portrait of C. S. Lewis; the Diaries of Major Warren Hamilton Lewis. LC 80-7756. (Illus.). Date not set. 14.95 (ISBN 0-06-065244-6, HarpR). Har-Row.
Kilby, Clyde S. Christian World of C. S. Lewis. 1964. pap. 2.95 (ISBN 0-8028-6028-1). Eerdmans.
Kilby, Clyde S. & Gilbert, Douglas. C. S. Lewis: Images of His World. (Illus.). 192p. 1973. pap. 11.95 (ISBN 0-8028-1622-3). Eerdmans.
Lewis, W. H., ed. The Letters of C. S. Lewis. LC 74-13416. (Illus.). 308p. 1975. pap. 4.95 (ISBN 0-15-650870-2, HB300, Harv). HarBraceJ.
Lindskoog, Kathryn. The Lion of Judah in Never-Never Land: God, Man & Nature in C. S. Lewis's Narnia Tales. 1973. pap. 1.95 (ISBN 0-8028-1495-6). Eerdmans.
Lindskoog, Kay. C. S. Lewis: Mere Christian. rev. ed. LC 81-3771. 192p. 1981. pap. 6.95 (ISBN 0-87784-466-6). Inter-Varsity.
Meilaender, Gilbert. The Taste for the Other: The Social & Ethical Thought of C. S. Lewis. 1978. pap. 6.95 (ISBN 0-8028-1751-3). Eerdmans.
Schakel, Peter J., ed. Longing for a Form: Essays on the Fiction of C. S. Lewis. 1979. pap. 5.95 (ISBN 0-8010-8160-2). Baker Bk.
Smith, Robert H. Patches of Godlight: The Pattern of Thought of C. S. Lewis. LC 80-14132. 288p. 1981. 18.00x (ISBN 0-8203-0528-6). U of Ga Pr.
Tripp, R. P., Jr., ed. Man's Natural Powers: Essays for & About C.S. Lewis. (Orig.). 1975. 4.00 (ISBN 0-905019-01-6). Soc New Lang Study.
Urang, Gunnar. Shadows of Heaven: Religion & Fantasy in the Writing of C. S. Lewis, Charles Williams & J. R. R. Tolkien. LC 73-153998. 208p. 1971. 7.95 (ISBN 0-8298-0197-9). Pilgrim NY.
Walsh, Chad. C. S. Lewis: Apostle to the Skeptics. LC 78-689. 1974. Repr. of 1949 ed. lib. bdg. 20.00 (ISBN 0-8414-9647-1). Folcroft.
--The Literary Legacy of C. S. Lewis. LC 78-22275. 1979. pap. 4.95 (ISBN 0-15-652785-5, Harv). HarBraceJ.
LEWIS, GEORGE, 1900-1968
Bethell, Tom. George Lewis: A Jazzman from New Orleans. LC 76-3872. 1977. 15.95 (ISBN 0-520-03212-8). U of Cal Pr.
LEWIS, JOHN LLEWELLYN, 1880-1969
Dubofsky, Melvyn & Van Tine, Warren. John L. Lewis. LC 76-50819. (Illus.). 1977. 20.00 (ISBN 0-8129-0673-X). Times Bks.
John L. Lewis. (Labor Studies Ser.). (gr. 7 up). 1972. 0.75 (ISBN 0-89550-026-4). RIM.
John L. Lewis: Mini-Play. (People of Conscience Ser). (gr. 8 up). 1978. 3.00 (ISBN 0-89550-311-5). RIM.
Kurland, Gerald. John L. Lewis: Labor's Strong-Willed Organizer. Rahmas, D. Steve, ed. (Outstanding Personalities Ser.). 32p. 1973. lib. bdg. 2.95 incl. catalog cards (ISBN 0-87157-555-8); pap. 1.50 vinyl laminated covers (ISBN 0-87157-055-6). SamHar Pr.
McFarland, C. K. Roosevelt, Lewis & the New Deal: 1933-1940. LC 73-98123. (History & Culture Monograph Ser., No.7). 1970. 0.75 (ISBN 0-912646-06-3). Tex Christian.
Niermann, Eleanor, ed. Papers of John L. Lewis: Guide to a Microfilm Edition. (Guides to Historical Resources Ser.). 1970. pap. 1.00 (ISBN 0-87020-182-4). State Hist Soc Wis.
Wechsler, James A. Labor Baron: A Portrait of John L. Lewis. LC 72-143312. 278p. 1972. Repr. of 1944 ed. lib. bdg. 15.75x (ISBN 0-8371-5968-7, WELB). Greenwood.
LEWIS, M. W.
Life Story of Doctor M. W. Lewis. 2nd ed. (Illus.). 1977. pap. 1.50 (ISBN 0-87612-191-1). Self Realization.
LEWIS, MATTHEW GREGORY, 1775-1818
Conger, Syndy M. Matthew G. Lewis, Charles Robert Maturin & the Germans: An Interpretative Study of the Influence of German Literature on Two Gothic Novels. Varma, Devendra P., ed. LC 79-8448. (Gothic Studies & Dissertations Ser.). 1980. Repr. of 1977 ed. lib. bdg. 28.00x (ISBN 0-405-12652-2). Arno.
Irwin, Joseph J. M. G. Lewis. LC 76-26062. (English Author Ser.: No. 198). 1976. lib. bdg. 10.95 (ISBN 0-8057-6670-7). Twayne.
Parreaux, Andre. The Publication of the Monk. 1960. Repr. 40.00 (ISBN 0-8274-3225-9). R West.
Peck, Louis F. Life of Matthew G. Lewis. LC 61-11067. (Illus.). 1961. 16.50x (ISBN 0-674-53200-7). Harvard U Pr.
Reno, Robert P. The Gothic Visions of Ann Radcliffe & Matthew G. Lewis. Varma, Devendra P., ed. LC 79-8473. (Gothic Studies & Dissertations Ser.). 1980. lib. bdg. 25.00x (ISBN 0-405-12648-4). Arno.
Summers, Montague. Gothic Quest: A History of the Gothic Novel. LC 64-8919. (Illus.). 1964. Repr. of 1938 ed. 15.00 (ISBN 0-8462-0522-X). Russell.
LEWIS, MERIWEATHER, 1774-1809
Allen, John L. Passage Through the Garden: Lewis & Clark & the Image of the American Northwest. LC 74-14512. (Illus.). 360p. 1975. 24.95 (ISBN 0-252-00397-7). U of Ill Pr.
Fisher, Vardis. Suicide or Murder. 1978. pap. 2.95 (ISBN 0-918522-57-9). O L Holmes.
Snyder, Gerald S. & National Geographic Society. In the Footsteps of Lewis & Clark. LC 77-125338. (Special Publications Ser.). (Illus.). 1970. 6.95, avail. only from natl. geog. (ISBN 0-87044-087-X). Natl Geog.
LEWIS, SINCLAIR, 1885-1951
Derleth, August. Three Literary Men: A Memoir of Sinclair Lewis, Sherwood Anderson & Edgar Lee Masters. LC 78-11518. Repr. of 1963 ed. lib. bdg. 10.00 (ISBN 0-8414-3686-X). Folcroft.
Dooley, D. J. Art of Sinclair Lewis. LC 65-17173. 1967. pap. 4.25x (ISBN 0-8032-5051-7, BB 199, Bison). U of Nebr Pr.
--Art of Sinclair Lewis. LC 65-17173. 1967. pap. 4.25x (ISBN 0-8032-5051-7, BB 199, Bison). U of Nebr Pr.
Fleming, Robert E. & Fleming, Esther. Sinclair Lewis: A Reference Guide. 1980. lib. bdg. 18.50 (ISBN 0-8161-8094-6). G K Hall.
Grebstein, Sheldon N. Sinclair Lewis. (Twayne's United States Authors Ser). 1962. pap. 3.45 (ISBN 0-8084-0278-1, T14, Twayne). Coll & U Pr.
--Sinclair Lewis. (U. S. Authors Ser.: No. 14). lib. bdg. 9.95 (ISBN 0-8057-0448-5). Twayne.
Harrison, Oliver. Sinclair Lewis. LC 73-3461. 1925. lib. bdg. 8.50 (ISBN 0-8414-2065-3). Folcroft.
Light, Martin. The Quixotic Vision of Sinclair Lewis. LC 74-82792. 176p. 1975. 6.50 (ISBN 0-911198-40-7). Purdue.
Lundquist, James. Sinclair Lewis. LC 72-76774. (Modern Literature Ser.). 10.95 (ISBN 0-8044-2562-0). Ungar.
Milch, Robert J. Babbitt Notes. (Orig.). pap. 1.75 (ISBN 0-8220-0219-1). Cliffs.
Monarch Notes on Lewis' Arrowsmith. (Orig.). pap. 1.95 (ISBN 0-671-00682-7). Monarch Pr.
Monarch Notes on Lewis' Babbitt. (Orig.). pap. 1.75 (ISBN 0-671-00683-5). Monarch Pr.
Monarch Notes on Lewis' Main Street. (Orig.). pap. 1.75 (ISBN 0-671-00684-3). Monarch Pr.
Paley, Alan L. Sinclair Lewis, Twentieth Century American Author & Nobel Prize Winner. Rahmas, D. Steve, ed. LC 73-87626. (Outstanding Personalities Ser.: No. 67). 32p. (Orig.). (gr. 7-12). 1974. lib. bdg. 2.95 incl. catalog cards (ISBN 0-686-05493-8); pap. 1.50 vinyl laminated covers (ISBN 0-87157-067-X). SamHar Pr.
Parrington, Vernon. Sinclair Lewis: Our Own Diogenes. LC 73-11205. (American Literature Ser., No. 49). 1974. lib. bdg. 49.95 (ISBN 0-8383-1720-0). Haskell.
Parrington, Vernon L. Sinclair Lewis: Our Own Diogenes. LC 77-9602. 1977. Repr. of 1930 ed. lib. bdg. 7.50 (ISBN 0-8414-6794-3). Folcroft.
Royster, Salibelle. Arrowsmith Notes. (Orig.). pap. 1.95 (ISBN 0-8220-0201-9). Cliffs.
--Main Street Notes. (Orig.). pap. 2.25 (ISBN 0-8220-0798-3). Cliffs.
Schorer, Mark. Sinclair Lewis. (Pamphlets on American Writers Ser: No. 27). (Orig.). 1963. pap. 1.25x (ISBN 0-8166-0290-5, MPAW27). U of Minn Pr.
Sherman, Stuart P. Significance of Sinclair Lewis. LC 73-16169. 1922. lib. bdg. 8.50 (ISBN 0-8414-7693-4). Folcroft.
LEWIS, WYNDHAM, 1884-1957
Cookson, William, ed. Agenda: Wyndham Lewis Special Issue. 1977. Repr. of 1970 ed. lib. bdg. 15.00 (ISBN 0-8495-0010-9). Arden Lib.

Grigson, G. A Master of Our Time. LC 72-3175. (English Literature Ser., No. 33). 1972. Repr. of 1951 ed. lib. bdg. 22.95 (ISBN 0-8383-1534-8). Haskell.
Grigson, Geoffrey. A Master of Our Time: A Study of Wyndham Lewis. LC 73-13534. 1951. lib. bdg. 6.50 (ISBN 0-8414-4428-5). Folcroft.
--A Master of Our Time: Wyndham Lewis. 59.95 (ISBN 0-87968-010-5). Gordon Pr.
Jameson, Fredric. Fables of Aggression: Wyndham Lewis, the Modernist As Fascist. LC 78-64462. 1979. 14.95x (ISBN 0-520-03792-8); pap. 5.95 (ISBN 0-520-04398-7, CAL 496). U of Cal Pr.
Kenner, Hugh. Wyndham Lewis: A Critical Guidebook. LC 54-9869. 1954. pap. 4.25 (ISBN 0-8112-0077-9, NDP167). New Directions.
Lewis, W. Wyndham Lewis the Artist. LC 74-173843. (English Literature Ser., No. 33). 1971. Repr. of 1939 ed. lib. bdg. 35.95 (ISBN 0-8383-1348-5). Haskell.
Materer, Timothy. Vortex: Pound, Eliot, & Lewis. LC 79-13009. (Illus.). 1979. 17.50x (ISBN 0-8014-1225-0). Cornell U Pr.
--Wyndham Lewis the Novelist. LC 75-29310. 189p. 1976. text ed. 12.50x (ISBN 0-8143-1544-5). Wayne St U Pr.
Meyers, Jeffrey. Wyndham Lewis: A Revaluation. 1980. 33.95 (ISBN 0-7735-0516-4). McGill-Queens U Pr.
Michel, Walter. Wyndham Lewis: Paintings & Drawings. LC 69-11616. (Illus.). 1970. 65.00x (ISBN 0-520-01612-2). U of Cal Pr.
Morrow, Bradford & Lafourcade, Bernard. A Bibliography of the Writings of Wyndham Lewis. (Illus.). 350p. 1978. 30.00 (ISBN 0-87685-419-6). Black Sparrow.
Porteus, H. Wyndham Lewis: A Discursive Explosion. 59.95 (ISBN 0-8490-1341-0). Gordon Pr.
Pound, Omar & Grover, Philip. Wyndham Lewis: A Descriptive Bibliography. (Illus.). 1978. 20.00 (ISBN 0-208-01725-9, Archon). Shoe String.
Richards, I. A., et al, eds. Essays on Wyndham Lewis. 1974. 20.00 (ISBN 0-685-43450-8). Norwood Edns.
Wagner, Geoffrey. Wyndham Lewis: A Portrait of the Artist As the Enemy. LC 72-12320. 363p. 1973. Repr. of 1957 ed. lib. bdg. 17.00x (ISBN 0-8371-6692-6, WAWK). Greenwood.

LEWIS AND CLARK COLLEGE
Montague, Martha F. Lewis & Clark College: Eighteen Sixty-Seven to Nineteen Sixty-Seven. LC 68-28925. (Illus.). 1968. 8.95 (ISBN 0-8323-0037-3). Binford.

LEWIS AND CLARK EXPEDITION
Allen, John L. Passage Through the Garden: Lewis & Clark & the Image of the American Northwest. LC 74-14512. (Illus.). 360p. 1975. 24.95 (ISBN 0-252-00397-7). U of Ill Pr.
Berthold, Mary P. Including Two Captains: A Later Look. LC 75-13400. 1975. 6.00 (ISBN 0-8187-0023-8). Harlo Pr.
Burroughs, Raymond D., ed. Natural History of the Lewis & Clark Expedition. 1961. 7.50 (ISBN 0-87013-058-7). Mich St U Pr.
Chuinard, Eldon G. Only One Man Died: The Medical Aspects of the Lewis & Clark Expedition. 2nd ed. LC 78-73417. (Western Frontiermen Ser.: No. 19). (Illus.). 444p. 1980. 29.00 (ISBN 0-87062-128-9). A H Clark.
Cutright, Paul R. A History of the Lewis & Clark Journals. LC 74-28244. (Illus.). 311p. 1976. 17.50 (ISBN 0-8061-1246-8). U of Okla Pr.
De Kay, Ormonde, Jr. Adventures of Lewis & Clark. (Step-up Bks). (Illus.). (gr. 3-4). 1968. (BYR); PLB 4.99 (ISBN 0-394-90069-3). Random.
De Voto, Bernard. Journals of Lewis & Clark. 1953. 22.50 (ISBN 0-395-07607-2). HM.
Eide, Ingvard H. American Odyssey: The Journey of Lewis & Clark. LC 71-77805. (Illus.). 1979. pap. 9.95 (ISBN 0-528-88017-9). Rand.
First Across the Continent: The Story of the Exploring Expedition of Lewis & Clark in 1803-4-5. Repr. of 1901 ed. 35.00 (ISBN 0-8492-9999-3). R West.
Flandrau, Grace. Glance at the Lewis & Clark Expedition. (Illus.). 29p. Repr. pap. 4.50 (ISBN 0-8466-0211-3, SJS211). Shorey.
--Lewis & Clark Expedition. (Illus.). Repr. of 1927 ed. pap. 7.50 (ISBN 0-8466-0210-5, SJS210). Shorey.
Grant, Matthew G. Lewis & Clark. LC 73-14582. 1974. PLB 5.95 (ISBN 0-87191-277-5). Creative Ed.
Hawke, David F. Those Tremendous Mountains: The Story of the Lewis & Clark Expedition. (Illus.). 1980. 12.95 (ISBN 0-393-01305-7). Norton.
Jackson, Donald, ed. Letters of the Lewis & Clark Expedition with Related Documents, 1783-1854. LC 78-15288. 1979. 39.95 (ISBN 0-252-00697-6). U of Ill Pr.
Laut, Agnes C. Pathfinders of the West. LC 74-90651. (Essay Index Reprint Ser). 1904. 25.00 (ISBN 0-8369-1220-9). Arno.
Lewis, Meriwether & Clark, William. History of the Expedition Under the Command of Lewis & Clark, 3 Vols. Coues, E., ed. (Illus.). Set. 35.00 (ISBN 0-8446-2468-3); 11.75 ea. Peter Smith.
--The History of the Lewis & Clark Expedition, 3 vols. Coues, Elliot, ed. (Illus.). 1508p. 1979. pap. 6.00 ea. Vol. 1 (ISBN 0-486-21268-8). Vol. 2 (ISBN 0-486-21269-6). Vol. 3 (ISBN 0-486-21270-X). Dover.
--Journals of Lewis & Clark. De Voto, Bernard, ed. (Illus.). 1963. pap. 8.95 (ISBN 0-395-08380-X, 31, SenEd). HM.
--Journals of Lewis & Clark: A New Selection. Bakeless, John, ed. (Orig.). 1964. pap. 1.95 (ISBN 0-451-61665-0, MJ1665, Ment). NAL.
Lewis, Meriwether, et al. History of the Expedition Under the Command of Captains Lewis & Clarke, 3 vols. LC 72-2820. (Illus.). Repr. of 1922 ed. Set. 78.50 (ISBN 0-404-54920-9). AMS Pr.
Mirsky, Jeannette. Westward Crossings: Balboa, Mackenzie, Lewis & Clark. LC 70-116434. 1970. pap. 3.45 (ISBN 0-226-53181-3, P370, Phoen). U of Chicago Pr.
Murphy, Dan. Lewis & Clark: Voyage of Discovery. DenDooven, Gweneth R., ed. LC 76-57451. (Illus.). 1977. 7.95 (ISBN 0-916122-19-0); pap. 3.75 (ISBN 0-916122-50-6). KC Pubns.
Neuberger, Richard L. Lewis & Clark Expedition. (Landmark Ser: No. 15). (Illus.). (gr. 4-6). 1951. PLB 5.99 (ISBN 0-394-90315-3, BYR). Random.
Salisbury, Albert P. Two Captains West. LC 50-8706. 1950. 10.95 (ISBN 0-87564-319-1). Superior Pub.
Satterfield, Archie. Lewis & Clark Country. LC 78-8324. (Illus.). 144p. 1978. 27.50 (ISBN 0-915796-12-0). Beautiful Am.
--The Lewis & Clark Trail. LC 77-17631. (Illus.). 224p. 1978. 12.95 (ISBN 0-8117-0935-3). Stackpole.
Stein, R. Conrad. The Story of the Lewis & Clark Expedition. LC 78-4648. (Cornerstones of Freedom Ser.). (Illus.). (gr. 3-6). 1978. PLB 7.95 (ISBN 0-516-04620-9); pap. 2.50 (ISBN 0-516-44620-7). Childrens.
--The Story of the Lewis & Clark Expedition. LC 78-4648. (Cornerstones of Freedom Ser.). (Illus.). (gr. 3-6). 1978. PLB 7.95 (ISBN 0-516-04620-9); pap. 2.50 (ISBN 0-516-44620-7). Childrens.
Thwaites, Rueben G., ed. Original Journals of the Lewis & Clark Expedition, 8 Vols. LC 72-88223. Repr. of 1904 ed. Set. 160.00 (ISBN 0-405-00030-8). Arno.
Wheeler, Olin D. The Trail of Lewis & Clark: 1804-1904, 2 vols. LC 75-177829. Repr. of 1904 ed. Set. 57.50 (ISBN 0-404-06926-6). AMS Pr.

LEWIS AND CLARK EXPEDITION–FICTION
Snyder, Gerald S. & National Geographic Society. In the Footsteps of Lewis & Clark. LC 77-125338. (Special Publications Ser.). (Illus.). 1970. 6.95, avail. only from natl. geog. (ISBN 0-87044-087-X). Natl Geog.

LEWIS FAMILY
Hindman, Juanita L. Postpioneers. LC 73-75069. 1973. 6.95 (ISBN 0-87706-023-1). Branch-Smith.

LEX COMMISSORIA (RECISSION)
see Sales, Conditional

LEXICOGRAPHY
see also Encyclopedias and Dictionaries–History and Criticism; Language and Languages–Etymology
Botha, Rudolf P. Function of the Lexicon in Transformational Generative Grammar. (Janua Linguarum, Ser. Major: No. 38). 1968. text ed. 44.10x (ISBN 90-2790-688-2). Mouton.
Carlton, Charles M. Studies in Romance Lexicography Based on a Collection of Late Latin Documents from Ravenna (A.D. 445-700) (Studies in the Romance Languages & Literatures). (Orig.). 1966. pap. 7.50x (ISBN 0-8078-9054-5). U of NC Pr.
Glossarium Harlemense: Circa 1440. (Monumenta Lexicographica Neelandica, Ser. I: Vol. I). 422p. 1973. text ed. 150.00x (ISBN 0-686-27746-5). Mouton.
Hayashi, Tetsuro. The Theory of English Lexicography 1530-1791. xii, 168p. 1978. 21.00 (ISBN 90-272-0956-1, SIHOL 18). Benjami Ns North Am.
Henne, Helmut. Semantik und Lexikographie: Untersuchungen zur lexikalischen Kodifikation der deutschen Sprache. (Studia Linguistia Germanica Vol. 7). 1972. 45.00x (ISBN 3-11-003528-6). De Gruyter.
Householder, Fred W. & Saporta, Sol, eds. Problems in Lexicography. 3rd ed. LC 62-62699. (General Publications Ser: Vol. 21). (Orig.). 1975. pap. text ed. 8.00x (ISBN 0-87750-113-0). Res Ctr Lang Semiotic.
Leclercq, R. Aufgaben Methode und Geschichte der Wissenschaftlichen Reimlexikographie. (Amsterdamer Publikationen Zur Sprache und Literatur: No. 23). 276p. (Ger.). 1976. pap. text ed. 24.00x (ISBN 90-6203-169-2). Humanities.
Lehrer, Adrienne. Semantic Fields & Lexical Structure. (North-Holland Linguistics Ser.: Vol. 11). 1974. pap. 19.50 (ISBN 0-444-10653-7, North-Holland). Elsevier.
Mathias, Jim & Kennedy, Thomas L., eds. Computers, Language Reform, & Lexicography in China. vii, 76p. (Orig.). 1980. pap. 5.00 (ISBN 0-87422-015-7). Wash St U Pr.
Steiner, Roger J. Two Centuries of Spanish & English Bilingual Lexicography, 1590-1800. LC 74-110958. (Janua Linguarum, Ser. Practica: No. 108). (Orig.). 1970. pap. text ed. 21.25x (ISBN 90-2790-743-9). Mouton.
Trump, Fred. Lincoln's Little Girl. LC 77-11026. 7.50 (ISBN 0-686-14375-2). Heritage Kansas.
Weinbrot, Howard D., ed. New Aspects of Lexicography: Literary Criticism, Intellectual History, & Social Change. LC 73-156780. 223p. 1972. 9.95x (ISBN 0-8093-0515-1). S Ill U Pr.
Wells, Ronald A. Dictionaries & the Authoritarian Tradition: A Study in English Usage & Lexicography. 1973. pap. text ed. 23.75x (ISBN 0-686-22569-4). Mouton.
Zgusta, Ladislav, ed. Theory & Methodology in Lexicography. 1980. pap. 5.75 (ISBN 0-686-64344-5). Hornbeam Pr.
Zgusta, Ladislav, et al. Manual of Lexicography. (Janua Linguarum, Ser. Major: No. 39). 360p. 1971. text ed. 62.00x (ISBN 90-2791-921-6). Mouton.

LEXICOLOGY
see also Semantics; Vocabulary
Apresjan, Yuri D. Lexical Semantics. Lehrman, Alexander, tr. from Rus. (Linguistica Extranea: Studia: No. 13). 450p. 1981. 35.00 (ISBN 0-89720-039-X); pap. 22.50 (ISBN 0-89720-040-3). Karoma.
Doroszewski, Witold. Elements of Lexicology & Semiotics. Taylor, Iain, tr. from Pol. (Approaches to Semiotics Ser.: No. 46). 314p. 1973. text ed. 30.00x (ISBN 90-2792-699-9). Mouton.
Dyen, Isidore. Linguistic Subgrouping & Lexicostatistics. LC 73-82418. (Janua Linguarum, Series Minor: No. 175). (Illus.). 251p. 1975. pap. text ed. 46.25x (ISBN 90-2793-054-6). Mouton.
Dyen, Isidore, ed. Lexicostatistics in Genetic Linguistics: Proceedings of the Yale Conference, Yale University, April 3-4, 1971. (Janua Linguarum Series Maior: No. 69). 1973. 36.25x (ISBN 0-686-21262-2). Mouton.
Guilbert, Louis. La Creativite lexicale. (Collection langue et langage). 285p. (Fr.). 1975. pap. 23.95 (ISBN 2-03-070340-0). Larousse.
Seymour, P. H. Human Visual Cognition. 1979. 25.00x (ISBN 0-312-39966-9). St Martin.
Smeaton, B. Hunter. Lexical Expansion Due to Technical Change: As Illustrated by the Arabic of Al Hasa, Saudi Arabia. (Language Science Monographs Ser: Vol. 10). 260p. 1973. pap. text ed. 12.00x (ISBN 0-87750-167-X). Res Ctr Lang Semiotic.

LEXINGTON, BATTLE OF, 1775
Beach, Stewart. Lexington & Concord in Color. (Profiles of America Ser.). 1970. 7.95 (ISBN 0-8038-4269-4, 8038-4269-4). Hastings.
Coburn, Frank W. Battle of April Nineteenth, Seventeen Seventy-Five. LC 70-120872. (American Bicentennial Ser). 1970. Repr. of 1922 ed. 13.50 (ISBN 0-8046-1265-X). Kennikat.
French, Allen. The Day of Concord & Lexington: The Nineteenth of April, 1775. LC 68-58325. (Illus.). 1969. Repr. of 1925 ed. 16.50 (ISBN 0-87152-051-6). Reprint.
--General Gage's Informers: New Material Upon Lexington & Concord, Benjamin Thompson As Loyalist & the Treachery of Benjamin Church, Jr. LC 68-54420. (Illus.). 1968. Repr. of 1932 ed. lib. bdg. 14.25x (ISBN 0-8371-0431-9, FRGI). Greenwood.
Murdock, Harold. The Nineteenth of April, 1775: Concord & Lexington. LC 68-58327. (Illus.). 1969. Repr. of 1923 ed. 15.00 (ISBN 0-87152-053-2). Reprint.
Provincial Congress of Massachusetts Colony, 1775. Narrative of the Excursions & Ravages of the King's Troops Under Command of General Gage. LC 67-29008. (Eyewitness Accounts of the American Revolution Ser., No. 1). 1968. Repr. of 1775 ed. 9.50 (ISBN 0-405-01119-9). Arno.
Tomlinson, A. Military Journals of Two Private Soldiers, 1758-1775. LC 75-146146. (Era of the American Revolution Ser). 1971. Repr. of 1855 ed. lib. bdg. 17.50 (ISBN 0-306-70134-0). Da Capo.
Tomlinson, Abraham, ed. Military Journals of Two Private Soldiers, 1758-1775. facs. ed. LC 70-117895. (Select Bibliographies Reprint Ser). 1854. 13.00 (ISBN 0-8369-5348-7). Arno.
Tourtellot, Arthur B. Lexington & Concord. (Illus.). 1963. pap. 5.95 (ISBN 0-393-00194-6, Norton Lib). Norton.

LEXINGTON, BATTLE OF, 1775–FICTION
Cullen, Maurice R. Battle Road: Birthplace of the American Revolution. LC 72-111381. (Illus.). 1970. pap. 3.95 (ISBN 0-85699-012-4). Chatham Pr.
MacKenzie, Frederick. British Fusilier in Revolutionary Boston. French, Allen, ed. LC 79-102237. (Select Bibliographies Reprint Ser). 1926. 17.00 (ISBN 0-8369-5122-0). Arno.

LEXINGTON, KENTUCKY
Coleman, J. Winston. The Squires Sketches of Lexington. 1972. 6.95 (ISBN 0-87642-009-9). Henry Clay.
Ranck, George W. History of Lexington, Kentucky. 428p. 1971. Repr. of 1872 ed. 10.95 (ISBN 0-87642-007-2). Henry Clay.

LEYH, GEORG, 1877-1968
Dosa, Marta L., tr. Libraries in the Political Scene: Georg Leyh & German Librarianship, 1933-53. LC 72-5218. (Contributions in Librarianship & Information Science: No. 7). 256p. 1973. lib. bdg. 16.95 (ISBN 0-8371-6443-5, DGL/). Greenwood.

LEYTE GULF, BATTLE OF, 1944
see Philippine Sea, Battles of The, 1944

LHASA APSO (DOG)
see Dogs–Breeds–Lhasa Apso

LI, FEI-KAN, 1905-
Munoz, V. Li Pei Kan & Chinese Anarchism: A Chronology. 59.95 (ISBN 0-87700-242-8). Revisionist Pr.

LI, HUNG-CHANG, 1823-1901
Folsom, Kenneth E. Friends, Guests & Colleagues: The Mufu System of the Late Ch'ing Period. LC 67-26479. 1968. 21.50x (ISBN 0-520-00425-6). U of Cal Pr.

LI, SHANG-YIN, 813-858
Liu, James J. Poetry of Li Shang-Yin, Ninth-Century Baroque Chinese Poet. LC 68-30695. 1969. 12.00x (ISBN 0-226-48690-7). U of Chicago Pr.

LI, TA-CHAO, 1888-1927
Meisner, Maurice. LiTa-Chao & the Origins of Chinese Marxism. LC 67-10904. 1970. pap. text ed. 5.95x (ISBN 0-689-70221-3, 154). Atheneum.

LI PO, 705-762
Waley, Arthur. The Poetry & Career of Li Po. (Ethical & Religious Classics of East & West Ser.). 1951. 13.50 (ISBN 0-04-895012-2). Allen Unwin.

LIABILITY (LAW)
see also Administrative Responsibility; Criminal Liability; Employers' Liability; Government Liability; Insurance, Liability; Liability for School Accidents; Liability for Traffic Accidents; Negligence; Proximate Cause (Law); Suretyship and Guaranty; Torts
American Institute for Property & Liability Underwriters. Code of Professional Ethics. 1979. write for info. (CPCU 10). IIA.
Baldwin, Scott, et al. The Preparation of a Products Liability Case. 1054p. 1981. write for info. (ISBN 0-316-07923-5). Little.
Beasley, James E. Products Liability & the Unreasonably Dangerous Requirement. pap. write for info. ALI-ABA.
Blalock, Joyce. Civil Liability of Law Enforcement Officers. 248p. 1974. photocopy ed. spiral 15.75 (ISBN 0-398-02864-8). C C Thomas.
Bodenheimer, Edgar. Philosophy of Responsibility. LC 79-26020. x, 147p. 1980. text ed. 18.50x (ISBN 0-8377-0309-3). Rothman.
California Trial Lawyers Association. Liability Seminar. 169p. 1966. 5.00 (ISBN 0-913338-04-4). Trans-Media Pub.
Company Programs to Reduce Products Liability Hazards: A Transcript of a MAPI Seminar. non-members 15.00 (ISBN 0-686-11597-X); members 10.00 (ISBN 0-686-11598-8). M & A Products.
Conference on Product Liability in Europe, Amsterdam, Sept. 1975. Proceedings. 155p. (Orig.). 1975. pap. text ed. 17.95x (ISBN 0-903393-23-9). Rothman.
Davis, Philip E., ed. Moral Duty & Legal Responsibility: A Philosophical-Legal Casebook. 2nd ed. (Orig.). 1981. 18.50x (ISBN 0-8290-0681-8). Irvington.
Epstein, Richard A. Defenses & Subsequent Pleas in a System of Strict Liability. (Research Contribution Ser.: No. 3). 1974. Repr. pap. 2.00 (ISBN 0-685-48017-8). Am Bar Foun.
--Modern Products Liability Law. LC 80-11486. (Quorum Bk.). 210p. 1980. lib. bdg. 25.00 (ISBN 0-89930-002-2, EPL/, Quorum). Greenwood.
Gaunt, Larry D. & Williams, Numan A. Commercial Liability Underwriting. 1978. write for info. (UND 63). IIA.
Harding, Arthur L., ed. Responsibility in Law & in Morals. LC 60-8677. (Studies in Jurisprudence: No. 7). 1960. 4.00 (ISBN 0-87074-070-9). SMU Press.

Howell, Edward B. & Howell, Richard P. Untangling the Web of Professional Liability. 3rd ed. LC 78-104786. 231p. 1980. 20.00 (ISBN 0-932056-03-2). Risk Analysis.
Knepper, William E. Liability of Corporate Officers & Directors. 3rd ed. 1979. text ed. 45.00 (ISBN 0-87473-118-6). A Smith Co.
Levin, Bruce A. & Coyne, Robert, eds. Tort Reform & Related Proposals: Annotated Bibliographies on Product Liability & Medical Malpractice. 300p. 1979. pap. 30.00 (ISBN 0-686-65427-7). Am Bar Foun.
Magarick, Pat. Excessive Liability - Duties & Responsibilities of the Insurer. LC 75-44308. 1976. with 1978 suppl. 30.00 (ISBN 0-87632-157-0). Boardman.
Malecki, Donald S., et al. Commercial Liability Risk Management & Insurance, 2 vols. 1978. write for info. (CPCU 4). IIA.
Middendorf. What Every Engineer Should Know About Product Liability. (What Every Engineer Should Know Ser.: Vol. 2). 1979. 12.75 (ISBN 0-8247-6876-0). Dekker.
Morris, Herbert, ed. Freedom & Responsibility: Readings in Philosophy & Law. 1961. 15.00x (ISBN 0-8047-0067-2). Stanford U Pr.
Noel, Dix & Phillips, Jerry J. Products Liability in a Nutshell. 2nd ed. LC 80-39726. (Nutshell Ser.). 341p. 1981. pap. text ed. 6.95 (ISBN 0-8299-2121-4). West Pub.
Page, Joseph A. The Law of Premises Liability with 1980 Supplement. LC 76-11993. 1976. text ed. 42.50 (ISBN 0-686-77435-3). Anderson Pub Co.
Peltzer, Martin & Treumann, Walter. Produzentenhaftpflicht in USA und Deutschland: Product Liability in Germany & the USA. 2nd ed. German American Chamber of Commerce, ed. Fischer-Theurer, Anette, tr. 54p. (Ger. & Eng.). 1981. pap. 15.00 (ISBN 0-86640-002-8). German Am Chamber.
Products Liability & Reliability: Some Management Considerations. non-members 15.00 (ISBN 0-686-11605-4); members 7.50 (ISBN 0-686-11606-2). M & A Products.
RADCO Staff, ed. Protecting Corporate Officers & Directors Against Liability. 1971. 29.50x (ISBN 0-8422-9001-X). Irvington.
Rheingold, Paul D. & Birnbaum, Sheila L., eds. Product Liability: Law, Practice, Science. 2nd ed. 1975. 25.00 (ISBN 0-685-85390-X, H3-2932). PLI.
Shapo, Marshall S. Cases & Materials on Products Liability. LC 80-11639. (University Casebook Ser.). 906p. 1980. text ed. write for info. (ISBN 0-88277-001-2). Foundation Pr.
Singewald, Karl. The Doctrine of Non-Suability of the State in the United States. LC 78-63936. (Johns Hopkins University. Studies in the Social Sciences. Twenty-Eighth Ser. 1910: 3). Repr. of 1910 ed. 15.50 (ISBN 0-404-61185-0). AMS Pr.
Sullivan, Gene. Products Liability: Who Needs It? LC 78-70485. 1979. text ed. 12.75 (ISBN 0-87218-003-4). Natl Underwriter.
Tebbens, H. Duintjer. International Product Liability. 480p. 1979. 37.50x (ISBN 90-286-0469-3). Sijthoff & Noordhoff.
Vanbiervliet, Alan & Sheldon-Wildgen, Jan. Liability Issues in Community-Based Programs: Legal Principles, Problem Areas, & Recommendations. LC 81-245. 224p. 1981. pap. text ed. 10.95 (ISBN 0-933716-08-7). P H Brookes.
Yiannopoulos, Athanassios N. Negligence Clauses in Ocean Bills of Lading: Conflict of Laws & the Brussels Convention of 1924, a Comparative Study. LC 62-10479. 1962. 15.00x (ISBN 0-8071-0840-5). La State U Pr.

LIABILITY, CRIMINAL
see Criminal Liability

LIABILITY, EMPLOYERS'
see Employers' Liability

LIABILITY FOR CONDITION AND USE OF LAND
Bradshaw, A. D. & Chadwick, M. J. The Restoration of the Land: The Ecology & Reclamation of Derelict & Degraded Land. LC 79-64658. (Blackwell Ecology Ser.: Vol. 6). 1981. 27.50 (ISBN 0-520-03961-0). U of Cal Pr.

LIABILITY FOR MARINE ACCIDENTS
see also Accident Law; Admiralty; Collisions at Sea

LIABILITY FOR NUCLEAR DAMAGES
Insurance for Nuclear Installations. (Legal Ser.: No. 6). (Illus., Orig., Eng. & Fr.). 1970. pap. 13.00 (ISBN 92-0-076070-8, ISP274, IAEA). Unipub.
International Conventions on Civil Liability for Nuclear Damage. (Legal Series: No. 4). (Orig.). 1976. pap. 26.00 (ISBN 0-685-74380-2, ISP430, IAEA). Unipub.
Nuclear Third Party Liability, 1976: Nuclear Legislation. (Analytical Study Ser.). 1977. 12.50x (ISBN 92-64-11619-2). OECD.
Shrader-Frechette, K. S. Nuclear Power & Public Policy: The Social & Ethical Problems of Fission Technology. (Pallas Paperbacks Ser.: No. 15). 220p. 1980. lib. bdg. 20.00 (ISBN 90-277-1054-6, Pub. by Reidel Holland); pap. 10.50 (ISBN 90-277-1080-5). Kluwer Boston.
Sills, David L., et al, eds. Accident at Three Mile Island: The Human Dimensions. 200p. (Orig.). Oct., 1981. lib. bdg. 20.00x (ISBN 0-86531-165-X); Sept., 1981. pap. text ed. 12.00x (ISBN 0-86531-187-0). Westview.

LIABILITY FOR PERSONAL INJURIES
see Personal Injuries

LIABILITY FOR SCHOOL ACCIDENTS
see also Tort Liability of School Districts; Unsatisfied Judgment Funds (Traffic Accidents)
Kigin, Denis J. Teacher Liability in School-Shop Accidents. rev. ed. LC 72-93864. 1973. 6.50x (ISBN 0-911168-28-1); pap. 4.50x (ISBN 0-911168-29-X). Prakken.
Leibee, Howard C. Tort Liability for Injuries to Pupils. (Illus.). 1965. pap. 2.75 (ISBN 0-87506-009-9). Campus.
Poe, Arthur C. School Liability for Injuries to Pupils. LC 79-177156. (Columbia University. Teachers College. Contributions to Education: No. 828). Repr. of 1941 ed. 17.50 (ISBN 0-404-55828-3). AMS Pr.

LIABILITY FOR TRAFFIC ACCIDENTS
see also Traffic Violations
Ross, H. L. Settled Out of Court. 2nd ed. 1980. 19.95x (ISBN 0-686-65269-X); pap. 7.95 class lots of twenty or more (ISBN 0-202-30296-2). Aldine Pub.

LIABILITY INSURANCE
see Insurance, Liability

LIABILITY OF THE STATE
see Government Liability

LIANG CH'I-CH'AO, 1873-1929
Chang, Hao. Liang Ch'i-Ch'ao & Intellectual Transition in China, 1890-1907. LC 75-162635. (East Asian Ser: No. 64). 1971. 16.50x (ISBN 0-674-53009-8). Harvard U Pr.
--Liang Ch'i-Ch'ao & Intellectual Transition in China, 1890-1907. LC 75-162635. (East Asian Ser: No. 64). 1971. 16.50x (ISBN 0-674-53009-8). Harvard U Pr.

LIAPUNOV, ALEKSANDR, MIKHAILOVICH, 1857-1918
Krasovskii, Nikolai N. Stability of Motion: Applications of Lyapunov's Second Method to Differential Systems & Equations with Delay. Brenner, J. L., tr. 1963. 10.00x (ISBN 0-8047-0098-2). Stanford U Pr.

LIAPUNOV FUNCTIONS
Kushner, Harold J. Stochastic Stability & Control. (Mathematics in Science & Engineering Ser.: Vol. 33). 1967. 29.50 (ISBN 0-12-430150-9). Acad Pr.
Stability Theory by Liapunov's Direct Method. LC 77-7285. (Applied Mathematical Sciences: Vol. 22). (Illus.). 1977. 19.30 (ISBN 0-387-90258-9). Springer-Verlag.

LIAR PARADOX
see also Logic; Paradox; Semantics (Philosophy)
Martin, Robert L., ed. The Paradox of the Liar. 1979. lib. bdg. 21.00 (ISBN 0-917930-30-4); pap. text ed. 6.00x (ISBN 0-917930-10-X). Ridgeview.

LIAS
see Geology, Stratigraphic–Jurassic

LIBEL AND SLANDER
see also Blasphemy; Liberty of Speech; Liberty of the Press; Press Law; Privacy, Right Of
Anderson, Douglas A. Washington Merry-Go-Round of Libel Actions. LC 79-18126. 1980. 19.95x (ISBN 0-686-77796-4); pap. 9.95 (ISBN 0-88229-746-5). Nelson-Hall.
Ashley, Paul P. Say It Safely: Legal Limits in Publishing, Radio, & Television. 5th, rev. ed. LC 75-40878. 252p. 1976. 11.50 (ISBN 0-295-95499-X). U of Wash Pr.
Carter-Ruck, Peter. Libel & Slander. xxx, 448p. 1973. 27.50 (ISBN 0-208-01321-0, Archon). Shoe String.
--Libel & Slander. xxx, 448p. 1973. 27.50 (ISBN 0-208-01321-0, Archon). Shoe String.
Cooper, Thomas. Treatise on the Law of Libel & the Liberty of the Press, Showing the Origin, Use & Abuse of the Law of Libel. LC 78-125688. (American Journalists Ser). 1970. Repr. of 1830 ed. 15.00 (ISBN 0-405-01665-4). Arno.
Eldredge, Laurence H. The Law of Defamation. 1978. 36.00 (ISBN 0-672-81587-7, Bobbs-Merrill Law). Michie-Bobbs.
Father of Candor. An Enquiry into the Doctrine, Lately Propagated, Concerning Libels, Warrants, & the Seizure of Papers. facsimile ed. LC 76-121100. (Civil Liberties in American History Ser.). 136p. Repr. of 1764 ed. 17.50 (ISBN 0-306-71970-3). Da Capo.
Hanson, Arthur B. Libel & Related Torts, Vols. 1 & 2. 1969. 48.00 set, incl. 1976 supplements to both vols. (ISBN 0-686-16545-4); supplements alone 10.00 set (ISBN 0-686-16546-2). Am Newspaper.
Kettle, Michael. Salome's Last Veil: The Libel Case of the Century. 320p. 1977. 12.95x (ISBN 0-8464-1131-8). Beekman Pubs.
Lawhorne, Clifton O. Defamation & Public Officials: The Evolving Law of Libel. LC 76-93884. (New Horizons in Journalism Ser). 373p. 1971. 15.00x (ISBN 0-8093-0454-6). S Ill U Pr.
--The Supreme Court & Libel. LC 80-21161. (New Horizons in Journalism Ser.). 176p. 1981. 19.95 (ISBN 0-8093-0998-X). S Ill U Pr.
Nelson, Jerome L. Libel: A Basic Program for Beginning Journalists. 100p. (Prog. Bk.). 1974. pap. text ed. 6.95x (ISBN 0-8138-0950-9). Iowa St U Pr.
Phelps, Robert H. & Hamilton, E. Douglas. Libel: Rights, Risks, Responsibilities. LC 77-86709. 1978. pap. 6.95 (ISBN 0-486-23595-5). Dover.
Sack, Robert D. Libel, Slander, & Related Problems. 697p. 1980. text ed. 50.00 (ISBN 0-686-68826-0, G1-0658). PLI.
Sanford, Bruce W. Synopsis of the Law of Libel & the Right of Privacy. 1980. pap. 1.95 (ISBN 0-915106-19-1). Newspaper Ent.
Sparrow, Gerald. Great Defamers. (Crime in Fact Ser.). 1971. 13.50x (ISBN 0-392-00956-0, LTB). Sportshelf.
Speeches at Full Length in the Cause of the People Against Harry Croswell. LC 78-125716. (American Journalists Ser). 1970. Repr. of 1804 ed. 8.00 (ISBN 0-405-01697-2). Arno.
Steigleman, Walter A. Newspaperman & the Law. LC 74-141419. 1971. Repr. of 1950 ed. lib. bdg. 18.25x (ISBN 0-8371-3059-X, STNE). Greenwood.
Thomas, E. C. Law of Libel and Slander. 3rd rev. ed. LC 73-12791. (Legal Almanac Ser.: No. 15). 128p. 1973. lib. bdg. 5.95 (ISBN 0-379-11093-8). Oceana.
Winfield, Richard N. Libel Litigation Nineteen Eighty-One. (Nineteen Eighty-Nineteen Eighty-One Patents, Copyrights, Trademarks & Literary Property Course Handbook Ser. Subscription). 564p. 1981. pap. text ed. 25.00 (ISBN 0-686-75081-0, G4-3688). PLI.
Wittenberg, Philip. The Protection of Literary Property. rev. ed. LC 77-14370. 1978. 12.95 (ISBN 0-87116-110-9). Writer.

LIBEL AND SLANDER–GREAT BRITAIN
Berkowitz, David S. & Thorne, Samuel E., eds. An Enquiry into the Doctrine Concerning Libels, Warrants, & the Seizure of Papers. LC 77-86678. (Classics of English Legal History in the Modern Era Ser.: Vol. 52). 99p. 1979. lib. bdg. 40.00 (ISBN 0-8240-3151-2). Garland Pub.
Carter-Ruck, Peter. Libel & Slander. xxx, 448p. 1973. 27.50 (ISBN 0-208-01321-0, Archon). Shoe String.
Cooper, Thomas. Treatise on the Law of Libel & the Liberty of the Press, Showing the Origin, Use & Abuse of the Law of Libel. LC 78-125688. (American Journalists Ser). 1970. Repr. of 1830 ed. 15.00 (ISBN 0-405-01665-4). Arno.
--Treatise on the Law of Libel & the Liberty of the Press. LC 71-107408. (Civil Liberties in American History Ser). 1970. Repr. of 1833 ed. lib. bdg. 19.50 (ISBN 0-306-71892-8). Da Capo.
Father of Candor. An Enquiry into the Doctrine, Lately Propagated, Concerning Libels, Warrants, & the Seizure of Papers. facsimile ed. LC 76-121100. (Civil Liberties in American History Ser.). 136p. Repr. of 1764 ed. 17.50 (ISBN 0-306-71970-3). Da Capo.
Holt, Francis L. The Law of Libel, in Which Is Contained a General History of This Law in the Ancient Codes, & of Its Introduction, & Successive Alterations in the Law of England, Comprehending a Digest of All the Leading Cases Upon Libels. Berkowitz, David & Thorne, Samuel, eds. LC 77-89192. (Classics of English Legal History in the Modern Era Ser.: Vol. 115). 1979. Repr. of 1812 ed. lib. bdg. 40.00 (ISBN 0-8240-3152-0). Garland Pub.
Lloyd, H. The Legal Limits of Journalism. 1968. pap. 4.20 (ISBN 0-08-012914-5). Pergamon.

LIBERACE, 1919-
Liberace. The Things I Love. 1.95 (ISBN 0-448-12718-0, MSP). G&D.

LIBERAL, THE, (LONDON, 1822-23)
Pickering, Leslie. The Liberal: Lord Byron, Leigh Hunt & the Liberal. LC 68-763. (Studies in Byron, No. 5). 1972. lib. bdg. 49.95 (ISBN 0-8383-0609-8). Haskell.

LIBERAL CATHOLIC CHURCH
Sheehan, Edmund W. Teaching & Worship of the Liberal Catholic Church. Pitkin, William H., ed. 1978. pap. 2.00 (ISBN 0-918980-07-0). St Alban Pr.

LIBERAL EDUCATION
see Education, Humanistic

LIBERAL JUDAISM
see Reform Judaism

LIBERAL PARTY (CANADA)
Courtney, John C. The Selection of National Party Leaders in Canada. xii, 268p. 1973. 18.50 (ISBN 0-208-01393-8, Archon). Shoe String.
Thomas, Lewis G. Liberal Party in Alberta: A History of Politics in the Province of Alberta, 1905-1921. LC 60-122. 1959. 17.50x (ISBN 0-8020-5083-2). U of Toronto Pr.

LIBERAL PARTY (GREAT BRITAIN)
Bentley, M. The Liberal Mind 1914-1929. LC 76-11072. (Cambridge Studies in the History & Theory of Politics). 1977. 36.00 (ISBN 0-521-21243-X). Cambridge U Pr.
Cook, Christopher. A Short History of the Liberal Party, 1900-1975. 192p. 1976. 19.95x (ISBN 0-312-72065-3). St Martin.
Cross, Colin. The Liberals in Power: 1905-1914. LC 75-40998. 1976. Repr. of 1963 ed. lib. bdg. 18.25x (ISBN 0-8371-8706-0, CRLP). Greenwood.
Dangerfield, George. Strange Death of Liberal England. 7.50 (ISBN 0-8446-1890-X). Peter Smith.
Douglas, Roy. The History of the Liberal Party: 1895-1970. LC 70-169814. 331p. 1971. 20.00 (ISBN 0-8386-1056-0). Fairleigh Dickinson.
--The History of the Liberal Party: 1895-1970. LC 70-169814. 331p. 1971. 20.00 (ISBN 0-8386-1056-0). Fairleigh Dickinson.
Emy, H. V. Liberals, Radicals & Social Politics, 1892-1914. LC 72-85435. 320p. 1973. 32.50 (ISBN 0-521-08740-6). Cambridge U Pr.
McCallum, Ronald B. Liberal Party from Earl Grey to Asquith. (Men & Ideas Ser.: No. 3). 1963. text ed. 3.75x (ISBN 0-575-01058-4). Humanities.
Matthew, H. C. The Liberal Imperialists: The Ideas & Politics of a Post-Gladstonian Elite. (Oxford Historical Monographs). 1973. 36.00x (ISBN 0-19-821842-7). Oxford U Pr.
Morgan, Kenneth O. The Age of Lloyd George: The Liberal Party & British Politics, 1880-1929. (Historical Problems: Studies & Documents). 1971. pap. text ed. 9.95x (ISBN 0-04-942093-3). Allen Unwin.
Oxford Liberal Group & McCallum, R. B. Radical Alternative: Studies in Liberalism. Watson, George, ed. LC 75-3869. 190p. 1975. Repr. of 1962 ed. lib. bdg. 15.00 (ISBN 0-8371-8085-6, OXRA). Greenwood.
Rasmussen, Jorgen S. Retrenchment & Revival: A Study of the Contemporary British Liberal Party. LC 64-17263. 1964. 2.00 (ISBN 0-8165-0079-7). U of Ariz Pr.
Robertson, John M. Meaning of Liberalism. 2nd ed. LC 71-102582. 1971. Repr. of 1925 ed. 12.00 (ISBN 0-8046-0742-7). Kennikat.
Vincent, J. R. The Formation of the British Liberal Party: 1857-1868. 2nd ed. LC 76-7171. 300p. 1976. text ed. 22.50x (ISBN 0-06-497213-5). B&N.
Williams, W. E. The Rise of Gladstone to the Leadership of the Liberal Party, 1859-1868. LC 73-17482. 189p. 1973. Repr. of 1934 ed. lib. bdg. 13.50x (ISBN 0-374-98614-2). Octagon.

LIBERAL REPUBLICAN PARTY
Ross, Earle D. Liberal Republican Movement. LC 71-137286. Repr. of 1919 ed. 8.00 (ISBN 0-404-05407-2). AMS Pr.

LIBERAL THEOLOGY
see Liberalism (Religion)

LIBERALISM
see also Laissez-Faire
Abbott, Philip. Furious Fancies: American Political Thought in the Post-Liberal Era. LC 79-7469. (Contributions in Political Science: No. 35). 1980. lib. bdg. 23.95 (ISBN 0-313-20945-6, AFF/). Greenwood.
--The Shotgun Behind the Door: Liberalism & the Problem of Political Obligation. LC 74-84590. 212p. 1975. 12.50x (ISBN 0-8203-0359-3). U of Ga Pr.
Ackerman, Bruce A. Social Justice in the Liberal State. LC 80-12618. 408p. 1981. pap. 6.95x (ISBN 0-300-02757-5, Y-401). Yale U Pr.
Alexander, Edward. Matthew Arnold & John Stuart Mill. LC 65-14321. 313p. 1965. 16.00x (ISBN 0-231-02786-9). Columbia U Pr.
Barnes, Harry E. The Chickens of the Interventionist Liberals Have Come to Roost. 59.95 (ISBN 0-87700-194-4). Revisionist Pr.
Barran, D. H., et al. Rebuilding the Liberal Order. (Institute of Economic Affairs, Occasional Papers Ser.: No. 27). pap. 2.50 (ISBN 0-255-69646-9). Transatlantic.
Bease, W. Lyon. A Short History of English Liberalism. 1976. lib. bdg. 59.95 (ISBN 0-8490-2600-8). Gordon Pr.
Bentley, M. The Liberal Mind 1914-1929. LC 76-11072. (Cambridge Studies in the History & Theory of Politics). 1977. 36.00 (ISBN 0-521-21243-X). Cambridge U Pr.
Bixler, Julius S. Conversations with an Unrepentant Liberal. LC 72-85298. 128p. 1973. Repr. of 1946 ed. 12.00 (ISBN 0-8046-1713-9). Kennikat.
Bowles, Chester. The Conscience of a Liberal. LC 74-15558. 351p. 1975. Repr. of 1962 ed. lib. bdg. 21.00x (ISBN 0-8371-7826-6, BOCO). Greenwood.

Bramsted, E. K. & Melhuish, K. J., eds. Western Liberalism: A History in Documents from Locke to Croce. 1978. text ed. 31.00x (ISBN 0-582-48830-3); pap. text ed. 16.95x (ISBN 0-582-48831-1). Longman.
Brown, Marshall G. & Stein, Gordon. Freethought in the United States: A Descriptive Bibliography. LC 77-91103. 1978. lib. bdg. 17.50 (ISBN 0-313-20036-X, BFT/). Greenwood.
Buchanan, Patrick J. Conservative Votes, Liberal Victories. LC 75-8302. 256p. 1975. 7.95 (ISBN 0-8129-0582-2). Times Bks.
--Conservative Votes, Liberal Vistories. 184p. Date not set. 5.00 (ISBN 0-686-31153-1). Concord Pr.
Burnham, James. Suicide of the West. LC 64-14211. 1970. Repr. of 1964 ed. 10.00 (ISBN 0-87000-056-X). Arlington Hse.
Caditz, J. White Liberals in Transition. LC 76-21339. 1976. 12.50 (ISBN 0-470-15182-X). Halsted Pr.
Callcott, Wilfrid H. Liberalism in Mexico, 1857-1929. (Illus.). 1965. Repr. of 1931 ed. 25.00 (ISBN 0-208-00278-2, Archon). Shoe String.
Chamberlain, John. Farewell to Reform: The Rise, Life & Decay of the Progressive Mind in America. 1972. pap. 2.95 (ISBN 0-8129-6020-3, QP19). Times Bks.
Charry, George L. Early English Liberalism. 10.95 (ISBN 0-685-60122-6, Pub by Twayne). Cyrco Pr.
Cherry, George. Early English Liberalism. LC 62-19359. 325p. 1962. text ed. 24.50x (ISBN 0-8290-0167-0). Irvington.
Clarke, P. Liberals & Social Democrats. LC 78-6970. 1978. 36.00 (ISBN 0-521-22171-4). Cambridge U Pr.
Cohen, Morris R. Faith of a Liberal. facsimile ed. LC 76-111820. (Essay Index Reprint Ser). 1946. 26.00 (ISBN 0-8369-1598-4). Arno.
Coleman, Frank M. Hobbes & America: Exploring the Constitutional Foundations. LC 76-46434. 1977. 17.50 (ISBN 0-8020-5359-9); pap. 6.50 (ISBN 0-8020-6374-8). U of Toronto Pr.
Commager, Henry Steele. Freedom & Order. LC 66-15755. 1966. 6.50 (ISBN 0-8076-0384-8). Braziller.
Courthope, W. J. Liberal Movement in English Literature. LC 72-194105. 1885. lib. bdg. 12.50 (ISBN 0-8414-2395-4). Folcroft.
Courthope, William J. Liberal Movement in English Literature. LC 72-458. Repr. of 1885 ed. 19.50 (ISBN 0-404-01784-3). AMS Pr.
Cox, C. B. The Free Spirit: A Study of Liberal Humanism in the Novels of George Eliot, Henry James, E. M. Forster, Virginia Woolf, Angus Wilson. LC 80-13281. 195p. 1980. Repr. of 1963 ed. lib. bdg. 18.00x (ISBN 0-313-22449-8, COFS). Greenwood.
Cumming, Robert D. Human Nature & History: A Study of the Development of Liberal Political Thought, 2 Vols. LC 68-54081. 1969. Set. 30.00x (ISBN 0-226-12364-2). U of Chicago Pr.
Dabney, Virginius. Liberalism in the South. LC 77-128983. (BCL Ser. II). Repr. of 1932 ed. 21.50 (ISBN 0-404-00146-7). AMS Pr.
Dangerfield, George. Strange Death of Liberal England. 7.50 (ISBN 0-8446-1890-X). Peter Smith.
De Ruggiero, Guido. History of European Liberalism. Collingwood, R. C., tr. 15.00 (ISBN 0-8446-1970-1). Peter Smith.
--The History of European Liberalism. Collingwood, R. G., tr. 1977. lib. bdg. 59.95 (ISBN 0-8490-1975-3). Gordon Pr.
Doudna, Martin K. Concerned About the Planet: The Reporter Magazine & American Liberalism, 1949-1968. LC 77-10048. (Contributions in American Studies: No. 32). 1977. lib. bdg. 16.95 (ISBN 0-8371-9698-1, DCA/). Greenwood.
Ekirch, Arthur A., Jr. Decline of American Liberalism. LC 67-13171. 1967. pap. text ed. 5.95x (ISBN 0-689-70069-5, 111). Atheneum.
Essays in Liberalism: Being the Lectures & Papers Which Were Delivered at the Liberal Summer School at Oxford. facs. ed. LC 68-16929. (Essay Index Reprint Ser). 1922. 15.00 (ISBN 0-8369-0426-5). Arno.
Everett, Edwin M. Party of Humanity: The Fortnightly Review & Its Contributors, 1865-1874. LC 70-139919. 1971. Repr. of 1939 ed. 16.00 (ISBN 0-8462-1538-1). Russell.
Ferguson, Kathy E. Self, Society, & Womankind: The Dialectic of Liberation. LC 79-6831. (Contributions in Women's Studies: No. 17). xii, 200p. 1980. lib. bdg. 22.95 (ISBN 0-313-22245-2, FSS/). Greenwood.
Fisher, Herbert A. The Republican Tradition in Europe. facsimile ed. LC 75-179519. (Select Bibliographies Reprint Ser). Repr. of 1911 ed. 19.00 (ISBN 0-8369-6648-1). Arno.
Foley, Michael. The New Senate: Liberal Influence on a Conservation Institution. LC 79-27751. 360p. 1980. 20.00x (ISBN 0-300-02440-1). Yale U Pr.
Freeden, Michael. The New Liberalism: An Ideology of Social Reform. 1978. 37.50x (ISBN 0-19-822463-X). Oxford U Pr.
Gerber, William. American Liberalism. LC 74-32118. (World Leaders Ser.: No. 51). 1975. lib. bdg. 10.95 (ISBN 0-8057-3604-2). Twayne.
Goldstene, Paul N. The Collapse of Liberal Empire: Science & Revolution in the Twentieth Century. LC 76-27367. 1977. 13.50x (ISBN 0-300-02029-5). Yale U Pr.
--The Collapse of Liberal Empire: Science & the Revolution in the Twentieth Century. (Political Science Ser.). 160p. 1980. pap. 5.95 (ISBN 0-88316-540-6). Chandler & Sharp.
Grampp, William. Economic Liberalism, 2 vols. Incl. Vol. 1. The Beginnings; Vol. 2. The Classical View. 6.50 ea. (ISBN 0-8446-2151-X). Peter Smith.
Gutmann, Amy. Liberal Equality. LC 79-27258. 320p. 1980. 34.95 (ISBN 0-521-22828-X); pap. 10.95 (ISBN 0-521-29665-X). Cambridge U Pr.
Hale, Charles A. Mexican Liberalism in the Age of Mora, 1821-1853. LC 68-13908. (Caribbean Ser.: No. 11). 1968. 30.00x (ISBN 0-300-00531-8). Yale U Pr.
Hartz, Louis. Liberal Tradition in America: An Interpretation of American Political Thought Since the Revolution. LC 55-5242. 1962. pap. 4.95 (ISBN 0-15-651269-6, HB53, Harv). HarBraceJ.
Hobhouse, L. T. Liberalism. 1911. pap. text ed. 3.95x (ISBN 0-19-500332-2). Oxford U Pr.
--Liberalism. 1979. Repr. lib. bdg. 12.50 (ISBN 0-8495-2283-8). Arden Lib.
Hobhouse, Leonard T. Liberalism. LC 80-10822. 130p. 1980. Repr. of 1911 ed. lib. bdg. 16.50x (ISBN 0-313-22332-7, HOLI). Greenwood.
Hobson, John A. The Crisis of Liberalism: New Issues of Democracy. Clarke, P. F., ed. (Society & the Victorians). 1974. text ed. 14.00x (ISBN 0-06-492913-2). Humanities.
Hoernle, Reinhold F. South African Native Policy & the Liberal Spirit. LC 75-97367. Repr. of 1939 ed. 10.50x (ISBN 0-8371-2428-X). Greenwood.
Holsworth, Robert D. Public Interest Liberalism & the Crisis of Affluence: Reflections on Nader, Environmentalism, & the Politics of a Sustainable Society. (Reference Bks.). 1980. lib. bdg. 17.50 (ISBN 0-8161-9032-1). G K Hall.
Hoover, Kenneth R. A Politics of Identity: Liberation & the Natural Community. LC 75-8797. 180p. 1975. 12.50 (ISBN 0-252-00436-1). U of Ill Pr.
Hughes, Emmet J. Church & the Liberal Society. 1961. pap. 1.95x (ISBN 0-268-00046-8). U of Notre Dame Pr.
Humes, D. Joy. Oswald Garrison Villard, Liberal of the 1920's. LC 77-23783. (Men & Movements Ser.). (Illus.). 1977. Repr. of 1960 ed. lib. bdg. 20.25x (ISBN 0-8371-9752-X, HUOGV). Greenwood.
Jackman, Sydney W., ed. English Reform Tradition Seventeen Ninety to Nineteen Ten. 5.50 (ISBN 0-8446-2295-8). Peter Smith.
Kariel, Henry S. Beyond Liberalism. LC 76-48302. 160p. 1977. 8.00 (ISBN 0-88316-526-0). Chandler & Sharp.
Kaufman, Arnold S. Radical Liberal. 1970. pap. 1.95 (ISBN 0-671-20576-5, Touchstone Bks). S&S.
Kayser, Elmer L. Grand Social Enterprise: A Study of Jeremy Bentham in His Relation to Liberal Nationalism. LC 32-31698. (Columbia University Studies in the Social Sciences: No. 377). Repr. of 1932 ed. 12.50 (ISBN 0-404-51377-8). AMS Pr.
Kehde, Ned, ed. American Left Nineteen Fifty-Five to Nineteen-Seventy: A National Union Catalog of Pamphlets Published in the United States & Canada. LC 76-8002. 526p. (Orig.). 1976. lib. bdg. 27.00 (ISBN 0-8371-8282-4, KTA/). Greenwood.
LaRouche, Lyndon H., Jr. How to Defeat Liberalism & William F. Buckley. LC 79-6749. 222p. 1979. pap. 3.95 (ISBN 0-933488-03-3). New Benjamin.
Laski, Harold J. The Rise of European Liberalism. (Unwin Bks.). 1966. pap. 2.95 (ISBN 0-04-329001-9). Allen Unwin.
Lazarus, Simon. The Genteel Populists. LC 76-25227. 1976. pap. 3.95 (ISBN 0-07-036793-0, SP). McGraw.
Libros, Harold. Hard-Core Liberals: A Sociological Analysis of the Philadelphia Americans for Democratic Action. LC 74-20487. 147p. 1975. text ed. 13.25x (ISBN 0-87073-148-3). Schenkman.
Lowi, Theodore S. The End of Liberalism: The Second Republic of the United States. 2nd ed. (Illus.). 1979. 15.00 (ISBN 0-393-05710-0); pap. text ed. 9.95x (ISBN 0-393-09000-0). Norton.
Ludovici, A. M. Specious Origins of Liberalism. 59.95 (ISBN 0-8490-1106-X). Gordon Pr.
McAuliffe, Mary S. Crisis on the Left: Cold War Politics & American Liberals, 1947-1954. LC 77-73479. 1978. 12.50x (ISBN 0-87023-241-X). U of Mass Pr.
McGrath, Michael J. Liberalism & the Modern Polity. (Political Science; a Comprehensive Publication Program Ser.: Vol. 5). 1978. 14.75 (ISBN 0-8247-6699-7). Dekker.
Manning, D. J. Liberalism. LC 76-15053. (Modern Ideologies Ser.). 1976. text ed. 14.95x (ISBN 0-312-48300-7); pap. text ed. 5.95 (ISBN 0-312-48335-X). St Martin.
Mansfield, Harvey C., Jr. The Spirit of Liberalism. LC 78-7809. 1978. 13.50x (ISBN 0-674-83312-0). Harvard U Pr.
Marcuse, Herbert. Negations: Essays in Critical Theory. Shapiro, Jeremy J., tr. LC 68-12842. 1969. pap. 4.95x (ISBN 0-8070-1553-9, BP320). Beacon Pr.
Martin, James J. American Liberalism & World Politics, 2 vol. set. 1963. 22.50 (ISBN 0-8159-5005-5). Devin.
Mises, Ludwig Von. Liberlaism: A Socio-Economic Exposition. 1978. write for info. NYU Pr.
Murray, Gilbert. Liberality & Civilization: Lectures Given at the Invitation of the Hibbert Trustees in the Universities of Bristol, Glasgow & Birmingham. LC 77-27139. (Hibbert Lectures Ser.). Repr. of 1938 ed. 14.50 (ISBN 0-404-60430-7). AMS Pr.
Nott, Kathleen. The Good Want Power: An Essay in the Psychological Possibilities of Liberalism. LC 76-43390. 1977. 13.50x (ISBN 0-465-02692-3). Basic.
Orton, William A. Liberal Tradition. LC 79-86051. (Essay & General Literature Index Reprint Ser). 1969. Repr. of 1945 ed. 13.75 (ISBN 0-8046-0583-1). Kennikat.
Pangle, Thomas L. Montesquieu's Philosophy of Liberalism. 1974. 15.00x (ISBN 0-226-64543-6). U of Chicago Pr.
Peacock, Alan. The Credibility of Liberal Economics. (Institute of Economic Affairs Occasional Paper Ser.: 50). 1977. pap. 2.50 (ISBN 0-255-36092-4). Transatlantic.
Pennock, James R. Liberal Democracy: Its Merits & Prospects. LC 77-13903. 1978. Repr. of 1950 ed. lib. bdg. 32.25x (ISBN 0-8371-9865-8, PELD). Greenwood.
Perkins, Dexter. American Way. facs. ed. LC 77-128285. (Essay Index Reprint Ser). 1957. 15.00 (ISBN 0-8369-2011-2). Arno.
--American Way. (YA) (gr. 9-12). 1959. pap. 4.95 (ISBN 0-8014-9017-0, CP17). Cornell U Pr.
Read, Leonard E. Elements of Libertarian Leadership. 183p. 1962. pap. 1.00 (ISBN 0-910614-07-5). Foun Econ Ed.
Riker, William H. Liberalism Against Populism. (Illus.). 1981. text ed. price not set (ISBN 0-7167-1245-8); pap. text ed. price not set (ISBN 0-7167-1246-6). W H Freeman.
Robertson, John M. Meaning of Liberalism. 2nd ed. LC 71-102582. 1971. Repr. of 1925 ed. 12.00 (ISBN 0-8046-0742-7). Kennikat.
Salvadori, Massimo. The Liberal Heresy: Origins & Historical Development. LC 77-82859. 1978. 19.95x (ISBN 0-312-48250-7). St Martin.
Salvany, Felix S. Liberalism Is a Sin. 1977. Repr. 4.50 (ISBN 0-913558-13-3). Educator Pubns.
Sampson, Geoffrey. Liberty & Language. 1979. 17.95 (ISBN 0-19-215951-8). Oxford U Pr.
Savelle, Max. Is Liberalism Dead? & Other Essays. LC 65-23913. 224p. 1967. 10.50 (ISBN 0-295-74004-3). U of Wash Pr.
Schapiro, J. Salwyn. Condorcet & the Rise of Liberalism. 1963. lib. bdg. 16.00x (ISBN 0-374-97068-8). Octagon.
--Liberalism & the Challenge of Fascism. 1964. lib. bdg. 20.00x (ISBN 0-374-97087-4). Octagon.
Sheehan, James J. German Liberalism in the Nineteenth Century. LC 77-25971. 1978. lib. bdg. 27.00x (ISBN 0-226-75207-0). U of Chicago Pr.
Sosna, Morton. In Search of the Silent South: Southern Liberals & the Race Issue. LC 77-4965. (Contemporary American History Ser.). 1977. 17.50x (ISBN 0-231-03843-7). Columbia U Pr.
Spender, Stephen. Forward from Liberalism. 1979. Repr. of 1937 ed. lib. bdg. 25.00 (ISBN 0-8482-6212-3). Norwood Edns.
--Forward from Liberalism. 1977. Repr. of 1937 ed. lib. bdg. 27.50 (ISBN 0-8495-4819-5). Arden Lib.
Spitz, David. The Liberal Idea of Freedom. LC 63-11972. 1964. 2.00 (ISBN 0-8165-0051-7). U of Ariz Pr.
Strauss, Leo. Liberalism, Ancient & Modern. LC 68-54139. 1968. 15.00x (ISBN 0-465-03928-6). Basic.
Takemoto, Toru. Failure of Liberalism in Japan: Shidehara Kijuro's Encounter with Anti-Liberals. LC 78-68695. 1979. pap. text ed. 10.50 (ISBN 0-8191-0698-4). U Pr of Amer.
Talmadge, Irving D., ed. Whose Revolution? LC 75-346. (The Radical Tradition in America Ser). 314p. 1975. Repr. of 1941 ed. 21.50 (ISBN 0-88355-250-7). Hyperion Conn.
Tsongas, Paul. The Road from Here: Liberalism & Reality in the 1980's. LC 81-47511. 256p. 1981. 12.95 (ISBN 0-394-52035-1). Knopf.
Unger, Roberto M. Knowledge & Politics. LC 74-15369. (Illus.). 1975. 12.95 (ISBN 0-02-932840-3). Free Pr.
Vanderhofen, Martinius. The Insuperable Opposition Between Catholicism & Liberalism. (Illus.). 107p. 1980. 49.55 (ISBN 0-930582-78-0). Gloucester Art.
Von Mises, Ludwig. Liberalism, a Socio-Economic Exposition. Raico, Ralph, tr. from Ger. LC 78-8457. (Studies in Economic Theory). 207p. 1979. 15.00x (ISBN 0-8362-5107-5); pap. 5.00x (ISBN 0-8362-5106-7). NYU Pr.
Waligorski, Conrad & Hone, Thomas, eds. Anglo-American Liberalism: A Collection of Readings in Political Economy. LC 81-4008. 330p. 1981. text ed. 20.95x (ISBN 0-88229-617-5); pap. text ed. 10.95x (ISBN 0-88229-785-6). Nelson-Hall.
Walter, Edward. The Immorality of Limiting Growth. LC 81-166. 220p. 1981. 33.50x (ISBN 0-87395-478-5, WAIL); pap. 10.95x (ISBN 0-87395-479-3, WAIL-P). State U NY Pr.
Warren, Frank A. Liberals & Communism: The "Red Decade" Revisited. LC 75-45488. 276p. 1976. Repr. of 1966 ed. lib. bdg. 16.75x (ISBN 0-8371-8738-9, WALC). Greenwood.
Wilkinson, Paul. Terrorism & the Liberal State. LC 78-53992. 1979. pap. 8.50x usa (ISBN 0-8147-9184-0). NYU Pr.
Wolfe, Alan. The Limits of Legitimacy: Contradictions of Contemporary Capitalism. LC 76-51567. 1977. 14.95 (ISBN 0-02-935570-2). Free Pr.
Wolff, Robert P. Poverty of Liberalism. LC 68-29314. 1969. pap. 4.50x (ISBN 0-8070-0583-5, BP346). Beacon Pr.
Wood, Ellen. Mind & Politics: An Approach to the Meaning of Liberal & Socialist Individualism. LC 74-153556. 224p. 1972. 22.75x (ISBN 0-520-02029-4). U of Cal Pr.

LIBERALISM (RELIGION)

Ayala, Francisco. El Problema De Liberalismo. 2nd ed. pap. 4.35 (ISBN 0-8477-2402-6). U of PR Pr.
Bonino, Jose M. Doing Theology in a Revolutionary Situation. Lazareth, William H., ed. LC 74-80424. (Confrontation Bks). 208p. 1975. pap. 4.50 (ISBN 0-8006-1451-8, 1-1451). Fortress.
Boys, Don. Liberalism: A Rope of Sand. 1979. 4.95 (ISBN 0-686-25591-7). Freedom U Pr.
Collini, Stefan. Liberalism & Sociology: Lt. Hobhouse & Political Argument in English 1880-1914. LC 78-23779. 1979. 32.95 (ISBN 0-521-22304-0). Cambridge U Pr.
Jedin, Hubert & Dolan, John P., eds. The Church in the Age of Liberalism. (History of the Church: Vol. 8). 1981. 37.50 (ISBN 0-8245-0011-3). Crossroad NY.
McCann, Dennis P. Christian Realism & Liberation Theology: Practical Theologies in Creative Conflict. LC 80-23163. 256p. (Orig.). 1981. pap. 9.95 (ISBN 0-88344-086-5). Orbis Bks.
Machen, J. Gresham. Christianity & Liberalism. 1923. pap. 4.95 (ISBN 0-8028-1121-3). Eerdmans.
Opton, Frank. Liberal Religion: Principles & Practices. LC 81-81129. (Library of Liberal Religion). 300p. 1981. 15.95 (ISBN 0-87975-155-X). Prometheus Bks.
Perrens, Francois T. Libertins en France au Dix-Septieme Siecle. LC 72-168701. 428p. (Fr.). 1973. Repr. of 1896 ed. lib. bdg. 29.00 (ISBN 0-8337-2728-1). B Franklin.
Reardon, B. Liberalism & Tradition. LC 75-7214. 320p. 1975. 42.00 (ISBN 0-521-20776-2). Cambridge U Pr.
Richesin, L. Dale, ed. The Challenge of Liberation Theology: A First World Response. Mahan, Brian. LC 81-9527. 192p. (Orig.). 1981. pap. 7.95 (ISBN 0-88344-092-X). Orbis Bks.
Rochester, Stuart I. American Liberal Disillusionment in the Wake of World War I. LC 76-47613. 1977. 16.50 (ISBN 0-271-01233-1). Pa St U Pr.
Rupp, George. Culture-Protestantism: German Liberal Theology at the Turn of the Twentieth Century. LC 77-13763. (American Academy of Religion. Studies in Religion: No. 15). 1977. pap. 7.50 (ISBN 0-89130-197-6, 010015). Scholars Pr Ca.
Sandmel, Samuel. The Several Israels. 1971. 10.00x (ISBN 0-87068-160-5). Ktav.
Sarda y Salvany, Felix. What Is Liberalism? Pallen, Conde B., tr. from Span. LC 79-87552. Orig. Title: Liberalism Isa Sin. 176p. 1979. pap. 2.00 (ISBN 0-89555-088-1, 130). Tan Bks Pubs.

Tambasco, Anthony J. The Bible for Ethics: Juan Luis Segundo & First-World Ethics. LC 80-6253. 286p. (Orig.). 1981. lib. bdg. 19.25 (ISBN 0-8191-1556-8); pap. text ed. 10.50 (ISBN 0-8191-1557-6). U Pr of Amer.

LIBERATOR (BOMBERS)
see B-Twenty-Four Bomber

LIBERIA

American Colonization Society. Annual Reports: First to Ninety First, Ninety Third. LC 77-90128. (Illus.). 1818-1910. Repr. 180.00x (ISBN 0-8371-2476-X, Pub. by Negro U Pr). Greenwood.

Anderson, R. Earle. Liberia, America's African Friend. LC 76-24842. (Illus.). 305p. 1976. Repr. of 1952 ed. lib. bdg. 21.50x (ISBN 0-8371-8999-3, ANLI). Greenwood.

Bacon, Leonard. A Discourse Preached in the Center Church. facsimile ed. LC 78-168507. (Black Heritage Library Collection). Repr. of 1828 ed. 9.50 (ISBN 0-8369-8861-2). Arno.

Boone, Clinton C. Liberia As I Know It. LC 73-106867. (Illus.). Repr. of 1929 ed. 10.50x (ISBN 0-8371-3284-3, Pub. by Negro U Pr). Greenwood.

Brawley, Benjamin G. Social History of the American Negro: Being a History of the Negro Problem in the United States. (Basic Afro-American Reprint Library). Repr. of 1921 ed. 19.50 (ISBN 0-384-05580-X). Johnson Repr.

Buell, Raymond L. Liberia: A Century of Survival Eighteen Forty-Seven to Nineteen Forty-Seven. LC 47-1714. 1969. Repr. of 1947 ed. 12.00 (ISBN 0-527-13400-7). Kraus Repr.

Cassell, Abayomi. Liberia: History of the First African Republic, Vol. 1. (Illus.). 457p. 10.00 (ISBN 0-685-41741-7). Fountainhead.

Cook, David R. The Water Mites of Liberia. (Memoirs Ser: No. 6). (Illus.). 418p. 1966. 25.00 (ISBN 0-686-17144-6). Am Entom Inst.

Crummell, Alexander. Future of Africa. LC 78-79770. Repr. of 1862 ed. 15.50x (ISBN 0-8371-0972-8, Pub. by Negro U Pr). Greenwood.

--Future of Africa. LC 79-92424. 1862. 13.00 (ISBN 0-403-00156-0). Scholarly.

Johnston, Harry H. Liberia, 2 Vols. LC 71-78372. (Illus.). Repr. of 1906 ed. 76.00x (ISBN 0-8371-3897-3, Pub. by Negro U Pr). Greenwood.

Liberia, Republic of. Reports & Opinions of the Attorney General of the Republic of Liberia: December 1922-July 1930. 448p. 1969. 30.00x (ISBN 0-8014-0530-0). Cornell U Pr.

Liberian Studies Journal, 6 vols. Incl. Vol. 1. 1968-1969; Vol. 2. 1969-1970; Vol. 3. 1970-1971; Vol. 4. 1971-1972; Vol. 5. 1972-1974; Vol. 6. 1975. 8.00 ea. Liberian Studies.

Maugham, Reginald C. Republic of Liberia. LC 79-90123. Repr. of 1920 ed. 17.75x (ISBN 0-8371-2018-7). Greenwood.

Nesbit, William & Williams, Samuel. Two Black Views of Liberia: Four Months in Liberia, or African Colonization Exposed Four Years in Liberia, a Sketch of the Life of Rev. Samuel Williams. LC 70-92234. (American Negro: His History & Literature, Ser. No. 3). 1970. Repr. of 1855 ed. 9.00 (ISBN 0-405-01936-X). Arno.

Report to the Government of Liberia on Conservation Management & Utilization of Wildlife Resources. 1969. pap. 7.50x (ISBN 2-88032-044-5, IUCN61, IUCN). Unipub.

Von Gnielinski, Stefan, ed. Liberia in Maps. LC 72-80411. (Graphic Perspectives of Developing Countries Ser.). (Illus.). 111p. 1972. text ed. 29.50x (ISBN 0-8419-0126-0, Africana). Holmes & Meier.

Williams, George W. History of the Negro Race in America from 1619 to 1880, 2 vols. LC 69-19636. (American Negro: His History & Literature Ser.., No. 1). 1968. Repr. of 1883 ed. Set. 39.00 (ISBN 0-405-01844-4). Arno.

Young, James C. Liberia Rediscovered. LC 74-15109. Repr. of 1934 ed. 15.00 (ISBN 0-404-12157-8). AMS Pr.

LIBERIA-BIBLIOGRAPHY

Holsoe, Svend E. Bibliography on Liberia: Part Two. (Liberian Studies Research Working Papers: No. 3). 1971. 2.50 (ISBN 0-686-11768-9). Liberian Studies.

Holsoe, Svend E., ed. Bibliography on Liberia: Part Three. (Liberian Research Working Papers: No. 5). 1976. 6.00 (ISBN 0-686-17779-7). Liberian Studies.

LIBERIA-DESCRIPTION AND TRAVEL

Becker-Donner, Etta. Hinterland Liberia. LC 74-15030. Repr. of 1939 ed. 27.50 (ISBN 0-404-12037-7). AMS Pr.

Brittan, Harriett G. Scenes & Incidents of Everyday Life in Africa. LC 70-75541. Repr. of 1860 ed. 16.00x (ISBN 0-8371-0981-7). Greenwood.

Greene, Graham. Journey Without Maps. 1978. pap. 3.25 (ISBN 0-14-003280-0). Penguin.

Harvard African Expedition. African Republic of Liberia & the Belgian Congo, Based on the Observations Made & Material Collected During the Harvard African Expediton, 1926-1927, 2 Vols. Strong, Richard P., ed. Repr. of 1930 ed. Set. lib. bdg. 86.50x (ISBN 0-8371-2480-8, HAAE). Greenwood.

Schulze, Willi. A New Geography of Liberia. (Illus.). 222p. 1974. pap. text ed. 9.50x (ISBN 0-582-60255-6). Longman.

LIBERIA-ECONOMIC CONDITIONS

Clower, Robert W., et al. Growth Without Development: An Economic Survey of Liberia. (Northwestern University African Studies Ser.: No. 16). 1966. 15.95x (ISBN 0-8101-0065-7). Northwestern U Pr.

LIBERIA-HISTORY

Alexander, Archibald. History of Colonization of the Western Coast of Africa. 2nd facs. ed. LC 71-149861. (Black Heritage Library Collection Ser). 1849. 27.25 (ISBN 0-8369-8743-8). Arno.

--History of Colonization on the Western Coast of Africa. LC 70-82319. Repr. of 1846 ed. 28.00x (ISBN 0-8371-1652-X, Pub. by Negro U Pr). Greenwood.

Azikiwe, Nnamdi. Liberia in World Politics. LC 71-107503. Repr. of 1934 ed. 20.50 (ISBN 0-8371-3774-8, Pub. by Negro U Pr). Greenwood.

Buell, Raymond L. Liberia: A Century of Survival, Eighteen Forty-Seven to Nineteen Forty-Seven. (African Handbooks Ser.: Vol. 7). (Illus.). 1947. 3.00 (ISBN 0-686-24090-1). Univ Mus of U.

Foote, Andrew H. Africa & the American Flag. LC 71-82050. Repr. of 1854 ed. 17.75x (ISBN 0-8371-1543-4, Pub. by Negro U Pr). Greenwood.

Guannu, Joseph S. Liberian History Before Eighteen Fifty-Seven: A Reference for Elementary Pupils. 1977. 6.00 (ISBN 0-682-48868-2). Exposition.

Gurley, Ralph R. Life of Jehudi Ashmun. facs. ed. LC 73-149867. (Black Heritage Library Collection Ser). 1835. 20.50 (ISBN 0-8369-8749-7). Arno.

--Life of Jehudi Ashmun, Late Colonial Agent in Liberia. LC 76-75532. Repr. of 1835 ed. 21.00x (ISBN 0-8371-1101-3, Pub. by Negro U Pr). Greenwood.

Henries, A. D. Short History of the Liberian Nation. 1966. text ed. 3.00 (ISBN 0-02-974080-0). Macmillan.

Innes, William, ed. Liberia: Or, Early History & Signal Preservation of the American Colony of Free Negroes on the Coast of Africa. facs. ed. LC 76-154078. (Black Heritage Library Collection Ser). 1831. 14.00 (ISBN 0-8369-8789-6). Arno.

McPherson, J. H. History of Liberia. pap. 7.00 (ISBN 0-685-30639-9). Johnson Repr.

McPherson, John H. History of Liberia. LC 78-63806. (Johns Hopkins University. Studies in the Social Sciences. Ninth Ser. 1891: 10). Repr. of 1891 ed. 11.50 (ISBN 0-404-61069-2). AMS Pr.

Murdza, Peter J., Jr., ed. Immigrants to Liberia, 1865-1904: An Alphabetical Listing. (Liberian Studies Research Working Papers: No. 4). 1975. 4.00 (ISBN 0-686-17780-0). Liberian Studies.

Shick, Tom. Emigrants to Liberia 1820-1843. (Liberian Studies Research Working Papers: No. 2). 1971. 4.00 (ISBN 0-686-11769-7). Liberian Studies.

Shick, Tom W. Behold the Promised Land: A History of Afro-American Settler Society in 19th Century Liberia. LC 79-22960. (Studies in Atlantic History & Culture). 1980. text ed. 16.00x (ISBN 0-8018-2309-9). Johns Hopkins.

Sundiata, I. K. Black Scandal: America & the Liberian Labor Crisis, 1929-1936. LC 79-25601. (Illus.). 1980. 15.95 (ISBN 0-915980-96-7). Inst Study Human.

A Third of A Century with George Way Harley in Liberia. (Liberian Studies Monograph Ser: No. 2). 1973. 4.00 (ISBN 0-916712-00-1). Liberian Studies.

Walker, Thomas H. History of Liberia. LC 76-109989. Repr. of 1921 ed. 10.25x (ISBN 0-8371-4127-3, Pub. by Negro U Pr). Greenwood.

LIBERIA-JUVENILE LITERATURE

Henries, A. D. Heroes & Heroines of Liberia. 1962. pap. 1.85 (ISBN 0-02-974090-8). Macmillan.

LIBERIA-POLITICS AND GOVERNMENT

Best, Kenneth Y. Cultural Policy in Liberia. (Studies & Documents on Cultural Policies). (Illus.). 59p. 1974. pap. 5.00 (ISBN 92-3-101160-X, U132, UNESCO). Unipub.

Clapham, C. Liberia and Sierra Leone. LC 75-32447. (African Studies: No.20). (Illus.). 160p. 1976. 19.95 (ISBN 0-521-21095-X). Cambridge U Pr.

Guannu, Joseph S., compiled by. The Inaugural Addresses of the Presidents of Liberia: From Joseph Jenkins Robert to William Richard Tolbert Jr., 1848 to 1976. 1980. 20.00 (ISBN 0-682-49444-5). Exposition.

Henries, A. D. Civics for Liberian Schools. 1966. 3.75 (ISBN 0-02-974070-3). Macmillan.

Hlope, Stephen S. Class, Ethnicity & Politics in Liberia: Analysis of Power Struggles in the Tubman & Tolbert Administrations from 1944-1975. LC 79-63261. 1979. pap. text ed. 11.25 (ISBN 0-8191-0721-2). U Pr of Amer.

Liebenow, J. Gus. Liberia: The Evolution of Privilege. LC 69-18359. (Africa in the Modern World Ser.). (Illus.). 247p. 1969. 19.50x (ISBN 0-8014-0506-8); pap. 5.95 (ISBN 0-8014-9096-0, CP96). Cornell U Pr.

Lowenkopf, Martin. Politics in Liberia: The Conservative Road to Development. LC 75-27010. (Publications Ser.: No. 151). 260p. 1976. 11.95 (ISBN 0-8179-6511-4). Hoover Inst Pr.

Nimley, Anthony J. The Liberian Bureaucracy: An Analysis & Evaluation of the Environment, Structures & Functions. LC 79-63561. 1979. pap. text ed. 11.25 (ISBN 0-8191-0732-8). U Pr of Amer.

Press Division, Executive Mansion. Presidential Papers (Liberia), 1973-74. (Illus.). 1975. 15.00x (ISBN 0-8002-1830-2). Intl Pubns Serv.

Reeve, Henry F. Black Republic: Liberia, Its Political & Social Conditions Today. LC 70-78586. (Illus.). Repr. of 1923 ed. 13.50x (ISBN 0-8371-1412-8, Pub. by Negro U Pr). Greenwood.

Sundiata, I. K. Black Scandal: America & the Liberian Labor Crisis, 1929-1936. LC 79-25601. (Illus.). 1980. 15.95 (ISBN 0-915980-96-7). Inst Study Human.

Wreh, Tuan. The Love of Liberty: The Rule of President William V. S. Tubman in Liberia 1944-1971. LC 76-17361. (Illus.). 1976. 12.00x (ISBN 0-87663-275-4). Universe.

LIBERIA-SOCIAL CONDITIONS

Hlope, Stephen S. Class, Ethnicity & Politics in Liberia: Analysis of Power Struggles in the Tubman & Tolbert Administrations from 1944-1975. LC 79-63261. 1979. pap. text ed. 11.25 (ISBN 0-8191-0721-2). U Pr of Amer.

Reeve, Henry F. Black Republic: Liberia, Its Political & Social Conditions Today. LC 70-78586. (Illus.). Repr. of 1923 ed. 13.50x (ISBN 0-8371-1412-8, Pub. by Negro U Pr). Greenwood.

Sundiata, I. K. Black Scandal: America & the Liberian Labor Crisis, 1929-1936. LC 79-25601. (Illus.). 1980. 15.95 (ISBN 0-915980-96-7). Inst Study Human.

Wiley, Bell I., ed. Slaves No More: Letters from Liberia, 1833-1869. LC 79-4015. (Illus.). 360p. 1980. 21.50x (ISBN 0-8131-1388-1). U Pr of Ky.

LIBERIA-SOCIAL LIFE AND CUSTOMS

Becker-Donner, Etta. Hinterland Liberia. LC 74-15030. Repr. of 1939 ed. 27.50 (ISBN 0-404-12037-7). AMS Pr.

Dennis, Benjamin G. The Gbandes: A People of the Liberian Hinterland. LC 72-88580. 1973. 22.95x (ISBN 0-911012-50-8). Nelson-Hall.

Harvard African Expedition. African Republic of Liberia & the Belgian Congo, Based on the Observations Made & Material Collected During the Harvard African Expediton, 1926-1927, 2 Vols. Strong, Richard P., ed. Repr. of 1930 ed. Set. lib. bdg. 86.50x (ISBN 0-8371-2480-8, HAAE). Greenwood.

Siegmann, William C. & Schmidt, Cynthia E. Rock of the Ancestors. (Illus.). 1977. pap. text ed. 6.50 (ISBN 0-686-10538-9). Liberian Studies.

LIBERIAN TALES
see Tales, Liberian

LIBERTARIANISM
see also Anarchism and Anarchists; Individualism; Liberty

Challenge: A Libertarian Weekly, Vols. 1-2, No. 18. 1938-39. Repr. lib. bdg. 65.00x (ISBN 0-8371-9138-6, CH00). Greenwood.

Strauss, Erwin S. The Case Against a Liberatarian Political Party. 1980. pap. 4.50 (ISBN 0-686-29514-5). Loompanics.

LIBERTY
see also Anarchism and Anarchists; Assembly, Right Of; Civil Rights; Conformity; Equality; Freedom of Association; Freedom of Movement; Liberalism; Libertarianism; Liberty of Contract; Political Rights; Religious Liberty; Social Control; Teaching, Freedom Of

Acton, Lord. Essays on Freedom & Power. 8.75 (ISBN 0-8446-0000-8). Peter Smith.

Adams, James L. On Being Human, Religiously: Selected Essays of James Luther Adams. Stackhouse, Max L., ed. LC 75-36037. 288p. 1976. 9.95 (ISBN 0-8070-1122-3). Beacon Pr.

Adler, Mortimer J. Freedom: A Study of the Development of the Concept in the English & American Traditions of Philosophy. (Overview Studies). (Orig.). 1968. pap. 0.50x (ISBN 0-87343-007-7). Magi Bks.

--The Idea of Freedom, 2 vols. LC 72-7872. 1973. Repr. lib. bdg. 54.00x (ISBN 0-8371-6547-4, ADIF). Greenwood.

Almond, Gabriel, et al. Freedom & Development. 4.75x (ISBN 0-210-22595-5). Asia.

Anderson, Gillian B., ed. Freedom's Voice in Poetry & Song. LC 77-78353. 1977. 55.00 (ISBN 0-8420-2124-8). Scholarly Res Inc.

Anscel, E. The Delemmas of Freedom. 1978. 10.50 (ISBN 0-9960009-0-9, Pub. by Kaido Hungary). Heyden.

Aptheker, Herbert. The Nature of Democracy, Freedom & Revolution. 2nd ed. 128p. (Orig.). 1981. pap. 1.95 (ISBN 0-7178-0137-3). Intl Pub Co.

Archer, Peter & Lord Reay. Freedom at Stake. LC 67-15647. (Background Ser.). 1967. 6.25 (ISBN 0-8023-1118-0). Dufour.

Aron, Arthur. Free Ourselves: Forgotten Goals of the Revolution. (Illus.). 64p. (Orig.). 1972. pap. 1.35 (ISBN 0-87810-018-0). Times Change.

Arrow, Kenneth J. Social Choice & Individual Values. 2nd ed. (Cowles Foundation Monograph: No. 12). 1970. 15.00x (ISBN 0-300-01363-9); pap. 3.95x (ISBN 0-300-01364-7, Y233). Yale U Pr.

Barth, Karl. Humanity of God. Weiser, Thomas & Thomas, John N., trs. LC 60-3479. 1960. pap. 4.95 (ISBN 0-8042-0612-0). John Knox.

Bates, Ernest. This Land of Liberty. LC 73-19817. (Civil Liberties in American History Ser.). 383p. 1974. Repr. of 1930 ed. lib. bdg. 35.00 (ISBN 0-306-70597-4). Da Capo.

Bay, Christian. The Structure of Freedom. rev. ed. LC 58-10475. 1970. 17.50x (ISBN 0-8047-0539-9); pap. 6.95 (ISBN 0-8047-0540-2, SP120). Stanford U Pr.

Bennett, J. F. The Way to Be Free. 1980. pap. 6.95 (ISBN 0-87728-491-1). Weiser.

Bentham, Jeremy & Mill, John S. The Utilitarians. Incl. Principles of Morals & Legislation. Bentham; Utilitarianism & on Liberty. Mill, John S. LC 62-2159. pap. 3.50 (ISBN 0-385-08256-8, C265, Anch). Doubleday.

Berger, Morroe, et al. Freedom & Control in Modern Society. 1964. lib. bdg. 17.50x (ISBN 0-374-90608-4). Octagon.

Bergmann, Frithjof. On Being Free. LC 77-89760. 1979. pap. text ed. 4.95x (ISBN 0-268-01493-0). U of Notre Dame Pr.

--On Being Free. LC 77-89760. 1977. text ed. 10.00x (ISBN 0-268-01492-2). U of Notre Dame Pr.

Berlin, Isaiah. Four Essays on Liberty. 1970. 14.95 (ISBN 0-19-501242-9). Oxford U Pr.

--Four Essays on Liberty. 1968. pap. 4.95 (ISBN 0-19-500272-5, GB). Oxford U Pr.

Bettelheim, Bruno. Informed Heart. 1971. pap. 2.75 (ISBN 0-380-01302-9, 52704, Discus). Avon.

--Informed Heart: Autonomy in a Mass Age. 1960. 12.95 (ISBN 0-02-903200-8). Free Pr.

Bhattacharrya, K. C. Search for the Absolute in Neo-Vedanta. Burch, George B., ed. LC 75-17740. 212p. 1976. text ed. 12.00x (ISBN 0-8248-0296-9). U Pr of Hawaii.

Biddle, Francis. Fear of Freedom. LC 76-138496. (Civil Liberties in American History Ser). 1971. Repr. of 1951 ed. lib. bdg. 37.50 (ISBN 0-306-70073-5). Da Capo.

Bidney, David, ed. Concept of Freedom in Anthropology. (Studies in General Anthropology). 1963. text ed. 32.75x (ISBN 90-2790-316-6). Mouton.

Boller, Paul F., Jr. Freedom & Fate in American Thought: From Edwards to Dewey. LC 78-5813. (Bicentennial Ser. in American Studies: No. 7). 1978. 15.00 (ISBN 0-87074-169-1). SMU Press.

Bossong, Ken & Denman, Scott. Nuclear Power & Civil Liberties: Can We Have Both? 2nd ed. 150p. 1981. 7.50 (ISBN 0-89988-071-1). Citizens Energy.

Bowie, Norman E. & Simon, R. L. The Individual & the Political Order: An Introduction to Social & Political Philosophy. 1977. pap. text ed. 11.95 (ISBN 0-13-457143-6). P-H.

Brackenridge, Hugh H. The Standard of Liberty, an Occasional Paper. 1976. Repr. 21.00 (ISBN 0-685-71963-4, Regency). Scholarly.

Buchanan, James M. The Limits of Liberty: Between Anarchy & Leviathan. LC 74-11616. 1977. pap. 4.95 (ISBN 0-226-07820-5, P714, Phoen). U of Chicago Pr.

Busha, Charles H., ed. An Intellectual Freedom Primer. LC 77-7887. 1977. 20.00x (ISBN 0-87287-172-X). Libs Unl.

Cardozo, Benjamin N. Paradoxes of Legal Science. LC 76-104241. Repr. of 1928 ed. lib. bdg. 15.00x (ISBN 0-8371-3263-0, CALS). Greenwood.

Carmer, Carl L. For the Rights of Men. facs. ed. LC 75-86740. (Essay Index Reprint Ser). 1947. 13.00 (ISBN 0-8369-1175-X). Arno.

Carrier, Herve. L' Universite Entre L'engagement et la Liberte. (Fr.). 1972. pap. 7.00 (ISBN 0-8294-0322-1, Pub. by Gregorian U Pr). Loyola.

Carson, Clarence B. American Tradition. 306p. 1970. pap. 4.00 (ISBN 0-910614-17-2). Foun Econ Ed.
--Fateful Turn: From Individual Liberty to Collectivism, 1880-1960. 255p. 1963. 3.50 (ISBN 0-910614-32-6). Foun Econ Ed.
Cary, Joyce. Power in Men. LC 63-18741. 320p. 1963. 7.50 (ISBN 0-295-73890-1). U of Wash Pr.
Caudwell, Christopher, pseud. Liberty, a Study in Bourgeois Illusion. 1970. Repr. pap. 0.75 (ISBN 0-88211-002-0). S A Russell.
Chafee, Zechariah. The Blessings of Liberty. LC 72-8237. 350p. 1973. Repr. of 1956 ed. lib. bdg. 15.75x (ISBN 0-8371-6536-9, CHBL). Greenwood.
Charvet, John. A Critique of Freedom & Equality. (Cambridge Studies in the History & Theory of Politics). 224p. Date not set. 36.00 (ISBN 0-521-23727-0). Cambridge U Pr.
Clifton, Merritt. Freedom Comes from Human Beings. 80p. (Orig.). 1980. pap. 4.00 (ISBN 0-686-28738-X). Samisdat.
Cohen, Monroe D., ed. Personal Liberty & Education. LC 76-2511. 288p. 1976. 8.95 (ISBN 0-590-07462-8, Citation); pap. text ed. 4.95 (ISBN 0-590-09406-8). Schol Bk Serv.
--Personal Liberty & Education. LC 76-2511. 288p. 1976. 8.95 (ISBN 0-590-07462-8, Citation); pap. text ed. 4.95 (ISBN 0-590-09406-8). Schol Bk Serv.
Cole, Franklin P. They Preached Liberty. LC 76-26327. 1976. 5.95 (ISBN 0-913966-16-9, Liberty Press); pap. 1.25 (ISBN 0-913966-20-7). Liberty Fund.
Commager, Henry S. Freedom, Loyalty, Dissent. 1954. 10.95 (ISBN 0-19-500510-4). Oxford U Pr.
Commager, Henry S., et al. Civil Liberties Under Attack: Publications of the William J. Cooper Foundation, Swarthmore College. facs. ed. LC 68-14899. (Essay Index Reprint Ser). 1951. 15.00 (ISBN 0-8369-0308-0). Arno.
Committee for the Bicentennial National Conference of Catholic Bishops. Liberty & Justice for All: A Discussion Guide. 1.50, 10 copies 1.25 (ISBN 0-686-11440-X). US Catholic.
Conference On The Scientific Spirit And Democratic Faith - 2nd. Authoritarian Attempt to Capture Education. facs. ed. (Essay Index Reprint Ser). 1945. 13.00 (ISBN 0-8369-1819-3). Arno.
Conference On The Scientific Spirit And Democratic Faith - 3rd. Science for Democracy. facs. ed. LC 70-121459. (Essay Index Reprint Ser). 1946. 16.00 (ISBN 0-8369-1793-6). Arno.
Conference On The Scientific Spirit And Democratic Faith - 1st - New York - 1943. Scientific Spirit & Democratic Faith. facs. ed. LC 72-121457. (Essay Index Reprint Ser). 1944. 12.00 (ISBN 0-8369-1872-X). Arno.
Corwin, Edward S. Liberty Against Government: The Rise, Flowering, & Decline of a Famous Judicial Concept. LC 77-4090. 1978. Repr. of 1948 ed. lib. bdg. 19.75x (ISBN 0-8371-9589-6, COLAG). Greenwood.
Coulton, G. G. Inquisition & Liberty. 8.00 (ISBN 0-8446-0560-3). Peter Smith.
Cowan, Z. Individual Liberty & the Law. 1977. 10.00 (ISBN 0-379-00597-2). Oceana.
Croce, Benedetto. History As Story of Liberty. pap. 2.65 (ISBN 0-89526-980-5). Regnery-Gateway.
Crocker, Lawrence H. Positive Liberty: An Essay in Normative Political Philosophy. (Melbourne International Philosophy Ser.: Vol. 7). 156p. 1980. lib. bdg. 29.00 (ISBN 90-247-2291-8, Pub. by Martinus Nijhoff Netherlands). Kluwer Boston.
Dahrendorf, Ralf. The New Liberty: Survival & Justice in a Changing World. LC 75-186. x, 112p. 1975. 7.50x (ISBN 0-8047-0882-7). Stanford U Pr.
D'Angelo, Edward. Problem of Freedom & Determinism. LC 68-63295. 1968. 6.00x (ISBN 0-8262-7713-6). U of Mo Pr.
D'Antonio, William V. & Ehrlich, Howard J., eds. Power & Democracy in America. 1961. pap. 1.50x (ISBN 0-268-00368-8). U of Notre Dame Pr.
Davenport, Russell W. The Dignity of Man. LC 72-10694. 338p. 1973. Repr. of 1955 ed. lib. bdg. 20.00x (ISBN 0-8371-6614-4, DADI). Greenwood.
Davis, Roy E. Freedom Is New. 189p. 1980. pap. 3.95 (ISBN 0-87707-221-3). CSA Pr.
De Jouvenel, Bertrand. Sovereignty: An Inquiry into the Political Good. Huntington, J. F., tr. LC 57-9548. 1957. 10.00x (ISBN 0-226-14161-6). U of Chicago Pr.
Del Rio, Angel, ed. Responsible Freedom in the Americas. Repr. of 1955 ed. lib. bdg. 27.75x (ISBN 0-8371-0199-9, RIFA). Greenwood.
De Robigne, Bennel. Trial of D. M. Bennett: Upon the Charge of Depositing Prohibited Matter in the Mail. LC 72-8110. (Civil Liberties in American History Ser). 202p. 1973. Repr. of 1879 ed. lib. bdg. 22.50 (ISBN 0-306-70525-7). Da Capo.
De Ruggiero, Guido. History of European Liberalism. Collingwood, R. C., tr. 15.00 (ISBN 0-8446-1970-1). Peter Smith.
Deutsch, Monroe E. Letter & the Spirit: A Selection from His Addresses. facs. ed. (Essay Index Reprint Ser). 1943. 18.00 (ISBN 0-8369-0372-2). Arno.
Donald, David H. Liberty & Union. 1978. pap. text ed. 10.95x (ISBN 0-669-01152-5). Heath.
Douglas, William O. The Anatomy of Liberty. pap. 1.95 (ISBN 0-671-03281-X, Touchstone Bks). S&S.
Drew, Philip. The Meaning of Freedom. 460p. 38.50 (ISBN 0-08-025743-7). Pergamon.
Eden, A. Freedom & Order: Selected Speeches, 1939-1946. Repr. of 1948 ed. 18.00 (ISBN 0-527-26320-6). Kraus Repr.
Edwards, Jonathan. A Dissertation Concerning Liberty & Necessity. LC 73-21786. 1974. Repr. of 1797 ed. lib. bdg. 22.50 (ISBN 0-8337-1003-6). B Franklin.
Ewing, David W. Freedom Inside the Organization: Bringing Civil Liberties to the Workplace. 1978. pap. 3.95 (ISBN 0-07-019847-0, SP). McGraw.
Ferguson, Kathy E. Self, Society, & Womankind: The Dialectic of Liberation. LC 79-6831. (Contributions in Women's Studies: No. 17). xii, 200p. 1980. lib. bdg. 22.95 (ISBN 0-313-22245-2, FSS/). Greenwood.
Feyerabend, Paul. Erkenntnis Fuer Freie Menschen. rev. ed. (Edition Suhrkamp. Neue Folge: es.NF 11). 270p. (Ger.). 1980. pap. text ed. 6.50 (ISBN 3-518-11011-X, Pub. by Suhrkamp Verlag Germany). Suhrkamp.
Foldvary, Fred E. The Soul of Liberty: The Universal Ethic of Freedom & Human Rights. LC 79-56782. (Illus.). 330p. 1980. pap. 6.75 (ISBN 0-9603872-1-8). Gutenberg.
Foster, Genevieve. Birthdays of Freedom: From Early Egypt to July 4, 1776. new ed. LC 73-5183. (Illus.). 128p. (gr. 4-7). 1973. reinforced bdg. 6.95 (ISBN 0-684-13496-9, ScribJ). Scribner.
Freedom or Order: Must We Choose? (Crucial Issues in American Government Ser.). (gr. 9-12). 1976. pap. text ed. 4.96 (ISBN 0-205-04905-2, 7649053). Allyn.
Friedrich, Carl J., ed. Liberty. (Nomos Ser: No. 4). 352p. 1962. 15.00x (ISBN 0-88311-034-2). Lieber-Atherton.
Fromm, Erich. Sane Society. 1955. pap. 5.95 (ISBN 0-03-018446-0). HR&W.
--Sane Society. 320p. 1977. pap. 2.95 (ISBN 0-449-30821-9, Prem). Fawcett.
Gastil, Raymond D. Freedom in the World: Political Rights & Civil Liberties, 1979. LC 79-87596. (Illus.). 1979. lib. bdg. 20.00 (ISBN 0-932088-01-5). Freedom Hse.
--Freedom in the World: Political Rights & Civil Liberties, 1978. LC 78-53867. (Illus.). 1978. lib. bdg. 20.00 (ISBN 0-932088-00-7). Freedom Hse.
Gibbs, Benjamin. Freedom & Liberation. LC 76-12234. 1976. 15.95 (ISBN 0-312-30415-3). St Martin.
--Freedom & Liberation. (Philosophy Now). 1976. pap. text ed. 4.50x (ISBN 0-85621-063-3). Humanities.
Gotesky, Rubin. Personality: The Need for Liberty & Rights. 1967. 3.50 (ISBN 0-87212-012-0). Libra.
Green, T. H. The Political Theory of T. H. Green: Selected Writings. Rodman, John R., ed. LC 64-20106. (Crofts Classics Ser.). 1964. pap. text ed. 1.25x (ISBN 0-88295-040-1). Harlan Davidson.
Griffiths, Julia, ed. Voices of Freedom. LC 77-155390. Repr. 15.50x (ISBN 0-8371-6080-4). Greenwood.
Hadley, Arthur T. Conflict Between Liberty & Equality. facs. ed. LC 79-84310. (Essay Index Reprint Ser). 1925. 14.75 (ISBN 0-8369-1083-4). Arno.
--The Relations Between Freedom & Responsibility in the Evolution of Democratic Government. LC 73-19151. (Politics & People Ser.). 186p. 1974. Repr. 10.00x (ISBN 0-685-49686-4). Arno.
Haksar, Vinit. Equality, Liberty & Perfectionism. (Clarendon Library of Logic & Philosophy Ser.). 310p. 1979. text ed. 24.95x (ISBN 0-19-824418-5). Oxford U Pr.
Halevy, Elie. The Era of Tyrannies: Essays on Socialism & War. Webb, R. K., tr. LC 66-24089. 1966. 10.95x (ISBN 0-8147-0177-9). NYU Pr.
Hand, Learned. The Spirit of Liberty. 3rd enl ed. Dilliard, Irving, ed. 1977. pap. 4.95 (ISBN 0-226-31544-4, P712, Phoen). U of Chicago Pr.
Handa, R. L. History of Freedom Struggle in Princely States. LC 68-16276. 1968. 12.50x (ISBN 0-8002-0648-7). Intl Pubns Serv.
Handlin, Oscar & Handlin, Mary. Dimensions of Liberty. LC 61-16694. 1966. pap. text ed. 1.75x (ISBN 0-689-70087-3, 84). Atheneum.
Handlin, Oscar & Handlin, Mary F. Dimensions of Liberty. LC 61-16694. (Center for the Study of the History of Liberty in America Ser). 1961. 12.50x (ISBN 0-674-20750-5, Belknap Pr). Harvard U Pr.
Harding, Arthur L., ed. Free Man Versus His Government. LC 58-9270. (Studies in Jurisprudence: No. 5). 1958. 4.00 (ISBN 0-87074-067-9). SMU Press.
Hare, A. Paul & Blumberg, Herbert H., eds. Liberation Without Violence: A Third Party Approach. 368p. 1978. 21.50x (ISBN 0-87471-998-4). Rowman.
Hayek, F. A. Law, Legislation, & Liberty: Vol. 1: Rules & Order. 15.00 (ISBN 0-226-32080-4). U of Chicago Pr.
--Law, Legislation, & Liberty: Vol. 3: the Political Order of a Free People. pap. 7.50 (ISBN 0-226-32090-1). U of Chicago Pr.
Hayek, Friedrich A. Constitution of Liberty. LC 59-11618. 1960. 25.00x (ISBN 0-226-32073-1); pap. 10.95 (ISBN 0-226-32084-7, P796, Phoen). U of Chicago Pr.
--Law, Legislation & Liberty: Rules & Order, Vol. 1. LC 73-82488. 1978. pap. 4.45 (ISBN 0-226-32086-3, P763, Phoen). U of Chicago Pr.
Haynes, E. S. The Decline of Liberty in England. 59.95 (ISBN 0-8490-0013-0). Gordon Pr.
Henderson, George. To Live in Freedom: Human Relations Today & Tomorrow. (Illus.). 243p. 1972. 12.95x (ISBN 0-8061-1017-1); pap. 7.95x (ISBN 0-8061-1037-6). U of Okla Pr.
Herbert, Auberon. The Right & Wrong of Compulsion by the State, & Other Essays. LC 78-4879. 1978. 9.00 (ISBN 0-913966-41-X); pap. 3.50 (ISBN 0-913966-42-8). Liberty Fund.
Himmelfarb, Gertrude. On Liberty & Liberalism: The Case of John Stuart Mill. 1974. 8.95 (ISBN 0-394-49028-2). Knopf.
Hollywood Arts Science & Professions Council. Thought Control in the U.S.A. Kupelnick, Bruce S., ed. LC 76-52131. (Classics of Film Literature Ser.). 1978. lib. bdg. 25.00 (ISBN 0-8240-2895-3). Garland Pub.
Hook, Sidney. Heresy, Yes - Conspiracy, No. LC 72-9049. 283p. 1973. Repr. of 1953 ed. lib. bdg. 15.00 (ISBN 0-8371-6562-8). Greenwood.
--The Paradoxes of Freedom. LC 62-16335. 1962. 12.75x (ISBN 0-520-00568-6); pap. 4.95x (ISBN 0-520-00569-4, CAL100). U of Cal Pr.
Hunold, A., ed. Freedom & Serfdom: An Anthology of Western Thought. Stevens, R. H., tr. from Ger. 288p. 1961. lib. bdg. 29.00 (ISBN 90-277-0007-9, Pub. by Reidel Holland). Kluwer Boston.
Hurd, Rollin Carlos. A Treatise on the Right of Personal Liberty & on Writ of Habeas Corpus. LC 77-37767. (American Constitutional & Legal History Ser). 670p. 1972. Repr. of 1876 ed. lib. bdg. 59.50 (ISBN 0-306-70431-5). Da Capo.
Hurst, J. Willard. Law & the Conditions of Freedom in the Nineteenth-Century United States. 150p. 1956. pap. 5.45 (ISBN 0-299-01363-4). U of Wis Pr.
Jackson, J. H. Unholy Shadows & Freedom's Holy Light. LC 67-29805. 1967. 5.00 (ISBN 0-935990-05-4). Townsend Pr.
Jackson, Thomas A. Trials of British Freedom: Being Some Studies in the History of the Fight for Democratic Freedom in Britain. LC 68-56759. (Research & Source Works Ser.: No. 244). 1968. Repr. of 1940 ed. 17.00 (ISBN 0-8337-1816-9). B Franklin.
Jaffa, Harry V. The Conditions of Freedom: Essays in Political Philosophy. LC 74-24389. 296p. 1975. 20.00x (ISBN 0-8018-1631-9). Johns Hopkins.
Johnson, Paul. The Recovery of Freedom. 232p. 1980. 19.95x (ISBN 0-631-12562-0, Pub. by Basil Blackwell England). Biblio Dist.
Johnson, Thomas H., ed. Return to Freedom. LC 75-134104. (Essay Index Reprint Ser). 1944. 16.00 (ISBN 0-8369-1966-1). Arno.
Jordan, Bill. Freedom & the Welfare State. 1978. pap. 6.95 (ISBN 0-7100-8910-4). Routledge & Kegan.
Kallen, Horace M. Liberty, Laughter & Tears: Reflections on the Relation of Comedy & Tragedy to Human Freedom. LC 68-26268. 380p. 1968. 8.50 (ISBN 0-87580-006-8). N Ill U Pr.
--A Study of Liberty. LC 72-7964. 151p. 1973. Repr. of 1959 ed. lib. bdg. 15.00x (ISBN 0-8371-6554-7, KASL). Greenwood.
Kallen, Horace M., ed. Freedom in the Modern World. facs. ed. LC 70-84313. (Essay Index Reprint Ser). 1928. 15.75 (ISBN 0-8369-1085-0). Arno.
Kaplan, Morton A. On Historical & Political Knowing: An Inquiry into Some Problems of Universal Law & Human Freedom. LC 79-131879. 1971. 7.50x (ISBN 0-226-42420-0). U of Chicago Pr.
Katz, Fred E. Autonomy & Organization: The Limits of Social Control. 1968. text ed. 6.95x (ISBN 0-685-19686-0). Phila Bk Co.
Kerenskii, A. F. The Crucifixion of Liberty. Repr. of 1934 ed. 22.00 (ISBN 0-527-49106-3). Kraus Repr.
King, Preston. Fear of Power: An Analysis of Anti-Statism in Three French Writers. 1967. text ed. 6.25x (ISBN 0-391-01977-5). Humanities.
Konvitz, Milton R. Expanding Liberties: Freedom's Gains in Postwar America. LC 76-7523. 1976. Repr. of 1966 ed. lib. bdg. 26.00x (ISBN 0-8371-8843-1, KEEL). Greenwood.
Konvitz, Milton R. & Rossiter, Clinton, eds. Aspects of Liberty: Essays Presented to Robert E. Cushman. Repr. of 1958 ed. 23.00 (ISBN 0-384-30170-3). Johnson Repr.
Labadie, Laurance. Reflections on Liberty. (Men & Movements in the History & Philosophy of Anarchism Ser.). 1979. lib. bdg. 59.95 (ISBN 0-685-96413-2). Revisionist Pr.
--Selected Essays. LC 78-78149. (Libertarian Broadsides: No. 7). (Illus.). 1978. pap. 1.50 (ISBN 0-87926-022-X). R Myles.
Lamont, Corliss. Freedom Is As Freedom Does. LC 74-171384. (Civil Liberties in American History Ser.). 1972. Repr. of 1956 ed. lib. bdg. 35.00 (ISBN 0-306-70498-6). Da Capo.
Lane, Rose W. Discovery of Freedom: Man's Struggle Against Authority. LC 73-172216. (Right Wing Individualist Tradition in America Ser). 1972. Repr. of 1943 ed. 16.00 (ISBN 0-405-00425-7). Arno.
Laski, Harold J. Liberty in the Modern State. rev. ed. LC 77-122064. Repr. of 1949 ed. 12.50x (ISBN 0-678-03166-5). Kelley.
Leder, Lawrence. Liberty & Authority: Early American Political Ideology, 1689-1763. 176p. 1976. pap. 2.95x (ISBN 0-393-00800-2, Norton Lib). Norton.
Lee, David G. The Complete Guide to Freedom & Survival. (Illus.). 1980. pap. text ed. 6.95 (ISBN 0-686-28071-7). Live Free.
Lees, et al. Freedom, or Free for All. 2.50 (ISBN 0-255-69531-4). Transatlantic.
Leoni, Bruno. Freedom & the Law. LC 71-167535. 204p. 1972. 7.50 (ISBN 0-8402-1215-1); pap. 4.95 (ISBN 0-89617-041-1). Inst Humane.
--Freedom & the Law. (Humane Studies). 204p. 1980. text ed. 7.50x (ISBN 0-8402-1215-1); pap. text ed. 4.95x (ISBN 0-8402-1215-1). Humanities.
Lewis, Hywel D. Freedom & History. 1962. text ed. 10.00x (ISBN 0-04-323007-5). Humanities.
Liebknecht, Karl. Libertarian Anthology. 59.95 (ISBN 0-8490-0517-5). Gordon Pr.
Lines, Patricia M. People Power Papers: A New Birth of Freedom. 1977. pap. text ed. 7.50 (ISBN 0-8191-0343-8). U Pr of Amer.
Locke, John. Of Civil Government, 2nd Essay. 1960. pap. 2.95 (ISBN 0-89526-921-X). Regnery-Gateway.
--The Second Treatise of Government & A Letter Concerning Toleration. 3rd ed. Gough, J. W., ed. 1976. Repr. of 1966 ed. 15.00x (ISBN 0-06-494349-6). B&N.
--Treatise of Civil Government & a Letter Concerning Toleration. Sherman, Charles L., ed. 1965. pap. text ed. 6.95x (ISBN 0-89197-519-5). Irvington.
--Two Treatises of Government. Laslett, Peter, ed. 1960. 39.95 (ISBN 0-521-06903-3). Cambridge U Pr.
Loemker, Leroy E. Struggle for Synthesis: The Seventeenth Century Background of Leibniz's Synthesis of Order & Freedom. LC 72-79308. 529p. 1972. 16.50x (ISBN 0-674-84545-5). Harvard U Pr.
Macek, Vladko. In the Struggle for Freedom. LC 68-8182. (Illus.). 1968. 15.95x (ISBN 0-271-00069-4). Pa St U Pr.
MacIver, R. M., ed. Great Expressions of Human Rights. LC 68-26196. (Essay & General Literature Index Reprint Ser). Repr. of 1950 ed. 12.50 (ISBN 0-8046-0227-1). Kennikat.
McKillop, Alan D. The Background of Thomson's Liberty. 123p. 1980. Repr. of 1951 ed. lib. bdg. 15.00 (ISBN 0-8482-1742-X). Norwood Edns.
--The Background of Thomson's Liberty. LC 79-14973. 1973. lib. bdg. 15.00 (ISBN 0-8414-6349-2). Folcroft.
McMillen, Wheeler. Why the United States Is Rich. LC 63-18183. (Illus., Orig.). 1963. pap. 1.00 (ISBN 0-87004-096-0). Caxton.
Macmurray, John. Conditions of Freedom: Being the Second Lectures on the Chancellor Dunning Rust, Delivered at Queen's University Kingston, Ont. 1949. 1978. pap. text ed. 3.95x (ISBN 0-920550-08-8). Humanities.
--Freedom in the Modern World. 1968. pap. text ed. 2.75x (ISBN 0-571-08622-5). Humanities.
MacSwiney, Terence. Principles of Freedom. LC 73-102616. (Irish Culture & History Ser). 1970. Repr. of 1921 ed. 12.50 (ISBN 0-8046-0793-1). Kennikat.

Marcuse, Herbert. Essay on Liberation. 1969. pap. 2.95 (ISBN 0-8070-0595-9, BP319). Beacon Pr.

Maritain, Jacques. Freedom & the Modern World. O'Sullivan, Richard, tr. LC 77-150414. 1971. Repr. of 1936 ed. text ed. 9.00 (ISBN 0-87752-147-6). Gordian.

--Rights of Man & Natural Law. LC 74-150416. 1971. Repr. of 1943 ed. text ed. 7.50 (ISBN 0-87752-146-8). Gordian.

Martin, Everett D. Liberty. 1930. 10.00 (ISBN 0-686-17703-7). Quality Lib.

Maxwell, Allen, ed. Present Danger: Four Essays on American Freedom. LC 53-12256. 1953. 2.00 (ISBN 0-87074-096-2). SMU Press.

May, Rollo. Freedom & Destiny. 1981. 14.95 (ISBN 0-393-01477-0). Norton.

Mayer, Milton, ed. Tradition of Freedom. LC 57-12989. (Orig.). 1957. 10.00 (ISBN 0-379-11701-0). Oceana.

Meiklejohn, Donald. Freedom & the Public: Public & Private Morality in America. LC 65-23650. 1965. 12.00x (ISBN 0-8156-2084-5). Syracuse U Pr.

Mendelson, Wallace. American Constitution & Civil Liberties. 487p. 1981. 21.00x (ISBN 0-256-02551-7). Dorsey.

Mill, J. S. On Liberty. Himmelfarb, Gertrude, ed. (Classics Ser.). (Orig.). 1975. pap. 1.95 (ISBN 0-14-040028-1, Pelican). Penguin.

Mill, John S. On Liberty. Shields, Currin V., ed. 1956. pap. 3.95 (ISBN 0-672-60234-2, LLA61). Bobbs.

--On Liberty. Spitz, David, ed. (Critical Editions Ser.). 1975. pap. text ed. 3.95x (ISBN 0-393-09252-6). Norton.

--On Liberty. Castell, Alburey, ed. LC 47-3494. (Crofts Classics Ser.). 1947. pap. text ed. 2.50x (ISBN 0-88295-056-8). Harlan Davidson.

--On Liberty. Rapaport, Elizabeth, ed. LC 77-26848. 1978. lib. bdg. 12.50 (ISBN 0-915144-44-1); pap. text ed. 2.75x (ISBN 0-915144-43-3). Hackett Pub.

--Utilitarianism. Piest, Oskar, ed. 1957. pap. 2.95 (ISBN 0-672-60164-8, LLA1). Bobbs.

Mishan, E. J. Pornography, Psychedelics & Technology: Essays on the Limits to Freedom. 184p. 1980. text ed. 22.50x (ISBN 0-04-300081-9). Allen Unwin.

Molnar, Thomas. Authority & Its Enemies. LC 76-8506. 1976. 7.95 (ISBN 0-87000-340-2). Arlington Hse.

Murphy, Paul L. World War One & the Origin of Civil Liberties in the United States. 1980. 16.95x (ISBN 0-393-01226-3); pap. 3.95x (ISBN 0-393-95012-3). Norton.

Nash, Ronald H. Freedom, Justice, & the State. LC 80-8145. 243p. 1980. lib. bdg. 17.75 (ISBN 0-8191-1195-3); pap. text ed. 9.25 (ISBN 0-8191-1196-1). U Pr of Amer.

Nearing, Scott. Freedom: Promise & Menace. 4.00 (ISBN 0-685-83851-X); pap. 2.00 (ISBN 0-685-83852-8). Soc Sci Inst.

Neville, Robert C. The Cosmology of Freedom. LC 73-86912. 416p. 1974. 25.00x (ISBN 0-300-01672-7). Yale U Pr.

Nevinson, Henry W. Essays in Freedom. 1977. Repr. lib. bdg. 20.00 (ISBN 0-8492-1913-2). R West.

--The Growth of Freedom. 1978. Repr. lib. bdg. 10.00 (ISBN 0-89760-602-7, Telegraph). Dynamic Learn Corp.

Norton, Thomas J. Losing Liberty Judicially: Prohibitory & Kindred Laws Examined. xiv, 252p. 1981. Repr. of 1928 ed. lib. bdg. 24.00x (ISBN 0-8377-0907-5). Rothman.

Osipova, Nonna. Articles Not to the Common Taste. (Illus.). 57p. (Orig., Rus.). 1980. pap. 3.00 (ISBN 0-935500-27-8). Am Samizdat.

Ould, Hermon, ed. Freedom of Expression. LC 73-111309. 1970. Repr. of 1944 ed. 12.50 (ISBN 0-8046-0968-3). Kennikat.

Paine, Thomas. The Rights of Man. (Pelican Classics Ser.). 1976. pap. 2.50 (ISBN 0-14-040011-7, Pelican). Penguin.

Palmer, George H. Problem of Freedom. LC 75-173487. Repr. of 1911 ed. 18.50 (ISBN 0-404-04868-4). AMS Pr.

Park, James. Loneliness & Existential Freedom. (Existential Freedom Ser.: No. 4). 1974. pap. 2.00x (ISBN 0-89231-004-9). Existential Bks.

Paterson, James. Commentaries on the Liberty of the Subject & the Laws of England Relating to the Security of the Person, 2 vols. 1010p. 1980. Repr. of 1877 ed. Set. lib. bdg. 75.00x (ISBN 0-8377-1005-7). Rothman.

Perry, Charner M., ed. Philosophy of American Democracy. LC 71-132089. (Essay & General Literature Index Reprint Ser). 1971. Repr. of 1943 ed. 12.50 (ISBN 0-8046-1417-2). Kennikat.

Persecution & Liberty: Essays in Honor of George Lincoln Burr. facs. ed. LC 68-26467. (Essay Index Reprint Ser). 1968. Repr. of 1931 ed. 17.50 (ISBN 0-8369-0783-3). Arno.

Plamenatz, J. P. Consent, Freedom & Political Obligation. 2nd ed. 1968. pap. 3.95 (ISBN 0-19-881143-8, 258, GB). Oxford U Pr.

Polanyi, Michael. The Logic of Liberty: Reflections & Rejoinders. LC 51-8809. (Midway Reprint Ser.). 1981. 9.00x (ISBN 0-226-67296-4). U of Chicago Pr.

Pollack, Harriet & Smith, Alexander B. Civil Liberties & Civil Rights in the United States. LC 78-5892. 299p. 1978. text ed. 14.95 (ISBN 0-8299-2003-X). West Pub.

Pollock, Lansing R. The Freedom Principle. 130p. 1981. text ed. 14.95 (ISBN 0-87975-157-6). Prometheus Bks.

Potter, David M. Freedom & Its Limitations in American Life. Fehrenbacher, Don E., ed. LC 76-17786. 112p. 1976. 6.50x (ISBN 0-8047-0933-5); pap. 2.95 (ISBN 0-8047-1009-0, SP147). Stanford U Pr.

Read, Leonard E. Accent on the Right. 126p. 1968. 2.00 (ISBN 0-910614-35-0). Foun Econ Ed.

--Anything That's Peaceful. 243p. 1964. 3.00 (ISBN 0-910614-36-9). Foun Econ Ed.

--Awake for Freedom's Sake. new ed. 192p. 1977. 3.00 (ISBN 0-910614-58-X). Foun Econ Ed.

--Comes the Dawn. 168p. 1976. 3.00 (ISBN 0-910614-57-1). Foun Econ Ed.

--Coming Aristocracy. 192p. 1969. 3.00 (ISBN 0-910614-37-7); pap. 1.00 (ISBN 0-910614-12-1). Foun Econ Ed.

--Having My Way. xiii, 176p. 1974. 3.00 (ISBN 0-910614-49-0). Foun Econ Ed.

--Let Freedom Reign. 167p. 1969. 3.00 (ISBN 0-910614-40-7); pap. 1.00 (ISBN 0-910614-22-9). Foun Econ Ed.

--Liberty: Legacy of Truth. 128p. 1978. 3.00 (ISBN 0-910614-60-1). Foun Econ Ed.

--The Love of Liberty. 172p. 1975. pap. 1.00 (ISBN 0-910614-54-7). Foun Econ Ed.

--Then Truth Will Out. 177p. 1971. 3.00 (ISBN 0-910614-27-X); pap. 1.00 (ISBN 0-910614-26-1). Foun Econ Ed.

--Who's Listening? 208p. 1973. 3.00 (ISBN 0-910614-48-2). Foun Econ Ed.

Reghaby, Heydar. Philosophy & Freedom. LC 71-104386. 1970. 3.75 (ISBN 0-8022-2324-9). Philos Lib.

Reitman, Alan, ed. Price of Liberty: Perspectives on Civil Liberties by Member of the A.C.L.U. 1968. 6.95x (ISBN 0-393-05284-2, Norton Lib); pap. 1.95x, 1969 (ISBN 0-393-00505-4). Norton.

Rice, Charles E. Freedom of Association. LC 62-16636. 202p. 1962. 10.00x (ISBN 0-8147-0360-7). NYU Pr.

Richmond, Bruce L. The Pattern of Freedom. 266p. 1980. Repr. of 1911 ed. lib. bdg. 25.00 (ISBN 0-8492-7732-9). R West.

Riegel, E. C. The New Approach to Freedom. new, rev. ed. MacCallum, Spencer H., ed. LC 76-24987. (Illus.). 1977. 11.95 (ISBN 0-9600300-7-7). Heather Foun.

Rossiter, Clinton. Political Thought of the American Revolution. rev. ed. LC 63-24720. 1963. pap. 2.95 (ISBN 0-15-672680-7, HB66, Harv). HarBraceJ.

--Seedtime of the Republic. LC 53-5647. 1953. 14.95 (ISBN 0-15-180111-8). HarBraceJ.

Rothbard, Murray N. The Ethics of Liberty. 250p. 1981. text ed. 10.00x (ISBN 0-391-02371-3). Humanities.

Ryan, Alan, ed. The Idea of Freedom: Essays in Honour of Isaiah Berlin. 1979. 17.95x (ISBN 0-19-215859-7). Oxford U Pr.

Ryan, John A. Declining Liberty, & Other Papers. facs. ed. LC 68-8491. (Essay Index Reprint Ser). 1927. 18.00 (ISBN 0-8369-0845-7). Arno.

Saraydarian, Haroutiun. Science of Becoming Oneself. 1969. 10.00 (ISBN 0-911794-26-3); pap. 8.00 (ISBN 0-911794-27-1). Aqua Educ.

Savonarola, Gerolamo. Liberty & Tyranny in the Government of Men. (Illus.). 1977. 44.15 (ISBN 0-89266-019-8). Am Classical Coll Pr.

Schelling, Friedrich W. Of Human Freedom. Gutmann, James, tr. 128p. 1936. 12.95 (ISBN 0-87548-024-1); pap. 4.95 (ISBN 0-87548-025-X). Open Court.

Schrag, Peter. Mind Control. LC 77-15077. 1978. 10.00 (ISBN 0-394-40759-8). Pantheon.

Schroeder, Theodore. A New Concept of Liberty. 59.95 (ISBN 0-8490-0720-8). Gordon Pr.

Scimecca, Joseph A. Society & Freedom: An Introduction to Humanist Sociology. 250p. 1981. text ed. 14.95x (ISBN 0-312-73806-4); pap. text ed. 7.95x (ISBN 0-686-71653-1). St Martin.

Scrimshaw, Frederic. The Dog & the Fleas, by One of the Dogs. 1976. lib. bdg. 59.95 (ISBN 0-8490-1729-7). Gordon Pr.

Seldes, G. You Can't Do That. LC 70-37287. (Civil Liberties in American History Ser). 308p. 1972. Repr. of 1938 ed. lib. bdg. 27.50 (ISBN 0-306-70201-0). Da Capo.

Shuster, George N., ed. Freedom & Authority in the West. 1967. 8.50x (ISBN 0-268-00106-5). U of Notre Dame Pr.

Simon, William E. A Time for Truth. LC 77-25465. 1978. 12.50 (ISBN 0-07-057378-6, GB). McGraw.

Simon, Yves. Freedom & Community. O'Donnell, Charles P., ed. LC 68-13310. 1968. 15.00 (ISBN 0-8232-0790-0). Fordham.

Simon, Yves R. A General Theory of Authority. LC 72-9920. 167p. 1973. Repr. of 1962 ed. lib. bdg. 15.00 (ISBN 0-8371-6609-8, SITA). Greenwood.

Singhvi, L. M., ed. Horizons of Freedom. 1969. 10.00x (ISBN 0-8426-1541-5). Verry.

Smith, Gerard. Truth That Frees. (Aquinas Lecture). 1956. 6.95 (ISBN 0-87462-121-6). Marquette.

Spitz, David. The Liberal Idea of Freedom. LC 63-11972. 1964. 2.00 (ISBN 0-8165-0051-7). U of Ariz Pr.

Sprading, Charles T., ed. Liberty & the Great Libertarians: An Anthology on Liberty, a Handbook of Freedom. LC 77-172233. (Right Wing Individualist Tradition in America Ser). 1972. Repr. of 1913 ed. 25.00 (ISBN 0-405-00442-7). Arno.

Staddon, John E. Limits to Action: The Allocation of Individual Behavior. LC 79-6794. 1980. 24.00 (ISBN 0-12-662650-2). Acad Pr.

Starr, Isidore. The Idea of Liberty. LC 78-1655. (Great Ideas in the Law Ser.). (Illus.). 1978. pap. text ed. 4.00 (ISBN 0-8299-1017-4). West Pub.

Steiner, Rudolf. The Philosophy of Freedom. 1972. Repr. of 1894 ed. lib. bdg. 59.95 (ISBN 0-8490-0825-5). Gordon Pr.

Stouffer, Samuel A. Communism, Conformity, & Civil Liberties Study, 1954: Cross-Section Sample. 1974. codebk. 8.00 (ISBN 0-89138-071-X). ICPSR.

--Communism, Conformity, & Civil Liberties Study, 1954: Leadership Sample. 1974. codebk. 8.00 (ISBN 0-89138-070-1). ICPSR.

Strackbein, Oscar R. Freedom's Holy Light. 372p. 1978. 9.95 (ISBN 0-8119-0299-4). Fell.

Sugar, Maurice. Ford Hunger March. LC 80-81137. (Studies in Law & Social Change: No.1). 1980. pap. 5.00 (ISBN 0-913876-15-1). Meiklejohn Civil Lib.

Sweet, Esther. Civil Liberties in America: A Casebook. 368p. 1966. pap. 5.50 (ISBN 0-442-08097-2, Pub. by Van Nos Reinhold). Krieger.

Swomley, J. Liberation Ethics. 1972. pap. 1.95 (ISBN 0-02-089620-4, Collier). Macmillan.

Taylor, Harold. On Education & Freedom. LC 53-13096. 320p. 1967. lib. bdg. 7.00x (ISBN 0-8093-0245-4). S Ill U Pr.

--On Education & Freedom. LC 53-13096. (Arcturus Books Paperbacks). 320p. 1967. pap. 2.65 (ISBN 0-8093-0246-2). S Ill U Pr.

Ten, C. L. Mill on Liberty. 464p. 1980. 36.00 (ISBN 0-19-824643-9); pap. 14.95 (ISBN 0-19-824644-7). Oxford U Pr.

Teplitsky, A. & Hyman, R. It's a Free Country. 1976. pap. text ed. 3.92 (ISBN 0-13-506600-X). P-H.

Thomas, Norman. The Test of Freedom. LC 73-19431. 211p. 1974. Repr. of 1954 ed. lib. bdg. 15.00x (ISBN 0-8371-7333-7, THTF). Greenwood.

Towards Liberty, 2 vols. Set. write for info. (ISBN 0-89617-039-X); Vol. 1. write for info (ISBN 0-89617-037-3); Vol. 2. write for info (ISBN 0-89617-038-1). Inst Humane.

Tucker, Benjamin & Hubbard, Elbert. Libertarian Anthology. 1980. lib. bdg. 59.95 (ISBN 0-8490-3076-5). Gordon Pr.

Tucker, Benjamin R. & Robertson, Thomas. Social Relation & Freedom. 1980. lib. bdg. 59.95 (ISBN 0-8490-3084-6). Gordon Pr.

Tucker, Benjamin R., ed. Liberty: A Journal of Anarchist Thought, 17 vols. 1980. lib. bdg. 49.95 ea. Revisionist Pr.

United Nations Educational, Scientific & Cultural Organization. Freedom & Culture. facsimile ed. LC 78-156725. (Essay Index Reprint Ser). Repr. of 1950 ed. 17.00 (ISBN 0-8369-2381-2). Arno.

Von Mises, Ludwig. Planning for Freedom. 4th, enl. ed. LC 80-10765. 296p. 1980. pap. 6.00 (ISBN 0-910884-13-7). Libertarian.

Wallich, Henry C. The Cost of Freedom: A New Look at Capitalism. LC 78-27775. 1979. Repr. of 1960 ed. lib. bdg. 16.00x (ISBN 0-313-20935-9, WACF). Greenwood.

Wasby, Stephen, ed. Civil Liberties & Free Speech Policy. 1975. pap. 5.00 (ISBN 0-918592-13-5). Policy Studies.

Watkins, Renee N., ed. Humanism & Liberty: Writings on Freedom from Fifteenth-Century Florence. LC 78-6588. 1978. lib. bdg. 14.95x (ISBN 0-87249-360-1). U of SC Pr.

Way, H. F. Liberty in the Balance. 4th ed. (Foundations of American Government Ser). 1976. 6.95 (ISBN 0-07-068659-9, C). McGraw.

Weaver, Henry G. Mainspring of Human Progress. 279p. 1953. 4.00 (ISBN 0-910614-42-3); pap. 0.95 (ISBN 0-910614-02-4). Foun Econ Ed.

Weiss, Paul. Man's Freedom. LC 67-23318. (Arcturus Books Paperbacks). 335p. 1967. pap. 8.95 (ISBN 0-8093-0277-2). S Ill U Pr.

Whipple, L. Story of Civil Liberty in the United States. LC 72-107419. (Civil Liberties in American History Ser). 1970. Repr. of 1927 ed. lib. bdg. 35.00 (ISBN 0-306-71879-0). Da Capo.

Whipple, Leon. Our Ancient Liberties. LC 73-175723. (Civil Liberties in American History Ser.). 1972. Repr. lib. bdg. 15.00 (ISBN 0-306-70419-6). Da Capo.

--Story of Civil Liberties in the U. S. 69.95 (ISBN 0-8490-1130-2). Gordon Pr.

White, Ben B. In Pursuit of Liberty. 88p. 1981. 5.95 (ISBN 0-8059-2810-3). Dorrance.

The Will to Bondage: Etienne De la Boetie(Discours De la Servitude Volontaire) LC 74-27714. (Libertarian Broadsides Ser.: No. 6). (Illus., Eng. & Fr.). 1974. pap. 3.25 (ISBN 0-87926-018-1). R Myles.

Williams, Roger J. Free & Unequal: The Biological Basis of Individual Liberty. LC 78-25671. (Illus.). 1979. 8.00 (ISBN 0-913966-52-5, Liberty Press); pap. 3.50 (ISBN 0-913966-53-3). Liberty Fund.

Williamson, H. R. Who Is for Liberty. 59.95 (ISBN 0-8490-1294-5). Gordon Pr.

Wilson, Everett P. Constitution of the United States of America, a Bulwark of Liberty. LC 55-32084. 1955. pap. 1.50 (ISBN 0-87004-174-6). Caxton.

Winstanley, Gerrard. The Law of Freedom in a Platform: Or, True Magistracy Restored. Kenny, Robert W., ed. LC 72-95902. 1973. 12.00x (ISBN 0-8052-3503-5). Schocken.

Wirszubski, Chaim. Libertas As a Political Idea at Rome. (Cambridge Classical Studies). 1950. 17.95 (ISBN 0-521-06848-7). Cambridge U Pr.

Wollstonecraft, Mary. A Vindication of the Rights of Men. LC 60-5073. 192p. 1975. Repr. of 1790 ed. lib. bdg. 20.00x (ISBN 0-8201-1164-3). Schol Facsimiles.

Wringe, Colin. Children's Rights: A Philosophical Study. (International Library of the Philosophy of Education). 192p. 1981. price not set (ISBN 0-7100-0852-X). Routledge & Kegan.

LIBERTY–JUVENILE LITERATURE

Jennings, Jerry E. & Hertel, Margaret F. Inquiring About Freedom: Civil Rights & Individual Responsibilities. LC 78-54258. (Fideler Social Studies). (Illus.). 212p. (gr. 8 up). 1979. text ed. 9.93 5 or more copies 7.94 ea. (ISBN 0-88296-411-9). tchrs' ed. 7.94 (ISBN 0-88296-417-8). Fideler.

Stevens, William O. Footsteps to Freedom. (gr. 9 up). 1954. 5.95 (ISBN 0-396-03635-X). Dodd.

LIBERTY (THEOLOGY)

see Freedom (Theology)

LIBERTY BELL

Boland, Charles M. Ring in the Jubilee: The Story of America's Liberty Bell. LC 72-80407. (Illus.). 96p. (gr. 6 up). 1973. pap. 3.95 (ISBN 0-85699-055-8). Chatham Pr.

Kramer, Justin. Cast in America. new ed. LC 74-15405. (Illus.). 1974. 10.00 (ISBN 0-87832-016-4). Piper.

LIBERTY IN LITERATURE

Anderson, Gillian B., ed. Freedom's Voice in Poetry & Song. LC 77-78353. 1977. 55.00 (ISBN 0-8420-2124-8). Scholarly Res Inc.

DeJean, Joan. Libertine Strategies: Freedom & the Novel in Seventeenth Century France. LC 81-38431. 240p. 1981. 17.50x (ISBN 0-8142-0325-6). Ohio St U Pr.

Martin, G. C. Poets of the Democracy. LC 79-113342. 1970. Repr. of 1917 ed. 10.00 (ISBN 0-8046-1048-7). Kennikat.

LIBERTY OF ASSOCIATION

see Freedom of Association

LIBERTY OF CONSCIENCE

see also Conscientious Objectors; Dissenters; Free Thought; Persecution; Public Opinion; Religious Liberty

Cox, Archibald. Freedom of Expression. LC 81-4374. 96p. 1981. 6.95 (ISBN 0-674-31912-5); pap. 2.95 (ISBN 0-674-31913-3). Harvard U Pr.

Hall, Gus. The Sakharov-Solzhenitsyn Fraud: What's Behind the Hue & Cry for Intellectual Freedom. 32p. 1973. pap. 0.40 (ISBN 0-87898-102-0). New Outlook.

Haring, Bernard. Liberty of the Children of God. LC 66-16472. 1966. 2.95 (ISBN 0-8189-0075-X). Alba.

Putnam, George H. Censorship of the Church of Rome & Its Influence Upon the Production & Distribution of Literature, 2 Vols. LC 67-12455. 1967. Repr. of 1906 ed. 40.00 (ISBN 0-405-08869-8). Arno.

Regan, Richard J. Private Conscience & Public Law: The American Experience. LC 72-77602. 245p. 1972. 17.50 (ISBN 0-8232-0945-8). Fordham.

Sibley, Mulford Q. Obligation to Disobey. LC 72-128194. (Special Studies Ser.). 1970. pap. 2.00 (ISBN 0-87641-209-6). Coun Rel & Intl.

Swancara, Frank. Obstruction of Justice by Religion: A Treatise on Religious Barbarities of the Common Law, & a Review of Judicial Oppressions of the Non-Religious in the U.S. LC 70-139581. (Civil Liberties in American History Ser). (Illus.). 1970. Repr. of 1936 ed. lib. bdg. 29.50 (ISBN 0-306-71964-9). Da Capo.

LIBERTY OF CONTRACT

see also Contracts

Atiyah, Patrick S. The Rise & Fall of Freedom of Contract. 804p. 1979. 59.00x (ISBN 0-19-825342-7). Oxford U Pr.

Hurst, J. Willard. Law & the Conditions of Freedom in the Nineteenth-Century United States. 150p. 1956. pap. 5.45 (ISBN 0-299-01363-4). U of Wis Pr.

LIBERTY OF INFORMATION

see Freedom of Information

LIBERTY OF RELIGION

see Religious Liberty

LIBERTY OF SPEECH

see also Blasphemy; Freedom of Information; Libel and Slander; Liberty of the Press

Auerbach, Jerold S. Labor & Liberty: The La Follette Committee & the New Deal. LC 66-28233. 1966. 18.50x (ISBN 0-672-51153-3). Irvington.

Barron, Jerome A. & Dienes, C. Thomas. Handbook of Free Speech & Free Press. 1979. text ed. 45.00 (ISBN 0-316-08230-9). Little.

Bartlett, Jonathan, ed. The First Amendment in a Free Society. (Reference Shelf Ser.: Vol. 50, No. 6). 1979. 6.25 (ISBN 0-8242-0627-4). Wilson.

Beman, Lamar T., compiled by. Selected Articles on Censorship of Speech & the Press. LC 76-98813. 1971. Repr. of 1930 ed. lib. bdg. 17.75x (ISBN 0-8371-3073-5, BECE). Greenwood.

Beman, Lamar T., ed. Selected Articles on Censorship of Speech & the Press. LC 77-95404. (BCL Ser. I). 1969. Repr. of 1930 ed. 14.00 (ISBN 0-404-00747-3). AMS Pr.

Berger, Fred R. Freedom of Expression. 224p. 1979. pap. text ed. 8.95x (ISBN 0-534-00749-X). Wadsworth Pub.

Berninghausen, David K. The Flight from Reason: Essays on Intellectual Freedom in the Academy, the Press, & the Library. LC 74-23236. 189p. 1975. pap. text ed. 7.50 (ISBN 0-8389-0192-1). ALA.

Berns, Walter. Freedom, Virtue & the First Amendment. LC 79-90470. Repr. of 1957 ed. lib. bdg. 15.00x (ISBN 0-8371-2143-4, BEFV). Greenwood.

Blount, Charles, et al. A Just Vindication of Learning. Berkowitz, David S. & Thorne, Samuel E., eds. LC 77-86655. (Classics of English Legal History in the Modern Era Ser.: Vol. 39). 109p. 1979. lib. bdg. 40.00 (ISBN 0-8240-3088-5). Garland Pub.

Bollan, William. The Freedom of Speech & Writing Upon Public Affairs Considered. LC 75-107346. (Civil Liberties in American History Ser). 1970. Repr. of 1766 ed. lib. bdg. 20.00 (ISBN 0-306-71878-2). Da Capo.

Bosmajian, Haig. Justice Douglas & Freedom of Speech. LC 79-26635. 377p. 1980. lib. bdg. 17.50 (ISBN 0-8108-1276-2). Scarecrow.

Bosmajian, Haig A., ed. The Principles & Practices of Free Speech. LC 80-2900. Repr. of 1971 ed. 42.50 (ISBN 0-404-18083-3). AMS Pr.

Chafee, Zechariah. The Inquiring Mind. LC 74-699. (American Constitutional & Legal History Ser.). 276p. 1974. Repr. of 1928 ed. lib. bdg. 27.50 (ISBN 0-306-70641-5). Da Capo.

Committee on Education & Labor, U.S. Senate, 76th Congress, 3rd Session. Violations of Free Speech & Rights of Labor: Hearings Before a Subcommittee on Education & Labor, 3 vols. in 1. facsimile ed. McCurry, Dan C. & Rubenstein, Richard E., eds. LC 74-30659. (American Farmers & the Rise of Agribusiness Ser.). 1975. Repr. of 1941 ed. 66.00x (ISBN 0-405-06836-0). Arno.

Cox, Archibald. Freedom of Expression. LC 81-4374. 96p. 1981. 6.95 (ISBN 0-674-31912-5); pap. 2.95 (ISBN 0-674-31913-3). Harvard U Pr.

Haiman, Deanklyn S. Speech & Law in a Free Society. LC 81-7546. 480p. 1981. lib. bdg. 22.50x (ISBN 0-226-31213-5). U of Chicago Pr.

Hemmer, Joseph J., Jr. Communication Under Law: Vol. I, Free Speech. LC 79-19166. 307p. 1979. 16.50 (ISBN 0-8108-1248-7). Scarecrow.

Hentoff, Nat. The First Freedom: The Tumultuous History of Free Speech in America. LC 78-72860. (gr. 7 up). 1980. 9.95 (ISBN 0-440-03850-2). Delacorte.

Hook, Sidney. Heresy, Yes - Conspiracy, No. LC 72-9049. 283p. 1973. Repr. of 1953 ed. lib. bdg. 15.00 (ISBN 0-8371-6562-8). Greenwood.

Johnson, Chalmers A. Communist Policies Toward the Intellectual Class. LC 72-10698. 139p. 1973. Repr. of 1970 ed. lib. bdg. 15.00x (ISBN 0-8371-6613-6, JOCP). Greenwood.

Kalven, Harry, Jr. Negro & the First Amendment. LC 66-29115. 1966. pap. 2.45 (ISBN 0-226-42315-8, P240, Phoen). U of Chicago Pr.

King, Jerome B. Law V. Order: Legal Process & Free Speech in Contemporary France. 206p. 1975. 17.50 (ISBN 0-208-01514-0, Archon). Shoe String.

Kurland, Philip B. Free Speech & Association: The Supreme Court & the First Amendment. 1976. pap. 6.95 (ISBN 0-226-46403-2). U of Chicago Pr.

Lieberman, Jethro K. Free Speech, Free Press, & the Law. LC 79-22483. (gr. 7 up). 1980. 7.95 (ISBN 0-688-41928-3); PLB 7.63 (ISBN 0-688-51928-8). Lothrop.

Meiklejohn, Alexander. Political Freedom: The Constitutional Powers of the People. LC 78-27616. 1979. Repr. of 1960 ed. lib. bdg. 16.00x (ISBN 0-313-20907-3, MEPF). Greenwood.

Murphy, Paul. The Meaning of Freedom of Speech. LC 72-133500. (Contributions in American History: No. 15). 401p. 1972. lib. bdg. 18.50 (ISBN 0-8371-5176-7, MCL/); pap. 6.95 (ISBN 0-8371-8925-X). Greenwood.

National Association of Broadcasters. Broadcasting & the Bill of Rights: Statements on the White Bill. 322p. 1972. Repr. of 1947 ed. 20.50 (ISBN 0-8337-4299-X). B Franklin.

O'Neil, Robert M. Free Speech: Responsible Communication Under Law. 2nd ed. LC 71-182877. (Orig.). 1972. pap. 3.95 (ISBN 0-672-61301-8, SC11). Bobbs.

Owen, Bruce M. Economics & Freedom of Expression: Media Structure & the First Amendment. LC 75-26645. 1975. text ed. 17.50 (ISBN 0-88410-044-8). Ballinger Pub.

Roberts, R. Imprisoned Tongues. 222p. 1968. 12.00x (ISBN 0-7190-0596-5, Pub. by Manchester U Pr England). State Mutual Bk.

Rogge, O. John. First & the Fifth. LC 71-140377. (Civil Liberties in American History Ser). 1971. Repr. of 1960 ed. lib. bdg. 35.00 (ISBN 0-306-70087-5). Da Capo.

Schroeder, Theodore A. Constitutional Free Speech Defined & Defended. LC 72-106497. (Civil Liberties in American History Ser). 1970. Repr. of 1919 ed. lib. bdg. 45.00 (ISBN 0-306-71872-3). Da Capo.

--Free Speech Bibliography. 1969. 24.00 (ISBN 0-8337-3171-8). B Franklin.

--Free Speech for Radicals. LC 68-56791. (Research & Source Works Ser.: No. 281). 1970. Repr. of 1916 ed. lib. bdg. 22.50 (ISBN 0-8337-3172-6). B Franklin.

Shuman, Samuel I., ed. Law & Disorder: The Legitimation of Direct Action As an Instrument of Social Policy. LC 78-130426. (Leo M. Franklin Memorial Lectures in Human Relations Ser: Vol. 19). 1971. text ed. 8.95x (ISBN 0-8143-1436-8). Wayne St U Pr.

Stephen, L. Essays on Freethinking & Plainspeaking. LC 75-41262. Repr. of 1905 ed. 25.50 (ISBN 0-404-14789-5). AMS Pr.

Worton, Stanley N. Freedom of Speech & Press. (American Issues in Perspective Ser.). 144p. 1975. pap. text ed. 4.50x (ISBN 0-8104-6012-2). Hayden.

LIBERTY OF SPEECH IN THE CHURCH

Rahner, Karl. Free Speech in the Church. LC 79-8717. Orig. Title: Das Freie Wort in der Kirche. 112p. 1981. Repr. of 1959 ed. lib. bdg. 17.50x (ISBN 0-313-20849-2, RAFS). Greenwood.

Seaton, Alexander A. The Theory of Toleration Under the Later Stuarts. 1972. lib. bdg. 17.50x (ISBN 0-374-97233-8). Octagon.

LIBERTY OF THE PRESS

see also Blasphemy; Censorship; Condemned Books; Expurgated Books; Freedom of Information; Libel and Slander; Press; Press Law; Prohibited Books; Public Opinion

Barron, Jerome A. & Dienes, C. Thomas. Handbook of Free Speech & Free Press. 1979. text ed. 45.00 (ISBN 0-316-08230-9). Little.

Bechtel, Edwin D. Freedom of the Press & L'Association Mensuelle: Philipon Versus Louis-Philippe. (Illus.). 40p. 1952. 14.00x (ISBN 0-8139-0452-8, Grolier Club). U Pr of Va.

Beman, Lamar T., compiled by. Selected Articles on Censorship of Speech & the Press. LC 76-98813. 1971. Repr. of 1930 ed. lib. bdg. 17.75x (ISBN 0-8371-3073-5, BECE). Greenwood.

Beman, Lamar T., ed. Selected Articles on Censorship of Speech & the Press. LC 77-95404. (BCL Ser. I). 1969. Repr. of 1930 ed. 14.00 (ISBN 0-404-00747-3). AMS Pr.

Berninghausen, David K. The Flight from Reason: Essays on Intellectual Freedom in the Academy, the Press, & the Library. LC 74-23236. 189p. 1975. pap. text ed. 7.50 (ISBN 0-8389-0192-1). ALA.

Bollan, William. The Freedom of Speech & Writing Upon Public Affairs Considered. LC 75-107346. (Civil Liberties in American History Ser). 1970. Repr. of 1766 ed. lib. bdg. 20.00 (ISBN 0-306-71878-2). Da Capo.

Calvocoressi, Peter & Bristow, Ann. Freedom to Publish: A Report on the Obstacles to Freedom in Publishing Prepared for the Congress International Publishers Association, Stockholm, May 1980. 1980. pap. text ed. 15.50x (ISBN 0-391-01949-X). Humanities.

Chenery, William L. Freedom of the Press. LC 77-14294. 1978. Repr. of 1955 ed. lib. bdg. 24.50x (ISBN 0-8371-9835-6, CHFP). Greenwood.

Cobbett, William. Democratic Judge Or, the Equal Liberty of the Press. LC 70-125686. (American Journalists Ser). 1970. Repr. of 1798 ed. 9.00 (ISBN 0-405-01663-8). Arno.

Cox, Archibald. Freedom of Expression. LC 81-4374. 96p. 1981. 6.95 (ISBN 0-674-31912-5); pap. 2.95 (ISBN 0-674-31913-3). Harvard U Pr.

Devol, Kenneth S., ed. Mass Media & the Supreme Court. rev. 2nd ed. (Communication Arts Bks.). 1976. pap. text ed. 9.50x (ISBN 0-8038-4684-3). Hastings.

Diderot, Denis & Proust, Jacques. Sur la Liberte de la Presse. 1975. 5.95 (ISBN 0-686-56031-0). French & Eur.

Duniway, Clyde A. The Development of Freedom of the Press in Massachusetts. LC 68-58770. 202p. 1906. Repr. 21.00 (ISBN 0-8337-0957-7). B Franklin.

Ernst, M. L. & Seagle, W. To the Pure: A Study of Obscenity & the Censor. LC 28-30424. 1928. 17.00 (ISBN 0-527-27650-2). Kraus Repr.

Fisk, Theophilus. Orations on the Freedom of the Press. LC 73-125692. (American Journalists Ser). 1970. Repr. of 1837 ed. 11.00 (ISBN 0-405-01669-7). Arno.

Franklin, Benjamin. An Apology for Printers. Goodman, Randolph, ed. LC 72-12396. (Illus.). 40p. 1973. Repr. pap. 3.95 (ISBN 0-87491-146-X). Acropolis.

Friendly, Fred. Minnesota Rag: The Dramatic Story of the Landmark Supreme Court Case That Gave New Meaning to Freedom of the Press. 1981. 12.95 (ISBN 0-394-50752-5). Random.

Goodale, James C., ed. The New York Times Co. v. U. S. Pentagon Papers Litigation, 2 vols. LC 72-173288. 75.00 (ISBN 0-405-00100-2). Arno.

Gora, Joel M. The Rights of Reporters. 1974. pap. 1.75 (ISBN 0-380-00188-8, 38836, Discus). Avon.

Hachten, William A. Supreme Court on Freedom of the Press: Decisions & Dissents. facsimile ed. 1968. pap. text ed. 14.40x (ISBN 0-8138-2330-7). Iowa St U Pr.

Hay, George. Essay on the Liberty of the Press. LC 71-125697. (American Journalists Ser). 1970. Repr. of 1799 ed. 11.00 (ISBN 0-405-01676-X). Arno.

--Two Essays on the Liberty of the Press. LC 75-112703. (Civil Liberties in American History Ser). 1970. Repr. of 1803 ed. lib. bdg. 15.00 (ISBN 0-306-71918-5). Da Capo.

Hocking, William E. Freedom of the Press. LC 77-39587. (Civil Liberties in American History Ser). 240p. 1972. Repr. of 1947 ed. lib. bdg. 22.50 (ISBN 0-306-70231-2). Da Capo.

--Freedom of the Press. LC 77-39587. (Civil Liberties in American History Ser). 240p. 1972. Repr. of 1947 ed. lib. bdg. 22.50 (ISBN 0-306-70231-2). Da Capo.

Hoyt, Olga G. & Hoyt, Edwin P. Freedom of the News Media. LC 72-93809. 192p. (gr. 6 up). 1973. 6.95 (ISBN 0-395-28910-6, Clarion). HM.

Johnson, Gerald W. Peril & Promise. LC 73-14034. 110p. 1974. Repr. of 1958 ed. lib. bdg. 15.00x (ISBN 0-8371-7143-1, JOPP). Greenwood.

Leigh, Robert D. A Free & Responsible Press, a General Report on Mass Communication: Newspapers, Radio, Motion Pictures, Magazines & Books. Commission on Freedom of the Press, ed. LC 46-13. (Midway Reprint Ser.). 139p. 1947. pap. text ed. 4.50x (ISBN 0-226-47135-7). U of Chicago Pr.

Lewis, Wyndham. The Writer & the Absolute. LC 75-7240. 202p. 1975. Repr. of 1952 ed. lib. bdg. 15.00x (ISBN 0-8371-8098-8, LEWR). Greenwood.

Lieberman, Jethro K. Free Speech, Free Press, & the Law. LC 79-22483. (gr. 7 up). 1980. 7.95 (ISBN 0-688-41928-3); PLB 7.63 (ISBN 0-688-51928-8). Lothrop.

Lofton, John. The Press As Guardian of the First Amendment. LC 80-10617. 358p. 1980. 14.95 (ISBN 0-87249-389-X). U of SC Pr.

McClellan, Grant S., ed. Censorship in the United States. (Reference Shelf Ser: Vol. 39, No. 3). 1967. 6.25 (ISBN 0-8242-0096-9). Wilson.

McCormick, Robert. Freedom of the Press. LC 77-125705. (American Journalists). 1970. Repr. of 1936 ed. 9.50 (ISBN 0-405-01686-7). Arno.

McCoy, Ralph E. Freedom of the Press: A Bibliocyclopedia. Ten Year Supplement (1967-1977) LC 78-16573. 544p. 1979. 42.50x (ISBN 0-8093-0844-4). S Ill U Pr.

--Freedom of the Press: An Annotated Bibliography. LC 67-10032. 576p. 1968. 32.50x (ISBN 0-8093-0335-3). S Ill U Pr.

Mill, James. Essays on Jurisprudence Government, Liberty of the Press, Law of Nations, Education, Colony & Prison Discipline. LC 66-21685. Repr. of 1825 ed. 17.50x (ISBN 0-678-00297-5). Kelley.

Milton, John. Areopagitica. 80p. 1972. Repr. of 1644 ed. 7.50x (ISBN 0-87556-219-1). Saifer.

Padover, Saul K., ed. Karl Marx on Freedom of the Press & Censorship. LC 78-172260. (Karl Marx Library: Vol. 4). 264p. 1974. 10.00 (ISBN 0-07-048077-X, GB). McGraw.

Putnam, George H. Books & Their Makers During the Middle Ages, 2 Vols. 1962. Set. text ed. 42.50x (ISBN 0-391-01060-3). Humanities.

--Censorship of the Church of Rome & Its Influence Upon the Production & Distribution of Literature, 2 Vols. LC 67-12455. 1967. Repr. of 1906 ed. 40.00 (ISBN 0-405-08869-8). Arno.

Report of the Twentieth Century Fund Task Force on the Government & the Press & Graham, Fred. Freedoms Under Pressure. LC 72-80586. 1972. pap. free on request (ISBN 0-87078-125-1). Twentieth Fund.

Rips, Geoffrey. Unamerican Activities: The Campaign Against the Underground Press in the United States, 1960-1979. 160p. 1981. 4.95 (ISBN 0-87286-127-9); pap. 4.95 (ISBN 0-87286-127-9). City Lights.

Ruckelshaus, William, et al. Freedom of the Press. 1976. pap. 3.75 (ISBN 0-8447-2075-5). Am Enterprise.

Rucker, Bryce W. First Freedom. LC 68-11651. (New Horizons in Journalism Ser.). 340p. 1968. 15.00x (ISBN 0-8093-0297-7). S Ill U Pr.

--First Freedom. LC 68-11651. (Arcturus Books Paperbacks). 340p. 1971. pap. 9.95 (ISBN 0-8093-0498-8). S Ill U Pr.

Rutherford, Livingston. John Peter Zenger, His Press, His Trial & a Bibliography of Zenger Imprints. LC 4-8588. (American Biography Ser). Repr. of 1904 ed. 14.50 (ISBN 0-384-52620-9). Johnson Repr.

Rutherfurd, L. John Peter Zenger: His Press, His Trial, & a Bibliography of Zenger Imprints. (With reprint of the first edition of his trial). 7.50 (ISBN 0-8446-1394-0). Peter Smith.

Rutherford, Livingston. John Peter Zenger, His Press, His Trial & a Bibliography of Zenger Imprints. LC 77-125713. (American Journalists). (Illus.). 1970. Repr. of 1904 ed. 20.00 (ISBN 0-405-01694-8). Arno.

Schmidt, Benno C., Jr. Freedom of the Press Vs. Public Access. LC 75-19818. (Special Studies). 1976. text ed. 26.95 (ISBN 0-275-01620-X); pap. text ed. 11.95 (ISBN 0-275-89430-4). Praeger.

Schroeder, Theodore. Obscene Literature & Constitutional Law. 59.95 (ISBN 0-8490-0745-3). Gordon Pr.

Schroeder, Theodore A. Free Speech Bibliography. 1969. 24.00 (ISBN 0-8337-3171-8). B Franklin.

--Free Speech for Radicals. LC 68-56791. (Research & Source Works Ser.: No. 281). 1970. Repr. of 1916 ed. lib. bdg. 22.50 (ISBN 0-8337-3172-6). B Franklin.

--Obscene Literature & Constitutional Law. LC 72-116913. (Civil Lib. in Am. Hist. Ser.). 440p. 1972. Repr. of 1911 ed. lib. bdg. 25.00 (ISBN 0-306-70156-1). Da Capo.

Seldes, G. Freedom of the Press. LC 73-146159. (Civil Liberties in American History Ser). 1971. Repr. of 1935 ed. lib. bdg. 35.00 (ISBN 0-306-70125-1). Da Capo.

Seldes, George. You Can't Print That: The Truth Behind the News. 1968. Repr. of 1929 ed. 32.00 (ISBN 0-403-00061-0). Scholarly.

Siebert, Fredrick S. The Rights & Privileges of the Press. LC 70-100243. xvii, 429p. Repr. of 1934 ed. lib. bdg. 17.75x (ISBN 0-8371-4021-8, SIRP). Greenwood.

Sinclair, William R. Press Freedom; Where to Now? 1980. 15.00 (ISBN 0-686-27951-4). CLCB Pr.

Thomson, John. Enquiry Concerning the Liberty & Licentiousness of the Press. LC 79-107418. (Civil Liberties in American History Ser). 1970. Repr. of 1801 ed. lib. bdg. 14.00 (ISBN 0-306-71880-4). Da Capo.

Twentieth Century Fund. Task Force Report for a National News Council. A Free & Responsive Press. Balk, Alfred, ed. LC 72-97796. 96p. pap. 8.00 (ISBN 0-527-02812-6). Kraus Repr.

Weinberger, Harry. The Liberty of the Press. 59.95 (ISBN 0-8490-0518-3). Gordon Pr.

Wickwar, William H. The Struggle for Freedom of the Press, 1819-1832. Repr. of 1928 ed. 23.00 (ISBN 0-384-68281-2). Johnson Repr.

Wortman, Tunis. Treatise Concerning Political Enquiry & the Liberty of the Press. LC 78-122162. (Civil Liberties in American History Ser). 1970. Repr. of 1800 ed. lib. bdg. 35.00 (ISBN 0-306-71967-3). Da Capo.

LIBERTY OF THE PRESS–EUROPE

Belin, Jean P. Commerce des livres prohibes a Paris de 1750 a 1789. (Illus.). 1962. Repr. of 1913 ed. 19.00 (ISBN 0-8337-0219-X). B Franklin.

Fliess, Peter J. Freedom of the Press in the German Republic, 1918-1933. LC 71-90507. Repr. of 1955 ed. lib. bdg. 15.00x (ISBN 0-8371-2208-2, FLFP). Greenwood.

Lea, Henry C. Chapters from the Religious History of Spain Connected with the Inquisition. LC 68-56760. (Research & Source Work Ser.: No. 245). 1967. Repr. of 1890 ed. 26.00 (ISBN 0-8337-2035-X). B Franklin.

Rodmell, Graham E. Memoires Sur la Librairie et Sur la Libertie De la Presse. (Studies in the Romance Languages & Literatures: No. 213). 384p. 1980. pap. 19.00 (ISBN 0-8078-9213-0). U of NC Pr.

Shackleton, Robert. Censure & Censorship: Impediments to Free Publication in the Age of Enlightenment. LC 72-619567. (Bibliographical Monograph: No.8). 1975. 5.95 (ISBN 0-87959-051-3). U of Tex Hum Res.

LIBERTY OF THE PRESS–GREAT BRITAIN

Bentham, Jeremy. Elements of the Art of Packing As Applied to Special Juries Particularly in Cases of Libel Law. Berkowitz, David & Thorne, Samuel, eds. LC 77-86672. (Classics of English Legal History in the Modern Era Ser.: Vol. 116). 1979. Repr. of 1821 ed. lib. bdg. 40.00 (ISBN 0-8240-3153-9). Garland Pub.

Blount, Charles, et al. A Just Vindication of Learning. Berkowitz, David S. & Thorne, Samuel E., eds. LC 77-86655. (Classics of English Legal History in the Modern Era Ser.: Vol. 39). 109p. 1979. lib. bdg. 40.00 (ISBN 0-8240-3088-5). Garland Pub.

Clyde, William M. Struggle for the Freedom of the Press from Caxton to Cromwell. LC 70-122223. (Research & Source Works: No. 479). 1970. Repr. of 1934 ed. lib. bdg. 23.50 (ISBN 0-8337-0606-3). B Franklin.

Collet, Collet D. History of Taxes on Knowledge: Their Origin & Repeal. LC 75-142565. 1971. Repr. 22.00 (ISBN 0-8103-3615-4). Gale.

A Decree of Starre-Chamber, Concerning Printing. LC 70-25951. (English Experience Ser.: No. 190). 1969. Repr. of 1637 ed. 8.00 (ISBN 9-0221-0190-8). Walter J Johnson.

Siebert, Fredrick S. Freedom of the Press in England, 1476-1776: The Rise & Decline of Government Controls. LC 52-5892. 1965. pap. 8.95 (ISBN 0-252-72431-3). U of Ill Pr.

LIBERTY OF THE WILL

see Free Will and Determinism

LIBERTY PARTY

Smith, Theodore C. Liberty & Free Soil Parties in the Northwest. LC 76-28555. (Anti-Slavery Crusade in America Ser). 1969. Repr. of 1897 ed. 15.00 (ISBN 0-405-00661-6). Arno.

--Liberty & Free-Soil Parties in the Northwest. LC 66-24761. (Illus.). 1967. Repr. of 1897 ed. 8.50 (ISBN 0-8462-0968-3). Russell.

LIBRARIANS

see also Bibliographers; Government Librarians; Library Science–Vocational Guidance

Abell, Millicent, ed. Collective Bargaining in Higher Education. (ACRL Publications in Librarianship Ser.: No. 38). 170p. 1977. pap. 7.50 (ISBN 0-8389-3189-8). ALA.

Armour, Richard. The Happy Bookers: A Playful History of Librarians & Their World from the Stone Age to the Distant Future. LC 75-28313. 1976. 6.95 (ISBN 0-07-002303-4, GB). McGraw.

Ash, Lee, ed. Biographical Directory of Librarians in the United States & Canada. 5th ed. LC 79-118854. 1970. 45.00 (ISBN 0-8389-0084-4). ALA.

Ash, Lee, et al. Who's Who in Library Service: A Biographical Directory of Professional Librarians in the United States & Canada. 4th ed. 1966. 27.50 (ISBN 0-208-00598-6). Shoe String.

Chicago, Illinois Regional Library Council. Directory of Human Resources in Libraries. 2nd ed. 1981. pap. write for info. (ISBN 0-917060-13-X). Ill Regional Lib Coun.

Cohen, Aaron & Cohen, Elaine. Designing & Space Planning for Libraries: A Behavioral Guide. LC 79-12478. (Illus.). 1979. 24.95 (ISBN 0-8352-1150-9). Bowker.

Cole, J. Ainsworth Rand Spofford: Bookman & Librarian. Harris, Michael H., ed. LC 75-31517. (Heritage of Librarianship: No. 2). 208p. 1975. PLB 20.00x (ISBN 0-87287-117-7). Libs Unl.

Cooper, Michael D. California's Demand for Librarians: Projecting Future Requirements. LC 78-8919. 1978. pap. 6.50x (ISBN 0-87772-256-0). Inst Gov Stud Berk.

Corrigan, John T., ed. Today's Youth-Today's Librarian. (Catholic Library Assn. Studies in Librarianship: No. 3). 64p. 1980. pap. 5.00 (ISBN 0-87507-007-8). Cath Lib Assn.

Cutler, Wayne & Harris, Michael H., eds. Justin Winsor: Scholar-Librarian. LC 80-19310. (Heritage of Librarianship Ser.: No. 5). 196p. 1980. lib. bdg. 25.00x (ISBN 0-87287-200-9). Libs Unl.

Dudley, E., ed. S. R. Ranganathan: Papers Given at Memorial Meeting in January, 1973. 1974. pap. 5.50x (ISBN 0-85365-197-3, Pub. by Lib Assn England). Oryx Pr.

Goff, Frederick R. The Delights of a Rare Book Librarian. 1975. 3.00 (ISBN 0-89073-001-6). Boston Public Lib.

Harrison, H. Picture Librarianship. 1981. 34.50 (ISBN 0-85365-912-5); pap. 18.50 (ISBN 0-85365-693-2). Oryx Pr.

James, Montague R. Ancient Libraries of Canterbury & Dover. 59.95 (ISBN 0-87968-628-6). Gordon Pr.

Johnston, Mary T. & Lipscomb, Elizabeth J. Amelia Gayle Gorgas: A Biography. LC 77-18889. 191p. 1978. 12.95x (ISBN 0-8173-5235-X). U of Ala Pr.

Josey, E. J., ed. & intro. by. Black Librarian in America. LC 79-17850. 1970. 10.00 (ISBN 0-8108-0362-3). Scarecrow.

Kroll, Morton, ed. Libraries & Librarians of the Pacific Northwest. LC 60-9873. (PNLA Library Development Project Reports, Ser.: Vol. 4). 281p. 1960. 10.50 (ISBN 0-295-73827-8). U of Wash Pr.

Lee, W. Storrs, ed. Partridge in a Swamp: The Journals of Viola C. White. 1979. 12.95 (ISBN 0-914378-40-6). Countryman.

Lubans, John, Jr. Educating the Library User. LC 74-11794. (Illus.). 435p. 1974. 17.95 (ISBN 0-8352-0674-2). Bowker.

Lyle, Guy R. Beyond My Expectation: A Personal Chronicle. LC 81-5071. 244p. 1981. 12.50 (ISBN 0-8108-1426-9). Scarecrow.

Metcalf, Keyes D. Random Recollections of an Anachronism. 401p. 1980. 14.95 (ISBN 0-918414-02-4). Readex Bks.

Mitchell, P. M. Halldor Hermannsson. LC 77-14665. (Islandica Ser.: XLI). (Illus.). 1978. 24.50x (ISBN 0-8014-1085-1). Cornell U Pr.

Mugnier, Charlotte. Paraprofessional & the Professional Job Structure. 164p. 1980. pap. text ed. 7.00 (ISBN 0-8389-0303-7). ALA.

Myers, Margaret & Scarborough, Mayra, eds. Women in Librarianship: Melvil's Rib Symposium. (Issues in Library & Information Sciences Ser.: No. 2). 1975. pap. text ed. 4.95x (ISBN 0-8135-0807-X). Rutgers U Slis.

Nunn, G. Raymond. Asian Libraries & Librarianship: An Annotated Bibliography of Selected Books & Periodicals & a Draft Syllabus. LC 73-6629. 1973. 10.00 (ISBN 0-8108-0633-9). Scarecrow.

Olle, J. G. Ernest A. Savage: Librarian Extraordinary. 1977. lib. bdg. 27.00x (ISBN 0-85365-459-X, Pub. by Lib Assn England). Oryx Pr.

O'Reilly, Robert C. & O'Reilly, Marjorie I. Librarians & Labor Relations: Employment Under Union Contracts. LC 80-1049. (Contributions in Librarianship & Information Science Ser.: No. 35). xiv, 191p. 1981. lib. bdg. 25.00 (ISBN 0-313-22485-4, OLL/). Greenwood.

Reeves, William J. Librarians As Professionals: The Occupation's Impact on Library Work Arrangements. LC 79-2389. (Illus.). 192p. 1980. 19.95x (ISBN 0-669-03163-1). Lexington Bks.

Shaffer, Dale E. Creativity for Librarians: A Management Guide to Encourage Creative Thinking. 39p. 1973. pap. 3.00 (ISBN 0-915060-07-8). D E Shaffer.

--Criteria for Improving the Professional Status of Librarianship. 49p. 1980. pap. text ed. 4.25 (ISBN 0-915060-15-9). D E Shaffer.

Shores, Louis. Quiet World: A Librarian's Crusade for Destiny. viii, 309p. (Orig.). 1975. 19.50 (ISBN 0-208-01477-2, Linnet). Shoe String.

Stevens, Norman D., ed. Essays for Ralph Shaw. LC 75-6664. 219p. 1975. 10.00 (ISBN 0-8108-0815-3). Scarecrow.

Stone, Elizabeth W. Factors Related to the Professional Development of Librarians. LC 75-7741. (Illus.). 1969. 10.00 (ISBN 0-8108-0274-0). Scarecrow.

Stone, Elizabeth W., ed. New Directions in Staff Development. LC 72-171618. 70p. 1971. 3.00 (ISBN 0-8389-3130-8). ALA.

Szigethy, Marion. Maurice Falcolm Tauber: A Biobibliography 1934-1973. LC 74-7401. 1974. 10.00 (ISBN 0-8108-0725-4). Scarecrow.

Thomas, Diana M., et al. The Effective Reference Librarian. (Library & Information Science). 1981. 17.50 (ISBN 0-12-688720-9). Acad Pr.

Thompson, A. Meilleur: Mobility of Employment International for Librarians in Europe. (Research Publication Ser.: No. 20). 1977. pap. 17.25x (ISBN 0-85365-660-6, Pub. by Lib Assn England). Oryx Pr.

Tunley, M. Library Structures & Staffing Systems. (Management Pamphlet Ser.). 1979. pap. 9.25x (ISBN 0-85365-771-8, Pub. by Lib Assn England). Oryx Pr.

Walbank, F. Alan. Queens of the Circulating Library. (Women Ser.). 1950. 30.00 (ISBN 0-685-43857-0). Norwood Edns.

Warren, G. Garry. The Handicapped Librarian: A Study in Barriers. LC 79-21811. 155p. 1979. 10.00 (ISBN 0-8108-1259-2). Scarecrow.

Wynar, Bohdan S., et al, eds. Dictionary of American Library Biography. LC 77-28791. 1978. lib. bdg. 85.00x (ISBN 0-87287-180-0). Libs Unl.

LIBRARIANS–CERTIFICATION

Rudman, Jack. Junior Librarian. (Career Examination Ser.: C-1820). (Cloth bdg, avail. on request). 1977. pap. 8.00 (ISBN 0-685-78626-9). Natl Learning.

Woellner, Elizabeth H. Requirements for Certification of Teachers, Counselors, Librarians, Administrators: 1980-81. 45th ed. (LC a43-1905). 1980. lib. bdg. 17.00x (ISBN 0-226-90465-2). U of Chicago Pr.

--Requirements for Certification of Teachers, Counselors, Librarians, Administrators: 1978-79. 43rd ed. LC 43-1905. 1978. lib. bdg. 17.00x (ISBN 0-226-90463-6). U of Chicago Pr.

LIBRARIANS–CONGRESSES

see Library Conferences

LIBRARIANS–DIRECTORIES

see also Libraries–Directories

Blunt, Adrian. Law Librarianship. (Outlines of Modern Librarianship Ser.). 1979. text ed. 12.00 (ISBN 0-89664-434-0). K G Saur.

Jaques Cattell Press, ed. The Librarians Phone Book 1981. 2nd ed. 445p. 1980. pap. 9.95 (ISBN 0-8352-1321-8). Bowker.

Li, Tze-Chung & Chang, Roy. Directory of Chinese American Librarians. LC 77-373584. 1977. pap. 5.00 (ISBN 0-686-24156-8). CHCUS Inc.

LIBRARIANS–SALARIES, PENSIONS, ETC.

ACRL Committee. Faculty Status for Academic Librarians. LC 75-29403. 62p. 1975. pap. text ed. 4.00 (ISBN 0-8389-5458-8). ALA.

Guyton, Theodore L. Unionization: The Viewpoint of Librarians. LC 74-19164. 218p. 1975. pap. 10.00 (ISBN 0-8389-0187-5). ALA.

New York State Library Association. Public Libraries in New York State: A 1977 Salary Survey. 1978. pap. text ed. 3.00 (ISBN 0-931658-00-4). NY Lib Assn.

Vignone, Joseph A. Collective Bargaining Procedures for Public Library Employees. LC 79-160579. 1971. 10.00 (ISBN 0-8108-0412-3). Scarecrow.

LIBRARIANS, AFRO-AMERICAN

see Afro-American Librarians

LIBRARIANS, INTERCHANGE OF

Interlibrary Loan Codes, 1981. 16p. pap. 1.50 (ISBN 0-8389-5587-8). ALA.

LIBRARIANS, TRAINING OF

see Library Schools and Training

LIBRARIANSHIP

see Library Science

LIBRARIES

see also Archives; Audio-Visual Library Service; Bibliographical Centers; Information Services; Public Libraries

Aldrich, Ella V. Using Books & Libraries. 5th ed. (gr. 9-12). 1967. pap. 5.95 (ISBN 0-13-939223-8). P-H.

American Library Association Centennial Celebration. Libraries & the Life of the Mind in America: Addresses. LC 77-3288. 1977. 8.00 (ISBN 0-8389-0238-3). ALA.

American Library Association, Library Administration Division, Buildings & Equipment Section, Buildings for College & University Libraries Committee. Running Out of Space: What Are the Alternatives. LC 78-1796. 1978. pap. 15.00 (ISBN 0-8389-3215-0). ALA.

Baeckler, Virginia & Larson, Linda. Go, Pep, & Pop: Two Hundred Fifty Tested Ideas for Lively Libraries. LC 75-20328. 1976. pap. 4.50 (ISBN 0-916444-01-5). UNABASHED Lib.

Bahr, Alice H. Book Theft & Library Security Systems, 1978-79. LC 77-25284. (Professional Librarian Ser.). (Illus.). 1978. pap. 24.50x (ISBN 0-914236-14-8). Knowledge Indus.

Baker, W. S. Bibliotheca Washingtoniana. 59.95 (ISBN 0-87968-746-0). Gordon Pr.

Berelson, Bernard & Ansheim, Lester. The Library's Public: A Report of the Public Library Inquiry. LC 75-31430. 174p. 1976. Repr. of 1949 ed. lib. bdg. 21.50x (ISBN 0-8371-8499-1, BELP). Greenwood.

Bishop, William W. Backs of Books, & Other Essays in Librarianship. facs. ed. LC 68-54328. (Essay Index Reprint Ser). 1968. Repr. of 1926 ed. 16.00 (ISBN 0-8369-0215-7). Arno.

Bloomfield, Masse. How to Use a Library. (Illus.). 1970. pap. 3.00x (ISBN 0-87881-000-5). Mojave Bks.

Boaz, Martha, ed. A Living Library. LC 58-8970. 84p. 1957. pap. 2.25 (ISBN 0-88474-006-4). U of S Cal Pr.

Bostwick, Arthur E. Librarian's Open Shelf: Essays on Various Subjects. facs. ed. LC 67-23182. (Essay Index Reprint Ser). 1920. 18.00 (ISBN 0-8369-0226-2). Arno.

Bowker Annual of Library & Book Trade Information 1981. 26th ed. LC 55-12434. (Illus.). 700p. 1981. 32.50 (ISBN 0-8352-1343-9). Bowker.

Brooks, James & Draper, James. Interior Designs for Libraries. (Orig.). 1979. pap. text ed. 12.50x (ISBN 0-8389-0282-0). ALA.

Burton, Margaret H. & Vosburgh, Marion E. A Bibliography of Librarianship: A Classified & Annotated Guide to the Library Literature of the World. LC 72-79206. 176p. 1934. Repr. 25.00 (ISBN 0-403-08910-7). Somerset Pub.

Clark, Robert L, Jr., ed. Archive-Library Relations. LC 76-18806. 1976. 18.50 (ISBN 0-8352-0770-6). Bowker.

Closurdo, Janette S., ed. Library Management 1979, Vol. 1. 1980. pap. 8.50 (ISBN 0-686-77554-6). SLA.

Coughlin, R. E., et al. Urban Analysis for Branch Library System Planning. LC 71-133496. (Contributions in Librarianship & Information Science: No. 1). 1972. lib. bdg. 15.95 (ISBN 0-8371-5161-9, CLP/). Greenwood.

Cowley, John, ed. Libraries in Higher Education: The User Approach to Service. 163p. (Orig.). 1975. 14.50 (ISBN 0-208-01371-7, Linnet). Shoe String.

Dana, John C. Libraries: Addresses & Essays. facs. ed. LC 67-22088. (Essay Index Reprint Ser). 1916. 18.00 (ISBN 0-8369-1329-9). Arno.

Dolnick, Sandy, ed. Friends of Libraries Sourcebook. LC 80-24643. 176p. 1980. pap. 6.00 (ISBN 0-8389-3245-2). ALA.

Downs, Robert B. American Library Resources: A Bibliographical Guide Supplement 1961-1970. LC 51-11156. 1972. text ed. 20.00 (ISBN 0-8389-0116-6). ALA.

Driver, Clive E. Early American Maps & Views. write for info. (ISBN 0-939084-12-0, Pub. by Rosenbach Mus & Lib). U Pr of Va.

Duchein, Michael. Archive Buildings & Equipment. (ICA Handbook Ser.: Vol. 1). 201p. 1977. pap. text ed. 25.00 (ISBN 3-7940-3780-4, Pub. by K G Saur). Gale.

Edwards, Edward. Memoirs of Libraries: Including a Handbook of Libraries & a Handbook of Library Economy, 2 vols. LC 72-79251. 1859. Repr. 43.00 (ISBN 0-403-04170-8). Somerset Pub.

Edwards, G. Memoirs of Libraries. 1976. lib. bdg. 59.95 (ISBN 0-8490-2224-X). Gordon Pr.

Essays Offered to Herbert Putnam by His Colleagues & Friends on His Thirtieth Anniversary As Librarian of Congress, April 5, 1929. facs. ed. LC 67-23214. (Essay Index Reprint Ser). 1929. 21.50 (ISBN 0-8369-0430-3). Arno.

Estabrook, Leigh, ed. Libraries in Post-Industrial Society. LC 77-8928. (A Neal-Schuman Professional Bk). 1977. lib. bdg. 18.50 (ISBN 0-912700-00-9). Oryx Pr.

Fiske, Majorie. Book Selection & Censorship: A Study of School & Public Libraries in California. LC 59-10464. (California Library Reprint Series: No. 1). 1968. 17.75x (ISBN 0-520-00418-3). U of Cal Pr.

Fussler, Herman H. & Simon, Julian. Patterns in the Use of Books in Large Research Libraries. 2nd ed. LC 72-79916. (Chicago Studies in Library Science Ser). 1969. 11.00x (ISBN 0-226-27556-6). U of Chicago Pr.

Gage-Babcock & Associates, Inc. Protecting the Library & Its Resources: A Guide to Physical Protection & Insurance. (LTP Publications Ser.: No. 7). (Illus.). 338p. 1963. 7.00 (ISBN 0-8389-3064-6). ALA.

Gates, Jean K. Introduction to Librarianship. 2nd ed. (Library Education Ser.). (Illus.). 1977. text ed. 13.95 (ISBN 0-07-022977-5, C). McGraw.

Gerard, David, ed. Libraries & the Arts. 1970. 15.00 (ISBN 0-208-01057-2, Archon). Shoe String.

Getz, Malcolm. Public Libraries: An Economic View. LC 80-10651. 208p. 1980. text ed. 12.50x (ISBN 0-8018-2395-1). Johns Hopkins.

Goldschmidt, Eva M., ed. Champion of a Cause: Essays & Addresses on Librarianship by Archibald MacLeish. LC 70-150577. 1971. 9.50 (ISBN 0-8389-0091-7). ALA.

Gordon, Charlotte. How to Find What You Want in the Library. LC 77-12534. 1979. pap. 4.50 (ISBN 0-8120-0696-8). Barron.

Gordon, Raoul, ed. The Libraries of Puerto Rico. 1976. lib. bdg. 59.95 (ISBN 0-8490-0519-1). Gordon Pr.

Gore, Daniel, ed. Farewell to Alexandria: Solutions to Space, Growth & Performance Problems of Libraries. LC 75-35345. 224p. 1976. lib. bdg. 15.00 (ISBN 0-8371-8587-4, GGP/). Greenwood.

Guild, Reuben A. The Librarian's Manual: A Treatise on Bibliography, Comprising a Select & Descriptive List of Bibliographical Works; to Which Are Added, Sketches of Public Libraries. LC 70-174942. (Illus.). x, 304p. 1972. Repr. of 1858 ed. 26.00 (ISBN 0-8103-3811-4). Gale.

Guthman, Judith D. Metropolitan Libraries: The Challenge & the Promise. (Public Library Reporter Ser.: No. 15). 64p. 1969. pap. 2.00 (ISBN 0-8389-3095-6). ALA.

Hansen, Linda Rose. The Public Library Service in Selected States: An Analysis of Some Patterns in System Formation. (Illinois Regional Library Council Occasional Papers Ser.: No. 2). 80p. 1978. soft cover 7.50 (ISBN 0-917060-04-0). Ill Regional Lib Coun.

Henry, William E. My Own Opinions Upon Libraries & Librarianship. facs. ed. LC 67-23231. (Essay Index Reprint Ser). 1931. 16.00 (ISBN 0-8369-0536-9). Arno.

Hoadley, Irene B. & Clark, Alice S., eds. Quantitative Methods in Librarianship: Standards, Research, Management. LC 73-149962. (Contributions in Librarianship & Information Science: No. 4). 256p. 1972. lib. bdg. 17.95 (ISBN 0-8371-6061-8, HOQ/). Greenwood.

Houghton, Bernard. Out of the Dinosaurs: The Evolution of the National Lending Library for Science & Technology. (Management of Change Ser.). 160p. 1972. 14.50 (ISBN 0-208-01183-8, Linnet). Shoe String.

International Conference, Kingston, Jamaica, April 24-29, 1972. Libraries & the Challenge of Change: Proceedings. Ingram, K. E. & Jefferson, Albertina A., eds. LC 76-351890. 276p. 1975. 20.00 (ISBN 0-7201-0523-4, Pub. by Mansell England). Merrimack Bk Serv.

Johnson, Edward R. & Mann, Stuart H. Organization Development for Academic Libraries: An Evaluation of the Management Review & Analysis Program. LC 79-8289. (Contributions in Librarianship & Information Science: No. 28). (Illus.). 1980. lib. bdg. 19.95 (ISBN 0-313-21373-9, JMA/). Greenwood.

Katz, William A. & Schwartz, Joel J., eds. Library Lit. The Best of 1970. LC 78-154842. 1971. 13.00 (ISBN 0-8108-0418-2). Scarecrow.

Keep, Austin B. The Library in Colonial New York. 1967. Repr. of 1909 ed. 19.50 (ISBN 0-8337-1902-5). B Franklin.

Knight, Hattie M. One-Two-Three Guide to Libraries. 5th ed. 88p. 1976. write for info. plastic comb (ISBN 0-697-06301-1). Wm C Brown.

Kroll, Morton, ed. Libraries & Librarians of the Pacific Northwest. LC 60-9873. (PNLA Library Development Project Reports, Ser.: Vol. 4). 281p. 1960. 10.50 (ISBN 0-295-73827-8). U of Wash Pr.

Lancaster, F. W. The Measurement & Evaluation of Library Services. LC 77-72081. (Illus.). 1977. text ed. 29.95 (ISBN 0-87815-017-X). Info Resources.

Lancaster, John H. The Use of the Library by Student Teachers: Some Factors Related to the Use of the Library by Student Teachers in Thirty-One Colleges in the Area of the North Central Association. LC 77-176973. (Columbia University. Teachers College. Contributions to Education: No. 849). Repr. of 1941 ed. 17.50 (ISBN 0-404-55849-6). AMS Pr.

Lang, Andrew. Library. 1973. lib. bdg. 15.00 (ISBN 0-8414-5774-3). Folcroft.

Lee, Joel M. & Hamilton, Beth A., eds. As Much to Learn As to Teach: Essays in Honor of Lester Asheim. 1979. 14.50 (ISBN 0-208-01751-8, Linnet). Shoe String.

Lee, Sul H. Emerging Trends in Library Organization: What Influences Change. LC 78-56102. (Library Management Ser.: No. 4). 1978. 14.95 (ISBN 0-87650-093-9). Pierian.

Levy, Frank S., et al. Urban Outcomes: Schools, Streets, & Libraries. (The Oakland Project). 1974. 24.50x (ISBN 0-520-02546-6); pap. 7.95x (ISBN 0-520-03045-1). U of Cal Pr.

Libraries in the Therapeutic Society. LC 76-164360. 1971. pap. 1.00 (ISBN 0-8389-5243-7). ALA.

Lockwood, Deborah, compiled by. Library Instruction: A Bibliography. LC 78-20011. 1979. lib. bdg. 16.50x (ISBN 0-313-20720-8, LLI/). Greenwood.

Lyman, Helen H. Literacy & the Nations's Libraries. LC 77-4450. 1977. 15.00 (ISBN 0-8389-0244-8). ALA.

Lynes, A. How to Organize a Local Collection. (Grafton Books on Library Science). 1977. lib. bdg. 8.75x (ISBN 0-233-96452-5). Westview.

McClellan, A. W. The Reader, the Library, & the Book. 150p. 1973. 13.50 (ISBN 0-208-01198-6, Linnet). Shoe String.

Machlup, Fritz & Leeson, Kenneth W. Information Through the Printed Word. Incl. Vol. 1. Book Publishing. 28.95 (ISBN 0-03-047401-9); Vol. 2. Journals. 30.95 (ISBN 0-03-047406-X); Vol. 3. Libraries. 25.95 (ISBN 0-03-047411-6). LC 78-19460. 1978. Praeger.

Mathews, Virginia H. Libraries for Today & Tomorrow. 1976. Repr. of 1976 ed. lib. bdg. 13.00x (ISBN 0-374-95314-7). Octagon.

Mount, Ellis, ed. Planning the Special Library. LC 72-85956. 1972. pap. 9.75 (ISBN 0-87111-205-1). SLA.

Munby, A. N. Essays & Papers. Barker, Nicolas, ed. (Illus.). 256p. 1978. 25.00x (ISBN 0-85967-349-9, Pub. by Scolar Pr England). Biblio Dist.

Orr, J. M. Libraries As Communication Systems. LC 76-8739. (Contributions in Librarianship & Information Science: No. 17). 240p. 1977. lib. bdg. 16.95 (ISBN 0-8371-8936-5, ORL/). Greenwood.

Parkes, M. B. & Watson, Andrew G., eds. Medieval Scribes, Manuscripts & Libraries: Essays Presented to N. R. Ker. (Illus.). 408p. 1978. 80.00x (ISBN 0-85967-450-9, Pub. by Scolar Pr England). Biblio Dist.

Pater, Alan F. & Pater, Jason R., eds. The Great Libraries of America---A Pictorial History. Date not set. 35.00 (ISBN 0-917734-03-3). Monitor.

Penland & Mathai. The Future Library As a Learning Service, Vol. 24. (Books in Library). 1978. 26.50 (ISBN 0-8247-6750-0). Dekker.

Penland, P. R. & Mathai, A. Library As a Learning Center. (Books in Library & Information Science Ser.: Vol. 24). 1978. 26.50 (ISBN 0-8247-6750-0). Dekker.

Peterson, Violet E. Library Instruction Guide: Suggested Courses for Use by Librarians & Teachers in Junior & Senior High Schools. 4th ed. 1974. 10.00 (ISBN 0-208-01418-7, Archon). Shoe String.

Plotnik, Arthur. Library Life - American Style: A Journalist's Field Report. LC 75-16280. (Illus.). 226p. 1975. 10.00 (ISBN 0-8108-0852-8). Scarecrow.

Pollett, Dorothy & Haskell, Peter C. Sign Systems for Libraries: Solving the Wayfinding Problem. LC 79-11138. (Illus.). 1979. 24.95 (ISBN 0-8352-1149-5). Bowker.

The Prince Library. 1870. 15.00 (ISBN 0-89073-023-7). Boston Public Lib.

Protection of Library Collection. (Eight Hundred&Nine Hundred Ser). 1970. pap. 2.00 (ISBN 0-685-58217-5, 910). Natl Fire Prot.

Robotham, John S. & LaFleur, Lydia. Library Programs: How to Select, Plan & Produce Them. LC 76-2033. 307p. 1976. 14.50 (ISBN 0-8108-0911-7). Scarecrow.

Rockwell, Anne. I Like the Library. LC 77-6365. (ps-4). 1977. 7.95 (ISBN 0-525-32528-X). Dutton.

Rosenlof, George W. Library Facilities in Teacher-Training Institutions. LC 76-177210. (Columbia University. Teachers College. Contributions to Education: No. 347). Repr. of 1929 ed. 17.50 (ISBN 0-404-55347-8). AMS Pr.

Schad, Jasper & Tanis, Norman E. Problems in Developing Academic Library Collections. LC 72-1944. (Problem-Centered Approaches to Librarianship Ser.). 183p. 1974. 18.50 (ISBN 0-8352-0551-7). Bowker.

Smith, Ruth S. Setting up a Library: How to Begin or Begin Again. LC 79-15630. (Guide Ser.: No. 1). 1979. pap. 2.50x (ISBN 0-915324-16-4). CSLA.

Steele, Colin. Major Libraries of the World: A Selective Guide. (Illus.). 512p. 1976. 26.00 (ISBN 0-85935-012-6). Bowker.

Stephen, Leslie. Hours in a Library. 1977. lib. bdg. 49.95 (ISBN 0-8490-2018-2). Gordon Pr.

Symbols of American Libraries. 1975. lib. bdg. 79.95 (ISBN 0-8490-1168-X). Gordon Pr.

Weber, Olga S., ed. Literary & Library Prizes. 10th ed. 1980. 24.95 (ISBN 0-8352-1249-1). Bowker.

Wedgeworth, Robert, ed. ALA Yearbook 1978. LC 76-647548. 1978. text ed. 35.00 (ISBN 0-8389-0261-8). ALA.

Wheatley, Henry B. How to Form a Library. LC 76-41922. 1976. Repr. of 1886 ed. lib. bdg. 25.00 (ISBN 0-8414-9494-0). Folcroft.

Wheatley, J. How to Form a Library. 1976. lib. bdg. 69.95 (ISBN 0-8490-2022-0). Gordon Pr.

Wilson, Patrick. Public Knowledge, Private Ignorance: Toward a Library & Information Policy. LC 76-52327. (Contributions in Librarianship & Information Sciences: No. 10). 1977. lib. bdg. 15.00x (ISBN 0-8371-9485-7, WPN/). Greenwood.

Woolard, Wilma L. B. Combined School - Public Libraries: A Survey with Conclusions & Recommendations. LC 80-36742. 204p. 1980. 11.00 (ISBN 0-8108-1335-1). Scarecrow.

LIBRARIES–ACCESSION DEPARTMENTS

see Acquisitions (Libraries)

LIBRARIES–ACCOUNTING

see Library Finance

LIBRARIES–ADMINISTRATION

see Library Administration; Library Science

LIBRARIES–ADVERTISING

see Advertising–Libraries

LIBRARIES–ARRANGEMENT OF BOOKS ON SHELVES

see Classification–Books

LIBRARIES–AUTOMATION

see also Information Storage and Retrieval Systems; MARC System

Balmforth, C. K. & Cox, N. S., eds. Interface: Library Automation with Special Reference to Computing Activity. 1971. 19.95x (ISBN 0-262-02084-X). MIT Pr.

Butler, Brett & Martin, Susan K., eds. Library Automation Two. LC 75-20168. 200p. 1975. pap. text ed. 7.50 (ISBN 0-8389-3152-9). ALA.

Christian, Roger W. The Electronic Library: Bibliographic Data Bases, 1978-79. 2nd ed. LC 78-18408. (Professional Librarian Ser.). 1978. pap. 24.50x (ISBN 0-914236-15-6). Knowledge Indus.

Clinic on Library Applications of Data Processing Proceedings, 1976. The Economics of Library Automation. Divilbiss, J. L., ed. LC 77-75153. 163p. 1977. 8.00x (ISBN 0-87845-046-7). U of Ill Lib Info Sci.

Cohn, Aaron & Cohn, Elaine. Automation Planning & Space Management: A Blueprint for Libraries. 264p. 1981. 29.95 (ISBN 0-8352-1398-6). Bowker.

Computer Science and Engineering Board. Libraries & Information Technology: A System Challenge. 96p. (Orig.). 1972. pap. text ed. 3.50 (ISBN 0-309-01938-9). Natl Acad Pr.

Corbin, John. Developing Computer-Based Library Systems. (Neal-Schuman Professional Bk). 1981. lib. bdg. 22.50 (ISBN 0-912700-10-6). Oryx Pr.

Cox, Nigel S. & Grose, Mitchel, eds. Organization & Handling of Bibliographic Records by Computer. LC 67-30792. 1967. 19.50 (ISBN 0-208-00237-5, Archon). Shoe String.

Crank, Lawrence J., ed. Automating the Archives. (Professional Librarian Ser.). 150p. 1980. pap. text ed. 24.50x (ISBN 0-914236-86-5). Knowledge Indus.

Davis, Jinnie Y. & Abrera, Joseta B. Monographic Searching on the OCLC Terminal: A Programmed Text with Teacher's Guide. (Illus.). 136p. 1981. pap. 14.50x (ISBN 0-208-01843-3, Linnet). Shoe String.

Divilbiss, J. L., ed. Clinic on Library Applications of Data Processing, Proceedings: 1977: Negotiating for Computer Services. LC 78-13693. 117p. 1978. 9.00x (ISBN 0-87845-048-3). U of Ill Lib Info Sci.

Gore, Daniel, et al, eds. Requiem for the Card Catalog: Management Issues in Automated Cataloging. LC 78-7129. (New Directions in Librarianship: No. 2). 1979. lib. bdg. 18.95 (ISBN 0-313-20608-2, GMI/). Greenwood.

Guild, Reuben A. The Librarian's Manual: A Treatise on Bibliography, Comprising a Select & Descriptive List of Bibliographical Works; to Which Are Added, Sketches of Public Libraries. LC 70-174942. (Illus.). x, 304p. 1972. Repr. of 1858 ed. 26.00 (ISBN 0-8103-3811-4). Gale.

Henley, J. P. Computer-Based Library & Information Systems. 2nd ed. (Computer Monograph Ser). 1972. text ed. 18.95 (ISBN 0-444-19584-X). Elsevier.

Hewitt, J. OCLC: Impact & Use. 1977. pap. 10.50 (ISBN 0-88215-043-X). Ohio St U Lib.

Kimber, Richard T. & Boyd, A. Automation in Libraries. 2nd ed. 1974. text ed. 28.00 (ISBN 0-08-017969-X). Pergamon.

King, Donald W., et al. Telecommunications & Libraries. (Professional Librarian Ser.). 160p. 1981. text ed. 32.50 (ISBN 0-914236-88-1); pap. text ed. 24.50 (ISBN 0-914236-51-2). Knowledge Indus.

Knowledge Industry Publication Editors. The Professional Librarian's Reader in Library Automation & Technology. LC 80-11636. (Professional Librarian Ser.). (Illus.). 256p. 1980. 24.50 (ISBN 0-914236-59-8); pap. 17.50 (ISBN 0-914236-57-1). Knowledge Indus.

Markuson, Barbara & Woolls, Blanche, eds. Networks for Networkers: Critical Issues in Cooperative Library Development. LC 79-24054. 1980. 17.95x (ISBN 0-918212-22-7). Neal-Schuman.

Mathies, M. Lorraine & Watson, Peter G. Computer Based Reference Services. LC 73-9967. 270p. 1973. pap. text ed. 11.00 (ISBN 0-8389-0156-5). ALA.

Matthews, Joseph R. Choosing an Automated Library System: A Planning Guide. LC 80-17882. 128p. 1980. 11.00 (ISBN 0-8389-0310-X). ALA.

Pitkin, Gary M. Serials Automation in the United States: A Bibliographic History. LC 76-18116. 1976. 10.00 (ISBN 0-8108-0955-9). Scarecrow.

Richardson, Arlene Z. & Hannah, Sheila, eds. Introduction to Visual Resource Library Automation. (Mid-America College Art Association Visual Resources Guides). 178p. 1981. 7.00 (ISBN 0-938852-08-6). Mid-Am Coll.

Rowley, Jennifer E. Computers for Libraries. (Outlines of Modern Librarianship Ser.). Date not set. text ed. 12.00 (ISBN 0-89664-016-7). K G Saur.

Ryans, Cynthia C., ed. The Card Catalog: Current Issues. LC 81-720. 336p. 1981. 16.00 (ISBN 0-8108-1417-X). Scarecrow.

Salmon, S. R. Library Automation Systems. 2nd ed. (Library & Information Ser.: Vol. 15). 1975. 29.75 (ISBN 0-8247-6358-0). Dekker.

Salmon, Stephen R., ed. Library Automation: A State of the Art Review. LC 73-77283. (Orig.). 1969. pap. 7.50 (ISBN 0-8389-3091-3). ALA.

Shera, Jesse H. Documentation & the Organization of Knowledge. Foskett, D. J., ed. & intro. by. 1966. 15.00 (ISBN 0-208-00083-6, Archon). Shoe String.

Swihart, Stanley J. & Hefley, Beryl F. Computer Systems in the Library: Handbook for Manager & Designer. LC 73-603. (Information Sciences Ser.). (Illus.). 338p. 1973. 33.95 (ISBN 0-471-83995-7, Pub. by Wiley-Interscience). Wiley.

Wasserman, Paul. Librarian & the Machine. LC 65-25320. 1965. 12.00 (ISBN 0-8103-0164-4). Gale.

LIBRARIES–BIBLIOGRAPHY

Abdul Huq, A. M. & Aman, Mohammed M. Librarianship & the Third World. LC 76-30916. (Reference Library of Social Science Ser.: Vol. 40). 1977. lib. bdg. 37.00 (ISBN 0-8240-9897-8). Garland Pub.

Davinson, Donald. Bibliographic Control. rev., 2nd ed. 128p. 1981. Repr. of 1975 ed. 11.00 (ISBN 0-208-01930-8, Linnet). Shoe String.

Downs, Robert B. American Library Resources: A Bibliographical Guide Supplement 1961-1970. LC 51-11156. 1972. text ed. 20.00 (ISBN 0-8389-0116-6). ALA.

Jordan, Anne H. & Jordan, Melbourne, eds. Cannons' Bibliography of Library Economy, 1876-1920: An Author Index with Citations. LC 76-3711. 481p. 1976. 22.00 (ISBN 0-8108-0918-4). Scarecrow.

World Guide to Libraries. 5th rev. ed. 1500p. 1980. 225.00 (ISBN 0-89664-043-4, Pub. by K G Saur). Gale.

Young, Margaret L. & Young, Harold C., eds. Subject Directory of Special Libraries & Information Centers, 5 vols. 6th rev. ed. Incl. Vol. 1. Business & Law Libraries (ISBN 0-8103-0300-0); Vol. 2. Education & Information Science Libraries, Including Audiovisual, Picture, Publishing, Rare Book, & Recreational Libraries (ISBN 0-8103-0301-9); Vol. 3. Health Sciences Libraries, Including All Aspects of Basic & Applied Medical Sciences (ISBN 0-8103-0302-7); Vol. 4. Social Sciences & Humanities Libraries, Including Aera-Ethnic, Art, Geography-Map, History, Music Religion-Theology, Theatre, & Urban-Regional Planning Libraries (ISBN 0-8103-0303-5); Vol. 5. Science & Technology Libraries Including Agriculture, Energy, Environment-Conservation, & Food Sciences Libraries (ISBN 0-8103-0304-3). LC 79-21711. 163p. 1981. Set. 350.00 set (ISBN 0-8103-0305-1); 80.00 ea. Gale.

LIBRARIES–BIBLIOGRAPHICAL SEARCHING

see Searching, Bibliographical

LIBRARIES–BOARDS

see Libraries–Trustees

LIBRARIES–BRANCHES, DELIVERY STATIONS, ETC.

see also Bookmobiles; Direct Delivery of Books

Branch Library Service. LC 77-17557. 66p. 1977. 5.00 (ISBN 0-913578-17-7). Inglewood Ca.

Brown, Eleanor F. Modern Branch Libraries & Libraries in Systems. LC 77-12808. (Illus.). 1970. 17.00 (ISBN 0-8108-0276-7). Scarecrow.

Service Points in Sparsely Populated Areas. 1976. pap. text ed. 6.85x (ISBN 0-85365-189-2, Pub. by Lib Assn England). Oryx Pr.

Yorke, D. A. Marketing the Library Service. (Management Pamphlet Ser.). 1977. 5.75x (ISBN 0-85365-590-1, Pub. by Lib Assn England). Oryx Pr.

LIBRARIES–CATALOGS

see Library Catalogs

LIBRARIES–CENSORSHIP

American Library Association Committee On Intellectual Freedom - 1st Conference - New York - 1952. Freedom of Communication: Proceedings. facsimile ed. Dix, William & Bixler, Paul, eds. LC 71-104989. (Essay Index Reprint Ser). 1954. 16.00 (ISBN 0-8369-1439-2). Arno.

Anderson, A. J. Problems in Intellectual Freedom & Censorship. LC 74-7106. (Problem-Centered Approaches to Librarianship Ser.). 195p. 1974. 18.50 (ISBN 0-8352-0677-7). Bowker.

Oboler, Eli M. Defending Intellectual Freedom: The Library & the Censor. LC 79-8585. (Contributions in Librarianship & Information Science: No. 32). xix, 246p. 1980. lib. bdg. 22.95 (ISBN 0-313-21472-7, ODF/). Greenwood.

Thompson, Anthony H. Censorship in Public Libraries in the United Kingdom During the 20th Century. 236p. 1976. 17.95 (ISBN 0-85935-019-3). Bowker.

LIBRARIES–CHILDREN'S ROOMS

see Libraries, Children's

LIBRARIES–CIRCULATION, LOANS
see also Direct Delivery of Books; Exchanges, Literary and Scientific; Libraries–Branches, Delivery Stations, etc.
Circulation Procedures. 2nd ed. 75p. 1972. 3.00 (ISBN 0-913578-02-9). Inglewood Ca.
Daiute, Robert J. & Gorman, Kenneth A. Library Operations Research: Computer Programming of Circulation. LC 73-20303. 1974. 28.50 (ISBN 0-913338-01-X). Oceana.
Edge, Sharon M., ed. Acquisitions-Circulation Interface. 104p. 1981. pap. 10.75 (ISBN 0-08-026761-0). Pergamon.
Kaser, David. A Book for a Sixpense. LC 79-4298. (Beta Phi Mu Chapbook: No. 14). (Illus.). 1980. 9.00 (ISBN 0-910230-14-5). Beta Phi Mu.
O.S.U. Libraries. Library Circulation System User's Guide. rev. ed. 1974. pap. 5.00 (ISBN 0-88215-029-4). Ohio St U Lib.

LIBRARIES–CLASSIFICATION
see Classification–Books

LIBRARIES–CONGRESSES
see Library Conferences

LIBRARIES–DIRECTORIES
see also Libraries, Special–Directories
American National Standards Institute, Standards Committee Z39 on Library Work, Documentation & Related Publishing Practices. American National Standard Directories of Libraries & Information Centers. rev. ed. 1977. 4.00 (ISBN 0-686-01887-7, Z39.10). ANSI.
Anders, Mary E. Libraries & Library Services in the Southeast: A Report of the Southeastern States Cooperative Library Survey, 1972-1974. LC 75-44140. (Illus.). 272p. 1976. 18.50x (ISBN 0-8173-9705-1). U of Ala Pr.
Catholic Library Association. C L A: Handbook & Membership Directory. 20.00 ea. Cath Lib Assn.
Directory of Documentation Libraries & Archives in Africa. (Documentation, Libraries & Archives, Bibliographies & Reference Work: No. 5). 1978. 22.50 (ISBN 92-3-001479-6, U824, UNESCO). Unipub.
IFLA Directory 1979. 1978. pap. 17.50 (ISBN 0-89664-065-5). K G Saur.
Jacques Cattell Press, compiled by. American Library Directory. 34th ed. 1914p. 1981. 59.95 (ISBN 0-8352-1358-7). Bowker.
Jaques Cattell Press, ed. American Library Directory 1980. 33rd ed. LC 23-3581. 1836p. 1980. 54.95 (ISBN 0-8352-1251-3). Bowker.
Jennings, Margaret, ed. Library & Reference Facilities in the Area of the District of Columbia. 10th ed. LC 44-11159. (American Society for Information Science Ser.). 1979. softcover 19.50x (ISBN 0-914236-35-0). Knowledge Indus.
Kent, A., et al, eds. Encyclopedia of Library & Information Science, Vols. 29-31. 45.00 ea. Vol. 29 (ISBN 0-8247-2129-2). Vol. 30 (ISBN 0-8247-2130-6). Vol. 31 (ISBN 0-8247-2131-4). Dekker.
Library Association Yearbooks, 1980. 1980. pap. 21.00x (ISBN 0-85365-971-0, Pub. by Lib Assn England). Oryx Pr.
Nitecki, Joseph Z., ed. Directory of Library Reprographic Services. 6th ed. 184p. 1976. pap. text ed. 9.95x (ISBN 0-913672-04-1). Microform Rev.
Symbols of American Libraries. 1975. lib. bdg. 79.95 (ISBN 0-8490-1168-X). Gordon Pr.
Thorpe, James. Gifts of Genius: Treasures of the Huntington Library. LC 80-80077. (Illus.). 214p. 1980. 10.00 (ISBN 0-87328-110-1). Huntington Lib.
Walker, G., ed. Directory of Libraries & Special Collections on Eastern Europe & U.S.S.R. 1971. 15.00 (ISBN 0-208-01260-5, Archon). Shoe String.
Wedgeworth, Robert, ed. ALA Yearbook, 1981. 432p. 1981. 55.00 (ISBN 0-8389-0335-5). ALA.
World Guide to Libraries. 5th rev. ed. 1500p. 1980. 225.00 (ISBN 0-89664-043-4, Pub. by K G Saur). Gale.
Young, Margaret L., et al, eds. Directory of Special Libraries & Information Centers: Vol. 2-Geographic & Personnel Indexes. 6th ed. LC 79-16788. 1979. 140.00 (ISBN 0-8103-0298-5). Gale.

LIBRARIES–EXHIBITIONS
see Library Exhibits

LIBRARIES–FICTION
see Fiction in Libraries

LIBRARIES–HANDBOOKS, MANUALS, ETC.
Baker, Robert K. Introduction to Library Research in French Literature. LC 77-18074. (A Westview Special Study Ser.). 1978. lib. bdg. 23.75x (ISBN 0-89158-060-3); pap. text ed. 9.00 (ISBN 0-89158-082-4). Westview.
Chirgwin, F. J. & Oldfield, P. The Library Assistant's Manual. 1978. 12.00 (ISBN 0-208-01666-X, Linnet). Shoe String.
Cleary, Florence D. Discovering Books & Libraries. 2nd ed. 1977. pap. 6.00 (ISBN 0-8242-0594-4). Wilson.
Corcoran, Eileen. Gaining Skills in Using the Library. (Illus.). 1980. pap. 2.50x (ISBN 0-88323-158-1, 247). Richards Pub.
Downs, Robert B. & Keller, Clara D. How to Do Library Research. 2nd ed. LC 74-28301. 153p. 1975. pap. 3.45 (ISBN 0-252-00535-X). U of Ill Pr.
Gates, Jean K. Guide to the Use of Books & Libraries. 3rd ed. (McGraw-Hill Series in Library Science). (Illus.). 288p. 1973. text ed. 10.95 (ISBN 0-07-022984-8, C); pap. text ed. 6.95 (ISBN 0-07-022983-X). McGraw.
--Guide to the Use of Books & Libraries. 4th ed. (Illus.). 1979. text ed. 9.95 (ISBN 0-07-022986-4, C); pap. text ed. 6.95 (ISBN 0-07-022985-6). McGraw.
Herring, James E. Teaching Library Skills in Schools. (General Ser.). 1979. pap. text ed. 11.75x (ISBN 0-85633-171-6, NFER). Humanities.
Hoover, Ryan, ed. Library & Information Manager's Guide to Online Services. (Professional Librarian Ser.). (Illus.). 269p. 1980. 29.50x (ISBN 0-914236-60-1); pap. 24.50x (ISBN 0-914236-52-0). Knowledge Indus.
Katz, William. Your Library: A Reference Guide. LC 78-21993. 1979. 15.95 (ISBN 0-03-048361-1, HoltC); pap. text ed. 8.95 (ISBN 0-03-043801-2). HR&W.
Lolley, John L. Your Library -- What's in It for You? LC 73-18293. (Self-Teaching Guides Ser.). 1974. pap. text ed. 4.95 (ISBN 0-471-54365-9). Wiley.
Mallett, Jerry J. Library Skills Activities Kit: Puzzles, Games, Bulletin Boards & Other Interest Rousers for the Elementary School Library. 1980. 24.95 (ISBN 0-87628-535-3). Ctr Appl Res.
Margrabe, Mary. Media Magic: Games & Activities for Total Curriculum Involvement. LC 78-5120. (Illus.). 1979. pap. 7.95 (ISBN 0-87491-213-X). Acropolis.
Miller, Jerome K. Applying the New Copyright Law: A Guide for Educators & Librarians. LC 79-4694. 1979. pap. 11.00 (ISBN 0-685-97224-0). ALA.
Montgomery, A. C., ed. Acronyms & Abbreviations in Library & Information Work. (Library Association Bks.). 1975. pap. text ed. 7.95x (ISBN 0-85365-218-X, Pub. by Lib Assn England). Oryx Pr.
Mortimer, E. A. Library Books: Their Care & Repair. 1981. 9.00x (ISBN 0-86025-904-8, Pub. by Ian Henry Pubns England). State Mutual Bk.
Percival, A. E., ed. The English Association Handbook of Societies & Collections. 1977. pap. 5.50x (ISBN 0-85365-449-2, Pub. by Lib Assn England). Oryx Pr.
Seeking & Finding Manual. 1970. pap. 6.75 (ISBN 0-913308-03-X). Fordham Pub.
Seeking & Finding Workbook. 1970. pap. 17.50 (ISBN 0-913308-02-1). Fordham Pub.
Spirt, Diana L. Library-Media Manual. 1979. 6.00 (ISBN 0-8242-0615-0). Wilson.
Stepping Stones to the Library. 1972. pap. 6.95 (ISBN 0-913308-04-8). Fordham Pub.
Taylor, L. J., ed. A Librarian's Handbook, Vol. 1. 1977. pap. 46.00x (ISBN 0-85365-079-9, Pub. by Lib Assn England). Oryx Pr.
--A Librarian's Handbook, Vol. 2. 1980. pap. 57.50x (ISBN 0-85365-651-7, Pub. by Lib Assn England). Oryx Pr.
Todd, Alden. Finding Facts Fast. LC 79-8516. (Illus.). 1979. 7.95 (ISBN 0-89815-013-2); pap. 3.95 (ISBN 0-89815-012-4). Ten Speed Pr.
Whatley, A., ed. International & Comparative Librarianship Group (ICLG) Handbook. (ICLG). 1977. pap. 10.95x (ISBN 0-85365-790-4, Pub. by Lib Assn England). Oryx Pr.
Wheatley, Henry B. How to Form a Library. 248p. 1980. Repr. of 1886 ed. lib. bdg. 25.00 (ISBN 0-8495-5819-0). Arden Lib.
Whipple, Alan L. Research & the Library: A Student Guide to Basic Techniques. 120p. (Orig.). (gr. 8-11). 1974. pap. text ed. 2.95x (ISBN 0-88334-062-3). Ind Sch Pr.
Wolf, Carolyn & Wolf, Richard. Basic Library Skills: A Short Course. LC 81-4865. 137p. 1981. pap. 8.95x (ISBN 0-89950-018-8). McFarland & Co.

LIBRARIES–HISTORY
Armour, Richard. The Happy Bookers: A Playful History of Librarians & Their World from the Stone Age to the Distant Future. LC 75-28313. 1976. 6.95 (ISBN 0-07-002303-4, GB). McGraw.
Bishop, William W. & Keogh, Andrew. Essays Offered to Herbert Putnam by His Colleagues & Friends on His 30th Anniversary As Librarian of Congress, 5 April Nineteen Twenty-Nine. 1929. 20.00x (ISBN 0-686-51379-7). Elliots Bks.
Bonn, George S. & Faibisoff, Sylvia G., eds. Changing Times: Changing Libraries. LC 78-1283. (Allerton Part Institutes Ser.: No. 22). 166p. 1978. 8.00x (ISBN 0-87845-047-5). U of Ill Lib Sci.
Clark, John W. Care of Books: An Essay on the Development of Libraries. 1973. Repr. of 1901 ed. lib. bdg. 35.00 (ISBN 0-8414-3502-2). Folcroft.
--The Care of Books: An Essay on the Development of Libraries & Their Fittings, from the Earliest Times to the End of the 18th Century. 442p. 1980. 50.00x (ISBN 0-902089-78-1, Pub. by Variorum England). State Mutual Bk.
Compton, Charles H., et al. Twenty-Five Crucial Years of the St. Louis Public Library, 1927 to 1952. 1953. 5.00 (ISBN 0-937322-00-8). St Louis Pub Lib.
Dale, Doris C., ed. Carl H. Milam & the United Nations Library. LC 76-14866. 149p. 1976. 10.00 (ISBN 0-8108-0941-9). Scarecrow.
Dumont, Rosemary R. Reform & Reaction: The Big City Public Library in American Life. LC 77-71864. (Contributions in Librarianship & Information Science: No. 21). 1977. lib. bdg. 15.00x (ISBN 0-8371-9540-3, DRR/). Greenwood.
Edwards, Edward. Libraries & Founders of Libraries. LC 68-58475. (Bibliography & Reference Ser: No. 260). 1969. Repr. of 1865 ed. 26.00 (ISBN 0-8337-1004-4). B Franklin.
Gaskell, P. Trinity College Library: The First 150 Years. LC 79-41415. (Illus.). 256p. 1981. 67.50 (ISBN 0-521-23100-0). Cambridge U Pr.
Gasquet, Francis C. Old English Bible & Other Essays. LC 68-26209. 1969. Repr. of 1897 ed. 14.50 (ISBN 0-8046-0166-6). Kennikat.
Goldstein, Harold, ed. Milestones to the Present: Papers from Library History Seminar V. 1978. 15.00 (ISBN 0-915794-21-7, 6561). Gaylord Prof Pubns.
Harris, Michael H, ed. Reader in American Library History. LC 71-165293. (Reader Ser. in Library & Information Science: No. 5). 1971. 16.00 (ISBN 0-910972-10-9). IHS-PDS.
Held, Ray E. Rise of the Public Library in California. LC 73-12719. 325p. 1973. text ed. 15.00 (ISBN 0-8389-0124-7). ALA.
Hessel, Alfred. History of Libraries. LC 57-2485. 1955. 10.00 (ISBN 0-8108-0058-6). Scarecrow.
Hoskin, Beryl. A History of the Santa Clara Mission Library. (California Heritage Ser.: Vol. 48). 1961. 15.00 (ISBN 0-686-14202-0). Sullivan Bks.
Jackson, Sidney, et al, eds. A Century of Service. LC 76-41815. 1976. text ed. 25.00 (ISBN 0-8389-0220-0). ALA.
Jackson, Sidney L. Brief History of Libraries & Librarianship in the West. (Illus.). 1974. text ed. 22.00 (ISBN 0-07-032118-3, C). McGraw.
Johnson, Elmer D. Communication: An Introduction to the History of Writing, Printing, Books & Libraries. 4th ed. LC 73-83. 1973. 11.00 (ISBN 0-8108-0588-X). Scarecrow.
Johnson, Elmer D. & Harris, Michael H. History of Libraries in the Western World. 3rd ed. LC 76-25422. 1976. 12.00 (ISBN 0-8108-0949-4). Scarecrow.
Kaser, David. A Book for a Sixpense. LC 79-4298. (Beta Phi Mu Chapbook: No. 14). (Illus.). 1980. 9.00 (ISBN 0-910230-14-5). Beta Phi Mu.
Keep, Austin B. The Library in Colonial New York. 1976. lib. bdg. 59.95 (ISBN 0-8490-2158-8). Gordon Pr.
Kibre, Pearl. Library of Pico Della Mirandola. LC 36-7980. Repr. of 1936 ed. 17.50 (ISBN 0-404-03667-8). AMS Pr.
Kirchhoff, Albrecht. Handschriftenhandler Des Mittelalters. 2nd ed. 1853. 22.50 (ISBN 0-8337-1929-7). B Franklin.
Loomis, Albertine. The Best of Friends: The Story of Hawaii's Libraries & Their Friends, 1879-1979. Pagliaro, Penny, ed. (Illus.). 1979. pap. 3.95 (ISBN 0-916630-10-2). Pr Pacifica.
Merryweather, F. Somner. Bibliomania in the Middle Ages. rev. ed. Copinger, H. B., ed. LC 72-83748. Repr. of 1933 ed. 15.00 (ISBN 0-405-08787-X, Pub. by Blom). Arno.
Morison, Samuel E. Intellectual Life of Colonial New England. 288p. (YA) (gr. 9-12). 1960. pap. 7.95 (ISBN 0-8014-9011-1, CP11). Cornell U Pr.
Olle, James G. Library History. (Outlines of Modern Librarianship Ser.). 114p. 1979. text ed. 12.00 (ISBN 0-85157-271-5, Pub. by Bingley England). Shoe String.
--Library History: An Examination Guidebook. 2nd ed. (Examination Guide Ser.). 1971. 14.00 (ISBN 0-208-01051-3). Shoe String.
Peebles, Margaret & Howell, J. B., eds. History of Mississippi Libraries. 437p. 1975. 10.00 (ISBN 0-88289-190-1). Pelican.
Reichmann, Felix. The Sources of Western Literacy: The Middle Eastern Civilizations. LC 79-8292. (Contributions in Librarianship & Information Science: No. 29). 274p. 1980. lib. bdg. 25.00 (ISBN 0-313-20948-0, RWL/). Greenwood.
Ribera Y Tarrago, Julian. Bibliofilos y Bibliotecas En la Espana Musulmana: Disertacion Leida En la Facultad De Medicina y Ciencias. 2nd ed. 1967. Repr. of 1896 ed. 16.50 (ISBN 0-8337-2977-2). B Franklin.
Rider, Alice D. A Story of Books & Libraries. LC 76-7596. 183p. 1976. 10.00 (ISBN 0-8108-0930-3). Scarecrow.
Savage, Ernest A. Old English Libraries. LC 68-26177. (Illus.). 1968. Repr. of 1912 ed. 26.00 (ISBN 0-8103-3179-9). Gale.
--Story of Libraries & Book Collecting. 1969. Repr. of 1909 ed. 20.00 (ISBN 0-8337-3130-0). B Franklin.
--Story of Libraries & Book Collecting. 1909. 15.00 (ISBN 0-8274-3519-3). R West.
Stone, Elizabeth W., ed. American Library Development: 1600 - 1899. 1977. 45.00 (ISBN 0-8242-0418-2). Wilson.
Thompson, James. A History of the Principles of Librarianship. 1977. 17.50 (ISBN 0-208-01661-9, Linnet). Shoe String.
Thompson, James W. Medieval Library. 1967. Repr. of 1939 ed. 19.25 (ISBN 0-02-853430-1). Hafner.
Vervliet, ed. Annual Bibliography of the History of the Printed Book & Libraries. Incl. Publications of 1973. 1975. pap. 56.00 (ISBN 90-247-1758-2); Publications of 1974. 1976. pap. 52.00 (ISBN 90-247-1753-1); Publications of 1975. 1977. pap. 54.00 (ISBN 90-247-1963-1). Pub. by Martinus Nijhoff Netherlands). Kluwer Boston.
Winger, Howard W., ed. American Library History: 1876-1976. (Library Trends Ser: Vol. 25, No. 1). 416p. 1976. 8.00x (ISBN 0-87845-045-9). U of Ill Lib Info Sci.
Wright, H. Curtis. The Oral Antecedents of Greek Librarianship. LC 77-73645. 1977. 19.95x (ISBN 0-8425-0623-3). Brigham.

LIBRARIES–HISTORY–BIBLIOGRAPHY
Harris, Michael H. A Guide to Research in American Library History. 2nd ed. LC 74-17113. 1974. 10.00 (ISBN 0-8108-0744-0). Scarecrow.
Harris, Michael H. & Davis, Donald G., Jr. American Library History: A Bibliography. LC 77-25499. 280p. 1978. 20.00x (ISBN 0-292-70332-5). U of Tex Pr.
Olle, James G. Library History: An Examination Guidebook. 2nd ed. (Examination Guide Ser.). 1971. 14.00 (ISBN 0-208-01051-3). Shoe String.

LIBRARIES–INFORMATION NETWORKS
see Library Information Networks

LIBRARIES–JUVENILE LITERATURE
Baker, Donna. I Want to Be a Librarian. LC 77-16221. (I Want to Be Ser.). (Illus.). (gr. k-4). 1978. PLB 7.35 (ISBN 0-516-01715-2). Childrens.
Barr, Jene. Miss Terry at the Library. rev. ed. LC 62-13170. (Career Awareness-Community Helpers Ser.). (Illus.). (gr. k-2). 1967. 5.25g (ISBN 0-8075-5168-6). A. Whitman.
Charles, Donald. Calico Cat Meets Bookworm. LC 78-6557. (Illus.). (ps-3). PLB 8.65 (ISBN 0-516-03441-3). Childrens.
De Leeuw, Adele. With a High Heart. (gr. 7 up). 1964. 9.95 (ISBN 0-02-728440-9). Macmillan.
Hardendorff, Jeanne B. Libraries & How to Use Them. LC 78-12992. (First Bks.). (Illus.). (gr. 4 up). 1979. PLB 6.90 s&l (ISBN 0-531-02259-5). Watts.
Matez, Beth & Fielden, Moreen. Library & Research Skills. new ed. (Get Ahead for Kids). (Illus.). (gr. 4-12). 1978. pap. 2.95 (ISBN 0-933048-03-3). Matez Fielden.
Mathews, Virginia H. Libraries for Today & Tomorrow. LC 75-25440. (Illus.). 200p. (gr. 5 up). 1976. pap. 3.95 (ISBN 0-385-05564-1). Doubleday.
Numeroff, Laura J. Beatrice Doesn't Want to. (Easy-Read Story Bks.). (Illus.). 32p. (gr. k-3). 1981. 3.95 (ISBN 0-686-76377-7); PLB 7.40 (ISBN 0-531-04299-5). Watts.
Ringstad, M. Adventures on Library Shelves. LC 68-16398. (Illus.). (gr. 2 up). 1967. PLB 7.99 prebound (ISBN 0-87783-001-0); pap. 2.75 (ISBN 0-87783-156-4). Oddo.
Rockwell, Anne. I Like the Library. LC 77-6365. (ps-4). 1977. 7.95 (ISBN 0-525-32528-X). Dutton.
Shapiro, Lillian L. Teaching Yourself in Libraries. 1978. 6.00 ea. (ISBN 0-8242-0628-2); 25 or more copies 4.00 ea. Wilson.
Vreeken, Elizabeth. Ramon's Adventures in the Library. LC 67-31108. (gr. 1-3). 1967. 3.95 (ISBN 0-379-00243-4). Oceana.

LIBRARIES–LAW AND LEGISLATION
see Library Legislation

LIBRARIES–MECHANICAL AIDS
Whitestone, Patricia. Photocopying in Libraries: The Librarians Speak. LC 77-8924. (Professional Librarian Ser.). 1977. pap. 24.50x (ISBN 0-914236-08-3). Knowledge Indus.

LIBRARIES–ORDER DEPARTMENT
see Acquisitions (Libraries)

LIBRARIES–ORGANIZATION
see Libraries; Library Administration; Library Science

LIBRARIES–PUBLIC RELATIONS
see Public Relations–Libraries
LIBRARIES–REFERENCE BOOKS
see Reference Books
LIBRARIES–REFERENCE DEPARTMENT
see also Reference Services (Libraries)

Foskett, D. J. Information Service in Libraries. rev. ed. 1967. 13.50 (ISBN 0-208-00373-8, Archon). Shoe String.

Grogan, Denis. Practical Reference Work. (Outlines of Modern Librarianship Ser.). 144p. 1979. text ed. 12.00 (ISBN 0-85157-275-8, Pub. by Bingley England). Shoe String.

LIBRARIES–SECURITY MEASURES

Gandert, Slade R. Protecting Your Collection: A Handbook, Survey, & Guide for the Security of Rare Books, Manuscripts, Archives, Works of Art, & the Circulating Library Collection. (Library & Archival Security Ser.: No. 4). 192p. 1981. text ed. 19.95 (ISBN 0-917724-78-X). Haworth Pr.

LIBRARIES–SHELVING
see Shelving (For Books)
LIBRARIES–SOCIETIES, ETC.
see Library Associations
LIBRARIES–SPECIAL COLLECTIONS
Here are entered works on the methods used to acquire, process and maintain special collections in libraries. Works describing the resources and special collections in libraries which are available for research in various fields are entered under Library Resources.

Cave, Roderick. Rare Book Librarianship. 176p. 1976. 15.00 (ISBN 0-208-01360-1, Linnet). Shoe String.

Chibnall, Bernard. The Organisation of Media. 96p. 1976. 11.50 (ISBN 0-208-01525-6, Linnet). Shoe String.

Chicago, Illinois Regional Library Council. Directory of Local History Collections in Northern Illinois. 42p. 1981. pap. 6.00 (ISBN 0-917060-11-3). Ill Regional Lib Coun.

Corbett, Edmund V. Illustrations Collection: Its Formation, Classification & Exploitation. LC 72-164185. (Illus.). 1971. Repr. of 1941 ed. 22.00 (ISBN 0-8103-3786-X). Gale.

Florida Atlantic University Conference. Management Problems in Serials Work: Proceedings. Spyers Duran, Peter & Gore, Daniel, eds. LC 73-10775. 1974. lib. bdg. 15.00x (ISBN 0-8371-7050-8, SSW/). Greenwood.

Ford, Stephen. Acquisition of Library Materials. LC 73-9891. 350p. 1973. text ed. 12.00 (ISBN 0-8389-0145-X). ALA.

Foster, Donald L. Prints in the Public Library. LC 72-13056. (Illus.). 1973. 10.00 (ISBN 0-8108-0579-0). Scarecrow.

French Revolutionary Collections in the British Library. 1981. pap. 24.00x (ISBN 0-904654-21-4, Pub. by Brit Lib England). State Mutual Bk.

Gebhardt, Walter. Special Collections in German Libraries. 1977. 92.00x (ISBN 3-11-005839-1). De Gruyter.

Grove, Pearce S., ed. Nonprint Media in Academic Libraries. LC 74-23972. (ACRL Publications in Librarianship: No. 34). 239p. 1975. pap. 10.00 (ISBN 0-8389-0153-0). ALA.

Guide to the Department of Oriental Manuscripts & Printed Books. 1981. pap. 6.00x (ISBN 0-7141-0658-5, Pub. by Brit Lib England). State Mutual Bk.

Harleston, Rebekah M. & Stoffle, Carla J. Administration of Government Documents Collections. LC 74-81960. 1974. lib. bdg. 15.00x (ISBN 0-87287-086-3). Libs Unl.

Holloway, A. H., et al. Information Work with Unpublished Reports. LC 76-43366. (Institute of Information Scientists Monograph Ser.). (Illus.). 1978. lib. bdg. 29.75x (ISBN 0-89158-717-9). Westview.

Josey, E. J. & Shockley, A. A., eds. Handbook of Black Librarianship. LC 77-21817. 1977. lib. bdg. 25.00x (ISBN 0-87287-179-7). Libs Unl.

Kane, Betty Ann. Widening Circle: The Story of the Folger Shakespeare Library & Its Collection. (Special Piublications). 3.95x (ISBN 0-918016-47-9). Folger Bks.

Korty, Margaret B. Audio-Visual Materials in the Church Library: How to Select, Catalog, Process, Store, Circulate & Promote. LC 77-74780. (Illus.). 1977. spiral bdg. 4.95 (ISBN 0-9603060-0-5). Church Lib.

Lane, Margaret T. State Publications & Depository Libraries: A Reference Handbook. LC 80-24688. (Illus.). 560p. 1981. lib. bdg. 49.95 (ISBN 0-313-22118-9, LSP/). Greenwood.

Library Service to the Spanish Speaking. LC 77-22847. 51p. 1977. 5.00 (ISBN 0-913578-16-9). Inglewood Ca.

Luciw, Jurij A. Building Slavic Collections. 63p. 1980. pap. text ed. 3.75 (ISBN 0-686-63318-0). Slavia Lib.

Nakata, Yuri, et al. Organizing a Local Government Documents Collection. 1979. pap. 5.00 (ISBN 0-8389-0284-7). ALA.

Nonbook Materials: The Organization of Integrated Collections. 2nd ed. 142p. 1980. 8.00 (ISBN 0-8389-3244-4). ALA.

Parker, J. Carlyle, ed. Library Service for Genealogists. LC 80-26032. (The Gale Genealogy & Local History Ser.: Vol. 15). 285p. 1981. 36.00 (ISBN 0-8103-1489-4). Gale.

Robotham, John S. & LFleur, Lydia. Library Programs: How to Select, Plan & Produce Them. LC 81-2149. 366p. 1981. 17.50 (ISBN 0-8108-1422-6). Scarecrow.

Thompson, James. English Studies: A Guide for Librarians to the Sources & Their Organisation. (Guides to Subject Literature Ser.). 1971. 14.50 (ISBN 0-208-01176-5, Linnet). Shoe String.

Tsien, T. H. & Winger, H. W., eds. Area Studies & the Library. LC 66-13891. (Studies in Library Science Ser). 1966. 8.50x (ISBN 0-226-81414-9). U of Chicago Pr.

Walker, G. P. Russian for Librarians. 128p. 1973. 12.50 (ISBN 0-208-01199-4, Linnet). Shoe String.

LIBRARIES–STATISTICAL METHODS
see Library Statistics
LIBRARIES–SUPPLIES
see Library Fittings and Supplies
LIBRARIES–TRUSTEES

Bommer, Michael R. W. & Chorba, Ronald W. Decision Making for Library Management. (Professional Librarian). 180p. 1981. 34.50 (ISBN 0-86729-001-3); pap. 27.50 (ISBN 0-86729-000-5). Knowledge Indus.

McClure, Charles R. & Samuels, Alan R. Strategies for Library Administration: Concepts & Approaches. 300p. 1981. lib. bdg. price not set (ISBN 0-87287-265-3). Libs Unl.

Prentice, Ann E. The Public Library Trustee: Image & Performance on Funding. LC 73-1648. 1973. 10.00 (ISBN 0-8108-0597-9). Scarecrow.

Taylor, David C. Managing the Serials Explosion: The Issues for Publisers & Libraries. (Professional Librarian). 175p. 1981. professional 34.95 (ISBN 0-914236-94-6); pap. 27.50 professional (ISBN 0-914236-54-7). Knowledge Indus.

Young, Virginia. Trustee of a Small Public Library. (Small Public Library Ser.). 12p. 1978. pap. text ed. 1.00 (ISBN 0-8389-5514-2). ALA.

Young, Virginia G. Library Trustee: A Practical Guidebook. 3rd ed. 1978. 15.95 (ISBN 0-8352-1068-5). Bowker.

LIBRARIES–AFRICA

Directory of Documentation Libraries & Archives in Africa. (Documentation, Libraries & Archives, Bibliographies & Reference Work: No. 5). 1978. 22.50 (ISBN 92-3-001479-6, U824, UNESCO). Unipub.

Maack, Mary N. Libraries in Senegal: Continuity & Change in an Emerging Nation. LC 81-1600. 294p. 1981. pap. 20.00 (ISBN 0-8389-0321-5). ALA.

Makerere University College Library, ed. Directory of East African Libraries. 2nd, rev. ed. 113p. 1969. 5.00x (ISBN 0-8002-0561-8). Intl Pubns Serv.

Standing Conference on Library Materials on Africa: Theses on Africa. 74p. 1964. pap. 24.00x (ISBN 0-7146-2991-X, F Cass Co). Biblio Dist.

Vervliet, H. D., ed. Resource Sharing of Libraries in Developing Countries. (IFLA Publications: No. 14). 286p. 1979. 19.00 (ISBN 0-89664-114-7, Pub. by K G Saur). Shoe String.

Wallenius, Anna B. Libraries in East Africa. LC 70-163924. 200p. 1971. text ed. 19.50x (ISBN 0-8419-0091-4, Africana). Holmes & Meier.

LIBRARIES–AFRICA, SOUTH

Taylor, L. E. South African Libraries. (Comparative Library Studies Ser.). (Illus.). 1967. 12.00 (ISBN 0-208-00549-8, Archon). Shoe String.

LIBRARIES–ASIA

Vervliet, H. D., ed. Resource Sharing of Libraries in Developing Countries. (IFLA Publications: No. 14). 286p. 1979. 19.00 (ISBN 0-89664-114-7, Pub. by K G Saur). Shoe String.

Welch, Theodore F. Toshokan: Libraries in Japanese Society. 1976. 15.00 (ISBN 0-8389-0172-7, Co-Pub by C Bingley). ALA.

Wijasuriya, D. K., et al. The Barefoot Librarian: Library Developments in Southeast Asia with Special Reference to Malaysia. (Comparative Library Studies). (Illus.). 112p. (Orig.). 1975. 12.50 (ISBN 0-208-01366-0, Linnet). Shoe String.

LIBRARIES–AUSTRALIA

Balnaves, John & Biskup, Peter. Australian Libraries. 2nd ed. (Comparative Library Studies). 192p. (Orig.). 1975. 15.00 (ISBN 0-208-01361-X, Linnet). Shoe String.

Borchardt, D. H. & Horacek, J. Librarianship in Australia, New Zealand & Oceania. 1976. 10.25 (ISBN 0-08-019920-8); pap. text ed. write for info. (ISBN 0-08-019752-3). Pergamon.

Bryan, Harrison & Greenwood, Gordon, eds. Design for Diversity: Library Services for Higher Education & Research in Australia. (Illus.). 1977. 39.95x (ISBN 0-7022-1314-4). U of Queensland Pr.

Downs, Robert S. Australian & New Zealand Library Resources. 1979. 33.30 (ISBN 0-7201-0913-2, Pub. by Mansell England). Merrimack Bk Serv.

Stockdale, H. & Graneek, J. J. Rationalization of Library Resources in Australia. 1967. pap. 2.00x (ISBN 0-424-05440-X, Pub. by Sydney U Pr). Intl Schol Bk Serv.

Watson, Elizabeth A. & Ashcroft, Tony. Study of Costs of the Interlibrary Loan System at ANU. (ANU Library Occasional Paper: No. 1). pap. text ed. 7.95 (ISBN 0-686-14474-0, Pub. by ANUP Australia). Bks Australia.

Wicks, V. M. Directory of Special Libraries in Australia. 3rd ed. LC 74-182516. 202p. 1976. 30.00x (ISBN 0-909915-11-3). Intl Pubns Serv.

LIBRARIES–CANADA

Canadian Library Association Directory. rev. ed. 115p. (Orig.). 1979. pap. text ed. 24.00 (ISBN 0-89664-082-5, Pub. by K G Saur). Gale.

Henderson, Diane. Guide to Basic Reference Materials for Canadian Libraries. 6th ed. 1980. looseleaf 16.50x (ISBN 0-8020-2410-6). U of Toronto Pr.

Jackson, Sidney, et al, eds. A Century of Service. LC 76-41815. 1976. text ed. 25.00 (ISBN 0-8389-0220-0). ALA.

LIBRARIES–CHINA

China Library Series, 28 vols. 1973. Set. 520.00 (ISBN 0-8420-2103-5). Scholarly Res Inc.

Fang, Josephine R. Chinas Libraries on the New Long March. Date not set. price not set (ISBN 0-89664-268-2). K G Saur.

LIBRARIES–EAST (FAR EAST)

Chandler, George. Libraries in the East: An International & Comparative Study. (International Bibliographical & Library Ser.). 214p. 1971. 31.00 (ISBN 0-12-785104-6). Acad Pr.

Directory of Libraries in Singapore. 165p. 1969. 12.50x (ISBN 0-8002-0757-2). Intl Pubns Serv.

Nunn, G. Raymond. Asian Libraries & Librarianship: An Annotated Bibliography of Selected Books & Periodicals & a Draft Syllabus. LC 73-6629. 1973. 10.00 (ISBN 0-8108-0633-9). Scarecrow.

Winkelman, John H. The Imperial Library in Southern Sung China, 1127-1279: A Study of the Organization & Operation of the Scholarly Agencies of the Central Government. LC 74-84370. (Transactions Ser.: Vol. 64, Pt. 8). (Illus.). 1974. pap. 5.00 (ISBN 0-87169-648-7). Am Philos.

LIBRARIES–EUROPE

Hamlin, Talbot. Some European Architectural Libraries: Their Methods, Equipment & Administration. LC 39-2757. Repr. of 1939 ed. 19.00 (ISBN 0-404-03090-4). AMS Pr.

Lewanski, Richard C., ed. Guide to Polish Libraries & Archives. (East European Monographs: No. 6). 220p. 1974. 12.50x (ISBN 0-231-03896-8). East Eur Quarterly.

Loeschburg, Winifred. Historic Libraries of Europe. (Illus.). 140p. 1976. wrappers 12.50 (ISBN 0-685-75698-X). Adler.

Thompson, A. Meilleur: Mobility of Employment International for Librarians in Europe. (Research Publication Ser.: No. 20). 1977. pap. 17.25x (ISBN 0-85365-660-6, Pub. by Lib Assn England). Oryx Pr.

LIBRARIES–EUROPE–BIBLIOGRAPHY

Lewanski, Richard C. Eastern Europe & Russia: A Handbook of Western European Archival & Library Resources. 471p. 1980. 60.00 (ISBN 0-89664-092-2). K G Saur.

Lewanski, Richard C., ed. Subject Collections in European Libraries. 2nd ed. LC 77-72343. 1978. 57.00 (ISBN 0-85935-011-8). Bowker.

LIBRARIES–FRANCE

Delisle, Leopold V. Le Cabinet Des Manuscripts De la Bibliotheque Imperiale, 4 vols. LC 78-125018. 1974. lib. bdg. 206.00 (ISBN 0-8337-0819-8, 0-8337-0819). B Franklin.

Dibdin, Thomas F. Bibliographical, Antiquarian, & Picturesque Tour in France & Germany, 3 Vols. 2nd ed. LC 76-111768. Repr. of 1829 ed. Set. 80.00 (ISBN 0-404-02130-1). AMS Pr.

Ferguson, John. Libraries in France. (Comparative Library Studies Ser). 1971. 12.50 (ISBN 0-208-01058-0, Linnet). Shoe String.

LIBRARIES–GERMANY

Andrews, John S & Walker, Gregory, trs. Libraries in the Federal Republic of Germany. (Illus.). 310p. 1972. pap. 12.00 (ISBN 0-8389-0135-2). ALA.

Catalogues of the Library of Deutsches Museum, Munich, 20 vols. Set. 5645.00 (ISBN 0-685-96558-9). K G Saur.

Dibdin, Thomas F. Bibliographical, Antiquarian, & Picturesque Tour in France & Germany, 3 Vols. 2nd ed. LC 76-111768. Repr. of 1829 ed. Set. 80.00 (ISBN 0-404-02130-1). AMS Pr.

Dosa, Marta L., tr. Libraries in the Political Scene: Georg Leyh & German Librarianship, 1933-53. LC 72-5218. (Contributions in Librarianship & Information Science: No. 7). 256p. 1973. lib. bdg. 16.95 (ISBN 0-8371-6443-5, DGL/). Greenwood.

Forschungsgemeinschaft, Deutsche, ed. Studies on the Organizational Structure & Services in National & University Libraries in the Federal Republic of Germany & in the United Kingdom. 227p. 1980. text ed. 27.00 (ISBN 0-686-64606-1). K G Saur.

Union List of Conference Proceedings in Libraries of the Federal Republic of Germany Including Berlin (West, 2 vols. 907p. 1978. Set. 375.00 (ISBN 3-7940-3004-4, Dist by Gale Research Co). K G Saur.

LIBRARIES–GREAT BRITAIN

Astbury, Raymond, ed. Libraries & the Book Trade in Britain. 194p. 1968. 18.00 (ISBN 0-208-00635-4). Shoe String.

Botfield, Beriah. Notes on the Cathedral Libraries of England. LC 68-23138. 1969. Repr. of 1849 ed. 39.00 (ISBN 0-8103-3174-8). Gale.

British Library General Catalogue of Printed Books to 1975, 360 vols. new ed. 1980. Set. 24,480.00 (ISBN 3-5983-0200-2, Pub. by K G Saur). Gale.

Burkett, J., ed. Government & Related Library & Information Services in the U. K. 3rd rev. ed. 1974. pap. 21.85 (ISBN 0-85365-127-2, Pub. by Lib Assn England). Oryx Pr.

Catalogue of Books in the Hirsch Library. 548p. 1980. 90.00x (ISBN 0-7141-0115-X, Pub. by Brit Lib England). State Mutual Bk.

Chaplin, A. H., ed. The British Library & AACR, Nineteen Sixty-Seven: A Study. 1973. pap. 13.25x (ISBN 0-85365-286-4, Pub. by Lib Assn England). Oryx Pr.

Esdaile, Arundell. The British Museum Library: A Short History & Survey. LC 78-31145. (Library Association Ser.). 1979. Repr. of 1948 ed. lib. bdg. 26.00x (ISBN 0-313-20940-5, ESBM). Greenwood.

Forschungsgemeinschaft, Deutsche, ed. Studies on the Organizational Structure & Services in National & University Libraries in the Federal Republic of Germany & in the United Kingdom. 227p. 1980. text ed. 27.00 (ISBN 0-686-64606-1). K G Saur.

Great Britain, Parliament, House of Commons, Select Committee on Public Libraries. Report from the Select Committee on Public Libraries, 23 July 1849. LC 74-366370. Date not set. Repr. of 1849 ed. lib. bdg. 27.50x (ISBN 0-678-05231-X). Kelley.

Hamilton, F. J., ed. Libraries in the United Kingdom & the Republic of Ireland. 9th ed. 1981. pap. 21.95x (ISBN 0-85365-803-X, Pub. by Lib Assn England). Oryx Pr.

--Libraries in the United Kingdom & the Republic of Ireland. 8th ed. 1979. pap. 10.95 (ISBN 0-85365-741-6, Pub. by Lib Assn England). Oryx Pr.

Harrison, K. C. The Library & the Community. (Grafton Books on Library Service). 1977. lib. bdg. 15.00x (ISBN 0-233-96875-X). Westview.

Kaufman, Paul. Community Library: A Chapter in English Social History. LC 67-28642. (Transactions Ser.: Vol. 57, Pt. 7). (Illus.). 1967. pap. 1.00 (ISBN 0-87169-577-4). Am Philos.

Keeling, D. F. British Library History, Nineteen Sixty-Nine to Nineteen Seventy-Two. (Bibliographic Ser.). 1975. 13.50x (ISBN 0-85365-417-4, Pub. by Lib Assn England). Oryx Pr.

Keeling, D. F., ed. British Library History, Nineteen Seventy-Three to Nineteen Seventy-Six. (Bibliographic Ser.). 15.50x (ISBN 0-85365-781-5, Pub. by Lib Assn England). Oryx Pr.

--British Library History, Nineteen Sixty-Two to Nineteen Sixty-Eight. (Bibliographic Ser.). 1972. 13.50x (ISBN 0-85365-345-3, Pub. by Lib Assn England). Oryx Pr.

Kelly, T. Early Public Libraries: A History of Public Libraries in Great Britain Before 1850. 1966. lib. bdg. 21.00x (ISBN 0-85365-381-X, Pub. by Lib Assn England). Oryx Pr.

--History of Public Libraries in Great Britain, 1845 to 1975. 2nd ed. 1977. 34.00x (ISBN 0-85365-239-2, Pub. by Lib Assn England). Oryx Pr.

Ker, N. H., ed. Medieval Libraries of Great Britain: A List of Surviving Books. 2nd ed. (Royal Historical Society Ser.). 424p. 1964. 18.50x (ISBN 0-8476-1345-3). Rowman.

Ker, Neil R., ed. Medieval Manuscripts in British Libraries: Abbotsford - Keele. Vol. II. (Illus.). 1977. pap. text ed. 89.00x (ISBN 0-19-818162-0). Oxford U Pr.

Montgomery, J. W., tr. A Seventeenth-Century View of European Libraries: Lomeier's De Bibliothecis Chapter X. (U. C. Publ. in Librarianship: Vol. 3). 1962. pap. 7.95x (ISBN 0-520-09206-6). U of Cal Pr.

Moore, George. Literature at Nurse. Fletcher, Ian & Stokes, John, eds. Bd. with A Mere Accident. LC 76-20110. (Decadent Consciousness Ser.). 1978. lib. bdg. 38.00 (ISBN 0-8240-2769-8). Garland Pub.

--Literature at Nurse, or, Circulating Morals: A Polemic on Victorian Censorship. (Society & the Victorians). 96p. 1976. Repr. of 1885 ed. text ed. 5.25x (ISBN 0-391-00588-X). Humanities.

Morton, Leslie T. How to Use a Medical Library. 6th ed. 1979. pap. 11.95x (ISBN 0-433-22451-7). Intl Ideas.

Pemberton, J. E. Politics & Public Libraries in England & Wales, 1850 - 1970. 1977. 17.25x (ISBN 0-85365-109-4, Pub. by Lib Assn England). Oryx Pr.

Penney, B., ed. Music in British Libraries: A Directory of Resources. 3rd ed. 1981. pap. 34.50 (ISBN 0-85365-981-8, Pub. by Lib Assn England). Oryx Pr.

Saunders, W. L., ed. British Librarianship Today. 1978. pap. 12.50 (ISBN 0-85365-498-0, 6506). Gaylord Prof Pubns.

Savage, E. A. Old English Libraries. 59.95 (ISBN 0-8490-0757-7). Gordon Pr.

Savage, Ernest A. Old English Libraries. LC 68-26177. (Illus.). 1968. Repr. of 1912 ed. 26.00 (ISBN 0-8103-3179-9). Gale.

Streeter, Burnett N. Chained Library. 1970. Repr. of 1931 ed. text ed. 25.50 (ISBN 0-8337-3431-8). B Franklin.

Usherwood, Bob. Libraries & Leisure: The Role of the Librarian in Leisure Management. 1981. 10.00x (ISBN 0-902248-07-3, Pub. by AALSED England). State Mutual Bk.

Ward, P. L. & Burkett, J., eds. Introductory Guide to Research in Librarianship & Information Studies in the U. K. (Pamphlet Ser.: No. 37). 1975. pap. 9.85x (ISBN 0-85365-058-6, Pub. by Lib Assn England). Oryx Pr.

Whatley, H. A., ed. British Librarianship & Information Science: Nineteen Sixty-Six to Nineteen Seventy. (Library Association Bk.). 1972. lib. bdg. 34.50x (ISBN 0-85365-175-2, Pub. by Lib Assn England). Oryx Pr.

LIBRARIES-INDIA

Trehan, G. L. Administration & Organization of College Libraries in India. 252p. 1969. 8.25x (ISBN 0-8426-1571-7). Verry.

LIBRARIES-ITALY

The Pittsburgh Bibliophiles Pilgrimage to Italy, 1976. (Illus.). 107p. 1978. ltd. ed. of 500 hand-numbered copies 36.00x (ISBN 0-686-65645-8). Hunt Inst Botanical.

LIBRARIES-IRELAND

Hamilton, F. J., ed. Libraries in the United Kingdom & the Republic of Ireland. 9th ed. 1981. pap. 21.95x (ISBN 0-85365-803-X, Pub. by Lib Assn England). Oryx Pr.

--Libraries in the United Kingdom & the Republic of Ireland. 8th ed. 1979. pap. 10.95 (ISBN 0-85365-741-6, Pub. by Lib Assn England). Oryx Pr.

McCarthy, Muriel. All Graduates & Gentlemen: Marsh's Library. (Illus.). 239p. 1980. 22.50x (ISBN 0-8476-3141-9). Rowman.

LIBRARIES-LATIN AMERICA

Thompson, Lawrence S. Essays in Hispanic Bibliography. LC 75-96729. 1970. 15.00 (ISBN 0-208-00978-7, Archon). Shoe String.

Vervliet, H. D., ed. Resource Sharing of Libraries in Developing Countries. (IFLA Publications: No. 14). 286p. 1979. 19.00 (ISBN 0-89664-114-7, Pub. by K G Saur). Shoe String.

LIBRARIES-MEXICO

Puttick & Simpson. Bibliotheca Mejicana. LC 71-168027. Repr. of 1869 ed. 15.00 (ISBN 0-404-02388-6). AMS Pr.

LIBRARIES-NEW ZEALAND

Borchardt, D. H. & Horacek, J. Librarianship in Australia, New Zealand & Oceania. 1976. 10.25 (ISBN 0-08-019920-8); pap. text ed. write for info. (ISBN 0-08-019752-3). Pergamon.

Downs, Robert S. Australian & New Zealand Library Resources. 1979. 33.30 (ISBN 0-7201-0913-2, Pub. by Mansell England). Merrimack Bk Serv.

LIBRARIES-OCEANICA

Borchardt, D. H. & Horacek, J. Librarianship in Australia, New Zealand & Oceania. 1976. 10.25 (ISBN 0-08-019920-8); pap. text ed. write for info. (ISBN 0-08-019752-3). Pergamon.

LIBRARIES-RUSSIA

Chandler, George. Libraries, Documentation & Bibliography in the USSR Nineteen Seventeen to Nineteen Seventy-One. LC 72-84273. (International Bibliographical & Library Ser). 1973. 31.00 (ISBN 0-12-785105-4). Acad Pr.

Francis, Simon, ed. Libraries in the U.S.S.R. (Comparative Library Studies Ser.). 1971. 14.50 (ISBN 0-208-01059-9, Linnet). Shoe String.

Horecky, Paul L. Libraries & Bibliographic Centers in the Soviet Union. LC 59-63389. (Russian & East European Ser.: No. 16). (Illus.). 308p. 1959. pap. 3.45x (ISBN 0-253-39016-8). Ind U Pr.

Lewanski, Richard C. Eastern Europe & Russia: A Handbook of Western European Archival & Library Resources. 471p. 1980. 60.00 (ISBN 0-89664-092-2). K G Saur.

Raymond, Boris. Krupskaia & Soviet Russian Librarianship: 1917-1939. LC 79-1041. 1979. 13.00 (ISBN 0-8108-1209-6). Scarecrow.

LIBRARIES-SCOTLAND

Roberts, Stephen, et al. Research Libraries & Collections in the United Kingdom: A Selective Inventory & Guide. 1978. 25.00 (ISBN 0-208-01667-8, Linnet). Shoe String.

Treasures of the National Library of Scotland. 1980. 12.00x (ISBN 0-902220-29-2, Pub. by Natl Lib Scotland). State Mutual Bk.

LIBRARIES-SOUTH AMERICA

McCarthy, Cavan. Developing Libraries in Brazil: with a Chapter on Paraguay. LC 74-23681. 1975. 10.00 (ISBN 0-8108-0750-5). Scarecrow.

National Library of Peru. Author Catalog of the Peruvian Collection of the National Library of Peru, 6 vols. De Gaviria, Maria C., ed. 1979. Set. lib. bdg. 655.00 (ISBN 0-8161-0250-3). G K Hall.

LIBRARIES-SPAIN

Foulche-Delbosc, Raymond & Barrau-Dihigo, L. Manuel De L'Hispanisant, 2 Vols. LC 20-16867. 1920-1925. Set. 48.00 (ISBN 0-527-30700-9). Kraus Repr.

Ribera Y Tarrago, Julian. Bibliofilos y Bibliotecas En la Espana Musulmana: Disertacion Leida En la Faculdad De Medicina y Ciencias. 2nd ed. 1967. Repr. of 1896 ed. 16.50 (ISBN 0-8337-2977-2). B Franklin.

LIBRARIES, ARCHITECTURAL

see Architectural Libraries

LIBRARIES, ART

see Art Libraries

LIBRARIES, BRANCH

see Libraries-Branches, Delivery Stations, etc.

LIBRARIES, BUSINESS

see Business Libraries

LIBRARIES, CATHOLIC

Brown, James, et al. The Relationship of the Library to Instructional Systems. Corrigan, John T., ed. (Catholic Library Association Studies in Librarianship: No. 2). 1978. pap. 3.00 (ISBN 0-87507-006-X). Cath Lib Assn.

Cashel Diocesan Library. County Tipperary, Republic of Ireland. Catalogue of the Cashel Diocesan Library. 1973. 95.00 (ISBN 0-8161-1065-4). G K Hall.

Harvey, John F., ed. Church & Synagogue Libraries. LC 80-11736. 299p. 1980. 15.00 (ISBN 0-8108-1304-1). Scarecrow.

Pilley, Catherine M. & Wilt, Matthew R., eds. Catholic Subject Headings. rev. ed. 257p. 1981. pap. 25.00x (ISBN 0-87507-009-4). Cath Lib Assn.

LIBRARIES, CHILDREN'S

see also Books and Reading for Children; Children's Literature (Collections); Libraries, Young People's; Libraries and Schools; School Libraries

Barnes, Donald L. & Burgdorf, Arlene. Study Skills for Information Retrieval, Bk. 1. (gr. 4-8). 1979. pap. text ed. 4.40 (ISBN 0-205-06436-1, 4964365); tchrs'. ed. 4.80 (ISBN 0-205-06440-X, 4964403). Allyn.

--Study Skills for Information Retrieval, Bk. 2. (gr. 4-8). 1979. pap. text ed. 4.40 (ISBN 0-205-06437-X, 4964373); tchrs'. ed. 4.80 (ISBN 0-205-06441-8, 4964411). Allyn.

--Study Skills for Information Retrieval, Bk. 3. (gr. 4-8). 1979. pap. text ed. 4.40 (ISBN 0-205-06438-6, 496438-1); tchrs'. ed. 4.80 (ISBN 0-205-06442-6, 496442-X). Allyn.

--Study Skills for Information Retrieval, Bk. 4. (gr. 4-8). 1974. pap. text ed. 4.40 (ISBN 0-205-03994-4, 4939948); tchrs. ed. 4.80 (ISBN 0-205-03995-2, 4939956). Allyn.

Baskins, Barbara & Harris, Karen, eds. Special Child & the Library. 1976. pap. text ed. 10.00 (ISBN 0-8389-0222-7). ALA.

Broderick, Dorothy M. Introduction to Children's Work in Public Libraries. 1965. 6.00 (ISBN 0-8242-0027-6). Wilson.

Broderick, Dorothy M., ed. Library Work with Children. 1977. 10.00 (ISBN 0-8242-0620-7). Wilson.

Currie, Dorothy H. How to Organize a Children's Library. LC 65-14215. 1965. 10.00 (ISBN 0-379-00233-7). Oceana.

Dyer, Esther R. Cooperation in Library Service to Children. LC 77-28190. 1978. 10.00 (ISBN 0-8108-1111-1). Scarecrow.

Educational Research Council of America. Children's Librarian. Keck, Florence & Marchak, John P., eds. (Real People at Work Ser: A). (Illus.). 1974. pap. text ed. 2.25 (ISBN 0-89247-003-8). Changing Times.

Fleet, A. Children's Libraries. (Grafton Books on Library Science). 1977. lib. bdg. 12.00x (ISBN 0-233-96229-8). Westview.

Foster, Joan, ed. Reader in Children's Librarianship. LC 78-26669. (Readers in Librarianship & Information Science: No. 27). (Illus.). 1979. text ed. 22.00 (ISBN 0-910972-89-3). IHS-PDS.

Gross, Elizabeth H. Public Library Service to Children. LC 67-24347. 1967. 9.00 (ISBN 0-379-00309-0). Oceana.

Harrod, L. M. Library Work with Children. (Grafton Books in Library Science). 1977. lib. bdg. 17.00x (ISBN 0-233-95994-7). Westview.

Johnson, Ferne, ed. Start Early for an Early Start: You & the Young Child. LC 76-44237. 1976. pap. 8.00 (ISBN 0-8389-3185-5). ALA.

Libraries Are for Children. rev. ed. 1971. pap. 6.95 (ISBN 0-913308-01-3). Fordham Pub.

Library Service to Schools & Children. (Documentation, Libraries & Archives - Studies & Research: No. 10). 1979. pap. 7.00 (ISBN 92-3-101640-7, U938, UNESCO). Unipub.

Long, Harriet G. Public Library Service to Children: Foundation & Development. LC 70-8592. 1970. 10.00 (ISBN 0-8108-0291-0). Scarecrow.

--Rich the Treasure: Public Library Service to Children. LC 53-9660. 1953. pap. 2.00 (ISBN 0-8389-0052-6). ALA.

Polette, Nancy & Hamlin, Marjorie. Reading Guidance in a Media Age. LC 75-26833. (Illus.). 1975. 12.00 (ISBN 0-8108-0873-0). Scarecrow.

Ray, Colin, ed. Library Service to Children: An International Survey, Vol. 12. (IFLA Publications Ser.). 1978. 24.50 (ISBN 0-89664-004-3, Pub. by K G Saur). Shoe String.

Rees, Gwendolen. Libraries for Children. (Library Science Ser.). 1980. lib. bdg. 55.00 (ISBN 0-8490-3131-1). Gordon Pr.

Richardson, Selma K., ed. Children's Services of Public Libraries. LC 78-11503. (Allerton Park Institutes Ser.: No. 23). 178p. 1978. 9.00x (ISBN 0-87845-049-1). U of Ill Lib Info Sci.

Sayers, William C. A Manual of Children Libraries. 1980. lib. bdg. 59.95 (ISBN 0-8490-3116-8). Gordon Pr.

Smith, Lillian H. The Unreluctant Years: A Critical Approach to Children's Literature. 194p. 1953. 5.00 (ISBN 0-8389-0065-8). ALA.

World Book-Childcraft International Inc., ed. Childcraft-the How & Why Library, 15 vols. Incl. Vol. 1. Poems & Rhymes; Vol. 2. Stories & Fables; Vol. 3. Children Everywhere; Vol. 4. World & Space; Vol. 5. About Animals; Vol. 6. The Green Kingdom; Vol. 7. How Things Work; Vol. 8. About Us; Vol. 9. Holidays & Birthdays; Vol. 10. Places to Know; Vol. 11. Make & Do; Vol. 12. Look & Learn; Vol. 13. Mathemagic; Vol. 14. About Me; Vol. 15. Guide for Parents. (Illus.). (gr. k-6). 1981. PLB write for info. (ISBN 0-7166-0181-8). World Bk Child.

LIBRARIES, CHILDREN'S-GERMANY (FEDERAL REPUBLIC, 1949-)

Lepman, Jella. Bridge of Children's Books. McCormick, Edith, tr. LC 68-54215. 1969. 5.00 (ISBN 0-8389-0070-4). ALA.

LIBRARIES, CHURCH

Barber, Cyril J. Minister's Library. 1973. 13.95 (ISBN 0-8010-0598-1). Baker Bk.

Brown, Charles C. Small Church Library. 1980. 0.75 (ISBN 0-686-28794-0). Forward Movement.

Deitrick, Bernard E. A Basic Book List for Church Libraries. rev. ed. LC 77-4093. 1979. pap. 1.75x (ISBN 0-915324-10-5). CSLA.

Dotts, Maryann J. The Church Resource Library: How to Start It & Make It Grow. LC 75-28087. 1976. pap. 2.95 (ISBN 0-687-08345-1). Abingdon.

Harvey, John F., ed. Church & Synagogue Libraries. LC 80-11736. 299p. 1980. 15.00 (ISBN 0-8108-1304-1). Scarecrow.

John, Erwin E. Key to a Successful Church Library. rev. ed. LC 58-13940. (Orig.). 1967. pap. 2.50 (ISBN 0-8066-0711-4, 10-3684). Augsburg.

Johnson, Marian S. Promoting Your Church Library. LC 68-25805. 1968. pap. 3.95, spiral bdg (ISBN 0-8066-0831-5, 10-5280). Augsburg.

Kohl, Rachel & Rodda, Dorothy. Church & Synagogue Library Resources. 3rd ed. LC 75-1178. 1979. pap. 2.50x (ISBN 0-915324-08-3). CSLA.

Korty, Margaret B. Audio-Visual Materials in the Church Library: How to Select, Catalog, Process, Store, Circulate & Promote. LC 77-74780. (Illus.). 1977. spiral bdg. 4.95 (ISBN 0-9603060-0-5). Church Lib.

McMichael, Betty. The Library & Resource Center in Christian Education. 1977. 12.95 (ISBN 0-8024-4895-X). Moody.

Merryweather, F. Somner. Bibliomania in the Middle Ages. rev. ed. Copinger, H. B., ed. LC 72-83748. Repr. of 1933 ed. 15.00 (ISBN 0-405-08787-X, Pub. by Blom). Arno.

Newton, LaVose. Church Library Handbook. rev. ed. LC 76-189488. 1972. pap. text ed. 4.95 (ISBN 0-930014-02-2). Multnomah.

Saul, Arthur K. One Hundred & Twenty One Ways Toward a More Effective Church Library. 204p. 1980. pap. 4.50 (ISBN 0-88207-171-8). Victor Bks.

Scheer, Gladys E. The Church Library: Tips & tools. (Orig.). 1973. pap. 2.50 (ISBN 0-8272-0435-3). Bethany Pr.

Smith, Ruth S. Workshop Planning. rev. ed. LC 78-24240. (Guide Ser.: No. 3). (Illus.). 1979. pap. 6.50x (ISBN 0-915324-15-6). CSLA.

Standards for Church & Synagogue Libraries. LC 77-6634. (Guide Ser.: No. 6). pap. 3.75x (ISBN 0-915324-12-1). CSLA.

Towns, Elmer J. & Barber, Cyril L. Successful Church Libraries. 1971. pap. 3.50 (ISBN 0-8010-8768-6). Baker Bk.

Walls, Francine E. The Church Library Workbook. 144p. 1980. pap. 7.95 (ISBN 0-89367-048-0). Light & Life.

LIBRARIES, COLLEGE

see Libraries, University and College

LIBRARIES, COMMERCIAL

see Commercial Libraries

LIBRARIES, EDUCATION

see Education Libraries

LIBRARIES, FILM

see Moving-Picture Film Collections

LIBRARIES, GOVERNMENTAL, ADMINISTRATIVE, ETC.

see also Government Librarians

Benton, Mildred, compiled by. Federal Library Resources: A User's Guide to Research Collections. 1973. 10.00 (ISBN 0-87837-002-1). Sci Assoc Intl.

Burkett, J., ed. Government & Related Library & Information Services in the U. K. 3rd rev. ed. 1974. pap. 21.85 (ISBN 0-85365-127-2, Pub. by Lib Assn England). Oryx Pr.

Grayson, L. Library & Information Services to Local Government. 1978. pap. 15.75x (ISBN 0-85365-810-2, Pub. by Lib Assn England). Oryx Pr.

Guide to Government Department & Other Libraries. 1981. 15.00x (ISBN 0-902914-54-5, Pub. by Brit Lib England). State Mutual Bk.

Simmler, Otto, ed. World Directory of Administrative Directories. 474p. 1976. 32.25 (ISBN 3-7940-4427-4, Pub. by K G Saur). Shoe String.

Taylor, Raymond M. Federal Court Libraries, 2 vols. LC 81-81758. 2089p. 1980. lib. bdg. 90.00 (ISBN 0-89941-100-2). W S Hein.

Worldwide Directory of Federal Libraries. 1st ed. LC 72-75955. 1973. 29.50 (ISBN 0-87876-029-6). Marquis.

LIBRARIES, HIGH-SCHOOL

see School Libraries (High School)

LIBRARIES, HOSPITAL

see Hospital Libraries

LIBRARIES, INSTITUTION

see Institution Libraries

LIBRARIES, JOURNALISTIC

see Newspaper Office Libraries

LIBRARIES, JUNIOR COLLEGE

see Junior College Libraries

LIBRARIES, LAW

see Law Libraries

LIBRARIES, MEDICAL

see Medical Libraries

LIBRARIES, MUSIC

see Music Libraries

LIBRARIES, NATIONAL

Davinson, Donald. Academic & Legal Deposit Libraries. 2nd ed. (Examination Guide Ser). 1969. 14.50 (ISBN 0-208-00879-9, Archon). Shoe String.

National Library of Anthropology & History, Mexico City. Catalogo de la Biblioteca Nacional de Antropologia y Historia - Catalogs of the National Library of Anthropology & History, 10 vols. 1972. Set. lib. bdg. 840.00 (ISBN 0-8161-0918-4). G K Hall.

Symposium of National Libraries, Vienna, 1958. National Libraries: Their Problems & Prospects. 1960. pap. 4.00 (ISBN 92-3-100442-5, U399, UNESCO). Unipub.

Thompson, Anthony, ed. National Library Buildings. 144p. 1975. 15.00 (ISBN 3-7940-4422-3, Pub. K G Saur). Shoe String.

LIBRARIES, NEWSPAPER OFFICE

see Newspaper Office Libraries

LIBRARIES, PARISH

see Libraries, Church

LIBRARIES, PHONORECORD

see Phonorecord Libraries

LIBRARIES, PRIVATE

see also Book Collecting; Book Collectors

Byrd, William. Writings of Colonel William Byrd. Bassett, J. S., ed. LC 76-125631. (Research & Source Ser.: No. 518). (Illus.). 1970. Repr. of 1901 ed. lib. bdg. 32.00 (ISBN 0-8337-0442-7). B Franklin.

Edwards, Edward. Libraries & Founders of Libraries. LC 68-58475. (Bibliography & Reference Ser: No. 260). 1969. Repr. of 1865 ed. 26.00 (ISBN 0-8337-1004-4). B Franklin.

Garner, Richard L. & Henderson, Donald C. Columbus & Related Family Papers, 1451-1902: An Inventory of the Boal Collection. LC 74-12303. (Penn State Studies: No. 37). 96p. 1974. pap. 3.50 (ISBN 0-271-01174-2). Pa St U Pr.
Latham, Robert, ed. Catalogue of the Pepys Library, Vol. 1. (Printed Bks.). 201p. 1978. 89.50x (ISBN 0-87471-819-8). Rowman.
Maxwell, M. Shaping a Library: William L. Clements As Collector. (Illus.). 1973. 32.50 (ISBN 9-0607-2631-6). Heinman.
Shaver, Chester L. & Shaver, Alice C. Wordsworth's Library: A Catalogue. LC 77-83348. (Reference Library of Humanities Ser.). 1979. lib. bdg. 40.00 (ISBN 0-8240-9842-0). Garland Pub.
Taylor, Archer. Problems in German Literary History of the Fifteenth & Sixteenth Centuries. 1939. pap. 13.00 (ISBN 0-527-89056-1). Kraus Repr.

LIBRARIES, PUBLIC
see Public Libraries

LIBRARIES, RESEARCH
see Research Libraries

LIBRARIES, RURAL
see also Libraries–Branches, Delivery Stations, etc.

LIBRARIES, SCHOOL
see School Libraries

LIBRARIES, SCIENTIFIC
see Scientific Libraries

LIBRARIES, SPECIAL
see also Business Libraries; Libraries–Special Collections;
also types of special libraries, e.g. Music Libraries

American Numismatic Society, New York. Dictionary & Auction Catalogues of the Library of the American Numismatic Society: First Supplement 1962-67. 1967. lib. bdg. 105.00 (ISBN 0-8161-0788-2). G K Hall.
Bailey, Martha J. The Special Librarian As a Supervisor or Middle Manager. LC 77-5021. (State-of-the-Art Review: No. 6). 1977. pap. 6.00 (ISBN 0-87111-249-3). SLA.
Boyle, Deirdre, ed. Expanding Media. LC 77-23335. (A Neal-Schuman Professional Bk). 1977. lib. bdg. 17.50 (ISBN 0-912700-03-3). Oryx Pr.
Burkett, Jack, ed. Trends in Special Librarianship. 1969. 13.50 (ISBN 0-208-00856-X, Archon). Shoe String.
Christianson, Elin B., ed. New Special Libraries: A Summary of Research. LC 80-11507. 1980. 7.25 (ISBN 0-87111-271-X). SLA.
Collins, Marcia R. & Anderson, Linda. Libraries for Small Museums. 3rd ed. Feldman, Lawrence, ed. LC 78-620740. (Miscellaneous Publications in Anthropology Ser.: No. 4). 1977. pap. text ed. 2.50x (ISBN 0-913134-90-2). Mus Anthro Mo.
Directory of Special Libraries Japan 1973. LC 73-169808. 500p. 1973. 45.00x (ISBN 0-8002-0561-8). Intl Pubns Serv.
Elazar, David H. & Elazar, Daniel J. A Classification System for Libraries of Judaica. 2nd ed. LC 79-111109. 1979. 18.00x (ISBN 965-20-0011-6, Pub by Turtledove Pub Ltd Israel). Intl Schol Bk Serv.
Gibson, Robert W., ed. The Special Library Role in Networks: Proceedings of a Conference. spiral bdg. 10.50 (ISBN 0-87111-279-5). SLA.
Guide to Government Department & Other Libraries. 1981. 15.00x (ISBN 0-902914-54-5, Pub. by Brit Lib England). State Mutual Bk.
Guidelines Subcommittee, SLA Networking Committee. Getting into Networking: Guidelines for Special Libraries. LC 76-58875. (State-of-the-Art Review: No. 5). 1977. pap. 6.00 (ISBN 0-685-85830-8). SLA.
The Hispanic Society of America: Catalogue of the Library, 10 vols. 1962. Set. 810.00 (ISBN 0-87535-131-X); first supplement, 1970. 4 vols 395.00 (ISBN 0-87535-132-8). Hispanic Soc.
International Labour Office, Central Library, Geneva. International Labour Documentation, Cumulative Edition, 1965-1969, 8 vols. 5334p. 1970. Set. lib. bdg. 510.00 (ISBN 0-8161-0902-8). G K Hall.
Jackson, Eugene B., ed. Special Librarianship: A New Reader. LC 80-11530. 773p. 1980. 27.50 (ISBN 0-8108-1295-9). Scarecrow.
Kane, Betty Ann. Widening Circle: The Story of the Folger Shakespeare Library & Its Collection. (Special Piublications). 3.95x (ISBN 0-918016-47-9). Folger Bks.
King, David E. Special Libraries: A Guide for Management. 2nd ed. 1981. write for info. (ISBN 0-87111-258-2). SLA.
Kroll, Morton, ed. College, University, & Special Libraries of the Pacific Northwest. LC 60-9873. (PNLA Library Development Project Reports: Vol. 3). 320p. 1961. 11.50 (ISBN 0-295-73745-X). U of Wash Pr.
Library & Information Services for Special Groups. 1974. 22.50 (ISBN 0-87837-003-X). Sci Assoc Intl.
Mount, Ellis, ed. Planning the Special Library. LC 72-85956. 1972. pap. 9.75 (ISBN 0-87111-205-1). SLA.
Musiker, Reuben. Special Libraries: A General Survey with Particular Reference to South Africa. 1970. 10.00 (ISBN 0-8108-0310-0). Scarecrow.
Reichardt, Gunther, ed. Special Libraries - Worldwide: A Collection of Papers Prepared for the Section of Special Libraries. 360p. 1974. 36.50 (ISBN 3-7940-4421-5, Pub. by K G Saur). Shoe String.
Rush, N. Orwin, et al. Special Collections: What They Mean to Librarians, Professors, & Collectors. LC 72-93783. 1972. 5.00 (ISBN 0-686-02404-4). Friends Fla St.
Slater, Frank, ed. Cost Reduction for Special Libraries and Information Centers. LC 73-81388. 1973. 12.50 (ISBN 0-87715-104-0). Am Soc Info Sci.
Strable, Edward G., ed. Special Libraries: A Guide for Management. rev. ed. LC 74-19252. 1975. 8.00 (ISBN 0-87111-228-0). SLA.
Van Halm, John. The Development of Special Libraries As an International Phenomenon. LC 78-13188. (State-of-the-Art Review Ser.: No. 4). 1979. pap. 19.50 (ISBN 0-87111-245-0). SLA.
Wilson, T. D. & Stephenson, J. Dissemination of Information. 2nd ed. (Examination Guide Ser.). 1969. 10.50 (ISBN 0-208-00862-4, Archon). Shoe String.

LIBRARIES, SPECIAL–DIRECTORIES
Here are entered directories of special libraries or of special collections in other libraries.

Ash, Lee. Subject Collections. 5th ed. LC 74-19331. 1978. 72.50 (ISBN 0-8352-0924-5). Bowker.
Bramley, Gerald. Outreach: Library Services for the Institutionalized, the Elderly, & the Physically Handicapped. 1978. 14.50 (ISBN 0-208-01663-5, Linnet). Shoe String.
Institutions Where SLA Members Are Employed: An SLA Directory. 1977. 15.50 (ISBN 0-87111-238-8). SLA.
Young, Margaret L., et al, eds. Directory of Special Libraries & Information Centers: Vol. 1-Special Libraries & Information Centers in the United States & Canada. 6th ed. LC 79-16966. 1979. 175.00 (ISBN 0-8103-0297-7). Gale.
--Directory of Special Libraries & Information Centers: Vol. 3-New Special Libraries. 6th ed. 1979. pap. text ed. 150.00 (ISBN 0-8103-0281-0). Gale.

LIBRARIES, STORAGE

Fussler, Herman H. & Simon, Julian. Patterns in the Use of Books in Large Research Libraries. 2nd ed. LC 72-79916. (Chicago Studies in Library Science Ser). 1969. 11.00x (ISBN 0-226-27556-6). U of Chicago Pr.

LIBRARIES, SUNDAY-SCHOOL
see also Libraries, Church

LIBRARIES, TECHNICAL
see Technical Libraries

LIBRARIES, THEOLOGICAL
see Theological Libraries

LIBRARIES, TRAVELING
see also Bookmobiles

LIBRARIES, UNIVERSITY AND COLLEGE
see also Junior College Libraries; Research Libraries

Adams, Herbert B. Seminary Libraries & University Extension. Repr. of 1887 ed. pap. 7.00 (ISBN 0-384-00328-1). Johnson Repr.
--Seminary Libraries & University Extension. LC 78-63777. (Johns Hopkins University. Studies in the Social Sciences. Fifth Ser. 1887: 11). Repr. of 1887 ed. 11.50 (ISBN 0-404-61043-9). AMS Pr.
Allen, Kenneth W. Use of Community College Libraries. 1971. 12.50 (ISBN 0-208-01143-9, Linnet). Shoe String.
Allen, Kenneth W. & Allen, Loren. Organization & Administration of the Learning Resources Center in the Community College. 187p. 1973. 14.00 (ISBN 0-208-01306-7, Linnet). Shoe String.
Association of College & Research Libraries & American Library Association. Books for College Libraries, 6 vols. 2nd ed. LC 74-13743. 2000p. 1975. pap. 70.00 set (ISBN 0-8389-0178-6). ALA.
Baker, Leigh R. Development of University Libraries in Papua New Guinea. LC 80-26936. 410p. 1981. 20.00 (ISBN 0-8108-1393-9). Scarecrow.
Baumol, William J. & Marcus, Matityahu. Economics of Academic Libraries. 112p. 1973. 6.50 (ISBN 0-8268-1257-0). ACE.
Beazley, Richard M. Library Statistics of College & Universities, 1976 Institutional Data (IIBGIS EEGIS XI) (Monograph: No. 16). 184p. 1979. pap. 5.00x (ISBN 0-87845-061-0, NCES 78-234). U of Ill Lib Info Sci.
Braden, Irene A. Undergraduate Library. LC 75-80834. (A.C.R.L. Monograph Ser: No. 31). (Orig.). 1970. pap. 9.00 (ISBN 0-8389-3097-2). ALA.
Branscomb, Harvie. Teaching with Books: A Study of College Libraries. xvii, 239p. 1974. Repr. of 1940 ed. 18.00 (ISBN 0-208-01411-X). Shoe String.
Branscomb, Lewis C. Case for the Faculty Status for Academic Librarians. LC 75-118198. (A.C.R.L. Monograph Ser.: No. 33). 1970. pap. 5.00 (ISBN 0-8389-3114-6). ALA.
Breivik, Patricia S. Open Admissions & the Academic Library. LC 77-5816. 1977. pap. 8.50 (ISBN 0-8389-3195-2). ALA.
Bryan, Harrison. University Libraries in Britain: A New Look. 1976. 14.50 (ISBN 0-208-01532-9, Linnet). Shoe String.
Buck, Paul. Libraries & Universities: Addresses & Reports. Williams, E. E., ed. LC 64-25053. 1964. 9.00x (ISBN 0-674-53050-0, Belknap Pr). Harvard U Pr.
Burlingame, Dwight F., et al. The College Learning Resource Center. LC 78-13716. 1978. lib. bdg. 18.50x (ISBN 0-87287-189-4). Libs Unl.
Cammack, Floyd M., et al. Community College Library Instruction: Training for Self-Reliance in Basic Library Use. (Illus.). 283p. 1979. 17.50 (ISBN 0-208-01825-5, Linnet). Shoe String.
Cornell University, New York State School of Industrial & Labor Ralations. Library Catalog of the Martin P. Catherwood Library of the New York State School of Industrial & Labor Relations, 12 vols. 1967. Set. lib. bdg. 1140.00 (ISBN 0-8161-0757-2). G K Hall.
Cornell University, New York State School of Industrial & Labor Relations. Library Catalog of the Martin P. Catherwood Library of the New York State School of Industrial & Labor Relations, First Supplement. 873p. 1967. lib. bdg. 110.00 (ISBN 0-8161-0772-6). G K Hall.
--Library Catalog of the Martin P. Catherwood Library of the New York State School of Industrial & Labor Relations, Second Supplement. 1968. lib. bdg. 120.00 (ISBN 0-8161-0844-7). G K Hall.
--Library Catalog of the Martin P. Catherwood Library of the New York State School of Industrial & Labor Relations, Third Supplement. 1969. lib. bdg. 120.00 (ISBN 0-8161-0878-1). G K Hall.
--Library Catalog of the Martin P. Catherwood Library of the New York State School of Industrial & Labor Relations, Fourth Supplement. 1970. lib. bdg. 120.00 (ISBN 0-8161-0911-7). G K Hall.
--Library Catalog of the Martin P. Catherwood Library of the New York State School of Industrial & Labor Relations, Fifth Supplement. 1972. 120.00 (ISBN 0-8161-0986-9). G K Hall.
Czarnecki, Jan, compiled by. Soviet Union, 1917-1967: An Annotated Bibliography of Soviet Semicentennial Publications in the Collection of the University of Miami at Coral Gables, Florida. LC 74-14893. 1974. 10.00x (ISBN 0-87024-273-3). U of Miami Pr.
Davies, David. The Evergreen Tree. 1971. 3.75 (ISBN 0-910330-18-2). Grant Dahlstrom.
Davinson, Donald. Academic & Legal Deposit Libraries. 2nd ed. (Examination Guide Ser). 1969. 14.50 (ISBN 0-208-00879-9, Archon). Shoe String.
Dougherty, Richard M. & Blomquist, Laura L. Improving Access to Library Resources. LC 73-20482. (Illus.). 1974. 10.00 (ISBN 0-8108-0637-1). Scarecrow.
Dougherty, Richard M. & Maier, Joan M. Centralized Processing for Academic Libraries. LC 73-155716. 1971. 16.50 (ISBN 0-8108-0381-X). Scarecrow.
Durey, Peter. Staff Management in University & College Libraries. Chandler, C., ed. 144p. 1976. text ed. 16.00 (ISBN 0-08-019718-3). Pergamon.
Farber, Evan I. Classified List of Periodicals for the College Library. 5th rev. ed. LC 72-76264. (The Useful Reference Ser. of Library Bks: Vol. 99). 1972. lib. bdg. 15.00x (ISBN 0-87305-099-1). Faxon.
Farber, Evan I. & Walling, Ruth. The Academic Library: Essays in Honor of Guy R. Lyle. LC 74-2098. 1974. 10.00 (ISBN 0-8108-0712-2). Scarecrow.
Fisher, R. K. Libraries of University Departments of Adult Education & Extra-Mural Studies. 1974. pap. 10.95x (ISBN 0-85365-377-1, Pub. by Lib Assn England). Oryx Pr.
Forschungsgemeinschaft, Deutsche, ed. Studies on the Organizational Structure & Services in National & University Libraries in the Federal Republic of Germany & in the United Kingdom. 227p. 1980. text ed. 27.00 (ISBN 0-686-64606-1). K G Saur.
Fussler, Herman H. & Simon, Julian. Patterns in the Use of Books in Large Research Libraries. 2nd ed. LC 72-79916. (Chicago Studies in Library Science Ser). 1969. 11.00x (ISBN 0-226-27556-6). U of Chicago Pr.
Fussler, Herman H., ed. Function of the Library in the Modern College: Nineteenth Annual Conference of the Graduate Library School. LC 67-28464. 1954. Repr. 7.00x (ISBN 0-226-27555-8). U of Chicago Pr.
Futas, Elizabeth, ed. Library Acquisition Policies & Procedures. LC 77-7275. (A Neal-Schuman Professional Bk). 1977. lib. bdg. 19.50x (ISBN 0-912700-02-5). Oryx Pr.
Gelfand, Morris A. University Libraries for Developing Countries. (Manuals for Libraries, Vol. 14). (Photos). 1971. pap. 7.00 (ISBN 92-3-100654-1, U708, UNESCO). Unipub.
Grove, Pearce S., ed. Nonprint Media in Academic Libraries. LC 74-23972. (ACRL Publications in Librarianship: No. 34). 239p. 1975. pap. 10.00 (ISBN 0-8389-0153-0). ALA.
Hamlin, Arthur. The University Library in the United States: Its Origins & Development. 1981. 25.00x (ISBN 0-8122-7795-3). U of Pa Pr.
International Seminar on Approval & Gathering Plans in Large & Medium Size Academic Libraries, 3rd. Economics of Approval Plans: Proceedings. Spyers-Duran, Peter & Gore, Daniel, eds. LC 72-836. 134p. 1972. lib. bdg. 15.00x (ISBN 0-8371-6405-2, SAJ/). Greenwood.
Jefferson, G. & Smith-Burnett, G. C. The College Library: A Collection of Essays. 1978. 15.00 (ISBN 0-208-01665-1, Linnet). Shoe String.
John Carter Brown Library. Bibliotheca Americana: Catalogue of the John Carter Brown Library in Brown University, Short-Title List of Additions, Books Printed 1471-1700. LC 73-7121. 73p. 1973. text ed. 10.00x (ISBN 0-87057-141-9). U Pr of New Eng.
--Bibliotheca Americana: Catalogue of the John Carter Brown Library in Brown University, Books Printed 1675-1700. LC 73-7120. 516p. 1973. text ed. 50.00x (ISBN 0-87057-140-0, Pub. by Brown U Pr). U Pr of New Eng.
Kroll, Morton, ed. College, University, & Special Libraries of the Pacific Northwest. LC 60-9873. (PNLA Library Development Project Reports: Vol. 3). 320p. 1961. 11.50 (ISBN 0-295-73745-X). U of Wash Pr.
Lyle, Guy R. Administration of the College Library. 4th ed. 1974. 10.00 (ISBN 0-8242-0552-9). Wilson.
McClure, Charles R. Information for Academic Library Decision Making: The Case for Organizational Information Management. LC 79-8412. (Contributions in Librarianship & Information Science; No. 31). (Illus.). xvi, 227p. 1980. lib. bdg. 23.95 (ISBN 0-313-21398-4, MCA/). Greenwood.
McCullough, Kathleen, et al. Approval Plans & Academic Libraries. LC 77-8514. (Neal-Schuman Professional Bk). 1977. lib. bdg. 16.50x (ISBN 0-912700-05-X). Oryx Pr.
McGill University, Blacker - Wood Library of Zoology & Ornithology. A Dictionary Catalogue of the Blacker - Wood Library of Zoology & Ornithology, 9 vols. 6300p. 1966. Set. lib. bdg. 655.00 (ISBN 0-8161-0719-X). G K Hall.
Marchant, Maurice P. Participative Management in Academic Libraries. LC 76-8740. (Contributions in Librarianship & Information Science: No. 16). 320p. 1977. lib. bdg. 18.95 (ISBN 0-8371-8935-7, MPM/). Greenwood.
Merrill, Irving R. & Drob, Harold A. Criteria for Planning the College & University Learning Resources Center. Wallington, Clint, ed. LC 77-2612. 1977. pap. 6.45 (ISBN 0-89240-003-X). Assn Ed Comm Tech.
Miller, William & Rockwood, D. Stephen, eds. College Librarianship. LC 80-25546. 290p. 1981. 15.00 (ISBN 0-8108-1383-1). Scarecrow.
Morrison, Perry D. Career of the Academic Librarian: A Study of the Social Origins, Educational Attainments, Vocational Experience & Personality Characteristics of a Group of American Academic Librarians. LC 68-24079. (A.C.R.L. Monograph Ser.: No. 29). 1969. pap. 4.50x (ISBN 0-8389-3089-1). ALA.
Mount, Ellis. University Science & Engineering Libraries. LC 74-34562. (Contributions in Librarianship & Information Science: No. 15). (Illus.). 214p. 1975. lib. bdg. 17.95 (ISBN 0-8371-7955-6, MSE/). Greenwood.
Oboler, Eli M. Ideas & the University Library: Essays of an Unorthodox Academic Librarian. LC 77-11. (Contributions in Librarianship & Information Science: No. 20). 1977. lib. bdg. 14.95x (ISBN 0-8371-9531-4, OIS/). Greenwood.
Overhage, Carl F. & Harman, R. Joyce, eds. INTREX: The Report of a Planning Conference on Information Transfer Experiments. 1965. 14.50x (ISBN 0-262-15004-2). MIT Pr.
Palmour, Vernon E., et alcompiled by. A Study of the Characteristics, Costs, & Magnitude of Interlibrary Loans in Academic Libraries. LC 70-39344. 1972. lib. bdg. 15.00 (ISBN 0-8371-6340-4, PIL/). Greenwood.
Platt, P. Libraries in Colleges of Education. 2nd ed. 1972. 23.00x (ISBN 0-85365-335-6, Pub. by Lib Assn England). Oryx Pr.
Poole, Herbert, ed. Academic Libraries by the Year 2000: Essays Honoring Jerrold Orne. LC 77-81880. 1977. 18.50 (ISBN 0-8352-0993-8). Bowker.

The Right Wing Collection of the University of Iowa Libraries, 1918-1977: A Guide to the Microform Edition. 175p. 1978. pap. 95.00 (ISBN 0-667-00520-X). Microfilming Corp.
Schad, Jasper & Tanis, Norman E. Problems in Developing Academic Library Collections. LC 72-1944. (Problem-Centered Approaches to Librarianship Ser.). 183p. 1974. 18.50 (ISBN 0-8352-0551-7). Bowker.
Sharma, Hari K. Organization & Administration of College Libraries: India. 1977. text ed. 10.50x (ISBN 0-8426-1011-1). Verry.
Stevens, Norman D., ed. Essays from the New England Academic Librarians' Writing Seminar. LC 80-21502. 230p. 1980. 12.50 (ISBN 0-8108-1365-3). Scarecrow.
Thompson, James. An Introduction to University Library Administration. 3rd ed. (Illus.). 160p. 1979. 18.75 (ISBN 0-208-01352-0, Linnet). Shoe String.
Thomson, Sarah K. Interlibrary Loan Involving Academic Libraries, Acrl. LC 70-124575. (A.C.R.L. Monograph Ser.: No. 32). 1970. pap. text ed. 5.00 (ISBN 0-8389-3010-7). ALA.
Tsuneishi, Warren, et al, eds. Issues in Library Administration. 140p. 1974. 12.50x (ISBN 0-231-03818-6). Columbia U Pr.
University Of Tennessee. Library in the University: University of Tennessee Library Lectures, 1949-1966. (Contributions to Library Literature Ser.: No. 7). 1967. 18.50 (ISBN 0-208-00318-5, Archon). Shoe String.
Wasserman, Paul. Librarian & the Machine. LC 65-25320. 1965. 12.00 (ISBN 0-8103-0164-4). Gale.
Wheeler, Helen R. Community College Library: A Plan for Action. 1965. 14.50 (ISBN 0-208-00232-4). Shoe String.
Wilson, Louis R., et al. The Library in College Instruction. LC 73-7383. 347p. 1973. Repr. of 1951 ed. lib. bdg. 17.75x (ISBN 0-8371-6928-3, WILC). Greenwood.
Young, Harold C. Planning, Programming, Budgeting Systems in Academic Libraries: An Exploratory Study of PPBS in University Libraries Having Membership in the Association of Research Libraries. LC 76-10667. 180p. 1976. 30.00 (ISBN 0-8103-0264-0). Gale.

LIBRARIES, YOUNG PEOPLE'S
see also Libraries, Children's
American Library Association, Young Adult Services Division, Services Statement Development Committee. Directions for Library Service to Young Adults. 30p. 1978. pap. 2.50 (ISBN 0-8389-3204-5). ALA.
Boston Public Library. Young Adult Catalog of the Boston Public Library, 2 vols. 1112p. 1972. Set. lib. bdg. 145.00 (ISBN 0-8161-1028-X). G K Hall.
Ellis, Alec. Library Services for Young People in England & Wales, 1830-1970. 1971. 26.00 (ISBN 0-08-016586-9). Pergamon.
--Library Services for Young People in England & Wales, 1830-1970. 1971. 26.00 (ISBN 0-08-016586-9). Pergamon.
Munson, Amelia H. Ample Field: Books & Young People. 1950. 3.00 (ISBN 0-8389-0008-9). ALA.
YASD Committee, ed. Look, Listen, Explain. 28p. 1975. pap. text ed. 2.00 (ISBN 0-8389-3171-5). ALA.

LIBRARIES AND ADULT EDUCATION
Adams, Herbert B. Seminary Libraries & University Extension. Repr. of 1887 ed. pap. 7.00 (ISBN 0-384-00328-1). Johnson Repr.
Library Association, London. Adult Education in Public Libraries in the Nineteen Eighties. 96p. 1980. pap. text ed. 13.25x (ISBN 0-85365-662-2, Pub by Lib Assn England). Oryx Pr.
Schuster, Marie. The Library-Centered Approach to Learning. LC 76-54328. 1977. 8.95 (ISBN 0-88280-047-7). ETC Pubns.

LIBRARIES AND AFRO-AMERICANS
see Afro-Americans and Libraries

LIBRARIES AND COMMUNITY
see also Public Relations–Libraries
Becker, Carol A. Community Information Service: A Directory of Public Library Involvement. LC 74-620019. (Student Contribution Ser.: No. 5). 1974. pap. 5.00 (ISBN 0-911808-09-4). U of Md Lib Serv.
Bostwick, Arthur E., ed. Library & Society. facs. ed. LC 68-54330. (Essay Index Reprint Ser). 1921. 19.50 (ISBN 0-8369-0227-0). Arno.
Brooks, Jean S. & Reich, David L. The Public Library in Non-Traditional Education. LC 73-21903. (Illus.). 256p. 1974. 10.00 (ISBN 0-88280-008-6). ETC Pubns.
Bundy, Mary L. & Goodstein, Sylvia, eds. Library's Public Revisited. (Student Contribution Ser.: No. 1). 1967. pap. 3.00 (ISBN 0-911808-01-9). U of Md Lib Serv.
Campbell, H. C. Public Libraries in the Urban Metropolitan Setting. (Management of Change Ser.). 298p. 1973. 18.50 (ISBN 0-208-01193-5, Linnet). Shoe String.
Conant, Ralph W. & Molz, R. Kathleen, eds. The Metropolitan Library. 256p. 1973. 17.50x (ISBN 0-262-03041-1). MIT Pr.
Davies, David W. Public Libraries As Culture & Social Centers: The Origin of the Concept. LC 74-8420. 1974. 10.00 (ISBN 0-8108-0738-6). Scarecrow.
Garrison, Guy, ed. Total Community Library Service. LC 73-4310. 1973. pap. 5.00 (ISBN 0-8389-0149-2). ALA.
Gocek, Matilda A. The Tuxedo Park Library: Social Aspects of Growth, 1901-1940. LC 68-58969. (Illus.). 1968. 6.75 (ISBN 0-912526-00-9). Lib Res.
Goldstein, Harold, ed. The Changing Environment for Library Services in the Metropolitan Area. (Allerton Park Institute Ser.: No. 12). 158p. 1966. pap. 4.00x (ISBN 0-87845-007-6). U of Ill Lib Info Sci.
Harrison, Colin. Communication in Library Management. 1981. 12.00x (ISBN 0-902248-05-7, Pub. by AALSED England). State Mutual Bk.
Howard, Edward N. Local Power & the Community Library. LC 78-13493. (Public Library Reporter: No. 18). 1978. pap. 5.00 (ISBN 0-8389-0274-X). ALA.
Kronus, Carol L. & Crowe, Linda, eds. Libraries & Neighborhood Information Centers. LC 78-81002. (Allerton Park Institutes: No. 17). 142p. 1972. 6.00x (ISBN 0-87845-034-3). U of Ill Lib Info Sci.
Library Association-the Working Party on Community Information, ed. Community Information: What Libraries Can Do. 1980. pap. 11.50x (ISBN 0-85365-872-2, Pub. by Lib Assn England). Oryx Pr.
Library Community Services. LC 77-28184. 98p. 1977. 6.00 (ISBN 0-913578-18-5). Inglewood Ca.
McKinney, Eleanor & Baechtold, Marquerite. Libraries & Family Development. (Orig.). 1981. price not set (ISBN 0-208-01856-5, Lib Prof Pubns); pap. price not set (ISBN 0-208-01855-7). Shoe String.
Martin, Lowell. Library Response to Urban Change: A Study of the Chicago Public Library. LC 76-104040. 1969. 8.50 (ISBN 0-8389-0077-1). ALA.
Palmour, Vernon E., et al. A Planning Process for Public Libraries. LC 80-13107. 320p. 1980. pap. 12.00 (ISBN 0-8389-3246-0). ALA.
Wilson, Pauline. Community Elite & the Public Library: Uses of Information in Leadership. LC 76-15336. (Contributions in Librarianship & Information Science: No. 18). 1977. lib. bdg. 16.95 (ISBN 0-8371-9031-2, WCE/). Greenwood.

LIBRARIES AND MOVING-PICTURES
see also Moving-Picture Film Collections
Rehrauer, George. The Film User's Handbook: A Basic Manual for Managing Library Film Services. LC 75-15584. (Illus.). 301p. 1975. 21.50 (ISBN 0-8352-0659-9). Bowker.

LIBRARIES AND NEGROES
This heading discontinued January 1976. See Afro-Americans and Libraries for later materials.
Josey, E. J. What Black Librarians Are Saying. LC 72-5372. 1972. 10.00 (ISBN 0-8108-0530-8). Scarecrow.

LIBRARIES AND NEW LITERATES
Lyman, Helen H. Library Materials in Service to the Adult New Reader. LC 72-11668. 1973. pap. 10.00 (ISBN 0-8389-0147-6). ALA.
--Literacy & the Nations's Libraries. LC 77-4450. 1977. 15.00 (ISBN 0-8389-0244-8). ALA.
--Reading & the Adult New Reader. LC 76-44431. 1977. text ed. 15.00 (ISBN 0-8389-0228-6). ALA.

LIBRARIES AND PICTURES
see also Libraries and Moving-Pictures
Evans, Hilary. The Art of Picture Research: A Guide to Current Practice, Procedure, Techniques & Resources. (Illus.). 33.00 (ISBN 0-7153-7763-9). David & Charles.
--Picture Librarianship. (Outlines of Modern Librarianship Ser.). 1980. text ed. 12.00 (ISBN 0-85157-294-4, Pub. by Bingley England). Shoe String.
Green, Stanford J. Classification & Cataloging of Pictures & Slides. 1980. pap. 3.95 (ISBN 0-89185-197-6). Anthelion Pr.
Ireland, Norma O. The Picture File in School, College & Public Libraries. rev. enl. ed. LC 75-35464. (The Useful Reference Ser. of Library Bks: Vol. 81). 1952. lib. bdg. 9.00x (ISBN 0-87305-081-9). Faxon.
Shaffer, Dale E. The Library Picture File: A Complete System of How to Process & Organize. 1972. pap. 1.00 (ISBN 0-915060-01-9). D E Shaffer.

LIBRARIES AND PUBLISHING
Fang, Josephine R. Modern Publishing & Librarianship. 1980. write for info. (ISBN 0-89664-021-3). K G Saur.
Fry, Bernard M. & White, Herbert S. Publishers & Libraries: The Study of Scholarly & Research Journals. (Illus.). 1976. 18.95 (ISBN 0-669-00886-9). Lexington Bks.
Turow, Joseph G. Getting Books to Children: An Exploration of Publisher-Market Relations. LC 78-24103. 1979. pap. 9.00 (ISBN 0-8389-0276-6). ALA.
Wright, Louis B. Folger Library, Two Decades of Growth: An Informal Account. (Special Publication Ser). 1978. 15.00x (ISBN 0-686-16062-2). Folger Bks.

LIBRARIES AND READERS
see also Fiction in Libraries; Libraries and Adult Education; Library Rules and Regulations
Aldrich, Ella V. Using Books & Libraries. 5th ed. (gr. 9-12). 1967. pap. 5.95 (ISBN 0-13-939223-8). P-H.
Benge, Ronald. Libraries & Cultural Change. 1970. 17.50 (ISBN 0-208-00882-9, Linnet). Shoe String.
Bloomberg, Marty. Introduction to Public Services for Library Technicians. 2nd ed. LC 76-45779. (Library Science Text Ser.). 1977. lib. bdg. 13.50x (ISBN 0-87287-126-6). Libs Unl.
Buckland, Michael K. Book Availability & the Library User. LC 74-8682. 220p. 1975. text ed. 21.00 (ISBN 0-08-017709-3); pap. text ed. 11.50 (ISBN 0-08-018160-0). Pergamon.
Bundy, Mary L. Metropolitan Public Library Users. 1968. pap. 3.50 (ISBN 0-911808-03-5). U of Md Lib Serv.
Collison, Robert L. Library Assistance to Readers. rev. 4th ed. LC 75-141261. (Illus.). 139p. 1972. Repr. of 1963 ed. lib. bdg. 15.00x (ISBN 0-8371-5858-3, COLA). Greenwood.
Compton, Charles H. Who Reads What? facs. ed. LC 69-18923. (Essay Index Reprint Ser). 1934. 12.00 (ISBN 0-8369-0012-X). Arno.
Corcoran, Eileen. Gaining Skills in Using the Library. (Illus.). 1980. pap. 2.50x (ISBN 0-88323-158-1, 247). Richards Pub.
Library Service to the Spanish Speaking. LC 77-22847. 51p. 1977. 5.00 (ISBN 0-913578-16-9). Inglewood Ca.
Santa, Beauel M. & Hardy, Lois L. How to Use the Library. 2nd ed. LC 55-6606. (Illus., Orig.). (gr. 7-12). 1966. text ed. 5.95x (ISBN 0-87015-144-4); pap. text ed. 3.95x (ISBN 0-87015-145-2). Pacific Bks.
Tancer, Jack. Our Reader. (Illus.). 1964. pap. 2.00x (ISBN 0-88323-060-7, 158). Richards Pub.
Vosper, R. G. & Koops, Willem R., eds. Libraries Meet with Their Users, Vol. 15. (IFLA Publications). 1980. write for info. (ISBN 0-89664-115-5). K G Saur.
Whittaker, Kenneth. Using Libraries. LC 64-9555. 6.00 (ISBN 0-8022-1879-2). Philos Lib.
Wyandt, Christine R. A Librarian's Hints for Students. 1980. 5.50 (ISBN 0-682-49487-9). Exposition.

LIBRARIES AND READERS–PROGRAMMED INSTRUCTION
Hopkinson, Shirley L. Instructional Materials for Teaching the Use of the Library. 5th ed. LC 76-369147. 1975. pap. 4.50x (ISBN 0-913860-03-4). Claremont House.

LIBRARIES AND SCHOOLS
see also Books and Reading for Children; Children's Literature (Collections); Libraries, Children's; School Libraries
Cassata, Mary B. & Totten, Herman L., eds. The Administrative Aspects of Education for Librarianship: A Symposium. LC 75-15726. 425p. 1975. 17.50 (ISBN 0-8108-0829-3). Scarecrow.
Hostrop, Richard W. Education Inside the Library Media Center. xiii, 178p. 1973. 15.00 (ISBN 0-208-01324-5, Linnet). Shoe String.
Kuhlthaw. School Librarian's Grade-by-Grade Activities Program. 1981. 22.95x (ISBN 0-87628-744-5). Ctr Appl Res.
Schuster, Marie. The Library-Centered Approach to Learning. LC 76-54328. 1977. 8.95 (ISBN 0-88280-047-7). ETC Pubns.
Trinkner, Charles L., ed. Teaching for Better Use of Libraries. LC 73-99445. (Contributions to Library Literature Ser.: No. 9). 1970. 17.50 (ISBN 0-208-00975-2). Shoe String.

LIBRARIES AND SOCIETY
Benge, Ronald. Cultural Crisis & Libraries in the Third World. 255p. 1979. 17.50 (ISBN 0-208-01668-6, Linnet). Shoe String.
Estabrook, Leigh, ed. Libraries in Post-Industrial Society. LC 77-8928. (A Neal-Schuman Professional Bk). 1977. lib. bdg. 18.50 (ISBN 0-912700-00-9). Oryx Pr.
Gerard, David E., ed. Libraries in Society: A Reader. 1979. 17.50 (ISBN 0-89664-402-2, Pub. by K G Saur). Shoe String.
Hanna, Patricia B. People Make It Happen: The Possibilities of Outreach in Every Phase of Public Library Service. LC 78-5923. 1978. lib. bdg. 10.00 (ISBN 0-8108-1136-7). Scarecrow.
Josey, E. J., ed. Libraries in the Political Process. (Neal-Schuman Professional Books Ser.). 1980. lib. bdg. 18.95x (ISBN 0-912700-25-4). Oryx Pr.
Lancaster, F. Wilfrid, ed. Clinic on Library Applications of Data Processing, Proceedings, 1979: The Role of the Library in an Electronic Society. LC 79-19449. 200p. 1980. 9.00x (ISBN 0-87845-053-X). U of Ill Lib Info Sci.
Library Community Services. LC 77-28184. 98p. 1977. 6.00 (ISBN 0-913578-18-5). Inglewood Ca.
Schnexaydre, Linda & Robins, Kaylyn. Workshops for Jail Library Service: A Planning Manual. 160p. 1981. pap. 15.00 (ISBN 0-8389-3259-2). ALA.

LIBRARIES AND STATE
see also Libraries and Community; Library Legislation
Koos, F. H. State Participation in Public School Library Service. LC 76-176946. (Columbia University. Teachers College. Contributions to Education: No. 265). Repr. 17.50 (ISBN 0-404-55265-X). AMS Pr.
Penna, et al. National Library & Information Services: A Handbook for Planners. 1977. 16.95 (ISBN 0-408-70818-2). Butterworth.
Wellisch, J. B., et al, eds. The Public Library & Federal Policy. LC 73-20302. 1974. lib. bdg. 15.00 (ISBN 0-8371-7334-5, PLF/). Greenwood.

LIBRARIES AND STUDENTS
Guild, Reuben A. The Librarian's Manual: A Treatise on Bibliography, Comprising a Select & Descriptive List of Bibliographical Works; to Which Are Added, Sketches of Public Libraries. LC 70-174942. (Illus.). x, 304p. 1972. Repr. of 1858 ed. 26.00 (ISBN 0-8103-3811-4). Gale.
Penland, P. R. & Mathai, A. Library As a Learning Center. (Books in Library & Information Science Ser.: Vol. 24). 1978. 26.50 (ISBN 0-8247-6750-0). Dekker.
Sears, Donald A. Harbrace Guide to the Library & the Research Paper. 3rd ed. (Orig.). 1973. pap. text ed. 7.95 (ISBN 0-15-535064-1, HC). HarBraceJ.
Sutherland, Zena, ed. Children in Libraries: Patterns of Access to Materials & Services in Schools & Public Libraries. LC 80-53135. (Studies in Library Science). 128p. 1981. lib. bdg. 10.00x (ISBN 0-226-78063-5). U of Chicago Pr.

LIBRARIES AND THE PHYSICALLY HANDICAPPED
Bramley, Gerald. Outreach: Library Services for the Institutionalized, the Elderly, & the Physically Handicapped. 1978. 14.50 (ISBN 0-208-01663-5, Linnet). Shoe String.
Cylke, Frank K., ed. Library Service for the Blind & Physically Handicapped: An International Approach. 106p. 1979. 19.50 (ISBN 3-598-20377-2, Pub. by K G Saur). Shoe String.
Davis, Emmett A. & Davis, Catherine M. Mainstreaming Library Services for Disabled People. LC 80-12280. 208p. 1980. 11.00 (ISBN 0-8108-1305-X). Scarecrow.
Going, Mona E., ed. Hospital Libraries & Work with the Disabled in the Community. 311p. 1981. lib. bdg. 28.75x (ISBN 0-686-73903-5, Pub. by Lib Assn England). Oryx Pr.
Lewis, M. J. Libraries for the Handicapped. 1969. pap. 6.75x (ISBN 0-85365-281-3, Pub. by Lib Assn England). Oryx Pr.
Library Service to the Disadvantaged. Directory of Outreach Services. 640p. 1980. pap. text ed. 25.00 (ISBN 0-8389-3242-8). ALA.
Petrie, Joyce A. Mainstreaming in the Media Center. 1981. lib. bdg. write for info. (ISBN 0-89774-006-8). Oryx Pr.
Thomas, Carol H. & Thomas, James L. Academic Library Facilities & Services for the Handicapped. 900p. 1981. text ed. 55.00x (ISBN 0-912700-95-5). Oryx Pr.
Velleman, Ruth A. Serving Physically Disabled People: An Information Handbook for All Libraries. LC 79-17082. 382p. 1979. 17.50 (ISBN 0-8352-1167-3). Bowker.

LIBRARIES AND THE SOCIALLY HANDICAPPED
Bramley, Gerald. Outreach: Library Services for the Institutionalized, the Elderly, & the Physically Handicapped. 1978. 14.50 (ISBN 0-208-01663-5, Linnet). Shoe String.
Brown, Eleanor F. Library Service to the Disadvantaged. LC 78-162668. (Illus.). 1971. 18.50 (ISBN 0-8108-0437-9). Scarecrow.
Hanna, Patricia B. People Make It Happen: The Possibilities of Outreach in Every Phase of Public Library Service. LC 78-5923. 1978. lib. bdg. 10.00 (ISBN 0-8108-1136-7). Scarecrow.
Martin, William J., ed. Library Services to the Disadvantaged. 185p. 1975. 15.00 (ISBN 0-208-01372-5, Linnet). Shoe String.
Pearlmen, Della. No Choice: Library Services for the Mentally Handicapped. 64p. 1981. lib. bdg. 15.00x (ISBN 0-686-73902-7, Pub. by Lib Assn England). Oryx Pr.

LIBRARIES FOR THE BLIND
see Blind, Libraries for the

LIBRARY ACQUISITIONS
see Acquisitions (Libraries)

LIBRARY ADMINISTRATION
see also Libraries–Trustees
Altman, Ellen. Local Public Library Administration. 2nd ed. 260p. 1981. 20.00 (ISBN 0-8389-0307-X). ALA.

American Library Association. Task Analysis Survey Instrument. 1969. pap. text ed. 1.00 (ISBN 0-8389-5227-5). ALA.
American Library Association, Library Administration Division, Personnel Administration Section. The Personnel Manual: An Outline for Libraries. LC 77-5539. 1977. pap. 3.00 (ISBN 0-8389-0239-1). ALA.
Baeckler, Virginia & Larson, Linda. Go, Pep, & Pop: Two Hundred Fifty Tested Ideas for Lively Libraries. LC 75-20328. 1976. pap. 4.50 (ISBN 0-916444-01-5). UNABASHED Lib.
Bahr, Alice H. Book Theft & Library Security Systems: 1981-82. 2nd ed. LC 77-25284. (Illus.). 156p. 1980. pap. 24.50 (ISBN 0-914236-71-7). Knowledge Indus.
Bailey, Martha J. Supervisory & Middle Managers in Libraries. LC 80-23049. 218p. 1981. 12.00 (ISBN 0-8108-1400-5). Scarecrow.
Boaz, Martha, ed. Current Concepts in Library Management. LC 79-20734. 1979. lib. bdg. 25.00x (ISBN 0-87287-204-1). Libs Unl.
Brophy, Peter, et al, eds. Reader in Operations Research for Libraries. LC 75-8053. (Reader Ser in Librarianship & Information Science: Vol. 19). 1976. 21.00 (ISBN 0-910972-46-X). IHS-PDS.
Brown, Royston. Public Library Administration. (Outlines of Modern Librarianship Ser.). 95p. 12.00 (ISBN 0-89664-419-7). K G Saur.
Bruemmer, Alice. Library Management in Review. 1981. write for info. SLA.
Cargill, Jennifer S. & Alley, Brian. Keeping Track of What You Spend: The Librarian's Guide to Simple Bookkeeping. 1981. write for info. (ISBN 0-912700-79-3). Oryx Pr.
--Library Technical Services Management: Alternatives for Technical Services Librarians. 1981. write for info. (ISBN 0-912700-55-6). Oryx Pr.
--Practical Approval Plan Management. 1980. lib. bdg. 14.00x (ISBN 0-912700-52-1). Oryx Pr.
Chen, Ching-Chin. Applications of Operations Research Models to Libraries: A Case Study in the Use of Monographs in the Francis A. Countway Library of Medicine, Harvard University. LC 75-28210. 192p. 1976. text ed. 20.00x (ISBN 0-262-03056-X). MIT Pr.
Chicago, Illinois Regional Library Council. Directory of Human Resources in Libraries. 2nd ed. 1981. pap. write for info. (ISBN 0-917060-13-X). Ill Regional Lib Coun.
Closurdo, Janette S., ed. Library Management 1979, Vol. 1. 1980. pap. 8.50 (ISBN 0-686-77554-6). SLA.
Conroy, Barbara. Library Staff Development Profile Pages. 52p. (Orig.). 1979. 12.00 (ISBN 0-686-27541-1). B Conroy.
Corbett, E. V. The Fundamentals of Library Organisation & Administration: A Practical Guide. 1978. 31.50x (ISBN 0-85365-540-5, Pub. by Lib Assn England); pap. text ed. 15.50x (ISBN 0-85365-840-4). Oryx Pr.
Creth, Sheila & Duda, Fred. Personnel Management in Libraries. 300p. 1980. 17.95x (ISBN 0-918212-25-1). Neal-Schuman.
Creth, Sheila & Duda, Frederick, eds. Personnel Administration in Libraries. 350p. 1981. 19.95x (ISBN 0-918212-25-1). Neal-Schuman.
Dougherty, Richard M. & Heinritz, Fred. J. Scientific Management of Library Operations. LC 66-13741. 1966. 10.00 (ISBN 0-8108-0132-9). Scarecrow.
Durey, Peter. Staff Management in University & College Libraries. Chandler, C., ed. 144p. 1976. text ed. 16.00 (ISBN 0-08-019718-3). Pergamon.
Emery, Richard. Staff Communication in Libraries. 213p. 1975. 15.00 (ISBN 0-208-01364-4, Linnet). Shoe String.
Gandert, Slade R. Protecting Your Collection: A Handbook, Survey, & Guide for the Security of Rare Books, Manuscripts, Archives, Works of Art, & the Circulating Library Collection. (Library & Archival Security Ser.: No. 4). 192p. 1981. text ed. 19.95 (ISBN 0-917724-78-X). Haworth Pr.
Goldberg, Robert L. A Systems Approach to Library Program Development. LC 76-18157. 1976. 10.00 (ISBN 0-8108-0944-3). Scarecrow.
Goodell, John S. Libraries & Work Sampling. Kemper, Robert E., ed. LC 74-79026. (Challenge to Change - Library Applications of New Concepts Ser.: No. 1). 72p. 1975. pap. 5.00 (ISBN 0-87287-087-1). Libs Unl.
Gore, Daniel, et al, eds. Requiem for the Card Catalog: Management Issues in Automated Cataloging. LC 78-7129. (New Directions in Librarianship: No. 2). 1979. lib. bdg. 18.95 (ISBN 0-313-20608-2, GMI/). Greenwood.
Harrison, Colin. Communication in Library Management. 1981. 12.00x (ISBN 0-902248-05-7, Pub. by AALSED England). State Mutual Bk.
Harvey, Joan. Business Administration for Librarians. 1980. 15.00 (ISBN 0-85157-174-3). K G Saur.
Heintze, Ingeborg. Organization of the Small Public Library. 1963. pap. 2.50 (ISBN 92-3-100523-5, U442, UNESCO). Unipub.
Hicks, Warren B. & Tillin, Alma M., eds. Managing Multimedia Libraries. LC 76-49116. 1977. 16.25 (ISBN 0-8352-0628-9). Bowker.
Hoadley, Irene B. & Clark, Alice S., eds. Quantitative Methods in Librarianship: Standards, Research, Management. LC 73-149962. (Contributions in Librarianship & Information Science: No. 4). 256p. 1972. lib. bdg. 17.95 (ISBN 0-8371-6061-8, HOQ/). Greenwood.
Holroyd, Gileon, ed. Studies in Library Management, Vol. 2. (Illus.). 167p. 1975. 12.50 (ISBN 0-208-01357-1, Linnet). Shoe String.
--Studies in Library Management, Vol. 3. 176p. (Orig.). 1976. 12.50 (ISBN 0-208-01526-4, Linnet). Shoe String.
--Studies in Library Management, Vol. 4. 1977. 15.00 (ISBN 0-208-01547-7, Linnet). Shoe String.
Hubbard, William. Stack Management: A Practical Guide to Shelving & Maintaining Collections. LC 80-28468. 110p. 1981. pap. 7.00 (ISBN 0-8389-0319-3). ALA.
Jefferson, George. Public Library Administration. 2nd ed. (Examination Guide Ser). 1969. 12.50 (ISBN 0-208-00877-2, Archon). Shoe String.
--Public Library Administration. 1966. 4.75 (ISBN 0-8022-0796-0). Philos Lib.
Jenkins, Harold R. The Management of a Public Library. Stueart, Robert D., ed. LC 76-13957. (Foundations in Library & Information Science: Vol. 8). 1980. lib. bdg. 32.50 (ISBN 0-89232-038-9). Jai Pr.
Kies, Cosette. Problems in Library Public Relations. LC 74-4062. (Problem-Centered Approaches to Librarianship Ser.). 179p. 1974. 18.50 (ISBN 0-8352-0678-5). Bowker.
Lock, R. N. Library Administration. 3rd ed. 200p. 1973. 10.95x (ISBN 0-8464-0566-0). Beekman Pubs.
Lock, R. Northwood, ed. Manual of Library Economy. 1977. 22.50 (ISBN 0-208-01538-8, Linnet). Shoe String.
Lock, Reginald N. Library Administration. 1965. 4.75 (ISBN 0-8022-0985-8). Philos Lib.
Lowell, Mildred H. Library Management Cases. LC 75-23077. 1975. 10.00 (ISBN 0-8108-0845-5). Scarecrow.
--The Management of Libraries & Information Centers, 3 vols. Incl. Vol. 1. The Case Method in Teaching Library Management. 10.00 (ISBN 0-8108-0089-6); Vol. 2. The Process of Managing: Syllabus & Cases. 12.00 (ISBN 0-8108-0090-X); Vol. 4. Role Playing & Other Management Cases. 1971. 16.50 (ISBN 0-8108-0424-7). LC 68-12642. (Illus.). 1968. Scarecrow.
Lundy, Kathryn R. Women View Librarianship: Nine Perspectives. LC 80-23611. (ACRL Publications in Librarianship: No. 41). 108p. 1980. pap. 7.00 (ISBN 0-8389-3251-7). ALA.
Lyle, Guy R. Administration of the College Library. 4th ed. 1974. 10.00 (ISBN 0-8242-0552-9). Wilson.
McClure, Charles R., ed. Planning for Library Services: A Guide to Utilizing Planning Methods for Library Management. (Journal of Library Administration Ser.: Vol. 2, No. 2). 1981. 19.95 (ISBN 0-917724-84-4, B84). Haworth Pr.
Maloney, R. Kay, ed. Personnel Development in Libraries. (Issues in Library & Information Sciences: No. 3). 1977. pap. text ed. 6.00 (ISBN 0-8135-0843-6). Rutgers U Slis.
Martin, Murray S. Budgetary Control in Academic Libraries, Vol. 5. LC 76-5648. (Foundations in Library & Information Science Ser.). 1978. lib. bdg. 32.50 (ISBN 0-89232-010-9). Jai Pr.
Moore, N. Manpower Planning in Libraries. (A Library Association Management Pamphlet Ser.). 1980. pap. 8.95x (ISBN 0-85365-532-4, Lib Assn England). Oryx Pr.
Myers, Gerald E. Insurance Manual for Libraries. LC 77-24524. 1977. pap. 5.00 (ISBN 0-8389-0236-7). ALA.
Nyren, Dorothy, ed. Community Service. LC 77-137361. (Public Library Reporter: No. 16). 1970. pap. 2.00 (ISBN 0-8389-3117-0). ALA.
Palmour, Vernon E., et al. A Planning Process for Public Libraries. LC 80-13107. 320p. 1980. pap. 12.00 (ISBN 0-8389-3246-0). ALA.
Phillips, B. J., et al. Public Libraries: Legislation, Administration, & Finance. 1977. pap. text ed. 8.65x (ISBN 0-85365-750-5, Pub. by Lib Assn England). Oryx Pr.
Plate, Kenneth H. Management Personnel in Libraries. 1970. 7.95x (ISBN 0-685-03095-4). Am Faculty Pr.
Pratt, Allan D. The Information of the Image. (Libraries & Librarianship Ser.). 300p. 1981. 15.00 (ISBN 0-89391-055-4). Ablex Pub.
Renford, Beverly & Hendrickson, Linnea. Bibliographic Instruction: A Handbook. LC 80-12300. 192p. 1980. pap. 14.95x (ISBN 0-918212-24-3). Neal-Schuman.
Reynolds, Linda & Barrett, Stephen. Library Signs & Guiding: A Practical Guide to Design & Production. 120p. 1981. 32.50 (ISBN 0-208-01927-8, Linnet). Shoe String.
Rizzo, John R. Management for Librarians: Fundamentals & Issues. LC 79-8950. (Contributions in Librarianship & Information Science: No. 33). (Illus.). xvii, 339p. 1980. lib. bdg. 35.00 (ISBN 0-313-21990-7, RML/). Greenwood.
Rochell, Carlton, ed. Wheeler & Goldhor's Practical Administration of Public Libraries. rev. ed. LC 79-3401. (Illus.). 480p. 1981. 27.50 (ISBN 0-06-013601-4, HarpT). Har-Row.
Rogers, Rutherford D. & Weber, David C. University Library Administration. (Illus.). 1971. 20.00 (ISBN 0-8242-0417-4). Wilson.
Setty, K. Umapathy. Problems in Library Management. 1976. 10.50 (ISBN 0-7069-0439-7). Intl Bk Dist.
--Problems in Library Management for Developing Countries. 240p. 1976. 14.00x (ISBN 0-7069-0439-7). Intl Pubns Serv.
Shaffer, Dale E. A Guide to Writing Library Job Descriptions: Examples Covering Major Work Areas. 49p. 1981. pap. 4.25 (ISBN 0-915060-17-5). D E Shaffer.
--Management Concepts for Improving Libraries: A Guide for the Professional Librarian. 1979. pap. text ed. 3.95 (ISBN 0-915060-14-0). D E Shaffer.
Shaffer, Kenneth R. Decision Making: A Seminar in Public Library Management. LC 70-150395. 1971. pap. 12.50 (ISBN 0-208-01207-9, Linnet). Shoe String.
Shimmon, Ross. A Reader in Library Management. 216p. 1976. 13.50 (ISBN 0-208-01378-4, Linnet). Shoe String.
Shuman, Bruce A. The River Bend Casebook: Problems in Public Library Service. 1981. pap. text ed. 18.00 (ISBN 0-912700-57-2). Oryx Pr.
Steele, Colin, ed. Steady-State, Zero Growth & the Academic Library: A Collection of Essays. 1978. 12.50 (ISBN 0-208-01680-5, Linnet). Shoe String.
Stevens, Rolland E., ed. Supervision of Employees in Libraries. LC 79-10860. (Allerton Park Institute Ser: No. 24). 113p. 1979. 9.00 (ISBN 0-87845-051-3). U of Ill Lib Info Sci.
Strauss, Lucille J., et al. Scientific & Technical Libraries: Their Organization & Administration. 2nd ed. LC 71-173679. 450p. 1972. 30.95 (ISBN 0-471-83312-6, Pub. by Wiley-Interscience). Wiley.
Stueart, Robert D. & Eastlick, John T. Library Management. 2nd ed. LC 80-22895. (Library Science Text Ser.). 292p. 1981. text ed. 25.00x (ISBN 0-87287-241-6); pap. text ed. 16.50x (ISBN 0-87287-243-2). Libs Unl.
--Library Management. LC 76-49568. (Library Science Text Ser.). 1977. lib. bdg. 15.00x (ISBN 0-87287-127-4). Libs Unl.
Thompson, James. An Introduction to a University Library Administration. 3rd rev. ed. 256p. 1979. 18.75 (ISBN 0-85157-288-X, Pub. by Bingley England). Shoe String.
Trehan, G. L. Administration & Organization of College Libraries in India. 252p. 1969. 8.25x (ISBN 0-8426-1571-7). Verry.
Tunley, M. Library Structures & Staffing Systems. (Management Pamphlet Ser.). 1979. pap. 9.25x (ISBN 0-85365-771-8, Pub. by Lib Assn England). Oryx Pr.
Urquhart, J. A. & Urquhart, N. C. Relegation & Stock Control in Libraries. 1976. 27.50 (ISBN 0-85362-162-4, Oriel). Routledge & Kegan.
Van Zant, Nancy, ed. Personnel Policies in Libraries. LC 80-11734. 334p. 1980. 19.95x (ISBN 0-918212-26-X). Neal-Schuman.
Vaughan, Anthony, ed. Studies in Library Management, Vol. 5. 176p. 1979. 14.00 (ISBN 0-89664-400-6). K G Saur.
Wasserman, Paul, ed. Reader in Library Administration. Bundy, Mary Lee. LC 68-28324. (Reader Ser. in Library & Information Science: Vol. 1). 1969. 17.00 (ISBN 0-910972-16-8). IHS-PDS.
Wilson, A. Planning Approach to Library Management. (Management Pamphlet Ser.). 1979. pap. text ed. 8.95x (ISBN 0-85365-522-7, Pub. by Lib Assn England). Oryx Pr.
Withers, E. N. Standards for Library Service: An International Survey. (Documentation, Libraries & Archives, Studies & Research Ser., No. 6). 421p. (Orig.). 1974. pap. 19.75 (ISBN 92-3-101177-4, U637, UNESCO). Unipub.
Young, Harold C. Planning, Programming, Budgeting Systems in Academic Libraries: An Exploratory Study of PPBS in University Libraries Having Membership in the Association of Research Libraries. LC 76-10667. 180p. 1976. 30.00 (ISBN 0-8103-0264-0). Gale.

LIBRARY ADULT EDUCATION
see Libraries and Adult Education

LIBRARY ADVERTISING
see Advertising–Libraries

LIBRARY ARCHITECTURE

Baumann, Charles H. The Influence of Angus Snead MacDonald & the Snead Bookstack on Library Architecture. LC 74-171928. (Illus.). 1972. 11.00 (ISBN 0-8108-0390-9). Scarecrow.
Clark, John W. Care of Books: An Essay on the Development of Libraries. 1973. Repr. of 1901 ed. lib. bdg. 35.00 (ISBN 0-8414-3502-2). Folcroft.
Holt, Raymond M., ed. Architectural Strategy for Change: Remodeling & Expanding for Contemporary Public Library Needs. LC 76-7965. 162p. 1976. pap. text ed. 12.50 (ISBN 0-8389-0210-3). ALA.
Library Buildings Institute And Alta Workshop - Detroit - 1965. Libraries: Building for the Future: Proceedings. Shaw, Robert J., ed. LC 67-23001. (Illus.). 1967. pap. 5.00 (ISBN 0-8389-0035-6). ALA.
Library Buildings Institute, San Francisco, June, 1967. Library Buildings, Innovation for Changing Needs: Proceedings. LC 73-39011. (Illus.). 302p. 1972. pap. 10.00 (ISBN 0-8389-3132-4). ALA.
Lushington, Nolan & Mills, Willis N., Jr. Libraries Designed for Users: A Planning Handbook. (Illus.). 1980. 24.50 (ISBN 0-208-01888-3, Lib Prof Pubns). Shoe String.
Mason, Ellsworth. Mason on Library Buildings. LC 80-12029. 348p. 1980. 25.00 (ISBN 0-8108-1291-6). Scarecrow.
Miletich, John J. Employee Absenteeism in Both the Public & Private Sectors: An Annotated Bibliography to 1979. (Public Administration Ser.: Bibliographies: P-639). 53p. 1981. pap. 8.25 (ISBN 0-686-28985-4). Vance Biblios.
Morris, John. Managing the Library Fire Risk. 2nd ed. LC 78-22603. (Illus.). 1979. 14.00 (ISBN 0-9602278-1-4). U Cal Risk Management.
Orr, J. M. Designing Library Buildings for Activity. (Grafton Books on Library Science). 1977. lib. bdg. 16.00x (ISBN 0-233-96230-1). Westview.
Pater, Alan F. & Pater, Jason R., eds. The Great Libraries of America---A Pictorial History. Date not set. 35.00 (ISBN 0-917734-03-3). Monitor.
Schell, Hal B., ed. Reader on the Library Building. LC 73-93967. (Reader Ser in Librarianship & Information Science: Vol. 15). (Illus.). 1975. 22.00 (ISBN 0-910972-11-7). IHS-PDS.
Thompson, Anthony, ed. National Library Buildings. 144p. 1975. 15.00 (ISBN 3-7940-4422-3, Pub. K G Saur). Shoe String.
Thompson, Godfrey. Planning & Design of Library Buildings. 2nd ed. LC 77-137. (Illus.). 1977. 27.50 (ISBN 0-89397-019-0). Nichols Pub.
Ward, H., ed. New Library Buildings: Nineteen Seventy-Four. 1974. pap. 22.50x (ISBN 0-85365-397-6, Pub. by Lib Assn England). Oryx Pr.
--New Library Buildings: Nineteen Seventy-Six. 1976. pap. 36.00x (ISBN 0-85365-089-6, Pub. by Lib Assn England). Oryx Pr.
Weis, Ina J. The Design of Library Areas & Buildings. (Architecture Ser.: Bibliography: A-413). 80p. 1981. pap. 12.00 (ISBN 0-686-28984-6). Vance Biblios.

LIBRARY ASSOCIATION, LONDON

Conference Proceedings: Library Association National Conference, 1976. 1976. Scarborough. 7.75x (ISBN 0-85365-199-X, Pub. by Lib Assn England). Oryx Pr.
Conference Proceedings: Library Association National Conference, 1977. 1977. London Centenary. 7.75x (ISBN 0-85365-820-X, Pub. by Lib Assn England). Oryx Pr.
Library Association Yearbooks, 1975. 1975. pap. 19.75x (ISBN 0-85365-487-5, Pub. by Lib Assn England). Oryx Pr.
Library Association Yearbooks 1976. 1976. pap. 19.75x (ISBN 0-85365-398-4, Pub. by Lib Assn England). Oryx Pr.
Library Association Yearbooks 1977. 1977. pap. 19.75x (ISBN 0-85365-309-7, Pub. by Lib Assn England). Oryx Pr.
Library Association Yearbooks 1978. 1978. pap. 19.75x (ISBN 0-85365-880-3, Pub. by Lib Assn England). Oryx Pr.
Library Association Yearbooks 1979. 1979. pap. 19.75x (ISBN 0-85365-751-3, Pub. by Lib Assn England). Oryx Pr.
Munford, W. A. History of the Library Association, 1877 to 1977. 1976. lib. bdg. 17.65x (ISBN 0-85365-488-3, Pub. by Lib Assn England); pap. text ed. 6.95x (ISBN 0-85365-600-2). Oryx Pr.

LIBRARY ASSOCIATIONS

Cambio, Edward P. The International Federation of Library Associations & Institutions: A Selected List of References. 51p. 1977. 10.25 (ISBN 3-7940-4431-2, Pub. by K G Saur). Shoe String.
Conference Proceedings: Library Association National Conference, 1978. 1978. Brighton. lib. bdg. 7.75 (ISBN 0-85365-601-0, Pub. by Lib Assn England). Oryx Pr.

Davis, Donald G., Jr. The Association of American Library Schools, 1915-1968: An Analytical History. LC 73-16014. 1974. 15.00 (ISBN 0-8108-0642-8). Scarecrow.

LIBRARY AUTOMATION
see Libraries-Automation

LIBRARY BOARDS
see Libraries-Trustees

LIBRARY BUILDINGS
see Library Architecture

LIBRARY CATALOGS
see also Catalogs, Card; Catalogs, Classified; Catalogs, Dictionary; Catalogs, Subject; Catalogs, Union

Alpine Association Library, Munich. Kataloge der Alpenvereins Bucherei: Catalogs of the Alpine Association Library, 2 pts. Incl. Pt. 1. Autorenkatalog,Author Catalog, 3 vols. 265.00 (ISBN 0-8161-0849-8); Pt. 2. Sachkatalog,Subject Catalog, 3 vols. 215.00 (ISBN 0-8161-0101-9). 1970. G K Hall.

American Journal of Nursing, New York. Catalog of the Sophia F. Palmer Memorial Library of the American Journal of the Nursing Coompany, 2 vols. 1973. Set. lib. bdg. 180.00 (ISBN 0-8161-1066-2). G K Hall.

American Library Association. Book Catalogs Committee, RTSD. Guidelines for Book Catalogs. LC 77-1248. 1977. pap. text ed. 3.50 (ISBN 0-8389-3190-1). ALA.

American School of Classical Studies at Athens. Catalogue of the Gennadius Library. American School of Classical Studies at Athens, First Supplement. 1973. lib. bdg. 120.00 (ISBN 0-8161-0835-8). G K Hall.

Arctic Institute of North America, Montreal. Catalogue of the Library of the Arctic Institute of North America, Third Supplement. 1980. lib. bdg. 395.00 (ISBN 0-8161-1162-6). G K Hall.

Barnett, L. D. Panjabi Printed Books in the British Museum: A Supplementary Catalogue. 132p. 1981. 40.00x (ISBN 0-7141-0624-0, Pub. by Brit Lib England). State Mutual Bk.

Baxtresser, Betty, ed. Catalogs of the Bureau of the Census Library: First Supplement, 5 vols. (Library Catalogs Bib.Guides). 1979. Set. lib. bdg. 595.00 (ISBN 0-8161-0296-1). G K Hall.

Benson, Nettie L. Catalogue of "Martin Fierro" Materials in the University of Texas Library. LC 72-97224. (Ilas Guides & Bibliographies Ser.: No. 6). 147p. 1973. pap. 4.50x (ISBN 0-292-71009-7). U of Tex Pr.

Berman, Sanford. Joy of Cataloging. 1981. lib. bdg. 22.50 (ISBN 0-912700-51-3); pap. 18.50 (ISBN 0-912700-94-7). Oryx Pr.

Bibliotheque Forney. Davis Catalog of the Catalogs of Sales of Art, 2 vols. 1972. Set. lib. bdg. 190.00 (ISBN 0-8161-0962-1). G K Hall.

Birkby, Elizabeth & Fitch, Canon J.compiled by. Suffolk Parochial Libraries: A Catalogue. 1977. lib. bdg. 31.50 (ISBN 0-7201-0704-0, Pub. by Mansell England). Merrimack Bk Serv.

Birrell, T. A. The Library of John Morris: The Reconstruction of a Seventeenth-Century Collection. 108p. 1980. 50.00x (ISBN 0-7141-0365-9, Pub. by Brit Lib England). State Mutual Bk.

Bishop, William W. Practical Handbook of Modern Library Cataloging. (Library Science Ser.). 1980. lib. bdg. 59.95 (ISBN 0-8490-3179-6). Gordon Pr.

Boston Public Library. Canadian Manuscripts in the Boston Public Library: A Descriptive Catalog. 1971. lib. bdg. 65.00 (ISBN 0-8161-0930-3). G K Hall.

Boston University Libraries. Index to the Classed Catalog of the Boston University Libraries, 2 vols. 3rd. rev ed. 1187p. 1972. Set. lib. bdg. 150.00 (ISBN 0-8161-1029-8). G K Hall.

British Library General Catalogue of Printed Books to 1975, 360 vols. new ed. 1980. Set. 24,480.00 (ISBN 3-5983-0200-2, Pub. by K G Saur). Gale.

Bromley, John, ed. The Clockmakers' Library: The Catalogue of the Books & Manuscripts in the Library of the Worshipful Company of Clockmakers. (Illus.). 136p. 1977. 52.50x (ISBN 0-85667-033-2, Pub. by Sotheby Parke Bernet England). Biblio Dist.

Brown, P. A. Modern British & American Private Presses (1850-1965) 216p. 1980. 60.00x (ISBN 0-7141-0367-5, Pub. by Brit Lib England). State Mutual Bk.

Buenos Aires, Universidad Nacional, Facultad de Derecho y Ciencias Sociales Biblioteca. Catalogo Metodico De la Biblioteca De la Facultad De Derecho y Ciencias Sociales De Buenos Aires Seguidode De una Table Alfabetica De Autores. 1976. lib. bdg. 134.95 (ISBN 0-8490-1584-7). Gordon Pr.

Cashel Diocesan Library. County Tipperary, Republic of Ireland. Catalogue of the Cashel Diocesan Library. 1973. 95.00 (ISBN 0-8161-1065-4). G K Hall.

Catalog of Special & Private Presses in the Rare Book Division, the Research Libraries of the New York Public Library, 2 vols. (Printed Book Catalogs). 1978. Set. lib. bdg. 170.00 (ISBN 0-8161-0097-7). G K Hall.

Catalog of the Kristine Mann Library of the Analytical Psychology Club of New York, Inc. (Reference Catalog Ser.). 1978. lib. bdg. 190.00 (ISBN 0-8161-0085-3). G K Hall.

Catalogue of Books in the Hirsch Library. 548p. 1980. 90.00x (ISBN 0-7141-0115-X, Pub. by Brit Lib England). State Mutual Bk.

Catalogues of the Library of Deutsches Museum, Munich, 20 vols. Set. 5645.00 (ISBN 0-685-96558-9). K G Saur.

Catalogues of the Library of the Marine Biological Association of the United Kingdom. Catalogues of the Library of the Marine Biological Association of the United Kingdom. 1978. lib. bdg. 1250.00 (ISBN 0-8161-0076-4). G K Hall.

Chibbett, D. G., et al. A Descriptive Catalogue of the Pre-1868 Japanese Books, Manuscripts, & Prints in the Library of the School of Oriental & African Studies. (Illus.). 192p. (Annotated entries). 1976. 34.50x (ISBN 0-19-713586-2). Oxford U Pr.

Columbia University. Catalog of the Avery Memorial Architectural Library, Columbia University, Second Supplement, 4 vols. 1975. Set. lib. bdg. 420.00 (ISBN 0-8161-1070-0). G K Hall.

--Catalog of the Avery Memorial Architectural Library, First Supplement, 4 vols. 3166p. 1973. Set. lib. bdg. 420.00 (ISBN 0-8161-0780-7). G K Hall.

--Dictionary Catalog of the Library of the School of Library Service, 1st Suppl, 4 vols. 1976. Set. lib. bdg. 460.00 (ISBN 0-8161-1166-9). G K Hall.

--Dictionary Catalog of the Teachers College Library, First Supplement, 5 vols. 1971. Set. lib. bdg. 525.00 (ISBN 0-8161-0958-3). G K Hall.

--Dictionary Catalog of the Teachers College Library, Second Supplement, 2 vols. 1973. Set. lib. bdg. 260.00 (ISBN 0-8161-1039-5). G K Hall.

Cornell University, Martin P. Catherwood Library. Cumulation of the Library Catalog Supplements of the New York State School of Industrial and Labor Relations, First Supplement. 1977. lib. bdg. 120.00 (ISBN 0-8161-0055-1). G K Hall.

Cornell University, New York State School of Industrial & Labor Relations. Library Catalog of the Martin P. Catherwood Library of the New York State School of Industrial & Labor Relations, Sixth Supplement. 1973. lib. bdg. 120.00 (ISBN 0-8161-1072-7). G K Hall.

Davis, Richard C. & Miller, Linda A., eds. Guide to the Cataloged Collections in the Manuscript Department of the William R. Perkins Library, Duke University. LC 79-28688. 1005p. 1980. lib. bdg. 47.50 (ISBN 0-87436-299-7). Abc-Clio.

Diaz, Albert, ed. Microforms & Library Catalogs: A Reader. (Microform Review Series in Library Micrographics Management: No. 3). 1978. 20.95x (ISBN 0-913672-16-5). Microform Rev.

Dolby, J. L. Evaluation of the Utility & Cost of Computerized Library Catalogues. 1969. 18.50x (ISBN 0-262-04023-9). MIT Pr.

Doucet, Jacques. Cataloguede Manuscritsde la Bibliotheque Litteraire Jacques Doucet, Paris, France. 1972. 94.00 (ISBN 0-8161-0950-8). G K Hall.

Dryander, Jonas. Catalogus Bibliothecae Historico-Naturalis Josephi Banks, 5 vols. Incl. Vol. 1. Scriptores Generalis. Repr. of 1798 ed. 28.00 (ISBN 0-384-13081-X); Vol. 2. Zoologici. Repr. of 1796 ed. 43.00 (ISBN 0-384-13082-8); Botanici. Repr. of 1797 ed. 54.00 (ISBN 0-384-13083-6); Mineralogi. Repr. of 1799 ed. 32.50 (ISBN 0-384-13084-4); Supplementum & Index Auctorum. 20.00 (ISBN 0-384-13085-2); Index Auctorum. 18.25 (ISBN 0-685-27510-8). 1796-1800. Repr. Set. 172.50 (ISBN 0-384-13086-0). Johnson Repr.

Ecole Biblique et Archeologique Francaise. Jerusalem. Catalogue De la Bibliotheque De L'ecole Biblique et Archeologique Francaise (Catalog of the Library of the French Biblical & Archaeological School, 13 vols. 1975. lib. bdg. 1350.00 (ISBN 0-8161-1154-5). G K Hall.

Engineering Societies Library, New York. Classed Subject Catalog of the Engineering Societies Library, New York City, 8th Supplement. 1972. lib. bdg. 105.00 (ISBN 0-8161-0982-6). G K Hall.

Folger Shakespeare Library, Washington, D. C. Catalog of Manuscripts of the Folger Shakespeare Library, 3 vols. (Library Catalogs Ser.). 1970. Set. lib. bdg. 215.00 (ISBN 0-8161-0888-9). G K Hall.

--Catalog of Printed Books of the Folger Shakespeare Library, 28 vols. 1970. Set. lib. bdg. 1845.00 (ISBN 0-8161-0887-0). G K Hall.

Fondation Nationale des Sciences Politiques. Bibliographie Courante d'Articles de Periodiques Posterieurs a 1944 sur les Problemes Politiques. Economiques et Sociaux, 17 Vols. 1968. Set. lib. bdg. 1420.00 (ISBN 0-8161-0769-6); first suppl., 1969, 2 vols. 215.00 (ISBN 0-8161-0803-X); second suppl., 1970, 2 vols. 215.00 (ISBN 0-8161-0917-6); third suppl., 1971, 2 vols. 215.00 (ISBN 0-8161-0981-8); fourth suppl., 1972, 2 vols. 215.00 (ISBN 0-8161-1056-5). G K Hall.

Fortescue, G. K. & Brodhurst, A. C. French Revolutionary Collections in the British Library. 88p. 1980. 40.00x (ISBN 0-904654-21-4, Pub. by Brit Lib England). State Mutual Bk.

Gaur, Albertine. Catalogue of Malayalam Books in the British Museum. 324p. 1981. 150.00 (ISBN 0-7141-0623-2, Pub. by Brit Lib England). State Mutual Bk.

Gore, Daniel, et al, eds. Requiem for the Card Catalog: Management Issues in Automated Cataloging. LC 78-7129. (New Directions in Librarianship: No. 2). 1979. lib. bdg. 18.95 (ISBN 0-313-20608-2, GMI/). Greenwood.

Grenoble Catalog of Printed Books to 1900, 12 vols. (Illus.). 12000p. (Fr.). 1981. Set. 2400.00 (ISBN 3-598-10160-0, Pub. by K G Saur). Gale.

Harvard University, Graduate School of Business Administration. Subject Catalog of the Baker Library, 10 vols. 1971. Set. 1020.00 (ISBN 0-8161-0186-8). G K Hall.

Harvard University, Gray Herbarium. Gray Herbarium Index, 10 Vols. 1968. Set. lib. bdg. 675.00 (ISBN 0-8161-0754-8). G K Hall.

Harvard University Library. Reference Collections Shelved in the Reading Room & Acquisitions Department: Classified & Alphabetical Listings. LC 77-128715. (Widener Library Shelflist Ser: No. 33). 1971. 10.00x (ISBN 0-674-75201-5). Harvard U Pr.

Hoffman, Herbert H. What Happens in Library Filing? (Illus.). 176p. 1976. 12.00 (ISBN 0-208-01557-4, Linnet). Shoe String.

Information Science & Automation Institutes on the Catalog, 1975 & 1977. The Nature & Future of the Catalog: Proceedings. Freedman, Maurice J., ed. Malinconico, S. Michael. (Neal-Schuman Professional Bk.). 1979. lib. bdg. 19.50x (ISBN 0-912700-08-4). Oryx Pr.

Institute for World Economics, Kiel, Germany. Catalog of the Library of the Institute for World Economics, 7 pts. Incl. Pt. 1. Bibliographical Catalog of Persons, 30 vols. 1966. Set. 2615.00 (ISBN 0-8161-0677-0); Pt. 2. Catalog of Administrative Authorities, 10 vols. 1967. Set. 825.00 (ISBN 0-8161-0189-2); Pt. 3. Catalog of Corporations, 13 vols. 1967. Set. 1100.00 (ISBN 0-8161-0190-6); Pt. 4. Regional Catalog, 52 vols. 1967. Set. 4400.00 (ISBN 0-8161-0191-4); Pt. 5. Subject Catalog, 83 vols. 1968. Set. 5775.00 (ISBN 0-8161-0192-2); Pt. 6. Shelf List of Periodical Holdings, 6 vols. 4734p. 1968. Set. 550.00 (ISBN 0-8161-0193-0); Pt. 7. Title Catalog, 13 vols. 1968. Set. 1100.00 (ISBN 0-8161-0194-9). G K Hall.

Jayne, Sears & Johnson, Francis R., eds. The Lumley Library: The Catalogue of 1609. 386p. 1980. 50.00x (ISBN 0-7141-0224-5, Pub. by Brit Lib England). State Mutual Bk.

Johann Gottfried Herder-Instituts, Marburg, Lahn. Alphabetischer Katalog der Bibliothek, 5 Vols. 1964. Set. lib. bdg. 380.00 (ISBN 0-8161-0698-3); First Suppl. 1971. 2 Vol. Set. lib. bdg. 215.00 (ISBN 0-8161-0808-0). G K Hall.

Junior High School Library Catalog. 4th ed. 1980. 62.00 (ISBN 0-8242-0652-5). Wilson.

Kynaston, W. H., compiled by. Catalogue of Foreign Books in the Chapter Library of Lincoln Cathedral. 82p. 1972. Repr. of 1937 ed. 8.00x (ISBN 0-87471-351-X). Rowman.

Lewin, Evans. Subject Catalogue of the Library of the Royal Empire Society 1930-1937, 4 vols. Incl. Vol. 1. British Empire. 850p. Repr. of 1930 ed; Vol. 2. Australia, New Zealand, South Pacific, Antarctic. 770p. Repr. of 1931 ed; Vol. 3. Canada, Newfoundland, West Indies, Colonial America. 830p. Repr. of 1932 ed; Vol. 4. Mediterranean Colonies, Middle East, Indian Empire, Far East. 820p. Repr. of 1937 ed. 1967. 40.00 ea.; 160.00x set (ISBN 0-8464-0894-5). Beekman Pubs.

Library Catalog of the Martin P. Catherwood Library of the New York State School of Industrial & Labor Relations: Second Supplement to the Cumulation. (Reference Publications). 1978. lib. bdg. 140.00 (ISBN 0-8161-0093-4). G K Hall.

Library of Congress Catalog of Printed Cards. Incl. General Works, 6 vols. 180.00 (ISBN 0-686-11717-4); Philosophy, Psychology, 4 vols. 120.00 (ISBN 0-686-11718-2); Religion, 8 vols. 240.00 (ISBN 0-686-11719-0); History, 4 vols. 120.00 (ISBN 0-686-11720-4); History, 12 vols. 360.00 (ISBN 0-686-11721-2); American History, 10 vols. 300.00 (ISBN 0-686-11722-0); Geography Anthropology, 2 vols. 60.00 (ISBN 0-686-11723-9); Social Science, 24 vols. 720.00 (ISBN 0-686-11724-7); Political Science, 10 vols. 300.00 (ISBN 0-686-11725-5); Law, 2 vols. 60.00 (ISBN 0-686-11726-3); Education, 6 vols. 180.00 (ISBN 0-686-11727-1); Music, 8 vols. 240.00 (ISBN 0-686-11728-X); Fine Arts, 4 vols. 120.00 (ISBN 0-686-11729-8); Language & Literature, 24 vols. 720.00 (ISBN 0-686-11730-1); Science, 12 vols. 360.00 (ISBN 0-686-11731-X); Medicine, 4 vols. 120.00 (ISBN 0-686-11732-8); Agriculture, 6 vols. 180.00 (ISBN 0-686-11733-6); Technology, 14 vols. 420.00 (ISBN 0-686-11734-4); Military Science, 2 vols. 60.00 (ISBN 0-686-11735-2); Naval Science, 2 vols. 60.00 (ISBN 0-686-11736-0); Bibliography, 8 vols. 240.00 (ISBN 0-686-11737-9). Biblio Pr.

Lista De Encabezamientos De Materia Para Bibliotecas, 3 Vols. y Suplementos-1967. (Manuales Del Bibliotecario Ser: No. 6). (Span.). 1977. Set. 25.00 (ISBN 0-686-76837-X). Vol. 1 (ISBN 0-8270-3105-X). Vol. II (ISBN 0-8270-3115-7). Supl. 1 (ISBN 0-8270-3125-4). Supl. 2 (ISBN 0-8270-3130-0). OAS.

Los Angeles Public Library. Catalog of the Police Library of the Los Angeles Public Library, 2 vols. 1972. Set. lib. bdg. 175.00 (ISBN 0-8161-0964-8). G K Hall.

McGill University, Montreal, Institute of Islamic Studies. The Library Catalogue of the Institute of Islamic Studies. Date not set. lib. bdg. price not set (ISBN 0-8161-1136-7). G K Hall.

Mackechnie, John, compiled by. Catalogue of Gaelic Manuscripts in Selected Libraries in Great Britain & Ireland, 2 vols. 1973. Set. 230.00 (ISBN 0-8161-0832-3). G K Hall.

Marine Biological Laboratory & Woods Hole Oceanographic Institution, Woods Hole, Massachusetts. Catalog of the Library of the Marine Biological Laboratory & the Woods Hole Oceanographic Institution, 12 vols. 1971. lib. bdg. 1060.00 set (ISBN 0-8161-0937-0); journal catalog 55.00 (ISBN 0-8161-0115-9). G K Hall.

Marx Memorial Library, London. Catalog of the Marx Memorial Library. 1979. lib. bdg. 275.00 (ISBN 0-8161-0280-5). G K Hall.

Massachusetts Horticultural Society, Boston. Dictionary Catalog of the Library of the Massachusetts Horticultural Society, First Supplement. 465p. 1972. lib. bdg. 60.00 (ISBN 0-8161-1038-7). G K Hall.

Menninger Foundation, Topeka, Kansas. Catalog of the Menninger Clinic Library, 4 vols. 1972. Set. lib. bdg. 325.00 (ISBN 0-8161-0961-3). G K Hall.

Moss, Cyril. Catalogue of Syriac Printed Books & Related Literature in the British Museum. 832p. 1981. 100.00x (ISBN 0-7141-0635-6, Pub. by Brit Lib England). State Mutual Bk.

Name Authority Control for Card Catalogs in the General Libraries. (Contributions to Librarianship Ser.: No. 5). 1981. pap. 10.00 (ISBN 0-930214-07-2). U TX Austin Gen Libs.

National Gallery of Canada. (Ottawa) Catalogue of the Library of the National Gallery of Canada. 1973. Eight Vols. lib. bdg. 725.00 (ISBN 0-8161-1043-3). G K Hall.

New York Public Library Research Libraries. Catalog of the Theatre & Drama Collections, Pt. 3. 30 Vols. Non-book Collection. 1976. lib. bdg. 3485.00 (ISBN 0-8161-1195-2). G K Hall.

New York Public Library, Research Libraries. Dictionary Catalog of the Music Collection, 33 Vols. 1964. Set. lib. bdg. 2400.00 (ISBN 0-8161-0709-2). G K Hall.

--Dictionary Catalog of the Schomburg Collection of Negro Literature & History, 9 Vols. 1962. Set. 795.00 (ISBN 0-8161-0632-0); 1st suppl. 1967, 2 vols. 115.00 (ISBN 0-8161-0735-1); 2nd suppl., 1972, 4 vols. 350.00 (ISBN 0-8161-0820-X). G K Hall.

O.C.L.C. Design of Formats & Packs of Catalog Cards. LC 73-620151. 1973. 4.00 (ISBN 0-88215-036-7). Ohio St U Lib.

Peschl, Otto, ed. Catalog of Holdings in Slavonic Philology Including Belles-Lettres, University of Library Vienna: Katalog der Bestande auf dem Gebiet der Slawischen Philologie Einschliesslich der Belle Tristik. 1972. lib. bdg. 65.00 (ISBN 0-8161-0996-6). G K Hall.

Pontifical Institute of Medieval Studies, Ontario. Dictionary Catalogue of the Library of the Pontifical Institute of Medieval Studies, 5 vols. 3952p. 1973. Set. lib. bdg. 485.00 (ISBN 0-8161-0970-2). G K Hall.

Population Council. Catalogue of the Population Council Library. 1979. lib. bdg. 280.00 (ISBN 0-8161-0278-3). G K Hall.
Princeton University. Dictionary Catalog of the Princeton University Plasma Physics Laboratory Library, 4 vols. 1970. Set. lib. bdg. 325.00 (ISBN 0-8161-0881-1). G K Hall.
Provincial Archives of British Columbia, Victoria. Dictionary Catalogue of the Library of the Provincial Archives of British Columbia, 8 vols. 1971. Set. lib. bdg. 660.00 (ISBN 0-8161-0912-5). G K Hall.
Public Archives of Canada. Catalogue of the Public Archives of Canada: Collection of Published Material with a Chronological List of Pamphlets. 1979. lib. bdg. 1200.00 (ISBN 0-8161-0316-X). G K Hall.
Radcliffe College, the Arthur & Elizabeth Schlesinger Library on the History of Women in America. Manuscripts Inventory & the Catalogs of the Manuscripts, Books & Pictures, 3 vols. 1973. lib. bdg. 235.00 book catalog (ISBN 0-8161-1053-0). G K Hall.
Ranganathan, S. R. Library Catalogue: Fundamentals & Procedures. (Library Science Ser.). 1980. lib. bdg. 75.00 (ISBN 0-8490-3168-0). Gordon Pr.
Research Catalog of the Library of the American Museum of Natural History: Classed Catalog. 1978. 1010.00 (ISBN 0-8161-0238-4). G K Hall.
Rowland, Arthur R. Catalog & Cataloging. (Contributions to Library Literature Ser.: No. 8). 1969. 17.50 (ISBN 0-208-00441-6, Archon). Shoe String.
Ryan, E. D., compiled by. A Bibliographical Checklist of the Library of Cooper K. Ragan. Date not set. 7.50 (ISBN 0-685-66044-3). Jenkins.
Ryans, Cynthia C., ed. The Card Catalog: Current Issues. LC 81-720. 336p. 1981. 16.00 (ISBN 0-8108-1417-X). Scarecrow.
Ryskamp, Charles, ed. & pref. by. Seventeenth Report to the Fellows of the Pierpont Morgan Library: 1972-1974. (Illus.). 1976. 25.00 (ISBN 0-87598-064-3). Pierpont Morgan.
Senior High School Library Catalog. 11th ed. 1977. 50.00 (ISBN 0-8242-0619-3). Wilson.
Shaver, Chester L. & Shaver, Alice C. Wordsworth's Library: A Catalogue. LC 77-83348. (Reference Library of Humanities Ser.). 1979. lib. bdg. 40.00 (ISBN 0-8240-9842-0). Garland Pub.
Short-Title Catalogue of Books Printed in Italy & of Italian Books Printed in Other Countries from 1465 to 1600 Now in the British Museum. 1000p. 1981. 40.00x (ISBN 0-7141-0269-5, Pub. by Brit Lib England). State Mutual Bk.
Short-Title Catalogue of Books Printed in the German-Speaking Countries & of German Books Printed in Other Countries from 1455 to 1600 Now in the British Museum. 1232p. 1980. 40.00x (ISBN 0-7141-0268-7, Pub. by Brit Lib England). State Mutual Bk.
Short-Title Catalogue of Books Printed in the Netherlands & Belgium & of Dutch & Flemish Books Printed in Other Countries from 1470 to 1600 in the British Museum. 284p. 1981. 35.00x (ISBN 0-7141-0270-9, Pub. by Brit Lib England). State Mutual Bk.
Simoni, Anna E. Publish & Be Free: A Catalogue of Clandestine Books Printed in the Netherlands 1940-1945 in the British Library. 302p. 1980. pap. 30.00x (ISBN 90-247-1764-7, Pub. by Brit Lib England). State Mutual Bk.
Simonton, Wesley & McClaskey, Marilyn J. AACR 2 & the Catalog: Theory-Structure-Changes. LC 81-11757. 78p. 1981. pap. 8.50x (ISBN 0-87287-267-X). Libs Unl.
Smithsonian Institution, Washington, D. C. Dictionary Catalog of the Library of the Freer Gallery of Art, 6 Vols. 1967. Set. lib. bdg. 430.00 (ISBN 0-8161-0799-8). G K Hall.
Stanford University, Hoover Institution on War, Revolution & Peace. Catalog of the Chinese Collection First Supplement, 2 vols. 1376p. 1972. Set. lib. bdg. 280.00 (ISBN 0-8161-1046-8). G K Hall.
Stanford University, Hoover Institution on War, Revolution, & Peace. The Catalog of the Chinese Collection: Second Supplement, 2 vols. 1977. Set. lib. bdg. 260.00 (ISBN 0-8161-0039-X). G K Hall.
Stanford University, Hoover Institution on War, Revolution & Peace. Catalog of the Japanese Collection, First Supplement. 581p. 1972. lib. bdg. 120.00 (ISBN 0-8161-1051-4). G K Hall.
Stanford University, Hoover Institution on War, Revolution, & Peace. Catalog of the Japanese Collection: Second Supplement. 1977. lib. bdg. 130.00 (ISBN 0-8161-0040-3). G K Hall.
Stanford University, Hoover Institution on War, Revolution & Peace. Catalog of the Western Language Collections, First Supplement, 5 vols. 2627p. 1972. Set. lib. bdg. 700.00 (ISBN 0-8161-1019-0). G K Hall.
--The Catalog of the Western Language Collections: Second Supplement, 6 vols. 1977. Set. lib. bdg. 840.00 (ISBN 0-8161-0037-3). G K Hall.
Strawn, Richard R. Topics, Terms, & Research Techniques: Self-Instruction in Using Library Catalogs. LC 80-12569. 98p. 1980. 10.00 (ISBN 0-8108-1308-4). Scarecrow.
Strout, Ruth French, ed. Library Catalogs: Changing Dimensions. LC 64-19840. (University of Chicago Studies in Library Science Ser). 1964. 7.50x (ISBN 0-226-77731-6). U of Chicago Pr.
Tavistock Joint Library, London. Catalogue of the Tavistock Joint Library, London, England, 2 vols. 1975. Set. lib. bdg. 105.00 (ISBN 0-8161-1167-7). G K Hall.
Towner, Lawrence W. An Uncommon Collection of Uncommon Collections: The Newberry Library. rev. ed. (Illus.). 36p. (Orig.). 1977. pap. 1.50 (ISBN 0-685-92873-X). Newberry.
U. S. Department of Health, Education & Welfare, Washington, D. C. Author-Title Catalog of the Department Library: First Supplement. Incl. Author-Title Catolog, 7 vols. lib. bdg. 735.00 (ISBN 0-8161-1109-X). 1973. G K Hall.
U. S. Department of Labor. Washington D. C. Catalog of the United States Department of Labor Library (Washington, D.C., 38 vols. 1975. Set. lib. bdg. 3800.00 (ISBN 0-8161-1165-0). G K Hall.
U. S. Department of the Interior, Washington, D. C. Dictionary Catalog of the Department Library, 37 Vols. 1967. Set. 3515.00 (ISBN 0-8161-0715-7). G K Hall.
--Dictionary Catalog of the Department Library 2nd Supplement, 2 vols. 1971. Set. lib. bdg. 210.00 (ISBN 0-8161-0845-5). G K Hall.
University of California - Berkeley. Dictionary Catalog of the Giannini Foundation of Agricultural Economics Library, 12 vols. 1971. 1140.00 (ISBN 0-8161-0908-7). G K Hall.
University of Illinois at Urbana-Champaign - University Library. Catalog of the Rare Book Room, 11 vols. 1972. Set. 1090.00 (ISBN 0-8161-0938-9). G K Hall.
University of London - Warburg Institute. Catalog of the Warburg Institute Library, First Supplement. 1971. 105.00 (ISBN 0-8161-0909-5). G K Hall.
University of Michigan. Catalogs of the Asia Library, the University of Michigan, 25 vols. 1978. Set. 2350.00 (ISBN 0-8161-0096-9). G K Hall.
University of Michigan, Ann Arbor, William L. Clements Library. Author-Title & Chronological Catalogs of Americana, 1493-1860, in the William L. Clements Library, 7 vols. 1970. Set. 620.00 (ISBN 0-8161-0874-9). G K Hall.
University of Texas, Austin. Catalog of the Latin American Collection of the University of Texas Library: Second Supplement, 3 vols. 1973. Set. lib. bdg. 325.00 (ISBN 0-8161-0979-6). G K Hall.
University of the West Indies, Imperial College of Tropical Agriculture, Trinidad. Catalogue of the Imperial College of Tropical Agriculture, 8 vols. 1975. Set. lib. bdg. 720.00 (ISBN 0-8161-1190-1). G K Hall.
University of Washington at Seattle. The Dictionary Catalog of the Pacific Northwest Collection of the University of Washington Libraries, 6 vols. 1972. Set. lib. bdg. 640.00 (ISBN 0-8161-0985-0). G K Hall.
University of Wurzburg, Library. Catalog of the Schoenleiniana Collection on Epidemics (Katalog der Sammlung Schoenlein) 1972. lib. bdg. 45.00 (ISBN 0-8161-1017-4). G K Hall.
U.S. Department of the Interior, Washington D.C. Dictionary Catalog of the Department Library, First Supp, 4 vols. 1969. Set. lib. bdg. 420.00 (ISBN 0-8161-0751-3). G K Hall.
Watson, A. G. The Library of Sir Simonds d'Ewes. 396p. 1981. 40.00x (ISBN 0-7141-0446-9, Pub. by Brit Lib England). State Mutual Bk.
Weiser, Frederick S. & Heaney, Howell J., eds. The Pennsylvania German Fraktur of the Free Library of Philadelphia: An Illustrated Catalogue, Vol. 1. Neff, Larry M., tr. from Ger. LC 76-13357. (Illus.). 250p. 1976. 30.00 (ISBN 0-911122-32-X). Penn German Soc.
--The Pennsylvania German Fraktur of the Free Library of Philadelphia: Illustrated Catalogue, Vol. 2. Neff, Larry M., tr. from Ger. LC 76-13357. (Illus.). 1977. 30.00 (ISBN 0-911122-33-8). Penn German Soc.
William Andrews Clark Memorial Library-Los Angeles. Dictionary Catalog of William Andrews Clark Memorial Library, 15 vols. 1974. Set. 1350.00 (ISBN 0-8161-1049-2). G K Hall.
World Council of Churches, Geneva, Switzerland. Classified Catalog of the Ecumenical Movement, 2 vols. 1972. lib. bdg. 190.00 (ISBN 0-8161-0925-7). G K Hall.
Wright, Mildred S., compiled by. Tyrrell Historical Library, Beaumont, Texas: A Catalog of the Genealogical Collection, February 14, 1978. LC 78-56570. 1978. lib. bdg. 12.50 (ISBN 0-917016-11-4); pap. 7.50 (ISBN 0-917016-10-6). M S Wright.

LIBRARY CATALOGS–BIBLIOGRAPHY

Collison, Robert, ed. Published Library Catalogues: An Introduction to Their Content & Use. LC 72-95007. 184p. 1974. 18.95 (ISBN 0-7201-0369-X, Co-Pub. by Mansell Info England). Bowker.
University of London - School of Oriental & African Studies. Library Catalogue of the School of Oriental & African Studies: 2nd Supplement, 16 vols. 1973. Set. lib. bdg. 1680.00 (ISBN 0-8161-0841-2). G K Hall.
Williams, William P. A Descriptive Catalog of Seventeenth Century Religious Literature in the Kansas State University Library. 1966. 1.50 (ISBN 0-686-20809-9). KSU.

LIBRARY CATALOGS–UNION CATALOGS

see Catalogs, Union

LIBRARY CENSORSHIP

see Libraries–Censorship

LIBRARY CLASSIFICATION

see Classification–Books

LIBRARY CONFERENCES

Foskett, D. J., et al, eds. Library Systems & Information Services. (Illus.). 1970. pap. 13.50 (ISBN 0-208-00984-1, Archon). Shoe String.
Fusonie, Alan & Moran, Leila, eds. International Agricultural Librarianship: Continuity & Change. LC 78-67916. 1979. lib. bdg. 18.95 (ISBN 0-313-20640-6, AIA/). Greenwood.
Goldstein, Harold, ed. Milestones to the Present: Papers from Library History Seminar V. 1978. 15.00 (ISBN 0-915794-21-7, 6561). Gaylord Prof Pubns.
International Federation of Library Associations Conference 1961. International Conference on Cataloguing Principles Report: Proceedings. 1969. Repr. of 1963 ed. 15.00 (ISBN 0-208-00875-6, Archon). Shoe String.
Koops, R. H., et al, eds. I F L A Annual 78. 197p. 1979. pap. 30.00 (ISBN 0-89664-112-0). K G Saur.
Pennsylvania University Library. Changing Patterns of Scholarship & the Future of Research Libraries. facs. ed. LC 68-14910. (Essay Index Reprint Ser). 1951. 15.00 (ISBN 0-8369-0782-5). Arno.
Subject Retrieval in the Seventies New Directions, an International Symposium. LC 70-183149. (Contributions in Librianship & Information Science: No. 3). 210p. 1972. lib. bdg. 14.00 (ISBN 0-8371-6322-6, SRS/, Pub. with U. of Md. Lib. Serv). Greenwood.

LIBRARY CONSORTIA

see Library Cooperation

LIBRARY CONSULTANTS

Change Institute. University of Maryland. Frontiers in Librarianship: Proceedings of Change Institute 1969. Wasserman, Paul, ed. LC 78-149958. (Contributions in Librarianship & Information Science: No. 2). 1972. lib. bdg. 17.50 (ISBN 0-8371-5823-0, WPC/). Greenwood.
Garrison, Guy, ed. The Changing Role of State Library Consultants. (Monograph: No. 9). 98p. 1968. 4.00x (ISBN 0-87845-031-9). U of Ill Lib Info Sci.
Pyeatt, Nancy. The Consultant's Legal Guide. (The Consultant's Library). 146p. 1980. text ed. 30.00 (ISBN 0-930686-09-8). Bermont Bks.

LIBRARY COOPERATION

see also Catalogs, Union; Intellectual Cooperation; Libraries, Storage; Library Information Networks; Periodicals–Bibliography–Union Lists

Brewster, Beverly J. American Overseas Library Technical Assistance, 1940-1970. LC 75-23006. 1976. 21.00 (ISBN 0-8108-0827-7). Scarecrow.
Carnovsky, Leon, ed. Library Networks-Promise & Performance. LC 78-77977. (Studies in Library Science Ser.). 1969. 6.50x (ISBN 0-226-09406-5). U of Chicago Pr.
Clinic on Library Applications of Data Processing Proceedings, 1973. Networking & Other Forms of Cooperation. Lancaster, F. W., ed. LC 65-1841. 185p. 1973. 7.00x (ISBN 0-87845-038-6). U of Ill Lib Info Sci.
Filon, S. P. The National Central Library: An Experiment in Library Cooperation 1916 - 1974. 300p. 1977. lib. bdg. 28.75x (ISBN 0-85365-249-X, Pub. by Lib Assn England). Oryx Pr.
Gregory, Ruth & Stoffel, Lester. Public Libraries in Cooperative Systems. LC 78-172295. 324p. 1971. 12.00 (ISBN 0-8389-0110-7). ALA.
Guidelines Subcommittee, SLA Networking Committee. Getting into Networking: Guidelines for Special Libraries. LC 76-58875. (State-of-the-Art Review: No. 5). 1977. pap. 6.00 (ISBN 0-685-85830-8). SLA.
Hamilton, Beth A. & Ernst, William, Jr. Multitype Library Cooperation. LC 77-24092. 1977. 21.50 (ISBN 0-8352-0980-6). Bowker.
Jefferson, George. Library Cooperation. (Grafton Books on Library Science). 1977. lib. bdg. 24.75 (ISBN 0-233-96851-2). Westview.
Kent, Allen & Galvin, Thomas J., eds. Library Resource Sharing: Proceedings of the 1976 Conference on Resource Sharing in Libraries, Pittsburgh, Pennsylvania. LC 77-5399. (Books in Library & Information Science: Vol. 21). 1977. 36.75 (ISBN 0-8247-6605-9). Dekker.
Knievel, Helen A., ed. Cooperative Services: A Guide to Policies & Procedures in Library Systems. 275p. 1981. 19.95x (ISBN 0-918212-56-1). Neal-Schuman.
Myrick, William J., Jr. Coordination: Concept or Reality? A Study of Libraries in a University System. LC 74-22456. 1975. 10.00 (ISBN 0-8108-0776-9). Scarecrow.
Planning National Infrastructures for Documentation, Libraries, & Archives. 328p. 1975. pap. 14.50 (ISBN 92-3-101144-8, U454, UNESCO). Unipub.
Reynolds, Michael M., ed. Reader in Library Cooperation. LC 72-86635. (Reader Ser. in Library & Information Science: Vol. 11). 1973. 17.00 (ISBN 0-910972-22-2). IHS-PDS.
--Reader in Library Cooperation. LC 72-86635. (Reader Ser. in Library & Information Science: Vol. 11). 1973. 17.00 (ISBN 0-910972-22-2). IHS-PDS.
Richardson, Ernest C. Some Aspects of International Library Cooperation. 1977. lib. bdg. 75.00 (ISBN 0-8490-2624-5). Gordon Pr.
Simsova, S. & Mackee, M. Handbook of Comparative Librarianship. 2nd ed. (Comparative Library Studies). 548p. (Orig.). 1975. 27.50 (ISBN 0-208-01355-5, Linnet). Shoe String.
Stenstrom, Ralph H. Cooperation between Types of Libraries, 1940-1968: An Annotated Bibliography. 168p. 1970. pap. 4.00 (ISBN 0-8389-0094-1). ALA.
Thomassen, Cora E., ed. Cooperation Between Types of Libraries: The Beginnings of a State Plan for Library Services in Illinois. LC 72-625423. (Allerton Park Institute Ser.: No. 15). 100p. 1969. 5.00x (ISBN 0-87845-010-6). U of Ill Lib Info Sci.

LIBRARY EDUCATION

Alvarez, Octavio, et al. Report on Library & Information Science Education in the United States. LC 75-620121. (Student Contribution Ser.: No. 7). 1975. pap. 5.00 (ISBN 0-911808-11-6). U of Md Lib Serv.
Anderson, A. J. Problems in Intellectual Freedom & Censorship. LC 74-7106. (Problem-Centered Approaches to Librarianship Ser.). 195p. 1974. 18.50 (ISBN 0-8352-0677-7). Bowker.
Applebaum, Edward L., ed. Reader in Technical Services. LC 72-87717. (Reader Ser. in Library & Information Science: Vol. 7). 1973. 17.00 (ISBN 0-910972-21-4). IHS-PDS.
Barr, Larry, ed. Library Education 2000 A.D. & After. 38p. 1977. 3.00x (ISBN 0-931510-05-8). Hi Willow.
A Basic Library Test for Four Year Colleges. 1977. pap. 7.00 (ISBN 0-88385-423-6). Math Assn.
Beeler, Richard J., ed. Evaluating Library Use Instruction. LC 75-677. (Library Orientation Ser.: No. 4). 1975. 14.95 (ISBN 0-87650-062-9). Pierian.
Bell, Irene W. & Wieckert, Jeanne E. Basic Classroom Skills Through Games. LC 80-351. 1980. 17.50 (ISBN 0-87287-207-6). Libs Unl.
--Basic Media Skills Through Games. LC 79-941. 1979. 17.50 (ISBN 0-87287-194-0). Libs Unl.
Bolner, Mary, ed. Planning & Developing a Library Orientation Program: Proceedings. LC 75-676. (Library Orientation Ser.: No. 3). 1975. 14.95 (ISBN 0-87650-061-0). Pierian.
Bramley, G. A. History of Library Education. 1969. 13.50 (ISBN 0-208-00868-3, Archon). Shoe String.
Bramley, Gerald. World Trends in Library Education. 234p. (Orig.). 1975. 17.50 (ISBN 0-208-01368-7, Linnet). Shoe String.
Burgard, Andrea, ed. Directory of Educational Programs in Information Science: Supplement for 1972/1973. LC 70-179373. 38p. 1972. pap. 3.00 (ISBN 0-87715-601-8). Am Soc Info Sci.
Carey, R. J. Library Guiding: A Program for Exploiting Library Resources. 1974. 14.50 (ISBN 0-208-01350-4, Linnet). Shoe String.
Chirgwin, F. J. & Oldfield, P. The Library Assistant's Manual. 1978. 12.00 (ISBN 0-208-01666-X, Linnet). Shoe String.
Churchwell, Charles D. Shaping of American Library Education. LC 74-22987. (ACRL Publications in Librarianship: No. 36). 138p. 1975. pap. text ed. 9.00 (ISBN 0-8389-0170-0). ALA.
A Comprehensive Program of User Education for the General Libraries: The University of Texas at Austin. (Contributions to Librarianship: No. 1). 101p. 1977. pap. 5.00 (ISBN 0-930214-01-3). U TX Austin Gen Libs.
Conant, Ralph W. The Conant Report: A Study of the Education of Librarians. 1980. text ed. 20.00x (ISBN 0-262-03072-1). MIT Pr.

Conroy, Barbara. Library Staff Development & Continuing Education: Principles & Practices. LC 78-18887. 1978. 23.50x (ISBN 0-87287-177-0). Libs Unl.
Croghan, Anthony. Manual & Code of Rules for Simple Cataloging. 2nd ed. 1974. pap. 6.95x plus 24 audio cassettes (ISBN 0-9501212-6-6). J Norton Pubs.
Davinson, Donald. Reference Service. 1980. text ed. 17.50 (ISBN 0-85157-291-X, Pub. by Bingley England). Shoe String.
Educating Library Users in Secondary Schools. 1981. 18.00x (ISBN 0-905984-31-5, Pub. by Brit Lib England). State Mutual Bk.
Fenner, Peter. Research: A Practical Guide to Finding Information. (Illus.). 250p. pap. 7.95 (ISBN 0-86576-010-1). W Kaufmann.
Finn, D., et al. Teaching Manual for Tutor Librarians. 1978. 13.25x (ISBN 0-85365-830-7, Pub. by Lib Assn England). Oryx Pr.
Fjallbrant, Nancy & Stevenson, Malcolm B. User Education in Libraries: Problems & Practice. 1978. 12.50 (ISBN 0-208-01664-3, Linnet). Shoe String.
Fleischer, Eugene & Goodman, Helen. Cataloguing Audiovisual Materials: A Manual Based on the AACR II. LC 80-18782. (Illus.). 387p. 1981. pap. 19.95x (ISBN 0-918212-39-1). Neal-Schuman.
Gardner, Richard K. Library Collections: Their Origin, Selection, & Development. (Library Education Ser.). 384p. 1981. text ed. 15.95 (ISBN 0-07-022850-7, C). McGraw.
Gwin, Sherry. The Library: What's in It for You? 1973. text ed. 0.40x (ISBN 0-8134-1579-9, 1579). Interstate.
Kirkendall, Carolyn B. Improving Library Instruction. LC 79-87707. (Library Orientation Ser.: No. 9). 1979. 14.95 (ISBN 0-87650-109-9). Pierian.
Kirkendall, Carolyn B., ed. Putting Library Instruction in Its Place: In the Library & in the Library School. LC 78-53996. (Library Orientation Ser.: No. 8). 1978. 14.95 (ISBN 0-87650-092-0). Pierian.
Kortendick, James J. & Stone, Elizabeth W. Job Dimensions & Educational Needs in Librarianship. LC 70-157141. 510p. 1971. text ed. 15.00 (ISBN 0-8389-3126-X). ALA.
Learning Technology Inc, ed. Library Skills: A Program for Self-Instruction. 1970. text ed. 8.50 (ISBN 0-07-051376-7). McGraw.
Library Association Working Pary on Training. Guidelines for Training in Libraries. 74p. 1980. spiral bound 7.50x (ISBN 0-85365-883-8, Pub by Lib Assn England). Oryx Pr.
Library Studies Duplicating Masters, 2 vols. 1976. 5.95 ea. Vol. 1 (ISBN 0-89273-537-6). Vol. 2 (ISBN 0-89273-538-4). Educ Serv.
Library User Education - Are New Approaches Needed? 1981. 21.00x (ISBN 0-905984-45-5, Pub. by Brit Lib England). State Mutual Bk.
Lubans, John, ed. Progress in Educating the Library User. 1978. 16.95 (ISBN 0-8352-1102-9). Bowker.
Malley, I., ed. Educating the User. 1979. pap. 13.25x (ISBN 0-85365-761-0, Pub. by Lib Assn England). Oryx Pr.
Manthorne, Jane, et al, eds. Idea Sourcebook for Young Adult Programs. 1973. 2.00 (ISBN 0-89073-015-6). Boston Public Lib.
Meder, Marylouise D., ed. Library School Review, Vol. 19. 1980. pap. 2.00 (ISBN 0-686-31205-8). Sch Lib Sci.
Mews, Hazel. Reader Instruction in Colleges & Universities: Teaching the Use of the Library. Orig. Title: Library Instruction in Colleges & Universities. 1972. 12.50 (ISBN 0-208-01174-9, Linnet). Shoe String.
Miller, William & Rockwood, D. Stephen, eds. College Librarianship. LC 80-25546. 290p. 1981. 15.00 (ISBN 0-8108-1383-1). Scarecrow.
Morehead, Joe. Theory & Practice in Library Education: The Teaching-Learning Process. LC 80-17431. (Research Studies in Library Science: No. 16). 1980. lib. bdg. 25.00x (ISBN 0-87287-215-7). Libs Unl.
Nassif, Ricardo. Methods of Teaching Librarianship. 1969. pap. 6.00 (ISBN 92-3-100758-0, U384, UNESCO). Unipub.
Rader, H., ed. Faculty Involvement in Library Instruction. LC 76-21914. (Library Orientation Ser.: No. 6). 1976. 14.95 (ISBN 0-87650-070-X). Pierian.
Rader, Hannelore B. A Guide to Academic Library Instruction. Stueart, Robert D., ed. LC 77-2107. (Foundations in Library & Information Science Ser.: Vol. 7). Date not set. lib. bdg. 25.00 (ISBN 0-89232-073-7). Jai Pr.
Rader, Hannelore B., ed. Academic Library Instruction: Objectives, Programs, & Faculty Involvement. LC 75-678. (Library Orientation Ser.: No. 5). 1975. 14.95 (ISBN 0-87650-063-7). Pierian.
--Library Instruction in the Seventies: State of the Art. LC 77-75678. (Library Orientation Ser.: No. 7). 1977. 14.95 (ISBN 0-87650-078-5). Pierian.
Renford, Beverly & Hendrickson, Linnea. Bibliographic Instruction: A Handbook. LC 80-12300. 192p. 1980. pap. 14.95x (ISBN 0-918212-24-3). Neal-Schuman.
Rice, James, Jr. Teaching Library Use: A Guide for Library Instruction. LC 80-21337. (Contributions in Librarianship & Information Service Ser.: No. 37). (Illus.). 216p. 1981. lib. bdg. 25.00 (ISBN 0-313-21485-9, RTL/). Greenwood.
Rogers, JoAnn V. Libraries & Young Adults: Media, Services, & Librarianship. LC 79-15. 1979. 17.50x (ISBN 0-87287-195-9). Libs Unl.
School Library Association Of California. Library Skills. rev ed. LC 73-78275. 1973. pap. 4.95 (ISBN 0-8224-4300-7). Pitman Learning.
Shinn, Duane. The Library Book: How to Mine the Wealth in Your Public Library. (Illus.). 1977. spiral bdg. 6.95 (ISBN 0-912732-25-3). Duane Shinn.
Simpson, N., ed. Training in Libraries: Report of the Library Association Working Party on Training. 1977. pap. 2.75x (ISBN 0-85365-339-9, Pub. by Lib Assn England). Oryx Pr.
Stone, Elizabeth. Continuing Library Education As Viewed in Relation to Other Continuing Professional Education Movements. LC 74-21737. 1974. 25.00 (ISBN 0-87715-108-3). Am Soc Info Sci.
Stone, Elizabeth W., et al. Continuing Library & Information Science Education: Final Report to the National Commission on Libraries & Information Science. LC 74-21738. 478p. 1974. lexhide 10.00 (ISBN 0-87715-109-1). Am Soc Info Sci.
Swanson, Don R., ed. Intellectual Foundations of Library Education. LC 65-2702. (University of Chicago Studies in Library Science Ser). 1965. 5.75x (ISBN 0-226-78467-3). U of Chicago Pr.
--Intellectual Foundations of Library Education. LC 65-2702. (University of Chicago Studies in Library Science Ser). 1965. 5.75x (ISBN 0-226-78467-3). U of Chicago Pr.
Teaching Library Skills in Freshman English: An Undergraduates Library's Experience. (Contributions to Librarianship Ser.: No. 6). 1981. pap. 15.00 (ISBN 0-930214-09-9). U TX Austin Gen Libs.
Tucker, John M. Articles on Library Instruction in Colleges & Universities,1876-1932. 45p. 1980. 3.00 (ISBN 0-686-31462-X). U of Ill Lib Sci.
Vann, Sarah K. Williamson Reports: A Study. LC 75-149992. 1971. 10.00 (ISBN 0-8108-0375-5). Scarecrow.
Ward, M. L. Readers & Library Users. 1977. 10.95x (ISBN 0-85365-479-4, Pub. by Lib Assn England). Oryx Pr.
What Shall I Read? 2nd ed. 1978. 17.25x (ISBN 0-85365-560-X, Pub. by Lib Assn England). Oryx Pr.
White, Carl. Historical Introduction to Library Education: Problems & Progress to 1951. LC 75-28086. 1976. 13.50 (ISBN 0-8108-0874-9). Scarecrow.
Williams, Nyal Z. & Tsukamoto, Jack T., eds. Library Instruction & Faculty Development. (Library Orientation Ser.: No. 11). 1980. 14.95 (ISBN 0-87650-125-0). Pierian.
Woodbury, Marda. Selecting Materials for Instruction: Issues & Policies. LC 79-18400. (Illus.). 1979. lib. bdg. 22.50 (ISBN 0-87287-197-5). Libs Unl.
--Selecting Materials for Instruction: Subject Areas & Implementation. LC 79-18400. (Illus.). 1980. lib. bdg. 22.50x (ISBN 0-87287-213-0). Libs Unl.

LIBRARY EXHIBITS

Here are entered works on exhibits illustrating the administration of libraries, their buildings, furniture, catalogs, etc.
see also Bibliographical Exhibitions

Baeckler, Virginia & Larson, Linda. Go, Pep, & Pop: Two Hundred Fifty Tested Ideas for Lively Libraries. LC 75-20328. 1976. pap. 4.50 (ISBN 0-916444-01-5). UNABASHED Lib.
Coplan, Kate. Effective Library Exhibits. rev., 2nd ed. LC 74-4428. (Illus.). 160p. 1974. lib. bdg. 12.50 (ISBN 0-379-00265-5). Oceana.
Franklin, Linda C. Library Display Ideas. LC 80-17036. (Illus.). 244p. 1980. lib. bdg. 12.95x (ISBN 0-89950-008-0); pap. 9.95x (ISBN 0-89950-009-9). McFarland & Co.
Garvey, Mona. Library Displays. LC 79-86918. 1969. 10.00 (ISBN 0-8242-0395-X). Wilson.
New York Public Library. Sixty-Four Treasures. (Illus.). 1964. pap. 2.00 (ISBN 0-87104-162-6). NY Pub Lib.

LIBRARY EXTENSION

see also Direct Delivery of Books

Library Service to the Spanish Speaking. LC 77-22847. 51p. 1977. 5.00 (ISBN 0-913578-16-9). Inglewood Ca.
Patrick, Ruth J., et al. A Study of Library Cooperatives, Networks & Demonstration Projects, 2 vols. in 1. 280p. 1980. Set. 39.80 (ISBN 0-208-01942-1, Linnet). Vol. 1: Findings & Recomendations. Vol. 2: Case Study Reports. Shoe String.

LIBRARY FINANCE

see also Taxation, Exemption From

Alley, B. & Cargill, J. S. Keeping Track of What You Spend: A Librarian's Guide to Simple Bookkeeping. 1981. write for info. (ISBN 0-912700-79-3). Oryx Pr.
Baumol, William J. & Marcus, Matityahu. Economics of Academic Libraries. 112p. 1973. 6.50 (ISBN 0-8268-1257-0). ACE.
Boss, Richard W. Grant Money & How to Get It: A Handbook for Librarians. 1st ed. 138p. 1980. 19.95 (ISBN 0-8352-1274-2). Bowker.
Breivik, Patricia S. & Gibson, E. Burr. Funding Alternatives for Libraries. LC 78-27865. 1979. pap. 10.00 (ISBN 0-8389-0273-1). ALA.
Brown, Eleanor F. Cutting Library Costs: Increasing Productivity & Raising Revenues. LC 79-19448. 274p. 1979. 13.50 (ISBN 0-8108-1250-9). Scarecrow.
Chen, Ching-Chih. Zero-Base Budgeting in Library Management: A Manual for Librarians. (Neal-Schuman Professional Books). 1980. lib. bdg. 25.00x (ISBN 0-912700-18-1). Oryx Pr.
Compton, Charles H., et al. Twenty-Five Crucial Years of the St. Louis Public Library, 1927 to 1952. 1953. 5.00 (ISBN 0-937322-00-8). St Louis Pub Lib.
Curran, Charles C., ed. Library Research Round Table Nineteen Seventy-Seven Research Forums: Proceedings: Meetings Held at the Annual Conference of the American Library Association, 96th, Detroit, Michigan, July 17-23, 1977. LC 79-15300. (Orig.). 1979. pap. 19.75 (ISBN 0-8357-0424-6, SS-00098). Univ Microfilms.
Drake, Miriam A. User Fees: A Practical Perspective. LC 81-6032. 142p. 1981. lib. bdg. 17.50x (ISBN 0-87287-244-0). Libs Unl.
Frase, Robert W. Library Funding & Public Support. LC 73-17396. 2.00 (ISBN 0-8389-3150-2). ALA.
Koenig, Michael, ed. Budgeting Techniques for Libraries & Information Centers. LC 80-27698. (Professional Development Ser.: No. 1). 1980. pap. 7.50 (ISBN 0-87111-278-7). SLA.
Krummel, Donald W., ed. Organizing the Library's Support: Donors, Volunteers, Friends. LC 80-14772. (Allerton Park Institute Ser.: No. 25). 119p. 1980. 10.00 (ISBN 0-87845-054-8). U of Ill Lib Info Sci.
Lee, Sul H., ed. Library Budgeting: Critical Challenges for the Future. LC 77-85231. (Library Management Ser.: No. 3). 1977. 14.95 (ISBN 0-87650-083-1). Pierian.
Martin, Murray S. Budgetary Control in Academic Libraries, Vol. 5. LC 76-5648. (Foundations in Library & Information Science Ser.). 1978. lib. bdg. 32.50 (ISBN 0-89232-010-9). Jai Pr.
Mitchell, Betty Jo, et al. Cost Analysis of Library Functions: A Total System Approach, Vol. 6. Stueart, Robert D., ed. LC 77-2110. (Foundations in Library & Information Science). 1978. lib. bdg. 32.50 (ISBN 0-89232-072-9). Jai Pr.
Moore, Evelyn, ed. Budgeting & Financing for Libraries. 20.00 (ISBN 0-86656-118-8, B118). Haworth Pr.
Phillips, B. J., et al. Public Libraries: Legislation, Administration, & Finance. 1977. pap. text ed. 8.65x (ISBN 0-85365-750-5, Pub. by Lib Assn England). Oryx Pr.
Prentice, Ann E. Public Library Finance. LC 77-9096. 1977. pap. 7.00 (ISBN 0-8389-0240-5). ALA.
Quirk, Dantia & Whitestone, Patricia. The Shrinking Library Dollar. (Communications Library). 160p. 1981. professional 24.95 (ISBN 0-914236-74-1). Knowledge Indus.
Ring, Daniel F., ed. Studies in Creative Partnership: Federal Aid to Public Libraries During the New Deal. LC 80-15762. 154p. 1980. 10.00 (ISBN 0-8108-1319-X). Scarecrow.
Speller, Benjamin F., Jr. Zero Based Budgeting for Libraries & Information Centers: A Continuing Education Manual. 1979. 11.00x (ISBN 0-931510-03-1). Hi Willow.
Tanis, Norman E. Fiscal & Acquisition Implications of the Tax Reform Act of 1969 for Research Libraries. 1977. pap. 10.00 (ISBN 0-937048-14-3). CSUN.

LIBRARY FITTINGS AND SUPPLIES

see also Bookmobiles; Shelving (For Books)

American Library Association. Library Furniture & Equipment: Proceedings of a Three - Day Institute, June 14-16, 1962. LC 63-18322. 1963. pap. 3.00 (ISBN 0-8389-3044-1). ALA.
American National Standards Institute, Standards Committee Z39 on Library Work, Documentation & Related Publishing Practices. American National Standard Criteria for Price Indexes for Library Materials, Z39.20. 1974. 4.00 (ISBN 0-686-15228-X). ANSI.
Library Equipment Institute - New York - July 7-9 1966. Procurement of Library Furnishings: Specifications, Bid Documents, & Evaluation: Proceedings. Poole, Frazer G. & Trezza, Alphonse E., eds. LC 70-77274. (Orig.). 1969. pap. 4.00 (ISBN 0-8389-3093-X). ALA.

LIBRARY INFORMATION NETWORKS

Allison, Anne M. & Allan, Ann G., eds. OCLC: A National Library Network. LC 78-11948. (Illus.). 1979. pap. 16.95 (ISBN 0-89490-019-6). Enslow Pubs.
Brelsford, William M. & Relles, Daniel A. Statlib: A Statistical Computing Library. 448p. 1981. text ed. 17.50 (ISBN 0-13-846220-8). P-H.
Burnett, D. & Cumming, E. E., eds. International Library & Information Programmes. 1978. pap. 15.65x (ISBN 0-85365-591-X, Pub. by Lib Assn England). Oryx Pr.
Casey, Genevieve. The Public Library in the Network Mode: A Preliminary Investigation. (Illinois Regional Council Occasional Papers Ser.: No. 3). 51p. 1978. soft cover 7.50 (ISBN 0-917060-01-6). Ill Regional Lib Coun.
Ching-Chih Chen & Hernon, Peter. Information Seeking: Assessing & Anticipating User Needs. 200p. 1981. 19.95x (ISBN 0-918212-50-2). Neal-Schuman.
Cope, Gabriele E. & Hoffman, Kay Y. Coping with the OCLC Subsystem. 2nd ed. LC 78-108748. 1979. pap. 8.40 (ISBN 0-933540-01-9). Ego Bks.
Davis, Charles H. & Lundeen, Gerald W. Illustrative Computer Programming for Libraries: Selected Examples for Information Specialists. 2nd ed. LC 81-1128. (Contributions in Librarianship & Information Science Ser.: No. 39). (Illus.). 120p. 1981. lib. bdg. 15.00 (ISBN 0-313-22151-0, DAD/). Greenwood.
Guidelines Subcommittee, SLA Networking Committee. Getting into Networking: Guidelines for Special Libraries. LC 76-58875. (State-of-the-Art Review: No. 5). 1977. pap. 6.00 (ISBN 0-685-85830-8). SLA.
Hoover, Ryan, ed. Library & Information Manager's Guide to Online Services. (Professional Librarian Ser.). (Illus.). 269p. 1980. 29.50x (ISBN 0-914236-60-1); pap. 24.50x (ISBN 0-914236-52-0). Knowledge Indus.
Jones, Clara S., ed. Public Library Information & Referral Service. 265p. 1981. pap. 14.50 (ISBN 0-915794-06-3, Lib Prof Pubns). Shoe String.
Kent & Galvin, eds. The Structure of Governance of Library Networks, Vol. 27. (Bks. in Library & Information Science). 1979. 43.75 (ISBN 0-8247-6866-3). Dekker.
Kent, Allen & Galvin, Thomas J., eds. Library Resource Sharing: Proceedings of the 1976 Conference on Resource Sharing in Libraries, Pittsburgh, Pennsylvania. LC 77-5399. (Books in Library & Information Science: Vol. 21). 1977. 36.75 (ISBN 0-8247-6605-9). Dekker.
Markuson, Barbara & Woolls, Blanche, eds. Networks for Networkers: Critical Issues in Cooperative Library Development. LC 79-24054. 1980. 17.95x (ISBN 0-918212-22-7). Neal-Schuman.
Martin, Susan K. Library Networks: 1981-1982. 4th ed. LC 78-10666. (Professional Librarian Ser.). 176p. 1980. text ed. 29.50x (ISBN 0-914236-55-5); pap. text ed. 24.50x (ISBN 0-914236-66-0). Knowledge Indus.
Networking in Sci-Tech & Information Centers. (Science & Technology Libraries Ser.: Vol. 1, No. 2). 1981. pap. 15.00 (ISBN 0-917724-72-0, B72). Haworth Pr.
A New Governance Structure for OCLC: Principles & Recommendations. LC 78-2099. 1978. pap. 10.00 (ISBN 0-8108-1146-4). Scarecrow.
Overington, M. A. The Subject Departmentalized Public Library. 1969. 11.25x (ISBN 0-85365-051-9, Pub. by Lib Assn England). Oryx Pr.
Patrick, R., et al. Study of Library Co-Operatives Networks & Demonstration Projects, 2 vols. 470p. 1980. text ed. 39.80 (ISBN 0-89664-313-1). K G Saur.
Patrick, Ruth J., et al. A Study of Library Cooperatives, Networks & Demonstration Projects, 2 vols. in 1. 280p. 1980. Set. 39.80 (ISBN 0-208-01942-1, Linnet). Vol. 1: Findings & Recomendations. Vol. 2: Case Study Reports. Shoe String.
Reynolds, Michael M. & Daniel, Evelyn H., eds. Reader in Library & Information Services. LC 73-94310. (Reader Ser. in Library & Information Science: Vol. 14). 1974. 20.00 (ISBN 0-910972-25-7). IHS-PDS.
Rouse, William B. & Rouse, Sandra H. Management of Library Networks: Policy Analysis, Implementation, & Control. LC 80-12644. (Information Sciences Ser.). 288p. 1980. 28.95 (ISBN 0-471-05534-4, Pub. by Wiley Interscience). Wiley.

Shaw, Debra & Prentice, Ann E., eds. Public Library Networking & Inter-Library Co-Operation. (Public Library Quarterly Ser.: Vol. 2, Nos. 3-4). 1981. 20.00 (ISBN 0-86656-116-1, B116). Haworth Pr.

Whatley, H. A., ed. British Librarianship & Information Science 1971-1975. 1977. 32.50x (ISBN 0-85365-099-3, Pub. by Lib Assn England). Oryx Pr.

LIBRARY LEGISLATION

see also Librarians–Certification

American Library Laws: First Supplement-1973 to 1974. 4th ed. LC 73-14863. 252p. 1975. text ed. 15.00 (ISBN 0-8389-0202-2). ALA.

Bosmajian, Haig A., compiled by. Censorship, Libraries, & the Law. 220p. 1981. 14.95x (ISBN 0-918212-56-1). Neal-Schuman.

Ladenson, Alex. American Library Laws. 4th ed. LC 73-14863. 1000p. 1973. 40.00 (ISBN 0-8389-0158-1). ALA.

Ladenson, Alex, ed. American Library Laws: Second Supplement 1975-1976. 4th ed. LC 73-14863. 1977. text ed. 15.00 (ISBN 0-8389-0253-7). ALA.

--American Library Laws: Third Supplement, 1977 to 1978. 4th ed. LC 73-14863. 248p. 1980. 15.00 (ISBN 0-8389-0304-5). ALA.

Ladley, Winifred, ed. Federal Legislation for Libraries. (Allerton Park Institute Ser.: No. 13). 104p. 1967. 4.00x (ISBN 0-87845-008-4). U of Ill Lib Info Sci.

Laundy, P. Parliamentary Librarianship in the English Speaking World. 1980. lib. bdg. 33.25x (ISBN 0-85365-731-9, Pub. by Lib Assn England). Oryx Pr.

Lukac, George J., ed. Copyright: The Librarian & the Law. (Issues in Library & Information Sciences Ser.: No. 1). 1972. pap. text ed. 3.95 (ISBN 0-8135-0746-4). Rutgers U Slis.

Molz, R. Kathleen. Federal Policy & Library Support. LC 76-17102. 1976. 16.00x (ISBN 0-262-13120-X). MIT Pr.

Pemberton, J. E. Politics & Public Libraries in England & Wales, 1850 - 1970. 1977. 17.25x (ISBN 0-85365-109-4, Pub. by Lib Assn England). Oryx Pr.

Phillips, B. J., et al. Public Libraries: Legislation, Administration, & Finance. 1977. pap. text ed. 8.65x (ISBN 0-85365-750-5, Pub. by Lib Assn England). Oryx Pr.

Schlipf, Frederick L., ed. Collective Bargaining in Libraries. LC 75-25240. (Allerton Park Institute Ser.: No. 20). 179p. 1975. 8.00x (ISBN 0-87845-042-4). U of Ill Lib Info Sci.

LIBRARY NETWORKS

see Library Information Networks

LIBRARY OF CONGRESS

see United States–Library of Congress

LIBRARY OF CONGRESS CLASSIFICATION

see Classification, Library of Congress

LIBRARY PROCESSING

see Processing (Libraries)

LIBRARY PUBLICITY

see Public Relations–Libraries

LIBRARY RESEARCH

see Library Science–Research

LIBRARY RESOURCES

Here are entered works describing the resources and special collections in libraries which are available for research in various fields. Works describing the resources and special collections in a particular field are entered under the subject with subdivision Library Resources, e.g. Africa–Library Resources. Works on the methods used to acquire, process, and maintain special collections in libraries are entered under Libraries–Special Collections.

Baker, D. Phillip & Bender, David R. Library Media Programs & the Special Learner. 400p. 1981. 18.50 (ISBN 0-208-01852-2, Lib Prof Pubns); pap. text ed. 14.50x (ISBN 0-208-01846-8, Lib Prof Pubns). Shoe String.

Baker, Robert K. Doing Library Research: An Introduction for Community College Students. (Westview Guides to Library Research Ser.). 260p. 27.50x (ISBN 0-89158-778-0). Westview.

Banks, Paul N. Preservation of Library Materials. 1978. pap. 1.75 (ISBN 0-686-53822-6). Newberry.

Bolte, Charles G. Libraries & the Arts & Humanities. pap. 14.50 (ISBN 0-915794-13-6). Gaylord Prof Pubns.

Booth, Marcella, ed. A Catalogue of the Louis Zukofsky Manuscript Collection. LC 70-38572. (Tower Bibliographical Ser.: No. 11). (Illus.). 1975. 18.50 (ISBN 0-87959-038-6). U of Tex Hum Res.

Boverie, Edward. Audio Service in Public Libraries. (Illus.). 175p. (Orig.). Date not set. spiral 7.50 (ISBN 0-913578-21-5). Inglewood CA.

Branyon, Brenda. Outstanding Women Who Promoted the Concept of the Unified School Library & Audio Visual Program. 375p. 1981. 25.00 (ISBN 0-686-69458-9). Hi Willow.

Cabeceiras, James. The Multimedia Library: Materials Selection & Use. 275p. 1978. tchrs' ed. 14.00 (ISBN 0-12-153950-4). Acad Pr.

Chernik, Barbara E. Introduction to Library Services for Library Technicians. (Illus.). 250p. 1982. text ed. price not setx (ISBN 0-87287-275-0). Libs Unl.

Cooke, Bette, et al. Manual & Exercises for Library Usage. 1978. pap. text ed. 6.95 (ISBN 0-8403-2211-9, 402211-01). Kendall-Hunt.

Eastern Europe & Russia-Soviet Union: Handbook of West European Archival & Library Resources. 1981. 75.00 (ISBN 0-686-69415-5, Dist. by Gale Research). K G Saur.

Fothergill, Richard & Butchart, Ian. Non-Book Materials in Libraries: A Practical Guide. 1978. 17.50 (ISBN 0-208-01673-2, Linnet). Shoe String.

Gill, Suzanne L. File Management & Information Retrieval Systems: A Manual for Managers & Technicians. LC 80-22785. (Illus.). 193p. 1981. lib. bdg. 18.50x (ISBN 0-87287-229-7). Libs Unl.

Hewitt, Vauneen J. Toys & Games in Libraries. 96p. 1981. pap. text ed. 10.95x (ISBN 0-85365-963-X, Pub. by Lib Assn England). Oryx Pr.

Higham, Norman. The Library in the University: Observations on a Service. (Grafton Books on Library & Information Sciences). 192p. 1980. lib. bdg. 23.25x (ISBN 0-86531-053-X, Pub. by Andre Deutsch). Westview.

Hunter, Frederick J., ed. A Guide to the Theater & Drama Collections at the University of Texas. LC 67-65517. (Tower Bibliographical Ser). (Illus.). 1967. 7.50 (ISBN 0-87959-040-8); pap. 4.00 (ISBN 0-87959-041-6). U of Tex Hum Res.

Irvine, Betty J. & Fry, P. Eileen. Slide Libraries: A Guide for Academic Institutions, Museums, & Special Collections. 2nd ed. LC 79-17354. (Illus.). 1979. lib. bdg. 22.50 (ISBN 0-87287-202-5). Libs Unl.

Jennings, Margaret, ed. Library & Reference Facilities in the Area of the District of Columbia. 10th ed. LC 44-41159. (American Society for Information Science Ser.). 1979. softcover 19.50x (ISBN 0-914236-35-0). Knowledge Indus.

Katz, Bill, ed. Library Lit. Ten: The Best of 1979. LC 78-154842. 512p. 1980. 13.00 (ISBN 0-686-65869-8). Scarecrow.

Kaufman, Paul, ed. Libraries & Their Users: Collective Papers in Library History. 233p. 1981. lib. bdg. 21.95x (ISBN 0-85365-171-X, Pub. by Lib Assn England). Oryx Pr.

Kent. Use of Library Materials: University of Pittsburgh Study. (Books in Library & Information Science Ser.: Vol. 26). 1979. 29.75 (ISBN 0-8247-6807-8). Dekker.

Koops, Willeur R. & Stellingwerf, Johannes. Developments in Collection Building in University Libraries in Western Europe. 109p. 1977. text ed. 17.00 (ISBN 3-7940-7020-8, Pub. by K G Saur). Shoe String.

Library Resource Provision in Schools: Guidelines & Recommendations. 1977. pap. 5.75x (ISBN 0-85365-700-9, Pub. by Lib Assn England). Oryx Pr.

Library Resources Market Place 1980. 300p. 1980. pap. 27.50 (ISBN 0-8352-1290-4). Bowker.

Marshall, Margaret. The Librarian & the Handicapped Child. LC 80-51349. (Grafton Books on Library & Information Science). 160p. 1981. lib. bdg. 26.75x (ISBN 0-86531-056-4, Pub. by Andre Deutsch). Westview.

Morehouse, Ward, ed. Foreign Area Studies & the College Library. (Occasional Publication). 80p. 1965. pap. 1.00 (ISBN 0-89192-134-6). Interbk Inc.

Osburn, Charles B. Academic Research & Library Resources: Changing Patterns in America. LC 78-20017. (New Directions in Librarianship: No. 3). (Illus.). 1979. lib. bdg. 18.95 (ISBN 0-313-20722-4, OAR/). Greenwood.

Petrie, Joyce A. Mainstreaming in the Media Center. 1981. lib. bdg. write for info. (ISBN 0-89774-006-8). Oryx Pr.

Preston, Jenny. Collection Development in St. Louis Area Libraries: A Survey. 1975. 1.50 (ISBN 0-937322-04-0). St Louis Pub Lib.

Robotham, John & Shields, Gerald. Freedom of Access to Library Materials. 250p. 1982. 16.95 (ISBN 0-918212-31-6). Neal-Schuman.

Rogers, JoAnn V. Libraries & Young Adults: Media, Services, & Librarianship. LC 79-15. 1979. 17.50x (ISBN 0-87287-195-9). Libs Unl.

Russell, Joyce, ed. Preservation of Library Materials. LC 80-20706. 1980. pap. 9.50 (ISBN 0-87111-270-1). SLA.

Sackton, Alexander, compiled by. The T. S. Eliot Collection of the University of Texas at Austin. LC 70-169270. (Tower Bibliographical Ser: No. 9). (Illus.). 1975. 20.00 (ISBN 0-87959-042-4). U of Tex Hum Res.

Stappenbeck, Herb, compiled by. A Catalogue of the Joseph Hergesheimer Collection at the University of Texas. LC 78-169267. (Tower Bibliographical Ser.: No. 10). (Illus.). 1974. 12.95 (ISBN 0-87959-043-2). U of Tex Hum Res.

Stueart, Robert D. & Miller, George. Collection Development in Libraries, Pts. A & B, Vol. 10. LC 79-93165. (Foundations in Library & Information Science Monographs). (Orig.). 1980. Set. lib. bdg. 60.00 (ISBN 0-686-64266-X); lib. bdg. 30.00 ea. Pt. A (ISBN 0-89232-106-7). Pt. B (ISBN 0-89232-162-8). Jai Pr.

Supply of & Demand for Qualified Librarians: Report of the Commission. 1977. pap. text ed. 8.75x (ISBN 0-85365-870-6, Pub. by Lib Assn England). Oryx Pr.

Swartzburg, Susan G. Preserving Library Materials: A Manual. LC 80-11742. 1980. 12.50 (ISBN 0-8108-1302-5). Scarecrow.

Taylor, Mary M., ed. School Library and Media Center Acquisitions Policies & Procedures. 1981. lib. bdg. 17.50 (ISBN 0-912700-70-X). Oryx Pr.

Todd, Alden. Finding Facts Fast. LC 79-8516. (Illus.). 1979. 7.95 (ISBN 0-89815-013-2); pap. 3.95 (ISBN 0-89815-012-4). Ten Speed Pr.

Upon the Objectives to Be Attained by the Establishment of a Public Library: Report of the Trustees of the Public Library of the City of Boston, 1852. Repr. 3.50 (ISBN 0-686-70431-2). Boston Public Lib.

Van Orden, Phyllis & Phillips, Edith B., eds. Background Readings in Building Library Collections. 2nd ed. LC 78-31263. 1979. 13.50 (ISBN 0-8108-1200-2). Scarecrow.

Walker, Gregory, ed. Resources for Soviet, East European & Slavonic Studies in British Libraries. rev. ed. Orig. Title: Directory of Libraries & Special Collections on Eastern Europe. 176p. 1981. lib. bdg. 43.00 (ISBN 0-7201-1589-2, Pub. by Mansell England). Merrimack Bk Serv.

Weiser, Frederick S., compiled by. The Pennsylvania German Fraktur of the Free Library of Philadelphia: An Illustrated Catalogue, Vols. 1 & 2. (Illus.). 1976. Set. 60.00x (ISBN 0-911122-32-X, Pub. with Penn. Ger. Soc.). Phila Free Lib.

Woodbury, Marda. Selecting Materials for Instruction: Issues & Policies. LC 79-18400. (Illus.). 1979. lib. bdg. 22.50 (ISBN 0-87287-197-5). Libs Unl.

Wright, Eugene P., ed. A Catalogue of the Joanna Southcott Collection AtThe University of Texas. LC 68-65505. (Tower Bibliographical Ser.: No. 7). (Illus.). 1968. 10.00 (ISBN 0-87959-045-9). U of Tex Hum Res.

Yang, Teresa S., et al. East Asian Resources in American Libraries. LC 77-87442. 1978. pap. text ed. 8.95 (ISBN 0-8188-0111-5). Paragon.

LIBRARY RULES AND REGULATIONS

see also Libraries and Readers

Hoadley, Irene B. & Clark, Alice S., eds. Quantitative Methods in Librarianship: Standards, Research, Management. LC 73-149962. (Contributions in Librarianship & Information Science: No. 4). 256p. 1972. lib. bdg. 17.95 (ISBN 0-8371-6061-8, HOQ/). Greenwood.

Murphy, Marcy & Johns, Claude J. Handbook of Library Regulations. (Library & Information Science Ser.: Vol. 20). 1977. 24.75 (ISBN 0-8247-6498-6). Dekker.

LIBRARY SCHOOL EDUCATION

see Library Education

LIBRARY SCHOOLS

see also Library Education

Davis, Donald G., Jr. The Association of American Library Schools, 1915-1968: An Analytical History. LC 73-16014. 1974. 15.00 (ISBN 0-8108-0642-8). Scarecrow.

Meder, Marylouise D., ed. Library School Review, Vol. 16. 1976. pap. 1.50 (ISBN 0-686-18269-3). Sch Lib Sci.

--Library School Review, Vol. 19. 1980. pap. 2.00 (ISBN 0-686-31205-8). Sch Lib Sci.

White, Carl. Historical Introduction to Library Education: Problems & Progress to 1951. LC 75-28086. 1976. 13.50 (ISBN 0-8108-0874-9). Scarecrow.

LIBRARY SCHOOLS AND TRAINING

Borko, Harold. Targets for Research in Library Education. LC 72-9923. 1973. text ed. 10.00 (ISBN 0-8389-0098-4). ALA.

Chicago University - Graduate Library School. Education for Librarianship. facs. ed. LC 71-117776. (Essay Index Reprint Ser). 1949. 19.50 (ISBN 0-8369-1701-4). Arno.

Evans, G. Edward. Developing Library Collections. LC 78-27303. (Library Science Text Ser.). 1979. lib. bdg. 19.50x (ISBN 0-87287-145-2); pap. text ed. 13.50x (ISBN 0-686-77127-3). Libs Unl.

Goldhor, Herbert, ed. Education for Librarianship: The Design of the Curriculum of Library Schools. LC 78-633332. (Monograph: No. 11). 195p. 1971. 5.00x (ISBN 0-87845-033-5). U of Ill Lib Info Sci.

Grosch, Audrey N. Minicomputers in Libraries, 1981-82. (Professional Librarian). 160p. 1981. professional 34.50 (ISBN 0-914236-96-2); pap. 27.50 professional (ISBN 0-914236-92-X). Knowledge Indus.

Schorr, Alan E., ed. Government Reference Books 76-77: A Biennial Guide to U.S. Government Publications. LC 76-146307. 1978. lib. bdg. 25.00x (ISBN 0-87287-192-4). Libs Unl.

World Guide to Library Schools & Training Courses in Documentation. 245p. 1973. 12.25 (ISBN 92-3-001024-3, UNESCO). Unipub.

LIBRARY SCIENCE

see also Audio-Visual Library Service; Bibliography; Cataloging; Classification–Books; Information Storage and Retrieval Systems; Processing (Libraries)

also headings beginning with the word Library

Adamovich, Shirley G., ed. Reader in Library Technology. LC 75-8051. (Reader Ser. in Library & Information Science: Vol. 17). 1975. 20.00 (ISBN 0-910972-52-4). IHS-PDS.

Allen, Walter C., ed. Serial Publications in Large Libraries. LC 74-629637. (Allerton Park Institute Ser.: No. 16). 194p. 1970. 6.00x (ISBN 0-87845-011-4). U of Ill Lib Info Sci.

Amadi, Adolphe O. African Libraries: Western Tradition & Colonial Brainwashing. LC 80-29593. xii, 265p. 1981. 14.00 (ISBN 0-8108-1409-9). Scarecrow.

American Association for Information Science Annual Meeting 1979. Information Choices & Policies: Proceedings, Vol.16. Tally, Roy D., compiled by. LC 64-8303. 1979. 19.50 (ISBN 0-914236-47-4). Knowledge Indus.

American National Standards Institute, Standards Committee Z39 on Library Work, Documentation & Related Publishing Practices. American National Standard for the Preparation of Scientific Papers for Written or Oral Presentation, Z39.16. 1979. 4.50 (ISBN 0-686-05270-6). ANSI.

Anderson, A. J. Problems in Library Management. LC 81-8153. (Library Science Text Ser.). 282p. 1981. text ed. 22.50x (ISBN 0-87287-261-0); pap. text ed. 13.50x (ISBN 0-87287-264-5). Libs Unl.

Asheim, Lester & Fenwick, Sara I., eds. Differentiating the Media. (Studies in Library Science). vi, 74p. 1975. 10.00x (ISBN 0-226-02964-6). U of Chicago Pr.

Ashworth, Wilfred. Special Librarianship. 120p. 1979. 17.50 (ISBN 0-89664-405-7). K G Saur.

Atherton, P., et al. The Unisist Guidelines. pap. text ed. 35.00x (ISBN 0-87837-014-5). Sci Assoc Intl.

Baer, Eleanora A. Titles in Series: A Handbook for Librarians & Students, 4 vols. 3rd ed. LC 78-14452. 1978. Set. 99.50 (ISBN 0-8108-1043-3). Scarecrow.

Bahr, Alice H. Automated Library Circulation Systems, 1979-1980. LC 79-16189. (Professional Librarian Ser.). (Illus.). 1979. softcover 24.50x (ISBN 0-914236-34-2). Knowledge Indus.

Balkema, John, ed. Services for the Aging: Source & Resource. 1980. pap. 29.95 (ISBN 0-915794-19-5, 9315/78). Gaylord Prof Pubns.

Ballard, Harlan. Adventures of a Librarian. 59.95 (ISBN 0-87968-579-4). Gordon Pr.

Ballard, Jan. If Young Adult Is the Answer, What Is the Question? (Neal-Schuman Professional Bk.). Date not set. cancelled (ISBN 0-912700-14-9). Oryx Pr.

Banks, Paul N. Preservation of Library Materials. 1978. pap. 1.75 (ISBN 0-686-53822-6). Newberry.

Barr, K. P. & Line, M. B., eds. Essays on Information & Libraries: A Festschrift for Donald Urquhart. 211p. 1975. 15.00 (ISBN 0-208-01370-9, Linnet). Shoe String.

Baumann, Roland M., ed. A Manual of Archival Techniques. (Illus.). 127p. 1979. pap. 4.00 (ISBN 0-89271-000-4). Pa Hist & Mus.

Becker, Joseph, ed. Interlibrary Communications & Information Networks. LC 70-185963. 1972. 15.00 (ISBN 0-8389-3123-5). ALA.

Berman, Sanford. Joy of Cataloging. 1981. lib. bdg. 22.50 (ISBN 0-912700-51-3); pap. 18.50 (ISBN 0-912700-94-7). Oryx Pr.

Bernhardt, Frances S. Introduction to Library Technical Services. 1979. 15.00 (ISBN 0-8242-0637-1). Wilson.

Beswick, Norman. Resource-Based Learning. 1977. text ed. 25.50x (ISBN 0-435-80077-9). Heinemann Ed.

Bishop, William W. Backs of Books, & Other Essays in Librarianship. facs. ed. LC 68-54328. (Essay Index Reprint Ser). 1968. Repr. of 1926 ed. 16.00 (ISBN 0-8369-0215-7). Arno.

Bishop, William W. & Keogh, Andrew. Essays Offered to Herbert Putnam by His Colleagues & Friends on His 30th Anniversary As Librarian of Congress, 5 April Nineteen Twenty-Nine. 1929. 20.00x (ISBN 0-686-51379-7). Elliots Bks.

Bone, Larry E., ed. Library School Teaching Methods: Courses in the Selection of Adult Materials. LC 77-625419. 137p. 1969. 5.00x (ISBN 0-87845-022-X). U of Ill Lib Info Sci.

Borko, Harold & Bernier, C. L. Abstracting Concepts & Methods. (Library & Information Science Ser.). 250p. 1975. 19.50 (ISBN 0-12-118650-4). Acad Pr.

Boss, Richard W. The Library Manager's Guide to Automation. LC 79-3057. (Professional Librarian Ser.). 1979. 29.50x (ISBN 0-914236-33-4); softcover 24.50x (ISBN 0-914236-38-5). Knowledge Indus.

Bostwick, A. E. Classics of American Librarianship, 8 vols. 1500.00 (ISBN 0-87968-879-3). Gordon Pr.

Bostwick, Arthur E. Library Essays. facs. ed. LC 71-84299. (Essay Index Reprint Ser). 1920. 20.00 (ISBN 0-8369-1076-1). Arno.

Bowerman, George F. Censorship & the Public Library, with Other Papers. facs. ed. LC 67-30199. (Essay Index Reprint Ser). 1931. 16.00 (ISBN 0-8369-0232-7). Arno.

Branyon, Brenda. Outstanding Women Who Promoted the Concept of the Unified School Library & Audio Visual Program. 375p. 1981. 25.00 (ISBN 0-686-69458-9). Hi Willow.

Broadus, Robert, ed. The Role of the Humanities in the Public Library. LC 79-24117. 1980. 20.00 (ISBN 0-8389-0297-9). ALA.

Buckman, Thomas, et al. University & Research Libraries in Japan & the United States. LC 76-178155. 1972. text ed. 20.00 (ISBN 0-8389-3111-1). ALA.

Butler, Pierce. Introduction to Library Science. LC 33-16039. (Library Science Ser.). 1961. pap. 4.00x (ISBN 0-226-08421-3, Phoen). U of Chicago Pr.

Carlson, William H. In a Grand & Awful Time. LC 67-16715. 1967. pap. 7.95 (ISBN 0-87071-309-4). Oreg St U Pr.

Carpenter, Michael A. Corporate Authorship: Its Role in Library Cataloging. LC 80-1026. (Contributions in Librarianship & Information Science Ser.: No. 34). x, 200p. 1981. lib. bdg. 27.50 (ISBN 0-313-22065-4, CAU/). Greenwood.

Carter, Jane R. Public Librarianship: A Reader. 400p. 1981. lib. bdg. 35.00 (ISBN 0-87287-246-7). Libs Unl.

Chamberlin, E. R. Librarian & His World. 1969. 6.00 (ISBN 0-8022-2265-X). Philos Lib.

Charlton, H. B. The Art of Literary Study. Repr. of 1924 ed. lib. bdg. 15.00 (ISBN 0-8414-1271-5). Folcroft.

Chen, Ching-Chih. Library Management Without Bias. Stueart, Robert D., ed. LC 80-82482. (Foundations in Library & Information Sciences Ser.: Vol. 13). 300p. (Orig.). 1981. 32.50 (ISBN 0-89232-163-6). Jai Pr.

Chicago Illinois Regional Library Council. Illinois Libraries & Information Centers. 1981. pap. write for info. (ISBN 0-917060-14-8). Ill Regional Lib Coun.

Chisholm, Margaret, ed. Reader in Media, Technology & Libraries. LC 75-8050. (Reader Ser in Librarianship Information Science: Vol. 18). 55p. 1976. 22.00 (ISBN 0-910972-51-6). IHS-PDS.

Clark, John W. The Care of Books: An Essay on the Development of Libraries & Their Fittings, from the Earliest Times to the End of the 18th Century. 442p. 1980. 50.00x (ISBN 0-902089-78-1, Pub. by Variorum England). State Mutual Bk.

Cohen, Nathan M. Library Science Dissertations, Nineteen Twenty-Five to Nineteen Sixty: An Annotated Bibliography of Doctoral Studies. (Library Science Ser.). 1980. lib. bdg. 55.00 (ISBN 0-8490-3167-2). Gordon Pr.

Collison, Robert L., ed. Progress in Library Science, 1966. 1967. 17.50 (ISBN 0-208-00176-X). Shoe String.

--Progress in Library Science, 1967. 1968. 17.50 (ISBN 0-208-00670-2). Shoe String.

Colloquium, June 27-28, 1980. An Information Agenda for the Nineteen Eighties: Proceedings. Rochell, Carlton, ed. LC 80-28685. 154p. 1981. pap. 7.50 (ISBN 0-8389-0336-3). ALA.

Comaromi, John P. Book Numbers: A Historical Study & Practical Guide to Their Use. 250p. 1981. lib. bdg. 23.50x (ISBN 0-87287-251-3). Libs Unl.

Cooke, Bette, et al. Manual & Exercises for Library Usage. 1978. pap. text ed. 6.95 (ISBN 0-8403-2211-9, 402211-01). Kendall-Hunt.

Corbett, E. V. The Fundamentals of Library Organisation & Administration: A Practical Guide. 1978. 31.50x (ISBN 0-85365-540-5, Pub. by Lib Assn England); pap. text ed. 15.50x (ISBN 0-85365-840-4). Oryx Pr.

--Introduction to Librarianship. 1968. 12.00 (ISBN 0-8022-0303-5). Philos Lib.

Corrigan, John T. Librarian-Educator Interdependence. 1976. 3.00 (ISBN 0-87507-002-7). Cath Lib Assn.

Corrigan, John T., ed. What Today's Youth Is Reading & Why. (CLA Studies in Librarianship). 46p. 5.00 (ISBN 0-87507-022-1); pap. 5.00 (ISBN 0-87507-022-1). Cath Lib Assn.

Coughlin, Caroline M., ed. Recurring Library Issues: A Reader. LC 79-14966. 543p. 1979. 19.00 (ISBN 0-8108-1227-4). Scarecrow.

Croghan, Anthony. Code for Cataloging Non Book Media. (Orig.). 1972. pap. 8.50x (ISBN 0-9501212-4-X). J Norton Pubs.

Cuadra, Carlos & Luke, Ann W., eds. The Annual Review of Information Science & Technology, Vol. 5, 1970. LC 66-25096. 1970. 35.00 (ISBN 0-85229-156-6). Knowledge Indus.

Cuadra, Carlos A. The Annual Review of Information Science & Technology, Vol 10, 1975. Luke, Ann W., ed. LC 66-25096. 1975. 35.00 (ISBN 0-686-67625-4). Knowledge Indus.

Cuadra, Carlos A., ed. The Annual Review of Information Science & Technology, Vol. 3, 1968. LC 66-25096. (Illus.). 1968. 35.00 (ISBN 0-685-94669-X). Knowledge Indus.

Cuadra, Carlos A. & Luke, Ann W., eds. The Annual Review of Information Science & Technology, Vol. 4, 1969. LC 66-25096. 1969. 35.00 (ISBN 0-85229-147-7). Knowledge Indus.

--The Annual Review of Information Science & Technology, Vol. 7, 1972. LC 66-25096. (Illus.). 1972. 35.00 (ISBN 0-87715-206-3). Knowledge Indus.

--The Annual Review of Information Science & Technology, Vol. 8, 1973. LC 66-25096. 1973. 35.00 (ISBN 0-87715-208-X). Knowledge Indus.

--The Annual Review of Information Science & Technology, Vol. 9, 1974. LC 66-25096. (Illus.). 1974. 35.00 (ISBN 0-87715-209-8). Knowledge Indus.

Curley, Marie T. The Buckram Syndrome: A Critical Essay on Paperbacks in Public Libraries of the United States. (Public Library Reporter: No. 13). 76p. 1968. pap. 2.00 (ISBN 0-8389-3086-7). ALA.

Curriculum Development in Librarianship & Information Science. 1981. pap. 27.00x (ISBN 0-905984-21-8, Pub. by Brit Lib England). State Mutual Bk.

Currie, Clifford. Prospects in Librarianship. 6.00 (ISBN 0-685-78047-3). Philos Lib.

Dana, John C. Libraries: Addresses & Essays. facs. ed. LC 67-22088. (Essay Index Reprint Ser). 1916. 18.00 (ISBN 0-8369-1329-9). Arno.

Danton, J. Periam. Between M.L.S. & Ph.D. LC 74-133380. 1970. pap. 4.00 (ISBN 0-8389-0089-5). ALA.

--Dimensions of Comparative Librarianship. LC 73-7935. 1973. text ed. 8.00 (ISBN 0-8389-0154-9). ALA.

Datta, Bimal K. Practical Guide to Library Procedure. 4.00x (ISBN 0-210-33724-9). Asia.

Developments in the Organisation of Non-Book Materials: Proceedings of a Joint Aslib-CET-LS Conference. 1977. pap. 7.00x (ISBN 0-686-64056-X, Pub. by Lib Assn England). Oryx Pr.

Dima-Dragan, Cornelius. Studia Bibliologica. 1980. 15.00 (ISBN 0-917944-02-X). Am Inst Writing Res.

Dobie, J. Frank. J. Frank Dobie on Libraries. (Illus.). 8p. 1970. pap. 3.00 (ISBN 0-87959-031-9). U of Tex Hum Res.

DuMont, Rosemary. Assessing the Effectiveness of Library Services. 1981. 3.00 (ISBN 0-686-31465-4). U of Ill Lib Sci.

Durnell, Jane B. & Stevens, Norman D., eds. The Librarian: Selections from the Column of That Name by Edmund L. Pearson. LC 75-35725. 1976. 27.50 (ISBN 0-8108-0851-X). Scarecrow.

Eastlick, John T., ed. The Changing Environment of Libraries. 86p. 1971. pap. 2.50 (ISBN 0-8389-0113-1). ALA.

Edwards, Ronald J. In-Service Training in British Libraries: Its Development & Present Practice. 1978. pap. 10.00 (ISBN 0-85365-219-8, 6508). Gaylord Prof Pubns.

Elman, Natalie M. & Ginsburg, Janet H. The Resource Room Primer. (Illus.). 320p. 1981. text ed. 15.95 (ISBN 0-13-774406-4). P-H.

Elrod, J. McRee. Choice of Main & Added Entries: Updated for Use with AACR2. 3rd ed. LC 80-23724. (Modern Library Practices Ser.: No. 4). 90p. 1980. pap. text ed. 5.50 (ISBN 0-8108-1339-4). Scarecrow.

--Choice of Subject Headings. 3rd ed. LC 80-23719. (Modern Library Practices Ser.: No. 5). 1980. pap. text ed. 5.50 (ISBN 0-686-73806-3). Scarecrow.

--Classification: For Use with LC or Dewey. 3rd ed. LC 80-23718. (Modern Library Practices Ser.: No. 3). 87p. 1980. pap. text ed. 5.50 (ISBN 0-8108-1338-6). Scarecrow.

--Construction & Adaption of the Unit Card. 3rd ed. LC 80-18903. (Modern Library Practices Ser.: No. 1). 80p. 1980. pap. text ed. 5.50 (ISBN 0-8108-1336-X). Scarecrow.

--Filing in the Public Catalogue & Shelf List. 3rd ed. LC 80-23723. (Modern Library Practices Ser.: No. 2). 89p. 1981. pap. text ed. 12.00 (ISBN 0-8108-1337-8). Scarecrow.

Esdaile, Arundell. Esdaile's Manual of Bibliography. 4th, rev. ed. Stokes, Roy, ed. (Illus.). 1974. Repr. of 1967 ed. 18.50x (ISBN 0-06-492032-1). B&N.

Essays Offered to Herbert Putnam by His Colleagues & Friends on His Thirtieth Anniversary As Librarian of Congress, April 5, 1929. facs. ed. LC 67-23214. (Essay Index Reprint Ser). 1929. 21.50 (ISBN 0-8369-0430-3). Arno.

Evans, G. E. Management Techniques for Librarians. (Library & Information Science Ser.). 276p. 1976. 17.00 (ISBN 0-12-243850-7). Acad Pr.

Fenner, Peter. Research. 250p. (Orig.). 1981. pap. 7.95 (ISBN 0-86576-010-1). W Kaufmann.

FLA Theses: From 1964. 1981. pap. 21.00x (ISBN 0-904654-20-6, Pub. by Brit Lib England). State Mutual Bk.

Foskett, D. J, ed. Reader in Comparative Librarianship. LC 76-10124. (Readers in Librarianship & Information Science Ser.: Vol. 23). (Illus.). 1976. 21.00 (ISBN 0-910972-61-3, 1422B). IHS-PDS.

Foster, Joan, ed. Reader in Children's Librarianship. LC 78-26669. (Readers in Librarianship & Information Science: No. 27). (Illus.). 1979. text ed. 22.00 (ISBN 0-910972-89-3). IHS-PDS.

Gabriel, Michael R. & Roselle, William C. The Microform Revolution in Libraries, Vol. 3. Stueart, Robert D., ed. LC 76-5646. (Foundations in Library & Information Science Ser.). 1980. lib. bdg. 32.50 (ISBN 0-89232-008-7). Jai Pr.

Galvin, Thomas J., et al, eds. Excellence in School Media Programs: Essays Honoring Elizabeth T. Fast. LC 79-26944. 238p. 1980. 12.50 (ISBN 0-8389-3239-8). ALA.

Gapen, D. Kaye & Library & Information Technology Association, eds. Authority Control: Proceedings of the LITA Institute. 1981. price not set (ISBN 0-912700-85-8). Oryx Pr.

Garnett, R. Essays in Librarianship & Bibliography. 1976. lib. bdg. 59.95 (ISBN 0-8490-1784-X). Gordon Pr.

Garnett, Richard. Essays in Librarianship & Bibliography. LC 79-122839. (Bibliography & Reference Ser.: No. 355). 1970. Repr. of 1899 ed. 22.50 (ISBN 0-8337-1282-9). B Franklin.

Gidwani, N. N., ed. Comparative Librarianship. 1973. 10.50 (ISBN 0-686-20202-3). Intl Bk Dist.

--Comparative Librarianship: Essays in Honour of Professor D. N. Marshall. 1973. text ed. 12.50x (ISBN 0-7069-0233-5). Verry.

Giljarevskij, R. S. International Distribution of Catalogue Cards: Present Situation & Future Prospects. (Orig.). 1968. pap. 3.25 (ISBN 92-3-100764-5, U326, UNESCO). Unipub.

Glover, Janice. Lighter Side of the Library. LC 74-75520. 128p. 1974. 4.95 (ISBN 0-88492-003-8). W S Sullwold.

Goldhor, Herbert. An Introduction to Scientific Research in Librarianship. LC 79-631732. (Monograph: No. 12). 201p. 1972. 5.00x (ISBN 0-87845-036-X). U of Ill Lib Info Sci.

Gore, Daniel. To Know a Library: Essays & Annual Reports, 1970-1976. LC 77-84769. (New Directions in Librarianship: No. 1). 1978. lib. bdg. 19.95 (ISBN 0-8371-9881-X, GTK/). Greenwood.

Gover, Harvey R. Keys to Library Research on the Graduate Level: A Guide to Guides. LC 80-5841. 75p. 1981. pap. text ed. 5.75 (ISBN 0-8191-1370-0). U Pr of Amer.

Harper, H. H. Library Essays. 59.95 (ISBN 0-8490-0520-5). Gordon Pr.

Harris, Jessica L., et al, eds. Cumulative Index to the Annual Review of Information Science & Technology, Vols.1-10, 1966-1975. LC 66-25096. 1976. 35.00 (ISBN 0-87715-211-X). Knowledge Indus.

Harris, Michael H., ed. Advances in Librarianship, Vol. 9. LC 79-88675. 1979. 26.50 (ISBN 0-12-785009-0); lib. ed. 34.00 (ISBN 0-12-785021-X); microfiche 22.00 (ISBN 0-12-785022-8). Acad Pr.

--Advances in Librarianship, Vol. 10. 1980. 23.00 (ISBN 0-12-785010-4); lib. ed. 30.00 (ISBN 0-12-785023-6); microfiche ed. 16.00 (ISBN 0-12-785024-4). Acad Pr.

Harris, Michael J. & Voight, Melvin J., eds. Advances in Librarianship, 8 vols. Incl. Vol. 1. 294p. 1970. 43.00 (ISBN 0-12-785001-5); Vol. 2. 388p. 1971. 43.00 (ISBN 0-12-785002-3); Vol. 3. 275p. 1972. 43.00 (ISBN 0-12-785003-1); Vol. 4. 1974. 43.00 (ISBN 0-12-785004-X); Vol. 5. 1975. 43.00 (ISBN 0-12-785005-8); lib ed. 55.00 (ISBN 0-12-785012-0); microfiche 31.50 (ISBN 0-12-785013-9); Vol. 6. 1976. 32.50 (ISBN 0-12-785006-6); lib ed. 40.50 (ISBN 0-12-785014-7); microfiche 24.00 (ISBN 0-12-785015-5); Vol. 7. 1977. lib ed. 51.50 (ISBN 0-12-785016-3); 40.50 (ISBN 0-12-785007-4); microfiche 29.50 (ISBN 0-12-785017-1); Vol. 8. 29.50 (ISBN 0-12-785008-2); lib. ed. 37.50 (ISBN 0-12-785018-X); microfiche 22.00 (ISBN 0-12-785019-8). LC 79-88675. Acad Pr.

Harrison, C. & Oakes, R. Basics of Librarianship. 1981. pap. 12.50x (ISBN 0-85365-523-5, Pub. by Lib Assn England). Oryx Pr.

Harvey, James. Librarians Censorship, & Intellectual Freedom. LC 72-7737. pap. 2.00 (ISBN 0-8389-3139-1). ALA.

Hauer, Mary, et al. Books, Libraries, & Research. 1978. pap. text ed. 5.95 (ISBN 0-8403-1953-3, 40195301). Kendall-Hunt.

Henry, William E. My Own Opinions Upon Libraries & Librarianship. facs. ed. LC 67-23231. (Essay Index Reprint Ser). 1931. 16.00 (ISBN 0-8369-0536-9). Arno.

Ho, Lucy C., ed. Exhibition Catalogue Manual in Use in the Library of the Metropolitan Museum of Art. (Illus.). 40p. 1974. 2.50 (ISBN 0-87099-099-3). Metro Mus Art.

Hoole, W. Stanley. According to Hoole: The Collected Essays & Tales of a Scholar-Librarian & Literary Maverick. LC 74-148688. 336p. 1973. 19.95x (ISBN 0-8173-7102-8). U of Ala Pr.

Information Systems Office - Library Of Congress. Format Recognition Process for MARC Records. LC 70-139250. 1970. pap. 10.00 (ISBN 0-8389-3122-7). ALA.

INIS: Authority List for Corporate Entries & Report Number Prefixes. 472p. 1980. pap. 29.75 (ISBN 92-0-178280-2, IN6-R13, IAEA). Unipub.

INIS: Descriptive Cataloguing Rules. 72p. 1980. pap. 5.50 (ISBN 92-0-178180-6, IN/R5, IAEA). Unipub.

Jackson, Miles M., ed. Comparative & International Librarianship. LC 77-98710. 1970. lib. bdg. 16.00x (ISBN 0-8371-3327-0, JAL/). Greenwood.

--International Handbook of Contemporary Developments in Librarianship. LC 80-27306. (Illus.). 672p. 1981. lib. bdg. 65.00 (ISBN 0-313-21372-0, JIH/). Greenwood.

Jackson, Sidney L. Brief History of Libraries & Librarianship in the West. (Illus.). 1974. text ed. 22.00 (ISBN 0-07-032118-3, C). McGraw.

Jefferson, George. Public Library Administration. 1966. 4.75 (ISBN 0-8022-0796-0). Philos Lib.

Jeffreys, A. E., ed. The Art of the Librarian: A Collection of Original Papers from the Library of the University of Newcastle Upon Tyne. 200p. 1976. 14.95 (ISBN 0-85362-151-9, Oriel). Routledge & Kegan.

Josey, E. J., ed. Information Society: Issues & Answers. LC 78-17708. (Neal-Schuman Professional Bk). 1978. lib. bdg. 16.50x (ISBN 0-912700-16-5). Oryx Pr.

Karetzky, Stephen. Reading Research & Librarianshop: A History & Anaylsis. LC 80-1715. (Contributions in Librarianship & Information Science Ser.: No. 36). (Illus.). 448p. 1981. lib. bdg. 37.50 (ISBN 0-313-22226-6, KRR/). Greenwood.

Katz, William A., ed. Library Lit. Nine: The Best of 1978. LC 78-154842. 1979. 13.00 (ISBN 0-8108-1213-4). Scarecrow.

--Library Lit. Seven: The Best of 1976. LC 78-154842. 1977. 13.00 (ISBN 0-8108-1017-4). Scarecrow.

--Library Lit. Six: The Best of 1975. LC 78-154842. 1976. 13.00 (ISBN 0-8108-0923-0). Scarecrow.

Katz, William A. & Schwartz, Joel J., eds. Library Lit. The Best of 1970. LC 78-154842. 1971. 13.00 (ISBN 0-8108-0418-2). Scarecrow.

Kent, et al. Encyclopedia of Library & Information Science, Vol. 31. 512p. 1981. 45.00 (ISBN 0-8247-2031-8). Dekker.

Kirk, Thomas. Course-Related Library & Literature-Use Instruction. LC 79-64352. (Micropapers Editions Ser.). 1979. 14.95x (ISBN 0-88432-013-8). J Norton Pubs.

Kirkendall, Carolyn A., ed. Directions for the Decade: Library Instruction in the 1980's. LC 81-80191. (Library Orientation Ser.: No. 12). 1981. 14.95 (ISBN 0-87650-131-5). Pierian.

Kirkendall, Carolyn B. Improving Library Instruction. LC 79-87707. (Library Orientation Ser.: No. 9). 1979. 14.95 (ISBN 0-87650-109-9). Pierian.

Knievel, Helen A., ed. Cooperative Services: A Guide to Policies & Procedures in Library Systems. 275p. 1981. 19.95x (ISBN 0-918212-56-1). Neal-Schuman.

Koops, Willeur R. & Stellingwerf, Johannes. Developments in Collection Building in University Libraries in Western Europe. 109p. 1977. text ed. 17.00 (ISBN 3-7940-7020-8, Pub. by K G Saur). Shoe String.

Lee, Joel M. & Hamilton, Beth A., eds. As Much to Learn As to Teach: Essays in Honor of Lester Asheim. 1979. 14.50 (ISBN 0-208-01751-8, Linnet). Shoe String.

Lee, Sul H., ed. A Challenge for Academic Libraries: How to Motivate Students to Use the Library. LC 73-78295. (Library Orientation Ser.: No. 2). 1973. 14.95 (ISBN 0-87650-039-4). Pierian.

--Planning-Programming-Budgeting System (PPBS) Implications for Library Management. LC 73-78314. (Library Management Ser.: No. 1). 1973. 14.95 (ISBN 0-87650-040-8). Pierian.

Librarianship & the Franciscan Library. (Franciscan Educational Conferences Ser). 1947. pap. 3.75 (ISBN 0-685-77546-1). Franciscan Herald.
Library & Information Technology Association. The Closing the Catalog: Proceedings of the LITA Institute. Gapen, D. Kaye & Juergens, Bonnie, eds. 1980. lib. bdg. 18.50x (ISBN 0-912700-56-4). Oryx Pr.
Library Objectives, Goals, & Activities. LC 73-22178. 105p. 1973. 5.00 (ISBN 0-913578-05-3). Inglewood Ca.
Liebaers, Herman. Mostly in the Line of Duty: Thirty Years with Books. 1980. lib. bdg. 29.00 (ISBN 90-247-2228-4, Pub. by Martinus Nijhoff Netherlands). Kluwer Boston.
Lock, Reginald N. Library Administration. 1965. 4.75 (ISBN 0-8022-0985-8). Philos Lib.
Luciw, Wasyl. Tvortsi Netlinnoi Krasy. (Ukra.). 1972. pap. text ed. 8.00 (ISBN 0-918884-05-5). Slavia Lib.
Lushington, H. N. Libraries Designed for Users. 1979. 22.50 (ISBN 0-915794-29-2, 6559). Gaylord Prof Pubns.
McClure, Charles R. Information for Academic Library Decision Making: The Case for Organizational Information Management. LC 79-8412. (Contributions in Librarianship & Information Science: No. 31). (Illus.). xvi, 227p. 1980. lib. bdg. 23.95 (ISBN 0-313-21398-4, MCA/). Greenwood.
McCrimmon, Barbara, ed. American Library Philosophy: An Anthology. (Contributions to Library Literature Ser.). xxiv, 248p. (Orig.). 1975. 15.00 (ISBN 0-208-01503-5). Shoe String.
Madan, Falconer. Books in Manuscript. LC 68-25315. (Reference Ser., No. 44). (Illus.). 1972. Repr. of 1893 ed. lib. bdg. 29.95 (ISBN 0-8383-0213-0). Haskell.
Malinconico, S. Michael & Fasana, Paul. The Future of the Catalog: The Library's Choices. LC 79-16619. (Professional Librarian Ser.). 1979. softcover 24.50x (ISBN 0-914236-32-6). Knowledge Indus.
Marshall, John D. Of, by & for Librarians: Second Series. (Contributions to Library Literature Ser). x, 242p. 1974. 16.50 (ISBN 0-208-01333-4). Shoe String.
Martin, Murray S. Issues in Personnel Management, Vol. 14. Stueart, Robert D., ed. LC 81-81649. (Foundations in Library & Information Sciences). 250p. 1981. 32.50 (ISBN 0-89232-136-9). Jai Pr.
Mason, Robert M. & Crepps, John E., eds. Information Services: Economics, Management, & Technology. (Westview Special Studies in Information Management). 200p. 1980. lib. bdg. 27.75x (ISBN 0-89158-938-4). Westview.
Matarazzo, James M. Library Problems in Science & Technology. LC 70-164033. (Problem-Centered Approaches to Librarianship Ser.). 167p. 1971. 18.50 (ISBN 0-8352-0486-3). Bowker.
Meder, Marylouise D., ed. Library School Review, Vol. 17. 1978. pap. 2.00 (ISBN 0-686-23580-0). Sch Lib Sci.
Miksa, Francis, ed. Charles Ammi Cutter: Library Systematizer. LC 76-58870. (Heritage of Librarianship: No. 3). 1977. lib. bdg. 20.00x (ISBN 0-87287-112-6). Libs Unl.
Miller, Shirley. The Vertical File & Its Satellites: A Handbook of Acquisition, Processing, & Organization. 2nd ed. LC 79-13773. (Library Science Text Ser.). 1979. lib. bdg. 17.50x (ISBN 0-87287-164-9). Libs Unl.
Milne, A. T., ed. Librarianship & Literature. 1970. text ed. 17.75x (ISBN 0-485-11117-9, Athlone Pr). Humanities.
Morehead, Joe. Introduction to U. S. Public Documents. 2nd ed. LC 78-16866. (Library Science Text). (Illus.). 1978. lib. bdg. 22.50x (ISBN 0-87287-186-X); pap. text ed. 13.50x (ISBN 0-87287-190-8). Libs Unl.
Naude, Gabriel. Advice on Establishing a Library. LC 76-1855. 110p. 1976. Repr. of 1950 ed. lib. bdg. 15.00x (ISBN 0-8371-8746-X, NAAE). Greenwood.
New, Peter. Education for Librarianship. 1978. 15.00 (ISBN 0-208-01548-5, Linnet). Shoe String.
New York University Libraries. Fales Library Checklist: First Supplement. LC 71-122494. 1973. 47.50 (ISBN 0-404-11203-X). AMS Pr.
Nichols, Harold. Local Studies Librarianship. 128p. 1979. 12.00 (ISBN 0-89664-415-4). K G Saur.
Nordenstreng, Kaarle. Mass Media Declaration of UNESCO. (Communications & Information Science Ser.). 250p. 1981. text ed. 22.50 (ISBN 0-89391-077-5). Ablex Pub.
Orr, J. M. Libraries As Communication Systems. LC 76-8739. (Contributions in Librarianship & Information Science: No. 17). 240p. 1977. lib. bdg. 16.95 (ISBN 0-8371-8936-5, ORL/). Greenwood.
Palmer, B. I. From Little Acorns: The Library Profession in Britain. 1967. 5.00x (ISBN 0-210-27190-6). Asia.
Penna, C. V. Planning of Library & Documentation Services. 2nd ed. Sewell, P. H. & Liebaers, Herman, eds. (UNESCO Manuals for Libraries Ser.). 1970. Orig. Title: Planning Library Services. 1970. pap. 7.25 (ISBN 92-3-100814-5, U455, UNESCO). Unipub.
Petru, William C., ed. The Library: An Introduction for Library Assistants. LC 66-29578. 1967. 5.00 (ISBN 0-87111-175-6). SLA.
Polette, Nancy. The Vodka in the Punch & Other Notes from a Library Supervisor. 153p. (Orig.). 1975. 13.50 (ISBN 0-208-01494-2, Linnet). Shoe String.
Powell, Judith W. & LeLieuvre, Robert B. Peoplework: Communications Dynamics for Librarians. 152p. 1980. pap. 6.50 (ISBN 0-8389-0290-1). ALA.
Preksto, Peter W., Jr. Library Skills. (Basic Skills Library). (Illus.). (gr. 4 up). 1979. PLB 5.95 (ISBN 0-87191-714-9). Creative Ed.
Professional & Non-Professional Duties in Libraries. 1974. pap. text ed. 8.25x (ISBN 0-85365-307-0, Pub. by Lib Assn England). Oryx Pr.
Ray, Sheila. Children's Librarianship. 12.00 (ISBN 0-89664-413-8). K G Saur.
Rayward, W. Boyd, ed. Variety in Librarianship: Essays in Honor of John Wallace Metcalfe. 1979. 20.00 (ISBN 0-8389-3226-6). ALA.
Reilly, Jane A. Public Librarian As Adult Learners' Advisor: An Innovation in Human Services. LC 80-27307. (Contributions in Librarianship & Information Science Ser.: No. 38). (Illus.). 184p. 1981. lib. bdg. 25.00 (ISBN 0-313-22134-0, REP/). Greenwood.
Renfro, Nancy. Puppet Corner in Every Library. (Illus.). 110p. 1977. pap. 8.95 (ISBN 0-931044-01-4). Renfro Studios.
Research Librarianship: Essays in Honor of Robert B. Downs. LC 78-163902. 162p. 1971. 14.95 (ISBN 0-8352-0487-1). Bowker.
Reynolds, Michael M., ed. Reader in Library Cooperation. LC 72-86635. (Reader Ser. in Library & Information Science: Vol. 11). 1973. 17.00 (ISBN 0-910972-22-2). IHS-PDS.
--Reader in the Academic Library. LC 71-112300. (Reader Ser. in Library & Information Science: Vol. 3). 374p. 1970. 16.00 (ISBN 0-910972-00-1). IHS-PDS.
Riggs, Donald E., ed. Visualizing the Future: A Guide to Library Leadership. 1981. lib. bdg. price not set (ISBN 0-912700-64-5). Oryx Pr.
Rochell, Carlton, ed. Wheeler & Goldhor's Practical Administration of Public Libraries. rev. ed. LC 79-3401. (Illus.). 480p. 1981. 27.50 (ISBN 0-06-013601-4, HarpT). Harper Row.
Ruoss, Martin. A Policy & Procedure Manual for Church & Synagogue Libraries: A Do-It-Yourself Guide. LC 79-28676. 1980. pap. 3.75 (ISBN 0-915324-17-2). CSLA.
Sable, Martin H. International & Area Studies Librarianship: Case Studies. LC 73-5547. 1973. 10.00 (ISBN 0-8108-0622-3). Scarecrow.
Samore, Theodore. Acquisition of Foreign Materials for U.S. Libraries. LC 73-4314. 1973. 13.00 (ISBN 0-8108-0614-2). Scarecrow.
Schurr, Sandra. Library Lingo. (Choose-a-Card Ser.). (Illus.). 32p. (gr. 3-6). 1981. pap. text ed. 5.95 (ISBN 0-86530-037-2, IP 372). Incentive Pubns.
Shaffer, Dale E. A Handbook of Library Ideas: 150 Innovative Practices for the Creative Librarian. 1977. pap. 3.50 (ISBN 0-915060-12-4). D E Shaffer.
Shera, Jesse H. Documentation & the Organization of Knowledge. Foskett, D. J., ed. & intro. by. 1966. 15.00 (ISBN 0-208-00083-6, Archon). Shoe String.
--An Introduction to Library Science: Basic Elements of Library Services. LC 76-21332. (Library Science Text Ser.). 1976. lib. bdg. 13.50x (ISBN 0-87287-173-8). Libs Unl.
--Knowing Books & Men; Knowing Computers, Too. LC 73-85553. 363p. 1973. lib. bdg. 17.50x (ISBN 0-87287-073-1). Libs Unl.
Shores, Louis. Mark Hopkins' Log & Other Essays. Marshall, J. D., ed. 1965. 19.50 (ISBN 0-208-00029-1). Shoe String.
Smith, Josephine M. Chronology of Librarianship. LC 67-12062. 1968. 10.00 (ISBN 0-8108-0024-1). Scarecrow.
Smith, Ruth S. Workshop Planning. rev. ed. LC 78-24240. (Guide Ser.: No. 3). (Illus.). 1979. pap. 6.50x (ISBN 0-915324-15-6). CSLA.
Soergel, Dagobert. Indexing Languages & Thesauri: Construction & Maintenance. LC 73-20301. (Information Sciences Ser.). 800p. 1974. 51.50 (ISBN 0-471-81047-9, Pub. by Wiley-Interscience). Wiley.
Spyers-Duran, Peter & Mann, Thomas, Jr., eds. Shaping Library Collections for the 1980s. 1981. lib. bdg. 18.50 (ISBN 0-912700-58-0). Oryx Pr.
Stevens, Norman D., ed. Essays from the New England Academic Librarians' Writing Seminar. LC 80-21502. 230p. 1980. 12.50 (ISBN 0-8108-1365-3). Scarecrow.
Stevens, Rolland E., ed. Supervision of Employees in Libraries. LC 79-10860. (Allerton Park Institute Ser: No. 24). 113p. 1979. 9.00 (ISBN 0-87845-051-3). U of Ill Lib Info Sci.
Stevenson, Grace T. Southwestern Library Association Project Report: ALA Chapter Relationships-National, Regional & State. 160p. 1971. pap. 2.50 (ISBN 0-8389-0101-8). ALA.
Studies in Comparative Librarianship: Three Sevensma Prize Essays. 1973. pap. 13.25x (ISBN 0-85365-306-2, Pub. by Lib Assn England). Oryx Pr.
Stueart, Robert, ed. Academic Librarianship: Trends & Issues. 250p. 1981. 19.95x (ISBN 0-918212-52-9). Neal-Schuman.
Swanson, Don R., ed. The Role of Libraries in the Growth of Knowledge. LC 79-5467. 1980. lib. bdg. 10.00x (ISBN 0-226-78468-1). U of Chicago Pr.
Swanson, Don R. & Bookstein, Abraham, eds. Operations Research: Implications for Libraries (35th Annual Conference of the Graduate Library School, August 2-4, 1971) LC 73-185760. (University of Chicago Studies in Library Science). (Illus.). 160p. 1972. lib. bdg. 10.00 (ISBN 0-226-78466-5). U of Chicago Pr.
Swarthout, Arthur W. Selecting Library Materials. rev. ed. LC 74-10504. (Guide Ser.: No. 4). 1978. pap. 2.50x (ISBN 0-915324-07-5). CSLA.
Tauber, Maurice F. Technical Services in Libraries. LC 54-10328. (Columbia Library Service Studies, No. 7). 1954. 25.00x (ISBN 0-231-02054-6). Columbia U Pr.
Taylor, Mary M., ed. School Library and Media Center Acquisitions Policies & Procedures. 1981. lib. bdg. 17.50 (ISBN 0-912700-70-X). Oryx Pr.
Thomassen, Cora E., ed. CATV & Its Implications for Libraries. LC 74-620101. (Allerton Park Institute: No. 19). 91p. 1974. 7.00x (ISBN 0-87845-040-8). U of Ill Lib Info Sci.
Thompson, James. A History of the Principles of Librarianship. 1977. 17.50 (ISBN 0-208-01661-9, Linnet). Shoe String.
Totterdell, B., et al, eds. The Effective Library. 1976. 34.50x (ISBN 0-85365-248-1, Pub. by Lib Assn England). Oryx Pr.
University of Chicago - Graduate Library School - 25th Conference. Persistent Issues in American Librarianship. Asheim, Lester, ed. 1961. 7.00x (ISBN 0-226-02960-3). U of Chicago Pr.
Use of Machine: Readable Data from External Sources in Large Research Libraries & Library Systems. (IFLA Publicaton: Vol. 16). 1980. write for info. (ISBN 0-89664-062-0). K G Saur.
Vann, Sarah K. Melvil Dewey: His Enduring Presence in Librarianship. LC 77-21852. (Heritage of Librarianship Ser.: No. 4). 1978. lib. bdg. 20.00x (ISBN 0-87287-134-7). Libs Unl.
Venkatappaiah, V., ed. March of Library Science. 1979. text ed. 37.50x (ISBN 0-7069-0482-6, Pub. by Vikas India). Advent NY.
Vishwanathan, C. G. Public Library Operations & Services. 2nd rev. ed. 5.50x (ISBN 0-210-33927-6). Asia.
Vosper, Robert & Newkirk, Leone, eds. National & International Library of Planning. 168p. 1976. 20.50 (ISBN 0-686-74469-1, Pub. by K G Saur). Shoe String.
Wallis, M. Industrial Relations & the Library Manager. (A Library Association Management Pamplet Ser.). 1981. pap. 8.95x (ISBN 0-85365-542-1, Pub. by Lib Assn Ehgland). Oryx Pr.
Wasserman, Paul, et al, eds. LIST: Library & Information Services Today, Vol. 5. LC 74-7634. 633p. 1975. 52.00 (ISBN 0-8103-0387-6). Gale.
--LIST: Library & Information Services Today, an International Registry of Research & Innovation, Vol. 4. LC 74-7634. 548p. 1974. 52.00 (ISBN 0-8103-0386-8). Gale.
Wedgeworth, Robert, ed. ALA Yearbook 1977. LC 76-647548. 1977. 35.00 (ISBN 0-8389-0233-2). ALA.
--ALA Yearbook, 1980. 432p. 1980. 55.00 (ISBN 0-8389-0306-1). ALA.
Wedgeworth, Robert, et al, eds. ALA World Encyclopedia of Library & Information Services. LC 80-10912. 624p. 1980. 85.00 (ISBN 0-8389-0305-3). ALA.
Weibel, Kathleen & Heim, Kathleen M., eds. The Role of Women in Librarianship, 1876-1976: The Entry, Advancement & Struggle for Equalization in One Profession. LC 78-27302. (Neal-Schuman Professional Bk). 1979. lib. bdg. 19.50x (ISBN 0-912700-01-7). Oryx Pr.
White, Brenda. Sourcebook of Planning Information. (Guides to Subject Literature Ser.). 1971. 22.50 (ISBN 0-208-01079-3, Linnet). Shoe String.
White, C. M. Bases of Modern Librarianship. 1964. 22.00 (ISBN 0-08-010627-7). Pergamon.
Wilkinson, Billy R., ed. Reader in Undergraduate Libraries. LC 78-9504. (Reader in Librarianship & Information Science: No. 25). 1978. text ed. 22.00 (ISBN 0-910972-76-1). IHS-PDS.
Williams, Martha E., ed. The Annual Review of Information Science & Technology, Vol. 11, 1976. LC 66-25096. (Illus.). 1976. 42.50 (ISBN 0-87715-212-8). Knowledge Indus.
--Annual Review of Information Science & Techology 1979, Vol. 14. LC 66-25096. 1979. 42.50 (ISBN 0-914236-44-X). Knowledge Indus.
Williamson, Charles C. The Williamson Reports of Nineteen Twenty-One & Nineteen Twenty-Three: Including Training for Library Work & Training for Library Service. LC 78-25204. 1971. 13.50 (ISBN 0-8108-0417-4). Scarecrow.
Wilson, A. Planning Approach to Library Management. (Management Pamphlet Ser.). 1979. pap. text ed. 8.95x (ISBN 0-85365-522-7, Pub. by Lib Assn England). Oryx Pr.
Wilson, Louis R. Education & Libraries: Selected Papers by Louis Round Wilson. Tauber, Maurice F. & Orne, Jerrold, eds. 1966. 18.50 (ISBN 0-208-00034-8). Shoe String.
Winger, Howard & Smith, Richard. Deterioration & Preservation of Library Materials. LC 78-115971. (Studies in Library Science Ser). 1970. 12.00x (ISBN 0-226-90201-3). U of Chicago Pr.
Wisdom, Aline C. Introduction to Library Services for Library Media Technical Assistants. (Illus.). 416p. 1974. 12.95 (ISBN 0-07-071140-2, G); instructors' manual 2.50 (ISBN 0-07-071141-0). McGraw.
Wright, Kieth C. Library & Information Services for Handicapped Individuals. LC 78-26472. 1979. lib. bdg. 17.50x (ISBN 0-87287-129-0). Libs Unl.

LIBRARY SCIENCE–BIBLIOGRAPHY

Burton, Margaret. Bibliography of Librarianship: Classified & Annotated Guide to the Library Literature of the World Excluding Slavonic & Oriental Languages. 1970. 22.50 (ISBN 0-8337-0429-X). B Franklin.
Burton, Margaret & Vosburgh, Marion. A Bibliography of Librarianship. 1976. lib. bdg. 59.95 (ISBN 0-8490-1499-9). Gordon Pr.
Burton, Margaret & Vosburgh, Marion E. A Bibliography of Librarianship: Classified & Annotated Guide to the Library Literature of the World. 176p. 1934. Repr. 32.00 (ISBN 0-403-01777-7). Scholarly.
Busha, Charles H., ed. A Library Science Research Reader & Bibliographic Guide. LC 80-22507. 201p. 1981. lib. bdg. 22.50 (ISBN 0-87287-237-8). Libs Unl.
Cannons, Harry G. Bibliography of Library Economy. LC 73-122221. (Bibliography & Reference Ser.: No. 350). 1971. Repr. of 1920 ed. lib. bdg. 41.50 (ISBN 0-8337-0458-3). B Franklin.
Columbia University. Dictionary Catalog of the Library of the School of Library Service, 7 Vols. 1962. Set. lib. bdg. 665.00 (ISBN 0-8161-0634-7). G K Hall.
Committee of the Young Adult Services Division, ALA. Media & the Young Adult: A Selected Bibliography 1950-1972. LC 77-699. 1977. pap. 5.00 (ISBN 0-8389-3188-X). ALA.
Cope, Gabriele E. Librarianship at a Four Year University. (Orig.). 1981. pap. 15.95 (ISBN 0-686-74617-1). Ego Bks.
Educational Resources Information Center. Library & Information Sciences, an ERIC Bibliography. LC 72-82741. 1972. 11.50 (ISBN 0-02-468630-1). Macmillan Info.
Johann gottfried herder institut. Alphabetischer Katalog der Bibliothek des Johann gottfried herder-Instituts: Second Supplement. (Library Catalogs-Supplements Ser.). 1981. lib. bdg. 350.00 (ISBN 0-8161-0277-5). G K Hall.
Katz, William A., ed. Library Lit. Eight: The Best of 1977. LC 78-154842. 1978. lib. bdg. 13.00 (ISBN 0-8108-1125-1). Scarecrow.
--Library Lit. Two: The Best of 1971. LC 78-154842. 1972. 13.00 (ISBN 0-8108-0519-7). Scarecrow.
Lengenfelder, Helga, ed. International Bibliography of the Book Trade & Librarianship 1976-79. 12th ed. (Handbook of International Documentation & Information Ser.: Vol. 2). 800p. 1981. 95.00 (ISBN 3-598-20504-X, Dist. by Gale Research). K G Saur.
Lilley, Dorothy B. & Badough, Rose M., eds. Library & Information Sciences: A Guide to Information Sources. (Bks., Libraries, & Publishing Information Guide Ser.: Vol. 5). 200p. 1981. 36.00 (ISBN 0-8103-1501-7). Gale.
Magnotti, Shirley. Master's Theses in Library Science 1970-1974: Supplement. LC 75-8232. 1976. 10.50x (ISBN 0-87875-100-9). Whitston Pub.
--Masters Theses in Library Science 1960-1969. LC 75-8232. 306p. 1975. 18.00x (ISBN 0-87875-074-6). Whitston Pub.

Michael, Mary E. Continuing Professional Education in Librarianship & Other Fields: A Classified & Annotated Bibliography, 1965-1974. LC 75-8998. (Reference Library of Humanities: Vol. 16). 224p. 1975. lib. bdg. 25.00 (ISBN 0-8240-1085-X). Garland Pub.
New York Public Library, Research Libraries & Library of Congress. Bibliographic Guide to Conference Publications: 1977. 1977. lib. bdg. 100.00 (ISBN 0-8161-6836-9). G K Hall.
Pantelidis, Veronica S. The Arab World: Libraries & Librarianship 1960-1976; a Bibliography. 1979. pap. 14.50 (ISBN 0-7201-0821-7, Pub. by Mansell England). Merrimack Bk Serv.
Research Libraries of the New York Public Library & the Library of Congress. Bibliographic Guide to Conference Publication: 1980. (Library Catalogs-Bib. Guides Ser.). 1981. lib. bdg. 130.00 (ISBN 0-8161-6884-9). G K Hall.
Schutze, Gertrude. Documentation Source Book. LC 65-13551. 1965. 18.50 (ISBN 0-8108-0271-6). Scarecrow.
--Information & Library Science Source Book: Supplement to Documentation Source Book. LC 72-1157. 1972. 16.50 (ISBN 0-8108-0466-2). Scarecrow.
Vervliet, Hendrik D., ed. Annual Bibliography of the History of the Printed Book & Libraries. 1978. pap. 89.50 (ISBN 90-247-2062-1, Pub. by Martinus Nijhoff Netherlands). Kluwer Boston.

LIBRARY SCIENCE–CONGRESSES

see Library Conferences

LIBRARY SCIENCE–DATA PROCESSING

Atherton, Pauline & Christian, Roger W. Librarians & Online Services. LC 77-25275. (Professional Librarian Ser.). 1977. 24.50x (ISBN 0-914236-13-X). Knowledge Indus.
Brelsford, William M. & Relles, Daniel A. Statlib: A Statistical Computing Library. 448p. 1981. text ed. 17.50 (ISBN 0-13-846220-8). P-H.
Chicago, Illinois Regional Library Council. INFOPASS-DATAPASS: Procedures Manual & Directory. 3rd ed. 16p. 1981. pap. 10.00 (ISBN 0-917060-12-1). Ill Regional Lib Coun.
Clinic on Library Applications of Data Processing Proceedings, 1974. Applications of Minicomputers to Library & Related Problems. Lancaster, F. W., ed. LC 65-1841. 195p. 1974. 7.00x (ISBN 0-87845-041-6). U of Ill Lib Info Sci.
Clinic on Library Applications of Data Processing Proceedings, 1970. MARC Uses & Users. Henderson, Kathryn L., ed. LC 65-1841. 113p. 1971. 7.00x (ISBN 0-87845-019-X). U of Ill Lib Info Sci.
Clinic on Library Applications of Data Processing, 1964. Proceedings. Goldhor, Herbert, ed. 117p. 1965. pap. 4.00x (ISBN 0-87845-013-0). U of Ill Lib Info Sci.
Clinic on Library Applications of Data Processing, 1968. Proceedings. Carroll, Dewey E., ed. LC 65-1841. 235p. 1969. 7.00x (ISBN 0-87845-017-3). U of Ill Lib Info Sci.
Clinic on Library Applications of Data Processing, 1969. Proceedings. Carroll, Dewey E., ed. LC 65-1841. 149p. 1970. 7.00x (ISBN 0-87845-018-1). U of Ill Lib Info Sci.
Clinic on Library Applications of Data Processing, 1980. Public Access to Library Automation: Proceedings. Divilbiss, J. L., ed. 1981. 10.00 (ISBN 0-87845-065-3). U of Ill Lib Info Sci.
Computerized Circulation Systems, 6 issues, Vol. 1. Incl. No. 1. Computerized Circulation Systems at the University of Arizona. Peters, Charles, ed. 1974. 7.50 ea., non-members 10.00; 41.25 set, non-members 55.00 (ISBN 0-685-45893-8); pap. 6.00 ea., non-members 8.00; pap. 33.00 set, non-members 44.00 (ISBN 0-685-45895-4). Lib Auto Res Con.
Davis, Charles H. Illustrative Computer Programming for Libraries: Selected Examples for Information Specialists. LC 74-22. (Contributions in Librarianship & Information Science: No. 12). (Illus.). 1974. lib. bdg. 15.00x (ISBN 0-8371-7354-X, DAC/). Greenwood.
Electronic Data Processing in Libraries. 1975. text ed. 19.50 (ISBN 3-7940-5214-5). K G Saur.
Eyre, John & Tonks, Peter. Computers & Systems: An Introduction for Librarians. 1971. 12.50 (ISBN 0-208-01073-4, Linnet). Shoe String.
Gellatly, Peter, ed. The Management of Serials Automation: Current Technology & Strategies for Future Planning. (The Serials Librarian Ser.: Vol. 5). 325p. 1981. 45.00 (ISBN 0-917724-37-2, B37). Haworth Pr.
Gough, Chester R. & Srikantaiah, Taverekere. Systems Analysis in Libraries: A Question & Answer Approach. (Illus.). 1978. 11.50 (ISBN 0-208-01753-4, Linnet). Shoe String.
Grosch, Audrey N. Minicomputers in Libraries, 1981-82. (Professional Librarian). 160p. 1981. professional 34.50 (ISBN 0-914236-96-2); pap. 27.50 professional (ISBN 0-914236-92-X). Knowledge Indus.
Hayes, Robert M. & Becker, Joseph. Handbook of Data Processing for Libraries. 2nd ed. LC 74-9690. (Information Sciences Ser). 712p. 1974. 39.95 (ISBN 0-471-36483-5, Pub. by Wiley-Interscience). Wiley.
Hoover, Ryan, ed. Library & Information Manager's Guide to Online Services. (Professional Librarian Ser.). (Illus.). 269p. 1980. 29.50x (ISBN 0-914236-60-1); pap. 24.50x (ISBN 0-914236-52-0). Knowledge Indus.
How to Go on-Line: Guidelines for the Establishment of on-Line Services in Public Libraries. 1981. 15.00x (ISBN 0-905984-57-9, Pub. by Brit Lib England). State Mutual Bk.
Juergens, Bonnie. Self Instruction to the OCLC Models 100 & 105 Terminals, No. 1. rev., 2nd ed. Duffy, Michelle, ed. (AMIGOS Training Series: No. 1). 40p. 3 hole punch, stapled 10.00 (ISBN 0-938288-00-8). AMIGOS Biblio.
Kaplan, Louis, ed. Reader in Library Services & the Computer. LC 70-149298. (Reader Ser. in Library & Information Science: Vol. 4). 1971. 16.00 (ISBN 0-910972-01-X). IHS-PDS.
Kent & Galvin. The On Line Revolution in Libraries. (Library Science Ser.: Vol. 23). 1978. 36.75 (ISBN 0-8247-6754-3). Dekker.
Lancaster, F. W., ed. Clinic on Library Applications of Data Processing, Proceedings, 1978: Problems & Failures in Library Automation. LC 73-31801. 109p. 1979. 9.00 (ISBN 0-87845-050-5). U of Ill Lib Info Sci.
Library Applications of Data Processing Clinic, 1980. Public Access to Library Automation: Proceedings. Divilbiss, J. L., ed. 1981. write for info. (ISBN 0-87845-065-3). U of Ill Lib Sci.
Library Applications of Data Processing Clinic, 1979. The Role of the Library in an Electronic Society: Proceedings. Lancaster, F. W., ed. LC 79-19449. 200p. 1980. 9.00 (ISBN 0-87845-053-X). U of Ill Lib Info Sci.
Library Applications of Dataprocessing Clinic, 1979. Role of the Library in an Electronic Society: Proceedings. Lancaster, F. W., ed. LC 79-19449. 200p. 1980. 9.00 (ISBN 0-87845-053-X). U of Ill Lib Sci.
Marcal: Manual Para la Automatizacion De las Reglas Catalograficas Para America Latina. (Manuales del Bibliotecario Ser.). 1978. pap. text ed. 4.00 (ISBN 0-8270-3085-1). OAS.
Mott, Thomas H., Jr., et al. Introduction to PL-1 Programming for Library & Information Science. (Library & Information Science Ser.). 239p. 1972. text ed. 19.95 (ISBN 0-12-508750-0). Acad Pr.
Murphy, Marcy. On-Line Services. 1981. 3.00 (ISBN 0-686-31464-6). U of Ill Lib Sci.
On-Line Experiments in Public Libraries. 1981. 15.00x (ISBN 0-905984-56-0, Pub. by Brit Lib England). State Mutual Bk.
Palmer, Richard P. Case Studies in Library Computer Systems. LC 73-17008. (Problem-Centered Approaches to Librarianship Ser.). 214p. 1973. 18.50 (ISBN 0-8352-0642-4). Bowker.
Rowley, Jennifer E. Computers for Libraries. (Outlines of Modern Librarianship Ser.). Date not set. text ed. 12.00 (ISBN 0-89664-016-7). K G Saur.
--Mechanized In-House Information Systems. 1979. 20.50 (ISBN 0-85157-259-6, Pub. by Bingley England). Shoe String.
Salton, Gerard. Dynamic Information & Library Processing. (Illus.). 416p. 1975. ref. ed. 27.95 (ISBN 0-13-221325-7). P-H.
Simonton, Wesley & McClaskey, Marilyn J. AACR 2 & the Catalog: Theory-Structure-Changes. LC 81-11757. 78p. 1981. pap. 8.50x (ISBN 0-87287-267-X). Libs Unl.
Tedd, L. A. Introduction to Computer-Based Library Systems. 1977. 25.00 (ISBN 0-85501-221-8). Heyden.

LIBRARY SCIENCE–DICTIONARIES

American Library Association. A. L. A. Glossary of Library Terms: With a Selection of Terms in Related Fields. Thompson, Elizabeth H., ed. LC 43-51241. 1943. 5.00 (ISBN 0-8389-0000-3). ALA.
Diccionario de Bibliotecologia. 2nd ed. 458p. (Span.). 1976. 44.95 (ISBN 0-686-56656-4, S-12239). French & Eur.
Harrod, L. M. Librarian's Glossary & Reference Book. LC 76-52489. 1977. lib. bdg. 46.25x (ISBN 0-89158-727-6). Westview.
Kent & Lancour. Encyclopedia of Library & Information Science, Vol. 28. 1980. 45.00 (ISBN 0-8247-2028-8). Dekker.
Kent, et al. Encyclopedia of Library & Information Science, Vol. 29. 450p. 1980. 45.00 (ISBN 0-8247-2029-6). Dekker.
--Encyclopedia of Library & Information Science, Vol. 32. 416p. 1981. 55.00 (ISBN 0-686-72689-8). Dekker.
--Encyclopedia of Library & Information Science, Vol. 33. 400p. 1981. price not set (ISBN 0-8247-2033-4). Dekker.
Kent, A., et al. Encyclopedia of Library & Information Science. (Vol. 25). 1978. 45.00 (ISBN 0-8247-2125-X). Dekker.
Kent, A., et al, eds. Encyclopedia of Library & Information Science, Vol. 26. 1978. 45.00 (ISBN 0-8247-2126-8). Dekker.
Kent, Allen, ed. Encyclopedia of Library & Information Science, Vol. 18. 1976. 45.00 (ISBN 0-8247-2118-7). Dekker.
--Encyclopedia of Library & Information Science, Vol. 20. 1977. 45.00 (ISBN 0-8247-2120-9). Dekker.
--Encyclopedia of Library & Information Science, Vol. 21. 1977. 45.00 (ISBN 0-8247-2121-7). Dekker.
Kent, Allen & Lancour, Harold, eds. Encyclopedia of Library & Information Science, Vol. 17. 1976. 45.00 (ISBN 0-8247-2117-9). Dekker.
--Encyclopedia of Library & Information Science, Vol. 19. 1976. 45.00 (ISBN 0-8247-2119-5). Dekker.
Kent, Allen, et al, eds. Encyclopedia of Library & Information Science, Vol. 1. 1968. 45.00 (ISBN 0-8247-2101-2). Dekker.
--Encyclopedia of Library & Information Science, Vol. 2. 1969. 45.00 (ISBN 0-8247-2102-0). Dekker.
--Encyclopedia of Library & Information Science, Vol. 3. 1970. 45.00 (ISBN 0-8247-2103-9). Dekker.
--Encyclopedia of Library & Information Science, Vol. 4. 1970. 45.00 (ISBN 0-8247-2104-7). Dekker.
--Encyclopedia of Library & Information Science, Vol. 5. 1971. 45.00 (ISBN 0-8247-2105-5). Dekker.
--Encyclopedia of Library & Information Science, Vol. 6. 1971. 45.00 (ISBN 0-8247-2106-3). Dekker.
--Encyclopedia of Library & Information Science, Vol. 7. 1972. 45.00 (ISBN 0-8247-2107-1). Dekker.
--Encyclopedia of Library & Information Science, Vol. 8. 1972. 45.00 (ISBN 0-8247-2108-X). Dekker.
--Encyclopedia of Library & Information Science, Vol. 9. 1973. 45.00 (ISBN 0-8247-2109-8). Dekker.
--Encyclopedia of Library & Information Science, Vol. 10. 1973. 45.00 (ISBN 0-8247-2110-1). Dekker.
--Encyclopedia of Library & Information Science, Vol. 11. 1974. 45.00 (ISBN 0-8247-2111-X). Dekker.
--Encyclopedia of Library & Information Science, Vol. 12. 1974. 45.00 (ISBN 0-8247-2112-8). Dekker.
--Encyclopedia of Library & Information Science, Vol. 13. 1975. 45.00 (ISBN 0-8247-2113-6). Dekker.
--Encyclopedia of Library & Information Science, Vol. 14. 1975. 45.00 (ISBN 0-8247-2114-4). Dekker.
--Encyclopedia of Library & Information Science, Vol. 15. 1975. 45.00 (ISBN 0-8247-2115-2). Dekker.
--Encyclopedia of Library & Information Science, Vol. 16. 1975. 45.00 (ISBN 0-8247-2116-0). Dekker.
--Encyclopedia of Library & Information Science, Vol. 22. 1977. 45.00 (ISBN 0-8247-2122-5). Dekker.
--Encyclopedia of Library & Information Science, Vol. 23. 1977. 45.00 (ISBN 0-8247-2123-3). Dekker.
--Encyclopedia of Library & Information Science, Vol. 24. 1978. 45.00 (ISBN 0-8247-2124-1). Dekker.
Kunze, Horst. Lexikon des Bibliothekswesens, 2 vols, Vols. 1 & 2. 2nd ed. (Ger.). 1974. 82.00 (ISBN 3-7940-4210-7, M-7209). French & Eur.
Pipics, Z. Woerterbuch Des Bibliothekars in 22 Sprachen. 6th rev. ed. 385p. (Librarian's Practical Dictionary in 22 Languages). 1974. 95.00 (ISBN 3-7940-4109-7, M-7540, Pub. by Vlg. Dokumentation). French & Eur.
Pipics, Zoltan. Librarians Practical Dictionary in 22 Languages (Worterbuch Des Bibliothekars in 22 Sprachen) 6th ed. LC 73-695. 1974. 64.50 (ISBN 3-7940-4109-7, Pub by Verlag Dokumentation). Bowker.
Vaillancourt, Pauline M. International Directory of Acronyms in Library, Information & Computer Sciences. 1980. 45.00 (ISBN 0-8352-1152-5). Bowker.

LIBRARY SCIENCE–EXAMINATIONS, QUESTIONS ETC.

Arco Editorial Board. Librarian. 4th ed. LC 75-37087. (Orig.). 1975. lib. bdg. 14.00 o. p. (ISBN 0-668-01403-2); pap. 10.00 (ISBN 0-668-00060-0). Arco.
Rudman, Jack. Assistant Library Director. (Career Examination Ser.: C-1108). (Cloth bdg. avail. on request). pap. 10.00 (ISBN 0-8373-1108-X). Natl Learning.
--Assistant Library Director 1. (Career Examination Ser.: C-2783). (Cloth bdg. avail. on request). 1980. pap. 12.00 (ISBN 0-8373-2783-0). Natl Learning.
--Assistant Library Director 2. (Career Examination Ser.: C-2784). (Cloth bdg. avail. on request). 1980. pap. 12.00 (ISBN 0-8373-2784-9). Natl Learning.
--Assistant Library Director 3. (Career Examination Ser.: C-2785). (Cloth bdg. avail. on request). 1980. pap. 14.00 (ISBN 0-8373-2785-7). Natl Learning.
--Assistant Library Director 4. (Career Examination Ser.: C-2786). (Cloth bdg. avail. on request). 1980. pap. 16.00 (ISBN 0-8373-2786-5). Natl Learning.
--Assistant Library Director 5. (Career Examination Ser.: C-2787). (Cloth bdg. avail. on request). 1980. pap. 18.00 (ISBN 0-8373-2787-3). Natl Learning.
--Department Librarian. (Career Examination Ser.: C-194). (Cloth bdg. avail. on request). pap. 8.00 (ISBN 0-8373-0194-7). Natl Learning.
--Department Library Aide. (Career Examination Ser.: C-206). (Cloth bdg. avail. on request). pap. 8.00 (ISBN 0-8373-0206-4). Natl Learning.
--Director of Library. (Career Examination Ser.: C-1254). (Cloth bdg. avail. on request). pap. 10.00 (ISBN 0-8373-1254-X). Natl Learning.
--Librarian. (Career Examination Ser.: C-438). (Cloth bdg. avail. on request). pap. 8.00 (ISBN 0-8373-0438-5). Natl Learning.
--Librarian Trainee. (Career Examination Ser.: C-2864). (Cloth bdg. avail. on request). 1980. pap. 8.00 (ISBN 0-8373-2864-0). Natl Learning.
--Librarian 1. (Career Examination Ser.: C-2788). (Cloth bdg. avail. on request). 1980. pap. 10.00 (ISBN 0-8373-2788-1). Natl Learning.
--Librarian 2. (Career Examination Ser.: C-2789). (Cloth bdg. avail. on request). 1980. pap. 12.00 (ISBN 0-8373-2789-X). Natl Learning.
--Librarian 3. (Career Examination Ser.: C-2790). (Cloth bdg. avail. on request). 1980. pap. 12.00 (ISBN 0-8373-2790-3). Natl Learning.
--Librarian 4. (Career Examination Ser.: C-2791). (Cloth bdg. avail. on request). 1980. pap. 14.00 (ISBN 0-8373-2791-1). Natl Learning.
--Librarian 5. (Career Examination Ser.: C-2792). (Cloth bdg. avail. on request). 1980. pap. 16.00 (ISBN 0-8373-2792-X). Natl Learning.
--Library Assistant. (Career Examination Ser.: C-1345). (Cloth bdg. avail. on request). pap. 8.00 (ISBN 0-8373-1345-7). Natl Learning.
--Library Clerk. (Career Examination Ser.: C-1931). (Cloth bdg. avail. on request). pap. 8.00 (ISBN 0-8373-1931-5). Natl Learning.
--Library Director 1. (Career Examination Ser.: C-1929). (Cloth bdg. avail. on request). pap. 10.00 (ISBN 0-8373-1929-3). Natl Learning.
--Library Director 2. (Career Examination Ser.: C-2779). (Cloth bdg. avail. on request). 1980. pap. 12.00 (ISBN 0-8373-2779-2). Natl Learning.
--Library Director 3. (Career Examination Ser.: C-2780). (Cloth bdg. avail. on request). 1980. pap. 14.00 (ISBN 0-8373-2780-6). Natl Learning.
--Library Director 4. (Career Examination Ser.: C-2781). (Cloth bdg. avail. on request). 1980. pap. 16.00 (ISBN 0-8373-2781-4). Natl Learning.
--Library Director 5. (Career Examination Ser.: C-2782). (Cloth bdg. avail. on request). 1980. pap. 18.00 (ISBN 0-8373-2782-2). Natl Learning.
--Library, Elementary School. (Teachers License Examination Ser.: T-38). (Cloth bdg. avail. on request). pap. 10.00 (ISBN 0-8373-8038-3). Natl Learning.
--Library, Secondary School. (Teachers License Examination Ser.: T-39). (Cloth bdg. avail. on request). pap. 10.00 (ISBN 0-8373-8039-1). Natl Learning.
--Principal Library Clerk. (Career Examination Ser.: C-1932). (Cloth bdg. avail. on request). pap. 10.00 (ISBN 0-8373-1932-3). Natl Learning.
--Professional Library Examination. (Career Examination Ser.: C-623). (Cloth bdg. avail. on request). pap. 10.00 (ISBN 0-8373-0623-X). Natl Learning.
--Public Librarian. (Career Examination Ser.: C-989). (Cloth bdg. avail. on request). pap. 8.00 (ISBN 0-8373-0989-1). Natl Learning.
--Senior Librarian. (Career Examination Ser.: C-1011). (Cloth bdg. avail. on request). pap. 10.00 (ISBN 0-8373-1011-3). Natl Learning.
--Senior Librarian 1. (Career Examination Ser.: C-1821). (Cloth bdg. avail. on request). pap. 10.00 (ISBN 0-8373-1821-1). Natl Learning.
--Senior Library Clerk. (Career Examination Ser.: C-1930). (Cloth bdg. avail. on request). pap. 10.00 (ISBN 0-8373-1930-7). Natl Learning.

LIBRARY SCIENCE–MATHEMATICAL MODELS

Williams, James G & Pope, Elspeth. Simulation Activities in Library Communication & Information Science. (Communication Science & Technology Ser.: Vol. 6). 1976. 34.75 (ISBN 0-8247-6376-9). Dekker.

LIBRARY SCIENCE–PERIODICALS

Bourne, R., ed. Handbook on Serials Librarianship. 1981. 23.00x (ISBN 0-85365-631-2, Pub. by Lib Assn England); pap. text ed. 13.50x (ISBN 0-85365-721-1). Oryx Pr.

Cannons, Harry G. Bibliography of Library Economy. LC 73-122221. (Bibliography & Reference Ser.: No. 350). 1971. Repr. of 1920 ed. lib. bdg. 41.50 (ISBN 0-8337-0458-3). B Franklin.

Mayes, Paul, ed. Periodicals Administration in Libraries: A Collection of Essays. 1978. 14.50 (ISBN 0-208-01675-9, Linnet). Shoe String.

Meder, Marylouise D., ed. Library School Review, Vol. 18. 1979. 2.00 (ISBN 0-686-26897-0). Emporia State.

--Library School Review, Vol. 18. 1979. pap. 2.00 (ISBN 0-686-29386-X). Sch Lib Sci.

Tuttle, Marcia & Smith, Lynn. Introduction to Serials Management, Vol. 11. Stueart, Robert D., ed. LC 81-81658. (Foundations in Library & Information Sciences). 250p. 1981. 32.50 (ISBN 0-89232-107-5). Jai Pr.

LIBRARY SCIENCE–PERIODICALS–INDEXES

Kilgour. The Library & Information Science CumIndex, Vol. 7. LC 72-86076. 1976. 55.00 (ISBN 0-88274-006-7). R & D Pr.

LIBRARY SCIENCE–PROGRAMMED INSTRUCTION

Bohlool, Janet. Library Orientation: Syllabus. 2nd ed. 1975. pap. text ed. 5.45 (ISBN 0-89420-080-1, 216788); cassette recordings 101.35 (ISBN 0-89420-161-1, 140800). Natl Book.

McGarry, K. J. & Burrell, T. W. Communications Studies. (Programmed Texts in Library & Information Science Ser.). 128p. 1973. 13.50 (ISBN 0-208-01186-2, Linnet). Shoe String.

LIBRARY SCIENCE–RESEARCH

Atkins, Thomas V. & Langstaff, Eleanor D. Access to Information Library Research Methods. 1979. pap. text ed. 10.95 (ISBN 0-686-62264-2). Collegium Bk Pubs.

Baker, Robert K. Doing Library Research: An Introduction for Community College Students. (Westview Guides to Library Research Ser.). 260p. 27.50x (ISBN 0-89158-778-0). Westview.

Bundy, Mary L., ed. Reader in Research Methods for Librarianship. Wasserman, Paul. LC 70-86858. (Reader Ser. in Library & Information Science: Vol. 2). 1970. 17.00 (ISBN 0-910972-42-7). IHS-PDS.

Busha, Charles H., ed. A Library Science Research Reader & Bibliographic Guide. LC 80-22507. 201p. 1981. lib. bdg. 22.50 (ISBN 0-87287-237-8). Libs Unl.

Busha, Charles H. & Harter, Stephen P., eds. Research Methods in Librarianship: Techniques & Interpretation. LC 79-8864. (Library & Information Science Ser.). 432p. 1980. tchrs' ed. 19.50 (ISBN 0-12-147550-6). Acad Pr.

Campbell, H. C. Canadian Libraries. 2nd ed. (Comparative Library Studies Ser). 1971. 13.50 (ISBN 0-208-01064-5, Linnet). Shoe String.

Christianson, Elin B., ed. New Special Libraries: A Summary of Research. LC 80-11507. 1980. 7.25 (ISBN 0-87111-271-X). SLA.

Frick, Elizabeth. Library Research Guide to History. (Library Research Guides Ser.: No. 4). 1980. 12.50 (ISBN 0-87650-119-6); pap. 5.95 (ISBN 0-87650-123-4). Pierian.

Gover, Harvey R. Keys to Library Research on the Graduate Level: A Guide to Guides. LC 80-5841. 75p. 1981. pap. text ed. 5.75 (ISBN 0-8191-1370-0). U Pr of Amer.

Hoadley, Irene B. & Clark, Alice S., eds. Quantitative Methods in Librarianship: Standards, Research, Management. LC 73-149962. (Contributions in Librarianship & Information Science: No. 4). 256p. 1972. lib. bdg. 17.95 (ISBN 0-8371-6061-8, HOQ/). Greenwood.

McMillan, Patricia & Kennedy, James R., Jr. Library Research Guide to Sociology. (Library Research Guides Ser.: No. 5). 1980. 12.50 (ISBN 0-87650-121-8); pap. 5.95 (ISBN 0-87650-122-6). Pierian.

Morse, Grant W. Concise Guide to Library Research. rev. ed. LC 74-21358. 200p. 1975. 14.50x (ISBN 0-8303-0143-7, Acad Edns); pap. 6.95x (ISBN 0-8303-0148-8). Fleet.

New York Public Library Research Libraries & Library of Congress. Bibliographic Guide to Conference Publications. 1979. lib. bdg. 130.00 (ISBN 0-8161-6866-0). G K Hall.

Objectives & Administration of Library Research: 1971 Seminar Papers. (Research Publication Ser.: No. 11). 1973. pap. text ed. 7.00x (ISBN 0-85365-296-1, Pub. by Lib Assn England). Oryx Pr.

Place, Linna F., et al. Aging & the Aged: An Annotated Bibliography & Research Guide. (Westview Guides to Library Research). 175p. 1980. lib. bdg. 17.50x (ISBN 0-89158-934-1). Westview.

Rorvig, Mark E. Microcomputers & Libraries: A Guide to Technology, Products & Applications. (Professional Librarian). (Illus.). 160p. 1981. pap. 27.50 professional (ISBN 0-914236-67-9). Knowledge Indus.

Simpson, Antony E. Guide to Library Research in Public Administration. 1976. bdg. 5.95 (ISBN 0-686-17549-2). Natl Ctr Public Prod.

Srikantaiah, Taverekere & Hoffman, Herbert H. Introduction to Quantitative Research Methods for Librarians. 2nd ed. 223p. 1978. pap. 8.00x (ISBN 0-89537-002-6). Headway Pubns.

Stevens, Rolland E., ed. Research Methods in Librarianship: Historical & Bibliographical Methods in Library Research. LC 79-631732. (Monograph: No. 10). 140p. 1971. 5.00x (ISBN 0-87845-032-7). U of Ill Lib Info Sci.

Voight, Melvin. Advances in Librarianship, Vol. 11. 1981. price not set (ISBN 0-12-785011-2); price not set lib. ed. (ISBN 0-12-785025-2); price not set microfiche (ISBN 0-12-785026-0). Acad Pr.

Ward, P. L. & Burkett, J., eds. Introductory Guide to Research in Librarianship & Information Studies in the U. K. (Pamphlet Ser.: No. 37). 1975. pap. 9.85x (ISBN 0-85365-058-6, Pub. by Lib Assn England). Oryx Pr.

LIBRARY SCIENCE–SOCIETIES, ETC.

see Library Associations

LIBRARY SCIENCE–STUDY AND TEACHING

see Library Education

LIBRARY SCIENCE–VOCATIONAL GUIDANCE

Atkinson, Frank L. Librarianship: An Introduction to the Profession. (Illus.). 112p. 1974. 12.50 (ISBN 0-686-75605-3). Shoe String.

Gates, Jean K. Introduction to Librarianship. 2nd ed. (Library Education Ser.). (Illus.). 1977. text ed. 13.95 (ISBN 0-07-022977-5, C). McGraw.

Josey, E. J. & Peeples, Kenneth E., Jr. Opportunities for Minorities in Librarianship. LC 77-375. 1977. 10.00 (ISBN 0-8108-1022-0). Scarecrow.

Michael, Mary E. Continuing Professional Education in Librarianship & Other Fields: A Classified & Annotated Bibliography, 1965-1974. LC 75-8998. (Reference Library of Humanities: Vol. 16). 224p. 1975. lib. bdg. 25.00 (ISBN 0-8240-1085-X). Garland Pub.

Munthe, Wilhelm. American Librarianship from a European Angle: An Attempt at the Evaluation of Policies & Activities. 1964. Repr. of 1939 ed. 15.00 (ISBN 0-208-00116-6). Shoe String.

Myers, Alpha & Temkin, Sara. Your Future in Library Careers. LC 75-29605. (Career Guidance Ser.). 160p. 1976. pap. 3.95 (ISBN 0-668-03913-2). Arco.

--Your Future in Library Careers. LC 73-77670. (Careers in Depth Ser). (Illus.). (gr. 7-12). 1976. PLB 5.97 (ISBN 0-8239-0282-X). Rosen Pr.

Noble, Valerie, ed. A Librarians Guide to Personal Development. LC 80-17485. (Bibliography Ser.: No. 7). 1980. pap. 4.50 (ISBN 0-87111-272-8). SLA.

Redfern, Brian, ed. Studies in Library Management, Vol. 1. 1972. 14.00 (ISBN 0-208-01071-8, Linnet). Shoe String.

Sellan, Betty-Carol. What Else Can You Do with a Library Degree? LC 79-14852. 380p. pap. 14.95 (ISBN 0-915794-46-2). Gaylord Prof Pubns.

Sellen, Betty-Carol, ed. What Else Can You Do with a Library Degree. 350p. 1980. 14.95x (ISBN 0-915794-46-2). Neal-Schuman.

Simpson, N., ed. Training in Libraries: Report of the Library Association Working Party on Training. 1977. pap. 2.75x (ISBN 0-85365-339-9, Pub. by Lib Assn England). Oryx Pr.

Sullivan, Peggy. Opportunities in Library & Information Science. LC 76-42887. (Illus.). (YA) (gr. 8 up). 1977. PLB 6.60 (ISBN 0-685-77770-7); pap. 4.95 (ISBN 0-8442-6533-0). Natl Textbk.

University of Chicago - Graduate Library School - 26th Conference. Seven Questions About the Profession of Librarianship. Ennis, Philip H. & Winger, Howard W., eds. LC 62-994. 1962. 7.50x (ISBN 0-226-21027-8). U of Chicago Pr.

LIBRARY SERVICE, MAIL

see Direct Delivery of Books

LIBRARY SERVICE TO THE PHYSICALLY HANDICAPPED

see Libraries and the Physically Handicapped

LIBRARY SERVICE TO THE SOCIALLY HANDICAPPED

see also Libraries and the Socially Handicapped

Appalachian Adult Education Center. Library Service Guides. 1977. 25.00 set (ISBN 0-8389-6325-0). ALA.

LIBRARY SKILLS

see Libraries–Handbooks, Manuals, etc.; Libraries and Readers

LIBRARY STATISTICS

Here are entered works on the compilation and study of statistics of libraries, or collections of general library statistics.

American National Standards Institute, Standards Committee Z39 on Library Work, Documentation & Related Publishing Practices. American National Standard Library Statistics. rev. ed. 1974. 6.50 (ISBN 0-686-01884-2, Z39.7). ANSI.

Carpenter, Ray L. Statistical Methods for Librarians. LC 78-3476. 1978. 14.00 (ISBN 0-8389-0256-1). ALA.

Ching-Chih Chen, ed. Quantitative Measurement & Dynamic Library Service. LC 78-13066. (Neal-Schuman Professional Bk.). 1978. 19.50x (ISBN 0-912700-17-3). Oryx Pr.

Hoadley, Irene B. & Clark, Alice S., eds. Quantitative Methods in Librarianship: Standards, Research, Management. LC 73-149962. (Contributions in Librarianship & Information Science: No. 4). 256p. 1972. lib. bdg. 17.95 (ISBN 0-8371-6061-8, HOQ/). Greenwood.

Simpson, I. S. Basic Statistics for Librarians. 113p. (Orig.). 1975. 12.50 (ISBN 0-208-01365-2, Linnet). Shoe String.

LIBRARY SUPPLIES

see Library Fittings and Supplies

LIBRARY SURVEYS

Here are entered works on the technique employed, and reports, etc., of individual surveys.

Beeler, M. Fancher, et al. Measuring the Quality of Library Service: A Handbook. LC 74-12107. (Illus.). 1974. 10.00 (ISBN 0-8108-0732-7). Scarecrow.

Berelson, Bernard & Ansheim, Lester. The Library's Public: A Report of the Public Library Inquiry. LC 75-31430. 174p. 1976. Repr. of 1949 ed. lib. bdg. 21.50x (ISBN 0-8371-8499-1, BELP). Greenwood.

Lancaster, John H. The Use of the Library by Student Teachers: Some Factors Related to the Use of the Library by Student Teachers in Thirty-One Colleges in the Area of the North Central Association. LC 77-176973. (Columbia University. Teachers College. Contributions to Education: No. 849). Repr. of 1941 ed. 17.50 (ISBN 0-404-55849-6). AMS Pr.

McCullough, Kathleen, et al. Approval Plans & Academic Libraries. LC 77-8514. (Neal-Schuman Professional Bk). 1977. lib. bdg. 16.50x (ISBN 0-912700-05-X). Oryx Pr.

Rosenlof, George W. Library Facilities in Teacher-Training Institutions. LC 76-177210. (Columbia University. Teachers College. Contributions to Education: No. 347). Repr. of 1929 ed. 17.50 (ISBN 0-404-55347-8). AMS Pr.

Tauber, Maurice F. & Stephens, Irlene R., eds. Library Surveys. LC 67-25304. (Columbia Library Service Studies: No. 16). 1967. 22.50x (ISBN 0-231-03056-8). Columbia U Pr.

LIBRARY TECHNICIANS

Bloomberg, Marty. Introduction to Public Services for Library Technicians. 2nd ed. LC 76-45779. (Library Science Text Ser.). 1977. lib. bdg. 13.50x (ISBN 0-87287-126-6). Libs Unl.

Bloomberg, Marty & Evans, G. Edward. Introduction to Technical Services for Library Technicians. 4th ed. LC 81-798. (Library Science Text Ser.). (Illus.). 363p. 1981. lib. bdg. 23.50 (ISBN 0-87287-228-9); pap. text ed. 16.50x (ISBN 0-87287-248-3). Libs Unl.

--Introduction to Technical Services for Library Technicians. 3rd ed. LC 76-43294. (Library Science Text Ser.). 1976. lib. bdg. 15.00x (ISBN 0-87287-125-8). Libs Unl.

Chirgwin, F. J. & Oldfield, P. The Library Assistant's Manual. 1978. 12.00 (ISBN 0-208-01666-X, Linnet). Shoe String.

Wisdom, Aline C. Introduction to Library Services for Library Media Technical Assistants. (Illus.). 416p. 1974. 12.95 (ISBN 0-07-071140-2, G); instructors' manual 2.50 (ISBN 0-07-071141-0). McGraw.

Wright, Alice E. Library Clerical Workers & Pages. v, 82p. (Orig.). 1973. pap. 9.50 (ISBN 0-208-01330-X, Linnet). Shoe String.

LIBRARY TRUSTEES

see Libraries–Trustees

LIBRETTISTS

Craig, Warren. Great Songwriters of Hollywood. LC 79-87793. 256p. 1980. 14.95 (ISBN 0-498-02439-3). A S Barnes.

Jenkins, Newell & Churgin, Bathia, eds. Thematic Catalogue of the Works of Giovanni Battista Sammartini. 1977. 35.00x (ISBN 0-674-87735-7). Harvard U Pr.

Murata, Margaret. Operas for the Papal Count: Sixteen Thirty-One to Sixteen Sixty-Eight. Buelow, George, ed. (Studies in Musicology: No. 39). 1981. 61.95 (ISBN 0-8357-1122-6, Pub. by UMI Res Pr). Univ Microfilms.

Pearson, Hesketh. Gilbert: His Life & Strife. LC 78-3698. 1978. Repr. of 1957 ed. lib. bdg. 21.50x (ISBN 0-313-20364-4, PEGI). Greenwood.

LIBRETTO

Bach, Johann S. Six Great Secular Cantatas in Full Score. 288p. (Orig.). 1980. pap. 7.95 (ISBN 0-486-23934-9). Dover.

Drummond, Andrew H. American Opera Librettos. LC 72-8111. 1973. 10.00 (ISBN 0-8108-0553-7). Scarecrow.

Eckelmeyer, Judith A., tr. The Magic Flute: Seventeen Ninety-One Libretto by Emanuel Schikaneder. LC 79-67268. xxix, 65p. 1980. pap. 6.95 (ISBN 0-88946-955-5). E Mellen.

Engel, Lehman. Words with Music. 300p. 6.95 (ISBN 0-02-870370-7). Macmillan.

Gilbert, W. S. Gilbert Without Sullivan. LC 81-43017. (Illus.). 112p. 1981. 12.95 (ISBN 0-670-34010-3, Studio). Viking Pr.

Hassall, Christopher. Troilus & Cressida: An Opera in Three Parts (Musical Score by Sir William Walton) 52p. (Orig.). 1976. pap. 3.75 (ISBN 0-19-338603-8). Oxford U Pr.

Smith, Patrick J. Tenth Muse: A Historical Study of the Opera Libretto. LC 73-111254. (Illus.). 1970. 12.95 (ISBN 0-394-44822-7). Knopf.

LIBRO DE ALIXANDRE

Willis, Raymond S., Jr. The Debt of the Spanish Libro De Alexandre to the French Roman D'Alexandre. (Elliott Monographs: Vol. 33). 1935. pap. 5.00 (ISBN 0-527-02636-0). Kraus Repr.

--Relationship of the Spanish Libro De Alexandre to the Alexandreis of Gautier De Chatillon. (Elliott Monographs: Vol. 31). 1934. pap. 7.00 (ISBN 0-527-02634-4). Kraus Repr.

LIBYA

Arif, I. M. & Ansell, M. O. Libyan Civil Code. 45.00 (ISBN 0-902675-00-1). Oleander Pr.

--Libyan Revolution: A Sourcebook of Legal & Historical Documents, Vol. 1, Sept. 1, 1969 to Aug. 30, 1970. 1971. 22.50 (ISBN 0-902675-10-9). Oleander Pr.

Askew, William C. Europe Italy's Acquisition of Libya, Nineteen Eleven to Nineteen Twelve. LC 73-93628. (Illus.). xi, 317p. Date not set. Repr. of 1942 ed. cancelled (ISBN 0-8462-1783-X). Russell.

Carvely, A. Institutionalizing Revolution: Egypt & Libya. Date not set. price not set (ISBN 0-686-11964-9). Bks Intl DH-TE.

Fathaly, Omar I. & Palmer, Monte. Political Development & Social Change in Libya. LC 77-712. 240p. 1980. 22.95 (ISBN 0-669-01427-3). Lexington Bks.

Fathaly, Omar I., et al. Political Development & Bureaucracy in Libya. LC 77-713. 1977. 15.95 (ISBN 0-669-01426-5). Lexington Bks.

First, Ruth. Libya: The Elusive Revolution. LC 75-9944. 294p. 1975. text ed. 25.00x (ISBN 0-8419-0211-9, Africana). Holmes & Meier.

Hahn, Lorna & Muirragui, Maureen. Historical Dictionary of Libya. LC 81-5728. (African Historical Dictionaries: No. 33). 132p. 1981. 10.00 (ISBN 0-8108-1442-0). Scarecrow.

Hester, James J. & Hobler, Philip M. Prehistoric Settlement Patterns in the Libyan Desert. (Nubian Ser.: No. 4). Repr. of 1969 ed. 44.00 (ISBN 0-404-60692-X, UAP NO. 92). AMS Pr.

Khadduri, Majid. Modern Libya: A Study in Political Development. 404p. 1963. 26.00x (ISBN 0-8018-0335-7). Johns Hopkins.

Latron, Andre. La Vie rurale en Syrie et au Liban: Etude d'economie sociale. LC 77-87618. Repr. of 1936 ed. 36.50 (ISBN 0-404-16439-0). AMS Pr.

Mason, John P. Island of the Blest: Islam in a Libyan Oasis Community. LC 77-620016. (Papers in International Studies: Africa: No. 31). (Illus.). 1977. pap. 10.00x (ISBN 0-89680-063-6). Ohio U Ctr Int.

Pelt, Adrian. Libyan Independence & the United Nations: A Case of Planned Decolonization. LC 72-99836. (Illus.). 1970. 65.00x (ISBN 0-300-01216-0). Yale U Pr.

Sabki, Hisham M. The United Nations & the Pacific Settlement of Disputes: A Case Study of Lybia. LC 77-962867. 207p. 1973. 10.00x (ISBN 0-8002-2122-2). Intl Pubns Serv.

Waddams, Frank C. The Libyan Oil Industry. LC 80-13939. (Illus.). 352p. 1980. text ed. 30.00x (ISBN 0-8018-2431-1). Johns Hopkins.

LIBYA–BIBLIOGRAPHY

Al-Barbar, Aghil M. Government & Politics in Libya, Nineteen Sixty-Nine to Nineteen Seventy-Eight: A Bibliography. (Public Administration Ser.: Bibliography P-388). 139p. 1979. pap. text ed. 14.50 (ISBN 0-686-26954-3). Vance Biblios.

Schluter, Hans. Bibliography of Libya, Nineteen Seventy to Nineteen Seventy-Five. (Reference Bks.). 1979. lib. bdg. 22.95 (ISBN 0-8161-8076-8). G K Hall.

Schluter, Hans, compiled by. Index Libycus: Bibliography of Libya 1957-1969 with Supplementary Material 1915-1956. (Seventy Ser.). 312p. 1972. 19.50 (ISBN 0-8161-0939-7). G K Hall.

Schuter, Hans & Magar, Kurt. Index Libycus: A Cumlative Index to Bibliography of Libya,Nineteen Fifteen to Nineteen Seventy-Five. (Reference Books Ser.). 1981. 25.00 (ISBN 0-8161-8534-4). G K Hall.

LIBYA-DESCRIPTION AND TRAVEL

Ward, Philip. Sabratha: A Guide for Visitors. (Illus.). 6.50 (ISBN 0-902675-05-2). Oleander Pr.

--Tripoli: Portrait of a City. (Illus.). 6.50 (ISBN 0-902675-06-0). Oleander Pr.

Ward, Philip & Pesce, Angelo. Motoring to Nalut. (Illus.). 2.50 (ISBN 0-902675-03-6). Oleander Pr.

Ward, Phillip. Touring Libya: The Southern Provinces. 8.50 (ISBN 0-571-08703-5). Transatlantic.

--Touring Libya: The Western Provinces. 8.50 (ISBN 0-571-08667-5). Transatlantic.

LIBYAN LANGUAGES

see Berber Languages

LIBYANS

see also Berbers

Bates, Oric. Eastern Libyans. (Illus.). 298p. 1970. Repr. of 1914 ed. 37.50x (ISBN 0-7146-1634-6, F Cass Co). Biblio Dist.

Behnke, Roy H., Jr. The Herders of Cyrenaica: Ecology, Economy, & Kinship Among the Bedouin of Eastern Libya. LC 79-10605. (Studies in Anthropology Ser.: No. 12). (Illus.). 1980. 14.50 (ISBN 0-252-00729-8). U of Ill Pr.

Goldberg, H. E. Cave Dwellers & Citrus Growers. LC 70-174260. (Illus.). 200p. 1972. pap. 23.95 (ISBN 0-521-08431-8). Cambridge U Pr.

Reynolds, Joyce, ed. Libyan Studies. 1975. 39.95 (ISBN 0-236-17680-3, Pub. by Paul Elek). Merrimack Bk Serv.

Ward, Philip. Apuleius on Trial at Sabratha. 2.50 (ISBN 0-902675-09-5). Oleander Pr.

LICE

Caldwell, John S. The Jumping Plant-Lice of Ohio (Homoptera: Chermidae) 1938. 1.00 (ISBN 0-686-30307-5). Ohio Bio Survey.

Cendrars, Blaise. Lice. LC 80-9058. 189p. 1981. 12.95 (ISBN 0-8128-2815-1). Stein & Day.

Sutton, S. Woodlice. (Illus.). 144p. 1980. 12.00 (ISBN 0-08-025942-1). Pergamon.

Zinsser, Hans. Rats, Lice & History. (gr. 9 up). 1935. 8.95 (ISBN 0-316-98890-1, Pub. by Atlantic Monthly Pr). Little.

LICENSE SYSTEM

see also Liquor Laws; Liquor Problem

Finnegan, Marcus B., ed. Licensing Law Handbook. 1980. softcover 17.50 (ISBN 0-87632-326-3). Boardman.

Licensing - Certification of Appraisers, with a Suggested Model Bill. LC 72-76987. (ASA Monograph: No. 5). 1972. 5.00 (ISBN 0-937828-14-9). Am Soc Appraisers.

Rudman, Jack. License Investigator (Spanish Speaking) (Career Examination Ser.: C-2286). (Cloth bdg. avail. on request). 1977. pap. 10.00 (ISBN 0-8373-2286-3). Natl Learning.

Standard Clauses in a Licensing Agreement. 47p. (Orig.). 1981. pap. text ed. 12.50x (ISBN 0-911378-37-5). Sheridan.

LICENSED BEVERAGE INDUSTRY

see Distilling Industries

LICENSED PRACTICAL NURSES

see Practical Nursing

LICENSES

see also Business Tax

Angel, Juvenal L. Directory of Professional & Occupational Licensing in the United States. 1969. 25.00 (ISBN 0-671-17685-4). Monarch Pr.

Brazell, D. Edmunds. Licensing Check Lists. 49p. (Orig.). 1981. pap. 12.50x (ISBN 0-911378-37-5). Sheridan.

Carrow, Milton M. Licensing Power in New York City. LC 68-58863. (Illus.). 223p. 1968. pap. 12.50x (ISBN 0-8377-0401-4). Rothman.

Committee of Experts on Restrictive Business Practices. Restrictive Business Practices Relating to Patents & Licenses. (Document Ser.). 56p. 1972. 1.75x (ISBN 92-64-11001-1). OECD.

Connors, John J. Price Guide to American & Canadian Chauffeur Badges. (Illus.). 1977. 5.25x (ISBN 0-686-20480-8). J J Connors.

Farley, Mike. Who's Who Behind Personalized California License Plates. Minard, Jeff, ed. LC 79-51013. (Illus.). 1979. 14.95 (ISBN 0-933850-00-X); pap. 6.95 (ISBN 0-686-25744-8). M Farley.

Finnegan, Marcus B. & Goldscheider, Robert. The Law & Business of Licensing, 4 vols. LC 75-22337. 1977. Set. looseleaf with 1979 suppl. 250.00 (ISBN 0-87632-136-8). Boardman.

Fretz, Bruce R. & Mills, David H. Licensing & Certification of Psychologists & Counselors: A Guide to Current Policies, Procedures, & Legislation. LC 80-8011. (Social & Behavioral Science Ser.). 1980. text ed. 14.95x (ISBN 0-87589-470-4). Jossey-Bass.

Hogan, Daniel B. The Regulation of Psychotherapists II: A Handbook of State Licensure Laws. LC 77-28991. (Regulation of Psychotherapists Ser.). 1978. 30.00 (ISBN 0-88410-523-7). Ballinger Pub.

Licensed Departments Rates, Policies & Expenses in Departent & Specialty Stores. 1977. pap. 9.00 (ISBN 0-685-86703-X, C14677). Natl Ret Merch.

Licensing Guide for Developing Countries. 1978. pap. 25.00 (ISBN 0-685-65238-6, WIPO 53, WIPO). Unipub.

Matsunaga, Yoshio. Successful Licensing to & from Japan. (Illus.). 1974. 30.00 (ISBN 0-685-51745-4). Sadtler Res.

Melville, Leslie W. Forms & Agreements on Intellectual Property & International Licensing. 3rd ed. LC 78-17576. 1979. looseleaf with 1979 rev. pages 75.00 (ISBN 0-686-57648-9). Boardman.

Practical & Legal Considerations in the International Licensing of Technology, Part III, Folio 8. pap. write for info. ALI-ABA.

Rottenberg, Simon, ed. Occupational Licensure & Regulation. 1981. 16.25 (ISBN 0-686-73719-9); pap. 8.25 (ISBN 0-8447-2193-X). Am Enterprise.

Rudman, Jack. Federation Licensing Examination (FLEX) (Admission Test Ser.: ATS-31). (Cloth bdg. avail. on request). pap. 17.95 (ISBN 0-8373-5131-6). Natl Learning.

--License Inspector. (Career Examination Ser.: C-439). (Cloth bdg. avail. on request). pap. 8.00 (ISBN 0-8373-0439-3). Natl Learning.

--Senior License Investigator. (Career Examination Ser.: C-2530). (Cloth bdg. avail). pap. 12.00 (ISBN 0-8373-2530-7). Natl Learning.

--Supervisor of Licensing. (Career Examination Ser.: C-2191). (Cloth bdg. avail. on request). pap. 10.00 (ISBN 0-8373-2191-3). Natl Learning.

--Supervisor of Professional Licensing. (Career Examination Ser.: C-1029). (Cloth bdg. avail. on request). pap. 8.00 (ISBN 0-8373-1029-6). Natl Learning.

Shimberg, Benjamin, et al. Occupational Licensing. 1973. 7.50 (ISBN 0-8183-0143-0). Pub Aff Pr.

LICHENS

Acharius, E. Lichenographia Universalis. 696p. 1981. 125.00x (ISBN 0-85546-195-0, Pub. by Richmond Pub England). State Mutual Bk.

--Synopsis Methodica Lichenum. 424p. 1981. 125.00x (ISBN 0-85546-202-7, Pub. by Richmond Pub England). State Mutual Bk.

Ahmadjian, Vernon & Hale, Mason E., eds. The Lichens. 1974. 58.50 (ISBN 0-12-044950-1). Acad Pr.

Ainsworth, G. C. Ainsworth & Bisby's Dictionary of the Fungi, Including the Lichens. 6th ed. LC 74-883641. (Illus.). 673p. 1971. 27.50x (ISBN 0-85198-075-9). Intl Pubns Serv.

Alvin, Kenneth. Observer's Book of Lichens. (Observer Bks.). (Illus.). 1977. 4.95 (ISBN 0-684-15202-9, ScribT). Scribner.

Asahina & Shibata. Chemistry of Lichen Substances. (Illus.). 1972. 43.00 (ISBN 90-6123-218-X). Lubrecht & Cramer.

Awasthi, D. D. Catalogue of the Lichens from India, Nepal, Pakistan & Ceylon. 1965. 20.00 (ISBN 3-7682-5417-8). Lubrecht & Cramer.

Awasthi, D. D. A Monograph of the Lichen Genus Dirinaria. 1975. 20.00 (ISBN 3-7682-0957-1). Lubrecht & Cramer.

Awasthi, Dharani D. A Monograph of the Lichen Genus Dirinaria. (Bibliotheca Lichenologica Ser.: Vol. 2). (Illus.). 116p. 1975. pap. 20.00x (ISBN 0-686-67201-1, Pub. by J. Cramer). Intl Schol Bk Serv.

Beltman, H. A. Vegetative Strukturen der Parmeliaceae und Ihre Entwickelung. (Bibliotheca Lichenologica Ser.: No. 11). (Illus.). 1978. lib. bdg. 30.00x (ISBN 3-7682-1199-1). Lubrecht & Cramer.

Bland, John. Forests of Lilliput: The Realm of Mosses & Lichens. LC 70-143811. (Natural History Ser). (Illus.). 1971. 9.95 (ISBN 0-13-326868-3). P-H.

Bolton, Eileen. Lichens for Vegetable Dyeing. (Illus.). 6.95 (ISBN 0-686-09830-7). Robin & Russ.

Brown, et al, eds. Lichenology: Progress & Problems. 634p. 1976. 90.00 (ISBN 0-12-136750-9). Acad Pr.

Buschardt, A. Zur Fletchtenflora der Inneralpinen Trockentaeler unter Besonderer Beruecksichtinhung des Vinschgaus. (Bibliotheca Lichenologica 10). 1979. lib. bdg. 40.00x (ISBN 3-7682-1226-2). Lubrecht & Cramer.

Culberson, Chicita F. Chemical & Botanical Guide to Lichen Products. 1979. pap. text ed. 45.00 (ISBN 3-87429-165-0). Lubrecht & Cramer.

Dahl, Eilif & Krog, Hildur. Macrolichens of Denmark, Finland, Norway, & Sweden. (Scandinavian University Books). (Illus.). 180p. 1973. 24.00 (ISBN 82-00-01898-9, Dist. by Columbia U Pr). Universitet.

De Wit, Toke. Epiphytic Lichens & Air Pollution in the Netherlands. 1974. 30.00 (ISBN 3-7682-1059-6). Lubrecht & Cramer.

Dobson, F. S. Lichens: An Illustrated Guide. 340p. 1981. pap. 25.50x (ISBN 0-85546-203-5, Pub. by Richmond Pub England). State Mutual Bk.

Dodge, C. W. Some Lichens of Tropical Africa IV: Dermatocarpaceae to Pertusariaceae. 1964. pap. 40.00 (ISBN 3-7682-5412-7). Lubrecht & Cramer.

--Some Lichens of Tropical Africa V: Lecanoraceae to Physiaceae. 1971. pap. 50.00 (ISBN 3-7682-5438-0). Lubrecht & Cramer.

Dodge, Carroll W. Lichen Flora of the Antarctic Continent & Adjacent Islands. LC 73-82976. 496p. 1973. 40.00 (ISBN 0-914016-01-6). Phoenix Pub.

Duncan, Ursula K. & James, P. W. Introduction to British Lichens. 292p. 1981. 23.00x (ISBN 0-85546-187-X, Pub. by Richmond Pub England). State Mutual Bk.

Eigler, G. Studien Zur Gliederung der Flechtengattung Lecanora. (Illus.). 15.00 (ISBN 3-7682-0628-9). Lubrecht & Cramer.

Evans, Alexander W. Supplementary Report on the Cladoniae of Connecticut. (Connecticut Academy of Arts & Sciences Transaction: Vol. 35). 1944. pap. 12.00 (ISBN 0-208-00890-X). Shoe String.

Grumann, V. Biographisch-bibliographisches Handbuch der Lichenologie. Nach dem Tode des Verfassers ed. by O. Klement. 1979. lib. bdg. 125.00x (ISBN 3-7682-0907-5). Lubrecht & Cramer.

Grumann, Vitus & Klement, Oscar, eds. Biographisch-Bibliographisches Handbuch der Lichenologie. (Illus.). 1975. deluxe ed. 100.00x (ISBN 3-7682-0907-5, Pub. by J. Cramer). Intl Schol Bk Serv.

Hale, Mason E. The Biology of Lichens. 2nd ed. LC 74-12607. (Contempory Biology Ser.). 181p. 1975. pap. text ed. 11.95 (ISBN 0-444-19530-0). Univ Park.

--How to Know the Lichens. 2nd ed. (Pictured Key Nature Ser.). 1979. write for info. wire coil (ISBN 0-697-04763-6); text ed. 8.95x (ISBN 0-697-04762-8). Wm C Brown.

Hawksworth, D. L. & Seaward, M. R. Lichenology in the British Isles, 1568-1975: An Historical & Bibliographical Survey. 240p. 1981. 70.00x (ISBN 0-85546-200-0, Pub. by Richmond Pub England). State Mutual Bk.

Jorgensen, Per M. Foliose & Frutcose Lichens from Tristan Da Cunha. 1975. 9.00x (ISBN 82-00-01644-7). Universitet.

Jurging, P., ed. Epiphytische Flechten Als Bioindikatoren der Luftverunreinigung. (Bibliotheca Lichenologica Ser.: Vol. 4). (Illus.). 164p. (Ger.). 1975. pap. 25.00x (ISBN 3-7682-0964-4, Pub. by J. Cramer). Intl Schol Bk Serv.

Lindau, Gustav. Thesaurus Litteraturae Mycologicae et Lichenologicae, 5 Vols. Repr. of 1917 ed. 231.00 (ISBN 0-384-32706-0); pap. 192.50 (ISBN 0-384-32707-9). Johnson Repr.

Mathey, A. Contribution a L'Etude Du Genre Siphula (Lichens) En Afrique. (Illus.). 84p. (Fr.). 1975. pap. 20.00 (ISBN 3-7682-0942-3, Pub. by J. Cramer). Intl Schol Bk Serv.

Mayrhofer, '. & Poelt, J. Die Saxicolen Arten der Flechtengattung Rinodina in Europa. (Bibliotheca Lichenologica: No. 12). (Illus., Ger.). 1979. lib. bdg. 30.00 (ISBN 3-7682-1237-8). Lubrecht & Cramer.

Mueller, J. Gesammelte Lichenologische Schriften, 2 vols. Incl. Vol. 1. Lichenologische Beitraege 1-XXXV. 1967. 220.00 set (ISBN 3-7682-0440-5). Lubrecht & Cramer.

Nylander, W. Collected Lichenological Papers: Collected Lichenological Papers. Incl. Vol. 4. Papers 1888-1900 (ISBN 3-7682-0434-0); Vol. 5. Synopsis Lichenum et Supplementum 1858-1869. (Illus.) (ISBN 3-7682-0435-9); Vol. 6. Prodromus Licherographiae Galliae et Algeriae 1857. Lichens Scandinaviae sive Prodomus... 1861. Supplementum: Lichens Lapponicae orientalis 1866. (Illus.) (ISBN 3-7682-0436-7). Date not set. 75.00 ea. Lubrecht & Cramer.

--Prodromus Lichenographiae Galliae et Algeriae. 1968. pap. 30.00 (ISBN 3-7682-0343-3). Lubrecht & Cramer.

Nylander, William. Lichenes Scandinaviae. 1968. pap. 34.00 (ISBN 3-7682-0459-6). Lubrecht & Cramer.

Poelt, J. Bestummingsschluessel Europaeischer Flechten. (Illus.). 1969. pap. 40.00 (ISBN 3-7682-0159-7). Lubrecht & Cramer.

Poelt, J. & Vezda, A. Bestimmungsschluessel Europaeischer Flechten, 1 suppl. (Bibliotheca Lichenologica Ser.: No. 9). 1977. lib. bdg. 25.00x (ISBN 3-7682-1162-2). Lubrecht & Cramer.

Rodenborg, L. Epilithische Vegetation in einem alten Waldgebiet auf Mittel-Oeland, Schweden. (Bibliotheca Lichenologica Ser.: No. 8). (Illus.). 1977. pap. text ed. 15.00x (ISBN 3-7682-1151-7). Lubrecht & Cramer.

Rogers, Roderick W. The Genera of Australian Lichens: (Lichenized Fungi) (Illus.). 124p. 1981. text ed. 24.25x (ISBN 0-7022-1579-1). U of Queensland Pr.

Roux, Claude. Etude Ecologique et Phytosociologique des Peuplements Licheniques Saxicoles-Calcicoles du Sud-Est de la France. (Bibliotheca Lichenologica: Vol. 15). (Illus.). 558p. (Fr.). 1981. text ed. 75.00x (ISBN 3-7682-1301-3, Pub. by Cramer Germany). Lubrecht & Cramer.

Schneider, Gotthard. Die Flechtengattung Psora Sensu Zahlbruckner. (Bibliotheca Lichenologica: 13). (Illus.). 308p. (Ger.). 1980. lib. bdg. 40.00x (ISBN 3-7682-1257-2). Lubrecht & Cramer.

Seaward, M. R., ed. Lichen Ecology. 1978. 79.00 (ISBN 0-12-634350-0). Acad Pr.

Smith, A. L. Handbook of the British Lichens. 1964. Repr. of 1921 ed. 6.00 (ISBN 3-7682-0215-1). Lubrecht & Cramer.

--Lichens. 1981. 35.00x (ISBN 0-85546-192-6, Pub. by Richmond Pub England). State Mutual Bk.

--A Monograph of the British Lichens: 1918-1926, 2 vols. 2nd ed. (Illus.). 1970. 100.00 (ISBN 90-6123-140-X). Lubrecht & Cramer.

Taylor, Conan J. Lichens of Ohio, Pt. II: Fruticose & Cladoniform. 1968. 4.00 (ISBN 0-686-30335-0). Ohio Bio Survey.

Thomson, J. W. The Lichen Genus Physcia in North America. (Illus.). 1963. pap. 30.00 (ISBN 3-7682-5407-0). Lubrecht & Cramer.

Thomson, John W. Lichen Genus Cladonia in North America. LC 68-85084. (Illus.). 1967. 20.00x (ISBN 0-8020-1486-0). U of Toronto Pr.

--Lichens of the Alaskan Arctic Slope. LC 78-31899. (Illus.). 1979. 35.00x (ISBN 0-8020-5428-5). U of Toronto Pr.

Tuckerman, E. Collected Lichenological Papers, 2 vols. Culberson, W. L., ed. 1964. Vol. 1. 45.00 (ISBN 3-7682-0221-6); Vol. 2. 54.00 (ISBN 3-7682-0222-4); Set. 99.00 (ISBN 3-7682-0220-8). Lubrecht & Cramer.

Turner, Dawson & Barrer, William. Specimen of a Lichenographia Britannica. 204p. 1981. 80.00x (ISBN 0-85546-204-3, Pub. by Richmond Pub England). State Mutual Bk.

Vobis, G. Bau und Entwicklung der Flechtenpycnidien und Ihrer Goniedien. (Bibliotheca Lichenologica: No. 14). 200p. (Ger.). 1981. pap. text ed. 25.00x (ISBN 3-7682-1270-X). Lubrecht & Cramer.

Wainio, E. A. Monographia Cladaoniarum Universalis, 3 vols. 1278p. (Lat. & Fr.). 1978. Set. lib. bdg. 200.00x (ISBN 3-87429-135-9). Lubrecht & Cramer.

Weber, W. A. & Wetmore, C. M. Catalogue of Lichens of Australia: Exclusive of Tasmania. 1972. 20.00 (ISBN 3-7682-5441-0). Lubrecht & Cramer.

Westhafer, Marj. Lichens. (Illus.). 48p. 1981. 24.00 (ISBN 0-686-74850-6). Mosaic Pr.

Wolfe, John N. A Catalog of the Lichens of Ohio. 1940. 1.00 (ISBN 0-686-30309-1). Ohio Bio Survey.

Zahlbruckner, Alexander. Catalogus Lichenum Universalis, 10 vols. Set. 500.50 (ISBN 0-384-70700-9). Johnson Repr.

LICHNOWSKY, KARL MAX, PRINCE, 1860-1928

Young, Harry F. Prince Lichnowsky & the Great War. LC 75-11448. (Illus.). 256p. 1977. 15.00x (ISBN 0-8203-0385-2). U of Ga Pr.

LICHTENSTEIN, ROY, 1923-

Cowart, Jack. Roy Lichtenstein Nineteen Seventy to Nineteen Eighty. LC 80-28348. (Illus.). 176p. 1981. 35.00 (ISBN 0-933920-14-8); pap. 15.00 museum distribution only (ISBN 0-933920-15-6). Hudson Hills.

Glenn, Constance W. Roy Lichtenstein Ceramic Sculpture. (Illus.). 64p. (Orig.). 1977. pap. 8.00 (ISBN 0-936270-05-5). Art Mus Gall.

LIE ALGEBRAS

see also Groups, Continuous; Lie Groups

Ado, I. D., et al. Lie Groups. (Translations, Ser.: No. 1, Vol. 9). 1962. 38.00 (ISBN 0-8218-1609-8, TRANS 1-9). Am Math.

Aleksandrov, A. D., et al. Nine Papers on Topology, Lie Groups, & Differential Equations. LC 51-5559. (Translations Ser.: No. 2, Vol. 21). 1962. 28.00 (ISBN 0-8218-1721-3, TRANS 2-21). Am Math.

Auslander, Louis & Moore, C. C. Unitary Representations of Solvable Lie Groups. LC 52-42839. (Memoirs: No. 62). 1971. pap. 9.60 (ISBN 0-8218-1262-9, MEMO-62). Am Math.

Azencott, R. & Wilson, E. N. Homogenous Manifolds with Negative Curvature II. LC 76-44403. (Memoirs: No. 178). 1976. 11.20 (ISBN 0-8218-2178-4, MEMO178). Am Math.

Belinfante, Johan G. & Kolman, Bernard. Lie Groups & Lie Algebras. LC 72-77081. 1972. text ed. 13.25 (ISBN 0-89871-044-8). Soc Indus-Appl Math.

Borel, Armand, et al. Lie Algebras & Lie Groups. LC 52-42839. (Memoirs: No. 14). 1972. pap. 8.00 (ISBN 0-8218-1214-9, MEMO-14). Am Math.

Brezin, Jonathan. Unitary Representation Theory for Solvable Lie Groups. LC 52-42839. (Memoirs: No. 79). 1968. pap. 7.20 (ISBN 0-8218-1279-3, MEMO-79). Am Math.
Chevalley, Claude. Theory of Lie Groups. (Mathematical Ser.: Vol. 8). 1946. 17.50 (ISBN 0-691-08052-6). Princeton U Pr.
Chow, S. Y. General Theory of Lie Algebra, 2 vols. 1978. 2-vol. set 93.00 (ISBN)-677-03890-9). Gordon.
D'Atri, J. E. & Ziller, W. Naturally Reductive Metrics & Einstein Metrics on Compact Lie Groups. LC 79-7. (Memoirs: No. 215). 1979. 8.00 (ISBN 0-8218-2215-2). Am Math.
De la Harpe, P. Classical Banach-Lie Algebras & Banach-Lie Groups of Operators in Hilbert Space. LC 72-88729. (Lecture Notes in Mathematics: Vol. 285). 160p. 1972. pap. 6.30 (ISBN 0-387-05984-9). Springer-Verlag.
Drucker, Daniel. Exceptional Lie Algebras & the Structure of Hermitian Symmetric Spaces. LC 78-15619. (Memoirs: No. 208). 1978. 12.40 (ISBN 0-8218-2208-X). Am Math.
Gilmore, Robert. Lie Groups, Lie Algebras & Some of Their Applications. LC 73-10030. 587p. 1974. 46.00x (ISBN 0-471-30179-5, Pub. by Wiley-Interscience). Wiley.
Gotto & Grosshan. Semisimple Lie Algebras. (Lecture Notes: Vol. 38). 1978. 49.75 (ISBN 0-8247-6744-6). Dekker.
Hausner, Melvin & Schwartz, Jacob T. Lie Groups, Lie Algebras. LC 66-28064. (Notes on Mathematics & Its Application Ser.). 1968. 31.50x (ISBN 0-677-00280-7). Gordon.
Hermann, Robert. Fourier Analysis on Groups & Partial Wave Analysis. (Math Lecture Notes Ser.: No. 32). 1969. 19.50 (ISBN 0-8053-3940-X, Adv Bk Prog); pap. 9.50 (ISBN 0-8053-3941-8, Adv Bk Prog). Benjamin-Cummings.
--Lie Algebras & Quantum Mechanics. (Math Lecture Notes Ser.: No. 46). 1970. 19.50 (ISBN 0-8053-3942-6, Adv Bk Prog). Benjamin-Cummings.
--Lie Groups for Physicists. (Mathematical Physics Monographs: No. 5). 1966. pap. 11.50 (ISBN 0-8053-3951-5, Adv Bk Prog). Benjamin-Cummings.
Hochschild, G. H. Basic Theory of Algebraic Groups & Lie Algebras. (Graduate Texts in Mathematics Ser.: Vol. 75). 350p. 1981. 32.00 (ISBN 0-387-90541-3). Springer-Verlag.
Humphreys, J. E. Algebraic Groups & Modular Lie Algebras. LC 52-42839. (Memoirs: No. 71). 1967. pap. 7.20 (ISBN 0-8218-1271-8, MEMO-71). Am Math.
--Introduction to Lie Algebras & Representation Theory. LC 72-85951. (Graduate Texts in Mathematics: Vol. 9). (Illus.). 170p. 1978. pap. text ed. 13.00 (ISBN 0-387-90052-7). Springer-Verlag.
--Introoduction to Lie Algebras & Representation Theory. rev., 3rd ed. (Graduate Texts to Mathematics Ser.: Vol. 9). (Illus.). 171p. 1981. 18.80 (ISBN 0-387-90053-5). Springer-Verlag.
Jacobson, N. Exceptional Lie Algebras. (Lecture Notes in Pure & Applied Mathematics Ser.: Vol. 1). 1971. 15.75 (ISBN 0-8247-1326-5). Dekker.
Jacobson, Nathan. Lie Algebras. LC 79-52006. 1979. pap. 5.00 (ISBN 0-486-63832-4). Dover.
Kamber, Franz W. & Tondeur, Philippe. Invariant Differential Operators & Cohomology of Lie Algebra Sheaves. LC 52-42839. (Memoirs: No. 113). 1971. pap. 7.20 (ISBN 0-8218-1813-9, MEMO-113). Am Math.
Kaplansky, Irving. Lie Algebras & Locally Compact Groups. LC 76-136207. (Chicago Lectures in Mathematics Ser). 1971. pap. 7.00x (ISBN 0-226-42453-7). U of Chicago Pr.
Kolman, Bernard. Lie Algebras: Applications & Computational Methods. (Illus.). 1974. text ed. 16.50 (ISBN 0-89871-153-3). Soc Indus-Appl Math.
Kumpera, Antonio & Spenser, Donald. Lie Equations, Vol. 1: General Theory. LC 77-39055. (Annals of Mathematics Studies: No. 73). 300p. 1972. 15.00 (ISBN 0-691-08111-5). Princeton U Pr.
McKay, W. G. & Patera, J. Tables of Dimensions, Indices, & Branching Rules for Representations of Simple Lie Algebras. (Lecture Notes in Pure & Applied Mathematics Ser.: Vol. 69). (Illus.). 336p. 1981. 39.75 (ISBN 0-8247-1227-7). Dekker.
Miller, Willard, Jr. On Lie Algebras & Some Special Functions of Mathematical Physics. LC 52-42389. (Memoirs: No. 50). 1969. pap. 7.20 (ISBN 0-8218-1250-5, MEMO-50). Am Math.
Samelson, Hans. Notes on Lie Algebras. (Mathematical Studies: No. 23). 1969. pap. text ed. 6.50x (ISBN 0-442-07341-0, MS23). Van Nos Reinhold.
Seligman, G. B. Modular Lie Algebras. LC 67-28452. (Ergebnisse der Mathematik & Ihrer Grenzgebiete: Vol. 40). 1967. 29.40 (ISBN 0-387-03782-9). Springer-Verlag.
Seligman, George. Rational Methods in Lie Algebras. (Lecture Notes in Pure and Applied Mathematics Ser: Vol. 17). 1976. 43.50 (ISBN 0-8247-6480-3). Dekker.
Serre, Jean-Pierre. Lie Algebras & Lie Groups. LC 65-20357. (Math Lecture Notes Ser.: No. 2). 256p. 1965. pap. 13.50 (ISBN 0-8053-8703-X, Adv Bk Prog). Benjamin-Cummings.
Slodowy, P. Simple Singularities & Simple Algebraic Groups. (Lecture Notes in Mathematics: Vol. 815). 175p. 1980. pap. 11.80 (ISBN 0-387-10026-1). Springer-Verlag.
Stewart, I. Lie Algebras Generated by Infinite-Dimensional Ideals. (Research Notes in Mathematics Ser.: No. 2). 154p. 1975. pap. text ed. 15.95 (ISBN 0-273-00142-6). Pitman Pub MA.
Stewart, I. N. Lie Algebras. LC 73-117720. (Lecture Notes in Mathematics: Vol. 127). 1970. pap. 10.70 (ISBN 0-387-04916-9). Springer-Verlag.
Van Der Kollen, W. L. Infinitesimally Central Extensions of Chevalley Groups. (Lecture Notes in Mathematics: Vol. 356). 147p. 1973. pap. 9.10 (ISBN 0-387-06559-8). Springer-Verlag.
Varadarajian, V. S. Lie Groups, Lie Algebras, & Their Representations. (Modern Analysis Ser.). 496p. 1974. ref. ed. 28.95 (ISBN 0-13-535732-2). P-H.
Wan-Z-Xian. Lie Algebras. LC 74-13832. 244p. 1976. text ed. 37.00 (ISBN 0-08-017952-5). Pergamon.
Winter, David J. Abstract Lie Algebras. 1972. 20.00x (ISBN 0-262-23051-8). MIT Pr.

LIE DETECTORS AND DETECTION

Abrams, Stanley. Polygraph Handbook for Attorneys. LC 77-6074. (Illus.). 1977. 19.95 (ISBN 0-669-01598-9). Lexington Bks.
Academy for Scientific Interrogation. Academy Lectures on Lie Detection, Vol.I. (Police Science Ser.). 112p. 1957. ed. spiral bdg. 18.75photocopy (ISBN 0-398-00005-0). C C Thomas.
Academy Lectures on Lie Detection. Academy for Scientific Interrogation, Vol. II. (Police Science Ser.). 168p. 1958. ed. spiral bdg. 18.75photocopy (ISBN 0-398-04182-2). C C Thomas.
Ansley, Norman, ed. Legal Admissibility of the Polygraph. (Illus.). 348p. 1975. 43.00 (ISBN 0-398-02954-7). C C Thomas.
Ferguson, Robert J., Jr. The Polygraph in Private Industry. (Illus.). 352p. 1966. pap. 27.75 photocopy ed. spiral (ISBN 0-398-00557-5). C C Thomas.
Ferguson, Robert J., Jr. & Miller, Allan L. Polygraph for the Defense. 312p. 1974. ed. spiral bdg. 24.50photocopy (ISBN 0-398-02877-X). C C Thomas.
Ferguson, Robert T., Jr. & Miller, Allan L. The Polygraph in Court. (Illus.). 372p. 1973. pap. 28.75 photocopy ed. spiral (ISBN 0-398-02679-3). C C Thomas.
Lykken, David T A Tremor in the Blood: Uses & Abuses of the Lie Detector. LC 80-10697. 320p. 1980. 14.95 (ISBN 0-07-039210-2). McGraw.
Matte, James A. The Art & Science of the Polygraph Technique. (Illus.). 296p. 1980. 29.50 (ISBN 0-398-04044-3). C C Thomas.
Reid, John E. & Inbau, Fred E. Truth & Deception. 2nd ed. (Illus.). 360p. 1977. 36.00 (ISBN 0-683-07224-2). Williams & Wilkins.

LIE GROUPS

see also Lie Algebras

Ackerman, M. & Hermann, Robert. Sophus Lie's Eighteen Eighty Transformation Group Paper. LC 75-17416. (Lie Groups: History, Frontiers on Applications Ser.: No. 1). 1975. 45.00 (ISBN 0-915692-10-4). Math Sci Pr.
Ash, A., et al. Smooth Compactification of Locally Symmetric Varieties. LC 75-38142. (Lie Groups: History, Frontiers & Applications Ser.: No. 4). 1975. 15.00 (ISBN 0-915692-12-0). Math Sci Pr.
Atiyah, M. F. Elliptic Operators & Compact Groups. (Lecture Notes in Mathematics Ser.: Vol. 401). v, 93p. 1974. pap. 9.90 (ISBN 3-540-06855-4). Springer-Verlag.
Atiyah, M. F., et al. Representation Theory of Lie Groups. LC 78-73820. (London Mathematical Society Lecture Note: No. 34). 1980. pap. 29.50x (ISBN 0-521-22636-8). Cambridge U Pr.
Auslander, L. & Tolimieri, R. Abelian Harmonic Analysis, Theta Functions & Functional Analysis on a Nilmanifold. (Lecture Notes in Mathematics Ser.: Vol. 436). v, 99p. 1975. pap. 10.00 (ISBN 0-387-07134-2). Springer-Verlag.
Azencott, R. & Wilson, E. N. Homogenous Manifolds with Negative Curvature II. LC 76-44403. (Memoirs: No. 178). 1976. 11.20 (ISBN 0-8218-2178-4, MEMO178). Am Math.
Bailey, W. L., Jr., et al. Discrete Subgroups of Lie Groups & Applications to Moduli. (Tata Institute of Fundamental Research Studies in Mathematics Ser.). (Illus.). 360p. 1976. pap. 13.75x (ISBN 0-19-560525-X). Oxford U Pr.
Belinfante, Johan G. & Kolman, Bernard. Lie Groups & Lie Algebras. LC 72-77081. 1972. text ed. 13.25 (ISBN 0-89871-044-8). Soc Indus-Appl Math.
Boothby, W. M. & Weiss, G. L., eds. Symmetric Spaces: Short Courses Presented at Washington University. (Pure & Applied Mathematics Ser: Vol. 8). 504p. 1972. 48.75 (ISBN 0-8247-1047-9). Dekker.
Borel, Armand, et al. Lie Algebras & Lie Groups. LC 52-42839. (Memoirs: No. 14). 1972. pap. 8.00 (ISBN 0-8218-1214-9, MEMO-14). Am Math.
Bourbaki, Nocolas. Elements of Mathematics: Lie Groups & Lie Algebras, Part 1. 1975. pap. 57.50 (ISBN 0-201-00643-X, Adv Bk Prog). A-W.
Bredon, Glen E. Introduction to Compact Transformation Groups. (Pure & Applied Mathematics Ser). 1972. 56.00 (ISBN 0-12-128850-1). Acad Pr.
Carter, R. W. Simple Groups of Lie Type. LC 72-39228. (Pure & Applied Mathematics Ser.). 280p. 1972. 48.95 (ISBN 0-471-13735-9, Pub. by Wiley-Interscience). Wiley.
D'Atri, J. E. & Ziller, W. Naturally Reductive Metrics & Einstein Metrics on Compact Lie Groups. LC 79-7. (Memoirs: No. 215). 1979. 8.00 (ISBN 0-8218-2215-2). Am Math.
De la Harpe, P. Classical Banach-Lie Algebras & Banach-Lie Groups of Operators in Hilbert Space. LC 72-88729. (Lecture Notes in Mathematics: Vol. 285). 160p. 1972. pap. 6.30 (ISBN 0-387-05984-9). Springer-Verlag.
Dieudonne, J. Introduction to the Theory of Formal Groups. (Pure & Applied Mathematics Ser: Vol. 20). 288p. 1973. 34.75 (ISBN 0-8247-6011-5). Dekker.
Dieudonne, Jean. Special Functions & Linear Representations of Lie Groups. (CBMS Regional Conference Ser. in Mathematics: No. 42). 1980. 9.40 (ISBN 0-8218-1692-6). Am Math.
Gaal, S. A. Linear Analysis & Representation Theory. LC 72-95686. (Die Grundlehren der Mathematischen Wissenschaften: Vol. 198). ix, 688p. 1973. 67.40 (ISBN 0-387-06195-9). Springer-Verlag.
Gilmore, Robert. Lie Groups, Lie Algebras & Some of Their Applications. LC 73-10030. 587p. 1974. 46.00x (ISBN 0-471-30179-5, Pub. by Wiley-Interscience). Wiley.
Glasner, M. S. Proximal Flows. (Lecture Notes in Mathematics: Vol. 517). 1976. pap. 9.90 (ISBN 0-387-07689-1). Springer-Verlag.
Harish-Chandra. Automorphic Forms on Semisimple Lie Groups. (Lecture Notes in Mathematics: Vol. 62). 1968. pap. 10.70 (ISBN 0-387-04232-6). Springer-Verlag.
Hausner, Melvin & Schwartz, Jacob T. Lie Groups, Lie Algebras. LC 66-28064. (Notes on Mathematics & Its Application Ser.). 1968. 31.50x (ISBN 0-677-00280-7). Gordon.
Helgason, Sigurdur. Analysis on Lie Groups & Homogeneous Spaces. LC 72-10153. (CBMS Regional Conference Series in Mathematics: Vol. 14). 64p. 1977. pap. text ed. 8.80 (ISBN 0-8218-1664-0, CBMS-14). Am Math.
Hermann, Robert & Ackerman, M. Sophus Lie's Eighteen Eighty Transformation Group Paper. LC 75-43189. (Lie Groups: History Frontiers & Applications Ser.: No. 3). 1976. 26.00 (ISBN 0-915692-13-9). Math Sci Pr.
Humphreys, J. E. Algebraic Groups & Modular Lie Algebras. LC 52-42839. (Memoirs: No. 71). 1967. pap. 7.20 (ISBN 0-8218-1271-8, MEMO-71). Am Math.
Jensen, G. Higher Order Contact of Submanifolds of Homogeneous Spaces. LC 77-14394. (Lecture Notes in Mathematics: Vol. 610). 1977. pap. text ed. 10.70 (ISBN 0-387-08433-9). Springer-Verlag.
Kaplansky, Irving. Lie Algebras & Locally Compact Groups. LC 76-136207. (Chicago Lectures in Mathematics Ser). 1971. pap. 7.00x (ISBN 0-226-42453-7). U of Chicago Pr.
Karras, U., et al. Cutting and Pasting of Manifolds: SK-Groups. LC 73-76374. (Mathematics Lecture Ser: No. 1). 70p. 1973. pap. 3.00 (ISBN 0-914098-10-1). Publish or Perish.
Kumpera, Antonio & Spenser, Donald. Lie Equations, Vol. 1: General Theory. LC 77-39055. (Annals of Mathematics Studies: No. 73). 300p. 1972. 15.00 (ISBN 0-691-08111-5). Princeton U Pr.
Lazarov, Conner & Wasserman, Arthur. Complex Actions of Lie Groups. LC 73-18039. (Memoirs: No. 137). 84p. 1973. pap. 8.40 (ISBN 0-8218-1837-6, MEMO-137). Am Math.
Miller, Willard, Jr. Symmetry Groups & Their Applications. (Pure & Applied Mathematics Ser.: Vol. 50). 1972. 47.00 (ISBN 0-12-497460-0). Acad Pr.
Non-Spherical Principle Series Representations of a Semisimple Lie Group. LC 79-10157. (Memoirs: No. 216). 1979. 8.00 (ISBN 0-8218-2216-0). Am Math.
Omori, H. Infinite Dimensional Lie Transformation Groups. LC 74-23625. (Lecture Notes in Mathematics: Vol. 427). xi, 149p. 1975. pap. 11.70 (ISBN 0-387-07013-3). Springer-Verlag.
Orlik, P. Seifert Manifolds. LC 72-90184. (Lecture Notes in Mathematics: Vol. 291). 155p. 1972. pap. 6.30 (ISBN 0-387-06014-6). Springer-Verlag.
Price, John F. Lie Groups & Compact Groups. LC 76-14034. (London Mathematical Society Lecture Notes Ser.: No. 25). 1977. pap. 16.95x (ISBN 0-521-21340-1). Cambridge U Pr.
Raghunathan, M. S. Discrete Subgroups of Lie Groups. LC 71-189389. (Ergebnisse der Mathematik und Ihrer Grenzgebiete: Vol. 68). 240p. 1972. 27.20 (ISBN 0-387-05749-8). Springer-Verlag.
Stein, Elias M. Topics in Harmonic Analysis Related to the Littlewood-Paley Theory. LC 72-83688. (Annals of Mathematics Studies: No. 63). 1969. 15.00 (ISBN 0-691-08067-4). Princeton U Pr.
Symposia in Pure Mathematics, Vol. 26. Harmonic Analysis on Homogeneous Spaces: Proceedings. Moore, Calvin C., ed. LC 73-10456. 480p. 1973. 35.60 (ISBN 0-8218-1426-5, PSPUM-26). Am Math.
Tondeur, Philippe. Introduction to Lie Groups & Transformation Groups. 2nd ed. LC 78-99012. (Lecture Notes in Mathematics: Vol. 7). 1969. pap. 10.70 (ISBN 0-387-04599-6). Springer-Verlag.
Varadarajian, V. S. Lie Groups, Lie Algebras, & Their Representations. (Modern Analysis Ser.). 496p. 1974. ref. ed. 28.95 (ISBN 0-13-535732-2). P-H.
Wallach, N. Symplectic Geometry & Fourier Analysis. Hermann, Robert, ed. LC 76-43503. (Lie Groups: History, Frontiers & Applications: Vol. 5). 1977. pap. 24.00 (ISBN 0-915692-15-5). Math Sci Pr.
Wallach, Nolan. Harmonic Analysis on Homogeneous Spaces. (Pure & Applied Mathematics Ser: Vol. 19). 384p. 1973. 39.75 (ISBN 0-8247-6010-7). Dekker.
Warner, Frank W. Foundations of Differentiable Manifolds & Lie Groups. 1971. 21.95x (ISBN 0-673-05737-2). Scott F.
Warner, G. Harmonic Analysis on Semi-Simple Lie Groups, Pt. 1. LC 70-160590. (Die Grundlehren der Mathematischen Wissenschaften: Vol. 188). (Illus.). 600p. 1972. 41.50 (ISBN 0-387-05468-5). Springer-Verlag.
--Harmonic Analysis on Semi-Simple Lie Groups, Pt. 2. (Die Grundlehren der Mathematischen Wissenschaften: Vol. 189). 600p. 1972. 41.50 (ISBN 0-387-05469-3). Springer-Verlag.
Wolf, J. A. Unitary Representations of Maximal Parabolic Subgroups of the Classical Groups. LC 76-44397. (Memoirs: No. 180). 1976. 13.20 (ISBN 0-8218-2180-6, MEMO-180). Am Math.
Wolf, J. A., et al, eds. Harmonic Analysis & Representations of Semi-Simple Lie Groups. (Mathematical Physics & Applied Mathematics: No. 5). 508p. 1980. lib. bdg. 66.00 (ISBN 90-277-1042-2, Pub. by Reidel Holland). Kluwer Boston.
Wolf, Joseph A. Unitary Representations on Partially Holomorphic Cohomology Spaces. LC 73-21505. (Memoirs: No. 138). 156p. 1974. pap. 8.80 (ISBN 0-8218-1838-4, MEMO-138). Am Math.
Zelobenko, D. P. Compact Lie Groups & Their Representations. LC 73-17185. (Translations of Mathematical Monographs: Vol. 40). 464p. 1973. 38.80 (ISBN 0-8218-1590-3, MMONO-40). Am Math.

LIEBER, FRANCIS, 1800-1872

Brown, Bernard E. American Conservatives: The Political Thought of Francis Lieber & John W. Burgess. LC 78-181923. (Columbia University Studies in the Social Sciences: No. 565). Repr. of 1951 ed. 17.50 (ISBN 0-404-51565-7). AMS Pr.
Freidel, Frank. Francis Lieber: Nineteenth-Century Liberal. (Illus.). 8.00 (ISBN 0-8446-0632-4). Peter Smith.
Harley, Lewis R. Francis Lieber: His Life & Political Philosophy. LC 70-126659. Repr. of 1899 ed. 19.50 (ISBN 0-404-03128-5). AMS Pr.
Root, Elihu. Addresses on International Subjects. facs. ed. LC 74-86780. (Essay Index Reprint Ser). 1916. 22.00 (ISBN 0-8369-1191-1). Arno.

LIEBIG, BARON JUSTUS VON, 1803-1873

Rossiter, Margaret W. The Emergence of Agricultural Science: Justus Liebig & the Americans, 1840-1880. LC 74-29737. (Studies in the History of Science & Medicine Ser.: No. 9). 288p. 1975. 20.00x (ISBN 0-300-01721-9). Yale U Pr.

LIEBKNECHT, KARL, 1871-1919

Burns, E. Karl Liebknecht. 59.95 (ISBN 0-8490-0469-1). Gordon Pr.

LIECHTENSTEIN–DESCRIPTION AND TRAVEL

Evans, Craig. On Foot Through Europe: A Trail Guide to Austria, Switzerland & Liechtenstein. Whitney, Stephen, ed. (Illus.). 416p. 1980. lib. bdg. 12.95 (ISBN 0-933710-07-0); pap. 6.95 (ISBN 0-933710-06-2). Foot Trails.

LIENS

see also Debtor and Creditor; Mechanics' Liens; Mortgages; Sales, Conditional

Eurich, Alvin C., ed. Major Transitions in the Human Life Cycle. LC 81-47067. 1981. write for info. (ISBN 0-669-04559-4). Lexington Bks.

NACM, ed. Mechanics Lien Laws & Federal Tax Lien Law. 1981. pap. 4.50 (ISBN 0-934914-39-7). NACM.

LIFE

see also Conduct of Life; Death; Ethics; Old Age; Ontology; Philosophical Anthropology

Agerskov, Michael, ed. Questions & Answers: First & Second Supplement to "Toward the Light". LC 79-9594. Orig. Title: Sporgsmaal Og Svar. 244p. 1979. pap. 6.95 (ISBN 87-87871-52-1). Toward the Light.

Atkins, Gaius G. Resources for Living. facs. ed. LC 77-117756. (Essay Index Reprint Ser). 1938. 17.00 (ISBN 0-8369-1741-3). Arno.

Attenborough, David. Life on Earth. 1981. 22.50 (ISBN 0-316-05745-2). Little.

Bacon, Francis. The Historie of Life & Death: Observations Naturall and Experimentall for the Prolonging of Life. Kastenbaum, Robert, ed. LC 76-19558. (Death and Dying Ser.). 1977. Repr. of 1638 ed. lib. bdg. 22.00x (ISBN 0-405-09554-6). Arno.

Baines, Gwendolyn L. People in the Web of Life. 1978. 5.00 (ISBN 0-682-48832-1). Exposition.

Beaubier, Jeff. High Life Expectancy on the Island of Paros, Greece. LC 75-22948. (Illus.). 160p. 1976. 10.00 (ISBN 0-8022-2172-6). Philos Lib.

Beers, Gilbert V. The Book of Life. 6000p. 1980. 299.00x (ISBN 0-310-79908-2). Zondervan.

Bendit, Laurence J. Mirror of Life & Death. 1965. pap. 1.35 (ISBN 0-8356-0411-X, Quest). Theos Pub Hse.

Bergson, Henri L. Creative Evolution. Mitchell, Arthur, tr. LC 74-28524. 453p. 1975. Repr. of 1944 ed. lib. bdg. 25.00x (ISBN 0-8371-7917-3, BECEV). Greenwood.

Bichat, Xavier. Physiological Researches on Life & Death. Gold, F., tr. from Fr. Bd. with Outlines of Phrenology; Phrenology Examined. (Contributions to the History of Psychology, Vol. II, Pt. E: Physiological Psychology). 1978. Repr. of 1827 ed. 30.00 (ISBN 0-89093-175-5). U Pubns Amer.

Blechschmidt, E. The Beginnings of Human Life. Transemantics, Inc., tr. from Ger. LC 77-16658. (Heidelberg Science Library). (Illus.). 1977. pap. 8.80 (ISBN 0-387-90249-X). Springer-Verlag.

Bohle, Bruce W., ed. Human Life: Controversies & Concerns. (Reference Shelf Ser.). 1979. 6.25 (ISBN 0-8242-0636-3). Wilson.

Bohn, Georges. Les Problems De la Vie et De la Mort. 1925. 20.00 (ISBN 0-8274-4187-8). R West.

Bradford, Gamaliel. Life & I, an Autobiography of Humanity. LC 68-54987. (Illus.). 1968. Repr. of 1928 ed. lib. bdg. 14.50x (ISBN 0-8371-0324-X, BRLI). Greenwood.

Britton, K. Philosophy & the Meaning of Life. LC 69-12926. 1969. 27.95 (ISBN 0-521-07456-8); pap. 7.95x (ISBN 0-521-09593-X, 593). Cambridge U Pr.

Chaudhuri, Haridas. Mastering the Problems of Living. new ed. LC 75-4172. 222p. 1975. pap. 2.75 (ISBN 0-8356-0463-2, Quest). Theos Pub Hse.

Cousteau, Jacques, intro. by. The Adventure of Life. LC 74-23940. (Ocean World of Jacques Cousteau Ser.: Vol. 14). (Illus.). 144p. 1975. 9.95 (ISBN 0-8109-0588-4). Abrams.

Crews, William. Four Causes of Reality. LC 69-14354. 1969. 5.50 (ISBN 0-8022-2268-4). Philos Lib.

Croce, Benedetto. Conduct of Life. facs. ed. Livingston, A., tr. LC 67-30204. (Essay Index Reprint Ser). 1924. 16.00 (ISBN 0-8369-0351-X). Arno.

De Vinck, Jose. The Yes Book. 1976. pap. 3.75 (ISBN 0-685-77499-6). Franciscan Herald.

--The Yes Book: An Answer to Life (a Manual for Chritian Existentialism) LC 77-190621. (Illus.). 200p. 1972. 8.75 (ISBN 0-911726-12-8); pap. 6.75 (ISBN 0-911726-11-X). Alleluia Pr.

Dillett, Eric S. Why Were We Born? 1980. 6.00 (ISBN 0-682-49534-4). Exposition.

Dinsmore, Charles A. Great Poets & the Meaning of Life. facs. ed. LC 68-58786. (Essay Index Reprint Ser). 1937. 16.00 (ISBN 0-8369-0109-6). Arno.

Dobschiner, Johanna R., tr. Destinada a Viver. (Portugese Bks.). (Port.). 1979. 1.60 (ISBN 0-8297-0655-0). Life Pubs Intl.

Dunne, John S. Time & Myth. LC 74-32289. 128p. 1975. pap. 3.45 (ISBN 0-268-01828-6). U of Notre Dame Pr.

Erskine, John. Complete Life. facs. ed. LC 74-134073. (Essay Index Reprint Ser). 1943. 19.50 (ISBN 0-8369-2153-4). Arno.

Gaskell, Augusta. What Is Life? 324p. 1929. ed. spiral bdg. 26.75photocopy (ISBN 0-398-04262-4). C C Thomas.

Giammatteo, Michael C. Circles of Life. (Illus., Orig.). 1973. pap. 5.00 (ISBN 0-918428-01-7). Sylvan Inst.

Greenberg, Sidney. Hidden Hungers. 244p. 1973. 10.00x (ISBN 0-87677-151-7). Hartmore.

Greg, William R. Enigmas of Life. LC 72-323. (Essay Index Reprint Ser.). Repr. of 1879 ed. 19.00 (ISBN 0-8369-2794-X). Arno.

Gregory, Robert L. Rays of Hope. LC 69-20332. 1969. 7.00 (ISBN 0-8022-2291-9). Philos Lib.

Halcane, John S. Mechanism, Life & Personality. LC 72-7966. 152p. 1973. Repr. of 1923 ed. lib. bdg. 15.00x (ISBN 0-8371-6557-1, HAML). Greenwood.

Hall, C. Margaret. Vital Life. LC 72-96976. 80p. 1973. 4.95 (ISBN 0-8158-0302-8). Chris Mass.

Halle, Louis J. Out of Chaos. 1977. 20.00 (ISBN 0-395-25357-8). HM.

Hamblin, Dora Jane. That Was the LIFE. (Illus.). 1977. 10.00 (ISBN 0-393-08764-6). Norton.

Hancock, Maxine. Vidas En Formacion. (Span.). Date not set. 2.25 (ISBN 0-686-76349-1). Life Pubs Intl.

--Vidas En Formacion. Mercado, Benjamin, ed. Sipowicz, Edwin, tr. from Eng. 212p. (Span.). 1979. pap. 1.90 (ISBN 0-8297-0653-4). Life Pubs Intl.

Hendren, Bob. Life Without End. LC 80-54164. (Journey Bks.). 144p. (Orig.). 1981. pap. 2.95 (ISBN 0-8344-0118-5). Sweet.

Heubach, Paul. Life's Greatest Values. (Flame Ser.). 1976. pap. 0.95 (ISBN 0-8127-0121-6). Review & Herald.

Hocking, Brian. Biology or Oblivion: Lessons from the Ultimate Science. rev ed. 150p. 1972. 5.50 (ISBN 0-87073-802-X); pap. text ed. 3.50 (ISBN 0-87073-803-8). Schenkman.

Hocking, William E. The Meaning of Immortality in Human Experience, Including Thoughts on Death & Life. rev. ed. 263p. 1973. Repr. of 1957 ed. lib. bdg. 15.75x (ISBN 0-8371-6621-7, HOMI). Greenwood.

Howe, Reuel L. Live All Your Life. LC 74-82655. 1976. pap. 4.50 (ISBN 0-87680-853-4, 98081). Word Bks.

Humphreys, Gertrude. Adventures in Good Living. (Illus.). 1972. 5.50 (ISBN 0-87012-133-2). McClain.

Inspiration for Living. 1971. 2.95 (ISBN 0-442-82271-5). Peter Pauper.

Jacks, Lawrence P. The Challenge of Life: Three Lectures. LC 77-27147. (Hibbert Lectures Ser.). Repr. of 1924 ed. 15.00 (ISBN 0-404-60423-4). AMS Pr.

Jaffe, Aniela. Myth of Meaning. 1975. pap. 2.25 (ISBN 0-14-003990-2). Penguin.

Jenks, Ward B. Purpose of Man. LC 65-26972. 1966. 3.50 (ISBN 0-8022-0799-5). Philos Lib.

Kallen, Horace M. William James & Henri Bergson: A Study in Contrasting Theories of Life. LC 75-3213. (Philosophy in America Ser.). Repr. of 1914 ed. 24.50 (ISBN 0-404-59209-0). AMS Pr.

Kaufmann, Walter. Life at the Limits. (Illus.). 1978. pap. 10.00 (ISBN 0-07-033315-7, GB). McGraw.

--Man's Lot. (Illus.). 1978. 60.00 (ISBN 0-07-033314-9, GB). McGraw.

Kevorkian, Jack. Beyond Any Kind of God. LC 66-18485. 1967. 3.75 (ISBN 0-8022-0847-9). Philos Lib.

Khan, R., et al. Story of Life. 6.50x (ISBN 0-210-27034-9). Asia.

Klemke, E. D., ed. The Meaning of Life. 288p. 1981. pap. text ed. 6.95x (ISBN 0-19-502871-6). Oxford U Pr.

Krishnamurti, J. The Wholeness of Life. LC 78-19495. 256p. 1981. pap. 6.95 (ISBN 0-06-064868-6, RD362, HarpR). Har-Row.

Ladd, George T. Knowledge, Life & Reality. 1918. 34.50x (ISBN 0-685-69836-X). Elliots Bks.

Latimer, Paul R. The Psychology of Life & the Psychology of Death. (Illus.). 1979. 27.75 (ISBN 0-89920-000-1). Am Inst Psych.

Lawson, Brian C. Life, Death, Eternity & the Secret of the Universe. (Illus.). 1979. 27.45 (ISBN 0-89266-207-7). Am Classical Coll Pr.

Levinson, Daniel, et al. The Seasons of a Man's Life. 1979. pap. 5.95 (ISBN 0-345-28258-2). Ballantine.

Lifton, Robert. The Broken Connection. 1980. pap. 7.95 (ISBN 0-671-41386-4, Touchstone). S&S.

Lindbergh, Anne M. Gift from the Sea. LC 55-5065. 1955. pap. 5.00 (ISBN 0-394-42629-0). Pantheon.

Luria, S. E., et al. A View of Life. 1981. 24.95 (ISBN 0-8053-6648-2); instr.'s guide 3.95 (ISBN 0-8053-6649-0). A-W.

Mandelbaum, Bernard. Choose Life. 1972. pap. 3.95 (ISBN 0-8197-0006-1). Bloch.

Mann, John A. Secrets of Life Extension. (Illus.). 256p. (Orig.). 1980. 14.00 (ISBN 0-936602-06-6); pap. 7.95 (ISBN 0-915904-47-0). Harbor Pub CA.

Marias, Julian. Metaphysical Anthropology: The Empirical Structure of Human Life. Lopez-Morillas, Frances M., tr. LC 78-127386. 1971. 15.75x (ISBN 0-271-01139-4). Pa St U Pr.

Markun, Alan F. Philosophy for the New Age. LC 79-169243. 1972. 7.50 (ISBN 0-8022-2066-5). Philos Lib.

Marquand, Josephine. Life: Its Nature, Origins, & Distribution. (Contemporary Science Library). (Illus.). 1971. pap. 1.65x (ISBN 0-393-00589-5). Norton.

Murchie, Guy. The Seven Mysteries of Life: An Exploration in Science & Philosophy. (Illus.). 1978. 17.95 (ISBN 0-395-26310-7). HM.

Nagel, T. Mortal Questions. LC 78-58797. 1979. 29.95 (ISBN 0-521-22360-1); pap. 7.95x (ISBN 0-521-29460-6). Cambridge U Pr.

Ney, Albert C. Seeing into Life: Sociological Essays. 1969. 5.50 (ISBN 0-87164-008-2). William-F.

Nicoll, W. R. Letters on Life. 15.00 (ISBN 0-8274-2851-0). R West.

O'Connor, John J. In Defense of Life. 1980. 4.00 (ISBN 0-686-74344-X); pap. 3.00 (ISBN 0-8198-3601-X). Dghtrs St Paul.

Orr, Leonard. The Truth About Psychology. Orig. Title: Unraveling the Birth-Death Cycle. 1976. pap. 2.00 (ISBN 0-686-15470-3). L Orr.

Pankin, B. Seven Essays on Life & Literature. 256p. 1979. 8.40 (ISBN 0-8285-1089-X, Pub. by Progress Pubs Russia). Imported Pubns.

The Philosophy of Life & the Philosophy of Death: Considerations & Anticipations of the Future Universe & of Man's Existence in It. 2nd ed. (Illus.). 1977. 27.25 (ISBN 0-89266-058-9). Am Classical Coll Pr.

Portugal, Pamela R. & Portugal, Nancy. A Place for Human Beings. LC 78-11533. (Illus.). 1978. pap. 6.95 (ISBN 0-9601088-5-8). Wide World-Tetra.

Pretto, G., et al. Life on Earth. Orlandi, Enzo & Marcolungo, G., eds. Pleasance, Simon, tr. from Ital. LC 77-78800. Orig. Title: Il Mondo Della Natura. 1977. 19.95 (ISBN 0-88225-251-8). Newsweek.

Rappoport, A. S. The Psalms in Life, Legend & Literature. 1935. 30.00 (ISBN 0-8414-7408-7). Folcroft.

Reeve, Bryant. Advent of the Cosmic Viewpoint. 1965. 3.50 (ISBN 0-910122-10-5). Amherst Pr.

Roderey, Nicholas A. Way of Power. LC 69-14358. 1969. 6.00 (ISBN 0-8022-2298-6). Philos Lib.

Rogers, Carl R. Therapist's View of Personal Goals. LC 60-11607. (Orig.). 1960. pap. 0.95x (ISBN 0-87574-108-8). Pendle Hill.

Rosenkranz, Samuel. Meaning in Your Life. 1958. 3.00 (ISBN 0-8022-1375-8). Philos Lib.

Ruane, Gerald P. Birth to Birth: The Life-Death. LC 75-40300. (Illus.). 99p. 1976. pap. 3.95 (ISBN 0-8189-0326-0). Alba.

Sanders, Steven & Cheny, David. The Meaning of Life: Questions, Answers & Analysis. 1980. pap. text ed. 7.95 (ISBN 0-13-567438-7). P-H.

Schlegel, F. Von. The Philosophy of Life & Philosophy of Language, in a Course of Lectures. Morrison, A. J., tr. 1847. Repr. 35.00 (ISBN 0-8274-3132-5). R West.

Schlitt, Dorothy M., et al. Life: A Question of Survival. (Illus., Orig.). (gr. 7-11). 1972. pap. text ed. 6.64x (ISBN 0-913688-03-7); teacher's guide 5.32x (ISBN 0-913688-04-5). Pawnee Pub.

Schutz, Alfred & Luckmann, Thomas. The Structures of the Life-World. Zaner, Richard & Engelhardt, Tristram, Jr., trs. from Ger. (Studies in Phenomenology & Existential Philosophy). 1973. text ed. 18.95x (ISBN 0-8101-0395-8); pap. 8.95 (ISBN 0-8101-0622-1). Northwestern U Pr.

Sinsheimer. The Book of Life. 1976. 1.50 (ISBN 0-201-07026-X). A-W.

Smith, O. C., Jr. The First Collected Insights of the Prophet O. C. 1978. 4.00 (ISBN 0-682-48784-8). Exposition.

Steiner, Rudolf. Philosophy of Freedom. Wilson, Michael, tr. from Ger. 226p. 1973. pap. 5.50 (ISBN 0-910142-52-1). Anthroposophic.

Sweeting, George. Living in a Dying World. 1972. 3.95 (ISBN 0-8024-4942-5). Moody.

Taylor, Richard W., ed. Life, Language, Law: Essays in Honor of Arthur F. Bentley. LC 56-8248. (Illus.). 1957. 6.00x (ISBN 0-87338-074-6). Kent St U Pr.

Teilhard De Chardin, Pierre. Activation de l'Energie. 1963. 21.50 (ISBN 0-685-10980-1). French & Eur.

Temkin, Owsei, et al. Respect for Life in Medicine, Philosophy, & the Law. LC 76-47366. (Thalheimer Lecture Ser.). 1977. text ed. 8.95x (ISBN 0-8018-1942-3). Johns Hopkins.

Tranter, John. The Livin' Is Easy. 9.95 (ISBN 0-392-03808-0, ABC). Sportshelf.

Trinkaus, Charles. Adversity's Noblemen. rev. ed. 1965. lib. bdg. 11.50x (ISBN 0-374-97999-5). Octagon.

Tully, Mary Jo. A Family Book of Praise: Or Would You Rather Be a Hippopotamus? (Illus.). 128p. (Orig.). 1980. 7.95 (ISBN 0-8215-6543-5); pap. 5.95 (ISBN 0-8215-6542-7). Sadlier.

Van Den Berg, J. H. Divided Existence & Complex Society: An Historical Approach. Jacobs, M., tr. from Dutch. LC 72-90634. 1974. text ed. 12.50x (ISBN 0-391-00320-8). Duquesne.

Von Schlegel, Friedrich. Philosophy of Life & Philosophy of Language. Morrison, A. J., tr. LC 70-147991. Repr. of 1847 ed. 27.50 (ISBN 0-404-08249-1). AMS Pr.

Wegerif, J. H. New Philosophy of Life. LC 68-10746. 1968. 7.95 (ISBN 0-8022-1841-5). Philos Lib.

White, Joseph L. Flight Pattern to Eternity. LC 67-24576. 1968. 4.00 (ISBN 0-8022-1861-X). Philos Lib.

White, R. W. The Enterprise of Living: A View of Personal Growth. 2nd ed. LC 75-38846. 1976. text ed. 17.95 (ISBN 0-03-089522-7, HoltC); instructor's manual avail. (ISBN 0-03-089759-9). HR&W.

Williams, R. H., ed. To Live & to Die: When, Why, & How. LC 73-2868. (Illus.). 1974. 9.10 (ISBN 0-387-90097-7). Springer-Verlag.

Zaner, Richard M. The Context of Self: A Phenomenological Inquiry Using Medicine As a Clue. LC 80-18500. (Continental Thought Ser.: Vol. 1). (Illus.). xiv, 282p. 1981. 18.95x (ISBN 0-8214-0443-1); pap. 8.95x (ISBN 0-8214-0600-0). Ohio U Pr.

LIFE–ORIGIN

see also Man–Origin; Spontaneous Generation

Abel, Ernest L. Ancient Views on the Origins of Life. LC 72-656. 93p. 1973. 10.00 (ISBN 0-8386-1198-2). Fairleigh Dickinson.

Adler, Irving. How Life Began. rev. ed. LC 76-16161. (Illus.). (gr. 7 up). 1977. 8.95 (ISBN 0-381-99603-4, JD-J). Har-Row.

Asimov, Isaac. Life & Times. 1979. pap. 2.50 (ISBN 0-380-47944-3, 47944, Discus). Avon.

Bastian, H. Charlton. The Origin of Life: Being an Account of Experiments with Certain Superheated Saline Solutions in Hermetically Sealed Vessels. 1979. Repr. of 1911 ed. lib. bdg. 20.00 (ISBN 0-8414-9836-9). Folcroft.

Bhaktivedanta, Swami A. C. Life Comes from Life. LC 75-39756. (Illus.). 1979. 5.95 (ISBN 0-912776-84-6); text ed. 5.95 (ISBN 0-685-70923-X). Bhaktivedanta.

Blechschmidt, E. The Beginnings of Human Life. Transemantics, Inc., tr. from Ger. LC 77-16658. (Heidelberg Science Library). (Illus.). 1977. pap. 8.80 (ISBN 0-387-90249-X). Springer-Verlag.

Bliss, Richard B. & Parker, Gary E. Origin of Life. LC 78-58477. (Illus.). 1978. pap. 4.95x (ISBN 0-89051-053-9). CLP Pubs.

Brooks, J. & Shaw, G. Origin & Development of Living Systems. 1972. 42.00 (ISBN 0-12-135740-6). Acad Pr.

Brooks, Noel. Let There Be Life. 3.95 (ISBN 0-911866-71-X); pap. 2.95 (ISBN 0-911866-88-4). Advocate.

Buvet, R. & Ponnamperuma, C., eds. Chemical Evolution & the Origin of Life. LC 75-146189. (Molecular Evolution Ser.: Vol. 1). (Illus.). 571p. 1971. 39.00 (ISBN 0-444-10093-8, North-Holland). Elsevier.

Chand, Bool. Our Earth & the Universe. 3.50x (ISBN 0-210-33909-8). Asia.

Cook, John S., ed. Biogenesis & Turnover of Membrane Macromolecules. LC 75-25111. (Society of General Physiologists Ser.: Vol. 31). 232p. 1976. 27.00 (ISBN 0-89004-092-3). Raven.

Dillon, L. S. The Genetic Mechanism & the Origin of Life. LC 78-4478. (Illus.). 573p. 1978. 39.50 (ISBN 0-306-31090-2, Plenum Pr). Plenum Pub.

Dose, K., et al, eds. The Origin of Life & Evolutionary Biochemistry. LC 74-10703. 476p. 1974. 39.50 (ISBN 0-306-30811-8, Plenum Pr). Plenum Pub.

Eccles, Sir John. The Human Mystery. LC 78-12095. (Illus.). 1979. 19.70 (ISBN 0-387-09016-9). Springer-Verlag.

Fourth International Conference on the Origin of Life, 1973, Invited Papers & Contributed Papers, et al. Cosmochemical Evolution & the Origins of Life, 2 vols. Oro, J. & Miller, S. L., eds. LC 74-77967. vii, 755p. 1974. Vol. 1. lib. bdg. 59.00 (ISBN 90-277-0519-4, Pub. by Reidel Holland); Vol. 2. lib. bdg. 36.00 (ISBN 9-0277-0518-6). Kluwer Boston.

Fox, Sidney W. & Dose, Klaus. Molecular Evolution & the Origins of Life. 2nd expanded ed. (Biology--a Ser. of Textbooks: Vol. 2). 1977. 23.50 (ISBN 0-8247-6619-9). Dekker.

Gallant, Roy A. Beyond Earth: The Search for Extraterrestrial Life. LC 77-5790. (gr. 7 up). 1977. 8.95g (ISBN 0-590-07437-7, Four Winds). Schol Bk Serv.
Gish, Duane T. Speculations & Experiments Related to the Origin of Life: A Critique. (ICR Technical Monograph: No. 1). (Illus.). 41p. 1972. pap. 4.50 (ISBN 0-89051-010-5). CLP Pubs.
Goldsmith, Donald. The Quest for Extraterrestrial Life: A Book of Readings. LC 79-57423. (Illus.). 308p. 1980. 18.00 (ISBN 0-935702-08-3); pap. text ed. 12.00 (ISBN 0-935702-02-4). Univ Sci Bks.
Gribbin, John. Genesis. 240p. 1981. 17.50x (ISBN 0-460-04505-9, Pub. by J. M. Dent England). Biblio Dist.
Hocking, Brian. Biology or Oblivion: Lessons from the Ultimate Science. rev ed. 150p. 1972. 5.50 (ISBN 0-87073-802-X); pap. text ed. 3.50 (ISBN 0-87073-803-8). Schenkman.
Hoyle, Fred & Wickramsinghe, N. C. Lifecloud: The Origin of Life in the Universe. LC 78-20167. (Illus.). 1979. 10.95 (ISBN 0-06-011954-3, HarpT). Har-Row.
Hyndman, Olan R. Origin of Life & Evolution of Living Things. 1952. 8.75 (ISBN 0-8022-0768-5). Philos Lib.
Interdisciplinary Conference - 2nd. Origins of Life: Proceedings, Vol. 2. Margulis, Lynn, ed. 1971. 46.25x (ISBN 0-677-13630-7). Gordon.
Jastrow, Robert. Red Giants & White Dwarfs. (Illus.). 1979. 14.95 (ISBN 0-393-85002-1). Norton.
--Red Giants & White Dwarfs: Man's Descent from the Stars. 1971. pap. 1.95 (ISBN 0-451-08270-2, J8270, Sig). NAL.
--Until the Sun Dies. (Illus.). 1977. 12.95 (ISBN 0-393-06415-8). Norton.
Kenyon, D. & Steinman, G. D. Biochemical Predestination. (Illus.). 1969. text ed. 14.50 (ISBN 0-07-034126-5, HP). McGraw.
Kvenvolden, K. A., ed. Geochemistry & the Origin of Life. LC 74-24685. (Benchmark Papers in Geology Ser: Vol. 14). 500p. 1975. 47.00 (ISBN 0-12-786895-X). Acad Pr.
Locker, A., ed. Biogenesis-Evolution-Homeostasis: A Symposium by Correspondence. LC 72-96743. (Illus.). 190p. 1973. pap. 28.90 (ISBN 0-387-06134-7). Springer-Verlag.
Margulis, L. Origins of Life, 2 vols. 1971. Vol. 1, 410 Pp. 67.25 (ISBN 0-677-13320-0); Vol. 2, 246 Pp. 46.25 (ISBN 0-677-13630-7). Gordon.
Matthew, William D. Outline & General Principles of the History of Life: University of California Syllabus Series, No. 213. Gould, Stephen J., ed. LC 79-8335. (The History of Paleontology Ser.). (Illus.). 1980. Repr. of 1928 ed. lib. bdg. 19.00x (ISBN 0-405-12719-7). Arno.
Miller, Stanley L. & Orgel, Leslie E. The Origins of Life on the Earth. (Concepts of Modern Biology Ser). (Illus.). 208p. 1974. pap. 12.95x ref. ed. (ISBN 0-13-642074-5). P-H.
Moore, Benjamin. The Origin & Nature of Life. 12.50 (ISBN 0-8274-4241-6). R West.
Noda, Haruhiko. Origin of Life. 1979. 63.00x (ISBN 0-89955-132-7, Pub. by Japan Sci Soc). Intl Schol Bk Serv.
Oparin, A. I. Genesis & Evolutionary Development of Life. 1969. 26.00 (ISBN 0-12-527446-7). Acad Pr.
Oparin, Alexander I. Origin of Life. 2nd ed. 1953. pap. 4.00 (ISBN 0-486-60213-3). Dover.
Orgel, L. E. The Origins of Life: Molecules & Natural Selection. LC 72-10534. 144p. 1973. 11.95 (ISBN 0-471-65693-3). Wiley.
Osborn, Henry F. The Origin & Evolution of Life: On the Theory of Action, Reaction & Interaction of Energy. Gould, Stephen J., ed. LC 79-8340. (The History of Paleontology Ser.). (Illus.). 1980. Repr. of 1917 ed. lib. bdg. 29.00x (ISBN 0-405-12728-6). Arno.
Oster, G. F., et al, eds. Irreversible Thermodynamics & the Origin of Life. new ed. 82p. 1974. 29.25x (ISBN 0-677-14270-6). Gordon.
Ponnamperuma, C. Exobiology. 1972. 56.00 (ISBN 0-444-10110-1, North-Holland). Elsevier.
Reich, Wilhelm. The Bion Experiments: On the Origin of Life. Jordan, Derek & Jordan, Inge, trs. (Octagon edition). 1979. 22.50 (ISBN 0-374-96768-7); pap. 8.95 (ISBN 0-374-51446-1). FS&G.
--The Bion Experiments: On the Origin of Life. Jordan, Derek & Jordan, Inge, trs. 1979. 18.50x (ISBN 0-374-96768-7). Octagon.
Rohlfing, Duane & Oparin, A. I., eds. Molecular Evolution: Prebiological & Biological. 481p. 1972. 39.50 (ISBN 0-306-30719-7, Plenum Pr). Plenum Pub.
Rutten, M. G. The Origin of Life. LC 73-118255. (Illus.). 440p. 1969. 75.75 (ISBN 0-444-40887-8). Elsevier.
Sagan, Carl. The Cosmic Connection: An Extraterrestrial Perspective. LC 73-81117. 288p. 1973. 8.95 (ISBN 0-385-00457-5, Anch). Doubleday.
Watson, David C. The Great Brain Robbery. 1976. pap. 1.50 (ISBN 0-8024-3303-0). Moody.

LIFE (BIOLOGY)

see also Biology; Biosphere; Death (Biology); Dormancy (Biology); Genetics; Longevity; Mechanism (Philosophy); Old Age; Protoplasm; Reproduction

Asimov, Isaac. Wellspring of Life. (Illus.). pap. 1.50 (ISBN 0-451-61619-7, MW1619, Ment). NAL.
Axelrod, A. Reanimacion Sin Sensaciones. 155p. (Span.). 1977. pap. 1.95 (ISBN 0-8285-1699-5, Pub. by Mir Pubs Russia). Imported Pubns.
Bell, Michael C., et al. Investigating Living Systems, Pt. I. 203p. (Orig.). 1980. pap. 9.95x lab manual (ISBN 0-89459-078-2). Hunter NC.
--Investigating Living Systems, Pt. II. 178p. (Orig.). 1981. pap. 9.95x lab manual (ISBN 0-89459-089-8). Hunter NC.
Bichat, Marie F. Physiological Researches on Life & Death. Kastenbaum, Robert, ed. Gold, F. & Magendie, F., trs. LC 76-19561. (Death & Dying Ser.). 1977. Repr. lib. bdg. 22.00x (ISBN 0-405-09557-0). Arno.
Bonner, John T. Size & Cycle: An Essay on the Structure of Biology. (Illus.). 1965. 17.50 (ISBN 0-691-08033-X). Princeton U Pr.
Brooks, J. & Shaw, G. Origin & Development of Living Systems. 1972. 42.00 (ISBN 0-12-135740-6). Acad Pr.
Brown, Walter R. & Anderson, Norman D. Life Science: A Search for Understanding. rev. ed. 1977. text ed. 11.20 (ISBN 0-397-43741-2); tchrs ed. 13.20 (ISBN 0-397-43742-0). Har-Row.
Clowes, Royston. The Structure of Life. (Illus.). 7.50 (ISBN 0-8446-1873-X). Peter Smith.
Corliss, William R. Incredible Life: A Handbook of Biological Mysteries. LC 80-53971. (Illus.). 1050p. 1981. 22.50 (ISBN 0-915554-07-0). Sourcebook.
Crick, Francis. Life Itself: Its Origins & Nature. 1981. 13.95 (ISBN 0-671-25562-2). S&S.
--Of Molecules & Men. LC 66-26994. (Jesse & John Danz Lecture Ser.). 118p. 1967. pap. 3.95 (ISBN 0-295-97869-4, WP-26). U of Wash Pr.
Crile, George W. Bipolar Theory of Living Processes. 2nd ed. 1981. Repr. of 1955 ed. 12.95x (ISBN 0-686-76728-4). Regent House.
Deperet, Charles. The Transformations of the Animal World: Being the Authorized Translation of "les Transformations Du Monde Animal. Gould, Stephen J., ed. LC 79-8330. (The History of Paleontology Ser.). 1980. Repr. of 1909 ed. lib. bdg. 28.00x (ISBN 0-405-12711-1). Arno.
Driesch, Hans A. The Science & Philosophy of the Organism, 2 vols. LC 77-27217. (Gifford Lectures: 1907-08). Repr. of 1908 ed. Set. 62.50 (ISBN 0-404-60500-1). AMS Pr.
Folsome, Clair E., intro. by. Life: Origin & Evolution: Readings from Scientific American. LC 78-15129. (Illus.). 1979. text ed. 16.95x (ISBN 0-7167-1033-1); pap. text ed. 8.95x (ISBN 0-7167-1032-3). W H Freeman.
Geist, V. Life Strategies, Human Evolution, Environmental Design: Toward a Biological Theory of Health, Vol. I. LC 78-10807. (Illus.). 1979. 31.30 (ISBN 0-387-90363-1). Springer-Verlag.
Gibor, Aharon, intro. by. Conditions for Life: Readings from Scientific American. LC 76-22196. (Illus.). 1976. text ed. 19.95x (ISBN 0-7167-0480-3); pap. text ed. 9.95x (ISBN 0-7167-0479-X). W H Freeman.
Hall, Eric J. Radiation & Life. 1976. 25.00 (ISBN 0-08-020599-2); pap. 9.75 (ISBN 0-08-020598-4). Pergamon.
Heidcamp, W. The Nature of Life. 1978. 11.95 (ISBN 0-8391-1280-7). Univ Park.
Jennings, Herbert S. The Universe & Life. facsimile ed. (Select Bibliographies Reprint Ser). Repr. of 1933 ed. 12.00 (ISBN 0-8369-6695-3). Arno.
Kendig, Frank & Hutton, Richard. Life Spans: Or, How Long Things Last. LC 79-15952. 288p. (Orig.). 1980. 12.95 (ISBN 0-03-053261-2); pap. 5.95 (ISBN 0-03-040876-8). HR&W.
Kennedy, J. F. Proteoglycans-Biological & Chemical Aspects in Human Life. (Studies in Organic Chemistry: Vol. 2). 490p. 1980. 80.50 (ISBN 0-444-41794-X). Elsevier.
Loeb, Jacques. Mechanistic Conception of Life. Fleming, Donald, ed. LC 64-13426. (The John Harvard Library). (Illus.). 1964. 10.00x (ISBN 0-674-55950-9). Harvard U Pr.
Mader, Sylia S. Inquiry into Life. 2nd ed. 750p. 1979. study guide 7.95x (ISBN 0-697-04564-1); text ed. 16.95x (ISBN 0-697-04563-3); lab. man. 8.95 (ISBN 0-697-04567-6); pap. instr. man. 3.00 (ISBN 0-686-60834-8); 50 transparencies 50.00x (ISBN 0-697-04573-0). Wm C Brown.
Metchnikoff, Elie. The Nature of Man: Studies in Optimistic Philosophy. Kastenbaum, Robert, ed. Mitchell, P. Chalmers, tr. LC 76-19582. (Death & Dying Ser.). (Illus.). 1977. Repr. of 1910 ed. lib. bdg. 21.00x (ISBN 0-405-09578-3). Arno.
Murchie, Guy. The Seven Mysteries of Life: An Exploration in Science & Philosophy. (Illus.). 1978. 17.95 (ISBN 0-395-26310-7). HM.
Nelson, Gideon E., Jr. Biological Principles with Human Perspectives. 1980. text ed. 19.95 (ISBN 0-471-02194-6). Wiley.
Palmeri, Rosario. Sources of Instinctive Life. LC 65-27461. 1966. 3.00 (ISBN 0-8022-1260-3). Philos Lib.
Phillips, John. Life on Earth: Its Origin & Succession. Gould, Stephen J., ed. LC 79-8343. (The History of Paleontology Ser.). 1980. Repr. of 1860 ed. lib. bdg. 18.00x (ISBN 0-405-12733-2). Arno.
Platt, Rutherford. River of Life. 1962. pap. 1.75 (ISBN 0-671-62451-2, Touchstone Bks). S&S.
Reich, Wilhelm. Ether, God & Devil & Cosmic Superimposition. Pol, Therese, tr. (Illus.). 260p. 1972. 10.00 (ISBN 0-374-14907-0); pap. 5.95 (ISBN 0-374-50991-3). FS&G.
--The Murder of Christ: The Emotional Plague of Mankind. 228p. 1953. 5.95 (ISBN 0-374-21625-8); pap. 3.95 (ISBN 0-374-50476-8, N290). FS&G.
Riedl, R. Order in Living Organisms: A Systems Analysis of Evolution. LC 77-28245. 1979. 47.50 (ISBN 0-471-99635-1, Pub. by Wiley-Interscience). Wiley.
Roller-Massar, Ann. Discovering the Basis of Life: An Introduction to Molecular Biology. (Illus.). 320p. 1973. pap. text ed. 8.95 (ISBN 0-07-053564-7, C). McGraw.
Rusche, Franz. Blut, Leben und Seele, Ihr Verhaeltnis Nach Auffassung der Griechischen und Hellenistischen Antike, der Bibel und der Alten Alexandrinischen Theologen. Repr. of 1930 ed. pap. 28.00 (ISBN 0-384-52515-6). Johnson Repr.
Scientific American Magazine Editors. Physics & Chemistry of Life. (Orig.). 1956. pap. 1.95 (ISBN 0-671-57050-1, Fireside). S&S.
Sherrington, Charles S. Man on His Nature. 1951. 39.95 (ISBN 0-521-06436-8); pap. 11.95x (ISBN 0-521-09203-5). Cambridge U Pr.
Simon, Michael A. Matter of Life: Philosophical Problems of Biology. LC 74-158142. 1971. 17.50x (ISBN 0-300-01500-3). Yale U Pr.
Smallwood, W. L. Life Science. 1972. 13.84 (ISBN 0-07-058415-X); tchr's. ed. 16.92 (ISBN 0-07-058416-8); work study guide, pupil's ed. 3.72 (ISBN 0-07-058418-4); work study guide, tchr's ed. 4.80 (ISBN 0-07-058419-2); tests 34.00 (ISBN 0-07-058417-6). McGraw.
Steinberg, Laurence D. The Life Cycle: Readings in Human Development. LC 81-3806. (Illus.). 432p. 1982. text ed. 25.00x (ISBN 0-231-05110-7); pap. 12.50x (ISBN 0-231-05111-5). Columbia U Pr.
Stephens, Charles A. Natural Salvation: The Message of Science, Outlining the First Principles of Immortal Life on the Earth. Kastenbaum, Robert, ed. LC 76-19588. (Death & Dying Ser.). 1977. Repr. of 1905 ed. lib. bdg. 14.00x (ISBN 0-405-09583-X). Arno.
Sweetser, William. Human Life: Considered in Its Present Condition & Future Developments. Kastenbaum, Robert, ed. LC 78-22219. (Aging & Old Age Ser.). 1979. Repr. of 1867 ed. lib. bdg. 22.00x (ISBN 0-405-11832-5). Arno.
Sze, William S., ed. Human Life Cycle. LC 75-4783. 750p. 1975. 30.00x (ISBN 0-87668-199-2). Aronson.
Szent-Gyorgyi, Albert. The Living State with Remarks on Cancer. 1972. 21.00 (ISBN 0-12-680960-7). Acad Pr.
Thompson, Paul D. Abiogenesis: From Molecule to Cell. LC 78-82399. (Introducing Modern Science Ser). (Illus.). (gr. 7 up). 1969. 6.95 (ISBN 0-397-31054-4). Lippincott.
Tocquet, R. L' Aventure de la vie. (Encyclopedie Larousse De Poche). (Illus., Fr.). pap. 3.50 (ISBN 0-685-13805-4). Larousse.
Virchow, Rudolf L. Disease, Life, & Man: Selected Essays. Rather, Lelland J., tr. 1958. 12.50x (ISBN 0-8047-0557-7). Stanford U Pr.
Yalon, Reuven. Man & Animal; Life Cycle. (B'yad Halashon). (Illus.). 40p. (Heb.). 1973. pap. 0.80 (ISBN 0-912022-74-4). EMC.

LIFE, FUTURE

see Future Life

LIFE, JEWISH WAY OF

see Jewish Way of Life

LIFE, ORIGIN OF

see Life–Origin

LIFE, SPIRITUAL

see Spiritual Life

LIFE AFTER DEATH

see Future Life; Immortality

LIFE-BOATS

Block, Richard A., ed. Able Seaman & Lifeboatman: All Grades. rev. ed. (Illus.). 338p. 1978. pap. 21.00 (ISBN 0-934114-04-8). Marine Educ.
Daunt, Achilles. Our Sea Coast Heroes: Stories of the Wreck & Rescue, Origin, History & Principles of the Construction of the Lightboat. 1977. lib. bdg. 69.95 (ISBN 0-8490-2393-9). Gordon Pr.
Farr, A. D. Let Not the Deep: Story of the Royal National Lifeboat Institution. (Illus.). 1973. 15.00x (ISBN 0-901311-27-8). Intl Pubns Serv.
Middleton, E. W. Lifeboats of the World. LC 77-26247. (Arco Color Ser.). (Illus.). 1978. 8.95 (ISBN 0-668-04470-5); pap. 6.95 (ISBN 0-668-04481-0). Arco.
Shanks, Ralph C., Jr. & Shanks, Janetta T. Lighthouses & Lifeboats on the Redwood Coast. LC 77-93457. (Illus.). 1978. 14.95 (ISBN 0-930268-04-0); pap. 8.95 (ISBN 0-930268-03-2). Costano.

LIFE INSURANCE

see Insurance, Life

LIFE INSURANCE STOCKS

Belth, Joseph M. Participating Life Insurance Sold by Stock Companies. 1965. 8.25x (ISBN 0-256-00639-3). Irwin.
Olson, Alden C. Impact of Valuation Requirements on the Preferred Stock Investment Policies of Life Insurance Companies. LC 64-63572. 1964. pap. 2.50 (ISBN 0-87744-036-0). Mich St U Busn.
Stock Life Insurance Companies. (Industry Audit Guides). 1972. pap. 7.00 (ISBN 0-685-58487-9). Am Inst CPA.

LIFE-LONG EDUCATION

see Adult Education

LIFE ON OTHER PLANETS

Here are entered works on the question of life in outer space. Works on the biology of man or other earth life while in outer space are entered under Space Biology.

see also Interstellar Communication; Plurality of Worlds; Religion and Astronautics

Azimov, Isaac. Extraterrestrial Civilization. 1979. 10.00 (ISBN 0-517-53075-9). Crown.
Barlowe, Wayne D. & Summers, Ian. Barlowe's Guide to Extraterrestrials. LC 79-64782. (Illus.). 1979. 14.95 (ISBN 0-89480-113-9); pap. 7.95 (ISBN 0-89480-112-0). Workman Pub.
Berrill, N. J. Worlds Without End. 1964. 5.95 (ISBN 0-02-510340-7). Macmillan.
Billingham, J. & Pesek, R., eds. Communication with Extraterrestrial Intelligence. (Astronautica: Vol. 6, Nos. 1-2). 1979. 47.00 (ISBN 0-08-024727-X). Pergamon.
Billingham, John, et al, eds. Life in the Universe. 400p. 1981. text ed. 20.00 (ISBN 0-262-02155-2); pap. text ed. 12.50x (ISBN 0-262-52062-1). MIT Pr.
Bracewell, Ronald N. The Galactic Club: Intelligent Life in Outer Space. (Illus.). 160p. 1979. Repr. of 1976 ed. pap. text ed. 3.95x (ISBN 0-393-95022-0). Norton.
--The Galactic Club: Intelligent Life in Outer Space. LC 76-1920. (The Portable Stanford Ser.). (Illus.). 1976. 8.95 (ISBN 0-913374-40-7); pap. 4.95 (ISBN 0-913374-41-5). SF Bk Co.
C O S P A R, 11th Plenary Meeting, Tokyo, 1968. Life Sciences & Space Research: Proceedings, Vol. 7. Vishniac, W. & Favorite, F. G., eds. LC 63-6132. (Illus.). 1969. text ed. 20.00x (ISBN 0-7204-1367-2, Pub. by North Holland). Humanities.
Cameron, A. G. W., ed. Interstellar Communication: The Search for Extraterrestrial Life. (Illus.). 1963. pap. 9.50 (ISBN 0-8053-1751-1, Adv Bk Prog). Benjamin-Cummings.
Chandler, David L. Life on Mars. 1979. 9.95 (ISBN 0-525-14560-5). Dutton.
Christian, James L. Extra-Terrestrial Intelligence: The First Encounter. 1976. pap. 6.00 (ISBN 0-87980-350-9). Wilshire.
Christian, James L., ed. Extra-Terrestrial Intelligence: The First Encounter. LC 76-25328. (Critiques of the Paranormal Ser.). 303p. 1976. 15.95 (ISBN 0-87975-063-4); pap. 6.95 (ISBN 0-87975-064-2). Prometheus Bks.
Edelson, Edward. Who Goes There: The Search for Intelligent Life in the Universe. (Illus.). 228p. 1980. pap. 4.95 (ISBN 0-07-018986-2, SB). McGraw.
Ehrensvard, Gosta. Man on Another World. LC 65-17287. (Illus.). 1965. 7.50x (ISBN 0-226-19259-8). U of Chicago Pr.
Feinberg, Gerald & Schapiro, Robert. Life Beyond Earth: The Intelligent Earthling's Guide to Extraterrestrial Life. LC 80-14009. (Illus.). 480p. 1980. 16.95 (ISBN 0-688-03642-2, Quill); pap. 9.95 (ISBN 0-688-08642-X, Quill). Morrow.
Fort, Charles. New Lands. Del Rey, Lester, ed. LC 75-409. (Library of Science Fiction). 1975. lib. bdg. 17.50 (ISBN 0-8240-1413-8). Garland Pub.
Freundlich, M. M. & Wagner, B. M., eds. Exobiology: The Search for Extraterrestrial Life. (Science & Technology Ser.: Vol. 19). (Illus.). 1969. 20.00 (ISBN 0-87703-047-2). Am Astronaut.

Fuller, John G. The Interrupted Journey. 1980. pap. 2.50 (ISBN 0-425-04388-6). Berkley Pub.
Goldsmith, D. & Owen, T. The Search for Life in the Universe. 1980. pap. 12.95 (ISBN 0-8053-3325-8). A-W.
Goldsmith, Donald. The Quest for Extraterrestrial Life: A Book of Readings. LC 79-57423. (Illus.). 308p. 1980. 18.00 (ISBN 0-935702-08-3); pap. text ed. 12.00 (ISBN 0-935702-02-4). Univ Sci Bks.
Hall, Marie B. Inquiry into the Nature of Space & of Life in Space. (Illus.). 1970. 8.50 (ISBN 0-938760-01-7). Veritat Found.
Hanrahan, J. S., ed. Search for Extraterrestrial Life. (Advances in the Astronautical Sciences Ser.: Vol. 22). 1967. 30.00 (ISBN 0-87703-025-1); microfiche suppl. 5.00 (ISBN 0-87703-132-0). Am Astronaut.
Hart, Michael H. & Zuckerman, Ben, eds. Extraterrestrials-Where Are They? (Illus.). 180p. 1981. 22.51 (ISBN 0-08-026342-9); pap. 9.51 (ISBN 0-08-026341-0). Pergamon.
Hoyle, Fred & Wickramasinghe, Chandra. Space Travellers: The Bringers of Life. 192p. 1981. text ed. 15.95 (ISBN 0-89490-061-7). Enslow Pubs.
Jonas, Doris & Jonas, David. Other Senses, Other Worlds. LC 75-11816. 224p. 1976. 25.00x (ISBN 0-8128-1841-5); pap. 3.95 (ISBN 0-8128-2471-7). Stein & Day.
Mark-Age. Visitors from Other Planets. LC 73-90880. 334p. 1974. 10.00 (ISBN 0-912322-04-7). Mark-Age.
Mathes, J. H. & Huett, Lenora. The Amnesia Factor. LC 75-9446. 1975. pap. 4.95 (ISBN 0-89087-023-3). Celestial Arts.
Moche, Dinah. Search for Life Beyond Earth. (Impact Bks.). (Illus.). (gr. 7 up). 1978. lib. bdg. 7.45 (ISBN 0-531-02204-8). Watts.
Moche, Dinah L. Life in Space. LC 79-51841. (Illus., Orig.). 1979. pap. 10.95 (ISBN 0-89104-155-9). A & W Pubs.
Moore, Patrick & Jackson, Francis. Life on Mars. (Illus.). 1966. 4.50 (ISBN 0-393-05225-7). Norton.
Mueller, Wolfgang D. Man Among the Stars. (Illus.). 1956. 10.95 (ISBN 0-87599-079-7). S G Phillips.
NASA. The Search for Extraterrestrial Intelligence. Morrison, Philip, et al, eds. 8.00 (ISBN 0-8446-5797-2). Peter Smith.
National Aeronautics & Space Administration. The Search for Extraterrestrial Intelligence. (Illus.). 190p. 1980. pap. 3.00 (ISBN 0-486-23890-3). Dover.
Norman, Ruth E. Decline & Destruction of the Orion Empire, Vol. 2. 375p. 1981. pap. 7.95 (ISBN 0-932642-54-3). Unarius.
--Decline & Destruction of the Orion Empire, Vol. 3. 375p. 1981. pap. 7.95 (ISBN 0-932642-55-1). Unarius.
--Decline & Destruction of the Orion Empire, Vol. 4. 368p. 1981. pap. 7.95 (ISBN 0-932642-64-0). Unarius.
Owen, Tobias & Goldsmith, Donald. The Search for Life in the Universe. 1979. 12.95 (ISBN 0-8053-3325-8). Benjamin-Cummings.
Ponnamperuma, C. Exobiology. 1972. 56.00 (ISBN 0-444-10110-1, North-Holland). Elsevier.
Ponnamperuma, Cyril, ed. Chemical Evolution of the Giant Planets. 1976. 24.00 (ISBN 0-12-561350-4). Acad Pr.
Puharich, Andrija. Time No Longer. LC 78-5096. 1980. 11.95 (ISBN 0-8128-2690-6). Stein & Day.
Ridpath, Ian. Messages from the Stars. LC 78-2160. 1979. pap. 3.95 (ISBN 0-06-090734-7, CN-734, CN). Har-Row.
--Messages from the Stars. LC 78-2160. (Illus.). 1978. 10.95 (ISBN 0-06-013589-1, HarpT). Har-Row.
--Worlds Beyond: A Report on the Search for Life in Space. LC 75-30344. (Illus.). (YA) 1976. pap. 6.95 (ISBN 0-06-013568-9, TD-251, HarpT). Har-Row.
Rood, Robert T. & Trefil, James S. Are We Alone? The Possibility of Extraterrestrial Civilizations. 1981. 14.95 (ISBN 0-684-16826-X, ScribT). Scribner.
Sagan, Carl. The Cosmic Connection: An Extraterrestrial Perspective. LC 73-81117. 288p. 1973. 8.95 (ISBN 0-385-00457-5, Anch). Doubleday.
Sagan, Carl & Shklovskii, I. S. Intelligent Life in the Universe. LC 64-18404. 1978. pap. text ed. 12.50x (ISBN 0-8162-7913-6). Holden-Day.
Sagan, Carl & Shklovsky, I. S. Intelligent Life in the Universe. 1968. pap. 3.95 (ISBN 0-440-54056-9, Delta). Dell.
Shklovski, I. S. Universo, Vida, Intelecto. 383p. (Span.). 1977. 4.50 (ISBN 0-8285-1700-2, Pub. by Mir Pubs Russia). Imported Pubns.
Space Science Board. Biology & the Exploration of Mars. 1966. 8.75 (ISBN 0-309-01296-1). Natl Acad Pr.
Spencer, John W. No Earthly Explanation. 1974. 6.95 (ISBN 0-686-10168-5). Phillips Pub Co.
Story, Ronald. The Space Gods Revealed: A Close Look at the Theories of Erich Von Daniken. LC 75-30347. (Illus.). 192p. (YA) 1976. 10.95 (ISBN 0-06-014141-7, HarpT). Har-Row.
Tocquet, Robert. La Vida En los Planetas. (Span.). 1967. 3.00 (ISBN 0-914326-07-4). Orbiting Bk.
Von Daniken, Erich. Chariots of the Gods: Unsolved Mysteries of the Past. (Illus.). 1970. 8.95 (ISBN 0-399-10128-4). Putnam.
Von Daniken, Frich. Chariots of the Gods? 1980. pap. 2.50 (ISBN 0-425-04381-9). Berkley Pub.
Woodrew, Greta. On a Slide of Light. 224p. 1981. 12.95 (ISBN 0-02-631390-1). Macmillan.

LIFE ON OTHER PLANETS–JUVENILE LITERATURE

Angrist, Stanley W. Other Worlds, Other Beings. LC 70-171001. (Illus.). (gr. 6-9). 1973. 8.95 (ISBN 0-690-60205-7, TYC-J). Har-Row.
Aylesworth, Thomas G. Who's Out There? The Search for Extraterrestrial Life. (gr. 9-12). 1975. PLB 6.95 (ISBN 0-07-002637-8, GB). McGraw.
Engdahl, Sylvia L. The Planet-Girded Suns. LC 73-84825. (Illus.). 208p. (gr. 8 up). 1974. 7.50 (ISBN 0-689-30135-9). Atheneum.
Gallant, Roy A. Beyond Earth: The Search for Extraterrestrial Life. LC 77-5790. (gr. 7 up). 1977. 8.95g (ISBN 0-590-07437-7, Four Winds). Schol Bk Serv.
Kraske, Robert. Is There Life in Outer Space? LC 76-929. (Illus.). 128p. (gr. 5 up). 1976. 6.95 (ISBN 0-15-239190-8, HJ). HarBraceJ.
Moche. The Star Wars Question & Answer Book About Space. (Illus.). (gr. 4). Date not set. pap. cancelled (ISBN 0-590-30065-2, Schol Pap). Schol Bk Serv.
Naha, E. Aliens. 1977. pap. 7.95 (ISBN 0-931064-03-1). Starlog.
Olesky, Walter. Visitors from Outer Space: Is There Life on Other Planets? (Illus.). (gr. 7 up). 1979. 7.95 (ISBN 0-399-20668-X). Putnam.
Stilley, Frank. The Search: Our Quest for Intelligent Life in Outer Space. LC 76-54149. (Illus.). (gr. 6-8). 1977. 7.95 (ISBN 0-399-20587-X). Putnam.
Woods, Geraldine & Woods, Harold. Is There Life on Other Planets? LC 80-12900. (Monsters & Mysteries Ser.). (gr. 4-10). 1980. pap. 1.95 (ISBN 0-88436-762-2). EMC.

LIFE-SAVING

see also Search and Rescue Operations; Survival (After Airplane Accidents, Shipwrecks, etc.)

American Red Cross, ed. Lifesaving, Rescue & Water Safety. 240p. 1974. pap. 2.25 (ISBN 0-385-06349-0). Doubleday.
Biggs, Howard. The Sound of Maroons. (Illus.). 1979. 16.50 (ISBN 0-900963-83-2, Pub. by Terence Dalton England). State Mutual Bk.
Giambarba, Paul. Surfmen & Lifesavers. (Illus.). (gr. 3-7). 1967. 2.95 (ISBN 0-87155-203-5); pap. 2.95 (ISBN 0-87155-103-9). Scrimshaw.
Jarvis, Margaret A. Your Book of Survival Swimming & Lifesaving. (gr. 6 up). 9.50 (ISBN 0-571-06438-8). Transatlantic.
Lifesaving. 64p. (gr. 6-12). 1980. pap. 0.70x (ISBN 0-8395-3278-4, 3278). BSA.
Nalty, Bernard C., et al, eds. Wrecks, Rescues & Investigations: Selected Documents of the U. S. Coast Guard & Its Predecessors. new ed. LC 78-12312. (Illus.). 1978. lib. bdg. 49.50 (ISBN 0-8420-2130-2). Scholarly Res Inc.
Noble, Dennis R. & O'Brien, T. Michael. Sentinels of the Rocks: From 'Graveyard Coast' to National Lakeshore. LC 79-83666. (Illus.). 1979. 5.75 (ISBN 0-918616-03-4); pap. 4.75 (ISBN 0-686-66735-2). Northern Mich.
Osborne, Ernest L. & West, Victor. Men of Action: A History of the U. S. Life Saving Service on the Pacific Coast. LC 80-69563. (Illus.). 150p. (Orig.). 1981. pap. 10.00 (ISBN 0-932368-05-0). Bandon Hist.
Pelta, Kathy. What Does a Lifeguard Do? LC 76-53440. (What Do They Do Ser.). (Illus.). (gr. 4 up). 1977. 5.95 (ISBN 0-396-07406-5). Dodd.
Silvia, Charles E. Lifesaving & Water Safety Today. (Illus.). 1965. pap. 3.95 (ISBN 0-8096-1595-9, Assn Pr). New Century.
Smith, Bradley & Stevens, Gus. The Emergency Book: You Can Save a Life. (Illus.). 1979. 8.95 (ISBN 0-671-24115-X). S&S.
United States Lifesaving Assoc. Lifesaving & Marine Safety. (Illus.). 320p. 1981. pap. 14.95 (ISBN 0-8329-0113-X). New Century.

LIFE-SAVING APPARATUS

Lewis, J. H. Life Saving Appliance Manual. 80p. 1976. pap. 5.50x (ISBN 0-540-07286-9). Sheridan.

LIFE SCIENCE ENGINEERING

see Bioengineering

LIFE SCIENCES

see also Agriculture; Biology; Medicine

Advances in the Biosciences, Vol. 29. 65.00 (ISBN 0-08-026400-X). Pergamon.
Barr, Bonnie & Leyden, Michael. Life Science. (gr. 7-8). 1980. text ed. 14.64 (ISBN 0-201-00312-0, Sch Div); tchrs'. materials 17.56 (ISBN 0-201-00313-9, Sch Div). A-W.
Burghes, D. N. Mathematical Models in the Social, Management & Life Sciences. LC 79-40989. (Mathematics & Its Applications Ser.). 287p. 1980. pap. 21.95 (ISBN 0-470-27073-X). Halsted Pr.
Claflin, William E. Collecting, Culturing, & Caring for Living Materials: A Guide for the Teacher, Student & Hobbyist. LC 80-69329. 110p. 1981. perfect bdg. 8.50 (ISBN 0-86548-026-5). Century Twenty One.
Cloud, Preston. Cosmos, Earth & Man: A Short History of the Universe. LC 78-2666. (Illus.). 1978. 22.50x (ISBN 0-300-02146-1); pap. 7.95 (ISBN 0-300-02594-7). Yale U Pr.
Colodny, Robert G., ed. Logic, Laws, & Life: Some Philosophical Complications. LC 76-50886. (Philosophy of Science Ser.). 1977. 15.95x (ISBN 0-8229-3346-2). U of Pittsburgh Pr.
Communications Research Machines, Inc. Essentials of Life & Health. 2nd ed. (CRM Bks.). 1977. pap. text ed. 11.95x (ISBN 0-394-31191-4). Random.
Crick, Francis. Life Itself: Its Origins & Nature. 1981. 13.95 (ISBN 0-671-25562-2). S&S.
Davis, Mikol & Lane, Earle. Rainbows of Life. (Illus., Orig.). 1978. pap. 6.95 (ISBN 0-06-090624-3, CN 624, CN). Har-Row.
Day, Stacey, ed. A Companion to the Life Sciences, Vol. 1. 1979. text ed. 24.50x (ISBN 0-442-22010-3). Van Nos Reinhold.
De Sapio, Rodolfo. Calculus for the Life Sciences. LC 77-21312. (Illus.). 1978. text ed. 22.95x (ISBN 0-7167-0371-8). W H Freeman.
Fritschen, L. J. & Gay, L. W. Environmental Instrumentation. (Springer Advanced Texts in Life Sciences). (Illus.). 1980. 22.80 (ISBN 0-387-90411-5). Springer-Verlag.
Hall, C. Margaret. Pilgrim: Explorations in Life Science. LC 77-91663. 1978. 6.00 (ISBN 0-87212-083-X). Libra.
Kane, J. W. & Sternheim, M. M. Life Science Physics. 644p. 1978. 26.50 (ISBN 0-471-03137-2). Wiley.
Kilburn, Robert E. & Howell, Peter S. Exploring Life Science. (Junior High Science Program Ser.). (gr. 7-9). 1981. text ed. 15.52 (ISBN 0-205-06728-X, 6967280); tchrs'. ed. with tests 9.96 (ISBN 0-205-06729-8, 696739-0); record bk. 7.20 (ISBN 0-686-77504-X, 6967302). Allyn.
Kosterlitz, H. W. & Terenius, L. Y., eds. Pain & Society. (Dahlem Workshop Reports, Life Sciences Research Report Ser.: No. 17). (Illus.). 523p. (Orig.). 1980. pap. text ed. 39.40 (ISBN 0-89573-099-5). Verlag Chemie.
Lewis, R., ed. Computers in Life Sciences. 128p. 1980. 25.00x (ISBN 0-686-69926-2, Pub. by Croom Helm England). State Mutual Bk.
Lygre, David G. Life Manipulation. 177p. 1980. pap. 7.95 (ISBN 0-8027-7162-9). Walker & Co.
--Life Manipulation. 177p. 1980. pap. 7.95 (ISBN 0-8027-7162-9). Walker & Co.
McGraw-Hill Editors. Dictionary of the Life Sciences. new ed. (Illus.). 1976. 19.95 (ISBN 0-07-045262-8, P&RB). McGraw.
Magner. A History of the Life Sciences. 1979. 23.50 (ISBN 0-8247-6824-8). Dekker.
Marion, Jerry B. General Physics with Bioscience Essays. LC 78-4487. 1979. text ed. 26.95x (ISBN 0-471-56911-9); tchrs. manual avail. (ISBN 0-471-03672-2); study guide avail. (ISBN 0-471-03673-0). Wiley.
Martin, Sue. Dictionary of the Life Sciences. LC 76-41041. 22.00x (ISBN 0-686-73283-9). Universe.
Matthews, D. E., ed. Mathematics & the Life Sciences: Selected Lectures, Canadian Mathematical Congress, Aug.1975. LC 77-11151. (Lect. Notes in Biomathematics: Vol. 18). 1977. pap. text ed. 18.30 (ISBN 0-387-08351-0). Springer-Verlag.
Medawar, P. B. & Medawar, J. S. The Life Science. 1978. pap. 3.45 (ISBN 0-06-090609-X, CN 609, CN). Har-Row.
Olinick, Michael. Introduction to Mathematical Models in the Social & Life Sciences. LC 77-77758. (Illus.). 1978. text ed. 22.95 (ISBN 0-201-05448-5). A-W.
Oparin, Alexander I. The Chemical Origin of Life. (American Lecture Living Chemistry). (Illus.). 152p. 1964. photocopy ed. spiral 14.75 (ISBN 0-398-01426-4). C C Thomas.
Poti, S. J. Quantitive Studies in Life Science. 250p. 1981. text ed. 25.00x (ISBN 0-7069-1247-0, Pub by Vikas India). Advent NY.
R. B Uleck Associates. Life Sciences Jobs Handbook. (Illus., Orig.). 1979. pap. 9.95 (ISBN 0-937562-01-7). Uleck Assoc.
Schima. Magic of Life. 1977. 4.25 (ISBN 0-13-545020-9). P-H.
Smith, et al. Smith's Guide to the Literature of the Life Sciences. 9th ed. LC 79-55580. 223p. 1980. pap. 12.95x (ISBN 0-8087-3576-4). Burgess.
Stable Isotopes in the Life Sciences. 1978. pap. 48.75 (ISBN 92-0-011077-0, ISP 442, IAEA). Unipub.
Wilson, Samuel & Roe, Richard, eds. Biology Anthology: Readings in the Life Sciences. LC 74-2810. 320p. 1974. pap. text ed. 9.95 (ISBN 0-8299-0019-5). West Pub.
Winchester, A. M. & Jaques, H. E. How to Know the Living Things. 2nd ed. 190p. 1981. write for info. wire coil (ISBN 0-697-04780-6). Wm C Brown.
Wong & Bernstein. Ideas & Investigations in Science: Life Science. 2nd ed. 1977. 14.64 (ISBN 0-13-449991-3). lab data bk. 4.72 (ISBN 0-685-78778-8). P-H.

LIFE SPAN PROLONGATION

see Longevity

LIFE SUPPORT SYSTEMS (SPACE ENVIRONMENT)

see also Project Apollo; Project Mercury; Space Ships

LIFT (AERODYNAMICS)

see also Drag (Aerodynamics)

LIFT FANS

see also Ground-Effect Machines

LIFT STATIONS

see Pumping Stations

LIFTING AND CARRYING

see also Weight Lifting

Adkins, Jan. Moving Heavy Things. (gr. 5 up). 1980. reinforced bdg. 6.95 (ISBN 0-395-29206-9). HM.
Ionescu Tulcea, A. & Ionescu Tulcea, C. Topics in the Theory of Lifting. (Ergebnisse der Mathematik: Vol. 48). 1969. 22.20 (ISBN 0-387-04471-X). Springer-Verlag.

LIFTS

see Elevators; Hoisting Machinery

LIGAMENTS

see also Cartilage

Chapchal, George, ed. Injuries of the Ligaments & Their Repair: Hand-Knee-Foot. LC 77-76624. (Illus.). 252p. 1977. 32.50 (ISBN 0-88416-133-1). Wright-PSG.

LIGAND FIELD THEORY

Busch, Daryl H., ed. Reactions of Coordinated Ligands & Homogeneous Catalysis. LC 63-13314. (Advances in Chemistry Ser: No. 37). 1963. pap. 14.00 (ISBN 0-8412-0038-6). Am Chemical.
Figgis, B. N. Introduction to Ligand Fields. 351p. 1966. 35.50 (ISBN 0-470-25880-2). Wiley.
Gerloch, M. & Slade, R. C. Ligand-Field Parameters. LC 72-93139. (Illus.). 250p. 1973. 42.50 (ISBN 0-521-20137-3). Cambridge U Pr.
Konig, E. & Kemer, S. Ligand Field Energy Diagrams. (Illus.). 454p. 1977. 49.50 (ISBN 0-306-30946-7, Plenum Pr). Plenum Pub.
Kragten, J. Atlas of Metal-Ligand Equilibria in Aqueous Solution. LC 77-12168. 1978. 159.95 (ISBN 0-470-99309-X). Halsted Pr.
Langford, C. H. & Gray, Harry B. Ligand Substitution Processes. 1966. pap. 8.50 (ISBN 0-8053-5822-6, Adv Bk Prog). Benjamin-Cummings.
McAuliffe & Levason. Transition Metal Complexes of Phosphorus Arsenic & Antimony Ligands. 1978. write for info. (ISBN 0-685-84734-9). Elsevier.
Sugano, Satoru, et al. Multiplets of Transition-Metal Ions in Crystals. (Pure & Applied Physics Ser.: Vol. 33). 1970. 55.00 (ISBN 0-12-676050-0). Acad Pr.
Travis, Jeffrey C. Fundamentals of RIA & Other Ligand Assays: A Programmed Text. (Illus.). 1977. 22.50 (ISBN 0-930914-05-8). Sci Newsletters.
Triggle, D. J., et al, eds. Cholinergic Ligand Interactions. 1971. 29.50 (ISBN 0-12-700450-5). Acad Pr.

LIGATURE (MUSIC)

see Musical Notation

LIGHT

see also Color; Doppler Effect; Electroluminescence; Interference (Light); Lasers; Light Filters; Luminescence; Optics; Photobiology; Photometry; Photons; Polarization (Light); Radiation; Radioactivity; Reflection (Optics); Refraction; Spectrum Analysis; X-Rays

American Institute of Physics. Photodetectors. (Physics of Technology Project Ser). (Illus.). 88p. 1976. pap. text ed. 4.00 (ISBN 0-07-001734-4, G). McGraw.
Babbitt, Edwin D. Principles of Light & Color. (Illus.). 578p. Date not set. 27.00 (ISBN 0-89540-060-X). Sun Pub.
Babbitt, Edwin S. The Principles of Light and Color. 1980. pap. text ed. 7.95 (ISBN 0-8065-0748-9). Lyle Stuart.
Birkhauser, Kaspar. Light from the Darkness. Wertenschlag, Eva, ed. 80p. 1980. pap. 18.00 (ISBN 0-686-74189-7). Birkhauser.
Branley, Franklyn M. Light & Darkness. LC 74-23938. (A Let's Read & Find Out Science Bk). (Illus.). 40p. (gr. k-3). 1975. (TYC-J); PLB 8.79 (ISBN 0-690-01122-9). Har-Row.
Brill, Thomas B. Light: Its Interaction with Art & Antiquities. (Illus.). 300p. 1980. 29.50 (ISBN 0-306-40416-8, Plenum Pr). Plenum Pub.

Broad, C. D. Perception, Physics & Reality: An Enquiry into the Information That Physical Science Can Supply About the Real. LC 79-180606. 388p. 1972. Repr. of 1914 ed. 19.00 (ISBN 0-8462-1639-6). Russell.
De Waters, Lillian. Light. (Atomic Ser). pap. 0.95 (ISBN 0-686-05724-4). L De Waters.
Ditchburn, R. W. Light, 3 vols. 3rd. ed. 1977. Vol. 1. pap. 23.00 (ISBN 0-12-218101-8); Vol. 2. pap. 20.50 (ISBN 0-12-218102-6); Vol. 3. 84.50 (ISBN 0-12-218150-6). Acad Pr.
Elementary Science Study. Light & Shadows. 2nd ed. 1975. tchr's. guide 6.40 (ISBN 0-07-018582-4, W). McGraw.
Essen, L. & Froome, K. D. Velocity of Light. 1970. 25.50 (ISBN 0-12-242850-1). Acad Pr.
Evans, G. C., et al, eds. Light As an Ecological Factor 2: Proceedings. LC 76-921. 1976. 60.95 (ISBN 0-470-15043-2). Halsted Pr.
The Facts of Light. 1977. 3.98 (ISBN 0-917102-13-4). Ortho.
Freeman, Mae & Freeman, Ira. Fun with Light. (Learning with Fun Ser.). (Illus.). (gr. 5 up). 1971. 12.50x (ISBN 0-7182-0070-5, SpS). Sportshelf.
Henderson, S. T. Daylight & Its Spectrum. 2nd ed. LC 77-88254. 1978. 40.95 (ISBN 0-470-99328-6). Halsted Pr.
Henry, Dennis C. & Nelson, Edward B. Experiments in Light, Electricity, & Modern Physics, Laboratory Manual. 1978. pap. text ed. 7.50 (ISBN 0-8403-1889-8). Kendall-Hunt.
Jaffe, Bernard. Michelson & the Speed of Light. LC 78-25969. (Illus.). 1979. Repr. of 1960 ed. lib. bdg. 16.75x (ISBN 0-313-20777-1, JAMI). Greenwood.
Kantor, Wallace. Relativistic Propagation of Light. 1976. 10.00x (ISBN 0-87291-084-9); pap. 6.95x (ISBN 0-685-74222-9). Coronado Pr.
Light & Color: Images from New Mexico. (Illus.). 1980. pap. 8.95 (ISBN 0-89013-134-1). Museum NM Pr.
Marat, J. P. Decouvertes Sur le Feau, L'electricite et la Lumiere Constatees Par une Suite D'experiences Nouvelles Qui Viennent D'etre Verifiees Par Mm. les Commissaires De L'academie Des Sciences. Repr. of 1779 ed. 20.00 (ISBN 0-8287-0568-2). Clearwater Pub.
Minnaert, M. The Nature of Light & Colour in the Open Air. LC 54-10021. 1954. lib. bdg. 11.50 (ISBN 0-88307-651-9). Gannon.
--Nature of Light & Colour in the Open Air. 1948. pap. text ed. 5.00 (ISBN 0-486-20196-1). Dover.
Newton, Isaac. Opticks, or a Treatise of the Reflections, Refractions, Inflections & Colours of Light. 11.00 (ISBN 0-8446-5799-9). Peter Smith.
Ott, John N. The Dynamics of Color & Light: How They Affect Human Health & Behavior. (Illus.). 256p. 1981. 10.00 (ISBN 0-8159-5314-3). Devin.
Perina, Jan. Coherence of Light. 1972. 24.50x (ISBN 0-442-06342-3). Van Nos Reinhold.
Priestly, Joseph. History & Present State of Discoveries Relating to Vision, Light, & Colours. Cohen, I. Bernard, ed. LC 80-2142. (Development of Science Ser.). (Illus.). 1981. lib. bdg. 70.00x (ISBN 0-405-13897-0). Arno.
Rainwater, Clarence. Light & Color. (Illus.). (gr. 9 up). 1971. PLB 10.38 (ISBN 0-307-63540-6, Golden Pr). Western Pub.
Ronchi, Vasco. Nature of Light: An Historical Survey. Barocas, V., tr. from It. (Illus.). 1970. 16.00x (ISBN 0-674-60526-8). Harvard U Pr.
Sabra, A. I. Theories of Light from Descartes to Newton. LC 81-6108. (Illus.). 380p. Date not set. price not set (ISBN 0-521-24094-8); pap. price not set (ISBN 0-521-28436-8). Cambridge U Pr.
Sanders, J. M. The Velocity of Light. 1965. 15.00 (ISBN 0-08-011315-X); pap. 7.50 (ISBN 0-08-011314-1). Pergamon.
Seliger, Howard H. & McElroy, W. D. Light: Physical & Biological Action. (U. S. Atomic Energy Commission Monographs). 1965. 22.50 (ISBN 0-12-635850-8). Acad Pr.
Shapiro, S. L., ed. Ultrashort Light Pulses. LC 77-2402. (Topics in Applied Physics: Vol. 18). 1977. 54.30 (ISBN 0-387-08103-8). Springer-Verlag.
Skobel'tsyn, D. V., ed. Physical Acoustics & Optics: Molecular Scattering of Light. (P. N. Lebedev Physics Institute Ser.: Vol. 72). (Illus.). 210p. 1975. 42.50 (ISBN 0-306-10918-2, Consultants). Plenum Pub.
Tyler, John E., ed. Light in the Sea. (Benchmark Paper in Optics Ser.: Vol. 3). 1977. 44.50 (ISBN 0-12-787595-6). Acad Pr.
Tyndall, John. Lectures on Light: Delivered in the United States in Eighteen Seventy-Two - Eighteen Seventy-Three. Cohen, I. Bernard, ed. LC 79-8003. (Three Centuries of Science in America Ser.). (Illus.). 1980. Repr. of 1873 ed. lib. bdg. 14.00x (ISBN 0-405-12592-5). Arno.
Walker, Jearl, intro. by. Light & Its Uses: Making & Using Lasers, Holograms, Interferometers & Instruments of Dispersion - Readings from Scientific American. LC 79-27551. (Illus.). 1980. pap. text ed. 8.95x (ISBN 0-7167-1185-0). W H Freeman.
Warren, Eugene. Geometries of Light. (The Wheaton Literary Ser.). 108p. 1981. pap. 3.95 (ISBN 0-87788-300-9). Shaw Pubs.
Wood, Elizabeth A. Crystals & Light. LC 76-27458. 1977. lib. bdg. 9.50 (ISBN 0-88307-650-0). Gannon.

LIGHT–CHEMICAL ACTION
see Photochemistry

LIGHT–JUVENILE LITERATURE
Adler, Irving. Story of Light. LC 79-93519. (Story of Science Ser). (Illus.). (gr. 5-8). 1971. PLB 7.29 (ISBN 0-8178-4752-9). Harvey.
Anderson, L. W. Light & Color. LC 77-27460. (Read About Science Ser.). (Illus.). (gr. k-3). 1978. PLB 11.15 (ISBN 0-8393-0077-8). Raintree Child.
Beeler, Nelson F. & Branley, Franklyn M. Experiments with Light. LC 58-5591. (Illus.). (gr. 5-11). 1957. 8.95 (ISBN 0-690-28217-6, TYC-J). Har-Row.
Crews, Donald. Light. LC 80-20273. (Illus.). 32p. (ps-1). 1981. 8.95 (ISBN 0-688-00303-6); lib. bdg. 8.59 (ISBN 0-688-00310-9). Greenwillow.
Feravolo, Rocco V. Light. LC 61-5489. (Junior Science Ser.). (Illus.). (gr. 2-5). 1961. PLB 6.09 (ISBN 0-8116-6156-3). Garrard.
Heuer, Kenneth. Rainbows, Halos, & Other Wonders: Light & Color in the Atmosphere. LC 77-16865. (Illus.). (gr. 5 up). 1978. 5.95 (ISBN 0-396-07557-6). Dodd.
Kohn, Bernice. Light. LC 78-64429. (Illus.). (gr. 2-5). 1979. 3.50 (ISBN 0-89799-121-4); pap. 1.50 (ISBN 0-89799-043-9). Dandelion Pr.
Levin, Edith. The Penetrating Beam, Reflections on Light. (gr. 7-12). 1979. PLB 7.97 (ISBN 0-8239-0416-4). Rosen Pr.
Schwalberg, Carol. Light & Shadow. LC 73-174587. (Finding-Out Book). 64p. (gr. 2-4). 1972. PLB 7.95 (ISBN 0-8193-0538-3). Enslow Pubs.

LIGHT–PHYSIOLOGICAL EFFECT
see also Color–Physiological Effect; Photoperiodism; Phototherapy; Plants, Effect of Light On
Allen, Mary B., ed. Comparative Biochemistry of Photoreactive Systems. 1960. 59.50 (ISBN 0-12-051750-7). Acad Pr.
Blum, H. F. Photodynamic Action & Diseases Caused by Light. rev. ed. 1964. Repr. of 1941 ed. 13.75 (ISBN 0-02-841560-4). Hafner.
Giese, A. C., ed. Photophysiology. Incl. Vol. 1. General Principles - Action of Light on Plants. 1964. 53.50 (ISBN 0-12-282601-9); Vol. 2. Action of Light on Animals & Microorganisms, Photobiochemical Mechanisms, Bioluminescence. 1964. 53.50 (ISBN 0-12-282602-7); Vols. 3 & 4. Current Topics. 1968. Vol. 3. 53.50 (ISBN 0-12-282603-5); Vol. 4. 53.50 (ISBN 0-12-282604-3); Vols. 5-7. Current Topics in Photobiology & Photochemistry. 1970-72. Vol. 5. 53.50 (ISBN 0-12-282605-1); Vol. 6. 53.50 (ISBN 0-12-282606-X); Vol. 7. 53.50 (ISBN 0-12-282607-8); Vol. 8. 1973. 53.50 (ISBN 0-686-77187-7). Acad Pr.
Herman, Peter S. & Sams, W. Mitchell, Jr. Soap Photodermatitis: Photosensitivity to Halogenated Salicylanilides. (Illus.). 192p. 1972. 18.75 (ISBN 0-398-02312-3). C C Thomas.
Hollwich, F. The Influence of Ocular Light Perception on Metabolism in Man & Animal. LC 78-17076. (Topics in Environmental Physiology & Medicine). (Illus.). 1979. 39.40 (ISBN 0-387-90315-1). Springer-Verlag.
McElroy, William D. & Glass, Bentley, eds. Light & Life. (McCallum Pratt Institute Symposium Ser). (Illus.). 920p. 1961. 40.00x (ISBN 0-8018-0411-6). Johns Hopkins.
Ott, John. Health & Light. 1976. pap. 2.50 (ISBN 0-671-80537-1). PB.
Ott, John N. Health & Light. 1981. 20.00x (ISBN 0-7224-0200-7, Pub. by Watkins England). State Mutual Bk.
--Health & Light: The Effects of Natural & Artificial Light on Man & Other Living Things. (Illus.). 224p. 1973. 7.50 (ISBN 0-8159-5703-3). Devin.
--My Ivory Cellar. (Illus.). 6.50 (ISBN 0-8159-6217-7). Devin.
Thomas, J. B. Primary Photoprocesses in Biology. 1965. 19.50 (ISBN 0-444-10285-X, North-Holland). Elsevier.
Williams, Theodore P. & Baker, B. N., eds. The Effect of Constant Light on Visual Processes. LC 79-26293. 465p. 1980. 45.00 (ISBN 0-306-40328-5, Plenum Pr). Plenum Pub.

LIGHT–SCATTERING
Balkanski, M. L., et al, eds. Light Scattering in Solids. 973p. 1976. 51.00 (ISBN 0-470-15034-3, Pub. by Wiley). Krieger.
Bendow, Bernard, et al, eds. Theory of Light Scattering in Condensed Matter. LC 76-47492. 540p. 1976. 45.00 (ISBN 0-306-30993-9, Plenum Pr). Plenum Pub.
Bergman, Werner & Heller, Wilfried. Angular Light Scattering Maxima & Minima in Monodisperse & Heterodisperse Systems of Spheres. LC 77-6931. (Illus.). 1977. 31.75 (ISBN 0-8143-1584-4, IS-00031, Pub. by Wayne State University Press). Univ Microfilms.
Berne, Bruce J. & Pecora, Robert. Dynamic Light Scattering: With Applications to Chemistry, Biology & Physics. LC 75-19140. 376p. 1976. 42.50 (ISBN 0-471-07100-5, Pub. by Wiley-Interscience). Wiley.
Birman, et al, eds. Light Scattering in Solids. 535p. 1979. 55.00 (ISBN 0-306-40313-7, Plenum Pr). Plenum Pub.
Buckingham, A. D., et al. Light Scattering in Physics, Chemistry & Biology. (Royal Society Ser.). (Illus.). 261p. 1980. Repr. of 1979 ed. text ed. 71.00x (ISBN 0-85403-127-8, Pub. by Royal Society London). Scholium Intl.
Cardona, M., ed. Light Scattering in Solids. LC 75-20237. (Topics in Applied Physics Ser.: Vol. 8). (Illus.). 250p. 1975. 48.20 (ISBN 0-387-07354-X). Springer-Verlag.
Crosignani, Bruno & Di Porto, Paolo. Statistical Properties of Scattered Light. (Quantum Electronics Ser.). 1975. 40.00 (ISBN 0-12-199050-8). Acad Pr.
Degiorgio, V., et al, eds. Light Scattering in Liquids & Macromolecular Solutions. 290p. 1980. pap. 35.00 (ISBN 0-306-40558-X, Plenum Pr). Plenum Pub.
Fabelinskii, I. L. Molecular Scattering of Light. LC 67-10534. 622p. 1968. 47.50 (ISBN 0-306-30308-6, Plenum Pr). Plenum Pub.
Hayes, William & Loudon, Rodney. Scattering of Light by Crystals. LC 78-9008. 1978. 38.50 (ISBN 0-471-03191-7, Pub. by Wiley-Interscience). Wiley.
Heller, Wilfried & Bergman, Werner. Angular Light Scattering Maxima & Minima in Monodisperse & Heterodisperse Systems of Spheres. 1977. write for info. (ISBN 0-8143-1584-4). Wayne St U Pr.
Heller, Wilfried, et al. Tables of Angular Scattering Functions for Heterodisperse Systems of Spheres. LC 68-57471. 1969. 50.00x (ISBN 0-8143-1364-7). Wayne St U Pr.
--Depolarization & Related Ratios of Light Scattering by Spheroids. LC 74-13816. 105p. 1974. 12.00 (ISBN 0-8143-1527-5). Wayne St U Pr.
Huglin, M. B., ed. Light Scattering from Polymer Solutions. (Physical Chemistry Ser.: Vol. 27). 1972. 121.50 (ISBN 0-12-361050-8). Acad Pr.
International Conference on Light Scattering Spectra of Solids, New York University, New York, 1968. Proceedings. Wright, G. B., ed. (Illus.). 1969. 105.00 (ISBN 0-387-04645-3). Springer-Verlag.
Kerker, Milton. Scattering of Light & Other Electromagnetic Radiation. (Physical Chemistry Ser.: Vol. 16). 1969. 78.50 (ISBN 0-12-404550-2). Acad Pr.
McCartney, Earl J. Optics of the Atmosphere: Scattering by Molecules & Particles. LC 76-10941. (Pure & Applied Optics Ser). 1976. 43.00 (ISBN 0-471-01526-1, Pub. by Wiley-Interscience). Wiley.
McIntyre, Donald & Gornick, F., eds. Light-Scattering from Dilute Polymer Solutions. (International Science Review Ser.). (Illus.). 1964. 49.00 (ISBN 0-677-00510-5). Gordon.
Pangonis, William J. & Heller, Wilfried. Angular Scattering Functions for Spherical Particles. LC 60-8930. (Illus.). 1960. pap. 9.50x (ISBN 0-8143-1117-2). Wayne St U Pr.
Schuerman, D. W., ed. Light Scattering by Irregularly Shaped Particles. 345p. 1980. 39.50 (ISBN 0-306-40421-4, Plenum Pr). Plenum Pub.
Sobolev, V. V. Light Scattering in Planetary Atmospheres. Irvine, W. M., tr. 1974. text ed. 46.00 (ISBN 0-08-017934-7). Pergamon.
Stevenson, Arthur F. & Heller, Wilfried. Tables of Scattering Functions for Heterodisperse Systems. LC 61-8315. 1961. pap. 9.95x (ISBN 0-8143-1135-0). Wayne St U Pr.
U. S.-Japan Seminar or Inelastic Light Scattering, Santa Monica, California. January 22-25, 1979. Inelastic Light Scattering: Proceedings. Burstein, E. & Kawamura, H., eds. 124p. 1980. 23.00 (ISBN 0-08-025425-X). Pergamon.
Van de Hulst, H. C. Light Scattering by Small Particles. x, 470p. 1982. pap. price not set (ISBN 0-486-64228-3). Dover.

LIGHT–TABLES, ETC.
see Optics–Tables, etc.

LIGHT, COLORED
see Light–Physiological Effect; Phototherapy

LIGHT, ELECTRIC
see Electric Lighting; Photometry; Phototherapy

LIGHT, ELECTROMAGNETIC THEORY OF
see Electromagnetic Theory

LIGHT, INNER
see Inner Light

LIGHT, INVISIBLE
see Spectrum, Infra-Red; Spectrum, Ultra-Violet

LIGHT, WAVE THEORY OF
see also Electromagnetic Theory; Optics, Physical
Chapple, M. A Level Physics: Wave Motion-Sound & Light, Vol. 2. 2nd ed. (Illus.). 240p. (Orig.). 1979. pap. text ed. 10.95x (ISBN 0-7121-0155-1, Pub. by Macdonald & Evans England). Intl Ideas.
Fresnel, Augustin J. Oeuvres Completes, 3 vols. (Lat.). Repr. of 1866 ed. 131.00 (ISBN 0-384-16770-5). Johnson Repr.
Frish, S. Problems of Wave Optics. 69p. 1976. pap. 1.50 (ISBN 0-8285-0831-3, Pub. by Mir Pubs Russia). Imported Pubns.
Home, Roderick W. The Effluvial Theory of Light. Cohen, I. Bernard, ed. LC 80-2317. (Development of Science Ser.). (Illus.). 1981. lib. bdg. 26.00x (ISBN 0-405-13965-9). Arno.
Waldron, R. A. The Wave & Ballistic Theories of Light: A Critical Review. (Illus.). 1977. text ed. 25.00x (ISBN 0-584-10148-1). Humanities.
Webb, Robert H. Elementary Wave Optics. 1969. text ed. 22.95 (ISBN 0-12-739550-4). Acad Pr.

LIGHT AMPLIFICATION BY STIMULATED EMISSION OF RADIATION
see Lasers

LIGHT AND SHADE
see Shades and Shadows

LIGHT BRIGADE, CHARGE OF
see Balaklava, Battle Of, 1854

LIGHT FILTERS
see also Light; Optics; Photographic Optics
Eastman Kodak Company. Filters & Lens Attachments for Black-&-White & Color Pictures. 1975. pap. 2.95 (ISBN 0-87985-254-2, AB-1). Eastman Kodak.
How to Use Filters. 1981. 2.50 (ISBN 0-88284-143-2). Alfred Pub.
Smith, Robb. Amphoto Guide to Filters. (Illus.). 1979. 10.95 (ISBN 0-8174-2458-X); pap. 6.95 (ISBN 0-8174-2132-7). Amphoto.
Voogel, Emile & Keyzer, Peter. Two Hundred Filter & Lens Tips. (Illus.). 1978. pap. 6.50x (ISBN 0-85242-612-7). Intl Pubns Serv.

LIGHT METALS
see also Alkali Metals; Alkaline Earth Metals; Aluminum; Aluminum Alloys; Magnesium
Elliott, William Y., et al. International Control in the Non-Ferrous Metals. Bruchey, Stuart & Bruchey, Eleanor, eds. LC 76-5007. (American Business Abroad Ser.). (Illus.). 1976. Repr. of 1937 ed. 49.00x (ISBN 0-405-09276-8). Arno.

LIGHT PRODUCTION IN ANIMALS AND PLANTS
see Bioluminescence

LIGHT QUANTUM
see Photons

LIGHT-SHIPS
Adams, William H. Lighthouses & Lightships: A Descriptive & Historical Account of Their Mode of Construction & Organization. 1976. Repr. of 1870 ed. 30.00 (ISBN 0-403-05775-2, Regency). Scholarly.
Armstrong, Warren. True Book About Lighthouses & Light Ships. Date not set. 10.75x (ISBN 0-392-09138-0, SpS). Sportshelf.

LIGHT THERAPY
see Phototherapy

LIGHTER THAN AIR CRAFT
see Air-Ships

LIGHTHOUSES
see also Light-Ships
Adams, William H. Lighthouses & Lightships: A Descriptive & Historical Account of Their Mode of Construction & Organization. 1976. Repr. of 1870 ed. 30.00 (ISBN 0-403-05775-2, Regency). Scholarly.
Armstrong, Warren. True Book About Lighthouses & Light Ships. Date not set. 10.75x (ISBN 0-392-09138-0, SpS). Sportshelf.
Beaver, Patrick. A History of Lighthouses. (Illus.). 182p. 1973. 7.95 (ISBN 0-8065-0368-8). Citadel Pr.
--A History of Lighthouses. (Illus.). 158p. 1976. pap. 4.95 (ISBN 0-8065-0256-8). Citadel Pr.
Behrens, June & Brower, Pauline. Lighthouse Family. LC 78-12707. (Living Heritage Ser.). (Illus.). (gr. 1-4). 1979. PLB 9.25 (ISBN 0-516-08755-X, Golden Gate). Childrens.
De Gast, Robert. The Lighthouses of the Chesapeake. LC 73-8216. (Illus.). 176p. 1973. 15.00 (ISBN 0-8018-1548-7). Johns Hopkins.
Gibbs, James A. Sentinels of Solitude: West Coast Lighthouses. (Illus.). 88p. (Orig.). 1981. pap. 9.95 (ISBN 0-912856-72-6). Graphic Arts Ctr.
--Sentinels of the North Pacific. (Illus.). 1955. 8.95 (ISBN 0-8323-0011-X). Binford.
--Tillamook Light: A True Account of Oregon's Tillamook Rock Lighthouse. LC 79-65015. (Illus.). 1979. pap. 5.95 (ISBN 0-8323-0334-8). Binford.
Glunt, Ruth R. Lighthouses & Legends of the Hudson River. LC 74-84583. (Illus.). 154p. 1975. 10.95 (ISBN 0-912526-14-9). Lib Res.
Greene, Carla. Let's Learn About Lighthouses. LC 69-20292. (Let's Learn About Ser). (Illus.). (gr. 2-5). 1969. PLB 5.39 (ISBN 0-8178-4462-7). Harvey.

Holland, Francis R., Jr. America's Lighthouses. rev. ed. (Illus.). 240p. 1981. pap. 19.95 (ISBN 0-8289-0441-3). Greene.
Holland, Ross. Lighthouses of the Pacific Coast. 1980. write for info (ISBN 0-87046-029-3). Trans-Anglo.
Jackson, Derrick. Lighthouses of England & Wales: Including the Channel Islands & the Isle of Man. LC 75-18685. (Illus.). 128p. 1976. 13.95 (ISBN 0-7153-6902-4). David & Charles.
Jones, Stephen. Harbor of Refuge. (Illus.). 1981. 24.95 (ISBN 0-393-01417-7). Norton.
Munro, W. R. Scottish Lighthouse. (Illus.). 340p. 1981. 25.00 (ISBN 0-906191-32-7, Pub. by Findhorn-Thule Scotland). Hydra Bk.
Munro, William. Scottish Lighthouses. (Illus.). 240p. 1980. 22.50 (ISBN 0-906191-32-7, Pub. by Thule Pr England). Intl Schol Bk Serv.
Nordhoff, Charles. The Lighthouses of the United States in Eighteen Seventy-Four. Jones, William R., ed. (Illus.). 64p. 1981. pap. 3.95 (ISBN 0-89646-073-8). Outbooks.
Parker, Tony. Lighthouse. LC 76-11056. 1976. 8.95 (ISBN 0-8008-4853-5). Taplinger.
Ross, John. Lighthouses of New Zealand. (Illus.). 155p. 1975. 10.50x (ISBN 0-8002-0468-9). Intl Pubns Serv.
Shanks, Ralph C., Jr. & Shanks, Janetta T. Lighthouses & Lifeboats on the Redwood Coast. LC 77-93457. (Illus.). 1978. 14.95 (ISBN 0-930268-04-0); pap. 8.95 (ISBN 0-930268-03-2). Costano.
Shattuck, Clifford. The Nubble: Cape Neddick Lightstation, York, Maine. LC 79-53507. (Illus.). 1979. pap. 4.95 (ISBN 0-87027-195-4). Wheelwright.
Smith, Arthur. Lighthouses. LC 79-98515. (Illus.). (gr. 3-7). 1971. 4.95 (ISBN 0-395-12371-2). HM.
Stick, David. North Carolina Lighthouses. (Illus.). 85p. (Orig.). 1980. 6.00 (ISBN 0-86526-144-X); pap. 2.50 (ISBN 0-86526-138-5). NC Archives.
Weiss, George. The Lighthouse Service: Its History, Activities & Organization. LC 72-3056. (Brookings Institution. Institute for Government Research. Service Monographs of the U.S. Government: No. 40). Repr. of 1926 ed. 19.50 (ISBN 0-404-57140-9). AMS Pr.
Wood, Pamela. The Salt Book. LC 76-53419. 480p. 1977. pap. 5.95 (ISBN 0-385-11423-0, Anchor Pr); pap. 5.95 (ISBN 0-385-11423-0, Anch). Doubleday.

LIGHTING
see also Acetylene; Candles; Electric Lighting; Lamps; Lighting, Architectural and Decorative; Stage Lighting
Allphin, Willard. Primer of Lamps & Lighting. 3rd ed. LC 72-12250. (Illus.). 240p. 1973. 12.50 (ISBN 0-201-00170-5). A-W.
Boyce, P. R. Human Factors in Lighting. (Illus.). 420p. 1981. 45.00 (ISBN 0-02-514140-6). Macmillan.
--Human Factors in Lighting. (Illus.). xiii, 420p. 1981. 52.00x (ISBN 0-686-28903-X). Burgess-Intl Ideas.
Committee on Interior Lighting for Public Conveyances of the IES. Interior Lighting of Public Conveyances: Road & Rail. new ed. (Illus.). 20p. 1974. tech. manual 6.50 (ISBN 0-87995-004-8, IES CP-12). Illum Eng.
Early Lighting. (Americana Books Ser.). (Illus.). 1975. 1.50 (ISBN 0-911410-39-2). Applied Arts.
Early Lighting: A Pictorial Guide. 2nd ed. LC 78-68597. 1979. 18.75 (ISBN 0-917422-03-1). Rushlight Club.
Gladstone, Bernard. Complete Book of Garden & Outdoor Lighting. LC 56-7386. (Illus.). 1956. 2.95 (ISBN 0-8208-0001-5). Hearthside.
Hayward, Arthur H. Colonial & Early American Lighting. 3rd ed. 1962. pap. 4.50 (ISBN 0-486-20975-X). Dover.
--Colonial Lighting. 3rd enl. ed. (Illus.). 8.75 (ISBN 0-8446-2224-9). Peter Smith.
Helms, R. Illumination Engineering for Energy Efficient Luminous Environments. 1980. 29.95 (ISBN 0-13-450809-2). P-H.
Hopkinson, R. G. & Kay, J. D. The Lighting of Building. 318p. 1972. 16.95 (ISBN 0-571-04770-X, Pub. by Faber & Faber). Merrimack Bk Serv.
IES Committee on Office Lighting. American National Standard Practice for Office Lighting A132.1-1973. rev. ed. (Illus.). 42p. 1973. 6.50 (ISBN 0-87995-002-1). Illum Eng.
Illuminating Engineering Society Industrial Lighting Committee. American National Standard Practice for Industrial Lighting. rev. ed. (Illus.). 48p. 1973. 6.50 (ISBN 0-685-34578-5, RP7). Illum Eng.
Kaufman, John E. & Christensen, Jack F., eds. Lighting Handbook. 5th ed. LC 77-186864. (Illus.). 770p. 1972. members 30.00 (ISBN 0-87995-000-5); non-members 40.00 (ISBN 0-685-23764-8). Illum Eng.
Lynes, J. A., ed. Developments in Lighting, Vol. 1. (Illus.). 1978. text ed. 48.30x (ISBN 0-85334-774-3, Pub. by Applied Science). Burgess-Intl Ideas.
Lyons. Handbook of Industrial Lighting. 1981. text ed. write for info. (ISBN 0-408-00525-4). Butterworth.
Lyons, S. L. Exterior Lighting for Industry & Security. (Illus.). xiv, 320p. 1980. 50.00x (ISBN 0-85334-879-0, Pub. by Applied Science). Burgess-Intl Ideas.
Patented Lighting. 1976. 6.50 (ISBN 0-917422-02-3). Rushlight Club.
Pownall, Glen. Lighting Craft. (New Crafts Ser.). 84p. 1980. 8.25 (ISBN 0-85467-022-X, Pub. by Viking Sevenseas New Zealand). Intl Schol Bk Serv.
Pritchard, D. C. Lighting. 2nd ed. (Environmental Physics Ser.). (Illus.). 1978. pap. text ed. 12.95x (ISBN 0-582-41083-5). Longman.
Rudman, Jack. Assistant Supervisor (Lighting) (Career Examination Ser.: C-2006). (Cloth bdg. avail. on request). pap. 10.00 (ISBN 0-8373-2006-2). Natl Learning.
--Foreman of Lighting. (Career Examination Ser.: C-271). (Cloth bdg. avail. on request). pap. 8.00 (ISBN 0-8373-0271-4). Natl Learning.
--Lighting Inspector. (Career Examination Ser.: C-2134). (Cloth bdg. avail. on request). 1977. pap. 8.00 (ISBN 0-8373-2134-4). Natl Learning.
Sorcar, Prafulla C. Rapid Lighting Design & Cost Estimating. LC 79-4690. (Illus.). 1979. 28.50 (ISBN 0-07-059651-4). McGraw.
Stevens, W. R. Building Physics: Lighting. 1969. 25.00 (ISBN 0-08-006370-5); pap. 13.25 (ISBN 0-08-006369-1). Pergamon.
Zimmermann, Ralf. Dictionary of Lighting. 362p. 1980. 70.00x (ISBN 0-569-08526-8, Pub. by Collet's). State Mutual Bk.

LIGHTING, ARCHITECTURAL AND DECORATIVE
Cooke, Lawrence S., ed. Lighting in America: From Colonial Rushlights to Victorian Chandeliers. LC 75-39889. (Antiques Magazine Library Ser.). (Illus.). 160p. 1976. 12.95x (ISBN 0-87663-253-3, Main Street-Universe); pap. 7.95 (ISBN 0-87663-924-4, Main Street-Universe). Universe.
DeBoer, J. B. & Fischer, D. Interior Lighting. (Philips Technical Library). (Illus.). 1978. text ed. 62.50x (ISBN 0-333-25670-0). Scholium Intl.
Early Twentieth Century Lighting Fixtures. (Illus.). 1980. pap. 11.95 (ISBN 0-89145-143-9). Collector Bks.
Editors of Hudson Home Magazine. Practical Guide to Home Lighting. 144p. 1980. 12.95 (ISBN 0-442-22853-8). Van Nos Reinhold.
Evans, Benjamin. Daylight in Architecture. LC 80-26066. (Illus.). 204p. 1981. 29.95 (ISBN 0-07-019768-7, Architectural Rec Bks). McGraw.
Frazier, A. Eugene. Glamorize with Lighting. Ide, Arthur F., ed. LC 79-9441. (Good Taste Begins with You Ser.). (Illus.). iii, 50p. 1980. Repr. of 1969 ed. pap. text ed. 5.00 (ISBN 0-86663-224-7). Ide Hse.
Gilliatt, Mary & Baker, Douglas. Lighting Your Home: A Practical Guide. LC 79-1884. 1979. 17.95 (ISBN 0-394-50151-9). Pantheon.
Kaufman, John E., ed. IES Lighting Handbook-1981: Application Volume. (Illus.). 532p. 1981. 50.00 (ISBN 0-87995-008-0). Illum Eng.
--IES Lighting Handbook-1981: Reference Volume. (Illus.). 488p. 1981. 50.00 (ISBN 0-87995-007-2). Illum Eng.
Lambeth, et al. Solar Four. 96p. 1981. softcover 14.95 (ISBN 0-9601678-7-0). Lambeth.
Lighting Fixtures. (Home & Office Furnishings). 1981. 350.00 (ISBN 0-686-31551-0). Busn Trend.
Nuckolls, James L. Interior Lighting for Environmental Designers. LC 75-40413. 371p. 1976. 37.50 (ISBN 0-471-65163-X, Pub. by Wiley-Interscience). Wiley.
Pownall, Glen. Lighting Crafts. (Creative Leisure Ser.). (Illus.). 84p. 1974. 7.50x (ISBN 0-85467-022-X). Intl Pubns Serv.
Smithson, Alison & Smithson, Peter. Ordinariness & Light. (Illus.). 1970. 14.50x (ISBN 0-262-19082-6). MIT Pr.
Traditional Guide to Home Lighting. (Bantam Hudson Plan Bk.). 1980. pap. 6.95 (ISBN 0-553-01234-7). Bantam.
Traister, John E. Practical Lighting Applications for Building Construction. 200p. 1981. text ed. price not set (ISBN 0-442-24727-3). Van Nos Reinhold.

LIGHTING, DECORATIVE
see Lighting, Architectural and Decorative

LIGHTING, GARDEN
see Garden Lighting

LIGHTNING
see also Atmospheric Electricity; Transients (Electricity)
Barry, James D. Ball Lightning & Bead Lightning: Extreme Forms of Atmospheric Electricity. (Illus.). 240p. 1980. 29.50 (ISBN 0-306-40272-6, Plenum Pr). Plenum Pub.
Golde, R. H. Lightning Protection. 1973. 30.00 (ISBN 0-8206-0226-4). Chem Pub.
Harward, Simon. A Discourse of Lightnings. LC 75-171762. (English Experience Ser.: No. 385). 24p. 1971. Repr. of 1607 ed. 7.00 (ISBN 90-221-0385-4). Walter J Johnson.
Lightning Protection Code. (Seventy Ser.). 59p. 1968. pap. 2.00 (ISBN 0-685-46076-2, 78). Natl Fire Prot.
Ritchie, Donald J. Ball Lightning. LC 61-15177. 70p. 1961. 17.50 (ISBN 0-306-10509-8, Consultants). Plenum Pub.
Salanave, Leon E. Lightning & Its Spectrum: An Atlas of Photographs. LC 80-18882. (Illus.). 1980. 25.00x (ISBN 0-8165-0374-5). U of Ariz Pr.
Singer, Stanley. The Nature of Ball Lightning. LC 70-128512. 169p. 1971. 24.50 (ISBN 0-306-30494-5, Plenum Pr). Plenum Pub.
Uman, Martin A. Understanding Lightning. LC 70-150762. (Illus.). 166p. 1971. 6.50x (ISBN 0-685-23654-4). Bek Tech.
Viemeister, Peter E. The Lightning Book. (Illus.). 316p. 1972. pap. 3.95 (ISBN 0-262-72004-3). MIT Pr.

LIGHTNING–JUVENILE LITERATURE
Cutts, David. I Can Read About Thunder & Lightning. new ed. LC 78-66273. (Illus.). (gr. 2-6). 1979. pap. 1.25 (ISBN 0-89375-217-7). Troll Assocs.
Zim, Herbert S. Lightning & Thunder. (Illus.). (gr. 3-7). 1952. PLB 6.00 (ISBN 0-688-31481-3). Morrow.

LIGHTNING (FIGHTER PLANES)
Gurney, Gene. P-Thirty Eight Lightning. LC 70-76218. (Famous Aircraft Ser). (Illus., Orig.). 1969. pap. 4.95 (ISBN 0-668-02015-6). Arco.
McDowell, Ernest. Lockheed P-38 Lightning. Ward, Richard, ed. & illus. LC 70-93932. (Aircam Aviation Ser). (Illus., Orig.). 1969. pap. 2.95 (ISBN 0-668-02113-6). Arco.

LIGHTNING ARRESTERS
Lightning Protection Code. (Seventy Ser.). 59p. 1968. pap. 2.00 (ISBN 0-685-46076-2, 78). Natl Fire Prot.

LIGHTNING CONDUCTORS
see also Fire Prevention; Lightning

LIGHTNING WAR
see also Military Art and Science; Tactics
Rutherford, Ward. Blitzkrieg Nineteen Forty. (Illus.). 1980. 16.95 (ISBN 0-399-12391-1). Putnam.

LIGHTS, FEAST OF
see Hanukkah (Feast of Lights)

LIGHTWEIGHT CONSTRUCTION
see also Sandwich Construction; Sheet-Metal Work

LIGHTWEIGHT STRUCTURES
see also Air-Supported Structures
Otto, Frei. IL Eleven: Lightweight & Energy Technics. Burkhardt, Berthold, et al, eds. (Information of the Institute for Lightweight Structures Ser.). (Illus., Orig., Ger., Eng.). 1978. pap. 32.50x (ISBN 0-8150-0743-4). Wittenborn.
--IL Fifteen: Air Hall Handbook. Burkhardt, Berthold, ed. (Information of the Institute for Lightweight Structures Ser.). (Illus., Orig., Ger., Eng.). Date not set. pap. price not set (ISBN 0-8150-0744-2). Wittenborn.
--IL Sixteen: Tents One. Burkhardt, Berthold, et al, eds. (Information of the Institute for Lightweight Structures Ser). (Illus., Orig., Ger., Eng.). 1976. pap. 20.00x (ISBN 0-8150-0745-0). Wittenborn.
Otto, Frei, et al. IL Twelve: Convertible Pneus. Burkhardt, Berthold & Schaur, Eda, eds. (Information of the Institute for Lightweight Structures Ser.). (Illus., Orig., Eng. & Ger.). 1976. pap. 17.50x (ISBN 0-8150-0774-4). Wittenborn.

LIGNIN
see also Wood–Chemistry
Brauns, Friedrich E. & Brauns, Dorothy A. Chemistry of Lignin: Suppl. Vol. Covering Literature for 1949-58. 1960. 78.00 (ISBN 0-12-127861-1). Acad Pr.
Crawford, Ronald L. Lignin Biodegradation & Transformation. LC 80-39557. 154p. 1981. 30.00 (ISBN 0-471-05743-6, Pub. by Wiley-Interscience). Wiley.
Freudenberg, K. & Neish, A. C. Constitution & Biosynthesis of Lignin. (Molecular Biology, Biochemistry & Biophysics: Vol. 2). 1968. 20.40 (ISBN 0-387-04274-1). Springer-Verlag.
Kirk, T. Kent, et al. Lignin Biodegradation: Microbiology, Chemistry & Potential Applications, 2 vols. 1980. Vol. 1, 256 Pgs. 66.95 (ISBN 0-8493-5459-5); Vol. 2, 272 Pgs. 69.95 (ISBN 0-8493-5460-9). CRC Pr.
Marton, Joseph, ed. Lignin Structure & Reactions. LC 66-28847. (Advances in Chemistry Ser: No. 59). 1966. 23.00 (ISBN 0-8412-0060-2). Am Chemical.
Sarkanen, K. V. & Ludwig, Charles H. Lignins: Occurrence, Formation, Structure & Reactions. LC 79-148456. (Illus.). 1971. 73.50 (ISBN 0-471-75422-6, Pub. by Wiley-Interscience). Wiley.
Schubert, Walter J. Lignin Biochemistry. 1965. 26.50 (ISBN 0-12-630950-7). Acad Pr.

LIGNITE
see also Coal
LBJ School of Public Affairs. Public Policies Affecting Lignite Developement in Texas. LC 77-620046. (Policy Research Report Ser.: No. 20). 1977. 3.00 (ISBN 0-89940-613-0). LBJ Sch Public Affairs.
Nowacki, Perry, ed. Lignite Technology. LC 79-26051. (Energy Technology Review Ser. No. 53; Chemical Technology Review Ser.: No. 146). (Illus.). 1980. 42.00 (ISBN 0-8155-0783-6). Noyes.

LIGURIA
Banks, Francis R. Your Guide to the Italian Riviera Dei Fiori. LC 66-412. (Your Guide Ser). (Illus.). 1964. 5.25x (ISBN 0-8002-0792-0). Intl Pubns Serv.

LIGURIAN RACE
see Mediterranean Race

LILBURNE, JOHN, 1614?-1657
Gregg, Pauline. Free-Born John: A Biography of John Lilburne. LC 73-22752. (Illus.). 424p. 1974. Repr. of 1961 ed. lib. bdg. 20.00x (ISBN 0-8371-7346-9, GRFJ). Greenwood.
Haller, William & Davies, Godfrey, eds. The Leveller Tracts 1647-1653: 1647-1653. 1964. 8.50 (ISBN 0-8446-1218-9). Peter Smith.
Pease, T. C. The Leveller Movement. 8.00 (ISBN 0-8446-1345-2). Peter Smith.

LILIES
Masters, Charles O. Encyclopedia of the Water-Lily. (Illus.). 512p. 1974. text ed. 14.95 (ISBN 0-87666-168-1, H-944). TFH Pubns.
Synge, Patrick M., compiled by. Lilies: A Revision of Elwes' Monograph of the Genus Lilium & Its Supplements. LC 79-9682. (Illus.). 280p. 1980. 59.50x (ISBN 0-87663-340-8). Universe.

LILIUOKALANI, QUEEN OF HAWAII, 1838-1917
Malone, Mary. Liliuokalani: Queen of Hawaii. LC 75-6783. (Discovery Ser.). (Illus.). 84p. (gr. 2-5). 1975. PLB 6.09 (ISBN 0-8116-6320-5). Garrard.

LILLIE, GORDON WILLIAM, 1860-1942
Shirley, Glenn. Pawnee Bill: A Biography of Major Gordon W. Lillie. LC 58-6870. (Illus.). 1965. pap. 5.95 (ISBN 0-8032-5185-8, BB 331, Bison). U of Nebr Pr.

LILLO, GEORGE, 1693-1739
Hudson, William H. Quiet Corner in a Library. facs. ed. LC 68-16940. (Essay Index Reprint Ser). 1915. 15.00 (ISBN 0-8369-0550-4). Arno.

LILLY, BENJAMIN VERNON, 1856-1936
Dobie, J. Frank. The Ben Lilly Legend. 253p. 1981. pap. 6.95 (ISBN 0-292-70728-2). U of Tex Pr.
--Ben Lilly Legend. (Illus.). 1950. 10.95 (ISBN 0-316-18792-5). Little.

LIMA
Lloyd, P. The Young Towns of Lima. LC 79-51826. (Urbanization in Developing Countries Ser.). (Orig.). 1980. 34.50 (ISBN 0-521-22871-9); pap. 9.95 (ISBN 0-521-29688-9). Cambridge U Pr.

LIMA-HAMILTON CORPORATION
Cook, Richard J. Super Power Steam Locomotives. LC 66-29787. (Illus.). 144p. 1966. 16.95 (ISBN 0-87095-010-X). Golden West.

LIMBA
Lewis, I. M. Peoples of the Horn of Africa: Somali, Afar & Saho. LC 76-489322. (International African Institute Ser.). 1969. 16.50x (ISBN 0-8002-0273-2). Intl Pubns Serv.

LIMBIC SYSTEM
DiCara, Leo V., ed. Limbic & Autonomic Nervous Systems Research. LC 74-17327. (Illus.). 428p. 1975. 27.50 (ISBN 0-306-30786-3, Plenum Pr). Plenum Pub.
Hamilton, Leonard W., ed. Basic Limbic System Anatomy of the Rat. LC 76-46401. (Illus.). 150p. 1976. 17.95 (ISBN 0-306-30925-4, Plenum Pr). Plenum Pub.
Hockman, Charles H., ed. Limbic System Mechanisms & Autonomic Function. (Illus.). 312p. 1972. 36.25 (ISBN 0-398-02315-8). C C Thomas.
Isaacson, Robert L. The Limbic System. LC 74-8298. (Illus.). 292p. 1974. 22.50 (ISBN 0-306-30773-1, Plenum Pr). Plenum Pub.
Kelly, Desmond. Anxiety & Emotions: Physiological Basis & Treatment. (Objective Psychiatry Ser.). (Illus.). 424p. 1980. text ed. 24.75 (ISBN 0-398-03893-7). C C Thomas.
Livingston, K. E. & Hornykiewicz, O., eds. Limbic Mechanisms: The Continuing Evolution of the Limbic System Concept. LC 78-1542. 558p. 1978. 34.50 (ISBN 0-306-31135-6, Plenum Pr). Plenum Pub.

LIMBS (ANATOMY)
see Extremities (Anatomy)

LIMBS, ARTIFICIAL
see Artificial Limbs

LIMBUS (ASIATIC PEOPLE)

Caplan, Lionel. Land & Social Change in East Nepal: A Study of Hindu-Tribal Relations. LC 73-81801. 1970. 20.00x (ISBN 0-520-01400-6). U of Cal Pr.

LIME

see also Cement

Boynton, Robert S. Chemistry & Technology of Lime & Limestone. 2nd ed. LC 79-16140. 1980. 62.00 (ISBN 0-471-02771-5, Pub. by Wiley-Interscience). Wiley.

LIMERICKS

see also Nonsense-Verses

Aquila, Richard E. Rhyme or Reason: A Limerick History of Philosophy. LC 81-40013. 126p. (Orig.). 1981. lib. bdg. 11.50 (ISBN 0-8191-1562-2); pap. text ed. 5.00 (ISBN 0-8191-1563-0). U Pr of Amer.

Asimon, Isaac & Ciardi, John. Limericks: Too Gross. 1978. 9.95 (ISBN 0-393-04522-6); pap. write for info. (ISBN 0-393-04530-7). Norton.

Asimov, Isaac. Asimov's Sherlockian Limericks. LC 77-92791. 1978. 7.50 (ISBN 0-89296-039-6). Mysterious Pr.

--Lecherous Limericks. LC 75-7922. (Illus.). 96p. 1975. pap. 3.95 (ISBN 0-8027-7096-7). Walker & Co.

--More Lecherous Limericks. (Illus.). 1976. pap. 3.95 (ISBN 0-8027-7102-5). Walker & Co.

--Still More Lecherous Limericks. LC 76-56688. (Illus.). 1977. 3.95 (ISBN 0-8027-7106-8). Walker & Co.

Baring-Gould, William S. Lure of the Limerick. (Illus.). 1967. 8.95 (ISBN 0-517-08323-X); pap. 4.95 (ISBN 0-517-53856-3). Potter.

Bashor, Richard U. Prime Ribaldry. 1980. 5.95 (ISBN 0-533-04656-4). Vantage.

Bibby, Cyril. The Art of the Limerick. (Illus.). 1978. 16.50 (ISBN 0-208-01761-5, Archon). Shoe String.

Billington, Ray A. Limericks Historical & Hysterical: Plagiarized, Arranged, Annotated & Some Written by Ray Allen Billington. 1981. 9.95 (ISBN 0-393-01453-3). Norton.

Bodecker, N. M. A Person from Britain & Other Limericks. LC 79-22779. (Illus.). 64p. (gr. 3 up). 1980. 7.95 (ISBN 0-689-50152-8, McElderry Bk). Atheneum.

Brock, H. I., ed. Little Book of Limericks. facsimile ed. LC 71-84351. (Granger Index Reprint Ser). 1947. 15.00 (ISBN 0-8369-6053-X). Arno.

Hart, Harold H., compiled by. Limericks Lewd & Lusty. 352p. 1981. pap. 3.95 (ISBN 0-89104-196-6). A & W Pubs.

Kabronsky, V., ed. Uncensored Russian Limericks. LC 78-65600. (Prints & Reprints Ser.). 1978. pap. 6.95 (ISBN 0-89830-001-0). Russica Pubs.

The Limerick: The Paris Edition. 1979. pap. 6.95 (ISBN 0-8065-0713-6). Citadel Pr.

Livingston, Myra C. A Lollygag of Limericks. LC 77-18060. (Illus.). 48p. (gr. 5 up). 1978. 7.95 (ISBN 0-689-50104-8, McElderry Bk). Atheneum.

Nichols, Elizabeth. Tune into Limericks. 1979. 5.00 (ISBN 0-913650-05-6). Volkwein Bros.

Potz, Veronica & Babin, Lawrence J. Limericks for Children. (See-Hear-Color Me Book Ser.). Date not set. cancelled (ISBN 0-912492-15-5). Pyquag.

Reed, Langford. The Complete Limerick Book: The Origin, History & Achievements of the Limerick. LC 78-175778. (Illus.). 147p. 1974. Repr. of 1925 ed. 19.00 (ISBN 0-8103-3974-9). Gale.

Superior, Irving. Superior Limericks. Carr, Sally B., ed. LC 76-9007. 1976. 7.95 (ISBN 0-87949-067-5). Ashley Bks.

Wells, Carolyn. Carolyn Wells' Book of American Limericks. LC 77-174140. (Tower Bks). (Illus.). viii, 91p. 1972. Repr. of 1925 ed. 22.00 (ISBN 0-8103-3929-3). Gale.

World's Best Limericks. 1955. 2.95 (ISBN 0-442-82471-8). Peter Pauper.

LIMERICKS–JUVENILE LITERATURE

Brewton, John E. & Blackburn, Lorraine A., eds. They've Discovered a Head in the Box for the Bread & Other Laughable Limericks. LC 77-26598. (Illus.). (gr. 3-7). 1978. (TYC-J); PLB 9.89 (ISBN 0-690-03883-6). Har-Row.

Brewton, Sara & Brewton, John E., eds. Laughable Limericks. LC 65-16179. (Illus.). (gr. 2 up). 1965. 10.95 (ISBN 0-690-48667-7, TYC-J). Har-Row.

Corbett, Scott. Jokes to Read in the Dark. LC 79-23129. (Illus.). 80p. (gr. 5-9). 1980. 7.95 (ISBN 0-525-32796-7); pap. 2.95 (ISBN 0-525-45052-1). Dutton.

O'Hare, Colette. What Do You Feed Your Donkey on? LC 77-17155. (Illus.). (ps-8). 1978. 6.95 (ISBN 0-00-183703-6); PLB 6.99 (ISBN 0-00-183734-6). Philomel.

Oliver, Hugh & MacMillan, Keith. The American Limerick Book. LC 80-21813. (Illus.). 96p. 1981. 9.95 (ISBN 0-8253-0001-0). Beaufort Bks NY.

Sawyer, Paul. There Once Was a Book of Limericks. LC 77-27109. (Games & Activities Ser.). (Illus.). (gr. k-3). 1978. PLB 10.65 (ISBN 0-8172-1168-3). Raintree Pubs.

LIMESTONE

Boynton, Robert S. Chemistry & Technology of Lime & Limestone. 2nd ed. LC 79-16140. 1980. 62.00 (ISBN 0-471-02771-5, Pub. by Wiley-Interscience). Wiley.

Cayeux, L. Carbonate Rocks, Limestone & Dolmites, Sedimentary Rocks of France. Carozzi, A. V., tr. (Illus.). 1969. Repr. 46.75 (ISBN 0-02-842660-6). Hafner.

Fischer, Alfred G., et al. Electron Micrographs of Limestones & Their Nannofossils. (Monographs in Geology & Palentology Ser). (Illus.). 1967. 14.00 (ISBN 0-691-07953-6); pap. 6.50x (ISBN 0-691-07954-4). Princeton U Pr.

Gwinner, M. P. Origin of the Upper Jurassic Limestones of the Swabian Alb (Southwest Germany) Fuechtbauer, H., ed. (Contributions to Sedimentology Ser.: Vol. 5). (Illus.). 75p. (Orig.). 1976. pap. 37.50x (ISBN 3-510-57005-7). Intl Pubns Serv.

Heckel, Philip H. Nature, Origin, & Significance of the Tully Limestone. LC 72-82612. (Special Paper: No. 138). (Illus.). 160p. (Orig.). 1973. pap. 11.00x (ISBN 0-8137-2138-5). Geol Soc.

Johnson, J. Harlan. Limestone-Building Algae & Algal Limestones. 1961. 6.75 (ISBN 0-918062-11-X). Colo Sch Mines.

Rodda, P. U., et al. Limestone & Dolomite Resources: Lower Cretaceous Rocks, Texas. (Illus.). 286p. 1966. 4.50 (ISBN 0-686-29338-X, RI 56). Bur Econ Geology.

Schneider, Jurgen. Biological & Inorganic Factors in the Destruction of Limestone Coasts. Sadler, Peter, tr. LC 77-480279. (Contributions to Sedimentology: Vol. 6). (Illus.). 112p. (Orig.). 1976. pap. 45.00x (ISBN 3-510-57006-5). Intl Pubns Serv.

Smith, D. I. & Drew, D. P., eds. Limestones & Caves of the Mendip Hills. LC 74-76186. 1975. 22.50 (ISBN 0-7153-6572-X). David & Charles.

Stringfield, V. T. & LeGrand, H. E. Hydrology of Limestone Terranes in the Coastal Plain of the Southeastern United States. LC 66-30771. (Special Paper: No. 93). (Illus., Orig.). 1966. pap. 3.00x (ISBN 0-8137-2093-1). Geol Soc.

Waltham, A. C., ed. Limestones & Caves of North-West England. (Illus.). 1974. 11.50 (ISBN 0-7153-6181-3). David & Charles.

LIMIT ANALYSIS (THEORY OF STRUCTURES)

see Plastic Analysis (Theory of Structures)

LIMITATIONS OF ACTIONS

see also Adverse Possession

LIMITATION OF ARMAMENT

see Disarmament

LIMITATIONS (LAW)

see Estates (Law); Real Property

LIMITATIONS, CONSTITUTIONAL

see Constitutional Law

LIMITATIONS, CONTRACTUAL

see Contracts

LIMITED ACCESS HIGHWAYS

see Express Highways

LIMITED COMPANIES

see Corporations

LIMITED LIABILITY

see also Carriers; Limited Partnership

LIMITED PARTNERSHIP

Fessler, Daniel W. Alternatives to Incorporation for Persons in Quest of Profit: Cases & Materials on Partnerships, Joint Ventures & Related Agency Concepts. LC 80-18481. (American Casebook Ser.). 284p. 1980. pap. text ed. 8.95 (ISBN 0-8299-2102-8). West Pub.

Hamilton, Robert W. Cases & Materials on Corporations: Including Partnerships & Limited Partnerships. 2nd ed. LC 81-4507. (American Casebook Ser.). 1100p. 1981. text ed. write for info. West Pub.

Private Real Estate Limited Partnerships: Structuring-Drafting-Marketing, 2 vols. (Vols. 133 & 134). 1977. Sets. pap. 20.00 (ISBN 0-685-85333-0, N6-3393). PLI.

LIMITS (MATHEMATICS)

see Calculus

LIMNOCHARES

Illies, Joachim, ed. Limnofauna Europaea: A Checklist of the Animals Inhabiting European Inland Waters, with Accounts of Their Distribution & Ecology (Except Protozoa) 532p. 1978. text ed. 120.00 (ISBN 90-265-0275-3, Pub. by Swets Pub Serv Holland). Swets North Am.

LIMNOLOGY

see also Fresh-Water Biology; Paleolimnology; ; Water Chemistry

Allanson, B. R., ed. Lake Sibaya. (Monographiae Biologicae: No. 36). 1980. lib. bdg. 68.50 (ISBN 90-6193-088-X, Pub. by Junk Pubs Netherlands). Kluwer Boston.

Beadle, L. C. The Inland Waters of Tropical Africa: An Introduction to Tropical Limnology. 2nd ed. (Illus.). 420p. 1982. text ed. 70.00x (ISBN 0-582-46341-6). Longman.

Britt, N. Wilson, et al. Limnological Studies of the Island Area of Western Lake Erie. 1973. 3.00 (ISBN 0-686-30328-8). Ohio Bio Survey.

Cole, Gerald A. Textbook of Limnology. 2nd ed. LC 78-24532. (Illus.). 1979. text ed. 19.95 (ISBN 0-8016-1016-8). Mosby.

Division Of Biology And Agriculture. Eutrophication: Causes, Consequences, Correctives. LC 68-62704. 1969. text ed. 14.75 (ISBN 0-309-01700-9). Natl Acad Pr.

Egerton, Frank N., 3rd, ed. Limnology in Wisconsin: An Original Anthology. LC 77-74203. (History of Ecology Ser.). (Illus.). 1978. lib. bdg. 43.00x (ISBN 0-405-10373-5). Arno.

Fraser, J. C. Determining Discharges for Fluvial Resources. (Fisheries Technical Paper: No. 143). (Illus.). 102p. 1976. pap. 7.50 (ISBN 0-685-68950-6, F873, FAO). Unipub.

Frey, David G., ed. Limnology in North America. (Illus.). 752p. 1963. 35.00x (ISBN 0-299-02760-0). U of Wis Pr.

Golterman. Physiological Limnology. LC 74-21857. (Developments in Water Science). 489p. 1975. 66.00 (ISBN 0-444-41270-0). Elsevier.

Hutchinson, G. Evelyn. A Treatise on Liminology, 3 vols. Incl. Vol. 1, 2 pts. 1975. Set. 29.95 (ISBN 0-471-42567-2); Pt. 1. Geography & Physics of Lakes. 672p. 17.95 (ISBN 0-471-42567-2); Pt. 2. Chemistry of Lakes. 474p. 16.50 (ISBN 0-471-42569-9); Vol. 2. Introduction to Lake Biology & the Limnoplankton. 1957. 79.50 (ISBN 0-471-42572-9); Vol. 3. Limnological Biology. 704p. 1975. 43.50 (ISBN 0-471-42574-5). LC 57-8888 (Pub. by Wiley-Interscience). Wiley.

Lind, Owen T. Handbook of Common Methods in Limnology. 2nd ed. LC 78-21173. (Illus.). 1979. pap. text ed. 12.95 (ISBN 0-8016-3019-3). Mosby.

Loffler, H., ed. Neusiedlersee: The Limnology of a Shallow Lake in Central Europe. (Monographiae Biologicae Ser.: No. 37). (Illus.). x, 559p. 1980. lib. bdg. 103.00 (ISBN 90-6193-089-8, Pub. by Junk Pubs Netherlands). Kluwer Boston.

Mackereth, F. J., et al. Water Analysis: Some Revised Methods for Limnologists. 1978. 25.00x (ISBN 0-900386-31-2, Pub. by Freshwater Bio). State Mutual Bk.

McLusky, Donald S. Ecology of Estuaries. (Scholarship Ser. in Biology). 1971. text ed. 9.50x (ISBN 0-435-61600-5). Heinemann Ed.

--Estuarine Ecosystem. LC 80-28199. (Tertiary Level Biology Ser.). 150p. 1981. 29.95 (ISBN 0-470-27127-2). Halsted Pr.

Murray, John & Pullar, Laurence. Bathymetrical Survey of the Scottish Fresh Water Lochs, Vol. 1. Egerton, Frank N., 3rd, ed. LC 77-74243. (History of Ecology Ser.). (Illus.). 1978. Repr. of 1910 ed. lib. bdg. 49.00x (ISBN 0-405-10412-X). Arno.

Russell-Hunter, W. D. Aquatic Productivity: An Introduction to Some Basic Aspects of Biological Oceanography & Limnology. (Illus.). 1970. text ed. 9.95x (ISBN 0-685-04258-8); pap. 8.95 (ISBN 0-02-404920-4). Macmillan.

Ruttner, Franz. Fundamentals of Limnology. 3rd ed. Frey, D. G. & Fry, F. E., trs. LC 64-919. (Illus.). 1963. 8.50x (ISBN 0-8020-2028-3). U of Toronto Pr.

Rzoska, Julian. On the Nature of Rivers: With Case Stories of the Nile, Zaire, & Amazon. 1978. pap. 10.50 (ISBN 90-6193-589-X, Pub. by Junk Pubs Netherlands). Kluwer Boston.

Salanki. Limnology of Shallow Waters. 1975. 22.00 (ISBN 0-9960001-1-9, Pub. by Kaido Hungary). Heyden.

Stamm, Douglas R. Under Water: The Northern Lakes. 128p. 1977. pap. 7.95 (ISBN 0-299-07264-9). U of Wis Pr.

Symposium of Limnology of Shallow Waters, 1973. Limnology of Shallow Water: Proceedings. Salanki, J., ed. 304p. 1975. 25.00x (ISBN 963-05-0427-8). Intl Pubns Serv.

Welch, Paul S. Limnological Methods. (Illus.). 1948. text ed. 24.50 (ISBN 0-07-069175-4, C). McGraw.

Wetzel, Robert G. Limnology. LC 74-31839. (Illus.). 625p. 1975. text ed. 19.95 (ISBN 0-7216-9240-0). Saunders.

LIMU

see Algae; Mosses

LIN, PIAO, 1908-

Van Ginneken, Jaap. The Rise & Fall of Lin Piao. 1977. pap. 2.50 (ISBN 0-380-00988-9, 32656, Discus). Avon.

LIN, TSE-HSU, 1785-1850

Chang, Hsin-Pao. Commissioner Lin & the Opium War. 1970. pap. 5.95 (ISBN 0-393-00521-6, Norton Lib). Norton.

Chen, Gideon. Lin Tse-Hsu: Pioneer Promoter of the Adoption of the Western Means of Maritime Defense in China. LC 67-31401. (Illus.). 1961. pap. 4.00 (ISBN 0-8188-0017-8). Paragon.

--Series of Monographs on Lin Tse-Hsu, Tso Tsung T'ang, & Tseng Kuo-Fan. 1968. 14.50 (ISBN 0-8188-0016-X). Paragon.

LIN, YU-TANG, 1895-

Lin Yutang. Memoirs of an Octogenarian. 86p. 1980. 2.50x (ISBN 0-89955-168-8, Pub. by Mei Ya China); pap. 1.95 (ISBN 0-686-64523-5). Intl Schol Bk Serv.

LINACRE, THOMAS, 1460-1524

Maddison, Francis & Pelling, Margaret, eds. Linacre Studies: Essays on the Life & Work of Thomas Linacre. (Illus.). 1977. 79.00x (ISBN 0-19-858150-5). Oxford U Pr.

LINCOLN, ABRAHAM, PRES. U. S., 1809-1865

Abraham Lincoln Fact Book & Teacher's Guide. 64p. Date not set. pap. 1.95 (ISBN 0-915992-07-8). Eastern Acorn.

Ander, O. F., ed. Lincoln Images: Augustana College Centennial Essays. LC 60-12543. (Augustana College Library Ser.: No. 31). (Illus.). 1960. 6.95 (ISBN 0-910182-29-9). Augustana Coll.

Anderson, David D. Abraham Lincoln. (U. S. Authors Ser.: No. 153). 1970. lib. bdg. 9.95 (ISBN 0-8057-0452-3). Twayne.

Angle, Paul M., ed. The Lincoln Reader. LC 80-25663. (Illus.). xii, 564p. 1981. Repr. of 1947 ed. lib. bdg. 49.50x (ISBN 0-313-22757-8, ANLR). Greenwood.

Arnold, Isaac N. History of Abraham Lincoln: & Overthrow of Slavery. facs. ed. LC 72-154069. (Black Heritage Library Collection Ser). 1866. 30.50 (ISBN 0-8369-8780-2). Arno.

Baringer, William. Lincoln's Rise to Power. (Illus.). 1971. Repr. of 1937 ed. 36.00 (ISBN 0-403-00853-0). Scholarly.

Barrett, Joseph H. Life of Abraham Lincoln. 842p. 1981. Repr. of 1865 ed. lib. bdg. 125.00 (ISBN 0-89987-070-8). Darby Bks.

--Life of Abraham Lincoln. 1865. Repr. 100.00 (ISBN 0-8274-2917-7). R West.

Bartlett, David W. Life & Public Services of Hon. Abraham Lincoln, with a Portrait on Steel, to Which Is Added a Biographical Sketch of Hon. Hannibal Hamlin. facsimile ed. LC 78-95064. (Select Bibliographies Reprint Ser). 1860. 26.00 (ISBN 0-8369-5066-6). Arno.

Barton, William E. Abraham Lincoln & His Books. LC 76-5911. 1976. Repr. lib. bdg. 10.00 (ISBN 0-8414-3346-1). Folcroft.

--Abraham Lincoln & Walt Whitman. LC 65-18601. 1928. Repr. 12.00 (ISBN 0-8046-0018-X). Kennikat.

Basler, Roy P. Lincoln. 192p. 1976. Repr. of 1961 ed. lib. bdg. 14.00x (ISBN 0-374-90454-5). Octagon.

--The Lincoln Legend. LC 70-75989. (Illus.). 1969. Repr. of 1935 ed. lib. bdg. 17.50x (ISBN 0-374-90456-1). Octagon.

--A Touchstone for Greatness: Essays, Addresses & Occasional Pieces About Abraham Lincoln. LC 72-781. (Contributions in American Studies: No. 4). 1973. lib. bdg. 14.75 (ISBN 0-8371-6135-5, BTG/). Greenwood.

Bassett, Margaret. Abraham & Mary Todd Lincoln. (Illus.). 64p. 1974. 3.75 (ISBN 0-87027-153-9); pap. 2.50 (ISBN 0-87027-148-2). Wheelwright.

Bell, I. E. & Chambers, J. D. Story of Lincoln. (Illus.). 1971. 14.95x (ISBN 0-8464-0887-2). Beekman Pubs.

Bestor, Arthur E., et al. Three Presidents & Their Books: The Reading of Jefferson, Lincoln, & Franklin D. Roosevelt. LC 54-12305. (Windsor Ser: No. 5). 1955. pap. 4.95 (ISBN 0-252-72686-3). U of Ill Pr.

Boritt, Gabor S. Lincoln & the Economics of the American Dream. LC 78-2926. 1978. 16.95x (ISBN 0-87870-043-9). Memphis St Univ.

Brogan, D. W. Abraham Lincoln. rev. ed. 145p. 1974. 16.00x (ISBN 0-7156-0865-7, Pub. by Duckworth England). Biblio Dist.

Brooks, Noah. Abraham Lincoln & the Downfall of American Slavery. LC 73-14436. (Heroes of the Nation Ser.). Repr. of 1894 ed. 30.00 (ISBN 0-404-58254-0). AMS Pr.

Browne, Ray B., ed. Lincoln-Lore: Lincoln in the Popular Mind. 500p. 1975. 20.00 (ISBN 0-87972-035-2). Bowling Green Univ.

Bruce, Robert V. Lincoln & the Tools of War. LC 73-15241. (Illus.). 368p. 1974. Repr. of 1956 ed. lib. bdg. 17.25x (ISBN 0-8371-7167-9, BRLS). Greenwood.

Carpenter, Francis B. Six Months with Lincoln in the White House. LC 60-15560. 6.00 (ISBN 0-87282-017-3). Century Hse.

Catton, William & Catton, Bruce. Two Roads to Sumter. 1971. pap. 4.95 (ISBN 0-07-010255-4, SP). McGraw.

Country Beautiful Editors, ed. Lincoln: His Words & His World. (Home Library Ser.). (Illus.). 1976. 9.95 (ISBN 0-87294-088-8). Country Beautiful.

Cox, Earnest S. Lincoln's Negro Policy. 1968. 3.00 (ISBN 0-911038-13-2). Noontide.
--Lincoln's Negro Policy. 1.50 (ISBN 0-686-24164-9). Liberty Lobby.
Cox, LaWanda. Lincoln & Black Freedom: A Study in Presidential Leadership. 275p. 1981. 14.95 (ISBN 0-87249-400-4). U of SC Pr.
Crocker, Lionel. An Analysis of Lincoln & Douglas As Public Speakers & Debaters. (Illus.). 568p. 1968. ed. spiral bdg. 54.50photocopy (ISBN 0-398-00366-1). C C Thomas.
Current, Richard N. Lincoln & the First Shot. (Critical Periods of History Ser). (Orig.). 1963. pap. text ed. 6.50 scp (ISBN 0-397-47044-4, HarpC). Har-Row.
--The Lincoln Nobody Knows. LC 80-16138. x, 314p. 1980. Repr. of 1958 ed. lib. bdg. 25.00x (ISBN 0-313-22450-1, CULN). Greenwood.
--The Lincoln Nobody Knows. 314p. 1963. pap. 5.25 (ISBN 0-8090-0059-8, AmCen). Hill & Wang.
--The Political Thought of Abraham Lincoln. LC 67-30069. 1967. pap. 6.95 (ISBN 0-672-60068-4, AHS46). Bobbs.
Davis, Cullom, et al, eds. The Public & the Private Lincoln: Contemporary Perspectives. LC 79-9803. 192p. 1979. 18.95x (ISBN 0-8093-0921-1). S Ill U Pr.
Davis, Michael. The Image of Lincoln in the South. LC 73-158115. 1971. 11.50x (ISBN 0-87049-133-4). U of Tenn Pr.
--The Image of Lincoln in the South. LC 73-158115. 1971. 11.50x (ISBN 0-87049-133-4). U of Tenn Pr.
Dell, Christopher. Lincoln & the War Democrats: The Grand Erosion of Conservative Tradition. LC 73-21227. 704p. 1975. 22.50 (ISBN 0-8386-1466-3). Fairleigh Dickinson.
Dodd, William E. Lincoln or Lee. 1964. 5.00 (ISBN 0-8446-1155-7). Peter Smith.
Donald, David. Lincoln Reconsidered. 1956. pap. 3.95 (ISBN 0-394-70190-9). Knopf.
--Lincoln Reconsidered: Essays on the Civil War Era. pap. 2.95 (ISBN 0-394-70190-9, V-190, Vin). Random.
Donald, David H. Lincoln Reconsidered: Essays on the Civil War Era. LC 80-22804. (Illus.). xiii, 200p. 1981. Repr. of 1956 ed. lib. bdg. 23.50x (ISBN 0-313-22575-3, DOLR). Greenwood.
Dye, John S. History of the Plots & Crimes of the Great Conspiracy to Overthrow Liberty in America. facs. ed. LC 76-75508. (Select Bibliographies Reprint Ser). 1866. 25.00 (ISBN 0-8369-5006-2). Arno.
Farr, Naunerle C. Abraham Lincoln-Franklin D. Roosevelt. (Pendulum Illustrated Biography Ser.). (Illus.). (gr. 4-12). 1979. text ed. 5.00 (ISBN 0-88301-366-5); pap. text ed. 1.95 (ISBN 0-88301-354-1); wkbk. 1.25 (ISBN 0-88301-378-9). Pendulum Pr.
Fehrenbacher, Don E. The Leadership of Abraham Lincoln. LC 77-114013. (Problems in American History Ser.). 194p. 1970. pap. text ed. 9.95 (ISBN 0-471-25689-7). Wiley.
--Prelude to Greatness: Lincoln in the 1850's. 1962. 10.00x (ISBN 0-8047-0119-9); pap. 3.75 (ISBN 0-8047-0120-2, SP109). Stanford U Pr.
Fehrenbacher, Don E., ed. Abraham Lincoln: A Documentary Portrait Through His Speeches & Writings. LC 76-53865. 1964. 10.00x (ISBN 0-8047-0942-4); pap. 3.85x (ISBN 0-8047-0946-7). Stanford U Pr.
Findley, Paul. A. Lincoln: The Crucible of Congress. 1979. 14.95 (ISBN 0-517-53436-3). Crown.
Fleckles, Elliot. Willie Speaks Out. LC 73-23123. 250p. 1974. 7.95 (ISBN 0-87542-233-0). Llewellyn Pubns.
Forgie, George B. Patricide in the House Divided: A Psychological Interpretation of Lincoln & His Age. 1979. 14.95x (ISBN 0-393-05695-3). Norton.
Gammans, Harold. Lincoln Names & Epithets. (Orig.). pap. 5.00 (ISBN 0-8283-1389-X). Branden.
Griggs, Edward H. American Statesmen: An Interpretation of Our History & Heritage. LC 76-121474. (Essay Index Reprint Ser). 1927. 19.50 (ISBN 0-8369-1810-X). Arno.
Hamilton, Holman. The Three Kentucky Presidents: Lincoln, Taylor, Davis. LC 77-92922. (Kentucky Bicentennial Bookshelf Ser.). (Illus.). 96p. 1978. 6.95 (ISBN 0-8131-0246-4). U Pr of Ky.
Handlin, Oscar & Handlin, Lilian. Abraham Lincoln & the Union. (Library of American Biography). 224p. (Orig.). 1980. 10.95 (ISBN 0-316-34315-3); pap. 4.95 (ISBN 0-316-34314-5). Little.
Harkness, David J. & McMurtry, R. Gerald. Lincoln's Favorite Poets. LC 59-9718. 1959. 7.50x (ISBN 0-87049-026-5). U of Tenn Pr.
Hay, John. Lincoln & the Civil War in the Diaries & Letters of John Hay. LC 79-135598. 348p. 1972. Repr. of 1939 ed. text ed. 19.25x (ISBN 0-8371-5190-2, Pub. by Negro U Pr). Greenwood.
Hesseltine, William B. Lincoln's Plan of Reconstruction. 7.00 (ISBN 0-8446-1236-7). Peter Smith.
--Lincoln's Plan of Reconstruction. 1972. pap. 1.95 (ISBN 0-8129-6046-7). Times Bks.
Horgan, Paul. Abraham Lincoln: Citizen of New Salem. 90p. 1961. 2.98 (ISBN 0-686-74487-X). Macmillan.
--Citizen of New Salem. LC 61-9893. (Illus.). 332p. (gr. 7 up). 1962. 3.75 (ISBN 0-374-31320-2). FS&G.
Horner, Harlan H. Lincoln & Greeley. LC 74-135247. viii, 432p. Repr. of 1953 ed. lib. bdg. 20.00x (ISBN 0-8371-5166-X, HOLG). Greenwood.
Johnson, William J. Abraham Lincoln the Christian. (Great American Christian Ser.). (Illus.). 1976. pap. 3.25 (ISBN 0-915134-13-6). Mott Media.
Jones, Edgar D. Lincoln & the Preachers. (Biography Index Reprint Ser). 1948. 19.00 (ISBN 0-8369-8018-2). Arno.
Keckley, Elizabeth H. Behind the Scenes or Thirty Years a Slave, & Four Years in the White House. LC 68-29006. (American Negro: His History & Literature, Ser. No. 1). 1968. Repr. of 1868 ed. 11.00 (ISBN 0-405-01824-X). Arno.
King, Willard L. Lincoln's Manager, David Davis. (Midway Reprint Ser.). 1960. pap. 12.00x (ISBN 0-226-43699-3). U of Chicago Pr.
Kranz, Henry B., ed. Abraham Lincoln: A New Portrait. LC 72-279. (Essay Index Reprint Ser.). Repr. of 1959 ed. 16.00 (ISBN 0-8369-2798-2). Arno.
Larned, Josephus N. Study of Greatness in Men. facsimile ed. LC 73-156677. (Essay Index Reprint Ser). Repr. of 1911 ed. 18.00 (ISBN 0-8369-2557-2). Arno.
Lewis, Joseph. Lincoln the Atheist. 1979. pap. 3.00 (ISBN 0-686-70314-6). Am Atheist.
Lewis, Lloyd. Myths After Lincoln. 8.50 (ISBN 0-8446-4023-9). Peter Smith.
Lincoln, Abraham. Life & Writings of Abraham Lincoln. Van Stern, P. & Nevins, A., eds. 1942. 5.95 (ISBN 0-394-60720-1, G20). Modern Lib.
--Lincoln Dictionary. Winn, Ralph, ed. pap. 1.45 (ISBN 0-685-19407-8, 43, WL). Citadel Pr.
--The Lincoln Encyclopedia: The Spoken & Written Words of A. Lincoln Arranged for Ready Reference. Shaw, Archer H., ed. LC 80-12651. xii, 395p. 1980. Repr. of 1950 ed. lib. bdg. 39.75x (ISBN 0-313-22471-4, SHLE). Greenwood.
Lincoln, Abraham, Pres. U. S. Collected Works Supplement 1832-1865. LC 53-6295. (Contributions in American Studies: No. 7). 1974. lib. bdg. 19.95 (ISBN 0-8371-6492-3, BAL/). Greenwood.
Lloyd, John A. Snowbound with Mr. Lincoln. 1979. 6.95 (ISBN 0-533-03859-6). Vantage.
Lodge, Henry C. Democracy of the Constitution, & Other Addresses & Essays. facs. ed. LC 67-22101. (Essay Index Reprint Ser). 1915. 16.00 (ISBN 0-8369-0623-3). Arno.
Ludwig, Emil. Abraham Lincoln. (Black & Gold Lib). (Illus.). 1949. 7.95 (ISBN 0-87140-884-8). Liveright.
Luthin, Reinhard H. The First Lincoln Campaign. 1964. 8.50 (ISBN 0-8446-1292-8). Peter Smith.
Macartney, Clarence E. Lincoln & His Generals. facsimile ed. LC 70-124241. (Select Bibliographies Reprint Ser). (Illus.). Repr. of 1925 ed. 16.00 (ISBN 0-8369-5429-7). Arno.
McCrary, Peyton. Abraham Lincoln & Reconstruction: The Louisiana Experiment. LC 78-51181. 1978. 30.00 (ISBN 0-691-04660-3). Princeton U Pr.
Mearns, David C. Lincoln Papers: The Story of the Collection with Selections to July 4, 1861, 2 Vols in 1. LC 48-9019. 1968. Repr. of 1948 ed. 26.00 (ISBN 0-527-62580-9). Kraus Repr.
Merriam, Charles E. Four American Party Leaders: Henry Ward Beecher Foundation Lectures, Amherst College. facs. ed. LC 67-23247. (Essay Index Reprint Ser). 1926. 11.50 (ISBN 0-8369-0702-7). Arno.
Miller, Francis T. Portrait Life of Lincoln. facsimile ed. LC 76-133528. (Select Bibliographies Reprint Ser). Repr. of 1910 ed. 23.00 (ISBN 0-8369-5560-9). Arno.
Minear. Abraham Lincoln & Emancipation: A Man's Dialogue with His Times. 1976. 3.40 (ISBN 0-201-04740-3). A-W.
Mitgang, Herbert. Lincoln As They Saw Him. 1980. Repr. of 1956 ed. lib. bdg. 27.50x (ISBN 0-374-95801-7). Octagon.
--Mister Lincoln. 72p. 1981. price not set (ISBN 0-8093-1034-1). S Ill U Pr.
Monaghan, James. The Man Who Elected Lincoln. LC 73-7310. (Illus.). 334p. 1973. Repr. of 1956 ed. lib. bdg. 15.75x (ISBN 0-8371-6920-8, MOMW). Greenwood.
Monaghan, Jay. Diplomat in Carpet Slippers: Abraham Lincoln Deals with Foreign Affairs. LC 79-39200. (Select Bibliographies Reprint Ser.). Repr. of 1945 ed. 31.00 (ISBN 0-8369-6802-6). Arno.
Morse, John T., Jr. Abraham Lincoln, 2 Vols. LC 73-128958. (American Statesman: Nos. 25, 26). Repr. of 1899 ed. Set. 47.00 (ISBN 0-404-50892-8); 23.50 ea. AMS Pr.
Musmanno, Michael A. The Glory & the Dream. LC 67-30690. 6.45 (ISBN 0-912806-23-0). Long Hse.
Nadal, Ehrman S. Virginian Village, & Other Papers. facs. ed. LC 68-20324. (Essay Index Reprint Ser). 1917. 15.50 (ISBN 0-8369-0733-7). Arno.
Neely, Mark E., Jr. The Abraham Lincoln Encyclopedia. (Louis A. Warren Lincoln Library). (Illus.). 416p. 1981. 39.95 (ISBN 0-07-046145-7, P&RB). McGraw.
Nichols, David A. Lincoln & the Indians: Civil War Policy & Politics. LC 77-12196. 1978. 16.00x (ISBN 0-8262-0231-4). U of Mo Pr.
Nicolay, John G. & Hay, John. Abraham Lincoln: A History. Angle, Paul M., ed. LC 66-20590. (Orig.). 1966. pap. 4.50 (ISBN 0-226-58332-5, P236, Phoen). U of Chicago Pr.
Oates, Stephen B. Our Fiery Trial: Abraham Lincoln, John Brown, & the Civil War Era. LC 78-16286. 1979. 11.50 (ISBN 0-87023-261-4). U of Mass Pr.
--With Malice Toward None: The Life of Abraham Lincoln. LC 76-12058. (Illus.). (YA) 1977. 15.95 (ISBN 0-06-013283-3, HarpT). Har-Row.
--With Malice Toward None: The Life of Abraham Lincoln. (Illus.). 1978. pap. 3.50 (ISBN 0-451-61932-3, ME1932, Ment). NAL.
Patton, William W. President Lincoln & the Chicago Memorial of Emancipation. LC 72-14411. (Maryland Historical Society. Fund-Publications: No. 27). Repr. of 1888 ed. 7.50 (ISBN 0-404-57627-3). AMS Pr.
Phelan, Mary K. Mr. Lincoln's Inaugural Journey. LC 76-175110. (Illus.). (gr. 5-8). 1972. 8.95 (ISBN 0-685-24997-2, TYC-J). Har-Row.
Pickett, William P. Negro Problem: Abraham Lincoln's Solution. LC 76-92757. Repr. of 1909 ed. 24.75x (ISBN 0-8371-2200-7, Pub. by Negro U Pr). Greenwood.
Potter, David M. Lincoln & His Party in the Secession Crisis. LC 75-41216. Repr. of 1942 ed. 27.00 (ISBN 0-404-14809-3). AMS Pr.
Potter, John M. Thirteen Desperate Days. 1964. 7.50 (ISBN 0-8392-1114-7). Astor-Honor.
Randall, J. G. Lincoln the Liberal Statesman. 5.00 (ISBN 0-8446-0863-7). Peter Smith.
--Lincoln, the President: Springfield to Gettysburg, 2 vols. 16.00 set (ISBN 0-8446-0864-5). Peter Smith.
--Mr. Lincoln. Current, Richard N., ed. 5.00 (ISBN 0-8446-0865-3). Peter Smith.
Randall, James G. Constitutional Problems Under Lincoln. rev. ed. 1950. 12.50 (ISBN 0-8446-1376-2). Peter Smith.
--Lincoln & the South. LC 80-22084. (The Walter Lynwood Fleming Lectures in Southern History, L. S. U.). (Illus.). viii, 161p. 1980. Repr. of 1946 ed. lib. bdg. 18.75x (ISBN 0-313-22843-4, RALS). Greenwood.
Rawley, James A. Lincoln & Civil War Politics. 6.25 (ISBN 0-8446-0870-X). Peter Smith.
Rawley, James A., ed. Lincoln & Civil War Politics. LC 77-8812. (American Problem Studies Ser.). 136p. 1977. pap. text ed. 5.50 (ISBN 0-88275-576-5). Krieger.
Rice, Allen T., ed. Reminiscences of Abraham Lincoln. LC 72-13766. (Concordance Ser., No. 37). 1971. Repr. of 1888 ed. lib. bdg. 69.95 (ISBN 0-8383-1227-6). Haskell.
Riddle, Donald W. Congressman Abraham Lincoln. LC 79-11614. 1979. Repr. of 1957 ed. lib. bdg. 21.00x (ISBN 0-8371-9307-9, RIAL). Greenwood.
Robinson, Luther E. Abraham Lincoln As a Man of Letters. LC 74-11355. 1974. Repr. of 1918 ed. lib. bdg. 22.50 (ISBN 0-8414-7327-7). Folcroft.
Sandburg, Carl. Abraham Lincoln. LC 74-8388. (Illus.). 800p. 1974. pap. 5.95 (ISBN 0-15-602611-2, HB297, Harv). HarBraceJ.
--Abraham Lincoln: The Prairie Years. LC 28-5762. Boxed Set. 40.00 (ISBN 0-15-100779-9). HarBraceJ.
--Abraham Lincoln, the Prairie Years & the War Years, 3 Vols. Set. pap. 6.95 (ISBN 0-440-30008-8, LE). Dell.
--Abraham Lincoln: The Prairie Years & the War Years. 6 vols. 120.00 (ISBN 0-15-102570-3). HarBraceJ.
--Abraham Lincoln: The Prairie Years & the War Years. rev. ed. LC 74-122389. (Illus.). 640p. (One vol.). 14.00 (ISBN 0-15-100640-7). HarBraceJ.
--Abraham Lincoln: The War Years, 4 Vols. LC 39-27998. Set. 80.00 (ISBN 0-15-101610-0); Vols. 1 & 2. 40.00 (ISBN 0-15-101608-9); Vols. 3 & 4. 40.00 (ISBN 0-15-101609-7). HarBraceJ.
Schluter, Herman. Lincoln, Labor & Slavery. LC 65-17920. 1965. Repr. of 1913 ed. 7.50 (ISBN 0-8462-0570-X). Russell.
Scripps, John L. Life of Abraham Lincoln. Basler, Roy P. & Dunlap, Lloyd A., eds. LC 68-56041. (Illus.). 1968. Repr. of 1961 ed. lib. bdg. 15.00 (ISBN 0-8371-0650-8, SCAL). Greenwood.
Slicer, Thomas R. From Poet to Premier: The Centennial Cycle, 1809-1909 - Poe, Lincoln, Holmes, Darwin, Tennyson, Gladstone. 1977. Repr. of 1909 ed. lib. bdg. 25.00 (ISBN 0-8495-4820-9). Arden Lib.
Starr, John W., Jr. Lincoln & the Railroads. Bruchey, Stuart, ed. LC 80-1346. (Railroads Ser.). 1981. Repr. of 1927 ed. lib. bdg. 32.00x (ISBN 0-405-13817-2). Arno.
Stoddard, William O. Abraham Lincoln: The True Story of a Great Life, the Inner Growth, Special Training, & Fitness of the Man. 1979. Repr. of 1884 ed. lib. bdg. 100.00 (ISBN 0-8495-4904-3). Arden Lib.
--Abraham Lincoln: The True Story of a Great Life. 1884. Repr. 50.00 (ISBN 0-8274-1813-2). R West.
Tarbell, Ida M. He Knew Lincoln. 1973. Repr. of 1907 ed. 17.50 (ISBN 0-8274-0424-7). R West.
--In the Footsteps of the Lincolns. 1973. Repr. of 1924 ed. 35.00 (ISBN 0-8274-0425-5). R West.
--The Life of Abraham Lincoln, 2 vols. 1973. Repr. of 1908 ed. 50.00 set (ISBN 0-8274-0423-9). R West.
Thomas, Benjamin P. Abraham Lincoln. (Illus.). (YA) 1952. 15.00 (ISBN 0-394-43334-3). Knopf.
--Abraham Lincoln: A Biography. 1968. Repr. of 1965 ed. 5.95 (ISBN 0-394-60764-3). Modern Lib.
--Portrait for Posterity: Lincoln & His Biographers. LC 72-38318. (Biography Index Reprint Ser). (Illus.). Repr. of 1947 ed. 18.25 (ISBN 0-8369-8130-8). Arno.
Thurow, Glen E. Abraham Lincoln & American Political Religion. LC 76-12596. 1976. 12.95 (ISBN 0-87395-334-7). State U NY Pr.
Trueblood, Elton. Abraham Lincoln: Theologian of American Anguish. LC 72-79955. 160p. 1973. 6.95 (ISBN 0-06-068511-5, HarpR). Har-Row.
Villard, Henry. Lincoln on the Eve of '61: A Journalist's Story. Villard, Henry & Villard, Osward G., eds. LC 73-16631. 105p. 1974. Repr. of 1941 ed. lib. bdg. 15.00 (ISBN 0-8371-7202-0, VILI). Greenwood.
Warren, Louis A. Lincoln's Youth: Indiana Years, Seven to Twenty-One, 1816-1830. LC 75-26223. (Illus.). 298p. 1976. Repr. of 1959 ed. lib. bdg. 22.75x (ISBN 0-8371-8408-8, WALY). Greenwood.
Welles, Gideon. Lincoln & Seward. facsimile ed. LC 79-85082. (Select Bibliographies Reprint Ser). 1874. 22.00 (ISBN 0-8369-5081-X). Arno.
Wheare, Kenneth C. Lincoln. Orig. Title: Abraham Lincoln & the United States. 1966. pap. 1.25 (ISBN 0-02-038300-2, Collier). Macmillan.
Whitlock, Brand. Abraham Lincoln. 1979. Repr. of 1908 ed. lib. bdg. 15.00 (ISBN 0-8495-5715-1). Arden Lib.
Wilbur, Henry W. President Lincoln's Attitude Toward Slavery & Emancipation. 1914. 12.00x (ISBN 0-8196-0267-1). Biblo.
Williams, T. Harry. Lincoln & His Generals. 1967. pap. 3.45 (ISBN 0-394-70362-6, Vin). Random.
--Lincoln & the Radicals. (Illus.). 432p. 1941. pap. 8.95x (ISBN 0-299-00274-8). U of Wis Pr.
Wilson, R. R., ed. Lincoln in Caricature. (Illus.). 1981. pap. 14.95 (ISBN 0-8180-0825-3). Horizon.
Woldman, Albert A. Lincoln & the Russians. LC 78-110297. ix, 311p. Repr. of 1952 ed. lib. bdg. 14.00x (ISBN 0-8371-4503-1, WOLR). Greenwood.
Wolf, William J. Lincoln's Religion. LC 70-123035. Orig. Title: Almost Chosen People. 1970. pap. 2.25 (ISBN 0-8298-0181-2). Pilgrim NY.
Wright, John S. Lincoln & the Politics of Slavery. LC 74-113811. xiii, 215p. 1970. 6.00 (ISBN 0-87417-027-3). U of Nev Pr.
Zornow, William F. Lincoln & the Party Divided. LC 73-152619. 264p. 1972. Repr. of 1954 ed. lib. bdg. 17.00x (ISBN 0-8371-6054-5, ZOLP). Greenwood.

LINCOLN, ABRAHAM, PRES. U. S., 1809-1865–ANECDOTES

Angle, Paul M., ed. Abraham Lincoln, by Some Men Who Knew Him. facsimile ed. LC 78-90601. (Essay Index Reprint Ser). 1950. 11.00 (ISBN 0-8369-1242-X). Arno.
Carpenter, Francis B. Six Months with Lincoln in the White House. LC 60-15560. 6.00 (ISBN 0-87282-017-3). Century Hse.
Eaton, John. Grant, Lincoln & the Freedman. LC 70-78763. (Illus.). Repr. of 1907 ed. 17.50x (ISBN 0-8371-1388-1, Pub. by Negro U Pr). Greenwood.

Lincoln's Own Yarns & Stories. 1980. pap. write for info (ISBN 0-935650-00-8). Bengal Pr.
McGinnis, Ralph Y. Quotations from Abraham Lincoln. LC 77-24595. (Illus.). 1978. 18.95x (ISBN 0-88229-316-8); pap. 9.95 (ISBN 0-88229-507-1). Nelson-Hall.
Neill, Edward D. Abraham Lincoln & His Mailbag: Two Documents by Edward D. Neill. Blegen, Theodore C., ed. LC 64-23313. 50p. 1964. 3.00 (ISBN 0-87351-021-6); pap. 1.75 (ISBN 0-87351-022-4). Minn Hist.
Stein, Max, ed. Abe Lincoln's Jokes: Wit & Humor, History, Chronology. pap. 1.50 (ISBN 0-685-02602-7, 00545119). Stein Pub.

LINCOLN, ABRAHAM, PRES. U. S., 1809-1865–ASSASSINATION

Balsiger, David W. & Sellier, Charles E., Jr. The Lincoln Conspiracy. (Illus.). 1977. pap. 2.25 (ISBN 0-917214-03-X). Schick Sunn.
Bates, Finis L. The Escape & Suicide of John Wilkes Booth: The First True Account of Lincoln's Assassination, Containing a Complete Confession of Booth Many Years After His Crime. 1979. Repr. of 1907 ed. 28.00 (ISBN 0-403-06413-9, Regency). Scholarly.
Buckingham, J. E., Sr. Reminiscences & Souvenirs of the Assassination of Abraham Lincoln. LC 80-128964. (Illus.). 89p. 22.50 (ISBN 0-939128-01-2); pap. 17.50 (ISBN 0-939128-02-0). J L Barbour.
Clarke, Asia. Unlocked Book: A Memoir of John Wilkes Booth by His Sister. LC 74-88533. (Illus.). 1938. 15.00 (ISBN 0-405-08363-7, Blom Pubns). Arno.
Dewitt, David M. Assassination of Abraham Lincoln & Its Expiation. facs. ed. (Select Bibliographies Reprint Ser). 1909. 17.00 (ISBN 0-8369-5574-9). Arno.
--Judicial Murder of Mary E. Surratt. LC 71-108472. 1970. Repr. of 1895 ed. 32.00 (ISBN 0-403-00423-3). Scholarly.
Ferguson, W. J. I Saw Booth Shoot Lincoln. LC 70-20379. (Illus.). 8.50 (ISBN 0-8363-0052-1). Jenkins.
Herold, David E. The Assassination of President Lincoln & the Trial of the Conspirators: The Courtroom Testmony As Originally Compiled by Benn Pitman. LC 73-8568. 1974. Repr. of 1954 ed. lib. bdg. 33.00 (ISBN 0-8371-6963-1, HEAP). Greenwood.
Lattimer, John K. Lincoln & Kennedy: Medical & Ballistic Comparisons of Their Assassinations. LC 80-7963. 1980. 19.95 (ISBN 0-15-152281-2). HarBraceJ.
McCarthy, Burke. The Suppressed Truth About the Assassination of Abraham Lincoln. 255p. 1976. 7.50 (ISBN 0-685-66405-8). Chedney.
McCarty, Burke. The Suppressed Truth About the Assassination of Abraham Lincoln. 255p. 1960. Repr. of 1870 ed. 10.00 (ISBN 0-686-29301-0, Pub. by Chedney). Alpine Ent.
--The Suppressed Truth About the Assassination of Lincoln. 69.95 (ISBN 0-87968-169-1). Gordon Pr.
Matheny, H. E. Major General Thomas Maley Harris, Including Roster of 10th West Virginia Volunteer Infantry Regiment, 1861-1865. 1963. 12.50 (ISBN 0-87012-003-4). McClain.
Weichmann, Louis J. A True History of the Assassination of Abraham Lincoln & the Conspiracy of 1865. Risvald, Floyd, ed. (Illus.). 1975. 16.95 (ISBN 0-394-49319-2). Knopf.
Whitman, Maxwell, intro. by. While Lincoln Lay Dying: A Facsimile Reproduction of the First Testimony Taken in Connection with the Assassination of President Abraham Lincoln. LC 68-19803. (Illus.). 1971. 10.00 (ISBN 0-915810-02-6). Union League PA.

LINCOLN, ABRAHAM, PRES. U. S., 1809-1865–BIBLIOGRAPHY

Angle, Paul M. A Shelf of Lincoln Books. LC 72-6403. 142p. 1972. Repr. of 1946 ed. lib. bdg. 15.00 (ISBN 0-8371-6491-5, ANLB). Greenwood.
Basler, Roy P. The Lincoln Legend. LC 70-75989. (Illus.). 1969. Repr. of 1935 ed. lib. bdg. 17.50x (ISBN 0-374-90456-1). Octagon.
Thomas, Benjamin P. Portrait for Posterity: Lincoln & His Biographers. LC 72-38318. (Biography Index Reprint Ser). (Illus.). Repr. of 1947 ed. 18.25 (ISBN 0-8369-8130-8). Arno.

LINCOLN, ABRAHAM, PRES. U. S., 1809-1865–DRAMA

Abraham Lincoln: Mini-Play, 2 pts. (U.S. History Ser). (gr. 8 up). 1978. 3.00 ea.; Pt. 1. (ISBN 0-89550-317-4); Pt. 2. (ISBN 0-89550-325-5). RIM.

LINCOLN, ABRAHAM, PRES. U. S., 1809-1865–FICTION

Lancaster, Bruce. For Us the Living. (Illus.). 556p. 1975. Repr. of 1940 ed. lib. bdg. 24.90x (ISBN 0-89190-882-X). Am Repr-Rivercity Pr.
Stone, Irving. Love Is Eternal. LC 54-9678. 9.95 (ISBN 0-385-02040-6). Doubleday.

LINCOLN, ABRAHAM, PRES. U. S., 1809-1865–GETTYSBURG ADDRESS

Barton, William E. Lincoln at Gettysburg: What He Intended to Say; What He Said; What He Was Reported to Have Said; What He Wished He Had Said. (Illus.). 8.00 (ISBN 0-8446-1059-3). Peter Smith.
Berns, Laurence, et al. Abraham Lincoln: The Gettysburg Address & American Constitutionalism. DeAlvarez, Leo P., ed. 1976. pap. 7.95 (ISBN 0-685-77625-5). U of Dallas Pr.
Musmanno, Michael A. The Glory & the Dream. LC 67-30690. 6.45 (ISBN 0-912806-23-0). Long Hse.
Richards, Kenneth. Story of the Gettysburg Address. LC 70-82962. (Cornerstones of Freedom Bks). (Illus.). (gr. 3-5). 1969. PLB 10.00 (ISBN 0-516-04615-2); pap. 2.95 (ISBN 0-516-44615-0). Childrens.

LINCOLN, ABRAHAM, PRES. U. S., 1809-1865–JUVENILE LITERATURE

Abraham Lincoln: Mini-Play, 2 pts. (U.S. History Ser). (gr. 8 up). 1978. 3.00 ea.; Pt. 1. (ISBN 0-89550-317-4); Pt. 2. (ISBN 0-89550-325-5). RIM.
Anderson, LaVere. Abe Lincoln & the River Robbers. LC 79-148089. (Regional American Stories Ser.). (Illus.). 64p. (gr. 3-6). 1971. PLB 6.09 (ISBN 0-8116-4251-8). Garrard.
Baber, Adin. Sarah & Abe in Indiana. LC 73-99295. (Illus.). (gr. 4-7). 1970. 9.95 (ISBN 0-87716-016-3, Pub. by Moore Pub Co). F Apple.
Bulla, Clyde R. Lincoln's Birthday. LC 65-27291. (Holiday Ser.). (Illus.). (gr. 1-3). 1966. PLB 7.89 (ISBN 0-690-49450-5, TYC-J). Har-Row.
Cary, Barbara. Meet Abraham Lincoln. (Step-up-Books Ser.). (Illus.). (gr. 2-6). 1965. 3.95 (ISBN 0-394-80057-5, BYR); PLB 4.99 (ISBN 0-394-90057-X). Random.
Chorpenning, Charlotte B. Abe Lincoln: New Salem Days. (Children's Theatre Playscript Ser.). 1954. pap. 2.00x (ISBN 0-88020-006-5). Coach Hse.
Collins, David R. Abraham Lincoln. LC 76-2456. (Sower Series). (Illus.). (gr. 3-6). 1976. 6.95 (ISBN 0-915134-09-8). Mott Media.
Colver, Anne. Abraham Lincoln. (Illus.). (gr. 1-7). 1966. pap. 0.95 (ISBN 0-440-40001-5, YB). Dell.
--Abraham Lincoln: For the People. LC 60-7079. (Discovery Books Ser.). (gr. 2-5). 1960. PLB 6.09 (ISBN 0-8116-6253-5). Garrard.
Coolidge, Olivia. The Apprenticeship of Abraham Lincoln. LC 74-11713. (Illus.). (gr. 7 up). 1974. 6.95 (ISBN 0-684-14003-9, ScribJ). Scribner.
--The Statesmanship of Abraham Lincoln. LC 76-14863. (Illus.). 237p. (gr. 6 up). 1976. 7.95 (ISBN 0-684-14677-0, ScribJ). Scribner.
D'Aulaire, Ingri & D'Aulaire, Edgar Parin. Abraham Lincoln. rev. ed. (gr. k-4). 1957. 10.95a (ISBN 0-385-07669-X); PLB (ISBN 0-385-07674-6). Doubleday.
Davidson, Margaret, ed. Abraham Lincoln. (ps-3). 1976. pap. 1.25 (ISBN 0-590-00096-9, Schol Pap). Schol Bk Serv.
Davis, Burke. Mr. Lincoln's Whiskers. LC 77-29208. (Illus.). (gr. 3-5). 1979. 6.95 (ISBN 0-698-20455-7). Coward.
De Regniers, Beatrice S. Abraham Lincoln Joke Book. (Illus.). (gr. 4-7). 1965. PLB 4.69 (ISBN 0-394-91079-6, BYR). Random.
Douglas, Spencer & Johnson, Ann D. Value of Respect. (Value Tales Ser.). (gr. 1-5). 1979. PLB 10.69 (ISBN 0-307-69956-0, Golden Pr). Western Pub.
Elliot, I., ed. Abraham Lincoln, Eighteen Nine to Eighteen Sixty-Five: Chronology, Documents, Bibliographical Aids. LC 75-111217. (Presidential Chronology Ser.). 1970. 8.00 (ISBN 0-379-12072-0). Oceana.
Foster, Genevieve. Abraham Lincoln's World. (Illus.). (gr. 5-11). 1944. lib. rep. ed. 20.00x (ISBN 0-684-14855-2, ScribJ). Scribner.
Gross, Ruth B. True Stories About Abraham Lincoln. (gr. k-3). 1974. pap. 1.25 (ISBN 0-590-03533-9, Schol Pap). Schol Bk Serv.
Hays, Wilma P. Abe Lincoln's Birthday. (Illus.). (gr. 3-5). 1961. PLB 5.59 (ISBN 0-698-30001-7). Coward.
Horgan, Paul. Citizen of New Salem. LC 61-9893. (Illus.). 332p. (gr. 7 up). 1962. 3.75 (ISBN 0-374-31320-2). FS&G.
Johnson, Ann D. The Value of Respect: The Story of Abraham Lincoln. LC 77-12455. (ValueTales Ser). (Illus.). (gr. k-6). 1977. 6.95 (ISBN 0-916392-14-7, Dist. by Oak Tree Pubns). Value Comm.
Lee, Susan D. Abraham Lincoln. LC 77-20125. (Heroes of the Civil War Ser.). (Illus.). (gr. 2-6). 1978. PLB 7.95 (ISBN 0-516-04701-9). Childrens.
Le Sueur, Meridel. River Road: A Story of Abraham Lincoln. (Illus.). (gr. 5 up). 1954. PLB 5.39 (ISBN 0-394-91551-8). Knopf.
McNeer, May. America's Abraham Lincoln. (Illus.). (gr. 4-8). 1957. Dolphin bdg. 3.57 (ISBN 0-395-06917-3). HM.
Miers, Earl S. & Angle, Paul M. Abraham Lincoln in Peace & War. LC 64-22350. (American Heritage Junior Library). (Illus.). 153p. (gr. 5 up). 1964. 9.95 (ISBN 0-06-024195-0, Dist. by Har-Row). Am Heritage.
Miller, Natalie. Story of the Lincoln Memorial. LC 66-10304. (Cornerstones of Freedom Bks). (Illus.). (gr. 2-5). 1966. PLB 7.95 (ISBN 0-516-04623-3). Childrens.
North, Sterling. Abe Lincoln: Log Cabin to White House. (Landmark Ser: No. 61). (Illus.). (gr. 5-11). 1956. PLB 5.99 (ISBN 0-394-90361-7, BYR). Random.
Ostendorf, Lloyd. Abraham Lincoln: The Boy, the Man. LC 62-11065. (Illus.). (gr. 3 up). 1977. PLB 4.50 (ISBN 0-88308-014-1). Lamplight Pub.
Richards, Dorothy F. Abe Lincoln, Make It Right! LC 78-7690. (Illus.). (gr. k-4). 1978. PLB 5.95 (ISBN 0-89565-033-9). Childs World.
Roche, A. Even the Promise of Freedom: In the Words of Abraham Lincoln. (gr. 4-12). 1970. PLB 4.75 (ISBN 0-13-292235-5). P-H.
Sandburg, Carl. Abe Lincoln Grows Up. LC 28-21008. (Illus.). (gr. 7-9). 1931. 6.95 (ISBN 0-15-201037-8, HJ). HarBraceJ.
--Abe Lincoln Grows up. LC 74-17180. (Illus.). 222p. (gr. 7 up). 1975. pap. 1.95 (ISBN 0-15-201039-4, AVB92, VoyB). HarBraceJ.
Waber, Bernard. Just Like Abraham Lincoln. (Illus.). (gr. 1-5). 1964. reinforced bdg. 6.95 (ISBN 0-395-20107-1). HM.

LINCOLN, ABRAHAM, PRES. U. S., 1809-1865–POETRY

Harrington, Mildred P. & Thomas, Josephine H., eds. Our Holidays in Poetry. 1929. 9.00 (ISBN 0-8242-0039-X). Wilson.
Horgan, Paul. Songs After Lincoln. 74p. 1965. 4.95 (ISBN 0-374-26664-6). FS&G.
Miller, Della C. Abraham Lincoln: A Biographic Trilogy in Sonnet Sequence, 3 Vols., Vol. 1. Boy, Vol. 2. Man, Vol. 3. President. 1964. Set. 10.50 (ISBN 0-8158-0148-3); 4.00 ea. Chris Mass.
Plotts, J. N., ed. Poetical Tributes to the Memory of Abraham Lincoln. 1972. Repr. of 1865 ed. lib. bdg. 20.00 (ISBN 0-8422-8105-3). Irvington.
Williams, A. Dallas, ed. Praise of Lincoln. LC 77-108590. (Granger Index Reprint Ser). 1911. 17.00 (ISBN 0-8369-6118-8). Arno.

LINCOLN, ABRAHAM, PRES. U. S., 1809-1865–PORTRAITS

Frazier, Carl & Frazier, Rosalie. The Lincoln Country-In Pictures. (Illus.). (gr. 4-6). 1963. 5.95 (ISBN 0-8038-4238-4). Hastings.
Lincoln: A Picture Story of His Life. (Illus.). 1981. 14.95 (ISBN 0-918058-04-X). Authors Edn.
Mellon, James. The Face of Lincoln. (Illus.). 1980. 75.00 (ISBN 0-670-30433-6, Studio). Viking Pr.

LINCOLN, MARY (TODD) 1818-1882

Anderson, LaVere. Mary Todd Lincoln: President's Wife. LC 74-18303. (Discovery Ser). (Illus.). 80p. (gr. 2-5). 1975. PLB 6.09 (ISBN 0-8116-6316-7). Garrard.
Bassett, Margaret. Abraham & Mary Todd Lincoln. (Illus.). 64p. 1974. 3.75 (ISBN 0-87027-153-9); pap. 2.50 (ISBN 0-87027-148-2). Wheelwright.
Keckley, Elizabeth H. Behind the Scenes or Thirty Years a Slave, & Four Years in the White House. LC 68-29006. (American Negro: His History & Literature, Ser. No. 1). 1968. Repr. of 1868 ed. 11.00 (ISBN 0-405-01824-X). Arno.
Ostendorf, Lloyd. The Photographs of Mary Todd Lincoln. 1969. 3.50 (ISBN 0-912226-00-5). Ill St Hist Soc.
Randall, Ruth P. Mary Lincoln: Biography of a Marriage. (Illus.). 1953. 12.50 (ISBN 0-316-73359-8). Little.
Turner, Justin G. & Turner, Linda L., eds. Mary Todd Lincoln: Her Life & Letters. 1972. 17.50 (ISBN 0-394-46643-8). Knopf.

LINCOLN, MARY (TODD) 1818-1882–FICTION

Stone, Irving. Love Is Eternal. LC 54-9678. 9.95 (ISBN 0-385-02040-6). Doubleday.

LINCOLN, NANCY (HANKS), 1784-1818

Wilson, Dorothy C. Lincoln's Mothers. LC 80-950. 432p. 1981. 13.95 (ISBN 0-385-15146-2, Galilee). Doubleday.

LINCOLN, ROBERT TODD, 1843-1926

Mearns, David C. Lincoln Papers: The Story of the Collection with Selections to July 4, 1861, 2 Vols in 1. LC 48-9019. 1968. Repr. of 1948 ed. 26.00 (ISBN 0-527-62580-9). Kraus Repr.

LINCOLN, SARAH (BUSH) JOHNSTON, MRS., 1788-1869

Wilson, Dorothy C. Lincoln's Mothers. LC 80-950. 432p. 1981. 13.95 (ISBN 0-385-15146-2, Galilee). Doubleday.

LINCOLN, ENGLAND–HISTORY

Bowker, Margaret. The Henrician Reformation: The Diocese of Lincoln Under John Longland 1521-1547. LC 80-41655. (Illus.). 256p. Date not set. price not set (ISBN 0-521-23639-8). Cambridge U Pr.
Hill, J. W. F. Victorian Lincoln. LC 73-82661. (Illus.). 350p. 1974. 48.00 (ISBN 0-521-20334-1). Cambridge U Pr.
Mann, Jenny E. Clay Tobacco Pipes from Excavations in Lincoln, 1970-1974. (Lincoln Archeological Trust Monograph: Vol. 16). 60p. 1977. pap. text ed. 11.95x (ISBN 0-686-74105-6, Pub. by Coun Brit Archaeology). Humanities.

LINCOLN, COUNTY, NEW MEXICO–HISTORY

Fulton, Maurice G. History of the Lincoln County War. Mullin, Robert N., ed. LC 68-13544. (Illus.). 384p. 1968. pap. 12.50x (ISBN 0-8165-0052-5). U of Ariz Pr.

LINCOLN-DOUGLAS DEBATES, 1858

Bauer, Charles. The Lincoln-Douglas Triangle. 1980. 9.50 (ISBN 0-87164-094-5). William-F.
Sigelschiffer, Saul. The American Conscience. (Illus.). 1973. 12.95 (ISBN 0-8180-0811-3). Horizon.

LINCOLN ELECTRIC COMPANY

Lincoln, James F. A New Approach to Industrial Economics. 1961. 4.50 (ISBN 0-8159-6301-7). Devin.

LINCOLNSHIRE, ENGLAND

Marsden, Walter. Lincolnshire. 1977. 19.95 (ISBN 0-7134-0683-6, Pub. by Batsford England). David & Charles.
Yates, Jack & Thorold, Henry. Lincolnshire: A Shell Guide. (Shell Guide Ser.). (Illus.). 160p. 1968. 14.95 (ISBN 0-571-06297-0, Pub. by Faber & Faber). Merrimack Bk Serv.

LINCOLNSHIRE, ENGLAND–GUIDEBOOKS

White, William. History, Gazetteer & Directory of Lincolnshire. LC 74-9029. Repr. of 1856 ed. lib. bdg. 27.50x (ISBN 0-678-05500-9). Kelley.

LIND-GOLDSCHMIDT, JENNY MARIA, 1820-1887

Cavanah, Frances. Jenny Lind & Her Listening Cat. LC 61-15483. (Illus.). (gr. 3-6). 1961. 6.95 (ISBN 0-8149-0289-8). Vanguard.
Holland, Henry & Rockstro, W. S. Memoir of Madame Jenny Lind-Goldschmidt: Her Early Art-Life & Dramatic Career 1820-1851, 2 vols. LC 77-90799. 1978. Repr. of 1891 ed. lib. bdg. 60.00 (ISBN 0-89341-416-6). Longwood Pr.
Maude, Jenny M. The Life of Jenny Lind. Farkas, Andrew, ed. LC 76-29953. (Opera Biographies). (Illus.). 1977. Repr. of 1926 ed. lib. bdg. 16.00 (ISBN 0-405-09694-1). Arno.
--The Life of Jenny Lind: Briefly Told by Her Daughter. LC 74-24149. (Illus.). Repr. of 1926 ed. 17.50 (ISBN 0-404-13041-0). AMS Pr.
Wagenknecht, Edward C. Jenny Lind. (Music Ser.). 1980. Repr. of 1931 ed. 22.50 (ISBN 0-306-76045-2). Da Capo.
Ware, Porter & Lockard, Thaddeus. P. T. Barnum Presents Jenny Lind. LC 80-1150. 320p. 1980. 20.00 (ISBN 0-8071-0687-9). La State U Pr.
Weber, Erwin. Jenny Lind Chapel. LC 75-316870. (Augustana College Library Occasional Paper: No. 12). 1975. pap. 1.00 (ISBN 0-910182-35-3). Augustana Coll.

LINDBERGH, ANNE (MORROW), 1906-

Lindberg, Ann M. War Within & Without: Diaries & Letters 1939-1944. 464p. 1981. pap. 3.50 (ISBN 0-425-05084-X). Berkley Pub.
Lindbergh, Anne M. The Flower & the Nettle: Diaries & Letters, 1936-1939. LC 75-25708. (A Helen & Kurt Wolff Bk). (Illus.). 640p. 1976. 12.95 (ISBN 0-15-131501-9). HarBraceJ.
--Hour of Gold, Hour of Lead. LC 72-88792. 1973. 7.95 (ISBN 0-15-142176-5). HarBraceJ.
--War Within & Without: Diaries & Letters, Nineteen Thirty-Nine to Nineteen Forty-Four. 1980. 14.95 (ISBN 0-15-194661-2). HarBraceJ.

LINDBERGH, CHARLES AUGUST, 1859-1924

Eubank, Nancy. The Lindberghs: Three Generations. LC 75-12517. (Minnesota Historic Sites Pamphlet Ser: No. 12). (Illus.). 1975. pap. 1.50 (ISBN 0-87351-094-1). Minn Hist.
Gill, Brendan. Lindbergh Alone. LC 76-54288. (Illus.). 1977. 11.95 (ISBN 0-15-152401-7). HarBraceJ.
Larson, Bruce L. Lindbergh of Minnesota: A Political Biography. LC 73-6596. 1973. 14.50 (ISBN 0-15-152400-9). HarBraceJ.

LINDBERGH, CHARLES AUGUSTUS, 1902-1974

Cole, Wayne S. Charles A. Lindbergh & the Battle Against American Intervention in World War Two. LC 73-22247. (Illus.). 320p. 1974. 10.00 (ISBN 0-15-118168-3). HarBraceJ.
Collins, David R. Charles Lindbergh: Hero Pilot. LC 77-13956. (Discovery Ser.). (Illus.). (gr. 2-5). 1978. PLB 6.09 (ISBN 0-8116-6322-1). Garrard.

Crouch, Tom D. Charles A. Lindbergh: An American Life. LC 77-14537. (Illus.). 128p. 1977. 10.95 (ISBN 0-87474-342-7); pap. 5.95 (ISBN 0-87474-343-5). Smithsonian.

Eubank, Nancy. The Lindberghs: Three Generations. LC 75-12517. (Minnesota Historic Sites Pamphlet Ser: No. 12). (Illus.). 1975. pap. 1.50 (ISBN 0-87351-094-1). Minn Hist.

Farr, Naunerle C. & Fago, John N. Amelia Earhart - Charles Lindbergh. (Pendulum Illustrated Biography Ser.). (Illus.). (gr. 4-12). 1979. text ed. 5.00 (ISBN 0-88301-361-4); pap. text ed. 1.95 (ISBN 0-88301-349-5); wkbk. 1.25 (ISBN 0-88301-373-8). Pendulum Pr.

Grierson, John. I Remember Lindbergh. LC 77-76436. (Illus.). 192p. (gr. 7 up). 1977. 8.95 (ISBN 0-15-238895-8, HJ). HarBraceJ.

Gross, Ruth B. Dangerous Adventure: Linbergh's Famous Flight. new ed. (gr. k-3). 1977. pap. 1.25 (ISBN 0-590-08582-4, Schol Pap). Schol Bk Serv.

--Dangerous Adventure! Lindbergh's Famous Flight. LC 77-79269. (Illus.). (gr. 2-6). 1977. 5.95 (ISBN 0-8027-6309-X); reinf. o.s.i. 5.85 (ISBN 0-8027-6310-3). Walker & Co.

Kurland, Gerald. Lindbergh Flies the Atlantic. new ed. Rahmas, D. Steve, ed. (Events of Our Time Ser.). 32p. 1975. lib. bdg. 2.95 incl. catalog cards (ISBN 0-686-11243-1); pap. 1.50 vinyl laminated covers (ISBN 0-686-11244-X). SamHar Pr.

Lindbergh, Charles A. Boyhood on the Upper Mississippi: A Reminiscent Letter. LC 75-75804. 64p. 1972. 4.50 (ISBN 0-87351-069-0). Minn Hist.

--Wartime Journals of Charles A. Lindbergh. LC 78-124830. 1970. 12.95 (ISBN 0-15-194625-6). HarBraceJ.

Miller, Francis T. Lindbergh: His Story in Pictures. Gilbert, James, ed. LC 79-7286. (Flight: Its First Seventy-Five Years Ser.). (Illus.). 1979. Repr. of 1929 ed. lib. bdg. 29.00x (ISBN 0-405-12195-4). Arno.

Mosley, Leonard. Lindbergh: A Biography. LC 75-40736. 400p. 1976. 12.95 (ISBN 0-385-09578-3). Doubleday.

Ross, Walter. The Last Hero: Charles A. Lindbergh. 1979. pap. 1.75 (ISBN 0-532-17119-5). Woodhill.

LINDBERGH, CHARLES AUGUSTUS, JR. 1930-1932

Haring, J. Vreeland. Hand of Hauptmann: The Handwriting Expert Tells the Story of the Lindbergh Case. (Illus.). 1937. 10.00 (ISBN 0-87585-702-7). Patterson Smith.

Lindbergh, Anne M. Hour of Gold, Hour of Lead. 288p. (RL 10). 1974. pap. 1.75 (ISBN 0-451-05825-9, E5825, Sig). NAL.

Wright, Theon. In Search of the Lindbergh Baby. 1981. pap. 2.50 (ISBN 0-505-51631-4). Tower Bks.

LINDEMAN, EDUARD CHRISTIAN, 1885-1953

Konopka, Gisela. Eduard C. Lindeman & Social Work Philosophy. LC 58-9162. 1958. 7.50x (ISBN 0-8166-0161-5). U of Minn Pr.

LINDENMAYER DEVELOPMENTAL LANGUAGES

see L Systems

LINDENMAYER SYSTEMS

see L Systems

LINDISFARNE ABBEY

Backhouse, Janet. The Lindisfarne Gospels. LC 81-65990. (Cornell Phaidon Bks.). (Illus.). 96p. 1981. 25.00 (ISBN 0-8014-1354-0, Pub. by Phaidon England). Cornell U Pr.

Dunleavy, Gareth W. Colum's Other Island: The Irish at Lindisfarne. (Illus.). 160p. 1960. 11.50x (ISBN 0-299-02120-3). U of Wis Pr.

LINDNER, RICHARD

Kramer, Hilton. Richard Lindner. LC 74-78458. (Illus.). 256p. 1975. 42.50 (ISBN 0-8212-0513-7, 743224). NYGS.

LINDSAY, JOHN VLIET, 1921-

Buckley, William F., Jr. The Unmaking of a Mayor. (Illus.). 1977. Repr. of 1966 ed. 9.95 (ISBN 0-87000-391-7). Arlington Hse.

Citron, Casper. John V. Lindsay. LC 65-26494. (Illus.). 1965. 6.95 (ISBN 0-8303-0045-7). Fleet.

LINDSAY, NICHOLAS VACHEL, 1879-1931

Davison, Edward L. Some Modern Poets, & Other Critical Essays. facs. ed. LC 68-16926. (Essay Index Reprint Ser). 1968. Repr. of 1928 ed. 16.00 (ISBN 0-8369-0366-8). Arno.

Flanagan, John T. Profile of Vachel Lindsay. LC 79-130279. (Literary Profiles Ser.). 1970. pap. text ed. 2.95x (ISBN 0-675-09287-6). Merrill.

Harris, Mark. City of Discontent: An Interpretive Biography of Vachel Lindsay, Being Also the Story of Springfield, Illinois, USA. 403p. 1975. Repr. of 1952 ed. lib. bdg. 20.00x (ISBN 0-374-93676-5). Octagon.

Masters, Edgar L. Vachel Lindsay: A Poet in America. LC 68-56452. (Illus.). 1969. Repr. of 1935 ed. 17.00x (ISBN 0-8196-0239-6). Biblo.

Wolfe, Glenn J. Vachel Lindsay: The Poet As Film Theorist. LC 72-554. (Dissertations on Film Ser). 250p. 1972. 15.00 (ISBN 0-405-04097-0). Arno.

LINDSEY, BENJAMIN BARR, 1869-1943

Larsen, Charles. The Good Fight: The Life & Times of Ben B. Lindsey. 1972. 10.00 (ISBN 0-8129-0237-8). Times Bks.

LINE (ART)

Lerner, Sharon. Straight Is a Line: A Book About Lines. LC 70-91671. (Art Concept Bks). (Illus.). (gr. k-3). 1970. PLB 4.95g (ISBN 0-8225-0273-9). Lerner Pubns.

Ludlow, Norman H., Jr. The Potpourri Clip Book of Line Artwork. (Illus.). 1979. pap. 8.95x (ISBN 0-916706-17-6). N H Ludlow.

MacAgy, Douglas & MacAgy, Elizabeth. Going for a Walk with a Line: A Step into the World of Modern Art. LC 59-5899. (gr. 1 up). 1959. pap. 1.95 (ISBN 0-385-05246-4). Doubleday.

Morris, Victoria S. Line & Color. (Illus.). 1977. pap. text ed. 3.00 (ISBN 0-914318-07-1). V S Morris.

LINE-ENGRAVING

see Engraving

LINE GEOMETRY

see also Algebras, Linear; Complexes

Bronstein, E. Lines & Half Planes. (Finite Math Text Ser.). write for info. (ISBN 0-685-84473-0). J W Wills.

Jessop, Charles H. Treatise on the Line Complex. LC 68-55945. 1969. Repr. of 1903 ed. 11.95 (ISBN 0-8284-0223-X). Chelsea Pub.

Timerding, H. Emil. Geometrie der Krafte. (Bibliotheca Mathematica Teubneriana, 33). (Ger). Repr. of 1908 ed. 23.00 (ISBN 0-384-60640-7). Johnson Repr.

Vasilyev, N. & Gutenmacher, V. Straight Lines & Curves. 1980. 4.00 (ISBN 0-8285-1792-4, Pub. by Mir Pubs Russia). Imported Pubns.

LINE OF BALANCE (MANAGEMENT)

Dogramaci, A. Productivity Analysis: A Range of Perspectives. (Studies in Productivity Analysis: Vol. 1). 208p. 1980. lib. bdg. 19.95 (ISBN 0-89838-039-1, Pub. by Martinus Nijhoff Netherlands). Kluwer Boston.

Doll, John P. & Orazem, Frank. Production Economics: Theory with Applications. LC 76-41478. (Agricultural Economics Ser.). 1978. text ed. 25.00 (ISBN 0-88244-118-3). Grid Pub.

Koopmans, Tjalling, ed. Activity Analysis of Production & Allocation. (Cowles Foundation Monograph: No. 13). 424p. 1972. Repr. of 1951 ed. 30.00x (ISBN 0-300-01539-9). Yale U Pr.

Tokel, F. Essays on the Asiatic Mode of Production. 1981. 40.00x (ISBN 0-686-73052-6, Pub. by Collet's). State Mutual Bk.

LINEAR A INSCRIPTIONS

see Inscriptions, Linear A

LINEAR ACCELERATORS

Radiological Safety Aspects of the Operation of Electron Linear Accelerators. (Technical Reports Ser.: No. 188). 1979. pap. 44.75 (ISBN 92-0-125179-3, IDC188, IAEA). Unipub.

LINEAR ALGEBRAS

see Algebras, Linear

LINEAR B INSCRIPTIONS

see Inscriptions, Linear B

LINEAR COMPLEXES

see Complexes

LINEAR DIFFERENTIAL EQUATIONS

see Differential Equations, Linear

LINEAR DIGITAL FILTERS (MATHEMATICS)

see Digital Filters (Mathematics)

LINEAR ELLIPTIC DIFFERENTIAL EQUATIONS

see Differential Equations, Elliptic

LINEAR FREE ENERGY RELATIONSHIP

Chapman, N. B. & Shorter, J., eds. Advances in Linear Free-Energy Relationships. LC 78-161305. 448p. 1972. 45.00 (ISBN 0-306-30566-6, Plenum Pr). Plenum Pub.

Johnson, C. D. The Hammett Equation. LC 72-93140. (Chemistry Texts Ser). (Illus.). 180p. 1973. 28.95 (ISBN 0-521-20138-1). Cambridge U Pr.

LINEAR INPUT LOGIC

see Threshold Logic

LINEAR MAPS

see Linear Operators

LINEAR NORMED SPACES

see Normed Linear Spaces

LINEAR OPERATORS

Akheizer, N. I. Theory of Linear Operators in Hilbert Space, 2 vols. Everitt, N., ed. Dawson, E. R., tr. (Monographs & Studies: No. 10). 1980. Vol. I, 352p. text ed. 79.95 (ISBN 0-273-08495-X); Vol. II, 272p. text ed. 69.95 (ISBN 0-273-08496-8). Pitman Pub MA.

Beals, Richard. Topics in Operator Theory. LC 70-147095. (Chicago Lectures in Mathematics Ser). (Orig.). 1971. pap. 6.00x (ISBN 0-226-03985-4). U of Chicago Pr.

Boumans, P. W., ed. Line Coincidence Tables for Inductively Coupled Plasma Atomic Emission Spectrometry, 2 vols. (Illus.). 941p. (Fr.). 1981. 250.00 (ISBN 0-08-026269-4). Pergamon.

--Line Coincidence Tables for Inductively Coupled Plasma Atomic Emission Spectrometry, 2 vols. (Illus.). 941p. (Span.). 1981. 250.00 (ISBN 0-08-026270-8). Pergamon.

Brodskii, M. S. Triangular & Jordan Representations of Linear Operators. LC 74-162998. (Translations of Mathematical Monographs: Vol. 32). 1972. 28.80 (ISBN 0-8218-1582-2, MMONO-32). Am Math.

Coddington, Earl A. Extension Theory of Formally Normal & Symmetric Subspaces. LC 73-7870. (Memoirs: No. 134). 1973. pap. 8.40 (ISBN 0-8218-1834-1, MEMO-134). Am Math.

Cristescu, Romulus. Ordered Vector Spaces & Linear Operators. 1976. 47.50x (ISBN 0-85626-090-8, Pub by Abacus Pr). Intl Schol Bk Serv.

De Vore, R. A. The Approximation of Continuous Functions by Positive Linear Operators. LC 72-91891. (Lecture Notes in Mathematics: Vol. 293). viii, 289p. 1972. pap. 9.40 (ISBN 0-387-06038-3). Springer-Verlag.

Diestel & Uhl. Vector Measures. LC 77-9625. (Mathematical Surveys Ser.: No. 15). 1977. 30.80 (ISBN 0-8218-1515-6, SURV15). Am Math.

Dubinsky, Ed & Ramanujan, M. S. On Lambda Nuclearity. LC 72-4515. (Memoirs: No. 128). 1972. pap. 7.60 (ISBN 0-8218-1828-7, MEMO-128). Am Math.

Ernest, John. Charting the Operator Terrain. LC 76-3583. (Memoirs: No. 171). 1976. 13.60 (ISBN 0-8218-1871-6, MEMO-171). Am Math.

Faris, W. G. Self-Adjoint Operators. (Lecture Notes in Mathematics Ser.: Vol. 433). vii, 115p. 1975. pap. 10.00 (ISBN 0-387-07030-3). Springer-Verlag.

Gohberg, I. & Goldberg, S. Basic Operator Theory. 350p. 1981. 14.50 (ISBN 3-7643-3028-7). Birkhauser.

Gohberg, I. C. & Fel'dman, I. A. Convolution Equations & Projection Methods for Their Solution. LC 73-22275. (Translations of Mathematical Monographs: Vol. 41). 262p. 1974. 48.40 (ISBN 0-8218-1591-1, MMONO-41). Am Math.

Gohberg, I. C. & Krein, M. G. Introduction to the Theory of Linear Nonselfadjoint Operators. LC 67-22348. (Translations of Mathematical Monographs: Vol. 18). 1969. 31.20 (ISBN 0-8218-1568-7, MMONO-18). Am Math.

Grabiner, Sandy. Derivations & Automorphisms of Banach Algebras of Power Series. LC 74-7124. (Memoirs: No. 146). 124p. 1974. pap. 8.80 (ISBN 0-8218-1846-5, MEMO-146). Am Math.

Groetsch, C. W. Generalized Inverses of Linear Operators: Representation & Approximation. (Pure & Applied Math: Vol. 37). 1977. 24.50 (ISBN 0-8247-6615-6). Dekker.

Helmberg, Gilbert M. Introduction to Spectral Theory in Hilbert Space. (Applied Mathematics & Mechanics Ser: Vol. 6). 1969. 39.00 (ISBN 0-444-10211-6, North-Holland). Elsevier.

Hofmann, K. H., ed. Lectures on Operator Algebras: Tulane University Ring & Operator Theory Year, 1970-71, Vol. 2. (Lecture Notes in Mathematics: Vol. 247). 786p. 1972. pap. 15.40 (ISBN 0-387-05729-3). Springer-Verlag.

Istratescu, V. Introduction to Linear Operator Theory. (Pure & Applied Mathematics Ser.: Vol. 65). 1981. 32.50 (ISBN 0-686-73818-7). Dekker.

Kaashoek, M. A. & West, T. Locally Compact Semi-Algebras. (Mathematics Studies Ser.: Vol. 9). 102p. 1974. pap. text ed. 17.00 (ISBN 0-444-10609-X, North-Holland). Elsevier.

Larsen, Ronald. Multiplier Problem. LC 74-97959. (Lecture Notes in Mathematics: Vol. 105). 1969. pap. 14.70 (ISBN 0-387-04624-0). Springer-Verlag.

Mayer, D. H. The Ruelle-Araki Transfer Operator in Classical Statistical Mechanics, (Lecture Notes in Physics: Vol. 123). 154p. 1980. pap. 12.00 (ISBN 0-387-09990-5). Springer-Verlag.

Newman, Isadore & Benz, Carolyn. Multiple Linear Regression: A Workbook, Syllabus, Readings; Problems & Exams. 1979. pap. text ed. 7.25 (ISBN 0-917180-07-0). I Newman.

Nikol'skii, N. K., ed. Investigations in Linear Operators & Function Theory, Pt. 1. LC 74-37620. (Seminars in Mathematics Ser.: Vol. 19). 138p. 1972. 25.00 (ISBN 0-306-18819-8, Consultants). Plenum Pub.

Pearcy, C., ed. Topics in Operator Theory. LC 74-8254. (Mathematical Surveys Ser.: No. 13). 1979. 26.80 (ISBN 0-8218-1513-X, SURV-13). Am Math.

Pietsch, A. Nuclear Locally Convex Spaces. Ruckle, U. H., tr. from Ger. LC 78-178753. (Ergebnisse der Mathematik und Ihrer Grenzgebiete: Vol. 66). 205p. 1972. 23.20 (ISBN 0-387-05644-0). Springer-Verlag.

Plesner, A. I. Spectral Theory of Linear Operators, 2 Vols. Nestell, Merlynd & Gibbs, Alan G., trs. LC 68-20524. 1969. Vol. 1. 18.00 (ISBN 0-8044-4767-5); Vol. 2. 18.00 (ISBN 0-8044-4768-3). Ungar.

Reuter, G. E. Elementary Differential Equations & Operators. (Library of Mathematics). 1971. pap. 3.00 (ISBN 0-7100-4342-2). Routledge & Kegan.

Saeks, R. Resolution Space, Operators & Systems. (Lecture Notes in Economics & Mathematical Systems: Vol. 82). 267p. 1973. pap. 12.20 (ISBN 0-387-06155-X). Springer-Verlag.

Sinclair, A. M. Automatic Continuity of Linear Operators. LC 74-31804. (London Mathematical Society Lecture Note Ser.: No. 21). 120p. 1976. 14.50x (ISBN 0-521-20830-0). Cambridge U Pr.

Smirnov, V. I., ed. Linear Operators & Operator Equations. LC 68-28092. (Problems in Mathematical Analysis Ser.: Vol. 2). 129p. 1971. 25.00 (ISBN 0-306-18702-7, Consultants). Plenum Pub.

Soule, J. L. Linear Operators in Hilbert Space. (Notes on Mathematics & Its Applications Ser). (Orig.). 1968. 18.75 (ISBN 0-677-30170-7). Gordon.

--Operateurs Lineaires Dans l'Espace d'Hilbert. (Cours & Documents de Mathematiques & de Physique Ser.). (Orig., Fr). 1967. 18.75x (ISBN 0-677-50170-6). Gordon.

Steklov Institute of Mathematics, No. 120. Selected Problems of Weighted Approximation & Spectral Analysis: Proceedings. LC 76-46375. 1976. 58.40 (ISBN 0-8218-3020-1, STEKLO-120). Am Math.

LINEAR PERSPECTIVE

see Perspective

LINEAR PROGRAMMING

see also Interindustry Economics; Recursive Programming

Althoen, Steven C. & Bumcrot, Robert J. Matrix Methods in Finite Mathematics: An Introduction with Applications to Business & Industry. new ed. 350p. 1976. text ed. 14.95x (ISBN 0-393-09192-9). Norton.

Anderson, David, et al. Linear Programming for Decision Making: An Applications Approach. LC 74-1138. 280p. 1974. text ed. 23.95 (ISBN 0-8299-0008-X); tchrs. manual avail. (ISBN 0-8299-0014-4). West Pub.

Anton, Howard & Rorres, Chris. Applications of Linear Algebra. 2nd ed. 1979. pap. text ed. 10.95 (ISBN 0-471-05337-6). Wiley.

Aronofsky, J. S., et al. Managerial Planning with Linear Programming: In Process Industry Operations. 379p. 1978. 46.50 (ISBN 0-471-03360-X, Pub. by Wiley-Interscience). Wiley.

Barsov, A. S. Que el la Programacion Lineal. 112p. (Span.). 1977. pap. 1.60 (ISBN 0-8285-1458-5, Pub. by Mir Pubs Russia). Imported Pubns.

Bazaraa, Mokhtar S. & Jarvis, John J. Linear Programming & Network Flows. LC 76-42241. 565p. 1977. text ed. 32.95 (ISBN 0-471-06015-1). Wiley.

Bazilevic, I. E., et al. Thirteen Papers on Algebra, Topology, Complex Variables, & Linear Programming. LC 51-5559. (Translations Ser.: No. 2, Vol. 71). 1968. 26.80 (ISBN 0-8218-1771-X, TRANS 2-71). Am Math.

Beneke, Raymond R. & Winterboer, Ronald D. Linear Programming Applications to Agriculture. LC 72-2298. (Illus.). 251p. 1973. text ed. 12.95 (ISBN 0-8138-1035-3). Iowa St U Pr.

Bonini, Charles P. Computer Models for Decision Analysis. (Illus.). 148p. (Orig.). 1980. pap. text ed. 12.50x (ISBN 0-89426-042-1); tchrs'. ed. 12.50x (ISBN 0-89426-043-X). Scientific Pr.

Bradley, Stephen P., et al. Applied Mathematical Programming. LC 76-10426. (Illus.). 1977. text ed. 23.95 (ISBN 0-201-00464-X). A-W.

Campbell, Hugh G. Introduction to Matrices, Vectors & Linear Programming. 2nd ed. LC 76-22757. (Illus.). 1977. text ed. 18.95 (ISBN 0-13-487439-0). P-H.

Childress, Robert L. Sets, Matrices & Linear Programmings. LC 73-17313. (Illus.). 224p. 1974. ref. ed. 12.95 (ISBN 0-13-806737-6). P-H.

Conference on Research in Income & Wealth. Input-Output Analysis: An Appraisal. LC 75-19705. (National Bureau of Economic Research Ser.). (Illus.). 1975. Repr. of 1955 ed. 21.00x (ISBN 0-405-07585-5). Arno.

Csepinszky, A. Input-Output Techniques. 1976. 27.50x (ISBN 963-05-0891-5). Intl Pubns Serv.

Dano, S. Linear Programming in Industry, Theory & Applications: An Introduction. rev. ed. LC 73-13172. (Illus.). 180p. 1974. pap. 21.20 (ISBN 0-387-81189-3). Springer-Verlag.

Dantzig, George B. Linear Programming & Extensions. (Rand Corporation Research Studies). 1963. 30.00 (ISBN 0-691-08000-3). Princeton U Pr.

Ford, Lester R., Jr. & Fulkerson, D. R. Flows in Networks. (Rand Corp. Research Studies Ser.). 1962. 14.00 (ISBN 0-691-07962-5). Princeton U Pr.

Fryer, M. J. An Introduction to Linear Programming & Matrix Game Theory. LC 77-13371. 1977. pap. text ed. 10.95 (ISBN 0-470-99327-8). Halsted Pr.

Gal, Tomas. Postoptimal Analyses, Parametric Programming, & Related Topics. 1979. text ed. 54.50 (ISBN 0-07-022679-2, C). McGraw.

Gale, David. Theory of Linear Economic Models. 1960. 27.50 (ISBN 0-07-022728-4, P&RB). McGraw.

Gass, Saul I. Illustrated Guide to Linear Programming. 1970. 19.75 (ISBN 0-07-022960-0, P&RB). McGraw.

--Linear Programming. 4th ed. (Illus.). 480p. 1975. 27.50 (ISBN 0-07-022968-6, P&RB). McGraw.

Hackworth, Robert D. & Howland, Joseph. Introductory College Mathematics: Linear Programming. LC 75-23630. 66p. 1976. pap. text ed. 2.95 (ISBN 0-7216-4423-6). HR&W.

Hadley, George. Linear Programming. (Illus.). 1962. 18.95 (ISBN 0-201-02660-0). A-W.

Heady, Earl O. & Candler, Wilfred C. Linear Programming Methods. facsimile ed. (Illus.). 1958. pap. 19.50 (ISBN 0-8138-2460-5). Iowa St U Pr.

Heady, Earl O., et al. Future Farm Programs: Comparative Costs & Consequences. LC 79-137095. 1972. 12.95x (ISBN 0-8138-0675-5). Iowa St U Pr.

Hu, T. C. Integer Programming & Network Flows. (Mathematics Ser). 1969. text ed. 19.95 (ISBN 0-201-03003-9). A-W.

Hughes, Ann J. & Grawoig, Dennis E. Linear Programming: An Emphasis on Decision Making. LC 72-1938. 1973. text ed. 19.95 (ISBN 0-201-03024-1). A-W.

Ignizio, James P. Linear Programming in Single & Multiple Objective Systems. (Illus.). 576p. 1982. 29.95 (ISBN 0-13-537027-2). P-H.

Jaasklainen. Linear Programming & Budgeting. 1977. pap. 9.95x (ISBN 0-442-80433-4). Van Nos Reinhold.

Kall, P. Stochastic Linear Programming. (Econometrics & Operations Research: Vol. 21). 120p. 1976. 22.40 (ISBN 0-387-07491-0). Springer-Verlag.

Koehler, G. J., et al, eds. Optimization Over Leontief Substitution Systems. LC 74-28992. 1975. 29.50 (ISBN 0-444-10956-0, North-Holland). Elsevier.

Kolman, Bernard & Beck, Robert. Elementary Linear Programming with Applications. (Computer Science & Applied Mathematics Ser.). 1980. text ed. 19.95 (ISBN 0-12-417860-X). Acad Pr.

Kwak, N. K. Mathematical Programming with Business Applications. (Illus.). 384p. 1972. text ed. 21.50 (ISBN 0-07-035717-X, C); instructor's manual 4.95 (ISBN 0-07-035718-8). McGraw.

Loomba, N. Paul. Linear Programming. 2nd ed. (Illus.). 1976. text ed. 20.95 (ISBN 0-02-371630-4). Macmillan.

Luenberger, David G. Introduction to Linear & Nonlinear Programming. LC 72-186209. 1973. text ed. 19.50 (ISBN 0-201-04347-5). A-W.

Martin, Wainwright E., Jr. Plaid for Linear Programming. 1974. pap. 5.50 (ISBN 0-256-01594-5, 15-1086-00). Learning Syst.

Meisels, Kurt. A Primer of Linear Programming. LC 62-10307. (Illus.). 1962. 7.95x (ISBN 0-8147-0297-X). NYU Pr.

Morishima, Michio. Equilibrium, Stability, & Growth: A Multi-Sectoral Analysis. 1964. 29.95x (ISBN 0-19-828145-5). Oxford U Pr.

Mueller-Merbach, H. On Round-off Errors in Linear Programming. LC 76-137141. (Lecture Notes in Operations Research & Mathematical Systems: Vol. 37). 1970. pap. 10.70 (ISBN 0-387-04960-6). Springer-Verlag.

Murtagh, Bruce A. Advanced Linear Programming. (Illus.). 232p. 1981. text ed. 39.50 (ISBN 0-07-044095-6). McGraw.

Murty, Katta G. Linear & Combinatorial Programming. LC 76-7047. 560p. 1976. 34.95 (ISBN 0-471-57370-1). Wiley.

Painter, Richard J. & Yantis, Richard C. Elementary Matrix Algebra with Applications. 2nd ed. 1977. text ed. write for info. (ISBN 0-87150-227-5, PWS 1801). Prindle.

Rothnberg, Ronald I. Linear Programming. 1979. 22.95 (ISBN 0-686-70737-0, North Holland). Elsevier.

Salkin, H. M. & Saha, J., eds. Studies in Linear Programming. LC 74-28998. (Studies in Management Science & Systems: Vol. 2). 322p. 1975. 27.00 (ISBN 0-444-10884-X, North-Holland). Elsevier.

Schlottmen, Alan M. Environmental Regulation & the Allocation of Coal: A Regional Analysis. LC 76-56841. (Special Studies). 1977. text ed. 21.95 (ISBN 0-275-24090-8). Praeger.

Schneeweiss, C. A. Inventory-Production Theory: A Linear Policy Approach. LC 77-13254. (Lecture Notes in Economics & Mathematical Systems: Vol. 151). 1977. pap. text ed. 10.70 (ISBN 0-387-08443-6). Springer-Verlag.

Schrage, Linus. Linear Programming Models: Lindo. (Illus.). 288p. (Orig.). 1981. pap. text ed. 15.50x (ISBN 0-89426-031-6); tchrs'. ed. 16.00x (ISBN 0-89426-033-2). Scientific Pr.

Simmons, Donald M. Linear Programming for Operations Research. LC 70-188129. 1972. text ed. 23.95x (ISBN 0-8162-7986-1). Holden-Day.

Sposito, Vincent A. Linear & Nonlinear Programming. (Illus.). 264p. 1975. text ed. 13.95x (ISBN 0-8138-1015-9). Iowa St U Pr.

Swanson, Leonard W. Linear Programming: Basic Theory & Applications. LC 79-10092. (Quantitative Methods for Management Ser.). (Illus.). 1979. 22.00 (ISBN 0-07-062580-8, C); instructor's manual 4.95 (ISBN 0-07-062581-6). McGraw.

Thie, Paul R. An Introduction to Linear Programming & Game Theory. LC 78-15328. 335p. 1979. text ed. 23.95 (ISBN 0-471-04248-X); tchr's. manual avail. (ISBN 0-471-04267-6). Wiley.

Thompson, Gerald E. Linear Programming: An Elementary Introduction. LC 79-89205. 1979. pap. text ed. 12.00 (ISBN 0-8191-0799-9). U Pr of Amer.

Trustrum, Kathleen. Linear Programming. (Library of Mathematics). 1971. pap. 5.00 (ISBN 0-7100-6779-8). Routledge & Kegan.

Vajda, S. Linear Programming: Algorithms & Applications. 1981. pap. 9.95x (ISBN 0-412-16430-2, Pub. by Chapman & Hall). Methuen Inc.

--Mathematics of Manpower Planning. LC 77-26104. 1978. 43.75 (ISBN 0-471-99627-0, Pub. by Wiley-Interscience). Wiley.

Vajda, Steven. Problems in Linear & Non-Linear Programming. LC 74-2565. 1974. 18.50 (ISBN 0-02-854070-0). Hafner.

Van De Panne, C. Linear Programming & Related Techniques. 1976. pap. text ed. 31.75 (ISBN 0-7204-3059-3, North-Holland). Elsevier.

--Methods for Linear & Quadratic Programming. LC 73-87371. (Studies on Mathematical & Managerial Economics: Vol. 17). 477p. 1975. 58.75 (ISBN 0-444-10589-1, North-Holland). Elsevier.

Wu, Nesa & Coppins, Richard. Linear Programming & Extensions. (Industrial Engineering & Management Science Ser.). (Illus.). 480p. 1981. 27.95 (ISBN 0-07-072117-3, C); solutions manual 8.95 (ISBN 0-07-072118-1). McGraw.

Zaremba, Joseph, ed. Mathematical Economics & Operations Research: A Guide to Information Sources. LC 73-17586. (Economics Information Guide Ser.: Vol. 10). 1978. 36.00 (ISBN 0-8103-1298-0). Gale.

Zeleny, M. Linear Multiobjective Programming. LC 73-22577. (Lecture Notes in Economics & Mathematical Systems: Vol. 95). (Illus.). x, 220p. 1974. pap. 11.20 (ISBN 0-387-06639-X). Springer-Verlag.

Zionts, Stanley. Linear & Integer Programming. (Illus.). 528p. 1974. text ed. 22.95 (ISBN 0-13-536763-8). P-H.

LINEAR SPACES

see Vector Spaces

LINEAR SYSTEM THEORY

see System Analysis

LINEAR TOPOLOGICAL SPACES

see also Distributions, Theory of (Functional Analysis); Topological Algebras

Adasch, N., et al. Topological Vector Spaces: The Theory Without Convexity Conditions. (Lecture Notes in Mathematics: Vol. 639). 1978. pap. 10.50 (ISBN 0-387-08662-5). Springer-Verlag.

Engelking, R. Dimension Theory. (North Holland Mathematics Studies: Vol. 19). 1979. 49.00 (ISBN 0-444-85176-3, North Holland). Elsevier.

Froelicher, A. & Bucher, W. Calculus in Vector Spaces Without Norm. (Lecture Notes in Mathematics). (Orig.). 1966. pap. 10.70 (ISBN 0-387-03612-1). Springer-Verlag.

Graves, William H. Conference on Integration, Topology and Geometry in Linear Spaces: Proceedings, Vol. 2. LC 80-25417. (Contemporary Mathematics Ser.). 1980. 16.00 (ISBN 0-8218-5002-4, CONM-2). Am Math.

Hirsch, Morris W. & Mazur, Barry. Smoothings of Piecewise Linear Manifolds. LC 74-2967. (Annals of Mathematics Studies: No. 80). 165p. 1974. 11.00x (ISBN 0-691-08145-X). Princeton U Pr.

Hudson, J. F. Piecewise Linear Topology. (Math Lecture Notes Ser.: No. 33). 1969. pap. 9.50 (ISBN 0-8053-4551-5, Adv Bk Prog). Benjamin-Cummings.

Husain, T. & Khaleelulla, S. M. Barrelledness in Topological & Ordered Vector Spaces. (Lecture Notes in Mathematics: Vol. 692). 1979. pap. 16.50 (ISBN 0-387-09096-7). Springer-Verlag.

Husain, Taqdir. The Open Mapping & Closed Graph Theorems in Topological Vector Spaces. LC 76-10334. 118p. 1976. Repr. of 1965 ed. 6.95 (ISBN 0-88275-412-2). Krieger.

Kelly, J. & Namioka, I. Linear Topological Spaces. LC 75-41498. (Graduate Texts in Mathematics: Vol. 36). 270p. 1976. 19.70 (ISBN 0-387-90169-8). Springer-Verlag.

Koethe, G. Topological Vector Space Two. LC 78-84831. (Grundlehren der Mathematischen Wissenschaften: Vol. 237). 1979. 41.80 (ISBN 0-387-90400-X). Springer-Verlag.

--Topological Vector Spaces One. Garling, D. J. H., tr. (Grundlehren der Mathematischen Wissenshaften: Vol. 159). 1969. 43.50 (ISBN 0-387-04509-0). Springer-Verlag.

Larsen, Ronald. Multiplier Problem. LC 74-97959. (Lecture Notes in Mathematics: Vol. 105). 1969. pap. 14.70 (ISBN 0-387-04624-0). Springer-Verlag.

Marti, J. T. Introduction to the Theory of Bases. LC 73-83680. (Springer Tracts in Natural Philosophy: Vol. 18). 1969. 20.90 (ISBN 0-387-04716-6). Springer-Verlag.

Nachbin, L. Topology in Spaces of Holomorphic Mappings. LC 68-29710. (Ergebnisse der Mathematik, und Ihrer Grenzgebiete: Vol. 47). 1969. 15.40 (ISBN 0-387-04470-1). Springer-Verlag.

Nachbin, Leopoldo. Elements of Approximation Theory. LC 76-48. 132p. 1976. Repr. of 1967 ed. 9.50 (ISBN 0-88275-388-6). Krieger.

Namioka, Isaac. Partially Ordered Linear Topological Spaces. LC 52-42389. (Memoirs: No. 24). 1974. pap. 9.60 (ISBN 0-8218-1224-6, MEMO-24). Am Math.

Noverraz, Ph. Pseudo-Convexite, Convexite Polynomiale et Domaines D'holomorphie En Dimension Infinie. (Mathematics Studies: Vol. 3). 1975. pap. 19.50 (ISBN 0-444-10692-8, North-Holland). Elsevier.

Parthasarathy, T. Selection Theorems & Their Applications. LC 72-78192. (Lecture Notes in Mathematics: Vol. 263). 108p. 1972. pap. 6.30 (ISBN 0-387-05818-4). Springer-Verlag.

Pietsch, A. Nuclear Locally Convex Spaces. Ruckle, U. H., tr. from Ger. LC 78-178753. (Ergebnisse der Mathematik und Ihrer Grenzgebiete: Vol. 66). 205p. 1972. 23.20 (ISBN 0-387-05644-0). Springer-Verlag.

Robertson, A. P. & Robertson, Wendy. Topologial Vector Spaces. 2nd ed. LC 72-89805. (Cambridge Tracts in Mathematics Ser: No. 53). 1980. pap. 10.95 (ISBN 0-521-29882-2). Cambridge U Pr.

Schaefer, H. H. Branach Lattices & Positive Operators. (Die Grundlehren der Mathematischen Wissenschaften Ser.: Vol. 215). xi, 376p. 1975. 51.00 (ISBN 0-387-06936-4). Springer-Verlag.

--Topological Vector Spaces. LC 65-24692. (Graduate Texts in Mathematics: Vol. 3). 1971. text ed. 24.00 (ISBN 0-387-90026-8); pap. text ed. 10.00 (ISBN 0-387-05380-8). Springer-Verlag.

Summer School on Topological Vector Spaces. Proceedings. Waelbroeck, L., ed. LC 73-83244. (Lecture Notes in Mathematics: Vol. 331). vi, 226p. (2 contributions in French). 1973. pap. 12.20 (ISBN 0-387-06367-6). Springer-Verlag.

Treves, Francois. Topological Vector Spaces, Distributions & Kernels. 1967. 48.00 (ISBN 0-12-699450-1). Acad Pr.

Treves, Franxois. Locally Convex Spaces & Linear Partial Differential Equations. LC 67-25286. (Grundlehren der Mathematischen Wissenschaften: Vol. 146). 1967. 24.10 (ISBN 0-387-03833-7). Springer-Verlag.

Vulikh, B. Z. Introduction to the Theory of Partially Ordered Spaces. 1967. 76.00x (ISBN 0-677-61330-X). Gordon.

Waelbroeck, L. Topological Vector Spaces & Algebras. (Lecture Notes in Mathematics: Vol. 230). 158p. 1971. pap. 8.20 (ISBN 0-387-05650-5). Springer-Verlag.

Wilansky, Albert. Modern Methods in Topological Vector Spaces. 1978. text ed. 34.50 (ISBN 0-07-070180-6, C). McGraw.

Wong, Yau-Chuen & Ng, Kung-Fu. Partially Ordered Topological Vector Spaces. (Oxford Mathematical Monographs Ser.). 217p. 1974. 54.00x (ISBN 0-19-853523-6). Oxford U Pr.

LINEAR VECTOR SPACES

see Vector Spaces

LINEN

All Sorts of Good Sufficient Cloth. LC 79-92225. (Illus.). 1979. 7.95 (ISBN 0-686-28439-9). Merrimack Vall Textile.

Gallagher, Constance. Linen Heirlooms. (Illus.). 210p. 1969. 13.95 (ISBN 0-8231-5018-6). Branford.

Warden, A. J. Linen Trade: Ancient & Modern. 745p. 1967. Repr. of 1864 ed. 30.00x (ISBN 0-7146-1114-X, F Cass Co). Biblio Dist.

LINERS

see Ocean Liners

LINGALA LANGUAGE

see Bangala Language

LINGARD, JOHN, 1771-1851

Shea, Donald F. English Ranke: John Lingard. 1970. text ed. 4.50x (ISBN 0-391-00630-4). Humanities.

LINGERIE

see also Underwear

Caldwell, Doreen. And All Was Revealed. (Illus.). 144p. 1981. 8.95 (ISBN 0-312-03613-2). St Martin.

Ewing, Elizabeth. Dress & Undress: A History of Women's Underwear. LC 78-16819. (Illus.). 1978. text ed. 12.95x (ISBN 0-89676-000-6). Drama Bk.

Gray, Mitchell & Kennedy, Mary. The Lingerie Book. (Illus.). 96p. 1980. 19.95 (ISBN 0-312-48701-0). St Martin.

Reger, Janet & Clarke, Brian. Chastity in Focus. (Illus.). 128p. 1981. 30.00 (ISBN 0-7043-2151-3, Pub. by Quartet England). Charles River Bks.

Rothacher, Nanette. The Undies Book. LC 75-41522. (Gladstone Bks.). (Illus.). 144p. 1976. 7.95 (ISBN 0-684-14605-3, ScribT). Scribner.

LINGUA FRANCA

see Languages, Mixed

LINGUISTIC ANALYSIS

see Analysis (Philosophy)

LINGUISTIC CHANGE

Anderson, James M. Structural Aspects of Language Change. (Linguistics Library Ser.). (Illus.). 1973. text ed. 14.95x (ISBN 0-582-55032-7); pap. text ed. 10.95x (ISBN 0-582-55033-5). Longman.

Baron, N. S. Language Acquisition & Historical Change. (North-Holland Linguistic Ser: Vol. 36). 1978. 36.75 (ISBN 0-444-85077-5, North-Holland). Elsevier.

Blount, Ben G. & Sanches, Mary, eds. Sociocultural Dimensions of Language Change. 1977. 39.50 (ISBN 0-12-107450-1). Acad Pr.

Bright, William. Variation & Change in Language: Essays by William Bright. Dil, A. S., ed. LC 76-23370. (Language Science & National Development Ser.). 304p. 1976. 10.95x (ISBN 0-8047-0926-2). Stanford U Pr.

Goodenough, Ward H. A Similarity in Cultural & Linguistic Change. (PDR Press Publication in Linguistic Change Ser.: No. 1). 1975. pap. text ed. 1.00x (ISBN 90-316-0052-0). Humanities.

Haas, Mary R. Prehistory of Languages. LC 76-75689. (Janua Linguarum, Ser. Minor: No. 57). 1978. pap. text ed. 14.50 (ISBN 90-279-0681-5). Mouton.

Lehmann, Winfred P. & Malkiel, Yakov, eds. Directions for Historical Linguistics: A Symposium. 213p. 1968. 12.00x (ISBN 0-292-78355-8). U of Tex Pr.

Liles, Bruce L. Linguistics & the English Language: A Transformational Approach. LC 71-187700. 320p. 1972. pap. text ed. 11.50 (ISBN 0-87620-529-5). Goodyear.

Myers, Sarah K. Language Shift Among Migrants to Lima, Peru. LC 73-78730. (Department of Geography Research Paper Ser.: No. 147). (Illus.). 203p. 1973. pap. 8.00 (ISBN 0-89065-054-3). U Chicago Dept Geog.

Samuels, M. L. Linguistic Evolution with Special Reference to English. LC 72-176255. (Cambridge Studies in Linguistics: No. 5). (Illus.). 256p. 1973. 32.50 (ISBN 0-521-08385-0); pap. 9.95x (ISBN 0-521-09913-7). Cambridge U Pr.

Stockwell, Robert P. & Macaulay, Ronald K., eds. Linguistic Change & Generative Theory. LC 70-180483. (History & Theory of Linguistics Ser). 320p. 1972. 12.50x (ISBN 0-253-33440-3). Ind U Pr.

Sturtevant, Edgar. Linguistic Change. LC 63-9732. 1961. pap. 2.45 (ISBN 0-226-77915-7, P60, Phoen). U of Chicago Pr.

Williams, E. B. From Latin to Portuguese. 69.95 (ISBN 0-8490-0204-4). Gordon Pr.

LINGUISTIC GEOGRAPHY

Allen, Harold B. Linguistic Atlas of the Upper Midwest, Vol. 1. LC 72-96716. (Illus.). 448p. 1973. 25.00x (ISBN 0-8166-0686-2). U of Minn Pr.

Gerbing, L. Die Flurnamen des Herzogtums Gotha und Die Forstnamen des Thurigerwaldes. (Ger.). 1910. pap. text ed. 26.00x (ISBN 90-6041-024-6). Humanities.

Iordan, Iorgu. Introduction to Romance Linguistics, Its Schools & Scholars. Orr, John, ed. Repr. of 1937 ed. lib. bdg. 18.50x (ISBN 0-8371-4244-X, IORL). Greenwood.

Masica, Colin P. Defining a Linquistic Area: South Asia. LC 74-16677. 256p. 1976. lib. bdg. 16.00x (ISBN 0-226-50944-3). U of Chicago Pr.

Navarro Tomas, Tomas. El Espanol En Puerto Rico: Contribucion Ala Geografia Linguistica De Hispanoamerica. 3rd ed. 6.25 (ISBN 0-8477-0516-1); pap. 5.00 (ISBN 0-8477-0517-X). U of PR Pr.

Taylor, Isaac. Words & Places: Or, Etymological Illustrations of History, Ethnology & Geography. 1977. Repr. of 1888 ed. lib. bdg. 30.00 (ISBN 0-8492-2607-4). R West.

Wakelin, Martyn F. Language & History in Cornwall. (Illus.). 1975. text ed. 20.00x (ISBN 0-7185-1124-7, Leicester). Humanities.

LINGUISTIC RESEARCH

see also Speech–Research

Aarsleff, Hans. Study of Language in England, Seventeen Eighty to Eighteen Sixty. LC 78-13573. 1979. Repr. of 1967 ed. lib. bdg. 19.75x (ISBN 0-313-21046-2, AASL). Greenwood.

Aman, Reinhold, ed. Maledicta 1979. LC 77-649633. (Maledicta: International Journal of Verbal Aggression Ser.: Vol. 3, Nos. 1-2). (Illus.). 320p. (Orig.). 1980. pap. 20.00 (ISBN 0-916500-54-3). Maledicta.

Association For Supervision And Curriculum Development. Interpreting Language Arts Research for the Teacher. LC 78-161581. 1971. pap. 4.00 (ISBN 0-87120-034-1, 611-17846). Assn Supervision.

Brame, Michael. Essays on Binding & Fusion. (Linguistics Research Monograph: Vol. 4). 1982. text ed. 32.00x (ISBN 0-932998-04-6). Noit Amrofer.

Charbonneau, Rene. Etude Sur les Voyelles Nasales Du Francais Canadien. (Langue & Litterature Francaises Au Canada Ser.: No. 7). (Illus.). 408p. (Fr.). 1971. pap. 13.50x (ISBN 2-7637-6427-4, Pub. by Laval). Intl Schol Bk Serv.

Child, Clarence G. Palatal Diphthongization of Stem Vowels in the Old English Dialects. LC 73-12892. 1903. lib. bdg. 25.00 (ISBN 0-8414-3392-5). Folcroft.

Chomsky, Noam. Current Issues in Linguistic Theory. (Janua Linguarum, Ser. Minor: No. 38). (Orig.). 1964. pap. text ed. 13.75x (ISBN 90-2790-700-5). Mouton.

Fant, Gunnar. Speech Sounds & Features. (Current Studies in Linguistics Ser: No. 4). 224p. 1974. 17.50x (ISBN 0-262-06051-5). MIT Pr.

Herdan, G. Advanced Theory of Language As Choice & Chance. (Communication & Cybernetics Ser.: Vol. 4). (Illus.). 1966. 40.70 (ISBN 0-387-03584-2). Springer-Verlag.

Hockett, Charles F. State of the Art. (Janua Linguarum, Ser. Minor: No. 73). 1968. pap. text ed. 18.75x (ISBN 90-2793-396-0). Mouton.

Hymes, Dell. Pidginization & Creolization of Languages: Proceedings. LC 77-123672. 1971. pap. 14.95x (ISBN 0-521-09888-2). Cambridge U Pr.

Ivic, H. Trends in Linguistics. Heppel, Muriel, tr. (Janua Linguarum, Ser. Minor: No. 42). (Orig.). 1965. pap. text ed. 27.50x (ISBN 0-686-22473-6). Mouton.

Juliard, Pierre. Philosophies of Language in 18th Century France. LC 77-111622. (Janua Linguarum Ser: No. 18). (Orig.). 1970. pap. text ed. 16.25x (ISBN 0-686-22419-1). Mouton.

Kavanagh, James F. & Strange, Winifred, eds. Speech & Language in the Laboratory, School & Clinic. 1978. 29.95x (ISBN 0-262-11065-2). MIT Pr.

Krashen, Stephen D., et al, eds. Child-Adult Differences in Second Language Acquisition. (Issues in Second Language Research Ser.). 336p. 1982. pap. text ed. 16.95 (ISBN 0-88377-206-X). Newbury Hse.

Lass, Norman J., ed. Speech & Language: Advances in Basic Research & Practice, Vol. 4. 1980. 35.00 (ISBN 0-12-608604-4). Acad Pr.

Lieberman, Philip. On the Origin of Languages: An Introduction to the Evolution of Human Language. 1975. pap. 11.95 (ISBN 0-02-370690-2). Macmillan.

Milivojevic, Dragan D. Current Russian Phonemic Theory 1952-1962. LC 75-108142. (Janua Linguarum, Ser. Minor: No. 78). (Orig.). 1970. pap. text ed. 11.75x (ISBN 0-686-22412-4). Mouton.

Miller, Robert L. Linguistic Relativity Principle & Humboldtian Ethnolinguistics. LC 68-13340. (Janua Linguarum Ser). 1968. pap. text ed. 20.75x (ISBN 90-2790-595-9). Mouton.

Moore, Timothy E., ed. Cognitive Development & the Acquisition of Language. 1973. 29.00 (ISBN 0-12-505850-0). Acad Pr.

Prucha, Jan. Soviet Psycholinguistics. (Janua Linguarum, Ser. Minor: No. 143). 117p. (Orig.). 1972. pap. text ed. 20.75x (ISBN 90-2792-317-5). Mouton.

Quirk, Randolph & Svartik, Jan. Investigating Linguistic Acceptability. (Janua Linguarum, Ser. Minor: No. 54). (Orig.). 1966. pap. text ed. 20.00x (ISBN 90-2790-585-1). Mouton.

Rauch, Irmengard & Scott, Charles T., eds. Approaches in Linguistic Methodology. 168p. 1967. 17.50x (ISBN 0-299-04240-5). U of Wis Pr.

Robins, Robert H. Ancient & Mediaeval Grammatical Theory in Europe. LC 71-113296. (Classics Ser). 1971. Repr. of 1951 ed. 10.50 (ISBN 0-8046-1202-1). Kennikat.

Saltarelli, Mario & Wanner, Dieter, eds. Diachronic Studies in Romance Linguistics. (Janua Linguarum, Series Practica: No. 207). 1975. pap. text ed. 52.50x (ISBN 90-2793-473-8). Mouton.

Samarin, William J. Field Linguistics: A Guide to Linguistic Field Work. LC 67-11823. (Illus.). 1967. 29.50x (ISBN 0-8290-0387-8); pap. text ed. 16.95x (ISBN 0-89197-758-9). Irvington.

Scarcella, Robin C. & Krashen, Stephen D., eds. Research in Second Language Acquisition: Selected Papers of the Los Angeles Second Language Acquisition Research Forum. (Issues in Second Language Research Ser.). 1981. pap. 15.95 (ISBN 0-88377-143-8). Newbury Hse.

Sedelow, Walter A., Jr. & Sedelow, Sally Y., eds. Computers in Language Research. (Trends in Linguistic Ser.). 1979. pap. text ed. 40.00x (ISBN 90-279-7846-8). Mouton.

Singh, Sadanand, ed. Measurement Proceedures in Speech, Hearing & Language. (Illus.). 300p. 1976. 22.50 (ISBN 0-8391-0753-6). Univ Park.

Smith, Frank & Miller, George, eds. Genesis of Language: A Psycholinguistic Approach. 1966. pap. 4.95 (ISBN 0-262-69022-5). MIT Pr.

Smith, Raoul N. Probabilistic Performance Models of Language. 1973. pap. text ed. 15.00x (ISBN 90-2792-414-7). Mouton.

Strawson, P. F. Logico-Linguistic Papers. 1974. pap. 11.95x (ISBN 0-416-70300-3). Methuen Inc.

Vachek, Josef, ed. Travaux Linguistiques De Prague, 4 vols. LC 66-63492. (Illus.). 280p. 1961-72. Vol. 1. 20.00x (ISBN 0-8173-0001-5); Vol. 2. 20.00x (ISBN 0-8173-0002-3); Vol. 3. 20.00x (ISBN 0-8173-0003-1); Vol. 4. 20.00x (ISBN 0-8173-0004-X). U of Ala Pr.

Von Raffler-Engel, Walburga & Hutcheson, Robert H. Language Intervention Programs in the United States, 1960-1974: Theoretical Issues, Experimental Research & Practical Application. 92p. (Orig.). 1975. pap. text ed. 12.00x (ISBN 90-232-1284-3). Humanities.

Whitney, William D. Selected Writings of William Dwight Whitney. Silverstein, Michael, ed. 1971. 20.00x (ISBN 0-262-19087-7). MIT Pr.

Wurm, S. A. Linguistic Fieldwork Methods in Australia. (AIAS Manuals: No. 3). 1967. pap. text ed. 2.50x (ISBN 0-85575-102-9). Humanities.

LINGUISTIC TABOO

see Taboo, Linguistic

LINGUISTICS

Here are entered works dealing with the scientific study of human speech, including phonetics, phonemics, morphology, and syntax. Works dealing with language in general, the origin and history of language and surveys of languages, are entered under the heading Language and Languages.

see also Grammar, Comparative and General; Historical Linguistics; Mathematical Linguistics; Phonetics; Sociolinguistics; Structural Linguistics; Tagmemes; Typology (Linguistics)

Adelung, J. Mithridates, oder allgemeine Sprachenkunde, 6 vols. (Linguistics 13th-18th Centuries Ser.). (Fr.). 1974. Repr. of 1806 ed. Set. lib. bdg. 815.50x, order nos. 71-5019 to 71-5024 (ISBN 0-8287-0006-0). Clearwater Pub.

Akhmanova, Olga. Linguostylistics: Theory & Method. (Janua Linguarum, Ser. Minor: No. 181). 1976. pap. text ed. 22.35x (ISBN 9-0279-3175-5). Mouton.

Alatis, James E. & Tucker, Richard, eds. Georgetown University Round Table on Languages & Linguistics: Language in Public Life. LC 58-31607. (Georgetown Univ. Round Table Ser.). 310p. 1980. pap. 6.95 (ISBN 0-87840-114-8). Georgetown U Pr.

Alexander, Christopher. The Timeless Way of Building. 1979. 27.50 (ISBN 0-19-502402-8). Oxford U Pr.

Allen, J. P. B. & Davies, Alan. The Edinburgh Course in Applied Linguistics: Testing and Experimental Methods. (Language and Language Learning Series: Vol. 4). 256p. 1977. 17.75x (ISBN 0-19-437125-5); pap. 13.25x (ISBN 0-19-437060-7). Oxford U Pr.

Allen, Trevor R. Vocabulario Resigaro. (Documentos De Trabajo: No. 16). 151p. (Orig.). 1979. pap. 4.00 (ISBN 0-88312-673-7); microfiche 1.60 (ISBN 0-88312-371-1). Summer Inst Ling.

Allighieri, Dante. De Vulgari Eloquentia, Sive Idiomate. (Linguistics 13th-18th Centuries Ser.). 212p. (Fr.). 1974. Repr. of 1878 ed. lib. bdg. 60.00x (ISBN 0-8287-0248-9, 5002). Clearwater Pub.

Althaus, Hans. Lexikon der Grammatischen Linguistik. (Ger.). 1973. 85.00 (ISBN 3-484-10186-5, M-7256). French & Eur.

Aman, Reinhold, ed. Ernest Borneman Festschrift. LC 77-649633. (Maledicta: the International Journal of Verbal Aggression: Vol. III, No. 1). (Illus.). 1979. pap. 10.00 (ISBN 0-916500-53-5). Maledicta.

--Maledicta 1978. LC 77-649633. (Maledicta: International Journal of Verbal Aggression Ser.: Vol. 2, No. 1-2). (Illus.). 1979. pap. 20.00 (ISBN 0-916500-52-7). Maledicta.

Ammon, Ulrich, ed. Dialect & Standard in Highly Industrialized Societies. (International Journal of the Sociology of Language: No. 21). 1979. text ed. 21.25x (ISBN 90-279-7858-1). Mouton.

Amos, Ashley C. Linguistic Means of Determining the Dates of Old English Literary Texts. 1980. 20.00 (ISBN 0-910956-70-7). Medieval Acad.

Anderson, John M., et al, eds. Historical Linguistics, 2 vols. 1974. (North-Holland); Set. pap. 53.75 (ISBN 0-444-10675-8). Elsevier.

Anttila. Analogy. (Trends in Linguistics: No. 10). 1977. 25.30 (ISBN 9-0279-7975-8). Mouton.

Apresjan, Ju. D. Principles & Methods of Contemporary Structural Linguistics. Crockett, Dina B., tr. from Dutch. LC 72-94441. (Janua Linguarum, Ser. Minor: No. 144). (Illus.). 349p. (Orig.). 1973. pap. text ed. 38.25x (ISBN 90-2792-386-8). Mouton.

Arlotto, Anthony. Introduction to Historical Linguistics. LC 80-6309. 284p. 1981. lib. bdg. 19.75 (ISBN 0-8191-1459-6); pap. text ed. 10.25 (ISBN 0-8191-1460-X). U Pr of Amer.

Aronoff, Mark. Word Formation in Generative Grammar. (Linguistic Inquiry Monographs). 134p. 1976. pap. text ed. 12.00x (ISBN 0-262-51017-0). MIT Pr.

Aschmann, Herman & Aschmann, Bessie. Diccionario Totonaco De Papantla. (Vocabularios Indigenas Ser.: No. 16). 1973. pap. 5.00 (ISBN 0-88312-750-4); microfiche 2.20 (ISBN 0-88312-585-4). Summer Inst Ling.

Ashby, William J. Clitic Inflection in French: An Historical Perspective. 1977. pap. text ed. 14.25x (ISBN 90-6203-469-1). Humanities.

Austerlitz, Roberg, ed. The Scope of American Linguistics. 1977. text ed. 10.25x (ISBN 90-316-0003-2). Humanities.

Austing, John F. & Austing, June. Semantics of Omie Discourse. (Language Data-Asia Pacific Ser.: No. 11). (Orig.). 1977. pap. text ed. 3.50x (ISBN 0-88312-211-1); microfiche 1.00 (ISBN 0-88312-311-8). Summer Inst Ling.

Bach, Kent & Harnish, Robert M. Linguistic Communication & Speech Acts. (Illus.). 1979. text ed. 19.95x (ISBN 0-262-02136-6). MIT Pr.

Baer, Phil & Merrifield, William R. Two Studies on the Lacandones of Mexico. (Publications in Linguistics & Related Fields Ser.: No. 33). 274p. 1971. pap. 4.00x (ISBN 0-88312-035-6); microfiche 1.60 (ISBN 0-88312-435-1). Summer Inst Ling.

Bailey, Charles-James N. Variation & Linguistic Theory. LC 73-84648. 1973. pap. 9.25x (ISBN 0-87281-032-1). Ctr Appl Ling.

Baldi, Philip & Werth, Ronald N., eds. Readings in Historical Phonology: Chapters in the Theory of Sound Change. LC 77-13895. 1978. lib. bdg. 16.50x (ISBN 0-271-00525-4); pap. text ed. 10.00x (ISBN 0-271-00539-4). Pa St U Pr.

Barcia, J., et al. Lengua y Cultura. LC 72-90216. 1973. 18.95 (ISBN 0-03-083624-7, HoltC). HR&W.

Bar-Hillel, Yehoshua. Aspects of Language: Essays & Lectures on Philosophy of Language, Linguistic Philosophy & Methodology of Linguistics. 1970. text ed. 30.00x (ISBN 0-7204-6033-6, Pub. by North Holland). Humanities.

Bartsch, R. & Vennemann, T. Linguistics & Neighboring Disciplines, Vol. 4. LC 74-24347. (North-Holland Linguistics Ser.). 250p. 1975. 29.50 (ISBN 0-444-10891-2, North-Holland); pap. 19.95 (ISBN 0-444-10786-X). Elsevier.

Bateman, Barbara D. Interpretation of the Nineteen Sixty-One Illinois Test of Psycholinguistic Abilities. LC 68-57926. (Orig.). 1968. pap. 5.00x (ISBN 0-87562-012-4). Spec Child.

Baur, Rupprecht S., et al. Resumierende Auswahlbibliographie Zur Neuren Sowjetischen Sprachlehrforschung (Gesteuerter Fremdsprachenerwerb, Vol. 3. (Linguistic & Lterary Studies in Eastern Europe). 318p. 1980. 39.00 (ISBN 90-272-1504-9). Benjamins North Am.

Bennett, J. Linguistic Behavior. LC 75-44575. 260p. 1976. 31.95 (ISBN 0-521-21168-9). Cambridge U Pr.

--Linguistic Behaviour. LC 75-44575. 1979. pap. 11.50x (ISBN 0-521-29751-6). Cambridge U Pr.

Bennett, W. A. Aspects of Language & Language Teaching. (Illus., Orig.). 1968. pap. 6.95x (ISBN 0-521-09512-3, 512). Cambridge U Pr.

Benveniste, Emile. Indo-European Language & Society. Palmer, Elizabeth, tr. from Fr. LC 73-77119. (Miami Linguistics Ser: No. 12). (Illus.). 579p. 1973. 29.50x (ISBN 0-87024-250-4). U of Miami Pr.

Berlin, Brent. Tzeltal Numerical Classifiers: A Study in Ethnographic Semantics. (Janua Linguarum, Ser. Practica: No. 70). (Orig.). 1968. pap. text ed. 52.50x (ISBN 0-686-22422-1). Mouton.

Berry, Margaret. Introduction to Systemic Linguistics, Vol. 1. LC 74-83966. 224p. 1975. 17.95 (ISBN 0-312-43365-4). St Martin.

--Introduction to Systemic Linguistics: Levels & Links, Vol. 2. LC 74-83966. 1977. text ed. 16.95 (ISBN 0-312-43400-6). St Martin.

Bezauzee, N. Grammaire Generale, 2 vols. (Linguistics 13th-18th Centuries Ser.). (Fr.). 1974. Repr. of 1767 ed. Set. lib. bdg. 323.00x (ISBN 0-8287-0087-7). Vol. 1 (71-5025). Vol. 2 (71-5026). Clearwater Pub.

Bibliander. De Ratione Omnium Linguarum et Litterarum Commentarius. (Linguistics 13th-18th Centuries Ser.). 235p. (Fr.). 1974. Repr. of 1548 ed. lib. bdg. 65.00x (ISBN 0-8287-0089-3, 71-5004). Clearwater Pub.

Bickerton, Derek, et al. The Genesis of Language: The First Michigan Colloquium, 1979. Hill, Kenneth C., ed. 159p. 1979. 15.50 (ISBN 0-89720-024-1); pap. 12.50 (ISBN 0-89720-025-X). Karoma.

Bierwisch, Manfred. Modern Linguistics, Its Development Methods & Problems. (Janua Linguarum, Ser. Minor: No. 110). 103p. 1971. pap. text ed. 15.30x (ISBN 90-2791-657-8). Mouton.

Bierwisch, Manfred & Heidolph, Karl E., eds. Progress in Linguistics: A Collection of Papers. LC 78-123127. (Janua Linguarum Ser.: No. 43). 1970. text ed. 48.25x (ISBN 90-2790-723-4). Mouton.

Binh, Duong T. Tagmemic Comparison of the Structure of English & Vietnamese Sentences. LC 74-123126. (Janua Linguarum, Ser. Practica: No. 110). (Orig.). 1971. pap. text ed. 51.75x (ISBN 90-2791-598-9). Mouton.

Birnbaum, Henrik, et al, eds. Studia Linguistica Alexandro Vasilii Filio Issatschenko a Collegis Amicisque Oblata. 1978. pap. text ed. 70.50x (ISBN 0-685-59424-6). Humanities.

Bloomfield, Leonard. A Leonard Bloomfield Anthology. Hockett, Charles F., ed. LC 78-98981. (History & Theory of Linguistics Ser). 592p. 1970. 24.95x (ISBN 0-253-33327-X). Ind U Pr.

Bloomfield, Morton W. & Newmark, Leonard. Linguistic Introduction to the History of English. LC 79-4563. (Illus.). 1979. Repr. of 1963 ed. lib. bdg. 25.50x (ISBN 0-313-20936-7, BLLI). Greenwood.

Bolinger, Dwight. Degree Words. (Janua Linguarum, Ser. Major: No. 53). 1972. text ed. 51.75x (ISBN 0-686-22528-7). Mouton.

Bolinger, Dwight & Sears, Donald A. Aspects of Language. 3rd ed. 352p. 1981. pap. text ed. 9.95 (ISBN 0-15-503872-9). HarBraceJ.

Bougeant, R. P. Amusement Philosophique sur le Langage des Betes. (Linguistics 13th-18th Centuries Ser). 160p. (Fr.). 1974. Repr. of 1739 ed. lib. bdg. 48.50 (ISBN 0-8287-0124-5, 71-5027). Clearwater Pub.

Brame, Michael K. Base Generated Syntax. LC 78-70404. (Linguistics Research Monograph Ser.). 1978. text ed. 26.00x (ISBN 0-932998-00-3). Noit Amrofer.

--Essays Toward Realistic Syntax. new ed. LC 79-67347. (Linguistics Research Monograph: Vol. 2). 1979. text ed. 32.00x (ISBN 0-932998-01-1). Noit Amrofer.

Brandreth, Gyles. Pears Book of Words. 204p. 1981. 13.95 (ISBN 0-7207-1186-X, Pub. by Michael Joseph). Merrimack Bk Serv.

Brekle, Herbert E., ed. Wortbildung Syntax & Morphologie: Festschrift Zum 60 Geburstag Von Hans Marchand Am, Oktober 1967. (Janua Linguarum, Ser. Major: No. 36). 1968. text ed. 51.75x (ISBN 90-2790-687-4). Mouton.

Brend. Advances in Tagmemics. LC 73-81526. (North Holland Linguistic Ser.: Vol. 9). 600p. 1974. 27.00 (ISBN 0-444-10534-4, North-Holland). Elsevier.

Brend, Ruth M. & Pike, Kenneth L., eds. The Summer Institute of Linguistics: Its Works & Contributions. 1977. pap. 26.75x (ISBN 90-279-3355-3). Mouton.

Brosses. Traite de la Formation Mecanique des Langues, 2 vols. (Linguistics 13th-18th Centuries Ser.). (Fr.). 1974. Repr. of 1765 ed. Set. lib. bdg. 269.50x (ISBN 0-8287-0146-6). Vol. 1 (71-5028). Vol. 2 (71-5029). Clearwater Pub.

Brown, Cecil H. Wittgensteinian Linguistics. Scheok, Thomas A., ed. LC 74-78289. (Approaches to Semiotics Ser.: No. 12). 135p. 1974. pap. text ed. 16.75x (ISBN 0-686-22582-1). Mouton.

Brown, G. Phonological Rules & Dialect Variation: A Study of the Phonology of Lumasaaba. LC 70-184904. (Studies in Linguistics: No. 7). (Illus.). 200p. 1972. 34.50 (ISBN 0-521-08485-7); pap. 10.95x (ISBN 0-521-29063-5). Cambridge U Pr.

Brown, Roger L. Wilhelm Von Humboldt's Conception of Linguistic Relativity. LC 67-30542. (Janua Linguarum, Ser. Minor: No. 65). (Orig.). 1967. pap. text ed. 20.00x (ISBN 90-2790-593-2). Mouton.

Buelow, Edeltraud & Schmitter, Peter, eds. Integrale Linguistik. (Illus.). xiv, 817p. 1979. 73.00 (ISBN 90-272-2001-8). Benajamins North Am.

Burghardt, Wolfgang & Hoelker, Klaus, eds. Text Processing. (Research in Text Theory Ser.). 466p. 1979. text ed. 92.00x (ISBN 3-11-007565-2). De Gruyter.

Bursill-Hall, G. L., ed. Grammatica Speculativa of Thomas of Erfurt. (The Classics of Linguistics Ser). 340p. 1972. text ed. 25.00x (ISBN 0-582-52495-4). Longman.

Butts, Robert E. & Hintikka, Jaakko, eds. Basic Problems in Methodology & Linguistics. (Western Ontario Ser: No. 11). 1977. lib. bdg. 53.00 (ISBN 90-277-0829-0, Pub. by Reidel Holland). Kluwer Boston.

Cachia, Pierre. Al-Arif: A Dictionary of Grammatical Terms-Arabic-English, English-Arabic. 1974. 15.00x (ISBN 0-86685-119-4). Intl Bk Ctr.

California Linguistics Association Conference, Sixth. Proceedings. Underhill, Robert, ed. LC 77-83490. 1977. 5.50x (ISBN 0-916304-38-8). Campanile.

Campbell, Lyle. Quichean Linguistic Pre-History. (Publications in Linguistics: Vol. 81). 1977. 12.50x (ISBN 0-520-09531-6). U of Cal Pr.

Campeau, Lucien. Premiere Mission D'Acadie, 1602-16. (Cahiers De Psychomecanique Du Langage). (Fr). 1967. 23.75x (ISBN 2-7637-6307-3, Pub. by Laval). Intl Schol Bk Serv.

Caninius. Institutiones...Linguae Syriacae, Assyriacae. (Linguistics 13th-18th Centuries Ser.). 93p. (Fr.). 1974. Repr. of 1554 ed. lib. bdg. 34.00x (ISBN 0-8287-0158-X, 71-5005). Clearwater Pub.

Cantrall, William R. Viewpoint, Reflexives & the Nature of Noun Phrases. LC 74-81555. (Janua Linguarum, Ser. Practica: No. 210). (Illus.). 178p. 1974. pap. text ed. 37.50x (ISBN 90-2793-102-X). Mouton.

Cassin, Elena & Glassner, Jean-Jacques. Anthroponymie et Anthropologie De Nuzi. (Les Anthroponymes Ser.: Vol. 1). 187p. (Fr.). 1977. 40.00 (ISBN 0-89003-024-3). Undena Pubns.

Castle, William E. The Effect of Selective Narrow-Band Filtering on the Perception of Certain English Vowels. (Janua Linguarum, Series Practica: No. 13). pap. 40.00x (ISBN 0-686-20926-5). Mouton.

Center for Applied Linguistics, Washington D.C. Dictionary Catalog of the Library of the Center for Applied Linguistics, Washington, D. C, 4 vols. 1974. Set. lib. bdg. 355.00 (ISBN 0-8161-1114-6). G K Hall.

Chafe, Wallace, ed. American Indian Languages & American Linguistics. 1976. pap. text ed. 9.25x (ISBN 90-316-0086-5). Humanities.

Chafe, Wallace L. Meaning & the Structure of Language. LC 79-114855. 1971. text ed. 18.00x (ISBN 0-226-10055-3). U of Chicago Pr.

Chandola, Anoop. Situation to Sentence: An Evolutionary Method for Descriptive Linguistics. LC 78-7125. 1978. 10.95 (ISBN 0-404-16038-7). AMS Pr.

Chesneau Du Marsais, C. Logique et Principes de Grammaire: Nouvelle Edition Plus Traite d'Inversion, 2 vols. (Linguistics 13th-18th Centuries Ser.). (Fr.). 1974. Repr. of 1792 ed. Set. lib. bdg. 204.00x (ISBN 0-8287-0187-3). Clearwater Pub.

--Veritables Principes de la Grammaire. (Linguistics 13th-18th Centuries Ser.). 56p. (Fr.). 1974. Repr. of 1729 ed. 18.00x (ISBN 0-8287-0188-1, 71-5042). Clearwater Pub.

Chisholm, William S., Jr. Elements of English Linguistics. (English & Humanities Ser.). 192p. (Orig.). 1981. text ed. 14.95x (ISBN 0-582-28080-X); training manual free (ISBN 0-582-28282-9). Longman.

Chiu, Rosaline K. Language Contact & Language Planning in China: 1900-1967. (Fr). 1970. pap. 7.50x (ISBN 2-7637-6456-8, Pub. by Laval). Intl Schol Bk Serv.

Chomsky, Noam. Cartesian Linguistics: A Chapter in the History of Rationalist Thought. 1966. text ed. 22.50 scp (ISBN 0-06-041275-5, HarpC). Har-Row.

--Reflections on Language. 1976. 12.95 (ISBN 0-394-49956-5); pap. 4.95 (ISBN 0-394-73123-9). Pantheon.

--Strukturen der Syntax. (Janua Linguarum, Series Minor: No. 182). 1973. pap. 15.75x (ISBN 90-2792-490-2). Mouton.

Chomsky, Noam & Miller, George A. Analyse Formelle Des Langues Naturelles. (Mathematiques et Sciences De L'homme: No. 8). 1971. pap. text ed. 13.50x (ISBN 90-2796-796-2). Mouton.

Chomsky, Noam, et al. Explorations in the Biology of Language. Walker, Edward, ed. LC 78-18352. (Higher Mental Processes Ser.). (Illus.). 256p. 1980. text ed. 22.50x (ISBN 0-262-23110-7, Pub. by Bradford). MIT Pr.

Christie, William M., Jr. Preface to a Neo-Firthian Linguistics. LC 80-21016. (Edward Sapir Monograph Series in Language, Culture, & Cognition: No. 7). viii, 70p. (Orig.). 1980. pap. 6.00x (ISBN 0-933104-11-1). Jupiter Pr.

--A Stratificational View of Linguistic Change. LC 79-115787. (Edward Sapir Monograph Ser. in Language, Culture & Cognition: No. 4). viii, 71p. (Orig.). 1977. pap. 5.00x (ISBN 0-933104-04-9). Jupiter Pr.

Chvany, Catherine V. & Brecht, Richard D., eds. Morphosyntax in Slavic. (Illus.). v, 316p. (Orig.). 1981. pap. 12.95 (ISBN 0-89357-070-2). Slavica.

Clark, Lawrence. Sayula Popoluca Texts. (Publications in Linguistics & Related Fields Ser.: No. 6). 216p. 1961. microfiche 2.20 (ISBN 0-88312-406-8). Summer Inst Ling.

Clark, Lawrence & Clark, Nancy. Vocabulario Popoluca de Sayula. (Vocabularios Indigenas Ser.: No. 4). 165p. 1960. pap. 3.00x (ISBN 0-88312-663-X); microfiche 1.60 (ISBN 0-88312-365-7). Summer Inst Ling.

Cohen, D. & Wirth, J. R., eds. Testing Linguistic Hypotheses. LC 74-14163. 227p. 1975. text ed. 12.50 (ISBN 0-470-16419-0). Halsted Pr.

Cohen, David. Etudes De Linguistique Semitique Et Arabe. (Janua Linguarum, Ser. Practica: No. 81). (Orig.). 1970. pap. text ed. 45.00x (ISBN 90-2790-732-3). Mouton.

--Explaining Linguistic Phenomena. LC 74-12463. 1974. 12.95 (ISBN 0-470-16425-5). Halsted Pr.

Cohen, David, ed. Explaining Linguistic Phenomena. LC 74-12463. 207p. 1974. 12.95 (ISBN 0-470-16425-5, Pub. by Wiley). Krieger.

Cohen, Marcel. Language: Its Structure & Evolution. Muller, Leonard R., tr. LC 78-102695. (Miami Linguistics Ser: No. 7). 1970. 9.95x (ISBN 0-87024-154-0). U of Miami Pr.

Cohen, Murray. Sensible Words: Linguistic Practice in England, 1640-1785. LC 77-1856. (Illus.). 1977. text ed. 14.00x (ISBN 0-8018-1924-5). Johns Hopkins.

Cole, Roger W., ed. Current Issues in Linguistic Theory. LC 76-26427. (Illus.). 312p. 1977. 17.50x (ISBN 0-253-31608-1); pap. 9.95x (ISBN 0-253-11262-1). Ind U Pr.

Collinge, N. E. Collectanea Linguistica: Essays in General & Genetic Linguistics. LC 76-129298. (Janua Linguarum, Ser. Minor: No. 21). (Orig.). 1971. pap. text ed. 20.25x (ISBN 0-686-22392-6). Mouton.

Collins, Harold R. The New English of the Onitsha Chapbooks. LC 78-630645. (Papers in International Studies: Africa: No. 1). 1968. pap. 3.00 (ISBN 0-89680-035-0). Ohio U Ctr Intl.

Comrie, B. Aspect. (Textbooks in Linguistics). 180p. 1976. 34.95 (ISBN 0-521-21109-3); pap. 9.95x (ISBN 0-521-29045-7). Cambridge U Pr.

Condillac, E. B. De. Principes Generaux de Grammaire pour Toutes les Langues. (Linguistics 13th-18th Centuries Ser.). 368p. (Fr.). 1974. Repr. of 1798 ed. lib. bdg. 95.00x (ISBN 0-8287-0217-9, 71-5038). Clearwater Pub.

Conference on Pragmatics, Urbino, July 8-14, 1979. Possibilities & Limitations of Pragmatics: Proceedings. Parret, H., et al, eds. (Studies in Language Companion). 1980. text ed. 77.00x (ISBN 90-272-3007-2). Humanities.

Congresso Internazionale di Linguistica e Filologia Romanza, 14th Napoli, 15-20 Aprile 1974. Atti, Vol. 3. Varvaro, Alberto, ed. 561p. 1980. pap. text ed. 69.50x (ISBN 90-272-0944-8). Humanities.

Cooper, William S. Foundations of Logico-Linguistics. (Synthese Language Library: No. 2). 1978. lib. bdg. 34.00 (ISBN 90-277-0864-9, Pub. by Reidel Holland); pap. text ed. 16.00 (ISBN 90-277-0876-2, Pub. by Reidel Holland). Kluwer Boston.

Copeland, James E. Stepmatricial Generative Phonology of German. 1970. pap. text ed. 15.50x (ISBN 0-686-22396-9). Mouton.

Coppieters, Frank & Goyvaerts, Didier, eds. Functional Studies in Language & Literature. 1978. pap. text ed. 33.50x (ISBN 0-391-01600-8). Humanities.

Cornulier, Benoit De. Meaning Detachment. (Pragmatics & Beyond Ser.: No. 7). 124p. 1981. pap. text ed. 17.25x (ISBN 90-272-2502-8, Pub. by Benjamins Holland). Humanities.

Court de Gebelin, A. Histoire Naturelle de la Parole. (Linguistics 13th-18th Centuries Ser.). 400p. (Fr.). 1974. Repr. of 1772 ed. lib. bdg. 102.00 (ISBN 0-8287-0233-0, 71-5039). Clearwater Pub.

Crane, et al. An Introduction to Linguistics. 320p. (Orig.). 1981. pap. text ed. 12.95 (ISBN 0-316-16015-6). Little.

Crawford, John C. Totontepec Mixe Phonotagmemics. (Publications in Linguistics & Related Fields Ser.: No. 8). 197p. 1963. pap. 3.00x (ISBN 0-88312-008-9); 2.20 (ISBN 0-88312-408-4). Summer Inst Ling.

Cresswell, M. J. Die Sprachen der Logik und Die Logik der Sprache. (Grundlagen der Kommunikation De Gruyter Studienbuch). 1979. 19.00x (ISBN 3-11-004923-6). De Gruyter.

Creswell, Thomas J. Usage in Dictionaries & Dictionaries of Usage. McDavid, Virginia & McMillan, James B., eds. (Publication of the American Dialect Society: Nos. 63-64). (Illus.). 1978. pap. 9.80x (ISBN 0-8173-0662-5). U of Ala Pr.

Crystal, David. Directions in Applied Linguistics. (Applied Language Studies). 1981. 25.00 (ISBN 0-12-198420-6). Acad Pr.

--Linguistics. 1972. pap. 2.95 (ISBN 0-14-021332-5, Pelican). Penguin.

Culler, Jonathan. Ferdinand De Saussure. (Modern Masters Ser.). 1977. pap. 3.95 (ISBN 0-14-004369-1). Penguin.

--Structuralist Poetics: Structuralism, Linguistics & the Study of Literature. LC 74-11608. 1975. 22.50x (ISBN 0-8014-0928-4); pap. 6.95 (ISBN 0-8014-9155-X). Cornell U Pr.

Daly, Richard T. Applications of the Mathematical Theory of Linguistics. (Janua Linguarum Ser. Minor: No. 185). 1974. pap. text ed. 20.75x (ISBN 90-2792-684-0). Mouton.

Damerau, Frederick J. Markov Models & Linguistic Theory: An Experimental Study of a Model for English. LC 78-135666. (Janua Linguarum, Ser. Minor: No. 95). (Orig.). 1971. pap. text ed. 28.75x (ISBN 90-2791-707-8). Mouton.

Davidson, D. & Harman, G., eds. Semantics of Natural Language. 2nd ed. LC 73-76427. (Synthese Library: No. 40). 769p. 1973. lib. bdg. 50.00 (ISBN 90-277-0304-3, Pub. by Reidel Holland); pap. 18.50 (ISBN 90-277-0310-8, Pub. by Reidel Holland). Kluwer Boston.

Davis, Philip W. Modern Theories of Language. (Illus.). 496p. 1973. 15.95 (ISBN 0-13-598987-6). P-H.

De Beaugrande, Robert. Text, Discourse, & Process: Toward a Multidisciplinary Science of Texts. (Advances in Discourse Processes Ser.). 1980. text ed. 29.50 (ISBN 0-89391-033-3). Ablex Pub.

De Cornulier, Benoit. Meaning Detatchment. vi, 124p. 1980. pap. 14.00 (ISBN 90-272-2502-8, P & B 7). Benjamins North Am.

De Cortraco, Sigerus. Summa Modorum Significande; Sophismata. (Studies in the History of Linguistics: No. 14). 1977. text ed. 25.50x (ISBN 0-391-01671-7). Humanities.

DeGuzman, Videa P. Syntactic Derivation of Tagalog Verbs. LC 78-11029. (Oceanic Linguistic Special Publication: No. 16). 1978. pap. text ed. 12.50x (ISBN 0-8248-0627-1). U Pr of Hawaii.

Deibler, Ellis. Semantic Relationships of Gahuku Verbs. (SIL Linguistic & Related Fields Ser.: No. 48). 1976. pap. 8.00x (ISBN 0-88312-058-5); microfiche 1.60 (ISBN 0-88312-458-0). Summer Inst Ling.

DeJoia, Alex & Stenton, Adrian. Terms in Systemic Linguistics. LC 80-5089. 1980. 17.95 (ISBN 0-312-79180-1). St Martin.

Delancey, Robert W. Linguistics & Teaching. 1965. pap. text ed. 1.50 (ISBN 0-930348-01-X). NY St Eng Coun.

Denisov, P. N. Principles of Constructing Linguistic Models. LC 72-88205. (Janua Linguarum, Ser. Minor: No. 91). 173p. (Orig.). 1973. pap. text ed. 31.25x (ISBN 90-2792-376-0). Mouton.

De Saussure, Ferdinand. Course in General Linguistics. Baskin, Wade, tr. 1966. pap. 4.95 (ISBN 0-07-016524-6, SP). McGraw.

Devoto, Giacimo. Linguistics & Literary Criticism. Edgerton, M. F., Jr., tr. 1963. 6.00x (ISBN 0-913298-08-5). S F Vanni.

Dieth, Eugen. Vademekum der Phonetik. 2nd ed. (Ger.). 1968. 30.00 (ISBN 3-7720-0292-7, M-7135). French & Eur.

Dillon, Myles. Celts & Aryans. 1977. text ed. 10.50x (ISBN 0-8426-1049-9). Verry.

Dilts, R., et al. Neuro-Linguistic Programming, Vol. 1. LC 80-50147. 1980. limited boxed ed. 24.00x (ISBN 0-916990-07-9). Meta Pubns.

Dingwall, William O. A Survey of Linguistic Science. LC 78-60709. 1976. 16.95x (ISBN 0-89223-014-2); pap. text ed. 10.00x (ISBN 0-89223-015-0). Greylock Pubs.

Dinneen, Francis P. An Introduction to General Linguistics. LC 78-1323. 452p. 1978. pap. text ed. 10.95 (ISBN 0-87840-172-5). Georgetown U Pr.

--An Introduction to General Linguistics. LC 67-10941. 1980. 34.50x (ISBN 0-8290-0375-4); pap. text ed. 18.50x (ISBN 0-8290-0376-2). Irvington.

Doerfer, Gerhard. Khalaj Materials. LC 70-630301. (Uralic & Altaic Ser: Vol. 115). (Illus., Orig.). 1971. pap. text ed. 10.00x (ISBN 0-87750-150-5). Res Ctr Lang Semiotic.

Donaldson, T. Ngiyambaa: The Language of the Wangaaybuwan. LC 79-7646. (Cambridge Studies in Linguistics: No. 29). (Illus.). 320p. 1980. 59.50 (ISBN 0-521-22524-8). Cambridge U Pr.

Dowty, David R. Word Meaning & Montague Grammar. (Synthese Language Library: No. 7). 1979. lib. bdg. 47.00 (ISBN 90-277-1008-2, Pub. by Reidel Holland); pap. 18.00 (ISBN 90-277-1009-0). Kluwer Boston.

Drake, Glendon F. The Role of Prescriptivism in American Linguistics 1820-1970. x, 130p. 1977. 19.00 (ISBN 90-272-0954-5, SIHO L 13). Benjamins North Am.

Drange, Theodore. Type Crossings: Sentential Meaninglessness in the Border Area of Linguistics & Philosophy. (Janua Linguarum, Ser. Minor: No. 44). (Orig.). 1966. pap. text ed. 30.00x (ISBN 90-2790-578-9). Mouton.

Dressler, Wolfgang U., ed. Current Trends in Textlinguistics. (Research in Text Theory: Vol. 2). 1978. 40.00x (ISBN 3-11-006518-5). De Gruyter.

Dubois, J. & Giacomo, M. Dictionnaire de linguistique. 516p. (Fr.). 1974. 27.50 (ISBN 2-03-020299-1, 1002). Larousse.

Dubois-Charlier, Francoise. Comment d'initier a la linguistique, 5 livrets in 1 vol. new ed. 319p. (Fr.). 1975. pap. 19.95 (ISBN 2-03-041307-0, 4541). Larousse.

Dunlap, Howard G. Social Aspects of a Verb Form: Native Atlanta Fifth-Grade Speech--the Present Tense of "Be". (Publications of the American Dialect Society: Nos. 61 & 62). 120p. 1978. pap. 8.50x (ISBN 0-8173-0661-7). U of Ala Pr.

D'Urfey, Thomas. Songs of Thomas D'Urfey. Day, Cyrus L., ed. (Harvard Studies in English). 1969. Repr. of 1933 ed. 19.50 (ISBN 0-384-11020-7). Johnson Repr.

Eastman, Carol M. Aspects of Language & Culture. LC 74-28741. (Publications in Anthropology Ser.). (Illus.). 168p. 1975. pap. text ed. 5.95x (ISBN 0-88316-514-7). Chandler & Sharp.

Eckman, Fred R., ed. Current Themes in Linguistics: Bilingualism, Experimental Linguistics, & Language Typologies. LC 77-5934. 1977. 19.95 (ISBN 0-470-99171-2). Halsted Pr.

Eglin, Peter. Talk & Taxonomy. x, 125p. 1980. pap. 14.00 (ISBN 90-272-2510-9, P & B 8). Benjamins North Am.

Elgin, S. What Is Linguistics? 2nd ed. 1979. pap. 9.95 (ISBN 0-13-952333-2). P-H.

Ellis, Jeffrey. Towards a General Comparative Linguistics. (Janua Linguarum, Ser. Minor: No. 52). (Orig.). 1966. pap. text ed. 26.25x (ISBN 90-2790-584-3). Mouton.

Empson, William. Structure of Complex Words. 3rd. ed. 450p. 1979. Repr. of 1951 ed. 22.50x (ISBN 0-8476-6207-1). Rowman.

Encyclopedie Thematique Weber, 14: Linguistique, Litterature Universelle. 360p. (Fr.). 59.95 (ISBN 0-686-57180-0, M-6247). French & Eur.

England, Nora C., ed. Papers in Mayan Linguistics. (Miscellaneous Publications in Anthropology No. 6; Studies in Mayan Linguistics: No. 2). v, 310p. 1978. pap. 12.00 (ISBN 0-913134-87-2). Mus Anthro Mo.

English Linguistics Fifteen Hundred to Eighteen Hundred. 1975. 2500.00 set (ISBN 0-8277-3700-9). British Bk Ctr.

Enkvist, Nils E. Linguistic Stylistics. (Janua Linguarum Ser. Critica: No. 5: No. 5). 1973. pap. text ed. 20.00x (ISBN 90-2792-382-5). Mouton.

Esper, Erwin A. Technique for the Experimental Investigation of Associative Interference in Artifical Linguistic. 1925. pap. 6.00 (ISBN 0-527-00805-2). Kraus Repr.

Espy, Willard. Have a Word on Me. 1981. 13.95 (ISBN 0-671-25255-0). S&S.

Estienne, H. Traite de la Confirmite du Francais avec le Grec. (Linguistics 13th-18th Centuries Ser.). 190p. (Fr.). 1974. Repr. of 1565 ed. lib. bdg. 55.00x (ISBN 0-8287-0320-5, 71-5006). Clearwater Pub.

Ewton, Ralph W. & Ornstein, Jacob, eds. Studies in Language & Linguistics 1972-73. LC 79-97794. viii, 252p. 1972. pap. text ed. 5.00 (ISBN 0-87404-018-3). Tex Western.

Ewton, Ralph W., Jr. & Ornstein, Jacob. Studies in Language & Linguistics, 1969-70. pap. 5.00 (ISBN 0-87404-019-1). Tex Western.

Falk, Julia S. Language & Linguistics: Bases for a Curriculum. (Language in Education Ser.: No. 10). 1978. pap. text ed. 3.25x (ISBN 0-87281-088-7). Ctr Appl Ling.

--Linguistics & Language: A Survey of Basic Concepts & Implications. 2nd ed. LC 77-22927. 1978. pap. text ed. 15.95 (ISBN 0-471-02529-1). Wiley.

Fant, G. & Scully, C., eds. The Larynx & Language. (Phonetica: Vol. 34, No. 4). (Illus.). 1977. 14.50 (ISBN 3-8055-2809-4). S Karger.

Fasold, Ralph W. & Shuy, Roger W., eds. Teaching Standard English in the Inner City. LC 72-120748. (Urban Language Ser). (Orig.). 1970. pap. 5.00 (ISBN 0-87281-001-1). Ctr Appl Ling.

Faust, Norma. Lecciones para el Aprendizage del Idioma Shipibo-Conibo. (Peruvian Working Papers Ser.: No. 1). 1973. pap. 3.00 (ISBN 0-88312-783-0); microfiche 1.60 (ISBN 0-88312-353-3). Summer Inst Ling.

Ferre, Frederick. Language, Logic, & God: With a New Preface. LC 80-27305. viii, 184p. 1981. pap. text ed. 6.50x (ISBN 0-226-24456-3). U of Chicago Pr.

Fisher, John C. Linguistics in Remedial English. (Janua Linguarum, Ser. Practica: No. 47). (Orig.). 1966. pap. text ed. 16.25x (ISBN 90-2790-659-9). Mouton.

Fisiak, Jacek, ed. Historical Morphology: Papers Prepared for the Conference, Held at Boszkovo, Poland, March 1978. (Trends in Linguistics, Studies & Monographs: No. 17). 1980. text ed. 79.50 (ISBN 90-279-3038-4). Mouton.

--Theoretical Issues in Contrastive Linguistics. x, 430p. 1980. 44.00 (ISBN 90-272-3502-3, CILT 12). Benjamins N Orth Am.

Fodor, Janet D. The Linguistic Description of Opaque Contexts. Hankamer, Jorge, ed. LC 78-66537. (Outstanding Dissertations in Linguistics Ser.). 1979. lib. bdg. 42.00 (ISBN 0-685-94397-6). Garland Pub.

Fortescue, Michael. A Discourse Production Model for "Twenty" Questions". x, 137p. 1980. pap. 14.00 (ISBN 90-272-2505-2, P & B 2). Benjamins North Am.

Fowler, Roger. Understanding Language: An Introduction to Linguistics. 1974. 12.50x (ISBN 0-7100-7755-6); pap. 7.95 (ISBN 0-7100-7756-4). Routledge & Kegan.

Frain Du Tremblay. Traite des Langues Ou L'on donne des Principes et des Regles pour Juger du Merite et de l'Excellence de Chaque Langue et en particulier de la Langue Francaise. (Linguistics 13th-18th Centuries Ser.). 288p. (Fr.). 1974. Repr. of 1703 ed. lib. bdg. 77.00x (ISBN 0-8287-0353-1, 71-5015). Clearwater Pub.

Fraser, Hugh & O'Donnell, W. R., eds. Applied Linguistics & the Teaching of English. (Education Today Ser). (Orig.). 1969. pap. text ed. 3.50x (ISBN 0-582-55070-X). Humanities.

Freeman, D. C. Linguistics & Literary Style. LC 74-101157. 1970. pap. text ed. 9.95 (ISBN 0-03-080800-6, HoltC). HR&W.

Friedrich, Paul. Language, Context, & the Imagination: Essays by Paul Friedrich. Dil, Anwar S., ed. LC 78-65328. (Language Science & National Development Ser.). 1979. 17.50x (ISBN 0-8047-1022-8). Stanford U Pr.

Fries, Charles C. Linguistics & Reading. LC 63-14410. (Illus.). 1981. Repr. of 1963 ed. 24.50x (ISBN 0-8290-0684-2). Irvington.

Fromkin, Victoria A. & Rodman, R. An Introduction to Language. 2nd ed. LC 77-16616. 1978. pap. text ed. 15.95 (ISBN 0-03-089947-8, HoltC). HR&W.

Fromkin, Victoria A., ed. Speech Errors As Linguistic Evidence. LC 73-78443. (Janua Linguarum, Ser. Major: No. 77). (Illus.). 269p. 1973. text ed. 46.75x (ISBN 90-2792-668-9). Mouton.

Fujiwara, Yoichi. A Linguistic Atlas of the Seto Inland Sea - Explanation: A Dialect-Geographical Study of the Seto Island Dialects, Vol. 3. (Eng. & Japanese.). 1977. 28.50x (ISBN 0-86008-173-7, Pub. by U of Tokyo Pr). Intl Schol Bk Serv.

Gaeng, Paul A. Introduction to the Principles of Language. 1971. pap. text ed. 16.50 scp (ISBN 0-06-042218-1, HarpC). Har-Row.

Gal, Susan. Language Shift: Social Determinants of Linguistic Change in Bilingual Austria. (Language, Thought & Culture Ser.). 1979. 24.00 (ISBN 0-12-273750-4). Acad Pr.

Gannon, Peter & Czerniewska, Pam. Using Linguistics: An Educational Focus. (Illus.). 224p. 1981. pap. text ed. 16.50x (ISBN 0-7131-6294-5). Intl Ideas.

Garcia, E. The Role of Theory in Linguistic Analysis. (N-H Linguistic Ser.: Vol. 19). 522p. 1975. pap. 34.25 (ISBN 0-444-10940-4, North-Holland). Elsevier.

Gardiner, Alan H. The Theory of Speech & Language. LC 79-4125. 1979. Repr. of 1951 ed. lib. bdg. 22.50x (ISBN 0-313-20987-1, GATS). Greenwood.

Garmonsway, G. N., ed. Aelfric's Colloquy. rev. ed. 64p. 1978. pap. text ed. 3.25x (ISBN 0-85989-098-8, Pub. by U Exeter England). Humanities.

Garvin, Paul L. On Linguistic Method: Selected Papers. LC 75-182468. (Janua Linguarum, Ser. Minor: No. 30). (Illus.). 199p. (Orig.). 1972. pap. text ed. 23.75x (ISBN 90-2792-005-2). Mouton.

Garvin, Paul L., ed. Method & Theory in Linguistics. LC 75-110950. (Janua Linguarum, Ser. Major: No. 40). 1970. text ed. 56.50x (ISBN 90-2790-722-6). Mouton.

Geach, Peter T. Reference & Generality: An Examination of Some Medieval & Modern Theories. 3rd ed. LC 80-10977. (Contempory Philosophy Ser.). 256p. 1980. 19.50x (ISBN 0-8014-1315-X). Cornell U Pr.

Gellner, Ernest. Words & Things: An Examination of, & an Attack on, Linguistic Philosophy. 1979. 24.00 (ISBN 0-7100-0260-2); pap. 12.50 (ISBN 0-7100-0285-8). Routledge & Kegan.

Gerver, D. & Sinaiko, H. W., eds. Language Interpretation & Communication. LC 78-15195. (NATO Conference Ser.: Series III, Human Factors, Vol. 6). 437p. 1978. 35.00 (ISBN 0-306-40051-0, Plenum Pr). Plenum Pub.

Gething, Thomas W. Aspects of Meaning in Thai Nominals: A Study in Structural Semantics. (Janua Linguarum, Ser. Practica: No. 141). (Illus.). 104p. (Orig.). 1972. pap. text ed. 26.25x (ISBN 90-2792-339-6). Mouton.

Ghils, Paul. Language & Thought: A Survey of the Problem. 80p. 1980. 5.95 (ISBN 0-533-02649-0). Vantage.

Ghosh, Samir K., ed. Man, Language & Society: Contributions to the Sociology of Language. (Janua Linguarum, Ser. Minor: No. 109). 1972. pap. text ed. 32.50x (ISBN 90-2792-120-2). Mouton.

Gleason, G. H. Introduction a la linguistique. (Sciences humaines et sociales). (Fr). pap. 20.95 (ISBN 2-03-070351-6, 3652). Larousse.

Glover, Warren. Sememic and Grammatical Structures in Gurung. (SIL Linguistics and Related Fields Ser: No. 49). 1974. 8.75x (ISBN 0-88312-059-3); microfiche 2.20 (ISBN 0-88312-459-9). Summer Inst Ling.

Goody, Esther N. Questions & Politeness. LC 77-6577. (Cambridge Papers in Social Anthropology Ser: No. 8). 1978. 32.50 (ISBN 0-521-21749-0); pap. 10.95x (ISBN 0-521-29250-6). Cambridge U Pr.

Goospeed, Robert C. From Greek to Graffiti: English Words That Survive & Thrive. (Illus.). 308p. (Orig.). 1981. 15.00 (ISBN 0-682-49696-0, University); pap. 10.00 (ISBN 0-682-49706-1, University). Exposition.

Goyvaerts, D. L. Present Day Historical & Comparative Linguistics, No. 2. 1980. pap. text ed. write for info. (ISBN 0-391-01599-0). Humanities.

--Present-Day Historical & Comparative Linguistics: An Introductory Guide to Theory & Method Part One General Background-Phonological Change. 231p. 1975. pap. text ed. 21.75x (ISBN 0-391-01588-5). Humanities.

Gradon, P. O. Cynewulf's Elene. 115p. Date not set. pap. text ed. 5.00x (ISBN 0-85989-087-2, Pub. by U Exeter England). Humanities.

Grady, Michael. Syntax & Semantics of the English Verb Phrase. LC 75-118277. (Janua Linguarum, Ser. Practica: No. 112). (Illus., Orig.). 1970. pap. text ed. 15.00x (ISBN 90-2790-745-5). Mouton.

Grannes, Alf. Loan Compounds in Bulgarian Reflecting the Turkish Indefinite Izafet-Construction. 70p. 1980. pap. 16.00x (ISBN 82-00-01951-9). Universitet.

Greenbaum, Sidney. Studies in English Adverbial Usage. LC 70-90047. (Miami Linguistics Ser: No. 5). 1969. 13.95x (ISBN 0-87024-137-0). U of Miami Pr.

Greenberg, Joseph H. A New Invitation to Linguistics. LC 76-42422. 1977. pap. 2.95 (ISBN 0-385-07550-2, Anch). Doubleday.

Greenberg, Joseph H., et al, eds. Universals of Human Language, 4 vols. Incl. Vol. I. Method & Theory. 15.00x (ISBN 0-8047-0965-3); Vol. II. Phonology. 25.00x (ISBN 0-8047-0966-1); Vol. III. Word Structure. 25.00x (ISBN 0-8047-0968-8); Vol. IV. Syntax. 25.00x (ISBN 0-8047-0969-6). LC 77-89179. 1978. Set. 90.00x (ISBN 0-8047-1012-0). Stanford U Pr.

Gregory, Michael & Carroll, Susanne. Language & Situation: Language Varieties & Their Social Contexts. (Language & Sociaty Ser). 1978. 12.50x (ISBN 0-7100-8756-X); pap. 7.95 (ISBN 0-7100-8773-X). Routledge & Kegan.

Griffiths, Glyn & Griffiths, Cynthia. Aspects of the Kadiweu Language. 222p. 1976. pap. 5.20x (ISBN 0-88312-369-X). Summer Inst Ling.

Grimes, Joseph E. Network Grammars. (SIL Linguistic & Related Fields Ser: No. 45). 199p. 1975. 8.50x (ISBN 0-88312-055-0); microfiche 2.20 (ISBN 0-88312-455-6). Summer Inst Ling.

Grinder, John T. On Deletion Phenomena in English. (Janua Linguarum, Series Minor: No. 221). (Illus.). 1976. pap. text ed. 27.50x (ISBN 90-2793-005-8). Mouton.

Gudschinsky, Sarah C. Literacy: The Growing Influence of Linguistics. (Trends in Linguistics: State-of-the-Art Report: No. 2). (Orig.). 1976. pap. text ed. 17.00x (ISBN 0-686-22623-2). Mouton.

Gudschinsky, Sarah C., et al. Estudos Sobre Linguas e Culturas Indigenas. (Eng. & Port.). 1971. pap. 5.00 (ISBN 0-88312-760-1); microfiche 2.20 (ISBN 0-88312-346-0). Summer Inst Ling.

Gulstad, Daniel E. A Modern Theory of 'Langue' LC 73-82004. (Janua Linguarum, Ser. Minor: No. 180). 141p. 1973. pap. text ed. 23.95x (ISBN 90-2792-540-2). Mouton.

Gumb, Raymond D. Rule-Governed Linguistic Behavior. (Janua Linguarum, Ser. Minor: No. 141). 139p. 1972. pap. text ed. 20.00x (ISBN 90-2792-316-7). Mouton.

Gusmani, Roberto. Lydisches Woerterbuch. (Ger.-Lyd.). 1964. 49.95 (ISBN 3-533-00655-7, M-7546, Pub. by Carl Winter). French & Eur.

Gyarmathy, S. Affinitas Linguae Hungaricae cum Linguis Fennicae Originis Grammatice Demonstrata. (Linguistics 13th-18th Centuries). 406p. (Fr.). 1974. Repr. of 1799 ed. lib. bdg. 103.00 (ISBN 0-8287-0412-0, 71-5043). Clearwater Pub.

Hagege, Claude. Critical Reflections on Transformational Grammar. rev. ed. Makkai, Valerie B., tr. from Fr. Orig. Title: La Grammaire Generative: Reflexions Critiques. 1981. pap. 12.00 (ISBN 0-933104-09-X). Jupiter Pr.

Hagman, Roy S. Nama Hottentot Grammar. (Language Science Monographs: No. 15). 1977. pap. text ed. 15.00x (ISBN 0-87750-212-9). Res Ctr Lang Semiotic.

Hall, Robert A., Jr. Language, Literature & Life: Selected Essays by Robert A. Hall, Jr. LC 79-26478. (Edward Sapir Monographs in Language, Culture & Cognition: No. 5). (Illus.). viii, 295p. 1978. pap. 8.00x (ISBN 0-933104-07-3). Jupiter Pr.

Halle, Morris. Sound Pattern of Russian: A Linguistic & Acoustical Investigation. (D a C S R Ser: No. 1). 1971. Repr. of 1959 ed. text ed. 36.25x (ISBN 0-686-22395-0). Mouton.

Halle, Morris, et al, eds. Linguistic Theory & Psychological Reality. LC 77-29054. (MIT Bicentennial Studies Ser.: NO. 4). 1978. 22.50x (ISBN 0-262-08095-8); pap. 7.95 (ISBN 0-262-58043-8). MIT Pr.

Halliday, N. A. & Martin, J. R., eds. Readings in Systemic Linguistics. 320p. 1981. 45.00 (ISBN 0-7134-3677-8, Pub. by Batsford England); pap. 25.00 (ISBN 0-7134-3678-6). David & Charles.

Hammarstroem, G. Linguistic Units & Items. LC 75-9679. (Communications & Cybernetics Ser.: Vol. 9). 135p. 1975. 20.80 (ISBN 0-387-07241-1). Springer-Verlag.

Hamp, Eric L. Glossary of American Technical Linguistic Usage, 1925-1950. 3rd ed. 1966. 10.50x (ISBN 0-8002-1460-9). Intl Pubns Serv.

Hamp, Eric P., ed. Themes in Linguistics: The 1970s. LC 72-94473. (Janua Linguarum, Ser. Minor: No. 172). (Illus.). 129p. 1973. pap. text ed. 15.75x (ISBN 90-2792-365-5). Mouton.

Hari, Anna M. An Investigation of the Tones of Lhasa Ribetan. (Language Data Asia-Pacifica Ser.: No. 13). 232p. (Orig.). pap. 5.50 (ISBN 0-88312-213-8); micro fiche 2.20 (ISBN 0-88312-313-4). Summer Inst Ling.

Harris, James. Hermes: Or, a Philosophical Inquiry Concerning Universal Grammar. (Linguistics, 13th-18th Centuries Ser.). 464p. (Fr.). 1974. Repr. of 1801 ed. lib. bdg. 115.50 (ISBN 0-8287-0415-5, 5044). Clearwater Pub.

--Philological Inquiries. (Linguistics 13th-18th Centuries Ser.). 338p. (Fr.). 1974. Repr. of 1801 ed. lib. bdg. 88.00x (ISBN 0-8287-0416-3, 5045). Clearwater Pub.

Harris, Roy. The Language-Makers. LC 79-6029. 1980. 19.50x (ISBN 0-8014-1317-6). Cornell U Pr.

Harris, Z. S. Papers in Structural & Transformational Linguistics. LC 74-118128. (Formal Linguistics Ser: No. 1). 850p. 1970. lib. bdg. 71.00 (ISBN 90-277-0026-5, Pub. by Reidel Holland). Kluwer Boston.

Harris, Zellig S. Structural Linguistics. LC 51-4864. (Orig.). 1960. pap. 7.00x (ISBN 0-226-31771-4, P52, Phoen). U of Chicago Pr.

Hartmann, Peter. Dimensionierugg Als Wissenschaftliche Teilaufgabe in der Textlinguistik. (PDR Press Publication in Textual Linguistic Ser.: 1). 1975. pap. text ed. 1.50x (ISBN 9-0316-0015-6). Humanities.

Hartmann, R. R. & Stork, F. C., eds. Dictionary of Language & Linguistics. LC 72-6251. 1976. 36.95 (ISBN 0-470-35667-7); pap. 29.95 (ISBN 0-470-15200-1). Halsted Pr.

Haudricourt, Andre & Juilland, Alphonse. Essai Pour une Histoire Structurale Du Phonetisme Francais. (Janua Linguarum, Ser. Practica: No. 115). (Fr). 1971. pap. text ed. 23.75x (ISBN 90-2791-550-4). Mouton.

Hayes, Curtis W., et al. ABC's of Languages & Linguistics. LC 77-75915. 1977. pap. text ed. 9.95 (ISBN 0-88499-066-4). Inst Mod Lang.

Hehn, Victor. Cultivated Plants & Domesticated Animals in Their Migration from Asia to Europe: Historico-Linguistic Studies (1870) xxv, 523p. 1976. 57.00 (ISBN 90-272-0878-6, ACIL 7). Benjamins North Am.

Hempel, Carl G. Aspekte Wissenschaftlicher Erklaerung. (Grundlagen der Kommunikation De Gruyter Studienbuch). 1977. 17.75x (ISBN 3-11-004630-X). De Gruyter.

Henne, Helmut & Rehbock, Helmut. Einfuehrung in Die Gespraechsanalyse. (Sammlung Goeschen: No. 2212). 1979. 9.90 (ISBN 3-1100-7846-5). De Gruyter.

Herbst, Thomas, et al. Grimm's Grandchildren: Current Topics in German Linguistics. (Longman Linguistics Library). (Illus.). 1980. text ed. 27.00x (ISBN 0-582-55487-X); pap. text ed. 15.95x (ISBN 0-582-55489-6). Longman.

Herder, J. G. Abhandlung uber den Ursprung der Sprache. (Linguistics 13th-18th Centuries). 154p. (Fr.). 1974. Repr. of 1789 ed. lib. bdg. 47.00 (ISBN 0-8287-0001-X, 5046). Clearwater Pub.

Hervas Y Panduro, L. Catalogo delle Lingue Conosciute e Notizia della Loro Affinita e Diversita. (Linguistics 13th-18th Centuries Ser.). 260p. (Fr.). 1974. Repr. of 1784 ed. lib. bdg. 70.50 (ISBN 0-8287-0427-9, 71-5047). Clearwater Pub.

Hickerson, Nancy P. Linguistic Anthropology. LC 79-28328. 168p. 1980. pap. text ed. 6.95 (ISBN 0-03-006956-4, HoltC). HR&W.

Higgins, F. R. The Pseudo-Cleft Construction in English. Hankamer, Jorge, ed. LC 78-66547. (Outstanding Dissertations in Linguistics Ser.). 1979. lib. bdg. 44.00 (ISBN 0-8240-9683-5). Garland Pub.

Hintikka, K. J. & Suppes, P., eds. Information & Inference. LC 70-118132. (Synthese Library: No. 28). 336p. 1970. lib. bdg. 37.00 (ISBN 90-277-0155-5, Pub. by Reidel Holland). Kluwer Boston.

Hockett, Charles F. Course in Modern Linguistics. (Illus.). 1958. text ed. 17.50x (ISBN 0-02-355090-2). Macmillan.

Hoenigswald, H. M. Studies in Formal Historical Linguistics. LC 72-95891. (Formal Linguistics Ser: No. 3). 63p. 1973. lib. bdg. 16.00 (ISBN 90-277-0270-5, Pub. by Reidel Holland). Kluwer Boston.

Hoenigswald, Henry M. Language Change & Linguistic Reconstruction. LC 59-12287. 1959. pap. 4.50x (ISBN 0-226-34741-9). U of Chicago Pr.

Hoffman, Richard L. & Myers, L. M. Companion to the Roots of Modern English. 2nd ed. 1979. pap. 7.95 (ISBN 0-316-36836-9). Little.

Hogg, Richard. English Quantifier Systems. (North-Holland Linguistics Ser.: Vol. 34). 1977. 27.00 (ISBN 0-444-85001-5, North-Holland). Elsevier.

Holec, Henri. Structures Lexicales et Enseignement Du Vocabulaire. (Janua Linguarum Ser.: No. 5). pap. 17.00x (ISBN 90-2793-272-7). Mouton.

Holtzmann, Adolf. Ueber Den Umlaut: Abhandlungen (1843), & Ueber Den Ablaut (1844) xxix, 129p. 1977. 22.00 (ISBN 0-686-31498-0, ACIL 12). Benjamins North Am.

Honti, Laszlo. System Derparadigmatischen Suffixmorpheme Des Wogulischen Dialektes an der Tawda.Aus Dem Ungarischen Ubersetzt Von Regina Hessky. (Janua Linguarum Ser.: No. 246). pap. 28.75x (ISBN 90-2793-406-1). Mouton.

Hopper, Paul J., ed. Studies in Descriptive & Historical Linguistics. x, 502p. 1977. 46.00 (ISBN 90-272-0905-7, CILT 4). Benjami Ns North Am.

Hornstein, N. & Lightfoot, D. Explanation in Linguistics: The Logical Problem of Language Acquistion. (Linguistics Library). (Illus.). 1981. text ed. 25.00x (ISBN 0-582-29114-3); pap. text ed. 13.95x (ISBN 0-582-29115-1). Longman.

House, Juliane. A Model for Translation Quality Assessment. 1977. pap. 30.00x (ISBN 3-87808-088-3). Intl Pubns Serv.

Householder, Fred W. Linguistics Speculations. LC 78-145601. (Illus.). 1971. 39.95 (ISBN 0-521-07986-1). Cambridge U Pr.

Hovdhaugen, Even, ed. The Nordic Languages & Modern Linguistics. 392p. 1981. 40.00x (ISBN 82-00-05569-8). Universitet.

Hungerford, Harold, et al. English Linguistics: An Introductory Reader. 1970. pap. 7.95x (ISBN 0-673-05296-6). Scott F.

Hutchins, W. J. Generation of Syntactic Structures from a Semantic Base. LC 78-146187. (Linguistics Ser: No. 2). (Illus., Orig.). 1971. pap. text ed. 17.25x (ISBN 0-7204-6182-0, Pub. by North Holland). Humanities.

Inkey, Peter & Szepe, Gyorgy, eds. Modern Linguistics & Language Teaching. Society for the Popularization of Sciences T.I.T: Federation Internationale Des Professeurs De Langues Vivantes-F.I.P.L.V. (Janua Linguarum Ser.: No. 87). 1975. 76.25x (ISBN 90-2793-161-5). Mouton.

International Conference on Historical Linguistics; 2nd, Tucson Ariz. & Christie, William M. Current Progress in Historical Linguistics. LC 76-26132. (North-Holland Linguistic Ser.: Vol. 31). 1976. pap. 49.00 (ISBN 0-7204-0533-5, North-Holland). Elsevier.

International Conference on Historical Linguistics, 3rd, Hamburg 22-26 August, 1977. Proceedings. (Current Issues in Linguistic Theory). 1980. text ed. 45.75x (ISBN 0-391-01653-9). Humanities.

Introduccion al Idioma Aguarana. (Peruvian Working Papers Ser.: No. 3). 1974. 5.25x (ISBN 0-88312-775-X). Summer Inst Ling.

Itkonen, Esa. Grammatical Theory & Metascience: A Critical Investigation into the Methodological & Philosophical Foundations of "Autonomous" Linguistics. x, 355p. 1978. 39.00 (ISBN 90-272-0906-5, CILT 5). Benjamins North Am.

Jackendoff, Ray. X Syntax: A Study of Phrase Structure, No. 2. (Linguistic Inquiry Mongraph). 249p. 1977. pap. text ed. 12.50x (ISBN 0-262-60009-9). MIT Pr.

Jackson, Howard. Analyzing English: An Introduction to Descriptive Linguistics. (Pergamon Institute of English). (Illus.). 1980. pap. 11.95 (ISBN 0-08-024556-0). Pergamon.

Jacobs, Roderick A. & Rosenbaum, Peter S., eds. Transformations, Style, & Meaning. LC 70-138978. (Orig.). 1971. pap. text ed. 10.95x (ISBN 0-471-00285-2). Wiley.

Jacobson, Rodolfo. London Dialect of the Late Fourteenth Century: A Transformational Analysis in Historical Linguistics. LC 73-104465. (Janua Linguarum Ser: No. 97). (Illus., Orig.). 1970. pap. text ed. 40.75x (ISBN 90-2790-739-0). Mouton.

Jakobson, Roman. Framework of Language. (Michigan Studies in the Humanities: No. 1). 1980. pap. 4.00 (ISBN 0-936534-00-1). Mich Slavic Pubns.

--Selected Writings, 3 vols. Incl. Vol. 1. Phonological Studies. 2nd ed. 1971 (ISBN 90-2791-662-4); Vol. 2. Word & Language. 1971 (ISBN 90-2791-766-3); Vol. 4. Slavic Epic Studies. 1966 (ISBN 90-2791-003-0). 80.00x ea. Mouton.

Jakway, Martha & De Davis, Patricia M. La Educacion Bilingue y los Cambios En el Diario Vivir y Confeccionando Cartillas. (Comumidades y Culturas Ser.: No. 1, Vol. 1). 36p. 1973. pap. 1.50 (ISBN 0-88312-754-7). Summer Inst Ling.

Jankowsky, Kurt R. The Neogrammarians: A Re-Evaluation of Their Place in the Development of Linguistic Science. LC 71-189705. (Janua Linguarum, Ser. Minor: No. 116). 275p. (Orig.). 1972. pap. text ed. 31.25x (ISBN 0-686-22539-2). Mouton.

Jansen, Frank, ed. Studies on Fronting. 1978. pap. text ed. 10.25x (ISBN 90-316-0163-2). Humanities.

Jazayery, Mohammad A., et al, eds. Linguistic & Literary Studies: In Honor of Archibald A. Hill, Vol. 2: Descriptive Linguistics. (Trends in Linguistics, Studies & Monographs: No. 10). 1978. text ed. 50.00x (ISBN 90-279-7727-5). Mouton.

--Linguistics & Literary Studies: In Honor of Archibald A. Hill, Vol. 4: Linguistics & Literature, Sociolinguistics & Applied Linguistics. (Trends in Linguistics, Studies & Monographs: No. 10). 1979. text ed. 50.00x (ISBN 90-279-7747-X). Mouton.

Jazayery, Mohammad L. & Polome, Edgar, eds. Linguistics & Literary Studies: In Honor of Archibald A. Hill, Vol. 3: Historical & Comparative Linguistics. (Trends in Linguistics, Studies & Monographs: No. 10). 1978. text ed. 50.00x (ISBN 90-279-7737-2). Mouton.

Jazayery, Mohammed Ali, et al, eds. Linguistic & Literary Studies in Honor of Archibald A. Hill: General & Theoretical Linguistics, Vol. I. (Trends in Linguistics Studies & Monographs: No. 7). 1978. 50.00 (ISBN 90-279-7717-8). Mouton.

Jehan, L. F. Dictionnaire de Linguistique et de Philologie Comparee. Migne, J. P., ed. (Troisieme et Derniere Encyclopedie Theologique Ser.: Vol. 34). 724p. (Fr.). Date not set. Repr. of 1864 ed. lib. bdg. 92.50x (ISBN 0-89241-313-1). Caratzas Bros.

Jenish, Daniel. Philosophisch-Kritische-Vergleichung und Wurdigung von vierzehn altern und neuren SPRACHENS EUROPENS. (Linguistics 13th-18th Centuries Ser.). 504p. (Ger.). 1974. Repr. of 1796 ed. lib. bdg. 114.00 (ISBN 0-8287-0464-3, 5048). Clearwater Pub.

Johnson, D. Barton. Transformations & Their Use in the Resolution of Syntactic Homomorphy, Prepositional of Constructions in Contemporary Standard Russian. (Janua Linguarum, Ser. Practica: No. 95). (Orig.). 1970. pap. text ed. 33.75x (ISBN 90-2791-525-3). Mouton.

Johnson, Marta K., ed. & tr. from Czech. Recycling the Prague Linguistic Circle. (Linguistica Extranea Ser.: Studia 6). 103p. 1978. pap. 5.50 (ISBN 0-89720-010-1). Karoma.

Joly, Andre. Negation, the Comparative Particle in English. (Cahiers De Psychomecanique Du Langage). 4.50x (ISBN 2-7637-6338-3, Pub. by Laval). Intl Schol Bk Serv.

Juilland, Alphonse. Transformational & Structural Morphology. (Stanford French & Italian Studies: No. 5). 1978. pap. 15.00 (ISBN 0-915838-33-8). Anma Libri.

Juilland, Alphonse & Edwards, P. M. Rumanian Verb System. LC 66-15853. (Janua Linguarum, Ser. Practica: No. 28). (Orig.). 1971. pap. text ed. 54.00x (ISBN 90-2791-605-5). Mouton.

Juilland, Alphonse & Roceric, Alexandra. The Decline of the Word. (Studia Linguistica et Philologica: No. 1). 1976. pap. 15.00 (ISBN 0-915838-40-0). Anma Libri.

Juilland, Alphonse, ed. Linguistic Studies Presented to Joseph Greenberg on the Occasion of His Sixtieth Birthday. (Studia Linguistica et Philologica: No. 4). 1977. pap. 60.00 (ISBN 0-915838-43-5). Anma Libri.

Juneau, Marcel. La Jument Qui Crote de L'Argent. (Illus.). 1977. pap. 11.50x (ISBN 2-7637-6769-9, Pub. by Laval). Intl Schol Bk Serv.

Kaplan, Robert, ed. Annual Review of Applied Linguistics. 216p. 1981. lib. bdg. 17.95 (ISBN 0-88377-201-9). Newbury Hse.

Kaplan, Robert B., ed. On the Scope of Applied Linguistics. 1980. pap. text ed. 6.95 (ISBN 0-88377-140-3). Newbury Hse.

Katicic, Radoslav. Contribution to the General Theory of Comparative Linguistics. LC 77-110956. (Janua Linguarum, Ser. Minor: No. 83). (Orig.). 1970. pap. text ed. 20.00x (ISBN 0-686-22411-6). Mouton.

Katz, Jerrold J. Language & Other Abstract Objects. 1981. 25.00x (ISBN 0-8476-6912-2); pap. 9.95x (ISBN 0-8476-6913-0). Rowman.

Katz, Jerrold J. & Postal, Paul M. An Integrated Theory of Linguistic Descriptions. LC 64-17356. 1978. pap. text ed. 5.95x (ISBN 0-262-61021-3). MIT Pr.

Kehoe, M., ed. Applied Linguistics: A Survey for Language Teachers. 1968. pap. text ed. 2.60 (ISBN 0-02-977490-X). Macmillan.

Keiler, Allan R. Phonological Study of the Indo-European Laryngeals. LC 72-110952. (Janua Linguarum, Ser. Practica: No. 76). (Orig.). 1970. pap. text ed. 25.00x (ISBN 90-2790-729-3). Mouton.

Kerns, J. A. & Schwartz, Benjamin. A Sketch of the Indo-European Finite Verb. (Monographs on Mediterranean Antiquity). 83p. 1972. 12.50x (ISBN 0-8147-4556-3). NYU Pr.

Kevelson, Roberta. Style Symbolic Language Structure & Syntactic Change: Intransitivity and the Perception of 'is' in English. (PDR Press Publication on Semiotics of Language: No. 2). (Orig.). 1976. pap. text ed. 4.25x (ISBN 90-316-0125-X). Humanities.

Khlennikova, Irina B. The Conjunctive Mood in English As a Problem in General Linguistics. (Janua Linguarum Ser: No. 212). 139p. (Orig.). 1976. pap. text ed. 23.50x (ISBN 90-2793-404-5). Mouton.

Kibrik, A. E. The Methodology of Field Investigation in Linguistics (Setting up the Problem) (Janua Linguarum Ser. Minor: No. 142). (Illus.). 1977. pap. text ed. 23.50x (ISBN 90-279-3076-7). Mouton.

Kiefer, F., ed. Trends in Soviet Theoretical Linguistics. LC 72-95890. (Foundations of Language Supplementary Ser: No. 18). 1973. lib. bdg. 66.00 (ISBN 90-277-0274-8, Pub. by Reidel Holland). Kluwer Boston.

Kimenyi, Alexandre. Linguistics: A Relational Grammar of Kinyarwanda. (UC Publications in Linguistics: Vol. 91). 1980. 14.50x (ISBN 0-520-09598-7). U of Cal Pr.

Kloss, Heinz, ed. Linguistic Composition of the Nations of the World (Composition Linguistique des Nations du Monde), Vol. 1: Central & Western South Asia. 405p. (Fr. - Eng.). 1974. pap. 24.00x (ISBN 2-7637-6710-9, Pub. by Laval). Intl Schol Bk Serv.

Koerner, E., et al, eds. Studies in Medieval Linguistic Thought. (Studies in the History of Linguistics: Vol. 26). 321p. 1981. text ed. 54.25x (ISBN 90-272-4508-8, Pub. by Benjamins Holland). Humanities.

Koerner, E. F. Contribution Au Debat Post-Saussurien Dur le Signe Linguistique: Introduction Generale et Bibliographie Annotee. (Approaches to Semiotics Ser.: No. 2). 103p. (Orig., Fr.). 1972. pap. text ed. 13.75x (ISBN 90-2792-301-9). Mouton.

Koerner, E. Konrad. The Importance of Techner's "Internationale Zeitschrift Fur Allgemeine Sprachwissenshaft" in the Development of General Linguistics. vii, 76p. 1973. 19.00 (ISBN 90-272-0892-1, SIHOL 1); pap. 14.00 (ISBN 0-686-31500-6). Benjamins North Am.

--Toward a Histroriography of Linguistics: Selected Essays. xx, 222p. 1978. 25.00 (ISBN 90-272-0960-X, SIHOL 19). Benjamins North Am.

--Western Jistories of Linguistic Thought: An Annotated Chronological Bibliography, 1822-1976. x, 113p. 1978. 16.00 (ISBN 90-272-0952-9, SIHOL 11). Benjamins North Am.

Koerner, E. Konrad, ed. Progress in Linguistic Historiography: Papers from the International Conference on the History of the Language Sciences, Ottowa, 28-31 August 1978. xiv, 421p. 1980. 41.00 (ISBN 90-272-4501-0, SIHOL 20). Benjamins North Am.

--The Transformational-Generative Paradigm & Modern Linguistic Theory. viii, 462p. 1975. 46.00 (ISBN 90-272-0902-2, CILT 1); pap. 41.00 (ISBN 0-686-31501-4). Benjamins North Am.

Koerner, Kohrad, et al, eds. Studies in Medieval Linguistic Thought, Vol. 26. (Studies in the History of Linguistics). vi, 321p. 1980. 41.00 (ISBN 90-272-4508-8). Benjamins North Am.

Komlev, N. G. Components of the Content Structure of the Word. LC 74-80542. (Janua Linguarum, Series Minor: No. 138). 227p. 1976. pap. text ed. 40.00x (ISBN 90-2793-364-2). Mouton.

Kotey, Paul F. Directions in Ghanaian Linguistics: A Brief Survey. LC 71-630646. (Papers in International Studies: Africa: No. 2). 1969. pap. 2.50x (ISBN 0-89680-036-9). Ohio U Ctr Intl.

Kraak, A. Linguistics in the Netherlands. 280p. 1974. text ed. 13.75x (ISBN 90-232-1251-7). Humanities.

Kramerae, Cheris. Women & Men Speaking. (Orig.). 1981. pap. text ed. 11.95 (ISBN 0-88377-179-9). Newbury Hse.

Kress, Gunther. Language As Ideology. 1981. pap. 9.75 (ISBN 0-7100-0795-7). Routledge & Kegan.

Kress, Gunther & Hodge, Robert. Language As Ideology. 1979. 20.00x (ISBN 0-7100-0215-7). Routledge & Kegan.

Kruijsen, Joep, ed. Liber Amicorum Weijnen: A Collection on Essays Presented to Professor Dr. A. Weijnen on the Occasion of His Seventieth Birthday. 396p. 1980. pap. text ed. 42.75 (ISBN 90-232-1749-7). Humanities.

Kuroda, S. Y. The Whole of the Doughnut. (Studies in Generative Linguistic Analysis: No. 1). 258p. 1980. text ed. 62.25x (ISBN 90-6439-161-0). Humanities.

Kutschera, Franz Von. Einfuehrung in Die Intensionale Semantik. (Grundlagen der Kommunikation). 1976. pap. 17.75x (ISBN 3-11-006684-X). De Gruyter.

Labov, William. What Is a Linguistic Fact? (PDR Press Publication in Linguistic Theory: No. 1). 1975. pap. text ed. 3.50x (ISBN 90-316-0075-X). Humanities.

Labov, William, ed. Locating Language in Time & Space, Vol. I. LC 80-757. (Quantitative Analysis of Linguistic Structure Ser.). 1980. 24.50 (ISBN 0-12-432060-0). Acad Pr.

Ladefoged, Peter. Preliminaries to Linguistic Phonetics. pap. 5.00 (ISBN 0-226-46787-2). U of Chicago Pr.

Ladusaw, William A. & Hankamer, Jorge. Polarity Sensitivity As Inherent Scope Relations. LC 79-6614. (Outstanding Dissertations in Linguistics Ser.). 236p. 1980. lib. bdg. 27.50 (ISBN 0-8240-4555-6). Garland Pub.

La Follette, James E. Etude Linguistique De Quatre Contes Folkloriques Du Canada Francais. (Folkloriques Du Canada Francais). 9.50x (ISBN 2-7637-6092-9, Pub. by Laval). Intl Schol Bk Serv.

Lamb, Pose. Linguistics in Proper Perspective. 2nd ed. (Elementary Education Ser.). 1977. pap. text ed. 5.95x (ISBN 0-675-08596-9). Merrill.

Lamy, B. De l'Art de Parler. (Linguistics 13th-18th Centuries Ser.). 288p. (Fr.). 1974. Repr. of 1675 ed. lib. bdg. 77.00x (ISBN 0-8287-0502-X, 71-5016). Clearwater Pub.

Lancelot, G. & Arnauld, A. Grammaire Generale et Raisonnee. (Linguistics 13th-18th Centuries Ser.). 226p. (Fr.). 1974. Repr. of 1754 ed. lib. bdg. 63.00x (ISBN 0-8287-0503-8, 71-5017). Clearwater Pub.

Landerman, Peter. Vocabulario Quechua del Pastaza. (Peruvian Linguistic Ser.: No. 8). 165p. 1973. pap. 2.50x (ISBN 0-88312-664-8); microfiche 1.60 (ISBN 0-88312-366-5). Summer Inst Ling.

Langacker, Ronald W. Language & Its Structure: Some Fundamental Linguistic Concepts. 2nd ed. LC 68-27167. 1973. pap. text ed. 13.95 (ISBN 0-15-549192-X, HC). HarBraceJ.

Language in Education: Ethnolinguistic Essays. (Language & Ethnography Ser.: No. 1). 1980. pap. 10.50x (ISBN 0-87281-134-4). Ctr Appl Ling.

Language, Man & Society, 23 titles in 31 vols. Repr. of 1916 ed. Set. 927.50 (ISBN 0-404-08490-7); sep. vols. avail. (ISBN 0-685-02384-2). AMS Pr.

Larsen-Freeman, Diane, ed. Discourse Analysis in Second Language Research. 283p. (Orig.). 1981. pap. text ed. 11.95 (ISBN 0-88377-163-2). Newbury Hse.

Lass, R. & Anderson, J. M. Studies in Old English Phonology. LC 74-80360. (Studies in Linguistics: No. 14). 352p. 1975. 49.50 (ISBN 0-521-20531-X). Cambridge U Pr.

Lass, Roger. On Explaining Language Change. LC 79-51825. (Studies in Linguistics Ser.: No. 27). (Illus.). 1980. 29.95 (ISBN 0-521-22836-0). Cambridge U Pr.

Lee, Berta G. Linguistics Evidence for the Priority of the French Text of the Ancrene Wisse. LC 74-77155. (Janua Linguarum, Ser. Practica: No. 242). 90p. 1974. pap. text ed. 22.50x (ISBN 90-2793-332-4). Mouton.

Lee, Don Y. An Introduction to East Asian & Tibetan Linquistics & Cultures. LC 81-67770. 300p. 1981. 22.00 (ISBN 0-939758-01-6). Eastern Pr.

Leech, G. N. & Short, M. H. Style in Fiction. (English Language Ser.). 384p. 1981. text ed. 32.00x (ISBN 0-582-29102-X); pap. text ed. 16.95x (ISBN 0-582-29103-8). Longman.

Leech, Geoffrey N. Explorations in Semantics & Pragmatics. viii, 133p. 1980. pap. 14.00 (ISBN 90-272-2506-0, P & B 5). Benjamins North Am.

Lehmann, Winfred P. Historical Linguistics: An Introduction. 2nd ed. LC 72-10305. 1973. text ed. 15.95 (ISBN 0-03-078370-4, HoltC). HR&W.

Lehmann, Winifred P. Descriptive Linguistics: An Introduction. 2nd ed. 288p. 1976. text ed. 10.95 (ISBN 0-394-30265-6, RanC); wkbk. 5.50 (ISBN 0-686-76936-8). Random.

Leib, Hans-Heinrich. Intergrational Linguistics: Volume 5, Morphology & Morphosemant-Tics. (Current Issues in Linguistic Theory Ser.: No. 17). 250p. 1981. text ed. 28.50x (ISBN 90-272-3508-2). Humanities.

Levelt, W. J. Formal Grammars in Linguistics & Psycholinguistics: An Introduction to the Theory of Formal Languages & Automata, Vol. 1. Barnas, Andrew, tr. from Dutch. (Janua Linguarum, Ser. Minor: No. 192). (Illus.). 143p. 1974. pap. text ed. 21.25x (ISBN 90-2792-666-2). Mouton.

--What Became of L (Anguage) a (Cquistion) D (Evice) (PDR Press Publication in Cognition: No. 1). 1977. pap. text ed. 1.50x (ISBN 90-316-0019-9). Humanities.

Levin, Samuel R. Linguistic Structures in Poetry. (Janua Linguarum, Ser. Minor: No. 23). 1973. pap. text ed. 12.50x (ISBN 90-2790-678-5). Mouton.

Lewin, Bernhard. A Vocabulary of the Hudailian Poems. (Acta Regiae Societatis Scientarum et Litterarum Goteborg, Humaniora: No. 13). 1978. pap. text ed. 28.00x (ISBN 91-85252-16-6). Humanities.

Lewis, E. Glyn. Linguistics & Second Language Pedagogy: A Theoretical Study. LC 73-79891. (Janua Linguarum, Ser. Didactica: No. 10), 137p. (Orig.). 1974. pap. text ed. 20.75x (ISBN 90-2792-707-3). Mouton.

Liefrink, Frans. Semantico-Syntax. (Linguistics Library Ser). 192p. 1974. text ed. 15.95x (ISBN 0-582-55035-1). Longman.

Liles, Bruce L. An Introduction to Linguistics. 368p. 1975. ref. ed. o.p. 14.50 (ISBN 0-13-486134-5); pap. text ed. 11.95 (ISBN 0-13-486126-4). P-H.

--Linguistics & the English Language: A Transformational Approach. LC 71-187700. 320p. 1972. pap. text ed. 11.50 (ISBN 0-87620-529-5). Goodyear.

Lindblom, Bjorn & Ohman, Sven, eds. Frontiers of Speech Communication Research. 1979. 50.00 (ISBN 0-12-449850-7). Acad Pr.

Lindemann, J. W. Old English Preverbal GE, Its Meaning. LC 79-130689. 88p. 1970. pap. 5.00x (ISBN 0-8139-0320-3). U Pr of Va.

Linguistic Theories & Their Application. LC 70-370137. (Modern Languages in Europe Ser). 1967. pap. 6.00x (ISBN 0-8002-1679-2). Intl Pubns Serv.

Linguistique-Linguistics: Catalogues et Inventaires. (Maison Des Sciences De L'homme, Service D'echange D'information Scientifiques, Publications Serie C: No. 4). 1971. pap. 19.50 (ISBN 0-686-21807-8). Mouton.

Longacre, R. E. Discourse Grammers: Studies in Indiginous Languages of Columbia, Panama & Equador, 3 vols. (SIL Ser: No. 52). 1977. Vol. I. pap. 7.50 (ISBN 0-88312-063-1); Vol. II. pap. 5.50 (ISBN 0-88312-064-X); Vol. III. pap. 7.00 (ISBN 0-88312-065-8); Set. pap. 18.00 (ISBN 0-88312-062-3); microfiche vol. 1 3.40 (ISBN 0-88312-463-7); microfiche vol. 2 2.80 (ISBN 0-88312-464-5); microfiche vol. 3 2.80 (ISBN 0-88312-465-3); microfiche set 9.00 (ISBN 0-88312-447-5). Summer Inst Ling.

Lopez-Morales, Humberto, ed. Corrientes Actuales En la Dialectologia Del Caribe Hispanico: Actas De un Simposio. LC 77-12823. 1978. pap. 7.00 (ISBN 0-8477-3186-3). U of PR Pr.

Loss, Eugene, ed. Estudios Panos I. (Peruvian Linguistic Ser.: No. 10). 1973. pap. 3.75 (ISBN 0-88312-759-8); microfiche 2.20 (ISBN 0-88312-342-8). Summer Inst Ling.

Lotman, J. M. Theses on the Semiotic Study of Culture: As Applied to Slavic Texts. (Semiotics of Culture 2). 1975. pap. text ed. 2.00x (ISBN 90-316-0032-6). Humanities.

Loukotka, Cestmir. Classification of South American Indian Languages. LC 67-65490. (Reference Ser.: Vol. 7). 1968. pap. 15.00 (ISBN 0-87903-107-7). UCLA Lat Am Ctr.

Lyons, John. Introduction to Theoretical Linguistics. (Illus., Orig.). 1968. 49.50 (ISBN 0-521-05617-9); pap. text ed. 13.95x (ISBN 0-521-09510-7). Cambridge U Pr.

--Language & Linguistics. LC 80-42002. (Illus.). 280p. 1981. 24.95 (ISBN 0-521-23034-9); pap. 8.95 (ISBN 0-521-29775-3). Cambridge U Pr.

Lyons, John, ed. Linguistique generale. (Langue et langage). (Fr). 1970. pap. 20.25 (ISBN 0-685-13970-0, 3635). Larousse.

Macaulay, Ronald. Generally Speaking: How Children Learn Language. (Orig.). 1980. pap. text ed. 6.95 (ISBN 0-88377-162-4). Newbury Hse.

McDavid, Raven I. & O'Cain, Raymond K. Linguistic Atlas of the Middle & South Atlantic States: Fascicles 1 & 2. LC 79-24748. (Illus.). 1980. No. 1. pap. 15.00x (ISBN 0-226-55742-1); No. 2. pap. 15.00x (ISBN 0-226-55744-8). U of Chicago Pr.

McDermott, A. Charlene. Godfrey of Fontaine's Abridgement of Boethius of Dacia's Modi Significandi Sive Quaestiones Super Priscianum Maiorem. (Studies in the History of Lnguistics: Vol. 22). 237p. 1980. 30.00 (ISBN 90-272-4504-5, SIHOL). Benjamins North Am.

McElhanon, K. A. & Voorhoeve, C. L. The Trans-New Guinea Phylum: Explorations in Deep Level Genetic Relationships. 107p. 1970. pap. 5.50x (ISBN 0-88312-650-8); microfiche 1.60 (ISBN 0-88312-361-4). Summer Inst Ling.

McNeill, David. Acquisition of Language: The Study of Developmental Psycholinguistics. (Holtzman Ser). (Illus.). 183p. 1970. pap. text ed. 11.50 scp (ISBN 0-06-044379-0, HarpC). Har Row.

McQuown, Norman A. American Indian Linguistics in New Spain. 1976. pap. text ed. 1.75x (ISBN 90-316-0082-2). Humanities.

Major, Diana. The Acquisition of Modal Auxiliaries in the Language of Children. (Janua Linguarum Ser. Minor: No. 195). 1974. pap. text ed. 15.00x (ISBN 90-2792-664-6). Mouton.

Makkai, Adam & Lockwood, David G. Readings in Stratificational Linguistics. LC 76-169497. 288p. 1972. 18.95x (ISBN 0-8173-0200-X). U of Ala Pr.

Makkai, Adam, ed. Toward a Theory of Context in Linguistics & Literature: Proceedings of a Conference of the Kelemen Mikes Hungarian Cultural Society, Maastricht, September 21-25, 1971. (De Proprietatibus Litterarum Ser. Minor: No. 18). pap. 32.50x (ISBN 90-2793-273-5). Mouton.

Makkai, Adam, et al. Linguistics at the Crossroads. LC 79-312499. viii, 502p. 1977. pap. 27.00x (ISBN 0-933104-02-2). Jupiter Pr.

Malkiel, Yakov. Linguistics & Philology in Spanish America: A Survey (1925-1970) (Janua Linguarum, Ser. Minor: No. 97). 179p. (Orig.). 1972. pap. text ed. 28.75x (ISBN 90-2792-313-2). Mouton.

Malmberg, Bertil. Linguistique Generale et Romane: Etudes En Allemand, Anglais, Espagnol et Francais. (Janua Linguarum, Series Maior: No. 66). 1973. 91.50x (ISBN 90-2792-429-5). Mouton.

--Phonetique Generale et Romane: Etudes En Allemand, Anylais, Es Paynol et Francais. LC 75-141182. (Janua Linguarum, Ser. Major: No. 42). 478p. 1971. text ed. 92.50x (ISBN 90-2791-790-6). Mouton.

Maquet, J., ed. On Linguistic Anthropology: Essays in Honor of Harry Hoijer, 1979. LC 80-50214. (Other Realities Ser.: Vol. 2). 139p. text ed. cancelled (ISBN 0-686-70972-1); pap. text ed. 9.00 (ISBN 0-89003-062-6). Undena Pubns.

Maquet, Jacques, ed. On Linguistic Anthropology: Essays in Honor of Harry Hoijer, 1979. LC 79-67375. (Other Realities Ser.: Vol. 2). 108p. (Orig.). 1980. pap. 8.30 (ISBN 0-89003-041-3). Undena Pubns.

Marouzeau, Jules. Lexique De la Terminologie Linguistique. 3rd ed. LC 53-5692. 280p. (Fr., Ger., Eng., Ital.). 1969. Repr. of 1951 ed. 7.50x (ISBN 0-8002-0840-4). Intl Pubns Serv.

Marten, Rainer. Existieren, Wahrsein, und Verstehen: Untersuchung zur ontologischen Basis sprachlicher Verstaendigung. 376p. 1972. 48.75x (ISBN 3-11-003583-9). De Gruyter.

Martin, Laura. Papers in Mayan Linguistics. 7.95 (ISBN 0-686-71052-5). Lucas.

Martin, R. M. Semiotics & Linguistic Structure. LC 78-6873. 1978. 33.00 (ISBN 0-87395-381-9). State U NY Pr.

Martin, Richard M. Pragmatics, Truth, & Language. (Boston Studies in Philosophy of Science: No. XXXVIII). 1979. lib. bdg. 42.00 (ISBN 90-277-0992-0, Pub. by Reidel Holland); pap. 14.50 (ISBN 90-277-0993-9, Pub. by Reidel Holland). Kluwer Boston.

Martin, Wallace, ed. Language, Logic, & Genre: Papers from the Poetics & Literary Theory Section, Modern Language Association. 54p. 1974. 8.00 (ISBN 0-8387-1446-3). Bucknell U Pr.

Martinet, Andre. Elements of General Linguistics. Palmer, Elisabeth, tr. LC 64-19845. 1964. 5.00 (ISBN 0-226-50873-0). U of Chicago Pr.

Mather, J. Y. & Speitel, H. M., eds. The Linguistic Atlas of Scotland, Scots Section, Vol. 1. (Illus.). 428p. (Orig.). 1975. 75.00 (ISBN 0-208-01475-6, Archon). Shoe String.

Mather, J. Y., et al, eds. The Linguistic Atlas of Scotland: Scots Section, Vol. 2. (Illus., With Indices for Volumes 1 & 2). 1977. 65.00 (ISBN 0-208-01571-X, Archon). Shoe String.

Mathiot, Madeleine, ed. Ethnolinguistics: Boas, Sapir, & Whorf Revisited. (Contributions to the Society of Language Ser.: No. 27). 1979. text ed. 47.00x (ISBN 0-686-27021-5). Mouton.

Matisoff, James A. Variational Semantics in Tibeto-Burman: The "Organic" Approach to Linguistic Comparison. LC 77-28921. (Occasional Papers of the Wolfenden Society on Tibeto-Burman Linguistics Ser.: Vol. 6). (Illus.). 1978. text ed. 21.95x (ISBN 0-915980-85-1). Inst Study Human.

Matthews, P. H. Generative Grammar & Linguistic Competence. (Illus.). 1979. text ed. 18.95x (ISBN 0-04-410002-7). Allen Unwin.

Mayrhofer, Manfred. Kurzgefasstes Etymologisches Woerterbuch Des Altindischen, Vol. 2. (Ger. & Sans.). 1963. 92.00 (ISBN 3-533-00657-3, M-7530, Pub. by Carl Winter). French & Eur.

--Kurzgefasstes Etymologisches Woerterbuch Des Altindischen, Vol. 3. (Ger. & Sans.). 1976. 130.00 (ISBN 3-533-02466-0, M-7531, Pub. by Carl Winter). French & Eur.

Meetham, A. R. Encyclopedia of Linguistics, Information & Control. 1969. 115.00 (ISBN 0-08-012337-6). Pergamon.

Meier, P., et al. A Grammar of Izi. (SIL Linguistics & Related Fields Ser: No. 47). 184p. 1975. 9.00 (ISBN 0-88312-057-7); microfiche 2.00 (ISBN 0-88312-457-2). Summer Inst Ling.

Meillet, A. Comparative Method in Historical Linguistics. Ford, G. B., Jr., tr. 1967. pap. 7.50 (ISBN 0-685-00758-8). Adler.

Mendeloff, Henry. A Manual of Comparative Romance Linguistics. 1970. 9.95 (ISBN 0-8132-0262-0). Cath U Pr.

Merrifield, William, ed. Studies in Otomanguean Phonology. (SIL Publications in Linguistics: No. 54). 1977. 8.00x (ISBN 0-88312-067-4); microfiche 1.60 (ISBN 0-88312-467-X). Summer Inst Ling.

Mey, Jacob L., ed. Pragmalinguistics: Theory & Practice. (Janua Linguarum, Series Maior: No. 85). 1979. text ed. 42.50 (ISBN 90-279-7757-7). Mouton.

Meyerstein, R. S. Functional Load: Descriptive Limitations, Alternative Assessments & Extensions of Application. LC 70-126053. (Janua Linguarum, Ser. Minor: No. 99). (Orig.). 1970. pap. text ed. 10.50x (ISBN 0-686-22415-9). Mouton.

Milan, William G., et al, eds. Colloquium on Spanish & Portuguese Linguistics: 1974. LC 75-28427. 148p. 1975. pap. 5.25 (ISBN 0-87840-040-0). Georgetown U Pr.

Millardet, George. Petit Atlas Linguistique D'une Region Des Landes. Repr. of 1910 ed. 35.50 (ISBN 0-384-38882-5). Johnson Repr.

Mixco, Mauricio J. Cochimi & Proto-Yuman: Lexical & Syntactic Evidence for a New Language Family in Lower Calif. (University of Utah Anthropological Papers: No. 101). 1979. pap. text ed. 10.00x (ISBN 0-87480-150-8). U of Utah Pr.

Monboddo, James B. Of the Origin & Progress of Language, 6 vols. LC 76-147982. Repr. of 1809 ed. Set. 195.00 (ISBN 0-404-08260-2); 32.50 ea. AMS Pr.

Montgomery, Martin & Coulthard, Malcolm, eds. Studies in Discourse Analysis. 1981. pap. price not set (ISBN 0-7100-0510-5). Routledge & Kegan.

Morag, Shelomo. The Vocalization Systems of Arabic, Hebrew & Aramaic: Their Phonetic & Phonemic Principles. (Janua Linguarum, Ser. Minor: No. 13). 1972. pap. text ed. 13.75x (ISBN 0-686-22534-1). Mouton.

Moravcsik, J. M. Logic & Philosophy for Linguists: A Book of Readings. 347p. 1974. pap. text ed. 34.50x (ISBN 90-2793-097-X). Mouton.

Morris, Marshall. Saying & Meaning in Puerto Rico: Some Problems in the Ethnography of Discourse. (Language & Communication Library: Vol. 1). 186p. 1981. 19.50 (ISBN 0-08-025822-0). Pergamon.

Moulton, Janice & Robinson, George M. Organization of Language. LC 80-19052. 400p. 1981. 42.50 (ISBN 0-521-23129-9); pap. 14.95 (ISBN 0-521-29851-2). Cambridge U Pr.

Mounin. Dicccionario De Linguistica. (Espn.). pns (ISBN 84-335-4004-1, S-50062). French & Eur.

Murane, Elizabeth. Daga Grammar. (Publications in Linguistics & Related Fields: No. 43). 1974. pap. 14.00x (ISBN 0-88312-053-4); microfiche 3.40 (ISBN 0-88312-453-X). Summer Inst Ling.

Nagy, Gregory. Greek Dialects & the Transformation of an Indo-European Process. LC 69-12730. (Loeb Classical Monographs Ser). 1970. text ed. 10.00x (ISBN 0-674-36226-8). Harvard U Pr.

Napoli, Donna J., ed. Elements of Tone, Stress, & Intonation. LC 78-4961. 173p. 1978. pap. text ed. 5.25 (ISBN 0-87840-211-X). Georgetown U Pr.

Nash. Multinlingual Lexicon of Linguistics & Philology. (Miami Linguistic Ser.). (Polyglot.). 52.50 (ISBN 0-685-36678-2). French & Eur.

Nash, Rose & Alleyne, M. Lexique Multiligue De la Linguistique et De la Philogie: Anglais-Russe-Allemand-Francais. 416p. (Eng., Fr., Rus. & Ger.). 1968. pap. 69.95 (ISBN 0-686-57056-1, M-6422). French & Eur.

Nash, Walter. Design in Prose. (English Language Ser.). (Illus.). 240p. 1980. text ed. 25.00x (ISBN 0-582-29100-3); pap. text ed. 13.50x (ISBN 0-582-29101-1). Longman.

Nasr, Raja T. The Essentials of Lingiustic Science. (Applied Linguistics & Language Study Ser.). 1980. pap. text ed. 7.50x (ISBN 0-582-74609-4). Longman.

N'Diaye, Genevieve. Structure Du Dialecte Basque De Maya. (Fr). 1970. pap. text ed. 36.75x (ISBN 0-686-22400-0). Mouton.

Needham, Rodney. Belief, Language, & Experience. 288p. 1973. 11.50x (ISBN 0-226-56993-4). U of Chicago Pr.

Neuenswander, Helen & Arnold, Dean. Cognitive Studies in Southern Mesoamerica. 1977. 10.95x (ISBN 0-88312-152-2); microfiche 2.80 (ISBN 0-88312-250-2). Summer Inst Ling.

Newmeyer, Frederick J. Linguistic Theory in America: The First Quarter Century of Transformational Generative Grammar. LC 79-27195. 1980. 23.00 (ISBN 0-12-517150-1). Acad Pr.

Nobel, Barry L. Linguistics for Bilinguals. 320p. 1981. pap. text ed. 11.95 (ISBN 0-88377-200-0). Newbury Hse.

Nogle, Lawrence E. Method & Theory in the Semantics & Cognition of Kinship Terminology. LC 73-91400. (Janua Linguarum, Ser. Minor: No. 205). 110p. 1974. pap. text ed. 20.00x (ISBN 90-2793-402-9). Mouton.

North, Eric M. The Book of a Thousand Tongues. LC 73-174087. (Tower Bks). 386p. 1972. Repr. of 1938 ed. 26.00 (ISBN 0-8103-3948-X). Gale.

Norton, B. Linguistic Framework & Ontology. 1977. 24.50x (ISBN 90-279-3337-5). Mouton.

Nott, Kathleen. A Soul in the Quad: The Use of Language in Philosophy & Literature. 1969. 25.00 (ISBN 0-7100-6502-7). Routledge & Kegan.

Nuessel, Frank H., Jr., ed. Linguistic Approaches to the Romance Lexicon. LC 78-12654. 123p. 1978. pap. text ed. 4.95 (ISBN 0-87840-046-X). Georgetown U Pr.

O'Brien, Richard J., ed. Linguistics: Developments of the Sixties-Viewpoints for the Seventies: Developments of the Sixties-Viewpoints for the Seventies. LC 58-31607. (Georgetown Univ. Round Table Ser.). 316p. 1971. pap. 5.00 (ISBN 0-87840-106-7). Georgetown U Pr.

Odmark, John, ed. Language, Literature & Meaning II: Current Trends in Literary Research, Vol. 2. (Linguistic & Literary Studies in Eastern Europe). 1980. 57.00 (ISBN 90-272-1503-0). Benjamins North Am.

O'Donnell, W. R. & Todd, Loreto. Variety in Contemporary English. (Illus.). 176p. (Orig.). 1980. 25.00x (ISBN 0-04-421005-1); pap. 8.50 (ISBN 0-04-421006-X). Allen Unwin.

Ohnesorg, Karel, ed. Colloquium Paedolinguisticum. (Janua Linguarum, Ser. Minor: No. 133). 1972. pap. text ed. 42.50x (ISBN 90-2792-315-9). Mouton.

Okby, Mamud M. Verbal Cues of Organizational Information in Message Decoding: An Integrative Approach to Linguistic Structure. LC 75-189706. (Janua Linguarum, Ser. Minor: No. 127). (Illus.). 168p. (Orig.). 1972. pap. text ed. 12.25x (ISBN 0-686-22500-7). Mouton.

Okreglak, Ludmila & Taylor, Marcia E., eds. Periodicals in the Field of Applied Linguistics: An International Survey. LC 74-21509. (Orig.). 1974. pap. 2.50 (ISBN 0-87281-036-4). Ctr Appl Ling.

Olmstead, D. L. Ethnolinguistics So Far. 1950. pap. 3.00 (ISBN 0-384-43285-9). Johnson Repr.

Olmsted, D. L. Out of the Mouth of Babes: Earliest Stages in Language Learning. LC 70-17001. (Janua Linguarum, Ser. Minor: No. 117). (Illus.). 260p. (Orig.). 1971. pap. text ed. 36.25x (ISBN 90-2791-892-9). Mouton.

Olson, Michael L. Barai Sentence Structure & Embedding. (Language Data, Asian-Pacific Ser.: No. 3). 1973. pap. 3.00x (ISBN 0-88312-303-7); microfiche 1.00x (ISBN 0-685-48708-3). Summer Inst Ling.

Oltrogge, David & Rensch, Calvin. Two Studies in Middle American Comparative Linguistics. (SIL Publications in Linguistics: No. 55). 1977. 5.00x (ISBN 0-88312-068-2); microfiche 1.60 (ISBN 0-88312-474-2). Summer Inst Ling.

Ortiz, Alejandro & Zierer, Ernesto. Set Theory & Linguistics. (Janua Linguarum, Ser. Minor: No. 70). (Orig.). 1968. pap. text ed. 12.00x (ISBN 90-2790-597-5). Mouton.

Orton, Harold, et al, eds. The Linguistic Atlas of England. (Illus.). 1977. text ed. 85.00x (ISBN 0-391-00759-9). Humanities.

Osgood, Charles E. Focus on Meaning: Vol. 2, from Words to Sentences. (Janua Linguarum, Series Minor: 225-2). 1979. pap. text ed. 22.25x (ISBN 90-279-7786-0). Mouton.

Padley, G. A. Grammatical Theory in Western Europe 1500-1700. LC 75-44573. 320p. 1976. 47.50 (ISBN 0-521-21079-8). Cambridge U Pr.

Pak, Ty. An Axiomatic Theory of Language with Applications to English. LC 80-12010. (Edward Sapir Monograph Ser. in Language, Culture & Cognition: No. 6). vi, 129p. (Orig.). 1979. pap. 6.00x (ISBN 0-933104-08-1). Jupiter Pr.

Palmer, Leonard R. Descriptive & Comparative Linguistics. 430p. 1972. 22.50x (ISBN 0-8448-0114-3). Crane-Russak Co.

--Descriptive & Comparative Linguistics. new ed. 432p. 1979. pap. 8.95 (ISBN 0-571-10690-0, Pub. by Faber & Faber). Merrimack Bk Serv.

Palumbo, E. The Literary Use of Formulas in Guthlac II & Their Relation to Felix's Vita Sancti Guthlaci. (De Proprietatibus Litterarum Ser. Practica: No. 37). 1977. 15.50x (ISBN 90-279-7695-3). Mouton.

Paper, Herbert H., ed. Language & Texts: The Nature of Linguistic Evidence. LC 75-36885. 204p. (Orig.). 1975. pap. 10.00 (ISBN 0-915932-02-4). Trillium Pr.

Paret, Herman, et al, Le Langage En Contexte: Etudes Philosophiques et Linguistiques De Pragmatique. iv, 790p. 1980. 69.00 (ISBN 90-272-3112-5, LIS 3). Benjamins North Am.

Parret, Herman, ed. History of Linguistic Thought & Contemporary Linguistics: Foundations of Communication. 816p. 1975. 112.00x (ISBN 3-11-005818-9). De Gruyter.

Pattanayak, D. P. Aspects of Applied Linguistics. 5.00x (ISBN 0-210-98168-7). Asia.

Pearson, Bruce L. Introduction to Linguistic Concepts. 1977. pap. text ed. 9.95 (ISBN 0-394-31122-1); wkbk. 5.50 (ISBN 0-394-31295-3). Knopf.

Pei, Mario & Gaynor, Frank. Dictionary of Linguistics. (Quality Paperback: No. 177). 1980. pap. 4.95 (ISBN 0-8226-0177-X). Littlefield.

Pei, Mario & Gaynor, Frank, eds. Dictionary of Linguistics. 1960. 6.00 (ISBN 0-685-77553-4). Philos Lib.

Pei, Mario A. Glossary of Linguistic Terminology. LC 66-21013. 299p. 1966. 20.00x (ISBN 0-231-03012-6). Columbia U Pr.

Peinovich, M. P. Old English Noun Morphology: A Diachronic Study. (Linguistic Ser.: Vol. 41). 1979. 27.00 (ISBN 0-444-85287-5, North Holland). Elsevier.

Pelc, Jerzy. Studies in Functional Logical Semiotics of Natural Languages. (Janua Linguarum, Ser. Minor: No. 90). 1971. text ed. 28.75x (ISBN 90-2791-599-7). Mouton.

Pensinger, Brenda. Diccionario Mixteco del Este De Jamiltepec. (Vocabularios Indigenas Ser.: No. 18). 1974. 8.00 (ISBN 0-88312-751-2); microfiche 1.60 (ISBN 0-88312-586-2). Summer Inst Ling.

Perry, Thomas, ed. Evidence & Argumentation in Linguistics. (Grundlagen der Kommunikation). 1979. 75.00x (ISBN 3-11-007272-6). De Gruyter.
Peters, Stanley, ed. Goals of Linguistic Theory. 288p. (Reference ed.). 1972. 13.95 (ISBN 0-13-357095-9). P-H.
Petrey, Sandy. Hisltory in the Text "Quatrevingt-Treize" & the French Revolution. viii, 125p. 1980. 19.00 (ISBN 90-272-1713-0, PUMRL 3). Benjamins North Am.
Pickering, Wilbur. A Framework for Discourse Analysis. (SIL Publications in Linguistics). 1980. pap. 10.95 (ISBN 0-88312-076-3); microfiche 1.60 (ISBN 0-88312-484-X). Summer Inst Ling.
Pierce, Joe E. The Bitter Winds. LC 77-71932. 1977. 3.50 (ISBN 0-913244-12-0). Hapi Pr.
--Development of Linguistic System in English Speaking American Children, Vol. 2. 185p. (Orig.). 1981. pap. cancelled (ISBN 0-913244-51-1). Hapi Pr.
--How English Really Works. LC 79-202. (Illus.). 1979. pap. 12.95 (ISBN 0-913244-18-X). Hapi Pr.
--Languages & Linguistics: An Introduction. (Janua Linguarum Series Didactica: No. 4). 188p. (Orig.). 1975. pap. text ed. 35.00x (ISBN 90-2793-371-5). Mouton.
Pike, K. L. & Pike, E. G. Grammatical Analysis. rev. ed. (Publications in Linguistics & Related Fields Ser.: No. 51). 1981. pap. 15.00x (ISBN 0-88312-066-6); microfiche 4.00 (ISBN 0-686-67824-9). Summer Inst Ling.
Pilch, Herbert. Empirical Linguistics. 1978. 14.75x (ISBN 3-7720-1090-3). Adler.
Pizer, Vernon. Take My Word for It. 128p. (gr. 7 up). 1981. PLB 8.95 (ISBN 0-396-07986-5). Dodd.
Polivanov, E. D. Selected Works: Articles on General Linguistics. Armstrong, Daniel, tr. from Rus. LC 73-83930. (Janua Linguarum, Ser. Major: No. 72). (Illus.). 386p. 1974. text ed. 88.75x (ISBN 0-686-22573-2). Mouton.
Popp, Daniel. Asbjornsen's Linguistic Reform, Vol. 1. 1977. pap. 8.00x (ISBN 82-00-01595-5, Dist. by Columbia U Pr). Universitet.
Posner, Roland, ed. & intro. by. Kategorialgrammatik. (Grundlagen der Kommunikation). pap. text ed. write for info. (ISBN 3-11-004478-1). De Gruyter.
Potter, S. Modern Linguistics. (Andre Deutsch Language Library). 1977. lib. bdg. 12.50x (ISBN 0-233-95546-1). Westview.
Press, Margaret L. Chemehuevi: A Grammar & Lexicon. (U. C. Publications in Linguistics Ser.: Vol. 92). 1980. pap. 13.50x (ISBN 0-520-09600-2). U of Cal Pr.
Prideaux, G. Experimental Linguistics: Integration of Theories & Applications. (Story-Scientia Linguistics Ser.: No. 3). 1980. text ed. 57.75x (ISBN 90-6439-164-5). Humanities.
Prideaux, Gary D. Syntax of Japanese Honorifics. (Janua Linguarum, Ser. Practica: No. 102). 1970. pap. text ed. 23.75x (ISBN 90-2790-741-2). Mouton.
Prideaux, Gary D., ed. Perspectives in Experimental Linguistics: Papers from the University of Alberta Conference on Experimental Linguistics, Edmonton, 13-14 Oct. 1978. xi, 176p. 1979. 21.00 (ISBN 90-272-3503-1, CILT 10). Benjamins North Am.
Probleme der Sprachwissenschaft. Beitraege zur Linguistik. (Janua Linguarum, Ser. Minor: No. 118). 1971. pap. text ed. 52.50x (ISBN 90-2791-797-3). Mouton.
Pulgram, Ernst. Syllable, Word, Nexus, Cursus. (Janua Linguarum Ser: No. 81). 1970. pap. text ed. 18.75x (ISBN 90-2790-706-4). Mouton.
Queneau, Raymond. Exercises in Style. 2nd ed. Wright, Barbara, tr. from Fr. LC 80-26102. Orig. Title: Exercises De Style. (Illus.). 208p. 1981. 12.95 (ISBN 0-8112-0803-6); pap. 4.95 (ISBN 0-8112-0789-7, ND513). New Directions.
Rallides, Charles. The Tense Aspect System of the Spanish Verb As Used in Cultivated Bogata Spanish. LC 73-147933. (Janua Linguarum, Ser. Practica: No. 119). 66p. 1971. pap. text ed. 10.00x (ISBN 0-686-22488-4). Mouton.
Ramat. Linguistic Reconstruction & Indo-European Syntax. (Current Issues of Linguistic Theory Ser.: No. 19). 236p. 1981. text ed. 34.25x (ISBN 90-272-3512-0, Pub. by Benjamins Holland). Humanities.
Rameh, Clea. Georgetown University Round Table on Languages & Linguistics: Semantics-Theory & Application. LC 58-31607. (Georgetown Univ. Round Table Ser.: 1976). (GURT 1976). 1976. pap. 6.00 (ISBN 0-87840-111-3). Georgetown U Pr.
Rastier, Francois. Ideologie et Theorie des Signes. (Approaches to Semiotics Ser.). (Illus.). 168p. 1972. text ed. 30.00x (ISBN 90-2792-114-8). Mouton.
Rauch, Irmengard & Carr, Gerald F., eds. Linguistic Method: Essays in Honor of Herbert Penzl. (Janua Linguarum, Series Maior: No. 79). 1979. text ed. 72.00x (ISBN 90-279-7767-4). Mouton.
Richards, Jack. Error Analysis: Perspectives on Second Language Acquisition. (Applied Linguistics & Language Study Ser.). 1974. pap. text ed. 9.00x (ISBN 0-582-55044-0). Longman.
Ricoeur, Paul. Interpretation Theory: Discourse & the Surplus of Meaning. LC 76-29604. 1976. pap. 7.00 (ISBN 0-912646-25-X). Tex Christian.
Robins, R. H. General Linguistics: An Introductory Survey. 3rd ed. (Longman Linguistics Library). (Illus.). 1980. text ed. 30.00x (ISBN 0-582-55363-6); pap. text ed. 14.95x (ISBN 0-582-55364-4). Longman.
--A Short History of Linguistics. 2nd ed. (Longman Linguistics Library). (Illus.). 1980. text ed. 23.00x (ISBN 0-582-55289-3); pap. text ed. 12.50x (ISBN 0-582-55288-5). Longman.
Rochester, S. R. & Martin, J. R. Crazy Talk: A Study of Discourse of Schizophrenic Speakers. LC 79-11978. (Cognition & Language, a Series in Psycholinguistics). (Illus.). 241p. 1979. 25.00 (ISBN 0-306-40236-X, Plenum Pr). Plenum Pub.
Rosenberg, J. F. Linguistic Representation. LC 74-26886. (Philosophical Studies: No. 1). 166p. 1975. lib. bdg. 27.50 (ISBN 90-277-0533-X); pap. 10.50 (ISBN 90-277-0946-7). Kluwer Boston.
Rosenberg, Samuel N. Modern French CE: The Neuter Pronoun in Adjectival Predication. (Janua Linguarum, Ser. Practica: No. 116). 1970. pap. text ed. 38.75x (ISBN 90-2790-747-1). Mouton.
Rosenbianz, Bernhard. Vergleichende Untersuchungen der Altanatolischen Sprachen. (Trends in Linguistics State-of-the-Art Reports: No. 8). 1978. pap. 35.25x (ISBN 90-279-7696-1). Mouton.
Rosetti, A. Etudes Linguistiques. (Janua Linguarum, Series Maior: No. 95). 1973. 54.00x (ISBN 90-2792-596-8). Mouton.
Rossi-Landi, Ferruccio. Ideologies of Linguistic Relativity. LC 72-94502. (Approach to Semiotics Paperback Ser.: No. 4). 101p. 1974. pap. text ed. 12.50x (ISBN 90-2792-594-1). Mouton.
--Linguistics & Economics. (Janua Linguarum Ser. Maior: No. 81). 240p. 1977. pap. text ed. 22.50x (ISBN 90-279-3243-3). Mouton.
Roulet, E. Linguistic Theory, Linguistic Description & Language Teaching. Candlin, Christopher N., tr. LC 75-326964. (Applied Linguistics & Language Study Ser.). 112p. 1975. pap. text ed. 9.00x (ISBN 0-582-55075-0). Longman.
Rozencveig, V. Ju. Linguistic Interference & Convergent Change. (Janual Linguarum, Series Minor: No. 99). (Illus.). 58p. 1976. pap. text ed. 12.50x (ISBN 90-2793-414-2). Mouton.
Runte, Hans R. & Valdman, Albert, eds. Identite Culturelle et Francophonie Dans les Ameriques. (Indiana University Publications: Collogue 2). (Fr.). 1976. pap. text ed. 15.00x (ISBN 0-87750-201-3). Res Ctr Lang Semiotic.
Sacy, L. Sylvestre De. Principe de Grammaire Generale Mis a la Portee des Enfants. (Linguistics 13th-18th Centuries Ser.). 197p. (Fr.). 1974. Repr. of 1799 ed. lib. bdg. 57.00x (ISBN 0-8287-0747-2, 5049). Clearwater Pub.
Safarewicz, Jan. Linguistic Studies. (Janua Linguarum, Ser. Major: No. 76). 395p. 1974. text ed. 69.00x (ISBN 90-2793-003-1). Mouton.
Salisbury, Rachel. Better Language & Thinking. LC 55-6420. 1955. 28.50x (ISBN 0-89197-537-3). Irvington.
Salmon, Vivian. The Study of Language in 17th-Century England. x, 218p. 1979. 30.00 (ISBN 90-272-0958-8, SIHOL 17). Benjamins North Am.
Saltarelli, Mario. Phonology of Italian in a Generative Grammar. (Janua Linguarum, Ser. Practica: No. 93). (Orig.). 1970. pap. text ed. 22.50x (ISBN 90-2790-737-4). Mouton.
Salus, Peter H. Linguistics. LC 69-13632. (Speech Communication Ser). 1969. pap. 2.95 (ISBN 0-672-61084-1, SC14). Bobbs.
Sampson, Geoffrey. The Form of Language. (Illus.). 236p. 1980. 14.95x (ISBN 0-8464-0987-9). Beekman Pubs.
--Liberty & Language. 1979. 17.95 (ISBN 0-19-215951-8). Oxford U Pr.
--Making Sense. 224p. 1980. text ed. 16.95x (ISBN 0-19-215950-X). Oxford U Pr.
--Schools of Linguistics. LC 80-81140. 272p. 1980. 23.50x (ISBN 0-8047-1084-8). Stanford U Pr.
--Stratificational Grammar: A Definition & an Example. LC 74-118282. (Janua Linguarum, Ser. Minor: No. 88). (Illus., Orig.). 1970. pap. text ed. 12.50x (ISBN 90-2790-712-9). Mouton.
Sankoff, David, ed. Linguistic Variation: Models & Methods. 1978. 22.50 (ISBN 0-12-618850-5). Acad Pr.
Sankoff, Gillian. The Social Life of Language. LC 79-5048. (Conduct & Communication Ser.). 352p. 1980. 35.00x (ISBN 0-8122-7771-6); pap. 12.00x (ISBN 0-686-77492-2). U of Pa Pr.
Sapir, E. Takelma Texts. (Anthropological Publications Ser.: Vol. 2-1). 1909. 3.50 (ISBN 0-686-24096-0). Univ Mus of U.
Saumjan, S. K. Principles of Structural Linguistics. Miller, James, tr. (Janua Linguarum, Ser. Major). 359p. 1971. text ed. 72.00x (ISBN 90-2791-658-6). Mouton.
Saville-Troike, Muriel, ed. Georgetown University Round Table on Languages & Linguistics: Linguistics & Anthropology. (Georgetown Univ. Round Table Ser.: 1977). 1977. 6.75 (ISBN 0-87840-112-1). Georgetown U Pr.
Schach, Paul, ed. Languages in Conflict: Linguistic Acculturation on the Great Plains. LC 80-12710. xii, 186p. 1981. 17.50x (ISBN 0-8032-2106-1). U of Nebr Pr.
Schank, R. C. Conceptual Information Processing. LC 74-84874. (Fundamental Studies in Computer Science: Vol. 3). 374p. 1975. 36.75 (ISBN 0-444-10773-8, North-Holland). Elsevier.
Schlegel, Friedrich. Ueber Die Sprache und Weisheit der Indier: Ein Beitrag Zur Begrundung der Altertumskunde. vii, 192p. 1977. 32.00 (ISBN 90-272-0872-7, ACIL 1). Benjamins North Am.
Schmalstieg, William R. Indo-European Linguistics: A New Synthesis. LC 79-65827. 224p. 1980. text ed. 16.75x (ISBN 0-271-00240-9). Pa St U Pr.
Schmidt-Radefeldt, J. Reading in Portuguese Linguistics. new ed. (North Holland Linguistics Ser.: Vol. 22). 1976. pap. 39.00 (ISBN 0-444-10910-2, North-Holland). Elsevier.
Scholes, Robert J. Acoustic Cues for Constituent Structure: A Series of Experiments on the Nature of Spoken Sentence Structures. (Janua Linguarum, Ser. Minor: No. 121). 80p. 1971. pap. text ed. 13.75x (ISBN 90-2791-855-4). Mouton.
Schultink, H. Output Conditions in Word Formation. (PDR Press Publication in Word Formation: No. 1). 1975. pap. text ed. 1.00x (ISBN 90-316-0028-5). Humanities.
Sciarone, A. G. Place De L'adjectif En Italien Moderne. (Janua Linguarum, Ser. Practica: No. 149). (Fr). 1971. pap. text ed. 25.00x (ISBN 90-2791-560-1). Mouton.
Searle, John R., et al, eds. Speech Act Theory & Pragmatics. (Synthese Language Library: No. 10). xii, 312p. 1980. lib. bdg. 39.50 (ISBN 90-277-1043-0, Pub. by Reidel Holland); pap. 19.50 (ISBN 90-277-1045-7). Kluwer Boston.
Sebeok, Thomas A., ed. Current Trends in Linguistics, 14 vols. Incl. Vol. 1. Soviet & East European Linguistics. 1963. text ed. 108.00x (ISBN 90-2791-242-4); Vol. 2. Linguistics in East Asia & Southeast Asia. 1967. text ed. 165.00x (ISBN 0-686-22480-9); Vol. 3. Theoretical Foundations. Ferguson, Charles A., et al, eds. 1966. text ed. 95.00x (ISBN 90-2791-243-2); Vol. 4. Ibero-American Caribbean Linguistics. 1968. text ed. 117.50x (ISBN 90-2790-024-8); Vol. 5. Linguistics in South Asia. 1969. text ed. 145.00x (ISBN 90-2790-435-9); Vol. 6. Linguistics in South West Asia & North Africa. 1971. text ed. 142.50x (ISBN 90-2791-627-6); Vol. 7. Linguistics in Sub-Saharan Africa. 1971. text ed. 165.00x (ISBN 90-2791-721-3); Vol. 8. Linguistics in Oceania, 2 pts. 1971. text ed. 218.75x (ISBN 90-2791-914-3); Vol. 9. Linguistics in Western Europe, Pts. 1-2. 1972. text ed. 312.50x (ISBN 0-686-22481-7); Vol. 10. Linguistics in North America, 2 vols. Set. text ed. 282.50x (ISBN 90-2792-518-6); Vol. 11. Diachronic, Areal & Typological Linguistics. text ed. 109.00x (ISBN 90-2792-521-6); Vol. 12. Linguistics & Adjacent Arts & Sciences, 4 pts. 1974. Pt. 1. text ed. 132.00x (ISBN 90-2793-172-0); Pt. 2. text ed. 159.50x (ISBN 90-2793-182-8); Pt. 3. text ed. 145.00 (ISBN 90-2793-192-5); Pt. 4. text ed. 159.50x (ISBN 0-686-22482-5); Vol. 13. Historiography of Linguistics. 1975. text ed. 305.00x (ISBN 90-2793-224-7); Vol. 14. Indexes 1976. 263.00x (ISBN 90-2793-056-2). Mouton.
Seebold, Elmar. Vergleichendes und Etymologisches Worterbuch der Germanischen Starken Verben. (Janua Linguarum, Ser. Practica: No. 85). (Ger.). 1970. pap. text ed. 109.00x (ISBN 0-686-22397-7). Mouton.
Shafer, Robert, ed. Applied Linguistics & Reading. (Orig.). 1979. pap. text ed. 6.00 (ISBN 0-87207-722-5, 722). Intl Reading.
Shapiro, M. Asymmetry. (North Holland Linguistic Ser: Vol. 26). 1976. pap. 24.50 (ISBN 0-7204-0415-0, North-Holland). Elsevier.
Shaumyan, Sebastian K. Applicational Grammar As a Semantic Theory of Natural Language. Miller, James E., tr. from Rus. LC 77-4432. (Illus.). 1977. lib. bdg. 14.00x (ISBN 0-226-75102-3). U of Chicago Pr.
Shuy, Roger W., ed. Linguistic Theory: What Can It Say About Reading? LC 77-1834. (Orig.). 1977. pap. 6.50 (ISBN 0-87207-720-9). Intl Reading.
Shuy, Roger W. & Bailey, Charles-James N., eds. Toward Tomorrow's Linguistics. LC 73-92303. 351p. 1973. pap. 6.95 (ISBN 0-87840-204-7). Georgetown U Pr.
Sigerus De Cortraco. Summa Modorum Significandi: Sophismata. 1977. 21.00 (ISBN 90-272-0955-3). Benjamins North Am.
Simpson, J. M. A First Course in Linguistics. 364p. 1979. 20.00x (ISBN 0-85224-319-7, Pub. by Edinburgh U Pr Scotland); pap. 10.00x (ISBN 0-85224-376-6, Pub. by Edinburgh U Pr Scotland). Columbia U Pr.
Smaby, R. M. Paraphrase Grammars. LC 76-13504. (Formal Linguistics Ser: No. 2). 145p. 1971. lib. bdg. 21.00 (ISBN 90-277-0178-4, Pub. by Reidel Holland). Kluwer Boston.
Smith, Adam. Essai sur la Primiere Formation des Langues et sur la Difference du Genie. (Linguistics 13th-18th Centuries Ser.). 258p. (Fr.). 1974. Repr. of 1809 ed. lib. bdg. 70.00x (ISBN 0-8287-0779-0, 5050). Clearwater Pub.
Smith, James R. English Linguistics. 1978. 2.50 (ISBN 0-8403-1436-1). Kendall-Hunt.
Smith, Neil & Wilson, Deirdre. Modern Linguistics: The Results of Chomsky's Revolution. LC 78-20405. (Midland Bks.: No. 255). 336p. 1980. pap. 6.95x (ISBN 0-253-20255-8). Ind U Pr.
--Modern Linguistics: The Results of Chomsky's Revolution. LC 78-20405. 336p. 1979. 17.50x (ISBN 0-253-19457-1). Ind U Pr.
Snorre, Sturleson. Edda. Deuxieme Partie: Tractatus Philogicus et Addimenta ex Lodicibus Manuscripts. (Linguistics 13th-18th Centuries Ser.). 260p. (Fr.). 1974. Repr. of 1852 ed. lib. bdg. 71.00x (ISBN 0-8287-0781-2, 71-5003). Clearwater Pub.
Southworth, Franklin C. & Daswani, Chander J. Foundations of Linguistics. LC 73-9137. (Illus.). 1974. text ed. 14.95 (ISBN 0-02-930300-1). Free Pr.
Spade, Paul V. Peter of Ailly: Concepts & Insolubles: An Annotated Translation. (Synthese Historical Library: No. 19). 193p. 1980. lib. bdg. 31.50 (ISBN 90-277-1079-1, Pub. by Reidel Holland). Kluwer Boston.
Spolsky, Bernard. Educational Linguistics. LC 78-2904. 1978. pap. 10.95 (ISBN 0-88377-094-6). Newbury Hse.
Stearns, MacDonald, Jr. Crimean Gothic. (Studia Linguistica et Philologica: No. 6). 1978. pap. 20.00 (ISBN 0-915838-45-1). Anma Libri.
Steele, Susan, et al. An Encyclopedia of Aux: A Study in Cross-Linguistic Equivalence. (Linguistic Inquiry Monographs). 380p. 1981. 30.00x (ISBN 0-262-19197-0); pap. 15.00x (ISBN 0-262-69074-8). MIT Pr.
Steible, Daniel J., ed. Concise Handbook of Linguistics. LC 67-11578. 1967. 6.00 (ISBN 0-8022-1635-8). Philos Lib.
Steinitz, Wolfgang. Ostjakologische Arbeiten, Bpd. 2. 1977. 46.25x (ISBN 90-279-3314-6). Mouton.
Stewart, Ann H. Graphic Representation of Models in Linguistic Theory. LC 75-5285. 208p. 1976. 11.50x (ISBN 0-253-32624-9). Ind U Pr.
Stoudt, Betty. Vocabulario Mixteco de San Miguel el Grande. (Vocabularios Indigenas Ser.: No. 12). 1965. pap. 3.00 (ISBN 0-88312-660-5); write for info. microfiche (ISBN 0-88312-580-3). Summer Inst Ling.
Strawson, P. F. Subject & Predicate in Logic & Grammar. (University Paperbacks Ser.). 144p. 1974. 22.00x (ISBN 0-416-82190-1); pap. 9.95x (ISBN 0-416-82200-2). Methuen Inc.
Streng, Alice. Syntax, Speech & Hearing: Applied Linguistics for Teachers of Children with Language & Hearing Disabilities. LC 72-1072. 288p. 1972. 28.25 (ISBN 0-8089-0756-5). Grune.
Stross, Brian. Variation & Natural Selection As Factors in Linguistic & Cultural Change. (PDR Press Publication in Linguistic Change: No. 2). 1977. pap. text ed. 2.00x (ISBN 90-316-0062-8). Humanities.
Studies in Linguistics, Vol. 1-17. Repr. Set. 300.00 (ISBN 0-384-58682-1); Set. pap. 205.00 (ISBN 0-685-02166-1). Johnson Repr.
Sturtevant, E. H. Linguistic Change. 183p. 1980. Repr. of 1942 ed. lib. bdg. 30.00 (ISBN 0-89987-765-6). Darby Bks.
Sturtevant, Edgar H. An Introduction to Linguistic Science. LC 75-41267. Repr. of 1947 ed. 16.50 (ISBN 0-404-14807-7). AMS Pr.
Suner, Margarita, ed. Contemporary Studies in Romance Linguistics. LC 78-13028. 402p. 1978. pap. text ed. 7.50 (ISBN 0-87840-044-3). Georgetown U Pr.

Sutton, Peter & Walsh, Michael. Linguistic Fieldwork Manual. (AIAS New Ser.). 1979. pap. text ed. 6.50x (ISBN 0-391-00992-3). Humanities.
Svelmoe, Gordon & Svelmoe, Thelma. Notes on Mansaka Grammar. (Language Data Asian-Pacific Ser.: No. 6). 1974. pap. 3.75 (ISBN 0-88312-206-5); microfiche 1.50 (ISBN 0-88312-306-1). Summer Inst Ling.
Tanahashi, Miyoko. Synchronicities. 1976. pap. 2.00 (ISBN 0-936072-02-4). Soc New Lang Study.
Tavakolian, Susan, ed. Language Acquisition & Linguistic Theory. (Illus.). 304p. 1981. text ed. 19.95x (ISBN 0-262-20039-2). MIT Pr.
Taylor, Daniel J. Declinatio: A Study of the Linguistic Theory of Marcous Terentius Varro. xv, 131p. 1974. 21.00 (ISBN 90-272-0893-X, SIHOL 2). Benjamins North Am.
Taylor, Talbot J. Linguistic Theory & Structural Stylistics. (Language & Communication Library: Vol. 2). 140p. 1981. 17.00 (ISBN 0-08-025821-2). Pergamon.
Thayer, James E. The Deep Structure of the Sentence in Sara-Ngambay Dialogues. (Linguistics & Related Fields Ser.: No. 57). 1978. 10.00x (ISBN 0-88312-071-2); microfiche 2.00 (ISBN 0-88312-470-X). Summer Inst Ling.
Tinkler, John D. Vocabulary & Syntax of the Old English Version in the Paris Psalter. LC 68-29824. (Janua Linguarum, Ser. Practica: No. 67). (Illus.). 92p. (Orig.). 1971. pap. text ed. 20.00x (ISBN 90-2791-895-3). Mouton.
Trager, G. I. The Field of Linguistics. Repr. of 1949 ed. pap. 3.00 (ISBN 0-384-61330-6). Johnson Repr.
Trager, George L. An Outline of English Structure. Repr. of 1957 ed. pap. 4.00 (ISBN 0-384-61335-7). Johnson Repr.
Traugott, Elizabeth C. & Pratt, Mary L. Linguistics for Students of Literature. 444p. 1980. pap. text ed. 12.95 (ISBN 0-15-551030-4, HC). HarBraceJ.
Traugott, Elizabeth C., et al, eds. Papers from the Fourth International Conference on Historical Linguistics, Stanford, March 26-30, 1979. x, 437p. 1980. 44.00 (ISBN 90-272-3501-5, CILT 14). Benjamins North Am.
Trubetzkoy, N. S. N. S. Trubetzkoy's Letters & Notes. Jakobson, Roman, et al, eds. (Janua Linguarum, Series Major: No. 47). (Illus.). 1975. 132.00x (ISBN 90-2793-181-X). Mouton.
Tsuzaki, Stanley M. English Influence on Mexican Spanish in Detroit. (Janua Linguarum, Ser. Practica: No. 107). 1970. pap. text ed. 20.75x (ISBN 90-2791-565-2). Mouton.
Tumins, Valerie A. Tsar Ivan Fourth's Reply to Jan Roktya. LC 79-114575. (Slavistic Printings & Reprintings Ser.: No. 84). (Illus.). 1971. text ed. 113.00x (ISBN 90-2791-764-7). Mouton.
Turner, Geoffrey J. & Mohan, Bernard A. A Linguistic Description & Computer Program for Children's Speech. LC 78-158825. 238p. 1971. 15.00 (ISBN 0-8039-0123-2). Sage.
Uitti, Karl D. Linguistics & Literary Theory. new ed. 264p. 1974. pap. text ed. 5.95x (ISBN 0-393-09293-3). Norton.
Ulrich, W. Woerterbuch - Linguistische Grundbegriffe. 2nd ed. (Ger.). 1975. pap. 12.95 (ISBN 3-554-80336-7, M-6914). French & Eur.
Vago, Robert, ed. Issues in Vowel Harmony: Proceedings of the CUNY Linguistics Conference on Vowel Harmony, May 14 1977. xx, 340p. 1980. 39.00 (ISBN 90-272-3005-6). Benjamins North Am.
Valdman, Albert, ed. Pidgin & Creole Linguistics. LC 76-48496. (Illus.). 384p. 1977. 17.50x (ISBN 0-253-34495-6). Ind U Pr.
Valin, Roch. Methode Comparative En Linguistique Historique et En Psychomecanique Du Langage. (Cahiers De Psychomecanique Du Langage). (Fr). 1964. pap. 3.75x (ISBN 2-7637-6118-6, Pub. by Laval). Intl Schol Bk Serv.
--Petite Introduction a la Psychomecanique Du Langage. 2nd ed. (Fr). 1967. pap. 6.00x (ISBN 2-7637-6119-4, Pub. by Laval). Intl Schol Bk Serv.
Van Alkemade, Dick, et al, eds. Linguistic Studies Offered to Berthe Siertsema. (Costerus Ser.). 1980. pap. text ed. 31.00x (ISBN 90-6203-731-3). Humanities.
Van Den Broecke, M. P. Hierarchies & Rank Orders in Distinctive Features. (Illus., Orig.). 1976. pap. text ed. 19.00x (ISBN 90-232-1369-6). Humanities.
Van Dijk, T. A. Pragmatics of Language & Literature. LC 75-31589. (Studies in Theoretical Poetics: Vol. 2). 236p. 1976. pap. 24.50 (ISBN 0-444-10897-1, North-Holland). Elsevier.
Varvaro, Alberto, ed. Congresso, XIV, Internationale Di Linguistica E Filologia Romanza, 5 vols. 1974. pap. 287.00 (ISBN 90-272-0941-3). Benjamins North Am.
Verschueren, Jef. Jef Verschuren: An Annotated Bibliography with Particular Reference to Speech Act Theory. xvi, 270p. 1978. 30.00 (ISBN 90-272-0995-2, LISL 2). Benjamins North Am.
Vetter, Harold J. Language Behavior & Communication: An Introduction. LC 68-57969. 1969. text ed. 9.95 (ISBN 0-87581-012-8). Peacock Pubs.
Vogt, Hans. Grammaire de la Langue Georgienne. (Institutt for Sammenlignende Kulturforskning Serie B.: No. 58). 278p. 1971. 27.00x (ISBN 8-200-08720-4, Dist. by Columbia U Pr). Universitet.
Vogt, Joann. The Linguistic Work of Friedrich Karl Fulda. LC 74-77154. (Janua Linguarum, Ser. Minor: No. 199). 160p. 1974. pap. text ed. 27.50x (ISBN 90-2793-053-8). Mouton.
Von Humboldt, Wilhelm. Linguistic Variability & Intellectual Development. LC 75-81614. 1972. pap. 5.95x (ISBN 0-8122-1028-X, Pa Paperbks). U of Pa Pr.
Wallwork, J. F. Language & Linguistics. 1969. pap. text ed. 8.00x (ISBN 0-435-10916-2); wkbk. 4.00x (ISBN 0-435-10917-0). Heinemann Ed.
--Language & People. 1978. pap. text ed. 8.95x (ISBN 0-435-10918-9). Heinemann Ed.
Wanner, Eric. On Remembering, Forgetting, & Understanding Sentences: A Study of the Deep Structure Hypothesis. LC 73-84695. (Janua Linguarum, Ser. Minor: No. 170). 160p. (Orig.). 1974. pap. 17.25x (ISBN 0-686-22572-4). Mouton.
Ward, Kendall K. & Kaltenborn, Arthur L. Guides for American-English Proninciation. (Illus.). 256p. 1971. photocopy ed. spiral 19.75 (ISBN 0-398-02019-1). C C Thomas.
Wardhaugh, Ronald. Introduction to Linguistics. 2nd ed. (Illus.). 1977. pap. text ed. 11.50 (ISBN 0-07-068152-X, C). McGraw.
Wardhaugh, Ronald & Brown, H. Douglas, eds. A Survey of Applied Linguistics. LC 75-31053. 1976. pap. 7.95x (ISBN 0-472-08959-5). U of Mich Pr.
Warneck, Joh. Toba-Batak-Deutsches Worterbuch. (Royal Institute of Linguistics & Anthropology-Leiden). 1977. lib. bdg. 40.50 (ISBN 90-247-201-84, Pub. by Martinus Nijhoff Netherlands). Kluwer Boston.
Waterman, John T. Leibniz & Ludolf on Things Linguistic: Excerpts from Their Correspondence, (1688-1703) (Publications in Linguistics: No. 88). 1978. pap. 11.00x (ISBN 0-520-09586-3). U of Cal Pr.
--Perspectives in Linguistics. 2nd ed. LC 63-9732. 1970. 3.50x (ISBN 0-226-87460-5). U of Chicago Pr.
Waugh, Linda R. Roman Jakobson's Science of Language. (PDR Press Publications on Roman Jakobson: No. 2). (Orig.). 1977. pap. text ed. 10.25x (ISBN 90-316-0112-8). Humanities.
Weigl, Egon. Neuropsychology & Neurolinguistics. (Janua Linguarum, Ser. Maior: No. 78). 1980. text ed. 75.00x (ISBN 90-279-7956-1). Mouton.
Weijnen, A. Outlines for an Interlingual European Dialectology: Essais De Dialectologie Interlinguale. (No. 1). 1978. pap. text ed. 11.75x (ISBN 90-232-1595-8). Humanities.
Weijnen, A., ed. Atlas Linguarum Europae-Ale. 216p. 1980. text ed. 22.50 (ISBN 90-232-1697-0). Humanities.
Weil, Henri. The Order of Words in the Ancient Languages Compared with That of the Modern Languages. Super, Charles W., tr. xxxix, 114p. 1978. 21.00 (ISBN 90-272-0975-8, ACIL 14). Benjamins North Am.
Weiler, Gershon. Mauthner's Critique of Language. LC 76-114605. 1971. 42.00 (ISBN 0-521-07861-X). Cambridge U Pr.
Weinstock, John, ed. The Hollander Festschrift: Saga Og Sprak. 15.00 (ISBN 0-8363-0086-6). Jenkins.
Weinstock, John M., ed. The Nordic Languages & Modern Linguistics, Vol. 3. 560p. 1978. text ed. 35.00x (ISBN 0-292-75513-9). U of Tex Pr.
Wexler, Kenneth & Culicover, Peter W. Formal Principles of Language Acquisition. 1980. 35.00x (ISBN 0-262-23099-2). MIT Pr.
Wheatley, Jon. Language & Rules. LC 70-95011. (Janua Linguarum, Ser. Minor: No. 80). (Orig.). 1970. pap. text ed. 7.80x (ISBN 0-686-22416-7). Mouton.
Whitelock, Dorothy, ed. Sermo Lupi Ad Anglos. rev. ed. 91p. 1980. pap. text ed. 5.00x (ISBN 0-85989-071-6, Pub. by U Exeter England). Humanities.
Whitney, William. Language & the Study of Language. 1867. 30.00 (ISBN 0-8274-3877-X). R West.
Whitney, William D. Life & Growth of Language. LC 79-53017. 1980. pap. text ed. 5.00 (ISBN 0-486-23866-0). Dover.
Widdowson, H. G. Discovering Discourse. (Orig.). 1979. pap. text ed. 5.95x (ISBN 0-19-451355-6); ed. 8.95xtchr's (ISBN 0-19-451356-4). Oxford U Pr.
--Explorations in Applied Linguistics. 1979. pap. text ed. 10.95x (ISBN 0-19-437080-1). Oxford U Pr.
Wilkins, John. Essay Towards a Real Character & a Philosophical Language. (Linguistics 13th-18th Centuries Ser.). 612p. (Fr.). 1974. Repr. of 1668 ed. lib. bdg. 148.50x (ISBN 0-8287-0884-3, 71-5018). Clearwater Pub.
Williams, Frederick. Language & Speech: Introductory Perspectives. 1972. pap. text ed. 8.95 (ISBN 0-13-522789-5). P-H.
Williamson, Robert C. & Van Eerde, John A., eds. Language Maintenance & Language Shift. (International Journal of the Sociology of Language Ser.: No. 25). 124p. 1980. 20.00 (ISBN 90-279-3068-6). Mouton.
Wilson, James. The Dialect of Robert Burns As Spoken in Central Ayrshire. LC 74-13196. 1974. Repr. of 1923 ed. lib. bdg. 25.00 (ISBN 0-8414-9543-2). Folcroft.
Wirth, Jessica R., ed. Assessing Linguistic Arguments. LC 76-25529. 1976. 14.95 (ISBN 0-470-98916-5). Halsted Pr.
Wise, Mary R., ed. Vocablos y Expresiones Medicos Mas Usuales En Veinte Idiomas Vernaculos Peruanos. (Peruvian Working Papers Ser.: No. 2). 1973. pap. 3.00x (ISBN 0-88312-652-4). Summer Inst Ling.
Wolfenden, Elmer. A Description of Hiligaynon Syntax. (Linguistics & Related Fields Ser: No. 46). 1975. 8.00x (ISBN 0-88312-056-9); microfiche 1.60 (ISBN 0-88312-456-4). Summer Inst Ling.
Wolfle, Dael L. Relation Between Linguistic Structure & Associative Interference in Artificial Linguistic Material. 1932. pap. 6.00 (ISBN 0-527-00815-X). Kraus Repr.
Wolfram, Walt. Speech Pathology & Dialect Differences. (Dialects & Educational Equity Ser.: No. 3). 1979. pap. 2.75x (ISBN 0-87281-122-0). Ctr Appl Ling.
Workshop on Grammar & Semantics, Stanford, 1970. Approaches to Natural Language: Proceedings. Hintikka, K. J., et al, eds. LC 72-179892. (Synthese Library: No. 49). (Illus.). 526p. 1973. lib. bdg. 60.50 (ISBN 90-277-0220-9, Pub. by Reidel Holland); pap. text ed. 29.00 (ISBN 90-277-0233-0). Kluwer Boston.
Wunderlich, D. Foundations of Linguistics. Lass, R., tr. from Ger. LC 77-82526. (Cambridge Studies in Linguistics Monographs: No. 22). 1979. 59.95 (ISBN 0-521-22007-6); pap. 17.50x (ISBN 0-521-29334-0). Cambridge U Pr.
Wundt, Wilhelm. The Language of Gestures. Sebeok, Thomas A., ed. LC 73-84206. (Approaches to Semiotics Ser.). 149p. 1973. pap. text ed. 26.25x (ISBN 90-2792-486-4). Mouton.
Youngren, William. Semantics, Linguistics & Criticism. 1971. pap. text ed. 3.95x (ISBN 0-685-47631-6). Phila Bk Co.
Zierer, Ernesto. Theory of Graphs in Linguistics. LC 71-129294. (Janua Linguarum, Ser. Minor: No. 94). 1970. pap. text ed. 11.25x (ISBN 90-2791-277-7). Mouton.
Ziff, Paul. Understanding Understanding. LC 72-4573. 170p. 1972. 14.50x (ISBN 0-8014-0744-3). Cornell U Pr.
Zirin, Ronald A. Phonological Basis of Latin Prosody. LC 71-118284. (Janua Linguarum, Ser. Practica: No. 99). (Orig.). 1971. pap. text ed. 21.25x (ISBN 90-2791-526-1). Mouton.
Zonneveld, Wim, ed. Linguistics in the Netherlands, 1974-1976. (Illus.). 1978. pap. text ed. 16.00x (ISBN 90-316-0159-4). Humanities.
Zsilka, Janos. Sentence Patterns & Reality. 1973. pap. text ed. 36.25x (ISBN 90-2792-447-3). Mouton.
Zwicky, Arnold M., et al. Language Development, Grammar, Semantics: The Contribution of Linguistics to Bilingual Education. LC 79-57530. (Bilingual Ed. Ser.: No. 7). 89p. 1980. text ed. 7.25x (ISBN 0-87281-111-5). Ctr Appl Ling.

LINGUISTICS–ADDRESSES, ESSAYS, LECTURES

Abraham, Werner. Ut Videam: Contributions to an Understanding of Linguistics. 1975. pap. text ed. 33.00x (ISBN 90-316-0002-4). Humanities.
Allen, J. P. & Corder, S. Pit, eds. The Edinburgh Course in Applied Linguistics: Techniques in Applied Linguistics, Vol. 3. (Language & Language Learning Ser). 386p. 1974. pap. text ed. 13.95x (ISBN 0-19-437059-3). Oxford U Pr.
Allwood, J., et al, eds. Logic in Linguistics. LC 76-46855. (Cambridge Textbooks in Linguistics Ser.). (Illus.). 1977. 29.95 (ISBN 0-521-21496-3); pap. 9.50 (ISBN 0-521-29174-7). Cambridge U Pr.
Austin, William M., ed. Papers in Linguistics in Honor of Leon Dostert. (Janua Linguarum, Ser. Major: No. 25). 1967. text ed. 34.10x (ISBN 90-2790-616-5). Mouton.
Bastide, Roger, ed. Sens et Usages Du Terme Structure Dans les Sciences Humaines et Sociales. 2nd ed. (Janua Linguarum, Series Minor: No. 16). 165p. (Fr.). 1972. pap. text ed. 26.25x (ISBN 90-2792-312-4). Mouton.
Bennett, Michael, et al. Papers in Cognitive-Stratificational Linguistics. Copeland, James E. & Davis, Philip W., eds. (Rice University Studies: Vol. 66, No. 2). (Illus.). 208p. (Orig.). 1980. pap. 5.50x (ISBN 0-89263-245-3). Rice Univ.
Blok, D. P., ed. Proceedings of the Eighth International Congress of Onomastic Sciences, Amsterdam, 1963. (Janua Linguarum Series Major: No. 17). 1966. 135.30x (ISBN 90-2790-609-2). Mouton.
Centre for Information on Language Teaching & Research, ed. Language Teaching & Linguistics. LC 77-88671. 1978. 11.95 (ISBN 0-521-21926-4). Cambridge U Pr.
Cohen, David, ed. Melanges Marcel Cohen: Etudes De Linguistique, Ethnographie & Sciences Connexes Offertes Par Ses Amis & Ses Eleves a L'occasion De Son 80eme Anniversaire. (Janua Linguarum, Series Maior: No. 27). 1970. 140.50x (ISBN 0-686-21253-3). Mouton.
Colloquium of Linguistics Assn. of Great Britain, Historical Section, Univ. of London, March 18-20, 1970. Hamito-Semitica: Proceedings. Bynon, James & Bynon, Theodora, eds. LC 74-81134. (Janua Linguarum, Series Practica: No. 200). (Illus.). 518p. (Orig.). 1975. 105.50x (ISBN 0-686-22584-8). Mouton.
Cooper, David E. Knowledge of Language. 196p. 1975. text ed. 15.50x (ISBN 0-391-00382-8); pap. text ed. 10.50x (ISBN 0-391-00383-6). Humanities.
Cowan, J. L., ed. Studies in Thought & Language. LC 75-89620. 220p. 1970. 2.00 (ISBN 0-8165-0189-0). U of Ariz Pr.
Danesi, Marcel, ed. Issues in Language: Studies in Honor of Robert J. Di Pietro Presented to Him by His Students. (Edward Sapir Monograph in Language, Culture, & Cognition: No. 9). viii, 165p. (Orig.). 1981. pap. 8.00x (ISBN 0-933104-13-8). Jupiter Pr.
Dubois, Jean. Diccionario de Linguistica. (Espn.). 1979. pap. pns (S-50086). French & Eur.
Dyen, Isidore. Linguistic Subgrouping & Lexicostatistics. LC 73-82418. (Janua Linguarum, Series Minor: No. 175). (Illus.). 251p. 1975. pap. text ed. 46.25x (ISBN 90-2793-054-6). Mouton.
Ebihara, May & Gianutsos, Rosamond, eds. Papers in Anthropology & Linguistics. (Annals of the New York Academy of Sciences: Vol. 318). (Orig.). 1978. pap. 19.00x (ISBN 0-89072-077-0). NY Acad Sci.
Emeneau, Murray B. Language & Linguistic Area: Essays by Murray B. Emeneau. Dil, Anwar S., ed. LC 79-66058. (Language Science & National Development Ser.). 1980. 15.00x (ISBN 0-8047-1047-3). Stanford U Pr.
Greenbaum, S., et al, eds. Studies in English Linguistics: For Randolph Quirk. LC 79-41023. (Illus.). 304p. 1980. text ed. 45.00x (ISBN 0-582-55079-3). Longman.
Greenberg, Joseph H. Essays in Linguistics. LC 57-6273. 1963. pap. 1.95 (ISBN 0-226-30615-1, P119, Phoen). U of Chicago Pr.
--Language, Culture, & Communication: Essays by Joseph H. Greenberg. Dil, A. S., ed. LC 72-150323. (Language Science & National Development Ser). 1971. 15.00x (ISBN 0-8047-0781-2). Stanford U Pr.
Haas, Mary R. Language, Culture, & History: Essays by Mary R. Haas. Dil, Anwar S., ed. LC 78-59373. (Language Science & National Development Series). 1978. 15.00x (ISBN 0-8047-0983-1). Stanford U Pr.
Halliday, M. A. K. Halliday: System & Function in Language: Selected Papers. Kress, Gunther, ed. (Language & Language Learning Ser.). 256p. 1976. pap. text ed. 11.00x (ISBN 0-19-437062-3). Oxford U Pr.
Halliday, Michael A. Explorations in the Functions of Language. new ed. LC 76-57229. 1977. 8.95 (ISBN 0-444-00201-4, North Holland). Elsevier.
Hamp, Eric P., et al, eds. Readings in Linguistics Two. LC 66-8391. (Midway Reprint Ser.). 1980. pap. text ed. 19.00x (ISBN 0-226-31532-0). U of Chicago Pr.
Hankamer, Jorge, ed. Deletion in Coordinate Structures. LC 78-67738. (Outstanding Dissertations in Linguistics Ser.). 1979. lib. bdg. 41.00 (ISBN 0-8240-9669-X). Garland Pub.
Hockett, C. F. The View from Language: Selected Essays, 1948-1974. LC 75-3818. 360p. 1977. 20.00x (ISBN 0-8203-0381-X). U of Ga Pr.
International Congress of Linguistics, 9th. Proceedings. Lunt, Horace G., ed. (Janua Linguarum, Ser. Major: No. 12). 1174p. 1964. text ed. 165.00x (ISBN 0-686-27756-2). Mouton.

Joos, Martin, ed. Readings in Linguistics One: The Development of Descriptive Linguistics in America, 1925-1956. 4th ed. LC 58-13036. 1966. 26.00x (ISBN 0-226-41026-9). U of Chicago Pr.

Kachru, Braj B., et al, eds. Issues in Linguistics: Papers in Honor of Henry & Renee Kahane. LC 72-88807. 940p. 1973. 32.50 (ISBN 0-252-00246-6). U of Ill Pr.

Kinkade, M. Dale & Hale, Kenneth, eds. Linguistics & Anthropology: In Honor of C. F. Voegelin. 1977. pap. text ed. 60.00x (ISBN 90-316-0079-2). Humanities.

Kramsky, J. Papers in General Linguistics. (Janua Linguarum Series Minor: No. 209). 207p. (Orig.). 1976. pap. text ed. 32.50x (ISBN 90-2793-131-3). Mouton.

Lencek, R. L. & Unbegaun, B., eds. Xenia Slavica: Papers Presented to Gojko Ruzicic on the Occasion of His 75th Birthday, February 2, 1969. (Slavistic Printings & Reprintings Ser.: No. 279). 237p. 1975. text ed. 52.50x (ISBN 90-2793-017-1). Mouton.

Linguistic Association of Canada & the U.S. The First LACUS Forum: Proceedings. Makkai, Adam & Makkai, Valerie, eds. pap. text ed. 10.95 (ISBN 0-685-69725-8). Hornbeam Pr.

--The Fourth LACUS Forum: Proceedings. Paradis, Michel, ed. 1978. pap. text ed. 10.95 (ISBN 0-685-38955-3). Hornbeam Pr.

--The Second LACUS Forum: Proceedings. Reich, Peter A., ed. pap. text ed. 10.95 (ISBN 0-685-69722-3). Hornbeam Pr.

--Third LACUS Forum: Proceedings. Di Pietro, Robert J. & Blansitt, Edward L., Jr., eds. pap. text ed. 10.95 (ISBN 0-685-82432-2). Hornbeam Pr.

Malkiel, Yakov. Essays on Linguistic Themes. LC 68-15588. 1968. 22.75x (ISBN 0-520-00798-0). U of Cal Pr.

Malmberg, Bertil, ed. Readings in Modern Linguistics: An Anthology. 384p. (Orig.). 1972. pap. text ed. 41.25x (ISBN 90-2792-429-5). Mouton.

Melanges De Linguistics et De Litterature Offerts a Lein Geschiere Par Ses Amis, Collegues et Elves. 297p. (Fr.). 1975. pap. text ed. 40.00x (ISBN 90-6203-209-5). Humanities.

Michigan Linguistic Society. Papers, Vol. II. LC 76-1372. 1976. 10.75 (ISBN 0-8357-0160-3, IS-00004, Pub by Michigan Linguistic Society). Univ Microfilms.

Nash, Rose, ed. Readings in Spanish-English Contrastive Linguistics, Vol. 1. LC 73-85939. 249p. 1973. 13.50 (ISBN 0-913480-19-3); pap. 4.50 (ISBN 0-913480-20-7). Inter Am U Pr.

Nickel, Gerhard, ed. Papers in Contrastive Linguistics. LC 78-149434. (Illus.). 1971. 19.95 (ISBN 0-521-08091-6). Cambridge U Pr.

Ninth International Congress of Linguists, Cambridge, Mass., August, 1962. Proceedings. Lunt, Horace G., ed. (Janua Linguarum Series Maior: No. 12). 1964. 132.25x (ISBN 0-686-21811-6). Mouton.

Osgood, C. E. Lectures on Language Performance. (Springer Ser. in Language & Communication: Vol. 7). (Illus.). 368p. 1980. 22.00 (ISBN 0-387-09901-8). Springer-Verlag.

Perren, G. E. & Trim, J. L., eds. Applications of Linguistics: Selected Papers on the Second International Congress of Applied Linguistics, Cambridge. (Illus.). 1972. 69.50 (ISBN 0-521-08088-6). Cambridge U Pr.

Pike, Kenneth L. Selected Writings: To Commemorate the 60th Birthday of Kenneth Lee Pike. Brend, Ruth M., ed. (Janua Linguarum, Series Maior: No. 55). (Illus.). 1972. 64.00x (ISBN 0-686-21824-8). Mouton.

Raymond, James C. & Russell, I. Willis, eds. James B. McMillan: Essays in Linguistics by His Friends & Colleagues. LC 77-7169. 1978. 15.50x (ISBN 0-8173-0503-3). U of Ala Pr.

Rosetti, Alexander. Linguistica. (Janua Linguarum, Ser. Major: No. 16). (Fr). 1965. text ed. 54.00x (ISBN 90-2790-608-4). Mouton.

Roy, Gerard-Raymond. Contribution a L'Analyse Du Syntagme Verbal Etude Morpho-Syntaxique et Statistique Des Coverbes. (Bibliotheque Francaise et Romane Ser.: Ser. A). 1977. pap. 18.00x (ISBN 2-7637-6789-3, Pub. by Laval). Intl Schol Bk Serv.

Sebeok, Thomas A., ed. Selected Writings of Gyula Laziczius. (Janua Linguarum, Series Minor: No. 55). 1966. pap. 40.00x (ISBN 90-2790-603-3). Mouton.

Smith, Henry L., Jr. Linguistic Science & the Teaching of English. LC 55-11607. (Inglis Lectures Ser: 1954). 1956. 6.95x (ISBN 0-674-53500-6). Harvard U Pr.

Smith, M. E., ed. Studies in Linguistics in Honor of George L. Trager. (Janua Linguarum, Series Maior: No. 52). 1972. 101.25 (ISBN 90-2792-309-4). Mouton.

Transactions of the Philological Society 1980. 162p. 1980. pap. 35.00x (ISBN 0-631-12574-4, Pub. by Basil Blackwell). Biblio Dist.

Vachek, Josef. Selected Writings in English & General Linguistics. (Janual Linguarum, Series Maior: No. 92). 451p. 1976. text ed. 83.75x (ISBN 0-686-22609-7). Mouton.

Valdman, Albert, ed. Papers in Linguistics & Phonetics to the Memory of Pierre Delattre. (Janua Linguarum, Ser. Major: No. 54). (Illus.). 513p. 1972. text ed. 109.00x (ISBN 90-2792-310-8). Mouton.

Valin, Roch, ed. Lecons De Linguistique De Gustave Guillaume, Vol. 4, 1949-1950. (Structure Semiologique et Structure Physique De la Langue Francaise: No. 2, Serie A). 223p. (Fr.). 1974. pap. 9.00x (ISBN 2-7637-6701-X, Pub. by Laval). Intl Schol Bk Serv.

Wescott, Roger W. Sound & Sense: Linguistic Essays on Phonosemic Subjects. (Edward Sapir Monograph Series in Language, Culture, & Cognition, No. 3). 405p. (Orig.). 1980. pap. 10.00x (ISBN 0-933104-12-X). Jupiter Pr.

LINGUISTICS–BIBLIOGRAPHY

Allen, Harold B. Linguistics & English Linguistics. 2nd ed. LC 75-42974. (Goldentree Bibliographies in Language & Literature Ser.). 1977. pap. text ed. 12.95x (ISBN 0-88295-558-6). Harlan Davidson.

Beylsmit, J. & Rijlaarsdam, J. C., eds. Linguistic Bibliography for the Year 1976. xlviii, 736p. 1980. lib. bdg. 103.00 (ISBN 90-247-2242-X, Martinus Nijhoff Pubs). Kluwer Boston.

Center for Applied Linguistics, Washington D.C. Dictionary Catalog of the Library of the Center for Applied Linguistics, Washington, D. C, 4 vols. 1974. Set. lib. bdg. 355.00 (ISBN 0-8161-1114-6). G K Hall.

Crystal, David. A First Dictionary of Linguistics & Phonetics. (Language Library Ser.). 404p. 1980. lib. bdg. 33.75x (ISBN 0-86531-051-3, Pub. by Andre Deutsch); pap. text ed. 12.00 (ISBN 0-86531-050-5). Westview.

Gazdar, Gerald, et al. A Bibliography of Contemporary Linguistic Research. LC 77-83358. (Library of Humanities Reference Bks.: No. 119). lib. bdg. 42.00 (ISBN 0-8240-9852-8). Garland Pub.

Hammer, John H. & Rice, Frank A., eds. Bibliography of Contrastive Linguistics. LC 65-29014. (Orig.). 1965. pap. 2.00 (ISBN 0-87281-005-4). Ctr Appl Ling.

Healey, Phyllis M., ed. Bibliography of the Summer Institute of Linguistics (Papua New Guinea Branch, 2 vols. Incl. Linguistics, Literacy & Anthropology. pap. 0.75 ea.. 1973. Summer Inst Ling.

Intl Comm. of Linguists, ed. Linguistic Bibliography for the Year..-Bibliographic Linguistique Del'annee... Incl. Vol. 1. 1946-1948. pap. 45.00x (ISBN 0-8002-1652-0); Vol. 2. 1947-1949. pap. 30.00x (ISBN 0-8002-1653-9); Vols. 3-7. pap. 30.00x ea.; Vol. 3, 1948-1950. pap. (ISBN 0-8002-1654-7); Vol. 4, 1949-1951. pap. (ISBN 0-8002-1655-5); Vol. 5, 1950-1952. pap. (ISBN 0-8002-1656-3); Vol. 6, 1951-1953. pap. (ISBN 0-8002-1657-1); Vol. 7, 1952-1954. pap. (ISBN 0-8002-1658-X); Vols. 9 & 11-16. pap. 30.00x ea. Vol. 9, 1954-1956 (ISBN 0-8002-1659-8). pap. (ISBN 0-8002-1660-1). Vol. 11, 1956-1958. Vol. 12, 1957-1959. pap. (ISBN 0-8002-1662-8); Vol. 13, 1958-1960. pap. (ISBN 0-8002-1663-6); Vol. 14, 1959-1961. pap. (ISBN 0-8002-1664-4); Vol. 15, 1960-1962. pap. (ISBN 0-8002-1665-2); Vol. 16, 1961-1963. pap. (ISBN 0-8002-1666-0); Vol. 17. 1962-1964. pap. 35.00x (ISBN 0-8002-1667-9); Vol. 18. 1963-1965. pap. 42.50x (ISBN 0-8002-1668-7); Vol. 19. 1964-1966. pap. 47.50x (ISBN 0-8002-1669-5); Vol. 20, 1965-1967. pap. 47.50x (ISBN 0-8002-1670-9); Vol. 21,1966-1968. pap. 47.50x (ISBN 0-8002-1671-7); Vol. 22. 1967-1969. pap. 37.50x (ISBN 0-8002-1672-5); Vol. 23. 1968-1970. pap. 47.50x (ISBN 0-8002-1673-3); Vol. 24. 1969-1972. pap. 55.00x (ISBN 0-8002-1674-1); Vol. 25, 1970-1973. pap. 60.00x (ISBN 0-8002-1675-X); Vol. 26, 1971-1974. pap. 87.50x (ISBN 0-8002-1676-8); Vol. 27. 1972-1975. pap. 87.50x (ISBN 0-8002-1677-6); Vol. 28. 1973-1976. pap. 95.00x (ISBN 0-8002-1678-4); Vol. 29. 1974. 1977. pap. 102.50x (ISBN 0-8002-2385-3). Intl Pubns Serv.

Juilland, Alphonse & Roceric, Alexandria. The Linguistic Concept of Word: Analytic Bibliography. (Janua Linguarum, Ser. Minor: No. 130). 118p. 1972. pap. text ed. 17.00x (ISBN 90-2792-188-1). Mouton.

Linguistics: World List of Specialized Periodicals. (Maison des Sciences de l'Homme Catalogues & Inventaires Ser: Vol. 4). (Illus.). 243p. (Orig.). 1971. pap. text ed. 19.50x (ISBN 90-2796-929-9). Mouton.

McCormack, William G. & Izzo, Herbert J., eds. Sixth LACUS Forum Proceedings, Linguistic Association of Canada & the U.S. pap. 10.95 (ISBN 0-686-64345-3). Hornbeam Pr.

Wares, Alan C., ed. Bibliography of the Summer Institute of Linguistics. 7th ed. 1974. pap. 2.50x (ISBN 0-88312-913-2); microfiche 2.80x (ISBN 0-88312-999-X). Summer Inst Ling.

Wawrzyszko, Aleksandra. Bibliography of General Linguistics, English & American. LC 75-150766. 1971. 15.00 (ISBN 0-208-01203-6, Archon). Shoe String.

Wise, Mary R. & Powlison, Paul. Bibliografia del Instituto Linguistico de Verano en el Peru: Junio 1946-Junio 1976. 1978. pap. 5.50x (ISBN 0-88312-740-7). Summer Inst Ling.

LINGUISTICS–DATA PROCESSING

see also Machine Translating; Mathematical Linguistics; Speech Processing Systems

Abramson, Harvey. Theory & Application of a Bottom-up Syntax-Directed Translator. (ACM Monograph Ser.). 1973. 28.00 (ISBN 0-12-042650-1). Acad Pr.

Automated Education Center. Automatic Language Processing. 19.50 (ISBN 0-686-02009-X). Mgmt Info Serv.

Borko, Harold. Automated Language Processing. LC 66-26735. 386p. 1967. 23.50 (ISBN 0-471-08950-8, Pub. by Wiley). Krieger.

Carvell, H. T. & Svartvik, J. Computational Experiments in Grammatical Classification. LC 68-23805. (Janua Linguarum, Ser. Minor: No. 61). (Orig.). 1969. pap. text ed. 36.25x (ISBN 90-2790-682-3). Mouton.

Freeman, Robert R., et al, eds. Information in the Language Sciences. (Mathematical Linguistics & Automatic Language Processing: Vol. 5). 1969. 21.95 (ISBN 0-444-00036-4, North Holland). Elsevier.

Heaps, H. S. Introduction to Computer Languages. LC 70-163864. (Automatic Computation Ser). (Illus.). 1972. ref. ed. 19.95 (ISBN 0-13-479584-9). P-H.

Herdan, G. Quantitative Linguistics. 1964. 18.50 (ISBN 0-208-00196-4, Archon). Shoe String.

Kelly, E. & Stone, P., eds. Computer Recognition of English Word Senses. (Linguistic Ser: Vol. 13). 269p. 1975. pap. 24.50 (ISBN 0-444-10831-9, North-Holland). Elsevier.

Kolers, Paul A., et al, eds. Processing of Visible Language, Vol. 2. 620p. 1980. 49.50 (ISBN 0-306-40576-8, Plenum Pr). Plenum Pub.

Litwiller, Bonnie & Duncan, David. Activities for the Maintenance of Computational Skills. 1980. pap. 3.20 (ISBN 0-87353-169-8). NCTM.

Minsky, Marvin L., ed. Semantic Information Processing. LC 68-18239. 1969. 27.50x (ISBN 0-262-13044-0). MIT Pr.

National Computing Centre Ltd., ed. Elements of BASIC. (Computers & the Professional Ser.). 100p. 1972. pap. 15.00x (ISBN 0-85012-213-9). Intl Pubns Serv.

Papp, Ferenc & Szepe, Gyorgy, eds. Papers in Computational Linguistics. (Janua Linguarum, Ser. Major: No. 91). 585p. text ed. 120.00x (ISBN 90-279-3285-9). Mouton.

Ritchie, Graeme D. Computational Grammar: An Artificial Intelligence Approach to Linguistic Description. (Harvester Studies in Cognitive Science: No. 15). 1980. 26.50x (ISBN 0-389-20048-4). B&N.

Rosen, A. & Frelden, R. Word Processing. 1977. text ed. 16.95 (ISBN 0-13-963504-1). P-H.

Sedelow, Walter A., Jr. Bibliography for a Science of Language: Computer Studies in the Humanities & Verbal Behavior. (No. V, 1-4). 1975. pap. 30.25x (ISBN 90-2797-537-X). Mouton.

Shelly, Gary B. & Cashman, Thomas J. OS Job Control Language. pap. text ed. 11.95x (ISBN 0-88236-290-9). Anaheim Pub Co.

Stindlova, Jitka, ed. Machines Dans La Linguistique. (Janua Linguarum, Ser. Major: No. 30). 1968. text ed. 64.00x (ISBN 90-2790-617-3). Mouton.

Webber, Bonnie L. A Formal Approach to Discourse Anaphora. Hankamer, Jorge, ed. LC 78-67737. (Outstanding Dissertations in Linguistics Ser.). 1979. lib. bdg. 24.00 (ISBN 0-8240-9670-3). Garland Pub.

Wheatley, Jon. Language & Rules. LC 70-95011. (Janua Linguarum, Ser. Minor: No. 80). (Orig.). 1970. pap. text ed. 7.80x (ISBN 0-686-22416-7). Mouton.

Wilks, Yorick A. Grammar, Meaning & the Machine Analysis of Language. 1971. 15.00x (ISBN 0-7100-7035-7). Routledge & Kegan.

Winograd, Terry. Understanding Natural Language. 1972. 25.00 (ISBN 0-12-759750-6). Acad Pr.

--Understanding Natural Language. 1972. 25.00 (ISBN 0-12-759750-6). Acad Pr.

Wisbey, R. A. Computer in Literary & Linguistic Research. LC 70-152645. (Publications of the Literary & Linguistic Computing Centre: No. 1). 1971. 49.50 (ISBN 0-521-08146-7). Cambridge U Pr.

LINGUISTICS–PROGRAMMED INSTRUCTION

De Beaugrande, R. & Dressler, W. Introduction to Text Linguistics. (Longman Linguistics Library). (Illus.). 288p. 1981. text ed. 25.00x (ISBN 0-582-55486-1); pap. text ed. 14.95x (ISBN 0-582-55485-3). Longman.

Stork, F. C. & Widdowson, J. D. Learning About Linguistics. 1980. pap. text ed. 11.25x (ISBN 0-09-118061-9, Hutchinson U Lib). Humanities.

LINGUISTICS–STUDY AND TEACHING

Alatis, James E., ed. Georgetown University Round Table on Languages & Linguistics: Linguistics & the Teaching of Standard English to Speakers of Other Languages or Dialects. LC 58-31607. (Georgetown Univ. Round Table Ser.: 1969). 267p. 1969. pap. 5.25 (ISBN 0-87840-104-0). Georgetown U Pr.

Allen, J. P. & Corder, S. Pit, eds. The Edinburgh Course in Applied Linguistics, Vol. 2. (Language & Language Learning Ser). 388p. 1975. pap. text ed. 17.00x (ISBN 0-19-437058-5). Oxford U Pr.

--The Edinburgh Course in Applied Linguistics: Readings for Applied Linguistics, Vol. 1. (Language & Language Learning Ser.). 284p. 1973. pap. 9.00x (ISBN 0-19-437057-7). Oxford U Pr.

Association for Supervision and Curriculum Development. Linguistics & the Classroom Teacher. LC 67-27469. 1967. pap. 2.75 (ISBN 0-87120-040-6, 611-17720). Assn Supervision.

Bell, Roger T. An Introduction to Applied Linguistics: Approaches & Methods in Language Teaching. 1981. 25.00x (ISBN 0-312-42547-3). St Martin.

Berry, Mildred F. Teaching Linguistically Handicapped Children. 1980. text ed. 18.95 (ISBN 0-13-893545-9). P-H.

Boulton, Marjorie. The Anatomy of Language: Saying What We Mean. 1971. pap. 7.95 (ISBN 0-7100-6351-2). Routledge & Kegan.

Bradley, C. Henry. A Linguistic Sketch of Jicaltepec Mixtec. (Publications in Linguistics & Related Fields Ser.: No. 25). 97p. 1970. pap. 3.00x (ISBN 0-88312-027-5); microfiche 1.60 (ISBN 0-686-66936-3). Summer Inst Ling.

Brend, Ruth M., ed. Kenneth L. Pike: Selected Writings. (Janua Linguarum, Ser. Major: No. 55). 336p. 1972. text ed. 51.75x (ISBN 0-686-22544-9). Mouton.

Briere, Eugene J. Psycholinguistic Study of Phonological Interference. LC 68-13339. (Janua Linguarum, Ser. Minor: No. 66). 1968. pap. text ed. 15.00x (ISBN 90-2790-594-0). Mouton.

Broderick, J. P. Modern English Linguistics: A Structural & Transformational Grammar. 1975. text ed. 15.50 scp (ISBN 0-690-00067-7, HarpC). Har-Row.

Bynon, Theodora. Historical Linguistics. LC 76-62588. (Cambridge Textbooks in Linguistics). (Illus.). 1977. 39.95 (ISBN 0-521-21582-X); pap. 9.95 (ISBN 0-521-29188-7). Cambridge U Pr.

Crisafulli, Allesandro S., ed. Linguistic & Literary Studies in Honor of Helmut A. Hatzfeld. 1964. 25.00 (ISBN 0-8132-0333-3, Pub. by Cath U Pr). Intl Schol Bk Serv.

Dinneen, F. P., ed. Georgetown University Round Table on Languages & Linguistics: Linguistics-Teaching & Interdisciplinary Relations. LC 58-31607. (Georgetown Univ. Round Table Ser.: 1969). 197p. (GURT 1974). 1974. pap. 4.50 (ISBN 0-87840-109-1). Georgetown U Pr.

Fisiak, Jacek. Contrastive Linguistics & the Language Teacher. 160p. 1981. pap. 9.95 (ISBN 0-08-027230-4). Pergamon.

Gonzalez, Joe R. & Zufelt, David L., eds. Cognates: Vocabulary Enrichment for Bilinguals. (Span. - Eng.). 1973. pap. text ed. 8.95x (ISBN 0-8422-0311-7). Irvington.

Jakobson, Roman. Studies on Child Language & Aphasia. (Janua Linguarum, Ser. Minor: No. 114). (Orig.). 1971. pap. text ed. 17.00x (ISBN 90-2791-640-3). Mouton.

Lado, Robert. Linguistics Across Cultures: Applied Linguistics for Language Teachers. 1957. pap. 4.95x (ISBN 0-472-08542-5). U of Mich Pr.

Lupas, Liana. Phonologie du Grec Attique. (Janua Linguarum, Ser. Practica: No. 164). 186p. (Orig., Fr.). 1972. pap. text ed. 40.00x (ISBN 90-2792-325-6). Mouton.

Marckwardt, Albert H., ed. Linguistics in School Programs. LC 76-13494. (National Society for the Study of Education Yearbooks Ser: No. 69, Pt. 2). 1970. 8.00x (ISBN 0-226-60102-1). U of Chicago Pr.

National Computing Center. Computers in Language Studies. Turnbull, J. J., ed. (Computers & People Ser.). 48p. 1973. pap. 10.00x (ISBN 0-85012-096-9). Intl Pubns Serv.

Pierce, Joe E. Linguistic Method of Teaching Second Languages. 2nd ed. 1972. pap. 6.95 (ISBN 0-913244-05-8). Hapi Pr.

Postman, Neil & Weingartner, Charles. Linguistics. 1966. pap. 2.95 (ISBN 0-440-54844-6, Delta). Dell.

Savage, John F. Linguistics for Teachers. LC 72-97928. 1973. pap. text ed. 9.95 (ISBN 0-574-17965-8, 13-0965). SRA.

Schwartz, Judy J. Teaching the Linguistically Diverse. (New York State English Council Monographs). 1980. text ed. 8.50 (ISBN 0-930348-08-7). NY St Eng Coun.
Valin, Roch. Lecons De Linguistique De Gustave Guillaume, Vols. 1, 2 & 3. (Fr.). 1971. Vol. 1, Structure Semiologique Et Structure Psychique De La Langua Francaise 1, Serie A 1948-1949. 11.50x (ISBN 2-7637-6651-X, Pub by Laval); Vol. 2, Psycho-systematique Du Language: Principles, Methods Et Applications 1, Serie B 1948-1949. 10.00x (ISBN 0-7746-6444-4); Vol. 3, 1948-1949. 12.50x (ISBN 0-7746-6651-X). Intl Schol Bk Serv.
--Principes De Linguistique Theorique De Gustave Guillaume. (Fr.). 1972. 14.50x (ISBN 2-7637-6639-0, Pub by Laval). Intl Schol Bk Serv.
Van Alkemade, Dick, et al, eds. Lingusitic Studies Offered to Berthe Siertsema. (Costerus New Ser.: No. XXV). 1980. pap. text ed. 31.00x (ISBN 90-6203-731-3). Humanities.
Whitman, R. L. English & English Linguistics. LC 74-19403. 1975. pap. text ed. 8.95 (ISBN 0-03-010391-6, HoltC). HR&W.

LINGUISTICS, MATHEMATICAL
see Mathematical Linguistics

LINGUISTICS, STRUCTURAL
see Structural Linguistics

LINGUISTS
see also Philologists
Bell, Aubrey F. Baltazar Gracian. (Illus.). 1921. 2.00 (ISBN 0-87535-005-4). Hispanic Soc.
Harris, Roy. The Language-Makers. LC 79-6029. 1980. 19.50x (ISBN 0-8014-1317-6). Cornell U Pr.
Jankowsky, Kurt R. The Neogrammarians: A Re-Evaluation of Their Place in the Development of Linguistic Science. LC 71-189705. (Janua Linguarum, Ser. Minor: No. 116). 275p. (Orig.). 1972. pap. text ed. 31.25x (ISBN 0-686-22539-2). Mouton.
Moravcsik, J. M., ed. Logic & Philosophy for Linguists: A Book of Readings. 1979. pap. text ed. 25.00x (ISBN 0-391-00399-2). Humanities.
Osselton, N. E. The Dumb Linguists. (Publications of Sir Thomas Browne Institute Ser: No. 5). 1973. lib. bdg. 24.00 (ISBN 90-6021-166-9). Kluwer Boston.
Parret, Herman. Discussing Language: Dialogues with N. Chomsky, A. J. Greimas, M. A. K. Holiday, et al. 1974. pap. text ed. 40.75x (ISBN 0-686-22558-9). Mouton.
Sebeok, Thomas A., ed. Portraits of Linguists, 2 vols. LC 75-45352. (Indiana University Studies in the History 2nd Theory of Linguistics,1746-1963). 1976. Repr. of 1966 ed. lib. bdg. 66.00x (ISBN 0-8371-8731-1, SEPL). Greenwood.
Waterman, John T. Leibniz & Ludolf on Things Linguistic: Excerpts from Their Correspondence, (1688-1703) (Publications in Linguistics: No. 88). 1978. pap. 11.00x (ISBN 0-520-09586-3). U of Cal Pr.

LINGVO INTERNACIA (ARTIFICIAL LANGUAGE)
see Esperanto (Artificial Language)

LINKAGE (GENETICS)
see also Chromosomes
Shahshahani, S. A New Mathematical Framework for the Study of Linkage & Selection. LC 78-23487. (Memoirs: No. 211). 1979. 7.60 (ISBN 0-8218-2211-X). Am Math.

LINKLETTER, ARTHUR GORDON, 1912-
Linkletter, Art & Bishop, George. Hobo on the Way to Heaven. 212p. 9.95 (ISBN 0-89191-337-8, 53371). Cook.
--I Didn't Do It Alone: The Autobiography of Art Linkletter. (Illus.). 220p. 1980. 10.95 (ISBN 0-89803-040-4). Caroline Hse.

LINKS AND LINK-MOTION
Chironis, Nicholas P. Mechanisms, Linkages, & Mechanical Controls. 1965. 30.00 (ISBN 0-07-010775-0, P&RB). McGraw.
Hartenberg, Richard S. & Denavit, Jacques. Kinematic Synthesis of Linkages. (Mechanical Engineering Ser.). 1964. text ed. 26.95 (ISBN 0-07-026910-6, C). McGraw.
Jones, L., ed. Mechanical Handling with Precision Conveyor Chain. 1971. 9.95 (ISBN 0-09-106990-4, Pub. by Hutchinson). Merrimack Bk Serv.

LINKS, GOLF
see Golf Courses

LINLITHGOW, JOHN ADRIAN LOUIS HOPE, 1ST MARQUIS OF, 1860-1908
La Nauze, J. Hopetown Blunder. pap. 2.00x (ISBN 0-424-05480-9, Pub. by Sydney U Pr). Intl Schol Bk Serv.

LINNE, CARL VON, 1707-1778
Broberg, Gunnar, ed. Linnaeus: Progress & Prospects in Linnaean Research. (Illus.). 318p. 1980. 49.50x (ISBN 0-913196-31-2). Hunt Inst Botanical.
Larson, James L. Reason & Experience: The Representation of Natural Order in the Work of Carl von Linne. LC 70-632164. 1971. 20.00x (ISBN 0-520-01834-6). U of Cal Pr.
Soulsby, Basil H. A Catalogue of the Works of Linnaeus Preserved in the Libraries of the British Museum (Natural History) 2nd ed. (Illus.). 1933-36. Set. 36.50x (ISBN 0-686-25779-0, Pub. by Brit Mus Nat Hist). Catalogue, 1933 (ISBN 0-565-00104-3). Index, 1936 (ISBN 0-565-00066-7). Sabbot-Natural Hist Bks.
Stearn, W. T. Three Prefaces on Linnaeus & Robert Brown. (Illus.). 1962. pap. 8.00 (ISBN 3-7682-0099-X). Lubrecht & Cramer.

LINNE, CARL VON, 1707-1778-BIBLIOGRAPHY
Rudolph, G. A. & Williams, Evan. Linnaeana. 1970. 5.00 (ISBN 0-686-20815-3). KSU.

LINNELL, JOH, 1792-1882
Hayward, Helena & Kirkham, Pat. William & John Linnel: 18th Century London Furniture-Makers, 2 vols. LC 80-51404. (Illus.). 400p. 1980. slipcased 125.00 (ISBN 0-8478-0325-2). Rizzoli Intl.

LINOLEUM BLOCK-PRINTING
Kafka, Francis J. Batik, Tie Dyeing, Stenciling, Silk Screen, Block Printing. 9.00 (ISBN 0-8446-5707-7). Peter Smith.
--Batik, Tie Dying, Stenciling, Silk Screen, Block Printing. LC 73-80948. 1973. lib. bdg. 10.50 (ISBN 0-88307-652-7). Gannon.
--Linoleum Block Printing. (Illus.). 76p. 1972. pap. 3.00 (ISBN 0-486-20308-5). Dover.
McLean, Ruari, intro. by. Edward Bawden: A Book of Cuts. (Illus.). 84p. 1979. 15.00 (ISBN 0-85967-456-8, Pub. by Scholars Pr England); pap. 7.95 (ISBN 0-85967-457-6, Pub. by Scolor Pr England). Biblio Dist.

LINOTYPE
Barnett, George E. Chapters on Machinery & Labor. LC 68-25563. (Masterworks in Industrial Relations Ser.). 191p. 1969. Repr. of 1926 ed. 6.95x (ISBN 0-8093-0397-3). S Ill U Pr.
Thompson, John S. The Mechanism of the Linotype. Bidwell, John, ed. Bd. with History of Composing Machines. LC 78-74413. (Nineteenth Century Book Arts & Printing History Ser.: Vol. 23). (Illus.). 1980. lib. bdg. 38.00 (ISBN 0-8240-3897-5). Garland Pub.

LINTON, WILLIAM JAMES, 1812-1897
Smith, Francis B. Radical Artisan: William James Linton 1812-1897. LC 73-1933. (Illus.). 254p. 1973. 17.50x (ISBN 0-87471-180-0). Rowman.

LIONEL OF ANTWERP, DUKE OF CLARENCE, 1338-1368
Cook, Albert S. Last Months of Chaucer's Earliest Patron. LC 72-1000. Repr. of 1916 ed. 14.50 (ISBN 0-404-01698-7). AMS Pr.

LIONEL CORPORATION
Greenberg, Bruce. Greenberg's Price Guide to Lionel Trains: 1901-1942. (Illus.). 1978. 12.95 (ISBN 0-517-53796-6). Crown.
--Greenberg's Price Guide to Lionel Trains: 0 & 0-27 Trains, 1945-1978. (Illus.). 1978. 13.95 (ISBN 0-517-53795-8). Crown.
Hollander, Ron. All Aboard: Josh Cowen's Great American Lionel Train Company. (Illus.). 224p. 1981. pap. 9.95 (ISBN 0-89480-184-8). Workman Pub.
Shanter, Stan. Greenberg's Operating & Repair Manual for Lionel-Fundimensions Trains, 1970-78. (Illus.). 1978. pap. 3.95 (ISBN 0-517-53797-4). Crown.

LIONS
Adamson, Joy. Born Free: A Lioness of Two Worlds. (Illus.). (gr. 9 up). 1960. 7.95 (ISBN 0-394-41743-7); PLB 7.99 (ISBN 0-394-90500-8). Pantheon.
--Forever Free. LC 63-8081. (Helen & Kurt Wolff Bk.). (Illus.). (gr. 10 up). 1963. 9.50 (ISBN 0-15-132550-2). HarBraceJ.
--Living Free. LC 61-15810. (Helen & Kurt Wolff Bk.). (Illus.). (gr. 10 up). 1961. 12.95 (ISBN 0-15-152925-6). HarBraceJ.
McBride, Chris. Operation White Lion. (Illus.). 198p. 1981. 15.95 (ISBN 0-312-58680-9). St Martin.
--The White Lions of Timbavati. Date not set. Repr. pap. cancelled (ISBN 0-553-11737-8). Bantam.
--The White Lions of Timbavati. LC 77-4896. 1977. 10.95 (ISBN 0-448-22677-4). Paddington.
McKenna, Virginia & Travers, Bill. On Playing with Lions. LC 66-25625. (Helen & Kurt Wolff Bk). (Illus.). 1967. 3.95 (ISBN 0-15-169954-2). HarBraceJ.
Overbeck, Cynthia. Lions. LC 81-1962. (Lerner Natural Science Bks.). (Illus.). (gr. 4-10). 1981. PLB 7.95 (ISBN 0-8225-1463-X, AACR2). Lerner Pubns.
Rudnai, Judith A. The Social Life of the Lion. (Illus.). 1973. 19.50 (ISBN 0-685-48358-4, 0-852-00053-7). Univ Park.
Schaller, George & Schaller, Kay. Wonders of Lions. (Wonders Series). (gr. 4 up). 1977. 5.95 (ISBN 0-396-07409-X). Dodd.
Schaller, George B. The Serengeti Lion: A Study in Predator-Prey Relations. LC 78-180043. (Wildlife Behavior & Ecology Ser). (Illus.). 1972. 20.00x (ISBN 0-226-73639-3). U of Chicago Pr.
--The Serengeti Lion: A Study of Predator-Prey Relations. LC 78-180043. (Wildlife Behavior & Ecology Ser.). (Illus.). 472p. 1976. pap. 12.95 (ISBN 0-226-73640-7, P661, Phoen). U of Chicago Pr.

LIONS-JUVENILE LITERATURE
Arundel, Jocelyn. Lions & Tigers. Bourne, Russell & Rifkin, Natalie S., eds. LC 74-80049. (Ranger Rick's Best Friends Ser.: No. 3). (Illus.). 32p. (gr. 1-6). 1974. 2.00 (ISBN 0-912186-12-7). Natl Wildlife.
Chipperfield, Mary. Lions. LC 77-13039. (Animals of the World Ser.). (Illus.). (gr. 4-8). 1977. PLB 11.95 (ISBN 0-8172-1075-X). Raintree Pubs.
Hamsa, Bobbie. Your Pet Lion. (Far-Fetched Pets Ser.). (Illus.). (ps-3). 1981. PLB 8.65 (ISBN 0-516-03366-2); pap. 2.95 (ISBN 0-516-43366-0). Childrens.
Johnson, Sylvia A. The Lions of Africa. Hammarberg, Dyan, tr. from Fr. LC 76-29474. (Animal Friends Books). (Illus.). (gr. k-4). 1977. PLB 4.95g (ISBN 0-87614-081-9). Carolrhoda Bks.
Michel, Anna. Little Wild Lion Cub. LC 79-17509. (I Am Reading Book Ser.). (Illus.). 48p. (gr. 1-4). 1980. 4.95 (ISBN 0-394-84352-5); PLB 5.99 (ISBN 0-394-94352-X). Pantheon.
Peet, Bill. Randy's Dandy Lions. (Illus.). (gr. k-3). 1964. reinforced bdg. 10.95 (ISBN 0-395-18507-6). HM.
Pluckrose, Henry, ed. Small World of Lions & Tigers. (Small World Ser.). (Illus.). 1979. (gr. 5-8) 2.95 (ISBN 0-531-03446-1); PLB 6.45 s&l (gr. k-3) (ISBN 0-531-03410-0). Watts.
Schaller, George & Schaller, Kay. Wonders of Lions. (Wonders Series). (gr. 4 up). 1977. 5.95 (ISBN 0-396-07409-X). Dodd.
Schick, Alice. Serengeti Cats. LC 77-812. (gr. 4 up). 1977. 6.95 (ISBN 0-397-31757-3, JBL-J). Har-Row.

LIPAN INDIANS
see Indians of North America-Southwest, New

LIPID METABOLISM
American Physiological Society. Disturbances in Lipid & Lipoprotein Metabolism. Dietschy, John M., ed. (American Physiological Society Monograph Ser.). 1978. 25.00 (ISBN 0-683-02557-0). Williams & Wilkins.
Bernsohn, Joseph & Grossman, Herbert J., eds. Lipid Storage Diseases: Enzymatic Defects & Clinical Implications. LC 70-137623. 1971. 38.50 (ISBN 0-12-092850-7). Acad Pr.
Christie, W. W., ed. Lipid Metabolism in Ruminant Animals. (Illus.). 464p. 1981. 70.00 (ISBN 0-08-023789-4). Pergamon.
Gatt, Shimon, et al, eds. Enzymes of Lipid Metabolism. LC 78-886. 805p. 1978. 59.50 (ISBN 0-306-40002-2, Plenum Pr). Plenum Pub.
Gunstone, F. D. Topics in Lipid Chemistry, Vol. 1. 451p. 1970. 37.95 (ISBN 0-471-33340-9). Halsted Pr.
--Topics in Lipid Chemistry, Vol. 2. 313p. 1971. 34.95 (ISBN 0-471-33350-6). Halsted Pr.
Holmes, W. L., et al. Drugs Affecting Lipid Metabolism. LC 77-76508. (Advances in Experimental Medicine & Biology Ser.: Vol. 4). 681p. 1969. 45.00 (ISBN 0-306-39004-3, Plenum Pr). Plenum Pub.
Holmes, W. L., et al, eds. Pharmacological Control of Lipid Metabolism. LC 72-82746. (Advances in Experimental Medicine & Biology Ser.: Vol. 26). 359p. 1972. 39.50 (ISBN 0-306-39026-4, Plenum Pr). Plenum Pub.
King, H. K. The Chemistry of Lipids in Health & Disease: A Review of Our Present Knowledge of Lipids; Their Chemical Structure; Their Breakdown & Synthesis in Living Organisms; Their Place in Human Nutrition; & Their Abnormalities of Metabolism in Disease. (American Lecture Living Chemistry). (Illus.). 120p. 1960. ed. spiral bdg. 13.50photocopy (ISBN 0-398-04310-8). C C Thomas.
Kritchevsky, David, et al, eds. Drugs, Lipid Metabolism, & Atherosclerosis. LC 78-14222. (Advances in Experimental Medicine & Biology: Vol. 109). 453p. 1978. 37.50 (ISBN 0-306-40052-9, Plenum Pr). Plenum Pub.
Levine, R. & Pfeiffer, E. F., eds. Lipid Metabolism, Obesity & Diabetes Mellitis. 1974. 28.50 (ISBN 0-12-445350-3). Acad Pr.
MacDonald, I., ed. Effect of Carbohydrates on Lipid Metabolism. (Progress in Biochemical Pharmacology: Vol. 8). (Illus.). 1973. 86.25 (ISBN 3-8055-1600-2). S Karger.
Masoro, E. J., ed. Pharmacology of Lipid Transport & Atherosclerotic Processes. 1974. text ed. 105.00 (ISBN 0-08-017762-X). Pergamon.
Paoletti, Rodolfo, ed. Lipid Pharmacology. (Medicinal Chemistry: Vol. 2). 1964. 56.00 (ISBN 0-12-544950-X). Acad Pr.
Snyder, Fred, ed. Lipid Metabolism in Mammals, 2 vols. Incl. Vol. 1. 402p (ISBN 0-306-35802-6); Vol. 2. 390p (ISBN 0-306-35803-4). LC 77-913. (Monographs in Lipid Research). (Illus.). 1977. 42.50 ea. (Plenum Pr). Plenum Pub.
Volk, Bruno W. & Schneck, Larry, eds. Current Trends in Sphingolipidoses & Allied Disorders. LC 76-2586. (Advances in Experimental Medicine & Biology Ser.: Vol. 68). 612p. 1976. 45.00 (ISBN 0-306-39068-X, Plenum Pr). Plenum Pub.
Wakil, Salih J., ed. Lipid Metabolism, Vol. 1. 1970. 60.50 (ISBN 0-12-730950-0). Acad Pr.

LIPIDOSIS
Aronson, S. M. & Volk, B. W., eds. Inborn Disorders of Sphingolipid Metabolism. 1967. 64.00 (ISBN 0-08-012038-5). Pergamon.
Schwandt, Med P. Preventing Arterial Lipidoses. 300p. 1981. 27.50 (ISBN 0-87527-232-0). Green.
Schwandt, P. Risk & Prevention of Arterial Lipidoses. 300p. 1981. 27.50 (ISBN 0-87527-232-0). Green.

LIPIDS
see also Lipid Metabolism; Lipoproteins; Steroids
Adachi, M., et al. Sphingolipidoses & Allied Disorders, Vol. 1. Horrobin, D. F., ed. (Annual Research Reviews). 1979. 26.00 (ISBN 0-88831-055-2). Eden Med Res.
Asselineau, Jean. The Bacterial Lipids. Lederer, Edgar, ed. LC 66-26033. (Chemistry of Natural Products Ser.). 372p. 1966. 50.00x (ISBN 0-8002-0682-7). Intl Pubns Serv.
Bazan, N. G., et al, eds. Function & Biosynthesis of Lipids. LC 77-6831. (Advances in Experimental Medicine & Biology: Vol. 83). 646p. 1977. 59.50 (ISBN 0-306-39083-3, Plenum Pr). Plenum Pub.
Biochemical Society Symposium, 35th. Current Trends in the Biochemistry of Lipids: Proceedings. Ganguly, J. & Smellie, R. M., eds. 1973. 73.50 (ISBN 0-12-274250-8). Acad Pr.
Christie, W. W. Lipid Analysis. 1973. text ed. 42.00 (ISBN 0-08-017753-0). Pergamon.
Ciba Foundation. Lipids, Malnutrition, & the Developing Brain. (Ciba Foundation Symposium: No. 3). 1972. 23.50 (ISBN 0-444-10372-4, Excerpta Medica). Elsevier.
Copinschi, G. & Jaquet, P., eds. Lipo-Corticotropic Hormones & Cushing's Disease. (Journal: Hormone Research Ser.: Vol. 13, No. 4-5). (Illus.). 148p. 1981. pap. 39.75 (ISBN 3-8055-3082-X). S Karger.
DeLuca, H. F., ed. Handbook of Lipid Research, Vol. 2: The Fat-Soluble Vitamins. LC 78-2009. (Illus.). 399p. 1978. 27.50 (ISBN 0-306-33582-4, Plenum Pr). Plenum Pub.
Eisenman, George, ed. Membranes,, Vol. 2: Lipid Bilayers & Antibiotics. 576p. 1973. 65.00 (ISBN 0-8247-6049-2). Dekker.
Erwin, Joseph A., ed. Lipids & Biomembranes of Eukaryotic Microorganisms. (Cell Biology Ser.). 1973. 52.50 (ISBN 0-12-242050-0). Acad Pr.
Fondu, M., ed. Lipids & Lipoproteins. (Journal: Nutrition & Metabolism: Vol. 24, Supplement 1). (Illus.). iv, 212p. 1980. 29.50 (ISBN 3-8055-1266-X). S Karger.
Galli, C., et al, eds. Dietary Lipids & Postnatal Development. LC 73-79580. (Illus.). 286p. 1973. 27.00 (ISBN 0-911216-50-2). Raven.
Galliard, T. & Mercer, E., eds. Recent Advanes in the Chemistry & Biochemistry of Plant Lipids. (Annual Proceedings of the Phytochemical Society Ser.). 1975. 63.00 (ISBN 0-12-274050-5). Acad Pr.
Gurr, A. I. & James, A. T. Lipid Biochemistry: An Introduction. 3rd ed. LC 75-20294. 244p. 1975. 34.00x (ISBN 0-412-22620-0, Pub. by Chapman & Hall England); pap. 16.95x (ISBN 0-412-22630-8). Methuen Inc.
Gurr, M. I. & James, A. T. Lipid Biochemistry: An Introduction. 3rd ed. 1980. 34.00x (ISBN 0-412-22620-0, Pub. by Chapman & Hall); pap. 16.95x (ISBN 0-412-22630-8). Methuen Inc.
Hitchcock, C. & Nichols, B. W. Plant Lipid Biochemistry. (Experimental Botany Ser.: Vol. 4). 1971. 61.50 (ISBN 0-12-349650-0). Acad Pr.
Holman, R. T., ed. Progress in Lipid Research, Vol. 17. 396p. 1980. 68.75 (ISBN 0-08-023797-5). Pergamon.
--Progress in Lipid Research, Vol. 18. (Illus.). 180p. 1981. 75.00 (ISBN 0-08-027129-4). Pergamon.
Holman, Ralph T., ed. New Concepts in Lipid Research in Honor of Stina & Einar Stenhagen, Vol. 16. new ed. (Progress in the Chemistry of Fats & Other Lipids). 1978. text ed. 71.00 (ISBN 0-08-022663-9). Pergamon.

Holman, Ralph T., et al, eds. Progress in the Chemistry of Fats & Other Lipids, Vols. 5-14. Incl. Vol. 5. Advances in Technology. 1958. 50.00 (ISBN 0-08-009098-2); Vol. 6. 1963. 50.00 (ISBN 0-08-009863-0); Vol. 7. Pt. 1, 1964. pap. 15.50 (ISBN 0-08-010087-2); Vol. 8. 1965. Vol. 8, Pt. 2. pap. 15.50 (ISBN 0-686-57466-4); Vol. 9, Pt. 1. Polyunsaturated Acids. 1966. pap. 15.50 (ISBN 0-08-011797-X); Vol. 9, Pts. 2-5. pap. 20.00 ea.; Pt. 2, 1968. pap. (ISBN 0-08-012632-4); Pt. 3. 1967. pap. (ISBN 0-08-013239-1); Pt. 4. 1968. pap. (ISBN 0-08-015971-0); Pt. 5, 1970. pap. (ISBN 0-08-016111-1); Vol. 9, Complete, 1971 Cloth. 62.50 (ISBN 0-08-016041-7); Complete, 1970. Cloth. 50.00 (ISBN 0-08-016040-9); Vol. 10, 1-4. pap. 15.50 ea.; Pt. 1, 1967. pap. (ISBN 0-08-012292-2); Pt. 2, 1969. pap. (ISBN 0-08-012996-X); Pt. 3, 1969. pap. (ISBN 0-08-012997-8); Pt. 4, 1969. 62.50 (ISBN 0-08-013990-6); Complete, 1972. Cloth. 50.00 (ISBN 0-08-016795-0); Vol. 11, Pts. 1-3. pap. 15.50 ea.; Pt. 1, 1970. pap. (ISBN 0-08-015847-1); Pt. 2, 1970. pap. (ISBN 0-08-016150-2); Pt. 3, 1971. pap. (ISBN 0-08-016571-0); Vol. 12. 1972. 50.00 (ISBN 0-08-016758-6); Complete. Cloth. 50.00 (ISBN 0-08-017146-X); Vol. 13, Pts. 1-4. pap. 15.50 ea.; Pt. 1. pap. (ISBN 0-08-016942-2); Pt. 2. pap. (ISBN 0-08-017043-9); Pt. 3. pap. (ISBN 0-08-017176-1); Pt. 4. 62.50 (ISBN 0-08-017129-X); Vol. 14, Pt. 1. pap. 15.50 (ISBN 0-08-017130-3); Vol. 14, Pt. 2. Lipids of Fungi. pap. 15.50 (ISBN 0-08-017880-4); Vol. 14, Pt. 3. Infrared Absorption Spectroscopy of Normal & Substituted Long-Chain Fatty Acids & Esters in Solid State. Fischmeister. pap. 15.00 (ISBN 0-08-018073-6); Vol. 14, Pt. 4. Lipid Metabolism Membrane Functions of the Mammary Gland. Patton, S. & Jensen, R. G. pap. 15.50 (ISBN 0-08-018222-4); Vol. 14, Complete. 1975. 50.00 (ISBN 0-08-017808-1). LC 53-22998. Pergamon.

International Congress On Clinical Chemistry - 7th. Hormones Lipids & Miscellaneous: Proceedings. Felber, J. P. & Scheidegger, J. J., eds. (Clinical Chemistry Ser.: Vol. 3). 1971. 29.50 (ISBN 0-8391-0591-6). Univ Park.

International Symposium of Biochemistry & Physiology of Plant Lipids. Advances in the Biochemistry & Physiology of Plant Lipids: Proceedings. Appelcvist, L. A. & Liljenberg, C., eds. (Development in Plant Biology: Vol. 3). 1979. 61.00 (ISBN 0-444-80129-4, Biomedical Pr). Elsevier.

Jain, Mahendra K. The Bimolecular Lipid Membrane: A System. 1972. 24.50x (ISBN 0-442-24086-4). Van Nos Reinhold.

Kates, M. Techniques of Lipidology. (Laboratory Techniques in Biochemistry & Molecular Biology: Vol. 3, Pt. 2). 1972. pap. 24.50 (ISBN 0-444-10350-3, North-Holland). Elsevier.

King, H. K. The Chemistry of Lipids in Health & Disease: A Review of Our Present Knowledge of Lipids; Their Chemical Structure; Their Breakdown & Synthesis in Living Organisms; Their Place in Human Nutrition; & Their Abnormalities of Metabolism in Disease. (American Lecture Living Chemistry). (Illus.). 120p. 1960. ed. spiral bdg. 13.50photocopy (ISBN 0-398-04310-8). C C Thomas.

Kritchevky, David, et al, eds. Lipids, Lipoproteins, & Drugs. LC 75-31790. (Advances in Experimental Medicine & Biology Ser.: Vol. 63). 520p. 1975. 42.50 (ISBN 0-306-39063-9, Plenum Pr). Plenum Pub.

Kritchevsky, David & Paoletti, Rodolfo, eds. Advances in Lipid Research, Vol. 17. LC 63-22330. (Serial Publication). 1980. 31.00 (ISBN 0-12-024917-0); lib ed. 40.50 (ISBN 0-12-024980-4); microfiche 20.50 (ISBN 0-12-024981-2). Acad Pr.

Kuksis, A., ed. Handbook of Lipid Research, Vol. 1: Fatty Acids & Glycerides. LC 77-25277. (Illus.). 487p. 1978. 35.00 (ISBN 0-306-33581-6, Plenum Pr). Plenum Pub.

Laskin, Allen I. & Lechevalier, Hubert, eds. Handbook of Microbiology, CRC, Vol. 4: Microbial Composition: Carbohydrates, Lipids & Minerals. 2nd ed. 720p. 1981. 64.95 (ISBN 0-8493-7204-6). CRC Pr.

Lewis, Clara M. Nutrition: Proteins Carbohydrates & Lipids. LC 75-43830. (Illus.). 1978. pap. text ed. 7.00 (ISBN 0-8036-5621-1). Davis Co.

Marinetti, Guido, ed. Lipid Chromatographic Analysis, Vol. 1. rev. ed. 1976. 44.50 (ISBN 0-8247-6355-6). Dekker.

--Lipid Chromatographic Analysis, Vol. 2. rev. ed. 1976. 44.50 (ISBN 0-8247-6356-4). Dekker.

Nanda, B. S., et al. Aging Pigment: Current Research, Vol. 1. 191p. 1974. text ed. 25.50x (ISBN 0-8422-7197-X). Irvington.

Nes, William R. & Nes, W. David. Lipids in Evolution. (Monographs in Lipid Research Ser.). (Illus.). 255p. 1980. 29.50 (ISBN 0-306-40393-5, Plenum Pr). Plenum Pub.

Paoletti, R. & Kritchevsky, D., eds. Advances in Lipid Research, Vols. 1-16. Incl. Vol. 1. 1964. 52.00 (ISBN 0-12-024901-4); Vol. 2. 1964. 52.00 (ISBN 0-12-024902-2); Vol. 3. 1965. 52.00 (ISBN 0-12-024903-0); Vol. 4. 1967. 52.00 (ISBN 0-12-024904-9); Vol. 5. 1967. 52.00 (ISBN 0-12-024905-7); Vol. 6. 1968. 52.00 (ISBN 0-12-024906-5); Vol. 7. 1969. 52.00 (ISBN 0-12-024907-3); Vol. 8. 1970. 52.00 (ISBN 0-12-024908-1); Vol. 9. 1971. 52.00 (ISBN 0-12-024909-X); Vol. 10. 1972. 52.00 (ISBN 0-12-024910-3); Vol. 11. 1973. 52.00 (ISBN 0-12-024911-1); Vol. 12. 1974. 52.00 (ISBN 0-12-024912-X); Vol. 13. 1975. 52.00 (ISBN 0-12-024913-8); Vol. 14. 1976. 52.00 (ISBN 0-12-024914-6); lib ed. 67.00 (ISBN 0-12-024974-X); microfiche 37.50 (ISBN 0-12-024975-8); Vol. 15. 1977. 45.50 (ISBN 0-12-024915-4); lib ed. 58.00 (ISBN 0-12-024976-6); microfiche 33.00 (ISBN 0-12-024977-4); Vol. 16. 1978. 42.50 (ISBN 0-12-024916-2); lib. ed. 54.00 (ISBN 0-12-024978-2); microfiche 31.00 (ISBN 0-12-024979-0). LC 63-22330. Acad Pr.

Paoletti, R., et al, eds. Lipids: Proceedings, 2 vols. Incl. Vol. 1. Biochemistry. LC 75-21982. 298p. 37.50 (ISBN 0-89004-028-1); Vol. 2. Technology. LC 75-26387. 286p. 37.50 (ISBN 0-89004-029-X). 1975. Set. 68.50 (ISBN 0-685-61106-X). Raven.

Paoletti, Rodolfo & Guleck, Charles J., eds. Lipid Pharmacology, Vol. 2. 1976. 48.00 (ISBN 0-12-544952-6). Acad Pr.

Rommel, K. & Bohmer, R., eds. Lipid Absorption: Biochemical & Clinical Aspects. (Illus.). 1976. 39.50 (ISBN 0-8391-0933-4). Univ Park.

Shapiro, David. Chemistry of Sphingolipids. LC 70-451052. (Chemistry of Natural Products Ser.). 111p. 1969. 18.50x (ISBN 0-8002-0293-7). Intl Pubns Serv.

Simons, Leon A. Lipids. 84p. pap. text ed. 13.95 (ISBN 0-8391-1496-6). Univ Park.

Snyder, Fred L., ed. Ether Lipids: Chemistry & Biology. 1972. 60.50 (ISBN 0-12-654150-7). Acad Pr.

Supran, Michael K., ed. Lipids As a Source of Flavor. LC 78-9739. (ACS Symposium Ser.: No. 75). 1978. 17.50 (ISBN 0-8412-0418-7). Am Chemical.

Sweeley, Charles C, ed. Cell Surface Glycolipids. LC 80-15283. (ACS Symposium Ser.: No. 128). 1980. 44.50 (ISBN 0-8412-0556-6). Am Chemical.

Tevini, M. & Lichtenthaler, H. K., eds. Lipids & Lipid Polymers in Higher Plants. 1977. 52.70 (ISBN 0-387-08201-8). Springer-Verlag.

Thompson, Guy A. Regulation of Membrane Lipid Metabolism. 256p. 1980. 64.95 (ISBN 0-8493-5427-7). CRC Pr.

Vaczi, L. The Biological Role of Bacterial Lipids. Geder, L., tr. LC 73-174901. 1973. 7.50x (ISBN 0-8002-0691-6). Intl Pubns Serv.

Walborg, E. F., Jr. Glycoproteins & Glycolipids in Disease Processes. LC 78-11920. (ACS Symposium Ser.: No. 80). 1978. 33.50 (ISBN 0-8412-0452-7). Am Chemical.

Weete, John D. Fungal Lipid Biochemistry. LC 94-8457. (Monographs in Lipid Research: Vol. 1). (Illus.). 393p. 1974. 35.00 (ISBN 0-306-35801-8, Plenum Pr). Plenum Pub.

Weete, John D. & Weber, Darrell J. Lipid Biochemistry of Fungi & Other Organisms. 400p. 1980. 45.00 (ISBN 0-306-40570-9, Plenum Pr). Plenum Pub.

LIPOIDOSIS

see Lipidosis

LIPOPROTEINS

American Physiological Society. Disturbances in Lipid & Lipoprotein Metabolism. Dietschy, John M., ed. (American Physiological Society Monograph Ser.). 1978. 25.00 (ISBN 0-683-02557-0). Williams & Wilkins.

Bremner, W. Fraser. The Hyperlipoproteinaemias & Atherosclerosis: Current Understanding of Their Inter-Relationships, Vol. 1. Horrobin, D. F., ed. (Annual Research Reviews). 1979. 26.00 (ISBN 0-88831-056-0). Eden Med Res.

Capaldi, Roderick A., ed. Membrane Proteins & Their Interaction with Lipids. (Membranes: Structure & Techniques). 1977. 39.75 (ISBN 0-8247-6595-8). Dekker.

Day. High Denstity Lipoproteins. 728p. 1981. 65.00 (ISBN 0-8247-1220-X). Dekker.

Day, Charles E. & Levy, Robert S., eds. Low Density Lipoproteins. LC 76-25840. (Illus.). 445p. 1976. 42.50 (ISBN 0-306-30934-3, Plenum Pr). Plenum Pub.

Dienstfrey. Protides of the Biological Fluids: Proceedings, Colloquium on Protides of the Biological Fluids, 25th. LC 58-5908. 1978. text ed. 150.00 (ISBN 0-08-021524-6). Pergamon.

Eisenberg, S., ed. Lipoprotein Metabolism. (Progress in Biochemical Pharmacology: Vol. 15). (Illus.). 1979. 77.25 (ISBN 3-8055-2985-6). S Karger.

Gotto, A. M., et al, eds. High Density Lipoproteins & Atherosclerosis: Proceedings of the 3rd Argenteuil Symposium Held Under the Auspices of the Foundation Cardiologique Princesse Liliane in Waterloo, Belgium, Nov., 1977. 1978. 36.75 (ISBN 0-444-80047-6, Biomedical Pr). Elsevier.

Greten, H., ed. Lipoprotein Metabolism. (Illus.). 180p. 1976. pap. 15.30 (ISBN 0-387-07635-2). Springer-Verlag.

Hessel, L. W. & Krans, J. M., eds. Lipoprotein Metabolism & Endocrine Regulation. (Developments in Endocrinology: Vol. 4). 1979. 48.50 (ISBN 0-444-80102-2, Biomedical Pr). Elsevier.

Kritchevky, David, et al, eds. Lipids, Lipoproteins, & Drugs. LC 75-31790. (Advances in Experimental Medicine & Biology Ser.: Vol. 63). 520p. 1975. 42.50 (ISBN 0-306-39063-9, Plenum Pr). Plenum Pub.

Nelson, Gary J., ed. Blood Lipids & Lipoproteins: Quantitation, Composition & Metabolism. LC 78-9098. 992p. 1979. Repr. of 1972 ed. lib. bdg. 52.50 (ISBN 0-88275-695-8). Krieger.

Palkovic, M. Hormones, Lipoproteins & Atherosclerosis: Proceedings of a Satelite Symposium of the 28th International Congress of Physiological Sciences, Bratislava, Czechoslovakia, 1980. LC 80-41926. (Advances in Physiological Sciences Ser.: Vol. 35). (Illus.). 300p. 1981. 40.00 (ISBN 0-08-027357-2). Pergamon.

Papahadjopoulos, Demetrios, ed. Liposomes & Their Uses in Biology & Medicine. (Annals of the New York Academy of Sciences: Vol. 308). 462p. 1978. pap. 57.00x (ISBN 0-89072-064-9). NY Acad Sci.

Peeters, Hubert, ed. The Lipoprotein Molecule. (NATO Advanced Study Institutes Ser.: Series A, Life Sciences, Vol. 15). 301p. 1978. 32.50 (ISBN 0-306-35615-5, Plenum Pr). Plenum Pub.

Scanu, Angelo M. & Landsberger, Frank R., eds. Lipoprotein Structure. (Annals of the New York Academy of Sciences: Vol. 348). 436p. 1980. 76.00x (ISBN 0-89766-082-X); pap. 76.00x (ISBN 0-89766-083-8). NY Acad Sci.

LIPPI, FRA FILIPPO, 1412-1469

Neilson, Katharine B. Filippino Lippi, a Critical Study. LC 77-138168. (Illus.). 235p. 1972. Repr. of 1938 ed. lib. bdg. 28.25x (ISBN 0-8371-5625-4, NEFL). Greenwood.

Strutt, Edward C. Fra Filippo Lippi. 1971. Repr. of 1901 ed. 19.00 (ISBN 0-403-00732-1). Scholarly.

--Fra Filippo Lippi. LC 78-176460. Repr. of 1901 ed. 11.50 (ISBN 0-404-06299-7). AMS Pr.

LIPPIZANER HORSE

Froissard, Jean. Lipizzaners & the Spanish Riding School. pap. 2.50 (ISBN 0-87980-198-0). Wilshire.

Rossi, Emilio, et al. Lipizzaner: The Story of the Horses Lipica: Commemorating the 400th Anniversary of the Lippizaner. Espeland, Pamela, ed. LC 80-28576. (Illus.). 215p. 1981. 18.95 (ISBN 0-89893-172-X). CDP.

LIPPMANN, WALTER, 1889-

Adams, Larry L. Walter Lippmann. (World Leaders Ser.: No. 58). 1977. lib. bdg. 10.95 (ISBN 0-8057-7709-1). Twayne.

Dam, Hari N. The Intellectual Odyssey of Walter Lippmann. 1973. 69.95 (ISBN 0-87968-057-1). Gordon Pr.

Luskin, John. Lippmann, Liberty & the Press. LC 72-4060. 224p. 1972. 15.50x (ISBN 0-8173-4722-4). U of Ala Pr.

Schapsmeier, Edward & Schapsmeier, Frederick. Walter Lippmann, Philosopher-Journalist. 1969. 8.00 (ISBN 0-8183-0218-6). Pub Aff Pr.

Steel, Ronald. Walter Lippmann & the American Century. (Illus.). 640p. 1980. 19.95 (ISBN 0-316-81190-4). Little.

Syed, Anwar H. Walter Lippmann's Philosophy of International Politics. LC 64-12626. 1963. 12.00x (ISBN 0-8122-7432-6). U of Pa Pr.

Weingast, David E. Walter Lippmann, a Study in Personal Journalism. Repr. of 1949 ed. lib. bdg. 15.00 (ISBN 0-8371-2970-2, WEWL). Greenwood.

Wellborn, Charles. Twentieth Century Pilgrimage: Walter Lippmann & the Public Philosophy. LC 69-17624. 1969. 15.00x (ISBN 0-8071-0303-9). La State U Pr.

LIP-READING

see Deaf–Means of Communication

LIPS–ABNORMALITIES AND DEFORMITIES

see also Harelip

LIPSIUS, JUSTUS, 1547-1606

Anderton, Basil. Sketches from a Library Window. facs. ed. LC 68-16903. (Essay Index Reprint Ser). 1923. 13.00 (ISBN 0-8369-0154-1). Arno.

LIQUEFACTION OF GASES

see Gases–Liquefaction

LIQUEFIED GASES

see also Liquefied Natural Gas

Bruggeling, Ir A. Prestressed Concrete for the Storage of Liquefied Gas. Van Amerongen, C., tr. from Dutch. (Viewpoint Ser.). (Illus.). 111p. 1981. pap. text ed. 45.00x (ISBN 0-7210-1187-X, Pub. by C & CA London). Scholium Intl.

LIQUEFIED NATURAL GAS

Davis, Lee N. Frozen Fire: Where Will It Happen Next? LC 78-74808. 1979. pap. 6.95 (ISBN 0-913890-30-8). Friends Earth.

Faridany, Edward. LNG: 1974-1990, Marine Operations & Market Prospects for Liquefied Natural Gas. LC 75-301911. 1974. 67.50x (ISBN 0-8002-0884-6). Intl Pubns Serv.

Liquefied Natural Gas, Production, Storage & Handling. (Fifty Ser.). 64p. 1972. pap. 2.00 (ISBN 0-685-46072-X, 59A). Natl Fire Prot.

Properties of Materials for Liquified Natural Gas Tankage. 1975. 39.75 (ISBN 0-686-52043-2, 04-579000-30). ASTM.

LIQUEFIED PETROLEUM GAS

Clark, William W. LP-Gas Guide for Architects, Engineers & Builders. (Illus.). 1977. pap. 2.50 (ISBN 0-685-85068-4). Natl LP Gas.

Huges, John R. The Storage & Handling of Petroleum Liquids. 2nd ed. (Illus.). 331p. 1978. pap. text ed. 42.95x (ISBN 0-85264-251-2, Pub. by Charles Griffin & Co Ltd England). Lubrecht & Cramer.

Liquefied Petroleum Gases at Utility Gas Plants. (Fifty Ser.). 53p. 1974. pap. 3.00 (ISBN 0-685-46071-1, 59). Natl Fire Prot.

Liquefied Petroleum Gases, Storage & Handling. (Fifty Ser.). 53p. 1974. pap. 4.00 (ISBN 0-685-46070-3, 58). Natl Fire Prot.

LP-Gas Engine Fuels. 140p. 1973. 4.75 (ISBN 0-8031-0104-X, STP525). ASTM.

Williams, A. F. & Lom, W. L. Liquified Petroleum Gases: A Guide to Properties, Applications & Usage of Propane & Butane. LC 73-15141. (Illus.). 403p. 1973. 72.95 (ISBN 0-470-94850-7). Halsted Pr.

LIQUEURS

Cocconi, Emilio. Liqueurs for All Seasons. Kulla, Frank & Kulla, Patricia S., eds. LC 75-26065. (Illus.). 9.95 (ISBN 0-915336-04-9); pap. 5.95 (ISBN 0-915336-24-3). Lyceum Bks.

DeWulf, Lucienne & Fourestier, Marie-Francoise. Adventures with Liqueurs. LC 78-74589. (Illus.). 1979. text ed. 14.95 (ISBN 0-916728-14-5). Bks in Focus.

Farrell, John P. Making Cordials & Liqueurs at Home. LC 74-1805. (Illus.). 156p. 1974. 9.95 (ISBN 0-06-011238-7, HarpT). Har-Row.

Hallgarten, Peter. Liqueurs. (Illus.). 8.50x (ISBN 0-685-72749-1). Corner.

--Spirits & Liqueurs. LC 79-670238. 192p. 1979. 16.95 (ISBN 0-571-10114-3, Pub. by Faber & Faber). Merrimack Bk Serv.

Hebert, Malcolm. Codially Yours. (Illus.). 160p. (Orig.). 1981. pap. 4.95 (ISBN 0-89037-129-6). Anderson World.

Herzbrum, Robert. The Perfect Martini Book. LC 79-1858. (Illus.). 1979. pap. 5.95 (ISBN 0-15-644642-1, Harv). HarBraceJ.

Keers, John H., Jr. How to Make Liqueurs at Home. 192p. (Orig.). 1973. pap. 1.25 (ISBN 0-532-12174-0). Woodhill.

Meilach, Dona & Meilach, Mel. Homemade Liqueurs. (Illus.). 1979. 9.95 (ISBN 0-8092-7137-0); pap. 6.95 (ISBN 0-8092-7582-1). Contemp Bks.

Price, Pamela V. Penguin Book of Spirits & Liqueurs. (Handbook Ser.). 1981. pap. 4.95 (ISBN 0-14-046335-6). Penguin.

LIQUID AMMONIA

Jolly, William L., ed. Metal Ammonia Solutions. LC 72-80134. (Benchmark Papers in Inorganic Chemistry Ser.). 1972. 47.00 (ISBN 0-12-786785-6). Acad Pr.

Nicholls, D. Inorganic Chemistry in Liquid Ammonia. (Topics in Inorganic & General Chemistry Ser.: Vol. 17). 1979. 53.75 (ISBN 0-444-41774-5). Elsevier.

LIQUID ASSETS

see Liquidity (Economics)

LIQUID CHROMATOGRAPHY

Bristow, P. A. Liquid Chromatography in Practice. 28.00 (ISBN 0-9504833-1-1); pap. 20.00 (ISBN 0-9504833-0-3); microfiche 10.00 (ISBN 0-9504833-2-X). Lab Data Control.

Brown, Phyllis R. High Pressure Liquid Chromatography: Biochemical & Biomedical Applications. 1973. 27.00 (ISBN 0-12-136950-1). Acad Pr.

Cazes. Liquid Chromatography of Polymers & Related Materials, Part III. 232p. 1981. write for info. (ISBN 0-8247-1514-4). Dekker.

Cazes & De La Marre. Liquid Chromatography of Polymers & Related Materials II. (Chromatographic Science Ser.: Vol. 13). 232p. 1980. 35.00 (ISBN 0-8247-6985-6). Dekker.

Cazes, J. Liquid Chromatography of Polymers & Related Materials. (Chromatgraphic Science Ser.: Vol. 8). 1977. 26.50 (ISBN 0-8247-6592-3). Dekker.

Deyl, Z. & Kopecky, J. Bibliography of Column Liquid Chromatography Nineteen Seventy-One to Nineteen Seventy-Three, Vol. 6. (Journal of Chromatography Supplement). 1977. 126.50 (ISBN 0-444-41469-X). Elsevier.

Deyl, Z., et al, eds. Liquid Column Chromatography: A Survey of Modern Techniques & Applications. (Journal of Chromatography Library: Vol. 3). 1176p. 1975. 141.50 (ISBN 0-444-41156-9). Elsevier.

Dixon, P. F., et al, eds. High Pressure Liquid Chromatography in Clinical Chemistry. 1976. 33.50 (ISBN 0-12-218450-5). Acad Pr.

Done, J. N., et al. Applications of High-Speed Liquid Chromatography. LC 74-16148. 1975. 43.75 (ISBN 0-471-21784-0, Pub. by Wiley-Interscience). Wiley.

Engelhardt, H. High Performance Liquid Chromatography. Gutnikov, G., tr. from Ger. LC 78-22002. (Chemical Laboratory Practice). (Illus.). 1979. 29.80 (ISBN 0-387-09005-3). Springer-Verlag.

Hamilton, R. J. & Sewell, P. A. Introduction to High Performance Liquid Chromatography. LC 77-8634. 183p. 1977. 24.95x (ISBN 0-412-13400-4, Pub. by Chapman & Hall England). Methuen Inc.

Hawk. Biological-Biomedical Applications of Liquid Chromatography. 1979. 45.00 (ISBN 0-8247-6784-5). Dekker.

--Biological-Biomedical Applications of Liquid Chromatography, II. (Chromatographic Science Ser.: Vol. 12). 1979. 49.75 (ISBN 0-8247-6915-5). Dekker.

Hawk, Gerald L., ed. Biological-Biomedical Applications of Liquid Chromatography. (Chromatographic Science Ser.: Vol. 18). (Illus.). 420p. 1981. 49.75 (ISBN 0-8247-1297-8). Dekker.

Horvath, Csaba, ed. High-Performance Liquid Chromatography: Advances & Perspectives, Vol. 1. (Serial Publication Ser.). 1980. 35.00 (ISBN 0-12-312201-5). Acad Pr.

--High Performance Liquid Chromatography: Advances & Perspectives, Vol. 2. 1980. 39.50 (ISBN 0-12-312202-3). Acad Pr.

Kabra, Pokar & Marton, Laurence J., eds. Liquid Chromatography in Clinical Analysis. LC 80-84083. (Biological Methods Ser.). 496p. 1981. 55.00 (ISBN 0-89603-026-1). Humana.

Knox, John H. High Performance Liquid Chromatography. 205p. 1981. pap. 17.00x (ISBN 0-85224-383-9, Pub. by Edinburgh U Pr Scotland). Columbia U Pr.

Krstulovic, Ante M. & Brown, Phyllis R. Reversed-Phase High Performance Liquid Chromatography: Theory, Practice, & Biomedical Applications. 272p. 1981. 22.50 (ISBN 0-471-05369-4, Pub. by Wiley Interscience). Wiley.

Lawrence, J. F. & Frei, R. W. Chemical Derivatization in Liquid Chromatography. (Journal of Chromatography Library: Vol. 7). 1976. 44.00 (ISBN 0-444-41429-0). Elsevier.

Lawrence, James F. Organic Trace Analysis by Liquid Chromatography. 1981. 34.00 (ISBN 0-12-439150-8). Acad Pr.

Liquid Chromatographic Data Compilation. 1975. pap. 15.00 (ISBN 0-686-51995-7, 10-041000-39). ASTM.

Majors, R. E. & Abbott, S. R. Column Selection in High Performance Liquid Chromatography. Date not set. price not set (ISBN 0-685-84728-4). Elsevier.

O A S General Secretariat. Cromatografia Liquida Alta Presion: Monografia, No. 10. (Serie de Quimica). (Illus.). 72p. (Span.). 1980. pap. 2.00 (ISBN 0-8270-1229-2). OAS.

Parris, N. A. Instrumental Liquid Chromatography. (Journal of Chromatography Library: Vol. 5). 1976. 49.00 (ISBN 0-444-41427-4). Elsevier.

Pattison, J. B. A Programmed Introduction to Gas-Liquid Chromatography. 1973. 24.50 (ISBN 0-85501-068-1). Heyden.

Practical High Performance Liquid Chromatography. 310p. Date not set. 18.50 (ISBN 0-686-76115-4, 13-106000-39). ASTM.

Pryde, A. & Gilbert, M. T. Application of High Performance Liquid Chromatography. LC 78-7950. 255p. 1979. 29.95x (ISBN 0-412-14220-1, Pub. by Chapman & Hall England). Methuen Inc.

Runser, Dennis J. Maintaining & Troubleshooting HPLC Systems: A Users Guide. LC 80-25444. 163p. 1981. 27.50 (ISBN 0-471-06479-3, Pub. by Wiley Interscience). Wiley.

Scott, R., ed. Contemporary Liquid Chromotography. LC 74-15553. (Techniques of Chemistry Ser.: Vol. XI). 1976. 38.50 (ISBN 0-471-92900-X, Pub. by Wiley-Interscience). Wiley.

Simpson, C. F. Practical High Performance Liquid Chromatography. 1976. 42.00 (ISBN 0-85501-089-4). Heyden.

Snyder, L. R. & Kirkland, J. J. Introduction to Modern Liquid Chromatography. 2nd ed. LC 79-4537. 1979. 39.00 (ISBN 0-471-03822-9, Pub. by Wiley-Interscience). Wiley.

Yau, W. W., et al. Modern Size-Exclusion Liquid Chromatography: Practice of Gel Permeation & Gel Filtration Chromatography. LC 79-12739. 1979. 31.75 (ISBN 0-471-03387-1, Pub. by Wiley-Interscience). Wiley.

LIQUID CRYSTALS

Bata, L., ed. Advances in Liquid Crystal Research & Applications: Proceedings of the Third Liquid Crystal Conference of the Socialist Countries, Budapest, 27-31 August 1979. 1000p. 1981. 195.00 (ISBN 0-08-026191-4). Pergamon.

Blumstein, Alexandre, ed. Mesomorphic Order in Polymers & Polymerization in Liquid Crystalline Media. LC 78-9470. (ACS Symposium Ser.: No. 74). 1978. 25.50 (ISBN 0-8412-0419-5). Am Chemical.

Brown, Glen H. & Labes, M. M., eds. Liquid Crystals Three: Proceedings, 2 pts. 1972. Set. 252.50 (ISBN 0-677-15010-5). Gordon.

Brown, Glen H., et al, eds. Liquid Crystals One: Proceedings. 1967. 104.00x (ISBN 0-677-11840-6). Gordon.

--Liquid Crystals Two: Proceedings, 2 pts. 1969. 54.50x (ISBN 0-677-13830-X, PT. 1); 186.00x (ISBN 0-677-13840-7, PT. 2). Gordon.

Brown, Glenn H. & Wolken, Jerome J. Liquid Crystals & Biological Stuctures. LC 78-67873. 1979. 25.50 (ISBN 0-12-136850-5). Acad Pr.

Brown, Glenn H., ed. Advances in Liquid Crystals, 3 vols. Incl. Vol. 1. 1975. 56.00 (ISBN 0-12-025001-2); lib ed. 72.00 (ISBN 0-12-025074-8); microfiche 40.50 (ISBN 0-12-025075-6); Vol. 2. 1976. 55.00 (ISBN 0-12-025002-0); lib ed. 70.00 (ISBN 0-12-025076-4); microfiche 39.50 (ISBN 0-12-025077-2); Vol. 3. 1978. 42.50 (ISBN 0-12-025003-9); lib ed. 54.50 (ISBN 0-12-025078-0); microfiche 31.00 (ISBN 0-12-025079-9). LC 74-17973. Acad Pr.

--Advances in Liquid Crystals, Vol. 4. (Serial Publication). 1979. 32.00 (ISBN 0-12-025004-7); lib. ed. 40.50 (ISBN 0-12-025080-2); microfiche 23.50 (ISBN 0-12-025081-0). Acad Pr.

Bulthuis, Jakob. NMR in Liquid Crystalline Solvents: Complications in Determining Molecular Geometries. (Illus.). 104p. (Orig.). 1974. pap. text ed. 12.00x (ISBN 90-6203-111-0). Humanities.

Chandrasekhar, S. Liquid Crystals. LC 75-32913. (Cambridge Monographs in Physics). (Illus.). 1977. 71.50 (ISBN 0-521-21149-2). Cambridge U Pr.

Chandrasenkhar, S. Liquid Crystals. (Cambridge Monographs in Physics). (Illus.). 352p. 1980. pap. 22.95 (ISBN 0-521-29841-5). Cambridge U Pr.

Chandresekhar. International Liquid Crystals Conf., Bangalore 1979: Proceedings. 1980. 84.00 (ISBN 0-85501-163-7). Heyden.

De Gennes, P. G. The Physics of Liquid Crystals. (International Series of Monographs on Physics). 1980. pap. 22.00x (ISBN 0-19-852004-2). Oxford U Pr.

--The Physics of Liquid Crystals. (International Series of Monographs on Physics). (Illus.). 367p. 1974. 74.00x (ISBN 0-19-851285-6). Oxford U Pr.

De Jeu, W. H. Physical Properties of Liquid Crystalline Materials. 140p. 1980. 35.25 (ISBN 0-677-04040-7). Gordon.

Demus, D. & Richter, L. Textures of Liquid Crystals. (Illus.). 1978. 108.90 (ISBN 0-89573-015-4). Verlag Chemie.

Friberg, Stig, ed. Lyotropic Liquid Crystals & the Structure of Biomembranes. LC 76-18704. (Advances in Chemistry Ser.: No. 152). 1976. 23.00 (ISBN 0-8412-0269-9). Am Chemical.

Gray, G. W. & Goodby, G. W. Liquid Crystals: Identification, Classification & Structure. (Illus.). 250p. 87.00 (ISBN 0-08-025299-0). Pergamon.

Gray, G. W. & Winsor, P. A., eds. Liquid Crystals & Plastic Crystals, Vol. 1: Preparation, Constitution & Applications. LC 73-11504. (Illus.). 383p. 1974. 65.95 (ISBN 0-470-32339-6). Halsted Pr.

--Liquid Crystals & Plastic Crystals, Vol. 2: Physico-Chemical Properties & Methods of Investigation. LC 73-11505. (Illus.). 314p. 1974. 65.95 (ISBN 0-470-32340-X). Halsted Pr.

Helfreich, W. & Heppke, G. Liquid Crystals of One- & Two-Dimensional Order: Proceedings. (Springer Series in Chemical Physics: Vol. 11). (Illus.). 416p. 1981. 40.80 (ISBN 0-387-10399-6). Springer-Verlag.

International Handbook of Liquid Crystal Displays 1975-1976. 2nd ed. 1976. 85.00x (ISBN 0-903969-14-9). Scholium Intl.

Johnson, Julian & Porter, Roger, eds. Liquid Crystals & Ordered Fluids. Incl. Vol. 1. LC 76-110760. 494p. 1970. 42.50 (ISBN 0-306-30466-X); Vol. 2. LC 74-1269. 783p. 1974. 49.50 (ISBN 0-306-35182-X); Vol. 3. 559p. 1978. 45.00 (ISBN 0-306-35183-8). Plenum Pr). Plenum Pub.

Kallard, Thomas, ed. Liquid Crystal Devices. LC 73-78006. (State of the Art Review Ser: Vol. 7). (Illus.). 350p. 1973. pap. 15.00 (ISBN 0-87739-007-X). Optosonic Pr.

Kelker, H. & Hatz, R. Handbook of Liquid Crystals. 1980. 262.50 (ISBN 0-89573-008-1). Verlag Chemie.

Khetrapal, C. L. Lyotropic Liquid Crystals. (NMR (Nuclear Magnetic Resonance) Ser.). (Illus.). 180p. 1975. 20.90 (ISBN 0-387-07303-5). Springer-Verlag.

Luckhurst, G. R. & Gray, G. W., eds. The Molecular Physics of Liquid Crystals. 1979. 53.00 (ISBN 0-12-458950-2). Acad Pr.

Meier, G., et al. Applications of Liquid Crystals. (Illus.). 160p. 1975. pap. 33.10 (ISBN 0-387-07302-7). Springer-Verlag.

Molecular Crystals & Liquid Crystals: Special Topics of the 6th International Liquid Crystal Conference, Kent State Univ., Aug. 1976, 4 pts. 1977. Set. 457.75x (ISBN 0-677-40275-9). Gordon.

Porter, Roger S. & Johnson, Julian F., eds. Ordered Fluids & Liquid Crystals. LC 67-28847. (Advances in Chemistry Ser: No. 63). 1967. 25.75 (ISBN 0-8412-0064-5). Am Chemical.

Priestly, E. B., et al. Introduction to Liquid Crystals. 356p. 1975. 22.50 (ISBN 0-306-30858-4, Plenum Pr). Plenum Pub.

Saeva. Liquid Crystals. 1979. 55.00 (ISBN 0-8247-6813-2). Dekker.

Sprokel, Gerald J., ed. The Physics & Chemistry of Liquid Crystal Devices. (IBM Research Symposia Ser.). 362p. 1980. 42.50 (ISBN 0-306-40440-0, Plenum Pr). Plenum Pub.

Tiddy, G. J. Lyotropic Liquid Crystals. cancelled (ISBN 0-677-04260-4). Gordon.

Zhdanov, S. I., ed. Liquid Crystal Chemistry & Physics. (Illus.). 300p. 1981. 60.00 (ISBN 0-08-026207-4). Pergamon.

LIQUID FUEL ROCKETS

see Liquid Propellant Rockets

LIQUID FUELS

see also Gasoline; Liquefied Petroleum Gas; Petroleum As Fuel; Petroleum Products

Ellington, R. T., ed. Liquid Fuels from Coal. 1977. 27.00 (ISBN 0-12-237250-6). Acad Pr.

H. Clarkson, Ltd., ed. Liquid Gas Carrier Register 1979. LC 75-644549. 1979. 80.00x (ISBN 0-8002-2204-0). Intl Pubns Serv.

The Potential for Liquid Fuels from Agriculture & Forestry in Australia. 147p. 1979. pap. 9.00 (ISBN 0-686-71840-2, CO 25, CSIRO). Unipub.

Steele, Henry B. Economic Potentialities of Synthetic Liquid Fuels from Oil Shale. Bruchey, Stuart, ed. LC 78-22751. (Energy in the American Economy Ser.). (Illus.). 1979. lib. bdg. 35.00x (ISBN 0-405-12015-X). Arno.

Stewart, G. A. The Potential for Liquid Fuels from Agriculture & Forestry in Australia. 147p. 1980. 35.00x (ISBN 0-643-00353-3, Pub. by CSIRO Australia). State Mutual Bk.

Stewart, G. A., et al. The Potential for Liquid Fuels from Agriculture & Forestry in Australia. 147p. 1980. pap. 7.50 (ISBN 0-643-00353-3, Pub. by SIRO Australia). Intl Schol Bk Serv.

Williams, Alan. The Combustion of Sprays of Liquid Fuels. 1975. pap. 9.95x (ISBN 0-236-31044-5, Pub. by Paul Elek). Merrimack Bk Serv.

Williams, D. A. & Jones, G. Liquid Fuels. 1963. pap. 9.75 (ISBN 0-08-010385-5). Pergamon.

LIQUID HELIUM

see also Superfluidity

Allen, J. F. Super-Fluid Helium. 1966. 48.50 (ISBN 0-12-051150-9). Acad Pr.

Bennemann, Karl H. & Ketterson, J. B., eds. Physics of Liquid & Solid Helium, 2 pts. LC 75-20235. (Interscience Monographs & Texts in Physics & Astronomy). 589p. Pt. 1, 1976, 608p. 46.50 (ISBN 0-471-06600-1, Pub. by Wiley-Interscience); Pt. 2, 1978, 750 Pgs. 92.50 (ISBN 0-471-06601-X). Wiley.

Careri, G., ed. Liquid Helium. (Italian Physical Society: Course 21). 1964. 57.00 (ISBN 0-12-368821-3). Acad Pr.

Keller, William E. Helium-Three & Helium-Four. LC 68-25382. (International Cryogenics Monographs). (Illus.). 431p. 1969. 42.50 (ISBN 0-306-30346-9, Plenum Pr). Plenum Pub.

Liquid Helium Technology. 1966. pap. 21.50 (ISBN 0-685-99152-0, IIR47, IIR). Unipub.

Wilks, John. Introduction to Liquid Helium. (Oxford Library of the Physical Sciences). (Illus.). 1970. pap. 12.95x (ISBN 0-19-851420-4). Oxford U Pr.

--Properties of Liquid & Solid Helium. (International Series of Monographs on Physics). 1967. 89.00x (ISBN 0-19-851245-7). Oxford U Pr.

LIQUID HYDROGEN

Liquid Hydrogen. 1965. pap. 17.75 (ISBN 0-685-99153-9, IIR23, IIR). Unipub.

Liquified Hydrogen Systems at Consumer Sites. (Fifty Ser). 1973. pap. 2.00 (ISBN 0-685-58092-X, 50B). Natl Fire Prot.

LIQUID METALS

see also Mercury

Chow, Brian G. The Liquid Metal Fast Breeder Reactor: An Economic Analysis. LC 75-39899. 1975. pap. 4.25 (ISBN 0-8447-3192-7). Am Enterprise.

Draley, J. E. & Weeks, J. R. Corrosion by Liquid Metals. LC 75-119057. 615p. 1970. 49.50 (ISBN 0-306-30482-1, Plenum Pr). Plenum Pub.

Dwyer, O. E. Boiling Liquid-Metal Heat Transfer. LC 75-11012. (Nuclear Science Technology Ser.). (Illus.). 1976. text ed. 37.95 (ISBN 0-89448-000-6). Am Nuclear Soc.

Faber, T. E. Introduction to the Theory of Liquid Metals. LC 76-184903. (Cambridge Monographs in Physics). (Illus.). 600p. 1972. 71.50 (ISBN 0-521-08477-6). Cambridge U Pr.

Gubanov, Alexsandr I. Quantum Electron Theory of Amorphous Conductors. LC 65-10526. 277p. 1965. 35.00 (ISBN 0-306-10703-1, Consultants). Plenum Pub.

International Conference, 2nd, Tokyo, 1972. The Properties of Liquid Metals: Proceedings. Takeuchi, S. & Takeuchi, S., eds. LC 73-1286. 640p. 1973. 46.95 (ISBN 0-470-84414-0). Halsted Pr.

Jackson, Carey B., ed. Liqid-Metals Handbook: Sodium-NaK Supplement. 445p. 1955. pap. 54.40 (ISBN 0-686-75851-X); microfilm 27.20 (ISBN 0-686-75852-8). DOE.

Kirko, Igor M. Magnetohydrodynamics of Liquid Metals. LC 65-17789. 80p. 1965. 25.00 (ISBN 0-306-10732-5, Consultants). Plenum Pub.

Knof, Hans. Thermodynamics of Irreversible Processes in Liquid Metals. 1966. 6.75x (ISBN 0-408-00131-3). Transatlantic.

Kutateladze, S. S., et al. Liquid-Metal Heat Transfer Media. LC 59-9228. 155p. 1959. 27.50 (ISBN 0-306-10548-9, Consultants). Plenum Pub.

Liquid Metal Fast Breeder Reactors: A Bibliography, January to December 1977. (DOE Technical Information Center Ser.). 518p. 1978. write for info. DOE.

Liquid Metal Fast Breeder Reactors: A Bibliography, Supplement 6, January 1978 to August 1980, 2 vols. (DOE Technical Information Center Ser.). 1980. write for info. DOE.

Liquid Metals Nineteen Seventy-Six: Bristol. (Institute of Physics Conference Ser.: No. 30). 1977. 80.00 (ISBN 0-9960030-9-6, Pub. by Inst Physics England). Heyden.

Luscher, E. & Coufal, H., eds. Liquid & Amorphous Metals: Mechanics of Plastic Solids. (NATO-Advanced Study Institute Ser.). 672p. 1980. 75.00x (ISBN 9-0286-0680-7). Sijthoff & Noordhoff.

Lyon, R. N., ed. Liquid-Metals Handbook. 2nd ed. 269p. 1952. pap. 33.50 (ISBN 0-686-75849-8); microfilm 16.80 (ISBN 0-686-75850-1). DOE.

Proposed Section XI-Division 3, Rules for Inspection & Testing of Components of Liquid Metal Cooled Plants. 1977. pap. text ed. 15.00 (ISBN 0-685-86877-X, E00123). ASME.

Ubbelohde, A. R. The Molten State of Matter: Melting & Crystal Structure. LC 77-28300. 454p. 1979. 87.50 (ISBN 0-471-99626-2). Wiley.

LIQUID PROPELLANT ROCKETS

Bollinger, Loren E., et al, eds. Liquid Rockets & Propellants. (Progress in Astronautics & Aeronautics: Vol. 2). 1960. 22.00 (ISBN 0-12-535102-X). Acad Pr.

LIQUID-VAPOR EQUILIBRIUM

see Vapor-Liquid Equilibrium

LIQUIDATION

Here are entered works on the winding up of companies or of the affairs of an individual.

Lenin, V. I. Against Liquidationism. 346p. 1973. 2.80 (ISBN 0-8285-0068-1, Pub. by Progress Pubs Russia). Imported Pubns.

LIQUIDITY (ECONOMICS)

see also Cash Flow; International Liquidity; Monetary Policy

Bryan, William H. Trading Asset Management. (New Horizons Ser.: No. 1). 40p. 1975. pap. 1.90 (ISBN 0-934914-23-0). NACM.

Chase, Samuel, Jr. Asset Prices in Economic Analysis. LC 63-13588. (California Library Reprint Series: No. 22). 1971. 21.50x (ISBN 0-520-01928-8). U of Cal Pr.

Hewson, John. Liquidity Creation & Distribution in the Eurocurrency Markets. LC 75-2804. 208p. 1975. 19.50 (ISBN 0-669-99556-8). Lexington Bks.

Mateer, William H. Checkless Society: Its Cost Implications for the Firm. LC 76-627114. 1969. 7.00 (ISBN 0-87744-091-3). Mich St U Busn.

Meigs, A. James. Free Reserves & the Money Supply. LC 62-17136. (Economic Research Studies Ser). 1962. 10.00x (ISBN 0-226-51901-5). U of Chicago Pr.

Morrison, George R. Liquidity Preferences of Commercial Banks. LC 66-13882. (Economic Research Studies Ser.). 1966. 10.50x (ISBN 0-226-54065-0). U of Chicago Pr.

Powell, Enoch J. Exchange Rates & Liquidity. (Institute of Economic Affairs, Occasional Papers Ser.: No. 18). pap. 2.50 (ISBN 0-255-69624-8). Transatlantic.

Willett, Thomas D. International Liquidity Issues. 1980. pap. 5.25 (ISBN 0-8447-3388-1). Am Enterprise.

LIQUIDS

see also Brownian Movements; Hydraulics; Hydrodynamics; Hydrostatics; Liquid Metals; Permeability; Quantum Liquids; Surface Tension

Bienestock, ed. Liquids & Amorphous Materials. pap. 7.50 (ISBN 0-686-60381-8). Polycrystal Bk Serv.

Blom, G. M., ed. Liquid Phase Epitaxy (from J. Crystal Growth, Vol. 27, 1974) Blank, S., et al. 332p. 1975. Repr. 78.00 (ISBN 0-444-10821-1, North-Holland). Elsevier.

Bretsznajder, S. Prediction of Transport and Other Physical Properties of Fluids. 424p. 1971. text ed. 46.00 (ISBN 0-08-013412-2). Pergamon.

Buckingham, A. D., et al. Organic Liquids: Structure, Dynamics & Chemical Properties. LC 78-8462. 1978. 62.95 (ISBN 0-471-99673-4, Pub. by Wiley-Interscience). Wiley.

Croxton, C. Introduction to Liquid State Physics. LC 74-13153. 283p. 1975. 42.00x (ISBN 0-471-18933-2, Pub. by Wiley-Interscience); pap. 21.25x (ISBN 0-471-18934-0). Wiley.

Croxton, Clive A. Statistical Mechanics of the Liquid Surface. LC 79-40819. 287p. 1980. 75.00 (ISBN 0-471-27663-4, Pub. by Wiley-Interscience). Wiley.

Croxton, Clive A., ed. Progress in Liquid Physics. LC 76-40166. 1978. 109.25 (ISBN 0-471-99445-6). Wiley.

D'Ans, J., et al. Densities of Binary Aqueous Systems & Heat Capacities of Liquid Systems. LC 62-53136. (Landolt-Boernstein Group IV: Vol. 1, Pt. B). (Illus.). 1978. 188.80 (ISBN 0-387-08272-7). Springer-Verlag.

Dupuy, J. & Dianioux, A. J., eds. Microscopic Structure & Dynamics of Liquids. (NATO Advanced Study Institutes Ser.: Series B, Physics, Vol. 33). 534p. 1978. 49.50 (ISBN 0-306-35733-X, Plenum Pr). Plenum Pub.

Dyer, A. Liquid Scintillation Counting, Vol.4. 1976. 55.50 (ISBN 0-85501-209-9). Heyden.

Francis, Albert W. Liquid-Liquid Equilibrium. (Interscience Library of Chemical Engineering & Processing: Vol. 3). 288p. 1963. text ed. 16.00 (ISBN 0-470-27435-2, Pub. by Wiley). Krieger.

Frisch, Harry L. & Salsburg, Z. W. Simple Dense Fluids. LC 67-23159. 1968. 62.00 (ISBN 0-12-268650-0). Acad Pr.

Gerrard, W. Solubility of Gases & Liquids...a Graphic Approach. (Illus.). 275p. 1976. 45.00 (ISBN 0-306-30866-5, Plenum Pr). Plenum Pub.

Halley, J. W., ed. Correlation Functions & Quasiparticle Interactions in Condensed Matter. (NATO Advanced Study Institute Ser.: Series B, Physics, Vol. 35). 644p. 1978. 59.50 (ISBN 0-306-40018-9, Plenum Pr). Plenum Pub.

Hansen, J. P. & McDonald, I. R. The Theory of Simple Liquids. 1977. 62.50 (ISBN 0-12-323850-1). Acad Pr.

Harrison, G. Dynamic Properties of Super-Cooled Liquids. 1976. 31.50 (ISBN 0-12-328150-4). Acad Pr.

Hirschfelder, Joseph O., et al. Molecular Theory of Gases & Liquids. LC 54-7621. 1964. 75.00 (ISBN 0-471-40065-3, Pub. by Wiley-Interscience). Wiley.

Holland, F. A. & Chapman, F. S. Liquid Mixing & Processing in Stirred Tanks. (Illus.). 1966. 19.50 (ISBN 0-442-35139-9). Van Nos Reinhold.

Influence of Organic Liquids on Rubber Materials. 89p. Date not set. 18.00 (ISBN 0-686-76106-5, 13-413001-20). ASTM.

Kirkwood, John G. Theory of Liquids. Alder, B., ed. (Documents on Modern Physics Ser.). (Illus., Orig.). 1968. 31.50x (ISBN 0-677-00350-1). Gordon.

Kobayashi, Yutaka & Maudsley, David V. Biological Applications of Liquid Scintillation Counting. 1974. 32.50 (ISBN 0-12-417250-4). Acad Pr.

Kohler, Friedrich. The Liquid State. LC 75-185277. (Monographs in Modern Chemistry: Vol. 1). (Illus.). 1972. 49.50 (ISBN 3-527-25390-4). Verlag Chemie.

Kruus, Peeter. Liquids & Solutions: Structure & Dynamics. 1977. 59.50 (ISBN 0-8247-6427-7). Dekker.

March, N. H. & Tosi, M. P. Atomic Dynamics in Liquids. LC 76-16040. 330p. 1977. 65.95 (ISBN 0-470-15145-5). Halsted Pr.

Marcus, Y. Introduction to Liquid State Chemistry. LC 76-40230. 1977. 48.25 (ISBN 0-471-99448-0, Pub. by Wiley-Interscience). Wiley.

Muus, L. T. & Atkins, P. W., eds. Electron Spin Relaxation in Liquids. LC 72-76022. 530p. 1972. 49.50 (ISBN 0-306-30588-7, Plenum Pr). Plenum Pub.

Noakes, G. R., ed. Sources of Physics Teaching: Gravity. Liquids. Gases, Vol. 5. 1970. pap. text ed. 12.95x (ISBN 0-85066-040-8). Intl Ideas.

Nyvlt, J. Solid-Liquid Phase Equilibria. 1977. 39.00 (ISBN 0-444-99850-0). Elsevier.

Oldshue, James Y. Liquid Mixing Technology. (Chemical Engineering Ser.). 400p. 1981. 27.50 (ISBN 0-07-047685-3, P&RB). McGraw.

Rabinovich, I. B. Influence of Isotopy on the Physicochemical Properties of Liquids. LC 69-17695. 304p. 1970. 42.50 (ISBN 0-306-10835-6, Consultants). Plenum Pub.

Rowlinson, J. S. Liquids & Liquid Mixtures. 2nd ed. LC 79-75522. 371p. 1969. 37.50 (ISBN 0-306-30694-8, Plenum Pr). Plenum Pub.

Skripov, V. P. Metastable Liquids. Slutzkin, D., ed. Kondor, R., tr. from Rus. LC 73-16416. 300p. 1974. 55.95 (ISBN 0-470-79546-8). Halsted Pr.

Societe De Chimie Physique, 24th, Paris-Orsay, July 2-6, 1973. Molecular Motions of Liquids: Proceedings. Lascombe, J., ed. LC 73-91947. 1974. lib. bdg. 105.00 (ISBN 90-277-0431-7, Pub. by Reidel Holland). Kluwer Boston.

Tabor, D. Gases, Liquids & Solids. 2nd ed. LC 78-26451. (Illus.). 1980. 57.50 (ISBN 0-521-22383-0); pap. 15.95 (ISBN 0-521-29466-5). Cambridge U Pr.

Tank Vehicles for Flammable & Combustible Liquids. (Thirty Ser). 1974. pap. 2.50 (ISBN 0-685-58035-0, 385). Natl Fire Prot.

Temperley, H. N. & Trevena, D. H. Liquids & Their Properties: A Molecular & Microscopic Treatise. LC 77-8177. 1978. 65.95 (ISBN 0-470-99203-4). Halsted Pr.

Toglia, Joseph U. Electronystagmography: Technical Aspects & Atlas. (Illus.). 168p. 1976. 18.50 (ISBN 0-398-03537-7). C C Thomas.

Tompkins, F. C., ed. Thin Liquid Films & Boundary Layers: Special Discussion of the Faraday Society. 1971. 43.50 (ISBN 0-12-694550-0). Acad Pr.

Trevena, D. H. & Cooke, R. J. The Liquid Phase. LC 75-19034. (Wykeham Science Ser.: No. 37). 1975. 9.95x (ISBN 0-8448-1164-5). Crane-Russak Co.

Vargaftik, N. B. Tables on the Thermophysical Properties of Liquids & Gases: In Normal & Dissociated States. 2nd ed. LC 75-14260. (Advances in Thermal Engineering Ser.). 758p. 1975. 49.50 (ISBN 0-470-90310-4). Halsted Pr.

Watts, R. O. & McGee, I. J. Liquid State Chemical Physics. LC 76-21793. 350p. 1976. 35.50 (ISBN 0-471-91240-9). Krieger.

Weber, A. Raman Spectroscopy of Gases & Liquids. (Topics in Current Physics Ser.: Vol. 11). (Illus.). 1979. 31.00 (ISBN 0-387-09036-3). Springer-Verlag.

Wilson, A. C. Insulating Liquids: Their Uses, Manufacture & Properties. (IEE Electrical & Electronics Materials & Devices). (Illus.). 1980. 37.00 (ISBN 0-906048-23-0). Inst Elect Eng.

LIQUIDS-COMPRESSIBILITY

see Compressibility

LIQUIDS-DIFFUSION

see Diffusion

LIQUIDS-VISCOSITY

see Viscosity

LIQUIDS, KINETIC THEORY OF

Babuel-Peyrissac, Jean-Paul. Equations Cinetiques Des Fluides & Des Plasmas. (Cours & Documents de Mathematiques & de Physique Ser.). 306p. 1975. 101.75 (ISBN 0-677-50630-9). Gordon.

Croxton, C. A. Liquid State Physics. LC 72-89803. (Physics Monographs). (Illus.). 400p. 1974. 57.50 (ISBN 0-521-20117-9). Cambridge U Pr.

Liboff, Richard L. Introduction to the Theory of Kinetic Equations. corr. ed. LC 76-30383. (Illus.). 410p. 1979. Repr. of 1969 ed. lib. bdg. 20.50 (ISBN 0-88275-496-3). Krieger.

Nozdrev, V. F. Application of Ultrasonics in Molecular Physics. (Russian Monographs Ser). (Illus.). 1963. 104.00 (ISBN 0-677-20360-8). Gordon.

Resibois, P. & De Leener, M. F. Classical Kinetic Theory of Fluids. LC 76-58852. 1977. 42.50 (ISBN 0-471-71694-4, Pub. by Wiley-Interscience). Wiley.

Temperley, H. N., et al, eds. Physics of Simple Liquids. 1968. 78.00 (ISBN 0-444-10281-7, North-Holland). Elsevier.

LIQUOR INDUSTRY

see Distilling Industries; Liquor Traffic

LIQUOR INDUSTRY AND TRADE

see also Brewing; Hotels, Taverns, Etc.

Arco Editorial Board. Beverage Control Investigator. 2nd ed. LC 64-8814. (Orig.). 1964. pap. 4.00 (ISBN 0-668-00150-X). Arco.

Guideline Publishing Co. Staff. The California Retail Liquor Store. 54p. (Orig.). 1972. pap. 9.95 (ISBN 0-917474-00-7). Guideline Pub.

Newman, Peter. King of the Castle, the Making of a Dynasty: Seagram's & the Bronfman Empire. LC 78-65198. 1979. 11.95 (ISBN 0-689-10963-6). Atheneum.

Shanken, Marvin R. The Impact American Beer Market Review & Forecast. 2nd ed. (Illus.). 60p. 1981. pap. 100.00 (ISBN 0-918076-15-3). M Shanken Comm.

--The Impact American Distilled Spirits Market Review & Forecast. 6th ed. (Illus.). 60p. 1981. pap. 100.00 (ISBN 0-918076-14-5). M Shanken Comm.

--The Impact American Distilled Spirits Market Review & Forecast. 5th ed. (Illus.). 1980. pap. 75.00 (ISBN 0-918076-08-0). M Shanken Comm.

--The Impact American Distilled Spirits Market Review & Forecast. 4th ed. (Illus.). 1979. pap. 75.00 (ISBN 0-918076-04-8). M Shanken Comm.

--The Impact American Distilled Spirits Review & Forecast. 3rd ed. 1978. 75.00 (ISBN 0-918076-02-1). M Shanken Comm.

--The Impact American Wine Market Review & Forecast. 7th ed. (Illus.). 60p. 1981. pap. 100.00 (ISBN 0-918076-13-7). M Shanken Comm.

Shanken, Marvin R., ed. The Impact American Distilled Spirits Market Review & Forecast. 2nd ed. (Illus.). 1977. 75.00 (ISBN 0-918076-05-6). M Shanken Comm.

LIQUOR INDUSTRY AND TRADE-SCOTLAND

Moss, Michael S. & Hume, John R. The Making of Scotch Whiskey. LC 81-3145. 296p. 1981. 49.50x (ISBN 0-8448-1393-1). Crane-Russak Co.

LIQUOR LAWS

see also Prohibition

Arco Editorial Board. Beverage Control Investigator. 2nd ed. LC 64-8814. (Orig.). 1964. pap. 4.00 (ISBN 0-668-00150-X). Arco.

Brown, Everett S. Ratification of the Twenty-First Amendment to the Constitution of the United States. LC 78-114757. (American Constitutional & Legal History Ser). 1970. Repr. of 1938 ed. 65.00 (ISBN 0-306-71928-2). Da Capo.

Engelmann, Larry. Intemperance: The Lost War Against Liquor. LC 79-7103. (Illus.). 1979. 10.95 (ISBN 0-02-909520-4). Free Pr.

Merz, Charles. Dry Decade. LC 71-8894. (Americana Library Ser.: No. 13). 364p. 1970. pap. 3.45 (ISBN 0-295-95099-4). U of Wash Pr.

Pearson, Charles C. & Hendricks, James E. Liquor & Anti-Liquor in Virginia, 1619-1919. LC 67-18530. (Illus.). 1967. 14.75 (ISBN 0-8223-0133-4). Duke.

Rudman, Jack. Beverage Control Inspector. (Career Examination Ser.: C-83). (Cloth bdg. avail. on request). pap. 8.00 (ISBN 0-8373-0083-5). Natl Learning.

Sites, Clement M. Centralized Administration of Liquor Laws in the American Commonwealths. LC 68-56687. (Columbia University. Studies in the Social Sciences: No. 28). Repr. of 1899 ed. 16.50 (ISBN 0-404-51028-0). AMS Pr.

Wechsler, Henry, ed. Minimum-Drinking-Age Laws: An Evaluation. LC 79-3133. 208p. 1980. 18.95x (ISBN 0-669-03380-4). Lexington Bks.

LIQUOR PROBLEM

see also Alcohol and Youth; Alcoholics; Alcoholism; Hotels, Taverns, etc.; Prohibition; Temperance

Barker, John M. Saloon Problem & Social Reform. LC 76-112521. (Rise of Urban America). 1970. Repr. of 1905 ed. 17.00 (ISBN 0-405-02434-7). Arno.

Berry, Ralph E. & Boland, James P. The Economic Cost of Alcohol Abuse. LC 76-19642. (Illus.). 1977. 13.95 (ISBN 0-02-903080-3). Free Pr.

Blakey, Leonard S. Sale of Liquor in the South. LC 74-94922. (Columbia University Studies in the Social Sciences: No. 127). Repr. of 1912 ed. 15.00 (ISBN 0-404-51127-9). AMS Pr.

Bruun, Kettil, et al. The Gentlemen's Club: International Control of Drugs & Alcohol. LC 74-21343. (Studies in Crime & Justice Ser). xiv, 338p. 1975. 17.50x (ISBN 0-226-07777-2, Phoen); pap. 5.95 (ISBN 0-226-07778-0). U of Chicago Pr.

Cahalan, Don. Problem Drinkers: A National Survey. LC 73-133617. (Social & Behavioral Science Ser.). 1970. 16.95x (ISBN 0-87589-080-6). Jossey-Bass.

Cahalan, Don, et al. American Drinking Practices: A National Study of Drinking Behavior & Attitudes. LC 70-626701. (Rutgers Center of Alcohol Studies: Monograph No. 6). 1969. pap. 9.50x (ISBN 0-911290-37-0). Rutgers Ctr Alcohol.

Calkins, Raymond. Substitutes for the Saloon: An Investigation Originally Made for the Committee of Fifty. LC 75-137181. (Poverty U.S.A. Historical Record Ser). 1971. Repr. of 1919 ed. 19.00 (ISBN 0-405-03119-X). Arno.

Committee Of Fifty. Liquor Problem: A Summary of Investigations Conducted by the Committee of Fifty, 1893-1903. LC 70-112533. (Rise of Urban America). 1970. Repr. of 1905 ed. 12.00 (ISBN 0-405-02444-4). Arno.

Ewing, John A. & Rouse, Beatrice A., eds. Drinking. LC 76-47522. 1978. 23.95x (ISBN 0-88229-129-7); pap. text ed. 11.95x (ISBN 0-88229-569-1). Nelson-Hall.

Fairchild, Daniel, et al. Everything You Always Wanted to Know About Drinking Problems & Then a Few Things You Didn't Want to Know. cancelled (ISBN 0-932194-04-4). Green Hill.

Follmann, Joseph F., Jr. Alcoholics & Business: Problems, Costs, Solutions. new ed. LC 75-40270. 256p. 1976. 12.95 (ISBN 0-8144-5410-0). Am Mgmt.

Fort, Joel. Alcohol: Our Biggest Drug Problem. (Illus.). 180p. 1973. 10.95 (ISBN 0-07-021598-7, C); pap. 6.95 (ISBN 0-07-021599-5). McGraw.

Goshen, Charles E. Drinks, Drugs, & Do-Gooders. LC 72-93309. (Illus.). 1973. 10.95 (ISBN 0-02-912620-7). Free Pr.

Grob, Gerald N., ed. Public Policy & the Problem of Addiction: Four Studies, 1914 to 1924, An Original Anthology. LC 70-1208. (Addiction in America Ser.). 1981. lib. bdg. 15.00x (ISBN 0-405-13564-5). Arno.

Hamer, John & Steinbring, Jack, eds. Alcohol & Native Peoples of the North. LC 80-8301. 323p. lib. bdg. 19.75 (ISBN 0-8191-1197-X); pap. text ed. 11.50 (ISBN 0-8191-1198-8). U Pr of Amer.

Jessor, Richard, et al. Society, Personality & Deviant Behavior: A Study of a Tri-Ethnic Community. 512p. 1975. Repr. of 1968 ed. 20.50 (ISBN 0-88275-339-8). Krieger.

Keller, Mark, ed. International Bibliography of Studies on Alcohol, 3 vols. Incl. Vol. 1. References, 1901-1950. Jordy, Sarah S., compiled by. 1966. 50.00x (ISBN 0-911290-34-6); Vol. 2. Indexes, 1901-1950. Efron, Vera & Jordy, Sarah S. 1968. 50.00x (ISBN 0-911290-35-4); Vol. 3. References, 1951-1960; Indexes, 1951-1960. Jordy, Sarah S., et al. 1980. 100.00x (ISBN 0-686-66592-9). LC 60-14437. Set Of Vols. 1 & 2. 95.00x (ISBN 0-911290-07-9). Rutgers Ctr Alcohol.

Lolli, Giorgio, et al. Alcohol in Italian Culture: Food & Wine in Relation to Sobriety Among Italians & Italian Americans. LC 58-9167. (Rutgers Center of Alcohol Studies: Monograph No. 3). 1958. 7.50x (ISBN 0-911290-27-3). Rutgers Ctr Alcohol.

--Alcohol in Italian Culture. 1958. 6.00x (ISBN 0-8084-0411-3). Coll & U Pr.

MacAndrew, Craig & Edgerton, Robert B. Drunken Comportment: A Social Explanation. LC 68-8154. 1969. 18.95x (ISBN 0-202-30095-1). Aldine Pub.

McCarthy, Raymond G., ed. Drinking & Intoxication: Selected Readings in Social Attitudes & Controls. LC 59-5289. 1963. pap. 8.50x (ISBN 0-911290-28-1). Rutgers Ctr Alcohol.

--Drinking & Intoxication: Selected Readings in Social Attitudes & Controls. 1959. pap. 8.50 (ISBN 0-8084-0409-1, B11). Coll & U Pr.

Patrick, Clarence H. Alcohol, Culture & Society. LC 73-112941. Repr. of 1952 ed. 18.00 (ISBN 0-404-04906-0). AMS Pr.

Pearson, Charles C. & Hendricks, James E. Liquor & Anti-Liquor in Virginia, 1619-1919. LC 67-18530. (Illus.). 1967. 14.75 (ISBN 0-8223-0133-4). Duke.

Plaut, Thomas F., ed. Alcohol Problems: A Report to the Nation by the Cooperative Commission on the Study of Alcoholism. 1967. 11.95 (ISBN 0-19-500060-9). Oxford U Pr.

--Alcohol Problems: A Report to the Nation by the Cooperative Commission on the Study of Alcoholism. LC 67-25647. (Orig.). 1967. pap. 3.95 (ISBN 0-19-500776-X, 262, GB). Oxford U Pr.

Robinson, David, ed. Alcohol Problems: Reviews, Research & Recommendations. LC 79-13367. 1980. text ed. 27.50x (ISBN 0-8419-0524-X). Holmes & Meier.

Rubington, Earl. Alcohol Problems & Social Control. LC 72-86515. 1973. pap. text ed. 6.95x (ISBN 0-675-09046-6). Merrill.

Sadoun, Roland, et al. Drinking in French Culture. LC 65-22389. (Rutgers Center of Alcohol Studies: Monograph No. 5). 1965. 7.50x (ISBN 0-911290-33-8). Rutgers Ctr Alcohol.

--Drinking in French Culture. 1965. 6.00x (ISBN 0-8084-0410-5). Coll & U Pr.

Stivers, Richard. A Hair of the Dog: Irish Drinking & American Stereotype. LC 75-27233. 300p. 1976. 14.95 (ISBN 0-271-01219-6). Pa St U Pr.

Surveys of Drinking & Abstaining: Urban, Suburban & National Studies. (Journal of Studies on Alcohol: Suppl. No. 6). 1972. 9.00x (ISBN 0-911290-01-X). Rutgers Ctr Alcohol.

Trice, Harrison M. Alcoholism in America. LC 77-2665. 168p. 1978. pap. 5.95 (ISBN 0-88275-479-3). Krieger.

LIQUOR PROBLEM-GREAT BRITAIN

Harrison, Brian. Drink & the Victorians: The Temperance Question in England, 1815-1872. LC 70-141765. 1971. 19.95 (ISBN 0-8229-3223-7). U of Pittsburgh Pr.

Stivers, Richard. A Hair of the Dog: Irish Drinking & American Stereotype. LC 75-27233. 300p. 1976. 14.95 (ISBN 0-271-01219-6). Pa St U Pr.

LIQUOR TRAFFIC

see also Brewing Industry; Distilling, Illicit

Warburton, Clark. Economic Results of Prohibition. LC 68-58634. (Columbia University. Studies in the Social Sciences: No. 379). Repr. of 1932 ed. 22.50 (ISBN 0-404-51379-4). AMS Pr.

LIQUORS

see also Brewing; Distillation; Hangover Cures; also names of liquors, e.g. Brandy

Arthur, Stanley C. Famous New Orleans Drinks & How to Mix'em. 1977. pap. 2.95 (ISBN 0-88289-132-4). Pelican.

Erdos, Richard. One Thousand Remarkable Facts About Booze. 192p. 1981. pap. 5.95 (ISBN 0-8317-0958-8, Rutledge Pr). Smith Pubs.

Hogg, Anthony. Cocktails & Mixed Drinks. (Illus.). 128p. 1981. 7.95 (ISBN 0-600-32028-6, 8179). Larousse.

Ray, Cyril. The Complete Book of Spirits & Liqueurs. 1978. 12.95 (ISBN 0-02-601150-6). Macmillan.

Shepard, John S. Shepard's Wine & Liquor Pricing Guide. (Foodservice Guides Ser.). 1981. spiral bdg. 15.00 (ISBN 0-89047-034-0). Herman Pub.

Stewart, Hilary. Wild Teas, Coffees, & Cordials. (Illus.). 128p. 1981. pap. 7.95 (ISBN 0-295-95804-9). U of Wash Pr.

United Kingdom Bartender's Guild. International Guide to Drinks. 7th ed. 1979. pap. 4.95 (ISBN 0-09-134811-0, Pub. by Hutchinson). Merrimack Bk Serv.

Waugh, Alec. Wines & Spirits. LC 68-55300. (Foods of the World Ser). (Illus.). (gr. 6 up). 1968. PLB 14.94 (ISBN 0-8094-0061-8, Time-Life). Silver.

--Wines & Spirits. (Foods of the World Ser). (Illus.). 1968. 14.95 (ISBN 0-8094-0034-0). Time-Life.

LISA, MANUEL, 1772-1820

Douglas, Walter B. Manuel Lisa. Nasatir, Abraham P., ed. (Illus.). 1964. Repr. of 1911 ed. 12.50 (ISBN 0-87266-006-0). Argosy.

LISBOA, ANTONIA FRANCISCO, 1730-1814

Mann, Hans & Mann, Graciela. The Twelve Prophets of Aleijadinho. (Illus.). 131p. 1967. 18.50x (ISBN 0-292-73654-1). U of Tex Pr.

LISBON

Arthur Frommer's Guide to Lisbon-Madrid, 1981-82. 224p. 1981. pap. 2.95 (ISBN 0-671-41433-X). Frommer-Pasmantier.

Wright, Carol. Lisbon. (Illus.). 1971. 5.00x (ISBN 0-460-03962-8). Intl Pubns Serv.

LISBON-SIEGE, 1147

David, Charles W., ed. De Expugnatione Lyxbonensi. (Illus., Lat. & Eng.). 1969. lib. bdg. 17.00x (ISBN 0-374-92071-0). Octagon.

LISP (COMPUTER PROGRAM LANGUAGE)

Anatomy of LISP. (Computer Science Ser). (Illus.). 1978. 19.95 (ISBN 0-07-001115-X, C). McGraw.

Friedman, Daniel P. The Little LISPer. LC 73-91284. 64p. 1974. pap. text ed. 3.95 (ISBN 0-574-19165-8, 13-2165). SRA.

McCarthy, John. LISP 1.5 Programmer's Manual. 1962. 6.95x (ISBN 0-262-13011-4). MIT Pr.

Maurer, W. D. The Programmers Introduction to Lisp. (Computer Monograph Ser). 1972. 16.95 (ISBN 0-444-19572-6). Elsevier.

Meehan, James R., ed. The New UCI LISP Manual. 336p. 1979. pap. text ed. 14.95x (ISBN 0-89859-012-4). L Erlbaum Assocs.

Siklossy, Laurent. Let's Talk Lisp. ref. ed. 456p. 1976. 19.95 (ISBN 0-13-532762-8). P-H.

Tracton, Ken. Programmer's Guide to LISP. (Illus.). 1979. 10.95 (ISBN 0-8306-9761-6); pap. 6.95 (ISBN 0-8306-1045-6, 1045). TAB Bks.

Weissman, Clark. LISP One-Point-Five Primer. (Orig.). 1967. pap. 18.95x (ISBN 0-8221-1050-4). Dickenson.

Winograd, Terry. Understanding Natural Language. 1972. 25.00 (ISBN 0-12-759750-6). Acad Pr.

LISSITZKY, EL

Lissitzky-Kuppers, Sophie. El Lissitzky. 1980. 47.50 (ISBN 0-500-23090-0). Thames Hudson.

LIST, FRIEDRICH, 1789-1846

Hirst, Margaret E. Life of Friedrich List & Selections from His Writings. LC 65-16266. Repr. of 1909 ed. 17.50x (ISBN 0-678-00068-9). Kelley.

Westerby, Herbert. Liszt Composer & His Piano Works. lib. bdg. 14.00 (ISBN 0-403-01718-1). Scholarly.

LIST PROCESSING (ELECTRONIC COMPUTERS)

Bowen & Behr. The Logical Design of Multiple Microprocessor Systems. (Illus.). 272p. 1980. text ed. 22.95 (ISBN 0-13-539908-4). P-H.

Griswold, Ralph C. String & List Processing in Snobol 4: Techniques & Applications. (Illus.). 304p. 1975. text ed. 14.95 (ISBN 0-13-853010-6). P-H.

LISTENING

Anastasi, Thomas E., Jr. Listen! Techniques for Improving Communication Skills. 112p. 1981. pap. text ed. 8.95 (ISBN 0-8436-0864-1). CBI Pub.

Astmann, Herbert K. Four Big Steps to Success: Reading, Writing, Speaking, Listening. 1978. pap. text ed. 7.95 (ISBN 0-8403-1916-9). Kendall-Hunt.

Atwater, Eastwood. I Hear You: Listening Skills to Make You a Better Manager. 224p. 1981. 12.95 (ISBN 0-13-450684-7); pap. 4.95 (ISBN 0-13-450676-6). P-H.

Bamberger, Jeanne S. & Brofsky, Howard. The Art of Listening: Developing Musical Perception. 4th ed. LC 78-20837. 1979. pap. text ed. 16.50 scp (ISBN 0-06-040943-6, HarpC); inst. manual free (ISBN 0-06-360966-5); Set Of 5 Records. scp 26.50 (ISBN 0-06-040981-9). Har-Row.

Banville, Thomas G. How to Listen-How to Be Heard. LC 77-17961. 1978. 14.95x (ISBN 0-88229-332-X); pap. 8.95 (ISBN 0-686-68003-0). Nelson-Hall.

Barbara, Dominick A. Art of Listening. (Illus.). 208p. 1974. 9.25 (ISBN 0-398-00086-7). C C Thomas.

Berman, Michael. Materials for Listening Comprehension & Note Taking in English. 1980. pap. 3.95 (ISBN 0-08-025316-4). Pergamon.

Carin. Creative Questioning & Sensitivity: Listening Techniques. 2nd ed. 1978. text ed. 7.95 (ISBN 0-675-08421-0); media 115.00 (ISBN 0-675-08485-7). Merrill.

Cassie, Dhyan. Auditory Training Handbook for Good Listeners. LC 75-26439. 1976. pap. text ed. 2.95x (ISBN 0-8134-1762-7, 1762). Interstate.

Cronkhite, Gary. Public Speaking & Critical Listening. LC 77-87452. 1978. 12.95 (ISBN 0-8053-1901-8). Benjamin-Cummings.

Crum, J. K. Art of Inner Listning. 1975. pap. 1.25 (ISBN 0-89129-092-3, PV092). Jove Pubns.

Ernst, Franklin H., Jr. Outline of the Activity of Listening. 3rd ed. 1973. softbound 1.95x (ISBN 0-916944-09-3). Addresso'set.

--Who's Listening - Handbook of the Listening Activity. LC 73-84380. 1973. 9.95x (ISBN 0-916944-15-8). Addresso'set.

Faber, Carl A. On Listening. LC 80-4512. 1976. 4.95 (ISBN 0-918026-02-4). Perseus Pr.

Fantel, Hans. Better Listening: A Practical Guide to Stereo Equipment for the Home. (Illus.). 192p. 1982. 14.95 (ISBN 0-686-76565-6, ScribT). Scribner.

Geeting, Baxter & Geeting, Corinne. How to Listen Assertively. (Illus.). 1978. pap. 3.95 (ISBN 0-671-18336-2). Monarch Pr.

Girzaitis, Loretta. Listening: A Response Ability. LC 72-77722. (Illus.). 1972. pap. 3.25 (ISBN 0-88489-047-3). St Marys.

Goldstein, H. Reading & Listening Comprehension at Various Controlled Rates. LC 71-176812. (Columbia University. Teachers College. Contributions to Education: No. 821). Repr. of 1940 ed. 17.50 (ISBN 0-404-55821-6). AMS Pr.

Hughes, Ted. Poetry in the Making. 124p. 1967. pap. 4.95 (ISBN 0-571-09076-1, Pub. by Faber & Faber). Merrimack Bk Serv.

Ihde, Don. Listening & Voice: A Phenomenology of Sound. LC 76-8302. (Illus.). x, 188p. 1979. pap. 4.95x (ISBN 0-8214-0563-2). Ohio U Pr.

Ilyin, Donna. Listening Comprehension Group Test: Examiner's Test Manual. (Listening Comprehension Group Test Ser.). 32p. 1981. pap. text ed. 4.99 (ISBN 0-88377-212-4); write for info. ICWT answer sheets (50) (ISBN 0-88377-214-0); write for info. answer sheets (50) & keys ICPT (ISBN 0-88377-213-2). Newbury Hse.

--Listening Comprehension Group Tests: Student Picture Booklet. (Listening Comprehension Group Test Ser.). 32p. (gr. 8-12). 1981. pap. text ed. 1.99 (ISBN 0-88377-210-8). Newbury Hse.

Ilyin, Donna & Rubin, Susan. LCGT Technical Guide. (Listening Comprehension Group Test Ser.). 24p. 1981. pap. text ed. 3.99 (ISBN 0-88377-211-6). Newbury Hse.

Johnson, Ida Mae. Developing the Listening Skills. 1974. 4.50 (ISBN 0-914296-18-3). Activity Rec.

Kerman, Joseph. Listen. 3rd ed. 1980. 16.95x (ISBN 0-87901-127-0); single record 3.95 (ISBN 0-686-31791-2); 10 record set 26.95 (ISBN 0-686-31792-0). H S Worth.

Koile, Earl. Listening As a Way of Becoming. LC 76-48520. 1977. 5.95 (ISBN 0-87680-510-1, 61001). Word Bks.

Kratoville, Betty L. Listen, My Children, & You Shall Hear, Bk. 1. LC 68-29770. 1968. pap. 3.25x (ISBN 0-8134-1044-4, 1044); pkg. of 20 extra grading sheets 0.75 (ISBN 0-8134-1045-2, 1045). Interstate.

--Listen My Children, & You Shall Hear, Bk. 3. LC 68-29770. 1979. pap. 3.25x (ISBN 0-8134-2057-1, 2057). Interstate.

Langs, Robert. The Listening Process. LC 78-68010. 1978. 35.00x (ISBN 0-87668-341-3). Aronson.

Lenard, Grace. Don't Just Hear-Listen. pap. 4.95 (ISBN 0-685-24816-X). Lawrence.

Lundsteen, Sara W. Listening: Its Impact at All Levels on Reading & Other Language Arts. LC 79-14249. (Illus.). 1979. pap. text ed. 8.00 (ISBN 0-8141-2949-8, ERIC-RCS). NCTE.

Mills, Ernest P. Listening: Key to Communication. (Vardamann Management & Communication Ser.). (Illus.). 128p. 1974. pap. 5.95x (ISBN 0-442-80021-5). Van Nos Reinhold.

Montgomery, Robert L. Listening Made Easy: How to Improve Listening on the Job, at Home & in the Community. 128p. 1981. 10.95 (ISBN 0-8144-5650-2). Am Mgmt.

Morley, Joan. Improving Aural Comprehension: Student's Workbook, Teacher's Book of Readings. LC 70-185904. 1972. tchrs.' bk. of readings 3.95x, free with adoption of students wkbk. (ISBN 0-472-08666-9); student's wkbk 5.95x (ISBN 0-472-08665-0). U of Mich Pr.

Nichols, R. & Stevens, L. A. Are You Listening? 1957. 12.95 (ISBN 0-07-046475-8, GB). McGraw.

Northcott, Winifred H., ed. I Heard That! A Developmental Sequence of Listening Activities for the Young Child. 40p. 1978. 3.75 (ISBN 0-88200-120-5, D2552). Alexander Graham.

Oakland, Thomas & Williams, Fern C. Auditory Perception: Diagnosis & Development for Language & Reading Abilities. LC 79-158860. (Orig.). 1971. pap. 9.00x (ISBN 0-87562-028-0). Spec Child.

Plaister, T. Developing Listening Comprehension for ESL Students: The Kingdom of Kochen. 1976. pap. 8.95 (ISBN 0-13-204479-X); tapes 125.00 (ISBN 0-13-204495-1). P-H.

Rubin, Irwin & Rose, Earl. The Power of Listening. (Illus.). 1978. leader's guide 10.00 (ISBN 0-07-054177-9); wkbk 6.95 (ISBN 0-07-054176-0). McGraw.

Russell, David H. & Russell, Elizabeth F. Listening Aids Through the Grades: Two Hundred Thirty-Two Listening Activities. rev ed. Hennings, Dorothy G., ed. LC 79-607. 1979. pap. text ed. 5.95x (ISBN 0-8077-2558-7). Tchrs Coll.

Sims, J. & Peterson, P. Better Listening Skills. (Illus.). 128p. 1981. pap. 6.95 (ISBN 0-13-074815-3). P-H.

Stocker, Claudell S. Listening for the Visually Impaired: A Teaching Manual. 192p. 1974. pap. 11.75 (ISBN 0-398-02936-9). C C Thomas.

Wakefield, Norman. Listening. 120p. 1981. pap. 4.95 (ISBN 0-8499-2920-2). Word Bks.

Weaver, Carl H. Human Listening. LC 75-182878. (Speech Communication Ser.). 1972. pap. text ed. 4.50 (ISBN 0-672-61234-8, SC18). Bobbs.

Wicks, Robert J. Helping Others: Ways of Listening, Sharing & Counseling. LC 79-11710. 1979. 9.95 (ISBN 0-8019-6777-5). Chilton.

Wolvin, Andrew & Coakley, Carolyn. Listening. 256p. 1981. pap. text ed. price not set (ISBN 0-697-04192-1); instr.'s manual avail. Wm C Brown.

LISTENING-PROGRAMMED INSTRUCTIONS

Erway, E. Listening: A Programmed Approach. 1969. text ed. 7.95 (ISBN 0-07-019655-9, C); tchr's. guide 4.95 (ISBN 0-07-019656-7); cassettes 115.00 (ISBN 0-07-075008-4). McGraw.

Oakland, Thomas & Williams, Fern C. Auditory Perception: Diagnosis & Development for Language & Reading Abilities. LC 79-158860. (Orig.). 1971. pap. 9.00x (ISBN 0-87562-028-0). Spec Child.

Rose, Michael A. & Stratton, Robert K. Listening in the Real World: Clues to English Conversation. 144p. 1978. pap. text ed. 5.95 (ISBN 0-940264-00-5); 49.50 (ISBN 0-940264-01-3). Lingual Hse Pub.

Teaching Your Child to Listen. Date not set. price not set (ISBN 0-939418-19-3). Ferguson-Florissant.

LISTENING DEVICES-LAW AND LEGISLATION

see Eavesdropping

LISTER, JOSEPH LISTER, BARON, 1827-1912

Fisher, Richard. Joseph Lister. LC 76-50614. (Illus.). 1977. 35.00x (ISBN 0-8128-2156-4). Stein & Day.

Mechnikov, et al. Founders of Modern Medicine. facs. ed. Berger, D., tr. LC 78-142669. (Essay Index Reprint Ser). 1939. 19.00 (ISBN 0-8369-2111-9). Arno.

LISTERIOSIS

Seeliger, Heinz P. Listeriosis. 2nd ed. 1961. 15.50 (ISBN 0-02-852020-3). Hafner.

Woodbine, M., ed. Problems of Listeriosis: Proceedings of the 5th International Symposium. (Illus.). 320p. 1975. text ed. 16.25x (ISBN 0-7185-1143-3, Leicester). Humanities.

LISZT, FRANZ, 1811-1886

Corder, Frederick. Ferencz (Francois) Liszt. LC 74-24062. Repr. of 1925 ed. 18.50 (ISBN 0-404-12888-2). AMS Pr.

Friedheim, Arthur. Life & Liszt. Bullock, Theodore L., ed. LC 61-15656. (Illus.). 1961. 6.00 (ISBN 0-685-20505-3). Taplinger.

Hueffer, Francis. Half a Century of Music in England 1837-1887: Essays Towards a History. LC 76-22335. 1976. Repr. of 1889 ed. lib. bdg. 25.00 (ISBN 0-89341-025-X). Longwood Pr.

Huneker, James G. Franz Liszt. LC 79-137245. (Illus.). Repr. of 1924 ed. 24.50 (ISBN 0-404-03387-3). AMS Pr.

--Mezzotints in Modern Music. 3rd ed. LC 72-137246. Repr. of 1905 ed. 24.50 (ISBN 0-404-03389-X). AMS Pr.

Liszt, Franz. Letters of Franz Liszt, 2 vols. 1980. Repr. Set. lib. bdg. 69.00 (ISBN 0-403-00360-1). Scholarly.

--The Letters of Franz Liszt to Olga von Meyendorff, 1871-1886, in the Mildred Bliss Collection at Dumbarton Oaks. Tyler, William R., tr. (Illus.). 553p. 1979. text ed. 30.00x (ISBN 0-88402-078-9). Harvard U Pr.

Mason, Daniel G. Romantic Composers. LC 73-119654. Repr. of 1906 ed. 14.00 (ISBN 0-404-04223-6). AMS Pr.

--Romantic Composers. Repr. of 1906 ed. lib. bdg. 15.75x (ISBN 0-8371-4096-X, MARC). Greenwood.

Newman, Ernest. Man Liszt. LC 74-119622. 1970. 10.00 (ISBN 0-8008-5095-5). Taplinger.

Nohl, Louis. Life of Liszt. LC 70-140402. 1970. Repr. of 1889 ed. 22.00 (ISBN 0-8103-3610-3). Gale.

Perenyi, Eleanor. Liszt: The Artist As Romantic Hero. (Illus.). 1974. 15.00 (ISBN 0-316-69910-1, Pub. by Atlantic Monthly Pr). Little.

Rostand, Claude. Liszt. Victor, John, tr. LC 77-143541. (Illus.). 192p. 1972. 7.95x (ISBN 0-670-43022-6); pap. 3.95x (ISBN 0-670-43023-4). Vienna Hse.

Searle, Humphrey. Music of Liszt. (Illus.). 1966. pap. 3.50 (ISBN 0-486-21700-0). Dover.

Seroff, Victor I. Franz Liszt. facs. ed. LC 77-136652. (Biography Index Reprint Ser.). 1966. 16.00 (ISBN 0-8369-8047-6). Arno.

Sitwell, S. Liszt. 59.95 (ISBN 0-8490-0543-4). Gordon Pr.

Sitwell, Sacheverell. Liszt. (Illus.). pap. 5.00 (ISBN 0-486-21702-7). Dover.

Stasov, Vladimir. Selected Essays on Music: Berlioz, Liszt, & Schumann. Jonas, Florene, tr. from Russian. 1968. text ed. 14.95x (ISBN 0-8464-0832-5). Beekman Pubs.

Tyler, William R., tr. Letters of Franz Liszt to Olga Von Megendorff: 1871-1886, in the Mildred Bliss Collection at Dumbarton Oaks. (Illus.). 554p. 1979. 30.00x (ISBN 0-88402-078-9, Ctr Landscape Arch). Dumbarton Oaks.

Westerby, Herbert. Liszt, Composer, & His Piano Works. LC 73-97337. (Illus.). xxii, 336p. Repr. of 1936 ed. lib. bdg. 15.75x (ISBN 0-8371-4365-9, WELI). Greenwood.

--Liszt, Composer, & His Piano Works. LC 77-75232. 1977. Repr. of 1936 ed. lib. bdg. 25.00 (ISBN 0-89341-087-X). Longwood Pr.

Winklhofer, Sharon. Liszt's Sonata in B Minor: A Study of Autograph Sources & Documents. Buelow, George, ed. LC 80-22524. (Studies in Musicology: No. 29). 361p. 1980. 34.95 (ISBN 0-8357-1119-6, Pub. by UMI Res Pr). Univ Microfilms.

LITERACY

see Illiteracy; New Literates, Writing For

LITERACY ETHICS

Paull, H. M. Literary Ethics: A Study in the Growth of the Literary Conscience. LC 68-26282. 1968. Repr. of 1928 ed. 13.75 (ISBN 0-8046-0349-9). Kennikat.

LITERARY AGENTS

see also Authors and Publishers

Higham, David. Literary Gent. LC 78-6488. 1978. 12.50 (ISBN 0-698-10852-3). Coward.

Literary Agents: A Complete Guide. LC 78-23329. (Illus.). 1978. pap. 3.95 (ISBN 0-913734-08-X). Poets & Writers.

Reynolds, Paul R. Middle Man: The Adventures of a Literary Agent. 1972. 6.95 (ISBN 0-688-00119-X). Morrow.

Watson, Graham. Book Society. LC 79-55587. 1980. 10.95 (ISBN 0-689-11060-X). Atheneum.

LITERARY ANACHRONISMS

see Errors and Blunders, Literary

LITERARY CALENDARS
see also Birthday Books

Dickinson, Emily. An Emily Dickinson Year Book. LC 76-52440. 1977. lib. bdg. 7.50 (ISBN 0-8414-2959-6). Folcroft.

Kuerschners Deutscher Literaturkalender. 1978. 130.00x (ISBN 3-11-006952-0). De Gruyter.

Palmer, Cecil. The Thomas Hardy Calendar. LC 73-557. 1973. lib. bdg. 12.50 (ISBN 0-8414-1518-8). Folcroft.

Shaw, George B. The G. B. S. Calendar: A Quotation from the Works of George Bernard Shaw for Every Day in the Year. Selected by Marion Nixon. LC 72-191622. 1973. Repr. of 1908 ed. lib. bdg. 10.00 (ISBN 0-8414-0854-8). Folcroft.

LITERARY CHARACTERS
see Characters and Characteristics in Literature

LITERARY CRITICISM
see Criticism

LITERARY CURIOSA
see also Literary Forgeries and Mystifications

Bombaugh, Charles C. Gleanings for the Curious from the Harvest Fields of Literature: A Melange of Excerpta. LC 68-23465. 1970. Repr. of 1875 ed. 37.00 (ISBN 0-8103-3086-5). Gale.

LITERARY ERRORS AND BLUNDERS
see Errors and Blunders, Literary

LITERARY EXCHANGES
see Exchanges, Literary and Scientific

LITERARY FORGERIES AND MYSTIFICATIONS
see also Imprints (In Books), Fictitious

Carter, John & Pollard. Enquiry into the Nature of Nineteen Century Pamphlets. LC 76-164659. (English Literature Ser., No. 33). 1971. Repr. of 1934 ed. lib. bdg. 49.95 (ISBN 0-8383-1261-6). Haskell.

Chambers, Edmund K. The History & Motives of Literary Forgeries Being the Chancellor's English Essay for 1891. LC 68-56729. (Research & Source Works Ser: No. 209). 1968. Repr. of 1891 ed. 12.50 (ISBN 0-8337-0522-9). B Franklin.

--History & Motives of Literary Forgeries. 1891. lib. bdg. 10.00 (ISBN 0-8414-3397-6). Folcroft.

Farrer, James A. Literary Forgeries. LC 68-23156. 1969. Repr. of 1907 ed. 19.00 (ISBN 0-8103-3305-8). Gale.

Hamilton, Charles. Great Forgers & Famous Fakes: The Manuscript Forgers of America & How They Duped the Experts. (Illus.). 288p. 1980. 12.95 (ISBN 0-517-54076-2, Michelman Bks). Crown.

Lang, Andrew. Books & Bookmen. LC 76-115093. (Illus.). Repr. of 1886 ed. 10.00 (ISBN 0-404-03818-2). AMS Pr.

Paull, H. M. Literary Ethics: A Study in the Growth of the Literary Conscience. LC 68-26282. 1968. Repr. of 1928 ed. 13.75 (ISBN 0-8046-0349-9). Kennikat.

Tannenbaum, Samuel A. Shakespearian Scraps & Other Elizabethan Fragments. LC 66-25947. (Illus.). Repr. of 1933 ed. 11.50 (ISBN 0-8046-0459-2). Kennikat.

Thomas, Ralph. Handbook of Fictitious Names. LC 70-90248. 1969. Repr. of 1868 ed. 22.00 (ISBN 0-8103-3145-4). Gale.

LITERARY FORM
see also specific forms, e.g. Drama

Agostini de del Rio, Amelia. Gramatica y Teoria Literaria: Guion Para el Estudiante. 2nd ed. 6.25 (ISBN 0-8477-3104-9). U of PR Pr.

Colie, Rosalie. The Resources of Kind: Genre-Theory in the Renaissance. LC 72-95307. 1974. 17.50x (ISBN 0-520-02397-8). U of Cal Pr.

Giroux, James A. & Williston, Glenn R. Appreciation of Literary Forms: Advanced Level. Spargo, Edward, ed. (Comprehension Skills Ser). (Illus.). 1974. pap. text ed. 2.40x (ISBN 0-89061-018-5). Jamestown Pubs.

Marcus, Millicent. An Allegory of Form: Literary Self-Conciousness in the "Decameron". (Stanford French & Italian Studies: No. 18). 1979. pap. 20.00 (ISBN 0-915838-21-4). Anma Libri.

Moran, Gary. The Boundaries of Genre: Dostoevsky's Diary of a Writer & the Traditions of Literary Utopia. (University of Texas Press Slavic Ser.: No. 4). 230p. 1981. 25.00 (ISBN 0-292-70732-0). U of Tex Pr.

Norden, Hugo. Form: The Silent Language. LC 66-27691. (Illus.). 1968. 7.50 (ISBN 0-8283-1131-5). Branden.

Partridge, Eric. The Shaggy Dog Story. facsimile ed. LC 72-117910. (Select Bibliographies Reprint Ser). Repr. of 1953 ed. 12.50 (ISBN 0-8369-5363-0). Arno.

Ptolemy, Claudius. Tetrabiblos. LC 76-41123. 1974. 7.95 (ISBN 0-912504-31-5); pap. 3.50 (ISBN 0-912504-24-2). Sym & Sign.

Reaske, Christopher R. College Writer's Guide to the Study of Literature. (Orig.). 1970. pap. text ed. 2.95x (ISBN 0-685-19712-3). Phila Bk Co.

Smitten, Jeffrey R. & Daghistany, Ann, eds. Spatial Form in Narrative. LC 81-3244. (Illus.). 304p. 1981. 19.50x (ISBN 0-8014-1375-3). Cornell U Pr.

Springer, Mary D. Forms of the Modern Novella. LC 75-9055. x, 198p. 1976. lib. bdg. 14.00x (ISBN 0-226-76986-0). U of Chicago Pr.

Strelka, Joseph P., ed. Theories of Literary Genre, Vol. 8. LC 76-41807. (Yearbook of Contemporary Criticism). 1978. text ed. 16.00x (ISBN 0-271-01243-9). Pa St U Pr.

Weston, Harold. Form in Literature: A Theory of Technique & Construction. LC 74-31015. 1973. Repr. of 1932 ed. lib. bdg. 15.00 (ISBN 0-8414-9580-7). Folcroft.

Williston, Glenn R. Appreciation of Literary Forms: Middle Level. (Comprehension Skills Ser.). (Illus.). 64p. 1976. pap. text ed. 2.40x (ISBN 0-89061-070-3, CB7M). Jamestown Pubs.

Wright, Rose E. Critique of Teaching Literary Forms. (Educational Ser.). 1941. Repr. 17.50 (ISBN 0-685-43634-9). Norwood Edns.

--Critique of Teaching Literary Forms: A Digest for Teachers & Students. 1978. Repr. of 1941 ed. lib. bdg. 27.50 (ISBN 0-8495-5640-6). Arden Lib.

LITERARY LANDMARKS
see also Cities and Towns in Literature

Allbut, R. Rambles in Dickens' Land. LC 76-52947. (Studies in Dickens, No. 52). 1977. lib. bdg. 48.95 (ISBN 0-8383-2139-9). Haskell.

Baildon, H. B. Homes Haunts of Famous Authors. 1979. Repr. of 1906 ed. lib. bdg. 25.00 (ISBN 0-8495-0542-9). Arden Lib.

Beckford, William. Recollections of an Excursion to the Monasteries of Alcobaca & Baltalha. LC 72-13457. 1974. Repr. of 1835 ed. lib. bdg. 20.00 (ISBN 0-8414-1187-5). Folcroft.

Benedict, Steward, ed. The Literary Guide to the U. S. (Illus.). 256p. 1981. 15.95 (ISBN 0-87196-304-3). Facts on File.

Bidwell, Alice T. & Rosenstiel, Isabelle D. Places of English Literature. LC 77-105765. 1970. Repr. of 1924 ed. 10.95 (ISBN 0-8046-0940-3). Kennikat.

Chapman, Mary L., ed. Literary Landmarks: A Guide to Homes & Memorials of American Writers Which Are Open to the Public. LC 73-92467. (Illus.). 175p. 1974. pap. 2.95 (ISBN 0-915588-01-3). Literary Sketches.

Daiches, David & Flower, John. Literary Landscapes of the British Isles: A Narrative Atlas. LC 78-11446. (Illus.). 1979. 12.95 (ISBN 0-448-22205-1). Paddington.

Dexter, Walter. Kent of Dickens. LC 72-2105. (Studies in Dickens, No. 52). 1972. Repr. of 1924 ed. lib. bdg. 49.95 (ISBN 0-8383-1482-1). Haskell.

--Mr. Pickwick's Pilgrimages. LC 72-3637. (Studies in Dickens, No. 52). 1972. Repr. of 1926 ed. lib. bdg. 40.95 (ISBN 0-8383-1587-9). Haskell.

Drennan, Robert E., ed. The Alquonquin Wits. (Illus.). 176p. 1975. pap. 2.95 (ISBN 0-8065-0464-1). Citadel Pr.

Eagle, Dorothy & Carnell, Hilary. The Oxford Literary Guide to the British Iles. (Illus.). 464p. 1980. pap. 8.95 (ISBN 0-19-285098-9, GB 617). Oxford U Pr.

--The Oxford Literary Guide to the British Isles. LC 76-47430. (Illus.). 1977. 14.95 (ISBN 0-19-869123-8). Oxford U Pr.

Faude, Wilson H. Renaissance of Mark Twain's House. 1977. lib. bdg. 20.00x (ISBN 0-89244-074-0). Queens Hse.

Goode, Clement T. & Shannon, Edgar F. An Atlas of English Literature. 1979. Repr. of 1925 ed. lib. bdg. 20.00 (ISBN 0-8495-2022-3). Arden Lib.

Harting, Emilie C. A Literary Tour Guide to England & Scotland. LC 75-22189. 192p. 1978. 6.95 (ISBN 0-688-02971-X); pap. 4.95 (ISBN 0-688-07971-7). Morrow.

Holland, C. Hardy's Wessex Scene. LC 79-119090. (Studies in Thomas Hardy, No. 14). 1970. Repr. of 1948 ed. lib. bdg. 29.95 (ISBN 0-8383-1086-9). Haskell.

Howitt, William. Homes & Haunts of the Most Eminent British Poets, 2 Vols. (Belles Lettres in English Ser). 1969. Repr. of 1847 ed. Set. 69.50 (ISBN 0-384-24520-X). Johnson Repr.

--Homes & Haunts of the Most Eminent British Poets. 1978. Repr. of 1849 ed. lib. bdg. 35.00 (ISBN 0-8414-4794-2). Folcroft.

Hubbard, Elbert. Little Journeys to the Homes of American Authors. Repr. of 1896 ed. 20.00 (ISBN 0-686-19836-0). Ridgeway Bks.

Hutton, Laurence. Literary Landmarks of Edinburgh. 1973. Repr. of 1898 ed. 20.00 (ISBN 0-8274-0372-0). R West.

Johnstone, Arthur. Recollections of Robert Louis Stevenson in the Pacific. LC 74-23652. 1974. Repr. of 1905 ed. lib. bdg. 25.00 (ISBN 0-8414-5324-1). Folcroft.

Jolly, William. Burns at Mossgiel. LC 76-52433. (English Literature Ser, No. 33). 1977. lib. bdg. 47.95 (ISBN 0-8383-2144-5). Haskell.

Kent, William. London for Dickens Lovers. LC 72-2106. (Studies in Dickens, No. 52). 1972. Repr. of 1935 ed. lib. bdg. 32.95 (ISBN 0-8383-1480-5). Haskell.

Kilpatrick, James. Literary Landmarks of Glasgow. 1973. Repr. of 1898 ed. 20.00 (ISBN 0-8274-0270-8). R West.

Kilpatrick, James A. Literary Landmarks of Glasgow. 298p. 1981. Repr. of 1898 ed. lib. bdg. 35.00 (ISBN 0-89987-453-3). Darby Bks.

Kraft, Stephanie. No Castles on Main Street: American Authors & Their Homes. LC 79-9816. (Illus.). 1979. 9.95 (ISBN 0-528-81828-7). Rand.

Lea, Hermann. Thomas Hardy's Wessex. LC 76-58449. 1977. Repr. of 1913 ed. lib. bdg. 72.50 (ISBN 0-8414-5736-0). Folcroft.

Le Clair, Robert C. Three American Travellers in England: James Russell Lowell, Henry Adams, Henry James. LC 77-19341. 1978. Repr. of 1945 ed. lib. bdg. 19.75x (ISBN 0-313-20190-0, LETA). Greenwood.

Masson, David. In the Footsteps of the Poets. LC 72-192501. 1893. lib. bdg. 20.00 (ISBN 0-8414-6492-8). Folcroft.

Moreland, Arthur. Dickens Landmarks in London. LC 72-6291. (Studies in Dickens, No. 52). (Illus.). 1972. Repr. of 1931 ed. lib. bdg. 36.95 (ISBN 0-8383-1625-5). Haskell.

Rogers, Neville. Keats, Shelley & Rome. LC 72-186989. Repr. of 1949 ed. lib. bdg. 20.00 (ISBN 0-8414-0352-X). Folcroft.

--Keats, Shelley & Rome. LC 75-22076. (English Literature Ser, No. 33). 1975. lib. bdg. 29.95 (ISBN 0-8383-2080-5). Haskell.

Scherman, David E. & Redlich, Rosemarie. Literary America: A Chronicle of American Writers from 1607-1952. LC 75-76. (Illus.). 1978. Repr. of 1952 ed. lib. bdg. 25.50x (ISBN 0-8371-8017-1, SCLA). Greenwood.

Thomas, Edward. Literary Pilgrim in England. facs. ed. LC 69-17591. (Essay Index Reprint Ser). 1917. 17.00 (ISBN 0-8369-0094-4). Arno.

Thum, Marcella. Exploring Literary America. LC 78-13297. (gr. 5 up). 1979. 11.95 (ISBN 0-689-30668-7). Atheneum.

Timbs, John. Clubs & Club Life in London with Anecodotes of Its Famous Coffee-Houses, Hostelries, & Taverns from the Seventeenth Century to the Present Time. LC 66-28045. 1967. Repr. of 1872 ed. 19.00 (ISBN 0-8103-3262-0). Gale.

Tindall, William Y. The Joyce Country. new ed. LC 72-83501. (Illus.). 174p. 1972. pap. 3.95 (ISBN 0-8052-0347-8). Schocken.

LITERARY LIFE
see Litterateurs

LITERARY PIRACY
see Copyright–Unauthorized Reprints

LITERARY PRIZES
see also Caldecott Medal Books; Newbery Medal Books

Bufkin, E. C. Foreign Literary Prizes: Romance & Germanic Languages. 1980. 24.95 (ISBN 0-8352-1243-2). Bowker.

Crouch, M. & Ellis, A., eds. Chosen for Children. 3rd ed. 1977. 15.50x (ISBN 0-85365-349-6, Pub. by Lib Assn England). Oryx Pr.

Gadney, Alan. How to Enter & Win Fiction Writing Contests. 1981. 12.95 (ISBN 0-87196-519-4); pap. 5.95 (ISBN 0-87196-552-6). Facts on File.

Henderson, Bill, ed. The Pushcart Prize: Best of the Small Presses. LC 75-40812. 1976. pap. 5.95 (ISBN 0-916366-01-4). Pushcart Pr.

--Pushcart Prize IV: Best of the Small Presses 1979-1980 Edition. 1979. 16.50 (ISBN 0-916366-06-5). Pushcart Pr.

--Pushcart Prize, No. 2: Best of the Small Presses. 1977-78 ed. LC 76-58675. 1977. 12.50 (ISBN 0-916366-02-2). Pushcart Pr.

Scherf, Walter, ed. Children's Prize Books. new ed. 1979. write for info. (ISBN 0-89664-094-9). K G Saur.

Wasserman, Paul, ed. Awards, Honors & Prizes: United States & Canada, Vol. 1. 5th ed. 600p. 1981. 78.00 (ISBN 0-8103-0380-9). Gale.

Weber, Olga S., ed. Literary & Library Prizes. 10th ed. 1980. 24.95 (ISBN 0-8352-1249-1). Bowker.

LITERARY PROPERTY
see Copyright

LITERARY RECREATIONS
see also Bible Games and Puzzles; Charades; Crossword Puzzles; Riddles; Word Games

Chacksfield, K. M., et al. Music & Language with Young Children. (Illus.). 190p. 1975. 18.50x (ISBN 0-631-15330-6, Pub. by Basil Blackwell). Biblio Dist.

Dorry, Gertrude N. Games for Second Language Learning. 1966. 1.75 (ISBN 0-07-017653-1, I). McGraw.

Kaplan, Sandra N., et al. The Big Book of Writing: Games & Activities. 2nd ed. (Illus.). 1979. spiral bdg. 16.95 (ISBN 0-87620-124-9). Goodyear.

LITERARY RESEARCH

Altick, Richard D. The Art of Literary Research. 3rd ed. 1981. price not set (ISBN 0-393-95176-6). Norton.

--Art of Literary Research. 2nd, rev. ed. 11.95x (ISBN 0-393-09227-5, NortonC). Norton.

--Scholar Adventurers. 1966. pap. text ed. 7.95 (ISBN 0-02-900580-9). Free Pr.

Bateson, F. W. The Scholar-Critic: An Introduction to Literary Research. 1972. 12.50x (ISBN 0-7100-7214-7). Routledge & Kegan.

Hutton, R. H. Literary Studies. 1892. Repr. 20.00 (ISBN 0-8274-2961-4). R West.

Kehler, Dorothea & Dickinson, Fidelia. Problems in Literary Research: A Guide to Selected Reference Works. LC 75-16427. 169p. 1975. 10.00 (ISBN 0-8108-0841-2); tchrs. index incl. (ISBN 0-8108-0842-0). Scarecrow.

Modern Language Association of America. Research Opportunities in Renaissance Drama: The Reports of the Modern Language Association Conferences, 20 nos. in 8 vols. Incl. Vol. 1, No. 1. Chicago Conference, 1955; Vol. 1, No. 2. Washington Conference, 1956; Vol. 1, No. 3. Madison Conference, 1957; Vol. 2, No. 4. New York Conference, 1958; Vol. 2, No. 5. Chicago, 1959 & Philadelphia, 1960, Conferences; Vol. 2, No. 6. Chicago, 1961 & Washington, 1962, Conferences. Repr. of 1962 ed. Set. 282.50 (ISBN 0-404-08063-4). AMS Pr.

Patterson, Margaret C., ed. Literary Research Guide. LC 75-13925. 1976. 32.00 (ISBN 0-8103-1102-X). Gale.

Sears, Donald A. The Discipline of English: A Guide to Literary Research. LC 73-13416. 152p. 1973. Repr. of 1963 ed. lib. bdg. 15.00 (ISBN 0-8371-7130-X, SEDE). Greenwood.

Thorpe, James. The Use of Manuscripts in Literary Research: Problems of Access & Literary Property Rights. 2nd ed. LC 79-87584. 40p. 1979. pap. 5.00x (ISBN 0-87352-085-8). Modern Lang.

LITERARY SKETCH
see Essay

LITERARY SOCIETIES

Deffand, Madame du. Letters to & from Madame Du Deffand & Julie De Lespinasse. limited ed. Smith, W. H., ed. 1938. 24.50x (ISBN 0-685-69810-6). Elliots Bks.

Hesselgrave, Ruth A. Lady Miller & Batheaston Literary Circle. 1927. Limited Ed. 27.50x (ISBN 0-685-69826-2). Elliots Bks.

McElroy, Davis D. Scotland's Age of Improvement: A Survey of Eighteenth-Century Literary Clubs & Societies. 1969. pap. 4.00 (ISBN 0-87422-010-6). Wash St U Pr.

Petersen, William A. Interrogating the Oracle: A History of the London Browning Society. 290p. 1979. 4.40x (ISBN 0-686-64109-4, Pub. by Browning Inst). Pub Ctr Cult Res.

Sanchez, Jose. Academias y Sociedades Literarias de Mexico. (Studies in the Romance Languages & Literatures: No. 18). 1951. pap. 13.50x (ISBN 0-8078-9018-9). U of NC Pr.

Shappard, Roger & Shappard, Judith, eds. Literary Societies for Bookmen. 80p. 1980. 15.00 (ISBN 0-8390-0251-3). Allanheld & Schram.

Williams, Harold H. Book Clubs & Printing Societies of Great Britain & Ireland. LC 68-26622. 1971. Repr. of 1929 ed. 26.00 (ISBN 0-8103-3749-5). Gale.

LITERARY STYLE
see Style, Literary

LITERARY TERMS
see Literature–Terminology

LITERARY TRANSMISSION
see Transmission of Texts

LITERATURE
Here are entered works dealing with literature in general, not limited to Esthetics, Philosophy, history or any one aspect.
see also Anthologies; Art and Literature; Authorship; Autobiography; Aztec Literature; Biobibliography; Biography (As a Literary Form); Books and Reading; Burlesque (Literature); Catholic Literature; Children's Literature (Collections); Christian Literature, Early; Classical Literature (Collections); College Readers; Copyright; Creation (Literary, Artistic, etc.); Criticism; Drama; Epic Literature; Erotic Literature; Errors and Blunders, Literary; Essays; Fables; Fairy Tales; Fantastic Fiction; Feminism and Literature; Fiction; Folk Literature; Gothic Literature; Humanism; Legends; Letters; Literary Forgeries and Mystifications; Modernism (Literature); Negro Literature; Orations; Parodies; Pastoral Literature; Picaresque Literature; Plagiarism; Plots (Drama, Novel, etc.); Poetry; Primitivism in Literature; Prose Literature; Quotations; Realism in Literature; Religious Literature; Romances; Romanticism; Sagas; Style, Literary; Tales; Wit and Humor

also Bible in Literature; Children in Literature; Love in Literature; Trees in Literature; and similar headings; also national literatures, e.g. English Literature

Abacarian, Richard & Klotz, Marvin, eds. Literature: The Human Experience. 2nd ed. LC 77-86004. 1978. pap. text ed. 10.95x (ISBN 0-312-48790-8). St Martin.

Abercrombie, Lascelles. Speculative Dialogues. 1971. Repr. of 1913 ed. 25.00 (ISBN 0-403-00799-2). Scholarly.

Adelphus, Johannes. Johannes Adelphus: Ausgewaehlte Schriften, 4 vols, Vol. 1, Barbarosssa. Gotzkowsky, Bodo, ed. (Ausgaben Deutscher Literatur des XV Bis XVIII Jahrhunderts). 1974. 123.50x (ISBN 3-11-003382-8). De Gruyter.

American Library Association. An Index to General Literature: The ALA Index. facs ed. LC 72-165612. (Essay Index Reprint Ser.). 40.00 (ISBN 0-8369-2382-0). Arno.

Arnold, Matthew. Literature & Dogma. Repr. of 1873 ed. lib. bdg. 20.00 (ISBN 0-8414-3076-4). Folcroft.

Arvine, Kazlitt. Cyclopedia of Anecdotes of Literature. LC 67-14020. 1967. Repr. of 1851 ed. 26.00 (ISBN 0-8103-3296-5). Gale.

Belyaev, A. The Ideological Struggle & Literature. 308p. 1978. 6.60 (ISBN 0-8285-1083-0, Pub. by Progress Pubs Russia). Imported Pubns.

Bombaugh, Charles C. Facts & Fancies for the Curious: From the Harvest-Fields of Literature. 1979. Repr. of 1905 ed. lib. bdg. 65.00 (ISBN 0-8482-3414-6). Norwood Edns.

Brandes, George. Don Quixote & Hamlet. 59.95 (ISBN 0-8490-0056-4). Gordon Pr.

Burroughs, John. Literary Values, & Other Papers. facsimile ed. LC 76-156624. (Essay Index Reprint Ser). Repr. of 1902 ed. 17.00 (ISBN 0-8369-2347-2). Arno.

Cappon, J. Bliss Carman & the Literary Currents & Influences of His Time. 59.95 (ISBN 0-87968-759-2). Gordon Pr.

Cartier, N. R. Aquila, Vol. 3. (Aquila Chestnut Hill Studies in Modern Languages & Literatures). 1976. pap. 34.00 (ISBN 90-247-1797-3). Kluwer Boston.

Chicorel, Marietta, ed. Chicorel Index to the Spoken Arts: Discs, Tapes & Cassettes, Vol. 7B. LC 71-106198. 500p. 1974. 85.00 (ISBN 0-934598-61-4). Am Lib Pub Co.

Clutton-Brock, Arthur. Essays on Literature & Life. facs. ed. LC 68-54339. (Essay Index Reprint Ser). 1927. 15.00 (ISBN 0-8369-0317-X). Arno.

Colby, J. Rose. Literature & Life in School. (Educational Ser.). 1906. Repr. 6.50 (ISBN 0-685-43004-9). Norwood Edns.

Colquitt, Betsy F., ed. Studies in Medieval, Renaissance, American Literature: A Festschrift. LC 78-165852. 200p. 1971. pap. 1.00 (ISBN 0-912646-19-5). Tex Christian.

Corti, Maria. An Introduction to Literary Semiotics. Bogat, Margherita & Mandelbaum, Allen, trs. from It. LC 77-23650. (Advances in Semiotics Ser.). 192p. 1978. 12.50x (ISBN 0-253-33118-8). Ind U Pr.

Cox, John H. Literature in the Common Schools. 1911. 20.00 (ISBN 0-932062-41-5). Sharon Hill.

Daiches, David. Two Studies. 32p. 1980. Repr. of 1958 ed. lib. bdg. 10.00 (ISBN 0-8492-4225-8). R West.

Davidson, Clifford, ed. Torquato Tasso's Aminta Englisht: The Henry Reynolds Translation of 1628. LC 72-78233. (North American Mentor Texts Ser: No. 1). (Illus.). 80p. 1972. pap. 10.00 (ISBN 0-87423-007-1). Westburg.

Davison, Peter, et al, eds. Uses of Literacy: Media. LC 77-90618. (Literary Taste, Culture & Mass Communications Ser: Vol. 9). 1978. lib. bdg. 44.00x (ISBN 0-914146-52-1). Somerset Hse.

Dube, Anthony, et al. Structure & Meaning: An Introduction to Literature. LC 75-31038. (Illus.). 1152p. 1976. text ed. 15.95 (ISBN 0-395-21967-1); inst. manual 1.00 (ISBN 0-395-21968-X). HM.

Earnest, Ernest P. Foreword to Literature. LC 75-167335. (Essay Index Reprint Ser.). Repr. of 1945 ed. 21.00 (ISBN 0-8369-2767-2). Arno.

Elton, Oliver. Literary Fame: A Renaissance Study. LC 74-12470. lib. bdg. 5.50 (ISBN 0-8414-3970-2). Folcroft.

Erskine, John. Literary Discipline. LC 70-131697. 1971. Repr. of 1923 ed. 13.00 (ISBN 0-403-00584-1). Scholarly.

--Literary Discipline. LC 74-90635. (Essay Index Reprint Ser). 1923. 16.00 (ISBN 0-8369-1257-8). Arno.

Escarpit, Robert & Pick, E., trs. Sociology of Literature. 104p. 1971. 25.00x (ISBN 0-7146-2729-1, F Cass Co). Biblio Dist.

Essay & General Literature Index: Works Indexed 1900-1969. 16.00 (ISBN 0-8242-0503-0). Wilson.

Fisher, Dexter, ed. Minority Language & Literature: Retrospective & Perspective. 160p. 1977. pap. 6.50x (ISBN 0-87352-350-4). Modern Lang.

Freeman, William. The Human Approach to Literature. 1973. lib. bdg. 12.50 (ISBN 0-8414-4282-7). Folcroft.

Frost, David, intro. by. The Bluffer's Guides, 6 bks. Incl. Bluff Your Way in Art. Lampitt, L; Bluff Your Way in Cinema. Wlaschin, Ken; Bluff Your Way in Literature. Seymoursmith, Martin; Bluff Your Way in Music. Gammond, Peter; Bluff Your Way in Opera. Coleman, Francis; Bluff Your Way in Wine. Clark, Wick. 64p. 1971. pap. 1.00 ea. Crown.

Frye, Northrop. The Educated Imagination. LC 64-18815. (Midland Bks.: No. 88). 160p. 1964. pap. 3.95x (ISBN 0-253-20088-1). Ind U Pr.

Gardiner, J. H. The Forms of Prose Literature. 1973. lib. bdg. 20.00 (ISBN 0-8414-4633-4). Folcroft.

Gibb, Carson. Exposition & Literature. 1971. pap. text ed. 6.25x (ISBN 0-02-341700-5, 34170). Macmillan.

Goethe, Johann W. Elective Affinities. (Penguin Classic Ser.). 1978. pap. 3.50 (ISBN 0-14-044242-1). Penguin.

Graham, David. Common Sense & the Muses. 1925. lib. bdg. 20.00 (ISBN 0-8414-4665-2). Folcroft.

Gray, Bennison. The Phenomenon of Literature. LC 74-77353. (De Proprietatibus Litterarum, Ser. Maior: No. 36). 594p. 1975. pap. text ed. 75.00x (ISBN 0-686-22585-6). Mouton.

Greenway, John. Literature Among the Primitives. LC 64-13289. xviii, 346p. 1964. Repr. of 1964 ed. 26.00 (ISBN 0-8103-5001-7). Gale.

Grierson, Herbert J. Criticism & Creation. LC 78-58259. (Essay Index in Reprint Ser.). 1978. 17.50x (ISBN 0-8486-3021-1). Core Collection.

Harris, Max. Angry Eye: A Comment on Life & Letters. 1974. text ed. 16.00 (ISBN 0-08-017373-X). Pergamon.

Hartman, Geoffrey H. Saving the Texts: Literature-Derrida-Philosophy. LC 80-21748. (Illus.). 190p. 1981. text ed. 12.95x (ISBN 0-8018-2452-4). Johns Hopkins.

Hess, Karen M. Appreciating Literature: As You Read It. LC 78-6871. (Self-Teaching Guides Ser.). 1978. pap. text ed. 5.95 (ISBN 0-471-03199-2). Wiley.

Hurst, George. Sacred Literature. LC 74-3454. Repr. lib. bdg. 10.00 (ISBN 0-8414-4813-2). Folcroft.

Jarrett-Kerr, Martin. Studies in Literature & Belief. facsimile ed. LC 74-134101. (Essay Index Reprint Ser). Repr. of 1954 ed. 16.00 (ISBN 0-8369-1978-5). Arno.

Jordan, Furneaux. Moral Nerve & the Error of Literary Verdicts. 1973. lib. bdg. 12.50 (ISBN 0-8414-5432-9). Folcroft.

Kearns, George, ed. Literature of the World. 2nd ed. (Illus.). 416p. (gr. 10). 1974. pap. text ed. 11.72 (ISBN 0-07-033437-4, W). McGraw.

Kellett, E. E. The Appreciation of Literature. LC 73-15899. 1973. lib. bdg. 12.50 (ISBN 0-8414-5479-5). Folcroft.

Kennedy, X. J. Literature: An Introduction to Fiction, Poetry & Drama. 2nd ed. 1979. text ed. 15.95 (ISBN 0-316-48867-4); instr's manual free (ISBN 0-316-48868-2). Little.

Korshin, Paul J., et al, eds. The Widening Circle: Essays on the Circulation of Literature in Eighteenth-Century Europe. 1976. 18.00x (ISBN 0-8122-7717-1). U of Pa Pr.

Lang, Andrew. Letters on Literature. 1973. lib. bdg. 9.95 (ISBN 0-8414-5772-7). Folcroft.

Lang, Elsie M. Literary London. 1973. lib. bdg. 20.00 (ISBN 0-685-37920-5). Folcroft.

Lee, Dennis. Savage Fields: An Essay in Literature & Cosmology. 125p. 1977. 14.95 (ISBN 0-88784-059-0, Pub. by Hse Anansi Pr Canada); pap. 6.95 (ISBN 0-88784-058-2). U of Toronto Pr.

Lehmann, Winfred P., et al. Introduction to Scholarship in Modern Languages & Literatures. Gibaldi, Joseph, ed. LC 81-1254. xi, 143p. 1981. 11.75x (ISBN 0-87352-092-0); pap. 6.25x (ISBN 0-87352-093-9). Modern Lang.

Literature & Ideas. 1949. pap. 6.00 (ISBN 0-527-01712-4, YFS NO. 4). Kraus Repr.

Lovejoy, Arthur O. Essays in the History of Ideas. LC 78-17473. 1978. Repr. of 1948 ed. lib. bdg. 29.50 (ISBN 0-313-20504-3, LOEH). Greenwood.

Lucas, Edward V. Reading, Writing, & Remembering: A Literary Record. (Illus.). 1971. Repr. of 1932 ed. 29.00 (ISBN 0-403-01076-4). Scholarly.

MacCarthy, Desmond. The European Tradition in Literature from 1600 Onwards. 858p. 1980. Repr. of 1937 ed. lib. bdg. 12.50 (ISBN 0-8492-1747-4). R West.

Mackenzie, Compton. Literature in My Time. 254p. 1981. Repr. of 1933 ed. lib. bdg. 30.00 (ISBN 0-89987-578-5). Darby Bks.

Magill, Frank L., ed. The Contemporary Literary Scene. LC 74-29200. 25.00 (ISBN 0-89356-173-8). Salem Pr.

Magill, Frank N. & Beacham, Walton, eds. Contemporary Literary Scene II. LC 74-29200. 1979. lib. bdg. 25.00 (ISBN 0-89356-174-6). Salem Pr.

Magnus, Laurie. A General Sketch of European Literature. 1973. lib. bdg. 30.00 (ISBN 0-8414-6443-X). Folcroft.

Martin, Ernest, ed. Le Roman De Renart, 3 vols. 1476p. 1973. Repr. of 1891 ed. 236.75x (ISBN 3-11-003337-2). De Gruyter.

Matthews, Brander. Recreations of an Anthologist. facs. ed. LC 67-26766. (Essay Index Reprint Ser). 1904. 14.75 (ISBN 0-8369-0699-3). Arno.

Moulton, Richard G. World Literature. LC 79-1409. 1973. lib. bdg. 40.00 (ISBN 0-8414-6336-0). Folcroft.

Naumann, Manfred, et al, eds. Society, Literature, Reading: The Reception of Literature Considered in Its Theoretical Context. (Linguistic & Literary Studies in Eastern Europe). 550p. 1980. text ed. 85.50x (ISBN 90-272-1509-X). Humanities.

Page, H. A. Vers De Societe & Parody. 1973. Repr. of 1882 ed. lib. bdg. 30.00 (ISBN 0-8414-9238-7). Folcroft.

Palfrey, Thomas R. Panorama Litteraire De l'Europe 1833-1834. LC 73-128990. (Northwestern Humanities Ser.: No. 22). (Fr). Repr. of 1950 ed. 16.50 (ISBN 0-404-50722-0). AMS Pr.

Partridge, Eric. Literary Sessions. facsimile ed. LC 70-117904. (Select Bibliographies Reprint Ser). Repr. of 1932 ed. 17.00 (ISBN 0-8369-5357-6). Arno.

Payn, James. Some Literary Recollections. 1884. 25.00 (ISBN 0-8274-3457-X). R West.

Purnell, Thomas. Literature & Its Professors. 1973. lib. bdg. 25.00 (ISBN 0-8414-9275-1). Folcroft.

Rascoe, Burton. Prometheans: Ancient & Moderns. LC 70-156707. (Essay Index Reprint Ser.). Repr. of 1933 ed. 18.00 (ISBN 0-8369-2855-5). Arno.

Reichert, John. Making Sense of Literature. LC 77-24455. 1978. lib. bdg. 6.95 (ISBN 0-226-70769-5). U of Chicago Pr.

Reynolds, George F. & Garland, Greever. The Facts & Backgrounds of Literature. 1924. Repr. 15.00 (ISBN 0-8274-2326-8). R West.

Richardson, William L. & Owen, Jessie M. Literature of the World. 1973. lib. bdg. 30.00 (ISBN 0-8414-7434-6). Folcroft.

Righter, William. Myth & Literature. (Concepts of Literature Ser.). 1975. 12.50x (ISBN 0-7100-8137-5). Routledge & Kegan.

Roloff, Leland H. The Perception & Evocation of Literature. 1973. text ed. 11.95x (ISBN 0-673-07550-8). Scott F.

Rothstein, Eric, ed. Literary Monographs, Vol. 3. LC 66-25869. 234p. 1970. 15.00 (ISBN 0-299-05780-1). U of Wis Pr.

Rudman, Jack. Literature. (Undergraduate Program Field Test Ser.: UPFT-14). (Cloth bdg. avail. on request). pap. 9.95 (ISBN 0-8373-6014-5). Natl Learning.

Saraf, D. N. Handicrafts of India. (Illus.). 60.00 (ISBN 0-7069-0735-3, Pub. by Vikas India). Advent NY.

Sartre, Jean-Paul. What Is Literature. 7.50 (ISBN 0-8446-2867-0). Peter Smith.

Schaff, Philip. Literature & Poetry. 1973. Repr. of 1890 ed. 20.00 (ISBN 0-8274-0923-0). R West.

Schucking, Levin L. The Sociology of Literary Taste. rev. ed. Battershaw, Brian, tr. LC 66-12708. (Midway Reprint Ser). viii, 112p. 1974. pap. text ed. 6.50x (ISBN 0-226-74100-1). U of Chicago Pr.

Schultz, Alfred P. Race or Mongrel. 1977. lib. bdg. 69.95 (ISBN 0-8490-2497-8). Gordon Pr.

Scott-James, R. A. Personality in Literature 1913-1931. 1973. lib. bdg. 17.50 (ISBN 0-8414-8148-2). Folcroft.

Shaw, Bernard. Bernard Shaw's Nondramatic Literary Criticism. Weintraub, Stanley, ed. LC 70-149739. (Regents Critics Ser). xxviii, 246p. 1972. 16.50x (ISBN 0-8032-0466-3); pap. 3.95x (ISBN 0-8032-5466-0, BB 414, Bison). U of Nebr Pr.

Sherman, Stuart P. On Contemporary Literature. LC 75-105037. (Essay Index Reprint Ser). 1917. 18.00 (ISBN 0-8369-1480-5). Arno.

Shorter, Clement. Victorian Literature: Sixty Years of Books & Bookmen. 1973. lib. bdg. 14.00 (ISBN 0-8414-8080-X). Folcroft.

Sieveking, Lance. The Eye of the Beholder: G. K. Chesterton, Bernard Shaw, Hilaire Belloc, H. G. Wells, Max Beerbohm, G. M. Hopkins. 1957. Repr. 17.50 (ISBN 0-8274-2324-1). R West.

Sisson, C. H. The Avoidance of Literature. Schmidt, Michael, ed. & 1979. 20.00 (ISBN 0-85635-229-2, Pub. by Carcanet New Pr England). Persea Bks.

Smith, Logan P. Prospects of Literature. 1927. lib. bdg. 7.50 (ISBN 0-8414-7857-0). Folcroft.

Solzhenitsyn, Alexandr I. The Nobel Lecture on Literature. Whitney, Thomas P., tr. from Rus. LC 72-9890. 48p. (YA) 1972. 5.95 (ISBN 0-06-013943-9, HarpT). Har-Row.

Some Lake Country Figures. 1911. Repr. 17.50 (ISBN 0-8274-3456-1). R West.

Spence, Joseph. Anecdotes, Observations & Characters of Books & Men: Collected from the Conversation of Mr. Pope & Other Eminent Persons of His Time. LC 65-10024. (Centaur Classics Ser.). 308p. 1964. 15.00x (ISBN 0-8093-0167-9). S Ill U Pr.

Spring, Powell. The Spirit of Literature. 1945. Repr. 10.00 (ISBN 0-8274-3494-4). R West.

Stanley, Julia P. & Wolfe, Susan J., eds. The Coming Out Stories. LC 79-27073. 286p. (Orig.). 1980. pap. text ed. 6.95 (ISBN 0-930436-03-2). Persephone.

Steeves, Harrison R. Literary Aims & Art. 1973. lib. bdg. 20.00 (ISBN 0-8414-7959-3). Folcroft.

Sticca, Sanduo, ed. Historical & Literary Perspectives: Essays & Studies in Honor of Albert D. Menut. 234p. 1973. 10.00x (ISBN 0-87291-065-2). Coronado Pr.

Summers, M. Gothic Quest. 59.95 (ISBN 0-8490-0254-0). Gordon Pr.

Symons, Arthur. Studies in Two Literatures. LC 72-193757. 1924. lib. bdg. 20.00 (ISBN 0-8414-8003-6). Folcroft.

Tayler, Edward W. Nature & Art in Renaissance Literature. LC 64-20484. (Illus.). 1964. 15.00x (ISBN 0-231-02718-4). Columbia U Pr.

Tennessee Studies in Literature. Incl. Vol. 1. 1956; Vol. 2. 1957; Vol. 3. 1958; Vol. 4. 1959. pap. (ISBN 0-87049-025-7); Vol. 5. 1960. pap. (ISBN 0-87049-027-3); Vol. 6. 1961. pap. (ISBN 0-87049-033-8); Vol. 7. 1962. pap. (ISBN 0-87049-036-2); Vol. 8. 1963. pap. (ISBN 0-87049-043-5); Vol. 9. 1964; Vol. 10. 1965; Vol. 11. 1966. pap. (ISBN 0-87049-062-1); Vol. 12. 1967. pap. (ISBN 0-87049-076-1); Vol. 13. 1968. pap. (ISBN 0-87049-084-2); Vol. 14. 1969. pap. (ISBN 0-87049-104-0); Vol. 15. 1970. (ISBN 0-87049-117-2); pap. (ISBN 0-87049-240-3); Vol. 16. 1971. (ISBN 0-87049-132-6); pap. (ISBN 0-87049-241-1); Vol. 17. 1972. (ISBN 0-87049-142-3); Vol. 18. 1973. (ISBN 0-87049-148-2); pap. (ISBN 0-87049-243-8); Vol. 19. 1974. (ISBN 0-87049-154-7); pap. (ISBN 0-87049-244-6); Vol. 20. 1975. (ISBN 0-87049-172-5); Vol. 21. 1976. pap. (ISBN 0-87049-246-2); Vol. 22. 1977. (ISBN 0-87049-212-8); pap. (ISBN 0-87049-236-5); Vol. 23. 1978. (ISBN 0-87049-249-7); pap. (ISBN 0-87049-250-0); Index. pap. 1.00x (ISBN 0-87049-075-3). LC 58-63252. 9.50x ea.; pap. 5.00x ea. U of Tenn Pr.

Thorndike, Ashley H. Outlook for Literature. LC 74-90686. (Essay Index Reprint Ser). 1931. 16.00 (ISBN 0-8369-1235-7). Arno.

Todorov, Tzvetan. Litterature et signification. (Fr). pap. 12.25 (ISBN 0-685-13971-9, 3636). Larousse.

Traubel, Horace. At the Graveside of Walt Whitman. 35.00 (ISBN 0-87968-674-X). Gordon Pr.

Tucker, T. G. Judgement & Appreciation of Literature. LC 76-40254. 1926. lib. bdg. 12.50 (ISBN 0-8414-8621-2). Folcroft.

Very, Alice, ed. Comprehensive Index of Poet Lore, 1889-1963, Vols. 1-58. 1966. 27.50 (ISBN 0-8283-1170-6). Branden.

Wagenknecht, Edward C. Preface to Literature. LC 54-6623. 1969. Repr. of 1954 ed. 14.00 (ISBN 0-527-93700-2). Kraus Repr.

Watt, Laughlan M. Burns. 1972. Repr. lib. bdg. 12.50 (ISBN 0-8414-9657-9). Folcroft.

Waugh, Alec. Modern Prose Literature: A Critical Survey. LC 74-23877. 1973. lib. bdg. 10.00 (ISBN 0-8414-9577-7). Folcroft.

Wendell, Barrett. The Traditions of European Literature. lib. bdg. 17.50 (ISBN 0-8414-9667-6). Folcroft.

Whipple, Edwin P. The Literature of the Age of Elizabeth. 1973. lib. bdg. 25.00 (ISBN 0-8414-9673-0). Folcroft.

Williams, William E. The Craft of Literature. 1973. lib. bdg. 8.50 (ISBN 0-8414-9740-0). Folcroft.

Winslow, Helen M. Little Journeys in Literature. 1973. lib. bdg. 17.50 (ISBN 0-8414-9777-X). Folcroft.

Wolfram, Von Eschenbach. Parzival: Eine Auswahl mit Anmerkungen und Woerterbuch. 4th ed. Jantzen, Hermann & Kolb, Herbert, eds. (Sammlung Goeschen 5021). 128p. 1973. pap. 6.25x (ISBN 3-11-004615-6). De Gruyter.

Woodberry, George E. Appreciation of Literature. 1907. lib. bdg. 10.00 (ISBN 0-8414-9784-2). Folcroft.

--Appreciation of Literature. LC 68-8200. (Essay & General Literature Index Reprint Ser). 1969. Repr. of 1907 ed. 10.50 (ISBN 0-8046-0509-2). Kennikat.

--The Appreciation of Literature. 1978. Repr. of 1922 ed. lib. bdg. 20.00 (ISBN 0-89760-905-0, Telegraph). Dynamic Learn Corp.

--Studies of a Litterateur. 1973. lib. bdg. 9.50 (ISBN 0-8414-9791-5). Folcroft.

Wordsworth, J. C. Adventures in Literature. 1973. lib. bdg. 20.00 (ISBN 0-8414-9798-2). Folcroft.

Worsfold, W. Basil. Principles of Criticism. LC 75-105857. 1970. Repr. of 1902 ed. 11.00 (ISBN 0-8046-0991-8). Kennikat.

Wulker, Richard. Geschichte der Englischen Litteratur. 1978. Repr. of 1896 ed. lib. bdg. 75.00 (ISBN 0-89760-902-6, Telegraph). Dynamic Learn Corp.

Zitner, Sheldon P., et al. Preface to Literary Analysis. 1964. pap. 6.95x (ISBN 0-673-05216-8). Scott F.

LITERATURE–ADDRESSES, ESSAYS, LECTURES

see also Literature–History and Criticism

Adams, J. D. Literary Frontiers. LC 51-9613. Repr. of 1951 ed. 10.00 (ISBN 0-527-00440-5). Kraus Repr.

Adams, Robert M. Strains of Discord. facs. ed. LC 75-142601. (Essay Index Reprint Ser). 1958. 16.00 (ISBN 0-8369-1917-3). Arno.

Aldington, Richard. Literary Studies & Reviews. facs. ed. LC 68-16901. (Essay Index Reprint Ser). 1924. 15.00 (ISBN 0-8369-0143-6). Arno.

Altrocchi, Rudolph. Sleuthing in the Stacks. LC 68-26239. 1968. Repr. of 1944 ed. 12.50 (ISBN 0-8046-0009-0). Kennikat.

Angoff, Charles, ed. & frwd. by. Twenty Years of the Literary Review: Essays, Stories, Poems, Plays, Epigrams. LC 77-92563. 500p. 1981. 18.00 (ISBN 0-8386-2221-6). Fairleigh Dickinson.

Arnold, Matthew. Four Essays on Life & Letters. Brown, E. K., ed. LC 47-4419. (Crofts Classics Ser.). 1947. pap. text ed. 1.25x (ISBN 0-88295-006-1). Harlan Davidson.

Auden, W. H. Forewords & Afterwords. 1973. 19.95 (ISBN 0-394-48359-6). Random.

--Forewords & Afterwords. 1973. pap. 2.95 (ISBN 0-394-71887-9, Vin). Random.

Auerbach, Erich. Scenes from the Drama of European Literature: Six Essays. 8.75 (ISBN 0-8446-5834-0). Peter Smith.

Bancroft, Hubert H. Literary Industries. LC 67-29422. (Works of Hubert Howe Bancroft Ser.). 1967. Repr. of 1888 ed. 25.00x (ISBN 0-914888-43-9). Bancroft Pr.

Barthes, Roland. Essais Critiques. 1964. 16.95 (ISBN 0-686-53934-6). French & Eur.

Benjamin, Walter. Illuminations. LC 68-24382. 1969. pap. 5.50 (ISBN 0-8052-0241-2). Schocken.

Bett, Henry. Studies in Literature. LC 68-8220. 1929. Repr. of 1929 ed. 9.50 (ISBN 0-8046-0028-7). Kennikat.

Bickersteth, Geoffrey L. The Golden World of King Lear: A Lecture. LC 73-9789. lib. bdg. 5.50 (ISBN 0-8414-3174-4). Folcroft.

Bloomfield, Morton W. Essays & Explorations: Studies in Ideas, Language, & Literature. LC 70-106956. (Illus.). x, 321p. 1970. 16.50x (ISBN 0-674-26425-8). Harvard U Pr.

Bond, Richard W. Studia Otiosa. facsimile ed. LC 71-99683. (Essay Index Reprint Ser). 1938. 16.00 (ISBN 0-8369-1341-8). Arno.

Borges, Jorge L. Other Inquisitions. Simms, Ruth L., tr. from Span. (Texas Pan American Ser.). Orig. Title: Otros inquisiciones. 223p. 1964. 9.95 (ISBN 0-292-73322-4); pap. 4.95 (ISBN 0-292-76002-7). U of Tex Pr.

Boyers, Robert. Excursions: Selected Literary Essays. (Literary Criticism Ser). 1976. 15.00 (ISBN 0-8046-9148-7, Natl U). Kennikat.

Burdett, Osbert. Critical Essays. facsimile ed. LC 79-99685. (Essay Index Reprint Ser). 1925. 16.00 (ISBN 0-8369-1346-9). Arno.

Burke, Kenneth. Counter Statement. 2nd rev. ed. 1953. 4.95 (ISBN 0-910720-01-0). Hermes.

--Counter-Statement. 1968. pap. 5.95x (ISBN 0-520-00196-6, CAL160). U of Cal Pr.

--Language As Symbolic Action: Essays on Life, Literature, & Method. LC 66-27655. 1966. 25.00x (ISBN 0-520-00191-5); pap. 9.95x (ISBN 0-520-00192-3, CAL166). U of Cal Pr.

--Perspectives by Incongruity. Hyman, Stanley E. & Karmiller, Barbara, eds. LC 64-18818. (Midland Bks.: No. 63). 208p. 1964. pap. 2.45x (ISBN 0-253-20063-6). Ind U Pr.

--The Philosophy of Literary Form. 1974. pap. 8.95x (ISBN 0-520-02483-4). U of Cal Pr.

--Terms for Order. Hyman, Stanley E. & Karmiller, Barbara, eds. LC 64-18818. (Midland Bks: No. 64). 208p. (Orig.). 1964. pap. 2.45x (ISBN 0-253-20064-4). Ind U Pr.

Burton, Richard. Literary Likings. facsimile ed. LC 79-37510. (Essay Index Reprint Ser). Repr. of 1898 ed. 21.00 (ISBN 0-8369-2538-6). Arno.

Butler, Samuel. The Humour of Homer & Other Essays. Streatfeild, R. A., ed. 1978. Repr. of 1913 ed. lib. bdg. 20.00 (ISBN 0-8492-3547-2). R West.

Camden, Carroll, ed. Literary Views: Critical & Historical Essays. LC 64-13715. 1964. 8.50x (ISBN 0-226-09213-5). U of Chicago Pr.

Canby, Henry S., et al. Saturday Papers, Essays on Literature from the Literary Review. 1969. Repr. of 1921 ed. 11.50 (ISBN 0-384-07310-7). Johnson Repr.

Carlyle, Thomas. Lectures on the History of Literature Delivered by Thomas Carlyle: April to July 1838. Greene, J. Reay, ed. 1978. Repr. of 1892 ed. lib. bdg. 25.00 (ISBN 0-8495-0754-5). Arden Lib.

Chancellor, E. Beresford. Literary Types, Being Essays in Criticism. 192p. 1979. Repr. lib. bdg. 22.50 (ISBN 0-8414-9989-6). Folcroft.

Chapman, John J. Emerson & Other Essays. LC 75-108126. 1970. Repr. of 1899 ed. 19.50 (ISBN 0-404-00619-1). AMS Pr.

Cheuse, Alan & Koffler, Richard, eds. The Rarer Action: Essays in Honor of Francis Fergusson. LC 70-127050. 1970. 23.00 (ISBN 0-8135-0670-0). Rutgers U Pr.

Clark, Arthur M. Studies in Literary Modes. LC 76-58436. 1946. lib. bdg. 20.00 (ISBN 0-8414-3428-X). Folcroft.

Clutton-Brock, Arthur. More Essays on Books. facs. ed. LC 68-57313. (Essay Index Reprint Ser). 1921. 13.00 (ISBN 0-8369-0315-3). Arno.

Connolly, Cyril. Condemned Playground: Essays, Nineteen Twenty-Seven to Forty-Four. LC 79-51238. (Essay Index in Reprint Ser.). Date not set. Repr. of 1946 ed. 24.50x (ISBN 0-8486-3038-6). Core Collection.

Cook, Edward T. More Literary Recreations. facsimile ed. LC 76-105005. (Essay Index Reprint Ser). 1919. 24.00 (ISBN 0-8369-1457-0). Arno.

Cooper, Lane. Evolution & Repentance: Mixed Essays & Addresses. facsimile ed. LC 78-152166. (Essay Index Reprint Ser). Repr. of 1935 ed. 16.00 (ISBN 0-8369-2222-0). Arno.

Creeley, Robert. Was That a Real Poem & Other Essays. Allen, Donald, ed. LC 78-16254. (Writing: 39). 150p. 1979. 12.00 (ISBN 0-87704-041-9); pap. 5.00 (ISBN 0-87704-042-7). Four Seasons Foun.

Crees, J. H. Meredith Revisited & Other Essays. LC 67-30813. (Studies in Fiction, No. 34). 1969. Repr. of 1921 ed. lib. bdg. 28.95 (ISBN 0-8383-0713-2). Haskell.

Cromer, Evelyn B. Political & Literary Essays: 1st Series. facs. ed. LC 68-8453. (Essay Index Reprint Ser). 1913. 21.25 (ISBN 0-8369-1058-3). Arno.

Dahlberg, Edward. Those Who Perish. LC 75-41070. Repr. of 1934 ed. 15.00 (ISBN 0-404-14528-0). AMS Pr.

Daiches, David. A Study of Literature for Readers & Critics. LC 71-152593. 240p. 1972. Repr. of 1948 ed. lib. bdg. 24.25x (ISBN 0-8371-6026-X, DARC). Greenwood.

Darrow, Clarence. A Persian Pearl & Other Essays. LC 74-1199. (American Literature Ser., No. 49). 1974. lib. bdg. 32.95 (ISBN 0-8383-1770-7). Haskell.

De Gaury, Gerald & Winstone, H. V. The Spirit of the East. 17.50 (ISBN 0-7043-2230-7, Pub. by Quartet England). Charles River Bks.

De La Mare, Walter J. Private View: Essays on Literature. LC 78-14114. 1979. Repr. of 1953 ed. 22.00 (ISBN 0-88355-786-X). Hyperion Conn.

Department of Romanic Languages of the University of California Members. Literary & Philological Studies. 1978. Repr. of 1919 ed. lib. bdg. 50.00 (ISBN 0-8414-0060-1). Folcroft.

Dixon, W. Macneile. An Apology for the Arts (Chatterton, English & Scottish Ballads, Wordsworth, Scott, Thomas Campbell, Tolstoy) LC 76-17899. 1973. lib. bdg. 17.50 (ISBN 0-8414-3734-3). Folcroft.

Donnelly, Francis P. Literature the Leading Educator. LC 79-107694. (Essay Index Reprint Ser). 1938. 17.00 (ISBN 0-8369-1497-X). Arno.

Egoff, Sheila, et al, eds. Only Connect: Readings on Children's Literature. 2nd ed. (Illus.). 496p. 1980. pap. text ed. 8.95x (ISBN 0-19-540309-6). Oxford U Pr.

Eliot, George. Early Essays. 71p. 1980. Repr. of 1919 ed. lib. bdg. 15.00 (ISBN 0-8492-0787-8). R West.

--Essays. Pinney, Thomas, ed. LC 63-20344. 476p. 1963. 20.00x (ISBN 0-231-02619-6). Columbia U Pr.

Eliot, T. S. On Poetry & Poets. 1957. pap. 7.95 (ISBN 0-374-50185-8, N214). FS&G.

--On Poetry & Poets. LC 75-10985. xii, 308p. 1975. Repr. of 1957 ed. lib. bdg. 16.50x (ISBN 0-374-92530-5). Octagon.

--Selected Essays. rev. ed. LC 32-24259. 1950. 12.50 (ISBN 0-15-180387-0). HarBraceJ.

Elton, Oliver. Modern Studies. LC 72-194354. 1907. lib. bdg. 12.50 (ISBN 0-8414-3997-4). Folcroft.

--Sheaf of Papers. LC 72-194754. 1923. lib. bdg. 15.00 (ISBN 0-8414-3917-6). Folcroft.

Enright, D. J. Conspirators & Poets: Reviews & Essays. LC 66-78655. 1979. 8.95 (ISBN 0-7011-0658-1, Pub. by Chatto Bodley Jonathan). Merrimack Bk Serv.

Essays & Studies in Honor of Carleton Brown. facsimile ed. LC 79-99693. (Essay Index Reprint Ser). 1940. 18.25 (ISBN 0-8369-1408-2). Arno.

Fausset, Hugh L. Poets & Pundits: Essays & Addresses. LC 67-25261. Repr. of 1947 ed. 12.50 (ISBN 0-8046-0139-9). Kennikat.

Fothergill, Brian, ed. Essays by Divers Hands: Being the Transactions of the Royal Society of Literature. (New Series: Vol. XLI). 147p. 1980. 22.50x (ISBN 0-8476-3530-9). Rowman.

Frye, Northrop. Spiritus Mundi: Essays on Literature, Myth, & Society. LC 76-12364. 320p. 1976. 12.50x (ISBN 0-253-35432-3). Ind U Pr.

Frye, Northrop, et al. Myth & Symbol: Critical Approaches & Applications. Slote, Bernice, ed. LC 63-9960. 1963. pap. 4.25x (ISBN 0-8032-5065-7, BB 141, Bison). U of Nebr Pr.

Frye, Prosser H. Visions & Chimeras. LC 66-23517. 1929. 9.00x (ISBN 0-8196-0179-9). Biblo.

Gardiner, Harold C., ed. Great Books: A Christian Appraisal, 4 Vols. Set. 12.00 (ISBN 0-685-08819-7); Vols. 1-4. 4.50 ea. Vol. 1 (ISBN 0-8159-5610-X). Vol. 2 (ISBN 0-8159-5611-8). Vol. 3 (ISBN 0-8159-5612-6). Vol. 4 (ISBN 0-8159-5613-4). Devin.

Gardner, W. H. Language, Literature, & Human Values. 1977. Repr. of 1966 ed. lib. bdg. 6.50 (ISBN 0-8482-0978-8). Norwood Edns.

Garnett, Richard. Essays of an Ex-Librarian. LC 74-107702. (Essay Index Reprint Ser). 1901. 18.00 (ISBN 0-8369-1503-8). Arno.

Garrod, H. W. The Study of Good Letters. Jones, John, ed. LC 75-9845. (Illus.). 221p. 1975. Repr. of 1963 ed. lib. bdg. 15.00x (ISBN 0-8371-8119-4, GAGL). Greenwood.

Garrod, Herbert B. Dante, Goethe's Faust, & Other Lectures. 1913. lib. bdg. 25.00 (ISBN 0-8414-4639-3). Folcroft.

Gass, William. The World Within the Word. LC 79-52634. 1979. pap. 6.95 (ISBN 0-87923-298-6, Nonpareil Bks.). Godine.

Gildersleeve, Basil L. Essays & Studies. (American Studies). 1968. Repr. of 1890 ed. 31.00 (ISBN 0-384-18501-0). Johnson Repr.

Godley, A. D. The Casual Word: Academic & Other Oddments (the Novel) 1978. Repr. of 1912 ed. lib. bdg. 25.00 (ISBN 0-89760-304-4, Telegraph). Dynamic Learn Corp.

Goodman, Paul. Creator Spirit Come: The Literary Essays of Paul Goodman. Stoehr, Taylor, ed. LC 77-71942. 1977. 11.95 (ISBN 0-914156-19-5). Free Life.

Gosse, Edmund. Continuity of Literature. LC 76-28547. lib. bdg. 4.50 (ISBN 0-8414-4516-8). Folcroft.

--More Books on the Table. 1914. Repr. 21.50 (ISBN 0-8274-2763-8). R West.

Gosse, Edmund W. Books on the Table. facsimile ed. LC 74-156653. (Essay Index Reprint Ser). Repr. of 1921 ed. 20.00 (ISBN 0-8369-2365-0). Arno.

--Leaves & Fruit. LC 70-105017. (Essay Index Reprint Ser). 1927. 19.50 (ISBN 0-8369-1505-4). Arno.

--More Books on the Table. LC 71-93340. (Essay Index Reprint Ser). 1923. 22.00 (ISBN 0-8369-1410-4). Arno.

--Silhouettes. facsimile ed. LC 78-156654. (Essay Index Reprint Ser). Repr. of 1925 ed. 22.00 (ISBN 0-8369-2399-5). Arno.

Gras, Vernon W., ed. European Literary Theory & Practice. (Orig.). 1973. pap. 2.95 (ISBN 0-440-52381-8, Delta). Dell.

Gregor, Ian. Reading the Victorian Novel: Detail into Form. (Critical Studies). (Illus.). 1980. text ed. 27.50x (ISBN 0-06-492542-0). B&N.

Grizzard, Lewis. Won't You Come Home Billy Bob Bailey. 240p. 1980. 8.95 (ISBN 0-931948-10-X). Peachtree Pubs.

Hardwick, Elizabeth. A View of My Own: Essays in Literature & Society. 1980. Repr. lib. bdg. 13.00x (ISBN 0-374-93661-7). Octagon.

Harper, George M. Spirit of Delight. facs. ed. LC 78-76902. (Essay Index Reprint Ser). 1928. 16.00 (ISBN 0-8369-0016-2). Arno.

Harper, Howard. Library Essays. LC 72-8899. 1972. Repr. of 1924 ed. lib. bdg. 25.00 (ISBN 0-8414-0412-7). Folcroft.

--Library Essays. LC 72-8899. 1972. Repr. of 1924 ed. lib. bdg. 25.00 (ISBN 0-8414-0412-7). Folcroft.

Harrison, Frederic. Among My Books. LC 74-105018. (Essay Index Reprint Ser). 1912. 24.00 (ISBN 0-8369-1470-8). Arno.

--Realities & Ideals: Social, Political, Literary & Artistic. LC 78-117803. (Essay Index Reprint Ser). 1908. 24.00 (ISBN 0-8369-1708-1). Arno.

Hartman, Geoffrey H. Beyond Formalism: Literary Essays, Nineteen Fifty-Eight to Nineteen Seventy. LC 79-115371. 1970. 27.50x (ISBN 0-300-01327-2); pap. 6.95 (ISBN 0-300-01515-1). Yale U Pr.

Hearn, Lafcadio. Books & Habits, from the Lectures of Lafcadio Hearn. facs. ed. Erskine, J., ed. LC 68-20308. (Essay Index Reprint Ser). 1921. 18.00 (ISBN 0-8369-0524-5). Arno.

--Essays in European & Oriental Literature. facs. ed. Mordell, A., ed. LC 68-58795. (Essay Index Reprint Ser). 1923. 14.75 (ISBN 0-8369-0077-4). Arno.

--Essays in European & Oriental Literature. Mordell, Alberrt, ed. 1977. Repr. of 1923 ed. 30.00 (ISBN 0-8495-2210-2). Arden Lib.

--Life & Literature. facs. ed. Erskine, J., ed. LC 78-90644. (Essay Index Reprint Ser). 1917. 22.00 (ISBN 0-8369-1206-3). Arno.

--Talks to Writers. facs. ed. Erskine, J., ed. LC 67-23230. (Essay Index Reprint Ser). 1967. Repr. of 1920 ed. 16.00 (ISBN 0-8369-0528-8). Arno.

House, Humphry. All in Due Time: Collected Essays & Broadcast Talks. LC 78-18897. 1955. lib. bdg. 17.50 (ISBN 0-8414-4962-7). Folcroft.

Huneker, James G. Unicorns. LC 72-6581. Repr. of 1917 ed. 22.50 (ISBN 0-404-10529-7). AMS Pr.

Hunt, Leigh. Essays: Selected. 1971. Repr. of 1929 ed. 22.00 (ISBN 0-403-03590-2). Scholarly.

--Men, Women, & Books. 1891. Repr. lib. bdg. 25.00 (ISBN 0-8414-5233-4). Folcroft.

--One Hundred Romances of Real Life. Repr. lib. bdg. 20.00 (ISBN 0-8414-5234-2). Folcroft.

Johnson, Lionel P. Post Liminium: Essays & Critical Papers. facs. ed. LC 68-20312. (Essay Index Reprint Ser). 1912. 16.00 (ISBN 0-8369-0573-3). Arno.

Johnson, Samuel. Samuel Johnson's Literary Criticism. Stock, R. D., ed. LC 73-91398. (Regents Critics Ser). xvi, 286p. 1974. 17.95x (ISBN 0-8032-0469-8); pap. 4.95x (ISBN 0-8032-5467-9, BB 415, Bison). U of Nebr Pr.

Kazin, Alfred. The Inmost Leaf. LC 79-10363. 1979. pap. 4.95 (ISBN 0-15-644398-8, Harv). HarBraceJ.

Kellett, E. E. Suggestions, Literary Essays. 1979. Repr. of 1923 ed. lib. bdg. 20.00 (ISBN 0-8492-1482-3). R West.

Kellett, Ernest E. Fashion in Literature. 369p. 1980. Repr. of 1931 ed. lib. bdg. 30.00 (ISBN 0-8482-4751-5). Norwood Edns.

Kelman, John. Among Famous Books. facs. ed. LC 68-57326. (Essay Index Reprint Ser). 1912. 18.00 (ISBN 0-8369-0587-3). Arno.

Ker, William P. Collected Essays, 2 Vols. facs. ed. LC 67-28736. (Essay Index Reprint Ser). 1925. 35.00 (ISBN 0-8369-0591-1). Arno.

Kittredge, George L. Anniversary Papers by Colleagues & Pupils of G. L. Kittredge. LC 66-24717. (Illus.). 1967. Repr. of 1913 ed. 11.00 (ISBN 0-8462-1025-8). Russell.

Knickerbocker, William, ed. Twentieth Century English. LC 75-107721. (Essay Index Reprint Ser). 1946. 25.00 (ISBN 0-8369-1668-9). Arno.

Knight, G. Wilson. Neglected Powers: Essays on Nineteenth & Twentieth Century Literature. 1970. 24.75 (ISBN 0-7100-6681-3). Routledge & Kegan.

Knox, Ronald A. Literary Distractions. LC 74-20678. 232p. 1975. Repr. of 1958 ed. lib. bdg. 14.75x (ISBN 0-8371-7840-1, KNLD). Greenwood.

Kostelanetz, Richard, ed. On Contemporary Literature. 1st ed. LC 72-156674. 1978. 50.00 (ISBN 0-932360-01-7); pap. 10.00 (ISBN 0-932360-00-9). RK Edns.

--On Contemporary Literature: An Anthology of Critical Essays on the Major Movements & Writings of Contemporary Literature. facsimile ed. LC 72-156674. (Essay Index Reprint Ser). Repr. of 1964 ed. 36.00 (ISBN 0-8369-2406-1). Arno.

Lehmann, John. Open Night. facsimile ed. LC 72-142654. (Essay Index Reprint Ser). Repr. of 1952 ed. 13.00 (ISBN 0-8369-2407-X). Arno.

Lemon, Lee T., ed. Approaches to Literature. 1969. pap. text ed. 4.95x (ISBN 0-19-500949-5). Oxford U Pr.

Levin, Harry. Grounds for Comparison. LC 72-75402. (Studies in Comparative Literature: No. 32). (Illus.). 448p. 1972. 20.00x (ISBN 0-674-36335-3). Harvard U Pr.

Levith, Murray J., ed. Renaissance & Modern: Essays in Honor of Edwin M. Moseley. 180p. 1976. 11.95x (ISBN 0-8156-2177-9). Syracuse U Pr.

Lewes, George H. Literary Criticism of George Henry Lewes. Kaminsky, Alice R., ed. LC 64-17230. (Regents Critics Ser). 1965. 12.95x (ISBN 0-8032-0456-6); pap. 2.75x (ISBN 0-8032-5455-5, BB 402, Bison). U of Nebr Pr.

Lewis, C. S. Essays Presented to Charles Williams. 1966. pap. 2.95 (ISBN 0-8028-1117-5). Eerdmans.

Litz, Walton A., Jr. & Lipking, Lawrence I., eds. Modern Literary Criticism: 1900-1970. LC 71-152045. 1972. pap. text ed. 12.95 (ISBN 0-689-10419-7). Atheneum.

Lodge, David, ed. Twentieth Century Literary Criticism: A Reader. 1977. pap. text ed. 14.95x (ISBN 0-582-48422-7). Longman.
Lowell, James R. Function of the Poet. LC 72-193720. 1920. lib. bdg. 11.50 (ISBN 0-8414-5894-4). Folcroft.
--Function of the Poet & Other Essays. Mordell, A. K., ed. LC 67-27621. 1968. Repr. of 1920 ed. 12.00 (ISBN 0-8046-0280-8). Kennikat.
--Literary Essays, 6 vols. 1981. Repr. of 1864 ed. Set. lib. bdg. 100.00 (ISBN 0-89984-315-8). Century Bookbindery.
--Literary Essays, 2 vols. LC 72-5803. (Essay Index Reprint Ser). 1972. Repr. of 1890 ed. Set. 45.00 (ISBN 0-8369-2998-5). Arno.
Lyall, Alfred C. Studies in Literature & History. facs. ed. LC 68-29227. (Essay Index Reprint Ser). 1968. Repr. of 1915 ed. 19.50 (ISBN 0-8369-0637-3). Arno.
Lynch, Thomas T. Essays on Some of the Forms of Literature. 1979. Repr. of 1853 ed. lib. bdg. 30.00 (ISBN 0-8492-1598-6). R West.
Lynd, Robert. Books & Authors. facs. ed. LC 73-90659. (Essay Index Reprint Ser). 1923. 17.00 (ISBN 0-8369-1209-8). Arno.
Mabie, Hamilton W. Essays in Literary Interpretation. LC 72-293. (Essay Index Reprint Ser.). Repr. of 1892 ed. 16.00 (ISBN 0-8369-2802-4). Arno.
Maccarthy, Desmond. Criticism. LC 78-97710. (Essay Index Reprint Ser). 1932. 19.50 (ISBN 0-8369-1360-4). Arno.
--Criticism. LC 72-194346. 1932. lib. bdg. 20.00 (ISBN 0-8414-6230-5). Folcroft.
Mackail, John W. Studies in Humanism. facs. ed. LC 73-84322. (Essay Index Reprint Ser). 1938. 15.75 (ISBN 0-8369-1092-3). Arno.
MacLean, Malcolm S. & Holmes, Elizabeth. Men & Books. LC 78-58261. (Essay Index in Reprint Ser.). 1978. Repr. 33.50x (ISBN 0-8486-3023-8). Core Collection.
Magill, Frank N., ed. Magill's Literary Annual: 1979, 2 vols. LC 77-99209. 1979. 50.00 (ISBN 0-89356-279-3). Salem Pr.
Makkai, Adam, ed. Toward a Theory of Context in Linguistics & Literature: Proceedings of a Conference of the Kelemen Mikes Hungarian Cultural Society, Maastricht, September 21-25, 1971. (De Proprietatibus Litterarum Ser. Minor: No. 18). pap. 32.50x (ISBN 90-2793-273-5). Mouton.
Mandelstam, Osip. Osip Mandelstam: Selected Essays. Monas, Sidney, tr. LC 76-22456. 271p. 1977. text ed. 15.95x (ISBN 0-292-76006-X). U of Tex Pr.
Martin, Harold. Cats, Dogs, Children & Other Small Creatures. 224p. 1980. 8.95 (ISBN 0-931948-12-6). Peachtree Pubs.
Masson, David. Three Devils: Luther's, Milton's & Goethe's. LC 78-128340. Repr. of 1874 ed. 18.45 (ISBN 0-404-04247-3). AMS Pr.
Matthews, Brander. Books & Play-Books: Essays on Literature & the Drama. facsimile ed. LC 71-37795. (Essay Index Reprint Ser). Repr. of 1895 ed. 17.00 (ISBN 0-8369-2612-9). Arno.
--Gateways to Literature: And Other Essays. facsimile ed. LC 70-142667. (Essay Index Reprint Ser). Repr. of 1912 ed. 18.00 (ISBN 0-8369-2414-2). Arno.
--Historical Novel, & Other Essays. facs. ed. LC 68-20320. (Essay Index Reprint Ser). 1968. Repr. of 1901 ed. 15.50 (ISBN 0-8369-0695-0). Arno.
Maugham, W. Somerset. Points of View: Five Essays. LC 69-10132. 1969. Repr. of 1959 ed. lib. bdg. 15.00 (ISBN 0-8371-0564-1, MAPV). Greenwood.
--Points of View: Five Essays. LC 75-25374. (Works of W. Somerset Maugham Ser.). 1977. Repr. of 1959 ed. 15.00x (ISBN 0-405-07827-7). Arno.
--Selected Prefaces & Introductions. LC 75-25375. (Works of W. Somerset Maugham Ser.). 1977. Repr. of 1963 ed. 15.00x (ISBN 0-405-07828-5). Arno.
Miller, James E., Jr., ed. Myth & Method: Modern Theories of Fiction. LC 60-12941. 1960. pap. 2.45x (ISBN 0-8032-5134-3, BB 105, Bison). U of Nebr Pr.
Mills, Howard, ed. Thomas Love Peacock: Memoirs of Shelley & Other Essays & Reviews. LC 76-129350. 1970. 10.00x (ISBN 0-8147-5354-X). NYU Pr.
Mudrick, Marvin. On Culture & Literature. 1970. pap. 3.95 (ISBN 0-8180-1156-4). Horizon.
Muir, Edwin. Essays on Literature & Society. rev. & enl. ed. LC 65-2483. 1965. 12.50x (ISBN 0-674-26700-1). Harvard U Pr.
Mumford, Lewis, et al. Arts in Renewal. facs. ed. LC 70-84296. (Essay Index Reprint Ser). 1951. 14.50 (ISBN 0-8369-1121-0). Arno.
Murphy, James J., et al. Rhetorical Essays & Modern Writing: Essays Toward the Re-Marriage of Literature & Literacy. 300p. 1982. 14.50x (ISBN 0-87352-097-1); pap. 8.50x (ISBN 0-87352-098-X). Modern Lang.
Murry, John M. John Clare & Other Studies. 1968. Repr. of 1950 ed. 14.00 (ISBN 0-527-65960-6). Kraus Repr.
--Pencillings. facs. ed. LC 70-90666. (Essay Index Reprint Ser). 1925. 17.00 (ISBN 0-8369-1229-2). Arno.
Nandakumar, Prema. The Glory & the Good: Essays on Literature. 1978. Repr. of 1965 ed. lib. bdg. 35.00 (ISBN 0-89760-601-9, Telegraph). Dynamic Learn Corp.
Nobel Foundation. Nobel Lectures in Literature, 1901-1967. Frenz, Horst, ed. 1969. 29.50 (ISBN 0-444-40685-9). Elsevier.
Noyes, Alfred. Opalescent Parrot: Essays. facs. ed. (Essay Index Reprint Ser). 1929. 16.00 (ISBN 0-8369-0748-5). Arno.
Oates, Joyce C. Contraries: Essays. 192p. 1981. 15.00 (ISBN 0-19-502884-8). Oxford U Pr.
O'Connor, Frank. Towards an Appreciation of Literature. LC 74-6482. (Studies in Comparative Literature, No. 35). 1974. lib. bdg. 40.95 (ISBN 0-8383-1907-6). Haskell.
O'Connor, Michael. Towards an Appreciation of Literature. LC 74-11154. 1945. 7.75 (ISBN 0-8414-6511-8). Folcroft.
O'Donovan, Michael. Towards an Appreciation of Literature. LC 70-105818. 1970. Repr. of 1945 ed. 9.00 (ISBN 0-8046-0967-5). Kennikat.
Ong, Walter J. Barbarian Within, & Other Fugitive Essays & Studies. 1962. 9.95 (ISBN 0-02-593260-8). Macmillan.
Orage, Alfred R. Readers & Writers. LC 72-99714. (Essay Index Reprint Ser). 1922. 15.00 (ISBN 0-8369-1367-1). Arno.
Papini, Giovanni. Four & Twenty Minds. LC 76-174357. Repr. of 1922 ed. 18.00 (ISBN 0-405-08832-9, Blom Pubns.). Arno.
Pearson, Hesketh. A Persian Critic. 106p. 1981. Repr. of 1923 ed. lib. bdg. 25.00 (ISBN 0-89984-393-X). Century Bookbindery.
Peck, Harry T. Studies in Several Literatures. facs. ed. LC 68-16967. (Essay Index Reprint Ser). 1909. 16.00 (ISBN 0-8369-0781-7). Arno.
Peterson, Houston. The Lonely Debate: Dilemmas from Hamlet to Hans Castrop. 1938. 30.00 (ISBN 0-8274-2981-9). R West.
Peyre, Henri M., ed. Essays in Honor of Albert Feuillerat. facs. ed. LC 75-99633. (Essay Index Reprint Ser). 1943. 19.50 (ISBN 0-8369-1650-6). Arno.
Phelps, William L. Essays on Things. 1979. Repr. of 1930 ed. lib. bdg. 20.00 (ISBN 0-8495-4377-0). Arden Lib.
Plowman, Max. The Right to Live. 319p. 1981. Repr. of 1942 ed. lib. bdg. 30.00 (ISBN 0-89984-392-1). Century Bookbindery.
Pound, Ezra. Literary Essays. Eliot, T. S., ed. LC 54-7905. 1968. pap. 6.95 (ISBN 0-8112-0157-0, NDP250). New Directions.
--Make It New: Essays. LC 71-145243. 1971. Repr. of 1935 ed. 29.00 (ISBN 0-403-01158-2). Scholarly.
Pound, Ezra L. Polite Essays. facs. ed. LC 67-22111. (Essay Index Reprint Ser). 1937. 18.00 (ISBN 0-8369-0796-5). Arno.
Powys, John C. Suspended Judgments, Essays on Books & Sensations. LC 76-29700. 1916. lib. bdg. 17.50 (ISBN 0-8414-6786-2). Folcroft.
--Visions & Revisions: A Book of Literary Devotions. LC 78-58263. (Essay Index in Reprint Ser.). 1978. Repr. 23.75x (ISBN 0-8486-3025-4). Core Collection.
Primeau, Ronald, ed. Influx: Essays on Literary Influence. (Literary Criticism Ser). 1977. 14.50 (ISBN 0-8046-9151-7, Natl U). Kennikat.
Pritchett, V. S. The Tale Bearers: Essays on English, American & Other Writers. 1980. 11.95 (ISBN 0-394-50486-0). Random.
Rahv, Philip. Essays on Literature & Politics 1932-1972. Porter, Arabel J. & Dvosin, Andrew J., eds. 1978. 15.00 (ISBN 0-395-27270-X). HM.
Rankin, T. E., et al. Fred Newton Scott Anniversary Papers, Contributed by Former Students & Colleagues of Professor Scott & Presented to Him in Celebration of His Thirty-Eighth Year of Distinguished Service in the University of Michigan, 1888-1926. facs. ed. LC 68-29205. (Essay Index Reprint Ser). 1968. Repr. of 1929 ed. 17.00 (ISBN 0-8369-0459-1). Arno.
Rascoe, Burton. Titans of Literature from Homer to the Present. LC 76-121502. (Essay Index Reprint Ser). 1932. 19.50 (ISBN 0-8369-1775-8). Arno.
Read, Herbert E. Nature of Literature. LC 74-105034. (Essay Index Reprint Ser). 1938. 22.00 (ISBN 0-8369-1478-3). Arno.
Richards, I. A. Complementarities: I. A. Richards Uncollected Essays. Russo, John P., ed. 1976. 15.00x (ISBN 0-674-15520-3). Harvard U Pr.
Robbins, Jack A., ed. James T. Farrell - Literary Essays, 1954-1974. (Literary Criticism Ser.). 1976. 11.50 (ISBN 0-8046-9125-8, Natl U). Kennikat.
Rosenfeld, Paul. By Way of Art: Criticisms of Music, Literature, Painting, Sculpture & the Dance. facs. ed. LC 67-30230. (Essay Index Reprint Ser). 1928. 16.00 (ISBN 0-8369-0835-X). Arno.
Sainte-Beuve, Charles A. Literary Criticism of Sainte-Beuve. Marks, Emerson R., ed. LC 75-132560. (Regents Critics Ser). 1971. 10.00x (ISBN 0-8032-0465-5). U of Nebr Pr.
Sartre, Jean-Paul. Situations, Vol. 1. 338p. 1947. 11.95 (ISBN 0-686-54992-9). French & Eur.
--Situations, Vol. 2. 336p. 1948. 15.95 (ISBN 0-686-54993-7). French & Eur.
--Situations, Vol. 3. 320p. 1949. 22.50 (ISBN 0-686-54994-5). French & Eur.
--Situations: Autour de 1968, Vol. 8. 481p. 1972. 16.95 (ISBN 0-686-54999-6). French & Eur.
--Situations: Colonialisme et Neo-Colonialisme, Vol. 5. 256p. 1964. 6.95 (ISBN 0-686-54996-1). French & Eur.
--Situations: Melanges, Vol. 9. 369p. 1972. 13.95 (ISBN 0-686-55000-5). French & Eur.
--Situations: Politique et Autobiographie, Vol. 10. 232p. 1976. 14.95 (ISBN 0-686-55001-3). French & Eur.
--Situations: Portraits, Vol. 4. 464p. 1964. 16.95 (ISBN 0-686-54995-3). French & Eur.
--Situations: Problemes du Marxisme, Pt. 1, Vol. 6. 392p. 1964. 24.95 (ISBN 0-686-54997-X). French & Eur.
--Situations: Problemes du Marxisme, Pt. 2, Vol. 7. 352p. 1965. 9.95 (ISBN 0-686-54998-8). French & Eur.
Saxl, Fritz. Volume of Memorial Essays. Gordon, D., ed. 1957. 19.50 (ISBN 0-8337-3131-9). B Franklin.
Sayers, Dorothy, et al. Essays Presented to Charles Williams. LC 77-142623. (Essay Index Reprint Ser.). Repr. of 1947 ed. 15.00 (ISBN 0-8369-2768-0). Arno.
Schelling, Felix E. Schelling Anniversary Papers, by His Former Students. LC 66-24755. (Illus.). 1967. Repr. of 1923 ed. 8.75 (ISBN 0-8462-1018-5). Russell.
Schlegel, Augustus W. A Course of Lectures on Dramatic Art & Literature. Black, John, tr. from Ger. LC 11-18702. Repr. of 1846 ed. 29.50 (ISBN 0-404-05605-9). AMS Pr.
Scott, Fred N. Fred Newton Scott Anniversary Papers. LC 72-192324. 1929. lib. bdg. 20.00 (ISBN 0-8414-8156-3). Folcroft.
Scott-James, Rolfe A. Personality in Literature. facs. ed. LC 68-22945. (Essay Index Reprint Ser). 1968. Repr. of 1932 ed. 15.00 (ISBN 0-8369-0858-9). Arno.
Sedgwick, Henry D. Essays on Great Writers. facs. ed. LC 68-29245. (Essay Index Reprint Ser). 1968. Repr. of 1903 ed. 18.00 (ISBN 0-8369-0861-9). Arno.
Sherman, Stuart P. Shaping Men & Women: Essay on Literature and Life. Zeitlin, Jacob, ed. LC 69-10153. 1969. Repr. of 1928 ed. lib. bdg. 16.25x (ISBN 0-8371-0221-9, SHEL). Greenwood.
Solzhenitsyn, Alexander. Nobel Lecture. bi-lingual ed. Reeve, F. D., tr. from Rus. 80p. 1973. 4.00 (ISBN 0-374-22300-9); pap. 1.95 (ISBN 0-374-51063-6). FS&G.
Spender, John A. Last Essays. LC 79-51247. (Essay Index in Reprint Ser.). Date not set. Repr. of 1944 ed. 18.50x (ISBN 0-8486-3046-7). Core Collection.
Stallknecht, Newton P. & Frenz, Horst, eds. Comparative Literature: Method & Perspective. rev. ed. LC 71-83780. 384p. 1971. 10.00x (ISBN 0-8093-0046-X). S Ill U Pr.
Steiner, George. Language & Silence: Essays on Language, Literature & the Inhuman. LC 67-14332. 1970. pap. text ed. 4.95x (ISBN 0-689-70226-4, 158). Atheneum.
Stoll, Elmer E. Poets & Playwrights: Shakespeare, Jonson, Spenser, Milton. 1930. pap. 2.95x (ISBN 0-8166-0440-1, Mp1). U of Minn Pr.
Strachey, Giles L. Characters & Commentaries. LC 78-23722. 1979. Repr. of 1933 ed. lib. bdg. 21.25x (ISBN 0-313-20763-1, STCCO). Greenwood.
Strong, Archibald T. Peradventure. LC 74-118416. 1971. Repr. of 1925 ed. 11.00 (ISBN 0-8046-1193-9). Kennikat.
Sturzl, Erwin A., ed. Essays in Honour of Professor Tyrus Hillway. (Salzburg Studies in English Literature, Romantic Reassessment Ser.: No. 65). (Illus.). 1977. pap. text ed. 25.00x (ISBN 0-391-01539-7). Humanities.
Swallow, Alan. Editor's Essays of Two Decades. LC 66-12521. 401p. 1962. 8.95 (ISBN 0-8040-0073-5). Swallow.
Symons, Arthur. Figures of Several Centuries. LC 77-99726. (Essay Index Reprint Ser). 1916. 22.00 (ISBN 0-8369-1383-3). Arno.
Tate, Allen. Hovering Fly & Other Essays. facs. ed. LC 68-22948. (Essay Index Reprint Ser). 1968. Repr. of 1949 ed. 16.00 (ISBN 0-8369-0923-2). Arno.
--Reason in Madness: Critical Essays. facs. ed. LC 68-26479. (Essay Index Reprint Ser). 1968. Repr. of 1941 ed. 17.00 (ISBN 0-8369-0925-9). Arno.
Thompson, Elbert N. Literary Bypaths of the Renaissance. facs. ed. LC 68-20343. (Essay Index Reprint Ser). 1968. Repr. of 1924 ed. 13.00 (ISBN 0-8369-0933-X). Arno.
Thompson, James W. Byways in Bookland. facs. ed. LC 73-88033. (Essay Index Reprint Ser.). 1935. 15.00 (ISBN 0-8369-1158-X). Arno.
Townsend, James L. Dear Heart. 224p. 1980. 8.95 (ISBN 0-931948-13-4). Peachtree Pubs.
Traill, H. D. New Fiction. LC 73-105843. 1970. Repr. of 1897 ed. 13.00 (ISBN 0-8046-0985-3). Kennikat.
Trent, William P. Greatness in Literature, & Other Papers. facs. ed. LC 67-26790. (Essay Index Reprint Ser). 1905. 15.00 (ISBN 0-8369-0949-6). Arno.
Tuell, Anne K. Victorian at Bay. facs. ed. LC 67-22123. (Essay Index Reprint Ser). 1932. 13.00 (ISBN 0-8369-0952-6). Arno.
Vidal, Gore. Matters of Fact & of Fiction: Essays, 1973-1976. 1978. pap. 3.95 (ISBN 0-394-72516-6, Vin). Random.
Vivas, Eliseo. Artistic Transaction & Essays on Theory of Literature. LC 63-15650. 1963. 6.75 (ISBN 0-8142-0126-1). Ohio St U Pr.
Von Goethe, Johann W. Literary Essays: A Selection in English. facs. ed. Springarn, J. E., ed. (Essay Index Reprint Ser). 1921. 16.00 (ISBN 0-8369-0478-8). Arno.
Washington University, St. Louis. Studies in Honor of Frederick W. Shipley, by His Colleagues. Washington Univ. Studies NS No. 14. facs. ed. LC 68-20341. (Essay Index Reprint Ser). 1942. 18.00 (ISBN 0-8369-0914-3). Arno.
Waugh, Arthur. Reticence in Literature & Other Papers. 1977. Repr. of 1915 ed. lib. bdg. 22.00 (ISBN 0-8492-3009-8). R West.
Wellek, Rene. Discriminations: Further Concepts of Criticism. LC 73-99847. 1970. 30.00x (ISBN 0-300-01230-6). Yale U Pr.
Wellek, Rene & Ribeiro, Alvaro, eds. Evidence in Literary Scholarship: Essays in Memory of James Marshall Osborn. (Illus.). 1979. 39.00x (ISBN 0-19-812612-3). Oxford U Pr.
West, Herbert F. Mind of the Wing. facs. ed. LC 75-134155. (Essay Index Reprint Ser). 1947. 17.00 (ISBN 0-8369-2087-2). Arno.
Whibley, Charles. Studies in Frankness. LC 79-122969. 1970. Repr. of 1898 ed. 12.50 (ISBN 0-8046-1350-8). Kennikat.
Whipple, Edwin. Literature & Life. LC 72-8540. (Essay Index Reprint Ser.). 1972. Repr. of 1899 ed. 20.00 (ISBN 0-8369-7340-2). Arno.
White, E. B. One Man's Meat. 1978. pap. 1.95 (ISBN 0-06-080420-3, P 420, PL). Har-Row.
Whitman, Walt. Rivulets of Prose. Wells, C., ed. LC 78-88037. (Essay Index Reprint Ser). 1928. 17.50 (ISBN 0-8369-1163-6). Arno.
Wilder, Thornton. American Characteristics & Other Essays. Gallup, Donald, ed. LC 79-1692. 1979. 14.95 (ISBN 0-06-014639-7, HarpT). Har-Row.
Will, Frederic. The Fact of Literature: Three Essays on Public Material. 215p. (Orig.). 1973. pap. text ed. 20.00x (ISBN 9-0620-3377-6). Humanities.
--The Knife in the Stone: Essays in Literary Theory. LC 72-94513. (De Proprietatibus Litterarum, Ser. Minor: No. 9). 162p. 1973. pap. text ed. 20.75x (ISBN 90-2792-534-8). Mouton.
Wilson, Edmund. The Triple Thinkers: 12 Essays on Literary Subjects. 288p. 1976. pap. 3.95 (ISBN 0-374-51322-8, N523). FS&G.
Wimsatt, William K. Hateful Contraries: Studies in Literature & Criticism. LC 65-11823. 280p. 1965. 17.00x (ISBN 0-8131-1099-8); pap. 6.00 (ISBN 0-8131-0110-7). U Pr of Ky.
Woolf, Leonard & Woolf, Virginia, eds. Hogarth Essays. LC 70-121478. (Essay Index Reprint Ser). 18.00 (ISBN 0-8369-1709-X). Arno.
Wordsworth, Elizabeth. Essays, Old & New. 160p. 1980. Repr. of 1919 ed. lib. bdg. 17.50 (ISBN 0-8492-2996-0). R West.
Wordsworth, J. C. Adventures in Literature. LC 78-105855. 1970. Repr. of 1919 ed. 13.50 (ISBN 0-8046-1366-4). Kennikat.
Wyndham, George. Essays in Romantic Literature. facs. ed. LC 68-54370. (Essay Index Reprint Ser). 1919. 20.50 (ISBN 0-8369-1013-3). Arno.

LITERATURE–ANTHOLOGIES
see Anthologies

LITERATURE–BIBLIOGRAPHY

Adler, Betty. H. L. M. The Mencken Bibliography, a Ten Year Supplement. 1971. 3.50 (ISBN 0-910556-02-4). Enoch Pratt.
American Library Association. American Library Association Index to General Literature, 3 vols. Incl. Vol. 1. Basic Volume. 65.00 (ISBN 0-87650-017-3); Vol. 2. Supplement. 30.00 (ISBN 0-87650-018-1); Vol. 3. Author Index. (Cumulative Author Index Ser., No. 4). 1971. 30.00 (ISBN 0-87650-019-X). LC 79-143240. 110.00 set (ISBN 0-685-24375-3). Pierian.
American Society of Appraisers. The Bibliography of Appraisal Literature. LC 73-92529. 769p. 1974. 30.00 (ISBN 0-937828-18-1). Am Soc Appraisers.
Armitage, Andrew D. & Tudor, Nancy, eds. Canadian Essay & Literature Index 1974. LC 75-7703. 1976. 40.00 (ISBN 0-8020-4525-1). U of Toronto Pr.

Balukhatyi, Sergei D. Teoriia Literatury: Annotirovannaia Bibliografiia. 15.50 (ISBN 0-384-03170-6). Johnson Repr.
Billick, David J. Jose De Espronceda: An Annotated Bibliography, 1834 to 1978. LC 80-8514. 200p. 1981. lib. bdg. 25.00 (ISBN 0-8240-9470-0). Garland Pub.
Bond, Donald F., compiled by. The Eighteenth Century. LC 74-28590. (Goldentree Bibliographies in Language & Literature Ser). (Orig.). 1975. pap. 12.95x (ISBN 0-88295-547-0). Harlan Davidson.
Brunton, David W., ed. Index to the Contemporary Scene, Vol. 1. LC 73-645955. 122p. 1973. 28.00 (ISBN 0-8103-1056-2). Gale.
Chicorel, Marietta, ed. & intro. by. Chicorel Index to the Spoken Arts on Discs, Tapes, & Cassettes, Vol 7. 500p. 1973. 85.00 (ISBN 0-934598-62-2). Am Lib Pub Co.
Cirtautas, Arista M., compiled by. Nicholas Poppe: A Bibliography of Publications from 1924-1977. (Parerga Ser.: No. 4). 62p. 1978. pap. 3.75 (ISBN 0-295-95601-1). U of Wash Pr.
Danielson, Henry. Arthur Machen: A Bibliography. LC 73-13506. 1923. lib. bdg. 15.00 (ISBN 0-8414-3683-5). Folcroft.
Erdman, David V., et al, eds. The Romantic Movement: A Selective & Critical Bibliography for Nineteen Seventy-Nine. LC 80-8494. 350p. 1980. lib. bdg. 35.00 (ISBN 0-8240-9512-X). Garland Pub.
Essay & General Literature Index: Works Indexed 1900-1969. 16.00 (ISBN 0-8242-0503-0). Wilson.
Faculty of Comparative Literature, Livingston College. A Syllabus of Comparative Literature. 2nd ed. McCormick, John O., ed. LC 72-8502. 1972. 10.00 (ISBN 0-8108-0555-3). Scarecrow.
Fomin, Aleksandr G. Putevoditel' Po Bibliografii. Repr. of 1934 ed. 19.50 (ISBN 0-384-16350-5). Johnson Repr.
Fuller, George W., ed. A Bibliography of Bookplate Literature. LC 72-178635. 151p. 1971. Repr. of 1926 ed. 28.00 (ISBN 0-8103-3190-X). Gale.
Grimes, Janet & Daims, Diva. Novels in English by Women, 1891 to 1920: A Preliminary Checklist. Robinson, Doris, ed. LC 79-7911. (Reference Library of Humanities Ser.: Vol. 202). 805p. 1981. lib. bdg. 100.00 (ISBN 0-8240-9522-7). Garland Pub.
Halkett & Laing. A Dictionary of Anonymous & Pseudonymous Publications in the English Language: Vol. 1, 1475-1640. Horden, John, ed. 1980. 150.00 (ISBN 0-582-55521-3). Longman.
Hall, Vernon, compiled by. Literary Criticisms: Plato Through Johnson. LC 76-123515. (Goldentree Bibliographies in Language & Literature Ser). (Orig.). 1970. pap. 6.95x (ISBN 0-88295-516-0). Harlan Davidson.
Harris, William J. First Printed Translations into English of the Great Foreign Classics. LC 76-40014. 1909. lib. bdg. 11.95 (ISBN 0-8414-4924-4). Folcroft.
Harvard University Library. Literature, General & Comparative: Classified, Alphabetical, & Chronological Listings. LC 68-15926. (Widener Library Shelflist Ser: No. 18). 1968. 10.00x (ISBN 0-674-53650-9). Harvard U Pr.
Jakobson, Roman. Roman Jakobson: A Bibliography of His Writings. LC 70-180723. (Janua Linguarum, Ser. Minor: No. 134). 60p. 1971. pap. text ed. 11.25x (ISBN 90-2791-816-3). Mouton.
Johnson, Robert O. An Index to Literature in the New Yorker, 1955-1970, Vols. 31-45. LC 71-7740. 1971. 20.50 (ISBN 0-8108-0413-1). Scarecrow.
Kesavan, B. S. The National Bibliography of Indian Literature, 1901-1953, 4 vols. 1962-1974 ed. Incl. Vol. 1. Assamese-Bengali-English-Gujaratt. Kulkarni, V. Y., ed; Vol. 2. Hindi-Jannada-Kashmiri-Malayalam. Mulay, Y. M., ed; Vol. 3. Marathi-Oriya-Panjabi-Sanskrit; Vol. 4. Sindhi-Tamil-Teleyu-Urdu. 1978. 150.00 set (ISBN 0-685-85184-2); 40.00 ea. Heinman.
List of Serial Publications in the British Museum (Natural History, 3 vols. 3rd ed. 1436p. 1980. Set. 125.00x (ISBN 0-565-00823-4). U Pr of Va.
Magill, Frank N., ed. Magill Books Index. LC 80-53597. 800p. 1980. 35.00 (ISBN 0-89356-200-9). Salem Pr.
Mais, S. P. From Shakespeare to O. Henry: Studies in Literature. 317p. 1981. Repr. of 1923 ed. lib. bdg. 25.00 (ISBN 0-8495-3854-8). Arden Lib.
Meserole, Harrison T., compiled by. MLA International Bibliography of Books & Articles on the Modern Languages & Literatures, 1971. 834p. 1973. 150.00x (ISBN 0-87352-213-3). Modern Lang.
--MLA International Bibliography of Books & Articles on the Modern Languages & Literatures, 1972. 955p. 1974. 150.00x (ISBN 0-87352-221-4). Modern Lang.
--MLA International Bibliography of Books & Articles on the Modern Languages & Literatures, 1969. 723p. 1970. 150.00x (ISBN 0-87352-409-8). Modern Lang.
MLA Directory of Periodicals: A Guide to Journals & Series in Languages & Literatures. 541p. 1979. 65.00x (ISBN 0-87352-414-4). Modern Lang.
MLA International Bibliography of Books & Articles on the Modern Languages & Literatures, 1979. LC 64-20773. 1061p. 1980. 150.00x (ISBN 0-87352-418-7). Modern Lang.
MLA International Bibliography of Books & Articles on the Modern Languages & Literatures, 1978. LC 64-20773. 1045p. 1979. 150.00x (ISBN 0-87352-413-6). Modern Lang.
MLA International Bibliography of Books & Articles on the Modern Languages & Literatures, 1976. LC 64-20773. 902p. 1978. 150.00x (ISBN 0-87352-403-9). Modern Lang.
Modern Language Association. Bibliography on the Relations of Literature & the Other Arts. LC 68-58407. Repr. of 1967 ed. 18.00 (ISBN 0-404-04348-8). AMS Pr.
Moore, Ernest R. Bibliografia De Novelistas De la Revolucion Mexicana. LC 72-82322. 189p. 1973. Repr. of 1941 ed. 18.50 (ISBN 0-8337-4661-8). B Franklin.
Patterson, Margaret C., ed. Author Newsletters & Journals. LC 79-63742. (American Literature, English Literature, & World Literature in English Information Guide Ser.: Vol. 19). 1979. 36.00 (ISBN 0-8103-1432-0). Gale.
Radcliffe, Elsa J. Gothic Novels of the Twentieth Century: An Annotated Bibliography. LC 78-24357. 291p. 1979. lib. bdg. 13.00 (ISBN 0-8108-1190-1). Scarecrow.
Sadleir, Michael. Excursions in Victorian Bibliography. LC 72-194779. 1922. lib. bdg. 20.00 (ISBN 0-8414-7510-5). Folcroft.
Salomon, Brownell. Critical Analyses in Renaissance Drama: A Bibliographic Guide. 1979. 13.00 (ISBN 0-87972-127-8); pap. 6.95 (ISBN 0-87972-125-1). Bowling Green Univ.
Seidel, Alison P., compiled by. Literary Criticism & Authors' Biographies: An Annotated Index. LC 78-11857. 1978. 11.00 (ISBN 0-8108-1172-3). Scarecrow.
Terry, Garth M. East European Languages & Literatures: A Subject & Name Index to Articles in English-Language Journals, 1900-1977. 275p. 1978. 47.50 (ISBN 0-903450-21-6). ABC-Clio.
Tucker, Lena L. A Bibliography of Fifteenth Century Literature. LC 73-138541. 1974. Repr. of 1928 ed. lib. bdg. 17.50 (ISBN 0-8414-8528-3). Folcroft.
--Bibliography of Fifteenth Century Literature, with Special Reference to the History of English Culture. 1974. lib. bdg. 49.95 (ISBN 0-87968-738-X). Gordon Pr.
Turner, Mary C., ed. Libros En Venta Supplement 1978. 1980. 42.50 (ISBN 0-8352-1278-5). Bowker.
Ward, Philip. A Lifetime's Reading: Five Hundred Great Classics of World Literature for a Private Library. (Oleander Reference Bks.: Vol. 5). 388p. 1981. 29.95 (ISBN 0-900891-73-4); pap. 25.00 (ISBN 0-900891-74-2). Oleander Pr.
Weber, J. Sherwood. Good Reading: A Guide for Serious Readers. rev. ed. 1980. pap. 3.50 (ISBN 0-451-61909-9, ME1909, Ment). NAL.
Welch, Jeffrey. Liturature & Film: An Annotated Bibliography, 1900 to 1977. LC 80-8509. 350p. 1981. lib. bdg. 40.00 (ISBN 0-8240-9478-6). Garland Pub.
Worthington, Greville. A Bibliography of the Waverly Novels. 143p. 1980. Repr. of 1931 ed. lib. bdg. 30.00 (ISBN 0-8495-5655-4). Arden Lib.
Wyatt, Andrea. Bibliography of the Works of Larry Eigner. 1970. 4.50 (ISBN 0-685-04666-4, Pub. by Oyez). SBD.
Zahorski, Kenneth J. & Boyer, Robert H. Lloyd Alexander, Evangeline Walton Ensley & Kenneth Morris: A Primary & Secondary Bibliography. (Reference Bks). 1981. lib. bdg. 23.00 (ISBN 0-8161-8055-5). G K Hall.

LITERATURE–BIO-BIBLIOGRAPHY

Havlice, Patricia P. Index to Literary Biography, 2 vols. LC 74-8315. 1975. Set. 47.50 (ISBN 0-8108-0745-9). Scarecrow.
Langnas, I. A. & List, Jacob S., eds. Concise Dictionary of Literature. LC 60-15958. 1963. 6.00 (ISBN 0-8022-0924-6). Philos Lib.
Langnas, Isaac A. & List, Jacob S. Major Writers of the World. (Quality Paperback: No. 148). 1963. pap. 4.95 (ISBN 0-8226-0148-6). Littlefield.
Richardson, Kenneth, ed. Twentieth Century Writing: A Reader's Guide to Contemporary Literature. 1970. 20.00 (ISBN 0-693-01700-7). Transatlantic.
Tod, T. M. Necrology of Literary Celebrities Thirteen Twenty One to Nineteen Forty Three. LC 72-195326. 1947. lib. bdg. 10.00 (ISBN 0-8414-8426-0). Folcroft.

LITERATURE–BIOGRAPHY

see Authors

LITERATURE–COLLECTIONS

Here are entered general collections. For collections limited to specific periods see subdivisions below, e.g. Literature, Medieval; Literature, Modern.

Abramowitz, Isidore, ed. Great Prisoners: The First Anthology of Literature Written in Prison. facsimile ed. LC 74-38782. (Essay Index Reprint Ser). Repr. of 1946 ed. 40.00 (ISBN 0-8369-2563-7). Arno.
Addison, Joseph & Steele, Richard. Selections from The Tatler & The Spectator. 2nd ed. LC 79-97857. (Rinehart Editions). 1970. pap. text ed. 5.95 (ISBN 0-03-080790-5, HoltC). HR&W.
Alta. The Shameless Hussy: Selected Prose & Poetry. LC 80-15551. (The Crossing Press Feminist Ser.). 1980. 10.95 (ISBN 0-89594-035-3); pap. 5.95 (ISBN 0-89594-036-1). Crossing Pr.
Altenbernd, Lynn. Exploring Literature: Fiction, Poetry, Drama & Criticism. 1970. pap. text ed. 8.95 (ISBN 0-02-302050-4, 30205). Macmillan.
Altenbernd, Lynn & Lewis, Leslie L. Introduction to Literature: Stories. 3rd ed. 1980. pap. 8.95 (ISBN 0-02-302070-9). Macmillan.
Alvis, John & West, Thomas, eds. Shakespeare As Political Thinker. LC 79-51946. 220p. 1980. lib. bdg. write for info. (ISBN 0-89089-097-8). Carolina Acad Pr.
America in Literature. Incl. The Midwest. Szymanski, Ronald, ed. LC 79-4078 (ISBN 0-684-16137-0); The Northeast. Lape, James, ed. LC 78-25617 (ISBN 0-684-16063-3); The Small Town. Schultheiss, Flory J., ed. LC 79-4209 (ISBN 0-684-16138-9); The South. Marshall, Sara, ed. LC 78-25615 (ISBN 0-684-16136-2); The West. Monahan, Peter, ed. LC 78-24512 (ISBN 0-684-16087-0). (gr. 9-12). 1979. pap. 6.50 ea. (ScribC). Scribner.
Anderson, George K. & Warnock, Robert. The World in Literature. 1967. pap. 8.95x ea.; Bk. 3. (ISBN 0-673-05653-8); Bk. 4. (ISBN 0-673-05654-6). Scott F.
Ashton, Thomas L., ed. Heath Ten Short Novels. 704p. 1978. pap. text ed. 10.95 (ISBN 0-669-01029-4). Heath.
Bain, Carl, et al. Norton Introduction to Literature: Combined Shorter Ed. 1248p. 1973. pap. 7.95x (ISBN 0-393-09334-4). Norton.
Bain, Carl E., et al, eds. The Norton Introduction to Literature. 3rd ed. 1536p. 1981. pap. text ed. 11.95x (ISBN 0-393-95146-4); classroom guide 2.95x (ISBN 0-393-95158-8). Norton.
Baring, Maurice. Lost Lectures. LC 76-118411. (Essay & General Literature Index Reprint Ser). 1971. Repr. of 1932 ed. 13.50 (ISBN 0-8046-1399-0). Kennikat.
Barrows, Marjorie. One Thousand Beautiful Things. (Library of Beautiful Things: Vol. 1). (gr. 7 up). 1955. 9.95 (ISBN 0-8015-5562-0, Hawthorn). Dutton.
Beardsley, Monroe C., et al, eds. Theme & Form: An Introduction to Literature. 4th ed. 704p. 1975. text ed. 18.95 (ISBN 0-13-912972-3). P-H.
Beatty, J. L. & Johnson, Oliver A. Heritage of Western Civilization, 2 vols. 4th ed. LC 76-14894. (Illus.). 1977. Vol. 1. pap. text ed. 10.95 (ISBN 0-13-387209-2); Vol. 2. pap. 10.95 (ISBN 0-13-387217-3). P-H.
Beckett, Samuel, et al. New Writers Thirteen. (New Writing & Writers Ser.). 1976. text ed. 11.25x (ISBN 0-7145-3552-4). Humanities.
Berry, Paul. The Essential Self: An Introduction to Literature. (Illus.). 480p. 1975. pap. text ed. 9.50 (ISBN 0-07-005048-1, C); pap. text ed. 3.95 instructors' manual (ISBN 0-07-005049-X). McGraw.
Bishop, Morris, ed. Romantic Storybook. (Illus.). 1971. 14.50 (ISBN 0-8014-0658-7). Cornell U Pr.
Bland, Peter. Passing Gods. 1970. pap. 2.00 (ISBN 0-686-02018-9, Pub. by Ferry Pr); pap. 11.00 signed ltd. ed. with holograph poem (ISBN 0-686-02019-7). SBD.
Boll, Heinrich, et al. New Writing & Writers Fifteen. (Illus.). 1978. text ed. 10.00x (ISBN 0-7145-3554-0). Humanities.
Bond, Otto F., et al, eds. Graded Russian Readers, 5 bks. Incl. Bk. 1. Taman. Lermontov, Mihail L; Bk. 2. Two Stories. Pushkin, Alexander; Bk. 3. Lermontov's Bela. Lermonton, Mihail. o. p. (ISBN 0-685-24361-3); Bk. 4. Three Short Stories. Turgenev, Ivan; Bk. 5. The Provincial Lady. Turgenev, Ivan. 1961. pap. text ed. 8.95x five vols. in one (ISBN 0-669-30676-2). Heath.
Braziller, Michael & Braziller, Karen, eds. Persea Three. 152p. (Orig.). 1981. pap. 3.95 (ISBN 0-89255-057-0). Persea Bks.
Brown, Ashley & Kimmey, John L. Comedy. LC 69-10745. 1968. pap. text ed. 3.25x (ISBN 0-675-09591-3). Merrill.
--Romance. LC 69-10742. 1968. pap. text ed. 3.25x (ISBN 0-675-09587-5). Merrill.
Brown, Calvin, et al, eds. Masterworks of World Literature, 2 vols. 3rd ed. Incl. Vol. 1. Homer to Cervantes. text ed. 18.95x (ISBN 0-8290-0130-1); Vol. II. Shakespeare to Sartre. text ed. 18.95x (ISBN 0-8290-0131-X). LC 75-92884. 1970. Irvington.
Brown, Estelle P., ed. Twice Fifteen: An Anthology. (Also for Slow HS Students). (gr. 7-10). pap. text ed. 5.50 (ISBN 0-684-51504-0, SSP30, ScribC). Scribner.
Burns, Alan, et al. Red Dust Two: New Writing. LC 72-127954. (Orig.). 1972. 5.25 (ISBN 0-87376-019-0); pap. 3.00 (ISBN 0-87376-020-4). Red Dust.
Burrows, David J., et al. Myths & Motifs in Literature. LC 72-90546. 448p. (Orig.). 1973. pap. text ed. 8.95 (ISBN 0-02-905030-8). Free Pr.
Cairns, Huntington, ed. Limits of Art, 1 vol. ed. (Bollingen Ser.: No. 12). 1948. 30.00 (ISBN 0-691-09781-X). Princeton U Pr.
--Limits of Art, Vol. 1: From Homer to Chaucer. (Bollingen Ser.: No. 12). 1969. pap. 9.95 (ISBN 0-691-01755-7). Princeton U Pr.
--Limits of Art, Vol. 2: From Villon to Gibbon. (Bollingen Ser.: No. 12). 1970. pap. 9.95 (ISBN 0-691-01765-4). Princeton U Pr.
--Limits of Art, Vol. 3: From Goethe to Joyce. (Bollingen Ser.: No. 12). pap. 9.95 (ISBN 0-691-01768-9). Princeton U Pr.
Carlsen, G. R. & Gilbert, Miriam. British & Western Literature. 3rd ed. (Themes & Writers Ser). (Illus.). 1979. text ed. 15.84 (ISBN 0-07-009871-9); tchr's. ed. 13.12 (ISBN 0-07-009872-7); tests 72.00 (ISBN 0-07-009873-5). McGraw.
Carlsen, G. Robert. Encounters: Themes in Literature. 3rd ed. (Themes & Writers Ser.). (Illus.). (gr. 10). 1979. text ed. 14.64 (ISBN 0-07-009863-8, W); tchr's. resource guide 12.60 (ISBN 0-07-009864-6); tests 64.00 (ISBN 0-07-009865-4). McGraw.
--Perception: Themes in Literature. 3rd ed. Rothermich, John A., ed. (Themes & Writers Ser.). (Illus.). (gr. 8). 1979. text ed. 13.20 (ISBN 0-07-009855-7, W); resource guide 12.60 (ISBN 0-07-009856-5); tests 64.00 (ISBN 0-07-009857-3). McGraw.
Carlsen, G. Robert & Tovatt, A. Insights: Themes in Literature. 3rd ed. (Themes & Writers Ser). (Illus.). 1979. pap. text ed. 14.40 (ISBN 0-07-009859-X, W); tchr's. resource guide 13.80 (ISBN 0-07-009860-3); tests 64.00 (ISBN 0-07-009861-1). McGraw.
Carlsen, G. Robert, et al. Western Literature: Themes & Writers. 2nd ed. (Themes & Writers Ser). (Illus.). 768p. (gr. 12). 1975. text ed. 15.84 (ISBN 0-07-009906-5, W); tchr's. resource guide 6.32 (ISBN 0-07-009912-X). McGraw.
Carlsen, G. Robert, et al, eds. Encounters: Themes in Literature. 2nd ed. Tovatt. (Themes & Writers Ser). (Illus.). 768p. (gr. 10). 1972. text ed. 14.64 (ISBN 0-07-009904-9, W); tchr's. resource guide 6.32 (ISBN 0-07-009910-3). McGraw.
Cattan, Henry. The Garden of Joys. 11.95 (ISBN 0-7043-2219-6, Pub. by Quartet England). Charles River Bks.
Chandler, Frank W. The Literature of Roguery, 2 vols. 1977. Repr. of 1907 ed. lib. bdg. 85.00 set (ISBN 0-8495-0707-3). Arden Lib.
Charles Scribner's Sons Editorial Staff, ed. Stories by Foreign Authors, 10 vols in 5. 1972. Repr. of 1896 ed. lib. bdg. 90.00 set (ISBN 0-685-36671-5); Vols 1-2. Fr. (ISBN 0-8422-8152-5); Vols 3-4. Fr. - Ger. (ISBN 0-8422-8153-3); Vols 5-6. Ger. - It. (ISBN 0-8422-8154-1); Vols. 7-8. Rus.-Scand. (ISBN 0-8422-8155-X); Vols. 9-10. Span. & Polish (ISBN 0-8422-8156-8); lib. bdg. 25.00 ea., 5 individual vols. Irvington.
Cheney, L. J. The World of Man: Prose Passages from the Works of the Great Historians, Classical & English. 1933. 15.00 (ISBN 0-686-17674-X). Quaker City.
Chesterton, G. K. All Is Grist: A Book of Essays. 1971. Repr. of 1932 ed. 19.00 (ISBN 0-403-00902-2). Scholarly.
Christy, Arthur E. & Wells, Henry W., eds. World Literature. facs. ed. LC 77-149100. (Granger Index Reprint Ser). 1947. 58.00 (ISBN 0-8369-6225-7). Arno.
Clark, Bruce B. & Thomas, Robert K. Favorite Selections from Out of the Best Books. LC 79-12533. 1979. 7.95 (ISBN 0-87747-757-4). Deseret Bk.
Clark, C. E., Jr. & Bruccoli, Matthew J., eds. Pages: The World of Books, Writers & Writing, Vol. 1. LC 76-20369. (Illus.). 1976. 24.00 (ISBN 0-8103-0925-4). Gale.
Clark, David R. That Black Day: The Manuscripts of 'Crazy Jane on the Day of Judgement' (New Years Papers Ser.: No. XVIII). (Illus.). 56p. 1980. pap. text ed. 11.75x (ISBN 0-85105-355-6, Dolmen Pr). Humanities.

Cole, Toby, ed. Venice: A Portable Reader. LC 78-19857. 1979. 12.00 (ISBN 0-88208-097-0); pap. 6.95 1980 (ISBN 0-88208-107-1). Lawrence Hill.
Columbia University Course in Literature, Based on the World's Best Literature, 18 Vols. facs. ed. LC 68-58779. (Essay Index Reprint Ser). 1929. Set. 450.00 (ISBN 0-8369-0037-5). Arno.
Conroy, Jack & Johnson, Curt, eds. Writers in Revolt: The Anvil Anthology, 1933-1940. LC 73-81748. 256p. 1973. 8.95 (ISBN 0-88208-025-3); pap. 4.95 (ISBN 0-88208-026-1). Lawrence Hill.
Coser, Lewis A. Sociology Through Literature. 2nd ed. 544p. 1972. pap. text ed. 11.95 (ISBN 0-13-821538-3). P-H.
Crane, Stephen. Red Badge of Courage, with Reader's Guide. (AMSCO Literature Program). (gr. 9-12). 1971. pap. text ed. 4.17 (ISBN 0-87720-811-5); tchrs. ed. 2.70 (ISBN 0-87720-911-1). AMSCO Sch.
Curley, Daniel, et al, eds. Accent: An Anthology, 1940-60. LC 73-76274. 544p. 1973. 22.50 (ISBN 0-252-00349-7). U of Ill Pr.
Curtius, Ernst R. Essays on European Literature. Kowal, Michael, tr. from Ger. 484p. 1973. 35.00 (ISBN 0-691-06252-8); pap. 12.50 (ISBN 0-691-10010-1). Princeton U Pr.
Davis, Joseph K., et al. Literature. 1977. text ed. 13.95x (ISBN 0-673-15009-7). Scott F.
Deluxe Classics, 14 vols. 1976. 77.00 set (ISBN 0-8277-4975-9). British Bk Ctr.
DeMoss, Arthur, ed. The Family Album: 1978 Edition. DeMoss, Nancy. (Illus.). 1977. 8.95 (ISBN 0-87981-086-6). Holman.
Denton Senior Citizens. I Remember: A Collection of the Writings of Denton Senior Citizens. Emery, Sarah & Cloud, Josie H., eds. LC 81-66721. (Illus.). xii, 123p. (Orig.). 1981. pap. 5.00 (ISBN 0-9606146-0-5). Denton Senior Ctr.
De Tocqueville, Alexis, et al. Bitch-Goddess Success. LC 68-15189. 1968. 5.95x (ISBN 0-87130-000-1). Eakins.
Dodd Mead & Co. One Hundred Twenty Fifth Anniversary Anthology. 1964. 5.00 (ISBN 0-396-05035-2). Dodd.
Downs, Robert B. Famous American Books. LC 72-172256. 394p. 1971. 12.95 (ISBN 0-07-017665-5, P&RB). McGraw.
Edwards, Eleanor M., compiled by. Great Mystery Stories. LC 60-6578. (The Lion Classics Ser). (Illus.). 160p. (YA) 1981. lib. bdg. 6.98 (ISBN 0-87460-194-0); pap. 1.95 (ISBN 0-87460-195-9). Lion Bks.
--Great Stories About Animals. LC 67-17991. (Illus.). 160p. (YA) 1979. PLB 6.98 (ISBN 0-87460-198-3); pap. 1.95 (ISBN 0-87460-199-1). Lion Bks.
--Great Stories About Horses. new ed. LC 63-18759. (Illus.). 160p. (YA) 1972. PLB 6.98 (ISBN 0-87460-202-5); pap. 1.95 (ISBN 0-87460-203-3). Lion Bks.
Ezzo, Elsie B. Bought for a Dollar & Other Exciting Stories of China. 1969. pap. 1.25 (ISBN 0-88243-505-1, 02-0505). Gospel Pub.
Fadiman, Clifton. Reading I've Liked. 1958. pap. 3.50 (ISBN 0-671-60750-2, Fireside). S&S.
Fadiman, Clifton, ed. Fantasia Mathematica. pap. 2.95 (ISBN 0-671-24451-5, Fireside). S&S.
--Mathematical Magpie. 1964. pap. 1.95 (ISBN 0-671-45511-7, Fireside). S&S.
Ferretti, Val S. & Scott, David L. Death in Literature. (Patterns in Literary Art Ser). (gr. 10-12). 1977. pap. text ed. 6.12 (ISBN 0-07-020633-3, W). McGraw.
Freeman, E. M., ed. Campfire Chillers. LC 79-28318. (Illus.). 192p. (Orig.). 1980. pap. 6.95 (ISBN 0-686-26886-5). East Woods.
Frome, J. & Spenser, D. Moods: An Anthology of Prose & Verse. 1977. Repr. 25.00 (ISBN 0-89984-183-X). Century Bookbindery.
Frye, Northrop, et al. The Practical Imagination: Stories, Poems, Plays. 1980. text ed. 17.50 scp (ISBN 0-06-040455-8, HarpC); instructor's manual free. Har-Row.
Galloway, D., et al. New Writers 12. (New Writing & Writers Ser). 1976. text ed. 11.25x (ISBN 0-7145-3542-7). Humanities.
Gant, Roland, ed. & intro. by. Edward Thomas in the Countryside. 1977. 14.95 (ISBN 0-571-10799-0, Pub. by Faber & Faber); pap. 6.95 (ISBN 0-571-11779-1). Merrimack Bk Serv.
Garnett, Richard, et al, eds. The International Library of Famous Literature, 20 vols. 1977. Repr. lib. bdg. 500.00 (ISBN 0-8414-2023-8). Folcroft.
Garrett, Horder W. The Sunlit Road: Readings in Verse & Prose for Every Day. 1978. Repr. of 1908 ed. lib. bdg. 20.00 (ISBN 0-8492-5242-3). R West.
Gass, Sherlock B. Criers of the Shops. facs. ed. LC 74-142633. (Essay Index Reprint Ser). 1925. 18.00 (ISBN 0-8369-2049-X). Arno.
Gillespie, Sheena & Stanley, Linda. The Treehouse: An Introduction to Literature. (Illus.). 352p. 1974. pap. text ed. 9.95x (ISBN 0-87626-878-5). Winthrop.
Goddard, Harold C. Alphabet of the Imagination. Worthen, Eleanor, ed. 257p. 1974. text ed. 10.00x (ISBN 0-391-00250-3). Humanities.
Greenberg, Sidney S., ed. Treasury of Comfort. pap. 4.00 (ISBN 0-87980-167-0). Wilshire.
Grossinger, Richard & Hough, Lindy, eds. Ethnoastronomy. (Illus.). 210p. 1971. pap. 6.00 (ISBN 0-913028-08-8). North Atlantic.
Gulliveriana, No. 1. Incl. A Trip to the Moon. McDermot, Murtagh. Repr. of 1728 ed; A Trip to the Moon. Lunatic, Humphrey. Repr. of 1764 ed. LC 73-133329. 220p. 1970. 25.00x (ISBN 0-8201-1084-1). Schol Facsimiles.
Guth, Hans P. Literature. 2nd ed. (Orig.). 1968. pap. 14.95x (ISBN 0-534-00667-1). Wadsworth Pub.
Haining, Peter, ed. A Thousand Afternoons: Anthology of Bullfighting. 15.00x (ISBN 0-8464-0924-0). Beekman Pubs.
Halberstam, B. J., et al, eds. The Collected Works of Harold Davenport, Vol. I. 1978. 64.00 (ISBN 0-12-099301-5). Acad Pr.
Haldeman-Julius, E. A. A Miscellany of the Little Blues Books. 2700.00 (ISBN 0-87968-290-6). Gordon Pr.
Hardison, O. B., Jr. & Mills, Jerry L. Forms of Imagination: An Anthology of Poetry, Fiction & Drama. 1972. pap. text ed. 10.95 (ISBN 0-13-329516-8). P-H.
Harter, Penny & Higginson, William J., eds. Between Two Rivers: Union County Literature Today. 112p. (Orig.). 1980. pap. 4.95 (ISBN 0-89120-017-7). From Here.
Hawthorne, Julian. Masterpieces & the History of Literature Analysis, 10 vols. Hawthorne, Julian, et al, eds. LC 73-115245. 1972. Repr. of 1899 ed. Set. 395.00 (ISBN 0-403-03641-0). Scholarly.
Hawthorne, Julian, et al, eds. The Literature of All Nations & All Ages (History, Character, & Incident, 10 vols. 1978. Repr. of 1899 ed. Set. lib. bdg. 300.00 (ISBN 0-8482-4410-9). Norwood Edns.
Henry, N., compiled by. A Round of Tales from Washington Irving to Algernon Blackwood. 192p. 1981. Repr. of 1924 ed. lib. bdg. 20.00 (ISBN 0-89987-049-X). Darby Bks.
Herman, Jan, ed. Something Else Yearbook 1974. LC 72-90050. (Illus.). 1973. pap. 9.00 (ISBN 0-87110-091-6). Ultramarine Pub.
Hibbard, Addison & Frenz, Horst, eds. Writers of the Western World. 2nd ed. LC 67-6008. 1967. text ed. 21.50 (ISBN 0-395-04601-7, 3-24495). HM.
Hough, G. Selected Essays. LC 77-85692. 1978. 32.50 (ISBN 0-521-21901-9). Cambridge U Pr.
Howe, Irving, et al, eds. Literature As Experience: An Anthology. 1104p. 1979. pap. text ed. 11.95 (ISBN 0-15-551113-0, HC); instructor's manual avail. (ISBN 0-15-551114-9). HarBraceJ.
Howells, William D. My Literary Passions. LC 74-131753. 1970. Repr. of 1895 ed. 8.00 (ISBN 0-403-00640-6). Scholarly.
Hrabal, Bohmil. Closely Watched Trains. (Writers from the Other Europe Ser). 1981. pap. 4.95 (ISBN 0-14-005808-7). Penguin.
Hudson, W. H. South American Romances: The Purple Lane; Green Mansions; el Ombu. 823p. 1981. Repr. of 1930 ed. lib. bdg. 40.00 (ISBN 0-89987-368-5). Darby Bks.
Hutchins, Robert M. & Adler, Mortimer, eds. Great Books of the Western World, 54 Vols. (YA) (gr. 9 up). 1952. write for info. (ISBN 0-85229-163-9). Ency Brit Ed.
The Jackdaw's Nest: A Fivefold Anthology. 1977. Repr. of 1929 ed. 20.00 (ISBN 0-89984-158-9). Century Bookbindery.
John, D. A., ed. Virgil's Georgics: Selections. (Illus.). 152p. (Orig.). 1973. pap. 4.50 (ISBN 0-571-09731-6, Pub. by Faber & Faber). Merrimack Bk Serv.
Kimmey, John & Brown, Ashley, eds. The World of Tragedy. 1981. pap. 4.50 (ISBN 0-451-61991-9, ME1991, Ment). NAL.
Kittredge, Bill & Krauzer, Steven M., eds. Great Action Stories. (RL 9). 1977. pap. 1.95 (ISBN 0-451-61915-3, MJ1915, Ment). NAL.
Knickerbocker, K. L. & Reninger, H. W. Interpreting Literature: Preliminaries to Literary Judgment. 6th ed. LC 77-24453. 1978. text ed. 14.95 (ISBN 0-03-020331-7, HoltC); inst. manual avail. (ISBN 0-03-023006-3). HR&W.
Laughlin, J., et al, eds. New Directions Forty-One: Anthology. LC 37-1751. 192p. 1980. 15.95 (ISBN 0-8112-0770-6); pap. 5.95 (ISBN 0-8112-0771-4, NDP505). New Directions.
Laughlin, James, ed. New Directions in Prose & Poetry 24. LC 37-1751. 224p. 1972. pap. 3.45 (ISBN 0-8112-0127-9, NDP332). New Directions.
Lehmann, John. New Writing in Europe. 1977. Repr. of 1940 ed. 15.00 (ISBN 0-89984-212-7). Century Bookbindery.
Levitas, G. B., ed. The World of Psychology, 2 Vols. 17.50, boxed set (ISBN 0-8076-0208-6). Braziller.
Levy, Howard S., tr. Translation from Po Chu-I's Collected Works, 2 vols. Incl. Vol. 1. The Old Style Poems. 13.50 (ISBN 0-685-27137-4); Vol. 2. The Regular Poems. 10.00 (ISBN 0-685-27138-2). 540p. 1971. Paragon.
Lister, Raymond. Little Treasury of Familiar Prose. (Little Treasury Ser.). 1964. 2.50 (ISBN 0-212-35942-8). Dufour.
Les Litteratures Populaires de Toutes les Nations: Conteurs et Poetes de Tous Pays, 53 vols. Set. 695.00 (ISBN 0-685-34000-7). French & Eur.
Litz, A. Walton, ed. The Scribner Quarto of Modern Literature. LC 77-13423. 1978. text ed. 14.95x (ISBN 0-684-15336-X, ScribC). Scribner.
London, Ephraim, ed. World of Law, 2 Vols. 1960. Set. 25.00 (ISBN 0-671-82936-X). S&S.
London, Jack. Call of the Wild with Reader's Guide. (Literature Program). (gr. 10-12). 1970. pap. text ed. 3.92 (ISBN 0-87720-804-2); tchrs' ed. 2.60 (ISBN 0-87720-904-9). AMSCO Sch.
--Martin Eden with Reader's Guide. (AMSCO Literature Program Ser). (gr. 10-12). 1971. pap. text ed. 4.33 (ISBN 0-87720-812-3); tchr's ed. 2.80 (ISBN 0-87720-912-X). AMSCO Sch.
Macaulay, Thomas B. Prose & Poetry: Selected by G. M. Young. (Reynard Library). 864p. 1952. pap. text ed. 7.95x (ISBN 0-674-71631-0). Harvard U Pr.
McFarland, Philip, et al. Perceptions in Literature. (Literature Ser.). (Illus.). (gr. 10). 1972. text ed. 10.18 (ISBN 0-395-11200-1, 2-26536); tchr's resource bk. 5.40 (ISBN 0-395-12621-5, 2-26537). HM.
McFarland, Philip J., et al. Focus on Action. LC 76-53136. (Focus on Literature Ser.). (Illus.). (gr. 7). 1977. text ed. 9.39 (ISBN 0-395-24966-X); tchr's guide 3.09 (ISBN 0-395-24964-3). HM.
--Focus on America. LC 76-53136. (Focus on Literature Ser.). (Illus.). (gr. 11). 1977. text ed. 15.32 (ISBN 0-395-24962-7); tchr's guide 5.76 (ISBN 0-395-24961-9). HM.
--Focus on Forms. LC 76-53136. (Focus on Literature Ser.). (Illus., Gr. 10). 1977. text ed. 14.80 (ISBN 0-395-24970-8); teachers guide 5.24 (ISBN 0-395-24963-5). HM.
--Focus on Ideas. LC 76-53136. (Focus on Literature Ser.). (Illus., Gr. 12). 1977. text ed. 15.32 (ISBN 0-395-24960-0); teachers guide 5.76 (ISBN 0-395-24959-7). HM.
--Focus on People. LC 76-53136. (Focus on Literature Ser.). (Illus.). (gr. 8). 1977. text ed. 9.39 (ISBN 0-395-24965-1); tchr's guide 3.09 (ISBN 0-395-24967-8). HM.
--Focus on Viewpoints. LC 76-53136. (Focus on Literature Ser.). (Illus., Gr. 9). 1977. text ed. 14.80 (ISBN 0-395-24968-6); tcr's guide 5.24 (ISBN 0-395-24969-4). HM.
McGinn, Donald J. & Howerton, G., eds. Literature As a Fine Art. LC 66-29576. (Illus.). 1967. Repr. of 1959 ed. 12.50 (ISBN 0-87752-069-0). Gordian.
Mack, Maynard, et al, eds. The Norton Anthology of World Masterpieces, 2 vols. 4th ed. 1979. text ed. 18.95x (ISBN 0-393-95036-0); Vol II. text ed. 18.95x (ISBN 0-393-95040-9); Vol I. pap. text ed. 15.95x (ISBN 0-393-95045-X); Vol II. pap. text ed. 15.95x (ISBN 0-393-95050-6). Norton.
--World Masterpieces, 2 vols. rev. ed. (Orig.). 1965. Vol. 1. text ed. 9.95x (ISBN 0-393-09624-6); Vol. 2. text ed. 9.45x (ISBN 0-393-09661-0); Vol. 1. pap. 8.25x (ISBN 0-393-09659-9); Vol. 2. pap. 7.75x (ISBN 0-393-09547-9). Norton.
--World Masterpieces, 2 vols. 3rd ed. 1973. text ed. 13.95x ea. Vol. 1 (ISBN 0-393-09421-9). Vol. 2 (ISBN 0-393-09658-0). pap. text ed. 10.95x ea.; Vol. 1. pap. (ISBN 0-393-09616-5); Vol. 2. pap. (ISBN 0-393-09717-X). Norton.
Marvin, Frederic R. Last Words (Real & Traditional) of Distinguished Men & Women. LC 72-140424. 1971. Repr. of 1910 ed. 22.00 (ISBN 0-8103-3187-X). Gale.
Miller, Ernest R., compiled by. Harvest of Gold. LC 72-92720. (Illus.). 96p. 1973. boxed 4.95 (ISBN 0-8378-1760-9). Gibson.
Miller, Ruth. Black American Literature: 1760 to the Present. 1971. pap. text ed. 17.95x (ISBN 0-02-476420-5, 47642). Macmillan.
Mirikitani, Janice, et al, eds. Time to Greez! Incantations from the Third World. LC 75-355. (Illus.). 224p. (Orig.). 1975. pap. 4.95 (ISBN 0-912078-44-8). New Glide.
Monroe, Lewis B., ed. Miscellaneous Readings. LC 71-38603. (Granger Reprint Ser). 1872. 19.00 (ISBN 0-8369-6335-0). Arno.
Moore, Arthur K. Contestable Concepts of Literary Theory. LC 73-77654. 256p. 1973. 17.50 (ISBN 0-8071-0057-9). La State U Pr.
Morris, Alton C., et al. Imaginative Literature. 3rd ed. 1978. text ed. 11.95 (ISBN 0-15-540729-5, HC); instructor's manual avail.; study guide 5.95 (ISBN 0-15-540731-7). HarBraceJ.
Morris, Audrey S. One Thousand Inspirational Things. (Library of Beautiful Things: Vol. 2). (YA) (gr. 9-12). 1956. 9.95 (ISBN 0-8015-5568-X, Hawthorn). Dutton.
Muggeridge, Malcolm. Things Past. Hunter, Ian A., ed. LC 78-71376. 1979. 9.95 (ISBN 0-688-03445-4). Morrow.
Mukarovsky, Jan. The Word & Verbal Art: Selected Essays by Jan Mukarovsky. Steiner, Peter & Steiner, Peter, eds. LC 76-49733. (Yale Russian & East European Ser.: No. 13). 1977. 18.50x (ISBN 0-300-01573-9). Yale U Pr.
Mulliken, Robert S. Selected Papers of Robert S. Mulliken. Hinze, J. & Ramsay, D. A., eds. LC 74-11633. xvi, 1128p. 1975. lib. bdg. 47.50x (ISBN 0-226-54847-3). U of Chicago Pr.
Neider, Charles. Short Novels of the Masters. enl. ed. LC 77-152908. 1972. text ed. 7.95 (ISBN 0-03-083051-6, HoltC). HR&W.
New Statesman. New Statesmanship. Hyams, E., ed. LC 72-128281. (Essay Index Reprint Ser). 1963. 19.00 (ISBN 0-8369-1891-6). Arno.
New Writing & Writers Fifteen. 1978. pap. 4.95 (ISBN 0-7145-3561-3). Riverrun NY.
Norris, Faith G. & Springer, Sharon J., eds. Men in Exile. LC 73-3485. (Illus.). 1973. 10.00 (ISBN 0-87071-319-1); pap. 6.00 (ISBN 0-87071-321-3). Oreg St U Pr.
Northouse, Cameron, ed. Concept: An Anthology of Contemporary Writing. (Orig.). 1979. pap. 9.95 (ISBN 0-89683-014-4). New London Pr.
Parrish, Paul A. Celebration: An Introduction to Literature. 1977. pap. text ed. 13.95 (ISBN 0-87626-113-6). Winthrop.
Partridge, Eric, ed. Ixion in Heaven & Endymion: Disraeli's Skit & Aytoun's Burlesque. facs. ed. LC 76-117903. (Select Bibliographies Reprint Ser). 1927. 12.00 (ISBN 0-8369-5356-8). Arno.
Partridge, Eric, et al, eds. Martial Medley. facs. ed. LC 73-117905. (Select Bibliographies Reprint Ser). 1931. 24.00 (ISBN 0-8369-5358-4). Arno.
Perrine, Laurence. Story & Structure. 5th ed. 1978. pap. text ed. 9.95 (ISBN 0-15-583786-9, HC); instructor's manual avail. (ISBN 0-15-583787-7). HarBraceJ.
Picano, Felice, ed. A True Likeness: An Anthology of Lesbian and Gay Writing Today. 320p. 1980. pap. 9.95 (ISBN 0-686-77525-2) (ISBN 0-933322-04-6). Sea Horse.
Plimpton, George, ed. Writers at Work, Vol. 5. (Writers at Work Ser.). 416p. 1981. pap. 8.95 (ISBN 0-14-005818-4). Penguin.
Porter, Peter. After Martial. 1972. pap. 4.00 (ISBN 0-19-211814-5). Oxford U Pr.
--Preaching to the Converted. 63p. 1972. pap. 4.00 (ISBN 0-19-211821-8). Oxford U Pr.
Pound, Ezra. Translations. rev. ed. LC 53-11965. 1953. pap. 7.95 (ISBN 0-8112-0164-3, NDP145). New Directions.
Praga, Anthony. Great Books Retold As Short Stories. 223p. 1981. Repr. of 1932 ed. lib. bdg. 45.00 (ISBN 0-89987-663-3). Darby Bks.
Praz, Mario. Conversation Pieces: A Survey of the Informal Group Portrait in Europe & America. LC 76-127380. (Illus.). 32.50 (ISBN 0-271-00132-1). Pa St U Pr.
Proffer, Carl R., ed. Glagol II: Al'manakh "Ardisa". (Rus.). 1978. 15.00 (ISBN 0-88233-360-7); pap. 4.00 (ISBN 0-88233-361-5). Ardis Pubs.
Proffer, Carl R. & Proffer, Ellendea, eds. Glagol III: Al'manakh "Ardisa". (Rus.). 1981. 15.00 (ISBN 0-88233-477-8); pap. 5.00 (ISBN 0-88233-478-6). Ardis Pubs.
Quinn, Edward G. & Dolan, Paul J. Relevants. 1970. pap. text ed. 5.95 (ISBN 0-02-925600-3). Free Pr.
Raeburn, Ben, ed. Treasury for the Free World. LC 72-5771. (Essay Index Reprint Ser). 1972. Repr. of 1946 ed. 25.00 (ISBN 0-8369-7293-7). Arno.
Reed, John. The Education of John Reed: Selected Writings. Stuart, John, ed. 224p. 1972. pap. 1.45 (ISBN 0-7178-0354-6). Intl Pub Co.
Rich, Mabel I., ed. Study of the Types of Literature. rev. ed. (Illus.). 1950. text ed. 38.50x (ISBN 0-89197-433-4). Irvington.
Rogers, Katharine M., ed. Before Their Time: Six Women Writers of the Eighteenth Century. LC 78-20942. 1979. 11.50 (ISBN 0-8044-2742-9); pap. 4.95 (ISBN 0-8044-6746-3). Ungar.
Rosset, Barney, ed. Evergreen Review Reader: Vol. 1. 1957-1961. LC 79-52055. (Illus.). 400p. 1979. pap. 8.95 (ISBN 0-394-17095-4, E733, Ever). Grove.
Rosten, Leo. Infinite Riches. 1979. 14.95 (ISBN 0-07-053983-9, GB). McGraw.
Rubinoff, Lionel, ed. Faith & Reason: Essays in the Philosophy of Religion by R. G. Collingwood. LC 67-21641. 352p. 1972. pap. 2.85 (ISBN 0-8129-6073-4, QP106). Times Bks.
Runes, Dagobert D., ed. Treasury of World Literature. Repr. of 1961 ed. lib. bdg. 41.00x (ISBN 0-8371-2110-8, RUWL). Greenwood.

--Treasury of World Literature. 1956. 15.00 (ISBN 0-8022-1454-1). Philos Lib.

Runte, Roseann, ed. Studies in Eighteenth-Century Culture, Vol. 8. 1979. 25.00 (ISBN 0-299-07740-3). U of Wis Pr.

Ryder, F. G. & McCormick, E. A. Lebendige Literatur: Deutsches Lesebuch Fur Anfanger. 1974. pap. text ed. 9.15 (ISBN 0-395-13826-4). HM.

Samson, Jack, ed. The Best of Corey Ford. LC 74-15474. (Illus.). 288p. 1975. 10.00 (ISBN 0-03-013501-X). HR&W.

Schmitz, Elizabeth. Dichtung Aus Osterreich, 4 pts. 6 vols. Incl. Pt. 1. Drama. 119.00 (ISBN 0-8044-0526-3); Pt. 2. Prose, 2 vols. 119.00 (ISBN 0-8044-0527-1); Pt. 3. Poetry, 2 vols. 119.00 (ISBN 0-8044-0529-8); Pt. 4. Radio Plays. 59.00 (ISBN 0-8044-0530-1). Set. 415.00 (ISBN 0-8044-0532-8). Ungar.

Scholes, Robert, et al, eds. Elements of Literature: Essay, Fiction, Poetry, Drama, Film. (Illus.). 1978. pap. text ed. 12.95x (ISBN 0-19-502265-3). Oxford U Pr.

Schwartz, Jacob. The Writings of Alfred Edgar Coppard. LC 73-10415. 1973. lib. bdg. 22.50 (ISBN 0-8414-7572-5). Folcroft.

Serpent's Egg: A Collection of Literature & Art. LC 79-84549. 1979. pap. 10.00 (ISBN 0-931350-02-6). Moonlight Pubns.

Shaw, Patick W. Literature: A College Anthology. LC 76-19905. (Illus.). 1976. text ed. 15.50 (ISBN 0-395-24841-8); instructors' manual 1.25 (ISBN 0-395-24842-6). HM.

Sheed, F. J. The Guest-Room Book. 1977. Repr. of 1948 ed. 10.00 (ISBN 0-89984-116-3). Century Bookbindery.

Shoemaker, J. W., ed. Shoemaker's Best Selections, No. 2. facs. ed. LC 79-116415. (Granger Index Reprint Ser). 1875. 13.00 (ISBN 0-8369-6185-4). Arno.

--Shoemaker's Best Selections, No. 5. facs. ed. LC 79-116415. (Granger Index Reprint Ser). 1877. 12.00 (ISBN 0-8369-6175-7). Arno.

--Shoemaker's Best Selections, No. 6. facs. ed. LC 79-116415. (Granger Index Reprint Ser). 1880. 13.00 (ISBN 0-8369-6186-2). Arno.

--Shoemaker's Best Selections, No. 7. facs. ed. LC 79-116415. (Granger Index Reprint Ser). 1880. 12.00 (ISBN 0-8369-6176-5). Arno.

Simonson, Harold P. Trio: A Book of Stories, Plays, & Poems. 5th ed. (Illus.). 1980. pap. text ed. 10.95 scp (ISBN 0-06-046186-1, HarpC); instrs.' manual free. Har-Row.

Sklar, Morty, intro. by. Cross-Fertilization: The Human Spirit As Place. (Contemporary Anthology Ser.: No. 3). (Illus.). 64p. 1980. pap. 2.50 (ISBN 0-930370-10-4) (ISBN 0-930370-10-4). Spirit That Moves.

Solomon, Barbara, ed. The Short Fiction of Mary Wilkins Freeman & Sarah Orne Jewett. (Orig.). 1979. pap. 2.95 (ISBN 0-451-51192-1, CE1192, Sig Classics). NAL.

Soyinka, Wole. Interpreters. (African American Library). 1970. pap. 1.50 (ISBN 0-02-053900-2, Collier). Macmillan.

Stegner, Wallace & Scowcroft, Richard, eds. Twenty Years of Stanford Short Stories. 1966. 15.00x (ISBN 0-8047-0394-9). Stanford U Pr.

Stegner, Wallace & Stegner, Mary, eds. Great American Short Stories. pap. 2.25 (ISBN 0-440-33060-2, LE). Dell.

Stern, Adele, ed. America in Literature: The City. (gr. 9-12). 1979. pap. text ed. 6.50 (ISBN 0-684-16139-7). Scribner.

Stillman, Peter R. Introduction to Myth. (Literature Ser.). (gr. 10 up). 1977. pap. text ed. 6.95x (ISBN 0-8104-5890-X). Hayden.

Sutherland, James, ed. The Oxford Book of Literary Anecdotes. 1976. pap. 2.95 (ISBN 0-671-80587-8). PB.

Szladits, Lola L. Nineteen Twenty-Two: a Vintage Year: A Selection of Works from the Berg Collection. (Illus.). 36p. 1972. 5.00 (ISBN 0-87104-234-7). NY Pub Lib.

Tennant, Emma. Bananas. 4.95 (ISBN 0-7043-3176-4, Pub. by Quartet England). Charles River Bks.

Thompson, Sydney. Solo Scenes from Great Writers. 80p. 1947. 4.50 (ISBN 0-573-60075-9). French.

Tomlinson, Charles. Written on Water. 54p. 1972. pap. 4.00 (ISBN 0-19-211820-X). Oxford U Pr.

Trevor, William. Lovers of Their Time. 288p. 1980. pap. 4.50 (ISBN 0-14-005140-6). Penguin.

Trilling, Lionel. Experience of Literature: Brief Ed. LC 69-19907. 1969. pap. text ed. 13.95 (ISBN 0-03-080056-0, HoltC). HR&W.

Trocchi, Alexander, et al. New Writers Three. (New Writing & Writers Ser.). 1965. pap. text ed. 6.00x (ISBN 0-7145-0401-7). Humanities.

Troupe, Quincy & Shulte, Rainer, eds. Giant Talk: An Anthology of Third World Writings. 1975. pap. 6.95 (ISBN 0-394-71443-1, V-443, Vin). Random.

Vestdijk, Simon, et al. New Writers Two. (New Writing & Writers Ser.). 1963. pap. text ed. 6.00x (ISBN 0-7145-0399-1). Humanities.

Walpole, Hugh. Famous Stories of Five Centuries. (Illus.). 1021p. 1980. Repr. lib. bdg. 25.00 (ISBN 0-8495-5818-2). Arden Lib.

Warner, Charles D., ed. Library of the World's Best Literature, 30 vols. 1975. lib. bdg. 3500.00 (ISBN 0-87968-365-1). Gordon Pr.

Watson, Lillian E. Light from Many Lamps. 1951. 10.95 (ISBN 0-671-42300-2). S&S.

White, Margaret B. & Quigley, Robert N., eds. How the Other Third Lives. LC 77-22499. 1977. 9.95 (ISBN 0-88344-190-X); pap. 4.95 (ISBN 0-88344-191-8). Orbis Bks.

Wignesian, T. Bunga Emas: An Anthology of Contemporary Malaysian Literature. 1964. lib. bdg. 20.00 (ISBN 0-8414-9731-1). Folcroft.

Wise, A. R. & Smith, Reginald A., eds. Voices on the Green: Anthology of Literature About Children. 1979. Repr. of 1945 ed. lib. bdg. 25.00 (ISBN 0-8482-7056-8). Norwood Edns.

Within & Without: Anthology of Prison Literature. 1978. pap. 2.00 (ISBN 0-931350-04-2). Moonlight Pubns.

Woods, Ralph L., ed. Treasury of the Familiar. 1942. 16.95 (ISBN 0-02-631490-8). Macmillan.

Wright, C. Kent. Nectar in a Nutshell. 1977. Repr. of 1944 ed. 10.00 (ISBN 0-89984-138-4). Century Bookbindery.

Zuntz, Gunther. Opuscula Selecta: Classics, Hellenistica, Christiana. 322p. 1972. 21.50x (ISBN 0-87471-095-2). Rowman.

Zytaruk, George J., ed. The Quest for Rananim: D.H. Lawrence's Letters to S.S. Koteliansky, 1914-1930. 1970. 14.00 (ISBN 0-7735-0054-5). McGill-Queens U Pr.

LITERATURE–COMPETITIONS

see also Floral Games

LITERATURE–DICTIONARIES

see also Fiction–Dictionaries

Bede, Jean-Albert & Edgerton, William, eds. Columbia Dictionary of Modern European Literature. 2nd ed. 800p. 1980. 5.00 (ISBN 0-231-03717-1). Columbia U Pr.

Benet, William R., ed. Reader's Encyclopedia. 2nd ed. LC 65-12510. (Illus.). 1965. 15.95 (ISBN 0-690-67128-8); thumb indexed 17.95 (ISBN 0-690-67129-6). T Y Crowell.

Bombaugh, Charles C. Gleanings for the Curious from the Harvest Fields of Literature: A Melange of Excerpta. LC 68-23465. 1970. Repr. of 1875 ed. 37.00 (ISBN 0-8103-3086-5). Gale.

--Oddities & Curiosities of Words & Literature. Gardner, M., ed. Orig. Title: Gleanings for the Curious. 1961. pap. 4.50 (ISBN 0-486-20759-5). Dover.

Bombaugh, Charles C., ed. Facts & Fancies for the Curious from the Harvest-Fields of Literature. LC 68-23464. 1968. Repr. of 1905 ed. 25.00 (ISBN 0-8103-3085-7). Gale.

Bondanella, Peter, ed. Dictionary of Italian Literature. Bondanella, Julia C. LC 78-4022. 1978. lib. bdg. 39.95x (ISBN 0-313-20421-7, BDI/). Greenwood.

Brewer, E. Cobham. Brewer's Dictionary of Phrase & Fable. Evans, Ivor H., ed. LC 79-107024. (Centenary ed.). 1971. 22.95 (ISBN 0-06-010466-X, HarpT). Har-Row.

--Reader's Handbook: Famous Names in Fiction, Allusions, References, Proverbs, Plots, Stories, & Poems, 3 vols. LC 71-134907. 1966. Repr. of 1899 ed. Set. 78.00 (ISBN 0-8103-0153-9). Gale.

Browning, D. S. Everyman's Dictionary of Literary Biography. 5th ed. (Everyman's Reference Library). 812p. 1970. 13.50x (ISBN 0-460-03008-6, Pub. by J. M. Dent England). Biblio Dist.

Capdevila Font, Juan. Diccionario de la Literatura Universal. 536p. (Espn.). 1977. 22.50 (ISBN 84-85117-41-7, S-50261). French & Eur.

Cuddon, J. A. A Dictionary of Literary Terms. LC 76-47853. 1977. 17.95 (ISBN 0-385-12713-8). Doubleday.

Daisne, John. Filmographic Dictionary of World Literature: Supplement A-Z. 1978. text ed. 96.00x (ISBN 0-391-01587-7). Humanities.

De Clarac, Pierre, ed. Dictionnaire Universel Des Lettres. 23.00 (ISBN 0-685-11144-X). French & Eur.

Diccionario Literario de Obras y Personajes de Todos los Tiempos y Paises, 12 vols. 2nd ed. De Riquer, M., ed. 11000p. (Espn.). 1972. Set. 430.00 (ISBN 84-274-0506-5, S-12328). French & Eur.

Diccionario Rioduero: Literatura, 2 vols. 648p. (Espn.). 1977. Set. 23.50 (ISBN 84-220-0820-3, S-50164). French & Eur.

Duffy, Charles & Petit, Henry. Dictionary of Literary Terms. rev. ed. pap. 2.00 (ISBN 0-910294-02-X). Brown Bk.

Encyclopedie Thematique Weber, 14: Linguistique, Litterature Universelle. 360p. (Fr.). 59.95 (ISBN 0-686-57180-0, M-6247). French & Eur.

Essay & General Literature Index, 8 vols. 1900-1979. 125.00 ea.; published semiannually incl. a bound permanent annual 5-year cumulation 50.00 (ISBN 0-686-76912-0). Wilson.

Fitzgerald, Percy. The Pickwickian Dictionary & Cyclopedia. LC 74-7473. Repr. of 1900 ed. lib. bdg. 50.00 (ISBN 0-8414-4179-0). Folcroft.

Frenzel, Elisabeth. Diccionario De Argumentos De la Literatura Universal. 496p. (Espn.). 1976. pap. 29.95 (ISBN 84-249-3140-8, S-29899). French & Eur.

--Diccionario De Argumentos De la Literatura Universal. 496p. (Espn.). 1976. 35.95 (ISBN 84-249-3141-6, S-50151). French & Eur.

Frey, Albert R. Sobriquets & Nicknames. LC 66-22671. 1966. Repr. of 1888 ed. 22.00 (ISBN 0-8103-3003-2). Gale.

Gonzalez Porto-Bompiani. Diccionario Literario De Obras y Perssonajes De Todos los Tiempos y Paises, 2 vols. 1538p. (Espn.). 1979. Set. 100.00 (ISBN 0-686-57356-0, S-50244). French & Eur.

Helmut, H. Woerterbuch des Buches. (Ger.). 1976. pap. 15.95 (ISBN 3-465-00186-9, M-6937). French & Eur.

Holden, John A. The Bookman's Glossary. 1975. Repr. of 1925 ed. 20.00 (ISBN 0-8274-4083-9). R West.

Hornstein, Lillian H., et al, eds. The Reader's Companion to World Literature. rev. ed. 1973. pap. 2.95 (ISBN 0-451-61841-6, ME1841, Ment). NAL.

Langnas, I. A. & List, Jacob S., eds. Concise Dictionary of Literature. LC 60-15958. 1963. 6.00 (ISBN 0-8022-0924-6). Philos Lib.

Langnas, Isaac A. & List, Jacob S. Major Writers of the World. (Quality Paperback: No. 148). 1963. pap. 4.95 (ISBN 0-8226-0148-6). Littlefield.

Magill, Frank N., ed. Cyclopedia of Literary Characters. 1964. 22.50 (ISBN 0-06-003990-6, HarpT); PLB 19.79 o.p (ISBN 0-06-003991-4, HarpT). Har-Row.

Magnus, Laurie. Dictionary of European Literature, Designed As a Companion to English Studies. rev. ed. (Library of Literature, Drama & Criticism Ser). Repr. of 1927 ed. 38.50 (ISBN 0-384-35050-X). Johnson Repr.

--A Dictionary of European Literature, Designed As a Companion to English Studies. rev. ed. LC 74-6269. xii, 605p. 1975. Repr. of 1927 ed. 39.00 (ISBN 0-8103-4014-3). Gale.

Mueller, U. Herder - Lexikon Literatur: Biographisches Woerterbuch. (Ger.). 1975. 15.95 (ISBN 3-451-16462-0, M-7442, Pub. by Herder). French & Eur.

--Herder - Lexikon Literatur: Sachwoerterbuch. (Ger.). 1975. 15.95 (ISBN 3-451-16464-7, M-7443, Pub. by Herder). French & Eur.

Parnaso. Diccionario Sopena De Literatura. 1820p. (Espn.). 54.00 (ISBN 84-303-0247-6, S-50140). French & Eur.

Perez Rioja, Jose A. Diccionario Literario Universal. 1024p. (Espn.). 1977. 47.95 (ISBN 84-309-0690-8, S-31441). French & Eur.

Ruediger, Horst. Kleines Literarisches Lexikon, Vol. 26. 4th ed. (Ger.). 1972. 19.95 (ISBN 3-7720-0953-0, M-7695, Pub. by Francke). French & Eur.

--Kleines Literarisches Lexikon: Autoren 1, Von Den Anfaengen Bis Zum 19. Jahrhundert, Vol. 1. 4th ed. (Ger.). 1969. 22.95 (ISBN 3-7720-0601-9, M-7503, Pub. by Francke). French & Eur.

--Kleines Literarisches Lexikon: Autoren 2, 20 Jahrhundert, Vol 2a. 4th ed. (Ger.). 1972. 19.95 (ISBN 0-686-56621-1, M-7504, Pub. by Francke). French & Eur.

--Kleines Literarisches Lexikon: Sachbegriffe, Vol. 4. 4th ed. (Ger.). 1966. 12.95 (ISBN 0-686-56622-X, M-7505, Pub. by Francke). French & Eur.

Ruttkowski, W. & Blake, R. Literaturwoerterbuch. 68p. (Ger., Eng. & Fr., Dictionary of Literature). 1969. pap. 7.95 (ISBN 3-7720-0591-8, M-7543, Pub. by A. Francke). French & Eur.

Shipley, Joseph T. Diccionario de la Literatura Mundial. 2nd ed. 564p. (Espn.). 1974. 37.50 (ISBN 84-233-0781-6, S-12359). French & Eur.

Southwick, Albert P. Wisps of Wit & Wisdom, or Knowledge in a Nutshell. LC 68-30582. 1968. Repr. of 1892 ed. 19.00 (ISBN 0-8103-3095-4). Gale.

Ungar, Frederick & Mainiero, Lina, eds. Encyclopedia of World Literature in the 20th Century, Vol. IV, Supplement & Index. LC 67-13615. 1976. 50.00 (ISBN 0-8044-3095-0). Ungar.

Van Tiegham, P. & Josserand, P., eds. Dictionnaire des litteratures, 3 Vols. 1968. Set. each 43.50 (ISBN 0-685-05207-9). Adler.

Van Tieghem, Philippe. Dictionnaire des Litt e01ratures, 2: G-N. 1436p. (Fr.). 1968. 47.50 (ISBN 0-686-57242-4, M-6546). French & Eur.

--Dictionnaire des Litt e01ratures, 3: O-Z. 1456p. (Fr.). 1968. write for info (M-6547). French & Eur.

Van Tieghen, Philippe. Dictionnaire des Litt e01ratures, 1: A-F. 1436p. (Fr.). 1968. 47.50 (ISBN 0-686-57241-6, M-6545). French & Eur.

Vega, Vincente. Diccionario Ilustrado De Frases Celebres y Citas Literarias. 939p. (Espn.). 1973. pap. 20.50 (ISBN 84-252-0128-4, S-50280). French & Eur.

Wahba, Magdi. A Dictionary of Literary Terms (English-French-Arabic) 1974. 30.00x (ISBN 0-86685-117-8). Intl Bk Ctr.

Wheeler, William A. Who Wrote It. LC 68-30667. 1968. Repr. of 1881 ed. 19.00 (ISBN 0-8103-3228-0). Gale.

--Who Wrote It? Wheeler, C. G., ed. (English Literary Reference Ser). Repr. of 1881 ed. 10.00 (ISBN 0-384-67860-2). Johnson Repr.

Wilpert, G. Sachwoerterbuch der Literatur. 873p. (Ger.). 1974. pap. 17.50 (ISBN 3-520-23105-0, M-7616, Pub. by A. Kroener). French & Eur.

Wilpert, Gero von. Lexikon der Weltliteratur: Biographisch - Bibliographisches Handwoerterbuch, Vol. 1. 2nd ed. (Ger.). 1975. 120.00 (ISBN 3-520-80702-5, M-7212). French & Eur.

--Lexikon der Weltliteratur: Werke, Vol. 2. 2nd ed. (Ger.). 1968. 77.00 (ISBN 3-520-80801-3, M-7211). French & Eur.

LITERATURE–ESTHETICS

see also Style, Literary

Barthes, Roland. Le Plaisir du Texte. 1973. 7.95 (ISBN 0-686-53940-0). French & Eur.

--The Pleasure of the Text. Miller, Richard, tr. from Fr. 80p. 1975. 5.95 (ISBN 0-8090-7722-1); pap. 3.95 (ISBN 0-8090-1380-0). Hill & Wang.

Bennett, Arnold. Literary Taste: How to Form It. LC 74-16487. (Collected Works of Arnold Bennett: Vol. 47). 1976. Repr. of 1909 ed. 18.25 (ISBN 0-518-19128-1). Arno.

Brightfield, Myron F. Issue in Literary Criticism. LC 68-23278. 1968. Repr. of 1932 ed. lib. bdg. 16.75x (ISBN 0-8371-0029-1, BRLC). Greenwood.

Burns, Gerald. Toward a Phenomenology of Written Art. LC 79-15699. 1979. 12.50 (ISBN 0-914232-36-3); pap. 4.95 (ISBN 0-914232-35-5). Treacle.

Falk, Eugene H. The Poetics of Roman Ingarden. LC 79-29655. 272p. 1980. 20.00x (ISBN 0-8078-1436-9); pap. 11.00x (ISBN 0-8078-4068-8). U of NC Pr.

Ingarden, Roman. Cognition of the Literary Work of Art. Crowley, Ruth A. & Olson, Kenneth R., trs. from Ger. LC 73-80117. (Studies in Phenomenology & Existential Philosophy Ser.). 440p. 1974. text ed. 21.95x (ISBN 0-8101-0424-5); pap. 10.95x (ISBN 0-8101-0599-3). Northwestern U Pr.

Kallen, Horace M. Art & Freedom: A Historical & Bibliographical Interpretation of the Relations Between the Ideas of Beauty, Use & Freedom in Western Civilization from the Greeks to the Present Day. Repr. of 1942 ed. lib. bdg. 32.25x (ISBN 0-8371-2507-3, KAAF). Greenwood.

Lukacs, Georg. Soul & Form. Bostock, Anna, tr. LC 74-12828. 1974. pap. 5.95 (ISBN 0-262-62034-0). MIT Pr.

McGinn, Donald J. & Howerton, G., eds. Literature As a Fine Art. LC 66-29576. (Illus.). 1967. Repr. of 1959 ed. 12.50 (ISBN 0-87752-069-0). Gordian.

Maritain, Jacques. Situation de la Poesie. 2nd ed. 144p. 1964. 4.95 (ISBN 0-686-56369-7). French & Eur.

Maritain, Raissa & Maritain, Jacques. Situation of Poetry: Four Essays on the Relations Between Poetry, Mysticism, Magic & Knowledge. Suther, Marshall, tr. LC 54-13505. 1968. Repr. of 1955 ed. 11.00 (ISBN 0-527-61400-9). Kraus Repr.

Paget, Violet. The Beautiful: An Introduction to Psychological Aesthetics. LC 74-22079. 1974. lib. bdg. 15.00 (ISBN 0-8414-5673-9). Folcroft.

Richter, Jean Paul. Horn of Oberon: Jean Paul Richter's School for Aesthetics. Hale, Margaret R., tr. from Ger. & intro. by. LC 72-6735. 550p. 1974. text ed. 19.95x (ISBN 0-8143-1500-3). Wayne St U Pr.

Schlobin, Roger, ed. The Aesthetics of Fantasy Literature. LC 81-40446. 288p. 1982. text ed. 19.95 (ISBN 0-268-00598-2); pap. text ed. 7.95 (ISBN 0-268-00600-8). U of Notre Dame Pr.

Schmid, Wolf. Der Asthetische Inhalt: Zur Semantischen Funktion Poetischer Verfahren. (Utrecht Slavic Studies in Literary Theory: No. 1). (Orig.). 1977. pap. text ed. 7.75x (ISBN 90-316-0128-4). Humanities.

Spirit Lamp: An Aesthetic, Literary & Critical Magazine, Vols. 1-4, No. 2. LC 79-8081. (Clothbound in vol. 1). Repr. of 1892 ed. 36.00 (ISBN 0-404-18390-5). AMS Pr.

Squire, John C. Flowers of Speech; Being Lectures in Words - Forms in Literature. facs. ed. LC 67-28769. (Essay Index Reprint Ser). 1935. 13.00 (ISBN 0-8369-0899-6). Arno.

Vivante, Leone. English Poetry & Its Contribution to the Knowledge of a Creative Principle. LC 75-35818. 1975. Repr. of 1950 ed. lib. bdg. 25.00 (ISBN 0-8414-9153-4). Folcroft.

Vivas, Eliseo. Creation & Discovery. 1966. pap. 4.95 (ISBN 0-89526-952-X). Regnery-Gateway.
Wellek, Rene & Warren, Austin. Theory of Literature. rev. ed. 1956. pap. 5.95 (ISBN 0-15-689084-4, HB75, Harv). HarBraceJ.
Wells, Henry W. Realm of Literature. LC 65-27135. Repr. of 1927 ed. 9.00 (ISBN 0-8046-0494-0). Kennikat.

LITERATURE–EVALUATION
see Bibliography–Best Books; Books and Reading; Criticism; Literature–History and Criticism

LITERATURE–EXAMINATIONS, QUESTIONS, ETC.
Arco Editorial Board. Literature: Advanced Test for the G. R. E. rev. ed. LC 72-94374. (Orig.). 1973. pap. 3.95 (ISBN 0-668-01073-8). Arco.
Killikelly, S. H. Curious Questions in History, Literature, Art & Social Life, 3 vols. Set. 300.00 (ISBN 0-87968-979-X). Gordon Pr.
Mordell, Albert. The Shifting of Literary Values. 1912. Repr. lib. bdg. 10.00 (ISBN 0-8414-6637-8). Folcroft.
Rudman, Jack. General Literature. (Teachers License Examination Ser.: G-3). (Cloth bdg. avail. on request). pap. 8.00 (ISBN 0-685-18739-X). Natl Learning.
Sohl, Marcia & Dackerman, Gerald. Around the World in Eighty Days: Student Activity Book. (Now Age Illustrated Ser.). (Illus.). (gr. 4-12). 1976. wkbk. 1.25 (ISBN 0-88301-285-5). Pendulum Pr.

LITERATURE–HANDBOOKS, MANUALS, ETC.
Barnet, Sylvan. A Short Guide to Writing About Literature. 4th ed. 256p. 1979. pap. text ed. 5.95 (ISBN 0-316-08159-0). Little.
Borger, Rykle. Handbuch der Keilschriftliteratur, Vol. 1: Repertorium. (Ger). 1967. 48.75x (ISBN 3-11-000125-X). De Gruyter.
Czermak, Herberth. Kafka's Short Stories Notes. 98p. 1973. pap. 1.95 (ISBN 0-8220-0700-2). Cliffs.
Kantindex Allgemeiner zu Kants Gesammelten Schriften, 21 vols. Incl. Vols. 16 & 17. Wortindex Zu Band 1-9. viii, 1100p. 1967. 123.25x (ISBN 3-11-005180-X); Vol. 20, Sect. 3. Personenindex zu Kants Gesammelten Schriften. Holger, Katharina, et al, eds. viii, 142p. 1969. 26.50x (ISBN 3-11-002557-4). (Ger.). De Gruyter.
Monarch Notes on Albee's Who's Afraid of Virginia Wolf? & Other Works. pap. 2.25 (ISBN 0-671-00907-9). Monarch Pr.
Nadel & Sherrer, Jr. Writing Themes About Literature. Markman, ed. Date not set. pap. 2.95 (ISBN 0-8120-0595-3). Barron.
Pickering, Hoeper. Concise Companion to Literature. 1980. pap. 7.95 (ISBN 0-686-71597-7). Macmillan.
Silk, Agnes K. & Fanning, Clara E., eds. Index to Dramatic Readings. LC 70-145299. 1971. Repr. of 1925 ed. 32.00 (ISBN 0-403-01211-2). Scholarly.
Stein, Charlotte M. Communal Dialogue Programs. rev. ed. 1981. Vol. 1. 2.95 (ISBN 0-916634-21-3). Double M Pr.

LITERATURE–HISTORY AND CRITICISM
see also Authors; Literary Landmarks; Literature–Addresses, Essays, Lectures; Transmission of Texts
Aaron, Daniel. Writers on the Left: Episodes in American Literary Communism. LC 73-19759. 460p. 1974. Repr. of 1961 ed. lib. bdg. 25.00x (ISBN 0-374-90005-1). Octagon.
Abcarian, Richard & Klotz, Marvin, eds. Literature: The Human Experience. 780p. 1980. pap. text ed. 8.95x (ISBN 0-312-48793-2); write for info. instructor's manual (ISBN 0-312-48794-0). St Martin.
Acton, Lord. Collected Works. 600.00 (ISBN 0-87968-883-1). Gordon Pr.
Adams, Stephen. The Homosexual As Hero in Contemporary Fiction. (Critical Studies Ser.). 1980. text ed. 23.50x (ISBN 0-06-490018-5). B&N.
Adams, William, et al, eds. Afro-American Literature: Nonfiction. (Afro-American Literature Ser). (gr. 9-12). 1970. pap. 5.32 (ISBN 0-395-01979-6, 2-00206). HM.
Adams, William D. By-Ways in Bookland. Repr. of 1889 ed. 15.00 (ISBN 0-8274-3803-6). R West.
Allen, Gay W. & Clark, Harry H., eds. Literary Criticism: Pope to Croce. LC 61-12267. (Waynebooks Ser: No. 2). 1962. 9.95x (ISBN 0-8143-1157-1); pap. 6.50x (ISBN 0-8143-1158-X). Wayne St U Pr.
Allen, L. David. Detective in Fiction. (Orig.). pap. 2.50 (ISBN 0-8220-0388-0). Cliffs.
Allen, P. S. The Romanesque Lyric: Studies in Its Background & Development from Petronius to the Cambridge Songs. 1969. Repr. of 1928 ed. text ed. 10.00x (ISBN 0-391-02040-4). Humanities.
Alves, Robert. Sketches of a History of Literature. LC 67-18714. 1967. Repr. of 1794 ed. 33.00x (ISBN 0-8201-1002-7). Schol Facsimiles.
Ampere, Jean J. Melanges D'Histoire Litteraire et De Litterature, 2 Vols. (Classics in Art & Literary Criticism Ser). (Fr). Repr. of 1867 ed. Set. lib. bdg. 77.00 (ISBN 0-384-01203-5). Johnson Repr.
Amur, G. S. Images & Impressions. 1980. text ed. 11.00x (ISBN 0-391-01917-1). Humanities.
Anderson, George K. & Warnock, Robert. The World in Literature, 2 vols. rev. ed. 1967. 15.95x ea. Vol. 1 (ISBN 0-673-05636-8). Vol. 2 (ISBN 0-673-05637-6). Scott F.
Anderson, Margaret, ed. Little Review Anthology. 1970. 10.00 (ISBN 0-8180-1123-8); pap. 4.95 (ISBN 0-8180-1154-8). Horizon.
Anderson, Ruth I., et al. Word Finder. 4th ed. (gr. 9-12). 1974. text ed. 4.50 (ISBN 0-8224-3330-3); pap. 3.50 (ISBN 0-8224-3355-9). Pitman Learning.
Andrew, Samuel O. Postscript on Beowulf. LC 70-77668. 1969. Repr. of 1948 ed. 8.00 (ISBN 0-8462-1341-9). Russell.
Anozie, Sunday O. Structural Models & African Poetics: Towards a Pragmatic View of Literature. 220p. 1981. 37.50 (ISBN 0-7100-0467-2). Routledge & Kegan.
Archer, Thomas. The Highway of Letters & Its Echoes of Famous Footsteps. 1973. Repr. of 1893 ed. 30.00 (ISBN 0-8274-1548-6). R West.
Arnold, Julian B. Giants in Dressing Gowns: Swinburne, Ruskin, Emerson, Browning, Arnold. 1973. Repr. of 1945 ed. 12.50 (ISBN 0-8274-1483-8). R West.
Arrom, Jose J. Historia De la Literatura Dramatica Cubana. LC 73-38491. (Yale Romanic Studies: No. 23). Repr. of 1944 ed. 14.00 (ISBN 0-404-53223-3). AMS Pr.
Arvine, K. Cyclopedia of Anecdotes of Literature & the Fine Arts. 75.00 (ISBN 0-87968-982-X). Gordon Pr.
Ashton, J. Humor, Wit & Satire of the Seventeenth Century. 59.95 (ISBN 0-8490-0377-6). Gordon Pr.
Atkinson, Geoffrey. Relations de voyages du Dixieme siecle a l'evolution des idees. LC 79-166450. (Research & Source Works Ser.: No. 785). 1971. Repr. of 1924 ed. lib. bdg. 22.50 (ISBN 0-8337-3948-4). B Franklin.
Aubrey, John. Three Prose Works. Buchanan-Brown, John, ed. Incl. Miscelanies; Remaines of Gentilisme & Judaisme; Observations. LC 77-183306. (Centaur Classics Ser.). 624p. 1972. 35.00x (ISBN 0-8093-0567-4). S Ill U Pr.
Auerbach, Erich. Mimesis: The Representation of Reality in Western Literature. Trask, W. R., tr. 1953. 23.00 (ISBN 0-691-06078-9); pap. 5.95 (ISBN 0-691-01269-5, 124). Princeton U Pr.
Augustin, Aurelius. King Alfred's Old English Version of St. Augustine's Soliloquies Turned into Modern English. 59.95 (ISBN 0-8490-0471-3). Gordon Pr.
Austen, Jane. Plan of a Novel According to Hints from Various Quarters. LC 72-188492. 1973. lib. bdg. 8.50 (ISBN 0-8414-1677-X). Folcroft.
Bach, Hans. Jean Pauls Hesperus. 21.50 (ISBN 0-384-02935-3); pap. 18.50 (ISBN 0-685-02214-5). Johnson Repr.
Baer, Joachim T. Vladimir Ivanovicdal As a Belletrist. LC 72-88190. (Slavistic Printings & Reprintings Ser: No. 276). 204p. 1972. text ed. 37.50x (ISBN 90-2792-334-5). Mouton.
Bagehot. Estimations in Criticism, 2 vols. LC 73-4485. 1973. lib. bdg. 50.00 (ISBN 0-8414-1756-3). Folcroft.
Bailey, Albert E. Notes on the Literary Aspects of Tennyson's Princess. LC 73-18307. Repr. of 1897 ed. lib. bdg. 5.00 (ISBN 0-8414-9897-0). Folcroft.
Baker, James. Literary & Biographical Studies. 1973. Repr. of 1908 ed. 25.00 (ISBN 0-8274-1492-7). R West.
Baker, Joseph E. Critical Studies in Arnold, Emerson, & Newman. 1973. lib. bdg. 15.00 (ISBN 0-8414-1662-1). Folcroft.
Baker, Josephine T. The Literary Workshop. 1973. Repr. of 1918 ed. 6.50 (ISBN 0-8274-1487-0). R West.
Balch, Marstons S. Jacobean Miscellany, Vol. 2. Hogg, James, ed. (Jacobean Drama Ser.: No. 95). 104p. 1981. pap. text ed. 25.00x (ISBN 0-391-02344-6, Pub. by Salzburg Austria). Humanities.
Banerja, J. R. Rhetoric & Prosody. 1973. Repr. of 1967 ed. 7.50 (ISBN 0-8274-1443-9). R West.
Banta, Martha & Satterwhite, Joseph N. Discovery & Response: Drama, Fiction & Poetry with an Appendix on Writing & Reading. 1970. pap. 7.95 (ISBN 0-02-305750-5, 30575). Macmillan.
Barbellion, W. N. Enjoying Life & Other Literary Remains. 75.00 (ISBN 0-87968-257-4). Gordon Pr.
--Journal of a Disappointed Man. lib. bdg. 75.00 (ISBN 0-87968-150-0). Gordon Pr.
Barlow, F., et al. Leofric of Exeter. 55p. 1972. pap. text ed. 3.75x (ISBN 0-900771-33-X, Pub. by U Exeter England). Humanities.
Barnet, et al. An Introduction to Literature. 7th ed. 1981. pap. text ed. 11.95 (ISBN 0-316-08211-2); tchrs'. manual free (ISBN 0-316-08212-0). Little.
Barteau, F. Les Romans de Tristan et Iseut: Introduction a une lecture plurielle. new ed. (Collection L). 288p. (Orig., Fr.). 1972. pap. 19.95 (ISBN 2-03-036007-4). Larousse.
Barthes, Roland. Writing Degree Zero. Laver & Smith, trs. 94p. 1977. 8.95 (ISBN 0-8090-9865-2); pap. 4.50 (ISBN 0-8090-1384-3). Hill & Wang.
Barthes, Roland, et al. Ecrire Pour Quoi? Pour Qui. 1974. 6.95 (ISBN 0-686-53932-X). French & Eur.
Bartlett, John R. The Literature of the Rebellion. 59.95 (ISBN 0-8490-0545-0). Gordon Pr.
Barzun, Jacques. The Energies of Art: Studies of Authors Classic & Modern. LC 74-3686. 355p. 1975. Repr. of 1956 ed. lib. bdg. 22.75 (ISBN 0-8371-6856-2, BAEA). Greenwood.
Bataille, Georges. Literature & Evil. Hamilton, Alastair, tr. 1981. 12.95 (ISBN 0-89396-013-6); pap. 7.95 (ISBN 0-89396-014-4). Urizen Bks.
--Literature & Evil. Hamilton, Alastair, tr. from Fr. (Signature Ser.). 179p. 1973. text ed. 10.00x (ISBN 0-7145-0345-2). Humanities.
Bates, Arlo. Talks on the Study of Literature. 1973. Repr. of 1897 ed. 20.00 (ISBN 0-8274-1677-6). R West.
Bates, Katharine L. From Gretna to Land's End. 1973. Repr. of 1907 ed. 20.00 (ISBN 0-8274-1673-3). R West.
Bayne, Peter. Essay in Biography & Criticism: Second Series. LC 73-39681. (Essay Index Reprint Ser.). Repr. of 1858 ed. 23.00 (ISBN 0-8369-2744-3). Arno.
Baynes, Thomas S. Shakespeare Studies & an Essay on English Dictionaries. 1973. Repr. of 1894 ed. 17.45 (ISBN 0-8274-1674-1). R West.
Beaumont, Charles. A Modest Proposal. LC 70-79858. (Literary Casebook Ser.). 1969. pap. text ed. 2.95x (ISBN 0-675-09441-0). Merrill.
Beckson, Karl, ed. Aesthetes & Decadents of the 1890's. (Illus.). 317p. 1981. pap. 6.95 (ISBN 0-89733-044-7). Academy Chi Ltd.
Beerbohm Tree, Herbert. The Imaginative Faculty. LC 75-25559. 1973. lib. bdg. 10.00 (ISBN 0-8414-8613-1). Folcroft.
Beja, Morris. Film & Literature. 1979. pap. text ed. 11.95x (ISBN 0-582-28094-X). Longman.
Bell, H. Idris. Literature & Life: Addresses to the English Association, 2 vols. 1973. Repr. of 1948 ed. 30.00 (ISBN 0-8274-1288-6). R West.
Benedikz, B. S., ed. On the Novel: A Present for Walter Allen on His 60th Birthday from His Friends & Colleagues. 239p. 1971. 12.50x (ISBN 0-87471-410-9). Rowman.
Berkman, Alexander. The Anti-Climax. 59.95 (ISBN 0-87968-647-2). Gordon Pr.
Bett, Henry. Studies in Literature. 1929. Repr. 6.95 (ISBN 0-8274-3537-1). R West.
Biasin, Gian-Paolo. Literary Diseases: Theme & Metaphor in the Italian Novel. LC 74-30345. 188p. 1975. 12.50x (ISBN 0-292-74614-8). U of Tex Pr.
Bibliotheque Nationale. Catalogue General Des Livres Imprimes: Auteurs, Collectivites, Auteurs Anonymes (1960-1969, 15 tomes. Set. 1350.00 (ISBN 0-685-35975-1). French & Eur.
Bieder, Maryellen. Narrative Perspective in the Post-Civil War Novels of Francisco Ayala: Muertes de Perro & El Fondo del Vaso. (Studies in the Romance Languages & Literatures: No. 207). 1979. 10.00x (ISBN 0-8078-9207-6). U of NC Pr.
Binion, Rudolph. Soundings: Psychohistorical & Psycholiterary. 164p. 1981. 18.95 (ISBN 0-914434-16-0); pap. 8.95 (ISBN 0-914434-17-9). Psychohistory Pr.
Binns, Harold. Outlines of the World's Literature. 1973. Repr. of 1914 ed. 35.00 (ISBN 0-8274-1473-0). R West.
Birnbaum, Henrik & Eekman, Thomas. Fiction & Drama in Eastern & Southeastern Europe: Evolution & Experiment in the Postwar Period. (UCLA Slavic Studies: Vol. 1). ix, 463p. 1980. 24.95 (ISBN 0-89357-064-8). Slavica.
Bjorkman, Edwin A. Voices of to-Morrow, Critical Studies of the New Spirit in Literature. Repr. of 1913 ed. 23.00 (ISBN 0-384-04540-5). Johnson Repr.
Bjornson, Bjornstjerne. Synnove Solbakken. Sutter, Julie, tr. LC 79-38341. (Select Bibliographies Reprint Ser.). 1894. 16.00 (ISBN 0-8369-6758-5). Arno.
Black, Landbroke. Some Queer People: Margaret Fuller, Poe, Beddoes. 1973. 35.00 (ISBN 0-8274-1477-3). R West.
Blackmore, Simon A. The Riddles of Hamlet & the Newest Answers. LC 73-4188. 1973. lib. bdg. 35.00 (ISBN 0-8414-1762-8). Folcroft.
Blackmur, Richard P. Expense of Greatness. Repr. of 1940 ed. 27.00 (ISBN 0-403-04062-0). Somerset Pub.
Blair, Hugh. Lectures on Rhetoric & Belles Lettres. 1824. 50.00 (ISBN 0-8274-1468-4). R West.
Blair, John G. The Confidence Man in Modern Fiction: A Rogue's Gallery of Six Portraits. LC 79-50928. (Critical Studies). 142p. 1979. text ed. 22.50x (ISBN 0-06-490449-0). B&N.
Blatchford, Robert. My Favourite Books. 1973. 12.50 (ISBN 0-8274-1475-7). R West.
Blocker, H. Gene. The Metaphysics of Absurdity. LC 78-78399. 1979. pap. text ed. 9.00 (ISBN 0-8191-0712-3). U Pr of Amer.
Bloom, Harold. Poetry & Repression: Revisionism from Blake to Stevens. LC 75-18165. 304p. 1980. 20.00x (ISBN 0-300-01923-8, Y-378); pap. 6.95 (ISBN 0-300-02604-8). Yale U Pr.
Blunden, Edmund. Chaucer to "B. V." with an Additional Paper on Herman Melville (A Selection of Lecture Given Chiefly at Tokyo University) 1978. Repr. of 1950 ed. lib. bdg. 30.00 (ISBN 0-89760-029-0, Telegraph). Dynamic Learn Corp.
Boas, Frederick S. Shakespeare & His Predecessors. 1969. Repr. of 1904 ed. 15.00 (ISBN 0-403-00109-9). Scholarly.
Boas, Ralph P. The Study & Appreciation of Literature. 1931. Repr. 20.00 (ISBN 0-8274-3546-0). R West.
Bolitho, Hector. Older People: Shaw, Lawrence, Maurice Baring. 1973. Repr. of 1935 ed. 25.00 (ISBN 0-8274-1466-8). R West.
Bombaugh, C. C. Gleanings for the Curious from Literature. 59.95 (ISBN 0-8490-0237-0). Gordon Pr.
Booth, James. Writers & Politics in Nigeria. LC 80-17670. (Writers & Politics Ser.). 128p. 1981. text ed. 24.50x (ISBN 0-8419-0650-5, Africana); pap. text ed. 14.25x (ISBN 0-8419-0651-3). Holmes & Meier.
Bornstein, George, ed. Romantic & Modern: Revaluations of Literary Tradition. LC 76-6658. 1976. 12.95x (ISBN 0-8229-3322-5). U of Pittsburgh Pr.
Bostwick, Arthur E. Earmarks of Literature. facs. ed. LC 67-22074. (Essay Index Reprint Ser). 1914. 15.00 (ISBN 0-8369-1319-1). Arno.
Bradbury, Malcolm & Palmer, David, eds. Contemporary Criticism. (Stratford-Upon-Avon Studies: No. 12). 219p. 1979. pap. text ed. 14.25x (ISBN 0-8419-5818-1). Holmes & Meier.
Bradford, Gamaliel. Naturalist of Souls. LC 75-85995. (Essay & General Literature Index Reprint Ser). 1969. Repr. of 1926 ed. 14.00 (ISBN 0-8046-0543-2). Kennikat.
Brandes, George. Main Currents in Nineteenth Century Literature, 6 vols. LC 72-3577. (Studies in European Literature, No. 56). 1972. Repr. of 1923 ed. Set. lib. bdg. 275.00 (ISBN 0-8383-1574-7). Haskell.
Bree, Germaine. World of Marcel Proust. LC 66-5642. 1966. pap. text ed. 5.50 (ISBN 0-395-04229-1, 3-05950, RivSL). HM.
Britt, Albert. Great Biographers. facs. ed. LC 71-84300. (Essay Index Reprint Ser). 1936. 15.50 (ISBN 0-8369-1077-X). Arno.
Brooks, Cleanth, ed. Tragic Themes in Western Literature: Seven Essays by Bernard Knox, Maynard Mack, Chauncey B. Tinker, Henri Peyre, Richard B. Sewall, Konstantin Reichardt, & Louis Martz. 1955. 17.50x (ISBN 0-300-00328-5). Yale U Pr.
Brown, Ivor. A Rhapsody of Words. 1972. 5.95 (ISBN 0-370-00333-0). Transatlantic.
Browne, William. The Whole Works: 2 Vols. in 1. Hazlitt, W. C., ed. (English Literary Reference Ser). 1969. Repr. of 1869 ed. 31.00 (ISBN 0-384-06015-3). Johnson Repr.
Bryant, Frank E. On the Limits of Descriptive Writings Apropos of Lessings Laocoon. LC 76-58443. Repr. of 1906 ed. 8.50 (ISBN 0-8414-1654-0). Folcroft.
Buchan, John. The Man & the Book. 1925. Repr. 10.00 (ISBN 0-8274-2669-0). R West.
Buck, Gertrude. The Social Criticism of Literature. LC 73-472. 1974. Repr. of 1916 ed. lib. bdg. 10.00 (ISBN 0-8414-1496-3). Folcroft.
Buckler, William E. The Victorian Imagination: Essays in Aesthetic Exploration. (The Gotham Library). 384p. 1980. 22.50x (ISBN 0-8147-1032-8); pap. 10.50x (ISBN 0-8147-1033-6). NYU Pr.
Buckley, Theodore A. The Dawnings of Genius. 1973. Repr. of 1853 ed. 50.00 (ISBN 0-8274-1447-1). R West.
Bullen, A. H. The Works of Dr. Thomas Campion. 1973. Repr. of 1889 ed. lib. bdg. 35.00 (ISBN 0-8414-2519-1). Folcroft.
Burke, Kenneth. Counter-Statement. 2nd rev. ed. 1953. 12.95 (ISBN 0-910720-01-0). Archive Pr.
Burr, Anna R. The Autobiography: A Critical & Comparative Study. LC 73-504. 1972. Repr. of 1909 ed. lib. bdg. 30.00 (ISBN 0-8414-1468-8). Folcroft.
--Weir Mitchell: His Life & Works. 1973. Repr. of 1930 ed. 45.00 (ISBN 0-8274-1423-4). R West.

Burt, Mary E. Literary Landmarks. 1973. Repr. of 1889 ed. 10.00 (ISBN 0-8274-1509-5). R West.
--Literary Landmarks: A Guide to Good Reading for Young People. 1977. lib. bdg. 59.95 (ISBN 0-8490-2170-7). Gordon Pr.
Burton, John H. Book Hunter. Slater, Herbert J., ed. LC 79-78122. 1971. Repr. of 1895 ed. 20.00 (ISBN 0-8103-3607-3). Gale.
Butler, George P., ed. Best Sermons, 1946. LC 74-134065. (Essay Index Reprint Ser.). 1946. Repr. of 1946 ed. 19.50 (ISBN 0-8369-2757-5). Arno.
Byrd, Max. Visits to Bedlam: Madness & Literature in the Eighteenth Century. LC 73-19855. (Illus.). xx, 210p. 1974. 14.95x (ISBN 0-87249-312-1). U of SC Pr.
Cahiers Elisabethains: Etudes sur la Pre-Renaissance et la Renaissance Anglaises, 3 vols. Incl. Vol. 1. Nos. 1-6, 1972-74; Vol. 2. Nos. 7-10, 1975-76; Vol. 3. Nos. 11-15, 1977-79. Set. 142.50 (ISBN 0-686-61430-5); 47.50 ea. AMS Pr.
Caird, Edward. Essays on Literature. LC 68-8224. 1968. Repr. of 1909 ed. 11.50 (ISBN 0-8046-0060-0). Kennikat.
--Essays on Literature & Philosophy, 2 Vols. in 1. LC 11-16433. 1968. Repr. of 1892 ed. 30.00 (ISBN 0-527-14110-0). Kraus Repr.
--Essays on Literature: Dante, Goethe, Rousseau, Carlyle, Wordsworth. 1973. Repr. of 1909 ed. 30.00 (ISBN 0-8274-1541-9). R West.
Cairns, Huntington, ed. Limits of Art, 1 vol. ed. (Bollingen Ser.: No. 12). 1948. 30.00 (ISBN 0-691-09781-X). Princeton U Pr.
--Limits of Art, Vol. 1: From Homer to Chaucer. (Bollingen Ser.: No. 12). 1969. pap. 9.95 (ISBN 0-691-01755-7). Princeton U Pr.
--Limits of Art, Vol. 2: From Villon to Gibbon. (Bollingen Ser.: No. 12). 1970. pap. 9.95 (ISBN 0-691-01765-4). Princeton U Pr.
--Limits of Art, Vol. 3: From Goethe to Joyce. (Bollingen Ser.: No. 12). pap. 9.95 (ISBN 0-691-01768-9). Princeton U Pr.
Caldecott, Alfred. Selections from the Literature of Theism. 1973. Repr. of 1904 ed. 45.00 (ISBN 0-8274-1540-0). R West.
Calhoun, Thomas & Potter, John. The Garden. LC 73-126736. (Literary Casebook Ser.). 1970. pap. text ed. 2.50x (ISBN 0-675-09301-5). Merrill.
California University - Department Of English. Essays in Criticism: First Series. facs. ed. LC 67-22083. (Essay Index Reprint Ser). 1929. 16.00 (ISBN 0-8369-0272-6). Arno.
Calverton, Victor F. The Newer Spirit: A Sociological Criticism of Literature. 1972. lib. bdg. 17.50x (ISBN 0-374-91246-7). Octagon.
Canby, Henry S. American Estimates. LC 68-26247. 1968. Repr. of 1929 ed. 11.50 (ISBN 0-8046-0064-3). Kennikat.
Canfield, J. Douglas. Nicholas Rowe & Christian Tragedy. LC 76-39917. 1977. 8.50 (ISBN 0-8130-0545-0). U Presses Fla.
Canning, Albert S. Philosophy of the Waverly Novels. 1973. Repr. of 1879 ed. 25.00 (ISBN 0-8274-1784-5). R West.
Cantor, Jay. The Space Between: Literature & Politics. LC 81-47600. 160p. 1982. text ed. 10.95x (ISBN 0-8018-2672-1). Johns Hopkins.
Capri. (Panorama Books Collection). (Fr.). 3.95 (ISBN 0-685-36095-4). French & Eur.
Carrier, Warren & Oliver, Kenneth, eds. Guide to World Literature. 237p. (Orig.). 1980. pap. 10.50 (ISBN 0-8141-1949-2). NCTE.
Carroll, Lewis. Feeding the Mind. 1973. Repr. of 1907 ed. lib. bdg. 10.00 (ISBN 0-8414-1818-7). Folcroft.
Caserio, Robert L. Plot, Story, & the Novel: From Dickens & Poe to the Modern Period. LC 79-4321. 1979. 18.50 (ISBN 0-691-06382-6). Princeton U Pr.
Cawelti, John G. Apostles of the Self-Made Man. LC 65-25123. 1968. pap. 4.95 (ISBN 0-226-09865-6, P292, Phoen). U of Chicago Pr.
Cazamian, Louis F. Criticism in the Making. LC 77-1286. 1977. lib. bdg. 20.00 (ISBN 0-8414-3588-X). Folcroft.
Cerna, Z., et al. Rise & Development of Modern Literatures in Asia. No. 3. (Oriental Institute Czechoslovakia Dissertationes Orientales, Vol. 28). 1970. 6.00x (ISBN 0-685-27143-9). Paragon.
Cesaire, Aime. Textes. Mercier, R. & Battestini, M., eds. (Classique du Monde, Litterature Africaine). pap. 3.50 (ISBN 0-685-35627-2). French & Eur.
Chadbourne, Richard & Dahlie, Hallvard, eds. The New Land: Studies in Literary Theme. 160p. 1978. pap. text ed. 5.75 (ISBN 0-88920-065-3, Pub. by Laurier U Pr Canada). Humanities.
Champigny, Robert. Ontology of the Narrative. (De Proprietatibus Litterarum, Ser. Minor: No. 12). 1972. pap. text ed. 18.25x (ISBN 90-2792-366-3). Mouton.
Chancellor, E. Beresford. Literary Types. 1973. Repr. of 1895 ed. 15.00 (ISBN 0-8274-0597-9). R West.
Chandler, Frank W. Literature of Roguery, 2 vols. in 1. 1966. Repr. of 1907 ed. 35.50 (ISBN 0-8337-0526-1). B Franklin.
Chapman, Elizabeth R. A Companion to "in Memoriam". 1973. lib. bdg. 12.50 (ISBN 0-8414-1150-6). Folcroft.
Chapman, Guy. A Bibliography of William Beckford of Fonthill. 1973. lib. bdg. 25.00 (ISBN 0-8414-1812-8). Folcroft.
Chapman, R. W. Johnson, Boswell, & Mrs. Piozzi: A Supressed Passage Restored. 1973. lib. bdg. 8.50 (ISBN 0-8414-3569-3). Folcroft.
Chertsey. The Chertsey Worthies Library, 14 vols. Grosart, Alexander B., ed. Incl. The Complete Works of Joshua Sylvester, 2 vols. Repr. of 1876 ed. 45.00 (ISBN 0-685-27643-0); The Complete Poems of Henry More. Repr. of 1878 ed. 18.50 (ISBN 0-685-27644-9); The Complete Works of John Davies, 2 vols. Repr. of 1878 ed. 39.50 (ISBN 0-685-27645-7); The Works in Verse & Prose of Nicholas Breton, 2 vols. Repr. of 1879 ed. 45.00 (ISBN 0-685-27646-5); The Complete Poems of Joseph Beaumont, 2 vols. Repr. of 1880 ed. 39.50 (ISBN 0-685-27647-3); The Complete Works in Prose & Verse of Francis Quarles, 3 vols. Repr. of 1881 ed. 67.50 (ISBN 0-685-27648-1); The Complete Works in Verse & Prose of Abraham Cowley, 2 vols. Repr. of 1881 ed. 45.00 (ISBN 0-685-27649-X). Set. 295.00 (ISBN 0-404-50290-3). AMS Pr.
Chesterton, G. K. As I Was Saying. 1973. lib. bdg. 20.00 (ISBN 0-8414-3020-9). Folcroft.
--Heretics. 1973. lib. bdg. 25.00 (ISBN 0-8414-3021-7). Folcroft.
--Miscellany of Men. 1973. lib. bdg. 25.00 (ISBN 0-8414-3023-3). Folcroft.
--Uses of Diversity. 1973. 25.00 (ISBN 0-8274-0086-1). R West.
Church, Alfred J. Memories of Men & Books. 1973. Repr. of 1908 ed. 20.00 (ISBN 0-8274-1539-7). R West.
Church, R. W. An Essay on Critical Appreciation. 1973. Repr. of 1938 ed. 20.00 (ISBN 0-8274-1538-9). R West.
--Miscellaneous Essays. 1973. Repr. of 1888 ed. 10.00 (ISBN 0-8274-1534-6). R West.
--Occasional Papers, 2 vols. 1973. Repr. of 1897 ed. 20.00 set (ISBN 0-8274-1533-8). R West.
Clark, B. The Past, Present, & Future in Prose & Poetry. LC 72-947. Repr. of 1867 ed. 16.25 (ISBN 0-404-00015-0). AMS Pr.
Clark, Cumberland. Shakespeare & National Character. LC 76-181002. (Studies in Shakespeare, No. 24). 308p. 1972. Repr. of 1932 ed. lib. bdg. 41.95 (ISBN 0-8383-1371-X). Haskell.
Clark, Thomas A. Some Particulars. 1971. pap. 3.50 (ISBN 0-912330-12-0, Dist. by Gnomon Pr). Jargon Soc.
Classen, E. Lectures on Style & Composition. 1973. Repr. of 1917 ed. 15.00 (ISBN 0-8274-1528-1). R West.
Cleaveland, Elizabeth W. A Study of Tindale's Genesis: Compared with the Genesis of Coverdale & of the Authorized Version. (Yale Studies in English Ser.: No. 43). xliii, 258p. 1972. Repr. of 1911 ed. 19.50 (ISBN 0-208-01126-9, Archon). Shoe String.
Clinton, Jerome W. The Divan of Manuchihri Damghani: A Critical Study. LC 72-87873. (Studies in Middle Eastern Literatures Ser: No. 1). 1972. pap. 15.00x (ISBN 0-88297-001-1). Bibliotheca.
Cohen, B. Bernard. Writing About Literature. rev ed. 256p. 1973. pap. 5.95x (ISBN 0-673-07653-9). Scott F.
Cole, G. D. Politics & Literature. LC 73-1577. 1973. Repr. of 1929 ed. lib. bdg. 15.00 (ISBN 0-8414-1806-3). Folcroft.
Coleman, John. Charles Reade As I Knew Him. 1973. Repr. of 1903 ed. 50.00 (ISBN 0-8274-1424-2). R West.
Coleridge, Hartley. Essays & Marginalia, 2 vols. LC 72-13289. (Essay Index Reprint Ser.). Repr. of 1851 ed. Set. 37.50 (ISBN 0-8369-8151-0). Arno.
Colles, William M. Literature & the Pension List. 1973. Repr. of 1889 ed. 17.50 (ISBN 0-8274-1656-3). R West.
Collet, Stephen. Relics of Literature. 1973. Repr. of 1823 ed. 45.00 (ISBN 0-8274-1664-4). R West.
Collins, A. S. The Profession of Letters. 1973. Repr. of 1928 ed. 12.00 (ISBN 0-8274-1654-7). R West.
Collins, Christopher. Uses of Observation: A Study of the Correspondential Vision in the Writings of Emerson, Thoreau & Whitman. LC 72-169993. (Studies in American Literature: Vol. 12). 125p. 1971. text ed. 13.50x (ISBN 0-686-22498-1). Mouton.
Colonna, Francesco. Hypnerotomachia: The Strife of Love in a Dreame (1592). Dallington, Robert, tr. from Latin. LC 73-16223. 208p. 1973. Repr. lib. bdg. 25.00x (ISBN 0-8201-1124-4). Schol Facsimiles.
Columbia University. Lectures on Literature. facs. ed. LC 67-22059. (Essay Index Reprint Ser). 1911. 18.00 (ISBN 0-8369-0329-3). Arno.
Comprone, Joseph. A Concise Guide to Writing About Literature. (Illus.). 104p. 1974. text ed. 3.75 (ISBN 0-685-53503-7). Collegiate Pub.
Compton-Rickett, Arthur. Personal Forces in Modern Literature. 1973. lib. bdg. 15.00 (ISBN 0-8414-2373-3). Folcroft.
Consolo, Dominick. Out of the Cradle, Endlessly Rocking. LC 70-138465. (Literary Casebook Ser.). 1971. pap. text ed. 2.95x (ISBN 0-675-09254-X). Merrill.
Cook, Albert S. The Authorized Version & Its Influence. LC 76-41905. Repr. of 1910 ed. lib. bdg. 8.50 (ISBN 0-8414-3559-6). Folcroft.
Cook, Edward. More Literary Recreations. 1973. Repr. of 1919 ed. 23.50 (ISBN 0-8274-1660-1). R West.
Cooper, Frederic T. The Craftsmanship of Writing. 1973. Repr. of 1911 ed. 12.50 (ISBN 0-8274-1665-2). R West.
Cornford, L. Cope. Interpretations: W. E. Henley, Dante, Victor Hugo Moliere, Scott, Shakespeare. 1926. Repr. 20.00 (ISBN 0-8274-3857-5). R West.
Costa del Sol. (Panorama Books Collection). (Fr.). 3.95 (ISBN 0-685-36096-2). French & Eur.
Costich, Julia F. The Poetic Structure of Change: A Study of the Surrealist Work of Benjamin Peret. (Studies in the Romance Languages & Literatures). 1979. 10.50x (ISBN 0-8078-9206-8). U of NC Pr.
Courtney, Janet E. Recollected in Tranquillity. 1973. Repr. of 1926 ed. 20.00 (ISBN 0-8274-1525-7). R West.
Courtney, W. L. The Feminine Note in Fiction. LC 73-4563. 1973. lib. bdg. 20.00 (ISBN 0-8414-1840-3). Folcroft.
--Studies at Leisure. 1973. Repr. of 1892 ed. 20.00 (ISBN 0-8274-1523-0). R West.
Coutinho, Alfranio. An Introduction to Literature in Brazil. Rabassa, Gregory, tr. from Portugese. LC 69-15569. 1969. 20.00x (ISBN 0-231-02993-4). Columbia U Pr.
Cowden-Clark, Mary. My Long Life: An Autobiographic Sketch. 1973. lib. bdg. 25.00 (ISBN 0-8414-2399-7). Folcroft.
Cox, C. B. The Free Spirit: A Study of Liberal Humanism in the Novels of George Eliot, Henry James, E. M. Forster, Virginia Woolf, Angus Wilson. LC 80-13281. 195p. 1980. Repr. of 1963 ed. lib. bdg. 18.00x (ISBN 0-313-22449-8, COFS). Greenwood.
Cox, Stephen D. The Stranger Within Thee: Concepts of the Self in Late-Eighteenth-Century Literature. LC 80-5252. (Illus.). 195p. 1980. 14.95x (ISBN 0-8229-3424-8). U of Pittsburgh Pr.
Craig, David & Egan, Michael. Extreme Situations: Literature & Crisis from the Great War to the Atom Bomb. LC 79-54651. 1980. text ed. 27.50x (ISBN 0-06-491305-8). B&N.
Crane, R. S. Critical & Historical Principles of Literary History. LC 75-159832. 1971. pap. 1.75 (ISBN 0-226-11826-6, P442, Phoen). U of Chicago Pr.
Crane, Ronald S., et al, eds. Critics & Criticism: Ancient & Modern. abr ed. LC 52-7330. 1957. pap. 5.00x (ISBN 0-226-11793-6, P15, Phoen). U of Chicago Pr.
Crawford, Charles. Collectanea Second Series: Montaigne, Webster, Marston, Donne. 1973. Repr. of 1907 ed. 40.00 (ISBN 0-8274-1776-4). R West.
Crawshaw, W. H. The Interpretation of Literature. 1973. Repr. of 1902 ed. 15.00 (ISBN 0-8274-1521-4). R West.
Crichton-Browne, James & Carlyle, Alexander. The Nemesis of Froude. 1973. Repr. of 1903 ed. 20.00 (ISBN 0-8274-1764-0). R West.
Croce, Benedetto. Benedetto Croce's Poetry & Literature: An Introduction to Criticism & History. Gullace, Giovanni, tr. from Ital. & intro. by. LC 80-19511. 272p. 1981. 24.95x (ISBN 0-8093-0982-3). S Ill U Pr.
Cronin, Vincent, ed. Essays by Divers Hands L: Innovation in Contemporary Literature. (Being the Transactions of a Royal Society of Literature, New Ser.: Vol. XL). 162p. 1979. 21.50x (ISBN 0-8476-3043-9). Rowman.
Cropper, Margaret. Flame Touches Flame: George Herbert, Nicholas Ferrar, Henry Vaughan, Jeremy Taylor, Margaret Godolphin, Thomas Ken. 1973. Repr. of 1951 ed. 20.00 (ISBN 0-8274-1522-2). R West.
Crosman, Inge K. Time Metaphors in a la Recherche Du Temps Perdu. (Studies in the Romance Languages & Literatures). 1978. 14.50x (ISBN 0-8078-9204-1). U of NC Pr.
Crothers, Samuel M. By the Christmas Fire. 1973. Repr. of 1908 ed. 15.00 (ISBN 0-8274-1592-3). R West.
--The Gentle Reader. 1973. Repr. of 1903 ed. 15.00 (ISBN 0-8274-1591-5). R West.
--Gentle Reader. LC 71-39162. (Essay Index Reprint Ser.). Repr. of 1903 ed. 18.00 (ISBN 0-8369-2684-6). Arno.
--Pardoner's Wallet. LC 78-39161. (Essay Index Reprint Ser.). Repr. of 1905 ed. 18.00 (ISBN 0-8369-2685-4). Arno.
Crouch, Marcus. The Nesbit Tradition: Children's Novels 1945-1972. (Illus.). 239p. 1972. 13.75x (ISBN 0-87471-146-0). Rowman.
Curtius, E. R. European Literature & the Latin Middle Ages. Trask, Willard R., tr. LC 52-10619. (Bollingen Ser., Vol. 36). 682p. 1953. 36.00 (ISBN 0-691-09739-9); pap. 8.50 (ISBN 0-691-01793-X). Princeton U Pr.
Daemmrich, Horst. The Shattered Self: E. T. A. Hoffmann's Tragic Vision. LC 72-11451. 144p. 1973. text ed. 9.95x (ISBN 0-8143-1493-7). Wayne St U Pr.
Daiches, David. Literature & Society. Repr. of 1938 ed. 25.00 (ISBN 0-403-04155-4). Somerset Pub.
Daniels, R. Balfour. Some Seventeenth-Century Worthies in a Twentieth-Century Mirror. LC 78-102486. 1971. Repr. of 1940 ed. 10.50 (ISBN 0-8462-1493-8). Russell.
Dante. Dante's Vita Nuova: A Translation & an Essay. new ed. Musa, Mark, tr. from It. LC 72-79905. (Midland Bks.: No. 162). 224p. 1973. 8.50x (ISBN 0-253-31620-0); pap. 4.50x (ISBN 0-253-20162-4). Ind U Pr.
--The Vita Nuova. Martin, Theodore, tr. & intro. by. Martin, Theodore. LC 74-39195. (Select Bibliographies Reprint Ser). Repr. of 1861 ed. 15.00 (ISBN 0-8369-6797-6). Arno.
Danziger, Marlies K. & Johnson, Wendell S. The Critical Reader: Analyzing & Judging Literature. LC 78-4302. 1978. 10.95 (ISBN 0-8044-2135-8); pap. 4.95 (ISBN 0-8044-6096-5). Ungar.
Dark, Sidney. Books & the Man. 1973. Repr. of 1921 ed. 15.00 (ISBN 0-8274-1649-0). R West.
--Twelve Bad Men. 1973. lib. bdg. 11.50 (ISBN 0-8414-2437-3). Folcroft.
Darton, F. Harvey. Essays of the Year 1933-1934. 1973. Repr. of 1934 ed. 20.00 (ISBN 0-8274-1645-8). R West.
Dassonville, Michel. L' Analyse De Texte. (Fr). 1957. pap. 3.95x (ISBN 2-7637-6150-X, Pub. by Laval). Intl Schol Bk Serv.
--Dissertation Litteraire, Conseils Pratiques Aux Futurs Bacheliers. 2nd ed. 1960. pap. 2.50x (ISBN 2-7637-6104-6, Pub. by Laval). Intl Schol Bk Serv.
--Initiation a la Recherche Litteraire. (Fr). 1961. pap. 3.00x (ISBN 2-7637-6103-8, Pub. by Laval). Intl Schol Bk Serv.
Davidson, Chris. New Writing & Writers, Seventeen. 1980. text ed. 12.50x (ISBN 0-7145-3693-8). Humanities.
Davies, Robertson. One Half of Robertson Davies. 1978. 12.95 (ISBN 0-670-52608-8). Viking Pr.
Davies, Stevie. Renaissance Views of Man. (Literature in Context Ser.). 1979. text ed. 21.50x (ISBN 0-06-491621-9). B&N.
Davis, Herbert. Nineteenth-Century Studies. LC 72-194751. 1973. Repr. of 1940 ed. lib. bdg. 20.00 (ISBN 0-8414-2444-6). Folcroft.
Davis, Madeleine & Wallbridge, David. Boundary & Space: An Introduction to the Work of D. W. Winnicott. 212p. 1981. 17.50 (ISBN 0-87630-251-7). Brunner-Mazel.
Davis, Robert C., ed. The Fictional Father: Lacanian Readings of the Text. LC 80-26222. 224p. 1981. lib. bdg. 15.00x (ISBN 0-87023-111-1). U of Mass Pr.
Day, Lewis C. Notable Images of Virtue: Emily Bronte, George Meredith, W. B. Yeats. LC 74-3179. 1973. lib. bdg. 8.50 (ISBN 0-8414-5724-7). Folcroft.
--We're Not Going to Do Nothing. LC 74-4379. 1973. lib. bdg. 6.50 (ISBN 0-8414-3741-6). Folcroft.
Defoe, Daniel. A System of Magick. (Illus.). 403p. 1973. Repr. of 1728 ed. 17.50x (ISBN 0-87471-426-5). Rowman.
De La Bruyere, Jean. Caracteres, 2 Vols. (Documentation thematique). (Illus., Fr.). pap. 2.95 ea. Larousse.
Delavenay, Emile. D. H. Lawrence & Edward Carpenter: A Study in Edwardian Transition. LC 79-143224. (Illus.). 1971. 15.00 (ISBN 0-8008-2180-7). Taplinger.
Del Re, Arundell. Bridges' The Testament of Beauty Introduction. 1973. lib. bdg. 20.00 (ISBN 0-8414-2460-8). Folcroft.
DeVitis, A. A. Anthony Burgess. (English Authors Ser.: No. 132). lib. bdg. 10.95 (ISBN 0-8057-1068-X). Twayne.
Dictionnaire des auteurs de tous les temps et de tous les pays, 2 tomes. Set. 109.50 (ISBN 0-685-36080-6). French & Eur.
Diderot. Diderot's Letters to Sophie Volland: A Selection. France, Peter, tr. 225p. 1972. 12.00x (ISBN 0-19-212551-6). Oxford U Pr.
Dietrich, Richard, ed. Realities of Literature. LC 70-136507. 1971. pap. text ed. 11.95 short ed. (ISBN 0-471-00123-6). Wiley.
Di Girolamo, Costanzo. A Critical Theory of Literature. 160p. 1981. 15.00 (ISBN 0-299-08120-6). U of Wis Pr.
Dinsmore, Charles A. Atonement in Literature & Life. 1973. Repr. of 1906 ed. 25.00 (ISBN 0-8274-1637-7). R West.

Disraeli, Isaac. Amenities of Literature, Consisting of Sketches & Characters of English Literature, 2 vols. 1973. Repr. of 1859 ed. 30.00 (ISBN 0-8274-1639-3). R West.

--The Calamities & Quarrels of Authors with Some Inquiries Respecting Their Moral & Literary Characters. 1973. Repr. of 1860 ed. 24.75 (ISBN 0-8274-1638-5). R West.

--The Literary Character: Or the History of Men of Genius. 1973. Repr. of 1868 ed. 40.00 (ISBN 0-8274-1696-2). R West.

--Miscellanies of Literature: A New Edition, Revised & Corrected. 1973. Repr. of 1840 ed. 50.00 (ISBN 0-8274-1640-7). R West.

Dixon, W. Macneile. The Human Situation. 1973. lib. bdg. 40.00 (ISBN 0-8414-2476-4). Folcroft.

Dobell, Bertram. Laureate of Pessimism. 1973. Repr. of 1910 ed. 4.95 (ISBN 0-8274-1657-1). R West.

Dobson, E. J. The Origins of Ancrene Wisse. 454p. 1976. 54.00x (ISBN 0-19-811864-3). Oxford U Pr.

Donne, John. Devotions Upon Emergent Occasions. LC 72-10115. 1973. lib. bdg. 25.00 (ISBN 0-8414-0650-2). Folcroft.

Downey, Edmund. Twenty Years Ago: A Book of Anecdote Illustrating Literary Life in London-Hardy, Etc. 1973. Repr. of 1905 ed. 25.00 (ISBN 0-8274-1699-7). R West.

Downs, Robert B. In Search of New Horizons. LC 78-13656. 1978. text ed. 15.00 (ISBN 0-8389-0269-3). ALA.

Doyle, F. H. Lectures Delivered Before the University of Oxford: Matthew Arnold Etc. 1973. Repr. of 1869 ed. 30.00 (ISBN 0-8274-1692-X). R West.

Dreiser, Theodore. Fine Furniture. LC 76-28778. 1973. lib. bdg. 7.50 (ISBN 0-8414-3708-4). Folcroft.

Du Bos, Charles. What Is Literature? LC 76-40044. Repr. of 1940 ed. lib. bdg. 15.00 (ISBN 0-8414-3810-2). Folcroft.

Duffield, A. J. Don Quixote: His Critics & Commentators. 1973. Repr. of 1881 ed. 25.00 (ISBN 0-8274-1415-3). R West.

Duhamel, Georges. In Defense of Letters. 1973. 8.00 (ISBN 0-8274-1728-4). R West.

Duncan, P. B. Literary Conglomerate; or a Combination of Various & Facts on Various Thoughts. 1973. Repr. of 1839 ed. 45.00 (ISBN 0-8274-1693-8). R West.

Dutt, William A. Some Literary Associations of East Anglia: George Borrow, George Crabbe, John Evelyn, Edward Fitzgerald, Charles Lamb, Lord Tennyson & William Wordsworth. 1978. Repr. of 1907 ed. 35.00 (ISBN 0-8492-0689-8). R West.

Dyson, Henry V. & Butt, John E. Augustans & Romantics, Sixteen Eighty-Nine to Eighteen Thirty. 2nd rev. ed. Repr. of 1950 ed. 29.00 (ISBN 0-403-03061-7). Somerset Pub.

Earl, Herbert L. Lectures Given at the Torquay Natural History Museum: Shakespeare, Sir Walter Raleigh, Voltaire. 1973. Repr. of 1939 ed. 25.00 (ISBN 0-8274-1389-0). R West.

Eaton, J. W. The German Influence on Danish Literature. 1973. Repr. of 1929 ed. 30.00 (ISBN 0-8274-1388-2). R West.

Echeruo, Michael J. The Conditioned Imagination from Shakespeare to Conrad. LC 77-11081. 1978. text ed. 25.50x (ISBN 0-8419-0330-1). Holmes & Meier.

Echeruo, Michael J. C. Joyce Cary & the Dimensions of Order. 1979. text ed. 22.50x (ISBN 0-06-491875-0). B&N.

Edwards, E. W. The Orlando Furioso & Its Predecessor. 1973. Repr. of 1924 ed. 20.00 (ISBN 0-8274-1683-0). R West.

Efron, Edith & Chambers, Clytia. How CBS Tried to Kill a Book. 240p. 1973. pap. 1.50 (ISBN 0-532-15115-1). Woodhill.

Ehrenpreis, Irvin. The "Types Approach" to Literature. LC 73-19263. 1945. lib. bdg. 15.00 (ISBN 0-685-44515-1). Folcroft.

Elliott, Robert C. The Shape of Utopia: Studies in a Literary Genre. LC 78-103136. 1970. 9.00x (ISBN 0-226-20500-2). U of Chicago Pr.

Ellis, Henry. Original Letters of Eminent Literary Men. 1973. Repr. of 1843 ed. 75.00 (ISBN 0-8274-1685-7). R West.

Ellsworth, William. A Golden Age of Authors. 1973. Repr. of 1919 ed. 20.00 (ISBN 0-8274-1681-4). R West.

Elstob, Peter, ed. The Survival & Ecouragement of Literature in Present Day Society. 94p. (Orig.). 1979. pap. 12.50x (ISBN 0-85591-003-8). Intl Pubns Serv.

Elton, Oliver. Modern Studies. facs. ed. LC 67-26739. (Essay Index Reprint Ser). 1907. 18.00 (ISBN 0-8369-0414-1). Arno.

Elwin, Malcolm. Old Gods Falling. 1973. Repr. of 1939 ed. 30.00 (ISBN 0-8274-1283-5). R West.

Elwin, Whitwell. Some Eighteenth Century Men of Letters, 2 vols. 1973. Repr. of 1902 ed. 44.50 set (ISBN 0-8274-0598-7). R West.

Emerson, Ralph W. Parnassus. 1973. Repr. of 1874 ed. 35.00 (ISBN 0-8274-0590-1). R West.

--Uncollected Lectures. Ghodes, Clarence, ed. LC 74-13155. 1973. lib. bdg. 10.00 (ISBN 0-8414-3977-X). Folcroft.

Engels, John. Studies in Paterson. 1971. pap. text ed. 2.50x (ISBN 0-675-09212-4). Merrill.

Enright, D. J. The Apothecary's Shop. LC 75-15663. 236p. 1975. Repr. of 1957 ed. lib. bdg. 14.00x (ISBN 0-8371-8222-0, ENAS). Greenwood.

Ensor, Allison R. & Heffernan, Thomas J., eds. Tennessee Studies in Literature, Vol. 24. LC 58-63252. 1979. text ed. 9.50x (ISBN 0-87049-271-3); pap. text ed. 5.00x (ISBN 0-87049-272-1). U of Tenn Pr.

--Tennessee Studies in Literature, Vol. 25. LC 58-63252. 1980. lib. bdg. 9.50x (ISBN 0-87049-277-2); pap. text ed. 5.00x (ISBN 0-87049-278-0). U of Tenn Pr.

Erskine, John. The Delight of Great Books. Repr. of 1928 ed. 25.00 (ISBN 0-403-02285-1). Somerset Pub.

--The Delight of Great Books. 1973. 25.00 (ISBN 0-8274-0412-3). R West.

--The Kinds of Poetry & Other Essays. 1978. Repr. of 1920 ed. lib. bdg. 25.00 (ISBN 0-89760-203-X, Telegraph). Dynamic Learn Corp.

--The Literary Discipline. LC 23-8332. Repr. of 1924 ed. 9.50 (ISBN 0-384-14600-7). Johnson Repr.

--Literary Discipline. 1973. lib. bdg. 11.95 (ISBN 0-8414-4009-3). Folcroft.

--The Literary Discipline. 1978. Repr. of 1925 ed. lib. bdg. 30.00 (ISBN 0-89760-202-1, Telegraph). Dynamic Learn Corp.

Escott, T. H. Club Makers & Club Members. 1973. Repr. of 1914 ed. 40.00 (ISBN 0-8274-0544-8). R West.

--Politics & Letters. 1973. Repr. of 1886 ed. 35.00 (ISBN 0-8274-1682-2). R West.

Escott, Thomas H. Edward Bulwer. 1973. lib. bdg. 10.95 (ISBN 0-8414-4010-7). Folcroft.

Essays in Honour of Gilbert Murray. LC 72-322. (Essay Index Reprint Ser.). Repr. of 1936 ed. 15.00 (ISBN 0-8369-2792-3). Arno.

Estess, Ted L. Elie Wiesel. LC 80-5337. (Modern Literature Ser.). 160p. 1980. 10.95 (ISBN 0-8044-2184-6). Ungar.

Evans, J. Martin. America: The View from Europe. 1979. pap. 3.95 (ISBN 0-393-00955-6). Norton.

Faguet, Emile. Initation into Literature. 1913. Repr. 25.00 (ISBN 0-8274-2572-4). R West.

--Initiation into Literature. Home Gordon, Bart, tr. 220p. (Fr.). 1980. Repr. of 1913 ed. lib. bdg. 25.00 (ISBN 0-89987-253-0). Darby Bks.

Farrar, Frederick W. Great Books. LC 72-6859. (Essay Index Reprint Ser.). Repr. of 1898 ed. 20.00 (ISBN 0-8369-7261-9). Arno.

Farrar, John C. Literary Spotlight. 1924. Repr. 13.50 (ISBN 0-685-43365-X). Norwood Edns.

Farrer, James A. Literary Forgeries. 1973. lib. bdg. 9.00 (ISBN 0-8414-4017-4). Folcroft.

Fenelon, Francois. Lettre a l'Academie. (Classiques Larousse). (Illus., Fr.). pap. 2.95 (ISBN 0-685-13967-0, 97). Larousse.

Ferguson, Francis. The Human Image in Dramatic Literature: Essays. 6.75 (ISBN 0-8446-0620-0). Peter Smith.

Fergusson, Francis. Literary Landmarks: Essays on the Theory & Practice of Literature. 1975. 11.00 (ISBN 0-8135-0815-0). Rutgers U Pr.

Feydel, Gabriel. Un Cahier D'histoire Litteraire. Repr. of 1818 ed. 28.00 (ISBN 0-8287-0341-8). Clearwater Pub.

Fish, Stanley E. Self-Consuming Artifacts: The Experience of Seventeenth-Century Literature. LC 76-187747. 1973. pap. 3.95 (ISBN 0-520-02764-7); pap. 3.95 (ISBN 0-520-02764-7). U of Cal Pr.

Fitch, George H. Comfort in Good Old Books: Shakespeare, Milton, Dr. Johnson, Cervantes. 1973. Repr. of 1911 ed. 17.50 (ISBN 0-8274-0665-7). R West.

--The Critic in the Occident. 1973. Repr. of 1913 ed. 20.00 (ISBN 0-8274-0666-5). R West.

Fitzgerald, Edward. Letters, 2 vols. Wright, William A., ed. LC 72-5597. (Select Bibliographies Reprint Ser.). 1972. Repr. of 1894 ed. 42.00 (ISBN 0-8369-6906-5). Arno.

Fitzgerald, Percy. The Book Fancier or the Romance of Book Collecting. 1973. Repr. of 1887 ed. 35.00 (ISBN 0-8274-0663-0). R West.

--The Garrick Club. 1973. Repr. of 1904 ed. 45.00 (ISBN 0-8274-0664-9). R West.

--Principles of Comedy & Dramatic Effeot. LC 76-7982. 1973. Repr. of 1870 ed. lib. bdg. 25.00 (ISBN 0-8414-4221-5). Folcroft.

--Recreations of a Literary Man. 1973. Repr. of 1883 ed. 35.00 (ISBN 0-8274-0661-4). R West.

Fleischmann, W. B., ed. Encyclopedia of World Literature in the 20th Century, 4 vols. rev. & enl ed. Incl. Vol. 1. A-F. (Illus.). 425p. 50.00 (ISBN 0-8044-3092-6); Vol. 2. G-N. 469p. 50.00 (ISBN 0-8044-3093-4); Vol. 3. 0-Z. 590p. 50.00 (ISBN 0-8044-3094-2); Vol. 4. Supplement & Index. Ungar, Frederick & Mainiero, Lina, eds. 50.00 (ISBN 0-8044-3095-0). LC 67-13615. Set. 210.00 (ISBN 0-8044-3091-8). Ungar.

Forastieri-Braschi, Eduardo & Guiness, Gerald. On Text & Context: Methodological Approaches to the Context of Literature. LC 79-18001. 1980. pap. 12.00 (ISBN 0-8477-3194-4). U of PR Pr.

Ford, Ford M. Portraits from Life. 256p. 1980. pap. 4.95 (ISBN 0-395-29911-X). HM.

Ford, John. The Broken Heart. Spencer, T. J. P., ed. 256p. 1981. 22.00 (ISBN 0-8018-2479-6). Johns Hopkins.

Fowlie, Wallace. Clown's Grail, Study of Love in Its Literary Expression. LC 73-11380. 1947. lib. bdg. 17.50 (ISBN 0-8414-1981-7). Folcroft.

Frane, Jeff. Fritz Leiber. (Starmont Reader's Guide Ser.: No. 8). 64p. 1980. lib. bdg. 9.95 (ISBN 0-89370-039-8). Borgo Pr.

Freeman, John. Moderns: Essays in Literary Criticism. 1973. Repr. of 1917 ed. 10.75 (ISBN 0-8274-0593-6). R West.

Friedman, Maurice. Problematic Rebel: Melville, Dostoievsky, Kafka, Camus. rev. ed. LC 72-101360. 1970. 15.00x (ISBN 0-226-26395-9). U of Chicago Pr.

Friedson, Anthony M. Literature Through the Ages. 1978. Repr. of 1964 ed. lib. bdg. 15.00 (ISBN 0-8482-0814-5). Norwood Edns.

Friswell, Laura H. In the Sixties & Seventies. 1973. Repr. of 1905 ed. 45.00 (ISBN 0-8274-0655-X). R West.

Frye, Northrop. The Critical Path: An Essay on the Social Context of Literary Criticism. LC 70-143246. (Midland Bks.: No. 158). 176p. 1971. 8.95x (ISBN 0-253-31568-9); pap. 3.50x (ISBN 0-253-20158-6). Ind U Pr.

Frye, Prosser H. Literary Reviews & Criticisms. facs. ed. LC 68-8462. (Essay Index Reprint Ser). 1968. Repr. of 1908 ed. 16.00 (ISBN 0-8369-0465-6). Arno.

Furst, Lilian R. The Contours of European Romanticism. LC 79-15141. xvi, 158p. 1980. 21.50x (ISBN 0-8032-1954-7). U of Nebr Pr.

Fyvie, John. Some Literary Eccentrics. 1973. Repr. of 1906 ed. 30.00 (ISBN 0-8274-0193-0). R West.

Galdon, Joseph A. Typology & Seventeenth-Century Literature. (De Proprietatibus Litterarum Series: Major 28). 164p. 1975. text ed. 35.00x (ISBN 90-2793-366-9). Mouton.

Garfield, Evelyn P. Julio Cortazar. LC 74-78440. (Modern Literature Ser.). 184p. 1975. 10.95 (ISBN 0-8044-2224-9). Ungar.

Garnett, R. S. Some Book-Hunting Adventures. 1973. Repr. of 1931 ed. 30.00 (ISBN 0-8274-0197-3). R West.

Garvin, Harry, ed. Romanticism, Modernism, Postmodernism: Vol. 25, No. 2. LC 79-50103. (Bucknell Review Ser.). 192p. 1980. 12.00 (ISBN 0-8387-5004-4). Bucknell U Pr.

Gass, William. Fiction & the Figures of Life. LC 78-58453. 1978. pap. 6.95 (ISBN 0-87923-254-4, Nonpareil Bk). Godine.

--The World Within the Word. LC 79-52634. 1979. pap. 6.95 (ISBN 0-87923-298-6, Nonpareil Bks.). Godine.

Gawsworth, John. Backwaters: Excursions in the Shades. 1973. Repr. of 1932 ed. 20.00 (ISBN 0-8274-0196-5). R West.

Geiger, Don. The Age of the Splendid Machine: Eliot, Pound, Melville, Wallace Stevens, Tolstoy. 1973. Repr. of 1961 ed. 35.00 (ISBN 0-8274-0636-3). R West.

George, W. L. Literary Chapters. 1973. Repr. of 1918 ed. 25.00 (ISBN 0-8274-0202-3). R West.

Ghose, Zulfikar. Hamlet, Prufrock & Language. 1978. 9.95x (ISBN 0-312-35723-0). St Martin.

Giamatti, A. Bartlett. Western Literature, 3 vols. Incl. Vol. 1. The Ancient World. Von Staden, Heinrich, ed. pap. (ISBN 0-15-595276-5); Vol. 2. The Middle Ages, Renaissance, Enlightenment. Hollander, Robert, ed. pap. (ISBN 0-15-595277-3); Vol. 3. The Modern World. Brooks, Peter, ed. pap. (ISBN 0-15-595278-1). 1971. pap. text ed. 8.95 ea. (HC); instructor's manual avail. (ISBN 0-15-595279-X, HC). HarBraceJ.

Gillis, James M. False Prophets. 1929. Repr. 25.00 (ISBN 0-8274-2330-6). R West.

Glasgow, George. From Dawes to Locarno. LC 72-7101. (Select Bibliographies Reprint Ser.). 1972. Repr. of 1925 ed. 19.50 (ISBN 0-8369-6935-9). Arno.

Glicksberg, Charles I. Modern Literary Perspectivism. LC 79-125979. 1970. 5.95 (ISBN 0-87074-061-X). SMU Press.

Glyph Seven: Textual Studies. 1980. 16.50x (ISBN 0-8018-2365-X); pap. 5.95 (ISBN 0-8018-2366-8). Johns Hopkins.

Goble, Neil. Asimov Analyzed. LC 73-169988. 1972. 5.95 (ISBN 0-88358-113-2). Mirage Pr.

Godley, A. D. Reliquiae, 2 vols. Fletcher, C. R., ed. 1973. Repr. of 1926 ed. 75.00 (ISBN 0-8274-0201-5). R West.

Goldberg, Issac. The Fine Art of Living: An Approach to Life & the Arts. 1973. Repr. of 1930 ed. 20.00 (ISBN 0-8274-0736-X). R West.

Goldberg, S. L. An Essay on King Lear. LC 73-84318. 212p. 1974. 33.50 (ISBN 0-521-20200-0); pap. 10.50x (ISBN 0-521-09831-9). Cambridge U Pr.

Golther, Wolfgang. Nordische Literaturgeschichte. (Ger.). 1973. Repr. of 1905 ed. 30.00 (ISBN 0-8274-0200-7). R West.

Goodman, Paul. Structure of Literature. LC 54-9577. 1962. pap. 2.45 (ISBN 0-226-30327-6, P91, Phoen). U of Chicago Pr.

Gorky, Maxim. On Literature. 397p. 1975. 12.00x (ISBN 0-8464-0684-5). Beekman Pubs.

Gosse, E. Aspects & Impressions. 1973. Repr. of 1922 ed. 9.50 (ISBN 0-8274-0383-6). R West.

Gosse, Edmund. Books on the Table. 1921. Repr. 19.50 (ISBN 0-8274-1965-1). R West.

--Critical Kit Kats. 1913. Repr. 20.00 (ISBN 0-8274-3841-9). R West.

--Father & Son. 1916. Repr. 25.00 (ISBN 0-8274-2340-3). R West.

--Northern Studies. 1973. Repr. of 1890 ed. 11.50 (ISBN 0-8274-0384-4). R West.

--Questions at Issue. LC 72-3465. (Essay Index Reprint Ser.). Repr. of 1893 ed. 18.00 (ISBN 0-8369-2902-0). Arno.

--Silhouettes. 1973. Repr. of 1925 ed. 25.00 (ISBN 0-8274-0382-8). R West.

Gosse, Edmund W. Aspects & Impressions. (English Literary Reference Ser). Repr. of 1922 ed. 14.00 (ISBN 0-384-19320-X). Johnson Repr.

--A History of Eighteenth Century Literature Sixteen Sixty to Seventeen Eighty. Repr. of 1930 ed. 27.00 (ISBN 0-403-04100-7). Somerset Pub.

--Selected Essay, Second Series. 1973. Repr. of 1928 ed. 14.50 (ISBN 0-8274-0619-3). R West.

--Selected Essays, First Series. 1973. Repr. of 1928 ed. 14.50 (ISBN 0-8274-0618-5). R West.

--Some Diversions of a Man of Letters. 1973. Repr. of 1919 ed. 17.50 (ISBN 0-8274-0620-7). R West.

Gottlieb, Darcy. No Witness But Ourselves. LC 73-85459. 1973. 5.00x (ISBN 0-8262-0154-7). U of Mo Pr.

Graff, Gerald. Literature Against Itself: Literary Ideas in Modern Society. LC 78-9879. x, 250p. 1981. pap. 5.95 (ISBN 0-226-30598-8). U of Chicago Pr.

Graham, Henry G. Literary & Historical Essays. 1973. Repr. of 1908 ed. 30.00 (ISBN 0-8274-0198-1). R West.

Graham, Stephen. The Death of Yesterday. 1973. Repr. of 1930 ed. 25.00 (ISBN 0-8274-0209-0). R West.

Gratcap, L. P. The Substance of Literature. 1973. Repr. of 1913 ed. 20.00 (ISBN 0-8274-0205-8). R West.

Green, Martin. Dreams of Adventure, Deeds of Empire. LC 78-73766. (Lust for Power Ser.: Vol. 2). 1979. 15.00 (ISBN 0-465-01718-5). Basic.

Greenlaw, Edwin. Province of Literary History. LC 68-26279. 1968. Repr. of 1931 ed. 12.00 (ISBN 0-8046-0180-1). Kennikat.

Greenwood, R. R. A Preface to Literature. 1978. Repr. of 1930 ed. lib. bdg. 10.00 (ISBN 0-8495-1914-4). Arden Lib.

Griffin, G. W. Studies in Literature. 1973. Repr. of 1870 ed. 20.00 (ISBN 0-8274-0204-X). R West.

--Studies in Literature (Shakespeare, Hawthorne, Shelley, Thackeray, Dante, Hugo) 1978. Repr. of 1870 ed. lib. bdg. 20.00 (ISBN 0-8414-2007-6). Folcroft.

Griffith, Dudley. The Origin of the Griselda Story. 1973. Repr. of 1931 ed. 12.50 (ISBN 0-8274-0195-7). R West.

Grigson, Geoffrey. The Contrary View: Glimpses of Fudge & Gold. 243p. 1974. 17.50x (ISBN 0-87471-152-5). Rowman.

Grimm, Herman. Essays on Literature. 1973. Repr. of 1888 ed. 25.00 (ISBN 0-8274-0216-3). R West.

Grossinger, Richard & Hough, Lindy, eds. Anima Mundi. (Earth Geography Booklet Ser: No. 4). (Illus.). 256p. (Orig.). 1973. pap. 4.00 (ISBN 0-913028-17-7). North Atlantic.

Guches, Richard C. Sequel: A Self-Paced Program for the Critical Analysis of Literature. LC 79-88953. (Orig.). 1979. pap. 7.95 (ISBN 0-917962-64-8). Peek Pubns.

Guerber, Helene A. The Book of the Epic: The World's Greatest Epics Told in Story. 1973. Repr. of 1913 ed. 50.00 (ISBN 0-8274-1385-8). R West.

Guillaume De Palerne. The Ancient English Romance of William & the Werwolf. Madden, Frederick, ed. LC 73-80173. (Literature & Criticism Ser). 1971. Repr. of 1832 ed. 29.50 (ISBN 0-8337-2178-X). B Franklin.

Gunton, Sharon, ed. Contemporary Literacy Criticism: Exerpts from Criticism of the Works of Today's Novelists, Poets, Playwrights & Other Creative Writers, Vol. 21. LC 76-38938. (Contemporary Literary Criticism Ser.). 600p. 1982. 66.00 (ISBN 0-8103-0117-2). Gale.

--Contemporary Literary Criticism: Excerpts from the Criticism of the Works of Today's Novelists, Poets,, Playwrights & Other Creative Writers, 15 vols. Incl. Vol. 1. 1973. (ISBN 0-8103-0100-8); Vol. 2. 1974. (ISBN 0-8103-0102-4); Vol. 3. 1975. (ISBN 0-8103-0104-0); Vol. 4. 1975. (ISBN 0-8103-0106-7); Vol. 5. 1976. (ISBN 0-8103-0108-3); Vol. 6. 1976. (ISBN 0-8103-0110-5); Vol. 7. 1977. (ISBN 0-8103-0112-1); Vol. 8. 1978. (ISBN 0-8103-0114-8); Vol. 9. 1978. (ISBN 0-685-92122-0); Vol. 10. 1979. (ISBN 0-8103-0118-0); Vol. 11. 1979 (ISBN 0-8103-0120-2); Vol. 12. 1979 (ISBN 0-8103-0122-9); Vol. 13. 1979 (ISBN 0-8103-0124-5); Vol. 14. 1980 (ISBN 0-8103-0101-6); Vol. 15. 1980 (ISBN 0-8103-0103-2). LC 76-38938. (Contemporary Literary Criticism Ser.). 62.00 ea. Gale.

Gwynn, Stephen. For Second Reading. 1973. Repr. of 1918 ed. 20.00 (ISBN 0-8274-0184-1). R West.

Haber, R. Burns, ed. Two Centuries of Anecdotes. 1973. Repr. of 1932 ed. 17.50 (ISBN 0-8274-0211-2). R West.

Habluetzel, Margrit. Die Bildwelt Thomas Deloneys. 1973. Repr. of 1946 ed. 25.00 (ISBN 0-8274-0210-4). R West.

Hackett, Francis. Horizons: A Book of Criticism. 1973. Repr. of 1918 ed. 25.00 (ISBN 0-8274-0389-5). R West.

Hall, Robert A., Jr. Language, Literature & Life: Selected Essays by Robert A. Hall, Jr. LC 79-26478. (Edward Sapir Monographs in Language, Culture & Cognition: No. 5). (Illus.). viii, 295p. 1978. pap. 8.00x (ISBN 0-933104-07-3). Jupiter Pr.

Hall, Sharon, ed. Twentieth-Century Literary Criticism. (Twentieth-Century Literary Criticism Ser.: Vol. 4). 650p. 1981. 62.00 (ISBN 0-8103-0178-4). Gale.

Hall, Sharon & Mendelson, Phyllis C., eds. Twentieth-Century Literary Criticism, Vol. 1. LC 76-46132. 1978. 62.00 (ISBN 0-8103-0175-X). Gale.

Hallam, Henry. Introduction to the Literature of Europe in the Fifteenth, Sixteenth, & Seventeenth Centuries. (Illus.). 1973. 45.00 (ISBN 0-8274-0219-8). R West.

Halle, Louis J. The Search for an Eternal Norm: As Represented by Three Classics. LC 80-5793. 220p. 1981. lib. bdg. 18.75 (ISBN 0-8191-1444-8); pap. text ed. 9.75 (ISBN 0-8191-1445-6). U Pr of Amer.

Hallwas, John E. & Reader, Dennis J., eds. The Vision of This Land: Studies of Vachel Lindsay, Edgar Lee Masters, & Carl Sandburg. LC 76-4350. 1976. pap. 5.00 (ISBN 0-934312-00-1). Essays in Lit W Ill U.

Ham, Roswell G. Otway & Lee: Biography from a Baroque Age. LC 31-4706. (Illus.). 1969. Repr. of 1931 ed. lib. bdg. 14.50x (ISBN 0-8371-0462-9, HAOL). Greenwood.

Hammerton, J. A. Outline of Great Books. 1973. Repr. of 1937 ed. 20.00 (ISBN 0-8274-0218-X). R West.

Haney, John L. The Story of Our Literature. 1973. Repr. of 1923 ed. 15.00 (ISBN 0-8274-0217-1). R West.

Hardison, O. B., Jr., ed. Modern Continental Literary Criticism. (Orig.). 1962. pap. text ed. 6.95 (ISBN 0-13-590802-7). P-H.

Hardy, William J. Book-Plates. 2nd ed. LC 72-5514. (Select Bibliographies Reprint Set). 1972. Repr. of 1896 ed. 20.00 (ISBN 0-8369-6914-6). Arno.

Harland, Marion. Where Ghosts Walk: The Haunts of Familiar Characters in History & Literature. 1973. Repr. of 1899 ed. 20.00 (ISBN 0-8274-0228-7). R West.

Harper, Howard. Library Essays. LC 72-8899. 1972. Repr. of 1924 ed. lib. bdg. 25.00 (ISBN 0-8414-0412-7). Folcroft.

--The Romance of Mary W. Shelley, John Howard Payne & Washington Irving. LC 72-7323. 1973. lib. bdg. 15.00 (ISBN 0-8414-0324-4). Folcroft.

Harris, Frank. Contemporary Portraits. (First Ser.). 1973. 25.00 (ISBN 0-8274-0396-8). R West.

Harris, J. Henry. Cornish Saints & Sinners. 1973. Repr. of 1926 ed. 35.00 (ISBN 0-8274-0226-0). R West.

Harrison, Frederic. Among My Books. 1973. lib. bdg. 20.00 (ISBN 0-8414-5002-1). Folcroft.

--Choice of Books & Other Literary Pieces. 1973. Repr. of 1925 ed. 20.00 (ISBN 0-8274-0224-4). R West.

--Literary Estimates. 1973. lib. bdg. 9.50 (ISBN 0-8414-5005-6). Folcroft.

Harrison, G. Elsie. Methodist Good Companions. Repr. of 1935 ed. lib. bdg. 20.00 (ISBN 0-8414-5009-9). Folcroft.

Hartman, Geoffrey H. Criticism in the Wilderness: The Study of Literature Today. LC 80-13491. (Illus.). 336p. 1980. 18.00x (ISBN 0-300-02085-6). Yale U Pr.

--The Fate of Reading & Other Essays. LC 74-11624. xiv, 352p. 1975. 15.00x (ISBN 0-226-31844-3). U of Chicago Pr.

Hatteras, Owen, pseud. Pistols for Two. LC 77-4002. 1973. lib. bdg. 10.00 (ISBN 0-8414-4910-4). Folcroft.

Hauser, Arnold. Social History of Art, 4 vols. Incl. Vol. 1. Prehistoric to Middle Ages. 1957. (ISBN 0-394-70114-3, V114); Vol. 2. Renaissance to Baroque. 1957. (ISBN 0-394-70115-1, V115); Vol. 3. Rococco to Romanticism. 1958. (ISBN 0-394-70116-X, V116); Vol. 4. Naturalism of the Film Age. 1958. (ISBN 0-394-70117-8, V117). pap. 2.95 ea. (Vin). Random.

Haverford Essays, Studies in Modern Literature Prepared by Some Former Pupils of Prof. Francis B. Gummere in Honor of the Completion of the Twentieth Year of His Teaching in Haverford College. facs. ed. LC 67-23227. (Essay Index Reprint Ser). 1909. 15.50 (ISBN 0-8369-0519-9). Arno.

Hawthorne, Julian. Confessions & Criticisms. 1973. lib. bdg. 11.45 (ISBN 0-8414-5023-4). Folcroft.

Hawthorne, Nathaniel. House of the Seven Gables. Gross, Seymour L., ed. (Critical Editions). (Annotated). (gr. 9-12). 1967. pap. text ed. 4.95x (ISBN 0-393-09705-6, 9705, NortonC). Norton.

Haynes, E. S. Fritto Misto. 1973. Repr. of 1924 ed. 20.00 (ISBN 0-8274-0234-1). R West.

--Personalia. 1973. Repr. of 1918 ed. 20.00 (ISBN 0-8274-0233-3). R West.

Hayward, A. Biographical & Critical Essays, 2 vols. 1973. Repr. of 1858 ed. Set. 85.00 (ISBN 0-8274-0232-5). R West.

Hazeltine, Mayo W. Chats About Books, Poets, & Novelists. 1973. Repr. of 1883 ed. 30.00 (ISBN 0-8274-0231-7). R West.

Hazlitt, William. Characteristics in the Manner of Rochefoueault's Maxims. LC 73-14721. 1927. Repr. lib. bdg. 20.00 (ISBN 0-8414-4760-8). Folcroft.

Heinrich von Kleist Studies. LC 79-8846. (Hofstra University Cultural & Intercultural Studies: Vol. 3). 24.50 (ISBN 0-404-61653-4). AMS Pr.

Heinzelman, Kurt. The Economics of the Imagination. LC 79-4019. 1980. lib. bdg. 18.50x (ISBN 0-87023-274-6). U of Mass Pr.

Heitner, Jack. The Search for the Real Self: Humanistic Psychology & Literature. LC 78-62174. 1978. pap. text ed. 8.75 (ISBN 0-8191-0474-4). U Pr of Amer.

Hemmings, F. W., ed. The Age of Realism. 1978. Repr. of 1974 ed. text ed. 27.50x (ISBN 0-391-00817-X). Humanities.

Henderson, Philip. And Morning in His Eyes. 1973. lib. bdg. 15.50 (ISBN 0-8414-5039-0). Folcroft.

Hendrickson, Robert. The Literary Life & Other Curiosities. LC 81-65262. (Illus.). 352p. 1981. 20.00 (ISBN 0-670-43029-3). Viking Pr.

Heninger, S. K., Jr. Touches of Sweet Harmony: Pythagorean Cosmology & Renaissance Poetics. LC 73-78049. (Illus.). 1974. 20.00 (ISBN 0-87328-063-6). Huntington Lib.

Hennequin, Emile. Critique Scientifique. (Classics in Art & Literary Criticism Ser). (Fr). 1970. Repr. of 1888 ed. 23.00 (ISBN 0-384-22340-0). Johnson Repr.

Henrion, Pierre. Gulliver's Secret. Incl. Le Secret De Gulliver. LC 72-171908. Repr. of 1962 ed. lib. bdg. 15.00 (ISBN 0-8414-5043-9). Folcroft.

Hermand, Jost & Beck, Evelyn T. Interpretive Synthesis: The Task of Literary Scholarship. LC 75-10102. 246p. 1976. 12.00 (ISBN 0-8044-2035-1). Ungar.

Hermant, Abel. L' Art D'ecrire. 1973. Repr. of 1926 ed. 15.00 (ISBN 0-8274-0230-9). R West.

Herts, B. Russell. Depreciations. 1973. 25.00 (ISBN 0-8274-0229-5). R West.

Hevesi, J. L. Essays on Language & Literature. 1973. Repr. of 1947 ed. 25.00 (ISBN 0-8274-0243-0). R West.

Heydrick, Benjamin. How to Study Literature. 1973. Repr. of 1901 ed. 15.00 (ISBN 0-8274-0242-2). R West.

Hibbard, Addison & Frenz, Horst, eds. Writers of the Western World. 2nd ed. LC 67-6008. 1967. text ed. 21.50 (ISBN 0-395-04601-7, 3-24495). HM.

Hicks, Seymour. Between Ourselves. 1973. Repr. of 1930 ed. 15.00 (ISBN 0-8274-0241-4). R West.

Higgins, Dick. Die Fabelhafte Getraume Von Taifun-Willi. LC 74-135054. 1970. pap. 2.00 (ISBN 0-911856-04-8). Abyss.

--Towards the Seventies. LC 79-129807. 1969. pap. 0.75 (ISBN 0-911856-00-5). Abyss.

Higginson, Thomas W. Book & Heart. 1973. Repr. of 1897 ed. 20.00 (ISBN 0-8274-0240-6). R West.

--Book & Heart: Essays on Literature & Life. LC 72-4549. (Essay Index Reprint Ser.). Repr. of 1897 ed. 16.00 (ISBN 0-8369-2949-7). Arno.

--Cheerful Yesterdays. 1973. Repr. of 1898 ed. 20.00 (ISBN 0-8274-0237-6). R West.

--Contemporaries. 1973. Repr. of 1899 ed. 25.00 (ISBN 0-8274-0239-2). R West.

--Malbone: An Oldport Romance. 1973. Repr. of 1882 ed. 25.00 (ISBN 0-8274-0238-4). R West.

--Out-Door Papers. 1973. Repr. of 1863 ed. 25.00 (ISBN 0-8274-0235-X). R West.

--Outdoor Studies. 1973. Repr. of 1900 ed. 25.00 (ISBN 0-8274-0251-1). R West.

--Part of a Man's Life. 1973. Repr. of 1905 ed. 25.00 (ISBN 0-8274-0236-8). R West.

--Studies in History & Letters. 1973. Repr. of 1900 ed. 25.00 (ISBN 0-8274-0249-X). R West.

--Women & Men. 1973. Repr. of 1888 ed. 25.00 (ISBN 0-8274-0250-3). R West.

Highet, Gilbert. Explorations. 1971. 15.95 (ISBN 0-19-501450-2). Oxford U Pr.

Hill, George B. Writers & Readers. 1973. Repr. of 1892 ed. 30.00 (ISBN 0-8274-0247-3). R West.

Hind, C. Lewis. Diary of a Looker-on. 1973. Repr. of 1908 ed. 20.00 (ISBN 0-8274-0246-5). R West.

--Life & I. 1973. Repr. of 1923 ed. 20.00 (ISBN 0-8274-0245-7). R West.

Hine, Reginald L. Hitchin Worthies. 1973. Repr. of 1932 ed. 35.00 (ISBN 0-8274-0244-9). R West.

Hines, John. Elements of Literature: A Student's Summary. 2d rev. ed. LC 77-1886. 1977. pap. text ed. 2.50 (ISBN 0-8477-3181-2). U of PR Pr.

Hirsch, Eric D., Jr. Validity in Interpretation. 1973. pap. 5.25x (ISBN 0-300-01692-1, Y259). Yale U Pr.

Hoare, Frederick R. Eight Decisive Books of Antiquity. 1973. Repr. of 1952 ed. 25.00 (ISBN 0-8274-0335-6). R West.

Hobhouse, John C. Historical Illustrations of the Fourth Canto of Childe Harold. LC 75-29435. 1973. Repr. of 1818 ed. lib. bdg. 45.00 (ISBN 0-8414-4880-9). Folcroft.

Hoge, James O. & West, James L., eds. Review Three. 1981. price not set (ISBN 0-8139-0910-4). U Pr of Va.

Holdom, Lynne. Capsule Reviews. LC 80-20445. 51p. 1980. Repr. of 1977 ed. lib. bdg. 9.95 (ISBN 0-89370-056-8). Borgo Pr.

Holland, Henry S. A Bundle of Memories. 1973. Repr. of 1915 ed. 20.00 (ISBN 0-8274-0334-8). R West.

--Personal Studies. 1973. Repr. of 1905 ed. 20.00 (ISBN 0-8274-0333-X). R West.

--Some Essays & Lectures. 1973. Repr. of 1893 ed. 20.00 (ISBN 0-8274-0332-1). R West.

Holland, Robert C. Men & Books & Cities. 1973. Repr. of 1919 ed. 12.50 (ISBN 0-8274-0255-4). R West.

Holman, C. Hugh. A Handbook to Literature. 4th ed. LC 79-10061. 1980. 12.95 (ISBN 0-672-61477-4); pap. 8.95 (ISBN 0-672-61441-3). Bobbs.

Hooker, Edward N., ed. The Critical Works of John Dennis, 2 vols. 1965. Set. 60.00x (ISBN 0-8018-0279-2). Johns Hopkins.

Hope, Quentin M. Saint-Evremond: The Honnete Homme As Critic. LC 62-62963. (Humanities Ser.: No. 51). 152p. 1962. pap. 5.00x (ISBN 0-253-38651-9). Ind U Pr.

Horn, Andras. Das Literarische Formalistische Versuche Zu Seiner Bestimmung. 1978. 37.75 (ISBN 3-11-007600-4). De Gruyter.

Houghton, Lord. Monographs Personal & Social. 1973. Repr. of 1873 ed. 35.00 (ISBN 0-8274-0337-2). R West.

Howarth, R. G. Literary Particles. LC 72-105796. 1970. Repr. of 1946 ed. 12.00 (ISBN 0-8046-0957-8). Kennikat.

Howe, Irving. Decline of the New. 336p. pap. 5.95 (ISBN 0-8180-1160-2). Horizon.

Howe, Irving, ed. The Idea of the Modern in Literature & the Arts. 1977. pap. 5.95 (ISBN 0-8180-1183-1). Horizon.

Howells, William D. Annie Kilburn. 1973. lib. bdg. 25.00 (ISBN 0-8414-5134-6). Folcroft.

--My Literary Passions. LC 4-15782. 1968. Repr. of 1895 ed. 10.00 (ISBN 0-527-42750-0). Kraus Repr.

--My Literary Passions. 1973. lib. bdg. 30.00 (ISBN 0-8414-5147-8). Folcroft.

--Pair of Patient Lovers. 1973. lib. bdg. 25.00 (ISBN 0-8414-5148-6). Folcroft.

Hughes, Langston, ed. The Best Short Stories by Negro Writers. 1967. 12.50 (ISBN 0-316-38032-6); pap. 6.95 (ISBN 0-316-38031-8). Little.

Hughes, Richard. The Lively Image: Four Myths in Literature. 1975. pap. text ed. 6.95 (ISBN 0-87626-500-X). Winthrop.

Huneker, James. Ivory, Apes & Peacocks. 1973. Repr. of 1915 ed. 25.00 (ISBN 0-8274-0049-7). R West.

Hurst, H. Norman. Four Elements in Literature. 1973. Repr. of 1936 ed. 20.00 (ISBN 0-8274-0351-8). R West.

Hutcheon, Linda. Narcissistic Narrative: The Metafictional Paradox, Vol. 5. Dimic, Milan V., ed. (Library of the Canadian Review of Comparative Literature). 168p. 1980. text ed. 10.75 (ISBN 0-88920-102-1, Pub. by Laurier U Pr Canada). Humanities.

Hutmacher, William F. Wynkyn De Worde & Chaucer's Canterbury Tales: A Transcription & Collation of the 1498 Edition with Caxton from the General Proloque Through the Knights Tale. (Costerus, New Ser.: No. 10). 1978. pap. text ed. 23.00x (ISBN 90-6203-502-7). Humanities.

Hutton, John A. Ancestral Voices. 1973. Repr. of 1915 ed. 20.00 (ISBN 0-8274-0349-6). R West.

--Pilgrims in the Region of Faith (Amiel, Tolstoy, Pater, Newman) 1973. lib. bdg. 20.00 (ISBN 0-8414-5241-5). Folcroft.

Hutton, Laurence. From the Books of Laurence Hutton. 1973. Repr. of 1892 ed. 20.00 (ISBN 0-8274-0348-8). R West.

--Literary Landmarks. Incl. Edinburgh. Repr. of 1891 ed; Florence. Repr. of 1897 ed; Jerusalem. Repr. of 1895 ed; London. Repr. of 1897 ed; Rome. Repr. of 1897 ed; Venice. Repr. of 1896 ed. 1973. 25.00 (ISBN 0-8274-0380-1). R West.

Hutton, Richard H. Literary Essays. 1973. Repr. of 1908 ed. 25.00 (ISBN 0-8274-0052-7). R West.

--Richard Holt Hutton of "The Spectator". 1973. Repr. of 1899 ed. 25.00 (ISBN 0-8274-0356-9). R West.

Huxley, Aldous L. Olive Tree. LC 72-167361. (Essay Index Reprint Ser.). Repr. of 1937 ed. 18.00 (ISBN 0-8369-2456-8). Arno.

Huxley, Thomas H. Critiques & Addresses. LC 72-3358. (Essay Index Reprint Ser.). Repr. of 1873 ed. 15.50 (ISBN 0-8369-2908-X). Arno.

Hyde, G. M. D. H. Lawrence & the Art of Translation. 128p. 1981. 24.50x (ISBN 0-389-20077-8). B&N.

Hyman, Stanley Edgar. The Critic's Credentials. LC 77-88902. 1978. 12.95 (ISBN 0-689-10847-8). Atheneum.

Ideas of Order in Literature & Film: Selected Papers from the 4th Annual Florida State University Conferenceon Literature & Film. LC 80-26017. viii, 136p. (Orig.). 1981. pap. 8.00 (ISBN 0-8130-0699-6). U Presses Fla.

Irving, H. B. Occasional Papers. 1973. Repr. of 1907 ed. 25.00 (ISBN 0-8274-0361-5). R West.

Jack, Adolphus A. Essays on the Novel: As Illustrated by Scott & Jane Austen. 1973. lib. bdg. 9.00 (ISBN 0-8414-5350-0). Folcroft.

Jackson, Holbrook. Essays of Today & Yesterday. 1973. Repr. of 1927 ed. 12.50 (ISBN 0-8274-0359-3). R West.

Jackson, William T. Anatomy of Love: A Study of the Tristan of Gottfried Von Strassburg. LC 70-154859. 1971. 16.00x (ISBN 0-231-03504-7). Columbia U Pr.

Jacobs, Carol. The Dissimulating Harmony: The Image of Interpretation in Nietzsche, Rilke, Artaud & Benjamin. LC 77-18392. (Illus.). 1978. text ed. 10.00x (ISBN 0-8018-2040-5). Johns Hopkins.

James, C., ed. Great Fights in Literature. 1978. Repr. of 1926 ed. lib. bdg. 25.00 (ISBN 0-8495-2714-7). Arden Lib.

James, Henry. Master Eustace. 1973. lib. bdg. 30.00 (ISBN 0-8414-5360-8). Folcroft.

--Notes & Reviews. facs. ed. LC 68-22100. (Essay Index Reprint Ser). 1968. Repr. of 1921 ed. 16.00 (ISBN 0-8369-0565-2). Arno.

--Partial Portraits. 1973. lib. bdg. 30.00 (ISBN 0-8414-5361-6). Folcroft.

--Real Thing & Other Tales. 1973. lib. bdg. 35.00 (ISBN 0-8414-5362-4). Folcroft.

--Selected Literary Criticism. Shapira, Morris, ed. LC 80-49685. 350p. Date not set. pap. 15.95 (ISBN 0-521-28365-5). Cambridge U Pr.

--Sense of the Past. 1973. lib. bdg. 45.00 (ISBN 0-8414-5363-2). Folcroft.

--The Siege of London. 1973. lib. bdg. 45.00 (ISBN 0-8414-5364-0). Folcroft.

--Soft Side. 1973. lib. bdg. 35.00 (ISBN 0-8414-5365-9). Folcroft.

--Terminations. 1973. lib. bdg. 40.00 (ISBN 0-8414-5366-7). Folcroft.

James, W. P. Romantic Professions. 1973. Repr. of 1894 ed. 30.00 (ISBN 0-8274-0256-2). R West.

Jameson, Anna B. Legends of the Madonna, As Represented in the Fine Arts. 1973. lib. bdg. 35.00 (ISBN 0-8414-5370-5). Folcroft.

--Sacred & Legendary Art, 2 vols. 1973. lib. bdg. 50.00 (ISBN 0-8414-5371-3). Folcroft.

Jebb, Richard C. Essays & Addresses. 1973. Repr. of 1907 ed. 30.00 (ISBN 0-8274-0363-1). R West.

Jenkins, MacGregor. Literature with a Large L. 1973. Repr. of 1919 ed. 10.00 (ISBN 0-8274-0260-0). R West.
Jennings, Henry J. Curiosities of Criticism. 1973. Repr. of 1881 ed. 25.00 (ISBN 0-8274-0258-9). R West.
Jerrold, Douglas. Georgian Adventure. 1973. Repr. of 1938 ed. 25.00 (ISBN 0-8274-0259-7). R West.
Joad, C. E. The Bookmark. 1973. Repr. of 1926 ed. 20.00 (ISBN 0-8274-0257-0). R West.
Johnson, Carol. The Disappearance of Literature. (Costerus New Ser.: Vol. 24). 123p. 1980. pap. text ed. 14.25x (ISBN 90-6203-761-5). Humanities.
Johnson, Lemuel A. Devil, the Gargoyle, & the Buffoon: The Negro As Metaphor in Western Literature. LC 76-139355. 1971. 12.00 (ISBN 0-8046-9006-5, Natl U); pap. 7.95 (ISBN 0-8046-9047-2). Kennikat.
Johnson, Samuel. Critical Opinions of Samuel Johnson. Brown, Joseph E., ed. LC 60-6035. 1961. Repr. of 1926 ed. 24.00 (ISBN 0-8462-0140-2). Russell.
--Johnson's Proposals for Printing Bibliotheca Harleiana 1742. LC 74-30045. Repr. of 1926 ed. lib. bdg. 6.50 (ISBN 0-8414-3556-1). Folcroft.
--Prologues Written by Samuel Johnson & Spoken by David Garrick at a Benefit Performance of Comus. LC 77-13301. Repr. of 1925 ed. 5.00 (ISBN 0-8414-5401-9). Folcroft.
--Proposals for the Publisher Seventeen Hundred & Forty-Four. Repr. of 1930 ed. 6.50 (ISBN 0-8414-5389-6). Folcroft.
--Samuel Johnson on Literature. Danziger, Marlies K., ed. LC 78-20936. (Milestones of Thought Ser.). 1979. pap. text ed. 3.95 (ISBN 0-8044-6097-3). Ungar.
Jones, Eldred D. Wole Soyinka. (World Authors Ser.: Nigeria: No. 256). 1971. lib. bdg. 10.95 (ISBN 0-8057-2852-X). Twayne.
Jones, Llewellyn. How to Criticize Books. 1973. Repr. of 1928 ed. 25.00 (ISBN 0-8274-0263-5). R West.
Jones, Peter. Philosophy & the Novel. 250p. 1975. pap. text ed. 4.95x (ISBN 0-19-824533-5). Oxford U Pr.
Jones, William M. Protestant Romance: Patterns of Reality in the Prose of Sir Giovanni Francesco Biondi. 131p. 1980. 10.00 (ISBN 0-87291-138-1). Coronado Pr.
Jordan, John E., ed. De Quincey As Critic. (Critics Ser.). 500p. 1973. 27.00x (ISBN 0-7100-7558-8). Routledge & Kegan.
Jordan-Smith, Paul. On Strange Altars: A Book of Enthusiasms. 59.95 (ISBN 0-8490-0762-3). Gordon Pr.
Kalwies, Howard. Hugues Salel: His Life & Works. Parent, David J., ed. LC 79-27150. (Applied Literature Press Medieval Studies: Vol. 4). 286p. 1979. 22.00 (ISBN 0-8357-0500-5, IS-00104, Pub by Applied Lit Pr). Univ Microfilms.
Katz, William A. & Klaessig, Janet, eds. Library Lit. Three: The Best of 1972. LC 78-15482. 1973. 13.00 (ISBN 0-8108-0613-4). Scarecrow.
Kaufmann, Walter. From Shakespeare to Existentialism. facsimile ed. LC 70-152180. (Select Bibliographies). Repr. of 1960 ed. 25.00 (ISBN 0-8369-5805-5). Arno.
Kawin, Bruce F. Telling It Again & Again: Repetition in Literature & Film. LC 75-37753. 208p. 1972. 14.50x (ISBN 0-8014-0698-6). Cornell U Pr.
Kazin, Alfred. Contemporaries, from the Nineteenth Century to the Present. rev. ed. 500p. 1981. 16.95 (ISBN 0-8180-1131-9); pap. 9.95 (ISBN 0-8180-1132-7). Horizon.
Kellett, E. E. Fashion in Literature: A Study of Changing Taste. LC 79-4409. 1979. Repr. of 1931 ed. lib. bdg. 30.00 (ISBN 0-8414-5482-5). Folcroft.
--Literary Quotation & Allusion. LC 70-86030. 1969. Repr. of 1933 ed. 10.00 (ISBN 0-8046-0619-6). Kennikat.
Kelman, John. Among Famous Books. 1973. Repr. of 1912 ed. 25.00 (ISBN 0-8274-0268-6). R West.
Kemble, James. Idols & Invalids (Byron) 1973. Repr. of 1933 ed. 35.00 (ISBN 0-8274-0266-X). R West.
Kent, Armine T. Otia: Poems, Essays, & Reviews. 1973. Repr. of 1905 ed. 20.00 (ISBN 0-8274-0272-4). R West.
Ker, William P. Collected Essays of W. P. Ker, 2 Vols. Whibley, Charles, ed. LC 68-15131. (Illus.). 1968. Repr. of 1925 ed. Set. 22.50 (ISBN 0-8462-1106-8). Russell.
Kermode, Frank. The Classic: Literary Images of Permanence & Change. LC 75-4824. 141p. 1975. 7.95 (ISBN 0-670-22508-8). Viking Pr.
Kernahan, Coulson. In Good Company. 1973. Repr. of 1917 ed. 20.00 (ISBN 0-8274-0323-2). R West.
Khrapchenko, M. The Writers of Creative Individuality & the Development of Literature. 420p. 1977. 8.00 (ISBN 0-8285-1095-4, Pub. by Progress Pubs Russia). Imported Pubns.
Kimpton, Edith. Book Ways: An Introduction to the Study of Literature. 1973. Repr. of 1913 ed. 12.50 (ISBN 0-8274-0093-4). R West.
Kincaid, Joseph J. Cristobal de Villalon. (World Authors Ser.: Spain: No. 264). 1971. lib. bdg. 10.95 (ISBN 0-8057-2963-1). Twayne.
Kingsmill, Hugh. The Sentimental Journey (Dickens) LC 72-13526. 1973. Repr. of 1934 ed. lib. bdg. 20.00 (ISBN 0-8414-1228-6). Folcroft.
Kirsch, Robert. Lives, Works & Transformations: A Quarter Century of Book Reviews & Essays. Rolens, Linda, ed. 1979. pap. 4.95 (ISBN 0-88496-086-2). Capra Pr.
Kleinau, Marion & McHughes, Janet. Theatres for Literature. LC 79-24492. 314p. 1980. pap. 11.50 (ISBN 0-88284-096-7). Alfred Pub.
Kleiser, Grenville. Similes & Their Use. 1973. Repr. of 1925 ed. 30.00 (ISBN 0-8274-0092-6). R West.
--Training for Authorship. 1973. Repr. of 1925 ed. 20.00 (ISBN 0-8274-0090-X). R West.
Knight, Everett. The Novel As Structure & Praxis: From Cervantes to Malraux. 1981. text ed. 8.50x (ISBN 0-391-00938-9). Humanities.
Knott, John R., Jr. & Reaske, Christopher R. Mirrors: An Introduction to Literature. 2nd ed. 1976. pap. text ed. 15.50 scp (ISBN 0-06-384701-9, HarpC); tchr's ed. free (ISBN 0-06-373614-4). Har-Row.
Kojecky, Roger. T. S. Eliot's Social Criticism. 255p. 1972. 7.95 (ISBN 0-374-27243-3). FS&G.
Koppen, Erwin. Dekadenter Wagnerismus: Studien zur europaeischen Literatur des Fin de siecle. (Komparatistische Studien 2, Beihefte Zur Zeitschrift Arcadia). 1973. 68.25x (ISBN 3-11-004388-2). De Gruyter.
Kostelanetz, Richard. In the Beginning. LC 73-186985. 1972. pap. 3.00 (ISBN 0-911856-05-6). Abyss.
Kostelanetz, Richard, ed. Aural Literature Criticism. (Precisely Ser.). 192p. (Orig.). 1981. 15.00 (ISBN 0-686-71636-1); pap. 6.00 (ISBN 0-686-73686-9). RK Edns.
--On Contemporary Literature. 1st ed. LC 72-156674. 1978. 50.00 (ISBN 0-932360-01-7); pap. 10.00 (ISBN 0-932360-00-9). RK Edns.
Kovacevic, Ivanka. Fact into Fiction: English Literature & the Industrial Scene 1750-1850. 416p. 1975. text ed. 19.50x (ISBN 0-7185-1130-1, Leicester). Humanities.
Krailsheimer, A. J., ed. Continental Renaissance, Fifteen Hundred to Sixteen Hundred. (Pelican Guides to European Literature). 1978. Repr. of 1971 ed. text ed. 28.50x (ISBN 0-391-00816-1). Humanities.
Krieger, Murray. Classic Vision: The Retreat from Extremity in Modern Literature. LC 77-167984. (Illus.). 1971. 16.50x (ISBN 0-8018-1312-3). Johns Hopkins.
Kronegger, Maria E. Literary Impressionism. 1973. pap. 2.95x (ISBN 0-8084-0365-6, L24). Coll & U Pr.
Kronenberger, Louis, ed. Atlantic Brief Lives: A Biographical Companion to the Arts. LC 73-154960. 1971. 15.00 (ISBN 0-316-50451-3, Pub by Atlantic Monthly Pr); pap. 6.95 (ISBN 0-316-50457-2). Little.
Krutch, Joseph W. Five Masters: A Study in the Mutations of the Novel. 7.75 (ISBN 0-8446-0750-9). Peter Smith.
Kurrik, Maire J. Literature & Negation. LC 79-15949. (Illus.). 1979. 25.00x (ISBN 0-231-04342-2). Columbia U Pr.
Laird, Charlton G., ed. World Through Literature. LC 77-99639. (Essay Index Reprint Ser). 1951. 30.00 (ISBN 0-8369-1359-0). Arno.
Landor, Walter S. The Sculptured Garland. LC 74-23824. Repr. of 1948 ed. lib. bdg. 10.00 (ISBN 0-8414-5709-3). Folcroft.
Lang, Andrew. Letters on Literature. LC 68-54277. Repr. of 1889 ed. 10.00 (ISBN 0-404-03836-0). AMS Pr.
Larg, David. Trial by Virgins. 1973. Repr. of 1933 ed. 30.00 (ISBN 0-8274-0316-X). R West.
Laughlin, James, et al, eds. New Directions in Prose & Poetry 26. LC 37-1751. 192p. 1973. 9.75 (ISBN 0-8112-0476-6); pap. 2.95 (ISBN 0-8112-0477-4, NDP353). New Directions.
Laurenson, Diana, ed. The Sociology of Literature: Applied Studies. (Sociological Review Monograph: No. 26). 284p. 1978. pap. 28.00x (ISBN 0-8476-2299-1). Rowman.
Lavrin, Janko. Studies in European Literature. LC 74-103230. 1970. Repr. of 1929 ed. 12.00 (ISBN 0-8046-0867-9). Kennikat.
Lawrence, Robert G., ed. Jacobean & Caroline Comedies. (Rowman & Littlefield University Library). 241p. 1973. 10.00x (ISBN 0-87471-402-8); pap. 4.50x (ISBN 0-87471-393-5). Rowman.
Lawton, William C. The Soul of the Anthology. 1973. Repr. of 1923 ed. 25.00 (ISBN 0-8274-0152-3). R West.
Leacock, Stephen B. Here Are My Lectures & Stories. LC 72-14188. (Essay Index Reprint Ser.). Repr. of 1937 ed. 16.25 (ISBN 0-518-10017-0). Arno.
Lemaitre, Jules. Literary Impressions. LC 77-105801. 1971. Repr. of 1921 ed. 13.50 (ISBN 0-8046-1360-5). Kennikat.
--Literary Impressions. 1973. Repr. of 1921 ed. 25.00 (ISBN 0-8274-0157-4). R West.
Lenz, Millicent & Mahood, Ramona, eds. Young Adult Literature: Background & Criticisms. LC 80-23489. 524p. 1980. 30.00 (ISBN 0-8389-0302-9). ALA.
Lessing, Doris. A Small Personal Voice: Essays, Reviews, Interviews. 1975. pap. 2.45 (ISBN 0-394-71685-X, Vin). Random.
Levin, Harry. Contexts of Criticism. LC 57-7613. 1963. pap. 1.65 (ISBN 0-689-70123-3, 29). Atheneum.
Levin, Harry T., ed. Perspectives of Criticism. LC 76-81459. 1970. Repr. of 1950 ed. 11.00 (ISBN 0-8462-1364-8). Russell.
Lewald, H. Ernest, ed. The Cry of Home: Cultural Nationalism & the Modern Writer. LC 76-173656. 1972. 17.50 (ISBN 0-87049-135-0). Lib Soc Sci.
Lewis, C. S. Hamlet: The Prince or the Poem. LC 73-18199. lib. bdg. 5.00 (ISBN 0-8414-5708-5). Folcroft.
Lewis, Clive S. Rehabilitations. 1973. Repr. of 1939 ed. 25.00 (ISBN 0-8274-1286-X). R West.
Lewisohn, L. Creative Life. LC 24-9372. 1924. 12.00 (ISBN 0-527-56800-7). Kraus Repr.
Literature (Predecessor of Times Literary Supplement, 9 vols. LC 74-3197. (Illus.). 1974. Repr. of 1897 ed. Set. 500.00 (ISBN 0-405-00698-5, Co Pub by New York Times); 65.00 ea. Arno.
Little, Charles J. Biographical & Literary Studies. 1973. Repr. of 1916 ed. 30.00 (ISBN 0-8274-0154-X). R West.
Les Livres de l'Annee. annual (Cercle de la Librairie). 1967 55.00 (ISBN 0-685-35968-9); 1968 57.50 (ISBN 0-685-35969-7); 1970 61.00 (ISBN 0-685-35970-0); 1970 75.00 (ISBN 0-685-35971-9). French & Eur.
Lodge, David. Novelist at the Crossroads & Other Essays on Fiction & Criticism. LC 77-163130. 308p. 1971. 17.50x (ISBN 0-8014-0674-9). Cornell U Pr.
--Working with Structuralism: Essays & Reviews on Nineteenth & Twentieth-Century Literature. 240p. 1981. 30.00 (ISBN 0-7100-0658-6). Routledge & Kegan.
Loliee, Frederic. Short History of Comparative Literature. Power, Douglas, tr. LC 74-105803. 1970. Repr. of 1906 ed. 16.50 (ISBN 0-8046-1361-3). Kennikat.
Lord, David N. The Characteristics & Laws of Figurative Language. 1973. Repr. of 1855 ed. 30.00 (ISBN 0-8274-0169-8). R West.
Low, Sidney. Masters of Literature: DeQuincey. 1973. Repr. of 1911 ed. 35.00 (ISBN 0-8274-1047-6). R West.
Low, Will H. A Chronicle of Friendships. 1973. Repr. of 1908 ed. 25.00 (ISBN 0-8274-1048-4). R West.
Lowe, E. A., ed. Codices Latini Antiquiores - Supplement. (Illus.). 1971. 49.00x (ISBN 0-19-818218-X). Oxford U Pr.
Lowell, James R. Among My Books. LC 75-126666. 1970. 11.50 (ISBN 0-404-04039-X). AMS Pr.
--Latest Literary Essays. 1973. Repr. of 1891 ed. 20.00 (ISBN 0-8274-0164-7). R West.
Lowell, Percival. The Soul of the Far East. 1973. Repr. of 1888 ed. 35.00 (ISBN 0-8274-1046-8). R West.
Lower, Mark A. Contributions to Literature: Historical, Antiquarian & Metrical. 1978. Repr. of 1854 ed. lib. bdg. 40.00 (ISBN 0-8492-1592-7). R West.
Lowery, Robert G., ed. Essays on Sean O'Casey's Autobiographies. 268p. 1981. text ed. 22.50x (ISBN 0-389-20180-4). B&N.
Lubbock, John. The Pleasures of Life. 1973. Repr. of 1899 ed. 20.00 (ISBN 0-8274-0163-9). R West.
Lucas, Dolores D. Emily Dickinson & Riddle. LC 73-76428. 151p. 1969. 8.50 (ISBN 0-87580-011-4). N Ill U Pr.
Lucas, Frank L. Authors Dead & Living. facs. ed. LC 68-29226. (Essay Index Reprint Ser). 1968. Repr. of 1926 ed. 16.00 (ISBN 0-8369-0633-0). Arno.
Lucas, John. The Literature of Change: Studies in the Nineteenth Century Provincial Novel. 2nd ed. 217p. 1980. 22.50x (ISBN 0-389-20020-4); pap. 11.50x (ISBN 0-389-20021-2). B&N.
Lucas, John, ed. The Nineteen Thirties: A Challenge to Orthodoxy. LC 78-67473. (Illus.). 1978. text ed. 23.50x (ISBN 0-06-494399-2). B&N.
Lu Hsun. Selected Stories of Lu Hsun. Yang, Hsien-Yi & Yang, Gladys, trs. from Chinese. LC 72-92717. (Illus.). 1973. 8.50 (ISBN 0-88211-042-X). S A Russell.
Lutyens, David B. The Creative Encounter. 200p. 1980. Repr. of 1960 ed. lib. bdg. 30.00 (ISBN 0-89987-506-8). Darby Bks.
Lyall, Alfred C. Studies in Literature. 1978. Repr. of 1915 ed. lib. bdg. 30.00 (ISBN 0-8495-3230-2). Arden Lib.
Lynch, Arthur. Moments of Genius. 1973. Repr. of 1919 ed. 17.50 (ISBN 0-8274-0108-6). R West.
Lynd, Robert. Books & Authors. 1973. Repr. of 1923 ed. 25.00 (ISBN 0-8274-0728-9). R West.
--Old & New Masters. 1973. Repr. of 1919 ed. 25.00 (ISBN 0-8274-0727-0). R West.
MacAndrew, Elizabeth. The Gothic Tradition. LC 79-9447. 1980. 20.00x (ISBN 0-231-04674-X). Columbia U Pr.
McCallion, Barry. Art Maxims in a Bronx Fedora. 1973. pap. 1.75 (ISBN 0-911856-06-4). Abyss.
McCarthy, D. Memories. 1973. Repr. of 1953 ed. 25.00 (ISBN 0-8274-1037-9). R West.
MacCarthy, Desmond. European Tradition in Literature from 1600 Onwards. LC 73-16195. 1938. lib. bdg. 8.50 (ISBN 0-8414-6087-6). Folcroft.
Macdonald, Duncan B. Hebrew Literary Genius: An Interpretation; Being an Introduction to the Reading of the Old Testament. LC 68-25676. 1968. Repr. of 1933 ed. 8.50 (ISBN 0-8462-1166-1). Russell.
McFarland, Philip, et al. Themes in World Literature. (Literature Ser.). 1970. text ed. 11.16 (ISBN 0-395-02875-2, 2-26380); tchrs' resource bk. 4.56 (ISBN 0-395-02876-0, 2-26382). HM.
--Themes in World Literature. (Literature Ser.). (Illus.). 1975. text ed. 13.98 (ISBN 0-395-20156-X); tchr's resource bk 5.61 (ISBN 0-395-20157-8). HM.
McHale, Frank, compiled by. Pieces That Have Won Prizes: Also Many Encore Pieces; Enlarged Edition. LC 79-39381. (Granger Index Reprint Ser.). Repr. of 1930 ed. 19.00 (ISBN 0-8369-6346-6). Arno.
MacIver, R. M., ed. Great Moral Dilemmas. (Religion & Civilization Ser). 189p. 1964. Repr. of 1956 ed. 19.50x (ISBN 0-8154-0145-0). Cooper Sq.
Mackenzie, A. S. The Evolution of Literature. 1977. Repr. of 1911 ed. lib. bdg. 25.00 (ISBN 0-8414-6221-6). Folcroft.
McLaughlin, Edward T. Studies in Mediaeval Life & Literature. LC 74-39101. (Essay Index Reprint Ser.). Repr. of 1894 ed. 15.00 (ISBN 0-8369-2701-X). Arno.
Macleod, Joseph G. Beauty & the Beast. 1973. Repr. of 1927 ed. 20.00 (ISBN 0-8274-0747-5). R West.
McMurtry, Jo. Victorian Life & Victorian Fiction: A Companion for the American Reader. (Illus.). 1978. 17.50 (ISBN 0-208-01744-5, Archon). Shoe String.
Macy, John. A Guide to Reading. 1973. Repr. of 1913 ed. 20.00 (ISBN 0-8274-0743-2). R West.
Magill, Frank N., ed. Magill's Bibliography of Literary Criticism. LC 79-63017. 1979. 200.00 (ISBN 0-89356-188-6). Salem Pr.
--Magill's Literary Annual: 1978, 2 vols. LC 77-99209. 1978. lib. bdg. 50.00 (ISBN 0-89356-278-5). Salem Pr.
--Magill's Literary Annual: 1979, 2 vols. LC 77-99209. 1979. 50.00 (ISBN 0-89356-279-3). Salem Pr.
Magill, Frank N., et al, eds. Magill's Literary Annual: 1977, 2 vols. LC 77-99209. 1977. lib. bdg. 50.00 (ISBN 0-89356-077-4). Salem Pr.
--Thirteen Hundred Critical Evaluations of Selected Novels & Plays. LC 78-55387. 1978. 150.00 (ISBN 0-89356-043-X). Salem Pr.
Magnus, Laurie. A General Sketch of European Literature in the Centuries of Romance. 1977. lib. bdg. 59.95 (ISBN 0-8490-1878-1). Gordon Pr.
--History of European Literature. LC 75-103233. 1970. Repr. of 1934 ed. 13.50 (ISBN 0-8046-0870-9). Kennikat.
Maier, Norman R. A Psychological Approach to Literary Criticism. 154p. 1980. Repr. of 1933 ed. lib. bdg. 20.00 (ISBN 0-8495-3797-5). Arden Lib.
Main, Alexander. Wise, Witty & Tender Sayings. 1973. Repr. of 1893 ed. 25.00 (ISBN 0-8274-1030-1). R West.
Mais, S. P. The Best in Their Kind. 1973. Repr. of 1949 ed. 20.00 (ISBN 0-8274-0766-1). R West.
--Book & Their Writers. 1973. Repr. of 1920 ed. 25.00 (ISBN 0-8274-1031-X). R West.
--Delight in Books. 1973. Repr. of 1931 ed. 20.00 (ISBN 0-8274-0764-5). R West.
--Some Books I Like. 1973. Repr. of 1932 ed. 20.00 (ISBN 0-8274-0765-3). R West.
--The Writing of English. 1973. Repr. of 1935 ed. 15.00 (ISBN 0-8274-0763-7). R West.
Mais, Stuart P. Why We Should Read. 1973. Repr. of 1921 ed. 20.00 (ISBN 0-8274-0116-7). R West.
Mallock, W. H. Memoirs of Life & Literature. 1973. Repr. of 1920 ed. 30.00 (ISBN 0-8274-0760-2). R West.
Mallory, H. S. Backgrounds of Book Reviewing. 59.95 (ISBN 0-87968-693-6). Gordon Pr.
Malone, Kemp, ed. Deor. rev. ed. 41p. 1979. pap. text ed. 2.50x (ISBN 0-85989-066-X, Pub. by U Exeter England). Humanities.

Man Literature Series: Level 1, Bk. 1. Incl. Man in the Poetic Mode. Zweigler (ISBN 0-88343-002-9); Man in the Fictional Mode. Haupt (ISBN 0-88343-001-0); Man in the Expository Mode. Solotaroff (ISBN 0-88343-003-7); Man in the Dramatic Mode. Heston (ISBN 0-88343-004-5). (gr. 7 up). 1971. pap. text ed. 3.72 ea.; tchr's. manual 3.90 (ISBN 0-88343-005-3). McDougal-Littell.

Man Literature Series: Level 2, Bk. 2. Incl. Man in the Fictional Mode. Haupt (ISBN 0-88343-011-8); Man in the Poetic Mode. Zweigler (ISBN 0-88343-012-6); Man in the Expository Mode. Solotaroff (ISBN 0-88343-013-4); Man in the Dramatic Mode. Heston (ISBN 0-88343-014-2). (gr. 8 up). 1971. pap. text ed. 3.72 ea.; tchr's manual 3.90 (ISBN 0-88343-015-0). McDougal-Littell.

Man Literature Series: Level 3, Bk. 3. Incl. Man in the Fictional Mode. Haupt (ISBN 0-88343-021-5); Book 3. Man in the Poetic Mode. Sweigler (ISBN 0-88343-022-3); Man in the Expository Mode. Solotaroff (ISBN 0-88343-023-1); Man in the Dramatic Mode. Heston (ISBN 0-88343-024-X). (gr. 9-12). 1970. pap. text ed. 3.72 ea.; tchr's manual 3.90 (ISBN 0-88343-025-8). McDougal-Littell.

Man Literature Series: Level 4, Bk. 4. Incl. Man in the Fictional Mode. Haupt (ISBN 0-88343-031-2); Man in the Poetic Mode (ISBN 0-88343-032-0); Man in the Expository Mode. Solotaroff (ISBN 0-88343-033-9); Man in the Dramatic Mode. Heston (ISBN 0-88343-034-7). (gr. 10-12). 1970. pap. text ed. 3.72 ea.; tchrs'. manual 3.90 (ISBN 0-686-57949-6). McDougal-Littell.

Man Literature Series: Level 5, Bk. 5. Incl. Man in He Fictional Mode. Haupt (ISBN 0-88343-041-X); Man in the Poetic Mode. Sweigler (ISBN 0-88343-042-8); Man in the Expository Mode. Solotaroff (ISBN 0-88343-043-6); Man in the Dramatic Mode. Heston (ISBN 0-88343-044-4). (gr. 11-12). 1970. pap. text ed. 3.72 ea.; tchr's manual 3.90 (ISBN 0-88343-045-2). McDougal-Littell.

Man Literature Series: Level 6, Bk. 6. Incl. Man in the Fictional Mode. Haupt (ISBN 0-88343-051-7); Man in the Poetic Mode. Sweigler (ISBN 0-88343-052-5); Man in the Expository Mode. Solotaroff (ISBN 0-88343-053-3); Man in the Dramatic Mode. Heston (ISBN 0-88343-054-1). (gr. 12 up). 1970. pap. text ed. 3.72 ea.; tchr's manual 3.90 (ISBN 0-88343-055-X). McDougal-Littell.

Mansfield, Katherine. Novels & Novelists. Repr. of 1930 ed. 29.00 (ISBN 0-403-02290-8). Somerset Pub.

Marble, Annie. Nobel Prize Winners in Literature, 1901-1931. facs. ed. LC 70-84324. (Essay Index Reprint Ser). 1932. 25.00 (ISBN 0-8369-1185-7). Arno.

Marble, Annie R. Pen Names & Personalities. 256p. 1980. Repr. of 1930 ed. lib. bdg. 30.00 (ISBN 0-89987-563-7). Century Bookbindery.

Marples, Morris. Shank's Pony. 1973. Repr. of 1960 ed. 15.00 (ISBN 0-8274-0759-9). R West.

Marti, Jose. The Critic: Writings on Art & Literature. Foner, Philip S., ed. Randall, Elinor, tr. LC 81-81697. 1981. 18.00 (ISBN 0-85345-589-9, CL5899). Monthly Rev.

Martin, Graham. The Architecture of Experience. 256p. 1981. 26.50x (ISBN 0-85224-409-6, Pub. by Edinburgh U Pr Scotland). Columbia U Pr.

Martindale, Colin. The Romantic Progression: Psychology of Literary History. LC 74-26559. 225p. 1975. 17.50x (ISBN 0-470-57365-1). Halsted Pr.

--Romantic Progression: The Psychology of Literary History. LC 74-26559. 225p. 1975. 17.50 (ISBN 0-470-57365-1, Pub. by Wiley). Krieger.

Martinez-Bonati, Felix. Fictive Discourse & the Structures of Literature: A Phenomenological Approach. rev. exp. ed. Silver, Philip W., tr. from Span. LC 80-23628. (Illus.). 200p. 1981. 15.00x (ISBN 0-8014-1308-7). Cornell U Pr.

Martz, Louis L. & Williams, Aubrey, eds. The Author in His Work: Essays on a Problem in Criticism. LC 77-16309. 1978. 30.00x (ISBN 0-300-02179-8). Yale U Pr.

Marvin, F. S. The Century of Hope. 1973. Repr. of 1919 ed. 25.00 (ISBN 0-8274-0757-2). R West.

Marvin, Frederic R. The Companionship of Books. 1973. Repr. of 1950 ed. 20.00 (ISBN 0-8274-0756-4). R West.

Mason, Eugene. A Book of References in Literature. 1973. Repr. of 1915 ed. 20.00 (ISBN 0-8274-0755-6). R West.

--Considered Writers Old & New. 1925. lib. bdg. 15.00 (ISBN 0-8414-6487-1). Folcroft.

Matthews, Brander. Books & Play-Books: Essays on Literature & the Drama. facsimile ed. LC 71-37795. (Essay Index Reprint Ser). Repr. of 1895 ed. 17.00 (ISBN 0-8369-2612-9). Arno.

Matthews, W. R. The Adventures of Gabriel in His Search for Mr. Shaw. 1973. Repr. of 1933 ed. 12.50 (ISBN 0-8274-1033-6). R West.

Matthews, William. Hours with Men & Books. 1973. Repr. of 1882 ed. 20.00 (ISBN 0-8274-0777-7). R West.

--Literary Style. 1973. Repr. of 1881 ed. 25.00 (ISBN 0-8274-0778-5). R West.

Mauriac, Francois. Second Thoughts: Reflections on Literature & on Life. LC 72-13201. (Essay Index Reprint Ser.). Repr. of 1961 ed. 10.50 (ISBN 0-8369-8169-3). Arno.

Maurois, Andre. The Art of Writing. Hopkins, Gerard, tr. LC 72-3375. (Essay Index Reprint Ser.). Repr. of 1960 ed. 18.00 (ISBN 0-8369-2914-4). Arno.

Mazzeo, Joseph A. Varieties of Interpretation. LC 78-51518. 1978. text ed. 13.95x (ISBN 0-268-00589-3). U of Notre Dame Pr.

Megroz, R. L. The Real Robinson Crusoe Being the Life & Strange Surprising Adventures of Alexander Selkirk of Largo, Fife, Mariner. 1973. 35.00 (ISBN 0-8274-1014-X). R West.

--Rhys Davies: A Critical Sketch. 1973. Repr. of 1932 ed. 20.00 (ISBN 0-8274-0775-0). R West.

Megroz, Rodolphe L. Five Novelists Poets of to-Day. 1973. Repr. of 1933 ed. 25.00 (ISBN 0-8274-1294-0). R West.

Mellor, Anne K. Blake's Human Form Divine. LC 72-161995. (Illus.). 1974. 34.00x (ISBN 0-520-02065-0). U of Cal Pr.

Melvill, David. The Melvill Book of Roundels. Bantock, Granville & Anderton, H. Orsmond, eds. LC 78-80256. (Research & Source Works Ser.: No. 839). (Illus.). 1972. Repr. of 1916 ed. lib. bdg. 25.50 (ISBN 0-8337-2349-9). B Franklin.

Mendilow, A. A. Time & the Novel. 244p. 1972. Repr. of 1952 ed. text ed. 15.00x (ISBN 0-391-00220-1). Humanities.

Menon, V. K. A Theory of Laughter. LC 78-21711. 1972. Repr. of 1931 ed. lib. bdg. 20.00 (ISBN 0-8414-6329-8). Folcroft.

Merton, Thomas. Raids on the Unspeakable. LC 66-17823. 1970. pap. 3.95 (ISBN 0-8112-0101-5, NDP213). New Directions.

Meyers, Jeffrey. Homosexuality & Literature: 1890-1930. 1977. lib. bdg. 13.95x (ISBN 0-7735-0300-5). McGill-Queens U Pr.

Middleton, R. D. Dr. Routh. 1973. Repr. of 1938 ed. 25.00 (ISBN 0-8274-1120-0). R West.

Miller, Henry. Books in My Life. LC 71-88728. 1969. pap. 5.95 (ISBN 0-8112-0108-2, NDP280). New Directions.

Mintz, Samuel I., et al, eds. From Smollett to James: Studies in the Novel & Other Essays Presented to Edgar Johnson. LC 79-25865. 1981. 24.95x (ISBN 0-8139-0663-6). U Pr of Va.

Mitford, Mary R. Recollection of a Literary Life: Or, Books, Places & People, 3 vols. 1973. Repr. of 1852 ed. 50.00 set (ISBN 0-8274-1202-9). R West.

Moir, D. M. Sketches of the Political Literature of the Past Half-Century. 1973. Repr. of 1851 ed. 45.00 (ISBN 0-8274-1201-0). R West.

Molina, N. de. On Literary Intention. 1975. 16.00x (ISBN 0-85224-275-1, Pub. by Edinburgh U Pr Scotland). Columbia U Pr.

Moore, T. Sturge. Art & Life (Flaubert, William Blake, Etc.) 1973. Repr. of 1910 ed. 30.00 (ISBN 0-8274-1199-5). R West.

Mordell, Albert. The Literature of Ecstasy. 1979. Repr. of 1921 ed. lib. bdg. 30.00 (ISBN 0-8495-3759-2). Arden Lib.

Morell, J. R. A History of European Literature. 1973. Repr. of 1874 ed. 25.00 (ISBN 0-8274-1197-9). R West.

Morgan, Louise. Writers at Work (W. B. Yeats, Richard Aldington, Sinclair Lewis, Wyndham Lewis, Somerset Maugham Etc.) LC 72-10206. Repr. of 1931 ed. lib. bdg. 20.00 (ISBN 0-8414-0625-1). Folcroft.

Morison, William. Andrew Melville. 1973. Repr. of 1899 ed. 20.00 (ISBN 0-8274-1418-8). R West.

Morley, Edith J., ed. Henry Crabb Robinson on Books & Their Writers, 3 vols. 1938. 70.00 set (ISBN 0-8274-2482-5). R West.

Morley, Henry. Journal of a London Playgoer. (Victorian Library Ser.). 348p. 1974. Repr. of 1866 ed. text ed. 14.00x (ISBN 0-7185-5031-5, Leicester). Humanities.

Morris, H. N. Flaxman, Blake, Coleridge, & Other Men of Genius Influenced by Swedenborg. 1973. Repr. of 1915 ed. lib. bdg. 20.00 (ISBN 0-8414-1515-3). Folcroft.

Morton, Andrew O. Literary Detection: How to Prove Authorship & Fraud in Literature & Documents. 1979. 17.50 (ISBN 0-684-15516-8, ScribT). Scribner.

Morton, Arthur L. Everlasting Gospel. 1973. Repr. of 1958 ed. lib. bdg. 8.50 (ISBN 0-8274-1559-1). R West.

Mottram, R. H. Vanities & Verities. 1973. Repr. of 1958 ed. 20.00 (ISBN 0-8274-1196-0). R West.

Moulton, Richard G. World Literature. 1973. Repr. of 1921 ed. 45.00 (ISBN 0-8274-1025-5). R West.

Mudford, Peter. The Art of Celebration. LC 67-581. 1979. 27.00 (ISBN 0-571-10852-0, Pub. by Faber & Faber). Merrimack Bk Serv.

Mueller, Gustar E. Philosophy of Literature. LC 72-14195. (Essay Index Reprint Ser.). Repr. of 1948 ed. 16.75 (ISBN 0-518-10021-9). Arno.

Muir, Edwin. Structure of the Novel. LC 29-3271. 1969. pap. 1.65 (ISBN 0-15-685688-3, Hbgr, H077). HarBraceJ.

Mulhern, Francis. The Moment of Scrutiny. 1979. 24.00 (ISBN 0-86091-007-5, Pub. by NLB). Schocken.

Murdoch, Walter. Speaking Personally. 1973. Repr. of 1930 ed. 25.00 (ISBN 0-8274-1192-8). R West.

Murray, Les. The Peasant Mandarin: Prose Pieces. 1979. 19.95x (ISBN 0-7022-1217-2); pap. 12.00x (ISBN 0-7022-1317-9). U of Queensland Pr.

Murry, J. Middleton. Heaven & Earth. 1973. Repr. of 1938 ed. 40.00 (ISBN 0-8274-0138-8). R West.

Murry, John M. Poets, Critics, Mystics: A Selection of Criticisms Written Between 1919 & 1955. LC 78-83668. (Crosscurrents-Modern Critiques Ser.). 190p. 1970. 6.95 (ISBN 0-8093-0414-7). S Ill U Pr.

Mursell, Walter. Byways in Bookland. 1973. Repr. of 1914 ed. 20.00 (ISBN 0-8274-1173-1). R West.

Mutschmann, Heinrich. The Origin & Meaning of Young's Night Thoughts. 22p. 1980. Repr. of 1939 ed. lib. bdg. 8.50 (ISBN 0-8492-6754-4). R West.

Myers, Elizabeth. The Basilisk of St. James (Swift) 1973. Repr. of 1945 ed. 20.00 (ISBN 0-8274-1003-4). R West.

Myers, F. W. Essays, Classical & Modern, 2 vols. in 1. LC 72-13467. (Essay Index Reprint Ser.). Repr. of 1883 ed. 25.00 (ISBN 0-8369-8170-7). Arno.

Nadel & Sherrer. Barron's How to Prepare for the CLEP Subject Exams - Analysis & Interpretations of Literature. 1982. pap. 4.95 (ISBN 0-8120-0619-4). Barron.

Narasimhaiah, C. D., ed. Awakened Conscience: Studies in Commonwealth Literature. 1978. 28.50x (ISBN 0-391-00920-6). Humanities.

Nathan, George J. Art of the Night. LC 75-120099. 296p. 1972. 12.00 (ISBN 0-8386-7965-X). Fairleigh Dickinson.

--Autobiography of an Attitude. LC 76-145204. 1971. Repr. of 1926 ed. 24.00 (ISBN 0-403-00758-5). Scholarly.

Nemerov, Howard. Figures of Thought: Speculations on the Meaning of Poetry & Other Essays. LC 77-78361. 1978. 15.00 (ISBN 0-87923-212-9). Godine.

Nettleship, Henry. Lectures & Essays, Second Series. Haverfield, F., ed. LC 72-336. (Essay Index Reprint Ser.). Repr. of 1895 ed. 18.00 (ISBN 0-8369-2812-1). Arno.

Neuburg, Victor E. Popular Literature: A History & Guide. (Illus.). 302p. 1977. 22.50x (ISBN 0-7130-0158-5, Pub. by Woburn Pr England). Biblio Dist.

Nevinson, Henry. Between the Wars. 1973. Repr. of 1936 ed. 12.95 (ISBN 0-8274-1166-9). R West.

Nevinson, Henry W. Books & Personalities. facs. ed. LC 68-16962. (Essay Index Reprint Ser). 1968. Repr. of 1905 ed. 15.50 (ISBN 0-8369-0738-8). Arno.

New Writing & Writers, Vol. 17. 1980. pap. 5.95 (ISBN 0-7145-3695-4). Riverrun NY.

Newbigging, Thomas. Literary Bypaths & Vagaries. 1973. Repr. of 1910 ed. 30.00 (ISBN 0-8274-1169-3). R West.

Nisbett, J. F. The Insanity of Genius. LC 72-8931. 1972. Repr. of 1900 ed. lib. bdg. 30.00 (ISBN 0-8414-0433-X). Folcroft.

Nitchie, Elizabeth. The Criticism of Literature. 1928. 40.00 (ISBN 0-8274-2120-6). R West.

Nolan, Rita. Foundations for an Adequate Theory of Paraphrase. LC 70-95011. (Janua Linguarum, Ser. Minor: No. 84). 1970. pap. text ed. 7.80x (ISBN 0-686-22414-0). Mouton.

Norman, Sylva. Contemporary Essays. 1973. Repr. of 1933 ed. 30.00 (ISBN 0-8274-1298-3). R West.

Nunn, M. E. Selected Prose of Julian Del Casal. 144p. 1949. pap. 2.50 (ISBN 0-8173-8550-9). U of Ala Pr.

Nyiroe, L., ed. Literature & Its Interpretation. (De Proprietatibus Litteraruum, Series Minor: No. 24). 1979. pap. text ed. 41.25x (ISBN 90-279-3387-1). Mouton.

Oates, Joyce Carol. The Edge of Impossibility: Tragic Forms in Literature. LC 77-188692. 1972. 10.95 (ISBN 0-8149-0675-3). Vanguard.

Odmark, John, ed. Language, Literature & Meaning II: Current Trends in Literary Research, Vol. 2. (Linguistic & Literary Studies in Eastern Europe). 1980. 57.00 (ISBN 90-272-1503-0). Benjamins North Am.

O'Leary, R. D. The Essay. 1973. Repr. of 1928 ed. 30.00 (ISBN 0-8274-1145-6). R West.

Olson, Charles F. Muthologos: Collected Lectures & Interviews, Vol. II. Butterick, George F., ed. LC 77-1955. (Writing Ser.: No. 35). 1979. 12.00 (ISBN 0-87704-039-7); pap. 6.00 (ISBN 0-87704-040-0). Four Seasons Foun.

Omond, Thomas S. The Romantic Triumph. LC 74-38364. (Select Bibliographies Reprint Ser.). Repr. of 1900 ed. 21.00 (ISBN 0-8369-6781-X). Arno.

Osborn, E. B. Literature & Life. 1973. Repr. of 1921 ed. 20.00 (ISBN 0-8274-1147-2). R West.

Osborne, W. A. Essays & Studies: Scientific Errors in Literature & Art, Vowel, Assonance, Signatism in English, on Translating, Some Brief Shakespeare Commentaries. 1973. Repr. of 1946 ed. 30.00 (ISBN 0-8274-1144-8). R West.

Oswald, Eugene. The Legend of Fair Helen. 1973. Repr. of 1905 ed. 35.00 (ISBN 0-8274-1142-1). R West.

Ovid. Tristia. Lind, L. R., tr. LC 73-88363. 177p. 1975. 10.00x (ISBN 0-8203-0330-5). U of Ga Pr.

Owen, C. A. Landmarks in Literary History. 1973. Repr. of 1915 ed. 20.00 (ISBN 0-8274-1143-X). R West.

Owlett, F. C. The Spacious Days & Other Essays. 1973. Repr. of 1937 ed. 15.00 (ISBN 0-8274-1138-3). R West.

Paget, John. The New Examen. 1973. Repr. of 1934 ed. 35.00 (ISBN 0-8274-1252-5). R West.

Pagnol, Marcel. Critique des Critiques. (Coll. Litterature). pap. 3.95 (ISBN 0-685-37001-1). French & Eur.

Painter, F. V. Elementary Guide to Literary Criticism. 1973. Repr. of 1903 ed. 20.00 (ISBN 0-8274-1254-1). R West.

Palestine Pilgrims' Text Society. The Library of the Palestine Pilgrims' Text Society. Stewart, Aubrey, et al, trs. Incl. Vol. 1, 1887-1891, 5 pts. Repr. of 1887 ed. 16.25 (ISBN 0-404-04891-9); Vol. 2, 1890-1897, 4 pts. Repr. of 1896 ed. 16.25 (ISBN 0-404-04892-7); Vol. 3, 1893-1897, 4 pts. Repr. of 1893 ed. 16.25 (ISBN 0-404-04893-5); Vol. 4, 1893-1897, 3 pts. Repr. of 1895 ed. 16.25 (ISBN 0-404-04894-3); Vol. 5, 1896-1897, 5 pts. Repr. of 1896 ed. 16.25 (ISBN 0-404-04895-1); Vol. 6, 1894-1897, 4 pts. Repr. of 1894 ed. 16.25 (ISBN 0-404-04896-X); Vols. 7-10, 1892-1897, 4 pts. in 2 vols. Repr. 32.50 ea. Vols. 7-10, Pts. 1 & 2 (ISBN 0-404-04897-8). Set. 65.00 (ISBN 0-404-09140-7); Vol. 11, 1895-1897, 2 pts. Repr. of 1896 ed. 16.25 (ISBN 0-404-04901-X); Vol. 12, 1895-1897, 3 pts. Repr. of 1895 ed. 16.25 (ISBN 0-404-04902-8); Vol. 13, 1897. Repr. of 1897 ed. 16.25 (ISBN 0-404-04903-6). Set. 211.25 (ISBN 0-404-04890-0). AMS Pr.

Palmer, W. Scott & Haggard, A. M. Michael Fairless. 1973. Repr. of 1913 ed. 20.00 (ISBN 0-8274-1427-7). R West.

Palmer de Dueno, Rosa M. Sentido, Forma y Estilo De "Redentores" De Manuel Zeno Gandia. (UPREX, E. Literarios: No. 34). pap. 1.85 (ISBN 0-8477-0034-8). U of PR Pr.

Pancoast, Henry S. Study Lists Chronological Tables & Maps. 1973. Repr. of 1908 ed. 12.50 (ISBN 0-8274-1245-2). R West.

Pantucek, S. La Literature Algerienne. (Oriental Institute Czechoslovakia Dissertationes Orientales, Vol. 22). 1969. 6.00x (ISBN 0-685-27155-2). Paragon.

Parrinder, Patrick & Philmus, Robert, eds. H. G. Wells's Literary Criticism. 261p. 1980. 27.50x (ISBN 0-389-20035-2). B&N.

Parry, Adam. Studies in Fifth-Century Thought & Literature. LC 71-166948. (Yale Classical Studies: No. 22). 260p. 1972. 36.00 (ISBN 0-521-08305-2). Cambridge U Pr.

Parry, Edward. Concerning Many Things. 1973. Repr. of 1929 ed. 20.00 (ISBN 0-8274-1241-X). R West.

Partridge, Eric. Adventuring Among Words. LC 76-39202. (Select Bibliographies Reprint Ser.). Repr. of 1961 ed. 10.00 (ISBN 0-8369-6804-2). Arno.

--A Charm of Words: Essays & Papers on Language. LC 73-167400. (Essay Index Reprint Ser.). Repr. of 1960 ed. 15.00 (ISBN 0-8369-2707-9). Arno.

--Name into Word. facsimile 2nd ed. LC 77-117906. (Select Bibliographies Reprint Ser). Repr. of 1950 ed. 36.00 (ISBN 0-8369-5361-4). Arno.

--Robert Eyres Landor: A Biographical Sketch. 1973. lib. bdg. 12.00 (ISBN 0-8414-9247-6). Folcroft.

--Words at War, Words at Peace: Essays on Language in General & Particular Words. 1973. lib. bdg. 8.50 (ISBN 0-8414-9248-4). Folcroft.

--Words, Words, Words. 1973. lib. bdg. 10.50 (ISBN 0-8414-9249-2). Folcroft.

Pascal, Roy. The Dual Voice: Free Indirect Speech & Its Functioning in the Nineteenth Century European Novel. 150p. 1977. 13.75x (ISBN 0-87471-927-5). Rowman.

Paston, George. At John Murray's: Records of a Literary Circle 1843-1892. 1973. Repr. of 1932 ed. 50.00 (ISBN 0-8274-1239-8). R West.
Pater, Walter. Appreciations. 1973. Repr. of 1889 ed. 25.00 (ISBN 0-8274-1080-8). R West.
Pater, Walter H. Emerald Uthwart. LC 73-498. 1973. lib. bdg. 10.00 (ISBN 0-8414-1415-7). Folcroft.
Patmore, Derek. The Life & Times of Coventry Patmore. 1973. Repr. of 1949 ed. 30.00 (ISBN 0-8274-1082-4). R West.
Patrides, C. A. & Waddington, Raymond B., eds. The Age of Milton: Backgrounds to Seventeenth-Century Literature. (Illus.). 438p. 1980. 33.50x (ISBN 0-389-20051-4); pap. 14.00x (ISBN 0-389-20052-2). B&N.
Paul, Herbert W. Men & Letters. 1973. Repr. of 1901 ed. 25.00 (ISBN 0-8274-0613-4). R West.
Paull, H. M. Literary Ethics: A Study in the Growth of the Literary Conscience. 1973. Repr. of 1929 ed. 10.95 (ISBN 0-8274-1234-7). R West.
Paulus. D. I. R. T. Y. Darned, Insulting, Rotten, Terrible Yarns. (Terrible Yarns Ser.: Vol. 1). 180p. 1973. 6.95 (ISBN 0-87881-006-4). Mojave Bks.
Payn, James. The Backwater of Life or Essays of a Literary Veteran. 1973. Repr. of 1899 ed. 25.00 (ISBN 0-8274-1235-5). R West.
Payne, William M. Little Leaders. 1973. Repr. of 1895 ed. 20.00 (ISBN 0-8274-1231-2). R West.
Peacock, Markham L., Jr. Critical Opinions of William Wordsworth. LC 70-86282. 1969. Repr. of 1950 ed. lib. bdg. 22.50x (ISBN 0-374-96327-4). Octagon.
Pearce, Charles E. Polly Peachum: The Story of Lavinia Fenton & the Beggar's Opera. 1973. 25.00 (ISBN 0-8274-1083-2). R West.
Pearson, Charles H. Literary & Biographical Essays. 1973. Repr. of 1908 ed. 30.00 (ISBN 0-8274-1230-4). R West.
--Reviews & Critical Essays. 1973. Repr. of 1896 ed. 30.00 (ISBN 0-8274-1232-0). R West.
Peck, Harry T. The Personal Equation. LC 79-39121. (Essay Index Reprint Ser.). Repr. of 1897 ed. 20.00 (ISBN 0-8369-2709-5). Arno.
--Studies in Several Literatures. 1973. Repr. of 1909 ed. 30.00 (ISBN 0-8274-1228-2). R West.
Peguy, Charles P. Basic Verities: Prose & Poetry. Green, Ann & Green, Julian, trs. LC 72-4493. (Essay Index Reprint Ser.). Repr. of 1943 ed. 14.50 (ISBN 0-8369-2967-5). Arno.
Penniman, James H. Books & How to Make the Most of Them. 1973. Repr. of 1911 ed. 15.00 (ISBN 0-8274-1224-X). R West.
Permewan, William & Permewan, Phillippa. Reviews & Essays. 1973. Repr. of 1929 ed. 20.00 (ISBN 0-8274-1225-8). R West.
Peyre, Henri. Literature & Sincerity. LC 78-6243. (Yale Roman Studies Second Ser: No. 9). 1978. Repr. of 1963 ed. lib. bdg. 21.75x (ISBN 0-313-20454-3, PELS). Greenwood.
Phillips, Henry A. Art in Story Narration. LC 73-4410. 1973. lib. bdg. 12.50 (ISBN 0-8414-2459-4). Folcroft.
Platt, Arthur. Nine Essays. facs. ed. LC 68-16969. (Essay Index Reprint Ser). 1968. Repr. of 1927 ed. 15.00 (ISBN 0-8369-0793-0). Arno.
Plautus, T. Maccius. Miles Gloriosus. 2nd ed. rev. ed. Hammond, Mason, et al, eds. LC 73-122213. 1970. 9.50x (ISBN 0-674-57436-2). Harvard U Pr.
Pocock, Guy. Brush up Your Reading. 1973. Repr. of 1942 ed. 10.00 (ISBN 0-8274-1130-8). R West.
Poe, Edgar A. Anastatic Printing. LC 73-13697. 1973. lib. bdg. 7.50 (ISBN 0-8414-1481-5). Folcroft.
Poggioli, Renato. Spirit of the Letter: Essays in European Literature. LC 65-22064. 1965. 18.50x (ISBN 0-674-83310-4). Harvard U Pr.
Poirier, Richard. Performing Self: Compositions & Decompositions in the Language of Contemporary Life. (Orig.). 1971. pap. 3.95 (ISBN 0-19-501369-7, GB). Oxford U Pr.
Pollak, Gustav. International Perspective in Criticism. 1973. Repr. of 1914 ed. 9.25 (ISBN 0-8274-1078-6). R West.
Pollard, A. F. Political Pamphlets. 1973. Repr. of 1897 ed. 45.00 (ISBN 0-8274-1636-9). R West.
Pope, Randolph D., ed. The Analysis of Literary Texts: Current Trends in Methodology (Third & Fourth York College Colloquia) LC 79-54144. (Studies in Literary Analysis). 336p. 1980. lib. bdg. 15.95x (ISBN 0-916950-14-X); pap. text ed. 9.95x (ISBN 0-916950-13-1). Bilingual Pr.
Pope-Hennessy, Una B. F. Durham Company. LC 70-36167. (Essay Index Reprint Ser.). Repr. of 1941 ed. 17.00 (ISBN 0-8369-2714-1). Arno.
Porter, Bern. Eighty-Nine Offenses. 1974. pap. 0.50 (ISBN 0-911856-11-0). Abyss.
Porter, Noah. Books & Reading: Or, What Books Shall I Read & How Shall I Read Them. 1973. 14.45 (ISBN 0-8274-1129-4). R West.
Postgate, J. P. That Devil Wilkes. 1973. Repr. of 1929 ed. 35.00 (ISBN 0-8274-1125-1). R West.
Potter, Stephen, ed. The Muse in Chains: A Study in Education. LC 73-4564. 1973. lib. bdg. 20.00 (ISBN 0-8414-2471-3). Folcroft.
Pound, Ezra. ABC of Reading. LC 60-30304. 1960. pap. 4.25 (ISBN 0-8112-0151-1, NDP89). New Directions.
--Pound - Joyce: Letters & Essays. LC 66-27616. 1970. pap. 5.45 (ISBN 0-8112-0159-7, NDP296). New Directions.
Powell, John W. The Confessions of a Browning Lover. 1973. Repr. of 1918 ed. 30.00 (ISBN 0-8274-1076-X). R West.
Pownall, David E., compiled by. Articles on Twentieth Century Literature: An Annotated Bibliography 1954-1970, 8 vols. LC 73-6588. Set. lib. bdg. 400.00 (ISBN 0-527-72150-6). Kraus Intl.
Praz, Mario. The Flaming Heart: Essays on Cranshaw, Machiavelli & Other Studies from Chaucer to T. S. Eliot. 1958. 8.00 (ISBN 0-8446-1365-7). Peter Smith.
Prescott, William H. Biographical & Critical Miscellanies. 1973. Repr. of 1875 ed. 30.00 (ISBN 0-8274-1124-3). R West.
Price, Reynolds. The Wings of the Dove: (Standard Ed.) LC 75-133743. 1970. pap. text ed. 2.50x (ISBN 0-675-09334-1). Merrill.
Queneau, Raymond. Histoire des Litteratures: Litteratures Anciennes, Orientales et Orales, Vol. 1. (Historique Ser.). 2024p. 82.50 (ISBN 0-686-56447-2). French & Eur.
--Histoire des Litteratures: Litteratures Occidentales, Vol. 2. (Historique Ser.). 2156p. 53.95 (ISBN 0-686-56448-0). French & Eur.
Quiller-Couch, A. T. Adventures in Criticism: Robinson Crusoe, Charles Reade, Henry Kingsley, George Moore. 428p. 1981. Repr. of 1896 ed. lib. bdg. 30.00 (ISBN 0-89760-724-4). Telegraph Bks.
--From a Cornish Window. 1906. 10.00 (ISBN 0-8274-2378-0). R West.
--Studies in Literature. (Third Ser.). 1919. 2.00 (ISBN 0-8274-3538-X). R West.
Quiller-Couch, Arthur. On the Art of Writing. LC 78-8305. Repr. of 1916 ed. lib. bdg. 20.00 (ISBN 0-8414-6918-0). Folcroft.
--Studies in Literature. (Second Series). 1973. 30.00 (ISBN 0-8274-0979-6). R West.
--Studies in Literature. 1973. Repr. of 1919 ed. 30.00 (ISBN 0-8274-0981-8). R West.
Raabe, Wilhelm. Else Von der Tanne: A Translation & Commentary with an Introduction to Wilhelm Raabe's Life & Work. O'Flaherty, James C. & King, Janet K., trs. LC 78-181895. 160p. 1972. 10.95x (ISBN 0-8173-8554-1); pap. 4.50 (ISBN 0-8173-8557-6). U of Ala Pr.
Rabkin, Eric S. Narrative Suspense: 'When Slim Turned Sidways...' LC 72-93403. (Illus.). 216p. 1973. 7.95 (ISBN 0-472-75400-9). U of Mich Pr.
Radcliffe, Susan M. Sir Joshua's Nephew. 1973. Repr. of 1930 ed. 35.00 (ISBN 0-8274-1399-8). R West.
Radford, G. H. Shylock & Others: Eight Studies. LC 72-13311. (Essay Index Reprint Ser.). Repr. of 1894 ed. 14.00 (ISBN 0-8369-8172-3). Arno.
Raine, Kathleen. The Land Unknown. LC 75-10995. 208p. 1975. 6.95 (ISBN 0-8076-0800-9). Braziller.
Raleigh, Walter. On Writing & Writers. 1973. Repr. of 1926 ed. 8.25 (ISBN 0-8274-0976-1). R West.
Raleigh, Walter A. Some Authors. facs. ed. LC 68-55855. (Essay Index Reprint Ser). 1923. 18.00 (ISBN 0-8369-0807-4). Arno.
Ralli, Augustus J. Later Critiques. 1973. Repr. of 1933 ed. 20.00 (ISBN 0-8274-0468-9). R West.
Ramaswami, S. & Seturaman, V. S. The English Critical Tradition: An Anthology of English Literary Criticism, Vol. 2. 746p. 1980. pap. text ed. 9.00x (ISBN 0-391-01769-1). Humanities.
Randall, Helen W. The Critical Theory of Lord Kames. 1973. Repr. of 1941 ed. 20.00 (ISBN 0-8274-0974-5). R West.
Rannie, David W. The Elements of Style: An Introduction to Literary Criticism. Repr. of 1915 ed. lib. bdg. 35.00 (ISBN 0-8414-7405-2). Folcroft.
Ransome, Arthur. A History of Story-Telling. LC 73-789. 1972. Repr. of 1909 ed. lib. bdg. 25.00 (ISBN 0-8414-1621-4). Folcroft.
Ratliff, William F. Creaciones y Creadores: A Basic Literary Reader. 128p. 1981. pap. text ed. 7.95 (ISBN 0-686-77385-3). Random.
Raymond, Ernest. Through Literature to Life. LC 76-42307. 1976. Repr. of 1928 ed. lib. bdg. 25.00 (ISBN 0-8414-7276-9). Folcroft.
Read, Herbert. A Coat of Many Colours. 1973. lib. bdg. 30.00 (ISBN 0-8414-7413-3). Folcroft.
Read, Herbert E. Collected Essays in Literary Criticism. LC 78-14137. 1980. Repr. of 1951 ed. 26.50 (ISBN 0-88355-811-4). Hyperion Conn.
Reed, Henry. Lectures on English History & Tragic Poetry As Illustrated by Shakespeare. 1973. Repr. of 1855 ed. 17.95 (ISBN 0-8274-1054-9). R West.
Rees, J. Rogers. The Brotherhood of Letters. 1973. Repr. of 1889 ed. 25.00 (ISBN 0-8274-0968-0). R West.
--With Friend & Book in the Study & the Fields. 1973. Repr. of 1892 ed. 25.00 (ISBN 0-8274-0966-4). R West.
Rehder, Jessie. The Nature of Fiction. Repr. of 1948 ed. lib. bdg. 6.50 (ISBN 0-8495-4531-5). Arden Lib.
Reid, Forrest. Pirates of the Spring. 1973. lib. bdg. 25.00 (ISBN 0-8414-7418-4). Folcroft.
Renard, Georges. La Methode Scientifique De L'Histoire Literaire. (French.). 1978. Repr. of 1900 ed. 65.00 (ISBN 0-8492-2371-7). R West.
Rendall, Gerald H. Shakespeare: Handwriting & Spelling. LC 76-169107. (Studies in Shakespeare, No. 24). 1971. Repr. of 1931 ed. lib. bdg. 40.95 (ISBN 0-8383-1335-3). Haskell.
Repplier, Agnes. Essays in Miniature. LC 70-112790. Repr. of 1892 ed. 9.50 (ISBN 0-404-05279-7). AMS Pr.
--Essays in Miniature. Repr. of 1892 ed. lib. bdg. 15.00x (ISBN 0-8371-1452-7, REMI). Greenwood.
Rhoads, Howard G. Wm. Hawkins' Apollo Shroving. 1973. Repr. of 1936 ed. 25.00 (ISBN 0-8274-0963-X). R West.
Rhondda, Viscountess. Notes on the Way. 1973. Repr. of 1937 ed. 15.00 (ISBN 0-8274-0964-8). R West.
Rhys, Ernest. Everyman Remembers. 1973. 30.00 (ISBN 0-8274-0956-7). R West.
--Letters from Limbo with 63 Reproductions of Letters. 1973. Repr. of 1936 ed. 15.00 (ISBN 0-8274-0961-3). R West.
--Literary Pamphlets, 2 vols. 1973. Repr. of 1897 ed. Set. 50.00 (ISBN 0-8274-0962-1). R West.
Rice, William G. The Carillon in Literature. 1977. lib. bdg. 59.95 (ISBN 0-8490-1576-6). Gordon Pr.
Richardson, Frederika. The Iliad of the East. 1973. Repr. of 1870 ed. 30.00 (ISBN 0-8274-0952-4). R West.
Rickward, Edell. Scrutinies by Various Writers (T. S. Eliot, Aldous Huxley, James Joyce, D. H Lawrence, Wyndham Lewis, the Sitwells, Virginia Woolf, Vol. II. LC 76-23331. 1973. lib. bdg. 20.00 (ISBN 0-8414-7241-6). Folcroft.
Rickword, Edgell. Essays & Opinions Nineteen Twenty-One to Nineteen Thirty-One. Young, Alan, ed. 326p. (Orig.). 1980. pap. 10.95 (ISBN 0-85635-293-4, Pub. by Carcanet New Pr England). Persea Bks.
Ridley, Maurice R. Studies in Three Literatures: English, Latin, & Greek Contrasts & Comparisons. LC 78-42. 1978. Repr. of 1962 ed. lib. bdg. 17.25x (ISBN 0-313-20189-7, RISTL). Greenwood.
Rigney, Barbara H. Madness & Sexual Politics in the Feminist Novel: Studies in Bronte, Woolf, Lessing & Atwood. LC 78-53291. 1978. 20.00 (ISBN 0-299-07710-1); pap. 5.95 (ISBN 0-299-07714-4). U of Wis Pr.
Roberts, Edgar V. Writing Themes About Literature (Brief Edition) (Illus.). 224p. 1982. pap. 6.95 ref. ed. (ISBN 0-686-76595-8). P-H.
Roberts, Thomas J. When Is Something Fiction? LC 79-188698. (Crosscurrents-Modern Critiques Ser.). 157p. 1972. 6.95 (ISBN 0-8093-0578-X). S Ill U Pr.
Roberts, William. History of Letter-Writing from the Earliest Period to the Fifth Century. 1973. 50.00 (ISBN 0-8274-0946-X). R West.
Robertson, D. W., Jr. Essays in Medieval Culture. LC 79-3228. (Illus.). 1980. 35.00x (ISBN 0-691-06429-6); pap. 12.95 (ISBN 0-691-10091-8). Princeton U Pr.
Robertson, Frederick W. Lectures, Addresses & Other Literary Remains. 1973. Repr. of 1876 ed. 17.50 (ISBN 0-8274-0945-1). R West.
Robertson, John G. Essays & Address on Literature. 1973. lib. bdg. 15.50 (ISBN 0-8414-7460-5). Folcroft.
Robinson, Christopher. Lucian & His Influence in Europe. 1979. 20.00x (ISBN 0-8078-1404-0). U of NC Pr.
Rogers, Pat. Eighteenth-Century Encounters: Essays on Literature & Society in the Age of Walpole. 220p. 1982. 21.00x (ISBN 0-389-20090-5). B&N.
Rogers, Robert. Metaphor: A Psychoanalytic View. LC 77-80477. 1978. 14.95x (ISBN 0-520-03548-8). U of Cal Pr.
Rogers, Robert E. The Fine Art of Reading. 1973. Repr. of 1929 ed. 20.00 (ISBN 0-8274-0942-7). R West.
Rolleston, James. Kafka's Narrative Theater. LC 73-6881. 228p. 1974. 16.50x (ISBN 0-271-01121-1, Penn State). Pa St U Pr.
Roseberry. Wallace Burns Stevenson. 1973. Repr. of 1905 ed. 20.00 (ISBN 0-8274-1420-X). R West.
Roseberry, Lord. Appreciations & Addresses. 1973. Repr. of 1898 ed. 20.00 (ISBN 0-8274-0941-9). R West.
--Miscellanies, 2 vols. 1973. Repr. of 1921 ed. 50.00 set (ISBN 0-8274-0938-9). R West.
Rosenblatt, Louise M. Literature As Exploration. 3rd ed. 304p. 1976. pap. 2.20x (ISBN 0-8107-6027-4). Modern Lang.
--The Reader, the Text, the Poem: The Transactional Theory of the Literary Work. LC 78-16335. 214p. 1978. 11.95x (ISBN 0-8093-0883-5). S Ill U Pr.
Ross, E. Denison. Eastern Art & Literature. 1973. Repr. of 1928 ed. 20.00 (ISBN 0-8274-0939-7). R West.
Rothstein, Eric, ed. Literary Monographs, Vol. 4. LC 66-25869. 234p. 1971. 15.00 (ISBN 0-299-05860-3). U of Wis Pr.
--Literary Monographs, Vol. 5. LC 72-7994. 220p. 1973. 15.00 (ISBN 0-299-06310-0). U of Wis Pr.
Routh, Jane & Wolff, Janet, eds. The Sociology of Literature: Theoretical Approaches. (Sociological Review Monograph: No. 25). 180p. 1977. pap. 18.50x (ISBN 0-8476-2298-3). Rowman.
Rowe, Nicholas. The Tragedy of Lady Jane Gray. Sherry, Richard J., ed. (SSEL - Poetic Drama Ser.: No. 59). (Orig.). 1980. pap. text ed. 22.75x (ISBN 0-391-01955-4). Humanities.
Rowley, Charles. A Paradise & Other Papers. 1973. Repr. of 1905 ed. 25.00 (ISBN 0-8274-0937-0). R West.
Ruskin, John. Literary Criticism. Bloom, Harold, ed. 10.00 (ISBN 0-8446-1691-5). Peter Smith.
--Ruskin As Literary Critic: Selections. Ball, A. H., ed. Repr. of 1928 ed. lib. bdg. 14.25x (ISBN 0-8371-1149-8, RULC). Greenwood.
Russell, A. P. Characteristics: Sketches & Essays. 1973. Repr. of 1883 ed. 25.00 (ISBN 0-8274-0935-4). R West.
Russell, Addison P. Library Notes. new rev. ed. LC 72-4599. (Essay Index Reprint Ser.). Repr. of 1879 ed. 20.00 (ISBN 0-8369-2971-3). Arno.
Russell, Edward R. & Standing, P. C. Ibsen on His Merits. LC 79-181000. (Studies in European Literature, No. 56). 1972. Repr. of 1897 ed. lib. bdg. 32.95 (ISBN 0-8383-1370-1). Haskell.
Russell, George W. E. Selected Essays on Literary Subjects. 1973. 20.00 (ISBN 0-8274-0932-X). R West.
Ruyslinck, Ward. The Depraved Sleepers & Golden Ophelia. Powell, R. B. & Smith, David, trs. (International Studies & Translations Program). 1978. lib. bdg. 10.95 (ISBN 0-8057-8158-7). Twayne.
Sadleir, Michael. Things Past. 1973. Repr. of 1944 ed. 25.00 (ISBN 0-8274-0929-X). R West.
Saha, Subhas C. Insights. (Writers Workshop Greybird Ser.). 109p. 1975. 8.00 (ISBN 0-88253-568-4); pap. text ed. 4.00 (ISBN 0-88253-567-6). Ind-US Inc.
Said, Edward W. Beginnings: Intention & Method. LC 77-17259. 432p. 1978. pap. 5.95 (ISBN 0-8018-2085-5). Johns Hopkins.
--Beginnings: Intention & Method. LC 74-78306. 1975. 18.95x (ISBN 0-465-00580-2). Basic.
Sainte-Beuvel, Charles A. Selected Essays. Steegmuller, Francis & Guterman, Norbert, eds. Steegmuller, Francis & Guterman, Norbert, trs. LC 76-167409. (Essay Index Reprint Ser.). Repr. of 1963 ed. 19.00 (ISBN 0-8369-2919-5). Arno.
Saintsbury, George. A History of Nineteenth Century Literature. 1973. 35.00 (ISBN 0-8274-1069-7). R West.
Saintsbury, George E. Collected Essays & Papers 1875-1920, 4 Vols. (English Literary Reference Ser). Repr. of 1924 ed. Set. 65.50 (ISBN 0-384-53070-2). Johnson Repr.
Sakkut, Hamdi. The Egyptian Novel & Its Main Trends 1913-1952. LC 73-149126. 1971. 13.00 (ISBN 0-89410-053-X, Pub. by American Univ in Cairo Egypt). Three Continents.
Salis, Richard & Larsen, Egon, eds. Motives. Larsen, Egon, tr. from Ger. 228p. 1975. text ed. 10.00x (ISBN 0-85496-056-2). Humanities.
Saltzmann, L. F. Mediaeval Byways. 1973. Repr. of 1913 ed. 20.00 (ISBN 0-8274-0928-1). R West.
Sampson, George. Seven Essays. 1973. lib. bdg. 20.00 (ISBN 0-8414-8165-2). Folcroft.
Sanborn, Kate. My Literary Zoo. LC 72-4751. (Essay Index Reprint Ser.). Repr. of 1896 ed. 15.00 (ISBN 0-8369-2973-X). Arno.
Sanders, Charles. Synthesis: Responses to Literature. text ed. write for info. (ISBN 0-685-55635-2, 31044). Phila Bk Co.
Sanders, Lloyd. The Holland House Circle. 1973. Repr. of 1908 ed. 35.00 (ISBN 0-8274-0927-3). R West.
Sappington, Joe. Joe Sap's Tales. Bennett, A. L., ed. (Illus.). 1969. 5.95 (ISBN 0-8363-0053-X). Jenkins.

Sarkar, Himansu B. Literary Heritage of Southeast Asia. 1980. 11.50x (ISBN 0-8364-0606-0, Pub. by Mukhopadhyay India). South Asia Bks.
Sartre, Jean-Paul. Literary Essays. 1978. pap. 2.25 (ISBN 0-8065-0647-4). Citadel Pr.
Sawyer, Newell W. Comedy of Manners from Sheridan to Maugham. LC 68-25059. 1969. Repr. of 1931 ed. 10.00 (ISBN 0-8462-1214-5). Russell.
Schiffhorst, Gerald, ed. The Triumph of Patience: Medieval & Renaissance Studies. LC 77-12732. (Illus.). 1978. 10.00 (ISBN 0-8130-0590-6). U Presses Fla.
Schlegel, Frederick. Lectures on the History of Literature, Ancient & Modern. 1977. Repr. of 1885 ed. lib. bdg. 40.00 (ISBN 0-8414-7936-4). Folcroft.
Scholes, Robert. Structuralism in Literature: An Introduction. LC 73-90578. 250p. 1974. 15.00x (ISBN 0-300-01750-2); pap. 5.25 (ISBN 0-300-01850-9). Yale U Pr.
Schroeder, William L. The Divine Element in Art & Literature. 1973. Repr. of 1916 ed. 25.00 (ISBN 0-8274-0922-2). R West.
Scott, S. H. The Exemplary Mr. Day. 1973. Repr. of 1935 ed. 25.00 (ISBN 0-8274-0920-6). R West.
Scott, Wilbur S., ed. Five Approaches to Literary Criticism. 1962. pap. 2.95 (ISBN 0-02-053680-1, Collier). Macmillan.
Scott-James, R. A. Making of Literature. 1973. Repr. of 1930 ed. 20.00 (ISBN 0-8274-1281-9). R West.
Segre, Cesare. Structures & Time: Narration, Poetry, Models. Meddemmen, John, tr. LC 79-68. 1979. Repr. of 1974 ed. lib. bdg. 19.50x (ISBN 0-226-74476-0). U of Chicago Pr.
Seidel, Alison P., compiled by. Literary Criticism & Authors' Biographies: An Annotated Index. LC 78-11857. 1978. 11.00 (ISBN 0-8108-1172-3). Scarecrow.
Seiler, R. M., ed. Walter Pater: The Critical Heritage. (The Critical Heritage Ser.). 1980. 32.50x (ISBN 0-7100-0380-3). Routledge & Kegan.
Selden, John. Table Talk, 2 vols. 1973. Repr. of 1868 ed. Set. 50.00 (ISBN 0-8274-1299-1). R West.
Seyler & Wilan. Introduction to Literature. LC 80-22488. 926p. 1981. 10.95 (ISBN 0-88284-113-0). Alfred Pub.
Seymour-Smith, Martin. A Reader's Guide to Fifty European Novels. (A Reader's Guide Ser.). 528p. 1980. 21.50x (ISBN 0-389-20138-3). B&N.
Shanks, Edward B. First Essays on Literature. 1973. lib. bdg. 15.50 (ISBN 0-8414-8114-8). Folcroft.
Shapiro, Karl. A Bibliography of Modern Prosody. LC 76-42289. 1973. lib. bdg. 10.00 (ISBN 0-8414-7598-9). Folcroft.
Sharp, William. Studies & Appreciations. facs. ed. Sharp, Mrs. W., ed. LC 67-26783. (Essay Index Reprint Ser). 1912. 17.00 (ISBN 0-8369-0871-6). Arno.
Shaylor, Joseph. The Pleasure of Literature & the Solace of Books. 1973. Repr. of 1898 ed. 10.00 (ISBN 0-8274-0912-5). R West.
Sheherbina, Vladimir. Lenin & the Problems of Literature: Twentieth Century Progress in the Arts & Aesthetic Ideas & Literary Phenomena. 396p. 1975. 16.00x (ISBN 0-8464-0556-3). Beekman Pubs.
Shepard, Leslie. History of Street Literature: The Story of Broadside Ballads, Chapbooks, Proclamations, News-Sheets, Etc. LC 72-12953. (Illus.). 240p. 1973. 28.00 (ISBN 0-8103-2006-1). Gale.
Shepard, William. The Best Criticisms on the Best Authors. 1973. Repr. of 1885 ed. 20.00 (ISBN 0-8274-0909-5). R West.
Shillan, David. Exercises in Criticism. 1973. Repr. of 1938 ed. 15.00 (ISBN 0-8274-0904-4). R West.
Shipley, Joseph T. The Quest for Literature: A Survey of Literary Criticism & Theories of the Literary Forms. 1977. Repr. of 1931 ed. lib. bdg. 25.00 (ISBN 0-8414-7947-X). Folcroft.
Shroff, Homai J. The Eighteenth Century Novel: The Idea of the Gentleman. 1978. text ed. 13.50x (ISBN 0-391-01067-0). Humanities.
Siegel, Eli. Aesthetic Realism: Three Instances. 1961. 0.25 (ISBN 0-911492-01-1). Aesthetic Realism.
Siegel, Paul N. Revolution & the Twentieth Century Novel. Stanton, Frederick, ed. 1979. lib. bdg. 14.00 (ISBN 0-913460-71-0); pap. 4.95 (ISBN 0-913460-72-9). Monad Pr.
Simnett, W. E. Books & Reading. 1973. Repr. of 1926 ed. 20.00 (ISBN 0-8274-0902-8). R West.
Simon, Pierre-Henri. Temoins de L'homme La Condition Humaine dans la Litterature Contemporaine. (Cahiers de la Fondat. Nat. Sc. Polit.). pap. 8.75 (ISBN 0-685-36580-8). French & Eur.
Sinclair, Upton B. Mammonart: An Essay in Economic Interpretation. LC 75-345. (The Radical Tradition in America Ser.). 396p. 1975. Repr. of 1925 ed. 23.50 (ISBN 0-88355-249-3). Hyperion Conn.
Sismandi, Simonde De. Historical View of the Literature of the South of Europe, 2 vols. 1973. Repr. of 1848 ed. 45.00 (ISBN 0-8274-0899-4). R West.
Sitwell, Edith. The Shadow of Cain. LC 77-7598. 1977. Repr. of 1947 ed. lib. bdg. 8.50 (ISBN 0-8414-7755-8). Folcroft.
Skinner, Robert T. Figures & Figureheads. 1973. Repr. of 1931 ed. 25.00 (ISBN 0-8274-0896-X). R West.
Skira, Albert & Teriade, E., eds. Minotaure, Vol. 2. (Illus.). 332p. (Fr.). 1981. 85.00 (ISBN 0-8478-5341-1). Rizzoli Intl.
Smalley, George W. Studies of Men. 1973. Repr. of 1895 ed. 25.00 (ISBN 0-8274-0895-1). R West.
Smith, A. H., ed. The Parker Chronicle: 832-900. rev. ed. 72p. 1980. pap. text ed. 3.75x (ISBN 0-85989-099-6, Pub. by U Exeter England). Humanities.
Smith, Alexander. Dreamthorp: A Book of Essays Written in the Country. LC 72-5690. (Essay Index Reprint Ser.). Repr. of 1864 ed. 19.00 (ISBN 0-8369-7289-9). Arno.
Smith, Anne, ed. The Novels of Thomas Hardy. (Critical Studies Ser.). 1979. text ed. 22.50x (ISBN 0-06-496379-9). B&N.
Smith, Goldwin. Lectures & Essays. 1973. Repr. of 1881 ed. 30.00 (ISBN 0-8274-0892-7). R West.
Smith, James H. & Parks, Edd W., eds. Great Critics. 3rd ed. 1977. 10.95x (ISBN 0-393-09074-4, NortonC). Norton.
Smith, Logan P. Fine Writing. 1973. lib. bdg. 7.50 (ISBN 0-8414-7775-2). Folcroft.
Smith, Naomi R. The State of Mind of Mrs. Sherwood. 1973. Repr. of 1946 ed. 25.00 (ISBN 0-8274-0887-0). R West.
Smith, William, Jr. Abbotsford. 1973. Repr. of 1905 ed. 25.00 (ISBN 0-8274-0629-0). R West.
Smith-Dampier, J. L. Carthusian Worthies. 1973. Repr. of 1940 ed. 45.00 (ISBN 0-8274-0888-9). R West.
Snell, F. J. The Celtic Borderland. 1973. 25.00 (ISBN 0-8274-0885-4). R West.
Snell, Frederick J. The Age of Transition, 2 vols. 1973. lib. bdg. 35.00 (ISBN 0-8414-1563-3). Folcroft.
Spalding, P. A. In the Margin. 1973. Repr. of 1957 ed. 10.00 (ISBN 0-8274-0883-8). R West.
Spencer, Herbert. Various Fragments. LC 72-14180. (Essay Index Reprint Ser.). Repr. of 1897 ed. 18.50 (ISBN 0-518-10025-1). Arno.
Spencer, Richard A., ed. Orientation by Disorientation: Studies on Literary Criticism & Biblical Literary Criticism Presented in Honor of William A. Beardslee. (Pittsburgh Theological Monograph Ser.: No. 35). 1980. pap. text ed. 14.00 (ISBN 0-915138-44-1). Pickwick.
Spender, J. A. New Lamps & Ancient Lights. 1973. Repr. of 1940 ed. 15.00 (ISBN 0-8274-0880-3). R West.
Spingarn, Joel E. Creative Criticism: Essays on the Unity of Genius & Taste. LC 78-14147. 1979. Repr. of 1931 ed. 19.50 (ISBN 0-88355-819-X). Hyperion Conn.
--History of Literary Criticism in the Renaissance. LC 76-27737. 1976. lib. bdg. 24.75 (ISBN 0-8371-9025-8, SPLC). Greenwood.
Sprich, Robert & Noland, Richard W., eds. The Whispered Meanings: Selected Essays of Simon O. Lesser. LC 77-73480. 1977. 12.50x (ISBN 0-87023-243-6); pap. 5.95x (ISBN 0-87023-244-4). U of Mass Pr.
Stanford, Derek. Inside the Forties; Literary Memoirs 1937-1957. (Illus.). 1976. text ed. 19.95x (ISBN 0-8464-0517-2). Beekman Pubs.
Stark, Barbara. Comparison & Criticism. 1968. pap. text ed. 3.50x (ISBN 0-435-18845-3). Heinemann Ed.
Stauffer, Donald A. Art of Biography in 18th Century England: With Bibliographical Supplement, 2 Vols. LC 78-83850. 1970. Repr. of 1941 ed. Set. 27.50 (ISBN 0-8462-1400-8). Russell.
Stearns, Harold. The Street I Know. 1973. Repr. of 1935 ed. 25.00 (ISBN 0-8274-0875-7). R West.
Stein, Getrude. Narration. LC 77-24699. 1973. lib. bdg. 8.50 (ISBN 0-8414-7932-1). Folcroft.
Sternbeck, Alfred. Filibusters & Buccaneers. LC 79-39105. (Essay Index Reprint Ser.). Repr. of 1942 ed. 21.00 (ISBN 0-8369-2723-0). Arno.
Stevenson, E. Early Reviews of Great Writers (1786-1832) 1973. lib. bdg. 25.00 (ISBN 0-8414-7963-1). Folcroft.
Stewart, Grace. A New Mythos: The Novel of the Artist As Heroine 1877 - 1977. 2nd ed. 208p. 1981. pap. 8.95 (ISBN 0-920792-11-1). EPWP.
Stewart, Herbert L. From a Library Window. 1973. Repr. of 1940 ed. 17.50 (ISBN 0-8274-0865-X). R West.
Stirling-Maxwell, William. Miscellaneous Essays & Addresses. 1973. Repr. of 1891 ed. 45.00 (ISBN 0-8274-0864-1). R West.
Stokes, H. F. Perseus or of Dragons. 1973. Repr. of 1925 ed. 6.50 (ISBN 0-8274-0862-5). R West.
Stonier, George W. Gog Magog, & Other Critical Essays. facs. ed. LC 67-22120. (Essay Index Reprint Ser). 1933. 13.00 (ISBN 0-8369-0907-0). Arno.
Story, Alfred. Books That Are the Hearts of Men. 1973. Repr. of 1906 ed. 15.00 (ISBN 0-8274-0858-7). R West.
Story, William W. Excursions in Art & Letters. 1973. Repr. of 1891 ed. 20.00 (ISBN 0-8274-0859-5). R West.
Strelka, Joseph P., ed. Anagogic Qualities of Literature. LC 79-136962. (Yearbook of Comparative Criticism, Vol. 4). (Illus.). 1971. 16.00x (ISBN 0-271-01145-9). Pa St U Pr.
Strong, Isobel & Osbourne, Lloyd. Memories of Vailima. 1973. Repr. of 1903 ed. 20.00 (ISBN 0-8274-0421-2). R West.
Strong, S. Arthur. Critical Studies & Fragments. 1973. Repr. of 1905 ed. Set. 25.00 (ISBN 0-8274-0852-8). R West.
Stuckey, W. J. The Pulitzer Prize Novels: A Critical Backward Look. LC 80-5244. 281p. 14.95 (ISBN 0-8061-1665-X). U of Okla Pr.
Sturtevant, Edgar H., et al, eds. T. Macci Plauti Pseudolus. 1978. Repr. of 1932 ed. lib. bdg. 20.00 (ISBN 0-89760-802-X, Telegraph). Dynamic Learn Corp.
Sumner, Laura. The Weddynge of Sir Gawen & Dame Ragnell. LC 76-43031. 1924. lib. bdg. 10.00 (ISBN 0-8414-7763-9). Folcroft.
Sutro, Alfred. Celebrities & Simple Souls. 1973. Repr. of 1933 ed. 20.00 (ISBN 0-8274-0847-1). R West.
Swain, Barbara. Fools & Folly During the Middle Ages & the Renaissance. LC 76-43313. 1973. lib. bdg. 20.00 (ISBN 0-8414-7718-3). Folcroft.
Swayne, Josephine L. The Story of Concord. 1973. Repr. of 1939 ed. 40.00 (ISBN 0-8274-0849-8). R West.
Swinburne, A. C. Essays & Studies. 1973. 20.00 (ISBN 0-8274-0518-9). R West.
Swinburne, Algernon C. Essays & Studies. 3rd ed. LC 72-13306. (Essay Index Reprint Ser.). Repr. of 1888 ed. 19.00 (ISBN 0-8369-8174-X). Arno.
Symonds, John A. Essays, Speculative & Suggestive, 2 vols. 1973. lib. bdg. 24.50 (ISBN 0-8414-7998-4). Folcroft.
--In the Key of Blue. 1973. lib. bdg. 9.95 (ISBN 0-8414-7999-2). Folcroft.
Symons, Arthur. Studies in Prose & Verse. LC 78-148315. Repr. of 1922 ed. 14.50 (ISBN 0-404-07827-3). AMS Pr.
Szladits, Lola L. Documents, Famous & Infamous: Selected from the Berg Collection of English & American Literature. (Illus.). 34p. 1972. pap. 3.00 (ISBN 0-87104-240-1). NY Pub Lib.
Talfourd, T. Noon. Critical & Miscellaneous Writings. 1973. Repr. of 1942 ed. 40.00 (ISBN 0-8274-0841-2). R West.
Tan, H. G. La Matiere De Don Juan et les Genre Litterairies. (Publications Romanes De L'Universite De Leyde Ser: Vol. 20). 1976. lib. bdg. 21.00 (ISBN 90-6021-215-0, Pub. by Leiden Univ. Holland). Kluwer Boston.
Tanaka, Ronald. Systems Models for Literary Macro-Theory. (PDR Press Publication in Literary Systems: No. 1). 1976. pap. text ed. 5.00x (ISBN 90-316-0085-7). Humanities.
Telleen, John M. Milton Dans la Litterature Francaise. LC 75-189895. ii, 151p. (Fr.). 1972. Repr. of 1904 ed. lib. bdg. 18.50 (ISBN 0-8337-4446-1). B Franklin.
Terry, Ellen. The Story of My Life. 1973. Repr. of 1908 ed. 25.00 (ISBN 0-8274-0426-3). R West.
Thomas, Edward. Last Sheaf: Essays. 1973. lib. bdg. 12.50 (ISBN 0-8414-8041-9). Folcroft.
Thomas, Gilbert. Builders & Makers. 1973. Repr. of 1944 ed. 20.00 (ISBN 0-8274-0834-X). R West.
Thompson, Denys, ed. Matthew Arnold: Selected Poems & Prose. (The Poetry Bookshelf Ser.). 1971. pap. text ed. 6.50x (ISBN 0-435-15063-4). Heinemann Ed.
Thompson, Edward. Cock Robin's Decease. 1973. Repr. of 1928 ed. 12.50 (ISBN 0-8274-0833-1). R West.
Thompson, Francis. Literary Criticisms. Connolly, Terence L., ed. LC 74-30927. 1975. Repr. of 1948 ed. lib. bdg. 37.00x (ISBN 0-8371-7888-6, THLC). Greenwood.
Thorndike, Ashley H. Outlook for Literature. 1973. Repr. of 1931 ed. 15.00 (ISBN 0-8274-1748-9). R West.
Thorn-Drury, G. Covent Garden Drollery. 1973. Repr. of 1928 ed. lib. bdg. 20.00 (ISBN 0-8414-7294-7). Folcroft.
Thorold, Algar. Six Masters in Disillusionment. 1973. Repr. of 1909 ed. 20.00 (ISBN 0-8274-0831-5). R West.
Thorpe, Peter. Why Literature Is Bad for You. 1980. text ed. 15.95x (ISBN 0-88229-486-5); pap. 7.95x (ISBN 0-88229-745-7). Nelson-Hall.
Thrall, W. F. & Hibbard, A. A Handbook to Literature. 582p. 1980. Repr. lib. bdg. 40.00 (ISBN 0-89987-807-5). Darby Bks.
Thurber, Carryl N. Sir Robert Howard's Comedy "The Committee". 1978. Repr. of 1921 ed. lib. bdg. 35.00 (ISBN 0-89760-877-1, Telegraph). Dynamic Learn Corp.
Tillyard, E. M. Lamb's Criticism: A Selection from the Literary Criticism of Charles Lamb. 112p. 1980. Repr. of 1923 ed. lib. bdg. 20.00 (ISBN 0-8495-5158-7). Arden Lib.
Toe Tunk. Histoire Universelle de la Litterature, 3 tomes. Set. 57.50 (ISBN 0-685-35931-X). French & Eur.
Tollemache, Lionel. Safe Studies. 1973. Repr. of 1884 ed. 40.00 (ISBN 0-8274-0828-5). R West.
Tolstoy, Leo. Essays & Letters. Maude, Aylmer, tr. LC 73-2691. (Select Bibliographies Reprint Ser.). 1973. Repr. of 1909 ed. 22.00 (ISBN 0-8369-7171-X). Arno.
Torgovnick, Marianna. Closure in the Novel. LC 80-8581. 272p. 1981. 16.50x (ISBN 0-691-06464-4). Princeton U Pr.
Townsend, George H. The Everyday Book of Modern Literature. 1973. 20.00 (ISBN 0-8274-0830-7). R West.
Tracey, A. G. The Appreciation of Literature. 1973. Repr. of 1921 ed. 20.00 (ISBN 0-8274-0826-9). R West.
Trevelyan, George M. Walking. 1973. Repr. of 1928 ed. 10.00 (ISBN 0-8274-0824-2). R West.
Trilling, Lionel. Prefaces to the Experience of Literature. LC 79-1850. 320p. 1981. pap. 8.95 (ISBN 0-15-673810-4). HarBraceJ.
--Prefaces to the Experience of Literature. Trilling, Diana, ed. LC 79-1850. 1979. 12.95 (ISBN 0-15-173915-3); pap. write for info. HarBraceJ.
Tripp, Raymond P., Jr. Beyond Canterbury: Chaucer, Humanism, & Literature. 1977. pap. 7.00 (ISBN 0-905019-03-2). Soc New Lang Study.
Trory, Ernie. Mainly About Books. 1973. Repr. of 1945 ed. 20.00 (ISBN 0-8274-0825-0). R West.
Ts'ai T'ung-Kan, tr. Chinese Poems in English Rhyme. LC 32-31028. (Illus.). 1969. Repr. of 1932 ed. lib. bdg. 15.00x (ISBN 0-8371-1159-5, TSCP). Greenwood.
Tschumi, Raymond. Philosophy of Literature. 1962. 7.95 (ISBN 0-8023-1102-4). Dufour.
Tucker, Nathaniel. The Complete Published Poems of Nathaniel Tucker, Together with Columbinus: A Mask (1783) LC 73-12391. 192p. 1973. lib. bdg. 25.00x (ISBN 0-8201-1121-X). Schol Facsimiles.
Tucker, T. G. The Judgment & Appreciation of Literature. 1926. Repr. 20.00 (ISBN 0-8274-2639-9). R West.
Tunney, Hubert J. Home's Douglas. 1973. Repr. of 1924 ed. 25.00 (ISBN 0-8492-9961-6). R West.
Twain, Mark. Stolen White Elephant, Ect. 1973. lib. bdg. 20.00 (ISBN 0-685-35503-9). Folcroft.
Uhlig, Claus. Hofkritik im England des Mittelalters und der Renaissance: Studien zu einem Gemeinplatz der Europaeischen Moralistik. LC 73-75495. (Quellen und Forschungen zur Sprach - und Kulturgeschichte der germanischen Voelker N. F. 56). 1973. 75.00x (ISBN 3-11-004501-X). De Gruyter.
Underhill, George. Literary Epochs: Chapters on Noted Periods of Intellectual Activity. 1973. Repr. of 1887 ed. 30.00 (ISBN 0-8274-0807-2). R West.
Valentine, Kristin B. & Valentine, D. E. Interlocking Pieces: Twenty Questions for Understanding Literature. 2nd ed. 1980. pap. text ed. 5.50 (ISBN 0-8403-2131-7). Kendall-Hunt.
Van Dyke, Henry. Camp-Fires & Guide Posts: A Book of Essays & Excursions. 1973. Repr. of 1921 ed. 20.00 (ISBN 0-8274-0801-3). R West.
--Days off & Other Digressions. 1973. Repr. of 1929 ed. 17.50 (ISBN 0-8274-0802-1). R West.
--Fisherman's Luck. 1973. Repr. of 1900 ed. 17.50 (ISBN 0-8274-0803-X). R West.
--The Unknown Quantity: A Book of Romance & Some Half-Told Truths. 1973. Repr. of 1927 ed. 20.00 (ISBN 0-8274-0799-8). R West.
--The Valley of Vision. 1973. Repr. of 1927 ed. 20.00 (ISBN 0-8274-0800-5). R West.
Van Dyke, John C. The Meaning of Pictures. 1973. 25.00 (ISBN 0-8274-0798-X). R West.
Vivas, Eliseo. Creation & Discovery. 1966. pap. 4.95 (ISBN 0-89526-952-X). Regnery-Gateway.

--Creation & Discovery: Essays in Criticism & Aesthetics. LC 72-3365. (Essay Index Reprint Ser.). Repr. of 1955 ed. 18.00 (ISBN 0-8369-2931-4). Arno.

Von Klenze, Camillo. Charles Timothy Brooks: Translator from the German & Genteel Tradition. 1973. Repr. of 1937 ed. 20.00 (ISBN 0-8274-0780-7). R West.

--The Interpretation of Italy During the Last Two Centuries. 1907. 25.00 (ISBN 0-8274-2579-1). R West.

Wackenroder, W. H. Wilhelm Heinrich Wackenroder's Confessions & Fantasies. Schubert, Mary H., tr. LC 73-136958. (Illus.). 1972. 14.95x (ISBN 0-271-01150-5). Pa St U Pr.

Waggoner, Diane. The Hills of Faraway: A Guide to Fantasy. LC 76-900. 1978. 16.95 (ISBN 0-689-10846-X). Atheneum.

Walley, H. & Wilson, J. The Anatomy of Literature. 1934. Repr. 20.00 (ISBN 0-8274-3788-9). R West.

Walser, Richard. Literary North Carolina: A Brief Historical Survey. (Illus.). 1970. 5.00 (ISBN 0-686-76833-7); pap. 2.00 (ISBN 0-86526-048-6). NC Archives.

Ward, A. C. Landmarks in Western Literature. 1979. Repr. of 1932 ed. lib. bdg. 15.00 (ISBN 0-8492-2991-X). R West.

--Landmarks in Western Literature. LC 70-105845. 1971. Repr. of 1932 ed. 10.50 (ISBN 0-8046-1365-6). Kennikat.

Ward, Adolphus W. In Memoriam: Adolphus William Ward, Master at Peterhouse 1900-1924. 1973. Repr. of 1924 ed. 25.00 (ISBN 0-8274-0819-6). R West.

Ward, David. Jonathan Swift: An Introductory Essay. 216p. 1973. pap. 9.95x (ISBN 0-416-76480-0). Methuen Inc.

Ward, Philip. A Lifetime's Reading: Five Hundred Great Classics of World Literature for a Private Library. (Oleander Reference Bks.: Vol. 5). 388p. 1981. 29.95 (ISBN 0-900891-73-4); pap. 25.00 (ISBN 0-900891-74-2). Oleander Pr.

Warner, Charles O. A Roundabout Journey. 1973. Repr. of 1883 ed. 15.00 (ISBN 0-8274-0793-9). R West.

Warner, Charles W. A Little Journey in the World. 1973. Repr. of 1899 ed. 10.00 (ISBN 0-8274-0791-2). R West.

Wasserstrom, William, ed. Van Wyck Brooks: The Critic & His Critics. (National University Publications, Literary Criticism Ser). 1979. 15.00 (ISBN 0-8046-9245-9). Kennikat.

Waters, W. G. Norfolk in Literature. 1973. 20.00 (ISBN 0-8274-0787-4). R West.

Watson, E. Lacon. The Unconscious Humourist: And Other Essays. LC 72-13313. (Essay Index Reprint Ser.). Repr. of 1896 ed. 14.75 (ISBN 0-8369-8177-4). Arno.

Watson, William. Pencraft: A Plea for the Older Ways. 1973. Repr. of 1917 ed. 10.00 (ISBN 0-8274-0784-X). R West.

Watt, L. Maclean. The Hills of Home. 1973. Repr. of 1914 ed. 20.00 (ISBN 0-8274-0436-0). R West.

Watts, Harold H. Hound & Quarry(Wallace Stevens, Maxwell Anderson, Robinson Jeffers, Thomas Mann, W. B. Yeats, T. S. Eliot, Hilda Doolittle) 1973. Repr. of 1953 ed. 30.00 (ISBN 0-8274-0782-3). R West.

Watts, Neville H. The Vision Splendid (Hardy, Housman) LC 74-16122. 1974. Repr. of 1946 ed. lib. bdg. 20.00 (ISBN 0-8414-9548-3). Folcroft.

Weathers, Winston. The Broken Word: Communication Pathos in Modern Literature. 238p. 1981. write for info. Gordon.

--The Tyger. LC 72-84930. (Literary Casebook Ser.). 1969. pap. text ed. 2.50x (ISBN 0-675-09443-7). Merrill.

Webb, Eugene. The Dark Dove: The Sacred & Secular in Modern Literature. LC 74-28210. 292p. 1975. 12.50 (ISBN 0-295-95377-2). U of Wash Pr.

Weber, Brom, ed. Sense & Sensibility in Twentieth-Century Writing: A Gathering in Memory of William Van O' Conner. LC 75-112395. (Crosscurrents-Modern Critiques Ser.). 191p. 1970. 6.95 (ISBN 0-8093-0448-1). S Ill U Pr.

Weekly, Ernest. Saxo Grammaticus or First Aid for the Best Seller. 1973. Repr. of 1930 ed. lib. bdg. 12.50 (ISBN 0-8414-9663-3). Folcroft.

Weimann, Robert. Structure & Society in Literary History: Studies in the History & Theory of Historical Criticism. LC 75-17719. 1976. 15.00x (ISBN 0-8139-0628-8). U Pr of Va.

Weinberg, Robert. The Annotated Guide to Robert E. Howard's Sword & Sorcery. LC 80-19169. 160p. 1980. Repr. of 1976 ed. lib. bdg. 13.95x (ISBN 0-89370-030-4). Borgo Pr.

Weiss, Daniel, et al, eds. The Critic Agonistes. 1982. price not set. U of Wash Pr.

Welch, John S. Literature in the School. 1973. Repr. of 1910 ed. 15.00 (ISBN 0-8274-0689-4). R West.

Wellek, Rene. Concepts of Criticism. Nichols, Stephen G., Jr., ed. (Orig.). 1963. 30.00x (ISBN 0-300-01033-8); pap. 6.95 (ISBN 0-300-00255-6, Y86). Yale U Pr.

Weller, Rene. Geschichte der Literaturkritik 1750-1950, 4 vols. Incl. Vol. 1. Das Spate 18. Jahrhundert-Das Zeitalter der Romantik. 1978. 73.50x (ISBN 3-11-005914-2); Vol. 2. Das Zeitalter Es Uebergangs. 37.75x (ISBN 3-11-005915-0); Vol. 3. Das Spaete 19. Jahrhundert. 61.00x (ISBN 3-11-005916-9). (Komparatistische Studien: Nos. 5 & 6). 1977. De Gruyter.

Wells, Henry W. New Poets from Old: A Study in Literary Genetics. LC 64-20676. 1964. Repr. of 1940 ed. 9.00 (ISBN 0-8462-0410-X). Russell.

Wendell, Barrett. Essays in Memory of Barrett Wendell. Castle, William R., Jr. & Kaufman, Paul, eds. LC 66-27178. 1967. Repr. of 1926 ed. 8.50 (ISBN 0-8462-0891-1). Russell.

--The Traditions of European Literature from Homer to Dante, 2 vols. Incl. Vol. 1. The Traditions of Greece & Rome. 350p (ISBN 0-8044-6977-6); Vol. 2. The Traditions of Christianity & the Middle Ages. 322p (ISBN 0-8044-6978-4). LC 64-15702. Set. pap. 7.90 (ISBN 0-8044-6976-8); pap. 3.95 ea. Ungar.

Wescott, Glenway. Images of Truth: Remembrances & Criticism. LC 77-167436. (Essay Index Reprint Ser.). Repr. of 1962 ed. 18.00 (ISBN 0-8369-2730-3). Arno.

Wessels, Abram. Scarlet Letter Guides. Zimmerman, Diane, ed. (LifeView: a Christian Approach to Literature Studies Ser.). (gr. 10-12). 1977. pap. 0.85 student guide (ISBN 0-915134-31-4); tchrs. ed. 1.50 (ISBN 0-915134-35-7). Mott Media.

West, Henry S. The Versification of King Horn. LC 76-39981. Repr. of 1907 ed. lib. bdg. 15.00 (ISBN 0-8414-9526-2). Folcroft.

Westwood, Thomas. A Literary Friendship: Lamb, Browning, Tennyson. 1973. Repr. of 1914 ed. 25.00 (ISBN 0-8274-0685-1). R West.

Weygandt, Cornelius. Time of Yeats: English Poetry of To-Day Against an American Background. LC 68-25053. 1969. Repr. of 1937 ed. 12.50 (ISBN 0-8462-1187-4). Russell.

Whibley, Charles. Book of Scoundrels. 1973. lib. bdg. 13.50 (ISBN 0-8414-9671-4). Folcroft.

Whitman, Sarah W. Letters of Sarah Wyman Whitman. 1973. Repr. of 1907 ed. 20.00 (ISBN 0-8274-0684-3). R West.

Wilde, Oscar. Essays. Pearson, Hesketh, ed. & intro. by. LC 72-364. (Essay Index Reprint Ser.). Repr. of 1950 ed. 18.00 (ISBN 0-8369-2832-6). Arno.

--Literary Criticism of Oscar Wilde. Weintraub, Stanley, ed. LC 68-22414. (Regents Critics Ser). 1969. 17.50x (ISBN 0-8032-0462-0). U of Nebr Pr.

Wilding, Michael. Political Fictions. 1980. 25.00x (ISBN 0-7100-0457-5). Routledge & Kegan.

Will, Frederic. Belphagor. 1977. pap. text ed. 12.75x (ISBN 90-6203-348-2). Humanities.

Willey, Basil. Tendencies in Renaissance Literary Theory. LC 73-12884. 1922. lib. bdg. 8.50 (ISBN 0-8414-9422-3). Folcroft.

--Tendencies in Renaissance Literary Theory. 1979. 24.50 (ISBN 0-685-67818-0). Porter.

Williams, William E. Craft of Literature. facs. ed. LC 67-28773. (Essay Index Reprint Ser). 1925. 12.50 (ISBN 0-8369-1001-X). Arno.

Williams-Ellis, Amabel. The Exquisite Tragedy. 1973. Repr. of 1929 ed. 30.00 (ISBN 0-8274-0565-0). R West.

Williamson, George. Senecan Amble: A Study in Prose Form from Bacon to Collier. Repr. of 1951 ed. 20.00 (ISBN 0-403-04260-7). Somerset Pub.

Willis, N. P. Famous Persons & Famous Places. 1973. Repr. of 1854 ed. 30.00 (ISBN 0-8274-0562-6). R West.

Willis, Nathaniel P. Famous Persons & Places. LC 72-5769. (Essay Index Reprint Ser.). Repr. of 1854 ed. 26.00 (ISBN 0-8369-7279-1). Arno.

Wilson, Edmund. The Wound & the Bow: Seven Studies in Literature. 1978. pap. 4.95 (ISBN 0-374-51480-1). FS&G.

Wilson, H. Schutz. Studies in History, Legend & Literature. 1977. Repr. of 1884 ed. lib. bdg. 35.00 (ISBN 0-8492-2884-0). R West.

Wilson, June. Green Shadows (John Clare) 1973. Repr. of 1951 ed. 25.00 (ISBN 0-8274-0556-1). R West.

Wilson, S. Law. The Theory of Modern Literature: Browning, G. Eliot, Hardy, Meredith. 1973. Repr. of 1899 ed. 30.00 (ISBN 0-8274-0675-4). R West.

Wimsatt, William K. & Brooks, Cleanth. Literary Criticism: A Short History (in Two Volumes) LC 78-55046. 1978. pap. 6.95 ea. (Phoen); Vol. I. (ISBN 0-226-90173-4, P797); Vol. II. (ISBN 0-226-90174-2, P798). U of Chicago Pr.

Winchester, Caleb T. Old Castle. 1973. Repr. of 1922 ed. 30.00 (ISBN 0-8274-0605-3). R West.

--Some Principles of Literary Criticism. 1973. lib. bdg. 25.00 (ISBN 0-8414-9723-0). Folcroft.

Winter, William. Old Friends: Longfellow, Dickens, Wilkie Collins, Artemus Ward, J. R. Lowell. 1973. Repr. of 1909 ed. 16.50 (ISBN 0-8274-0673-8). R West.

--Old Shrines & Ivy: Shakespeare, Sheridan, Farquhar, Longfellow, Cooper. 1973. Repr. of 1898 ed. 20.00 (ISBN 0-8274-0674-6). R West.

Winters, Yvor. Function of Criticism: Problems & Exercises. LC 57-1652. 200p. 1957. pap. 5.95x (ISBN 0-8040-0130-8). Swallow.

Woodberry, George E. Studies in Letters & Life. 1890. lib. bdg. 20.00 (ISBN 0-8414-9791-5). Folcroft.

--Torch. facs. ed. LC 73-84349. (Essay Index Reprint Ser). 1905. 14.50 (ISBN 0-8369-1115-6). Arno.

Woolf, Virginia. The Captain's Death Bed & Other Essays. LC 50-7411. 248p. 1973. pap. 2.95 (ISBN 0-15-615395-5, HB253, Harv). HarBraceJ.

Yeazell, Ruth B. Language & Knowledge in the Late Novels of Henry James. LC 75-46538. viii, 144p. 1980. lib. bdg. 6.00x (ISBN 0-226-95095-6). U of Chicago Pr.

Zabel, Morton D. Literary Opinion in America: Essays Illustrating the Status, Methods & Problems of Criticism in the United States in the Twentieth Century, 2 vols. 18.00 (ISBN 0-8446-1487-4). Peter Smith.

Zangwill, I. Without Prejudice. LC 72-13302. (Essay Index Reprint Ser.). Repr. of 1896 ed. 19.25 (ISBN 0-8369-8183-9). Arno.

Zekowski, Arlene. Seasons of the Mind. 304p. 1973. pap. 3.75 (ISBN 0-8180-0617-X). Horizon.

Zeller, Rosmarie. Spiel und Konversation im Barock: Untersuchungen Zu Harsdoerffers Gespraechspielen. LC 73-75496. (Quellen und Forschungen zur Sprach-und Kulturgeschichte der Germanischen Voelker N. F. 58). 198p. 1974. 42.25x (ISBN 3-11-004245-2). De Gruyter.

LITERATURE–INFLUENCE

see Literature and Morals

LITERATURE–MISCELLANEA

see also Literary Recreations

Boas, Ralph P. Enjoyment of Literature. 1952. Repr. 20.00 (ISBN 0-8274-2277-6). R West.

Clouston, W. A. Literary Coincidences: A Bookstall Bargain. LC 73-11482. 1973. lib. bdg. 15.00 (ISBN 0-8414-3386-0). Folcroft.

--Literary Curiosities & Eccentries. 1977. lib. bdg. 25.00 (ISBN 0-8414-1832-2). Folcroft.

D'Alembert, Jean. Miscellaneous Pieces in Literature, History, Philosophy. 59.95 (ISBN 0-8490-0642-2). Gordon Pr.

Dobree, Bonamy. Rochester: A Conversation Between Sir George Etherege & Mister Fitzjames. LC 73-13531. 1926. lib. bdg. 6.50 (ISBN 0-8414-3672-X). Folcroft.

Eglinton, John. Letters to George Moore. LC 77-1316. 1942. lib. bdg. 12.50 (ISBN 0-8414-3980-X). Folcroft.

Erens, Pat. Masterpieces. LC 79-88242. 1979. pap. 5.95 (ISBN 0-914090-75-5). Chicago Review.

Evelyn, John. Devotionaries Book. LC 73-3159. 1936. lib. bdg. 17.50 (ISBN 0-8414-1903-5). Folcroft.

Forman, M. Buxton. Some Letters & Miscellanea of Charles Brown, the Friend of John Keats & Thomas Richards. LC 76-26940. 1937. lib. bdg. 15.00 (ISBN 0-8414-4205-3). Folcroft.

Franklin, James T. Mid-Day Gleanings: A Book for Home & Holiday Readings. LC 76-168134. Repr. of 1893 ed. 16.00 (ISBN 0-404-00052-5). AMS Pr.

Greenwood, R. R. A Preface to Literature. 1930. Repr. 10.00 (ISBN 0-8274-3199-6). R West.

House, Humphry. All in Due Time: Collected Essays & Broadcast Talks. LC 78-18897. 1955. lib. bdg. 17.50 (ISBN 0-8414-4962-7). Folcroft.

Mackail, John. Coleridge's Literary Criticism. 1908. Repr. lib. bdg. 25.00 (ISBN 0-8414-5997-5). Folcroft.

Marvin, Frederic R. Companionship of Books & Other Papers. LC 75-90662. (Essay Index Reprint Ser). 1905. 17.00 (ISBN 0-8369-1227-6). Arno.

Salter, Christopher & Lloyd, William. Landscape in Literature. Natoli, Salvatore J., ed. LC 76-29268. (Resource Papers for College Geography Ser.). 1977. pap. text ed. 4.00 (ISBN 0-89291-118-2). Assn Am Geographers.

Walsh, William S. Handy-Book of Literary Curiosities. LC 68-24370. 1966. Repr. of 1892 ed. 48.00 (ISBN 0-8103-0162-8). Gale.

LITERATURE–MORAL AND RELIGIOUS ASPECTS

see Literature and Morals; Religion and Literature

LITERATURE–OUTLINES, SYLLABI, ETC.

Arnez, Nancy Levi. Moll Flanders Notes. pap. text ed. 1.95 (ISBN 0-8220-0854-8). Cliffs.

Goodman, Roland A. Plot Outlines of One Hundred Famous Novels: The First 100. 6.00 (ISBN 0-8446-0652-9). Peter Smith.

Smaridge, Norah. Sense & Sensibility Notes. pap. text ed. 2.25 (ISBN 0-8220-1174-3). Cliffs.

Tindall, William Y. A Reader's Guide to James Joyce. 1971. lib. bdg. 15.00x (ISBN 0-374-97947-2). Octagon.

Willison, George. Federalist Notes. (Orig.). 1970. pap. 1.95 (ISBN 0-8220-0488-7). Cliffs.

Zeiger, Arthur. Encyclopedia of English. LC 59-8821. (Orig.). 1957. pap. 3.95 (ISBN 0-685-06490-5). Arco.

LITERATURE–PHILOSOPHY

Armstrong, Daniel & Schooneveld, C. H., eds. Roman Jakobson: Echoes of His Scholarship. 1977. pap. text ed. 68.50x (ISBN 90-316-0147-0). Humanities.

Brightfield, Myron F. Issue in Literary Criticism. LC 68-23278. 1968. Repr. of 1932 ed. lib. bdg. 16.75x (ISBN 0-8371-0029-1, BRLC). Greenwood.

Burke, Kenneth. The Philosophy of Literary Form. 1974. pap. 8.95x (ISBN 0-520-02483-4). U of Cal Pr.

Burks, Don M., ed. Rhetoric, Philosophy, & Literature: An Exploration. LC 77-92712. 1978. 7.50 (ISBN 0-911198-52-0). Purdue.

Craig, Hardin. The Enchanted Glass: The Elizabethan Mind in Literature. LC 75-11492. 293p. 1975. Repr. of 1952 ed. lib. bdg. 16.75x (ISBN 0-8371-8200-X, CREG). Greenwood.

Curtius, E. R. European Literature & the Latin Middle Ages. Trask, Willard R., tr. LC 52-10619. (Bollingen Ser., Vol. 36). 682p. 1953. 36.00 (ISBN 0-691-09739-9); pap. 8.50 (ISBN 0-691-01793-X). Princeton U Pr.

Donoghue, Denis. The Sovereign Ghost: Studies in Imagination. LC 75-27923. 1977. 15.95x (ISBN 0-520-03134-2). U of Cal Pr.

Eaton, Trevor. Semantics of Literature. (De Proprietatibus Litterarum Ser. Minor: No. 1). (Orig.). 1966. pap. text ed. 12.00x (ISBN 90-2790-084-1). Mouton.

Ellmann, Richard & Feidelson, Charles, Jr., eds. Modern Tradition: Backgrounds of Modern Literature. 1965. 25.00 (ISBN 0-19-500542-2). Oxford U Pr.

Ermolaev, Herman. Soviet Literary Theories 1917-1934: The Genesis of Socialist Realism. 1977. Repr. of 1963 ed. lib. bdg. 15.50x (ISBN 0-374-92625-5). Octagon.

Foerster, Norman, ed. Humanism & America: Essays on the Outlook of Modern Civilization. LC 67-27598. 1967. Repr. of 1930 ed. 12.50 (ISBN 0-8046-0154-2). Kennikat.

Foucault, Michel. Language, Counter-Memory, Practice: Selected Essays and Interviews. Bouchard, Donald F., ed. & tr. from Fr. LC 77-4561. (Illus.). 1977. 18.50x (ISBN 0-8014-0979-9). Cornell U Pr.

Freund, Philip. Art of Reading the Novel. 1965. pap. 1.50 (ISBN 0-02-050990-1, Collier). Macmillan.

Gary, Romain. Pour Sganarelle. 480p. 1965. 11.95 (ISBN 0-686-55884-7). French & Eur.

Giorgi, Rubina. Figure Di Nessuno. LC 75-4966. 131p. 1976. pap. 7.95 (ISBN 0-915570-02-5). Oolp Pr.

Hernadi, Paul, ed. What is Literature? LC 77-23640. 288p. 1978. 17.50x (ISBN 0-253-36505-8). Ind U Pr.

Ingarden, Roman. Cognition of the Literary Work of Art. Crowley, Ruth A. & Olson, Kenneth R., trs. from Ger. LC 73-80117. (Studies in Phenomenology & Existential Philosophy Ser.). 440p. 1974. text ed. 21.95x (ISBN 0-8101-0424-5); pap. 10.95x (ISBN 0-8101-0599-3). Northwestern U Pr.

--The Literary Work of Art. Grabowicz, George G., tr. (Studies in Phenomenology & Existential Philosophy). 1974. text ed. 21.95x (ISBN 0-8101-0418-0); pap. 10.95x (ISBN 0-8101-0537-3). Northwestern U Pr.

Kermode, Frank. Sense of an Ending: Studies in the Theory of Fiction. (YA) (gr. 10 up). 1968. pap. 5.95 (ISBN 0-19-500770-0, GB). Oxford U Pr.

Liu, James J. Chinese Theories of Literature. LC 74-11631. 208p. 1975. 15.00x (ISBN 0-226-48692-3). U of Chicago Pr.

McElroy, Davis D. Study of Literature. LC 65-11950. 1965. 3.50 (ISBN 0-8022-1015-5). Philos Lib.

Mackenzie, Agnes M. The Process of Literature. 1929. Repr. 35.00 (ISBN 0-8274-3208-9). R West.

Marghescour, Mircea. Le Concept de Litterarite: Essai sur les Possibilities Theoriques d'une Science de la Litterature. (De Proprietatibus Litterarum, Ser. Minor: No. 23). 119p. (Fr.). 1975. pap. text ed. 13.75x (ISBN 90-2793-372-3). Mouton.

Medina, Angel. Reflection, Time & the Novel. (International Library of Phenomenology & Moral Sciences). 1979. 20.00x (ISBN 0-7100-0273-4). Routledge & Kegan.

Olsen, Stein H. The Structure of Literary Understanding. LC 77-77719. 1978. 28.50 (ISBN 0-521-21731-8). Cambridge U Pr.

Peckham, Morse. Man's Rage for Chaos: Biology, Behavior, & the Arts. LC 65-22544. (Illus.). 1967. pap. 4.95 (ISBN 0-8052-0142-4). Schocken.

Phillips, Daniel E. Human Element in Literature. LC 70-93068. 1969. Repr. of 1940 ed. 12.00 (ISBN 0-8046-0681-1). Kennikat.
Pollock, Thomas C. Nature of Literature: Its Relation to Science, Language & Human Experiences. LC 65-25135. 1965. Repr. of 1942 ed. 9.00 (ISBN 0-87752-086-0). Gordian.
Salm, Peter. Three Modes of Criticism: The Literary Theories of Scherer, Walzel, & Staiger. 1968. 15.00 (ISBN 0-8295-0128-2). UPB.
Sartre, Jean-Paul. Literature & Existentialism. 1962. pap. 3.95 (ISBN 0-8065-0105-7). Citadel Pr.
Smith, Barbara H. On the Margins of Discourse: The Relation of Literature to Language. LC 78-18274. 1979. 14.00x (ISBN 0-226-76452-4). U of Chicago Pr.
Spanos, William V., ed. Martin Heidegger & the Question of Literature: Toward a Postmodern Literary Hermeneutics. LC 79-84261. (Studies in Phenomenology & Existential Philosophy). 352p. 1980. 15.00x (ISBN 0-253-17575-5). Ind U Pr.
Steiner, George. Language & Silence: Essays on Language, Literature & the Inhuman. LC 67-14332. 1970. pap. text ed. 4.95x (ISBN 0-689-70226-4, 158). Atheneum.
Tschumi, Raymond. Philosophy of Literature. 1962. 7.95 (ISBN 0-8023-1102-4). Dufour.
--Philosophy of Literature. 7.50 (ISBN 0-87556-338-4). Saifer.
Turquet-Milnes, G. From Pascal to Proust. LC 76-52955. (Studies in French Literature, No. 45). 1977. lib. bdg. 32.95 (ISBN 0-8383-2131-3). Haskell.
Uitti, Karl D. Linguistics & Literary Theory. new ed. 264p. 1974. pap. text ed. 5.95x (ISBN 0-393-09293-3). Norton.
Weiss, Paul. Nine Basic Arts. LC 61-7164. (Arcturus Books Paperbacks). 247p. 1966. pap. 5.95 (ISBN 0-8093-0199-7). S Ill U Pr.
Wellek, Rene & Warren, Austin. Theory of Literature. rev. ed. 1956. pap. 5.95 (ISBN 0-15-689084-4, HB75, Harv). HarBraceJ.
Weston, Harold. Form in Literature: A Theory of Technique & Construction. LC 74-31015. 1973. Repr. of 1932 ed. lib. bdg. 15.00 (ISBN 0-8414-9580-7). Folcroft.
Wicker, Brian. The Story-Shaped World: Fiction & Metaphysics: Some Variations on a Theme. LC 74-27889. 238p. 1976. text ed. 12.95x (ISBN 0-268-01669-0); pap. 3.95x (ISBN 0-268-01671-2). U of Notre Dame Pr.
Zekowski, Arlene. Image Breaking Images. LC 76-21886. 1976. 15.00 (ISBN 0-8180-1168-8); pap. 4.95 (ISBN 0-8180-1169-6). Horizon.
--Image Breaking Images: A New Mythology of Language. LC 75-36890. (Archives of Post-Modern Literature). 1976. 15.00 (ISBN 0-913844-28-4); pap. 6.00 (ISBN 0-913844-03-9). Am Canadian.

LITERATURE–PRIZES

see Literary Prizes

LITERATURE–PSYCHOLOGY

see also Esthetics; Literature–Philosophy

Basler, Roy P. Sex, Symbolism & Psychology in Literature. 1967. lib. bdg. 15.00x (ISBN 0-374-90437-5). Octagon.
Bodkin, Maud. Archetypal Patterns in Poetry: Psychological Studies of Imagination. (Oxford Paperbacks Ser). pap. 8.95x (ISBN 0-19-281018-9). Oxford U Pr.
Harris, Jay & Harris, Jean. The Roots of Artifice: On the Origin & Development of Literary Creativity. 320p. 1981. 24.95 (ISBN 0-89885-004-5). Human Sci Pr.
Holland, Norman N. The Dynamics of Literary Response. 400p. 1975. pap. 6.95 (ISBN 0-393-00790-1, N790, Norton Lib). Norton.
--Poems in Persons: An Introduction to the Psychoanalysis of Literature. 192p. 1975. pap. 3.95 (ISBN 0-393-00776-6, Norton Lib). Norton.
Humphrey, Robert. Stream of Consciousness in the Modern Novel. LC 54-6673. (Perspectives in Criticism: No. 3). 1954. pap. 2.95 (ISBN 0-520-00585-6, CAL14). U of Cal Pr.
Lee, Vernon. The Handling of Words & Other Studies in Literary Psychology. 5.25 (ISBN 0-8446-2442-X). Peter Smith.
Lindauer, Martin S. The Psychological Study of Literature: Limitations, Possibilities & Accomplishments. LC 73-80499. 250p. 1974. 17.95x (ISBN 0-911012-74-5). Nelson-Hall.
Maier, Norman & Reninger, H. W. Psychological Approach to Literary Criticism. LC 72-191682. 1933. lib. bdg. 15.00 (ISBN 0-8414-6448-0). Folcroft.
Martindale, Colin. The Romantic Progression: Psychology of Literary History. LC 74-26559. 225p. 1975. 17.50x (ISBN 0-470-57365-1). Halsted Pr.
Ragland, Mary E. Rabelais & Panurge: A Psychological Approach to Literary Character. 1976. pap. text ed. 20.00x (ISBN 90-6203-339-3). Humanities.
Strelka, Joseph P., ed. Literary Criticism & Psychology. LC 75-27285. (Yearbook of Comparative Criticism: Vol. 7). 240p. 1976. 17.50x (ISBN 0-271-01228-8). Pa St U Pr.
Van Kaam, Adrian & Healy, K. The Demon & the Dove: Personality Growth Through Literature. 1967. text ed. 7.50x (ISBN 0-8207-0092-4, J26039). Duquesne.
Von Franz, Marie-Louise. A Psychological Interpretation of 'the Golden Ass of Apuleius' Hillman, James, ed. (Seminar Ser.). 188p. 1980. pap. text ed. 9.50 (ISBN 0-88214-103-1). Spring Pubns.
Wormhoudt, Arthur. Demon Lover. facs. ed. LC 68-29256. (Essay Index Reprint Ser). 1949. 12.25 (ISBN 0-8369-1011-7). Arno.

LITERATURE–QUESTIONS

see Literature–Examinations, Questions, etc.

LITERATURE–RESEARCH

see Literary Research

LITERATURE–SELECTIONS

see Literature–Collections

LITERATURE–STORIES, PLOTS, ETC.

Carlsen, G. Robert, et al, eds. Insights: Themes in Literature. 2nd ed. (Themes & Writers Ser). (Illus.). (gr. 9). 1972. text ed. 14.40 (ISBN 0-07-009903-0); tchr's resource guide 6.32 (ISBN 0-07-009909-X). McGraw.
Koehmstedt, Carol L. Plot Summary Index. LC 72-13726. 1973. 11.50 (ISBN 0-8108-0584-7). Scarecrow.
Kolar, Carol K., compiled by. Plot Summary Index. 2nd rev. & enl. ed. LC 80-27112. 544p. 1981. 25.00 (ISBN 0-8108-1392-0). Scarecrow.
Magill, Frank N., ed. Cyclopedia of Literary Characters. 1964. 22.50 (ISBN 0-06-003990-6, HarpT); PLB 19.79 o.p (ISBN 0-06-003991-4, HarpT). Har-Row.
--Masterpieces of World Literature in Digest Form, 4 vols. Incl. Series 1. 1952; Series 2. 1956. lib. bdg. 19.79 (ISBN 0-06-003900-0); Series 3. 1960. 22.50 (ISBN 0-06-003750-4); Series 4. 1969. 22.50 (ISBN 0-06-003751-2); lib. bdg. 19.79 (ISBN 0-06-003752-0). HarpT). Har-Row.
Rohrberger, Mary. Story to Anti-Story. LC 78-69581. 1978. pap. text ed. 8.50 (ISBN 0-395-26387-5); inst. manual 0.45 (ISBN 0-395-26388-3). HM.

LITERATURE–STUDY AND TEACHING

Ackerman, James S., et al. Teaching the Old Testament in English Classes. LC 72-93907. (English Curriculum Study Ser.). 512p. 1973. 15.00x (ISBN 0-253-35785-3); pap. 5.95x (ISBN 0-253-28850-9). Ind U Pr.
Altenbernd, Lynn & Lewis, Leslie L. An Introduction to Literature: Plays. 2nd ed. 1969. pap. 8.95 (ISBN 0-02-302040-7, 30204). Macmillan.
Barricelli, Jean-Pierre, et al. Interrelations of Literature. Gibaldi, Joseph, ed. 352p. 1982. 15.00x (ISBN 0-87352-090-4); pap. 8.50x (ISBN 0-87352-091-2). Modern Lang.
Bleich, David. Readings & Feelings: An Introduction to Subjective Criticism. LC 74-84482. 120p. 1975. pap. 5.00 (ISBN 0-8141-3921-3). NCTE.
Boas, Ralph P. & Smith, Edwin. An Introduction to the Study of Literature. 1977. Repr. of 1925 ed. lib. bdg. 20.00 (ISBN 0-8492-0344-9). R West.
Bolenius, Emma M. Teaching Literature in the Grammar Grades & High School. (Educational Ser.). 1915. Repr. 20.00 (ISBN 0-685-43090-1). Norwood Edns.
Boulton, Marjorie. The Anatomy of Prose. 1968. pap. 7.95 (ISBN 0-7100-6089-0). Routledge & Kegan.
Byron, George G. Fugitive Pieces. LC 72-3567. (Studies in Byron, No. 5). 1972. Repr. of 1933 ed. lib. bdg. 43.95 (ISBN 0-8383-1553-4). Haskell.
Carlsen, G. Robert, et al, eds. Insights: Themes in Literature. 2nd ed. (Themes & Writers Ser). (Illus.). (gr. 9). 1972. text ed. 14.40 (ISBN 0-07-009903-0); tchr's resource guide 6.32 (ISBN 0-07-009909-X). McGraw.
Cohen, Ralph, ed. New Directions in Literary History. LC 73-8115. 272p. 1974. 18.00x (ISBN 0-8018-1549-5). Johns Hopkins.
Committee on Literature in the Elementary Language Arts & Lamme, Linda. Learning to Love Literature: Preschool Through Grade Three. (Illus.). 1981. price not set (ISBN 0-8141-2787-8). NCTE.
Conference On The Teaching Of World Literature - University Of Wisconsin - 1959. Teaching of World Literature: Proceedings. Block, Haskell M., ed. 1960. 9.50 (ISBN 0-384-04730-0). Johnson Repr.
Cooper, Lane. Methods & Aims in the Study of Literature. 239p. 1981. Repr. of 1915 ed. lib. bdg. 35.00 (ISBN 0-89760-120-3). Telegraph Bks.
Cox, John H. Literature in the Common Schools. (Educational Ser.). 1911. Repr. 10.00 (ISBN 0-685-43519-9). Norwood Edns.
Craig, Hardin. Literary Study & the Scholarly Profession. facs. ed. LC 72-84303. (Essay Index Reprint Ser.). 1944. 14.75 (ISBN 0-8369-1079-6). Arno.
Culler, Jonathan. Structuralist Poetics: Structuralism, Linguistics & the Study of Literature. LC 74-11608. 1975. 22.50x (ISBN 0-8014-0928-4); pap. 6.95 (ISBN 0-8014-9155-X). Cornell U Pr.
Dickinson, L. T. A Guide to Literary Study. 1959. pap. text ed. 6.50 (ISBN 0-03-008270-6, HoltC). HR&W.
Dogherty, Marian A. Literature in the Schools. (Educational Ser.). 1927. Repr. 7.50 (ISBN 0-685-43007-3). Norwood Edns.
Dowden, Edward. New Studies in Literature. 1973. lib. bdg. 50.00 (ISBN 0-8414-3854-4). Folcroft.
Elkins, Deborah. Teaching Literature: Designs for Cognitive Development. new ed. (Secondary Education Ser.). 384p. 1976. text ed. 14.95x (ISBN 0-675-08653-1). Merrill.
Fernandez, T. L., ed. Oral Interpretation & the Teaching of English: A Collection of Readings. LC 75-91828. 1969. pap. 3.85 (ISBN 0-8141-3475-0). NCTE.
Frye, Northrop. The Educated Imagination. LC 64-18815. (Midland Bks.: No. 88). 160p. 1964. pap. 3.95x (ISBN 0-253-20088-1). Ind U Pr.
Gibaldi, Joseph & Mirollo, James V., eds. The Teaching Apprentice Program in Language & Literature. LC 81-1159. (Options for Teaching Ser.: No. 4). vi, 133p. (Orig.). 1981. pap. 7.00x (ISBN 0-87352-303-2). Modern Lang.
Gillespie, Bryan. Independent Study & Research in Literature. LC 75-2175. 1975. 3.50 (ISBN 0-912112-07-7). Everett-Edwards.
Greenlaw, Edwin. Province of Literary History. LC 68-26279. 1968. Repr. of 1931 ed. 12.00 (ISBN 0-8046-0180-1). Kennikat.
Hill, Knox C. Interpreting Literature: History, Drama, Fiction, Philosophy, Rhetoric. LC 66-13873. (Midway Reprint Ser). x, 194p. 1975. pap. text ed. 3.95x (ISBN 0-226-33492-9); 6.50x (ISBN 0-226-33491-0). U of Chicago Pr.
Hill, Leslie A. Advanced Stories for Reproduction. 62p. 1965. pap. 3.25x (ISBN 0-19-432543-1). Oxford U Pr.
--Elementary Stories for Reproduction. 64p. 1965. pap. 3.25x (ISBN 0-19-432541-5). Oxford U Pr.
--Intermediate Stories for Reproduction. 68p. 1965. pap. 3.25x (ISBN 0-19-432542-3). Oxford U Pr.
Hogins, James B. Literature: Fiction. LC 73-90125. (Illus.). 368p. 1974. pap. text ed. 5.95 (ISBN 0-574-19130-5, 13-2130). SRA.
Hosic, James F. Empirical Studies in School Reading; with Special Reference to the Evaluation of Literary Reading Books. LC 75-176880. (Columbia University. Teachers College. Contributions to Education: No. 114). Repr. of 1921 ed. 17.50 (ISBN 0-404-55114-9). AMS Pr.
Hudson, William H. An Introduction to the Study of Literature. 1973. lib. bdg. 20.00 (ISBN 0-8414-5191-5). Folcroft.
Jones, Henry. Essays on Literature & Education. LC 74-176123. 1974. Repr. of 1924 ed. lib. bdg. 25.00 (ISBN 0-8414-5314-4). Folcroft.
Kitzhaber, Albert R. Concepts in Literature. Incl. Elements of Literature. (gr. 7). text ed. 10.60 (ISBN 0-03-088197-8); tchr's guide 10.36 (ISBN 0-03-089376-3); Patterns in Literature. (gr. 8). text ed. 9.32 (ISBN 0-03-088198-6); tchr's guide 10.36 (ISBN 0-03-089377-1); Themes in Literature. (gr. 9). text ed. 13.40 (ISBN 0-03-088199-4); tchr's guide 7.00 (ISBN 0-03-089371-2); Viewpoints in Literature. (gr. 10). text ed. 13.72 (ISBN 0-03-088200-1); tchr's guide 7.00 (ISBN 0-03-089345-3); Forms of Literature. (gr. 11). text ed. 13.72 (ISBN 0-03-088201-X); tchr's guide 7.04 (ISBN 0-03-089372-0); The Craft of Literature. (gr. 12). text ed. 13.72 (ISBN 0-03-088202-8); tchr's guide 6.80 (ISBN 0-03-089373-9). (gr. 7-12). 1974 (HoltE). HR&W.
--Literature, Bk. 2. 1968. text ed. 13.92 (ISBN 0-03-071400-1, HoltE); tchr's guide 5.80 (ISBN 0-03-071405-2). HR&W.
--Literature, Bk. 5. 1970. text ed. 14.56 (ISBN 0-03-084422-3, HoltE). HR&W.
--Literature, Bk. 6. 1970. text ed. 14.56 (ISBN 0-03-084423-1, HoltE). HR&W.
Knapton, J. & Evans, B. Teaching a Literature-Centered English Program. 7.50 (ISBN 0-8446-2389-X). Peter Smith.
Knapton, James & Evans, Bertrand. Teaching a Literature-Centered English Program. (Orig.). 1967. pap. text ed. 3.65 (ISBN 0-685-19776-X). Phila Bk Co.
Learning in Language & Literature. Incl. Insistent Tasks in Language Learning. MacKinnon, A. R. (Burton Lectures Ser: 1962); The Developing Imagination. Frye, Northrop. (Inglis Lectures Ser: 1962). LC 63-13811. 62p. 1963. 5.95x (ISBN 0-674-52000-9). Harvard U Pr.
Leavis, Frank R. How to Teach Reading. LC 74-12156. 1932. lib. bdg. 7.50 (ISBN 0-8414-5741-7). Folcroft.
Lefevere, Andre. Literary Knowledge: A Polemical & Programmatic Essay on Its Nature, Growth, Relevance & Transmission. 1977. pap. text ed. 9.00x (ISBN 90-232-1498-6). Humanities.
Lynn, Kenneth S., ed. Houghton Books in Literature. Incl. Designs for Reading, 4 bks. pap. 4.80 ea.; tchr's guide 4.80 (ISBN 0-395-11195-1); Plays (ISBN 0-395-02790-X); Poems (ISBN 0-395-02786-1); Short Stories (ISBN 0-395-02780-2); Nonfiction Prose (ISBN 0-395-02788-8); Range of Literature, 4 bks. tchr's guide 4.80 (ISBN 0-685-59075-5); Drama. pap. 6.48 (ISBN 0-395-02782-9); Poetry. pap. 4.80 (ISBN 0-395-02784-5); Fiction. pap. 5.60 (ISBN 0-395-02792-6); Nonfiction Prose. pap. 5.60 (ISBN 0-395-02794-2); Level 3, 4 bks. tchr's guide 4.80 (ISBN 0-395-13709-8); Five Comedies. pap. 6.96 (ISBN 0-395-12049-7); Tunnel & the Light: Readings in Modern Fiction. pap. 7.52 (ISBN 0-395-13452-8); Twentieth Century Poetry. pap. 6.48 (ISBN 0-395-12357-7); Scene Seventy: Recent Non Fiction. pap. 7.52 (ISBN 0-395-12505-7). HM.
McFarland, Philip, et al. Perceptions in Literature. (Literature Ser.). (Illus.). (gr. 10). 1975. text ed. 10.98 (ISBN 0-395-20075-X); tchr's resource bk 5.40 (ISBN 0-395-20080-6). HM.
McGuire, Richard L. Passionate Attention: An Introduction to Literary Study. 1973. 3.95x (ISBN 0-393-09324-7). Norton.
Marcus, Mordecai. The Assistant Notes. 1972. pap. 1.95 (ISBN 0-8220-0214-0). Cliffs.
Miller, Bruce E. Teaching the Art of Literature. (Orig.). 1980. pap. 5.50 (ISBN 0-8141-5192-2, 51922). NCTE.
Mirrielees, Lucia B. Teaching Composition & Literature in Junior & Senior High School. rev. ed. LC 71-95128. Repr. of 1952 ed. lib. bdg. 22.50x (ISBN 0-8371-2461-1, MITC). Greenwood.
Moody, H. L. The Teaching of Literature. (Longman Handbooks for Language Teachers). 1974. pap. text ed. 5.50x (ISBN 0-582-52602-7). Longman.
Morize, Andre. Problems & Methods of Literary History. LC 66-13475. 1922. 12.00x (ISBN 0-8196-0168-3). Biblo.
Moulton, Richard G. The Modern Study of Literature. LC 78-27804. 1973. lib. bdg. 35.00 (ISBN 0-8414-6333-6). Folcroft.
Nicholas, David & Ritchie, Maureen. Literature & Bibliometrics. 1978. 15.00 (ISBN 0-208-01541-8, Linnet). Shoe String.
Northman, Alan. Literature As an Aid to Teaching. LC 76-105817. 1970. Repr. of 1906 ed. 8.50 (ISBN 0-8046-0966-7). Kennikat.
Pound, Ezra. ABC of Reading. LC 60-30304. 1960. pap. 4.25 (ISBN 0-8112-0151-1, NDP89). New Directions.
Purves, A. C., et al, eds. Literature Education in Ten Countries. LC 73-8044. (International Studies in Evaluation Ser.: Vol. 2). 428p. 1973. pap. 16.95 (ISBN 0-470-70229-X). Halsted Pr.
Purves, Alan C. & Beach, Richard. Literature & the Reader: Research in Response to Literature, Reading Interests & the Teaching of Literature. LC 72-89632. 200p. (Orig.). 1972. pap. 7.00 (ISBN 0-8141-2969-2). NCTE.
Roberts, Edgar V. Writing Themes About Literature. 4th ed. 1977. pap. text ed. 7.95 (ISBN 0-13-970582-1). P-H.
Rodrigues, Raymond J. & Badaczewski, Dennis. A Guidebook for Teaching Literature. new ed. 1978. pap. text ed. 19.95 (ISBN 0-205-06068-4). Allyn.
Sastri, P. S., ed. Studies in Elizabeth Literature: Festschrift to Prof. G. C. Bannerjee. 112p. 1973. text ed. 6.75x (ISBN 0-8426-0514-2). Verry.
Scholes, Robert. Structuralism in Literature: An Introduction. LC 73-90578. 250p. 1974. 15.00x (ISBN 0-300-01750-2); pap. 5.25 (ISBN 0-300-01850-9). Yale U Pr.
Scott, Louise B. Developing Communication Skills: A Guide for the Classroom Teacher. 1971. text ed. 15.60 (ISBN 0-07-055828-0, W). McGraw.
Shapiro, Jon E., ed. Using Literature & Poetry Affectively. (Orig.). 1979. pap. text ed. 5.00 (ISBN 0-87207-489-7, 489). Intl Reading.
Sharwood-Smith, J. On Teaching Classics. (Students Library of Education). 1977. 10.00x (ISBN 0-7100-8580-X). Routledge & Kegan.
Shoemaker, F. Aesthetic Experience & the Humanities. LC 70-176013. Repr. of 1943 ed. 21.00 (ISBN 0-404-05987-2). AMS Pr.
Slatoff, Walter J. With Respect to Readers: Dimensions of Literary Response. LC 77-123995. 1970. 12.50x (ISBN 0-8014-0580-7). Cornell U Pr.
Sloan, Glenna. The Child As Critic: Teaching Literature in the Elementary School. LC 75-23360. 1975. pap. text ed. 6.50x (ISBN 0-8077-2482-3). Tchrs Coll.

Spaethling, Robert & Weber, Eugene, eds. Literature One: Supplementary Readings with Exercises. (Ger). 1972. pap. text ed. 4.95 (ISBN 0-19-501550-9); tapes set 29.95 (ISBN 0-19-501703-X). Oxford U Pr.

Strindberg, August. By the Open Sea. LC 72-3561. (Studies in Fiction, No. 34). 1972. Repr. of 1913 ed. lib. bdg. 37.95 (ISBN 0-8383-1547-X). Haskell.

Taylor, J. F., et al. Introduction to Literature & the Fine Arts. (Illus.). 418p. 1950. text ed. 10.00x (ISBN 0-87013-037-4). Mich St U Pr.

Von Scoy, Karen & Whitehead, Robert. Literature Games. 1971. pap. 3.95 (ISBN 0-8224-4310-4). Pitman Learning.

Walden, James, ed. Oral Language & Reading. LC 76-78447. 1969. pap. 3.75 (ISBN 0-8141-3485-8). NCTE.

Wantling, William. Seven on Style. 1975. pap. 2.50 (ISBN 0-915016-02-8). Second Coming.

Weisinger, Herbert & Joyaux, Georges. Rene Etiemble: The Crisis in Comparative Literature. xxiv, 62p. 1966. 3.00 (ISBN 0-87013-099-4). Mich St U Pr.

Welch, Carolyn R. Steppenwolf & Siddhartha Notes. 81p. 1973. pap. text ed. 2.25 (ISBN 0-8220-1224-3). Cliffs.

Wellek, Rene & Warren, Austin. Theory of Literature. rev. ed. 1956. pap. 5.95 (ISBN 0-15-689084-4, HB75, Harv). HarBraceJ.

Widdowson, Henry G. Stylistics & the Teaching of Literature. 2nd ed. (Applied Linguistics & Language Study Ser.). (Illus.). 144p. 1975. pap. text ed. 8.75x (ISBN 0-582-55076-9). Longman.

Wilkinson, Sylvia & Campbell, Ed, eds. Change: A Handbook for the Teaching of English & Social Studies. 225p. 1971. 3.00 (ISBN 0-686-15542-4). Learning Inst NC.

Zitner, Sheldon P., et al. Preface to Literary Analysis. 1964. pap. 6.95x (ISBN 0-673-05216-8). Scott F.

LITERATURE–STYLE

see Style, Literary

LITERATURE–TERMINOLOGY

Anderson, Robert & Eckhard, Ronald. Lexicon of Literary Terms. 160p. 1975. pap. 3.50 (ISBN 0-671-18749-X). Monarch Pr.

Barnet, Sylvan, et al. A Dictionary of Literary, Dramatic, & Cinematic Terms. 2nd ed. 124p. 1971. pap. 4.95 (ISBN 0-316-08194-9). Little.

Lemon, Lee T. Glossary for the Study of English. 1971. pap. text ed. 3.95x (ISBN 0-19-501387-5). Oxford U Pr.

Loane, George G. Short Handbook of Literary Terms. LC 72-188273. 1972. lib. bdg. 15.00 (ISBN 0-8414-0600-6). Folcroft.

Murray, Patrick. Literary Criticism: A Glossary of Major Terms. 208p. 1978. pap. text ed. 7.95x (ISBN 0-582-35247-9). Longman.

Scott, A. F., ed. Current Literary Terms. 324p. Repr. of 1980 ed. lib. bdg. 14.95x (ISBN 0-312-17956-1). St Martin.

Shaw, Harry. Concise Dictionary of Literary Terms. (McGraw-Hill Paperbacks). Orig. Title: Dictionary of Literary Terms. 224p. 1976. pap. 3.95 (ISBN 0-07-056483-3, SP). McGraw.

--Dictionary of Literary Terms. LC 72-179884. 418p. 1972. 18.95 (ISBN 0-07-056490-6, P&RB). McGraw.

Yelland, H. L., et al. Handbook of Literary Terms. LC 79-14512. 1980. bds. 10.00 laminated (ISBN 0-87116-118-4). Writer.

LITERATURE–TRANSLATING

see Translating and Interpreting

LITERATURE–TRANSLATIONS

see Translations

LITERATURE–YEARBOOKS

Friederich, Werner P. & Frenz, Horst, eds. Yearbook of Comparative & General Literature, 1952-1962, 11 vols. Incl. Vols. 1-9. 1952-1960. Ed. by Werner P. Friederich. Vol. 1 (ISBN 0-8462-0557-2). Vol. 2 (ISBN 0-8462-0558-0). Vol. 3 (ISBN 0-8462-0559-9). Vol. 4 (ISBN 0-8462-0604-8). Vol. 5 (ISBN 0-8462-0605-6). Vol. 6 (ISBN 0-8462-0606-4). Vol. 7 (ISBN 0-8462-0699-4). Vol. 8 (ISBN 0-8462-0700-1). Vol. 9 (ISBN 0-8462-0701-X); Vols. 10-11. 1961-62. Ed. by Horst Frenz. Vol. 10 (ISBN 0-8462-0885-7). Vol. 11 (ISBN 0-8462-1135-1). LC 65-22672. (1965-1968 repr. of 1952-62 eds.). 8.50 ea. Russell.

Kabakoff, Jacob, ed. Jewish Book Annual, Vol. 38. 1980. 15.00 (ISBN 0-914820-33-8). JWB Jewish Bk Coun.

Magill, Frank N., ed. Magill's Literary Annual, 1980: Books of 1979, 2 vols. LC 77-99209. 900p. 1980. 50.00 (ISBN 0-89356-080-4). Salem Pr.

LITERATURE, ANCIENT

see also Classical Literature (Collections)

Atchity, Kenneth J. Homer's Iliad: The Shield of Memory. LC 77-17065. (Literary Structures Ser.). 367p. 1978. 17.50x (ISBN 0-8093-0809-6). S Ill U Pr.

Mercer, Samuel A. & Hallock, Frank H., eds. The Tell El-Amarna Tablets, 2 vols. LC 78-72764. (Ancient Mesopotamian Texts & Studies). Repr. of 1939 ed. 87.50 set (ISBN 0-404-18216-X). AMS Pr.

Quackenbos, J. D. Ancient Literature: Oriental & Classical. 30.00 (ISBN 0-8274-3974-1). R West.

Webster, T. B. From Mycenae to Homer: A Study in Early Greek Literature & Art. (Illus.). 1977. Repr. of 1958 ed. 28.50x (ISBN 0-87471-882-1). Rowman.

LITERATURE, ANCIENT–HISTORY AND CRITICISM

Hoare, Frederick R. Eight Decisive Books of Antiquity. LC 73-99638. (Essay Index Reprint Ser). 1952. 19.50 (ISBN 0-8369-1414-7). Arno.

Ullman, Berthold L. Ancient Writing & Its Influence. (Medieval Academy Reprints for Teaching Ser.). 260p. 1981. pap. 7.50x (ISBN 0-8020-6435-3). U of Toronto Pr.

Wilkins, A. S. Roman Literature. Repr. of 1890 ed. 10.00 (ISBN 0-686-20109-4). Quality Lib.

LITERATURE, APOCALYPTIC

see Apocalyptic Literature

LITERATURE, BAROQUE

see Baroque Literature

LITERATURE, CLASSICAL

see Classical Literature (Collections)

LITERATURE, COMIC

see Burlesque (Literature); Comedy; Commedia Dell'Arte; Farce; Parody; Satire

LITERATURE, COMPARATIVE

Alphonso-Karkala, John B. Comparative World Literature: Seven Essays. 98p. 1976. lib. bdg. 9.95 (ISBN 0-89253-048-0). Ind-US Inc.

Armato, Rosario P. & Spalek, John M., eds. Medieval Epic to the Epic Theater of Brecht. LC 68-29169. (University of Southern California Studies in Comparative Literature Ser: No. 1). 1968. 7.95x (ISBN 0-912158-00-X). Hennessey.

Baldensperger, Fernand & Friederich, Werner P. Bibliography of Comparative Literature. LC 60-5279. 1960. Repr. of 1950 ed. 30.00 (ISBN 0-8462-0114-3). Russell.

Betz, L. P. Litterature Comparee. LC 68-25307. (Studies in Comparative Literature, No. 35). 1969. Repr. of 1904 ed. lib. bdg. 44.95 (ISBN 0-8383-0911-9). Haskell.

Betz, Louis P. La Litterature Comparee: Essai Bibliographique. LC 69-13826. (Fr). Repr. of 1904 ed. lib. bdg. 15.00x (ISBN 0-8371-1072-6, BELC). Greenwood.

Brewer, Wilmon. Ovid's Metamorphoses in European Culture, 2 vols. (Illus.). 1978. Set. 10.00 (ISBN 0-685-14287-6); Vol. I. (ISBN 0-685-99059-1); Vol. II. (ISBN 0-685-99060-5). M Jones.

Buck, Philo M. Social Forces in Modern Literature. LC 76-58444. 1913. lib. bdg. 12.50 (ISBN 0-8414-1651-6). Folcroft.

Bulman, Joan. Strindberg & Shakespeare: Shakespeare's Influence on Strindberg's Historical Drama. LC 73-153482. (Studies in Comparative Literature, No. 35). 1971. Repr. of 1933 ed. lib. bdg. 36.95 (ISBN 0-8383-1239-X). Haskell.

Chatterji, Suniti K., ed. Some Aspects of Indo-Iranian Literary & Cultural Traditions. (Illus.). 1977. 36.00x (ISBN 0-686-22674-7). Intl Bk Dist.

Clements, Robert J. Comparative Literature As Academic Discipline: A Statement of Principles, Praxis, Standards. LC 77-91123. 342p. 1978. 20.00x (ISBN 0-87352-375-X); pap. 9.50x (ISBN 0-87352-376-8). Modern Lang.

--The Peregrine Muse: Studies in Comparative Renaissance Literature. (Studies in the Romance Languages & Literatures: No. 82). 1969. pap. 11.00x (ISBN 0-8078-9082-0). U of NC Pr.

Collins, John C. Illustrations of Tennyson. LC 77-148765. Repr. of 1891 ed. 9.00 (ISBN 0-404-08738-8). AMS Pr.

Comparative Literature Symposium, No. 12. Shakespeare's Art from a Comparative Perspective: Proceedings. Aycock, Wendell M., ed. (Proceedings of the Comparative Literature Symposium). (Illus.). 197p. (Orig.). 1981. pap. 17.50 (ISBN 0-89672-081-0). Tex Tech Pr.

Crane, Thomas F. Italian Social Customs of the Sixteenth Century & Their Influence on the Literatures of Europe. LC 70-143873. 1971. Repr. of 1920 ed. 20.00 (ISBN 0-8462-1535-7). Russell.

Damiani, Bruno M., et al, eds. Hispano-Italic Studies, No. 1. 1976. pap. 4.00 (ISBN 0-87840-250-0). Georgetown U Pr.

Desai, Rupin W. Sir John Falstaff Knight. LC 75-5210. (Comparative Literature Studies Ser). 133p. pap. 10.00 (ISBN 0-87423-013-6). Westburg.

Eckenstein, Lina. Comparative Studies in Nursery Rhymes. LC 68-23469. 1968. Repr. of 1906 ed. 19.00 (ISBN 0-8103-3479-8). Gale.

Eoff, Sherman H. The Modern Spanish Novel: Comparative Essays Examining the Philosophical Impact of Science on Fiction. LC 61-11261. (Gotham Library). 1961. pap. 4.95x (ISBN 0-8147-0139-6). NYU Pr.

Fauriel, C. C. History of Provencal Poetry. LC 68-753. (Studies in French Literature, No. 45). 1969. Repr. of 1860 ed. lib. bdg. 59.95 (ISBN 0-8383-0546-6). Haskell.

Ferguson, John D. American Literature in Spain. LC 74-168017. Repr. of 1916 ed. 22.00 (ISBN 0-404-02377-0). AMS Pr.

Fitz-Gerald, J. D. & Taylor, P., eds. Todd Memorial Volumes: Philological Studies, 2 Vols. facs. ed. LC 68-22950. (Essay Index Reprint Ser). 1968. Repr. of 1930 ed. 28.00 (ISBN 0-8369-0948-8). Arno.

Fourth Congress of the International Comparative Literature Association, Fribourg, 1964. Actes Du IVe Congres De L'association Internationle De Litterature Comparee: Proceedings, 2 vols. Jost, Francois, ed. 1966. 229.00x (ISBN 0-686-20909-5). Mouton.

Friederich, Werner P. & Frenz, Horst, eds. Yearbook of Comparative & General Literature, 1952-1962, 11 vols. Incl. Vols. 1-9. 1952-1960. Ed. by Werner P. Friederich. Vol. 1 (ISBN 0-8462-0557-2). Vol. 2 (ISBN 0-8462-0558-0). Vol. 3 (ISBN 0-8462-0559-9). Vol. 4 (ISBN 0-8462-0604-8). Vol. 5 (ISBN 0-8462-0605-6). Vol. 6 (ISBN 0-8462-0606-4). Vol. 7 (ISBN 0-8462-0699-4). Vol. 8 (ISBN 0-8462-0700-1). Vol. 9 (ISBN 0-8462-0701-X); Vols. 10-11. 1961-62. Ed. by Horst Frenz. Vol. 10 (ISBN 0-8462-0885-7). Vol. 11 (ISBN 0-8462-1135-1). LC 65-22672. (1965-1968 repr. of 1952-62 eds.). 8.50 ea. Russell.

Friederich, Werner P., et al. Challenge of Comparative Literature: And Other Addresses. De Sua, William J., ed. (Studies in Comparative Literature Ser.: No. 51). 1970. 11.50x (ISBN 0-8078-7051-X). U of NC Pr.

Gifford, Henry. Comparative Literature. (Concepts of Literature Ser.). 1969. pap. 4.50 (ISBN 0-7100-6377-6). Routledge & Kegan.

Harkins, William E. Russian Folk Epos in Czech Literature: 1800-1900. LC 76-141414. 1971. Repr. of 1951 ed. lib. bdg. 15.00 (ISBN 0-8371-4687-9, HACL). Greenwood.

Hart, George L., III. The Poems of Ancient Tamil: Their Milieu & Their Sanskrit Counterparts. LC 73-91667. 300p. 1975. 26.50x (ISBN 0-520-02672-1). U of Cal Pr.

Hervieux, A. Leopold. Les Fabulistes Latins Depuis le Siecle d'Auguste Jusqu'a la Fin Du Moyen Age, 5 Vols. 1964. Set. 210.00 (ISBN 0-8337-1685-9). B Franklin.

International Comparative Literature Association - Second Congress - Chapel Hill - N. C. - 1958. Comparative Literature: Proceedings, 2 Vols. Friedrich, Werner P., ed. (North Carolina University, Studies in Comparative Literature Ser: Vols. 23,24). 1970. Repr. of 1959 ed. Set. 54.00 (ISBN 0-685-13392-3, B33). Johnson Repr.

Irwin, Agnes. Studies in English & Comparative Literature by Former & Present Students at Radcliffe College. LC 72-194993. 1910. lib. bdg. 15.00 (ISBN 0-8414-5065-X). Folcroft.

Jones, Joseph. Radical Cousins: Nineteenth Century American & Australian Writers. 1977. 15.00x (ISBN 0-7022-1223-7). U of Queensland Pr.

Jost, Francois. Essais De Litterature Comparee, Tome Deux: Europaeana. (Fr.). 1969. pap. 14.95 (ISBN 0-252-00039-0). U of Ill Pr.

--Introduction to Comparative Literature. LC 73-19849. 1974. 14.95 (ISBN 0-672-63657-3). Pegasus.

Kurtz, Benjamin P. Studies in the Marvellous. LC 77-164580. (Studies in Comparative Literature, No. 35). 1972. Repr. of 1910 ed. lib. bdg. 49.95 (ISBN 0-8383-1326-4). Haskell.

Lasater, Alice E. Spain to England: A Comparative Study of Arabic, European, & English Literature of the Middle Ages. LC 73-94277. 1974. 2.00 (ISBN 0-87805-056-6). U Pr of Miss.

Lee, Sidney. Elizabethan & Other Essays. Boas, F. S., ed. LC 78-133811. Repr. of 1929 ed. 11.00 (ISBN 0-404-03928-6). AMS Pr.

--Elizabethan & Other Essays. facs. ed. Boas, F. S., ed. LC 68-22108. (Essay Index Reprint Ser). 1929. 18.00 (ISBN 0-8369-0614-4). Arno.

Levin, Harry. Refractions: Essays in Comparative Literature. 1968. pap. 5.95 (ISBN 0-19-500771-9, GB). Oxford U Pr.

Levy, Gertrude R. The Sword from the Rock: An Investigation into the Origins of Epic Literature & the Development of the Hero. LC 76-47642. (Illus.). 1977. Repr. of 1953 ed. lib. bdg. 18.50x (ISBN 0-8371-9300-1, LESFR). Greenwood.

Loliee, Frederic. Short History of Comparative Literature. Power, Douglas, tr. LC 74-105803. 1970. Repr. of 1906 ed. 16.50 (ISBN 0-8046-1361-3). Kennikat.

Lord, Albert B. The Singer of Tales. (Harvard Studies in Comparative Literature Ser.: No. 24). 325p. 1981. pap. text ed. 5.95x (ISBN 0-674-80881-9). Harvard U Pr.

Magnus, Laurie. English Literature in Its Foreign Relations, 1300-1800. LC 68-20238. 1968. Repr. of 1927 ed. 15.00 (ISBN 0-405-08775-6). Arno.

--History of European Literature. LC 75-103233. 1970. Repr. of 1934 ed. 13.50 (ISBN 0-8046-0870-9). Kennikat.

Mais, S. P. From Shakespeare to O. Henry: Studies in Literature. 1977. Repr. of 1932 ed. lib. bdg. 17.50 (ISBN 0-8495-3708-8). Arden Lib.

Matthiessen, Francis O. Translation: An Elizabethan Art. 1965. lib. bdg. 15.00x (ISBN 0-374-95377-5). Octagon.

Meres, Francis. Palladis Tamia. LC 39-10093. 1978. Repr. of 1598 ed. 35.00 (ISBN 0-8201-1188-0). Schol Facsimiles.

Neff, Emery. A Revolution in European Poetry, 1660-1900. LC 73-19762. 279p. 1974. Repr. lib. bdg. 15.00x (ISBN 0-374-96040-2). Octagon.

Nitze, William A. Arthurian Romance & Modern Poetry & Music. LC 76-122995. (Arthurian Legend & Literature Ser., No. 1). 1970. Repr. of 1940 ed. lib. bdg. 27.95 (ISBN 0-8383-1128-8). Haskell.

Nordau, Max. Degeneration. LC 68-17664. 1968. Repr. 22.50 (ISBN 0-86527-039-2). Fertig.

Partridge, Eric. Critical Medley. facsimile ed. LC 73-148894. (Select Bibliographies Reprint Ser). Repr. of 1926 ed. 17.00 (ISBN 0-8369-5680-X). Arno.

Posnett, Hutcheson M. Comparative Literature. LC 11-19750. 1971. Repr. of 1886 ed. 23.00 (ISBN 0-384-47330-X). Johnson Repr.

Rhein, Phillip H. & Schultz, Hans J., eds. Comparative Literature: The Early Years. (Studies in Comparative Literature Ser.: No. 55). 16.50x (ISBN 0-8078-7055-2). U of NC Pr.

Routh, Harold V. God, Man & Epic Poetry: A Study in Comparative Literature, 2 Vols. LC 69-10152. (Illus.). 1968. Repr. of 1927 ed. lib. bdg. 32.50x (ISBN 0-8371-0206-5, ROEP). Greenwood.

Ruediger, Horst, et al, eds. Zur Theorie der Vergleichenden Literaturwissenschaft. 87p. 1971. 10.50x (ISBN 3-11-003622-3). De Gruyter.

Schelling, Felix E. Foreign Influences in Elizabethan Plays. LC 70-124765. Repr. of 1923 ed. 14.50 (ISBN 0-404-05579-6). AMS Pr.

Schludermann, Brigitte, et al, eds. Deutung und Bedeutung: Studies in German & Comparative Literature Presented to Karl-Werner Maurer. (De Proprietatibus Litterarum, Series Maior: No. 25). 1973. 78.75x (ISBN 90-2792-479-1). Mouton.

Schofield, William. English Literature from the Norman Conquest to Chaucer. LC 68-24917. (Studies in Chaucer, No. 6). 1969. Repr. of 1906 ed. lib. bdg. 50.95 (ISBN 0-8383-0239-4). Haskell.

Schofield, William H. English Literature, from the Norman Conquest to Chaucer. Repr. of 1906 ed. lib. bdg. 18.00x (ISBN 0-8371-4100-1, SCEL). Greenwood.

--English Literature from the Norman Conquest to Chaucer. LC 78-76535. 1968. Repr. of 1931 ed. 12.50 (ISBN 0-87753-034-3). Phaeton.

Sheppard, J. T. Aeschylus & Sophocles: Their Work & Influence. LC 63-10270. (Our Debt to Greece & Rome Ser). 1930. 7.50x (ISBN 0-8154-0205-8). Cooper Sq.

Sherwood, Margaret P. Undercurrents of Influence in English Romantic Poetry. LC 70-155612. Repr. of 1934 ed. 9.50 (ISBN 0-404-05959-7). AMS Pr.

Snyder, Edward D. The Celtic Revival in English Literature Seventeen Sixty-Eighteen Hundred. 1923. 7.50 (ISBN 0-8446-1415-7). Peter Smith.

Stallknecht, Newton P. & Frenz, Horst, eds. Comparative Literature: Method & Perspective. rev. ed. LC 71-83780. 384p. 1971. 10.00x (ISBN 0-8093-0046-X). S Ill U Pr.

--Comparative Literature: Method & Perspective. LC 73-12636. (Arcturus Books Paperbacks). 384p. 1973. pap. 2.85 (ISBN 0-8093-0660-3). S Ill U Pr.

Stark, Barbara. Comparison & Criticism. 1968. pap. text ed. 3.50x (ISBN 0-435-18845-3). Heinemann Ed.

Strich, Fritz. Goethe & World Literature. Sym, C. A., tr. from Ger. LC 71-138188. 1971. Repr. of 1949 ed. lib. bdg. 17.75x (ISBN 0-8371-5645-9, STGO). Greenwood.

--Goethe & World Literature. LC 75-159710. 1971. Repr. of 1949 ed. 15.00 (ISBN 0-8046-1648-5). Kennikat.

Tillyard, Eustace M. The English Epic & Its Background. LC 75-2543. 548p. 1976. Repr. of 1966 ed. lib. bdg. 35.25x (ISBN 0-8371-8781-8, TIEE). Greenwood.

Tufte, Virginia. The Poetry of Marraige: The Epithalamium in Europe & Its Development in England. LC 68-28173. (University of Southern California Studies in Comparative Literature Ser: No. 2). 12.50x (ISBN 0-912158-52-2). Hennessey.

Vaganay, Hugues. Sonnet En Italie et En France Au Seizieme Siecle, 2 Vols. 1962. Repr. of 1903 ed. 40.50 (ISBN 0-8337-3608-6). B Franklin.

Valency, Maurice J. Tragedies of Herod & Mariamne. LC 70-8450. Repr. of 1940 ed. 19.50 (ISBN 0-404-06750-6). AMS Pr.

Weisinger, Herbert & Joyaux, Georges. Rene Etiemble: The Crisis in Comparative Literature. xxiv, 62p. 1966. 3.00 (ISBN 0-87013-099-4). Mich St U Pr.

Wright, H. G. Studies in Anglo-Scandinavian Literary Relations. LC 72-10784. 1973. Repr. of 1919 ed. lib. bdg. 20.00 (ISBN 0-8414-0716-9). Folcroft.

Yohannan, John D. Persian Poetry in England & America: A Two Hundred Year History. LC 75-22418. (Persian Studies Ser.). 400p. 1977. lib. bdg. 25.00x (ISBN 0-88206-006-6). Caravan Bks.

LITERATURE, COMPARATIVE-BIBLIOGRAPHY

Betz, Louis P. Litterature Comparee. LC 77-101092. (BCL Ser. I). (Fr). 1969. Repr. of 1904 ed. 10.00 (ISBN 0-404-00793-7). AMS Pr.

Gaudin, Lois S. Bibliography of Franco-Spanish Literary Relations Until the Nineteeth Century. LC 74-178937. (Institute of French Studies Publications). 71p. 1973. Repr. of 1930 ed. lib. bdg. 18.50 (ISBN 0-8337-4125-X). B Franklin.

LITERATURE, COMPARATIVE-THEMES, MOTIVES

see also Fairy Tales-Classification; Folk Literature-Themes, Motives;
also specific subjects in Literature e.g. Negroes in Literature; Social Problems in Literature; names of literary themes, e.g. Perceval (Romances, etc.)

Brown, Arthur C. Origin of the Grail Legend. LC 65-17878. 1966. Repr. of 1943 ed. 14.00 (ISBN 0-8462-0655-2). Russell.

Buchan, John. The Novel & the Fairy Tale. LC 77-28042. 1931. 6.50 (ISBN 0-8414-0055-5). Folcroft.

Cole, Howard C. The All's Well Story from Boccaccio to Shakespeare. LC 81-2474. 192p. 1981. 12.50 (ISBN 0-252-00883-9). U of Ill Pr.

Duggan, George C. Stage Irishman. LC 70-91899. (Illus.). 1937. 18.00 (ISBN 0-405-08468-4, Blom Pubns). Arno.

Egan, M. F. The Ghost in Hamlet & Other Essays in Comparative Literature. 59.95 (ISBN 0-8490-0232-X). Gordon Pr.

Gardner, Edmund G. Arthurian Legend in Italian Literature. LC 78-120255. 1970. Repr. lib. bdg. 18.50x (ISBN 0-374-92999-8). Octagon.

Greene, Thomas M. The Descent from Heaven: A Study in Epic Continuity. LC 63-7934. 434p. 1975. pap. 6.45x (ISBN 0-300-01873-8, Y-279). Yale U Pr.

Griffith, Dudley. Origin of the Griselda Story. LC 73-9823. 1931. lib. bdg. 12.50 (ISBN 0-8414-2042-4). Folcroft.

Hahn, Juergen S. The Origins of the Baroque Concept of Peregrinatio. (Studies in the Romance Languages & Literatures: No. 131). 1973. pap. 10.50x (ISBN 0-8078-9131-2). U of NC Pr.

Hartveit, Lars. The Art of Persuasion: A Study of Six Novels. 1977. text ed. 10.00x (ISBN 8-2000-1668-4, Dist. by Columbia U Pr). Universitet.

Hayward, C. The Courtesan: The Part She Has Played in Classical & Modern Literature & in Life. Winick, Charles, ed. LC 78-60872. (Prostitution Ser.: Vol. 7). (Illus.). 492p. 1979. lib. bdg. 40.00 (ISBN 0-8240-9721-1). Garland Pub.

Jones, W. P. The Pastourelle. LC 73-3478. 244p. 1973. Repr. of 1931 ed. lib. bdg. 14.50x (ISBN 0-374-94333-8). Octagon.

Kirkconnell, Watson. Awake the Courteous Echo: The Themes of Comus, Lycidas, & Paradise Regained in World Literature with Translations of the Major Analogues. LC 78-185721. 340p. 1973. 20.00x (ISBN 0-8020-5266-5). U of Toronto Pr.

--Celestial Cycles: The Theme of Paradise Lost in World Literature with Translations of the Major Analogues. LC 67-30308. 1967. Repr. of 1952 ed. 17.50 (ISBN 0-87752-058-5). Gordian.

Loomis, Roger S., ed. Arthurian Literature in the Middle Ages: A Collaborative History. 1959. 72.00x (ISBN 0-19-811588-1). Oxford U Pr.

Mabie, Hamilton W. Short Studies in Literature. 1973. lib. bdg. 15.00 (ISBN 0-8414-6381-6). Folcroft.

Mohl, Ruth. Three Estates in Medieval & Renaissance Literature. LC 62-10897. 1962. 8.50 (ISBN 0-8044-2636-8). Ungar.

Nitze, William A. Arthurian Romance & Modern Poetry & Music. LC 72-105816. 1970. Repr. of 1940 ed. 10.00 (ISBN 0-8046-1049-5). Kennikat.

Schlauch, Margaret. Chaucer's Constance & Accused Queens. LC 71-93253. 1970. Repr. of 1927 ed. 6.50 (ISBN 0-87752-097-6). Gordian.

Severs, J. Burke. Literary Relationships of Chaucer's Clerkes Tale. (Yale Studies in English Ser.: No. 96). 1972. Repr. of 1942 ed. 18.50 (ISBN 0-208-01138-2, Archon). Shoe String.

Shipley, Joseph T. Literary Isms. LC 77-7150. 1931. lib. bdg. 10.00 (ISBN 0-8414-7757-4). Folcroft.

Smith, Charles G. Spenser's Theory of Friendship. 1939. lib. bdg. 11.00 (ISBN 0-8414-1579-X). Folcroft.

Soudek, Ernst. Studies in the Lancelot Legend. (Rice University Studies: Vol. 58, No. 1). 60p. 1972. pap. 3.25x (ISBN 0-89263-211-9). Rice Univ.

Stanford, William B. Ulysses Theme. 1968. pap. 4.95 (ISBN 0-472-06143-7, 143, AA). U of Mich Pr.

Stevenson, David L. Love-Game Comedy. Repr. of 1946 ed. 14.50 (ISBN 0-404-06263-6). AMS Pr.

Todorov, Tzvetan. The Fantastic: A Structural Approach to a Literary Genre. Howard, Richard, tr. from Fr. LC 72-87175. 186p. 1973. 15.00 (ISBN 0-8295-0245-9). UPB.

Van Roosbroeck, G. L. Persian Letters Before Montesquieu. 1932. 19.00 (ISBN 0-8337-4458-5). B Franklin.

Weiss, Adelaide M. Merlin in German Literature. LC 73-140017. (Catholic University Studies in German Ser.: No. 3). Repr. of 1933 ed. 16.00 (ISBN 0-404-50223-7). AMS Pr.

Zabara, Joseph B. Book of Delight. Hadas, Moses, tr. 1969. lib. bdg. 14.00x (ISBN 0-374-93344-8). Octagon.

LITERATURE, COMPARATIVE-AMERICAN AND CLASSICAL

Fairclough, Henry R. Classics & Our Twentieth-Century Poets. LC 75-168001. (Stanford University. Stanford Studies in Language & Literature: Vol. 2, Pt. 2). Repr. of 1927 ed. 14.00 (ISBN 0-404-51804-4). AMS Pr.

Pritchard, John P. Return to the Fountains. 1966. lib. bdg. 15.00x (ISBN 0-374-96650-8). Octagon.

LITERATURE, COMPARATIVE-AMERICAN AND ENGLISH

Cairns, William B. British Criticism of American Writings 1815-1833: A Contribution to the Study of Anglo-American Literary Relationships. 1972. Repr. of 1922 ed. lib. bdg. 20.00 (ISBN 0-8414-0079-2). Folcroft.

Eidson, John O. Tennyson in America: His Reputation & Influence from 1827 to 1858. LC 43-1265. 262p. 1943. 15.00x (ISBN 0-8203-0177-9). U of Ga Pr.

Frontain, Raymond-Jean & Wojcik, Jan, eds. The David Myth in Western Literature. LC 78-69904. (Illus.). 1980. 10.95 (ISBN 0-911198-55-5). Purdue.

Gohdes, Clarence. American Literature in Nineteenth-Century England. LC 63-9473. (Arcturus Books Paperbacks). 202p. 1963. pap. 1.65 (ISBN 0-8093-0086-9). S Ill U Pr.

Green, Martin. Transatlantic Patterns: Cultural Comparisons of England with America. LC 74-78305. 1977. 11.95 (ISBN 0-465-08688-8). Basic.

Heilman, Robert B. America in English Fiction, 1760-1800. 1968. lib. bdg. 25.00x (ISBN 0-374-93781-8). Octagon.

Leonard, William E. Byron & Byronism in America. LC 65-24997. 1965. Repr. of 1907 ed. 6.50 (ISBN 0-87752-062-3). Gordian.

Michaels, Walter B., ed. Glyph Eight. LC 76-47370. (Glyph: Johns Hopkins Textual Studies). 256p. 1981. text ed. 16.50x (ISBN 0-8018-2481-8); pap. text ed. 6.95 (ISBN 0-8018-2482-6). Johns Hopkins.

Power, J. Shelley in America in the Nineteenth Century. LC 65-15892. (Studies in Shelley, No. 25). 1969. Repr. of 1940 ed. lib. bdg. 33.95 (ISBN 0-8383-0611-X). Haskell.

Power, Julia. Shelley in America in the Nineteenth Century. LC 70-90370. 1969. Repr. of 1940 ed. text ed. 8.50 (ISBN 0-87752-088-7). Gordian.

Raiziss, Sona. Metaphysical Passion: Seven Modern American Poets & the Seventeenth Century Tradition. Repr. of 1952 ed. lib. bdg. 15.00x (ISBN 0-8371-3343-2, RAMP). Greenwood.

Raleigh, John H. Matthew Arnold & American Culture. 1962. 5.00 (ISBN 0-8446-2777-1). Peter Smith.

--Matthew Arnold & American Culture. 1957. pap. 1.95 (ISBN 0-520-01046-9, CAL51). U of Cal Pr.

LITERATURE, COMPARATIVE-AMERICAN AND FRENCH

Benamou, Michel. Wallace Stevens & the Symbolist Imagination. LC 66-11962. (Princeton Essays in Literature Ser.). 156p. 1972. 16.50 (ISBN 0-691-06225-0). Princeton U Pr.

Cambiare, C. P. Influence of Poe in France. LC 71-92954. (Studies in Comparative Literature, No. 35). 1970. Repr. of 1927 ed. lib. bdg. 36.95 (ISBN 0-8383-0963-1). Haskell.

Falb, Lewis. American Drama in Paris, 1945-1970: A Study of Its Critical Reception. (Studies in Comparative Literature Ser.: No. 54). 13.00x (ISBN 0-8078-7054-4). U of NC Pr.

French-American Literary Relationships. 1952. pap. 6.00 (ISBN 0-527-01718-3, YFS 10). Kraus Repr.

Salvan, Albert J. Zola Aux Etats-Unis. 1943. 12.00 (ISBN 0-527-78650-0). Kraus Repr.

LITERATURE, COMPARATIVE-AMERICAN AND GERMAN

Hatfield, James T. New Light on Longfellow: With Special Reference to His Relations with Germany. LC 70-114097. (Illus.). 1970. Repr. of 1933 ed. text ed. 8.50 (ISBN 0-87752-050-X). Gordian.

Matenko, Percy. Ludwig Tieck & America. LC 54-62860. (North Carolina University. Studies in the Germanic Languages & Literatures: No. 12). Repr. of 1954 ed. 18.50 (ISBN 0-404-50912-6). AMS Pr.

Pochmann, Henry A. German Culture in America: Philosophical & Literary Influences 1600-1900. LC 78-5337. 1978. Repr. of 1957 ed. lib. bdg. 80.00x (ISBN 0-313-20378-4, POGC). Greenwood.

Price, Lawrence M. Reception of United States Literature in Germany. (Studies in Comparative Literature: No. 39). 1967. 16.50x (ISBN 0-8078-7039-0). U of NC Pr.

Shelley, Phillip A., et al, eds. Anglo-German & American-German Crosscurrents, Vol. 1. (University of North Carolina Studies in Comparative Literature: No. 19). 1969. Repr. of 1957 ed. 23.00 (ISBN 0-384-55110-6). Johnson Repr.

Vogel, Stanley M. German Literary Influences on the American Transcendentalists. LC 77-91192. (Yale Studies in English Ser.: No. 127). 1970. Repr. of 1955 ed. 16.00 (ISBN 0-208-00927-2, Archon). Shoe String.

Walz, John A. German Influence in American Education & Culture. facsimile ed. LC 70-99672. (Select Bibliographies Reprint Ser). 1936. 15.00 (ISBN 0-8369-5101-8). Arno.

Wellek, Rene. Confrontations: Studies in the Intellectual & Literary Relations Between Germany, England, & the U. S. During the 19th Century. 17.50x (ISBN 0-691-06017-7); pap. 4.95 (ISBN 0-691-01253-9). Princeton U Pr.

LITERATURE, COMPARATIVE-AMERICAN AND ORIENTAL

Christy, Arthur. Orient in American Transcendentalism: A Study of Emerson, Thoreau & Alcott. 1963. lib. bdg. 20.00x (ISBN 0-374-91539-3). Octagon.

Miner, Earl. The Japanese Tradition in British & American Literature. LC 76-3698. 312p. 1976. Repr. of 1958 ed. lib. bdg. 20.75 (ISBN 0-8371-8818-0, MIJT). Greenwood.

LITERATURE, COMPARATIVE-AMERICAN AND SPANISH

Englekirk, John E. Edgar Allan Poe in Hispanic Literature. LC 73-184231. xiv, 504p. 1972. Repr. of 1934 ed. 22.00 (ISBN 0-8462-1655-8). Russell.

Roades, M. T. Cervantes & Mark Twain. 59.95 (ISBN 0-87968-830-0). Gordon Pr.

LITERATURE, COMPARATIVE-ANGLO-SAXON AND LATIN

Haber, Tom B. Comparative Study of the Beowulf & the Aeneid. LC 68-29338. 1968. Repr. of 1931 ed. 7.50 (ISBN 0-87753-019-X). Phaeton.

LITERATURE, COMPARATIVE-ASSYROBABYLONIAN AND HEBREW

Cumming, Charles G. Assyrian & Hebrew Hymns of Praise. LC 34-3318. (Columbia University. Oriental Studies: No. 12). Repr. of 1934 ed. 16.50 (ISBN 0-404-50502-3). AMS Pr.

Stummer, Friedrich. Summerisch - Akkadische Parallelen Zum Aufbau Alttestamentlicher Psalmen. Repr. of 1922 ed. pap. 12.50 (ISBN 0-384-58710-0). Johnson Repr.

LITERATURE, COMPARATIVE-CLASSICAL AND ITALIAN

Moore, Edward. Studies in Dante, First Series: Scriptures & Classical Authors in Dante. LC 68-57627. (Illus.). 1969. Repr. of 1896 ed. lib. bdg. 15.25x (ISBN 0-8371-0909-4, MODF). Greenwood.

--Studies in Dante, Second Series: Miscellaneous Essays. LC 68-57628. (Illus.). 1969. Repr. of 1899 ed. lib. bdg. 15.25x (ISBN 0-8371-0908-6, MOSD). Greenwood.

--Studies in Dante, Third Series: Miscellaneous Essays. LC 68-57629. (Illus.). 1969. Repr. of 1903 ed. lib. bdg. 15.25x (ISBN 0-8371-0917-5, MODT). Greenwood.

LITERATURE, COMPARATIVE-CLASSICAL AND MODERN

Burlingame, Anne E. Battle of the Books in Its Historical Setting. LC 68-54230. 1969. Repr. of 1920 ed. 9.00x (ISBN 0-8196-0224-8). Biblo.

Fairclough, Henry R. Classics & Our Twentieth-Century Poets. LC 75-168001. (Stanford University. Stanford Studies in Language & Literature: Vol. 2, Pt. 2). Repr. of 1927 ed. 14.00 (ISBN 0-404-51804-4). AMS Pr.

Hamburger, Kate. From Sophocles to Sartre: Figures from Greek Tragedy, Classical & Modern. Sebba, Helen, tr. LC 68-31451. 1969. 10.50 (ISBN 0-8044-2340-7). Ungar.

Highet, Gilbert. Classical Tradition. 1949. 22.50 (ISBN 0-19-500570-8). Oxford U Pr.

Lemmi, Charles W. Classic Deities in Bacon. LC 70-120639. 1970. Repr. lib. bdg. 14.00x (ISBN 0-374-94929-8). Octagon.

Rigault, Hippolyte. Histoire de la Querelle des Anciens et des Modernes. 1859. 29.00 (ISBN 0-8337-2995-0). B Franklin.

Zweig, Paul. The Heresy of Self-Love: A Study of Subversive Individualism. LC 79-5482. 288p. 1980. 17.50x (ISBN 0-691-06431-8); pap. 4.95 (ISBN 0-691-01371-3). Princeton U Pr.

LITERATURE, COMPARATIVE-CZECH AND RUSSIAN

Harkins, William E. Russian Folk Epos in Czech Literature: 1800-1900. LC 76-141414. 1971. Repr. of 1951 ed. lib. bdg. 15.00 (ISBN 0-8371-4687-9, HACL). Greenwood.

Jakobson, Roman. Ocheshskomstikhe,preimushches nnovsopostavleniisrusskim. LC 68-8623. (Slavic Reprint Ser.: No. 6). 145p. (Rus). 1969. pap. text ed. 4.00x (ISBN 0-87057-119-2, Pub. by Brown U Pr). U Pr of New Eng.

Souckova, Milada. Literary Satellite: Czechoslovak-Russian Literary Relations. LC 79-99772. 1970. 8.75x (ISBN 0-226-76840-6). U of Chicago Pr.

LITERATURE, COMPARATIVE-ENGLISH AND CELTIC

Snyder, Edward D. The Celtic Revival in English Literature Seventeen Sixty-Eighteen Hundred. 1923. 7.50 (ISBN 0-8446-1415-7). Peter Smith.

LITERATURE, COMPARATIVE-ENGLISH AND CHINESE

Chang, H. Allegory & Courtesy in Spenser. 1955. lib. bdg. 10.00 (ISBN 0-8414-3351-8). Folcroft.

Chang, Hsin. Allegory & Courtesy in Spenser. LC 75-30924. (English Literature Ser., No. 33). 1975. lib. bdg. 33.95 (ISBN 0-8383-2100-3). Haskell.

Deeney, John J., ed. Chinese-Western Comparative Literature Theory & Strategy. 220p. 1981. 17.50 (ISBN 0-295-95810-3, Pub. by Chinese Univ Hong Kong). U of Wash Pr.

Tay, William, ed. China & the West: Comparative Literature Studies. (New Asia Economic Bulletin Ser.). 306p. 1980. 18.95 (ISBN 0-295-95694-1, Pub. by Chinese Univ Hong Kong). U of Wash Pr.

LITERATURE, COMPARATIVE-ENGLISH AND CLASSICAL

Bush, Douglas. Mythology & the Renaissance Tradition in English Poetry. rev. ed. 1963. pap. 3.45x (ISBN 0-393-00187-3, Norton Lib). Norton.

Charlton, H. B. Shakespeare's Recoil from Romanticism. 1931. lib. bdg. 5.00 (ISBN 0-8414-3493-X). Folcroft.

Chislett, William, Jr. Classical Influence in English Literature. LC 74-8491. 1918. lib. bdg. 25.00 (ISBN 0-8414-3503-0). Folcroft.

Driver, Tom F. The Sense of History in Greek & Shakespearean Drama. LC 59-15146. 1960. pap. 6.00x (ISBN 0-231-08576-1). Columbia U Pr.

Gordon, George S., ed. English Literature & the Classics. LC 68-15126. 1969. Repr. of 1912 ed. 8.50 (ISBN 0-8462-1258-7). Russell.

Houghton, Ralph E. Influence of the Classics on the Poetry of Matthew Arnold. LC 76-26648. 1923. lib. bdg. 8.50 (ISBN 0-8414-4931-7). Folcroft.

Jepsen, Laura. Ethical Aspects of Tragedy. LC 79-153332. Repr. of 1953 ed. 14.95 (ISBN 0-404-03566-3). AMS Pr.

Lemmi, Charles W. Classic Deities in Bacon. LC 70-120639. 1970. Repr. lib. bdg. 14.00x (ISBN 0-374-94929-8). Octagon.

Lord, George D. Heroic Mockery: Variations on Epic Themes from Homer to Joyce. LC 76-13930. 162p. 1977. 11.50 (ISBN 0-87413-117-0). U Delaware Pr.

McEuen, Kathryn A. Classical Influence Upon the Tribe of Ben. 1968. lib. bdg. 15.00x (ISBN 0-374-95472-0). Octagon.

Montagu, Elizabeth. Essay on the Writings & Genius of Shakespeare Compared with the Greek & French Dramatic Poets. 6th ed. LC 17-29281. Repr. of 1810 ed. 19.75 (ISBN 0-404-04358-5). AMS Pr.
Papenheim, Wilhelm. Die Charakterschilderungen Im Tatler, Spectator, und Guardian. Repr. of 1930 ed. pap. 6.00 (ISBN 0-384-44720-1). Johnson Repr.
Ridley, Maurice R. Studies in Three Literatures: English, Latin, & Greek Contrasts & Comparisons. LC 78-42. 1978. Repr. of 1962 ed. lib. bdg. 17.25x (ISBN 0-313-20189-7, RISTL). Greenwood.
Samuel, Irene. Plato & Milton. 1965. pap. 3.95 (ISBN 0-8014-9092-8, CP92). Cornell U Pr.
Starnes, DeWitt T. & Talbert, Ernest W. Classical Myth & Legend in Renaissance Dictionaries. LC 73-11753. (Illus.). 517p. 1973. Repr. of 1955 ed. lib. bdg. 39.75x (ISBN 0-8371-7086-9, STCM). Greenwood.
Swardson, Harold R. Poetry & the Fountain of Light: Observations on the Conflict Between Christian & Classical Traditions in Seventeenth-Century Poetry. LC 62-9993. 1962. 4.50x (ISBN 0-8262-0015-X). U of Mo Pr.
Thomson, James A. Shakespeare & the Classics. 1978. Repr. of 1966 ed. lib. bdg. 22.75x (ISBN 0-313-20388-1, THSC). Greenwood.
Watt, Laughlan M. Attic & Elizabethan Tragedy. LC 67-27661. 1968. Repr. of 1908 ed. 14.00 (ISBN 0-8046-0490-8). Kennikat.

LITERATURE, COMPARATIVE–ENGLISH AND DUTCH

Scherpbier, H. Milton in Holland. LC 76-41928. 1933. lib. bdg. 17.50 (ISBN 0-8414-7580-6). Folcroft.

LITERATURE, COMPARATIVE–ENGLISH AND FRENCH

Bastide, Charles. Anglo-French Entente in the 17th Century. LC 78-146136. (Research & Source Works Ser.: No. 825). 1971. Repr. of 1914 ed. lib. bdg. 21.00 (ISBN 0-8337-0185-1). B Franklin.
Braddy, Haldeen. Chaucer & the French Poet Graunson. LC 68-16278. 1968. Repr. of 1947 ed. 9.50 (ISBN 0-8046-0039-2). Kennikat.
Brett-James, Anthony. The Triple Stream: Four Centuries of English, French & German Literature 1531-1930. LC 74-13161. 1973. lib. bdg. 17.50 (ISBN 0-8414-5306-3). Folcroft.
Brown, Huntington. Rabelais in English Literature. 1967. Repr. lib. bdg. 17.50x (ISBN 0-374-91027-8). Octagon.
Cestre, Charles. La Revolution Francaise et les Poetes Anglais, 1789-1809. 1972. Repr. of 1906 ed. lib. bdg. 50.00 (ISBN 0-8414-0108-X). Folcroft.
Clark, Alexander F. Boileau & the French Classical Critics in England, 1660-1830. LC 65-18796. 1965. Repr. of 1925 ed. 11.50 (ISBN 0-8462-0637-4). Russell.
De Mourgues, Odette. Metaphysical Baroque & Precieux Poetry. LC 73-1144. 1953. lib. bdg. 20.00 (ISBN 0-8414-1850-0). Folcroft.
Devonshire, Marian G. English Novel in France, Eighteen Thirty to Eighteen Seventy. 1967. lib. bdg. 17.50x (ISBN 0-374-92147-4). Octagon.
Ferguson, Walter D. Influence of Flaubert on George Moore. LC 74-10999. 1934. lib. bdg. 10.00 (ISBN 0-8414-4220-7). Folcroft.
Green, Frederick C. Literary Ideas in Eighteenth Century France & England: A Critical Survey. LC 65-23576. 1965. 18.00 (ISBN 0-8044-2299-0). Ungar.
--Minuet: A Critical Survey of French & English Literary Ideas in the 18th Century. LC 75-158504. 1971. Repr. of 1935 ed. 35.00 (ISBN 0-403-01296-1). Scholarly.
Gregory, Allene. French Revolution & the English Novel. LC 68-764. (Studies in Comparative Literature, No. 35). 1969. Repr. of 1915 ed. lib. bdg. 51.95 (ISBN 0-8383-0560-1). Haskell.
--French Revolution & the English Novel. LC 65-27134. 1965. Repr. of 1915 ed. 12.00 (ISBN 0-8046-0183-6). Kennikat.
Hancock, Albert E. French Revolution & the English Poets: Study in Historical Criticism. LC 67-27605. 1967. Repr. of 1899 ed. 12.50 (ISBN 0-8046-0193-3). Kennikat.
Havens, George R. Abbe Prevost & English Literature. LC 65-15884. (Studies in Comparative Literature, No. 35). 1969. Repr. of 1921 ed. lib. bdg. 48.95 (ISBN 0-8383-0568-7). Haskell.
--Abbe Prevost & English Literature. (Elliott Monographs: Vol. 9). 1921. pap. 9.00 (ISBN 0-527-02613-1). Kraus Repr.
Hooker, Kenneth W. Fortunes of Victor Hugo in England. LC 39-3325. Repr. of 1938 ed. 12.50 (ISBN 0-404-03328-8). AMS Pr.
Kinne, Willard A. Revivals & Importations of French Comedies in England, 1749-1800. LC 40-3880. Repr. of 1939 ed. 24.50 (ISBN 0-404-03705-4). AMS Pr.
Lee, Sidney. French Renaissance in England. 1968. lib. bdg. 27.50x (ISBN 0-374-94865-8). Octagon.
Lockitt, Charles H. The Relations of French & English Society (1763-1793) (Perspectives in European History Ser.: No. 21). 136p. Repr. of 1920 ed. lib. bdg. 13.50x (ISBN 0-87991-506-4). Porcupine Pr.
Lockwood, Helen D. Tools & the Man. LC 21-12534. Repr. of 1927 ed. 14.75 (ISBN 0-404-03999-5). AMS Pr.
Miles, Dudley H. Influence of Moliere on Restoration Comedy. LC 71-159247. 1971. Repr. lib. bdg. 15.00x (ISBN 0-374-95652-9). Octagon.
Montagu, Elizabeth. Essay on the Writings & Genius of Shakespeare Compared with the Greek & French Dramatic Poets. 6th ed. LC 17-29281. Repr. of 1810 ed. 19.75 (ISBN 0-404-04358-5). AMS Pr.
Painter, William. Palace of Pleasure: Elizabethan Versions of Italian & French Novels, 3 Vols. 4th ed. Jacobs, Joseph, ed. 10.00 ea. (ISBN 0-8446-2694-5). Peter Smith.
Papenheim, Wilhelm. Die Charakterschilderungen Im Tatler, Spectator, und Guardian. Repr. of 1930 ed. pap. 6.00 (ISBN 0-384-44720-1). Johnson Repr.
Partridge, Eric. French Romantics' Knowledge of English Literature: 1820-1848. (Research & Source Works Ser.: No. 201). 1968. Repr. of 1924 ed. 22.50 (ISBN 0-8337-2676-5). B Franklin.
Rickard, P. Britain in Medieval French Literature, 1100-1500. 1956. 14.00 (ISBN 0-527-75250-9). Kraus Repr.
Sabin, Margery. English Romanticism & the French Tradition. 1976. 15.00x (ISBN 0-674-25686-7, SAER). Harvard U Pr.
Scales, D. Aldous Huxley & French Literature. (Australian Humanities Research Council Monograph: No. 13). 1969. pap. 6.50x (ISBN 0-424-05900-2, Pub by Sydney U Pr). Intl Schol Bk Serv.
Sells, Iris E. Matthew Arnold & France. rev ed. LC 69-15236. 1969. Repr. lib. bdg. 18.50x (ISBN 0-374-97278-8). Octagon.
Starkie, Enid. From Gautier to Eliot: The Influence of France on English Literature, 1851-1939. LC 73-158509. 1971. 24.00 (ISBN 0-403-01303-8). Scholarly.
Stendhal. Racine et Shakespeare: Etudes sur le romantisme. (Coll GF). pap. 3.95 (ISBN 0-685-35016-9). French & Eur.
Stewart, Jean. Poetry in France & England. LC 73-15819. 1973. lib. bdg. 15.00 (ISBN 0-8414-7687-X). Folcroft.
Taylor, George C. Shakespeare's Debt to Montaigne. LC 68-58441. 1968. Repr. of 1925 ed. 5.00 (ISBN 0-87753-039-4). Phaeton.
Upham, Alfred H. French Influence in English Literature. 1965. lib. bdg. 24.00x (ISBN 0-374-98057-8). Octagon.
Van Der Vat, Daniel G. Fabulous Opera. LC 67-30820. (Studies in Comparative Literature, No. 35). 1969. Repr. of 1936 ed. lib. bdg. 48.95 (ISBN 0-8383-0724-8). Haskell.
Wheatley, Katherine E. Racine & English Classicism. Repr. of 1956 ed. lib. bdg. 15.00 (ISBN 0-8371-3161-8, WHRC). Greenwood.
Whiting, B. J. Proverbs in the Earlier English Drama. LC 70-86290. 1969. Repr. of 1938 ed. lib. bdg. 25.00x (ISBN 0-374-98513-8). Octagon.
Wilcox, John. Relation of Moliere to the Restoration Comedy. LC 64-14719. 1938. 15.00 (ISBN 0-405-09078-1). Arno.

LITERATURE, COMPARATIVE–ENGLISH AND GERMAN

Beyer, Werner W. Keats & the Daemon King. LC 76-86270. 1969. Repr. of 1947 ed. lib. bdg. 20.00x (ISBN 0-374-90627-0). Octagon.
Blassneck, Marce. Frankreich Als Vermittler Englisch-Deutscher Einflusse Im Siebzehnten und Achtzehnten Jahrhundert. 1934. pap. 10.00 (ISBN 0-384-04685-1). Johnson Repr.
Bradley, Andrew C. English Poetry & German Philosophy in the Age of Wordsworth. LC 73-16150. 1909. lib. bdg. 4.50 (ISBN 0-685-09976-8). Folcroft.
Brett-James, Anthony. The Triple Stream: Four Centuries of English, French & German Literature 1531-1930. LC 74-13161. 1973. lib. bdg. 17.50 (ISBN 0-8414-5306-3). Folcroft.
Elson, Charles. Wieland & Shaftesbury. LC 79-166024. (Columbia University. Germanic Studies, Old Ser.: No. 16). Repr. of 1913 ed. 22.50 (ISBN 0-404-50416-7). AMS Pr.
Ewen, Frederic. Prestige of Schiller in England, 1788-1859. Repr. of 1932 ed. 22.50 (ISBN 0-404-02364-9). AMS Pr.
Fouquet, K. Jakob Ayrers Sidea, Shakespeares Tempest und das Maerchen. pap. 7.00 (ISBN 0-384-16500-1). Johnson Repr.
Fuerst, Norbert. Victorian Age of German Literature: Eight Essays. LC 65-23845. 1965. 14.95x (ISBN 0-271-73107-9). Pa St U Pr.
Garvin, Wilhelma C. Development of the Comic Figure in German Drama. LC 72-119091. (Studies in Comparative Literature, No. 35). 1970. Repr. of 1923 ed. lib. bdg. 22.95 (ISBN 0-8383-1087-7). Haskell.
Hemminghaus, Edgar H. Mark Twain in Germany. LC 40-30032. (North Carolina. University. Studies in the Germanic Languages & Literatures: No. 9). Repr. of 1939 ed. 19.00 (ISBN 0-404-50459-0). AMS Pr.
Herford, Charles H. Studies in the Literary Relations of England & Germany in the Sixteenth Century. 1966. lib. bdg. 22.50x (ISBN 0-374-93819-9). Octagon.
Hewett-Thayer, Harvey W. Laurence Sterne in Germany. LC 5-33194. (Columbia University. Germanic Studies. Old Series: No. 5). Repr. of 1905 ed. 19.00 (ISBN 0-404-50405-1). AMS Pr.
Howe, Susanne. Wilhelm Meister & His English Kinsmen. LC 30-1541. Repr. of 1930 ed. 17.00 (ISBN 0-404-03367-9). AMS Pr.
Liptzin, Solomon. Shelley in Germany. LC 24-14279. (Columbia University. Germanic Studies, Old Series: No. 27). Repr. of 1924 ed. 17.00 (ISBN 0-404-50427-2). AMS Pr.
Macintosh, W. Scott & Goethe. LC 71-113340. 1970. Repr. of 1925 ed. 12.00 (ISBN 0-8046-1026-6). Kennikat.
Orrick, James. Matthew Arnold & Goethe. LC 70-179267. (Studies in Comparative Literature, No. 35). 1972. Repr. of 1928 ed. lib. bdg. 40.95 (ISBN 0-8383-1368-X). Haskell.
Pompen, Aurelius. English Versions of the Ship of Fools. 1967. lib. bdg. 12.00x (ISBN 0-374-96518-8). Octagon.
Price, Lawrence M. Reception of English Literature in Germany. LC 68-21223. 1968. Repr. of 1932 ed. 28.00 (ISBN 0-405-08863-9). Arno.
Robertson, John G. Goethe & Byron. LC 77-23089. 1925. lib. bdg. 12.50 (ISBN 0-8414-7386-2). Folcroft.
Shaffer, E. S. Kubla Kahn & the Fall of Jerusalem. LC 74-79141. 320p. 1975. 54.00 (ISBN 0-521-20478-X). Cambridge U Pr.
Shears, Lambert A. Influence of Walter Scott on the Novels of Theodor Fontane. LC 22-10118. (Columbia University. Germanic Studies, Old Ser.: No. 25). Repr. of 1922 ed. 11.50 (ISBN 0-404-50425-6). AMS Pr.
Shelley, Phillip A., et al, eds. Anglo-German & American-German Crosscurrents, Vol. 1. (University of North Carolina Studies in Comparative Literature: No. 19). 1969. Repr. of 1957 ed. 23.00 (ISBN 0-384-55110-6). Johnson Repr.
Stockley, Violet A. German Literature As Known in England, 1750-1830. LC 70-93073. 1969. Repr. of 1929 ed. 14.50 (ISBN 0-8046-0686-2). Kennikat.
Vail, Curtis C. Lessing's Relation to the English Language & Literature. LC 36-30041. (Columbia University. Germanic Studies, New Series: No. 3). Repr. of 1936 ed. 27.00 (ISBN 0-404-50453-1). AMS Pr.
Waterhouse, Gilbert. Literary Relations of England & Germany in the 17th Century. LC 68-818. (Studies in Comparative Literature, No. 35). 1969. Repr. of 1914 ed. lib. bdg. 33.95 (ISBN 0-8383-0689-6). Haskell.
Wellek, Rene. Confrontations: Studies in the Intellectual & Literary Relations Between Germany, England, & the U. S. During the 19th Century. 17.50x (ISBN 0-691-06017-7); pap. 4.95 (ISBN 0-691-01253-9). Princeton U Pr.
Willoughby, Leonard A. Dante Gabriel Rossetti & German Literature. LC 77-23086. 1912. lib. bdg. 8.50 (ISBN 0-8414-9614-5). Folcroft.

LITERATURE, COMPARATIVE–ENGLISH AND GREEK

Bhattacharya, Mohinimohana. Platonic Ideas in Spenser. LC 72-187921. 1935. lib. bdg. 12.50 (ISBN 0-8414-1643-5). Folcroft.
Collins, John C. Greek Influence on English Poetry. LC 72-3186. 1910. lib. bdg. 15.00 (ISBN 0-8414-2362-8). Folcroft.
Ridley, M. R. Studies in Three Literatures: English, Latin, Greek Contrasts & Comparisons. 1979. Repr. of 1962 ed. lib. bdg. 30.00 (ISBN 0-8495-4602-8). Arden Lib.
Rutland, William R. Swinburne: A Nineteenth Century Hellene. LC 72-187516. 1931. lib. bdg. 30.00 (ISBN 0-8414-7497-4). Folcroft.

LITERATURE, COMPARATIVE–ENGLISH AND ICELANDIC

Hoare, Dorothy M. The Works of Morris & of Yeats in Relation to Early Saga Literature. LC 72-139476. 1971. Repr. of 1937 ed. 11.00 (ISBN 0-8462-1382-6). Russell.
--Works of Morris & Yeats in Relation to Early Saga Literature. LC 72-193501. 1973. lib. bdg. 10.95 (ISBN 0-8414-5087-0). Folcroft.
Nordby, Conrad H. Influence of Old Norse Literature Upon English Literature. LC 3-19188. (Columbia University. Germanic Studies, Old Ser.: No. 3). Repr. of 1901 ed. 14.00 (ISBN 0-404-50403-5). AMS Pr.

LITERATURE, COMPARATIVE–ENGLISH AND ITALIAN

Barnes, C. L. Parallels in Dante & Milton. LC 74-3180. 1917. lib. bdg. 5.00 (ISBN 0-8414-9926-8). Folcroft.
Brand, Charles P. Torquato Tasso. 1965. 57.50 (ISBN 0-521-04311-5). Cambridge U Pr.
Collison-Morley, Lacy. Shakespeare in Italy. LC 67-23862. Repr. of 1916 ed. 11.00 (ISBN 0-405-08373-4, Blom Pubns). Arno.
Cummings, H. M. Indebtedness of Chaucer's Works to the Italian Works of Boccacio. LC 65-21098. (Studies in Comparative Literature, No. 35). 1969. Repr. of 1916 ed. lib. bdg. 27.95 (ISBN 0-8383-0534-2). Haskell.
Cummings, Hubertis M. Indebtedness of Chaucer's Work to the Italian Works of Boccaccio. LC 67-30901. 1967. Repr. of 1916 ed. 8.00 (ISBN 0-87753-011-4). Phaeton.
Jeffery, Violet M. John Lyly & the Italian Renaissance. LC 68-25080. 1969. Repr. of 1928 ed. 7.50 (ISBN 0-8462-1262-5). Russell.
Kroeber, Karl. Artifice of Reality: Poetic Style in Wordsworth, Foscolo, Keats, & Leopardi. 1964. 21.50 (ISBN 0-299-03230-2). U of Wis Pr.
Lea, Kathleen M. Italian Popular Comedy: A Study in the Commedia Dell'Arte, 1560-1620, with Special Reference to the English Stage, 2 vols. in 1. LC 62-10692. (Illus.). 1962. Repr. of 1934 ed. 25.00 (ISBN 0-8462-0226-3). Russell.
Lee, Sidney. Shakespeare & the Italian Renaissance. 1915. lib. bdg. 5.00 (ISBN 0-8414-5785-9). Folcroft.
Marshall, Roderick. Italy in English Literature. LC 72-190937. 1934. lib. bdg. 25.00 (ISBN 0-8414-0875-0). Folcroft.
Murray, J. Ross. Influence of Italian Upon English Literature During the Sixteenth & Seventeenth Centuries. LC 70-138743. Repr. of 1886 ed. 11.45 (ISBN 0-404-04544-8). AMS Pr.
Painter, William. Palace of Pleasure: Elizabethan Versions of Italian & French Novels, 3 Vols. 4th ed. Jacobs, Joseph, ed. 10.00 ea. (ISBN 0-8446-2694-5). Peter Smith.
Praz, Mario. The Flaming Heart: Essays on Cranshaw, Machiavelli & Other Studies from Chaucer to T. S. Eliot. 1958. 8.00 (ISBN 0-8446-1365-7). Peter Smith.
Scott, Mary A. Elizabethan Translations from the Italian. 1969. 32.50 (ISBN 0-8337-3210-2). B Franklin.
Sells, Arthur L. Italian Influence in English Poetry from Chaucer to Southwell. LC 76-136893. 1971. Repr. of 1955 ed. lib. bdg. 17.75x (ISBN 0-8371-5336-0, SEIF). Greenwood.
Smith, Winifred. Commedia Dell'Arte. rev. ed. LC 64-14715. (Illus.). 23.00 (ISBN 0-405-08984-8, Pub. by Blom). Arno.

LITERATURE, COMPARATIVE–ENGLISH AND JAPANESE

Miner, Earl. The Japanese Tradition in British & American Literature. LC 76-3698. 312p. 1976. Repr. of 1958 ed. lib. bdg. 20.75 (ISBN 0-8371-8818-0, MIJT). Greenwood.

LITERATURE, COMPARATIVE–ENGLISH AND LATIN

Aiken, Pauline. Influence of the Latin Elegists on English Lyric Poetry 1600-1650. LC 78-91345. 1970. Repr. of 1932 ed. 7.00 (ISBN 0-87753-002-5). Phaeton.
Duckett, Eleanor S., ed. Catullus in English Poetry. LC 76-173518. 1972. Repr. of 1925 ed. 13.00 (ISBN 0-8462-1661-2). Russell.
Goad, Caroline. Horace in the English Literature of 18th Century. LC 67-30804. (Studies in Comparative Literature, No. 35). 1969. Repr. of 1918 ed. lib. bdg. 49.95 (ISBN 0-8383-0701-9). Haskell.
Grierson, Herbert. Verse Translation. LC 77-4114. 1948. lib. bdg. 6.00 (ISBN 0-8414-4478-1). Folcroft.
McPeek, James A. Catullus in Strange & Distant Britain. LC 76-173550. 1972. Repr. of 1939 ed. 20.00 (ISBN 0-8462-1634-5). Russell.
Nitchie, Elizabeth. Vergil & the English Poets. LC 19-9760. Repr. of 1919 ed. 16.45 (ISBN 0-404-04778-5). AMS Pr.
Ridley, M. R. Studies in Three Literatures: English, Latin, Greek Contrasts & Comparisons. 1979. Repr. of 1962 ed. lib. bdg. 30.00 (ISBN 0-8495-4602-8). Arden Lib.
Thayer, Mary R. Influence of Horace on the Chief English Poets of the Nineteenth Century. LC 68-842. (Studies in Comparative Literature, No. 35). 1969. Repr. of 1912 ed. lib. bdg. 48.95 (ISBN 0-8383-0633-0). Haskell.
--Influence of Horace on the Chief English Poets of the Nineteenth Century. LC 67-18297. 1967. Repr. of 1916 ed. 5.75 (ISBN 0-8462-1131-9). Russell.
Whipple, Thomas K. Martial & English Epigram from Sir Thomas Wyatt to Ben Jonson. LC 70-90362. 1970. Repr. of 1925 ed. 7.50 (ISBN 0-87753-043-2). Phaeton.

Wise, Boyd A. Influence of Statius Upon Chaucer. LC 67-30907. 1967. Repr. of 1911 ed. 7.50 (ISBN 0-87753-045-9). Phaeton.

LITERATURE, COMPARATIVE–ENGLISH AND LATIN (MODERN)

Crane, Dougall. Johannes Secundus, His Life, Work, & Influence on English Literature. 1931. pap. 6.00 (ISBN 0-384-10100-3). Johnson Repr.

LITERATURE, COMPARATIVE–ENGLISH AND RUSSIAN

Davie, Donald, ed. Russian Literature & Modern English Fiction. (Patterns of Literary Criticism Ser). 1965. 8.50x (ISBN 0-226-13747-3); pap. 1.95 (ISBN 0-226-13748-1, PLC3). U of Chicago Pr.

Muchnic, Helen. Dostoyevsky's English Reputation: 1881-1936. LC 77-86281. 1969. Repr. of 1939 ed. lib. bdg. 14.00x (ISBN 0-374-95985-4). Octagon.

Phelps, Gilbert. Russian Novel in English Fiction. LC 79-158907. 1971. Repr. of 1956 ed. 19.00 (ISBN 0-403-01301-1). Scholarly.

--Russian Novel in English Fiction. LC 79-158907. 1971. Repr. of 1956 ed. 19.00 (ISBN 0-403-01301-1). Scholarly.

Simmons, Ernest J. English Literature & Culture in Russia, 1553-1840. 1964. lib. bdg. 17.50x (ISBN 0-374-97448-9). Octagon.

LITERATURE, COMPARATIVE–ENGLISH AND SPANISH

Hagedorn, Maria. Reformation und Spanische Andachtsliteratur. 1934. pap. 10.00 (ISBN 0-384-20770-7). Johnson Repr.

Hume, M. Spanish Influences on English Literature. LC 65-15903. (Studies in Comparative Literature, No. 35). 1969. Repr. of 1905 ed. lib. bdg. 33.95 (ISBN 0-8383-0573-3). Haskell.

Patchell, Mary. Palmerin Romances in Elizabethan Prose Fiction. LC 47-30744. Repr. of 1947 ed. 17.00 (ISBN 0-404-04889-7). AMS Pr.

Underhill, John G. Spanish Literature in the England of the Tudors. LC 70-131496. Repr. of 1899 ed. 28.50 (ISBN 0-404-06702-6). AMS Pr.

Ungerer, Gustav. Anglo-Spanish Relations in Tudor Literature. LC 73-138944. Repr. of 1956 ed. 21.00 (ISBN 0-404-06704-2). AMS Pr.

LITERATURE, COMPARATIVE–ENGLISH AND SWEDISH

Bulman, Joan. Strindberg & Shakespeare: Shakespeare's Influence on Strindberg's Historical Drama. LC 73-153482. (Studies in Comparative Literature, No. 35). 1971. Repr. of 1933 ed. lib. bdg. 36.95 (ISBN 0-8383-1239-X). Haskell.

Wright, H. G. Studies in Anglo-Scandinavian Literary Relations. LC 72-10784. 1973. Repr. of 1919 ed. lib. bdg. 20.00 (ISBN 0-8414-0716-9). Folcroft.

LITERATURE, COMPARATIVE–FRENCH AND CLASSICAL

Peyre, Henri. L' Influence des litteratures antiques sur la litterature francaise moderne. LC 72-1699. (Yale Romanic Studies: No. 19). Repr. of 1941 ed. 11.00 (ISBN 0-404-53219-5). AMS Pr.

LITERATURE, COMPARATIVE–FRENCH AND ENGLISH

Bastide, Charles. Anglo-French Entente in the 17th Century. LC 78-146136. (Research & Source Works Ser.: No. 825). 1971. Repr. of 1914 ed. lib. bdg. 21.00 (ISBN 0-8337-0185-1). B Franklin.

Brownell, W. C. French Traits: An Essay in Comparative Criticism. 1977. Repr. of 1916 ed. lib. bdg. 20.00 (ISBN 0-8414-1749-0). Folcroft.

Green, Frederick C. Minuet: A Critical Survey of French & English Literary Ideas in the 18th Century. LC 75-158504. 1971. Repr. of 1935 ed. 35.00 (ISBN 0-403-01296-1). Scholarly.

Miles, Dudley H. Influence of Moliere on Restoration Comedy. LC 71-159247. 1971. Repr. lib. bdg. 15.00x (ISBN 0-374-95652-9). Octagon.

Sabin, Margery. English Romanticism & the French Tradition. 1976. 15.00x (ISBN 0-674-25686-7, SAER). Harvard U Pr.

Starkie, Enid. From Gautier to Eliot: The Influence of France on English Literature, 1851-1939. LC 73-158509. 1971. 24.00 (ISBN 0-403-01303-8). Scholarly.

Stewart, Jean. Poetry in France & England. LC 73-15819. 1973. lib. bdg. 15.00 (ISBN 0-8414-7687-X). Folcroft.

LITERATURE, COMPARATIVE–FRENCH AND GERMAN

Barth, Bruno. Liebe und Ehe Im Altfranzosischen Fabel und in der Mittelhochdeutschen Novelle. Repr. of 1910 ed. 21.50 (ISBN 0-384-03465-9); pap. 18.50 (ISBN 0-685-02215-3). Johnson Repr.

Furst, Lillian R. Counterparts: The Dynamics of Franco-German Literary Relationships, 1770-1895. LC 77-2407. 1977. text ed. 13.50x (ISBN 0-8143-1582-8). Wayne St U Pr.

Kommerell, M. Jean Pauls Verhaltnis Zu Rousseau. Repr. of 1924 ed. pap. 15.50 (ISBN 0-384-30120-7). Johnson Repr.

Pusey, William W. Louis-Sebastien Mercier in Germany. LC 39-31447. (Columbia University. Germanic Studies, New Ser.: No. 8). Repr. of 1939 ed. 19.00 (ISBN 0-404-50458-2). AMS Pr.

Rachbauer, M. A. Wolfram Von Eschenbach. LC 73-140041. (Catholic University Studies in German Ser.: No. 4). Repr. of 1934 ed. 22.00 (ISBN 0-404-50224-5). AMS Pr.

Richardson, Frank C. Kleist in France. LC 62-64205. (North Carolina. University. Studies in the Germanic Languages & Literatures: No. 35). Repr. of 1962 ed. 18.50 (ISBN 0-404-50935-5). AMS Pr.

Root, Winthrop H. German Criticism of Zola, 1875-1893, with Special Reference to the Rougon-Macquart Cycle & the Roman Experimental. LC 31-32036. (Columbia University. Germanic Studies, Old Ser.: No. 35). Repr. of 1931 ed. 15.00 (ISBN 0-404-50435-3). AMS Pr.

LITERATURE, COMPARATIVE–FRENCH AND GREEK

Egger, E. L' Hellenisme En France, 2 Vols. 1964. Repr. of 1869 ed. 50.50 (ISBN 0-8337-1022-2). B Franklin.

Hutton, James. Greek Anthology in France & in the Latin Writers of the Netherlands to the Year 1800. 1946. 58.00 (ISBN 0-384-25150-1). Johnson Repr.

LITERATURE, COMPARATIVE–FRENCH AND ITALIAN

Pieri, Marius. Petrarquisme Au Seizieme Siecle: Petrarque et Ronsard, Ou l'Influence De Petrarque Sur la Pleiade Francaise. (Research & Source Works Ser: No. 179). 1967. Repr. of 1896 ed. 22.50 (ISBN 0-8337-2763-X). B Franklin.

Pirazzini, Agide. Influence of Italy on the Literary Career of Alphonse De Lamartine. LC 18-2055. (Columbia University. Studies in Romance Philology & Literature). Repr. of 1917 ed. 17.50 (ISBN 0-404-50622-4). AMS Pr.

LITERATURE, COMPARATIVE–FRENCH AND LATIN

Faral, Edmond. Recherches Sur les Sources Latines Des Contes et Romans Courtois Du Moyen Age. LC 72-178580. Repr. of 1913 ed. 27.50 (ISBN 0-404-56600-6). AMS Pr.

May, Georges. D'Ovid a Racine. (Yale Romanic Studies). 1949. pap. 27.50x (ISBN 0-685-69841-6). Elliots Bks.

LITERATURE, COMPARATIVE–FRENCH AND RUSSIAN

Von Mohrenschildt, Dimitri S. Russia in the Intellectual Life of Eighteenth-Century France. LC 71-159255. x, 326p. 1971. Repr. of 1936 ed. lib. bdg. 16.00x (ISBN 0-374-98088-8). Octagon.

LITERATURE, COMPARATIVE–FRENCH AND SCOTTISH

Smith, Janet M. The French Background of Middle Scots Literature. LC 76-28971. 1976. Repr. of 1934 ed. lib. bdg. 27.50 (ISBN 0-8414-7712-4). Folcroft.

LITERATURE, COMPARATIVE–FRENCH AND SPANISH

Gaudin, Lois S. Bibliography of Franco-Spanish Literary Relations Until the Nineteeth Century. LC 74-178937. (Institute of French Studies Publications). 71p. 1973. Repr. of 1930 ed. lib. bdg. 18.50 (ISBN 0-8337-4125-X). B Franklin.

Segall, Jacob B. Corneille & the Spanish Drama. LC 77-85907. (Columbia University. Studies in Romance Philology & Literature: No. 3). Repr. of 1902 ed. 16.00 (ISBN 0-404-50603-8). AMS Pr.

Spell, Jefferson. Rousseau in the Spanish World Before 1833. LC 70-76009. 1969. Repr. of 1938 ed. lib. bdg. 14.00x (ISBN 0-374-97543-4). Octagon.

Spell, Jefferson R. Rousseau in the Spanish World Before 1833: A Study in Franco-Spanish Literary Relations. LC 76-93257. 1969. Repr. of 1938 ed. text ed. 9.00 (ISBN 0-87752-104-2). Gordian.

Willis, Raymond S., Jr. The Debt of the Spanish Libro De Alexandre to the French Roman D'Alexandre. (Elliott Monographs: Vol. 33). 1935. pap. 5.00 (ISBN 0-527-02636-0). Kraus Repr.

--Relationship of the Spanish Libro De Alexandre to the Alexandreis of Gautier De Chatillon. (Elliott Monographs: Vol. 31). 1934. pap. 7.00 (ISBN 0-527-02634-4). Kraus Repr.

LITERATURE, COMPARATIVE–GERMAN AND GREEK

Knight, Arthur H. Some Aspects of the Life & Work of Nietzsche. LC 66-27192. 1967. Repr. of 1933 ed. 8.00 (ISBN 0-8462-1026-6). Russell.

LITERATURE, COMPARATIVE–GERMAN AND INDO-IRANIAN

Remy, Arthur F. Influence of India & Persia on the Poetry of Germany. LC 12-28753. (Columbia University. Germanic Studies, Old Series: No. 44). Repr. of 1901 ed. 14.50 (ISBN 0-404-50404-3). AMS Pr.

LITERATURE, COMPARATIVE–GERMAN AND ITALIAN

Rusack, Hedwig H. Gozzi in Germany. LC 31-2392. (Columbia University. Germanic Studies, Old Ser.: No. 34). Repr. of 1930 ed. 19.00 (ISBN 0-404-50434-5). AMS Pr.

LITERATURE, COMPARATIVE–GERMAN AND RUSSIAN

Birnbaum, Henrik. Dokter Faustur und "Dokter Schiwago". Versuch ueber zwei Zeitromane aus Exilsicht. 1976. pap. text ed. 4.75x (ISBN 90-316-0092-X). Humanities.

LITERATURE, COMPARATIVE–GREEK AND LATIN

Hutton, James. Greek Anthology in France & in the Latin Writers of the Netherlands to the Year 1800. 1946. 58.00 (ISBN 0-384-25150-1). Johnson Repr.

Ridley, M. R. Studies in Three Literatures: English, Latin, Greek Contrasts & Comparisons. 1979. Repr. of 1962 ed. lib. bdg. 30.00 (ISBN 0-8495-4602-8). Arden Lib.

LITERATURE, COMPARATIVE–HEBREW AND MEDIEVAL

Zabara, Joseph B. Book of Delight. Hadas, Moses, tr. 1969. lib. bdg. 14.00x (ISBN 0-374-93344-8). Octagon.

LITERATURE, COMPARATIVE–NORWEGIAN AND SPANISH

Gregersen, H. Ibsen & Spain: A Study in Comparative Drama. 1936. pap. 14.00 (ISBN 0-527-01108-8). Kraus Repr.

LITERATURE, COMPARATIVE–RUSSIAN AND SPANISH

Turkevich, Ludmilla B. Cervantes in Russia. LC 75-31685. 1975. Repr. of 1950 ed. 10.00 (ISBN 0-87752-175-1). Gordian.

LITERATURE, CRIME IN

see Crime in Literature

LITERATURE, EPIC

see Epic Literature

LITERATURE, EROTIC

see Erotic Literature

LITERATURE, IMMORAL

see also Censorship; Erotic Literature; Literature and Morals; Obscenity (Law); Sex in Literature

Comstock, Anthony. Frauds Exposed; or, How People Are Deceived & Robbed, & Youth Corrupted. LC 69-16234. (Criminology, Law Enforcement, & Social Problems Ser.: No. 79). (Illus.). 1969. Repr. of 1880 ed. 25.00 (ISBN 0-87585-079-0). Patterson Smith.

--Traps for the Young. Bremner, Robert H., ed. LC 67-17306. (The John Harvard Library). (Illus.). 1967. 15.00x (ISBN 0-674-90555-5). Harvard U Pr.

Craig, Alec. Above All Liberties. facsimile ed. LC 70-37839. (Essay Index Reprint Ser). Repr. of 1942 ed. 16.00 (ISBN 0-8369-2587-4). Arno.

Ernst, M. L. & Seagle, W. To the Pure: A Study of Obscenity & the Censor. LC 28-30424. 1928. 17.00 (ISBN 0-527-27650-2). Kraus Repr.

Goldstein, Michael J., et al. Pornography & Sexual Deviance. LC 72-97753. 1973. 20.00x (ISBN 0-520-02406-0); pap. 2.45 (ISBN 0-520-02619-5). U of Cal Pr.

Hewitt, Cecil R., ed. Does Pornography Matter? facsimile ed. LC 71-152175. (Essay Index Reprint Ser). Repr. of 1961 ed. 13.00 (ISBN 0-8369-2651-X). Arno.

Holbrook, David, ed. The Case Against Pornography. LC 72-5279. 294p. 1973. 17.50 (ISBN 0-912050-28-4, Library Pr); pap. 5.95 (ISBN 0-686-77013-7). Open Court.

King, Francis. Sexuality, Magic & Perversion. (Illus.). 1972. 6.95 (ISBN 0-8065-0289-4). Citadel Pr.

Lewis, Felice F. Literature, Obscenity, & Law. LC 75-42094. 310p. 1976. 12.50 (ISBN 0-8093-0749-9). S Ill U Pr.

Sussman, C. & Sussman, I. How to Read a Dirty Book. 3.95 (ISBN 0-8199-0359-0, L38294). Franciscan Herald.

LITERATURE, LEGAL

see Legal Literature

LITERATURE, MEDIEVAL

see also Christian Literature, Early; Romances; also subdivisions referring to Medieval Literature under specific national literatures, e.g. English Literature–Middle English; French Literature–Old French

Baldwin, C. S. Renaissance Literary Theory & Practice. 1959. 7.50 (ISBN 0-8446-1042-9). Peter Smith.

Brook, G. L. & Leslie, R. F., eds. Lazamon: Brut, Vol. 2. (Early English Text Society, Original Ser.). 1978. 39.50x (ISBN 0-19-722279-X). Oxford U Pr.

Chaytor, H. J. From Script to Print: An Introduction to Medieval Vernacular Literature. pap. 5.95 (ISBN 0-686-10843-4). British Am Bks.

Cunliffe, John W., ed. Early English Classical Tragedies. 1971. Repr. of 1912 ed. 35.00 (ISBN 0-403-00913-8). Scholarly.

De La Sale, Antoine. Little John of Saintre. Gray, Irvine, tr. LC 76-48432. (Library of World Literature Ser.). (Illus.). 1978. Repr. of 1931 ed. 23.50 (ISBN 0-88355-560-3). Hyperion Conn.

Eliot, Elizabeth A. The Crowned Knot of Fire. LC 79-67045. 1980. 8.95 (ISBN 0-533-04425-1). Vantage.

Gollancz, Israel, ed. Medieval Library, 28 vols. Repr. of 1926 ed. write for info. Cooper Sq.

Gossman, Lionel. Medievalism & the Ideologies of the Enlightenment: The World & Work of la Curne de Sainte-Palaye. LC 68-16274. 377p. 1968. 25.00x (ISBN 0-8018-0227-X). Johns Hopkins.

Grunmann-Gaudet, Minnette & Jones, Robin F., eds. The Nature of Medieval Narrative. LC 80-66330. (French Forum Monographs: No. 22). 218p. (Orig.). 1980. pap. 12.50 (ISBN 0-917058-21-6). French Forum.

Halsall, Maureen. The Old English Rune Poem: A Critical Edition. (McMaster Old English Studies and Texts). 224p. 1980. 20.00x (ISBN 0-8020-5477-3). U of Toronto Pr.

Hauser, Arnold. Social History of Art, 4 vols. Incl. Vol. 1. Prehistoric to Middle Ages. 1957. (ISBN 0-394-70114-3, V114); Vol. 2. Renaissance to Baroque. 1957. (ISBN 0-394-70115-1, V115); Vol. 3. Rococo to Romanticism. 1958. (ISBN 0-394-70116-X, V116); Vol. 4. Naturalism of the Film Age. 1958. (ISBN 0-394-70117-8, V117). pap. 2.95 ea. (Vin). Random.

Holmes, Urban T., Jr. Mediaevel Studies in Honor of Urban Tigner Holmes, Jr. Mahoney, John & Keller, John E., eds. LC 73-84754. (Illus.). 219p. Date not set. Repr. of 1965 ed. cancelled (ISBN 0-8462-1735-X). Russell.

Holzknecht, Karl J. Literary Patronage in the Middle Ages. 1967. lib. bdg. 14.50x (ISBN 0-374-93933-0). Octagon.

Howard, Donald R. Writers & Pilgrims: Medieval Pilgrimage Narratives & Their Posterity. LC 79-64480. (A Quantum Bk.). 100p. 1980. 10.95 (ISBN 0-520-03926-2). U of Cal Pr.

Lasater, Alice E. Spain to England: A Comparative Study of Arabic, European, & English Literature of the Middle Ages. LC 73-94277. 1974. 2.00 (ISBN 0-87805-056-6). U Pr of Miss.

Lee, Berta G. Linguistics Evidence for the Priority of the French Text of the Ancrene Wisse. LC 74-77155. (Janua Linguarum, Ser. Practica: No. 242). 90p. 1974. pap. text ed. 22.50x (ISBN 90-2793-332-4). Mouton.

Loomis, Laura A. Adventures in the Middle Ages: A Memorial Collection of Essays & Studies. 1962. 22.50 (ISBN 0-8337-2143-7). B Franklin.

Loomis, Roger S., ed. Studies in Medieval Literature: A Memorial Collection of Essays. LC 73-135508. (Research & Source Works Ser.: No. 599). (Bibl. of loomis's writings by ruth roberts). 1970. Repr. 23.50 (ISBN 0-8337-4733-9). B Franklin.

Maitland, S. R. Dark Ages: Essays Illustrating the State of Religion & Literature in the Ninth, Tenth, Eleventh & Twelfth Centuries, 2 Vols. LC 68-8242. 1969. Repr. of 1889 ed. 23.50 (ISBN 0-8046-0297-2). Kennikat.

Matthews, William, ed. Medieval Secular Literature: Four Essays. (UCLA Center for Medieval & Renaissance Studies). 1965. 18.50x (ISBN 0-520-00832-4). U of Cal Pr.

Mermier, Guy R. & DuBruck, Edelgard E., eds. Fifteenth Century Studies, Vol. 1. LC 78-5176. 1978. pap. 21.00 (ISBN 0-8357-0312-6, SS-00064). Univ Microfilms.

Moore, Philip S., et al. Sententiae Petri Pictaviensis 2. (Mediaeval Studies Ser: No. 11). (Lat). 1950. pap. 10.95x (ISBN 0-268-00391-2). U of Notre Dame Pr.

Morley, Henry, intro. by. Medieval Tales. 1977. Repr. of 1884 ed. lib. bdg. 25.00 (ISBN 0-8495-3714-2). Arden Lib.

Morse, Charlotte C. The Pattern of Judgement in the "Queste" & "Cleanness". LC 77-25158. (Illus.). 1978. 16.50x (ISBN 0-8262-0242-X). U of Mo Pr.

Petit, H., et al, eds. Annuale Mediaevale, Vol. 20. 122p. 1981. pap. text ed. 13.50x (ISBN 0-686-73232-4). Humanities.

Plummer, John F. & Plummer, John F., eds. Vox Feminae: Studies in Medieval Woman's Songs. LC 81-3981. (Studies in Medieval Culture XV). viii, 223p. (Orig.). 1981. pap. 10.95 (ISBN 0-918720-12-5). Medieval Inst.

Quiggin, E. C., ed. Essays & Studies Presented to William Ridgeway on His Sixtieth Birthday, 6 August 1913. facs. ed. LC 67-22093. (Essay Index Reprint Ser). 1913. 35.00 (ISBN 0-8369-0421-4). Arno.

Reinhard, John R., tr. Medieval Pageant. LC 75-129969. (Studies in European Literature, No. 56). 1970. Repr. of 1939 ed. lib. bdg. 52.95 (ISBN 0-8383-1166-0). Haskell.

Rigg, George, ed. Editing Medieval Texts. LC 76-52722. (Conference on Editorial Problems Ser.: Vol. 12). 1977. lib. bdg. 16.50 (ISBN 0-8240-2426-5). Garland Pub.
Robertson, D. W. Preface to Chaucer: Studies in Medieval Perspectives. (Illus.). 1969. 36.00x (ISBN 0-691-06099-1); pap. 7.95 (ISBN 0-691-01294-6). Princeton U Pr.
Salzmann, L. F. More Medieval Byways. 1926. Repr. 20.00 (ISBN 0-8274-2765-4). R West.
Schmidt, A. V. & Jacobs, Nicolas, eds. Medieval English Romances, Part 1. LC 79-48002. (The London Medieval & Renaissance Ser.). 210p. 1981. text ed. 29.50x (ISBN 0-8419-0604-1). Holmes & Meier.
Segar, Mary G. A Mediaeval Anthology. 132p. 1980. Repr. of 1915 ed. lib. bdg. 17.50 (ISBN 0-8482-6219-0). Norwood Edns.
--A Mediaeval Anthology. LC 74-18417. 1974. Repr. of 1915 ed. lib. bdg. 15.00 (ISBN 0-8414-7827-9). Folcroft.
Shackford, Martha H. Legends & Satires from Mediaeval Literature. 1979. Repr. of 1913 ed. lib. bdg. 22.50 (ISBN 0-8492-8115-6). R West.
Southeastern Institute of Medieval & Renaissance Studies. Medieval & Renaissance Studies: Proceedings. Wenzel, Siegfried, ed. LC 66-25361. (Medieval & Renaissance Ser.: No. 7). 1978. 11.00x (ISBN 0-8078-1311-7). U of NC Pr.
Spence, Lewis. Dictionary of Medieval Romance & Romance Writers. LC 76-27530. 1976. Repr. of 1913 ed. lib. bdg. 40.00 (ISBN 0-89341-050-0). Longwood Pr.
Studies in French Language & Mediaeval Literature. facs. ed. LC 70-84340. (Essay Index Reprint Ser). 1939. 24.25 (ISBN 0-8369-1109-1). Arno.
Thompson, P. M. The Shen Tzu Fragments. (London Oriental Ser.). (Illus.). 1979. 125.00x (ISBN 0-19-713579-X). Oxford U Pr.
Thomson, R. M., ed. The Chronicle of the Election of Hugh, Abbot of Bury St. Edmunds & Later Bishop of Ely. (Oxford Medieval Texts Ser). 244p. 1974. 34.50x (ISBN 0-19-822227-0). Oxford U Pr.
Tupper, Frederick. Types of Society in Medieval Literature. (English Literary Reference Ser). Repr. of 1926 ed. 9.00 (ISBN 0-384-61990-8). Johnson Repr.
Van Duzee, Mabel. A Medieval Romance of Friendship: Eger & Grime. LC 67-3001. (Essays in Literature & Criticism Ser.: No. 2). 198p. 1972. lib. bdg. 23.50 (ISBN 0-8337-3614-0). B Franklin.
Waldron, R. A., ed. Sir Gawain & the Green Knight. LC 75-129568. (York Medieval Texts Ser). 1970. text ed. 9.95 (ISBN 0-8101-0327-3). Northwestern U Pr.
Wallace-Hadrill, J. M., tr. The Fourth Book of the Chronicle of Fredegar with Its Continuations. LC 80-28086. (Medieval Classics Ser.). (Illus.). lxvii, 137p. 1981. Repr. of 1960 ed. lib. bdg. 27.50x (ISBN 0-313-22741-1, WAFRE). Greenwood.
Walpole, Ronald N. An Anonymous Old French Translation of the Pseudo-Turpin "Chronicle". 1979. 18.00 (ISBN 0-910956-68-5). Medieval Acad.
Walsh, James J. A Golden Treasury of Medieval Literature. LC 73-11328. 1973. lib. bdg. 25.00 (ISBN 0-8414-9385-5). Folcroft.
Wright, Thomas. Essays on Subjects Connected with the Literature, Popular Superstitions, & History of England in the Middle Ages, 2 vols. LC 70-80262. (Research & Source Works Ser.: No. 404). 1970. Repr. of 1846 ed. lib. bdg. 36.00 (ISBN 0-8337-3889-5). B Franklin.

LITERATURE, MEDIEVAL-BIBLIOGRAPHY

Goldschmidt, E. P. Medieval Texts & Their First Appearance in Print. LC 68-54232. 1969. Repr. of 1943 ed. 9.50x (ISBN 0-8196-0226-4). Biblo.
Little, Andrew G. Initia Operum Latinorum, Quae Saeculis Treizieme Quatorzieme Quinzieme Attribuuntur, Secundum Ordinem Alphabeti Disposita. (Victoria Univ. of Manchester). 1904. 26.50 (ISBN 0-8337-2118-6). B Franklin.
Martin, Lynn S. King Arthur in the Middle Ages: A Topical Bibliography. LC 75-5133. (Reference Library of the Humanities: Vol. 15). 880p. 1975. lib. bdg. 70.00 (ISBN 0-8240-1097-3). Garland Pub.

LITERATURE, MEDIEVAL-DICTIONARIES, INDEXES, ETC.

Corbett, James A., ed. Catalog of Medieval & Renaissance Manuscripts of the University of Notre Dame. 1978. text ed. 25.00x (ISBN 0-268-00723-3). U of Notre Dame Pr.

LITERATURE, MEDIEVAL-HISTORY AND CRITICISM

Alexander, J. J. G. & Gibson, M. T., eds. Medieval Learning & Literature: Essays Presented to Richard William Hunt. (Illus.). 500p. 1976. 67.00x (ISBN 0-19-822402-8). Oxford U Pr.
Allen, Judson B. The Ethical Poetic of the Later Middle Ages: A Decorum of Convenient Discussion. 360p. 1981. 35.00x (ISBN 0-8020-2370-3). U of Toronto Pr.
Approaches to Medieval Romance. (YFS, No. 51). 1974. pap. 6.00 (ISBN 0-527-03205-0). Kraus Repr.
Bakere, Jane A. The Cornish Ordinalia: A Critical Study. 191p. 1980. text ed. 50.00x (ISBN 0-7083-0745-0). Verry.
Baldwin, C. S. Medieval Rhetoric & Poetic to 1400. 1959. 7.50 (ISBN 0-8446-1043-7). Peter Smith.
Baldwin, Charles S. Medieval Rhetoric & Poetic to Fourteen Hundred. LC 71-144865. xvii, 321p. 1972. Repr. of 1928 ed. 29.00 (ISBN 0-403-00852-2). Scholarly.
Barefield, James P., et al. Medieval & Other Studies: In Honor of Floyd Seyward Lear. (Rice University Studies: Vol. 60, No. 4). (Illus.). 111p. (Orig.). 1975. pap. 3.25x (ISBN 0-89263-222-4). Rice Univ.
Barto, P. S. Tannhauser & the Mountain of Venus: A Study in the Legend of the Germanic Paradise. 1977. lib. bdg. 59.95 (ISBN 0-8490-2731-4). Gordon Pr.
Benson, Larry D., ed. The Learned & the Lewed: Studies in Chaucer & Medieval Literature. LC 74-78719. (English Studies: No. 5). 448p. 1974. pap. 6.95x (ISBN 0-674-51888-8). Harvard U Pr.
Benson, Larry D & Leyerle, John, eds. Chivalric Literature: Essays on Relations Between Literature and Life in the Later Middle Ages. LC 80-17514. (Studies in Medieval Culture: XIV). (Illus.). 176p. (Orig.). 1980. 18.80 (ISBN 0-918720-08-7); pap. 10.80 (ISBN 0-918720-09-5). Medieval Inst.
Berington, Joseph. The Literary History of the Middle Ages: Comprehending an Account of the State of Learning, from the Close of the Reign of Augustus, to Its Revival in the 15th Century. 1977. Repr. of 1846 ed. lib. bdg. 45.00 (ISBN 0-8495-0326-4). Arden Lib.
Bethurum, Dorothy, ed. Critical Approaches to Medieval Literature. LC 60-13104. (Essays of the English Institute Ser.). 1960. 15.00x (ISBN 0-231-02417-7). Columbia U Pr.
Boyce, Gray C., compiled by. Literature of Medieval History: 1930-1975: a Supplement to Louis John Paetow's "Guide to the Study of Medieval History", 5 vols. LC 80-28773. 1981. lib. bdg. 595.00 (ISBN 0-527-10462-0). Kraus Intl.
Boyd, James. Ulrich Fuetrer's Parzival: Material & Sources. 1977. lib. bdg. 59.95 (ISBN 0-8490-2782-9). Gordon Pr.
Bregy, Katherine M. From Dante to Jeanne D'Arc: Adventures in Medieval Life & Letters. LC 78-774. (Science & Culture Ser.). 1978. Repr. of 1933 ed. lib. bdg. 14.50x (ISBN 0-313-20290-7, BRFD). Greenwood.
Campbell, Anna M. Black Death & Men of Learning. LC 31-29792. Repr. of 1931 ed. 18.50 (ISBN 0-404-01368-6). AMS Pr.
Chaytor, Henry J. From Script to Print. LC 74-16460. 1974. Repr. of 1966 ed. lib. bdg. 20.00 (ISBN 0-685-51256-8). Folcroft.
Clements, Robert J. & Gibaldi, Joseph. The Anatomy of the Novella: The European Tale Collection from Boccaccio & Chaucer to Cervantes. LC 76-52548. 1977. 20.00x (ISBN 0-8147-1369-6); pap. 9.00x (ISBN 0-8147-1370-X). NYU Pr.
Coleman, Janet. Medieval Readers & Writers: Literature & Society, 1350-1400. 320p. 1981. 25.00x (ISBN 0-231-05364-9). Columbia U Pr.
Curtius, E. R. European Literature & the Latin Middle Ages. Trask, Willard R., tr. LC 52-10619. (Bollingen Ser., Vol. 36). 682p. 1953. 36.00 (ISBN 0-691-09739-9); pap. 8.50 (ISBN 0-691-01793-X). Princeton U Pr.
Davidson, Clifford, ed. Drama in the Middle Ages: Essays from Comparative Drama. (AMS Studies in the Middle Ages). 380p. 1981. 24.50 (ISBN 0-404-61431-0). AMS Pr.
Dronke, P. The Medieval Lyric. 1978. 28.50 (ISBN 0-521-21944-2); pap. 8.95x (ISBN 0-521-29319-7). Cambridge U Pr.
Eckhardt, Caroline D., ed. Essays in the Numerical Criticism of Medieval Literature. LC 76-55822. (Illus.). 240p. 1979. 17.50 (ISBN 0-8387-2019-6). Bucknell U Pr.
Edwardes, Marian. Summary of the Literatures of Modern Europe from the Origins to 1400. LC 7-20970. 1968. Repr. of 1907 ed. 30.00 (ISBN 0-527-26400-8). Kraus Repr.
Ferrante, Joan M. Woman As Image in Medieval Literature: From the Twelfth Century to Dante. LC 74-26652. 166p. 1975. 12.00x (ISBN 0-231-03929-8). Columbia U Pr.
Ferrante, Joan M. & Economou, George D., eds. In Pursuit of Perfection: Courtly Love in Medieval Literature. LC 74-80596. 1975. 15.00 (ISBN 0-8046-9092-8, Natl U). Kennikat.
Fisher, John H., ed. The Medieval Literature of Western Europe: A Review of Research, Mainly 1930-1960. LC 66-22346. 1966. 12.50x (ISBN 0-8147-0150-7). NYU Pr.
Fleming, John V. An Introduction to the Franciscan Literature of the Middle Ages. 1977. 10.95 (ISBN 0-8199-0651-4). Franciscan Herald.
Fletcher, Robert. Arthurian Material in the Chronicles of Great Britain & France. LC 68-2114. (Arthurian Legend & Literature Ser., No. 1). 1969. Repr. of 1906 ed. lib. bdg. 51.95 (ISBN 0-8383-0551-2). Haskell.
Fletcher, Robert H. Arthurian Material in the Chronicles, Especially Those of Great Britain & France... Expanded by a Bibliography & Critical Essay for the Period 1905-1965 by Roger Sherman Loomis. new ed. LC 66-20679. 344p. 1973. lib. bdg. 28.50 (ISBN 0-8337-1153-9). B Franklin.
Flinn, John. Roman de Renart dans la Litterature Francaise et dans les Litteratures Etrangeres au Moyen Age. LC 65-3080. (Fr). 1964. 40.00x (ISBN 0-8020-7050-7). U of Toronto Pr.
Fraser, Russell. The Dark Ages & the Age of Gold. LC 70-29786. 472p. 1973. 28.50x (ISBN 0-691-06216-1). Princeton U Pr.
Friedman, John B. Orpheus in the Middle Ages. LC 71-111484. (Illus.). 1970. 12.50x (ISBN 0-674-64490-5). Harvard U Pr.
Goedicke, Hans. The Protocol of Neferyt. LC 76-47371. (Near East Studies). 1977. text ed. 14.00x (ISBN 0-8018-1905-9). Johns Hopkins.
Henderson, Ingeborg. Strickers Daniel Von Dem Bluhenden Tal: Welstruktur und Interpretation. viii, 206p. 1979. 21.00 (ISBN 90-272-0961-8, GLLM 1). Benjamins North Am.
Hexter, Ralph J. Equivocal Oaths & Ordeals in Medieval Literature. (LeBaron Russell Briggs Prize Honors Essays in English Ser: 1974). 70p. 1975. pap. text ed. 3.25x (ISBN 0-674-26036-8). Harvard U Pr.
Jackson, William T. Literature of the Middle Ages. LC 60-13153. 1960. 20.00x (ISBN 0-231-02429-0). Columbia U Pr.
--Medieval Literature: A History & a Guide. (Orig.). 1966. pap. 1.50 (ISBN 0-02-052290-8, Collier). Macmillan.
Ker, William P. The Dark Ages. LC 78-27533. 1979. Repr. of 1955 ed. lib. bdg. 22.50x (ISBN 0-313-20933-2, KEDA). Greenwood.
--The Dark Ages. LC 78-59027. 1979. Repr. of 1955 ed. 26.50 (ISBN 0-88355-700-2). Hyperion Conn.
Kilgour, Raymond L. The Decline of Chivalry, As Shown in the French Literature of the Late Middle Ages. 1937. 8.50 (ISBN 0-8446-1262-6). Peter Smith.
Knapp, Peggy A. & Stugrin, Michael A., eds. Assays: Critical Approaches to Medieval & Renaissance Texts, Vol. 1. LC 80-54059. 200p. 1981. 12.95x (ISBN 0-8229-3439-6). U of Pittsburgh Pr.
Kostelanetz, Richard, ed. Visual Literature Criticism: A New Collection. LC 79-18457. (Illus.). 194p. 1980. 12.50 (ISBN 0-8093-0950-5). S Ill U Pr.
Laistner, Max L. & King, H. H. Thought & Letters in Western Europe, A.D. 500 to 900. 2nd ed. 416p. 1966. 20.00x (ISBN 0-8014-0243-3); pap. 7.95 (ISBN 0-8014-9037-5, CP37). Cornell U Pr.
Lawrence, William W. Medieval Story & the Beginnings of the Social Ideals of English-Speaking People. 2nd ed. LC 63-11333. 1963. 10.50 (ISBN 0-8044-1535-8). Ungar.
Leclercq, Jean. Monks & Love in Twelfth-Century France: Psycho-Historical Essays. 156p. 1979. text ed. 28.50x (ISBN 0-19-822546-6). Oxford U Pr.
Lewis, Clive S. Discarded Image. LC 64-21555. (Orig.). 1968. 29.95 (ISBN 0-521-05551-2); pap. 7.50 (ISBN 0-521-09450-X). Cambridge U Pr.
Loomis, Laura A. Medieval Romance in England: A Study of the Sources and Analogues of the Non-Cyclic Metrical Romances. new ed. 1969. 23.50 (ISBN 0-8337-2144-5). B Franklin.
Lutz, Cora E. Essays on Manuscripts & Rare Books. (Illus.). 177p. (Orig.). 1975. 15.00 (ISBN 0-208-01513-2, Archon). Shoe String.
MacDowall, M. W. Epics & Romances of the Middle Ages. Anson, W. S., ed. LC 77-94600. 1979. Repr. of 1883 ed. lib. bdg. 50.00 (ISBN 0-89341-188-4). Longwood Pr.
Mohl, Ruth. Three Estates in Medieval & Renaissance Literature. LC 62-10897. 1962. 8.50 (ISBN 0-8044-2636-8). Ungar.
Murdoch, Brian O. The Recapitulated Fall: A Comparative Study in Medieval Literature. LC 73-91188. (Amsterdamer Publikationen Zur Sprache und Literatur: No. 11). 207p. (Orig.). 1974. pap. text ed. 20.00x (ISBN 90-6203-021-1). Humanities.
Patch, Howard R. Goddess Fortuna in Medieval Literature. 1968. Repr. lib. bdg. 13.00x (ISBN 0-374-96308-8). Octagon.
Pickering, F. P. Literature & Art in the Middle Ages. LC 79-102698. (Illus.). 1970. 17.95x (ISBN 0-87024-152-4). U of Miami Pr.
Preminger, Alex, et al, eds. Classical & Medieval Literary Criticism: Translations & Interpretations. LC 73-84722. 1974. 35.00 (ISBN 0-8044-3257-0). Ungar.
Quinn, Esther C. Quest of Seth for the Oil of Life. LC 62-18120. (Illus.). 1962. 10.00x (ISBN 0-226-70087-9). U of Chicago Pr.
Rand, Edward K. Founders of the Middle Ages. 1928. pap. 5.00 (ISBN 0-486-20369-7). Dover.
Rosenberg, Bruce A. & Mandel, Jerome, eds. Medieval Literature & Folklore Studies. LC 70-127053. 1971. 27.50 (ISBN 0-8135-0676-X). Rutgers U Pr.
Rothwell, W., et al. Studies in Medieval Literature and Languages. 404p. 1973. 51.00x (ISBN 0-7190-0550-7, Pub. by Manchester U Pr England). State Mutual Bk.
Ruggiers, Paul G. Versions of Medieval Comedy. LC 77-6384. 1977. pap. 5.95 (ISBN 0-8061-1438-X). U of Okla Pr.
Sackville-West, Edward. Inclinations. LC 76-55779. 1976. Repr. of 1949 ed. lib. bdg. 20.00 (ISBN 0-8414-7832-5). Folcroft.
Saintsbury, George E. Flourishing of Romance & the Rise of Allegory. LC 72-193752. 1907. lib. bdg. 35.00 (ISBN 0-8414-7519-9). Folcroft.
Schmidt, A. V. & Jacobs, Nicolas, eds. Medieval English Romances, Part 2. (London Medieval & Renaissance Ser.). 285p. 1981. text ed. 32.50x (ISBN 0-686-75481-6). Holmes & Meier.
Shackford, M. H., ed. Legends & Satires from Medieval Literature. 1977. lib. bdg. 59.95 (ISBN 0-8490-2144-8). Gordon Pr.
Shackford, Martha H. Legends & Satires from Medieval Literature. LC 77-7379. 1913. lib. bdg. 20.00 (ISBN 0-8414-7588-1). Folcroft.
Singleton, Charles S. An Essay on the Vita Nuova. LC 77-5263. 1977. pap. text ed. 5.00x (ISBN 0-8018-2004-9). Johns Hopkins.
Smith, Gregory G. The Transition Period. 1979. Repr. of 1927 ed. lib. bdg. 40.00 (ISBN 0-8414-8024-9). Folcroft.
Sola-Sole, Josep M., et al, eds. Studies in Honor of Tatiana Fotitch. 1973. 12.00 (ISBN 0-8132-0527-1). Cath U Pr.
Staines, David. Tennyson's Camelot: The Idylls of the King & Its Medieval Sources. 252p. 1981. text ed. 11.50x (ISBN 0-88920-115-3, Pub. by Laurier U Pr). Humanities.
Thiebaux, Marcelle. The Stag of Love: The Chase in Medieval Literature. LC 73-14396. (Illus.). 256p. 1974. 22.50x (ISBN 0-8014-0792-3). Cornell U Pr.
Tupper, Frederick. Types of Society in Medieval Literature. LC 67-29555. 1968. Repr. of 1926 ed. 7.00x (ISBN 0-8196-0212-4). Biblo.
Voigt, Max. Beitrage Zur Geschichte der Visionenliteratur Im Mittelalter. 21.50 (ISBN 0-384-64831-2); pap. 18.50 (ISBN 0-384-64830-4). Johnson Repr.
Wagner, W. Epics & Romances of the Middle Ages. Anson, W. S., ed. 1978. Repr. of 1892 ed. lib. bdg. 65.00 (ISBN 0-8492-2955-3). R West.
Walsh, James J. A Golden Treasury of Medieval Literature. LC 73-11328. 1973. lib. bdg. 25.00 (ISBN 0-8414-9385-5). Folcroft.
Yunck, John A. Lineage of Lady Meed: The Development of Mediaeval Venality-Satire. (Mediaeval Studies Ser.: No. 17). 1963. 12.95x (ISBN 0-268-00157-X). U of Notre Dame Pr.

LITERATURE, MEDIEVAL-TRANSLATIONS

see Translations-Literature, Medieval

LITERATURE, MODERN (COLLECTIONS)

Beckett, Samuel, et al. New Writing & Writers Thirteen. 1980. pap. 6.00 (ISBN 0-7145-3541-9). Riverrun NY.
Boll, Heinrich, et al. New Writing & Writers Fifteen. 1980. pap. 6.00 (ISBN 0-7145-3561-3). Riverrun NY.
Burroughs, William, et al. New Writing & Writers Sixteen. 1980. pap. 6.00 (ISBN 0-7145-3638-5). Riverrun NY.
Campbell, Kathleen W. Poems on Several Occasions Written in the 18th Century. 1971. Repr. of 1934 ed. 16.00 (ISBN 0-403-00543-4). Scholarly.
Carlsen, G. Robert. Perception: Themes in Literature. 3rd ed. Rothermich, John A., ed. (Themes & Writers Ser.). (Illus.). (gr. 8). 1979. text ed. 13.20 (ISBN 0-07-009855-7, W); resource guide 12.60 (ISBN 0-07-009856-5); tests 64.00 (ISBN 0-07-009857-3). McGraw.
Domandi, Agnes K., ed. Modern German Literature, 2 vols. LC 70-160436. (Library of Literary Criticism Ser.). Set. 55.00 (ISBN 0-8044-3075-6). Ungar.
The Faber Popular Reciter. 256p. 1979. 17.95 (ISBN 0-571-11287-0, Pub. by Faber & Faber); pap. 7.95 (ISBN 0-571-11339-7). Merrimack Bk Serv.
Gosse, Edmund. Aspects & Impressions. 1979. Repr. of 1928 ed. lib. bdg. 20.00 (ISBN 0-8495-2027-4). Arden Lib.
Gosse, Edmund W. Aspects & Impressions. LC 73-145048. 1971. Repr. of 1922 ed. 9.00 (ISBN 0-403-00992-8). Scholarly.

Hudson, Anne, ed. Selections from English Wycliffite Writings. LC 77-1506. 234p. 1981. pap. 17.95 (ISBN 0-521-28258-6). Cambridge U Pr.

Johnson, Gertrude E. Modern Literature for Oral Interpretation. 1926. Repr. 20.00 (ISBN 0-8274-2752-2). R West.

Kazin, Alfred. The Inmost Leaf: A Selection of Essays. LC 73-17921. 273p. Repr. of 1955 ed. lib. bdg. 15.75x (ISBN 0-8371-7281-0, KAIN). Greenwood.

Lewis, Sinclair. Free Air. 1971. Repr. of 1919 ed. 25.00 (ISBN 0-403-01071-3). Scholarly.

Magill, Frank N. Magill's Literary Annual 1981: 1981, 2 vols. Magill, G. N., ed. LC 77-99209. 900p. 1981. 50.00 (ISBN 0-89356-281-5). Salem Pr.

Pattison, Walter T. & Bleznick, Donald W., eds. Representative Spanish Authors, Vol. 1: From the Middle Ages Through the Eighteenth Century. 3rd ed. 1971. text ed. 15.95x (ISBN 0-19-501326-3). Oxford U Pr.

Rice, Cale Y. Selected Plays & Poems. LC 27-16490. xviii, 786p. 1972. Repr. of 1926 ed. 45.00 (ISBN 0-403-01174-4). Scholarly.

Rochester, John W. Collected Works of John Wilmont, Second Earl of Rochester. 1971. Repr. of 1926 ed. 32.00 (ISBN 0-403-01184-1). Scholarly.

Schulte, Rainer, ed. Contemporary Writing from the Continents: Retrospective. 450p. 1981. pap. 20.00 (ISBN 0-939378-01-9). Mundus Artium.

Smollett, Tobias. Shakespeare Head Edition of Smollett's Novel, 11 Vols. 1971. Repr. of 1925 ed. Set. 345.00 (ISBN 0-403-01220-1). Scholarly.

Stern, Richard. Honey & Wax: Pleasures & Powers of Narrative. LC 66-13889. 1969. pap. 3.95 (ISBN 0-226-77313-2, P346, Phoen). U of Chicago Pr.

Stern, Richard, ed. Honey & Wax: Pleasures & Powers of Narrative. LC 66-13889. (Illus.). 1966. 10.00x (ISBN 0-226-77312-4). U of Chicago Pr.

Van Der Zee, John & Jacobson, Boyd. Imagined City: San Francisco in the Minds of Its Writers. Larrick, Gail, ed. LC 80-65977. (Illus.). 96p. (Orig.). 1980. pap. 4.95 (ISBN 0-89395-043-2). Cal Living Bks.

Varady, Tibor, et al. New Writing & Writers Eighteen. 1980. pap. 6.00 (ISBN 0-7145-3815-9). Riverrun NY.

White, James P., ed. New & Experimental Literature. 1975. pap. 5.95 (ISBN 0-916092-04-6). Tex Ctr Writers.

White, Margaret B. & Quigley, Robert N., eds. How the Other Third Lives. LC 77-22499. 1977. 9.95 (ISBN 0-88344-190-X); pap. 4.95 (ISBN 0-88344-191-8). Orbis Bks.

LITERATURE, MODERN (COLLECTIONS)-15TH AND 16TH CENTURIES

Cullen, Patrick & Roche, Thomas P., Jr., eds. Spenser Studies: A Renaissance Poetry Annual, Vol. II. (Illus.). 320p. 1981. 24.95x (ISBN 0-8229-3433-7). U of Pittsburgh Pr.

Erasmus. The Collected Works of Erasmus: Literary & Educational Writings, Vol. 23 & Vol. 24. Thompson, Craig R., ed. LC 78-6904. (Antibarbari, De Copia, De Rationae Studii, Parabolae). 1978. 45.00x (ISBN 0-8020-5395-5). U of Toronto Pr.

Goldberg, Jonathan. Endlesse Worke: Spenser & the Structure of Discourse. LC 81-4906. 208p. 1981. text ed. 14.50x (ISBN 0-8018-2608-X). Johns Hopkins.

Haydn, Hiram C. & Nelson, John C., eds. Renaissance Treasury. LC 69-10105. 1969. Repr. of 1953 ed. lib. bdg. 22.25x (ISBN 0-8371-0100-X, HARW). Greenwood.

Quinones, Ricardo J. The Renaissance Discovery of Time. LC 70-182815. (Studies in Comparative Literature: No. 31). 979p. 1972. 25.00x (ISBN 0-674-76025-5). Harvard U Pr.

Ross, James B. & McLaughlin, Mary M., eds. Portable Renaissance Reader. rev. ed. (Viking Portable Library: No. 61). (Orig.). 1958. 10.00 (ISBN 0-670-59411-3). Viking Pr.

--Portable Renaissance Reader. (Viking Portable Library: No. 61). 1977. pap. 5.95 (ISBN 0-14-015061-7). Penguin.

Shaaber, M. A. Sixteenth Century Imprints in Libraries of the University of Pennsylvania. (Haney Foundation Ser). 672p. 1976. 16.00x (ISBN 0-8122-7698-1). U of Pa Pr.

Stabler, Arthur, ed. Four French Renaissance Plays. (Illus.). 1978. pap. 10.00 (ISBN 0-87422-014-9). Wash St U Pr.

LITERATURE, MODERN (COLLECTIONS)-17TH CENTURY

Schelling, Felix E., ed. A Book of Seventeenth Century Lyrics. 1977. Repr. of 1899 ed. lib. bdg. 25.00 (ISBN 0-8492-2473-X). R West.

LITERATURE, MODERN (COLLECTIONS)-20TH CENTURY

Abood, Edward F. Underground Man. LC 72-97331. 189p. 1973. pap. 5.95 (ISBN 0-88316-048-X). Chandler & Sharp.

Bishop, Elizabeth & Brasil, Emanuel, eds. An Anthology of Twentieth-Century Brazilian Poetry. Blackburn, Paul, et al, trs. from Port. LC 75-184359. 224p. (Orig.). 1972. pap. 7.50x (ISBN 0-8195-6023-5, Pub. by Wesleyan U Pr). Columbia U Pr.

Bloom, Edward A. & Bloom, Lillian D., eds. The Variety of Fiction: A Critical Anthology. LC 75-79102. 1969. pap. 7.50 (ISBN 0-672-63137-7). Odyssey Pr.

Bowler, Christine, et al. Red Dust One: New Writing. LC 78-127954. 180p. 1971. 5.25 (ISBN 0-87376-016-6); pap. 3.00 (ISBN 0-87376-017-4). Red Dust.

Burroughs, W., et al. New Writing & Writers, No. 16. (Illus.). 1979. pap. text ed. 11.50x (ISBN 0-7145-3635-0). Humanities.

Dobie, B., et al. Growing up in Texas. (Illus.). 170p. 1972. 7.95 (ISBN 0-88426-000-3). Encino Pr.

Eliot, T. S., et al. Poetry in Prose. LC 78-64019. (Des Imagistes: Literature of the Imagist Movement). Repr. of 1921 ed. 11.00 (ISBN 0-404-17090-0). AMS Pr.

Hanes, E. & McCoy, M. Readings in Contemporary Literature. Repr. of 1936 ed. lib. bdg. 12.50 (ISBN 0-8414-4989-9). Folcroft.

Harrison, Gilbert A., ed. The Critic As Artist: Essays on Books 1920-1970. 464p. 1972. 12.00 (ISBN 0-87140-544-X); pap. 3.95 (ISBN 0-87140-060-X). Liveright.

Hartmann, Sadakichi. Collected Works, 6 vols. 600.00 (ISBN 0-87968-890-4). Gordon Pr.

Katz, William A. & Gaherty, Sherry, eds. Library Lit. Four: The Best of 1973. 1974. 13.00 (ISBN 0-8108-0702-5). Scarecrow.

Kostelanetz, Richard, ed. Breakthrough Fictioneers. LC 72-75710. (Illus.). 1973. 12.45 (ISBN 0-87110-087-8); pap. 3.95 (ISBN 0-87110-088-6). Ultramarine Pub.

Kumanitu. 1974. pap. 2.50 (ISBN 0-916912-17-5, Bonewhistle Pr). Hellcoal Pr.

Laqueur, Walter. The Guerrilla Reader: A Historical Anthology. 1977. pap. 5.95 (ISBN 0-452-00460-8, F460, Mer). NAL.

Laughlin, James & Glassgold, Peter, eds. New Directions in Prose & Poetry 31. LC 37-1751. 192p. 1975. 9.95 (ISBN 0-8112-0587-8); pap. 3.75 (ISBN 0-8112-0588-6, NDP404). New Directions.

Laughlin, James, et al, eds. New Directions in Prose & Poetry 28. LC 37-1751. (Prose & Poetry Ser). 192p. 1974. 9.95 (ISBN 0-8112-0525-8); pap. 2.95 (ISBN 0-8112-0526-6, NDP371). New Directions.

--New Directions in Prose & Poetry 30. LC 37-1751. 192p. 1975. 9.95 (ISBN 0-8112-0572-X); pap. 3.75 (ISBN 0-8112-0573-8, NDP395). New Directions.

Magill, Frank N. Survey of Contemporary Literature, 12 vols. new ed. LC 77-79874. 1977. 320.00 set (ISBN 0-89356-050-2). Salem Pr.

Mueller, Lothar W., ed. Harlo's Anthology of Modern-Day Poets & Authors 1974. LC 74-27876. 152p. 1974. 6.00 (ISBN 0-8187-0016-5). Harlo Pr.

Mulisch, H., et al, eds. New Writing & Writers, Vol. 18. 1981. text ed. 15.50x (ISBN 0-7145-3773-X, Pub. by Calder England). Humanities.

New Writers, No. 1. Incl. Catfish. Lange, Monique & Burns, Alan.; Scala Scare. Buzzati, Dino. 1967. 4.50 (ISBN 0-7145-0397-5); pap. 2.45 (ISBN 0-7145-0397-5). Transatlantic.

New Writers, No. 2. Incl. My Brown Friend. Vestdijk, Simon; Return. Johnstone, Keith; Lovers. Bulatovic, Miodrag; The Old Tune. Pinget, Robert. 4.50 (ISBN 0-685-24472-5); pap. 2.45 (ISBN 0-685-24473-3). Transatlantic.

New Writers, No. 3. Incl. Four Stories. Trocchi, Alexander; Texts. Rawson, Nick; Four Poems. Belles, Sinclair; Long Crawl Through Time. Mercer, David. 4.50 (ISBN 0-7145-0400-9); pap. 2.45 (ISBN 0-7145-0400-9). Transatlantic.

New Writers, No. 4. Incl. Plays & Happenings. Nimma, E. C., et al.. 4.50 (ISBN 0-7145-0402-5). Transatlantic.

New Writers, No. 5. Incl. Unlikely Meeting. Castelain, Daniel; Which Land Is Mine. Nour, Nazli; Before the Undertaker Comes. Naish, Alex. 4.50 (ISBN 0-7145-0404-1); pap. 2.45 (ISBN 0-7145-0405-X). Transatlantic.

New Writers, No. 6. Incl. Infatuation. Burns, Carol; Road. Dooley, J. A; Excusable Vengence. Shuttle, Penelope. 4.50 (ISBN 0-7145-0406-8); pap. 2.45 (ISBN 0-7145-0407-6). Transatlantic.

Norman, C. H. Revolutionary Spirit in Modern Literature & Drama & the Class War in Europe: 1918-36. 1937. lib. bdg. 6.50 (ISBN 0-8414-6659-9). Folcroft.

Quinn, Kerker & Shattuck, Charles, eds. Accent Anthology: Selections from Accent, a Quarterly of New Literature, 1940-1945. facsimile ed. LC 70-156601. (Essay Index Reprint Ser). Repr. of 1946 ed. 35.00 (ISBN 0-8369-2302-2). Arno.

Sklar, Morty & Mulac, Jim, eds. Editor's Choice: Literature & Graphics from the U. S. Small Press, 1965-1977. LC 79-64861. (Contemporary Anthology Ser.: No. 2). (Illus.). 501p. 1980. 14.50 (ISBN 0-930370-05-8); pap. 9.50 (ISBN 0-930370-04-X); signed, numbered ed. 25.00 (ISBN 0-930370-06-6). Spirit That Moves.

Thorburn, David, ed. Initiation: Stories & Short Novels on Three Themes. 2nd ed. 1976. pap. text ed. 9.95 (ISBN 0-15-541512-3, HC). HarBraceJ.

Weinstock, E. B. & Arthur, Robert P. New Gothic Restaurant. 1978. pap. text ed. 9.25 (ISBN 0-8191-0369-1). U Pr of Amer.

LITERATURE, MODERN-ADDRESSES, ESSAYS, LECTURES

Beach, Joseph W. American Fiction, Nineteen Twenty to Nineteen Forty. LC 60-8197. 1972. pap. text ed. 3.25x (ISBN 0-689-70289-2, 172). Atheneum.

Bennett, Arnold. Books & Persons: Being Comments on a Past Epoch, 1908-1911. LC 69-10069. 1969. Repr. of 1917 ed. lib. bdg. 17.00x (ISBN 0-8371-0018-6, BEBP). Greenwood.

Boyle, Edward. Biographical Essays, 1790-1890. facs. ed. LC 68-54331. (Essay Index Reprint Ser). 1936. 16.00 (ISBN 0-8369-0237-8). Arno.

Brod, Richard I. & Fisher, Dexter, eds. Profession Eighty. 60p. (Orig.). 1980. pap. 4.00x (ISBN 0-87352-315-6). Modern Lang.

Canby, Henry S. Seven Years Harvest. LC 66-25902. Repr. of 1936 ed. 12.00 (ISBN 0-8046-0065-1). Kennikat.

Chapman, John J. Emerson & Other Essays. LC 75-108126. 1970. Repr. of 1899 ed. 19.50 (ISBN 0-404-00619-1). AMS Pr.

Clark, Barrett H. Intimate Portraits. LC 77-93059. (Essay & General Literature Index Reprint Ser). 1970. Repr. of 1951 ed. 12.00 (ISBN 0-8046-0672-2). Kennikat.

Cook, Edward T. Literary Recreations. facs. ed. LC 68-54340. (Essay Index Reprint Ser). 1918. 16.00 (ISBN 0-8369-0331-5). Arno.

Courtney, William L. Development of Maurice Maeterlinck. LC 74-118408. 1971. Repr. of 1904 ed. 12.50 (ISBN 0-8046-1185-8). Kennikat.

Crawford, Virginia M. Studies in Foreign Literature. LC 70-103221. 1970. Repr. of 1899 ed. 12.50 (ISBN 0-8046-0858-X). Kennikat.

De Casseres, Benjamin. Forty Immortals. 59.95 (ISBN 0-8490-0184-6). Gordon Pr.

Dowden, Edward. Essays, Modern & Elizabethan. facs. ed. LC 71-117784. (Essay Index Reprint Ser). 1910. 19.50 (ISBN 0-8369-1647-6). Arno.

Drake, William A., ed. American Criticism, Nineteen Twenty-Six. facs. ed. LC 67-28734. (Essay Index Reprint Ser). 1926. 18.00 (ISBN 0-8369-0389-7). Arno.

Elton, Oliver. Essays & Addresses. facs. ed. LC 77-86746. (Essay Index Reprint Ser). 1939. 17.00 (ISBN 0-8369-1179-2). Arno.

--Essays & Addresses. LC 72-193944. 1939. lib. bdg. 14.00 (ISBN 0-8414-3996-6). Folcroft.

--Essays & Addresses. 1978. Repr. of 1939 ed. lib. bdg. 25.00 (ISBN 0-8495-1310-3). Arden Lib.

Enright, D. J. Literature for Man's Sake. LC 72-192045. 1955. lib. bdg. 15.00 (ISBN 0-8414-3971-0). Folcroft.

Frye, Prosser H. Literary Reviews & Criticisms. LC 68-59378. 1968. Repr. of 1908 ed. 8.50 (ISBN 0-87752-040-2). Gordian.

Garzilli, Enrico. Circles Without Center: Paths to the Discovery & Creation of Self in Modern Literature. LC 77-182814. 260p. 1972. 10.00x (ISBN 0-674-13165-7). Harvard U Pr.

Goodheart, Eugene. Cult of the Ego: The Self in Modern Literature. LC 68-9847. 1968. 11.00x (ISBN 0-226-30286-5). U of Chicago Pr.

Gosse, Edmund W. Aspects & Impressions. LC 77-105016. (Essay Index Reprint Ser). 1922. 17.00 (ISBN 0-8369-1469-4). Arno.

--Critical Kit-Kats. 1971. Repr. of 1914 ed. 14.00 (ISBN 0-403-00993-6). Scholarly.

Grant, Percy S. Essays. facs. ed. LC 68-22916. (Essay Index Reprint Ser). 1968. Repr. of 1922 ed. 13.00 (ISBN 0-8369-0492-3). Arno.

Grimm, Herman. Literature. facsimile ed. LC 76-37520. (Essay Index Reprint Ser). Repr. of 1885 ed. 18.00 (ISBN 0-8369-2551-3). Arno.

Guthrie, William N. Modern Poet Prophets. 1979. Repr. of 1897 ed. lib. bdg. 30.00 (ISBN 0-8495-2032-0). Arden Lib.

Hackett, Francis. On Judging Books: In General & in Particular. facsimile ed. LC 79-156657. (Essay Index Reprint Ser.). Repr. of 1947 ed. 18.00 (ISBN 0-8369-2400-2). Arno.

Hart, Walter M. Five Galey Lectures Nineteen Forty Seven to Nineteen Fifty Four. LC 72-13954. 1954. lib. bdg. 20.00 (ISBN 0-8414-1315-0). Folcroft.

Henderson, Archibald. Interpreters of Life & the Modern Spirit. facs. ed. LC 68-54348. (Essay Index Reprint Ser.). 1911. 17.00 (ISBN 0-8369-0534-2). Arno.

Howe, Irving. World More Attractive. LC 70-134096. (Essay Index Reprint Ser). 1963. 18.00 (ISBN 0-8369-1958-0). Arno.

Hyman, Stanley, ed. William Troy: Selected Essays. 1967. 19.00 (ISBN 0-8135-0553-4). Rutgers U Pr.

James, Henry. Essays in London & Elsewhere. LC 72-658. (Essay Index Reprint Ser.). Repr. of 1893 ed. 18.00 (ISBN 0-8369-2796-6). Arno.

Lynd, Robert. Books & Writers. LC 71-105028. (Essay Index Reprint Ser). 1952. 24.00 (ISBN 0-8369-1525-9). Arno.

--Old & New Masters. LC 79-111845. (Essay Index Reprint Ser). 1919. 16.00 (ISBN 0-8369-1616-6). Arno.

Monkhouse, Allan. Books & Plays. LC 72-292. (Essay Index Ser.). Repr. of 1894 ed. 15.00 (ISBN 0-8369-2807-5). Arno.

Murry, John M. Aspects of Literature. LC 79-128280. (Essay Index Reprint Ser). 1920. 16.00 (ISBN 0-8369-1838-X). Arno.

--Countries of the Mind: Essays in Literary Criticism, 1st Ser. facsimile ed. LC 68-22111. (Essay Index Reprint Ser). 1931. 14.00 (ISBN 0-8369-0729-9). Arno.

--Countries of the Mind: Essays in Literary Criticism, 2nd Ser. facs. ed. LC 68-22112. (Essay Index Reprint Ser). 1931. 14.75 (ISBN 0-8369-0730-2). Arno.

Nicholson, Hubert. A Voyage to Wonderland &Other Essays. 1977. Repr. of 1947 ed. lib. bdg. 20.00 (ISBN 0-8414-6308-5). Folcroft.

Norman, C. H. Revolutionary Spirit in Modern Literature & Drama. LC 74-95335. 1971. Repr. of 1937 ed. 9.50 (ISBN 0-8046-1346-X). Kennikat.

Pater, Walter. Uncollected Essays. LC 72-192016. 1903. lib. bdg. 20.00 (ISBN 0-8414-9201-8). Folcroft.

Pattee, Fred L. Tradition & Jazz. facs. ed. LC 68-22937. (Essay Index Reprint Ser). 1968. Repr. of 1925 ed. 18.00 (ISBN 0-8369-0776-0). Arno.

Pritchett, Victor S. Books in General. LC 70-110378. 258p. Repr. of 1953 ed. lib. bdg. 15.00x (ISBN 0-8371-4582-1, PRBG). Greenwood.

--In My Good Books. LC 79-105823. 1970. Repr. of 1942 ed. 10.00 (ISBN 0-8046-0971-3). Kennikat.

Read, Herbert E. In Defence of Shelley & Other Essays. facs. ed. LC 68-26470. (Essay Index Reprint Ser). 1968. Repr. of 1936 ed. 16.00 (ISBN 0-8369-0813-9). Arno.

Repplier, Agnes. Points of View. 1979. Repr. of 1895 ed. lib. bdg. 20.00 (ISBN 0-8495-4605-2). Arden Lib.

Robertson, John G. Essays & Addresses on Literature. facs. ed. LC 68-26471. (Essay Index Reprint Ser). 1968. Repr. of 1935 ed. 16.00 (ISBN 0-8369-0828-7). Arno.

Rolland, Romain. Compagnons de Route. 256p. 1961. 4.95 (ISBN 0-686-55243-1). French & Eur.

Romains, Jules. Saints de Notre Calendrier. 256p. 1952. 4.95 (ISBN 0-686-55290-3). French & Eur.

Sherman, Stuart P. On Contemporary Literature. LC 75-127905. Repr. of 1917 ed. 12.50 (ISBN 0-404-05958-9). AMS Pr.

Smith, Logan P. Reperusals & Re-Collections. facs. ed. LC 68-29249. (Essay Index Reprint Ser). 1968. Repr. of 1937 ed. 18.00 (ISBN 0-8369-0884-8). Arno.

Sollers, Philippe. Logiques. 1968. 15.95 (ISBN 0-686-55013-7). French & Eur.

Strachey, Lytton. Books & Characters: French & English. 1976. lib. bdg. 59.95 (ISBN 0-8490-1535-9). Gordon Pr.

Tate, Allen. On the Limits of Poetry: 1928-1948. LC 74-105042. (Essay Index Reprint Ser). 1948. 23.00 (ISBN 0-8369-1484-8). Arno.

Thomson, G. W. Mirrors of Modernity (Goethe, Dostoyevsky, Whitman, Ibsen, Strindberg) LC 73-13843. 1974. Repr. of 1933 ed. lib. bdg. 20.00 (ISBN 0-8414-8523-2). Folcroft.

Torrey, Bradford. Friends on the Shelf. LC 70-108709. (Essay & General Literature Index Reprint Ser). 1970. Repr. of 1906 ed. 13.00 (ISBN 0-8046-0927-6). Kennikat.

Trilling, Lionel. The Liberal Imagination: Essays on Literature & Society. 1979. 10.00 (ISBN 0-15-151197-7). HarBraceJ.

Weisinger, Herbert. Agony & the Triumph: Papers on the Use & Abuse of Myth. x, 283p. 1964. 5.00 (ISBN 0-87013-081-1). Mich St U Pr.

Whibley, Charles. Literary Studies. facsimile ed. LC 70-90693. (Essay Index Reprint Ser). 1919. 19.50 (ISBN 0-8369-1238-1). Arno.

Wilson, Edmund. Shores of Light. 814p. 1952. pap. 9.95 (ISBN 0-374-50616-7). FS&G.

LITERATURE, MODERN-BIBLIOGRAPHY

Dobelis, M. C. Anonymous & Pseudononymous Publications of Twentieth Century Authors. Date not set. 16.95x (ISBN 0-918230-06-3). Barnstable.

Drummond, H. J., compiled by. A Short-Title Catalogue of Books Printed on the Continent of Europe, Fifteen Hundred to Sixteen Hundred, in Aberdeen University Library. 326p. 1979. text ed. 65.00x (ISBN 0-19-714106-4). Oxford U Pr.
Freeman, Ronald E., ed. Bibliographies of Studies in Victorian Literature: For the Ten Years 1965-1974. LC 79-8838. 1981. 47.50 (ISBN 0-404-18032-9). AMS Pr.
Hatzfeld, Helmut A. A Critical Bibliography of the New Stylistics Applied to the Romance Literatures, 1900-1952. (North Carolina Studies in Comparative Literature Ser: No. 5). 1971. Repr. of 1953 ed. 18.50 (ISBN 0-384-21770-2). Johnson Repr.
Krawitz, Henry. A Post-Symbolist Bibliography. LC 73-1181. 1973. 10.00 (ISBN 0-8108-0594-4). Scarecrow.
Paris. Universite. Bibliotheque. Catalogue De la Reserve Seizieme Siecle, De la Bibliotheque De l'Universite De Paris 1501-1540, 2 vols. Beauliaux, Charles, ed. LC 68-58474. (Bibliography & Reference Ser.: No. 258). (Fr). 1969. Repr. of 1910 ed. 39.00 (ISBN 0-8337-0204-1). B Franklin.
Shaaber, M. A. Sixteenth Century Imprints in Libraries of the University of Pennsylvania. (Haney Foundation Ser). 672p. 1976. 16.00x (ISBN 0-8122-7698-1). U of Pa Pr.
Slack, Robert C., ed. Bibliographies of Studies in Victorian Literature: For the Ten Years 1955-1964. LC 79-8839. Repr. of 1967 ed. 47.50 (ISBN 0-404-18033-7). AMS Pr.
Stonehill, C. A. & Stonehill, H. W. Bibliographies of Modern Authors: Second Series. LC 72-6241. 1925. lib. bdg. 17.50 (ISBN 0-8414-0091-1). Folcroft.

LITERATURE, MODERN–BIOBIBLIOGRAPHY

Kunitz, Stanley J. & Colby, Vineta, eds. European Authors, One Thousand to Nineteen Hundred. (Illus.). 1967. 28.00 (ISBN 0-8242-0013-6). Wilson.
Kunitz, Stanley J. & Haycraft, Howard, eds. Twentieth Century Authors. (Illus.). 1942. 35.00 (ISBN 0-8242-0049-7); 1st suppl. 1955. 27.00 (ISBN 0-8242-0050-0). Wilson.

LITERATURE, MODERN–DICTIONARIES, INDEXES, ETC.

Beckson, Karl & Ganz, Arthur. Literary Terms: A Dictionary. rev. ed. 228p. 1975. 10.00 (ISBN 0-374-18800-9); pap. 3.95 (ISBN 0-374-51225-6). FS&G.
Brunton, David W., ed. Index to the Contemporary Scene, Vol. 2. xvi, 120p. 1975. 28.00 (ISBN 0-8103-1057-0). Gale.
Concise Encyclopedia of Modern World Literature. 20.00x (ISBN 0-8277-0358-9). British Bk Ctr.
Tennyson, G. B. & Tennyson, Elizabeth J., eds. Index to Nineteenth-Century Fiction: 1945-1975, Vols. 1-30. 1978. 21.50x (ISBN 0-520-03334-5). U of Cal Pr.

LITERATURE, MODERN–HISTORY AND CRITICISM

see also Baroque Literature–History and Criticism

Artz, Frederick B. From the Renaissance to Romanticism: Trends in Style in Art, Literature, & Music 1300-1830. LC 62-20021. 1962. 12.50x (ISBN 0-226-02837-2). U of Chicago Pr.
--From the Renaissance to Romanticism: Trends in Style, in Art, Literature & Music, 1300-1830. LC 62-20021. 1962. pap. 3.95 (ISBN 0-226-02838-0, P186, Phoen). U of Chicago Pr.
Baldwin, C. S. Renaissance Literary Theory & Practice. 1959. 7.50 (ISBN 0-8446-1042-9). Peter Smith.
Bartlett, Lee. The Beats: Essays in Criticism. LC 80-28179. 205p. 1981. lib. bdg. 19.95x (ISBN 0-89950-026-9). McFarland & Co.
Bate, Walter J. Criticism: The Major Texts. enl. ed. 1970. text ed. 19.95 (ISBN 0-15-516148-2, HC). HarBraceJ.
Baudelaire, Charles P. Selected Critical Studies of Baudelaire. Parmee, D., ed. LC 76-29452. Repr. of 1949 ed. 21.00 (ISBN 0-404-15300-3). AMS Pr.
Boyd, Ernest. Studies from Ten Literatures. LC 68-16289. 1968. Repr. of 1925 ed. 12.50 (ISBN 0-8046-0038-4). Kennikat.
Boyd, Ernest A. Studies from Ten Literatures. (English Literary Reference Ser). Repr. of 1927 ed. 14.00 (ISBN 0-384-05330-0). Johnson Repr.
--Studies from Ten Literatures. facs. ed. LC 68-20287. (Essay Index Reprint Ser). 1925. 18.00 (ISBN 0-8369-0236-X). Arno.
Bradbury, Malcolm & McFarlane, James, eds. Modernism: 1890-1930. (Pelican Guides to European Literature). 1978. Repr. of 1974 ed. text ed. 28.50x (ISBN 0-391-00818-8). Humanities.
Brooks, Peter. The Melodramatic Imagination: Balzac, Henry James, Melodrama & the Mode of Excesss. LC 75-43305. 1976. 20.00x (ISBN 0-300-02001-5). Yale U Pr.
Buck, Philo M. Social Forces in Modern Literature. LC 76-58444. 1913. lib. bdg. 12.50 (ISBN 0-8414-1651-6). Folcroft.
--Social Forces in Modern Literature. 1979. Repr. of 1913 ed. lib. bdg. 25.00 (ISBN 0-8495-0393-0). Arden Lib.
Chesterton, G. K. Handful of Authors. Collins, Dorothy, ed. Repr. of 1953 ed. 12.00 (ISBN 0-527-16600-6). Kraus Repr.
Chiari, Joseph. Realism & Imagination. LC 74-131248. 1970. Repr. of 1960 ed. text ed. 9.00 (ISBN 0-87752-019-4). Gordian.
Colum, Mary. From These Roots: The Ideas That Have Made Modern Literature. LC 67-25260. Repr. of 1937 ed. 13.50 (ISBN 0-8046-0084-8). Kennikat.
Compton-Rickett, Arthur. Personal Forces in Modern Literature. LC 72-973. Repr. of 1906 ed. 19.25 (ISBN 0-404-01649-9). AMS Pr.
Davies, Trevor H. Spiritual Voices in Modern Literature. LC 78-14335. 1978. Repr. lib. bdg. 25.00 (ISBN 0-8414-1860-8). Folcroft.
Friedberg, Maurice. A Decade of Euphoria: Western Literature in Post-Stalin Russia, 1954-1964. LC 76-11932. 384p. 1977. 17.50x (ISBN 0-253-31675-8). Ind U Pr.
Gorky, Maxim. On Literature. 347p. 1979. 9.00 (ISBN 0-8285-1713-4, Pub. by Progress Pubs Russia). Imported Pubns.
--On Literature. LC 72-11682. 400p. 1975. pap. 3.95 (ISBN 0-295-95453-1). U of Wash Pr.
Guthrie, William N. Modern Poet Prophets. 1979. Repr. of 1897 ed. lib. bdg. 30.00 (ISBN 0-8495-2032-0). Arden Lib.
Hallam, Henry. Introduction to the Literature of Europe in the 15th, 16th, & 17th Centuries, 4 Vols. (Classics in Art & Literary Criticism Ser). 1970. Repr. of 1837 ed. Set. 154.00 (ISBN 0-384-21020-1). Johnson Repr.
--Introduction to the Literature of Europe in the 15th, 16th, & 17th Centuries, 3 Vols. LC 74-118869. 1970. Repr. of 1873 ed. Set. 75.00 (ISBN 0-8044-2331-8). Ungar.
Harper, George M. John Morley, & Other Essays. facs. ed. LC 68-22094. (Essay Index Reprint Ser). 1920. 15.00 (ISBN 0-8369-0511-3). Arno.
Hazard, Paul. European Mind, Sixteen Eighty to Seventeen Fifteen. 10.00 (ISBN 0-8446-2225-7). Peter Smith.
Hern, Nicholas. Peter Handke. LC 76-190349. (Modern Literature Ser.). 1972. 10.95 (ISBN 0-8044-2380-6). Ungar.
James, Henry. Selected Literary Criticism. LC 78-5588. 1978. Repr. of 1964 ed. lib. bdg. 27.75x (ISBN 0-313-20389-X, JALC). Greenwood.
Jameson, Fredric. The Prison-House of Language: A Critical Account of Structuralism & Russian Formalism. LC 78-173757. (Princeton Essays in Literature Ser.). 228p. 1972. 17.50 (ISBN 0-691-06226-9); pap. 5.95 (ISBN 0-691-01316-0). Princeton U Pr.
Kennedy, William J. Rhetorical Norms in Renaissance Literature. LC 78-7391. 1978. 17.50x (ISBN 0-300-02263-8). Yale U Pr.
Kral, O., et al. Rise & Development of Modern Literatures in Asia, No. 2. (Oriental Institute Czechoslovakia Dissertationes Orientales, Vol. 15). 1969. 6.00x (ISBN 0-685-27160-9). Paragon.
Krieger, Murray. The Classic Vision: The Retreat from Extremity, Vol. 2. LC 77-167984. (Illus.). 390p. 1973. pap. 4.45 (ISBN 0-8018-1551-7). Johns Hopkins.
--The Tragic Vision: The Confrontation of Extremity, Vol. 1. LC 60-7935. (Visions of Extremity in Modern Literature Ser). 295p. 1974. pap. 3.95x (ISBN 0-8018-1550-9). Johns Hopkins.
--Visions of Extremity in Modern Literature. Incl. Vol. 1. The Tragic Vision: The Confrontation of Extremity. 295p. 1973. pap. 3.95x (ISBN 0-8018-1550-9); Vol. II. The Classic Vision: The Retreat from Extremity. 390p. 1973. pap. 4.95 (ISBN 0-8018-1551-7). Johns Hopkins.
Kuhn, R. The Demon of Noontide: Ennui in Western Literature. 1976. 32.50 (ISBN 0-691-06311-7); pap. 11.50 (ISBN 0-691-10047-0). Princeton U Pr.
Lewis, Wyndham. Men Without Art. LC 64-13930. 1964. Repr. of 1934 ed. 20.00 (ISBN 0-8462-0433-9). Russell.
Lowenthal, Leo. Literature & the Image of Man. LC 78-134110. (Essay Index Reprint Ser). 1957. 17.00 (ISBN 0-8369-1982-3). Arno.
Lukacs, Georg. Soul & Form. Bostock, Anna, tr. LC 74-12828. 1974. pap. 5.95 (ISBN 0-262-62034-0). MIT Pr.
Lunacharsky, A. On Literature & Art. 298p. 1973. 4.20 (ISBN 0-8285-1088-1, Pub. by Progress Pubs Russia). Imported Pubns.
McElroy, Davis D. Existentialism & Modern Literature. LC 63-18056. 1963. 3.75 (ISBN 0-8022-1016-3). Philos Lib.
--Existentialism & Modern Literature: An Essay in Existential Criticism. LC 68-8087. (Illus.). 1968. Repr. of 1963 ed. lib. bdg. 15.00 (ISBN 0-8371-0179-4, MCEL). Greenwood.
MacNeice, Louis. Varieties of Parable. 1966. 28.50 (ISBN 0-521-05654-3). Cambridge U Pr.
Madden, David & Powers, Richard. Writers' Revisions: An Annotated Bibliography of Articles & Books About Writers' Revisions & Their Comments on the Creative Process. LC 80-22942. 254p. 1981. 13.50 (ISBN 0-8108-1375-0). Scarecrow.
Mentor Book CV. 1969. 3.50 (ISBN 0-312-52990-2). St Martin.
Mudrick, Marvin. The Man in the Machine. LC 75-5994. 192p. 1977. 9.95 (ISBN 0-8180-1164-5). Horizon.
Oliphant, Ernest H. Plays of Beaumont & Fletcher: An Attempt to Determine Their Respective Shares & the Shares of Others. 1971. Repr. of 1927 ed. 11.00 (ISBN 0-403-01138-8). Scholarly.
Oxford University. Taylor Institution. Studies in European Literature, Being the Taylorian Lectures 1920-1930. LC 76-90673. (Essay Index Reprint Ser). 1930. 22.00 (ISBN 0-8369-1232-2). Arno.
Pankin, B. Seven Essays on Life & Literature. 256p. 1979. 8.40 (ISBN 0-8285-1089-X, Pub. by Progress Pubs Russia). Imported Pubns.
Paul, Sherman, ed. Criticism & Culture. (Papers of the Midwest Modern Language Association: No. 2). 123p. (Orig.). 1972. pap. 6.50x (ISBN 0-87352-171-4). Modern Lang.
Pfleger, Karl. Wrestlers with Christ. facs. ed. Watkin, E. I., tr. LC 68-16968. (Essay Index Reprint Ser). 1936. 18.00 (ISBN 0-8369-0785-X). Arno.
Plottel, Jeanine P. & Charney, Hanna, eds. Intertextuality: New Perspectives in Criticism. LC 77-18628. (Illus., Orig.). 1978. pap. text ed. 12.50 (ISBN 0-931196-01-9). NY Lit Forum.
Poulet, Georges. The Metamorphoses of the Circle. Dawson, Carley & Coleman, Elliott, trs. LC 66-24405. 427p. 1967. 22.50x (ISBN 0-8018-0538-4). Johns Hopkins.
Pugh, Anthony R. From Montaigne to Chateaubriand: An Introduction to the Works of Major French Prose Writers of 17th & 18th Centuries. 1966. text ed. 4.25x (ISBN 0-333-04314-6). Humanities.
Quiller-Couch, Arthur T. Adventures in Criticism. LC 12-37963. 1969. Repr. of 1896 ed. 19.00 (ISBN 0-403-00064-5). Scholarly.
Raymond, Ernest. Through Literature to Life: An Enthusiams & an Anthology. 212p. 1980. Repr. of 1928 ed. lib. bdg. 22.50 (ISBN 0-8492-7707-8). R West.
Reade, Arthur R. Main Currents in Modern Literature. 223p. 1980. Repr. of 1935 ed. lib. bdg. 25.00 (ISBN 0-8492-7708-6). R West.
Robbins, J. Albert, ed. American Literary Scholarship: An Annual, 1969. LC 65-19450. 1971. 14.75 (ISBN 0-8223-0248-9). Duke.
Robertson, J. M. Modern Humanists Reconsidered. LC 72-3443. (English Literature Ser., No. 33). 1972. Repr. of 1927 ed. lib. bdg. 32.95 (ISBN 0-8383-1556-9). Haskell.
Routh, H. V. Money, Morals & Manners As Revealed in Modern Literature. 59.95 (ISBN 0-8490-0662-7). Gordon Pr.
Ruland, Richard. America in Modern European Literature: From Image to Metaphor. LC 74-29376. 197p. 1976. 19.50x (ISBN 0-8147-7364-8). NYU Pr.
Saintsbury, George E. English Novel. 1971. Repr. of 1913 ed. 14.00 (ISBN 0-403-01192-2). Scholarly.
Sartre, Jean-Paul. Critiques Litteraires, Vol. 1. 416p. 1975. 4.95 (ISBN 0-686-54976-7). French & Eur.
Schoenbaum, Samuel. Middleton's Tragedies. LC 71-128191. 1970. Repr. of 1955 ed. text ed. 10.00 (ISBN 0-87752-132-8). Gordian.
Schug, Charles. The Romantic Genesis of the Modern Novel. LC 78-26484. (Critical Essays in Modern Lierature Ser.). 1979. 14.95 (ISBN 0-8229-3397-7). U of Pittsburgh Pr.
Sherman, Stuart P. Critical Woodcuts, Essays on Writers & Writing. LC 67-27647. Repr. of 1926 ed. 11.25 (ISBN 0-8046-0415-0). Kennikat.
Spitzer, Leo. Linguistics & Literary History. LC 62-10235. 1962. Repr. of 1948 ed. 8.00 (ISBN 0-8462-0278-6). Russell.
Steadman, John M. The Lamb & the Elephant: Ideal Imitation & the Context of Renaissance Allegory. LC 73-93874. 1974. 18.50 (ISBN 0-87328-062-8). Huntington Lib.
Strachey, John. Literature & Dialectical Materialism. LC 74-6468. (Studies in Comparative Literature, No. 35). 1974. lib. bdg. 22.95 (ISBN 0-8383-1938-6). Haskell.
Strauss, Walter A. Descent & Return: The Orphic Theme in Modern Literature. LC 70-131461. 1971. 15.00x (ISBN 0-674-19830-1). Harvard U Pr.
Thompson, Elbert N. Literary Bypaths of the Renaissance. LC 73-176152. Repr. of 1924 ed. 12.00 (ISBN 0-404-06399-3). AMS Pr.
Trent, W. P., et al. Cambridge History of American Literature, 3 Vols in 1. 1943. 12.50 (ISBN 0-02-520930-2). Macmillan.
Twentieth-Century Literary Criticism, Vol. 2. LC 76-46132. 1979. 58.00 (ISBN 0-8103-0176-8). Gale.
Weber, Samuel & Sussman, Henry, eds. Glyph Four. LC 76-47370. (The Johns Hopkins Textual Studies). 229p. 1978. text ed. 13.50x (ISBN 0-8018-2143-6). Johns Hopkins.
Wellek, Rene. A History of Modern Criticism: Seventeen Fifty to Nineteen Fifty, 4 vols. Incl. Vol. 1. The Late Eighteenth Century. (Illus.). vii, 358p. 1955. 27.50x (ISBN 0-300-01034-6); Vol. 2. The Romantic Age. v, 459p. 1955. 30.00x (ISBN 0-300-01035-4); Vol. 3. The Age of Transition. (Illus.). xvi, 389p. 1965. 30.00x (ISBN 0-300-01036-2); Vol. 4. The Late Nineteenth Century. (Illus.). vi, 671p. 1965. 35.00x (ISBN 0-300-01037-0). Yale U Pr.
White, Allon. The Uses of Obscurity: The Fiction of Early Modernism. 180p. 1981. 30.00 (ISBN 0-7100-0751-5). Routledge & Kegan.
Widmer, Kingsley. Literary Rebel. LC 65-12389. (Crosscurrents-Modern Critiques Ser.). 271p. 1965. 7.95 (ISBN 0-8093-0157-1). S Ill U Pr.
Wiley, Paul L., compiled by. British Novel: Conrad to the Present. LC 79-178291. (Goldentree Bibliographies in Language & Literature Ser). (Orig.). 1973. pap. 6.95x (ISBN 0-88295-530-6). Harlan Davidson.
Wood, Frank. Rainer Maria Rilke: The Ring of Forms. LC 78-120681. 1970. Repr. lib. bdg. 14.50x (ISBN 0-374-98715-7). Octagon.
Woolf, Virginia. Common Reader: First Series. LC 25-10098. 1955. pap. 3.95 (ISBN 0-15-619805-3, HB10, Harv). HarBraceJ.

LITERATURE, MODERN–HISTORY AND CRITICISM–15TH AND 16TH CENTURIES

Campbell, Lily B. Divine Poetry & Drama in 16th Century England. LC 79-148614. 1972. Repr. of 1959 ed. text ed. 10.00 (ISBN 0-87752-143-3). Gordian.
Clements, Robert J. The Peregrine Muse: Studies in Comparative Renaissance Literature. (Studies in the Romance Languages & Literatures: No. 82). 1969. pap. 11.00x (ISBN 0-8078-9082-0). U of NC Pr.
Hannay, David. The Later Renaissance. 1898. 18.50 (ISBN 0-8337-1566-6). B Franklin.
--Later Renaissance. LC 73-12460. 1898. lib. bdg. 35.00 (ISBN 0-8414-4734-9). Folcroft.
Jones, William M., ed. The Present State of Scholarship in Sixteenth-Century Literature. LC 78-50810. 1978. text ed. 19.00x (ISBN 0-8262-0253-5). U of Mo Pr.
Knapp, Peggy A. & Stugrin, Michael A., eds. Assays: Critical Approaches to Medieval & Renaissance Texts, Vol. 1. LC 80-54059. 200p. 1981. 12.95x (ISBN 0-8229-3439-6). U of Pittsburgh Pr.
Levin, Harry. Myth of the Golden Age in the Renaissance. 167p. 1972. pap. 4.95 (ISBN 0-19-501602-5, GB). Oxford U Pr.
Mohl, Ruth. Three Estates in Medieval & Renaissance Literature. LC 62-10897. 1962. 8.50 (ISBN 0-8044-2636-8). Ungar.
Parry, Adam. Studies in Fifth-Century Thought & Literature. LC 71-166948. (Yale Classical Studies: No. 22). 260p. 1972. 36.00 (ISBN 0-521-08305-2). Cambridge U Pr.
Phillips, James E. Images of a Queen: Mary Stuart in Sixteenth-Century Literature. 1964. 25.00x (ISBN 0-520-01007-8). U of Cal Pr.
Rebhorn, Wayne A. Courtly Performances: Masking & Festivity in Castiglione's "Book of the Courtier". LC 77-17066. 1978. text ed. 16.95x (ISBN 0-8143-1587-9). Wayne St U Pr.
Smith, Gregory G. The Transition Period. 1979. Repr. of 1927 ed. lib. bdg. 40.00 (ISBN 0-8414-8024-9). Folcroft.
Tuve, Rosemond. Allegorical Imagery: Some Medieval Books & Their Posterity. (Illus.). 1966. 30.00x (ISBN 0-691-06002-9); pap. 8.95 (ISBN 0-691-01339-X). Princeton U Pr.

LITERATURE, MODERN–HISTORY AND CRITICISM–17TH CENTURY

Golden, Morris. The Self Observed: Swift, Johnson, Wordsworth. LC 70-179137. 199p. 1972. 14.00x (ISBN 0-8018-1289-5). Johns Hopkins.
Gosse, Edmund. Seventeenth Century Studies. 1897. Repr. 10.95 (ISBN 0-8274-3366-2). R West.
Grierson, Herbert. First Half of the Seventeenth Century. LC 76-40232. 1906. lib. bdg. 30.00 (ISBN 0-8414-4419-6). Folcroft.
--Seventeenth Century Studies Presented to Sir Herbert Grierson. 1967. Repr. lib. bdg. 18.50x (ISBN 0-374-93268-9). Octagon.
Marcus, Leah S. Childhood & Cultural Despair: A Theme & Variations in Seventeenth-Century Literature. LC 77-15733. 1978. 14.95 (ISBN 0-8229-3367-5). U of Pittsburgh Pr.
Miner, Earl, ed. Illustrious Evidence: Approaches to Early Seventeenth-Century Literature. 1975. 18.50x (ISBN 0-520-02782-5). U of Cal Pr.
Mulder, John R. Temple of the Mind: Education & Literary Taste in Seventeenth-Century England. LC 79-79059. 1969. 24.50x (ISBN 0-672-53602-1). Irvington.

Praz, Manrio. Studies in Seventeenth Century Imagery, 2 vols. in 1. LC 40-3654. Repr. 59.00 (ISBN 0-403-07208-5). Somerset Pub.
Roth, Maria C. Der Philotheus Des Laurentius Von Schnuffis (1633-1702). LC 79-26552. 156p. (Orig.). 1979. pap. 15.75 (ISBN 0-8357-0488-2, SS-00118). Univ Microfilms.
Thompson, Elbert N. Literary Bypaths of the Renaissance. LC 73-176152. Repr. of 1924 ed. 12.00 (ISBN 0-404-06399-3). AMS Pr.

LITERATURE, MODERN–HISTORY AND CRITICISM–18TH CENTURY

Benson, Mary S. Women in Eighteenth-Century America: A Study of Opinion & Social Usage. LC 75-41025. (BCL Ser. II). 1976. Repr. of 1935 ed. 18.50 (ISBN 0-404-51405-7). AMS Pr.
Bredvold, Louis I., et al, eds. Eighteenth Century Prose, 2 vols. 942p. Repr. of 1932 ed. 49.00 (ISBN 0-403-04040-X). Somerset Pub.
Dobson, Austin. Eighteenth Century Studies. 1978. Repr. lib. bdg. 15.00 (ISBN 0-8482-0630-4). Norwood Edns.
--Eighteenth Century Vignettes, 3 Vols. LC 73-115237. (Illus.). 1971. Repr. of 1923 ed. Set. 45.00 (ISBN 0-686-57480-X); 17.50 ea. Scholarly.
Donohue, J. W., Jr. Dramatic Character in the English Romantic Age. 1970. 28.00 (ISBN 0-691-06187-4). Princeton U Pr.
Frei, Hans W. The Eclipse of Biblical Narrative: A Study in Eighteenth & Nineteenth Century Hermeneutics. LC 73-86893. 384p. 1974. 25.00x (ISBN 0-300-01623-9); pap. 7.95 (ISBN 0-300-02602-1). Yale U Pr.
Gosse, Edmund. A History of Eighteenth Century Literature. 1891. lib. bdg. 30.00 (ISBN 0-8414-4663-6). Folcroft.
Ker, W. P. The Eighteenth Century. 1978. 18.50 (ISBN 0-685-86100-7). Porter.
Lyons, John O. The Invention of the Self: The Hinge of Consciousness in the Eighteenth Century. LC 77-27103. (Illus.). 277p. 1978. 15.95x (ISBN 0-8093-0815-0). S Ill U Pr.
Mc Kenzie, Gordon. Critical Responsiveness. 1949. Repr. lib. bdg. 35.00 (ISBN 0-8414-6346-8). Folcroft.
Millar, J. H. Mid-Eighteenth Century. 1902. lib. bdg. 30.00 (ISBN 0-8414-6343-3). Folcroft.
Miller, Samuel. Brief Retrospect of the Eighteenth Century, 2 Vols. LC 70-132812. 1970. Repr. of 1803 ed. Set. 54.50 (ISBN 0-8337-2395-2). B Franklin.
Morgan, P., ed. Jeffrey's Criticism. 200p. 1981. 17.00x (ISBN 0-7073-0300-1, Pub. by Scottish Academic Pr Scotland). Columbia U Pr.
Preston, John. The Created Self: The Reader's Role in Eighteenth-Century Fiction. 1970. pap. text ed. 7.50x (ISBN 0-435-18721-X). Heinemann Ed.
Reynolds, Joshua. Portraits: Character Sketches of Oliver Goldsmith, Samuel Johnson, & David Garrick. 1979. Repr. of 1952 ed. lib. bdg. 25.00 (ISBN 0-8495-4604-4). Arden Lib.

LITERATURE, MODERN–HISTORY AND CRITICISM–19TH CENTURY

Adams, Robert M. Nil: Episodes in the Literary Conquest of Void During the Nineteenth Century. LC 66-22257. 1970. pap. 3.50 (ISBN 0-19-500797-2, 303, GB). Oxford U Pr.
Arac, Jonathan. Commissioned Spirits: The Shaping of Social Motion in Dickens, Carlyle, Melville, & Hawthorne. 1979. 15.00 (ISBN 0-8135-0874-6). Rutgers U Pr.
Becker, George J. Realism in Modern Literature. LC 79-4833. 1980. 14.50 (ISBN 0-8044-2031-9). Ungar.
Bjorkman, Edwin A. Voices of Tomorrow: Critical Studies of the New Spirit in Literature. LC 74-98818. Repr. of 1913 ed. lib. bdg. 14.25x (ISBN 0-8371-2962-1, BJVT). Greenwood.
Brandes, Georg M. Creative Spirits of the Nineteenth Century. facs. ed. Anderson, R. B., tr. LC 67-26719. (Essay Index Reprint Ser). 1923. 25.00 (ISBN 0-8369-0245-9). Arno.
Coustillas, Pierre, ed. Politics in Literature in the Nineteenth Century. 1974. pap. text ed. 10.00x (ISBN 0-685-41700-X). Humanities.
Croce, Benedetto. European Literature in the Nineteenth Century. LC 67-30822. (Studies in Comparative Literature, No. 35). 1969. Repr. of 1924 ed. lib. bdg. 49.95 (ISBN 0-8383-0735-3). Haskell.
Dana, William F. The Optimism of Ralph Waldo Emerson. LC 76-46925. 1976. Repr. of 1886 ed. lib. bdg. 10.00 (ISBN 0-8414-3806-4). Folcroft.
De Mille, A. B. Literature in the Century. 1973. lib. bdg. 35.00 (ISBN 0-8414-2463-2). Folcroft.
Frei, Hans W. The Eclipse of Biblical Narrative: A Study in Eighteenth & Nineteenth Century Hermeneutics. LC 73-86893. 384p. 1974. 25.00x (ISBN 0-300-01623-9); pap. 7.95 (ISBN 0-300-02602-1). Yale U Pr.
Gorman, Herbert S. Procession of Masks. LC 77-99698. (Essay Index Reprint Ser). 1923. 17.00 (ISBN 0-8369-1352-3). Arno.
Hayter, Alethea. Opium & the Romantic Imagination. LC 68-29700. 1968. pap. 3.45 (ISBN 0-520-01746-3, CAL194). U of Cal Pr.
James, Henry. Partial Portraits. Repr. of 1888 ed. lib. bdg. 16.50x (ISBN 0-8371-2797-1, JAPA). Greenwood.
--Partial Portraits. LC 68-24939. (Studies of Henry James, No. 17). 1969. Repr. of 1911 ed. lib. bdg. 49.95 (ISBN 0-8383-0208-4). Haskell.
Kennard, Jean E. Victims of Convention. 1978. 16.50 (ISBN 0-208-01659-7, Archon). Shoe String.
Larkin, Maurice. Man & Society in Nineteenth-Century Realism: Determinism & Literature. 201p. 1977. 22.75x (ISBN 0-87471-956-9). Rowman.
Lavrin, Janko. Aspects of Modernism, from Wilde to Pirandello. facs. ed. LC 68-22107. (Essay Index Reprint Ser). 1968. Repr. of 1935 ed. 16.00 (ISBN 0-8369-0611-X). Arno.
Lowell, James R. Literary Criticism of James Russell Lowell. Smith, Herbert F., ed. LC 69-10408. (Regents Critics Ser.). 1969. 17.50x (ISBN 0-8032-0457-4). U of Nebr Pr.
MacCarthy, Desmond. Portraits. 1979. Repr. of 1931 ed. lib. bdg. 30.00 (ISBN 0-8495-3511-5). Arden Lib.
Mackenzie, Compton. Literature in My Time. facs. ed. LC 67-28758. (Essay Index Reprint Ser). 1934. 14.25 (ISBN 0-8369-0654-3). Arno.
Matthews, Brander. Inquiries & Opinions. facs. ed. LC 68-22930. (Essay Index Reprint Ser). 1968. Repr. of 1907 ed. 15.50 (ISBN 0-8369-0696-9). Arno.
Pater, Walter. Sketches & Reviews. LC 72-195890. 1919. lib. bdg. 20.00 (ISBN 0-8414-9200-X). Folcroft.
Pater, Walter H. Sketches & Reviews. LC 77-99718. (Essay Index Reprint Ser). 1919. 15.00 (ISBN 0-8369-1371-X). Arno.
Pollak, Gustav. International Minds & the Search for the Restful. LC 73-107734. (Essay Index Reprint Ser). 1919. 15.00 (ISBN 0-8369-1532-1). Arno.
Pollard, Percival. Their Day in Court. (American Studies). 1970. Repr. of 1909 ed. 27.00 (ISBN 0-384-47170-6). Johnson Repr.
Rahv, Philip. Image & Idea: Fourteen Essays on Literary Themes. LC 77-26061. 1978. Repr. of 1949 ed. lib. bdg. 17.75x (ISBN 0-313-20082-3, RAII). Greenwood.
Saintsbury, George E. Later Nineteenth Century. LC 72-194338. 1907. lib. bdg. 30.00 (ISBN 0-8414-7521-0). Folcroft.
Sheridan, Susan S., ed. Matthew Arnold: Essays in Criticism. 175p. 1980. lib. bdg. 10.00 (ISBN 0-89760-821-6, Telegraph). Dynamic Learn Corp.
Spender, Stephen. The Creative Element: A Study of Vision, Despair, & Orthodoxy Among Some Modern Writers. LC 70-164628. (Select Bibliographies Reprint Ser.). Repr. of 1953 ed. 18.00 (ISBN 0-8369-5911-6). Arno.
Thwaite, Anthony. Victorian Voices. 1980. pap. 9.95 (ISBN 0-19-211937-0). Oxford U Pr.
Tillotson, Geoffrey. A View of Victorian Literature. 1978. 19.95 (ISBN 0-19-812044-3). Oxford U Pr.
Willcocks, Mary P. Between the Old World & the New: Being Studies in Literary Personality from Goethe & Balzac to Anatole France & Thomas Hardy. facs. ed. LC 67-28772. (Essay Index Reprint Ser). 1926. 17.00 (ISBN 0-8369-0999-2). Arno.
Williams, Roger L. The Horror of Life. LC 79-26641. 1980. 22.50 (ISBN 0-226-89918-7). U of Chicago Pr.
Wilson, Edmund. Axel's Castle. 1931. 6.95 (ISBN 0-684-10672-8, ScribC); pap. text ed. 5.95x (ISBN 0-684-15490-0, ScribC). Scribner.
Wolff, Robert L. Strange Stories: Explorations in Victorian Fiction. LC 70-144338. (Illus.). 1971. 12.50 (ISBN 0-87645-047-8). Gambit.

LITERATURE, MODERN–HISTORY AND CRITICISM–20TH CENTURY

see also Dadaism

Anderson, Sherwood. The Modern Writer. LC 76-40963. 1976. Repr. of 1925 ed. lib. bdg. 10.00 (ISBN 0-8414-2992-8). Folcroft.
Balakian, Nona. Critical Encounters: Literary Views & Reviews 1953-1977. LC 77-15421. 1978. 10.95 (ISBN 0-672-52341-8). Bobbs.
Barrett, William. Time of Need: Forms of Imagination in the Twentieth Century. (Illus.). 416p. 1973. pap. 4.95x (ISBN 0-06-131754-3, TB 1754, Torch). Har-Row.
Becker, George J. Realism in Modern Literature. LC 79-4833. 1980. 14.50 (ISBN 0-8044-2031-9). Ungar.
Bennett, Arnold. The Evening Standard Years 'Books & Persons' 1926-1931. Mylett, Andrew, ed. 512p. (Orig.). 1974. 25.00 (ISBN 0-208-01444-6, Archon). Shoe String.
Berne, Stanley. Future Language. LC 76-21885. 1976. 15.00 (ISBN 0-8180-1166-1); pap. 6.00 (ISBN 0-8180-1167-X). Horizon.
Bjorkman, Edwin A. Voices of Tomorrow: Critical Studies of the New Spirit in Literature. LC 74-98818. Repr. of 1913 ed. lib. bdg. 14.25x (ISBN 0-8371-2962-1, BJVT). Greenwood.
Blackmur, Richard P. Anni Mirabiles, Nineteen Twenty-One to Twenty-Five. LC 72-13511. 1974. Repr. of 1956 ed. lib. bdg. 6.50 (ISBN 0-8414-1196-4). Folcroft.
Bond, et al. New Writing & Writers, No. 14. text ed. 13.00x (ISBN 0-7145-3562-1). Humanities.
Braungart, Richard G. Family Status, Socialization & Student Politics: A Multivariate Analysis. LC 79-22685. (Illus.). 375p. (Orig.). 1979. pap. 23.25 (ISBN 0-8357-0478-5, SS-00115). Univ Microfilms.
Brower, Reuben, ed. Twentieth Century Literature in Retrospect. LC 76-168430. (English Studies: No. 2). viii, 363p. 1971. pap. 5.95x (ISBN 0-674-91424-4). Harvard U Pr.
Buck, Philo M. Directions in Contemporary Literature. LC 75-58254. (Essay Index in Reprint Ser.). 1978. Repr. 26.75x (ISBN 0-8486-3016-5). Core Collection.
Butler, Christopher. After the Wake: An Essay on the Contemporary Avant-Garde. (Illus.). 192p. 1980. 24.50x (ISBN 0-19-815766-5). Oxford U Pr.
Canby, Henry S. Seven Years Harvest. LC 66-25902. Repr. of 1936 ed. 12.00 (ISBN 0-8046-0065-1). Kennikat.
City Literary Institute Of London. Tradition & Experiment in Present-Day Literature. facs. ed. LC 68-20290. (Essay Index Reprint Ser). 1968. Repr. of 1929 ed. 13.00 (ISBN 0-8369-0307-2). Arno.
Davidson, A. E. & Davidson, C. N., eds. The Art of Margaret Atwood: Essays in Criticism. 250p. 1981. 18.95 (ISBN 0-88784-080-9, Pub. by Hse Anansi Pr Canada). U of Toronto Pr.
Decker, Clarence R. The Victorian Conscience. LC 77-8021. 1977. Repr. of 1952 ed. lib. bdg. 17.25x (ISBN 0-8371-9684-1, DEVC). Greenwood.
Dibernard, Barbara. Alchemy & Finnegans Wake. LC 79-22809. 1980. lib. bdg. 24.95 (ISBN 0-87395-388-6); pap. 7.95 (ISBN 0-87395-429-7). State U NY Pr.
Duhamel, P. Albert. After Strange Fruit: Changing Literary Tastes in Post-World-War II Boston. write for info. Boston Public Lib.
Durant, Will & Durant, Ariel. Interpretations of Life. 1976. pap. 4.95 (ISBN 0-671-22424-7, Touchstone Bks). S&S.
Eastman, Max. Literary Mind: Its Place in an Age of Science. LC 72-75992. 1969. Repr. of 1931 ed. lib. bdg. 17.50x (ISBN 0-374-92451-1). Octagon.
Eliot, T. S. Tradition & Experiment in Present Day Literature. lib. bdg. 69.95 (ISBN 0-87968-044-X). Gordon Pr.
Ellmann, Richard & Feidelson, Charles, Jr., eds. The Modern Tradition: Backgrounds of Modern Literature. 1965. text ed. 19.95x (ISBN 0-19-500876-6). Oxford U Pr.
Fletcher, John. New Directions in Literature: A Critical Approach to a Contemporary Phenomenon. 1968. text ed. 7.75x (ISBN 0-7145-0004-6). Humanities.
Fokkema, D. W. & Kunne-Ibsch, Elrud. Theories of Literature in the Twentieth Century. LC 77-608292. 1978. 18.95x (ISBN 0-312-79643-9). St Martin.
Frank, Joseph. The Widening Gyre: Crisis & Mastery in Modern Literature. LC 68-27360. (Midland Bks.: No. 120). 296p. 1968. pap. 2.65x (ISBN 0-253-20120-9). Ind U Pr.
Friedman, Melvin J. & Vickery, John B., eds. Shaken Realist: Essays in Modern Literature in Honor of Frederick J. Hoffman. LC 77-108199. 1970. 22.50x (ISBN 0-8071-0933-9). La State U Pr.
Frye, Northrop. Northrop Frye on Culture & Literature: A Collection of Review Essays. Denham, Robert D., intro. by. LC 77-12917. 1980. pap. 5.50 (ISBN 0-226-26648-6, P867, Phoen). U of Chicago Pr.
Garcia Ponce, Juan. Entry into Matter: Modern Literature & Reality. Parent, David J. & Bruce-Novoa, Juan, trs. from Spanish. LC 76-43514. (Illinois Language & Culture Ser.: Vol.2). 1976. 25.25 (ISBN 0-8357-0186-7, IS-00015, Pub. by Applied Literature Press). Univ Microfilms.
Glicksberg, Charles I. Literature & Religion: A Study in Conflict. LC 77-23753. 1977. Repr. of 1960 ed. lib. bdg. 19.75x (ISBN 0-8371-9753-8, GLLR). Greenwood.
--Self in Modern Literature. LC 63-18887. 1963. 12.95x (ISBN 0-271-73101-X). Pa St U Pr.
--Tragic Vision in Twentieth-Century Literature. LC 63-8904. (Crosscurrents-Modern Critiques Ser.). 205p. 1963. 7.95 (ISBN 0-8093-0091-5). S Ill U Pr.
Gomori, George & Newman, Charles, eds. New Writing of East Europe. LC 68-19073. 1972. 6.95 (ISBN 0-8129-0067-7). Times Bks.
Gorman, Herbert S. Procession of Masks. LC 77-99698. (Essay Index Reprint Ser). 1923. 17.00 (ISBN 0-8369-1352-3). Arno.
Gross, Harvey. Contrived Corridor: History & Fatality in Modern Literature. LC 74-163621. 1972. 7.95 (ISBN 0-472-39390-1). U of Mich Pr.
Hall, Sharon, ed. Twentieth Century Literary Criticism, Vol. 5. LC 76-46132. (Illus.). 700p. 1981. 62.00 (ISBN 0-8103-0179-2). Gale.
Hall, Sharon K., ed. Twentieth-Century Literary Criticism. LC 76-46132. (Twentieth-Century Literary Criticism Ser.: Vol. 3). 600p. 1980. 62.00 (ISBN 0-8103-0177-6). Gale.
Hamalian, Leo & Yohannan, John D., eds. New Writing from the Middle East. LC 78-4411. 1978. 16.50 (ISBN 0-8044-2338-5). Ungar.
Hassan, Ihab. Paracriticisms: Seven Speculations of the Times. LC 74-19108. 200p. 1975. 15.00 (ISBN 0-252-00469-8). U of Ill Pr.
Henderson, Philip. Novel Today. LC 73-12887. 1936. lib. bdg. 20.00 (ISBN 0-8414-4750-0). Folcroft.
Henry, Ralph L. & Salisbury, Rachel. Current Thinking & Writing. (Seventh Ser.). 1976. pap. 9.95 (ISBN 0-13-195693-0). P-H.
Hibbard, Addison. The South in Contemporary Literature. LC 73-7753. 1930. Repr. lib. bdg. 8.50 (ISBN 0-8414-4702-0). Folcroft.
Hoffman, Frederick J. Freudianism & the Literary Mind. 1977. Repr. of 1957 ed. lib. bdg. 26.75 (ISBN 0-8371-9713-9, HOFL). Greenwood.
Howe, Irving. Decline of the New. LC 78-95876. 1970. 7.50 (ISBN 0-15-124510-X). HarBraceJ.
Langbaum, Robert. The Mysteries of Identity: A Theme in Modern Literature. LC 76-42657. 1977. 17.95 (ISBN 0-19-502189-4). Oxford U Pr.
Lavrin, Janko. Aspects of Modernism, from Wilde to Pirandello. facs. ed. LC 68-22107. (Essay Index Reprint Ser). 1968. Repr. of 1935 ed. 16.00 (ISBN 0-8369-0611-X). Arno.
Lewis, Wyndham. Men Without Art. LC 64-13930. 1964. Repr. of 1934 ed. 20.00 (ISBN 0-8462-0433-9). Russell.
Longyear, Christopher R. Linguistically Determined Categories of Meanings: A Comparative Analysis of Meanings in the Snows of Kilimanjaro. (Janua Linguarum, Ser. Practica: No. 92). 169p. (Orig.). 1971. pap. text ed. 37.50x (ISBN 90-2791-948-8). Mouton.
MacCarthy, Desmond. Portraits. 1979. Repr. of 1931 ed. lib. bdg. 30.00 (ISBN 0-8495-3511-5). Arden Lib.
Mackenzie, Compton. Literature in My Time. facs. ed. LC 67-28758. (Essay Index Reprint Ser). 1934. 14.25 (ISBN 0-8369-0654-3). Arno.
Martin, E. W. New Spirit: Tolstoy, Faulkner, Joyce, D. H. Lawrence. LC 77-4667. 1946. lib. bdg. 15.00 (ISBN 0-8414-6182-1). Folcroft.
Moulton, Richard G. The Modern Study of Literature. 530p. 1980. Repr. of 1915 ed. lib. bdg. 40.00 (ISBN 0-8482-5013-3). Norwood Edns.
Oates, Joyce C. New Heaven, New Earth: The Visionary Experience in Literature. LC 74-76438. 308p. 1974. 10.00 (ISBN 0-8149-0743-1). Vanguard.
Pence, Raymond W. Readings in Present-Day Writers. 1933. 12.50 (ISBN 0-8274-3249-6). R West.
Pfleger, Karl. Wrestlers with Christ. facs. ed. Watkin, E. I., tr. LC 68-16968. (Essay Index Reprint Ser). 1936. 18.00 (ISBN 0-8369-0785-X). Arno.
Piercy, Josephine K., ed. Modern Writers at Work. 993p. 1981. Repr. of 1930 ed. lib. bdg. 65.00 (ISBN 0-8495-3874-2). Arden Lib.
Pierssens, Michel. Literal Violence. Lingua Press Staff, ed. (Paperplay Mini-Bks: Vol. 8). 16p. 1978. saddle-stitched 2.60 (ISBN 0-939044-14-5). Lingua Pr.
Rahv, Philip. Image & Idea: Fourteen Essays on Literary Themes. LC 77-26061. 1978. Repr. of 1949 ed. lib. bdg. 17.75x (ISBN 0-313-20082-3, RAII). Greenwood.
Reader's Index to the Twentieth Century Views in Literary Criticism Series, Vols. 1-100. 20.00 (ISBN 0-13-753384-5, Spec). P-H.
Robbins, Rae G. The Bloomsbury Group: A Selective Bibliography. 219p. 1978. 17.00 (ISBN 0-685-70087-9). Price Guide.
Rose, William & Isaacs, Jacob, eds. Contemporary Movements in European Literature. facs. ed. (Essay Index Reprint Ser). 1929. 16.00 (ISBN 0-8369-0833-3). Arno.
Rosenfeld, Paul. Men Seen: Twenty Four Modern Authors. facs. ed. LC 67-26776. (Essay Index Reprint Ser). 1925. 20.00 (ISBN 0-8369-0836-8). Arno.
Russell, Charles, ed. The Avant-Garde Today. LC 80-23922. 1981. 17.95x (ISBN 0-252-00851-0); pap. 7.95 (ISBN 0-252-00852-9). U of Ill Pr.
Scholes, Robert, ed. Learners & Discerners: A Newer Criticism. LC 64-13303. 1964. 10.95x (ISBN 0-8139-0213-4). U Pr of Va.
Sontag, Susan. Against Interpretation. 1967. pap. 5.95 (ISBN 0-440-50038-9, Delta). Dell.
--Against Interpretation. 146p. 1966. 6.95 (ISBN 0-374-10224-4). FS&G.

Spencer, Sharon. Space, Time & Structure in the Modern Novel. LC 76-142375. 251p. 1971. pap. 6.95x (ISBN 0-8040-0334-3). Swallow.
Spender, Stephen. The Creative Element: A Study of Vision, Despair, & Orthodoxy Among Some Modern Writers. LC 70-164628. (Select Bibliographies Reprint Ser.). Repr. of 1953 ed. 18.00 (ISBN 0-8369-5911-6). Arno.
Spradley, James P. & McDonough, George E. Anthropology Through Literature: Cross-Cultural Perspectives. 432p. (Orig.). 1973. pap. text ed. 7.95 (ISBN 0-316-80760-5). Little.
Stern, Guy. War, Weimar, & Literature: The Story of the Neue Merkur, 1914-1925. LC 71-136960. (Illus.). 1971. 16.50x (ISBN 0-271-01147-5). Pa St U Pr.
Stonier, George W. Gog Magog, & Other Critical Essays. facs. ed. LC 67-22120. (Essay Index Reprint Ser). 1933. 13.00 (ISBN 0-8369-0907-0). Arno.
Sypher, Wylie. Loss of the Self: In Modern Literature & Art. LC 78-11790. 1979. Repr. of 1962 ed. lib. bdg. 15.25x (ISBN 0-313-20759-3, SYLS). Greenwood.
Trotsky, Leon. Leon Trotsky on Literature & Art. 2nd ed. Siegel, Paul N., ed. LC 72-795611. 1972. 17.00 (ISBN 0-87348-180-1); pap. 5.45 (ISBN 0-87348-373-1). Path Pr NY.
Val Baker, Denys. Writers of Today, Vol. 1. LC 72-13043. 1973. Repr. of 1946 ed. lib. bdg. 20.00 (ISBN 0-8414-1162-X). Folcroft.
--Writers of Today, Vol. 2. Repr. of 1948 ed. lib. bdg. 20.00 (ISBN 0-685-25811-4). Folcroft.
Vernon, John. The Garden & the Map: Schizophrenia in 20th Century Literature & Culture. LC 72-85612. 1973. 8.95x (ISBN 0-252-00256-3). U of Ill Pr.
Waldman, M. The Propaganda Novel. 59.95 (ISBN 0-8490-0900-6). Gordon Pr.
Ward, A. C. Longman Companion to Twentieth Century Literature. 608p. 1981. text ed. 30.00x (ISBN 0-582-35307-6). Longman.
--Longman Companion to Twentieth Century Literature. 3rd ed. 1981. text ed. 30.00x (ISBN 0-582-35307-6). Longman.
Wickham, Harvey. Impuritans. LC 72-84346. (Essay Index Reprint Ser). 1929. 18.00 (ISBN 0-8369-1587-9). Arno.
Williams, A. Indo-Anglian Literature, 1880-1970: A Survey. 1977. 7.50x (ISBN 0-88386-996-9). South Asia Bks.
Wilson, Edmund. Axel's Castle. 1931. 6.95 (ISBN 0-684-10672-8, ScribC); pap. text ed. 5.95x (ISBN 0-684-15490-0, ScribC). Scribner.
--The Thirties. Edel, Leon, ed. 800p. 1980. 17.50 (ISBN 0-374-27572-6). FS&G.
Wilson, Robert N. The Writer As Social Seer. LC 79-455. 1979. 14.00x (ISBN 0-8078-1363-X). U of NC Pr.

LITERATURE, MODERN–OUTLINES, SYLLABI, ETC.

Brett-James, Antony. The Triple Stream. 1978. Repr. of 1954 ed. lib. bdg. 25.00 (ISBN 0-8495-0351-5). Arden Lib.

LITERATURE, MODERN–TRANSLATIONS

see Translations–Literature, Modern

LITERATURE, PASTORAL

see Pastoral Literature

LITERATURE, PICARESQUE

see Picaresque Literature

LITERATURE, PRIMITIVE

see Folk Literature

LITERATURE, UNDERGROUND

see Underground Literature

LITERATURE AND ART

see Art and Literature

LITERATURE AND COMMUNISM

see Communism and Literature

LITERATURE AND HISTORY

Barthes, Roland. New Critical Essays. Howard, Richard, tr. from Fr. 121p. 1980. 10.95 (ISBN 0-8090-7257-2). Hill & Wang.
Bremner, Robert H., ed. Essays on History & Literature. LC 66-22733. 1966. 5.00 (ISBN 0-8142-0029-X). Ohio St U Pr.
Crane, Ronald S. Idea of the Humanities, & Other Essays Critical & Historical, 2 Vols. LC 66-30214. 1967. 17.50x (ISBN 0-226-11825-8). U of Chicago Pr.
Dumezil, Georges. From Myth to Fiction. Coltman, Derek, tr. from Fr. 1973. 12.50x (ISBN 0-226-16972-3). U of Chicago Pr.
Garvin, Harry, ed. Literature & History. LC 77-74403. 186p. 1977. 12.00 (ISBN 0-8387-2139-7). Bucknell U Pr.
Gross, Harvey. Contrived Corridor: History & Fatality in Modern Literature. LC 74-163621. 1972. 7.95 (ISBN 0-472-39390-1). U of Mich Pr.
Miller, John C. Los Testimonios Literarios De la Guerra Espanol-Marroqui. LC 78-23740. 1978. pap. 16.50 (ISBN 0-8357-0338-X, SS-00073). Univ Microfilms.
Morris, Wesley. Toward a New Historicism. LC 77-166384. 228p. 1972. 18.00x (ISBN 0-691-06223-4). Princeton U Pr.
Neff, Emery. The Poetry of History: The Contributions of Literature & Literary Scholarship to the Writing of History Since Voltaire. 1979. Repr. of 1947 ed. lib. bdg. 17.00x (ISBN 0-374-96039-9). Octagon.
Neff, Emery E. The Poetry of History: The Contribution of Literature & Literary Scholarship to the Writing of History Since Voltaire. LC 47-30933. 1947. pap. 6.00x (ISBN 0-231-08525-7). Columbia U Pr.
Peyre, Henri. Historical & Critical Essays. LC 68-12702. 1968. 18.50x (ISBN 0-8032-0145-1). U of Nebr Pr.
Shaw, Leroy R. Playwright & Historical Change: Dramatic Strategies in Brecht, Hauptmann, Kaiser, & Wedekind. LC 75-106042. 194p. 1970. 17.50x (ISBN 0-299-05500-0). U of Wis Pr.
Williams, Kenny J. Prairie Voices: A Literary History of Chicago from the Frontier to Eighteen Ninety-Three. LC 79-27237. (Illus.). 529p. 1980. 16.95 (ISBN 0-935990-00-3). Townsend Pr.

LITERATURE AND LAW

see Law and Literature

LITERATURE AND MORALS

see also Censorship; Literature, Immoral

Bastiaenen, J. A. Moral Tone of Jacobean & Caroline Drama. LC 68-951. (Studies in Drama, No. 39). 1969. Repr. of 1930 ed. lib. bdg. 27.95 (ISBN 0-8383-0507-5). Haskell.
Baum, Helena W. Satiric & the Didactic in Ben Jonson's Comedy. LC 70-139900. 1971. Repr. of 1947 ed. 12.00 (ISBN 0-8462-1550-0). Russell.
Carlisle, Janice. The Sense of an Audience: Dickens, Thackeray & George Eliot at Mid-Century. LC 81-435. 262p. 1981. 19.50 (ISBN 0-8203-0559-6). U of Ga Pr.
Clark, Glenn. God's Voice in the Folklore. 3.50 (ISBN 0-910924-06-6). Macalester.
Farrell, J. T. Literature & Morality. LC 47-4577. Repr. of 1947 ed. 17.00 (ISBN 0-527-28400-9). Kraus Repr.
Jepsen, Laura. Ethical Aspects of Tragedy. LC 79-153332. Repr. of 1953 ed. 14.95 (ISBN 0-404-03566-3). AMS Pr.
Lewis, Felice F. Literature, Obscenity, & Law. LC 75-42094. 310p. 1978. pap. 8.95 (ISBN 0-8093-0870-3). S Ill U Pr.
MacIver, R. M., ed. Great Moral Dilemmas. (Religion & Civilization Ser). 189p. 1964. Repr. of 1956 ed. 19.50x (ISBN 0-8154-0145-0). Cooper Sq.
Nettleship, Henry. The Moral Influence of Literature. LC 74-19150. 1974. lib. bdg. 6.50 (ISBN 0-8414-6277-1). Folcroft.
--The Moral Influence of Literature. 1978. Repr. of 1890 ed. lib. bdg. 8.50 (ISBN 0-8495-4011-9). Arden Lib.
Rist, Ray C., ed. Pornography Controversy: Changing Moral Standards in American Life. LC 73-92813. (Social Policy Ser.). 225p. 1974. pap. 4.95 (ISBN 0-87855-587-0). Transaction Bks.
Routh, H. V. Money, Morals & Manners As Revealed in Modern Literature. 59.95 (ISBN 0-8490-0662-7). Gordon Pr.
Sacks, Sheldon. Fiction & the Shape of Belief: A Study of Henry Fielding - with Glances at Swift, Johnson, & Richardson. LC 79-24436. 1980. pap. 5.95 (ISBN 0-226-73337-8, P877, Phoen). U of Chicago Pr.
Tanner, Tony. Adultry in the Novel: Contact & Transgression. LC 79-4948. 384p. 1981. pap. 7.95 (ISBN 0-8018-2471-0). Johns Hopkins.
Wickham, Harvey. Impuritans. LC 72-84346. (Essay Index Reprint Ser). 1929. 18.00 (ISBN 0-8369-1587-9). Arno.
Will, Frederic. Belphagor. 1977. pap. text ed. 12.75x (ISBN 90-6203-348-2). Humanities.
Winters, Yvor. Primitivism & Decadence. LC 70-92994. (Studies in Comparative Literature, No. 35). 1969. Repr. of 1937 ed. lib. bdg. 32.95 (ISBN 0-8383-1213-6). Haskell.

LITERATURE AND MUSIC

see Music and Literature

LITERATURE AND PSYCHOANALYSIS

see Psychoanalysis and Literature

LITERATURE AND RELIGION

see Religion and Literature

LITERATURE AND REVOLUTIONS

Farrell, John P. Revolution As Tragedy: The Dilemma of the Moderate from Scott to Arnold. LC 79-26000. (Illus.). 1980. 17.50x (ISBN 0-8014-1278-1). Cornell U Pr.
Swingewood, Alan. The Novel & Revolution. LC 75-21103. 288p. 1975. text ed. 23.50x (ISBN 0-06-496682-8). B&N.

LITERATURE AND SCIENCE

see also Literature and Technology; Science Fiction (Collections)

Barber, Otto. H. G. Wells' Verhaltnis Zum Darwinismus. pap. 6.00 (ISBN 0-384-03380-6). Johnson Repr.
Barksdale, E. C. Cosmologies of Consciousness. 148p. 1980. text ed. 16.50x (ISBN 0-87073-969-7); pap. text ed. 11.25x (ISBN 0-87073-970-0). Schenkman.
Beaver, Joseph C. Walt Whitman, Poet of Science. 1972. lib. bdg. 14.00x (ISBN 0-374-90514-2). Octagon.
Buchanan, Scott. Poetry & Mathematics. (Midway Reprint Ser). 156p. 1975. pap. text ed. 4.95x (ISBN 0-226-07821-3). U of Chicago Pr.
Bush, Douglas. Science & English Poetry: A Historical Sketch, 1590-1950. LC 80-18161. (The Patten Lectures Ser., 1949, Indiana Univ.). viii, 166p. 1980. Repr. of 1950 ed. lib. bdg. 18.75x (ISBN 0-313-22654-7, BUSC). Greenwood.
Ceccio, Joseph F., ed. Medicine in Literature: An Anthology for Reading & Writing. LC 77-17721. (English & Humanities Ser.). 1978. pap. text ed. 9.95x (ISBN 0-582-28051-6). Longman.
Crum, Ralph B. Scientific Thought in Poetry. LC 31-29142. Repr. of 1931 ed. 16.50 (ISBN 0-404-01868-8). AMS Pr.
Cunliffe, John W. Leaders of the Victorian Revolution. LC 69-1648. Repr. of 1934 ed. 12.50 (ISBN 0-8046-0521-1). Kennikat.
--Leaders of the Victorian Revolution. LC 64-10700. 1963. Repr. of 1934 ed. 9.50 (ISBN 0-8462-0404-5). Russell.
Dingle, Herbert. Science & Literary Criticism. 184p. 1980. Repr. of 1949 ed. lib. bdg. 20.00 (ISBN 0-8492-4212-6). R West.
--Science & Literary Criticism. LC 74-16039. 1974. Repr. of 1949 ed. lib. bdg. 12.50 (ISBN 0-8414-3799-8). Folcroft.
Dobree, Bonamy. The Broken Cistern. LC 72-6790. (Studies in Comparative Literature, No. 35). 1972. Repr. of 1955 ed. lib. bdg. 48.95 (ISBN 0-8383-1664-6). Haskell.
Duncan, Carson S. The New Science & English Literature in the Classical Period. LC 74-173520. iii, 191p. 1972. Repr. of 1913 ed. 14.00 (ISBN 0-8462-1654-X). Russell.
--The New Science & English Literature in the Classical Period. LC 74-173520. iii, 191p. 1972. Repr. of 1913 ed. 14.00 (ISBN 0-8462-1654-X). Russell.
Eastman, Max. Literary Mind: Its Place in an Age of Science. LC 72-75992. 1969. Repr. of 1931 ed. lib. bdg. 17.50x (ISBN 0-374-92451-1). Octagon.
Elster, Ernst. Prinzipien Der Literaturwissenschaft: Einfuhrung Von Herman Salinger und Alois Arnoldner, 2 Vols. in 1. 1972. 61.50 (ISBN 0-384-14280-X). Johnson Repr.
Evans, B. Ifor. Literature & Science. LC 74-23911. 1954. lib. bdg. 12.50 (ISBN 0-8414-3941-9). Folcroft.
Foerster, Norman. American Scholar. LC 65-18604. 1965. Repr. of 1929 ed. 8.50 (ISBN 0-8046-0155-0). Kennikat.
Gode, Alexander. Natural Science in German Romanticism. LC 70-168170. (Columbia University. Germanic Studies, New Ser.: No. 11). Repr. of 1941 ed. 19.00 (ISBN 0-404-50461-2). AMS Pr.
Grabo, Carl A. Newton Among Poets: Shelley's Use of Science in Prometheus Unbound. LC 68-19138. 1968. Repr. of 1930 ed. 8.50x (ISBN 0-8154-0085-3). Cooper Sq.
Grabo, Carl H. Newton Among Poets: Shelly's Use of Science in Prometheus Unbound. LC 68-24046. 1968. Repr. of 1930 ed. 6.50 (ISBN 0-87752-044-5). Gordian.
Henkin, Leo J. Darwinism in the English Novel, 1860-1910. LC 63-9505. 1963. Repr. of 1940 ed. 13.00 (ISBN 0-8462-0355-3). Russell.
Isaacs. Darwin to Double Helix: The Biological Theme in Science Fiction. (Siscon Ser.). 1977. 3.95 (ISBN 0-408-71302-X). Butterworth.
Johnson, Francis R. Astronomical Thought in Renaissance England. LC 68-27334. (Illus.). 1968. lib. bdg. 17.50x (ISBN 0-374-94218-8). Octagon.
Levere, Trevor H. Poetry Realized in Nature: Samuel Taylor Coleridge & Early Nineteenth-Century Science. LC 81-1930. 272p. Date not set. price not set (ISBN 0-521-23920-6). Cambridge U Pr.
McBryde, John M. Profitable Company in Literature & Science. 1934. 15.00 (ISBN 0-8274-3209-7). R West.
Nicholl, Charles. The Chemical Theatre. 272p. 1980. 35.00 (ISBN 0-7100-0515-6). Routledge & Kegan.
Nicholson, Marjorie H. Newton Demands the Muse: Newton's "Opticks" & the Eighteenth Century Poets. LC 78-13146. 1979. Repr. of 1966 ed. lib. bdg. 16.75x (ISBN 0-313-21044-6, NIND). Greenwood.
Richards, I. A. Poetries & Sciences. LC 68-22862. 1970. 6.00x (ISBN 0-393-04308-8); pap. 2.25x (ISBN 0-393-00652-2). Norton.
Roberts, Michael. Modern Mind. facs. ed. LC 68-29241. (Essay Index Reprint Ser). 1968. Repr. of 1937 ed. 15.00 (ISBN 0-8369-0827-9). Arno.
Stocker, R. Dimsdale. Poetry & the Scientific Spirit. 1978. Repr. lib. bdg. 22.50 (ISBN 0-89760-807-0, Telegraph). Dynamic Learn Corp.
Sussman, Herbert L. Victorians & the Machine: Literary Response to Technology. LC 68-14274. (Illus.). 1968. 10.00x (ISBN 0-674-93705-8). Harvard U Pr.

LITERATURE AND SOCIETY

Berger, Morroe. Real & Imagined Worlds: The Novel & Social Science. 1977. 16.00x (ISBN 0-674-74941-3). Harvard U Pr.
Bergonzi, Bernard. Reading the Thirties: Texts & Contexts. LC 78-4262. (Critical Essays in Modern Literature). 1978. 9.95 (ISBN 0-8229-1135-3). U of Pittsburgh Pr.
Bertaux, Daniel, ed. Biography & Society: The Life History Approach in the Social Sciences. (Sage Studies in International Sociology: Vol. 23). 308p. 1981. 22.50 (ISBN 0-8039-9800-7); pap. 9.95 (ISBN 0-8039-9801-5). Sage.
Borenstein, Audrey. Redeeming the Sin: Social Science & Literature. LC 78-9332. 269p. 1978. 17.50x (ISBN 0-231-04430-5). Columbia U Pr.
Bowra, M. Poetry & Politics. 1966. 29.95x (ISBN 0-521-04294-1). Cambridge U Pr.
Carter, Paul A. The Creation of Tomorrow: Fifty Years of Magazine Science Fiction. LC 77-5606. (Illus.). 318p. 1977. 16.00x (ISBN 0-231-04210-8); pap. 6.95 (ISBN 0-231-04211-6). Columbia U Pr.
Cazamian, Louis. The Social Novel in England 1830-1850: Dickens, Disraeli, Mrs. Gaskell, Kingsley. Fido, Martin, ed. & tr. 1973. 22.00 (ISBN 0-7100-7282-1). Routledge & Kegan.
Craig, David. The Real Foundation: Literature & Social Change. 318p. 1974. 8.95 (ISBN 0-19-519752-6). Oxford U Pr.
Davison, Peter, et al, eds. Literature & Society. LC 77-90613. (Literary Taste, Culture & Mass Communication Ser.: Vol. 5). 1978. lib. bdg. 40.00x (ISBN 0-914146-48-3). Somerset Hse.
--The Sociology of Literature. LC 77-90614. (Literary Taste, Culture & Mass Communication Ser.: Vol. 6). 1978. lib. bdg. 49.00x (ISBN 0-914146-49-1). Somerset Hse.
Dickinson, H. T., ed. Politics & Literature in the Eighteenth Century. (Rowman & Littlefield University Library). 234p. 1974. 9.50x (ISBN 0-87471-405-2); pap. 4.50x (ISBN 0-87471-400-1). Rowman.
Dixon, Bob. Catching Them Young: Sex, Race & Class in Children's Fiction, Vol. 1. 160p. 1980. text ed. 13.95 (ISBN 0-904383-51-2); pap. 5.95 (ISBN 0-904383-50-4). Pluto Pr.
Donaldson, Ian. World Upside-Down: Comedy from Jonson to Fielding. (Illus.). 1970. pap. 19.50x (ISBN 0-19-812065-6). Oxford U Pr.
Drinkwater, John. Patriotism in Literature. 1980. Repr. of 1924 ed. lib. bdg. 25.00 (ISBN 0-8482-0649-5). Norwood Edns.
Dunham, Vera S. In Stalin's Time. LC 75-10238. 368p. 1976. 36.00 (ISBN 0-521-20949-8); pap. 9.95 (ISBN 0-521-29650-1). Cambridge U Pr.
Emrich, Wilhelm. Literary Revolution & Modern Society & Other Essays. LC 70-125963. 1971. 10.50 (ISBN 0-8044-2169-2, 2169-2). Ungar.
Frye, Northrop. The Critical Path: An Essay on the Social Context of Literary Criticism. LC 70-143246. (Midland Bks.: No. 158). 176p. 1971. 8.95x (ISBN 0-253-31568-9); pap. 3.50x (ISBN 0-253-20158-6). Ind U Pr.
Goldmann, Lucien. Essays on Method in the Sociology of Literature. Boelhower, William Q., tr. from Fr. LC 79-89567. 1980. lib. bdg. 14.00 (ISBN 0-914386-19-0); pap. 4.50 (ISBN 0-914386-20-4). Telos Pr.
--Toward a Sociology of the Novel. 1975. pap. 10.95x (ISBN 0-422-76350-0, Pub. by Tavistock). Methuen Inc.
Guerard, Albert L. Literature & Society. LC 74-135271. 451p. 1971. Repr. of 1935 ed. lib. bdg. 16.50x (ISBN 0-8154-0364-X). Cooper Sq.
Jain, Ravindra K., ed. Text & Context: The Social Anthropology of Tradition. LC 77-842. (Asa Essays in Social Anthropology Ser.: Vol. 2). (Illus.). 256p. 1977. text ed. 14.95x (ISBN 0-915980-03-7). Inst Study Human.
Larkin, Maurice. Man & Society in Nineteenth-Century Realism: Determinism & Literature. 201p. 1977. 22.75x (ISBN 0-87471-956-9). Rowman.
Laurenson, Diana T. & Swingewood, Alan. The Sociology of Literature. LC 72-79743. 281p. 1972. 12.00x (ISBN 0-8052-3457-8). Schocken.
Lewis, C. Day. Revolution in Writing. 1979. 28.50 (ISBN 0-685-94343-7). Porter.
Little, Kenneth. The Sociology of Urban Women's Image in African Literature. 174p. 1980. 27.50x (ISBN 0-8476-6290-X). Rowman.
Loftis, John. Comedy & Society from Congreve to Fielding. LC 76-51940. (Stanford Studies in Language & Literature: 19). Repr. of 1959 ed. 16.50 (ISBN 0-404-51829-X). AMS Pr.
Lowenthal, Leo. Literature & the Image of Man. LC 78-134110. (Essay Index Reprint Ser). 1957. 17.00 (ISBN 0-8369-1982-3). Arno.
--Literature, Popular Culture & Society. LC 61-13532. (Pacific Books Paperbounds, PB-4). 1968. pap. 3.95x (ISBN 0-87015-166-5). Pacific Bks.

Lukacs, Georg. Realism in Our Time: Literature & the Class Struggle. 6.75 (ISBN 0-8446-4576-1). Peter Smith.

Lynn, Kenneth S. Visions of America: Eleven Literary Historical Essays. (Contributions in American Studies: No. 6). 205p. 1973. lib. bdg. 15.00 (ISBN 0-8371-6386-2, LYV/). Greenwood.

Marshall, Thomas F. Literature & Society, 1956-1960. LC 77-942. 1977. lib. bdg. 12.50 (ISBN 0-8414-6057-4). Folcroft.

Marx, Karl & Engels, Frederick. Karl Marx & Frederick Engels on Literature & Art. Baxandall, Lee & Morawski, Stefan, eds. (Documents on Marxist Aesthetics: Vol.I). 192p. 1974. 10.00 (ISBN 0-88477-000-1); pap. 4.50 (ISBN 0-88477-001-X). Intl General.

Miller, James E., Jr. & Herring, Paul D., eds. Arts & the Public. LC 67-26094. 1967. 8.50x (ISBN 0-226-52607-0). U of Chicago Pr.

Mills, Gordon. Hamlet's Castle: The Study of Literature As a Social Experience. LC 76-8020. 372p. 1976. 17.50x (ISBN 0-292-73005-5). U of Tex Pr.

Milne, Gordon. The Sense of Society: A History of the American Novel of Manners. 305p. 1977. 15.00 (ISBN 0-8386-1927-4). Fairleigh Dickinson.

Moore, T. Inglis. Social Patterns in Australian Literature. LC 71-133027. 1971. 25.00x (ISBN 0-520-01828-1). U of Cal Pr.

Norman, C. H. Revolutionary Spirit in Modern Literature & Drama. LC 74-95335. 1971. Repr. of 1937 ed. 9.50 (ISBN 0-8046-1346-X). Kennikat.

Redmond, J., ed. Drama in Society. LC 77-54723. (Themes in Drama: No. 1). (Illus.). 1979. 29.50 (ISBN 0-521-22076-9). Cambridge U Pr.

Rickword, Edgell. Literature in Society: Essays & Opinions II, 1931-1978. Young, Alan, ed. 1978. text ed. 17.25x (ISBN 0-85635-254-3). Humanities.

Rutherford, John. Mexican Society During Revolution. 352p. 1971. 29.95x (ISBN 0-19-827183-2). Oxford U Pr.

Said, Edward, ed. Literature & Society: Selected Papers from the English Institute, 1978. LC 79-17484. 1980. text ed. 7.50x (ISBN 0-8018-2294-7). Johns Hopkins.

Snell, Bruno. Poetry & Society: The Role of Poetry in Ancient Greece. LC 73-165808. (Select Bibliographies Reprint Ser.). Repr. of 1961 ed. 12.00 (ISBN 0-8369-5965-5). Arno.

Soyinka, W. Myth, Literature & the African World. LC 75-38184. 180p. 1976. 27.50 (ISBN 0-521-21190-5); pap. 8.95 (ISBN 0-521-29394-4). Cambridge U Pr.

Strelka, Joseph P., ed. Literary Criticism & Sociology. LC 72-136963. (Yearbook of Comparative Criticism Ser., Vol. 5). 307p. 1973. 16.50x (ISBN 0-271-01152-1). Pa St U Pr.

Terry, Edward D., ed. Artists & Writers in the Evolution of Latin America. LC 69-16097. 240p. 1969. 12.95x (ISBN 0-8173-5060-8). U of Ala Pr.

Trilling, Lionel. The Liberal Imagination: Essays on Literature & Society. 1979. 10.00 (ISBN 0-15-151197-7). HarBraceJ.

Wilson, Robert N. The Writer As Social Seer. LC 79-455. 1979. 14.00x (ISBN 0-8078-1363-X). U of NC Pr.

Ziff, Larzer. Literary Democracy: The Declaration of Cultural Independence in America 1837-1861. LC 80-54082. 1981. 20.00 (ISBN 0-670-43026-9). Viking Pr.

LITERATURE AND STATE

see also Authors and Patrons; State Encouragement of Science, Literature, and Art

Coustillas, Pierre, ed. Politics in Literature in the Nineteenth Century. 1974. pap. text ed. 10.00x (ISBN 0-685-41700-X). Humanities.

Davison, Peter, et al, eds. The Writer & Politics. LC 77-90620. (Literary Taste, Culture & Mass Communications Ser: Vol. 11). 1978. 42.00x (ISBN 0-914146-54-8). Somerset Hse.

Eastman, Max. Artists in Uniform. 1972. lib. bdg. 15.00x (ISBN 0-374-92453-8). Octagon.

Knights, L. C. Public Voices: Literature & Politics with Special Reference to the 17th Century. the Clark Lectures for 1970-71. 133p. 1972. 8.50x (ISBN 0-87471-081-2). Rowman.

McDonald, William C. & Goebel, Ulrich. German Medieval Literary Patronage from Charlemagne to Maximilian the First: A Critical Commentary with Special Emphasis on Imperial Promotion of Literature. LC 73-82154. (Amsterdamer Publikationen Zur Sprache und Literatur: No. 10). 220p. (Orig.). 1973. pap. text ed. 23.00x (ISBN 90-6203-201-X). Humanities.

Reavey, George. Soviet Literature Today. Repr. of 1947 ed. lib. bdg. 15.00x (ISBN 0-8371-2297-X, RESL). Greenwood.

Underwood, John C. Literature & Insurgency. 1914. 17.50x (ISBN 0-8196-0160-8). Biblo.

Vickery, Walter N. The Cult of Optimism. LC 62-63205. (Indiana University Humanities Ser.: No. 52). Repr. of 1963 ed. 14.00 (ISBN 0-527-93100-4). Kraus Repr.

Williams, Raymond. Marxism & Literature. (Marxist Introductions Ser.). 1977. 12.95x (ISBN 0-19-876056-6). Oxford U Pr.

LITERATURE AND TECHNOLOGY

Carter, Paul A. The Creation of Tomorrow: Fifty Years of Magazine Science Fiction. LC 77-5606. (Illus.). 318p. 1977. 16.00x (ISBN 0-231-04210-8); pap. 6.95 (ISBN 0-231-04211-6). Columbia U Pr.

LITERATURE AND WAR

see War and Literature

LITERATURE AS A PROFESSION

see Authors; Authorship; Journalism; Journalists; Litterateurs

LITHIUM

Berner, P., et al, eds. Current Perspectives in Lithium Prophilaxis. (Bibliotheca Psychiatrica Ser.: Vol. 161). (Illus.). viii, 248p. 1981. pap. 52.75 (ISBN 3-8055-1753-X). S Karger.

Dubrova, Sara K. Vitreous Lithium Silicates: Their Properties & Field of Application. 46p. 1964. 20.00 (ISBN 0-306-10679-5, Consultants). Plenum Pub.

Fishwick, J. H. Applications of Lithium in Ceramics. (Illus.). 176p. 1974. 24.95 (ISBN 0-8436-0611-8). CBI Pub.

Freyhan, F. A., ed. Lithium: Clinical & Biological Aspects. (International Pharmacopsychiatry: Vol. 5, No. 2-4). (Illus.). 192p. 1971. pap. 35.50 (ISBN 3-8055-1277-5). S Karger.

Gershon, Samuel & Shopsin, Baron. Lithium: Its Role in Psychiatric Research & Treatment. LC 72-91021. (Illus.). 350p. 1973. 25.00 (ISBN 0-306-30720-0, Plenum Pr). Plenum Pub.

Jefferson, James W & Greist, John H. Primer of Lithium Therapy. 233p. 1977. pap. 14.00 (ISBN 0-683-04466-4). Williams & Wilkins.

Johnson, F. N. Lithium Research & Therapy. 1975. 89.00 (ISBN 0-12-386550-6). Acad Pr.

Johnson, F. Neil. Handbook of Lithium Therapy. 453p. text ed. 39.50 (ISBN 0-8391-1478-8). Univ Park.

Johnson, Susan, ed. Lithium in Medical Practice. LC 77-18031. 1978. 39.50 (ISBN 0-8391-1210-6). Univ Park.

Logan, Joshua. Josh: My up & Down in & Out Life. 1976. 10.00 (ISBN 0-440-04235-6). Delacorte.

Rossof, Arthur H. & Robinson, William A., eds. Lithium Effects of Granulopiesis & Immune Function. (Advances in Experimental Medicine & Biology Ser.: Vol. 127). 470p. 1980. 47.50 (ISBN 0-306-40359-5). Plenum Pub.

Schou, M. Lithium Treatment of Manic-Depressive Illness. (Illus.). viii, 72p. 1980. pap. 14.50 (ISBN 3-8055-0392-X). S Karger.

Smith, Donald F. Lithium & Animal Behavior. (Lithium Research Review Ser.: Vol. 2). 1981. 12.95 (ISBN 0-89885-075-4). Human Sci Pr.

--Lithium & Animal Behavior. Horrobin, D. F., ed. (Lithium Research Review Ser.: Vol. I). 66p. 1980. Repr. of 1977 ed. 12.95 (ISBN 0-87705-961-6). Human Sci Pr.

LITHOGRAPHERS

Library of Congress. Charles Fenderich: Lithographer of American Statesmen. Miller, Lillian B., ed. (Illus.). 1978. text ed. 25.00 incl. microfiche (ISBN 0-226-69243-4). U of Chicago Pr.

--Charles Fenderich: Lithographer of American Statesmen. LC 76-24470. includes 3 black & white fiches 25.00 (ISBN 0-226-69243-4, Chicago Visual Lib). U of Chicago Pr.

Peters, Harry T. America on Stone: The Other Printmakers to the American People. LC 75-22832. (America in Two Centuries Ser). (Illus.). 1976. Repr. of 1931 ed. 150.00x (ISBN 0-405-07703-3). Arno.

--California on Stone. LC 75-22833. (America in Two Centuries Ser). (Illus.). 1976. Repr. of 1935 ed. 150.00x (ISBN 0-405-07704-1). Arno.

Rudman, Jack. Lithographic Pressman. (Career Examination Ser.: C-445). (Cloth bdg. avail. on request). pap. 8.00 (ISBN 0-8373-0445-8). Natl Learning.

LITHOGRAPHS

see also Printing As a Graphic Art

Bloch, E. Maurice, intro. by. Tamarind: A Renaissance of Lithography. LC 79-158627. (Illus.). 1971. soft bdg 4.50 (ISBN 0-88397-066-X). Intl Exhibit Foun.

Daphne & Nelson, eds. Beauty Unknown Color Lithographs. (New Age Ser.: No. 502). 1976. 12.00 (ISBN 0-89007-502-6). C Stark.

Daumier, Honore-Victorin. Daumier: One Hundred & Twenty Great Lithographies. Ramus, Charles F., ed. 12.50 (ISBN 0-8446-5675-5). Peter Smith.

Durieux, Caroline & Cox, Richard. Caroline Durieux Lithographs of the Thirties & Forties. LC 77-16525. (Illus.). 1977. 14.95 (ISBN 0-8071-0372-1). La State U Pr.

Field, Richard S. The Lithographs & Etchings of Philip Pearlstein. LC 78-52835. (Illus., Orig.). 1978. pap. text ed. 12.95x (ISBN 0-934306-01-X). Springfield.

Guerin, Marcel. Forain Lithographe. rev. ed. (Illus.). 208p. (Fr.). 1980. 75.00 (ISBN 0-915346-39-7). A Wofsy Fine Arts.

Leiris, Michael & Mourlot, Fernand. Joan Miro, Lithographs, Vol. 1. (Illus.). 231p. 1972. 150.00x (ISBN 0-8148-0494-2, Pub. by Tudor). Hennessey.

Levy, Lester S. Picture the Songs: Lithographs from the Sheet Music of 19th Century America. LC 76-13518. (Illus.). 232p. 1976. 25.00 (ISBN 0-8018-1814-1). Johns Hopkins.

Monthan, Doris. R. C. Gorman: The Lithographs. LC 78-58469. (Illus.). 1978. 35.00 (ISBN 0-87358-179-2). Northland.

Olson, Nancy. Garvarni's Carnival Lithographs. (Illus.). 1979. write for info. (ISBN 0-89467-009-3). Yale Art Gallery.

Peters, Harry T. Currier & Ives: Printmakers to the American People, 2 vols. LC 75-22834. (America in Two Centuries Ser). (Illus.). 1976. Repr. of 1929 ed. 300.00x (ISBN 0-405-07741-6); 150.00x ea. Vol. 1 (ISBN 0-405-07742-4). Vol. 2 (ISBN 0-405-07743-2). Arno.

Reps, John W. Cities on Stone: Nineteenth Century Lithograph Images of the Urban West. LC 76-12313. (Illus.). 100p. 1976. lib. bdg. 14.95 (ISBN 0-88360-024-2); pap. 9.95 (ISBN 0-88360-051-X). Amon Carter.

Ross, John & Romano, Clare. The Complete Screen Print & the Lithograph. LC 74-2696. 1974. pap. text ed. 9.95 (ISBN 0-02-927380-3). Free Pr.

Savory, Jerold J. The Vanity Fair Gallery: A Collector's Guide to the Caricatures. LC 78-353. (Illus.). 209p. 1978. 30.00 (ISBN 0-87982-023-3). Art Alliance.

Stuckey, Ronald & Stuckey, Joan. The Lithographs of Stow Wengenroth, 1931-1972. (Illus.). 1974. 25.00 (ISBN 0-89073-035-0). Boston Public Lib.

LITHOGRAPHS–CATALOGS

Ball, Maudette Ww. Nathan Oliveira Print Retrospective 1949-1980. (Illus.). 72p. (Orig.). 1980. pap. 10.00 (ISBN 0-936270-00-4). Art Mus Gall.

Brabyn, Howard, tr. Daumier's Hunting & Fishing. (Illus.). 140p. 1975. 25.00 (ISBN 0-8148-0642-2). L Amiel Pub.

Delteil, Loys, ed. Le Peintre-Graveur Illustre, 32 vols, Vols. 1-16. Incl. Vol. 1. J. F. Millet, Th. Rousseau, Jules Dupre, J. Barthold Jongkind. 20.00 (ISBN 0-306-78501-3); Vol. 2. Charles Meryon. 35.00 (ISBN 0-306-78502-1); Vol. 3. J. A. D. Ingres & Eugene Delacroix. 60.00 (ISBN 0-306-78503-X); Vol. 4. Anders Zorn. 45.00 (ISBN 0-306-78504-8); Vol. 5. C. Corot. 35.00 (ISBN 0-306-78505-6); Vol. 6. Rude, Barye, Carpeaux, Rodin. 20.00 (ISBN 0-306-78506-4); Vol. 7. Paul Huet. 20.00 (ISBN 0-306-78507-2); Vol. 8. Eugene Carriere. 25.00 (ISBN 0-306-78508-0); Vol. 9. Edgar Degas. 35.00 (ISBN 0-306-78509-9); Vols. 10 & 11. Toulouse-Lautrec. Set. 140.00 (ISBN 0-685-24299-4); Vol. 10. 70.00 ea. (ISBN 0-306-78510-2). Vol. 11 (ISBN 0-306-78511-0); Vol. 12. Gustave Leheutre. 25.00 (ISBN 0-306-78512-9); Vol. 13. Charles-Francois Daubigny. 40.00 (ISBN 0-306-78513-7); Vols. 14 & 15. Francisco Goya. Set. 140.00 (ISBN 0-685-24300-1). Vol. 14 (ISBN 0-306-78514-5). Vol. 15 (ISBN 0-306-78515-3); Vol. 16. Jean-Francois Raffaeli. 35.00 (ISBN 0-306-78516-1). LC 68-27720. (Graphic Art Ser). Set Of 32 Vols. Da Capo.

--Le Peintre-Graveur Illustre, 32 vols, Vols. 17-32. Incl. Vol. 17. Camille Pissaro, Alfred Sisley, Auguste Renoir. 75.00 (ISBN 0-306-78517-X); Vol. 18. Theodore Gericault. 35.00 (ISBN 0-306-78518-8); Vol. 19. Henri Leys, Henri de Braekeleer, James Ensor. 50.00 (ISBN 0-306-78519-6); Vols. 20-29. Honore Daumier. Set. 550.00 (ISBN 0-306-78520-X); Vol. 30. Albert Besnard. 40.00 (ISBN 0-306-78530-7); Vol. 31. Jean Frelaut. 45.00 (ISBN 0-686-66647-X); Vol. 32. Appendix. Wechsler, Herman J. 30.00 (ISBN 0-306-78532-3). LC 68-27720. (Graphic Art Ser). Set Of 32 Vols. 980.00 (ISBN 0-306-78500-5). Da Capo.

Monthan, Doris. R. C. Gorman: The Lithographs. LC 78-58469. (Illus.). 1978. 35.00 (ISBN 0-87358-179-2). Northland.

Olson, Nancy. Garvarni's Carnival Lithographs. (Illus.). 1979. write for info. (ISBN 0-89467-009-3). Yale Art Gallery.

White, Robert R. Lithographs & Etchings of E. Martin Hennings. (Illus.). 1978. pap. 1.25 (ISBN 0-89013-117-1). Museum NM Pr.

LITHOGRAPHY

see also Chromolithography; Color-Printing; Offset Printing; Photolithography

Antreasian, Garo Z. & Adams, Clinton. Tamarind Book of Lithography: Art & Techniques. LC 76-121328. (Illus.). 1971. 37.50 (ISBN 0-8109-0496-9); pap. 19.95 (ISBN 0-8109-9017-2). Abrams.

Arnold, Grant. Creative Lithography & How to Do It. (Illus.). 7.50 (ISBN 0-8446-1552-8). Peter Smith.

--Creative Lithography & How to Do It. (Illus.). 1941. pap. 3.50 (ISBN 0-486-21208-4). Dover.

Bibliotheque Nationale & Farwell, Beatrice. French Popular Lithographic Imagery, 1815-1870: Lithographs & Literature, Vol. I. (Illus.). 100p. 1981. price not set text-fiche (ISBN 0-226-69011-3). U of Chicago Pr.

Cate, Dennis & Hitchings, Sinclair Hamilton. The Color Revolution: Color Lithography in France, 1890-1900. 1978. 9.95 (ISBN 0-87905-032-2). Boston Public Lib.

Cate, Phillip D. & Hitchings, Sinclair. The Color Revolution. LC 78-13809. (Illus.). 1978. pap. 9.95 (ISBN 0-87905-032-2). Peregrine Smith.

Dennis, Ervin A. Lithographic Technology. LC 79-16756. 1980. 19.95 (ISBN 0-672-97164-X); tchr's manual 6.67 (ISBN 0-672-97165-8); student manual 7.95 (ISBN 0-672-97166-6). Bobbs.

Eichenberg, Fritz. Lithography & Silkscreen: Art & Technique. LC 77-20263. (Illus.). 1978. pap. 7.95 (ISBN 0-8109-2095-6). Abrams.

Faux, Ian. Modern Lithography. (Illus.). 352p. 1978. pap. 15.95x (ISBN 0-7121-1294-4, Pub. by Macdonald & Evans England). Intl Ideas.

--Modern Lithography. 2nd ed. (Illus.). 1979. pap. 20.00 (ISBN 0-7121-1294-4). Transatlantic.

Freeman, Larry. Louis Prang, Color Lithographer. LC 70-145867. (Library of Victorian Culture Ser.). (Illus.). 1971. 25.00 (ISBN 0-87282-050-5, 87282). Century Hse.

Hird. Introduction to Photo-Offset Lithography. 1981. text ed. 10.00 (ISBN 0-87002-336-5). Bennett IL.

Hoagland, H. E. Collective Bargaining in the Lithographic Industry. LC 73-76708. (Columbia University. Studies in the Social Sciences: No. 176). Repr. of 1917 ed. 16.50 (ISBN 0-404-51176-7). AMS Pr.

Hullmandel, Charles J. The Art of Drawing on Stone, Giving a Full Explanation of the Various Styles of the Different Methods to Be Employed to Ensure Success, & of the Modes of Correcting, As Well As of the Several Causes of Failure. LC 78-74392. (Nineteenth-Century Book Arts & Printing History Ser.: Vol. 7). 1980. lib. bdg. 22.00 (ISBN 0-8240-3881-9). Garland Pub.

Jones, Stanley. Lithography for Artists. (Oxford Paperbacks Handbooks for Artists). 1967. pap. 4.00x (ISBN 0-19-289902-3). Oxford U Pr.

Kampmann, Lothar. Picture Printing. 1970. 19.95 (ISBN 0-7134-2280-7, Pub. by Batsford England). David & Charles.

Knigin, Michael & Zimiles, Murray. Techniques of Fine Art Lithography. rev. ed. 1977. pap. 7.95 (ISBN 0-442-24479-7). Van Nos Reinhold.

Munson, Fred C. Labor Relations in the Lithographic Industry. LC 63-10872. (Wertheim Publications in Industrial Relations Ser). (Illus.). 290p. 1963. 16.00x (ISBN 0-674-50850-5). Harvard U Pr.

Peters, Harry T. America on Stone: The Other Printmakers to the American People. LC 75-22832. (America in Two Centuries Ser). (Illus.). 1976. Repr. of 1931 ed. 150.00x (ISBN 0-405-07703-3). Arno.

--California on Stone. LC 75-22833. (America in Two Centuries Ser). (Illus.). 1976. Repr. of 1935 ed. 150.00x (ISBN 0-405-07704-1). Arno.

Prust, Z. A. Photo-Offset Lithography. (Illus.). 160p. 1981. 9.96 (ISBN 0-87006-240-9). Goodheart.

Rudman, Jack. Offset Lithography. (Occupational Competency Examination Ser.: OCE-27). (Cloth bdg. avail. on request). pap. 9.95 (ISBN 0-8373-5727-6). Natl Learning.

Senefelder, Alois. A Complete Course of Lithography. LC 68-27721. (Graphic Art Ser). (Illus.). 1968. Repr. of 1819 ed. lib. bdg. 35.00 (ISBN 0-306-71155-9). Da Capo.

--A Complete Course of Lithography. LC 68-27721. 1977. pap. 7.95 (ISBN 0-306-80053-5). Da Capo.

Twyman, Michael. Lithography Eighteen Hundred to Eighteen Fifty: The Techniques of Drawing on Stone in England & France & Their Application in Works of Topography. 1970. 26.00x (ISBN 0-19-215168-1). Oxford U Pr.

Weber. Histoire de la Lithographie. 65.75 (ISBN 0-685-35922-0). French & Eur.

LITHOLOGY

see Petrology

LITHOPHYTES

see Corals

LITHOPRINTING

see Offset Printing

LITHUANIA

Daumantas, Juozas L. Fighters for Freedom. 1975. 9.95 (ISBN 0-87141-049-4). Manyland.

Gerutis, Albertas, et al. Lithuania: Seven Hundred Years. 5th ed. Budreckis, Algirdas, tr. LC 75-80057. 1969. 15.00 (ISBN 0-87141-028-1). Manyland.

Kaslas, Bronis. USSR - German Aggression Against Lilhuania: 1918-1945. Orig. Title: Documentary History of Lithuania's Foreign Policy. 15.00 (ISBN 0-8315-0135-9). Speller.

Lukaszewicz, Joseph. Girys I Biruta: Poemat Z Dawnych Czasow Litewskich. (Polish). 1964. 2.75 (ISBN 0-685-09284-4). Endurance.
Melamed, Frances. Janova: Portrait of a Lithuanian Village in Revolutionary & Communist Russia 1914-1920. LC 75-38045. (Illus.). 229p. 1976. 12.50 (ISBN 0-917294-01-7). Janova Pr.
Pajaujis-Javis, Joseph. Soviet Genocide in Lithuania. 1980. 10.95 (ISBN 0-87141-060-5). Manyland.
Senn, Alfred E. The Emergence of Modern Lithuania. LC 74-14028. 272p. 1975. Repr. of 1959 ed. lib. bdg. 16.50x (ISBN 0-8371-7780-4, SEML). Greenwood.
Vardys, V. Stanley. The Catholic Church, Dissent & Nationality in Soviet Lithuania. (East European Monographs: No. 43). 1978. 18.00x (ISBN 0-914710-36-2). East Eur Quarterly.

LITHUANIAN LANGUAGE

Dambriunas, L. A. Introduction to Modern Lithuanian. 2nd, rev. ed. 1972. 20.00 (ISBN 0-685-47301-5). Heinman.
Peteraitis, Vilius. Lithuanian-English Dictionary. 22.50 (ISBN 0-87559-037-3); thumb indexed 26.00 (ISBN 0-87559-038-1). Shalom.
Robinson, David F. Lithuanian Reverse Dictionary. 1976. soft cover 11.95 (ISBN 0-89357-034-6). Slavica.
Senn, Alfred. Lithuanian Dialectology. Repr. of 1947 ed. pap. 6.00 (ISBN 0-384-54870-9). Johnson Repr.
Wood, Frederic T. Accentuation of Nominal Compounds in Lithuanian. 1930. pap. 6.00 (ISBN 0-527-00753-6). Kraus Repr.

LITHUANIAN LITERATURE

Ford, G. B. The Old Lithuanian Catechism of Mazvydas. 1971. 21.65x (ISBN 90-232-0565-0, Pub by Van Gorcum). Intl Schol Bk Serv.
Fraenkel, Ernst. Litauisches Etymologisches Woerterbuch, Vol. 1. (Lith. & Ger.). 1960. 152.00 (ISBN 3-533-00650-6, M-7541, Pub. by Westdeutscher Verlag/VVA). French & Eur.
--Litauisches Etymologisches Woerterbuch, Vol. 2. (Lith. & Ger.). 1965. 195.00 (ISBN 3-533-00651-4, M-7542, Pub. by Westdeutscher Verlag/VVA). French & Eur.
Skrupskelis, Alina, ed. Lithuanian Writers in the West: An Anthology. LC 79-83800. (Ethnic Encyclopedia of Lithuanaina Culture in USA Ser.). (Illus.). 388p. 1979. 20.00 (ISBN 0-932042-05-8, Co-Pub. by Loyola). Lithuanian Lib.
Zobarskas, Stepas, ed. Lithuanian Short Story: Fifty Years. 1977. 12.50 (ISBN 0-87141-035-4). Manyland.

LITHUANIANS IN THE UNITED STATES

Braude, Michael. The First Thirty Odd Years. 224p. 1976. 8.95 (ISBN 0-8180-0228-X). Horizon.
Budreckis, Algirdas, ed. The Lithuanians in America: A Chronology & Fact Book. LC 76-6680. (Ethnic Chronology Ser). 1976. lib. bdg. 8.50 (ISBN 0-379-00517-4). Oceana.
Fainhaus, David. Lithuanians in Multi-Ethnic Chicago Until World War II. LC 76-5693. 1977. 20.00 (ISBN 0-8294-0370-1). Loyola.
Greene, Victor. For God & Country: The Rise of Polish & Lithuanian Ethnic Consciousness in America, 1860-1910. LC 75-19017. (Illus.). 202p. 1975. 17.50 (ISBN 0-87020-155-7). State Hist Soc Wis.
Kezys, A., ed. A Lithuanian Cemetery. LC 75-21496. 1977. 19.95 (ISBN 0-8294-0279-9). Loyola.
Vengris, Vitolis E. Lithuanian Bookplates. (Ethnic Encyclopedia of Lithuanian Culture in USA Ser.). (Illus.). 248p. 1980. 20.00 (ISBN 0-932042-06-6). Lithuanian Lib.

LITIGATION, GOVERNMENT

see Government Litigation

LITTER (TRASH)

Kundell, James E. Litter Abatement Measures. 74p. 1979. spiral bdg. 5.00 (ISBN 0-89854-062-3). U of GA Inst Govt.
Smaridge, Norah. Litterbugs Come in Every Size. (Illus.). (ps-4). 1972. PLB 7.62 (ISBN 0-307-60455-1, Golden Pr). Western Pub.

LITTERATEURS

see also Authors; Dramatists; Poets;
also subdivision Intellectual Life under names of countries, cities, etc.

Britton, Burt. Self Portrait: Book People Picture Themselves. 1976. pap. 6.95 (ISBN 0-394-73104-2). Random.
MacFarlane, Charles. Reminiscences of a Literary Life. LC 74-18318. 1974. Repr. of 1917 ed. lib. bdg. 30.00 (ISBN 0-8414-6174-0). Folcroft.
Magill, Frank L., ed. The Contemporary Literary Scene. LC 74-29200. 25.00 (ISBN 0-89356-173-8). Salem Pr.
Scott, Dixon. Men of Letters. 1977. Repr. of 1923 ed. lib. bdg. 20.00 (ISBN 0-8414-7948-8). Folcroft.

LITTERING

see Litter (Trash)

LITTLE, MALCOLM, 1925-1965

Adoff, Arnold. Malcolm X. LC 70-94787. (Biography Ser.). (Illus.). (gr. 2-5). 1970. (TYC-J); PLB 8.79 (ISBN 0-690-51414-X). Har-Row.
Breitman, George. The Last Year of Malcolm X: The Evolution of a Revolutionary. LC 67-20467. 1970. 12.00 (ISBN 0-87348-003-1); pap. 3.45 (ISBN 0-87348-004-X). Path Pr NY.
Breitman, George, et al. The Assassination of Malcolm X. Miah, Malik, ed. (Illus.). 1977. 9.00 (ISBN 0-87348-472-X); pap. 2.45 (ISBN 0-87348-473-8). Path Pr NY.
Curtis, Richard. Life of Malcolm X. (Illus.). (gr. 7up). 1971. 6.25 (ISBN 0-8255-2786-4). Macrae.
Fowler, James W. & Lovin, Robin W. Trajectories in Faith: Five Life Stories. LC 79-20485. 1980. pap. 6.50 (ISBN 0-687-42480-1). Abingdon.
Goldman, Peter L. The Death & Life of Malcolm X. 2nd ed. LC 79-18105. 1979. pap. 7.95 (ISBN 0-252-00774-3). U of Ill Pr.
Lomax, Louis. To Kill a Black Man. LC 68-8400. (Orig.). 1968. pap. 0.95 (ISBN 0-87067-160-X, BH160). Holloway.
Maglangbayan, Shawna. Garvey, Lumumba, Malcolm: Black Nationalist-Separatists. 1972. 4.95 (ISBN 0-88378-022-4); pap. 2.95 (ISBN 0-88378-079-8). Third World.
Malcolm X: A Bibliography. (Bibliographies in Black Studies). 1981. lib. bdg. 15.00 (ISBN 0-937954-02-0). Chi Ctr Afro-Am Stud.
Malcolm X. Autobiography of Malcolm X. 1977. pap. 2.75 (ISBN 0-345-29420-3). Ballantine.
--Malcolm X Speaks. Breitman, George, ed. LC 65-27410. 226p. 1976. 15.00 (ISBN 0-87348-461-4). Path Pr NY.
Paris, Peter J. Black Leaders in Conflict: Joseph H. Jackson, Martin Luther King Jr., Malcolm X, Adam Clayton Powell Jr. LC 78-3833. 1978. pap. 6.95 (ISBN 0-8298-0336-X). Pilgrim NY.
Phillips, Elizabeth. Monarch Notes on Malcolm X's Autobiography. 1975. pap. 1.95 (ISBN 0-671-00949-4). Monarch Pr.
Randall, Dudley & Burroughs, Margaret G., eds. For Malcolm: Poems on the Life & Death of Malcolm X. 2nd ed. 1969. 4.95 (ISBN 0-685-07543-5); pap. 2.95 (ISBN 0-910296-12-X). Broadside.
Rich, Andrea & Smith, Arthur L. Rhetoric of Revolution. LC 79-99291. 12.00 (ISBN 0-87716-010-4, Pub. by Moore Pub Co). F Apple.
White, Florence M. Malcolm X. (gr. k-6). 1980. pap. 1.25 (ISBN 0-440-45023-3, YB). Dell.
--Malcolm X: Black & Proud. LC 74-16264. (Americans All Ser). (Illus.). 96p. (gr. 3-6). 1975. PLB 6.48 (ISBN 0-8116-4582-7). Garrard.
Wolfenstein, Eugene V. The Victims of Democracy: Malcolm X & the Black Revolution. 600p. 1981. 16.95 (ISBN 0-520-03903-3). U of Cal Pr.

LITTLE BIG HORN, BATTLE OF THE, 1876

Brininstool, E. A. A Trooper with Custer & Other Historic Incidents of the Battle of the Little Big Horn. LC 74-12558. (Illus.). 214p. 1975. Repr. of 1926 ed. lib. bdg. 11.00x (ISBN 0-8154-0500-6). Cooper Sq.
Brown, Jesse & Willard, A. M. The Black Hills Trails: A History of the Struggles of the Pioneers... facsimile ed. LC 75-83. (Mid-American Frontier Ser.). (Illus.). 1975. Repr. of 1924 ed. 33.00x (ISBN 0-405-06852-2). Arno.
Carroll, John M. & Price, Byron. Roll Call on the Little Big Horn. (Source Custeriana Ser.: No. 3). 1974. 27.50 (ISBN 0-88342-033-3). Old Army.
Carroll, John M., ed. The Benteen-Goldin Letters on Custer & His Last Battle. 1974. 35.00 (ISBN 0-87140-580-6). Liveright.
--General Custer & the Battle of the Little Big Horn: The Federal View. LC 76-11331. (Illus.). 1978. 19.50 (ISBN 0-686-77344-6). Presidio Pr.
--The Two Battles of the Little Big Horn. (Illus.). 1974. 35.00 (ISBN 0-87140-586-5). Liveright.
Custer's Last Battle, 1876. (Illus.). 44p. 1976. Repr. of 1892 ed. pap. 3.50 (ISBN 0-89646-000-2). Outbooks.
Dippie, Brian W. Custer's Last Stand: The Anatomy of an American Myth. (Illus.). 1976. pap. 7.95 (ISBN 0-686-18656-7). U of MT Pubns Hist.
Kain, Robert C. In the Valley of the Little Big Horn. rev. ed. (Illus.). 117p. 1978. 7.95 (ISBN 0-917714-16-4). Beinfeld Pub.
Marquis, Thomas B. Keep the Last Bullet for Yourself: The True Story of Custer's Last Stand. new ed. Irvine, Keith & Faherty, Robert, eds. LC 75-39093. (Illus.). 192p. 1976. 12.50 (ISBN 0-917256-02-6); pap. 5.95 (ISBN 0-917256-14-X). Ref Pubns.
Marquis, Thomas B., tr. Wooden Leg: A Warrior Who Fought Custer. LC 31-10067. (Illus.). 1962. pap. 6.50 (ISBN 0-8032-5124-6, BB 126, Bison). U of Nebr Pr.
Masters, Joseph G. Shadows Fall Across the Little Horn: Custer's Last Stand. 62p. 1951. 20.00 (ISBN 0-932068-02-2). South Pass Pr.
Russell, Don. Custer's Last. LC 68-19219. (Illus.). 67p. 1968. 6.95 (ISBN 0-88360-016-1). Amon Carter.
Sandoz, Mari. The Battle of the Little Bighorn. LC 78-8733. (Illus.). 1978. pap. 3.95 (ISBN 0-8032-9100-0, BB 677, Bison). U of Nebr Pr.
Scudder, Ralph E. Custer Country. LC 62-21700. (Illus.). 1963. 6.50 (ISBN 0-8323-0042-X). Binford.

LITTLE COMMONWEALTH

Bazeley, E. T. Homer Lane & the Little Commonwealth. LC 69-19624. 1969. pap. 1.95 (ISBN 0-8052-0221-8). Schocken.

LITTLE ENTENTE, 1920-1939

Machray, Robert. The Little Entente. LC 68-9665. 1970. Repr. of 1929 ed. 25.00 (ISBN 0-86527-118-6). Fertig.

LITTLE FLOWER OF JESUS

see Therese De Lisieux, Saint, 1873-1897

LITTLE GIDDING

Williams, Alvin M., Jr. Conversations at Little Gidding. LC 78-85741. (Illus.). 1970. 58.00 (ISBN 0-521-07680-3). Cambridge U Pr.

LITTLE LEAGUE BASEBALL, INC

Einstein, Charles. How to Coach, Manage & Play Little League Baseball. LC 68-12167. 1969. pap. 3.95 (ISBN 0-671-20291-X, Fireside). S&S.
Lee, S. C. Little League Leader. LC 74-77738. (Super Star Ser.). 1974. 4.95 (ISBN 0-87397-046-2). Strode.
Reizer, John. Once in a Lifetime: The Story of a National Championship Little League Team. 1978. 5.95 (ISBN 0-533-03153-2). Vantage.
Shirts, Morris A. Warm up for Little League Baseball. (Illus.). (gr. 3-6). 1977. pap. 1.75 (ISBN 0-671-41135-7). PB.
--Warm up for Little League Baseball. 1981. pap. 1.95 (ISBN 0-671-42422-X). Archway.
Shirts, Morris A. & Myers, Kent E. Call It Right! Umpiring in the Little League. LC 76-51169. (Illus.). 1977. 7.95 (ISBN 0-8069-4108-1); lib. bdg. 7.49 (ISBN 0-8069-4109-X). Sterling.
Voigt, David Q. A Little League Journal. 96p. 1975. pap. 3.00 (ISBN 0-87972-102-2). Bowling Green Univ.
Yablonsky, Lewis & Brower, Jonathan J. The Little League Game: How Parents, Coaches & Kids Really Play It. LC 78-58179. 1979. 10.00 (ISBN 0-8129-0803-1). Times Bks.

LITTLE MAGAZINES

Fleet, Fred A., 2nd. Pertinent Facts About Self Publications. 1979. pap. 4.95 (ISBN 0-933542-50-X). F A Fleet.
Fulton, Len. International Directory of Little Magazines & Small Presses. 13th ed. 1977. 11.95 (ISBN 0-913218-05-7); pap. 8.95 (ISBN 0-913218-04-9). Dustbooks.
--Small Press Record of Books in Print. 5th ed. 1976. cloth 21.95 (ISBN 0-913218-69-3). Dustbooks.
--Small Press Record of Books in Print. 6th ed. 1977. pap. 8.95 (ISBN 0-913218-03-0). Dustbooks.
Fulton, Len, ed. International Directory of Little Magazines & Small Presses. 11th ed. 304p. 1975. 8.95 (ISBN 0-913218-16-2); pap. 5.95 (ISBN 0-913218-15-4). Dustbooks.
--International Directory of Little Magazines & Small Presses. 12th ed. 1976. 15.95 (ISBN 0-913218-12-X); pap. 19.95 (ISBN 0-913218-67-7). Dustbooks.
--Small Press Record of Books in Print, 1978. 7th ed. (Small Press Information Library). 1978. 10.95 (ISBN 0-913218-60-X). Dustbooks.
Fulton, Len & Ferber, Ellen, eds. Directory of Small Magazine Press Editors & Publishers. 10th ed. 1979. pap. 8.95 (ISBN 0-913218-90-1). Dustbooks.
--Directory of Small Magazine Press Editors & Publishers. 10th ed. 1979. pap. 8.95 (ISBN 0-913218-90-1). Dustbooks.
--International Directory of Little Magazines & Small Presses. 16th ed. (Dustbooks Small Press Info. Library). 580p. 1980. 17.95 (ISBN 0-913218-94-4); pap. 13.95 (ISBN 0-913218-93-6). Dustbooks.
--International Directory of Little Magazines & Small Presses. 15th ed. 1979. 15.95 (ISBN 0-913218-88-X); pap. 11.95 (ISBN 0-913218-87-1). Dustbooks.
--International Directory of Little Magazines & Small Presses, 1978-79. 14th ed. (Small Press Information Library). 1978. 13.95 (ISBN 0-913218-58-8); pap. 10.95 (ISBN 0-913218-57-X). Dustbooks.
--Small Press Record of Books in Print. 9th ed. (Dustbooks Small Press Info. Library). 680p. 1980. 17.95 (ISBN 0-913218-95-2). Dustbooks.
--Small Press Record of Books in Print. 8th ed. 1979. 11.95 (ISBN 0-913218-89-8). Dustbooks.
Fulton, Len & May, James B., eds. International Directory of Little Magazines & Small Presses. 10th ed. 200p. 1974. 7.95 (ISBN 0-913218-14-6); pap. 4.95 (ISBN 0-913218-13-8). Dustbooks.
McGilvery, Lynette, ed. An Index to the Paperback Little Magazines. 1980. pap. 6.95x (ISBN 0-910938-64-4). McGilvery.
Roeming, Robert F. Catalog of Little Magazines. LC 79-5414. 154p. 1979. 19.50 (ISBN 0-299-08180-X, IS-00097, Pub. by U of Wisc Pr). Univ Microfilms.
Sader, Marion, ed. Comprehensive Index to English-Language Little Magazines, 1890-1970, 8 vols. LC 74-11742. 1976. Set. 650.00 (ISBN 0-527-00370-0). Kraus Intl.

LITTLE PRESSES

Carrey, Dixieann W. Writer's Self-Publishing Procedures. Date not set. write for info (ISBN 0-931882-05-2). TIB Pubns.
Chickadel, Charles J. Publish It Yourself: The Complete Guide to Self-Publishing Your Own Book. 2nd ed. 1980. pap. 5.95 (ISBN 0-931314-02-X). Caroline Hse.
Doty, Betty. Publish Your Own Handbound Books. LC 80-67947. (Illus.). 127p. 1980. 8.95 (ISBN 0-930822-02-1); lib. bdg. 7.95 (ISBN 0-930822-03-X). Bookery.
Finney, Frederick M., ed. Small Press Publishing. LC 78-50210. 1978. 12.00 (ISBN 0-89421-015-7). Challenge Pr.
Fleet, Fred A., 2nd. Pertinent Facts About Self Publications. 1979. pap. 4.95 (ISBN 0-933542-50-X). F A Fleet.
Franklin, Walt. Encyclopedia of Self-Publishing: Complete Reference for Self-Publishing Writers. rev. ed. Walton, S. F., ed. (Illus.). 256p. 1979. 24.95 (ISBN 0-686-63393-8). Media Unltd.
Fulton, Len. International Directory of Little Magazines & Small Presses. 13th ed. 1977. 11.95 (ISBN 0-913218-05-7); pap. 8.95 (ISBN 0-913218-04-9). Dustbooks.
--Small Press Record of Books in Print. 5th ed. 1976. cloth 21.95 (ISBN 0-913218-69-3). Dustbooks.
--Small Press Record of Books in Print. 6th ed. 1977. pap. 8.95 (ISBN 0-913218-03-0). Dustbooks.
Fulton, Len, ed. International Directory of Little Magazines & Small Presses. 11th ed. 304p. 1975. 8.95 (ISBN 0-913218-16-2); pap. 5.95 (ISBN 0-913218-15-4). Dustbooks.
--International Directory of Little Magazines & Small Presses. 12th ed. 1976. 15.95 (ISBN 0-913218-12-X); pap. 19.95 (ISBN 0-913218-67-7). Dustbooks.
--International Directory of Little Magazines & Small Presses. 12th ed. 1976. 15.95 (ISBN 0-913218-12-X); pap. 19.95 (ISBN 0-913218-67-7). Dustbooks.
--Small Press Record of Books in Print, 1978. 7th ed. (Small Press Information Library). 1978. 10.95 (ISBN 0-913218-60-X). Dustbooks.
Fulton, Len & Ferber, Ellen, eds. Directory of Small Magazine Press Editors & Publishers. 10th ed. 1979. pap. 8.95 (ISBN 0-913218-90-1). Dustbooks.
--Directory of Small Magazine Press Editors & Publishers. 10th ed. 1979. pap. 8.95 (ISBN 0-913218-90-1). Dustbooks.
--International Directory of Little Magazines & Small Presses. 16th ed. (Dustbooks Small Press Info. Library). 580p. 1980. 17.95 (ISBN 0-913218-94-4); pap. 13.95 (ISBN 0-913218-93-6). Dustbooks.
--International Directory of Little Magazines & Small Presses. 16th ed. (Dustbooks Small Press Info. Library). 580p. 1980. 17.95 (ISBN 0-913218-94-4); pap. 13.95 (ISBN 0-913218-93-6). Dustbooks.
--International Directory of Little Magazines & Small Presses. 15th ed. 1979. 15.95 (ISBN 0-913218-88-X); pap. 11.95 (ISBN 0-913218-87-1). Dustbooks.
--International Directory of Little Magazines & Small Presses, 1978-79. 14th ed. (Small Press Information Library). 1978. 13.95 (ISBN 0-913218-58-8); pap. 10.95 (ISBN 0-913218-57-X). Dustbooks.
--Small Press Record of Books in Print. 9th ed. (Dustbooks Small Press Info. Library). 680p. 1980. 17.95 (ISBN 0-913218-95-2). Dustbooks.
--Small Press Record of Books in Print. 8th ed. 1979. 11.95 (ISBN 0-913218-89-8). Dustbooks.
Fulton, Len & May, James B., eds. International Directory of Little Magazines & Small Presses. 10th ed. 200p. 1974. 7.95 (ISBN 0-913218-14-6); pap. 4.95 (ISBN 0-913218-13-8). Dustbooks.
Henderson, Bill, ed. The Pushcart Prize V: Best of the Small Presses, 1980-1981 Edition. 1980. 17.95 (ISBN 0-916366-10-3). Pushcart Pr.
How to Print & Publish a Book Cheaply. pap. 7.50 (ISBN 0-935068-01-5). Meeker Pub.
Howard, Lee. How to Publish Your Own Book Successfully. 80p. 1980. pap. 10.00 (ISBN 0-912584-00-9). Selective.

Johnson, Christine L. & Straayer, A. Christine. A Book of One's Own: Guide to Self-Publishing. LC 79-89245. (Orig.). 1979. pap. 4.00 (ISBN 0-934816-03-4). Metis Pr Inc.
Nicanor, Precioso M. How to Establish Your Own Publishing Company & Publish - Promote - Sell Your Books Profitably. LC 78-71695. 1978. pap. 4.95 (ISBN 0-918458-01-3). Pre-Mer.
Passman, Jerome. Publish What You Write. Levy, Barbara, ed. LC 78-68780. (Orig.). 1979. pap. 5.95 (ISBN 0-933468-00-8). Graystone Pub Co.
Rather, Lois. Rather a Small Press. (Illus.). 1976. ltd. ed. 12.50 (ISBN 0-686-20625-8). Rather Pr.
Ross, Marilyn & Ross, Tom. The Encyclopedia of Self-Publishing: How to Successfully Write, Publish, Promote & Sell Your Own Work. 2nd ed. LC 79-4054. 216p. 1980. 29.95 (ISBN 0-918880-05-X). Comm Creat.
Shinn, Duane. How to Publish Your Own Book, Song, or Course, & Make It Go! 64p. 1974. 49.95 (ISBN 0-912732-15-6). Duane Shinn.
Thompson, Paul. How to Be Your Own Publisher & Get Your Book into Print. new ed. (Illus.). 1978. pap. 4.40 (ISBN 0-88409-055-8). Creative Bk Co.

LITTLE WOLFE, CHEYENNE CHIEF, d. 1904
Sandoz, Mari. Cheyenne Autumn. 1969. pap. 2.95 (ISBN 0-380-01094-1, 52621, Discus). Avon.

LITTLEFIELD, GEORGE WASHINGTON, 1842-1920
Haley, J. Evetts. George W. Littlefield, Texan. (Illus.). 287p. 1943. pap. 6.95 (ISBN 0-8061-1166-6). U of Okla Pr.

LITTLEFIELD LANDS COMPANY
Gracy, David B., 2nd. Littlefield Lands: Colonization on the Texas Plains, 1912-1920. (M. K. Brown Range Life Ser.: No. 8). (Illus.). 175p. 1968. 9.95 (ISBN 0-292-78359-0). U of Tex Pr.

LITTLE'S DISEASE
see Cerebral Palsy

LITTORAL DRIFT
see also Beach Erosion; Coast Changes

LITTORAL FLORA
see Coastal Flora

LITURGICAL APOSTOLATE
see Liturgical Movement-Catholic Church

LITURGICAL DRAMA
see also Mysteries and Miracle-Plays
Collins, Fletcher, Jr. Production of Medieval Church Music-Drama. LC 78-168610. (Illus.). 1972. 17.50x (ISBN 0-8139-0373-4). U Pr of Va.
Hardison, O. B., Jr. Christian Rite & Christian Drama in the Middle Ages: Essays in the Origin & Early History of Modern Drama. (Illus.). 344p. 1965. 22.00x (ISBN 0-8018-0254-7); pap. 4.95x (ISBN 0-8018-1044-2). Johns Hopkins.
Parker, Elizabeth C. The Descent from the Cross: Its Relation to the Extra-Liturgical Depositio Drama. LC 77-94713. (Outstanding Dissertations in the Fine Arts Ser.). 1978. lib. bdg. 34.00 (ISBN 0-8240-3245-4). Garland Pub.

LITURGICAL DRAMAS
Greenberg, Noah & Smoldon, W. L., eds. Play of Herod: A Twelfth-Century Musical Drama. (Illus.). 1965. pap. 4.25x (ISBN 0-19-385196-2). Oxford U Pr.

LITURGICAL LATIN
see Latin Language-Church Latin

LITURGICAL MOVEMENT
Here are entered works dealing with the revived interest in liturgical matters, which began about 1890 in Catholic circles and spread over to Protestantism.
Largo, Gerald A. Community & Liturgy: An Historical Overview. LC 80-1434. 151p. 1980. lib. bdg. 16.25 (ISBN 0-8191-1302-6); pap. text ed. 7.75 (ISBN 0-8191-1303-4). U Pr of Amer.

LITURGICAL MOVEMENT-CATHOLIC CHURCH
Del Mazza, Valentino. Good News for the Liturgical Community: Cycle C. rev. ed. 1981. 5.95 (ISBN 0-8198-0573-4); pap. 4.95 (ISBN 0-8198-3003-8). Dghtrs St Paul.

LITURGICAL YEAR
see Church Year

LITURGICS
see also Bible-Liturgical Use; Chants (Plain, Gregorian, etc.); Christian Art and Symbolism; Church Music; Church Vestments; Church Year; Fasts and Feasts; Liturgical Movement; Lord's Supper (Liturgy); Sacraments (Liturgy)
Avenary, Hanoch. Studies in the Hebrew Syrian and Greek Liturgical Recitative. LC 64-253. 1963. pap. 6.75 (ISBN 0-913932-34-5). Boosey & Hawkes.
Babin, David E. Celebration of Life: Our Changing Liturgy. LC 79-97262. 1969. 4.75 (ISBN 0-8192-1102-8). Morehouse.
Barrois, Georges A. Scripture Readings in Orthodox Worship. 1977. pap. 5.95 (ISBN 0-913836-41-9). St Vladimirs.
Beachy, Alvin J. Worship As Celebration of Covenant & Incarnation. LC 68-57497. 1968. pap. 2.00 (ISBN 0-87303-940-8). Faith & Life.
Bouyer, Louis. Rite & Man: Natural Sacredness & Christian Liturgy. (Liturgical Studies Ser: No. 7). 1963. 9.95x (ISBN 0-268-00233-9). U of Notre Dame Pr.
Deiss, Lucien. Springtime of the Liturgy: Liturgical Texts of the First Four Centuries. rev. ed. O'Connell, Matthew J., tr. from Fr. LC 79-15603. 1979. pap. 8.50 (ISBN 0-8146-1023-4). Liturgical Pr.
Del Mazza, Valentino. Good News for the Liturgical Community: Cycle B. 1980. 5.95 (ISBN 0-8198-3004-6); pap. 4.95 (ISBN 0-8198-3005-4). Dghtrs St Paul.
Elhen, Sr. Margaret A. Liturgy Activity Books. Incl. Remember. (gr. 6). pap. text ed. 2.40 (ISBN 0-02-642110-0, 64211); Sign. (gr. 7). pap. text ed. 2.40 (ISBN 0-02-642130-5, 64213); Celebrate. (gr. 8). pap. text ed. 2.40 (ISBN 0-02-642150-X, 64215). (gr. 6-8). 1975. pap. text ed. 2.96 ea. Benziger Pub Co.
Feuer, Avrohom C. Tashlich. (Art Scroll Mesorah Ser.). 64p. 1979. 5.95 (ISBN 0-89906-158-3); pap. 3.95 (ISBN 0-89906-159-1). Mesorah Pubns.
Fischer, Edward. Everybody Steals from God: Communication As Worship. LC 77-3711. 1977. text ed. 7.95x (ISBN 0-268-00904-X). U of Notre Dame Pr.
Gallen, John, ed. Christians at Prayer. LC 76-22407. (Liturgical Studies). 1977. pap. text ed. 4.95 (ISBN 0-268-00719-5). U of Notre Dame Pr.
Garrett, Thomas S. Christian Worship: An Introductory Outline. 2nd ed. 1963. 7.00x (ISBN 0-19-213210-5). Oxford U Pr.
Hovda, Robert. Strong, Loving & Wise: Presiding in Liturgy. LC 76-56474. 1976. pap. 8.75 (ISBN 0-918208-12-2). Liturgical Conf.
Hughes, Dom A., compiled by. Liturgical Terms for Music Students: A Dictionary. LC 70-166236. 1972. Repr. of 1940 ed. 14.00 (ISBN 0-403-01363-1). Scholarly.
Jones, Cheslyn & Wainwright, Geoffrey, eds. The Study of Liturgy. 1978. 23.95 (ISBN 0-19-520075-6); pap. 9.95 (ISBN 0-19-520076-4). Oxford U Pr.
Kern, Walter. New Liturgy & Old Devotions. LC 78-73623. (Illus., Orig.). 1979. pap. 3.50 (ISBN 0-8189-1151-4, 151, Pub. by Alba Bks). Alba.
Kucharek, Casimir. The Byzantine Slav Liturgy of St. John Chrysostom, Its Origin & Evolution. LC 74-147735. 840p. 1971. 18.75 (ISBN 0-911726-06-3, BSL). Alleluia Pr.
Leclercq, Dom H. & Marron, Henr i01. Dictionnaire d'Archeologie Chretienne et de Liturgie, 28 vols. (Fr.). 1903. Set. 1995.00 (ISBN 0-686-57001-4, M-6342). French & Eur.
Lehmann, Arnold D. Lehmann's Little Dictionary of Liturgical Terms. 1980. 3.75 (ISBN 0-8100-0127-6). Northwest Pub.
Liturgy of St. John Chrysostom. (Eng. & Arab.). 1978. pap. 3.00 (ISBN 0-911726-39-X). Alleluia Pr.
McKenna, Megan & Ducote, Darryl. Sacraments, Liturgy & Prayer. LC 78-71531. (Followers of the Way Ser.: Vol. 5). 221p. (gr. 9-12). 1979. 22.50 (ISBN 0-8091-9546-1); cassette 7.50 (ISBN 0-8091-7670-X). Paulist Pr.
Maxwell, Jack M. Worship & Reformed Theology: The Liturgical Lessons of Mercersburg. LC 75-45492. (Pittsburgh Theological Monographs: No. 10). 1976. pap. 8.50 (ISBN 0-915138-12-3). Pickwick.
Mossi, John P. Modern Liturgy Handbook: A Study and Planning Guide for Worship. LC 76-12648. 1976. pap. 7.95 (ISBN 0-8091-1952-8). Paulist Pr.
Neale, John M. Essays on Liturgiology & Church History. LC 70-173070. Repr. of 1863 ed. 32.50 (ISBN 0-404-04667-3). AMS Pr.
Schmidt, Herman. Liturgy, Self-Expression of the Church. LC 77-168650. (Concilium Ser.: Religion in the Seventies: Vol. 72). 1972. pap. 4.95 (ISBN 0-8245-0231-0). Crossroad NY.
Schmidt, Herman & Power, David. Liturgy & Cultural Religious Tradition. (Concilium Ser.: Vol. 102). 1977. pap. 4.95 (ISBN 0-8245-0262-0). Crossroad NY.
Schmidt, Herman & Power, David, eds. The Liturgical Experience of Faith. (Concilium Ser.: Religion in the Seventies: Vol. 82). 156p. 1973. pap. 4.95 (ISBN 0-8245-0241-8). Crossroad NY.
Searle, Mark, ed. Liturgy & Social Justice. 1980. pap. 5.50 (ISBN 0-8146-1209-1). Liturgical Pr.
Seasoltz, R. Kevin. New Liturgy, New Laws. 1980. pap. 7.95 (ISBN 0-8146-1077-3). Liturgical Pr.

LITURGICS-CATHOLIC CHURCH
Aitken, John. Compilations of Litanies & Vesper Hymns. 10.00x (ISBN 0-87556-004-0). Saifer.
Daughters of St. Paul. Sunday Liturgy Themes. 1975. 5.00 (ISBN 0-8198-0474-6); pap. 4.00 (ISBN 0-8198-0475-4). Dghtrs St Paul.
Devine, George. Liturgical Renewal. LC 73-12923. 199p. (Orig.). 1973. pap. 3.95 (ISBN 0-8189-0281-7). Alba.
Grail Simplified Documents. This Is the Liturgy. (Orig.). 1967. pap. 0.80 (ISBN 0-02-644230-2, 64423). Glencoe.
Krause, Frederick J. Liturgy in Parish Life: A Study of Worship & the Celebrating Community. LC 79-1971. (Orig.). 1979. pap. 5.95 (ISBN 0-8189-0383-X). Alba.
Miller, Charles E. Making Holy the Day: A Commentary in the Liturgy of the Hours. red flexible bdg. 0.95 (ISBN 0-686-14286-1, 410/04). Catholic Bk Pub.
Westerhoff, John H. & Willimon, William H. Liturgy & Learning Through the Life Cycle. 176p. 1980. 9.95 (ISBN 0-8164-0471-2). Seabury.

LITURGIES
see also Dedication Services; Funeral Service; Hours, Books of; Hymns; Installation Service (Church Officers); Liturgies; Marriage Service; Mass; Pastoral Prayers; Responsive Worship; Ritual; Worship Programs
also subdivision Liturgy and Ritual, or name of ritual, under names of churches, e.g. Catholic Church-Liturgy and Ritual; Church of England-Book of Common Prayer
Babbitt, Edmond H. Pastor's Pocket Manual for Hospital & Sickroom. 1949. 5.95 (ISBN 0-687-30265-X). Abingdon.
Bruck, Maria, ed. More Children's Liturgies. LC 81-80877. 256p. (Orig.). 1981. pap. 9.95 (ISBN 0-8091-2362-2). Paulist Pr.
Burgess, Stephen W. & Righter, James D. Celebrations for Today: Acts of Worship in Modern English Language. LC 76-46429. 1977. pap. 3.95 (ISBN 0-687-04804-4). Abingdon.
Celebrate. (Liturgy Activity Book Ser.). (gr. 8). 1.80 (ISBN 0-02-642160-7); tchr's ed. 2.22 (ISBN 0-686-67301-8). Benziger Pub Co.
Champlin, Joseph M. The Proper Balance. 144p. (Orig.). 1981. pap. write for info. (ISBN 0-87793-233-6). Ave Maria.
Christensen, James L. Minister's Service Handbook. 1960. 7.95 (ISBN 0-8007-0206-9). Revell.
Gelineau, Joseph. The Liturgy Today & Tomorrow. LC 78-58966. 1978. pap. 5.95 (ISBN 0-8091-2120-4). Paulist Pr.
Guerric of Igny Liturgical Sermons, 2 vols. Berkeley, Theodore, tr. from Latin. (Cistercian Father Ser.: No. 8 & No. 32). 378p. 1970-71. 15.00 set (ISBN 0-87907-400-0). Vol. 1, LC 75-148203 (ISBN 0-87907-408-6). Vol. 2, LC 79-152481 (ISBN 0-87907-432-9). Cistercian Pubns.
Herring, William. The Role of Music in the New Roman Liturgy. LC 75-14548. 1971. pap. 0.50 (ISBN 0-915866-01-3). Am Cath Pr.
Hilliard, Dick & Valenti-Hilliard, Beverly. Happenings. (Center Celebration Ser.). (Illus.). 60p. 1981. pap. text ed. 3.95 (ISBN 0-89390-033-8). Resource Pubns.
--Surprises. (Center Celebration Ser.). (Illus.). 60p. (Orig.). 1981. pap. text ed. 3.95 (ISBN 0-89390-031-1). Resource Pubns.
--Wonders. (Center Celebration Ser.). (Illus.). 60p. (Orig.). 1981. pap. text ed. 3.95 (ISBN 0-89390-032-X). Resource Pubns.
Hiscox, Edward T. Star Book for Ministers. rev. ed. 1967. 5.95 (ISBN 0-8170-0167-0). Judson.
Hobbs, James R. Pastor's Manual. 1940. 8.50 (ISBN 0-8054-2301-X). Broadman.
Hovda, Robert. Manual of Celebration. 170p. (Including supplement one). loose-leaf 9.95 (ISBN 0-686-61516-6). Liturgical Conf.
Huck, Gabe. Liturgy Needs Community Needs Liturgy. LC 73-84360. 1974. pap. 2.45 (ISBN 0-8091-1791-6). Paulist Pr.
Huse, Dennis & Watson, Geralyn. Speak Lord, I'm Listening. LC 80-70851. 176p. 1981. pap. 7.95 perfect bnd. (ISBN 0-87793-220-4). Ave Maria.
Ihli, Sr. Jan. Liturgies of the Word for Children. LC 79-90003. 1979. pap. 8.95 (ISBN 0-8091-2176-X). Paulist Pr.
Jamison, Andrew. Liturgies for Children. (Illus.). 120p. (gr. 6 up). 1975. pap. 2.45 (ISBN 0-912228-18-0). St Anthony Mess Pr.
Jeep, Elizabeth M. & Huck, Gabe. Celebrate Summer! Guidebook for Families & Congregations, 2 vols. 5.95 (ISBN 0-686-61515-8). Liturgical Conf.
Jung, Wolfgang. Liturgisches Woerterbuch. (Ger.). 1964. leatherette 13.50 (ISBN 3-87537-023-6, M-7544, Pub. by Merseburger Berlin). French & Eur.
Kenny, Bernadette. Children's Liturgies. LC 77-74582. 176p. 1977. pap. 7.95 (ISBN 0-8091-2030-5). Paulist Pr.
Klauser, Theodor. A Short History of the Western Liturgy. Halliburton, John, tr. from Ger. 1979. text ed. 14.95x (ISBN 0-19-213224-5); pap. text ed. 8.95x (ISBN 0-19-213223-7). Oxford U Pr.
LeBlanc, Etienne & Talbot, Sr. Mary Rose. How Green Is Green. LC 73-83350. 1973. pap. 3.95 (ISBN 0-87793-061-9). Ave Maria.
Lee, Frederick G. A Glossary of Liturgical & Ecclesiastical Terms. LC 76-174069. (Tower Bks). (Illus.). xl, 452p. 1972. Repr. of 1877 ed. 25.00 (ISBN 0-8103-3949-8). Gale.
Liturgies & Occasional Forms of Prayer Set Forth in the Reign of Queen Elizabeth. 1847. 46.00 (ISBN 0-384-32940-3). Johnson Repr.
Liturgy Planning Guide. LC 75-14546. (Illus.). 54p. 1974. pap. 2.95 (ISBN 0-915866-05-6). Am Cath Pr.
Miguens, Manuel. Gospels for Sundays & Feasts: Cycle C. 1980. 7.50 (ISBN 0-8198-3000-3); pap. 6.00 (ISBN 0-8198-3001-1). Dghtrs St Paul.
Morse, Kenneth I. Move in Our Midst: Looking at Worship in the Life of the Church. 1977. pap. 2.95 (ISBN 0-87178-583-8). Brethren.
Rezy, Carol. Liturgies for Little Ones: 38 Complete Celebrations for Kindergarten Through Third Grade. LC 78-59926. (Illus.). 160p. (gr. k-3). 1978. pap. 3.95 (ISBN 0-87793-160-7). Ave Maria.
Schmidt, Herman. Liturgy, Self-Expression of the Church. LC 77-168650. (Concilium Ser.: Religion in the Seventies: Vol. 72). 1972. pap. 4.95 (ISBN 0-8245-0231-0). Crossroad NY.
Sloyan, Virginia, ed. Signs, Songs & Stories: Another Look at Children's Liturgies. 160p. 8.75 (ISBN 0-686-61511-5). Liturgical Conf.
Sloyan, Virginia & Huck, Gabe, eds. Children's Liturgies. 220p. 10.25 (ISBN 0-686-61510-7). Liturgical Conf.
Swidler, Arlene, ed. Sistercelebrations: Nine Worship Experiences. LC 74-80414. 96p. (Orig.). 1974. pap. 0.50 (ISBN 0-8006-1084-9, 1-1084). Fortress.
Thompson, Bard. Liturgies of the Western Church. (Fount Paperback Ser). 4.95 (ISBN 0-529-02077-7, M345). Collins Pubs.
Thompson, Bard, ed. Liturgies of the Western Church. LC 80-8044. 448p. 1980. pap. 7.95 (ISBN 0-8006-1428-3, 1-1428). Fortress.
Thompson, Fred. Twenty-Four Seasonal Liturgies for the Young. (Illus.). 112p. 1981. pap. 7.95 (ISBN 0-89622-142-3). Twenty-Third.
Two Liturgies, A. D. Fifteen Forty-Nine, & A. D. Fifteen Fifty-Seven. 1844. 42.50 (ISBN 0-384-62140-6). Johnson Repr.
Ware, James H., Jr. Not with Words of Wisdom: Performative Language & Liturgy. LC 80-6239. 252p. (Orig.). 1981. lib. bdg. 21.00 (ISBN 0-8191-1706-4); pap. text ed. 11.00 (ISBN 0-8191-1707-2). U Pr of Amer.
Whyman, Patricia C. Worship with Hands. 12p. (Orig.). 1974. pap. 2.10 (ISBN 0-89536-259-7). CSS Pub.

LITURGIES-BIBLIOGRAPHY
Charles Louis De Bourbon. Bibliotheque liturgique, 2 vols. in 1. Ales, Anatole, ed. LC 72-130592. (Fr). 1970. Repr. of 1898 ed. lib. bdg. 40.50 (ISBN 0-8337-0036-7). B Franklin.
Zaccaria, Francesco A. Bibliotheca Ritualis, 2 vols. in 3. 1964. Repr. of 1781 ed. Set. 106.00 (ISBN 0-8337-3913-1). B Franklin.

LITURGIES, EARLY CHRISTIAN
see also Church Orders, Ancient
Bludau, August. Die Pilgerreise der Aetheria. pap. 18.50 (ISBN 0-384-04760-2). Johnson Repr.
Hamman, Adelbert. Mass: Ancient Liturgies & Patristic Texts. Halton, Thomas, ed. LC 67-15202. 1967. 4.95 (ISBN 0-8189-0086-5). Alba.
Jungmann, Josef A. Early Liturgy, to the Time of Gregory the Great. Brunner, Francis A., tr. (Liturgical Studies Ser.: No. 7). 1959. 10.95 (ISBN 0-268-00083-2). U of Notre Dame Pr.
Oesterley, William O. The Jewish Background of the Christian Liturgy. 1925. 8.50 (ISBN 0-8446-1329-0). Peter Smith.
Orthodox Eastern Church. Liturgies of Saints Mark, James, Clement, Chrysostom, & the Church of Malabar. LC 76-83374. Repr. of 1859 ed. 18.50 (ISBN 0-404-04658-4). AMS Pr.
--Liturgies of Saints Mark, James, Clement, Chrysostom, Basil. LC 79-80721. (Gr). 1969. Repr. of 1859 ed. 18.50 (ISBN 0-404-04657-6). AMS Pr.
Pink, Arthur W. Christians in Romans Seven. pap. 0.50 (ISBN 0-685-00738-3). Reiner.
Sarapion. Bishop Sarapion's Prayer Book: An Egyptian Sacramentary Dated Probably About A.D. 350-356. 1964. Repr. of 1923 ed. 13.50 (ISBN 0-208-00101-8, Archon). Shoe String.
Schermann, Theodor. Die Allgemeine Kirchenordnung Fruehchristliche Liturgien und Kirchliche Uberlieferung, 3 pts. Repr. of 1914 ed. Set. pap. 46.00 (ISBN 0-384-53740-5). Johnson Repr.
Warren, Frederick E. Liturgy & Ritual of the Ante-Nicene Church. 2nd rev. ed. LC 78-177851. Repr. of 1912 ed. 25.00 (ISBN 0-404-06847-2). AMS Pr.

LITURGY
see Liturgics

LITURGY AND DRAMA
see also Religious Drama
Cargill, Oscar. Drama & Liturgy. LC 73-86272. 1969. Repr. of 1930 ed. lib. bdg. 13.50x (ISBN 0-374-91292-0). Octagon.

De Coussemaker, Edmond, ed. Drames liturgiques du moyen age, texte et musique. (Illus.). 370p. (Fr., Lat.). 1964. Repr. of 1860 ed. 57.50x (ISBN 0-8450-1004-2). Broude.

LITURGY AND LITERATURE

Cabaniss, Allen. Liturgy & Literature: Selected Essays. LC 73-92653. 181p. 1970. 12.50x (ISBN 0-8173-7001-3). U of Ala Pr.

Weber, Sarah A. Theology & Poetry in the Middle English Lyric: A Study of Sacred History & Aesthetic Form. LC 68-18940. (Illus.). 1969. 10.00 (ISBN 0-8142-0128-8). Ohio St U Pr.

LITVINOV, MAKSIM MAKSIMOVICH, 1876-1951

Bishop, Donald G. Roosevelt-Litvinov Agreements: The American View. LC 65-15852. 1965. 16.95x (ISBN 0-8156-2077-2). Syracuse U Pr.

LIU, SHAO-CH'I, 1900-

Li, Tien-Min. Mao's First Heir-Apparent. LC 72-152427. (Special Project). 223p. 1975. 11.95 (ISBN 0-8179-4141-X). Hoover Inst Pr.

LIVE POLIOVIRUS VACCINE

see Poliomyelitis Vaccine

LIVER

Andrews. Liver. (Studies in Biology: No. 105). 1979. 5.95 (ISBN 0-8391-0255-0). Univ Park.

Arias, Irwin, et al, eds. The Liver: Biology & Pathobiology. Date not set. text ed. price not set (ISBN 0-89004-575-5). Raven.

Bartosek, I., et al, eds. Isolated Liver Perfusion & Its Applications. LC 72-95635. (Mario Negri Institute for Pharmacological Research Monographs). (Illus.). 1973. 25.50 (ISBN 0-911216-43-X). Raven.

Becker, Frederick F., ed. The Liver: Normal & Abnormal Functions, 2 pts. (Biochemistry of Disease Ser.: Vol. 5). 592p. 1975. Part A. 65.00 (ISBN 0-8247-6205-3); Part B. 55.00 (ISBN 0-8247-6214-2). Dekker.

Boyce, Frederick F. The Role of the Liver in Surgery. (Illus.). 365p. 1941. ed. spiral bdg. 34.75photocopy (ISBN 0-398-04217-9). C C Thomas.

Bruguera, Miquel, et al. Atlas of Laparoscopy & Biopsy of the Liver. Galambos, Joht T. & Jinich, Horacio, trs. LC 78-64703. (Illus.). 1979. text ed. 60.00 (ISBN 0-7216-2182-1). Saunders.

Chandra, R. K., ed. The Liver & Biliary Tract in Infants & Children. (Illus.). 1979. text ed. 59.50 (ISBN 0-443-01456-6). Churchill.

Ciba Foundation. CIBA Foundation Symposium 55: Hepatotrophic Factors & the Liver. 1978. 40.50 (ISBN 0-444-90018-7, Excerpta Medica). Elsevier.

David, H. Submicroscopic Ortho- & Patho-Morphology of the Liver. 1964. 195.00 (ISBN 0-08-010903-9). Pergamon.

Elias, H. & Sherrick, Joseph C. Morphology of the Liver. 1969. 59.75 (ISBN 0-12-237950-0). Acad Pr.

Fausto, Nelson, et al. Liver Regeneration, No. 2. LC 72-13504. (Illus.). 220p. 1973. text ed. 24.00x (ISBN 0-8422-7080-9). Irvington.

Ferguson, A. & MacSween, R. N., eds. Immunological Aspects of the Liver & Gastrointestinal Tract. (Illus.). 1976. 29.50 (ISBN 0-8391-0877-X). Univ Park.

Gall, Edward A. & Mostofi, F. K., eds. The Liver. 2nd ed. LC 79-28745. (I.A.P. Ser.). 540p. 1980. Repr. lib. bdg. cancelled (ISBN 0-89874-122-X). Krieger.

Gastaad Symposium, 1st International, Swiss Society for Gastroenlerology. The Liver: Quantitative Aspects of Structure & Function, Proceedings. Preisig, R. & Paumgartener, G., eds. (Illus.). 1973. 39.00 (ISBN 3-8055-1603-7). S Karger.

Gentilini, P., et al, eds. Intrahepatic Cholestasis. LC 75-10551. 199p. 1975. 24.50 (ISBN 0-89004-049-4). Raven.

Gram, T. E., ed. Extrahepatic Metabolism of Drugs & Other Foreign Compounds. (Monographs in Pharmacology & Physiology: Vol. 5). (Illus.). 470p. 1980. 55.00 (ISBN 0-89335-095-8). Spectrum Pub.

International Symposium on: HBsAg Containing Immune Complexes: Renal & Other Extra-Hepatic Manifestations: Italy, Sept. 1979, et al. Systematic Effects of HBsAg Immune Complexes: Proceedings. Chiandussi, L. & Sherlock, S., eds. 308p. 1981. text ed. 33.00 (ISBN 0-686-31134-5, Pub. by Piccin Italy). J K Burgess.

Javitt, N. Liver & Biliary Tract Physiology I. 1980. 34.50 (ISBN 0-8391-1554-7). Univ Park.

Kitani, K., ed. Liver & Aging: Proceedings of the Tokyo Symposium, Tokyo, Japan, Aug. 27-28-a Satellite Symposium of the 11th Congress of Gerontology. 1978. 57.00 (ISBN 0-444-80088-3, Biomedical Pr). Elsevier.

Kuster, Gustavo G. Hepatic Support in Acute Liver Failure. (Illus.). 320p. 1976. 31.75 (ISBN 0-398-03539-3). C C Thomas.

Lautt, W. Wayne, ed. Hepatic Circulation in Health & Disease. 1981. text ed. 39.00 (ISBN 0-89004-617-4). Raven.

Lesch, R., et al. Liver. Eichler, O., ed. (Handbook of Experimental Pharmacology: Bund 16). 1977. 130.80 (ISBN 0-387-07647-6). Springer-Verlag.

McGilvery, R. W. & Pogell, B. M., eds. Fructose-One, Six-Diphosphates & Its Role in Gluconeogenesis. 1964. 5.50 (ISBN 0-934454-40-X). Lubrecht & Cramer.

McNulty, James G. Radiology of the Liver. LC 77-75536. (Monographs in Clinical Radiology: 13). (Illus.). 1977. text ed. 32.00 (ISBN 0-7216-5969-1). Saunders.

Malkin, Leonard I., et al. Liver Regeneration, No. 1. (Illus.). 200p. 1973. text ed. 24.00x (ISBN 0-8422-7079-5). Irvington.

Motta, Pietro, et al. The Liver: An Atlas of Scanning Electron Microscopy. LC 77-95454. (Illus.). 1978. 46.00 (ISBN 0-89640-026-3). Igaku-Shoin.

Najarian, John S. Hepatic Biliary & Pancreatic Surgery. 1980. 69.95 (ISBN 0-8151-6331-2). Year Bk Med.

Orlandi, F. & Jezequel, A. M., eds. Liver & Drugs. 1972. 42.00 (ISBN 0-12-528350-4). Acad Pr.

Plaa, G. L. & Hewitt, W. R., eds. Liver Toxicology. (Target Organ Toxicology Ser.). 1982. text ed. price not set (ISBN 0-89004-584-4). Raven.

Powell, L. Metals & the Liver. (Liver; Normal Function & Disease Ser.: Vol. 1). 1978. 38.50 (ISBN 0-8247-6740-3). Dekker.

Rouiller, C., ed. The Liver: Morphology, Biochemistry, Physiology, 2 vols. 1963-64. 91.00 set (ISBN 0-686-66624-0); Vol. 1. 64.00 (ISBN 0-12-598901-6); Vol. 2. 64.00 (ISBN 0-12-598902-4). Acad Pr.

Sherlock, S. V. The Human Liver. Head, J. J., ed. LC 76-50844. (Carolina Biology Readers Ser.). (Illus.). (gr. 11 up). 1978. pap. 1.65 (ISBN 0-89278-283-8, 45-9683). Carolina Biological.

Sideman, Samuel & Chang, T. M., eds. Hemoperfusion: Kidney & Liver Support Detoxification, Pt. 2. 1982. text ed. price not set (ISBN 0-89116-211-9). Hemisphere Pub.

Sies, H. & Wondel, A., eds. Functions of Glutathione in Liver & Kidney. (Proceedings in Life Sciences). (Illus.). 1979. 34.10 (ISBN 0-387-09127-0). Springer-Verlag.

South African International Liver Conference, 1973. Liver: Proceedings. Saunders, S. J. & Terblanche, John, eds. (Illus.). 432p. 1973. pap. text ed. 20.00x (ISBN 0-8464-0575-X). Beekman Pubs.

Struin, Leo. The Liver & Anasthesia. LC 72-97914. (Major Problem in Anaesthesia: Vol. 3). (Illus.). 1976. text ed. 26.00 (ISBN 0-7216-8625-7). Saunders.

Tager, J. M., et al, eds. Use of Isolated Liver Cells & Kidney Tabules in Metabolic Studies: Proceedings. 1976. 58.75 (ISBN 0-444-10925-0, North-Holland). Elsevier.

Taylor, W., ed. The Hepatobiliary System: Fundamental & Pathological Mechanisms. LC 76-2486. (NATO Advanced Study Institutes Ser, Ser. A: Life Sciences: Vol. 7). 654p. 1976. 49.50 (ISBN 0-306-35607-4, Plenum Pr). Plenum Pub.

Van de Reis, L., ed. Enzymology of the Liver. (Frontiers of Gastrointestinal Research: Vol. 2). (Illus.). xii, 292p. 1976. 91.75 (ISBN 3-8055-2220-7). S Karger.

Williams, R. & Murray-Lyon, I. M. Artificial Liver Support. 1975. pap. text ed. 26.00x (ISBN 0-685-83069-1). State Mutual Bk.

Wisse, E. & Knook, D. L., eds. Kupffer Cells & Other Liver Sinusoidal Cells: Proceedings of the International Kupffer Cell Symposium, Noordwijderhout, the Netherlands, September, 1977. 1978. 77.00 (ISBN 0-444-80031-X, Biomedical Pr). Elsevier.

LIVER-DISEASES

see also Portal Hypertension

Adolph, A. L. & Lorenz, Rita. Enzyme Diagnosis in Diseases of the Heart, Liver & Pancreas. (Illus.). 128p. 1981. pap. 13.25 (ISBN 3-8055-3079-X). S Karger.

Adolph, L. & Lorenz, Rita. Diagnostico enzimatico En las Enfermedades De corazon, higado y Pancreas. (Illus.). 126p. 1980. soft cover 13.25 (ISBN 3-8055-0506-X). S Karger.

Alagille, Daniel & Odievre, Michel. Liver & Biliary Tract Disease in Children. LC 79-12254. 364p. 1979. 52.50 (ISBN 0-471-05256-6, Pub. by Wiley-Medical). Wiley.

Anderson, Robert J. & Schrier, Robert W. Clinical Uses of Drugs in Patients with Kidney & Liver Disease. (Illus.). 368p. Date not set. text ed. price not set (ISBN 0-7216-1239-3). Saunders.

Bannasch, P. Cytoplasm of Hepatocytes During Carcinogenesis: Electron & Lightmicroscopial Investigations of the Nitrosomorphiline-Intoxicated Rat Liver. LC 69-18017. (Recent Results in Cancer Research: Vol. 19). (Illus.). 1968. 21.70 (ISBN 0-387-04308-X). Springer-Verlag.

Becker, Frederick F., ed. The Liver: Normal & Abnormal Functions, 2 pts. (Biochemistry of Disease Ser.: Vol. 5). 592p. 1975. Part A. 65.00 (ISBN 0-8247-6205-3); Part B. 55.00 (ISBN 0-8247-6214-2). Dekker.

Berk, Paul D. & Chalmers, Thomas C., eds. Frontiers in Liver Disease. (Illus.). 300p. 1981. text ed. 42.00 (ISBN 0-86577-017-4). Thieme-Stratton.

Bianchi, L., et al, eds. Liver & Bile. 1978. 39.50 (ISBN 0-8391-1142-8). Univ Park.

Bolt, H., et al, eds. Primary Liver Tumors. 1978. 29.50 (ISBN 0-8391-1226-2). Univ Park.

Brown, Burnell R., Jr., ed. Anesthesia & the Patient with Liver Disease. LC 80-22088. (Contemporary Anesthesia Practice Ser.: Vol. 4). 190p. 1981. 24.00 (ISBN 0-8036-1268-0). Davis Co.

Brucer, Marshall. Liver Scans, Clearances & Perfusions: The Development of Nuclear Hepatology. LC 76-23126. 160p. 1977. 14.50 (ISBN 0-88275-458-0). Krieger.

Cameron, H. M., et al, eds. Liver Cell Cancer. 1976. 75.25 (ISBN 0-444-41542-4). Elsevier.

Chen, T. S. & Chen, P. S. Essential Hepatology. 1977. 29.95 (ISBN 0-409-95005-X). Butterworth.

Conn & Lieberthal. The Hepatic Coma Syndromes & Lactulose. (Illus.). 1979. 49.00 (ISBN 0-683-02100-1). Williams & Wilkins.

David, H. Submicroscopic Ortho- & Patho-Morphology of the Liver. 1964. 195.00 (ISBN 0-08-010903-9). Pergamon.

Davidson, Charles S., ed. Problems in Liver Diseases. LC 78-25654. (Illus.). 1979. text ed. 35.00 (ISBN 0-913258-58-X). Thieme-Stratton.

Demers, Laurence & Shaw, Leslie, eds. Evaluation of Liver Function: A Multifaceted Approach to Clinical Diagnosis. LC 78-13314. (Illus.). 222p. 1978. text ed. 19.50 (ISBN 0-8067-0400-4). Urban & S.

Eddleston, A. L., et al, eds. Immune Reactions in Liver Disease. Williams, Roger. (Illus.). 1979. text ed. 30.00 (ISBN 0-397-58246-3, JBL-Med-Nursing). Har-Row.

Eddleston, Adrian & Williams, Roger. Immune Reaction in Liver Disease. (Illus.). 1978. 24.95x (ISBN 0-8464-0503-2). Beekman Pubs.

Eliakim, M., ed. International Symposium on Hepatotoxicity. 1974. 28.50 (ISBN 0-12-237850-4). Acad Pr.

Elias, H. & Sherrick, Joseph C. Morphology of the Liver. 1969. 59.75 (ISBN 0-12-237950-0). Acad Pr.

Epstein, M., ed. The Kidney in Liver Disease. 1978. 32.50 (ISBN 0-444-00240-5, North Holland). Elsevier.

Farber & Fisher. Toxic Injury of the Liver, Pt. B. (Liver: Normal Function & Disease: Vol. 2). 1979. 39.75 (ISBN 0-8247-6839-6). Dekker.

--Toxic Injury of the Liver, Pt. A. 1979. 47.50 (ISBN 0-8247-6838-8). Dekker.

Foster, James H. & Berman, Martin M. Solid Liver Tumors. LC 76-28938. (Major Problems in Clinical Surgery Ser.: Vol. 22). 1977. text ed. 25.00 (ISBN 0-7216-3824-4). Saunders.

Galambos, John T. Cirrhosis. LC 78-65970. (Illus.). 1979. text ed. 25.00 (ISBN 0-7216-3987-9). Saunders.

Gerschenson, L. E. & Thompson, Brad E., eds. Gene Expression & Carcinogenesis in Cultured Liver. 1975. 42.50 (ISBN 0-12-281150-X). Acad Pr.

Gitnick, G. L. Current Hepatology, Vol. 2. 1981. 45.00 (ISBN 0-471-09516-8, Pub. by Wiley Med). Wiley.

--Practical Diagnosis: Gastrointestinal & Liver Didease. 318p. 1979. 22.00 (ISBN 0-471-09481-1, Pub. by Wiley Med). Wiley.

Gitnick, Gary L., ed. Current Gastroenterology & Hepatology. (Illus.). 510p. 1979. 45.00 (ISBN 0-471-09479-X, Pub. by Wiley Med). Wiley.

--Current Hepatology, Vol. 1. (Current Ser). (Illus.). 384p. 1980. 40.00 (ISBN 0-471-09518-4, Pub. by Wiley Med). Wiley.

Grases, Pedro J. & Beker G., Simon. Color Atlas of Liver Biopsy: A Clinical Pathological Guide. LC 80-28801. Orig. Title: Guia Practica De Biopsia Hepatica En el Adulto. (Illus.). 125p. 1981. 60.00 (ISBN 0-8451-0209-5). A R Liss.

Iio, M., et al. Nuclear Hepatology. 174p. 1973. 27.50 (ISBN 0-683-04289-0, Pub. by W & W). Krieger.

International Association for the Study of the Liver, Quadrennial Meeting, 5th, Acapulco, October 1974. Diseases of the Liver & Biliary Tract with Standardization of Nomenclature Diagnostic Criteria & Diagnostic Methodology: Proceedings. Leevy, C. M., ed. (Illus.). 250p. 1976. 36.00 (ISBN 3-8055-2276-2). S Karger.

International Symposium on Tirrenia, June 1974. New Trends in the Therapy of Liver Disease: Proceedings. Bertelli, A., ed. 300p. 1975. 35.50 (ISBN 3-8055-2118-9). S Karger.

Keppler, D., ed. Pathogenesis & Mechanisms of Liver Cell Necrosis. (Illus.). 280p. 1975. 39.50 (ISBN 0-8391-0837-0). Univ Park.

Kitani, K., ed. Liver & Aging: Proceedings of the Tokyo Symposium, Tokyo, Japan, Aug. 27-28-a Satellite Symposium of the 11th Congress of Gerontology. 1978. 57.00 (ISBN 0-444-80088-3, Biomedical Pr). Elsevier.

Koff, Raymond S. Liver Disease in Primary Care Medicine. (Illus.). 262p. 1980. 21.50x (ISBN 0-8385-5678-7). ACC.

Landolt, R., ed. Aktuelle Probleme der Paediatrischen Hepatologie. (Paediatrische Fortbildungskurse fuer die Praxis: Band 44). (Illus.). 1977. 14.50 (ISBN 3-8055-2662-8). S Karger.

Lapis, Karoly & Johannessen, Jan V., eds. Liver Carcinogenesis. LC 79-134. (Illus.). 1979. text ed. 40.00 (ISBN 0-89116-149-X, Co-Pub. by McGraw Intl). Hemisphere Pub.

Leevy & Popper. Diseases of the Liver & Biliary Tract. 212p. 1979. text ed. 30.00 (ISBN 0-7194-0006-6, Pub. by Castle Hse England). J K Burgess.

Leevy, Carroll M. Liver Regeneration in Man. (Amer. Lec. in Living Chemistry Ser.). (Illus.). 128p. 1973. 13.75 (ISBN 0-398-02776-5). C C Thomas.

Leevy, Carroll M., et al. Diseases of the Liver & Biliary Tract. 1977. 13.95 (ISBN 0-8151-5357-0). Year Bk Med.

Leevy, Carroll M., et al, eds. Diseases of the Liver & Billiary Tract: Standardization of Nomenclature, Diagnostic Criteria, Diagnostic Methodology. 1979. 40.00x (ISBN 0-7194-0006-6). Intl Ideas.

MacSween, Roderick, et al, eds. Pathology of the Liver. (Illus.). 1980. text ed. 75.00 (ISBN 0-443-01561-9). Churchill.

Meeting on Hemoperfusion, Kidney & Liver Supports & Detoxification, Haifa, Aug 25-26, 1979. Hemoperfusion: Kidney & Liver Support & Detoxification, Pt. 1. Sideman, Samuel & Chang, T. M., eds. LC 80-14154. 496p. 1980. text ed. 49.50 (ISBN 0-89116-152-X). Hemisphere Pub.

Melnick, J. L. & Maupas, P., eds. Hepatitis B Virus & Primary Liver Cancer. (Progress in Medical Virology Ser.: Vol. 27). (Illus.). viii, 212p. 1981. 75.00 (ISBN 3-8055-1784-X). S Karger.

Mowat, A. P. Liver Disorders in Childhood. Apley, J., ed. (Postgraduate Pediatric Ser.). 1979. text ed. 53.95 (ISBN 0-407-00163-8). Butterworth.

Newberne, Paul M. & Butler, W. H., eds. Rat Hepatic Neoplasia. 1978. text ed. 27.50x (ISBN 0-262-14029-2). MIT Pr.

Norgaard-Pederson. Human Alpha Feto-Protein. 1976. 6.95 (ISBN 0-8391-0987-3). Univ Park.

Okuda, Kunio & Peters, Robert L., eds. Hepatocellular Carcinoma. LC 76-6500. (Wiley Series on Diseases of the Liver). 512p. 1976. 64.95 (ISBN 0-471-65316-0, Pub. by Wiley Medical). Wiley.

Orr, Marsha E. Acute Pancreatic & Hepatic Dysfunction. (The Fleschner Series in Critical Care Nursing). (Illus.). 200p. (Orig.). 1981. pap. text ed. 9.95 (ISBN 0-937878-04-9). Fleschner.

Pack, G. T. & Islami, A. H., eds. Tumors of the Liver. LC 71-99868. (Recent Results in Cancer Research: Vol. 26). (Illus.). 1970. 37.20 (ISBN 0-387-04991-6). Springer-Verlag.

Perez-Soler, A. Inflamatory & Artresia-Inducing Disease of the Liver & Bile Ducts. (Monographs in Pediatrics: Vol. 8). (Illus.). 1976. 46.75 (ISBN 3-8055-2257-6). S Karger.

Popper, H. Membrane Alterations As Basis of Liver Injury. 1977. 34.50 (ISBN 0-8391-1141-X). Univ Park.

Popper, Hans P. & Schaffner, Fenton, eds. Progress in Liver Diseases, Vol. 3. 580p. 1969. 72.00 (ISBN 0-8089-0364-0). Grune.

--Progress in Liver Diseases, Vol. 5. LC 61-14102. (Illus.). 752p. 1976. 76.25 (ISBN 0-8089-0926-6). Grune.

--Progress in Liver Diseases, Vol. 6. 688p. 1979. 59.50 (ISBN 0-8089-1174-0). Grune.

Schiff, Leon, ed. Diseases of the Liver. 4th ed. LC 75-20047. (Illus.). 1450p. 1975. text ed. 90.00 (ISBN 0-397-50319-9, JBL-Med-Nursing). Har-Row.

Schwartz, Seymour I. Surgical Diseases of the Liver. 1964. 32.00 (ISBN 0-07-055774-8, HP). McGraw.

Sherlock, Sheila & Summerfield, John A. Color Atlas of Liver Disease. (Illus.). 1979. 47.95 (ISBN 0-8151-7644-9). Year Bk Med.

Sherlock, Shiela. Atlas a Color De Enfermedades Del Higado. 1981. 62.50 (ISBN 0-8151-7645-7). Year Bk Med.

Slater, T. F., ed. Biochemical Mechanisms of Liver Injury. 1979. 116.50 (ISBN 0-12-649150-X). Acad Pr.

Steigmann, Frederick & Clowdus, Bernard F., 2nd. Hepatic Encephalopathy. (Illus.). 214p. 1971. text ed. 18.75 (ISBN 0-398-01841-3). C C Thomas.

Symposium on Virus Hepatitis Antigens & Antiobodies, Munich, 1970. Australia Antigen: Hepatitis Associated Antigen & Corresponding Antibodies. Soulier, J. P., ed. (Vox Sanguinis: Vol. 19, Nos. 3-4). 1970. pap. 36.00 (ISBN 3-8055-1088-8). S Karger.

Tanikawa, K. Ultrastructural Aspects of the Liver & Its Disorders. (Illus.). 1968. 35.30 (ISBN 0-387-04357-8). Springer-Verlag.

Tanikawa, Kyuichi. Ultrastructural Aspects of the Liver & Its Disorders. 2nd ed. LC 79-84646. (Illus.). 1979. 62.50 (ISBN 0-89640-034-4). Igaku-Shoin.

Wepler, W. & Wildhirt, E. Clinical Histopathology of the Liver: An Atlas. Lowbeer, Leo, tr. LC 76-182156. 160p. 1972. 62.50 (ISBN 0-8089-0746-8). Grune.

White, Thomas T., et al. Liver, Bile Ducts & Pancreas. 1977. 54.75 (ISBN 0-8089-1002-7). Grune.

Williams, Roger & Murray-Lyon, Iain M., eds. Artificial Liver Support: Proceedings of an International Symposium on Artificial Support Systems for Acute Hepatic Failure-Sept., 1974. 367p. 1975. 17.45x (ISBN 0-8464-1076-1). Beekman Pubs.

Wright, Ralph. Immunology of Gastrointestinal & Liver Disease. (Current Topics in Immunology Ser.: Vol. 8). (Illus., Orig.). 1979. pap. 13.95 (ISBN 0-8151-9367-X). Year Bk Med.

Wright, Ralph, et al. Liver & Biliary Disease. LC 79-1531. (Illus.). 1345p. 1979. text ed. 69.50 (ISBN 0-7216-9609-0). Saunders.

Zimmerman, Hyman J. Hepatotoxicity: The Adverse Effects of Drugs & Other Chemicals on the Liver. (Illus.). 597p. 1978. 56.00 (ISBN 0-8385-3725-1). ACC.

Zuckerman, A. J. Virus Diseases of the Liver. 1970. 15.95 (ISBN 0-407-43700-2). Butterworth.

LIVER-SURGERY

Calne, R., et al. The Liver. (Surgical Forum Ser.). 1974. 10.95 (ISBN 0-407-10007-5). Butterworth.

Castaing, D., et al. Hepatic & Portal Surgery in the Rat. (Illus.). 184p. 1980. 37.50x (ISBN 0-89352-101-9). Masson Pub.

Fagarasanu, I. Surgery of the Liver & Intrahepatic Bile Ducts. Heimlich, Henry, ed. LC 77-86984. (Illus.). 490p. 1972. 32.50 (ISBN 0-87527-007-7). Green.

Foster, James H. & Berman, Martin M. Solid Liver Tumors. LC 76-28938. (Major Problems in Clinical Surgery Ser.: Vol. 22). 1977. text ed. 25.00 (ISBN 0-7216-3824-4). Saunders.

Najarian, John S. & Delaney, John P., eds. Hepatic, Biliary & Pancreatic Surgery. 1980. write for info. (ISBN 0-8151-6331-2). Symposia Special.

--Surgery of the Liver, Pancreas & Bilary Tract. LC 74-27862. (Illus.). 1975. 37.50 (ISBN 0-8151-6329-0, Pub. by Symposia Special). Year Bk Med.

Puestow, Charles B. Surgery of the Biliary Tract, Pancreas & Spleen. 4th ed. (Illus.). 1970. 30.00 (ISBN 0-8151-6882-9). Year Bk Med.

Scheuer, P. Liver Biopsy Interpretation. 3rd ed. 1980. text ed. 65.00 (ISBN 0-02-859180-1). Macmillan.

LIVERMORE, MARY ASHTON RICE, 1820-1905

Livermore, Mary A. The Story of My Life; or, the Sunshine & Shadow of Seventy Years...to Which Is Added Six of Her Most Popular Lectures. LC 74-3960. (Women in America Ser). (Illus.). 760p. 1974. Repr. of 1899 ed. 39.00x (ISBN 0-405-06108-0). Arno.

LIVERPOOL

Baines, Thomas. History of the Commerce, Company & Town of Liverpool. LC 68-55467. 1852. 37.50x (ISBN 0-678-00983-X). Kelley.

Channon, Howard. Portrait of Liverpool. LC 72-550617. (Portrait Books Ser). 1970. 10.50x (ISBN 0-7091-5575-1). Intl Pubns Serv.

Harris, John R., ed. Liverpool & Merseyside. LC 68-21449. (Illus.). 1969. 25.00x (ISBN 0-678-05016-3). Kelley.

--Liverpool & Merseyside: Essays in the Economic & Social History of the Port & Its Hinterland. 287p. 1969. 27.50x (ISBN 0-7146-1314-2, F Cass Co). Biblio Dist.

Hughes, F. Quentin. Seaport: Architecture & Townscape of Liverpool. 16.00 (ISBN 0-685-20625-4). Transatlantic.

Lucie-Smith, E. The Liverpool Scene. (Illus.). 7.50 (ISBN 0-8446-2495-0). Peter Smith.

Mackenzie-Grieve, Averil. Last Years of the English Slave Trade. LC 68-21439. (Illus.). Repr. of 1941 ed. 25.00 (ISBN 0-678-05070-8). Kelley.

Midwinter, Eric. Old Liverpool. (Old...Ser.). (Illus.). 200p. 1971. 6.50 (ISBN 0-7153-5335-7). David & Charles.

Vigier, Francois. Change & Apathy: Liverpool & Manchester During the Industrial Revolution. (Illus.). 1970. 15.00x (ISBN 0-262-22012-1). MIT Pr.

Williams, Gomer. History of the Liverpool Privateers & Letters of Marque. LC 66-24413. Repr. of 1897 ed. 24.00x (ISBN 0-678-00199-5). Kelley.

LIVERPOOL, ROBERT BANKS JENKINSON, 2ND EARL OF, 1770-1828

Brock, William R. Lord Liverpool & Liberal Toryism 1820-1827. 1967. Repr. of 1941 ed. 19.50 (ISBN 0-208-00428-9, Archon). Shoe String.

--Lord Liverpool & Liberal Toryism: 1820-27. 2nd ed. (Illus.). 300p. 1967. 26.00x (ISBN 0-7146-1457-2, F Cass Co). Biblio Dist.

Cookson, J. E. Lord Liverpool's Administration: The Crucial Years, 1815-1822. xii, 422p. (Orig.). 1975. 25.00 (ISBN 0-208-01495-0, Archon). Shoe String.

LIVERPOOL AND MANCHESTER RAILWAY

Booth, Henry. Account of the Liverpool & Manchester Railway. (Illus.). 104p. 1969. Repr. of 1830 ed. 22.50x (ISBN 0-7146-1433-5, F Cass Co). Biblio Dist.

Carlson, Robert E. Liverpool & Manchester Railway Project, 1821-1831. LC 76-86621. (Illus.). 1969. 15.00x (ISBN 0-678-05540-8). Kelley.

Fitzgerald, R. S. Liverpool Road Station, Manchester: An Historical & Archaeological Survey. 76p. 1980. 36.00x (ISBN 0-7190-0765-8, Pub. by Manchester U Pr England); pap. 18.00x (ISBN 0-7190-0790-9). State Mutual Bk.

Kemble, Frances A. Fanny Kemble's Ride on the Liverpool & Manchester Railway. (Illus.). 1980. pap. 1.50 (ISBN 0-912276-16-9). Comox.

Thomas, R. H. The Liverpool & Manchester Railway. LC 79-57313. (Illus.). 264p. 1980. 45.00 (ISBN 0-7134-0537-6, Pub. by Batsford England). David & Charles.

LIVERWORTS

Allison, K. W. Liverworts of New Zealand. LC 75-329568. (Illus.). 300p. 1975. 22.00x (ISBN 0-8002-0470-0). Intl Pubns Serv.

Bonner, C. E. Index Hepaticarum: An Index to the Liverworts of the World. Incl. Pt. 2. Achiton to Balantiopsis. 37.50 (ISBN 3-7682-0092-2); Pt. 3. Barbilophozia to Ceranthus. 37.50 (ISBN 3-7682-0093-0); Pt. 4. Ceratolejeunea to Crystolejeunea. 37.50 (ISBN 3-7682-0094-9); Pt. 5. Delavayella to Geothallus. 50.00 (ISBN 3-7682-0095-7); Pt. 6. Goebelliella to Jubula. 37.50 (ISBN 3-7682-0096-5). 1963-66. Lubrecht & Cramer.

--Index Hepaticarum, Index to the Liverworts of the World Part 7A: Supplement, Additions & Corrections to Parts 2-4. 1977. pap. text ed. 30.00 (ISBN 3-7682-0097-3). Lubrecht & Cramer.

--Index Hepaticarum. Index to the Liverworts of the World Part 8: Jungermannia. 1976. pap. text ed. 60.00 (ISBN 0-686-31698-3). Lubrecht & Cramer.

--Index Hepaticarum. Part 9: Jungermanniopsis-Lejeunea. 1978. pap. 50.00x (ISBN 0-686-31669-X). Lubrecht & Cramer.

Conard, Henry S. & Redfearn, Paul L., Jr. How to Know the Mosses & Liverworts. 2nd ed. (Pict. Key Nature Ser.). 1979. wire coil avail. (ISBN 0-697-04768-7); text ed. write for info. (ISBN 0-697-04769-5). Wm C Brown.

Crandall, B. J. Morphology & Development of Branches in the Leafy Hepaticae. (Illus.). 1970. 40.00 (ISBN 3-7682-5430-5). Lubrecht & Cramer.

Gottsche, K. M., et al. Synopsis Hepaticarum. 1967. Repr. of 1844 ed. 80.00 (ISBN 3-7682-0516-9). Lubrecht & Cramer.

Husnot, P. T. Hepatologia Gallica. 2nd ed. (Illus.). 1968. Repr. of 1922 ed. 20.60 (ISBN 90-6123-081-0). Lubrecht & Cramer.

Schuster, R. M. Boreal Hepaticae, a Manual of Liverworts of Minnesota & Adjacent Regions. (Bryophytorum Bibliotheca Ser.: No. 11). (Illus.). 1977. lib. bdg. 50.00x (ISBN 3-7682-1150-9). Lubrecht & Cramer.

Schuster, Rudolf M. Hepaticae & Anthocerotae of North America East of the Hundredth Meridian, 4 vols. LC 66-14791. 1966-74. 45.00x ea. Vol. 1 (ISBN 0-231-08981-3). Vol. 2 (ISBN 0-231-08982-1). Vol. 3 (ISBN 0-231-03567-5). Vol. 4. 85.00x (ISBN 0-231-04608-1). Columbia U Pr.

Steere, William C. Liverworts of Southern Michigan. LC 40-10272. (Bulletin Ser.: No. 17). (Illus.). 97p. (Orig.). 1940. pap. 3.00x (ISBN 0-87737-004-4, 17). Cranbrook.

Watson, E. Vernon. British Mosses & Liverworts. 2nd ed. LC 68-22665. (Illus.). 1968. 50.00 (ISBN 0-521-06741-3); pap. 29.50 (ISBN 0-521-29472-X). Cambridge U Pr.

LIVESTOCK

see also Cattle; Donkeys; Goats; Horses; Pastures; Range Management; Sheep

also headings beginning with the word Livestock

Alderson, Lawrence. The Chance to Survive: Rare Breeds in a Changing World. (Illus.). 1979. 19.95 (ISBN 0-8289-0376-X). Greene.

Animal Husbandry: Animal Diseases, How Animals Reproduce. (Better Farming Ser: No. 9). (Illus.). 33p. 1977. pap. 3.00 (ISBN 92-5-100148-0, F67, FAO). Unipub.

Animal Husbandry: Feeding & Care of Animals. (Better Farming Ser: No. 8). (Illus.). 38p. 1977. pap. 3.00 (ISBN 92-5-100147-2, F66, FAO). Unipub.

Annual Meeting Commission on Animal Management & Health, 28th, Brussels, August 1977. The Ethology & Ethics of Farm Animal Production: Proceedings. Folsch, Detlef W., ed. 1978. pap. text ed. 23.75x (ISBN 3-7643-1004-9). Renouf.

Banerjee, G. C. A Textbook of Animal Husbandry. 4th ed. 1981. 35.00x (ISBN 0-686-72968-4, Pub. by Oxford & IBH India). State Mutual Bk.

Battaglia & Mayrose. Handbook of Livestock Management Techniques. (Illus.). 570p. 1981. 24.95 (ISBN 0-686-76186-3). Burgess.

Belanger, Jerome. The Homesteader's Handbook to Raising Small Livestock. Stoner, Carol, ed. LC 73-88254. (Illus.). 250p. 1974. 10.95 (ISBN 0-87857-075-6). Rodale Pr Inc.

Bell, Hershel M. Rangeland Management for Livestock Production. (Illus.). 1978. pap. 7.95x (ISBN 0-8061-1473-8). U of Okla Pr.

Blakely & Bade. Science of Animal Husbandry. 3rd ed. 544p. 1982. text ed. 16.95 (ISBN 0-8359-6978-9); instr's. manual free (ISBN 0-8359-6979-7). Reston.

Bogart, Ralph. Scientific Farm Animal Production. LC 77-74745. 1977. text ed. 18.95x (ISBN 0-8087-2802-4). Burgess.

Boggs, Donald L. & Merkel, Robert A. Live Animal Carcass Evaluation & Selection Manual. 208p. (Orig.). 1979. pap. text ed. 11.50 (ISBN 0-8403-2036-1). Kendall-Hunt.

Briggs, Hilton M. & Briggs, Dinus M. Modern Breeds of Livestock. 4th ed. (Illus.). 1980. text ed. 24.95 (ISBN 0-02-314730-X). Macmillan.

Buckett, M. Introduction to Livestock Husbandry. 2nd ed. 1977. 23.00 (ISBN 0-08-021180-1); pap. 9.25 (ISBN 0-08-021179-8). Pergamon.

Bundy, Clarence E., et al. Livestock & Poultry Production. 4th ed. 1975. text ed. 23.00 (ISBN 0-13-538579-2). P-H.

Campbell, John R. & Lasley, John F. The Science of Animals That Serve Mankind. 2nd ed. (Agricultural Science Series). (Illus.). 736p. 1975. text ed. 20.00 (ISBN 0-07-009696-1, C). McGraw.

Chessmore, Roy A. Profitable Pasture Management. xvi, 424p. 1979. 13.95 (ISBN 0-686-74414-4); text ed. 13.95 (ISBN 0-686-74415-2). Interstate.

Church, D. C., et al. Livestock Feeds & Feeding. 1977. 17.00 (ISBN 0-686-26680-3). Dairy Goat.

Clemen, Rudolf A. The American Livestock & Meat Industry. abr. ed. (Illus.). 1923. 31.00 (ISBN 0-384-09305-1). Johnson Repr.

Cole, H. H., ed. Introduction to Livestock Production: Including Dairy & Poultry. 2nd ed. LC 66-16377. (Illus.). 1966. 26.95x (ISBN 0-7167-0812-4). W H Freeman.

Cole, H. H. & Garrett, W. N., eds. Animal Agriculture: The Biology, Husbandry, & Use of Domestic Animals. 2nd ed. LC 79-18984. (Animal Science Ser.). (Illus.). 1980. text ed. 22.95x (ISBN 0-7167-1099-4). W H Freeman.

Dick, Lila. An Introduction to Modern Nursery Stock Production. 225p. 1981. 35.00x (ISBN 0-686-75474-3, Pub. by Muller Ltd). State Mutual Bk.

Dickinson, Darol. Photographing Livestock: The Complete Guide. LC 79-88468. (Illus.). Date not set. 14.50 (ISBN 0-87358-199-7); pap. 7.95 (ISBN 0-87358-200-4). Northland.

Diggins, Ronald V. & Bundy, Clarence E. Beef Production. 3rd ed. 1971. text ed. 23.00 (ISBN 0-13-073288-5). P-H.

Ensminger, M. E. The Stockman's Handbook. 5th ed. LC 76-58206. 1978. 29.95 (ISBN 0-8134-1943-3, 1943). Interstate.

Ensminger, M. Eugene. Animal Science. 7th ed. LC 76-1512. (Illus.). 1977. 29.95 (ISBN 0-8134-1798-8, 1798). Interstate.

Fraser, Alistair & Thear, Katie, eds. Small Farmer's Guide to Raising Livestock & Poultry. (Illus.). 240p. 1981. 25.00 (ISBN 0-668-04687-2). Arco.

Gaal. Animal Husbandry in Hungary in the 19th - 20th Centuries. 1977. 29.00 (ISBN 0-9960000-1-1, Pub. by Kaido Hungary). Heyden.

Gasser, J. K., et al, eds. Effluents from Livestock. (Illus.). v, 712p. 1980. 80.00x (ISBN 0-85334-895-2). Burgess-Intl Ideas.

Gillespie, James. Modern Livestock & Poultry Production. LC 79-50918. (Agriculture Ser.). 1981. pap. 18.20 (ISBN 0-8273-1688-7); instr's guide 3.15 (ISBN 0-8273-1689-5). Delmar.

Guide to Statistics of Livestock & Livestock Products. 98p. 1976. pap. 11.75 (ISBN 0-685-68956-5, F928, FAO). Unipub.

Hafez, E. S., ed. Reproduction in Farm Animals. 4th ed. LC 80-10489. (Illus.). 627p. 1980. text ed. 31.00 (ISBN 0-8121-0697-0). Lea & Febiger.

Hart, Edward. Showing Livestock. LC 78-74086. 1979. 14.95 (ISBN 0-7153-7537-7). David & Charles.

Haynes, N. Bruce. Keeping Livestock Healthy: A Veterinary Guide. (Illus.). 1978. pap. 10.95 (ISBN 0-88266-134-5). Garden Way Pub.

Hoveland, Carl S., ed. The Role of Biological Nitrogen Fixation in Forage Livestock Systems. 1976. pap. 6.25 (ISBN 0-89118-046-X). Am Soc Agron.

Juergenson, E. M. Handbook of Livestock Equipment. 2nd ed. (Illus.). 266p. 1979. 14.00 (ISBN 0-8134-2030-X, 2030). Interstate.

Kays, John M. Basic Animal Husbandry. 1958. text ed. 19.95x ref. ed. (ISBN 0-13-056598-9). P-H.

Lasley, John F. Genetics of Livestock Improvement. 3rd ed. LC 77-22807. (Illus.). 1978. ref. ed. 25.95 (ISBN 0-13-351106-5). P-H.

Latham, Hiram. Trans-Missouri Stock Raising. Dykes, J. C., ed. 1962. Repr. of 1871 ed. 10.00 (ISBN 0-912094-02-8). Old West.

Lerner, I. M. & Donald, H. P. Modern Developments in Animal Breeding. 1966. 47.00 (ISBN 0-12-444350-8). Acad Pr.

Lerner, I. Michael. The Genetic Basis of Selection. LC 73-19295. (Illus.). 298p. 1974. Repr. of 1958 ed. lib. bdg. 20.25x (ISBN 0-8371-7315-9, LEGB). Greenwood.

Lush, Jay L. Animal Breeding Plans. facs. ed. (Illus.). 1945. pap. 14.50x (ISBN 0-8138-2345-5). Iowa St U Pr.

McCoy, John H. Livestock & Meat Marketing. 2nd ed. (Illus.). 1979. text ed. 28.50 (ISBN 0-87055-321-6). AVI.

McCurry, Dan C. & Rubenstein, Richard E., eds. Bankers & Beef: An Original Press Anthology. facsimile ed. LC 74-30618. (American Farmers & the Rise of Agribusiness Ser.). (Illus.). 1975. Repr. of 1975 ed. 22.00x (ISBN 0-405-06763-1). Arno.

Merkel, James A. Managing Livestock Wastes. (Illus.). 1981. text ed. 24.50 (ISBN 0-87055-373-9). AVI.

Midwest Plan Service Personnel. Livestock Waste Facilities Handbook. (Illus.). 1975. pap. 4.00 (ISBN 0-89373-012-2, MWPS-18). Midwest Plan Serv.

--Planning Grain-Feed Handling for Live-Stock & Cash-Grain Farms. (Illus.). 1974. pap. 4.00 (ISBN 0-89373-007-6, MWPS-13). Midwest Plan Serv.

Nelson, R. H. An Introduction to Feeding Farm Livestock. 2nd ed. 1979. text ed. 28.00 (ISBN 0-08-023757-6); pap. text ed. 9.75 (ISBN 0-08-023756-8). Pergamon.

Park, R. D., et al. Animal Husbandry. 2nd ed. (Illus.). 1970. pap. 16.95x (ISBN 0-19-859422-4). Oxford U Pr.

Peterson, Paul, et al. Working in Animal Science. Amberson, Max, ed. (Illus.). (gr. 9-10). 1978. pap. text ed. 6.96 (ISBN 0-07-000839-6, G). McGraw.

Plucknett, Donald A. Managing Pastures & Cattle Under Coconuts. (Tropical Agriculture Ser.). 1979. lib. bdg. 28.75x (ISBN 0-89158-299-1). Westview.

Rice, Victor A., et al. Breeding & Improvement of Farm Animals. 6th ed. (Agricultural Science Ser.). 1967. text ed. 19.50 (ISBN 0-07-052179-4, C). McGraw.

Ritchie, Harland D. Livestock Judging & Evaluation Manual. (Illus.). x, 205p. 1969. pap. 5.00 (ISBN 0-87013-152-4). Mich St U Pr.

Sainsbury, David & Sainsbury, Peter. Livestock Health & Housing. 2nd ed. 388p. 1979. pap. 27.50 (ISBN 0-8121-0751-9). Lea & Febiger.

Savage, William W., Jr. The Cherokee Strip Live Stock Association: Federal Regulation & the Cattleman's Last Frontier. LC 72-93932. (Illus.). 1973. 10.00x (ISBN 0-8262-0144-X). U of Mo Pr.

Scott, W. N., ed. The Care & Management of Farm Animals. 2nd ed. (Illus.). 254p. 1978. pap. 19.50 (ISBN 0-8121-0752-7). Lea & Febiger.

Shanklin, Eugenia & Berleant-Schiller, Riva, eds. Livestock Production & the Community. LC 81-65015. 170p. 1981. text ed. 25.00 (ISBN 0-86598-033-0). Allanheld.

Shepherd, William. Prairie Experiences in Handling Cattle & Sheep. facsimile ed. LC 70-165807. (Select Bibliographies Reprint Ser.). Repr. of 1885 ed. 16.00 (ISBN 0-8369-5964-7). Arno.

Sims, John A. & Johnson, Leslie E. Animals in the American Economy. (Illus.). 200p. 1972. text ed. 10.50 (ISBN 0-8138-0245-8). Iowa St U Pr.

Sorenson, Anton M., Jr. Animal Reproduction: Principles & Practice. Zappa, C. Robert, ed. (Agriculture Sciences Ser.). (Illus.). 1979. text ed. 19.50 (ISBN 0-07-059670-0). McGraw.

Swithi, G. R. & Chatrath, M. S. Improving Crop & Animal Productivity. 629p. 1981. 120.00x (ISBN 0-686-76645-8, Pub by Oxford & IBH India). State Mutual Bk.
Teutsch, Gotthard M. & Von Loeper, Eisenhart, eds. Intensivhaltung von Nutztieren aus ethischer, rechtlicher und ethologischer Sicht. (Tierhaltung-Animal Management: No. 8). 228p. (Ger.). 1979. pap. 18.00 (ISBN 3-7643-1119-3). Birkhauser.
Thomas, Steve. Backyard Livestock: How to Grow Meat for Your Family. (Illus.). 1978. pap. 5.95 (ISBN 0-684-15529-X, ScribT). Scribner.
Trevisick, Charles. Keep Your Own Livestock: A Practical Guide to Self-Sufficiency. (Illus.). 1978. 10.95 (ISBN 0-09-129460-6, Pub. by Hutchinson); pap. 6.50 (ISBN 0-09-129461-4). Merrimack Bk Serv.
Warwick, E. J. & Legates, J. E. Breeding & Improvement of Farm Animals. 7th ed. (Agricultural Sciences Ser). (Illus.). 1979. text ed. 22.95 (ISBN 0-07-068375-1, C). McGraw.
Wolf, Ray. Managing Your Personal Food Supply. LC 76-50569. 1977. 11.95 (ISBN 0-87857-121-3). Rodale Pr Inc.

LIVESTOCK-DISEASES
see Parasites-Domestic Animals; Veterinary Medicine

LIVESTOCK-EXHIBITIONS
see Livestock Exhibitions

LIVESTOCK-HOUSING
see also Farm Buildings; Stables
Clark, J. A. Environmental Aspects of Housing for Animal Production. 1981. text ed. price not set (ISBN 0-408-10688-3). Butterworth.
Leavy, Herbert T. Successful Small Farms: Building Plans & Methods. LC 78-7987. 1978. 14.00 (ISBN 0-912336-67-6); pap. 7.95 (ISBN 0-912336-68-4). Structures Pub.
Midwest Plan Service Personnel. Dairy Housing & Equipment Handbook. 3rd ed. (Illus.). 1976. pap. 5.00 (ISBN 0-89373-004-1, MWPS 7). Midwest Plan Serv.
--Horse Housing & Equipment Handbook. (Illus.). 1971. pap. 4.00 (ISBN 0-89373-009-2, MWPS-15). Midwest Plan Serv.
Sainsbury, David & Sainsbury, Peter. Livestock Health & Housing. 2nd ed. 388p. 1979. pap. 27.50 (ISBN 0-8121-0751-9). Lea & Febiger.
Some Environmental Problems of Livestock Housing. (Technical Note Ser.). (Illus.). 71p. (Orig.). 1973. pap. 15.00 (ISBN 0-685-34862-8, 325, WMO). Unipub.

LIVESTOCK-LAW AND LEGISLATION
see Animal Industry-Law and Legislation

LIVESTOCK-STUDY AND TEACHING
Commission On Education In Agriculture And Natural Resources. Undergraduate Teaching in the Animal Sciences. 1967. pap. 4.25 (ISBN 0-309-01486-7). Natl Acad Pr.

LIVESTOCK-CHINA
Taylor, George E. The Livestock of China. LC 78-74304. (The Modern Chinese Economy Ser.). 174p. 1980. lib. bdg. 22.00 (ISBN 0-8240-4286-7). Garland Pub.

LIVESTOCK-INDIA
Mishra, S. N. Livestock Planning in India. 1978. text ed. 15.00x (ISBN 0-7069-0574-1). Verry.
Ranjhan, S. K. Animal Nutrition & Feeding Practices in India. (Illus.). 339p. 1977. 11.00x (ISBN 0-7069-0509-1, Pub. by Croom Helm Ltd. England). Biblio Dist.
Singh, H. Domestic Animals. (India - Land & People Ser). (Illus.). 1966. 4.00x (ISBN 0-8426-1530-X). Verry.

LIVESTOCK-TROPICS
Sastry, N. S. Farm Animal Management. 400p. 1976. 13.00x (ISBN 0-7069-0454-0). Intl Pubns Serv.
Williamson, G. & Payne, W. J. An Introduction to Animal Husbandry in the Tropics. 3rd ed. (Tropical Agriculture Ser.). (Illus.). 1978. text ed. 31.00x (ISBN 0-582-46813-2). Longman.

LIVESTOCK BUILDINGS
see Livestock-Housing

LIVESTOCK EXHIBITIONS
Hart, Edward. Showing Livestock. LC 78-74086. 1979. 14.95 (ISBN 0-7153-7537-7). David & Charles.
Winogrand, Garry & Tyler, Ron. Stock Photographs: The Fort Worth Fat Stock Show & Rodeo. (Illus.). 128p. 1980. 19.95 (ISBN 0-292-72433-0). U of Tex Pr.

LIVING, COST OF
see Cost and Standard of Living

LIVING FOSSILS
see also names of living fossils, e.g Platypus
Aliki. The Long Lost Coelacanth & Other Living Fossils. LC 72-83773. (A Let's-Read-&-Find-Out Science Bk.). (Illus.). 40p. (gr. k-3). 1973. 7.95 (ISBN 0-690-50478-0, TYC-J). Har-Row.

LIVING ROOMS
Grow, Lawrence. The Old House Book of Living Rooms & Parlors. (The Old House Book Ser.). (Illus.). 150p. 1980. 15.00 (ISBN 0-446-51215-X); pap. 7.95 (ISBN 0-446-97552-4). Warner Bks.
Loftie, M. J., et al. The Dining Room & the Drawing Room & the Bedroom & the Boudoir. Stansky, Peter & Shewan, Rodney, eds. LC 76-18321. (Aesthetic Movement & the Arts & Crafts Movement Ser.). 1978. lib. bdg. 44.00x (ISBN 0-8240-2461-3). Garland Pub.

LIVINGSTON, EDWARD, 1764-1836
Hatcher, William. Edward Livingston: Jeffersonian Republican & Jacksonian Democrat. (Illus.). 8.00 (ISBN 0-8446-0684-7). Peter Smith.
Pound, Roscoe. Formative Era of American Law. 7.00 (ISBN 0-8446-1359-2). Peter Smith.

LIVINGSTON, ROBERT, 1654-1728
Leder, Lawrence H. Robert Livingston 1654-1728, & the Politics of Colonial New York. (Institute of Early American History & Culture Ser.). 1961. 21.00x (ISBN 0-8078-0805-9). U of NC Pr.

LIVINGSTON, WILLIAM, 1723-1790
Dillon, Dorothy R. New York Triumvirate: A Study of the Legal & Political Careers of William Livingston, John Morin Scott, & William Smith Jr. LC 68-58567. (Columbia University Studies in the Social Sciences: No. 548). Repr. of 1949 ed. 18.50 (ISBN 0-404-51548-7). AMS Pr.

LIVINGSTON FAMILY
Armes, Ethel, ed. Nancy Shippen: Her Journal. LC 68-21204. 1968. 20.00 (ISBN 0-405-08213-4, Pub. by Blom). Arno.

LIVINGSTONE, DAVID, 1813-1873
Blaikie, William G. Personal Life of David Livingstone. LC 69-19353. (Illus.). 1880. 22.00x (ISBN 0-8371-0518-8). Greenwood.
Buel, J. W. Heroes of the Dark Continent. facs. ed. LC 73-138333. (Black Heritage Library Collection Ser). 1889. 32.75 (ISBN 0-8369-8725-X). Arno.
Campbell, Reginald J. Livingstone. LC 77-138212. (Illus.). 295p. 1972. Repr. of 1930 ed. lib. bdg. 16.00x (ISBN 0-8371-5567-3, CALI). Greenwood.
Casada, James A. Dr. David Livingstone & Henry Morton Stanley: An Annotated Bibliography with Commentary. LC 75-24101. (Reference Library of Social Science: Vol. 21). 225p. 1975. lib. bdg. 25.00 (ISBN 0-8240-9967-2). Garland Pub.
Chambliss, J. E. Life & Labors of David Livingstone. LC 76-132642. (Illus.). Repr. of 1875 ed. 36.00x (ISBN 0-8371-3636-9, Pub. by Negro U Pr). Greenwood.
Charles, Elizabeth R. Three Martyrs of the Nineteenth Century. LC 73-77196. Repr. of 1886 ed. 15.00 (ISBN 0-8371-1296-6). Greenwood.
Coupland, Reginald. Kirk on the Zambesi: A Chapter of African History. Repr. of 1928 ed. 15.25x (ISBN 0-8371-2916-8, Pub. by Negro U Pr). Greenwood.
David Livingstone. (Ladybird Ser.). 1.49 (ISBN 0-686-70884-9). Chr Lit.
Latham, Robert O. Trail Maker (David Livingstone) 1973. pap. 1.95 (ISBN 0-87508-626-8). Chr Lit.
Livingstone, David. Family Letters: 1841-1856, 2 vols. LC 75-17198. (Illus.). 1975. Repr. of 1959 ed. Set. lib. bdg. 31.50x (ISBN 0-8371-8290-5, LIFL). Greenwood.
Martelli, George. Livingstone's River. LC 71-101881. 1970. 7.50 (ISBN 0-671-20466-1). S&S.
Ransford, Oliver. David Livingstone: The Dark Interior. LC 78-50673. 1978. 19.95 (ISBN 0-312-18379-8). St Martin.
Roberts, John S. Life & Explorations of David Livingstone. 1875. 24.00 (ISBN 0-403-00314-8). Scholarly.
Stanley, H. M. Finding of Dr. Livingstone. 1978. Repr. lib. bdg. 30.00 (ISBN 0-8495-4871-3). Arden Lib.
Stanley, Henry M. How I Found Livingston. LC 71-125717. (American Journalists Ser). 1970. Repr. of 1872 ed. 30.00 (ISBN 0-405-01698-0). Arno.
--How I Found Livingstone. LC 70-90137. (Illus.). Repr. of 1913 ed. 26.00x (ISBN 0-8371-1995-2, Pub. by Negro U Pr). Greenwood.
Worchester, J. H., Jr. David Livingstone. 128p. 1980. pap. 2.25 (ISBN 0-8024-4782-1). Moody.

LIVONIA
Kirchner, Walther. Rise of the Baltic Question. Repr. of 1954 ed. lib. bdg. 15.00x (ISBN 0-8371-3009-3, KIBQ). Greenwood.
Verne, Jules. Drama in Livonia. 3.95 (ISBN 0-685-27950-2). Assoc Bk.

LIVRE DU ROY MODUS
Madden, D. H. Chapter of Mediaeval History. LC 74-91048. 1969. Repr. of 1924 ed. 15.00 (ISBN 0-8046-0658-7). Kennikat.

LIVRES A CLEF
Walbridge, Earle F. Literary Characters Drawn from Life. LC 72-195653. 1974. Repr. of 1936 ed. lib. bdg. 17.50 (ISBN 0-8414-9556-4). Folcroft.

LIVY (LIVIUS, TITUS)
Briscoe, John. A Commentary on Livy, Bks, 31-33. 1973. 45.00x (ISBN 0-19-814442-3). Oxford U Pr.
Conway, Robert S. Harvard Lectures on the Vergilian Age. LC 67-13861. 1928. 9.50x (ISBN 0-8196-0182-9). Biblo.
Klotz, Alfred. Appians Darstellung Des Zweiten Punischen Krieges. Repr. of 1936 ed. pap. 6.00 (ISBN 0-384-29880-X). Johnson Repr.
Luce, T. J. Livy: The Composition of His History. LC 77-72126. 1977. text ed. 23.00 (ISBN 0-691-03552-0). Princeton U Pr.
Machiavelli, Niccolo. The Prince. Ricci, Luigi, tr. Bd. with The Discourses. (YA) 1950. pap. 3.95x (ISBN 0-394-30925-1, T25, Mod LibC). Modern Lib.
Mazzolani, Lidia S. Empire Without End: Three Historians of Rome. McConnell, Joan & Pel, Mario, trs. LC 76-20672. (A Helen & Kurt Wolff Bk). 1976. Repr. of 1972 ed. 10.95 (ISBN 0-15-128780-5). HarBraceJ.
Nissen, Heinrich. Kritische Untersuchungen Uber Die Quellen der Vierten und Funften Dekade Des Livius. LC 75-7332. (Roman History Ser.). (Ger.). 1975. Repr. 20.00x (ISBN 0-405-07109-4). Arno.
Ogilvie, Robert M. Commentary on Livy, Bks 1-5. 1965. 72.00x (ISBN 0-19-814432-6). Oxford U Pr.
Packard, David W. Concordance to Livy, 4 Vols. LC 68-29181. (Lat). 1968. Set. text ed. 175.00x (ISBN 0-674-15890-3). Harvard U Pr.
Sinclair, K. Melbourne Livy. 1961. pap. 3.00x (ISBN 0-424-05540-6, Pub. by Sydney U Pr). Intl Schol Bk Serv.
Walsh, P. G. Livy: His Historical Aims & Methods. 1961. 39.00 (ISBN 0-521-06729-4). Cambridge U Pr.

LIZARDS
see also Chameleons
Boulenger, G. A. Catalogue of the Lizards in the British Museum, 3 vols. in 2. (Illus.). 1964. 240.00 (ISBN 3-7682-0239-9). Lubrecht & Cramer.
Brenner, Barbara. We're off to See the Lizard. LC 76-10350. (Read to Myself Ser.). (Illus.). 32p. (gr. k-2). 1977. PLB 8.50 (ISBN 0-8172-0151-3). Raintree Pubs.
Hartman, Jane E. Looking at Lizards. LC 78-5357. (Illus.). (gr. 5-9). 1978. 7.95 (ISBN 0-8234-0330-0). Holiday.
Hopf, Alice L. Biography of a Komodo Dragon. (A Nature Biography Book). (Illus.). 64p. (gr. 7-11). 1981. PLB 6.99 (ISBN 0-399-61140-1). Putnam.
The Lizard. (Animal Environmet Ser.). Date not set. 4.95 (ISBN 0-8120-5379-6). Barron.
Milstead, William W., ed. Lizard Ecology: A Symposium. LC 66-17955. 1967. 14.00x (ISBN 0-8262-0058-3). U of Mo Pr.
Rieppel, Oliver. The Phylogeny of Anguinomorph Lizards. 88p. 1980. pap. text ed. 38.00 (ISBN 0-686-74190-0). Birkhauser.
Roberts, Mervin F. All About Chameleons & Anoles. (Illus.). 1977. pap. 2.50 (ISBN 0-87666-902-X, PS-310). TFH Pubns.
Roberts, Mervin F. & Roberts, Martha D. All About Iguanas. (Orig.). 1976. 2.50 (ISBN 0-87666-903-8, PS311). TFH Pubns.
Saiga Editors. Lizards & Frogs. 1981. 10.00x (ISBN 0-86230-004-5, Pub. by Saiga Pub). State Mutual Bk.
Smith, Hobart M. Handbook of Lizards: Lizards of the United States & Canada. (HANH Ser.). (Illus.). 578p. 1946. 32.50x (ISBN 0-8014-0393-6). Comstock.
Smith, Malcolm. The Fauna of British India, Including Ceylon & Burma: Reptilia & Amphibia, 2 vols. Incl. Vol. 1. Loricata, Testudines. 189p. Repr. of 1931 ed. Vol. 1. 15.00 (ISBN 0-88359-005-0); Vol. 2. Sauria. Repr. of 1935 ed. Vol. 2. 22.50 (ISBN 0-88359-006-9). (Illus.). 1973. Set. 35.00 (ISBN 0-88359-007-7). R Curtis Bks.

LLAMAS
Conklin, Gladys. The Llamas of South America. LC 74-18453. (Illus.). 64p. (gr. 3-7). 1975. 5.95 (ISBN 0-8234-0252-5). Holiday.
Earle, Olive L. Camels & Llamas. (Illus.). (gr. 3-7). 1961. PLB 6.48 (ISBN 0-688-31138-5). Morrow.
Perry, Roger. Wonders of Llamas. LC 77-6492. (Wonders Ser.). (Illus.). (gr. 5 up). 1977. 5.95 (ISBN 0-396-07460-X). Dodd.
Ruck, Ruth J. Along Came a Llama. (Illus.). 248p. 1978. 13.95 (ISBN 0-571-11277-3, Pub. by Faber & Faber). Merrimack Bk Serv.

LLANOS
see also Pampas; Prairies; Steppes; Tundras
Nesbitt, L. M. Desolate Marches: Travels in the Orinoco Llanos of Venezuela. 1936. 12.50 (ISBN 0-8495-4026-7). Arden Lib.

LLOYD, ALFRED HENRY, 1864-1927
Shirk, Evelyn U. Adventurous Idealism: Philosophy of Alfred Lloyd. 1968. Repr. of 1952 ed. lib. bdg. 14.50x (ISBN 0-8371-0223-5, SHAI). Greenwood.

LLOYD, CHARLES, 1735-1773
Father of Candor. An Enquiry into the Doctrine, Lately Propagated, Concerning Libels, Warrants, & the Seizure of Papers. facsimile ed. LC 76-121100. (Civil Liberties in American History Ser.). 136p. Repr. of 1764 ed. 17.50 (ISBN 0-306-71970-3). Da Capo.

LLOYD, DAVID, 1686-1731
Lokken, Roy N. David Lloyd, Colonial Lawmaker. LC 59-13419. (Publications in History). (Illus.). 319p. 1959. 9.50 (ISBN 0-295-73762-X). U of Wash Pr.

LLOYD, HAROLD CLAYTON, 1894-1971
McCaffrey, Donald W. Three Classic Silent Screen Comedies Starring Harold Lloyd. LC 74-4993. (Illus.). 264p. 1976. 18.00 (ISBN 0-8386-1455-8). Fairleigh Dickinson.
Reilly, Adam. Harold Lloyd: The King of Daredevil Comedy. (Illus.). 1977. pap. 9.95 (ISBN 0-02-036350-8, Collier). Macmillan.

LLOYD, HENRY DEMAREST, 1847-1903
Ham, F. Gerald, ed. The Papers of Henry Demarest Lloyd: Guide to a Microfilm Edition. LC 74-212656. (Guides to Historical Resources Ser.). 1971. pap. 1.00 (ISBN 0-87020-114-X). State Hist Soc Wis.
Jernigan, E. Jay. Henry Demarest Lloyd. LC 76-17104. (U.S. Authors Ser: No. 277). 1976. lib. bdg. 12.50 (ISBN 0-8057-7177-8). Twayne.

LLOYD GEORGE, DAVID LLOYD GEORGE, 1ST EARL, 1863-1945
Campbell, John. Lloyd George: The Goat in the Wilderness; 1922-1931. (Illus.). 383p. 1977. 27.50x (ISBN 0-87471-813-9). Rowman.
Cregier, Don M. Bounder from Wales: Lloyd George's Career Before the First World War. LC 76-4894. 1976. 17.50x (ISBN 0-8262-0203-9). U of Mo Pr.
Fry, Michael G. Lloyd George & Foreign Policy Volume I: The Education of a Statesman, 1890-1916. 1977. lib. bdg. 18.50x (ISBN 0-7735-0274-2). McGill-Queens U Pr.
George, W. R. The Making of Lloyd George. (Illus.). 1976. 17.50 (ISBN 0-208-01627-9, Archon). Shoe String.
Gilbert, M. Lloyd George. 1968. 8.95 (ISBN 0-13-353961-X, Spec); pap. 1.95 (ISBN 0-13-353953-9). P-H.
Grigg, John. Lloyd George: The People's Champion, 1902-1911. LC 77-91762. 1979. 32.50x (ISBN 0-520-03634-4). U of Cal Pr.
Lloyd George, D. War Memoirs of David Lloyd George, 6 vols. LC 75-41179. Repr. of 1936 ed. 165.00 set (ISBN 0-404-15040-3). AMS Pr.
Lloyd George, David. Memoirs of the Peace Conference, 2 vols. 1939. Set. 75.00x (ISBN 0-686-51415-7). Elliots Bks.
Maurice, Nancy, ed. The Maurice Case: From the Papers of Major-General Sir Fredrick Maurice. 240p. (Orig.). 1972. 17.50 (ISBN 0-208-00871-3, Archon). Shoe String.
Morgan, Kenneth. Consensus & Disunity: The Lloyd George Coalition Government, 1918 to 1922. 448p. 1979. text ed. 54.00x (ISBN 0-19-822497-4). Oxford U Pr.
Morgan, Kenneth O. The Age of Lloyd George: The Liberal Party & British Politics, 1880-1929. (Historical Problems: Studies & Documents). 1971. pap. text ed. 9.95x (ISBN 0-04-942093-3). Allen Unwin.
--David Lloyd George Eighteen Sixty-Three to Nineteen Forty-Fivw. (Bilingual Ser.). (Illus.). 91p. (Eng. & Welsh.). 1981. pap. 8.25x (ISBN 0-7083-0790-6). Verry.
Pike, E. Royston. Human Documents of the Lloyd George Era. (Illus.). 378p. 1972. 9.95 (ISBN 0-312-39900-6). St Martin.
Scally, Robert J. The Origins of the Lloyd George Coalition: The Politics of Social Imperialism, 1900-1918. LC 74-25608. (Illus.). 408p. 1975. 30.00x (ISBN 0-691-07570-0). Princeton U Pr.
Turner, J. Lloyd George's Secretariat. LC 79-50510. (Studies in the History & Theory of Politics). 1980. 27.50 (ISBN 0-521-22370-9). Cambridge U Pr.
Wrigley, C. J. David Lloyd George & the British Labour Movement: Peace & War. LC 75-41578. 298p. 1976. text ed. 17.50x (ISBN 0-06-497910-5). B&N.

LLOYDS BANK, LIMITED
Brown, Antony. Cuthbert Heath: The Maker of Modern Lloyds. LC 79-91476. (Illus.). 1980. 19.95 (ISBN 0-7153-7942-9). David & Charles.
Flower, Raymond & Jones, Michael W. Lloyd's of London: An Illustrated History. (Illus.). 1974. 16.50 (ISBN 0-8038-4290-2). Hastings.

LNG
see Liquefied Natural Gas

LOAD (ELECTRIC POWER)
see Electric Power-Plants-Load

LOAD-LINE
see also Ships-Cargo

LOADING AND UNLOADING
see also Bulk Solids Handling; Cargo Handling; Longshoremen

Cross, Framk L., Jr. & Forehand, David, eds. Air Pollution Emissions from Bulk Loading Facilities. LC 75-26079. (Environmental Monograph). (Illus.). 22p. 1976. 10.00x (ISBN 0-87762-179-9). Technomic.

Hulett, Malcolm. Unit Load Handling. 351p. 1970. 39.95 (ISBN 0-7161-0035-5). CBI Pub.

LOAN ASSOCIATIONS

see Building and Loan Associations

LOAN SHARKING

see Interest and Usury; Loans, Personal

LOANS

see also Debts, Public; Government Lending; Interest and Usury; Investments; Loans, Foreign; Loans, Personal; Mortgage Loans

A Banker's Guide to Commercial Loan Analysis. rev. ed. 1977. 6.00 (ISBN 0-89982-074-3, 160200). Am Bankers.

Behrens, Robert H. Commercial Problem Loans: How to Identify, Supervise & Collect the Problem Loan. LC 74-13733. (Bank Study Ser). 1974. pap. 20.00 (ISBN 0-87267-021-X). Bankers.

Business Borrowers Complete Success Kit, 7 bks. 1978. 99.50 (ISBN 0-685-83455-7). Intl Wealth.

Business Capital Sources. 150p. 1980. 20.00 (ISBN 0-686-62447-5). B Klein Pubns.

Clemens, J. H. Balance Sheets & the Lending Banker. 5th ed. LC 78-670081. 1977. 17.50x (ISBN 0-905118-15-4). Intl Pubns Serv.

Donaldson, T. H. Lending in International Commercial Banking. LC 79-15566. (International Banking Ser.). 187p. 1979. 27.95x (ISBN 0-470-26793-3). Halsted Pr.

Estes, Jack C. Handbook of Loan Payment Tables. 1976. 24.50 (ISBN 0-07-019682-6, P&RB). McGraw.

Financial Publishing Co. Yields If Prepaid, Seventy-Eight's Method No. 841. 15.00 (ISBN 0-685-02561-6). Finan Pub.

Financing Goods. LC 57-7094. 609p. 1957. text ed. 20.00 (ISBN 0-9605500-0-3). A G Sweetser.

Haney, Lewis H., et al. Brokers Loans: A Study in the Relation Between Speculative Credits & the Stock Market, Business & Banking. facsimile ed. LC 75-2638. (Wall Street & the Security Markets Ser.). 1975. Repr. of 1932 ed. 15.00x (ISBN 0-405-06963-4). Arno.

Hayes, Douglas A. Bank Lending Policies: Domestic & International. 2nd ed. (Michigan Business Studies, New Ser.: Vol. 1, No. 3). 1977. 12.50 (ISBN 0-87712-180-X). U Mich Busn Div Res.

Hayes, Rick S. Business Loans: A Guide to Money Sources & How to Approach Them Successfully. 2nd ed. 354p. 1980. pap. 12.50 (ISBN 0-8436-0786-6). CBI Pub.

--Business Loans: A Guide to Money Sources & How to Approach Them Successfully. 2nd ed. LC 80-10941. 1980. 24.95 (ISBN 0-8436-0786-6). CBI Pub.

Hoffman, Margaret A. & Fischer, Gerald C. Credit Department Management. LC 80-65026. (Illus.). 264p. 1980. 23.00 (ISBN 0-936742-00-3). R Morris Assocs.

How & Where to Get Capital. 158p. 1979. 25.00 (ISBN 0-686-62459-9). B Klein Pubns.

Hunt, Pearson. Portfolio Policies of Commercial Banks in the United States 1920-1939. Bruchey, Stuart, ed. LC 80-1187. (The Rise of Commercial Banking Ser.). 1981. Repr. of 1940 ed. lib. bdg. 12.00x (ISBN 0-405-13657-9). Arno.

Konopa, Leonard J. The Methods of Operation & the Credit Accomodations of a Commercial Bank to Small Business in the Pittsburgh Area. Bruchey, Stuart & Carosso, Vincent P., eds. LC 78-18966. (Small Business Enterprise in America Ser.). (Illus.). 1979. lib. bdg. 20.00x (ISBN 0-405-11470-2). Arno.

Loan Payment Tables. 224p. 1980. saddle stitched 2.95 (ISBN 0-930306-22-8). Delphi Info.

McGillivray, Robert E. How Do Bankers Measure Income. (Illus.). 250p. (Orig.). 1981. 29.95 (ISBN 0-86663-892-X); pap. 17.95 (ISBN 0-86663-893-8). Ide Hse.

Mathis, F. John, ed. Offshore Lending by U. S. Commercial Banks. 2nd ed. LC 80-83082. (Illus.). 366p. 1981. 22.00 (ISBN 0-936742-01-1). R Morris Assocs.

Riley, James C. International Government Finance & the Amsterdam Capital Market: 1740-1815. LC 79-152. (Illus.). 1980. 37.50 (ISBN 0-521-22677-5). Cambridge U Pr.

Roussakis, Emmanuel, ed. International Lending by U. S. Commercial Banks: A Casebook. 414p. 1981. 35.00 (ISBN 0-03-057586-9). Praeger.

Sampson, Anthony. The Money Lenders: Bankers & a World in Turmoil. LC 81-51910. 336p. 1982. 16.95 (ISBN 0-670-21106-0). Viking Pr.

Stephens, Ray G. Uses of Financial Information in Bank Lending Decisions. Dufey, Gunter, ed. (Research for Business Decisions: No. 15). 1980. 31.95x (ISBN 0-8357-1054-8, Pub. by UMI Res Pr). Univ Microfilms.

Sweetser, Albert G. Bank Loans Secured by Field-Warehouse Receipts. LC 57-7980. 112p. (Orig.). 1957. pap. 5.00 (ISBN 0-9605500-1-1). A G Sweetser.

Wood, J. H. Commercial Bank Loan & Investment Behavior. Walters, A. A., ed. LC 75-1192. (Monographs in Applied Econometrics Ser). 153p. 1975. 30.95 (ISBN 0-471-95998-7, Pub. by Wiley-Interscience). Wiley.

LOANS, FOREIGN

DeWitt, R. Peter, Jr. The Inter-American Development Bank & Political Influence: With Special Reference to Costa Rica. LC 77-2929. (Special Studies). 1977. text ed. 24.95 (ISBN 0-275-24460-1). Praeger.

Rubin, Seymour J., ed. Foreign Development Lending: Legal Aspects. LC 73-161939. (American Society of International Law Ser). 1976. lib. bdg. 27.50 (ISBN 0-379-00129-2). Oceana.

LOANS, FOREIGN–MATHEMATICAL MODELS

King, Benjamin B. Notes on the Mechanics of Growth & Debt. LC 68-8701. (World Bank Staff Occasional Papers Ser: No. 6). 69p. 1968. pap. 5.00x (ISBN 0-8018-0338-1). Johns Hopkins.

LOANS, GOVERNMENT

see Government Lending

LOANS, PERSONAL

see also Banks and Banking, Cooperative; Building and Loan Associations; Finance Charges; Pawnbroking

Chapman, John M. & Shay, Robert P. Licensed Lending in New York. LC 67-21693. (Graduate School of Business Report, Columbia University). 114p. 1970. 17.50x (ISBN 0-231-03416-4). Columbia U Pr.

Clark, Evans. Financing the Consumer. LC 75-39239. (Getting & Spending: the Consumer's Dilemma). (Illus.). 1976. Repr. of 1933 ed. 21.00x (ISBN 0-405-08016-6). Arno.

Cohen, Benjamin, ed. Banks & the Balance of Payments: Private Lending in the International Adjustment Process. 1981. 31.50 (ISBN 0-86598-038-1). Allanheld.

Curran, Barbara A. Trends in Consumer Credit Legislation. LC 65-17284. 1965. 13.50x (ISBN 0-226-12888-1). U of Chicago Pr.

The Fear Merchants: An Expose of Loan Companies. (Illus.). 1978. pap. 3.95 deluxe (ISBN 0-9602420-0-7). May Day Pr.

Financial Loan Tables. 1978. pap. 6.95 (ISBN 0-695-81141-X). Follett.

Financial Publishing Co. Truth-In-Lending Tables. 2nd ed. 5.00 (ISBN 0-685-02559-4). Finan Pub.

Financial Publishing Company Staff. The Cost of Personal Borrowing in the United States. 10th ed. Gushee, Charles H., ed. (Illus.). 1981. perfect bound 32.00 (ISBN 0-685-87665-9, 830). Finan Pub.

Follett Loan Payments Handbook. Date not set. pap. 6.95 (ISBN 0-695-81143-6). New Century.

Gibbs, Gerald. The Complete Guide to Credit & Loans. 1981. pap. 2.75 (ISBN 0-686-72911-0, 16931). Playboy Pbks.

Gross, Robin & Cullen, Jean. Help! The Basics of Borrowing Money. 160p. 1980. 9.95 (ISBN 0-8129-0899-6). Times Bks.

Havighurst, Clark C., ed. Consumer Credit Reform. LC 79-111218. (Law & Contemporary Problems Ser.). 1970. 10.00 (ISBN 0-379-11513-1). Oceana.

The Loan Calculator. 1979. pap. 3.95 (ISBN 0-930306-21-X). Delphi Info.

McConnell, J. Knox. How to Get a Loan from Your Bank, Credit Union, or Finance Company. 1975. 4.00 (ISBN 0-682-48442-3, Banner). Exposition.

Schlachter, Gail A. Directory of Financial Aids for Women. LC 77-78149. 16.95 (ISBN 0-918276-02-0). Ref Serv Pr.

Sherman, Michael. Add-on Interest Installment Loan Payment Tables. 1977. pap. 7.50 (ISBN 0-930306-03-1). Delphi Info.

Thorndike, David & Tarlow, Eric K. Consumer Credit Computation & Compliance Guide with Annual Percentage Rate Tables. LC 80-52857. pap. 48.00 (ISBN 0-88262-511-X). Warren.

Wood, Oliver G., Jr. & Barksdale, William C. How to Borrow Money. 144p. 1981. text ed. 13.95 (ISBN 0-442-25204-8). Van Nos Reinhold.

LOATHLY LADY (FOLK-LORE)

Maynadier, Gustavus. Wife of Bath's Tale: Its Sources & Analogues. LC 71-144526. (Grimm Library: No. 13). Repr. of 1901 ed. 10.00 (ISBN 0-404-53556-9). AMS Pr.

LOB TECHNIQUE

see Line of Balance (Management)

LOBACHEVSKI GEOMETRY

see Geometry, Hyperbolic

LOBBYING

Alderson, George & Sentman, Everett. How You Can Influence Congress: The Complete Handbook for the Citizen Lobbyist. 1979. 15.95 (ISBN 0-87690-306-5); pap. 9.95 (ISBN 0-87690-320-0). Dutton.

Ashworth, William. Under the Influence: Congress, Lobbies, & the American Park Barreling System. 1981. pap. 8.25 (ISBN 0-8015-5929-4, Hawthorn). Dutton.

Bailey, Stephen K. Education Interest Groups in the Nation's Capital. 87p. 1975. 7.50 (ISBN 0-8268-1265-1). ACE.

Bauer, Raymond A., et al. American Business & Public Policy: The Politics of Foreign Trade. 2nd ed. LC 63-8171. (Illus.). 1972. 34.95x (ISBN 0-202-24128-9); pap. 15.90x (ISBN 0-202-24129-7). Aldine Pub.

Burman, Ian D. Lobbying at the Illinois Constitutional Convention. LC 72-95000. (Studies in Illinois Constitution Making Ser). 130p. 1973. pap. 5.95 (ISBN 0-252-00336-5). U of Ill Pr.

Chase, Stuart. Democracy Under Pressure: Special Interest Vs. the Public Welfare. LC 68-8054. (Illus.). 1968. Repr. of 1945 ed. lib. bdg. 15.00x (ISBN 0-8371-0039-9, CHDP). Greenwood.

Crater, Flora. The Woman Activist Guide to Lobbying, 1977. rev. ed. 1977. pap. 1.00 (ISBN 0-917560-08-6). Woman Activist.

Crawford, Kenneth G. The Pressure Boys: The Inside Story of Lobbying in America. LC 73-19139. (Politics & People Ser.). 320p. 1974. Repr. 16.00x (ISBN 0-405-05864-0). Arno.

Deakin, James. Lobbyists. 1966. 6.00 (ISBN 0-8183-0180-5). Pub Aff Pr.

DeKieffer, Donald. How to Lobby Congress: A Guide for the Citizen Lobbyist. LC 81-4621. 228p. 1981. 12.95 (ISBN 0-396-07965-2); pap. 7.95 (ISBN 0-396-07969-5). Dodd.

Dexter, Lewis Anthony. How Organizations Are Represented in Washington. LC 69-15729. 1969. pap. 5.95 (ISBN 0-672-60748-4). Bobbs.

Directory of Registered Lobbyists & Lobbyist Legislation. 2nd ed. LC 75-27033. 645p. 1975. 44.50 (ISBN 0-8379-2402-2). Marquis.

Eastman, Hope. Lobbying: A Constitutionally Protected Right. LC 77-85166. 1977. pap. 4.25 (ISBN 0-8447-3267-2). Am Enterprise.

Farkas, Suzanne. Urban Lobbying: Mayors in the Federal Arena. LC 77-124523. 1971. 12.50x (ISBN 0-8147-2550-3). NYU Pr.

Green, Mark J. The Other Government: The Unseen Power of Washington Lawyers. new ed. 1978. pap. 3.45 (ISBN 0-393-00865-7, N865, Norton Lib). Norton.

Greenwald, Carol S. Group Power: Lobbying & Public Policy. LC 74-11921. 372p. 1977. pap. text ed. 10.95 (ISBN 0-03-038276-9, HoltC). HR&W.

Grupenhoff, John T. & Murphy, James J. Nonprofits' Handbook on Lobbying: The History & Impact of the New 1976 Lobbying Regulations on the Activities of Nonprofit Organizations. LC 77-80283. (Non-Profit Ability Ser.). 1977. pap. 9.95 (ISBN 0-914756-16-8). Taft Corp.

Hall, Donald R. Cooperative Lobbying: The Power of Pressure. LC 69-16328. 347p. 1969. pap. 2.00 (ISBN 0-8165-0202-1). U of Ariz Pr.

Hayes, Michael J. Lobbyists & Legislators: A Theory of Political Markets. 208p. 1981. 16.00 (ISBN 0-8135-0910-6). Rutgers U Pr.

Herring, Pendleton. Group Representation Before Congress. LC 66-24706. 1967. Repr. of 1929 ed. 9.00 (ISBN 0-8462-0871-7). Russell.

Hrebenar, Ronald J. & Scott, Ruth K. Interest Group Politics in America. (Illus.). 288p. (Orig.). 1982. pap. 9.95 (ISBN 0-13-469254-3). P-H.

Lane, Edgar. Lobbying & the Law: State Regulation of Lobbying. LC 64-16059. 1964. 18.50x (ISBN 0-520-00696-8). U of Cal Pr.

Latham, Earl. Group Basis of Politics. 1965. lib. bdg. 15.00x (ISBN 0-374-94807-0). Octagon.

McKean, Dayton D. Pressures on the Legislature of New Jersey. LC 66-27121. 1967. Repr. of 1938 ed. 8.00 (ISBN 0-8462-0850-4). Russell.

Marsh, Benjamin C. Lobbyist for the People. 1953. 3.50 (ISBN 0-8183-0235-6). Pub Aff Pr.

Melone, Albert P. Lawyers, Public Policy & Interest Group Politics. 265p. 1977. pap. text ed. 9.75 (ISBN 0-8191-0297-0). U Pr of Amer.

Milbrath, Lester. Washington Lobbyists Survey, 1956-1957. 1972. codebk. 8.00 (ISBN 0-89138-054-X). ICPSR.

Milbrath, Lester W. The Washington Lobbyists. LC 76-5789. (Illus.). 431p. 1976. Repr. of 1963 ed. lib. bdg. 28.75x (ISBN 0-8371-8802-4, MIWL). Greenwood.

Moriarty, Daniel P. Ten Ways to Lobby Your Representatives from Home. 1979. pap. 2.00 (ISBN 0-933968-03-5). D Moriarty.

Murphy, Thomas P. Pressures Upon Congress: Legislation by Lobby. Dillon, Mary E., ed. LC 72-7681. (Politics of Government Ser.). 1973. pap. 2.50 (ISBN 0-8120-0444-2). Barron.

Ornstein, Norman J. & Elder, Shirley. Interest Groups, Lobbying & Policymaking. LC 77-17492. (Politics & Public Policy Ser.). 1978. pap. text ed. 6.25 (ISBN 0-87187-134-3). Congr Quarterly.

Patterson, Samuel. Illinois Lobbyists Study, 1964. 2nd ed. LC 75-38490. 1975. Repr. of 1969 ed. codebk 8.00 (ISBN 0-89138-006-X). ICPSR.

Pym, Bridget. Pressure Groups & the Permissive Society. (People, Plans & Problems Ser.). 176p. 1974. 5.95 (ISBN 0-7153-6451-0). David & Charles.

Sagstetter, Karen. Lobbying. (American Government Ser.). (Illus.). (gr. 7 up). 1978. PLB 7.45 s&l (ISBN 0-531-01413-4). Watts.

Smith, Dorothy. In Our Own Interest: A Handbook for the Citizen Lobbyist in State Legislatures. LC 78-10625. 144p. 1979. pap. 4.95 (ISBN 0-914842-33-1). Madrona Pubs.

Truman, David B. Governmental Process: Political Interests & Public Opinion. 2nd ed. 1951. pap. text ed. 9.95 (ISBN 0-394-31554-5, KnopfC). Knopf.

Vogel, David. Lobbying the Corporation: Citizen Challenges to Business Authority. LC 78-54496. 1979. 14.95 (ISBN 0-465-04157-4). Basic.

Webster, George D. & Krebs, Frederick J. Associations & Lobbying Regulation. LC 79-89996. (Associations & Government Ser.). 75p. (Orig.). 1979. pap. 9.00 (ISBN 0-89834-014-4, 6137). Chamber Comm US.

Wilson, James Q. Political Organizations. LC 73-85991. 374p. 1973. text ed. 11.95x (ISBN 0-465-05936-8). Basic.

Wolf, Alvin. Lobbies & Lobbyists: In Whose Best Interest? Fraenkel, Jack, ed. (Crucial Issues in American Government Ser.). (gr. 9-12). 1976. pap. text ed. 4.96 (ISBN 0-205-04909-5, 7649096). Allyn.

Zeller, Belle. Pressure Politics in New York. LC 66-27184. 1967. Repr. of 1937 ed. 8.50 (ISBN 0-8462-0963-2). Russell.

LOBI (AFRICAN TRIBE)

see also Dagari (African Tribe)

Labouret, Henri. Les Tribus du Rameau Lobi. LC 74-15058. (Illus.). Repr. of 1931 ed. 95.00 (ISBN 0-404-12100-4). AMS Pr.

LOB-NOR

Przhevalskii, Nikolai M. From Kulja, Across the Tian Shan to Lob-Nor. Morgan, E. Delmar, tr. Repr. of 1879 ed. lib. bdg. 15.00x (ISBN 0-8371-3856-6, PRFK). Greenwood.

LOBOTOMY, FRONTAL

see Frontal Lobotomy

LOBSTER FISHERIES

Herrick, Francis H. Natural History of the American Lobster. Egerton, Frank N., 3rd, ed. LC 77-74228. (History of Ecology Ser.). (Illus.). 1978. Repr. of 1911 ed. lib. bdg. 17.00x (ISBN 0-405-10398-0). Arno.

Ipcar. The Lobsterman. (Illus.). (gr. 2-3). 1977. Repr. 2.95 (ISBN 0-89272-032-8). Down East.

McMillan, Bruce A. Finest Kind O'day: Lobstering in Maine. LC 77-3049. (gr. 2 up). 1977. 8.95 (ISBN 0-397-31763-8, JBL-J). Har-Row.

Stewart, Robert. A Living from Lobsters. 1978. 9.50x (ISBN 0-685-63431-0). State Mutual Bk.

Wood, Pamela. The Salt Book. LC 76-53419. 480p. 1977. pap. 5.95 (ISBN 0-385-11423-0, Anchor Pr); pap. 5.95 (ISBN 0-385-11423-0, Anch). Doubleday.

LOBSTERS

Carrick, Carol. The Blue Lobster. LC 74-18594. (Illus.). 32p. (gr. k-3). 1975. 6.95 (ISBN 0-8037-4482-X); PLB 6.46 (ISBN 0-8037-4483-8). Dial.

Cobb, J. Stanley & Phillips, Bruce F., eds. The Biology & Management of Lobsters: Vol. 1, Physiology & Behavior. LC 79-6803. 1980. 55.00 (ISBN 0-12-177401-5). Acad Pr.

--The Biology & Management of Lobsters: Vol. 2, Ecology & Management. LC 79-6803. 1980. 45.00 (ISBN 0-12-177402-3); Set. 89.50 (ISBN 0-686-65861-2). Acad Pr.

Cobb, Stanley J. The American Lobster: The Biology of Homarus Americanus. (Marine Technical Report Ser: No. 49). 1976. pap. 2.00 (ISBN 0-938412-01-9). URI MAS.

Cook, Joseph J. Nocturnal World of the Lobster. LC 70-143289. (Illus.). (gr. 3-7). 1972. PLB 5.95 (ISBN 0-396-06420-5). Dodd.

Merriam, Kendall A. Illustrated Dictionary of Lobstering. LC 78-61525. (Illus., Orig.). 1978. pap. 6.95 (ISBN 0-87027-192-X). Wheelwright.

Olsen, E. A. Lobster King. LC 68-16400. (Oceanography Ser.). (Illus.). (gr. 3 up). 1970. PLB 5.99 (ISBN 0-87783-024-X); pap. 2.75 deluxe ed. (ISBN 0-87783-099-1); cassette 7.95 (ISBN 0-87783-192-0). Oddo.

Philips, B. F. & Cobb, J. S. Workshop on Lobster & Rock Lobster Ecology & Physiology. 300p. 1981. 65.00x (ISBN 0-643-00243-X, Pub. by CSIRO Australia). State Mutual Bk.

Prudden, T. M. About Lobsters. LC 62-21299. (Illus.). 1973. pap. 5.95 (ISBN 0-87027-127-X). Wheelwright.

Recommended International Standard for Quick Frozen Lobsters. 1979. pap. 4.50 (ISBN 92-5-100648-2, F1568, FAO). Unipub.

Stewart, Robert. A Living from Lobsters. 2nd ed. (Illus.). 70p. 15.00 (ISBN 0-85238-099-2, FN 56, FNB). Unipub.

Synopsis of Biological Data on the Norway Lobster. (Fisheries Synopsis: No. 112). (Illus.). 97p. 1976. pap. 7.50 (ISBN 0-685-68967-0, F845, FAO). Unipub.

Synopsis of Biological Data on the Western Rock Lobster: Panulirus Cygnus. (FAO Fisheries Synopsis: No.128). 64p. 1980. pap. 7.50 (ISBN 92-5-101025-0, F2166, FAO). Unipub.

LOCAL ADMINISTRATION

see Local Government

LOCAL ANESTHESIA

Bennett, C. Richard. Monheim's Local Anesthesia & Pain Control in Dental Practice. 6th ed. LC 77-10994. (Illus.). 1978. text ed. 24.95 (ISBN 0-8016-0609-8). Mosby.

Bonica, John J. Regional Anesthesia: Recent Advances & Current Status. text ed. 10.00 (ISBN 0-8036-0990-6). Davis Co.

Covino, Benjamin G. & Vassallo, Helen G. Local Anesthetics: Mechanisms of Action & Clinical Use. LC 75-35749. 192p. 1976. 27.00 (ISBN 0-8089-0918-5). Grune.

De Jong, Rudolph H. Local Anesthetics. 2nd ed. (Illus.). 364p. 1977. 41.25 (ISBN 0-398-03611-X). C C Thomas.

Ehrlich, Ann. The Auxiliary's Role in the Administration of Local Anesthesia. (Illus.). 1978. 2.50 (ISBN 0-940012-02-2). Colwell Co.

Malamed, Stanley F. Handbook of Local Anesthesia. LC 80-17546. (Illus.). 249p. 1980. pap. text ed. 19.95 (ISBN 0-8016-3072-X). Mosby.

Moore, Daniel C. Regional Block: A Handbook for Use in the Clinical Practice of Medicine & Surgery. 4th ed. (Illus.). 1979. 23.75 (ISBN 0-398-01337-3). C C Thomas.

LOCAL COLOR IN LITERATURE

see also Poetry of Places; France in Literature; Italy in Literature

Lieberman, Elias. The American Short Story: A Study of the Influence of Locality in Its Development. 1979. Repr. of 1912 ed. lib. bdg. 17.50 (ISBN 0-8495-3317-1). Arden Lib.

Skaggs, Merrill M. The Folk of Southern Fiction. LC 76-190050. 293p. 1972. 15.00x (ISBN 0-8203-0294-5). U of Ga Pr.

Warfel, Harry R. & Orians, G. H., eds. American Local Color Stories. LC 72-127599. 1971. Repr. of 1941 ed. lib. bdg. 23.50x (ISBN 0-8154-0345-3). Cooper Sq.

LOCAL ELECTIONS

see Elections

LOCAL FINANCE

see also Local Taxation; Metropolitan Finance; Municipal Finance; School Districts-Finance; Finance

Burke, John & Mitchell, James. Local Government Budgeting: Financial Planning & Operational Control. 15.00 (ISBN 0-686-16235-8). MSU-Inst Comm Devel.

Chatters, C. H. & Hillhouse, A. M. Local Government Debt Administration. 1977. lib. bdg. 59.95 (ISBN 0-8490-2178-2). Gordon Pr.

Falcon, William. Improving Local Government Fiscal Management: Action Guidelines for Business Executives. LC 70-65826. (Illus.). pap. 10.00 per copy (ISBN 0-89834-005-5, 5908). Chamber Comm US.

Gardner, Wyland. Government Finance: National, State & Local. LC 77-3572. 1978. 19.95 (ISBN 0-13-360743-7). P-H.

Haskins & Sells Government Services Group. Implementing Effective Cash Management in Local Government: A Practical Guide. LC 76-52520. 1977. looseleaf with vinyl binder 10.00 (ISBN 0-89125-004-2). Municipal.

Lindholm, Richard W. & Wignjowijoto, Hortojo. Financing & Managing State & Local Government. LC 78-19227. (Illus.). 1979. 29.95 (ISBN 0-669-02434-1). Lexington Bks.

Lynn, Edward S. & Freeman, Robert J. Fund Accounting: Theory & Practice. 1974. ref. ed. 22.95 (ISBN 0-13-332379-X). P-H.

McWatters, Ann R. Financing Capital Formation for Local Governments. LC 79-10333. (Research Report: No. 79-3). 1979. pap. 3.00x (ISBN 0-87772-266-8). Inst Gov Stud Berk.

Marshall, A. H. Financial Management in Local Government. 1974. text ed. 42.50x (ISBN 0-04-352050-2); pap. text ed. 18.95x (ISBN 0-04-352051-0). Allen Unwin.

Meyer, M. W. Change in Public Bureaucracies. LC 76-47193. (Illus.). 1979. 22.50 (ISBN 0-521-22670-8). Cambridge U Pr.

Minge, David & Blevins, Audie, Jr. Effect of Law on County & Municipal Expenditures, As Illustrated by the Wyoming Experience. new ed. LC 75-19122. (Illus.). 217p. 1975. pap. 4.50 (ISBN 0-915876-02-7). Wyoming Law Inst.

Mueller, Keith J. Zero-Base Budgeting in Local Government: Attempts to Implement Administrative Reform. LC 80-5860. 149p. 1981. lib. bdg. 16.25 (ISBN 0-8191-1534-7); pap. text ed. 7.50 (ISBN 0-8191-1535-5). U Pr of Amer.

OECD Staff. Measuring Local Government Expenditure Needs: The Copenhagen Workshop. (Urban Management Studies: No. 4). 354p. (Orig.). 1981. pap. 19.00x (ISBN 92-64-12133-1). OECD.

Patitucci, Frank M. & Lichtenstein, Michael H. Improving Cash Management in Local Government: A Comprehensive Approach. LC 76-52518. (Illus.). 1977. pap. 6.00 (ISBN 0-89125-003-4). Municipal.

Portney, Paul R., ed. Economic Issues in Metropolitan Growth. LC 76-15906. (Resources for the Future Ser). 160p. 1977. 10.00x (ISBN 0-8018-1885-0). Johns Hopkins.

Rosentraub, Mark S., ed. Financing Local Government: New Approaches to Old Problems. LC 77-82727. 1977. 17.00 (ISBN 0-8357-0268-5, IS-00032, Pub. by Western Social Science Assoc., Colorado State Univ.). Univ Microfilms.

Schaller, Howard G., ed. Public Expenditure Decisions in the Urban Community. (Resources for the Future Ser). (Illus.). 208p. 1963. pap. 3.50x (ISBN 0-8018-0576-7). Johns Hopkins.

Snyder, James C. Fiscal Management & Planning in Local Government. LC 76-43218. 1977. 18.95 (ISBN 0-669-01055-3). Lexington Bks.

U.S. Senate Committee on Government Operations. The Effect of Inflation & Recession on State & Local Governments. LC 77-74957. 1977. lib. bdg. 10.00x (ISBN 0-405-10500-2). Arno.

LOCAL FINANCE–GREAT BRITAIN

Hepworth, N. P. Finance of Local Government. 6th rev. ed. (New Local Government Ser.: No. 6). 328p. 1981. pap. text ed. 18.95x (ISBN 0-04-352087-1). Allen Unwin.

Maynard, Alan K. & King, David N. Rates or Prices? a Study of the Economics of Local Government & Its Replacement by the Market. (Institute of Economic Affairs, Hobart Papers Ser.: No. 54). 1972. pap. 2.50 (ISBN 0-255-36030-4). Transatlantic.

LOCAL GOVERNMENT

Here are entered works which deal with local government of districts, counties, townships, etc. Works dealing with government of municipalities only are entered under Municipal Government; those dealing with government of counties only are entered under County Government.

see also Administrative and Political Divisions; Boroughs; Cities and Towns; County Government; Decentralization in Government; Elections; Mayors; Metropolitan Government; Municipal Government; Public Administration; Special Districts; Villages

Adams, Herbert B. The Germanic Origin of New England Towns. Repr. of 1882 ed. pap. 7.00 (ISBN 0-384-00331-1). Johnson Repr.

--Saxon Tithing-Men in America. Repr. of 1883 ed. pap. 7.00 (ISBN 0-384-00332-X). Johnson Repr.

--Saxon Tithing-Men in America. LC 78-63734. (Johns Hopkins University. Studies in the Social Sciences. First Ser. 1882-1883: 4). Repr. of 1883 ed. 11.50 (ISBN 0-404-61004-8). AMS Pr.

Adrian, Charles R. Governing Our Fifty States & Their Communities. 4th ed. LC 77-11933. (Illus.). 1978. pap. text ed. 6.95 (ISBN 0-07-000453-6, C). McGraw.

--State & Local Governments. 4th ed. 1976. 15.95 (ISBN 0-07-000450-1, C). McGraw.

Altshuler, Alan. Community Control: The Black Demand for Participation in Large American Cities. LC 72-110439. 1970. pap. 5.50 (ISBN 0-672-63517-8). Pegasus.

American Geographical Society. New England's Prospect: 1933. Adams, James T., et al, eds. LC 78-111763. Repr. of 1933 ed. 34.00 (ISBN 0-404-00354-0). AMS Pr.

Baine, Sean. Community Action & Local Government. 96p. 1975. pap. text ed. 8.75x (ISBN 0-7135-1842-1, Pub. by Bedford England). Renouf.

Baxter, Robert D. Local Government & Taxation, & Mr. Goschen's Report. 1976. Repr. of 1874 ed. 25.00 (ISBN 0-403-06440-6, Regency). Scholarly.

Bayley, Gordon. Local Government: Is Is Manageable? 1979. 15.00 (ISBN 0-08-024279-0). Pergamon.

Bemis, Edward W. Local Government in Michigan & the Northwest. Repr. of 1883 ed. pap. 7.00 (ISBN 0-384-03887-5). Johnson Repr.

--Local Government in Michigan & the Northwest. LC 78-63735. (Johns Hopkins University. Studies in the Social Sciences. First Ser. 1882-1883: 5). Repr. of 1883 ed. 11.50 (ISBN 0-404-61005-6). AMS Pr.

Bemis, Edward W., et al. Local Government in the South & Southwest. LC 78-63824. (Johns Hopkins University. Studies in the Social Sciences. Eleventh Ser. 1893: 11). Repr. of 1893 ed. 11.50 (ISBN 0-404-61085-4). AMS Pr.

Berkley, George & Fox, William J. Eighty Thousand Governments: The Politics of Subnational America. 1978. text ed. 19.95 (ISBN 0-205-06007-2). Allyn.

Berman, David R. State & Local Politics. 3rd ed. 336p. 1980. text ed. 18.95 (ISBN 0-205-07219-4, 767219-5). Allyn.

Bingham, Richard D. The Adoption of Innovation by Local Government. LC 75-41922. 1976. 22.95 (ISBN 0-669-00484-7). Lexington Bks.

Blair, George S. Government at the Grass-Roots. 3rd ed. LC 80-84554. (Illus.). 1981. 15.95 (ISBN 0-913530-25-5); pap. 10.95x (ISBN 0-913530-24-7). Palisades Pub.

Boy Scouts of America. Citizenship in the Community. LC 19-600. (Illus.). 48p. (gr. 6-12). 1972. pap. 0.70x (ISBN 0-8395-3253-9, 3253). BSA.

Bryan, Frank M. Politics in Rural America: People, Parties, & Policy. (Special Study Ser.). 320p. (Orig.). lib. bdg. 28.50x (ISBN 0-89158-561-3); pap. text ed. 10.95x (ISBN 0-89158-984-8). Westview.

Buell, Erwin C. & Brigman, William E. The Grass Roots: Readings in State & Local Government. 1968. pap. 7.95x (ISBN 0-673-05904-9). Scott F.

Burns, James M., et al. State & Local Politics: Government by the People. 3rd ed. (Illus.). 1981. 9.95f (ISBN 0-13-843516-2). P-H.

Channing, E. Town & County Government in the English Colonies of North America. 1973. Repr. of 1884 ed. pap. 7.00 (ISBN 0-384-08463-X). Johnson Repr.

Collins, W. P., ed. Perspectives on State & Local Politics. LC 74-5202. (Illus.). 288p. 1974. pap. text ed. 10.95 (ISBN 0-13-660548-6). P-H.

Committee for Economic Development. Improving Productivity in State & Local Government. LC 76-2408. 1976. lib. bdg. 4.00 (ISBN 0-87186-760-5); pap. 2.50 (ISBN 0-87186-060-0). Comm Econ Dev.

--Modernizing Local Government. LC 66-26939. 84p. 1966. lib. bdg. 2.50 (ISBN 0-87186-723-0); pap. 1.50 (ISBN 0-87186-023-6). Comm Econ Dev.

Computers & Local Government Workshop. 1977. Participant's Notebook, 170pp. & Instructor's Notebook, 472pp. 40.00 (ISBN 0-89854-004-6); set participant's materials 10.00 ea.; binders for participant's materials 5.00 ea. U of GA Inst Govt.

Daland, Robert T., ed. Comparative Urban Research. LC 69-18751. 368p. 1969. 20.00 (ISBN 0-8039-0012-0). Sage.

Daniels, Bruce C., ed. Town & County: Essays on the Structure of Local Government in the American Colonies. LC 77-14834. 1978. 20.00x (ISBN 0-8195-5020-5, Pub. by Wesleyan U Pr). Columbia U Pr.

Danielson, Michael N., et al. One Nation, So Many Governments: A Ford Foundation Report. LC 76-53868. 1977. 16.95 (ISBN 0-669-01293-9). Lexington Bks.

Davidson, Jeffrey L. Political Partnerships: Neighborhood Residents & Their Council Members. LC 79-13107. (The City & Society: Vol. 5). (Illus.). 231p. 1979. write for info. (ISBN 0-8039-1050-9). Sage.

--Political Partnerships: Neighborhood Residents & Their Council Members. LC 79-13107. (The City & Society: Vol. 5). (Illus.). 231p. 1979. pap. 9.95 (ISBN 0-8039-1051-7). Sage.

--Political Partnerships: Neighborhood Residents & Their Council Members. LC 79-13107. (City & Society Ser.: Vol. 5). (Illus.). 231p. 1979. 20.00 (ISBN 0-8039-1050-9); pap. 8.95 (ISBN 0-8039-1051-7). Sage.

Dye, Thomas R. Politics in States & Communities. 4th ed. (Illus.). 512p. 1981. text ed. 17.95 (ISBN 0-13-685131-2). P-H.

Eichner, James A. The First Book of Local Government. rev. ed. (First Bks.). (Illus.). 72p. (gr. 6-9). 1976. PLB 7.40 (ISBN 0-531-00571-2). Watts.

Flinn, Thomas A. Local Government & Politics: Analyzing Decision-Making Systems. 1970. pap. 6.95x (ISBN 0-673-05562-0). Scott F.

Foster, C. D., et al. Local Government Finance in a Unitary State. (Illus.). 640p. 1980. text ed. 60.00x (ISBN 0-04-336066-1). Allen Unwin.

Foster, W. E. Town Government in Rhode Island. 1973. pap. 7.00 (ISBN 0-384-16455-2). Johnson Repr.

Freeman, E. A. An Introduction to American Institutional History. 1973. pap. 7.00 (ISBN 0-384-16766-7). Johnson Repr.

Gargan, John J. & Coke, James G. Political Behavior & Public Issues in Ohio. LC 72-78408. 1972. 12.00x (ISBN 0-87338-124-6). Kent St U Pr.

Gertzog, Irvin N. Readings on State & Local Government. (Foundation of Modern Political Science Ser). 1970. pap. 10.95 ref. ed. (ISBN 0-13-761106-4). P-H.

Goehlert, Robert. Local Government: A Selected Bibliography of Journal Literature. (Public Administration Ser.: P 177). 1979. pap. 6.50 (ISBN 0-686-24635-7). Vance Biblios.

Goodnow, Frank J., ed. Comparative Administrative Law: An Analysis of the Administrative Systems of the U. S., England, France & Germany. 1970. Repr. of 1893 ed. Set. text ed. 44.50 (ISBN 0-8337-1384-1). B Franklin.

Grant, Daniel R. & Nixon, H. C. State & Local Government in America. 3rd ed. 608p. 1975. text ed. 18.95x (ISBN 0-205-04574-X, 7645740); instr's manual o.p. free (ISBN 0-205-05473-0). Allyn.

Greenwood, Royston, et al. Patterns of Management in Local Government. (Government & Administration Ser.). 192p. Date not set. 27.50x (ISBN 0-85520-244-0, Pub. by Martin Robertson England). Biblio Dist.

Gunlicks, Arthur B., ed. Local Government Reform & Reorganization: An International Perspective. (National University Publications, Political Science Ser.). 1981. 17.50 (ISBN 0-8046-9272-6). Kennikat.

Hambleton, Robin. Policy Planning & Local Government. LC 78-73593. (A Landmark Study). (Illus.). 384p. 1979. Repr. of 1978 ed. text ed. 22.00 (ISBN 0-916672-92-1). Allanheld.

Harris, George M. Local Government in Many Lands. LC 74-110907. 1970. Repr. of 1933 ed. 17.00 (ISBN 0-8046-0889-X). Kennikat.

Harvey, L. James & Rusten, Allan C. The ZBB Handbook for Local Governments. LC 77-78223. 1977. pap. 6.95 (ISBN 0-89103-018-2). Ireland Educ.

Hawkins, Robert B., Jr. Self Government by District: Myth & Reality. LC 76-20292. (Publication Ser.: No. 162). 1976. pap. 5.95 (ISBN 0-8179-6622-6). Hoover Inst Pr.

Heilbrun, James. Urban Economics & Public Policy. 2nd ed. 480p. 1981. text ed. 17.95x (ISBN 0-312-83441-1). St Martin.

Henry, Nicholas J. Governing at the Grassroots: State & Local Politics. (Illus.). 1980. text ed. 17.95 (ISBN 0-13-360602-3). P-H.

Herman, Harold. New York State & the Metropolitan Problem. LC 63-7856. 1963. 12.00x (ISBN 0-8122-7382-6). U of Pa Pr.

Highsaw, R. B. & Dyer, J. A. Conflict & Change in Local Government: Patterns of Cooperation. LC 65-16387. 176p. 1965. 11.95x (ISBN 0-8173-4713-5). U of Ala Pr.

Hoggart, Keith. Geography & Local Administration: A Bibliography. (Public Administration Ser.: Bibliography P-530). 84p. 1980. pap. 9.00 (ISBN 0-686-29051-8). Vance Biblios.

Holcomb, W. P. Pennsylvania Boroughs. 1973. Repr. of 1886 ed. pap. 7.00 (ISBN 0-384-24045-3). Johnson Repr.

Howard, George E. An Introduction to the Local Constitutional History of the United States: Vol. 1, Development of the Township, Hundred & Shire. LC 78-64249. (Johns Hopkins University. Studies in the Social Sciences. Extra Volumes: 4). Repr. of 1889 ed. 38.50 (ISBN 0-404-61353-5). AMS Pr.

Hutcheson, John D., Jr. & Shevin, Jann. Citizen Groups in Local Politics: A Bibliographic Review. LC 76-23441. 275p. 1976. text ed. 32.50 (ISBN 0-87436-231-8). ABC-Clio.

I C I S (Influence-Control Information System) Workplan for Local Government Administrators. 1975. 27.50 (ISBN 0-934752-08-7). Eckman Ctr.

Ingle, E. Local Institutions of Virginia. 1973. Repr. of 1885 ed. pap. 11.00 (ISBN 0-384-25741-0). Johnson Repr.

Jansiewicz, Donald R. The New Alexandria Simulation: A Serious Game of State & Local Politics. LC 73-11272. 108p. 1974. pap. text ed. 10.95 scp (ISBN 0-06-384255-6, HarpC); tchrs. ed. avail. (ISBN 0-06-373340-4). Har-Row.

Johnson, J. H. Old Maryland Manors with the Records of a Court Leet & a Court Baron. 1973. Repr. of 1883 ed. pap. 7.00 (ISBN 0-685-30635-6). Johnson Repr.

Jones, George, ed. New Approaches to the Study of Central-Local Government Relationships. 200p. 1980. text ed. 32.00x (ISBN 0-566-00332-5, Pub. by Gower Pr England). Renouf.

Kemp, Roger L. Coping with Proposition Thirteen. LC 80-8188. 1980. 21.95x (ISBN 0-669-03974-8). Lexington Bks.

Kraemer, Kenneth L., ed. Computers & Local Government: A Review of the Research, Vol. 2. King, John L. LC 77-23886. (Praeger Special Studies). 1978. 32.95 (ISBN 0-03-040761-3). Praeger.

Kraemer, Kenneth L. & King, John L., eds. Computers & Local Government: A Manager's Guide, Vol. 1. LC 77-23886. (Praeger Special Studies). 1977. 22.95 (ISBN 0-03-040846-6). Praeger.

Lamb, Curt. Political Power in Poor Neighborhoods. LC 75-19435. 1976. 21.50 (ISBN 0-470-51196-6); pap. 9.50x (ISBN 0-470-51197-4). Halsted Pr.

Lancaster, Lane W. Government in Rural America. 2nd ed. LC 74-2686. (Illus.). 375p. 1974. Repr. of 1952 ed. lib. bdg. 19.25x (ISBN 0-8371-7425-2, LAGR). Greenwood.

Lane, Frederick S., ed. Managing State & Local Government: Cases & Readings. 509p. (Orig.). 1980. text ed. 15.95x (ISBN 0-312-51241-4); pap. text ed. 8.95x (ISBN 0-312-51242-2); write for info. instructor's manual (ISBN 0-312-51243-0). St Martin.

Laudon, Kenneth C. Computers & Bureaucratic Reform. LC 74-9750. 344p. 1974. 17.00 (ISBN 0-471-51840-9, Pub. by Wiley). Krieger.

League of Women Voters Education Fund. Know Your Community. 1972. pap. 0.75 (ISBN 0-89959-056-X, 288). LWV US.

Lefcoe, George, ed. Respective Roles of State & Local Governments in Land Policy & Taxation. (Lincoln Institute Monograph: No. 80-7). 271p. 1980. pap. text ed. 12.00 (ISBN 0-686-31827-7). Lincoln Inst Land.

Levin, Melvin R. Community & Regional Planning: Issues in Public Policy. 3rd ed. LC 76-12862. (Special Studies). 1977. text ed. 29.95 (ISBN 0-275-23690-0); pap. 11.95 (ISBN 0-275-85740-9). Praeger.

Levitt, Morris J. & Feldbaum, Eleanor G. Of, by & for the People: State & Local Governments & Politics. 300p. 1981. lib. bdg. 26.25x (ISBN 0-89158-591-5); pap. text ed. 12.00x (ISBN 0-89158-896-5). Westview.

Lewis, Eugene & Anechiarico, Frank. Urban America: Politics & Policy. 2nd ed. 1981. text ed. 11.95 (ISBN 0-03-050391-4, HoltC). HR&W.

Lockard, Duane. Politics of State & Local Government. 2nd ed. (Illus.). 1969. text ed. 13.95x (ISBN 0-02-371520-0). Macmillan.

Lockard, Duane, ed. Governing the States & Localities: Selected Readings. (Illus.). 1969. pap. text ed. 6.75x (ISBN 0-02-371560-X). Macmillan.

Long, Norton E. The Polity. (Reprints in Sociology Ser). lib. bdg. 24.50x (ISBN 0-685-70258-8); pap. 6.95x (ISBN 0-685-70259-6). Irvington.

Maddox & Fuquay. State & Local Government. 4th ed. Date not set. pap. text ed. price not set (ISBN 0-442-24454-1). D Van Nostrand.

Maddox, Russell W. & Fuquay, Robert F. Issues in State & Local Government. 1965. pap. 6.50x (ISBN 0-442-05075-5). Van Nos Reinhold.

--State & Local Government. 3rd ed. 628p. 1975. text ed. 13.95x (ISBN 0-442-25078-9). D Van Nostrand.

--State & Local Government. 3rd ed. 628p. 1975. text ed. 13.95x (ISBN 0-442-25078-9). D Van Nostrand.

Magazine, Alan H. Environmental Management in Local Government: A Study of Local Response to Federal Mandate. LC 77-12818. (Praeger Special Studies). 1977. 22.95 (ISBN 0-03-040786-9). Praeger.

Mandelker, Daniel R. & Netsch, Dawn C. State & Local Government in a Federal System, Cases & Materials. (Contemporary Legal Education Ser.). 1977. 25.00 (ISBN 0-672-83047-7, Bobbs-Merrill Law). Michie-Bobbs.

Martin, Roscoe C. Grass Roots: Essays. LC 78-5058. 1978. Repr. of 1964 ed. lib. bdg. 15.00 (ISBN 0-8371-9347-8, MAGR). Greenwood.

Martin, Sigur. History of Our Local Gov., Etc. 1966. 30.00 (ISBN 0-685-42978-4). Claitors.

Marx, Herbert L., Jr., ed. State & Local Government. (Reference Shelf Ser: Vol. 34, No. 3). 1962. 6.25 (ISBN 0-8242-0071-3). Wilson.

Matthews, Byron S. Local Government: How to Get into It, How to Administer It Effectively. LC 78-110451. 1970. 16.95 (ISBN 0-911012-04-4). Nelson-Hall.

Morlan, Robert L. Capitol, Courthouse & City Hall. 5th ed. LC 76-13093. (Illus.). 384p. 1977. pap. text ed. 10.95 (ISBN 0-395-24331-9). HM.

Nandedkar, V. G. Local Government: Its Role in Development Administration. 1979. text ed. 12.50x (ISBN 0-686-61444-5). Humanities.

Noel, Bernard. Dictionnaire de la Commune, 1. (Fr.). 1978. pap. 6.95 (ISBN 0-686-57059-6, M-6428). French & Eur.

Ogg, Frederic A. & Ray, P. Orman. Ogg & Ray's Essentials of American State & Local Government. 10th ed. Young, William H., ed. (Illus.). 1969. pap. text ed. 9.95 (ISBN 0-13-633644-2). P-H.

Ott, David J., et al. State & Local Finances in the Last Half of the Seventies. 1975. pap. 5.25 (ISBN 0-8447-3157-9). Am Enterprise.

Pearce, Clifford. The Machinery of Change in Local Government: 1888-1974. (Institute of Local Government Studies). 240p. 1980. text ed. 37.50x (ISBN 0-04-352091-X). Allen Unwin.

Perry, James L. & Kraemer, Kenneth L., eds. Technological Innovation in American Local Governments: The Case of Computing. LC 78-26458. (Pergamon Policy Studies). (Illus.). 22.00 (ISBN 0-08-023707-X). Pergamon.

Peterson, Paul E. City Limits. LC 80-29043. 288p. 1981. lib. bdg. 27.50x (ISBN 0-226-66292-6); pap. 9.95 (ISBN 0-226-66293-4). U of Chicago Pr.

Pinkus, Charles E. & Dixson, Anne. Solving Local Government Problems: Practical Applications of Operations Research in Cities & Regions. (Illus.). 304p. 1981. text ed. 37.50x (ISBN 0-04-658232-0); pap. text ed. 17.95x (ISBN 0-04-658233-9). Allen Unwin.

Poister, Theodore H., et al. Applied Program Evaluation in Local Government. LC 78-20374. 240p. 1979. 23.95 (ISBN 0-669-02731-6). Lexington Bks.

Political Science & State & Local Government. 1973. pap. 3.75 (ISBN 0-915654-00-8). Am Political.

Purchasing for Local Governments. LC 76-150056. 75p. 1976. pap. 5.00 (ISBN 0-89854-017-8). U of GA Inst Govt.

Quiko, Eduard. The ABC's of State & Local Government in America. LC 81-51458. (Illus.). 70p. 1981. perfect bound 6.95 (ISBN 0-88247-602-5). R & E Res Assocs.

Ramage, Burr J. Local Government & Free Schools in South Carolina. 1973. Repr. of 1883 ed. pap. 7.00 (ISBN 0-384-49560-5). Johnson Repr.

--Local Government & Free Schools in South Carolina. LC 78-63741. (Johns Hopkins University. Studies in Social Sciences. First Ser. 1882-1883: 12). Repr. of 1883 ed. 11.50 (ISBN 0-404-61011-0). AMS Pr.

Richards, Peter G. Reformed Local Government System. 4th ed. (New Local Government Ser.). 192p. 1980. pap. text ed. 9.95 (ISBN 0-04-352090-1). Allen Unwin.

Robinson, M. Political Structure in a Changing Sinhalese Village. LC 74-31806. (South Asian Studies: No. 15). (Illus.). 368p. 1975. 39.95 (ISBN 0-521-20374-0). Cambridge U Pr.

Robson, William A. The Development of Local Government. 3rd rev. ed. LC 78-2840. 1978. Repr. of 1954 ed. lib. bdg. 31.00x (ISBN 0-313-20340-7, RODL). Greenwood.

Rodgers, Joseph L., Jr. Citizen Committees: A Guide to Their Use in Local Government. LC 76-56193. 1977. 12.50 (ISBN 0-88410-654-3). Ballinger Pub.

Rosentraub, Mark S., ed. Financing Local Government: New Approaches to Old Problems. LC 77-82727. 1977. 17.00 (ISBN 0-8357-0268-5, IS-00032, Pub. by Western Social Science Assoc., Colorado State Univ.). Univ Microfilms.

Rowat, Donald C., ed. International Handbook on Local Government Reorganization: Contemporary Developments. LC 79-54063. (Illus.). xv, 626p. 1980. lib. bdg. 45.00 (ISBN 0-313-21269-4, RHL/). Greenwood.

Rubinfeld, Daniel, ed. Essays on the Law & Economics of Local Governments. (Papers on Public Econmics Ser.: Vol. 3). 253p. (Orig.). 1980. pap. text ed. 10.00 (ISBN 0-87766-262-2, 27200). Urban Inst.

Rutter, Laurence. The Essential Community: Local Government in the Year 2000. LC 80-16901. (Municipal Management Ser.). (Illus.). 170p. (Orig.). 1980. pap. 15.00 (ISBN 0-87326-994-2). Intl City Mgt.

Saffell, David C. State & Local Government: Politics & Public Policies. LC 77-76119. (Political Science Ser.). 1978. pap. text ed. 11.95 (ISBN 0-201-06806-0); instr's manual & tests 1.50 (ISBN 0-201-06809-5). A-W.

Sato, Sho. State & Local Government Law. 2nd ed. 1165p. 1977. 26.00 (ISBN 0-316-77116-3). Little.

Schaller, Howard G., ed. Public Expenditure Decisions in the Urban Community. (Resources for the Future Ser). (Illus.). 208p. 1963. pap. 3.50x (ISBN 0-8018-0576-7). Johns Hopkins.

Schulz, Ann T. Local Politics & Nation-States: Case Studies in Politics & Policy. LC 79-11416. (Studies in International & Comparative Politics: No. 12). 234p. 1980. text ed. 23.50 (ISBN 0-87436-289-X). ABC-Clio.

Shaw, Albert. Local Government in Illinois. Bd. with Local Government in Pennsylvania. Gould, E. R. LC 78-63732. (Johns Hopkins University. Studies in the Social Sciences. First Ser. 1883: 3). Repr. of 1883 ed. 11.50 (ISBN 0-404-61003-X). AMS Pr.

Shrimp, William G. & Pines, Denniss, eds. Baldwin's Ohio Township Law, with Text & Forms. 4th rev. ed. (Baldwin's Ohio Practice Ser.). 1977. 90.00 (ISBN 0-8322-0019-0). Banks-Baldwin.

Sly, John F. Town Government in Massachusetts, 1620-1930. 1967. Repr. of 1930 ed. 17.50 (ISBN 0-208-00573-0, Archon). Shoe String.

Snider, Clyde F. Local Government in Rural America. LC 74-10652. (Illus.). 584p. 1974. Repr. of 1957 ed. lib. bdg. 32.00x (ISBN 0-8371-7648-4, SNLG). Greenwood.

Spencer, David E. Local Government in Wisconsin. Repr. of 1890 ed. pap. 7.00 (ISBN 0-384-57025-9). Johnson Repr.

--Local Government in Wisconsin. LC 78-63793. (Johns Hopkins University. Studies in the Social Sciences. Eighth Ser. 1890: 3). Repr. of 1890 ed. 11.50 (ISBN 0-404-61058-7). AMS Pr.

Sprigg, J. & Pandya, K. M. Performance Measurement in Local Government: Report of a Study of Five District Councils Including Epping Forest. 20p. 1976. write for info. Coun on Municipal.

Stanley, David T. Managing Local Government Under Union Pressure. (Studies of Unionism in Government). 1972. pap. 5.95 (ISBN 0-8157-8101-6). Brookings.

Stedman, M., Jr. State & Local Governments. 2nd ed. 1979. pap. 10.95 (ISBN 0-87626-821-1). Winthrop.

Stedman, Murray S., Jr. State & Local Governments. 3rd ed. (Illus.). 448p. 1981. pap. text ed. 12.95 (ISBN 0-686-73310-X, W8203-9); tchrs.'s manual free. Winthrop.

Stever, James A. Diversity & Order in State & Local Politics. (Illus.). 1980. text ed. 14.95 (ISBN 0-87249-387-3). U of SC Pr.

Stewart, Debra W., ed. Women in Local Politics. LC 80-14526. vi, 232p. 1980. 12.50 (ISBN 0-8108-1312-2). Scarecrow.

Straayer, John A. American State & Local Government. 2nd ed. (Political Science Ser.). 1977. pap. 11.50 (ISBN 0-675-08489-X). Merrill.

Stumpf, Harry P. Community Politics & Legal Services: The Other Side of the Law. LC 72-98049. (Sage Series on Politics & the Legal Order: Vol. 4). 320p. 1975. 20.00 (ISBN 0-8039-0127-5). Sage.

Tarrow, Sidney. Between Center & Periphery: Grassroots Politicians in Italy & France. LC 76-26642. 1977. 20.00x (ISBN 0-300-02047-3). Yale U Pr.

Valente, William D. Local Government Law, Cases & Materials. 2nd ed. LC 80-10272. (American Casebook Ser.). 1048p. 1980. text ed. 21.95 (ISBN 0-8299-2087-0). West Pub.

Valenzuela, Arturo. Political Brokers in Chile: Local Government in a Centralized Polity. LC 76-47225. 1977. 14.75 (ISBN 0-8223-0380-9). Duke.

Washnis, George J. Productivity Improvement Handbook for State & Local Government. LC 80-11254. 1492p. 1980. 56.00 (ISBN 0-471-04638-8, Pub. by Wiley-Interscience). Wiley.

Webb, Kenneth & Hatry, Harry P. Obtaining Citizen Feedback: The Application of Citizen Surveys to Local Governments. 1973. pap. 3.50 (ISBN 0-87766-055-7, 18000). Urban Inst.

Wickwar, W. Hardy. Political Theory of Local Government. LC 71-95258. 1970. 7.95x (ISBN 0-87249-174-9). U of SC Pr.

Wilhelm, L. W. Local Institutions of Maryland. Repr. of 1885 ed. pap. 11.00 (ISBN 0-384-68479-3). Johnson Repr.

Williams, Arthur R. Measuring Local Government Performance: Assessing Management, Decentralization, & Participation. (Occasional Papers Ser.). (Orig.). 1981. pap. 4.50 (ISBN 0-86731-054-5). RDC Ctr Intl Stud.

Winter. State & Local Government in Decentralized Republic. 1981. 17.95 (ISBN 0-686-73337-1). Macmillan.

Wooster, Ralph A. People in Power: Courthouse & Statehouse in the Lower South, 1850-1860. LC 69-20116. 1969. 12.50x (ISBN 0-87049-090-7). U of Tenn Pr.

--Politicians, Planters, & Plain Folk: Courthouse & Statehouse in the Upper South, 1850-1860. LC 75-32339. 204p. 1975. 12.50x (ISBN 0-87049-166-0). U of Tenn Pr.

Zimmerman, Joseph F. State & Local Government. 3rd ed. (Illus., Orig.). pap. 4.95 (ISBN 0-06-460181-1, CO 181, COS). Har-Row.

Zuckerman, Michael. Peaceable Kingdoms: New England Towns in the Eighteenth Century. 1978. pap. 5.95x (ISBN 0-393-00895-9, N895, Norton Lib). Norton.

LOCAL GOVERNMENT–AFRICA

Ashford, Douglas E. National Development & Local Reform: Political Participion in Morocco, Tunisia, & Pakistan. 1967. 28.00 (ISBN 0-691-07510-7). Princeton U Pr.

Burke, Fred G. Local Government & Politics in Uganda. LC 64-16919. 1964. 12.95x (ISBN 0-8156-2062-4). Syracuse U Pr.

Cowan, Laing G. Local Government in West Africa. LC 75-110429. (BCL Ser. I). Repr. of 1958 ed. 23.00 (ISBN 0-404-00144-0). AMS Pr.

Dryden, Stanley. Local Administration in Tanzania. LC 78-5710. (Illus.). 1968. 12.25x (ISBN 0-8002-0605-3). Intl Pubns Serv.

Fallers, Lloyd A. Bantu Bureaucracy: A Century of Political Evolution Among the Basoga of Uganda. LC 65-10270. 1965. 12.50x (ISBN 0-226-23678-1). U of Chicago Pr.

--Bantu Bureaucracy: A Century of Political Evolution Among the Basoga of Uganda. LC 65-10270. 1965. pap. 2.25 (ISBN 0-226-23680-3, P197, Phoen). U of Chicago Pr.

Nsarkoh, J. K. Local Government in Ghana. 1964. 3.40x (ISBN 0-19-713805-5). Oxford U Pr.

Tordoff, W. Administration in Zambia. 320p. 1981. 80.00x (ISBN 0-686-73055-0, Pub. by Manchester U Pr England). State Mutual Bk.

Wraith, Ronald. Local Administration in West Africa. rev. ed. LC 72-76471. 235p. 1972. text ed. 17.95x (ISBN 0-8419-0123-6, Africana). Holmes & Meier.

LOCAL GOVERNMENT–ASIA

Ashford, Douglas E. National Development & Local Reform: Political Participion in Morocco, Tunisia, & Pakistan. 1967. 28.00 (ISBN 0-691-07510-7). Princeton U Pr.

Ch'u T'ung-tsu. Local Government in China under the Ch'ing. LC 62-11396. (East Asian Ser: No. 9). 1962. 18.50x (ISBN 0-674-53675-4). Harvard U Pr.

Hall, John W. Government & Local Power in Japan: A Study Based on the Bizen Province, 500-1700. (Illus.). 446p. 1981. 30.00x (ISBN 0-691-03019-7); pap. 8.95 (ISBN 0-691-00780-2). Princeton U Pr.

Steiner, Kurt. Local Government in Japan. 1965. 18.50x (ISBN 0-8047-0217-9). Stanford U Pr.

LOCAL GOVERNMENT–AUSTRALIA

Mathews, Russell, ed. Local Government in Transition. 1978. pap. 10.95 (ISBN 0-7081-1576-4, Pub by ANUP Australia). Bks Australia.

LOCAL GOVERNMENT–CANADA

Bourinot, J. G. Local Government in Canada: A Historical Study. Repr. of 1887 ed. pap. 7.00 (ISBN 0-384-05311-4). Johnson Repr.

Bourinot, John G. Local Government in Canada: An Historical Study. LC 78-63771. (Johns Hopkins University. Studies in the Social Sciences. Fifth Ser. 1887: 5-6). Repr. of 1887 ed. 11.50 (ISBN 0-404-61038-2). AMS Pr.

LOCAL GOVERNMENT–EUROPE

Allen, William S. Nazi Seizure of Power: The Experience of a Single German Town, 1930-1935. (Illus.). 1965. pap. 6.95 (ISBN 0-531-06439-5). Watts.

Gruder, Vivian R. Royal Provincial Intendants: A Governing Elite in Eighteenth Century France. 1968. 22.50x (ISBN 0-8014-0164-X). Cornell U Pr.

Piekalkiewicz, Jaroslaw. Communist Local Government: A Study of Poland. LC 72-85539. xiv, 282p. 1975. 18.00x (ISBN 0-8214-0140-8). Ohio U Pr.

LOCAL GOVERNMENT–FRANCE

see also Intendants

Chapman, Brian. Introduction to French Local Government. LC 78-59010. (Illus.). 1979. Repr. of 1953 ed. 18.50 (ISBN 0-88355-685-5). Hyperion Conn.

--Introduction to French Local Government. LC 78-19030. (Illus.). 1978. Repr. of 1953 ed. lib. bdg. 22.25x (ISBN 0-313-20538-8, CHIF). Greenwood.

Gourevitch, Peter A. Paris & the Provinces: The Politics of Local Government Reform in France. LC 79-64666. 256p. 1981. 18.50x (ISBN 0-520-03971-8). U of Cal Pr.

Harding, Robert R. Anatomy of a Power Elite: The Provincial Governors of Early Modern France. LC 78-4125. (Historical Publications Ser.: No. 120). 1978. 25.00x (ISBN 0-300-02202-6). Yale U Pr.

Lagroye, Jacques & Wright, Vincent, eds. Local Government in Britain & France: Problems & Progress. (New Local Government Ser.: No. 18). (Illus.). 1979. text ed. 25.00x (ISBN 0-04-352081-2). Allen Unwin.

Machin, Howard. The Prefect in French Public Administration. LC 76-27185. 1977. 22.50x (ISBN 0-312-63805-1). St Martin.

Tarrow, Sidney. Between Center & Periphery: Grassroots Politicians in Italy & France. LC 76-26642. 1977. 20.00x (ISBN 0-300-02047-3). Yale U Pr.

LOCAL GOVERNMENT–GREAT BRITAIN

Bains, Malcolm A. Management Reform in English Local Government. (Centre for Research on Federal Financial Relations Research Monograph: No. 24). 1978. pap. 7.95 (ISBN 0-7081-1059-2, Pub by ANUP Australia). Bks Australia.

Cam, Helen. Hundred & the Hundred Rolls: An Outline of Local Government in Medieval England. 1960. Repr. of 1930 ed. 21.50 (ISBN 0-8337-0455-9). B Franklin.

Channing, E. Town & County Government in the English Colonies of North America. 1973. Repr. of 1884 ed. pap. 7.00 (ISBN 0-384-08463-X). Johnson Repr.

Clarke, John J. A History of Local Government of the United Kingdom. LC 77-23552. 1977. Repr. of 1955 ed. lib. bdg. 23.50x (ISBN 0-8371-9701-5, CLLG). Greenwood.

Cockburn, Cynthia. The Local State. 216p. text ed. 14.00 (ISBN 0-904383-49-0); pap. 5.95 (ISBN 0-904383-48-2). Pluto Pr.

Danziger, James N. Making Budgets: Public Resource Allocation. LC 79-2394. (Sage Library of Social Research: No. 63). 255p. 1978. 20.00x (ISBN 0-8039-0999-3); pap. 9.95x (ISBN 0-8039-1010-X). Sage.

Friend, John K. & Jessop, William N. Local Government & Strategic Choice: An Operational Research Approach to the Processes of Public Planning. 2nd ed. 1977. text ed. 27.00 (ISBN 0-08-021176-3); pap. text ed. 16.00 (ISBN 0-08-021451-7). Pergamon.

Godwin's Concise Guide to Local Authorities in England & Wales. LC 75-321333. 179p. 1974. 12.00x (ISBN 0-7114-3701-7). Intl Pubns Serv.

Green, Alice S. Town Life in the Fifteenth Century, 2 Vols. LC 70-171443. 920p. Repr. of 1894 ed. Set. 40.00 (ISBN 0-405-08575-3, Blom Pubns); 20.00 ea. Vol. 1 (ISBN 0-405-08576-1). Vol. 2 (ISBN 0-405-08577-X). Arno.

Gyford, John. Local Politics in Britain. 193p. 1976. 22.00x (ISBN 0-85664-319-X, Pub. by Croom Helm Ltd England). Biblio Dist.

Haynes, Robert J. Organization Theory & Local Government. (New Local Government Ser.: No. 19). (Illus.). 224p. (Orig.). 1980. text ed. 27.50x (ISBN 0-04-352088-X); pap. text ed. 12.95x (ISBN 0-04-352089-8). Allen Unwin.

Hepworth, N. P. Finance of Local Government. 6th rev. ed. (New Local Government Ser.: No. 6). 328p. 1981. pap. text ed. 18.95x (ISBN 0-04-352087-1). Allen Unwin.

Hill, Dilys M. Democratic Theory & Local Government. (New Local Government Ser.). 1974. pap. text ed. 9.95x (ISBN 0-04-352053-7). Allen Unwin.

Jackson, William Eric. The Structure of Local Government in England & Wales. 4th ed. LC 74-29792. 1976. Repr. of 1960 ed. lib. bdg. 18.50x (ISBN 0-8371-8001-5, JASL). Greenwood.

Keith-Lucas, Bryan. The Unreformed Local Government System. 173p. 1980. 27.00x (ISBN 0-85664-877-9, Pub. by Croom Helm Ltd England). Biblio Dist.

Lagroye, Jacques & Wright, Vincent, eds. Local Government in Britain & France: Problems & Progress. (New Local Government Ser.: No. 18). (Illus.). 1979. text ed. 25.00x (ISBN 0-04-352081-2). Allen Unwin.

Lambarde, William. William Lambarde & Local Government: His "Ephemeris" & Twenty-Nine Charges to Juries & Commissions. Read, Conyers, ed. (Document Ser). 1978. 12.95x (ISBN 0-918016-36-3). Folger Bks.

Laski, Harold J., et al. A Century of Municipal Progress, 1835-1935. Laski, H. J. & Jennings, W. Ivor, eds. LC 75-41171. Repr. of 1935 ed. 29.50 (ISBN 0-685-14561-1). AMS Pr.

Laski, Harold J., et al, eds. A Century of Municipal Progress, 1835-1935. LC 77-27362. 1978. Repr. of 1935 ed. lib. bdg. 33.75x (ISBN 0-313-20192-7, LACE). Greenwood.

Lee, J. M., et al. The Scope of Local Initiative: A Study of Cheshire County Council 1961-1974. 208p. 1974. 30.50x (ISBN 0-85520-059-6, Pub by Martin Robertson England). Biblio Dist.

Lucas, Bryan K. & Richards, Peter G. A History of Local Government in the 20th Century. (New Local Government Ser.). 1978. text ed. 25.00x (ISBN 0-04-352070-7); pap. text ed. 9.95x (ISBN 0-04-352071-5). Allen Unwin.

Maltbie, Milo R. English Local Government of To-Day: A Study of the Relations of Central & Local Government. LC 74-76664. (Columbia University. Studies in the Social Sciences: No. 23). Repr. of 1897 ed. 21.50 (ISBN 0-404-51023-X). AMS Pr.

Maynard, Alan K. & King, David N. Rates or Prices? a Study of the Economics of Local Government & Its Replacement by the Market. (Institute of Economic Affairs, Hobart Papers Ser.: No. 54). 1972. pap. 2.50 (ISBN 0-255-36030-4). Transatlantic.

Minogue, M., ed. Documents on Contemporary British Government: Local Government in Britain, Vol. 2. LC 76-26374. 1977. 39.95 (ISBN 0-521-21429-7); pap. 12.95x (ISBN 0-521-29147-X). Cambridge U Pr.

Poole, K. P. The Local Government Service: In England & Wales. (New Local Government Ser.). (Illus.). 1978. text ed. 25.00x (ISBN 0-04-352073-1); pap. text ed. 10.95x (ISBN 0-04-352074-X). Allen Unwin.

Richards, Peter G. The Local Government Act 1972: Problem of Implementation. (New Local Government Ser). 1975. text ed. 18.95x (ISBN 0-04-352058-8). Allen Unwin.

Sherman, T. D. O & M in Local Government. 1969. 22.00 (ISBN 0-08-013317-7); pap. 10.75 (ISBN 0-08-013309-6). Pergamon.

Stanyer, Jeffrey. Understanding Local Government. 320p. 1976. 30.50x (ISBN 0-85520-140-1, Pub. by Martin Robertson England). Biblio Dist.

Webb, Sidney & Webb, Beatrice. History of English Local Government, 11 vols. Incl. Vol. 1. 28.50x (ISBN 0-7146-1372-X); Vols. 2 & 3. 57.50x set (ISBN 0-7146-1373-8); Vol. 4. 28.50x (ISBN 0-7146-1374-6); Vol. 5. 29.50x (ISBN 0-7146-1375-4); Vol. 6. 28.50x (ISBN 0-7146-1376-2); Vol. 7; Vols. 8 & 9; Vol. 10. 27.50x (ISBN 0-7146-1379-7); Vol. 11. 27.50x (ISBN 0-7146-1380-0). 1963 (F Cass Co). Biblio Dist.

Wood, Bruce. The Process of Local Government Reform: 1966 - 1974. (New Local Government Ser.). 1976. text ed. 25.00x (ISBN 0-04-350052-8). Allen Unwin.

LOCAL GOVERNMENT-NEW ZEALAND

Bedggood, David. Rich & Poor in New Zealand. 200p. 1980. text ed. 21.00x (ISBN 0-86861-377-0); pap. text ed. 11.50x (ISBN 0-86861-385-1). Allen Unwin.

Bush, Graham. Local Government & Politics in New Zealand. 200p. 1980. text ed. 22.95x (ISBN 0-86861-074-7); pap. text ed. 14.95x (ISBN 0-86861-082-8). Allen Unwin.

Palmer, K. A. Local Government & Planning Law in New Zealand. 400p. 1976. 25.00x (ISBN 0-8002-1680-6). Intl Pubns Serv.

Tomasic, Roman, ed. Legislation & Society in Australia: Law & Society. (Law & Society Ser.). 448p. 1980. text ed. 25.95x (ISBN 0-86861-057-7); pap. text ed. 13.95x (ISBN 0-86861-065-8). Allen Unwin.

LOCAL GOVERNMENT-TANGANYIKA

Heussler, Robert. British Tanganyika. LC 78-142291. 1971. 8.75 (ISBN 0-8223-0247-0). Duke.

LOCAL GOVERNMENT BONDS

see Municipal Bonds

LOCAL HISTORY

Here are entered works on the writing and compiling of local histories. Works concerned with local history of specific areas are entered under names of countries, states, etc. with subdivision History, Local, or under names of places with or without the subdivision History.

Ai-Nai-Yim, Meir. Polychrome Historical Haggadah. (Illus.). 30.00 (ISBN 0-686-10317-3). J Freedman Liturgy.

Crouch, Milton & Raum, Hans, eds. Directory of State & Local History Periodicals. LC 77-4396. 1977. pap. 6.00 (ISBN 0-8389-0246-4). ALA.

Emmison, F. G. Archives & Local History. 2nd ed. (Illus.). 111p. 1974. bds. 15.00x (ISBN 0-8476-1283-X). Rowman.

Felt, Thomas E. Researching, Writing & Publishing Local History. LC 75-44027. (Illus.). 1976. pap. 6.00 (ISBN 0-910050-22-8). AASLH.

Gilbert, Karen D. Picture Indexing for Local History Materials. new ed. LC 73-91411. (Illus.). 36p. 1974. pap. text ed. 2.45 (ISBN 0-912526-12-2). Lib Res.

Kyvig, David E. & Marty, Myron A. Local & Community History. (Illus., Orig.). 1982. pap. text ed. 5.95 (ISBN 0-88295-802-X). Harlan Davidson.

Lincoln, R. I. Once in a Hundred Years: A Pictorial History. 1971. 6.00 (ISBN 0-685-67665-X). RI Hist Soc.

Parker, Donald D. Local History: How to Gather It, Write It, & Publish It. LC 78-11873. 1979. Repr. of 1944 ed. lib. bdg. 16.00x (ISBN 0-313-21100-0, PLAH). Greenwood.

Schreiner-Yantis, Netti, ed. Genealogical & Local History Books in Print. LC 75-4225. 1000p. 20.00 (ISBN 0-686-30194-3); pap. 15.00 (ISBN 0-89157-031-4). GBIP.

Stephens, W. B. Teaching Local History. 182p. 1977. 30.00x (ISBN 0-7190-0660-0, Pub. by Manchester U Pr England). State Mutual Bk.

Thompson, Enid T. Local History Collections: A Manual for Librarians. LC 77-28187. (Illus.). 1978. pap. 5.75 (ISBN 0-910050-33-3). AASLH.

Weitzman, David. My Backyard History Book. (A Brown Paper School Book). (Illus.). 128p. (gr. 4 up). 1975. 8.95 (ISBN 0-316-92901-8); pap. 5.95 (ISBN 0-316-92902-6). Little.

--Underfoot: A Guide to Exploring and Preserving America's Past. LC 76-11475. (Illus.). 192p. 1976. pap. 2.95 encore ed. (ISBN 0-684-16205-9, ScribT). Scribner.

LOCAL JUNIOR COLLEGES

see Community Colleges

LOCAL OFFICIALS AND EMPLOYEES

see also Municipal Officials and Employees

Bleakney, Thomas. Retirement Systems for Public Employees. 1972. 9.75x (ISBN 0-256-01407-8). Irwin.

Committee for Economic Development. Improving Management of the Public Work Force: The Challenge to State & Local Government. LC 78-11075. 1978. lib. bdg. 6.50 (ISBN 0-87186-767-2); pap. 5.00 (ISBN 0-87186-067-8). Comm Econ Dev.

Davidson, Jeffrey L. Political Partnerships: Neighborhood Residents & Their Council Members. LC 79-13107. (City & Society Ser.: Vol. 5). (Illus.). 231p. 1979. 20.00 (ISBN 0-8039-1050-9); pap. 8.95 (ISBN 0-8039-1051-7). Sage.

Ham, Randall E. The County & the Kingdom: Sir Herbert Croft & the Elizabethan State. 316p. 1977. pap. text ed. 11.75 (ISBN 0-8191-0260-1). U Pr of Amer.

Heginbotham, Stanley J. Cultures in Conflict: The Four Faces of Indian Bureaucracy. LC 74-31206. (Studies of the South Asia Institute). 236p. 1975. 17.50x (ISBN 0-231-03888-7). Columbia U Pr.

Mass, Jeffrey P. Warrior Government in Early Medieval Japan: A Study of the Kamakur Bakufu, Shugo, & Jito. LC 74-75875. 296p. 1974. 20.00x (ISBN 0-300-01756-1). Yale U Pr.

Stanley, David T. Managing Local Government Under Union Pressure. (Studies of Unionism in Government). 1972. pap. 5.95 (ISBN 0-8157-8101-6). Brookings.

Taylor, Vernon R. Employment of the Disadvantaged in the Public Service. 1971. 3.00 (ISBN 0-87373-283-9). Intl Personnel Mgmt.

LOCAL OPTION

see also Liquor Laws; Liquor Problem

LOCAL TAXATION

see also Income Tax, Municipal

Bingham, Richard D., et al. The Politics of Raising State & Local Revenue. LC 78-8392. 1978. 23.95 (ISBN 0-03-022306-7); pap. 9.95 (ISBN 0-03-041471-7). Praeger.

Dworak, Robert J. Taxpayers, Taxes, & Government Spending: Perspectives on the Taxpayers Revolt. 272p. 1980. 24.95 (ISBN 0-03-056111-6); pap. 9.95 (ISBN 0-03-056109-4). Praeger.

Hellerstein, Jerome R. & Hellerstein, Walter. Cases & Materials on State & Local Taxation. 4th ed. LC 78-2418. (American Casebook Ser.). 1041p. 1978. text ed. 21.95 (ISBN 0-8299-2000-5). West Pub.

Johnson, Harry L., ed. State & Local Tax Problems. LC 69-10113. 1969. 12.50x (ISBN 0-87049-089-3). U of Tenn Pr.

Lee, Eugene C. Local Taxation in Tanganyika. (Research Ser.: No. 6). 1965. pap. 1.00x (ISBN 0-87725-106-1). U of Cal Intl St.

Lefcoe, George, ed. Local Governments' Decisions & the Local Tax Base. 270p. 1979. pap. text ed. 7.00 (ISBN 0-686-28295-7). Lincoln Inst Land.

Newcomer, Mabel. Separation of State & Local Revenues in the United States. LC 68-56675. (Columbia University. Studies in the Social Sciences: No. 180). Repr. of 1917 ed. 17.50 (ISBN 0-404-51180-5). AMS Pr.

Phares, Donald. Who Pays State & Local Taxes? LC 80-15454. 240p. 1980. text ed. 22.50 (ISBN 0-89946-026-7). Oelgeschlager.

Quindry, Kenneth E. & Schoening, Niles. State & Local Tax Performance Nineteen Seventy-Eight. rev. ed. 1980. pap. 3.00 (ISBN 0-686-29037-2). S Regional Ed.

Schroeder, Larry D. & Sjoquist, David L. The Property Tax & Alternative Local Taxes: An Economic Analysis. LC 75-3751. (Special Studies). (Illus.). 128p. 1975. text ed. 22.95 (ISBN 0-275-07480-3). Praeger.

Shannon, John. Business Taxes in State & Local Governments. 1976. Repr. of 1972 ed. 15.00 (ISBN 0-527-89012-X). Kraus Repr.

Vineberg, Solomon. Provincial & Local Taxation in Canada. LC 70-76698. (Columbia University. Studies in the Social Sciences: No. 128). Repr. of 1912 ed. 16.50 (ISBN 0-404-51128-7). AMS Pr.

Weeks, J. Devereux. Handbook for Georgia Tax Commissioners. 2nd ed. LC 80-2. 80p. 1980. spiral bdg. 7.50 (ISBN 0-89854-056-9). U of GA Inst Govt.

White, Anthony G. Municipal Bonding & Taxation. LC 78-68296. (Reference Library of Social Sciences Ser.). 1979. lib. bdg. 20.00 (ISBN 0-8240-9761-0). Garland Pub.

LOCAL TRANSIT

see also Motor Bus Lines; Railroads, Elevated; Street-Railroads; Subways; Taxicabs

Anderson, J. Edward. Transit Systems Theory. LC 77-11856. (Illus.). 1978. 24.95 (ISBN 0-669-01902-X). Lexington Bks.

Burke, Catherine G. Innovation & Public Policy: The Case of Personal Rapid Transit. LC 79-2410. (Illus.). 416p. 1979. 23.95 (ISBN 0-669-03167-4). Lexington Bks.

Carson, Robert B. Whatever Happened to the Trolley? 1977. pap. text ed. 7.25 (ISBN 0-8191-0330-6). U Pr of Amer.

Cheape, Charles W. Moving the Masses: Urban Public Transit in New York, Boston, & Philadelphia, 1880 to 1912. LC 79-15875. (Harvard Studies in Business History: No. 31). (Illus.). 1980. text ed. 18.50x (ISBN 0-674-58827-4). Harvard U Pr.

Fischler, Stanley I. Moving Millions: An Inside Look at Mass Transit. LC 78-2133. (Illus.). 1979. 14.95 (ISBN 0-06-011272-7, HarpT). Har-Row.

Gray, G. & Hoel, L. Public Transportation: Planning, Operations & Management. 1979. 33.95 (ISBN 0-13-739169-2). P-H.

Hamer, Andrew, ed. Out of Cars - into Transit: Urban Transportation Planning Crisis. LC 76-7900. (Research Monograph: No. 65). 196p. 1976. pap. 12.00 (ISBN 0-88406-097-7). Ga St U Busn Pub.

Hamilton, Neil W. & Hamilton, Peter R. Governance of Public Enterprise: A Case Study of Urban Mass Transit. LC 80-5349. 1981. 18.95 (ISBN 0-686-77664-X). Lexington Bks.

Howson, Henry F. The Rapid Transit Railways of the World. (Illus.). 183p. 1971. 14.00x (ISBN 0-04-385056-1). Intl Pubns Serv.

Jansen, G. R., et al, eds. New Developments in Modelling Travel Demand & Urban Systems. 1979. 45.75x (ISBN 0-566-00269-8, Pub. by Gower Pub Co England). Renouf.

McCaleb, Charles S. Trolleys & Tribulations: A Mobile History of San Jose & the South Bay. Sebree, Mac, ed. (Interurbans Special Ser.: No. 78). (Illus.). 250p. 1981. 30.00 (ISBN 0-916374-48-3). Interurban.

McGuire, Bill & Teed, Charles. Fruit Belt Route: The Railways of Grand Junction, Colorado. (Illus.). 52p. (Orig.). 1981. pap. 4.95 (ISBN 0-939646-00-5). Natl Rail Rio Grande.

Meyer, John R., et al. Urban Transportation Problem. LC 65-13848. (Illus.). 1965. 20.00x (ISBN 0-674-93120-3); pap. 6.95x (ISBN 0-674-93121-1, HP37). Harvard U Pr.

Morris, Ben. Marketing the New Mass Transit. (Illus.). 179p. (Orig.). 1980. pap. text ed. 16.95 (ISBN 0-89894-034-6). Advocate Pub Group.

OECD, ed. Urban Public Transport: Evaluation of Performance. (Road Research Ser.). (Illus.). 76p. 1980. pap. 5.50x (ISBN 9-2641-2127-7, 77-80-04-1). OECD.

Pederson, E. O. Transportation in Cities. 1980. 12.50 (ISBN 0-08-024666-4). Pergamon.

Perry, James L. & Angle, Harold L. Labor-Management Relations & Public Agency Effectiveness: A Study of Urban Mass Transit. LC 80-10746. (Pergamon Policy Studies on Business). 208p. 1980. 24.00 (ISBN 0-08-025953-7). Pergamon.

Rallis, T. Intercity Transportation: Engineering & Planning. 1978. 43.95 (ISBN 0-470-01394-X). Halsted Pr.

Rudman, Jack. Transit Captain. (Career Examination Ser.: C-819). (Cloth bdg. avail. on request). pap. 12.00 (ISBN 0-8373-0819-4). Natl Learning.

--Transit Lieutenant. (Career Examination Ser.: C-820). (Cloth bdg. avail. on request). pap. 10.00 (ISBN 0-8373-0820-8). Natl Learning.

--Transit Management Analyst. (Career Examination Ser.: C-2028). (Cloth bdg. avail. on request). pap. 10.00 (ISBN 0-8373-2028-3). Natl Learning.

--Transit Management Analyst Trainee. (Career Examination Ser.: C-2095). (Cloth bdg. avail. on request). 1977. pap. 8.00 (ISBN 0-8373-2095-X). Natl Learning.

--Transit Patrolman. (Career Examination Ser.: C-821). (Cloth bdg. avail. on request). pap. 8.00 (ISBN 0-8373-0821-6). Natl Learning.

--Transit Sergeant. (Career Examination Ser.: C-822). (Cloth bdg. avail. on request). pap. 10.00 (ISBN 0-8373-0822-4). Natl Learning.

Trzyna, Thomas N. & Beck, Joseph R. Urban Mass Transit: A Guide to Organizations & Information Resources. LC 78-12497. (Who's Doing What Ser.: No. 5). 1979. pap. 25.00x (ISBN 0-912102-38-1). Cal Inst Public.

ULI Research Division & Gladstone Associates. Joint Development: Making the Real Estate-Transit Connection. LC 79-66189. (Illus.). 216p. 1979. pap. text ed. 25.75 (ISBN 0-87420-588-3). Urban Land.

U.S House Committee on Banking & Currency. Demonstration Cities Housing & Urban Development & Urban Mass Transit, 2 vols. in one. LC 77-74955. (American Federalism-the Urban Dimension). 1978. Repr. of 1966 ed. lib. bdg. 66.00x (ISBN 0-405-10499-5). Arno.

Vuchic, Vukan. Urban Public Transportation. (Illus.). 672p. 1981. text ed. 38.95 (ISBN 0-13-939496-6). P-H.

Willson, Beckles. The Story of Rapid Transit. (Illus.). 1979. Repr. of 1904 ed. lib. bdg. 20.00 (ISBN 0-8495-5809-3). Arden Lib.

Wingo, Lowdon, Jr. Transportation & Urban Land. LC 77-86416. (Resources for the Future, Inc. Publications). Repr. of 1961 ed. 16.00 (ISBN 0-404-60346-7). AMS Pr.

LOCALIZATION OF CEREBRAL FUNCTIONS

see Brain-Localization of Functions

LOCALIZATION OF SOUND

see Sound, Localization Of

LOCALLY COMPACT GROUPS

Argabright, Loren & De Lamadrid, Jesus G. Fourier Analysis of Unbounded Measures on Locally Compact Abelian Groups. LC 74-6499. (Memoirs: No. 145). 1974. pap. 7.60 (ISBN 0-8218-1845-7, MEMO-145). Am Math.

Berg, C. & Forst, G. Potential Theory on Locally Compact Abelian Groups. (Ergebnisse der Mathematik und Ihrer Grenzgebiete Ser.: Vol. 87). 240p. 1975. 32.30 (ISBN 0-387-07249-7). Springer-Verlag.

Gaal, S. A. Linear Analysis & Representation Theory. LC 72-95686. (Die Grundlehren der Mathematischen Wissenschaften: Vol. 198). ix, 688p. 1973. 67.40 (ISBN 0-387-06195-9). Springer-Verlag.

Morris, S. A. Pontryagin Duality & the Structure of Locally Compact Abelian Groups. LC 76-53519. (London Mathematical Society Lecture Note Ser.: No. 29). 1977. 16.95x (ISBN 0-521-21543-9). Cambridge U Pr.

Parthasarathy, K. R. Multipliers on Locally Compact Groups. LC 71-84142. (Lecture Notes in Mathematics: Vol. 93). (Orig.). 1969. pap. 10.70 (ISBN 0-387-04612-7). Springer-Verlag.

Reiter, H. L-Prime Algebras & Segal Algebras. LC 76-178758. (Lecture Notes in Mathematics: Vol. 231). 113p. 1971. pap. 8.20 (ISBN 0-387-05651-3). Springer-Verlag.

Stratila, S. V. & Voiculescu, D. V. Representations of AF-Algebras & of the Group U (Infinity) (Lecture Notes in Mathematics: Vol. 486). ix, 169p. 1975. pap. 10.50 (ISBN 0-387-07403-1). Springer-Verlag.

Symposia in Pure Mathematics, Vol. 26. Harmonic Analysis on Homogeneous Spaces: Proceedings. Moore, Calvin C., ed. LC 73-10456. 480p. 1973. 35.60 (ISBN 0-8218-1426-5, PSPUM-26). Am Math.

LOCATION OF FACTORIES

see Factories–Location

LOCATION OF INDUSTRIES

see Industries, Location Of

LOCATION OF STORES

see Store Location

LOCH NESS

see Ness, Loch

LOCKE, DAVID ROSS, 1833-1888

Austin, James C. Petroleum V. Nasby. (Twayne's United States Authors Ser). 1965. pap. 3.45 (ISBN 0-8084-0242-0, T89, Twayne). Coll & U Pr.

LOCKE, JOHN, 1632-1704

Aaron, Richard I. John Locke. 3rd ed. 1971. 42.00x (ISBN 0-19-824355-3). Oxford U Pr.

Acton, Henry. Religious Opinions & Example of Milton, Locke, & Newton. LC 71-158223. Repr. of 1833 ed. 11.50 (ISBN 0-404-00283-8). AMS Pr.

Alexander, Samuel. Locke. LC 73-102561. 1970. Repr. of 1908 ed. 9.00 (ISBN 0-8046-0717-6). Kennikat.

Barger, Bill D. Locke on Substance. (Orig.). 1976. pap. 11.00x (ISBN 0-917044-01-0). Sheffield Pr.

Bourne, Henry R. The Life of John Locke, 2 vols. 1969. Repr. of 1876 ed. Set. 65.00x (ISBN 3-511-03820-0). Intl Pubns Serv.

Boyd, William. From Locke to Montessori. 1976. Repr. 27.00 (ISBN 0-685-71143-9, Regency). Scholarly.

Brand, Reinhard, ed. John Locke: Symposium Wolfenbuttel 1979. 288p. 1980. 43.50 (ISBN 3-11-008266-7). De Gruyter.

--Locke: Symposium Wolfenbuttel, Nineteen Hundred Seventy-Nine. 288p. 1980. text ed. 48.75x (ISBN 3-11-008266-7). De Gruyter.

Calkins, Mary W., ed. & intro. by. Locke's Essay Concerning Human Understanding, Bks. II & IV. 1962. Repr. of 1905 ed. 19.95 (ISBN 0-87548-033-0). Open Court.

Chaudhuri, Joyotpaul, ed. The Non-Lockean Roots of American Democratic Thought. LC 77-15042. (Institute of Government Research Ser.). 1977. pap. text ed. 1.95x (ISBN 0-8165-0614-0). U of Ariz Pr.

Christophersen, H. O. A Bibliographical Introduction to the Study of John Locke. LC 72-79217. 134p. 1930. Repr. 21.00 (ISBN 0-403-03323-3). Somerset Pub.

Christophersen, Hans O. Bibliographical Introduction to the Study of John Locke. LC 68-56598. (Bibliography & Reference Ser: No. 11). 1969. Repr. of 1930 ed. 18.50 (ISBN 0-8337-0565-2). B Franklin.

Collins, James. British Empiricists: Locke, Berkeley, Hume. (Orig.). 1967. pap. 3.50 (ISBN 0-02-813460-5). Glencoe.

Cranston, Maurice. John Locke: A Biography. Mayer, J. P., ed. LC 78-67349. (European Political Thought Ser.). 1979. Repr. of 1957 ed. lib. bdg. 30.00x (ISBN 0-405-11690-X). Arno.

Danford, John W. Wittgenstein & Political Philosophy: A Re-Examination of the Foundation of Social Science. LC 78-6716. 1978. lib. bdg. 17.00x (ISBN 0-226-13593-4). U of Chicago Pr.

De Porte, Michael V. Nightmares & Hobbyhorses: Swift, Sterne, & Augustan Ideas of Madness. LC 73-78048. (Illus.). 1974. 12.50 (ISBN 0-87328-061-X). Huntington Lib.

Dunn, John. Political Thought of John Locke. 1969. 34.95 (ISBN 0-521-07408-8). Cambridge U Pr.

Eisenach, Eldon J. Two Worlds of Liberalism: Religion & Politics in Hobbes, Locke, & Mill. LC 80-27255. (Chicago Original Paperback Ser.). 272p. 1981. lib. bdg. 20.00x (ISBN 0-226-19533-3). U of Chicago Pr.

Fowler, Thomas. Locke. Morley, John, ed. LC 68-58378. (English Men of Letters). Repr. of 1888 ed. lib. bdg. 12.50 (ISBN 0-404-51710-2). AMS Pr.

--Locke. 1973. Repr. of 1880 ed. 12.00 (ISBN 0-8274-1339-4). R West.

Franklin, J. H. John Locke & the Theory of Sovereignty. LC 77-80833. (Studies in the History & Theory of Politics). 1978. 19.95 (ISBN 0-521-21758-X). Cambridge U Pr.

Fraser, Alexander C. Locke. LC 71-103188. 1970. Repr. of 1890 ed. 12.50 (ISBN 0-8046-0825-3). Kennikat.

Gay, Peter, ed. John Locke on Education. LC 64-14307. 1964. text ed. 8.75 (ISBN 0-8077-1419-4); pap. text ed. 4.00x (ISBN 0-8077-1416-X). Tchrs Coll.

Gough, J. W. John Locke's Political Philosophy: Eight Studies. 2nd ed. 238p. 1973. 36.00x (ISBN 0-19-827190-5). Oxford U Pr.

Green, Thomas H. Hume & Locke. 6.00 (ISBN 0-8446-2161-7). Peter Smith.

Hargreaves-Mawdsley, W. N. Oxford in the Age of John Locke. (Centers of Civilization Ser: Vol. 32). 160p. 1973. 6.95 (ISBN 0-8061-1038-4). U of Okla Pr.

James, D. G. The Life of Reason (Hobbes, Locke, Bolingbroke) 1978. Repr. of 1949 ed. lib. bdg. 27.50 (ISBN 0-89760-401-6, Telegraph). Dynamic Learn Corp.

James, David G. Life of Reason: Hobbes, Locke, Bolingbroke. facsimile ed. LC 76-38378. (Biography Index Reprint Ser. - English Augustans: Vol. 1). Repr. of 1949 ed. 17.75 (ISBN 0-8369-8122-7). Arno.

Johnson, Merwyn S. Locke on Freedom: An Incisive Study of the Thought of John Locke. LC 77-94130. 1978. pap. 8.25 (ISBN 0-9601590-5-3). M S Johnson.

Kang, Sugwon. Monarch Notes on Locke's & Hobbes' Philosophy. (Orig.). pap. 2.25 (ISBN 0-671-00531-6). Monarch Pr.

Kendall, Willmoore. John Locke & the Doctrine of Majority-Rule. LC 41-52730. (Studies in Social Science Ser: Vol. 26, No. 2). 1965. pap. 3.95 (ISBN 0-252-72499-2). U of Ill Pr.

Kendall, Willmore. John Locke & the Doctrine of Majority Rule. 4.75 (ISBN 0-8446-2364-4). Peter Smith.

Larkin, P. Property in the Eighteenth Century. LC 68-9655. 1969. Repr. of 1930 ed. 15.75 (ISBN 0-86527-160-7). Fertig.

Larkin, Paschal. Property in the Eighteenth Century. LC 75-86034. Repr. of 1930 ed. 12.00 (ISBN 0-8046-0622-6). Kennikat.

Locke, John. The Correspondence of John Locke, 2 vols. De Beer, E. S., ed. Incl. Letters 1-461, Covering the Years 1650-1679. Vol. 1 (ISBN 0-19-824396-0); Letters - 462-848 Covering the Years 1679-1686. Vol. 2 (ISBN 0-19-824559-9). 1976. 110.00 ea. Oxford U Pr.

--The Correspondence of John Locke, Vol. 4. De Beer, E. S., ed. (Clarendon Edition of the Works of John Locke). 1979. pap. write for info. (ISBN 0-19-824561-0). Oxford U Pr.

--Correspondence of John Locke & Edwin Clarke. LC 72-10623. (Select Bibliographies Reprint Ser.). 1973. Repr. of 1927 ed. 33.00 (ISBN 0-8369-7116-7). Arno.

--The Correspondence of John Locke: Vol. 5, Letters 1702-2198 Covering the Years 1694-1697. DeBeer, E. S., ed. 808p. 1979. text ed. 89.00x (ISBN 0-19-824562-9). Oxford U Pr.

--The Correspondence of John Locke: Volume 3, Letters 849-1241. De Beer, Gavin R., ed. (Clarendon Edition of the Works of John Locke). 1978. 110.00x (ISBN 0-19-824560-2). Oxford U Pr.

--An Essay Concerning Human Understanding. Nidditch, Peter H., ed. (Clarendon Edition of the Works of John Locke Ser). 928p. 1975. 75.00x (ISBN 0-19-824386-3). Oxford U Pr.

Mackie, J. L. Problems from Locke. (Illus.). 240p. 1976. text ed. 28.00x (ISBN 0-19-824555-6); pap. text ed. 8.95x (ISBN 0-19-875036-6); 13.95 (ISBN 0-19-824642-0). Oxford U Pr.

McLachlan, Herbert. The Religious Opinions of Milton, Locke & Newton. LC 74-20740. 1974. Repr. of 1941 ed. lib. bdg. 11.95 (ISBN 0-8414-5930-4). Folcroft.

MacLean, Kenneth. John Locke & English Literature of the Eighteenth Century. LC 62-10233. 1962. Repr. of 1936 ed. 15.00 (ISBN 0-8462-0239-5). Russell.

Macpherson, Crawford B. Political Theory of Possessive Individualism: Hobbes to Locke. (Oxford Paperbacks Ser). 1962. pap. 5.95x (ISBN 0-19-881084-9). Oxford U Pr.

Morris, Charles R. Locke, Berkeley, Hume. LC 79-17847. 1979. Repr. of 1931 ed. lib. bdg. 16.50x (ISBN 0-313-22091-3, MOLO). Greenwood.

Norris, John. Christian Blessedness (with) Reflections Upon a Late Essay Concerning Human Understanding. Wellek, Rene, ed. LC 75-11241. (British Philosophers & Theologians of the 17th & 18th Centuries Ser.). 1978. Repr. of 1690 ed. lib. bdg. 42.00 (ISBN 0-8240-1793-5). Garland Pub.

Parry, Geraint. John Locke. (Political Thinkers Ser.). 1978. pap. text ed. 8.95x (ISBN 0-04-320131-8). Allen Unwin.

Pickering, Samuel F., Jr. John Locke & Children's Books in Eighteenth Century England. LC 80-24899. (Illus.). 312p. 1981. 21.00x (ISBN 0-87049-290-X). U of Tenn Pr.

Quintana, Ricardo. Two Augustans: John Locke, Jonathan Swift. LC 77-91059. 156p. 1978. 17.50 (ISBN 0-299-07420-X). U of Wis Pr.

Rickaby, Joseph J. Free Will & Four English Philosophers. facs. ed. LC 74-84333. (Essay Index Reprint Ser). 1906. 15.50 (ISBN 0-8369-1103-2). Arno.

Sahakian, Mabel L. & Sahakian, William S. John Locke. (World Leaders Ser.: No. 40). 1975. lib. bdg. 9.95 (ISBN 0-8057-3539-9). Twayne.

Santayana, George. Some Turns of Thought in Modern Philosophy: Five Essays. facs. ed. LC 67-23268. (Essay Index Reprint Ser). 1933. 11.00 (ISBN 0-8369-0849-X). Arno.

Schouls, Peter A. The Imposition of Method: A Study of Descartes & Locke. 282p. 1980. text ed. 45.00x (ISBN 0-19-824613-7). Oxford U Pr.

Squadrito, Kathleen. John Locke. (English Authors Ser.: No. 271). 1979. 10.95 (ISBN 0-8057-6772-X). Twayne.

Squadrito, Kathleen M. Locke's Theory of Sensitive Knowledge. LC 78-62265. 1978. pap. text ed. 9.25 (ISBN 0-8191-0571-6). U Pr of Amer.

Steinberg, Jules. Locke, Rousseau, & the Idea of Consent: An Inquiry into the Liberal-Democratic Theory of Political Obligation. LC 77-91094. (Contributions in Political Science: No. 6). 1978. lib. bdg. 19.95x (ISBN 0-313-20052-1, SLR/). Greenwood.

Tagart, Edward. Locke's Writings & Philosophy Historically Considered. 1977. lib. bdg. 59.95 (ISBN 0-8490-2179-0). Gordon Pr.

Tucker, Josiah. A Treatise on Civil Government, 3 pts. Incl. Pt. 1. The Notion of Mr. Locke & His Followers, Concerning the Origin, Extent & End of Civil Government, Examined & Confuted; Pt. 2. The True Basis of Civil Government Set Forth; Pt. 3. England's Former Gothic Constitution Censured & Exposed. LC 65-26384. v, 428p. Repr. of 1781 ed. 22.50x (ISBN 0-678-00217-7). Kelley.

Tuveson, Ernest L. Imagination As a Means of Grace. LC 73-21543. 218p. 1973. Repr. of 1960 ed. 10.00 (ISBN 0-87752-173-5). Gordian.

Vaughn, Karen I. John Locke: Economist & Social Scientist. LC 79-17875. 1980. lib. bdg. 13.50x (ISBN 0-226-85166-4). U of Chicago Pr.

Villey-Desmeserets, Pierre. Influence De Montaigne Sur les Idees Pedagogiques De Locke & De Rousseau. LC 70-157527. (Research & Source Works Ser: No. 72). 1971. Repr. of 1911 ed. lib. bdg. 23.50 (ISBN 0-8337-4465-8). B Franklin.

Von Leyden, W. Hobbes & Locke: The Politics of Freedom & Obligation. 272p. 1981. 22.50x (ISBN 0-312-38824-1). St Martin.

White, Morton. Science & Sentiment in America: Philosophical Thought from Jonathan Edwards to John Dewey. 1972. 15.95 (ISBN 0-19-501519-3). Oxford U Pr.

Yolton, J. W. John Locke & the Way of Ideas. LC 80-2894. (BCL Ser.: No. II). Repr. of 1956 ed. 29.50 (ISBN 0-404-18076-0). AMS Pr.

Yolton, John W. John Locke & Education. 1971. pap. text ed. 2.95x (ISBN 0-685-04758-X). Phila Bk Co.

--Locke & the Compass of Human Understanding. LC 76-112477. 1970. 29.95 (ISBN 0-521-07838-5). Cambridge U Pr.

LOCKHART, JOHN GIBSON, 1794-1854

Carswell, Donald. Scott & His Circle. facsimile ed. LC 72-175692. (Select Bibliographies Reprint Ser). Repr. of 1930 ed. 19.00 (ISBN 0-8369-6607-4). Arno.

Grierson, Herbert. Lang, Lockhart & Biography. LC 73-14791. 1834. Repr. lib. bdg. 6.00 (ISBN 0-8414-4444-7). Folcroft.

Lang, Andrew. Life & Letters of John Gibson Lockhart, 2 Vols. LC 79-110131. 1970. Repr. of 1897 ed. 32.50 (ISBN 0-404-03849-2). AMS Pr.

Lockhead, Marian. John Gibson Lockhart. 324p. 1980. lib. bdg. 30.00 (ISBN 0-8482-1621-0). Norwood Edns.

Lockhead, Marion. John Gibson Lockhart. LC 78-845. Repr. of 1954 ed. lib. bdg. 25.00 (ISBN 0-8414-5835-9). Folcroft.

MacBeth, Gilbert. John Gibson Lockhart. 1935. Repr. lib. bdg. 30.00 (ISBN 0-8414-6385-9). Folcroft.

Ruddick, William, ed. John Gibson Lockhart: Petter's Letters to His Kinfolk. 1977. 12.50x (ISBN 0-7073-0135-1, Pub. by Scottish Academic Pr Scotland). Columbia U Pr.

LOCKHEED AIRPLANES

Arnold, Rhodes. Shooting Star, T-Bird & Starfire: A Famous Lockheed Family. (Illus.). 128p. 1981. pap. 12.95 (ISBN 0-89404-035-9). Aztex.

Lockheed Aircraft Corporation. Of Men & Stars: A History of Lockheed Aircraft Corporation. Gilbert, James, ed. LC 79-7280. (Flight: Its First Seventy-Five Years Ser.). (Illus.). 1979. Repr. of 1957 ed. lib. bdg. 21.00x (ISBN 0-405-12189-X). Arno.

Maloney, Edward T. Lockheed P-38. LC 68-31778. (Aero Ser.: Vol. 19). (Illus.). 1968. pap. 3.95 (ISBN 0-8168-0572-5). Aero.

LOCKOUTS

see Strikes and Lockouts

LOCKS AND KEYS

Alth, Max. All About Locks & Locksmithing. (Illus.). 1972. pap. 4.50 (ISBN 0-8015-0151-2, Hawthorn). Dutton.

Arnall, Franklin M. The Padlock Collector. 3rd ed. LC 77-74542. (Illus.). 1977. pap. 3.95 (ISBN 0-914638-02-5). Arnall.

Eddie The Wire. The Complete Guide to Lock Picking. 1981. pap. 7.95 (ISBN 0-686-30630-9). Loompanics.

--How to Make Your Own Professional Lock Tools. 1980. pap. 6.50 (ISBN 0-686-30628-7). Loompanics.

--How to Make Your Own Professional Lock Tools, Vol. 2. 1981. pap. 5.95 (ISBN 0-686-30629-5). Loompanics.

Gibbons, Gail. Locks & Keys. LC 79-7825. (Illus.). 32p. (gr. 1-4). 1980. 7.95 (ISBN 0-690-04058-X, TYC-J); PLB 7.89 (ISBN 0-690-04059-8). Har-Row.

Hobbs. Construction of Locks & Safes. 15.00 (ISBN 0-87556-126-8). Saifer.

Monk, Eric. Keys: Their History & Collection. (Illus.). 1975. pap. 5.00 (ISBN 0-912728-90-6). Newbury Bks.

Roper, C. A. Complete Handbook of Locks & Locksmithing. LC 76-43134. (Illus.). 1976. 12.95 (ISBN 0-8306-6920-5); pap. 7.95 (ISBN 0-8306-5920-X, 920). TAB Bks.

Russell, John L., 3rd. Involuntary Repossession or in the Steal of the Night. 3rd ed. LC 76-29796. (Illus.). 1979. pap. text ed. 10.95 (ISBN 0-933558-00-7). Russell Pubns.

Sloane, Eugene A. The Complete Book of Locks, Keys, Burglar & Smoke Alarms & Other Security Devices. 1979. pap. 2.95 (ISBN 0-451-08713-5, E8713, Sig). NAL.

--The Complete Book of Locks, Keys, Burglar & Smoke Alarms, & Other Security Devices. LC 76-30530. (Illus.). 1977. pap. 6.95 (ISBN 0-688-08189-4). Morrow.

Tobias, Marc W. Locks, Safes, & Security: A Handbook for Law Enforcement Personnel. (Illus.). 352p. 1971. photocopy ed. spiral 34.50 (ISBN 0-398-02155-4). C C Thomas.

LOCKSMITHING

Alth, Max. All About Locks & Locksmithing. (Illus.). 1972. pap. 4.50 (ISBN 0-8015-0151-2, Hawthorn). Dutton.

Crichton, Whitcomb. Practical Course in Modern Locksmithing. 1943. 14.95 (ISBN 0-911012-06-0). Nelson-Hall.

Eddie The Wire. How to Make Your Own Professional Lock Tools. 1980. pap. 6.50 (ISBN 0-686-30628-7). Loompanics.

--How to Make Your Own Professional Lock Tools, Vol. 2. 1981. pap. 5.95 (ISBN 0-686-30629-5). Loompanics.

Educational Research Council of America. Lock Master. Braverman, Jack R. & Marchak, John P., eds. (Real People at Work Ser: E). (Illus.). 1974. pap. text ed. 2.25 (ISBN 0-89247-036-4). Changing Times.

Lock Pick Design Manual. (Illus.). 1973. pap. 5.00 (ISBN 0-87364-081-0). Paladin Ent.

Mayers, Keith. A Dictionary of Locksmithing. 1980. pap. 6.50 (ISBN 0-686-27629-9). Mayers-Joseph.

Office of Strategic Services. OSS CIA Locks, Picks & Clicks. (Illus.). 70p. 1975. pap. 5.95 (ISBN 0-87364-040-3). Paladin Ent.

Robinson, Robert L. Complete Course in Professional Locksmithing. LC 73-174584. (Illus.). 300p. 1973. 42.95 (ISBN 0-911012-15-X). Nelson-Hall.

Roper, C. A. Complete Handbook of Locks & Locksmithing. LC 76-43134. (Illus.). 1976. 12.95 (ISBN 0-8306-6920-5); pap. 7.95 (ISBN 0-8306-5920-X, 920). TAB Bks.

Rudman, Jack. Foreman Locksmith. (Career Examination Ser.: C-2223). (Cloth bdg. avail. on request). pap. 8.00 (ISBN 0-8373-2223-5). Natl Learning.

--Locksmith. (Career Examination Ser.: C-1348). (Cloth bdg. avail. on request). pap. 6.00 (ISBN 0-8373-1348-1). Natl Learning.

--Maintenance Locksmith. (Career Examination Ser.: C-1353). (Cloth bdg. avail. on request). pap. 6.00 (ISBN 0-8373-1353-8). Natl Learning.

LOCKWOOD, BELVA ANN, 1830-1917

Dunnahoo, Terry. Before the Supreme Court: The Story of Belva Ann Lockwood. LC 73-22057. (Illus.). 192p. (gr. 4-7). 1974. 7.95 (ISBN 0-395-18520-3). HM.

LOCKYER, JOSEPH NORMAN, SIR, 1836-1920

Meadows, A. J. Science & Controversy: A Biography of Sir Norman Lockyer. 280p. 1972. 10.00 (ISBN 0-262-13079-3). MIT Pr.

LOCMARIAQUER, FRANCE

Clark, Eleanor. The Oysters of Locmariaquer. LC 77-82670. (Illus.). 1978. pap. 3.95 (ISBN 0-226-10763-9, P752, Phoen). U of Chicago Pr.

LOCOMOTION

see also Animal Locomotion; Automobiles; Boats and Boating; Coaching; Communication and Traffic; Cycling; Driving of Horse-Drawn Vehicles; Flight; Horsemanship; Human Locomotion; Navigation; Transportation

Bekker, M. G. Introduction to Terrain-Vehicle Systems. LC 68-29272. (Illus.). 1969. 27.50 (ISBN 0-472-04144-4). U of Mich Pr.

Dagg, A. I. & James, A. Running, Walking & Jumping: The Science of Locomotion. LC 77-15301. (Wykeham Science Ser.: No. 42). 1977. 14.95x (ISBN 0-8448-1169-6). Crane-Russak Co.

Jenkins, Farish A., ed. Primate Locomotion. 1974. 56.00 (ISBN 0-12-384050-3). Acad Pr.

Pauwels, F. Biomechanics of the Locomotor Apparatus. (Illus.). 520p. 1980. 175.90 (ISBN 0-387-09131-9). Springer-Verlag.

LOCOMOTIVE DIESELS

see Diesel Locomotives

LOCOMOTIVE ENGINEERS

Abdill, George. Locomotive Engineer Album. (Encore Ed.). (Illus.). 9.95 (ISBN 0-87564-534-8). Superior Pub.

Marshall, John. Biographical Dictionary of Railway Engineers. 1978. 15.95 (ISBN 0-7153-7489-3). David & Charles.

Nock, O. S. Out the Line. (Illus.). 1977. 9.95 (ISBN 0-236-40070-3, Pub. by Paul Elek). Merrimack Bk Serv.

Reynolds, Michael. Engine-Driving Life: Stirring Adventures & Incidents in the Lives of Locomotive Engine-Drivers. (Illus.). 1968. Repr. of 1880 ed. 4.50 (ISBN 0-8038-1877-7). Hastings.

Rolt, Lionel T. George & Robert Stephenson: The Railway Revolution. LC 77-22800. (Illus.). 1977. Repr. of 1960 ed. lib. bdg. 28.25x (ISBN 0-8371-9747-3, RORR). Greenwood.

LOCOMOTIVES

see also Diesel Locomotives; Electric Locomotives

Ahron, E. L. British Steam Railway Locomotive: Volume I, 1825-1925. 29.50x (ISBN 0-392-07695-0, SpS). Sportshelf.

American Locomotive Company: Rotary Snow Plows 1909. (Illus.). 1973. pap. 2.50 (ISBN 0-913556-05-X). Spec Pr NJ.

American Locomotive Company: USRA Locomotive 1919. (Illus.). 1973. pap. 3.00 (ISBN 0-913556-04-1). Spec Pr NJ.

Anderson, Norman E. & Macdermot, C. G. PA-Four Locomotive. LC 78-51249. (Illus.). 1978. 22.50 (ISBN 0-89685-035-8). Chatham Pub CA.

Baldwin Locomotive Works (BALDWIN) General Catalogue 1915. (Illus.). 1972. 9.00 (ISBN 0-913556-02-5); pap. 6.00 (ISBN 0-913556-03-3). Spec Pr NJ.

BALDWIN Logging Locomotives 1913. (Illus.). 1973. pap. 4.00 (ISBN 0-913556-09-2). Spec Pr NJ.

BALDWIN Narrow-Gauge Locomotives 1872-1876. (Illus.). 1973. 6.00 (ISBN 0-913556-35-1); pap. 4.00 (ISBN 0-913556-31-9). Spec Pr NJ.

Basic Steam Locomotive Maintenance. 21.95 (ISBN 0-686-75182-5). Chatham Pub CA.

Best, Gerald M. Promontory's Locomotives. LC 80-15895. (Illus.). 1981. 2.95 (ISBN 0-87095-082-7). Golden West.

Bowen Cooke, Charles J. British Locomotives: Their History, Construction & Modern Development. (Illus.). 381p. 1979. Repr. of 1893 ed. 20.00x (ISBN 0-905418-72-7). Intl Pubns Serv.

Bradley, D. L. Drummond Greyhounds of the LSWR. 1977. 14.95 (ISBN 0-7153-7329-3). David & Charles.

British Locomotive Names of the 20th Century. 16.95x (ISBN 0-392-07681-0, SpS). Sportshelf.

Cook, Richard J. Super Power Steam Locomotives. LC 66-29787. (Illus.). 144p. 1966. 16.95 (ISBN 0-87095-010-X). Golden West.

Dow, George. World Locomotive Models. (Illus.). 192p. 1973. 15.00 (ISBN 0-668-02973-0). Arco.

Evans, Martin. LBSC's Shop, Shed & Road. 2nd ed. 192p. (Orig.). 1979. pap. 12.50x (ISBN 0-85242-708-5). Intl Pubns Serv.

--Model Locomotive Construction. 2nd ed. (Illus.). 163p. 1978. pap. 9.50x (ISBN 0-85242-602-X). Intl Pubns Serv.

Fitt, William C., ed. Steam Locomotive Study Course, 4 vols. LC 79-65782. (Illus.). 1500p. 1980. Set. 100.00 (ISBN 0-914104-05-5). Wildwood Pubns MI.

Garratt, Colin. A Popular Guide to the Preserved Steam Railways of Britain. (Illus.). 1979. 12.95 (ISBN 0-7137-0978-2, Pub by Blandford Pr England). Sterling.

Halcroft, H. Locomotive Adventure, Vol. 2. 17.75x (ISBN 0-392-08040-0, SpS). Sportshelf.

Hauff, Steve & Gertz, Jim. Willamette Locomotive. LC 76-24498. 1977. 15.00 (ISBN 0-8323-0274-0). Binford.

Hirota, Naotaka. Steam Locomotives of Japan. LC 72-80748. (Illus.). 104p. 1972. 12.50 (ISBN 0-87011-185-X). Kodansha.

Hollingsworth, Brian. How to Drive a Steam Locomotive. 1979. 17.50x (ISBN 0-906525-03-9). Nichols Pub.

Instructions for the Care of Shay Geared Locomotives. 1972. pap. 3.00 (ISBN 0-87012-140-5). McClain.

Le Fleming, H. M. & Price, J. H. Russian Steam Locomotives. 5.95 (ISBN 0-7153-5495-7). David & Charles.

Locomotives of the Rio Grande. Date not set. 9.95 (ISBN 0-686-75188-4). Chatham Pub CA.

Motor Power of the Union Pacific. Date not set. 39.95 (ISBN 0-686-75190-6). Chatham Pub CA.

Nock, O. S. The Gresley Pacifics: Part 1 1922-1935. (Locomotive Monographs). 1973. 14.95 (ISBN 0-7153-6336-0). David & Charles.

--The Pocket Encyclopedia of British Steam Locomotives. (Illus.). 1964. 1.50 (ISBN 0-486-22936-X). Dover.

--Steam Railways of Britian. (Illus.). 1967. 1.50 (ISBN 0-486-22937-8). Dover.

Nock, Oswald S. Great Steam Locomotives of All Time. LC 76-56418. (Arco Color Books). (Illus.). 1977. 7.95 (ISBN 0-668-04209-5, 4209); pap. 5.95 (ISBN 0-668-04250-8, 4250). Arco.

--LWNR Precursor Family. LC 66-7430. (Illus.). 1966. 10.95x (ISBN 0-678-05716-8). Kelley.

--Steam Locomotive. 2nd ed. LC 73-38377. (Illus.). 1968. 12.95x (ISBN 0-678-06024-X). Kelley.

North British Locomotive Co. Catalogue of Narrow Gauge Locomotives. LC 70-99262. (Illus.). Repr. of 1912 ed. 11.95x (ISBN 0-678-05666-8). Kelley.

Reed, Brian. Locomotives. (Transport Source Book Ser). 1970. 4.00x (ISBN 0-7063-1227-9). Intl Pubns Serv.

Repair Parts for Shay Geared Locomotives. 1908. pap. 3.00 (ISBN 0-87012-026-3). McClain.

Sattler, Helen R. Train Whistles: A Language in Code. LC 77-2163. (Illus.). (ps-3). 1977. 8.25 (ISBN 0-688-41808-2); PLB 7.92 (ISBN 0-688-51808-7). Lothrop.

Shay Patent & Direct Locomotives by the Lima Locomotive & Machine Company. 1971. Repr. of 1901 ed. 3.00 (ISBN 0-87012-114-6). McClain.

Shays & Other Geared Locomotives from Catalogs & Cyclopedias. (Train Shed Cyclopedia Ser: No. 34). (Illus.). 64p. 1975. pap. 4.50 (ISBN 0-912318-65-1). N K Gregg.

Smith, David L. Locomotives of the Glasgow & Southwestern Railway. 1976. 6.95 (ISBN 0-7153-6960-1). David & Charles.

Southern Pacific Motive Power Annual, 1974-1976. (Illus.). 1976. 15.00 (ISBN 0-89685-008-0). Chatham Pub CA.

Southern Pacific Motive Power Annual, 1971. (Illus.). 1971. 12.50 (ISBN 0-89685-005-6). Chatham Pub CA.

Southern Pacific Motive Power Annual, 1972. (Illus.). 1973. 12.50 (ISBN 0-89685-006-4). Chatham Pub CA.

Southern Pacific Motive Power Annual, 1973. (Illus.). 1974. 12.50 (ISBN 0-89685-007-2). Chatham Pub CA.

The Sp 4300 4-8-2's. Date not set. 24.00 (ISBN 0-686-75209-0). Chatham Pub CA.

Tamburello, Adolfo. Japan. Nannicini, Giuliana & Bowman, John, eds. Mondadori, tr. from It. LC 71-179262. (Monuments of Civilization Ser.). Orig. Title: Giappone. (Illus.). 192p. 1973. 25.00 (ISBN 0-448-02022-X, MSP). G&D.

Tuplin, W. A. The Steam Locomotive. 1974. 10.00 (ISBN 0-684-13749-6, ScribT). Scribner.

Union Pacific Motor Power Review. Date not set. 11.95 (ISBN 0-686-75211-2). Chatham Pub CA.

Western Pacific Steam Locomotives. Date not set. 38.50 (ISBN 0-686-75214-7). Chatham Pub CA.

Why You Can Haul at Least Thirty per Cent More per Ton of Locomotive with the Modern Heisler. 1975. Repr. 3.00 (ISBN 0-87012-212-6). McClain.

Wright, Roy V., ed. Famous Passenger Trains from the 1943 Car Builder's Cyclopedia. (Train Shed Cyclopedia Ser., No. 16). (Illus.). 1974. pap. 3.95 (ISBN 0-912318-45-7). N K Gregg.

--Four-Eight-Four's & Other Heavy Passenger Locos, 1927-1941. (Train Shed Cyclopedia Ser., No. 14). (Illus.). 1973. pap. 3.95 (ISBN 0-912318-43-0). N K Gregg.

--Heavy Traction, 1922-1941. (Train Shed Cyclopedia Ser., No. 15). (Illus.). 1974. pap. 4.95 (ISBN 0-912318-44-9). N K Gregg.

--Industrial & Foreign Locomotives from the Nineteen Thirty Locomotive Cyclopedia. (Train Shed Cyclopedia Ser: No. 37). (Illus.). 72p. 1975. pap. 4.95 (ISBN 0-912318-68-6). N K Gregg.

--Locomotive Cabs and Fittings from the 1927 Locomotive Cyclopedia, Pt. 1. (Train Shed Cyclopedia Ser: No. 40). (Illus.). 40p. 1975. pap. 3.00 (ISBN 0-912318-71-6). N K Gregg.

--Locomotive Cabs and Fittings from Tne 1927 Locomotive Cyclopedia, Pt. 2. (Train Shed Cyclopedia Ser: No. 41). (Illus.). 40p. 1975. pap. 3.00 (ISBN 0-912318-72-4). N K Gregg.

--Locomotive Drawings & Boilers: Part 2. (Train Shed Ser.: No. 68). (Illus.). 1978. pap. 4.50 (ISBN 0-87962-074-9). N K Gregg.

--Locomotives from the Nineteen Sixteen Locomotive Dictionary. (Train Shed Cyclopedia Ser., No. 18). (Illus.). 1974. pap. 4.95 (ISBN 0-912318-47-3). N K Gregg.

--Locomotives from the Nineteen Twenty-Seven Locomotive Cyclopedia, Pt. 1, Pt. 1. (Train Shed Cyclopedia Ser: No. 31). (Illus.). 80p. 1975. pap. 5.50 (ISBN 0-912318-62-7). N K Gregg.

--Locomotives, Tenders and Trucks from the 1927 Locomotive Cyclopedia, Pt. 2. (Train Shed Cyclopedia Ser: No. 32). (Illus.). 80p. 1975. pap. 5.50 (ISBN 0-912318-63-5). N K Gregg.

--Steam Locomotives & Tenders from the 1938 Locomotive Cyclopedia: Part 2. 10th ed. (Train Shed Cyclopedia Ser., No. 23). (Illus.). 1974. pap. 4.50 (ISBN 0-912318-53-8). N K Gregg.

--Steam Locomotives from the 1919 Locomotive Dictionary & Cyclopedia, No. 52. (Train Shed Ser.). (Illus.). 1976. pap. 4.50 (ISBN 0-912318-84-8). N K Gregg.

--Steam Locomotives from the 1919 Locomotive Dictionary & Cyclopedia: Part 2, No. 53. (Train Shed Ser.). (Illus.). 1977. pap. 4.50 (ISBN 0-912318-85-6). N K Gregg.

--Steam Locomotives from the 1938 Locomotive Cyclopedia: Part 1. 10th ed. (Train Shed Cyclopedia Ser., No. 22). (Illus.). 1974. pap. 4.50 (ISBN 0-912318-52-X). N K Gregg.

LOCOMOTIVES–HISTORY

Articulated Steam Locomotive of North America. 45.00 (ISBN 0-686-70715-X). Chatham Pub CA.

BALDWIN Narrow-Gauge Locomotives 1872-1876. (Illus.). 1973. 6.00 (ISBN 0-913556-35-1); pap. 4.00 (ISBN 0-913556-31-9). Spec Pr NJ.

Burtt, F. Locomotives of the London, Brighton & South Coast Railway, 1839-1903. LC 76-373261. (Illus.). 1975. 11.00x (ISBN 0-901759-87-2). Intl Pubns Serv.

Cotton Belt Locomotives. 20.00 (ISBN 0-686-64894-3). Chatham Pub CA.

Crump, Spencer. Rail Car, Locomotive & Trolley Builders: An All-Time Directory. 1980. write for info. (ISBN 0-87046-032-3). Trans-Anglo.

Duke, Donald. Southern Pacific Steam Locomotives. LC 62-6982. (Illus.). 88p. 13.95 (ISBN 0-87095-012-6). Golden West.

Durrant, A. E. The Book of the Garratt Locomotive. LC 80-70298. (Illus.). 176p. 1981. 30.00 (ISBN 0-7153-7641-1). David & Charles.

--Steam Locomotives of Eastern Europe. LC 66-69115. (Illus.). 1966. 11.95x (ISBN 0-678-05663-3). Kelley.

Evans, Martin. Evening Star. (Illus.). 224p. (Orig.). 1980. pap. 16.50x (ISBN 0-85242-634-8). Intl Pubns Serv.

Fowler, George L., ed. Locomotive Dictionary. (Illus.). 684p. 1972. Repr. of 1906 ed. lib. bdg. 24.95 buckram (ISBN 0-912318-20-1). N K Gregg.

Hall, V. F. Industrial Steam Locomotives. 96p. 1981. 25.00x (ISBN 0-903485-34-6, Pub. by Moorland). State Mutual Bk.

Heiron, George F. The Majesty of British Steam. (Illus.). 104p. 1975. 20.00x (ISBN 0-7110-0482-X). Intl Pubns Serv.

Hilton, George W. Monon Route. 2nd ed. LC 78-52512. (Illus.). 468p. 1978. Repr. of 1978 ed. 30.00 (ISBN 0-8310-7115-X). Howell-North.

Holden, B. & Leech, K. Portraits of Castles. 112p. 1981. 30.00x (ISBN 0-903485-89-3, Pub. by Moorland). State Mutual Bk.

Jackman, Michael. Thirty Years at Bricklayers Arms: Southern Steam from the Footplate. LC 75-31329. (Illus.). 160p. 1976. 4.95 (ISBN 0-7153-6928-8). David & Charles.

Koenig, Karl R. Virginia & Truckee Locomotives. LC 80-67819. (Illus.). 88p. 1980. pap. 14.00 (ISBN 0-89685-102-8). Chatham Pub CA.

Locomotives from the Baldwin Catalog 1913 & Locomotive Stoker Catalog 1919, No. 44. (Train Shed Ser.). (Illus.). 1976. pap. 4.50 (ISBN 0-912318-76-7). N K Gregg.

Locos of the Forties & Fifties New Formulas: Electrics & Turbines, Part 10. (Train Shed Ser.: No. 66). (Illus.). 1978. pap. 4.50 (ISBN 0-87962-068-4). N K Gregg.

Middlemass, Thomas. Mainly Scottish Steam. (Illus.). 1974. 4.95 (ISBN 0-7153-6328-X). David & Charles.

Mohawk That Refused to Abdicate. 25.00 (ISBN 0-685-83356-9). Chatham Pub CA.

Nabarro, Gerald. Steam Nostalgia: Locomotive & Railway Preservation in Great Britain. (Illus.). 286p. 1972. 22.00 (ISBN 0-7100-7391-7); pap. 7.50 (ISBN 0-7100-8386-6). Routledge & Kegan.

Nock, Oswald S. Caledonian Dunalastairs & Associated Classes. LC 68-23835. (Illus.). 1968. 11.95x (ISBN 0-678-05619-6). Kelley.

--LNER Steam. LC 68-26165. (Illus.). 1969. 13.95x (ISBN 0-678-05520-3). Kelley.

--LWNR Precursor Family. LC 66-7430. (Illus.). 1966. 10.95x (ISBN 0-678-05716-8). Kelley.

--Midland Compounds. LC 65-2124. (Illus.). 1964. 10.95x (ISBN 0-678-05717-6). Kelley.

Olmsted, Robert. The Diesel Years. LC 75-17721. (Illus.). 170p. 1975. 19.95 (ISBN 0-87095-054-1). Golden West.

Pacific Coast Shay. 14.95 (ISBN 0-685-83366-6). Chatham Pub CA.

Reed, Brian. One-Hundred Fifty Years of British Steam Locomotives. LC 75-10514. (Illus.). 128p. 1975. 19.95 (ISBN 0-7153-7051-0). David & Charles.

Rogers, H. C. G. J. Churchward: A Locomotive Biography. 1974. 17.95 (ISBN 0-04-385061-8). Allen Unwin.

Stagner, Lloyd E. Steam Locomotives of the Frisco Line. (Illus.). 160p. 1976. 17.95 (ISBN 0-87108-097-4). Pruett.

Steam Locomotives of the Frisco Line. 17.95 (ISBN 0-685-83397-6). Chatham Pub CA.

Those Daylight 4-8-4's. 18.50 (ISBN 0-685-83407-7). Chatham Pub CA.

Treacy, Eric. Spell of Steam. (Illus.). 208p. 1975. 12.50x (ISBN 0-7110-0457-9). Intl Pubns Serv.

Tuplin, W. A. Great Central Steam. 1967. 6.95 (ISBN 0-04-385039-1). Allen Unwin.

--The Steam Locomotive. 1980. text ed. 20.75 (ISBN 0-239-00198-2). Humanities.

Tuplin, William A. British Steam Since Nineteen Hundred. LC 69-12249. (Illus.). 1968. 11.95x (ISBN 0-678-05637-4). Kelley.

Turbines Westward. 16.95 (ISBN 0-685-83410-7). Chatham Pub CA.

Webb, Brian. Deltic Locomotives of British Rail. LC 81-67013. (Illus.). 96p. 1982. 17.95 (ISBN 0-7153-8110-5). David & Charles.

--English Electric Main Line Diesels of British Rail. (Locomotive Studies Ser.). (Illus.). 96p. 1976. 6.95 (ISBN 0-7153-7158-4). David & Charles.

Westwood, J. N. Locomotive Designers in the Age of Steam. LC 77-90502. 285p. 1978. 18.00 (ISBN 0-8386-2220-8). Fairleigh Dickinson.

White, John H., Jr. A History of the American Locomotive, Its Development: 1830-1880. 17.50 (ISBN 0-8446-5828-6). Peter Smith.

--A History of the American Locomotive: Its Development, 1830-1880. (Illus.). 1980. pap. 10.00 (ISBN 0-486-23818-0). Dover.

White, John H., Jr., ed. Early American Locomotives. (Illus.). 6.50 (ISBN 0-8446-4838-8). Peter Smith.

Winkworth, D. W. Bulleid's Pacifics. 1974. 17.95 (ISBN 0-04-625005-0). Allen Unwin.

Wright, Roy V., ed. Box Stock & Refrigerator Cars from the 1931 Car Builders' Cyclopedia of American Practice. 13th ed. (Train Shed Cyclopedia Ser, No. 3). (Illus.). 1972. pap. 4.50 (ISBN 0-912318-27-9). N K Gregg.

--Gondolas & Hoppers from the Nineteen Forty Car Builders' Cyclopedia of American Practice. 15th ed. (Train Shed Cyclopedia Ser, No. 5). (Illus.). 1973. pap. 4.50 (ISBN 0-912318-29-5). N K Gregg.

--Locos of the Forties & Fifties New Formula from He Nineteen Forty-One Locomotive Cyclopedia of American Practice: Steam Part 3, No. 49. (Train Shed Ser.). (Illus.). 1976. pap. 4.50 (ISBN 0-912318-81-3). N K Gregg.

--Locos of the Forties & Fifties New Formula from He Nineteen Forty-One Locomotive Cyclopedia of American Practice: Steam Part 3, No. 49. (Train Shed Ser.). (Illus.). 1976. pap. 4.50 (ISBN 0-912318-81-3). N K Gregg.

--Locos of the Forties & Fifties New Formula from the Nineteen Forty-One Locomotive Cyclopedia of American Practice: Steam Part 1, No. 45. (Train Shed Ser.). (Illus.). 1976. pap. 4.50 (ISBN 0-912318-77-5). N K Gregg.

--Locos of the Forties & Fifties New Formula from the Nineteen Forty-One Locomotive Cyclopedia of American Practice: Steam Part 1, No. 45. (Train Shed Ser.). (Illus.). 1976. pap. 4.50 (ISBN 0-912318-77-5). N K Gregg.
--Locos of the Forties & Fifties New Formula from the Nineteen Forty-One Locomotive Cyclopedia of American Practice: Steam Part 2, No. 47. (Train Shed Ser.). (Illus.). 1976. pap. 4.50 (ISBN 0-912318-79-1). N K Gregg.
--Locos of the Forties & Fifties New Formula from the Nineteen Forty-One Locomotive Cyclopedia of American Practice: Steam Part 2, No. 47. (Train Shed Ser.). (Illus.). 1976. pap. 4.50 (ISBN 0-912318-79-1). N K Gregg.
--Locos of the Forties & Fifties New Formula from the Nineteen Forty-One Locomotive Cyclopedia of American Practice: Steam Part 4, No. 50. (Train Shed Ser.). (Illus.). 1976. pap. 4.50 (ISBN 0-912318-82-1). N K Gregg.
--Locos of the Forties & Fifties New Formula from the Nineteen Forty-One Locomotive Cyclopedia of American Practice: Steam Part 4, No. 50. (Train Shed Ser.). (Illus.). 1976. pap. 4.50 (ISBN 0-912318-82-1). N K Gregg.
--Locos of the Forties & Fifties New Formula from the Nineteen Forty-One Locomotive Cyclopedia of Amerian Practice: Steam Part 5, No. 51. (Train Shed Ser.). (Illus.). 1976. pap. 4.50 (ISBN 0-912318-83-X). N K Gregg.
--Locos of the Forties & Fifties New Formula from the Nineteen Forty-One Locomotive Cyclopedia of American Practice: Diesels Part 8, No. 60. (Train Shed Ser.). (Illus.). 1977. pap. 4.50 (ISBN 0-912318-95-3). N K Gregg.
--Locos of the Forties & Fifties Still More Diesels: Part 9. (Train Shed Ser.: No. 64). (Illus.). 1977. pap. 4.50 (ISBN 0-912318-99-6). N K Gregg.
--Locos of the 40's & 50's from the 1941 Locomotive Cyclopedia of American Practice: Diesels Part 7, No. 58. (Train Shed Ser.). (Illus.). 1977. pap. 4.50 (ISBN 0-912318-93-7). N K Gregg.
--Locos of the 40's & 50's New Formula from the 1941 Locomotive Cyclopedia of American Practice: Steam Part 6, No. 56. (Train Shed Ser.). (Illus.). 1977. pap. 4.50 (ISBN 0-685-78540-8). N K Gregg.
--Rail Motor Cars of the Nineteen Thirty's from the 1931 & 1937 Car Builders' Cyclopedias. (Train Shed Cyclopedia Ser, No. 10). (Illus.). 1973. pap. 4.50 (ISBN 0-912318-34-1). N K Gregg.
--Steam Locomotives from the 1927 Locomotive Cyclopedia. (Illus.). 1976. pap. 9.95 (ISBN 0-912318-86-4). N K Gregg.
--War & Standard Locomotives & Cars. (Train Shed Cyclopedia Ser, No. 9). (Illus.). 1973. pap. 4.50 (ISBN 0-912318-33-3). N K Gregg.

LOCOMOTIVES–MODELS

Ahern, John H. Miniature Locomotive Construction. (Illus.). 172p. 7.50x (ISBN 0-85344-075-1). Intl Pubns Serv.
Brown, R. A. The Brown Book. (Illus.). 11.95 (ISBN 0-686-75673-8). Darwin Pubns.
Evans, Martin. LBSC's Shop, Shed & Road. 2nd ed. 192p. (Orig.). 1979. pap. 12.50x (ISBN 0-85242-708-5). Intl Pubns Serv.
--Model Locomotive Construction. 2nd ed. (Illus.). 163p. 1978. pap. 9.50x (ISBN 0-85242-602-X). Intl Pubns Serv.
Evans, Martin, ed. Simple Model Locomotive Building: Introducing LBSC's Tich. rev. ed. 1976. 13.50x (ISBN 0-85242-457-4). Intl Pubns Serv.
Hambleton, F. C. Locomotives Worth Modelling. 1977. 10.50x (ISBN 0-85242-580-5). Intl Pubns Serv.
Maisie a Great Northern 4-4-2. (Illus.). 1977. pap. text ed. 8.50x (ISBN 0-85242-496-5). Intl Pubns Serv.
Pocket Diesel & Electric Guide. (Illus.). 1974. 5.00 (ISBN 0-913556-11-4). Spec Pr NJ.
Shay Instruction Sheets. 1975. Repr. 3.00 (ISBN 0-87012-238-X). McClain.

LOCOMOTIVES–PICTORIAL WORKS

Baxter, D. Victorian Locomotives. 129p. 1981. 25.00x (ISBN 0-903485-62-1, Pub. by Moorland England). State Mutual Bk.
Collias, Joe G. The Last of Steam. LC 60-14067. (Illus.). 1960. 20.00 (ISBN 0-8310-7018-8). Howell-North.
--The Search for Steam. LC 72-86957. (Illus.). 1972. 20.00 (ISBN 0-8310-7092-7). Howell-North.
Doherty, Douglas. The LMS Duchesses. (Illus.). 89p. 1973. 9.00x (ISBN 0-85242-325-X). Intl Pubns Serv.
Fitt, William C., ed. Union Pacific FEF-3 Class 4-8-4 Locomotive Drawings. LC 75-27822. (Illus.). 54p. 1975. pap. 15.50 (ISBN 0-914104-02-0). Wildwood Pubns MI.
Hill, Ronald C. Union Pacific Eight Thousand, Four Hundred Forty-Four. (Illus.). 1978. pap. 9.00 (ISBN 0-918654-28-9). CO RR Mus.
Last of Steam. 20.00 (ISBN 0-685-83344-5). Chatham Pub CA.
LeMassena, Robert A. Articulated Steam Locomotives of North America: A Catalogue of "Giant Steam". (Illus.). 416p. 1979. 45.00 (ISBN 0-913582-26-3). Sundance.
Maskelyne, John N. Locomotives I Have Known. Freezer, C. J., ed. 199p. 1980. Repr. of 1959 ed. 35.00x (ISBN 0-85242-636-4). Intl Pubns Serv.
Nock, O. S. Railways at the Zenith of Steam, 1920-1940. LC 71-115302. (Railways of the World in Color Ser.: Vol. 2). 1970. 8.95 (ISBN 0-02-589710-1). Macmillan.
Search for Steam. 20.00 (ISBN 0-685-83387-9). Chatham Pub CA.
White, John H., Jr. Early American Locomotives. LC 79-188951. (Illus.). 142p. (Orig.). 1972. pap. 5.00 (ISBN 0-486-22772-3). Dover.
Wright, Roy V., ed. Locomotive Photos: Part I. (Train Shed Ser.: No. 69). (Illus.). 1978. pap. 4.50 (ISBN 0-87962-071-4). N K Gregg.

LOCOMOTOR ATAXIA

see also Paraplegia

LOCUSTS

Application of Remote Sensing Techniques for Improving Desert Locust Survey & Control. (Illus.). 92p. 1977. pap. 10.50 (ISBN 92-5-100112-X, F 721, FAO). Unipub.
Barrass, Robert. The Locust. (Illus.). 73p. (gr. 10 up). 1975. 8.95x (ISBN 0-903330-11-3). Transatlantic.
Bronson, Wilfrid S. Grasshopper Book. LC 43-51236. (Illus.). (gr. 3-7). 1943. 4.95 (ISBN 0-15-232362-7, HJ). HarBraceJ.
Commission for Controlling the Desert Locust in the Eastern Region of Its Distribution Area in Southwest Asia, 12th Session. Report. 28p. 1978. pap. 7.50 (ISBN 0-685-20385-9, F1266, FAO). Unipub.
Dallinger, Jane. Grasshoppers. LC 80-27806. (Lerner Natural Science Bks.). (Illus.). (gr. 4-10). 1981. PLB 7.95 (ISBN 0-8225-1455-9). Lerner Pubns.
FAO Desert Locust Control Committee, Nineteenth Session,Rome,1975. Report. 32p. 1976. pap. 7.50 (ISBN 0-685-66347-7, F1127, FAO). Unipub.
Food & Agriculture Organization. Desert Locust Project: Final Report. (Orig.). 1968. pap. 16.50 (ISBN 0-685-09377-8, F114, FAO). Unipub.
Hogner, Dorothy C. Grasshoppers & Crickets. LC 60-9219. (Illus.). (gr. 2-5). 1960. 8.95 (ISBN 0-690-35035-X, TYC-J) (ISBN 0-690-35036-8). Har-Row.
Jones, Jack Colvard. The Anatomy of the Grasshopper: Romalea Microptera. (Illus.). 292p. 1981. pap. 27.50 spiral bdg. (ISBN 0-398-04126-1). C C Thomas.
Otte, Daniel. The North American Grasshoppers: Acrididae - Gomphocerinae & Acridinae, Vol. 1. (Illus.). 368p. 1981. text ed. 45.00 (ISBN 0-674-62660-5). Harvard U Pr.
Rainey, R. C. & Aspilden, C. Meteorology & the Migration of Desert Locusts. (Technical Note Ser.). 1963. pap. 25.00 (ISBN 0-685-22324-8, WMO). Unipub.
Report of the Conference of FAO: 19th Session. 1978. pap. 19.75 (ISBN 92-5-100547-8, F 1358, FAO). Unipub.
Report of the Seventh Session of the Commission for Controlling the Desert Locust in the Near East. 24p. 1977. pap. 7.50 (ISBN 92-5-100198-7, F1108, FAO). Unipub.
Report of the Twentieth Session of the FAO Desert Locust Control Committee. 41p. 1977. pap. 7.50 (ISBN 92-5-100191-X, F1128, FAO). Unipub.
Report of the Twenty-First Session of the FAO Desert Locust Control Committee. 41p. 1978. pap. 7.50 (ISBN 92-5-100492-7, F1344, FAO). Unipub.

LODAGAA (AFRICAN TRIBE)

see Dagari (African Tribe)

LODGE, HENRY CABOT, 1850-1924

Adams, Henry. The Life of George Cabot Lodge. LC 78-16619. 1978. Repr. of 1911 ed. 24.00x (ISBN 0-8201-1316-6). Schol Facsimiles.
Lodge, H. C. & Redmond, C. F., eds. Selections from the Correspondence of Theodore Roosevelt & Henry Cabot Lodge, 1884-1918, 2 Vols. LC 72-146156. (American Public Figures Ser). 1971. Repr. of 1925 ed. Set. lib. bdg. 95.00 (ISBN 0-306-70129-4). Da Capo.
Lodge, Henry C. Early Memories. facsimile ed. LC 75-1853. (Leisure Class in America Ser.). 1975. Repr. of 1913 ed. 22.00x (ISBN 0-405-06919-7). Arno.

LODGE, HENRY CABOT, 1902-

Miller, William J. Henry Cabot Lodge: A Biography. (Illus.). 1967. 8.50 (ISBN 0-685-11960-2). Heineman.
Widenor, William C. Henry Cabot Lodge & the Search for an American Foreign Policy. 1980. 19.95 (ISBN 0-520-03778-2). U of Cal Pr.

LODGE, THOMAS, 1558-1625

Ingleby, C. M. Was Thomas Lodge an Actor? An Exposition Touching the Social Status of the Playwright in the Time of Queen Elizabeth. Repr. of 1868 ed. lib. bdg. 5.50 (ISBN 0-8414-5077-3). Folcroft.
Rae, Wesley D. Thomas Lodge. LC 67-25185. (English Authors Ser.). 1967. lib. bdg. 6.95x (ISBN 0-89197-964-6). Irvington.
Sisson, Charles J. Thomas Lodge & Other Elizabethans. 1966. lib. bdg. 32.00x (ISBN 0-374-97467-5). Octagon.
Tenney, Edward A. Thomas Lodge. LC 68-25680. 1969. Repr. of 1935 ed. 8.00 (ISBN 0-8462-1182-3). Russell.
Walker, Alice. The Life of Thomas Lodge. LC 74-16101. 1974. Repr. of 1933 ed. lib. bdg. 8.50 (ISBN 0-8414-9552-1). Folcroft.

LODGES

see Secret Societies

LOEFFLER, CHARLES MARTIN TORNOV, 1861-1935

Gilman, Lawrence. Nature in Music, & Other Studies in the Tone Poetry of Today. facs. ed. LC 67-22096. (Essay Index Reprint Ser). 1914. 13.00 (ISBN 0-8369-0475-3). Arno.

LOESS

Krinitzsky, E. L. & Turnbull, W. J. Loess Deposits of Mississippi. LC 67-27058. (Special Paper: No. 94). (Illus., Orig.). 1967. pap. 4.50x (ISBN 0-8137-2094-X). Geol Soc.
Smalley, I. J., ed. Loess: Lithology & Genesis. LC 75-30690. (Benchmark Papers in Geology: Vol. 26). 448p. 1975. 51.00 (ISBN 0-12-787472-0). Acad Pr.

LOFOTEN ISLANDS–DESCRIPTION AND TRAVEL

Gosse, Edmund. Northern Studies. LC 75-103225. 1970. Repr. of 1890 ed. 11.50 (ISBN 0-8046-0862-8). Kennikat.

LOFTS

Weiss, Jeffrey. Lofts. (Illus.). 1979. 14.95 (ISBN 0-393-01290-5); pap. 7.95 (ISBN 0-393-00945-9). Norton.

LOG BOOKS

Loroch, Kim J. Vessel Voyage Data Analysis: A Comparative Study. LC 65-20766. (Illus.). 1966. 10.00x (ISBN 0-87033-131-0). Cornell Maritime.
Mariners Museum Library - Newport News - Virginia. Catalog of Maps, Ships' Papers & Logbooks. 1964. lib. bdg. 55.00 (ISBN 0-8161-0686-X). G K Hall.
Pilot's Work Book & Pilot's Log Book. Set. pap. 7.50 (ISBN 0-685-32975-5). Seven Seas.
Sherman, Stuart C. The Voice of the Whaleman: With an Account of the Nicholson Whaling Collection. LC 65-18564. (Illus.). 1965. 12.50x (ISBN 0-685-88515-1, Pub. by Providence Public Library). U Pr of Va.
Wright, Derek. Yacht Log. 120p. 1979. 14.95 (ISBN 0-686-74151-X). Superior Pub.

LOG CABINS

Angier, Bradford & Angier, Vena. How to Build Your Home in the Woods. (Illus.). 9.95 (ISBN 0-911378-10-3). Sheridan.
Bealer, Alex W. & Ellis, John O. The Log Cabin. (Illus.). 1978. 17.95 (ISBN 0-517-52892-4, Dist. by Crown); pap. 8.95 (ISBN 0-517-53379-0). Barre.
--The Log Cabin. (Illus.). 1978. 17.95 (ISBN 0-517-52892-4, Dist. by Crown); pap. 8.95 (ISBN 0-517-53379-0). Barre.
Beard, Daniel C. Shelters, Shacks, & Shanties. (Illus.). 1976. pap. 3.95 (ISBN 0-684-14541-3, SL632, ScribT). Scribner.
Building the Hewn Log House. Date not set. 13.95 (ISBN 0-685-54509-1); pap. 8.95 (ISBN 0-685-54510-5). Mountain Pub Servs.
Duncan, S. Blackwell. How to Build Your Own Log Home & Cabin from Scratch. (Illus.). 1978. 14.95 (ISBN 0-8306-9874-4); pap. 8.95 (ISBN 0-8306-1081-2, 1081). TAB Bks.
Flaccus, Edward. North Country Cabin. LC 78-21638. (Illus.). 122p. 1979. pap. 5.95 (ISBN 0-87842-111-4). Mountain Pr.
Gadd, Laurence. From Tent to Cabin. 1981. pap. 10.95 (ISBN 0-672-52687-5). Bobbs.
Goodall, Harrison & Friedman, Renee. Log Structures, Preservation & Problem-Solving. 120p. 1980. pap. 10.95 (ISBN 0-910050-46-5). AASLH.
Hard, Roger E. Build Your Own Low-Cost Log Home. (Illus.). 12.95 (ISBN 0-88266-098-5); pap. 8.95 (ISBN 0-88266-097-7). Garden Way Pub.
Hunt, W. Ben. How to Build & Furnish a Log Cabin. 1974. pap. 3.95 (ISBN 0-02-001670-0, Collier). Macmillan.
Jordan, Terry G. Texas Log Buildings: A Folk Architecture. LC 77-24559. (Illus.). 240p. 1978. 19.95 (ISBN 0-292-78023-0). U of Tex Pr.
Kramer, Jack. The Log House Book. (Illus., Orig.). 1979. pap. 5.95 (ISBN 0-452-25278-4, Z5278, Plume). NAL.
Leitch, William. Hand Hewn. LC 75-45418. (Illus.). 192p. 1976. pap. 4.95 (ISBN 0-87701-079-X). Chronicle Bks.
Mackie, B. Allan. Building with Logs. 1981. pap. 11.95 (ISBN 0-684-16959-2, ScribT). Scribner.
McRaven, Charles. Building the Hewn Log House. LC 78-22453. (Illus.). 1979. 14.95 (ISBN 0-690-01797-9); pap. 8.95 (ISBN 0-690-01827-4, TYC-T). T Y Crowell.
Mann, Dale & Skinulis, Richard. The Complete Log House Book. (Illus., Orig.). 1979. pap. 9.95 (ISBN 0-07-082817-2). McGraw.
Pfarr, Paul & Pfarr, Karyn. Build Your Own Log Cabin. (Illus.). 1979. 12.50 (ISBN 0-87691-249-8); pap. 8.95 (ISBN 0-87691-305-2). Winchester Pr.
Ritchie, James D. Successful Log Homes. LC 78-15308. 1978. 13.95 (ISBN 0-912336-71-4); pap. 6.95 (ISBN 0-912336-72-2). Structures Pub.
Roebuck, Alan D. How to Put up Your Own Post-Frame House & Cabin. (Illus.). 1979. pap. 8.95 (ISBN 0-8306-1154-1, 1154). TAB Bks.
Rutstrum, Calvin. Wilderness Cabin. (Illus.). 1961. 5.95 (ISBN 0-02-606350-6); rev. ed. 1972 o.p. 5.95 (ISBN 0-686-66488-4). Macmillan.
--Wilderness Cabin. rev. ed. 192p. 1972. pap. 2.95 (ISBN 0-02-098500-2, Collier). Macmillan.
U.S. Dept. of Agriculture. Vacation Homes & Cabins: Sixteen Complete Plans. (USDA Material Ser.). (Illus.). 1978. pap. 3.00 (ISBN 0-486-23631-5). Dover.
Walton, Harry. How to Build Your Cabin or Modern Vacation Home. (A Popular Science Skill Bk.). 1964. 5.95 (ISBN 0-06-007200-8, HarpT); (HarpT). Har-Row.

LOG SCALING

see Forests and Forestry–Mensuration

LOGAN, BEN, 1920-

Logan, Ben. The Land Remembers: The Story of a Farm & Its People. LC 74-6565. 320p. 1975. 8.95 (ISBN 0-670-41761-0). Viking Pr.

LOGAN, JAMES, 1674-1751

Penn, William. Correspondence Between William Penn & James Logan & Others, 2 Vols. Logan, Deborah & Armstrong, Edward, eds. LC 72-173943. Repr. of 1870 ed. Set. 57.50 (ISBN 0-404-04985-0). AMS Pr.
Tolles, Frederick B. James Logan & the Culture of Provincial America. Handlin, Oscar, ed. LC 77-2783. (The Library of American Biography). 1978. Repr. of 1957 ed. lib. bdg. 20.50x (ISBN 0-313-20197-8, TOJL). Greenwood.

LOGARITHMS

see also Functions, Exponential; Mathematics–Tables, etc.; Slide-Rule

Allen, Edward S. Six-Place Tables. 7th ed. 1947. 9.95 (ISBN 0-07-057751-X, P&RB). McGraw.
Attwood, C., ed. Practical Tables, Vol. 1: Six-Figure Trigonometrical Functions of Angles in Degrees & Minutes. 5th ed. 1965. 8.50 (ISBN 0-08-009894-0); pap. 4.20 (ISBN 0-08-009893-2). Pergamon.
Ball, W. Rouse, et al, eds. String Figures & Other Monographs, 4 vols. in 1. Incl. String Figures. Ball, W. R; History of the Slide Rule. Cajori, F; Non Euclidean Geometry. Carslaw, Horatio S; Methods Geometrical Construction. Petersen, Julius. LC 59-11780. 12.95 (ISBN 0-8284-0130-6). Chelsea Pub.
Bauschinger, J. & Peters, J. Logarithmic Trigonometrical Tables to 8 Decimal Places or Numbers 1-200,000 & Trigon: Functions for Sexagesmil Second of the Quadrant, 2vols. 3rd ed. 1971. 45.00 (ISBN 0-934454-57-4). Lubrecht & Cramer.
Bruhn, Karl C. Seven Figure Logarithmic Tables. 1947. 6.00 (ISBN 0-685-19499-X). Powner.
Bruhns. New Manual of Logarithms. 634p. 1941. 14.50 (ISBN 0-442-01145-8, Pub. by Van Nos Reinhold). Krieger.
Davis, Harold T. & Nelson, William F. Elements of Statistics with Application to Economic Data. rev. & enl. 2nd ed. LC 78-163681. Repr. of 1937 ed. 28.50 (ISBN 0-404-01994-3). AMS Pr.
Fienberg, Stephen. The Analysis of Cross-Classified Categorical Data. 2nd ed. 1980. text ed. 14.00x (ISBN 0-262-06071-X). MIT Pr.
Glover, James W. & Carver, Henry C. Tables of Compound Interest Functions & Logarithms of Compound Interest Functions. 1921. 3.00x (ISBN 0-685-21808-2). Wahr.
Goodall, Harrison & Friedman, Renee. Log Structures. 120p. 1980. pap. 10.95 (ISBN 0-910050-46-5). Liberty Pub.
Kells, Lyman M., et al. Log & Trig Tables. 1955. pap. 2.95 (ISBN 0-07-033601-6, SP). McGraw.
Merrill, Arthur A. Log Scale Construction. 29p. pap. 4.00 (ISBN 0-911894-31-4). Analysis.
Napier, John. A Description of the Admirable Table of Logarithmes. Wright, tr. LC 79-25885. (English Experience Ser.: No. 211). 1969. Repr. of 1616 ed. 16.00 (ISBN 90-221-0211-4). Walter J Johnson.
Nielsen, Kaj L. Logarithmic & Trigonometric Tables to Five Places. rev. ed. (Orig.). 1971. pap. 2.95 (ISBN 0-06-460044-0, CO 44, COS). Har-Row.
Norwood, Richard. Trigonometrie, or the Doctrine of Triangles, 2 pts. LC 78-171779. (English Experience Ser.: No. 404). 362p. 1971. Repr. of 1631 ed. 53.00 (ISBN 90-221-0404-4). Walter J Johnson.

Peters, J., et al. Ten-Place Logarithm Tables, 3 vols. Hyman, Charles J., tr. Incl. German Text with English Translations. LC 57-6794. Set. 60.00 (ISBN 0-8044-4748-9); German Text Only. LC 57-6795. Set. 45.00 (ISBN 0-8044-4752-7). Ungar.
Smoley, C. K. Logarithmic-Trigonometric Tables. rev. ed. Smoley, E. R. & Smoley, N. G., eds. 1971. fabricoid o.p. 3.50 (ISBN 0-911390-05-7); pap. 3.00 (ISBN 0-911390-06-5). Smoley.
--Parallel Tables of Logarithms & Squares. rev. ed. Smoley, E. R. & Smoley, N. G., eds. 1974. fabricoid 14.00 (ISBN 0-911390-02-2). Smoley.
--Segmental Functions, Text & Tables. rev. ed. Smoley, E. R. & Smoley, N. G., eds. 1974. fabricoid 14.00 (ISBN 0-911390-04-9). Smoley.
Spenceley, George W., et al. Smithsonian Logarithmic Tables: To Base e & Base Ten. LC 52-60707. 402p. 1960. 15.00x (ISBN 0-87474-004-5). Smithsonian.
Uhler, Horace S. Original Tables to One Hundred & Thirty-Seven Decimal Places of Natural Logarithms for Factors of the Form One Plus N Ten Minus P Enhanced by Auxiliary Tables of Logarithms of Small Integers. 1942. pap. 24.50x (ISBN 0-685-89769-9). Elliots Bks.
Vega, Georg, ed. Seven-Place Logarithmic Tables of Numbers & Trigonometrical Functions. 1971. Repr. 9.75 (ISBN 0-02-854120-0). Hafner.

LOGAU, FRIEDRICH VON, 1604-1655

Hempel, Paul. Kunst Friedrichs Von Logau. 1917. 21.50 (ISBN 0-384-22276-5); pap. 18.50 (ISBN 0-384-22275-7). Johnson Repr.

LOGBARA (AFRICAN TRIBE)

Middleton, John. Lugbara of Uganda. LC 65-11935. (Case Studies in Cultural Anthropology). (Orig.). 1965. pap. text ed. 5.95 (ISBN 0-03-049685-3, HoltC). HR&W.
--Lugbara Religion: Ritual & Authority Among an East African People. (International African Institute Ser). (Illus.). 1960. 34.95x (ISBN 0-19-724136-0). Oxford U Pr.
--Study of the Lugbara: Expectation & Paradox in Anthropological Research. LC 72-110498. (Studies in Anthropological Method). 1970. pap. text ed. 5.95 (ISBN 0-03-083985-8, HoltC). HR&W.

LOGGING

see Lumbering

LOGGING RAILROADS

BALDWIN Logging Locomotives 1913. (Illus.). 1973. pap. 4.00 (ISBN 0-913556-09-2). Spec Pr NJ.
Belcher, C. Francis. Logging Railroads of the White Mountains. (Illus.). 242p. (Orig.). 1981. pap. 8.95 (ISBN 0-910146-32-2). Appalach Mtn.
King, Frank. Minnesota Logging Railroads. (Illus.). 224p. 35.00 (ISBN 0-87095-076-2). Golden West.
Labbe, John T. & Goe, Vernon. Railroads in the Woods. LC 61-11373. (Illus.). 1961. 15.00 (ISBN 0-8310-7023-4). Howell-North.
Last of the Three-Foot Loggers. 14.95 (ISBN 0-686-70721-4). Chatham Pub CA.
Logging Railroads of the West. 9.95 (ISBN 0-685-83348-8). Chatham Pub CA.
Railroads in the Woods. 15.00 (ISBN 0-685-83374-7). Chatham Pub CA.
Spencer, James. The Northwest Loggers: Rayonier, Vol. 1. (Illus.). Date not set. price not set. Darwin Pubns.
Steam & Thunder in the Timber. Date not set. 15.00 (ISBN 0-686-75206-6). Chatham Pub CA.
They Felled the Redwoods. 15.00 (ISBN 0-686-70734-6). Chatham Pub CA.

LOGIC

see also A Priori; Abstraction; Definition (Logic); Dilemma; Evidence; Fallacies (Logic); Hypothesis; Identity; Induction (Logic); Intention (Logic); Judgment (Logic); Knowledge, Theory Of; Liar Paradox; Logic Machines; Logical Positivism; Modality (Logic); Nominalism; Nyaya; Predicate (Logic); Probabilities; Reasoning; Sufficient Reason; Syllogism; Thought and Thinking; Uniformity of Nature; Universals (Philosophy)

Abramov, L. M., et al. Fourteen Papers on Logic, Algebra, Complex Variables & Topology. LC 51-5559. (Translations Ser.: No. 2, Vol. 48). 1965. 26.80 (ISBN 0-8218-1748-5, TRANS 2-48). Am Math.
Adams, E. The Logic of Conditionals: An Application of Probability to Deductive Logic. LC 75-20306. (Synthese Library: No. 86). 140p. 1975. lib. bdg. 29.00 (ISBN 90-277-0631-X, Pub. by Reidel Holland). Kluwer Boston.
Albury, W. R. La Logique. Bonnot de Condillac, Etienne, tr. LC 77-86228. 1980. 20.00 (ISBN 0-913870-38-2). Abaris Bks.
Al-Hibri, Azizah. Deontic Logic: A Comprehensive Appraisal & a View Proposal. LC 78-66422. 1978. pap. text ed. 8.75 (ISBN 0-8191-0303-9). U Pr of Amer.
Andree, Josephine & Andree, Richard. Logic Unlocks. 1979. pap. 2.00 (ISBN 0-686-28235-3). Mu Alpha Theta.
Angeles, Peter A. Introduction to Sentential Logic: A Workbook Approach. new ed. (Philosophy Ser.). 128p. 1976. pap. text ed. 7.95x (ISBN 0-675-08665-5). Merrill.
Angell, Richard B. Reasoning & Logic. LC 63-16209. (Century Philosophy Ser.). (Illus.). 1964. 18.95x (ISBN 0-89197-375-3); pap. text ed. 7.95x (ISBN 0-89197-376-1). Irvington.
Aristotelian Society For The Systematic Study Of Philosophy. Logic & Reality: Proceedings, Supplmentary Vol. 20. Repr. of 1946 ed. 13.50 (ISBN 0-384-33395-8); pap. 7.25 (ISBN 0-384-33396-6). Johnson Repr.
--Psychical Research, Ethics & Logic: Proceedings, Supplementary Vol. 24. Repr. of 1950 ed. 13.50 (ISBN 0-685-92690-7); pap. 8.50 (ISBN 0-384-48086-1). Johnson Repr.
--Relativity, Logic & Mysticism: Proceedings, Supplementary Vol. 3. Repr. of 1923 ed. 12.00 (ISBN 0-384-50269-5); pap. 7.00 (ISBN 0-384-48086-1). Johnson Repr.
Arnauld, Antoine. Art of Thinking: Port-Royal Logic. Dickoff, James & James, Patricia, trs. LC 63-16933. (Orig.). 1964. pap. 10.95 (ISBN 0-672-60358-6, LLA144). Bobbs.
Bachhuber, Andrew H. Introduction to Logic. (Illus.). 1957. text ed. 12.50 (ISBN 0-13-487280-0). P-H.
Bacon, Francis. The Advancement of Learning. Kitchin, G. W., ed. (Rowman & Littlefield University Library). 246p. 1973. 11.50x (ISBN 0-87471-664-0); pap. 6.50x (ISBN 0-87471-665-9). Rowman.
Baldwin, James M. Thought & Things: Study of the Development & Meaning of Thought or Genetic Logic, 4 vols. in 2. LC 74-21397. (Classics in Child Development Ser). 1975. Repr. 78.00x (ISBN 0-405-06451-9). Arno.
Ballard, Keith E. Copi: Study Guide. 5th ed. 1972. pap. text ed. 7.50 (ISBN 0-02-305520-0, 30552). Macmillan.
Barker, Stephen F. Elements of Logic. 3rd ed. (Illus.). 1980. text ed. 14.95 (ISBN 0-07-003720-5); study guide 6.95 (ISBN 0-07-003722-1); instructor's manual 3.95 (ISBN 0-07-003721-3). McGraw.
Barnett, Peter. Tools of Thought: The Practical Foundations of Formal Reasoning. 256p. 1981. 16.95x (ISBN 0-87073-655-8); pap. text ed. 9.95x (ISBN 0-87073-656-6). Schenkman.
Barry, Vincent E. Practical Logic. 2nd ed. LC 80-21202. 1981. text ed. 15.95 (ISBN 0-686-72069-5, HoltC). HR&W.
Bastable, Patrick K. Logic: Depth Grammar of Rationality, a Textbook on the Science & History of Logic. 429p. 1975. text ed. 32.50x (ISBN 0-7171-0710-8). Humanities.
Baum, Robert. Logic. 2nd ed. 608p. 1980. text ed. 14.95 (ISBN 0-03-046396-3, HoltC); answer key avail. (ISBN 0-03-056878-1). HR&W.
Baynes, Thomas S. Essay on the New Analytic of Logical Forms. LC 73-168274. (Research & Source Works Ser.: No. 897). 170p. (Philosophy Monographs, No. 88). 1972. Repr. of 1850 ed. lib. bdg. 21.00 (ISBN 0-8337-0197-5). B Franklin.
Beardsley, Monroe. Practical Logic. 1950. text ed. 14.95 (ISBN 0-13-692111-6). P-H.
Beardsley, Monroe C. Thinking Straight: Principles of Reasoning for Readers & Writers. 4th ed. LC 74-16349. (Illus.). 1975. pap. text ed. 8.95 (ISBN 0-13-918227-6). P-H.
Bell, P. B. & Staines, P. J. Reasoning & Argument in Psychology. 228p. (Orig.). 1981. pap. 11.95 (ISBN 0-7100-0712-4). Routledge & Kegan.
Belnap, Nuel D. & Steel, Thomas B., Jr. The Logic of Questions & Answers. LC 75-27761. 1976. 17.50x (ISBN 0-300-01962-9). Yale U Pr.
Bennett, John B. Rational Thinking: A Study in Basic Logic. 1980. 18.95x (ISBN 0-88229-285-4); pap. 9.95x (ISBN 0-88229-739-2). Nelson-Hall.
Beonio-Brocchieri Fumagalli, M. T. The Logic of Abelard. Pleasance, Simon, tr. from It. (Synthese Library: No. 1). 101p. 1969. lib. bdg. 18.50 (ISBN 90-277-0068-0, Pub. by Reidel Holland). Kluwer Boston.
Berger, F. Studying Deductive Logic. 1977. pap. 8.95 (ISBN 0-13-858811-2). P-H.
Bergmann, Merrie, et al. The Logic Book. 608p. 1980. text ed. 17.95 (ISBN 0-394-32323-8). Knopf.
Beth, E. W. Aspects of Modern Logic. De Jongh, D. M. & De Jongh-Kearl, Susan, trs. from Dutch. LC 79-135102. (Synthese Library: No. 32). 176p. 1971. 26.00 (ISBN 90-277-0173-3, Pub. by Reidel Holland). Kluwer Boston.
Biswas, Nripendra U. Introduction to Logic & Switching Theory. new ed. 368p. 1975. 52.25x (ISBN 0-677-02860-1). Gordon.
Bittinger, M. S. Logic & Proof. 1970. pap. 5.95 (ISBN 0-201-00597-2). A-W.
Black, Max. Caveats & Critiques: Philosophical Essays in Language, Logic, & Art. LC 74-25365. (Illus.). 280p. 1975. 22.50x (ISBN 0-8014-0958-6). Cornell U Pr.
--Critical Thinking. 2nd ed. 1952. text ed. 16.95 (ISBN 0-13-194092-9). P-H.
Blumberg, Albert. Logic: A First Course. 1976. text ed. 18.95 (ISBN 0-394-31442-5); tchr's manual free (ISBN 0-394-31178-7). Knopf.
Bogoslovsky, B. B. The Technique of Controversy: Principles of Dynamic Logic. 1977. lib. bdg. 59.95 (ISBN 0-8490-1180-9). Gordon Pr.
Bohnert, Herbert G. Logic: Its Use & Basis. 1977. pap. text ed. 11.50 (ISBN 0-8191-0265-2). U Pr of Amer.
Bolzano, Bernhard. The Theory of Science, (Die Wissenschaftslehre Oder Versuch Einer Neuen Darstellung der Logik) George, Rolf, ed. & tr. LC 71-126765. 1972. 32.50x (ISBN 0-520-01787-0). U of Cal Pr.
Boolos, G. S. & Jeffrey, R. Computability & Logic. 2nd ed. LC 77-85710. (Illus.). 280p. 1981. 39.95 (ISBN 0-521-23479-4); pap. 13.95 (ISBN 0-521-29967-5). Cambridge U Pr.
Bosanquet, Bernard. Essentials of Logic: Being Ten Lectures on Judgment & Inference. LC 4-3994. 1968. Repr. of 1895 ed. 11.00 (ISBN 0-527-10006-4). Kraus Repr.
--Implication & Linear Inference. LC 20-20435. 1968. Repr. of 1920 ed. 12.00 (ISBN 0-527-10012-9). Kraus Repr.
--Knowledge & Reality. LC 14-924. 1968. Repr. of 1892 ed. 19.00 (ISBN 0-527-10018-8). Kraus Repr.
--Knowledge & Reality: A Criticism of Mr. F. H. Bradley's "Principles of Logic". 1976. Repr. of 1885 ed. 41.00 (ISBN 0-685-70634-6, Regency). Scholarly.
--Logic: Or, The Morphology of Knowledge, 2 vols. in 1. 2nd ed. LC 12-12390. 1968. Repr. of 1911 ed. 38.00 (ISBN 0-527-10024-2). Kraus Repr.
Bradley, Raymond & Swartz, Norman. Possible Worlds: An Introduction to Logic & Its Philosophy. LC 79-51037. (Illus.). 1979. lib. bdg. 25.00 (ISBN 0-915144-60-3); pap. text ed. 12.50 (ISBN 0-915144-59-X). Hackett Pub.
Broad, C. D. Induction Probability & Causation: Selected Papers. (Synthese Library). 296p. 1968. lib. bdg. 34.00 (ISBN 90-277-0012-5, Pub. by Reidel Holland). Kluwer Boston.
Buffalo Symposium on Modernist Interpretation of Ancient Logic, 21&22 April, 1972. Ancient Logic & Its Modern Interpretations: Proceedings. Corcoran, J., ed. LC 73-88589. (Synthese Historical Library: No. 9). 1974. lib. bdg. 42.00 (ISBN 90-277-0395-7, Pub. by Reidel Holland). Kluwer Boston.
Butrick, Richard. Deduction & Analysis. rev. ed. LC 80-6177. 121p. 1981. lib. bdg. 15.75 (ISBN 0-8191-1410-3); pap. text ed. 6.75 (ISBN 0-8191-1411-1). U Pr of Amer.
Cambridge University Library. Catalog of a Collection of Books on Logic Presented to the Library by John Venn. LC 74-165346. 1975. Repr. of 1889 ed. 29.50 (ISBN 0-8337-3624-8). B Franklin.
Cargile, J. Paradoxes. LC 78-67299. (Cambridge Studies in Philosophy). 1979. 32.95 (ISBN 0-521-22475-6). Cambridge U Pr.
Carmichael, Peter A. Reasoning: A Textbook of Elementary Logic. LC 77-80132. (Illus.). 1978. 12.50 (ISBN 0-8022-2206-4). Philos Lib.
Carney, James D. & Scheer, Richard K. Fundamentals of Logic. 3rd ed. (Illus.). 1980. text ed. 18.95 (ISBN 0-02-319480-4). Macmillan.
Carroll, Lewis. Symbolic Logic & the Game of Logic. pap. 3.95 (ISBN 0-486-20492-8). Dover.
Carter, Codell K. A Contemporary Introduction to Logic with Applications. 1977. text ed. 9.95 (ISBN 0-02-471500-X). Macmillan.
Casey, Helen & Clark, Mary T. Logic: A Practical Approach. (gr. 9-12). 1966. pap. text ed. 3.67 (ISBN 0-685-14109-8). Lawrence.
Ceitin, G. S., et al. Fourteen Papers on Logic, Geometry, Topology, & Algebra. LC 72-2350. (Translations Ser.: No. 2, Vol. 100). 1972. 42.00 (ISBN 0-8218-3050-3, TRANS 2-100). Am Math.
Chandra-Vidyabhusana, M. M. History of Indian Logic. 1970. 15.00 (ISBN 0-8426-0233-X). Verry.
Cheifetz & Avenoso. Logic & Set Theory. LC 76-126359. 1973. 6.95x (ISBN 0-916060-01-2). Math Alternatives.
Clarke, D. S., Jr. Deductive Logic: An Introduction to Evaluation Technique & Logical Theory. LC 73-10459. 255p. 1973. pap. 8.95x (ISBN 0-8093-0657-3). S Ill U Pr.
Coffey, Peter. Science of Logic, 2 vols. 9.00 ea. (ISBN 0-8446-1120-4). Peter Smith.
Cohen, M. R. Preface to Logic. 7.50 (ISBN 0-8446-1878-0). Peter Smith.
Cohen, Morris R. A Preface to Logic. LC 77-75235. 1977. Repr. of 1944 ed. pap. 3.50 (ISBN 0-486-23517-3). Dover.
Cohen, Morris R. & Nagel, Ernest. Introduction to Logic. LC 62-21468. 1962. pap. 2.95 (ISBN 0-15-645125-5, H008, Hbgr). HarBraceJ.
Copi, Irving M. Introduction to Logic. 6th ed. 1982. text ed. 18.95 (ISBN 0-686-75035-7). Macmillan.
--Introduction to Logic. 5th ed. (Illus.). 500p. 1978. text ed. 16.95 (ISBN 0-02-324880-7, 32486). Macmillan.
Copi, Irving M. & Gould, James A. Readings on Logic. 2nd ed. 1972. pap. 7.95 (ISBN 0-02-324910-2, 32491). Macmillan.
Davies, Martin. Meaning, Quantification, Necessity. (International Library of Philosophy). 260p. 1981. 32.00 (ISBN 0-7100-0759-0). Routledge & Kegan.
Davis, J. W., et al, eds. Philosophical Logic. (Synthese Library: No. 20). 277p. 1969. lib. bdg. 29.00 (ISBN 90-277-0075-3, Pub. by Reidel Holland). Kluwer Boston.
Degrood, David H. Dialectics & Revolution, Vol. 1. (Philosophical Currents Ser.: No. 21). 1978. pap. text ed. 23.00x (ISBN 90-6032-097-2). Humanities.
Dewey, John. Logic: Theory of Inquiry. 1981. Repr. of 1938 ed. 24.50x (ISBN 0-89197-831-3). Irvington.
The Dialectics Between Response to Exdogenous & Autochehonous Innovation in India in the Nineteenth & Twentieth Centuries with Special Reference to Modern Bengal. 38p. 1980. pap. 5.00 (ISBN 92-808-0109-0, TUNU 047, UNU). Unipub.
Ellis, Brian. Rational Belief Systems. (American Philosophical Quarterly Library of Philosophy). 118p. 1979. 16.00x (ISBN 0-8476-6108-3). Rowman.
Elster, Jon. Logic & Society: Contradictions & Possible Worlds. LC 77-9550. 1978. 42.00 (ISBN 0-471-99549-5, Pub. by Wiley-Interscience). Wiley.
Emmet, E. R. Handbook of Logic: The Use of Reason. 1966. 4.75 (ISBN 0-8022-0455-4). Philos Lib.
Emmet, Eric R. Handbook of Logic. (Quality Paperback: No. 178). 1974. pap. 4.95 (ISBN 0-8226-0178-8). Littlefield.
Englebretsen, G. Three Logicians. 120p. 1981. pap. text ed. 9.50x (ISBN 90-232-1815-9, Pub. by Van Gorcum Holland). Humanities.
Facione, Peter & Scherer, Donald. Logic & Logical Thinking. LC 77-24173. (Illus.). 1977. pap. text ed. 15.50 (ISBN 0-07-019884-5, C); instructor's manual 5.95x (ISBN 0-07-019885-3). McGraw.
--Logic & Logical Thinking. LC 77-24173. (Illus.). 1977. pap. text ed. 15.50 (ISBN 0-07-019884-5, C); instructor's manual 5.95x (ISBN 0-07-019885-3). McGraw.
Fairchild, David. Logic: A First Course. 201p. 1977. pap. text ed. 9.50 (ISBN 0-8191-0117-6). U Pr of Amer.
Faris, J. A. Quantification Theory. 2nd ed. (Monographs in Modern Logic). 1969. pap. 4.95 (ISBN 0-7100-3806-2). Routledge & Kegan.
Fay. Heidegger: The Critique of Logic. 1977. pap. 26.00 (ISBN 90-247-1931-3, Pub. by Martinus Nijhoff Netherlands). Kluwer Boston.
Finocchiaro, Maurice A. Galileo & the Art of Reasoning: Rhetorical Foundations of Logic & Scientific Method. (Philosophy of Science Studies: No. 61). 463p. 1980. lib. bdg. 42.00 (ISBN 90-277-1094-5, Pub. by Reidel Holland); pap. 21.00 (ISBN 90-277-1095-3). Kluwer Boston.
Fleischer, H. Kleines Textbuch der kommunistischen Ideologie: Auszuege aus dem Lehrbuch Osnovy Marksizma-Leninizma. (Sovietica Ser.: No. 11). 116p. (Ger.). 1963. 16.00 (ISBN 90-277-0052-4, Pub. by Reidel Holland). Kluwer Boston.
Flesch, Rudolf. The Art of Clear Thinking. 1951. 10.95 (ISBN 0-06-001440-7, HarpT). Har-Row.
Fogelin, Robert J. Understanding Arguments: An Introduction to Informal Logic. 1978. pap. text ed. 12.95 (ISBN 0-15-592860-0, HC); instructor's manual avail. (ISBN 0-15-592861-9). HarBraceJ.
Foss, Martin. Logic & Existence. LC 61-18687. 1962. 4.75 (ISBN 0-8022-0521-6). Philos Lib.
Frege, Gottlob. Posthumous Writings. Hermes, Hans, et al, eds. White, Roger & Long, Peter, trs. LC 79-10986. 1979. Repr. lib. bdg. 31.00x (ISBN 0-226-26199-9). U of Chicago Pr.
Frisch, Joseph C. Extension & Comprehension in Logic. LC 69-14355. 1969. 10.00 (ISBN 0-8022-2269-2). Philos Lib.
Frye, Albert M. & Levi, Albert W. Rational Belief: An Introduction to Logic. Repr. of 1941 ed. lib. bdg. 17.75x (ISBN 0-8371-2142-6, FRRB). Greenwood.
Gallin, D. Intensional & Higher-Order Model Logic. (North-Holland Mathematics Studies: Vol. 19). 1976. text ed. 24.50 (ISBN 0-444-11002-X, North-Holland). Elsevier.
Geach, P. T. Logic Matters. LC 72-138286. 1972. 21.50x (ISBN 0-520-01851-6, CAMPUS 222); pap. 6.95x (ISBN 0-520-03847-9). U of Cal Pr.

Geach, Peter T. Reference & Generality: An Examination of Some Medieval & Modern Theories. 3rd ed. LC 80-10977. (Contempory Philosophy Ser.). 256p. 1980. 19.50x (ISBN 0-8014-1315-X). Cornell U Pr.
Georgacarakos, George N. & Smith, Robin. Elementary Formal Logic. 1978. text ed. 14.95 (ISBN 0-07-023051-X, C); instructor's manual 3.95 (ISBN 0-07-023052-8). McGraw.
George, F. H. Precision, Language & Logic. 224p. 1977. text ed. 29.00 (ISBN 0-08-019650-0). Pergamon.
Giannoni, Carlo B. Conventionalism in Logic: A Study in the Linguistic Foundation of Logical Reasoning. (Janua Linguarum, Ser. Major: No. 46). 157p. 1971. text ed. 27.50x (ISBN 0-686-22486-8). Mouton.
Gochet, Paul. Outline of a Nominalist Theory of Propositions: An Essay in the Theory of Meaning & in the Philosophy of Logic. Jackson, Margareth & Dale, Anthony, trs. from Fr. (Synthese Library: No. 98). 204p. 1980. lib. bdg. 39.50 (ISBN 9-0277-1031-7, Pub. by Reidel Holland). Kluwer Boston.
Goddard, L. & Routley, R. The Logic of Significance & Context, Vol. 1. LC 73-8025. 641p. 1973. 49.95 (ISBN 0-470-30865-6). Halsted Pr.
Goekoop, V. The Logic of Invariable Concomitance in the Tattvacintamani: Gangesa's Amunitinirupana & Vyaptivada. 162p. 1967. lib. bdg. 24.00 (ISBN 90-277-0024-9, Pub. by Reidel Holland). Kluwer Boston.
Goldblatt, R. Topoi: The Categorial Analysis of Logic. (Studies in Logic & the Foundations of Mathematics Ser.: Vol. 98). 1980. 68.50 (ISBN 0-444-85207-7, North Holland). Elsevier.
Grayling, Tony. Introduction to Philosophical Logic. (Harvester Studies in Philosophy Ser.: No. 15). 1980. text ed. write for info. (ISBN 0-391-01791-8). Humanities.
Guttenplan, Sammuel D. & Tamny, Martin. Logic: A Comprehensive Introduction. rev. 2nd ed. LC 77-20418. 1978. 12.95x (ISBN 0-465-04161-2). Basic.
Haack, Susan. Deviant Logic. LC 74-76949. 208p. 1975. 23.95 (ISBN 0-521-20500-X). Cambridge U Pr.
--Philosophy of Logics. LC 77-17071. (Illus.). 1978. 42.00 (ISBN 0-521-21988-4); pap. 10.95x (ISBN 0-521-29329-4). Cambridge U Pr.
Hacking, Ian. Concise Introduction to Logic. (Orig.). 1971. pap. text ed. 10.95 (ISBN 0-394-31008-X). Random.
Hackstaff, I. H. Systems of Formal Logic. 354p. 1966. lib. bdg. 42.00 (ISBN 90-277-0077-X, Pub. by Reidel Holland). Kluwer Boston.
Handy, Rollo & Harwood, E. C. Useful Procedures of Inquiry. LC 72-93865. (Orig.). 1973. 10.00x (ISBN 0-913610-00-3). Behavioral Mass.
Hanna, Samuel C., et al. Sets & Logic. 1971. pap. 11.50x (ISBN 0-256-00230-4). Irwin.
Hasenjaeger, G. Introduction to the Basic Concepts & Problems of Modern Logic. Mays, E. G., tr. from Ger. LC 70-135108. 180p. 1972. 26.00 (ISBN 90-277-0206-3, Pub. by Reidel Holland). Kluwer Boston.
Hedge, Levi. Elements of Logick: Or a Summary of the Great Principles & Different Modes of Reasoning. LC 75-3173. Repr. of 1848 ed. 11.50 (ISBN 0-404-59177-9). AMS Pr.
Hegel, G. W. Hegel's Science of Logic: Muirhead Library of Philosophy. Miller, Arnold, tr. (Muirhead Library of Philosophy). 1976. Repr. of 1969 ed. text ed. 30.00x (ISBN 0-391-00675-4). Humanities.
Hegel, G. W. F. Hegel's Logic: Being Part One of the Encyclopedia of Philosophical Sciences (1830) 3rd ed. Wallace, William, tr. from German. 386p. 1975. 48.00x (ISBN 0-19-824502-5); pap. text ed. 4.95 (ISBN 0-19-824512-2). Oxford U Pr.
Hegel, Georg W. F. Encyclopedie Des Sciences Philosophiques, 1: La Science de la Logique. Bourgeois, Bernard, ed. 648p. (Fr.). 1970. pap. 45.00 (ISBN 0-686-57325-0, M-6312). French & Eur.
Hilpinen, R., ed. Deontic Logic: Introductory & Systematic Readings. LC 72-135103. (Synthese Library: No. 33). 182p. 1971. 24.00 (ISBN 90-277-0167-9, Pub. by Reidel Holland). Kluwer Boston.
Hinman, P. G. Recursion-Theoretic Hierarchies. (Perspectives in Mathematical Logic). 1977. 50.80 (ISBN 0-387-07904-1). Springer-Verlag.
Hintikka, J., et al, eds. Essays on Mathematical & Philosophical Logic. (Synthese Library: No. 122). 1978. lib. bdg. 50.00 (ISBN 90-277-0879-7, Pub. by Reidel Holland). Kluwer Boston.
Hintikka, Jaakko. Logic, Language-Games, & Information: Kantian Themes in the Philosophy of Logic. (Illus.). 305p. 1973. 45.00x (ISBN 0-19-824364-2). Oxford U Pr.
Hobbes, Thomas. Computatio Sive Logica - Logic: Part I of Elementorum Philosophiae Sectio Prima de Corpe. Martinich, Aloysius, tr. LC 77-86237. 449p. (Eng. & Latin.). 1981. 20.00 (ISBN 0-913870-36-6). Abaris Bks.
Hodges, Wilfred. Logic. 1980. 3.95 (ISBN 0-14-021985-4). Penguin.
Howell, Wilbur S. Eighteenth-Century British Logic & Rhetoric. LC 70-151531. 1971. 47.50 (ISBN 0-691-06203-X). Princeton U Pr.
--Logic & Rhetoric in England, 1500-1700. LC 56-6646. 1961. Repr. of 1956 ed. 19.00 (ISBN 0-8462-0204-2). Russell.
Hubig, Christoph. Dialektik und Wissenschaftslogik. (Grundlagen der Kommunikation). 1978. 24.00x (ISBN 3-11-007373-0). De Gruyter.
Hughes, G. E. & Cresswell, M. J. Einfuehrung in Die Modallogik. (Grundlagen der Kommunikation De Gruyter Studienbuch). 1978. 47.75x (ISBN 3-11-004609-1). De Gruyter.
Husserl. Formale und Transzedentale Logik. (Husserliana Ser: No. 17). 1974. lib. bdg. 58.00 (ISBN 90-247-5115-2, Pub. by Martinus Nijhoff Netherlands). Kluwer Boston.
--Logische Untersuchungen, Erster Band. (Husserliana Ser: No. 18). 1975. lib. bdg. 39.50 (ISBN 90-247-1722-1, Pub. by Martinus Nijhoff Netherlands). Kluwer Boston.
Husserl, Edmund. Logische Untersuchungen, 3 Vols. (Ger.). 1968. Repr. of 1913 ed. Set. 58.50 (ISBN 0-686-66271-7); pap. 30.00 (ISBN 3-4847-0118-8). Adler.
Ilyenkov, E. V. Dialectical Logic. 372p. 1977. 3.50 (ISBN 0-8285-0192-0, Pub. by Progress Pubs Russia). Imported Pubns.
Inhelder, Barbel & Piaget, Jean. Early Growth of Logic in the Child. (Illus.). 1969. pap. 4.45 (ISBN 0-393-00473-2, Norton Lib.). Norton.
--Growth of Logical Thinking: From Childhood to Adolescence. LC 58-6439. pap. text ed. 6.95x (ISBN 0-465-02772-5). Basic.
International Congress for Logic, Methodology, & Philosophy of Science, 4th, Bucharest, Sept. 1971. Logic, Language & Probability: Proceedings. Bogdan, R. J. & Niiniluoto, I., eds. LC 72-95892. (Synthese Library: No. 51). 316p. 1973. lib. bdg. 45.00 (ISBN 90-277-0312-4, Pub. by Reidel Holland). Kluwer Boston.
Iseminger, Gary. Introduction to Deductive Logic. LC 68-14984. (Century Philosophy Ser.). (Illus., Orig.). 1968. pap. text ed. 5.95x (ISBN 0-89197-239-0). Irvington.
Jackins, Harvey. La Homa Flanko De Homoj. (Esperanto.). 1974. pap. 3.00 (ISBN 0-911214-32-1). Rational Isl.
Jaques, Elliott, et al. Levels of Abstraction in Logic & Human Action. 1978. text ed. 15.00x (ISBN 0-435-82280-2). Heinemann Ed.
Jeffrey, Richard C. Formal Logic: Its Scope & Limits. 2nd ed. (Illus.). 256p. 1981. text ed. 17.95 (ISBN 0-07-032321-6, C); instr's manual 5.95 (ISBN 0-07-032322-4). McGraw.
--Formal Logic: Its Scope & Limits. 1967. text ed. 16.95 (ISBN 0-07-032316-X, C); instructor's manual 5.95 (ISBN 0-07-032317-8). McGraw.
Johnston, Frederick S., Jr. Logic of Relationship. LC 68-30747. 1969. 4.00 (ISBN 0-8022-2255-2). Philos Lib.
Jorgensen, Jorgen. Treatise of Formal Logic: Its Evolution & Main Branches, with Its Relations to Mathematics & Philosophy, 3 Vols. LC 62-10688. 1962. Repr. of 1931 ed. Set. 37.50 (ISBN 0-8462-0211-5). Russell.
Kahane, Howard. Logic & Philosophy. 3rd ed. 1978. text ed. 19.95x (ISBN 0-534-00555-1). Wadsworth Pub.
Kalish, Donald, et al. Logic: Techniques of Formal Reasoning. 2nd ed. 520p. 1980. text ed. 8.95 (ISBN 0-15-551181-5, HC). HarBraceJ.
Kaminsky, J. & Kaminsky, A. R. Logic: A Philosophical Introduction. 1974. 14.95 (ISBN 0-201-03576-6). A-W.
Kant, Immanuel. Kant's Introduction to Logic & His Essay on the Mistaken Subtilty of the Four Figures. Abbott, Thomas K., tr. LC 77-156197. 100p. 1963. Repr. lib. bdg. 15.00x (ISBN 0-8371-6148-7, KAIL). Greenwood.
Kantor, J. R. Psychology & Logic, 2 Vols. 1945-50. Set. 25.00 (ISBN 0-911188-36-3). Principia Pr.
Katz, Robert. A New Approach to Logic. 1978. pap. 15.00 (ISBN 0-685-03496-8). Mathco.
Kegley, Charles W. & Kegley, Jacquelyn A. Introduction to Logic. (Philosophy Ser.). 1978. text ed. 15.95 (ISBN 0-675-08358-3); media pkg. 75.00 (ISBN 0-675-08357-5); instructor's manual 3.95 (ISBN 0-686-67979-2); 5 sets 45.00 (ISBN 0-686-77338-1); 6 sets or more 35.00 (ISBN 0-686-77339-X). Merrill.
Kilgore, W. J. An Introductory Logic. 2nd ed. LC 78-26568. 1979. text ed. 18.95 (ISBN 0-03-022626-0, HoltC); inst. manual avail. (ISBN 0-03-045061-6). HR&W.
Kirwan, C. A. Logic & Argument. LC 78-53099. 299p. 1978. 29.50x (ISBN 0-8147-4568-7). NYU Pr.
Kneller, George F. Logic & Language of Education. 242p. 1966. text ed. 12.00 (ISBN 0-471-49518-2, Pub. by Wiley). Krieger.
Korner, Stephan, ed. Philosophy of Logic. LC 76-6020. 1976. 28.75x (ISBN 0-520-03235-7). U of Cal Pr.
Kowalski, R. Logic for Problem Solving. (Artificial Intelligence Ser.: Vol. 7). 295p. 1979. 18.95 (ISBN 0-444-00365-7, North Holland); pap. 9.95 (ISBN 0-444-00368-1). Elsevier.
Kreyche, Robert J. Logic for Undergraduates. 3rd ed. LC 70-97844. 1970. text ed. 17.95 (ISBN 0-03-078095-0, HoltC); wkbk. 5.95 (ISBN 0-03-079880-9). HR&W.
Kubinski, Taceusz. An Outline of the Logical Theory of Questions. 1980. 19.00 (ISBN 0-686-64311-9). Adler.
Lambert, K., ed. Philosophical Problems in Logic: Some Recent Developments. (Synthese Library: No. 29). 176p. 1970. lib. bdg. 25.00 (ISBN 90-277-0079-6, Pub. by Reidel Holland). Kluwer Boston.
Lamm, Zvi. Conflicting Theories of Instruction: Conceptual Dimensions. LC 76-9238. 1976. 18.40x (ISBN 0-8211-1112-4); text ed. 16.55x (ISBN 0-685-73826-4). McCutchan.
Langer, Jonas. The Origin of Logic: From Six to Twelve Months. LC 79-23266. (Developmental Psychology Ser.). 1980. 30.50 (ISBN 0-12-436150-1). Acad Pr.
Leblanc, Hugues & Wisdom, William. Deductive Logic. 2nd ed. 354p. 1976. text ed. 21.95 (ISBN 0-205-05496-X). Allyn.
Lemmon, E. J. Beginning Logic. LC 78-51926. 1979. 15.00 (ISBN 0-915144-66-2); pap. text ed. 7.95x (ISBN 0-915144-50-6). Hackett Pub.
Leonard, H. S. Principles of Reasoning: An Introduction to Logic, Methodology & the Theory of Signs. 5.75 (ISBN 0-8446-2452-7). Peter Smith.
Leplin, Jarrett. Propositional Logic. LC 79-63560. 1979. pap. text ed. 7.50 (ISBN 0-8191-0728-X). U Pr of Amer.
Lerman, M., et al, eds. Logic Year 1979-1980. (Lecture Notes in Mathematics Ser.: Vol. 859). 326p. 1981. pap. 18.00 (ISBN 0-387-10708-8). Springer-Verlag.
Lewis, David. Counterfactuals. LC 72-78430. 1973. 8.95x (ISBN 0-674-17540-9). Harvard U Pr.
Lewis, H. D., ed. Logic, Ontology & Action, Vol. 1. (Jadavpur Studies in Philosophy). 1980. text ed. write for info. (ISBN 0-391-01764-0). Humanities.
Leys, Wayne A. Ethics for Policy Decisions: The Art of Asking Deliberate Questions. LC 69-10118. (Illus.). 1968. Repr. of 1952 ed. lib. bdg. 18.75x (ISBN 0-8371-0146-8, LEPD). Greenwood.
Longley, Peter. Contemporary Logic. LC 80-1443. 178p. (Orig.). 1981. pap. text ed. 8.75 (ISBN 0-8191-1458-8). U Pr of Amer.
Lorenzen, P. Formal Logic. Crosson, Frederick J., tr. from Ger. (Synthese Library: Vol. 9). 123p. 1965. lib. bdg. 18.50 (ISBN 90-277-0080-X, Pub. by Reidel Holland). Kluwer Boston.
Lorenzen, Paul. Formale Logik. 4th ed. (Sammlung Goeschen, Vol. 1176-1176a). (Ger). 1970. 5.00x (ISBN 3-11-002772-0). De Gruyter.
Lotze, Hermann. Logic, 2 vols. Natanson, Maurice, ed. LC 78-66738. (Phenomenology Background, Foreground & Influences Ser.: Vol. 8). 1980. Set. lib. bdg. 77.00 (ISBN 0-8240-9562-6). Garland Pub.
Lutoslawski, Wincenty. The Origin & Growth of Plato's Logic: With an Account of Plato's Style & the Chronology of His Writings. (Classical Studies Ser.). Repr. of 1897 ed. lib. bdg. 30.00x (ISBN 0-697-00041-9). Irvington.
McArthur, Robert P. Tense Logic. 1976. lib. bdg. 21.00 (ISBN 90-277-0697-2, Pub. by Reidel Holland). Kluwer Boston.
McCurdy, Lyle B. & McHenry, Albert L. Digital Logic Design & Applications: An Experimental Approach. (Illus.). 144p. 1981. pap. text ed. 12.95 (ISBN 0-13-212381-9). P-H.
Machina, Kenton. Basic Applied Logic. 1981. text ed. 11.95x (ISBN 0-673-15359-2). Scott F.
McLaughlin, Joseph. Outline & Manual of Logic. 1932. 5.95 (ISBN 0-87462-401-0). Marquette.
McTaggart, John M. Commentary on Hegel's Logic. LC 64-10391. 1964. Repr. of 1910 ed. 18.00 (ISBN 0-8462-0425-8). Russell.
--Studies in the Hegelian Dialectic. 2nd ed. LC 64-10392. 1964. Repr. of 1922 ed. 20.00 (ISBN 0-8462-0420-7). Russell.
Makinson, D. C. Topics in Modern Logic. (University Paperback Ser.). 107p. 1973. pap. 4.95x (ISBN 0-416-78100-4). Methuen Inc.
Makrakis, Apostolos. Logic: An Orthodox Christian Approach. Orthodox Christian Educational Society, ed. Cummings, Denver, tr. from Hellenic. (The Logos & Holy Spirit in the Unity of Christian Thought Ser.: Vol. 3). 200p. 1977. pap. 3.50x (ISBN 0-938366-04-1). Orthodox Chr.
Mally, E. Logische Schriften: Grosses Logikfragment, Grundgesetze des Sollens. LC 73-135106. (Synthese Historical Library: No. 3). 347p. (Ger.). 1971. lib. bdg. 45.00 (ISBN 90-277-0174-1, Pub. by Reidel Holland). Kluwer Boston.
Manicas, Peter T. & Krugar, A. N. Logic: The Essentials. 1976. text ed. 16.50 (ISBN 0-07-039893-3, C); instructors' manual 3.95 (ISBN 0-07-039894-1). McGraw.
Mann, William E. The Language of Logic. LC 79-66151. 1979. pap. text ed. 9.50 (ISBN 0-8191-0795-6). U Pr of Amer.
Martin, R. M. Belief, Existence, & Meaning. LC 69-16344. 1969. 15.00x (ISBN 0-8147-0292-9). NYU Pr.
--Logic, Language & Metaphysics. LC 74-133025. 1971. 12.50x (ISBN 0-8147-5350-7). NYU Pr.
Martin, Richard. Primordiality, Science, & Value. LC 80-14724. 336p. 1980. lib. bdg. 34.00x (ISBN 0-87395-443-2); pap. text ed. 12.95x (ISBN 0-87395-444-0). State U NY Pr.
Meiland, Jack W. Talking About Particulars. (International Library of Philosophy & Scientific Method). 1970. text ed. 8.00x (ISBN 0-391-00056-X). Humanities.
Menne, A., ed. Logico-Philosophical Studies. Glover, Horace S., tr. 136p. 1962. lib. bdg. 21.00 (ISBN 90-277-0082-6, Pub. by Reidel Holland). Kluwer Boston.
Mill, J. S. John Stuart Mill's Philosophy of Scientific Method. (Library of Classics Ser.: No. 12). 1950. pap. text ed. 4.25 (ISBN 0-02-849250-1). Hafner.
Mill, John S. System of Logic: Ratiocinative & Inductive, 2 vols. Robson, J. M., ed. LC 73-78926. (Collected Works of John Stuart Mill Ser.). 1974. Set. 70.00x (ISBN 0-8020-1875-0). U of Toronto Pr.
Miller, Harlan. Arguments, Arrows, Trees & Truth: A First Book in Logic & Language. 2nd ed. 242p. 1980. pap. text ed. 8.65x (ISBN 0-89894-036-2). Advocate Pub Group.
Mohanty, J. N., ed. Readings on Edmund Hysserl's Logical Investigations. 1977. lib. bdg. 28.00 (ISBN 90-247-1928-3, Pub. by Martinus Nijhoff Netherlands). Kluwer Boston.
Moody, Ernest A. Logic of William of Ockham. LC 65-17914. 1965. Repr. of 1935 ed. 20.00 (ISBN 0-8462-0666-8). Russell.
--Truth & Consequence in Mediaeval Logic. LC 76-44307. (Studies in Logic & the Foundations of Mathematics). 1976. Repr. of 1953 ed. lib. bdg. 15.00 (ISBN 0-8371-9053-3, MOTC). Greenwood.
Moor, James & Nelson, Jack. A Manual for Bertie. 1979. pap. text ed. 4.95x (ISBN 0-933694-06-7). COMPress.
Morris, Charles R. Idealistic Logic. LC 76-102578. 1970. Repr. of 1933 ed. 14.00 (ISBN 0-8046-0738-9). Kennikat.
Munitz, Milton K. Existence & Logic. LC 74-10417. 220p. 1974. 18.50x (ISBN 0-8147-5365-5). NYU Pr.
Needham, Charles W. Cerebral Logic: Solving the Problem of Mind & Brain. (Illus.). 232p. 1978. 23.50 (ISBN 0-398-03754-X). C C Thomas.
Nicod, Jean. Geometry & Induction: Containing Geometry in the Sensible World & the Logical Problem of Induction. Bell, J. & Wood, M., trs. LC 70-107149. 1970. 16.00x (ISBN 0-520-01689-0). U of Cal Pr.
Norman, Edward & Earr, Murray. Logic, Proof, & Mathematical Structures. 1981. write for info. U Presses Fla.
Northrop, Filmer S. The Logic of the Sciences & the Humanities. LC 78-21524. 1979. Repr. of 1959 ed. lib. bdg. 26.00x (ISBN 0-313-21161-2, NOLS). Greenwood.
Novack, George. Introduction to the Logic of Marxism. rev. 5th ed. LC 76-87909. 1969. 12.00 (ISBN 0-87348-019-8); pap. 3.45 (ISBN 0-87348-018-X). Path Pr NY.
Nute, Donald. Topics in Conditional Logic. (Philosophical Studies Series in Philosophy: No. 20). 168p. 1980. lib. bdg. 31.50 (ISBN 90-277-1049-X, Pub. by Reidel Holland). Kluwer Boston.
Oesterle, John A. Logic: The Art of Defining & Reasoning. 2nd ed. 1963. pap. text ed. 11.95 (ISBN 0-13-539999-8). P-H.
Ong, Walter J. Ramus: Method, & the Decay of Dialogue. LC 73-19771. 408p. 1974. Repr. of 1958 ed. lib. bdg. 21.50x (ISBN 0-374-96148-4). Octagon.
Ortega Y Gasset, Jose. Idea of Principle in Leibnitz & the Evolution of Deductive Theory. LC 66-18068. 1971. 10.00x (ISBN 0-393-01086-4). Norton.

Otto, Herbert R. The Linguistic Basis of Logic Translation. LC 78-63261. 1978. pap. text ed. 9.25 (ISBN 0-8191-0617-8). U Pr of Amer.
Panfilov, V. Z. Grammar & Logic. LC 68-15535. (Janua Linguarum, Ser. Minor: No. 63). (Orig.). 1968. pap. text ed. 17.50x (ISBN 90-2790-591-6). Mouton.
Peirce, Charles S. Chance, Love & Logic. 317p. 1980. Repr. of 1923 ed. lib. bdg. 50.00 (ISBN 0-89984-386-7). Century Bookbindery.
Piaget, Jean. Logique et Connaissance Scientifique. (Methodique Ser.). 1360p. 55.95 (ISBN 0-686-56429-4). French & Eur.
Popper, Karl R. Logic of Scientific Discovery. rev. ed. pap. 6.95x (ISBN 0-06-130576-6, TB576, Torch). Har-Row.
Pospesel, Howard. Introduction to Logic: Propositional Logic. (Illus.). 224p. 1974. pap. text ed. 9.95 (ISBN 0-13-486217-1). P-H.
Pospesel, Howard & Marans, David. Arguments: Deductive Logic Exercises. 2nd ed. (Illus.). 1978. pap. text ed. 8.95 (ISBN 0-13-045880-5). P-H.
Prazak, Milos. Language & Logic. LC 76-141264. 154p. 1972. Repr. of 1963 ed. lib. bdg. 15.00x (ISBN 0-8371-5860-5, PRLL). Greenwood.
Prior, Arthur N. The Doctrine of Propositions & Terms. Geach, P. T. & Kenny, A. J., eds. LC 76-9375. 1976. 9.00x (ISBN 0-87023-214-2). U of Mass Pr.
--Formal Logic. 2nd ed. 1962. 35.00x (ISBN 0-19-824156-9). Oxford U Pr.
--Objects of Thought. Geach, P., ed. 1971. 29.95x (ISBN 0-19-824354-5). Oxford U Pr.
--Papers in Logic & Ethics. Geach, P. T. & Kenny, A. J., eds. LC 76-9376. 1976. 12.00x (ISBN 0-87023-213-4). U of Mass Pr.
Przelecki, Marian. The Logic of Empirical Theories. (Monographs in Modern Logic). 1969. 12.50 (ISBN 0-7100-6230-3). Routledge & Kegan.
Przexecki, Marian & Wojcicki, Ryszard, eds. Twenty-Five Years of Logical Methodology in Poland. LC 76-7064. (Synthese Library Set: No. 87). 1976. lib. bdg. 71.00 (ISBN 90-277-0601-8, Pub by Reidel Holland). Kluwer Boston.
Purtill, Richard L. Introduction to Logic: Argument, Refutation & Proof. 1979. text ed. 18.50 scp (ISBN 0-06-386900-4, HarpC); scp study guide 6.50 (ISBN 0-06-385439-2). Har-Row.
Quine, W. V. Elementary Logic. rev. ed. LC 80-81978. 144p. 1981. text ed. 7.95x (ISBN 0-674-24450-8); pap. text ed. 3.95x (ISBN 0-674-24451-6). Harvard U Pr.
--Philosophy of Logic. 1970. pap. 7.95x ref. ed. (ISBN 0-13-663625-X). P-H.
Reichenbach, Hans. Elements of Symbolic Logic. 444p. 1980. pap. 7.00 (ISBN 0-486-24004-5). Dover.
Rennie, M. K. Logic Theory & Practice. 1973. 19.95x (ISBN 0-7022-0840-X); pap. 9.95x (ISBN 0-7022-0853-1). U of Queensland Pr.
Rescher, N. Topics in Philosophical Logic. (Synthese Library: No. 17). 347p. 1968. lib. bdg. 42.00 (ISBN 90-277-0084-2, Pub. by Reidel Holland). Kluwer Boston.
Rescher, Nicholas. Introduction to Logic. 1964. text ed. 13.95 (ISBN 0-312-42875-8). St Martin.
--Many-Valued Logic. LC 69-11708. 1969. text ed. 17.50 (ISBN 0-07-051893-9, C). McGraw.
Resnik, Michael D. Elementary Logic. LC 69-13613. 1970. text ed. 18.00 (ISBN 0-07-051897-1, C). McGraw.
Rhodes, Charles M. Mastering the Decisive Power of Logical Thinking. (Illus.). 1980. deluxe ed. 39.75 (ISBN 0-89266-223-9). Am Classical Coll Pr.
Rodman, Alexius. An Introduction to Logic: Mastering the Powers of Logical Thinking. (Illus.). 1980. deluxe ed. 37.75 (ISBN 0-89266-228-X). Am Classical Coll Pr.
Rony, Peter R. Logic & Memory Experiments: Using TTL Integrated Circuits. Incl. Bk. 1. pap. 10.95 (ISBN 0-672-21542-X); Bk. 2. pap. 10.95 (ISBN 0-672-21543-8). LC 78-57209. 1978. Bks 1 & 2. pap. 19.95 (ISBN 0-672-21544-6). Sams.
Rosser, J. Barkley & Turquette, Atwell R. Many-Valued Logics. LC 77-405. (Studies in Logic & the Foundations of Mathematics). 1977. Repr. of 1952 ed. lib. bdg. 15.00x (ISBN 0-8371-9449-0, ROMV). Greenwood.
Royce, Josiah. Principles of Logic. (Orig.). pap. 0.95 (ISBN 0-685-19411-6, 114, WL). Citadel Pr.
Ruby, L. Logic & Critical Thinking. (Aspects of English). (gr. 10-12). 1970. pap. text ed. 3.40 (ISBN 0-03-072085-0, HoltC). HR&W.
Runes, Dagobert D., ed. Classics in Logic. LC 62-15033. 1962. 10.00 (ISBN 0-8022-1426-6). Philos Lib.
Runkle, Gerald. Good Thinking: An Introduction to Logic. 2nd ed. LC 80-29326. 1981. text ed. 12.95 (ISBN 0-03-058161-3, HoltC). HR&W.
Russell, Bertrand. Mysticism & Logic & Other Essays. 2nd ed. 168p. 1981. pap. 5.95x (ISBN 0-389-20135-9). B&N.
St. Aubyn, Giles. Art of Argument. LC 62-8865. (gr. 9 up). 1960. 8.95 (ISBN 0-87523-133-0). Emerson.
Salmon, Wesley C. Logic. 2nd ed. (Foundations of Philosophy Ser). (Illus.). 160p. 1973. pap. 7.95 ref. ed. (ISBN 0-13-540104-6). P-H.
Sartre, Jean-Paul. Critique of Dialectical Reason. (Illus.). 1976. 35.00 (ISBN 0-902308-01-7, Pub. by NLB). Schocken.
Scheler, Max. Logik I. (Elementa Schriften Zur Philosophie und Ihrer Problemgeschichte: No. 3). 295p. (Ger.). 1976. pap. text ed. 16.00x (ISBN 90-6203-229-X). Humanities.
Schiller, Ferdinand C. Formal Logic, a Scientific & Social Problem. LC 75-3345. Repr. of 1912 ed. 31.50 (ISBN 0-404-59344-5). AMS Pr.
Semenenko, M. I., et al. Twelve Papers in Logic & Algebra. Silver, Ben, ed. LC 79-9994. (American Mathematical Society Translations Ser. 2: Vol. 113). 1979. 29.60 (ISBN 0-8218-3063-5, TRANS 2-113). Am Math.
Sen, Pranab K. Logic, Induction & Ontology, Vol. 2. (Jadavpur Studies in Philosophy). 1980. text ed. write for info. (ISBN 0-391-01765-9). Humanities.
Simco, Nancy D. & James, Gene G. Elementary Logic. 1976. text ed. 17.95x (ISBN 0-8221-0156-4). Dickenson.
Simmons, E. D. Scientific Art of Logic. 1st ed. 1961. 4.80 (ISBN 0-02-829000-3). Glencoe.
Simonds, Roger T. Beginning Philosophical Logic. 1977. pap. text ed. 9.00 (ISBN 0-8191-0262-8). U Pr of Amer.
Smiley, T. J. & Shoesmith, D. J. Multiple-Conclusion Logic. LC 77-84003. (Illus.). 1978. 59.50 (ISBN 0-521-21765-2). Cambridge U Pr.
Smith, J. E., ed. Integrated Injection Logic. LC 80-18841. 1980. 34.95 (ISBN 0-87942-137-1). Inst Electrical.
Smullyan, Raymond. What Is the Name of This Book? The Riddle of Dracula & Other Logical Puzzles. LC 77-18692. 1978. 8.95 (ISBN 0-13-955088-7); pap. 4.95 (ISBN 0-13-955062-3). P-H.
Strawson, P. F. Introduction to Logical Theory. 1963. pap. 10.95 (ISBN 0-416-68220-0). Methuen Inc.
Strawson, P. F., ed. Philosophical Logic. (Oxford Readings in Philosophy Ser). (Orig.). 1967. pap. 4.95x (ISBN 0-19-500375-6). Oxford U Pr.
Sullivan, D. J. Fundamentals of Logic. 1963. text ed. 13.95 (ISBN 0-07-062338-4, C); tchr's. manual 2.95 (ISBN 0-07-062328-7). McGraw.
Suppes, Patrick. Introduction to Logic. (Illus.). 1957. text ed. 13.95x (ISBN 0-442-08072-7). Van Nos Reinhold.
Swain, M., ed. Induction, Acceptance, & Rational Belief. (Synthese Library: No. 26). 232p. 1970. lib. bdg. 26.00 (ISBN 90-277-0086-9, Pub. by Reidel Holland). Kluwer Boston.
Tammelo, I. Modern Logic in the Service of Law. 1978. pap. 16.70 (ISBN 0-387-81486-8). Springer-Verlag.
Tarski, Alfred. Logic, Semantics, Metamathematics. Corcoran, John, ed. Woodger, J. H., tr. from Polish. 1981. lib. bdg. 40.00 (ISBN 0-915144-75-1); pap. text ed. 19.50 (ISBN 0-915144-76-X). Hackett Pub.
Thomas, Norman L. Modern Logic: An Introduction. (Illus., Orig.). 1966. pap. 3.95 (ISBN 0-06-460103-X, CO 103, COS). Har-Row.
Toulmin, Stephen. Uses of Argument. 1958-1964. 32.95 (ISBN 0-521-06644-1); pap. 8.95x (ISBN 0-521-09230-2). Cambridge U Pr.
Toulmin, Stephen, et al. An Introduction to Reasoning. 1979. text ed. 16.95 (ISBN 0-02-421030-7). Macmillan.
Trusted, Jennifer. Logic of Scientific Inference: An Introduction. (Modern Introductions to Philosophy Ser.). 144p. 1980. text ed. 20.00x (ISBN 0-333-26669-2); pap. text ed. 10.00x (ISBN 0-333-26670-6). Humanities.
Tyrer, J. H. & Eadie, M. J. The Astute Physician: How to Think in Clinical Medicine. 1976. pap. text ed. 15.75 (ISBN 0-444-41425-8). Elsevier.
Udolf, Roy. Logic Design for Behavioral Scientists. LC 73-75622. 1973. 18.95x (ISBN 0-911012-54-0). Nelson-Hall.
Van Fraassen, B. C. Formal Semantics & Logic. 1971. text ed. 19.95x (ISBN 0-02-422690-4). Macmillan.
Veatch, Henry B. Two Logics: The Conflict Between Classical & Neo-Analytic Philosophy. LC 68-17734. 1969. 13.95x (ISBN 0-8101-0022-3). Northwestern U Pr.
Venn, John. Principles of Empirical or Inductive Logic. 2nd ed. LC 77-165344. 604p. 1973. Repr. of 1907 ed. 33.50 (ISBN 0-8337-3625-6). B Franklin.
--The Principles of Inductive Logic. 2nd ed. LC 72-119162. Orig. Title: The Principles of Empirical, or Inductive Logic. 624p. 1973. 18.50 (ISBN 0-8284-0265-5). Chelsea Pub.
Vidyabhusana, Satis Chandra. History of the Mediaeval School of Indian Logic. 2nd ed. LC 77-913386. 1977. 12.50x (ISBN 0-8002-0299-6). Intl Pubns Serv.
Volpe, Galvano D. Logic As a Positive Science. 288p. 1981. 19.95 (ISBN 0-8052-7096-5, Pub. by NLB England). Schocken.
Wald, Henri. Introduction to Dialectical Logic. (Philosophical Currents Ser: No. 14). 240p. 1975. pap. text ed. 29.00x (ISBN 90-6032-040-9). Humanities.
Wallace, William. The Logic of Hegel: Translated from the Encyclopedia of the Philosophical Sciences. with Prolegomena. 1979. Repr. of 1874 ed. lib. bdg. 100.00 (ISBN 0-8495-5718-6). Arden Lib.
--Prolegomena to the Study of Hegel's Philosophy, & Especially of His Logic. 2nd ed. LC 68-15169. 1968. Repr. of 1894 ed. 12.00 (ISBN 0-8462-1302-8). Russell.
Wells, D. G. Recreations in Logic. LC 79-51882. (Illus., Orig.). 1980. pap. 1.75 (ISBN 0-486-23895-4). Dover.
Whately, Richard. Elements of Logic. LC 75-17581. 360p. 1975. lib. bdg. 37.00x (ISBN 0-8201-1157-0). Schol Facsimiles.
Williams, Donald C. Ground of Induction. LC 63-15189. (Illus.). 1963. Repr. of 1947 ed. 6.00 (ISBN 0-8462-0368-5). Russell.
Wilson, John C. Statement & Inference: With Other Philosophical Papers. 1962. 98.00x (ISBN 0-19-824336-7). Oxford U Pr.
Windelband, Wilhelm. Theories in Logic. LC 61-15253. 1962. 2.75 (ISBN 0-8022-1899-7). Philos Lib.
Wittgenstein, Ludwig. Tractatus Logico-Philosophicus: German Text with English Translation. Ogden, C. K., tr. 208p. 1981. pap. price not set (ISBN 0-7100-0962-3). Routledge & Kegan.
Wright, Georg H. Von. Handlung,Norm und Intension: Untersuchungen Zur Deontischen Logik. Poser, Hans, ed. (De Gruyter Studienbuch). 1977. 17.75x (ISBN 3-11-004930-9). De Gruyter.
Yourgrau, Wolfgang & Breck, Allen D., eds. Physics, Logic, & History. LC 68-32135. 336p. 1970. 29.50 (ISBN 0-306-30360-4, Plenum Pr). Plenum Pub.
Ziehen, Theodor. Lehrbuch der Logik: Auf positivistischer Grundlage mit Beruecksichtigung der Geschichte der Logik. viii, 866p. 1974. Repr. of 1920 ed. 117.00x (ISBN 3-11-003305-4). De Gruyter.
Ziembinski, Zygmunt. Practical Logic: With the Appendix on Deontic Logic. Ter-Oganian, Leon, tr. LC 75-45254. 1976. lib. bdg. 43.00 (ISBN 90-277-0557-7, Pub. by Reidel Holland). Kluwer Boston.
Zierer, Ernesto. Formal Logic & Linguistics. LC 78-134547. (Janua Linguarum, Ser. Minor: No. 102). 92p. (Orig.). 1972. pap. text ed. 13.75x (ISBN 90-2792-009-5). Mouton.
Zinoviev, A. A., et al. Philosophical Problems of Many-Valued Logic. rev. ed. Kung, Guido & Comey, David, eds. Kung, Guido & Comey, David, trs. from Rus. (Synthese Library: No. 7). 155p. 1963. lib. bdg. 24.00 (ISBN 90-277-0091-5, Pub. by Reidel Holland). Kluwer Boston.

LOGIC–ADDRESSES, ESSAYS, LECTURES

Allwood, J., et al, eds. Logic in Linguistics. LC 76-46855. (Cambridge Textbooks in Linguistics Ser.). (Illus.). 1977. 29.95 (ISBN 0-521-21496-3); pap. 9.50 (ISBN 0-521-29174-7). Cambridge U Pr.
Beattie, James. Elements of Moral Science, 2 vols. Wellek, Rene, ed. LC 75-11195. (British Philosophers & Theologians of the 17th & 18th Centuries: Vol. 2). 1976. Repr. of 1793 ed. Set. lib. bdg. 84.00 (ISBN 0-8240-1751-X); lib. bdg. 42.00 ea. Garland Pub.
Berlin, Isaiah. Concepts & Categories. Hardy, Henry, ed. 1979. 12.95 (ISBN 0-670-23552-0). Viking Pr.
Black, Max. Margins of Precision: Essays in Logic & Language. LC 75-128369. 288p. 1970. 19.50x (ISBN 0-8014-0602-1). Cornell U Pr.
Blair, J. Antony & Johnson, Ralph H., eds. Informal Logic: The First International Symposium. LC 80-67674. 175p. (Orig.). 1980. pap. 9.95 (ISBN 0-918528-09-7). Edgepress.
Copi, Irving M. & Gould, James A., eds. Contemporary Philosophical Logic. LC 77-85986. 1978. pap. text ed. 8.95x (ISBN 0-312-16786-5). St Martin.
Dunn, J. Michael & Epstein, George, eds. Modern Uses of Multiple-Valued Logic. (Episteme: No. 2). 1977. lib. bdg. 55.00 (ISBN 90-277-0747-2, Pub. by Reidel Holland). Kluwer Boston.
Gandy, R. D. & Hyland, M. Logic Colloquium Seventy-Six. (Studies in Logic: Vol. 87). 1977. 44.00 (ISBN 0-7204-0691-9, North-Holland). Elsevier.
Hintikka, J. The Intention of Intentionality & Other New Models for Modalities. LC 75-31698. (Synthese Library: No. 90). 275p. 1975. lib. bdg. 44.75 (ISBN 90-277-0633-6); pap. 23.70 (ISBN 90-277-0634-4). Kluwer Boston.
Iseminger, Gary, ed. Logic & Philosophy: Selected Readings. (Century Philosophy Ser). 1980. text ed. 18.95x o. p. (ISBN 0-89197-829-1); pap. text ed. 8.95x (ISBN 0-89197-830-5). Irvington.
Kechris, A. S. & Moschovakis, Y. N., eds. Cabal Seminar Seventy Six-Seventy Seven: Proceedings, Caltech-UCLA Logic Seminar 1976-1977. (Lecture Notes in Mathematics: Vol. 689). 1979. pap. 16.50 (ISBN 0-387-09086-X). Springer-Verlag.
Leblanc, Hughes. Existence, Truth, & Probability. 1980. text ed. 45.00x (ISBN 0-87395-380-0); pap. text ed. 19.00x (ISBN 0-87395-450-5). State U NY Pr.
Logic Colloquium, Bristol, July 1973. Proceedings. Rose, H. E. & Shepherdson, J. C., eds. LC 74-79302. (Studies in Logic & the Foundations of Mathematics: Vol. 80). 513p. 1975. 63.50 (ISBN 0-444-10642-1, North-Holland). Elsevier.
Quine, Willard. From a Logical Point of View: Logico-Philosophical Essays. pap. 3.95x (ISBN 0-06-130566-9, TB566, Torch). Har-Row.
Quine, Willard V. From a Logical Point of View: Nine Logico-Philosophical Essays. 2nd rev. ed. LC 61-15277. 1961. 10.00x (ISBN 0-674-32350-5); pap. 3.95x (ISBN 0-674-32351-3). Harvard U Pr.
Ramsey, F. P., intro. by. Foundations: Essays in Philosophy, Logic, Mathematics & Economics. (International Library of Psychology, Philosophy & Scientific Method). 1978. text ed. 24.75x (ISBN 0-391-00814-5). Humanities.
Russell, Bertrand. Essays in Analysis. Lackey, Douglas, ed. LC 73-79346. 340p. 1973. 8.95 (ISBN 0-8076-0698-7); pap. 3.95 (ISBN 0-8076-0699-5). Braziller.
Schiller, Ferdinand C. Logic for Use: An Introduction to the Voluntarist Theory of Knowledge. LC 75-3346. (Philosophy of America Ser.). Repr. of 1929 ed. 37.50 (ISBN 0-404-59345-3). AMS Pr.
Seldin, J. P. & Hindley, R., eds. To H. B. Curry: Essays on Combinatory Logic, Lambda Calculus & Formalism. 1980. 64.00 (ISBN 0-12-349050-2). Acad Pr.
Von Wright, George H., ed. Logic & Philosophy. (International Institute of Philosophy Ser.). 96p. 1980. lib. bdg. 25.00 (ISBN 90-247-2271-3, Pub. by Martinus Nijhoff Netherlands). Kluwer Boston.
Waismann, Friedrich. How I See Philosophy. Harre, R., ed. LC 68-12306. 1968. 17.95 (ISBN 0-312-39515-9). St Martin.

LOGIC–DIAGRAMS

see Logic Diagrams

LOGIC–EARLY WORKS TO 1800

Aristotle. Posterior Analytics. Barnes, Jonathan, ed. (Clarendon Aristotle Ser). 1975. 19.95x (ISBN 0-19-872066-1); pap. 17.95x (ISBN 0-19-872067-X). Oxford U Pr.
Bacon, Francis. Two Books...of the Proficience & Advancement of Learning. LC 70-25525. (English Experience Ser.: No. 218). 236p. Repr. of 1605 ed. 39.00 (ISBN 90-221-0218-1). Walter J Johnson.
Blundeville, Thomas. The Art of Logike. Plainly Taught in the English Tongue. LC 71-26166. (English Experience Ser.: No. 102). 170p. 1969. Repr. of 1599 ed. 25.00 (ISBN 90-221-0102-9). Walter J Johnson.
Gyekye, Kwame, ed. & tr. Arabic Logic: Ibn Al-Tayyib on Porphyry's "Eisagoge". LC 76-4071. 1979. 30.00 (ISBN 0-87395-308-8); microfiche 30.00 (ISBN 0-87395-309-6). State U NY Pr.
La Ramee, Pierre de. The Logike of the Most Excellent Philosopher P. Ramus, Martyr. Makilmenaeus, Rolandus, tr. LC 77-26225. (English Experience Ser.: No. 107). 101p. 1969. Repr. of 1555 ed. 11.50 (ISBN 90-221-0107-X). Walter J Johnson.
Leibniz, Gottfried. Logical Papers: A Selection. Parkinson, G. H., tr. 1966. 27.00x (ISBN 0-19-824306-5). Oxford U Pr.
Mullally, Joseph, tr. Peter of Spain: Tractatus Syncategorematum. Bd. with Selected Anonymous Treatises. (Medieval Philosophical Texts in Translation: No. 13). pap. 5.95 (ISBN 0-87462-213-1). Marquette.
Paul Of Venice. Lociga Magna of Paul of Venice. (British Academy Ser: Fascicule 6). 1978. text ed. 37.50x (ISBN 0-19-725962-6). Oxford U Pr.
Simon, Yves R., et al, trs. Material Logic of John of St. Thomas, Basic Treatises. LC 54-11215. 1955. 20.00x (ISBN 0-226-75849-4). U of Chicago Pr.
Wade, Francis C. John of Saint Thomas: Outlines of Formal Logic. 2nd ed. (Medieval Philosophical Texts in Translation: No. 8). 1962. pap. 5.95 (ISBN 0-87462-208-5). Marquette.
Wilson, Thomas. The Rule of Reason. LC 75-25441. (English Experience Ser.: No. 261). 320p. 1970. Repr. of 1551 ed. 25.00 (ISBN 90-221-0261-0). Walter J Johnson.

LOGIC–HISTORY

Adamson, Robert. A Short History of Logic. Sorley, W. R., ed. (Reprints in Philosophy Ser.). Repr. of 1911 ed. lib. bdg. 24.50x (ISBN 0-697-00001-X). Irvington.

Ashworth, E. J. Language & Logic in the Post Medival Period. LC 74-76478. (Synthese Historical Library: No. 12). 350p. 1974. lib. bdg. 53.00 (ISBN 90-277-0464-3, Pub. by Junk Pubs Netherlands). Kluwer Boston.

Augustine. De Dialectica. Pinborg, Jan, ed. Jackson, B. Darell, tr. from Latin. LC 74-28325. (Synthese Historical Library: No. 16). 151p. 1975. lib. bdg. 34.00 (ISBN 90-277-0538-0, Pub. by Reidel Holland). Kluwer Boston.

Bochenski, Innocenty M. History of Formal Logic. 2nd ed. LC 72-113118. 1970. text ed. 16.95 (ISBN 0-8284-0238-8). Chelsea Pub.

Butts, Robert E. & Hintikka, Jaakko, eds. Historical & Philosophical Dimensions of Logic, Methodology & Philosophy of Science. (Western Ontario Ser: No. 12). 1977. lib. bdg. 56.00 (ISBN 90-277-0831-2, Pub. by Reidel Holland). Kluwer Boston.

Copi, Irving M. The Theory of Logical Types. (Monographs in Modern Logic). 1971. 11.50 (ISBN 0-7100-7026-8). Routledge & Kegan.

Dumitriu, Anton. History of Logic, 4 vols. 1977. Set. 79.50x (ISBN 0-85626-139-4, Pub. by Abacus Pr); 21.50x ea. Vol. 1 (ISBN 0-85626-140-8). Vol. 2 (ISBN 0-85626-141-6). Vol. 3 (ISBN 0-85626-142-4). Vol. 4 (ISBN 0-85626-143-2). Intl Schol Bk Serv.

Enriques, Federigo. Historic Development of Logic: The Principles & Structure of Science in the Conception of Mathematical Thinkers. Rosenthal, Jerome, tr. LC 68-10918. 1968. Repr. of 1929 ed. 9.50 (ISBN 0-8462-1120-3). Russell.

Geach, P. T. Logic Matters. LC 72-138286. 1972. 21.50x (ISBN 0-520-01851-6, CAMPUS 222); pap. 6.95x (ISBN 0-520-03847-9). U of Cal Pr.

Grattan-Guinness, I., ed. History & Philosophy of Logic. 252p. 1981. pap. 71.00x (ISBN 0-85626-189-0, Pub. by Abacus Pr England). Intl Schol Bk Serv.

Kapp, Ernst. Greek Foundations of Traditional Logic. LC 76-181936. Repr. of 1942 ed. 12.50 (ISBN 0-404-03637-6). AMS Pr.

Kneale, William & Kneale, Martha. Development of Logic. (Illus.). 1962. 49.50x (ISBN 0-19-824183-6). Oxford U Pr.

Spade, Paul V. Peter of Ailly: Concepts & Insolubles: An Annotated Translation. (Synthese Historical Library: No. 19). 193p. 1980. lib. bdg. 31.50 (ISBN 90-277-1079-1, Pub. by Reidel Holland). Kluwer Boston.

LOGIC–OUTLINES, SYLLABI, ETC.

McCall, Raymond J. Basic Logic: The Fundamental Principles of Formal Deductive Reasoning. 2nd ed. 1962. pap. 3.95 (ISBN 0-06-460052-1, CO 52, COS). Har-Row.

Moore, Wilbert E. Creative & Critical Thinking. LC 67-7864. 1967. text ed. 16.75 (ISBN 0-395-04939-3, 3-38340); instructor's manual. pap. 2.00 (ISBN 0-395-04940-7, 3-38342). HM.

Purtill, Richard L. Logical Thinking. (Illus.). 1972. pap. text ed. 9.50 scp (ISBN 0-06-045297-8, HarpC). Har-Row.

Sharvy, Robert. Logic: An Outline. (Quality Paperback: No. 80). (Orig.). 1977. pap. 2.50 (ISBN 0-8226-0080-3). Littlefield.

LOGIC–PROBLEMS, EXERCISES, ETC.

Berloquin, Pierre. One Hundred Games of Logic. LC 76-49947. (Illus.). 1977. 7.95 (ISBN 0-684-14860-9, ScribT). Scribner.

Moore, Wilbert E. Creative & Critical Thinking. LC 67-7864. 1967. text ed. 16.75 (ISBN 0-395-04939-3, 3-38340); instructor's manual. pap. 2.00 (ISBN 0-395-04940-7, 3-38342). HM.

Purtill, Richard L. Logical Thinking. (Illus.). 1972. pap. text ed. 9.50 scp (ISBN 0-06-045297-8, HarpC). Har-Row.

Segerberg, Krister. The Essence of Classical Propositional Operators: An Exercise in the Foundations of Logic. (Oxford Logic Guides Ser.). 150p. 1981. 29.95x (ISBN 0-19-853173-7). Oxford U Pr.

Summers, George J. Test Your Logic: Fifty Puzzles in Deductive Reasoning. LC 75-188244. 1972. lib. bdg. 9.50x (ISBN 0-88307-573-3). Gannon.

LOGIC, ANCIENT

Averroes. Averroes' Middle Commentary on Aristole's Categories. Kassem, Mahmoud M, et al, eds. (Corpus Commentariorum Averrois in Aristotelem Ser.: Vol. I). 180p. (Orig.). 1981. pap. 8.00 (ISBN 0-936770-04-X, Pub. by Am Res Ctr Egypt). Undena Pubns.

Averroes, Rushd Ibn. Averroes' Middle Commentary on Aristole's De Interpretations. Kassem, Mahmoud M., et al, eds. (Corpus Commentariorum Averroes in Aristotelem Ser.: Vol. 2). 150p. (Orig.). 1981. pap. 8.00 (ISBN 0-936770-05-8, Pub. by Am Res Ctr Egypt). Undena Pubns.

Hu Shih. Development of the Logical Method in Ancient China. 2nd ed. 1964. 10.00 (ISBN 0-8188-0046-1). Paragon.

Kleingunther, Adolf. Untersuchungen zur Geschichte Einer Fragestellung. facsimile ed. LC 75-13276. (History of Ideas in Ancient Greece Ser.). (Ger.). 1976. Repr. of 1933 ed. 9.00x (ISBN 0-405-07316-X). Arno.

Lear, Jonathan. Aristotle & Logical Theory. LC 79-20273. (Illus.). 1980. 17.50 (ISBN 0-521-23031-4). Cambridge U Pr.

Lloyd, Geoffrey E. Polarity & Analogy. 1966. 59.50 (ISBN 0-521-05578-4). Cambridge U Pr.

Prier, Raymond A. Archaic Logic: Symbol & Structure in Heraclitus Parmenides, & Empedocles. (De Proprietatibus Litterarum, Ser. Practica: No. 11). 1976. pap. text ed. 28.25x (ISBN 90-2793-155-0). Mouton.

LOGIC, BUDDHIST

see Buddhist Logic

LOGIC, DEDUCTIVE

see Logic

LOGIC, INDUCTIVE

see Induction (Logic)

LOGIC, MEDIEVAL

Boehner, P. Medieval Logic: An Outline of Its Development from 1250 to c. 1400. 1952p. 1952. 21.00x (ISBN 0-7190-0063-7, Pub. by Manchester U Pr England). State Mutual Bk.

De Rijk, Lambertus M. Logica Modernorum, Vol. 2. (Philos. Texts & Studies: Vol. 16). 1967. text ed. 116.50x (ISBN 90-232-0440-9). Humanities.

Durr, Karl. The Propositional Logic of Boethius. LC 80-18931. (Studies in Logic & the Foundations of Mathematics). 79p. 1980. Repr. of 1951 ed. lib. bdg. 14.75x (ISBN 0-313-21102-7, DUPL). Greenwood.

Henry, D. P. Medieval Logic & Metaphysics: A Modern Introduction. (Orig.). 1972. text ed. 7.50x (ISBN 0-09-110830-6, Hutchinson U Lib); pap. text ed. 6.75x (ISBN 0-09-110831-4, Hutchinson U Lib). Humanities.

Moody, Ernest. Studies in Medieval Philosophy, Science & Logic: Collected Papers, 1933-1969. LC 73-91661. 1975. 32.50x (ISBN 0-520-02668-3). U of Cal Pr.

Shirwood, William. William of Sherwood's Introduction to Logic. Kretzmann, Norman, tr. LC 75-3998. 187p. 1976. Repr. of 1966 ed. lib. bdg. 14.00x (ISBN 0-8371-7412-0, SHSI). Greenwood.

Wilson, Curtis. William Heytesbury: Medieval Logic & the Rise of Mathematical Physics. (Medieval Science Pubns., No. 3). 1956. 20.00x (ISBN 0-299-01350-2). U of Wis Pr.

LOGIC, SYMBOLIC AND MATHEMATICAL

see also Algebra, Abstract; Algebra, Boolean; Axiomatic Set Theory; Categories (Mathematics); Constructive Mathematics; Goedel's Theorem; Infinitary Languages; Logic Machines; Machine Theory; Metamathematics; Model Theory; Probabilities; Reasoning; Recursive Functions; Science–Methodology; Semantics (Philosophy); Set Theory; Switching Theory; Syllogism; Threshold Logic

Abramov, L. M., et al. Fifteen Papers on Topology & Logic. LC 51-5559. (Translations Ser.: No. 2, Vol. 39). 1964. 22.40 (ISBN 0-8218-1739-6, TRANS 2-39). Am Math.

--Fourteen Papers on Logic, Algebra, Complex Variables & Topology. LC 51-5559. (Translations Ser.: No. 2, Vol. 48). 1965. 26.80 (ISBN 0-8218-1748-5, TRANS 2-48). Am Math.

Adjan, S. I., ed. Mathematical Logic, the Theory of Algorithms & the Theory of Sets: Dedicated to Academician Petr Sergeevic Novikov. LC 77-3359. (Proceedings of the Steklov Institute of Mathematics: No. 133). 1977. 57.20 (ISBN 0-8218-3033-3, STEKLO 133). Am Math.

Aiserman, Mark A., et al. Logic, Automata & Algorithms. (Mathematics in Science & Engineering Ser). (Rus). 1971. 58.50 (ISBN 0-12-046350-4). Acad Pr.

Alchourron, C. E. & Bulygin, E. Normative Systems. LC 75-170895. (Library of Exact Philosophy: Vol. 5). (Illus.). 1971. 26.40 (ISBN 0-387-81019-6). Springer-Verlag.

Anderson, Alan R. & Belnap, Nuel D., Jr. Entailment: The Logic of Relevance & Necessity, Vol. 1. LC 72-14016. 567p. 1975. 35.00 (ISBN 0-691-07192-6). Princeton U Pr.

Anderson, Alan R., et al, eds. The Logical Enterprise. LC 74-20084. 288p. 1975. 20.00x (ISBN 0-300-01790-1). Yale U Pr.

Anscombe, G. E. Introduction to Wittgenstein's Tractatus. 3rd ed. 1967. pap. text ed. 4.00 (ISBN 0-09-051131-X, Hutchinson U Lib). Humanities.

Arruda, A. L., et al, eds. Mathematical Logic in South America. (Studis in Logic & the Foundations of Mathematics). 392p. 1979. 44.00 (ISBN 0-686-63095-5, North Holland). Elsevier.

Arson, I. S., et al. Eighteen Papers on Logic & Theory of Functions. LC 51-5559. (Translations, Ser.: No. 2, Vol. 83). 1969. 28.00 (ISBN 0-8218-1783-3, TRANS 2-83). Am Math.

Baranskii, V. A., et al. Sixteen Papers on Logic & Algebra. LC 51-5559. (Translations Ser.: No. 2, Vol. 94). 1970. 28.00 (ISBN 0-8218-1794-9, TRANS 2-94). Am Math.

Barnes, D. W. & Mack, J. M. An Algebraic Introduction to Mathematical Logic. LC 74-22241. (Graduate Texts in Mathematics Ser.: Vol. 22). (Illus.). 230p. 1975. 15.50 (ISBN 0-387-90109-4). Springer-Verlag.

Barwise, J., ed. Handbook of Mathematical Logic. (Studies in Logic: Vol. 90). 1977. 85.00 (ISBN 0-7204-2285-X, North-Holland). Elsevier.

Bell, J. & Machover, M. A Course in Mathematical Logic. 1977. text ed. 25.00 (ISBN 0-7204-2844-0, North-Holland). Elsevier.

Berman, S. D., et al. Nine Papers on Logic & Group Theory. LC 51-5559. (Translations Ser.: No. 2, Vol. 64). 1967. 28.80 (ISBN 0-8218-1764-7, TRANS 2-64). Am Math.

Beth, E. W. Formal Methods: An Introduction to Symbolic Logic & to the Study of Effective Operations in Arithmetic & Logic. (Synthese Library: No.4). 170p. 1962. lib. bdg. 26.00 (ISBN 90-277-0069-9, Pub. by Reidel Holland). Kluwer Boston.

--Formal Methods: An Introduction to Symbolic Logic. 170p. 1962. 29.25x (ISBN 0-677-00050-2). Gordon.

Beth, E. W. & Piaget, J. Mathematical Epistemology & Psychology. 1966. 56.75x (ISBN 0-677-01290-X). Gordon.

Biswas, Nripendra U. Introduction to Logic & Switching Theory. new ed. 368p. 1975. 52.25x (ISBN 0-677-02860-1). Gordon.

Black, Max. Nature of Mathematics. (Quality Paperback: No. 201). 219p. 1965. pap. 2.95 (ISBN 0-8226-0201-6). Littlefield.

Blanche, R. Axiomatics. Keene, G. B., tr. (Monographs in Modern Logic). 1967. pap. 5.00 (ISBN 0-7100-3802-X). Routledge & Kegan.

Bochenski, J. M. Precis of Mathematical Logic. (Illus.). 1962. 21.50x (ISBN 0-677-00070-7). Gordon.

--A Precis of Mathematical Logic. Bird, Otto, tr. from Fr & Ger. (Snthese Library: No.1). 100p. 1959. lib. bdg. 14.50 (ISBN 90-277-0073-7, Pub. by Reidel Holland). Kluwer Boston.

Boffa, M., et al, eds. Logic Colloquium Nineteen Seventy-Eight. (Studiesin Logic & the Foundations of Mathematics: Vol. 97). 550p. 1979. 58.75 (ISBN 0-444-85378-2, North Holland). Elsevier.

Boole, George. Investigation of the Laws of Thought. 9.50 (ISBN 0-8446-1699-0). Peter Smith.

--Laws of Thought. 1953. pap. 5.00 (ISBN 0-486-60028-9). Dover.

--Logical Works, 2 vols. Incl. Vol. 1. Studies in Logic & Probability. 500p. 22.50 (ISBN 0-87548-038-1); Vol. 2. Laws of Thought. xvi, 448p. 22.50 (ISBN 0-87548-039-X). 1952. Open Court.

Boyer, Robert S. & Moore, J. Strother, eds. A Computational Logic. LC 79-51693. (ACM Monograph Ser.). 1979. 29.50 (ISBN 0-12-122950-5). Acad Pr.

Brown, G. Spencer. Laws of Form. LC 72-80668. (Illus.). 176p. 1972. 9.00 (ISBN 0-517-52776-6). Crown.

Bukstein, Edward J. Practice Problems in Number Systems, Logic, & Boolean Algebra. 2nd ed. LC 77-72632. (Illus.). 1977. pap. 6.95 (ISBN 0-672-21451-2, 21451). Sams.

Bulloff, J. J., et al, eds. Foundations of Mathematics: Symposium Papers Commemorating the Sixtieth Birthday of Kurt Goedel. LC 68-28757. (Illus.). 1969. 27.10 (ISBN 0-387-04490-6). Springer-Verlag.

Butts, Robert E. & Hintikka, Jaakko, eds. Logic, Foundations of Mathematics & Computability Theory. (Western Ontario Ser: No. 9). 1977. lib. bdg. 53.00 (ISBN 90-277-0708-1, Pub. by Reidel Holland). Kluwer Boston.

Cambridge Summer School in Mathematical Logic, 1971. Proceedings. Mathias, A. R. & Rogers, H., eds. LC 73-12410. (Lecture Notes in Mathematics Ser: Vol. 337). ix, 660p. 1973. pap. 25.40 (ISBN 0-387-05569-X). Springer-Verlag.

Cardwell, Charles E. Argument & Inference: An Introduction to Symbolic Logic. (Philosophy Ser.). 1978. pap. text ed. 11.95x (ISBN 0-675-08368-0); instr. manual 3.95 (ISBN 0-686-67969-5). Merrill.

Carnap, Rudolf. Foundations of Logic & Mathematics. (Foundations of the Unity of Science Ser: Vol. 1, No. 3). 1937. pap. 3.00x (ISBN 0-226-57578-0, P402, Phoen). U of Chicago Pr.

--Introduction to Semantics & Formalization of Logic. LC 58-13846. 1959. 20.00x (ISBN 0-674-46200-9). Harvard U Pr.

--Introduction to Symbolic Logic & Its Applications. 1958. pap. 3.50 (ISBN 0-486-60453-5). Dover.

--Logical Syntax of Language. (International Library of Psychology & Philosophy & Scientific Method). 1964. text ed. 30.00x (ISBN 0-7100-3125-4). Humanities.

--Meaning & Necessity: A Study in Semantics & Modal Logic. 2nd ed. LC 56-9132. 1956. pap. 4.95 (ISBN 0-226-09346-8, P30, Phoen). U of Chicago Pr.

Carroll, Lewis. Lewis Carroll's Symbolic Logic: Part I & Part II. Bartley, W. W., ed. 1977. 14.95 (ISBN 0-517-52383-3); pap. 6.95 (ISBN 0-517-53363-4). Potter.

Castonguay, C. Meaning & Existence in Mathematics. LC 72-96052. (Library of Exact Philosophy: Vol. 9). 159p. 1973. 22.30 (ISBN 0-387-81110-9). Springer-Verlag.

Ceitin, G. S., et al. Five Papers on Logic & Foundations. new ed. LC 51-5559. (Translations Ser.: No. 2, Vol. 99). 280p. 1972. 28.00 (ISBN 0-8218-1799-X, TRANS 2-99). Am Math.

Chang, C. C. & Keisler, H. J. Model Theory. 2nd ed. (Studies in Logic & the Foundations of Mathematics Ser.: Vol. 73). 552p. 1977. 44.00 (ISBN 0-685-48940-X, North-Holland); pap. 25.00 (ISBN 0-7204-0692-7). Elsevier.

Chang, Chin-Liang & Lee, Richard C. Symbolic Logic & Mechanical Theorem Proving. (Computer Science & Applied Mathematics Ser). 1973. 39.50 (ISBN 0-12-170350-9). Acad Pr.

Church, Alonzo. Bibliography of Symbolic Logic. 12.00 (ISBN 0-685-64498-7, JSLBIBL). Am Math.

--Introduction to Mathematical Logic. (Mathematical Ser.: Vol. 17). 1956. 28.00 (ISBN 0-691-07984-6). Princeton U Pr.

--Introduction to Mathematical Logic, Pt. 1. 1944. pap. 17.00 (ISBN 0-527-02729-4). Kraus Repr.

Clifford, John E. Tense & Tense Logic. (Janua Linguarum, Ser. Minor: No. 215). 173p. (Orig.). 1975. pap. text ed. 28.75x (ISBN 90-2793-453-3). Mouton.

Cohen, Paul J. Set Theory & the Continuum Hypothesis. (Math Lecture Notes Ser.: No. 3). (Orig.). 1966. pap. 8.50 (ISBN 0-8053-2327-9, Adv Bk Prog). Benjamin-Cummings.

Colloquium - Manchester - Aug 1969. Summer School in Mathematical Logic: Proceedings. Gandy, R. O. & Yates, C. M., eds. LC 71-146188. (Studies in Logic & the Foundations of Mathematics: No. 61). 1971. text ed. 25.75x (ISBN 0-7204-2261-2). Humanities.

Conference in Mathematical Logic, London, 1970. Proceedings. Hodges, W., ed. (Lecture Notes in Mathematics: Vol. 255). 351p. 1972. pap. 10.20 (ISBN 0-387-05744-7). Springer-Verlag.

Cooper, William S. Foundations of Logico-Linguistics. (Synthese Language Library: No. 2). 1978. lib. bdg. 34.00 (ISBN 90-277-0864-9, Pub. by Reidel Holland); pap. text ed. 16.00 (ISBN 90-277-0876-2, Pub. by Reidel Holland). Kluwer Boston.

Copi, Irving M. Symbolic Logic. 5th ed. 1979. text ed. 19.95 (ISBN 0-02-324980-3). Macmillan.

Couturat, Louis. L' Algebre De la Logique. 116p. 1981. Repr. of 1905 ed. lib. bdg. 55.00 (ISBN 0-8287-1475-4). Clearwater Pub.

--La Logique de Leibniz d'apres des documents inedite. 622p. 1981. Repr. of 1901 ed. lib. bdg. 235.00 (ISBN 0-8287-1476-2). Clearwater Pub.

Craig, W. Logic in Algebraic Form: Three Languages & Theories. (Studies in Logic & the Foundations of Mathematics: Vol. 72). 190p. 1974. 24.50 (ISBN 0-444-10477-1, North-Holland). Elsevier.

Crossley, J. N., et al. What Is Mathematical Logic. (Opus 60 Ser.). 92p. 1972. pap. 3.95x (ISBN 0-19-888087-1). Oxford U Pr.

Curry, Haskell B. Foundations of Mathematical Logic. 10.00 (ISBN 0-8446-5568-6). Peter Smith.

--Foundations of Mathematical Logic. 2nd ed. 1977. pap. 6.00 (ISBN 0-486-63462-0). Dover.

--Theory of Formal Deducibility. (Orig.). 1957. pap. 2.25x (ISBN 0-268-00274-6). U of Notre Dame Pr.

Daegneauit, Aubert, ed. Studies in Algebraic Logic. LC 74-84580. (Studies in Mathematics: No. 9). 1975. 12.50 (ISBN 0-88385-109-1). Math Assn.

Dalen, D. van. Logic & Structure. (Universitext Ser.). 180p. 1980. pap. 12.80 (ISBN 3-540-09893-3). Springer-Verlag.

Defrancesco, Henry F. Quantitative Analysis Methods for Substantive Analysts. LC 80-11355. 448p. 1981. Repr. of 1975ed. lib. bdg. write for info. (ISBN 0-89874-139-4). Krieger.

DeLong, Howard. Profile of Mathematical Logic. (Intermediate Mathematics Geometry Topology Ser). 1970. text ed. 17.95 (ISBN 0-201-01499-8). A-W.

Detlovs, V. K., et al. Nine Papers on Logic & Quantum Electrodynamics. American Mathematical Society, tr. LC 51-5559. (Translations Ser.: No. 2, Vol. 23). 1963. 24.40 (ISBN 0-8218-1723-X, TRANS 2-23). Am Math.

Dinkines, Flora. Elementary Concepts of Modern Mathematics. Incl. Pt. 1. Elementary Theory of Sets. pap. text ed. 10.50 (ISBN 0-13-261875-3); Pt. 2. Introduction to Mathematical Logic. pap. text ed. 6.95 (ISBN 0-13-487470-6); Pt. 3. Abstract Mathematical Systems. pap. text ed. 4.50 (ISBN 0-13-000877-X). (Illus.). P-H.

Drake, F. R., et al, eds. Recursion Theory: Its Generalisations & Applications, Proceedings of Logic Colloquim '79, Leeds, Aug. 1979. (London Mathematical Society Lecture Notes Ser.: No. 45). 300p. 1980. pap. 24.50 (ISBN 0-521-23543-X). Cambridge U Pr.

Faddeev, D. K., et al. Five Papers on Logic, Algebra, & Number Theory. LC 51-5559. (Translations Ser.: No. 2, Vol. 3). 1956. 20.80 (ISBN 0-8218-1703-5, TRANS 2-3). Am Math.

Fairchild, David. Logic: A First Course. 201p. 1977. pap. text ed. 9.50 (ISBN 0-8191-0117-6). U Pr of Amer.

Fel'dman, N. I., et al. Twelve Papers on Logic & Algebra. LC 51-5559. (Translations Ser.: No. 2, Vol. 59). 1966. 31.20 (ISBN 0-8218-1759-0, TRANS 2-59). Am Math.

Fenstad, J. E. General Recursion Theory: An Axiomatic Approach. Gandy, R. O., et al, eds. LC 79-13099. (Perspectives in Mathematical Logic Ser.). 240p. 1980. 42.90 (ISBN 3-540-09349-4). Springer-Verlag.

Fitch, Frederick B. Symbolic Logic: An Introduction. 1952. 12.95 (ISBN 0-8260-3095-5). Wiley.

Fraisse, R. Course in Mathematical Logic, Vol. 1: Relation & Logical Formula. Louvish, D., tr. from Fr. LC 72-95893. (Synthese Library: No. 54). Orig. Title: Cours De Logique Mathematique, Tome 1. 210p. 1973. lib. bdg. 34.00 (ISBN 90-277-0268-3, Pub. by Reidel Holland); pap. 16.00 (ISBN 90-277-0403-1). Kluwer Boston.

--Course of Mathematical Logic: Model Theory, Vol. 2. Louvish, David, tr. from Fr. LC 72-95893. (Synthese Library: No. 69). Orig. Title: Cours De Logique Mathematique. 212p. 1974. lib. bdg. 34.00 (ISBN 90-277-0269-1); pap. text ed. 16.00 (ISBN 90-277-0510-0). Kluwer Boston.

Frege, Gottlob. Translations from the Philosophical Writings of Gottlob Frege. 3rd ed. Geach, Peter & Black, Max, eds. 228p. 1980. 25.00x (ISBN 0-8476-6286-1); pap. 10.95x (ISBN 0-8476-6287-X). Rowman.

Gandy, R. D. & Hyland, M. Logic Colloquium Seventy-Six. (Studies in Logic: Vol. 87). 1977. 44.00 (ISBN 0-7204-0691-9, North-Holland). Elsevier.

Gel'fand, M. S., et al. Twelve Papers on Logic & Differential Equations. LC 51-5559. (Translations Ser.: No. 2, Vol. 29). 1963. 26.00 (ISBN 0-8218-1729-9, TRANS 2-29). Am Math.

Gersting, Judith L. & Kuczkowski. Yes-No, Stop-Go: Some Patterns in Mathematic Logic. LC 76-46376. (Young Math Ser.). (Illus.). (gr. k-3). 1977. PLB 8.79 (ISBN 0-690-01130-X, TYC-J). Har-Row.

Godel, Kurt. Consistency of the Continuum Hypothesis. (Annals of Mathematics Studies, Vol. 3). (Orig.). 1940. pap. 10.50x (ISBN 0-691-07927-7). Princeton U Pr.

Goodstein, R. L. Development of Mathematical Logic. LC 74-167509. 1971. 13.70 (ISBN 0-387-91088-3). Springer-Verlag.

--Mathematical Logic. 2nd ed. 1965. text ed. 6.50x (ISBN 0-7185-1010-0, Leicester). Humanities.

Grandy, Richard E. Advanced Logic for Applications. (Pallas Paperbacks: No. 13). 1979. pap. 13.00 (ISBN 90-277-1034-1, Pub. by Reidel Holland). Kluwer Boston.

--Advanced Logic for Applications. (Synthese Library: No. 110). 1977. lib. bdg. 31.50 (ISBN 90-277-0781-2, Pub. by Reidel Holland). Kluwer Boston.

Greenstein, Carol. Dictionary of Logical Terms & Symbols. 1978. text ed. 13.95 (ISBN 0-442-22834-1). Van Nos Reinhold.

Griffin, Nicholas. Relative Identity. (Clarendon Library of Logic & Philosophy Ser.). 1977. 24.95x (ISBN 0-19-824409-6). Oxford U Pr.

Grzegorczyk, A. An Outline of Mathematical Logic: Fundamental Results & Notions Explained with All Details. LC 72-97956. (Synthese Library: No. 70). 1974. lib. bdg. 66.00 (ISBN 90-277-0359-0, Pub. by Reidel Holland); pap. text ed. 34.25 (ISBN 90-277-0447-3, Pub. by Reidel Holland). Kluwer Boston.

Gustason, W. Elementary Symbolic Logic. LC 73-237. 1973. text ed. 13.95 (ISBN 0-03-004616-5, HoltC). HR&W.

Hackstaff, L. H. Systems of Formal Logic. 1966. 48.50x (ISBN 0-677-01280-2). Gordon.

Hackworth, Robert D. & Howland, Joseph. Introductory College Mathematics: Sets & Logic. LC 75-23618. (Illus.). 77p. 1976. pap. text ed. 2.95 (ISBN 0-7216-4411-2). HR&W.

Hallerberg, Arthur E. Logic in Mathematics: An Elementary Approach. (Orig.). 1974. pap. 5.00 (ISBN 0-02-845671-8). Hafner.

Halmos, Paul R. Algebraic Logic. LC 61-17955. 1962. 9.95 (ISBN 0-8284-0154-3). Chelsea Pub.

Hamilton, A. G. Logic for Mathematicians. LC 77-84802. (Illus.). 1978. 57.50 (ISBN 0-521-21838-1); pap. 14.95x (ISBN 0-521-29291-3). Cambridge U Pr.

Hao, Wang. Popular Lectures on Mathematical Logic. 286p. 1981. text ed. 24.95 (ISBN 0-442-23109-1). Van Nos Reinhold.

Herbrand, J. Logical Writings. Goldfarb, Warren D., ed. LC 74-146963. 312p. 1971. lib. bdg. 39.50 (ISBN 90-277-0176-8, Pub. by Reidel Holland). Kluwer Boston.

Hermes, Hans. Introduction to Mathematical Logic. Schmidt, D., tr. LC 72-76760. 200p. 1973. pap. text ed. 16.50 (ISBN 0-387-05819-2). Springer-Verlag.

Heyting, A. Logic & Foundations of Mathematics. 1968. 39.00 (ISBN 0-677-61300-8). Gordon.

Hilbert, David & Ackermann, W. Principles of Mathematical Logic. LC 50-4784. 9.50 (ISBN 0-8284-0069-5). Chelsea Pub.

Hintikka, J., et al, eds. Essays on Mathematical & Philosophical Logic. (Synthese Library: No. 122). 1978. lib. bdg. 50.00 (ISBN 90-277-0879-7, Pub. by Reidel Holland). Kluwer Boston.

Hirst, K. E. & Rhodes, F. Conceptual Models in Mathematics. (Mathematical Studies). 1971. pap. text ed. 7.95x (ISBN 0-04-510035-7). Allen Unwin.

Howard, Delton T. Analytical Syllogistics: A Pragmatic Interpretation of the Aristotelian Logic. (Northwestern University. Humanities Ser.: No. 15). Repr. of 1946 ed. 17.50 (ISBN 0-404-50715-8). AMS Pr.

Hull, Clark L., et al. Mathematico-Deductive Theory of Rote Learning: A Study in Scientific Methodology. Repr. of 1940 ed. lib. bdg. 17.75x (ISBN 0-8371-3126-X, HURL). Greenwood.

Hunter, Geoffrey. Metalogic: An Introduction to the Metatheory of Standard First Order Logic. LC 71-131195. 1971. 20.00x (ISBN 0-520-01822-2); pap. 6.95x (ISBN 0-520-02356-0). U of Cal Pr.

Iglewicz, B. & Stoyle, J. Introduction to Mathematical Reasoning. 1973. pap. 8.95 (ISBN 0-02-359600-7). Macmillan.

International Congress of Logic, Methodology and Philosophy of Science - 1960. Logic, Methodology & Philosophy of Science: Proceedings. Nagel, Ernest, et al, eds. 1962. 25.00x (ISBN 0-8047-0096-6). Stanford U Pr.

Jevons, W. Stanley. Pure Logic & Other Minor Works. Adamson, R. & Jevons, H. A., eds. LC 71-160420. (Research & Source Works Ser.: No. 773). 1971. Repr. of 1890 ed. lib. bdg. 22.50 (ISBN 0-8337-1842-8). B Franklin.

Journal of Symbolic Logic Cumulative Indexes, Vol. 26. (Covers volumes 1-25). 1961. 25.00 (ISBN 0-686-73962-0). Am Math.

Journal of Symbolic Logic Cumulative Indexes, 27-45 vols, Vol. 45. Date not set. 25.00 (ISBN 0-686-73842-X). Am Math.

Kennedy, Hubert. Peano: Life & Works of Giuseppe Peano. (Studies in the History of Modern Science: No. 4). 227p. 1980. lib. bdg. 34.00 (ISBN 90-277-1067-8, Pub. by Reidel Holland); pap. 14.95 (ISBN 90-277-1068-6, Pub. by Reidel Holland). Kluwer Boston.

Kleene, Stephen. Mathematical Logic. LC 66-26747. 398p. 1967. 29.95 (ISBN 0-471-49033-4). Wiley.

Korfhage, R. R. Logic & Algorithms with Applications to the Computer & Information Sciences. LC 66-25225. 194p. 1966. 23.95x (ISBN 0-471-50365-7). Wiley.

Kueker, D. W., ed. Infinitary Logic: In Memoriam Carol Karp. (Lecture Notes in Mathematics: Vol. 492). vi, 206p. 1976. pap. 12.20 (ISBN 0-387-07419-8). Springer-Verlag.

Kuipers, Theo A. Studies in Inductive Probability & Rational Expectation. (Synthese Library: No. 123). 1978. lib. bdg. 26.00 (ISBN 90-277-0882-7, Pub. by Reidel Holland). Kluwer Boston.

Lakatos, E. Proofs & Refutations. Worrall, J., ed. LC 75-32478. 160p. 1976. 32.50 (ISBN 0-521-21078-X); pap. 8.95 (ISBN 0-521-29038-4). Cambridge U Pr.

Langdon, Glen G. Logic Design. 1974. 30.50 (ISBN 0-12-436550-7). Acad Pr.

Langer, Susanne K. Introduction to Symbolic Logic. 3rd ed. 1953. pap. text ed. 5.00 (ISBN 0-486-60164-1). Dover.

Latin American Symposium on Mathematical Logic, 3rd. Non-Classical Logics, Model Theory & Computability: Proceedings. Arruda, A., et al, eds. (Studies in Logic: Vol. 89). 1977. 34.25 (ISBN 0-7204-0752-4, North-Holland). Elsevier.

Leibniz, Gottfried. Logical Papers: A Selection. Parkinson, G. H., tr. 1966. 27.00x (ISBN 0-19-824306-5). Oxford U Pr.

Leisenring, A. C. Mathematical Logic & Hilbert's E-Symbol. 1969. 37.50x (ISBN 0-677-61790-9). Gordon.

Lemoine, Roy E. The Anagogic Theory of Wittgenstein's Tractatus. LC 74-80541. (Janua Linguarum Series Minor: No. 214). 215p. (Orig.). 1975. pap. text ed. 36.25x (ISBN 90-2793-393-6). Mouton.

Lieber, Hugh G. & Lieber, Lillian R. Education of T. C. Mits. (Illus.). 1944 7.95 (ISBN 0-393-06278-3); pap. 4.95 1978 (ISBN 0-393-00906-8). Norton.

Lightstone, A. H. Mathematical Logic: An Introduction to Model Theory. (Mathematical Concepts & Methods in Science & Engineering Ser.: Vol. 9). (Illus.). 352p. 1978. 22.50 (ISBN 0-306-30894-0, Plenum Pr). Plenum Pub.

Logic, Conference, Kiel, 1974. Proceedings. Muller, G. H., et al, eds. LC 75-40481. (Lecture Notes in Mathematics: Vol. 499). 1975. pap. 26.80 (ISBN 0-387-07534-8). Springer-Verlag.

Lynch, Edward P. Applied Symbolic Logic. LC 79-29718. 1980. 41.00 (ISBN 0-471-06256-1, Pub. by Wiley Interscience). Wiley.

McCall, Storrs, ed. Polish Logic 1920-1939. Grushman, B., et al, trs. 1967. 49.50x (ISBN 0-19-824304-9). Oxford U Pr.

MacIntyre, A. Logic Colloquium Seventy-Seven. (Studies in Logic & the Foundations of Mathematics: Vol. 96). 1978. 39.00 (ISBN 0-444-85178-X, North Holland). Elsevier.

McShane, Philip. Randomness, Statistics & Emergence. LC 78-122619. 1970. 9.00x (ISBN 0-268-00436-6). U of Notre Dame Pr.

Maley, Gerald A. & Earle, J. Logic Design of Transistor Digital Computers. (Illus.). 1963. 23.95 (ISBN 0-13-540054-6). P-H.

Malitz, J. Introduction to Mathematical Logic: Set Theory-Computable Functions-Model Theory. (Undergraduate Texts in Mathematics). (Illus.). 1979. 14.70 (ISBN 0-387-90346-1). Springer-Verlag.

Manaster, Alfred B. Completeness, Compactness & Undecidability: An Introduction to Mathematical Logic. (Illus.). 192p. 1975. ref. ed. 15.95x (ISBN 0-13-164624-9). P-H.

Manin, Y. I. A Course in Mathematical Logic. Koblitz, N., tr. from Russian. LC 77-1838. (Graduate Texts in Mathematics: Vol. 53). 1977. pap. text ed. 21.80 (ISBN 0-387-90243-0). Springer-Verlag.

Miller, Charles F., 3rd. On Group-Theoretic Decision Problems & Their Classification. (Annals of Mathematics Studies: No. 68). 1971. 11.50 (ISBN 0-691-08091-7). Princeton U Pr.

Monk, J. D. Mathematical Logic. LC 75-42416. (Graduate Texts in Mathematics: Vol. 37). 1976. 26.00 (ISBN 0-387-90170-1). Springer-Verlag.

Mostowski, A. Foundational Studies: Selected Works, Vols. 1 & 2. LC 77-18025. (Studies in Logic & the Foundations of Mathematics: Vol. 93). 1979. Set. 134.25 (ISBN 0-444-85104-6, North Holland). Elsevier.

Mounce, H. O. Wittgenstein's Tractatus: An Introduction. LC 81-40474. 144p. 1981. 19.00 (ISBN 0-226-54318-8). U of Chicago Pr.

--Wittgenstein's Tractatus: An Introduction. 1981. pap. 7.95 (ISBN 0-226-54319-6). U of Chicago Pr.

Muller, G. H. Sets & Classes on the Work by Paul Bernays. (Studies in Logic: Vol. 84). 1976. 58.75 (ISBN 0-444-10907-2, North-Holland). Elsevier.

Munroe, Marshall E. Introductory Real Analysis. 1965. 17.95 (ISBN 0-201-04905-8). A-W.

Novikov, P. S. Elements of Mathematical Logic. 1964. 12.75 (ISBN 0-201-05335-7, Adv Bk Prog). A-W.

Oglesby, Francis C. Examination of a Decision Procedure. LC 52-42839. (Memoirs: No. 44). 1971. pap. 8.80 (ISBN 0-8218-1244-0, MEMO-44). Am Math.

Polya, Gyorgy. Mathematics & Plausible Reasoning, 2 vols. Incl. Vol. 1. Induction & Analogy in Mathematics. 1954 (ISBN 0-691-08005-4); Vol. 2. Patterns of Plausible Inference. rev. ed. 1969 (ISBN 0-691-08006-2). 15.00 ea.; Set. 25.50 (ISBN 0-685-23091-0). Princeton U Pr.

Ponasse, Daniel. Mathematical Logic. LC 72-136738. (Notes on Mathematics & Its Applications Ser.). Orig. Title: Logique Mathematique. 144p. 1973. 24.75x (ISBN 0-677-30390-4). Gordon.

Pospesel, Howard. Introduction to Logic: Predicate Logic. (Illus.). 224p. 1976. text ed. 10.50 (ISBN 0-13-486225-2). P-H.

Post, Emil L. Two-Valued Iterative Systems of Mathematical Logic. 1941. pap. 6.00 (ISBN 0-527-02721-9). Kraus Repr.

Prior, Arthur. Past, Present & Future. 1967. 36.00x (ISBN 0-19-824311-1). Oxford U Pr.

Quine, Willard V. Algebraic Logic & Predicate Functors. LC 71-157092. 1971. pap. text ed. 1.25x (ISBN 0-672-61267-4). Irvington.

--Mathematical Logic. rev ed. LC 51-7541. 1951. 16.50x (ISBN 0-674-55450-7); pap. 8.95x (ISBN 0-674-55451-5). Harvard U Pr.

--Set Theory & Its Logic. rev. ed. LC 68-14271. 1969. 5.95 (ISBN 0-674-80207-1, Belknap Pr). Harvard U Pr.

--Word & Object. 1960. pap. 8.95 (ISBN 0-262-67001-1). MIT Pr.

Rao, A. Pampapathy. Classical Theory of First Order Logic. (Indian Institute of Advanced Study Monographs). 60p. 1970. 7.50x (ISBN 0-8002-0295-3). Intl Pubns Serv.

Rasiowa, H. An Algebraic Approach to Non-Classical Logics. (Studies in Logic & the Foundations of Mathematics: Vol. 78). 403p. 1974. 39.00 (ISBN 0-444-10489-5, North-Holland). Elsevier.

Rasiowa, Helen. Introduction to Modern Mathematics. LC 72-88575. 360p. 1973. 31.75 (ISBN 0-444-10435-6, North-Holland). Elsevier.

Rescher, N. & Urquhart, A. J. Temporal Logic. LC 74-141565. (Library of Exact Philosophy: Vol. 3). (Illus.). 1971. 33.90 (ISBN 0-387-80995-3). Springer-Verlag.

Rieger, Ladislav. Algebric Methods of Mathematical Logic. 1967. 32.50 (ISBN 0-12-588050-2). Acad Pr.

Rine, D., ed. Computer Science & Multiple-Valued Logic: Theory & Applications. 1977. 61.00 (ISBN 0-7204-0406-1, North-Holland). Elsevier.

Roethel, Louis & Weinstein, Abraham. Logic, Sets, & Numbers: A Positive Approach to Math. 2nd ed. 1976. 20.95x (ISBN 0-534-00491-1). Wadsworth Pub.

Rosser, John B. Logic for Mathematicians. 2nd ed. LC 77-7663. 1978. text ed. 19.95 (ISBN 0-8284-0294-9). Chelsea Pub.

Schroeder, Ernst. Algebra der Logik, 5 vols. in 3. 2nd ed. LC 63-11315. 2192p. (Ger.). 1980. Set. 75.00 (ISBN 0-8284-0171-3). Chelsea Pub.

Shearman, A. T. The Development of Symbolic Logic. (Reprints in Philosophy Ser.). Repr. of 1906 ed. lib. bdg. 26.50x (ISBN 0-697-00048-6). Irvington.

Shoenfield, J. R. Mathematical Logic. 1967. text ed. 19.95 (ISBN 0-201-07028-6). A-W.

Skolem, Thoralf, et al. Mathematical Interpretation of Formal Systems. (Orig.). 1955. bds. 7.25x (ISBN 0-7204-2226-4, Pub. by North Holland). Humanities.

Slisenko, A. O., ed. Studies in Constructive Mathematics & Mathematical Logic, Part 1. LC 69-12507. (Seminars in Mathematics Ser.: Vol. 4). 88p. 1969. 25.00 (ISBN 0-306-18804-X, Consultants). Plenum Pub.

Smith, Karl J. Introduction to Symbolic Logic. LC 73-87250. (Contemporary Undergrad Math Ser). 1974. pap. text ed. 5.95 (ISBN 0-8185-0115-4). Brooks-Cole.

Smullyan, R. M. First-Order Logic. LC 68-13495. (Ergebnisse der Mathematik und Ihrer Grenzgebiete: Vol. 43). 1968. Repr. 20.90 (ISBN 0-387-04099-4). Springer-Verlag.

Steklov Institute of Mathematics, Academy of Sciences, U S S R, No. 98. Calculi of Symbolic Logic: Proceedings I. Orevkov, V. P., ed. 1971. 40.00 (ISBN 0-8218-1898-8, STEKLO-98). Am Math.

Steklov Institute of Mathematics, Academy of Sciences, U S S R, No. 121. Logical & Logico-Mathematical Calculi, 2: Proceedings. Orebkov, V. P., ed. LC 74-8854. 1974. text ed. 41.20 (ISBN 0-8218-3021-X, STEKLO-121). Am Math.

Suppes, P., et al. Logic, Methodology & Philosophy of Science IV. (Studies in Logic & the Foundation of Mathematics: Vol. 74). 1974. 73.25 (ISBN 0-444-10491-7, North-Holland). Elsevier.

Symposium on Logic, Boston, 1972-73. Logic Colloquium. Parikh, R., ed. (Lecture Notes in Mathematics Ser.: Vol. 453). iv, 251p. (Orig.). 1975. pap. 13.80 (ISBN 0-387-07155-5). Springer-Verlag.

Takeuti, Gaisi. Two Applications of Logic to Mathematics. (Publications of the Mathematical Society of Japan: No. 13). 1978. 18.50x (ISBN 0-691-08212-X). Princeton U Pr.

Tapscott, Bangs L. Elementary Applied Symbolic Logic. (Illus.). 512p. 1976. text ed. 17.50 (ISBN 0-13-252940-8). P-H.

Tennant, N. Natural Logic. 206p. 1979. 13.00x (ISBN 0-85224-347-2, Pub. by Edinburgh U Pr Scotland). Columbia U Pr.

Thomas, James A. Symbolic Logic. (Philosophy Ser.). 1977. text ed. 14.50 (ISBN 0-675-08558-6); instructor's manual 3.95 (ISBN 0-686-67529-0). Merrill.

Thomas, R., ed. Kinetic Logic. (Lecture Notes in Biomathematics: Vol. 29). 507p. 1980. pap. 27.30 (ISBN 0-387-09556-X). Springer-Verlag.

Thomason, Richmond H. Symbolic Logic: An Introduction. (Illus.). 1970. text ed. 18.95 (ISBN 0-02-420210-X). Macmillan.

Troelstra, A. S. Principles of Intuitionism. LC 74-88182. (Lecture Notes in Mathematics: Vol. 95). 1969. pap. 10.70 (ISBN 0-387-04614-3). Springer-Verlag.

Van Heijenoort, Jean. Frege & Godel: Two Fundamental Texts in Mathematical Logic. abr. ed. LC 71-116736. 1970. 8.95x (ISBN 0-674-31844-7); pap. 5.95x (ISBN 0-674-31845-5). Harvard U Pr.

Van Heijenoort, Jean, ed. From Frege to Godel: A Source Book in Mathematical Logic, 1879-1931. LC 67-10905. (Source Books in the History of the Sciences Ser). 1967. 30.00x (ISBN 0-674-32450-1); pap. 13.95x (ISBN 0-674-32449-8). Harvard U Pr.

Venn, John. Logic of Chance. 4th ed. LC 62-11698. (YA) (gr. 7-12). 12.95 (ISBN 0-8284-0173-X). Chelsea Pub.

--Symbolic Logic. LC 70-165345. (Research & Source Works Ser.: No. 778). 1971. Repr. of 1894 ed. lib. bdg. 32.00 (ISBN 0-8337-3626-4). B Franklin.

--Symbolic Logic. LC 70-165345. (Research & Source Works Ser.: No. 778). 1971. Repr. of 1894 ed. lib. bdg. 32.00 (ISBN 0-8337-3626-4). B Franklin.

--Symbolic Logic. 2nd ed. LC 79-119161. 1971. text ed. 15.95 (ISBN 0-8284-0251-5). Chelsea Pub.

Von Wright, Georg H. The Logical Problem of Induction. 2nd ed. LC 78-24370. 1979. Repr. of 1957 ed. lib. bdg. 20.25x (ISBN 0-313-20830-1, WRLP). Greenwood.

Waddell, Ward, Jr. Structure of Laws As Represented by Symbolic Methods. 1961. pap. 2.75 (ISBN 0-9600130-0-8). Waddell.

Wang, Hao. From Mathematics to Philosophy. (International Library of Philosophy & Scientific Method). 420p. 1973. text ed. 29.25x (ISBN 0-391-00335-6). Humanities.

--Logic, Computers & Sets. LC 70-113155. Orig. Title: Survey of Mathematical Logic. 1970. Repr. of 1962 ed. text ed. 19.95 (ISBN 0-8284-0245-0). Chelsea Pub.

Whitehead, Alfred N. & Russell, Bertrand. Principia Mathematica, 3 Vols. Set. 270.00 (ISBN 0-521-06791-X). Cambridge U Pr.

--Principia Mathematica to Fifty-Six. 2nd ed. 1925-27. pap. 19.95x (ISBN 0-521-09187-X). Cambridge U Pr.

Wiatrowski, Claude A. & House, Charles H. Logic Circuits & Microcomputer Systems. Cerra, Frank J., ed. (McGraw-Hill Series in Electrical Engineering: Computer Engineering & Switching Theory-Electronics & Electronic Circuits). (Illus.). 512p. Date not set. text ed. 25.95 (ISBN 0-07-070090-7); price not set solutions manual (ISBN 0-07-070091-5). McGraw.

Wilson, N. L. Concept of Language. 1971. 12.50x (ISBN 0-8020-7026-4). U of Toronto Pr.

Wittgenstein, Ludwig. Philosophical Grammar. Kenny, A. J., tr. 1974. 32.50x (ISBN 0-520-02664-0); pap. 6.95 (ISBN 0-520-03725-1). U of Cal Pr.

--Prototractatus: An Early Version of Tractatus Logico-Philosophicus. McGuinness, B. F., et al, eds. Pears, D. F. & McGuinness, B. F., trs. LC 79-136737. 1971. 38.50x (ISBN 0-8014-0610-2). Cornell U Pr.

--Tractatus Logico-Philosophicus: German-English Text. 1963. text ed. 10.75x (ISBN 0-7100-3605-1). Humanities.

Woodger, Joseph H. Technique of Theory Construction. (Foundations of the Unity of Science Ser: Vol. 2, No. 5). 1939. pap. 1.95x (ISBN 0-226-57595-0, P414, Phoen). U of Chicago Pr.

Wright, C. Frege's Conception of Numbers As Objects. 150p. pap. 13.50 (ISBN 0-08-025726-7). Pergamon.

LOGIC, SYMBOLIC AND MATHEMATICAL–PROGRAMMED INSTRUCTION

Enderton, Herbert B. A Mathematical Introduction to Logic. 1972. 20.95 (ISBN 0-12-238450-4). Acad Pr.

Mates, Benson. Elementary Logic. 2nd ed. 1972. text ed. 9.95x (ISBN 0-19-501491-X). Oxford U Pr.

Schagrin, Morton L. The Language of Logic: A Self-Instruction Text. 2nd ed. 1978. pap. text ed. 7.95x (ISBN 0-394-31299-6). Random.

LOGIC, THRESHOLD

see Threshold Logic

LOGIC AND FAITH

see Faith and Reason

LOGIC AND LANGUAGE

see Logical Positivism

LOGIC DIAGRAMS

Friedman, Arthur D. Logical Design of Digital Systems. LC 74-82932. (Illus., Solutions manual avail. only to instructors for course adoptions). 1975. text ed. 19.95x (ISBN 0-914894-50-1). Computer Sci.

Mowle, Frederic J. Systematic Approach to Digital Logic Design. LC 75-18156. (A-W Series in Electrical Engineering). 500p. 1976. text ed. 25.95 (ISBN 0-201-04920-1); solution manual 5.95 (ISBN 0-201-04921-X). A-W.

Roberts, Don D. Existential Graphs of Charles S. Peirce. LC 73-85776. (Approaches to Semiotics Ser.: Vol. 27). (Illus.). 168p. 1973. text ed. 33.75x (ISBN 90-2792-523-2). Mouton.

LOGIC MACHINES

see also Artificial Intelligence

Beth, E. W. & Piaget, J. Mathematical Epistemology & Psychology. 1966. 56.75x (ISBN 0-677-01290-X). Gordon.

Streater, Jack W. How to Use Integrated Circuit Logic Elements. 3rd ed. LC 79-63819. 1979. pap. 5.95 (ISBN 0-672-21613-2). Sams.

LOGIC OF MATHEMATICS

see Mathematics–Philosophy

LOGIC STRUCTURE TABLES

see Decision Logic Tables

LOGICAL ANALYSIS

see Analysis (Philosophy)

LOGICAL POSITIVISM

see also Analysis (Philosophy); Semantics (Philosophy)

Ayer, Alfred J. Logical Positivism. LC 78-6321. 1978. Repr. of 1959 ed. lib. bdg. 32.50 (ISBN 0-313-20462-4, AYLP). Greenwood.

Ayer, Alfred J., ed. Logical Positivism. LC 58-6467. 1966. pap. text ed. 9.95 (ISBN 0-02-900130-7). Free Pr.

Ballmer, T. Logical Grammar. (North Holland Linguistic Ser.: Vol. 39). 1978. 42.75 (ISBN 0-444-85205-0, North Holland). Elsevier.

Bergmann, Gustav. Meaning & Existence. (Orig.). 1960. pap. 7.95x (ISBN 0-299-01984-5). U of Wis Pr.

--The Metaphysics of Logical Positivism. LC 78-28139. 1978. Repr. of 1967 ed. lib. bdg. 26.75x (ISBN 0-313-20235-4, BEML). Greenwood.

Carnap, Rudolf. The Logical Structure of the World & Pseudoproblems in Philosophy. George, Rolf A., tr. LC 66-13604. Orig. Title: Logische Aufbau der Welt. 1967. pap. 9.95x (ISBN 0-520-01417-0, CAL184). U of Cal Pr.

Copleston, Frederick. Contemporary Philosophy. rev. ed. Orig. Title: Contemporary Philosophy, Studies of Logical Positivism & Existentialism. 240p. 1972. pap. 4.95 (ISBN 0-8091-1757-6). Paulist Pr.

Cornforth, Maurice. Science Versus Idealism. LC 72-6924. 463p. 1975. Repr. of 1962 ed. lib. bdg. 25.50x (ISBN 0-8371-6501-6, COSV). Greenwood.

Ferre, Frederick. Language, Logic, & God. LC 77-9060. 1977. Repr. of 1961 ed. lib. bdg. 18.25x (ISBN 0-8371-9716-3, FELL). Greenwood.

Flew, A. G., ed. Logic & Language. (First Ser.). 206p. 1968. pap. 12.50x (ISBN 0-631-03420-X, Pub. by Basil Blackwell). Biblio Dist.

--Logic & Language. (Second Ser.). 242p. 1973. Repr. of 1953 ed. 12.50x (ISBN 0-631-03430-7, Pub. by Basil Blackwell England). Biblio Dist.

Hamm, Victor M. Language, Truth & Poetry. (Aquinas Lecture). 1960. 6.95 (ISBN 0-87462-125-9). Marquette.

Hanfling, Oswald. Logical Positivism. 208p. 1981. 20.00x (ISBN 0-231-05386-X). Columbia U Pr.

Hanfling, Oswald, ed. Essential Readings in Logical Positivism. 320p. 1981. pap. 14.95x (ISBN 0-631-12566-3, Pub. by Basil Blackwell England). Biblio Dist.

Hockney, Donald, et al, eds. Contemporary Research in Philosophical Logic & Linguistic Semantics. LC 74-34079. (Western Ontario Ser: No. 4). 330p. (Orig.). 1975. lib. bdg. 53.00 (ISBN 90-277-0511-9, Pub. by Reidel Holland); pap. 31.50 (ISBN 90-277-0512-7, Pub. by Reidel Holland). Kluwer Boston.

Joergensen, Joergen. Development of Logical Empiricism. LC 72-131573. (Foundations of the Unity of Science Ser.: Vol. 2, No. 9). 1951. pap. 2.50x (ISBN 0-226-57599-3, P418, Phoen). U of Chicago Pr.

Jorgensen, Jorgen. Development of Logical Empiricism. (International Encyclopedia of Unified Science Ser: Vol. 1 & 2). 1970. Repr. of 1951 ed. 8.00 (ISBN 0-384-27870-1). Johnson Repr.

Kazemier, B. H. & Vusje, D., eds. Logic & Language: Studies Dedicated to Professor Rudolf Carnap on the Occasion of His 70th Birthday. (Synthese Library: No. 5). 246p. 1962. lib. bdg. 26.00 (ISBN 90-277-0019-2, Pub. by Reidel Holland). Kluwer Boston.

Kraft, Viktor. The Vienna Circle, the Origin of Neo-Positivism. Pap, Arthur, tr. LC 70-75584. 209p. Repr. of 1953 ed. lib. bdg. 15.00x (ISBN 0-8371-0517-X, KRVC). Greenwood.

McCawley, James D. Everything That Linguists Have Always Wanted to Know About Logic: but Were Ashamed to Ask. LC 80-345. (Illus.). 528p. 1980. lib. bdg. 35.00x (ISBN 0-226-55617-4); pap. text ed. 12.50x (ISBN 0-226-55618-2). U of Chicago Pr.

Morris, Charles W. Logical Positivism, Pragmatism & Scientific Empiricism. LC 75-3285. Repr. of 1937 ed. 11.50 (ISBN 0-404-59273-2). AMS Pr.

Stebbing, L. Susan. Logical Positivism & Analysis. 1974. lib. bdg. 35.00 (ISBN 0-8490-2180-4). Gordon Pr.

Van Peursen, Cornelius A. Phenomenology & Analytical Philosophy. (Duquesne Philosophical Ser.: No. 28). 190p. 1972. text ed. 8.50x (ISBN 0-8207-0139-4). Duquesne.

Waismann, Friedrich. Ludwig Wittgenstein & the Vienna Circle: Conversations Recorded by Friedrich Waismann. McGuinness, Brian, ed. Schulte, Joachim & McGuiness, B., trs. LC 78-6452. (Illus.). 1979. text ed. 23.50x (ISBN 0-06-497310-7). B&N.

Wisdom, John. Logical Constructions. 1969. pap. text ed. 3.45 (ISBN 0-685-19743-3). Phila Bk Co.

LOGICIANS, POLISH

McCall, Storrs, ed. Polish Logic 1920-1939. Grushman, B., et al, trs. 1967. 49.50x (ISBN 0-19-824304-9). Oxford U Pr.

LOGISTICS

Blanchard, Benjamin S. Logistics Engineering & Management. 2nd ed. (P-H Ser. in Industrial & Systems Engineering). (Illus.). 464p. 1981. text ed. 25.95 (ISBN 0-13-540088-0). P-H.

--Logistics Engineering & Management. (Int'l. Series in Industrial Systems Engr.). (Illus.). 416p. 1974. ref. ed. 25.95 (ISBN 0-13-540047-3). P-H.

Fair, Marvin L. & Williams, Ernest W., Jr. Transportation & Logistics. rev. ed. 1981. 19.95x (ISBN 0-256-02308-5). Business Pubns.

Geisler, M. A. Logistics. LC 74-83269. (N-H-TIMS Studies in Management Sciences: Vol. 1). 184p. 1975. pap. 19.50 (ISBN 0-444-10873-4, North-Holland). Elsevier.

Johnson, James C. Readings in Contemporary Physical Distribution & Logistics. 4th ed. 352p. 1981. pap. text ed. 13.95 (ISBN 0-87814-154-5). Pennwell Pub.

Little, Wallace I. Transportation-Logistics Dictionary 1977. LC 77-79988. text ed. 10.00 (ISBN 0-87408-009-6). Traffic Serv.

Marlow, W. H., ed. Modern Trends in Logistics Research. LC 75-43617. 480p. 1976. text ed. 26.00x (ISBN 0-262-13122-6). MIT Pr.

Rose, Warren. Logistics Management: Systems & Components. 650p. 1979. text ed. write for info. (ISBN 0-697-08026-9); instrs.' manual avail. (ISBN 0-685-91872-6). Wm C Brown.

Van Creveld, Martin L. Supplying War: Logistics from Wallenstein to Patton. LC 77-5550. (Illus.). 1977. 27.50 (ISBN 0-521-21730-X). Cambridge U Pr.

LOGISTICS, INDUSTRIAL

see Shipment of Goods

LOGOS

see also Jesus Christ–Pre-Existence

Brinton, Howard H. Evolution & the Inward Light. LC 77-137101. (Orig.). 1970. pap. 0.70x (ISBN 0-87574-173-8). Pendle Hill.

Menard, Jacques E. L' Authentikos Logos. (Fr.). 1977. pap. 14.50x (ISBN 2-7637-6809-1, Pub. by Laval). Intl Schol Bk Serv.

Mills, Lawrence H. Zarathushtra, Philo, the Achaemenids & Israel. LC 74-21261. Repr. of 1906 ed. 34.50 (ISBN 0-404-12815-7). AMS Pr.

Pascher, Josef. Der Konigsweg Zu Wiedergeburt und Vergottung Bei Philon Von Alexandreia. Repr. of 1931 ed. pap. 18.50 (ISBN 0-384-45050-4). Johnson Repr.

Wavell, Bruce B. The Living Logos: A Philosophico-Religious Essay in Free Verse. LC 77-18478. 1978. pap. text ed. 8.75 (ISBN 0-8191-0324-1). U Pr of Amer.

LOHE, WILHELM, 1808-1872

Heintzen, Erich H. & Starr, Frank. Love Leaves Home. LC 72-94586. 1973. 2.50 (ISBN 0-570-03513-9, 14-2017). Concordia.

LOHENSTEIN, DANIEL KASPER VON, 1633-1683

Gillespie, Gerald E. Daniel Casper Von Lohenstein's Historical Tragedies. LC 65-18733. 1966. 6.25 (ISBN 0-8142-0053-2). Ohio St U Pr.

LOIRE RIVER AND VALLEY–DESCRIPTION AND TRAVEL

Blue Guide - Normandy, Brittany, Loire Valley. 1977. 28.95 (ISBN 0-528-84597-7); pap. 19.95 (ISBN 0-528-84598-5). Rand.

Chateaux of the Loire. write for info. (ISBN 2-06-013211-8). Michelin.

Cook, Theodore A. Old Touraine: The Life & History of the Chateaux of the Loire, 2 vols. 1978. Repr. of 1920 ed. lib. bdg. 60.00 (ISBN 0-8414-1847-0). Folcroft.

Delpal, Jacques-Louis. The Valley of the Loire Today. (Illus.). 256p. 1979. 14.95 (ISBN 2-8525-8034-9, Pub. by J A Editions France). Hippocrene Bks.

Dunlop, Ian. Chateaux of the Loire. LC 70-77983. 1969. 12.00 (ISBN 0-8008-1435-5). Taplinger.

Lanoux, Armand, ed. Dreams of the Chateaux of the Loire. (Illus.). 92p. 1967. 13.50x (ISBN 0-8002-0758-0). Intl Pubns Serv.

Michelin Green Travel Guide: Chateaux of the Loire. (Fr. & Eng.). 4.95 (ISBN 0-685-11374-4). French & Eur.

Myhill, Henry. The Loire Valley: Plantagenet & Valois. (Illus.). 160p. 1978. 14.95 (ISBN 0-571-10446-0, Pub. by Faber & Faber). Merrimack Bk Serv.

Ortzen, Len. Your Guide to the Loire Valley. LC 68-141018. (Your Guide Ser). 1968. 5.25x (ISBN 0-8002-0793-9). Intl Pubns Serv.

LOISEL, REGIS, d. 1804

Tabeau, Pierre-Antoine. Tabeau's Narrative of Loisel's Expedition to the Upper Missouri. (American Exploration & Travel Ser: No. 3). (Illus.). 1968. Repr. of 1939 ed. 14.95 (ISBN 0-8061-0080-X). U of Okla Pr.

LOLIGO

see Squids

LOLLARDS

Carrick, J. C. Wycliffe & the Lollards. 1977. lib. bdg. 59.95 (ISBN 0-8490-2824-8). Gordon Pr.

Gairdner, James. Lollardy & the Reformation in England: An Historical Survey, 4 Vols. 1965. Repr. of 1913 ed. 141.00 (ISBN 0-8337-1268-3). B Franklin.

Hudson, Anne, ed. Selections from English Wycliffite Writings. LC 77-1506. 1978. 38.50 (ISBN 0-521-21667-2). Cambridge U Pr.

Powell, Edgar & Trevelyan, G. M., eds. The Peasants' Rising & the Lollards. LC 78-63202. (Heresies of the Early Christian & Medieval Era: Second Ser.). Repr. of 1899 ed. 17.00 (ISBN 0-404-16238-X). AMS Pr.

Summers, William H. The Lollards of the Chiltern Hills. LC 80-12770. (Heresies of the Early Christian & Medieval Era: Second Ser.). Repr. of 1906 ed. 22.00 (ISBN 0-404-16245-2). AMS Pr.

Wycliffe, John. Apology for Lollard Doctrines, Attributed to Wycliffe. Repr. of 1842 ed. 21.00 (ISBN 0-404-50120-6). AMS Pr.

--Apology for Lollard Doctrines, Attributed to Wycliffe. 23.00 (ISBN 0-384-69838-7). Johnson Repr.

LOLME, JEAN LOUIS DE, 1740-1806

De Lolme, J. L. & Machelon, Jean-Pierre. The Constitution of England & les Idees Politliques De J.L. De Lolme: 1741-1806, 2 vols. in one. Mayer, J. P., ed. LC 78-67366. (European Political Thought Ser.). (Eng. & Fr.). 1979. Repr. of 1807 ed. lib. bdg. 44.00x (ISBN 0-405-11714-0). Arno.

LOLO LANGUAGE

Bradley, David. Proto-Lolish. (Scandanavian Institute of Asian Studies Monograph: No. 39). (Orig.). 1980. pap. text ed. 18.00x (ISBN 0-7007-0128-1). Humanities.

Matisoff, James A. The Loloish Tonal Split Revisited. (Research Monograph: No. 7). 1972. 7.50 (ISBN 0-686-23619-X, Ctr South & Southeast Asia Studies). Cellar.

LOLOS

see also Moso (Tribe)

LOMBARD, CAROLE, 1908-1942

Ott, Frederick W. The Films of Carole Lombard. (Illus.). 256p. 1974. pap. 7.95 (ISBN 0-8065-0449-8). Citadel Pr.

LOMBARD LOANS

see also Pawnbroking

LOMBARDI, VINCE THOMAS, 1913-1970

Etter, Les. Vince Lombardi: Football Legend. LC 74-18076. (Sports Library Ser.). (Illus.). 96p. (gr. 3-6). 1975. PLB 6.48 (ISBN 0-8116-6670-0). Garrard.

Fago, John N. Vincent Lombardi - Pele. (Pendulum Illustrated Biography Ser.). (Illus.). (gr. 4-12). 1979. text ed. 5.00 (ISBN 0-88301-370-3); pap. text ed. 1.95 (ISBN 0-88301-358-4); wkbk. 1.25 (ISBN 0-88301-382-7). Pendulum Pr.

Flynn, George L., ed. Vince Lombardi on Football. 352p. 1981. price not set (ISBN 0-442-22540-7). Van Nos Reinhold.

Myers, Hortense & Burnett, Ruth. Vincent Lombardi: Young Football Coach. (Childhood of Famous Americans Ser.). 200p. (gr. 3-7). 1971. 3.95 (ISBN 0-672-51623-3). Bobbs.

Olsen, James T. Vince Lombardi. LC 73-10289. (Creative Superstars Ser.). 1974. PLB 5.95 (ISBN 0-87191-261-9). Creative Ed.

Wells, Robert. Vince Lombardi: His Life & Times. LC 75-178223. (Illus.). 1971. 8.95 (ISBN 0-88361-002-7). Stanton & Lee.

Wells, Robert W. Vince Lombardi: His Life & Times. (Illus.). 1977. pap. 1.95 (ISBN 0-89041-168-9, 3168). Major Bks.

LOMBARDO, GUY, 1903-1977

Richman, Saul. Guy: The Life & Times of Guy Lombardo. (Illus.). 192p. 1980. 10.00 (ISBN 0-517-54000-2). Crown.

LOMBARDO-VENETIAN KINGDOM

Rath, R. John. The Provisional Austrian Regime in Lombardy-Venetia (1814-1815) LC 69-63009. 426p. 1969. 18.50x (ISBN 0-292-78385-X). U of Tex Pr.

LOMBARDS

see also Barbarian Invasions of Rome

LOMBARDY–HISTORY

Butler, William F. Lombard Communes. LC 68-25226. (World History Ser., No. 48). 1969. lib. bdg. 62.95 (ISBN 0-8383-0923-2). Haskell.

--Lombard Communes: A History of the Republics of North Italy. LC 69-13847. Repr. of 1906 ed. lib. bdg. 22.75x (ISBN 0-8371-2753-X, BULC). Greenwood.

Greenfield, Kent R. Economics & Liberalism in the Risorgimento: A Study of Nationalism in Lombardy, 1814-1848. LC 78-17674. 1978. Repr. of 1965 ed. lib. bdg. 22.25x (ISBN 0-313-20510-8, GREL). Greenwood.

Klang, Daniel M. Tax Reform in Eighteenth-Century Lombardy. (East European Monographs: No. 27). 1977. 10.00x (ISBN 0-914710-20-6). East Eur Quarterly.

Williams, W. K. Communes of Lombardy from the Sixth to the Tenth Century: An Investigation of the Causes Which Led to the Development of the Municipal Unity Among the Lombard Communes. Repr. of 1891 ed. pap. 7.00 (ISBN 0-384-68590-0). Johnson Repr.

LOMBARDY–HISTORY–FICTION

Bowen, Marjorie. Viper of Milan. (gr. 4-8). 1964. 5.00 (ISBN 0-8023-1014-1). Dufour.

LOMONOSOV, MIKHAIL VASILEVICH, 1711-1765

Menshutkin, Boris N. Russia's Lomonosov: Chemist, Courtier, Physicist, Poet. LC 79-100232. Repr. of 1952 ed. lib. bdg. 15.00 (ISBN 0-8371-3688-1, MELO). Greenwood.

LONDON, JACK, 1876-1916

Bamford, Georgia L. Mystery of Jack London. LC 73-15997. 1931. lib. bdg. 30.00 (ISBN 0-8414-9856-3). Folcroft.

Barltrop, Robert. Jack London: The Man, the Writer, & the Rebel. (Illus.). 244p. 1980. text ed. 10.00 (ISBN 0-904383-18-0); pap. 4.95 (ISBN 0-904383-19-9). Pluto Pr.

Bosworth Inc. Presents 'John Barleycorn' by Jack London. (Illus.). 4p. 1973. Repr. of 1914 ed. pap. 0.50 (ISBN 0-915046-13-X). Wolf Hse.

Etulain, Richard W., ed. Jack London on the Road: The Tramp Diary & Other Hobo Writings. 209p. 1979. 7.50 (ISBN 0-87421-098-4); pap. 4.50 (ISBN 0-87421-100-X). Utah St U Pr.

Feied, Frederick. No Pie in the Sky: The Hobo As American Cultural Hero in the Works of Jack London, John Dos Passos, & Jack Kerouac. (Orig.). 1964. pap. 1.50 (ISBN 0-8065-0088-3, 170). Citadel Pr.

Foner, Philip S. Jack London: American Rebel. new ed. 1969. pap. 5.95 (ISBN 0-8065-0112-X). Citadel Pr.

Gaer, Joseph. Jack London: Bibliography & Biographical Data. LC 75-131409. (Bibliography & Reference Ser.: No. 383). 1971. Repr. of 1934 ed. lib. bdg. 14.00 (ISBN 0-8337-1258-6). B Franklin.

Harmon, Robert, compiled by. First Editions of Jack London. (First Edition Pocket Guides Ser.). 19p. softcover 3.95 (ISBN 0-910720-17-7). Hermes.

Hensley, Dennis E. Jack London Masterplots. 1981. write for info (ISBN 0-918466-07-5). Quintessence.

Irvine, Alexander. Jack London at Yale. (Illus.). 28p. 1972. Repr. of 1906 ed. pap. 1.25 (ISBN 0-915046-09-1). Wolf Hse.

Jack London: A Sketch of His Life & Work. (Illus.). 15p. 1971. Repr. of 1905 ed. pap. 1.00 (ISBN 0-915046-00-8). Wolf Hse.

Jack London: Who He Is & What He Has Done. 16p. 1972. Repr. of 1908 ed. pap. 1.00 (ISBN 0-915046-06-7). Wolf Hse.

Kingman, Russ. A Pictoral Life of Jack London. 1981. pap. 9.95 (ISBN 0-517-54093-2). Crown.

--Pictorial Life of Jack London. 15.95 (ISBN 0-517-53163-1). Crown.

Labor, Earle. Jack London. (U. S. Authors Ser.: No. 230). 184p. 1974. lib. bdg. 10.95 (ISBN 0-8057-0455-8). Twayne.

Livingston, Leon R. From Coast to Coast with Jack London by A-NO. 1. LC 74-101741. (Illus.). 1969. Repr. of 1917 ed. 7.50 (ISBN 0-912382-01-5). Black Letter.

McClintock, James I. White Logic: Jack London's Short Stories. LC 74-84862. (Monograph Ser: No. 2). (Illus.). 208p. 1976. 12.00 (ISBN 0-915046-22-9). Wolf Hse.

McDevitt, William. Jack London's First. 32p. 1972. Repr. of 1946 ed. pap. 2.00 (ISBN 0-915046-08-3). Wolf Hse.

Monarch Notes on London's Call of the Wind. (gr. 7-12). pap. 1.95 (ISBN 0-671-00685-1). Monarch Pr.

Mosby, C. V. A Little Journey to the Home of Jack London. 20p. 1972. Repr. of 1917 ed. pap. 1.00 (ISBN 0-915046-04-0). Wolf Hse.

Ownbey, Ray W., ed. Jack London: Essays in Criticism. LC 78-26193. 1979. pap. 4.95 (ISBN 0-87905-053-5). Peregrine Smith.

Perry, John. Jack London: An American Myth. 356p. 1981. text ed. 21.95 (ISBN 0-88229-378-8); pap. 10.95 (ISBN 0-88229-794-5). Nelson-Hall.

Sherman, Joan. Jack London: A Reference Guide. (Reference Publications Ser.). 1977. lib. bdg. 22.00 (ISBN 0-8161-7849-6). G K Hall.

Sinclair, Andrew. Jack: A Biography of Jack London. (gr. 11-12). 1979. pap. 2.50 (ISBN 0-671-82299-3). PB.

Sisson, James E. & Martens, Robert W. Jack London First Editions. LC 78-63374. (Illus.). 1978. 25.50x (ISBN 0-932458-00-9). Star Rover.

Stone, Irving. Jack London: Sailor on Horseback. 1969. pap. 2.75 (ISBN 0-451-11164-8, AE1164, Sig). NAL.

Walcutt, Charles C. Jack London. (Pamphlets on American Writers Ser: No. 57). (Orig.). 1966. pap. 1.25x (ISBN 0-8166-0387-1, MPAW57). U of Minn Pr.

Walker, Dale L. Jack London & Conan Doyle: A Literary Kinship. LC 80-67698. (Sherlock Holmes Monograph). (Illus.). 70p. 1981. 8.95x (ISBN 0-934468-03-6). Gaslight.

Walker, Dale L., ed. Curious Fragments: Jack London's Tales of Fantasy Fiction. 1975. 12.95 (ISBN 0-8046-9114-2, Natl U). Kennikat.

Walker, Dale L., compiled by. The Fiction of Jack London: A Chronological Bibliography. LC 70-190575. (Illus.). 40p. 1972. 10.00 (ISBN 0-87404-044-2). Tex Western.

Walker, Franklin. Jack London & the Klondike: The Genesis of an American Writer. LC 66-20412. (Illus.). 1978. pap. 5.00 (ISBN 0-87328-022-9). Huntington Lib.

LONDON, JACK, 1876-1916–BIBLIOGRAPHY

Gaer, Joseph. Jack London: Bibliography & Biographical Data. LC 75-131409. (Bibliography & Reference Ser.: No. 383). 1971. Repr. of 1934 ed. lib. bdg. 14.00 (ISBN 0-8337-1258-6). B Franklin.

Woodbridge, H. C. Jack London: A Bibliography. rev. & enl. ed. LC 73-5921. 1973. 40.00 (ISBN 0-527-97860-4). Kraus Intl.

LONDON

see also Mayfair, London

Bardsley, Charles W. Romance of the London Directory. LC 72-78115. 1971. Repr. of 1879 ed. 22.00 (ISBN 0-8103-3782-7). Gale.

Becker, Bernard H. Scientific London. 340p. 1968. Repr. of 1847 ed. 25.00x (ISBN 0-7146-2328-8, F Cass Co). Biblio Dist.

Boynton, Percy H. London in English Literature. 346p. 1980. Repr. of 1913 ed. lib. bdg. 30.00 (ISBN 0-8414-9906-3). Folcroft.

Brewer, H. W. Old London Illustrated. (Illus.). 1962. deluxe ed. 14.95x (ISBN 0-89563-012-5). Intl Ideas.

Church, Richard. London in Color. (Illus.). 160p. 1980. 24.00 (ISBN 0-7134-0020-X, Pub. by Batsford England). David & Charles.

Dark, Sidney. London Town. Repr. 10.00 (ISBN 0-685-64775-7). Norwood Edns.

--London Town. 1976. 20.00 (ISBN 0-8495-1131-3). Arden Lib.

Dore, Gustave & Jerrold, Blanchard. London: A Pilgrimage. LC 68-56513. (Illus.). 1968. Repr. of 1872 ed. 40.00 (ISBN 0-405-08460-9, Blom Pubns). Arno.

Ebel, Suzanne & Impey, Doreen. London's Riverside. (Illus.). 256p. 1976. pap. 5.95 (ISBN 0-86002-137-8). Transatlantic.

Edwards, G. W. London. 59.95 (ISBN 0-8490-0552-3). Gordon Pr.

Foley, Donald L. Controlling London's Growth: Planning the Great Wen, 1940-1960. LC 63-19958. (Illus.). 1963. 21.50x (ISBN 0-520-00424-8). U of Cal Pr.

Gardiner, George. The Changing Life of London. 5.95 (ISBN 0-85468-409-3). David & Charles.

Gordon, W. J. The Horse-World of London, Eighteen Ninety-Three. (Illus.). 190p. 1971. Repr. 2.50 (ISBN 0-7153-5128-1). David & Charles.

Graunt, John. Natural & Political Observations Mentioned in a Following Index, & Made Upon the Bills of Mortality. LC 74-25754. (European Sociology Ser.). 110p. 1975. Repr. 9.00x (ISBN 0-405-06508-6). Arno.

Kemnitz, Milt. London & Back. 1977. 12.50 (ISBN 0-686-22822-7). M N Kemnitz.

Kerstin, A. F. Prospect of London. Date not set. 14.50 (ISBN 0-392-04294-0, SpS). Sportshelf.

Lodge, Thomas & Greene, Robert. Looking-Glass for London & England. LC 71-133697. (Tudor Facsimile Texts. Old English Plays: No. 67). Repr. of 1914 ed. 31.50 (ISBN 0-404-53367-1). AMS Pr.

Mitton, G. E. The Book of London: For Young People. 1978. Repr. of 1922 ed. lib. bdg. 25.00 (ISBN 0-89760-529-2, Telegraph). Dynamic Learn Corp.

Munro, John M. The Royal Aquarium: Failure of a Victorian Compromise. 1971. 10.00x (ISBN 0-8156-6033-2, Am U Beirut). Syracuse U Pr.

Reynolds, George W. The Mysteries of London, 4 vols. in 2. LC 79-8192. Repr. of 1848 ed. Set. 84.50 (ISBN 0-404-62106-6); Vol. 1. (ISBN 0-404-62107-4); Vol. 2. (ISBN 0-404-62108-2). AMS Pr.

Round, John H. Commune of London & Other Studies. 1971. Repr. of 1899 ed. 29.00 (ISBN 0-403-01187-6). Scholarly.

Timbs, John. Curiosities of London. rev. ed. LC 68-22056. 1968. Repr. of 1867 ed. 30.00 (ISBN 0-8103-3497-6). Gale.

Wynter, Andrew. Our Social Bees. LC 67-23950. (Social History Reference Ser.). (Illus.). 1969. Repr. of 1861 ed. 19.00 (ISBN 0-8103-3265-5). Gale.

LONDON–ANTIQUITIES

The Archaeology of London. LC 74-83860. (Illus.). 1975. 9.95 (ISBN 0-8155-5033-2, NP). Noyes.

Harrison, Michael. The London That Was Rome. 1971. 10.50 (ISBN 0-04-913011-0). Allen Unwin.

Marsden, Peter. Roman London. (Illus.). 224p. 1981. 19.95 (ISBN 0-500-25073-1). Thames Hudson.

Norman, Philip. London Signs & Inscriptions. LC 68-22039. (Camden Library Ser). (Illus.). 1968. Repr. of 1893 ed. 19.00 (ISBN 0-8103-3496-8). Gale.

Wheatley, Henry B. London, Past & Present: A Dictionary of Its History Associations & Traditions, 3 Vols. LC 68-17956. 1968. Repr. of 1891 ed. Set. 85.00 (ISBN 0-8103-3499-2). Gale.

LONDON–BARTHOLOMEW FAIR

Morley, Henry. Memoirs of Bartholomew Fair. LC 67-24348. 1968. Repr. of 1880 ed. 24.00 (ISBN 0-8103-3495-X). Gale.

LONDON–BIOGRAPHY

Defoe, Daniel. The History of the Life & Adventures of Mr. Duncan Campbell. LC 74-13463. (Illus.). Repr. of 1895 ed. 27.50 (ISBN 0-404-07914-8). AMS Pr.

Egan, Pierce. Life in London; or the Day & Night Scenes of Jerry Hawthorn, Esq. & Corinthian Tom. LC 79-8260. Repr. of 1821 ed. 44.50 (ISBN 0-404-61841-3). AMS Pr.

Kent, Elizabeth E. Goldsmith & His Booksellers. 1978. Repr. of 1933 ed. lib. bdg. 12.50 (ISBN 0-8495-3017-2). Arden Lib.

Smith, Richard. The Obituary of Richard Smith. 1849. 15.50 (ISBN 0-384-56145-4). Johnson Repr.

Sutherland, Lucy S. London Merchant. new ed. 164p. 1962. 24.00x (ISBN 0-7146-1515-3, F Cass Co). Biblio Dist.

Swinnerton, Frank. The Bookman's London. (Illus.). 161p. 1980. Repr. of 1951 ed. lib. bdg. 30.00 (ISBN 0-8492-8129-6). R West.

LONDON–CLUBS

Lejeune, Anthony. The Gentlemen's Clubs of London. LC 78-32161. (Illus.). 1979. 35.00 (ISBN 0-8317-3800-6, Mayflower Bks). Smith Pubs.

Timbs, John. Clubs & Club Life in London with Anecdotes of Its Famous Coffee-Houses, Hostelries, & Taverns from the Seventeenth Century to the Present Time. LC 66-28045. 1967. Repr. of 1872 ed. 19.00 (ISBN 0-8103-3262-0). Gale.

LONDON–CHURCHES

Brooke-Hunt, Violet. Story of Westminster Abbey. 1977. lib. bdg. 59.95 (ISBN 0-8490-2692-X). Gordon Pr.

Gray, Ronald. Christopher Wren & St. Paul's Cathedral. (Cambridge Topic Bks.). (Illus.). 52p. (gr. 6 up). 1981. PLB 5.95 (ISBN 0-8225-1222-X). Lerner Pubns.

Harvey, Barbara. Westminster Abbey & Its Estates in the Middle Ages. (Illus.). 1977. text ed. 57.00x (ISBN 0-19-822449-4). Oxford U Pr.

His Majesties Commission & Further Declaration Concerning the Reparation of Saint Pauls Church. LC 75-171754. (English Experience Ser.: No. 379). 1971. Repr. of 1633 ed. 7.00 (ISBN 90-221-0379-X). Walter J Johnson.

His Majesties Commission to Enquire of the Decayes of the Cathedral Church of St. Paul. LC 72-185. (English Experience Ser.: No. 355). 1971. Repr. of 1631 ed. 8.00 (ISBN 90-221-0355-2). Walter J Johnson.

Lethaby, William R. Westminster Abbey & the King's Craftsmen. LC 69-13243. (Illus.). Repr. of 1906 ed. 25.00 (ISBN 0-405-08745-4, Pub. by Blom). Arno.

--Westminster Abbey Re-Examined. LC 69-13244. (Illus.). Repr. of 1925 ed. 21.00 (ISBN 0-405-08744-6, Pub. by Blom). Arno.

London - St. Paul'S Cathedral. Documents Illustrating the History of St. Paul's Cathedral. Simpson, W. S., ed. 1880. 22.50 (ISBN 0-384-55530-6). Johnson Repr.

Pilkington, James. Works of James Pilkington, Lord Bishop of Durham. 1842. Repr. of 1842 ed. 46.00 (ISBN 0-384-46530-7). Johnson Repr.

Westminster Abbey. 1974. pap. 1.95 (ISBN 0-8277-3318-6). British Bk Ctr.

LONDON–COMMERCE

Ashton, R. The City & the Court: Sixteen Hundred & Three to Sixteen Forty-Three. LC 78-67296. 1979. 29.50 (ISBN 0-521-22419-5). Cambridge U Pr.

Brackenbury, M. C., et al, eds. Dealing on the London Metal Exchange & Commodity Markets. 1976. 22.50 (ISBN 0-9504936-0-0, Pub. by Kogan Pg). Nichols Pub.

Clay, C. J. & Wheble, B. S., eds. Modern Merchant Banking: A Guide to the Workings of the Accepting Houses of the City of London & Their Services to Industry & Commerce. 160p. 1980. pap. 12.50 (ISBN 0-85941-044-7). Herman Pub.

Claypoole, James. James Claypoole's Letter Book: London & Philadelphia, 1681-1684. Balderston, Marion, ed. LC 66-25063. 1967. 10.00 (ISBN 0-87328-027-X). Huntington Lib.

Colquhoun, Patrick. Treatise on the Commerce & Police of the River Thames. LC 69-14917. (Criminology, Law Enforcement, & Social Problems Ser.: No. 41). (Map). 1969. Repr. of 1800 ed. 30.00 (ISBN 0-87585-041-3). Patterson Smith.

Gibson-Jarvie, Robert. The City of London: A Financial & Commercial History. (Illus.). 128p. 1980. 17.50 (ISBN 0-85941-090-0). Herman Pub.

Heal, Ambrose. London Tradesmen's Cards of the XVIII Century. (Illus.). 8.75 (ISBN 0-8446-2227-3). Peter Smith.

Kemp's Commercial Guide of London, 1975. 1975. 17.50x (ISBN 0-8277-2840-9). British Bk Ctr.

Moholy-Nagy, L. & Benedetta, Mary. The Street Markets of London. LC 72-84542. (Illus.). Repr. of 1936 ed. 20.00 (ISBN 0-405-08792-6, Pub. by Blom). Arno.

Monier-Williams, R. Tallow Chandlers of London. Incl. Mystery in the Making; Vol. 2. Crown, the City & the Crafts. 11.00x (ISBN 0-7182-0900-1). 1972. Verry.

Thrupp, Sylvia L. Merchant Class of Medieval London. 1962. pap. 5.95 (ISBN 0-472-06072-4, 72, AA). U of Mich Pr.

Willan, Thomas S. Muscovy Merchants of 1555. LC 72-85754. Repr. of 1953 ed. 12.50x (ISBN 0-678-00929-5). Kelley.

LONDON–CRIES

Bridge, Frederick. The Old Cryes of London. LC 74-24050. 1976. Repr. of 1921 ed. 17.50 (ISBN 0-404-12872-6). AMS Pr.

--Old Cryes of London. LC 77-75209. 1977. Repr. of 1921 ed. lib. bdg. 12.50 (ISBN 0-89341-109-4). Longwood Pr.

Hindley, Charles. History of the Cries of London. LC 67-23948. 1969. Repr. of 1884 ed. 19.00 (ISBN 0-8103-0156-3). Gale.

LONDON–DESCRIPTION

AA Shopping in London. rev. ed. pap. 1.95 (ISBN 0-7095-0166-8, Pub. by B T A). Merrimack Bk Serv.

Adcock, A. Famous Houses & Literary Shrines of London. with Seventy-Four Illustrations by Frederick Adcock (Shakespeare, Pope, Hogarth, Goldsmith, Reynolds, Boswell, Blake, Johnson, Lamb, Dickens) 1912. Repr. 35.00 (ISBN 0-8274-2335-7). R West.

Barron, Caroline M. The Medieval Guildhall of London. 59p. 1975. text ed. 22.50x (ISBN 0-8426-0828-1). Verry.

Bates, L. M. The Spirit of London's River. 200p. 1979. 25.00x (ISBN 0-905418-43-3, Pub. by Gresham England). State Mutual Bk.

Bennett, Arnold. London Life. LC 74-16480. (Collected Works of Arnold Bennet: Vol. 48). 1976. Repr. of 1924 ed. 18.75 (ISBN 0-518-19129-X). Arno.

Boswell, James. Boswell's London. 1978. 13.50 (ISBN 0-7045-0259-3). State Mutual Bk.

Boynton, Percy H. London in English Literature. 1913. Repr. 35.00 (ISBN 0-8274-2979-7). R West.

Brewster, Dorothy. Virginia Woolf's London. LC 78-26590. 1979. Repr. of 1960 ed. lib. bdg. 15.00x (ISBN 0-313-20788-7, BRVW). Greenwood.

Byrd, Max. London Transformed: Images of the City in the Eighteenth Century. LC 77-11875. 1978. 17.50x (ISBN 0-300-02166-6). Yale U Pr.

Cadfryn-Roberts, John, ed. Old London. LC 79-81859. (Golden Ariels Ser). (Illus.). 1969. 3.95 (ISBN 0-8008-5690-2). Taplinger.

Cameron, Robert & Cooke, Alistair. Above London. LC 80-80944. 1980. 19.95 (ISBN 0-918684-10-2). Cameron & Co.

Chancellor, E. Beresford. The London of Thackeray. 1923. lib. bdg. 30.00 (ISBN 0-8414-9986-1). Folcroft.

Clark, Cumberland. Dickens' London. LC 73-9522. (Studies in Dickens, No. 52). 1973. Repr. of 1923 ed. lib. bdg. 29.95 (ISBN 0-8383-1714-6). Haskell.

Clunn, Harold. The Face of London. 1978. lib. bdg. 40.00 (ISBN 0-8482-7552-7). Norwood Edns.

Cocks, Barnett. A Mid-Victorian Masterpiece. (Illus.). 1978. 12.95 (ISBN 0-09-128260-8, Pub. by Hutchinson). Merrimack Bk Serv.

Collins, Henry G. Collin's Illustrated Atlas of London. (Victorian Library). 120p. 1973. Repr. of 1854 ed. text ed. 6.50x (ISBN 0-391-00156-6, Leicester). Humanities.

Crawford, D. The City of London: Its Architectural Heritage. 1977. soft 12.00 (ISBN 0-85941-043-9); cased 20.00 (ISBN 0-85941-049-8). State Mutual Bk.

Crawford, David. The City of London: Its Architectual Heritage. (Illus.). 144p. 1980. 15.00 (ISBN 0-85941-049-8); pap. 9.95 (ISBN 0-85941-043-9). Herman Pub.
Crookston, Peter. Village London. 190p. 1979. pap. 5.95 (ISBN 0-500-27150-X). Thames Hudson.
Defoe, Daniel. Tour Thro' London About the Year 1725. Beeton, Mayson M. & Chancellor, E. Beresford, eds. LC 68-56542. (Illus.). Repr. of 1929 ed. 30.00 (ISBN 0-405-08441-2, Blom Pubns). Arno.
Denney, Martyn. London's Waterways. 1977. 19.95 (ISBN 0-7134-0558-9, Pub. by Batsford England). David & Charles.
Denney, Maryn. London & South-East England. 124p. 1980. 25.00x (ISBN 0-903485-71-0, Pub. by Moorland England). State Mutual Bk.
Dore, Gustave & Jerrold, Blanchard. London: A Pilgrimage. (Illus.). 1970. pap. 6.00 (ISBN 0-486-22306-X). Dover.
Feeney, Leonard. London Is a Place. 1951. 6.00 (ISBN 0-911218-02-5). Ravengate Pr.
Field, John. Place-Names of Greater London. LC 79-56447. (Illus.). 168p. 1980. 19.95 (ISBN 0-7134-2538-5, Pub. by Batsford England). David & Charles.
Fitch, Robert. London, a Pictorial & Literary Map. 1952. 2.00 (ISBN 0-911218-04-1). Ravengate Pr.
Fletcher, Geoffrey. Portraits of London. (Illus.). 9.95 (ISBN 0-901571-95-4, Pub. by Kingsmead Pr England). State Mutual Bk.
Ford, Ford M. The Soul of London. LC 72-91. (English Literature Ser., No. 33). 1972. Repr. of 1911 ed. lib. bdg. 38.95 (ISBN 0-8383-1407-4). Haskell.
Godfrey, Walter H., ed. The Parish of St. Pancras, Part 4: King's Cross Neighbourhood. LC 76-37851. (London County Council. Survey of London: No. 24). Repr. of 1952 ed. 74.50 (ISBN 0-404-51674-2). AMS Pr.
Greater London Council. Survey of London. Incl. Vol. 31-32. St. James, Westminister, Pt. 2. text ed. 78.00x (ISBN 0-485-41831-2); Vol. 33-34. St. Anne, Soho. text ed. 91.00x (ISBN 0-485-48233-9); Vol. 35. Theatre Royal, Drury Lane, & the Royal Opera House, Covent Garden; Vol. 36. St. Paul, Covent Garden. text ed. 78.00x (ISBN 0-485-48236-3); Vol. 37. Northern Kensington. text ed. 78.00x (ISBN 0-485-48237-1). Athlone Pr). Humanities.
Hanff, Helene. The Duchess of Bloomsbury Street. LC 73-1801. 144p. 1973. 6.95 (ISBN 0-397-00976-3). Har-Row.
Hart, Douglas. Strategic Planning in London: The Rise & Fall of the Primary Road Network. Urban & Regional Planning Advisory Committee, ed. 239p. 1976. text ed. 18.75 (ISBN 0-08-019780-9). Pergamon.
Hauff, Helene. The Duchess of Bloomsbury Street. 1976. pap. 3.95 (ISBN 0-380-00634-0, 50385). Avon.
Hogg, Garry, ed. The Batsford Colour Book of London. 95p. 1971. 10.50x (ISBN 0-7134-0021-8). Intl Pubns Serv.
--The Batsford Colour Book of London. 95p. 1971. 10.50x (ISBN 0-7134-0021-8). Intl Pubns Serv.
Howard, Philip. London's River. LC 76-28032. (Illus.). 1977. 15.00 (ISBN 0-312-49595-1). St Martin.
Hyatt, Alfred H. The Charm of London. 1976. lib. bdg. 59.95 (ISBN 0-8490-1597-9). Gordon Pr.
James, Henry. A London Life, 4 vols. in one. Incl. The Patagonia; Mrs. Temperly. 1978. Repr. of 1889 ed. lib. bdg. 30.00 (ISBN 0-8495-2707-4). Arden Lib.
Jarvis, Stan. Around the Historic City of London. 128p. 1981. 25.00x (ISBN 0-7135-1249-0, Pub. by Bell & Hyman England). State Mutual Bk.
Jefferies, Greg. Port of London. (Jackdaw Ser: No. 81). 1970. 6.95 (ISBN 0-670-56532-6, Grossman). Viking Pr.
Kemnitz, Milton N. London & Back: A Book of Personal Drawings. (Illus.). 120p. 1977. 12.50 (ISBN 0-89824-009-3). Trillium Pr.
The Kennedys Abroad: Ann & Peter in London. Date not set. 9.50 (ISBN 0-392-08636-0, SpS). Sportshelf.
London at Dinner. LC 71-94356. Repr. of 1858 ed. 3.50x (ISBN 0-678-05658-7). Kelley.
London County Council. Survey of London, 36 Vols. Sheppard, F. W., et al, eds. Repr. of 1970 ed. write for info (ISBN 0-404-51650-5). AMS Pr.
London in 48 Hours. 1977. pap. 1.50 (ISBN 0-8277-5105-2). British Bk Ctr.
London Magazine. Coming to London. facsimile ed. Lehmann, John, ed. LC 73-152189. (Essay Index Reprint Ser). Repr. of 1957 ed. 15.00 (ISBN 0-8369-2409-6). Arno.
Lowe, David, ed. Thirty-Two Picture Postcards of Old London. (Dover Picture Postcard Ser.). (Illus.). 1978. pap. 2.25 (ISBN 0-486-23539-4). Dover.
Mace, Rodney. Trafalgar Square: Emblem of Empire. (Illus.). 1976. text ed. 20.00x (ISBN 0-85315-368-X). Humanities.
Macmillan, Iain & Baker, Roger. Book of London. LC 69-14436. (Illus.). 1969. 14.95 (ISBN 0-8008-0925-4). Taplinger.
Menen, Aubrey. London. (Great Cities Ser.). (Illus.). 1976. 14.95 (ISBN 0-8094-2254-9). Time-Life.
Moholy-Nagy, L. & Benedetta, Mary. The Street Markets of London. LC 72-84542. (Illus.). Repr. of 1936 ed. 20.00 (ISBN 0-405-08792-6, Pub. by Blom). Arno.
Newman, E. M. Seeing London. 59.95 (ISBN 0-8490-1017-9). Gordon Pr.
Nicholson Publications. Nicholson's American's London. 1978. pap. 2.95 (ISBN 0-684-15641-5, SL795, ScribT). Scribner.
--Nicholson's Complete London. 1978. pap. 5.95 (ISBN 0-684-15640-7, SL794, ScribT). Scribner.
Ordish, Thomas F. Shakespeare's London: A Study of London in the Reign of Queen Elizabeth. LC 72-144667. Repr. of 1897 ed. 18.45 (ISBN 0-404-07957-1). AMS Pr.
Palmer, Geoffrey & Lloyd, Noel. The Observer's Book of London. (The Observer Bks). (Illus.). 1979. 3.95 (ISBN 0-684-16027-7, ScribT). Scribner.
The Parish of Chelsea, Part 4: The Royal Hospital, Chelsea. LC 71-138271. (London County Council. Survey of London: No. 11). Repr. of 1927 ed. 74.50 (ISBN 0-404-51661-0). AMS Pr.
Pennell, Joseph. Haunts of Old London. facsimile ed. LC 71-164620. (Select Bibliographies Reprint Ser). Repr. of 1914 ed. 12.00 (ISBN 0-8369-5903-5). Arno.
Pocock, Tom. London Walks: Forty Walks Around London. 1981. 6.50 (ISBN 0-911268-37-5). Rogers Bk.
Shepherd, Thomas & Elmes, James. Metropolitan Improvements, Or, London in the Nineteenth Century. LC 67-13342. (Illus.). Repr. of 1828 ed. 20.00 (ISBN 0-405-08963-5). Arno.
Shepherd, Thomas H. & Elmes, James. London & Its Environs in the 19th Century. LC 67-13341. (Illus.). Repr. of 1829 ed. 20.00 (ISBN 0-405-08962-7). Arno.
Stephenson, Henry T. Shakespeare's London. LC 74-176435. Repr. of 1905 ed. 24.50 (ISBN 0-404-06258-X). AMS Pr.
Stow, John. Survey of London. 1956. 14.95x (ISBN 0-460-00589-8, Evman). Biblio Dist.
Summerson, John. The Architecture of Victorian London. LC 75-16130. (Illus.). 1976. 10.95x (ISBN 0-8139-0592-3). U Pr of Va.
Thompson, Godfrey. London's Statues. LC 70-871500. (Illus.). 1971. 6.50x (ISBN 0-460-03939-3). Intl Pubns Serv.
Turner, John H. London, Brighton & South Coast Railway, Vol. 1. 1977. 30.00 (ISBN 0-7134-0275-X, Pub. by Batsford England). David & Charles.
--London, Brighton & South Coast Railway, Vol. 2. 1978. 30.00 (ISBN 0-7134-1198-8, Pub. by Batsford England). David & Charles.
--London, Brighton & South Coast Railway, Vol. 3. 1979. 30.00 (ISBN 0-7134-1389-1, Pub. by Batsford England). David & Charles.
What Goes on in the City. 1977. cased 10.00 (ISBN 0-85941-040-4); 5.00 (ISBN 0-85941-018-8). State Mutual Bk.
Williams, Guy. Let's Look at London. (Illus.). 12.50x (ISBN 0-392-03730-0, LTB). Sportshelf.
--London Walks. 1981. 15.00x (ISBN 0-09-462740-1, Pub. by Constable Pubs). State Mutual Bk.

LONDON–DESCRIPTION–GUIDEBOOKS

AA-BTA Book of London. (Illus.). 196p. 1980. pap. 18.95 (ISBN 0-86145-020-5, Pub. by B T A). Merrimack Bk Serv.
AA London Map. rev. ed. pap. 2.95 (ISBN 0-901088-99-4, Pub. by B T A). Merrimack Bk Serv.
Alter, Richard C. The Tired Tourists Concise Guide to London. (Illus.). 96p. 1978. pap. 3.00 (ISBN 0-89726-002-3). Foldabook Pub.
Arthur Frommer's Guide to London, 1981-82. 224p. 1981. pap. 2.95 (ISBN 0-671-41434-8). Frommer-Pasmantier.
Automobile Association & British Tourist Authority. A-Z Visitors' London Atlas & Guide. (Illus.). 96p. 1981. pap. 3.50 3-copy minimum order (ISBN 0-85039-107-5, Pub. by Auto Assn-British Tourist Authority England). Merrimack Bk Serv.
Barish & Schla. Seeing the Real London. 1982. pap. 7.95 (ISBN 0-8120-2241-6). Barron.
Berger, Jason & Berger, Susanna. London in Your Pocket. Price, Diana, ed. (Grosset Travel Guide Ser.). 1979. pap. 1.95 (ISBN 0-448-16636-4). G&D.
Blue Guide - London. 1978. 25.95 (ISBN 0-528-84638-8); pap. 16.95 (ISBN 0-528-84637-X). Rand.
The Blue Jeans Guide to London. (Illus.). 176p. 1981. pap. 3.95 (ISBN 0-7064-1464-0, Pub. by Octopus). Smith Pubs.
Bowman, Leona, ed. The Indespensable Shopping Guide. Jenkins, Jo-An. McColl, Patricia, ed. LC 79-55613. 1980. pap. 8.95 (ISBN 0-689-11030-8). Atheneum.
British Tourist Authority. Discovering London's Villages. (Illus.). 72p. 1981. pap. 2.95 (ISBN 0-85263-451-X, Pub. by Auto Assn-British Tourist Authority England). Merrimack Bk Serv.
Byron, Arthur. A Guide to London's Statues. 1981. 15.00x (ISBN 0-09-463430-0, Pub. by Constable Pubs). State Mutual Bk.
Clarke, William M. Inside the City. 1979. 19.50 (ISBN 0-04-332070-8). Allen Unwin.
Color Guide to London. 1978. pap. 3.95 (ISBN 0-8277-5644-5). British Bk Ctr.
Colourmaster. London's Pageantry. (Travel in England Ser.). (Illus.). 64p. 1975. 7.95 (ISBN 0-85933-110-5). Transatlantic.
Complete London Guide. (Nicholson Guides Ser.). 1981. pap. 10.95 (ISBN 0-684-16975-4). Scribner.
Cruickshank, Dan & Wyld, Peter. London: The Art of Georgian Building. (Illus.). 256p. 1975. 40.00 (ISBN 0-8038-0143-2). Hastings.
Donald, Elsie B. London Shopping Guide. (Penguin Handbooks Ser.). (Illus.). 1978. pap. 2.95 (ISBN 0-14-046222-8). Penguin.
Fodor's London, 1981. 1981. 9.95 (ISBN 0-679-00705-9); pap. 5.95 (ISBN 0-679-00706-7). McKay.
Goddard, Donald. Blimey! Another Book About London. new ed. LC 72-188175. (Illus.). 214p. 1972. 7.95 (ISBN 0-8129-0269-6); pap. 4.95 (ISBN 0-8129-6210-9). Times Bks.
Kay, F. George. London. LC 79-89188. (A Rand McNally Pocket Guide). (Illus., Orig.). 1980. pap. 3.95 (ISBN 0-528-84288-9). Rand.
Kent, William. London for Americans. 1950. 20.00 (ISBN 0-89984-023-X). Century Bookbindery.
--London for Americans. 1979. Repr. of 1950 ed. lib. bdg. 20.00 (ISBN 0-8495-3033-4). Arden Lib.
Kutcher, Arthur. Looking at London: Illustrated Walks Through a Changing City. (Illus.). 1978. pap. 6.95 (ISBN 0-500-27124-0). Thames Hudson.
Lawson, Andrew. Discover Unexpected London. LC 77-82736. (Illus.). 1978. 8.95 (ISBN 0-8467-0369-6, Pub. by Two Continents). Hippocrene Bks.
London. 65th ed. (Red Guides Ser). (Illus.). 1972. 5.00x (ISBN 0-7063-5409-5). Intl Pubns Serv.
The London Fashion Guide: Spring 1976. 1976. pap. 5.95 (ISBN 0-8277-4679-2). British Bk Ctr.
London, Your Sightseeing Guide. rev. ed. (Illus.). 92p. 1980. pap. 2.95 (ISBN 0-7095-0147-1, Pub. by B T A). Merrimack Bk Serv.
London's Restaurants. (Nicholson Guides Ser.). 1981. pap. 4.95 (ISBN 0-684-16996-7). Scribner.
Magi, G. London: A Complete Guide for Visiting the City. (Illus.). 159p. (Orig.). 1978. pap. 9.00x (ISBN 88-7009-041-8). Intl Pubns Serv.
Meiland, Jack. First Time in London. LC 78-21547. 1979. pap. 5.95 (ISBN 0-684-16505-8, ScribT). Scribner.
Michelin. Michelin Green Guide London. 2nd ed. 1980. pap. 7.95 (ISBN 2-06-015431-6). Michelin.
Michelin Guides & Maps. Michelin Green Guide to Londres. 2nd ed. (Green Guide Ser.). (Fr.). 1976. pap. 7.95 (ISBN 2-06-005420-6). Michelin.
--Michelin Red Guide to London. (Red Guide Ser.). 1981. pap. 3.25 (ISBN 2-06-006601-8). Michelin.
Moldvay, Albert & Fabian, Erika. Photographing London. (Amphoto Travel Guide Ser.). (Illus.). 1980. pap. 5.95 (ISBN 0-8174-2125-4). Amphoto.
Nicholson Publications. Nicholson's Student's London. LC 72-12167. 1978. pap. 2.45 (ISBN 0-684-15639-3, ScribT). Scribner.
Nicholson's Publications. Nicholson's London Guide. rev. ed. (Illus.). 1978. pap. 3.45 (ISBN 0-684-15751-9, SL800, ScribT). Scribner.
Off-Beat Walks in London. rev. ed. 56p. 1980. pap. 2.95 (ISBN 0-85263-378-5, Pub. by B T A). Merrimack Bk Serv.
Plimmer, Charlotte & Plimmer, Denis. London: A Visitor's Companion. (Illus.). 1977. 10.95 (ISBN 0-393-04488-2). Norton.
Prowse, Philip. This Is London: Heinemann Guided Readers Ser. (Illus.). 1977. pap. 1.50x (ISBN 0-435-27045-1). Heinemann Ed.
Rickards, Maurice. Where They Lived in London: A Guide to Famous Doorsteps. LC 72-145542. (Illus.). 112p. 1972. 7.95 (ISBN 0-8008-8245-8). Taplinger.
Rubin, Cynthia & Rubin, Jerome. London Dining Out. LC 74-81275. (International Dining Out Ser.). (Orig.). 1974. pap. 2.50 (ISBN 0-88278-024-7). Emporium Pubns.
Vevers, Gwynne. London's Zoo. LC 76-363958. (Illus.). 1979. 12.50 (ISBN 0-370-10440-4, Pub. by Chatto Bodley Jonathan). Merrimack Bk Serv.
Visitor's London. (Nicholson Guides Ser.). 1981. pap. 3.95 (ISBN 0-684-16976-2). Scribner.
Warinner, Emily V. A Royal Journey to London. LC 75-28654. 1975. pap. 2.95 (ISBN 0-914916-11-4). Topgallant.
Wittich, John. Discovering London Street Names. (Discovering Ser.). 96p. (Orig.). (gr. 6 up). 1977. pap. 2.50 (ISBN 0-913714-09-7). Legacy Bks.

LONDON–DESCRIPTION–POETRY

Irving, William H. John Gay's London, Illustrated from the Poetry of the Time. (Illus.). 1968. Repr. of 1928 ed. 25.00 (ISBN 0-208-00618-4, Archon). Shoe String.

LONDON–DIRECTORIES

Balfour, Michael. Help Yourself in London: A Guide to Services, Facilities & Things to Do. 1970. 4.00x (ISBN 0-900391-37-5). Intl Pubns Serv.
Investors Chronicle. City Directory: An Investors Chronicle Guide to Financial & Professional Services Allied to the City of London. 376p. 1980. pap. 20.00x (ISBN 0-85941-083-8). Herman Pub.
Pygott, D., ed. The City Directory. 1977. soft 18.00 (ISBN 0-685-77759-6); cased 25.00 (ISBN 0-85941-046-3). State Mutual Bk.
Thomas, David J., intro. by. Three Victorian Telephone Directories. Incl. Bk. 1. The United Telephone Company's Professions & Trades Classified Directory of 1885; Bk. 2. The United Telephone Company's Instructions for the Use of Exchange Lines & the South of England Telephone Company's (Brighton) Directory of 1885; Bk. 3. The London & Globe Telephone & Maintainance Company's Directory 1884. LC 70-101259. Repr. of 1884 ed. 12.50x (ISBN 0-678-05678-1). Kelley.
Woodhead-Faulkner, ed. The City Directory 1980-81: An Investors Chronicle Guide to Financial & Professional Services Allied to the City of London. 432p. 1980. 45.00x (ISBN 0-85941-135-4, Pub. by Woodhead-Faulkner England); pap. 36.00x (ISBN 0-85941-136-2). State Mutual Bk.

LONDON–ECONOMIC CONDITIONS

Gibson-Jarvie, Robert. The City of London: A Financial & Commercial History. (Illus.). 128p. 1980. 17.50 (ISBN 0-85941-090-0). Herman Pub.
Hausman, William J. Public Policy & the Supply of Coal to London, 1700-1770. Bruchey, Stuart, ed. LC 80-2809. (Dissertations in European Economic History II). (Illus.). 1981. lib. bdg. 28.00x (ISBN 0-405-13993-4). Arno.
Morgan, E. Victor, et al. City Lights: Essays on Financial Institutions & Markets in the City of London, No. 19. (Orig.). 1979. technical 5.95 (ISBN 0-255-36119-X). Transatlantic.
Pendrill, Charles. London Life in the Fourteenth Century. LC 79-118495. 1971. Repr. of 1925 ed. 17.50 (ISBN 0-8046-1243-9). Kennikat.
Sheppard, Francis. London, Eighteen Eight Eighteen Seventy: The Infernal Wen. LC 71-142067. (History of London Series). (Illus.). 1971. 30.00x (ISBN 0-520-01847-8). U of Cal Pr.
Sutherland, Lucy S. London Merchant. new ed. 164p. 1962. 24.00x (ISBN 0-7146-1515-3, F Cass Co). Biblio Dist.
Woodhead-Faulkner, ed. The City Directory 1980-81: An Investors Chronicle Guide to Financial & Professional Services Allied to the City of London. 432p. 1980. 45.00x (ISBN 0-85941-135-4, Pub. by Woodhead-Faulkner England); pap. 36.00x (ISBN 0-85941-136-2). State Mutual Bk.

LONDON–FIRE, 1666

Bell, Walter G. Great Fire of London in 1666. LC 70-114464. (Illus.). 1971. Repr. of 1920 ed. lib. bdg. 20.00x (ISBN 0-8371-4774-3, BEGF). Greenwood.

LONDON–FIRE, 1666–FICTION

Ainsworth, W. Harrison. Old Saint Paul's. 1968. 5.00x (ISBN 0-460-00522-7, Evman). Biblio Dist.

LONDON–GALLERIES AND MUSEUMS

Early Netherlandish School. 1975. text ed. 10.00x (ISBN 0-8277-3173-6). British Bk Ctr.
French School. 1975. text ed. 5.95x (ISBN 0-8277-3174-4). British Bk Ctr.
Friedman, Winnifred H. Boydell's Shakespeare Gallery. LC 75-23791. (Outstanding Dissertations in the Fine Arts - 17th & 18th Century). (Illus.). 1976. lib. bdg. 45.00 (ISBN 0-8240-1987-3). Garland Pub.
Ragghianti, Carlo L. National Gallery: London. LC 73-109885. (Great Museums of the World Ser.). (Illus.). 1968. 16.95 (ISBN 0-88225-231-3). Newsweek.

LONDON–GREAT EXHIBITION OF THE WORKS OF INDUSTRY OF ALL NATIONS, 1851

Art-Journal. Crystal Palace Exhibition Illustrated Catalogue: London, 1851. Orig. Title: Art-Journal Illustrated Catalogue. (Illus.). 1970. pap. 7.95 (ISBN 0-486-22503-8). Dover.

Crystal Palace Exhibition: Illustrated Catalogue, London, 1851. (Unabr. republication of Art Journal). 7.50 (ISBN 0-8446-4532-X). Peter Smith.
Great Exhibition-London 1851: The Art Journal Illustrated Catalogue of the Industries of All Nations. (Bounty Bks). (Illus.). 1970. pap. 2.95 (ISBN 0-517-02792-5). Crown.
Langdon-Davies, John. Great Exhibition, Eighteen Fifty-One. (Jackdaw Ser: No. 43). (Illus.). 1968. 6.95 (ISBN 0-670-34888-0, Grossman). Viking Pr.

LONDON–HISTORIOGRAPHY

Rubinstein, Stanley. Historians of London: An Account of the Many Surveys, Histories, Perambulations, Maps & Engravings Made About the City & Its Environs, & of the Dedicated Londoners Who Made Them. (Illus.). 1968. 18.50 (ISBN 0-208-00660-5, Archon). Shoe String.

LONDON–HISTORY

Adburgham, Alison. Shopping in Style: London from the Restoration to Edwardian Elegance. (Illus.). 1979. 14.95 (ISBN 0-500-01205-9). Thames Hudson.
Altick, Richard D. The Shows of London. LC 77-2755. 1978. 35.00 (ISBN 0-674-80731-6, Belknap Pr). Harvard U Pr.
Aungier, George J., ed. Croniques de London. Bd. with The French Chronicle of London. LC 77-161712. (Camden Society First Ser.: No. 28). (Eng. & Fr.). Repr. of 1844 ed. 14.00 (ISBN 0-404-50128-1). AMS Pr.
Barker, Felix & Jackson, Peter. London: Two Thousand Years of a City & Its People. rev. ed. 388p. 1974. 27.50 (ISBN 0-02-507120-3). Macmillan.
Bermant, Chaim. Point of Arrival. LC 75-22453. (Illus.). 304p. 1976. 10.95 (ISBN 0-02-510090-4, 51009). Macmillan.
Besant, Walter. London. 1892. lib. bdg. 50.00 (ISBN 0-8492-3723-8). R West.
Betjeman, John. Victorian & Edwardian London. 1969. pap. 13.50 (ISBN 0-7134-2185-1, Pub. by Batsford England). David & Charles.
Blacker, Harry. Just Like It Was: Memoirs of the Mittel East. (Illus.). 192p. 1974. 14.50x (ISBN 0-85303-178-9, Pub. by Vallentine Mitchell England). Biblio Dist.
Broad, Lewis. The Friendships & Follies of Oscar Wilde. LC 79-8056. Repr. of 1954 ed. 29.50 (ISBN 0-404-18367-0). AMS Pr.
Brooke, Christopher. London, Eight Hundred to Twelve Sixteen: The Shaping of a City. LC 73-92620. (The History of London Ser). (Illus.). 1975. 35.00x (ISBN 0-520-02686-1). U of Cal Pr.
Brown, R. Douglas. The Port of London. (Illus.). 1979. 15.00x (ISBN 0-900963-87-5, Pub. by Terence Dalton England). State Mutual Bk.
Chancellor, E. Beresford. The London of Charles Dickens. 1976. lib. bdg. 59.95 (ISBN 0-8490-2182-0). Gordon Pr.
Chancellor, Edwin B. The London of Charles Dickens. LC 78-14818. 1978. Repr. of 1924 ed. lib. bdg. 35.00 (ISBN 0-8414-0053-9). Folcroft.
City of London Through Five Centuries. pap. 2.95 (ISBN 0-8277-2438-1). British Bk Ctr.
Compton-Rickett, Arthur. The London Life of Yesterday. 1979. Repr. of 1909 ed. lib. bdg. 40.00 (ISBN 0-8482-7573-X). Norwood Edns.
Croniques De London, Depuis L'an Quarante-Quatre Henry Trois' Jusqu'a L'an Dix-Sept Edward Trois' 1844. 15.50 (ISBN 0-384-10225-5). Johnson Repr.
Crookston, Peter. Village London. 190p. 1979. pap. 5.95 (ISBN 0-500-27150-X). Thames Hudson.
De Angeli, Marguerite. The Door in the Wall: Story of Medieval London. LC 64-7025. (gr. 3-6). 7.95a (ISBN 0-385-07283-X); PLB (ISBN 0-385-05743-1); pap. 1.95 (ISBN 0-385-07909-5). Doubleday.
Egan, Pierce. Life in London; or the Day & Night Scenes of Jerry Hawthorn, Esq. & Corinthian Tom. LC 79-8260. Repr. of 1821 ed. 44.50 (ISBN 0-404-61841-3). AMS Pr.
Fitz-Thedmar, Arnold. De Antiquis Legibus Liber. Repr. of 1846 ed. 46.00 (ISBN 0-384-15820-X). Johnson Repr.
Fredette, Raymond H. The Sky on Fire: The First Battle of Britain. LC 75-33909. 290p. 1976. pap. 5.25 (ISBN 0-15-682750-6, HB329, Harv). HarBraceJ.
Gairdner, James, ed. Historical Collections of a Citizen of London in the Fifteenth Century. Repr. of 1876 ed. 22.50 (ISBN 0-384-17560-0). Johnson Repr.
Gonzales, Manuel. London in Seventeen Thirty-One. Repr. of 1888 ed. 15.00 (ISBN 0-685-43202-5). Norwood Edns.
Gray, Robert. A History of London. LC 78-22605. 1979. 9.95 (ISBN 0-8008-3884-X); pap. 5.95 (ISBN 0-8008-3885-8). Taplinger.
Greater London Council. Survey of London, Vol. 39: The Grosvenor Estate in Mayfair, Part. 1, General History. (Survey of London Ser.). 1977. text ed. 78.00x (ISBN 0-485-48239-8, Athlone Pr). Humanities.
Hausman, William J. Public Policy & the Supply of Coal to London, 1700-1770. Bruchey, Stuart, ed. LC 80-2809. (Dissertations in European Economic History II). (Illus.). 1981. lib. bdg. 28.00x (ISBN 0-405-13993-4). Arno.
Heal, Ambrose. London Tradesmen's Cards of the XVIII Century. (Illus.). 8.75 (ISBN 0-8446-2227-3). Peter Smith.
Holme, Thea. Chelsea. LC 74-162963. (Illus.). 1972. 12.95 (ISBN 0-8008-1440-1). Taplinger.
Holmes, Thomas. London's Underworld. 1979. Repr. of 1912 ed. lib. bdg. 30.00 (ISBN 0-8482-4485-0). Norwood Edns.
Home, Gordon. A History of London. 1929. Repr. 10.00 (ISBN 0-685-43039-1). Norwood Edns.
Hoppe, E. O. The London of George VI. 1937. 20.00 (ISBN 0-686-17240-X). Scholars Ref Lib.
Howgego, James. London in the Twenties & Thirties from Old Photographs. (Illus.). 1978. 19.95 (ISBN 0-7134-3281-0, Pub. by Batsford England). David & Charles.
--Victorian & Edwardian City of London. 1977. 14.95 (ISBN 0-7134-0598-8, Pub. by Batsford England). David & Charles.
Humpherus, Henry. The History of the Origin & Progress of the Company of Watermen & Lightermen on the River Thames, 3 vols. 1500p. 1981. Repr. of 1886 ed. Set. lib. bdg. 150.00 (ISBN 0-88354-150-5, Pub. by EP Microform). Vol. I (ISBN 0-88354-151-3). Vol. II (ISBN 0-88354-152-1). Vol. III (ISBN 0-88354-153-X). Clearwater Pub.
James, Henry. The Siege of London. 59.95 (ISBN 0-8490-1053-5). Gordon Pr.
Kingsford, Charles L. Chronicles of London. 368p. 1977. Repr. of 1905 ed. 23.00x (ISBN 0-87471-984-4). Rowman.
Lewis, Wilmarth S. Three Tours Through London in the Years 1748, 1776, 1797. LC 77-104252. (Illus.). 1971. Repr. of 1941 ed. lib. bdg. 15.00x (ISBN 0-8371-3977-5, LETL). Greenwood.
Lindsay, Jack. The Monster City: Defoe's London, 1688-1730. LC 78-58316. 1978. 17.95x (ISBN 0-312-54612-2). St Martin.
McClure, Ruth K. Coram's Children: The London Foundling Hospital in the Eighteenth Century. LC 80-21375. (Illus.). 336p. 1981. text ed. 27.50 (ISBN 0-300-02465-7). Yale U Pr.
McDonnell, Kevin. Medieval London Suburbs. (Illus.). 196p. 1978. 21.00x (ISBN 0-8476-2266-5). Rowman.
Machin, Henry. Diary of Henry Machyn. Nichols, John G., ed. (Camden Society, London. Publications. First Ser.: No. 42). Repr. of 1848 ed. 42.00 (ISBN 0-404-50142-7). AMS Pr.
Margetson, Stella. Fifty Years of Victorian London. Date not set. 5.95 (ISBN 0-8038-7737-4). Hastings.
Mearns, Andrew. Bitter Cry of Outcast London. LC 76-11185. Repr. of 1883 ed. 6.50x (ISBN 0-678-08022-4). Kelley.
Metcalf, Priscilla. The Halls of the Fishmongers' Company: An Architectural History of a Riverside Site. (Illus.). 214p. 1977. 36.00x (ISBN 0-8476-1386-0). Rowman.
Mingay, G. E. Georgian London. 1975. 33.00 (ISBN 0-7134-3045-1, Pub. by Batsford England). David & Charles.
Myers, A. R. London in the Age of Chaucer. LC 73-177342. (Centers of Civilization Ser.: Vol. 31). 200p. 1972. 7.95 (ISBN 0-8061-0997-1). U of Okla Pr.
Olsen, Donald J. The Growth of Victorian London. LC 76-25164. (Illus.). 1976. text ed. 32.50x (ISBN 0-8419-0284-4). Holmes & Meier.
Ordish, T. P. Shakespeare's London. 59.95 (ISBN 0-8490-1043-8). Gordon Pr.
Parsons, F. The Earlier Inhabitants of London. 59.95 (ISBN 0-8490-0065-3). Gordon Pr.
Parsons, F. G. Earlier Inhabitants of London. LC 78-118492. 1971. Repr. of 1927 ed. 13.00 (ISBN 0-8046-1240-4). Kennikat.
Passingham, W. J. Romance of London's Underground. LC 72-80705. (Illus.). Repr. of 1932 ed. 25.00 (ISBN 0-405-08839-6). Arno.
Pearton, Maurice. The L. S. O. at Seventy: A History of the London Symphony Orchestra. (Illus.). 240p. 1974. 12.50x (ISBN 0-575-01763-5). Intl Pubns Serv.
Pendrill, Charles. London Life in the Fourteenth Century. LC 79-118495. 1971. Repr. of 1925 ed. 17.50 (ISBN 0-8046-1243-9). Kennikat.
--London Life in the Fourteenth Century. 1976. lib. bdg. 59.95 (ISBN 0-8490-2181-2). Gordon Pr.
Prothero, Iowerth. Artisans & Politics in Early Nineteenth-Century London: John Gast & His Times. LC 78-71958. 1979. 30.00x (ISBN 0-8071-0570-8). La State U Pr.
Ramsay, G. D. The City of London in International Politics at the Accession of Elizabeth Tudor. 310p. 1975. 22.50x (ISBN 0-87471-646-2). Rowman.
Rasmussen, Steen E. London: The Unique City. rev. ed. (Illus.). Date not set. pap. 9.95 (ISBN 0-262-68027-0). MIT Pr.
Rude, George. Hanoverian London, 1714-1808. LC 69-10590. (History of London Series). (Illus.). 1971. 25.00x (ISBN 0-520-01778-1). U of Cal Pr.
Salgado, Gamini. The Elizabethan Underworld. (Illus.). 221p. 1977. 12.50x (ISBN 0-87471-967-4). Rowman.
Samuel, Raphael, ed. East End Underworld, Vol. 2: The Life of Arthur Harding. (History Workshop Ser.). (Illus.). 400p. 1981. 32.00 (ISBN 0-7100-0725-6); pap. write for info. (ISBN 0-7100-0726-4). Routledge & Kegan.
Seaman, L. C. Life in Victorian London. 1973. 19.95 (ISBN 0-7134-1465-0, Pub. by Batsford England). David & Charles.
Service, Alastair. London, Nineteen Hundred. LC 78-68491. (Illus.). 1979. 40.00 (ISBN 0-8478-0214-0). Rizzoli Intl.
Sheppard, Francis. London, Eighteen Eight Eighteen Seventy: The Infernal Wen. LC 71-142067. (History of London Series). (Illus.). 1971. 30.00x (ISBN 0-520-01847-8). U of Cal Pr.
Stow, John. Survey of London. 1956. 14.95x (ISBN 0-460-00589-8, Evman). Biblio Dist.
Summerson, John. Georgian London. 3rd ed. (Illus.). 1978. 20.00 (ISBN 0-262-19173-3). MIT Pr.
--Georgian London. (Illus.). 1979. pap. 4.95 (ISBN 0-14-055138-7, Peregrine). Penguin.
The Parish of St. Mary Lambeth. The Parish of St. Mary Lambeth, Pt. 2. LC 74-6546. (London County Council Survey of London Ser.: No. 26). Repr. of 1956 ed. 74.50 (ISBN 0-404-51676-9). AMS Pr.
Thomas, A. H. & Thonley, I. D., eds. Great Chronicle of London. Repr. of 1938 ed. 47.50x (ISBN 0-678-00732-2). Kelley.
Tristan, Flora. Flora Tristan's London Journals. 1980. 20.00 (ISBN 0-89182-024-8). Charles River Bks.
Troyer, Howard W. Ned Ward of Grub Street: A Study of Sub-Literary London in the Eighteenth Century. (Illus.). 290p. 1968. 25.00x (ISBN 0-7146-1523-4, F Cass Co). Biblio Dist.
Walford, L. B. Memories of Victorian London. 1912. 25.00 (ISBN 0-8274-2719-0). R West.
Wheatley, H. B. London, Past & Present, 3 vols. 300.00 (ISBN 0-8490-0553-1). Gordon Pr.
Wheatley, Henry B. London, Past & Present: A Dictionary of Its History Associations & Traditions, 3 Vols. LC 68-17956. 1968. Repr. of 1891 ed. Set. 85.00 (ISBN 0-8103-3499-2). Gale.
Wohl, Anthony S. The Eternal Slum: Housing & Social Policy in Victorian London. (Studies in Urban History Ser.). (Illus.). 1977. lib. bdg. 29.95x (ISBN 0-7735-0311-0). McGill-Queens U Pr.
Wunderli, Richard M. London Church Courts & Society on the Eve of the Reformation: Ecclesiastical Courts in Pre-Reformation London. 1980. 12.50 (ISBN 0-686-64886-2, SAM7); pap. 5.00 (ISBN 0-910956-71-5). Medieval Acad.

LONDON–HOSPITALS

McClure, Ruth K. Coram's Children: The London Foundling Hospital in the Eighteenth Century. LC 80-21375. (Illus.). 336p. 1981. text ed. 27.50 (ISBN 0-300-02465-7). Yale U Pr.

LONDON–HOTELS, TAVERNS, ETC.

Robinson, Edward. The Early English Coffee House: With an Account of the First Use of Coffee. (Illus.). 240p. 1973. Repr. of 1893 ed. text ed. 9.00x (ISBN 0-85642-005-0). Humanities.
Timbs, John. Clubs & Club Life in London with Anecodotes of Its Famous Coffee-Houses, Hostelries, & Taverns from the Seventeenth Century to the Present Time. LC 66-28045. 1967. Repr. of 1872 ed. 19.00 (ISBN 0-8103-3262-0). Gale.

LONDON–INDUSTRIES

Dodd, George. Days at the Factories. LC 67-18569. (Illus.). Repr. of 1843 ed. 14.00x (ISBN 0-678-00262-2). Kelley.
--Days at the Factories; or, the Manufacturing Industry of Great Britain, Described & Illustrated by Numerous Engravings of Machines & Processes. (Illus.). 408p. 1975. Repr. of 1843 ed. 16.50x (ISBN 0-87471-620-9). Rowman.
Heal, Ambrose. The London Furniture Makers from the Restoration to the Victorian Era: 1660-1840. (Illus.). 11.00 (ISBN 0-8446-4752-7). Peter Smith.
Herbert, William. History of the Twelve Great Livery Companies of London, 2 Vols. LC 68-19812. Repr. of 1834 ed. 50.00x (ISBN 0-678-00365-3). Kelley.
Martin, John E. Greater London: An Industrial Geography. LC 66-21351. 1967. 9.50x (ISBN 0-226-50827-7). U of Chicago Pr.
Unwin, G., ed. Guilds & Companies of London. 4th ed. (Illus.). 401p. 1963. 27.50x (ISBN 0-7146-1366-5, F Cass Co). Biblio Dist.
Wilson, Aubrey. London's Industrial Heritage. LC 67-28482. (Illus.). 1967. 12.50x (ISBN 0-678-05747-8). Kelley.

LONDON–INTELLECTUAL LIFE

Klein, Hermann. Thirty Years of Musical Life in London. LC 78-2565. (Music Reprint Ser., 1978). (Illus.). 1978. Repr. of 1903 ed. lib. bdg. 32.50 (ISBN 0-306-77586-7). Da Capo.
Lang, Elsie M. Literary London: Addison, Boswell, Carlyle, Dickens, Goldsmith, Lamb, Johnson, Milton, Shakespeare, Thackeray. 1907. 25.00 (ISBN 0-8274-2956-8). R West.
Masson, David. Memories of London in the Forties. 1908. lib. bdg. 40.00 (ISBN 0-8414-6493-6). Folcroft.
Parsons, Florence M. Garrick & His Circle. LC 78-82837. (Illus.). 1906. 20.00 (ISBN 0-405-08836-1, Pub. by Blom). Arno.
Powell, Anthony. Messengers of Day. LC 78-4703. (Illus.). 1978. 10.95 (ISBN 0-03-020996-X). HR&W.
Rees, Thomas. Reminiscences of Literary London from 1779 - 1853. LC 68-24476. 1969. Repr. of 1896 ed. 19.00 (ISBN 0-8103-3888-2). Gale.
Robbins, Rae G. The Bloomsbury Group: A Selective Bibliography. 219p. 1978. 17.00 (ISBN 0-685-70087-9). Price Guide.
Rosenbaum, S. P., ed. The Bloomsbury Group: A Collection of Memoirs, Commentary & Criticism. 1975. 30.00x (ISBN 0-8020-2182-4); pap. 12.50 (ISBN 0-8020-6268-7). U of Toronto Pr.
Sanders, Lloyd. Holland House Circle. LC 70-82004. (Illus.). Repr. of 1908 ed. 20.00 (ISBN 0-405-08915-5). Arno.
Scholes, Percy A. Great Dr. Burney: His Life, His Travels, His Works, His Family & His Friends, 2 Vols. LC 74-104254. (Illus.). 1971. Repr. of 1948 ed. lib. bdg. 35.50x (ISBN 0-8371-4017-X, SCDB). Greenwood.
Weintraub, Stanley. The London Yankees: Portraits of American Writers & Artists in England, 1894-1914. Ellenboger, Eileen, tr. LC 78-22276. 1979. 14.95 (ISBN 0-15-152978-7). HarBraceJ.

LONDON–JUVENILE LITERATURE

De Mare, Eric. London's River: The Story of a City. (Illus.). 128p. 1978. 7.95 (ISBN 0-370-00846-4, Pub. by Chatto Bodley Jonathan). Merrimack Bk Serv.
Discovering London for Children. 88p. 1980. pap. 2.95 (ISBN 0-85263-429-3, Pub. by B T A). Merrimack Bk Serv.
Menen, Aubrey. London. (The Great Cities Ser.). (Illus.). (gr. 6 up). 1976. PLB 14.94 (ISBN 0-8094-2255-7, Pub by Time-Life). Silver.

LONDON–LIVERY COMPANIES

Hadley, Guy. Citizens & Founders: A History of the Worshipful Company of Founders, London 1365-1975. (Illus.). 199p. 1976. 45.00x (ISBN 0-8476-1385-2). Rowman.
Hazlitt, William C. Livery Companies of the City of London. LC 68-56529. (Illus.). 1969. Repr. of 1892 ed. 30.00 (ISBN 0-405-08504-4, Blom Pubns). Arno.
Kahl, William F. The Development of the London Livery Companies. (Kress Library of Business & Economics: No. 15). (Illus.). 1960. pap. 5.00x (ISBN 0-678-09910-3, Baker Lib). Kelley.

LONDON–MAPS

Automobile Association British Tourist Authority. A-Z London Map. (Illus.). 1981. pap. 2.95 3-copy minimum order (ISBN 0-85039-021-4, Pub. by Auto Assn-British Tourist Authority England). Merrimack Bk Serv.
Fitch, Robert. London, a Pictorial & Literary Map. 1952. 2.00 (ISBN 0-911218-04-1). Ravengate Pr.
Jones, E. & Sinclair, D. J. Atlas of London. 1969. 205.00 (ISBN 0-08-013255-3). Pergamon.
London: Two Maps. pap. 2.50 (ISBN 0-8277-2435-7). British Bk Ctr.
Pocket Atlas of Central London. pap. 1.95 (ISBN 0-8277-2437-3). British Bk Ctr.
Sugden, Edward H. Topographical Dictionary to the Works of Shakespeare & His Fellow Dramatists. 1969. Repr. of 1925 ed. 66.75 (ISBN 3-4870-2702-X). Adler.

LONDON–MARKETS

Dodd, George. The Food of London. LC 75-27635. (World Food Supply Ser). 1976. Repr. of 1856 ed. 31.00x (ISBN 0-405-07777-7). Arno.
King, Wilfred T. History of the London Discount Market. 355p. 1972. Repr. of 1936 ed. 32.50x (ISBN 0-7146-1231-6, F Cass Co). Biblio Dist.
The Lawes of the Market. LC 74-80198. (English Experience Ser.: No. 676). 22p. 1974. Repr. of 1595 ed. 3.50 (ISBN 90-221-0676-4). Walter J Johnson.
Moholy-Nagy, L. & Benedetta, Mary. The Street Markets of London. LC 72-84542. (Illus.). Repr. of 1936 ed. 20.00 (ISBN 0-405-08792-6, Pub. by Blom). Arno.

LONDON–MUSIC-HALLS (VARIETY-THEATERS, CABARETS, ETC.)

Short, Ernest H. & Compton-Rickett, Arthur. Ring up the Curtain. facsimile ed. LC 78-114895. (Select Bibliographies Reprint Ser). 1938. 20.00 (ISBN 0-8369-5299-5). Arno.

LONDON–PARKS

Cecil, Mrs. Evelyn. London Parks & Gardens. 1981. Repr. of 1907 ed. lib. bdg. 75.00 (ISBN 0-8495-0759-6). Arden Lib.

Saunders, Ann. Regent's Park. LC 69-11238. (Illus.). 1969. 12.95x (ISBN 0-678-05625-0). Kelley.

LONDON–PLAGUE

see Plague–London

LONDON–POLICE

Colquhoun, Patrick. Treatise on the Commerce & Police of the River Thames. LC 69-14917. (Criminology, Law Enforcement, & Social Problems Ser.: No. 41). (Map). 1969. Repr. of 1800 ed. 30.00 (ISBN 0-87585-041-3). Patterson Smith.

--Treatise on the Police of the Metropolis. 7th ed. LC 69-14918. (Criminology, Law Enforcement, & Social Problems Ser.: No. 42). 1969. Repr. of 1806 ed. 30.00 (ISBN 0-87585-042-1). Patterson Smith.

Garforth, John. A Day in the Life of a Victorian Policeman. (Victorian Day Ser.). 1974. pap. text ed. 5.95x (ISBN 0-04-942123-9). Allen Unwin.

Miller, Wilbur. Cops & Bobbies: Police Authority in New York & London, 1830-70. LC 76-27847. 1977. 16.00x (ISBN 0-226-52595-3). U of Chicago Pr.

Pearce, Philippa & Scott, Harold R. From Inside Scotland Yard. (Illus.). (gr. 4-7). 1965. 3.50 (ISBN 0-02-781360-6). Macmillan.

Scott, Harold. Scotland Yard. 1954. 25.00 (ISBN 0-89984-236-4). Century Bookbindery.

Select Committee on Police. Report from the Select Committee on Police of the Metropolis. LC 74-156286. (Police in Great Britain Ser). 1971. Repr. of 1828 ed. 22.00 (ISBN 0-405-03397-4). Arno.

Wilkes, J. The London Police in the Nineteenth Century. LC 76-57247. (Cambridge Introduction to the History of Mankind Ser.). (Illus.). 1977. 3.95 (ISBN 0-521-21406-8). Cambridge U Pr.

LONDON–POLITICS AND GOVERNMENT

Ashton, R. The City & the Court: Sixteen Hundred & Three to Sixteen Forty-Three. LC 78-67296. 1979. 29.50 (ISBN 0-521-22419-5). Cambridge U Pr.

Henderson, Alfred J. London & the National Government 1721-1742: A Study of City Politics & the Walpole Administration. LC 75-29086. (Perspectives in European History: No. 7). (Illus.). x, 242p. Repr. of 1945 ed. lib. bdg. 15.00x (ISBN 0-87991-609-5). Porcupine Pr.

Prothero, Iowerth. Artisans & Politics in Early Nineteenth-Century London: John Gast & His Times. LC 78-71958. 1979. 30.00x (ISBN 0-8071-0570-8). La State U Pr.

Ramsay, G. D. The City of London in International Politics at the Accession of Elizabeth Tudor. 310p. 1975. 22.50x (ISBN 0-87471-646-2). Rowman.

Rhodes, Gerald & Ruck, S. K. The Government of Greater London. (New Local Government Ser.). 1970. text ed. 18.95x (ISBN 0-04-352027-8); pap. text ed. 9.50x o. p. (ISBN 0-04-352028-6). Allen Unwin.

Rhodes, Gerald, ed. The New Government of London: The First Five Years. LC 73-79596. 548p. 1973. 20.00 (ISBN 0-87332-042-5). M E Sharpe.

Turner, John E. Labour's Doorstep Politics in London. LC 77-99160. 1978. 19.50x (ISBN 0-8166-0843-1). U of Minn Pr.

Young, Ken. Local Politics & the Rise of the Party. 256p. 1975. text ed. 19.50x (ISBN 0-7185-1140-9, Leicester). Humanities.

LONDON–POOR

Booth, Charles. Life & Labour of the People of London, First Series: Poverty, 5 Vols. rev. ed. LC 68-55487. (Illus.). Repr. of 1902 ed. Set. 95.00x (ISBN 0-678-00455-2). Kelley.

Godwin, George. Town Swamps & Social Bridges. (Victorian Library). 110p. 1972. Repr. of 1859 ed. text ed. 8.25x (ISBN 0-391-00158-2, Leicester). Humanities.

Humpherys, Anne. Travels into the Poor Man's Country: The Work of Henry Mayhew. LC 76-15346. 240p. 1977. 16.00 (ISBN 0-8203-0416-6). U of Ga Pr.

White, Jerry. Rothschild Buildings: Life in an East End Tenement Block 1887-1920. (History Workshop Ser.). 1980. 30.00 (ISBN 0-7100-0429-X); pap. 15.00 (ISBN 0-686-65998-8). Routledge & Kegan.

LONDON–POPULATION

Dench, Geoff. Maltese in London. 1975. 25.00x (ISBN 0-7100-8067-0). Routledge & Kegan.

Graunt, John. Natural & Political Observations Mentioned in a Following Index, & Made Upon the Bills of Mortality. LC 74-25754. (European Sociology Ser.). 110p. 1975. Repr. 9.00x (ISBN 0-405-06508-6). Arno.

LONDON–RAILWAY CLEARING HOUSE

Bagwell, Philip. Railway Clearing House in the British Economy 1842-1922. LC 71-355685. (Illus.). 1968. 15.00x (ISBN 0-678-06013-4). Kelley.

Head, Francis B. Stokers & Pokers. LC 69-10757. Repr. of 1949 ed. 12.50x (ISBN 0-678-05601-3). Kelley.

LONDON–RELIGION

Davies, Charles M. Heterodox London or Phases of Free Thought in the Metropolis, 2 Vols. in 1. LC 69-17494. Repr. of 1874 ed. 25.00x (ISBN 0-678-00469-2). Kelley.

--Unorthodox London or Phases of Religious Life in the Metropolis. LC 69-17495. Repr. of 1875 ed. 19.50x (ISBN 0-678-00470-6). Kelley.

Wunderli, Richard M. London Church Courts & Society on the Eve of the Reformation: Ecclesiastical Courts in Pre-Reformation London. 1980. 12.50 (ISBN 0-686-64886-2, SAM7); pap. 5.00 (ISBN 0-910956-71-5). Medieval Acad.

LONDON–ROYAL ACADEMY OF ARTS

Cave, Kathryn, ed. The Diary of Joseph Farington, R. A. Volumes 7 & 8: January 1805 Through December 1807. LC 78-7056. (Published for the Paul Mellon Center for Studies in British Art Ser.). 360p. 1981. text ed. 70.00x (ISBN 0-300-02768-0, Set). Yale U Pr.

Garlick & Macintyre. The Diary of Joseph Farington, R. A. LC 78-7056. 1979. text ed. 75.00x set (ISBN 0-300-02418-5). Vol. 4 (ISBN 0-300-02416-9). Vol. 5 (ISBN 0-300-02417-7). Yale U Pr.

Graves, Algernon. Royal Academy of Art: 1769-1904, 4 vols. Set. 160.00 (ISBN 0-87556-111-X). Saifer.

--The Royal Academy of Arts, 8 vols. Repr. of 1905 ed. Set. 250.00 (ISBN 0-685-76592-X). Norwood Edns.

--The Royal Academy of Arts, a Complete Dictionary of Contributors & Their Work from Its Foundation in 1769 to 1904, Compiled with the Sanction of the President & Council of the Royal Academy, 8 vols. in 4. LC 76-118750. 1972. Repr. of 1905 ed. Set. lib. bdg. 181.00 (ISBN 0-8337-1425-2). B Franklin.

Hutchison, Sidney C. History of the Royal Academy 1768-1968. LC 68-21819. (Illus.). 1968. 12.95 (ISBN 0-8008-3900-5). Taplinger.

Rossetti, William M. Notes on the Royal Academy Exhibition, 1868. LC 75-144681. Repr. of 1868 ed. 11.50 (ISBN 0-404-05418-8). AMS Pr.

Royal Academy Exhibitors 1905-1970: A Dictionary of Artists & Their Work in the Summer Exhibitions of the Royal Academy of Arts, 8 vols. 1974. text ed. 45.00x ea.; Set. text ed. 350.00x (ISBN 0-8277-2675-9); Vol. 1. (ISBN 0-8277-2684-8); Vol. 2. Vol. 3. (ISBN 0-8277-2677-5); Vol. 4. (ISBN 0-8277-2678-3); Vol. 5. (ISBN 0-8277-2680-5); Vol. 6. (ISBN 0-8277-2681-3); Vol. 7. (ISBN 0-8277-2682-1). British Bk Ctr.

Royal Academy Exhibitors 1905-1970: A Dictionary of Artists & Their Work in the Summer Exhibitions of the Royal Academy of Arts, Vol. 8. text ed. 45.00x (ISBN 0-8277-2683-X). British Bk Ctr.

The Royal Academy Catalogues. The Exhibition of the Royal Academy of Arts, 4 vol. (History & Literature of Art Ser.). 1975. Repr. of 1901 ed. Set. lib. bdg. 295.00 (ISBN 0-306-70644-X). Da Capo.

LONDON–ROYAL OPERA HOUSE

Rosenthal, Harold. Covent Garden. (Folio Miniature Ser.). 48p. 1979. 4.95 (ISBN 0-7181-1474-4, Pub. by Michael Joseph). Merrimack Bk Serv.

LONDON–SOCIAL CONDITIONS

Booth, Charles. Charles Booth on the City: Physical Pattern & Social Structure. Pfautz, Harold W., ed. LC 67-28466. (Heritage of Sociology Ser). (Illus.). 1967. pap. 3.45 (ISBN 0-226-06551-0, P282, Phoen). U of Chicago Pr.

--Life & Labour of the People of London, First Series: Poverty, 5 Vols. rev. ed. LC 68-55487. (Illus.). Repr. of 1902 ed. Set. 95.00x (ISBN 0-678-00455-2). Kelley.

Booth, Charles, et al. Life & Labour of the People in London, 1890-1900, 17 vols. LC 76-113561. Repr. of 1904 ed. Set. 502.50 (ISBN 0-404-00940-9). AMS Pr.

Donnison, David & Eversley, David, eds. London: Urban Patterns, Problems, & Policies. LC 73-80440. 452p. 1973. 37.50x (ISBN 0-8039-0270-0). Sage.

Eppel, Emanuel M. & Eppel, M. Adolescents & Morality: A Study of Some Moral Values & Dilemmas of Working Adolescents in the Context of a Changing Climate of Opinion. (International Library of Sociology & Social Reconstruction Ser.). (Illus.). 1966. text ed. 8.50x (ISBN 0-7100-3455-5). Humanities.

Godwin, George. Town Swamps & Social Bridges. (Victorian Library). 110p. 1972. Repr. of 1859 ed. text ed. 8.25x (ISBN 0-391-00158-2, Leicester). Humanities.

Greve, John. London's Homeless. 76p. 1964. pap. text ed. 3.75x (ISBN 0-686-70849-0, Pub. by Bedford England). Renouf.

Hill, Octavia & Mearns, Andrew. Homes of the London Poor: Bitter Cry of Outcast London. 1970. Repr. 23.50x (ISBN 0-7146-2419-5, F Cass Co). Biblio Dist.

Holmes, Thomas. London's Underworld. 1979. Repr. of 1912 ed. lib. bdg. 30.00 (ISBN 0-8482-4485-0). Norwood Edns.

Land, Hilarly. Large Families in London. 154p. 1969. pap. text ed. 6.25x (ISBN 0-7135-1577-5, Pub. by Bedford England). Renouf.

Madge, Charles & Willmott, Peter. Inner City Poverty in Paris & London. (Reports of the Institute of Community Studies Ser.). 144p. 1981. price not set (ISBN 0-7100-0819-8). Routledge & Kegan.

Mayhew, Augustus. Paved with Gold: The Romance & Reality of the London Street. 2nd ed. (Illus.). 408p. 1971. 25.00x (ISBN 0-7146-1412-2, F Cass Co). Biblio Dist.

Mayhew, Henry. London Labour & the London Poor, 4 vols. (Illus.). 1967. 165.00x (ISBN 0-7146-1148-4, F Cass Co). Biblio Dist.

Mayhew, Henry & Binny, J. Criminal Prisons of London. LC 68-18227. (Illus.). Repr. of 1862 ed. 22.50x (ISBN 0-678-05072-4). Kelley.

Mayhew, Henry & Binny, John. Criminal Prisons of London & Scenes of Prison Life. (Illus.). 634p. 1968. 35.00x (ISBN 0-7146-1411-4, F Cass Co). Biblio Dist.

Mearns, Andrew. Bitter Cry of Outcast London. LC 76-11185. Repr. of 1883 ed. 6.50x (ISBN 0-678-08022-4). Kelley.

Sheppard, Francis. London, Eighteen Eight Eighteen Seventy: The Infernal Wen. LC 71-142067. (History of London Series). (Illus.). 1971. 30.00x (ISBN 0-520-01847-8). U of Cal Pr.

Tristan, Flora. Flora Tristan's London Journals. 1980. 20.00 (ISBN 0-89182-024-8). Charles River Bks.

Troyer, Howard W. Ned Ward of Grub Street: A Study of Sub-Literary London in the Eighteenth Century. (Illus.). 290p. 1968. 25.00x (ISBN 0-7146-1523-4, F Cass Co). Biblio Dist.

Whore's Rhetoric: Calculated to the Meridian of London, & Rules of Art. 331p. 1960. 5.00x (ISBN 0-87556-162-4). Saifer.

LONDON–SOCIAL LIFE AND CUSTOMS

Aumonier, Stacy & Belcher, George F. Odd Fish. facs. ed. LC 71-116929. (Short Story Index Reprint Ser). 1923. 11.00 (ISBN 0-8369-3431-8). Arno.

Boulton, William B. Amusements of Old London, 2 Vols. in 1. LC 75-82820. (Illus.). 1901. 25.00 (ISBN 0-405-08295-9, Blom Pubns). Arno.

Burford, E. J. The Orrible Synne: A Look at London Lechery from Roman to Cromwellian Times. (Illus.). 256p. 1973. text ed. 12.50x (ISBN 0-7145-0978-7). Humanities.

Byrd, William. London Diary, 1717-1721 & Other Writings. Wright, Louis B. & Tinglin, Marion, eds. LC 77-141208. (Research Library of Colonial Americana). (Illus.). 1971. Repr. of 1958 ed. 29.00 (ISBN 0-405-03305-2). Arno.

Compton-Rickett, Arthur. The London Life of Yesterday. 1979. Repr. of 1909 ed. lib. bdg. 40.00 (ISBN 0-8482-7573-X). Norwood Edns.

Dore, Gustave & Jerrold, Blanchard. London: A Pilgrimage. (Illus.). 1970. pap. 6.00 (ISBN 0-486-22306-X). Dover.

Feeney, Leonard. London Is a Place. 1951. 6.00 (ISBN 0-911218-02-5). Ravengate Pr.

Greve, J., et al. Homelessness in London. 1971. 17.50x (ISBN 0-7073-0195-5, Pub. by Scottish Academic Pr Scotland). Columbia U Pr.

Hayward, Arthur L. Days of Dickens: A Glance at Some Aspects of Early Victorian Life in London. (Illus.). 1968. Repr. of 1926 ed. 18.50 (ISBN 0-208-00674-5, Archon). Shoe String.

Hibbard, George R., ed. Three Elizabethan Pamphlets. facs. ed. LC 74-80622. (Select Bibliographies Reprint Ser). 1951. 17.00 (ISBN 0-8369-5034-8). Arno.

Hindley, C. A History of the Cries of London, Ancient & Modern. 59.95 (ISBN 0-8490-0352-0). Gordon Pr.

Holmes, Urban T., Jr. Daily Living in the Twelfth Century: Based on the Observations of Alexander Neckam in London & Paris. (Illus.). 1952. pap. 7.95x (ISBN 0-299-00854-1). U of Wis Pr.

Irving, William H. John Gay's London, Illustrated from the Poetry of the Time. (Illus.), 1968. Repr. of 1928 ed. 25.00 (ISBN 0-208-00618-4, Archon). Shoe String.

Nadal, E. S. Impressions of London Social Life. 223p. 1980. Repr. of 1875 ed. lib. bdg. 30.00 (ISBN 0-89984-350-6). Century Bookbindery.

Parker, Hershel, ed. Gansevoort Melville's 1846 London Journal & Letters from England, 1845. LC 66-17838. (Orig.). 1966. pap. 5.00 (ISBN 0-87104-083-2). NY Pub Lib.

Pedicord, Harry W. Theatrical Public in the Time of Garrick. LC 53-12030. (Arcturus Books Paperbacks). 281p. 1966. lib. bdg. 7.00x (ISBN 0-8093-0221-7); pap. 2.65 (ISBN 0-8093-0222-5). S Ill U Pr.

Pendrill, Charles. London Life in the Fourteenth Century. LC 79-118495. 1971. Repr. of 1925 ed. 17.50 (ISBN 0-8046-1243-9). Kennikat.

Prothero, Iowerth. Artisans & Politics in Early Nineteenth-Century London: John Gast & His Times. LC 78-71958. 1979. 30.00x (ISBN 0-8071-0570-8). La State U Pr.

Raven, Charles. Underworld Nights: Tales of London Underworld. Date not set. 7.95 (ISBN 0-392-16400-0, SpS). Sportshelf.

Smith, Adolphe & Thompson, John. Street Life in London. LC 68-28169. (Illus.). 1968. Repr. of 1877 ed. 20.00 (ISBN 0-405-08982-1). Arno.

Smith, Charles M. Curiosities of London Life: Phases, Physiological & Social, of the Great Metropolis. 408p. 1972. Repr. of 1853 ed. 22.50x (ISBN 0-7146-2426-8, F Cass Co). Biblio Dist.

Thompson, C. J. Love, Marriage & Romance in Old London. LC 70-76076. (Illus.). 1971. Repr. of 1936 ed. 22.00 (ISBN 0-8103-3211-6). Gale.

Thrupp, Sylvia L. Merchant Class of Medieval London. 1962. pap. 5.95 (ISBN 0-472-06072-4, 72, AA). U of Mich Pr.

Timbs, John. Romance of London. LC 68-22058. 1968. Repr. of 1865 ed. 45.00 (ISBN 0-8103-3498-4). Gale.

Young, Michael & Willmott, Peter. Family & Kinship in East London. 7.50 (ISBN 0-8446-5103-6). Peter Smith.

--Family & Kinship in East London. 1963. pap. 2.95 (ISBN 0-14-020595-0, Pelican). Penguin.

Zwager, Nicolaas. Glimpses of Ben Jonson's London. 219p. 1980. Repr. of 1926 ed. lib. bdg. 30.00 (ISBN 0-8495-6205-8). Arden Lib.

LONDON–STOCK EXCHANGE

Burgon, John W. Life & Times of Sir Thomas Gresham, 2 Vols. (Illus.). 1965. Repr. of 1839 ed. Set. 53.00 (ISBN 0-8337-0422-2). B Franklin.

LONDON–THEATERS

Adams, Joseph Q. Conventual Buildings of Blackfriars, London, & the Playhouses Constructed Therein. LC 76-113537. Repr. of 1917 ed. 11.50 (ISBN 0-404-00289-7). AMS Pr.

--Shakespearean Playhouses: A History of English Theatres from the Beginning to the Reformation. (Illus.). 1959. 12.50 (ISBN 0-8446-1009-7). Peter Smith.

Amery, Colin. National Theatre: An Architectural Guide. (Illus.). 1977. 9.00 (ISBN 0-85139-442-6, Pub. by Architectural Pr). Nichols Pub.

Armstrong, William A. The Elizabethan Private Theatres. LC 76-52989. 1977. Repr. of 1958 ed. lib. bdg. 7.50 (ISBN 0-8414-2955-3). Folcroft.

Arundell, Dennis. The Story of Sadler's Wells, 1683-1977. 2nd ed. (Illus.). 352p. 1978. 16.50x (ISBN 0-8476-6138-5). Rowman.

Baker, Barton. History of the London Stage & Its Famous Players 1576-1903. LC 72-81971. (Illus.). Repr. of 1904 ed. 25.00 (ISBN 0-405-08231-2, Pub. by Blom). Arno.

Berry, Herbert, ed. The First Public Playhouse: The Theatre in Shoreditch, 1576-1598. 1979. pap. 9.95x (ISBN 0-7735-0340-4). McGill-Queens U Pr.

Bradbrook, M. C. The Living Monument. LC 76-7142. (Illus.). 1976. 38.00 (ISBN 0-521-21255-3); pap. 10.95 (ISBN 0-521-29530-0). Cambridge U Pr.

Ebers, John. Seven Years of the King's Theatre. LC 79-88490. Repr. of 1828 ed. 17.50 (ISBN 0-405-08481-1, Blom Pubns). Arno.

Fischer, Mildred. London Theatre Today: A Guide for Travelers. (Illus.). 144p. (Orig.). 1981. pap. 4.50 (ISBN 0-914846-09-4). Golden West Pub.

Graves, Thornton S. Court & the London Theatres During the Reign of Elizabeth. LC 72-194353. 1913. lib. bdg. 5.95 (ISBN 0-8414-4669-5). Folcroft.

Hotson, J. Leslie. Commonwealth & Restoration Stage. LC 62-10686. (Illus.). 1962. Repr. of 1928 ed. 12.50 (ISBN 0-8462-0203-4). Russell.

Isaacs, J. Production & Stage Management at the Blackfriars Theatre. LC 73-14939. Repr. of 1933 ed. lib. bdg. 6.00 (ISBN 0-8414-5052-8). Folcroft.

Kelly, Michael. Reminiscences of Michael Kelly. Hook, Theodore E., ed. LC 72-88491. Repr. of 1826 ed. 18.00 (ISBN 0-405-08688-1, Pub. by Blom). Arno.

--Reminiscences of Michael Kelly of the King's Theatre & Theatre Royal Drury Lane 2 Vols. 2nd ed. LC 68-16243. (Music Ser). 1968. Repr. of 1826 ed. lib. bdg. 45.00 (ISBN 0-306-71094-3). Da Capo.

Loftis, John C. Steele at Drury Lane. LC 72-6925. 260p. 1973. Repr. of 1952 ed. lib. bdg. 15.00x (ISBN 0-8371-6502-4, LOST). Greenwood.

London's Theatreland. 1975. pap. 1.95 (ISBN 0-8277-3434-4). British Bk Ctr.
MacCarthy, Desmond. Court Theatre, Nineteen Four to Nineteen Seven: A Commentary & Criticism. Weintraub, Stanley, ed. LC 66-27969. (Bks of the Theatre: No. 6). 1966. 9.95x (ISBN 0-87024-068-4). U of Miami Pr.
Mander, Raymond & Mitchenson, Joe. Lost Theatres of London. LC 68-29986. (Illus.). 1968. 12.00 (ISBN 0-8008-5025-4). Taplinger.
--The Theatres of London. LC 78-11808. 1979. Repr. of 1961 ed. lib. bdg. 19.75x (ISBN 0-313-21227-9, MATL). Greenwood.
Mason, Alfred E. Sir George Alexander & the St. James' Theatre. LC 72-84520. (Illus.). 1935. 15.00 (ISBN 0-405-08762-4, Pub. by Blom). Arno.
Reynolds, George F. Staging of Elizabethan Plays at the Red Bull Theatre, 1605-1625. 1940. pap. 13.00 (ISBN 0-527-75000-X). Kraus Repr.
Rhodes, Ernest L. Henslowe's Rose: The Stage & Staging. LC 73-80466. (Illus.). 352p. 1976. 26.00 (ISBN 0-8131-1305-9). U Pr of Ky.
Short, Ernest. Fifty Years of Vaudeville. LC 78-16385. (Illus.). 1978. Repr. of 1946 ed. lib. bdg. 27.75 (ISBN 0-313-20576-0, SHFY). Greenwood.
Sisson, C. J. The Boar's Head Theatre: An Inn-Yard Theatre of the Elizabethan Age. (Illus.). 1972. 15.00x (ISBN 0-7100-7252-X). Routledge & Kegan.
Smith, Irwin. Shakespeare's Blackfriars Playhouse: Its History & Its Design. LC 64-16902. (Illus.). 578p. 1964. 16.00x (ISBN 0-8147-0391-7); pap. 5.95x (ISBN 0-8147-0483-2). NYU Pr.
Thaler, Alwin. Shakespere to Sheridan. LC 63-23190. (Illus.). 1922. 18.00 (ISBN 0-405-09025-0). Arno.
Wallace, Charles W. Children of the Chapel at Blackfriars, 1597-1603. LC 75-115007. Repr. of 1908 ed. 14.50 (ISBN 0-404-06808-1). AMS Pr.
--Evolution of the English Drama up to Shakespeare: With a History of the First Blackfriars Theatre. LC 68-26276. 1968. Repr. of 1912 ed. 11.00 (ISBN 0-8046-0483-5). Kennikat.
Watson, Ernest B. Sheridan to Robertson: A Study of the Nineteenth-Century London Stage. LC 63-23191. (Illus.). 1926. 23.00 (ISBN 0-405-09055-2). Arno.

LONDON–TOWER OF LONDON
Hibbert, Christopher & Newsweek Editors, eds. Tower of London. LC 70-136436. (Illus.). 1971. 16.95 (ISBN 0-88225-002-7). Newsweek.
Johnson, David. The Tower of London. (Jackdaw Ser: No. 62). (Illus.). 1969. 6.95 (ISBN 0-670-72259-6, Grossman). Viking Pr.
Pottinger, Don. The Official Chart of the Tower of London. (Illus.). 1978. pap. 2.95 (ISBN 0-517-53412-6). Crown.
Prisoners in the Tower. 1975. pap. 1.95 (ISBN 0-8277-3438-7). British Bk Ctr.
Rowse, A. L. The Tower of London. (Folio Miniature Ser.). (Illus.). 48p. 1978. 4.95 (ISBN 0-7181-1544-9, Pub. by Michael Joseph). Merrimack Bk Serv.
Wilson, Derek. The Tower: The Tumultuous History of the Tower of London from 1078. (Illus.). 1979. 14.95 (ISBN 0-684-16261-X, ScribT). Scribner.

LONDON–TRANSIT SYSTEMS
Buchanan, Malcolm, et al. Transport Planning for Greater London. 315p. 1980. text ed. 42.75x (ISBN 0-566-00314-7, Pub. by Gower Pub Co England). Renouf.
Collins, Michael F. & Pharoah, Timothy M. Transport Organization in a Great City: The Case of London. LC 74-77339. 660p. 1974. 40.00 (ISBN 0-8039-0434-7). Sage.
Jackson, Alan. London's Local Railways. LC 77-85017. 1978. 19.00 (ISBN 0-7153-7479-6). David & Charles.
Passingham, W. J. Romance of London's Underground. LC 72-80705. (Illus.). Repr. of 1932 ed. 25.00 (ISBN 0-405-08839-6). Arno.

LONDON–WORKING-MEN'S COLLEGE
Davies, John L., ed. Working Men's College, 1854-1904. LC 75-144594. Repr. of 1904 ed. 21.50 (ISBN 0-404-01978-1). AMS Pr.

LONDON, UNIVERSITY OF
Goldsmiths'-Kress Library of Economic Literature: A Consolidated Guide to Segment I of the Microfilm Collection, 4 vols, Vols. 1, 2 & 3 (through 1800) 1976. Set. 575.00 (ISBN 0-89235-004-0). Res Pubns Conn.
University of London, Institute of Education. Catalogue of the Comparative Education Library, 1st Suppl, 3 vols. 1974. Set. lib. bdg. 315.00 (ISBN 0-8161-0988-5). G K Hall.

LONDON AND NORTHWESTERN RAILWAY
Head, Francis B. Stokers & Pokers. LC 69-10757. Repr. of 1949 ed. 12.50x (ISBN 0-678-05601-3). Kelley.
Nock, Oswald S. LNER Steam. LC 68-26165. (Illus.). 1969. 13.95x (ISBN 0-678-05520-3). Kelley.

LONDON AND SOUTH WESTERN RAILWAY COMPANY
Williams, R. A. The London & South Western Railway: Growth & Consolidation, Vol. 2. (Railway History Ser.). (Illus.). 1973. 7.00 (ISBN 0-7153-5940-1). David & Charles.
--The London & South Western Railway: The Formative Years, Vol. 1. (Railway History Ser.). (Illus.). 1968. 7.00 (ISBN 0-7153-4188-X). David & Charles.

LONDON BROWNING SOCIETY
Peterson, William S. Interrogating the Oracle: A History of the London Browning Society. LC 69-15916. (Illus.). xii, 276p. 1970. 16.00x (ISBN 0-8214-0056-8). Ohio U Pr.

LONDON METROPOLITAN AREA
Foley, Donald L. Governing the London Region: Reorganization & Planning in the 1960's. LC 76-157822. (Institute of Governmental Studies, UC Berkeley & Lane Studies in Regional Environment). 1972. 21.50x (ISBN 0-520-02040-5); pap. 6.95x (ISBN 0-520-02248-3, CAMPUS81). U of Cal Pr.

LONDON NAVAL CONFERENCE, 1930
O'Connor, Raymond G. Perilous Equilibrium: The United States & the London Naval Conference of 1930. LC 69-14014. 1969. Repr. of 1962 ed. lib. bdg. 15.00 (ISBN 0-8371-0595-1, OCEQ). Greenwood.

LONDON SCHOOL OF ECONOMICS AND POLITICAL SCIENCE
Beveridge, William H. & Bew, P. London School of Economics & Its Problems, 1919-1937. 1960. text ed. 6.50x (ISBN 0-391-02007-2). Humanities.

LONDON–STATIONERS' COMPANY
Blagden, Cyprian. The Stationers' Company: A History, 1403-1959. LC 75-48000. 1960. 17.50x (ISBN 0-8047-0935-1). Stanford U Pr.

LONDONDERRY, ROBERT STEWART, 2ND MARQUIS OF, 1769-1822
Kissinger, Henry A. World Restored: Europe After Napoleon. 8.00 (ISBN 0-8446-2384-9). Peter Smith.
Webster, Sir Charles. Foreign Policy of Castlereagh, 2 vols. Incl. Vol. 1. 1812-1815; Vol. 2. 1815-1822. 1963. Set. text ed. 19.25x (ISBN 0-391-00520-0). Humanities.

LONELINESS
see also Consolation; Solitude
Burke, Charles & Provost, Norman, eds. Loneliness. (Illus.). 101p. (Orig.). 1970. pap. 3.25 (ISBN 0-88489-022-8). St Marys.
Cruz, Nicky & Harris, Madalene. Lonely, but Never Alone. 192p. (Orig.). 1981. pap. 5.95 (ISBN 0-310-43361-4). Zondervan.
Dauw, Dean C. Stranger in Your Bed: A Guide to Emotional Intimacy. LC 78-23444. 1979. 13.95 (ISBN 0-88229-472-5). Nelson-Hall.
Ellison, Craig W. Loneliness: The Search for Intimacy. LC 79-55681. 1980. 8.95 (ISBN 0-915684-57-8). Christian Herald.
Gordon, Suzanne. Lonely in America. 1977. pap. 5.95 (ISBN 0-671-22754-8, Touchstone). S&S.
Greenwald, Jerry. Breaking Out of Loneliness. LC 79-67635. 1980. 12.95 (ISBN 0-89256-120-3). Rawson Wade.
Hall, Manly P. Ways of the Lonely Ones. pap. 3.00 (ISBN 0-89314-368-5). Philos Res.
Hartog, Joseph, et al, eds. Anatomy of Loneliness. LC 79-53591. 1980. text ed. 30.00 (ISBN 0-8236-0146-3). Intl Univs Pr.
Hulme, William E. Creative Loneliness. LC 76-27083. 1977. pap. 3.50 (ISBN 0-8066-1556-7, 10-1715). Augsburg.
Johnson, James. Loneliness Is Not Forever. 1979. 7.95 (ISBN 0-8024-4949-2). Moody.
Kennedy, Eugene. Loneliness. 1977. pap. 5.95 (ISBN 0-88347-023-3). Thomas More.
Killinger, John. The Loneliness of Children. LC 79-56378. 320p. 1980. 12.95 (ISBN 0-8149-0830-6). Vanguard.
Lauder, Robert E. Loneliness Is for Loving. LC 77-94033. (Illus.). 144p. 1978. pap. 2.75 (ISBN 0-87793-147-X). Ave Maria.
Lynch, James J. The Broken Heart: The Medical Consequences of Loneliness. LC 77-2173. 1979. 11.95 (ISBN 0-465-00772-4); pap. 4.95 (ISBN 0-465-00771-6). Basic.
Madden, James P., ed. Loneliness: Issues of Emotional Living in an Age of Stress for Clergy & Religious. LC 77-368127. 1977. pap. 2.95 (ISBN 0-89571-002-1). Affirmation.
Moustakas, Clark E. Loneliness. (Orig.). 1961. pap. 2.95 (ISBN 0-13-540161-5, Spec). P-H.
--Loneliness & Love. 1972. 8.95 (ISBN 0-13-540252-2, Spec); pap. 2.95 (ISBN 0-13-540245-X, S267, Spec). P-H.
Oles, Carole. The Loneliness Factor. LC 78-24746. 1979. 7.95 (ISBN 0-89672-072-1); pap. 3.95 (ISBN 0-89672-071-3). Tex Tech Pr.
Park, James. Loneliness & Existential Freedom. (Existential Freedom Ser.: No. 4). 1974. pap. 2.00x (ISBN 0-89231-004-9). Existential Bks.
Potts, Nancy. Loneliness: Living Between the Times. 1978. pap. 3.95 (ISBN 0-88207-630-2). Victor Bks.
Robert, Marc. Loneliness in the Schools. LC 73-78537. (Illus.). 1973. pap. 3.95 (ISBN 0-913592-18-8). Argus Comm.
Schmidt, Jay H. & Neimark, Paul. Good-Bye Loneliness. LC 77-16766. (Illus.). 192p. 1981. pap. 6.95 (ISBN 0-8128-6095-0). Stein & Day.
--Good-Bye Loneliness. LC 77-16766. 1979. 9.95 (ISBN 0-8128-2460-1). Stein & Day.
Schultz, Terri. Bittersweet: Surviving & Growing from Loneliness. 1978. pap. 2.50 (ISBN 0-14-004745-X). Penguin.
Schwarzrock, Shirley & Wrenn, C. Gilbert. Living with Loneliness. (Coping with Ser.). (Illus.). 31p. (gr. 7-12). 1970. pap. text ed. 1.30 (ISBN 0-913476-32-3). Am Guidance.
Skoglund, Elizabeth. Beyond Loneliness. LC 78-73194. 168p. 1980. 8.95 (ISBN 0-385-13192-5, Galilee). Doubleday.
--Loneliness. 32p. 1975. pap. 0.50 (ISBN 0-87784-150-0). Inter-Varsity.
Spence, Inez. Coping with Loneliness. (Direction Books). 112p. 1975. pap. 1.95 (ISBN 0-8010-8060-6). Baker Bk.
Stevens, Velma D. A Fresh Look at Loneliness. LC 81-65802. 1981. 5.95 (ISBN 0-8054-5297-4). Broadman.
Tanner, Ira J. Loneliness: The Fear of Love, An Application of Transactional Analysis. 160p. 1974. pap. 1.95 (ISBN 0-06-080333-9, P333, PL). Har-Row.
--Loneliness: The Fear of Love, An Application of Transactional Analysis. 160p. 1974. pap. 1.95 (ISBN 0-06-080333-9, P333, PL). Har-Row.
Wakin, Edward. Have You Ever Been Lonely? (Illus.). 1978. pap. 1.50 (ISBN 0-89570-148-0). Claretian Pubns.
Warlick, Harold C. Conquering Loneliness. 1979. 5.95 (ISBN 0-8499-0169-3). Word Bks.
Weiss, Robert S., ed. Loneliness. 240p. 1974. pap. 6.95 (ISBN 0-262-73041-3). MIT Pr.
Wellington, Paul A., ed. Loneliness. 1980. pap. 3.00 (ISBN 0-8309-0287-2). Herald Hse.
Wilkerson, Ralph. Loneliness: The World's Number One Killer. Tanner, Don, ed. LC 78-51901. (Illus.). 1978. pap. 1.45 (ISBN 0-918818-03-6). Melodyland.
Wood, Robert S. Goodbye Loneliness. 1976. pap. 3.45 (ISBN 0-440-53097-0, Delta). Dell.
Wright, Norman. An Answer to Loneliness. (Orig.). pap. 1.25 (ISBN 0-89081-077-X). Harvest Hse.

LONERGAN, BERNARD J. F.
Crowe, Frederick E. The Lonergan Enterprise. LC 80-51569. 120p. (Orig.). 1980. pap. 5.00 (ISBN 0-936384-02-6). Cowley Pubns.
Lamb, Matthew L., ed. Creativity & Method: Studies in Honor of Rev. Bernard Lonergan, S.J. 600p. 1981. 24.95 (ISBN 0-87462-533-5). Marquette.
McShane, Philip. Lonergan's Challenge to the University & the Economy. LC 79-3809. 1980. text ed. 16.75 (ISBN 0-8191-0933-9); pap. text ed. 9.00 (ISBN 0-8191-0934-7). U Pr of Amer.
Meynell, Hugo. An Introduction to the Philosophy of Bernard Lonergan. LC 75-39082. (Library of Philosophy & Religion Ser.). 201p. 1976. text ed. 25.00x (ISBN 0-06-494793-9). B&N.

LONG, CRAWFORD WILLIAMSON, 1815-1878
Radford, Ruby L. Prelude to Fame: Crawford Long's Discovery of Anaesthesia. LC 74-81776. (gr. 7 up). 1969. 4.95 (ISBN 0-87672-104-8). Geron-X.

LONG, EARL KEMP, 1895-1960
Liebling, A. J. Earl of Louisiana. LC 76-130664. 1970. 17.50x (ISBN 0-8071-0537-6); pap. text ed. 5.95x (ISBN 0-8071-0203-2). La State U Pr.
McCaughan, Richard. Socks on a Rooster. 1967. 6.00 (ISBN 0-685-08209-1). Claitors.

LONG, HUEY PIERCE, 1893-1935
Beals, Carleton. Story of Huey P. Long. LC 75-136054. 1971. Repr. of 1935 ed. lib. bdg. 21.50x (ISBN 0-8371-5204-6, BEHL). Greenwood.
--Story of Huey P. Long. LC 75-136054. 1971. Repr. of 1935 ed. lib. bdg. 21.50x (ISBN 0-8371-5204-6, BEHL). Greenwood.
Blain, Hugh M. Favorite Huey Long Stories. 1972. 3.00 (ISBN 0-685-08164-8); pap. 1.00 (ISBN 0-685-08165-6). Claitors.
Fineran, John K. Career of a Tinpot Napoleon: Political Biography of Huey P. Long. 2.50 (ISBN 0-685-08225-3). Claitors.
Harris, T. O. Kingfish: Huey P. Long. 1968. 5.00 (ISBN 0-685-08183-4). Claitors.
Kane, Harnett T. Louisiana Hayride. (Illus.). 1971. Repr. of 1941 ed. 10.00 (ISBN 0-911116-32-X). Pelican.
Sindler, Allan P. Huey Long's Louisiana: State Politics, 1920-1952. LC 56-11664. 316p. 1956. pap. 3.95x (ISBN 0-8018-0597-X). Johns Hopkins.
Williams, T. Harry. Huey Long. LC 69-10692. (Illus.). 1969. 22.50 (ISBN 0-394-42954-0). Knopf.
Zinman, David. Day Huey Long Was Shot. 1963. 7.95 (ISBN 0-8392-1024-8). Astor-Honor.

LONG, STEPHEN H., 1784-1864
Hafen, L. R., ed. Bell's Journal of the S. H. Long Expedition. (Illus.). 1973. 15.00 (ISBN 0-87062-033-9). A H Clark.
Kane, Lucile M. & Holmquist, June D., eds. The Northern Expeditions of Stephen H. Long: The Journals of 1817 & 1823 & Related Documents. (Illus.). 407p. 1978. 17.50 (ISBN 0-87351-129-8). Minn Hist.
Nichols, Roger & Halley, Patrick L. Stephen Long & America Frontier Expedition. LC 78-68878. (Illus.). 280p. 1980. 19.50 (ISBN 0-87413-149-9). U Delaware Pr.
Wood, Richard G. Stephen H. Long, 1784-1864. (Illus.). 1966. 12.50 (ISBN 0-87062-066-5). A H Clark.

LONG ISLAND
Garland, Joseph E. Boston's North Shore: Being an Account of Life Among the Noteworthy, Fashionable, Wealthy, Eccentric & Ordinary 1823-1890. 1978. 17.50 (ISBN 0-316-30425-5). Little.
Jaray, Cornell. Mills of Long Island. pap. 4.95 (ISBN 0-911660-18-6). Yankee Peddler.
Mannello, George. Our Long Island. 2nd ed. 1981. lib. bdg. write for info. (ISBN 0-88275-968-X). Krieger.
Murphy, Robert C. Fish-Shape Paumanok. LC 63-22603. (Memoirs Ser.: Vol. 58). (Illus.). 1964. 5.00 (ISBN 0-87169-058-6). Am Philos.
Seon, Manley. Long Island Discovery. 10.95 (ISBN 0-911660-19-4). Yankee Peddler.
Sterling, Dorothy. The Outer Lands: A Natural History Guide to Cape Cod, Martha's Vineyard, Nantucket, Block Island, & Long Island. (Illus.). 1978. 10.95 (ISBN 0-393-06438-7); pap. 5.95 (ISBN 0-393-06441-7). Norton.
Stevens, William. Discovering Long Island. 12.50 (ISBN 0-911660-14-3). Yankee Peddler.
Viemeister, August. An Architectural Journey Through Long Island. 1974. 9.95 (ISBN 0-8046-9109-6). Kennikat.
Wenig, Jeffrey. An Introduction to Environmental Science: The Ecology of Long Island. 1976. pap. 5.75 (ISBN 0-686-17783-5). Environ Pubns.

LONG ISLAND–DESCRIPTION AND TRAVEL
Albright, Rodney & Albright, Priscilla. Short Walks on Long Island. LC 74-75075. (Illus.). 128p. 1974. pap. 2.95 (ISBN 0-87106-143-0). Globe Pequot.
Angelillo, Phil. Short Bike Rides on Long Island. LC 76-45045. (Illus.). 1977. pap. 2.95 (ISBN 0-87106-071-X). Globe Pequot.
Clemente, Vince & Everett, Graham, eds. Paumanok Rising: An Anthology of Eastern Long Island Aesthetics. LC 81-50937. (Illus.). 216p. (Orig.). 1981. pap. 7.50 (ISBN 0-935252-27-4). Street Pr.
McCarthy, Mary A. Sappho by the Sea: An Illustrated Guide to the Hamptons. LC 76-21830. (Belvedere Bk.). (Illus.). 98p. 1980. Repr. of 1976 ed. 7.95 (ISBN 0-87754-252-X). Chelsea Hse.
Masters, James I., ed. The Hamptons Guidebook. 2nd ed. LC 81-67383. (Illus.). 386p. (YA) 1981. pap. 5.95 (ISBN 0-89808-006-1). Blue Claw.
--The Hamptons Guidebook. (Illus.). 398p. (Orig.). 1980. 6.95 (ISBN 0-89808-002-9). Blue Claw.
--North Fork & Shelter Island Guidebook. 3rd ed. LC 81-67384. (Illus.). 320p. (YA) 1981. pap. 4.95 (ISBN 0-89808-007-X). Blue Claw.
--North Fork & Shelter Island Guidebook. 2nd ed. LC 79-51477. (Illus.). 1979. pap. 4.95 (ISBN 0-89808-000-2). Blue Claw.
--North Fork & Shelter Island Guidebook. LC 77-77068. (Illus.). 1977. pap. 6.00 (ISBN 0-89808-001-0). Blue Claw.

LONG ISLAND–GENEALOGY
Bunker, Mary P. Long Island Genealogies. LC 76-11845. 1976. Repr. of 1895 ed. 15.00 (ISBN 0-8063-0529-0). Genealog Pub.

LONG ISLAND–HISTORIC HOUSES
Randall, Monica. The Mansions of Long Island's Gold Coast. (Illus.). 1979. 27.50 (ISBN 0-8038-2697-4). Hastings.

LONG ISLAND–HISTORY
Abbott, Katharine M. Old Paths & Legends of the New England Border: Connecticut, Deerfield, Berkshire. LC 72-75227. 1970. Repr. of 1907 ed. 22.00 (ISBN 0-8103-3562-X). Gale.
Bunce, James E. & Harmond, Richard P., eds. Long Island As America: A Documentary History. (Empire State Historical Publications Ser.). 1977. 12.95 (ISBN 0-8046-9171-1). Kennikat.
Case, Walter H. History of Long Beach & Vicinity. LC 73-2901. (Metropolitan America Ser.). (Illus.). 692p. 1974. Repr. 32.00x (ISBN 0-405-05387-8, Blom Pubns). Arno.
Des Grange, Jane. Long Island's Religious History. 3.95 (ISBN 0-911660-17-8). Yankee Peddler.
Diamond, Beatrice. Episode in American Journalism. LC 64-15546. 1964. 11.50 (ISBN 0-8046-0108-9). Kennikat.

Dyson, Verne. Anecdotes & Events in Long Island History. LC 70-8296. (Empire State Historical Publications Ser). 1969. 7.95 (ISBN 0-87198-079-7). Friedman.

Furman, Gabriel. Antiquities of Long Island. 8.50 (ISBN 0-911660-15-1). Yankee Peddler.

Halsey, William D. Sketches from Local History, Long Island, N. Y. 2nd ed. (Illus.). 1966. 15.00 (ISBN 0-911660-02-X). Yankee Peddler.

Rattray, Everett T. The South Fork: The Land & the People of Eastern Long Island. LC 78-23692. (Illus.). 1979. 10.00 (ISBN 0-394-41860-3). Random.

Smith, M. H. History of Garden City. 160p. 1980. 12.00 (ISBN 0-9604654-0-5). Garden City.

Tooker, William W. The Indian Place-Names on Long Island & Islands Adjacent with Their Probable Significations. Chamberlain, Alexander, ed. LC 62-13522. (Empire State Historical Publications). 1975. 12.50 (ISBN 0-8046-8006-X). Kennikat.

Waller, Henry D. History of the Town of Flushing, Long Island. LC 75-9678. 1975. Repr. of 1899 ed. 12.50 (ISBN 0-916346-12-9). Harbor Hill Bks.

Whitson, Skip, compiled by. Old Long Island. (Sun Historical Ser). (Illus., Orig.). 1976. pap. 3.50 (ISBN 0-89540-020-0, SB020). Sun Pub.

Wilson, Rufus. Historic Long Island. 11.00 (ISBN 0-911660-13-5). Yankee Peddler.

Wood, Simeon. A History of Hauppauge Long Island. 2nd ed. Werner, Charles J. & Marr, Jack J., eds. (Illus.). 115p. (Orig.). 1981. 15.95 (ISBN 0-9605854-0-0); pap. 7.95 (ISBN 0-9605854-1-9). J Marr.

Wyckoff, Edith H. The Fabled Past: Tales of Long Island. (Empire State Historical Publications Ser.). (Illus.). 1977. 9.95 (ISBN 0-8046-9146-0). Kennikat.

LONG ISLAND–IMPRINTS

McMurtrie, Douglas C. Historical Records Survey: Check List of the Imprints of Sag Harbor, L. I., 1791-1820, No. 12. 1939. pap. 6.00 (ISBN 0-527-01909-7). Kraus Repr.

LONG ISLAND, BATTLE OF, 1776

Johnston, H. P. Campaign of Seventeen Seventy-Six Around New York & Brooklyn. LC 74-157827. (Era of the American Revolution Ser). 1971. Repr. of 1878 ed. lib. bdg. 42.50 (ISBN 0-306-70169-3). Da Capo.

Manders, Eric. The Battle of Long Island. LC 78-72581. (Revolutionary War Bicentennial Ser). (Illus.). 1978. lib. bdg. 13.95 (ISBN 0-912480-14-9). Freneau.

LONG ISLAND HERALD

Diamond, Beatrice. Episode in American Journalism. LC 64-15546. 1964. 11.50 (ISBN 0-8046-0108-9). Kennikat.

LONG ISLAND RAILROAD

Kramer, Fred & Krause, John. Long Island Railroad. 1978. pap. text ed. 9.95 (ISBN 0-911868-34-8). Carstens Pubns.

LONG ISLAND SOUND

Koppelman, Lee E., et al. The Urban Sea: Long Island Sound. LC 74-3161. (Illus.). 1976. text ed. 29.95 (ISBN 0-275-09010-8). Praeger.

LONG ISLAND UNIVERSITY

Sparling, Edward J. Do College Students Choose Vocations Wisely? LC 74-177755. (Columbia University. Teachers College. Contributions to Education: No. 561). Repr. of 1933 ed. 17.50 (ISBN 0-404-55561-6). AMS Pr.

LONGEVITY

see also Aging; Immortalism; Middle Age; Old Age

Abbo, Fred E. Steps to a Longer Life. LC 78-31661. 191p. 1979. pap. 4.95 (ISBN 0-89037-211-X). Anderson World.

Aero, Rita. The Complete Book of Longevity. (Illus.). 1979. 16.95 (ISBN 0-399-12363-6); pap. 10.95 (ISBN 0-399-50401-X, Perigee). Putnam.

Bacon, Francis. The Historie of Life & Death: Observations Naturall and Experimentall for the Prolonging of Life. Kastenbaum, Robert, ed. LC 76-19558. (Death and Dying Ser.). 1977. Repr. of 1638 ed. lib. bdg. 22.00x (ISBN 0-405-09554-6). Arno.

--The Historie of Life & Death: With Observations Naturall & Experimentall. LC 68-54613. (English Experience Ser.: No.20). 324p. Repr. of 1638 ed. 21.00 (ISBN 90-221-0020-0). Walter J Johnson.

Baltes, P. B. & Brim, O. C., Jr., eds. Life-Span Development & Behavior, Vol. 3. 1980. 35.00 (ISBN 0-12-431803-7). Acad Pr.

Baltes, Paul B. & Brim, Orville G., eds. Life Span Development & Behavior, Vol. 2. (Serial Publication). 1979. 28.50 (ISBN 0-12-431802-9). Acad Pr.

Bee Pollen, the Miracle Food, Source of Youth, Vitality & Longevity. 25th ed. (Spanish ed. avail). 1979. 1.35 (ISBN 0-9600356-2-1). F Murat.

Brues, Austin M. & Sacher, G. A., eds. Aging & Levels of Biological Organization. LC 65-17281. (Illus.). 1965. 16.00x (ISBN 0-226-07712-8). U of Chicago Pr.

Cantor, Alfred U. Doctor Cantor's Longevity Diet: How to Slow Down Aging & Prolong Youth & Vigor. 1967. 12.95 (ISBN 0-13-216267-9, Parker). P-H.

Chen, Philip S. A Practical Guide to Longevity. 1978. 6.95 (ISBN 0-533-02927-9). Vantage.

Clark, Linda. Stay Young Longer. 1.50 (ISBN 0-686-29892-6). Cancer Bk Hse.

Cornaro, Luigi. The Art of Living Long. Kastenbaum, Robert, ed. LC 78-22195. (Aging & Old Age Ser.). (Illus.). 1979. Repr. of 1917 ed. lib. bdg. 14.00x (ISBN 0-405-11812-0). Arno.

Cutler, Charles L. How We Made It to One Hundred: Wisdom from the Super Old. LC 77-87771. 1978. 9.95 (ISBN 0-9601502-1-8). Rockfall Pr.

Deparcieux, Antoine. Essai Sur les Probabilitie De la Duree De la Vie Humaine. Repr. of 1760 ed. 46.00 (ISBN 0-8287-0260-8). Clearwater Pub.

Edds, Kevin. How to Live a Healthy One Hundred Years & More. Orig. Title: How to Live Hundreds of Years Without Disease. 1977. pap. 2.95 (ISBN 0-89036-089-8). Hawkes Pub Inc.

Fisher, Irving. National Vitality, Its Wastes & Conservation. LC 75-17221. (Social Problems & Social Policy Ser.). 1976. Repr. of 1909 ed. 8.00x (ISBN 0-405-07492-1). Arno.

Ford, Barbara. Why Does a Turtle Live Longer Than a Dog? A Report on Animal Longevity. LC 79-28159. (Illus.). (gr. 4-6). 1980. 6.95 (ISBN 0-688-22229-3); PLB 6.67 (ISBN 0-688-32229-8). Morrow.

Ford, Norman D. Secrets of Staying Young & Living Longer. 183p. 1979. 4.95 (ISBN 0-686-63831-X). Harian.

Georgakas, Dan. The Methuselah Factors: Living Long & Living Well. 1981. 14.95 (ISBN 0-671-24064-1). S&S.

Gomez, Joan. How Not to Die Young. LC 79-160343. 1972. 25.00x (ISBN 0-8128-1418-5). Stein & Day.

Gordon, Raoul. Go to Puerto Rico & Live to 85 Years of Age. 1978. lib. bdg. 75.00 (ISBN 0-8490-1892-7). Gordon Pr.

--How You Can Live a Long & Healthful Life in the Island of Longevity: Puerto Rico. 1978. lib. bdg. 75.00 (ISBN 0-8490-2024-7). Gordon Pr.

--Living the Good Life in Puerto Rico: Why People Live to a Ripe Old Age in Puerto Rico & How You Can Do It Too. 1978. lib. bdg. 75.00 (ISBN 0-8490-2177-4). Gordon Pr.

--Puerto Rico Land of Longevity: Living a Long Life in Puerto Rico. 1978. lib. bdg. 75.00 (ISBN 0-8490-2490-0). Gordon Pr.

Gruman, Gerald J. A History of Ideas About the Prolongation of Life: The Evolution of Prolongevity Hypotheses to 1800. Kastenbaum, Robert, ed. LC 76-19574. (Death & Dying Ser.). (Illus.). 1977. Repr. of 1966 ed. lib. bdg. 12.00x (ISBN 0-405-09572-4). Arno.

Halsell, Grace. People of Longevity. 1977. write for info. (ISBN 0-394-49404-0). Random.

Hill, Howard E. Nine Magic Secrets of Long Life. 1979. 10.95 (ISBN 0-13-622548-9, Parker). P-H.

Ho, Betty Y. A Chinese & Western Guide to Better Health & Longer Life. LC 74-12332. (Orig.). 1974. pap. 2.00 (ISBN 0-87576-046-5). Pilot Bks.

Hopf, Alice L. Animal & Plant Life Spans. LC 77-17571. (Illus.). (gr. 6 up). 1978. 6.95 (ISBN 0-8234-0320-3). Holiday.

Hufeland, Christoph W. Art of Prolonging Life. Wilson, Erasmus & Kastenbaum, Robert, eds. LC 78-22201. (Aging & Old Age Ser.). 1979. Repr. of 1854 ed. lib. bdg. 22.00x (ISBN 0-405-11817-1). Arno.

Johnson, Charles W., Jr. Fasting, Longevity, & Immortality. (Illus.). 213p. (Orig.). pap. 3.00 (ISBN 0-686-27081-9). Survival CT.

Kahn, Samuel. Essays on Longevity. LC 74-76592. 200p. 1974. 10.00 (ISBN 0-8022-2146-7). Philos Lib.

Kordel, Lelord. Stay Alive Longer. 2nd ed. 224p. 1977. pap. 1.50 (ISBN 0-532-15182-8). Woodhill.

Kugler, Hans. Seven Keys to a Longer Life. 2.25 (ISBN 0-686-29778-4). Cancer Bk Hse.

Kugler, Hans J. Your First Hundred Years of Health: A Practical Guide to Preventive Medicine. LC 78-56945. 1979. cancelled (ISBN 0-8128-2524-1). Stein & Day.

Leonard, Jon N., et al. Live Longer Now: The First One Hundred Years of Your Life. 256p. 1976. pap. 4.95 (ISBN 0-448-12262-6, Today Press). G&D.

Lessius, Leonard & Cornaro, Luigi. A Treatise of Health & Long Life with the Future Means of Attaining It. Kastenbaum, Robert, ed. Smith, Timothy, tr. LC 78-22206. (Aging & Old Age Ser.). 1979. Repr. of 1743 ed. lib. bdg. 12.00x (ISBN 0-405-11821-X). Arno.

Liben, Lynn S., et al, eds. Spatial Representation & Behavior: Application & Theory Across the Life Span. (Developmental Psychology Ser.). 1980. 27.50 (ISBN 0-12-447980-4). Acad Pr.

McQueen-Williams, Morvyth & Apisson, Barbara. A Diet for 100 Healthy Happy Years: Health Secrets from the Caucasus. Ober, Norman, ed. LC 76-30710. 1977. 9.95 (ISBN 0-13-211185-3). P-H.

Mann, John A. Secrets of Life Extension. LC 80-15479. 180p. 1980. pap. 7.95 (ISBN 0-915904-47-0). And-Or Pr.

Metchnikoff, Elie. The Prolongation of Life: Optimistic Studies. Kastenaum, Robert, ed. Mitchell, P. Chalmers, tr. LC 76-19583. (Death & Dying Ser.). (Illus.). 1977. Repr. of 1908 ed. lib. bdg. 23.00x (ISBN 0-405-09579-1). Arno.

Miller, Jonas E. Prescription for Total Health & Longevity. 1979. 2.95 (ISBN 0-88270-353-6). Logos.

Moral Responsibility in Prolonging Life Decisions. 200p. (Orig.). 1981. pap. text ed. write for info. (ISBN 0-935372-08-3). Pope John Ctr.

Parkinson, C. Northcote & LeCompte, Herman. The Law of Longer Life. (Illus.). 1980. 10.95x (ISBN 0-916624-31-5). TSU Pr.

Pelletier, Kenneth R. Longevity: Fulfilling Our Biological Potential. 1981. 14.95 (ISBN 0-440-05016-2, Sey Lawr). Delacorte.

Pohaska, Steve. Little Known Secrets: Health - Long Life. 1.45 (ISBN 0-686-29942-6). Cancer Bk Hse.

Richardson, Joseph G. Long Life & How to Reach It. Rosenkrantz, Barbara G., ed. LC 76-40640. (Public Health in America Ser.). 1977. Repr. of 1886 ed. lib. bdg. 12.00x (ISBN 0-405-09828-6). Arno.

Rosenfeld, Albert. Prolongevity. 1976. 11.95 (ISBN 0-394-48929-2). Knopf.

Sage, J. A. Live to Be One Hundred & Enjoy It. 128p. 1975. pap. 1.95 (ISBN 0-346-12202-3). Cornerstone.

ShuChin, Chuang & Deisher, J. Chinese Secrets of Longevity. 1978. pap. 2.95 (ISBN 0-8120-0945-2). Barron.

Thomas, William J. Human Longevity: Its Fact & Its Fiction. Kastenbaum, Robert, ed. LC 78-22220. (Aging & Old Age Ser.). 1979. Repr. of 1873 ed. lib. bdg. 20.00x (ISBN 0-405-11833-3). Arno.

Ticktin, George B. How to Be One Hundred Years Young. LC 78-12702. 144p. 1979. 9.95 (ISBN 0-8119-0318-4). Fell.

Veatch, Robert M., ed. Life Span: The Hastings Center Report on Values & Life-Extending Technologies. LC 78-3354. 1979. 12.95 (ISBN 0-06-250908-X, HarpR). Har-Row.

Volin, Michael. Challenging the Years: A Book of Ancient Wisdom & Modern Knowledge for Health & Long Life. LC 78-69624. (Illus.). 1979. 11.95 (ISBN 0-06-014469-6, HarpT). Har-Row.

West, Steven & Tyburn-Lombard, Donald. How to Live to Be a 100 & Enjoy It! (Illus.). 1977. 5.95 (ISBN 0-89519-004-4). AMW.

Woodruff, Diana S. Can You Live to Be One Hundred. LC 77-11997. 1977. 7.95 (ISBN 0-89456-001-8). Chatham Sq.

LONGFELLOW, HENRY WADSWORTH, 1807-1882

Aldrich, Mrs. Thomas B. Crowding Memories: Mark Twain, Browning, Longfellow. 1979. Repr. of 1920 ed. lib. bdg. 25.00 (ISBN 0-8495-0145-8). Arden Lib.

Arvin, Newton. Longfellow: His Life & Work. LC 77-1342. 1977. Repr. of 1963 ed. lib. bdg. 26.00 (ISBN 0-8371-9505-5, ARLO). Greenwood.

Austin, George L. Henry Wadsworth Longfellow. LC 73-12138. 1888. 40.00 (ISBN 0-8414-2889-1). Folcroft.

--Henry Wadsworth Longfellow: His Life, His Works & His Friendships. 419p. 1980. Repr. of 1888 ed. lib. bdg. 35.00 (ISBN 0-8492-3249-X). R West.

--Henry Wadsworth Longfellow: His Life, His Works, His Friendship. 1980. Repr. of 1888 ed. lib. bdg. 35.00 (ISBN 0-8495-0153-9). Arden Lib.

Bates, C. F. The Longfellow Birthday Book. 398p. 1980. Repr. lib. bdg. 30.00 (ISBN 0-89760-039-8, Telegraph). Dynamic Learn Corp.

Carpenter, George R. Henry Wadsworth Longfellow. 1901. lib. bdg. 10.00 (ISBN 0-8414-3471-9). Folcroft.

Chamberlain, Jacob C. A Bibliography of the First Editions in Book Form of the Writings of Henry Wadsworth Longfellow. LC 72-3116. (American Literature Ser., No. 49). 1972. Repr. of 1908 ed. lib. bdg. 32.95 (ISBN 0-8383-1513-5). Haskell.

Clarke, Helen A. Longfellow's Country. 1978. Repr. of 1909 ed. lib. bdg. 40.00 (ISBN 0-8495-0733-2). Arden Lib.

--Longfellow's Country. 1979. Repr. of 1909 ed. lib. bdg. 35.00 (ISBN 0-8492-4030-1). R West.

Country Beautiful Editors. America the Beautiful in the Words of Henry Wadsworth Longfellow. LC 65-16922. (America the Beautiful Ser). (Illus.). 98p. 1965. 9.95 (ISBN 0-87294-001-2). Country Beautiful.

Dexter, D. Gilbert. Life & Works of Henry Wadsworth Longfellow. 59.95 (ISBN 0-8490-0524-8). Gordon Pr.

Edwards, George T. The Youthful Haunts of Longfellow. 1907. Repr. 25.00 (ISBN 0-8274-3782-X). R West.

Goold, Nathan. The Wadsworth-Longfellow House: Longfellow's Old Home. Repr. of 1915 ed. lib. bdg. 17.50 (ISBN 0-8492-4907-4). R West.

Gorman, Herbert S. A Victorian American: Henry Wadsworth Longfellow. 1979. Repr. of 1926 ed. lib. bdg. 35.00 (ISBN 0-8492-4933-3). R West.

Hansen, Harry. Longfellow's New England. (Illus.). 192p. 1972. 8.75 (ISBN 0-8038-4279-1). Hastings.

Hatfield, James T. New Light on Longfellow: With Special Reference to His Relations with Germany. LC 70-114097. (Illus.). 1970. Repr. of 1933 ed. text ed. 8.50 (ISBN 0-87752-050-X). Gordian.

Herbin, John F. Grand-Pre: A Sketch of the Acadian Occupation of the Shores of the Basin of Minas. 1978. Repr. of 1900 ed. 25.00 (ISBN 0-8492-5312-8). R West.

Hilen, Andrew. Longfellow & Scandinavia: A Study of the Poet's Relationship with the Northern Languages & Literature. LC 76-91181. (Yale Studies in English Ser.: No. 107). 1970. Repr. of 1947 ed. 16.50 (ISBN 0-208-00921-3, Archon). Shoe String.

Holberg, Ruth L. American Bard: The Story of Henry Wadsworth Longfellow. LC 63-15090. (Illus.). (gr. 5-9). 1963. 5.95 (ISBN 0-690-05923-X, TYC-J). Har-Row.

Iannetta, Sabatino. Henry W. Longfellow & Montecassino. LC 72-10002. (American Literature Ser., No. 49). 1973. Repr. of 1938 ed. lib. bdg. 32.95 (ISBN 0-8383-1678-6). Haskell.

--Henry W. Longfellow & Montecassino, His Rhode Island Friendship, His Birthplace. LC 74-12262. 1974. Repr. of 1938 ed. lib. bdg. 8.75 (ISBN 0-8414-5060-9). Folcroft.

--Henry W. Longfellow & Montecassion, His Rhode Island Friendship, His Birthplace. 136p. 1980. Repr. of 1938 ed. lib. bdg. 15.00 (ISBN 0-8495-2613-2). Arden Lib.

Johnson, Carl L. Professor Longfellow of Harvard. LC 44-42422. 1944. pap. 1.00 (ISBN 0-87114-003-9). U of Oreg Bks.

--Three Notes on Longfellow. (American Literature Ser., No. 49). 1970. pap. 11.95 (ISBN 0-8383-0047-2). Haskell.

Johnson, L. W. The Longfellow Prose Birthday Book. 421p. 1980. Repr. of 1888 ed. lib. bdg. 30.00 (ISBN 0-89760-405-9, Telegraph). Dynamic Learn Corp.

Kennedy, W. Sloane. Henry W. Longfellow: Biography, Anecdote, Letters, Criticism. LC 72-3295. (American Biography Ser., No. 32). 1972. Repr. of 1882 ed. lib. bdg. 42.95 (ISBN 0-8383-1512-7). Haskell.

Livingston, Luther S. Bibliography of the First Editions in Book Form of the Writings of Henry Wadsworth Longfellow. 1908. 20.50 (ISBN 0-8337-2129-1). B Franklin.

Longfellow, Henry W. The Letters of Henry Wadsworth Longfellow, 4 vols. Hilen, Andrew R., ed. Incl. Vols. 1-2. 1814-36; 1837-43. 1967. Set. 50.00x (ISBN 0-674-52725-9); Vols. 3-4. 1844-1856; 1857-1865. 1972. Set. 50.00x (ISBN 0-674-52728-3). LC 66-18248 (Belknap Pr). Harvard U Pr.

--Life of Henry Wadsworth Longfellow, with Extracts from His Journals & Correspondence, 3 Vols. Longfellow, Samuel, ed. LC 4-17165. 1968. Repr. of 1891 ed. Set. 40.00 (ISBN 0-403-00078-5). Scholarly.

--The Poetical Works of Longfellow. rev. new ed. Monteiro, George, intro. by. (Cambridge Editions Ser.). 1975. 18.95 (ISBN 0-395-18487-8). HM.

Longfellow, Samuel, ed. Life of Henry Wadsworth Longfellow, with Extracts from His Journals & Correspondence, 3 Vols. LC 68-57619. (Illus.). 1969. Repr. of 1891 ed. Set. lib. bdg. 57.00x (ISBN 0-8371-1048-3, LOLO). Greenwood.

Macchetta, Blanche R. The Home Life of Henry W. Longfellow. LC 74-19094. 1974. Repr. of 1882 ed. lib. bdg. 22.50 (ISBN 0-8414-8604-2). Folcroft.

M'Ilwraith, J. N. A Book About Longfellow. 1900. Repr. 20.00 (ISBN 0-8274-1952-X). R West.

Murphy, Patrick. Henry Wadsworth Longfellow. LC 76-44808. 1976. Repr. of 1882 ed. lib. bdg. 10.00 (ISBN 0-8414-6055-8). Folcroft.

Norton, Charles E. Henry Wadsworth Longfellow. LC 72-191243. Repr. of 1906 ed. 12.50 (ISBN 0-8414-0866-1). Folcroft.

Robertson, Eric S. Life of Henry Wadsworth Longfellow. LC 70-160775. 1971. Repr. of 1887 ed. 11.00 (ISBN 0-8046-1607-8). Kennikat.

--Life of Henry Wadsworth Longfellow. 1887. Repr. lib. bdg. 10.50 (ISBN 0-8414-7451-6). Folcroft.

--Life of Henry Wadsworth Longfellow. Repr. of 1887 ed. lib. bdg. 20.00 (ISBN 0-8495-4535-8). Arden Lib.
Saintsbury, George E. Prefaces & Essays. LC 72-99722. (Essay Index Reprint Ser). 1933. 25.00 (ISBN 0-8369-1377-9). Arno.
Seiber, R. Timothy, Jr. Characters in Tales of a Wayside Inn. 199p. 1981. Repr. of 1939 ed. lib. bdg. 40.00 (ISBN 0-89760-928-X). Telegraph Bks.
Shepard, Odell. Longfellow. 371p. 1980. Repr. lib. bdg. 35.00 (ISBN 0-89987-754-0). Darby Bks.
Smeaton, Oliphant. Longfellow & His Poetry. 1913. lib. bdg. 7.50 (ISBN 0-8414-7706-X). Folcroft.
Smeaton, William H., ed. Longfellow & His Poetry. LC 76-120966. (Poetry & Life Ser.). Repr. of 1913 ed. 7.25 (ISBN 0-404-52533-4). AMS Pr.
Smith, A. H. A Longfellow Calendar. 1973. lib. bdg. 8.50 (ISBN 0-8414-1576-5). Folcroft.
Thompson, Lawrance. Young Longfellow, 1807-1843. 1969. lib. bdg. 24.50x (ISBN 0-374-97885-9). Octagon.
Underwood, Francis H. Henry Wadsworth Longfellow. LC 72-1974. (American Biography Ser., No. 32). 1972. Repr. of 1882 ed. lib. bdg. 38.95 (ISBN 0-8383-1449-X). Haskell.
--Henry Wadsworth Longfellow: A Biographical Sketch. 1978. Repr. of 1882 ed. lib. bdg. 25.00 (ISBN 0-8495-5400-4). Arden Lib.
Van Schaick, John, Jr. Characters in Tales of a Wayside Inn. LC 74-1159. (Henry W. Longfellow Ser., No. 58). 1974. lib. bdg. 37.95 (ISBN 0-8383-2028-7). Haskell.
Walters, Frank. Studies of Some of Longfellow's Poems. LC 77-22319. 1892. lib. bdg. 10.00 (ISBN 0-8414-9465-7). Folcroft.
Whitmore, Sandra J., illus. Scenes from Longfellow's Poems: A Coloring Book. (gr. 1-4). 1978. pap. 1.95 (ISBN 0-915592-31-2). Maine Hist.
Williams, Cecil B. Henry Wadsworth Longfellow. (Twayne's United States Authors Ser). 1964. pap. 3.45 (ISBN 0-8084-0155-6, T68, Twayne). Coll & U Pr.
--Henry Wadsworth Longfellow. (U. S. Authors Ser.: No. 68). 1964. lib. bdg. 9.95 (ISBN 0-8057-0456-6). Twayne.

LONGHORN CATTLE

Dobie, J. Frank. The Longhorns. (Illus.). 1941. 12.95 (ISBN 0-316-18796-8). Little.
Steele, Melba. Cowboy, Game Warden & Longhorns. 104p. 1981. 6.95 (ISBN 0-686-72645-6). Dorrance.

LONGITUDE

see also Time

Christy, Miller, ed. The Voyage of Captain Luke Foxe of Hull & Captain Thomas James of Bristol, in Search of a Northwest Passage, in 1631-32. (Hakluyt Society. Publications: Nos. 88-89). (Illus.). 1966. Repr. of 1894 ed. 63.00 (ISBN 0-8337-0568-7). B Franklin.
Howse, Derek. Greenwich Time & the Discovery of the Longitude. (Illus.). 1980. 24.95 (ISBN 0-19-215948-8). Oxford U Pr.
James, Thomas. The Strange & Dangerous Voyage of Captaine T. James. LC 68-54650. (English Experience Ser.: No. 58). 1968. Repr. of 1633 ed. 22.00 (ISBN 90-221-0058-8). Walter J Johnson.

LONGSHOREMEN

Barnes, Charles B. The Longshoremen. Stein, Leon, ed. LC 77-70482. (Work Ser.). (Illus.). 1977. Repr. of 1915 ed. lib. bdg. 25.00x (ISBN 0-405-10156-2). Arno.
Clark, Roy. The Longshoremen. 1974. 5.95 (ISBN 0-7153-6484-7). David & Charles.
Evans, A. A. Technical & Social Changes in the World's Ports. 2nd ed. (Studies & Reports, New Ser.: No. 74). 1971. 6.85 (ISBN 92-2-100009-5). Intl Labour Office.
Fairley, Lincoln. Facing Mechanization: The West Coast Longshore Plan. (Monograph Ser.: No. 23). 1979. 8.50 (ISBN 0-89215-101-3). U Cal LA Indus Rel.
Guide to Safety & Health in Dock Work. x, 287p. 1976. 18.55 (ISBN 92-2-101081-3). Intl Labour Office.
Hill, Stephen. The Dockers: Class & Tradition in London. 1976. text ed. 37.00x (ISBN 0-435-82416-3). Heinemann Ed.
Jackson, Michael P. Labor Relations on the Docks. 1973. 16.95 (ISBN 0-347-01002-4, 86579-6, Pub. by Saxon Hse). Lexington Bks.
Jensen, Vernon H. Decasualization & Modernization of Dock Work in London. LC 72-632773. (ILR Paperback Ser.: No. 9). 112p. 1971. pap. 2.50 (ISBN 0-87546-040-2); pap. 5.50 special hard bdg. (ISBN 0-87546-276-6). NY Sch Indus Rel.
--Hiring of Dock Workers & Employment Practices in the Ports of New York, Liverpool, London, Rotterdam, & Marseilles. LC 64-19587. (Wertheim Publications in Industrial Relations Ser). 1964. 17.50x (ISBN 0-674-39200-0). Harvard U Pr.
Larrowe, Charles P. Shape-up & Hiring Hall. LC 75-46614. (Illus.). 250p. 1976. Repr. of 1955 ed. lib. bdg. 15.25x (ISBN 0-8371-8750-8, LASU). Greenwood.
Pilcher, W. Portland Longshoremen. LC 72-84398. (Case Studies in Cultural Anthropology). 1972. pap. text ed. 5.95 (ISBN 0-03-091289-X, HoltC). HR&W.
Quin, Mike. The Big Strike. (Illus.). 1979. pap. 2.95 (ISBN 0-7178-0504-2). Intl Pub Co.
Theriault, Reg. Longshoring on the San Francisco Waterfront. (Singlejack Little Book Ser.). 32p. 1978. pap. 0.95 (ISBN 0-917300-02-5). Miles & Weir.
Ward, Estolv E. Harry Bridges on Trial. LC 74-22761. (Labor Movement in Fiction & Non-Fiction). 1976. Repr. of 1940 ed. 19.75 (ISBN 0-404-58514-0). AMS Pr.

LONGSTREET, JAMES, 1821-1904

Longstreet, H. D. Lee & Longstreet at High Tide: Gettysburg in the Light of the Official Records. 1904. write for info. (ISBN 0-527-58200-X). Kraus Repr.
Sanger, Donald B. & Hay, Thomas R. James Longstreet: Soldier, Politician, Officeholder, & Writer. 10.00 (ISBN 0-8446-0890-4). Peter Smith.
Thomas, Wilbur D. General James "Pete" Longstreet. 1979. 21.00 (ISBN 0-87012-330-0). McClain.

LONGUS, fl. 3RD or 4TH CENTURY A.D.

Longus. The Story of Daphnis & Chloe. Connor, W. R., ed. LC 78-18586. (Greek Texts & Commentaries Ser.). (Illus.). 1979. Repr. of 1908 ed. lib. bdg. 15.00x (ISBN 0-405-11428-1). Arno.
McCulloh, William E. Longus. LC 77-99541. (World Authors Ser.). 1970. lib. bdg. 12.95x (ISBN 0-8057-2540-7). Irvington.

LONGWAYS DANCE

see Country-Dance

LONGWORTH, ALICE ROOSEVELT, 1884-

Longworth, Alice R. Crowded Hours. Baxter, Annette K., ed. LC 79-8799. (Signal Lives Ser.). (Illus.). 1980. Repr. of 1933 ed. lib. bdg. 33.00x (ISBN 0-405-12846-0). Arno.
Teague, Michael. Mrs L. Conversations with Alice Roosevelt Longworth. LC 78-22360. (Illus.). 216p. 1981. 19.95 (ISBN 0-686-71768-6). Doubleday.
Teichmann, Howard. Alice: The Life & Times of Alice Roosevelt Longworth. LC 79-12512. (Illus.). 1979. 12.95 (ISBN 0-13-022210-0). P-H.

LOOKING-GLASSES

see Mirrors

LOOMS

Aitken, J. B. Automatic Weaving. 7.50 (ISBN 0-87245-000-7). Textile Bk.
Broudy, Eric. Book of Looms. 1979. 16.95 (ISBN 0-442-21105-8). Van Nos Reinhold.
Grae, Ida. Dressing the Loom. 1975. Repr. of 1953 ed. 5.00 (ISBN 0-686-11143-5). Robin & Russ.
Hjert, Jeri & Von Rosenstiel, Paul. Loom Construction. 1978. 11.95 (ISBN 0-442-23416-3); pap. 7.95 (ISBN 0-442-23417-1). Van Nos Reinhold.
Hooper, Luther. Hand Loom Weaving. LC 78-21372. (Illus.). 1979. pap. 9.95 (ISBN 0-8008-3805-X, Pentalic). Taplinger.
Kirby, Mary. Designing on the Loom. (Illus.). 1979. pap. 7.50 (ISBN 0-910458-11-1). Select Bks.
Kliot. The Vertical Loom: Principles & Construction. 2.00 (ISBN 0-916896-09-9). Lacis Pubns.
Redman, Jane. Frame-Loom Weaving. (Illus.). 144p. 1976. 14.50 (ISBN 0-442-26860-2). Van Nos Reinhold.
Reed, Tim. The Loom Book. LC 76-11108. pap. 5.95 (ISBN 0-684-14073-X, SL558, ScribT). Scribner.
Roth, H. Ling. Ancient Egyptian & Greek Looms. 1978. pap. 5.95 (ISBN 0-686-15716-8). Robin & Russ.
--Studies in Primitive Looms. 1977. pap. 7.95 (ISBN 0-686-19834-4). Robin & Russ.
Tidball, Harriet. Build or Buy a Loom, Pt. 1. Bd. with Pt. 2. Patterns for Pick-Ups. LC 76-24013. (Shuttle Craft Guild Monographs: No. 23). (Illus.). 38p. 1968. pap. 6.50 (ISBN 0-916658-23-6). HTH Pubs.

LOONS

Green, Ivah J. Loon. LC 65-22310. (Illus.). (gr. 4 up). 1968. PLB 5.99 (ISBN 0-87783-025-8). Oddo.

LOOPS, PHASE-LOCKED

see Phase-Locked Loops

LOPE DE VEGA

see Vega Carpio, Lope Felix De, 1562-1635

LOPEZ, AARON, 1731-1782

Chyet, Stanley F. Lopez of Newport: Colonial American Merchant Prince. LC 78-93898. 1970. 11.95x (ISBN 0-8143-1407-4). Wayne St U Pr.

LOPEZ, FERNAM, d. 1341

Bell, Aubrey F. Fernam Lopez. (Illus.). 1921. 2.00 (ISBN 0-87535-006-2). Hispanic Soc.

LOPEZ, MARTIN

Gardiner, Clinton H. Martin Lopez. Conquistador Citizen of Mexico. LC 73-19307. 193p. 1974. Repr. of 1958 ed. lib. bdg. 15.00x (ISBN 0-8371-7322-1, GAML). Greenwood.

LOPEZ, NANCY

Lopez, Nancy. The Education of a Woman Golfer. 192p. 1980. pap. 6.95 (ISBN 0-346-12492-1). Cornerstone.
Phillips, Betty L. The Picture Story of Nancy Lopez. LC 79-25344. (Illus.). 64p. (gr. 4-6). 1980. PLB 6.97 (ISBN 0-671-33050-0). Messner.

LORD HOWE ISLAND-HISTORY

Finch, Alan & Finch, Valerie. Lord Howe Island. (Illus.). 1967. 8.00x (ISBN 0-8426-1258-0). Verry.

LORD'S DAY

see Sabbath; Sunday

LORD'S PRAYER

Barclay, William. The Beatitudes & the Lord's Prayer for Everyman. LC 75-9309. 256p. 1975. pap. 4.95 (ISBN 0-06-060393-3, RD112, HarpR). Har-Row.
Bast, Henry. The Lord's Prayer. 2.50 (ISBN 0-686-23480-4). Rose Pub MI.
Bouley, Alan. From Freedom to Formula: The Evolution of the Eucharistic Prayer from Oral Improvisation to Written Text. (Studies in Christian Antiquity: Vol. 21). 288p. 1980. 25.00x (ISBN 0-8132-0554-9). Cath U Pr.
Brown, John. An Exposition of Our Lord's Intercessory Prayer. (Giant Summit Books). 1980. pap. 6.95 (ISBN 0-8010-0774-7). Baker Bk.
--The Intercessory Prayer of Our Lord Jesus Christ. 1978. 10.50 (ISBN 0-86524-961-X). Klock & Klock.
Cartwright, Colbert S. The Lord's Prayer Comes Alive. LC 73-2816. (Orig.). 1973. pap. 2.75 (ISBN 0-8272-2112-6). Bethany Pr.
Clark, Glenn. Lord's Prayer. pap. 0.50 (ISBN 0-910924-08-2). Macalester.
Cockman, Welda. Layman Looks at the Lord's Prayer: Leader's Guide. 1979. pap. 3.25 (ISBN 0-8024-4646-9). Moody.
Cottle, Ronald E. The Lord's Prayer. 48p. 1980. 0.95 (ISBN 0-88243-566-3, 02-0566). Gospel Pub.
Crosby, Michael H. Thy Will Be Done: Praying the Our Father As Subversive Activity. LC 77-5118. 1977. 8.95 (ISBN 0-88344-496-8); pap. 6.95 (ISBN 0-88344-497-6). Orbis Bks.
Dods, Marcus. The Prayer That Teaches to Pray. LC 80-82323. (Shepherd Illustrated Classics Ser.). (Illus.). 1980. pap. 5.95 (ISBN 0-87983-232-0). Keats.
Elliott, Norman. How to Be the Lord's Prayer. pap. 2.95 (ISBN 0-910924-26-0). Macalester.
Errico, Rocco A. The Ancient Aramaic Prayer of Jesus. (Illus.). 1978. pap. 3.95 (ISBN 0-911336-69-9). Sci of Mind.
Evely, Louis. We Dare to Say Our Father. 120p. 1975. pap. 1.45 (ISBN 0-385-06274-5, Im). Doubleday.
Hammarberg, Melvin A. & Nelson, Clifford A., eds. My Book of Prayers: A Personal Prayer Book. LC 56-10134. 192p. 1956. pap. 3.75 (ISBN 0-8006-0454-7, 1-454). Fortress.
Huffman, John A., Jr. Forgive Us Our Prayers. 1980. pap. 1.95 (ISBN 0-88207-519-5). Victor Bks.
Jeremias, Joachim. The Lord's Prayer. Reumann, John, ed. & tr. from Ger. LC 64-11859. (Facet Bks.). 56p. 1964. pap. 1.50 (ISBN 0-8006-3008-4, 1-3008). Fortress.
Keller, Phillip, tr. Meditacoes De Um Leigo. (Portugese Bks.). (Port.). 1979. 1.60 (ISBN 0-8297-0788-3). Life Pubs Intl.
Keller, W. Philip. Layman Looks at the Lord's Prayer. study ed 4.95 (ISBN 0-8024-4647-7). Moody.
--A Layman Looks at the Lord's Prayer. 1977. pap. 3.95 (ISBN 0-8024-4644-2). Moody.
Keller, W. Phillip. A Layman Looks at the Lord's Prayer. 1977. pap. 2.95 (ISBN 0-89066-003-4). World Wide Pubs.
Letchford, Peter. Help! I Don't Know How to Pray. LC 76-29332. 1976. 4.95 (ISBN 0-914850-75-X). Impact Tenn.
Marty, Martin E. Hidden Discipline. LC 62-21428. 1962. 3.50 (ISBN 0-570-03194-X, 12-2595). Concordia.
Maurice, Frederick D. The Prayer Book & the Lord's Prayer. 1977. Repr. of 1880 ed. 11.95 (ISBN 0-87921-038-9). Attic Pr.
Ogilvie, Heinrich. The Lord's Prayer. 1978. pap. 2.50 (ISBN 0-903540-09-6, Pub by Floris Books). St George Bk Serv.
Overduin, Daniel. Reflections on the Lord's Prayer. 1980. pap. 1.75 (ISBN 0-570-03815-4, 12-2783). Concordia.
Pink, Arthur W. Beatitudes & the Lord's Prayer. 1979. 5.95 (ISBN 0-8010-7043-0). Baker Bk.
Poovey, W. A. The Prayer He Taught: Seven Dramas & Meditations on the Lord's Prayer. LC 76-27077. 1977. pap. 3.50 (ISBN 0-8066-1564-8, 10-5077); drama bklet 1.50 (ISBN 0-8066-1563-X, 10-5078). Augsburg.
Prime, Derek. Tell Me About the Lord's Prayer. (Illus., Orig.). (gr. 4-6). 1967. pap. 1.50 (ISBN 0-8024-3620-X). Moody.
Rommel, Kurt. Our Father Who Art in Heaven. Cooperrider, Edward A., tr. from Ger. LC 80-2373. 64p. 1981. pap. write for info. (ISBN 0-8006-1448-8, 1-1448). Fortress.
Sikorsky, Igor I. Message of the Lord's Prayer. 1963. 4.95 (ISBN 0-8392-1068-X). Astor-Honor.
Snowden, Rita F. Lord's Prayer: The Living Word. (Illus.). 1968. pap. 1.00 (ISBN 0-87508-520-2). Chr Lit.
Thielicke, Helmut. The Prayer That Spans the World. Doberstein, J. W., tr. from Ger. 1978. 12.00 (ISBN 0-227-67671-8). Attic Pr.
Very, Alice. The Lord's Prayer. 1975. 3.75 (ISBN 0-8283-1629-5). Branden.
Wainwright, Geoffrey. Eucharist & Eschatology. 256p. 1981. pap. text ed. 6.95x (ISBN 0-19-520248-1); pap. 6.95 (ISBN 0-19-520249-X). Oxford U Pr.
Watson, Thomas. Lord's Prayer. 1978. 10.95 (ISBN 0-85151-145-7). Banner of Truth.

LORD'S PRAYER-EARLY WORKS TO 1800

Hill, Robert. The Pathway to Prayer & Pietie. LC 74-28864. (English Experience Ser.: No. 744). 1975. Repr. of 1613 ed. 26.50 (ISBN 90-221-0744-2). Walter J Johnson.

LORD'S PRAYER-JUVENILE LITERATURE

Lomasney, Eileen. My Book of the Lord's Prayer. (Illus.). 32p. (gr. k-4). 1976. 5.95 (ISBN 0-570-03456-6, 56-1290). Concordia.
Lucy, Reda, pseud. The Lord's Prayer for Children. (Illus.). 24p. (Orig.). (ps-3). 1981. pap. 1.95 (ISBN 0-87516-437-4). De Vorss.
Rostron, Hilda L. Lord's Prayer & Other Prayers. (Ladybird Ser.). (Illus.). (gr. 1-2). 1961. bds. 1.49 (ISBN 0-87508-848-1). Chr Lit.

LORD'S PRAYER-MEDITATIONS

Archilla, Rogelio. Meditaciones Sobre el Padrenuestro. 96p. (Span.). Date not set. pap. price not set (ISBN 0-311-40046-9, Edit Mundo). Casa Bautista.
Burghardt, W. J. & Lawler, T. C., eds. St. Gregory of Nyssa, the Lord's Prayer, the Beatitudes. LC 78-62466. (ACW Ser.: No. 18). 216p. 1954. 9.95 (ISBN 0-8091-0255-2). Paulist Pr.
Raymond, Francis & Line, Helen E. Blueprint for Living. 1977. pap. text ed. 1.95x (ISBN 0-8358-0360-0). Upper Room.

LORD'S PRAYER-SERMONS

Ebeling, Gerhard. On Prayer: The Lord's Prayer in Today's World. Leitch, James W., tr. from Ger. LC 78-5079. 112p. 1978. pap. 2.95 (ISBN 0-8006-1336-8, 1-1336). Fortress.
Thielicke, Helmut. Our Heavenly Father. (Minister's Paperback Library Ser.). 1974. pap. 3.95 (ISBN 0-8010-8814-3). Baker Bk.

LORD'S SUPPER

see also Agape; First Communion; Last Supper; Mass; Sacraments; Sacred Meals; Transubstantiation

Aelfric, Abbot. A Testimonie of Antique. LC 73-36208. (English Experience Ser.: No. 214). Repr. of 1567 ed. 13.00 (ISBN 90-221-0214-9). Walter J Johnson.
Bernadot, M. V. The Eucharist & the Trinity. 2.25 (ISBN 0-685-62267-3). M Glazier.
Bernier, Paul. Bread Broken & Shared. LC 81-67539. (Illus.). 144p. 1981. pap. 3.95 (ISBN 0-87793-232-8). Ave Maria.
Bothwell, H. Roger. My First Book About Communion. (My Church Teaches Ser.). (Illus.). (ps). 1978. pap. 1.25 (ISBN 0-8127-0180-1). Review & Herald.
Bradford, John. Writings of John Bradford...Martyr, 1555, 2 Vols. Repr. of 1853 ed. Set. 76.00 (ISBN 0-384-05440-4). Johnson Repr.
Brokamp, Sr. Marlene & Brokamp, Sr. Marilyn. Eucharist: God's Gift of Love. (Illus.). 28p. (Orig.). 1976. pap. 1.25 (ISBN 0-912228-25-3). St Anthony Mess Pr.
Champlin, Joseph M. An Important Office of Immense Love: A Handbook for Eucharistic Ministers. LC 80-80085. 152p. (Orig.). 1980. pap. 3.50 (ISBN 0-8091-2287-1). Paulist Pr.
Consultation on Church Union. World Bread Cup. 1978. 0.85 (ISBN 0-686-28801-7). Forward Movement.
Cullmann, Oscar & Leenhardt, Franz J. Essays on the Lord's Supper. LC 58-8979. 1958. pap. 3.95 (ISBN 0-8042-3748-4). John Knox.
Deiss, Lucien. It's the Lord's Supper: The Eucharist of Christians. LC 76-12649. 168p. 1976. pap. 4.95 (ISBN 0-8091-1954-4, Deus). Paulist Pr.
Drower, Ethel S. Water into Wine: A Study of Ritual Idiom in the Middle East. LC 77-87663. Repr. of 1956 ed. 23.50 (ISBN 0-404-16401-3). AMS Pr.
Elert, W. The Lord's Supper Today. (Contemporary Theology Ser. II). 1973. 2.95 (ISBN 0-570-06723-5, 12RT2562). Concordia.
Feeley-Harnick, Gillian. The Lord's Table: Eucharist & Passover in Early Christianity. 1981. text ed. 19.95x (ISBN 0-8122-7786-4). U of Pa Pr.

Gavin, F. Jewish Antecedents of the Christian Sacraments. 1929. 10.00x (ISBN 0-87068-056-0). Ktav.

Grabo, Norman S. Edward Taylor's Treatise Concerning the Lord's Supper. li, 263p. 1966. 7.50 (ISBN 0-87013-098-6). Mich St U Pr.

Greet, Brian A. Broken Bread in a Broken World. LC 70-172826. 1972. pap. 2.50 (ISBN 0-8170-0549-8). Judson.

Guzie, Tad W. Jesus & the Eucharist. LC 73-90069. 1974. pap. 4.95 (ISBN 0-8091-1858-0). Paulist Pr.

Habel, Norman C. Create in Me: A Form of the Eucharist in a Modern Idiom. 1978. 0.95 (ISBN 0-915644-14-2). Clayton Pub Hse.

Haffert, John M. World's Greatest Secret. 312p. 1968. 4.95 (ISBN 0-911988-21-1); pap. 1.50 (ISBN 0-911988-22-X). AMI Pr.

Hagerty, Cornelius. The Holy Eucharist. 77p. 1967. pap. 1.50 (ISBN 0-912414-12-X). Lumen Christi.

Hay, Camillus. The Eucharist in the Churches. 1976. pap. 2.50 (ISBN 0-685-77521-6). Franciscan Herald.

Hellwig, Monika. The Eucharist & the Hunger of the World. LC 76-18050. 100p. 1976. pap. 2.95 (ISBN 0-8091-1958-7). Paulist Pr.

Hooper, John. The Later Writings of Bishop Hooper. 1852. 46.00 (ISBN 0-384-24211-1). Johnson Repr.

Jaubert, Annie. Date of the Last Supper. LC 65-17975. 1965. 3.50 (ISBN 0-8189-0036-9). Alba.

Kay, Melissa. It Is Your Own Mystery: A Guide to the Communion Rite. (Illus.). 1977. pap. 5.00 (ISBN 0-918208-17-3). Liturgical Conf.

Keating, J. F. Agape & the Eucharist in the Early Church: Studies in the History of Christian Love Feasts. LC 71-79511. Repr. of 1901 ed. 19.50 (ISBN 0-404-03640-6). AMS Pr.

Kelly, George A. Sacrament of the Eucharist in Our Time. 1978. 3.75 (ISBN 0-8198-0553-X); pap. 2.25 (ISBN 0-8198-0554-8). Dghtrs St Paul.

Kilmartin, Edward J. Church, Eucharist & Priesthood: A Theological Commentary on "The Mystery & Worship of the Most Holy Eucharist". LC 81-81343. 112p. (Orig.). 1981. pap. 4.95 (ISBN 0-8091-2386-X). Paulist Pr.

Lemons, Frank W. In Remembrance of Me. 1975. 4.25 (ISBN 0-87148-430-7); pap. 2.95 (ISBN 0-87148-431-5). Pathway Pr.

Livermore, Penny. Called to His Supper: The Biblical Eucharist. 2.95 (ISBN 0-685-62268-1). M Glazier.

The Lord's Supper. 1979. 10.95 (ISBN 0-570-03275-X, 15-2720). Concordia.

Lubich, Chiara. The Eucharist. LC 77-82230. 1977. pap. 1.95 (ISBN 0-911782-30-3). New City.

McEachern, Alton H. Here at Thy Table Lord. LC 77-1024. 1978. pap. 3.50 (ISBN 0-8054-2310-9). Broadman.

Marty, Martin E. The Lord's Supper. LC 79-6550. 80p. (Orig.). 1980. pap. 2.25 (ISBN 0-8006-1386-4, 1-1386). Fortress.

Merton, Thomas. The Living Bread. 157p. 1956. 12.95 (ISBN 0-374-14613-6); pap. 5.95 (ISBN 0-374-51520-4). FS&G.

Miller, Ronald H. The Holy Eucharist: Study Guide. 1977. pap. 2.75x (ISBN 0-8192-4075-3). Morehouse.

Mitchell, Nathan. Cult & Controversy: The Worship of the Eucharist Outside Mass. Kavanagh, Aidan, ed. (Studies in the Reformed Rites of the Catholic Church: Vol. IV). 360p. (Orig.). 1981. pap. 11.95 (ISBN 0-916134-50-4). Pueblo Pub Co.

Murray, Andrew & Choy, Leona. Lord's Table. (Orig.). 1980. pap. 2.95 (ISBN 0-87508-380-3). Chr Lit.

Nevin, John W. Mystical Presence & Other Writings on the Eucharist. abr. ed. Thompson, Bard & Bricker, George M., eds. LC 66-16193. 1966. 9.95 (ISBN 0-8298-0093-X). Pilgrim NY.

Pope John Paul. Brazill - Journey in the Light of the Eucharist. 1980. 8.00 (ISBN 0-8198-1102-5); pap. 7.00 (ISBN 0-8198-1103-3). Dghtrs St Paul.

Rauch, William J. The Lord's Supper. 1971. 2.25 (ISBN 0-89536-136-1). CSS Pub.

Riggle, H. M. Christian Baptism, Feet Washing & the Lord's Supper. 264p. 3.50 (ISBN 0-686-29105-0). Faith Pub Hse.

Saunders, Landon B. The Power of Receiving. (Twentieth Century Sermons Ser.). 1979. 9.95 (ISBN 0-89112-312-1). Bibl Res Pr.

Sumrall, Lester. The Cup of Life. 180p. 1980. pap. 3.95 (ISBN 0-8407-5720-4). Nelson.

Toler, Thomas. Elder at the Lord's Table. 1953. pap. 2.50 (ISBN 0-8272-0800-6). Bethany Pr.

Tyndale, William. An Answer to Sir Thomas More's Dialogue, the Supper of the Lord After the True Meaning of John 6 & or. 11. Repr. of 1850 ed. 25.50 (ISBN 0-384-62240-2). Johnson Repr.

Voillaume, Rene. Source of Life: The Eucharist & Christian Living. Livingstone, Dinah, tr. from Fr. 1977. pap. 1.50 (ISBN 0-914544-17-9). Living Flame Pr.

Wallis, Charles L., ed. Complete Sourcebook for the Lord's Supper. (Sourcebooks for Ministers Ser.). 1978. pap. 4.95 (ISBN 0-8010-9606-5). Baker Bk.

Watkins, Keith. The Feast of Joy: Ministering the Lord's Supper in the Free Tradition. 1977. pap. 2.50 (ISBN 0-8272-1006-X). Bethany Pr.

Weber, Gerard P. Growth in the Eucharist. 2nd ed. 1978. pap. 2.64 (ISBN 0-02-647430-1); tchrs. ed. 4.80 (ISBN 0-02-647440-9); parent handbook 1.76 (ISBN 0-02-647450-6). Benziger Pub Co.

Willimon, William H. Sunday Dinner. 1981. pap. 0.50 (ISBN 0-8358-0429-1). Upper Room.

LORD'S SUPPER–ANGLICAN COMMUNION

Hill, Robert. The Pathway to Prayer & Pietie. LC 74-28864. (English Experience Ser.: No. 744). 1975. Repr. of 1613 ed. 26.50 (ISBN 90-221-0744-2). Walter J Johnson.

Hooper, John. The Early Writings of John Hooper. 1843. 42.50 (ISBN 0-384-24210-3). Johnson Repr.

Jewel, John. Works, 4 Vols. 1845-1850. Set. 170.00 (ISBN 0-384-27217-7). Johnson Repr.

LORD'S SUPPER–CATHOLIC CHURCH

Balasuriya, Tissa. The Eucharist & Human Liberation. LC 78-9160. 1979. pap. 6.95 (ISBN 0-88344-118-7). Orbis Bks.

Davies, Michael. Communion Under Both Kinds-an Ecumenical Surrender. 1980. pap. 1.00 (ISBN 0-89555-141-1). Tan Bks Pubs.

De Margerie, Bertrand. Remarried Divorcees & Eucharistic Communion. 1980. 3.00 (ISBN 0-8198-6400-5); pap. 1.95 (ISBN 0-8198-6401-3). Dghtrs St Paul.

Duckworth, Robin, ed. This Is the Word of the Lord: Year A: The Year of Matthew. 192p. 1980. pap. 8.95 (ISBN 0-19-213248-2). Oxford U Pr.

Fay, Bertrand. Church at Eucharist. LC 67-29589. 1967. 3.95 (ISBN 0-685-07620-2, 80217). Glencoe.

Krump, John. What a Modern Catholic Believes About Eucharist. 96p. (Orig.). 1974. pap. 5.95 (ISBN 0-88347-040-3). Thomas More.

Lussier, Ernest. Getting to Know the Eucharist. new ed. LC 74-3236. 192p. 1974. 4.95 (ISBN 0-8189-0289-2). Alba.

--Living the Eucharistic Mystery. LC 75-22027. 208p. 1976. 5.95 (ISBN 0-8189-0322-8). Alba.

Morse, A. It's All About Celebrating. (Winston Mine Editions). 1971. text ed. 2.50 (ISBN 0-685-26880-2, HoltC); tchr's manual 0.30 (ISBN 0-685-26881-0). HR&W.

O'Neill, Colman. New Approaches to the Eucharist. 1967. 3.95 (ISBN 0-8189-0100-4). Alba.

LORD'S SUPPER–FIRST COMMUNION

see First Communion

LORD'S SUPPER–HISTORY

Bouyer, Louis. Eucharist: Theology & Spirituality of the Eucharist Prayer. Quinn, Charles U., tr. LC 68-17064. 1968. 14.00x (ISBN 0-268-00091-3); pap. 7.95 (ISBN 0-268-00498-6). U of Notre Dame Pr.

Brooks, Peter. Thomas Cranmer's Doctrine of the Eucharist. LC 64-24369. 1965. text ed. 6.00x (ISBN 0-8401-0246-1). Allenson-Breckinridge.

Jasper, R. C. & Cuming, G. J., eds. Prayers of the Eucharist: Early & Reformed. 2nd ed. 1979. 12.95 (ISBN 0-19-520140-X); pap. 4.95 (ISBN 0-19-520141-8). Oxford U Pr.

Macdonald, Allan J. Berengar & the Reform of the Sacramental System. 444p. 1977. Repr. of 1930 ed. lib. bdg. 28.50x (ISBN 0-915172-25-9). Richwood Pub.

Marshall, I. Howard. Last Supper & Lord's Supper. (Orig.). 1981. pap. 6.95 (ISBN 0-8028-1854-4). Eerdmans.

Marxsen, Willi. Lord's Supper As a Christological Problem. Reumann, John, ed. Nieting, Lorenz, tr. from Ger. LC 79-81528. (Facet Bks). 64p. 1970. pap. 1.00 (ISBN 0-8006-3059-9, 1-3059). Fortress.

Rordorf, Willy, et al. The Eucharist of the Early Christians. O'Connell, Matthew J., tr. from Fr. 1978. pap. 8.95 (ISBN 0-916134-33-4). Pueblo Pub Co.

LORD'S SUPPER–MEDITATIONS

Buck, Carlton C. At the Lord's Table. 1956. 4.50 (ISBN 0-8272-0007-2). Bethany Pr.

Cowper, J. M. & Manning, Robert, eds. Mediations on the Supper of Our Lord. (EETS, OS Ser.: No. 60). Repr. of 1875 ed. pap. 4.00 (ISBN 0-527-00054-X). Kraus Repr.

Haring, Bernard. The Eucharist & Our Everyday Life. (Orig.). 1979. pap. 3.95 (ISBN 0-8245-0304-X). Crossroad NY.

Lussier, Ernest. The Eucharist: The Bread of Life. LC 77-3035. 248p. 1979. pap. 5.95 (ISBN 0-8189-0349-X). Alba.

Ogilvie, Lloyd. Cup of Wonder. 1976. 3.95 (ISBN 0-8423-0490-8). Tyndale.

Sala, John R. Command to Love. LC 70-127849. 1970. pap. 2.50 (ISBN 0-8272-0431-0). Bethany Pr.

Weber, Gerard P., et al. Unite at the Lord's Table. (The Word Is Life Ser.). 4p. (gr. 4). 1977. 3.92 (ISBN 0-02-658400-X); tchrs. ed. 8.00 (ISBN 0-02-658410-7); family handbook 1.00 (ISBN 0-02-658450-6). Benziger Pub Co.

LORD'S SUPPER–ORTHODOX EASTERN CHURCH

Ambrosius, Saint The Eucharist: Saint Ambrose on the Mysteries. 1977. pap. 1.00 (ISBN 0-686-19348-2). Eastern Orthodox.

LORD'S SUPPER–PRAYER BOOKS AND DEVOTIONS

Buck, Carlton C. Communion Thoughts & Prayers. new ed. 1977. 5.50 (ISBN 0-8272-0440-X). Bethany Pr.

Harrison, Russell F. Brief Prayers for Bread & Cup. 1976. pap. 2.95 (ISBN 0-8272-0211-3). Bethany Pr.

Mossi, John. Bread Blessed & Broken. LC 74-16844. 160p. 1974. pap. 7.95 (ISBN 0-8091-1855-6). Paulist Pr.

LORD'S SUPPER–SERMONS

Here are entered sermons on the Lord's Supper itself. Sermons preached at, or in preparation for a communion service are entered under the heading Communion Sermons.

Belford, William J. Special Ministers of the Eucharist. 1979. pap. 1.95 (ISBN 0-916134-39-3). Pueblo Pub Co.

Hutchinson, Roger. Works. 1842. 25.50 (ISBN 0-384-25120-X). Johnson Repr.

Spurgeon, Charles H. Twelve Sermons on the Lord's Supper. (Charles Spurgeon Library). 1980. pap. 2.95 (ISBN 0-8010-8178-5). Baker Bk.

LORD'S SUPPER (LITURGY)

see also Communion Service Music

Cook, Paul E. Communion Handbook. 96p. 1980. 4.95 (ISBN 0-8170-0877-2). Judson.

Frere, Walter H. Anaphora, or Great Eucharistic Prayer. (Church Historical Society Ser.: No. 25). 1938. 12.50x (ISBN 0-8401-5025-3). Allenson-Breckinridge.

Jasper, R. C. & Cuming, G. J., eds. Prayers of the Eucharist: Early & Reformed. 2nd ed. 1979. 12.95 (ISBN 0-19-520140-X); pap. 4.95 (ISBN 0-19-520141-8). Oxford U Pr.

Liesting, G. T. Sacrament of the Eucharist. 7.50 (ISBN 0-8091-0129-7). Paulist Pr.

Searle, Mark. Liturgy Made Simple. 96p. (Orig.). 1981. pap. 2.95 (ISBN 0-8146-1221-0). Liturgical Pr.

Wigan, Bernard, ed. Liturgy in English. 2nd ed. 1964. 7.25x (ISBN 0-19-213410-8). Oxford U Pr.

LORD'S SUPPER IN LITERATURE

Ross, Malcolm M. Poetry & Dogma. LC 78-86284. 1969. Repr. of 1954 ed. lib. bdg. 14.50x (ISBN 0-374-96973-6). Octagon.

LOREN, SOPHIA, 1934-

Crawley, Tony. The Films of Sophia Loren. 256p. 1976. 14.00 (ISBN 0-8065-0512-5). Citadel Pr.

--The Films of Sophia Loren. (Illus.). pap. 6.95 (ISBN 0-8065-0700-4). Citadel Pr.

Hotchner, A. E. Sophia: Living & Loving Her Own Story. (Illus.). 1980. pap. 2.75 (ISBN 0-553-13030-7). Bantam.

--Sophia Living & Loving: Her Own Story. LC 78-23858. (Illus.). 1979. 9.95 (ISBN 0-688-03428-4). Morrow.

LORENTZ, PARE

Snyder, Robert L. Pare Lorentz & the Documentary Film. LC 68-10301. (Illus.). 1968. 12.50x (ISBN 0-8061-0784-7). U of Okla Pr.

LORENZ, KONRAD

Montagu, Ashley. Man & Aggression. 2nd ed. 1973. pap. 4.50 (ISBN 0-19-501680-7, 250, GB). Oxford U Pr.

Nisbett, Alec. Konrad Lorenz: A Bibliography. LC 76-29116. (A Helen & Kurt Wolf Book). (Illus.). 1977. 10.00 (ISBN 0-15-147286-6). HarBraceJ.

LORICATA

Gutberlet, John E. On the Osteology of Some of the Loricati. (Illus.). pap. 5.50 (ISBN 0-384-20480-5). Johnson Repr.

LORIES

see Parrots

LORIS

see Lemurs

LORRAIN, CLAUDE

see Gelee, Claude, Called Claude Lorrain, 1600-1682

LORRAINE–HISTORY–SOURCES

Putnam, Ruth. Alsace & Lorraine from Caesar to Kaiser 58 B.C.-1871 A.D. facsimile ed. LC 75-160988. (Select Bibliographies Reprint Ser). Repr. of 1915 ed. 30.00 (ISBN 0-8369-5856-X). Arno.

LORRIES (MOTOR VEHICLES)

see Motor-Trucks

LOS ALAMOS, NEW MEXICO

Church, Peggy P. House at Otowi Bridge: The Story of Edith Warner & Los Alamos. LC 60-13408. (Zia Bks.). (Illus.). 149p. 1973. pap. 3.95 (ISBN 0-8263-0281-5). U of NM Pr.

Kunetka, James W. City of Fire: Los Alamos & the Atomic Age, 1943 to 1945. rev. ed. LC 79-4935. (Illus.). 1979. pap. 7.95 (ISBN 0-8263-0513-X). U of NM Pr.

LOS ANGELES

Adler, Pat. Bunker Hill Story. rev. ed. (Illus.). 1968. 1.00 (ISBN 0-910856-06-0). La Siesta.

Banham, Rayner. Los Angeles. 1973. pap. 3.95 (ISBN 0-14-021178-0, Pelican). Penguin.

Barron, Stephanie & Celant, Germano. Art in los Angeles -- the Museum As Site: Sixteen Projects. D'Andrea, Jeanne, et al, eds. (Orig., Sold as set with L. A.: The Sixties). 1981. pap. 16.95 (ISBN 0-87587-102-X). La Co Art Mus.

Catapusan, Benicio. The Filipino Occupational & Recreational Activities in Los Angeles. LC 74-83364. 1975. Repr. of 1934 ed. soft bdg. 8.00 (ISBN 0-88247-350-6). R & E Res Assoc.

Hagevik, George H. Decision-Making in Air Pollution Control. LC 72-112981. (Special Studies in U.S. Economic, Social, & Political Issues). 1970. 28.00x (ISBN 0-89197-723-6); pap. text ed. 12.50x (ISBN 0-89197-724-4). Irvington.

Henry, Sheila E. Cultural Persistence & Socio-Economic Mobility: A Comparative Study of Assimilation Among Armenians & Japanese in Los Angeles. LC 77-81011. 1978. soft cover 10.00 (ISBN 0-88247-489-8). R & E Res Assoc.

Kuehn, Gernot & Burnett, William L. Views of Los Angeles. 3rd ed. 1979. 21.95 (ISBN 0-9602274-1-5). Portriga Pubns.

Lavender, David. Los Angeles: Two Hundred. Blakey, Ellen S. & Silvey, Larry P., eds. LC 80-66342. (The American Portrait Ser.). (Illus.). 240p. 1980. 24.95 (ISBN 0-932986-08-0). Continent Herit.

Modell, John. The Economics & Politics of Racial Accomodation: The Japanese of Los Angeles, 1900-1942. LC 77-6749. 1977. 12.50 (ISBN 0-252-00622-4). U of Ill Pr.

Nelson, Howard J. & Clark, W. A. The Los Angeles Metropolitan Experience: Uniqueness, Generality & the Goal of the Good Life. LC 76-4795. (Contemporary Metropolitan Analysis Ser.). (Illus.). 1976. pap. text ed. 6.95 (ISBN 0-88410-438-9). Ballinger Pub.

Seidenbaum, Art. Los Angeles Two Hundred: A Bicentennial Celebration. (Illus.). 320p. 1980. 30.00 (ISBN 0-686-62686-9, 1257-0). Abrams.

Shevky, Eshref & Williams, Marilyn. The Social Areas of Los Angeles: Analysis & Typology. LC 72-138180. (Illus.). 172p. 1972. Repr. of 1949 ed. lib. bdg. 16.75x (ISBN 0-8371-5637-8, SHLA). Greenwood.

Tuchman, Maurice, et al. Art in los Angeles: Seventeen Artists in the Sixties. D'Andrea, Jeanne, et al, eds. (Illus.). 160p. (Orig., Sold as set with art in los angeles -- the museum as a site: fifteen projects). 1981. pap. 16.95 (ISBN 0-87587-101-1). La Co Art Mus.

LOS ANGELES–DESCRIPTION

Berger, Brian. Los Angeles: Commemorating Two Hundred Years. Shangle, Robert D., ed. LC 80-16824. 1980. 27.50 (ISBN 0-89802-176-6). Beautiful Am.

Brodsly, David. L. A. Freeway: An Appreciative Essay. LC 80-29620. (Illus.). 224p. 1981. 17.95 (ISBN 0-520-04068-6). U of Cal Pr.

Burnett, William, ed. Views of Los Angeles. rev. ed. (Illus.). 1979. 24.95 (ISBN 0-9602274-1-5); pap. 14.95 (ISBN 0-9602274-0-7). Portriga Pubns.

Cameron, Robert. Above Los Angeles. LC 76-28657. 1977. 19.95 (ISBN 0-918684-03-X). Cameron & Co.

Daniel, Glenda. Dune Country: A Guide for Hikers & Naturalists. LC 77-78782. (Illus.). 167p. 1977. pap. 6.95 (ISBN 0-8040-0757-8). Swallow.

Dash, Norman. Yesterday's Los Angeles. LC 76-21249. (Historic Cities Ser: No. 26). (Illus.). 208p. 1976. 12.95 (ISBN 0-912458-70-4). E A Seemann.

Dwan, Lois. Los Angeles Restaurant Guide. frev. & enl. ed. LC 76-24713. 1980. pap. 4.95 (ISBN 0-87477-152-8). J P Tarcher.

Gader, June R. L. A. Live: Profiles of a City. 256p. 1980. 10.95 (ISBN 0-312-46119-4). St Martin.

Gill, Brendan. The Dream Come True: Great Houses of Los Angeles. LC 80-7881. 216p. 1980. 40.00 (ISBN 0-690-01893-2); special ltd. ed. signed 100.00, (ISBN 0-690-01961-0). Har-Row.

Halpern, John. Los Angeles: Improbable City. (Illus.). 1979. 19.95 (ISBN 0-525-14890-6); pap. 10.95 (ISBN 0-525-47550-8). Dutton.

Harlow, Neal. Maps & Surveys of the Pueblo Lands of Los Angeles. LC 75-43213. (Illus.). 1976. 100.00 (ISBN 0-87093-173-3). Dawsons.

Kennelley, Joe & Hankey, Roy. Sunset Boulevard: America's Dream Street. (Illus.). Date not set. price not set. Darwin Pubns.

Kuehn, Gernot & Burnett, William L. Views of Los Angeles. 2nd ed. (Illus.). 1978. pap. 12.95 (ISBN 0-9602274-0-7). Portriga Pubns.

Los Angeles Times Glove Compartment Street Atlas of Los Angeles. new ed. (Illus., Orig.). 1978. pap. 5.95 wire bd. (ISBN 0-913040-51-7, Gousha Chek-Chart). H M Gousha.
Los Angeles Times Glove Compartment Street Atlas of Los Angeles & Orange County. new ed. (Illus., Orig.). 1978. pap. 9.95 wire bd. (ISBN 0-913040-50-9, Gousha Chek-Chart). H M Gousha.
Newsom, Joseph C. Artistic Buildings & Homes of Los Angeles. facsimile ed. LC 81-4762. (Illus.). 1981. Repr. of 1888 ed. pap. 9.95 (ISBN 0-939684-02-0). Calliope Pr.
Ord, Edward O. The City of the Angels & the City of the Saints or a Trip to Los Angeles & San Bernardino in 1856. Harlow, Neal, ed. LC 78-52566. (Illus.). 1978. pap. 7.50 (ISBN 0-87328-074-1). Huntington Lib.
Patridge, Barbara. Bargain Hunting in L. A. rev. & enl. ed. LC 76-24714. 1979. pap. 5.95 (ISBN 0-87477-100-5). J P Tarcher.
Peck, David & Fine, David. L. A. Culture Quiz. (Illus.). 96p. (Orig.). 1981. 5.95 (ISBN 0-935232-07-9); pap. 3.95 (ISBN 0-935232-06-0). Deep River Pr.
Robert Lang Adams & Associates, ed. The Los Angeles Job Bank: A Comprehensive Guide to Major Employers Throughout Southhern California. (Job Bank Ser.). 400p. (Orig.). 1981. pap. 9.95 (ISBN 0-937860-04-2). Adams Inc MA.
Walker, Derek, et al, eds. Los Angeles. (Architectural Design Profile Ser.). (Illus.). 170p. 1980. pap. 25.00 (ISBN 0-8478-5328-4). Rizzoli Intl.
Wilson, Robert S. Trolley Trails Through the West: Southern California, Vol. 8. (Illus., Orig.). 1980. pap. 4.00 (ISBN 0-934944-08-3). Wilson Bros.

LOS ANGELES–DESCRIPTION–GUIDEBOOKS

Ackland, Donald, ed. Los Angeles: The Complete Guide to Living, Going Out & Touring. LC 79-2414. (Illus.). Date not set. pap. cancelled (ISBN 0-8317-5640-3, Mayflower Bks). Smith Pubs.
Arthur Frommer's Guide to Los Angeles, 1981-82. 224p. 1981. pap. 2.95 (ISBN 0-671-41435-6). Frommer-Pasmantier.
California Critic Editors, ed. Best Restaurants of Los Angeles & Southern California. LC 78-18227. (Best Restaurants Ser.). (Illus.). 1978. pap. 3.95 (ISBN 0-89286-118-5). One Hund One Prods.
Camaro Editors. Official Visitors Guide: Los Angeles. 1981. 2.95 (ISBN 0-913290-30-0). Camaro Pub.
--Restaurant Phone Book: Los Angeles. 1981. 2.95 (ISBN 0-913290-29-7). Camaro Pub.
Christy, George. Los Angeles Underground Gourmet. LC 78-130469. 1970. 1.95 (ISBN 0-671-20661-3, Fireside). S&S.
Clark, David L. L. A. on Foot. (Illus.). 1976. 2.95 (ISBN 0-913290-03-3). Camaro Pub.
Cochran, Betty. Los Angeles Epicure. (Epicure Ser.). (Orig.). 1981. pap. 4.95 (ISBN 0-89716-095-9). Peanut Butter.
Curran, William C. Beautiful Los Angeles. Shangle, Robert D., ed. LC 79-12045. 72p. 1979. 14.95 (ISBN 0-89802-056-5); pap. 7.95 (ISBN 0-89802-055-7). Beautiful Am.
Federal Writers' Project. Los Angeles: A Guide to the City & Its Environs. 1941. Repr. 39.00 (ISBN 0-403-02202-9). Somerset Pub.
Gebhard, David & Winter, Robert. A Guide to Architecture in Los Angeles & Southern California. LC 7-7317. (Illus.). 1977. pap. 11.95 (ISBN 0-87905-049-7). Peregrine Smith.
Healy, Bridget, ed. Labyrinth: A Student's Guide to Los Angeles. 1976. pap. 2.95 (ISBN 0-88474-037-4). U of S Cal Pr.
Hodor, Sue. LAbyrinth. rev. ed. 140p. Date not set. pap. 1.95 (ISBN 0-88474-101-X). U of S Cal Pr.
Kadish, Ferne & Kirtland, Kathleen. Los Angeles on Five Hundred Dollars a Day: Tax & Gratuities Not Included. 256p. 1976. pap. 4.95 (ISBN 0-02-097770-0, Collier). Macmillan.
Little Restaurants of Los Angeles. (Illus.). 1977. 2.95 (ISBN 0-913290-01-7). Camaro Pub.
Lodge, Yvette & Morgan, Francis, eds. The Los Angeles Guide. (Double Decker Guides). (Illus.). 176p. (Orig.). 1981. pap. 5.95 (ISBN 0-938888-00-5). Double Decker.
Los Angeles. (On the Go Restaurant Guides Ser.). (Illus., Orig.). 1982. pap. 5.95 (ISBN 0-89416-006-0). Travel World.
Los Angeles. (On the Go Travel Guides Ser.). (Illus., Orig.). 1982. pap. 5.95 (ISBN 0-89416-007-9). Travel World.
Los Angeles Guide, 1978. (Illus.). pap. 2.50 (ISBN 0-528-84166-1). Rand.
MacConaugha, Carol. Five Hundred Things to Do in Los Angeles for Free. 140p. 1981. pap. 3.95 (ISBN 0-8329-1562-9). New Century.
Malin, Roni S. & Ruderman, Judy. Only in L. A. A Guide to Exceptional Services. LC 79-16877. (Illus., Orig.). 1979. pap. 5.95 (ISBN 0-87701-146-X). Chronicle Bks.
Marinacci, Barbara & Marinacci, Rudy. Take Sunset Boulevard: A Guide. (Illus., Orig.). 1980. pap. 7.95 (ISBN 0-89141-103-8). Presidio Pr.
Newell, Diana & Dunas, Avis. Singles Guide to Los Angeles. (Illus.). 1979. pap. 5.95 (ISBN 0-89554-023-1). Brasch & Brasch.
Simon, Bennet. Kosher Konnection: The los Angeles Dining Guide to the Best of Kosher, Delis & Natural Foods. LC 79-67671. (Orig.). 1980. pap. 4.95 (ISBN 0-935618-00-7). Rossi Pubns.
Spencer, J. E., ed. Day Tours in & Around Los Angeles. LC 79-10872. (Los Angeles Geographical Society Publication: No. 3). (Illus., Orig.). 1979. pap. 6.95 (ISBN 0-87015-230-0). Pacific Bks.
Spradling, David & Aries, Barbara. L. A. Brunch. LC 79-23187. 140p. (Orig.). 1980. pap. 5.95 (ISBN 0-87701-202-4). Chronicle Bks.
Stokell, Marjorie. A Visitor's Guide to L.A. Harper, Susan, ed. LC 80-67475. (Illus.). 224p. (Orig.). Date not set. pap. 6.95 (ISBN 0-89395-061-0). Cal Living Bks.
Weber, Francis J. Saint Vibiana's Cathedral: A Centennial History. 1976. 10.00 (ISBN 0-87093-307-8). Dawsons.
Welles, Annette. The Los Angeles Guidebook. 384p. 1971. pap. 4.95 (ISBN 0-8202-0074-3). Sherbourne.

LOS ANGELES–HISTORY

Antoniou, Mary. Welfare Activities Among the Greek People in Los Angeles: Thesis. LC 74-7650. 1974. Repr. of 1939 ed. soft bdg. 8.00 (ISBN 0-88247-283-6). R & E Res Assoc.
Aquino, Valentin R. The Filipino Community in Los Angeles: Thesis. LC 74-76502. 1974. Repr. of 1952 ed. soft bdg. 7.00 (ISBN 0-88247-272-0). R & E Res Assoc.
Bowman, Lynn. Los Angeles: Epic of a City. LC 74-16723. (Illus.). 400p. 1974. 10.00 (ISBN 0-8310-7109-5). Howell-North.
Burnett, William, ed. Views of Los Angeles. rev. ed. (Illus.). 1979. 24.95 (ISBN 0-9602274-1-5); pap. 14.95 (ISBN 0-9602274-0-7). Portriga Pubns.
Caughey, John & Caughey, LaRee. Los Angeles: Biography of a City. LC 75-17300. 1976. 16.95 (ISBN 0-520-03079-6); pap. 6.95 (ISBN 0-520-03410-4). U of Cal Pr.
Cleland, Robert G. & Putnam, Frank B. Isaias W. Hellman & the Farmers & Merchants Bank. LC 65-12230. (Huntington Library Classics). 136p. 1980. pap. 4.00 (ISBN 0-87328-018-0). Huntington Lib.
Dakin, Susanna B. A Scotch Paisano in Old Los Angeles: Hugo Reid's Life in California, 1832-1852. (Cal Ser.: No. 397). 1979. pap. 3.95 (ISBN 0-520-03717-0). U of Cal Pr.
Dash, Norman. Yesterday's Los Angeles. LC 76-21249. (Historic Cities Ser: No. 26). (Illus.). 208p. 1976. 12.95 (ISBN 0-912458-70-4). E A Seemann.
Diehl, Digby. Front Page Eighteen Eighty-One to Nineteen Eighty-One: One Hundred Years of the Los Angeles Times. (Illus.). 288p. 1981. 25.00 (ISBN 0-8109-0925-1). Abrams.
Doyle, Harrison. Boy's Eyeview of the Wild West. Doyle, R. H., ed. (Illus.). 1977. Repr. 7.95 (ISBN 0-918462-02-9). Hillside.
Flanner, Hildegarde. A Vanishing Land. 60p. (Orig.). 1980. pap. 6.00 (ISBN 0-931832-15-2). No Dead Lines.
Griswold del Castillo, Richard. Los Angeles Barrio, Eighteen Fifty to Eighteen Ninety: A Social History. LC 78-65460. 1980. 21.50x (ISBN 0-520-03816-9). U of Cal Pr.
Henstell, Bruce. Los Angeles: An Illustrated History. LC 80-7642. (Illus.). 224p. 1980. 25.00 (ISBN 0-394-50941-2). Knopf.
Mayer, R. Los Angeles: A Chronological & Documentary History, 1542-1976. (City Chronology Ser.). 160p. 1978. 8.50 (ISBN 0-379-00612-X). Oceana.
Melnick, Robert & Melnick, Mimi. Manhole Covers of Los Angeles. (L.A. Miscellany Ser.: No. 4). 1974. 12.50 (ISBN 0-87093-168-7). Dawsons.
Nadeau, Remi. City-Makers: The Story of Southern California's First Boom. 4th rev. ed. 15.00 (ISBN 0-87046-039-0). Trans-Anglo.
Robinson, John. Los Angeles in Civil War Days. (L.A. Miscellany Ser.: No. 8). 1977. 20.00 (ISBN 0-87093-174-1). Dawsons.
Robinson, W. W. Los Angeles from the Days of the Pueblo. Nunis, Doyce B., Jr., ed. (Orig.). 1981. pap. 6.95 (ISBN 0-87701-242-3). Chronicle Bks.
Rolle, Andrew. Los Angeles. LC 65-23495. (Orig.). 1965. pap. 2.95 (ISBN 0-8077-2056-9). Tchrs Coll.
Rolle, Andrew, Jr. Los Angeles. Hundley, Norris, Jr. & Schutz, John A., eds. LC 81-67252. (Golden State Ser.). (Illus.). 120p. 1981. pap. text ed. 4.95x (ISBN 0-87835-119-1). Boyd & Fraser.
Steiner, Rodney. Los Angeles: The Centrifugal City. LC 80-84456. 224p. 1981. pap. text ed. 12.95 (ISBN 0-8403-2333-6). Kendall-Hunt.
Tom, Kim F. Participation of Chinese in the Community Life of Los Angeles: Thesis. LC 73-82409. 1974. Repr. of 1944 ed. soft bdg. 8.00 (ISBN 0-88247-279-8). R & E Res Assoc.
Vickery, Oliver. Harbor Heritage. new ed. LC 79-89082. 1979. 15.00 (ISBN 0-89430-036-9). Morgan-Pacific.
Vogeth, Lamberta. Germans in Los Angeles County, 1850-1909. 1968. Repr. of 1933 ed. 6.00 (ISBN 0-685-40307-6). R & E Res Assoc.
Weaver, John. Los Angeles: The Enormous Village. 2nd ed. Orig. Title: El Pueblo Grande. (Illus.). 240p. 1980. 15.00 (ISBN 0-88496-158-3); pap. 8.95 (ISBN 0-88496-153-2). Capra Pr.

LOS ANGELES–POLICE

Police Department, Los Angeles. Law Enforcement in Los Angeles: Los Angeles Police Department Annual Report, 1924. facsimile ed. LC 74-3831. (Criminal Justice in America Ser.). 1974. Repr. of 1924 ed. 16.00x (ISBN 0-405-06151-X). Arno.
U. S. Committee On Education And Labor. Documents Relating to Intelligence Bureau or Red Squad of Los Angeles Police Department: Hearings Before a Subcommittee of the Committee on Education & Labor. LC 73-154593. (Police in America Ser). 1971. Repr. of 1940 ed. 9.00 (ISBN 0-405-03388-5). Arno.

LOS ANGELES–RIOTS, 1965

Crump, Spencer. Black Riot in Los Angeles: The Story of the Watts Tragedy. 17.95 (ISBN 0-87046-007-2). Trans-Anglo.
Fogelson, Robert, ed. Los Angeles Riots. LC 70-90205. (Mass Violence in America Ser). Repr. of 1969 ed. 12.00 (ISBN 0-405-01311-6). Arno.

LOS ANGELES–RIOTS, 1967

Balbus, Issac D. The Dialectics of Legal Repression: Black Rebels Before the American Criminal Courts. new ed. LC 75-44825. (Law & Society Ser.). 270p. 1977. pap. text ed. 4.95 (ISBN 0-87855-609-5). Transaction Bks.

LOS ANGELES, SIMON RODIA TOWERS

Kitzhaber, Albert R. Literature, Bk. 2. 1968. text ed. 13.92 (ISBN 0-03-071400-1, HoltE); tchr's guide 5.80 (ISBN 0-03-071405-2). HR&W.
--Literature, Bk. 5. 1970. text ed. 14.56 (ISBN 0-03-084422-3, HoltE). HR&W.
--Literature, Bk. 6. 1970. text ed. 14.56 (ISBN 0-03-084423-1, HoltE). HR&W.

LOS ANGELES BASEBALL CLUB (NATIONAL LEAGUE)

Holmes, Tommy. Baseball Dodgers. (Baseball's Great Teams Ser.). 1975. pap. 4.95 (ISBN 0-02-029390-9, Collier). Macmillan.
Kahn, Roger. The Boys of Summer. (RL 9). 1973. pap. 2.25 (ISBN 0-451-08493-4, E92880, Sig). NAL.
Roseboro, John & Libby, Bill. Glory Days with the Dodgers: And Other Days with Others. LC 77-23697. 1978. 9.95 (ISBN 0-689-10864-8). Atheneum.

LOS ANGELES COUNTY, CALIFORNIA

Basten, Fred E. Santa Monica Bay: The First Hundred Years. LC 76-17332. (Illus.). 1976. 16.50 (ISBN 0-913264-26-1). Douglas-West.
Doyle, Harrison. Boy's Eyeview of the Wild West. Doyle, R. H., ed. (Illus.). 1977. Repr. 7.95 (ISBN 0-918462-02-9). Hillside.
Los Angeles County Museum of Art-Curatorial Staff. Decade of Collecting, 1965-1975. LC 74-25968. (Illus.). 248p. 1975. pap. 10.00 (ISBN 0-87587-064-3). LA Co Art Mus.
McNamara, Patrick. Mexican-Americans in Los Angeles County: A Study in Acculturation. LC 75-167579. 1975. Repr. of 1957 ed. soft bdg. 8.00 (ISBN 0-88247-362-X). R & E Res Assoc.
Martin, Helen E. History of the Los Angeles County Hospital (1878-1968) & the Los Angeles County University of Southern California Medical Center (1968 - 1978) text ed. 20.00 (ISBN 0-88474-100-1). U of S Cal Pr.
Thompson & West. History of Los Angeles County & Orange County, California. LC 59-12776. (Illus.). 1959. Repr. of 1880 ed. 25.00 (ISBN 0-8310-7009-9). Howell-North.
Walker, E. F. Five Prehistoric Archeological Sites in Los Angeles County, California. (Illus.). 1951. 5.50 (ISBN 0-686-20676-2). Southwest Mus.

LOS ANGELES COUNTY MUSEUM, LOS ANGELES

Feinblatt, Ebria & Davis, Bruce. Los Angeles Prints: Eighteen Eighty-Three to Nineteen Eighty. (Illus.). 112p. (Orig.). 1980. pap. 10.00 (ISBN 0-87587-097-X). La Co Art Mus.
Feinblatt, Ebria, et al. Los Angeles County Museum of Art Bulletin, 1979, Vol. 25. LC 58-35949. (Illus.). 80p. (Orig.). 1980. pap. 6.00 (ISBN 0-87587-092-9). La Co Art Mus.
Museum Curatorial Staff. Los Angeles County Museum of Art Handbook. LC 77-78728. (Illus.). 1977. pap. 2.50 (ISBN 0-87587-081-3). LA Co Art Mus.
Museum Staff. Los Angeles County Museum of Art Report, July 1, 1977-June 30, 1979. D'Andrea, Jeanne & Hirsch, Alison, eds. LC 80-641019. (Illus.). 84p. (Orig.). 1980. pap. 2.00 (ISBN 0-87587-093-7). La Co Art Mus.
Pignatti, Terisio, et al. Los Angeles County Museum of Art Bulletin, 1975, Vol. 21. LC 58-35949. (Illus.). 1976. pap. text ed. 2.50 (ISBN 0-87587-069-4). LA Co Art Mus.
Wardwell, Anne, et al. Los Angeles County Museum of Art Bulletin: 1978, Vol. 24. LC 58-35949. (Illus.). 1979. pap. 6.00 (ISBN 0-87587-089-9). LA Co Art Mus.

LOS ANGELES METROPOLITAN AREA

Crouch, Winston W. & Dinerman, Beatrice. Southern California Metropolis: A Study in Development of Government for a Metropolitan Area. LC 63-21640. (Illus.). 1963. 25.75x (ISBN 0-520-00280-6). U of Cal Pr.
Pegrum, Dudley F. Residential Population & Urban Transport Facilities in the Los Angeles Metropolitan Area. (BBER Occasional Paper: No. 3). (Illus.). 1964. pap. 1.00 (ISBN 0-911798-13-7). UCLA Mgmt.

LOS ANGELES STAR

Rice, William B. Los Angeles Star, Eighteen Fifty-One to Eighteen Sixty-Four: The Beginnings of Journalism in Southern California. Caughey, John W., ed. Repr. of 1947 ed. lib. bdg. 14.75x (ISBN 0-8371-1148-X, RILA). Greenwood.

LOSEY, JOSEPH

Hirsch, Foster. Joseph Losey. (Theatrical Arts Ser.). 1980. lib. bdg. 12.95 (ISBN 0-8057-9257-0). Twayne.

LOSSES, BUSINESS

see Business Losses

LOST ARTICLES (LAW)

see also Treasure-Trove

LOST ARTS

see also Industrial Arts–History

LOST MINES

see Folk-Lore of Mines

LOST TRIBES OF ISRAEL

see also Anglo-Israelism; Mormons and Mormonism

Boudinot, Elias. Star in the West: A Humble Attempt to Discover the Long Lost Ten Tribes of Israel. facs. ed. LC 79-121499. (Select Bibliographies Reprint Ser). 1816. 17.00 (ISBN 0-8369-5457-2). Arno.
Brough, R. Clayton. The Lost Tribes: History Doctrine, Prophecies & Theories About Israel's Lost Ten Tribes. LC 79-89351. 1979. 7.50 (ISBN 0-88290-123-0). Horizon Utah.
Dickey, C. R. One Man's Destiny. 1942. 3.00 (ISBN 0-685-08811-1). Destiny.
Gerber, Israel J. The Heritage Seekers--Black Jews in Search of Identity. LC 77-2907. 1977. 9.95 (ISBN 0-8246-0214-5). Jonathan David.
--The Heritage Seekers: Black Jews in Search of Identity. David, Jonathan, ed. LC 77-2907. 1977. 9.95 (ISBN 0-8246-0214-5). Inst Jewish Stud.
Godbey, Allen H. Lost Tribes: A Myth. rev. ed. (Library of Biblical Studies). 1970. 35.00x (ISBN 0-87068-102-8). Ktav.
Gottwald, Norman K. The Tribes of Yahweh: A Sociology of the Religion of Liberated Israel, 1250-1050 B.C. LC 78-24333. 1979. 29.95 (ISBN 0-88344-498-4); pap. 19.95 (ISBN 0-88344-499-2). Orbis Bks.
Harriman, Joseph B. Israel & the World Crisis. 2nd ed. 1961. 1.25 (ISBN 0-910840-04-0). Kingdom.
Waskow, Arthur I. Godwrestling. LC 78-54389. 208p. 1980. pap. 4.95 (ISBN 0-8052-0645-0). Schocken.

LOST-WAX PROCESS

see Precision Casting

LOTI, PIERRE

see Viaud, Julien, 1850-1923

LOTTERIES

Ashton, John. History of English Lotteries. LC 67-23945. (Illus.). 1969. Repr. of 1893 ed. 22.00 (ISBN 0-8103-3250-7). Gale.
Ewen, C. L'Estrange. Lotteries & Sweepstakes. LC 72-80143. (Illus.). 1973. Repr. of 1932 ed. lib. bdg. 18.50 (ISBN 0-405-08493-5). Arno.
Jones, Jennifer J. Winning Sweepstakes! You Can Start Being a Winner Today! 1980. pap. 5.95 (ISBN 0-934832-22-6). Word Power.
Kaplan, H. Roy. Lottery Winners: How They Won & How Winning Changed Their Lives. LC 78-2143. 1978. 9.95 (ISBN 0-06-012257-9, HarpT). Har-Row.
Pavlik, Zdenek V. Lotto-Keno Supersystems: Winning Combinations & Systems for Lotto 6/40 & Keno Players. (Illus.). 73p. 1980. 6.00 (ISBN 0-682-49616-2). Exposition.
Rudman, Jack. Lottery Inspector. (Career Examination Ser.: C-451). (Cloth bdg. avail. on request). pap. 6.00 (ISBN 0-8373-0451-2). Natl Learning.
Sullivan, George. By Chance a Winner: The History of Lotteries. LC 70-183000. (Illus.). 160p. (gr. 7 up). 1972. 5.95 (ISBN 0-396-06499-X). Dodd.

Thomas, John L. Law of Lotteries, Frauds & Obscenity in the Mails. xviii, 358p. 1980. Repr. of 1903 ed. lib. bdg. 32.50x (ISBN 0-8377-1202-5). Rothman.

LOUD-SPEAKER CABINETS

Badmaieff, Alexis & Davis, Don. How to Build Speaker Enclosures. LC 66-29405. (Illus., Orig.). 1966. pap. 4.95 (ISBN 0-672-20520-3, 20520). Sams.

Robin, Christopher. Twenty-One Stereo Hi-Fi Stereo Speaker Cabinets You Can Build. (Illus.). 80p. 1980. pap. 4.95 (ISBN 0-8359-7896-6). Reston.

Weems, David B. Twenty One Custom Speaker Enclosure Projects You Can Build. (Illus.). 240p. (Orig.). 1980. 12.95 (ISBN 0-8306-9962-7); pap. 8.95 (ISBN 0-8306-1234-3, 1234). TAB Bks.

LOUD-SPEAKERS

see also Loud-Speaker Cabinets; Public Address Systems

Colloms, Martin. High Performance Loudspeakers. 2nd ed. LC 79-21318. 245p. 1979. 27.95x (ISBN 0-470-26875-1). Halsted Pr.

Crowhurst, Norman H. How to Select & Install Your Own Speakers. (Illus.). 1979. pap. 6.95 (ISBN 0-8306-1034-0, 1034). TAB Bks.

Gayford, M. L. Electroacoustics. (STC Monograph Ser). 1971. 25.00 (ISBN 0-444-19649-8). Elsevier.

Weems, David B. How to Design, Build & Test Complete Speaker Systems. (Illus.). 1978. 10.95 (ISBN 0-8306-9897-3); pap. 7.95 (ISBN 0-8306-1064-2, 1064). TAB Bks.

LOUDOUN, JOHN CAMPBELL, 4TH EARL OF, b. 1705

Pargellis, Stanley M. Lord Loudon in North America. (Illus.). 1968. Repr. of 1933 ed. 22.50 (ISBN 0-208-00195-6, Archon). Shoe String.

LOUDOUN COUNTY, VIRGINIA

Jewell, Aurelia M. Loundoun County, Virginia: Marriage Records to 1891. 100p. 1975. 12.50 (ISBN 0-685-65071-5). Va Bk.

LOUIS, SAINT OF TOULOUSE

Knox, W. F. The Court of a Saint: St. Louis of France. 1976. lib. bdg. 59.95 (ISBN 0-8490-1681-9). Gordon Pr.

LOUIS 1ST LE PIEUX, EMPEROR, KING OF THE FRANKS, 778-840

Cabaniss, Allen, ed. Son of Charlemagne: A Contemporary Life of Louis the Pious. LC 61-1398. 1961. 14.00x (ISBN 0-8156-2031-4). Syracuse U Pr.

LOUIS 7TH, LE JEUNE, KING OF FRANCE, 1119-1180

Odo of Deuil. De Profectione Ludovici VII in Orienteni: The Journey of Louis the Seventh to the East. Berry, Virginia G., ed. & tr. 1965. pap. 5.95x (ISBN 0-393-09662-9). Norton.

LOUIS 9TH, SAINT, KING OF FRANCE, 1214-1270

De Joinville, Jean. Histoire De Saint Louis. De Wailly, N., ed. 1868. 31.00 (ISBN 0-384-27721-7); pap. 27.00 (ISBN 0-384-27720-9). Johnson Repr.

Giles, John A. & Johnes, Thomas, trs. Chronicles of the Crusades. LC 73-84862. (Bohn's Antiquarian Library Ser). Repr. of 1848 ed. 27.50 (ISBN 0-404-50014-5). AMS Pr.

Guillaume De Berneville. La Vie De Saint Gilles. Paris, Gaston & Bos, Alphonse, eds. 28.00 (ISBN 0-384-20300-0); pap. 23.00 (ISBN 0-384-20285-3). Johnson Repr.

Jordan, William C. Louis the Ninth: The Challenge of the Crusade. LC 79-83996. (Illus.). 1979. 22.50 (ISBN 0-691-05285-9). Princeton U Pr.

Le Nain De Tillemont, Louis S. Vie De Saint Louis, Roi De France, 6 Vols. Repr. of 1851 ed. 212.50 (ISBN 0-384-32195-X); pap. 185.00 (ISBN 0-384-32196-8). Johnson Repr.

O'Connell, David, ed. The Teachings of Saint Louis: A Critical Text. (Studies in the Romance Languages & Literatures: No. 116). 1972. pap. 7.00x (ISBN 0-8078-9216-5). U of NC Pr.

Perry, Frederick. Saint Louis: Louis IX of France, the Most Christian King. LC 73-14462. Repr. of 1901 ed. 30.00 (ISBN 0-404-58280-X). AMS Pr.

LOUIS 11TH, KING OF FRANCE, 1423-1483

Basin, Thomas. Histoire Des Regnes De Charles VII et De Louis XI, 4 Vols. Repr. of 1855 ed. Set. 126.50 (ISBN 0-384-03510-8); Set. pap. 108.00 (ISBN 0-685-13455-5). Johnson Repr.

Champion, Pierre. Louis the Eleventh. facs. ed. Whale, Winifred S., tr. LC 73-109617. (Select Bibliographies Reprint Ser). 1929. 22.00 (ISBN 0-8369-5226-X). Arno.

Kendall, Paul M. Louis the Eleventh. LC 62-19011. (Illus.). 1971. 10.00 (ISBN 0-393-05380-6). Norton.

LOUIS 11TH, KING OF FRANCE, 1423-1483-FICTION

Tyrrell, Joseph M. Louis XI. (World Leaders Ser.: No. 82). 1980. lib. bdg. 12.50 (ISBN 0-8057-7728-8). Twayne.

LOUIS 12TH, KING OF FRANCE, 1462-1515

Bowen, Marjorie. Sundry Great Gentlemen: Some Essays in Historical Biography. facs. ed. LC 68-29192. (Essay Index Reprint Ser). 1968. Repr. of 1928 ed. 18.00 (ISBN 0-8369-0230-0). Arno.

Kendall, Paul M. Louis the Eleventh. LC 62-19011. (Illus.). 1971. 10.00 (ISBN 0-393-05380-6). Norton.

LOUIS 13TH, KING OF FRANCE, 1601-1643

Chapman, Hester W. Privileged Persons: Four Seventeenth-Century Studies. 1967. 6.00 (ISBN 0-688-61082-X). Reynal.

Ranum, Orest A. Richelieu & the Councillors of Louis XIII. LC 76-3762. 211p. 1976. Repr. of 1963 ed. lib. bdg. 15.00x (ISBN 0-8371-8803-2, RARI). Greenwood.

LOUIS 14TH, KING OF FRANCE, 1638-1715

Airy, Osmund. The English Restoration & Louis XIV. 1977. Repr. of 1900 ed. lib. bdg. 17.50 (ISBN 0-8492-0137-3). R West.

Church, William F. Louis the Fourteenth in Historical Thought. (Historical Controversies Ser.). 128p. 1976. pap. text ed. 2.95x (ISBN 0-393-09211-9). Norton.

Church, William F., ed. Greatness of Louis Fourteenth. 2nd ed. (Problems in European Civilization Ser.). 1972. pap. text ed. 4.95x (ISBN 0-669-82016-4). Heath.

Ekberg, Carl J. The Failure of Louis XIV's Dutch War. LC 78-21955. 20.00x (ISBN 0-8078-1347-8). U of NC Pr.

Gaxotte, Pierre. Age of Louis Fourteenth. Shaw, Michael, tr. 1970. Repr. of 1958 ed. 7.95 (ISBN 0-02-542880-2). Macmillan.

Goubert, Pierre. Louis the Fourteenth & the Twenty Million Frenchmen. 352p. 1972. pap. 3.95 (ISBN 0-394-71751-1, V751, Vin). Random.

Hall, Geoffrey F. Moths Round the Flame. LC 72-93343. (Essay Index Reprint Ser). 1935. 29.00 (ISBN 0-8369-1413-9). Arno.

Hassall, Arthur. Louis the Fourteenth & the Zenith of the French Monarchy. LC 72-2558. (Select Bibliography Reprint Ser). 1972. Repr. of 1895 ed. 43.00 (ISBN 0-8369-6856-5). Arno.

Hatton, Ragnhild. Europe in the Age of Louis XIV. (Library of World Civilization). 1979. pap. 5.95x (ISBN 0-393-95092-1). Norton.

Hatton, Ragnhild, ed. Louis the Fourteenth & Absolutism. LC 75-45158. (Illus.). 1976. 17.50x (ISBN 0-8142-0255-1). Ohio St U Pr.

Jordan, David P. The King's Trial: Louis XVI vs. the French Revolution. LC 78-54797. 1979. 14.95 (ISBN 0-520-03684-0); pap. 5.95 (ISBN 0-520-04399-5, CAL 497). U of Cal Pr.

King, James E. Science & Rationalism in the Government of Louis XIV: 1661-1683. LC 78-64207. (Johns Hopkins University. Studies in the Social Sciences. Sixty-Sixth Ser. 1948: 2). Repr. of 1949 ed. 12.50 (ISBN 0-404-61312-8). AMS Pr.

Klaits, J. Printed Propaganda Under Louis the Fourteenth: Absolute Monarchy & Public Opinion. 1976. 25.00 (ISBN 0-691-05238-7). Princeton U Pr.

Lewis, W. H. The Splendid Century. LC 53-9235. 1954. pap. 6.95 (ISBN 0-688-06009-9). Morrow.

Martin, Germain. Grande Industrie Sous le Regne De Louis Quatorze. LC 70-128843. (Research & Source Works Ser.: No. 527). 1971. Repr. of 1899 ed. lib. bdg. 30.50 (ISBN 0-8337-2265-4). B Franklin.

Mitford, Nancy. Sun King: Louis Fourteen at Versailles. LC 66-18954. (Illus.). 1966. 20.00 (ISBN 0-06-012988-3, HarpT); (HarpT). Har-Row.

Ogg, David. Louis the Fourteenth of France: 2nd ed. (Oxford Paperbacks University Ser). pap. 4.95x (ISBN 0-19-888021-9). Oxford U Pr.

Packard, L. B. The Age of Louis XIV. 1969. pap. text ed. 5.95 (ISBN 0-03-082838-4, HoltC). HR&W.

Rule, John C., ed. Louis the Fourteenth & the Craft of Kingship. LC 72-79845. (Illus.). 1970. 12.00 (ISBN 0-8142-0004-4). Ohio St U Pr.

Tilley, Arthur A. The Decline of the Age of Louis XIV, or French Literature 1687-1715. 458p. 1968. Repr. of 1929 ed. 15.00x (ISBN 0-87471-381-1). Rowman.

Wolf, John B. Louis the Fourteenth of France: LC 67-20618. (Illus., Orig.). 1974. pap. 7.95x (ISBN 0-393-00753-7, Norton Lib). Norton.

LOUIS 14TH, KING OF FRANCE, 1638-1715-FICTION

Auchincloss, Louis. The Cat & the King. 192p. 1981. 10.95 (ISBN 0-395-30225-0). HM.

LOUIS 15TH, KING OF FRANCE, 1710-1774

Gaxotte, P. Louis the Fifteenth & His Times. 69.95 (ISBN 0-8490-0558-2). Gordon Pr.

Gooch, George P. Louis the Fifteenth: The Monarchy in Decline. LC 75-36361. (Illus.). 1976. Repr. of 1956 ed. lib. bdg. 21.50x (ISBN 0-8371-8632-3, GOLO). Greenwood.

Kaplan, S. L. Bread, Politics & Political Economy in the Reign of Louis XV. (International Archives of the History of Ideas Ser: No. 86). 1977. lib. bdg. 105.00 (ISBN 90-247-1873-2, Pub. by Martinus Nijhoff Netherlands); Vol. 1 & 2. lib. bdg. 52.50 ea. Kluwer Boston.

LOUIS 16TH, KING OF FRANCE, 1754-1793

Beaucourt, Gaston L. Captivite et derniers moments de Louis seize, 2 Vols. LC 71-161732. Repr. of 1892 ed. Set. 35.00 (ISBN 0-404-07622-X); 18.00 ea. Vol. 1 (ISBN 0-404-07623-8). Vol. 2 (ISBN 0-404-07624-6). AMS Pr.

Padover, Saul K. Life & Death of Louis XVI. LC 63-18335. 1963. 7.50 (ISBN 0-8008-4776-8). Taplinger.

Webster, Nesta. Louis the Sixteenth & Marie Antoinette. 75.00 (ISBN 0-87968-364-3). Gordon Pr.

LOUIS 17TH, KING OF FRANCE, 1785-1795

Beauchesne, Alcide. Louis the Seventeenth, 2 vols. LC 78-161731. (Illus.). Repr. of 1855 ed. 64.00 (ISBN 0-404-07546-0). AMS Pr.

Francq, H. G. Louis the Seventeenth: The Unsolved Mystery. (Illus.). 1970. 25.00 (ISBN 0-685-25488-7). Heinman.

LOUIS PHILIPPE, KING OF FRANCE, 1773-1850

Bechtel, Edwin D. Freedom of the Press & L'Association Mensuelle: Philipon Versus Louis-Philippe. (Illus.). 40p. 1952. 14.00x (ISBN 0-8139-0452-8, Grolier Club). U Pr of Va.

LOUIS, JOE, 1914-

Libby, Bill. Joe Louis: The Brown Bomber. LC 80-12372. (Illus.). 224p. (gr. 5 up). 1980. 7.95 (ISBN 0-688-41968-2); PLB 7.63 (ISBN 0-688-51968-7). Lothrop.

Louis, Joe, et al. Joe Louis: My Life. LC 77-91341. (Illus.). 288p. 1978. 10.95 (ISBN 0-15-146375-1). HarBraceJ.

Louis, Joe, Jr. & Rust, Art. Joe Louis: My Life. 304p. 1981. pap. 2.95 (ISBN 0-425-04429-7). Berkley Pub.

Vitale, Rugio. Joe Louis: Biography of a Champion. (Orig.). 1979. pap. 1.95 (ISBN 0-87067-655-5, BH655). Holloway.

LOUISBURG-SIEGES, 1745, 1758

Bollan, William. The Importance & Advantage of Cape Breton. Repr. of 1698 ed. 11.00 (ISBN 0-384-04965-6). Johnson Repr.

Rawlyk, G. A. Yankees at Louisbourg. 1967. pap. 2.50 (ISBN 0-89101-015-7). U Maine Orono.

LOUISIANA

see also names of cities, counties, towns, etc. in Louisiana

Addison, Harry. Rfd No. 3. LC 77-23069. 1977. 5.95 (ISBN 0-88289-161-8). Pelican.

Calhoun, James & Kempe, Helen. Louisiana Almanac 1979-80. 10th ed. (Illus.). 1979. 11.95 (ISBN 0-88289-181-2); pap. 7.95 (ISBN 0-88289-182-0). Pelican.

Carter, Hodding, ed. Louisiana Almanac 1968. (Illus.). 1968. pap. 7.95 (ISBN 0-911116-48-6). Pelican.

--Louisiana Almanac, 1969. 1969. pap. 7.95 (ISBN 0-911116-49-4). Pelican.

Foote, L. B., compiled by. Bibliography of the Official Publications of Louisana, 1803-1934. (Historical Records Survey Ser: No. 19). Repr. of 1942 ed. 25.00 (ISBN 0-527-01916-X). Kraus Repr.

Fruge, J. C. Biographies of Judges of Louisiana. 1971. 12.50 (ISBN 0-685-42977-6). Claitors.

Looney, Ben E. Beau Sejour: Watercolors of Louisiana Plantation Country. 1972. 13.95 (ISBN 0-685-37717-2). Claitors.

Louisiana. 28.00 (ISBN 0-89770-094-5). Curriculum Info Ctr.

Lowery, George H., Jr. Louisiana Birds. 3rd ed. LC 74-77662. (Illus.). 720p. 1974. 25.00 (ISBN 0-8071-0087-0). La State U Pr.

McKoin, Florence S. Between the Rivers: A West Carroll Chronicle. 1971. 7.95 (ISBN 0-685-37718-0). Claitors.

Madden, John L. Federal & State Lands in Louisiana. 1972. 25.00x (ISBN 0-685-37719-9). Claitors.

Perrin, W. H. Southwest Louisiana. 1971. 15.00 (ISBN 0-685-00422-8). Claitors.

Port of Shreve Capter ABNA Shreveport, LA & Collins. Shreve's Landing. 1978. 7.50 (ISBN 0-918544-18-1). Wimmer Bks.

Prichard, Walter. Prichard's Outline of Louisiana Studies. abr ed. Eakin, Sue, ed. LC 72-84201. 160p. (Orig.). (gr. 8). 1972. pap. text ed. 8.95x (ISBN 0-911116-72-9). Pelican.

R. W. Norton Art Gallery. Louisiana Landscape & Genre Paintings of the 19th Century. LC 81-50951. (Illus.). 48p. 1981. pap. 5.75x (ISBN 0-913060-19-4). Norton.

Reeves, Miriam G. Governors of Louisiana. 3rd ed. Calhoun, James, ed. LC 72-89969. (Governors of the States Ser.). (Illus.). 160p. 1980. 12.95 (ISBN 0-911116-71-0). Pelican.

Schumacher, E. D. Adult Functional Illiteracy in Louisiana. 1973. 6.50 (ISBN 0-685-37724-5). Claitors.

Stoddard, Amos. Sketches, Historical & Descriptive, of Louisiana. LC 72-956. Repr. of 1812 ed. 27.50 (ISBN 0-404-06278-4). AMS Pr.

Vidrine, Mercedes. Louisiana Lagniappe. 1973. 6.95 (ISBN 0-685-37729-6). Claitors.

LOUISIANA-ANTIQUITIES

Ford, James A. Analysis of Indian Village Site Collections from Louisiana & Mississippi. LC 37-27887. 1975. Repr. of 1937 ed. 19.00 (ISBN 0-527-03231-X). Kraus Repr.

--Analysis of Indian Village Site Collections from Louisiana & Mississippi. LC 37-27887. 1975. Repr. of 1937 ed. 19.00 (ISBN 0-527-03231-X). Kraus Repr.

--Ceramic Decoration Sequence at an Old Indian Village Site Near Sicily Island, Louisiana. LC 36-19610. 1975. Repr. of 1935 ed. 10.00 (ISBN 0-527-03230-1). Kraus Repr.

Ford, James A. & Willey, Gordon. Crooks Site, a Marksville Period Burial Mound in the LaSalle Parish, Louisiana. LC 40-28710. 1975. Repr. of 1940 ed. 12.00 (ISBN 0-527-03232-8). Kraus Repr.

Sibley, J. A. Louisiana Ancients of Man. 1967. 6.00 (ISBN 0-685-08186-9). Claitors.

Walker, Winslow M. The Trayville Mounds-Catahoula Parish, Louisiana. Repr. of 1936 ed. 12.00 (ISBN 0-403-03714-X). Scholarly.

LOUISIANA-ECONOMIC CONDITIONS

Beard, Thomas R., ed. Louisiana Economy. LC 69-17622. (University Studies, Social Science Ser.: Vol. 15). (Illus.). 1969. 17.50x (ISBN 0-8071-0307-1). La State U Pr.

Surrey, Nancy M. Commerce of Louisiana During the French Regime, 1699-1763. LC 71-76702. (Columbia University. Studies in Social Sciences: No. 167). Repr. of 1916 ed. 20.00 (ISBN 0-404-51167-8). AMS Pr.

LOUISIANA-DESCRIPTION AND TRAVEL

Berger, Brian. Beautiful Louisiana. Shangle, Robert D., ed. (Illus.). 72p. 1981. 14.95 (ISBN 0-89802-111-1); pap. 7.95 (ISBN 0-89802-110-3). Beautiful Am.

Bossu, Jean B & Forster, Johann R. Travels Through That Part of North America Formerly Called Louisiana. 1976. Repr. of 1771 ed. 109.00 (ISBN 0-685-70607-9, Regency). Scholarly.

Browne, Turner, photos by. Louisiana Cajuns. LC 77-24171. (Illus.). 1977. 14.95 (ISBN 0-8071-0363-2); pap. 6.95 (ISBN 0-8071-0853-7). La State U Pr.

Calhoun, James, ed. Louisiana Sports Record Book. 104p. 1971. pap. 3.95 (ISBN 0-911116-55-9). Pelican.

Darby, William. A Geographical Description of the State of Louisiana, with an Account of the Characters & Manners of the Inhabitants. 1977. Repr. 25.00 (ISBN 0-403-07893-8). Scholarly.

Douglas, Neil H. Freshwater Fishes of Louisiana. 1974. 12.95 (ISBN 0-685-42666-1). Claitors.

Federal Writers' Project. Louisiana: A Guide to the State. 711p. 1941. Repr. 69.00 (ISBN 0-403-02169-3). Somerset Pub.

Feibleman, Peter. The Bayous. LC 73-84544. (American Wilderness Ser). (Illus.). (gr. 6 up). 1973. lib. bdg. 11.97 (ISBN 0-8094-1189-X, Pub. by Time-Life). Silver.

Hackett, Charles W., ed. Pichardo's Treatise on the Limits of Louisiana & Texas, 4 vols. facsimile ed. LC 72-157340. (Select Bibliographies Reprint Ser). Repr. of 1946 ed. 120.00 (ISBN 0-8369-5800-4). Arno.

Hansen, Harry & Federal Writers' Project, eds. Louisiana: A State Guide. rev. ed. (American Guide Ser.). 1971. 14.95 (ISBN 0-8038-4272-4). Hastings.

Jolly, Ellen R. & Calhoun, James. Pelican Guide to the Louisiana Capital. LC 78-21239. (Pelican Guide Ser.). (Illus.). 128p. 1980. pap. 3.95 (ISBN 0-88289-212-6). Pelican.

Kniffen, Fred B. Louisiana: Its Land & People. LC 68-13448. (Illus.). 1968. 14.95x (ISBN 0-8071-0549-X). La State U Pr.

Mills, Elizabeth S. Natchitoches: 1729-1803. LC 76-52880. 1977. pap. 20.00 (ISBN 0-686-10450-1). Polyanthos.

Morgan & Kerr. Louisiana Scenes: The Lower Mississippi Valley. 1962. 5.95 (ISBN 0-685-08188-5). Claitors.

Morgan, Elemore & East, Charles. Face of Louisiana. LC 78-86493. (Illus.). 1969. 14.95 (ISBN 0-8071-0913-4). La State U Pr.

Robin, C. C. Voyage to Louisiana: 1803-1805. 1966. Repr. of 1807 ed. 20.00 (ISBN 0-911116-20-6). Pelican.

Skeen, C. Edward, ed. Description of Louisiana by Thomas Jefferys: From His "Natural & Civil History of the French Dominions in North & South America". (Mississippi Valley Collection Bulletin, No. 6). (Illus.). 50p. 1973. pap. 5.95x facsimile ed. (ISBN 0-87870-082-X). Memphis St Univ.

State Industrial Directories Corp. Louisiana State Industrial Directory, Nineteen Eighty-One. Date not set. pap. price not set (ISBN 0-89910-047-3). State Indus D.

Stoddard, M. A. Sketches, Historical & Descriptive of Louisiana. 1974. Repr. of 1812 ed. 15.00 (ISBN 0-685-42672-6). Claitors.
Thomson, Bailey, ed. Historic Shreveport. LC 80-54715. (Illus.). 128p. (Orig.). 1980. pap. 6.95 (ISBN 0-939042-00-2). Shreveport Pub.
Tixier, Victor. Tixier's Travels on the Osage Prairies. McDermott, John, ed. Salvan, Albert, tr. (American Exploration & Travel Ser: No. 4). (Illus.). 1968. Repr. of 1940 ed. 16.95 (ISBN 0-8061-0087-7). U of Okla Pr.

LOUISIANA–GENEALOGY

Ardoin, Robert B. Louisiana Census Records, Vol. 2: Iberville, Natchitoches, Pointe Coupee, & Rapides Parishes, 1810 & 1820. LC 71-134170. (Illus.). 1972. 15.00 (ISBN 0-8063-0507-X). Genealog Pub.
Arthur & Kernion. Old Families of Louisiana. 1971. 12.50 (ISBN 0-685-27195-1). Claitors.
Cochran, E. M. The Fortier Family. 1963. 20.00 (ISBN 0-685-42976-8). Claitors.
Conrad, Glenn. First Families of la, 2 vols. 1969. Set. 25.00 (ISBN 0-685-27199-4). Claitors.
Forsyth, Alice D. Louisiana Marriages: Vol. 1: 1784-1806. 1977. 20.00 (ISBN 0-686-20419-0). Polyanthos.
Fruge, J. C. Fruges of Fakaitaic. 1971. pap. 4.00 (ISBN 0-685-27200-1). Claitors.
Jackson, Ronald V. & Teeples, Gary R. Louisiana Census Index 1810. LC 77-85938. (Illus.). lib. bdg. 17.00 (ISBN 0-89593-049-8). Accelerated Index.
--Louisiana Census Index 1820. LC 77-85939. (Illus.). lib. bdg. 22.00 (ISBN 0-89593-050-1). Accelerated Index.
--Louisiana Census Index 1830. LC 77-85941. (Illus.). lib. bdg. 23.00 (ISBN 0-89593-051-X). Accelerated Index.
--Louisiana Census Index 1840. LC 77-85942. (Illus.). lib. bdg. 30.00 (ISBN 0-89593-052-8). Accelerated Index.
--Louisiana Census Index 1850. LC 77-85960. (Illus.). lib. bdg. 35.00 (ISBN 0-89593-053-6). Accelerated Index.
King, Grace. Creole Families of New Orleans. 1971. 12.50 (ISBN 0-685-27201-X). Claitors.
Louisiana Pen Women. Louisiana Leaders. 1970. 12.50 (ISBN 0-685-00425-2). Claitors.
Madeull, Charles. New Orleans Marriage Contracts: 1804-1820. 1977. 17.50 (ISBN 0-686-20421-2). Polyanthos.
Marchand, Sidney A. Attempt to Re-Assemble the Old Settlers in Family Groups. 1965. 6.00 (ISBN 0-685-08143-5). Claitors.
Villere, Sidney L. The Canary Islands Migration to Louisiana, 1778-1783. LC 72-7239. (Illus.). 1972. Repr. of 1971 ed. 12.50 (ISBN 0-8063-0522-3). Genealog Pub.

LOUISIANA–HISTORIC HOUSES, ETC.

Calhoun, James. Pelican Guide to Plantation Homes of Louisiana. 5th ed. LC 75-162347. (Pelican Guide Ser.). (Illus.). 1980. pap. 3.95 (ISBN 0-911116-50-8). Pelican.
Desmond, John. Louisiana's Antebellum Architecture. 1970. 10.00 (ISBN 0-685-00417-1). Claitors.
Hays, M. S. Louisiana: Sketches of Historical Homes & Sights. 1973. 5.95 (ISBN 0-685-08189-3). Claitors.
Huber, Leonard & Wilson, Samuel, Jr. Baroness Pontalba's Buildings. 1973. pap. 3.95 (ISBN 0-911116-40-0). Pelican.
Louisiana Pen Women. Vignettes of Louisiana History. 12.50 (ISBN 0-685-08231-8). Claitors.
Morrison, Betty L. The Parish Court Houses of Louisiana. new ed. 1978. 20.00 (ISBN 0-930676-04-1). Her Pub Co.
Oszuscik, Philippe. Louisiana's Gothic Revival Architecture. 1973. 7.50 (ISBN 0-685-00421-X). Claitors.
Reeves, Miriam. Felicianas of Louisiana. 1967. 12.50 (ISBN 0-685-08166-4). Claitors.
Seebold, Herman. Old Louisiana Plantation Homes & Family Trees, Vol. 1. (Illus.). 1971. Repr. of 1941 ed. 30.00 (ISBN 0-911116-34-6). Pelican.
Stahls, Paul, Jr. Plantation Homes of the Lafourche Country. LC 76-9802. (Illus.). 1976. 12.95 (ISBN 0-88289-103-0). Pelican.
--Plantation Homes of the Teche Country. LC 78-24283. (Illus.). 96p. 1979. 12.95 (ISBN 0-88289-205-3). Pelican.
Swanson, Betsy. Historic Jefferson Parish. LC 74-23204. (Illus.). 176p. (Orig.). 1975. 20.95 (ISBN 0-88289-048-4). Pelican.

LOUISIANA–HISTORY

Arthur, Stanley C., compiled by. Index to the Dispatches of Spanish Governors of Louisiana: 1766-1792. 1975. 12.50 (ISBN 0-686-20876-5). Polyanthos.
Barbe-Marbois, Francois. The History of Louisiana, Particularly of the Cession of That Colony to the United States of America. Lyon, E. Wilson, ed. LC 77-5665. (Louisiana Bicentennial Reprint Ser.). 1977. 20.00x (ISBN 0-8071-0186-9). La State U Pr.
--The History of Louisiana, Particularly of the Cession of That Colony to the United States of America. Lyon, E. Wilson, ed. LC 77-5665. (Louisiana Bicentennial Reprint Ser.). 1977. 20.00x (ISBN 0-8071-0186-9). La State U Pr.
Barron, Bill, ed. Census of Pointe Coupee, Louisiana: 1745. LC 77-92116. 1978. pap. 12.50x (ISBN 0-686-09335-6). Polyanthos.
Becnel, Thomas. Labor, Church, & the Sugar Establishment Louisiana, 1887-1976. LC 80-10572. (Illus.). 276p. 1980. 20.00x (ISBN 0-8071-0660-7). La State U Pr.
Bergerie, Maurine. They Tasted Bayou Water: A Brief History of Iberia Parish. LC 80-66373. (Illus.). 1980. 10.00 (ISBN 0-686-27535-7). M Bergerie.
Blankenstein, M. E. Rotary in Baton Rouge 1918-1970. 10.00x (ISBN 0-685-00412-0). Claitors.
Bridges, L. T. Flags of Louisiana. (ps-8). 1971. 2.95 (ISBN 0-685-27197-8). Claitors.
Carter, Hodding. Doomed Road of Empire: The Spanish Trail of Conquest. (American Trails Library Ser). (Illus.). 1963. 10.95 (ISBN 0-07-010182-5, P&RB). McGraw.
Caskey, Willie M. Secession & Restoration of Louisiana. LC 78-75302. (American Scene Ser). (Illus.). 1970. Repr. of 1938 ed. lib. bdg. 32.50 (ISBN 0-306-71263-6). Da Capo.
Casso, Evans J. Louisiana Legacy: History of the National Guard. LC 76-10175. (Illus.). 300p. 1976. 15.00 (ISBN 0-88289-107-3); special ed. 75.00 (ISBN 0-88289-162-6). Pelican.
Caughey, John W. Bernardo De Galvez in Louisiana: 1776-1783. 2nd ed. LC 72-86562. (Illus.). 304p. 1972. Repr. of 1934 ed. 20.00 (ISBN 0-911116-78-8). Pelican.
Charlevoix, Pierre, et al. Charlevoix's Louisiana: Selections from the History & the Journal. O'Neill, Charles E. & Tregle, Joseph G., Jr., eds. LC 77-3343. (Louisiana Bicentennial Reprint Ser.). (Illus.). 1977. 15.00x (ISBN 0-8071-0250-4). La State U Pr.
Chidsey, Donald B. The Louisiana Purchase. (Illus.). 192p. 1972. 4.95 (ISBN 0-517-50740-4). Crown.
Childs, Marleta. North Louisiana Census Reports: Vol. 1, 1830 & 1840, Parishes of Union, Claiborne, Caldwell, Catahoula & Ouachita. 1975. 15.00 (ISBN 0-686-20886-2). Polyanthos.
Claiborne, William C. Official Letter Books, 1801 to 1816, 6 Vols. Rowland, Dunbar, ed. LC 72-980. Repr. of 1917 ed. Set. 165.00 (ISBN 0-404-01600-6); 27.50 ea. AMS Pr.
Coles, Harry L. A History of the Administration of Federal Land Policies & Land Tenure in Louisiana, 1803-1860. Bruchey, Stuart, ed. LC 78-56718. (Management in Public Lands in the U. S. Ser.). (Illus.). 1979. lib. bdg. 25.00x (ISBN 0-405-11327-7). Arno.
Craven, Avery O. Rachel of Old Louisiana. LC 74-15921. (Illus.). 128p. 1975. 9.95 (ISBN 0-8071-0095-1). La State U Pr.
Crete, Liliane. Daily Life in Louisiana, 1815-1830. Gregory, Patrick, tr. from Fr. 308p. 1981. text ed. 25.00x (ISBN 0-8071-0887-1). La State U Pr.
Cruise, Boyd. Index to the Louisiana Historical Quarterly, Vol. 1-33. 1956. 35.00, slip case (ISBN 0-911116-05-2). Pelican.
Dargo, George. Jefferson's Louisiana: Politics & the Clash of Legal Traditions. LC 74-25036. (Studies in Legal History). 272p. 1974. text ed. 15.00x (ISBN 0-674-47370-1). Harvard U Pr.
Davis, Edwin A. Louisiana - the Pelican State. 4th ed. LC 75-8468. 392p. 1975. 16.95 (ISBN 0-8071-0163-X). La State U Pr.
--Louisiana: A Narrative History. 3rd ed. 1971. 12.50 (ISBN 0-685-08184-2); text ed. 9.00x (ISBN 0-685-08185-0). Claitors.
--The Rivers & Bayous of Louisiana. (Illus.). 201p. 1968. 12.50 (ISBN 0-911116-96-6). Pelican.
--Story of Louisiana, 4 Vols. Vol. 1. 20.00x (ISBN 0-685-08213-X); Vol. 2. 25.00x (ISBN 0-685-08214-8); Vol. 3. 25.00x (ISBN 0-685-08215-6); Vol. 4. 35.00x (ISBN 0-685-08216-4); Set. 79.50x (ISBN 0-685-08217-2). Claitors.
Dawson, Sarah M. A Confederate Girl's Diary. Robertson, James I., Jr., ed. LC 70-170604. (Civil War Centennial Ser). 473p. 1972. Repr. of 1960 ed. lib. bdg. 26.00x (ISBN 0-8371-6250-5, DACG). Greenwood.
Deiler, J. Hanno. The Settlement of the German Coast of Louisiana. LC 67-28597. 1975. Repr. of 1909 ed. 12.50 (ISBN 0-8063-0092-2). Genealog Pub.
De Ville, Winston. Louisiana Recruits: 1752-1758. 12.50 (ISBN 0-686-20880-3). Polyanthos.
--Louisiana Troops, Seventeen Twenty-Seventeen-Seventy. LC 67-10538. (Illus.). 1965. pap. 10.00 (ISBN 0-8063-0463-4). Genealog Pub.
Ditto, Tanya. The Longest Street: A History of Lafourche Parish & Grandlsle. Woolfolk, Doug, ed. (Illus.). 136p. 1980. 13.00 (ISBN 0-86518-013-X). Moran Pub Corp.
Du Fossat, Guy. Synopsis of the History of Louisiana. 1975. 7.50 (ISBN 0-686-20898-6). Polyanthos.
Dufour, Charles L. Ten Flags in the Wind: The Story of Louisiana. LC 67-22497. (Regions of America Ser). (YA) 1967. 12.95 (ISBN 0-06-011107-0, HarpT). Har-Row.
Dunbar, Rowland, compiled by. Guide to the General Correspondence of Louisiana: 1678-1763. 1975. 15.00 (ISBN 0-686-20871-4). Polyanthos.
DuPratz, L. History of Louisiana. 1972. 15.00 (ISBN 0-685-37711-3). Claitors.
Edmonds, David C. Yankee Autumn in Acadiana: A Narrative of the Great Texas Overland Expedition Through Southwestern Louisiana. 2nd ed. LC 79-67333. (Illus.). 512p. 1980. Repr. 15.95 (ISBN 0-937614-01-7). Acadiana Pr.
Ellis, Frederick S. St. Tammany Parish: L'autre Cote du lac. LC 80-63. (Illus.). 1981. 19.95 (ISBN 0-88289-252-5). Pelican.
Ficklen, John R. History of Reconstruction in Louisiana (Through 1868) LC 78-63934. (Johns Hopkins University. Studies in the Social Sciences. Twenty-Eighth Ser. 1910: 1). Repr. of 1910 ed. 13.00 (ISBN 0-404-61183-4). AMS Pr.
Fischer, Roger A. The Segregation Struggle in Louisiana, 1862-77. LC 74-7230. 180p. 1974. 12.50 (ISBN 0-252-00394-2). U of Ill Pr.
Fortier, Alcee. History of Louisiana. rev. ed. Carrigan, J. A., ed. Vols. 1 & 2. 15.00 ea. Claitors.
Fortier, Gilbert J., Jr. Humorous Highlights of Louisiana History. 60p. pap. 1.95 (ISBN 0-911116-90-7). Pelican.
French, Benjamin F. Historical Collections of Louisiana, Embracing Rare & Valuable Documents Relating to the Natural, Civil, & Political History of That State, 5 vols. LC 72-14380. Repr. of 1853 ed. Set. 150.00 (ISBN 0-404-11050-9); 30.00 ea. Vol. 1 (ISBN 0-404-11051-7). Vol. 2 (ISBN 0-404-11052-5). Vol. 3 (ISBN 0-404-11053-3). Vol. 4 (ISBN 0-404-11054-1). Vol. 5 (ISBN 0-404-11055-X). AMS Pr.
French, Benjamin F., ed. Historical Collections of Louisiana & Florida, 2 vols. LC 72-14374. Repr. of 1875 ed. Set. 55.00 (ISBN 0-404-11096-7); 27.50 ea. Vol. 1 (ISBN 0-404-11097-5). Vol. 2 (ISBN 0-404-11098-3). AMS Pr.
Gaillardet, Frederic. Sketches of Early Texas & Louisiana. Shepard, James L., tr. from Fr. (Texas History Paperbacks Ser.: No. 13). 1966. pap. 2.95x (ISBN 0-292-70102-0). U of Tex Pr.
Gayaree, Charles. History of Louisiana, 4 vols. 4th ed. 1974. Repr. Set. 75.00 (ISBN 0-685-42677-7). Claitors.
Gayarre, Charles. History of Louisiana, 4 vols. 5th ed. (Illus.). 1974. Repr. 75.00 (ISBN 0-88289-041-7). Pelican.
Gayarre, Charles E. History of Louisiana, 4 Vols. 3rd ed. LC 70-168103. Repr. of 1885 ed. Set. 100.00 (ISBN 0-404-02770-9); 25.00 ea. Vol. 1 (ISBN 0-404-02771-7). Vol. 2 (ISBN 0-404-02772-5). Vol. 3 (ISBN 0-404-02773-3). Vol. 4 (ISBN 0-404-08000-6). AMS Pr.
Giraud, Marcel. A History of French Louisiana, Vol. 1: The Reign of Louis XIV, 1698-1715. LC 71-18156. (Illus.). 416p. 1974. 25.00x (ISBN 0-8071-0247-4). La State U Pr.
Griffin, Harry L. Attakapas Country. (Illus.). 263p. 1975. 15.00 (ISBN 0-88289-036-0). Pelican.
Hair, William I. Bourbonism & Agrarian Protest: Louisiana Politics, 1877-1900. LC 70-88741. (Illus.). 1969. 22.50 (ISBN 0-8071-0908-8); pap. text ed. 7.95 (ISBN 0-8071-0206-7). La State U Pr.
Heinrich, Pierre. Louisiane Sous la Compagnie Des Indes, 1717-1731. LC 75-129035. (Research & Source Works Ser.: No. 533). (Illus.). 1970. Repr. of 1908 ed. lib. bdg. 23.50 (ISBN 0-8337-1641-7). B Franklin.
Hepworth, George H. The Whip, Hoe, & Sword. Taylor, Joe G., ed. LC 78-10596. (Louisiana Bicentennial Reprint Ser.). 1979. 14.95x (ISBN 0-8071-0490-6). La State U Pr.
Houck, Louis. Spanish Regime in Missouri: A Collection of Papers & Documents Relating to Upper Louisiana Principally Within the Present Limits of Missouri During the Dominion of Spain, from the Archives of the Indies at Seville, 2 Vols. in 1. LC 70-146403. (First American Frontier Ser). (Illus.). 1971. Repr. of 1909 ed. 40.00 (ISBN 0-405-02860-1). Arno.
LeBlanc, J. Dudley. The Acadian Miracle. 1966. 7.50 (ISBN 0-685-27202-8). Claitors.
Le Clercq, Chretien. First Establishment of the Faith in New France, 2 Vols. LC 77-172312. Repr. of 1881 ed. Set. 55.00 (ISBN 0-404-03914-6); 28.00 ea. Vol. 1 (ISBN 0-404-03915-4). Vol. 2 (ISBN 0-404-03916-2). AMS Pr.
Le Page Du Pratz, Antoine S. History of Louisiana. Tregle, Joseph G., Jr., ed. & intro. by. LC 74-30512. (Louisana Bicentennial Ser.). (Illus.). 456p. 1975. 19.95x (ISBN 0-8071-0156-7). La State U Pr.
Lyon, E. Wilson. Louisiana in French Diplomacy: 1759-1804. LC 73-10603. 1974. 12.95x (ISBN 0-8061-0027-3); pap. 6.95x (ISBN 0-8061-1114-3). U of Okla Pr.
--The Man Who Sold Louisiana: The Career of Francois Barbe-Marbois. (Illus.). 1974. 10.95x (ISBN 0-8061-0104-0); pap. 5.95x (ISBN 0-8061-1149-6). U of Okla Pr.
Martin, Francois X. History of Louisiana. 3rd ed. LC 75-34820. (Illus.). 480p. 1976. Repr. of 1827 ed. 30.00 (ISBN 0-88289-042-5). Pelican.
Mills, Gary B. The Forgotten People: Cane River's Creoles of Color. LC 77-452. (Illus.). 1977. 20.00x (ISBN 0-8071-0279-2); pap. 8.95 (ISBN 0-8071-0287-3). La State U Pr.
Mims, Sam. Trail of the Pack Peddler. pap. 2.00 (ISBN 0-911116-45-1). Pelican.
Moody, Vernie A. Slavery on Louisiana Sugar Plantations. LC 74-22753. (Labor Movement in Fiction & Non-Fiction). Repr. of 1924 ed. 12.00 (ISBN 0-404-58505-1). AMS Pr.
Moore, John P. Revolt in Louisiana: The Spanish Occupation, 1766-1770. (Illus.). 1976. 17.50x (ISBN 0-8071-0180-X). La State U Pr.
Morgan, Cecil, ed. The First Constitution of the State of Louisiana. LC 75-9052. (Historic New Orleans Collection Monograph Series). (Illus.). 144p. 1975. 10.95x (ISBN 0-8071-0158-3). La State U Pr.
Newton, Lewis W. The Americanization of French Louisiana: A Study of the Process of Adjustment Between French & Anglo-American Population of Louisiana. Cordasco, Francesco, ed. LC 80-884. (American Ethnic Groups Ser.). 1981. lib. bdg. 25.00x (ISBN 0-405-13445-2). Arno.
Noggle, Burl. Working with History: The Historical Records Survey in Louisiana & the Nation, 1936-1942. LC 81-5789. 160p. 1981. text ed. 14.95x (ISBN 0-8071-0881-2). La State U Pr.
Phelps, Albert. Louisiana: A Record of Expansion. LC 72-3748. (American Commonwealths: No. 18). Repr. of 1905 ed. 27.50 (ISBN 0-404-57218-9). AMS Pr.
Pitot, James. Observations on the Colony of Louisiana from Seventeen Ninety-Six to Eighteen Hundred & Two. Bush, Robert D., ed. Pitot, Henry C., tr. LC 79-14897. (The Historic New Orleans Collection Monograph). (Illus.). 1979. text ed. 14.95x (ISBN 0-8071-0579-1). La State U Pr.
Pollard, Nora L. The Book of LeBlanc. 1973. 12.50x (ISBN 0-685-37722-9). Claitors.
Post, Lauren C. Cajun Sketches from the Prairies of Southwest Louisiana. 2nd ed. LC 74-83444. (Illus.). 232p. 1974. 11.95 (ISBN 0-8071-0703-4). La State U Pr.
Price, John M. Civil War Tax in Louisiana: 1865. 1975. 12.50 (ISBN 0-686-20860-9). Polyanthos.
Prud'Homme, Luclie & Christensen, Fern, eds. The Natchitoches Cemeteries: Transcriptions of Gravestones from the 18th, 19th, & 20th Centuries. LC 77-85632. 1978. pap. 17.50x (ISBN 0-686-09339-9). Polyanthos.
Reed, Germaine M. David French Boyd: Founder of Louisiana State University. LC 77-4460. (Southern Biography Ser). 1977. 22.50x (ISBN 0-8071-0266-0). La State U Pr.
Ripley, C. Peter. Slaves & Freedmen in Civil War Louisiana. LC 75-18043. 1976. 17.50x (ISBN 0-8071-0187-7). La State U Pr.
Robertson, James A., ed. Louisiana Under the Rule of Spain, France & the United States 1785-1807, 2 vols. facsimile ed. LC 72-102254. (Select Bibliographies Reprint Ser). 1911. Set. 56.00 (ISBN 0-8369-5139-5). Arno.
Robichaux, Albert. Louisiana Census & Militia Lists: 1770-1789. (Vol. 1). Repr. 17.50 (ISBN 0-686-20879-X). Polyanthos.
Robin, C. C. Voyage to Louisiana: 1803-1805. 1966. Repr. of 1807 ed. 20.00 (ISBN 0-911116-20-6). Pelican.
Roosevelt, Theodore. Winning of the West. Wish, Harvey, ed. & intro. by. 8.00 (ISBN 0-8446-2827-1). Peter Smith.
Ryan, Marah E. A Flower of France: A Story of Old Louisiana. LC 72-2930. (Black Heritage Library Collection Ser.). Repr. of 1894 ed. 18.25 (ISBN 0-8369-9078-1). Arno.
Shugg, Roger W. Origins of Class Struggle in Louisiana: A Social History of White Farmers & Laborers During Slavery & After, 1840-1875. LC 39-33962. (Illus.). 1968. 22.50x (ISBN 0-8071-0739-5); pap. text ed. 8.95x (ISBN 0-8071-0136-2). La State U Pr.
Sindler, Allan P. Huey Long's Louisiana: State Politics, 1920 to 1952. LC 80-19447. (Illus.). xv, 316p. 1980. Repr. of 1956 ed. lib. bdg. 25.00x (ISBN 0-313-22692-X, SIHL). Greenwood.

Skeen, C. Edward, ed. Description of Louisiana by Thomas Jefferys: From His "Natural & Civil History of the French Dominions in North & South America". (Mississippi Valley Collection Bulletin, No. 6). (Illus.). 50p. 1973. pap. 5.95x facsimile ed. (ISBN 0-87870-082-X). Memphis St Univ.

Smeal, Lee. Louisiana Historical & Biographical Index. LC 78-53698. (Illus.). Date not set. lib. bdg. price not set (ISBN 0-89593-183-4). Accelerated Index.

Stoddard, M. A. Sketches, Historical & Descriptive of Louisiana. 1974. Repr. of 1812 ed. 15.00 (ISBN 0-685-42672-6). Claitors.

Taylor, Joe G. Louisiana. LC 66-14673. (Orig.). 1966. pap. 2.95 (ISBN 0-8077-2254-5). Tchrs Coll.

--Louisiana: A Bicentennial History. (States & the Nation Ser.). (Illus.). 1976. 12.95 (ISBN 0-393-05602-3, Co-Pub by AASLH). Norton.

The Territory of Louisiana-Missouri, 1803-1806. (The Territorial Papers of the United States: Vol. 13). Repr. of 1948 ed. 69.50 (ISBN 0-404-01463-1). AMS Pr.

The Territory of Louisiana-Missouri, 1806-1814. (The Territorial Papers of the United States: Vol. 14). Repr. of 1949 ed. 69.50 (ISBN 0-404-01464-X). AMS Pr.

The Territory of Louisiana-Missouri, 1815-1821. (The Territorial Papers of the United States: Vol. 15). Repr. of 1951 ed. 69.50 (ISBN 0-404-01465-8). AMS Pr.

The Territory of Orleans, 1803-1812. (The Territorial Papers of the United States: Vol. 9). Repr. of 1940 ed. 69.50 (ISBN 0-404-01459-3). AMS Pr.

Valentine, Orpha. Lafayette: A Historical Perspective. Woolfolk, Doug, ed. (Illus.). 120p. 1980. 12.50 (ISBN 0-86518-014-8). Moran Pub Corp.

Vexler, R. I. Louisiana Chronology & Factbook, Vol. 18. 1978. 8.50 (ISBN 0-379-16143-5). Oceana.

Whitaker, Arthur P. The Mississippi Question, 1795-1803. 8.50 (ISBN 0-8446-1476-9). Peter Smith.

Whitson, Skip, compiled by. Louisiana-One Hundred Years Ago. (Sun Historical Ser). (Illus., Orig.). 1976. pap. 3.50 ea.; Vol. 1. pap. (ISBN 0-89540-026-X, SB026). Vol. 2 (ISBN 0-89540-027-8, SB027). Sun Pub.

Winters, John D. The Civil War in Louisiana. LC 63-9647. 552p. 1979. 30.00x (ISBN 0-8071-0834-0). La State U Pr.

Wood, Ted. History of Caldwell Parish. 1972. 6.95 (ISBN 0-685-27207-9). Claitors.

LOUISIANA–HISTORY–FICTION

Cable, George W. Strange True Stories of Louisiana. LC 78-116944. (Short Story Index Reprint Ser). 1889. 22.00 (ISBN 0-8369-3446-6). Arno.

Costain, Thomas B. High Towers. (Illus.). 1949. 6.95 (ISBN 0-385-04194-2). Doubleday.

St. Martin, Gerard L. & Voorhies, Jacqueline K. Ecrits Louisianais Du Dix-Neuvieme Siecle: Nouvelles, Contes, et Fables. LC 78-24295. 1979. 20.00x (ISBN 0-8071-0353-5). La State U Pr.

LOUISIANA–JUVENILE LITERATURE

Bailey, Bernadine. Picture Book of Louisiana. rev. ed. LC 54-9944. (Illus.). (gr. 3-5). 1967. 5.50g (ISBN 0-8075-9520-9). A Whitman.

Carpenter, Allan. Louisiana. new ed. LC 78-3390. (New Enchantment of America State Bks.). (Illus.). (gr. 4 up). 1978. PLB 10.60 (ISBN 0-516-04118-5). Childrens.

Duplantier, Kathleen B. & Marmillion, Norman. A Child's Louisiana. (Create & Color Ser.). (Illus.). 40p. (gr. k-8). 1981. wkbk., staple bound 3.95 (ISBN 0-936980-00-1). Pretzel Pr.

Fradin, Dennis. Louisiana: In Words & Pictures. LC 80-28609. (Young People's Stories of Our States Ser.). (Illus.). 48p. (gr. 2-5). 1981. PLB 9.25 (ISBN 0-516-03918-0). Childrens.

LOUISIANA–POLITICS AND GOVERNMENT

Beals, Carleton. Story of Huey P. Long. LC 75-136054. 1971. Repr. of 1935 ed. lib. bdg. 21.50x (ISBN 0-8371-5204-6, BEHL). Greenwood.

Caskey, Willie M. Secession & Restoration of Louisiana. LC 78-75302. (American Scene Ser). (Illus.). 1970. Repr. of 1938 ed. lib. bdg. 32.50 (ISBN 0-306-71263-6). Da Capo.

Civil Code of the State of Louisiana: By Authority. LC 74-19620. Repr. of 1825 ed. 94.50 (ISBN 0-404-12456-9). AMS Pr.

Clay, Floyd M. Coozan Dudley LeBlanc: From Huey Long to Hadacol. LC 73-14609. (Illus.). 1974. 10.00 (ISBN 0-911116-69-9). Pelican.

Constitution of the State of Louisiana. 1974. 5.00 (ISBN 0-685-42670-X); pap. 2.00 (ISBN 0-685-42671-8). Claitors.

Haskins, James. Pinckney Benton Stewart Pinchback: A Biography. (Illus.). 304p. 1973. 12.95 (ISBN 0-02-548890-2). Macmillan.

Howard, Perry H. Political Tendencies in Louisiana. rev. ed. LC 74-123205. (Illus.). 1971. 30.00x (ISBN 0-8071-0441-8). La State U Pr.

Kane, Harnett T. Louisiana Hayride. (Illus.). 1971. Repr. of 1941 ed. 10.00 (ISBN 0-911116-32-X). Pelican.

Liebling, A. J. Earl of Louisiana. LC 76-130664. 1970. 17.50x (ISBN 0-8071-0537-6); pap. text ed. 5.95x (ISBN 0-8071-0203-2). La State U Pr.

Long, Huey P. Every Man a King: Autobiography. 7.50 (ISBN 0-8446-2485-3). Peter Smith.

--Every Man a King: The Autobiography of Huey P. Long. (Illus.). 1972. pap. 3.45 (ISBN 0-8129-6012-2, QP8). Times Bks.

Lonn, Ella. Reconstruction in Louisiana After 1868. LC 66-24724. (Illus.). 1967. Repr. of 1918 ed. 12.50 (ISBN 0-8462-0832-6). Russell.

--Reconstruction in Louisiana After 1868. 1918. 8.00 (ISBN 0-8446-1289-8). Peter Smith.

McCrary, Peyton. Abraham Lincoln & Reconstruction: The Louisiana Experiment. LC 78-51181. 1978. 30.00 (ISBN 0-691-04660-3). Princeton U Pr.

Pugh, George W. Louisiana Evidence Law 1978 Supplement. 1978. pap. 19.50 (ISBN 0-672-83238-0). Bobbs.

Rogers, Murphy P. A State's Supervision of Its Elementary Schools. LC 73-177204. (Columbia University. Teachers College. Contributions to Education: No. 679). Repr. of 1936 ed. 17.50 (ISBN 0-404-55679-5). AMS Pr.

Seebold, Herman. Old Louisiana Plantation Homes & Family Trees, Vol. 1. (Illus.). 1971. Repr. of 1941 ed. 30.00 (ISBN 0-911116-34-6). Pelican.

Sindler, Allan P. Huey Long's Louisiana: State Politics, 1920-1952. LC 56-11664. 316p. 1956. pap. 3.95x (ISBN 0-8018-0597-X). Johns Hopkins.

Stephenson, Wendell H. Alexander Porter, Whig Planter of Old Louisiana. LC 69-19761. (American Scene Ser.). 1969. Repr. of 1934 ed. lib. bdg. 17.50 (ISBN 0-306-71254-7). Da Capo.

Taylor, Joe G. Louisiana Reconstructed, 1863-1877. LC 74-77327. (Illus.). 576p. 1974. 32.50x (ISBN 0-8071-0084-6). La State U Pr.

Vincent, Charles. Black Legislators in Louisiana During Reconstruction. LC 74-77328. (Illus.). 296p. 1976. 17.50x (ISBN 0-8071-0089-7). La State U Pr.

Warmoth, Henry C. War, Politics & Reconstruction: Stormy Days in Louisiana. LC 74-109364. Repr. of 1930 ed. 15.00x (ISBN 0-8371-3874-4). Greenwood.

Williams, T. Harry. Romance & Realism in Southern Politics. LC 61-9798. 1966. pap. text ed. 2.25x (ISBN 0-8071-0103-6). La State U Pr.

Woodward, M. Truman. Louisiana Notarial Manual: 1973 Supplement. 1973. 7.50 (ISBN 0-685-59739-3). A Smith Co.

LOUISIANA–POPULATION

Ardoin, Robert B. Louisiana Census Records, Vol. 1: Avoyelles & St. Landry Parishes, 1810 & 1820. LC 71-134170. 1970. 12.00 (ISBN 0-8063-0446-4). Genealog Pub.

Ardoin, Robert B., compiled by. Louisiana Census Records: Ascension, Assumption, T. Charles, St. Bernard, St. John the Baptist, St. James, East & West Baton Rouge, 1810-1820, Vol. III. 1977. 20.00 (ISBN 0-686-10449-8). Polyanthos.

Childs, Marleta & Ross, John. North Louisiana Census Reports. Incl. Vol. II. 1830 & 1840, Parishes of Caddo, Claiborne, & Natchitoches; Vol. III. 1850 & 1860, Union Parish. 1977. 20.00 (ISBN 0-686-20579-0). Polyanthos.

Maduell, Charles R., Jr. The Census Tables for the French Colony at Louisiana: From 1699 Through 1732. LC 76-183748. 181p. 1972. 12.50 (ISBN 0-8063-0490-1). Genealog Pub.

LOUISIANA–SOCIAL LIFE AND CUSTOMS

Barrow, Bennet H. Plantation Life in the Florida Parishes of Louisiana 1836-1846, As Reflected in the Diary of Bennet H. Barrow. Davis, Edwin A., ed. LC 74-163680. Repr. of 1943 ed. 29.50 (ISBN 0-404-01989-7). AMS Pr.

Crete, Liliane. Daily Life in Louisiana, 1815-1830. Gregory, Patrick, tr. from Fr. 308p. 1981. text ed. 25.00x (ISBN 0-8071-0887-1). La State U Pr.

Darby, William. A Geographical Description of the State of Louisiana, with an Account of the Characters & Manners of the Inhabitants. 1977. Repr. 25.00 (ISBN 0-403-07893-8). Scholarly.

Hallowell, Christopher L. People of the Bayou: Cajun Life in Lost America. (Illus.). 1979. 8.95 (ISBN 0-525-17728-0). Dutton.

Kennedy, R. Emmet. Mellows: A Chronicle of Unknown Singers. LC 78-32125. (Illus.). 1979. Repr. of 1925 ed. lib. bdg. 19.75x (ISBN 0-8371-5831-1, KME&). Greenwood.

Mugnier, George F. Louisiana Images, 1880-1920: A Photographic Essay. Kemp, John R. & King, Linda O., eds. LC 74-27199. (Illus.). 144p. 1975. pap. 8.95 (ISBN 0-8071-0151-6). La State U Pr.

Saucier. Traditions De la Paroisse Des Avoyelles En Louisiana. 1956. pap. 5.00 (ISBN 0-88289-031-X). Pelican.

Schweid, Richard. Hot Peppers: Cajuns & Capsicum in New Iberia la. LC 80-23160. 200p. 1980. 9.95 (ISBN 0-914842-50-1); pap. 6.95 (ISBN 0-914842-51-X). Madrona Pubs.

Zimmer, Maude F. Time to Remember. 3.95 (ISBN 0-8315-0005-0). Speller.

LOUISIANA PURCHASE

Barbe-Marbois, Francois. The History of Louisiana, Particularly of the Cession of That Colony to the United States of America. Lyon, E. Wilson, ed. LC 77-5665. (Louisiana Bicentennial Reprint Ser.). 1977. 20.00x (ISBN 0-8071-0186-9). La State U Pr.

Brown, Everett S. Constitutional History of the Louisiana Purchase, 1803-1812. LC 68-55492. Repr. of 1920 ed. 15.00x (ISBN 0-678-00742-X). Kelley.

Chase, John. Louisiana Purchase: America's Best Buy. 4.95 (ISBN 0-911116-24-9); pap. 1.00 (ISBN 0-911116-68-0). Pelican.

Chidsey, Donald B. The Louisiana Purchase. (Illus.). 192p. 1972. 4.95 (ISBN 0-517-50740-4). Crown.

Houck, Louis. Boundaries of the Louisiana Purchase: A Historical Study. LC 72-146401. (First American Frontier Ser). 1971. Repr. of 1901 ed. 9.00 (ISBN 0-405-02855-5). Arno.

Marshall, T. M. History of the Western Boundary of the Louisiana Purchase, 1819-1841. LC 73-87411. (American Scene Ser). (Illus.). 1970. Repr. of 1914 ed. lib. bdg. 27.50 (ISBN 0-306-71554-6). Da Capo.

Phelan, Mary K. The Story of the Louisiana Purchase. LC 78-22505. (Illus.). (gr. 4-6). 1979. 8.95 (ISBN 0-690-03955-7, TYC-J); PLB 8.79 (ISBN 0-690-03956-5). Har-Row.

Robertson, James A., ed. Louisiana Under the Rule of Spain, France & the United States 1785-1807, 2 vols. facsimile ed. LC 72-102254. (Select Bibliographies Reprint Ser). 1911. Set. 56.00 (ISBN 0-8369-5139-5). Arno.

Sprague, Marshall. So Vast So Beautiful a Land: Louisiana & the Purchase. LC 73-21943. 1974. 12.50 (ISBN 0-316-80766-4). Little.

Stoddard, Amos. Sketches, Historical & Descriptive, of Louisiana. LC 72-956. Repr. of 1812 ed. 27.50 (ISBN 0-404-06278-4). AMS Pr.

Tallant, Robert. Louisiana Purchase. (Landmark Ser: No. 24). (gr. 5-6). 1952. PLB 5.99 (ISBN 0-394-90324-2, BYR). Random.

LOUISIANA STATE UNIVERSITY AND AGRICULTURAL AND MECHANICAL COLLEGE

Taylor, H. Warren. Forty-Two Years on the Tiger Gridiron. 6.50x (ISBN 0-685-08174-5). Claitors.

LOUISVILLE, KENTUCKY

Bierman, Don E., ed. An Introduction to the Louisville Region: Selected Essays. (Illus.). 90p. 1980. pap. 2.50 (ISBN 0-89291-145-X). U of Louisville.

Lesy, Michael. Real Life: Louisville in the Twenties. LC 76-9977. 1976. pap. 7.95 (ISBN 0-394-73235-9). Pantheon.

Morgan, William. Louisville: Architecture & the Urban Environment. LC 79-631. 1979. 6.95 (ISBN 0-87233-050-8). Bauhan.

LOURDES

see also Bernadette, Saint (Bernadette Soubirous), 1844-1879

Bertrin, G. Lourdes: A History of Its Apparitions & Cures. 59.95 (ISBN 0-8490-0560-4). Gordon Pr.

Marnham, Patrick. Lourdes: A Modern Pilgrimage. (Illus.). 244p. 1981. 12.95 (ISBN 0-686-74811-5). Coward.

LOURDES–DESCRIPTION–VIEWS

Menotti, Giulia. Lourdes. Orling, Merry, tr. (Illus., Orig.). 1976. pap. 9.00x (ISBN 0-8002-0142-6). Intl Pubns Serv.

Zola, Emile. Mes Voyages: Lourdes, Rome. 1955. 8.95 (ISBN 0-686-55790-5). French & Eur.

LOURDES, NOTRE-DAME DE

Hutchinson, Gloria. Mary & Inner Healing. 112p. (Orig.). 1980. pap. 2.50 (ISBN 0-912228-76-8). St Anthony Mess Pr.

Walne, Damien & Flory, Joan. The Lady Said Come to Lourdes. (Illus.). 1978. pap. 3.95 (ISBN 0-8199-0753-7). Franciscan Herald.

LOUSE

see Lice

LOUVRE, PARIS

LaClotte, Michel. The Louvre. LC 79-57409. (Abbeville Library of Art: No. 3). (Illus.). 112p. 1980. pap. 4.95 (ISBN 0-89659-097-6). Abbeville Pr.

Laclotte, Michel & Cuzin, Jean-Pierre. One Hundred Favorite Old Master Paintings from the Louvre Museum, Paris. LC 79-64988. (Illus.). 160p. 1979. 17.95 (ISBN 0-89659-065-8). Abbeville Pr.

Ragghianti, Carlo L. Louvre: Paris. LC 68-19927. (Great Museums of the World Ser). (Illus.). 1968. 16.95 (ISBN 0-88225-229-1). Newsweek.

Schneider, Pierre. Louvre Dialogues. Southgate, Patsy, tr. from Fr. LC 72-135572. (Illus.). 1971. 10.00 (ISBN 0-689-10386-7). Atheneum.

LOUYS, PIERRE, 1870-1925

Clive, H. P. Pierre Louys Eighteen Seventy to Nineteen Twenty-Five: A Biography. 1978. 45.00x (ISBN 0-19-815751-7). Oxford U Pr.

LOVARI DIALECT

see Gipsies–Language

LOVASIK, LEO EDWARD, 1921-1943

Lovasik, Lawrence. Our Lady's Knight. 3.50 (ISBN 0-8198-0112-7). Dghtrs St Paul.

LOVE

see also Courtly Love; Courtship; Friendship; Marriage

Abarbanel, Judah. The Philosophy of Love. Friedeberg-Seeley, F. & Barnes, J. H., trs. 1977. lib. bdg. 59.95 (ISBN 0-8490-2433-1). Gordon Pr.

Ahlem, Lloyd H. Do I Have to Be Me? LC 73-79843. 208p. (Orig.). 1973. pap. 3.25 (ISBN 0-8307-0252-0, 54-098-02). Regal.

Alphabet of Love. 1967. 2.50 (ISBN 0-442-82137-9). Peter Pauper.

Amato, Antony & Edwards, Katherine. Affair. LC 77-20490. 1978. 7.95 (ISBN 0-399-12106-4). Putnam.

Amen, Carol. Love Is the Motive. LC 77-12655. (Better Living Ser.). 1977. pap. 0.95 (ISBN 0-8127-0153-4). Review & Herald.

Andreas Capellanus. Art of Courtly Love. Perry, John J., tr. 1969. pap. text ed. 5.95x (ISBN 0-393-09848-6, NortonC). Norton.

Andrews, Stephen P., Sr., et al. Love, Marriage, & Divorce. Shively, Charles, ed. 1975. 12.50x (ISBN 0-87730-010-0). M&S Pr.

Augsburger, David. Cherishable: Love & Marriage. LC 71-171536. 4.95 (ISBN 0-8361-1707-7). Herald Pr.

--Cherishable: Love & Marriage. 1975. pap. 1.25 (ISBN 0-89129-065-6, PV065). Jove Pubns.

Baker, Elizabeth. Love Around the House. 1979. pap. 2.95 (ISBN 0-88207-603-5). Victor Bks.

Bell, Joseph N. Love Theory in Later Hanbalite Islam. LC 78-5904. 1979. PLB 39.00 (ISBN 0-87395-244-8). State U NY Pr.

Bloomfield, Harold, et al. How to Survive the Loss of a Love. 1977. pap. 2.50 (ISBN 0-553-14839-7). Bantam.

Boom, Corrie T. Amazing Love. (Orig.). pap. 1.95 (ISBN 0-515-04898-4). Jove Pubns.

Botwin, Carol & Fine, Jerome L. The Love Crisis. LC 77-27698. 1979. 8.95 (ISBN 0-385-13482-7). Doubleday.

Branden, Nathaniel. The Psychology of Romantic Love. 288p. 1981. pap. 2.95 (ISBN 0-553-20001-1). Bantam.

--The Psychology of Romantic Love. LC 79-91763. 216p. 1980. 10.00 (ISBN 0-87477-124-2). J P Tarcher.

Branden, Nathaniel & Branden, E. Devers. The Romantic Love Question & Answer Book. 204p. 1981. 10.95 (ISBN 0-87477-184-6). J P Tarcher.

Bride's Magazine Editors & Calderone, Mary. Questions & Answers About Love & Sex. 144p. 1980. pap. 1.95 (ISBN 0-380-52977-7, 52977). Avon.

Bride's Magazine Editors & Editors of "Bride's Magazine". Questions & Answers About Love & Sex. LC 78-21401. 1979. 8.95 (ISBN 0-312-66041-3). St Martin.

Burton, Richard, tr. The Perfumed Garden of the Shaykh Nafzawi. 272p. 15.00x (ISBN 0-85435-363-1, Pub. by Spearman England). State Mutual Bk.

Buscaglia, Leo F. Love. LC 72-92810. 147p. 1972. 6.95 (ISBN 0-913590-07-X). C B Slack.

Capellanus, Andreas. Art of Courtly Love. abr ed. Locke, F. W., ed. Parry, John J., tr. LC 56-12400. (Milestones of Thought Ser.). 6.00 (ISBN 0-8044-2108-0); pap. 2.95 (ISBN 0-8044-6075-2). Ungar.

Carpenter, Edward. Love's Coming-of-Age. 1912. lib. bdg. 40.00 (ISBN 0-8414-1559-5). Folcroft.

Centers, Richard. Sexual Attraction & Love: An Instrumental Theory. (Illus.). 340p. 1975. 16.50 (ISBN 0-398-03187-8). C C Thomas.

Chauchard, Paul. Our Need of Love. (gr. 10 up). 1968. 4.95 (ISBN 0-02-831720-3, 83172). Kenedy.

Chervin, Ronda. Love & Your Everyday Life. 1977. pap. 1.50 (ISBN 0-89243-069-9, 288005). Liguori Pubns.

Choate, Carole. A Gentle & Tender Love. 1978. pap. 1.75 (ISBN 0-911336-72-9). Sci of Mind.

Cleckley, Hervey M. Caricature of Love. 10.00 (ISBN 0-911238-52-2). Regent House.

Colfax, Henry G. The Most Critical Stations in the Love Experience. (Illus.). 1979. deluxe ed. 47.45 (ISBN 0-930582-22-5). Gloucester Art.

Colman, Arthur D. & Colman, Libby L. Love & Ecstasy. LC 75-2136. 1975. 8.95 (ISBN 0-8164-9250-6). Continuum.

Constable, Benjamin. The Mystical Symbolism of Universal Love. (Illus.). 1978. 37.50 (ISBN 0-89266-113-5). Am Classical Coll Pr.

Cook, Mark & Wilson, Glenn, eds. Love & Attraction: An International Conference. LC 78-40286. 1979. text ed. 72.00 (ISBN 0-08-022234-X). Pergamon.
Cooper, Norman W. Love That Heals. 1977. pap. 3.00 (ISBN 0-87516-228-2). De Vorss.
Country Beautiful Editors. Love. LC 72-131399. (Illus.). 194p. 1970. 15.95 (ISBN 0-87294-021-7). Country Beautiful.
Country Beautiful Editors, ed. The Meaning & Mystery of Love. (Home Library Ser). (Illus.). Date not set. price not set (ISBN 0-87294-104-3). Country Beautiful.
Cowburn, John. Person & Love. 1967. 7.95 (ISBN 0-8189-0110-1). Alba.
Craigin, Elisabeth. Either Is Love. LC 75-12311. (Homosexuality). 1975. Repr. of 1937 ed. 9.00x (ISBN 0-405-07379-8). Arno.
Creed, Charles. The Art of the Affair. 80p. (Orig.). 1980. pap. 3.95 (ISBN 0-933180-10-1). Ellis Pr.
Crosby, John. Illusion & Disillusion: The Serf in Love & Marriage. 2nd ed. 1976. pap. text ed. 10.95x (ISBN 0-534-00450-4). Wadsworth Pub.
Curtin, Mary E., ed. Symposium on Love. LC 73-10475. 244p. 1973. text ed. 19.95 (ISBN 0-87705-116-X). Human Sci Pr.
Da Free John. Love of the Two-Armed Form. LC 78-57090. 1978. 10.95 (ISBN 0-913922-37-4). Dawn Horse Pr.
Davis, Genny W. & Davis, Bruce. Love & Wealth. (Illus.). 96p. 1981. 4.95 (ISBN 0-02-530010-5). Macmillan.
Davis, Georgia. Astrology & Love. 13th ed. 1977. pap. 1.50 (ISBN 0-685-11794-4, Argent Bks). Merit Pubns.
De Aragon, Ray J. The Great Lovers. (Non-Fiction Ser.). (Illus.). 104p. (Orig.). 1981. pap. 5.95 (ISBN 0-932906-10-9). Pan-Am Publishing Co.
Deaton, John. Love & Sex in Marriage: Doctor's Guide to the Sensual Union. 1978. 12.95 (ISBN 0-13-540856-3, Parker). P-H.
De Gourmont, Remy. Natural Philosophy of Love. Pound, Ezra, tr. (Black & Gold Lib). (Illus.). 1944. 6.95 (ISBN 0-87140-951-8, Co-Pub with Tudor). Liveright.
DeJong, Constance. Modern Love. 1978. pap. 4.95 (ISBN 0-918746-01-9). Urizen Bks.
Delfiore, Clarence T. Purity & the Carnal Element in Love: The Story of a Concrete Case. (Intimate Life of Man Library). (Illus.). 111p. 1981. 39.75 (ISBN 0-89266-298-0). Am Classical Coll Pr.
Dell, Floyd. Love in the Machine Age. 428p. 1981. Repr. of 1930 ed. lib. bdg. 30.00 (ISBN 0-89760-136-X). Telegraph Bks.
DeMarco, Ginilou. A Time to Love. 175p. 1981. pap. 4.95 (ISBN 0-86608-001-5). Impact Tenn.
Doherty, Catherine D. The Gospel Without Compromise. LC 75-28619. 152p. 1976. pap. 2.45 (ISBN 0-87793-104-6). Ave Maria.
Doi, Takeo. The Anatomy of Dependence. Bester, John, tr. from Jap. LC 72-76297. Orig. Title: Amae No Kozo. 1973. pap. 5.95 (ISBN 0-87011-299-6). Kodansha.
Drury, Michael. Advice to a Young Wife from an Old Mistress. LC 68-22668. 1968. 6.95 (ISBN 0-385-03632-9). Doubleday.
Dunkell, Samuel. Lovelives: How We Make Love. LC 78-7381. (Illus.). 1978. 8.95 (ISBN 0-688-03354-7). Morrow.
Eberle, Sarah. What Is Love? Sparks, Judith, ed. (A Happy Day Book). (Illus.). 24p. (gr. k-2). 1980. 0.98 (ISBN 0-87239-410-7, 3642). Standard Pub.
Ebertin, Elsbeth. Astrology & Romance. Nelson, D. G., tr. from Ger. LC 73-90428. (Illus.). 132p. 1973. Repr. of 1936 ed. 7.95 (ISBN 0-88231-002-X). ASI Pubs Inc.
Emerson, Ralph W. On Love & Friendship. 2.95 (ISBN 0-442-82199-9). Peter Pauper.
Finck, Henry T. Primitive Love & Love-Stories. 1976. lib. bdg. 75.00 (ISBN 0-8490-2476-5). Gordon Pr.
Fletcher, Jefferson B. Religion of Beauty in Woman: Essays on Platonic Love in Poetry & Society. LC 68-925. (Studies in Poetry, No. 38). 1969. Repr. of 1911 ed. lib. bdg. 49.95 (ISBN 0-8383-0550-4). Haskell.
Ford, Edward E. & Englund, Steven. Permanent Love: Practical Steps to a Lasting Relationship. 1979. 7.95 (ISBN 0-03-052696-5); pap. 4.95 (ISBN 0-03-051216-6). Winston Pr.
Fowlie, Wallace. Clown's Grail, Study of Love in Its Literary Expression. LC 73-11380. 1947. lib. bdg. 17.50 (ISBN 0-8414-1981-7). Folcroft.
Francisca, Beverly. Love, a Symposium. 1976. pap. 2.95 (ISBN 0-685-77530-5). New Age.
Fraser, Antonia, ed. Love Letters: An Anthology. 1977. 10.95 (ISBN 0-394-41278-8). Knopf.
Frazer, Louis D. Authentic Love Scenes from a Period When Love Was Real & Not the Fraud It Is Today. (Illus.). 1978. deluxe ed. 23.75 (ISBN 0-930582-15-2). Gloucester Art.
Fromm, Erich. The Art of Loving. 128p. 1974. pap. 2.95 (ISBN 0-06-080291-X, P291, PL). Har-Row.
--Art of Loving: An Enquiry into the Nature of Love. pap. 3.95 (ISBN 0-06-090001-6, CN 1, CN). Har-Row.
--Art of Loving: An Enquiry into the Nature of Love. LC 56-8750. (World Perspectives Ser.). 1956. 9.95 (ISBN 0-06-011375-8, HarpT). Har-Row.
Fromme, Allan. Ability to Love. pap. 5.00 (ISBN 0-87980-000-3). Wilshire.
Gallagher, Chuck, Fr., S.J. Love Is a Couple. 1978. pap. 2.95 (ISBN 0-385-13595-5, Im). Doubleday.
Gardner, John F. Love & the Illusion of Love. 1976. Repr. of 1973 ed. pap. 1.50 (ISBN 0-913098-12-4). Myrin Institute.
Gaylin, Willard. Caring. 1976. 9.95 (ISBN 0-394-49785-6). Knopf.
Gill, Brendan. Ways of Loving. 1974. 7.95 (ISBN 0-15-195312-0). HarBraceJ.
Goldberg, Jan, et al. The Statue of Liberty Is Cracking up: A Guide to Loving, Leaving, & Living Again. 1979. 8.95 (ISBN 0-15-184916-1). HarBraceJ.
Goodman, Linda. Linda Goodman's Love Signs: A New Approach to the Human Heart. LC 78-2141. 1978. 15.00 (ISBN 0-06-011550-5, HarpT). Har-Row.
Gormely, Sheila. Coupling: Personal Stories of Love That Lasts. LC 78-22631. 264p. 1981. 14.95 (ISBN 0-385-14477-6). Doubleday.
Gould, James A. & Iorio, John J. Love, Sex & Identity. LC 78-176093. 184p. 1972. pap. 5.95x (ISBN 0-87835-033-0). Boyd & Fraser.
Grant, Vernon. Falling in Love: The Psychology of the Romantic Emotion. LC 75-44446. 192p. 1976. text ed. 11.00 (ISBN 0-8261-1890-9); pap. text ed. 6.95 (ISBN 0-8261-1891-7). Springer Pub.
Grau, Joseph A. Morality & the Human Future in the Thought of Teilhard De Chardin: A Critical Study. LC 74-4976. 389p. 1976. 19.50 (ISBN 0-8386-1579-1). Fairleigh Dickinson.
Greene, John. Ciceronis Amor: Tullies Love (1589) & Quip for an Upstart (1592) LC 54-11901. 22.00x (ISBN 0-8201-1224-Ø). Schol Facsimiles.
Greene, Liz. Star Signs for Lovers. LC 80-5890. (Illus.). 480p. 1980. 14.95 (ISBN 0-8128-2765-1). Stein & Day.
Grossman, Jack H. The Promise of Love. 1977. pap. 1.45 (ISBN 0-87029-133-5, 20159). Abbey.
Guidepost Associates. Guideposts Treasury of Love. (Illus.). 352p. 1981. 12.95 (ISBN 0-385-14973-5). Doubleday.
Gutridge, D. Foster, II. Your Secret Power: Creating Love, Vol. 3. (Your Secret Power Ser.). 96p. (Orig.). 1981. pap. 5.95 (ISBN 0-938014-03-X, 2001C). Freedom Unltd.
Harlow, Harry F. Learning to Love. (Illus.). 1973. pap. 2.95 (ISBN 0-87843-606-5). Albion.
Harper, Ralph. Human Love-Existential & Mystical. 178p. 1966. 11.50x (ISBN 0-8018-0255-5). Johns Hopkins.
Hashagen, August. Let Us Have Love. rev. ed. 1967. pap. 1.50 (ISBN 0-910140-06-5). Anthony.
--Let Us Have Love. pap. 2.00 (ISBN 0-685-06573-1). Assoc Bk.
Haughton, Rosemary. The Mystery of Sexuality. LC 72-82768. 84p. (Orig.). 1972. pap. 2.45 (ISBN 0-8091-1736-3, Deus). Paulist Pr.
Hegeler, Inge & Hegeler, Sten. An ABZ of Love. 384p. 11.50x (ISBN 0-85435-333-X, Pub. by Spearman England). State Mutual Bk.
Helmlinger, Trudy. After You've Said Goodbye: How to Recover After Ending a Relationship. 292p. 1977. 8.95 (ISBN 0-87073-791-0). Schenkman.
Henke, Thomas R. How to Love...& Be Loved. Henke, Christina M., ed. LC 78-69809. (Illus.). 1978. 14.95 (ISBN 0-931190-01-0). Trans Traffic.
Hine, James R. What Comes After You Say, "I Love You"? LC 80-11277. (Illus.). 1980. 12.50 (ISBN 0-87015-231-9). Pacific Bks.
Hinmon, Dean. Loving. 1976. pap. 2.95 perfect bound (ISBN 0-685-79064-9). Awareness.
Hirschfeld, Magnus. Sex in Human Relationships. LC 72-9649. Repr. of 1935 ed. 21.00 (ISBN 0-404-57459-9). AMS Pr.
Hocking, David L. Love & Marriage. LC 81-413. (Orig.). 1981. pap. 4.95 (ISBN 0-89081-291-8). Harvest Hse.
Hoest, Bill. Of Course I Love You - What Do I Know? (Lockhorns Ser.: No. 6). (Orig.). 1981. pap. 1.75 (ISBN 0-451-09984-2, E9984, Sig). NAL.
Jampolsky, Gerald. Love Is Letting Go of Fear. 144p. 1981. pap. 2.50 (ISBN 0-553-14651-3). Bantam.
John Hadfield's Book of Love. 1981. 15.00x (ISBN 0-85115-139-6, Pub. by Boydell England). State Mutual Bk.
Johnson, Caesar, compiled by. Today, Tomorrow & Always. (Illus.). 1977. boxed 4.95 (ISBN 0-8378-1729-3). Gibson.
Jones, Gladys V. The Greek Love Mysteries. 1975. 6.95 (ISBN 0-87613-037-6). New Age.
Junke, N. Sex & Love Today. 536p. 25.00x (ISBN 0-85435-373-9, Pub. by Spearman England). State Mutual England.
Kaufman, Barry N. To Love Is to Be Happy with: The First Book of the Option Process. 1977. 8.95 (ISBN 0-698-10779-9). Coward.
Kenmare, Dallas. Love the Unknown. 8.95 (ISBN 0-85307-067-9). Transatlantic.
Kershner, H. E. How to Stay in Love with One Woman for 70 Years. LC 77-85444. pap. 3.95 (ISBN 0-87359-013-9). Northwood Inst.
Kiev, Ari. Active Loving. LC 79-7090. 1979. 8.95 (ISBN 0-690-01785-5). T Y Crowell.
Krantzler, Mel. Learning to Love Again: Beyond Creative Divorce. 1979. pap. 2.25 (ISBN 0-553-11831-5). Bantam.
Kristy, Norton F. Staying in Love: Reinventing Marriage & Other Realationships. (Orig.). pap. 2.75 (ISBN 0-515-05089-X). Jove Pubns.
Labadie, Joseph A. What Is Love? (Men & Movements in the History & Philosophy of Anarchism Ser.). 1979. lib. bdg. 59.95 (ISBN 0-686-51647-8). Revisionist Pr.
Lair, Jess. Sex-If I Didn't I'd Cry. LC 77-27678. 1979. pap. 5.95 (ISBN 0-385-13391-X). Doubleday.
Langone, John. Like, Love, Lust: A View of Sex & Sexuality. 144p. 1981. pap. 2.25 (ISBN 0-380-54189-0, 54189). Avon.
Larzelere, Bob. The Harmony of Love. LC 81-3189. 137p. (Orig.). 1982. pap. 6.95 (ISBN 0-932654-03-7). Context Pubns.
Lasswell, Marcia & Lobsenz, Norman. Styles of Loving: Why You Love the Way You Do. 192p. 1981. pap. 2.50 (ISBN 0-345-29228-6). Ballantine.
Lasswell, Marcia & Lobsenz, Norman M. The Styles of Loving: Why You Love the Way You Do. LC 78-22338. 1980. 9.95 (ISBN 0-385-13534-3). Doubleday.
LaViolette, Wesley. Love & Live. 3.95 (ISBN 0-87516-038-7). De Vorss.
Leavenworth, Carol. Love & Commitment: You Don't Have to Settle for Less. (Illus.). 192p. 1981. 10.95t (ISBN 0-13-540971-3, Spec); pap. 5.95 (ISBN 0-13-540963-2). P-H.
Lester, Gordon. Living & Loving. 1976. pap. 1.75 (ISBN 0-89243-063-X, 41470). Liguori Pubns.
Lewis, Clive S. Allegory of Love: A Study of Medieval Tradition. 1936. 22.00x (ISBN 0-19-811562-8); pap. 4.95x (ISBN 0-19-500343-8). Oxford U Pr.
--Four Loves. LC 60-10920. 1960. 9.95 (ISBN 0-15-132915-X). HarBraceJ.
Liebman, Monte H. What Is Love & How to Find It. (Counselor's Handbook Ser.). 1977. pap. 4.75 (ISBN 0-89769-002-8). Pine Mntn.
Lipke, Jean C. Loving. LC 72-104894. (Being Together Books). Orig. Title: Getting Ready for Marriage. (gr. 5-11). 1971. PLB 4.95 (ISBN 0-8225-0593-2). Lerner Pubns.
Lorrance, Arleen & Pike, Diane K. The Love Project Way. 216p. (Orig.). 1980. pap. 6.95 (ISBN 0-916192-15-6). L P Pubns.
Love & Marriage. 1967. 2.95 (ISBN 0-442-82323-1). Peter Pauper.
Love Is a Poem. 1962. 2.95 (ISBN 0-442-82328-2). Peter Pauper.
Love Is the Answer. 96p. 1978. pap. 3.50 (ISBN 0-911336-74-5). Sci of Mind.
The Love Test Book: Rate Your Compatibility, Romantic Style, Honesty, Assertiveness, Sexual Satisfaction, & Much More. LC 78-15730. 1978. lib. bdg. 12.90 (ISBN 0-89471-053-2); pap. 3.95 (ISBN 0-89471-052-4). Running Pr.
The Lover's Dictionary: How to Be Amorous in Five Delectable Languages. 1981. pap. 4.95 (ISBN 0-686-29648-6). Natl Textbk.
Ludwig, Emil. Of Life & Love. LC 72-128273. (Essay Index Reprint Ser). 1945. 16.00 (ISBN 0-8369-1984-X). Arno.
Mac Carthy, Denis Florence. Love the Greatest Enchantment: The Sorceries of Sin, the Devotion of the Cross. 1861. 50.00 (ISBN 0-8274-3002-7). R West.
McNair, Jim. Love & Gifts. LC 76-6555. 1976. 3.50 (ISBN 0-87123-328-2, 210328). Bethany Hse.
Mantegazza, Paolo. The Physiology & the Pathology of Love. (Illus.). 131p. 1981. Repr. of 1917 ed. 55.65 (ISBN 0-89901-035-0). Found Class Reprints.
--Physiology of Love. Robinson, Victor, ed. Alexander, Herbert, tr. from It. LC 78-22291. Repr. of 1936 ed. 22.50 (ISBN 0-404-61526-0). AMS Pr.
Marquis, Dave M. Making Love a Way of Life. LC 76-54490. 1977. pap. 3.95 (ISBN 0-913592-84-6). Argus Comm.
Mary. Love. 1959. pap. 0.75 (ISBN 0-87516-056-5). De Vorss.
Maurois, Andre. Seven Faces of Love. Repr. of 1944 ed. 15.75 (ISBN 0-518-10169-X). Arno.
May, Rollo. Love & Will. LC 66-12799. 1969. 14.95 (ISBN 0-393-01080-5). Norton.
--Love & Will. 1973. pap. 5.95 (ISBN 0-440-55027-0, Delta). Dell.
Mayer, Eve R. Let's Stay Lovers. 1981. 7.95 (ISBN 0-533-04917-2). Vantage.
Mellen, Sydney L. The Evolution of Love. LC 80-18028. 1981. text ed. 15.95x (ISBN 0-7167-1271-7); pap. text ed. 8.95x (ISBN 0-7167-1272-5). W H Freeman.
Melly, George. Great Lovers. 48p. 1981. 9.95 (ISBN 0-517-54537-3, Harmony). Crown.
Menninger, Karl A. Love Against Hate. LC 42-50183. 1959. pap. 3.50 (ISBN 0-15-653892-X, HB28, Harv). HarBraceJ.
Miller, Howard L. & Siegel, Paul S. Loving: A Psychological Approach. LC 72-3770. 224p. 1972. pap. 11.50 (ISBN 0-471-60390-2). Wiley.
Miller, Keith. Please Love Me. 1977. 8.95 (ISBN 0-87680-509-8). Word Bks.
Moncure, Jane B. Love. (Values to Live by Ser.). (Illus.). (ps-3). 1981. PLB 8.65 (ISBN 0-516-06525-4). Childrens.
--Love. LC 80-15771. (What Does the Bible Say? Ser.). (Illus.). 32p. (ps-2). 1980. PLB 4.95 (ISBN 0-89565-165-3). Childs World.
Montagu, A. The Practice of Love. 1975. pap. 2.95 (ISBN 0-13-694463-9, Spec). P-H.
Montagu, Ashley, ed. Meaning of Love. LC 72-11335. 248p. 1974. Repr. of 1953 ed. lib. bdg. 14.75x (ISBN 0-8371-6656-X, MOML). Greenwood.
Moore, John C. Love in Twelfth Century France. LC 75-170268. (Orig.). 1972. 12.00x (ISBN 0-8122-7648-5); pap. 5.95x (ISBN 0-8122-1027-1, Pa Paperbks). U of Pa Pr.
Moreno, Z. T. Love Songs to Life. 8.50 (ISBN 0-685-25823-8); pap. 6.00 (ISBN 0-685-25824-6). Beacon Hse.
Morin, David & Warnock, Jeanine. I in the Sky. 1979. 5.95 (ISBN 0-533-03696-8). Vantage.
Morris, Paul D. Love Therapy. 1975. pap. 2.95 (ISBN 0-8423-3861-6). Tyndale.
Mortimer, Geoffrey. Chapters on Human Love. 59.95 (ISBN 0-87968-836-X). Gordon Pr.
Mow, Anna B. The Secret of Married Love. (Trumpet Bks). 1976. pap. 1.50 (ISBN 0-87981-054-8). Holman.
Mueller-Lyer, Franz C. The Evolution of Modern Marriage: A Sociology of Sexual Relations. LC 72-11292. Repr. of 1930 ed. 20.50 (ISBN 0-404-57484-X). AMS Pr.
Murray, Andrew. Secret of Brotherly Love. (Secret Ser.). (Orig.). 1980. pap. 1.25 (ISBN 0-87508-390-0). Chr Lit.
Murstein, Bernard I. Love, Sex, & Marriage Through the Ages. LC 73-92201. 1974. text ed. 18.95 (ISBN 0-8261-1460-1); pap. text ed. 10.95 (ISBN 0-8261-1461-X). Springer Pub.
Murstein, Bernard I., et al. Theories of Attraction & Love. LC 77-172067. 1971. text ed. 8.95 (ISBN 0-8261-1290-0). Springer Pub.
Naevestad, Marie. The Colors of Rage & Love. 1979. 30.00x (ISBN 82-00-05173-0). Universitet.
Nanxe, Aline de. Diccionario Del Amor. 122p. (Espn.). 1969. pap. 3.50 (ISBN 84-290-1061-0, S-50136). French & Eur.
Niebuhr, Reinhold. Love & Justice: Selections from the Shorter Writings of Reinhold Niebuhr. Robertson, D. B., ed. 6.75 (ISBN 0-8446-2659-7). Peter Smith.
Ogilvie, Lloyd J. The Beauty of Love. LC 80-80465. (Orig.). 1980. pap. 4.95 (ISBN 0-89081-245-4). Harvest Hse.
Orage, Alfred R. On Love. LC 78-17779. pap. 2.50 (ISBN 0-87728-264-1). Weiser.
Partridge, Eric. Journey to the Edge of Morning. facs. ed. LC 77-84331. (Essay Index Reprint Ser). 1946. 11.25 (ISBN 0-8369-1101-6). Arno.
Pasle-Green, Jeanne & Haynes, Jim, eds. Hello, I Love You! Voices from Within the Sexual Revolution. LC 77-77389. (Orig.). 1977. pap. 4.50 (ISBN 0-87810-032-6). Times Change.
Peace, R. Learning to Love People. LC 68-12955. pap. 1.95 (ISBN 0-87784-454-2). Inter-Varsity.
Peele, Stanton & Brodsky, Archie. Love & Addiction. LC 74-5818. 1975. 9.95 (ISBN 0-8008-5041-6). Taplinger.
--Love & Addiction. 1976. pap. 2.25 (ISBN 0-451-06985-4, E6985, Sig). NAL.
Peirce, Charles S. Chance, Love & Logic. 317p. 1980. Repr. of 1923 ed. lib. bdg. 50.00 (ISBN 0-89984-386-7). Century Bookbindery.
Phillips, Debora & Judd, Robert. How to Fall Out of Love. 1980. pap. 2.50 (ISBN 0-445-04510-8). Popular Lib.
--How to Fall Out of Love. 1978. 6.95 (ISBN 0-395-27116-9). HM.
Ponder, Catherine. Prospering Power of Love. LC 66-25849. (Orig.). 1966. pap. 2.00 (ISBN 0-87159-129-4). Unity Bks.
Pope, Kenneth S., et al. On Love & Loving: Psychological Perspectives on the Nature & Experience of Romantic Love. LC 80-8012. (Social & Behavioral Science Ser.). 1980. text ed. 17.95x (ISBN 0-87589-479-8). Jossey-Bass.
Powell, John. The Secret of Staying in Love. LC 74-84712. (Illus.). 1974. pap. 3.95 (ISBN 0-913592-29-3). Argus Comm.

Querelle Des Amyes. Opuscules D'amour Par Heroet. 1970. Repr. of 1547 ed. 27.00 (ISBN 0-384-49035-2). Johnson Repr.

Rathana-Nakintara, Thaworn. Understanding Love: The Key to Growth & Fulfillment. LC 80-85428. (Illus.). 112p. (Orig.). 1981. pap. text ed. 7.95 (ISBN 0-939210-00-2). Intl Inst Psych.

Raudsepp, Eugene. Love & Loving. (Best Thoughts Ser.). (Illus.). 80p. 1981. pap. 2.50 (ISBN 0-8431-0389-2). Price Stern.

--Sex & Sexuality. (Best Thoughts Ser.). (Illus.). 80p. 1981. pap. 2.50 (ISBN 0-8431-0387-6). Price Stern.

Ray, Sondra. Loving Relationships. LC 79-55633. 1980. pap. 5.95 (ISBN 0-89087-244-9). Celestial Arts.

Reik, Theodor. Psychology of Sex Relations. LC 74-28525. 243p. 1975. Repr. of 1945 ed. lib. bdg. 21.00x (ISBN 0-8371-7916-5, RESR). Greenwood.

Rice, Mac M. & Rice, Vivian B. When Can I Say, "I Love You"? 1977. pap. 1.95 (ISBN 0-8024-9436-6). Moody.

Robb, Dale. Love & Living Together. LC 77-15242. 112p. (Orig.). 1978. pap. 3.50 (ISBN 0-8006-1326-0, 1-1326). Fortress.

Rohrlich, Jay B. Work & Love: The Crucial Balance. LC 80-14727. 254p. 1980. 10.95 (ISBN 0-671-40087-8). Summit Bks.

Rouner, Arthur A., Jr. You Can Find Love Again. (Christian Counseling Aids Ser.). 1977. pap. 0.75 ea. (ISBN 0-8010-7659-5). Baker Bk.

Rubin, Z. Liking & Loving: An Invitation to Social Psychology. LC 73-51. 1973. pap. text ed. 8.95 (ISBN 0-03-083003-6, HoltC). HR&W.

Safilios-Rothschild, Constantina. Love, Sex & Sex Roles. LC 76-44439. 1977. 9.95 (ISBN 0-13-540948-9, Spec); pap. 5.95 (ISBN 0-13-540930-6). P-H.

Sala-Molins, Louis. La Philosophie De L'amour Chez Raymond Lulle. (Illus.). 1974. pap. 32.50x (ISBN 90-2797-301-6). Mouton.

Saltus, Edgar. Gardens of Aphrodite. LC 70-182709. Repr. of 1920 ed. 17.50 (ISBN 0-404-05545-1). AMS Pr.

--Historia Amoris: A History of Love Ancient & Modern. LC 74-116001. Repr. of 1922 ed. 17.50 (ISBN 0-404-05547-8). AMS Pr.

San Pedro, Diego de. The Castle of Love. LC 51-634. Repr. of 1549 ed. 23.00x (ISBN 0-8201-1217-8). Schol Facsimiles.

Satre, Elizabeth D. The Story of Ellen: How Love Transforms a Troubled Child. LC 78-66952. 1979. pap. 2.95 (ISBN 0-8066-1691-1, 10-6045). Augsburg.

Sawyer, Alex. In a Time Meant for Love. LC 80-65678. 1980. 9.95 (ISBN 0-89754-017-4); pap. 2.95 (ISBN 0-89754-016-6). Dan River Pr.

Schier, A. Die Liebe in der Fruhromantik. Repr. of 1913 ed. pap. 15.50 (ISBN 0-384-53820-7). Johnson Repr.

Schilling, David E. For Lovers Only. 1980. 0.70 (ISBN 0-89536-425-5). CSS Pub.

Schmidt, Paul F. Rebelling, Loving & Liberation: A Metaphysics of the Concrete. LC 73-152513. 208p. 1971. 10.00 (ISBN 0-912998-00-8); pap. 4.00 (ISBN 0-912998-01-6). Hummingbird.

Seidenspinner-Nunez, Dayle. The Allegory of Love: Parodic Perspectivism in the Libro De Buon Amor. (U.C. Publications in Modern Philology: Vol. 112). 1981. pap. 12.00x (ISBN 0-520-09630-4). U of Cal Pr.

Seskin, Jane & Ziegler, Bette. Older Women-Younger Men. LC 78-69667. 1979. 7.95 (ISBN 0-385-13698-6, Anchor Pr). Doubleday.

Shain, Merle. When Lovers Are Friends. 1979. pap. 3.95 (ISBN 0-553-01203-7). Bantam.

Shedd, Charlie. The Best Dad Is a Good Lover. 1977. 5.95 (ISBN 0-8362-0660-6). Andrews & McMeel.

Shedd, Charlie & Shedd, Martha. How to Stay in Love. 160p. 1981. pap. 2.95 (ISBN 0-441-34513-1). Ace Bks.

Sheed, Charlie. How to Know If You're Really in Love. 176p. 1981. pap. 2.25 (ISBN 0-671-82841-X). PB.

Shibles, Warren. Rational Love. LC 77-93187. 1978. pap. 4.95 (ISBN 0-912386-13-4). Language Pr.

Siegel, Eli. Love & Reality. 1977. pap. 1.50 (ISBN 0-911492-22-4). Aesthetic Realism.

Simons, Joseph & Reidy, Jeanne. Risk of Loving. LC 68-54376. 1973. pap. 4.95 (ISBN 0-8164-9141-0). Continuum.

Singer, Irving. Mozart & Beethoven: The Concept of Love in Their Operas. LC 77-4551. 1977. text ed. 12.00x (ISBN 0-8018-1987-3). Johns Hopkins.

Skoglund, Elizabeth. Loving Begins with Me. LC 78-3364. 1979. 6.95 (ISBN 0-06-067393-1, HarpR). Har-Row.

Small, Dwight H. How Should I Love You? LC 78-20588. 1979. 7.95 (ISBN 0-06-067398-2, HarpR). Har-Row.

Smelser, Neil J. & Erikson, Erik H., eds. Themes of Work & Love in Adulthood. (Illus.). 307p. 1980. 15.00x (ISBN 0-674-87750-0). Harvard U Pr.

Solomon, Robert. Love: Emotion, Myth, & Metaphor. LC 81-43045. 216p. 1981. 15.95 (ISBN 0-385-14118-1, Anchor Pr). Doubleday.

Sorokin, P. A. Explorations in Altruistic Love & Behavior. Repr. of 1950 ed. 17.00 (ISBN 0-527-84806-9). Kraus Repr.

Spicer, Faith. Sex & the Love Relationship. 1972. 6.50 (ISBN 0-85078-044-6); pap. 3.75 (ISBN 0-85078-045-4). Technomic.

Steig, William. The Rejected Lovers. (Illus.). 153p. 1973. pap. 1.50 (ISBN 0-486-22956-4). Dover.

Stein, Charlotte M. The Pear Tree. Rubenstein, Nancy, ed. LC 79-54652. (Illus.). 214p. 1981. pap. 6.00 (ISBN 0-916634-03-5). Double M Pr.

Stevenson, David L. Love-Game Comedy. Repr. of 1946 ed. 14.50 (ISBN 0-404-06263-6). AMS Pr.

Strange de Jim. The Strange Experience: How to Become the World's Second Greatest Lover. LC 80-69868. (Illus.). 192p. (Orig.). 1980. perfect bdg. 6.95 (ISBN 0-9605308-1-9). Ash-Kar Pr.

Sullerot, Evelyne, compiled by. Women on Love. Lane, Helen, tr. 352p. 1981. 35.00x (ISBN 0-906908-13-2, Pub. by Norman England). State Mutual Bk.

Tennov, Dorothy. Love & Limerence. 1979. 11.95 (ISBN 0-8128-2328-1). Stein & Day.

--Love & Limerence: The Experience of Being in Love. LC 78-20117. (Illus.). 336p. 1981. pap. 7.95 (ISBN 0-8128-6134-5). Stein & Day.

Thompson, Paul J. Freedom-Love & Playing-Love & Other Special Kinds. LC 78-65331. 1977. 4.95 (ISBN 0-9601288-2-4); pap. 2.95 (ISBN 0-9601288-1-6). P J Thompson.

Thomson, Watson. Turning into Tomorrow. LC 66-18488. 1967. 3.75 (ISBN 0-8022-1718-4). Philos Lib.

Tillich, Paul. Love, Power & Justice. 1960. pap. 3.95 (ISBN 0-19-500222-9, GB). Oxford U Pr.

Toletana, Luisa S. Dialogues on the Arcana of Love & Venus. McKenzie, Donald A., tr. 174p. 1974. 10.00x (ISBN 0-87291-069-5). Coronado Pr.

Townley, John. Love Cycles. 196p. 1981. 7.95 (ISBN 0-89281-029-7, Destiny Bks.). Inner Tradit.

Trobisch, Walter. Love Is a Feeling to Be Learned. 1968. pap. 1.95 (ISBN 0-87784-314-7). Inter-Varsity.

Van de Vate, Dwight, Jr. Romantic Love: A Philosophical Inquiry. LC 81-47171. 176p. 1981. 15.75x (ISBN 0-271-00288-3). Pa St U Pr.

Vatsyayana. Kama Sutra of Vatsyayana: Classic Hindu Treatise on Love & Social Conduct. Burton, Sir Richard, tr. 1964. pap. 3.50 (ISBN 0-525-47139-1). Dutton.

Verene, D. P., ed. Sexual Love & Western Morality. pap. 6.95x (ISBN 0-06-131722-5, TB1722, Torch). Har-Row.

Von Hildebrand, Dietrich. The Role of Human Love. 1978. 0.65 (ISBN 0-8199-0719-7). Franciscan Herald.

Wallace, Frank R. Psychuous Sex. LC 75-24723. 1976. 25.00 (ISBN 0-911752-21-8); flexible bdg. 17.50 (ISBN 0-911752-20-X). I & O Pub.

Walley, Dean. A Love Story (Yours & Mine) 1979. pap. 2.50 (ISBN 0-8378-5031-2). Gibson.

--Missing You: You're Never Really Far from Me. 1979. pap. 2.50 (ISBN 0-8378-5019-3). Gibson.

Walsh, Anthony. Human Nature & Love: Biological, Intrapsychic & Social-Behavioral Perspectives. LC 80-6176. 342p. 1981. lib. bdg. 20.50 (ISBN 0-8191-1532-0); pap. text ed. 11.75 (ISBN 0-8191-1533-9). U Pr of Amer.

Wanderer, Dr. Zev & Cabot, Tracy. Letting Go: A Twelve Week Personal Action Program to Overcome a Broken Heart. LC 77-26616. 1978. 9.95 (ISBN 0-399-12136-6). Putnam.

West, Uta. If Love Is the Answer, What Is the Question? 1977. 8.95 (ISBN 0-07-069476-1, GB). McGraw.

--If Love Is the Answer, What Is the Question? 1979. pap. 1.95 (ISBN 0-671-82056-7). PB.

Willke, J. C. & Willke, Mrs. Sex & Love. 1979. pap. 2.95 (ISBN 0-910728-10-0). Hayes.

Wilson, Glenn & Nias, David. The Mystery of Love: The Hows & Whys of Sexual Attraction. LC 76-9711. (Illus.). 1976. 8.95 (ISBN 0-8129-0657-8). Times Bks.

Wilson, John. Love, Sex, Feminism. LC 79-24902. 1980. 18.95 (ISBN 0-03-056103-5). Praeger.

Words of Love. (Gifts of Gold Ser.). 1970. 3.50 (ISBN 0-442-82507-2). Peter Pauper.

Worth, Robert. Star Signs for Lovers. LC 78-57049. 1978. pap. 2.45 (ISBN 0-87754-075-6). Chelsea Hse.

LOVE–LITERARY COLLECTIONS

Bowman, Jayne, compiled by. You Are My Love: A Collection of Beautiful Writings. 1980. 3.00 (ISBN 0-8378-2026-X). Gibson.

Cawein, Madison, ed. Book of Love. facsimile ed. LC 79-116395. (Granger Index Reprint Ser). 1911. 17.00 (ISBN 0-8369-6136-6). Arno.

D'Avenant, William. Love & Honour & the Siege of Rhodes. Tupper, James W., ed. 1909. 30.00 (ISBN 0-8274-2999-1). R West.

Edgeworth, Mark. Beyond the Stars, Beyond the Heavens: A Book of Lines, Sayings & Verses of Love. LC 78-56835. 1980. 5.95 (ISBN 0-87212-103-8). Libra.

Hadfield, John, ed. A Book of Love: An Anthology of Words & Pictures. rev. ed. LC 78-56380. (Illus.). 1978. 10.00x (ISBN 0-87663-321-1). Universe.

Levin, Martin, ed. Love Stories. LC 75-8293. 600p. 1975. 12.50 (ISBN 0-8129-0516-4). Times Bks.

Schneider, Isidor, ed. The World of Love, 2 Vols. LC 64-12396. (Illus.). 1964. boxed 17.50 (ISBN 0-8076-0251-5). Braziller.

Smelyakov, Y. Work & Love. dual language ed. 229p. 1976. text ed. 2.75 (ISBN 0-8285-0639-6, Pub by Progress Pubs Russia). Imported Pubns.

Sutphen, Dick. Open Hand Love. LC 74-83815. (Illus.). 1974. pap. 3.95 (ISBN 0-911842-12-8). Valley Sun.

Teasdale, Sara, compiled by. The Answering Voice: Love Lyrics by Women. new facsimile ed. LC 76-37023. (Granger Index Reprint Ser.). Repr. of 1928 ed. 16.00 (ISBN 0-8369-6323-7). Arno.

Three Love Stories, 12 bks. 544p. 1981. pap. 2.95 ea. (100). Playmore & Prestige.

LOVE (THEOLOGY)

see also Agape; God–Love; God–Worship and Love; Identification (Religion); Self-Love (Theology)

Allen, Charles L. The Miracle of Love. LC 72-5430. 128p. 1972. 6.95 (ISBN 0-8007-0543-2). Revell.

Andrews, Stephen P., ed. Love, Marriage, & Divorce, & the Sovereignty of the Individual. LC 78-67573. (Free Love in America). Repr. of 1853 ed. 14.50 (ISBN 0-404-60962-7). AMS Pr.

Anglund, Joan W. Love One Another. (Illus.). 5.95 (ISBN 0-915696-45-2). Determined Prods.

Arnold, Eberhard. Love & Marriage in the Spirit. LC 64-24321. 1965. 7.95 (ISBN 0-87486-103-9). Plough.

Babris, Janina. The Covenant of Love. pap. 6.95 (ISBN 0-686-74587-6, 101-25). Prow Bks-Franciscan.

Benn, Douglas R. Love--God's Greatest Gift. 1981. pap. 4.00 (ISBN 0-682-49736-3). Exposition.

Bernard, Mary. How to Find Real Love & Keep It. 1981. 8.50 (ISBN 0-533-04684-X). Vantage.

Billheimer, Paul. Love Covers. 1981. pap. 3.95 (ISBN 0-87508-006-5). Chr Lit.

Boom, Corrie T. Amazing Love. 1976. pap. 1.95 (ISBN 0-89129-183-0). Jove Pubns.

Brown, Reuben R. Love Divine. 1979. 5.50 (ISBN 0-682-49299-X). Exposition.

Bucer, Martin. Instruction in Christian Love. write for info. John Knox.

Butler, Roy F. The Meaning of Agapao & Phileo in the Greek New Testament. 1977. 6.50x (ISBN 0-87291-089-X). Coronado Pr.

Butterworth, Eric. Life Is for Loving. LC 73-6326. 128p. 1974. 7.95 (ISBN 0-06-061268-1, HarpR). Har-Row.

Cardenal, Ernesto. Love. 160p. (Span.). 1981. pap. 4.95 (ISBN 0-8245-0043-1). Crossroad NY.

Chesser, Eustace. Love Without Fear. 192p. 1973. pap. 2.50 (ISBN 0-451-11057-9, AE1057, Sig). NAL.

Coleman, Bill & Coleman, Patty. Only Love Can Make It Easy, 2 vols. rev. ed. 1981. Complete Kit. pap. 39.95 (ISBN 0-686-75465-4); Couples' Wkbk. pap. 2.95 (ISBN 0-89622-131-8); Leader's Guide. pap. 8.50 (ISBN 0-89622-132-6). Twenty-Third.

Cowburn, John. Person & Love. 1967. 7.95 (ISBN 0-8189-0110-1). Alba.

De Coppens, Peter R. Spiritual Perspective II: The Spiritual Dimension & Implications of Love, Sex, & Marriage. LC 80-6302. 175p. (Orig.). 1981. pap. text ed. 7.50 (ISBN 0-8191-1512-6). U Pr of Amer.

Del Mastro, M. L., tr. Revelations of Divine Love: Juliana of Norwich. LC 76-52004. 1977. pap. 2.95 (ISBN 0-385-12297-7, Im). Doubleday.

Denninger, Richard. Anatomy of the Pure & of the Impure Love. (Intimate Life of Man Library Bk.). (Illus.). 1979. 31.75 (ISBN 0-89266-177-1); spiral bdg. 14.75 (ISBN 0-685-67718-4). Am Classical Coll Pr.

De Vinck, Jose. The Yes Book. 1976. pap. 3.75 (ISBN 0-685-77499-6). Franciscan Herald.

--The Yes Book: An Answer to Life (a Manual for Chritian Existentialism) LC 77-190621. (Illus.). 200p. 1972. 8.75 (ISBN 0-911726-12-8); pap. 6.75 (ISBN 0-911726-11-X). Alleluia Pr.

Dodson, Rita. Life, Love & God. Date not set. 4.95 (ISBN 0-533-04647-5). Vantage.

Dorita, la Nina Que Nadie Amaba. 1980. pap. 1.90 (ISBN 0-8297-1042-6). Life Pubs Intl.

Drummond, Henry. The Greatest Thing in the World. 64p. 1981. pap. 2.25 (ISBN 0-88368-100-5). Whitaker Hse.

--Greatest Thing in the World. 1959. 2.50 (ISBN 0-448-01642-7). G&D.

--Greatest Thing in the World. (Inspirational Classic Ser). 1968. 4.95 (ISBN 0-8007-1144-0); pap. 1.95 (ISBN 0-8007-8018-3, Spire Bks). Revell.

--Greatest Thing in the World. red leatheroid 1.95 (ISBN 0-00-410382-3, D2); 2.95 (ISBN 0-529-05676-3, F4). Collins Pubs.

Eberhard. Is It Love? LC 77-7527. 6.95 (ISBN 0-87747-632-2). Deseret Bk.

Elder, E. Rozanne, ed. The Way of Love. (Cistercian Fathers Ser.: No. 16). (Illus.). 1977. 7.95 (ISBN 0-87907-616-X); pap. 4.50 (ISBN 0-87907-966-5). Cistercian Pubns.

Evans, Colleen T. Love Is an Everyday Thing. 1977. pap. 1.50 (ISBN 0-8007-8271-2, Spire). Revell.

Finney, Charles G. Love Is Not a Special Way of Feeling. Orig. Title: Attributes of Love. 1963. pap. 2.50 (ISBN 0-87123-005-4, 200005). Bethany Hse.

Geisler, Norman L. The Christian Ethic of Love. 160p. 1973. 3.95 (ISBN 0-310-24921-X). Zondervan.

Getz, Gene A. Measure of a Church. LC 75-17160. (Orig.). 1975. pap. 2.25 (ISBN 0-8307-0398-5, 50-147-00). Regal.

Gillquist, Peter E. Love Is Now. new ed. 1970. 3.95 (ISBN 0-310-36941-X); study guide 0.75 (ISBN 0-310-25013-7). Zondervan.

Gocek, Matilda A. Love Is a Challenge. LC 78-12327. (Keepers of the Light Ser.). (Illus.). 72p. 1978. pap. 3.95 (ISBN 0-912526-22-X). Lib Res.

Goergen, Don. The Power of Love. 1979. 13.95 (ISBN 0-88347-108-6). Thomas More.

Goldsmith, Joel S. The Gift of Love. Sinkler, Lorraine, ed. LC 75-9330. 96p. (Gift format). 1975. 4.95 (ISBN 0-06-063172-4, HarpR). Har-Row.

Griffin, Robert. I Never Said I Didn't Love You. LC 76-24442. (Emmuas Book Ser.). 1977. pap. 1.95 (ISBN 0-8091-1989-7). Paulist Pr.

Heide, Florence P. & Heide, Roxanne. I Love Everypeople. (Concept Ser. II). (Illus.). (gr. 1-4). 1978. pap. 2.95 (ISBN 0-570-07785-0, 56-1308). Concordia.

Hong, Edna. El Luminoso Valle Del Amor. (Span.). Date not set. 2.00 (ISBN 0-686-76304-1). Life Pubs Intl.

Howe, Reuel L. Herein Is Love. pap. 3.95 (ISBN 0-8170-0263-4). Judson.

Johann, Robert. Meaning of Love. LC 66-22053. 162p. 1966. pap. 1.95 (ISBN 0-8091-1633-2). Paulist Pr.

Joyce, Mary R. Love Responds to Life: The Challenge of Humanae Vitae. pap. 3.25 (ISBN 0-686-74592-2, 101-8). Prow Bks-Franciscan.

Kelsey, Morton T. Caring: How Can We Love One Another? LC 80-84659. 208p. (Orig.). 1981. pap. 6.95 (ISBN 0-8091-2366-5). Paulist Pr.

Keyes, Frances P. Three Ways of Love. 1975. 6.00 (ISBN 0-8198-0477-0); pap. 5.00 (ISBN 0-8198-0478-9). Dghtrs St Paul.

King, Martin L. Strength to Love. (Fount Religious Paperback Ser.). 1977. pap. 2.95 (ISBN 0-529-05391-8, FT5391). Collins Pubs.

Lauder, Robert E. The Love Explosion: Human Experience & the Christian Mystery. (Orig.). 1979. pap. 2.50 (ISBN 0-914544-22-5). Living Flame Pr.

Leenhouts, Keith J. Une Course d'Amour. Date not set. 1.75 (ISBN 0-686-76392-0). Life Pubs Intl.

--Um Pai...Filho..Corrida De Amor. Date not set. 1.50 (ISBN 0-686-76445-5). Life Pubs Intl.

Lewis, Clive S. Four Loves. LC 60-10920. 1960. 9.95 (ISBN 0-15-132915-X). HarBraceJ.

Lewis, Samuel L. Talks of an American Sufi: Love, Sex & Relationships - the Path of Initiation. Klotz, Saadi, ed. (Bismillah Bks.: No. 2). 112p. (Orig.). 1981. pap. 4.50 (ISBN 0-915424-06-1, Prophecy Pressworks). Sufi Islamia Prophecy.

Lin, Jan. Living Out God's Love. 128p. 1981. pap. 4.95 (ISBN 0-8170-0897-7). Judson.

Lussier, Ernest. God Is Love: According to St. John. LC 76-57254. 1977. 5.95 (ISBN 0-8189-0339-2). Alba.

Mains, Karen B. Llave De un Corazon Amoroso. (Span.). Date not set. 2.00 (ISBN 0-686-76301-7). Life Pubs Intl.

Mann, Stella T. Change Your Life Through Love. 1971. pap. 4.95 (ISBN 0-87516-052-2). De Vorss.

Mason, Clarence. Love Song. 1977. pap. 2.25 (ISBN 0-8024-5025-3). Moody.

Mayers, Marvin K. & Koechel, David. Love Goes on Forever. 1977. pap. 4.95 (ISBN 0-310-28951-3). Zondervan.

Merchant, Jane. The Greatest of These. (Orig.). pap. 1.25 (ISBN 0-89129-175-X). Jove Pubns.

Moffatt, James. Love in the New Testament. 1978. Repr. of 1930 ed. lib. bdg. 40.00 (ISBN 0-8414-6245-3). Folcroft.

Moncure, Jane B. Love. rev. ed. LC 80-27479. (What Is It? Ser.). (Illus.). 32p. (gr. k-3). 1981. PLB 5.50 (ISBN 0-89565-205-6). Childs World.

Morris, Leon. Testaments of Love: A Study of Love in the Bible. (Orig.). 1981. 12.95 (ISBN 0-8028-3502-3). Eerdmans.

Moss, Jean D. Godded with God: Hendrik Niclaes & His Family of Love. LC 81-68192. (Transactions Ser.: Vol. 71, Pt. 8). 1981. 8.00 (ISBN 0-87169-718-1). Am Philos.

Mouton, Boyce. These Two Commandments. (Orig.). 1978. pap. 2.95 (ISBN 0-89900-138-6). College Pr Pub.

Murray, Andrew. Secret of Brotherly Love. (Secret Ser.). (Orig.). 1980. pap. 1.25 (ISBN 0-87508-390-0). Chr Lit.

Narada. Narada Bhakti Sutras: The Gospel of Divine Love. Tyagisananda, Swami, tr. (Sanskrit & Eng). pap. 3.95 (ISBN 0-87481-427-8). Vedanta Pr.

--Narada's Way of Divine Love: The Bhakti Sutras. 1st ed. Prabhavananda, Swami, tr. from Sansk. LC 75-161488. 1971. 7.95 (ISBN 0-87481-027-2). Vedanta Pr.

Newlands, George. Theology of the Love of God. LC 80-22547. 224p. 1981. 12.50 (ISBN 0-8042-0726-7); pap. 6.95 (ISBN 0-8042-0727-5). John Knox.

Nighswander, Ada. The Little Martins Learn to Love. 1981. 5.00 (ISBN 0-686-30775-5). Rod & Staff.

Ogilvie, Lloyd J. Loved & Forgiven. LC 76-29889. 1977. pap. 2.50 (ISBN 0-8307-0442-6, S313-1-03). Regal.

Orgill, Michael. Anchored in Love. 1976. pap. 1.50 (ISBN 0-89129-152-0). Jove Pubns.

Palmer, Earl F. Love Has Its Reasons. LC 76-19539. 1977. 5.95 (ISBN 0-87680-481-4, 80481). Word Bks.

Peace, R. Learning to Love Packet. pap. 5.50 (ISBN 0-87784-730-4). Inter Varsity.

Perkins, Dorothy. Separation & Suffering: Hindu & Christian Views of Love. (Orig.). 1980. pap. 4.00 (ISBN 0-9604742-0-X). D J Perkins.

Rouner, Arthur A., Jr. How to Love. (Contemporary Discussion Ser.). 1974. pap. 1.25 (ISBN 0-8010-7622-6). Baker Bk.

Ruiz, Juan. Libro De Buen Amor: Texte De Quatorzieme Siecle Publie Pour la Premiere Fois Avec les Lecons Des Trois Manuscrits Connus, Parjean Dueamin. Repr. of 1901 ed. 29.00 (ISBN 0-384-52550-4). Johnson Repr.

Saxton, Andrew. The Universal Symbolism of Love in Dramatic Representative Forms. (Illus.). 1978. deluxe ed. 37.75 (ISBN 0-930582-06-3). Gloucester Art.

Schmitt, Abraham. The Art of Listening with Love. LC 77-83296. 1977. pap. 5.95 (ISBN 0-8499-2883-4). Word Bks.

Scroggie, W. Graham. Love Life: I Cor. 13. LC 79-2551. (W. Graham Scroggie Library). 1980. pap. 2.50 (ISBN 0-8254-3733-4). Kregel.

Shastrim, Hari P. The Philosophy of Love, the Narada Sutras. 59.95 (ISBN 0-8490-0828-X). Gordon Pr.

Sheen, Fulton J. Power of Love. 1968. pap. 1.95 (ISBN 0-385-01090-7, D235, Im). Doubleday.

Siegel, Lee. Sacred & Profane Dimensions of Love in Indian Traditions As Exemplified in the Gitagovind of Jayadeva. 1978. text ed. 21.00x (ISBN 0-19-560807-0). Oxford U Pr.

Simpson, A. B. Walking in Love. 1975. Repr. 2.50 (ISBN 0-87509-040-0). Chr Pubns.

Small, Dwight H. How Should I Love You? LC 78-20588. 1979. 7.95 (ISBN 0-06-067398-2, HarpR). Har-Row.

Smith, Bob. Love Story... the Real Thing. LC 75-17111. (Discovery Bks.). 1975. pap. 2.95 (ISBN 0-87680-989-1, 98042). Word Bks.

Smith, Nelson M. What Is This Thing Called Love. 1970. 6.65 (ISBN 0-89137-505-8); pap. 3.10 (ISBN 0-89137-504-X). Quality Pubns.

Stafford, A. Tim. A Love Story. 1977. pap. 3.95 (ISBN 0-310-32938-8). Zondervan.

Steele. Love Enthroned. kivar 4.95 (ISBN 0-686-12891-5). Schmul Pub Co.

Swedenborg, Emanuel. Marital Love. LC 38-13542. 760p. 1974. trade ed. 8.25 (ISBN 0-87785-161-1); student ed. 6.50 (ISBN 0-87785-150-6). Swedenborg.

Sweeting, George. Love Is the Greatest. 144p. 1976. pap. 1.50 (ISBN 0-8024-5024-5). Moody.

Teves, Helen & Howard, Jenny. The I of Love. (Infinity Ser.: No. 14). 1972. text ed. 2.50 (ISBN 0-03-004131-7, 253); tchr's. guide by Joan Mitchell 1.15 (ISBN 0-03-004136-8, 254). Winston Pr.

Thomas Aquinas, Saint Saint Thomas Aquinas: On Charity. Kendzierski, Lotti H., tr. (Medieval Philosophical Texts in Translation: No. 10). 1960. pap. 5.95 (ISBN 0-87462-210-7). Marquette.

Thompson, Hugo W. Love-Justice. 1970. 6.95 (ISBN 0-8158-0032-0); pap. 3.95 (ISBN 0-8158-0242-0). Chris Mass.

Thurman, Howard. Mysticism & the Experience of Love. LC 61-13708. (Orig.). 1961. pap. 1.10x (ISBN 0-87574-115-0). Pendle Hill.

Tormey, John C. Tell Me Again You Love Me. LC 75-44675. (Illus.). 128p. 1976. pap. 1.65 (ISBN 0-8189-1128-X, Pub. by Alba Bks). Alba.

Toyotome, M. Three Kinds of Love. pap. 0.50 (ISBN 0-87784-132-2). Inter-Varsity.

Tully, Mary Jo & Hirstein, Sandra J. Focus on Loving. (Light of Faith Ser.). (Orig.). (gr. 1). 1981. pap. text ed. write for info. (ISBN 0-697-01763-X); tchrs.' ed. avail. (ISBN 0-697-01764-8). Wm C Brown.

Vanstone, W. H. The Risk of Love. 1978. 8.95 (ISBN 0-19-520053-5). Oxford U Pr.

Vent-Qui-Pleure. Mon Coeur Te Cherche. Date not set. 2.25 (ISBN 0-686-76406-4). Life Pubs Intl.

Von Hildebrand, Alice. Love & Selfishness. 54p. 1970. pap. 0.65 (ISBN 0-8199-0376-0). Franciscan Herald.

Von Hildebrand, D. Man & Woman. 4.50 (ISBN 0-8199-0068-0, L38412). Franciscan Herald.

Walker, Alan. Love in Action. (Fount Religious Paperback Ser.). 1977. pap. 2.50 (ISBN 0-00-625001-7, FA5001). Collins Pubs.

William Of St. Tierry. The Nature & Dignity of Love. Elder, E. R., ed. Davis, Thomas X., tr. from Lat. (Cistercian Fathers Ser.: No. 30). Orig. Title: De natura et dignitate amoris. 1981. 13.95 (ISBN 0-87907-330-6). Cistercian Pubns.

Williams, Daniel D. The Spirit & the Forms of Love. LC 81-40368. 316p. 1981. lib. bdg. 20.50 (ISBN 0-8191-1691-2); pap. text ed. 11.75 (ISBN 0-8191-1692-0). U Pr of Amer.

Wynkoop, Mildred B. The Theology of Love. 1972. 8.95 (ISBN 0-8341-0102-5, Beacon). Nazarene.

LOVE (THEOLOGY)–MEDITATIONS

Chapman, Ian M. Do a Loving Thing. LC 76-48750. 1977. pap. 2.75 (ISBN 0-8170-0717-2). Judson.

Elliot, Elisabeth. Love Has a Price Tag. LC 79-50944. 148p. 1981. pap. 4.95 (ISBN 0-915684-87-X). Christian Herald.

Lockyer, Herbert. Seven Words of Love. LC 74-28719. 1975. 5.95 (ISBN 0-87680-369-9). Word Bks.

Walley, Dean. So Many Kinds of Love. (Illus.). 1977. boxed 4.95 (ISBN 0-8378-1741-2). Gibson.

LOVE, COURTLY

see Courtly Love

LOVE, COURTS OF

see Courts of Love

LOVE, MATERNAL

see also Maternal Deprivation

Friday, Nancy. My Mother, My Self: The Daughter's Search for Identity. 1977. 9.95 (ISBN 0-440-06006-0). Delacorte.

Heffner, Elaine. Mothering: The Emotional Experience of Motherhood After Freud & Feminism. LC 77-82946. 1978. 7.95 (ISBN 0-385-12837-1). Doubleday.

Schwing, Gertrud. Way to the Soul of the Mentally Ill. Ekstein, Rudolf & Hall, Bernard H., trs. LC 54-7541. (Monograph Ser. on Schizophrenia: No. 4). (Illus.). 1954. text ed. 13.50 (ISBN 0-8236-6800-2). Intl Univs Pr.

LOVE, PERFECT

see Perfection

LOVE FEASTS

see also Agape

LOVE IN ART

Hartt, Frederick. Love in Baroque Art. LC 62-19124. (Illus.). 5.00 (ISBN 0-685-71752-6). J J Augustin.

Owen, D. D. R. Noble Lovers. LC 75-4303. (Illus.). 208p. 1975. cusa 17.50x (ISBN 0-8147-7365-6). NYU Pr.

Saxton, Andrew. The Universal Symbolism of Love in Dramatic Representative Forms. (Illus.). 1978. deluxe ed. 37.75 (ISBN 0-930582-06-3). Gloucester Art.

Stewart, Alison. Unequal Lovers. LC 77-86221. (Illus.). 1978. 49.50 (ISBN 0-913870-44-7). Abaris Bks.

LOVE IN LITERATURE

see also Erotic Literature; Sex in Literature

Allsup, James O. The Magic Circle: A Study of Shelley's Concept of Love. (Literary Criticism Ser.). 1976. 9.95 (ISBN 0-8046-9117-7, Natl U). Kennikat.

Barthes, Roland. A Lover's Discourse: Fragments. Howard, Richard, tr. from Fr. 224p. 1979. 10.00 (ISBN 0-8090-6689-0); pap. 5.95 (ISBN 0-8090-1388-6). Hill & Wang.

Brodwin, Leonora Leet. Elizabethan Love Tragedy: 1587-1625. LC 71-124519. 1971. 15.00x (ISBN 0-8147-0955-9). NYU Pr.

Dodd, William G. Courtly Love in Chaucer & Gower. 59.95 (ISBN 0-87968-956-0). Gordon Pr.

Fowlie, Wallace. Love in Literature: Studies in Symbolic Expression. facsimile ed. LC 70-37836. (Essay Index Reprint Ser). Repr. of 1965 ed. 16.00 (ISBN 0-8369-2589-0). Arno.

Furber, Donald & Callahan, Anne. Erotic Love in Literature from Medeival Legend to Romantic Illusion. 216p. 1981. 16.00x (ISBN 0-87875-219-6). Whitston Pub.

Gould, James A. & Iorio, John J. Love, Sex & Identity. LC 78-176093. 184p. 1972. pap. 5.95x (ISBN 0-87835-033-0). Boyd & Fraser.

Hagstrum, Jean H. Sex & Sensibility: Ideal & Erotic Love from Milton to Mozart. LC 79-20657. (Illus.). 1980. text ed. 30.00 (ISBN 0-226-31289-5). U of Chicago Pr.

Herford, Charles H. Normality of Shakespeare: Illustrated in His Treatment of Love & Marriage. 1920. lib. bdg. 5.00 (ISBN 0-8414-5048-X). Folcroft.

Holbrook, David. Quest for Love. LC 65-24879. 376p. 1965. 21.95x (ISBN 0-8173-7305-5). U of Ala Pr.

Lerner, Laurence. Love & Marriage: Literature & Its Social Context. 1979. 25.00x (ISBN 0-312-49938-8). St Martin.

Meader, William G. Courtship in Shakespeare. LC 78-120649. viii, 266p. 1970. Repr. of 1954 ed. lib. bdg. 15.00x (ISBN 0-374-95553-0). Octagon.

Phialas, Peter G. Shakespeare's Romantic Comedies: The Development of Their Form & Meaning. 1966. pap. 5.50x (ISBN 0-8078-4043-2, CHB43). U of NC Pr.

Riordan, Sr. Francis E. Concept of Love in the French Catholic Literary Revival. LC 76-94183. (Catholic University of America Studies in Romance Languages & Literature Ser: No. 42). Repr. of 1952 ed. 19.00 (ISBN 0-404-50342-X). AMS Pr.

Rose, Mark. Heroic Love: Studies in Sidney & Spenser. LC 68-29182. 1968. 8.95x (ISBN 0-674-39000-8). Harvard U Pr.

Scaglione, Aldo D. Nature & Love in the Middle Ages. LC 76-2688. (Illus.). 250p. 1976. Repr. of 1963 ed. lib. bdg. 20.75x (ISBN 0-8371-8768-0, SCNL). Greenwood.

Sherfan, Andrew D. Kahlil Gibran: Nature of Love. LC 70-136015. 1971. 4.75 (ISBN 0-685-77557-7). Philos Lib.

Smith, John H. The Gay Couple in Restoration Comedy. LC 74-159229. xii, 205p. 1971. Repr. of 1948 ed. lib. bdg. 13.50x (ISBN 0-374-97508-6). Octagon.

Stilling, Roger. Love & Death in Renaissance Tragedy. LC 74-27193. 1977. 20.00x (ISBN 0-8071-0188-5). La State U Pr.

Thurin, Erik I. Emerson As Priest of Pan: A Study in the Metaphysics of Sex. LC 81-4818. 208p. 1981. 20.00 (ISBN 0-7006-0216-X). Regents Pr Ks.

LOVE LETTERS

see also Courtship

Bowen, Marjorie, ed. Some Famous Love Letters. LC 78-14213. 1978. Repr. of 1937 ed. lib. bdg. 30.00 (ISBN 0-8414-1659-1). Folcroft.

Frazer Clark, C. E., Jr., frwd. by. Love Letters of Nathaniel Hawthorne. 17.00 (ISBN 0-685-77418-X). Bruccoli.

Krueger, Catherine M. Letters to Art. 1978. 5.95 (ISBN 0-533-03183-4). Vantage.

Kueck, Edwardine D. The Old Love Letters. 1979. 5.95 (ISBN 0-533-04112-0). Vantage.

Love Poems & Love Letters. 2.95 (ISBN 0-442-82332-0). Peter Pauper.

Megroz, R. L. Letters of Women in Love. (Women Ser.). 1929. 20.00 (ISBN 0-685-43732-9). Norwood Edns.

Merydew, J. T. Love Letters of Famous Men & Women of the Past & Present Century. Repr. of 1888 ed. 125.00 (ISBN 0-686-20657-6). Lib Serv Inc.

Tyard, Pontus De. Modeles de Phrases suivis d'un recueil de modeles de lettres d'amour. Lapp, John C., ed. (Studies in the Romance Languages & Literatures: No. 70). 1967. pap. 7.00x (ISBN 0-8078-9070-7). U of NC Pr.

Wyatt, E. A. The Love Letters of a Genius: (Being a Translation of Prosper Merimees "Lettres a une Inconnue." F. E. B. Doff, Intro. 1905. Repr. 45.00 (ISBN 0-8274-3000-0). R West.

LOVE OF SELF (THEOLOGY)

see Self-Love (Theology)

LOVE POETRY

see also Epithalamia; Minnesingers; Valentines

Betjeman, John & Taylor, Geoffrey, eds. English Love Poems. 220p. 1964. pap. 6.95 (ISBN 0-571-07065-5, Pub. by Faber & Faber). Merrimack Bk Serv.

Bullen, A. H. Speculum Amantis: Love Poems. Repr. of 1902 ed. lib. bdg. 15.00 (ISBN 0-8414-2518-3). Folcroft.

Bullen, Arthur H. Speculum Amantis: Love Poems. 1902. 25.00 (ISBN 0-89984-035-3). Century Bookbindery.

Caine, Ralph H. Love Songs of English Poets 1500-1800. 1892. lib. bdg. 10.00 (ISBN 0-8414-1550-1). Folcroft.

Chadwick, John W. & Chadwick, Annie H., eds. Out of the Heart. facsimile ed. LC 70-86795. (Granger Index Reprint Ser). 1891. 12.50 (ISBN 0-8369-6072-6). Arno.

Chang Ya-Hsiung. Love-Songs of Northwest China. (National Peking University & Chinese Assn. for Folklore, Folklore & Folkliterature Ser.: No. 94). (Chinese.). 8.00 (ISBN 0-89986-174-1). E Langstaff.

Chao Tzu-Yung. Yueh Eo, Early Cantonese Lovesongs. (National Peking University & Chinese Assn. for Folklore, Folklore & Folkliterature Ser.: No. 56). (Chinese.). 6.00 (ISBN 0-89986-147-4). E Langstaff.

Chung Ching-Wen. Tribal Love-Songs from Canton. (Folklore Series of National Sun Yat-Sen University: No. 16). (Chinese.). 5.50 (ISBN 0-89986-085-0). E Langstaff.

Edgeworth, Mark. Beyond the Stars, Beyond the Heavens: A Book of Lines, Sayings & Verses of Love. LC 78-56835. 1980. 5.95 (ISBN 0-87212-103-8). Libra.

Feng Meng-Lung. Love-Songs, Thirteen Sixty-Eight to Sixteen Forty-Six A.D. (National Peking University & Chinese Assn. for Folklore, Folklore & Folkliterature Ser.: No. 2). (Chinese.). 6.00 (ISBN 0-89986-102-4). E Langstaff.

Grigson, Geoffrey, ed. The Gambit Book of Love Poems. LC 74-84418. 407p. 1975. 9.95 (ISBN 0-87645-088-5). Gambit.

Gross, David C., ed. Love Poems from the Hebrew. 1976. 5.95 (ISBN 0-385-11136-3). Doubleday.

Husted, Helen, ed. Love Poems of Six Centuries. LC 70-86798. (Granger Index Reprint Ser). 1950. 21.00 (ISBN 0-8369-6105-6). Arno.

Japanese Love Poems, Vol. 10. (East Asian Poetry in Translation Ser.). 1977. pap. 4.00 (ISBN 0-89986-323-X). E Langstaff.

Knappert, Jan, ed. & tr. An Anthology of Swahili Love Poetry. 200p. (Orig.). 1972. pap. 3.50 (ISBN 0-520-02177-0, CAL245). U of Cal Pr.

Levy, Howard S., tr. Japanese Love Poems, No. 8. (East Asian Poetry in Translation Series). 1976. pap. 4.00 (ISBN 0-89986-304-3). E Langstaff.

--Japanese Love Poems, Vol. 9. (East Asian Poetry in Translation Ser.). 1977. pap. 4.00 (ISBN 0-89986-322-1). E Langstaff.

Li Chin-Fa. Love-Songs from Hakka in Mei-Hsien. (National Peking University & Chinese Assn. for Folklore, Folklore & Folkliterature Ser.: No. 4). (Chinese.). 6.00 (ISBN 0-89986-104-0). E Langstaff.

Li Lin-Ts'an. Love-Songs from the Kin Sha River. (National Peking University & Chinese Assn. for Folklore, Folklore & Folkliteratureser.: No. 35). (Chinese.). 6.00 (ISBN 0-89986-130-X). E Langstaff.

Li Po-Ying. Love Songs from the South of the Yang-Tzu River. (National Peking University & Chinese Assn. for Folklore, Folklore & Folkliterature Ser.: No. 53). (Chinese.). 6.00 (ISBN 0-89986-144-X). E Langstaff.

Lister, Raymond. Little Treasury of Love Lyrics. (Little Treasury Ser.). 1963. 2.50 (ISBN 0-685-09180-5). Dufour.

Lord, William S., compiled by. This Is for You. facs. ed. LC 78-121926. (Granger Index Reprint Ser). 1902. 15.00 (ISBN 0-8369-6167-6). Arno.

Love Poems & Love Letters. 2.95 (ISBN 0-442-82332-0). Peter Pauper.

Lucy, Sean, ed. Love Poems of the Irish. 182p. 1967. pap. 5.95 (ISBN 0-85342-103-X). Irish Bk Ctr.

Mabie, Hamilton W. A Book of Old English Love Songs. 1977. Repr. 10.00 (ISBN 0-89984-054-X). Century Bookbindery.

Mabie, Hamilton W., compiled by. Book of Old English Love Songs. facs. ed. LC 73-121930. (Granger Index Reprint Ser). 1897. 15.00 (ISBN 0-8369-6171-4). Arno.

Merwin, W. S. & Masson, J. Moussaiff, eds. Classical Sanskrit Love Poetry. LC 77-13407. 204p. 1977. 17.50x (ISBN 0-231-04282-5). Columbia U Pr.

Niu Lang. Love-Songs of the Hakka in Kwangtung. (National Peking University & Chinese Assn. for Folklore, Folklore & Folkliterature Ser.: No. 133). (Chinese.). 6.00 (ISBN 0-89986-207-1). E Langstaff.

Riley, Elizabeth, compiled by. Love Poems. facsimile ed. LC 68-58827. (Granger Index Reprint Ser). 1945. 12.00 (ISBN 0-8369-6040-8). Arno.

Sia Hoon-Seng. Love-Songs of Formosa. (Folklore Series of National Sun Yat-Sen University: No. 4). (Chinese.). 5.50 (ISBN 0-89986-074-5). E Langstaff.

Sidgwick, Frank, ed. Ballads & Lyrics of Love. LC 77-23536. 1977. Repr. of 1908 ed. lib. bdg. 25.00 (ISBN 0-89341-161-2). Longwood Pr.

Stallworthy, Jon, ed. A Book of Love Poetry. 385p. 1974. 17.95 (ISBN 0-19-519774-7). Oxford U Pr.

--The Penguin Book of Love Poetry. (Poets Ser.). 1976. pap. 3.95 (ISBN 0-14-042148-3). Penguin.
Teasdale, Sara, compiled by. The Answering Voice: Love Lyrics by Women. new facsimile ed. LC 76-37023. (Granger Index Reprint Ser.). Repr. of 1928 ed. 16.00 (ISBN 0-8369-6323-7). Arno.
Vance, Bruce. In & Out of Love. 1971. pap. 2.95 (ISBN 0-442-28911-1). Van Nos Reinhold.
Wharton, Edith & Norton, Robertcompiled by. Eternal Passion in English Poetry. facs. ed. LC 77-76950. (Granger Index Reprint Ser). 1939. 15.00 (ISBN 0-8369-6047-5). Arno.
Yaroslava, ed. I Like You & Other Poems for Valentine's Day. (Illus.). 33p. (gr. 3 up). 1976. reinforced bdg. 6.95 (ISBN 0-684-14746-7, ScribJ). Scribner.
Young, Augustus, tr. Danta Gradha: Love Poems from the Irish 13th-17th Centuries. 1975. sewn in wrappers 2.00 (ISBN 0-685-78976-4, Pub. by Menard Pr). SBD.

LOVE POETRY–HISTORY AND CRITICISM

Ball, Patricia M. The Heart's Events: The Victorian Poetry of Relationships. 240p. 1976. text ed. 21.50x (ISBN 0-485-11163-2, Athlone Pr). Humanities.
Chadwick, John W. & Chadwick, Annie H., eds. Lovers' Treasury of Verse. facs. ed. LC 70-139758. (Granger Index Reprint Ser). 1891. 16.00 (ISBN 0-8369-6212-5). Arno.
Donaldson-Evans, Lancelot K. Love's Fatal Glance: A Study of Eye Imagery in the Poets of the Ecole lyonnaise. LC 80-10415. (Romance Monographs: No. 39). 155p. 1980. 16.00 (ISBN 84-499-3694-2). Romance.
Dronke, Peter. Medieval Latin & the Rise of the European Love Lyric, 2 Vols. 2nd ed. (Latin). 1969. Set. 59.00x (ISBN 0-19-814346-X). Oxford U Pr.
Ferry, Anne. All in War with Time: Love Poetry in Shakespeare, Donne, Jonson, Marvell. LC 74-31995. 304p. 1975. text ed. 15.00x (ISBN 0-674-01630-0). Harvard U Pr.
Kelly, Douglas. Medieval Imagination: Rhetoric & the Poetry of Courtly Love. LC 78-3522. 346p. 1978. 32.50 (ISBN 0-299-07610-5). U of Wis Pr.
Minta, Stephen. Love Poetry in 16th Century France: A Study in Themes & Traditions. LC 77-16716. 1977. text ed. 21.25x (ISBN 0-391-00828-5). Humanities.
Pearson, Lu E. Elizabethan Love Conventions. LC 75-29044. 1976. 35.00 (ISBN 0-8414-6733-1). Folcroft.
Saiz, Prospero. Personae & Poiesis: The Poet & the Poem in Medieval Love Lyric. (De Proprietatibus Litterarum, Series Minor: No. 17). (Illus.). 1976. pap. text ed. 26.25x (ISBN 90-2793-494-0). Mouton.
Valency, Maurice. In Praise of Love: An Introduction to the Love-Poetry of the Renaissance. xi, 319p. 1976. Repr. of 1958 ed. lib. bdg. 18.50x (ISBN 0-374-98067-5). Octagon.

LOVECRAFT, HOWARD PHILLIPS, 1890-1937

Armand, Barton L. The Roots of Horror in the Fiction of H.P. Lovecraft. (Illus.). 1977. 12.50 (ISBN 0-686-23038-8). Dragon Pr.
Cook, W. Paul. Lovecraft: In Memoriam. 1977. pap. 4.95 (ISBN 0-686-19171-4). Necronomicon.
Derleth, August W. Some Notes on H. P. Lovecraft. 50p. 1980. Repr. of 1959 ed. lib. bdg. 10.00 (ISBN 0-8495-1059-7). Arden Lib.
Faig, Kenneth W., Jr. The Notes & Commonplace Book: His Life, His Work. 2.95 (ISBN 0-686-31244-9). Necronomicon.
Gatto, John T. The Major Works of H. P. Lovecraft. (Monarch Notes). (Orig.). 1977. pap. 1.50 (ISBN 0-671-00982-6). Monarch Pr.
Joshi, S. T. H. P. Lovecraft & Lovecraft Criticism: An Annotated Bibliography. LC 80-84662. (Serif Ser.: No. 38). 1981. 27.50x (ISBN 0-87338-248-X). Kent St U Pr.
Joshi, S. T., ed. H. P. Lovecraft: Four Decades of Criticism. LC 80-11535. xvi, 247p. 1980. 15.00 (ISBN 0-8214-0442-3, 0442E). Ohio U Pr.
Long, Frank B. Howard Phillips Lovecraft: Dreamer on the Nightside. LC 74-18652. 1975. 8.50 (ISBN 0-87054-068-8). Arkham.
Lovecraft, H. P. H. P. Lovecraft in "the Eyrie" (Weird Tales) 4.95 (ISBN 0-686-31243-0). Necronomicon.
Palmer, Doug, ed. Journal of the H. P. Lovecraft Society. pap. 2.00 (ISBN 0-937330-04-3, Pub. by Worthy Labor Pr). SBD.
Schweitzer, Darrell. The Dream Quest of H. P. Lovecraft. LC 78-891. (The Milford Ser: Popular Writers of Today: Vol. 12). 1978. lib. bdg. 8.95x (ISBN 0-89370-117-3); pap. 2.95 (ISBN 0-89370-217-X). Borgo Pr.
--Essays Lovecraftian. LC 80-19213. 120p. 1980. Repr. lib. bdg. 9.95x (ISBN 0-89370-096-7). Borgo Pr.
Shreffler, Philip A. The H. P. Lovecraft Companion. LC 76-52605. (Illus.). 1977. lib. bdg. 15.00 (ISBN 0-8371-9482-2, SHP/). Greenwood.

LOVEJOY, ELIJAH PARISH, 1802-1837

Beecher, E. Narrative of Riots at Alton. LC 70-115858. (Studies in Black History & Culture, No. 54). 1970. Repr. of 1838 ed. lib. bdg. 44.95 (ISBN 0-8383-1072-9). Haskell.
Dillon, Merton L. Elijah P. Lovejoy, Abolitionist Editor. LC 80-11000. ix, 190p. 1980. Repr. of 1961 ed. lib. bdg. 18.75x (ISBN 0-313-22352-1, DIEJ). Greenwood.
Lovejoy, Joseph C. & Lovejoy, Owen. Memoir of the Rev. Elijah P. Lovejoy. facsimile ed. LC 72-117882. (Select Bibliographies Reprint Ser). Repr. of 1838 ed. 19.00 (ISBN 0-8369-5335-5). Arno.
--Memoir of the Reverend Elijah P. Lovejoy. LC 72-90183. (Mass Violence in America Ser). Repr. of 1838 ed. 16.00 (ISBN 0-405-01323-X). Arno.
Tanner, Henry. Martyrdom of Lovejoy: An Account of the Life, Trials, & Perils of Rev. Elijah P. Lovejoy. LC 68-18603. (Illus.). Repr. of 1881 ed. lib. bdg. 15.00x (ISBN 0-678-00744-6). Kelley.

LOVELACE, RICHARD, 1618-1658

Hartman, Cyril H. Cavalier Spirit & Its Influence on the Life & Work of Richard Lovelace. LC 74-11254. 1925. lib. bdg. 17.50 (ISBN 0-8414-4830-2). Folcroft.
Hartmann, Cyril H. The Cavalier Spirit. LC 72-3666. (English Literature Ser., No. 33). 1972. Repr. of 1925 ed. lib. bdg. 33.95 (ISBN 0-8383-1560-7). Haskell.

LOW, DAVID, 1891-1963

Official Guide to Coin Collecting. LC 73-93248. (Illus.). 1979. pap. text ed. 2.95 (ISBN 0-87637-238-8). Hse of Collectibles.

LOW, SETH, 1830-1916

Kurland, Gerald. Seth Low: The Patrician As Social Reformer; the Patrician As Social Architect--a Biography. LC 76-125816. 415p. 1971. text ed. 29.50x (ISBN 0-8290-0205-7). Irvington.
Low, Benjamin R. Seth Low. LC 70-137256. Repr. of 1925 ed. 11.50 (ISBN 0-404-04037-3). AMS Pr.

LOW BLOOD PRESSURE

see also Hypotension

LOW BODY TEMPERATURE

see Hypothermia

LOW-CALORIE DIET

see also Cookery–Reducing Recipes; Low Carbohydrate Diet; Sugar-Free Diet

A to Z Diet Guide Calorie Counter. 23rd ed. 1977. pap. 1.25 (ISBN 0-89596-225-X). Merit Pubns.
B., Bill. Compulsive Overeater. 1981. 10.95 (ISBN 0-89638-046-7). CompCare.
Better Homes & Gardens Books, ed. Better Homes & Gardens Calorie Counter's Cook Book. LC 77-129266. (Illus.). 1970. text ed. 4.95 (ISBN 0-696-00493-3). BH&G.
Better Homes & Gardens Editors. Better Homes & Gardens Calorie Counter's Cookbook. 176p. 1981. pap. 2.50 (ISBN 0-553-14267-4). Bantam.
Betty Crocker's Low Calorie Cookbook. 1973. (Golden Pr); pap. 2.95 (ISBN 0-307-09922-9). Western Pub.
Black, Colette. Low-Calorie Cookbook. 1962. pap. 1.25 (ISBN 0-02-009210-5, Collier). Macmillan.
Bluestein, Bill & Bluestein, Enid. Mom, How Come I'm Not Thin? (Illus.). (gr. 2-5). 1981. 6.95 (ISBN 0-89638-044-0). CompCare.
Brand Name Calorie Counter & Diet Guide. 9th ed. 1977. pap. 1.50 (ISBN 0-89596-204-7, Success). Merit Pubns.
Carper, Jean & Krause, Patricia A. The All-in-One Calorie Counter. rev. ed. 304p. (Orig.). 1980. pap. 2.95 (ISBN 0-553-20339-8). Bantam.
Complete ABC Calorie Counter Diet Guide. 37th ed. 1977. pap. 1.75 (ISBN 0-89596-210-1, Success). Merit Pubns.
Consumer Guide Editors. The Dieter's Complete Guide to Calories, Carbohydrates, Sodium, Fats & Cholesterol. 192p. (Orig.). 1981. pap. 5.95 (ISBN 0-449-90050-9, Columbine). Fawcett.
Corbitt, Helen. Helen Corbitt Cooks for Looks: An Adventure in Low-Calorie Eating. 1967. 6.95 (ISBN 0-395-07575-0). HM.
De Salles, Frances. Doctor's Diet Cookbook. 5th ed. 1977. pap. 2.95 (ISBN 0-89596-213-6, Success). Merit Pubns.
Deutsch, Ronald M. The Fat Counter Guide. LC 77-21049. 1978. pap. 1.95 (ISBN 0-915950-16-2). Bull Pub.
Dwivedi, Basant K., ed. Low Calorie & Special Dietary Foods. (Uniscience Ser.). 1978. 46.95 (ISBN 0-8493-5249-5). CRC Pr.
Easy Calorie Counter Diet Guide. 15th ed. 48p. 1974. pap. 0.50 (ISBN 0-89596-239-X, Basic Hlth). Merit Pubns.
Eat & Be Slim. 2nd ed. 1970. pap. 0.50 (ISBN 0-89596-237-3, Better Hlth). Merit Pubns.
Eat & Lose Weight. 4th ed. 1972. pap. 0.50 (ISBN 0-89596-238-1, Better Hlth). Merit Pubns.
Eat, Drink & Lose Weight. 25th ed. 1977. pap. 1.25 (ISBN 0-89596-215-2, Basic Hlth). Merit Pubns.
Ernst, K. F. The Complete Calorie Counter for Dining Out. 288p. (Orig.). 1981. pap. 2.95 (ISBN 0-515-05500-X). Jove Pubns.
Everybody's Diet Guide. 10th ed. 1972. pap. 0.50 (ISBN 0-89596-240-3, Betterment). Merit Pubns.
Forbes, Evelyn. Recipe for Slimming. (Illus.). 1968. 5.25x (ISBN 0-8002-1904-X). Intl Pubns Serv.
Gerber, Albert B. The Joy of Dieting. 1976. 7.95 (ISBN 0-396-07138-4). Dodd.
Gibbons, Barbara. The International Slim Gourmet Cookbook. LC 78-2136. 1978. 15.95 (ISBN 0-06-011507-6, HarpT). Har-Row.
Good Housekeeping Slimmers' Cook Book. (Illus.). 240p. 1970. 9.50x (ISBN 0-85223-127-X). Intl Pubns Serv.
Guerard, Michael. Michael Guerard's Cuisine Minceur. Chamberlain, Narcisse & Brennan, Fanny, trs. LC 76-49719. (Illus.). 1976. 12.95 (ISBN 0-688-03142-0). Morrow.
Guia Dietetica. (Spanish.). 1967. pap. 0.60 (ISBN 0-89596-200-4). Merit Pubns.
Hirschberg, Leonard K., intro. by. Hollywood Star Diet Guide. 10th ed. 1969. pap. 0.50 (ISBN 0-89596-246-2, Basic Hlth). Merit Pubns.
Kowit, Mary, intro. by. Low Calorie Diet Cookbook. 6th ed. 1977. pap. 2.95 (ISBN 0-89596-218-7, Success). Merit Pubns.
Kraus, Barbara. Calories & Carbohydrates. 4th, rev. ed. 1981. pap. 5.95 (ISBN 0-686-77707-7, Z5267, Plume). NAL.
--Calories & Carbohydrates. 4th, rev. ed. (Orig.). 1981. pap. 3.50 (ISBN 0-451-09774-2, E9774, Sig). NAL.
Low Calorie Diet Recipes. 4th ed. 1977. pap. 2.95 (ISBN 0-89596-219-5, Success). Merit Pubns.
MacRae, Norma M. How to Have Your Cake & Eat It Too! Diet Cooking for the Whole Family: Diabetic, Hypoglycemic, Low-Cholesterol, Low-Fat, Low-Salt, Low-Calorie Diets. LC 75-41392. (Illus.). 1975. pap. 6.95 (ISBN 0-88240-025-8). Alaska Northwest.
Mart, Donald S. The Carbo-Calorie Diet. LC 72-92396. 120p. 1973. pap. 1.95 (ISBN 0-385-00615-2, Dolp). Doubleday.
Milo, Mary & Family Circle Food Staff. Diet & Exercise Guide. rev. ed. LC 73-11787. (Family Circle Books). (Illus.). 160p. 1976. 7.98x (ISBN 0-405-09844-8). Arno.
Pappas, Lou S. Gourmet Cooking: The Slim Way. 1977. 8.95 (ISBN 0-201-05670-4); pap. 4.95 (ISBN 0-201-05671-2). A-W.
Ross, Elaine. Low Calorie Menus for Entertaining. 1970. 7.75 (ISBN 0-8038-4271-6). Hastings.
Schoenberg, Hazel P. Good Housekeeping Cookbook for Calorie Watchers. LC 75-137516. (Illus.). 384p. 1971. 12.95 (ISBN 0-87851-004-4). Hearst Bks.
Simple Diet Guide Calorie Counter. 18th ed. 48p. 1974. pap. 0.50 (ISBN 0-89596-243-8, Basic Hlth). Merit Pubns.
Small, Marvin. The Low-Calorie Diet. pap. 2.25 (ISBN 0-671-82434-1). PB.
Stillman, Irwin & Baker, Sam. Doctor's Quick Weight Loss Diet Cookbook. 352p. 1973. pap. 2.50 (ISBN 0-553-14380-8). Bantam.
Stillman, Irwin & Baker, Samm S. Doctor's Quick Weight Loss Diet. LC 67-15182. 1967. 7.50 (ISBN 0-13-216879-0). P-H.
Stillman, Irwin M. & Baker, Samm. Doctor's Quick Inches-off Diet. 1970. pap. 1.95 (ISBN 0-440-12043-8). Dell.
Stuelke, Richard G. Thin for Life. LC 77-2469. 1977. 8.95 (ISBN 0-89437-000-6). Baronet.
Waldo, Myra. Diet Delight Cookbook. 1971. pap. 2.95 (ISBN 0-02-010410-3, Collier). Macmillan.
Weiss, Elizabeth & Wolfson, Rita. Cholesterol Counter. (Health Ser.). (Orig.). 1973. pap. 1.50 (ISBN 0-515-05689-8, P3208). Jove Pubns.

LOW CARBOHYDRATE DIET

see also Sugar-Free Diet

Brand Name Carbohydrate Diet. 13th ed. 1977. pap. 1.50 (ISBN 0-89596-205-5, Success). Merit Pubns.
Cholesterol Diet Guide Carbohydrate. 16th ed. 1974. pap. 0.60 (ISBN 0-89596-245-4, Basic Hlth). Merit Pubns.
Complete ABC Carbohydrate Diet Guide. 26th ed. 1977. pap. 1.25 (ISBN 0-89596-207-1, Success). Merit Pubns.
Consumer Guide Editors. The Dieter's Complete Guide to Calories, Carbohydrates, Sodium, Fats & Cholesterol. 192p. (Orig.). 1981. pap. 5.95 (ISBN 0-449-90050-9, Columbine). Fawcett.
Doctor's Carbohydrate Diet Guide. 14th ed. 1977. pap. 1.25 (ISBN 0-89596-214-4, Success). Merit Pubns.
Ernst, K. F. The Complete Carbohydrate Counter for Dining Out. 288p. (Orig.). 1981. pap. 2.95 (ISBN 0-515-05698-7). Jove Pubns.
Fiore, Evelyn L., ed. Low Carbohydrate Diet. (Orig.). 1965. pap. 1.95 (ISBN 0-448-01298-7). G&D.
Fredericks, Carlton. Dr. Carlton Fredericks Low Carbohydrate Diet. 192p. 1980. pap. 2.25 (ISBN 0-448-17202-X, Tempo). Ace Bks.
Kline, E. Lee, ed. Carbohydrate Diet Cookbook. 15th ed. 1977. pap. 2.95 (ISBN 0-89596-209-8). Merit Pubns.
Kraus, Barbara. The Basic Food & Brand-Name Carbohydrate Counter. 128p. 1974. pap. 2.95 (ISBN 0-448-11685-5, Today Press). G&D.
--Calories & Carbohydrates. 4th, rev. ed. 1981. pap. 5.95 (ISBN 0-686-77707-7, Z5267, Plume). NAL.
--Calories & Carbohydrates. 4th, rev. ed. (Orig.). 1981. pap. 3.50 (ISBN 0-451-09774-2, E9774, Sig). NAL.
Lindeman, Joanne. Low Carbohydrate Cookbook. LC 74-5249. (Illus.). 192p. (Orig.). 1974. pap. 4.95 (ISBN 0-911954-30-9). Nitty Gritty.
Lopez-Pereira. New Carbohydrate Diet Counter. pap. 1.50 (ISBN 0-87980-107-7). Wilshire.
Netzer, Corinne T. Brand Name Carbohydrate Gram Counter. 272p. 1973. pap. 1.95 (ISBN 0-440-11805-0). Dell.
Schumann, Dolly & Schumann, Jack. Low Carbohydrate Cookery. LC 66-13530. 1966. 6.95 (ISBN 0-8048-0388-9). C E Tuttle.
Tarr, Yvonne Y. Ten-Minute Gourmet Diet Cookbook. (Illus.). 1967. 5.95 (ISBN 0-8184-0125-7). Lyle Stuart.

LOW-CHOLESTEROL DIET

ABC Milligram Cholesterol Diet Guide. 18th ed. 1977. pap. 2.25 (ISBN 0-685-11818-5). Merit Pubns.
Alphabetical Diet Guide Cholesterol Ratings. 1st rev. ed. 1976. pap. 0.75 (ISBN 0-89596-201-2). Merit Pubns.
Betz, Eleanor P., et al. Holiday Eating for a Healthy Heart. 1981. pap. write for info. Rush-Presby-St Lukes.
--Summertime Eating for a Healthy Heart: Cook Out - Camp Out - Eat Out the Low Cholesterol Way. 60p. 1981. pap. 3.95 (ISBN 0-686-31628-2). Rush-Presby-St Lukes.
Board, Evelyn. Right Way to His Heart Cookbook. 7.50 (ISBN 0-392-05459-0, LTB). Sportshelf.
Caviani, Mable. Low Cholesterol Cooking: A Collection of Regional & Ethic Receipes. 1981. 12.95 (ISBN 0-8092-5945-1). Contemp Bks.
Cholesterol Diet Cookbook. 3rd ed. 1974. pap. 1.25 (ISBN 0-685-11799-5, Basic Hlth). Merit Pubns.
Cholesterol Diet Guide Carbohydrate. 16th ed. 1974. pap. 0.60 (ISBN 0-89596-245-4, Basic Hlth). Merit Pubns.
Evans, D. Wainwright & Greenfield, Meta A., eds. Cooking for Your Heart's Content: 250 Gourmet Recipes to Keep Your Heart Healthy. LC 77-5075. (Illus.). 1977. 8.95 (ISBN 0-448-23166-2). Paddington.
Grace, Vilma J. Latin American & Cholesterol Conscious Cooking. (Illus.). 1979. pap. 5.95 (ISBN 0-87491-280-6). Acropolis.
Jones, Jeanne. Diet for a Happy Heart. LC 75-6713. (Illus.). 192p. 1975. pap. 5.95 (ISBN 0-912238-57-7). One Hund One Prods.
Leviton, Roberta. The Jewish Low-Cholesterol Cookbook. LC 77-79243. 1978. 14.95 (ISBN 0-8397-4206-1). Eriksson.
McFarlane, Helen B. The Cholesterol Control Cookbook. 1977. pap. 1.50 (ISBN 0-89437-026-X). Baronet.
Roth, June. Low-Cholesterol Jewish Cookery: The Unsaturated Fat Way. LC 77-13968. 1978. pap. 2.95 (ISBN 0-668-04420-9). Arco.
Wayne, Doreen. The Healthy Gourmet: Low Calorie-Low Cholesterol-Low Cost Cookery. 1979. 14.95x (ISBN 0-8464-0055-3). Beekman Pubs.
Zelle, Ann H. The Enjoyment of Low Cholesterol. LC 73-80772. (Illus.). 87p. (Orig.). 1973. pap. 3.50 (ISBN 0-913514-02-0). Am Natl Pub.

LOW-FAT DIET

see also Cookery–Reducing Recipes

Bond, Clara-Beth Young, et al. Low Fat, Low Cholesterol Diet. rev. ed. LC 76-103741. 1971. 9.95 (ISBN 0-385-03905-0). Doubleday.
Brown, W. J., et al. Cook to Your Heart's Content: On a Low-Fat, Low-Salt Diet. rev ed. 160p. 1976. pap. 6.95 (ISBN 0-442-24812-1). Van Nos Reinhold.
Carper, Jean & Eyton, Audrey. The Revolutionary Seven-Unit Low-Fat Diet. LC 80-5982. 1981. 11.95 (ISBN 0-89256-156-4). Rawson Wade.
Consumer Guide Editors. The Dieter's Complete Guide to Calories, Carbohydrates, Sodium, Fats & Cholesterol. 192p. (Orig.). 1981. pap. 5.95 (ISBN 0-449-90050-9, Columbine). Fawcett.

Dayton, Seymour, et al. Controlled Clinical Trial of a Diet High in Unsaturated Fat in Preventing Complications of Atherosclerosis. (Monograph: Vol. 25). (Illus., Orig.). 1969. pap. text ed. 4.00 (ISBN 0-87493-005-7, 73-017A). Am Heart.

Dosti, Rose, et al. Light Style: The New American Cuisine. the Low Calorie, Low Salt, Low Fat Way to Good Food & Good Health. LC 79-1771. (Illus.). 1979. 12.95 (ISBN 0-06-250485-1, HarpR). Har-Row.

Evans, D. Wainwright & Greenfield, Meta A., eds. Cooking for Your Heart's Content: 250 Gourmet Recipes to Keep Your Heart Healthy. LC 77-5075. (Illus.). 1977. 8.95 (ISBN 0-448-23166-2). Paddington.

Faigel, Frayda. The Happy Heart Cookbook. LC 77-83876. (Orig.). 1977. pap. 1.95 (ISBN 0-89516-011-0). Condor Pub Co.

Forsythe, Elizabeth. The Low-Fat Gourmet. 156p. 1981. 14.95 (ISBN 0-7207-1226-2, Pub. by Michael Joseph). Merrimack Bk Serv.

Jones, Jeanne. Diet for a Happy Heart. LC 75-6713. (Illus.). 192p. 1975. pap. 5.95 (ISBN 0-912238-57-7). One Hund One Prods.

Lampen, Nevada. Fat-Free Recipes. 1977. pap. 4.95 (ISBN 0-571-11026-6, Pub. by Faber & Faber). Merrimack Bk Serv.

MacRae, Norma M. How to Have Your Cake & Eat It Too! Diet Cooking for the Whole Family: Diabetic, Hypoglycemic, Low-Cholesterol, Low-Fat, Low-Salt, Low-Calorie Diets. LC 75-41392. (Illus.). 1975. pap. 6.95 (ISBN 0-88240-025-8). Alaska Northwest.

Payne, Alma & Callahan, Dorothy. The Fat & Sodium Control Cookbook: A Handy & Authoritative Guide for Those on Sodium Restricted or Fat-Controlled Diets-Including Suggestions for Controlling Carbohydrate, Cholesterol & Saturated Fats. 4th rev ed. 1975. 9.95 (ISBN 0-316-69542-4). Little.

Stead, Evelyn & Warren, Gloria. Low-Fat Cookery. rev. ed. LC 74-14509. (Illus.). 420p. 1975. 8.95 (ISBN 0-07-060902-0, GB). McGraw.

Stead, Evelyn S. & Warren, Gloria K. Low-Fat Cookery. new, rev. ed. 1977. pap. 4.95 (ISBN 0-07-060903-9, SP). McGraw.

Stern, Ellen & Michaels, Jonathan. The Good Heart Diet Cookbook. 288p. 1982. 12.95 (ISBN 0-89919-053-7). Ticknor & Fields.

LOW GERMAN DRAMA-HISTORY AND CRITICISM

Heins, O. Johann Rist und das Niederdeutsche Drama des siebzehnten Jahrhunderts. 1930. pap. 15.00 (ISBN 0-384-22110-6). Johnson Repr.

LOW GERMAN LANGUAGE

see also Dutch Language-Early To 1500; Friesian Language

Goetsch, Charles. Phonology of the Low German Deeds in the Oldest Registy at Riga, Latvia. 1934. pap. 6.00 (ISBN 0-527-00819-2). Kraus Repr.

LOW INCOME HOUSING

see Housing; Public Housing

LOW-PROTEIN DIET

Krawitt, Laura P. & Weinberger, Emily K. Practical Low Protein Cookery. (Illus.). 128p. 1971. pap. 10.50 (ISBN 0-398-01049-8). C C Thomas.

Schuett, Virginia, ed. Low Protein Cookery for Phenylketonuria. LC 76-53656. 334p. 1977. 19.50 (ISBN 0-299-07320-3). U of Wis Pr.

LOW SODIUM DIET

see Salt-Free Diet

LOW SUGAR DIET

see Sugar-Free Diet

LOW TEMPERATURE BIOLOGY

see Cryobiology

LOW TEMPERATURE ENGINEERING

see also Gases-Liquefaction; Materials at Low Temperatures; Refrigeration and Refrigerating Machinery

Bailey, C. A. Advanced Cryogenics. LC 77-119158. (International Cryogenics Monographs Ser.). 527p. 1971. 49.50 (ISBN 0-306-30458-9, Plenum Pr). Plenum Pub.

Barron, Randall. Cryogenic Systems. (Mechanical Engineering Ser). 1966. text ed. 29.00 (ISBN 0-07-003820-1, C). McGraw.

Booth, Sterling & Vance, Robert W., eds. Applications of Cryogenic Technology, Vol. 8. LC 68-57815. (Cryogenic Society of America Applications of Cryogenic Technology Ser.). (Illus.). 1976. text ed. 25.00x (ISBN 0-87936-010-0). Scholium Intl.

Clark, A. F. & Reed, R. P., eds. Advances in Cryogenic Engineering (Materials, Vol. 26. 720p. 1981. 59.50 (ISBN 0-306-40531-8, Plenum Pr). Plenum Pub.

Conference of the Cryogenic Society of America, 5th, 1972. Application of Cryogenic Technology: Proceedings, Vol. 5. Carr, Robert H., ed. LC 68-57815. 352p. 1973. text ed. 20.00x (ISBN 0-87936-001-1). Scholium Intl.

Conference of the Cryogenic Society of America, 1973. Applications of Cryogenic Technology: Proceedings, Vol. 6. Vance, Robert H. & Booth, Sterling H., eds. LC 68-57815. (Illus.). 290p. 1974. text ed. 25.00x (ISBN 0-87936-003-8). Scholium Intl.

Cryogenic Conference, U. of Colorado, Boulder, Col., August 2-5, 1977. Advances in Cryogenic Engineering: Vol. 23, Proceedings. 765p. 1978. 49.50 (ISBN 0-306-38023-4, Plenum Pr). Plenum Pub.

Cryogenic Society of America, LNG Terminals & Safety Symposium. Applications of Cryogenic Technology: Proceedings, Vol. 9. Petsinger, Robert E. & Vance, Robert W., eds. LC 68-57815. 1979. 39.50x (ISBN 0-87936-014-3). Scholium Intl.

Cryoimmunology. 1976. pap. 21.50 (ISBN 0-685-99133-4, IIR39, IIR). Unipub.

Cryophysics & Cryoengineering. 1970. pap. 17.75 (ISBN 0-685-99134-2, IIR45, IIR). Unipub.

Developments in Cryogenic Technology in the 1-20 K Range. 1979. pap. 10.50 (ISBN 0-685-90708-2, IIR 18, IIR). Unipub.

Douzou, P. Cryobiochemistry: An Introduction. 1977. 45.50 (ISBN 0-12-221050-6). Acad Pr.

Frechette, V. D., et al, eds. Quality Assurance in Ceramic Industries. 1979. 39.50 (ISBN 0-306-40183-5, Plenum Pr). Plenum Pub.

Gottzman, C. F. Cryogenic Processes & Equipment in Energy Systems. 200p. 1980. 40.00 (ISBN 0-686-69847-9, H00164). ASME.

Hasselman, D. P. & Heller, R. A., eds. Thermal Stresses in Severe Environments. 750p. 1980. 75.00 (ISBN 0-306-40544-X, Plenum Pr). Plenum Pub.

Hill, A. W., et al. Handbook to BS 5337, 1976: The Structural Use of Concrete for Retaining Aqueous Liquids. (Viewpoint Publication Ser.). (Illus.). 60p. 1979. pap. text ed. 22.50x (ISBN 0-7210-1078-4, Pub. by C&CA London). Scholium Intl.

Law, Beverly, ed. Cryogenics Handbook. 1981. text ed. 39.00 (ISBN 0-86103-021-4). Butterworth.

Meaden, George T. Electrical Resistance of Metals. LC 64-23243. (International Cryogenics Monograph). 218p. 1965. 29.50 (ISBN 0-306-30207-1, Plenum Pr). Plenum Pub.

Rechowicz, Michael. Electric Power at Low Temperatures. (Monographs in Electrical & Electronic Engineering). (Illus.). 150p. 1975. 45.00x (ISBN 0-19-859312-0). Oxford U Pr.

Sheskin, Arlene. Cryonics: A Sociology of Death & Bereavement. LC 79-13402. 216p. 1979. 16.95x (ISBN 0-470-26786-0). Halsted Pr.

Timmerhaus, K. D. & Snyder, H. A., eds. Advances in Cryogenic Engineering, Vol. 25. (Illus.). 835p. 1980. 59.50 (ISBN 0-306-40504-0, Plenum Pr). Plenum Pub.

Vance, Robert W. & Weinstock, Harold, eds. Applications of Cryogenic Technology. LC 68-57815. (Illus.). 1969. 14.95 (ISBN 0-87252-011-0). Tinnon-Brown.

Zabetakis, M. G. Safety with Cryogenic Fluids. LC 66-12628. (International Cryogenics Monographs Ser.). 156p. 1967. 29.50 (ISBN 0-306-30285-3, Plenum Pr). Plenum Pub.

LOW TEMPERATURE MATERIALS

see Materials at Low Temperatures

LOW TEMPERATURE METALS

see Metals at Low Temperatures

LOW TEMPERATURE RESEARCH

see also Cold; Gases-Liquefaction; Thermomagnetism

Ashwood, M. J. & Farrant, Smith J. Low Temperature Preservation in Medicine & Biology. 323p. text ed. 39.50 (ISBN 0-8391-1492-3). Univ Park.

Freezing Frozen Storage & Freeze-Drying. 1979. pap. 28.75 (ISBN 0-685-90709-0, IIR 17, IIR). Unipub.

Lounasmas, O. V. Experimental Principles & Methods Below 1k. 1974. 55.50 (ISBN 0-12-455950-6). Acad Pr.

Shoenberg, David. Superconductivity. 2nd ed. (Cambridge Monographs on Physics). (Illus.). 1960-1965. pap. 5.00 (ISBN 0-521-09254-X). Cambridge U Pr.

LOW TEMPERATURES

see also Cold; Cryobiology; Low Temperature Engineering; Low Temperature Research; Materials at Low Temperatures; Quantum Liquids; Solid Helium; Superfluidity

Bailey, C. A. Advanced Cryogenics. LC 77-119158. (International Cryogenics Monographs Ser.). 527p. 1971. 49.50 (ISBN 0-306-30458-9, Plenum Pr). Plenum Pub.

Brewer, D. F. Progress in Low Temperature Physics, 2 vols, Vols. 7a & 7b. 1979. Set. 117.00 (ISBN 0-444-85210-7, North Holland); Vol. 7a. 66.00 (ISBN 0-444-85177-1); Vol. 7b. 66.00 (ISBN 0-444-85209-3). Elsevier.

Croft, A. J. Cryogenic Laboratory Equipment. LC 65-11337. (International Cryogenics Monographs Ser.). 182p. 1969. 29.50 (ISBN 0-306-30253-5, Plenum Pr). Plenum Pub.

Dugdale, John S. Entropy & Low Temperature Physics. (Orig.). pap. text ed. 3.50x (ISBN 0-09-078251-8, Hutchinson U Lib). Humanities.

Gopal, Erode S. Specific Heats at Low Temperatures. LC 65-11339. 240p. 1966. 30.00 (ISBN 0-306-30222-5, Plenum Pr). Plenum Pub.

Gorter, C. J., ed. Progress in Low Temperature Physics, Vols. 4-6. Vol. 4. 63.50 (ISBN 0-444-10205-1, North-Holland); Vol. 5. 39.00 (ISBN 0-444-10206-X); Vol. 6. 49.00 (ISBN 0-444-10011-3). Elsevier.

Hawthorne, J. & Rolfe, E. J., eds. Low Temperature Biology of Foodstuffs. 1969. 55.00 (ISBN 0-08-013294-4). Pergamon.

International Institute of Refrigeration. Progress in Refrigeration Science & Technology, 11th Conference, 3 Vols. 1965. Set. 180.00 (ISBN 0-08-011439-3). Pergamon.

Kruisius, M. & Vuorio, M. Low Temperature Physics, 5 vols. 1976. Set. 153.75 (ISBN 0-7204-9301-3, North-Holland). Elsevier.

Lounasmas, O. V. Experimental Principles & Methods Below 1k. 1974. 55.50 (ISBN 0-12-455950-6). Acad Pr.

O'Sullivan, W. J., et al, eds. Low Temperature Physics - LT-13, 4 vols. Incl. Vol. 1. Quantum Fluids. 669p. 47.50 (ISBN 0-306-35121-8); Vol. 2. Quantum Crystals & Magnetism. 668p. 52.50 (ISBN 0-306-35122-6); Vol. 3. Superconductivity. 834p. 52.50 (ISBN 0-686-66919-3); Vol. 4. Electronic Properties, Instrumentation, & Measurement. 684p. 52.50 (ISBN 0-306-35124-2). LC 73-81092. (Illus.). 1974 (Plenum Pr). Plenum Pub.

Turner, F. H. Concrete & Cryogenics. (Viewpoint Publication Ser.). (Illus.). 125p. 1979. pap. text ed. 27.50x (ISBN 0-7210-1124-1, Pub by C&CA London). Scholium Intl.

Vance, Robert W. Application of Cyrogenic Technology, Vol 2. 1970. 14.95 (ISBN 0-87252-026-9). Tinnon-Brown.

White, Guy K. Experimental Techniques in Low-Temperature Physics. 3rd ed. (Monographs on the Physics & Chemistry of Materials). (Illus.). 1979. 29.50x (ISBN 0-19-851359-3). Oxford U Pr.

Zemansky, Mark W. Temperatures Very Low & Very High. 144p. 1981. pap. 3.00 (ISBN 0-486-24072-X). Dover.

LOWDEN, FRANK ORREN, 1861-1943

Hutchinson, William T. Lowden of Illinois: The Life of Governor Frank O. Lowden, 2 vols. Incl. Vol. 1. xiv, 382p (ISBN 0-226-36245-0); Vol. 2. viii, 385p (ISBN 0-226-36246-9). LC 57-6274. (Midway Reprint Ser). 1975. pap. text ed. 12.50x ea. U of Chicago Pr.

LOWELL, AMY, 1874-1925

Damon, S. Foster. Amy Lowell: A Chronicle. (Illus.). 1966. Repr. of 1935 ed. 30.00 (ISBN 0-208-00150-6, Archon). Shoe String.

Flint, F. Cudworth. Amy Lowell. (Pamphlets on American Writers Ser: No. 82). (Orig.). 1969. pap. 1.25x (ISBN 0-8166-0544-0, MPAW82). U of Minn Pr.

Gould, Jean. Amy: The World of Amy Lowell & the Imagist Movement. LC 75-11563. 350p. 1975. 12.50 (ISBN 0-396-07022-1). Dodd.

Gregory, Horace. Amy Lowell. facs. ed. LC 69-16855. (Select Bibliographies Reprint Ser). 1958. 25.00 (ISBN 0-8369-5008-9). Arno.

Heymann, C. David. American Aristocracy: The Lives & Times of James Russell, Amy, & Robert Lowell. LC 79-9351. (Illus.). 1980. 17.95 (ISBN 0-396-07608-4). Dodd.

Hoskier, H. C. Bronze Horses, Comment on the Prose Poem of Amy Lowell. LC 76-23438. 1930. lib. bdg. 6.00 (ISBN 0-8414-4814-0). Folcroft.

Moore, Charles L. Incense & Iconoclasm. 343p. 1980. Repr. of 1915 ed. lib. bdg. 30.00 (ISBN 0-89987-573-4). Century Bookbindery.

Ruihley, Glenn R. The Thorn of a Rose: Amy Lowell Reconsidered. (Illus.). 191p. 1975. 17.50 (ISBN 0-208-01458-6, Archon). Shoe String.

Sargeant, George H. Amy Lowell: A Mosaic. 28p. 1980. Repr. of 1926 ed. lib. bdg. 10.00 (ISBN 0-8492-8125-3). R West.

Sargent, George H. Amy Lowell: A Mosaic. LC 77-10636. 1926. lib. bdg. 10.00 (ISBN 0-8414-7941-0). Folcroft.

Wood, Clement. Amy Lowell: Critical Study. LC 73-3300. 1926. lib. bdg. 20.00 (ISBN 0-8414-2815-8). Folcroft.

LOWELL, JAMES RUSSELL, 1819-1891

Beatty, Richmond C. James Russell Lowell. (Illus.). 1969. Repr. of 1942 ed. 19.50 (ISBN 0-208-00752-0, Archon). Shoe String.

Browne, E. E. Life of Lowell. Repr. 20.00 (ISBN 0-8274-2934-7). R West.

Burack, Irving. Etude Critique Des Poemes Inedits de James Russell Lowell. 1939. Repr. 30.00 (ISBN 0-8274-2315-2). R West.

Clark, H. H. & Foerster, Norman. Lowell. 498p. 1980. Repr. lib. bdg. 40.00 (ISBN 0-89987-108-9). Darby Bks.

Commemoration of the Centenary of the Birth of James Russell Lowell: Poet, Scholar, Diplomat. 88p. 1980. Repr. of 1919 ed. lib. bdg. 35.00 (ISBN 0-8495-3349-X). Arden Lib.

Cooke, George W. A Bibliography of James Russell Lowell. LC 77-13536. 1977. Repr. of 1906 ed. lib. bdg. 20.00 (ISBN 0-89341-453-0). Longwood Pr.

Emerson, Edward W. Life & Letters of Charles Russell Lowell. LC 71-137909. (American History & Culture in the Nineteenth Century Ser). 1971. Repr. of 1907 ed. 22.50 (ISBN 0-8046-1477-6). Kennikat.

Etude Critique Des Poemes Inedits De James Russell Lowell. 166p. 1981. Repr. of 1939 ed. lib. bdg. 75.00 (ISBN 0-89987-071-6). Darby Bks.

Greenslet, Ferris. James Russell Lowell. 1973. Repr. of 1905 ed. 9.50 (ISBN 0-8274-1338-6). R West.

--James Russell Lowell: His Life & Work. LC 77-77162. 1969. Repr. of 1905 ed. 22.00 (ISBN 0-8103-3893-9). Gale.

Hale, E. James Russell Lowell & His Friends. 59.95 (ISBN 0-8490-0434-9). Gordon Pr.

Hale, Edward E. James Russell Lowell. 128p. 1980. Repr. of 1899 ed. lib. bdg. 15.00 (ISBN 0-8495-2273-0). Arden Lib.

--James Russell Lowell. LC 80-20008. (American Men & Women of Letters Ser.). 310p. 1981. pap. 4.95 (ISBN 0-87754-168-X). Chelsea Hse.

--James Russell Lowell. LC 73-14571. 1899. lib. bdg. 20.00 (ISBN 0-8414-4764-0). Folcroft.

--James Russell Lowell & His Friends. LC 71-97165. Repr. of 1899 ed. 11.50 (ISBN 0-404-01946-3). AMS Pr.

Heymann, C. David. American Aristocracy: The Lives & Times of James Russell, Amy, & Robert Lowell. LC 79-9351. (Illus.). 1980. 17.95 (ISBN 0-396-07608-4). Dodd.

Howard, Leon. Victorian Knight-Errant: A Study of the Early Literary Career of James Russell Lowell. LC 72-136072. 1971. Repr. of 1952 ed. lib. bdg. 17.25x (ISBN 0-8371-5222-4, HOVK). Greenwood.

--Victorian Knight-Errant: A Study of the Early Literary Career of James Russell Lowell. LC 72-136072. 1971. Repr. of 1952 ed. lib. bdg. 17.25x (ISBN 0-8371-5222-4, HOVK). Greenwood.

Hudson, William H. Lowell & His Poetry. LC 78-120988. (Poetry & Life Ser.). Repr. of 1914 ed. 7.25 (ISBN 0-404-52517-2). AMS Pr.

--Lowell & His Poetry. LC 72-195247. 1911. lib. bdg. 7.50 (ISBN 0-8414-5194-X). Folcroft.

Le Clair, Robert C. Three American Travellers in England: James Russell Lowell, Henry Adams, Henry James. LC 77-19341. 1978. Repr. of 1945 ed. lib. bdg. 19.75x (ISBN 0-313-20190-0, LETA). Greenwood.

Livingston, Luther S. Bibliography of the First Editions in Book Form of the Writings of James Russell Lowell. 1914. 20.50 (ISBN 0-8337-2130-5). B Franklin.

Lowell, James R. Among My Books: Second Series. Repr. 20.00 (ISBN 0-8274-1861-2). R West.

--Letters of James R. Lowell, 2 vols. Repr. lib. bdg. 34.50 (ISBN 0-8414-5895-2). Folcroft.

McGlinchee, Claire. James Russell Lowell. (Twayne's United States Authors Ser). 1967. pap. 3.45 (ISBN 0-8084-0173-4, T120, Twayne). Coll & U Pr.

--James Russell Lowell. (U. S. Authors Ser.: No. 120). lib. bdg. 10.95 (ISBN 0-8057-0460-4). Twayne.

Nadal, Ehrman S. Virginian Village, & Other Papers. facs. ed. LC 68-20324. (Essay Index Reprint Ser). 1917. 15.50 (ISBN 0-8369-0733-7). Arno.

Scudder, Horace E. James Russell Lowell, 2 vols. 1973. Repr. of 1901 ed. 50.00 (ISBN 0-8274-1337-8). R West.

--James Russell Lowell: A Biography, 2 Vols. LC 1-24659. 1969. Repr. of 1901 ed. Set. 18.00 (ISBN 0-403-00063-7). Scholarly.

--James Russell Lowell: A Biography, 2 vols. LC 73-126665. Repr. of 1901 ed. Set. 27.50 (ISBN 0-404-05664-4). AMS Pr.

--James Russell Lowell: A Biography, 2 vols. LC 73-126665. Repr. of 1901 ed. Set. 27.50 (ISBN 0-404-05664-4). AMS Pr.

Underwood, Francis H. James Russell Lowell. Repr. 30.00 (ISBN 0-8274-2600-3). R West.

--The Poet & the Man: Recollections & Appreciations of James Russell Lowell. 1893. Repr. 30.00 (ISBN 0-8274-3161-9). R West.

Wagenknecht, Edward C. James Russell Lowell: Portrait of a Many-Sided Man. (Portraits of American Writers Ser). 1971. 11.95 (ISBN 0-19-501376-X). Oxford U Pr.

LOWELL, MRS. JOSEPHINE (SHAW) 1843-1905
Stewart, William R. Philanthropic Work of Josephine Shaw Lowell, Containing a Biographical Sketch of Her Life Together with a Selection of Her Public Papers & Private Letters. LC 71-172576. (Criminology, Law Enforcement, & Social Problems Ser.: No. 163). (Illus.). 1974. Repr. of 1911 ed. 20.00 (ISBN 0-87585-163-0). Patterson Smith.
LOWELL, ROBERT, 1917-1977
Axelrod, Steven G. Robert Lowell: Life of Art. LC 78-51155. (Illus.). 1978. text ed. 21.00 (ISBN 0-691-06363-X); pap. 7.95 (ISBN 0-691-01364-0). Princeton U Pr.
Cooper, Philip. Autobiographical Myth of Robert Lowell. 1970. 12.00x (ISBN 0-8078-1147-5). U of NC Pr.
Cosgrave, Patrick. Public Poetry of Robert Lowell. LC 72-183597. 1972. 7.95 (ISBN 0-8008-6559-6). Taplinger.
Fein, Richard J. Robert Lowell. 2nd ed. (United States Authors Ser.: No. 176). 1979. lib. bdg. 9.95 (ISBN 0-8057-7279-0). Twayne.
Heymann, C. David. American Aristocracy: The Lives & Times of James Russell, Amy, & Robert Lowell. LC 79-9351. (Illus.). 1980. 17.95 (ISBN 0-396-07608-4). Dodd.
Martin, Jay. Robert Lowell. (Pamphlets on American Writers Ser: No. 92). (Orig.). 1970. pap. 1.25x (ISBN 0-8166-0564-5, MPAW92). U of Minn Pr.
Meiners, R. K. Everything to Be Endured: An Essay on Robert Lowell & Modern Poetry. LC 75-105270. (Literary Frontiers Ser). (Orig.). 1970. pap. 5.00 (ISBN 0-8262-0093-1). U of Mo Pr.
Perloff, Marjorie G. The Poetic Art of Robert Lowell. LC 72-12412. 232p. 1973. 19.50x (ISBN 0-8014-0771-0). Cornell U Pr.
Price, Jonathan, ed. Critics on Robert Lowell. LC 78-161435. (Readings in Literary Criticism Ser: No. 17). 1972. 5.95x (ISBN 0-87024-210-5). U of Miami Pr.
Raffel, Burton. Robert Lowell. LC 81-40470. (Modern Literature Ser.). 160p. 1981. 10.95 (ISBN 0-8044-2707-0). Ungar.
Smith, Vivian. The Poetry of Robert Lowell. (Studies in Literature). 144p. 1974. 7.50x (ISBN 0-424-06510-X, Pub. by Sydney U Pr). Intl Schol Bk Serv.
Williamson, Alan. Pity the Monsters: The Political Vision of Robert Lowell. LC 73-93614. 225p. 1974. 17.50x (ISBN 0-300-01734-0). Yale U Pr.
Yenser, Stephen. Circle to Circle: The Poetry of Robert Lowell. LC 74-79778. 400p. 1976. 27.50x (ISBN 0-520-02790-6). U of Cal Pr.
LOWELL, MASSACHUSETTS
Arrow Pub Staff, ed. Arrow Street Guide of Lowell, Lawrence & Haverhill. 1976. pap. 2.50 (ISBN 0-913450-31-6). Arrow Pub.
Coolidge, John P. Mill & Mansion: A Study of Architecture & Society in Lowell, Massachusetts, 1820-1865. LC 66-27058. (Illus.). 1967. Repr. of 1942 ed. 27.00 (ISBN 0-8462-0866-0). Russell.
Josephson, Hannah. Golden Threads: New England's Mill Girls & Magnates. LC 66-27109. 1967. Repr. of 1949 ed. 15.00 (ISBN 0-8462-0873-3). Russell.
Scoresby, William. American Factories & Their Female Operatives: With an Appeal on Behalf of the British Factory Population & Suggestions for the Improvement of Their Condition. (Research & Source Works Ser.: No. 184). 1967. Repr. of 1845 ed. 19.00 (ISBN 0-8337-3206-4). B Franklin.
LOWELL, MASSACHUSETTS-HISTORY
Lowell Historical Society. Cotton Was King: A History of Lowell, Mass. Eno, Arthur L., Jr., ed. LC 76-11304. (Illus.). 1976. pap. 6.95 (ISBN 0-912274-61-1). NH Pub Co.
Miles, Henry A. Lowell, As It Was, & As It Is. LC 72-5063. (Technology & Society Ser.). (Illus.). 234p. 1972. Repr. of 1845 ed. 11.00 (ISBN 0-405-04714-2). Arno.
Robinson, Harriet H. Loom and Spindle. LC 75-46389. 144p. 1976. 5.95 (ISBN 0-916630-01-3); pap. 4.50 (ISBN 0-916630-02-1). Pr Pacifica.
LOWER SILURIAN PERIOD
see Geology, Stratigraphic-Ordovician
LOWER UMPQUA LANGUAGE
see Kuitsch Language
LOWIE, ROBERT HARRY, 1883-1957
Lowie, Robert H. Robert H. Lowie, Ethnologist: A Personal Record. (Illus.). 1959. 26.75x (ISBN 0-520-00775-1). U of Cal Pr.
Murphy, Robert F. Robert Lowie. LC 72-1969. (Leaders of Modern Anthropology Ser). (Illus.). 200p. 1972. 15.00x (ISBN 0-231-03375-3); pap. 6.00x (ISBN 0-231-03397-4). Columbia U Pr.
LOWRY, L. S.
Levy, Mervyn. The Drawings of L. S. Lowry: Public & Private. 352p. 1981. 39.00x (ISBN 0-904041-69-7, Pub. by Jupiter England). State Mutual Bk.
--The Paintings of L. S. Lowry: Oils & Watercolours. 192p. 1981. 39.00x (ISBN 0-904041-23-9, Pub. by Jupiter England). State Mutual Bk.
Levy, Mervyn, ed. Selected Paintings of L. S. Lowry: Oils & Watercolours. 128p. 1981. 18.00x (ISBN 0-904041-62-X, Pub. by Jupiter England). State Mutual Bk.
LOWRY, MALCOLM, 1909-1957
Beckoff, Samuel. Monarch Notes on Lowry's Under the Volcano. 1975. pap. 1.50 (ISBN 0-671-00968-0). Monarch Pr.
Bradbrook, Muriel C. Malcolm Lowry: His Art & Early Life. (Illus.). 170p. 1975. 28.50 (ISBN 0-521-20473-9); pap. 7.95x (ISBN 0-521-09985-4). Cambridge U Pr.
Cross, Richard K. Malcolm Lowry: A Preface to His Fiction. LC 79-16091. 1980. 12.50 (ISBN 0-226-12125-9). U of Chicago Pr.
Day, Douglas. Malcolm Lowry: A Biography. (Illus.). 1973. 16.95 (ISBN 0-19-501711-0). Oxford U Pr.
Dodson, Daniel B. Malcolm Lowry. LC 70-126542. (Columbia Essays on Modern Writers Ser.: No. 51). 48p. (Orig.). 1970. pap. 2.00 (ISBN 0-231-03244-7). Columbia U Pr.
Markson, David. Malcolm Lowry's Volcano. LC 77-92329. 1978. 12.95 (ISBN 0-8129-0751-5). Times Bks.
New, William H. Malcolm Lowry: A Reference Guide. (Reference Bks.). 1978. lib. bdg. 18.00 (ISBN 0-8161-7884-4). G K Hall.
Smith, Anne, ed. The Art of Malcolm Lowry. LC 78-62638. (Critical Studies Ser.). 1978. text ed. 20.00x (ISBN 0-06-496378-0). B&N.
LOYALISTS, AMERICAN
see American Loyalists
LOYALTY
Here are entered general works on loyalty as a virtue. Works on loyalty to the state are entered under the heading Allegiance.
see also Patriotism; Turncoats
Bloch, Herbert A. Concept of Our Changing Loyalties: An Introductory Study into the Nature of the Social Individual. LC 34-36571. (Columbia University Studies in the Social Sciences: No. 401). Repr. of 1934 ed. 22.50 (ISBN 0-404-51401-4). AMS Pr.
Gellhorn, Walter. Security, Loyalty & Science. Repr. of 1950 ed. 23.00 (ISBN 0-384-18000-0). Johnson Repr.
Hirschman, Albert O. Exit, Voice, & Loyalty: Responses to Decline in Firms, Organizations, & States. LC 77-99517. 1970. 8.95x (ISBN 0-674-27650-7); pap. 4.95x (ISBN 0-674-27660-4). Harvard U Pr.
MacDonald, William. To What Should We Be Loyal. 55p. pap. 0.75 (ISBN 0-937396-47-8). Walterick Pubs.
Royce, Josiah. The Philosophy of Loyalty. xiv, 409p. 1971. Repr. of 1908 ed. 18.00 (ISBN 0-02-851160-3). Hafner.
Sammon, Sean D., et al. Fidelity: Issues of Emotional Living in an Age of Stress for Clergy & Religious. Hart, Joseph L., ed. LC 81-533. 148p. (Orig.). 1981. pap. 5.00 (ISBN 0-89571-011-0). Affirmation.
Schrag, Peter. Test of Loyalty. LC 74-111. 416p. 1975. pap. 3.95 (ISBN 0-671-22021-7, Touchstone Bks). S&S.
Whyte, William H., Jr. Organization Man. 1957. 14.95 (ISBN 0-671-54330-X). S&S.
Young, George K. Who Is My Liege? A Study of Loyalty & Betrayal in Our Time. 200p. 1972. 12.50x (ISBN 0-85614-008-2). Intl Pubns Serv.
LOYALTY INVESTIGATIONS
see Loyalty-Security Program, 1947-
LOYALTY OATHS
Gardner, David P. The California Oath Controversy. LC 67-16840. 1967. 21.50x (ISBN 0-520-00455-8). U of Cal Pr.
Hyman, Harold M. Era of the Oath: Northern Loyalty Tests During the Civil War & Reconstruction. 1978. Repr. of 1954 ed. lib. bdg. 15.00x (ISBN 0-374-94083-5). Octagon.
LOYALTY-SECURITY PROGRAM, 1947-
see also Loyalty Oaths
Association of the Bar of the City of New York. Report of the Special Committee on the Federal Loyalty Security Program. LC 74-6494. (Civil Liberties in American History Ser.). 301p. 1974. Repr. of 1956 ed. lib. bdg. 32.50 (ISBN 0-306-70596-6). Da Capo.
Biddle, Francis. Fear of Freedom. LC 76-138496. (Civil Liberties in American History Ser). 1971. Repr. of 1951 ed. lib. bdg. 37.50 (ISBN 0-306-70073-5). Da Capo.
Bontecou, Eleanor. The Federal Loyalty-Security Program. LC 73-17628. 377p. 1974. Repr. of 1953 ed. lib. bdg. 17.00x (ISBN 0-8371-7256-X, BOFL). Greenwood.
Clubb, O. Edmund. The Witness & I. LC 74-11385. 314p. 1975. 16.00x (ISBN 0-231-03859-3). Columbia U Pr.
Fund for the Republic, Inc. Digest of the Public Record of Communism in the United States. Grob, Gerald, ed. LC 76-46078. (Anti-Movements in America). 1977. lib. bdg. 43.00x (ISBN 0-405-09951-7). Arno.
Wilcox, Laird M., compiled by. Bibliography on Loyalty & Security. (Orig.). 1981. pap. text ed. 9.95 (ISBN 0-933592-26-4). Edit Res Serv.
Yarmolinsky, Adam, compiled by. Case Studies in Personnel Security. LC 75-25606. 310p. 1975. Repr. of 1955 ed. lib. bdg. 24.00x (ISBN 0-8371-8318-9, YAPS). Greenwood.
LOYOLA, IGNACIO DE, SAINT, 1491-1556
Amey, Peter, et al. Luther, Erasmus & Loyola. Yapp, Malcolm, et al, eds. (World History Ser.). (Illus.). (gr. 10). 1980. lib. bdg. 5.95 (ISBN 0-89908-043-X); pap. text ed. 1.95 (ISBN 0-89908-018-9). Greenhaven.
Barthes, Roland. Sade, Fourier, Loyola. 1971. 14.95 (ISBN 0-686-53941-9). French & Eur.
Brodrick, James. Origin of the Jesuits. LC 70-138604. 1971. Repr. of 1940 ed. lib. bdg. 16.00x (ISBN 0-8371-5523-1, BROJ). Greenwood.
Clancy, Thomas H. The Conversational Word of God: A Commentary on the Doctrine of St. Ignatius of Loyola Concerning Spiritual Conversation, with Four Early Jesuit Texts. Ganss, George E., frwd. by. LC 78-51343. (Study Aids on Jesuit Topics: No. 8 in Ser. IV). 83p. 1978. 5.00 (ISBN 0-912422-33-5); pap. 2.50 smyth sewn (ISBN 0-912422-34-3). Inst Jesuit.
Fleming, David L. A Contemporary Reading of the Spiritual Exercises: A Companion to St. Ignatius' Text. 2nd ed. Ganss, George E., ed. LC 80-81812. (Study Aids on Jesuit Topics Ser.: No.2). 112p. 1980. pap. 3.00 (ISBN 0-912422-47-5); smyth sewn o.s.i. 4.00 (ISBN 0-912422-48-3). Inst Jesuit.
--The Spiritual Exercises of St. Ignatius: A Literal Translation & a Contemporary Reading. Ganss, George G., ed. LC 77-93429. (Study Aids on Jesuit Topics Ser.: No. 7). 290p. 1978. 12.00 (ISBN 0-912422-32-7); smythe sewn 8.00 (ISBN 0-912422-31-9); pap. 7.00 (ISBN 0-912422-28-9). Inst Jesuit.
Ganss, George E. Saint Ignatius' Idea of a Jesuit University. 2nd ed. (Illus.). 1956. pap. 9.95 (ISBN 0-87462-437-1). Marquette.
Hughes, Thomas A. Loyola & the Educational System of the Jesuits. 34.95 (ISBN 0-8490-0565-5). Gordon Pr.
Ignatius, Saint Spiritual Exercises of St. Ignatius of Loyola. Delmage, Lewis, tr. 1978. 4.00 (ISBN 0-8198-0557-2); pap. 2.25 (ISBN 0-8198-0558-0). Dghtrs St Paul.
Ignatius Of Loyala, Saint Letters of Saint Ignatius of Loyola. Young, William J., ed. LC 59-13459. 1959. 3.95 (ISBN 0-8294-0085-0). Loyola.
Joly, Henri. Saint Ignatius of Loyola. LC 70-170821. Repr. of 1899 ed. 21.00 (ISBN 0-404-03597-3). AMS Pr.
Leturia, Pedro. Inigo De Loyola. Owen, Aloysius J., tr. (Request Reprint). 1965. 3.50 (ISBN 0-8294-0046-X). Loyola.
Loyola, Ignatius. The Autobiography of Saint Ignatius Loyola. O'Callaghan, Joseph F., tr. 8.00 (ISBN 0-8446-5240-7). Peter Smith.
McNally, Robert E. Council of Trent, the Spiritual Exercises & the Catholic Reform. Anderson, Charles S., ed. LC 70-96863. (Facet Bks). 64p. 1970. pap. 1.00 (ISBN 0-8006-3056-4, 1-3056). Fortress.
Marcuse, Ludwig. Soldier of the Church: The Life of Ignatius Loyola. LC 70-172842. Repr. of 1939 ed. 23.00 (ISBN 0-404-04187-6). AMS Pr.
Olin, John C. The Autobiography of St. Ignatius Loyola, with Related Documents. O'Callaghan, Joseph F., tr. Date not set. 8.00 (ISBN 0-8446-5703-4). Peter Smith.
Olin, John C., ed. Autobiography of St. Ignatius Loyola. 1974. pap. 4.95x (ISBN 0-06-131783-7, TB1783, Torch). Har-Row.
Owen, Aloysius J. The Holy Spirit, Your Retreat Director: A Manual for a Direct-Retreat Based on the Ignatian Exercises. LC 79-14945. (Orig.). 1979. pap. 3.50 (ISBN 0-8189-0387-2). Alba.
Pousset, Edouard. Life in Faith & Freedom: An Essay Presenting Gaston Fessard's Analysis of the Dialectic of the Spiritual Exercises of St. Ignatius. Ganss, G. E., frwd. by. LC 79-84200. (Modern Scholarly Studies About Jesuits, in English Translation Ser.: No. 4). 286p. 1980. 9.00 (ISBN 0-912422-41-6); pap. 8.00 smythsewn (ISBN 0-912422-40-8); pap. 7.00 (ISBN 0-912422-39-4). Inst Jesuit.
Purcell, Mary. The First Jesuit. rev. ed. 225p. 1981. 10.00 (ISBN 0-8294-0371-X). Loyola.
Rahner, Hugo. The Spirituality of St. Ignatius Loyola: An Account of Its Historical Development. Smith, Francis J., tr. LC 53-5586. (Request Reprint). 1968. 3.50 (ISBN 0-8294-0066-4). Loyola.
Rahner, Karl & Imhof, Paul. Ignatius of Loyola. (Illus.). 1979. 14.95 (ISBN 0-529-05643-7, RB5643). Collins Pubs.
Toner, Jules J. A Commentary on Saint Ignatius' Rules for the Discernment of Spirits: A Guide to the Principles & Practice. LC 79-89606. 400p. 1982. 14.00 (ISBN 0-912422-43-2); pap. 12.00 smyth sewn paper (ISBN 0-912422-42-4). Inst Jesuit.
Van Dyke, Paul. Ignatius Loyola, the Founder of the Jesuits. LC 67-27659. Repr. of 1926 ed. 14.50 (ISBN 0-8046-0477-0). Kennikat.
Wulf, F., et al. Ignatius of Loyola: His Personality & Spiritual Heritage, 1556-1956, Studies on the 400th Anniversary of His Death. LC 77-16677. (Modern Scholarly Studies About the Jesuits,in English Translations Ser.: No. 2). 318p. 1977. pap. 7.00 (ISBN 0-912422-22-X). Inst Jesuit.
LOZI (AFRICAN TRIBE)
Gluckman, Max. Judicial Process Among the Barotse of Northern Rhodesia. (Rhodes Livingston Institute Bks). 1955. pap. text ed. 15.00x (ISBN 0-7190-1040-3). Humanities.
Reynolds, Barrie. Magic, Divination & Witchcraft Among the Barotse of Northern Rhodesia. (Illus.). 1963. 23.50x (ISBN 0-520-01063-9). U of Cal Pr.
LOZI LAW
see Law, Lozi
LPG
see Liquefied Petroleum Gas
LSD
see Lysergic Acid Diethylamide
LU-GANDA
see Ganda Language
LUANSHYA, NORTHERN RHODESIA
Epstein, Arnold L. Politics in an Urban African Community. 1958. pap. text ed. 10.25x (ISBN 0-7190-1041-1). Humanities.
Powdermaker, Hortense. Copper Town: Changing Africa, the Human Situation on the Rhodesian Copperbelt. 391p. 1973. Repr. of 1962 ed. lib. bdg. 21.00x (ISBN 0-8371-6632-2, POCT). Greenwood.
LUBIN, DAVID, 1849-1919
Agresti, Olivia R. David Lubin: A Study in Practical Idealism. 2nd ed. LC 41-53013. (Illus.). 1941. 5.00 (ISBN 0-911090-01-0). Pacific Bk Supply.
LUBITSCH, ERNST, 1892-1947
Carringer, Robert L. & Sabath, Barry, eds. Ernst Lubitsch: A Guide to References & Resources. (Reference & Resource Guide Ser.). 1978. lib. bdg. 20.00 (ISBN 0-8161-7895-X). G K Hall.
Huff, Theodore. An Index to the Films of Ernst Lubitsch. 1976. lib. bdg. 59.95 (ISBN 0-8490-2048-4). Gordon Pr.
Poague, Leland A. The Cinema of Ernst Lubitsch. LC 76-18481. (Illus.). 1978. 12.00 (ISBN 0-498-01958-6). A S Barnes.
Weinberg, Herman G. The Lubitsch Touch: A Critical Study. 3rd ed. 7.50 (ISBN 0-8446-5651-8). Peter Smith.
LUBRICATION AND LUBRICANTS
see also Bearings (Machinery); Fluid Film Bearings; Metal-Working Lubricants; Oils and Fats; Petroleum Products;
also names of lubricants
Applied Science Publishers Ltd London, ed. Metabolism of Hydrocarbons, Oils, Fuels & Lubricants. (Illus.). 1976. 50.40x (ISBN 0-85334-703-4). Intl Ideas.
BCC Staff. Fuel & Lubricant Additives. 1981. 950.00 (ISBN 0-89336-239-5, C-027). BCC.
Billett, M. G. A Handbook of Industrial Lubrication. 1979. 28.00 (ISBN 0-08-024232-4). Pergamon.
Boner, C. J. Gear & Transmission Lubricants. LC 64-18674. 510p. 1971. Repr. of 1964 ed. 25.00 (ISBN 0-88275-005-4). Krieger.
--Manufacture & Application of Lubricating Greases. LC 54-11031. 986p. 1971. Repr. of 1954 ed. 35.50 (ISBN 0-88275-006-2). Krieger.
--Modern Lubricating Greases. LC 75-18294. (Illus.). 250p. 1976. ref. ed. 35.00x (ISBN 0-87936-002-X). Scholium Intl.
Cameron, A. Principles of Lubrication. 2nd ed. Date not set. text ed. price not set (ISBN 0-582-47000-5). Longman.
Cameron, A., ed. Basic Lubrication Theory. 3rd ed. (Series in Engineering Science: Civil Engineering). 256p. 1981. 34.95 (ISBN 0-470-27187-6). Halsted Pr.
Cameron, Alastair. Basic Lubrication Theory. 2nd ed. LC 76-48204. 1977. 38.95 (ISBN 0-470-99020-1). Halsted Pr.
Cheng, H. S. & Keer, L. M., eds. Solid Contact & Lubrication. (AMD: Vol. 39). 248p. 1980. 30.00 (ISBN 0-686-69861-4, G00172). ASME.
Clauss, Francis J. Solid Lubricants & Self-Lubricating Solids. 1972. 39.00 (ISBN 0-12-176150-9). Acad Pr.
Drew, H. M. Metal-Based Lubricant Compositions. LC 75-2945. (Chemical Technology Review Ser: No. 48). (Illus.). 350p. (Index of patents, inventors, companies). 1975. 36.00 (ISBN 0-8155-0577-9). Noyes.
Fuller, Dudley D. Theory & Practice of Lubrication for Engineers. LC 56-6483. 1956. 46.00 (ISBN 0-471-28710-5, Pub. by Wiley-Interscience). Wiley.

Gross, William & Matsch, Lee A. Fluid Film Lubrication. Vohr, John H. & Wildman, Manfred, eds. LC 80-36889. 773p. 1980. 38.50 (ISBN 0-471-08357-7, Pub. by Wiley-Interscience). Wiley.
Halliday, Kenneth R. The Lubrication Pocket Handbook. 1980. pap. 6.95x cancelled (ISBN 0-87201-439-8). Gulf Pub.
Hersey, Mayo D. Theory & Research in Lubrication: Foundations for Future Developments. 488p. 1966. text ed. 24.50 (ISBN 0-471-37346-X, Pub. by Wiley). Krieger.
Institute of Marine Engineers, Ministry of Defense. Lubrication - Successes & Failures. (Illus.). 70p. 1973. limp bdg. 10.55 (ISBN 0-900976-12-8, Pub. by Inst Marine Eng). Intl Schol Bk Serv.
International Symposium on Rolling Contact Fatigue & Tourett. Performance Testing of Lubricants. 1977. 62.50 (ISBN 0-85501-301-X). Heyden.
Lubricants. (Industrial Equipment & Supplies Ser.). 130p. 1979. 295.00 (ISBN 0-686-31548-0). Busn Trend.
McConnell, B. D., ed. Assessment of Lubricant Technology. 142p. 1972. pap. text ed. 20.00 (ISBN 0-685-30776-X, G00001). ASME.
McCue, C. F., et al, eds. Performance Testing of Lubricants for Automotive Engines & Transmissions. (Illus.). 1974. 42.00x (ISBN 0-85334-468-X). Intl Ideas.
O'Connor, J. J. & Boyd, J. Standard Handbook of Lubrication Engineering. (Illus.). 1968. 46.50 (ISBN 0-07-047605-5, P&RB). McGraw.
Olds, W. J. Lubricants, Cutting Fluids & Coolants. LC 72-83305. 1973. 19.95 (ISBN 0-8436-0812-9). CBI Pub.
Postnikov, S. N. Electrophysical & Electrochemical Phenomena in Friction, Cutting, & Lubrication. Teague, Ben, tr. 1978. text ed. 21.50x (ISBN 0-442-26624-3). Van Nos Reinhold.
Ranney, M. W. Synthetic Oils & Greases for Lubricants-Recent Developments. LC 76-9487. (Chemical Technology Review: No. 72). (Illus.). 1976. 39.00 (ISBN 0-8155-0624-4). Noyes.
Rohde, S. M. & Cheng, H. S., eds. Surface Roughness Effects in Hydrodymanic & Mixed Lubrication. 211p. 1980. 30.00 (ISBN 0-686-69862-2, G00193). ASME.
Schilling, A. Automobile Engine Lubrication. (Illus.). 480p. 1972. text ed. 50.00x (ISBN 0-900645-00-8). Scholium Intl.
Single Cylinder Engine Tests for Evaluating Performance of Crankcase Lubricants. 1972. pap. 5.00 (ISBN 0-8031-0074-4, STP509). ASTM.
Synthetic Lubricants C-011. 1979. 650.00 (ISBN 0-89336-118-6). BCC.
Tipei, Nicolae. Theory of Lubrication: With Applications to Liquid & Gas-Film Lubrication. Gross, William A., ed. 1962. 22.00x (ISBN 0-8047-0028-1). Stanford U Pr.
Wills. Lubrication Fundamentals. (Mechanical Engineering Ser.: Vol. 3). 1980. 39.50 (ISBN 0-8247-6976-7). Dekker.
Zuidema, H. H. Performance of Lubricating Oils. 2nd ed. LC 52-8017. (ACS Monograph: No. 143). 1959. 22.00 (ISBN 0-8412-0283-4). Am Chemical.

LUCAN, GEORGE CHARLES BINGHAM, 3RD EARL OF, 1800-1888
Woodham-Smith, Cecil. Reason Why. 1960. pap. 5.50 (ISBN 0-525-47053-0). Dutton.

LUCANIA-SOCIAL LIFE AND CUSTOMS
Levi, Carlo. Christ Stopped at Eboli. Frenaye, Frances, tr. from It. 263p. 1947. pap. 5.95 (ISBN 0-374-50316-8, N250). FS&G.

LUCANUS, MARCUS ANNAEUS
Ahl, Frederick M. Lucan: An Introduction. LC 75-16926. (Studies in Classical Philology: Vol. 39). 416p. 1976. 27.50x (ISBN 0-8014-0837-7). Cornell U Pr.
Gotoff, Harold C. Transmission of the Text of Lucan in the Ninth Century. LC 72-133212. (Loeb Classical Monographs Ser). 1971. 12.50x (ISBN 0-674-90646-4). Harvard U Pr.

LUCAS, EDWARD VERRALL, 1868-1938
Lucas, Audrey. E. V. Lucas: A Portrait. LC 78-86040. (Illus.). 1969. Repr. of 1939 ed. 12.00 (ISBN 0-8046-0624-2). Kennikat.
--E. V. Lucas: A Portrait. 1939. Repr. 20.00 (ISBN 0-8274-2321-7). R West.

LUCCA
Meek, Christine. Lucca, Thirteen Sixty-Nine to Fourteen Hundred: Politics & Society in an Early Renaissance City-State. (Oxford Historical Monographs). 438p. 1978. text ed. 45.00x (ISBN 0-19-821866-4). Oxford U Pr.

LUCE, CLARE BOOTHE, 1903-
see Boothe, Clare, 1903-

LUCE, HENRY ROBINSON, 1898-1967
Cort, David. The Sin of Henry R. Luce: An Anatomy of Journalism. 480p. 1974. 12.50 (ISBN 0-8184-0201-6). Lyle Stuart.
Swanberg, W. A. Luce & His Empire: A Biography. LC 73-162778. (Illus.). 448p. 1975. 12.50 (ISBN 0-684-12592-7, ScribT). Scribner.

LUCERNE (PLANT)
see Alfalfa

LUCERNE, LAKE
Frei, Hans. Lake Lucerne. (Panorama Bks.). (Illus., Fr.). 1966. 3.95 (ISBN 0-685-11286-1). French & Eur.

LUCIANO, CHARLES
Powell, Hickman. Lucky Luciano: His Amazing Trial & Wild Witnesses. Orig. Title: Ninety Nine Times Guilty. 338p. 1975. Repr. of 1939 ed. 7.95 (ISBN 0-8065-0493-5). Citadel Pr.
--Ninety Times Guilty. LC 73-11909. (Metropolitan America Ser.). 356p. 1974. Repr. 17.00 (ISBN 0-405-05411-4). Arno.

LUCIANUS SAMOSATENSIS
Allinson, Francis G. Lucian, Satirist & Artist. LC 63-10286. (Our Debt to Greece & Rome Ser). Repr. of 1930 ed. 7.50x (ISBN 0-8154-0010-1). Cooper Sq.
Baldwin, Barry. Studies in Lucian. LC 73-83516. 1974. 12.00 (ISBN 0-88866-524-5). Samuel Stevens.
Craig, Hardin. Written Word & Other Essays. LC 78-86008. (Essay & General Literature Index Reprint Ser). 1969. Repr. of 1953 ed. 10.00 (ISBN 0-8046-0551-3). Kennikat.
Goebel, Ulrich. Wortindex zur Heidlaufschen Ausgabe Des Lucindarius. (Ger.). 1976. pap. text ed. 24.00x (ISBN 90-6203-467-5). Humanities.
Oden, Robert A., Jr. Studies in Lucian's De Syria Dea. LC 76-54988. (Harvard Semitic Monograph). (Illus.). 1977. pap. 7.50 (ISBN 0-89130-123-2, 040015). Scholars Pr Ca.

LUCKY LADY (U. S. BOMBER)
Midlam, Don S. Flight of the Lucky Lady. (Illus.). 1954. 6.50 (ISBN 0-8323-0091-8). Binford.

LUCRETIUS CARUS, TITUS
Deutsch, Rosamund E. The Pattern of Sound in Lucretius. Commager, Steele, ed. LC 77-70763. (Latin Poetry Ser.). 1979. Repr. of 1939 ed. lib. bdg. 21.00 (ISBN 0-8240-2967-4). Garland Pub.
Hadzsits, George D. Lucretius & His Influence. LC 63-10292. (Our Debt to Greece & Rome Ser). Repr. of 1930 ed. 27.50x (ISBN 0-8154-0106-X). Cooper Sq.
Holland, Louise A. Lucretius & the Transpadanes. LC 79-1415. 1979. 15.00 (ISBN 0-691-06401-6). Princeton U Pr.
Lucretius. De Rerum Natura. Kenney, Ed, ed. (Cambridge Greek & Latin Classics Ser.: Bk. 3). 42.00 (ISBN 0-521-08142-4); pap. 11.95x (ISBN 0-521-29177-1). Cambridge U Pr.
Minadeo, Richard. The Lyre of Science: Form & Meaning in Lucretius' De Rerum Natura. LC 68-28364. 1969. 10.95x (ISBN 0-8143-1361-2). Wayne St U Pr.
Nichols, James H., Jr. Epicurean Political Philosophy: The "De Rerum Nature" of Lucretius. LC 75-36993. 216p. 1976. 18.50x (ISBN 0-8014-0993-4). Cornell U Pr.
Roberts, Louis. A Concordance of Lucretius. Commager, Steele, ed. LC 77-70759. (Latin Poetry Ser.). 1977. lib. bdg. 39.00 (ISBN 0-8240-2978-X). Garland Pub.
Santayana, George. Three Philosophical Poets. LC 74-134467. 1971. Repr. of 1910 ed. lib. bdg. 11.00x (ISBN 0-8154-0361-5). Cooper Sq.
Sikes, Edward E. Lucretius, Poet & Philosopher. LC 76-139477. 1971. Repr. of 1936 ed. 12.00 (ISBN 0-8462-1410-5). Russell.
Snyder, Jane. Puns & Poetry in Lucretius De Rerum Natura. 1980. text ed. 28.50 (ISBN 90-6032-124-3). Humanities.

LUDDITES
Darvall, Frank O. Popular Disturbances & Public Order in Regency England. LC 68-58973. Repr. of 1934 ed. lib. bdg. 17.50x (ISBN 0-678-00458-7). Kelley.
The Luddites: Eighteen Twelve to Eighteen Thirty-Nine. LC 72-2533. (British Labour Struggles Before 1850 Ser). 18.00 (ISBN 0-405-04426-7). Arno.
Peel, F. Rising of the Luddites, Chartists and Plug-Drawers. 4th ed. (Illus.). 348p. 1968. 27.50x (ISBN 0-7146-1350-9, F Cass Co). Biblio Dist.
Peel, Frank. Risings of the Luddites, Chartists & Plug-Drawers. 3rd ed. LC 68-21440. (Illus.). Repr. of 1895 ed. 25.00x (ISBN 0-678-05013-9). Kelley.
Thomis, Malcolm I. The Luddites: Machine-Breaking in Regency England. LC 72-80042. (Studies in the Libertarian & Utopian Tradition). (Illus.). 196p. 1972. pap. 3.95 (ISBN 0-8052-0369-9). Schocken.

LUDENDORFF, ERICH VON, 1865-1937
Ludendorff, Erich Von. Ludendorff's Own Story, 2 vols. facsimile ed. LC 72-165647. (Select Bibliographies Reprint Ser). Repr. of 1920 ed. Set. 50.00 (ISBN 0-8369-5956-6). Arno.
Parkinson, Roger. Tormented Warrior. LC 78-24691. (Illus.). 1979. 12.95 (ISBN 0-8128-2597-7). Stein & Day.
Tschuppik, Karl. Ludendorff: The Tragedy of a Military Mind. Johnston, W. H., tr. from Ger. LC 74-14118. (Illus.). 1975. Repr. of 1932 ed. lib. bdg. 16.75x (ISBN 0-8371-7788-X, TSLU). Greenwood.

LUDI SAECULARES
see Secular Games

LUDICROUS, THE
see Comic, The; Wit and Humor

LUDLOW, JOHN MALCOLM FORBES, 1821-1911
Murray, A. D., ed. The Autobiography of John Ludlow, Christian Socialist. Date not set. 30.00x (ISBN 0-7146-3085-3, F Cass Co). Biblio Dist.

LUDRUK
Here are entered general works, and those that deal solely with the presentation of Ludruk plays on the stage.
Peacock, James L. Rites of Modernization: Symbolic & Social Aspects of Indonesian Proletarian Drama. LC 68-15931. (Symbolic Anthropology Ser: Vol. 1). (Illus.). 1968. 12.75x (ISBN 0-226-65130-4). U of Chicago Pr.

LUDWICK, CHRISTOPHER, 1720-1801
Rush, Benjamin. An Account of the Life & Character of Christopher Ludwick: Baker-General of the Army of the U.S. During the Revolutionary War. 1972. Repr. of 1831 ed. 15.50x (ISBN 0-8422-8133-9). Irvington.

LUDWIG, OTTO, 1813-1865
McClain, William H. Between Real & Ideal: Course of Otto Ludwig's Development As a Narrative Writer. LC 72-181951. (North Carolina. University. Studies in the Germanic Languages & Literatures: No. 40). Repr. of 1963 ed. 18.50 (ISBN 0-404-50940-1). AMS Pr.

LUESCHER TEST
see Luscher Test

LUGANDA LANGUAGE
see Ganda Language

LUGARD, FREDERICK JOHN DEALTRY, BARON, 1858-1945
Kirk-Greene, A H., ed. Lugard & the Amalgamation of Nigeria: A Documentary Record. 281p. 1968. 32.50x (ISBN 0-7146-1685-0, F Cass Co). Biblio Dist.

LUGBARA (AFRICAN TRIBE)
see Logbara (African Tribe)

LUIS DE GRANADA, 1504-1588
Brentano, Sr. Mary B. Nature in the Works of Fray Luis De Granada. LC 75-94164. (Catholic University. Studies in Romance Languages & Literatures: No. 15). Repr. of 1936 ed. 16.50 (ISBN 0-404-50315-2). AMS Pr.
Hagedorn, Maria. Reformation und Spanische Andachtsliteratur. 1934. pap. 10.00 (ISBN 0-384-20770-7). Johnson Repr.
Moore, John A. Fray Luis De Granada. (World Authors Ser.: No. 438). 1977. lib. bdg. 12.50 (ISBN 0-8057-6276-0). Twayne.

LUISENO LANGUAGE
Hyde, Villiana. An Introduction to the Luiseno Language. 1971. pap. 7.50 (ISBN 0-686-11772-7). Malki Mus Pr.

LUKACS, GEORG, 1885-1971
Arato, Andrew & Breines, Paul. The Young Lukacs & the Origins of Western Marxism. 1979. 16.50 (ISBN 0-8164-9359-6). Continuum.
Bahr, Ehrhard & Kunzer, Ruth G. Georg Lukacs. LC 70-190350. (Modern Literature Ser.). 1972. 10.95 (ISBN 0-8044-2014-9). Ungar.
Goldmann, Lucien. Lukacs & Heidegger: Towards a New Philosophy. Boelhower, William Q., tr. 1979. pap. 7.95 (ISBN 0-7100-8794-2). Routledge & Kegan.
--Lukacs & Heidegger: Towards a New Philosophy. Boelhower, William Q., tr. 15.00x (ISBN 0-7100-8625-3). Routledge & Kegan.
Kiralyfalvi, Bela. The Aesthetics of Gyorgy Lukacs. LC 74-22401. (Essays in Literature Ser.). 180p. 1975. 14.50 (ISBN 0-691-07205-1). Princeton U Pr.
Lowy, Michael. Georg Lukacs: From Romanticism to Bolshevism. 220p. 1980. 24.75 (ISBN 0-86091-003-2, Pub. by NLB). Schocken.
Meszaros, I. Lukacs' Concept of Dialectic: With Biography, Bibliography & Documents. (Illus.). 211p. 1972. text ed. 8.25x (ISBN 0-85036-159-1). Humanities.
Meszaros, Istvan. Lukacs' Concept of Dialect. (Illus.). pap. 4.95 (ISBN 0-686-23497-9, Merlin Pr). Carrier Pigeon.
Murphy, P. Writings by & About Georg Lukacs: A Bibliography. 1976. 1.00 (ISBN 0-89977-032-0). Am Inst Marxist.
Parkinson, George H. Georg Lukacs. 1977. 16.00x (ISBN 0-7100-8678-4). Routledge & Kegan.
Pinkus, Theo, ed. Conversations with Lukacs. LC 74-34021. 1975. pap. 4.95 (ISBN 0-262-66044-X). MIT Pr.

LUKE, FRANK, 1887-1918
Hall, Norman S. Balloon Buster: Frank Luke of Arizona. LC 70-169420. (Literature & History of Aviation Ser). 1972. Repr. of 1928 ed. 12.00 (ISBN 0-405-03765-1). Arno.

LUKE, SAINT
Brown, Robert. Luke: Doctor-Writer. (Illus.). (gr. 1-6). 1977. bds. 5.50 (ISBN 0-8054-4233-2). Broadman.
Hendriksen, William. Luke. (New Testament Commentary Ser.). 1978. 19.95 (ISBN 0-8010-4191-0). Baker Bk.
Jervell, Jacob. Luke & the People of God: A New Look at Luke-Acts. LC 72-78565. 208p. 1979. pap. 6.50 (ISBN 0-8066-1730-6, 10-4136). Augsburg.
Marshall, I. Howard. Luke: Historian & Theologian. (Contemporary Evangelical Perspective Ser). 1971. kivar 6.95 (ISBN 0-310-28761-8). Zondervan.
Ramsay, William M. Luke the Physician. (William M. Ramsay Library Ser.). 1979. pap. 6.95 (ISBN 0-8010-7683-8). Baker Bk.
Robertson, A. T. Luke the Historian in the Light of Research. 1977. pap. 3.95 (ISBN 0-8054-1365-0). Broadman.

LUKENS, THEODORE PARKER, 1848-1918
Sargent, Shirley. Theodore Parker Lukens: Father of Forestry. (Illus.). 1969. 10.00 (ISBN 0-87093-080-X). Dawsons.

LULL, RAMON, d. 1315
Brophy, Liam. So Great a Lover. 1960. 2.50 (ISBN 0-8199-0132-6, L38815). Franciscan Herald.
Hillgarth, J. N. Ramon Lull & Lullism in Fourteenth-Century France. (Oxford-Warburg Ser.). 1971. 75.00x (ISBN 0-19-824348-0). Oxford U Pr.
Peers, Edgar A. Ramon Lull: A Biography. LC 77-76019. (Bibliography & Reference Ser.: No. 266). 1969. Repr. of 1929 ed. 29.50 (ISBN 0-8337-2706-0). B Franklin.
--Ramon Lull, Biography. 1980. lib. bdg. 75.00 (ISBN 0-8490-3186-9). Gordon Pr.
Sala-Molins, Louis. La Philosophie De L'amour Chez Raymond Lulle. (Illus.). 1974. pap. 32.50x (ISBN 90-2797-301-6). Mouton.

LULLABIES
see Children'S Songs

LUMBAR PUNCTURE
see Spine-Puncture

LUMBER
see also Hardwoods; Sawmills; Timber; Wood; Woodwork;
also kinds of lumber
Hackenberg, Larry M. The Green Wood House: How to Build & Own a Beautiful,Inexpensive House. rev. ed. LC 75-33166. 1978. 9.75x (ISBN 0-8139-0646-6). U Pr of Va.
Handy Lumber Table. pap. 0.25 (ISBN 0-686-65405-6). Bennett IL.
More, Richard. The Carpenters Rule to Measure Ordinarie Timber. LC 74-26026. (English Experience Ser.: No. 252). 56p. 1970. Repr. of 1602 ed. 8.00 (ISBN 90-221-0252-1). Walter J Johnson.
Seddon, Leigh. Low-Cost Green Lumber Construction. (Illus.). 220p. 1981. pap. 8.95 (ISBN 0-88266-250-3). Garden Way Pub.
Willis, W. E. Timber from Forest to Consumer. LC 75-415006. (Illus.). 1968. 11.25x (ISBN 0-510-48011-X). Intl Pubns Serv.

LUMBER-TRANSPORTATION
see Logging Railroads

LUMBER CAMPS
Dye, Rex J. & Dye, Jacob. Lumber Camp Life in Michigan: An Autobiographical Account. 1975. 5.00 (ISBN 0-682-48102-5, Lochinvar). Exposition.

LUMBER TRADE
see also Lumbering; Timber; Woodwork
Amigo, Eleanor & Neuffer, Mark. Beyond the Adirondacks: The Story of St. Regis Paper Company. LC 80-1798. (Contributions in Economics & Economic History: No. 35). (Illus.). xi, 219p. 1980. lib. bdg. 22.95 (ISBN 0-313-22735-7, AFN/). Greenwood.
Carranco, Lynwood. The Redwood Lumber Industry of Northern California. (Illus.). 250p. 32.95 (ISBN 0-87095-084-3). Golden West.
Chaplin, R., et al. Centralia Case: Three Views of the Armistice Day Tragedy at Centralia, Washington, November 11, 1919. LC 77-160845. (Civil Liberties in American History Ser). 1971. Repr. of 1924 ed. lib. bdg. 29.50 (ISBN 0-306-70211-8). Da Capo.
Clawson, Marion. Decision Making in Timber Production, Harvest, & Marketing. LC 77-84930. (Resources for the Future, R-4 Research Paper). 1977. pap. text ed. 5.75x (ISBN 0-8018-2048-0). Johns Hopkins.
Economic Problems of the Lumber Industry. 1965. 0.65 (ISBN 0-686-20728-9). SUNY Environ.
Ficken, Robert E. Lumber & Politics: The Career of Mark E. Reed. LC 78-21756. (Illus.). 276p. 1980. 14.95 (ISBN 0-295-95655-0). U of Wash Pr.

Fickle, James E. The New South & the "New Competition". A Case Study of Trade Association Development in the Southern Pine Industry. LC 80-12420. 300p. 1980. 17.50 (ISBN 0-252-00788-3). U of Ill Pr.

Fox, William F. History of the Lumber Industry in the State of New York. LC 76-7561. (Illus.). 1976. Repr. of 1901 ed. 13.95 (ISBN 0-916346-23-4). Harbor Hill Bks.

Hanft, Robert M. Red River: Paul Bunyan's Own Lumber Company & Its Railroads. LC 79-53190. (Illus.). 304p. 32.50 (ISBN 0-9602894-5-3). CSU Ctr Busn Econ.

Heavrin, Charles A. Baskets, Boxes & Boards: A History of Anderson-Tully Company. (Illus.). 144p. 1981. 14.95 (ISBN 0-87870-206-7). Memphis St Univ.

Jensen, Vernon H. Lumber & Labor. LC 74-156444. (American Labor Ser., No. 2). 1971. Repr. of 1945 ed. 17.00 (ISBN 0-405-02928-4). Arno.

Lillard, Richard G. The Great Forest. LC 72-8129. (Illus.). 452p. 1973. Repr. of 1947 ed. lib. bdg. 39.50 (ISBN 0-306-70534-6). Da Capo.

Louden, Louise. Toxicity of Chemicals & Pulping Wastes to Fish. LC 79-64742. (Bibliographic Ser.: No. 265, Suppl. I). 1979. pap. 60.00 (ISBN 0-87010-058-0). Inst Paper Chem.

Lower, Arthur R. North American Assault on the Canadian Forest: A History of the Lumber Trade Between Canada & the United States. LC 68-57620. (Illus.). 1969. Repr. of 1938 ed. lib. bdg. 18.00x (ISBN 0-8371-0543-9, LOLT). Greenwood.

The Marketing of Tropical Wood: Wood Species from African Tropical Moist Forests. 60p. 1976. pap. 8.00 (ISBN 0-685-68962-X, F1029, FAO). Unipub.

Mead, Walter J. Competition & Oligopsony in the Douglas-Fir Lumber Industry. (Institute of Business & Economic Research, UC Berkeley). 1966. 25.00x (ISBN 0-520-00848-0). U of Cal Pr.

Moore, John H. Andrew Brown & Cypress Lumbering in the Old Southwest. LC 67-12216. (Illus.). 1967. 12.50x (ISBN 0-8071-0623-2). La State U Pr.

Outdoor Storage Forest Products. (Forty Ser). 1973. pap. 2.00 (ISBN 0-685-58157-8, 46). Natl Fire Prot.

Outdoor Storage of Logs. (Forty Ser). 1971. pap. 2.00 (ISBN 0-685-58159-4, 46B). Natl Fire Prot.

Outdoor Storage of Wood Chips. (Forty Ser). 1973. pap. 2.00 (ISBN 0-685-58158-6, 46A). Natl Fire Prot.

Production & Cost of Logging & Transport of Bamboo. (Swedish Funds-in-Trust Ser.: No. 157). (Illus.). 72p. 1975. pap. 7.50 (ISBN 0-685-57606-X, F1144, FAO). Unipub.

Retail & Wholesale Lumber Storage Yards. (Forty Ser). 1973. pap. 2.00 (ISBN 0-685-58156-X, 47). Natl Fire Prot.

Rumsey, Fay & Duerr, William A. Social Sciences in Forestry: A Book of Readings. LC 74-24518. (Illus.). 409p. 1975. pap. text ed. 9.95 (ISBN 0-7216-7839-4). HR&W.

Takeuchi, Kenji. Tropical Hardwood Trade in the Asia-Pacific Region. LC 74-4214. (World Bank Staff Occasional Paper Ser: No. 17). 108p. 1974. pap. 4.00x (ISBN 0-8018-1627-0). Johns Hopkins.

--Tropical Hardwood Trade in the Asia-Pacific Region. LC 74-4214. (World Bank Staff Occasional Paper Ser: No. 17). 108p. 1974. pap. 4.00x (ISBN 0-8018-1627-0). Johns Hopkins.

Thompson, Ben. A History of the Lumber Business at Davis, West Virginia. 1974. 3.00 (ISBN 0-87012-188-X). McClain.

Timber Trades Directory 1979. (Benn Directories Ser.). 1980. 56.00 (ISBN 0-510-49823-X, Pub by Benn Pubns). Nichols Pub.

Timber Trades Journal Special Issue 1980. (Benn Directories Ser.). 1980. 15.00 (ISBN 0-686-60669-8, Pub by Benn Pubns). Nichols Pub.

Timber Trades Journal Telephone Address Book 1980. (Benn Directories Ser.). 1980. write for info (Pub by Benn Pubns). Nichols Pub.

Todes, Charlotte. Labor & Lumber. facsimile ed. McCurry, Dan C. & Rubenstein, Richard E., eds. LC 74-30655. (American Farmers & the Rise of Agribusiness Ser.). (Illus.). 1975. Repr. of 1931 ed. 14.00x (ISBN 0-405-06830-1). Arno.

Van Syckle, Edwin. They Tried to Cut It All; Grays Harbor: Turbulent Years of Greed & Greatness. LC 80-16469. (Illus.). 308p. 1980. 17.95 (ISBN 0-9605152-0-8); pap. 9.95 (ISBN 0-9605152-1-6). Friends Aberdeen.

Williams, Richard L. The Loggers. (The Old West Ser.). (Illus.). 1976. 14.95 (ISBN 0-8094-1525-9). Time-Life.

Zaremba, Joseph. Economics of the American Lumber Industry. 1963. 7.95 (ISBN 0-8315-0025-5). Speller.

LUMBER TRADE–TABLES AND READY-RECKONERS

Moselle, Merritt. Practical Lumber Computer. 1956. pap. 4.00 (ISBN 0-910460-02-7). Craftsman.

LUMBERING

see also Lumber Camps; Lumber Trade; Woodworking Machinery

Allen, Alice B. Simon Benson: Northwest Lumber King. LC 77-157143. 1970. 12.50 (ISBN 0-8323-0047-0). Binford.

Andrews, Ralph W. Heroes of the Western Woods. (Illus.). 1979. pap. 6.95 (ISBN 0-87564-908-4). Superior Pub.

--This Was Logging. 1954. 17.95 (ISBN 0-87564-901-7). Superior Pub.

Birkeland, Torger. Echoes of Puget Sound: Fifty Years of Logging & Steamboating. (Illus.). 252p. pap. 20.00 (ISBN 0-8466-0315-2). Shorey.

Carranco, Lynwood & Labbe, John. Logging the Redwoods. LC 72-80989. (Illus.). 144p. 1975. boxed 17.95 (ISBN 0-87004-236-X). Caxton.

Cayford, John E. & Scott, Ronald E. Underwater Logging. LC 64-18585. (Illus.). 1964. pap. 3.00 (ISBN 0-87033-128-0). Cornell Maritime.

Clarkson, Roy B. Tumult on the Mountains: Lumbering in West Virginia,1770-1920. 1964. 18.00 (ISBN 0-87012-004-2). McClain.

Conway, Steve. Logging Practices: Principles of Timber Harvesting Systems. LC 74-20164. (A Forest Industries Book). (Illus.). 1976. 29.50 (ISBN 0-87930-038-8). Miller Freeman.

Davis, Richard C., compiled by. Inventory of the Records of the California State Council of Lumber & Sawmill Workers, AFL-CIO. 1976. pap. 1.25 (ISBN 0-89030-027-5). Forest Hist Soc.

Educational Research Council of America. Lumber Worker. rev. ed. Ferris, Theodore N. & Marchak, John P., eds. (Real People at Work Ser: K). (Illus.). 1980. pap. text ed. 2.25 (ISBN 0-89247-084-4). Changing Times.

Gibbs, Esther. We Went a Loggin' (Illus.). 128p. 1975. 4.95 (ISBN 0-87839-017-0); pap. 3.00 (ISBN 0-87839-021-9). North Star.

Hanlon, Howard A. Bull-Hunchers. (Illus.). 1970. 10.00 (ISBN 0-87012-042-5). McClain.

Hochschild, Harold K. Lumberjacks & Rivermen in the Central Adirondacks, 1850-1950. (Illus.). 1962. pap. 4.95 (ISBN 0-8156-8023-6, Pub. by Adirondack Museum). Syracuse U Pr.

Johnston, Hank. They Felled the Redwoods: A Saga of Rails and Flumes in the High Sierra. 3rd rev. ed. (Illus.). 1966. 15.00 (ISBN 0-87046-003-X). Trans-Anglo.

--Thunder in the Mountains. 15.00 (ISBN 0-87046-017-X). Trans-Anglo.

Knights of the Broadax. LC 79-57239. (Illus.). 198p. (Orig.). 1981. pap. 6.95 (ISBN 0-87004-283-1). Caxton.

Larson, Agnes M. History of the White Pine Industry in Minnesota. LC 72-2875. (Use & Abuse of America's Natural Resources Ser). (Illus.). 468p. 1972. Repr. of 1949 ed. 24.00 (ISBN 0-405-04516-6). Arno.

Lind, Carol J. Big Timber, Big Men: A History of Loggers in a New Land. (Resource Ser.). (Illus.). 1978. 15.00x (ISBN 0-87663-200-2, Pub. by Hancock Hse). Universe.

McCulloch, Walter F. Woods Words. 1977. pap. 9.95 (ISBN 0-88246-082-X). Oreg St U Bkstrs.

McGrail, Sean. Logboats of England & Wales with Comparative Material from European & Other Countries. (National Maritime Museum, Greenich, Archaeological Ser.: No. 2). 1978. 60.00x (ISBN 0-86054-026-X, Pub. by BAR). State Mutual Bk.

Marshall, Mel. Lumber, Plywood, Hardboards & Laminates -- How to Choose & Use Them. LC 79-4710. (A Popular Science Skill Bk.). (Illus.). 1980. pap. 4.95 (ISBN 0-06-090724-X, CN-724, HarpT). Har-Row.

Moore, John H. Andrew Brown & Cypress Lumbering in the Old Southwest. LC 67-12216. (Illus.). 1967. 12.50x (ISBN 0-8071-0623-2). La State U Pr.

Morton, James. The Enterprising Mr. Moody, the Bumptious Capt. Stamp: The Lives & Colourful Times of Vancouver's Lumber Pioneers. 14.50 (ISBN 0-88894-147-1, Pub. by Douglas & McIntyre). Intl Schol Bk Serv.

Nelligan, John E. White Pine Empire: The Life of a Lumberman. Sheridan, Charles M., ed. 1969. Repr. of 1927 ed. 7.50 (ISBN 0-87839-001-4). North Star.

Pearce, J. Kenneth & Stenzel, George. Logging & Pulpwood Production. 400p. 1972. 26.50 (ISBN 0-471-06839-X, Pub. by Wiley-Interscience). Wiley.

Pierre, Joseph H. When Timber Stood Tall. LC 79-21006. (Illus.). 192p. 1980. 19.95 (ISBN 0-87564-909-2). Superior Pub.

Pinchot, Gifford. Adirondack Spruce, a Study of the Forest in Ne-Ha-Sa-Ne Park. LC 77-125756. (American Environmental Studies). 1971. Repr. of 1907 ed. 10.00 (ISBN 0-405-02682-X). Arno.

Reports of the FAO-Norway Training Course on Logging Operations. 110p. 1980. pap. 8.00 (ISBN 0-686-68194-0, F1937, FAO). Unipub.

Resources for Freedom: A Report to the President by the President's Materials Policy Commission, June 1952, 2 vols. in 1. Bd. with Vol. 1. Foundations for Growth & Security; Vol. 4. The Promise of Technology. LC 72-2863. (Use & Abuse of America's Natural Resources Ser). 434p. 1972. Repr. of 1952 ed. 29.00 (ISBN 0-405-04533-6). Arno.

Shipping Marks on Timber 1979-81. (Benn Directories Ser.). 1979. 42.50 (ISBN 0-510-49824-8, Pub by Benn Pubns). Nichols Pub.

Smith, David C. A History of Lumbering in Maine, 1861-1960. 1972. 15.00 (ISBN 0-89101-024-6). U Maine Orono.

--Lumbering & the Maine Woods: A Bibliographical Guide. (Maine History Bibliographical Guide Ser.). 1971. pap. 4.00 (ISBN 0-915592-17-7). Maine Hist.

Swanholm, Marx. Lumbering in the Last of the White-Pine States. LC 78-14221. (Minnesota Historic Sites Pamphlet Ser.: No. 17). (Illus.). 34p. 1978. 2.00 (ISBN 0-87351-131-X). Minn Hist.

Taber, Thomas T. Logging Railroad Era of Lumbering in Pennsylvania, 3 vols. (Illus.). 1978. Set. 85.00x (ISBN 0-9603398-1-7). T T Taber.

Thunder in the Mountains. 17.95 (ISBN 0-685-83408-5). Chatham Pub CA.

Timber Trades Directory 1979. (Benn Directories Ser.). 1980. 56.00 (ISBN 0-510-49823-X, Pub by Benn Pubns). Nichols Pub.

Trzesniowski, A. Logging in the Mountains of Central Europe. (Illus.). 1976. pap. 7.50 (ISBN 0-685-68960-3, F1024, FAO). Unipub.

U. S. Dept. of Commerce & Labor-Bureau of Corporations. The Lumber Industry, 2 vols. in 1. Bd. with Pt. 1. Standing Timber. Repr. of 1913 ed; Pt. 2. Concentration of Timber Ownership in Important Selected Regions. Repr. of 1914 ed; Pt. 3. Land Holdings of Large Timber Owners (with Owner-Ship Maps) Repr. of 1914 ed. LC 72-2873. (Use & Abuse of America's Natural Resources Ser). 616p. 1972. Repr. of 1913 ed. 30.00 (ISBN 0-405-04540-9). Arno.

Wackerman, Albert E., et al. Harvesting Timber Crops. 2nd ed. (American Forestry Ser.). 1966. text ed. 20.00 (ISBN 0-07-067638-0, C). McGraw.

Webber, Bert. Swivel-Chair Logger. 1977. 12.00 (ISBN 0-87770-163-6); pap. 6.95 (ISBN 0-87770-174-1). Ye Galleon.

Whatcom Museum of History & Art. Green Gold Harvest: A History of Logging & Its Products. LC 72-10060. (Whatcom Museum Ser.). (Illus.). 78p. 1969. pap. 5.00 (ISBN 0-295-95577-5). U of Wash Pr.

When the Circus Came to Town. (Americana Books Ser.). (Illus.). 1969. 1.50 (ISBN 0-911410-23-6). Applied Arts.

Willis, W. E. Timber from Forest to Consumer. LC 75-415006. (Illus.). 1968. 11.25x (ISBN 0-510-48011-X). Intl Pubns Serv.

Wood, Richard G. A History of Lumbering in Maine, 1820-1861. 1972. 12.50 (ISBN 0-89101-023-8). U Maine Orono.

LUMBERING–JUVENILE LITERATURE

Abrams, Kathleen & Abrams, Lawrence. Logging & Lumbering. LC 80-19473. (Illus.). 96p. (gr. 4 up). 1980. PLB 7.79 (ISBN 0-671-34007-7). Messner.

John, Hughes. Larry the Logger. (People Working Today Ser). (Illus.). 40p. (gr. 7-12). 1975. pap. 1.85 (ISBN 0-915510-04-9). Janus Bks.

Newton, James R. Forest Log. LC 78-22515. (Illus.). 32p. (gr. 2-5). 1980. 6.95 (ISBN 0-690-04007-5, TYC-J); PLB 6.89 (ISBN 0-690-04008-3). Har-Row.

Williams, Richard. The Loggers. (The Old West). (Illus.). (gr. 5 up). 1976. kivar 12.96 (ISBN 0-8094-1527-5, Pub. by Time-Life). Silver.

LUMBERMEN

Allen, Ruth. East Texas Lumber Workers: An Economic & Social Picture, 1870-1950. (Illus.). 249p. 1961. 12.50x (ISBN 0-292-73219-8). U of Tex Pr.

Hochschild, Harold K. Lumberjacks & Rivermen in the Central Adirondacks, 1850-1950. (Illus.). 1962. pap. 4.95 (ISBN 0-8156-8023-6, Pub. by Adirondack Museum). Syracuse U Pr.

Hyman, Harold M. Soldiers & Spruce: Origins of the Loyal Legion of Loggers & Lumbermen. (Monograph Ser.: No. 10). 1963. 7.50 (ISBN 0-89215-011-4). U Cal LA Indus Rel.

Jensen, Vernon H. Lumber & Labor. LC 74-156444. (American Labor Ser., No. 2). 1971. Repr. of 1945 ed. 17.00 (ISBN 0-405-02928-4). Arno.

Knights of the Broadax. LC 79-57239. (Illus.). 198p. (Orig.). 1981. pap. 6.95 (ISBN 0-87004-283-1). Caxton.

Nelligan, John E. White Pine Empire: The Life of a Lumberman. Sheridan, Charles M., ed. 1969. Repr. of 1927 ed. 7.50 (ISBN 0-87839-001-4). North Star.

Pike, Robert E. Tall Trees, Tough Men. (Illus.). 1967. 14.95 (ISBN 0-393-07351-3). Norton.

Williams, Richard L. The Loggers. (The Old West Ser.). (Illus.). 1976. 14.95 (ISBN 0-8094-1525-9). Time-Life.

Wyman, Walker D. & Prentice, Lee. The Lumberjack Frontier. 88p. 1969. pap. 2.95 (ISBN 0-686-27296-X). U Pr Wisc River Falls.

LUMBERMEN–SONGS AND MUSIC

Fowke, Edith. Lumbering Songs from the Northern Woods. (American Folklore Society Memoir Ser.: No. 55). 246p. 1970. 9.95x (ISBN 0-292-70018-0). U of Tex Pr.

Ives, Edward D. Joe Scott, the Woodsman-Songmaker. LC 78-8149. (Music in American Life Ser.). 1978. 22.50 (ISBN 0-252-00683-6); cassette 6.95 (ISBN 0-252-00727-1). U of Ill Pr.

Morton, James. The Enterprising Mr. Moody, the Bumptious Capt. Stamp: The Lives & Colourful Times of Vancouver's Lumber Pioneers. 14.50 (ISBN 0-88894-147-1, Pub. by Douglas & McIntyre). Intl Schol Bk Serv.

LUMBWAS

see Kipsigis

LUMET, SIDNEY

Bowles, Stephen E. Sidney Lumet: A Guide to References & Resources. (Reference Books). 1979. lib. bdg. 15.50 (ISBN 0-8161-7938-7). G K Hall.

LUMINESCENCE

see also Bioluminescence; Electroluminescence; Fluorescence; Moessbauer Effect

Attix, Frank H., ed. Luminescence Dosimetry: Proceedings. LC 67-60038. (AEC Symposium Ser.). 532p. 1967. pap. 6.00 (ISBN 0-686-75828-5); microfiche 3.00 (ISBN 0-686-75829-3). DOE.

Barenboim, Grigory M., et al. Luminescence of Biopolymers & Cells. LC 68-26768. 229p. 1969. 29.50 (ISBN 0-306-30350-7, Plenum Pr). Plenum Pub.

Bowen, E. J., ed. Luminescence in Chemistry. (Physical Chemistry Ser). (Illus.). 1968. 16.95x (ISBN 0-442-00961-5). Van Nos Reinhold.

Cantow, H. J., et al, eds. Luminescence. (Advances in Polymer Science: Vol. 40). (Illus.). 200p. 1981. 42.90 (ISBN 0-387-10550-6). Springer-Verlag.

Dunitz, J. D., et al, eds. Luminescence & Energy Transfer. (Structure & Bonding Ser.: Vol. 42). (Illus.). 133p. 1981. 40.00 (ISBN 0-387-10395-3). Springer-Verlag.

Goldberg, Paul. Luminescence of Inorganic Solids. 1966. 81.00 (ISBN 0-12-287550-8). Acad Pr.

Hurtubise, Robert J. Solid Surface Luminescence Analysis. (Modern Monographs in Analytical Chemistry: Vol. 1). 288p. 1981. 37.50 (ISBN 0-8247-1265-X). Dekker.

International Conference on Luminescence, Budapest, 1966. Proceedings, 2 vols. 1968. Set. 75.00x (ISBN 0-8002-1848-5). Intl Pubns Serv.

International Symposium on Luminescence - the Physics & Chemistry of Scintillators, Munich, 1965. Proceedings. (Illus.). 1966. 25.00x (ISBN 0-8002-1870-1). Intl Pubns Serv.

Kemp, T. J. Luminescence Kinetics of Metal Complexes in Solution. (Illus.). 98p. 1980. pap. 20.50 (ISBN 0-08-027135-9). Pergamon.

Leverenz, Humboldt W. An Introduction to Luminescence of Solids. 8.50 (ISBN 0-8446-2456-X). Peter Smith.

Lumb, Michael, ed. Luminescence Spectroscopy. 1979. 70.50 (ISBN 0-12-459550-2). Acad Pr.

Mazing, M. A. Research on Spectroscopy & Luminescence, Part 2: On the Broadening & Shift of Spectral Lines in the Plasma of a Gaseous Discharge. LC 62-12860. (P. N. Lebedev Physics Institute Ser.: Vol. 15). 66p. 1962. 22.50 (ISBN 0-306-17042-6, Consultants). Plenum Pub.

Morawetz, Herbert & Steinberg, I. Z., eds. Luminescence from Biological & Synthetic Macromolecules. 414p. 1981. 80.00 (ISBN 0-89766-123-0); pap. write for info. (ISBN 0-89766-124-9). NY Acad Sci.

Shlyapintokh, V. Y., et al, eds. Chemiluminescence Techniques in Chemical Reactions. LC 68-16132. 222p. 1968. 32.50 (ISBN 0-306-10799-6, Consultants). Plenum Pub.

Skolbel'tsyn, D. V., ed. Soviet Researches on Luminescence. LC 64-7763. (P. N. Lebedev Phyiscs Institute Ser.: Vol. 23). 1964. 42.50 (ISBN 0-306-10685-X, Consultants). Plenum Pub.

Steiner, Robert F. & Weinryb, Ira, eds. Excited States of Proteins & Nucleic Acids. LC 75-138521. 478p. 1971. 49.50 (ISBN 0-306-30509-7, Plenum Pr). Plenum Pub.

Stepanov, B. I. & Gribkovskii, V. P. Theory of Luminescence. 1970. 89.25x (ISBN 0-677-61530-2). Gordon.

Sukhodrev, N. K. Research on Spectroscopy & Luminescence, Part 3: On Excitation Spectra in Spark Discharges. LC 62-12860. (P. N. Lebedev Physics Institute Ser.: Vol. 15). 53p. 1962. 22.50 (ISBN 0-306-17043-4, Consultants). Plenum Pub.

Waite, M. S. & Vecht, A. Phosphors. (Illus.). 320p. 1982. write for info. (Pub. by Peregrinus London). Inst Elect Eng.

Williams, E. W. & Hall, R. Luminescence & the Light Emitting Diode. LC 77-4427. 1978. text ed. 45.00 (ISBN 0-08-020442-2); pap. text ed. 17.00 (ISBN 0-08-020441-4). Pergamon.

Williams, Ferd, ed. Luminescence of Crystals, Molecules, & Solutions. LC 73-77339. 723p. 1973. 49.50 (ISBN 0-306-30736-7, Plenum Pr). Plenum Pub.

LUMINESCENCE ANALYSIS

see Fluorimetry; Phosphorimetry

LUMMI LANGUAGE

Gibbs, George. Alphabetical Vocabularies of the Clallam & Lumni. LC 75-168115. (Library of American Linguistics: No. 11). Repr. of 1863 ed. 10.00 (ISBN 0-404-50991-6). AMS Pr.

LUMMIS, CHARLES FLETCHER, 1859-1928

Bingham, Edwin R. Charles F. Lummis: Editor of the Southwest. LC 73-15058. (Illus.). 218p. 1974. Repr. of 1955 ed. lib. bdg. 12.25x (ISBN 0-8371-7149-0, BICL). Greenwood.

Fiske, Turbese L. & Lummis, Keith. Charles F. Lummis: The Man & His West. LC 74-15910. (Illus.). 250p. 1975. 17.50 (ISBN 0-8061-1228-X). U of Okla Pr.

Fleming, Robert E. Charles F. Lummis, No. 50. LC 81-67304. (Western Writers Ser.). (Illus.). 52p. (Orig.). 1981. pap. 2.00 (ISBN 0-88430-074-9). Boise St Univ.

Thrapp, Dan L., ed. Dateline Fort Bowie: Charles Fletcher Lummis Reports on an Apache War. LC 78-58091. (Illus.). 1979. 10.95 (ISBN 0-8061-1494-0). U of Okla Pr.

LUMPY SKIN DISEASE

Hanshaw, J. B. Cytomegloviruses. Bd. with Rinderpest Virus. Plowright, W; Lumpy Skin Disease. Weiss, K. E. (Virology Monographs: Vol. 3). (Illus.). iv, 131p. 1968. 19.50 (ISBN 0-387-80891-4). Springer-Verlag.

LUMUMBA, PATRICE, 1925-1961

Kanza, Thomas. The Rise & Fall of Patrice Lumumba. 386p. 1979. pap. text ed. 11.25x (ISBN 0-87073-901-8). Schenkman.

Maglangbayan, Shawna. Garvey, Lumumba, Malcolm: Black Nationalist-Separatists. 1972. 4.95 (ISBN 0-88378-022-4); pap. 2.95 (ISBN 0-88378-079-8). Third World.

Patrice Lumumba. 215p. 1976. pap. text ed. 4.95x (ISBN 0-8277-4841-8). British Bk Ctr.

LUNAR BASES

see also Moon–Exploration

Malina, F. J. Applied Sciences Research & Utilization of Lunar Resources. 1970. 50.00 (ISBN 0-08-015565-0). Pergamon.

LUNAR EXPEDITIONS

see Space Flight to the Moon

LUNAR EXPLORATION

see Moon–Exploration

LUNAR FLIGHT

see Space Flight to the Moon

LUNAR GEOLOGY

Analytical Methods Developed for Application to Lunar Sample Analysis. 156p. 1973. 15.00 (ISBN 0-8031-0124-4, 04-539000-38). ASTM.

Branley, Franklyn M. Pieces of Another World: The Story of Moon Rocks. LC 71-158684. (Illus.). (gr. 5-8). 1972. PLB 9.89 (ISBN 0-690-62566-9, TYC-J). Har-Row.

Chamberlain, Joseph, ed. Reviews of Lunar Sciences. 1977. pap. 15.00 (ISBN 0-87590-220-0). Am Geophysical.

Fielder, G. Geology & Physics of the Moon. 1972. 73.25 (ISBN 0-444-40924-6). Elsevier.

Frondel, Judith W. Lunar Mineralogy. LC 75-9786. 323p. 1975. 37.50 (ISBN 0-471-28289-8, Pub. by Wiley-Interscience). Wiley.

Gallob, Edward. City Rocks, City Blocks & the Moon. LC 73-1333. (Illus.). 48p. (gr. 3-7). 1973. reinforced bdg. 6.95 (ISBN 0-684-13542-6, ScribJ). Scribner.

Green, Jack, ed. Geological Problems in Lunar & Planetary Research. (Science & Technology Ser.: Vol. 25). (Illus.). 1971. lib. bdg. 45.00 (ISBN 0-87703-056-1). Am Astronaut.

--Interpretation of Lunar Probe Data. (Science & Technology Ser.: Vol. 14). 1967. 25.00 (ISBN 0-87703-042-1). Am Astronaut.

Guest, J. E. & Greeley, R. Geology on the Moon. LC 77-371984. (Wykeham Science Ser.: No. 43). 1977. 17.95x (ISBN 0-8448-1170-X); pap. 12.50x (ISBN 0-8448-1346-X). Crane-Russak Co.

Karr, Clarence, ed. Infrared & Raman Spectroscopy of Lunar & Terrestrial Minerals. 1975. 63.00 (ISBN 0-12-399950-2). Acad Pr.

Kopal, Z. & Goudas, C. L. Measure of the Moon. 1967. 96.75 (ISBN 0-677-11850-3). Gordon.

Levinson, A. A. & Taylor, Ross. Moon Rocks & Minerals. 240p. 1976. text ed. 31.00 (ISBN 0-08-016669-5). Pergamon.

Lindsay, J. Lunar Stratigraphy & Sedimentology. 1976. 46.50 (ISBN 0-444-41443-6). Elsevier.

Lunar & Flanetary Science Conference, 9th, Houston, 1978. Proceedings, 3 vols. Lunar & Planetary Institute, Houston, Texas, compiled by. (Geochimica et Cosmochimicha Acta: Suppl. 10). 1979. Set. 245.00 (ISBN 0-08-022966-2). Pergamon.

Lunar & Planetary Institute. Proceedings of the Conference on the Lunar Highlands Crust: Houston, Texas, USA, 14-16 November 1979. 550p. 1980. 52.00 (ISBN 0-08-026304-6). Pergamon.

Lunar & Planetary Institute, Houston, Texas, U. S. A., ed. Proceedings of the Conference on Multi-Ring Basins. 300p. 1981. 35.01 (ISBN 0-08-028045-5). Pergamon.

Lunar Science Conference, 8th, Houston, 1977. Proceedings. Lunar Science Institute, Houston, Texas, compiled by. (Lunar Science Ser.: No. 8). (Illus.). 1978. 255.00 (ISBN 0-08-022052-5). Pergamon.

Mutch, Thomas A. Geology of the Moon: A Stratigraphic View. rev. ed. LC 79-83687. 1973. 37.50x (ISBN 0-691-08110-7). Princeton U Pr.

Randall, Charles A., ed. Extra-Terrestrial Matter. LC 69-15447. (Illus.). 331p. 1969. 15.00 (ISBN 0-87580-009-2). N Ill U Pr.

Sekiguchi, Naosuke. Catalogue of Central Peaks & Floor Objects of the Lunar Craters on the Visible Hemisphere. (Illus.). 1972. 75.00 (ISBN 0-8391-0649-1). Univ Park.

Short, Nicholas M. Planetary Geology. (Illus.). 384p. 1975. ref. ed. 31.95 (ISBN 0-13-679290-1). P-H.

LUNAR PROBES

see also Project Ranger

Green, Jack, ed. Interpretation of Lunar Probe Data. (Science & Technology Ser.: Vol. 14). 1967. 25.00 (ISBN 0-87703-042-1). Am Astronaut.

LUNAR SOCIETY, BIRMINGHAM, ENGLAND

Priestley, Joseph. Scientific Correspondence: Ninety-Seven Letters. LC 5-5452. 1968. Repr. of 1892 ed. 18.00 (ISBN 0-527-72728-8). Kraus Repr.

LUNAR SURFACE VEHICLES

see Moon Cars

LUNAR THEORY

see Moon, Theory Of

LUNATIC ASYLUMS

see Psychiatric Hospitals

LUNCH ROOMS

see Restaurants, Lunchrooms, etc.

LUNCHEONS

Barbour, Beverly. Easy, Elegant Luncheon Menus. (Illus.). 1980. 14.95 (ISBN 0-8019-6831-3). Chilton.

Blair, Eulalia C. Luncheon & Supper Dishes for Foodservice Menu Planning. LC 72-92379. (Foodservice Menu Planning Ser.). 1973. 17.95 (ISBN 0-8436-0559-6). CBI Pub.

Durand, Pauline & Languirand, Yolande. Brunch: Great Ideas for Planning, Cooking & Serving. LC 77-21616. 1978. pap. text ed. 2.95 (ISBN 0-8120-0726-3). Barron.

Macpherson, Ruth. Discover Brunch: A New Way of Entertaining. new ed. (Illus.). 1977. spiral bdg. 6.95 (ISBN 0-8437-2110-3). Hammond Inc.

Ser-Vol-Tel Institute. Luncheon Cooking. (Foodservice Career Education Ser.). 1974. pap. 4.95 (ISBN 0-8436-2031-5). CBI Pub.

Smirnoff Brunch Book. 5.95 (ISBN 0-87502-017-8); pap. 1.95 (ISBN 0-87502-092-5). Benjamin Co.

Super Lunch. pap. 0.50 (ISBN 0-685-81432-7); tchrs' ed 0.50 (ISBN 0-685-81433-5). Folk Art.

LUND, ERIC

Lund, Doris. Eric. LC 74-7061. 1974. 11.95 (ISBN 0-397-01046-X). Har-Row.

LUNDA (BANTU TRIBE)

Bustin, Edouard. Lunda Under Belgian Rule: The Politics of Ethnicity. (Illus.). 462p. 1975. text ed. 16.50x (ISBN 0-674-53953-2). Harvard U Pr.

Cunnison, Ian G. Luapula Peoples of Northern Rhodesia. 1959. text ed. 18.25 (ISBN 0-7190-1015-2). Humanities.

LUNDY, BENJAMIN, 1789-1839

Dillon, Merton L. Benjamin Lundy & the Struggle for Negro Freedom. LC 66-15473. 1966. 17.50 (ISBN 0-252-72748-7). U of Ill Pr.

LUNG FUNCTION TESTS

see Pulmonary Function Tests

LUNGS

see also Respiration

Bohlig. Lung & Pleura. 1980. 12.95 (ISBN 0-8151-1016-2). Year Bk Med.

Bonsignore, G. & Cumming, G., eds. The Lung in Its Environment. (Ettore Majorana International Science (Life Sciences) Ser.: Vol. 6). 526p. 1981. text ed. price not set (ISBN 0-306-40742-6, Plenum Pr). Plenum Pub.

Bouhuys, A., ed. Lung Cells in Disease: Brooke Lodge Conference, 1976. 1976. 53.75 (ISBN 0-7204-0589-0, North-Holland). Elsevier.

Ciba Foundation. Lung Liquids. (CIBA Foundation Symposium Ser.: No. 38). 1976. 33.75 (ISBN 0-444-15204-0, Excerpta Medica). Elsevier.

Comroe, Julius H., Jr., et al. The Lung: Clinical Physiology & Pulmonary Function Tests. 2nd ed. (Illus.). 1962. 19.00 (ISBN 0-8151-1821-X). Year Bk Med.

Crystal, Ronald, ed. The Biochemical Basis of Pulmonary Function. (Lung Biology in Health & Disease: Vol.2). 560p. 1976. 57.50 (ISBN 0-8247-6363-7). Dekker.

Dempsey, Jerome A. & Reed, Charles E., eds. Exercise & the Lung. 1977. 35.00x (ISBN 0-299-07220-7). U of Wis Pr.

Edge, J. R., et al. The Aging Lung: Normal Function. LC 73-1458. 1974. 19.00x (ISBN 0-8422-7165-1). Irvington.

Forgacs, Paul. Lung Sounds. (Illus.). 1978. text ed. 15.95 (ISBN 0-02-857750-7). Macmillan.

Fraser, Robert G. & Pare, J. A. Organ Physiology: Structure & Function of the Lung with Emphasis on Roentgenology. 2nd ed. LC 76-20933. (Illus.). 1977. text ed. 9.50 (ISBN 0-7216-3859-7). Saunders.

Freundlich. Pulmonary Masses, Cysts & Cavities: A Radiologic Approach. Date not set. price not set (ISBN 0-8151-3330-8). Year Bk Med.

Frownfelter, Donna L. Chest Physical Therapy & Pulmonary Rehabilitation. (Illus.). 1978. 21.50 (ISBN 0-8151-3296-4). Year Bk Med.

Green, Jerry F. Mechanical Concepts in Cardiovascular & Pulmonary Physiology. LC 77-23965. (Illus.). 166p. 1977. pap. 10.00 (ISBN 0-8121-0598-2). Lea & Febiger.

Grodins, Fred S. & Yamashiro, Stanley M. Respiratory Function of the Lung & Its Control. (Illus.). 176p. 1978. text ed. 13.50 (ISBN 0-02-348190-0); pap. text ed. 9.95 (ISBN 0-686-71603-5). Macmillan.

--Respiratory Function of the Lung & Its Control. (Illus.). 1978. text ed. 13.50 (ISBN 0-02-348190-0); pap. text ed. 9.95 (ISBN 0-02-348120-X). Macmillan.

Hirsch, Edwin F. & Kaiser, George C. The Innervation of the Lung. (Illus.). 116p. 1969. photocopy ed. spiral 14.50 (ISBN 0-398-00842-6). C C Thomas.

Hodson, W. A. Development of the Lung. (Lung Biology in Health & Disease: Vol. 6). 1977. 55.00 (ISBN 0-8247-6377-7). Dekker.

Holman, B. L. Regional Pulmonary Function in Health & Disease. 1973. 44.50 (ISBN 0-8391-0542-8). Univ Park.

Hornbein. Regulation of Breathing, Pt. 1. (Lung Biology in Health & Disease Ser.: Vol. 17). 1981. 69.50 (ISBN 0-8247-6607-5). Dekker.

Hughes, G. M. The Vertebrate Lung. rev. ed. Head, J. J., ed. LC 77-75590. (Carolina Biology Readers Ser.). (Illus.). (gr. 11-12). 1979. pap. 1.65 (ISBN 0-89278-259-5, 45-9659). Carolina Biological.

Junod, Alain F. & DeHaller, Rodolphe, eds. Lung Metabolism: Proteolysis & Antiproteolysis, Biochemical Pharmacology, Handling of Bioactive Substances. 1976. 46.00 (ISBN 0-12-392250-X). Acad Pr.

Kirkpatrick & Reynolds. Immunologis & Infectious Reactions in the Lung. (Lung Biology in Health & Disease Ser.: Vol. 1). 1976. 62.50 (ISBN 0-8247-6306-8). Dekker.

Levitzky, M. G. Pulmonary Phusiology. 1982. price not set (ISBN 0-07-037431-7). McGraw.

Mandell, Charles H. Scintillation Camera Lung Imaging: An Anatomic Atlas & Guide. LC 76-16057. 208p. 1976. 49.00 (ISBN 0-8089-0960-6). Grune.

Miller, William S. The Lung. 2nd ed. (Illus.). 240p. 1950. photocopy ed. spiral 23.75 (ISBN 0-398-04363-9). C C Thomas.

Murray, John F. The Normal Lung: The Basis for Diagnosis & Treatment of Pulmonary Disease. LC 74-25480. (Illus.). 335p. 1976. text ed. 17.50 (ISBN 0-7216-6612-4). Saunders.

Nagaishi, C. Functional Anatomy & Histology of the Lung. (Illus.). 1975. 98.50 (ISBN 0-8391-0580-0). Univ Park.

Pickrell, John A., ed. Lung Connective Tissue: Location, Metabolism, & Response to Injury. 240p. 1981. 59.95 (ISBN 0-8493-5749-7). CRC Pr.

Randall, D. J., et al. The Evolution of Air Breathing in Vertebrates. LC 80-462. (Illus.). 176p. 1981. 27.50 (ISBN 0-521-22259-1). Cambridge U Pr.

Rhyne, Theodore L. Acoustic Instrumentation & Characterisation of Lung Tissue. (Ultrasound in Biomedicine Ser.: Vol. 2). (Illus.). 1977. pap. 30.25 (ISBN 0-471-27884-X). Res Stud Pr.

Simmons, D. H. Current Pulmonology, Vol. 3. LC 79-643614. 441p. 1981. 50.00 (ISBN 0-471-09505-2, Pub. by Wiley Med). Wiley.

Simmons, Daniel H., ed. Current Pulmonology, Vol. 1. (Illus.). 1979. 45.00 (ISBN 0-471-09495-1, Pub. by Wiley Med). Wiley.

Simon, Seymour. About Your Lungs. (Illus.). (gr. k-3). 1978. 6.95 (ISBN 0-07-057494-4, GB). McGraw.

Snider, Gordon L. Clinical Pulmonary Medicine. 1981. price not set (ISBN 0-316-80218-2). Little.

Staub, Norman C., ed. Lung Water & Solute Exchange. (Lung Biology in Health & Disease Ser.: Vol. 7). 1978. 56.50 (ISBN 0-8247-6379-3). Dekker.

Thurlbeck, ed. The Lung: Structure, Function & Disease, No. 19. International Academy of Pathology. (Illus.). 344p. 1978. 39.00 (ISBN 0-683-08274-4). Williams & Wilkins.

Turner-Warwick, Margaret. Immunology of the Lung. (Current Topics in Immunology Ser.: Vol. 10). (Illus.). 1979. 29.95 (ISBN 0-8151-8879-X). Year Bk Med.

LUNGS-CANCER

Frederick E. Jones Memorial Symposium in Thoracic Surgery, Columbus, Ohio, October 1976. Perspectives in Lung Cancer: Proceedings. Williams, T. E., et al, eds. (Illus.). 1977. 26.50 (ISBN 3-8055-2649-0). S Karger.

Greco, F. Anthony, ed. Small Cell Lung Cancer. (Clinical Oncology Monograph). (Illus.). 480p. 1981. 39.50 (ISBN 0-8089-1345-X). Grune.

Karbe, E. & Park, J. F., eds. Experimental Lung Cancer: Carcinogenesis & Bioassays. (Illus.). xiv, 662p. 1975. 46.80 (ISBN 0-387-06996-8). Springer-Verlag.

Livingston, Robert B., ed. Lung Cancer. (Cancer Treatment & Research Ser.: No. 1). (Illus.). 320p. 1981. PLB 47.50 (ISBN 90-247-2394-9, Pub. by Martinus Nijhoff Netherlands). Kluwer Boston.

McGrail, Joie H. Fighting Back: One Woman's Struggle Against Cancer. LC 76-26244. 1978. 10.95 (ISBN 0-06-012958-1, HarpT). Har-Row.

Muggia, Franco & Rozencweig, Marcel, eds. Lung Cancer: Progress in Therapeutic Research. LC 77-84552. (Progress in Cancer Research & Therapy Ser.: Vol. 11). 639p. 1978. 52.00 (ISBN 0-89004-223-3). Raven.

Peterson, B. E., ed. Cancer of the Lung. LC 76-3894. (Illus.). 296p. 1979. 23.00 (ISBN 0-88416-118-8). Wright-PSG.

Seale, Albert. Behold the Sun. LC 77-74169. (Illus.). 1977. 6.95 (ISBN 0-918464-08-0); pap. 3.95 (ISBN 0-918464-06-4). D Armstrong.

Shields, Thomas W. Bronchial Carcinoma. (American Lectures in Surgery Ser.). (Illus.). 200p. 1974. text ed. 17.50 (ISBN 0-398-03095-2). C C Thomas.

Tsuboi, Eitaka. Atlas of Transbronchial Biopsy: Early Diagnosis of Peripheral Pulmonary Carcinomas. (Illus.). 1970. 34.00 (ISBN 0-89640-004-2). Igaku-Shoin.

LUNGS-CIRCULATION

see Pulmonary Circulation

LUNGS-DISEASES

see also Auscultation; Bronchoscope and Bronchoscopy; Chest–Diseases; Cor Pulmonale; Cystic Fibrosis; Emphysema, Pulmonary; Lungs–Dust Diseases; Percussion; Pneumonia; Pulmonary Edema; Pulmonary Manifestations of General Diseases; Respiratory Insufficiency; Tuberculosis

Ahronson, E. F., et al, eds. Air Pollution & the Lung. LC 76-3488. 313p. Date not set. Repr. of 1976 ed. 51.00 (ISBN 0-470-15049-1). Krieger.

American Hospital Association. Staff Manual for Teaching Patients About Chronic Obstructive Pulmonary Diseases. LC 78-27387. (Illus.). 424p. 1979. pap. 39.75 (ISBN 0-87258-249-3, 1317). Am Hospital.

Avery, Mary E., et al. The Lung & Its Disorders in the Newborn Infant. 4th ed. (Major Problems in Clinical Pediatrics: Vol. 1). (Illus.). 560p. 1981. text ed. write for info. (ISBN 0-7216-1462-0). Saunders.

Bakhle, Y. S. & Vane, J. R., eds. Metabolic Functions of the Lung, Vol. 4. (Lung Biology in Health & Disease). 1977. 39.50 (ISBN 0-8247-6383-1). Dekker.

Barjon, J. Radio-Diagnosis of Pleuro-Pulmonary Affections. 1918. 47.50x (ISBN 0-685-89775-3). Elliots Bks.

Bates, David V., et al. Respiratory Function in Disease. 2nd ed. LC 78-135319. (Illus.). 1971. 30.00 (ISBN 0-7216-1591-0). Saunders.

Baum, Gerald L., ed. Textbook of Pulmonary Diseases. 2nd ed. 1974. 67.50 (ISBN 0-316-08385-2). Little.

Berte, John B. Pulmonary Emergencies. LC 77-21473. (Illus.). 1977. soft cover 19.50 (ISBN 0-397-50383-0, JBL-Med-Nursing). Har-Row.

Bone, Roger C. Pulmonary Disease Review, Vol. 1. (Pulmonary Disease Review Ser.). 581p. 1980. 40.00 (ISBN 0-471-05736-3, Pub. by Wiley Med). Wiley.

Bordow, Richard, et al, eds. Manual of Clinical Problems in Pulmonary Medicine. (Spiral Manual Ser.). 12.95 (ISBN 0-316-10264-4, Little Med Div). Little.

Bouhuys, A., ed. Lung Cells in Disease: Brooke Lodge Conference, 1976. 1976. 53.75 (ISBN 0-7204-0589-0, North-Holland). Elsevier.

Bouhuys, Arend, ed. The Physiology of Breathing: A Textbook for Medical Students. LC 76-46724. (Illus.). 368p. 1977. 19.50 (ISBN 0-8089-0984-3). Grune.

Brashear, Richard E. & Rhodes, Mitchell L. Chronic Obstructive Lung Disease: Clinical Treatment & Management. new ed. LC 77-18551. (Illus.). 1978. text ed. 38.50 (ISBN 0-8016-0753-1). Mosby.

Buechner, Howard A., ed. Management of Fungus Diseases of the Lungs. (Illus.). 248p. 1971. 22.50 (ISBN 0-398-00247-9). C C Thomas.
Comroe, Julius H., Jr., et al. The Lung: Clinical Physiology & Pulmonary Function Tests. 2nd ed. (Illus.). 1962. 19.00 (ISBN 0-8151-1821-X). Year Bk Med.
Davies, Geoffrey M. Office Diagnosis & Management of Chronic Obstructive Pulmonary Disease. LC 81-8386. (Illus.). 150p. 1981. pap. price not set (ISBN 0-8121-0823-X). Lea & Febiger.
Dosman, James A. & Cotton, David J., eds. Occupational Pulmonary Disease: Focus on Grain Dust & Health. 1980. 42.00 (ISBN 0-12-221240-1). Acad Pr.
Eskenasy, Alex. Immunomorphology & Immunopathology of the Lung. 1978. 42.00x (ISBN 0-85626-108-4, Pub. by Abacus Pr). Intl Schol Bk Serv.
Fazzini, Eugene P. Interpretation of Lung Biopsies. (Biopsy Interpretation Ser.). 1981. write for info. (ISBN 0-89004-332-9, 469). Raven.
Gimenez, P., ed. Muscular Exercise in Chronic Lung Disease: Proceedings of Meeting on Factors Limiting Exercise, Nancy, France, 13-15 Sept. 1978. LC 79-40806. (Special Issue of the Bulletin Europeen De Physiopathologie Respiratoire). (Illus.). 1980. 50.00 (ISBN 0-08-024930-2). Pergamon.
Gomez, Rafael A., et al. Solitary Nodular Lesions of the Lung: Contribution to Its Diagnosis & Management. (Illus.). 250p. 1981. 32.50 (ISBN 0-87527-245-2). Green.
Hall, William J. Pulmonary Disease Review. LC 77-11665. (Arco Medical Review Ser.). 1977. pap. text ed. 12.00 (ISBN 0-668-04008-4). Arco.
Heitzman, E. Robert. The Lung: Radiologic - Pathologic Correlations. LC 73-6926. (Illus.). 1973. 46.50 (ISBN 0-8016-2134-8). Mosby.
Hercules, Patricia R., et al. Pulmonary Restriction & Obstruction: A Programmed Text. (Illus.). 1979. 19.95 (ISBN 0-8151-4361-3). Year Bk Med.
Holman, Cranston W. & Muschenheim, Carl, eds. Bronchopulmonary Diseases & Related Disorders, 2 vols. (Illus.). 1972. 100.00x (ISBN 0-06-141273-2, Harper Medical). Harrow.
Huisman, P. H. & Schipperheypn, J. J. The Isolated Heart-Lung Preparation. (Illus.). 1978. pap. 16.00 (ISBN 90-247-2107-5, Pub. by Martinus Nijhoff Netherlands). Kluwer Boston.
International Titisee Conference, Titisee, October 19-21, 1978. Biomedical Engineering & Data Processing in Pneumonology. Matthys, H., ed. (Progress in Respiration Research: Vol. 11). (Illus.). 1979. 69.50 (ISBN 3-8055-3012-9). S Karger.
Johnson, H. Patterns of Pulmonary Interstitial Disease. (Illus.). 320p. 1981. 15.00 (ISBN 0-87527-218-5). Green.
Kehrer, James B. Oxygen Induced Lung Damage: The Chemistry of Oxygen Reduction. (Lectures in Toxicology: No. 4). (Illus.). 1981. 50.00 (ISBN 0-08-025706-2). Pergamon.
Key, Marcus M., et al, eds. Pulmonary Reactions to Coal Dust: A Review of the U. S. Experience. (Environmental Science Ser.). 1971. 35.50 (ISBN 0-12-405950-3). Acad Pr.
Kirby & Smith. Mechanical Ventilation of the Lungs. Date not set. text ed. write for info. (ISBN 0-443-08063-1). Churchill.
Lyons, Harold A. Vascular Diseases of the Lung. (Illus.). 212p. 1967. photocopy ed. spiral 19.75 (ISBN 0-398-01175-3). C C Thomas.
Macklem, P. T. & Permutt, S., eds. Lung in Transition Between Health & Disease. (Lung Biology in Health & Disease Ser.: Vol. 12). 1979. 45.50 (ISBN 0-8247-6380-7). Dekker.
Miller, Warren C. Chronic Obstructive Pulmonary Disease. LC 79-91977. (Discussions in Pateint Managemenrt Ser.). 1980. pap. 12.00 (ISBN 0-87488-872-7). Med Exam.
Mitchell, Roger S. Synopsis of Clinical Pulmonary Diseases. 2nd ed. LC 77-11024. (Illus.). 1978. pap. text ed. 15.95 (ISBN 0-8016-3430-X). Mosby.
Moser, et al. Better Living & Breathing: A Manual for Patients. 2nd ed. LC 80-17943. (Illus.). 94p. 1980. pap. text ed. 5.45 (ISBN 0-8016-3565-9). Mosby.
Moser, K. M. Pulmonary Vascular Diseases. (Lung Biology in Health & Disease Ser.: Vol. 14). 1979. 69.75 (ISBN 0-8247-6609-1). Dekker.
Murray, John F., ed. Lung Disease: State of the Art. Incl. 1976-77. 1978. 11.50 (ISBN 0-915116-02-2); 1977-78. 1979. 10.00 (ISBN 0-686-64034-9); (1978-79); 12.50 (ISBN 0-686-77610-0, 1980). Am Lung Assn.
Nadel, J., ed. Physiology & Pharmacology of the Airways. (Lung Biology in Health & Disease: Vol. 15). 1980. 44.50 (ISBN 0-8247-6382-3). Dekker.
Nair, Sreedhar, et al, eds. Computers in Critical Care & Pulmonary Medicine. (Computers in Biology & Medicine Ser.). 418p. 1980. 39.50 (ISBN 0-306-40449-4, Plenum Pr). Plenum Pub.
Oaks, Wilbur W. & Moyer, John H. Pre- & Postoperative Management of the Cardiopulmonary Patient. LC 70-78885. (The Nineteenth Hahnemann Symposium). 424p. 1970. 64.50 (ISBN 0-8089-0352-7). Grune.
Parkes, W. Raymond. Occupational Lung Disorders. 2nd ed. 1981. text ed. 159.95 (ISBN 0-407-33731-8). Butterworth.
Petty, Thomas E., ed. Chronic Obstructive Pulmonary Disease. (Lung Biology in Health & Disease: Vol. 9). 1978. 31.50 (ISBN 0-8247-6612-1). Dekker.
Piiper, J. & Scheid, P., eds. Gas Exchange Function of Normal & Diseased Lungs. (Progress in Respiration Research Ser.: Vol. 16). (Illus.). xvi, 320p. 1981. 118.75 (ISBN 3-8055-1638-X). S Karger.
Prichard, John S. Edema of the Lung. (Illus.). 456p. 1982. 45.75 (ISBN 0-398-04493-7). C C Thomas.
Putman, Charles E., ed. Pulmonary Diagnosis: Imaging & Other Techniques. 320p. 1981. 46.50 (ISBN 0-8385-8058-0). ACC.
Saccomanno, Geno. Diagnostic Pulmonary Cytology. LC 78-8285. (Illus.). 1978. text ed. 45.00 (ISBN 0-89189-050-5, 16-3-003-00). Am Soc Clinical.
Sackner. Diagnostic Techniques in Pulmonary Disease, Pt. 1. (Lung Biology in Health & Disease Ser.: Vol. 16). 746p. 1980. 49.50 (ISBN 0-8247-1059-2). Dekker.
--Diagnostic Techniques in Pulmonary Disease, Part 2. (Lung Biology in Health & Disease Ser.: Vol. 16). 480p. 1981. 49.50 (ISBN 0-8247-1182-3). Dekker.
Scarpelli, Emile M., et al, eds. Pulmonary Disease of the Fetus, Newborn & Child. LC 78-8762. (Illus.). 680p. 1978. text ed. 54.00 (ISBN 0-8121-0606-7). Lea & Febiger.
Sharnoff, J. G. The Prevention of Venous Thrombosis & Pulmonary Thromboembolism. (Medical Publicatons Ser.). 1980. lib. bdg. 25.00 (ISBN 0-8161-2223-7). G K Hall.
Simmons, Daniel E. Current Pulmonology, Vol. 2. (Current Pulmonology Ser.). (Illus.). 1980. text ed. 45.00 (ISBN 0-471-09496-X, Pub. by Wiley Med). Wiley.
Spencer, H. Pathology of the Lung. 3rd ed. 1976. text ed. 145.00 (ISBN 0-08-021021-X). Pergamon.
Spencer, Herbert. Pathology of the Lung, 2 vols. LC 76-56633. 1977. Set. text ed. 89.50 (ISBN 0-7216-8515-3). Saunders.
Stone, Daniel J., et al. Practical Points in Pulmonary Diseases. 1978. spiral bdg. 14.00 (ISBN 0-87488-724-0). Med Exam.
Tashkin, Donald P. & Cassan, Stanley M., eds. Guide to Pulmonary Medicine. (Monographs in Family Medicine). 384p. 1978. 29.00 (ISBN 0-8089-1088-4). Grune.
Thurlbeck, ed. The Lung: Structure, Function & Disease, No. 19. International Academy of Pathology. (Illus.). 344p. 1978. 39.00 (ISBN 0-683-08274-4). Williams & Wilkins.
Thurlbeck, William M. Chronic Airflow Obstruction in Lung Disease. LC 75-25278. (Major Problems in Pathology Ser.: No. 5). (Illus.). 450p. 1976. text ed. 20.00 (ISBN 0-7216-8859-4). Saunders.
Tisi, Gennaro M. Pulmonary Physiology in Clinical Medicine. (Illus.). 292p. 1980. lib. bdg. 25.00 (ISBN 0-683-08250-7). Williams & Wilkins.
Tysinger, D. S., Jr. The Clinical Physics & Physiology of Chronic Lung Disease, Inhalation Therapy, & Pulmonary Function Testing. (Illus.). 264p. 1973. text ed. 17.50 (ISBN 0-398-02777-3). C C Thomas.
Wagenvoort, C. A., et al. The Pathology of the Pulmonary Vasculature. (Illus.). 512p. 1964. photocopy ed. spiral 49.75 (ISBN 0-398-01998-3). C C Thomas.
Weiss, Leonard & Gilbert, Harvey. Pulmonary Metastasis. 1978. lib. bdg. 29.95 (ISBN 0-8161-2107-9). G K Hall.
West, John B. Pulmonary Pathophysiology: The Essentials. 1977. pap. text ed. 13.50 (ISBN 0-683-08934-X). Williams & Wilkins.
West, John B., ed. Bioengineering Aspects of the Lung. (Lung Biology & Health Ser.: Vol. 3). 1977. 59.75 (ISBN 0-8247-6378-5). Dekker.

LUNGS–DUST DISEASES

Berton, Alberta D., compiled by. Asbestosis: A Comprehensive Bibliography. (Biomedical Information Guides Ser.: Vol. 1). 395p. 1980. 85.00 (ISBN 0-306-65176-9, IFI). Plenum Pub.
British Occupational Hygiene Society, International Symposium. Inhaled Particles III: Proceedings, 2 vols. Walton, W. H., ed. 1977. 50.00 set (ISBN 0-685-87553-9). State Mutual Bk.
Internatioal Labour Office. Guidelines for the Use of ILO International Classification of Radiographs of Pneumoconioses. (Occupational Safety & Health Ser.: No. 22). (Orig.). 1980. pap. 250.00 (ISBN 92-2-102463-6). Intl Labour Office.
Lanza, Anthony J., ed. The Pneumoconioses. LC 62-20522. (Illus.). 160p. 1963. 29.50 (ISBN 0-8089-0252-0). Grune.
Walton, W. H., ed. Inhaled Particles IV, 2 vols. LC 76-55009. 1977. Set. text ed. 160.00 (ISBN 0-08-020560-7). Pergamon.
Zahorski, Witold W., ed. Coal Workers' Pneumoconiosis: A Critical Review. LC 73-92706. (National Library of Medicine). (Illus.). 120p. 1974. text ed. 12.00x (ISBN 0-87451-097-X). U Pr of New Eng.

LUNGS–RADIOGRAPHY

see Chest–Radiography

LUNT, ALFRED, 1892-1977

Runkel, Phillip M. Alfred Lunt & Lynn Fontanne: A Bibliography. (Illus.). 1978. pap. 4.50 (ISBN 0-916120-03-1). Carroll Coll.

LUO (NILOTIC TRIBE)

DuPre, Carole E. Luo of Kenya: An Annotated Bibliography. LC 68-8362. 2.95 (ISBN 0-911976-04-3); pap. 1.95 (ISBN 0-911976-05-1). ICR.
Ocholla-Ayayo, A. B. Traditional Ideology & Ethics Among the Southern Luo. 1976. pap. 14.00x (ISBN 0-8419-9719-5). Holmes & Meier.
Ogot, Bethwell A. History of the Southern Luo, Vol. 1, Migration & Settlement 1500-1900. (Illus.). 1967. 7.50x (ISBN 0-8002-1512-5). Intl Pubns Serv.
Parkin, David. The Cultural Definition of Political Response: Linear Destiny Among the Luo. (Language, Thought & Culture Ser.). 1978. 44.00 (ISBN 0-12-545650-6). Acad Pr.

LUPINO, IDA

Stewart, Lucy A. Ida Lupino As Film Director. Jowett, Garth S., ed. LC 79-6687. (Dissertations on Film, 1980). 1980. lib. bdg. 20.00x (ISBN 0-405-12919-X). Arno.

LUPUS

see also Phototherapy

LUPUS ERYTHEMATOSUS

Aladjem, Henrietta. The Sun Is My Enemy. LC 76-7733. 1977. pap. 4.95 (ISBN 0-8070-2171-7, BP537). Beacon Pr.
Blau, Sheldon Paul, M.D. & Schultz, Dodi. Lupus-The Body Against Itself. LC 76-40881. 1977. 7.95 (ISBN 0-385-04562-X). Doubleday.
Dubois, Edmund L. Lupus Erythematosus: A Review of the Current Status of Discoid & Systemic Lupus Erythematosus & Their Variants. rev. 2nd ed. LC 73-86882. 1976. 39.50 (ISBN 0-88474-000-5). U of S Cal Pr.
Fries, James F. & Holman, Halsted R. Systematic Lupus Erythematosus: A Clinical Analysis, Vol. 6. LC 74-31837. (Major Problems in Internal Medicine Ser.). (Illus.). 199p. 1975. text ed. 20.00 (ISBN 0-7216-3917-8). Saunders.
Fukase, Masaichi. Systemic Lupus Erythematosus. 418p. text ed. 39.50 (ISBN 0-8391-1633-0). Univ Park.
Ropes, Marian W. Systemic Lupus Erythematosus. 224p. 1976. text ed. 12.50x (ISBN 0-674-86255-4). Harvard U Pr.
Verbov, J. L., et al. Systemic Lupus Erythematosus: Clinical & Theoretical Aspects. (Illus.). 220p. 1973. text ed. 26.00x (ISBN 0-8422-7104-X). Irvington.

LURIA, ISSAC BEN SOLOMON, 1534-1572

Ashlag, Yehuda. An Entrance to the Tree of Life of Rabbi Isaac Luria. Berg, Philip S., ed. 11.00 (ISBN 0-686-21759-4). Res Ctr Kabbalah.

LUSCHER TEST

Luscher, Max. Luscher Color Test. 1980. pap. 2.95 (ISBN 0-671-83170-4). PB.

LUSITANIA (STEAMSHIP)

Bailey, Thomas A. & Ryan, Paul B. The Lusitania Disaster: An Episode in Modern Warfare & Diplomacy. LC 75-2806. (Illus.). 1975. 12.95 (ISBN 0-02-901240-6). Free Pr.
Simpson, Colin. The Lusitania. 1973. 14.95 (ISBN 0-316-79178-4). Little.

LUTE

Robinson, Thomas. The Schoole of Musicke, Wherein Is Taught the Perfect Method of True Fingering of the Lute, Pandora, Orpharion & Viol da Gamba. LC 73-6122. (English Experience Ser.: No. 589). 1973. Repr. of 1603 ed. 16.00 (ISBN 90-221-0589-X). Walter J Johnson.
Van Gulik, R. H. Hsi K'ang & His Poetical Essay on the Lute. LC 68-58913. 1969. 15.00 (ISBN 0-8048-0868-6). C E Tuttle.
Van Gulik, Robert H. The Lore of the Chinese Lute. LC 68-57056. (Illus.). 1969. 21.00 (ISBN 0-8048-0869-4). C E Tuttle.

LUTE MUSIC

Dowland, Robert. Varietie of Lute-Lessons. LC 79-84102. (English Experience Ser.: No. 921). 76p. 1979. Repr. of 1610 ed. lib. bdg. 14.00 (ISBN 90-221-0921-6). Walter J Johnson.
--Varietie of Lute Lessons. Hunt, Edgar, ed. 1958. 11.25 (ISBN 0-901938-45-9, 75-A10441). Eur-Am Music.
Holborne, Anthony. Complete Works, 2 vols. Kanazawa, Masakata, ed. Incl. Vol. 1. Music for Lute & Bandora. (Illus.). 1967. pap. 17.50x (ISBN 0-674-15500-9); Vol. 2. Music for Cittern. 1974. pap. 15.95x (ISBN 0-674-15512-2). LC 67-14341. (Publications in Music Ser: No. 1, 5). Harvard U Pr.

LUTEAL HORMONE

see Progesterone

LUTHER, MARTIN, 1483-1546

Adam, Karl. One & Holy. Hastings, Cecily, tr. LC 79-95111. Repr. of 1951 ed. lib. bdg. 15.00 (ISBN 0-8371-2470-0, ADOH). Greenwood.
Aland, Kurt. Four Reformers: Luther, Melanchthon, Zwingli, Calvin. Schaaf, James L., tr. LC 79-50091. 176p. 1979. pap. 4.95 (ISBN 0-8066-1709-8, 10-2364). Augsburg.
--Martin Luther's Ninety-Five Theses. LC 67-27726. 1967. 3.95 (ISBN 0-570-03757-3, 12-2665). Concordia.
Althaus, Paul. The Ethics of Martin Luther. Schultz, Robert C., tr. from Ger. LC 72-164552. 192p. 1972. 8.95 (ISBN 0-8006-0047-9, 1-47). Fortress.
--Theology of Martin Luther. Schultz, Robert C., tr. from Ger. LC 66-17345. 480p. 1966. 13.95 (ISBN 0-8006-0060-6, 1-60). Fortress.
Amey, Peter, et al. Luther, Erasmus & Loyola. Yapp, Malcolm, et al, eds. (World History Ser.). (Illus.). (gr. 10). 1980. lib. bdg. 5.95 (ISBN 0-89908-043-X); pap. text ed. 1.95 (ISBN 0-89908-018-9). Greenhaven.
Atkinson, James. Martin Luther & the Birth of Protestantism. LC 81-82356. 348p. 1981. pap. 9.95 (ISBN 0-8042-0941-3). John Knox.
Bacon, Thomas I. Martin Luther & the Drama. (Amsterdamer Pulkationen Zur Sprache und Literature: No. 25). 1976. text ed. 14.25x (ISBN 90-6203-359-8). Humanities.
Bainton, Roland H. Here I Stand: A Life of Martin Luther. pap. 2.50 (ISBN 0-451-61953-6, ME1953, Ment). NAL.
Barlow, William. A Dyaloge Descrybyng the Orygynall Ground of These Lutheran Saccyons, That Is, Faccyons. LC 74-80161. (English Experience Ser.: No. 641). 200p. 1974. Repr. of 1531 ed. 13.00 (ISBN 90-221-0641-1). Walter J Johnson.
Beard, Charles. Martin Luther & the Reformation in Germany Until the Close of the Diet of Worms. 1976. Repr. of 1889 ed. 63.00 (ISBN 0-403-06472-4, Regency). Scholarly.
Benson, Kathleen. A Man Called Martin Luther. 1980. 6.95 (ISBN 0-570-03625-9, 39-1067). Concordia.
Boehmer, Heinrich. Luther in the Light of Recent Research. 1977. lib. bdg. 59.95 (ISBN 0-8490-2189-8). Gordon Pr.
Bohmer, Heinrich. Road to Reformation: Martin Luther to the Year 1521. Doberstein, John W. & Tappert, Theodore G., trs. from Ger. (Illus.). Repr. of 1946 ed. lib. bdg. 25.00x (ISBN 0-87991-507-2). Porcupine Pr.
Bruce, Gustav M. Luther As an Educator. LC 77-114482. (Illus.). 318p. Repr. of 1928 ed. lib. bdg. 18.50x (ISBN 0-8371-4771-9, BRLD). Greenwood.
Chamberlin, R. C. Martin Luther. (Jackdaw Ser: No. 69). (Illus.). 1972. 6.95 (ISBN 0-670-45929-1, Grossman). Viking Pr.
Crawford, James L. Catalogue of a Collection of 1500 Tracts by Martin Luther & His Contemporaries, 1511-1598. 1965. Repr. of 1903 ed. 32.00 (ISBN 0-8337-1001-X). B Franklin.
D'Aubigne, J. H. Life & Times of Martin Luther. pap. 10.95 (ISBN 0-8024-4899-2). Moody.
Davey, Cyril. Monk Who Shook the World (Martin Luther) 1960. pap. 1.95 (ISBN 0-87508-614-4). Chr Lit.
Davies, Rupert E. The Problems of Authority in the Continental Reformers: A Study of Luther, Zwingli, & Calvin. LC 78-5871. 1978. Repr. of 1946 ed. lib. bdg. 18.00x (ISBN 0-313-20487-X, DAPA). Greenwood.
--Problems of Authority in the Continental Reformers: A Study of Luther, Zwingli, & Calvin. LC 78-59015. 1979. Repr. of 1946 ed. 14.50 (ISBN 0-88355-689-8). Hyperion Conn.
Davy, Yvonne. Frau Luther. LC 78-57355. (Destiny Ser.). 1979. pap. 4.95 (ISBN 0-8163-0235-9). Pacific Pr Pub Assn.
Ebeling, Gerhard. Luther: An Introduction to His Thought. Wilson, R. A., tr. from Ger. LC 77-99612. 288p. 1970. pap. 4.95 (ISBN 0-8006-1162-4, 1-1162). Fortress.
Edwards, Mark U., Jr. Luther and the False Brethren. LC 75-181. 1975. 12.50x (ISBN 0-8047-0883-5). Stanford U Pr.
Erikson, Erik H. Young Man Luther. 1958 6.50 (ISBN 0-393-07365-3); pap. 2.95 (ISBN 0-393-00170-9). Norton.
--Young Man Luther. 1958 6.50 (ISBN 0-393-07365-3); pap. 2.95 (ISBN 0-393-00170-9). Norton.

Fagerberg, Holsten. A New Look at the Lutheran Confession. Lund, Gene J., tr. 336p. 1981. 14.50 (ISBN 0-570-03223-7, 15-2121). Concordia.

Ferm, Vergilius. Cross-Currents in the Personality of Martin Luther. LC 71-189362. 192p. 1972. 6.50 (ISBN 0-8158-0277-3). Chris Mass.

Fife, Robert H. Young Luther. LC 79-131040. 1970. Repr. of 1928 ed. 19.50 (ISBN 0-404-02385-1). AMS Pr.

Forell, George W. Faith Active in Love. LC 15-5702. 1954. pap. 4.95 (ISBN 0-8066-0186-8, 10-2165). Augsburg.

Freytag, Gustav. Martin Luther. LC 78-144612. Repr. of 1897 ed. 17.50 (ISBN 0-404-02577-3). AMS Pr.

Froude, James A. A Comparative Analysis of the Philosophies of Erasmus & Luther. (Illus.). 133p. 1981. Repr. of 1868 ed. 59.85 (ISBN 0-89901-038-5). Found Class Reprints.

Gerrish, Brian A. Grace & Reason: A Study in the Theology of Luther. (Midway Reprints Ser.). 1979. pap. text ed. 11.00x (ISBN 0-226-28868-4). U of Chicago Pr.

Grisar, Hartmann. Martin Luther: His Life & Work. Preuss, Arthur, ed. LC 71-137235. Repr. of 1930 ed. 29.50 (ISBN 0-404-02935-3). AMS Pr.

--Martin Luther: His Life & Work. Preuss, Arthur, ed. LC 71-137235. Repr. of 1930 ed. 29.50 (ISBN 0-404-02935-3). AMS Pr.

Hacker, Paul. Ego in Faith: Martin Luther & the Origins of Anthropocentric Religion. Wicks, Jared, ed. LC 70-85506. (Das Ich Im Glauben Bei Martin Luther). 1971. 6.50 (ISBN 0-8199-0406-6). Franciscan Herald.

Haile, H. G. Luther: An Experiment in Biography. LC 79-6282. (Illus.). 456p. 1980. 14.95 (ISBN 0-385-15960-9). Doubleday.

Hatznung, Ruth. Martin Luther: Man for Whom God Had Great Plans. 1974. pap. 1.25 (ISBN 0-8100-0060-1, 16-0757). Northwest Pub.

Headley, John M. Luther's View of Church History. 1963. pap. 37.50x (ISBN 0-686-51413-0). Elliots Bks.

Hendrix, Scott H. Luther & the Papacy: Stages in a Reformation Conflict. LC 80-2393. 224p. 1981. 14.95 (ISBN 0-8006-0658-2, 1-658). Fortress.

Henry VIII. A Copy of the Letters, Wherein Kyng Henry the Eyght Made Answere into a Certayn Letter of Martyn Luther. LC 72-204. (English Experince Ser.: No. 322). 100p. 1971. Repr. of 1528 ed. 14.00 (ISBN 90-221-0322-6). Walter J Johnson.

Hoffman, Bengt, ed. The Theologia Germanica of Martin Luther. LC 80-50155. (Classics of Western Spirituality). 224p. 1980. 11.95 (ISBN 0-8091-0308-7); pap. 7.95 (ISBN 0-8091-2291-X). Paulist Pr.

Hoffman, Bengt R. Luther & the Mystics: A Re-Examination of Luther's Spiritual Experience & His Relationship to the Mystics. LC 75-22724. 264p. 1976. 9.95 (ISBN 0-8066-1514-1, 10-4140). Augsburg.

Holl, Karl. The Reconstruction of Morality. Adams, James L. & Bense, Walter F, eds. Meuser, Fred W. & Wietzke, Walter E., trs. LC 79-50098. 160p. 1979. pap. 4.95 (ISBN 0-8066-1720-9, 10-5440). Augsburg.

--What Did Luther Understand by Religion? Adams, James L. & Bense, Walter F., eds. Meuser, Fred W. & Wietzke, Walter R., trs. from Ger. LC 76-62611. 128p. 1977. pap. 4.25 (ISBN 0-8006-1260-4, 1-1260). Fortress.

Hyma, Albert. Luther's Theological Development from Erfurt to Augsburg. LC 76-137247. Repr. of 1928 ed. 12.50 (ISBN 0-404-03479-9). AMS Pr.

Jacobs, Henry E. Martin Luther, the Hero of the Reformation. LC 72-170838. Repr. of 1898 ed. 27.50 (ISBN 0-404-03544-2). AMS Pr.

Jensen, De Lamar. Confrontation at Worms: Martin Luther & the Diet of Worms. LC 73-5906. (Friends of the Brigham Young University Library Keepsake Ser.: No. 6). (Illus.). 120p. 1973. 3.95 (ISBN 0-8425-0286-6). Brigham.

Karant-Nunn, Susan C. Luther's Pastors: The Reformation in the Ernestine Countryside. LC 79-51539. (Transactions Ser.: Vol. 69, Pt. 8). 1979. 8.00 (ISBN 0-87169-698-3). Am Philos.

Kerr, Hugh T., Jr., ed. Compend of Luther's Theology. 1966. pap. 4.95 (ISBN 0-664-24729-6). Westminster.

Kiessling, Elmer C. Early Sermons of Luther & Their Relation to the Pre-Reformation Sermon. LC 75-171064. Repr. of 1935 ed. 14.45 (ISBN 0-404-03669-4). AMS Pr.

Kirchner, Hubert. Luther & the Peasants' War. Anderson, Charles S., ed. Jodock, Darrell, tr. from Ger. LC 73-171507. (Facet Bks.). 48p. (Orig.). 1972. pap. 1.00 (ISBN 0-8006-3068-8, 1-3068). Fortress.

Klingner, Erich. Luther und der Deutsche Volksaberglaube. Repr. of 1912 ed. 14.00 (ISBN 0-384-29830-3); pap. 11.00 (ISBN 0-685-02277-3). Johnson Repr.

Koenigsberger, H. G., ed. Luther: A Profile. (World Profiles Ser). 251p. 1973. 7.95 (ISBN 0-8090-6702-1); pap. 3.45 (ISBN 0-8090-1403-3). Hill & Wang.

Kohler, Walther. Zwingli und Luther, Ihr Streit Uber das Abendmahl Nach Seinen Politischen und Religiosen Beziehung En. (Ger). Repr. of 1924 ed. 53.00 (ISBN 0-384-30019-7); pap. 46.00 (ISBN 0-384-30018-9). Johnson Repr.

Kostlin, Julius. Life of Luther. 1883. Repr. 50.00 (ISBN 0-8274-2894-4). R West.

Leaver, Robin A. Luther on Justification. LC 74-11781. 1975. pap. 3.95 (ISBN 0-570-03188-5, 12-2590). Concordia.

Letis, Theodore P. Martin Luther & Charismatic Ecumenism. (Orig.). 1980. pap. 1.95 (ISBN 0-936592-00-1). Reformation Res.

Lindsay, Thomas M. Luther & the Germany Reformation. facsimile ed. LC 71-133524. (Select Bibliographies Reprint Ser). Repr. of 1900 ed. 16.00 (ISBN 0-8369-5556-0). Arno.

Loeschen, John R. Wrestling with Luther. LC 75-33815. 232p. 1976. 10.50 (ISBN 0-570-03256-3, 15-2164). Concordia.

Lotz, David W. Ritschl & Luther. LC 73-14962. 216p. 1974. 10.50 (ISBN 0-687-36449-3). Abingdon.

Ludwig, Martin. Religion und Sittlichkeit Bei Luther Bis Zum Sermon Von Den Guten Werken 1520. (Ger). 29.00 (ISBN 0-384-34151-9); pap. 23.00 (ISBN 0-384-34150-0). Johnson Repr.

Luther, Martin. Luther's Ninety-Five Theses. Jacobs, C. M., tr. 1957. pap. 0.95 (ISBN 0-8006-1265-5, 1-1265). Fortress.

--Luthers Werke in Auswahl, 8 vols. Clemen, Otto, ed. Incl. Vol. 1. Schriften von 1517 bis 1520. 6th rev. ed. (Illus.). xxxii, 512p. 1966. 17.75x (ISBN 3-11-003152-3); Vol. 2. Schriften von 1520 bis 1524. 6th rev. ed. vi, 464p. 1967. 17.75x (ISBN 3-11-002897-2); Vol. 3. Schriften von 1524 bis 1528. 6th rev. ed. vi, 516p. 1966. 17.75x (ISBN 3-11-003154-X); Vol. 4. Schriften von 1529 bis 1545. 6th rev. ed. vi, 428p. 1967. 15.75x (ISBN 3-11-003151-5); Vol. 5. Der Junge Luther. 3rd rev. ed. Vogelsang, Erich, ed. xi, 434p. 1963. 17.75 (ISBN 3-11-005609-7); Vol. 6. Luthers Briefe. 3rd rev. ed. Rueckert, Hanns, ed. xv, 451p. 1966. 20.00x (ISBN 3-11-005610-0); Vol. 7. Predigten. 3rd ed. Hirsch, Emanuel, ed. xii, 420p. 1962. 20.00x (ISBN 3-11-005611-9); Vol. 8. Tischreden. 3rd ed. Clemen, Otto, ed. x, 387p. 1962. 20.00x (ISBN 3-11-005612-7). De Gruyter.

Luther's Theology of the Cross. Bowman, Herbert J., tr. LC 75-2845. 1975. 9.95 (ISBN 0-8066-1490-0, 10-4232). Augsburg.

McGoldrick, J. E. Luther's English Connection. 1979. pap. 7.50 (ISBN 0-8100-0070-9, 15-0368). Northwest Pub.

Maritain, Jacques. Three Reformers. LC 70-112813. 1970. Repr. of 1928 ed. 12.75 (ISBN 0-8046-1080-0). Kennikat.

--Three Reformers: Luther-Descartes-Rousseau. Repr. of 1950 ed. lib. bdg. 15.00 (ISBN 0-8371-2825-0, MATR). Greenwood.

--Three Reformers: Luther, Descartes, Rousseau. 8.50 (ISBN 0-8446-0195-0). Peter Smith.

Masson, David. Essays Biographical & Critical: Chiefly on English Poets. 1856. lib. bdg. 50.00 (ISBN 0-8414-6491-X). Folcroft.

--Three Devils: Luther's, Milton's & Goethe's. LC 72-193946. 1874. lib. bdg. 17.50 (ISBN 0-8414-6495-2). Folcroft.

Montgomery, John W. In Defense of Martin Luther. (Illus.). 1970. 2.50 (ISBN 0-8100-0026-1, 12N0339). Northwest Pub.

More, St. Thomas. Responsio Ad Lutherum, 2 Vols. Headley, John M., ed. LC 63-7949. (Complete Works of St. Thomas More Ser.: No. 5). 1969. Set. 60.00x (ISBN 0-300-01123-7). Yale U Pr.

Nettl, Paul. Luther & Music. Best, Frida & Wood, Ralph, trs. LC 66-27133. 1967. Repr. of 1948 ed. 7.50 (ISBN 0-8462-1008-8). Russell.

Olivier, Daniel. The Trial of Luther. 1979. pap. 8.50 (ISBN 0-570-03785-9, 12-2743). Concordia.

O'Neill, Judith. Martin Luther. LC 74-12959. (Introduction to the History of Mankind). (Illus.). 48p. (gr. 6-11). 1975. pap. text ed. 3.95 (ISBN 0-521-20403-8). Cambridge U Pr.

Oswald, Hilton, ed. Luther's Works, Vol. 11. Bowman, Herbert J., tr. from Lat. LC 55-9893. 560p. 1976. 14.95 (ISBN 0-570-06411-2, 15-1753). Concordia.

Pascal, Roy. Social Basis of the German Reformation: Martin Luther & His Times. LC 68-30539. Repr. of 1933 ed. 15.000 (ISBN 0-678-00549-4). Kelley.

Pelikan, Jaroslav, ed. Luther the Expositor. 1959. 12.95 (ISBN 0-570-06431-7, 15-1741). Concordia.

Pelikan, Jaroslav, et al, trs. from Lat. Luther's Works, Vol. 15, Letters On Ecclesiastes, Song Of Solomon, & The Last Words Of David. LC 55-9893. 1971. 13.95 (ISBN 0-570-06415-5, 15-1757). Concordia.

Porter, J. M., ed. Luther: Selected Political Writings. new ed. LC 74-76931. 160p. (Orig.). 1974. pap. 3.50 (ISBN 0-8006-1079-2, 1-1079). Fortress.

Preus, Herman A. A Theology to Live By. 1977. pap. 7.95 (ISBN 0-570-03739-5, 12-2643). Concordia.

Preus, James S. Carlstadts Ordinaciones & Luther's Liberty. (Harvard Theological Review & Studies). 1974. pap. 6.00 (ISBN 0-89130-223-9, 020027). Scholars Pr Ca.

--From Shadow to Promise: Old Testament Interpretation from Augustine to the Young Luther. LC 69-12732. (Illus.). xii, 301p. 1969. 15.00x (ISBN 0-674-32610-5, Belkap Pr). Harvard U Pr.

Reu, Johann M. Thirty-Five Years of Luther Research. LC 27-460. (Illus.). Repr. of 1917 ed. 16.50 (ISBN 0-404-05284-3). AMS Pr.

Ritter, Gerhard. Luther: His Life & Work. Riches, John, tr. from Ger. LC 78-2717. 1978. Repr. of 1963 ed. lib. bdg. 24.25x (ISBN 0-313-20347-4, RILU). Greenwood.

Rudolph, Erwin P., ed. The Martin Luther Treasury. 1979. pap. 1.95 (ISBN 0-88207-518-7). Victor Bks.

Rupp, E. G. & Drewery, Benjamin, eds. Martin Luther. (Documents of Modern History Ser.). 1970. pap. text ed. 4.95 (ISBN 0-312-51660-6). St Martin.

Schenker, Walter. Die Sprache Huldrych Zwinglis Im Kontrast Zur Sprache Luthers. (Studia Linguistica Germanica: Vol. 14). (Illus.). 1977. 86.00x (ISBN 3-11-006605-X). De Gruyter.

Schreiber, Clara S. Katherine: Life of Luther. 1981. 6.95 (ISBN 0-8100-0144-6). Northwest Pub.

Schwiebert, E. G. Luther's Ninety-Five Theses. pap. 0.60 (ISBN 0-570-03519-8, 14-1253). Concordia.

Schwiebert, Ernest G. Luther & His Times: The Reformation from a New Perspective. (Illus.). (gr. 9 up). 1950. 21.95 (ISBN 0-570-03246-6, 15-1164). Concordia.

Sherman, Franklin & Lehman, Helmut T., eds. Luther's Works: The Christian in Society IV, Vol. 47. LC 55-9893. 1971. 8.00 (ISBN 0-8006-0347-8, 1-347). Fortress.

Sider, Ronald J., ed. Karlstadt's Battle with Luther: Documents in a Liberal-Radical Debate. LC 77-78642. 180p. (Orig.). 1978. pap. 5.95 (ISBN 0-8006-1312-0, 1-1312). Fortress.

Siggins, Ian. Luther & His Mother. LC 80-2386. 96p. (Orig.). 1981. pap. 4.95 (ISBN 0-8006-1498-4, 1-1498). Fortress.

Smith, Preserved. Luther's Table Talk. LC 78-127457. (Columbia University Studies in the Social Sciences: No. 69). 1970. Repr. of 1907 ed. 14.50 (ISBN 0-404-51069-8). AMS Pr.

Steinmetz, David C. Luther & Staupitz: An Essay in the Intellectual Origins of the Protestant Reformation. LC 80-23007. (Duke Monographs in Medieval & Renaissance Studies: No. 4). 1980. 16.75 (ISBN 0-8223-0447-3). Duke.

Strand, Kenneth A. Essays on Luther. pap. 2.75x (ISBN 0-89039-142-4). Ann Arbor Pubs.

Tierney, Brian, et al, eds. Martin Luther--Reformer or Revolutionary? 3rd ed. (Historical Pamphlets). 1977. pap. text ed. 1.95x (ISBN 0-394-32055-7). Random.

Volz, Hans. Die Lutherpredigten Des Johannes Mathesius. (Ger). 29.00 (ISBN 0-384-64913-0); pap. 23.00 (ISBN 0-384-64912-2). Johnson Repr.

Von Doellinger, Johann J. Luther. 1977. Repr. 19.00 (ISBN 0-403-08289-7). Scholarly.

Waring, Luther H. Political Theories of Martin Luther. LC 68-15837. 1968. Repr. of 1910 ed. 12.50 (ISBN 0-8046-0488-6). Kennikat.

Weidenschilling, J. M. Living with Luther. 1945. pap. text ed. 0.95 (ISBN 0-570-03523-6, 14-1155). Concordia.

Wicks, Jared, ed. Catholic Scholars Dialogue with Luther. LC 78-105429. (Orig.). 1970. pap. 3.00 (ISBN 0-8294-0181-4). Loyola.

Wolf, Ernst. Staupitz Und Luther. (Ger). Repr. of 1927 ed. 29.00 (ISBN 0-384-69019-X); pap. 23.00 (ISBN 0-384-69018-1). Johnson Repr.

Woolf, Bertram L., tr. Reformation Writings of Martin Luther, Vol. 2. 6.00 (ISBN 0-8022-1929-2). Philos Lib.

LUTHER, MARTIN, 1483-1546–DRAMA

Osborne, John. Luther. pap. 1.95 (ISBN 0-451-09626-6, J9626, Sig). NAL.

LUTHER, MARTIN, 1483-1546–JUVENILE LITERATURE

Fehlauer, Adolph. Life & Faith of Martin Luther. 1981. pap. 5.95 (ISBN 0-8100-0125-X). Northwest Pub.

Nohl, Frederick. Martin Luther: Hero of Faith. LC 62-14146. (Illus.). (gr. 4-6). 1962. pap. 4.50 (ISBN 0-570-03727-1, 12-2629). Concordia.

O'Neill, Judith. Martin Luther. LC 78-56804. (Cambridge Topic Bks). (Illus.). (gr. 5-10). 1978. PLB 4.95 (ISBN 0-8225-1215-7). Lerner Pubns.

LUTHERAN CHURCH

see also Augustana Evangelical Lutheran Church; Evangelical Lutheran Church

Bonhoeffer, Dietrich. The Way to Freedom. (Fount Religious Paperback Ser.). 1977. pap. 2.95 (ISBN 0-00-642842-8, FA2842). Collins Pubs.

Empie, Paul C. Lutherans & Catholics in Dialogue: Personal Notes for a Study. LC 80-69754. (Orig.). 1981. pap. 3.95 (ISBN 0-8006-1449-6, 1-1449). Fortress.

Hamsher, Paul O. This I Believe: My Lutheran Handbook. 1972. 3.25 (ISBN 0-89536-153-1). CSS Pub.

Inter-Lutheran Commission on Worship. Lutheran Book of Worship. 8.50 (ISBN 0-686-25963-7). Bd of Pubn LCA.

Kreider, Harry J. Lutheranism in Colonial New York. LC 78-38452. (Religion in America, Ser. 2). 184p. 1972. Repr. of 1942 ed. 11.00 (ISBN 0-405-04072-5). Arno.

--Lutheranism in Colonial New York. LC 78-38452. (Religion in America, Ser. 2). 184p. 1972. Repr. of 1942 ed. 11.00 (ISBN 0-405-04072-5). Arno.

Luther, Martin. Martin Luther: Selections from His Writings. LC 61-9503. pap. 3.95 (ISBN 0-385-09876-6, A271, Anch). Doubleday.

Meitler, Neal D. & La Porte, Linda M. Standard Accounting System for Lutheran Congregations. 1981. 4.50 (ISBN 0-8100-0129-2). Northwest Pub.

Melanchthon, Philipp. Opera Quae Supersunt Omnia, 28 Vols. (Corpus Reformatorum). Repr. of 1860 ed. Set. 1330.00 (ISBN 0-384-38050-6); 48.00 ea. Johnson Repr.

--Selected Writings. Flack, Elmer E. & Satre, Lowell J., eds. Hill, Charles L., tr. LC 78-5175. 1978. Repr. of 1962 ed. lib. bdg. 18.75x (ISBN 0-313-20384-9, MESW). Greenwood.

Neuhaus, Richard J. Lutherans. (Ecumenical Ser.). pap. 0.25 (ISBN 0-8091-5085-9). Paulist Pr.

Polack, W. G. The Handbook to the Lutheran Hymnal. 3rd rev. ed. 1975. Repr. of 1942 ed. lib. bdg. 13.95 (ISBN 0-8100-0003-2, 03-0700). Northwest Pub.

Smith, Clifford N. Nineteenth-Century Emigration of "Old Lutherans" from Eastern Germany (Mainly Pomerania & Lower Silesia) to Australia, Canada, & the United States. (German-American Genealogical Research Monograph: No. 7). 1979. pap. 12.50 (ISBN 0-915162-06-7). Westland Pubns.

Stauderman, Albert P. Facts About Lutherans. 1959. pap. 0.65 (ISBN 0-8006-1832-7, 1-1832). Fortress.

Tappert, Theodore G. & Lehmann, Helmut T., eds. Luther's Works: Table Talk, Vol. 54. Tappert, Theodore G., tr. LC 55-9893. 1967. 12.95 (ISBN 0-8006-0354-0, 1-354). Fortress.

LUTHERAN CHURCH–ADDRESSES, ESSAYS, LECTURES

Sittler, Joseph A. Grace Notes & Other Fragments. Herhold, Robert M. & Delloff, Linda M., eds. LC 80-8055. 128p. (Orig.). 1981. pap. 5.50 (ISBN 0-8006-1404-6, 1-1404). Fortress.

LUTHERAN CHURCH–CATECHISMS AND CREEDS

Allbeck, Willard D. Studies in the Lutheran Confessions. rev. ed. LC 68-11139. 336p. 1968. 6.50 (ISBN 0-8006-0095-9, 1-95). Fortress.

Anderson, Charles S. Faith & Freedom: The Christian Faith According to the Lutheran Confessions. LC 76-27087. 1977. pap. 3.95 (ISBN 0-8066-1558-3, 10-2170). Augsburg.

Bachmann, Theodore & Lehmann, Helmut T., eds. Luther's Works, Vol. 35: Word & Sacrament I. LC 55-9893. 426p. 1960. 14.50 (ISBN 0-8006-0335-4, 1-335). Fortress.

Backus, William & Malte, Paul. Perspective. pap. 4.85 (ISBN 0-933350-06-6). Morse Pr.

Bente, F. Historical Introduction to the Book of Concord. 1965. 9.95 (ISBN 0-570-03287-3, 15-1926). Concordia.

Fagerberg, Holsten. A New Look at the Lutheran Confession. Lund, Gene J., tr. 336p. 1981. 14.50 (ISBN 0-570-03223-7, 15-2121). Concordia.

Fischer, Robert H. & Lehmann, Helmut T., eds. Luther's Works, Vol. 37: Word & Sacrament III. LC 55-9893. 1961. 12.95x (ISBN 0-8006-0337-0, 1-337). Fortress.

Girgensohn, Herbert. Teaching Luther's Catechism, Vol. II. Doberstein, John W., tr. from Ger. LC 59-8463. 1960. 6.00 (ISBN 0-8006-0866-6, 1-866). Fortress.

Huggenvik, Theodore. We Believe. 1950. pap. 1.85 (ISBN 0-8066-0151-5, 15-7102). Augsburg.

Janzow, F. Samuel. Getting into Luther's Large Catechism. 1979. pap. 3.25 (ISBN 0-570-03783-2, 12-2737). Concordia.

Keller, Paul F. Studies in Lutheran Doctrine. LC 60-15574. (YA) (gr. 7-8). 1959. pap. 5.50 (ISBN 0-570-03517-1, 14-1265); correction & profile chart 0.40 (ISBN 0-570-03526-0, 14-1267); tests 0.45 (ISBN 0-570-03525-2, 14-1266). Concordia.

Kurth, Edwin W. Catechetical Helps. (gr. 4-12). 1981. pap. text ed. 4.50 (ISBN 0-570-03507-4, 14-1261). Concordia.

Kurth, Erwin, et al. Growing in Christ: Catechism. (Illus.). (gr. 4-6). 1953. text ed. 3.25 (ISBN 0-570-01517-0, 22-1097); wkbk. 1.15 (ISBN 0-570-01518-9, 22-1100). Concordia.

Luther, Martin. The Chiefe & Prycypall Articles of the Christian Faythe. LC 72-6080. (English Experience Ser.: No. 84). 248p. 1969. Repr. of 1548 ed. 21.00 (ISBN 90-221-0084-7). Walter J Johnson.

--The Large Catechism of Martin Luther. Fischer, Robert H., tr. from Ger. LC 61-3802. 112p. 1959. 4.95 (ISBN 0-8006-0885-2, 1-885). Fortress.

--Luther's Large Catechism. Lenker, J. M., tr. 1967. flexible bdg. 3.95 (ISBN 0-8066-0720-3, 10-4211). Augsburg.

--Luther's Works, Vol. 17. Bouman, Herbert J., tr. LC 55-9893. 1972. 15.95 (ISBN 0-570-06417-1, 15-1759). Concordia.

--Small Catechism in Contemporary English. 1963. pap. 0.30 (ISBN 0-8066-0324-0). Augsburg.

Preus, Robert. Getting into the Theology of Concord. 1978. pap. 2.75 (ISBN 0-570-03767-0, 12-2702). Concordia.

Tappert, Theodore G., ed. & tr. Book of Concord: The Confessions of the Evangelical Lutheran Church. LC 59-11369. 1959. 10.95 (ISBN 0-8006-0825-9, 1-825). Fortress.

Theiss, Herman C. Life with God. pap. 4.85 (ISBN 0-933350-05-8); tchrs. manual 1.65 (ISBN 0-933350-55-4). Morse Pr.

This We Believe. (Eng. & Ger.). pap. 0.75 (ISBN 0-8100-0004-0, 04-0622). Northwest Pub.

Wangerin, Walter M., ed. Concordia Catechism Ser. 4.25 (ISBN 0-570-08153-X, 22-1406). Concordia.

Wentz, Abdel R. & Lehmann, eds. Luther's Works, Vol. 36: Word & Sacrament II. LC 55-9893. 400p. 1959. 16.95 (ISBN 0-8006-0336-2, 1-336). Fortress.

LUTHERAN CHURCH–CLERGY

Behnken, John W. This I Recall. LC 64-24265. 1964. 3.95 (ISBN 0-570-03284-9, 15-1907). Concordia.

Hoard, Samuel L. Almost a Layman: Becoming a Black Lutheran Minister. 1978. 5.50 (ISBN 0-87164-046-5). William-F.

Lindberg, Duane R. Men of the Cloth & the Social-Cultural Fabric of the Norwegian Ethnic Community in North Dakota. Cordasco, Francesco, ed. LC 80-877. (American Ethnic Groups Ser.). 1981. lib. bdg. 35.00x (ISBN 0-405-13438-X). Arno.

LUTHERAN CHURCH–CONFIRMATION

see Confirmation–Lutheran Church

LUTHERAN CHURCH–DOCTRINAL AND CONTROVERSIAL WORKS

Bold in the Spirit: Erling Jorstad. LC 74-77681. (Lutheran Charismatic Renewal in America Today). 128p. (Orig.). 1974. pap. 3.50 (ISBN 0-8066-1432-3, 10-0780). Augsburg.

Chemnitz, Martin. Examination of the Council of Trent. Kramer, Fred, tr. from Lat. LC 79-143693. 1971. 15.95 (ISBN 0-570-03213-X, 15-2113). Concordia.

Duin, Edgar C. Lutheranism Under the Tsars & the Soviets, 2 vols. LC 75-37478. (Sponsored by the lutheran theological Seminary). 1975. Set. 62.50 (ISBN 0-8357-0157-3, SS-00005); Vol. 1. (ISBN 0-8357-0155-7); Vol. 2. (ISBN 0-8357-0156-5). Univ Microfilms.

Forde, Gerhard O. Where God Meets Man: Luther's Down-to-Earth Approach to the Gospel. LC 72-78569. 128p. 1972. pap. 3.95 (ISBN 0-8066-1235-5, 10-7060). Augsburg.

Forell, George W. & McCue, James F. Confessing One Faith: A Joint Commentary on the Augsburg Confession by Lutheran & Catholic Theologians. LC 80-65557. 368p. 1981. pap. 15.00 (ISBN 0-8066-1802-7, 10-1637). Augsburg.

Holl, Karl. What Did Luther Understand by Religion? Adams, James L. & Bense, Walter F., eds. Meuser, Fred W. & Wietzke, Walter R., trs. from Ger. LC 76-62611. 128p. 1977. pap. 4.25 (ISBN 0-8006-1260-4, 1-1260). Fortress.

Huggenvik, Theodore. We Believe. 1950. pap. 1.85 (ISBN 0-8066-0151-5, 15-7102). Augsburg.

Krauth, Charles P. Conservative Reformation & Its Theology. 1963. 15.00 (ISBN 0-8066-0315-1, 10-1665). Augsburg.

Pieper, Francis. Christian Dogmatics, 4 Vols. Engelder, Theodore, et al, trs. 1950-1957. Vol. 1. 13.95 (ISBN 0-570-06712-X, 15-1001); Vol. 2. 13.95 (ISBN 0-570-06713-8, 15-1002); Vol. 3. 13.95 (ISBN 0-570-06714-6, 15-1003); Vol. 4. 19.95 (ISBN 0-570-06711-1, 15-1000); Set. 58.95 (ISBN 0-570-06715-4, 15-1852). Concordia.

Prenter, Regin. Luther's Theology of the Cross. Anderson, Charles S., ed. LC 71-152368. (Facet Bks.). 32p. 1971. pap. 1.00 (ISBN 0-8006-3062-9, 1-3062). Fortress.

Preus, Robert D. Theology of Post-Reformation Lutheranism: A Study of Theological Prolegomena. LC 70-121877. 1970. 15.50 (ISBN 0-570-03211-3, 15-2110). Concordia.

Rudnick, Miltin L. Christianity Is for You. 1961. pap. 2.75 (ISBN 0-570-03503-1, 14-1271). Concordia.

Schmid, Heinrich. Doctrinal Theology of the Evangelical Lutheran Church. LC 66-13052. 1961. 15.00 (ISBN 0-8066-0107-8, 10-1930). Augsburg.

Three Tudor Dialogues. LC 78-14887. 1979. 20.00x (ISBN 0-8201-1319-0). Schol Facsimiles.

LUTHERAN CHURCH–EDUCATION

Backus, William & Malte, Paul R. Crossroad. pap. 4.45 (ISBN 0-933350-03-1); tchrs' ed. 1.65 (ISBN 0-933350-53-8). Morse Pr.

Backus, William, et al. Adventuring in the Church. pap. 4.85 (ISBN 0-933350-08-2); tchrs' ed. 1.95 (ISBN 0-933350-58-9). Morse Pr.

Basic Teacher's Guide. pap. 1.65 (ISBN 0-933350-51-1). Morse Pr.

Grams, Armin & Kurz, Graham. I Believe. pap. 1.95 (ISBN 0-933350-07-4). Morse Pr.

Malte, Paul R. & Saffen, Wayne. In Touch. pap. 1.95 (ISBN 0-933350-02-3). Morse Pr.

Montgomery, Mary & Montgomery, Herb. Together at the Lord's Supper: Preparation for Holy Communion. (Illus.). (gr. 5 up). 1977. pap. text ed. 3.25 (ISBN 0-03-021291-X, 141); parent bk. 1.75 (ISBN 0-03-021286-3, 192); leader's guide 4.95 (ISBN 0-03-021296-0, 193). Winston Pr.

Solberg, Richard W. & Strommen, Merton P. How Church-Related Are Church-Related Colleges? Answers Based on a Comprehensive Survey of Supporting Constituencies of 18 LCA Colleges. LC 80-13833. 96p. (Orig.). 1980. pap. 3.50 (ISBN 0-8006-1388-0, 1-1388). Fortress.

Strauss, Gerald. Luther's House of Learning: Indoctrination of the Young in the German Reformation. LC 77-18705. 1979. text ed. 20.00x (ISBN 0-8018-2051-0). Johns Hopkins.

Vala, Eduard. A Time, Place & Season. pap. 4.95 (ISBN 0-933350-15-5). Morse Pr.

LUTHERAN CHURCH–HISTORY

Bernheim, Gotthardt D. History of the German Settlements & of the Lutheran Church in North & South Carolina. LC 76-187361. 573p. 1972. Repr. of 1872 ed. 27.50 (ISBN 0-87152-089-3). Reprint.

Elert, Werner. Structure of Lutheranism: The Theology & Philosophy of Life of Lutheranism, 16th & 17th Centuries, Vol. 1. Hansen, Walter A., tr. LC 62-19955. 1974. pap. 12.95 (ISBN 0-570-03192-3, 12-2588). Concordia.

Erb, Peter. Johann Arndt: True Christianity. LC 78-72046. (Classics of Western Spirituality). 320p. 1979. 11.95 (ISBN 0-8091-0281-1); pap. 7.95 (ISBN 0-8091-2192-1). Paulist Pr.

Jungkuntz, Theodore R. Formulators of the Formula of Concord. 1977. pap. 6.95 (ISBN 0-570-03740-9, 12-2644). Concordia.

Klug, Eugene F. Getting into the Formula of Concord. 1977. pap. 2.75 (ISBN 0-570-03742-5, 12-2646). Concordia.

Ludolphy, Ingetraut. From Luther to 1580: A Pictorial Account. (Illus.). 1977. 14.95 (ISBN 0-570-03264-4, 15-2710). Concordia.

Reumann, John, ed. The Church Emerging: A U. S. Lutheran Case Study. LC 76-62618. 288p. 1977. pap. 9.95 (ISBN 0-8006-1259-0, 1-1259). Fortress.

Riforgiato, Leonard R. Missionary of Moderation: Henry Melchior Muhlenberg & the Lutheran Church in English America. LC 78-75203. 256p. Date not set. 19.50 (ISBN 0-8387-2379-9). Bucknell U Pr.

Rogness, Alvin N. The Story of the American Lutheran Church. LC 80-65555. 96p. (Orig.). 1980. pap. 3.50 (ISBN 0-8066-1800-0, 10-6038). Augsburg.

Scaer, David. Getting into the Story of Concord. 1978. pap. 2.75 (ISBN 0-570-03768-9, 12-2703). Concordia.

Schmucker, Samuel S. American Lutheran Church, Historically, Doctrinally, & Practically Delineated in Several Discourses. LC 72-83436. (Religion in American Ser). 1969. Repr. of 1851 ed. 14.50 (ISBN 0-405-00261-0). Arno.

Spitz, Lewis W. & Lohff, Wenzel, eds. Discord, Dialogue, & Concord: Studies in the Lutheran Reformation's Formula of Concord. LC 77-78644. 224p. 1977. 9.95 (ISBN 0-8006-0511-X, 1-511). Fortress.

Strauss, Gerald. Luther's House of Learning: Indoctrination of the Young in the German Reformation. LC 77-18705. 1979. text ed. 20.00x (ISBN 0-8018-2051-0). Johns Hopkins.

Vajta, Vilmos, ed. The Lutheran Church: Past & Present. LC 76-46120. 1977. pap. 9.50 (ISBN 0-8066-1573-7, 10-4160). Augsburg.

LUTHERAN CHURCH–HYMNS

see also Chorale; Chorales

Cavaille-Coll, A. Devis d'un grand orgue a trois claviers et un pedalier complets projete pour la vieille Eglise Lutherienne Evangelique a Amsterdam. (Bibliotheca Organologica Ser.: Vol. 45). 52p. 1980. Repr. of 1881 ed. wrappers 17.50 (ISBN 90-6027-193-9, Pub. by Frits Knuf Netherlands). Pendragon NY.

Leupold, Ulrich S. & Lehmann, Helmut T., eds. Luther's Works: Liturgy & Hymns, Vol. 53. LC 55-9893. 1965. 12.95 (ISBN 0-8006-0353-2, 1-353). Fortress.

Olson, Ruth L., ed. Hymns & Songs for Church Schools. LC 62-13898. (Illus.). 1962. 2.25 ea. (12-1500); 10-49 2.10 ea.; 50 or more 2.00 ea. Augsburg.

LUTHERAN CHURCH–LITURGY AND RITUAL

Kemper, Frederick W. A Change of Key. 1977. pap. 5.95 (ISBN 0-570-03761-1, 12-2683). Concordia.

Lutheran Book of Worship, 7 vols. Incl. Pew Edition. 8.50 (ISBN 0-685-92595-1, 12-2000); Ministers Edition. 35.00 (ISBN 0-685-92596-X, 12-2001); Accompaniment Edition, Liturgy. 15.00 (ISBN 0-685-92597-8, 12-2002); Organist Edition, Hymns. 10.00 (ISBN 0-685-92598-6, 12-2003); Ministers Desk Edition. 12.50 (ISBN 0-685-92599-4, 12-2004); Gift Edition. 19.50 (ISBN 0-686-52336-9, 12-2005); Pocket Edition. 17.50 (ISBN 0-686-52337-7, 12-2006). LC 77-92169. 1978. Augsburg.

McClean, Charles, ed. The Conduct of the Services. (Illus.). 138p. 1975. pap. 6.50 (ISBN 0-915644-04-5). Clayton Pub Hse.

Pfatteicher, Philip H. & Messerli, Carlos R. Manual on the Liturgy: Lutheran Book of Worship. LC 78-68179. 1979. 12.50 (ISBN 0-8066-1676-8, 12-2015). Augsburg.

LUTHERAN CHURCH–MEMBERSHIP

Rudnick, Miltin L. Christianity Is for You. 1961. pap. 2.75 (ISBN 0-570-03503-1, 14-1271). Concordia.

LUTHERAN CHURCH–MISSOURI SYNOD

see Evangelical Lutheran Synod of Missouri, Ohio and other states

LUTHERAN CHURCH–PRAYER-BOOKS AND DEVOTIONS

Brokering, Herbert F., ed. Luthers Prayers. Kistler, Charles E., tr. LC 67-25366. 1967. lea. bdg. 4.50 (ISBN 0-8066-0721-1, 10-4231). Augsburg.

Doerffler, Alfred. Treasures of Hope. 1945. pap. 6.95 (ISBN 0-570-03763-8, 12-2697). Concordia.

Gockel, Herman W. & Saleska, Edward J., eds. Child's Garden of Prayer. (Illus.). (gr. k-2). 1981. pap. 0.99 (ISBN 0-570-03412-4, 56-1016). Concordia.

Huxhold, Harry N. Family Altar. rev. ed. 1964. 0.95 (ISBN 0-570-03071-4, 6-1085). Concordia.

Kraus, George. By Word & Prayer. 1981. 8.95 (ISBN 0-570-03045-5, 6-1169). Concordia.

Lindemann, Herbert, ed. Daily Office. LC 65-26201. 1965. red vinyl 16.95 (ISBN 0-570-03060-9, 6-1086); red morr leather 25.00 (ISBN 0-570-03061-7, 6-1087). Concordia.

Little Folded Hands. rev. ed. LC 59-12074. (gr. 1-5). 1959. 2.50 (ISBN 0-570-03417-5, 56-1038); pap. 1.10 laminated (ISBN 0-570-03416-7, 56-1037). Concordia.

Lutheran Book of Prayer. rev. ed. LC 76-119916. 1970. 3.50 (ISBN 0-570-03005-6, 6-1141). Concordia.

Nelson, Ruth Y. God's Song in My Heart: Daily Devotions. LC 56-11912. 432p. 1957. 7.50 (ISBN 0-8006-0254-4, 1-254). Fortress.

Pfatteicher, Philip H. Festivals & Commemorations: Handbook to the Calendar in Lutheran Book of Worship. LC 79-54129. 336p. 15.00 (ISBN 0-8066-1757-8, 10-2295). Augsburg.

Syverud, Genevieve W. This Is My Song of Songs. (Orig.). 1966. pap. 1.50 (ISBN 0-8066-0613-4, 11-9495). Augsburg.

Wiencke, Gustav K. & Lehman, Helmut T., eds. Luther's Works: Devotional Writing II, Vol. 43. LC 55-9893. 1968. 15.95 (ISBN 0-8006-0343-5, 1-343). Fortress.

LUTHERAN CHURCH–RELATIONS–CATHOLIC CHURCH

Empie, Paul C., et al, eds. Lutherans & Catholics in Dialogue I-III. LC 74-83330. 1974. pap. 4.95 (ISBN 0-8066-1451-X, 10-4190). Augsburg.

Marty, Myron A. Lutherans & Roman Catholicism: The Changing Conflict, 1917-1963. 1968. 8.95x (ISBN 0-268-00162-6). U of Notre Dame Pr.

Quanbeck, Warren A. Search for Understanding: Lutheran Conversations with Reformed, Anglican, & Roman Catholic Churches. LC 72-90259. 112p. 1972. pap. 2.95 (ISBN 0-8066-1306-8, 10-5610). Augsburg.

LUTHERAN CHURCH–SERMONS

Augsburg Sermons: Gospels - Series C. LC 73-78262. 1973. 11.50 (ISBN 0-8066-9485-8, 10-0525). Augsburg.

Hillerbrand, Hans J. & Lehmann, Helmut T., eds. Luther's Works: Sermons II, Vol. 52. LC 55-9893. 416p. 1974. 15.95 (ISBN 0-8006-0352-4, 1-352). Fortress.

Hoffmann, Oswald. God Is No Island. LC 71-80998. 1969. 3.25 (ISBN 0-570-03000-5, 6-1136). Concordia.

Kierkegaard, Soren. For Self-Examination. Hong, Edna & Hong, Howard, trs. (Orig.). 1940. pap. 3.50 (ISBN 0-8066-0075-6, 10-2350). Augsburg.

--For Self-Examination & Judge for Yourselves. (American-Scandinavian Foundation). 16.50 (ISBN 0-691-07112-8); pap. 5.95 (ISBN 0-691-01952-5). Princeton U Pr.

Kiessling, Elmer C. Early Sermons of Luther & Their Relation to the Pre-Reformation Sermon. LC 75-171064. Repr. of 1935 ed. 14.45 (ISBN 0-404-03669-4). AMS Pr.

Kolb, Robert. Andreae & the Formula of Concord. 1977. pap. 7.50 (ISBN 0-570-03741-7, 12-2645). Concordia.

Lehmann, Helmut T. & Doberstein, John W., eds. Luther's Works: Sermons I, Vol. 51. Doberstein, John W., tr. LC 55-9893. 1959. 16.95 (ISBN 0-8006-0351-6, 1-353). Fortress.

Lejeune, R. Christoph Blumhardt & His Message. LC 63-15816. 1963. 7.95 (ISBN 0-87486-200-0). Plough.

Poovey, W. A. Celebrate with Drama: Dramas & Meditations for Six Special Days. LC 74-14172. 88p. (Orig.). 1975. pap. 3.50 (ISBN 0-8066-1456-0, 10-1010); drama bklet 1.50 (ISBN 0-8066-1457-9, 10-1011). Augsburg.

Schreibner, Vernon R. My Redeemer Lives: Messages from the Book of Job for Lent & Easter. LC 74-14170. 80p. 1974. pap. 2.50 (ISBN 0-8066-1453-6, 10-4600). Augsburg.

Steimle, Edmund A. God the Stranger: Reflections About Resurrection. LC 78-14674. 80p. 1979. pap. 3.50 (ISBN 0-8006-1354-6, 1-1354). Fortress.

Thielicke, Helmot. The Waiting Father. LC 75-12284. 192p. 1981. pap. 4.95 (ISBN 0-06-067991-3, RD 364, HarpR). Har-Row.

Thielicke, Helmut. How Modern Should Theology Be? Anderson, H. George, tr. from Ger. LC 69-14620. 96p. 1969. 3.50 (ISBN 0-8006-0287-0, 1-287). Fortress.

--How the World Began: Man in the First Chapters of the Bible. Doberstein, John W., tr. from Ger. LC 61-6756. 324p. 1961. pap. 5.50 (ISBN 0-8006-1894-7, 1-1894). Fortress.

--How to Believe Again. Anderson, H. George, tr. from Ger. LC 72-75656. 224p. 1972. pap. 4.75 (ISBN 0-8006-0123-8, 1-123). Fortress.

--Our Heavenly Father. (Minister's Paperback Library Ser.). 1974. pap. 3.95 (ISBN 0-8010-8814-3). Baker Bk.

Thompson, Orin D. Even If I'm Bad: Sermons for Children. (Orig.). 1966. pap. 2.95 (ISBN 0-8066-0616-9, 10-2108). Augsburg.

LUTHERAN CHURCH–YEARBOOKS

Pfatteicher, Philip H. Festivals & Commemorations: Handbook to the Calendar in Lutheran Book of Worship. LC 79-54129. 336p. 15.00 (ISBN 0-8066-1757-8, 10-2295). Augsburg.

Yearbook: Wisconsin Ev. Lutheran Synod, 1981. 4.25 (ISBN 0-8100-0137-3, 29-1419). Northwest Pub.

LUTHERAN CHURCH IN SCANDINAVIA

Wordsworth, John. National Church of Sweden. 1911. 12.50x (ISBN 0-8401-2821-5). Allenson-Breckinridge.

LUTHERAN CHURCH IN THE UNITED STATES

Bernheim, Gotthardt D. History of the German Settlements & of the Lutheran Church in North & South Carolina. LC 75-969. xvi, 557p. 1975. Repr. of 1872 ed. 20.00 (ISBN 0-8063-8001-2). Regional.

Graebner, Alan. Uncertain Saints. LC 75-1573. (Contributions in American History: No. 42). 320p. 1975. lib. bdg. 16.00 (ISBN 0-8371-7963-7, GUS/). Greenwood.

Groh, John E. & Smith, Robert H., eds. The Lutheran Church in North American Life: 1776-1976, 1580-1980. LC 78-71233. 1979. 5.95 (ISBN 0-915644-17-7, Clayton). Luth Acad.

Groh, John E., et al, eds. The Lutheran Church in North American Life: 1776-1976; 1580-1980. LC 78-71233. 1979. pap. 5.95 (ISBN 0-915644-17-7). Clayton Pub Hse.

Hart, Simon & Kreider, Harry J., trs. Lutheran Church in New York & New Jersey, 1722-1760. 1962. 11.00 (ISBN 0-913186-03-1). Monocacy.

Heintzen, Erich H. & Starr, Frank. Love Leaves Home. LC 72-94586. 1973. 2.50 (ISBN 0-570-03513-9, 14-2017). Concordia.

Kersten, Lawrence K. The Lutheran Ethic: The Impact of Religion on Laymen & Clergy. LC 71-102200. 1970. 10.95x (ISBN 0-8143-1416-3). Wayne St U Pr.

Knudsen, Johannes. The Formation of the Lutheran Church in America. LC 77-15235. 132p. 1978. 5.95 (ISBN 0-8006-0517-9, 1-517). Fortress.

Lindberg, Duane R. Men of the Cloth & the Social-Cultural Fabric of the Norwegian Ethnic Community in North Dakota. Cordasco, Francesco, ed. LC 80-877. (American Ethnic Groups Ser.). 1981. lib. bdg. 35.00x (ISBN 0-405-13438-X). Arno.

Schmucker, Samuel S. American Lutheran Church, Historically, Doctrinally, & Practically Delineated in Several Discourses. LC 72-83436. (Religion in American Ser). 1969. Repr. of 1851 ed. 14.50 (ISBN 0-405-00261-0). Arno.

Thorkelson, Willmar. Lutherans in the U. S. A. rev. ed. LC 77-84812. 1978. pap. 1.95 (ISBN 0-8066-1688-1, 10-4200). Augsburg.

Tietjen, John H. Which Way to Lutheran Unity? A History of Efforts to Unite the Lutherans of America. LC 66-25270. 176p. 1975. pap. text ed. 7.50 (ISBN 0-915644-01-0). Clayton Pub Hse.

Weisheit, Eldon. The Zeal of His House. LC 73-76988. 1973. 2.50 (ISBN 0-570-03516-3, 14-2020). Concordia.

LUTHERANS IN NORTH AMERICA

Groh, John E. & Smith, Robert H., eds. The Lutheran Church in North American Life: 1776-1976, 1580-1980. LC 78-71233. 1979. 5.95 (ISBN 0-915644-17-7, Clayton). Luth Acad.

Nelson, E. Clifford, ed. Lutherans in North America. rev. ed. LC 74-26337. (Illus.). 576p. 1980. o. p. 22.50x (ISBN 0-8006-0409-1); pap. 14.95 (ISBN 0-8006-1409-7, 1-1409). Fortress.

Tengbom, Mildred. No Greater Love. (Greatness with Faith Ser.). (Illus.). (gr. 5-8). 1978. 4.95 (ISBN 0-570-07878-4, 39-1203); pap. 2.95 (ISBN 0-570-07883-0, 39-1213). Concordia.

LUTZ, FRANK EUGENE, 1879-1943

Pallister, John C. In the Steps of the Great American Entomologist, Frank Eugene Lutz. Forbes, John R., ed. (In the Steps of the Great American Naturalists Ser.). (Illus.). 127p. 1976. Repr. of 1966 ed. 3.95 (ISBN 0-916544-10-9). Natural Sci Youth.

LUXATIONS

see Dislocations

LUXEMBURG, ROSA, 1870-1919

Bronner, Stephen, ed. The Letters of Rosa Luxemburg. 1979. lib. bdg. 25.25x (ISBN 0-89158-186-3); pap. text ed. 9.50 (ISBN 0-89158-188-X). Westview.

Ettinger, Elzbieta, ed. Comrade & Lover: Rosa Luxemburg's Letters to Leo Jogiches. 1979. 15.00 (ISBN 0-262-05021-8); pap. 4.95 (ISBN 0-262-62037-5). MIT Pr.

Frolich, Paul. Rosa Luxemburg. LC 68-9668. 1970. Repr. of 1940 ed. 23.50 (ISBN 0-86527-175-5). Fertig.

--Rosa Luxemburg: Her Life & Work. Hoornweg, Johanna, tr. from Ger. LC 72-81776. 352p. (Orig.). 1972. pap. 3.95 (ISBN 0-85345-260-1, PB-2601). Monthly Rev.

Geras, Norman. The Legacy of Rosa Luxemburg. 1976. 11.00 (ISBN 0-902308-28-9, Pub. by NLB). Schocken.

Luxemburg, Rosa. The National Question: Selected Writings. Davis, Horace B., ed. & tr. from Pol. LC 74-21468. 320p. 1976. 16.50 (ISBN 0-85345-355-1, CL3551). Monthly Rev.

LUXEMBURG

Riley, R. C. & Ashworth, Gregory. Benelux: An Economic Geography of Belgium, the Netherlands, & Luxembourg. LC 74-84586. (Illus.). 256p. 1975. text ed. 25.00 (ISBN 0-8419-0174-0). Holmes & Meier.

Taylor-Whitehead, W. J. Luxembourg: Land of Legends. 1976. lib. bdg. 59.95 (ISBN 0-8490-2190-1). Gordon Pr.

Van Houtte, J. A. An Economic History of the Low Countries 800-1800. LC 77-81397. (Illus.). 1977. 19.95x (ISBN 0-312-23320-5). St Martin.

LUXEMBURG-DESCRIPTION AND TRAVEL-GUIDEBOOKS

Evans, Craig. On Foot Through Europe: A Trail Guide to France & the Benelux Nations. Whitney, Stephen, ed. (Illus.). 496p. 1980. lib. bdg. 13.95 (ISBN 0-933710-17-8); pap. 7.95 (ISBN 0-933710-16-X). Foot Trails.

Fodor's Belgium & Luxembourg, 1981. 1980. 12.95 (ISBN 0-679-00671-0). McKay.

Michelin Guides & Maps. Michelin Green Guide Belgique et Grand Duche du Luxembourg. 1978. pap. 7.95 (ISBN 2-06-005100-2). Michelin.

Michelin Red Guide to Benelux: Michelin Guides & Maps. (Red Guide Ser.). 1981. 12.95 (ISBN 2-06-006301-9). Michelin.

LUXURY

Sekora, John. Luxury: The Concept in Western Thought, Eden to Smollett. LC 77-4545. 1978. text ed. 19.50x (ISBN 0-8018-1972-5). Johns Hopkins.

LUZAN, IGNACIO, 1702-1754

McClelland, Ivy L. Ignacio de Luzan. (World Authors Ser.: Spain: No. 221). lib. bdg. 10.95 (ISBN 0-8057-2552-0). Twayne.

LUZZATTO, SAMUELE DAVIDE, 1800-1865

Margolies, Morris B. Samual David Luzzatto: Traditionalist Scholar. Date not set. 15.00x (ISBN 0-87068-696-8). Ktav.

LUZON-SOCIAL LIFE AND CUSTOMS

Lava, Horacio C. Levels of Living in the Ilocos Region. LC 75-30066. (Institute of Pacific Relations). Repr. of 1938 ed. 11.50 (ISBN 0-404-59538-3). AMS Pr.

Scott, William F. The Discovery of the Igorots: Spanish Contacts with the Pagans of Northern Luzon. rev. ed. 1977. wrps. 11.75x (ISBN 0-686-18708-3). Cellar.

LYAPUNOV FUNCTIONS

see Liapunov Functions

LYAUTEY, HERBERT, 1854-1934

Maurois, Andre. Lyautey. 7.95 (ISBN 0-685-36945-5). French & Eur.

Scham, Alan. Lyautey in Morocco: Protectorate Administration, 1912-1925. LC 74-92680. 1970. 26.75x (ISBN 0-520-01602-5). U of Cal Pr.

LYCANTHROPY

see Werewolves

LYCEUMS

see also Chautauquas; Lectures and Lecturing

Bode, Carl. American Lyceum: Town Meeting of the Mind. LC 56-5163. 282p. 1968. Repr. of 1956 ed. lib. bdg. 7.00x (ISBN 0-8093-0318-3). S Ill U Pr.

--American Lyceum: Town Meeting of the Mind. LC 56-5163. (Arcturus Books Paperbacks). 282p. 1968. pap. 2.45 (ISBN 0-8093-0319-1). S Ill U Pr.

DaBoll, Raymond F. & DaBoll, Irene B. Recollections of the Lyceum & Chautauqua Circuits Plus Notes on Calligraphy & Scribal Writing. LC 66-19773. (Illus.). 188p. 1974. 16.95 (ISBN 0-87027-107-5); pap. 10.95 (ISBN 0-87027-133-4). Wheelwright.

Mead, Carl D. Yankee Eloquence in the Middle West: The Ohio Lyceum, 1850-1870. LC 77-5130. 1977. Repr. of 1951 ed. lib. bdg. 19.50x (ISBN 0-8371-9323-0, MEYE). Greenwood.

LYCOPERDON

see Puffballs

LYCOPDIUM

see Club-Mosses

LYDGATE, JOHN, 1370-1451

Buhler, Curt F. The Sources of the Court of Sapience. 1932. pap. 6.00 (ISBN 0-384-06235-0). Johnson Repr.

Gattinger, E. Die Lyrik Lydgates. 1965. pap. 10.00 (ISBN 0-384-17720-4). Johnson Repr.

Schirmer, Walter F. John Lydgate: A Study in the Culture of the XVth Century. Keep, Ann E., tr. from Ger. LC 78-12343. (Illus.). 1979. Repr. of 1961 ed. lib. bdg. 22.50x (ISBN 0-313-21216-3, SCJL). Greenwood.

LYELL, CHARLES, SIR, 1797-1875

Lyell, Charles. Life, Letters & Journals, 2 Vols. LC 72-1728. Repr. of 1881 ed. Set. 35.00 (ISBN 0-404-08156-8). AMS Pr.

--Travels in North America, the Years, 1841-2: Geological Observations on the United States, Canada, & Nova Scotia, 2 vols. in one. Albritton, Claude C., Jr., ed. LC 77-6525. (History of Geology Ser.). (Illus.). 1978. Repr. of 1845 ed. lib. bdg. 30.00x (ISBN 0-405-10447-2). Arno.

Wilson, Leonard G. Charles Lyell, the Years to Eighteen Forty One: The Revolution in Geology. LC 72-75212. (Illus.). 1972. 40.00x (ISBN 0-300-01486-4). Yale U Pr.

LYGAEIDAE

Usinger, R. L. Genus Nysius & Its Allies in the Hawaiian Islands. Repr. of 1942 ed. pap. 15.00 (ISBN 0-527-02281-0). Kraus Repr.

LYING

see Truthfulness and Falsehood

LYLY, JOHN, 1554-1606

Feuillerat, Albert. John Lyly: Contribution a Historie De La Renaissance. LC 70-145015. 661p. 1910. Repr. 38.00 (ISBN 0-403-00777-1). Scholarly.

--John Lyly: Contribution a l'Histoire de la Renaissance en Angleterre. LC 68-10917. (Orig., Fr.). 1968. Repr. of 1910 ed. 17.50 (ISBN 0-8462-1063-0). Russell.

Hunter, G. K. Lyle. Incl. Peele. Hunter, G. K. pap. 2.95 (ISBN 0-8277-6206-2, WTW206). British Bk Ctr.

Jeffery, Violet M. John Lyly & the Italian Renaissance. LC 68-25080. 1969. Repr. of 1928 ed. 7.50 (ISBN 0-8462-1262-5). Russell.

Rushton, William L. Shakespeare's Euphuism. LC 73-18333. 1973. lib. bdg. 6.45 (ISBN 0-8414-7281-5). Folcroft.

Saccio, Peter. Court Comedies of John Lyly: A Study in Allegorical Dramaturgy. LC 68-56320. 1969. 17.50x (ISBN 0-691-06159-9). Princeton U Pr.

Sisson, Charles J. Thomas Lodge & Other Elizabethans. 1966. lib. bdg. 32.00x (ISBN 0-374-97467-5). Octagon.

Wilson, John D. John Lyly. LC 68-24926. (English Biography Ser., No. 31). 1969. Repr. of 1905 ed. lib. bdg. 27.95 (ISBN 0-8383-0261-0). Haskell.

LYMAN BEECHER LECTURES

Jones, Edgar D. Royalty of the Pulpit. LC 79-134105. (Essay Index Reprint Ser). 1951. 25.00 (ISBN 0-8369-1979-3). Arno.

LYMPHANGIOGRAPHY

Fuchs, W. A., et al. Lymphography in Cancer. LC 76-84146. (Recent Results in Cancer Research: Vol. 23). 1969. 50.70 (ISBN 0-387-04685-2). Springer-Verlag.

Kuisk, Hans. Technique of Lymphography & Principles of Interpretation. LC 74-96986. (Illus.). 344p. 1971. 25.00 (ISBN 0-87527-046-8). Green.

LYMPH NODES

Robb-Smith, A. H. & Taylor, G. B. Lymph-Node Biopsy: A Diagnostic Atlas. (Illus.). 300p. 1981. text ed. 75.00x (ISBN 0-19-520247-3). Oxford U Pr.

Shields, Jack W. The Trophic Function of Lymphoid Elements. (Illus.). 456p. 1972. photocopy ed. sripal 44.75 (ISBN 0-398-02412-X). C C Thomas.

LYMPHATIC SYSTEM

see Lymphatics

LYMPHATICS

see also Hodgkin's Disease; Lymph Nodes; Sarcoidosis

Abramson, David I., ed. Blood Vessels & Lymphatics. 1962. 72.00 (ISBN 0-12-042550-5). Acad Pr.

Barrowman, J. A. Physiology of the Gastro-Intestinal Lymphatic System. LC 77-22823. (Physiological Society Monographs: No. 33). (Illus.). 1978. 59.50 (ISBN 0-521-21710-5). Cambridge U Pr.

Battezzati, M. & Donini, I. The Lymphatic System. LC 73-9924. 496p. 1974. 59.95 (ISBN 0-470-05706-8). Halsted Pr.

Bona, Constantin & Cazenave, Pierre-Andre. Lymphocytic Regulation by Antibodies. LC 80-17399. 324p. 1981. 49.50 (ISBN 0-471-05693-6, Pub. by Wiley-Interscience). Wiley.

Cohen, Stanley, et al, eds. Biology of the Lymphokines. LC 78-825. 1979. 45.50 (ISBN 0-12-178250-6). Acad Pr.

Cronkite, Eugene D. & Berliner, Robert W. Blood & Lymph & the Excretion of Urine. 84p. 1973. pap. 9.50 (ISBN 0-686-65352-1). Krieger.

De Weck, Alain L., et al, eds. Biochemical Characterization of Lymphokines: Proceedings of the Second International Lymphokine Workshop. LC 80-289. 1980. 39.50 (ISBN 0-12-213950-X). Acad Pr.

Fuchs, W. A., et al. Lymphography in Cancer. LC 76-84146. (Recent Results in Cancer Research: Vol. 23). 1969. 50.70 (ISBN 0-387-04685-2). Springer-Verlag.

Haagensen, Cushman D., et al. The Lymphatics in Cancer. LC 76-126454. (Illus.). 583p. 1972. 30.00 (ISBN 0-7216-4443-0). Saunders.

International Coloquim, Brussels. Lympho Kinetics: Proceedings. Leduc, Albert & Lievens, Pierre, eds. (Experientia Supplementum: No. 33). (Illus.). 123p. 1978. 29.50 (ISBN 3-7643-1029-4). Birkhauser.

Kampmeier, Otto F. Evolution & Comparative Morphology of the Lymphatic System. (Illus.). 636p. 1969. photocopy ed. spiral 59.50 (ISBN 0-398-00966-X). C C Thomas.

Krakauer, Randall S. & Clough, John D., eds. Suppressor Cells & Their Factors. 192p. 1981. 54.95 (ISBN 0-8493-6185-0). CRC Pr.

Lindahl-Kiessling, K., et al, eds. Morphological & Functional Aspects of Immunity. LC 75-148822. (Advances in Experimental Medicine & Biology Ser.: Vol. 12). 694p. 1971. 45.00 (ISBN 0-306-39012-4, Plenum Pr). Plenum Pub.

Malek, P. & Bartos, V., eds. Lymphology: Proceedings of the 6th International Conference. LC 78-24681. (Illus.). 532p. 1979. text ed. 49.50 (ISBN 0-88416-280-X). Wright-PSG.

Mayall, R. C. & White, Marlys H., eds. Progress in Lymphology. LC 76-46410. 389p. 1977. 45.00 (ISBN 0-306-30989-0, Plenum Pr). Plenum Pub.

Miller, Albert J. The Lymphatics of the Heart. 1981. text ed. 55.00 (ISBN 0-89004-604-2). Raven.

Molander, David W., ed. Lymphoproliferative Diseases. (Illus.). 592p. 1975. text ed. 52.75 (ISBN 0-398-03025-1). C C Thomas.

Pick, Edgar, ed. Lymphokine, Vol. 3. (Serial Publication Ser.). 1981. 49.50 (ISBN 0-12-432003-1). Acad Pr.

Symposia Angiologica Santoriana, 3rd Intl. Symposium, Fribourg, 1970. Physiology of Blood & Lymph Vessels: Proceedings, 2 pts. Comel, M. & Lastz, L., eds. Incl. Pt. 1. Angiologica, Vol. 8, Nos. 3-5; Pt. 2. Angiologica, Vol. 8, Additament. 1971. 1 vol. ed. reprint 46.50 (ISBN 3-8055-1263-5); Pt. 1. pap. text ed. 36.50 (ISBN 3-8055-2472-2); Pt. 2. pap. text ed. 24.75 (ISBN 3-8055-1289-9); Set. pap. text ed. 46.50 (ISBN 3-8055-1726-2). S Karger.

Van Der Putte, S. C. The Development of the Lymphatic System in Man. (Advances in Anatomy, Embryology & Cell Biology: Vol. 51, Pt. 1). (Illus.). 60p. 1975. pap. 22.50 (ISBN 0-387-07204-7). Springer-Verlag.

Weiss, Leonard, et al. Lymphatic System Metastasis. (Medical Publications Ser.). 1980. lib. bdg. 55.00 (ISBN 0-8161-2142-7). G K Hall.

Yoffey, J. M. & Coortice, F. C. Lymphatics, Lymph & the Lymphomyelard Complex. 1971. 112.00 (ISBN 0-12-772050-2). Acad Pr.

LYMPHOCYTES

Aiuti, F. & Wigzell, H., eds. Thymus, Thymic Hormones & T Lymphocytes. (Serono Symposia Ser.: No. 38). 1980. 57.50 (ISBN 0-12-046450-0). Acad Pr.

Arber, W., et al, eds. Current Topics in Microbiology & Immunology, Vols. 86-87. (Illus.). 1980. Vol. 86. 39.30 (ISBN 0-387-09432-6); Vol. 87. 37.40 (ISBN 0-387-09433-4). Springer-Verlag.

Bona, Constantin. Idiotypes & Lymphocytes. (Immunology: an International Ser. of Monographs & Treatise). 1981. price not set (ISBN 0-12-112950-0). Acad Pr.

Castellani, Amleto, ed. Lymphocyte Stimulation: Differential Sensitivity to Radiation, Biochemical & Immunological Processes. 185p. 1980. 27.50 (ISBN 0-306-40475-3, Plenum Pr). Plenum Pub.

Cold Spring Harbor Symposia on Quantitative Biology: Origins of Lymphocyte Diversity, 2 bk. set, Vol. 41. LC 34-8174. (Illus.). 1024p. 1977. Set. 85.00 (ISBN 0-87969-040-2). Cold Spring Harbor.

De Sousa, Maria. Lymphocyte Circulation: Experimental & Clinical Aspects. LC 80-40848. 259p. 1981. 54.95 (ISBN 0-471-27854-8, Pub. by Wiley-Interscience). Wiley.

De Weck, A. L., ed. Differentiated Lymphocyte Functions & Their Ontogeny. (Progress in Allergy Ser.: Vol. 28). (Illus.). x, 286p. 1981. 87.00 (ISBN 3-8055-1834-X). S Karger.

Epstein, M. A. & Achong, B. G., eds. The Epstein-Barr Virus. (Illus.). 1979. 69.30 (ISBN 0-387-09272-2). Springer-Verlag.

Escobar, M. R. & Friedman, H., eds. Macrophages & Lymphocytes: Nature, Functions & Interaction, Pt. B. (Advances in Experimental Medicine & Biology: Vol. 121B). 625p. 1980. 59.50 (ISBN 0-306-40286-6, Plenum Pr). Plenum Pub.

FEBS Meeting, 8th, et al. Immunoglobulins-Cell Bound Receptors & Humoral Antibodies: Proceedings, Vol. 26. Ballieux, R., ed. 1973. 11.00 (ISBN 0-444-10421-6, North-Holland). Elsevier.

Feldman, Michael & Globerson, Amiela, eds. Immune Reactivity of Lymphocytes: Development, Expression, & Control. LC 75-42123. (Advances in Experimental Medicine & Biology Ser.: Vol. 66). 732p. 1976. 49.50 (ISBN 0-306-39066-3, Plenum Pr). Plenum Pub.

Garland, P. B. & Crumpton, M. J., eds. The Lymphocyte Cell Surface. (Symposia Ser.: No. 45). 124p. 1981. 35.00x (ISBN 0-904498-10-7, Pub. by Biochemical England). State Mutual Bk.

Gottlieb, Arthur A., et al, eds. Developments in Lymphoid Cell Biology. new ed. LC 74-77918. (Uniscience Ser.). 176p. 1974. 42.50 (ISBN 0-87819-056-2). CRC Pr.

Haas, W. & Von Boehmer, H. Techniques for Separation & Selection of Specific Lymphocytes. (Current Topics in Microbiology & Immunology Ser.: Vol. 84). (Illus.). 1979. 30.50 (ISBN 0-387-09029-0). Springer-Verlag.

Hadden, John W. & Stewart, William E., eds. The Lymphokines. LC 80-85521. (Contemporary Immunology Ser.). (Illus.). 1981. 59.50 (ISBN 0-89603-012-1). Humana.

ICN-UCLA Symposia on Molecular & Cellular Biology, 1979. T & B Lymphocytes: Recognition & Function: Symposium, Vol. XVI. Bach, Fritz H., et al, eds. LC 79-26438. 1979. 45.50 (ISBN 0-12-069850-1). Acad Pr.

Katz, D. H. Lymphocyte Differentiation, Recognition & Regulation. 1977. 52.75 (ISBN 0-12-401640-5). Acad Pr.

Lehmann-Grube, F., ed. Lymphocytic Choriomeningitis. LC 70-167276. (Virology Monographs: Vol. 10). 1971. 23.20 (ISBN 0-387-81017-X). Springer-Verlag.

--Lymphocytic Choriomeningitis Virus & Other Arenaviruses. LC 73-10673. xiii, 339p. 1973. pap. 33.00 (ISBN 0-387-06403-6). Springer-Verlag.

Ling, N. R. & Kay, J. E., eds. Lymphocyte Stimulation. rev. 2nd ed. LC 74-83274. 397p. 1975. 73.25 (ISBN 0-444-10701-0, North-Holland). Elsevier.
Loor, F. & Roelants, G. E., eds. B & T Cells in Immune Recognition. LC 76-26913. 1977. 70.95 (ISBN 0-471-99438-3, Pub. by Wiley-Interscience). Wiley.
Lucas, D. O., ed. Regulatory Mechanism in Lymphocyte Activation. 1977. 60.00 (ISBN 0-12-458050-5). Acad Pr.
Lymphography: Clinical & Experimental, B. W. M. Gooneratne. 1974. 46.95 (ISBN 0-407-26140-0). Butterworth.
Marchalonis, John J., ed. The Lymphocyte: Structure & Function, Pt. 1. (Immunology Ser.: Vol. 5). 1977. 47.50 (ISBN 0-8247-6418-8). Dekker.
--The Lymphocyte: Structure & Function, Pt. 2. (Immunology Ser.: Vol. 5). 1977. 49.50 (ISBN 0-8247-6419-6). Dekker.
Mathe, G., et al, eds. Lymphocytes, Macrophages, & Cancer. LC 76-26538. (Recent Results in Cancer Research Ser.: Vol. 56). 1976. 29.10 (ISBN 3-540-07902-5). Springer-Verlag.
Melchers, F., et al, eds. Lymphocyte Hybridomas: Second Workshop. (Illus.). 1979. 17.20 (ISBN 0-387-09670-1). Springer-Verlag.
Natvig, ed. Lymphocytes: Fractionation, Isolation, & Characterization. 1977. 32.50 (ISBN 0-8391-0979-2). Univ Park.
Nossal, G. J. & Ada, G. L. Antigens, Lymphoid Cells & the Immune Response. LC 71-137602. (Monographs on Immunology: Vol. 1). 1971. 51.50 (ISBN 0-12-521950-4). Acad Pr.
Pernis, Benvenuto & Vogel, Henry J., eds. Regulatory T Lymphocytes. (P & S Biomedical Science Ser.). 1980. 47.50 (ISBN 0-12-551860-9). Acad Pr.
Sell, Kenneth W. & Miller, William V. The Lymphocyte. LC 81-2773. (Progress in Clinical & Biological Research Ser.: Vol. 58). 242p. 1981. 34.00 (ISBN 0-8451-0058-0). A R Liss.
Williams, Ralph C., Jr., ed. Lymphocytes & Their Interactions. 240p. 1975. text ed. 18.00 (ISBN 0-89004-052-4). Raven.

LYMPHOMA

see also Burkitt's Lymphoma; Hodgkin's Disease

Bachmann, Peter A., ed. Leukaemias, Lymphomas & Papillomas: Comparative Aspects. (Munich Symposia on Microbiology). (Illus.). 273p. (Orig.). 1980. pap. text ed. 26.00 (ISBN 0-85066-213-3, Pub. by Taylor & Francis England). J K Burgess.
Bluefarb, Samuel M. Cutaneous Manifestations of Malignant Lymphomas. (American Lecture Dermatology). (Illus.). 548p. 1959. ed. spiral bdg. 49.50photocopy (ISBN 0-398-00174-X). C C Thomas.
Chiappa, S., et al. Endolymphatic Radiotherapy in Malignant Lymphomas. LC 78-148260. (Recent Results in Cancer Research Ser.: Vol. 37). (Illus.). 1971. 28.60 (ISBN 0-387-05330-1). Springer-Verlag.
Clouse, Melvin E., ed. Lymphography. (Golden's Diagnostic Radiology Ser.: Section 7). (Illus.). 1977. 44.00 (ISBN 0-683-01883-3). Williams & Wilkins.
Fairley, G. Hamilton, et al. Leukemia & Lymphoma. LC 74-26642. 238p. 1974. Repr. 36.00 (ISBN 0-8089-0858-8). Grune.
Freireich, Emil J., et al, eds. Leukemia & Lymphoma. 368p. 1978. 36.00 (ISBN 0-8089-1166-X). Grune.
Goldstone, A. H., et al. Leukaemias, Lymphomas & Allied Disorders. LC 75-44603. (Illus.). 1976. text ed. 18.50 (ISBN 0-7216-4149-0). Saunders.
Graham-Pole, John, ed. Non-Hodgkin's Lymphomas in Children. LC 80-81990. (Masson Monographs in Pediatric Hematology - Oncology: Vol. 2). (Illus.). 192p. 1980. 26.50x (ISBN 0-89352-068-3). Masson Pub.
Jackson, J. R. The Histopathology of Lymphomas & Pseudolymphomas. 253p. text ed. 34.50 (ISBN 0-8391-1324-2). Univ Park.
Lee, Yeu-Tsu N. & Spratt, John S., Jr. Malignant Lymphoma: Nodal & Extranodal Diseases. (Modern Surgical Monographs). (Illus.). 384p. 1974. 44.75 (ISBN 0-8089-0824-3). Grune.
Lennert, K. Histopathology of Non-Hodgkin Lymphomas: Kiel Classification. (Illus.). 130p. 1981. 33.00 (ISBN 0-387-10445-3). Springer-Verlag.
--Malignant Lymphomas. 1977. 170.40 (ISBN 0-387-08020-1). Springer-Verlag.
Mathe, G., et al, eds. Lymphoid Neoplasias I: Classification, Categorization, Natural History. LC 78-19077. (Recent Results in Cancer Research: Vol. 64). (Illus.). 1978. 50.80 (ISBN 0-387-08830-X). Springer-Verlag.
Ngan, H. & James, K. W. Clinical Radiology of the Lymphomas. Trapnell, D. H., ed. (Radiology in Clinical Diagnosis Ser.: Vol. 7). Orig. Title: Radiology in Lymphomas. (Illus.). 1973. 14.95 (ISBN 0-407-13715-7). Butterworth.
Pochedly, Carl. Leukemia & Lymphoma in the Nervous System. (Illus.). 248p. 1977. 30.00 (ISBN 0-685-73596-6). C C Thomas.
Stone, Hoyt E. Yet Will I Serve Him. 1976. pap. 2.35 (ISBN 0-87148-931-7). Pathway Pr.
Stuart, A. E., et al, eds. Lymphomas Other Than Hodgkin's Disease. (Illus.). 80p. 1981. text ed. 39.50x (ISBN 0-19-261296-4). Oxford U Pr.
Symposium on the Epidemiology of Cancer, Lymphomas, Duesseldorf, Nov. 4-6, 1971. Current Problems in the Epidemiology of Cancer & Lymphomas. Grundmann, E. & Tulinius, H., eds. LC 72-81166. (Recent Results in Cancer Research: Vol. 39). (Illus.). 260p. 1972. 24.10 (ISBN 0-387-05860-5). Springer-Verlag.
Thierfelder, S., et al, eds. Immunological Diagnosis of Leukemias & Lymphomas. (Haematologie und Bluttransfusion: Vol. 20). 1977. soft cover 43.80 (ISBN 0-387-08216-6). Springer-Verlag.
Ultmann, J. E., et al, eds. Current Concepts in the Management of Lymphoma & Leukemia. LC 71-146232. (Recent Results in Cancer Research: Vol. 36). (Illus.). 1971. 28.60 (ISBN 0-387-05309-3). Springer-Verlag.
Van der Twell, J. G., et al, eds. Malignant Lymphoproliferative Diseases. (Boerhaave Ser. for Postgraduate Medical Education: No. 17). (Illus.). 520p. 1980. lib. bdg. 76.00 (ISBN 90-6021-451-X, Pub. by Leiden Univ. Holland). Kluwer Boston.

LYMPHOSARCOMA

see Hodgkin's Disease

LYMPHOID TISSUE

Carr, Ian, et al. Lymphoreticular Disease: An Introduction for the Pathologist & Oncologist. 1978. soft cover 21.95 (ISBN 0-397-60436-X, Pub. by Blackwell Scientific). Mosby.
Fiore-Donati, L. & Hanna, M. G. Lymphatic Tissue & Germinal Centers in Immune Response. LC 75-82374. (Advances in Experimental Medicine & Biology Ser.: Vol. 5). 529p. 1969. 42.50 (ISBN 0-306-39005-1, Plenum Pr). Plenum Pub.
Glick. Fundamentals of Human Lymphoid Cell Culture. 176p. 1980. 22.50 (ISBN 0-8247-6988-0). Dekker.
--Human Lymphoid Cell Cultures: The Fundamentals. 1980. 22.50 (ISBN 0-8247-6988-0). Dekker.
Jankovic, B. D. & Isakovic, K., eds. Microenvironmental Aspects of Immunity. LC 72-89487. (Advances in Experimental Medicine & Biology Ser.: Vol. 29). 726p. 1973. 55.00 (ISBN 0-306-39029-9, Plenum Pr). Plenum Pub.
Luriya, E. A., ed. Hematopoietic & Lymphoid Tissue in Cultures. LC 76-55703. (Studies in Soviet Science: Life Science). (Illus.). 181p. 1977. 42.50 (ISBN 0-306-10934-4, Consultants). Plenum Pub.
Mathe, G., et al, eds. Lymphoid Neplasias II: Clinical & Therapeutic Aspects. (Recent Results in Cancer Research: Vol. 65). (Illus.). 1978. 31.50 (ISBN 0-387-08831-8). Springer-Verlag.
Mori, Y. & Lennert, K. Electron Microscopic Atlas of Lymph Node Cytology & Pathology. Kuechemann, K., tr. LC 73-79750. (Illus.). 1969. 153.40 (ISBN 0-387-04662-3). Springer-Verlag.
Pick, Edgar, ed. Lymphokines: A Form for Immunoregulatory Cell Products, Vol. 4. (Serial Publication). 1981. price not set (ISBN 0-12-432004-X). Acad Pr.
Robb-Smith, A. H. & Taylor, G. B. Lymph-Node Biopsy: A Diagnostic Atlas. (Illus.). 300p. 1981. text ed. 75.00x (ISBN 0-19-520247-3). Oxford U Pr.
Shields, Jack W. The Trophic Function of Lymphoid Elements. (Illus.). 456p. 1972. photocopy ed. sripal 44.75 (ISBN 0-398-02412-X). C C Thomas.
Trnka, Z. & Cahill, R. N., eds. Essays on the Anatomy & Physiology of Lymphoid Tissues. (Monographs in Allergy: Vol. 16). (Illus.). 1979. pap. 87.00 (ISBN 3-8055-3059-5). S Karger.
Tuchel, V. Non-Specific Mesenteric Lymphadenitis. 1972. 38.50 (ISBN 3-8055-1251-1). S Karger.
Vianna, Nicholas J. Lymphoreticular Malignancies: Epidemiologic & Related Aspects. (Illus.). 144p. 1975. 34.50 (ISBN 0-8391-0813-3). Univ Park.

LYNCHING

see also Vigilance Committees

Addams, Jane & Wells, Ida B. Lynching & Rape: An Exchange of Views. Aptheker, Bettina, ed. 1977. 1.25 (ISBN 0-89977-023-1). Am Inst Marxist.
Ames, Jessie D. Changing Character of Lynching: Review of Lynching 1931-1941, with a Discussion of Recent Developments in This Field. LC 78-158249. Repr. of 1942 ed. 11.50 (ISBN 0-404-00134-3). AMS Pr.
Cameron, James. From the Inside Out: A Lynching in the North. LC 79-66608. 1981. 9.95 (ISBN 0-918270-05-7). That New Pub.
Chadbourn, James H. Lynching & the Law. LC 33-32207. (Basic Afro-American Reprint Library). 1970. Repr. of 1933 ed. 11.00 (ISBN 0-384-08205-X). Johnson Repr.
Cutler, James E. Lynch Law: An Investigation into the History of Lynching in the United States. LC 77-88428. Repr. of 1905 ed. 17.50x (ISBN 0-8371-1821-2, Pub. by Negro U Pr). Greenwood.
--Lynch-Law: An Investigation into the History of Lynching in the United States. LC 69-14920. (Criminology, Law Enforcement, & Social Problems Ser.: No. 70). (Illus.). 1969. Repr. of 1905 ed. 11.00 (ISBN 0-87585-070-7). Patterson Smith.
Grant, Donald L. Anti-Lynching Movement, Eighteen Eighty-Three to Nineteen Thirty-Two. LC 75-18122. 1975. soft bdg. 10.00 (ISBN 0-88247-348-4). R & E Res Assoc.
National Association For The Advancement Of Colored People. Thirty Years of Lynching in the United States, 1889-1918. LC 73-94142. (American Negro: His History & Literature, Ser. No. 3). 1970. Repr. of 1919 ed. 7.50 (ISBN 0-405-01932-7). Arno.
--Thirty Years of Lynching in the United States, 1889-1918. Repr. of 1919 ed. 10.00x (ISBN 0-8371-1950-2). Greenwood.
Patterson, William L., ed. We Charge Genocide: The Crime of Government Against the Negro People. LC 76-140208. 1970. 5.95 (ISBN 0-7178-0311-2); pap. 1.95 (ISBN 0-7178-0312-0). Intl Pub Co.
Raper, Arthur F. The Tragedy of Lynching. LC 77-110755. 1970. pap. 4.00 (ISBN 0-486-22622-0). Dover.
--Tragedy of Lynching. LC 72-90191. (Mass Violence in America Ser). Repr. of 1933 ed. 17.00 (ISBN 0-405-01334-5). Arno.
--Tragedy of Lynching. LC 69-16568. (Illus.). Repr. of 1933 ed. 20.75x (ISBN 0-8371-1145-5). Greenwood.
--Tragedy of Lynching. LC 69-14943. (Criminology, Law Enforcement, & Social Problems Ser.: No. 25). (With a new intro. by the author). 1969. Repr. of 1933 ed. 16.00 (ISBN 0-87585-025-1). Patterson Smith.
--The Tragedy of Lynching. 5.50 (ISBN 0-8446-0230-2). Peter Smith.
Shay, Frank. Judge Lynch: His First Hundred Years. LC 70-75359. 1969. Repr. of 1938 ed. 12.00x (ISBN 0-8196-0231-0). Biblo.
--Judge Lynch: His First Hundred Years. Bd. with Lynching & Racial Exploitation. Raper, Arthur F. LC 69-14945. (Criminology, Law Enforcement, & Social Problems Ser., No. 55). (With introductory essay). 1969. Repr. of 1938 ed. 11.00 (ISBN 0-87585-055-3). Patterson Smith.
Wells, Ida B. On Lynchings: A Red Record, Mob Rule in New Orleans: Southern Horrors. LC 72-75854. (American Negro: His History & Literature Ser., No. 2). 1969. 10.00 (ISBN 0-405-01849-5); pap. 1.95 (ISBN 0-405-01978-5). Arno.
White, Walter F. Rope & Faggot: Biography of Judge Lynch. LC 69-18545. (American Negro: His History & Literature Ser. No. 2). 1969. Repr. of 1929 ed. 12.00 (ISBN 0-405-01907-6). Arno.

LYNDHURST, JOHN SINGETON COPLEY, BARON, 1772-1863

Amory, Martha B. Domestic & Artistic Life of John Singleton Copley, R.A. facs. ed. LC 70-119925. (Select Bibliographies Reprint Ser). 1882. 25.00 (ISBN 0-8369-5368-1). Arno.
Benton, Josiah H. Warning Out in New England. facs. ed. LC 70-137370. (Select Bibliographies Reprint Ser). 1911. 11.00 (ISBN 0-8369-5571-4). Arno.

LYNDWOOD, WILLIAM, BP. OF ST. DAVID'S, 1375-1446

Ogle, Arthur. Canon Law in Mediaeval England: An Examination of William Lyndwood's Provinciale. LC 78-156390. (Research & Source Works Ser.: No. 731). 1971. Repr. of 1912 ed. lib. bdg. 20.50 (ISBN 0-8337-2603-X). B Franklin.

LYNN, JAMES JESSE, 1892-1955

Self-Realization Fellowship. Rajarsi Janakananda: A Great Western Yogi. (Illus.). 1977. pap. 1.50 (ISBN 0-87612-181-4). Self Realization.

LYNN, JANET

Morse, Ann. Janet Lynn. (Creative's Superstars Ser.). (Illus.). (gr. 3-9). 1975. PLB 5.95 (ISBN 0-87191-456-5). Creative Ed.

LYNX

see also Bobcat

LYON, JAMES

Sonneck, Oscar G. Francis Hopkinson, the First American Poet-Composer, & James Lyon, Patriot, Preacher, Psalmodist. 2nd ed. LC 65-23393. (Music Ser). 1966. Repr. of 1905 ed. lib. bdg. 19.50 (ISBN 0-306-70918-X). Da Capo.

LYON, MARY, 1797-1849

Banning, Evelyn I. Mary Lyons of Putnam Hill. LC 66-10683. (gr. 4 up). 1965. 6.95 (ISBN 0-8149-0269-3). Vanguard.

LYONS

Gascon, Richard. Grand Commerce et Vie Urbaine Au XVIe Siecle: Lyons et Ses Marchands (Environds De 1520-Environs De 1580, 2 vols. (Civilizations et Societes: No. 22). 1971. pap. 77.75x (ISBN 90-2796-967-1). Mouton.
Gueneau, Louis. Lyon et le Commerce de la Soie. LC 70-140977. 272p. (Fr.). 1973. Repr. of 1923 ed. lib. bdg. 26.50 (ISBN 0-8337-1483-X). B Franklin.
Sheridan, George J., Jr. The Social & Economic Foundations of Association Among the Silk Weavers of Lyons, 1852-1870. Bruchey, Stuart, ed. LC 80-2829. (Dissertations in European Economic History Ii). (Illus.). 1981. lib. bdg. 65.00x (ISBN 0-405-14013-4). Arno.
Wadsworth, James B. Lyons, Fourteen Seventy Three to Fifteen Three: The Beginnings of Cosmopolitanism. 1962. 9.00 (ISBN 0-910956-47-2). Medieval Acad.

LYRIC DRAMA

see Opera

LYRIC POETRY

see Poetry

LYSENKO, TROFIM DENISOVICH, 1898-

Huxley, Julian S. Heredity, East & West: Lysenko & World Science. LC 49-50254. 1969. Repr. of 1949 ed. 13.00 (ISBN 0-527-43810-3). Kraus Repr.
Lecourt, Dominique. Proletarian Science? The Case of Lysenko. 1978. 14.00 (ISBN 0-902308-69-6, Pub by NLB). Schocken.
Medvedev, Zhores A. The Rise & Fall of T. D. Lysenko. Lerner, I. Michael, tr. LC 79-77519. 284p. 1969. 16.00x (ISBN 0-231-03183-1). Columbia U Pr.

LYSERGIC ACID DIETHYLAMIDE

Alpert, Richard & Cohen, Sidney. LSD. pap. 2.95 (ISBN 0-452-25703-4, Z5703, Plume). NAL.
Barber, Theodore X. LSD, Marijuana, Yoga, & Hypnosis. LC 73-115935. 1970. 24.95x (ISBN 0-202-25004-0). Aldine Pub.
Barron, Frank. LSD, Man & Society. DeBold, Richard C. & Leaf, Russell C., eds. LC 73-15314. (Illus.). 219p. 1975. Repr. of 1967 ed. lib. bdg. 15.00 (ISBN 0-8371-7195-4, BALS). Greenwood.
Blum, Richard H., et al. Utopiates: The Use & Users of LSD-25. 1964. 10.95x (ISBN 0-202-26040-2). Beresford Bk Serv.
Cavanna, Roberto & Servadio, Emilio. ESP Experiments with LSD Twenty-Five & Psilocybin. LC 64-24271. (Parapsychological Monograph No. 5). 1964. pap. 3.00 (ISBN 0-912328-08-8). Parapsych Foun.
Cohen, Sidney. Beyond Within: The LSD Story. rev. ed. LC 64-25848. 1967. 6.95 (ISBN 0-689-10056-6). Atheneum.
Grof, Stanislav. LSD Psychotherapy. LC 79-65432. (Illus.). 1980. 24.95 (ISBN 0-89793-008-8). Hunter Hse.
Grof, Stanislav & Halifax, Joan. The Human Encounter with Death. 1978. pap. 3.95 (ISBN 0-525-47492-7). Dutton.
Hofmann. LSD: My Problem Child. Date not set. 9.95 (ISBN 0-07-029325-2). McGraw.
Krippner, Stanley & Cohen, Sidney, eds. LSD into the Eighties. (Illus.). 350p. 1981. 14.95 (ISBN 0-913300-22-5); pap. 7.95 (ISBN 0-913300-23-3). Unity Pr.
Ludwig, Arnold M. LSD & Alcoholism. (Illus.). 344p. 1970. photocopy ed. spiral 29.75 (ISBN 0-398-01162-1). C C Thomas.
Roseman, Bernard. LSD: The Age of Mind. pap. 2.00 (ISBN 0-87980-088-7). Wilshire.
Siva Sankar, D., et al. LSD-A Total Study. LC 72-95447. 1975. 39.75 (ISBN 0-9600290-3-6). PJD Pubns.
Ungerleider, J. Thomas, ed. The Problems & Prospects of LSD. (Illus.). 132p. 1972. 9.75 (ISBN 0-398-01952-5). C C Thomas.

LYSIAS, d. 380 B.C.

Adams, Charles D. Lysias. LC 79-123339. 1977. pap. 8.95x (ISBN 0-8061-1396-0). U of Okla Pr.
Dover, K. J. Lysias & the Corpus Lysiacum. LC 68-63337. (Sather Classical Lectures: No. 39). 1968. 23.50x (ISBN 0-520-00351-9). U of Cal Pr.
Lysias. Lysia Epitaphios, Pts. I & II. Connor, W. R., ed. LC 78-18608. (Greek Texts & Commentaries Ser.). 1979. Repr. of 1887 ed. lib. bdg. 10.00x (ISBN 0-405-11448-6). Arno.
--Lysias. Lamb, W. R., tr. LC 76-29460. Repr. of 1943 ed. 45.00 (ISBN 0-404-15315-1). AMS Pr.
Voegelin, Walter. Die Diabole bei Lysias. Vlastos, Gregory, ed. LC 78-14599. (Morals & Law in Ancient Greece Ser.). (Ger. & Gr.). 1979. Repr. of 1943 ed. lib. bdg. 12.00x (ISBN 0-405-11579-2). Arno.

LYSIPPUS (SCULPTOR)

Johnson, Franklin P. Lysippos. LC 68-29743. (Illus.). 1968. Repr. of 1927 ed. lib. bdg. 32.00x (ISBN 0-8371-0119-0, JOLY). Greenwood.

LYSOSOMES
Allison, A. C. Lysosomes. rev. ed. Head, J. J., ed. LC 76-29372. (Carolina Biology Readers Ser.). (Illus.). (gr. 11 up). 1977. pap. 1.65 (ISBN 0-89278-258-7, 45-9658). Carolina Biological.
Callahan, John W. & Lowden, J. Alexander, eds. Lysosomes & Lysosomal Storage Diseases. 455p. 1980. text ed. 50.00 (ISBN 0-89004-476-7). Raven.
Daems, W. T., et al, eds. Cell Biological Aspects of Disease: The Plasma Membrane & Lysosomes. (Boerhaave Series for Postgraduate Medical Education: No. 19). 330p. 1981. PLB 68.50 (ISBN 90-6021-466-8, Pub. by Leiden Univ Netherlands). Kluwer Boston.
Dingle, J. T. & Dean, R. T. Lysosomes in Biology & Pathology, Vol. 4. (Frontiers of Biology: Vol. 43). 1976. 102.00 (ISBN 0-444-10810-6, North-Holland). Elsevier.
Dingle, J. T., ed. Lysosomes: A Laboratory Handbook. 2nd ed. 1977. 66.50 (ISBN 0-7204-0627-7, North-Holland); pap. 35.75 (ISBN 0-7204-0628-5). Elsevier.
Dingle, J. T., et al, eds. Lyposomes in Applied Biology & Therapeutics. (Lyposomes in Biology & Pathology Ser.: Vol. 6). 714p. 1979. 109.50 (ISBN 0-686-63105-6, North Holland). Elsevier.
Hers, H. G. & Van Hoof, F., eds. Lysosomes & Storage Diseases. 1973. 81.00 (ISBN 0-12-342850-5). Acad Pr.
Holtzman, E. Lysosomes: A Survey. (Cell Biology Monographs: Vol. 3). (Illus.). 300p. 1976. 70.90 (ISBN 0-387-81316-0). Springer-Verlag.
Matile, P. The Lytic Compartment of Plant Cells. LC 75-5931. (Cell Biology Monographs: Vol. 1). (Illus.). xiii, 183p. 1975. 48.60 (ISBN 0-387-81296-2). Springer-Verlag.
Osserman, Elliot F., et al. Lysosome. 1974. 78.00 (ISBN 0-12-528950-2). Acad Pr.
Pitt, Dennis. Lysosomes & Cell Function. LC 75-308385. (Integrated Themes in Biology Ser). (Illus.). 160p. 1975. pap. text ed. 12.95x (ISBN 0-582-44344-X). Longman.
LYSSA
see Rabies
LYTLE, ANDREW NELSON, 1902-
Bradford, M. E., ed. The Form Discovered: Essays on the Achievement of Andrew Lytle. LC 73-86315. 128p. 1973. 1.00 (ISBN 0-87805-050-7). U Pr of Miss.
Wright, Stuart. Andrew Lytle: A Descriptive Bibliography of First Printings of His Works. Northouse, Cameron, ed. (First Printings Ser.). (Illus.). 60p. 1981. limited ed. 30.00 (ISBN 0-939722-05-4). Pressworks.
LYTTON, EDWARD GEORGE EARLE LYTTON BULWER-LYTTON, 1ST BARON, 1803-1873
Bulwer-Lytton, Edward. The Wit & Wisdom of E. Bulwer-Lytton. Bonney, C. L., ed. 1883. lib. bdg. 25.00 (ISBN 0-8414-2544-2). Folcroft.
Christensen, Allen C. Edward Bulwer-Lytton: The Fiction of New Regions. LC 74-27550. 268p. 1976. 16.00x (ISBN 0-8203-0387-9). U of Ga Pr.
Escott, T. H. Edward Bulwer. LC 75-113309. 1970. Repr. of 1910 ed. 13.50 (ISBN 0-8046-1016-9). Kennikat.
--Edward Bulwer: First Baron Lytton of Knebworth: A Social, Personal, & Political Monograph. 1977. Repr. of 1910 ed. lib. bdg. 30.00 (ISBN 0-8495-1305-7). Arden Lib.
Flower, S. J. Bulwer-Lytton. (Clarendon Biography Ser.). (Illus.). 1973. pap. 3.50 (ISBN 0-912728-60-4). Newbury Bks.
Lytton, Edward. Letters of the Late Edward Bulwer, Lord Lytton, to His Wife. LC 79-148815. Repr. of 1889 ed. 24.50 (ISBN 0-404-08884-8). AMS Pr.
Sadleir, Michael. Bulwer: A Panorama (Edward & Rosina 1803-1836) 1977. Repr. of 1931 ed. lib. bdg. 30.00 (ISBN 0-8414-7928-3). Folcroft.

M

M. G. AUTOMOBILE
see Automobiles, Foreign-Types-M. G.
MA-ATABELE
see Matabele
MA'DI (AFRICAN TRIBE)
see Logbara (African Tribe)
MAAS, PAUL
Dasnoy, A. Paul Maas: Catalog Raisonne. (Illus.). 277p. (Fr.). 1975. 65.00 (ISBN 0-912728-97-3). Newbury Bks.
MABINOGION
Griffith, W. Adventures of Pryderi: Taken from the Mabinogion. 1962. 7.50x (ISBN 0-7083-0418-4). Verry.
John, Ivor B. Mabinogion. LC 70-139174. (Popular Studies in Mythology, Romance & Folklore: No. 11). Repr. of 1901 ed. 5.50 (ISBN 0-404-53511-9). AMS Pr.
Jones, Gwyn. Kings, Beasts, & Heroes. 224p. 1972. 12.95 (ISBN 0-19-215181-9). Oxford U Pr.
MCALMON, ROBERT, 1896-1956
Knoll, Robert E. Robert McAlmon: Expatriate Publisher & Writer. LC 57-62784. 1959. pap. 2.95x (ISBN 0-8032-5226-9). U of Nebr Pr.
Smoller, Sanford J. Adrift Among Geniuses: Robert McAlmon, Writer & Publisher of the Twenties. LC 74-12257. 400p. 1974. 16.95 (ISBN 0-271-01173-4). Pa St U Pr.
MACAO
Coates, Austin. A Macao Narrative. LC 79-101322. (Asian Studies). 1978. pap. text ed. 6.50x (ISBN 0-686-65321-1, 00128). Heinemann Ed.
MACAQUES
Albrecht, Gene H. The Craniofacial Morphology of the Sulawesi Macaques: Multivariate Analysis As a Tool in Systematics. (Contributions to Primatology: Vol. 13). (Illus.). 1977. 44.50 (ISBN 3-8055-2694-6). S Karger.
Chevalier-Skolnikoff, Suzanne. The Ontogeny of Communication in the Stumptail Macaque. (Contributions to Primatology: Vol. 2). (Illus.). 174p. 1974. 44.50 (ISBN 3-8055-1647-9). S Karger.
Fedigan, L. M. A Study of Roles in the Arashiyama West Troop of Japanese Monkeys (Macaca Fuscata) Szalay, F. S., ed. (Contributions to Primatology: Vol. 9). (Illus.). 116p. 1976. 29.50 (ISBN 3-8055-2334-3). S Karger.
Kusama, T. & Mabuchi, M. Stereotaxic Atlas of the Brain of Macaca Fuscata. (Illus.). 1970. 125.00 (ISBN 0-8391-0011-6). Univ Park.
Lindburg, Donald G. The Macaques: Studies in Ecology, Behavior & Evolution. (Primate Behavior & Development Ser.). 400p. 1980. text ed. 22.50 (ISBN 0-442-24817-2). Van Nos Reinhold.
Winters, W. D., et al. A Stereotaxic Brain Atlas for Macaca Nemestrina. LC 69-16743. (Illus.). 1969. 55.00x (ISBN 0-520-01445-6). U of Cal Pr.
MACARIUS 3RD, PATRIARCH OF ANTIOCH, fl. 1636-1666
Ridding, Laura, ed. Travels of Macarius: Extracts from the Diary of the Travels of Macarius, Patriarch of Antioch. LC 77-115577. (Russia Observed Ser). 1971. Repr. of 1936 ed. 8.00 (ISBN 0-405-03089-4). Arno.
Spiritual Direction: Letters of Starets Macarius of Optina Monastery. pap. 1.50 (ISBN 0-686-00254-7). Eastern Orthodox.
MACARONI
see also Cookery (Macaroni)
The Pasta Market. (Food & Beverage Studies). 1979. 235.00 (ISBN 0-686-31528-6). Busn Trend.
MACARONI PRODUCTS
see also Cookery (Macaroni)
MACARONI WHEAT
see Wheat
MACARTHUR, DOUGLAS, 1880-1964
Devaney, John. Douglas MacArthur: Something of a Hero. LC 78-10820. (Illus.). (gr. 5-8). 1979. 8.95 (ISBN 0-399-20660-4). Putnam.
Gunther, John. The Riddle of MacArthur: Japan, Korea, & the Far East. LC 74-11880. 240p. 1974. Repr. of 1951 ed. lib. bdg. 17.75x (ISBN 0-8371-7701-4, GURM). Greenwood.
Hunt, Frazier. The Untold Story of Douglas MacArthur. 1977. pap. 2.25 (ISBN 0-532-22107-9). Woodhill.
James, D. Clayton. Years of MacArthur: Vol. 1. 1880-1941. 1970. 12.50 (ISBN 0-395-10948-5). HM.
--The Years of MacArthur 1941-1945, Vol. 2. LC 76-1086885. 960p. 1975. 15.00 (ISBN 0-395-20446-1). HM.
Langley, Michael. Inchon Landing: MacArthur's Last Triumph. LC 78-20688. 1979. 10.00 (ISBN 0-8129-0821-X). Times Bks.
--Inchon: Macarthur's Last Triumph. 1979. 24.00 (ISBN 0-7134-3346-9, Pub. by Batsford England). David & Charles.
Manchester, William. American Caesar: Douglas MacArthur 1880-1964. LC 78-8004. (Illus.). 15.00 (ISBN 0-316-54498-1). Little.
Mayer, S. L. The Biography of General of the Army Douglas Macarthur: The/Commanders Ser. (Illus.). 160p. 1981. 9.98 (ISBN 0-89196-105-4, Bk Value Intl). Quality Bks IL.
Newlon, Clarke. Fighting Douglas MacArthur. LC 65-16300. (Illus.). (gr. 9 up). 1965. 4.50 (ISBN 0-396-05141-3). Dodd.
Petillo, Carol M. Douglas MacArthur: The Philippine Years. LC 81-47166. (Illus.). 320p. 1981. 17.50x (ISBN 0-253-11248-6). Ind U Pr.
Phillips, William S., Jr. Douglas MacArthur: A Modern Knight-Errant. 77p. 1978. 5.00 (ISBN 0-8059-2539-2). Dorrance.
Steinberg, Rafael. The Return to the Philippines. Time-Life Books, ed. (World War Two Ser.). (Illus.). 1979. 14.95 (ISBN 0-8094-2514-9). Time-Life.
Whitney, Courtney. MacArthur: His Rendezvous with History. LC 77-2965. 1977. Repr. of 1956 ed. lib. bdg. 36.75 (ISBN 0-8371-9564-0, WHMA). Greenwood.
MACAULAY, THOMAS BABINGTON MACAULAY, 1ST BARON, 1800-1859
Beatty, Richard C. Lord Macaulay, Victorian Liberal. LC 72-116905. 1971. Repr. of 1938 ed. 22.50 (ISBN 0-208-01037-8, Archon). Shoe String.
Bryant, Arthur. Macaulay. 1933. Repr. 20.00 (ISBN 0-8274-2655-0). R West.
--Macaulay. 2nd rev. ed. LC 78-27536. (Illus.). 1979. Repr. of 1932 ed. text ed. 15.00x (ISBN 0-06-490761-9). B&N.
Burrow, John W. A Liberal Descent: Victorian Historians & the English Past. LC 81-3912. 336p. Date not set. price not set (ISBN 0-521-24079-4). Cambridge U Pr.
Clark, Perceval. Index to Trevelyan's Life & Letters of Lord Macaulay. LC 73-11257. 1881. lib. bdg. 15.00 (ISBN 0-8414-3408-5). Folcroft.
Clive, John. Macaulay: Shaping of the Historian. (Illus.). 1973. 15.00 (ISBN 0-394-47278-0). Knopf.
Firth, C. Commentary on Maculay's "History of England". 375p. 1964. 25.00x (ISBN 0-7146-1475-0, F Cass Co). Biblio Dist.
Gay, Peter. Style in History. LC 76-25490. (McGraw-Hill Paperbacks). 1976. pap. 3.95 (ISBN 0-07-023063-3, SP). McGraw.
Hassard, Albert R. A New Light on Lord Macaulay. LC 73-11367. 1918. Repr. lib. bdg. 12.50 (ISBN 0-8414-4716-0). Folcroft.
--A New Light on Lord McCaulay. 1978. Repr. of 1918 ed. lib. bdg. 12.50 (ISBN 0-8495-2306-0). Arden Lib.
Jones, Charles H. Lord Macaulay. 1880. Repr. 20.00 (ISBN 0-8274-2989-4). R West.
--Lord Macaulay: His Life & His Writings. 1978. Repr. of 1902 ed. lib. bdg. 20.00 (ISBN 0-8495-2734-1). Arden Lib.
Levine, George. Boundaries of Fiction: Carlyle, Macaulay, Newman. LC 68-11445. 1968. 20.00 (ISBN 0-691-06140-8). Princeton U Pr.
Macaulay, Thomas B. The Works of Lord Macaulay Complete: The Albany Edition, 12 vols. LC 76-42708. Repr. of 1898 ed. Set. 450.00 (ISBN 0-404-59480-8); 37.50 ea. AMS Pr.
Macauley, T. B. The Letters. Pinney, T., ed. 1977. Vol. 1. 72.00 (ISBN 0-521-20201-9); Vol. 2. 72.00 (ISBN 0-521-20202-7); Vol. 3. 72.00 (ISBN 0-521-21125-5); Vol. 4. 72.00 (ISBN 0-521-21126-3). Cambridge U Pr.
Maccaulay. Marginal Notes: Selected by Sir George Otto Trevelyan. Repr. of 1907 ed. lib. bdg. 12.50 (ISBN 0-8414-6391-3). Folcroft.
Millgate, Jane. Macaulay. (Routledge Author Guides Ser.). 1973. cased 14.50 (ISBN 0-7100-7663-0); pap. 6.95 (ISBN 0-7100-7685-1). Routledge & Kegan.
Morison, J. Cotter. Macaulay. 1909. Repr. 12.00 (ISBN 0-8274-2656-9). R West.
Pinney, T., ed. The Letters of Thomas Babington Macaulay, Vol. 5. LC 73-75860. (Illus.). 425p. Date not set. 95.00 (ISBN 0-521-22749-6). Cambridge U Pr.
--The Letters of Thomas Babington Macaulay, Vol. 6. LC 73-75860. (Illus.). 350p. Date not set. 95.00 (ISBN 0-521-22750-X). Cambridge U Pr.
Roberts, Sidney C. Lord Macaulay: The Pre-Eminent Victorian. LC 73-3472. 1973. lib. bdg. 8.50 (ISBN 0-8414-2561-2). Folcroft.
Roberts, Sydney C. Lord Macauley: The Pre-Eminent Victorian. 1978. Repr. of 1927 ed. lib. bdg. 6.00 (ISBN 0-8495-4524-2). Arden Lib.
St. Aubyn, Giles. Macaulay. 1978. Repr. of 1952 ed. lib. bdg. 15.00 (ISBN 0-8495-0119-9). Arden Lib.
Sedgwick, Henry D. Essays on Great Writers. facs. ed. LC 68-29245. (Essay Index Reprint Ser). 1968. Repr. of 1903 ed. 18.00 (ISBN 0-8369-0861-9). Arno.
Stirling, James H. Jerrold, Tennyson & Macaulay, with Other Critical Essays. LC 77-8713. Repr. of 1868 ed. lib. bdg. 22.50 (ISBN 0-8414-7561-X). Folcroft.
Trevelyan, George O. The Life & Letters of Lord Macaulay. 1978. pap. 14.95 (ISBN 0-19-822487-7). Oxford U Pr.
--The Life & Letters of Lord McCaulay. 1978. Repr. of 1893 ed. lib. bdg. 40.00 (ISBN 0-8492-2643-0). R West.
--Macaulay's Marginal Notes. LC 72-13757. 1907. lib. bdg. 10.00 (ISBN 0-8414-1284-7). Folcroft.
MCAULEY, JEREMIAH, 1839-1884
Offord, R. M., ed. Jerry McAuley, an Apostle to the Lost. facsimile ed. LC 75-124248. (Select Bibliographies Reprint Ser). (Illus.). Repr. of 1907 ed. 19.00 (ISBN 0-8369-5436-X). Arno.
MCCABE, HERB, 1936-
McCabe, Herb & McCabe, Sandra. Love Letters of Herb & Sandy McCabe. LC 73-78879. 271p. (YA) 1973. pap. 0.95 (ISBN 0-570-03159-1, 12-2544). Concordia.
MCCABE, SANDY
McCabe, Herb & McCabe, Sandra. Love Letters of Herb & Sandy McCabe. LC 73-78879. 271p. (YA) 1973. pap. 0.95 (ISBN 0-570-03159-1, 12-2544). Concordia.
MACCABEES
Farmer, William R. Maccabees, Zealots & Josephus. LC 73-15052. 239p. 1974. Repr. of 1956 ed. lib. bdg. 20.25x (ISBN 0-8371-7152-0, FAMA). Greenwood.
Hirsh, Marilyn. The Hanukkah Story. LC 77-22183. (Illus.). (gr. k-4). 1977. 7.95 (ISBN 0-88482-756-9, Bonim Bks). Hebrew Pub.
Shamir, Moshe. King of Flesh & Blood. Patterson, David, tr. from Hebrew. Date not set. pap. 4.95 (ISBN 0-85222-220-3, East & West Lib). Hebrew Pub.
MACCABEES-COMMENTARIES
Goldstein, Jonathan A., tr. & intro. by. Maccabees One. (Anchor Bible Ser.: Vol. 41). 14.00 (ISBN 0-385-08533-8, Anchor Pr). Doubleday.
MACCABEES, FEAST OF THE
see Hanukkah (Feast of Lights)
MCCALL FAMILY
McCall, Dorothy L. Ranch Under the Rimrock. LC 68-28923. (Illus.). 1971. 8.95 (ISBN 0-8323-0065-9). Binford.
MCCARTHY, EUGENE J., 1916-
Eisele, Albert. Almost to the Presidency. LC 76-187432. 1972. 15.00 (ISBN 0-87832-005-9). Piper.
McCarthy, Eugene. Frankly McCarthy. Rinzler, Carol E., ed. 1.00 (ISBN 0-8183-0169-4). Pub Aff Pr.
O'Brien, Michael. McCarthy & McCarthyism in Wisconsin. LC 80-16792. 288p. 1981. 22.00 (ISBN 0-8262-0319-1). U of Mo Pr.
MCCARTHY, GLENN
Davis, Wallace. Corduroy Road, Glenn McCarthy: Texas Oil Field Saga. (Illus.). 1951. 15.00 (ISBN 0-685-04999-X). A Jones.
MCCARTHY, JOSEPH RAYMOND, 1909-1957
Bayley, Edwin. Joe McCarthy & the Press. LC 81-50824. 256p. 1981. 18.95 (ISBN 0-299-08620-8). U of Wis Pr.
Crosby, Donald F. God, Church, & Flag: Senator Joseph R. McCarthy & the Catholic Church, 1950-1957. LC 77-14064. 1978. 19.50x (ISBN 0-8078-1312-5). U of NC Pr.
Days, G. D., ed. Threshold of the McCarthy Era & the McCarthy Era - Beginning of the End. 60p. 1980. pap. 19.95 includes cassettes (ISBN 0-918628-54-7, 54/7). Congeros Pubns.
Evans, Medford. Assassination of Joe McCarthy. LC 74-126921. 1970. 6.00 (ISBN 0-88279-217-2). Western Islands.
Latham, Earl, ed. Meaning of McCarthyism. 2nd ed. (Problems in American Civilization Ser). 1973. pap. text ed. 4.95x (ISBN 0-669-81851-8). Heath.
Lattimore, Owen. Ordeal by Slander. LC 72-138156. 1971. Repr. of 1950 ed. lib. bdg. 15.00x (ISBN 0-8371-5613-0, LAOS). Greenwood.
Matusow, Allen J. Joseph R. McCarthy. 1970. 8.95 (ISBN 0-13-566729-1, Spec); pap. 8.95 (ISBN 0-13-566711-9, S720, Spec). P-H.
Oshinsky, David M. Senator Joe McCarthy. LC 77-18474. 1981. cancelled (ISBN 0-02-923490-5). Free Pr.
--Senator Joseph McCarthy & the American Labor Movement. LC 75-23426. 192p. 1975. 12.50x (ISBN 0-8262-0188-1). U of Mo Pr.
Reeves, Thomas C. The Life & Times of Joe McCarthy. LC 79-3730. (Illus.). 592p. 1981. 19.95 (ISBN 0-8128-2337-0). Stein & Day.
Reeves, Thomas C., ed. McCarthyism. LC 78-2879. (American Problem Studies). (Illus.). 144p. 1978. pap. text ed. 5.50 (ISBN 0-88275-674-5). Krieger.
Rogin, Michael P. The Intellectuals & McCarthy: The Radical Specter. (Illus.). 366p. 1967. pap. 6.95x (ISBN 0-262-68015-7). MIT Pr.
Rorty, James. McCarthy & the Communists. LC 78-138179. 163p. 1972. Repr. of 1954 ed. lib. bdg. 15.00x (ISBN 0-8371-5636-X, ROCO). Greenwood.
Theoharis, Athan. Seeds of Repression: Harry S. Truman & the Origins of McCarthyism. LC 71-116089. 256p. 1971. 6.95 (ISBN 0-8129-0169-X); pap. 2.95 (ISBN 0-8129-6283-4). Times Bks.
MCCARTHY, MARY THERESE, 1912-
Goldman, Sherli E. Mary McCarthy: A Bibliography. LC 68-12574. 80p. 4.50 (ISBN 0-15-157775-7). HarBraceJ.
McKenzie, Barbara. Mary McCarthy. (Twayne's United States Authors Ser). 1966. pap. 3.45 (ISBN 0-8084-0215-3, T108, Twayne). Coll & U Pr.
Rovere, Richard. Senator Joe McCarthy. 1973. pap. 3.95 (ISBN 0-06-090345-7, CN345, CN). Har-Row.
Stock, Irvin. Mary McCarthy. LC 68-64755. (Pamphlets on American Writers Ser: No. 72). (Orig.). 1968. pap. 1.25x (ISBN 0-8166-0487-8, MPAW72). U of Minn Pr.

MCCLELLAN, GEORGE BRINTON, 1826-1885
Catton, Bruce. Mister Lincoln's Army. LC 62-1068. 10.95 (ISBN 0-385-04310-4). Doubleday.
Hassler, Warren W., Jr. General George B. McClellan, Shield of the Union. LC 74-9619. (Illus.). 350p. 1974. Repr. of 1957 ed. lib. bdg. 29.75x (ISBN 0-8371-7606-9, HAGG). Greenwood.
Myers, William S. The Mexican War Diary of General George B. McClellan. LC 71-87641. (The American Scene Ser). 98p. 1972. Repr. of 1917 ed. lib. bdg. 17.50 (ISBN 0-306-71789-1). Da Capo.
Williams, Thomas H. McClellan, Sherman, & Grant. LC 76-29654. (Illus.). 1976. Repr. of 1962 ed. lib. bdg. 15.00x (ISBN 0-8371-9280-3, WIMS). Greenwood.

MCCLOUD RIVER RAILROAD
Hanft, Robert. Pine Across the Mountain: California's McCloud River Railroad. LC 71-16462. (Illus.). 224p. 1970. 20.95 (ISBN 0-87095-038-X). Golden West.
Pine Across the Mountain. 20.95 (ISBN 0-685-83369-0). Chatham Pub CA.

MCCORMACK, JOHN, 1884-1945
Ledbetter, Gordon T. The Great Irish Tenor. (Encore Edition). (Illus.). 1978. 4.95 (ISBN 0-684-16360-8, ScribT). Scribner.
McCormack, John. John McCormack: His Own Life Story. Key, Pierre V., as told to. LC 72-93828. (Illus.). 443p. 1973. Repr. of 1918 ed. 16.50x (ISBN 0-8443-0092-6). Vienna Hse.
McCormack, Lily. I Hear You Calling Me. LC 75-20980. (Illus.). 201p. 1976. Repr. of 1949 ed. lib. bdg. 15.25x (ISBN 0-8371-8350-2, MCIH). Greenwood.
Roe, L. McDermott. The John McCormack Discography. 1972. pap. 5.00x (ISBN 0-85361-106-8). Intl Pubns Serv.
Strong, Leonard A. John McCormack. LC 76-181270. 309p. 1949. Repr. 29.00 (ISBN 0-403-01693-2). Scholarly.

MCCORMICK, CYRUS HALL, 1809-1884
Casson, Herbert N. Cyrus Hall McCormick: His Life & Work. LC 74-152977. (Select Bibliographies Reprint Ser.). 1972. Repr. of 1909 ed. 22.00 (ISBN 0-8369-5729-6). Arno.
Hutchinson, William T. Cyrus Hall Maccormick, 2 Vols. 2nd ed. LC 68-8127. (American Scene Ser). 1969. Repr. of 1935 ed. lib. bdg. 69.50 (ISBN 0-306-71162-1). Da Capo.
McCormick, Cyrus. The Century of the Reaper: An Account of Cyrus Hall McCormick, the Inventor of the Reaper, of the McCormick Harvesting Machine Company, the Business He Created & of the International Harvester Company, His Heir & Chief Memorial. LC 31-9940. Repr. of 1931 ed. 23.00 (ISBN 0-384-34740-1). Johnson Repr.

MCCORMICK, ROBERT RUTHERFORD, 1880-1955
Gies, Joseph. The Colonel of Chicago. (Illus.). 1979. 12.95 (ISBN 0-525-08267-0). Dutton.
Waldrop, Frank C. McCormick of Chicago. LC 74-1782. (Illus.). 328p. 1976. Repr. of 1966 ed. lib. bdg. 24.00 (ISBN 0-8371-7401-5, WAMO). Greenwood.

MCCORMICK FAMILY
Tebbel, John W. American Dynasty: Story of the Maccormicks, Medills & Pattersons. LC 68-10162. (Illus.). 1968. Repr. of 1947 ed. lib. bdg. 22.50x (ISBN 0-8371-0246-4, TEAD). Greenwood.

MCCOSH, JAMES, 1811-1894
Hoeveler, J. David, Jr. James McCosh & the Scottish Intellectual Tradition: From Glasgow to Princeton. LC 80-8553. (Illus.). 384p. 1981. 25.00x (ISBN 0-691-04670-0). Princeton U Pr.
Sloane, William M., ed. The Life of James McCosh: A Record Chiefly Autobiographical. LC 72-78832. 1896. Repr. 20.00 (ISBN 0-403-04148-1). Somerset Pub.

MCCOY, ISAAC, 1784-1846
Schultz, George A. An Indian Canaan: Isaac McCoy & the Vision of an Indian State. (Civilization of the American Indian Ser.: No. 121). (Illus.). 350p. 1972. 12.50 (ISBN 0-8061-1024-4); pap. 6.95 (ISBN 0-8061-1303-0). U of Okla Pr.

MCCULLERS, CARSON (SMITH) 1917-
Carr, Virginia Spencer. The Lonely Hunter: A Biography of Carson McCullers. LC 74-9478. 1976. pap. 5.95 (ISBN 0-385-12289-6, Anch). Doubleday.
Cook, Richard M. Carson McCullers. LC 75-2789. (Modern Literature Ser.). 160p. 1975. 10.95 (ISBN 0-8044-2128-5). Ungar.
Graver, Lawrence. Carson McCullers. (Pamphlets on American Writers Ser: No. 84). (Orig.). 1969. pap. 1.25x (ISBN 0-8166-0546-7, MPAW84). U of Minn Pr.
Kiernan, Robert F. Carson McCullers & Katherine Anne Porter: A Reference Guide. (Ser. Seventy). 1976. lib. bdg. 19.00 (ISBN 0-8161-7806-2). G K Hall.
McDowell, Margaret B. Carson McCullers. (United States Authors Ser.: No. 354). 1980. lib. bdg. 9.95 (ISBN 0-8057-7297-9). Twayne.
Shapiro, Adrian M., et al. Carson McCullers: A Descriptive Listing & Annotated Bibliography of Criticism. LC 79-7909. (Garland Reference Library of Humanities). 250p. 1980. lib. bdg. 35.00 (ISBN 0-8240-9534-0). Garland Pub.
Wikborg, Eleanor. Carson McCullers' The Member of the Wedding: Aspects of Structure & Style. (Gothenburg Studies in English Ser: No. 31). 200p. 1975. pap. text ed. 8.50x (ISBN 91-7346-005-2). Humanities.

MCCULLOCH, BEN, 1811-1862
Reid, Samuel C., Jr. Scouting Expeditions of McCulloch's Texas Rangers: Or, the Summer & Fall Campaign of the Army of the United States in Mexico 1846. facs. ed. LC 72-126252. (Select Bibliographies Reprint Ser). 1847. 16.00 (ISBN 0-8369-5479-3). Arno.

MCCULLOCH, JOHN, 1754?-1824
Spieseke, Alice W. The First Textbooks in American History & Their Compiler John M'culloch. LC 71-177749. (Columbia University. Teachers College. Contributions to Education: No. 744). Repr. of 1938 ed. 17.50 (ISBN 0-404-55744-9). AMS Pr.

MCCULLOUGH, JOHN, 1832-1885
McCullough, William W., Jr. John McCullough: Pioneer Presbyterian Missionary in Texas. (Illus.). 9.50 (ISBN 0-8363-0055-6). Jenkins.

MCDILL FAMILY
Tebbel, John W. American Dynasty: Story of the Maccormicks, Medills & Pattersons. LC 68-10162. (Illus.). 1968. Repr. of 1947 ed. lib. bdg. 22.50x (ISBN 0-8371-0246-4, TEAD). Greenwood.

MACDONAGH, THOMAS, 1878-1916
Norstedt, Johann A. Thomas MacDonagh: A Critical Biography. LC 78-31320. 1980. 12.95x (ISBN 0-8139-0786-1). U Pr of Va.

MACDONALD, FLORA (MACDONALD) 1722-1790
Vining, Elizabeth G. Flora: A Biography. LC 66-12343. (Illus.). 1966. 4.95 (ISBN 0-397-00427-3). Lippincott.

MACDONALD, GEORGE, 1824-1905
Macdonald, Greville. George Macdonald & His Wife. Repr. of 1924 ed. 38.50 (ISBN 0-384-34777-0, E240). Johnson Repr.
Reis, Richard H. George MacDonald. LC 71-125820. (English Authors Ser.). 1972. lib. bdg. 12.95x (ISBN 0-8057-1356-5). Irvington.
Wolff, Robert L. The Golden Key: A Study of the Fiction of George MacDonald. 1961. 34.50x (ISBN 0-686-51395-9). Elliots Bks.

MACDONALD, JAMES RAMSAY, 1866-1937
Hamilton, Mary A. J. Ramsay Macdonald. facsimile ed. LC 79-165638. (Select Bibliographies Reprint Ser). Repr. of 1929 ed. 18.00 (ISBN 0-8369-5947-7). Arno.
Marquand, David. Ramsay MacDonald. (Illus.). 903p. 1977. 37.50x (ISBN 0-87471-814-7). Rowman.

MACDONALD, JEANETTE
Castanza, Philip. The Films of Jeanette MacDonald & Nelson Eddy. (Illus.). 224p. 1981. pap. 7.95 (ISBN 0-8065-0771-3). Citadel Pr.

MACDONALD, JOHN ALEXANDER, SIR, 1815-1891
Pope, Joseph. Memoirs of the Right Honorable Sir John Alexander Macdonald, 2 Vols. LC 76-137271. Repr. of 1894 ed. 42.50 (ISBN 0-404-05085-9). AMS Pr.

MACDONALD, JOHN SANDFIELD, 1812-1872
Hodgins, Bruce. John Sandfield Macdonald, 1812-1872. (Canadian Biographical Studies). 1971. 5.50 (ISBN 0-8020-3248-6). U of Toronto Pr.

MACDONALD, RANALD, 1828-1894
Gowen, Herbert H. Five Foreigners in Japan. facs. ed. LC 67-28735. (Essay Index Reprint Ser). 1936. 18.00 (ISBN 0-8369-0491-5). Arno.

MACDONNELL, ALASTAIR RUADH, 1725-1761
Lang, Andrew. Pickle the Spy. LC 72-110132. Repr. of 1897 ed. 10.00 (ISBN 0-404-03853-0). AMS Pr.

MACDONNELL DOUGLAS AIRCRAFT CO.
Ingells, Douglas J. The McDonnell Douglas Story. LC 79-54064. 1979. 17.95 (ISBN 0-8168-4995-1). Aero.

MACDOWELL, EDWARD ALEXANDER, 1861-1908
Gilman, Lawrence. Edward MacDowell. 59.95 (ISBN 0-8490-0096-3). Gordon Pr.
--Edward MacDowell: A Study. 2nd ed. LC 67-27455. (Music Ser). 1969. Repr. of 1908 ed. lib. bdg. 17.50 (ISBN 0-306-70979-1). Da Capo.
Porte, John F. Edward MacDowell. 59.95 (ISBN 0-8490-0097-1). Gordon Pr.
Scholes, Percy A. Everyman & His Music. facs. ed. LC 72-76914. (Essay Index Reprint Ser). 1917. 15.00 (ISBN 0-8369-0029-4). Arno.
Sonneck, O. G. Catalogue of First Editions of Edward MacDowell, 1861-1908. LC 70-151053. (Library of Congress Publications in Reprint Ser). 1971. Repr. of 1917 ed. 6.00 (ISBN 0-405-03422-9). Arno.
Sonneck, Oscar G. Catalogue of First Editions of Edward MacDowell. LC 72-155232. (Music Ser). 1971. Repr. of 1917 ed. lib. bdg. 15.00 (ISBN 0-306-70161-8). Da Capo.

MACEDONIA
Bompois, H. F. Examen Chronologique des Monnais Frappes par la Communaute des Macedoniens Avant, Pendant et Apes la Conquete Romaine. (Illus.). 102p. (Fr.). 20.00 (ISBN 0-916710-77-7). Obol Intl.
Brailsford, H. N. Macedonia: Its Races & Their Future. LC 78-135796. (Eastern Europe Collection Ser). 1970. Repr. of 1906 ed. 20.00 (ISBN 0-405-02738-9). Arno.
Casson, Stanley. Macedonia, Thrace & Illyria: Their Relations to Greece from the Earliest Times Down to the Time of Philip, Son of Amyntas. LC 75-114495. (Illus.). 1971. Repr. of 1926 ed. lib. bdg. 22.00x (ISBN 0-8371-4727-1, CAMT). Greenwood.
Dordevic, Tikhomir R. Macedonia. LC 77-87529. Repr. of 1918 ed. 23.50 (ISBN 0-404-16586-9). AMS Pr.
Ellis, J. R. Philip Second & Macedonian Imperialism. (Aspects of Greek & Roman Life Ser.). (Illus.). 1977. 19.95 (ISBN 0-500-40028-8). Thames Hudson.
Gimbutas, Marija, ed. Neolithic Macedonia. LC 76-18606. (Monumenta Archaeologica Ser). (Illus.). 1976. 28.00 (ISBN 0-685-79156-4). U of S Cal Pr.
--Neolithic Macedonia. LC 76-18606. (Monumenta Archaeologica: No. 1). (Illus.). 1976. 28.00 (ISBN 0-917956-00-1). UCLA Arch.
Hammond, N. G. L. & Griffith, G. T. A History of Macedonia: Volume II: 550-336 B.C. (Illus.). 1979. 98.00x (ISBN 0-19-814814-3). Oxford U Pr.
Heurtley, W. A. Prehistoric Macedonia: An Archaeological Reconnaisance of Greek Macedonia (West of the Struma) in the Neolithic, Bronze & Early Iron Ages. LC 77-86430. Repr. of 1939 ed. 46.00 (ISBN 0-404-16646-6). AMS Pr.
Palmer, Stephen E., Jr. & King, Robert. Yugoslav Communism & the Macedonian Question. LC 79-116904. (Illus.). 1971. 18.50 (ISBN 0-208-00821-7, Archon). Shoe String.
Pribichevich, Stoyan. Macedonia: History, Culture & People. (Illus.). 1980. 14.95 (ISBN 0-915326-10-8). Cyrco Pr.
Tarn, William W. Antigonos Gonatas. 1913. 13.50x (ISBN 0-19-814275-7). Oxford U Pr.
Wust, Fritz R. Philipp Second: Von Makedonien und Griechenland in den Jahren von 346 bis 338. LC 72-7910. (Greek History Ser.). (Ger.). Repr. of 1938 ed. 13.00 (ISBN 0-405-04806-8). Arno.

MACEDONIAN QUESTION
see also Eastern Question (Balkan)
Barker, Elisabeth. Macedonia: Its Place in Balkan Power Politics. LC 80-16769. (Illus.). 129p. 1980. Repr. of 1950 ed. lib. bdg. 17.50x (ISBN 0-313-22587-7, BAMI). Greenwood.
Palmer, Stephen E., Jr. & King, Robert. Yugoslav Communism & the Macedonian Question. LC 79-116904. (Illus.). 1971. 18.50 (ISBN 0-208-00821-7, Archon). Shoe String.

MACFADDEN, BERNARR ADOLPHUS, 1868-1955
Wood, Clement. Bernarr Macfadden: A Study in Success. (American Newspapermen 1790-1933 Ser.). 316p. 1974. Repr. of 1929 ed. 18.00x (ISBN 0-8464-0001-4). Beekman Pubs.

MCGILL, RALPH EMERSON, 1898-1969
Logue, Calvin M. Ralph McGill, Editor & Publisher, 2 vols. Incl. Vol. 1. Biography. 256p. 10.95 (ISBN 0-87716-013-9); Vol. 2. Famous Speeches. 517p. 12.95 (ISBN 0-87716-014-7). LC 71-97784. 1969 (Pub. by Moore Pub Co). F Apple.

M'GILLIVRARY, SIMON
Halkett, John. Statement Respecting the Earl of Selkirk's Settlement Upon the Red River, in North America. 1817. 19.50 (ISBN 0-384-20980-7). Johnson Repr.

MCGLYNN, EDWARD, 1837-1900
Bell, Stephen. Rebel, Priest & Prophet: A Biography of Dr. Edward McGlynn. LC 75-301. (The Radical Tradition in America Ser). 303p. 1975. Repr. of 1937 ed. 22.50 (ISBN 0-88355-206-X). Hyperion Conn.

MCGOVERN, GEORGE STANLEY, 1922-
Hart, Gary. Right from the Start. LC 72-96438. 1973. 7.95 (ISBN 0-8129-0372-2). Times Bks.

MCGRAW, JOHN JOSEPH, 1873-1934
McGraw, John J. My Thirty Years in Baseball. LC 74-15746. (Popular Culture in America Ser.). (Illus.). 314p. 1975. Repr. 19.00x (ISBN 0-405-06381-4). Arno.

MACGREGOR, DUNCAN, CALLED LAIDUS OR LAUDASACH
Innes, Cosmo. Black Book of Taymouth. LC 79-170802. (Bannatyne Club, Edinburgh. Publications: No. 100). Repr. of 1855 ed. 75.00 (ISBN 0-404-52848-1). AMS Pr.

MACGREGOR, ROBERT, 1671-1734
Evans, Martin. Rob Roy. (Illus.). 160p. 1972. 13.50x (ISBN 0-85344-148-0). Intl Pubns Serv.

MACGREGOR, ROBERT, CALLED ROB ROY, 1671-1734–FICTION
Scott, Sir Walter. Rob Roy. 1973. 9.95x (ISBN 0-460-00142-6, Evman); pap. 4.50x (ISBN 0-460-01142-1, Evans). Biblio Dist.

MCGUFFEY, WILLIAM HOLMES, 1800-1873
Minnich, Harvey C. Williams Holmes McGuffey & His Readers. LC 74-19214. (Illus.). xii, 203p. 1975. Repr. of 1936 ed. 22.00 (ISBN 0-8103-4104-2). Gale.
Mosier, Richard D. Making the American Mind: Social & Moral Ideas in the McGuffey Readers. LC 65-18823. (With a new bibli.). 1965. Repr. of 1947 ed. 8.50 (ISBN 0-8462-0589-0). Russell.
Westerhoff, John H., 3rd. McGuffey & His Readers: Piety, Morality, & Education in Nineteenth-Century America. LC 77-23989. 1978. 9.95 (ISBN 0-687-23850-1). Abingdon.
Williams, Barbara. William H. McGuffey: Boy Reading Genius. LC 68-57788. (Childhood of Famous Americans Ser.). (Illus.). (gr. 3-7). 1968. 3.95 (ISBN 0-672-50190-2). Bobbs.

MACH, ERNST, 1839-1916
Bradley, J. Mach's Philosophy of Science. (Illus.). 240p. 1971. text ed. 29.25x (ISBN 0-485-11124-1, Athlone Pr). Humanities.
Cohen, R. S. & Seeger, R. J., eds. Boston Studies in the Philosophy of Science: Ernst Mach, Physicist & Philosopher, Vol. 6. (Synthese Library: No. 27). 295p. 1970. 29.00 (ISBN 90-277-0016-8, Pub. by Reidel Holland). Kluwer Boston.
McGuinness, Brian, ed. Ernst Mach: Knowledge & Error. Foulkes, Paul, tr. from Ger. LC 73-75641. (Vienna Circle Collection: Vol. 3). 432p. 1975. lib. bdg. 71.00 (ISBN 90-277-0281-0, Pub. by Reidel Holland); pap. 39.50 (ISBN 90-277-0282-9, Pub. by Reidel Holland). Kluwer Boston.

MACH NUMBER
see also Aerodynamics, Hypersonic

MACHADO, MANUEL, 1874-1947
Brotherston, J. Gordon. Manuel Machado: A Revaluation. LC 68-11281. (Illus.). 1968. 32.00 (ISBN 0-521-04334-4). Cambridge U Pr.

MACHADO DE ASSIS, JOACHIM MARIA, 1839-1908
Caldwell, Helen. Machado de Assis: The Brazilian Master & His Novels. LC 76-89891. 1970. 18.50x (ISBN 0-520-01608-4). U of Cal Pr.

MACHADO Y RUIZ, ANTONIO, 1875-1939
Cabrera, Vicente & Gonzalez-Del-Valle, Luis. Antonio Machado. LC 76-4181. (Span.). 1976. pap. 8.00 (ISBN 0-89294-000-X). Journal Span Stud.
Cobb, Carl W. Antonio Machado. (World Authors Ser.: Spain: No. 161). lib. bdg. 10.95 (ISBN 0-8057-2556-3). Twayne.
Hutman, Norma L. Machado: A Dialogue with Time: Nature As an Expression of Temporality in the Poetry of Antonio Machado. LC 70-78554. 207p. 1969. text ed. 21.50x (ISBN 0-8290-0186-7). Irvington.
Young, Howard T. Victorious Expression: A Study of Four Contemporary Spanish Poets, Unamuno, Machado, Jimenez, & Lorca. 1964. pap. 6.95x (ISBN 0-299-03144-6). U of Wis Pr.

MACHAQUILA, GUATEMALA
Lisi, Albert. Machaquila: Through the Mayan Jungle to a Lost City. (Photos). 1968. 7.75 (ISBN 0-8038-4600-2). Hastings.

MACHEN, ARTHUR, 1863-1947
Danielson, Henry. Arthur Machen: A Bibliography. LC 73-13506. 1923. lib. bdg. 15.00 (ISBN 0-8414-3683-5). Folcroft.
--Arthur Machen: A Bibliography. LC 79-149784. 1971. Repr. of 1923 ed. 19.00 (ISBN 0-8103-3682-0). Gale.
Danielsson, H. Arthur Machen: A Bibliography. LC 74-130267. (Reference Ser., No. 44). 1970. Repr. of 1923 ed. lib. bdg. 42.95 (ISBN 0-8383-1174-1). Haskell.
Goldstone, Adrian & Sweetser, Wesley D. A Bibliography of Arthur Machen. LC 72-6469. (English Literature Ser., No. 33). 180p. 1972. Repr. of 1965 ed. lib. bdg. 49.95 (ISBN 0-8383-1614-X). Haskell.
Michael, D. P. Arthur Machen. (Writers of Wales Ser.). 1971. pap. 4.50x (ISBN 0-8426-1385-4). Verry.

MACHIAVELLI, NICCOLO, 1469-1527
Barincou, Edmond. Machiavelli. Lane, Helen, tr. LC 75-11427. 192p. 1975. Repr. of 1962 ed. lib. bdg. 15.25x (ISBN 0-8371-8185-2, BAMA). Greenwood.
Barricelli, Jean-Pierre. The Prince: An Analysis of Machiavelli's Treatise on Power Politics. LC 74-1301. 1975. pap. 2.50 (ISBN 0-8120-0524-4). Barron.
Biskirk, Richard A. Modern Management & Machiavelli. 1975. pap. 2.25 (ISBN 0-451-61703-7, ME1703, Ment). NAL.
Bondanella, Peter E. Machiavelli & the Art of Renaissance History. LC 73-9729. 200p. 1973. text ed. 12.95x (ISBN 0-8143-1499-6). Wayne St U Pr.

Boughner, Daniel C. Devils Disciple. LC 67-24571. 1968. 5.95 (ISBN 0-8022-0159-8). Philos Lib.
--The Devil's Disciple: Ben Jonson's Debt to Machiavelli. LC 73-16606. 264p. 1975. Repr. of 1968 ed. lib. bdg. 14.50x (ISBN 0-8371-7183-0, BODD). Greenwood.
Buskirk, Richard H. Modern Management & Machiavelli. LC 74-11194. 291p. 1974. 13.95 (ISBN 0-8436-0734-3). CBI Pub.
Butterfield, Herbert. Statecraft of Machiavelli. 1962. pap. 0.95 (ISBN 0-02-072500-0, Collier). Macmillan.
Caranfa, Angelo. Machiavelli Rethought: A Critique of Strauss' Machiavelli. LC 77-94393. 1978. pap. text ed. 7.00 (ISBN 0-8191-0421-3). U Pr of Amer.
Crawford, R. Per Quale Iddio: Machiavelli's Second Thoughts. 1967. pap. 2.00x (ISBN 0-424-05750-6, Pub. by Sydney U Pr). Intl Schol Bk Serv.
Fester, Richard. Machiavelli. LC 77-143655. 204p. 1904. Repr. 21.00 (ISBN 0-8337-3154-8). B Franklin.
Fleisher, Martin, ed. Machiavelli & the Nature of Political Thought. LC 79-181461. 1972. pap. text ed. 4.95x (ISBN 0-689-70329-5, 189). Atheneum.
Gilbert, Felix. Machiavelli & Guicciardini: Politics & History in Sixteenth Century Florence. LC 63-23405. 1965. 22.50x (ISBN 0-691-05133-X); pap. 8.95 (ISBN 0-691-00771-3). Princeton U Pr.
Kempner, Nadja. Raleighs Staatstheoretische Schriften, Die Einfuehrung Des Machiavellismus in England. 1928. pap. 9.50 (ISBN 0-384-29190-2). Johnson Repr.
Luciani, Vincent, ed. Machiavelli: La Mandragola. 1979. pap. 3.25x (ISBN 0-913298-19-0). S F Vanni.
Machiavelli. The Portable Machiavelli. Bondanella, Peter & Musa, Mark, eds. (Portable Library Ser.: No. 92). 1979. 10.00 (ISBN 0-670-44522-3). Viking Pr.
Machiavelli, Niccolo. The Literary Works of Machiavelli: Mandragola, Clizia, a Dialogue on Language & Belfagor, with Selections from the Private Correspondence. Hale, John R., ed. LC 79-4216. 1979. Repr. of 1961 ed. lib. bdg. 19.75x (ISBN 0-313-21248-1, MALW). Greenwood.
--The Living Thoughts of Machiavelli. Sforza, Carlo, ed. LC 74-28758. (Illus.). 161p. 1975. Repr. of 1940 ed. lib. bdg. 15.00 (ISBN 0-8371-7923-8, MALIT). Greenwood.
--Machiavelli's Thoughts on the Management of Men. (Illus.). 1978. deluxe bdg. 47.45 (ISBN 0-918968-08-9). Inst Econ Finan.
Mansfield, Harvey C., Jr. Machiavelli's New Modes & Orders: A Study of the "Discourses on Livy". LC 79-12380. 1979. 32.50x (ISBN 0-8014-1182-3). Cornell U Pr.
Meyer, Edward. Machiavelli & the Elizabethan Drama. 59.95 (ISBN 0-8490-0572-8). Gordon Pr.
Meyer, Edward S. Machiavelli & the Elizabethan Drama. 1897. 20.50 (ISBN 0-8337-2380-4). B Franklin.
Morley, John. Machiavelli. LC 72-195763. 1897. lib. bdg. 6.00 (ISBN 0-8414-6647-5). Folcroft.
Muir, Dorothy E. Machiavelli & His Times. LC 74-30928. (Illus.). 262p. 1976. Repr. of 1936 ed. lib. bdg. 22.75 (ISBN 0-8371-7889-4, MUMA). Greenwood.
Pansini, Anthony J. Machiavelli & the United States, 6 vols. in 1. LC 70-108252. 1371p. (500th anniv. ed). 1969. 20.00 (ISBN 0-685-23384-7, 911876-02). Greenvale.
Pocock, J. G. The Machiavellian Moment: Florentine Political Thought & the Atlantic Republican Tradition. LC 73-2490. 576p. 1975. 40.00x (ISBN 0-691-07560-3); pap. 16.50 (ISBN 0-691-10029-2). Princeton U Pr.
Praz, Mario. Machiavelli & the Elizabethans. LC 72-12507. 1928. lib. bdg. 6.00 (ISBN 0-8414-1300-2). Folcroft.
Rawson, Judith A., ed. Machiavelli: The History of Florence & Other Selections. (Great History Ser). 1978. 10.95 (ISBN 0-685-60155-2, Pub by Twayne). Cyrco Pr.
Skinner, Quentin. Machiavelli. Thomas, Keith, ed. (Past Masters Ser.). 1981. 7.95 (ISBN 0-8090-6706-4); pap. 2.95 (ISBN 0-8090-1420-3). Hill & Wang.
Sobel, Robert. Monarch Notes on Machiavelli's the Prince. (Orig.). pap. 1.95 (ISBN 0-671-00565-0). Monarch Pr.
Strauss, Leo. Thoughts on Machiavelli. LC 78-55044. 1978. pap. 5.95 (ISBN 0-226-77702-2, P785, Phoen). U of Chicago Pr.
Thevenet, J. Idees Economiques D'un Homme D'Etat Dans la Florence Des Medicis. 1967. Repr. of 1922 ed. 18.50 (ISBN 0-8337-3504-7). B Franklin.
Vergani, Luisa. Prince Notes. (Orig.). pap. 1.95 (ISBN 0-8220-1093-3). Cliffs.
Villari, P. Life & Time of Niccolo Machiavelli. LC 68-25275. (World History Ser., No. 48). 1969. Repr. of 1892 ed. lib. bdg. 79.95 (ISBN 0-8383-0175-4). Haskell.
Villari, Pasquale. Life & Times of Niccolo Machiavelli, 2 Vols. Villari, Linda, tr. LC 68-31007. (Illus.). 1968. Repr. of 1892 ed. Set. lib. bdg. 41.00x (ISBN 0-8371-0732-6, VINM). Greenwood.
--Life & Times of Niccolo Machiavelli, 2 vols. Villari, Linda, tr. from It. LC 79-115284. (Illus.). 1058p. 1972. Repr. of 1929 ed. 33.00 (ISBN 0-403-00033-5). Scholarly.
--Life & Times of Niccolo Machiavelli. 1929. 35.00 (ISBN 0-8274-1336-X). R West.
Whitfield, John H. Machiavelli. LC 66-13175. 1965. Repr. of 1947 ed. 14.00 (ISBN 0-8462-0708-7). Russell.

MACHIAVELLIANISM (PSYCHOLOGY)

Christie, Richard, et al. Studies in Machiavellianism. (Social Psychology Ser). 1970. 37.50 (ISBN 0-12-174450-7). Acad Pr.
Dyer, Louis. Machiavelli & the Modern State. 69.95 (ISBN 0-8490-0573-6). Gordon Pr.
Mervil, Fritz L. The Political Philosophy of Niccolo' Macchiavelli As It Applies to Politics, the Management of the Firm & the Science of Living. (Illus.). 167p. 1981. 49.75 (ISBN 0-89266-270-0). Am Classical Coll Pr.
Skinner, Quentin. Machiavelli. Thomas, Keith, ed. (Past Masters Ser.). 1981. 7.95 (ISBN 0-8090-6706-4); pap. 2.95 (ISBN 0-8090-1420-3). Hill & Wang.

MACHINE ACCOUNTING

see also Accounting Machines; Calculating-Machines; Tabulating Machines

Rudman, Jack. Accounting Machine Operator. (Career Examination Ser.: C-1073). (Cloth bdg. avail. on request). pap. 8.00 (ISBN 0-8373-1073-3). Natl Learning.

MACHINE DATA STORAGE AND RETRIEVAL SYSTEMS

see Information Storage and Retrieval Systems

MACHINE DESIGN

see Machinery–Design

MACHINE EMBROIDERY

see Embroidery

MACHINE GUNS

see also Gatling Guns

Archer, Denis. Jane's Pocket Book of Rifles & Light Machine Guns. 1977. pap. 6.95 (ISBN 0-02-079980-2, Collier). Macmillan.
Archer, Denis, ed. Jane's Pocket Book of Pistols & Submachine Guns. (Jane's Pocket Book Ser.). 1977. pap. 6.95 (ISBN 0-02-079970-5, Collier). Macmillan.
Chamberlain, Peter & Gander, Terry. Machine Guns. (World War 2 Fact Files Ser.). (Illus.). 64p. 1975. 5.95 (ISBN 0-668-03506-4); pap. 3.95 (ISBN 0-668-03608-7). Arco.
--Submachine Guns & Automatic Rifles: World War 2 Facts Ser. LC 76-28423. 1976. pap. 3.95 (ISBN 0-668-04013-0). Arco.
Holmes, Bill. Home Workshop Guns for Defense & Resistance: The Submachine Gun, Vol. 1. Leifield, Timothy, ed. (Illus.). 144p. 1977. pap. 8.00 (ISBN 0-87364-085-3). Paladin Ent.
The World's Machine Pistols & Submachine Guns: Developments from 1963-1980, Vol. 2. 1980. 29.95 (ISBN 0-686-15933-0). TBN Ent.
The World's Submachine Guns: Developments from 1915 to 1963, Vol. I. rev. ed. 1980. 29.95 (ISBN 0-686-15931-4). TBN Ent.

MACHINE INDUSTRY

see Machinery–Trade and Manufacture

MACHINE INTELLIGENCE

see Artificial Intelligence

MACHINE LANGUAGE

see Programming Languages (Electronic Computers)

MACHINE PARTS

Collins, J. A. Failure of Materials in Mechanical Design: Analysis, Prediction, Prevention. LC 80-20674. 629p. 1981. 39.95 (ISBN 0-471-05024-5, Pub. by Wiley-Interscience). Wiley.
Stock Drive Products Staff Engineers. Handbook of Small Belt & Chain Drives, 2 vols. 1978. pap. 1.95 (ISBN 0-686-10242-8). Stock Drive.

MACHINE QUILTING

see Quilting

MACHINE-READABLE CATALOG SYSTEM

see MARC System

MACHINE-SHOP MATHEMATICS

see Shop Mathematics

MACHINE-SHOP PRACTICE

Amiss, John M. & Jones, Franklin D. The Use of Handbook Tables & Formulas. 21st ed. Ryffel, Henry H., ed. LC 75-10949. (Illus.). 224p. 1980. 8.00 (ISBN 0-8311-1131-3). Indus Pr.
Anderson, James & Tatro, Earl E. Shop Theory. 6th ed. (Illus.). 576p. (gr. 9-11). 1974. text ed. 15.70 (ISBN 0-07-001612-7, W). McGraw.
Black, Bruce J. Workshop Processes, Practices & Materials. (Illus.). 282p. 1979. pap. 13.95x (ISBN 0-7131-3409-7). Intl Ideas.
Bredin, Harold W. Tooling Methods & Ideas. LC 67-17406. (Illus.). 376p. 1967. 22.00 (ISBN 0-8311-1057-0). Indus Pr.
Engineering Industry Training Board, ed. Training for Operators of Numerically Controlled Machines, 17 vols. Incl. Vol. 1. Introduction to NC Machine Tool; Vol. 2. Rotating Tool; Vol. 3. Rotating Work; Vol. 4. Milling Cutters; Vol. 5. Tape NC Machines; Vol. 6. Automatic Tool & Work Exchanging; Vol. 7. X, Y, & Z Axes; Vol. 8. Positioning of the Tool & Workpiece; Vol. 9. Emergency Stop & Switching Operations; Vol. 10. Operation. 1973. Set. 37.50x (ISBN 0-89563-028-1). Intl Ideas.
Felker, Charles A. Machine Shop Technology. rev. ed. (gr. 9-12). 1962. text ed. 8.96 (ISBN 0-02-816210-2); ans. bk. 1.36 (ISBN 0-02-816230-7). Glencoe.
Heineman, Stephen S. & Genevro, George W. Machine Tools: Processes & Applications. 1979. text ed. 23.50 scp (ISBN 0-06-453305-0, HarpC); manual free (ISBN 0-06-453307-7). Har-Row.
Johnson, Harold V. General-Industrial Machine Shop. 1979. text ed. 18.60 (ISBN 0-87002-293-8); student guide 3.80 (ISBN 0-87002-295-4); visual masters 13.40 (ISBN 0-87002-054-4). Bennett IL.
Jones, Franklin D. Machine Shop Training Course, 2 Vols. 5th ed. (Illus.). (gr. 11-12). 1964. 14.00 ea. Vol. 1, 570 Pgs (ISBN 0-8311-1039-2). Vol. 2, 566 Pgs (ISBN 0-8311-1040-6). Indus Pr.
Kibbe, Richard R. & Neely, John E. Machine Tool Practices. 2nd ed. 1024p. 1982. text ed. 21.95 (ISBN 0-471-05788-6). Wiley.
Kibbe, Richard R., et al. Machine Tool Practices. LC 78-18533. 946p. 1979. text ed. 26.95x (ISBN 0-471-04331-1); tchrs. manual avail. (ISBN 0-471-05120-9). Wiley.
Knight, Roy E. Machine Shop Projects. (gr. 9 up). 1943. pap. text ed. 6.64 (ISBN 0-685-04225-1). McKnight.
Krar, Stephen F., et al. Technology of Machine Tools. 2nd ed. LC 77-3663. (Illus.). 1977. text ed. 18.50 (ISBN 0-07-035383-2, G); answer key to workbook 2.95 (ISBN 0-07-035384-0). McGraw.
Lazarenko, B. R., ed. Electrospark Machining of Metals, Vol. 2. LC 64-20561. 195p. 1964. 32.50 (ISBN 0-306-18242-4, Consultants). Plenum Pub.
Liebers, Arthur. You Can Be a Machinist. LC 75-16390. (A Vocations in Trades Book). (Illus.). 128p. (gr. 6 up). 1975. PLB 6.96 (ISBN 0-688-51719-6). Lothrop.
Ludwig, Oswald A. & McCarthy, Willard J. Metalwork Technology & Practice. rev. & 5th ed. (Illus.). (gr. 11-12). 1975. text ed. 17.28 (ISBN 0-87345-123-6); study guide 5.00 (ISBN 0-87345-118-X); ans key avail. (ISBN 0-685-04228-6). McKnight.
Machine Shop Trades. 1980. text ed. 7.95 (ISBN 0-686-65131-6, 66221); pap. text ed. 5.95 (ISBN 0-686-65132-4, 66213). Natl Textbk.
Moltrecht, K. H. Machine Shop Practice. 2nd ed. LC 79-91236. (Illus.). 1981. Vol. 1, 512 Pp. 19.95x (ISBN 0-8311-1126-7); Vol. 2, 528 Pp. 19.95x (ISBN 0-8311-1132-1). Indus Pr.
Neely, John E. Practical Machine Shop. LC 81-4537. 688p. 1982. text ed. 21.95 (ISBN 0-471-08000-4); price not set tchr.'s ed. (ISBN 0-471-86377-7). Wiley.
Olivo, C. Thomas. Advanced Machine Technology. 1982. text ed. 24.95 (ISBN 0-534-01040-7, Breton Pubs). Wadsworth Pub.
Opitz, H. A Classification System to Describe Workpieces, Classification System. Taylor, R. A., tr. LC 71-112891. 1970. Set. 64.00 (ISBN 0-08-015758-0). Pergamon.
Parsons, Noel R., ed. NC Machinability Data Systems. LC 74-153852. (Numerical Control Ser). 1971. text ed. 13.60x (ISBN 0-87263-029-3). SME.
Stern, Benjamin J. Opportunities in Machines Shop Trades. (gr. 8 up). 1976. PLB 6.60 (ISBN 0-685-65211-4); pap. 4.95 (ISBN 0-8442-6404-0). Natl Textbk.
Tobias, S. A. & Koenigsberger, F., eds. Proceedings of the Thirteenth International Machine Tool Design & Research Conference. LC 73-2955. 1973. 98.95 (ISBN 0-470-87529-1). Halsted Pr.
Vezzani, A. A. & Leuchtman, Alex. Use of the Mechanics' Handbooks. rev. ed. LC 68-59490. (gr. 9-12). 1969. pap. 5.95x (ISBN 0-911168-17-6); ans. bk. 2.00x (ISBN 0-911168-18-4). Prakken.
Walker, John R. Machining Fundamentals. LC 77-22648. (Illus.). 1977. text ed. 15.32 (ISBN 0-87006-236-0). Goodheart.
Wasiloff, T. Machine Shop Safety Kit: Set 1. 1974. Kit Set. 195.00 (ISBN 0-07-079410-3, G); instr's manual 1.95 (ISBN 0-07-068419-7); wkbk. 6.95 (ISBN 0-07-068413-8). McGraw.
Work Planning & Setup. (Machine Tool Ser.: Vol. 3). 1974. pap. text ed. 3.95x (ISBN 0-88462-244-4). Ed Methods.

MACHINE-SHOP PRACTICE–ESTIMATES AND COSTS

Nordhoff, William A. Machine Shop Estimating. 2nd ed. (Illus.). 1960. 31.00 (ISBN 0-07-047159-2, P&RB). McGraw.

MACHINE-SHOP PRACTICE–EXAMINATIONS, QUESTIONS, ETC.

Hoffman, E. Practical Problems in Mathematics for Machinists. LC 78-74432. (Mathematics Ser.). (gr. 8). 1980. 6.60 (ISBN 0-8273-1281-4); instr's guide 1.75 (ISBN 0-8273-1282-2). Delmar.
Rudman, Jack. Basin Machine Operator. (Career Examination Ser.: C-2517). (Cloth bdg. avail. on request). pap. 10.00 (ISBN 0-8373-2517-X). Natl Learning.
--Foreman Machinist. (Career Examination Ser.: C-1414). (Cloth bdg. avail. on request). pap. 8.00 (ISBN 0-8373-1414-3). Natl Learning.
--Machinist. (Career Examination Ser.: C-460). (Cloth bdg. avail. on request). pap. 8.00 (ISBN 0-8373-0460-1). Natl Learning.
--Machinist's Helper. (Career Examination Ser.: C-461). (Cloth bdg. avail. on request). pap. 8.00 (ISBN 0-8373-0461-X). Natl Learning.

MACHINE SHOPS–AUTOMATION

see also Machine Tools–Numerical Control

MACHINE-SHOPS–MANAGEMENT

Ashour, S. Sequencing Theory. LC 72-83014. (Lecture Notes in Economics & Mathematical Systems: Vol. 69). (Illus.). 138p. 1972. pap. 6.30 (ISBN 0-387-05877-X). Springer-Verlag.
Lascoe, Orville D., et al. Machine Shop Operations & Setups. 4th ed. (Illus.). 1973. 18.00 (ISBN 0-8269-1842-5). Am Technical.

MACHINE SHORTHAND

see Stenotypy

MACHINE THEORY

see also Artificial Intelligence; Automata; Coding Theory; Control Theory; Computers; Formal Languages; L Systems; Sequential Machine Theory; Switching Theory

Arbib, M. A., et al. A Basis for Theoretical Computer Science. (Computer Science Texts & Monographs). (Illus.). 224p. 1981. 17.50 (ISBN 0-387-90573-1). Springer-Verlag.
Arbib, Michael A. Algebraic Theory of Machines, Languages & Semigroups. LC 68-18654. 1968. 55.00 (ISBN 0-12-059050-6). Acad Pr.
Ausiello, G. & Lucertini, M., eds. Analysis & Design of Algorithms in Combinatorial Optimization. (CISM International Centre for Mechanical Sciences Ser.: Vol. 266). 209p. 1981. pap. 24.80 (ISBN 0-387-81626-7). Springer-Verlag.
Bobrow, Leonard S. & Arbib, Michael A. Discrete Mathematics: Applied Algebra for Computer & Information Science. LC 73-77936. (Illus.). 1974. 24.50 (ISBN 0-7216-1768-9). Hemisphere Pub.
Colloquium on Automata, Languages & Programming, 2nd, University of Saarbrucken, 1974. Proceedings. Loeckx, J., ed. (Lecture Notes in Computer Science Ser.: Vol. 14). viii, 611p. 1974. pap. 26.20 (ISBN 0-387-06841-4). Springer-Verlag.
Gill, Arthur. Applied Algebra for the Computer Sciences. (Illus.). 416p. 1976. 24.95 (ISBN 0-13-039222-7). P-H.
--Introduction to the Theory of Finite-State Machines: Electronic Systems Ser. 1962. text ed. 22.50 (ISBN 0-07-023243-1, P&RB). McGraw.
Ginsburg, Seymour. An Introduction to Mathematical Machine Theory. 1962 ed. (Illus.). 11.50 (ISBN 0-201-02390-3, Adv Bk Prog). A-W.
Ginzburg, Abraham. Algebraic Theory of Automata. LC 68-23492. (ACM Monograph Ser). 1968. 30.50 (ISBN 0-12-285050-5). Acad Pr.
Gruska, J., ed. Mathematical Foundations of Computer Science 1977: Proceedings, 6th Symposium, Tatranska Lmnica, Sept. 5-9, 1977. LC 77-10135. (Lecture Notes in Computer Science: Vol. 53). 1977. pap. 23.40 (ISBN 0-387-08353-7). Springer-Verlag.
Hartmanis, Juris. Feasible Computations & Provable Complexity Properties. (CBMS-NSF Regional Conference Ser.: Vol. 30). (Orig.). 1978. pap. text ed. 7.75 (ISBN 0-89871-027-8). Soc Indus-Appl Math.
Hopkin, D. & Moss, B. Automata. 1978. text ed. 17.95 (ISBN 0-444-00249-9, North-Holland). Elsevier.
Hu, Sze-Tsen. Mathematical Theory of Switching Circuits & Automata. LC 68-18370. (Illus.). 1968. 30.00x (ISBN 0-520-00581-3). U of Cal Pr.
International Symposium on Category Theory, 1st, San Francisco, 1974. Category Theory Applied to Computation & Control: Proceedings. Manes, E. G., ed. LC 74-34481. (Lecture Notes in Computer Science Ser.: Vol. 25). x, 245p. 1975. pap. 15.00 (ISBN 0-387-07142-3). Springer-Verlag.
Kain, Richard Y. Automata Theory: Machines & Language. LC 81-230. 320p. 1981. Repr. 27.50 (ISBN 0-89874-322-2). Krieger.

Kalman, Rudolph E., et al. Topics in Mathematical System Theory. LC 68-31662. (International Pure & Applied Mathematics Ser). 1969. text ed. 26.95 (ISBN 0-07-033255-X, C). McGraw.

Lazarev, V. G. & Zakrevskii, A. D., eds. Synthesis of Digital Automata. LC 69-12514. (Illus.). 172p. 1969. 35.00 (ISBN 0-306-10829-1, Consultants). Plenum Pub.

Milner, R. A Calculus of Communicating Systems. (Lecture Notes in Computer Science Ser.: Vol. 92). 260p. 1981. pap. 11.80 (ISBN 0-387-10235-3). Springer-Verlag.

Minsky, Marvin. Computation: Finite & Infinite Machines. 1967. ref. ed. 24.95 (ISBN 0-13-165563-9). P-H.

Sampson, J. R. Adaptive Information Processing: An Introductory Survey. LC 76-8470. (Texts & Monographs in Computer Science Ser.). (Illus.). 1976. 17.90 (ISBN 0-387-07739-1). Springer-Verlag.

Second GI Conference, Karlsruhe, May 20-23, 1975. Automata Theory & Formal Languages. Brakhage, H., ed. (Lecture Notes in Computer Science Ser.: Vol. 33). viii, 292p. 1975. pap. 14.70 (ISBN 0-387-07407-4). Springer-Verlag.

Starke, P. H. Abstract Automata. 1972. 41.50 (ISBN 0-444-10349-X, North-Holland); pap. 27.00 (ISBN 0-444-10354-6, North Holland). Elsevier.

Tsetlin, M. L. Automata Theory & Modeling of Biological Systems. (Mathematics in Science & Engineering Ser.). 1973. 51.00 (ISBN 0-12-701650-3). Acad Pr.

Wang, Hao. Logic, Computers & Sets. LC 70-113155. Orig. Title: Survey of Mathematical Logic. 1970. Repr. of 1962 ed. text ed. 19.95 (ISBN 0-8284-0245-0). Chelsea Pub.

Weihrauch, K., ed. Theoretical Computer Science: 4th GI Conference Aachen, March 26 - 28, 1979. (Lecture Notes in Computer Science: Vol. 67). 1979. pap. 16.80 (ISBN 0-387-09118-1). Springer-Verlag.

MACHINE-TOOLS

see also Jigs and Fixtures; Manufacturing Processes; Tool-Steel;
also specific machine tools, e.g. Planning Machines

Anderson, James & Tatro, Earl E. Shop Theory. 6th ed. (Illus.). 576p. (gr. 9-11). 1974. text ed. 15.70 (ISBN 0-07-001612-7, W). McGraw.

--Shop Theory. 5th ed. 1968. 12.80 (ISBN 0-07-001608-9, W). McGraw.

Basic Hand Tools. (Machine Tool Ser.: Vol. 2). 1974. pap. text ed. 3.95x (ISBN 0-88462-243-6). Ed Methods.

Boothroyd, Geoffrey. Fundamentals of Metal Machining & Machine Tools. (Illus.). 350p. 1975. text ed. 18.95 (ISBN 0-07-006498-9, C); solutions manual 3.95 (ISBN 0-07-006502-0). McGraw.

Bradley, Ian. History of Machine Tools. 1972. 12.50x (ISBN 0-85242-102-8). Intl Pubns Serv.

Bredin, Harold W. Tooling Methods & Ideas. LC 67-17406. (Illus.). 376p. 1967. 22.00 (ISBN 0-8311-1057-0). Indus Pr.

Broehl, Wayne G., Jr. Precision Valley: The Machine Tool Companies of Springfield, Vermont. LC 75-41748. (Companies & Men: Business Enterprises in America). (Illus.). 1976. Repr. of 1959 ed. 21.00x (ISBN 0-405-08065-4). Arno.

Brothwell, C., et al, eds. Maintenance of Numerically Controlled Machine Tools, 2 vols. 2nd ed. (Engineering Craftsmen: No. J27). (Illus.). 1973. Set. sprial bdg. 52.00x (ISBN 0-85083-155-5). Intl Ideas.

Dixon, Robert G. Benchwork. 2nd ed. LC 80-66607. (Machine Trades - Machine Shop Ser.). (Illus.). 208p. 1981. pap. text ed. 7.80 (ISBN 0-8273-1743-3); instr's. guide 1.10 (ISBN 0-8273-1744-1). Delmar.

Engineering Industry Training Board, ed. Training in Safe Working Practice for Power Press Tool Setters & Operators, 9 vols. Incl. Vol. 1. Introduction to Power Press; Vol. 3. Press Brakes; Vol. 4. Safety Tool Setting; Vol. 5. Guards; Vol. 6. Testing Press Guards; Vol. 7. Accident Prevention. 1973. Set. 21.00x (ISBN 0-89563-031-1). Intl Ideas.

Equipment Guide-Book Co. Machine Tool Value Guide: Grinding Machines, Vol. III. Husek, Jiri, ed. 600p. 1981. pap. cancelled (ISBN 0-89692-104-2). Equipment Guide.

Feirer, John L. Machine Tool Metalworking. 2nd ed. Gilmore, D. E., ed. LC 72-10166. (Illus.). 568p. (gr. 10-12). 1973. text ed. 14.75 (ISBN 0-07-020369-5). McGraw.

Floud, R. The British Machine-Tool Industry, 1850-1914. LC 75-46205. (Illus.). 180p. 1976. 29.95 (ISBN 0-521-21203-0). Cambridge U Pr.

Gough, P. J. Swarf & Machine Tools. 1970. 8.95 (ISBN 0-09-102240-1, Pub. by Hutchinson). Merrimack Bk Serv.

Heineman, Stephen S. & Genevro, George W. Machine Tools: Processes & Applications. 1979. text ed. 23.50 scp (ISBN 0-06-453305-0, HarpC); manual free (ISBN 0-06-453307-7). Har-Row.

Heritage, P., et al, eds. Machining for Toolmaking & Experimental Work, 3 vols. 2nd ed. (Engineering Craftsmen: No. H1). (Illus.). 1977. Set. spiral bdg. 36.50x (ISBN 0-85083-024-9). Intl Ideas.

Hine, Charles R. Machine Tools & Processes for Engineers. 634p. Date not set. Repr. of 1971 ed. lib. bdg. price not set (ISBN 0-89874-354-0). Krieger.

Kibbe, Richard R. & Neely, John E. Machine Tool Practices. 2nd ed. 1024p. 1982. text ed. 21.95 (ISBN 0-471-05788-6). Wiley.

Kibbe, Richard R., et al. Machine Tool Practices. LC 78-18533. 946p. 1979. text ed. 26.95x (ISBN 0-471-04331-1); tchrs. manual avail. (ISBN 0-471-05120-9). Wiley.

Koenigsberger, F. & Tlusty, J. Machine Tool Structures, Vol. 1. LC 79-84073. 1970. 94.00 (ISBN 0-08-013405-X). Pergamon.

Koenigsberger, T. & Tobias, S. A., eds. Proceedings of the Sixteenth Machine Tool Design & Research Conference. LC 76-5219. (International Machine Tool Design & Research Conference Ser.). 599p. 1976. text ed. 109.95 (ISBN 0-470-15100-5). Halsted Pr.

Krar, S. F. & Oswald, J. W. Turning Technology: Engine & Turret Lathes. LC 78-153723. 1971. pap. text ed. 11.60 (ISBN 0-8273-0206-1); instructor's guide 1.60 (ISBN 0-8273-0207-X). Delmar.

Krar, Stephen F., et al. Technology of Machine Tools. 2nd ed. LC 77-3663. (Illus.). 1977. text ed. 18.50 (ISBN 0-07-035383-2, G); answer key to workbook 2.95 (ISBN 0-07-035384-0). McGraw.

Machine Tool & Design Research International Conference, 14th. Proceedings. Tobias, S. A. & Tobias, S. A., eds. 1974. 114.95 (ISBN 0-470-49746-7). Halsted Pr.

Machine Tool Design & Research International Conference 15th. Proceedings. Tobias, S. A. & Koenigsberger, F., eds. LC 63-19240. 738p. 1975. 181.95 (ISBN 0-470-87532-1). Halsted Pr.

Matt, Stephen R. Machine Tool Operation: An Introduction. 1981. text ed. 19.95 (ISBN 0-534-01039-3, Breton Pubs). Wadsworth Pub.

National Research & Appraisal Co., compiled by. Machine Tool Value Guide: Milling Machines, Vol. 2. (Orig.). 1980. pap. 75.00 (ISBN 0-89692-103-4). Equipment Guide.

Olivo, C. Thomas. Advanced Machine Technology. 1982. text ed. 24.95 (ISBN 0-534-01040-7, Breton Pubs). Wadsworth Pub.

Ryder, G. H. Jigs, Fixtures, Tools & Gauges. 6th ed. Orig. Title: Jigs, Tools & Fixtures. (Illus.). 176p. 1973. text ed. 12.75x (ISBN 0-291-39432-9). Scholium Intl.

Schlesinger, G. Testing Machine Tools: For the Use of Machine Tool Makers, Users Inspectors & Plant Engineers. 8th ed. 1977. text ed. 18.00 (ISBN 0-08-021685-4). Pergamon.

Sigmon, D. L. A Framing Guide & Steel Square Book. rev. ed. 312p. 1958. 9.00 (ISBN 0-914760-01-7). Cline-Sigmon.

Simon, Wilhelm. The Numerical Control of Machine Tools. 2nd rev. ed. LC 72-89494. 1972. 55.00x (ISBN 0-8448-0117-8). Crane-Russak Co.

Steffy, Wilbert. Economics of Machine Tool Procurement. LC 77-90986. (Manufacturing Data Ser.). 1978. 12.75 (ISBN 0-87263-041-2). SME.

Tobias, S. A. & Koenigsbergen, T. Proceedings of the Seventeenth International Machine, Tool, Design & Research Conference. 1978. 120.95 (ISBN 0-470-99076-7). Halsted Pr.

Tobias, S. A. & Koenigsberger, F., eds. Proceedings of the Thirteenth International Machine Tool Design & Research Conference. LC 73-2955. 1973. 98.95 (ISBN 0-470-87529-1). Halsted Pr.

Wagoner, Harless D. U. S. Machine Tool Industry from 1900 to 1950. 1968. 25.00x (ISBN 0-262-23030-5). MIT Pr.

White, Warren T., et al. Machine Tools & Machining Practices, 2 vols. LC 76-27863. 1977. Vol. 1. text ed. 27.95 (ISBN 0-471-94035-6); Vol. 2. text ed. 27.95 (ISBN 0-471-94036-4). Wiley.

Woodbury, Robert S. Studies in the History of Machine Tools. (History of Science & Technology Ser). 625p. 1973. pap. 6.95 (ISBN 0-262-73033-2). MIT Pr.

Zim, Herbert S. & Skelly, James R. Machine Tools. LC 69-10403. (How Things Work Ser., No. 1). (Illus.). (gr. 3-7). 1960. pap. 1.25 (ISBN 0-688-26555-3). Morrow.

MACHINE-TOOLS–DESIGN

American Society of Tool & Manufacturing Engineers. Fundamentals of Tool Design. (Illus.). 1962. text ed. 23.95 (ISBN 0-13-344861-4). P-H.

Donaldson, Cyril & Le Cain, George. Tool Design. 3rd ed. (Illus.). 840p. 1973. text ed. 19.95 (ISBN 0-07-017531-4, G); answer key 2.50 (ISBN 0-07-017532-2). McGraw.

Hoover, T. W. & Schumacher, H. G. Tool & Die Drafting. LC 57-12844. 1968. 5.25x (ISBN 0-911168-09-5). Prakken.

International Machine Tool Design & Research Conference, 21st. Proceedings. Alexander, J. M., ed. 1981. text ed. 170.00x (ISBN 0-686-76762-4). Verry.

Machine Tool Design & Research International Conference, 12th. Proceedings. Koenigsberger, F. & Tobias, S. A., eds. LC 72-6276. 582p. 1972. 108.95 (ISBN 0-470-49745-9). Halsted Pr.

Tobias, S. A. & Koenigsbergen, T. Proceedings of the Seventeenth International Machine, Tool, Design & Research Conference. 1978. 120.95 (ISBN 0-470-99076-7). Halsted Pr.

MACHINE TOOLS–DICTIONARIES

Freeman, Henry G. Fachwoerterbuch Spanende Werkzeugmaschinen. 527p. (Ger. & Eng., Dictionary of Machine Tools). 1965. leatherette 72.00 (ISBN 3-7736-5090-6, M-7403, Pub. by Verlag W. Gerardet). French & Eur.

--Spanende Werkzeugmaschinen, Deutsch-Englische Begriffserlauterungen und Kommentare. 617p. (Machine Tools, German-English Explanations and Comments). 1973. 75.00 (ISBN 3-7736-5082-5, M-7624, Pub. by Verlag W. Girardet). French & Eur.

Lexicue Trilingue des Termes d'usage Courant En Machines Outils; les Tours, Pt. 1. 74p. (Trilingual Lexicon of Common Terms in Machine Tools; Wheels). 1961. pap. 12.50 (ISBN 0-686-56791-9, M-6374). French & Eur.

Lexique Trilinque des Termes d'Usage Courant En Machines Outils, les Perceuses, Pt. 2. 96p. (Trilingual Lexicon of Commonly Used Terms in Machine Tools; Drilling Tools). pap. 12.50 (ISBN 0-686-56792-7, M-6375). French & Eur.

MACHINE TOOLS–NUMERICAL CONTROL

Barron, C. H. Numerical Control for Machine Tools. 1971. 15.95 (ISBN 0-07-003824-4, G); answer key 2.00 (ISBN 0-07-003831-7). McGraw.

Childs, James J. Numerical Control Part Programming. LC 73-9766. (Illus.). 340p. 1973. 21.00 (ISBN 0-8311-1099-6). Indus Pr.

--Principles of Numerical Control. 2nd ed. LC 70-81756. (Illus.). 294p. (gr. 11 up). 1969. text ed. 18.00 (ISBN 0-8311-1051-1). Indus Pr.

Olesten, Nils O. Numerical Control. LC 78-105390. 1970. 51.00 (ISBN 0-471-65336-5, Pub. by Wiley-Interscience). Wiley.

Parsons, Noel R., ed. NC Machinability Data Systems. LC 74-153852. (Numerical Control Ser). 1971. text ed. 13.60x (ISBN 0-87263-029-3). SME.

Patton, William J. Numerical Control: Practice& Application. LC 72-85266. 432p. 1972. 15.95 (ISBN 0-87909-564-4). Reston.

Roberts, Arthur & Prentice, Richard. Programming for Numerical Control Machines. 2nd ed. (Illus.). 1978. text ed. 14.95 (ISBN 0-07-053156-0, G). McGraw.

MACHINE-TOOLS, AUTOMATIC

see Machine-Tools

MACHINE-TRACTOR STATIONS

Miller, Robert F. One Hundred Thousand Tractors: The MTS & the Development of Controls in Soviet Agriculture. LC 70-95929. (Russian Research Center Studies: No. 60). 1970. 20.00x (ISBN 0-674-63875-1). Harvard U Pr.

MACHINE TRADE

see Machinery–Trade and Manufacture

MACHINE TRANSLATING

see also Translating Machines

Akhmanova, O. S., et al. Exact Methods in Linguistic Research. Haynes, David G. & Mohr, Dolores V., trs. LC 63-19957. 1963. 24.50x (ISBN 0-520-00542-2). U of Cal Pr.

Bruderer, Herbert E. Handbook of Machine & Machine-Aided Translation. 1977. write for info. (ISBN 0-7204-0717-6, North-Holland). Elsevier.

Ceccato, Silvio, ed. Linguistic Analysis & Programming for Mechanical Translation. (Illus.). 1961. 36.25x (ISBN 0-677-00110-X). Gordon.

Garvin, Paul L. On Machine Translation. LC 79-182469. (Janua Linguarum Ser. Minor: No. 128). 142p. (Orig.). 1972. pap. text ed. 21.25x (ISBN 90-2792-004-4). Mouton.

Henisz-Dostert, Bozena, et al. Machine Translation. (Trends in Linguistics, Studies, & Monographs: No. 16). 1979. text ed. 44.25x (ISBN 90-279-7836-0). Mouton.

Ingerman, Peter Z. Syntax Oriented Translator. 1966. text ed. 10.95 (ISBN 0-12-370850-8). Acad Pr.

Locke, William N. & Booth, E. Donald, eds. Machine Translation of Languages: Fourteen Essays. LC 75-29339. 243p. 1976. Repr. of 1955 ed. lib. bdg. 15.25x (ISBN 0-8371-8434-7, LOMT). Greenwood.

Pronikov, A. S. Dependability & Durability of Engineering Products. 1973. text ed. 13.95 (ISBN 0-408-70383-0). Butterworth.

MACHINERY

see also Bearings (Machinery); Construction Equipment; Electric Engineering; Electric Machinery; Engines; Friction; Gearing; Hydraulic Machinery; Inventions; Locomotives; Lubrication and Lubricants; Machine-Tools; Mechanical Drawing; Mechanical Engineering; Mechanics; Patents; Power Transmission; Replacement of Industrial Equipment; Sealing (Technology); Shafting; Steam-Engines; Turning; Windmills also machinery used in particular industries or for special purposes, e.g. Agricultural Machinery; Calculating Machines

Appraisal of Machinery & Equipment. LC 73-97948. (ASA Monograph: No. 2). 1969. 5.00 (ISBN 0-937828-11-4). Am Soc Appraisers.

Babbage, Charles. On the Economy of Machinery & Manufactures. 4th ed. LC 74-22019. Repr. of 1835 ed. 17.50x (ISBN 0-678-00001-8). Kelley.

Barnett, George E. Chapters on Machinery & Labor. LC 68-25563. (Arcturus Books Paperbacks). 191p. 1969. pap. 2.25 (ISBN 0-8093-0398-1). S Ill U Pr.

The Book of Knowledge of Ingenious Mechanical Devices: Kitab Ft Ma 'rifat Al-Hiyal Al-Handasiyya. LC 72-92529. 286p. 1974. lib. bdg. 126.00 (ISBN 90-277-0329-9, Pub. by Reidel Holland). Kluwer Boston.

Burroughs, William. The Soft Machine. Bd. with Nova Express; The Wild Boys: Three Novels. LC 80-8062. 544p. (Orig.). 1981. pap. 5.95 (ISBN 0-394-17749-5, B 446, BC). Grove.

Charman, B. W. Special Purpose Production Machines. 1970. 7.50x (ISBN 0-258-96738-2). Transatlantic.

Ciupik, Larry A. & Seevers, James A. Space Machines. LC 78-26991. (Machine World Ser.). (Illus.). (gr. 2-4). 1979. PLB 11.15 (ISBN 0-8172-1325-2). Raintree Pubs.

Collacott, R. A. Mechanical Fault Diagnosis & Condition Monitoring. LC 77-397. 496p. 1977. 67.95x (ISBN 0-412-12930-2, Pub. by Chapman & Hall England). Methuen Inc.

Conference on Picture Language Machines. Proceedings. Kaneff, S., ed. 1971. 67.50 (ISBN 0-12-396250-1). Acad Pr.

Cooper, Grace R. The Sewing Machine: Its Invention & Development. LC 75-619415. (Illus.). 238p. 1977. 20.00x (ISBN 0-87474-330-3). Smithsonian.

Darack, Arthur. Outdoor Power Equipment: How It Works, How to Fix It. LC 77-70404. 1977. 9.95 (ISBN 0-8128-2344-3); pap. 4.95 (ISBN 0-8128-2276-5). Stein & Day.

Enger, Ronald L. Do It Yourself (At Home) Sewing Machine Care & Repair. (Illus.). 33p. 1978. pap. 3.95 (ISBN 0-685-59470-X). R L Enger.

Ewing, Kristine L. Mill Maintenance II: Large Machinery. LC 78-387. (Bibliographic Ser.: No. 281). 1978. pap. 13.00 (ISBN 0-87010-031-9). Inst Paper Chem.

--Mill Maintenance III: Instruments & Small Equipment. LC 78-387. (Bibliographic Ser.: No. 282). 1978. pap. 13.00 (ISBN 0-87010-032-7). Inst Paper Chem.

Ferguson, Eugene S., ed. The Various & Ingenious Machines of Captain Agostino Ramelli. Gnudi, Martha T., tr. from Fr. & It. LC 75-24985. (Studies in the History of Technology). (Illus.). 604p. 1976. 115.00x (ISBN 0-8018-1796-X). Johns Hopkins.

Follette, Daniel. Machining Fundamentals. Williams, Roy & Weller, E. J., eds. LC 80-51218. (Illus.). 400p. 1980. 27.50 (ISBN 0-87263-054-4). SME.

Gaskets. (Special Technical Publications Ser.). 42p. 1977. softcover 15.00x (ISBN 0-686-76052-2, 620, 04-620000-20). ASTM.

Gingrich, Harold W. Electrical Machinery, Transformers, & Control. (Illus.). 1978. ref. 21.95 (ISBN 0-13-247320-8). P-H.

Ham, C. W., et al. Mechanics of Machinery. 4th ed. (Mechanical Engineering Ser.). 1958. text ed. 22.95 (ISBN 0-07-025688-8, C). McGraw.

Handler, W. & Weizenbaum, J., eds. Display Use for Man-Machine Dialog. 1973. 22.50x (ISBN 0-8448-0783-4). Crane-Russak Co.

Holmes, Roy. The Characteristics of Mechanical Engineering Systems. 1977. text ed. 19.00 (ISBN 0-08-021033-3); pap. text ed. 8.50 (ISBN 0-08-021032-5). Pergamon.

International Directory of Machinery, Apparatus, Tools & Automated Production 1979. 45th ed. 1979. 30.00x (ISBN 0-8002-2373-X). Intl Pubns Serv.

James, Dilmus. Used Machinery & Economic Development. LC 72-619710. 216p. 1974. pap. 6.00 (ISBN 0-87744-114-6). Mich St U Busn.

Living with ERISA: A Current Review & a Look Ahead, a Transcript of a MAPI Conference. 1976. non-members 15.00, members 10.00 (ISBN 0-686-16743-0). M & A Products.

Liwschitz-Garik, M. & Whipple, C. C. A-C Machines. 2nd ed. 604p. 1961. 21.50 (ISBN 0-685-36895-5, Pub. by Van Nos Reinhold). Krieger.

Machinery Buyers Guide 1981. 52nd ed. LC 72-626509. 1500p. (Orig.). 1981. pap. 47.50x (ISBN 0-8002-2794-8). Intl Pubns Serv.
Machinery Maintenance. (Illus.). 140p. 1981. pap. text ed. 5.00 (ISBN 0-86691-002-6); write for info. Deere & Co.
Olivo, Thomas C. Basic Machine Technology. 1980. 19.95 (ISBN 0-672-97171-2); instructor's guide 6.67 (ISBN 0-672-97173-9). Bobbs.
Pick, Christopher C. Undersea Machines. LC 78-27420. (Machine World Ser.). (Illus.). (gr. 2-4). 1979. PLB 11.15 (ISBN 0-8172-1326-0). Raintree Pubs.
Raczkowski, George. Principles of Machine Dynamics. 110p. 1979. pap. 12.95x (ISBN 0-87201-440-1). Gulf Pub.
Rich, Mark. Earth Movers. LC 79-23494. (On the Move Ser.). (Illus.). 48p. (gr. 3-6). 1980. PLB 10.00 (ISBN 0-516-03884-2). Childrens.
Shigley, Joseph E. Dynamic Analysis of Machines. (Mechanical Engineering Ser.). 1961. text ed. 24.95 (ISBN 0-07-056858-8, C); solutions manual 3.50 (ISBN 0-07-056859-6). McGraw.
Shigley, Joseph E. & Uiker, John J. Theory of Machines & Mechanisms. (Mechanical Engineering Ser.). (Illus.). 576p. 1980. text ed. 27.95x (ISBN 0-07-056884-7); solutions manual 13.95 (ISBN 0-07-056885-5). McGraw.
Smith, Richard T. Analysis of Electrical Machines. (Illus.). 300p. 1981. 36.01 (ISBN 0-08-027174-X). Pergamon.
Smith, William. Ancient Machine & Contrivances, Greek & Roman. (Illus.). 68p. 1972. pap. 1.00x (ISBN 0-685-65321-8). Coronado Pr.
Tomlinson, Charles. The Matachines. 2.00 (ISBN 0-685-47005-9); signed 5.00 (ISBN 0-685-47006-7). San Marcos.
U. S. Navy Bureau of Naval Personnel. Basic Machines & How They Work. LC 77-153739. 1971. lib. bdg. 10.50 (ISBN 0-88307-633-0). Gannon.
U. S. Navy (Bureau of Naval Personnel) Basic Machines & How They Work. (Illus.). 1965. pap. 3.00 (ISBN 0-486-21709-4). Dover.
Walker, John R. Machining Fundmentals. 512p. 1981. 15.32 (ISBN 0-87006-331-6). Goodheart.
Weingartner, C., compiled by. Machinists' Ready Reference. rev., enl. ed. LC 81-81329. (Illus.). 1981. wire bdg. 6.95x (ISBN 0-911168-50-8). Prakken.
Wesolek, Mary K. Machine Book. (Illus., Orig.). 1978. pap. 3.95 (ISBN 0-8431-0459-7). Price Stern.
White, James. New Century of Inventions. (Illus.). 1967. Repr. of 1822 ed. 32.00 (ISBN 0-8337-3768-6). B Franklin.

MACHINERY-DESIGN

see also Human Engineering; Machinery-Models

American Society Of Mechanical Engineers. ASME Handbook: Metals Engineering-Design. 2nd ed. 1964. 53.50 (ISBN 0-07-001518-X, P&RB). McGraw.
--ASME Handbook: Metals Properties. (Illus.). 1956. 38.50 (ISBN 0-07-001513-9, P&RB). McGraw.
Black, Paul H. & Adams, O. Eugene, Jr. Machine Design. 3rd ed. LC 68-13623. 1968. text ed. 23.00 (ISBN 0-07-005524-6, C). McGraw.
Collins, J. A. Failure of Materials in Mechanical Design: Analysis, Prediction, Prevention. LC 80-20674. 629p. 1981. 39.95 (ISBN 0-471-05024-5, Pub. by Wiley-Interscience). Wiley.
Creamer, Robert H. Machine Design. 2nd ed. LC 75-12093. (Engineering Technology Ser.). (Illus.). 544p. 1976. text ed. 21.95 (ISBN 0-201-01178-6); instr's guide 1.50 (ISBN 0-201-01179-4). A-W.
Deutschman, Aaron D., et al. Machine Design: Theory & Practice. (Illus.). 768p. 1975. text ed. 27.95 (ISBN 0-02-329000-5, 32900). Macmillan.
Faires, Virgil M. Design of Machine Elements. 4th ed. 1965. text ed. 22.954 (ISBN 0-02-335950-1, 33595). Macmillan.
Faires, Virgil M. & Wingren, Roy M. Problems on the Design of Machine Elements. 4th ed. 1965. text ed. 5.95 (ISBN 0-02-335960-9, 33596). Macmillan.
Hall, A. S., et al. Machine Design. (Orig.). 1961. pap. 6.95 (ISBN 0-07-025595-4, SP). McGraw.
Johnson, Ray C. Mechanical Design Synthesis: Creative Design & Optimization. 2nd ed. LC 77-10974. 360p. 1978. lib. bdg. 19.50 (ISBN 0-88275-612-5). Krieger.
Juvinall, Robert C. Engineering Considerations of Stress, Strain, & Strength. (Illus.). 1967. text ed. 25.50 (ISBN 0-07-033180-4, C); instructor's manual 4.95 (ISBN 0-07-033181-2). McGraw.
Levinson, Irving. Machine Design. (Illus.). 1978. ref. 19.95 (ISBN 0-87909-461-3). Reston.
Leyer, Albert. Machine Design. 1974. 21.50x (ISBN 0-216-87457-2). Intl Ideas.
Parr, Robert E. Principles of Mechanical Design. (Illus.). 1969. text ed. 17.95 (ISBN 0-07-048512-7, G). McGraw.
Phelan, Richard M. Fundamentals of Mechanical Design. 3rd ed. LC 79-98487. 1970. text ed. 24.50 (ISBN 0-07-049776-1, C); solutions manual 2.50 (ISBN 0-07-049790-7). McGraw.
Rothbart, Harold A. Mechanical Design & Systems Handbook. 1964. 54.50 (ISBN 0-07-054019-5, P&RB). McGraw.
Ruiz, C. & Koenigsburger, F. Design for Strength & Production. 1970. 59.00x (ISBN 0-677-62050-0). Gordon.
Sharma, K. D. Fundamentals of Machine Design. 1971. 12.50x (ISBN 0-210-27015-2). Asia.
Shigley, Joseph E. Mechanical Engineering Design. 2nd ed. LC 74-167497. (Mechanical Engineering Ser.). (Illus.). 768p. 1972. text ed. 19.50 (ISBN 0-07-056869-3, C). McGraw.
--Mechanical Engineering Design. 3rd ed. (Mechanical Engineering Ser.). (Illus.). 1976. text ed. 27.50 (ISBN 0-07-056881-2); solutions manual 8.50 (ISBN 0-07-056882-0). McGraw.
Sors, L. Fatigue Design of Machine Components. 224p. 1971. text ed. 42.00 (ISBN 0-08-016138-3). Pergamon.
Spotts, M. F. Design of Machine Elements. 5th ed. (Illus.). 1978. ref. ed. 27.95 (ISBN 0-13-200576-X). P-H.
Stephenson, J. & Callander, R. A. Engineering Design. LC 73-5277. 705p. 1974. 44.95 (ISBN 0-471-82210-8, Pub. by Wiley-Interscience). Wiley.
Suh, C. H. & Radcliffe, C. W. Kinematics & Mechanisms Design. LC 77-7102. 434p. 1978. 35.95 (ISBN 0-471-01461-3). Wiley.
Walker, J. H. Large Synchronous Machines: Design, Manufacture & Operation. (Monographs in Electrical & Electronic Engineering). (Illus.). 250p. 1981. 65.00 (ISBN 0-19-859364-3). Oxford U Pr.

MACHINERY-DICTIONARIES

Diccionario Para Obras Publicas, Edificacion y Maquinaria en Obra. (Ger. -Span.). 1962. 86.00 (ISBN 3-7625-1160-8, M-7132). French & Eur.
Freeman, H. G. Special Dictionary Machinery. 8th ed. 207p. (Eng. & Ger.). 1971. 44.25 (ISBN 3-7736-5031-0). Adler.
Lanecki, Francois & Dupre, Celine. Vocabulaire Francais-Anglais De la Machine a Coudre Industrielle. 85p. (Fr.-Eng.). 1973. pap. 3.50 (ISBN 0-686-56991-1, M-6331). French & Eur.
Schlomann, A. Illustrierte Technische Woerterbucher: Maschinenelemente, Vol. 1. (Ger., Eng., Fr., Rus., Span. & It., Illustrated dictionary elements of machinery & tools). 1968. 59.95 (ISBN 0-686-56482-0, M-7469, Pub. by R. Oldenbourg). French & Eur.
Simons, Eric N. A Dictionary of Machining. (Illus.). 240p. 1973. 15.00 (ISBN 0-685-27907-3). Philos Lib.

MACHINERY-DRAWINGS

Grafstein, Paul & Schwarz, Otto M. Pictorial Handbook of Technical Devices. (Illus.). 1971. 14.00 (ISBN 0-8206-0234-5). Chem Pub.
Yankee, H. W. Machine Drafting & Related Technology. 2nd ed. 1981. 16.95 (ISBN 0-07-072252-8). McGraw.

MACHINERY-EXHIBITIONS

Johnson, Philip. Machine Art. LC 77-86423. (Museum of Modern Art Publications in Reprint Ser). (Illus.). 1970. Repr. of 1934 ed. 19.00 (ISBN 0-405-01542-9). Arno.

MACHINERY-HISTORY

Burstall, Aubrey F. Simple Working Models of Historic Machines. (Paperback Ser: No. 280). 1975. 5.95 (ISBN 0-262-52036-2). MIT Pr.
Calder, Ritchie. The Evolution of the Machine. LC 68-17249. (Illus.). 160p. 1968. 5.95 (ISBN 0-8281-0342-9, J04001, Co-Pub. by Smithsonian). Am Heritage.
Glynn, Joseph. Construction of Cranes & Machinery Circa 1850. (Illus.). Repr. of 1854 ed. 4.95 (ISBN 0-686-05396-6). British Am Bks.
Laithwaite. Exciting Electric Machine Inventions. pap. 3.95 (ISBN 0-08-017249-0). Pergamon.
Muslin, E. A. Machines of the Twentieth Century. 269p. 1974. pap. 1.75 (ISBN 0-8285-0824-0, Pub. by Mir Pubs Russia). Imported Pubns.
Roberts, Verne L. Machine Guarding: A Historical Perspective. LC 80-84798. (Illus.). 282p. 1980. text ed. 59.95 (ISBN 0-938830-00-7). Inst Product.
Strandh, Sigvard. A History of the Machine. LC 77-82279. (Illus.). 1979. 35.00 (ISBN 0-89479-025-0). A & W Pubs.

MACHINERY-INSPECTION

Town, H. C. & Moore, H. Inspection Machines: Measuring Systems & Instruments. 1978. 22.50 (ISBN 0-7134-0795-6); pap. 13.50 (ISBN 0-7134-0796-4). David & Charles.

MACHINERY-JUVENILE LITERATURE

Ackins, Ralph. Energy Machines. LC 79-27714. (Machine World Ser.). (Illus.). (gr. 2-4). 1980. PLB 11.15 (ISBN 0-8172-1336-8). Raintree Child.
Adkins, Jan. Heavy Equipment. LC 80-15213. (Illus.). 32p. (gr. 1-4). 1980. 8.95 (ISBN 0-684-16641-0). Scribner.
--Moving Heavy Things. (gr. 5 up). 1980. reinforced bdg. 6.95 (ISBN 0-395-29206-9). HM.
Aylesworth, Thomas G., ed. It Works Like This: A Collection of Machines from Nature & Science Magazine. LC 68-19350. (gr. 4-7). 1968. 4.95 (ISBN 0-385-03525-X). Natural Hist.
Boy Scouts Of America. Machinery. LC 19-600. (Illus.). 64p. (gr. 6-12). 1962. pap. 0.70x (ISBN 0-8395-3337-3, 3337). BSA.
Fenner, Sal. Sea Machines. LC 79-28586. (Machine World Ser.). (Illus.). (gr. 2-4). 1980. PLB 11.15 (ISBN 0-8172-1334-1). Raintree Child.
Gardner, Robert. This Is the Way It Works: A Collection of Machines. LC 79-7493. (Illus.). 1980. 8.95a (ISBN 0-385-14697-3); PLB (ISBN 0-385-14698-1). Doubleday.
Girard, Pat. Flying Machines. LC 79-28842. (Machine World Ser.). (Illus.). (gr. 2-4). 1980. PLB 11.15 (ISBN 0-8172-1333-3). Raintree Child.
Hahn, Christine. Amusement Park Machines. LC 78-26920. (Machine World Ser.). (Illus.). (gr. 2-4). 1979. PLB 11.15 (ISBN 0-8172-1330-9). Raintree Pubs.
Hancock, Ralph. Super Machines. LC 78-2202. (Illus.). (gr. 4-9). 1978. 5.95 (ISBN 0-670-68446-5). Viking Pr.
Howard, Sam. Communications Machines. LC 79-27715. (Machine World Ser.). (Illus.). 32p. (gr. 2-4). 1980. PLB 11.15 (ISBN 0-8172-1335-X). Raintree Child.
James, Elizabeth & Barkin, Carol. The Simple Facts of Simple Machines. LC 74-20664. (Illus.). 64p. (gr. 5 up). 1975. PLB 6.24 (ISBN 0-688-51685-8). Lothrop.
Kiley, Denise. Biggest Machines. LC 80-383. (Machine World Ser.). (Illus.). 32p. (gr. 2-4). 1980. PLB 11.15 (ISBN 0-8172-1332-5). Raintree Child.
Maloney, Cecelia. The Box Book. (Illus.). (gr. k-2). 1978. PLB 5.38 (ISBN 0-307-68910-7, Golden Pr). Western Pub.
Pine, Tillie S. & Levine, Joseph. Simple Machines & How We Use Them. (Illus.). (gr. 3-5). 1965. PLB 6.95 (ISBN 0-07-050067-3, GB). McGraw.
Rockwell, Anne. Machines. (Illus.). (ps-2). 1972. 9.95 (ISBN 0-02-777520-8). Macmillan.
Sharp, Elizabeth N. Simple Machines & How They Work. (Gateway Ser: No. 12). (gr. 3-5). 1959. PLB 5.99 (ISBN 0-394-90112-6, BYR). Random.
Stevens, Chris. Fastest Machines. LC 80-10227. (Machine World Ser.). (Illus.). 32p. (gr. 2-4). 1980. PLB 11.15 (ISBN 0-8172-1337-6). Raintree Child.
Stone, William D. Earth Moving Machines. LC 78-26947. (Machine World Ser.). (Illus.). (gr. 2-4). 1979. PLB 11.15 (ISBN 0-8172-1329-5). Raintree Pubs.
Zaffo, George. Airplanes & Trucks & Trains, Fire Engines, Boats & Ships, & Building & Wrecking Machines. (Illus.). (gr. k-3). 1968. 6.95 (ISBN 0-448-01887-X). G&D.

MACHINERY-MANUFACTURE

see Machinery-Trade and Manufacture

MACHINERY-MODELS

Atteberry, Pat H. Power Mechanics. LC 80-20581. (Illus.). 112p. 1980. text ed. 4.80 (ISBN 0-87006-307-3). Goodheart.
Burstall, Aubrey F. Simple Working Models of Historic Machines. (Paperback Ser: No. 280). 1975. 5.95 (ISBN 0-262-52036-2). MIT Pr.
Geers, T. L. & Tong, P., eds. Survival of Mechanical Systems in Transient Environments, Bk. No. G00153. LC 79-954424. (Applied Mechanics Division Ser.: Vol. 36). 196p. 1979. 24.00 (ISBN 0-686-62963-9). ASME.
Maginley, C. J. Historic Models of Early America, & How to Make Them. LC 47-11432. (Illus.). (gr. 4-6). 1947. 5.95 (ISBN 0-15-234689-9, HJ). HarBraceJ.
--Historic Models of Early America: & How to Make Them. LC 47-11432. (Illus.). (gr. 4-6). 1966. pap. 0.60 (ISBN 0-15-234691-0, AVB28, VoyB). HarBraceJ.

MACHINERY-SOUNDPROOFING

Diehl, George M. Machinery Acoustics. LC 73-12980. 204p. 1973. 28.00 (ISBN 0-471-21360-8, Pub. by Wiley-Interscience). Wiley.

MACHINERY-TESTING

Collacott, R. A. Mechanical Fault Diagnosis & Condition Monitoring. LC 77-397. 496p. 1977. 67.95x (ISBN 0-412-12930-2, Pub. by Chapman & Hall England). Methuen Inc.
Gibbs, W. J. Electric Machine Analysis Using Tensors. Date not set. 22.50x (ISBN 0-392-07759-0, SpS). Sportshelf.
Mitchell, John S. An Introduction to Machinery Analysis & Monitoring. 256p. 1981. 37.50 (ISBN 0-87814-145-6). Pennwell Pub.

MACHINERY-TRADE AND MANUFACTURE

see also Electric Machinery Industry

Brewer, Allen F. Effective Lubrication. LC 72-87324. 366p. 1974. lib. bdg. 18.50 (ISBN 0-88275-083-6). Krieger.
Cheng, Chu-Yan. Machine Building Industry in Communist China. (Committee on the Economy of China Monographs Ser.). 1971. 11.95x (ISBN 0-202-31016-7). Beresford Bk Serv.
Coe, W. E. Engineering Industry of the North of Ireland. LC 69-11234. (Illus.). 1969. 12.50x (ISBN 0-678-05589-0). Kelley.
Company Programs to Reduce Products Liability Hazards: A Transcript of a MAPI Seminar. non-members 15.00 (ISBN 0-686-11597-X); members 10.00 (ISBN 0-686-11598-8). M & A Products.
Equipment Guide-Book Co. Machine Tool Value Guide: Grinding Machines, Vol. III. Husek, Jiri, ed. 600p. 1981. pap. cancelled (ISBN 0-89692-104-2). Equipment Guide.
Granick, David. Soviet Metal-Fabricating & Economic Development: Practice Versus Policy. 382p. 1967. 22.50x (ISBN 0-299-04290-1). U of Wis Pr.
Ihne, Russel W. & Streeter, Walter E. Machine Trades Blueprint Reading. 6th ed. 1972. pap. 10.00 spiral bound (ISBN 0-8269-1862-X). Am Technical.
Moorsteen, Richard. Prices & Production of Machinery in the Soviet Union 1928-1958. LC 62-7336. (Rand Corporation Research Studies). 1962. 25.00x (ISBN 0-674-70450-9). Harvard U Pr.
Rudman, Jack. Machine Trades. (Occupational Competency Examination Ser.: OCE-22). 14.95 (ISBN 0-8373-5772-1); pap. 9.95 (ISBN 0-8373-5722-5). Natl Learning.
Walker, J. H. Large Synchronous Machines: Design, Manufacture & Operation. (Monographs in Electrical & Electronic Engineering). (Illus.). 250p. 1981. 65.00 (ISBN 0-19-859364-3). Oxford U Pr.
Who Makes Machinery? West Germany 1980. 42nd ed. LC 53-30391. 844p. (Orig.). pap. 15.00x (ISBN 3-87362-010-3). Intl Pubns Serv.

MACHINERY-VIBRATION

Arya, Suresh C., et al. Design of Structures & Foundations for Vibrating Machines. 200p. 1979. 29.95x (ISBN 0-87201-294-8). Gulf Pub.
Diehl, George M. Machinery Acoustics. LC 73-12980. 204p. 1973. 28.00 (ISBN 0-471-21360-8, Pub. by Wiley-Interscience). Wiley.
Jackson, Charles. The Practical Vibration Primer. (Illus.). 120p. 1979. 19.95x (ISBN 0-87201-891-1). Gulf Pub.
Mitropol'skii, Yu. A. & Mosenkov, B. I. Monofrequency Method in the Dynamic Analysis of Structures. LC 67-24736. 104p. 1967. 29.50 (ISBN 0-306-10797-X, Consultants). Plenum Pub.

MACHINERY, AUTOMATIC

see also Automation; Machine-Tools; Vending Machines

MACHINERY, KINEMATICS OF

see also Rolling Contact

Dijksman, E. A. Motion Geometry of Mechanism. LC 75-3977. (Illus.). 250p. 1976. 35.50 (ISBN 0-521-20841-6). Cambridge U Pr.
Esposito, Anthony. Kinematics for Technology. LC 72-96341. 1973. text ed. 20.95x (ISBN 0-675-09005-9); instructor's manual 3.95 (ISBN 0-686-66863-4). Merrill.
Faires, Virgil M. & Keown, Robert. Mechanism. 5th ed. 1960. text ed. 18.95 (ISBN 0-07-019899-3, C). McGraw.
Ham, C. W., et al. Mechanics of Machinery. 4th ed. (Mechanical Engineering Ser.). 1958. text ed. 22.95 (ISBN 0-07-025688-8, C). McGraw.
Hartenberg, Richard S. & Denavit, Jacques. Kinematic Synthesis of Linkages. (Mechanical Engineering Ser.). 1964. text ed. 26.95 (ISBN 0-07-026910-6, C). McGraw.
Jones, Franklin D., et al. Ingenious Mechanisms for Designers & Inventors, Vols. 1-4, 1930-67. LC 30-14992. (Illus.). Set. 80.00 (ISBN 0-685-12543-2); Vol. 1, 536 Pgs. 22.00 (ISBN 0-8311-1029-5); Vol. 2, 538 Pgs. 22.00 (ISBN 0-8311-1030-9); Vol. 3, 536 Pgs. 22.00 (ISBN 0-8311-1031-7); Vol. 4, 493 Pgs. 22.00 (ISBN 0-8311-1032-5). Indus Pr.
Lent, Deane. Analysis & Design of Mechanisms. 2nd ed. (Technology Ser). 1970. text ed. 17.95 (ISBN 0-13-032797-2). P-H.
Mabie, Hamilton H. & Ocvirk, Fred W. Mechanisms & Dynamics of Machinery. 3rd ed. LC 74-30405. 616p. 1975. text ed. 30.95 (ISBN 0-471-55935-0). Wiley.
Martin, George H. Kinematics & Dynamics of Machines. 2nd ed. (Illus.). 544p. 1982. text ed. 28.95x (ISBN 0-07-040657-X, C); write for info. solutions manual (ISBN 0-07-040658-8). McGraw.
--Kinematics & Dynamics of Machines. LC 69-12261. (Mechanical Engineering Ser). (Illus.). 1969. text ed. 24.95 (ISBN 0-07-040637-5, C); solutions manual 5.95 (ISBN 0-07-040638-3). McGraw.
Ramous, Arthur. Applied Kinematics. 348p. 1972. text ed. 19.95 (ISBN 0-13-041202-3). P-H.

Reuleaux, Franz. Kinematics of Machinery: Outlines of a Theory of Machines. Kennedy, Alexander B., tr. (Illus.). 1876. pap. text ed. 6.00 (ISBN 0-486-61124-8). Dover.

Rosenauer, N. & Willis, A. H. Kinematics of Mechanisms. pap. text ed. 4.00 (ISBN 0-486-61796-3). Dover.

Shigley, Joseph E. Kinematic Analysis of Mechanisms. 2nd ed. LC 68-9559. (Mechanical Engineering Ser). (Illus.). 1969. text ed. 24.95 (ISBN 0-07-056868-5, C); instructor's manual 4.50 (ISBN 0-07-056874-X). McGraw.

Sloane, Alvin. Engineering Kinematics. 5.00 (ISBN 0-8446-2953-7). Peter Smith.

Suh, C. H. & Radcliffe, C. W. Kinematics & Mechanisms Design. LC 77-7102. 434p. 1978. 35.95 (ISBN 0-471-01461-3). Wiley.

Szuladzinski, Gregory. Dynamics of Structures & Machinery: Problems & Solutions. 700p. 1981. 50.00 (ISBN 0-471-09027-1, Pub. by Wiley Interscience). Wiley.

Tao, D. C. Fundamentals of Applied Kinematics. (Illus.). 1967. 17.95 (ISBN 0-201-07451-6). sol. manual o.p. 1.50 (ISBN 0-686-66351-9). A-W.

MACHINERY AND CIVILIZATION

see Technology and Civilization

MACHINERY IN INDUSTRY

see also Automation; Division of Labor; Factory System; Labor Productivity; Technocracy; Technological Innovations; Technology–Philosophy; Unemployment, Technological

Anderson, Sherwood. Perhaps Women. LC 76-105301. 1970. Repr. of 1931 ed. 8.95 (ISBN 0-911858-05-9). Appel.

Barnett, George E. Chapters on Machinery & Labor. LC 68-25563. (Masterworks in Industrial Relations Ser.). 191p. 1969. Repr. of 1926 ed. 6.95x (ISBN 0-8093-0397-3). S Ill U Pr.

Braverman, Harry. Labor & Monopoly Capital: The Degradation of Work in the Twentieth Century. LC 74-7785. (Illus.). 448p. 1975. 12.50 (ISBN 0-85345-340-3, CL-3403). Monthly Rev.

--Labor & Monopoly Capital: The Degradation of Work in the Twentieth Century. LC 74-7785. (Modern Reader Paperbacks Ser.). (Illus.). 465p. 1976. pap. 6.50 (ISBN 0-85345-370-5, PB3705). Monthly Rev.

Chase, Stuart. Economy of Abundance. LC 75-137934. (Economic Thought, History & Challenge Ser). 1971. Repr. of 1934 ed. 14.50 (ISBN 0-8046-1439-3). Kennikat.

--The Economy of Abundance. facsimile ed. LC 79-37876. (Select Bibliographies Reprint Ser). Repr. of 1934 ed. 19.00 (ISBN 0-8369-6713-5). Arno.

Dahlberg, Arthur A. Jobs, Machines & Capitalism. LC 70-91296. (BCL Ser. I). Repr. of 1932 ed. 16.50 (ISBN 0-404-01917-X). AMS Pr.

Dodd, William. Labouring Classes of England. LC 68-55703. Repr. of 1847 ed. 13.50x (ISBN 0-678-00961-9). Kelley.

Gaskell, Peter. Artisans & Machinery. LC 68-28259. Repr. of 1836 ed. 30.00x (ISBN 0-678-05047-3). Kelley.

--The Manufacturing Population of England. LC 73-38266. (The Evolution of Capitalism Ser.). 374p. 1972. Repr. of 1833 ed. 19.00 (ISBN 0-405-04120-9). Arno.

Gillespie, Laroux K., ed. Deburring Capabilities & Limitations. LC 76-47179. (Illus.). text ed. 15.95 (ISBN 0-87263-038-2). SME.

Gyllenhammer, Pehr G. People at Work. LC 77-73067. (Illus.). 1977. 8.95 (ISBN 0-201-02499-3). A-W.

Holloman, J. Herbert. Technical Change & American Enterprise. LC 74-19049. 52p. 1974. 1.50 (ISBN 0-89068-013-2). Natl Planning.

Knight, Charles. Capital & Labor: Including the Results of Machinery. LC 76-38272. (The Evolution of Capitalism Ser.). 254p. 1972. Repr. of 1845 ed. 18.00 (ISBN 0-405-04125-X). Arno.

Knowles, Lillian C. Industrial & Commercial Revolutions in Great Britain During the Nineteenth Century. 4th ed. LC 67-27704. Repr. of 1961 ed. 17.50x (ISBN 0-678-06518-7). Kelley.

Land, Charles. Land's Industrial Machinery & Epuipment Pricing Guide. 1980. pap. text ed. 29.95 (ISBN 0-442-28820-4). Van Nos Reinhold.

Lexique Francais-Anglais et Anglais-Francais des Termes d'usage Courant en Machines Outils et Machines Similaires. 56p. (Fr., French-English, English-French Lexicon of Commonly Used Terms in Machine Tools and Similar Machines). 1960. pap. 6.95 (ISBN 0-686-56794-3, M-6365). French & Eur.

Nicholson, J. Shield. The Effects of Machinery on Wages. LC 72-38263. (The Evolution of Capitalism Ser.). 160p. 1972. Repr. of 1892 ed. 12.00 (ISBN 0-405-04129-2). Arno.

Sen, Amartya K. Choice of Techniques: An Aspect of the Theory of Planned Economic Development. 3rd ed. LC 68-3220. 1968. 12.50x (ISBN 0-678-06266-8). Kelley.

Smith, Elliot D. & Nyman, Richmond C. Technology & Labor: Study of the Human Problems of Labor Saving. Stein, Leon, ed. LC 77-70533. (Work Ser.). 1977. Repr. of 1939 ed. lib. bdg. 18.00x (ISBN 0-405-10201-1). Arno.

Soule, George. What Automation Does to Human Beings. Stein, Leon, ed. LC 77-70534. (Work Ser.). 1977. Repr. of 1956 ed. lib. bdg. 15.00x (ISBN 0-405-10202-X). Arno.

The Spread of Machinery, 1793-1806. LC 72-2545. (British Labour Struggles Before 1850 Ser). (5 pamphlets). 1972. 14.00 (ISBN 0-405-04437-2). Arno.

Todd, Arthur J. Industry & Society: Sociological Appraisal of Modern Industrialism. Stein, Leon, ed. LC 77-70540. (Work Ser.). 1977. Repr. of 1933 ed. lib. bdg. 39.00x (ISBN 0-405-10209-7). Arno.

Tozer, John. Mathematical Investigation of the Effect of Machinery on the Wealth of a Community & On the Effect Of the Non-Residence of Landlords On the Wealth of a Community. LC 66-21696. 1968. 9.00x (ISBN 0-678-00300-9). Kelley.

Walker, Charles R. Toward the Automatic Factory: A Case Study of Men & Machines. LC 76-45083. (Illus.). 1977. Repr. of 1957 ed. lib. bdg. 19.00x (ISBN 0-8371-9301-X, WATA). Greenwood.

Yellowitz, Irwin. Industrialization & the American Labor Movement, 1850-1900. 1976. 15.00 (ISBN 0-8046-9150-9, National University Pub). Kennikat.

MACHINES

see Machinery

MACHINES, LOGIC

see Logic Machines

MACHINING OF METALS

see Metal-Work

MACHINISTS

Arco Editorial Board. Machinist--Machinist's Helper. 3rd ed. LC 79-28693. 256p. 1980. pap. 8.00 (ISBN 0-668-04933-2). Arco.

Blueprint Reading for Machinists-Advanced. LC 75-138355. 86p. 1972. 8.60 (ISBN 0-8273-0087-5); instructor's guide 1.60 (ISBN 0-8273-0088-3). Delmar.

Blueprinting Reading for Machinists-Intermediate. LC 75-138355. 132p. 1971. 8.60 (ISBN 0-8273-0085-9); instructor's guide 1.60 (ISBN 0-8273-0086-7). Delmar.

Colvin, Fred H. New American Machinist's Handbook. 1955. 39.50 (ISBN 0-07-037065-6, P&RB). McGraw.

Educational Research Council of America. Machinist. rev. ed. Kunze, Linda J. & Marchak, John P., eds. (Real People at Work Ser: G). (Illus.). 1976. pap. text ed. 2.25 (ISBN 0-89247-057-7). Changing Times.

Frederick, Stella. I Can Be a Machinist. McFadden, S. Michele, ed. (Reach High Career Awareness Ser.). (Illus.). (gr. 1-4). 1979. pap. text ed. 4.95x (ISBN 0-89262-020-X). Career Pub.

Marshall, Oscar S. Journeyman Machinist En Route to the Stars. Douglas, Eva M., ed. LC 78-64614. (Illus.). 1979. 12.00 (ISBN 0-88492-025-9). W S Sullwold.

Rudman, Jack. Foreman Machinist. (Career Examination Ser.: C-1414). (Cloth bdg. avail. on request). pap. 8.00 (ISBN 0-8373-1414-3). Natl Learning.

--Machinist. (Career Examination Ser.: C-460). (Cloth bdg. avail. on request). pap. 8.00 (ISBN 0-8373-0460-1). Natl Learning.

--Maintenance Machinist. (Career Examination Ser.: C-1354). (Cloth bdg. avail. on request). pap. 8.00 (ISBN 0-8373-1354-6). Natl Learning.

MACHU PICCHU, PERU

Bingham, Hiram. Lost City of the Incas. LC 48-9227. (Illus.). 1963. pap. text ed. 3.95x (ISBN 0-689-70014-8, 33). Atheneum.

--Machu Pichu: A Citadel of the Incas. LC 79-83881. (Illus.). 1979. Repr. of 1930 ed. lib. bdg. 50.00 (ISBN 0-87817-252-1). Hacker.

Gemming, Elizabeth. Lost City in the Clouds: The Discovery of Machu Picchu. LC 78-31877. (Science Dicovery Ser.). (Illus.). (gr. 3-7). 1980. PLB 5.99 (ISBN 0-698-30698-8). Coward.

Waisbard, Simone. The Mysteries of Machu Picchu. 1979. pap. 2.75 (ISBN 0-380-43687-6, 43687). Avon.

MCINTIRE, SAMUEL, 1757-1811

Cousins, Frank & Riley, Phil M. Wood Carver of Salem: Samuel McIntire, His Life & Work. LC 74-119649. (BCL Ser. II). Repr. of 1916 ed. 20.00 (ISBN 0-404-01786-X). AMS Pr.

MCINTOSH, LACHLAN, 1725-1806

Jackson, Harvey H. Lachlan McIntosh & the Politics of Revolutionary Georgia. LC 78-8995. 256p. 1979. 16.00 (ISBN 0-8203-0459-X). U of Ga Pr.

MCINTYRE, OSCAR ODD, 1884-1938

Driscoll, Charles B. The Life of O. O. McIntyre. (American Newspapermen 1790-1933 Ser.). (Illus.). 344p. 1974. Repr. of 1938 ed. 17.50x (ISBN 0-8464-0022-7). Beekman Pubs.

MC JUNKIN, GEORGE

Folsom, Franklin. The Life & Legend of George McJunkin: Black Cowboy. LC 73-6446. (Illus.). 160p. (gr. 5 up). 1973. 7.95 (ISBN 0-525-66326-6). Elsevier-Nelson.

MACK FAMILY

Smith, Lucy M. Biographical Sketches of Joseph Smith, the Prophet & His Progenitors for Many Generations. LC 73-83439. (Religion in America, Ser. 1). 1969. Repr. of 1853 ed. 12.00 (ISBN 0-405-00264-5). Arno.

MCKAY, CLAUDE, 1890-1948

Bronz, Stephen H. Roots of Negro Racial Consciousness. 1964. 5.00 (ISBN 0-87212-019-8). Libra.

Gayle, Addison. Claude McKay: The Black Poet at War. (Broadside Critics Ser: No. 2). pap. 1.50 (ISBN 0-910296-76-6). Broadside.

Giles, James R. Claude McKay. LC 76-10154. (U.S. Authors Ser.: No. 271). 1976. lib. bdg. 10.95 (ISBN 0-8057-7171-9). Twayne.

MACKAY, HUGH, 1640-1692

Life of Lieut.-General Hugh Mackay. LC 74-172708. (Bannatyne Club, Edinburgh. Publications: No. 53). Repr. of 1836 ed. 27.50 (ISBN 0-404-52763-9). AMS Pr.

MACKAY, JOHN HENRY, 1864-1933

Riley, Thomas A. Germany's Poet-Anarchist: The Life & Work of John Henry Mackay. (Illus.). 336p. 1972. 69.95 (ISBN 0-87700-101-4). Revisionist Pr.

MCKAY, THOMAS, b. 1797–FICTION

Fraser, Hermia. Tall Brigade. 1956. 8.95 (ISBN 0-8323-0058-6); pap. 5.95 (ISBN 0-8323-0284-8). Binford.

MACKAYE, STEELE, 1842-1894

MacKaye, Percy. Epoch: The Life of Steele MacKaye Genius of the Theatre, in Relation to His Time & Contemporaries, a Memoir, 2 Vols. LC 27-25140. 1968. Repr. of 1927 ed. Set. 59.00 (ISBN 0-403-00077-7). Scholarly.

MCKELL, DAVID MCCANDLESS, 1881– LIBRARY

Fieler, Frank B., compiled by. The David McCandless McKell Collection: A Descriptive Catalog of Manuscripts, Early Printed Books & Children's Books. (Library Catalogs Ser.). 200p. 1973. lib. bdg. 32.00 (ISBN 0-8161-0993-1). G K Hall.

MCKENNA, JOSEPH, 1843-1926

McDevitt, Matthew. Joseph McKenna. LC 73-21874. (American Constitutional & Legal History Ser.). 250p. 1974. Repr. of 1946 ed. lib. bdg. 27.50 (ISBN 0-306-70632-6). Da Capo.

MACKENNA, ROBERT WILLIAM, 1874-1930

Mackenna, Robert W. As Shadows Lengthen: Later Essays. facs. ed. LC 67-26759. (Essay Index Reprint Ser). 1933. 14.25 (ISBN 0-8369-0653-5). Arno.

MCKENNEY, THOMAS LORAINE, 1785-1859

Viola, Herman J. Thomas L. McKenney, Architect of America's Early Indian Policy: 1816-1830. LC 74-18075. (Illus.). xii, 365p. (Orig.). 1981. pap. 8.95x (ISBN 0-8040-0669-5, SB). Swallow.

MACKENZIE, ALEXANDER, SIR, 1763-1820

Laut, Agnes C. Pathfinders of the West. LC 74-90651. (Essay Index Reprint Ser). 1904. 25.00 (ISBN 0-8369-1220-9). Arno.

Mirsky, Jeannette. Westward Crossings: Balboa, Mackenzie, Lewis & Clark. LC 70-116434. 1970. pap. 3.45 (ISBN 0-226-53181-3, P370, Phoen). U of Chicago Pr.

MACKENZIE, ALEXANDER, SIR, 1822-1892

Buckingham, W. & Ross, G. W. Honorable Alexander Mackenzie, His Life & Times. LC 68-25225. (English Biography Ser., No. 31). 1969. Repr. of 1892 ed. lib. bdg. 59.95 (ISBN 0-8383-0920-8). Haskell.

Buckingham, William & Ross, George W. Honorable Alexander Mackenzie, His Life & Times. LC 69-13844. Repr. of 1892 ed. lib. bdg. 22.50x (ISBN 0-8371-1074-2, BUAM). Greenwood.

MACKENZIE, COMPTON, SIR, 1883-

Dooley, D. J. Compton Mackenzie. (English Authors Ser.: No. 173). 176p. 1974. lib. bdg. 9.95 (ISBN 0-8057-1361-1). Twayne.

Robertson, Leo. Compton Mac Kenzie: An Appraisal of His Literary Work. 230p. 1980. Repr. of 1954 ed. lib. bdg. 25.00 (ISBN 0-8482-5864-9). Norwood Edns.

--Compton Mackenzie: An Appraisal of His Literary Work. 1954. Repr. 30.00 (ISBN 0-8274-2087-0). R West.

MACKENZIE, JOHN

Mackenzie, William D. John Mackenzie, South African Missionary & Statesman. LC 78-97373. Repr. of 1902 ed. 24.75x (ISBN 0-8371-2443-3, Pub. by Negro U Pr). Greenwood.

MACKENZIE DISTRICT–DESCRIPTION AND TRAVEL

Birket-Smith, Kaj. Geographical Notes on the Barren Grounds. LC 76-21642. (Thule Expedition, 5th, 1921-24: Vol. 1, No. 4). (Illus.). Repr. of 1933 ed. 32.50 (ISBN 0-404-58304-0). AMS Pr.

MACKENZIE KING, WILLIAM LYON

see King, William Lyon Mackenzie, 1874-1950

MACKENZIE RIVER

Aquilina, Alfred P. The Mackenzie: Yesterday & Beyond. (Illus.). 250p. 1981. pap. 7.95 (ISBN 0-87663-633-4, Pub. by Hancock Hse). Universe.

Lambie, Beatrice R. The Mackenzie: River to the Top of the World. LC 67-10040. (Rivers of the World Ser.). (Illus.). (gr. 4-7). 1967. PLB 3.68 (ISBN 0-8116-6369-8). Garrard.

Roberts, Leslie. The Mackenzie. LC 73-20906. 276p. 1974. Repr. of 1949 ed. lib. bdg. 14.25x (ISBN 0-8371-5864-8, ROMR). Greenwood.

MCKIM, CHARLES FOLLEN, 1847-1909

Granger, Alfred H. Charles Follen McKim: A Study of His Life & Work. LC 70-168178. Repr. of 1913 ed. 12.00 (ISBN 0-404-02890-X). AMS Pr.

--Charles Follen McKim: A Study of His Life & Work. LC 79-152623. (Illus.). Repr. of 1913 ed. 15.00 (ISBN 0-405-08570-2, Blom Pubns). Arno.

Hill, Frederick P. Charles F. McKim the Man. 1950. 3.00 (ISBN 0-8338-0026-4). M Jones.

Moore, Charles. Life & Times of Charles Follen McKim. LC 70-99857. (Architecture & Decorative Art Ser). (Illus.). 1970. Repr. of 1929 ed. lib. bdg. 32.50 (ISBN 0-306-71324-1). Da Capo.

MCKIM, MEAD AND WHITE

Reilly, C. H. McKim, Mead & White. LC 71-180028. (Illus.). Repr. of 1924 ed. 14.00 (ISBN 0-405-08877-9). Arno.

Roth, Leland M. The Architecture of McKim, Mead & White, 1870-1920: A Building List. LC 77-83368. (Library of Humanities Reference Bks.: No. 114). lib. bdg. 54.00 (ISBN 0-8240-9850-1). Garland Pub.

MACKINAC–ANTIQUITIES

Armour, David A. & Widder, Keith R. Michilimackinac: A Handbook to the Site. 1st ed. (Illus.). 48p. (Orig.). 1980. pap. 1.50 (ISBN 0-911872-39-6). Mackinac Island.

Petersen, Eugene T. Gentlemen on the Frontier. (Illus.). 68p. (Orig.). 1964. pap. 2.00 (ISBN 0-911872-26-4). Mackinac Island.

Stone, Lyle M. Archaeological Investigation of the Marquette Mission Site. Armour, David A., ed. LC 74-171070. (Reports in Mackinac History & Archaeology Ser: No. 1). (Illus.). 33p. (Orig.). 1972. pap. 2.00 (ISBN 0-911872-17-5). Mackinac Island.

MACKINAC–HISTORY

Armour, David A. & Widder, Keith R. Michilimackinac: A Handbook to the Site. 1st ed. (Illus.). 48p. (Orig.). 1980. pap. 1.50 (ISBN 0-911872-39-6). Mackinac Island.

Dunnigan, Brian L. The British Army at Mackinac, Eighteen Twelve - Eighteen Fifteen. Armour, David A., ed. (Reports in Mackinac History & Archaelogy Ser.: No. 7). (Illus.). 56p. (Orig.). 1981. pap. 5.00 (ISBN 0-911872-40-X). Mackinac Island.

--King's Men at Mackinac: The British Garrisons, 1780-1796. Armour, David A., ed. LC 74-172729. (Reports in Mackinac History & Archaeology Ser: No. 3). (Illus.). 38p. (Orig.). 1973. pap. 3.00 (ISBN 0-911872-19-1). Mackinac Island.

Hamilton, T. M. Firearms on the Frontier: Guns at Fort Michilimackinac 1715-1781. Armour, David A., ed. LC 76-624498. (Reports in Mackinac History & Archaeology: No 5). (Illus., Orig.). 1976. pap. 3.00 (ISBN 0-911872-21-3). Mackinac Island.

May, George. Doctor's Secret Journal. (Illus.). 1960. pap. 1.50 (ISBN 0-911872-30-2). Mackinac Island.

Petersen, Eugene T., et al. Mackinac History, Vol. 1. (Illus.). 80p. (Orig.). 1969. pap. 4.50 (ISBN 0-911872-35-3). Mackinac Island.

Peterson, Eugene T. The Preservation of History at Mackinac. Armour, David A., ed. LC 74-175853. (Reports on Mackinac History & Archaeology Ser: No. 2). (Illus.). 46p. (Orig.). 1972. pap. 2.00 (ISBN 0-911872-18-3). Mackinac Island.

Thwaites, Reuben G. How George Rogers Clark Won the Northwest, & Other Essays in Western History. facs. ed. LC 68-22949. (Essay Index Reprint Ser). 1903. 19.50 (ISBN 0-8369-0943-7). Arno.

Widder, Keith R. Mackinac National Park, 1875-1895. Armour, David A., ed. (Reports in Mackinac History & Archaeology Ser: No. 4). (Illus.). 48p. (Orig.). 1975. pap. 3.00 (ISBN 0-911872-20-5). Mackinac Island.

MACKINAC ISLAND

Armour, David. Fort Michilimackinac Sketch Book. (Illus.). 48p. (Orig.). 1975. pap. 1.50 (ISBN 0-911872-16-7). Mackinac Island.

Newton, Stanley D. Mackinac Island & Saulte St. Marie. LC 76-4405. (Illus.). 1976. pap. 6.00 (ISBN 0-912382-19-8). Black Letter.
Petersen, Eugene T. Mackinac Island: Its History in Pictures. LC 74-17184. (Illus.). 103p. (Orig.). 1973. 12.50 (ISBN 0-911872-13-2). Mackinac Island.

MCKINLEY, WILLIAM, PRES. U. S., 1843-1901

Gould, Lewis L. The Presidency of William McKinley. LC 80-16022. (The American Presidency Ser.). 298p. 1981. 15.00x (ISBN 0-7006-0206-2). Regents Pr KS.
Leech, Margaret. In the Days of McKinley. LC 75-16614. (Illus.). 686p. 1975. Repr. of 1959 ed. lib. bdg. 38.00x (ISBN 0-8371-8243-3, LEDM). Greenwood.
Morgan, H. Wayne. William McKinley. LC 63-19723. (Illus.). 1963. 16.95x (ISBN 0-8156-0032-1). Syracuse U Pr.
Olcott, Charles S. Life of William McKinley, 2 vols. LC 79-128946. (American Statesman: Nos. 38, 39). Repr. of 1916 ed. Set. 47.00 (ISBN 0-404-50893-6); 23.50 ea. Vol. 1 (ISBN 0-404-50888-X). Vol. 2 (ISBN 0-404-50889-8). AMS Pr.
Sievers, H. J. William McKinley, 1843-1901: Chronology, Documents, Bibliographical Aids. LC 72-116065. (Presidential Chronology Ser). 1970. text ed. 8.00 (ISBN 0-379-12074-7). Oceana.
Stern, Clarence A. Protectionist Republicanism: Republican Tariff Policy in the McKinley Period. 1971. pap. 1.50 (ISBN 0-9600116-4-1). Stern.
--Resurgent Republicanism: The Handiwork of Hanna. 1968. pap. 1.25 (ISBN 0-9600116-3-3). Stern.
Townsend, G. W. Memorial Life of William McKinley. 1978. Repr. of 1901 ed. lib. bdg. 25.00 (ISBN 0-8482-2723-9). Norwood Edns.

MCKINLEY, MOUNT

Davidson, Art. Minus One Hundred & Forty-Eight Degrees: The Winter Ascent of Mt. McKinley. (Illus.). 1979. pap. 4.95 (ISBN 0-89174-037-6). Comstock Edns.
Moore, Terris. Mt. McKinley: The Pioneer Climbs. LC 81-1002. (Illus.). 224p. 1981. pap. 8.95 (ISBN 0-89886-021-0). Mountaineers.
--Mt. McKinley: The Pioneer Climbs. (Illus.). 1977. 10.50 (ISBN 0-912006-03-X, Pub. by U of Alaska Pr); autographed ed. 13.00 (ISBN 0-686-22694-1). Intl Schol Bk Serv.
Mount McKinley: The Pioneer Climbs. write for info. (ISBN 0-912006-03-X); write for info. autographed ed. U of Alaska Pr.
Stuck, Hudson. The Ascent of Denali. LC 77-90371. (Illus.). 1977. pap. 6.95 (ISBN 0-916890-58-9). Mountaineers.

MACKLIN, CHARLES, 1697-1797

Cooke, William. Memoirs of Charles Macklin. LC 72-82822. 1804. 20.00 (ISBN 0-405-08378-5, Blom Pubns). Arno.

MCLAIN, GEORGE H., 1901-

Pinner, Frank A., et al. Old Age & Political Behavior: A Case Study. Stein, Leon, ed. LC 79-8678. (Growing Old Ser.). (Illus.). 1980. Repr. of 1959 ed. lib. bdg. 28.00x (ISBN 0-405-12796-0). Arno.

MACLAINE, SHIRLEY

Denis, Christopher. The Films of Shirley Maclaine. (Illus.). 1980. 14.95 (ISBN 0-8065-0693-8). Citadel Pr.

MCLANE, LOUIS, 1786-1857

Munroe, John A. Louis McLane: Federalist & Jacksonian. (Illus.). 768p. 1974. 45.00 (ISBN 0-8135-0757-X). Rutgers U Pr.

MACLEAN, JOHN, 1771-1814

Priestley, Joseph. Considerations on the Doctrine of Phlogiston, & the Decomposition of Water. Foster, William, ed. LC 30-8577. 1968. Repr. of 1929 ed. 12.00 (ISBN 0-527-72700-8). Kraus Repr.

MCLEAN, JOHN, 1785-1861

Weisenburger, Francis P. Life of John McLean. LC 76-150296. (American Constitutional & Legal History Ser.). 1971. Repr. of 1937 ed. lib. bdg. 29.50 (ISBN 0-306-70106-5). Da Capo.

MACLEISH, ARCHIBALD, 1892-

Falk, Signi L. Archibald MacLeish. (Twayne's United States Authors Ser). 1965. pap. 3.45 (ISBN 0-8084-0054-1, T93, Twayne). Coll & U Pr.
Mizener, Arthur. A Catalogue of the First Editions of Archibald MacLeish. LC 73-7719. 1938. Repr. lib. bdg. 12.50 (ISBN 0-8414-5941-X). Folcroft.
Mullaly, Edward J. Archibald Macleish: A Checklist. LC 72-619620. (Serif Ser.: No. 26). 100p. 1973. 7.00x (ISBN 0-87338-132-7). Kent St U Pr.
Smith, Grover. Archibald MacLeish. (Pamphlets on American Writers Ser: No. 99). (Orig.). 1971. 1.25x (ISBN 0-8166-0618-8, MPAW99). U of Minn Pr.

MCLOUGHLIN, JOHN, 1784-1857

Fogdall, Alberta B. Royal Family of the Columbia. (Illus.). 1978. 14.95 (ISBN 0-87770-168-7). Ye Galleon.
Johnson, Robert C. John McLoughlin: Father of Oregon. LC 58-11483. (Illus.). 330p. 1975. pap. 6.50 (ISBN 0-8323-0257-0). Binford.
Montgomery, Richard G. The White-Headed Eagle: John McLoughlin, Builder of an Empire. facsimile ed. LC 76-164616. (Select Bibliographies Reprint Ser). Repr. of 1934 ed. 22.00 (ISBN 0-8369-5900-0). Arno.
Morrison, Dorothy N. The Eagle & the Fort: The Story of John McLoughlin. LC 78-12911. (Illus.). (gr. 5-9). 1979. 7.95 (ISBN 0-689-30691-1). Atheneum.
Sampson, William R., ed. John McLoughlin's Business Correspondence, 1847-48. LC 73-8747. (Illus.). 232p. 1973. 16.50 (ISBN 0-295-95299-7). U of Wash Pr.
Smith, Helen K. Sitkum Siwash. LC 74-33825. (A Western Americana Book). (Illus.). 104p. (Orig.). 1976. pap. 5.50 (ISBN 0-913626-29-5). S S S Pub Co.

MCLUHAN, MARSHALL

Curtis, James M. Culture As Polyphony: An Essay on the Nature of Paradigms. LC 77-25242. 1978. text ed. 15.00 (ISBN 0-8262-0251-9). U of Mo Pr.
Theall, Donald F. The Medium Is the Rear View Mirror: Understanding McLuhan. 1971. 10.00x (ISBN 0-7735-0093-6); pap. 3.25 (ISBN 0-7735-0106-1). McGill-Queens U Pr.

MCMANIGAL, ORTIE E

Burns, William J. Masked War: The Story of a Peril That Threatened the United States. LC 76-90168. (Mass Violence in America Ser). Repr. of 1913 ed. 11.50 (ISBN 0-405-01303-5). Arno.

MACMANUS, SEUMAS

MacManus, Seumas. The Rocky Road to Dublin. 5.95 (ISBN 0-8159-6712-8). Devin.

MACMILLAN, HAROLD, 1894-

Hutchinson, George. The Last Edwardian at No. Ten: An Impression of Harold MacMillan. 12.95 (ISBN 0-7043-2232-3, Pub. by Quartet England). Charles River Bks.

MCNAMARA, ROBERT S., 1916-

Coulam, Robert F. Illusions of Choice: Robert McNamara, the F-111 & the Problem of Weapons Acquisition Reform. LC 76-24292. 1977. text ed. 31.50 (ISBN 0-691-07583-2). Princeton U Pr.
McNamara, Robert S. The McNamara Years at the World Bank: Major Policy Addresses of Robert S. McNamara, 1968-1981. 1981. text ed. 30.00x (ISBN 0-686-75328-3). Johns Hopkins.
Murdock, Clark A. Defense Policy Formation: A Comparative Analysis of the McNamara Era. LC 73-18032. 204p. 1974. 16.50 (ISBN 0-87395-252-9); microfiche 16.50 (ISBN 0-87395-253-7). State U NY Pr.

MCNEEL FAMILY

Edgar, Betsy J. McNeel Family Record. (Illus.). 1967. 15.00 (ISBN 0-87012-063-8). McClain.
--The McNeel Family Record. (Illus.). 1967. 12.50 (ISBN 0-87012-063-8). B J Edgar.

MACNEICE, LOUIS

Moore, D. B. The Poetry of Louis MacNeice. 272p. 1972. text ed. 11.50x (ISBN 0-7185-1105-0, Leicester). Humanities.

MACON, NATHANIEL, 1757-1837

Dodd, William E. Life of Nathaniel Macon 1757-1837. LC 78-130600. (Research & Source Works: No. 537). 1970. lib. bdg. 26.50 (ISBN 0-8337-0876-7). B Franklin.

MACON, GEORGIA

Anderson, Nancy. Macon: A Pictorial History. LC 79-24559. (Illus.). 1979. 16.95 (ISBN 0-915442-56-6); ltd. ed. 24.95 (ISBN 0-89865-026-7). Donning Co.

MACON COUNTY, GEORGIA

Writers Program, Georgia. The Macon Guide & Ocmulgee National Monument. LC 73-3607. (American Guide Ser). 1939. Repr. 18.50 (ISBN 0-404-57911-6). AMS Pr.

MACPHERSON, JAMES, 1736-1796

Bailey, Saunders. The Life & Letters of James Macpherson. 1979. Repr. of 1894 ed. lib. bdg. 30.00 (ISBN 0-89760-814-3, Telegraph). Dynamic Learn Corp.
Saunders, Thomas. Life & Letters of James Macpherson. LC 68-24916. (English Biography Ser., No. 31). 1969. lib. bdg. 46.95 (ISBN 0-8383-0238-6). Haskell.
Saunders, Thomas B. Life & Letters of James Macpherson. Repr. of 1894 ed. lib. bdg. 15.00x (ISBN 0-8371-2390-9, SAJM). Greenwood.
Smart, J. S. James Macpherson: An Episode in Literature. 1974. Repr. of 1905 ed. lib. bdg. 11.95 (ISBN 0-8414-7721-3). Folcroft.
Smart, John S. James Macpherson, an Episode in Literature. LC 71-177577. Repr. of 1905 ed. 12.00 (ISBN 0-404-08715-9). AMS Pr.
Thomson, Derick S. Gaelic Sources of Macpherson's Ossian. LC 73-905. 1951. lib. bdg. 15.00 (ISBN 0-8414-2650-3). Folcroft.

MCQUEEN, STEVE

McCoy, Malachy. Steve McQueen. Date not set. pap. 2.50 (ISBN 0-451-09930-3, E9930, Sig). NAL.
Nolan, William F. Steve McQueen: Star on Wheels. (Putnam Sports Shelf). (gr. 5 up). 1972. PLB 6.29 (ISBN 0-399-60778-1). Putnam.

MACRAME

Ames, Marjorie. Miniature Macrame for Dollhouses. 1981. pap. 2.00 (ISBN 0-486-23960-8). Dover.
Andes, Eugene. Far Beyond the Fringe: Three Dimensional Knotting Techniques Using Macrame & Nautical Ropework. (Illus.). 132p. 1973. pap. 8.95 (ISBN 0-442-20353-5). Van Nos Reinhold.
--Practical Macrame. 1971. pap. 5.95 (ISBN 0-442-20346-2). Van Nos Reinhold.
Barnes, Charles & Blake, David P. Creative Macrame Projects. LC 76-8115. (Illus.). 256p. 1976. pap. 3.00 (ISBN 0-486-23370-7). Dover.
Big-Knot Macrame. 1977. pap. 1.50 (ISBN 0-8277-5737-9). British Bk Ctr.
Boberg, Anne-Marie & Svennas, Elsie. Macrame. LC 74-14199. (Illus.). 104p. 1975. lib. bdg. 7.95 (ISBN 0-668-03753-9); pap. 3.95 (ISBN 0-668-03623-0). Arco.
Bogen, Constance. Macrame. 1973. 7.95 (ISBN 0-671-27108-3). Trident.
Bress, Helene. The Craft of Macrame. 1977. pap. 5.95 (ISBN 0-684-14723-8, SL671, ScribT). Scribner.
--The Macrame Book. LC 79-37222. (Illus.). 224p. 1972. 17.50 (ISBN 0-684-12756-3, ScribT). Scribner.
Close, Eunice. Macrame Made Easy. (Illus.). 88p. 1973. pap. 3.95 (ISBN 0-02-011170-3, Collier). Macmillan.
Creative Educational Society Editors. How to Have Fun with Macrame. LC 73-19667. (Creative Craft Bks.). (Illus.). 32p. (gr. 2-5). 1973. PLB 5.95 (ISBN 0-87191-290-2). Creative Ed.
Dodge, Jane. New Macreme. (Step by Step Craft Ser.). Date not set. pap. 2.95 (ISBN 0-307-42023-X, Golden Pr). Western Pub.
--Step-by-Step New Macrame. (Step-by-Step Goldencraft Ser.). 1979. pap. 2.95 (ISBN 0-307-42023-X, Golden Pr). Western Pub.
Hargreaves, Joyce. New Ways with Macrame. LC 81-81036. (Illus.). 144p. 1981. 14.95 (ISBN 0-88332-264-1, 8192). Larousse.
Harvey, Virginia. Macrame: The Art of Creative Knotting. (Illus.). 128p. 1967. 10.95 (ISBN 0-442-31186-9); pap. 6.95 (ISBN 0-442-23191-1). Van Nos Reinhold.
Harvey, Virginia I. Color & Design in Macrame. LC 80-25748. (Connecting Threads Ser.). (Illus.). 104p. (gr. 11-12). 1980. pap. 9.95 (ISBN 0-914842-55-2). Madrona Pubs.
Introducing Macrame. 1974. pap. 13.50 (ISBN 0-7134-2446-X, Pub. by Batsford England). David & Charles.
La Barge, Lura. Do Your Own Thing with Macrame. (Illus.). 152p. 1973. 15.95 (ISBN 0-8230-1354-5). Watson-Guptill.
La Croix, Grethe & Pesch, Imelda M. Macrame Macrame Macrame: Pb. LC 81-8865. (Illus.). 96p. (Orig.). 1981. pap. 5.95 (ISBN 0-8069-7538-5). Sterling.
Lightbody, Donna. Let's Knot: A Macrame Book. LC 72-1096. (Craft Ser.). (Illus.). 160p. (gr. 5-12). 1972. PLB 7.44 (ISBN 0-688-51528-2). Lothrop.
Macrame Jewellery. 1977. pap. 1.50 (ISBN 0-8277-5738-7). British Bk Ctr.
Macrame One. 1975. pap. 1.50 (ISBN 0-8277-4452-8). British Bk Ctr.
Macrame Two. 1975. pap. 1.50 (ISBN 0-8277-4453-6). British Bk Ctr.
Meilach, Dona Z. Macrame Accessories: Patterns and Ideas for Knotting. (Illus.). 1972. 5.95 (ISBN 0-517-50194-5); pap. 3.95 (ISBN 0-517-50009-4). Crown.
--Macrame: Creative Design in Knotting. (Arts & Crafts Ser). (Illus.). 1971. 9.95 (ISBN 0-685-00159-8, K07893); pap. 4.95 (ISBN 0-685-00160-1, K05874). Crown.
--Macrame Gnomes & Puppets: Creative Patterns & Ideas. (Illus.). 96p. 1980. pap. 7.95 (ISBN 0-517-54010-X). Crown.
Pesch, Imelda M. Macrame. LC 76-126848. (Little Craft Book Ser.). (gr. 6 up). 1970. 5.95 (ISBN 0-8069-5158-3); PLB 6.69 (ISBN 0-8069-5159-1). Sterling.
Phillips, Mary W. Macrame, Step by Step. (Step by Step Craft Ser). 1974. pap. 2.95 (ISBN 0-307-42005-1, Golden Pr). Western Pub.
Pownall, Glen. Knotting Crafts. (New Crafts Books Ser.). 76p. 1980. 8.25 (ISBN 0-85467-020-3, Pub. by Viking Sevenseas New Zealand). Intl Schol Bk Serv.
Pyman, Kit. Macrame Patterns. LC 79-56466. (Illus.). 120p. 1980. 19.95 (ISBN 0-7134-3307-8, Pub. by Batsford England). David & Charles.
Rack, Norman & Rack, Lilian. Macrame: Advanced Technique & Design. (Illus.). 6.75 (ISBN 0-8446-4455-2). Peter Smith.
Rainey, Sarita. Fiber Techniques: Knotting & Looping. LC 78-72194. (Illus.). 1979. 14.95 (ISBN 0-87192-107-3). Davis Mass.
Short, Jacqueline. Macrame - The Craft of Knotting. (Illus.). 1973. 5.95 (ISBN 0-7137-0626-0, Pub by Blandford Pr England). Sterling.
Solvit, Marie-Janine. Magnificent Macrame: 50 Projects You Can Create. LC 78-66295. (Illus.). 1979. 19.95 (ISBN 0-8069-5390-X); lib. bdg. 16.79 (ISBN 0-8069-5391-8). Sterling.
Stearns, Ann. Macrame. LC 74-25009. (Step-by-Step Ser.). (Illus.). 1975. 8.95 (ISBN 0-668-03669-9). Arco.
Sunset Editors. Macrame. 2nd ed. LC 75-6225. (Illus.). 80p. 1975. pap. 3.95 (ISBN 0-376-04544-2, Sunset Bks.). Sunset-Lane.
Willsmore, Heidy. Macrame: A Comprehensive Study. (Illus.). 208p. 1979. 23.00 (ISBN 0-571-11310-9, Pub. by Faber & Faber). Merrimack Bk Serv.

MACREADY, WILLIAM CHARLES, 1793-1873

Downer, Alan S. Eminent Tragedian: William Charles Macready. LC 66-14441. (Illus.). 1966. 20.00x (ISBN 0-674-25100-8). Harvard U Pr.

MACROBIOTIC COOKERY

see Macrobiotic Diet-Recipes

MACROBIOTIC DIET

Aihara, Herman. Learning from Salmon & Other Essays. Rothman, Sandy, ed. 157p. 1980. pap. 7.95 (ISBN 0-918860-37-7). G Ohsawa.
--Seven Macrobiotic Principles. 1973. 1.00 (ISBN 0-918860-16-4). G Ohsawa.
Kushi, Michio. The Book of Macrobiotics: The Universal Way of Health & Happiness. LC 76-29341. (Illus.). 176p. (Orig.). 1977. pap. 10.95 (ISBN 0-87040-381-8). Japan Pubns.
Lawson-Wood, D. & Lawson-Wood, J. Glowing Health Through Diet & Posture. 1980. 17.50x (ISBN 0-85032-190-5, Pub. by Daniel Co England). State Mutual Bk.
Ohsawa, George. Macrobiotics: An Invitation to Health & Happiness. 77p. 1971. pap. 3.95 (ISBN 0-918860-02-4). G Ohsawa.
--The Unique Principle: The Philosophy of Macrobiotics. (Orig.). 1973. pap. 4.95 (ISBN 0-918860-17-2). G Ohsawa.

MACROBIOTIC DIET-RECIPES

Abehsera, Michel. Zen Macrobiotic Cooking. 1971. pap. 3.95 (ISBN 0-8065-0254-1). Citadel Pr.
--Zen Macrobiotic Cooking. 1970. pap. 2.95 (ISBN 0-380-01483-1, 55426). Avon.
Ohsawa, Lima. Lima Ohsawa's Macrobiotic Cookbook: The Art of Just Cooking. Orig. Title: The Art of Just Cooking. (Illus.). 320p. 1981. pap. 3.95 (ISBN 0-914398-29-6). Autumn Pr.
Weber, Marces. Sweet Life! Macrobiotic Desserts. (Illus.). 1981. pap. 9.95 (ISBN 0-686-73716-4). Japan Pubns.

MACROBIOTICS

see Macrobiotic Diet

MACROCOSM AND MICROCOSM

see Microcosm and Macrocosm

MACROECONOMICS

Albrecht, W., Jr. Macroeconomic Principles. 1979. pap. 10.95 (ISBN 0-13-542738-X); study guide & wkbk. 11.95 (ISBN 0-13-227553-8). P-H.
Allen, Roy G. Macro-Economic Theory. LC 67-12508. 1968. pap. 8.50 (ISBN 0-312-50330-X). St Martin.
Aschheim, Joseph & Ching-Yao Hsieh. Macroeconomics: Income & Monetary Theory. LC 80-5519. 279p. 1980. pap. text ed. 10.25 (ISBN 0-8191-1128-7). U Pr of Amer.
Attiyeh, Richard & Lumsden, Keith. Macroeconomics: A Programmed Book. 4th ed. 256p. 1982. pap. text ed. 10.95 (ISBN 0-13-542704-5). P-H.
Attiyeh, Richard E., et al. Macroeconomics: A Programmed Book. 3rd ed. (Illus.). 272p. (Prog. Bk.). 1974. pap. 9.95 ref. ed. (ISBN 0-13-542662-6). P-H.
Ayatey, Siegfried B. Essentials of Economic Analysis: Vol. 2, Macroeconomics. LC 79-66234. 1979. pap. text ed. 9.00 (ISBN 0-8191-0804-9). U Pr of Amer.
Bach, George L. Macroeconomics: Analysis & Applications. 2nd ed. 1980. pap. text ed. 11.95 (ISBN 0-13-542712-6). P-H.
Bailey, M. J. National Income & the Price Level: A Study in Macroeconomic Theory. 2nd ed. 1970. text ed. 17.95 (ISBN 0-07-003221-1, C). McGraw.
Baird, Charles W. Elements of Macroeconomics. 1977. pap. text ed. 10.95 (ISBN 0-8299-0069-1). West Pub.
Baird, Charles W. & Cassuto, Alexander E. Macroeconomics. 2nd ed. 336p. 1980. text ed. 16.95 (ISBN 0-574-19400-2, 13-2400); instr's. guide avail. (ISBN 0-574-19401-0, 13-2401). SRA.
Barkley, Paul W. An Introduction to Macroeconomics. (Illus.). 1977. pap. text ed. 13.95 (ISBN 0-15-518816-X, HC); instructor's manual avail. (ISBN 0-15-518819-4); study guide by sam cordes 5.95 (ISBN 0-685-03548-4); test bklet avail. (ISBN 0-15-518825-9). HarBraceJ.

Barro, Robert J. Money, Expectations & Business Cycles: Essays in Macroeconomics. (Economic Theory, Econometrics & Mathematical Economic Ser.). 1981. 25.00 (ISBN 0-12-079550-7). Acad Pr.

Beenstock, M. A Neoclassical Analysis of Macroeconomic Policy. LC 79-8961. 1981. 32.50 (ISBN 0-521-23077-2). Cambridge U Pr.

Bhaskar, K. N. Macroeconomic Systems. 300p. 1976. 22.50x (ISBN 0-85664-295-9). Intl Pubns Serv.

Bowles, Roger A. & Whynes, David K. Macroeconomic Planning. (Studies in Economics). (Illus.). 1979. text ed. 25.00x (ISBN 0-04-330294-7); pap. text ed. 9.95x (ISBN 0-04-330295-5). Allen Unwin.

Bradley, Michael E. Macroeconomics. 1980. pap. text ed. 11.95x (ISBN 0-673-15336-3); study guide 5.95x (ISBN 0-673-15423-8). Scott F.

Branson, William H. Macroeconomic Theory & Policy. 2nd ed. (Illus.). 1979. text ed. 22.95 scp (ISBN 0-06-040936-3, HarpC). Har-Row.

Branson, William H. & Litvack, James M. Macroeconomics. 2nd ed. 407p. 1981. text ed. 20.50 scp (ISBN 0-06-040937-1, HarpC). Har-Row.

Branson, William H. & Litvak, James. Macroeconomia. (Span.). 1979. 13.20 (ISBN 0-06-310059-2, Pub. by HarLA Mexico). Har-Row.

Bronfenbrenner, Martin. Macroeconomic Alternatives. LC 79-50880. (Illus.). 1979. text ed. 17.95x (ISBN 0-88295-404-0). Harlan Davidson.

Brooks, John & Evans, Robert W. Macroeconomic Policy in Theory & Practice. (Economics & Society Ser). (Illus.). 1978. text ed. 17.95x (ISBN 0-04-339012-9); pap. text ed. 7.50x (ISBN 0-04-339013-7). Allen Unwin.

Brooman, Frederick & Jacoby, Henry D. Macroeconomics: An Introduction to Theory & Policy. LC 73-75979. 1970. 29.95x (ISBN 0-202-06026-8). Aldine Pub.

Buchanan, James M. Cost & Choice: An Inquiry in Economic Theory. LC 78-70150. (Midway Reprints Ser.). 1979. pap. text ed. 6.00x (ISBN 0-226-07818-3). U of Chicago Pr.

Burrows, Paul & Hitiris, Theodore. Macroeconomic Theory: A Mathematical Introduction. LC 73-2779. 1974. text ed. 21.75 (ISBN 0-471-12525-3, Pub. by Wiley-Interscience). Wiley.

Burton, Robert H. & Brunhild, Gordon. Macroeconomic Theory. (Illus.). 544p. 1973. ref. ed. 19.95x (ISBN 0-13-542639-1). P-H.

Campagna, Anthony S. Macroeconomics. 600p. 1981. text ed. 16.95x (ISBN 0-312-50333-4). St Martin.

Carson, Robert B. Macroeconomic Issues Today. 182p. (Orig.). 1980. text ed. 12.95 (ISBN 0-312-50324-5); pap. text ed. 5.95 (ISBN 0-312-50325-3); write for info. instructor's manual (ISBN 0-312-50326-1). St Martin.

Cavaco-Silva, Anibal A. Economic Effects of Public Debt. LC 77-74813. 1977. 16.95x (ISBN 0-312-23222-5). St Martin.

Cherry, Robert D. Macroeconomics. LC 79-3130. (Economics Ser.). 1980. text ed. 16.95 (ISBN 0-201-00911-0). A-W.

Chisholm, Roger & McCarty, Marilu. Principles of Macroeconomics. 2nd ed. 1981. pap. text ed. 11.95x (ISBN 0-673-15493-9). Scott F.

Chrystal, K. A. Controversies in British Macroeconomics. 1981. pap. text ed. 15.00x (ISBN 0-86003-123-3). Verry.

--Controversies in British Macroeconomics. 1979. 21.00x (ISBN 0-86003-022-9, Pub. by Allan Pubs England); pap. 10.50x (ISBN 0-86003-123-3). State Mutual Bk.

Cochrane, James L. Macroeconomics Before Keynes. 1970. pap. 5.95x (ISBN 0-673-05010-6). Scott F.

Cochrane, James L., et al. Macroeconomics: Analysis & Policy. 398p. 1974. text ed. 12.95x (ISBN 0-673-07639-3). Scott F.

Currie, David & Peel, David, eds. Macroeconomic Analysis: Current Problems & Theories in Macroeconomics & Econometrics. 500p. 1981. 44.00x (ISBN 0-686-30457-8, Pub. by Croom Helm Ltd England). Biblio Dist.

Currie, David, et al, eds. Microeconomic Analysis: Current Problems & Theories in Micro-Labour & Development Economics. 500p. 1981. 44.00x (ISBN 0-7069-0709-4, Pub. by Croom Helm Ltd England). Biblio Dist.

Cuthbertson, K. Macroeconomic Policy: New Cambridge, Keynesian and Monetarist Controversies. LC 79-12195. (New Studies in Economic Ser.). 209p. 1979. 30.95x (ISBN 0-470-26740-2). Halsted Pr.

Darby, McIhael. Intermediate Macroeconomics. (Illus.). 1979. text ed. 16.95 (ISBN 0-07-015348-5, C); write for info. instructor's manual (ISBN 0-07-015349-3). McGraw.

Dasgupta, Ajit K. & Hagger, A. J. Objectives of Macro-Economic Policy. 1971. text ed. 19.00x (ISBN 0-333-12396-4). Humanities.

David, Paul A. & Reder, Melvin W., eds. Nations & Households in Ecnomic Growth: Essays in Honor of Moses Abramovitz. 1973. 50.00 (ISBN 0-12-205050-9). Acad Pr.

Dernburg, Thomas & McDougall, Duncan. Macroeconomics. 6th ed. (Illus.). 1980. text ed. 17.95 (ISBN 0-07-016534-3). McGraw.

Diulio, Eugene. Macroeconomic Theory. 256p. (Orig.). 1974. pap. text ed. 4.95 (ISBN 0-07-017049-5, SP). McGraw.

Dolan, Edwin G. Basic Macroeconomics: Understanding National Income, Inflation & Unemployment. 400p. 1980. pap. text ed. 13.95 (ISBN 0-03-051276-X). Dryden Pr.

Dornbusch, Rudiger. Open Economy Macroeconomics. LC 80-66308. (Illus.). 293p. 1980. text ed. 17.95x (ISBN 0-465-05286-X). Basic.

Dornbusch, Rudiger & Fischer, Stanley. Macroeconomics. 2nd ed. (Illus.). 736p. 1980. text ed. 18.95 (ISBN 0-07-017754-6, C); instructor's manual 6.95 (ISBN 0-07-017755-4); study guide 6.95 (ISBN 0-07-017756-2). McGraw.

--Macroeconomics. (Illus.). 1978. text ed. 16.95 (ISBN 0-07-017751-1, C); instructor's manual 5.95 (ISBN 0-07-017752-X); suppl. to instructors' manual 4.95 (ISBN 0-07-017753-8). McGraw.

Edgmand, M. Macroeconomics: Theory & Policy. 1979. 19.95 (ISBN 0-13-542647-2). P-H.

Elliott, J. W. Macroeconomics Analysis. 1975. 15.95 (ISBN 0-87626-545-X). Winthrop.

Elliott, S. W. Macroecomonics Analysis. 2nd ed. 1979. 19.95 (ISBN 0-87626-540-9). Winthrop.

Evans, Michael K. Macroeconomic Activity: Theory, Forecasting, & Control. LC 69-11111. (Illus.). 1969. scp 36.50 (ISBN 0-06-041918-0, HarpC). Har-Row.

Fellner, William. Towards a Reconstruction of Macroeconomics. LC 76-21162. 1976. pap. 5.25 (ISBN 0-8447-1318-X). Am Enterprise.

Fels, Rendig, et al. Macroeconomic Problems & Policies. 4th ed. 1979. pap. text ed. 5.95 (ISBN 0-8299-0191-4). West Pub.

Focus: Macroeconomics. 2nd ed. LC 72-180264. (Annual Editions Ser.). 1977. pap. text ed. 5.25 (ISBN 0-87967-168-8). Dushkin Pub.

Frazer, William. Expectations, Forecasting & Control--a Provisional Textbook of Macroeconomics: Volume II, Prices, Market & Turning Points. LC 80-1361. 439p. 1980. lib. bdg. 25.50 (ISBN 0-8191-1290-9); pap. text ed. 16.25 (ISBN 0-8191-1291-7). U Pr of Amer.

--Expectations, Forecasting & Control: A Provisional Textbook of Macroeconomics, Vol. I: Monetary Matters, Keynesian & Other Models. LC 80-1361. 493p. 1980. lib. bdg. 25.50 (ISBN 0-8191-1144-9); pap. text ed. 16.75 (ISBN 0-8191-1145-7). U Pr of Amer.

Gallais-Hamonno, Janine. Langage de Macroeconomics. 2nd ed. 312p. (Eng.-Fr.). 1973. pap. 19.95 (ISBN 0-686-57188-6, M-6260). French & Eur.

Gershuny, J. After Industrial Society? The Emerging Self-Service Economy. 1978. text ed. 20.75x (ISBN 0-391-00837-4); pap. text ed. 7.75x (ISBN 0-391-00847-1). Humanities.

Glahe, Fred R. Macroeconomics: Theory & Policy. 2nd ed. (Illus.). 1977. text ed. 18.95 (ISBN 0-15-551266-8, HC). HarBraceJ.

Golladay, Frederick L. Macroeconomics: Problems, Principles, Priorities. LC 78-53018. 1978. 10.95 (ISBN 0-8053-3307-X). Benjamin-Cummings.

Gordon, Robert J. Macroecomomics. 2nd ed. 1981. text ed. 19.95 (ISBN 0-316-32125-7); wkbk. 6.95 (ISBN 0-316-32127-3). Little.

Gossling, W. F. Productivity Trends in a Sectoral Macroeconomic Model: A Study of American Agriculture & Supporting Industries, 1919-1964. 1972. lib. bdg. 37.50x (ISBN 0-678-08072-0). Kelley.

Gwartney, James D. & Stroup, Richard. Macroeconomics: Private & Public Choice. 2nd ed. 1980. pap. text ed. 12.95 (ISBN 0-12-311070-X). Acad Pr.

Hadjimichalakis, Michael G. Modern Macroeconomics: An Intermediate Text. (Illus.). 640p. 1982. text ed. 21.95 (ISBN 0-13-595074-0). P-H.

Haieh, Ching-yao, et al. A Short Introduction to Modern Growth Theory. LC 78-61916. 1978. pap. text ed. 9.00 (ISBN 0-8191-0628-3). U Pr of Amer.

Harcourt, G. C., et al. Economic Activity. 1967. 45.00 (ISBN 0-521-05199-1). Cambridge U Pr.

Harvey, J. & Johnson, M. An Introduction to Macro-Economics. 320p. 1971. text ed. 13.00x (ISBN 0-333-12509-6); pap. text ed. 6.00x (ISBN 0-333-12511-8). Humanities.

Hatten, Mary L. Macroeconomics for Management. (Illus.). 384p. 1981. text ed. 19.95 (ISBN 0-13-542498-4). P-H.

Havrilesky, Thomas M. & Boorman, John T. Monetary Macroeconomics. LC 77-85996. (Illus.). 1978. pap. text ed. 15.95x (ISBN 0-88295-401-6). Harlan Davidson.

Heesterman, A. R. Macro-Economic Market Regulation. LC 72-90322. 256p. 1974. 27.50x (ISBN 0-8448-0118-6). Crane-Russak Co.

Heyne, Paul & Johnson, Thomas. Toward Understanding Macroeconomics. LC 76-22501. 1976. pap. text ed. 11.95 (ISBN 0-574-19275-1, 13-2275); instr's guide avail. (ISBN 0-574-19256-5, 13-2256). SRA.

Horwich, George & Samuelson, Paul A., eds. Trade, Stability, & Macroeconomics: Essays in Honor of Lloyd A. Metzler. (Economic Theory & Mathematical Economics Ser.). 1974. 43.00 (ISBN 0-12-356750-5). Acad Pr.

Hosek, William R. Macroeconomic Theory. 1975. 18.50x (ISBN 0-256-01669-0). Irwin.

Johnson, Harry G. Macroeconomics & Monetary Theory. 214p. 1972. 16.95x (ISBN 0-202-06053-5). Aldine Pub.

Kelly, William A., Jr. Macroeconomics. (Illus.). 496p. 1981. text ed. 17.95 (ISBN 0-13-542761-4). P-H.

Kennedy, Peter E. Macroeconomics. 2nd ed. LC 16-65995. 1979. text ed. 20.95x (ISBN 0-205-06599-6); sol. manual avail. (ISBN 0-205-06606-2). Allyn.

Korliras, Panayotis G. & Thorn, Richard S. Modern Macroeconomics: Major Contributions to Contemporary Thought. 1979. text ed. 26.95 scp (ISBN 0-06-043764-2, HarpC). Har-Row.

Kuh, E. & Schmalensee, R. L. An Introduction to Applied Macroeconomics. 1973. 24.50 (ISBN 0-444-10390-2, North-Holland). Elsevier.

Kurihara, Kenneth K. Essays in Macrodynamic Economics. LC 74-171175. 1972. 12.00 (ISBN 0-87395-136-0). State U NY Pr.

Lachmann, L. M. Macro-Economic Thinking & the Market Economy. (Institute of Economic Affairs, Hobart Papers Ser.: No. 56). pap. 2.50 (ISBN 0-255-36043-6). Transatlantic.

Laidler, David E. Demand for Money: Theories & Evidence. 2nd ed. (Monetary Economic Ser). 128p. 1978. pap. text ed. 8.50 scp (ISBN 0-912212-07-1, HarpC). Har-Row.

Leijonhufvud, Axel. Information & Coordination: Essays in Macroeconomic Theory. (Illus.). 400p. 1981. text ed. 19.95x (ISBN 0-19-502814-7); pap. text ed. 11.95x (ISBN 0-19-502815-5). Oxford U Pr.

Leonard, Fred H. Macroeconomic Theory: Static & Dynamic Analyses. 1978. text ed. 15.95 (ISBN 0-394-31884-6). Random.

Lindauer, John. Macroeconomic Readings. LC 68-9816. (Orig.). 1968. pap. text ed. 9.95 (ISBN 0-02-919110-6). Free Pr.

--Macroeconomics: A Modern View. LC 77-79399. 1979. pap. text ed. cancelled (ISBN 0-7216-5780-X). HR&W.

Linder, Marc. The Anti-Samuelson. Incl. Vol. I. Macroeconomics: Basic Problems of Capitalist Economy (ISBN 0-916354-14-8) (ISBN 0-916354-15-6); Vol. II. Microeconomics: Money & Banking (ISBN 0-916354-16-4) (ISBN 0-916354-17-2). 1977. 20.00 ea.; pap. text ed. 6.95 ea. Urizen Bks.

Lindert, Peter H. Prices, Jobs & Growth: An Introduction to Macroeconomics. (Series in Economics). 1976. text ed. 9.95 (ISBN 0-316-52630-4); instr's manual free (ISBN 0-316-52631-2). Little.

Lipsey, Richard G. & Steiner, Peter O. Economics, Vol. I: Macroeconomics. 5th ed. LC 78-25646. 1979. pap. text ed. 14.95 scp (ISBN 0-06-043976-9, HarpC); scp study guide 6.50 (ISBN 0-06-043982-3). Har-Row.

Lovell, M. Macroeconomics: Measurement, Theory, & Policy. LC 75-2001. 541p. 1975. 25.50 (ISBN 0-471-54850-2). Wiley.

McClelland, Peter D. Introductory Macroeconomics Nineteen Eighty-One - Nineteen Eighty-Two: Readings on Contemporary Issues. LC 77-6193. 224p. 1981. pap. text ed. 8.95x (ISBN 0-8014-9878-3). Cornell U Pr.

McClelland, Peter D., ed. Focus on Macro Economics. (Annual Eds. Ser.). (Illus.). 224p. (gr. 11 up). 1975. pap. text ed. 4.50 (ISBN 0-87967-111-4); tchr's guide free (ISBN 0-685-51788-8). Dushkin Pub.

--Introductory Macroeconomics, 1980-81: Readings on Contemporary Issues. LC 80-66907. (Illus.). 224p. (Orig.). 1980. softcover 8.95x (ISBN 0-8014-9873-2). Cornell U Pr.

McDougall, Duncan & Quirk, James P. Macroeconomics. 1981. pap. text ed. 13.95 (ISBN 0-574-19415-0, 13-2415); instr's guide avail. (ISBN 0-574-19416-9, 13-2416). SRA.

McNown, Robert F. & Lee, Dwight R. Economics in Our Time: Macro Issues. LC 76-374. 224p. 1976. pap. text ed. 6.95 (ISBN 0-574-19260-3, 13-2260); instr's guide avail. (ISBN 0-574-19261-1, 13-2261). SRA.

Mansfield, Edwin. Principles of Macroeconomics. 400p. 1974. pap. text ed. 6.75x (ISBN 0-393-09275-5). Norton.

--Principles of Macroeconomics. (Illus.). 1977. pap. text ed. 9.95x (ISBN 0-393-09120-1); tchrs guide gratis (ISBN 0-393-09286-0); reading, issues & cases 4.95x (ISBN 0-686-77328-4); study guide 4.50x (ISBN 0-393-09114-7); transparency masters gratis (ISBN 0-393-95131-6); test item file gratis (ISBN 0-393-95125-1). Norton.

--Principles of Macroeconomics. 3rd ed. pap. text ed. 10.95x (ISBN 0-393-95120-0); instrs' manual free (ISBN 0-393-95124-3); study guide 3.95x (ISBN 0-393-95140-5); cases 4.95x (ISBN 0-393-95134-0); test item free (ISBN 0-393-95125-1); transparency masters free (ISBN 0-393-95131-6). Norton.

--Principles of Microeconomics. 3rd ed. 1980. pap. text ed. 10.95x (ISBN 0-393-95128-6); instrs' manual free (ISBN 0-393-95124-3); cases 4.95x (ISBN 0-393-95144-8); study guide 3.95x (ISBN 0-393-95147-2); test item free (ISBN 0-393-95125-1); transparency masters free (ISBN 0-393-95131-6). Norton.

Mansfield, Edwin, ed. Principles of Macroeconomics. 2nd ed. Incl. Reading, Issues, & Cases. 1974. pap. text ed. 3.25x (ISBN 0-393-09271-2). 1977. pap. text ed. 4.95x (ISBN 0-393-09108-2). Norton.

Martin, Leonard W. Principles of Economics: Macro. LC 79-12141. (Grid Series in Economics). 1980. pap. text ed. 10.95 (ISBN 0-88244-191-4). Grid Pub.

Meyer, Robert A. Problems in Macroeconomics. 352p. 1974. pap. 7.50 (ISBN 0-395-17824-X); instructors' manual 1.50 (ISBN 0-395-17825-8). HM.

Miller, Roger L. Economics of Macro Issues. 3rd ed. 1980. pap. text ed. 8.50 (ISBN 0-8299-0333-X). West Pub.

--The Economics of Macro Issues. 2nd ed. 1978. pap. text ed. 8.50 scp (ISBN 0-06-385471-6, HarpC); tchr's ed. free (ISBN 0-06-375617-X). Har-Row.

--Economics Today: Macro View. 3rd ed. 1979. pap. text ed. 14.95 scp (ISBN 0-06-385488-0, HarpC); scp study guide 5.50 (ISBN 0-06-388579-4); wkbk scp 6.50 (ISBN 0-06-385381-7); scp cassetts 1-14 175.00 (ISBN 0-06-385379-5). Har-Row.

Miller, Roger L. & Williams, Raburn M. Unemployment & Inflation: The New Economics of the Wage-Price Spiral. LC 74-1062. 100p. 1974. text ed. 11.95 (ISBN 0-8299-0009-8). West Pub.

Mitchell, William E., et al. Exercises in Macroeconomics: Development of Concepts. (Illus.). 432p. 1973. pap. text ed. 10.95 (ISBN 0-07-042511-6, C). McGraw.

--Readings in Macroeconomisc. (Illus.). 512p. 1974. pap. text ed. 9.50 (ISBN 0-07-042510-8, C). McGraw.

Morgenstern, Oskar. National Income Statistics: A Critique of Macroeconomic Aggregation. (Cato Papers Ser.: No.5). 64p. 1979. pap. 2.00x (ISBN 0-932790-04-6). Cato Inst.

Mueller, Max G., ed. Readings in Macroeconomics. 2nd ed. LC 72-139800. 1971. pap. text ed. 10.95 (ISBN 0-03-078475-1, HoltC). HR&W.

Mussa, M. A Study of Macroeconomics. LC 75-38905. (Studies in Monetary Economics: Vol. 3). 1976. 53.75 (ISBN 0-444-10908-0, North-Holland). Elsevier.

Nagatani, Keizo. Macroeconomic Dynamics. LC 80-28883. (Illus.). 250p. Date not set. price not set (ISBN 0-521-23515-4). Cambridge U Pr.

Negishi, T. Microeconomic Foundations of Keynesian Macroeconomics. (Studies in Mathematical & Managerial Economics: Vol. 27). 264p. 1980. 44.00 (ISBN 0-444-85225-5, North Holland). Elsevier.

Nickson, Jack W., Jr. Economics & Social Choice. 2nd ed. (Illus.). 352p. 1974. pap. text ed. 10.95 (ISBN 0-07-046523-1, C); tchrs' manual 4.95 (ISBN 0-07-046524-X). McGraw.

OECD. Macro-Economic Evaluation of Environmental Programmes. 194p. (Orig.). 1978. pap. 11.00x (ISBN 92-64-11751-2). OECD.

Okun, Arthur M. Prices & Quantities: A Macroeconomic Analysis. 400p. 1981. 19.95 (ISBN 0-8157-6480-4); pap. 7.95 (ISBN 0-8157-6479-0). Brookings.

Ott, David, et al. Macroeconomic Theory. (Illus.). 416p. 1975. text ed. 17.95 (ISBN 0-07-047918-6, C). McGraw.

Peston, M. H. Theory of Macroeconomic Policy. 224p. 1974. pap. 19.50x (ISBN 0-86003-113-6, Pub. by Allan Pubs England). State Mutual Bk.

--Whatever Happened to Macroeconomics. 66p. 1981. pap. 10.00x (ISBN 0-686-73072-0, Pub. by Manchester U Pr England). State Mutual Bk.

Phelps, Edmund S., ed. Studies in Macroeconomic Theory Taxation: Vol. 2 Redistribution & Growth. (Economic Theory, Econometrics & Mathematics Ser.). 1980. 21.00 (ISBN 0-12-554002-7). Acad Pr.

--Studies in Macroeconomics Theory: Employment & Inflation, Vol. 1. (Economic Theory Econometrics, & Mathematical Economics Ser.). 1979. 24.50 (ISBN 0-12-554001-9). Acad Pr.
Philpot, Gordon A. The National Economy: An Introduction to Macroeconomics. LC 80-20615. 188p. 1980. pap. text ed. 8.95 (ISBN 0-471-05591-3). Wiley.
Poindexter, J. Carl, Jr. Macroeconomics. 2nd ed. LC 79-51107. 560p. 1981. text ed. 21.95 (ISBN 0-03-050271-3). Dryden Pr.
Presley, J. R., et al. Case Studies in Macro-Economics. Maunder, Peter, ed. (Case Studies in Economic Analysis). 1977. 5.00x (ISBN 0-435-84473-3); tchr's ed. 8.50x (ISBN 0-435-84474-1). Heinemann Ed.
Presley, John R. Robertsonian Economics. LC 78-25958. 1979. 38.50 (ISBN 0-8419-0471-5). Holmes & Meier.
Reekie, W. Duncan. Macroeconomics for Managers. 160p. 1980. 18.00x (ISBN 0-86003-510-7, Pub. by Allan Pubs England); pap. 9.00x (ISBN 0-86003-610-3). State Mutual Bk.
Reynolds, Lloyd G. Macroeconomics: Analysis & Policy. 3rd. ed. 1979. 12.95x (ISBN 0-256-02173-2); review guide & wkbk. 6.50x (ISBN 0-256-02170-8). Irwin.
Rimmer, Douglas. Macromancy: The Ideology of Development Economics. (Institute of Economic Affairs, Hobart Papers Ser.: No. 55). 64p. 1973. pap. 2.50 (ISBN 0-255-36042-8). Transatlantic.
Rudman, Jack. Introductory Macroeconomics. (College Level Examination Ser.: CLEP-41). 14.95 (ISBN 0-8373-5391-2); pap. 9.95 (ISBN 0-8373-5341-6). Natl Learning.
--Introductory Micro- & Macroeconomics. (College Level Examination Ser.: CLEP-42). 1977. 14.95 (ISBN 0-8373-5342-4); pap. 9.95 (ISBN 0-8373-5392-0). Natl Learning.
Sanderson, Allen R., ed. DRI-McGraw-Hill Readings in Macroeconomics. (Illus.). 480p. 1981. pap. text ed. 7.95 (ISBN 0-07-054659-2). McGraw.
Sargent, Thomas. Macroeconomic Theory. LC 78-4803. (Economic Theory, Econometrics & Mathematical Economics Ser.). 1979. 24.50 (ISBN 0-12-619750-4). Acad Pr.
Shapiro, Edward. Macroeconomic Analysis. 4th ed. 1978. text ed. 18.95 (ISBN 0-15-551212-9, HC); wkbk. 7.95 (ISBN 0-15-551213-7). HarBraceJ.
Shaw, G. K. An Introduction to the Theory of Macro-Economic Policy. 3rd ed. 218p. 1980. bds. 30.50x (ISBN 0-85520-183-5, Pub. by Martin Robertson England); pap. 12.50x (ISBN 0-85520-182-7). Biblio Dist.
Sherman, Howard J. Stagflation: A Radical Theory of Unemployment & Inflation. (Illus.). 1976. pap. text ed. 10.50 scp (ISBN 0-06-046106-3, HarpC). Har-Row.
Siebrand, Jan C. Towards Operational Disequilibrium Macro Economics. 1979. lib. bdg. 34.00 (ISBN 90-247-2153-9, Pub. by Martinus Nijhoff Netherlands). Kluwer Boston.
Solmon, Lewis C. Macroeconomics. 3rd ed. LC 79-25516. 480p. 1980. pap. text ed. 12.95 (ISBN 0-201-07217-3); student guide avail. (ISBN 0-201-07220-3). A-W.
Spector, Lee C. & Kieffer, Richard J. Applying Macroeconomic Principles: A Student Guide to Analyzing Economic News. 1979. pap. text ed. 8.50 scp (ISBN 0-06-388576-X, HarpC). Har-Row.
--Applying Microeconomic Principles: A Student Guide to Analyzing Economic News. 1979. pap. text ed. 8.50 scp (ISBN 0-06-388577-8, HarpC). Har-Row.
Spencer, Milton H. Contemporary Macroeconomics. 4th ed. (Illus.). text ed. 13.95x (ISBN 0-87901-114-9); study guide 5.95 (ISBN 0-87901-110-6). H S Worth.
Surrey, M. J. C., ed. Macroeconomic Themes: Edited Readings in Macroeconomics. (Illus.). 1976. text ed. 37.50x (ISBN 0-19-877059-6); pap. text ed. 15.95x (ISBN 0-19-877060-X). Oxford U Pr.
Thomas, Robert P. Macroeconomic Applications. 256p. 1981. pap. text ed. 7.95x (ISBN 0-534-00963-8). Wadsworth Pub.
Thornton, et al. Principles of Microeconomics: Study Guide. 2nd ed. 1981. pap. text ed. 4.95x (ISBN 0-673-15495-5). Scott F.
Tobin, James. Asset Accumulation & Economic Activity: Reflections on Contemporary Macroeconomic Theory. LC 80-12844. 112p. 1980. lib. bdg. 13.00x (ISBN 0-226-80501-8). U of Chicago Pr.
Veiga, John F. & Yanouzas, John N. The Dynamics of Organization Theory: Gaining a Macro Perspective. (Illus.). 1979. text ed. 16.50 (ISBN 0-8299-0182-5); insts.' manual avail. (ISBN 0-8299-0578-2). West Pub.
Venieris, Y. P. & Sebold, F. D. Macroeconomic, Models & Policy. 1977. 26.95 (ISBN 0-471-90560-7). Wiley.
Vernon, Jack. Macroeconomics. 464p. 1980. text ed. 21.95 (ISBN 0-03-042336-8). Dryden Pr.
Veseth, Michael. Introductory Macroeconomics. 432p. 1981. 12.95 (ISBN 0-12-719552-1). Acad Pr.
Waud, Roger N. Macroeconomics. (Illus.). 1980. text ed. 14.95 scp (ISBN 0-06-046965-X, HarpC); scp study guide 6.50 (ISBN 0-06-046989-7). Har-Row.
Weintraub, E. R. Microfoundations. LC 78-16551. (Cambridge Surveys of Economic Literature Ser.). 1979. 26.50 (ISBN 0-521-22305-9); pap. 7.95x (ISBN 0-521-29445-2). Cambridge U Pr.
Westaway, A. J. & Weyman-Jones, T. G. Macroeconomics: Theory, Evidence, & Policy. LC 76-54984. (Modern Economics Ser.). (Illus.). 1977. text ed. 22.50x (ISBN 0-582-44666-X). Longman.
Williams, Harold R. Macroeconomics: Problems, Concepts & Self-Tests: Workbook to Accompany Income, Employment & Economic Growth by Wallace Peterson. 1967. pap. 3.95x (ISBN 0-393-09763-3, NortonC). Norton.
Wonnacott, Paul. Macroeconomics. rev. ed. 1978. 19.95x (ISBN 0-256-02032-9). Irwin.
Wykoff, Frank C. Macroeconomics: Theory, Evidence & Policy. 2nd ed. (Illus.). 640p. 1981. 19.95 (ISBN 0-13-543967-1). P-H.
Zahn, Frank. Macroeconomic Theory & Policy. (Illus.). 320p. 1975. 18.95 (ISBN 0-13-542555-7). P-H.
Zincone, Louis, et al. Principles of Microeconomics: Study Guide. 2nd ed. 1981. pap. text ed. 4.95x (ISBN 0-673-15496-3). Scott F.
Zolotov, Alan K. Elements of Macroeconomics. 1979. pap. text ed. 7.95 (ISBN 0-8403-2096-5). Kendall-Hunt.

MACROECONOMICS–MATHEMATICAL MODELS

Boorman, John T. & Havrilesky, Thomas M. Money Supply, Money Demand & Macroeconomic Models. LC 79-167998. 1972. pap. 13.95x (ISBN 0-88295-400-8). Harlan Davidson.
Fair, Ray C. A Model of Macroeconomic Activity: Vol. II: the Empirical Model. LC 74-12199. 316p. 1976. text ed. 20.00 (ISBN 0-88410-295-5). Ballinger Pub.
Kogiku, K. C. An Introduction to Macroeconomic Models. LC 78-11772. 256p. 1980. Repr. of 1968 ed. lib. bdg. 16.50 (ISBN 0-88275-769-5). Krieger.
Powell, Alan A. & Williams, Ross A. Econometric Studies of Macro & Monetary Relations. 1973. 34.25 (ISBN 0-444-10455-0, North-Holland). Elsevier.
Scarfe, Brian L. Cycles, Growth & Inflation. (Illus.). 1977. text ed. 27.00x (ISBN 0-07-055039-5, C). McGraw.
Taylor, Lance. Macro Models for Developing Countries. (Economic Handbook Ser). (Illus.). 1979. text ed. 26.50 (ISBN 0-07-063135-2, C). McGraw.
Turnovsky, S. J. Macroeconomic Analysis & Stabilization Policy. LC 76-46862. (Illus.). 1977. 44.50 (ISBN 0-521-21520-X); pap. 15.95x (ISBN 0-521-29187-9). Cambridge U Pr.
Van Duyne, Carl. Modsim: A Computer Program for Simulating Macroeconomic Models. Hepler, Molly L., ed. (Orig., User's man., 89 p.; instr's. man., 67 p.). 1980. User's Manual. pap. text ed. 5.00 (ISBN 0-686-27411-3); Instructor's Manual. 5.00 (ISBN 0-686-27412-1). Conduit.

MACROMOLECULES

Alexandrov, V. Y. Cells, Macromolecules, & Temperature. (Ecological Studies Ser: Vol. 21). 1977. 43.60 (ISBN 0-387-08026-0). Springer-Verlag.
Ansell, G. Macromolecules & Behavior. (Illus.). 1973. 29.50 (ISBN 0-8391-0575-4). Univ Park.
Baserga, Renato, et al, eds. Introduction of Macromolecules into Viable Mammalian Cells. LC 79-91743. (Wistar Symposium Ser.: Vol. 1). 354p. 1980. 26.00x (ISBN 0-8451-2000-X). A R Liss.
Bovey, Frank & Winslow, F. H., eds. Macromolecules: An Introduction to Polymer Science. LC 78-20041. 1979. 45.00 (ISBN 0-12-119755-7). Acad Pr.
Chance, Britton, et al, eds. Probes of Structure & Function of Macromolecules & Membranes, 2 Vols. 1971. Vol. 1. 49.50 (ISBN 0-12-167801-6); Vol. 2. 49.50 (ISBN 0-12-167802-4); Set. 81.00 (ISBN 0-685-02417-2). Acad Pr.
Clausen, J. Immunochemical Techniques for the Identification & Estimation of Macromolecules. (Lab Techiques in Biochemistry & Molecular Biology Vol. 1, Pt. 3). 1969. pap. 12.25 (ISBN 0-444-10160-8, North-Holland). Elsevier.
Cleveland Symposium on Macromolecules, 1st, Case Western Reserve Univ., Oct. 1976. Proceedings. Walton, A. G., ed. 1977. 53.75 (ISBN 0-444-41561-0). Elsevier.
Cold Spring Harbor Symposia on Quantitative Biology: Synthesis and Structure of Macromolecules, Vol. 28. LC 34-8174. (Illus.). 630p. 1964. 30.00 (ISBN 0-87969-027-5). Cold Spring Harbor.
Dillon, Lawrence S. Ultrastructure,Macromolecules, & Evolution. 750p. 1981. 69.50 (ISBN 0-306-40528-8, Plenum Pr). Plenum Pub.
Division of Chemistry and Chemical Technology. Characterization of Macromolecular Structure. (Illus.). 1968. 16.00 (ISBN 0-309-01573-1). Natl Acad Pr.
Dole, Malcolm, ed. The Radiation Chemistry of Macromolecules, 2 vols. 1972. Vol. 1. 56.50 (ISBN 0-12-219801-8); Vol. 2. 60.00 (ISBN 0-12-219802-6); Set. 95.50 (ISBN 0-685-36101-2). Acad Pr.
Eby, Ronald K., ed. Durability of Macromolecular Materials. LC 78-31777. (Symposium Ser.: No. 95). 1979. 34.00 (ISBN 0-8412-0485-3). Am Chemical.
Elias, H-G, ed. Trends in Macromolecular Science. LC 73-86253. (Midland Macromolecular Monographs Ser.). 132p. 1973. 19.75x (ISBN 0-677-15860-2). Gordon.
Elias, Hans-Georg. Macromolecules. Incl. Vol. 1, Structure & Properties. 532p (ISBN 0-306-35111-0); Vol. 2, Synthesis & Materials. 599p. 1977. 39.50 ea. Plenum Pub.
Everett. Ions in Macromolecular & Biological Systems. 1978. 39.50 (ISBN 0-8391-1290-4). Univ Park.
Fettes, Edward M., ed. Macromolecular Synthesis, Vol.7. LC 63-18627. (Macromolecular Synthesis Ser.). 1980. 28.50 (ISBN 0-471-05891-2, Pub. by Wiley-Interscience). Wiley.
Gaito, John, ed. Macromolecules & Behavior. LC 76-150497. 397p. 1972. 32.50 (ISBN 0-306-50025-6, Plenum Pr). Plenum Pub.
Hay, Elizabeth D., et al, eds. Macromolecules Regulating Growth & Development. 1974. 43.00 (ISBN 0-12-612973-8). Acad Pr.
Hopfinger, A. J. Conformational Properties of Macromolecules. (Molecular Biology Ser.). 1973. 55.50 (ISBN 0-12-355550-7). Acad Pr.
Hudson Symposium, 9th, Plattsburgh, N.Y., Apr. 1976. Homoatomic Rings, Chains & Macromolecules of Main Group Elements: Proceedings. Rheingold, A. L., ed. 1977. 95.25 (ISBN 0-444-41634-X). Elsevier.
International Symposium on Macromolecules. Proceedings. Mano, E. B., ed. 1974. 58.75 (ISBN 0-444-41278-6). Elsevier.
International Union of Pure & Applied Chemistry. International Congress of Pure & Applied Chemistry. 22nd Sydney, 1969. Proceedings. 294p. 1976. text ed. 52.00 (ISBN 0-08-020842-8). Pergamon.
--Macromolecular Chemistry: Proceedings. Incl. No. 1. Montreal, 1961. 1966. 15.50 (ISBN 0-08-020779-0); No. 2. Prague, 1965. 1966. 31.00 (ISBN 0-08-020780-4); No. 3. Tokyo & Kyoto, 1966. 1967. 22.00 (ISBN 0-08-020781-2); No. 4. Brussels-Louvain, 1967. 1968. 22.00 (ISBN 0-08-020782-0); No. 5. Prague, 1969. 1970. 28.00 (ISBN 0-08-020783-9); No. 6. Prague, 1970. Sedlacek, B., ed. 1971. 18.00 (ISBN 0-08-020784-7); No. 7. Leiden, 1970. Voorn, M., ed. 1971. 36.00 (ISBN 0-08-020785-5); No. 8. Helsinki, 1972. Saarela, K., ed. 1973. 77.50 (ISBN 0-08-020786-3); No. 9. Aberdeen, Scotland, 1973. 1974. 37.00 (ISBN 0-08-020787-1); No. 11. Jerusalem, 1975. Eisenberg, H., ed. 1976. 38.50 (ISBN 0-08-020975-0). Pergamon.
Ivin, K. J., ed. Structural Studies of Macromolecules by Spectroscopic Methods. LC 75-19355. 1976. 73.25 (ISBN 0-471-43120-6, Pub. by Wiley-Interscience). Wiley.
Jamieson & Rippon. Instrumental Methods for Characterization of Biological Macromolecules. 1980. write for info. (ISBN 0-685-84733-0). Elsevier.
Jirgensons, B. Optical Activities of Proteins & Other Macromolecules. rev. ed. (Molecular Biology, Biochemistry & Biophysics Ser.: Vol. 5). (Illus.). 199p. 1973. 34.90 (ISBN 0-387-06340-4). Springer-Verlag.
Kirkwood, John G. Macromolecules. Auer, P. L., ed. (Documents on Modern Physics Ser). (Orig.). 1967. 35.75x (ISBN 0-677-00340-4). Gordon.
Koch, Gerhard & Richter, Dietmar, eds. Regulation of Macromolecular Synthesis by Low Molecular Weight Mediators. LC 79-26279. 1979. 27.50 (ISBN 0-12-417580-5). Acad Pr.
Koruza, Colleen M. Macromolecular Science. (IRS Physical Chemistry Ser. Two: Vol. 8). 1975. 29.95 (ISBN 0-408-70607-4). Butterworth.
Loening, K. L., ed. Nomenclature of Regular Single-Strand Organic Polymers. 1977. pap. text ed. 10.00 (ISBN 0-08-021579-3). Pergamon.
Maaloe, O. & Kjeldgaard, N. O. Control of Macromolecular Synthesis: a Study of DNA RNA & Protein: A Study of Dna, Rna & Protein. (Microbial & Molecular Biology Ser.: No. 4). 1966. 17.50 (ISBN 0-8053-6680-6, Adv Bk Prog). Benjamin-Cummings.
Macromolecular Chemistry, 4 vols. Incl. Vol. 1. 340p. 1962. 32.50 (ISBN 0-306-35001-7); Vol. 2. 648p. 1966. 32.50 (ISBN 0-306-35002-5); Vol. 3. LC 68-25340. 300p. 1968. 32.50 (ISBN 0-306-35003-3); Vol. 4. LC 68-54464. 321p. 1968. 24.50 (ISBN 0-306-35004-1). LC 68-54464 (Plenum Pr). Plenum Pub.
Mandelkern, L. An Introduction to Macromolecules. LC 72-83670. (Heidelberg Science Library: Vol. 17). (Illus.). 176p. 1972. pap. 10.30 (ISBN 0-387-90045-4). Springer-Verlag.
Microsymposia on Macromolecules. Macromolecular Chemistry: Proceedings. Sedlacek, B., ed. Incl. No. 4-6. Prague, 1969. 1970. 22.50 (ISBN 0-686-67819-2); No. 7. Prague, 1970. 1971. 14.50 (ISBN 0-686-67820-6); No. 8 & 9. Prague, 1971. 37.00 (ISBN 0-08-020788-X); No. 10 & 11. Prague, 1972. 1974. 37.00 (ISBN 0-08-020789-8); No. 12 & 13. Prague, 1973. (Illus.). 1974. 36.00 (ISBN 0-08-020790-1). (International Union of Pure & Applied Chemistry). Pergamon.
Morawetz, Herbert & Steinberg, I. Z., eds. Luminescence from Biological & Synthetic Macromolecules. 414p. 1981. 80.00 (ISBN 0-89766-123-0); pap. write for info. (ISBN 0-89766-124-9). NY Acad Sci.
Mulvaney, James E., ed. Macromolecular Syntheses. LC 63-18627. (Macromolecular Syntheses Ser.: Vol. 6). 1977. 29.95 (ISBN 0-471-02131-8, Pub. by Wiley-Interscience). Wiley.
Nato Advanced Study Institute, No. C-4, Troy, N. Y., July, 1973. Reactions on Polymers: Proceedings. Moore, James A., ed. LC 73-91207. Orig. Title: Reactions of Molecules. 1973. lib. bdg. 53.00 (ISBN 90-277-0416-3, Pub. by Reidel Holland). Kluwer Boston.
Overberger, C. & Mark, H. International Symposium on Macromolecules. (JPS Symposium: No. 62). 1978. 44.95 (ISBN 0-471-05602-2, Pub by Wiley-Interscience). Wiley.
Pasika, W. M., ed. Advances in Macromolecular Chemistry. Vol. 1. 1968. 36.00 (ISBN 0-12-025201-5); Vol. 2. 1970. 25.00 (ISBN 0-12-025202-3). Acad Pr.
Pethig, Ronald. Dielectric & Electronic Properties of Biological Materials. LC 78-13694. 1979. 52.25 (ISBN 0-471-99728-5, Pub. by Wiley-Interscience). Wiley.
Poland, D. & Scheraga, H. A. Theory of Helix Coil Transitions in Biopolymers. (Molecular Biology). 1970. 55.50 (ISBN 0-12-559550-6). Acad Pr.
Reinisch, R. F., ed. Photochemistry of Macromolecules. LC 70-127936. 229p. 1970. 29.50 (ISBN 0-306-30499-6, Plenum Pr). Plenum Pub.
Roberts, Richard B., ed. Studies in Macromolecular Biosynthesis. (Illus.). 702p. 1964. 29.00 (ISBN 0-87279-635-3, 624). Carnegie Inst.
Salvatore, F., et al, eds. Macromolecules in the Functioning Cell. LC 78-27547. 351p. 1979. 35.00 (ISBN 0-306-40146-0, Plenum Pr). Plenum Pub.
Silverstein, S. C., ed. Transport of Macromolecules in Cellular Systems, LSRR 11. (Dahlem Workshop Reports Ser.: L.S.R.R. No. 11). 1978. pap. 42.40 (ISBN 0-89573-095-2). Verlag Chemie.
Societe de Chimie Physique, 23rd. Dynamic Aspects of Conformation Changes in Biological Macromolecules: Proceedings. Sadron, C., ed. LC 72-97962. 400p. 1973. lib. bdg. 79.00 (ISBN 90-277-0334-5, Pub. by Reidel Holland). Kluwer Boston.
Society for the Study of Development & Growth - Symposium. Cytodifferentiation & Macromolecular Synthesis: Proceedings. Locke, M., ed. 1963. 40.00 (ISBN 0-12-454156-9). Acad Pr.
Spragg, S. P. The Physical Behavior of Macromolecules with Biological Functions. LC 80-40280. (Biophysics & Biochemistry Monographs). 202p. 1980. 40.50 (ISBN 0-471-27784-3, Pub. by Wiley-Interscience). Wiley.
Tanford, Charles. Physical Chemistry of Macromolecules. LC 61-11511. 710p. 1961. 44.95 (ISBN 0-471-84447-0, Wiley-Interscience). Wiley.
Timasheff, S. N. & Fasman, G. D., eds. Structure & Stability of Biological Macromolecules. (Biological Macromolecules Ser: Vol. 2). 1969. 75.00 (ISBN 0-8247-1670-1). Dekker.
Tombs, M. & Peacocke, A. R. The Osmotic Pressure of Biological Macromolecules. (Monographs on Physical Biochemistry). (Illus.). 230p. 1975. 29.50x (ISBN 0-19-854606-8). Oxford U Pr.

Williams, J. W. Ultracentrifugation of Macromolecules: Modern Topics. 1973. 22.50 (ISBN 0-12-755160-3). Acad Pr.
Wilson, A. D. & Crisp, S. Organolithic Macromolecular Materials. (Illus.). 1977. 30.00x (ISBN 0-85334-699-2). Intl Ideas.
Wittbecker, Emerson L., ed. Macromolecular Syntheses, Vol. 5. LC 63-18627. 114p. 1974. 15.50 (ISBN 0-471-95770-4, Pub. by Wiley). Krieger.
Wold, Finn. Macromolecules: Structure & Function. (Modern Biochemistry Ser). (Illus.). 1971. ref. ed. 15.95 (ISBN 0-13-542613-8); pap. 12.95 ref. ed. (ISBN 0-13-542605-7). P-H.
Wunderlich, Bernard. Macromolecular Physics: Crystals, Structure, Morphology & Defects. 1973. Vol. 1, 1973. 60.50 (ISBN 0-12-765601-4); Vol. 2, 1976. 72.00 (ISBN 0-12-765602-2). Acad Pr.
Wunderlich, Bernhard. Macromolecular Physics: Vol. 3, Crystal Melting. LC 72-82632. 1980. 42.50 (ISBN 0-12-765603-0). Acad Pr.

MACROPHAGES

Carr, Ian. The Macrophage: A Review of Ultrastructure & Function. 1974. 32.00 (ISBN 0-12-160550-7). Acad Pr.
Chirigos, Michael A., et al, eds. Mediation of Cellular Immunity in Cancer by Immune Modifiers. (Progress in Cancer Research & Therapy Ser.). 1981. text ed. 31.50 (ISBN 0-89004-628-X). Raven.
Escobar, M. R. & Friedman, H., eds. Macrophages & Lymphocytes: Nature, Functions & Interaction, Pt. B. (Advances in Experimental Medicine & Biology: Vol. 121B). 625p. 1980. 59.50 (ISBN 0-306-40286-6, Plenum Pr). Plenum Pub.
Fink, Mary, ed. The Macrophage: Its Role in Tumor Immunology. 1976. 25.50 (ISBN 0-12-256950-4). Acad Pr.
Herscowitz, H. B. Manual of Macrophage Methodology. (Immunology Ser.: Vol. 13). 1981. 65.00 (ISBN 0-686-73817-9). Dekker.
Mathe, G., et al, eds. Lymphocytes, Macrophages, & Cancer. LC 76-26538. (Recent Results in Cancer Research Ser.: Vol. 56). 1976. 29.10 (ISBN 3-540-07902-5). Springer-Verlag.
Meeting of the Midwest Autumn Immunology Conference, 7th, Michigan, Nov. 1978. Immunologic Tolerance & Macrophage Function: Proceedings. Baram, R., et al, eds. LC 79-243. (Developments in Immunology Ser.: Vol. 4). 1979. 40.00 (ISBN 0-444-00316-9, North Holland). Elsevier.
Unanue, Emil R. & Rosenthal, Alan S., eds. Macrophage Regulation of Immunity. LC 79-24609. 1980. 27.50 (ISBN 0-12-708550-5). Acad Pr.
Wagner, W. H., et al, eds. Activation of Macrophages. (International Congress Ser.: No. 325). 354p. 1974. 65.50 (ISBN 0-444-15114-1, Excerpta Medica). Elsevier.

MACROPHOTOGRAPHY

see also Photomicrography
Hawken, William R. Close-up & Macro Zoom Photography. (Illus.). 128p. (Orig.). 1982. pap. 10.95 (ISBN 0-930764-33-1). Curtin & London.
Kruyt, W. Macro-Photography: Close up Photography Made Easy. (Illus.). 80p. 1972. pap. 5.00x (ISBN 0-85242-624-0). Intl Pubns Serv.

MACROPODIDAE

see Kangaroos

MACRORIE, KEN, 1918-

Macrorie, Ken. A Vulnerable Teacher. 192p. (Orig.). 1974. 6.95 (ISBN 0-8104-5936-1). Hayden.

MCTAGGART, JOHN MCTAGGART ELLIS, 1866-1926

Gale, Richard M. Language of Time. (International Library of Philosophy & Scientific Method). 1968. text ed. 14.50x (ISBN 0-7100-3637-X). Humanities.
Geach, P. T. Truth, Love, & Immortality: An Introduction to McTaggart's Philosophy. LC 78-62842. 1979. 17.95x (ISBN 0-520-03755-3). U of Cal Pr.

MACUMBA (CULTUS)

see Umbanda (Cultus)

MACY, ANNE (SULLIVAN)-1866-1936

Davidson, Margaret. Helen Keller's Teacher. (gr. 4-6). 1972. pap. 1.25 (ISBN 0-590-02224-5, Schol Pap). Schol Bk Serv.
Malone, Mary. Annie Sullivan. LC 71-121943. (See & Read Biographies). (Illus.). (gr. 2-4). 1971. PLB 5.99 (ISBN 0-399-60031-0). Putnam.
Waite, Helen E. Valiant Companions. (gr. 7-11). 1959. 6.25 (ISBN 0-8255-9060-4). Macrae.

MACY, ANNE (SULLIVAN)-1886-1936-DRAMA

Gibson, William. Miracle Worker. (YA) 1957. 8.95 (ISBN 0-394-40630-3). Knopf.

MADAGAMA, CEYLON

Obeyesekere, Gananath. Land Tenure in Village Ceylon. (Cambridge South Asian Studies: No. 4). 1967. 29.95 (ISBN 0-521-05854-6). Cambridge U Pr.

MADAGASCAR

Andriamirado, Sennen. Madagascar Today. 240p. 1979. 14.95 (ISBN 0-686-60755-4, Pub. by J A Editions France). Hippocrene Bks.
Bloch, Maurice. Placing the Dead: Tombs, Ancestral Villages, & Kinship Organization in Madagascar. LC 70-162375. (Seminar Studies in Anthropology). 242p. 1971. 37.00 (ISBN 0-12-785062-7). Acad Pr.
Brown, Mervyn. Madagascar Rediscovered: A History from Early Times to Independence. (Illus.). 1979. 17.50 (ISBN 0-208-01828-X, Archon). Shoe String.
--Madagascar Rediscovered: A History from Early Times to Independence. 1979. pap. text ed. cancelled (ISBN 0-9506284-0-9). Humanities.
Carpenter, Allan & Maginnis, Matthew. Malagasy Republic: Madagascar. LC 72-1460. (Enchantment of Africa Ser.). (Illus.). 96p. (gr. 5 up). 1972. PLB 10.60 (ISBN 0-516-04575-X). Childrens.
Conference Internationale Sur la Conservation De la Nature & De Ses Ressources a Madagascar. (Illus.). 1972. pap. 15.00x (ISBN 2-88032-046-1, IUCN32, IUCN). Unipub.
Copland, Samuel. History of the Island of Madagascar. LC 72-106856. Repr. of 1822 ed. 20.75x (ISBN 0-8371-3478-1, Pub. by Negro U Pr). Greenwood.
Dandoy, Gerard. Economics Villageoises De la Region De Vavatenina (Cote Orientale Malgache) (Atlas Des Structures Agraires a Madagascar: No. 1). (Illus.). 1974. pap. 25.50x (ISBN 90-2797-685-6). Mouton.
Drury, Robert. Madagascar: 0r, Robert Drury's Journal During Fifteen Years' Captivity on That Island, & a Furthur Description of Madagascar by Alexis Rochon. LC 69-19359. (Illus.). 1970. Repr. of 1890 ed. lib. bdg. 18.50x (ISBN 0-8371-1403-9, DRM&). Greenwood.
Ellis, William. Madagascar Revisited. LC 72-5541. (Black Heritage Library Collection Ser). 1972. Repr. of 1867 ed. 30.75 (ISBN 0-8369-9139-7). Arno.
--Three Visits to Madagascar. 1853-1856. 75.00 (ISBN 0-403-00412-8). Scholarly.
Gow, Bonar A. Madagascar & the Protestant Impact. LC 78-11216. (Dalhousie African Studies). 1979. text ed. 42.00x (ISBN 0-8419-0463-4, Africana). Holmes & Meier.
Grandidier, Alfred & Grandidier, Guillaume. Ethnographie de Madagascar, 4 vols. LC 77-87499. Repr. of 1928 ed. Set. 250.00 (ISBN 0-404-16720-9). AMS Pr.
Grandidier, Alfred, ed. Collection des ouvrages anciens concernant Madagascar, 9 vols. LC 74-15041. Repr. of 1920 ed. Set. 595.00 (ISBN 0-404-12063-6); 67.50 ea. AMS Pr.
Jolly, Alison. A World Like Our Own: Man & Nature in Madagascar. LC 80-11871. (Illus.). 1980. 29.95 (ISBN 0-300-02478-9). Yale U Pr.
Keller, Konrad. Madagascar, Mauritius, & the Other East-African Islands. LC 70-89005. (Illus.). Repr. of 1901 ed. 20.50x (ISBN 0-8371-1766-6, Pub. by Negro U Pr). Greenwood.
Kent, Raymond K. Early Kingdoms in Madagascar: 1500-1700. 352p. 1970. 11.50 (ISBN 0-03-084171-2, Pub. by HR&W). Krieger.
--From Madagascar to the Malagasy Republic. LC 75-25489. (Illus.). 182p. 1976. Repr. of 1962 ed. lib. bdg. 15.00x (ISBN 0-8371-8421-5, KEFM). Greenwood.
Koechlin, Bernard. Les Vezo du Sud-Ouest De Madagascar: Contribution a LEtude de L'Eco-Systeme de Semi-Nomades Marins. (Cahiers de L'Homme Nouvelle Ser: No. 15). (Illus.). 243p. (Fr.). 1975. pap. text ed. 16.25x (ISBN 0-686-22586-4). Mouton.
Kottak, Conrad P. The Past in the Present: History, Ecology, and Cultural Variation in Highland Madagascar. (Illus.). 406p. 1980. 18.95x (ISBN 0-472-09323-1); pap. 9.95x (ISBN 0-472-06323-5). U of Mich Pr.
Lavondes, Henri. Bekoropoka: Quelques Aspects De la Vie Familiale et Sociale D'un Village Malgache. (Cahiers De L'homme, Nouvelle Serie: No. 6). 1967. pap. 23.50x (ISBN 90-2796-065-8). Mouton.
Little, Henry W. Madagascar Its History & People. LC 70-129949. Repr. of 1884 ed. 20.75x (ISBN 0-8371-4996-7, Pub. by Negro U Pr). Greenwood.
McLeod, Lyons. Madagascar & Its People. LC 72-82061. (Illus.). Repr. of 1865 ed. 15.00x (ISBN 0-8371-1563-9, Pub. by Negro U Pr). Greenwood.
Marchal, Jean-Yves. La Petite Region dambohimanambola (Sous-Prefecture de Betafo) La Colonisation Agricole au Moyan-Quest Malgache. (Atlas des Structures Agraires au Sud de Madagascar Ser: No. 2). (Illus.). 122p. (Fr.). 1974. pap. text ed. 40.00x (ISBN 90-2797-935-9). Mouton.
Maude, Francis C. Five Years in Madagascar, with Notes on the Military Situation. LC 76-82062. (Illus.). Repr. of 1895 ed. 13.75x (ISBN 0-8371-1571-X, Pub. by Negro U Pr). Greenwood.
Mutibwa, Phares M. The Malagasy & the Europeans. (Ibadan History Ser). (Illus.). 395p. 1974. text ed. 18.00x (ISBN 0-391-00348-8). Humanities.
Oliver, Samuel P. True Story of the French Dispute in Madagascar. LC 77-77209. (Illus.). Repr. of 1885 ed. 14.00x (ISBN 0-8371-1282-6). Greenwood.
Phelps, John W. The Island of Madagascar: A Sketch, Descriptive & Historical. LC 72-4155. (Black Heritage Library Collection Ser.). Repr. of 1883 ed. 12.25 (ISBN 0-8369-9102-8). Arno.
Shaw, George A. Madagascar & France, with Some Account of the Island, Its People, Its Resources & Development. LC 73-82072. (Illus.). Repr. of 1885 ed. 17.00x (ISBN 0-8371-1562-0, Pub. by Negro U Pr). Greenwood.
Sibree, James. Great African Island. LC 76-82472. Repr. of 1880 ed. 16.50x (ISBN 0-8371-1642-2, Pub. by Negro U Pr). Greenwood.
--Madagascar Before the Conquest; the Island, the Country & the People. LC 74-15090. Repr. of 1896 ed. 27.50 (ISBN 0-404-12140-3). AMS Pr.
Sterling Publishing Company Editors. Madagascar: The Malagasy Republic in Pictures. LC 74-82331. (Visual Geography Ser). (Illus.). 64p. (gr. 5 up). 1974. PLB 4.99 (ISBN 0-8069-1189-1); pap. 2.95 (ISBN 0-8069-1188-3). Sterling.
Thompson, Virginia & Adloff, Richard. The Malagasy Republic: Madagascar Today. (Illus.). 1965. 20.00x (ISBN 0-8047-0279-9). Stanford U Pr.

MADEIRA

Nagel's Encyclopedia Guide: Portugal (Madiera, the Azores) (Illus.). 496p. 1974. 30.00 (ISBN 2-8263-0505-0). Masson Pub.
Pink, Annette & Watkins, Paul. See Madeira & the Canaries. (Format's Complete Guides). (Illus.). 144p. 1979. 7.95 (ISBN 0-903372-02-9, Pub by Format Bks England). Hippocrene Bks.
Rogers, Francis M. Atlantic Islanders of the Azores & Madeiras. LC 78-72837. (Illus.). 1979. 17.50 (ISBN 0-8158-0373-7). Chris Mass.
Thomas, Charles W. Adventures & Observations on the West Coast of Africa, & Its Islands. LC 69-18988. (Illus.). Repr. of 1860 ed. 21.50 (ISBN 0-8371-0988-4, Pub. by Negro U Pr). Greenwood.

MADERO, FRANCISCO INDALECIO, PRES. MEXICO, 1873-1913

Cumberland, Charles C. Mexican Revolution, Genesis Under Madero. LC 71-90495. Repr. of 1952 ed. lib. bdg. 19.25x (ISBN 0-8371-2126-4, CUMR). Greenwood.
Ross, Stanley R. Francisco I. Madero: Apostle of Mexican Democracy. LC 79-122591. Repr. of 1955 ed. 26.50 (ISBN 0-404-05409-9). AMS Pr.

MADISON, DOROTHY (PAYNE) TODD, 1768-1849

Arnett, Ethel S. Mrs. James Madison: The Incomparable Dolley. LC 78-183987. (Illus.). 240p. 1972. 10.95 (ISBN 0-911452-00-1). Straughan.
Goodwin, Maud W. Dolly Madison. LC 67-30157. 1967. Repr. of 1896 ed. 16.50 (ISBN 0-87152-039-7). Reprint.
Grant, Matthew G. Dolley Madison. LC 73-15848. 1974. PLB 5.95 (ISBN 0-87191-308-9). Creative Ed.
Johnson, Spencer. The Value of Understanding: The Story of Margaret Mead. LC 79-9800. (ValueTales Ser.). (Illus.). (gr. k-6). 1979. 6.95 (ISBN 0-916392-37-6, Dist. by Oak Tree Pubns). Value Comm.
Thane, Elswyth. Dolly Madison: Her Life & Times. LC 77-108148. (gr. 7 up). 1970. 8.95 (ISBN 0-02-789210-7, CCPr). Macmillan.

MADISON, JAMES, PRES. U. S., 1751-1836

Adams, Henry. History of the United States of America During the Administrations of Jefferson & Madison, 9 vols. 1980. lib. bdg. 995.00 (ISBN 0-8490-3148-6). Gordon Pr.
Burns, Edward M. James Madison, Philosopher of the Constitution. 1968. Repr. lib. bdg. 16.50x (ISBN 0-374-91121-5). Octagon.
Elliot, I., ed. James Madison, 1751-1836: Chronology, Documents, Bibliographical Aids. LC 76-90902. (Presidential Chronology Ser.). 1969. 8.00 (ISBN 0-379-12068-2). Oceana.
Fredman, Lionel E. James Madison, American President & Constitutional Author. Rahmas, D. Steve, ed. LC 74-14592. (Outstanding Personalities Ser.). 32p. 1974. lib. bdg. 2.95 incl. catalog cards (ISBN 0-686-11490-6); pap. 1.50 vinyl laminated covers (ISBN 0-686-11491-4). SamHar Pr.
Gay, Sydney H. James Madison. LC 80-25344. (American Statesmen Ser.). 350p. 1981. pap. 5.95 (ISBN 0-87754-196-5). Chelsea Hse.
--James Madison. Morse, John T., ed. LC 70-128976. (American Statesmen: No. 12). Repr. of 1898 ed. 19.50 (ISBN 0-404-50862-6). AMS Pr.
Hunt, Gaillard. Life of James Madison. LC 66-27105. 1968. Repr. of 1902 ed. 10.00 (ISBN 0-8462-1048-7). Russell.
Koch, Adrienne. Jefferson & Madison: The Great Collaboration. 1964. pap. 8.95 (ISBN 0-19-500420-5, GB). Oxford U Pr.
--Jefferson & Madison: The Great Collaboration. 7.50 (ISBN 0-8446-0743-6). Peter Smith.
--Madison's Advice to My Country. 1966. 17.00 (ISBN 0-691-04524-0); pap. 6.95 (ISBN 0-691-00559-1). Princeton U Pr.
Lecky, William. Historical & Political Essays. LC 76-99707. (Essay Index Reprint Ser). 1908. 18.00 (ISBN 0-8369-1973-4). Arno.
Lodge, Henry C. Historical & Political Essays. LC 72-282. (Essay Index Reprint Ser.). Repr. of 1892 ed. 15.00 (ISBN 0-8369-2801-6). Arno.
Meyers, Marvin, ed. Mind of the Founder: Sources of the Political Thought of James Madison. LC 72-158723. pap. text ed. 7.75x (ISBN 0-8290-0334-7). Irvington.
--The Mind of the Founder: Sources of the Political Thought of James Madison. rev. ed. LC 80-54466. 480p. 1981. pap. 10.00 (ISBN 0-87451-201-8). U Pr of New Eng.
Moore, Virginia. The Madisons: A Biography. 1979. 15.00 (ISBN 0-07-042903-0, P&RB). McGraw.
Rives, William C. History of the Life & Times of James Madison, 3 Vols. facs. ed. LC 76-126253. (Select Bibliographies Reprint Ser). Repr. of 1868 ed. Set. 90.00 (ISBN 0-8369-5480-7). Arno.
Rutland, Robert A. & Hobson, Charles F., eds. The Papers of James Madison: Vol. 11, 7 March 1788-1 March 1789. LC 62-9114. 1978. 15.00x (ISBN 0-8139-0739-X). U Pr of Va.
--The Papers of James Madison, Vol. 13: Twenty January Seventeen Ninety to Thirty-One March Seventeen Ninety-One. LC 62-9144. (Papers of James Madison). 1981. 20.00x (ISBN 0-8139-0861-2). U Pr of Va.
--The Papers of James Madison: Volume 12, 2 March 1789-20 January 1790. with a Supplement 24 October 1775-24 January 1789. LC 62-9114. 1979. 17.50x (ISBN 0-8139-0803-5). U Pr of Va.

MADISON, WISCONSIN

Edelson, Morris. A Madison Journal. 1978. pap. 1.50 (ISBN 0-9600306-0-3). Quixote.
Spielberg, Franklin. Transportation Improvements in Madison, Wisconsin: Preliminary Analysis of Pricing Programs for Roads & Parking in Conjunction with Transit Changes. (An Institute Paper). 65p. 1978. pap. 5.00 (ISBN 0-87766-234-7, 22400). Urban Inst.

MADISONVILLE, OHIO-ANTIQUITIES

Hooton, E. A. Indian Village Site & Cemetery Near Madisonville, Ohio. 1920. pap. 12.00 (ISBN 0-527-01212-2). Kraus Repr.

MADOG AB OWAIN GWYNEDD, 1150-1180?

Deacon, Richard. Madoc & the Discovery of America. LC 67-23398. (Illus.). 1967. 5.00 (ISBN 0-8076-0421-6). Braziller.
Pugh, Ellen. Brave His Soul. LC 70-117619. (Illus.). (gr. 7 up). 1970. 5.95 (ISBN 0-396-06190-7). Dodd.

MADONNA

see Mary, Virgin

MADRAS

Arnold, David. The Congress in Tamiland: Nationalist Politics in South India, Nineteen Nineteen to Nineteen Thirty-Seven. 1977. 12.00x (ISBN 0-88386-958-6). South Asia Bks.
Love, Henry D. Vestiges of Old Madras, 4 Vols. in 3. Repr. of 1913 ed. Set. 127.50 (ISBN 0-404-04060-8). Vol. 1 (ISBN 0-404-04061-6). Vol. 2 (ISBN 0-404-04062-4). Vol. 3 (ISBN 0-404-04063-2). AMS Pr.
Ramaswami, N. S. Founding of Madras. 1977. 5.50x (ISBN 0-8364-0404-1). South Asia Bks.
Washbrook, D. A. The Emergence of Provincial Politics: The Madras Presidency, 1870 to 1920. LC 75-36292. (South Asian Studies: No. 18). (Illus.). 368p. 1976. 39.95 (ISBN 0-521-20982-X). Cambridge U Pr.

MADRID

Kany, Charles E. Life & Manners in Madrid, 1750-1800. LC 70-124773. Repr. of 1932 ed. 31.50 (ISBN 0-404-03634-1). AMS Pr.
Launay, Andre & Pendered, Maureen. Madrid & Southern Spain. 19.95 (ISBN 0-7134-3081-8). David & Charles.
Mitchell, B. Viaje a Madrid. (Illus.). 1975. pap. text ed. 3.00x (ISBN 0-582-36463-9); tapes 19.50x (ISBN 0-582-37190-2); cassette 10.50x (ISBN 0-582-37359-X). Longman.
Williams, L. Toledo & Madrid. 1976. lib. bdg. 59.95 (ISBN 0-8490-2753-5). Gordon Pr.

MADRID-DESCRIPTION-GUIDEBOOKS

Arthur Frommer's Guide to Lisbon-Madrid, 1981-82. 224p. 1981. pap. 2.95 (ISBN 0-671-41433-X). Frommer-Pasmantier.

Beene, Gerrie & King, Lourdes. Dining in Spain: A Guide to Spanish Cooking with Recipes from Its Most Distinguished Restaurants. LC 69-13508. 1969. pap. 2.50 (ISBN 0-8048-0138-X). C E Tuttle.

Berlitz Travel Guide to Madrid. 1977. pap. 2.95 (ISBN 0-02-969340-3, Berlitz). Macmillan.

Gonzalez-Ruano, Cesar. Madrid. 7th ed. LC 66-4369. (Spanish Guide Ser). (Illus.). 1965. 4.50x (ISBN 0-8002-0847-1). Intl Pubns Serv.

MADRID-GALLERIES AND MUSEUMS

Harris, Enriqueta. The Prado, Treasure House of the Spanish Royal Collections. LC 40-322144. 136p. 1940. Repr. 20.00 (ISBN 0-403-04220-8). Somerset Pub.

Mercader, Gasper. El Prado De Valencia. Repr. of 1907 ed. 26.00 (ISBN 0-384-38150-2). Johnson Repr.

Ragghianti, Carlo L. Prado: Madrid. LC 68-20028. (Great Museums of the World Ser.). (Illus.). 1968. 16.95 (ISBN 0-88225-236-4). Newsweek.

MADRIGAL

see also Motet; Part-Songs

Barrett, William A. English Glee & Madrigal Writers. LC 77-75190. 1977. Repr. of 1877 ed. lib. bdg. 10.00 (ISBN 0-89341-089-6). Longwood Pr.

Cartledge, J. A., compiled by. List of Glees, Madrigals, Part-Songs, Etc. in the Henry Watson Music Library. LC 74-80247. (Bibliography & Reference Ser.: No. 362). 1970. Repr. of 1913 ed. lib. bdg. 24.50 (ISBN 0-8337-0483-4). B Franklin.

Chater, James. Luca Marenzio & the Italian Madrigal Fifteen Seventy-Seven to Fifteen Ninety-Three, 2 vols. Fortune, Nigel, ed. (British Studies in Musicology). 1981. Set. price not set (ISBN 0-8357-1242-7, Pub. by UMI Res Pr). Vol. 1 (ISBN 0-8357-1255-9). Vol. 2 (ISBN 0-8357-1256-7). Univ Microfilms.

Cox, Frederick A. English Madrigals in the Time of Shakespeare. LC 77-27932. 1899. 25.00 (ISBN 0-8414-1842-X). Folcroft.

Einstein, A. Italian Madrigal, 3 vols. 1971. Set. 85.00x (ISBN 0-691-09112-9). Princeton U Pr.

Einstein, Alfred, ed. The Golden Age of the Madrigal. Reese, Gustave, tr. LC 74-24074. Repr. of 1942 ed. 24.50 (ISBN 0-404-12902-1). AMS Pr.

Fellowes, Edmund H. English Madrigal Composers. 2nd ed. 1948. pap. 9.95x (ISBN 0-19-315144-8). Oxford U Pr.

Fellowes, Edmund H., ed. English Madrigal Verse: 1588-1632. 3rd ed. 1967. 83.00x (ISBN 0-19-811474-5). Oxford U Pr.

Harman, Alec, ed. Popular Italian Madrigals of the Sixteenth Century. 1977. pap. 9.95 (ISBN 0-19-343646-9). Oxford U Pr.

Lassus, Orlandus. Ten Madrigals. Arnold, Denis, ed. 88p. 9.95 (ISBN 0-19-343668-X). Oxford U Pr.

Ledger, Philip, ed. The Oxford Book of English Madrigals. 1979. pap. 9.95 (ISBN 0-19-343664-7). Oxford U Pr.

Lichtfield, Henry. The First Set of Madrigals of Five Parts. LC 70-38206. (English Experience Ser.: No. 472). 1972. Repr. of 1613 ed. 40.00 (ISBN 90-221-0472-9). Walter J Johnson.

Monteverdi, Claudio. Ten Madrigals. Stevens, Denis, ed. 1979. pap. 9.95 (ISBN 0-19-343676-0). Oxford U Pr.

Newcomb, Anthony. Madrigal at Ferrara, Fifteen Seventy-Nine to Fifteen Ninety-Seven, 2 vols. LC 78-573. (Studies in Music: No. 7). 1979. Set. 60.00x (ISBN 0-691-09125-0). Princeton U Pr.

Ravenscroft, Thomas. A Briefe Discourse of the True Use of Charact'ring the Degrees in Measurable Musicke, 2 pts. LC 70-171785. (English Experience Ser.: No. 409). 108p. 1971. Repr. of 1614 ed. Set. 9.50 (ISBN 90-221-0409-5). Walter J Johnson.

Rimbault, Edward F. Bibliotheca Madrigaliana: A Bibliographical Account of the Musical & Poetical Works Published in England During the 16th & 17th Centuries. 1847. 20.50 (ISBN 0-8337-2996-9). B Franklin.

Rowland, Daniel B. Mannerism - Style & Mood. 1964. 29.50x (ISBN 0-685-69860-2). Elliots Bks.

Scott, Charles K. Madrigal Singing. facsimile ed. LC 77-109634. (Select Bibliographies Reprint Ser). 1931. 15.00 (ISBN 0-8369-5243-X). Arno.

--Madrigal Singing. 2nd ed. Repr. of 1931 ed. lib. bdg. 15.00 (ISBN 0-8371-4330-6, SCMS). Greenwood.

Slim, H. Colin, ed. A Gift of Madrigals & Motets. LC 73-172799. (Illus.). 1973. Set Of 2 Vols. 37.50x (ISBN 0-226-76271-8); Vol. 2. pap. 8.75x (ISBN 0-226-76272-6). U of Chicago Pr.

Stevens, Denis. English Madrigals Five Voice. 1977. pap. 2.95 (ISBN 0-14-070837-5). Penguin.

Stevens, Denis, ed. The Penguin Book of English Madrigals for Four Voices. 1978. pap. 2.95 (ISBN 0-14-070833-2). Penguin.

--The Second Penguin Book of English Madrigals: For Five Voices. 1977. pap. 2.95 (ISBN 0-14-070837-5). Penguin.

Wilbye, John. The Second Set of Madrigales to 3, 4, 5, & 6. Parts Apt Both for Voyals & Voyces. LC 73-6171. (English Experience Ser.: No. 633). 1973. Repr. of 1609 ed. 27.00 (ISBN 90-221-0633-0). Walter J Johnson.

Willbye, John. The First Set of English Madrigals to 3, 4, 5 & 6 Voices, 6 pts. LC 75-38229. (English Experience Ser.: No. 493). 160p. 1972. Repr. of 1598 ed. 26.50 (ISBN 90-221-0493-1). Walter J Johnson.

Yonge, Nicholas. Musica Transalpina. Madrigales Translated 4, 5 & 6 Parts. LC 77-38232. (English Experience Ser.: No. 496). 346p. 1972. Repr. of 1588 ed. 58.00 (ISBN 90-221-0496-6). Walter J Johnson.

MAECENATISM

see Art Patronage; Authors and Patrons

MAETERLINCK, MAURICE, 1862-1949

Baily, Auguste. Maeterlinck. LC 74-6385. (Studies in French Literature, No. 45). 1974. lib. bdg. 31.95 (ISBN 0-8383-1877-0). Haskell.

Bithell, Jethro. Life & Writings of Maurice Maeterlinck. LC 71-160743. 1971. Repr. of 1913 ed. 12.50 (ISBN 0-8046-1556-X). Kennikat.

Clark, Macdonald. Maurice Maeterlinck Poet & Philosopher. 1916. Repr. 30.00 (ISBN 0-8274-2694-1). R West.

Ellehauge, Martin. Striking Figures Among Modern English Dramatists. LC 72-195909. 1931. lib. bdg. 15.00 (ISBN 0-8414-3895-1). Folcroft.

Flaccus, Louis W. Artists & Thinkers. facs. ed. LC 67-23218. (Essay Index Reprint Ser). 1916. 15.00 (ISBN 0-8369-0444-3). Arno.

Halls, W. D. Maurice Maeterlinck: A Study of His Life & Thought. LC 78-16379. 1978. Repr. of 1960 ed. lib. bdg. 17.50x (ISBN 0-313-20574-4, HAMM). Greenwood.

Hanse. Maeterlinck. 16.50 (ISBN 0-685-34935-7). French & Eur.

Harry, Gerard. Maurice Maeterlinck: A Biographical Study with Two Essays by M. Maeterlinck. 1910. Repr. 30.00 (ISBN 0-8274-2692-5). R West.

Heller, Otto. Prophets of Dissent: Essays on Maeterlinck, Strindberg, Nietzsche & Tolstoy. LC 68-26246. 1968. Repr. of 1918 ed. 12.00 (ISBN 0-8046-0200-X). Kennikat.

Knapp, Bettina L. Maurice Maeterlinck. (World Authors Ser.: France: No. 342). 1975. lib. bdg. 10.95 (ISBN 0-8057-2562-8). Twayne.

Mahony, P. Magic of Maeterlinck. LC 52-489. 1951. 14.00 (ISBN 0-527-60750-9). Kraus Repr.

Newman, Ernest. Musical Studies. LC 68-25297. (Studies in Music, No. 42). 1969. Repr. of 1910 ed. lib. bdg. 36.95 (ISBN 0-8383-0309-9). Haskell.

Rose, Henry. Maeterlinck's Symbolism: The Blue Bird. LC 74-10729. 1910. 12.50 (ISBN 0-8414-7315-3). Folcroft.

--On Maeterlinck. LC 73-21891. (Studies in French Literature, No. 45). 1974. lib. bdg. 49.95 (ISBN 0-8383-1829-0). Haskell.

Slosson, Edwin E. Major Prophets of To-Day. facs. ed. LC 68-8493. (Essay Index Reprint Ser). 1914. 18.00 (ISBN 0-8369-0882-1). Arno.

Taylor, Una. Maurice Maeterlinck, a Critical Study. LC 67-27657. Repr. of 1915 ed. 11.50 (ISBN 0-8046-0462-2). Kennikat.

Thomas, E. Maurice Maeterlinck. LC 73-21707. (Studies in French Literature, No. 45). 1974. lib. bdg. 43.95 (ISBN 0-8383-1826-6). Haskell.

Worth, Katharine. The Irish Drama of Europe from Yeats to Beckett. LC 78-18909. 1978. text ed. 35.25x (ISBN 0-391-00891-9, Athlone Pr). Humanities.

MAFIA

Abadinsky, Howard. The Mafia in America: An Oral History. 160p. 1981. 19.95 (ISBN 0-03-059587-8). Praeger.

Albini, Joseph L. American Mafia: Genesis of a Legend. LC 70-147120. (Orig.). 1979. Repr. of 1971 ed. 22.50x (ISBN 0-89197-013-4). Irvington.

Allen, Edward J. Merchants of Menace - the Mafia: A Study of Organized Crime. (Illus.). 344p. 1962. ed. spiral bdg. 24.50photocopy (ISBN 0-398-04187-3). C C Thomas.

Anderson, Annelise G. The Business of Organized Crime: A Cosa Nostra Family. (Publications 201 Ser.). (Illus.). 200p. 1979. 13.95 (ISBN 0-8179-7011-8). Hoover Inst Pr.

Blok, Anton. The Mafia of a Sicilian Village, 1860-1960. (State & Revolution Ser). 1974. pap. 4.95x (ISBN 0-06-131790-X, TB1790, Torch). Har-Row.

Bramanti, Edward. The Political Theory of the Italian, the Irish, & the Jewish Mafia, 2 vols. in one. (Illus.). 200p. 1976. 59.45 (ISBN 0-913314-78-1). Am Classical Coll Pr.

Campbell, Rodney. The Luciano Project: The Secret Wartime Collaboration of the Mafia & the U.S. Navy. 1977. 9.95 (ISBN 0-07-009674-0, GB). McGraw.

Catania, Enzo. Mafia. (Illus.). 136p. 1980. pap. 8.95 (ISBN 0-312-50402-0). St Martin.

Cressey, Donald R. Theft of the Nation: The Structure & Operations of Organized Crime in America. 1969. pap. 4.95x (ISBN 0-06-131934-1, TB1934, Torch). Har-Row.

Demaris, Ovid. The Last Mafioso. 560p. 1981. pap. 3.95 (ISBN 0-553-20230-8). Bantam.

--The Last Mafioso: The Treacherous World of Jimmy Fratianno. 1981. 15.00 (ISBN 0-8129-0955-0). Times Bks.

Eisenberg, Dennis, et al. Meyer Lansky: Mogul of the Mob. LC 79-15979. (Illus.). 1979. 11.95 (ISBN 0-448-22206-X). Paddington.

Hammer, Richard & Gosch, Marvin. The Last Testament of Lucky Luciano. 1981. pap. 3.50 (ISBN 0-440-14705-0). Dell.

Hanna, David. The Mafia: Two Hundred Years of Terror. (Orig.). 1980. pap. 2.25 (ISBN 0-532-23131-7). Woodhill.

Hayes, John P. Lonely Fighter: One Man's Battle with the United States Government. 1979. 10.00 (ISBN 0-8184-0270-9). Lyle Stuart.

Hess, Genner. Mafia & Mafiosi: The Structure of Power. Orig. Title: Mafia Power Structure. 1973. 18.50 (ISBN 0-347-01008-3, 86272-X, Pub. by Saxon Hse). Lexington Bks.

Ianni, Francis A. & Ianni, Elizabeth R. A Family Business: Kinship & Social Control in Organized Crime. LC 72-75320. 1972. 10.00 (ISBN 0-87154-396-6). Russell Sage.

Kwitny, Jonathan. Vicious Circles. 1979. 14.95 (ISBN 0-393-01188-7). Norton.

--Vicious Circles: The Mafia in the Marketplace. 432p. 1981. pap. 6.95 (ISBN 0-393-00029-X). Norton.

Mazzola, Reparata & Gibson, Sonny. Mafia Kingpin. LC 81-47703. (Illus.). 512p. 1981. 14.95 (ISBN 0-448-11990-0). G&D.

Servadio, Gaia. Mafioso: A History of the Mafia from Its Origins to the Present Day. LC 76-12980. (Illus.). 1976. 10.00 (ISBN 0-685-70108-5). Stein & Day.

Verra, Vincent L. Death in the Family: The Mafia Way. LC 75-32924. (Illus.). 192p. 1976. pap. 1.25 (ISBN 0-89041-047-X, 3047). Major Bks.

Yards, A. Mafia-Syndicate: Organized Crime - the Government Within the Government. LC 76-23355. 202p. 1977. pap. 4.95 (ISBN 0-686-22703-4). A Yards.

MAGARS

Hitchcock, John T. Magars of Banyan Hill. LC 66-11715. (Case Studies in Cultural Anthropology). (Illus.). 1966. pap. text ed. 5.95 (ISBN 0-03-055305-9, HoltC). HR&W.

MAGAZINE ADVERTISING

see Advertising, Magazine

MAGAZINES

see Periodicals

MAGELLAN, FERDINAND (FERNAO MAGALHAES) d. 1521

Harley, Ruth. Ferdinand Magellan. new ed. LC 78-18058. (Illus.). 48p. (gr. 4-7). 1979. PLB 5.89 (ISBN 0-89375-176-6); pap. 1.75 (ISBN 0-89375-168-5). Troll Assocs.

Nowell, Charles E., ed. Magellan's Voyage Around the World: Three Contemporary Accounts. (Illus.). 1962. 16.95x (ISBN 0-8101-0180-7). Northwestern U Pr.

Parr, Charles M. So Noble a Captain: The Life & Times of Ferdinand Magellan. LC 75-31439. (Illus.). 423p. 1976. Repr. of 1953 ed. lib. bdg. 29.75x (ISBN 0-8371-8521-1, PASN). Greenwood.

Pigafetta, Antonio. First Voyage Around the World by Magellan, 1581-1521. Stanley Of Alderly, ed. 1963. 32.00 (ISBN 0-8337-3363-X). B Franklin.

--Magellan's Voyage: A Narrative Account of the First Circumnavigation, 2 Vols. Skelton, R. A., tr. (Illus.). 1969. Set. slipcased 145.00x (ISBN 0-300-01164-4). Yale U Pr.

MAGELLAN, FERDINAND (FERNAO MAGALHAES) d. 1521-JUVENILE LITERATURE

Brownlee, W. D. The First Ships Around the World. LC 76-22430. (Cambridge Topic Bks). (Illus.). (gr. 5-10). 1977. PLB 5.95 (ISBN 0-8225-1204-1). Lerner Pubns.

Guillemard, Francis H. Life of Ferdinand Magellan & the First Circumnavigation of the Globe. LC 70-127901. Repr. of 1890 ed. 26.00 (ISBN 0-404-02947-7). AMS Pr.

Magellan. (gr. 1). 1974. pap. text ed. 2.80 (ISBN 0-205-03877-8, 8038775); tchrs'. ed. 12.00 (ISBN 0-205-03866-2, 803866X). Allyn.

Schecter, Darrow. I Can Read About Magellan. new ed. LC 78-73713. (Illus.). (gr. 3-6). 1979. pap. 1.25 (ISBN 0-89375-209-6). Troll Assocs.

Syme, Ronald. Magellan: First Around the World. (Illus.). (gr. 3-7). 1953. PLB 6.24 (ISBN 0-688-31594-1). Morrow.

Wilkie, Katherine. Ferdinand Magellan: Noble Captain. (gr. 4-6). 1963. pap. 2.44 (ISBN 0-395-01751-3, Piper). HM.

MAGELLAN, STRAIT OF

Sarmiento De Gamboa, Pedro. Narratives of the Voyages of Pedro Sarmiento De Gamboa to the Straits of Magellan. Markham, Clements R., ed. & tr. LC 74-136043. (Hakluyt Society First Ser: No. 91). 1970. lib. bdg. 32.00 (ISBN 0-8337-2239-5). B Franklin.

MAGELLANIC CLOUDS

Hodge, Paul W. & Wright, Frances W. The Small Magellanic Cloud. LC 76-49159. (Illus.). 80p. 1978. 55.00 (ISBN 0-295-95387-X). U of Wash Pr.

Symposium on the Magellanic Clouds, Santiago De Chile, March 1969. The Magellanic Clouds. Muller, A. B., ed. LC 73-154743. (Astrophysics & Space Science Library: No.23). 189p. 1971. lib. bdg. 26.00 (ISBN 90-277-0205-5, Pub. by Reidel Holland). Kluwer Boston.

MAGENDIE FRANCOIS, 1783-1855

Olmsted, J. M. D. Francois Magendie. Cohen, I. Bernard, ed. LC 80-2139. (Illus.). 1981. Repr. of 1944 ed. lib. bdg. 28.00 (ISBN 0-405-13894-6). Arno.

MAGI

Butler, E. M. The Myth of the Magus. LC 78-73950. 1979. 36.00 (ISBN 0-521-22564-7); pap. 8.95 (ISBN 0-521-29554-8). Cambridge U Pr.

Hill & Roberts. Secret of the Star. (Arch Bks: Set 3). 1966. laminated bdg. 0.79 (ISBN 0-570-06021-4, 59-1130). Concordia.

The Moost Excellent Treatise of the Thre Kynges of Coleyne. LC 74-80169. (English Experience Ser: No. 648). (Illus.). 91p. 1974. Repr. of 1499 ed. 9.50 (ISBN 9-0221-0648-9). Walter J Johnson.

O'Rourke, John J. & Greenburg, S. Thomas, eds. Symposium on the Magisterium: A Positive Statement. 1978. 5.95 (ISBN 0-8198-0559-9); pap. 4.50 (ISBN 0-8198-0560-2). Dghtrs St Paul.

Sturdevant, Winifred. The Misterio De los Reyes Magos, Its Position in the Development of the Mediaeval Legend of the Three Kings. Repr. of 1927 ed. 15.50 (ISBN 0-384-58735-6). Johnson Repr.

MAGI-FICTION

Atiyeh, Wadeeha. Fourth Wise Man. (gr. 4 up). 1959. pap. 1.50 (ISBN 0-8315-0038-7). Speller.

Blanco, Thomas. The Child's Gift: A Twelfth Night Tale. LC 75-46530. (Illus.). 1976. 8.95 (ISBN 0-664-32595-5). Westminster.

MAGIC

Here are entered works dealing with occult science (supernatural arts). Works on modern parlor magic, legerdemain, prestidigitation, etc. are entered under the heading Conjuring.

see also Alchemy; Amulets; Cabala; Charms; Conjuring; Crystal-Gazing; Divination; Idols and Images; Incantations; Indians of North America-Magic; Mana; Medicine, Magic, Mystic, and Spagiric; Occult Sciences; Symbolism of Numbers; Talismans; Tantrism; Witchcraft

Adams, William H. D. Witch, Warlock, & Magician. LC 73-5621. 1971. Repr. of 1889 ed. 37.00 (ISBN 0-8103-3619-7). Gale.

Agrippa, Henry C. The Philosophy of Natural Magic. 1974. 8.95 (ISBN 0-8216-0218-7). Univ Bks.

Agrippa, Nettesheim & Heinrich, Cornelius. Three Books of Occult Philosophy or Magic. LC 79-8222. (Illus.). Repr. of 1898 ed. 34.50 (ISBN 0-404-18401-4). AMS Pr.

Bandler, Richard & Grinder, John. Structure of Magic, Vol.1. LC 75-12452. 1975. 8.95 (ISBN 0-8314-0044-7). Sci & Behavior.

--Structure of Magic, Vol. 2. LC 75-12452. 1976. write for info. (ISBN 0-8314-0049-8). Sci & Behavior.

Baroja, Julio C. World of the Witches. Glendinning, O. N., tr. LC 64-15829. (Nature of Human Society Ser). 1965. 15.00x (ISBN 0-226-03762-2). U of Chicago Pr.

Benson, Robert H. The Necromancers. LC 75-36826. (Occult Ser.). 1976. Repr. of 1909 ed. 18.00x (ISBN 0-405-07939-7). Arno.

Bias, Clifford, compiled by. Ritual Book of Magic. 160p. 1981. pap. 6.95 (ISBN 0-87728-532-2). Weiser.

Blackman, James R. The Big Book of Tricks & Magic. (gr. 2 up). 1966. 2.95 (ISBN 0-394-80632-8, BYR). Random.

Blackstone, Harry. Blackstone's Secrets of Magic. pap. 2.00 (ISBN 0-87980-260-X). Wilshire.

--Secrets of Magic. 2.95 (ISBN 0-685-47574-3). Wehman.

Bode, Carl. Practical Magic: Poems. LC 80-17597. viii, 54p. 1981. 10.95x (ISBN 0-8040-0362-9); pap. 4.95 (ISBN 0-8040-0373-4). Swallow.

Bowness, Charles. Romany Magic. 96p. 1973. 4.50 (ISBN 0-87728-201-3). Weiser.

Bradley, Donald A. Picking Winners. 1981. pap. 2.00 (ISBN 0-87542-043-5). Llewellyn Pubns.

Braid, James. Magic, Witchcraft, Animal Magnetism, Hypnotism, & Electro-Biology. 1976. Repr. 25.00 (ISBN 0-685-71981-2, Regency). Scholarly.

Brockel, Ray & White, Laurence B., Jr. Abra-Ca-Dazzle: Easy Magic Tricks. Fay, Ann, ed. (Idea Bks.). (Illus.). 48p. (gr. 2 up). 1981. 6.95 (ISBN 0-8075-0121-2). A Whitman.
Brown, Handy N. Necromancer, Or, Voo-Doo Doctor. LC 77-39544. Repr. of 1904 ed. 13.50 (ISBN 0-404-00008-8). AMS Pr.
Buckley, Arthur H. Principles & Deceptions. (Illus.). 224p. 1973. pap. 4.00 (ISBN 0-911996-40-0). Gamblers.
Buckley, Arthur H. & Cook, John B. Gems of Mental Magic. 132p. 1973. pap. 4.00 (ISBN 0-911996-39-7). Gamblers.
Budge, E. Wallis. Egyptian Magic. 1971. pap. 3.50 (ISBN 0-486-22681-6). Dover.
Butler, E. M. Ritual Magic. LC 80-19324. 329p. 1980. Repr. of 1971 ed. lib. bdg. 10.95x (ISBN 0-89370-601-9). Borgo Pr.
--Ritual Magic. 1971. pap. 3.45 (ISBN 0-87877-001-1, W-1). Newcastle Pub.
--Ritual Magic. LC 78-73949. 1979. 36.00 (ISBN 0-521-22563-9); pap. 9.95 (ISBN 0-521-29553-X). Cambridge U Pr.
Butler, W. E. Magic: Its Ritual Power & Purpose. pap. 5.95 (ISBN 0-87728-157-2). Weiser.
Cavendish, Richard. A History of Magic. LC 76-56613. (Illus.). 1980. pap. 5.95 (ISBN 0-8008-3887-4). Taplinger.
Charney, David, ed. Magic: Secrets of the Great Illusions Revealed. LC 74-24286. (Strawberry-Hill Book). (Illus.). 247p. 1975. 9.95 (ISBN 0-8129-0512-1). Times Bks.
Christian, Paul. History & Practice of Magic. 1969. pap. 4.95 (ISBN 0-8065-0126-X). Citadel Pr.
Christopher, Milbourne. Panorama of Magic. (Illus., Orig.). 1962. pap. 4.95 (ISBN 0-486-20774-9). Dover.
Clodd, Edward. Magic in Names, & in Other Things. LC 67-23906. 1968. Repr. of 1920 ed. 19.00 (ISBN 0-8103-3024-5). Gale.
Clough, Nigel R. How to Make & Use Magic Mirrors. (Orig.). 1977. pap. 1.50 (ISBN 0-87728-314-1). Weiser.
Crow, W. B. Witchcraft, Magic & Occultism. pap. 5.00 (ISBN 0-87980-173-5). Wilshire.
Crowley, Aleister. Magick. Symonds, John & Grant, Kenneth, eds. LC 74-24002. (Illus.). 511p. 1974. Repr. of 1973 ed. 25.00 (ISBN 0-87728-254-4). Weiser.
--Magick in Theory & Practice. (Illus.). 480p. 1976. pap. 6.00 (ISBN 0-486-23295-6). Dover.
--Magick, in Theory & Practice. 10.00 (ISBN 0-8446-5476-0). Peter Smith.
--Vision & the Voice. 7.50 (ISBN 0-685-47278-7). Weiser.
Crowly, Aleister. Crowley on Magick. 1982. 35.00 (ISBN 0-87542-111-3). Llewellyn Pub.
David-Neel, Alexandra. Magic & Mystery in Tibet. (Illus.). 8.50 (ISBN 0-8446-0073-3). Peter Smith.
Davidson, Ronald H. & Day, Richard. Symbol & Realization: A Contribution to the Study of Magic & Healing. (Research Monograph: No. 12). 1974. 8.75 (ISBN 0-686-23615-7, Ctr South & Southeast Asia Studies). Cellar.
Davies, Thomas W. Magic, Divination & Demonology Among the Hebrews & Their Neighbors. 1898. 10.00x (ISBN 0-87068-051-X). Ktav.
De Claremont, Lewis. Ancients Book of Magic. 2.95 (ISBN 0-685-21876-7). Wehman.
Denning & Phillips. Apparel of High Magick. (Magickal Philosophy Ser.: Vol. 2). (Illus.). 200p. 1975. 10.00 (ISBN 0-87542-177-6). Llewellyn Pubns.
--Mysteria Magica. (Magical Philosphy Ser.: Vol. 5). 1981. 10.00 (ISBN 0-87542-180-6). Llewellyn Pubns.
--Robe & Ring. (Magickal Philosophy Ser.: Vol. 1). (Illus.). 1974. 10.00 (ISBN 0-87542-176-8). Llewellyn Pubns.
--Sword & Serpent. (Magickal Philosophy Ser.: Vol. 3). (Illus.). 250p. 1975. 10.00 (ISBN 0-87542-178-4). Llewellyn Pubns.
Denning, Melita & Phillips, Osborne. Llewellyn Practical Guide to the Evocation of the Gods. 1981. 5.95 (ISBN 0-686-73839-X). Llewellyn Pubns.
De Pascale, Marc. Book of Spells. LC 70-163218. (Illus.). 1971. 6.95 (ISBN 0-8008-0933-5). Taplinger.
Downs, Nelson T. The Art of Magic. Hilliard, John N., ed. 8.75 (ISBN 0-8446-5753-0). Peter Smith.
Downs, T. Nelson. The Art of Magic. Hilliard, John N., ed. Date not set. 8.75 (ISBN 0-8446-5753-0). Peter Smith.
Drury, Nevill. Don Juan, Mescalito & Modern Magic: The Mythology of Inner Space. 1978. pap. 7.95 (ISBN 0-7100-8582-6). Routledge & Kegan.
--Inner Visions: Explorations in Magical Consciousness. (Illus.). 1979. 15.95 (ISBN 0-7100-0257-2); pap. 9.95 (ISBN 0-7100-0184-3). Routledge & Kegan.
Elliot, Bruce. Classic Secrets of Magic. (Illus.). 226p. (Orig.). 1969. pap. 4.95 (ISBN 0-571-09019-2, Pub. by Faber & Faber). Merrimack Bk Serv.
Elliott, Robert C. Power of Satire: Magic, Ritual, Art. 1960. pap. 7.95 (ISBN 0-691-01276-8). Princeton U Pr.
Evans-Pritchard, Edward E. Witchcraft, Oracles & Magic Among the Azande. 1937. 52.50x (ISBN 0-19-823103-2). Oxford U Pr.
Fisher, John. Body Magic. LC 78-6387. (Illus.). 158p. 1980. pap. 6.95 (ISBN 0-8128-6088-8). Stein & Day.
Fitzkee, Dariel. The Card Expert Entertains. 10.00 (ISBN 0-685-36856-4). Borden.
--Magic by Misdirection. 13.50 (ISBN 0-685-36855-6). Borden.
--Showmanship for Magicians. 12.50 (ISBN 0-685-36854-8). Borden.
--The Trick Brain. 15.00 (ISBN 0-685-36853-X). Borden.
FitzSimons, Raymund. Death & the Magician. LC 80-21071. 1981. 10.95 (ISBN 0-689-11122-3). Atheneum.
Frazer, James G. Aftermath: A Supplement to The Golden Bough. LC 75-41104. Repr. of 1937 ed. 34.00 (ISBN 0-404-14543-4). AMS Pr.
--Golden Bough. abr ed. 19.95 (ISBN 0-02-095560-X); pap. 8.95 (ISBN 0-685-15196-4). Macmillan.
--New Golden Bough. abridged ed. Gaster, Theodor H., ed. LC 59-6125. 1959. 19.95 (ISBN 0-87599-036-3). S G Phillips.
Frederick, Guy. One Hundred One Best Magic Tricks. 1979. pap. 1.50 (ISBN 0-451-08956-1, W8956, Sig). NAL.
Gardner, G. B. High Magic's Aid. LC 74-84852. 1975. pap. 3.95 (ISBN 0-87728-278-1). Weiser.
Gibson, Walter B. Fell's Beginner's Guide to Magic. LC 76-17125. 160p. 1976. 8.95 (ISBN 0-8119-0271-4); pap. 4.95 (ISBN 0-8119-0364-8). Fell.
--New Magician's Manual. LC 73-87046. (Illus.). 144p. 1975. pap. 4.00 (ISBN 0-486-23113-5). Dover.
--Popular Card Tricks. pap. 3.50 (ISBN 0-685-36859-9). Borden.
--Professional Magic for Amateurs. (Illus.). 225p. 1974. pap. 3.50 (ISBN 0-486-23012-0). Dover.
--Professional Magic for Amateurs. (Illus.). 5.00 (ISBN 0-8446-5035-8). Peter Smith.
Gill, Robert, ed. Magic As a Performing Art: A Bibliography of Conjuring. 1976. 15.95 (ISBN 0-85935-038-X). Bowker.
Givry, Grillot De. Witchcraft, Magic & Alchemy. (Illus.). 11.00 (ISBN 0-8446-0113-6). Peter Smith.
Gleadow, Rupert. Magic & Divination. (Illus.). 308p. 1976. Repr. of 1941 ed. 17.50x (ISBN 0-87471-808-2). Rowman.
--Magic & Divination. (Illus.). 1977. Repr. of 1941 ed. 25.00x (ISBN 0-7158-1148-7). Charles River Bks.
Gonzalez-Wippler, Migene. The Complete Book of Spells, Ceremonies, & Magic. (Illus.). 1977. 12.95 (ISBN 0-517-52885-1). Crown.
Grant, Kenneth. Magical Revival. LC 72-185895. 7.95 (ISBN 0-87728-217-X). Weiser.
Gray, William G. Inner Traditions of Magic. 1978. pap. 5.95 (ISBN 0-87728-153-X). Weiser.
--Self Made by Magic. 1976. 10.00 (ISBN 0-87728-333-8). Weiser.
Gross, Henry. Pure Magic. (Illus.). 1979. pap. 7.95 (ISBN 0-684-15337-8, SL 751, ScribT). Scribner.
Haining, Peter, ed. The Black Magic Omnibus. LC 75-28511. (Illus.). 450p. 1976. 10.95 (ISBN 0-8008-0809-6). Taplinger.
Hall, Manly P. Magic: A Treatise on Esoteric Ethics. pap. 1.75 (ISBN 0-89314-384-7). Philos Res.
Hall, Trevor H. Old Conjuring Books. ltd. ed. 228p. 1973. 54.00x (ISBN 0-7156-0678-6, Pub. by Duckworth England). Biblio Dist.
Hartmann, Franz. Magic White & Black. 1971. pap. 4.95 (ISBN 0-87877-003-8, P-3). Newcastle Pub.
Hay, Henry. The Amateur Magician's Handbook. 3rd, rev. ed. LC 72-78265. (Illus.). 400p. 1972. 12.95 (ISBN 0-690-05711-3). T Y Crowell.
--Learn Magic. LC 74-80337. (Illus.). 320p. 1975. Repr. of 1947 ed. 3.95 (ISBN 0-486-21238-6). Dover.
Hay, Henry, ed. Cyclopedia of Magic. LC 74-27511. (Illus.). 512p. 1975. pap. 4.00 (ISBN 0-486-21808-2). Dover.
Hills, Christopher. White Magic: The Power of Consciousness. Massy, Robert, ed. LC 75-46096. (Illus.). Date not set. pap. 14.95 (ISBN 0-916438-20-1). Univ of Trees.
Houdini, Harry. Miracle Mongers & Their Methods: A Complete Expose. LC 80-84404. (Skeptic's Bookshelf Ser.). 240p. 1981. Repr. of 1920 ed. 13.95 (ISBN 0-87975-143-6). Prometheus Bks.
--The Right Way to Do Wrong. 96p. 1974. pap. 2.50 (ISBN 0-911996-43-5). Gamblers.
Hugard, Jean & Braue, Frederick. Royal Road to Card Magic. 304p. 1949. 7.95 (ISBN 0-571-11399-0, Pub. by Faber & Faber). Merrimack Bk Serv.
Hunderfund, Richard. Magic, Myths & Medicine. (Illus.). 1980. 13.95x (ISBN 0-89863-036-3). Star Pub CA.
James, Stewart. Abbott's Encyclopedia of Rope Tricks for Magicians. (Illus.). 6.75 (ISBN 0-8446-5206-7). Peter Smith.
James First King Of England. Daemonologie, in Forme of a Dialogue. (English Experience Ser.: No. 94). 1969. Repr. of 1597 ed. 13.00 (ISBN 90-221-0094-4). Walter J Johnson.
Jennings, Gary. Black Magic, White Magic. 160p. (YA) 1975. pap. 0.95 (ISBN 0-440-31037-7, LFL). Dell.
Kaufman, Hal & Schroeter, Bob. Hocus-Focus. (Orig.). 1981. pap. 1.75 (ISBN 0-451-09781-5, E9781, Sig). NAL.
Kaye, Marvin. The Handbook of Mental Magic. LC 75-9830. 1977. 5.95 (ISBN 0-8128-2253-6). Stein & Day.
--Stein & Day Handbook of Magic. LC 73-817930. 1975. pap. 3.95 (ISBN 0-8128-1803-2). Stein & Day.
King, Francis. Sexuality, Magic & Perversion. 208p. 15.00x (ISBN 0-686-75477-8, Pub. by Spearman England). State Mutual Bk.
King, Francis & Skinner, Stephen. Techniques of High Magic. pap. 6.95 (ISBN 0-89281-030-0, Destiny Bks). Inner Tradit.
Knight, G. Practice of Ritual Magic. (Paths to Inner Power Ser.). 1.25 (ISBN 0-685-01083-X). Weiser.
Kosky, Gerald. Magic of Gerald Kosky. 25.00 (ISBN 0-685-64527-4). Borden.
Kris, Ernst & Kurz, Otto. Legend, Myth, & Magic in the Image of the Artist: A Historical Experiment. LC 78-24024. (Illus.). 175p. 1981. pap. 5.95 (ISBN 0-300-02669-2, Y-386). Yale U Pr.
Lamb, Geoffrey. Illustrated Magic Dictionary. (Illus.). 160p. 1980. 7.95 (ISBN 0-525-66689-3). Elsevier-Nelson.
Lang, Andrew. Magic & Religion. LC 76-137255. Repr. of 1901 ed. 12.50 (ISBN 0-404-03857-3). AMS Pr.
Legeza, Laszlo. Tao Magic: The Chinese Art of the Occult. LC 75-10369. (Illus.). 128p. 1975. pap. 4.95 (ISBN 0-394-73125-5). Pantheon.
Leland, Charles G. Gypsy Sorcery & Fortune-Telling. (Illus.). 6.00 (ISBN 0-8446-0181-0). Peter Smith.
Leuba, James H. Psychological Study of Religion: Its Origin, Function, & Future. LC 75-98628. Repr. of 1912 ed. 24.50 (ISBN 0-404-03969-3). AMS Pr.
Levi, Eliphas. History of Magic. 75.00 (ISBN 0-8490-0332-6). Gordon Pr.
--Transcendental Magic. Waite, A. E., tr. from Fr. LC 72-16629. (Illus.). 1980. pap. 7.95 (ISBN 0-87728-079-7). Weiser.
Levy, Robert & Joseph, Joan. Robert Levy's Magic Book. LC 76-16016. (Illus.). 216p. (gr. 10 up). 1976. 5.95 (ISBN 0-87131-219-0). M Evans.
Lewin, Ronald. The American Magic. 1982. 15.95 (ISBN 0-374-10417-4). FS&G.
Lewis, Shari & Hurwitz, Abraham B. Magic for Non-Magicians. LC 75-17014. (Illus.). 160p. 1975. 5.95 (ISBN 0-87477-043-2). J P Tarcher.
Long, Max F. Tarot Card Symbology. 2nd ed. Wingo, E. Otha, ed. (Illus.). 1972. pap. 8.50x (ISBN 0-910764-03-4). Huna Res Inc.
Malak, Frater. The Mystic Grimoire of Mighty Spells & Rituals. 1976. 10.95 (ISBN 0-13-609107-5, Parker). P-H.
Maple, Eric. Deadly Magic. 1976. pap. 3.95 (ISBN 0-87728-354-0). Weiser.
Marechal, Greer. The Complete Magician. 8.95 (ISBN 0-498-01985-3); pap. 5.95 (ISBN 0-498-01974-8). A S Barnes.
Maria, Constantino de. Enciclopedia de la Magia y de la Brujeria. 660p. (Espn.). 1971. 35.95 (ISBN 84-315-0672-5, S-14961). French & Eur.
Marshall, Jay. How to Perform Instant Magic. rev. ed. 192p. 1981. pap. 8.95 (ISBN 0-89196-107-0, Domus Bks). Quality Bks IL.
Maskelyne, Nevil. Maskelyne on the Performance of Magic. LC 75-22648. 160p. 1976. pap. 2.00 (ISBN 0-486-23238-7). Dover.
--Maskelyne on the Performance of Magic. 4.25 (ISBN 0-8446-5221-0). Peter Smith.
Mathers, S. L. The Book of the Sacred Magic of Abramelin the Mage. LC 75-12248. 320p. 1975. pap. 4.50 (ISBN 0-486-23211-5). Dover.
Mauss, Marcel. A General Theory of Magic. Brain, Robert, tr. from Fr. 152p. 1972. 14.95 (ISBN 0-7100-7338-0). Routledge & Kegan.
--A General Theory of Magic. 160p. (Eng.). 1975. pap. 2.45 (ISBN 0-393-00779-0, Norton Lib). Norton.
Mulholland, John. Magic of the World. LC 65-21366. (Encore Edition). 1965. 2.95 (ISBN 0-684-15428-5, ScribT). Scribner.
Mumford, Jonn. Sexual Occultism. (Illus.). 150p. 1975. 10.00 (ISBN 0-87542-491-0). Llewellyn Pubns.
Murray, Margaret. God of the Witches. (Illus.). 1970. pap. 5.95 (ISBN 0-19-501270-4, GB). Oxford U Pr.
Nelms, H. Magic & Showmanship. 3.95 (ISBN 0-685-38463-2). Wehman.
Newall, Venetia, ed. The Witch Figure: Essays in Honor of Katharine M. Briggs. (Illus.). 1973. 19.95 (ISBN 0-7100-7696-7). Routledge & Kegan.
Norvell. The Miracle of Prosperity Magic. LC 80-29147. 214p. 1981. 12.95 (ISBN 0-13-585547-0, Parker). P-H.
O'Keefe, Daniel L. Stolen Lightening. 368p. 1981. 24.95 (ISBN 0-8264-0059-0). Continuum.
Ophiel. Art & Practice of Talismanic Magic. pap. 5.00 (ISBN 0-87728-445-8). Weiser.
Page, Patrick. The Big Book of Magic. (Illus.). (YA) 1976. 9.95 (ISBN 0-8037-0565-4). Dial.
Paulsen, Kathryn. The Complete Book of Magic & Witchcraft. rev. ed. 1980. pap. 1.75 (ISBN 0-451-09180-9, E9180, Sig). NAL.
Pecor, Charles J. Craft of Magic, Easy-to-Learn Illusions for Spectacular Performance. (Illus.). 1979. text ed. 14.95 (ISBN 0-13-188847-1, Spec); pap. 6.95 (ISBN 0-13-188839-0, Spec). P-H.
Perry, Margaret. Rainy Day Magic: The Art of Making Sunshine on a Rainy Day. LC 77-122817. 160p. (gr. 3 up). 1970. 5.95 (ISBN 0-87131-087-2). M Evans.
Perry, W. J. Origin of Magic & Religion. LC 73-118543. 1971. Repr. of 1923 ed. 13.00 (ISBN 0-8046-1168-8). Kennikat.
Proskauer, Julien J. Spook Crooks: Exposing the Secrets of the Propheteers Who Conduct Our Wickedest Industry. LC 70-162517. (Illus.). 1971. Repr. of 1932 ed. 22.00 (ISBN 0-8103-3760-6). Gale.
Redgrove, H. Stanley. Magic & Mysticism: Studies in Bygone Beliefs. 1970. 7.95 (ISBN 0-8216-0111-3). Univ Bks.
Redgrove, Herbert S. Bygone Beliefs: Being a Series of Excursions in the Byways of Thought. (Folklore & Society Ser). (Illus.). 1969. Repr. of 1920 ed. 23.00 (ISBN 0-384-50050-1). Johnson Repr.
Reed, Kathie. Enchanted Things. 1975. 3.95 (ISBN 0-87212-043-0). Libra.
Regardie, Israel. The Golden Dawn. 4th ed. 1978. Repr. of 1921 ed. 29.95 (ISBN 0-87542-664-6). Llewellyn Pubns.
--Middle Pillar. 154p. 1978. cancelled (ISBN 0-87542-665-4); pap. 4.95 (ISBN 0-87542-658-1). Llewellyn Pubns.
Roheim, Geza. Animism, Magic & the Divine King. LC 78-190281. 390p. 1972. Repr. of 1930 ed. text ed. 30.00 (ISBN 0-8236-0150-1). Intl Univs Pr.
Rohmer, Sax. The Romance of Sorcery. 1973. Repr. of 1914 ed. 22.00 (ISBN 0-685-70657-5). Gale.
Salverte, Eusebe. The Philosophy of Magic. large type ed. pap. 4.75 (ISBN 0-910122-41-5). Amherst Pr.
Scarne, John. One-Hundred Scarne's Magic Tricks. 1975. pap. 1.95 (ISBN 0-346-12206-6). Cornerstone.
Schindler, George. Presto! Magic for the Beginner. 1977. pap. 5.00 (ISBN 0-89515-000-X). Reiss Pub.
Scot, Reginald. The Discoverie of Witchcraft. (Illus.). xxxvii, 283p. 1972. pap. 3.50 (ISBN 0-486-22880-0). Dover.
--The Discoverie of Witchcraft. LC 75-171789. (English Experience Ser.: No. 299). 560p. 1971. Repr. of 1584 ed. 72.00 (ISBN 90-221-0299-8). Walter J Johnson.
Scott, C. Initiate. pap. 6.95 (ISBN 0-87728-361-3). Weiser.
--Initiate in the Dark Cycle. pap. 5.95 (ISBN 0-686-76832-9). Weiser.
--Initiate in the New World. pap. 5.95 (ISBN 0-87728-363-X). Weiser.
Severn, Bill. Bill Severn's Guide to Magic As a Hobby. (Illus.). 1979. pap. 9.95 (ISBN 0-679-51202-0). McKay.
--More Magic in Your Pockets. (Illus.). 1980. 8.95 (ISBN 0-679-20806-2). McKay.
Shah, Idries. Secret Lore of Magic. 1970. pap. 3.95 (ISBN 0-8065-0004-2). Citadel Pr.
Shah, Indries. Secret Lore of Magic. 9.95 (ISBN 0-685-22099-0). Wehman.
Shah, Sayed I., ed. Secret Lore of Magic. 1965. Repr. of 1957 ed. text ed. 11.50x (ISBN 0-584-10250-X). Humanities.
Simpson, Jacqueline, tr. Legends of Icelandic Magicians. (Folklore Society Mistletoe Ser). 120p. 1975. 11.50x (ISBN 0-87471-763-9). Rowman.
Tavenner, Eugene. Studies in Magic from Latin Literature. LC 16-25151. Repr. of 1916 ed. 16.50 (ISBN 0-404-06350-0). AMS Pr.
Terweil, Bareno J. Monks & Magic: An Analysis of Religious Ceremonies in Central Thailand. (Scandinavian Institute of Asian Studies Monographs: No. 24). (Orig.). 1976. pap. text ed. 13.75x (ISBN 0-7007-0091-9). Humanities.
Thurston, Howard. Fascinating Magic Tricks. 3.00 (ISBN 0-685-41931-2). Wehman.
--Four Hundred Fascinating Magic Tricks You Can Do. pap. 3.00 (ISBN 0-87980-257-X). Wilshire.

Turner, Robert, tr. from Latin. Arbatel of Magic. LC 79-88512. (Illus.). 1979. Repr. of 1655 ed. 10.00 (ISBN 0-935214-03-8). Heptangle.
Wagner, Bob & Adams, Howard. Magic Dungeon Mentallism. 7.50 (ISBN 0-685-36858-0). Borden.
Waite, Arthur E. Book of Ceremonial Magic. 1970. pap. 3.95 (ISBN 0-8065-0208-8). Citadel Pr.
Walker, D. P. Spiritual & Demonic Magic: From Ficino to Campanella. LC 74-34547. 244p. 1975. pap. 5.95x (ISBN 0-268-01670-4). U of Notre Dame Pr.
Webster, Hutton. Magic: A Sociological Study. LC 73-4244. xv, 524p. 1973. Repr. of 1948 ed. lib. bdg. 26.50x (ISBN 0-374-98318-6). Octagon.
Weinstein, Marion. Marion Weinstein's Earth Magic: A Dianic Book of Shadows. (Illus., Orig.). 1980. pap. 4.95 (ISBN 0-9604128-1-6). Earth Magic.
--Positive Magic. rev. ed. (Illus.). 320p. 1981. pap. 7.95 (ISBN 0-919345-00-X). Phoenix Pub WA.
Wells, Harold B. You Can Be a Magician. 128p. (Orig.). 1976. pap. 2.25 (ISBN 0-8024-9823-X). Moody.
Wels, Byron. Magic Made Easy. 1971. pap. 2.00 (ISBN 0-87980-090-9). Wilshire.
Whetmore, Edward J. The Magic Medium. 256p. 1981. pap. text ed. 11.95x (ISBN 0-534-00922-0). Wadsworth Pub.
White, Nelson & White, Anne. Secret Magick Revealed. LC 79-63571. (Illus.). 128p. (Orig.). 1979. pap. 25.00 (ISBN 0-686-30201-X, Magick Circle). Tech Group.
--Working High Magic. LC 81-51402. (Illus.). 125p. (Orig.). 1981. pap. 30.00 (ISBN 0-939856-15-8). Tech Group.
White, Nelson H. An Introduction to Magick. (Ritual Magick Ser.: No. 1). (Orig.). 1972. pap. 3.00 (ISBN 0-939856-00-X, Magick Circle). Tech Group.
--Magick & the Law, or, Getting What You Want from the Government, the Courts & Private Persons, Inc. Protecting What You Write & Say. LC 80-50273. (Magick & the Law Ser.: Vol. 3). (Illus.). 125p. (Orig.). 1980. pap. 15.00 (ISBN 0-939856-09-3, Magick Circle). Tech Group.
--Magick & the Law, or, How to Keep What You've Got & How to Protect Yourself from Assorted Crooks & Nuts. LC 80-50273. (Magick & the Law Ser.: Vol. 2). (Illus.). 100p. (Orig.). 1980. pap. 15.00 (ISBN 0-939856-08-5, Magick Circle). Tech Group.
--Magick & the Law, or, How to Organize & Operate Your Own Occult Church, Coven or Lodge. rev. ed. LC 76-7197. (Magick & the Law Ser.: Vol. 1). 48p. 1976. pap. 9.00 (ISBN 0-939856-02-6, Magick Circle). Tech Group.
Wilde, Jane. Ancient Cures, Charms & Usages of Ireland. 59.95 (ISBN 0-87968-626-X). Gordon Pr.
Witch Hunting, Magic & the New Philosophy: An Introduction to Debates of the Scientific Revolution, 1450-1750. (Harvester Studies in Philosophy: No. 14). (Illus.). 283p. 1981. 42.50 (ISBN 0-391-01806-X); pap. 16.50 (ISBN 0-391-01808-6). Humanities.
Woodman, David. White Magic & English Renaissance Drama. LC 72-423. 148p. 1973. 12.00 (ISBN 0-8386-1125-7). Fairleigh Dickinson.
Ziolkowski, Theodore. Disenchanted Images: A Literary Iconology. 1977. text ed. 20.00 (ISBN 0-691-06334-6). Princeton U Pr.

MAGIC–HISTORY

Bouisson, Maurice. Magic: Its History & Principal Rites. Almayrac, G., tr. from Fr. LC 79-8094. Repr. of 1961 ed. 31.00 (ISBN 0-404-18405-7). AMS Pr.
Bronowski, Jacob. Magic, Science, & Civilization. LC 78-1660. (Bampton Lectures in America: No. 20). 88p. 1978. 10.00 (ISBN 0-231-04484-4); pap. 4.95 (ISBN 0-231-04485-2). Columbia U Pr.
Butler, Eliza M. The Myth of the Magus. LC 78-14108. (Illus.). 1979. Repr. of 1948 ed. 23.50 (ISBN 0-88355-781-9). Hyperion Conn.
Cavendish, Richard. History of Magic. LC 76-56613. (Illus.). 1977. 9.95 (ISBN 0-8008-3886-6). Taplinger.
De Camp, L. Sprague & De Camp, Catherine C. Spirits, Stars, & Spells: The Profits & Perils of Magic. LC 65-25470. (Illus.). 348p. 1980. 17.00 (ISBN 0-913896-17-9). Owlswick Pr.
Ennemoser, Joseph. The History of Magic. large type ed. (Illus.). pap. 8.50 (ISBN 0-910122-45-8). Amherst Pr.
Evans, Henry. History of Conjuring & Magic. 59.95 (ISBN 0-8490-0322-9). Gordon Pr.
A History of White Magic. 1979. pap. 6.95 (ISBN 0-87728-482-2). Weiser.
Levi, Eliphas. History of Magic. 1980. pap. 7.95 (ISBN 0-87728-077-0). Weiser.
--The Key of the Mysteries. 1980. pap. 6.95 (ISBN 0-87728-078-9). Weiser.
Loomis, C. Grant. White Magic: An Introduction to the Folklore of Christian Legend. 1967. Repr. of 1948 ed. 8.00 (ISBN 0-910956-26-X). Medieval Acad.
Page, Peter L. Magic, Psychology & Spiritism. (Illus.). 1979. 47.50 (ISBN 0-930582-50-0). Gloucester Art.
Peters, Edward. The Magician, the Witch & the Law. LC 78-51341. (Middle Ages Ser.). 1978. 18.00x (ISBN 0-8122-7746-5). U of Pa Pr.
Ross, Thomas. A Book of Elizathan Magic: Thomas Hill's Naturall & Artificial Conclusions. 84p. 1974. 11.00 (ISBN 3-4180-0204-8). Adler.
Thompson, C. J. Mysteries & Secrets of Magic. LC 78-174119. (Tower Bks). (Illus.). 1971. Repr. of 1928 ed. 28.00 (ISBN 0-8103-3213-2). Gale.
Thorndike, Lynn. A History of Magic & Experimental Science, 8 vols. Incl. Vols. 1 & 2. The First Thirteen Centuries. 1923. Vol. 1. (ISBN 0-231-08794-2); Vol. 2. (ISBN 0-231-08795-0); Vols. 3 & 4. Fourteenth & Fifteenth Centuries. Vol. 3. (ISBN 0-231-08796-9); Vol. 4. (ISBN 0-231-08797-7); Vols. 5 & 6. The Sixteenth Century. 1941. Vol. 5. (ISBN 0-231-08798-5); Vol. 6. (ISBN 0-231-08799-3); Vols. 7 & 8. The Eighteenth Century. 1958. Vol. 7. (ISBN 0-231-08800-0); Vol. 8. (ISBN 0-231-08801-9). LC 23-2984. 30.00x ea. Columbia U Pr.
--Place of Magic in the Intellectual History of Europe. LC 70-177455. (Columbia University Studies in the Social Sciences: No. 62). Repr. of 1905 ed. 14.50 (ISBN 0-404-51062-0). AMS Pr.
Vetter, George B. Magic & Religion: Their Origins & Consequences. LC 73-82103. 1958. 6.00 (ISBN 0-8022-1776-1). Philos Lib.

MAGIC–JUVENILE LITERATURE

Adams, Pam, illus. Magic. (Imagination Ser.). (Illus.). 32p. (Orig.). 1978. 4.50 (ISBN 0-85953-104-X, Pub. by Child's Play England); pap. 3.00 (ISBN 0-85953-081-7). Playspaces.
Ames, Gerald & Wyler, Rose. Magic Secrets. LC 67-4229. (I Can Read Ser.). (Illus.). 1978. pap. 1.95 (ISBN 0-06-444007-9, Trophy). Har-Row.
Appel, Benjamin. Man & Magic. (Illus.). (gr. 7 up). 1966. PLB 5.69 (ISBN 0-394-91370-1). Pantheon.
Avent, Sue. Spells, Chants, & Potions. LC 77-22779. (Myth, Magic & Superstition Ser.). (Illus.). (gr. 4-5). 1977. PLB 10.65 (ISBN 0-8172-1035-0). Raintree Pubs.
Boyar, Jay. Be a Magician! How to Put on a Magic Show & Mystify Your Friends. LC 80-26799. (Illus.). 160p. (gr. 7 up). 1981. PLB 10.29 (ISBN 0-671-42273-1). Messner.
Broekel, Ray & White, Laurence. Now You See It: Easy Magic for Beginners. (Illus.). (gr. 1-3). 1979. 6.95 (ISBN 0-316-93595-6). Little.
Broekel, Ray & White, Laurence B., Jr. Now You See It: Easy Magic for Beginners. (Illus.). 64p. 1980. pap. 1.50 (ISBN 0-590-30876-9, Schol Pap). Schol Bk Serv.
Brown, Bob. How to Fool Your Friends. (Kids Paperbacks). (gr. 3 up). 1978. PLB 7.62 (ISBN 0-307-63435-3, Golden Pr); pap. 1.95 (ISBN 0-307-12082-1). Western Pub.
Cohen, Daniel. Ceremonial Magic. LC 78-20429. (Illus.). 160p. (gr. 7 up). 1979. 7.95 (ISBN 0-590-07466-0, Four Winds). Schol Bk Serv.
Educational Challenges, Inc. Magic Does the Trick. (Turning Point II Ser.). (Illus.). 32p. (gr. 7-12). 1978. pap. text ed. 2.80 (ISBN 0-8009-1961-0). McCormick-Mathers.
Eldin. Making Magic. (Glouster Press Ser.). (gr. 4 up). 1980. PLB 5.90 (ISBN 0-531-03422-4, B22). Watts.
Gardner, Robert. Magic Through Science. LC 77-76239. (gr. 3-5). 1978. 6.95 (ISBN 0-385-12437-6); PLB (ISBN 0-385-12438-4). Doubleday.
Gibson, Walter B. Junior Magic. LC 76-58624. (Illus.). (gr. 5 up). 1977. 7.95 (ISBN 0-8069-4546-X); PLB 7.49 (ISBN 0-8069-4547-8). Sterling.
Gilbert, George & Rydell, Wendy. Great Tricks of the Master Magicians. 1978. PLB 13.77 (ISBN 0-307-68606-X, Golden Pr); pap. 5.95 (ISBN 0-307-16806-9). Western Pub.
Glickman, Paul. Magic Tricks. (gr. 1-3). 1980. PLB 8.60 (ISBN 0-531-04141-7). Watts.
Goma, Eulalia. Diccionario Magico Infantil. 7th ed. 50p. (Espn.). 1978. 10.75 (ISBN 84-324-0190-0, S-26065). French & Eur.
--Diccionario Magico Infantil En Seis Lenguas. 2nd ed. 96p. (Span., Cata., Vasco, Galle., Fr. & Eng.). 1978. 20.25 (ISBN 84-324-0249-4, S-50028). French & Eur.
Heger, Robert & Polachek, Marianne. The Two-Sided Trick Book. (Illus.). (gr. 2-8). 1979. pap. text ed. 3.50x (ISBN 0-87879-216-3). Acad Therapy.
Herrmann, Charles F., III. The Trick Book. McCarthy, Pat, ed. (Pal Paperbacks Kit B Ser.). (Illus., Orig.). (gr. 7-12). 1974. pap. text ed. 1.25 (ISBN 0-8374-3514-5). Xerox Ed Pubns.
Kobs, Betty & Kobs, Douglas. Magic, Magic. LC 76-53540. (Games & Activities Ser.). (Illus.). (gr. k-5). 1977. PLB 10.65 (ISBN 0-8172-0070-3). Raintree Pubs.
Lewis, Shari. Magic Show in a Book. LC 79-23941. (Kids-Only Club Bks.). (Illus.). 96p. (Orig.). (gr. 3-6). 1980. pap. 3.95 (ISBN 0-03-049746-9). HR&W.
--Magic Show in a Box. (gr. 4-6). 1981. pap. 1.95 (ISBN 0-03-049731-0). HR&W.
Magic Wanda's Dynamite Magic Book. (gr. 5 up). 1978. pap. 1.50 (ISBN 0-590-11808-0, Schol Pap). Schol Bk Serv.
Marks, Burton. Magic Tricks. (Illus.). 32p. 1981. pap. 3.95 (ISBN 0-89844-078-5). Troubador Pr.
Miller, Jay & Miller, Frank. Magic Tricks. LC 74-11891. (Early Craft Bks.). (Illus.). 32p. (gr. 1-4). 1975. PLB 3.95 (ISBN 0-8225-0865-6). Lerner Pubns.
Olney, Ross R. & Olney, Pat. Easy to Make Magic. LC 79-97630. (Easy to Make Ser.). (Illus.). (gr. 1-3). 1979. PLB 5.79 (ISBN 0-8178-6330-3). Harvey.
Severn, Bill. Bill Severn's Big Book of Close-up Magic. (gr. 7 up). 1978. 8.95 (ISBN 0-679-20453-9). McKay.
--Bill Severn's Big Book of Magic. (Illus.). (gr. 7 up). 1980. pap. 4.95 (ISBN 0-679-20534-9). McKay.
Shalit, Nathan. Science Magic Tricks: Over 50 Fun Tricks That Mystify & Dazzle. LC 79-18645. (Illus.). 128p. (gr. 4-7). 1981. 8.95 (ISBN 0-03-047116-8); pap. 3.95 (ISBN 0-03-059269-0). HR&W.
Sleator, William. That's Silly. LC 80-21902. (Illus.). (gr. k-3). 1981. 8.25 (ISBN 0-525-40981-5, Smart Cat). Dutton.
Stoddard, Edward. The First Book of Magic. 1980. pap. 1.75 (ISBN 0-380-49221-0, 49221, Camelot). Avon.
Supraner, Robyn. Magic Tricks You Can Do! LC 80-19780. (Illus.). 48p. (gr. 1-5). 1981. PLB 6.92 (ISBN 0-89375-418-8); pap. 1.95 (ISBN 0-89375-419-6). Troll Assocs.
Walter, Marion. Another Magic Mirror Book. (gr. k-3). 1978. pap. 1.50 (ISBN 0-590-11826-9, Schol Pap). Schol Bk Serv.

MAGIC, AFRICAN

Friedrich, Adolf. Afrikanische Priestertuemer. pap. 31.00 (ISBN 0-384-16920-1). Johnson Repr.
Retel-Laurentin, Anne. Oracles et Ordalies Chez les Nzakara. (Le Monde D'outre-Mer Passe & Present, Etudes: No. 33). 1969. pap. 38.50x (ISBN 90-2796-269-3). Mouton.

MAGIC, ANGLO-SAXON

Briggs, Katherine M. Pale Hecates Team: Examination of the Beliefs on Witchcraft and Magic Among Shakespeare's Contemporaries & His Immediate Succesors. Dorson, Richard M., ed. LC 77-70582. (International Folklore Ser.). (Illus.). 1977. lib. bdg. 18.00x (ISBN 0-405-10083-3). Arno.
Storms, Godfrid. Anglo-Saxon Magic. LC 75-11736. (Limited 100 copies). 1975. Repr. of 1948 ed. lib. bdg. 35.00 (ISBN 0-8414-7842-2). Folcroft.

MAGIC, EGYPTIAN

Brier, Bob. Ancient Egyptian Magic. LC 80-15608. (Illus.). 322p. 1981. Repr. of 1980 ed. 14.95 (ISBN 0-688-03654-6); pap. price not set. Morrow.
Budge, E. Wallis. Egyptian Magic. (Illus.). 8.00 (ISBN 0-8446-0044-X). Peter Smith.
--Egyptian Magic. (Illus.). 1979. pap. 6.95 (ISBN 0-7100-0135-5). Routledge & Kegan.
Budge, Wallis. Egyptian Magic. 1978. pap. 3.95 (ISBN 0-8065-0629-6). Citadel Pr.
--Egyptian Magic. 1974. 5.95 (ISBN 0-8216-0176-8). Univ Bks.
David, Rosalie. Cult of the Sun: Myth & Magic in Ancient Egypt. (Illus.). 208p. 1980. 24.50x (ISBN 0-460-04284-X, Pub. by J M Dent England). Biblio Dist.
Leontianoff, Igor. The Cult of Magic in Ancient Egypt & Among the Jews. (Illus.). 141p. 1980. deluxe ed. 69.75 (ISBN 0-89266-258-1). Am Classical Coll Pr.

MAGIC, FILIPINO

Lieban, Richard W. Cebuano Sorcery: Malign Magic in the Philippines. 1967. 16.50x (ISBN 0-520-00749-2); pap. 4.95x (ISBN 0-520-03420-1). U of Cal Pr.

MAGIC, GERMANIC

Grimm, Jacob. Teutonic Mythology, 4 Vols. 4th ed. Stallybrass, James S., tr. Set. 50.00 (ISBN 0-8446-2168-4). Peter Smith.

MAGIC, GIPSY

Trigg, Elwood B. Gypsy Demons & Divinities: The Magic & Religion of the Gypsies. 256p. 1974. 7.95 (ISBN 0-8065-0379-3). Citadel Pr.

MAGIC, HAITIAN

Herskovits, Melville J. Life in a Haitian Valley. 1964. lib. bdg. 18.00x (ISBN 0-374-93857-1). Octagon.

MAGIC, HAWAIIAN

Long, Max F. Secret Science at Work. 1953. 8.50 (ISBN 0-87516-046-8). De Vorss.
--Secret Science Behind Miracles. 1948. pap. 6.50 (ISBN 0-87516-047-6). De Vorss.
Thompson, Vivian. Meet the Hawaiian Menehunes. (Illus.). 1967. pap. 3.25 (ISBN 0-912180-08-0). Petroglyph.

MAGIC, INDIAN

see Indians of North America–Magic

MAGIC, INDIC

McIver, Brady V. The Stupendous & Awful Powers of the Art of Magic in India. (Illus.). 147p. 1980. deluxe ed. 69.85 (ISBN 0-89920-015-X). Am Inst Psych.

MAGIC, JAPANESE

Davis, Winston. Dojo: Magic & Exorcism in Modern Japan. LC 79-64219. (Illus.). 1980. 18.50x (ISBN 0-8047-1053-8). Stanford U Pr.

MAGIC, JEWISH

Leontianoff, Igor. The Cult of Magic in Ancient Egypt & Among the Jews. (Illus.). 141p. 1980. deluxe ed. 69.75 (ISBN 0-89266-258-1). Am Classical Coll Pr.
Thompson, Campbell. Semitic Magic: Its Origin & Development. 19.95x (ISBN 0-87068-172-9). Ktav.
Thompson, Reginald C. Semitic Magic: Its Origins & Development. LC 73-18858. Repr. of 1908 ed. 24.50 (ISBN 0-404-11361-3). AMS Pr.

MAGIC, MALAYAN

Skeat, Walter W. Malay Magic: Being an Introduction to the Folklore & Popular Religion of the Malay Peninsula. LC 70-174437. (Illus.). 1973. Repr. of 1900 ed. lib. bdg. 28.00 (ISBN 0-405-08980-5). Arno.

MAGIC SQUARES

see also Mathematical Recreations

Benson, William H. & Jacoby, Oswald. New Recreations with Magic Squares. LC 74-28909. 192p. (Orig.). 1976. pap. 4.00 (ISBN 0-486-23236-0). Dover.
Benson, William H. & Oswald, Jacoby. Magic Cubes: New Recreations, 2 pts. (Illus.). 96p. (Orig.). 1981. pap. 4.00 (ISBN 0-486-24140-8). Dover.
Blaisdell, Frank E. Magical Fun with Magic Squares. Walker, Barbara, ed. (Illus.). 86p. (Orig.). 1978. pap. 10.00 (ISBN 0-915926-35-0). Magic Ltd.
Falkener, Edward. Games Ancient & Oriental & How to Play Them. (Illus.). 1892. pap. 4.00 (ISBN 0-486-20739-0). Dover.
Fults, John L. Magic Squares. LC 73-23041. (Illus.). 112p. 1974. 9.95 (ISBN 0-87548-317-8); pap. 2.95 (ISBN 0-87548-198-1). Open Court.

MAGICIANS

Berlinski, Allen. Purvis: The Newcastle Conjuror. (Illus.). 39p. (Orig.). 1981. pap. 10.00x (ISBN 0-916638-25-1). Meyerbooks.
Burlingame, Hardin J. Leaves from Conjurors' Scrap Books, Or, Modern Magicians & Their Works. LC 74-148349. 1971. Repr. of 1891 ed. 22.00 (ISBN 0-8103-3371-6). Gale.
Butler, Eliza M. The Myth of the Magus. LC 78-14108. (Illus.). 1979. Repr. of 1948 ed. 23.50 (ISBN 0-88355-781-9). Hyperion Conn.
Butler, W. E. Magician-His Training & Work. pap. 3.00 (ISBN 0-87980-212-X). Wilshire.
Church, Alfred J. Stories of the Magicians. Repr. of 1887 ed. 25.00 (ISBN 0-89987-109-7). Darby Bks.
Corey, Stephen. The Last Magician. LC 81-50605. (Illus.). 64p. (Orig.). 1981. 25.00 (ISBN 0-931956-06-4); pap. 6.50 (ISBN 0-931956-03-X); hand made paper jacket 10.00 (ISBN 0-931956-12-9); handbound 60.00 (ISBN 0-931956-10-2). Water Mark.
Edmonds, I. G. The Magic Brothers: Carl & Alexander Herrmann. LC 79-1516. (Illus.). 1979. 7.95 (ISBN 0-525-66644-3). Elsevier-Nelson.
--The Magic Makers: Magic & the Men Who Made It. LC 76-145. (Illus.). 192p. (gr. 6 up). 1976. 7.95 (ISBN 0-525-66476-9). Elsevier-Nelson.
Edwards, Anne. The Great Houdini. LC 76-8472. (See & Read Biographies). (Illus.). (gr. k-3). 1977. PLB 5.99 (ISBN 0-399-61020-0). Putnam.
Fortman, Jan. Houdini & Other Masters of Magic. LC 77-12638. (Myth, Magic & Superstition Ser.). (Illus.). (gr. 4-5). 1977. PLB 10.65 (ISBN 0-8172-1032-6). Raintree Pubs.
Furst, Arnold. Famous Magicians of the World. Date not set. pap. 3.00 (ISBN 0-685-55923-8). Borden.
--Famous Magicians of the World. 1957. 3.00 (ISBN 0-915926-08-3). Magic Ltd.
Gibson, Walter. Dunninger's Secrets. LC 73-76823. 220p. 1974. 7.95 (ISBN 0-8184-0166-4). Lyle Stuart.
Lamb, Geoffrey F. Magicians. LC 79-366524. (Pegasus Books: No. 15). (Illus.). 1968. 7.50x (ISBN 0-234-77022-8). Intl Pubns Serv.
Lovitt, Chip. Masters of Magic. (gr. 7-12). 1979. pap. 1.25 (ISBN 0-590-05754-5, Schol Pap). Schol Bk Serv.
Nelms, Henning. Magic & Showmanship: A Handbook for Conjurers. (Illus.). 6.00 (ISBN 0-8446-0818-1). Peter Smith.

MAGINN, WILLIAM, 1793-1842
Thrall, Miriam M. Rebellious Fraser's: Nol Yorke's Magazine in the Days of Maginn, Thackeray & Carlyle. LC 35-1070. Repr. of 1934 ed. 19.50 (ISBN 0-404-06458-2). AMS Pr.
MAGISTRATES
see Judges; Justices of the Peace
MAGNA CARTA
Ashley, Maurice. Magna Carta in the Seventeenth Century. LC 65-23456. (Illus., Orig.). 1965. pap. 1.95x (ISBN 0-8139-0014-X). U Pr of Va.
Browning, Charles H. Magna Charta Barons & Their American Descendants: Lineal Descents from Them of the Members of the Baronial Order of Runnemede. LC 69-17125. (Illus.). 1969. Repr. of 1915 ed. 17.50 (ISBN 0-8063-0056-6). Genealog Pub.
--Magna Charta Barons & Their American Descendants, Together with the Pedigrees of the Founders of the Order of Runnemede. LC 73-77634. (Illus.). 1969. Repr. of 1898 ed. 18.50 (ISBN 0-8063-0055-8). Genealog Pub.
Coke, Sir Edward. Coke on Magna Carta: The Common Law. 1979. lib. bdg. 75.00 (ISBN 0-8490-2885-X). Gordon Pr.
Goodhart, Arthur L. Law of the Land. LC 66-16914. 1966. pap. 1.95x (ISBN 0-8139-0108-1). U Pr of Va.
Jones, J. A. King John & the Magna Carta. (Illus.). 1971. pap. text ed. 5.50x (ISBN 0-582-31463-1). Longman.
McKechnie, William S. Magna Carta: A Commentary on the Great Charter of King John, with Historical Introduction. 2nd ed. 1914. 35.00 (ISBN 0-8337-2330-8). B. Franklin.
Magna Carta. 1981. 6.00x (ISBN 0-7141-0473-6, Pub. by Brit Lib England). State Mutual Bk.
Pallister, Anne. Magna Carta: The Heritage of Liberty. 144p. 1971. 22.50x (ISBN 0-19-827181-6). Oxford U Pr.
Thompson, Faith. First Century of Magna Carta: Why It Persisted As a Document. LC 66-27166. 1967. Repr. of 1925 ed. 7.50 (ISBN 0-8462-1033-9). Russell.
--Magna Carta: Its Role in the Making of the English Constitution, 1300-1629. LC 70-159233. x, 410p. 1971. Repr. of 1948 ed. lib. bdg. 20.00x (ISBN 0-374-97870-0). Octagon.
Wright, Louis B. Magna Carta & the Tradition of Liberty. Bourne, Russell, ed. LC 76-9244. (Illus.). 64p. 1976. pap. 1.50 (ISBN 0-916200-12-4). US Capitol Hist Soc.
MAGNESIUM
Aikawa, Jerry K. Magnesium: It's Biologic Significance. 144p. 1981. 44.95 (ISBN 0-8493-5871-X). CRC Pr.
--Relationship of Magnesium to Disease in Domestic Animals & in Humans. (Illus.). 160p. 1971. 16.75 (ISBN 0-398-02215-1). C C Thomas.
American Welding Society. Magnesium-Alloy Welding Rods & Bare Electrodes: A5.19-69. 3.50 (ISBN 0-685-65980-1). Am Welding.
Kenney, George B. An Analysis of the Energy Efficiency & Economic Viability of Expanded Magnesium Utilization. LC 78-75004. (Outstanding Dissertations on Energy Ser.). 1979. lib. bdg. 20.00 (ISBN 0-8240-3975-0). Garland Pub.
Magnesium Storage, Handling & Processing. (Forty Ser). 1974. pap. 2.50 (ISBN 0-685-58155-1, 48). Natl Fire Prot.
Seelig, Mildred S., ed. Magnesium Deficiency in the Pathogenesis of Disease. (Topics in Bone & Mineral Disorders Ser.). 500p. 1980. 39.50 (ISBN 0-306-40202-5, Plenum Pr). Plenum Pub.
Standard for the Manufacture of Aluminum or Magnesium Powder. (Sixty Ser). 1974. pap. 2.00 (ISBN 0-685-58073-3, 651). Natl Fire Prot.
Wacker, Warren E. Magnesium & Man. LC 80-14189. (Commonwealth Fund Ser.). 1980. text ed. 17.50x (ISBN 0-674-54225-8). Harvard U Pr.
MAGNESIUM METABOLISM
see also Grass Tetany
Cantin, Marc & Seelig, Mildred S., eds. Magnesium in Health & Disease. LC 78-13181. (Monographs of the Am College of Nutrition: Vol. 4). (Illus.). 1154p. 1980. 200.00 (ISBN 0-89335-055-9). Spectrum Pub.
MAGNESYN
see Synchros
MAGNETIC DOMAIN
see Domain Structure
MAGNETIC FIELDS
see also Electromagnetic Fields; Galvanomagnetic Effects; Hyperfine Interactions; Magnetic Resonance
Barnes, Thomas. Origin & Destiny of the Earth's Magnetic Field. LC 73-79065. (ICR Technical Monograph: No. 4). (Illus.). 64p. 1973. pap. 4.95 (ISBN 0-89051-013-X). CLP Pubs.
Barnothy, Madeline F., ed. Biological Effects of Magnetic Fields. Incl. Vol. 1. 324p. 1964. 35.00 (ISBN 0-306-37601-6); Vol. 2. 314p. 1969. 35.00 (ISBN 0-306-37602-4). Plenum Pr). Plenum Pub.
Canuto, V., ed. Role of Magnetic Fields in Physics & Astrophysics, Vol. 257. (Annals of the New York Academy of Sciences). 226p. 1975. 36.00x (ISBN 0-89072-012-6). NY Acad Sci.
Chari, M. V. & Silvester, P., eds. Finite Elements in Electrical & Magnetic Field Problems. LC 79-10377. (Wiley Series in Numerical Methods in Engineering). 1980. 42.25 (ISBN 0-471-27578-6, Pub. by Wiley-Interscience). Wiley.
Cheston, Warren B. Elementary Theory of Electric & Magnetic Fields. LC 64-17135. 1964. text ed. 22.50x (ISBN 0-471-15459-8). Wiley.
Davis, Albert R. & Rawls, Walter C., Jr. Magnetism & Its Effects on the Living System. LC 74-84423. 1974. 8.50 (ISBN 0-682-48087-8, University). Exposition.
Knoepfel, H. & Herlach, F., eds. Megagauss Magnetic Field Generation by Explosives & Related Experiments: Proceedings of the EUR-CNEN Association Meetings, Frascati, Italy, 1965. 1976. pap. text ed. 27.00 (ISBN 0-08-020449-X). Pergamon.
The Magnetic Circuit. (Siemens Programmed Instruction "pi" Self-Study Bks.: No. 4). 1978. 2.90 (ISBN 0-85501-504-7). Heyden.
The Magnetic Field. (Siemens Programmed Instruction "pi" Self-Study Bks.: No. 3). 1978. 2.90 (ISBN 0-85501-503-9). Heyden.
Miura, N. & Chikazumi, S., eds. Physics in High Magnetic Fields: Proceedings. (Springer Ser. in Solid-State Sciences: Vol. 24). (Illus.). 358p. 1981. 43.70 (ISBN 0-387-10587-5). Springer-Verlag.
Parkinson, David & Mulhall, Brian E. The Generation of High Magnetic Fields. LC 67-13568. (International Cryogenics Monographs Ser.). 165p. 1967. 24.50 (ISBN 0-306-30250-0, Plenum Pr). Plenum Pub.
Sheppard, Asher R. & Eisenbud, Merril. Biological Effects of Electric & Magnetic Fields of Extremely Low Frequency. LC 76-39695. 1977. 18.50x (ISBN 0-8147-2562-7). NYU Pr.
Skolbel'tsyn, D. V., ed. Physical Investigations in Strong Magnetic Fields. (P. N. Lebedev Physics Institute Ser.: Vol. 67). (Illus.). 167p. 1974. 37.50 (ISBN 0-306-10906-9, Consultants). Plenum Pub.
Tenforde, T. S., ed. Magnetic Field Effects on Biological Systems. LC 79-20739. 108p. 1979. 25.00 (ISBN 0-306-40312-9, Plenum Pr). Plenum Pub.
MAGNETIC FIELDS (COSMIC PHYSICS)
see also Magnetism, Terrestrial; Magnetohydrodynamics
Advanced Study Institute, Bergen, Norway, 1965. Radiation Trapped in the Earth's Magnetic Field: Proceedings. McCormac, B. M., ed. (Astrophysics & Space Library: No. 5). 901p. 1966. lib. bdg. 79.00 (ISBN 90-277-0130-X, Pub. by Reidel Holland). Kluwer Boston.
Advanced Summer Institute, Sheffield, England, 13-12 August, 1973. Magnetospheric Physics: Proceedings. McCormac, B. M., ed. LC 74-76472. (Astrophysics & Space Science Library: No. 44). 370p. 1974. lib. bdg. 66.00 (ISBN 90-277-0454-6, Pub. by Reidel Holland). Kluwer Boston.
IAU Symposium, No. 43, College de France, Paris, August 31-September 4, 1970. Solar Magnetic Fields: Proceedings. Howard, R., ed. LC 78-159656. (IAU Symposia). 361p. 1971. lib. bdg. 76.00 (ISBN 90-277-0201-2, Pub. by Reidel Holland). Kluwer Boston.
Knott, K., ed. Physics of Planetary Magnetospheres. (Illus.). 390p. 1981. pap. 46.00 (ISBN 0-08-027151-0). Pergamon.
Norvell, Anthony. Cosmic Magnetism: The Miracle of the Magic Power Circle. 1970. pap. 3.95 (ISBN 0-13-179119-2, Reward). P-H.
Parker, E. N. Cosmical Magnetic Fields: Their Origin & Their Activity. (International Series of Monographs on Physics). (Illus.). 1979. 98.00x (ISBN 0-19-851290-2). Oxford U Pr.
MAGNETIC FLUIDS
International Advanced Course & Workshop on Thermomechanics of Magnetic Fluids, Udine, Italy, Oct. 3-7, 1977. Thermomechanics of Magnetic Fluids: Theory & Applications, Proceedings. new ed. Berkovsky, Boris, ed. LC 78-15126. 1978. text ed. 45.00 (ISBN 0-89116-143-0, Co-Pub. by McGraw Intl). Hemisphere Pub.
MAGNETIC HEALING
see also Animal Magnetism; Mesmerism
Burke, Abbot G. Magnetic Therapy: Healing in Your Hands. LC 80-22941. (Illus.). 86p. (Orig.). 1980. pap. text ed. 4.95 (ISBN 0-932104-04-5). St George Pr.
Davis, Albert R. & Rawls, Walter C., Jr. The Magnetic Effect. 1975. 7.50 (ISBN 0-682-48312-5). Exposition.
Eden, Jerome. Animal Magnetism & the Life Energy. 1974. 8.50 (ISBN 0-682-48045-2). Exposition.
Sierra, Ralph. Power in a Magnet. 6.00 (ISBN 0-686-29962-0). Cancer Bk Hse.
Wade, Carlson. Magic Enzymes: Key to Youth & Health. 8.95 (ISBN 0-686-29985-X). Cancer Bk Hse.
MAGNETIC INDUCTION
see also Electromagnetism; Nuclear Induction
Hudson, Ralph P. Principles & Applications of Magnetic Cooling. 1972. 29.50 (ISBN 0-444-10392-9, North-Holland). Elsevier.
Lepley, Arthur R. & Closs, G. L., eds. Chemically Induced Magnetic Polarization. 426p. (Orig.). 1973. 27.50 (ISBN 0-471-52775-0). Krieger.
MAGNETIC MATERIALS
see also Ferrites (Magnetic Materials); Magnets
AIP Conference. Magnetism & Magnetic Materials: Proceedings, 2 pts, No. 18. Graham, C. D., Jr. & Rhyne, J. J., eds. LC 52-2468. 1974. 25.00x (ISBN 0-88318-117-7). Am Inst Physics.
AIP Conference, Chicago, 1971. Magnetism & Magnetic Materials 1971: Proceedings, 2 pts, No. 5. Graham, C. D., Jr & Rhyne, J. J., eds. LC 59-2468. 1573p. 1972. 22.00 (ISBN 0-88318-104-5). Am Inst Physics.
AIP Conference, Denver, 1972. Magnetism & Magnetic Materials 1972: Proceedings, 2 pts, No. 10. Graham, C. D., Jr & Rhyne, J. J., eds. LC 72-623469. 1714p. 1973. 24.00x (ISBN 0-88318-109-6). Am Inst Physics.
Annual Conference on Magnetic Materials, 22nd, Pittsburgh, June 15-18, 1976. Magnetism & Magnetic Materials - 1976: Proceedings. LC 76-47106. (AIP Conference Proceedings: No. 34). 1976. 19.50 (ISBN 0-88318-133-9). Am Inst Physics.
Becker, J. J., et al, eds. Magnetism & Magnetic Materials-1975. LC 76-10931. (AIP Conference Proceedings: No. 29). 693p. 1976. 30.00 (ISBN 0-88318-128-2). Am Inst Physics.
Boll, R. Soft Magnetic Materials. 34.00 (ISBN 0-85501-263-3). Heyden.
Conference on Magnetism & Magnetic Materials 20th, Dec 3-6, 1974 San Francisco. Magnetism & Magnetic Materials: Proceedings. Graham, C. D., Jr., et al, eds. LC 75-2647. (AIP Conference Proceedings: No. 24). 792p. 1975. 30.00 (ISBN 0-88318-123-1). Am Inst Physics.
Cullity, Berrard D. Introduction to Magnetic Materials. LC 71-159665. 1972. text ed. 27.95 (ISBN 0-201-01218-9). A-W.
Freeman, A. J. & Schuler, D., eds. Arbeitsgemeinschaft Magnetismus Conference, 1976: Held at Bad Nauheim, Ger., Mar. 1976. (Journal of Magnetism & Magnetic Materials: Vol. 4). 1977. 97.75 (ISBN 0-7204-0576-9, North-Holland). Elsevier.
Freeman, A. J. & Schuler, K., eds. Arbeitsgemeinschaft Magnetismus Conference: Proceedings, Munster, Federal Republic of Germany, March 1977. 1978. Repr. 88.00 (ISBN 0-444-85090-2, North-Holland). Elsevier.
Izyumov, Yu. A. & Medvedev, M. V. Magnetically Ordered Crystals Containing Impurities. LC 72-82625. (Illus.). 168p. 1973. 35.00 (ISBN 0-306-10874-7, Consultants). Plenum Pub.
Koenig, E. G. Magnetic Properties of Coordination & Organometallic Transition Metal Compounds: Supplement Three, (1971, 1972) (Landolt-Boernstein-Numerical Data & Functional Relationships in Science & Technology: Group II, Vol. 11 (Supplement to Vol. 2)). (Illus.). 800p. 1980. 702.10 (ISBN 0-387-09908-5). Springer-Verlag.
Magnetic Properties of Coordination & Organometallic Transition Metal Compounds. LC 62-53136. (Landolt-Boernstein Ser. Group Two: Vol. 10, Supplement 2). (Illus.). 1979. 542.80 (ISBN 0-387-08722-2). Springer-Verlag.
Magnetism & Magnetic Materials Digest. Incl. 1965. White, R. L. & Wickersheim, K. A., eds. 1965. 34.00 (ISBN 0-12-747150-2); 1966. Haas, Warren C. & Jarrett, H. S., eds. 1968. 43.50 (ISBN 0-12-312750-5); 1967. Doyle, W. D. & Harris, A. B., eds. 1967. 47.00 (ISBN 0-12-221550-8); 1968. Chang, H. & McGuire, T. R., eds. 1968. 50.00 (ISBN 0-12-170450-5). Acad Pr.
Sinha, Krityunjai P. & Kumar, Narendra. Interactions in Magnetically Ordered Solids. (Illus.). 192p. 1980. text ed. 45.00x (ISBN 0-19-851423-9). Oxford U Pr.
MAGNETIC MEMORY (CALCULATING-MACHINES)
Chang, H. Magnetic Bubble Memory Technology, Vol. 6. (Electrical Engineering & Electronics Ser.). 1978. 19.50 (ISBN 0-8247-6795-0). Dekker.
Electronics Magazine. Memory Design: Microcomputers to Mainframes. Altman, Laurence, ed. LC 77-26332. (Illus.). 180p. 1978. pap. text ed. 12.95 (ISBN 0-07-099718-7, R-732). McGraw.
Fuller, S. H. Analysis of Drum & Disk Storage Units. (Lecture Notes in Computer Science Ser.: Vol. 31). ix, 283p. 1975. pap. 15.40 (ISBN 0-387-07186-5). Springer-Verlag.
Further Planning of the Storage & Retrieval Service. (World Weather Watch Planning Report Ser.: No. 32). 1970. pap. 16.00 (ISBN 0-685-02475-X, WMO). Unipub.
MAGNETIC NEEDLE
see Compass
MAGNETIC RECORDERS AND RECORDING
see also Phonotapes in Education; Video Tape Recorders and Recording
Barsley, Michael. Tape Recording. Blishan, Bruce, ed. LC 75-7654. (Hobbies for Young People Ser). (gr. 9 up). 1967. 3.25x (ISBN 0-7181-0465-X). Intl Pubns Serv.
Burstein, Herman. Questions & Answers About Tape Recording. LC 73-89813. 1974. pap. 5.95 (ISBN 0-8306-2681-6, 681). TAB Bks.
Davidson, Homer. Servicing Cassette & Cartridge Tape Players. LC 74-25564. (Illus.). 294p. 1975. 10.95 (ISBN 0-8306-4716-3); pap. 6.95 (ISBN 0-8306-3716-8, 716). TAB Bks.
Dolan, Edward F., Jr. It Sounds Like Fun: How to Use & Enjoy Your Tape Recorder & Stereo. LC 81-296. (Illus.). 192p. (gr. 7 up). 1981. PLB 9.79 (ISBN 0-671-34053-0). Messner.
Earl, James. Cassette Tape Recorders. 1977. 12.50x (ISBN 0-85242-510-4). Intl Pubns Serv.
Everest, Alton. Handbook of Multichannel Recording. LC 75-20842. 322p. 1975. 13.95 (ISBN 0-8306-5781-9); pap. 9.95 (ISBN 0-8306-4781-3, 781). TAB Bks.
Gardner, J. Newnes Tape Recorder Servicing Manual, 2 vols. 2nd ed. 21.20 ea. (Pub. by Newnes-Butterworth). Vol. 1 (ISBN 0-408-00252-2, NB 42). Vol. 2 (ISBN 0-408-00253-0, NB 58). Hayden.
Gifford, F. Tape: a Radio News Handbook. (Communication Arts Bks.). 1977. 13.50 (ISBN 0-8038-7161-9); pap. text ed. 7.95x (ISBN 0-8038-7162-7). Hastings.
Jorgenson, Finn. The Complete Handbook of Magnetic Recording. (Illus.). 448p. (Orig.). 1980. 16.95 (ISBN 0-8306-9940-6); pap. text ed. 10.95 (ISBN 0-8306-1059-6, 1059). Tab Bks.
Lloyd, J. M. All in One Tape Recorder Book. 1970. pap. 7.95 (ISBN 0-240-44710-7). Focal Pr.
Lowman, Charles E. Magnetic Recording. (Illus.). 320p. 1972. 28.50 (ISBN 0-07-038845-8, P&RB). McGraw.
Margoschis, Richard. Recording Natural History Sounds. (Illus.). 1979. 8.95x (ISBN 0-913714-24-0); pap. 5.95x (ISBN 0-913714-25-9). Legacy Bks.
Middleton, Robert G. Tape Recorder Servicing Guide. 2nd ed. LC 79-62994. 1979. pap. 5.50 (ISBN 0-672-21594-2). Sams.
Paul, Norman. You & Your Tape Recorder. Date not set. 4.50x (ISBN 0-392-12282-0, SpS). Sportshelf.
Pear, C. B., Jr. Magnetic Recording in Science & Industry. 1967. 27.50x (ISBN 0-442-15579-4). Van Nos Reinhold.
Poteet, G. Howard. Workbench Guide to Tape Recorder Servicing. (Illus.). 1976. 12.95 (ISBN 0-13-965293-0, Busn). P-H.
Runstein, Robert E. Modern Recording Techniques. LC 73-90292. (Illus.). 1974. 10.50 (ISBN 0-672-21037-1). Sams.
Salm, Walter G. Cassette Tape Recorders-How They Work-Care & Repair. LC 73-86291. (Illus.). 204p. 1973. 8.95 (ISBN 0-8306-3689-7). TAB Bks.
Schroder, H. Tape Recorder Servicing Mechanics. (Illus.). 1968. 6.95x (ISBN 0-442-07416-6). Van Nos Reinhold.
Sinclair, I. Master Stereo Cassette Recording. (Illus.). (gr. 10 up). 1977. pap. 6.95 (ISBN 0-8104-0841-4). Hayden.
Tape Recording Made Easy: A Programmed Primer. 1978. 1-19 copies 3.75 ea. (ISBN 0-9601006-3-6); 20 or more copies 3.37 ea. G T Yeamans.
Tombs, David. Sound Recording: From Microphone to Master Tape. (Illus.). 192p. 1980. 24.00 (ISBN 0-7153-7954-2). David & Charles.
Zuckerman, Art. Tape Recording for the Hobbyist. 4th ed. LC 76-19692. (Illus.). 1977. pap. 4.95 (ISBN 0-672-21348-6). Sams.
MAGNETIC RECORDINGS (DATA STORAGE)
see Data Tapes
MAGNETIC RESONANCE
see also Electron Paramagnetic Resonance; Nuclear Magnetic Resonance
Berliner, Lawrence J. & Reuben, Jacques, eds. Biological Magnetic Resonance, Vol. 3. 263p. 1981. 35.00 (ISBN 0-306-40612-8, Plenum Pr). Plenum Pub.
Berlinger, L. J. & Reuben, J., eds. Biological Magnetic Resonance, Vol. 1. LC 78-16035. (Illus.). 359p. 1978. 35.00 (ISBN 0-306-38981-9, Plenum Pr). Plenum Pub.

Carrington, A. & McLachlan, A. D. Introduction to Magnetic Resonance: With Applications to Chemistry & Chemical Physics. LC 78-11738. 266p. 1979. pap. text ed. 17.95x (ISBN 0-412-21700-7, Pub. by Chapman & Hall England). Methuen Inc.

--Introduction to Magnetic Resonance with Applications to Chemistry & Chemical Physics. LC 78-11738. 1979. pap. 16.95 (ISBN 0-470-26572-8). Halsted Pr.

Caspers, W. J. Theory of Spin Relaxation. (Monographs in Statistical Physics & Thermodynamics Ser: Vol. 6). 160p. 1964. text ed. 12.75 (ISBN 0-470-14040-2, Pub. by Wiley). Krieger.

DePasquale, Nicholas P. & Bruno, Michael S. Cardiology Case Studies. 2nd ed. LC 79-91847. 1980. pap. 15.00 (ISBN 0-87488-001-7). Med Exam.

Fiat, D., ed. International Symposium on Magnetic Resonance, 4th, Rehovot-Jerusalem, 1971: Proceedings. 360p. 1976. 75.00 (ISBN 0-08-020791-X). Pergamon.

Fraissard, Jacques P. & Resing, Henry A., eds. Magnetic Resonance in Colloid & Interface Science. (NATO Advanced Study Institutes C. Mathematical & Physical Sciences Ser.: No. 61). 710p. 1980. lib. bdg. 76.00 (ISBN 90-277-1153-4, Pub. by Reidel Holland). Kluwer Boston.

Franconi, Cafiero. Magnetic Resonances in Biological Research. (Illus.). 420p. 1971. 83.75x (ISBN 0-677-14780-5). Gordon.

Hausser, K. H., et al, eds. International Symposium on Magnetic Resonance, 5th, Bombay, 1974: Proceedings. 276p. 1976. 50.00 (ISBN 0-08-020792-8). Pergamon.

Haws, E. S., et al. Interpretation of Proton Magnetic Resonance Spectra. 192p. 1979. 24.50 (ISBN 0-85501-063-0). Heyden.

Herak, J. N. & Adamic, K. J., eds. Magnetic Resonance in Chemistry & Biology. 576p. 1975. 55.75 (ISBN 0-8247-6119-7). Dekker.

Joint ISMAR-AMPERE International Conference on Magnetic Resonance. Proceedings. Smidt, J., ed. 1981. 60.00 (ISBN 0-686-77674-7). Franklin Inst Pr.

Kundla, E., et al. Magnetic Resonance & Related Phenomena. 606p. 1980. 21.30 (ISBN 0-387-09380-X). Springer-Verlag.

McDowell, C. A. Magnetic Resonance. (Mtp International Review of Science-Physical Chemistry Ser. 1: Vol. 4). (Illus.). 29.50, index vol. 12.50 (ISBN 0-685-02088-6). Univ Park.

--Magnetic Resonance, Vol. 4. (IRS Physical Chemistry Ser. Two). 1975. 29.95 (ISBN 0-408-70603-1). Butterworth.

McLauchlan, K. A. Magnetic Resonance. (Oxford Chemical Ser). 108p. 1972. pap. text ed. 7.95x (ISBN 0-19-855403-6). Oxford U Pr.

Mullen, K. & Pregosin, P. S. Fourier Transform Nuclear Magnetic Resonance Techniques: A Practical Approach. 1977. 28.00 (ISBN 0-686-75175-2). Acad Pr.

Poole, Charles P., et al. Relaxation in Magnetic Resonance: Dielectric & Mossbauer Applications. 1971. 54.00 (ISBN 0-12-561450-0). Acad Pr.

Resing, Henry A. & Wade, Charles G., eds. Magnetic Resonance in Colloid & Interface Science. LC 76-44442. (ACS Symposium Ser: No. 34). 1976. 30.50 (ISBN 0-8412-0342-3). Am Chemical.

Schumacher, Robert T. Introduction to Magnetic Resonance. (Modern Physics Monograph Ser.: No. 1). 1970. text ed. 17.50 (ISBN 0-8053-8504-5, Adv Bk Prog); pap. text ed. 9.50 (ISBN 0-8053-8505-3, Adv Bk Prog). Benjamin-Cummings.

Shulman, R. G., ed. Biological Applications of Magnetic Resonance. LC 79-16020. 1979. 37.50 (ISBN 0-12-640750-9). Acad Pr.

Simmons, Frank G. & Coombes, Susan E. Cardiopulmonary Technology Examination Review Book, Vol. 1. 1980. pap. 12.50 (ISBN 0-87488-473-X). Med Exam.

Slichter, C. P. Principles of Magnetic Resonance. 2nd rev ed. (Springer Series in Solid State Science: Vol 1). 1978. pap. 24.80 (ISBN 0-387-08476-2). Springer-Verlag.

Waugh, J. S., ed. Advances in Magnetic Resonance. Vol. 1, 1966. 60.00 (ISBN 0-12-025501-4); Vol. 2, 1967. 60.00 (ISBN 0-12-025502-2); Vol. 3, 1968. 60.00 (ISBN 0-12-025503-0); Vol. 4, 1970. 60.00 (ISBN 0-12-025504-9); Vol. 5, 1971. 60.00 (ISBN 0-12-025505-7); Vol. 6, 1973. 60.00 (ISBN 0-12-025506-5); Vol. 7, 1974. 60.00 (ISBN 0-12-025507-3); Vol. 8, 1976. 50.00 (ISBN 0-12-025508-1); Vol. 9, 1977. 60.50 (ISBN 0-12-025509-X). Acad Pr.

MAGNETIC RESONANCE, NUCLEAR
see Nuclear Magnetic Resonance

MAGNETIC RESONANCE ACCELERATOR
see Cyclotron

MAGNETIC SEPARATORS
see Calutron

MAGNETIC STORMS
see also Solar Activity

Akasofu, S. I. Polar & Magnetospheric Substorms. (Astrophysics & Space Science Library: No.11). 280p. 1968. lib. bdg. 37.00 (ISBN 90-277-0108-3, Pub. by Reidel Holland). Kluwer Boston.

MAGNETIC TAPE FILES
see Data Tapes

MAGNETISM
see also Animal Magnetism; Compass; Electricity; Electromagnetic Theory; Electromagnetism; Ferrimagnetism; Ferromagnetism; Magnetochemistry; Magnets; Nuclear Magnetism; Paramagnetism; Spin-Lattice Relaxation; Thermomagnetism
also headings beginning with the word Magnetic

AIP Conference. Magnetism & Magnetic Materials: Proceedings, 2 pts, No. 18. Graham, C. D., Jr. & Rhyne, J. J., eds. LC 52-2468. 1974. 25.00x (ISBN 0-88318-117-7). Am Inst Physics.

AIP Conference, Chicago, 1971. Magnetism & Magnetic Materials 1971: Proceedings, 2 pts, No. 5. Graham, C. D., Jr. & Rhyne, J. J., eds. LC 59-2468. 1573p. 1972. 22.00 (ISBN 0-88318-104-5). Am Inst Physics.

AIP Conference, Denver, 1972. Magnetism & Magnetic Materials 1972: Proceedings, 2 pts, No. 10. Graham, C. D., Jr. & Rhyne, J. J., eds. LC 72-623469. 1714p. 1973. 24.00x (ISBN 0-88318-109-6). Am Inst Physics.

Al'tov, et al, eds. Stabilization of Superconducting Magnetic Systems. LC 77-8618. (International Cryogenics Monographs Ser.). 338p. 1977. 39.50 (ISBN 0-306-30943-2, Plenum Pr). Plenum Pub.

Annual Book of ASTM Standards, 1981: Magnetic Properties & Magnetic Materials; Metallic Materials for Thermostats & for Electrical Resistance, Heating & Contacts; Temperature Measurement, Pt. 44. 1026p. 1981. 45.00 (ISBN 0-686-76012-3, 01-044081-40). ASTM.

Annual Conference on Magnetic Materials, 22nd, Pittsburgh, June 15-18, 1976. Magnetism & Magnetic Materials - 1976: Proceedings. LC 76-47106. (AIP Conference Proceedings: No. 34). 1976. 19.50 (ISBN 0-88318-133-9). Am Inst Physics.

Baran, Michael. Atlantis Reconsidered: A New Look at the Ancient Deluge Legends & an Analysis of Mysterious Modern Phenomena. 96p. 1981. 6.00 (ISBN 0-682-49761-4). Exposition.

Becker, J. J., et al, eds. Magnetism & Magnetic Materials-1975. LC 76-10931. (AIP Conference Proceedings: No. 29). 693p. 1976. 30.00 (ISBN 0-88318-128-2). Am Inst Physics.

Berkowitz, A. E. & Kneller, E., eds. Magnetism & Metallurgy, 2 Vols. Vol. 2 1969. 60.00 (ISBN 0-12-091702-5); 49.00 set (ISBN 0-685-05134-X). Acad Pr.

Birss, R. R. Symmetry & Magnetism. 2nd ed. (Selected Topics in Solid State Physics Ser.: Vol. 3). 1965. 31.75 (ISBN 0-444-10144-6, North-Holland). Elsevier.

Bleaney, B. I. & Bleaney, B. Electricity & Magnetism. 3rd ed. (Illus.). 1976. pap. 34.50x (ISBN 0-19-851141-8). Oxford U Pr.

Blitz, J., et al. Electrical, Magnetic & Visual Methods of Testing Materials. (Illus.). 1970. 12.00 (ISBN 0-8088-8350-X). Davey.

Bobeck, A. H. & Della Torre, E. Magnetic Bubbles. LC 74-79298. (Selected Topics in Solid State Physics: Vol. 14). 222p. 1975. 36.75 (ISBN 0-444-10658-8, North-Holland). Elsevier.

Breitsameter. Lexikon der Schulphysik: Elektrizitaet und Magnetismus A-K, Vol. 3A. (Ger.). 37.00 (ISBN 3-7614-0168-X, M-7224). French & Eur.

--Lexikon der Schulphysik: Elektrizitaet und Magnetismus L-Z, Vol. 3B. (Ger.). 37.00 (ISBN 3-7614-0169-8, M-7225). French & Eur.

Carlin, R. L. & Van Duyneveldt, A. J. Magnetic Properties of Transition Metal Compounds. LC 77-18002. (Inorganic Chemistry Concepts: Vol. 2). 1977. 24.00 (ISBN 0-387-08584-X). Springer-Verlag.

Chang, Hsu, ed. Magnetic Bubble Technology: Integrated Circuit Magnetics for Digital Storage & Processing. LC 73-87653. 1975. 37.95 (ISBN 0-87942-033-2). Inst Electrical.

Chikazumi, Sushin & Charap, Stanley H. Physics of Magnetism. LC 78-2315. 566p. 1978. Repr. of 1964 ed. lib. bdg. 29.75 (ISBN 0-88275-662-1). Krieger.

Conference on Magnetism & Magnetic Materials 20th, Dec 3-6, 1974 San Francisco. Magnetism & Magnetic Materials: Proceedings. Graham, C. D., Jr., et al, eds. LC 75-2647. (AIP Conference Proceedings: No. 24). 792p. 1975. 30.00 (ISBN 0-88318-123-1). Am Inst Physics.

Cullity, Berrard D. Introduction to Magnetic Materials. LC 71-159665. 1972. text ed. 27.95 (ISBN 0-201-01218-9). A-W.

Desirant, M., ed. Solid State Physics in Electronics & Telecommunications: Magnetic & Optical Properties. 1960. 87.50 (ISBN 0-12-211503-1); Vol. 4. Part 2. 64.50 (ISBN 0-12-211504-X). Acad Pr.

Direct-Current Magnetic Hysteresigraphs. 62p. 1973. pap. 6.00 (ISBN 0-8031-0118-X, STP526). ASTM.

Direct-Current Magnetic Measurements for Soft Magnetic Materials. 1970. pap. 6.25 (ISBN 0-686-52052-1, 04-371001-06). ASTM.

Eschenfelder, A. H. Magnetic Bubble Theory. 2nd corrected & updated ed. (Springer Ser. in Solid-State Sciences: Vol. 14). (Illus.). 364p. 1981. pap. 35.00 (ISBN 0-387-10790-8). Springer-Verlag.

Foner, S. Magnetism: Selected Topics. new ed. LC 72-121047. 768p. 1976. 141.50x (ISBN 0-677-15390-2). Gordon.

Freeman, A. J., ed. Arbeitsgemeinschaft Magnetismus: Proceedings, March 26-28. 503p. 1975. 68.50 (ISBN 0-444-10900-5, North-Holland). Elsevier.

Freeman, A. J. & Schuler, D., eds. Arbeitsgemeinschaft Magnetismus Conference, 1976: Held at Bad Nauheim, Ger., Mar. 1976. (Journal of Magnetism & Magnetic Materials: Vol. 4). 1977. 97.75 (ISBN 0-7204-0576-9, North-Holland). Elsevier.

Freeman, A. J. & Schuler, K., eds. Arbeitsgemeinschaft Magnetismus Conference: Proceedings, Munster, Federal Republic of Germany, March 1977. 1978. Repr. 88.00 (ISBN 0-444-85090-2, North-Holland). Elsevier.

Goodenough, John B. Magnetism & the Chemical Bond. LC 76-8393. 410p. 1976. Repr. of 1963 ed. 23.50 (ISBN 0-88275-384-3). Krieger.

Graf, Rudolf F. Safe & Simple Electrical Experiments. Orig. Title: Safe & Simple Book of Electricity. 1973. pap. 3.50 (ISBN 0-486-22950-5). Dover.

Gray, Andrew. Absolute Measurements in Electricity & Magnetism. 2nd ed. (Illus.). 1921. pap. text ed. 6.00 (ISBN 0-486-61787-4). Dover.

Hargraves, R. B., ed. Physics of Magmatic Processes. LC 80-7525. (Illus.). 800p. 1980. 40.00x (ISBN 0-691-08259-6); pap. 15.00x (ISBN 0-691-08261-8). Princeton U Pr.

Hooper, H. O. & De Graaf, A. M. Amorphous Magnetism. LC 72-96493. 443p. 1973. 42.50 (ISBN 0-306-30726-X, Plenum Pr). Plenum Pub.

Huebener, R. P. Magnetic Flux Structures in Superconductors. (Springer Ser. in Solid State Sciences: Vol. 6). (Illus.). 1979. 31.20 (ISBN 0-387-09213-7). Springer-Verlag.

International Conference on Magnetism '76. Proceedings. De Chatel, P. & Franse, J., eds. 1977. 231.75 (ISBN 0-7204-0733-8, North-Holland). Elsevier.

Jefimenko, Oleg D. Electricity & Magnetism: An Introduction to the Theory of Electric & Magnetic Fields. LC 65-12058. 591p. 1966. 35.00 (ISBN 0-306-50035-3, Plenum Pr). Plenum Pub.

Kalvius, G. M. & Tebble, R. S. Experimental Magnetism, Vol. 1. LC 79-50036. 346p. 1979. 64.25 (ISBN 0-471-99702-1, Pub. by Wiley-Interscience). Wiley.

Kemp, J. F. & Young, P. Electricity & General Magnetism. 2nd ed. (Kemp & Young Ser.). 142p. 1971. pap. 9.50x (ISBN 0-540-00366-2). Sheridan.

Kip, Arthur F. Fundamentals of Electricity & Magnetism. 2nd ed. (Fundamentals of Physics Ser.). 1968. text ed. 19.95 (ISBN 0-07-034780-8, C); instructor's manual 2.95 (ISBN 0-07-034781-6). McGraw.

Konig, E. & Konig, G. Magnetic Properties of Coordination & Organometallic Transition Metal Compounds: Supplement 1 1964-1968. (Landolt-Bornstein New Ser.: Group II, Vol. 8). 1977. 649.00 (ISBN 0-387-07441-4). Springer-Verlag.

Korth, Leslie. Healing Magnetism. LC 75-12014. 1975. pap. 1.25 (ISBN 0-87728-297-8). Weiser.

Lapuszanski, J. T., et al. Magnetism in Metals & Metallic Compounds. LC 75-20369. 622p. 1976. 57.50 (ISBN 0-306-30865-7, Plenum Pr). Plenum Pub.

Levy, R. A. & Hasegawa, eds. Amorphous Magnetism-II. LC 77-5377. 680p. 1977. 59.50 (ISBN 0-306-34412-2, Plenum Pr). Plenum Pub.

Magnaflux Corporation. Principles of Magnetic Particle Testing. LC 66-29699. (Illus.). 1966. 23.50x (ISBN 0-686-21417-X). Magnaflux.

Magnetic Properties, ASTM Standards on (A-6) 1976. pap. 9.75 (ISBN 0-686-52053-X, 03-106076-06). ASTM.

Magnetism & Magnetic Materials Digest. Incl. 1965. White, R. L. & Wickersheim, K. A., eds. 1965. 34.00 (ISBN 0-12-747150-2); 1966. Haas, Warren C. & Jarrett, H. S., eds. 1968. 43.50 (ISBN 0-12-312750-5); 1967. Doyle, W. D. & Harris, A. B., eds. 1967. 47.00 (ISBN 0-12-221550-8); 1968. Chang, H. & McGuire, T. R., eds. 1968. 50.00 (ISBN 0-12-170450-5). Acad Pr.

Maxwell, James C. Electricity & Magnetism, 2 Vols. (Illus.). 1891. pap. text ed. 6.50 ea.; Vol. 1. pap. text ed. (ISBN 0-486-60636-8); Vol. 2. pap. text ed. (ISBN 0-486-60637-6). Dover.

Mintz, Stephan & Perlmutter, Arnold, eds. New Pathways in High Energy Physics, Pt. 1: Magnetic Charge & Other Fundamental Approaches. (Studies in the Natural Sciences Ser.: Vol. 10). 1976. 45.00 (ISBN 0-306-36910-9, Plenum Pr). Plenum Pub.

Morrish, Allan H. The Physical Principles of Magnetism. LC 78-2480. 696p. 1980. Repr. of 1965 ed. lib. bdg. 29.50 (ISBN 0-88275-670-2). Krieger.

Mottelay, Paul F., ed. Bibliographical History of Electricity & Magnetism. LC 74-26277. (History, Philosophy & Sociology of Science Ser.). (Illus.). 1975. Repr. 40.00x (ISBN 0-405-06605-8). Arno.

Norvell. Cosmic Magnetism. pap. 3.95 (ISBN 0-13-179119-2). P-H.

O'Dell, T. H. Magnetic Bubbles. LC 74-12048. 159p. 1974. 38.95 (ISBN 0-470-65259-4). Halsted Pr.

Pugh, Emerson M. & Pugh, Emerson W. Principles of Electricity & Magnetism. 2nd ed. LC 70-87043. (Physics Ser). 1970. text ed. 22.95 (ISBN 0-201-06014-0). A-W.

Rado, George T. & Suhl, H., eds. Magnetism: A Treatise on Modern Theory & Materials, 5 vols. 1963-1973. Vol. 1. 63.00 (ISBN 0-12-575301-2); Vol. 2A. 55.50 (ISBN 0-12-575302-0); Vol. 2B. 55.50 (ISBN 0-12-575342-X); Vol. 3. 56.00 (ISBN 0-12-575303-9); Vol. 4. 52.00 (ISBN 0-12-575304-7); Vol. 5. 60.00 (ISBN 0-12-575305-5). Acad Pr.

Rawls, Walter, Jr. & Davis, Albert R. Magnetism & Its Effect on the Living System. 8.50 (ISBN 0-686-29946-9). Cancer Bk Hse.

Scott, William T. The Physics of Electricity & Magnetism. 2nd ed. LC 75-42235. 722p. 1977. Repr. of 1966 ed. 24.00 (ISBN 0-88275-375-4). Krieger.

Sears, Francis W. Electricity & Magnetism. (Illus.). 1951. 17.95 (ISBN 0-201-06900-8). A-W.

Sprott, Julien C. Electric Circuits & Electronics. LC 80-25366. 368p. 1981. text ed. 24.95 (ISBN 0-471-05840-8). Wiley.

Stacey, F. D. & Banerjee, S. K. Physical Principles of Rock Magnetism. LC 72-87965. (Developments in Solid Earth Geophysics Ser.: Vol. 5). 224p. 1974. 46.50 (ISBN 0-444-41084-8). Elsevier.

Still, Alfred. Soul of Lodestone: The Background of Magnetical Science. 1978. Repr. of 1946 ed. lib. bdg. 25.00 (ISBN 0-89760-811-9, Telegraph). Dynamic Learn Corp.

The Theory of Magnetism One: Statistics & Dynamics. (Springer Series in Solid-State Sciences: Vol. 17). (Illus.). 320p. 1981. 34.00 (ISBN 0-387-10611-1). Springer-Verlag.

Tyablikov, S. V. Methods in the Quantum Theory of Magnetism. LC 65-27345. 354p. 1967. 37.50 (ISBN 0-306-30263-2, Plenum Pr). Plenum Pub.

Van Vleck, John H. Theory of Electric & Magnetic Susceptibilities. (International Series of Monographs on Physics). (Illus.). 1932. pap. 37.50x (ISBN 0-19-851243-0). Oxford U Pr.

Von Reichenbach, Karl. Researches on Magnetism, Electricity, Heat, Light, Crystallization, & Chemical Attraction in Relation to the Vital Force. Gregory, William, tr. 1974. 10.00 (ISBN 0-8216-0216-0). Univ Bks.

Vonsovskii, S. V. Magnetism, 2 vols. Hardin, R., tr. from Rus. LC 73-16426. 1974. Set. 148.95 (ISBN 0-470-91193-X). Halsted Pr.

Vonsovsky, S. V. Magnetism of Elementary Particles. 295p. 1975. 4.80 (ISBN 0-8285-0792-9, Pub. by Mir Pubs Russia). Imported Pubns.

Wagner, D. Introduction to the Theory of Magnetism. 290p. 1972. text ed. 28.00 (ISBN 0-08-016595-8). Pergamon.

Watson, J. K. Applications of Magnetism. LC 79-20882. 1980. 29.50 (ISBN 0-471-03540-8, Pub. by Wiley-Interscience). Wiley.

Winkler. Magnetic Garnets. 1981. 76.00 (ISBN 0-9940013-3-9, Pub. by Vieweg & Sohn Germany). Heyden.

Yoder, H. S., Jr. Generation of Basaltic Magma. LC 76-29672. 1976. pap. text ed. 6.25 (ISBN 0-309-02504-4). Natl Acad Pr.

Zijlstra, H. Experimental Methods in Magnetism, 2 vols. (Selected Topics in Solid State Physics Ser.: Vol. 9). 1967. Set. 63.50 (ISBN 0-444-10327-9, North-Holland). Elsevier.

MAGNETISM–EARLY WORKS T0 1800

Barlow, William. A Briefe Discovery of the Idle Animadversions of Mark Ridley, Doctor of Phisicke. LC 71-38149. (English Experience Ser.: No. 429). 16p. 1972. Repr. of 1618 ed. 7.00 (ISBN 90-221-0429-X). Walter J Johnson.

--Magneticall Advertisements. LC 68-54616. (English Experience Ser.: No. 47). Repr. of 1616 ed. 14.00 (ISBN 90-221-0047-2). Walter J Johnson.

Home, R. W. Aepinus's Essay on the Theory of Electricity & Magnetism. Connor, P. J., tr. LC 78-10105. 1979. 37.50x (ISBN 0-691-08222-7). Princeton U Pr.

Norman, Robert. The Newe Attractive, Containing a Short Discourse of the Magnes or Lodestone, Etc. LC 73-6153. (English Experience Ser.: No. 616). (Illus.). 76p. 1973. Repr. of 1581 ed. 21.00 (ISBN 90-221-0616-0). Walter J Johnson.

MAGNETISM–JUVENILE LITERATURE

Bender, Alfred. Science Projects with Electrons & Computers. LC 76-55382. (Illus.). (gr. 6 up). 1977. lib. bdg. 6.95 (ISBN 0-668-04334-2); pap. 3.25 (ISBN 0-686-67874-5). Arco.

Yates, Raymond F. Boys' Book of Magnetism. rev. ed. LC 59-11731. (Illus.). (gr. 4 up). 1959. PLB 7.89 (ISBN 0-06-026676-7, HarpJ). Har-Row.

MAGNETISM, ANIMAL

see Animal Magnetism

MAGNETISM, HUMAN

see Animal Magnetism

MAGNETISM, TERRESTRIAL

Air Force Cambridge Research Laboratories - Boston College - 1967. Physics of the Magnetosphere: Proceedings. Carovillano, R. L., et al, eds. (Astrophysics & Space Science Library: Vol. 10). (Illus.). 1969. 44.00 (ISBN 0-387-91023-9). Springer-Verlag.

Chapman, F. Solar Plasma, Geomagnetism & Aurora. (Documents on Modern Physics Ser). (Illus.). 1964. 34.75x (ISBN 0-677-00130-4). Gordon.

Dubrov, A. P. The Geomagnetic Field & Life: Geomagnetobiology. (Illus.). 318p. 1978. 25.00 (ISBN 0-306-31072-4, Plenum Pr). Plenum Pub.

Fuller, M., et al, eds. Tectomagnetics & Local Geomagnetic Field Variations. (Advances in Earth & Planetary Sciences Ser.: No. 5). 140p. 1979. 22.50x (ISBN 0-89955-212-9, Pub. by Japan Sci Soc Japan). Intl Schol Bk Serv.

Jacobs, J. A. Geomagnetic Micropulsations. LC 70-107315. (Physics & Chemistry in Space: Vol. 1). (Illus.). 1970. 23.60 (ISBN 0-387-04986-X). Springer-Verlag.

Knott, K., et al, eds. Advances in Magnetospheric Physics with GEOS-1 & ISEE. 1979. lib. bdg. 68.50 (ISBN 0-686-25183-0, Pub. by Reidel Holland). Kluwer Boston.

Matsushita, S. & Campbell, W. H., eds. Physics of Geomagnetic Phenomena, 2 Vols. (International Geophysics Ser.: Vol. 11). 1967. Vol. 1. 67.50 (ISBN 0-12-480301-6); Vol. 2, 1968. 78.50 (ISBN 0-12-480302-4). Acad Pr.

Nishida, A. Geomagnetic Diagnosis of the Magnetosphere. (Physics & Chemistry in Space: Vol. 9). (Illus.). 1978. 44.80 (ISBN 0-387-08297-2). Springer-Verlag.

Rikitake, T. Electromagnetism & the Earth's Interior. (Developments in Solid Earth Geophysics Ser: Vol. 2). 1966. 61.00 (ISBN 0-444-40480-5). Elsevier.

Vacquier, Victor. Geomagnetism in Marine Geology. 1972. 44.00 (ISBN 0-444-41001-5). Elsevier.

Waynick, A. H., ed. Geomagnetism & Aeronomy. LC 65-60042. (Antarctic Research Ser.: Vol. 4). 1965. 10.00 (ISBN 0-87590-104-2). Am Geophysical.

Wienert, Karl A. Notes on Geomagnetic Observatory & Survey Practice. (Earth Sciences Ser., No. 5). (Illus.). 1969. pap. 17.25 (ISBN 92-3-100816-1, U432, UNESCO). Unipub.

MAGNETOCHEMISTRY

Mulay, L. N. Magnetic Susceptibility. (Illus.). 134p. 1963. pap. text ed. 6.25 (ISBN 0-470-62360-8, Pub. by Wiley). Krieger.

MAGNETOHYDRODYNAMIC GENERATORS

see also Plasma Rockets

Buende, R., et al. MHD Power Generation: Selected Problems of Combustion MHD Generation. Raeder, J., ed. (Illus.). 320p. 1975. pap. 64.90 (ISBN 0-387-07296-9). Springer-Verlag.

Caldirola, P. & Knoepfel, H., eds. Physics of High Energy Density. (Italian Physical Society: Course 48). 1971. 54.00 (ISBN 0-12-368848-5). Acad Pr.

Electricity from MHD 1968, 6 Vols. (Illus., Orig.). 1969. pap. 31.00 ea. (IAEA); Vol. 1. pap. (ISBN 92-0-030468-0, ISP191-1); Vol. 2. pap. (ISBN 92-0-030568-7, ISP191-2); Vol. 3. pap. (ISBN 92-0-030668-3, ISP191-3); Vol. 4. pap. (ISBN 92-0-030768-X); Vol. 5. pap. (ISBN 92-0-030868-6, ISP191-5); Vol. 6. pap. (ISBN 92-0-030968-2, ISP191-6). Unipub.

MAGNETOHYDRODYNAMICS

see also Cosmic Electrodynamics; Ion Flow Dynamics; Magnetohydrodynamic Generators; Plasma Dynamics; Plasma Instabilities; Rockets (Aeronautics); Van Allen Radiation Belts

Bateman, Glenn. MHD Instabilities. 1978. text ed. 27.50x (ISBN 0-262-02131-5). MIT Pr.

Branover, H. MHD Flows & Turbulence: Proceedings. 1977. 39.95 (ISBN 0-470-99061-9). Halsted Pr.

Branover, Herman. Magnetohydrodynamic Flow in Ducts. LC 78-67721. 1979. 43.95x (ISBN 0-470-26539-6). Halsted Pr.

Cabannes, Henri. Theoretical Magneto Fluid-Dynamics. LC 75-117095. (Applied Mathematics & Mechanics Ser.: Vol. 13). 1970. 42.00 (ISBN 0-12-153750-1). Acad Pr.

Chamberlain, Joseph W. Motion of Charged Particles in the Earth's Magnetic Field. (Documents on Modern Physics Ser). (Illus.). 1964. 12.75x (ISBN 0-677-00120-7). Gordon.

Chandrasekhar, S. Hydrodynamic & Hydromagnetic Stability. (Illus.). 704p. pap. 10.95 (ISBN 0-486-64071-X). Dover.

Chapman, F. Solar Plasma, Geomagnetism & Aurora. (Documents on Modern Physics Ser). (Illus.). 1964. 34.75x (ISBN 0-677-00130-4). Gordon.

Cowling, T. G. Magnetohydrodynamics. LC 76-38002. (Monographs on Astronomical Subjects). 1977. 39.50x (ISBN 0-8448-1060-6). Crane-Russak Co.

Eskinazi, Salamon, ed. Vector Mechanics of Fluids & Magneto-Fluids. 1967. 55.00 (ISBN 0-12-242558-8). Acad Pr.

Gundersen, Roy M. Linearized Analysis of One-Dimensional Magnetohydrodynamic Flows. (Springer Tracts in Natural Philosophy: Vol. 1). (Illus.). 1965. 15.40 (ISBN 0-387-03216-9). Springer-Verlag.

Jeffrey, Alan & Taniuti, T., eds. M H D Stability & Thermonuclear Containment. (Perspectives in Physics Ser.). 1966. 38.50 (ISBN 0-12-382550-4). Acad Pr.

Kirko, Igor M. Magnetohydrodynamics of Liquid Metals. LC 65-17789. 80p. 1965. 25.00 (ISBN 0-306-10732-5, Consultants). Plenum Pub.

Kolm, Henry, et al, eds. High Magnetic Fields. 1961. 37.50x (ISBN 0-262-11008-3). MIT Pr.

Krause, F. & Radler, K-H. Mean-Field Magnetohydrodynamics & Dynamo Theory. (Illus.). 270p. 1981. 36.00 (ISBN 0-08-025041-6). Pergamon.

Mather, N. W. & Sutton, G. W. Engineering Aspects of Magnetohydrodynamics. 1964. 128.25 (ISBN 0-677-10320-4). Gordon.

Pai Shih-I. Magnetogasdynamics & Plasma Dynamics. (Illus.). 1962. 29.00 (ISBN 0-387-80608-3). Springer-Verlag.

Roberts, Paul H. An Introduction to Magnetohydrodynamics. 1967. 21.50 (ISBN 0-444-19829-6). Elsevier.

Roederer, J. G. Dynamics of Geomagnetically Trapped Radiation. LC 73-109668. (Physics & Chemistry in Space: Vol. 2). (Illus.). 1970. 19.50 (ISBN 0-387-04987-8). Springer-Verlag.

Roos, Bernard W. Analytic Functions & Distributions in Physics & Engineering. 521p. 1969. text ed. 26.00 (ISBN 0-471-73334-2, Pub. by Wiley). Krieger.

Sturrock, P. A., ed. Plasma Astrophysics. (Italian Physical Society: Course 39). 1967. 55.00 (ISBN 0-12-368839-6). Acad Pr.

Symposia in Applied Mathematics - New York - 1965. Magneto-Fluid & Plasma Dynamics: Proceedings, Vol. 18. Grad, H., ed. LC 66-20436. 1967. 20.00 (ISBN 0-8218-1318-8, PSAPM-18). Am Math.

Wasserman, Robert H. & Wells, Charles P., eds. Fundamental Topics in Relativistic Fluid Mechanics & Magnetohydrodynamics: Proceedings. 1963. 32.50 (ISBN 0-12-736250-9). Acad Pr.

MAGNETOHYDRODYNAMICS–BIBLIOGRAPHY

Bethmann, Johannes. Untersuchungen Uber Die Mhd. 14.00 (ISBN 0-384-04083-7); pap. 11.00 (ISBN 0-685-02222-6). Johnson Repr.

MAGNETO-IONIC THEORY

see also Ionospheric Radio Wave Propagation

Budden, K. G. Lectures on Magnetoionic Theory. (Documents on Modern Physics Ser.). 1964. 23.25x (ISBN 0-677-00100-2). Gordon.

MAGNETO-OPTICS

see also Electromagnetic Theory; Electrons; Polarization (Light)

Conference on Magneto-Optics, Zurich, Sept. 1-3 1976. Proceedings. Wachter, P., ed. (Physica, Special Issue: Vol. 89 B & C). 1977. 46.50 (ISBN 0-7204-0737-0, North-Holland). Elsevier.

Devreese, J. T., ed. Theoretical Aspects & the New Developments in Magneto-Optics. (NATO Advanced Study Institutes Ser.: B Physics: Vol. 60). 635p. 1981. 69.50 (ISBN 0-306-40555-5, Plenum Pr). Plenum Pub.

MAGNETOSTATICS

see also Magnetic Fields

Akasofu, S. I., ed. Dynamics of the Magnetosphere. (Astrophysics & Space Science Library: No. 78). 1980. lib. bdg. 79.00 (ISBN 90-277-1052-X, Pub. by Reidel Holland). Kluwer Boston.

Brown, William F., Jr. Magnetoelastic Interactions. (Springer Tracts in Natural Philosophy: Vol. 9). (Illus.). 1966. 26.30 (ISBN 0-387-03674-1). Springer-Verlag.

MAGNETS

see also Solenoids

Baldock, C. R. & Hudson, E. D. Electrical Equipment for Tanks & Magnets. (National Nuclear Energy Ser.: Division I, Vol. 10). 401p. 1947. pap. 49.80 (ISBN 0-686-75761-0); microfilm 24.90 (ISBN 0-686-75762-9). DOE.

Brechna, H. Superconducting Magnet Systems. LC 72-96051. (Technische Physik in Einveldarstellungen: Vol. 18). (Illus.). 480p. 1973. 94.60 (ISBN 0-387-06103-7). Springer-Verlag.

McCaig, M. Permanent Magnets in Theory & Practice. LC 77-23949. 1977. 39.95 (ISBN 0-470-99269-7). Halsted Pr.

Mills, R. E. Critical Phenomena. (Materials Science & Engineering Ser.). 1971. 59.50 (ISBN 0-07-042365-2, P&RB). McGraw.

Moskowitz, Lester R. Permanent Magnet Design & Application Handbook. LC 75-28109. 1976. 49.95 (ISBN 0-8436-1800-0). CBI Pub.

Nesbitt, E. A. & Wernick, J. A. Rare Earth Permanent Magnets. (Materials Science Ser). 1973. 29.00 (ISBN 0-12-515450-X). Acad Pr.

Parker, Rollin J. & Studders, R. J. Permanent Magnets & Their Applications. LC 62-10930. 1962. 46.50 (ISBN 0-471-66264-X, Pub. by Wiley-Interscience). Wiley.

Wakerling, R. K., ed. Magnets & Magnetic Measuring Techniques. Guthrie, A. (National Nuclear Energy Ser.: Div.I, Vol.2). 213p. 1949. pap. 27.00 (ISBN 0-686-75870-6); microfilm(35mm) 13.50 (ISBN 0-686-75871-4); microfilm(16mm) 10.00 (ISBN 0-686-75872-2). DOE.

MAGNETS–JUVENILE LITERATURE

Feravolo, Rocco V. Magnets. LC 60-12079. (Junior Science Books Ser). (Illus.). (gr. 2-5). 1960. PLB 6.09 (ISBN 0-8116-6155-5). Garrard.

Freeman, Mae. The Real Magnet Book. (gr. k-3). 1970. pap. 1.50 (ISBN 0-590-01660-1, Schol Pap). Schol Bk Serv.

Keen, Martin L. Magnets & Magnetism. (How & Why Wonder Books Ser.). (gr. 4-6). pap. 1.00 (ISBN 0-448-05046-3). Wonder.

Kirkpatrick, Rena K. Look at Magnets. LC 77-26665. (Look at Science Ser.). (Illus.). (gr. k-3). 1978. PLB 11.15 (ISBN 0-8393-0063-8). Raintree Child.

Schneider, Herman & Schneider, Nina. Secret Magnets. (Illus.). (gr. k-3). 1979. pap. 1.50 (ISBN 0-590-05769-3, Schol Pap). Schol Bk Serv.

MAGNIFICAT (MUSIC)

De La Rue, Pierre. Magnificat Quinti Toni. Davison, Nigel, ed. LC 65-26095. (Penn State Music Series, No. 8). 19p. 1965. pap. 2.50x (ISBN 0-271-73081-1). Pa St U Pr.

Van Den Borren, Charles, ed. Polyphonia Sacra: A Continental Miscellany of the Fifteenth Century. LC 63-18891. 1963. 27.50x (ISBN 0-271-73092-7). Pa St U Pr.

MAGNOLIA

Treseder, Neil. Magnolias. (Illus.). 220p. 1978. 72.00 (ISBN 0-571-09619-0, Pub. by Faber & Faber). Merrimack Bk Serv.

MAGOON, CHARLES EDWARD, 1861-1920

Lockmiller, David A. Magoon in Cuba: A History of the Second Intervention, 1906-1909. Repr. of 1938 ed. lib. bdg. 15.00x (ISBN 0-8371-2210-4, LOMC). Greenwood.

MAGRITTE, RENE, 1898-1967

Breton, Andre. Magritte. (Illus.). 1964. pap. 3.50 (ISBN 0-914412-24-8). Inst for the Arts.

De Menil, Dominique, ed. Secret Affinities: Words & Images by Rene Magritte. LC 76-45518. 1976. 2.00 (ISBN 0-914412-12-4). Inst for the Arts.

Dopagne, Jacques. Magritte. (Masters of Art Ser.). (Illus.). 1979. pap. 3.95 (ISBN 0-8120-2154-1). Barron.

Gablik, Suzi. Magritte. LC 77-125894. (Illus.). 232p. 1973. pap. 9.95 (ISBN 0-8212-0520-X, 543772). NYGS.

Hammacher, A. M. Magritte. LC 73-13789. (Library of Great Painters). (Illus.). 160p. 1974. 40.00 (ISBN 0-8109-0278-8). Abrams.

Noel, Bernard. Magritte. (Q L P Art Ser.). 1977. 6.95 (ISBN 0-517-53009-0). Crown.

Passeron, Rene. Rene Magritte. (Filipacchi Art Bks). (Illus.). 96p. 1981. 25.00 (ISBN 2-8501-8098-X); pap. 9.95 (ISBN 2-8501-8099-8). Hippocrene Bks.

Schneede. Rene Magritte. (Pocket Art Ser.). 1982. pap. 3.50 (ISBN 0-8120-2187-8). Barron.

Torczyner, Harry, ed. Magritte: Ideas & Images. 1979. pap. 7.95 (ISBN 0-451-79963-1, G9963, Co-Pub. by Abrams). NAL.

MAGUIRES, MOLLY

see Molly Maguires

MAGYAR LANGUAGE

see Hungarian Language

MAGYAR LITERATURE

see Hungarian Literature (Collections)

MAGYAR MYTHOLOGY

see Mythology, Finno-Ugrian

MAGYAR TALES

see Tales, Magyar

MAGYARS

Dioszegi, Vilmos. Tracing Shamans in Siberia. Babo, A. R., tr. (Illus.). 1968. text ed. 15.00x (ISBN 90-623-4007-5). Humanities.

Erdy, Miklos. The Sumerian, Ural-Altaic, Magyar Relationship: A History of Research, Pt. 1, the 19th Century. LC 72-112303. (Studia Sumiro-Hungarica: Vol. 3). (Illus.). 530p. (Bilingual text). 1974. 15.00 (ISBN 0-914246-53-4). Gilgamesh Pub.

Erdy, Miklos, ed. Studia Sumiro-Hungarica, 3 vols. 1968-1974. Set. 39.00 (ISBN 0-914246-50-X). Gilgamesh Pub.

Feher, Matyas & Erdy, Miklos, eds. Studia Sumiro-Hungarica, 2 vols. Incl. A Sumir Kerdes (the Sumerian Question) Galgoczy, Janos. LC 79-7359. (Vol. 1). 270p (ISBN 0-914246-51-8); Szumirok Es Magyarok (Sumerians & Magyars) Somogyi, Ede. LC 70-7362. (Vol. 2). 270p (ISBN 0-914246-52-6). (Illus.). 1968. Repr. 12.00 ea. Gilgamesh Pub.

Macartney, C. A. The Magyars in the Ninth Century. 1978. lib. bdg. 59.95 (ISBN 0-8490-2198-7). Gordon Pr.

MAH JONG

Kanai, Shozo & Farrell, Margaret. Mah Jong for Beginners. LC 58-12108. (Illus.). bds. 5.25 (ISBN 0-8048-0391-9). C E Tuttle.

Li, Tze-Chung. Mah Jong: The Rules for Playing the Chinese Game. 1981. write for info. (ISBN 0-937256-02-1). CHCUS Inc.

Strauser, Kitty & Evans, Lucille. Mah Jong, Anyone. LC 64-16009. (Illus.). 1964. bds. 5.25 (ISBN 0-8048-0390-0). C E Tuttle.

Whitney, Eleanor N. Mah Jong Handbook: How to Play, Score, & Win the Modern Game. LC 64-17162. (Illus.). 1964. 8.75 (ISBN 0-8048-0392-7). C E Tuttle.

MAHABHARATA

Banerji, S. C. Indian Society in the Mahabharata. 1976. 14.00x (ISBN 0-88386-510-6). South Asia Bks.

Buck, William. Mahabarata. 1979. pap. 2.50 (ISBN 0-451-61783-5, MEM85, Ment). NAL.

--Mahabharata. (Illus.). 1974. 14.95 (ISBN 0-520-02017-0); pap. 6.95 (ISBN 0-520-04393-6). U of Cal Pr.

Goldman, Robert P. God's Priests & Warriors: The Bhrgus of the Mahabharata. LC 76-41255. (Studies in Oriental Culture). 195p. 1977. 15.00x (ISBN 0-231-03941-7). Columbia U Pr.

Gupta, S. P., ed. Mahabharata: Myth & Reality. LC 76-902982. 1976. 17.50x (ISBN 0-88386-856-3). South Asia Bks.

Hopkins, E. Washburn. Epic Mythology. rev. ed. LC 76-75358. 1968. Repr. of 1915 ed. 16.00x (ISBN 0-8196-0228-0). Biblo.

Lal, P. An Annotated Mahabharata Bibliography. 31p. 1973. 10.00 (ISBN 0-88253-306-1). Ind-US Inc.

--The Mahabharata. 352p. 1980. text ed. 25.00 (ISBN 0-7069-1033-8, Pub. by Vikas India); pap. 14.50 (ISBN 0-686-77530-9). Advent NY.

Lal, P., tr. from Sanskrit. The Mahabharata, Vols. 1-110. LC 73-900568. 3750p. 1972. Set. 465.00x (ISBN 0-8002-1684-9). Intl Pubns Serv.

Narasimhan, Chakravarthi V., tr. The Mahabharata. LC 64-10347. 254p. (English version based on selected verses). 1973. pap. 6.00 (ISBN 0-231-08321-1). Columbia U Pr.

Rameshwar Rao, S., tr. The Mahabharata. 2nd ed. Orig. Title: The Children's Mahabharata. 219p. 1976. pap. text ed. 2.85 (ISBN 0-89253-041-3). Ind-US Inc.

Roy, P. C., tr. Mahabharata, 12 vols. Incl. Adi Parva. 3rd ed. 13.50x (ISBN 0-8426-0748-X); Sabha Parva & Vana Parva, Pt. 1. 3rd ed. 13.50x (ISBN 0-8426-0749-8); Vana Parva, Pt. 2. 3rd ed; Virata & Udyoga Parva. 13.50x (ISBN 0-8426-0751-X); Bhishma Parva. 3rd ed. 13.50x (ISBN 0-8426-0752-8); Drona Parva. 13.50x (ISBN 0-8426-0753-6); Karna Parva, Salya Parva, Sauptika Parva, Stree Parva. 3rd ed. 22.50x (ISBN 0-8426-0754-4); Vol. 8. Santi Parva, Pt. 1. 22.50x (ISBN 0-8426-0978-4); Vol. 9. Santi Parva, Pt. 2. 13.50x (ISBN 0-8426-0755-2); Vol. 10. Santi Parva, Pt. 3 & Anusasana Parva, Pt. 1. 3rd ed; Vol. 11. Anusasana Parva, Pt. 2. 3rd ed. 22.50x (ISBN 0-8426-0980-6). Verry.

--Mahabharata: Aswamedha, Asramavasika, Mausala, Mahaprasthanika, & Swargarohanika Parvas, Vol. 12. 3rd ed. 1975. 22.50x (ISBN 0-8426-0982-2). Verry.
Sorensen, S. An Index to the Names in the Mahabharata. 1978. Repr. 34.50 (ISBN 0-89684-011-5, Pub. by Motilal Banarsidass India). Orient Bk Dist.
Van Buitenen, J. A. The Mahabharata: The Book of the Beginning. LC 72-97802. (Illus.). lii, 492p. 1980. pap. 9.95 (ISBN 0-226-84663-6, P879). U of Chicago Pr.
Van Buitenen, J. A., ed. & tr. from Sanskrit. The Mahabharata. Incl. Vol. 1. Book 1: The Book of the Beginning. 1974. 22.00x (ISBN 0-226-84648-2); Vol. II. Book 2: The Book of the Assembly Hall. 1976; Book 3: The Book of the Forest. 1976. LC 72-97802. lib. bdg. 36.00x set (ISBN 0-226-84649-0). U of Chicago Pr.
Van Buitenen, J. A., ed. & tr. The Mahabharata, Vol. 2, Bks. 2 & 3. LC 75-5067. 880p. 1981. Book 2 The Book Of The Assembly Hall. 15.00 (ISBN 0-226-84664-4, Phoen). Book 3 The Book Of The Forest. U of Chicago Pr.
Van Nooten, Barend A. Mahabharata. (World Authors Ser.: India: No. 131). lib. bdg. 10.95 (ISBN 0-8057-2564-4). Twayne.
Vyasa. Mahabharata. 6th ed. Rajagopalachari, Chakravarti, ed. Rajagapalachari, Chakravarti & Rao, N. R., trs. from Tamil. 332p. 1980. 5.00 (ISBN 0-934676-16-X). Greenlf Bks.

MAHABHARATA, BHAGAVADGITA

Arnold, Edwin, tr. The Song Celestial or Bhaggvad-Gita: From the Mahabharata, Being a Discourse Between Arjuna, Prince of India, & the Supreme Being Under the Form of Krishna. 1967. pap. 4.00 (ISBN 0-7100-6268-0). Routledge & Kegan.
Judge, William Q., ed. Bhagavad-Gita: Recension with Essays. LC 70-92964. 1977. 6.00 (ISBN 0-911500-27-8); pap. 3.50 (ISBN 0-911500-28-6). Theos U Pr.
Mahabharata. The Mahabharata: Critical Edition, 19 vols. in 22. Sukthankar, Vishnu S., et al, eds. LC 67-2016. (Illus.). 13000p. (Sanskrit.). 1967. Set. 900.00x (ISBN 0-8002-1685-7). Intl Pubns Serv.
Mahesh Yogi Maharishi, tr. Maharishi Mahesh Yogi on the Bhaqavad-Gita. (Orig.). 1969. pap. 3.95 (ISBN 0-14-002913-3). Penguin.
Pandit, M. P., ed. Light from the Gita. 1967. 3.50x (ISBN 0-8426-1462-1). Verry.
Srinivasachari, P. N. Ethical Philosophy of the Gita. 2.00 (ISBN 0-87481-454-5). Vedanta Pr.
Vaidya, P. L. Pratika-Index: Index of Quarter Verses in the Critical Edition of the Mahabharata, 6 vols. 1972. Set. 70.00x (ISBN 0-8002-1828-0). Intl Pubns Serv.

MAHAFFY, JOHN PENTLAND, 1839-1919

Stanford, W. B. & McDowell, R. B. Mahaffy: A Biography of an Anglo-Irishman. 1971. 12.95 (ISBN 0-7100-6880-8). Routledge & Kegan.

MAHAKA

see Tobacco

MAHAN, ALFRED THAYER, 1840-1914

Livezey, William E. Mahan on Sea Power. rev. ed. LC 79-6720. (Illus.). 389p. 1981. 15.95 (ISBN 0-8061-1569-6). U of Okla Pr.
Seager, Robert. Alfred Thayer Mahan: The Man & His Letters. LC 77-74158. 1977. 24.95x (ISBN 0-87021-359-8). Naval Inst Pr.
Seager, Robert, II & Maguire, Doris D., eds. Letters & Papers of Alfred Thayer Mahan, 3 vols. LC 73-91863. (Letters Ser., No. 4). 1975. 95.00x (ISBN 0-87021-339-3). Naval Inst Pr.

MAHARAJ JI, GURU

Downton, James V., Jr. Sacred Journeys: Conversion & Commitment to Divine Light Mission. LC 79-546. (Illus.). 1979. 15.00 (ISBN 0-231-04198-5). Columbia U Pr.

MAHARASHTRA, INDIA (STATE)

Antulay, A. R. Mahajan Report Uncovered. 1968. 5.00x (ISBN 0-8188-1011-4). Paragon.
Carter, A. T. Elite Politics in Rural India. LC 73-86043. (Studies in Social Anthropology: No. 9). (Illus.). 224p. 1974. 23.95 (ISBN 0-521-20366-X). Cambridge U Pr.
Cashman, Richard I. The Myth of the Lokamanya: Tilak & Mass Politics in Maharashtra. LC 72-97734. 1975. 23.75x (ISBN 0-520-02407-9). U of Cal Pr.
Deshpande, C. D. Geography of Maharashtra. (India; Land & People Ser.). (Illus.). 218p. 1973. 4.00x (ISBN 0-8426-0512-6). Verry.
McDonald, Ellen E. & Stark, Craig M. English Education, Nationalist Politics & Elite Groups in Maharashtra, 1885-1915. (Occasional Papers Ser.: No. 5). 1969. 8.00 (ISBN 0-686-23628-9, Ctr South & Southeast Asia Studies). Cellar.
Mathur, Kuleep. Administrative Response to Emergency: A Study of Scarcity Administration in Maharashtra. LC 75-904667. 1975. 7.00x (ISBN 0-88386-642-0). South Asia Bks.
Tucker, Richard P. Ranade & the Roots of Indian Nationalism. (Midway Reprint Ser.). pap. 11.00x (ISBN 0-226-81532-3). U of Chicago Pr.
Wagle, N. K., ed. Images of Maharashtra: A Regional Profile of India. 1981. pap. 12.00x (ISBN 0-8364-0713-X, Pub. by Curzon Pr). South Asia Bks.

MAHARISHI, THE GURU

see Mahesh Yogi, Maharishi

MAHASHAY, NAG

Chakravarty, Sarat C. Nag Mahasaya: A Saintly Householder Disciple of Sri Ramakrishna. 1978. pap. 2.25 (ISBN 0-87481-481-2). Vedanta Pr.

MAHAYANA BUDDHISM

Asvaghosha, B. Asvaghosha's Discourse on the Awakening of Faith in the Mahayana. lib. bdg. 59.95 (ISBN 0-87968-472-0). Krishna Pr.
Ch'an Master Hua. Dharma Flower Sutra, Vol. II. Bhikshuni Heng Yin, tr. (Illus.). 1978. pap. 7.95 (ISBN 0-917512-22-7). Buddhist Text.
Conze, Edward. Buddhist Thought in India. 1967. pap. 3.95 (ISBN 0-472-06129-1, 129, AA). U of Mich Pr.
Conze, Edward, ed. & tr. The Large Sutra on Perfect Wisdom, with the Divisions of the Abhisamayalankara. LC 71-189224. 1975. 39.50x (ISBN 0-520-02240-8). U of Cal Pr.
Cowell, E. B., et al. Buddhist Mahayana Texts. Mueller, F. Max, ed. LC 68-9450. (Sacred Books of the East Ser). 1969. pap. 6.50 (ISBN 0-486-22093-1). Dover.
Crowell, E. B. Buddhist Mahayana Texts. lib. bdg. 59.95 (ISBN 0-87968-499-2). Krishna Pr.
Dohanian, Diran D. The Mahayana Buddhist Sculpture of Ceylon. LC 76-23613. (Outstanding Dissertations in the Fine Arts). (Illus.). 1977. Repr. of 1964 ed. lib. bdg. 48.00 (ISBN 0-8240-2685-3). Garland Pub.
Dutt, Nalinaksha. Mahayana Buddhism. rev. ed. 1978. 10.00 (ISBN 0-89684-032-8, Pub. by Motilal Banarsidass India). Orient Bk Dist.
--Mahayana Buddhism. 1976. Repr. of 1973 ed. 11.00x (ISBN 0-8364-0430-0). South Asia Bks.
Getty, Alice. The Gods of Northern Buddhism. LC 62-15617. (Illus.). 1962. 39.50 (ISBN 0-8048-1129-6). C E Tuttle.
Gudmunsen, Chris. Wittgenstein & Buddhism. LC 76-19863. 1977. text ed. 22.50x (ISBN 0-06-492585-4). B&N.
Hurvitz, Leon, tr. from Chin & Sanskrit. Scripture of the Lotus Blossom of the Fine Dharma: The Lotus Sutra. LC 75-45381. 1976. 20.00x (ISBN 0-231-03789-9); pap. 10.00x (ISBN 0-231-03920-4). Columbia U Pr.
Jumsai, M. L. Understanding Thai Buddhism. 124p. 1971. 5.50x (ISBN 0-685-25238-8). Paragon.
Kato, Bunno, et al, trs. The Threefold Lotus Sutra. LC 74-23158. Orig. Title: Hokke Sambu-Kyo. 464p. 1975. 19.75 (ISBN 0-8348-0105-1); pap. 10.95 (ISBN 0-8348-0106-X). Weatherhill.
Kiyota, Minoru. Mahayana Buddhist Meditation: Theory & Practice. 1978. text ed. 15.00x (ISBN 0-8248-0556-9). U Pr of Hawaii.
Lama Mi-phan. Golden Zephyr. Kawamura, Leslie S., tr. from Tibetan. LC 75-5259. (Tibetan Translation Ser.: Vol.4). (Illus.). 192p. (Orig.). 1975. 12.95 (ISBN 0-913546-22-4); pap. 6.95 (ISBN 0-913546-21-6). Dharma Pub.
McGovern, William M. Introduction to Mahayana Buddhism. LC 70-149665. Repr. of 1922 ed. 17.00 (ISBN 0-404-04129-9). AMS Pr.
Reichelt, Karl L. Truth & Tradition in Chinese Buddhism. 2nd ed. Van Wagenen, Kathrina, tr. LC 68-59117. 1969. Repr. of 1934 ed. 11.50 (ISBN 0-8188-0074-7). Paragon.
Suzuki, Beatrice L. Mahayana Buddhism. 1969. pap. 1.45 (ISBN 0-02-089580-1). Macmillan.
Suzuki, Daisetz T. Studies in the Lankavatara Sutra: An Elucidation & Analysis of One of the Most Important Texts of Mahayana Buddhism, in Which Almost All Its Principal Tenets Are Presented Including the Teaching of Zen. 1968. Repr. of 1930 ed. 30.00 (ISBN 0-7100-6330-X). Routledge & Kegan.
Suzuki, Daisetz T., tr. The Lankavatara Sutra: A Mahayana Text. (Illus.). 1972. Repr. of 1932 ed. 26.00 (ISBN 0-7100-2165-8). Routledge & Kegan.
Thomas, E. J., tr. from Sanskrit. The Perfection of Wisdom: The Career of the Predestined Buddhas. LC 78-12005. 1979. Repr. of 1952 ed. lib. bdg. 15.00x (ISBN 0-313-20646-5, MAPWI). Greenwood.
Thurman, Robert A., tr. from Tibetan. The Holy Teaching of Vimalakirti: Mahayana Scripture. LC 75-27197. (Institute for Advanced Study of World Religions Ser.). 220p. 1976. 14.95 (ISBN 0-271-01209-9). Pa St U Pr.

MAHDI

Wingate, F. R. Mahdiism & Egyptian Sudan. 2nd ed. (Illus.). 618p. 1968. 37.50x (ISBN 0-7146-1738-5, F Cass Co). Biblio Dist.

MAHESH YOGI, MAHARISHI

Yogi, Maharishi Mahesh, tr. from Sanskrit. & commentary by. Maharishi Mahesh Yogi on the Bhagavad-Gita, Pts. 1-6. lib. bdg. 10.50x (ISBN 0-88307-290-4). Gannon.

MAHLER, GUSTAV, 1860-1911

Bauer-Lechner, Natalie. Recollections of Gustav Mahler. Franklin, P., ed. Newlin, D., tr. from Ger. LC 80-834. (Illus.). 241p. 1980. 22.50 (ISBN 0-521-23572-3). Cambridge U Pr.
Cooke, Deryck. Gustav Mahler: An Introduction to His Music. 1980. 19.95 (ISBN 0-521-23175-2); pap. 5.95 (ISBN 0-521-29847-4). Cambridge U Pr.
De La Grange, Henry-Louis. Mahler. LC 72-76147. 1008p. 1973. 17.50 (ISBN 0-385-00524-5). Doubleday.
Gartenberg, Egon. Mahler: The Man & His Music. LC 77-70274. (Illus.). 1979. pap. 6.95 (ISBN 0-02-871540-3). Schirmer Bks.
--Mahler: The Man & His Music. LC 77-70274. (Illus.). 1978. 14.95 (ISBN 0-02-870840-7). Schirmer Bks.
Holbrook, David. Gustav Mahler & the Courage to Be. (Illus.). 270p. 1981. Repr. of 1975 ed. lib. bdg. 27.50 (ISBN 0-306-76095-9). Da Capo.
Kennedy, Michael. Mahler. (Master Musicians Ser.: No. M161). (Illus.). 1977. pap. 7.95 (ISBN 0-8226-0714-X). Littlefield.
--Mahler. (Master Musicians Ser). (Illus.). 208p. 1974. 11.00x (ISBN 0-460-03141-4, Pub. by J. M. Dent England). Biblio Dist.
Martner, Knud & Mahler, Alma, eds. Selected Letters of Gustav Mahler. Wilkins, E., et al, trs. 1979. 30.00 (ISBN 0-374-25846-5). FS&G.
Mitchell, Donald. Gustav Mahler: The Early Years. Banks, Paul & Mathews, David, eds. LC 79-9694. 1980. 28.50 (ISBN 0-520-04141-0). U of Cal Pr.
--Gustav Mahler: The Wunderhorn Years. LC 79-9694. 1980. pap. 10.95 (ISBN 0-520-04220-4, CAL 442). U of Cal Pr.
Newlin, Dika. Bruckner-Mahler-Schoenberg. rev. ed. 1978. 14.95 (ISBN 0-393-02203-X); pap. write for info. (ISBN 0-393-00421-X). Norton.
Walter, Bruno. Gustav Mahler. Galston, James, tr. LC 78-87691. (Music Ser). 1970. Repr. of 1941 ed. lib. bdg. 19.50 (ISBN 0-306-71701-8). Da Capo.
--Gustav Mahler. Galston, James, tr. from Ger. LC 73-89928. (Studies of Composers). 256p. 1973. pap. 15.00x (ISBN 0-8443-0035-7). Vienna Hse.

MAHOMET THE PROPHET

see Mohammed, the Prophet, 570-632

MAHRATTA LANGUAGE

see Marathi Language

MAHRATTAS

see Marathas

MAIAKOVSKII, VLADIMIR VLADIMIROVICH, 1894-1930

Brown, Edward J. Mayakovsky: A Poet in Revolution. LC 72-14022. (Studies of the Russian Institute, Columbia University). 475p. 1973. 28.00x (ISBN 0-691-06255-2). Princeton U Pr.

MAI-CHI SHAN CAVES

Sullivan, Michael. The Cave Temples of Maichishan. LC 69-15829. (Illus.). 1969. 55.00x (ISBN 0-520-01448-0). U of Cal Pr.

MAIDEN AUNTS

see Single Women

MAIDU LANGUAGE

Dixon, Roland B. Maidu Texts. LC 73-3539. (American Ethnological Society. Publications: No. 4). Repr. of 1912 ed. 21.00 (ISBN 0-404-58154-4). AMS Pr.

MAIER, WALTER ARTHUR, 1893-1950

Maier, Paul L. The Best of Walter A. Maier. 1980. pap. 7.95 (ISBN 0-570-03823-5, 12-2786). Concordia.
--A Man Spoke, a World Listened. 1980. pap. 8.95 (ISBN 0-570-03822-7, 12-2762). Concordia.

MAIL BOATS

see Packets

MAIL LIBRARY SERVICE

see Direct Delivery of Books

MAIL-ORDER BUSINESS

see also Advertising-Direct-Mail; Sales Letters

Alexander, Ken. How to Start Your Own Mail Order Business. rev. ed. (Illus.). 1960. 6.95 (ISBN 0-87396-000-9). Stravon.
Arco Editorial Board. How to Win Success in the Mail Order Business. 2nd ed. LC 59-9294. 1966. pap. 5.00 (ISBN 0-668-02897-1). Arco.
B. P. Foundation. Mail Order Operation. 2.00 (ISBN 0-685-22025-7). Wehman.
Boyd, Margaret A. & Scott-Martin, Sue. Directory of Shop-by-Mail Bargain Sources. LC 77-17778. 1979. pap. 2.95 (ISBN 0-87576-063-5). Pilot Bks.
Brandell, Raymond J. & Brandell, Raymond E. The Dynamics of Making a Fortune in Mail Order. (Illus.). 368p. 1980. 19.95 (ISBN 0-8119-0325-7). Fell.
Brumbaugh, J. Frank. Mail Order....Starting up, Making It Pay. LC 78-14623. 1979. pap. 7.95 (ISBN 0-8019-6805-4). Chilton.
Cooklin, Lawrence. Profitable Mail Order Marketing. 1976. 18.95x (ISBN 0-434-90259-4). Intl Ideas.
Cooray, L. J. Conventions, the Australian Constitution & the Future. xix, 235p. 1979. 24.00x (ISBN 0-9596568-1-2). Rothman.
Corita Communications Editors. The Mail Order Guide: For the Beginner Interested in a Part or Full Time Business (in Mail Order) 1979. 9.95 (ISBN 0-933016-02-6). Corita Comm.
Cossman, E. Joseph. How I Made One Million Dollars in Mail Order. (Illus.). 1963. 9.95 (ISBN 0-13-397406-5). P-H.
Direct Mail Advertising & Selling for Retailers. 1978. text ed. 19.75 (ISBN 0-685-86701-3). Natl Ret Merch.
Direct Mail Databook. 3rd ed. 276p. 1980. text ed. 65.00x (ISBN 0-566-02177-3, Pub. by Gower Pub Co England). Renouf.
Directory of High-Discount Merchandise & Product Sources for Distributors & Mail-Order Wealth Builders. 1978. 17.50 (ISBN 0-685-83448-4). Intl Wealth.
Directory of Mailing List Houses: 1977 Edition. 232p. 30.00 (ISBN 0-686-62437-8). B Klein Pubns.
Du Vall, Dean F. The Du Vall Method for Acquiring Great Self-Publishing Wealth. 7th ed. 88p. 1980. pap. 25.00 (ISBN 0-931232-10-4). Du Vall Financial.
--Exactly How to Build a Fortune in Mail Order. 1978. pap. 10.00 (ISBN 0-931232-18-X). Du Vall Financial.
--The Princely Profits of Party Plan. 12th ed. 84p. 1980. pap. 10.00 (ISBN 0-931232-08-2). Du Vall Financial.
First Impressions. 92p. 1978. 14.00 (ISBN 0-686-62455-6). B Klein Pubns.
Foster, Lee. Just Twenty-Five Cents & Three Wheaties Boxtops. pap. 4.95 (ISBN 0-87465-041-0). Pacific Coast.
Gonzales, Andrew. Mail Order & Other Profitable Methods. pap. 4.75 (ISBN 0-686-19131-5). Gonzales.
Gottlieb, Richard, ed. Directory of Mail Order Catalogs. 1981. 85.00 (ISBN 0-87196-523-2). Facts on File.
--The Directory of Mail Order Catalogs. 360p. pap. 70.00 (ISBN 0-939300-00-1). Grey Hse Pub.
Harviston, Vernon L. How to Go into the Mail Order Business & Make a Fortune Out of It. (Illus.). 1979. deluxe ed. 37.50 (ISBN 0-918968-44-5). Inst Econ Finan.
Henck, Karl N. How to Start Your Own Microcomputer Based Mail Order Business. LC 81-65513. (Illus., Orig.). 1981. pap. 15.00 (ISBN 0-939258-00-5). Bork Res.
Hicks, Tyler G. Directory of High-Discount Merchandise & Product Sources for Distributors & Mail-Order Wealth Builders. 2nd ed. 150p. 1981. pap. 17.50 (ISBN 0-914306-58-8). Intl Wealth.
--How to Make a Fortune Through Export Mail-Order Riches. 2nd ed. 150p. 1981. pap. 17.50 (ISBN 0-914306-57-X). Intl Wealth.
--Mail Order Riches Success Kit. 2nd ed. 927p. 1981. pap. 99.50 (ISBN 0-914306-41-3). Intl Wealth.
Hodgson, Richard S. Direct Mail & Mail Order Handbook. 3rd ed. 1980. 52.50 (ISBN 0-85013-116-2). Dartnell Corp.
Hoge, Cecil C., Sr. Mail Order Moonlighting. LC 78-61866. 1978. 10.95 (ISBN 0-913668-95-8); pap. 7.95 (ISBN 0-913668-94-X). Ten Speed Pr.
Horchow, Roger. Elephants in Your Mailbox: How I Learned the Secrets of Mail-Order Marketing Despite Having Made 25 Horrendous Mistakes. 288p. 1980. 12.50 (ISBN 0-8129-0891-0). Times Bks.
How Mail Order Fortunes Are Made. 352p. 12.00 (ISBN 0-686-62460-2). B Klein Pubns.
How to Make Your Mail Order Fortune from Classified Ads. 76p. 1978. 12.00 (ISBN 0-686-62461-0). B Klein Pubns.
How You Too Can Make One Million in the Mail Order Business. 360p. 1978. 16.00 (ISBN 0-686-62463-7). B Klein Pubns.
Israel, Fred L., ed. Eighteen Ninety-Seven Sears Roebuck Catalogue. abr. ed. LC 80-69200. (Illus.). 256p. 1981. pap. 4.95 (ISBN 0-87754-138-8). Chelsea Hse.
Joffe, Gerardo. How You Too Can Make at Least One Million Dollars (But Probably Much More) in the Mail-Order Business. LC 77-92067. 1979. 19.95 (ISBN 0-930992-02-4, HarpT). Har-Row.
Jones, Jennifer. Coupon Power: How to Turn Your Mailbox into a Treasure Chest Using 10 Secrets of Refunding. (Illus.). 96p. (Orig.). 1981. pap. 5.95 (ISBN 0-934832-23-4). Word Power.
Kavanaugh, Kam. The Mailbox Emporium the Thinking Man's Comperhensive Guide to Selling by Mail. 120p. 1981. pap. 9.95 (ISBN 0-9605742-2-0). Kambrina.
Keup, Erwin J. Mail Order Legal Manual. LC 81-80335. 300p. 1981. 45.00 (ISBN 0-916378-14-4). PSI Res.
Lyons, Delphine C. Whole World Catalog. LC 73-79934. (Illus.). 356p. (Orig.). 1973. pap. 5.00 (ISBN 0-8129-0388-9). Times Bks.

Mail Order Blues. (Illus.). 1975. 3.00 (ISBN 0-937514-01-2, 633543). World Merch Import.
Mail Order Business Directory: 1980 Edition. 430p. 45.00 (ISBN 0-686-62435-1). B Klein Pubns.
Mail Order Flip-Flops. (Illus.). 5.00 (ISBN 0-937514-02-0, 579356). World Merch Import.
Marcus, Adrianne, et al. Carrion House. (Illus.). 64p. 1980. pap. 3.95 (ISBN 0-312-12265-9); pre-pack 39.50 (ISBN 0-312-12266-7). St Martin.
Martyn, Sean. How to Start & Run a Successful Mail Order Business. 1971. 12.95 (ISBN 0-679-50259-9). McKay.
Metallo, William R. A Fortune Awaits You in Mail Order. LC 79-54313. (Illus.). 1979. 14.95 (ISBN 0-9603192-0-4). Am Ent FL.
Miller, Lowell. The Wholesale-by-Mail Catalog. LC 78-21204. 1979. 11.95 (ISBN 0-312-87762-5); pap. 5.95 (ISBN 0-312-87763-3). St Martin.
Miller, Nelson A. & Rhoads, Joseph H. How to Grow Rich in Mail Order. rev., abr. ed. LC 81-68715. 113p. 1981. spiral bdg. 14.95 (ISBN 0-940902-00-1). Assoc Pubs NY.
O'Callaghan, Dorothy. Mail Order U. S. A. A Consumer's Guide to Over 2,000 Top Mail Order Catalogs in the United States & Canada. 3rd ed. LC 78-51830. 1981. pap. 7.00 (ISBN 0-914694-03-0). Mail Order.
Powers, Melvin. How to Get Rich in Mail Order. 1980. pap. 10.00 (ISBN 0-87980-373-8). Wilshire.
Print Project. The Unusual-by-Mail Catalog. (Illus.). 192p. 1980. 14.95 (ISBN 0-312-83374-1); pap. 7.95 (ISBN 0-312-83375-X). St Martin.
Rex, David. Mail Order Rules & Regulations: Facts Every Buyer & Seller Through the Mail Needs to Know. 110p. 1982. pap. write for info. (ISBN 0-940544-00-8). Briar Co.
Secrets & Top Tips of Mail Order Advertising. 1976. 1.00 (ISBN 0-937514-04-7, 706391). World Merch Import.
Shinn, Duane. How to Sell Your Product to Mail Order Houses by the Thousands. 1976. 19.95 (ISBN 0-912732-23-7). Duane Shinn.
Simon, Julian L. How to Start & Operate a Mail Order Business. 3rd. ed. LC 80-13807. (Illus.). 544p. 1980. 19.95 (ISBN 0-07-057417-0, P&RB). McGraw.
Smith, Don P. Mathematics of Mail Order, 3 vol. set. 1976. 8.00 (ISBN 0-937514-05-5, 764752, New Era). World Merch Import.
--Mr. Mel Order, 10 vols. (Big-Little Reports Ser.: Nos. 101-110). (Illus.). 1976. 3.00 set (ISBN 0-937514-06-3, 788783, New Era). World Merch Import.
--Shortest Route to "the" Ultimate Success in Mail Order, 3 vol set. (Illus.). 1976. 4.00 (ISBN 0-937514-07-1, 729275, New Era). World Merch Import.
Sparks, Howard. Amazing Mail Order Business & How to Succeed in It. LC 66-17336. 244p. 1966. 9.95 (ISBN 0-8119-0005-3). Fell.
Stern, Alfred. How Mail Order Fortunes Are Made. rev. ed. LC 70-106818. (Illus.). 352p. 1974. 12.95 (ISBN 0-685-41838-3). Selective.
Tilson, Ann & Weiss, Carol H. The Mail Order Food Guide. 1977. 10.95 (ISBN 0-671-22810-2); pap. 4.95 (ISBN 0-671-23077-8). S&S.
Vogel, Erwin. How to Start Minding Your Own (Mail Order, That Is) Business. (Business Reference Ser.). (Illus.). 54p. (Microfiche avail., ISBN 0-912392-06-1). (gr. 9 up). 1969. pap. 4.00 (ISBN 0-912392-02-9, MO1); pap. 5.50 incld. how to write collection letters that click & collect (ISBN 0-912392-07-X). Copy-Write.
Wilber, L. Perry. Money in Your Mailbox: How to Start & Operate a Mail Order Business. 1979. 14.95 (ISBN 0-8359-4631-2). Reston.
You Can Get Rich in Your Own Home Mail Order Business. (Illus.). 1981. pap. 9.95 (ISBN 0-686-73528-5). Menaid.

MAIL PLANES
see Transport Planes

MAIL SERVICE
see Postal Service

MAILER, NORMAN, 1923-

Adams, Laura. Existential Battles: The Growth of Norman Mailer. LC 74-27710. 192p. 1978. 12.95x (ISBN 0-8214-0182-3); pap. 5.25 (ISBN 0-8214-0401-6). Ohio U Pr.
--Norman Mailer: A Comprehensive Bibliography. LC 74-14163. (Author Bibliographies Ser.: No. 20). 1974. 10.00 (ISBN 0-8108-0771-8). Scarecrow.
Adams, Laura, ed. Will the Real Norman Mailer Please Stand up. LC 73-83259. 288p. 1974. 16.00 (ISBN 0-8046-9066-9). Kennikat.
Bailey, Jennifer. Norman Mailer: Quick-Change Artist. LC 79-14282. 1980. text ed. 24.50x (ISBN 0-06-490284-6). B&N.
Begiebing, Robert J. Acts of Regeneration: Allegory & Archetype in the Works of Norman Mailer. LC 80-50416. 224p. 1981. text ed. 20.00x (ISBN 0-8262-0310-8). U of Mo Pr.
Braudy, Leo, ed. Norman Mailer: A Collection of Critical Essays. 1972. pap. 1.95 (ISBN 0-13-545541-3, STC101, Spec). P-H.
Bufithis, Philip H. Norman Mailer. LC 74-78438. (Modern Literature Ser.). 1978. 10.95 (ISBN 0-8044-2097-1); pap. 4.95 (ISBN 0-8044-6064-7). Ungar.
Ehrlich, Robert. Norman Mailer: The Radical As Hipster. LC 78-14849. 1978. lib. bdg. 12.00 (ISBN 0-8108-1160-X). Scarecrow.
Gordon, Andrew. An American Dreamer: A Psychoanalytic Study of the Fiction of Norman Mailer. LC 77-79778. 240p. 1981. pap. 8.95 (ISBN 0-8386-3066-9). Fairleigh Dickinson.
Gordon, Andrew M. An American Dreamer: A Psychoanalytic Study of the Fiction of Norman Mailer. LC 77-89778. 240p. 1980. 18.00 (ISBN 0-8386-2158-9). Fairleigh Dickinson.
Gutman, Stanley T. Mankind in Barbary: The Individual & Society in the Novels of Norman Mailer. LC 75-18290. 238p. 1975. text ed. 15.00x (ISBN 0-87451-118-6). U Pr of New Eng.
Leeds, Barry H. The Structured Vision of Norman Mailer. LC 72-80067. (Gotham Library). 1969. 12.00x (ISBN 0-8147-0256-2); pap. 5.95 (ISBN 0-8147-0257-0). NYU Pr.
McConnell, Frank D. Four Postwar American Novelists: Bellow, Mailer, Barth, & Pynchon. LC 76-25638. 1978. pap. text ed. 4.50 (ISBN 0-226-55685-9, P800, Phoen). U of Chicago Pr.
Mailer, Norman. A Transit to Narcissus: A Facsimile of the Original Typescript. LC 77-24755. 1978. 100.00x (ISBN 0-86527-315-4). Fertig.
Merrill, Robert. Norman Mailer. (United States Authors Ser.: No. 322). 1978. 12.50 (ISBN 0-8057-7254-5). Twayne.
Poirier, Richard. Norman Mailer. Kermode, Frank, ed. LC 75-185983. (Modern Masters Ser). 128p. 1972. 6.95 (ISBN 0-670-51503-5). Viking Pr.
Radford, Jean. Norman Mailer: A Critical Study. LC 74-10479. 203p. 1975. text ed. 24.50x (ISBN 0-06-495759-4). B&N.
Sokoloff, B. A. Norman Mailer: A Comprehensive Bibliography. 1972. lib. bdg. 15.00 limited ed. (ISBN 0-8414-1614-1). Folcroft.
Weatherby, W. J. Squaring Off: Mailer vs. Baldwin. 1977. 9.95 (ISBN 0-442-80449-0). Van Nos Reinhold.

MAILING LISTS

Crown, P. Building Your Mailing Lists. LC 72-13927. (Business Almanac Ser: No. 20). 128p. 1973. 5.95 (ISBN 0-379-11220-5). Oceana.
The IRRI Computerized List System. (IRRI Research Paper Ser.: No. 51). 37p. 1981. pap. 5.00 (ISBN 0-686-69631-X, R134, IRRI). Unipub.

MAILLART, ROBERT

Billington, David P. Robert Maillart's Bridges: The Art of Engineering. LC 78-70279. (Illus.). 1979. 20.00 (ISBN 0-691-08203-0). Princeton U Pr.

MAILLOL, ARISTIDE JOSEPH BONAVENTURE, 1861-1944

Buffalo Fine Arts Academy. Aristide Maillol. Ritchie, Andrew C., ed. LC 71-184839. (Illus.). 128p. 1972. Repr. of 1945 ed. lib. bdg. 15.00x (ISBN 0-8371-6329-3, BFAM). Greenwood.
Maillol, Aristide. Maillol Woodcuts: Great Book Illustrations. (Illus.). 1979. pap. 4.00 (ISBN 0-486-23897-0). Dover.
Maillol, Aristide, illus. Maillol Nudes: Thirty-Five Lithographs by Aristide Maillol. (Dover Art Library). Orig. Title: The Dialogues of the Courtesans. (Illus.). 1980. pap. 2.00 (ISBN 0-486-24000-2). Dover.
Rewald, John. Aristide Maillol: 1861-1944. LC 75-42576. (Illus.). 140p. 1975. soft cover 9.50 (ISBN 0-89207-000-5). S R Guggenheim.
Wofsy, Alan. Aristide Maillol: The Artist & The Book. (Illus.). 1975. 2.50 (ISBN 0-915346-01-X). A Wofsy Fine Arts.

MAIMONIDES
see Moses ben Maimon, 1135-1204

MAINE, HENRY JAMES SUMTER, SIR, 1822-1888

Evans, Morgan O. Theories & Criticisms of Sir Henry Maine. viii, 93p. 1981. Repr. of 1896 ed. lib. bdg. 18.50x (ISBN 0-8377-0540-1). Rothman.
Grant Duff, M. E. Sir Henry Maine: A Brief Memoir of His Life. Stokes, Whitley, ed. vi, 451p. 1979. Repr. of 1892 ed. lib. bdg. 35.00x (ISBN 0-8377-0609-2). Rothman.
Holdsworth, William S. Historians of Anglo-American Law. 1966. Repr. of 1928 ed. 16.50 (ISBN 0-208-00347-9, Archon). Shoe String.
Lippincott, Benjamin E. Victorian Critics of Democracy. 1964. lib. bdg. 15.50x (ISBN 0-374-95035-0). Octagon.

MAINE

Bangor Public Library. Bibliography of the State of Maine. 1962. 95.00 (ISBN 0-8161-0636-3). G K Hall.
Brunelle, James. Maine Almanac. 2nd ed. (Illus., Orig.). 1979. pap. text ed. 4.95 (ISBN 0-930096-04-5). G Gannett.
Caldwell, Bill. Maine Magic. LC 79-88015. (Illus.). 334p. (Orig.). 1979. 12.95 (ISBN 0-930096-03-7). G Gannett.
Clifford, Harold. Maine & Her People, Suppl. on Aroostook County. rev ed. LC 57-14930. (Illus.). (YA) 1976. text ed. 8.50 (ISBN 0-87027-166-0). Wheelwright.
Cowger, Joel, ed. Public Access to Maine Shoreline: A Workshop Discussion. (Fisheries Information Ser.: No. 1). (Illus.). 1978. pap. write for info. (ISBN 0-89737-000-7). Maine Dept Marine.
Cowger, Joel D. Sources of Financial Assistance Available to the Maine Fishing Industry. (Fisheries Information Ser.: No. 2). 1979. pap. write for info (ISBN 0-89737-001-5). Maine Dept Marine.
Cramer, Carl, ed. State O' Maine Facts: 1981. (Illus.). 200p. 1981. pap. 4.95 (ISBN 0-89272-124-3). Down East.
Dodge, Ernest S. Morning Was Starlight: My Maine Boyhood. LC 80-82791. (Illus.). 216p. 1981. pap. 8.95 (ISBN 0-87106-047-7). Globe Pequot.
Greenleaf, Moses. Survey of the State of Maine in Reference to Its Geographical Features, Statistics & Political Economy. LC 71-128108. 1970. 14.00 (ISBN 0-913764-00-0). Maine St Mus.
Holmes, Edward M. Mostly Maine. Date not set. pap. 5.95 (ISBN 0-89101-035-1). U Maine Orono.
Letourneau, Gene. Sportsmen Say. 1977. 8.95 (ISBN 0-930096-01-0). G Gannett.
Maine. 23.00 (ISBN 0-89770-095-3). Curriculum Info Ctr.
Maine Register 1981-1982. 1300p. 1981. 65.00 (ISBN 0-89442-025-9). Tower Pub Co.
Mellon, Gertrud A. & Wilder, Elizabeth F., eds. Maine & Its Role in American Art: 1740-1963. (Illus.). 178p. 1963. 8.00 (ISBN 0-910394-09-1). Colby.
Plummer, Edward C. Reminiscences of a Yarmouth, Maine Schoolboy. (Illus.). 263p. 1926. 5.00x (ISBN 0-686-00235-0). O'Brien.
Pohl, William. The Voice of Maine. (Illus.). 176p. Date not set. 18.95 (ISBN 0-8159-7104-4). Devin.
Pullen, John. The Twentieth Maine. 1980. 17.50 (ISBN 0-686-68805-8). Pr of Morningside.
Ring, Elizabeth. Maine Bibliographies: A Bibliographical Guide. (Maine History Bibliographical Guide Ser.). 1973. pap. 4.00 (ISBN 0-915592-16-9). Maine Hist.
State Industrial Directories Corp. Maine State Industrial Directory 1977. (Maine State Industrial Directory Ser.). 1976. 20.00 (ISBN 0-916112-53-5). State Indus Dir.
Weber, Carl. Thomas Hardy in Maine. LC 75-22203. (Studies in Thomas Hardy, No. 14). 1975. lib. bdg. 40.95 (ISBN 0-8383-2077-5). Haskell.
Wilkins, Austin H. Ten Million Acres of Timber: The Remarkable Story of Forest Protection in the Maine Forestry District 1909-1972. (Illus.). xxiv, 312p. 1978. pap. 8.95 (ISBN 0-931474-03-5). TBW Bks.

MAINE–ANTIQUITIES

Camp, Helen. Archaeological Excavations at Pemaquid, Maine. LC 75-44753. (Illus.). 1976. 6.95x (ISBN 0-913764-07-8). Maine St Mus.
Casco Bay Steamboat Album. 1973. pap. 2.95 (ISBN 0-89272-003-4). Down East.
Moorehead, Warren K. A Report on the Archaeology of Maine: Being a Narrative of Explorations in That State, 1912-1920, Together with Work at Lake Champlain, 1917. LC 76-43788. (Phillips Academy, Dept of Anthropology). Repr. of 1922 ed. 49.50 (ISBN 0-404-15643-6). AMS Pr.
Soule, William H., ed. Prehistoric Peoples of Maine. (Illus.). 66p. 1970. looseleaf tchrs' ed. 2.00x (ISBN 0-913764-02-7). Maine St Mus.
Willoughby, C. C. Prehistoric Burial Places in Maine. (Harvard University Peabody Museum of Archaeology & Ethnology Papers). Repr. of 1898 ed. pap. 3.00 (ISBN 0-527-01188-6). Kraus Repr.
Willoughby, Charles C. Indian Antiquities of the Kennebec Valley. Spiess, Arthur E., ed. (Occasional Publications in Maine Archaeology: No. 1). (Illus.). 160p. 1980. 22.00 (ISBN 0-913764-13-2). Maine St Mus.

MAINE–DESCRIPTION AND TRAVEL

AMC Maine Mountain Guidebook Committee. AMC Katahdin Guide. (Illus., Orig.). Date not set. pap. price not set (ISBN 0-910146-27-6). Appalach Mtn.
AMC Maine Mountain Guidebook Committee, ed. AMC Maine Mountain Guide: A Guide to Trails in the Mountains of Maine. (Illus.). 1976. 6.95 (ISBN 0-910146-05-5). Appalach Mtn.
--AMC Trail Guide to Mount Desert Island & Acadia National Park. 2nd ed. (Illus.). 1975. pap. 2.50 (ISBN -0910146-04-7). Appalach Mtn.
Anderson, David. The Net in the Bay: Or, Journal of a Visit to Moose & Albany. 18.50 (ISBN 0-384-01401-1). Johnson Repr.
Attwood, Stanley B. Length & Breadth of Maine. 1973. pap. 3.95 (ISBN 0-89101-027-0). U Maine Orono.
Averill, Gerald. Ridge Runner. LC 79-14339. (Illus.). 1979. pap. 4.95 (ISBN 0-89621-030-8). Thorndike Pr.
Baxter, Percival P. Greatest Mountain: Kalahdin's Wilderness. Hakola, Judith & Hakola, John, eds. (Illus.). 114p. (Orig.). 1980. Repr. of 1972 ed. pap. 6.50 (ISBN 0-89272-030-1, 115). Down East.
Beiser, Karl. Twenty-Five Ski Tours in Maine: From Kittery to Caribou,A Cross - Country Skiers Guide. LC 79-64992. (Illus.). 1979. pap. 5.95 (ISBN 0-89725-006-0). NH Pub Co.
Berchen, William. Maine. (Illus.). 1973. 10.95 (ISBN 0-395-15457-X). HM.
Beston, Henry. Especially Maine: The Natural World of Henry Beston, from Cape Cod to the St. Lawrence. Coatsworth, Elizabeth, ed. LC 75-118226. 1976. pap. 6.95 (ISBN 0-8289-0267-4). Greene.
Butcher, Russell E. & Menzietti, Marie I. Maine Paradise. (Large Format Ser). (Illus.). 1976. pap. 5.95 (ISBN 0-14-004316-0). Penguin.
Caldwell, Bill. Enjoying Maine. LC 77-78126. 1978. 10.95 (ISBN 0-930096-01-0). G Gannett.
Catlett, Cloe. Fifty More Hikes in Maine. LC 79-92571. (Fifty Hikes Ser.). (Illus., Orig.). 1980. pap. 8.95 (ISBN 0-89725-017-6). NH Pub Co.
Chadbourne, Ava H. Cumberland County. (Maine County Place - Name Ser.). Date not set. pap. 4.95 (ISBN 0-87027-115-6). Wheelwright.
--Maine Place Names & the Peopling of Its Towns: Washington County. LC 77-115159. (Illus.). 1971. pap. 1.95 (ISBN 0-87027-114-8). Wheelwright.
--Maine Place Names & the Peopling of Its Towns: York County. LC 77-115159. (Illus., Orig.). 1971. pap. 1.95 (ISBN 0-87027-118-0). Wheelwright.
Conkling, Philip. Islands in Time. LC 80-70610. (Illus.). 280p. 1981. 14.95 (ISBN 0-89272-111-1). Down East.
--Islands in Time. LC 80-70610. (Illus.). 280p. 1981. 14.95 (ISBN 0-89272-111-1). Down East.
Cummings, O. R. Trolleys to Augusta, Maine. (Transportation Bulletin: No. 76). (Illus.). 1969. 5.00 (ISBN 0-910506-03-5). De Vito.
Dibner, Martin. Seacoast Maine: The People & Places. LC 72-98412. 192p. 1973. 12.50 (ISBN 0-385-08849-3). Doubleday.
Dietz. Touch of Wildness: A Maine Woods Journal. 1976. pap. 4.25 (ISBN 0-89272-021-2). Down East.
Eckstorm, Fannie H. Indian Place Names of the Penobscot Valley & the Maine Coast. 1974. pap. 4.95 (ISBN 0-89101-028-9). U Maine Orono.
Federal Writers' Project. Maine: A Guide Down East. 476p. 1936. Repr. 49.00 (ISBN 0-403-02170-7). Somerset Pub.
Gibson. Walking the Maine Coast. (Illus.). 1977. pap. 3.75 (ISBN 0-89272-028-X). Down East.
Gibson, John. Fifty Hikes in Maine. LC 74-33818. (Illus.). 160p. 1976. pap. 6.95 (ISBN 0-912274-48-4). NH Pub Co.
Grace, Patrick W. The Gulf of Maine. 1977. pap. 2.95 (ISBN 0-911764-18-6). Durrell.
Graham, Ada & Graham, Frank. Puffin Island. LC 79-22344. (Illus.). 140p. (gr. 6-10). 1979. PLB cancelled (ISBN 0-89621-052-9); pap. 5.95 (ISBN 0-89621-053-7). Thorndike Pr.
Grossinger, Richard. Book of the Cranberry Islands. 299p. Date not set. pap. 5.95 (ISBN 0-913028-88-6). North Atlantic.
Hakola, John W. Legacy of a Lifetime: The Story of Baxter State Park in Maine. (Illus.). 448p. 1981. 16.00 (ISBN 0-931474-18-3). TBW Bks.
Huber, J. Parker. The Wildest Country: A Guide to Thoreau's Maine. (Illus.). 200p. (Orig.). 1981. pap. 10.95 (ISBN 0-910146-34-9). Appalach Mtn.
Hunt, H. Draper. The Blaine House, Home of Maine's Governors. LC 73-86843. pap. 5.95 (ISBN 0-915592-12-6). Maine Hist.
Isaacson, Dorris A. Maine: A Guide Down East. 510p. 1970. 6.50 (ISBN 0-913954-01-2). Courier of Maine.
--Maine: A Guide Downeast. (Illus.). 1970. 6.50 (ISBN 0-913764-06-X). Maine St Mus.
Jennison, Keith. Green Mountains & Rock Ribs. (Illus.). 1979. pap. 5.95 (ISBN 0-911764-03-8). Durrell.
--Maine Idea. (Illus.). 1978. pap. 5.95 (ISBN 0-911764-04-6). Durrell.
--Remember Maine. LC 72-106943. (Illus., Orig.). 1978. pap. 5.95 (ISBN 0-911764-05-4). Durrell.
King, B. A. My Maine Thing. 1st ed. LC 81-65328. (Illus.). 80p. 1981. 19.95 (ISBN 0-939250-00-4); special limited ed. 150.00 (ISBN 0-939250-02-0). Black Ice.
Leavitt, H. Walter. Katahdin Skylines. 1970. pap. 2.75 (ISBN 0-89101-020-3). U Maine Orono.

Lewis, Gerald E. My Big Buck: Outdoor Stories of Maine. LC 78-26185. (Illus.). 1978. pap. 4.95 (ISBN 0-89621-020-0). Thorndike Pr.
Lewis, Paul M. Beautiful Maine. Shangle, Robert D., ed. (Illus.). 72p. (YA) 1981. 14.95 (ISBN 0-89802-307-6); pap. 7.95 (ISBN 0-89802-306-8). Beautiful Am.
Ludman, Allan, ed. Guidebook for Field Trips in Southeastern Maine & South Western New Brunswick. (Geological Bulletins). pap. text ed. 2.50 (ISBN 0-930146-05-0). Queens Coll Pr.
MacDougall, Arthur, Jr. Dud Dean, Maine Guide: Tales of Hunting & Fishing. 1976. pap. 3.95 (ISBN 0-87027-178-4). Wheelwright.
McLane, Charles B. Islands of the Mid-Maine Coast: Penobscot & Blue Hill Bays. (Illus.). 576p. 1981. 35.00 (ISBN 0-933858-00-0, Pub by Kennebec River Pr); signed & numbered limited ed 100.00 (ISBN 0-933858-01-9). TBW Bks.
Maine Historical Society. The Maine Bicentennial Atlas: An Historical Survey. (Illus.). 1976. 10.00 (ISBN 0-915592-24-X); pap. 6.00 (ISBN 0-915592-23-1). Maine Hist.
Maine Mountain Guide Committee (AMC) & Hakola, John, eds. AMC Maine Mountain Guide. 5th ed. (Illus.). Date not set. pap. 6.95 (ISBN 0-910146-25-X). Appalach Mtn.
Mallett, Richard. University of Maine at Farmington. LC 74-20199. (Illus.). 304p. 1975. 10.95 (ISBN 0-87027-157-1); pap. 6.95 (ISBN 0-87027-158-X). Wheelwright.
Miller, Dorcas S. The Maine Coast: A Nature Lover's Guide. LC 79-10290. (Illus.). 192p. 1978. pap. 6.95 (ISBN 0-914788-12-4). East Woods.
Photo. Maine Four Seasons. 1974. 10.95 (ISBN 0-89272-009-3). Down East.
Rand, John. People's Lewiston - Auburn, Maine 1875-1975. LC 75-7980. (Illus.). 128p. 1975. 9.95 (ISBN 0-87027-164-4); pap. 7.95 (ISBN 0-87027-165-2). Wheelwright.
Randall, Peter E. All Creation & the Isles of Shoals. (Illus.). 72p. (Orig.). 1980. pap. 4.95 (ISBN 0-89272-089-1). Down East.
Rich, Louise D. My Neck of the Woods. 255p. 1976. pap. 3.95 (ISBN 0-89272-026-3, 282). Down East.
Roberts, Kenneth. Trending into Maine. 1975. pap. 4.75 (ISBN 0-89272-022-0). Down East.
Rolde, Neil. York Is Living History. LC 74-28772. (Illus.). 96p. 1975. pap. 4.95 (ISBN 0-88448-003-8). Harpswell Pr.
Sadlier, Ruth & Sadlier, Paul. Short Walks Along the Maine Coast. LC 76-51125. (Illus.). 1977. pap. 3.50 (ISBN 0-87106-077-9). Globe Pequot.
Smith, Clyde. Portrait of Maine. (Portrait of America Ser.). (Illus.). 80p. (Orig.). 1981. pap. 6.95 (ISBN 0-912856-71-8). Graphic Arts Ctr.
Smith, Harry W. The ABC's of Maine. LC 79-67415. 60p. (ps-1). 1980. pap. 3.95 (ISBN 0-89272-070-0). Down East.
Steadman. One Hundred Country Inns of Maine. 1979. pap. 6.95 (ISBN 0-89272-061-1). Down East.
Teg, William. Almuchicoitt. 1950. 4.00 (ISBN 0-8158-0196-3). Chris Mass.
Thoreau, Henry D. Maine Woods. (Apollo Eds.). (YA) (gr. 9-12). pap. 4.95 (ISBN 0-8152-0117-6, A117). T Y Crowell.
Thorndike Press, ed. Maine Rivers. LC 79-12996. (Maine Nature Ser.). (Illus., Orig.). 1979. pap. 2.95 (ISBN 0-89621-038-3). Thorndike Pr.
Tower Publishing Company. Maine Marketing Directory Nineteen Eighty. 1980. pap. 12.50 (ISBN 0-89442-020-8). Tower Pub Co.
Wilson, Dorothy C. The Big-Little World of Doc Pritham. 1975. pap. 4.95 (ISBN 0-686-15955-1). Juniper Maine.
Writers Program, Maine. Augusta-Hallowell on the Kennebec. LC 73-3620. (American Guide Ser.). Repr. 10.00 (ISBN 0-404-57922-1). AMS Pr.
--Portland City Guide. LC 73-3621. (American Guide Ser.). 1940. Repr. 20.00 (ISBN 0-404-57923-X). AMS Pr.

MAINE–GENEALOGY

Flagg, Charles A. Alphabetical Index of Revolutionary Pensioners Living in Maine. LC 67-28604. 1967. Repr. of 1920 ed. 8.50 (ISBN 0-8063-0111-2). Genealog Pub.
Frost, John E. Maine Genealogy: A Bibliographical Guide. 1976. pap. 4.00 (ISBN 0-915592-25-8). Maine Hist.
House, Charles J. Names of Soldiers of the American Revolution from Maine: Who Applied for State Bounty Under Resolves of 1835 & 1836 As Appears of Record in Land Office. LC 67-28605. 1967. Repr. of 1893 ed. 7.50 (ISBN 0-8063-0184-8). Genealog Pub.
Jackson, Ronald V. & Teeples, Gary R. Maine Census Index 1810. LC 77-85947. (Illus.). lib. bdg. 24.00 (ISBN 0-89593-055-2). Accelerated Index.
--Maine Census Index 1820. LC 77-85948. (Illus.). lib. bdg. 28.00 (ISBN 0-89593-056-0). Accelerated Index.
--Maine Census Index 1830. LC 77-85949. (Illus.). lib. bdg. 41.00 (ISBN 0-89593-057-9). Accelerated Index.
--Maine Census Index 1840. LC 77-85951. (Illus.). lib. bdg. 46.00 (ISBN 0-89593-058-7). Accelerated Index.
--Maine Census Index 1850. LC 77-85952. (Illus.). lib. bdg. 58.00 (ISBN 0-89593-059-5). Accelerated Index.
Jacson, Ronald V. & Teeples, Gary R. Maine Census Index 1800. LC 77-85944. (Illus.). lib. bdg. 23.00 (ISBN 0-89593-054-4). Accelerated Index.
Noyes, Sybil, et al. Genealogical Dictionary of Maine & New Hampshire. LC 79-88099. 1979. Repr. of 1939 ed. 25.00 (ISBN 0-8063-0502-9). Genealog Pub.
Parsons, Nancy S., ed. Stockton Springs Vital Records Eighteen Fifty-Nine to Eighteen Ninety-One. LC 79-55454. (Orig.). 1979. pap. 12.95x (ISBN 0-918768-02-0). C & H Pub.
Pope, Charles H. Pioneers of Maine & New Hampshire, 1623 to 1660. LC 65-22477. 1973. Repr. of 1908 ed. 15.00 (ISBN 0-8063-0278-X). Genealog Pub.
U. S. Bureau of the Census. Heads of Families at the First Census of the United States Taken in the Year 1790: Maine. LC 73-8201. 1973. Repr. of 1908 ed. 12.50 (ISBN 0-8063-0569-X). Genealog Pub.
--Heads of Families at the First Census of the United States Taken in the Year 1790: Maine. LC 73-8201. 1973. Repr. of 1908 ed. 12.50 (ISBN 0-8063-0569-X). Genealog Pub.
--Heads of Families, First Census of the United States, 1790: Maine. LC 64-60351. 1961-64. Repr. of 1908 ed. 12.50 (ISBN 0-87152-014-1). Reprint.
Watson, S. M., ed. Maine Historical & Genealogical Recorder, 9 vols. in 3. LC 72-10614. (Illus.). 1973. Repr. of 1884 ed. 100.00 set (ISBN 0-8063-0536-3). Genealog Pub.

MAINE–HISTORY

Ames, Scribner. Marsden Hartley in Maine. 1972. 2.95 (ISBN 0-89101-025-4). U Maine Orono.
Baker, William A. Maine Shipbuilding: A Bibliographical Guide. (Maine History Bibliographical Guide Ser.). 1974. pap. 4.00 (ISBN 0-915592-09-6). Maine Hist.
Banks, Ronald F. Maine Becomes a State: The Movement to Separate Maine from Massachusetts, 1785-1820. LC 73-82845. 1973. pap. 6.95 (ISBN 0-915592-08-8). Maine Hist.
--Maine During the Federal & Jeffersonian Period: A Bibliographical Guide. (Maine History Biblopgraphical Guide Ser.). 1974. pap. 4.00 (ISBN 0-915592-13-4). Maine Hist.
Baxter, James P. Sir Ferdinando Gorges (1565-1647) & His Province of Maine, 3 vols. 1966. Set. 62.00 (ISBN 0-8337-0190-8). B Franklin.
Bennett, Dean B. & Young, Barbara E., eds. Maine Dirigo: I Lead. LC 80-68242. (Maine Studies Curriculum Project). (Illus.). 300p. 1980. text ed. 13.50 (ISBN 0-89272-103-0). Down East.
Boyle, Hal. Best of Boyle. (Illus.). 288p. (Orig.). 1980. pap. 7.95 (ISBN 0-930096-07-X). G Gannett.
Brown, Martin. A Maine Deeper In. LC 81-66264. (Illus.). 115p. 1981. pap. price not set (ISBN 0-89272-127-8). Down East.
Carroll, Gladys H. Dunnybrook. (Illus.). 1978. 11.95 (ISBN 0-393-08822-7). Norton.
Cayford, John E. Maine Firsts. LC 79-56551. (Orig.). (gr. 4-8). 1980. PLB 1.50 (ISBN 0-918768-03-9). C & H Pub.
Churchill, Edwin A. Maine Communities & the War for Independence. 1976. study guide 2.95x (ISBN 0-913764-08-6). Maine St Mus.
Clark, Charles E. Maine: A History. (State & the Nation Ser.). (Illus.). 1977. 12.95 (ISBN 0-393-05653-8, Co-Pub by AASLH). Norton.
--Maine During the Colonial Period: A Bibliographical Guide. (Maine History Bibliographical Guide Ser.). 1974. pap. 4.00 (ISBN 0-915592-14-2). Maine Hist.
Coffin, Robert P. Kennebec: Cradle of Americans. (Rivers of America Ser.). (Illus.). 292p. 1975. pap. 3.75 (ISBN 0-89272-012-3, 194). Down East.
Corliss, Augustus, compiled by. Old Times of North Yarmouth, Maine. LC 76-52883. (Illus.). 1977. 55.00 (ISBN 0-912274-72-7). NH Pub Co.
Day, Clarence A. Ezekiel Holmes, Father of Maine Agriculture. 1968. pap. 2.50 (ISBN 0-89101-016-5). U Maine Orono.
Detmer, Josephine & Pancoast, Patricia. Portland. Dibner, Martin, ed. LC 72-172820. (Illus.). 1973. collector's 25.00x (ISBN 0-9600612-0-7). Greater Portland.
Dietz, Lew. Night Train at Wiscasset Station: A Maine Retrospect. LC 76-52220. 1977. 14.95 (ISBN 0-385-12932-7). Doubleday.
Doolottle. Only in Maine. Repr. 3.75 (ISBN 0-89272-002-6). Down East.
Edwards, George T. Music & Musicians of Maine. LC 74-135736. Repr. of 1928 ed. 23.00 (ISBN 0-404-07231-3). AMS Pr.
Goold, Nathan. The Wadsworth-Longfellow House. (Illus.). 1969. pap. 3.00 (ISBN 0-915592-04-5). Maine Hist.
Haskell, John D., Jr., ed. Maine: A Bibliography of Its History. (Reference Publications Ser.). 1977. lib. bdg. 25.00 (ISBN 0-8161-8010-5). G K Hall.
Hutchinson, Vernal. A Maine Town in the Civil War. LC 67-16827. (Illus.). 1965. pap. 2.95 (ISBN 0-87027-119-9). Wheelwright.
Jordan, William B. Maine in the Civil War: A Bibliographical Guide. (Maine History Bibliographical Guide Ser.). 1976. pap. 4.00 (ISBN 0-915592-22-3). Maine Hist.
Lapham, William B. History of Bethel, Maine. 1981. Repr. of 1891 ed. 35.00 (ISBN 0-89725-023-0). NH Pub Co.
McLane, Charles B. Islands of the Mid-Maine Coast: Penobscot & Blue Hill Bays. (Illus.). 576p. 1981. 35.00 (ISBN 0-933858-00-0, Pub by Kennebec River Pr); signed & numbered limited ed 100.00 (ISBN 0-933858-01-9). TBW Bks.
McLellan, Hugh D. History of Gorham, Maine. 1000p. 1981. Repr. 45.00 (ISBN 0-89725-021-4). NH Pub Co.
Maine Historical Society. Collections of the Maine Historical Society, 10 vols. Incl. Set. 345.00 (ISBN 0-404-11059-2); 34.50 ea.; Vol. 1. (ISBN 0-404-11060-6); Vol. 2. (ISBN 0-404-11061-4); Vol. 3. (ISBN 0-404-11062-2); Vol. 4. (ISBN 0-404-11063-0). LC 72-14377. Repr. of 1831 ed. Vol. 5. (ISBN 0-404-11064-9); Vol. 6. (ISBN 0-404-11065-7); Vol. 7. (ISBN 0-404-11066-5); Vol. 8. (ISBN 0-404-11067-3); Vol. 9. (ISBN 0-404-11068-1); Vol. 10. (ISBN 0-404-11069-X). AMS Pr.
--The Maine Bicentennial Atlas: An Historical Survey. (Illus.). 1976. 10.00 (ISBN 0-915592-24-X); pap. 6.00 (ISBN 0-915592-23-1). Maine Hist.
--Province & Court Records of Maine. (Province & Court Records of Maine Ser.). (Earliest known records of Maine). Vol. 5, 1964. 18.00 (ISBN 0-915592-02-9); Vol. 6, 1975. 30.00 (ISBN 0-915592-03-7). Maine Hist.
Martin, Kenneth R. Whalemen & Whaleships of Maine. LC 74-28773. (Illus.). 72p. 1976. pap. 3.95 (ISBN 0-88448-005-4). Harpswell Pr.
Moody, Robert E., ed. The Letters of Thomas Gorges, Deputy Governor of the Province of Maine: 1640-1643. LC 78-52565. 1978. 20.00 (ISBN 0-915592-30-4). Maine Hist.
Nichols & Pachard. Maine One Hundred Years Ago. (Sun Historical Ser.). (Illus.). pap. 3.50 (ISBN 0-89540-049-9). Sun Pub.
North, James W. History of Augusta, Maine. LC 81-80137. 1000p. 1981. Repr. of 1870 ed. 55.00 (ISBN 0-89725-020-6). NH Pub Co.
Perry, Estelle. Story of Maine for Young Readers. rev. ed. LC 62-20544. (Illus.). 104p. (gr. 4). 1976. pap. 4.95 (ISBN 0-87027-160-1). Wheelwright.
Reid, John G. Acadia, Maine, & New Scotland: Marginal Colonies in the Seventeenth Century. 320p. 1981. 30.00x (ISBN 0-8020-5508-7). U of Toronto Pr.
--Maine, Charles II & Massachusetts: Governmental Relationships in Early Northern New England. LC 77-18562. (Maine Historical Society Research Ser.: No. 1). 1977. 28.00 (ISBN 0-915592-28-2, IS-00041, Pub. by Maine Historical Soc.). Univ Microfilms.
Rich, Louise D. State O' Maine. LC 64-12679. (Illus.). 1964. 12.50 (ISBN 0-06-013550-6, HarpT). Har-Row.
Smeal, Lee. Maine Historical & Biographical Index. LC 78-53701. (Illus.). Date not set. lib. bdg. price not set (ISBN 0-89593-184-2). Accelerated Index.
Smith, David C. Lumbering & the Maine Woods: A Bibliographical Guide. (Maine History Bibliographical Guide Ser.). 1971. pap. 4.00 (ISBN 0-915592-17-7). Maine Hist.
Snow, Helen. History of Damariscove Island in Maine, from Sixteen Fourteen. 170p. 1979. lib. bdg. 25.00 (ISBN 0-686-64039-X). H F Snow.
Spear, Arthur, ed. The Journals of Hezekiah Prince, Jr., 1822-1828. 1965. 6.50 (ISBN 0-915592-06-1). Maine Hist.
Spencer, Wilbur D. Pioneers on Maine Rivers. LC 72-10466. (Illus.). 1973. Repr. of 1930 ed. 18.50 (ISBN 0-8063-0532-0). Genealog Pub.
Stackpole, Everett S. History of Durham, Maine, Sixteen Eighty-Four to Eighteen Ninety-Nine. LC 79-57068. (Illus.). 1979. Repr. of 1899 ed. 35.00 (ISBN 0-89725-011-7). NH Pub Co.
--Old Kittery & Her Families. 850p. 1981. Repr. of 1903 ed. 45.00 (ISBN 0-89725-024-9). NH Pub Co.
Sullivan, James. History of the District of Maine. LC 71-128109. 1970. 14.00 (ISBN 0-913764-01-9). Maine St Mus.
Vexler, R. I. Maine Chronology & Factbook. 1978. 8.50 (ISBN 0-379-16144-3). Oceana.
Voices from the Past, Bangor the First Hundred Years. 1978. pap. 5.95 (ISBN 0-686-15957-8). Juniper Maine.
Willey, Austin. History of the Antislavery Cause in State & Nation. LC 69-18989. (Illus.). Repr. of 1886 ed. 23.75x (ISBN 0-8371-0991-4, Pub. by Negro U Pr). Greenwood.
Willis, William. History of Portland, Maine. (Illus.). 928p. 1972. 22.50 (ISBN 0-912274-24-7). O'Brien.

MAINE–HISTORY–FICTION

Daggett, Windsor P. A Down-East Yankee from the District of Maine. LC 20-21414. (Illus.). 1920. pap. 4.00 (ISBN 0-915592-07-X). Maine Hist.

MAINE–JUVENILE LITERATURE

Bailey, Bernadine. Picture Book of Maine. rev. ed. LC 57-7144. (Illus.). (gr. 3-5). 1967. 5.50g (ISBN 0-8075-9521-7). A Whitman.
Carpenter, Allan. Maine. new ed. LC 79-10804. (New Enchantment of America State Bks.). (Illus.). (gr. 4 up). 1979. PLB 10.60 (ISBN 0-516-04119-3). Childrens.
Fradin, Dennis. Maine: In Words & Pictures. LC 79-25122. (Young People's Stories of Our States Ser.). (Illus.). 48p. (gr. 2-5). 1980. PLB 9.25 (ISBN 0-516-03919-9). Childrens.
Lane, Paula. Maine Is Many Things. (Illus.). 32p. (Orig.). (gr. 3-6). 1976. pap. 1.95 (ISBN 0-89933-014-2). DeLorme Pub.
Radlauer, Ruth. Acadia National Park. LC 77-18056. (Parks for People Ser.). (Illus.). (gr. 3 up). 1978. PLB 10.00 (ISBN 0-516-07495-4, Elk Grove Bks). Childrens.

MAINE–SOCIAL LIFE AND CUSTOMS

Brace. Between Wind & Water. 1977. pap. 3.95 (ISBN 0-89272-029-8). Down East.
Chase, Mary E. A Goodly Heritage. LC 78-8180. 1978. pap. 4.95 (ISBN 0-89621-004-9). Thorndike Pr.
Coffin, Robert P. Maine Doings. LC 78-26413. 1978. pap. 4.95 (ISBN 0-89621-024-3). Thorndike Pr.
Gould, John. Last One In. (Illus.). 248p. 1979. pap. 3.95 (ISBN 0-89272-055-7, 171). Down East.
Grossinger, Richard. Book of the Cranberry Islands. 320p. (Orig.). 1974. 10.00 (ISBN 0-87685-211-8). Black Sparrow.
McKenzie, Scotty & Goode, Ruth. My Love Affair with the State of Maine. 1977. pap. 4.95 (ISBN 0-685-80278-7). Durrell.
Mitchell, Edwin V. It's an Old State of Maine Custom. LC 78-8102. 1978. pap. 4.95 (ISBN 0-89621-006-5). Thorndike Pr.
Morse, Kendall. Stories Told in the Kitchen. LC 81-8775. (Illus.). 96p. (Orig.). 1981. pap. 3.95 (ISBN 0-89621-064-2). Thorndike Pr.
Rich, Louise D. State O' Maine. LC 64-12679. (Illus.). 1964. 12.50 (ISBN 0-06-013550-6, HarpT). Har-Row.
Silber, Mark. Rural Maine. LC 72-75136. (Illus.). 60p. (Orig.). 1972. 12.50 (ISBN 0-87923-057-6); pap. 5.95 (ISBN 0-87923-056-8). Godine.
Standish, Marjorie. Cooking Down East. 1979. 8.95 (ISBN 0-930096-00-2). G Gannett.
Wood, Pamela. The Salt Book. LC 76-53419. 480p. 1977. pap. 5.95 (ISBN 0-385-11423-0, Anchor Pr); pap. 5.95 (ISBN 0-385-11423-0, Anch). Doubleday.

MAINE (BATTLESHIP)

Bronin, Andrew & Johnson, Cris. Remember the Maine. (Jackdaw Ser: No. A14). (Illus.). 1973. 6.95 (ISBN 0-670-59364-8, Grossman). Viking Pr.

MAINSTREAMING IN EDUCATION

Blackwell, Robert B. & Joynt, Robert R. Mainstreaming: What to Expect...What to Do. 1980. 15.95 (ISBN 0-87804-416-7). Mafex.
Blankenship, Colleen & Lilly, M. Stephen. Mainstreaming Students with Learning & Behavior Problems. 1981. pap. text ed. 9.95 (ISBN 0-03-046051-4, HoltC). HR&W.
Burbach, Harold J., ed. Mainstreaming: A Book of Readings & Resources for the Classroom Teacher. LC 80-81281. 224p. 1980. pap. text ed. 12.95 (ISBN 0-8403-2208-9). Kendall-Hunt.
Cohen, Sandra B. Resource Teaching: A Mainstreaming Simulation. 1978. pap. text ed. 4.95 (ISBN 0-675-08351-6); 125.00, 4 cassettes 4 filmstrips (ISBN 0-675-08444-X); 2-5 sets 75.00, 6 or more sets 60.00 (ISBN 0-686-67988-1). cards 3.95 (ISBN 0-686-67990-3). Merrill.
Fleming, Jo Ellen & Goplerud, Dena. Mainstreaming with Learning Sequences. 1980. pap. 10.95 (ISBN 0-8224-4260-4). Pitman Learning.
Haglund, E. & Stevens, V. L. A Resource Guide for Mainstreaming. (Illus.). 192p. 1980. 14.75 (ISBN 0-398-04003-6). C C Thomas.
Hart, Verna. Mainstreaming Children with Special Needs. (Illus.). 224p. (Orig.). 1980. pap. text ed. 8.95x (ISBN 0-582-28211-X). Longman.
Hasazi, Susan E., et al. Mainstreaming: Merging Regular & Special Education. LC 79-83629. (Fastback Ser.: No. 124). 1979. pap. 0.75 (ISBN 0-87367-124-4). Phi Delta Kappa.
Hein, Ronald D. & Bishop, Milo E. Bibliography on Mainstreaming, 2 vols. 1978. 20.00 set (ISBN 0-88200-130-2, N6249). Alexander Graham.

Herlihy, John G. & Herlihy, Myra T., eds. Mainstreaming in the Social Studies. LC 80-81636. (Bulletin Ser.: No. 62). 96p. (Orig.). 1980. pap. 6.95 (ISBN 0-87986-026-X, 498-15284). Coun Soc Studies.
Jarman, Ronald F. & Das, J. P. Issues in Developmental Disabilities. LC 80-12931. 136p. (Orig.). 1980. pap. 11.50 (ISBN 0-8357-0524-2, SS-00136). Univ Microfilms.
Jones, Reginald L., ed. Mainstreaming & the Minority Child. 1976. pap. text ed. 5.00x (ISBN 0-86586-051-3). Coun Exc Child.
Market Linkage Project for Special Education, ed. Educational Products for the Exceptional Child. 1981. 60.00 (ISBN 0-912700-84-X). Oryx Pr.
Mehlinger, Howard D. & Tucker, Jan L., eds. Teaching Social Studies in Other Nations. LC 79-53231. (Bulletin Ser.: No. 60). 104p. (Orig.). 1979. pap. 6.95 (ISBN 0-87986-024-3, 498-15280). Coun Soc Studies.
Ochoa, Anna S. & Shuster, Susan K. Social Studies in the Mainstreamed Classroom, K-6. LC 80-12323. 1980. pap. 11.95 (ISBN 0-89994-242-3). Soc Sci Ed.
Reynolds, Maynard C., ed. Mainstreaming: Origins & Implications. LC 76-16668. 1976. pap. text ed. 3.00x (ISBN 0-86586-053-X). Coun Exc Child.
Rodrigues, Raymond J. & White, Robert H. Mainstreaming the Non-English Speaking Student. (Theory & Research into Practice Ser.). 50p. (Orig.). 1981. 3.95 (ISBN 0-8141-3036-4, 30364). NCTE.
Special Learning Corporation. Readings in Mainstreaming. rev. ed. Sullivan, John M., ed. (Special Education Ser.). (Illus.). 224p. 1981. pap. text ed. 10.95 (ISBN 0-89568-293-1). Spec Learn Corp.
Special Learning Corporation, ed. Readings in Mainstreaming. rev. ed. (Special Education Ser.). 1978. pap. text ed. 10.95 (ISBN 0-89568-011-4). Spec Learn Corp.
Strain, Phillip S. & Kerr, Mary M. Mainstreaming of Children in Schools: Research & Programmatic Issues. LC 80-70666. (Educational Psychology Ser.). 1981. write for info. (ISBN 0-12-673460-7). Acad Pr.
Washburn, Winifred Y. Vocational Mainstreaming. 1979. pap. 6.00x (ISBN 0-87879-204-X). Acad Therapy.
Woodward, Dolores M. Mainstreaming the Learning Disabled Adolescent: A Manual of Strategies & Materials. LC 80-19566. 249p. 1981. text ed. 23.95 (ISBN 0-89443-299-0). Aspen Systems.

MAINTAINABILITY (ENGINEERING)
see also Reliability (Engineering)
Blanchard, B. B., Jr. & Lowery, E. Edward. Maintainability: Principles & Practices. LC 69-12772. (Illus.). 1969. 32.50 (ISBN 0-07-005855-5, P&RB). McGraw.
Feldman, Edwin B. Building Design for Maintainability. (Illus.). 256p. 1975. 19.95 (ISBN 0-07-020385-7, P&RB). McGraw.
Goldman, A. S. & Slattery, T. B. Maintainability: A Major Element of System Effectiveness. 2nd ed. LC 76-40242. 298p. 1977. Repr. of 1967 ed. 16.50 (ISBN 0-88275-292-8). Krieger.
Halpern, S. The Assurance Sciences: An Introduction to Quality Control & Reliability. 1978. 19.95 (ISBN 0-13-049601-4). P-H.
Patton, Joseph D., Jr. Maintainability & Maintenance Management. LC 80-82118. 480p. 1981. text ed. 35.00x (ISBN 0-87664-466-3). Instru Soc.

MAINTENANCE
see also Automatic Checkout Equipment; Plant Maintenance; Repairing
Arco Editorial Board. Maintainer's Helper, Group A & C: Transit Electrical Helper. 4th ed. LC 74-20378. 1974. pap. 6.00 (ISBN 0-668-00175-5). Arco.
Bell, Clint C. Maintenance Mechanics Qualification Program. (Illus.). 56p. 1981. pap. 44.95 (ISBN 0-89852-389-3, 01-01-R089). TAPPI.
Clifton, R. H. Principles of Planned Maintenance. 1974. pap. 14.95x (ISBN 0-7131-3317-1). Intl Ideas.
DC Symposium Houston, 1979. Instrument Maintenance Management: Proceedings, Vol. 13. LC 67-13017. 70p. 1979. pap. text ed. 10.00x (ISBN 0-87664-448-5). Instru Soc.
The Design of a Maintainance System. (Productivity Ser.: No. 14). 50p. 1979. pap. 8.25 (ISBN 92-833-1704-1, APO92, APO). Unipub.
Didactic Systems Staff. Planned Maintenance. (Simulation Game Ser.). 1969. pap. 24.90 (ISBN 0-89401-072-7); pap. 21.50 two or more (ISBN 0-685-78141-0). Didactic Syst.
Gertsbakh, I. B. Models of Preventive Maintenance. (Studies in Mathematical & Managerial Economics: Vol. 23). 1977. text ed. 41.50 (ISBN 0-7204-0465-7, North-Holland). Elsevier.
Heintzelman, J. Complete Handbook of Maintenance Management. 1976. 32.95 (ISBN 0-13-160994-7); pap. 9.95 (ISBN 0-13-160986-6). P-H.
Higgins, L. R. & Morrow, L. C. Maintenance Engineering Handbook. 3rd ed. 1977. 44.50 (ISBN 0-07-028755-4, P&RB). McGraw.
Mann, Lawrence. Maintenance Management. 320p. 1976. 24.95 (ISBN 0-669-00143-0). Lexington Bks.
Modifying the Calendar to Meet Business Needs. (Accounting Practice Report: No. 3). 2.50 (ISBN 0-686-09816-1, 5611). Natl Assn Accts.
Patton, Joseph D., Jr. Instructor's Resource Manual: Maintainability & Maintenance Management. LC 80-82118. 80p. 1980. pap. text ed. 5.00x (ISBN 0-87664-501-5). Instru Soc.
Preparation of Plant for Maintenance. 90p. 1981. 30.00x (ISBN 0-85295-130-2, Pub. by Inst Chem Eng England). State Mutual Bk.
Priel, V. Z. Systematic Maintenance. 288p. 1980. 24.00x (ISBN 0-7121-1926-4, Pub. by Macdonald & Evans). State Mutual Bk.
--Systematic Maintenance Organization. (Illus.). 274p. 1975. 22.50x (ISBN 0-7121-1926-4). Intl Pubns Serv.
Rudman, Jack. Director of Maintenance. (Career Examination Ser.: C-2812). (Cloth bdg. avail. on request). 1980. pap. 14.00 (ISBN 0-8373-2812-8). Natl Learning.
--Toll Equipment Maintenance Supervisor. (Career Examination Ser.: C-2547). (Cloth bdg. avail. on request). pap. 12.00 (ISBN 0-8373-2547-1). Natl Learning.
Schultz, Morton J. How to Fix It. (Illus.). 1978. pap. 4.95 (ISBN 0-07-055649-0, SP). McGraw.
White, E. N. Maintenance Planning, Control & Documentation. 1979. text ed. 37.25x (ISBN 0-566-02144-7, Pub. by Gower Pub Co England). Renouf.

MAINTENANCE (DOMESTIC RELATIONS)
see Support (Domestic Relations)

MAINTENANCE OF PRICES
see Price Maintenance

MAINTENON, FRANCOISE D'AUBIGNE, 1635-1719
Barnard, H. C. Madame de Maintenon & Saint-Cyr. 1977. Repr. of 1934 ed. 12.50x (ISBN 0-85409-702-3). Charles River Bks.

MAISTRE, JOSEPH MARIE, COMTE DE, 1753-1821
Bayle, Francis & Rohden, Peter R. Les Idees Politiques de Joseph de Maistre & Joseph de Maistre als Politischer Theoretiker, 2 vols. in one. Mayer, J. P., ed. LC 78-67331. (European Political Thought Ser.). (Fr. & Ger.). 1979. Repr. of 1929 ed. lib. bdg. 28.00x (ISBN 0-405-11677-2). Arno.
Lombard, Charles M. Joseph de Maistre. LC 76-13846. (World Authors Ser: No. 407). 1976. lib. bdg. 12.50 (ISBN 0-8057-6247-7). Twayne.

MAITLAND, FREDERIC WILLIAM, 1850-1906
Cameron, James R. Frederick William Maitland & the History of English Law. LC 77-677. 1977. Repr. of 1961 ed. lib. bdg. 17.75x (ISBN 0-8371-9499-7, CAFWM). Greenwood.
Delany, Vincent T., ed. Frederic William Maitland Reader. LC 57-10624. 1957. 7.50 (ISBN 0-379-11310-4); pap. 2.50 (ISBN 0-685-18990-2). Oceana.
Fifoot, C. H. Frederic William Maitland: A Life. LC 73-145892. (Studies in Legal History). 1971. 17.50x (ISBN 0-674-31825-0). Harvard U Pr.
Ogle, Arthur. Canon Law in Mediaeval England: An Examination of William Lyndwood's Provinciale. LC 78-156390. (Research & Source Works Ser.: No. 731). 1971. Repr. of 1912 ed. lib. bdg. 20.50 (ISBN 0-8337-2603-X). B Franklin.
Smith, A. L. Frederick William Maitland: Two Lectures & a Bibliography. LC 73-170960. (History, Economics & Social Science Ser.: No. 290). 1971. Repr. of 1908 ed. lib. bdg. 14.50 (ISBN 0-8337-4396-1). B Franklin.

MAITLAND, JOHN, BARON OF THIRLESTANE, 1543-1595
Lee, Maurice, Jr. John Maitland of Thirlestane & the Foundation of the Stewart Despotism in Scotland. (Studies in History: Vol. 11). (Illus.). 1959. 23.00 (ISBN 0-691-05129-1). Princeton U Pr.
Roberts, Morley. The Private Life of Henry Maitland. 1912. 40.00 (ISBN 0-8274-3205-4). R West.

MAITLAND, THOMAS, SIR
Dixon, C. Willis. Colonial Administration of Sir Thomas Maitland. 1968. Repr. of 1939 ed. 24.00x (ISBN 0-7146-1469-6, F Cass Co). Biblio Dist.
--Colonial Administrations of Sir Thomas Maitland. LC 74-94534. Repr. of 1939 ed. lib. bdg. 19.50x (ISBN 0-678-05099-6). Kelley.

MAITLAND CLUB, GLASGOW
Holland, Richard. Buke of the Howlat. LC 78-169476. (Bannatyne Club, Edinburgh. Publications: No. 3). Repr. of 1823 ed. 18.50 (ISBN 0-404-52703-5). AMS Pr.
Maitland Club. Catalogue of the Works Printed for the Maitland Club. LC 72-1043. (Maitland Club. Glasgow. Publications: No. 38). Repr. of 1836 ed. 10.00 (ISBN 0-404-53011-7). AMS Pr.

MAIZE
see Corn

MAJI MAJI UPRISING, 1905-1907
Mapunda, O. B. The Maji Maji War in Ungoni. LC 77-980908. 1969. 4.00x (ISBN 0-8002-1686-5). Intl Pubns Serv.

MAJOLICA
Barnes, Mark & May, Ron. Mexican Majolica in Northern New Spain. 1980. Repr. 4.95 (ISBN 0-686-62076-3). Acoma Bks.
Dansaert, Georges. Les Anciennes Faiences De Bruxelles: Histoire, Fabrication, Produits. Freitag, Wolfgang M., ed. LC 78-50320. (Ceramics & Glass Ser.: Vol. 5). (Illus.). 1979. lib. bdg. 40.00 (ISBN 0-8240-3391-4). Garland Pub.
Fortnum, Charles D. Maiolica: A Historical Treatise on the Glazed & Enamelled Earthenwares of Italy. Freitag, Wolfgang M., ed. LC 78-50321. (Ceramics & Glass Ser.: Vol. 7). (Illus.). 1979. lib. bdg. 55.00 (ISBN 0-8240-3393-0). Garland Pub.
Goggin, John M. Spanish Majolica in the New World: Types of the Sixteenth to Eighteenth Centuries. LC 68-24636. (Publications in Anthropology: No. 72). 1968. pap. 12.00 (ISBN 0-685-64466-9). Yale U Anthro.
Kube, Alfred N., intro. by. Italian Majolica XV-XVIII Centuries. Kolokolov, G. S., tr. Date not set. 50.00 (ISBN 0-89893-037-5). CDP.
May, Ronald V. An Evaluation of Mexican Majolica in Alta California. 1980. Repr. 4.95 (ISBN 0-686-31787-4). Acoma Bks.
Voit, Pal & Holl, Imre. Old Hungarian Stove Tiles. LC 79-15131. 1963. 7.50x (ISBN 0-8002-0875-7). Intl Pubns Serv.
Von Erdberg, Joan P. & Ross, Marvin C. Italian Majolica in the Walters Art Gallery. (Illus.). 1952. bds. 10.00 (ISBN 0-685-21827-9). Walters Art.

MAJOR ORDERS
see Bishops; Clergy

MAJORCA
Arielli, A. D. Majorca. (Illus.). 119p. 1962. 12.50x (ISBN 0-8002-1687-3). Intl Pubns Serv.
Hoffman, Ann. Majorca. (Island Ser.). 1978. 14.95 (ISBN 0-7153-7492-3). David & Charles.
Moore, Kenneth. Those of the Street: The Catholic Jews of Mallorca. LC 76-636. 224p. 1976. text ed. 11.95x (ISBN 0-268-01830-8). U of Notre Dame Pr.

MAJORCA-DESCRIPTION AND TRAVEL
Sand, George. Winter in Majorca. Graves, Robert, tr. from Fr. (Illus.). 1978. lib. bdg. 11.95 (ISBN 0-915864-69-X); pap. 5.00 (ISBN 0-915864-68-1). Academy Chi Ltd.
Thurson, Hazel. The Balearic Islands: Majorca, Minorca, Ibiza & Formentera. 1977. 19.95 (ISBN 0-7134-0882-0). David & Charles.

MAJORCA-DESCRIPTION AND TRAVEL-GUIDEBOOKS
Cox, Thornton. Majorca. rev. ed. (Thornton Cox's Travellers' Guide Ser.). Date not set. pap. 5.95 (ISBN 0-8038-7205-4). Hastings.
--Thornton Cox Traveller's Guide to Majorca. rev. ed. 1973. 5.95 (ISBN 0-8038-7205-4). Hastings.

MAJORITIES
see also Minorities
Farley, John E. Majority-Minority Relations. (Illus.). 384p. 1982. 19.95 (ISBN 0-13-545574-X). P-H.
Hermens, Ferdinand A. Democracy or Anarchy: A Study of Proportional Representation. LC 41-11446. 1972. Repr. of 1941 ed. 38.50 (ISBN 0-384-22485-7). Johnson Repr.
Packard, H. Jeremy. Minority-Majority Confrontation in America. (gr. 11-12). 1977. pap. 4.95x (ISBN 0-88334-088-7). Ind Sch Pr.

MAJORITY LOGIC
see Threshold Logic

MAJURO, MARSHALL ISLANDS
Spoehr, Alexander. Majuro, a Village in the Marshall Islands. (Illus.). 1949. pap. 12.00 (ISBN 0-527-01895-3). Kraus Repr.

MAKAH INDIANS
see Indians of North America-Northwest, Pacific

MAKARENKO, ANTON SEMENIVICH, 1888-1939
Bowen, James. Soviet Education: Anton Makarenko & the Years of Experiment. 244p. 1962. pap. 4.75x (ISBN 0-299-02644-2). U of Wis Pr.
Gorky, M., et al. Anton Makarenk: His Life and His Work in Education. 393p. 1976. 3.60 (ISBN 0-686-74555-8, Pub. by Progress Pubs Russia). Imported Pubns.

MAKARIOS 3RD, ARCHBISHOP, 1913-1977
Mayes, Stanley. Makarios. LC 80-13765. 300p. 1981. 20.00x (ISBN 0-312-50488-8). St Martin.

MAKAROVA, NATALIA
Austin, Richard. Natalia Makarova, Ballerina. LC 77-94038. (Illus.). 1978. 15.95 (ISBN 0-87127-103-6). Dance Horiz.
Makarova, Natalia. A Dance Autobiography. Smakov, Gennady, ed. LC 78-20621. (Illus.). 1979. 30.00 (ISBN 0-394-50141-1). Knopf.

MAKE-UP (COSMETICS)
see Cosmetics

MAKE-UP (TYPOGRAPHY)
see Printing, Practical-Make-Up

MAKE-UP, THEATRICAL
see also Masks
Albarella, Jacqueline. The Basic Make-up Workbook. (Illus.). 1980. pap. 4.00 (ISBN 0-914620-03-7). Alpha Pr.
Baird, John. Make-Up. rev. ed. 132p. 1941. 4.50 (ISBN 0-573-69031-6). French.
Baker, James W. Elements of Stagecraft. LC 77-25899. 241p. 1978. pap. text ed. 11.50x (ISBN 0-88284-053-3). Alfred Pub.
Barwell, Eve. Disguises You Can Make. LC 77-24998. (Lothrop Craft Ser.). (Illus.). (gr. 3-7). 1977. PLB 7.92 (ISBN 0-688-51810-9). Lothrop.
Baygan, Lee. Makeup for Theatre, Film & Television: A Step by Step Photographic Guide. LC 81-1911. (Illus.). 206p. 1981. 22.95x (ISBN 0-89676-023-5). Drama Bk.
Bruun-Rasmussen, Ole & Petersen, Grete. Make up, Costumes & Masks for the Stage. LC 76-19803. (Illus.). (gr. 5 up). 1976. 10.95 (ISBN 0-8069-7024-3); PLB 9.87 (ISBN 0-8069-7025-1). Sterling.
Buchman, Herman. Film & Television Makeup. LC 79-190513. (Illus.). 224p. 1972. 19.95 (ISBN 0-8230-1784-2). Watson-Guptill.
--Stage Makeup. 1971. 21.50 (ISBN 0-8230-4910-8). Watson-Guptill.
Corey, Irene. The Mask of Reality: An Approach to Design for Theatre. (Illus.). 1968. 22.50 (ISBN 0-87602-007-4); pap. 17.50 (ISBN 0-87602-006-6). Anchorage.
Corson, Richard. Stage Makeup. 6th ed. (Illus.). 464p. 1981. text ed. 23.95 (ISBN 0-13-840512-3). P-H.
Emerald, Jack. Make-up in Amateur Movies, Drama & Photography. LC 67-73158. (Illus.). 125p. 1966. 7.50x (ISBN 0-85242-096-X). Intl Pubns Serv.
Jones, Eric. Make-up for School Plays. 1969. 16.95 (ISBN 0-7134-2063-4, Pub. by Batsford England). David & Charles.
Kehoe, Vincent J. The Technique of Film & Television Make-up: For Color & Black & White. rev. ed. (Library of Communication Techniques). 29.50 (ISBN 0-8038-7087-6). Hastings.
Liszt, Rudolph. The Last Word in Make-up: A Practical Illustrated Handbook. rev. ed. (Illus.). 1980. 6.00 (ISBN 0-686-68849-X). Dramatists Play.
Ormsby, Alan. Movie Monsters: Monster Make-up & Monster Shows to Put on. (gr. 4-7). 1975. pap. 1.25 (ISBN 0-590-02175-3, Schol Pap). Schol Bk Serv.
Smith, C. Ray, ed. Theatre Crafts Book of Makeup, Masks & Wigs. Theatre Craft Editors. LC 72-94992. (Illus.). 1974. pap. 6.95 (ISBN 0-87857-058-6). Rodale Pr Inc.
Taylor, Al & Roy, Sue. Making a Monster: The Creation of Screen Characters by the Great Make-up Artists. (Illus.). 1979. 14.95 (ISBN 0-517-52862-2). Crown.
Terry, Ellen & Anderson, Lynne. Theatre Student: Makeup & Masks. LC 78-139744. (gr. 7 up). 1971. PLB 7.97 (ISBN 0-8239-0232-3). Rosen Pr.
Thomas, Charles. Make-Up: The Dramatic Student's Approach. 2nd ed. 1968. pap. 4.95 (ISBN 0-87830-560-2). Theatre Arts.
Westmore, Michael G. The Art of Theatrical Makeup for Stage & Screen. (Illus.). 1972. pap. text ed. 11.50 (ISBN 0-07-069485-0, G). McGraw.

MAKHORKA
see Tobacco

MAKONDE (BANTU TRIBE)
Sharma, Krishan. The Konds of Orissa. 1979. text ed. 10.00x (ISBN 0-391-01816-7). Humanities.

MALABAR, INDIA
Barbosa, Duarte. Description of the Coasts of East Africa & Malabar in the Beginning of the Sixteenth Century. LC 4-40434. (Landmarks in Anthropology Ser). Repr. of 1866 ed. 19.50 (ISBN 0-384-03405-5, L121). Johnson Repr.
Mayer, Adrian C. Land & Society in Malabar. LC 73-13032. 158p. 1974. Repr. of 1952 ed. lib. bdg. 15.00x (ISBN 0-8371-7103-2, MASM). Greenwood.

MALABAR RITES
see also Chinese Rites

MALABSORPTION SYNDROMES
see also Celiac Disease
Csaky, T. Z., ed. Intestinal Absorption & Malabsorption. LC 74-80532. 318p. 1975. 27.00 (ISBN 0-89004-020-6). Raven.
Losowsky, M. S., et al. Malabsorption in Clinical Practice. LC 73-83852. 1974. 30.00 (ISBN 0-443-01007-2). Churchill.

Sleisenger, Marvin H. & Brandborg, Lloyd L. Malabsorption. LC 76-41543. (Major Problems in Internal Medicine: Vol. XIII). (Illus.). 1977. text ed. 14.00 (ISBN 0-7216-8361-4). Saunders.

MALACOLOGY
see Mollusks

MALACOSTRACA
see also Amphipoda; Isopoda

MALADJUSTED CHILDREN
see Problem Children

MALADJUSTMENT (PSYCHOLOGY)
see also Adjustment (Psychology)

MALAGA, SPAIN-DESCRIPTION-GUIDEBOOKS

Fitton, Mary. Malaga: The Biography of a City. (Illus.). 1971. 12.50x (ISBN 0-04-946006-4). Intl Pubns Serv.

Souviron, Jose M. Malaga & Costa Del Sol. 2nd ed. LC 66-5035. (Spanish Guide Ser). (Illus.). 1964. 4.50x (ISBN 0-8002-0846-3). Intl Pubns Serv.

MALAGASY LANGUAGE

Arthus, Gothard. Dialogues in the English & Malaiane Languages. Spalding, A., tr. LC 74-80160. (English Experience Ser.: No. 640). 1974. Repr. of 1614 ed. 8.00 (ISBN 90-221-0640-3). Walter J Johnson.

MALAMUD, BERNARD

Astro, Richard & Benson, Jackson, eds. The Fiction of Bernard Malamud. LC 77-23232. 1977. text ed. 10.95 (ISBN 0-87071-446-5). Oreg St U Pr.

Avery, Evelyn. Rebels & Victims: The Fiction of Richard Wright & Bernard Malamud. (National Univ. Pubns. Literary Criticism Ser.). 1979. 10.00 (ISBN 0-8046-9234-3). Kennikat.

Field, Joyce & Field, Leslie, eds. Bernard Malamud: A Collection of Critical Essays. (Twentieth Century Views Ser). 192p. 1975. 10.95 (ISBN 0-13-548032-9, Spec). P-H.

Field, Leslie A. & Field, Joyce W., eds. Bernard Malamud & His Critics. LC 70-133016. 1970. 18.50x (ISBN 0-8147-2552-X); pap. 9.00x (ISBN 0-8147-2553-8). NYU Pr.

The Good Man's Dilemma: Social Criticism in the Fiction of Bernard Malamud. LC 79-8836. (AMS Studies in Modern Literature Ser.: No. 5). 1981. 19.50 (ISBN 0-404-18038-8). AMS Pr.

Hershinow, Sheldon J. Bernard Malamud. LC 79-4877. (Modern Literature Ser.). 160p. 1980. 10.95 (ISBN 0-8044-2377-6). Ungar.

Kosofsky, Rita N. Bernard Malamud: An Annotated Checklist. LC 75-626236. (Serif Ser.: No. 7). 1969. 6.00x (ISBN 0-87338-037-1). Kent St U Pr.

Richman, Sidney. Bernard Malamud. (Twayne's United States Authors Ser). 1966. pap. 3.45 (ISBN 0-8084-0060-6, T109, Twayne). Coll & U Pr.

--Bernard Malamud. (U. S. Authors Ser.: No. 109). 1966. lib. bdg. 9.95 (ISBN 0-8057-0472-8). Twayne.

MALARIA
see also Mosquitoes-Extermination

Ackerknecht, Erwin H. Malaria in the Upper Mississippi Valley: 1760-1900. Rosenkrantz, Barbara G., ed. LC 76-25650. (Public Health in America Ser.). (Illus.). 1977. Repr. of 1945 ed. lib. bdg. 11.00x (ISBN 0-405-09805-7). Arno.

Bilharziasis & Malaria. (Bulletin of WHO: Vol. 35, No. 3). 178p. 1966. pap. 3.60 (ISBN 0-686-09213-9). World Health.

Bruce-Chwatt, L. J. & DeZulueta, Julian. The Rise & Fall of Malaria in Europe: A Historico-Epidemiological Study. (Illus.). 224p. 1980. text ed. 36.00x (ISBN 0-19-858168-8). Oxford U Pr.

Celli, Angelo. The History of Malaria in the Roman Campagna from Ancient Times. Celli-Fraentzel, Anna, ed. LC 75-23694. Repr. of 1933 ed. 19.00 (ISBN 0-404-13243-X). AMS Pr.

Childs, St. Julien R. Malaria & Colonization in the Carolina Low Country, 1526-1696. LC 78-64178. (Johns Hopkins University. Studies in the Social Sciences. Fifty-Eighth Ser. 1940: 1). Repr. of 1940 ed. 25.50 (ISBN 0-404-61286-5). AMS Pr.

Covell, G., et al. Chemotherapy of Malaria. (Monograph Ser: No. 27). 123p. (Eng. & Fr.). 1955. pap. 5.60 (ISBN 92-4-140027-7). World Health.

Harrison, Gordon. Mosquitoes, Malaria & Man: A History of the Hostilities Since 1880. 320p. 1980. 40.00x (ISBN 0-7195-3580-8, Pub. by Murray Pubs England). State Mutual Bk.

Holstein, M. H. Biology of Anopheles Gambiae: Research in French West Africa. (Monograph Ser: No. 9). 172p. 1954. pap. 3.60 (ISBN 92-4-140009-9). World Health.

Information on Malaria Risk for International Travellers. 2nd ed. (Also avail. in French). 1976. pap. 2.40 (ISBN 92-4-058004-2). World Health.

Jones, William H. Malaria & Greek History. LC 75-23729. Repr. of 1909 ed. 17.50 (ISBN 0-404-13287-1). AMS Pr.

Killick-Kendrick, R. & Peters, W., eds. Rodent Malaria. 1978. 65.00 (ISBN 0-12-407150-3). Acad Pr.

Kreier, Julius P., ed. Malaria: Epidemiology, Chemotherapy, Morphology & Metabolism, Vol. 1. LC 80-530. 1980. 49.00 (ISBN 0-12-426101-9). Acad Pr.

--Malaria: Pathology, Vector Studies & Culture, Vol. 2. LC 80-530. 1980. 38.50 (ISBN 0-12-426102-7). Acad Pr.

Malaria & Insecticides. Incl. Vol. 27, No. 2. 122p. 1962; Vol. 28, No. 1. 138p. 1963; Vol. 29, No. 2. 158p. 1963; Vol. 30, No. 1. 151p. 1964; Vol. 31, No. 5. 131p. 1964. (Bulletin of WHO). (Eng. & Fr.). pap. 3.60 ea. World Health.

Manual on Personal & Community Protection Against Malaria. (Offset Pub.: No. 10). (Also avail. in French). 1974. pap. 5.60 (ISBN 92-4-170010-6). World Health.

Pampana, Emilio. Textbook of Malaria Eradication. 2nd ed. 1969. 24.00x (ISBN 0-19-264212-X). Oxford U Pr.

Peters, W. Chemotherapy & Drug Resistance in Malaria. 1971. 114.00 (ISBN 0-12-552750-0). Acad Pr.

Spira, Dan T. & Greenblatt, Charles L., eds. Malaria-Immunology & Immunopathology. 1978. pap. 35.50 (ISBN 3-8055-2940-6). S Karger.

Swaroop, S. Statistical Methods in Malaria Eradication. Gilroy, A. B. & Uemura, K., eds. (Monograph Ser: No. 51). (Illus.). 164p. (Eng, Fr, Rus, & Span.). 1966. 8.00 (ISBN 0-686-09185-X, 92-4-140051). World Health.

Symposium on Malaria Research. Rabat, Morocco. April 1-5, 1974. Malaria Research. (WHO Bulletin: Vol. 50, No. 3-4). (Summary in French). 1974. pap. 7.20 (ISBN 0-686-16793-7). World Health.

Terminology of Malaria & of Malaria Eradication: Report of a Drafting Committee. 127p. (Eng, Fr, Rus, & Span.). 1963. pap. 6.40 (ISBN 92-4-154014-1). World Health.

Thompson, Paul E. & Werbel, Leslie M. Antimalarial Agents: Chemistry & Pharmacology. 1972. 60.00 (ISBN 0-12-688950-3). Acad Pr.

WHO Expert Committee. Geneva, 1973, 16th. WHO Expert Committee on Malaria: Report. (Technical Report Ser.: No. 549). (Also avail. in French & Spanish). 1974. pap. 2.80 (ISBN 92-4-120549-0). World Health.

WHO Expert Committee on Malaria. Report. Incl. 15th Report, Geneva, 1970. (Technical Report Ser: No. 467). 59p. (Eng. Fr. & Span.). 1971. pap. 2.00 (ISBN 92-4-120467-2, 1078); 14th Report, Geneva, 1967. (Technical Report Ser: No. 382). 50p. (Eng., Fr., Rus. & Span.). 1968. pap. 2.00 (ISBN 92-4-120382-X, 1077). World Health.

WHO Interregional Conference. Brazzaville, 1972. Malaria Control in Countries Where Time-Limited Eradication Is Impracticable at Present: Report. (Technical Report Ser.: No. 537). (Also avail. in French & Spanish). 1974. pap. 2.40 (ISBN 92-4-120537-7). World Health.

WHO Scientific Group, Geneva, 1967. Immunology of Malaria: A Report. (Technical Report Ser: No. 396). 50p. 1968. pap. 2.00 (ISBN 92-4-120396-X, 1102). World Health.

WHO Scientific Group. Geneva, 1972. Chemotherapy of Malaria & Resistance to Antimalarials: Report. (Technical Report Ser.: No. 529). (Also avail. in French & Spanish). 1973. pap. 2.80 (ISBN 92-4-120529-6). World Health.

WHO Scientific Group. Geneva, 1975. Developments in Malaria Immunology: Report. (Technical Report Ser.: No. 579). (Also avail. in French & Spanish). 1975. pap. 2.80 (ISBN 92-4-120579-2). World Health.

WHO Scientific Group, Teheran, 1968. Parasitology of Malaria: A Report. (Technical Report Ser: No. 433). 70p. 1969. pap. 2.00 (ISBN 92-4-120433-8, 1085). World Health.

MALARIA-AFRICA

Carlson, Dennis G. African Fever: A Study of British Science, Technology, and Politics in West Africa, 1787-1864. Date not set. price not set. N Watson.

MALARIAL FEVER
see Malaria

MALAWI

Agnew, Swanzie & Stubbs, Michael, eds. Malawi in Maps. LC 74-654433. (Graphic Perspectives of Developing Countries Ser). (Illus.). 141p. 1972. text ed. 29.50x (ISBN 0-8419-0127-9, Africana). Holmes & Meier.

Boeder, Robert B. Malawi. (World Bibliographical Ser.). 165p. 1980. 28.50 (ISBN 0-903450-22-4). ABC Clio.

Brown, Edward F., et al. A Bibliography of Malawi. (Foreign & Comparative Studies-Eastern African Bibliographic Ser.: No. 1). 161p. 1965. pap. 5.00x (ISBN 0-686-70994-2). Syracuse U Foreign Comp.

Carpenter, Allan & DeLany, Milan. Malawi. LC 76-52908. (Enchantment of Africa Ser.). (Illus.). (gr. 5 up). 1977. PLB 10.60 (ISBN 0-516-04573-3). Childrens.

Crosby, Cynthia A. Historical Dictionary of Malawi. LC 80-18. (African Historical Dictionaries Ser.: No. 25). 280p. 1980. lib. bdg. 14.00 (ISBN 0-8108-1287-8). Scarecrow.

Dean, Edwin. Supply Responses of African Farmers: Theory & Measurement in Malawi. (Orig.). 1966. text ed. 14.00x (ISBN 0-7204-3138-7, Pub. by North Holland). Humanities.

Deane, Phyllis. Colonial Social Accounting. xv, 360p. 1973. Repr. of 1953 ed. 22.00 (ISBN 0-208-01316-4, Archon). Shoe String.

Fraser, Donald. African Idylls: Portraits & Impressions of Life on a Central African Mission Station. LC 78-94477. (Illus.). Repr. of 1923 ed. 12.25x (ISBN 0-8371-2354-2, Pub. by Negro U Pr). Greenwood.

Johnston, Harry H. British Central Africa. LC 78-88439. Repr. of 1897 ed. 51.00x (ISBN 0-8371-1910-3, Pub. by Negro U Pr). Greenwood.

Jones, P. J. The Malatesta of Rimini & the Papal State. LC 72-87178. (Illus.). 360p. 1974. 49.95 (ISBN 0-521-20042-3). Cambridge U Pr.

McCracken, J. Politics & Christianity in Malawi 1875-1940. LC 76-27905. (Cambridge Commonwealth Ser.). (Illus.). 1977. 39.00 (ISBN 0-521-21444-0). Cambridge U Pr.

McMaster, Carolyn. Malawi: Foreign Policy & Development. LC 74-80653. 288p. 1974. 18.95 (ISBN 0-312-50925-1). St Martin.

Morrison, James H. Streams in the Desert: A Picture of Life in Livingstonia. LC 79-12172. Repr. of 1919 ed. 10.50x (ISBN 0-8371-2780-7, Pub. by Negro U Pr). Greenwood.

Mwase, George Simeon. Strike a Blow & Die: A Narrative of Race Relations in Colonial Africa. rev. ed. Rotberg, Robert I., ed. LC 66-21342. (Center for International Affairs Ser). (Illus.). xlviii, 135p. 1970. 8.95x (ISBN 0-674-84345-2). Harvard U Pr.

Pachai, Bridglal. Land & Politics in Malawi, Ca. 1875-1975. (Modern Africa Ser.: No. 2). (Illus.). 1978. 10.50x (ISBN 0-919642-82-9); pap. 5.50 (ISBN 0-919642-83-7). Limestone Pr.

Rafael, B. R. A Short History of Malawi. (Illus.). 120p. (Orig.). (gr. 9-12). 1980. pap. 5.00x (ISBN 0-686-64604-5). Three Continents.

Read, Margaret. Children of Their Fathers: Growing up Among the Ngoni of Malawi. Spindler, George & Spindler, Louise, eds. 112p. pap. text ed. 6.95x (ISBN 0-8290-0320-7). Irvington.

Rotberg, Robert I. Rise of Nationalism in Central Africa: The Making of Malawi & Zambia, 1873-1964. LC 65-19829. (Center for International Affairs Ser). (Illus.). 1965. 16.50x (ISBN 0-674-77190-7); pap. 4.95x (ISBN 0-674-77191-5, HP39). Harvard U Pr.

Short, Philip. Banda. 358p. 1974. 20.00 (ISBN 0-7100-7631-2). Routledge & Kegan.

Sterling Publishing Company Editors. Malawi in Pictures. LC 72-95206. (Visual Geography Ser.). (Illus.). 64p. (gr. 6 up). 1973. pap. 2.95 (ISBN 0-8069-1166-2). Sterling.

Van Der Post, Laurens. Venture to the Interior. LC 73-13411. 253p. 1973. Repr. of 1951 ed. lib. bdg. 15.00 (ISBN 0-8371-7058-3, VAVI). Greenwood.

Williams, T. David. Malawi: The Politics of Despair. LC 77-90915. (Africa in the Modern World Ser). 1978. 22.50x (ISBN 0-8014-1149-1). Cornell U Pr.

Wills, A. J. An Introduction to the History of Central Africa. 3rd ed. (Illus.). 450p. 1973. pap. text ed. 8.95x (ISBN 0-19-215649-7). Oxford U Pr.

MALAY ARCHIPELAGO
see also Malay Peninsula

Crawfurd, John. History of the Indian Archipelago, 3 Vols. LC 68-89362. Repr. of 1820 ed. 80.00x (ISBN 0-678-05164-X). Kelley.

Forbes, Henry O. A Naturalist's Wanderings in the Eastern Archipelago: A Narrative of Travel & Exploration from 1878 to 1883. LC 77-86991. (Illus.). Repr. of 1885 ed. 41.50 (ISBN 0-404-16708-X). AMS Pr.

Schrieke, Bertram J., ed. Effect of Western Influence on Native Civilisations in the Malay Archipelago. LC 77-86982. Repr. of 1929 ed. 30.75 (ISBN 0-404-16778-0). AMS Pr.

Wallace, Alfred R. The Malay Archipelago. 1978. pap. 6.95 (ISBN 0-486-20187-2). Dover.

MALAY LANGUAGE
see also Indonesian Language

Alisjahbana, Takdir S. Language Planning for Modernization: The Case of Indonesian & Malaysian. (Contributions to the Sociology of Language Ser.: No. 14). 1976. pap. text ed. 20.00x (ISBN 90-279-7712-7). Mouton.

Arthus, Gothard. Dialogues in the English & Malaiane Languages. Spalding, A., tr. LC 74-80160. (English Experience Ser.: No. 640). 1974. Repr. of 1614 ed. 8.00 (ISBN 90-221-0640-3). Walter J Johnson.

Bodman, N. C. & Su-Chu, Wu. Spoken Taiwanese. (Spoken Language Ser.). 208p. (Taiwanese.). 1980. pap. 10.00x (ISBN 0-87950-460-9); cassettes 9 dual track 60.00x (ISBN 0-87950-461-7); text & cassettes 65.00x (ISBN 0-87950-462-5). Spoken Lang Serv.

Hendon, Rufus S. The Phonology & Morphology of Ulu Muar Malay. LC 65-4001. (Publications in Anthropology: No. 70). 1966. pap. 7.00 (ISBN 0-685-64467-7). Yale U Anthro.

Learn Malay for English Speakers. pap. 5.00 (ISBN 0-685-90822-4). Saphrograph.

Lewis. Teach Yourself Malay. (Teach Yourself Ser.). 1978. pap. 3.95 (ISBN 0-679-10187-X). McKay.

Marsden, William. Malay-English Dictionary. 1976. Repr. of 1958 ed. 92.00 (ISBN 0-518-19003-X). Arno.

Reid, Lawrence A. Central Bontoc: Sentence, Paragraph & Discourse. (Publications in Linguistics & Related Fields Ser.: No. 27). 185p. 1970. pap. 3.25x (ISBN 0-88312-029-1); microfiche 1.50x (ISBN 0-88312-429-7). Summer Inst Ling.

Scott-Ross, Marcus. Learn Malay the Easy Way: Book 1. 1978. pap. 3.00 (ISBN 0-8048-1284-5). C E Tuttle.

--Learn Malay the Easy Way: Book 2. 1978. pap. 3.00 (ISBN 0-8048-1285-3). C E Tuttle.

MALAY LITERATURE-HISTORY AND CRITICISM

Hamilton, Arthur W. Malay Proverbs. LC 77-87030. Repr. of 1957 ed. 14.00 (ISBN 0-404-16825-6). AMS Pr.

Sweeney, Amin. Authors & Audiences in Traditional Malay Literature. (Monograph: No. 20). 86p. 1981. pap. 7.00x (ISBN 0-686-28990-0, Pub. by U Cal Ctr S&SE Asian Stud). Cellar.

MALAY PENINSULA

Clifford, Hugh C. In a Corner of Asia. facsimile ed. LC 77-106265. (Short Story Index Reprint Ser.). 1926. 15.00 (ISBN 0-8369-3302-8). Arno.

Evans, Ivor H. Studies in Religion, Folklore & Custom in British North Borneo & the Malay Peninsula. (Illus.). 299p. 1970. Repr. of 1923 ed. 35.00x (ISBN 0-7146-2007-6, F Cass Co). Biblio Dist.

Mills, Lennox A. British Rule in Eastern Asia: A Study of Contemporary Government & Economic Development in British Malaya & Hong Kong. LC 76-83863. (Illus.). 1970. Repr. of 1942 ed. 17.50 (ISBN 0-8462-1415-6). Russell.

Skeat, Walter W. Malay Magic: An Introduction to the Folklore & Popular Religion of the Malay Peninsular. (Illus.). 685p. 1965. Repr. 37.50x (ISBN 0-7146-2026-2, F Cass Co). Biblio Dist.

Skeat, Walter W. & Blagden, Charles O. Pagan Races of the Malay Peninsula, 2 vols. new ed. (Illus.). 1966. 75.00x set (ISBN 0-7146-2027-0, F Cass Co). Biblio Dist.

Wallace, A. R. The Malay Archipelago. 12.50 (ISBN 0-8446-3129-9). Peter Smith.

Wheatley, Paul. The Golden Khersonese. LC 73-1841. (Illus.). 388p. 1973. Repr. of 1961 ed. lib. bdg. 33.25x (ISBN 0-8371-6808-2, WHGH). Greenwood.

Wheeler, Leonard R. The Modern Malay. LC 77-87033. Repr. of 1928 ed. 24.00 (ISBN 0-404-16877-9). AMS Pr.

MALAY PENINSULA-HISTORY

Sweeney, Amin. Reputations Live on: An Early Malay Autobiography. 150p. 1980. 20.00x (ISBN 0-520-04073-2). U of Cal Pr.

Wilkinson, Richard J. A History of the Penisular Malays, with Chapters on Perak & Selangor. 3rd rev. ed. LC 74-179252. Repr. of 1923 ed. 12.50 (ISBN 0-404-54878-4). AMS Pr.

MALAY POETRY-TRANSLATIONS INTO ENGLISH

Wilkinson, Richard J. & Winstedt, Richard O., eds. Pantun Melayu. LC 77-87058. Repr. of 1957 ed. 18.50 (ISBN 0-404-16880-9). AMS Pr.

MALAY-POLYNESIAN LANGUAGES
see Austronesian Languages

MALAY RACE
see also Dyaks

Djamour, Judith. Malay Kinship & Marriage in Singapore. (Monographs on Social Anthropology: No. 21). (Orig.). 1959. pap. text ed. 10.50x (ISBN 0-485-19621-2, Athlone Pr). Humanities.

Nakhoda Muda. Memoirs of a Malayan Family. (Oriental Translation Fund Ser: No. 11). 1969. pap. 8.00 (ISBN 0-384-40830-3). Johnson Repr.

Sweeney, Amin. Reputations Live on: An Early Malay Autobiography. 150p. 1980. 20.00x (ISBN 0-520-04073-2). U of Cal Pr.

MALAYA
see also Malay Peninsula

Clarkson, James D. The Cultural Ecology of a Chinese Village: Cameron Highlands, Malaysia. LC 67-28490. (Research Papers Ser.: No. 114). 174p. 1968. pap. 8.00 (ISBN 0-89065-022-5). U Chicago Dept Geog.
Curle, Richard. Into the East: Notes on Burma & Malaya. Repr. of 1923 ed. 20.00 (ISBN 0-686-19872-7). Ridgeway Bks.
Evans, Ivor H. Negritos of Malaya. (Illus.). 325p. 1968. Repr. of 1937 ed. 32.50x (ISBN 0-7146-2006-8, F Cass Co). Biblio Dist.
Kawaguchi, Keizaburo & Kyuma, Kazutake. Lowland Rice Soils in Malaya. (Center for Southeast Asian Studies Monographs, Kyoto University). 1969. text ed. 10.00x (ISBN 0-8248-0374-4). U Pr of Hawaii.
Lim, John. At Grandmother's House. LC 77-79548. (Illus.). (gr. 1-6). 1977. 12.95 (ISBN 0-912766-82-4). Tundra Bks.
Ooi Jin-Bee. Peninsular Malaysia. 2nd ed. LC 75-42166. (Geographies for Advanced Study). 1976. text ed. 23.00x (ISBN 0-582-48185-6). Longman.
Robequain, Charles. Malaya, Indonesia, Borneo, & the Philippines: A Geographical, Economic, & Political Description of Malaya, the East Indies, the Philippines. Labrde, E. D., tr. LC 75-30078. Repr. of 1954 ed. 29.50 (ISBN 0-404-59555-3). AMS Pr.
Ryan, N. J. Cultural Heritage of Malaya. 2nd ed. (Illus.). 1971. 4.50x (ISBN 0-582-72417-1). Intl Pubns Serv.
Thompson, Virginia. Postmortem on Malaya. Repr. of 1943 ed. 25.00 (ISBN 0-89987-024-4). Darby Bks.
Wright, Leigh R. & Allen, J. Dev. A Collection of Agreements & Other Documents Affecting the States of Malaya, 1761-1763, 2 vols. 1979. 85.00 set (ISBN 0-379-00781-9). Oceana.

MALAYA–DESCRIPTION AND TRAVEL

Annandale, Nelson & Robinson, H. C. Fasciculi Malayeneses: Anthropological & Zoological Results of an Expedition to Perak & the Siamese Malay States, 1901-1902. LC 77-87478. 1977. Repr. of 1904 ed. 22.50 (ISBN 0-404-16791-8). AMS Pr.
Hamilton, Arthur W., ed. Malay Pantuns. LC 77-87028. Repr. of 1956 ed. 14.50 (ISBN 0-404-16824-8). AMS Pr.

MALAYA–ECONOMIC CONDITIONS

Courtenay, P. P. A Geography of Trade & Development in Malaya. (Illus.). 298p. 1972. 12.50x (ISBN 0-7135-1624-0). Intl Pubns Serv.
--A Geography of Trade & Development in Malaya. (Advanced Economic Geography Ser.). 1972. lib. bdg. 23.25 (ISBN 0-7135-1624-0). Westview.
International Bank for Reconstruction & Development. Economic Development of Malaya. LC 77-86377. Repr. of 1960 ed. 57.50 (ISBN 0-404-60305-X). AMS Pr.
Mills, Lennox A. Malaya: A Political & Economic Appraisal. LC 72-12499. 234p. 1973. Repr. of 1958 ed. lib. bdg. 16.00x (ISBN 0-8371-6746-9, MIMA). Greenwood.
Tan Sri Lim Swee Aun. Rubber & the Malaysian Economy: Implications of Declining Prices. (Papers in International Studies: Southeast Asia: No. 11). (Illus.). 1969. pap. 4.00 (ISBN 0-89680-005-9). Ohio U Ctr Intl.

MALAYA–HISTORY

Andaya, Barbara W. Perak, the Abode of Grace: A Study of an Eighteen-Century Malay State. (East Asian Historical Monographs). 1979. 34.00x (ISBN 0-19-580385-X). Oxford U Pr.
Brown, C. C., tr. Sejarah Melayu or Malay Annals. (Oxford in Asia Historical Reprints). 310p. 1970. 10.50x (ISBN 0-19-638106-1). Oxford U Pr.
Butcher, John G. The British in Malaya, Eighteen Eighty to Nineteen Forty-One: The Social History of a European Community in Colonial South-East Asia. (Illus.). 314p. 1979. 34.95x (ISBN 0-19-580419-8). Oxford U Pr.
Mills, Lennox A. British Malaya 1824-1867. LC 74-172732. Repr. of 1925 ed. 26.45 (ISBN 0-404-04345-3). AMS Pr.
O'Ballance, Edgar. Malaya: The Communist Insurgent War, 1948-1960. (Illus.). 1966. 15.00 (ISBN 0-208-00468-8, Archon). Shoe String.
Robertson, Eric. The Japanese File. 1979. pap. text ed. 11.95x (ISBN 0-686-58246-2, 00113). Heinemann Ed.
Ryan, N. J. The Cultural Heritage of Malaya. 2nd ed. (Illus.). 184p. 1971. pap. text ed. 3.25x (ISBN 0-582-72417-1). Humanities.
Sidhu, Jagjit S. Administration in the Federated Malay States: Eighteen Ninety-Six-Nineteen Twenty. (East Asian Historical Monographs). 250p. 1981. 25.00x (ISBN 0-19-580432-5). Oxford U Pr.
Swettenham, Frank A. British Malaya. LC 74-179244. Repr. of 1948 ed. 34.00 (ISBN 0-404-54870-9). AMS Pr.
Tweedie, Michael W. The Stone Age in Malaya. LC 77-87514. (Journal of the Royal Asiatic Society, Malayan Branch: Vol. 26). Repr. of 1953 ed. 15.00 (ISBN 0-404-16872-8). AMS Pr.
Winstedt, Richard. The Malays: A Cultural History. 6th ed. (Illus.). 1961. 20.00x (ISBN 0-7100-2312-X). Routledge & Kegan.
Winstedt, Richard O. A History of Malaya. (Perspectives in Asian History: No. 11). (Illus.). Repr. of 1935 ed. lib. bdg. 17.50x (ISBN 0-87991-603-6). Porcupine Pr.

MALAYA–POLITICS AND GOVERNMENT

Ampalavanar, Rajeswary. The Indian Minority & Political Change in Malaya: 1945-1957. (East Asian Historical Monographs). (Illus.). 256p. 1981. 37.50 (ISBN 0-19-580473-2). Oxford U Pr.
Heussler, Robert. The Administration of British Malaya: A Bibliographical & Biographical Compendium. 1981. lib. bdg. 30.00 (ISBN 0-8240-9369-0). Garland Pub.
--British Rule in Malaya: The Malayan Civil Service & Its Predecessors, Eighteen Sixty-Seven to Nineteen Forty-Two. LC 80-658. (Contributions in Comparative Colonial Studies: No. 6). (Illus.). xx, 356p. 1981. lib. bdg. 37.50 (ISBN 0-313-22243-6, HBM/). Greenwood.
Institute of Pacific Relations. American Council. The Development of Self-Rule & Independence in Burma, Malaya & the Philippines: An Interim Report in a Study of Progress Toward Self-Government & Independence in Southeast Asia. LC 77-8717. Repr. of 1948 ed. 18.00 (ISBN 0-404-16829-9). AMS Pr.
Middlebrook, Stanley M. & Pinnick, Alfred W. How Malaya Is Governed. 2nd ed. LC 73-179225. (Illus.). Repr. of 1949 ed. 16.00 (ISBN 0-404-54852-0). AMS Pr.
Mills, Lennox A. Malaya: A Political & Economic Appraisal. LC 72-12499. 234p. 1973. Repr. of 1958 ed. lib. bdg. 16.00x (ISBN 0-8371-6746-9, MIMA). Greenwood.
Nash, Manning. Peasant Citizens: Politics, Religion, & Modernization in Kelantan, Malaysia. LC 62-620027. (Papers in International Studies: Southeast Asia: No. 31). 1977. pap. 12.00x (ISBN 0-89680-018-0). Ohio U Ctr Intl.
Purcell, Victor W. Malaya: Communist or Free? LC 75-30076. (Institute of Pacific Relations). Repr. of 1954 ed. 23.00 (ISBN 0-404-59553-7). AMS Pr.
Pye, Lucian W. Guerrilla Communism in Malaya: Its Social & Political Meaning. LC 81-4591. xvi, 369p. 1981. Repr. of 1956 ed. lib. bdg. 29.75x (ISBN 0-313-23017-X, PYGC). Greenwood.
Rabushka, Alvin. Race & Politics in Urban Malaya. LC 72-91040. (Studies: No. 35). 150p. 1973. 7.95 (ISBN 0-8179-3351-4). Hoover Inst Pr.
Sidhu, Jagjit S. Administration in the Federated Malay States: Eighteen Ninety-Six-Nineteen Twenty. (East Asian Historical Monographs). 250p. 1981. 25.00x (ISBN 0-19-580432-5). Oxford U Pr.

MALAYA–SOCIAL CONDITIONS

Golomb, Louis. Brokers of Morality: Thai Ethnic Adaptation in a Rural Malaysian Setting. LC 78-4141. (Asian Studies at Hawaii: No. 23). 1979. pap. text ed. 10.75 (ISBN 0-8248-0629-8). U Pr of Hawaii.
Hodder, B. W. Man in Malaya. LC 72-11329. (Illus.). 144p. 1973. Repr. of 1959 ed. lib. bdg. 15.00 (ISBN 0-8371-6654-3, HOMM). Greenwood.
Marsden, William, tr. Memoirs of a Malayan Family: Written by Themselves. LC 77-87032. Repr. of 1830 ed. 12.50 (ISBN 0-404-16842-6). AMS Pr.
Rogers, Marvin L. Sungai Raya: A Sociopolitical Study of a Rural Malay Community. (Research Monograph: No. 15). 1977. 8.00 (ISBN 0-686-23612-2, Ctr South & Southeast Asia Studies). Cellar.
Stevens, Mark. Light to Darkness. 1981. 7.95 (ISBN 0-533-04956-3). Vantage.
Wilken, George A. The Sociology of Malayan Peoples: Being Three Essays on Kinship, Marriage & Inheritance in Indonesia. Hunt, G., tr. LC 77-87034. Repr. of 1921 ed. 23.00 (ISBN 0-404-16879-5). AMS Pr.
Wilson, Peter J. Malay Village & Malaysia: Social Values & Rural Development. LC 66-27877. (Behavior Science Monographs). x, 171p. 1968. pap. 7.50x (ISBN 0-87536-322-9). HRAFP.

MALAYA–SOCIAL LIFE AND CUSTOMS

Alwi Bin Alhady, Syed. Malay Customs & Traditions. LC 77-87477. Repr. of 1962 ed. 21.50 (ISBN 0-404-16789-6). AMS Pr.
Comber, Leon. Chinese Magic & Superstitions in Malaya. LC 77-87023. (Illus.). 104p. Repr. of 1960 ed. 16.50 (ISBN 0-404-16808-6). AMS Pr.
Gimlette, John D. Malay Poisons & Charm Cures. 2nd ed. LC 77-87027. Repr. of 1923 ed. 22.00 (ISBN 0-404-16821-3). AMS Pr.
Hill, R. D. Rice in Malaya: A Study in Historical Geography. 1978. 39.50x (ISBN 0-19-580335-3). Oxford U Pr.
Marsden, William, tr. Memoirs of a Malayan Family: Written by Themselves. LC 77-87032. Repr. of 1830 ed. 12.50 (ISBN 0-404-16842-6). AMS Pr.
Winstedt, Richard. The Malays: A Cultural History. 6th ed. (Illus.). 1961. 20.00x (ISBN 0-7100-2312-X). Routledge & Kegan.
Winstedt, Richard O. The Circumstances of Malay Life. LC 77-87516. Repr. of 1909 ed. 16.00 (ISBN 0-404-16882-5). AMS Pr.

MALAYALAM LANGUAGE

see also Tamil Language

MALAYALAM LITERATURE

Asher, R. E. & Radharkrishnan, R. Tamil Prose Reader. LC 73-93705. 1971. text ed. 38.50 (ISBN 0-521-07214-X). Cambridge U Pr.
Chaitanya, Krishna. A History of Malayalam Literature. 1971. 17.50 (ISBN 0-8046-8805-2). Kennikat.

MALAYAN FOLK-LORE

see Folk-Lore, Malayan

MALAYAN LANGUAGES

see also Austronesian Languages; Indonesian Language; Javanese Language; Malagasy Language; Malay Language; Philippine Languages

Dyen, Isidore. Spoken Malay. Incl. Units 1-12. v, 192p. pap. 10.00x (ISBN 0-87950-160-X); Bk. 2, Units 13-30. 324p. pap. o.s.i (ISBN 0-87950-161-8); Cassettes, Six Dual Track. 60.00x (ISBN 0-87950-165-0); Cassette Course - Bk. & Cassettes. pap. 65.00 (ISBN 0-87950-166-9). LC 74-176207. (Spoken Language Ser.). (Prog. Bk.). 1974. Spoken Lang Serv.
McManus, Edwin G., et al. Palauan-English Dictionary. LC 76-9058. (Pali Language Texts: Micronesia). 1977. pap. text ed. 14.50x (ISBN 0-8248-0450-3). U Pr of Hawaii.

MALAYAN MAGIC

see Magic, Malayan

MALAYS

see Malay Race

MALAYSIA

Allen, Betty M. Common Malaysian Fruits. (Malaysian Nature Handbooks). (Illus.). 1975. 7.50x (ISBN 0-582-72409-0). Intl Pubns Serv.
Anand, Sudhir. Inequality & Poverty in Malaysia: Measurement & Decomposition. (WBRP Ser.). (Illus.). 228p. 1981. text ed. 14.95x (ISBN 0-19-520153-1); pap. text ed. 5.95x (ISBN 0-19-520154-X). Oxford U Pr.
Arasaratnam, Sinnappah. Indians in Malaysia & Singapore. 1980. pap. 8.95x (ISBN 0-19-580427-9). Oxford U Pr.
Asia Pacific Centre. The Markets of Asia Pacific. 1981. Malaysia. 75.00 (ISBN 0-87196-585-2); Singapore. 75.00 (ISBN 0-87196-584-4); Thailand. 75.00 (ISBN 0-87196-586-0); Set. avail. (ISBN 0-87196-596-8); as part of set 49.95 ea. Facts on File.
Aun, Wu M. & Vohrah, Beatrix. The Commercial Law of Malaysia. (Orig.). 1979. pap. text ed. 14.95x (ISBN 0-686-74437-3, 00141). Heinemann Ed.
Bailey, Conner. Broker, Mediator, Patron, & Kinsman: An Historical Analysis of Key Leadership Roles in a Rural Malaysian District. LC 75-620141. (Papers in International Studies, Southeast Asia Ser.). 89p. 1980. pap. 9.00 (ISBN 0-89680-024-5). Ohio U Ctr Intl.
Bhanoji Rao, V. V. Malaysia: Development Pattern & Policy, 1947-1971. 270p. 1981. pap. 12.00 (ISBN 9971-69-026-8, Pub. by Singapore U Pr). Ohio U Pr.
Boyce, P. Malaysia & Singapore in International Diplomacy: Documents & Commentaries. 1968. 12.50x (ISBN 0-424-05660-7, Pub by Sydney U Pr). Intl Schol Bk Serv.
Brown, Charles C. Perak Malays. LC 77-87481. Repr. of 1921 ed. 17.00 (ISBN 0-404-16797-7). AMS Pr.
Carey, Iskandar. Orang Asli: The Aboriginal Tribes of Peninsular Malaysia. 1976. 24.95x (ISBN 0-19-580270-5). Oxford U Pr.
Carlson. Sevinc Malaysia. LC 75-13846. (The Washington Papers: No. 25). 80p. 1975. 4.00 (ISBN 0-8039-0563-7). Sage.
Clammer, John R. Straits Chinese Society: Studies in the Sociology of the Baba Communities of Malaysia & Singapore. 1981. 18.00 (ISBN 9971-69-009-8, Pub. by Singapore U Pr); pap. 8.95 (ISBN 9971-69-015-2, Pub. by Singapore U Pr). Ohio U Pr.
Conservation in Malaysia: A Manual on the Conservation of Malaysia's Renewable Natural Resources. (Illus.). 1969. pap. 12.00x (ISBN 2-88032-047-X, IUCN33, IUCN). Unipub.
De Silva, Judith C., ed. Malaysia Official Year Book 1977. 17th ed. LC 62-41053. (Illus.). 576p. (Orig.). 1979. pap. 15.00x (ISBN 0-8002-2453-1). Intl Pubns Serv.
Dunn, Miriam. Let's Look at Malaysia. pap. 1.25 (ISBN 0-85363-096-8). OMF Bks.
Duza, M. Badrud & Baldwin, C. Stephen. Nuptiality & Population Policy: An Investigation in Tunisia, Sri Lanka, & Malaysia. LC 77-23888. 1977. pap. text ed. 4.50 (ISBN 0-87834-028-9). Population Coun.
Fishing in Troubled Waters: Research on the Chinese Fishing Industry in West Malaysia. (Asian Folklore & Social Life Monographs: Vol. 100). 1977. 9.00 (ISBN 0-89986-319-1). E Langstaff.
Fletcher, Nancy M. Separation of Singapore from Malaysia. (Data Paper Ser.: No. 73). 1969. pap. text ed. 2.50 (ISBN 0-87727-073-2). Cornell SE Asia.
Grenfell, Newell. Switch on: Switch off: The Mass Media Audiences of Malaysia. (Illus.). 1979. 34.00x (ISBN 0-19-580407-4). Oxford U Pr.
Gullick, J. M. Malaysia & Its Neighbours. (World Studies). 1967. 9.75x (ISBN 0-7100-4141-1). Routledge & Kegan.
Gullick, John. Malaysia: Economic Expansion & National Unity. (Illus.). 272p. 1981. lib. bdg. 30.00x (ISBN 0-86531-089-0). Westview.
Hai, Tan Soo & Sendut, Hamzah, eds. Public & Private Housing in Malaysia. 1979. text ed. 27.50x (ISBN 0-686-26358-8, 00109). Heinemann Ed.
Hanna, Willard A. Formation of Malaysia. LC 64-19390. 1964. 6.50 (ISBN 0-910116-57-1). Am U Field.
Hirschman, C., et al. Malaysian Studies: Present Knowledge & Research Trends. Lent, John A., ed. (Occasional Paper Ser.: No. 7). 461p. 1979. pap. text ed. 14.25x (ISBN 0-686-26880-6, Pub. by U Cal Ctr SSE Asian Stud). Cellar.
Ho, Lisa. Some Observations on Consumer Behavior in the Third World: The Case of a Suburban New Town in Malaysia. (Griffith Asian Papers: No.2). (Illus., Orig.). 1981. pap. text ed. 19.95 (ISBN 0-86857-098-2, 0152, Pub. by ANUP Australia). Bks Australia.
Hoffmann, Lutz & Ee, Tan S. Industrial Growth, Employment & Foreign Investment in Peninsular Malaysia. (East Asian Social Science Monograph). 325p. 1980. 42.00x (ISBN 0-19-580415-5). Oxford U Pr.
Industrialization Strategy, Regional Development & the Growth Centre Approach: A Case Study of West Malaysia. 160p. 1975. pap. 6.00 (ISBN 0-686-75487-5, CRD056, UNCRD). Unipub.
Koentjaraningrat, R. M. Introduction to the Peoples & Cultures of Indonesia & Malaysia. LC 75-4078. 1975. pap. 6.95 (ISBN 0-8465-1670-5). Benjamin-Cummings.
Kuchiba, Masuo, et al, eds. Three Malay Villages: A Sociology of Paddy Growers in West Malaysia. LC 79-573. (Monographs of the Center for Southeast Asian Studies, Kyoto University). 1979. text ed. 22.00x (ISBN 0-8248-0665-4); pap. text ed. 13.00x (ISBN 0-8248-0666-2). U Pr of Hawaii.
Lent, John A., ed. Cultural Pluralism in Malaysia: Polity, Military, Mass Media, Education, Religion & Social Class. (Special Report Ser.: No. 14). wrps. 6.00x (ISBN 0-686-09455-7). Cellar.
Lim, David. Economic Growth & Development in West Malaysia 1947-1970. (East Asian Social Science Monographs). (Illus.). 367p. 1973. 22.50x (ISBN 0-19-638218-1). Oxford U Pr.
McKie, Ronald. The Emergence of Malaysia. LC 72-13868. (Illus.). 310p. 1973. Repr. of 1963 ed. lib. bdg. 15.00x (ISBN 0-8371-6763-9, MCEM). Greenwood.
Malaysia Nineteen Seventy Six: Official Year Book. 16th ed. LC 62-41053. (Illus.). 1976. 15.00x (ISBN 0-8002-0413-1). Intl Pubns Serv.
Malaysian National Bibliography, 4 vols. annual Incl. Vol. 1, 1967. 141p. 1968 (ISBN 0-8002-1689-X); Vol. 2, 1968. 195p. 1969 (ISBN 0-8002-1690-3); Vol. 3, 1969. 1970 (ISBN 0-8002-1691-1); Vol. 4, 1970. 1971. pap. 7.50x ea. Intl Pubns Serv.
Malaysian National Bibliography Nineteen Seventy-Eight. 252p. (Orig.). 1979. pap. 30.00x (ISBN 0-8002-2471-X). Intl Pubns Serv.
Malaysian National Bibliography Nineteen Seventy-Seven. 241p. (Orig.). 1978. pap. 30.00 (ISBN 0-8002-2470-1). Intl Pubns Serv.
Mazumdar, Dipak. Urban Labor Market & Income Distribution. (World Bank Research Publications Ser.). (Illus.). 392p. 1981. 19.95 (ISBN 0-19-520213-9); pap. 7.95 (ISBN 0-19-520214-7). Oxford U Pr.
Meerman, Jacob P. Public Expenditure in Malaysia: Who Benefits & Why. (World Bank Research Publications Ser.). (Illus.). 1979. 24.00x (ISBN 0-19-520096-9); pap. 9.95x (ISBN 0-19-520097-7). Oxford U Pr.
Milne, R. S. & Ratnam, K. J. Malaysia: New States in a New Nation. 512p. 1973. 32.50x (ISBN 0-7146-2988-X, F Cass Co). Biblio Dist.
Morais, J. Victor, ed. Who's Who in Malaysia & Singapore 1979-80. 13th ed. (Illus.). 761p. 1980. 60.00x (ISBN 0-8002-2469-8). Intl Pubns Serv.
Naidu, Ratna. The Communal Edge to Plural Societies: India & Malaysia. 1978. text ed. 14.00x (ISBN 0-7069-0922-4). Humanities.

Ness, Gayl D. Bureaucracy & Rural Development in Malaysia. 1967. 24.00x (ISBN 0-520-00922-3). U of Cal Pr.

New Straits Times Directory of Malaysia 1979. LC 53-30515. 1979. 58.50x (ISBN 0-8002-2389-6). Intl Pubns Serv.

Osborn, James. Area, Development Policy, & the Middle City in Malaysia. LC 73-92650. (Research Papers Ser.: No. 153). (Illus.). 273p. 1974. pap. 8.00 (ISBN 0-89065-060-8). U Chicago Dept Geog.

Pelzer, Karl J. West Malaysia & Singapore: A Selected Bibliography. LC 72-87853. (Behavior Science Bibliographies Ser.). vi, 394p. 1971. 18.00x (ISBN 0-87536-235-4). HRAFP.

Pettelkay, Harald. Malaysia. LC 74-29566. (This Beautiful World Ser.: Vol. 52). (Illus.). 150p. (Orig.). 1975. pap. 4.95 (ISBN 0-87011-245-7). Kodansha.

Rao, V. Bhanoji. National Accounts of West Malaysia 1947-1971. 1976. text ed. 14.50x (ISBN 0-686-60455-5, 00111). Heinemann Ed.

Singh, Jaginder, et al. Credit & Security in West Malaysia: The Legal Problems of Development Finance. (Law & Development Finance in Asia Ser.). (Illus.). 497p. 1980. text ed. 48.50x (ISBN 0-7022-1350-0). U of Queensland Pr.

Singh, Nihal S. Malaysia: A Commentary. 1972. 13.50 (ISBN 0-686-20271-6). Intl Bk Dist.

Stephens, Harold. Malaysia. Black, Star & Hoefer, Hans, eds. (Apa Photo Guides Ser.). (Illus.). 1978. pap. 14.00x (ISBN 0-686-23211-9). Intl Learn Syst.

Strange, Heather. Rural Malay Women in Traditional Transition. 288p. 1981. 24.95 (ISBN 0-03-052616-7). Praeger.

Tee, Lim H. Malaysia. (World Bibliographical Ser.: No. 12). 1981. write for info. (ISBN 0-903450-23-2). Abc-Clio.

Thoburn, John T. Primary Commodity Exports & Economic Development: Theory, Evidence, & a Study of Malaysia. LC 76-26337. 310p. 1977. 36.95 (ISBN 0-471-99441-3, Pub. by Wiley-Interscience). Wiley.

Tugby, Donald. Cultural Change & Identity: Mandailing Immigrants in West Malaysia. (Illus.). 1977. 20.00x (ISBN 0-7022-1361-6). U of Queensland Pr.

University Of Singapore Library. Catalogue of the Singapore-Malaysia Collection. 1968. lib. bdg. 125.00 (ISBN 0-8161-0818-8). G K Hall.

Wegelin, E. A. Urban Low-Income Housing & Development: A Case Study in Peninsular Malaysia. 1978. lib. bdg. 23.00 (ISBN 90-207-0729-9, Pub. by Martinus Nijhoff Netherlands). Kluwer Boston.

Wiebe, Paul & Mariappan, S. Indian Malaysians: The View from the Plantation. LC 77-88660. 1979. 12.00 (ISBN 0-89089-078-1). Carolina Acad Pr.

Yee, Lo S. The Development Performance of West Malaysia, Nineteen Fifty-Five to Nineteen Sixty-Seven. 1972. pap. text ed. 5.95x (ISBN 0-686-60348-6, 00110). Heinemann Ed.

Young, Kevin, et al. Malaysia: Growth & Equity in a Multiracial Society. LC 79-3677. (A World Bank Country Economic Report Ser.). (Illus.). 368p. 1980. text ed. 25.00x (ISBN 0-8018-2384-6); pap. text ed. 7.95x (ISBN 0-8018-2385-4). Johns Hopkins.

MALAYSIA-FOREIGN RELATIONS-INDONESIA

Hyde, Douglas. Confrontation in the East. (Background Ser). 1965. 6.25 (ISBN 0-8023-1062-1). Dufour.

Mackie, J. A. Konfrontasi: The Indonesia-Malaysia Dispute 1963-1966. (Illus.). 384p. 1974. 34.50x (ISBN 0-19-638247-5). Oxford U Pr.

Mezerik, Avrahm G., ed. Malaysia-Indonesia Conflict. 1965. pap. 15.00 (ISBN 0-685-13205-6, 86). Intl Review.

MALAYSIA-HISTORY

Bedlington, Stanley S. Malaysia & Singapore: The Building of New States. Kahin, G. M., ed. LC 77-3114. (Politics & International Relations of Southeast Asia Ser.). 1978. 19.50x (ISBN 0-8014-0910-1); pap. 6.95x (ISBN 0-8014-9864-3). Cornell U Pr.

Bhanoji Rae, V. V. Malaysia: Development Patterns & Policy, 1947 to 1971. 270p. 1981. 21.95x (ISBN 0-8214-0512-8); pap. 12.00x (ISBN 0-686-77598-8). Swallow.

Endicott, Kirk. Batek Negrito Religion: The World-View & Rituals of a Hunting & Gathering People of Peninsular Malaysia. (Illus.). 1979. 45.00x (ISBN 0-19-823197-0). Oxford U Pr.

Ghee, Lim T. Peasants & Their Agricultural Economy in Colonial Malaya, 1874-1941. (East Asian Historical Monographs). (Illus.). 1978. 27.50x (ISBN 0-19-580338-8). Oxford U Pr.

Hanna, Willard A. Sequel to Colonialism: The Nineteen Fifty-Seven to Nineteen Sixty Foundations for Malaysia. LC 65-12895. 1965. 7.50 (ISBN 0-910116-59-8). Am U Field.

Jackson, J. C. & Rudner, M. Issues in Malaysian Development. (Orig.). 1980. pap. text ed. 15.95x (ISBN 0-686-71776-7, 00136). Heinemann Ed.

Moore, Russell F. Thailand - Malaysia - Singapore. LC 74-27959. 1975. 6.95 (ISBN 0-915806-01-0). Thai-Am-Pubs.

Shaw, W. S. Tun Razak: His Life & Times. (Illus.). 1976. text ed. 14.50x (ISBN 0-582-72414-7). Longman.

MALAYSIA-HISTORY-SOURCES

Boestamam, Ahmad. Carving the Path to the Summit. Roff, William R., tr. from Malayan. LC 79-11174. (Southeast Asia Translation Ser.: Vol. 2). xxxii, 149p. 1980. 12.95x (ISBN 0-8214-0397-4); pap. 6.50x (ISBN 0-8214-0409-1). Ohio U Pr.

MALAYSIA-JUVENILE LITERATURE

Caldwell, John C. Let's Visit Malaysia. LC 68-26341. (Let's Visit Ser). (Illus.). (gr. 3-7). 1968. PLB 7.89 (ISBN 0-381-99887-8, A43030, JD-J). Har-Row.

MALAYSIA-POLITICS AND GOVERNMENT

Bailey, Conner. Broker, Mediator, Patron, & Kinsman: An Historical Analysis of Key Leadership Roles in a Rural Malaysian District. LC 75-620141. (Papers in International Studies: Southeast Asia: No. 38). (Illus.). 1976. pap. 9.00 (ISBN 0-89680-024-5). Ohio U Ctr Intl.

Bedlington, Stanley S. Malaysia & Singapore: The Building of New States. Kahin, G. M., ed. LC 77-3114. (Politics & International Relations of Southeast Asia Ser.). 1978. 19.50x (ISBN 0-8014-0910-1); pap. 6.95x (ISBN 0-8014-9864-3). Cornell U Pr.

Bhanoji Rao, V. V. Malaysia: Development Pattern & Policy, 1947-1971. 270p. 1981. pap. 12.00 (ISBN 9971-69-026-8, Pub. by Singapore U Pr). Ohio U Pr.

Esman, Milton J. Administration & Development in Malaysia: Institution Building & Reform in a Plural Society. LC 71-173991. 357p. 1972. 25.00x (ISBN 0-8014-0685-4). Cornell U Pr.

Funston, John. Malay Politics in Malaysia: A Study of Umno & Pas. 1981. pap. text ed. 12.95x (ISBN 0-686-31818-8, 00116). Heinemann Ed.

Jackson, J. C. & Rudner, M. Issues in Malaysian Development. (Orig.). 1980. pap. text ed. 15.95x (ISBN 0-686-71776-7, 00136). Heinemann Ed.

Means, Gordon P. Malaysian Politics. LC 78-91692. 1970. 15.00x (ISBN 0-8147-0469-7). NYU Pr.

--Malaysian Politics. 484p. 1976. text ed. 20.50x (ISBN 0-340-18186-9). Verry.

Mills, Lennox A. British Rule in Eastern Asia: A Study of Contemporary Government & Economic Development in British Malaya & Hong Kong. LC 76-83863. (Illus.). 1970. Repr. of 1942 ed. 17.50 (ISBN 0-8462-1415-6). Russell.

Norris, M. W. Local Government in Peninsular Malaysia. 121p. 1980. text ed. 27.00x (ISBN 0-566-00283-3, Pub. by Gower Pr England). Renouf.

Puthucheary, Mavis. The Politics of Administration: The Malaysian Experience. 1978. 29.00x (ISBN 0-19-580386-8). Oxford U Pr.

Rao, Chandriah A., et al. Issues in Contemporary Malaysia. LC 79-670083. 1977. pap. text ed. 5.50x (ISBN 0-686-60442-3, 00105). Heinemann Ed.

Sheridan, Lionel A. & Groves, H. E. The Constitution of Malaysia. LC 66-25577. 1967. 22.50 (ISBN 0-379-00209-4). Oceana.

Singh, Jaginder, et al. Credit & Security in West Malaysia: The Legal Problems of Development Finance. (Law & Development Finance in Asia Ser.). (Illus.). 497p. 1980. text ed. 48.50x (ISBN 0-7022-1350-0). U of Queensland Pr.

Snodgrass, Donald R. Inequality & Economic Development in Malaysia. (East Asian Social Science Monographs). (Illus.). 340p. 1980. 34.95x (ISBN 0-19-580431-7); pap. 19.95 (ISBN 0-19-580442-2). Oxford U Pr.

Strauch, Judith. Chinese Village Politics in the Malaysian State. LC 80-20519. (Harvard East Asian Ser.: No. 95). (Illus.). 208p. 1981. text ed. 22.50x (ISBN 0-674-12570-3). Harvard U Pr.

Suffian, Tun M., et al, eds. The Constitution of Malaysia: Its Development, Nineteen Fifty-Seven to Nineteen Seventy-Seven. 1979. 29.00x (ISBN 0-19-580406-6). Oxford U Pr.

Tan Sri Haji Khalid. Malaysia: An Anthology. 1978. 6.95 (ISBN 0-533-03382-9). Vantage.

Vasil, Raj K. Ethnic Politics in Malaysia. (Illus.). 234p. 1980. text ed. 16.00x (ISBN 0-391-01770-5). Humanities.

Von Vorys, Karl. Democracy Without Consensus: Communalism & Political Stability in Malaysia. 512p. 1975. 31.00x (ISBN 0-691-07571-9). Princeton U Pr.

MALAYSIAN LITERATURE

Abdullah, M. Mansur. Permata-Permata Di Lumpur. (Karyawan Malaysia Ser.). (Malay.). 1979. pap. text ed. 3.25x (ISBN 0-686-60458-X, 00354). Heinemann Ed.

Ahmad, Shahnon. Selesai Sudah. (Karyawan Malaysia Ser.). (Malay.). 1979. pap. text ed. 3.25x (ISBN 0-686-60467-9, 00352). Heinemann Ed.

--Seluang Menodak Baung. (Karyawan Malaysia Ser.). (Malay.). 1979. pap. text ed. 5.50x (ISBN 0-686-60468-7, 00355). Heinemann Ed.

Busu, Fatimah. Ombak Bukan Biru. (Karyawan Malaysia Ser.). (Malay.). 1979. pap. text ed. 5.50x (ISBN 0-686-60457-1, 00350). Heinemann Ed.

Johns, Anthony H. Cultural Options & the Role of Tradition: A Collection of Essays on Modern Indonesian & Malaysian Literature. LC 78-74666. 1979. pap. text ed. 9.95 (ISBN 0-7081-0341-3, Faculty of Asian Studies in Association with Australian Natn'l). Bks Australia.

MALCOLM X

see Little, Malcolm, 1925-1965

MALDIVE ISLANDS

Maloney, Clarence. The People of the Maldive Islands. 1981. 20.00x (ISBN 0-8364-0682-6, Orient Longman). South Asia Bks.

MALDON, BATTLE OF, 991

Gordon, E. V., ed. The Battle of Maldon. (Old English Ser.). 1966. pap. text ed. 1.95x (ISBN 0-89197-565-9). Irvington.

--The Battle of Maldon, with a Supplement. Scragg, D. G. LC 76-28820. (Old and Middle English Texts Ser.). 1976. pap. text ed. 6.75x (ISBN 0-06-492494-7). B&N.

MALE NURSES

see Men Nurses

MALE PHOTOGRAPHY

see Photography of Men

MALE SEX HORMONE

see Hormones, Sex

MALE STERILITY

see Sterility, Male

MALEBRANCHE, NICOLAS, 1638-1715

Church, Ralph W. Study in the Philosophy of Malebranche. LC 74-102564. 1970. Repr. of 1931 ed. 14.50 (ISBN 0-8046-0724-9). Kennikat.

Luce, A. A. Berkeley & Malebranche: A Study in the Origins of Berkeley's Thought. 1934. 34.95x (ISBN 0-19-824319-7). Oxford U Pr.

MALEDICTION

see Blessing and Cursing

MALEMBA LANGUAGE

see Congo Language

MALESHERBES, CHRETIEN GUILLAUME DE LAMOIGNON DE, 1721-1794

Shaw, Edward P. Problems & Policies of Malesherbes As Directeur De la Librarie in France, 1750-1763. LC 66-63787. 1966. 12.00 (ISBN 0-87395-018-6); microfiche 12.00 (ISBN 0-87395-118-2). State U NY Pr.

MALFORMATIONS, CONGENITAL

see Abnormalities, Human

MALGACHE LANGUAGE

see Malagasy Language

MALGONKAR, MANOHAR, 1913-

Amur, G. S. Manohar Malgonkar. (Indian Writers Ser: No. 3). 155p. (Orig.). 1973. pap. text ed. 2.75x (ISBN 0-391-00428-X). Humanities.

--Manohar Malgonkar. (Indian Writers Ser.). 1976. 8.50 (ISBN 0-89253-506-7). Ind-US Inc.

Dayananda, James Y. Manohar Malgonkar. (World Authors Ser.: India: No. 340). 1975. lib. bdg. 12.50 (ISBN 0-8057-2566-0). Twayne.

MALHERBE, FRANCOISE DE, 1555-1628

Brunot, Ferdinand. Doctrine de Malherbe d'apres son commentaire sur Desportes. 1971. Repr. of 1891 ed. lib. bdg. 34.50 (ISBN 0-8337-0405-2). B Franklin.

Gosse, Edmund. Malherbe & the Classical Reaction in the Seventeenth Century. LC 73-503. 1973. lib. bdg. 5.00 (ISBN 0-8414-1543-9). Folcroft.

--Malherbe & the Classical Rendition in the Seventeenth Century. 1978. Repr. of 1920 ed. lib. bdg. 6.50 (ISBN 0-8495-1923-3). Arden Lib.

Rubin, David L. Higher, Hidden Order: Design & Meaning in the Odes of Malherbe. (Studies in the Romance Languages & Literatures: No. 117). 1972. pap. 7.50x (ISBN 0-686-77166-4). U of NC Pr.

MALI

Carpenter, Allan, et al. Mali: Enchantment of Africa. (gr. 5 up). 1975. 10.60 (ISBN 0-516-04574-1). Childrens.

Ernst, Klaus. Tradition & Progress in the African Village: Non-Capitalist Reform of Rural Communities in Mali - The Sociological Problems. LC 74-22292. 350p. 1977. 27.50x (ISBN 0-312-81235-3). St Martin.

Imperato, Pascal J., ed. Historical Dictionary of Mali. LC 76-55775. (African Historical Dictionaries Ser: No. 11). (Illus.). 1977. 12.00 (ISBN 0-8108-1004-2). Scarecrow.

Jones, William I. Planning & Economic Policy: Socialist Mali & Her Neighbors. LC 76-8048. (Illus.). 1976. cased 18.00 (ISBN 0-914478-70-2); pap. 10.00 (ISBN 0-914478-71-0). Three Continents.

Levtzion, Nehemia. Ancient Ghana & Mali. LC 79-27281. 1980. text ed. 21.50x (ISBN 0-8419-0431-6, Africana); pap. text ed. 9.75x (ISBN 0-8419-0432-4). Holmes & Meier.

Savonnet, Georges. Les Birifor De Diepla et Sa Region Insulaires Du Rameau Lobi (Haute-Volta) (Atlas Des Structures Agraires Au Sud Du Sahara: No. 12). (Fr.). 1976. pap. text ed. 38.75x (ISBN 90-2797-823-9). Mouton.

MALICIOUS MISCHIEF

see also Sabotage

MALINOWSKI, BRONISLAW, 1884-1942

Firth, Raymond, ed. Man & Culture: An Evaluation of the Work of Bronislaw Malinowski. 292p. 1980. 27.50x (ISBN 0-7100-1376-0, Pub. by Routledge England). Humanities.

MALL, E. JANE, 1920-

Mall, E. Jane. How Am I Doing God? LC 72-97343. 176p. 1973. pap. 2.25 (ISBN 0-570-03150-8, 12-2535). Concordia.

MALLARME, STEPHANE, 1842-1898

Block, Haskell M. Mallarme & the Symbolist Drama. LC 77-9242. (Wayne State University Study of Language & Literature: No. 14). 1977. Repr. of 1963 ed. lib. bdg. 15.00x (ISBN 0-8371-9706-6, BLMS). Greenwood.

Bowie, M. Mallarme & the Art of Being Difficult. LC 77-82488. 1978. 29.95 (ISBN 0-521-21813-6). Cambridge U Pr.

Chiari, Joseph. Symbolisme from Poe to Mallarme: The Growth of a Myth. LC 76-114096. 1970. Repr. of 1956 ed. text ed. 9.00 (ISBN 0-87752-020-8). Gordian.

Chisholm, A. Mallarme's "L'Apres-Midi D'un Faune". 1958. pap. 2.00x (ISBN 0-424-05450-7, Pub. by Sydney U Pr). Intl Schol Bk Serv.

Cohn. Mallarme's Masterwork. (Coll. De Proprietatibus Litterarum, Ser. Pratica). 22.50 (ISBN 0-685-34939-X). French & Eur.

Cohn, Robert G. Mallarme: Igitur. 150p. 1981. 5.95x (ISBN 0-520-04188-7). U of Cal Pr.

--Mallarme's Un coup de des: An Exegesis. LC 77-10256. Repr. of 1949 ed. 27.50 (ISBN 0-404-16311-4). AMS Pr.

--Toward the Poems of Mallarme. 1965. 12.50x (ISBN 0-520-00250-4); pap. 5.95x (ISBN 0-520-03846-0). U of Cal Pr.

Cohn, Robert G., Jr. Mallarme's Masterwork: New Findings. (De Proprietatibus l' Herarum Ser. Practica: No. 1). 1966. pap. text ed. 20.00x (ISBN 90-2790-089-2). Mouton.

Cooperman, Hasye. Aesthetics of Stephane Mallarme. rev. ed. LC 75-152535. (Illus.). 1971. Repr. of 1933 ed. 18.00 (ISBN 0-8462-1603-5). Russell.

Dujardin, Edouard. Mallarme par un des siens. LC 77-10259. Repr. of 1936 ed. 27.50 (ISBN 0-404-16314-9). AMS Pr.

Ellis, Arthur. Stephane Mallarme. LC 77-790. 1977. Repr. of 1927 ed. lib. bdg. 20.00 (ISBN 0-8414-3982-6). Folcroft.

Fowlie, Wallace. Mallarme. LC 53-9931. (Illus.). 1953. 10.00x (ISBN 0-226-25880-7). U of Chicago Pr.

--Mallarme. LC 53-9931. (Illus.). 1962. pap. 2.45 (ISBN 0-226-25881-5, P93, Phoen). U of Chicago Pr.

--Mallarme. 1953. Repr. 15.00 (ISBN 0-8274-2667-4). R West.

Franklin, Ursula. Anatomy of Poesis: The Prose Poems of Stephane Mallarme. (Studies in the Romance Languages & Literatures Ser: No. 167). 1976. pap. 14.00x (ISBN 0-8078-9167-3). U of NC Pr.

Frey, John A. Motif Symbolism in the Disciples of Mallarme. LC 73-94193. (Catholic University of America Studies in Romance Languages & Literatures Ser: No. 55). Repr. of 1957 ed. 17.50 (ISBN 0-404-50355-1). AMS Pr.

Gill, Austin. The Early Mallarme: Vol. 1, Parentage, Early Years & Juvenilia. (Illus.). 286p. 1979. text ed. 29.00x (ISBN 0-19-815726-6). Oxford U Pr.

Kravis, Judy. The Prose of Mallarme. LC 75-22977. 272p. 1976. 42.00 (ISBN 0-521-20921-8). Cambridge U Pr.

Lewis, Paula G. The Aesthetics of Stephane Mallarme in Relation to His Public. LC 74-5898. 260p. 1976. 15.00 (ISBN 0-8386-1615-1). Fairleigh Dickinson.

Mallarme, Stephane. Mallarme et le symbolisme, auteurs et oeuvres. (Nouveaux Classiques Larousse). (Illus., Fr.). pap. 2.95 (ISBN 0-685-13978-6, 165). Larousse.

--Stephane Mallarme. 159p. 1980. Repr. of 1927 ed. lib. bdg. 20.00 (ISBN 0-8492-6835-4). R West.

Mauron, Charles. Introduction to the Psychoanalysis of Mallarme. McLendon, Will & Henderson, Archibald, Jr., trs. (Perspectives in Criticism: No. 10). 1963. 20.00x (ISBN 0-520-00833-2). U of Cal Pr.

Michaud, Guy. Mallarme. Collins, Marie & Humez, Bertha, trs. LC 65-10766. (Orig.). 1965. 8.50x (ISBN 0-8147-0304-6); pap. 3.95 (ISBN 0-8147-0305-4). NYU Pr.
Morris, D. Hampton. Stephane Mallarme, Twentieth-Century Criticism, 1901-1971. rev. ed. LC 77-708. (Romance Monographs: No. 25). 1977. 19.00x (ISBN 84-399-6423-4). Romance.
Ragusa, Olga. Mallarme in Italy: Literary Influence & Critical Response. 1957. 7.50x (ISBN 0-913298-34-4). S F Vanni.
St. Aubyn, Fredric C. Stephane Mallarme. (World Authors Ser.: No. 52). 10.95 (ISBN 0-8057-2568-7). Twayne.
Valery, Paul. Ecrits Divers sur Stephane Mallarme. pap. 8.75 (ISBN 0-685-36612-X). French & Eur.
Wills, Ludmilla M. Le Regard Contemplatif Chez Valery et Mallarme. (Orig., Fr.). 1976. pap. text ed. 14.50x (ISBN 90-620-3407-1). Humanities.
Woolley, Grange. Stephane Mallarme 1842-1898. LC 77-11499. (Illus.). 264p. Repr. of 1942 ed. 31.50 (ISBN 0-404-16358-0). AMS Pr.

MALLEA, EDVARDO

Lewald, H. Ernest. Eduardo Mallea. (World Authors Ser.: No. 433). 1977. lib. bdg. 12.50 (ISBN 0-8057-6273-6). Twayne.
Pintor Genaro, Mercedes. Eduardo Mallea, Novelista. LC 76-6545. (Coleccion Mente y Palabra). (Span.). 1976. 6.25 (ISBN 0-8477-0524-2); pap. text ed. 5.00 (ISBN 0-8477-0525-0). U of PR Pr.
Shaw, D. L., ed. Eduardo Mallea: Todo verdor perecera. 1968. 8.30 (ISBN 0-08-012868-8); pap. 5.75 (ISBN 0-08-012867-X). Pergamon.

MALLET DU PAN, JACQUES, 1749-1800

Acomb, Frances. Mallet Du Pan (Seventeen Forty-Nine-Eighteen Hundred: A Career in Political Journalism. LC 72-96985. 330p. 1973. 14.75 (ISBN 0-8223-0295-0). Duke.

MALMESBURY, JAMES HARRIS, 1ST EARL OF, 1746-1820

Cobban, Alfred. Ambassadors & Secret Agents: The Diplomacy of the First Earl of Malmesbury at the Hague. LC 78-59012. (Illus.). 1979. Repr. of 1954 ed. 21.00 (ISBN 0-88355-687-1). Hyperion Conn.

MALNUTRITION

see also Deficiency Diseases; Starvation

Alleyne, G. A., et al. Protein-Energy Malnutrition. (Illus.). 1977. text ed. 25.00 (ISBN 0-8151-0116-3). Year Bk Med.
Austin, James E. Confronting Urban Malnutrition: The Design of Nutrition Programs. LC 79-3705. 1980. pap. 6.50x (ISBN 0-8018-2261-0). Johns Hopkins.
Austin, James E., ed. Global Malnutrition & Cereal Grain Fortification. LC 78-21224. 1979. reference 27.50 (ISBN 0-88410-366-8). Ballinger Pub.
Balderston, Judith, et al. Malnourished Children of the Rural Poor: The Web of Food, Health, Education, Fertility, & Agricultural Production. LC 81-3483. 206p. 1981. 19.95 (ISBN 0-86569-071-5). Auburn Hse.
Billions More to Feed. 1978. pap. 6.00 (ISBN 92-5-100229-0, F90, FAO). Unipub.
Bower, Fay L. Nutrition in Nursing. LC 79-10562. (Nursing Concept Modules Ser.). 1979. pap. 12.50 (ISBN 0-471-04124-6, Pub. by Wiley Med). Wiley.
Brown, Roy E. Starving Children: The Tyranny of Hunger. LC 73-92195. (Illus.). 1977. text ed. 14.95 (ISBN 0-8261-1690-6). Springer Pub.
Cravioto, Joaquin, et al, eds. Early Malnutrition & Mental Development. (Symposia of the Swedish Nutrition Foundation Ser.: No. 12). 1974p. 1974. text ed. 25.00x (ISBN 91-2200-271-5). Humanities.
Eckholm, Erik P. & Record, Francis. The Two Faces of Malnutrition. LC 76-47787. (Worldwatch Papers). 1976. pap. 2.00 (ISBN 0-916468-08-9). Worldwatch Inst.
Gardner, L. I. & Amacher, P., eds. Endocrine Aspects of Malnutrition: Marasmus, Kwashiorkor & Psychosocial Deprivation. LC 73-88110. 538p. 1973. 27.00 (ISBN 0-685-48386-X). Raven.
Greene, Lawrence S., ed. Malnutrition, Behavior & Social Organization. 1977. 34.00 (ISBN 0-12-298050-6). Acad Pr.
Gyorgy, P. & Kline, O. L., eds. Malnutrition Is a Problem of Ecology. (Bibliotheca Nutritio et Dieta: No. 14). 1970. pap. 20.50 (ISBN 3-8055-0164-1). S Karger.
Hoorweg, J. C. Protein-Energy Malnutrition & Intellectual Abilities: A Study of Teenage Ugandan Children. (Communications, Ser.: No. 5). 1976. pap. text ed. 12.25x (ISBN 90-2797-752-6). Mouton.
Levitsky, David A., ed. Malnutrition, Environment, & Behavior: New Perspectives. LC 78-58016. 1979. 22.50x (ISBN 0-8014-1045-2). Cornell U Pr.
Lloyd-Still, J. D. Malnutrition and Intellectual Development. LC 76-17432. (Illus.). 202p. 1976. 19.50 (ISBN 0-88416-181-1). Wright-PSG.
Malnutrition & Mental Development in Man, 2 vols. Incl. Vol. 1. Hermann, Harold W., et al, eds. 164p (ISBN 0-8422-7259-3); Vol. 2. Kallen, David J., et al, eds. 169p. 1976. text ed. 21.50x ea. Irvington.
Manocha, Sohan L. Malnutrition & Retarded Human Development. (Illus.). 400p. 1972. 39.50 (ISBN 0-398-02548-7). C C Thomas.
May, Jacques M. & McLellan, Donna L., eds. Studies in Medical Geography, 14 vols. Incl. Vol. 2. Studies in Disease Ecology. (Illus.). 1961. 24.25 (ISBN 0-02-848980-2); Vol. 3. The Ecology of Malnutrition in the Far & Near East. (Illus.). 1961. 21.75 (ISBN 0-02-849010-X); Vol. 4. The Ecology of Malnutrition in Five Countries of Eastern & Central Europe: East Germany,Poland, Yugoslavia, Albania, Greece. (Illus.). 1964. 16.25 (ISBN 0-02-848970-5); Vol. 5. The Ecology of Malnutrition in Middle Africa: Ghana, Nigeria, Republic of the Congo, Rwanda & Burundi & the Former French Equatorial Africa. (Illus.). 1965. 14.25 (ISBN 0-02-848990-X); Vol. 6. The Ecology of Malnutrition in Central & Southern Europe: Austria, Hungary, Romania, Bulgaria & Czechoslovakia. (Illus.). 1966. 16.25 (ISBN 0-02-849000-2); Vol. 7. The Ecology of Malnutrition in Northern Africa: Libya, Tunisia, Algeria, Morocco, Spanish Sahara & Ifni, Mauretania. (Illus.). 1967. 16.25 (ISBN 0-02-848950-0); Vol. 8. The Ecology of Malnutrition in the French-Speaking Countries of West Africa & Madagascar: Senegal, Guinea, Ivory Coast, Togo, Dahomey, Cameroon, Niger, Mali, Upper Volta, & Madagascar. (Illus.). 1968. 18.50 (ISBN 0-02-848960-8); Vol. 9. The Ecology of Malnutrition in Eastern Africa: Equatorial Guinea, the Gambia, Liberia, Sierra Leone, Malawi, Rhodesia, Zambia, Kenya, Tanzania, Uganda, Ethiopia, the French Territory of the Atars & Issas, the Somali Republic & Sudan. 1970. 28.50 (ISBN 0-02-849020-7); Vol. 10. The Ecology of Malnutrition in Seven Countries of Southern Africa and in Portuguese Guinea: The/Republic of South Africa, South West Africa (Namibia), Botswana, Lesotho, Swaziland, Mozambique, Angola, Portuguese Guinea. 1971. 24.00 (ISBN 0-02-848940-3); Vol. 11. The Ecology of Malnutrition in Mexico & Central America. 1972. 21.75 (ISBN 0-02-848930-6); Vol. 12. The Ecology of Malnutrition in the Caribbean. 1973. 26.25 (ISBN 0-02-848920-9); Vol. 13. The Ecology of Malnutrition in Eastern South America. 1975. 36.25 (ISBN 0-02-849060-6); Vol. 14. The Ecology of Malnutrition in Western South America. 1975. 28.50 (ISBN 0-02-849070-3). Hafner.
Morley, David C. & Woodland, Margaret. See How They Grow: Monitoring Child Growth for Appropriate Health Care in Developing Countries. (Illus.). 1980. text ed. 15.95x (ISBN 0-19-520160-4). Oxford U Pr.
Nestle Foundation Symposium. Protein-Calorie Malnutrition: Proceedings. Von Muralt, A., ed. (Illus.). 1971. Repr. of 1969 ed. 34.90 (ISBN 0-387-04677-1). Springer-Verlag.
Pollitt, Ernesto. Poverty & Malnutrition in Latin America: Early Childhood Intervention Programs. LC 80-18811. 150p. 1980. 22.95 (ISBN 0-03-058031-5). Praeger.
Prescott, James W., ed. Brian Function & Malnutrition: Neuropsychological Methods of Assessment. LC 74-26971. 449p. (Orig.). 1975. 28.50 (ISBN 0-471-69673-0). Krieger.
Ramsey, Frank C. Protein-Energy Malnutrition in Barbados: The Role of Continuity of Care. new ed. LC 79-88999. (Illus.). 1979. pap. 4.00 (ISBN 0-914362-28-3). J Macy Foun.
Robson, John R., et al. Malnutrition, Its Causation & Control. Set. 63.75x (ISBN 0-677-03140-8). Gordon.
Roche, Alex F. & Falkner, Frank. Nutrition & Malnutrition: Identification & Measurement. LC 74-13950. (Advances in Experimental Medicine & Biology Ser.: Vol. 49). 365p. 1974. 37.50 (ISBN 0-306-39049-3, Plenum Pr). Plenum Pub.
Simon, Arthur. Bread for the World. 179p. 1975. pap. 2.95 (ISBN 0-8028-1602-9). Eerdmans.
Somogyi, J. C., ed. Early Signs of Nutritional Deficiencies. (Bibliotheca Nutritio et Dieta: No. 23). (Illus.). 150p. 1976. 58.75 (ISBN 3-8055-2314-9). S Karger.
Stein, Zena, et al. Famine & Human Development: The Dutch Hunger Winter 1944-1945. (Illus.). 425p. 1974. text ed. 14.95x (ISBN 0-19-501811-7). Oxford U Pr.
Suskind, Robert M., ed. Malnutrition & the Immune Response. LC 75-14589. 1977. 43.50 (ISBN 0-89004-060-5). Raven.
Winick, Myron. Hunger Disease: Studies by the Jewish Physicians in the Warsaw Ghetto. LC 78-26397. (Current Concepts in Nutrition Ser.: Vol. 7). 1979. 24.00 (ISBN 0-471-05003-2, Pub. by Wiley-Interscience). Wiley.
--Malnutrition & Brain Development. (Illus.). 176p. 1976. text ed. 13.95x (ISBN 0-19-501983-0). Oxford U Pr.
Wurtman, Richard J. & Wurtman, Judith J., eds. Control of Feeding Behavior, & Biology of the Brain in Protein-Calorie Malnutrition. LC 75-14593. (Nutrition & the Brain Ser: Vol. 2). 323p. 1977. 31.50 (ISBN 0-89004-046-X). Raven.

MALONE, EDMOND, 1741-1812

Ireland, Samuel. Investigation into Mister Malone's Claim to the Charter of Scholar. 162p. 1970. Repr. of 1796 ed. 28.00x (ISBN 0-7146-2512-4, F Cass Co). Biblio Dist.
--Investigation of Mr. Malone's Claim to the Character of Scholar. LC 72-149663. Repr. of 1797 ed. 21.00 (ISBN 0-404-03505-1). AMS Pr.
--Investigation of Mr. Malone's Claim to the Character of Scholar, or Critic. LC 71-96369. (Eighteenth Century Shakespeare). Repr. of 1797 ed. lib. bdg. 25.00x (ISBN 0-678-05136-4). Kelley.
Mason, J. M. Comments on the Several Editions of Shakespeare's Plays, Extended to Those of Malone & Steevens. LC 77-172852. Repr. of 1807 ed. 39.75 (ISBN 0-404-04226-0). AMS Pr.

MALORY, THOMAS, SIR, 15TH CENTURY

Beardsley, Aubrey. Illustrations for le Morte Darthur. 250p. 1972. pap. 4.50 (ISBN 0-486-22348-5). Dover.
Benson, Larry D. Malory's Morte d'Arthur: A 15th Century Chivalric Romance. 256p. 1976. 15.00x (ISBN 0-674-54393-9). Harvard U Pr.
Chambers, Edmund K. Sir Thomas Malory. Repr. of 1922 ed. lib. bdg. 6.50 (ISBN 0-8414-3431-X). Folcroft.
Dillon, Bert, ed. A Malory Handbook. (Reference Publications). 1978. lib. bdg. 18.00 (ISBN 0-8161-7964-6). G K Hall.
Gardner, John C. Morte Darthur Notes. (Orig.). 1967. pap. 1.95 (ISBN 0-8220-0726-6). Cliffs.
Hicks, Edward. Sir Thomas Malory: His Turbulent Career, a Biography. LC 78-120630. 1970. Repr. of 1928 ed. lib. bdg. 14.50x (ISBN 0-374-93885-7). Octagon.
Hissiger, P. F. Le Morte Arthur: A Critical Edition. (Studies in English Literature: No. 96). 184p. 1975. pap. text ed. 31.25x (ISBN 90-2793-386-3). Mouton.
Kato, Tomomi, ed. Concordance to the Works of Sir Thomas Malory. 1500p. 1974. 160.00x (ISBN 0-86008-100-1, Pub. by U of Tokyo Pr). Intl Schol Bk Serv.
Ker, N. R., intro. by. The Winchester Malory: A Facsimile. (Early English Text Society Ser.: Supplementary No. 4). 1976. pap. 149.00x (ISBN 0-19-722404-0). Oxford U Pr.
Kittredge, George L. Sir Thomas Malory. LC 74-17474. 1974. Repr. of 1925 ed. lib. bdg. 4.00 (ISBN 0-8414-5516-3). Folcroft.
Knight, S. Structure of Sir Thomas Malory's Arthuriad. (Australian Humanities Research Council Monograph: No. 14). 1969. pap. 6.50x (ISBN 0-424-05960-6, Pub. by Sydney U Pr). Intl Schol Bk Serv.
Krishna, Valerie S., ed. The Alliterative Morte Arthure: A Critical Edition. new ed. 400p. 1976. lib. bdg. 21.50 (ISBN 0-89102-039-X). B Franklin.
Life, Page W. Sir Thomas Malory & the Morte Darthur: A Survey of Scholarship & Annotated Bibliography. LC 80-16180. 1980. 13.50x (ISBN 0-8139-0868-X). U Pr of Va.
Stugrin, Michael. Monarch Notes on Malory's Mote D'Arthur. 1975. pap. 1.50 (ISBN 0-671-00961-3). Monarch Pr.
Takamiya, Toshiyuki & Brewer, Derek, eds. Aspects of Malory. (Arthurian Studies: No. I). (Illus.). 240p. 1981. 35.00x (ISBN 0-8476-7013-9). Rowman.
Vinaver, Eugene. Malory. LC 77-23499. 1977. lib. bdg. 27.50 (ISBN 0-8414-9179-8). Folcroft.
--Rise of Romance. 1971. 12.95 (ISBN 0-19-501446-4). Oxford U Pr.
Wilson, Robert H. Characterization in Malory. LC 72-187875. 1934. lib. bdg. 8.50 (ISBN 0-8414-9721-4). Folcroft.

MALOZI

see Lozi (African Tribe)

MALPIGHI, MARCELLO, 1628-1694

Adelmann, Howard B. Marcello Malpighi & the Evolution of Embryology, 5 Vols. (History of Science Ser.). 1966. Set. boxed 200.00x (ISBN 0-8014-0004-X). Cornell U Pr.
Adelmann, Howard B., ed. & tr. from It. The Correspondence of Marcello Malpighi, 5 vols. Incl. Vol. 1. 1-214 Letters, 1658-1669; Vol. 2. 214-431 Letters, 1670-1683; Vol. 3. 432-724 Letters, 1684-1688; Vol. 4. 725-824 Letters, 1689-1692; Vol. 5. 825-1050 Letters, 1693-1694. LC 73-9867. (History of Science Ser). 2316p. 1975. boxed set 95.00x (ISBN 0-8014-0802-4). Cornell U Pr.

MALPRACTICE

Adriani, John & Eaton, Allen. The Law & Health Professionals: Fundamentals of the Law & Malpractice. 144p. 1981. 10.50x (ISBN 0-87527-189-8). Green.
Alton, Walter G., Jr. Malpractice: A Trial Lawyer's Advice for Physicians. 1977. 12.95 (ISBN 0-316-03500-9). Little.
Bermont, Hubert. The Consultant's Malpractice Avoidance Manual. (The Consultant's Library). 70p. (Orig.). 1981. pap. 19.00 (ISBN 0-930686-15-2). Bermont Bks.
Bertolet, Mary M. & Goldsmith, Lee S., eds. Hospital Liability: Law & Tactics. 4th ed. LC 79-92666. 789p. 1980. text ed. 45.00 (ISBN 0-686-65589-3). PLI.
Cohen, Ronald J. Malpractice: A Guide for Mental Health Professionals. LC 78-72147. 1979. 13.95 (ISBN 0-02-905790-6). Free Pr.
Corea, Gena. The Hidden Malpractice. 1978. pap. 1.95 (ISBN 0-515-04522-5). Jove Pubns.
Daly, John C., et al. Medical Malpractice Dilemma. 1977. pap. 3.75 (ISBN 0-8447-2095-X). Am Enterprise.
Dawidoff, Donald J. The Malpractice of Psychiatrists: Malpractice in Psychoanalysis, Psychotherapy & Psychiatry. (American Lecture in Behavioral Science & Law Ser.). 184p. 1973. 16.75 (ISBN 0-398-02711-0). C C Thomas.
Dunlap, J. Medical Negligence Malpractice: The Uncontrolled Killer. 1976. 8.95 (ISBN 0-686-17451-8). World Intl.
--Medical Negligence: The Uncontrolled Killer. rev. ed. 1979. 10.75 (ISBN 0-686-24851-1). World Intl.
--Medical Negligence: The Uncontrolled Killer. 1978. softcover 2.95 (ISBN 0-686-10225-8). World Intl.
Dunlap, James. Malpractice of Dentists, Psychiatrists & Chiropractors. 1978. pap. 2.25 (ISBN 0-686-22705-0). World Intl.
--Malpractice of Dentists, Psychiatrists, Chiropractors. 1977. 8.95 (ISBN 0-686-18980-9). World Intl.
Furrow, Barry R. Malpractice in Psychotherapy. LC 79-3253. 192p. 1980. 18.95x (ISBN 0-669-03399-5). Lexington Bks.
Gots, Ronald E. Truth About Medical Malpractice: The Patient's Rights, the Doctor's Rights. LC 75-11801. 1975. 7.95 (ISBN 0-8128-1831-8); pap. 4.95 (ISBN 0-8128-6000-4). Stein & Day.
Harney, David M. Medical Malpractice. 1973. text ed. 42.50 including 1980 suppl. (ISBN 0-87473-069-4). A Smith Co.
--Medical Malpractice: 1980 Supplement. 1980. 15.00 (ISBN 0-685-59738-5). A Smith Co.
Hogan, Daniel B. The Regulation of Psychotherapists, Vol. III: A Review of Malpractice Suits in the U.S. LC 78-23778. (The Regulation of Psychotherapists Ser.). 1979. reference 25.00 (ISBN 0-88410-524-5). Ballinger Pub.
Holder, Angela R. Medical Malpractice Law. 2nd ed. LC 77-27288. 1978. 41.95 (ISBN 0-471-03882-2, Pub. by Wiley Medical). Wiley.
Hutzler, Laurie H. Attorney's Malpractice Prevention Manual. 4th ed. (Illus.). 1979. 35.00x (ISBN 0-937542-00-8); pap. 19.95x (ISBN 0-937542-01-6). Legal Mgmt Serv.
Institute of Medicine. Beyond Malpractice: Compensation for Medical Injuries. LC 78-58382. 1978. pap. text ed. 6.50 (ISBN 0-309-02765-9). Natl Acad Pr.
Jacobs, H. Barry. The Spectre of Malpractice. Bennett, Clifford A., et al, eds. LC 77-88921. (Illus.). 1978. 17.95 (ISBN 0-917188-14-4). Nationwide Pr.
Kindregan, Charles P. Malpractice & the Lawyer. LC 78-16754. 85p. 1981. 10.95 (ISBN 0-686-31600-2). Natl Prac Inst.
Kramer, Charles. Medical Malpractice. 4th ed. 1976. 15.00 (ISBN 0-685-85392-6, H1-0833). PLI.
Lander, Louise. Defective Medicine: Risk, Anger, & the Malpractice Crisis. LC 78-5577. 242p. 1978. 10.00 (ISBN 0-374-13627-0); pap. 4.95 (ISBN 0-374-51509-3). FS&G.
Laufman, Alan K. The Law of Medical Malpractice in Texas: A Primer for the Medical Community. LC 77-420. (Illus.). 136p. 1977. 10.00 (ISBN 0-292-74620-2). U of Tex Pr.
Law, Sylvia & Polan, Stephen. Pain & Profit: The Politics of Malpractice. LC 77-11535. 1978. 14.95 (ISBN 0-06-012546-2, HarpT). Har-Row.
Lawyers Co-Op Editorial Staff. Medical Malpractice: ALR 20 Cases & Annotations, 3 vols. LC 70-1405. 1966. 105.00 (ISBN 0-686-14517-8). Lawyers Co-Op.
Levin, Bruce A. & Coyne, Robert, eds. Tort Reform & Related Proposals: Annotated Bibliographies on Product Liability & Medical Malpractice. 300p. 1979. pap. 30.00 (ISBN 0-686-65427-7). Am Bar Foun.
Levine, M. Surgical Malpractice. 554p. 1970. 22.00 (ISBN 0-913338-11-7). Trans-Media Pub.
Lipton, Dean. Malpractice: Autobiography of a Victim. LC 77-84574. (Illus.). 1978. 9.95 (ISBN 0-498-02185-8). A S Barnes.

Lubliner, Jerry & Bednarski, Mary W. An Introduction to Medical Malpractice. (Learning Packages in Policy Issues: No. 1). 52p. 1976. pap. text ed. 1.50 (ISBN 0-936826-10-X). Pol Stud Assocs.
Ludlam, James E. Informed Consent. LC 78-24495. 96p. (Orig.). 1978. 8.75 (ISBN 0-87258-243-4, 1160). Am Hospital.
Making Your Practice More Malpractice-Proof. 1975. pap. 3.50 (ISBN 0-87489-059-4). Med Economics.
Meisel, David J. Attorney Malpractice: Law & Procedure, Vol.1. LC 79-89562. 1980. 47.50 (ISBN 0-686-29229-4). Lawyers Co-Op.
Moore, Robert P. The Medical Malpractice Controversy. 14.00 (ISBN 0-686-52512-4). Fountainhead.
Morris, William O. Dental Litigation. 2nd ed. 1977. 25.00 (ISBN 0-87215-198-0). Michie-Bobbs.
O'Connell, Jeffrey. The Lawsuit Lottery: Only the Lawyers Win. LC 79-7579. 1979. 10.95 (ISBN 0-02-923280-5). Free Pr.
Orlikoff, James E., et al. Malpractice Prevention & Liability Control for Hospitals. Greeley, Hugh P., ed. (Orig.). 1981. price not set (ISBN 0-87258-359-7, 1467). Am Hospital.
Pegalis, Steven & Wachsman, Harvey. American Law of Medical Malpactice, 2 vols. LC 79-90712. 1980. 95.00 (ISBN 0-686-29235-9). Lawyers Co-Op.
Redish, Martin H. The Constitutionality of Medical Malpractice Reform Legislation: A Supplemental Report. LC 78-17281. 40p. (Orig.). 1978. pap. 9.00 (ISBN 0-87258-239-6, 2002). Am Hospital.
--Legislative Response to the Medical Malpractice Crisis: Constitutional Implications. LC 77-6381. 76p. (Orig.). 1977. pap. 13.25 (ISBN 0-87258-216-7, 2001). Am Hospital.
Roady, Thomas G., Jr. & Andersen, William R., eds. Professional Negligence. LC 60-8216. 1960. 11.50 (ISBN 0-8265-1055-8). Vanderbilt U Pr.
Rosenblatt, Stanley M., ed. Malpractice & Other Malfeasances. 1977. 10.00 (ISBN 0-8184-0234-2). Lyle Stuart.
Rottenberg, Simon, ed. The Economics of Medical Malpractice. 1978. 15.25 (ISBN 0-8447-2112-3); pap. 7.25 (ISBN 0-8447-2111-5). Am Enterprise.
Shoecraft, Billee. Sue the Bastards! (Expose-Herbicides) 6.00 (ISBN 0-686-29959-0). Cancer Bk Hse.
Smith, Jeffery M. Preventing Legal Malpractice. LC 80-26759. 156p. 1981. pap. text ed. 7.95 (ISBN 0-8299-2118-4). West Pub.
Speiser, Stuart & Krause, Charles. Aviation Tort Law, 3 vols. LC 78-55326. 1980. 180.00 (ISBN 0-686-29236-7). Lawyers Co-Op.
Stone, Alan A. Malpractice & the Mental Health Professions. LC 78-19812. Date not set. 15.00 (ISBN 0-465-04329-1). Basic.
Sumner, Michael. The Dollars & Sense of Hospital Malpractice Insurance. LC 78-67846. 1979. text ed. 22.50 (ISBN 0-89011-517-6). Abt Assoc.
Wecht, Cyril H., ed. Exploring the Medical Malpractice Dilemma. (Illus.). 1972. 25.00 (ISBN 0-8151-9160-X, Pub. by Symposia Special). Year Bk Med.

MALRAUX, ANDRE, 1901-1976

Blumenthal, Gerda. Andre Malraux: The Conquest of Dread. LC 78-12576. 1979. Repr. of 1960 ed. lib. bdg. 15.00x (ISBN 0-313-21194-9, BLAM). Greenwood.
Dorenlot, Francoise & Braun, Micheline T., eds. Andre Malraux: Metamorphosis & Imagination. LC 77-18629. (New York Literary Forum Ser.). (Illus., Orig.). 1979. pap. text ed. 12.50 (ISBN 0-931196-02-7). NY Lit Forum.
Flanner, Janet. Men & Monuments. facs. ed. LC 73-121468. (Essay Index Reprint Ser). 1957. 19.50 (ISBN 0-8369-1876-2). Arno.
Frohock, Wilbur. Andre Malraux. LC 74-1198. (Columbia Essays on Modern Writers Ser.: No. 71). 48p. 1974. pap. 2.00 (ISBN 0-231-03441-5). Columbia U Pr.
Frohock, Wilbur M. Andre Malraux & the Tragic Imagination. 1952. 12.50x (ISBN 0-8047-0441-4); pap. 2.95 (ISBN 0-8047-0442-2, SP42). Stanford U Pr.
Greenlee, James W. Malraux's Heroes & History. LC 74-12819. 222p. 1975. 15.00 (ISBN 0-87580-051-3). N Ill U Pr.
Hewitt, James R. Andre Malraux. LC 70-15661. (Modern Literature Ser.). 1978. 10.95 (ISBN 0-8044-2379-2). Ungar.
Hiddleston, J. A. Malraux: La Condition Humaine. (Studies in French Literature). 1973. pap. text ed. 3.95x (ISBN 0-7131-5673-2). Dynamic Learn Corp.
Horvath, Violet M. Andre Malraux: The Human Adventure. LC 75-80065. (Gotham Library Ser.). 1969. 12.00x (ISBN 0-8147-0203-1); pap. 3.95 (ISBN 0-8147-0204-X). NYU Pr.
Kline, Thomas J. Andre Malraux & the Metamorphosis of Death. 197p. 1973. 15.00x (ISBN 0-231-03608-6). Columbia U Pr.
Malraux, Andre. La Corde et les Souris: Avec: Les Hotes de Passage, Les Chenes qu'on abat (Version Difinitive), La Tete d'Obsidienne (Version Definitive), Lazare. 1976. 4.95 (ISBN 0-686-56322-0). French & Eur.
--Etre et Dire: Neocritique. 1976. 19.95 (ISBN 0-686-56324-7). French & Eur.
--Les Hotes de Passage: Comprend les 3 Premiers Chapitres du Tome 2 de Le Memoir des Limbes. 240p. 1975. 17.50 (ISBN 0-686-56326-3). French & Eur.
--Lazarus. Kilmartin, Terence, tr. from Fr. LC 78-3184. 1978. pap. 2.95 (ISBN 0-394-17068-7, E719, Ever). Grove.
--Le Miroir des Limbes: Edition Definitive. rev. ed. 1011p. 1976. 33.95 (ISBN 0-686-56331-X). French & Eur.
Michalczyk, John J. Andre Malraux's Espoir: The Propaganda-Art Film & the Spanish Civil War. LC 77-7308. (Romance Monographs: No. 27). 1977. 18.00x (ISBN 84-399-6811-6). Romance.
Passion & the Intellect, or Andre Malraux. 1956. pap. 6.00 (ISBN 0-527-01726-4). Kraus Repr.
Romeiser, John B. Critical Reception of Andre Malraux's l'Espoir in the French Press: December 1937-June 1940. LC 79-19837. (Romance Monographs, Inc.: No. 37). 176p. 1980. 18.00x (ISBN 84-499-3368-4). Romance.
Savage, Catharine. Malraux, Sartre, & Aragon As Political Novelists. LC 65-63876. (U of Fla. Humanities Monographs: No. 17). 1964. pap. 2.75 (ISBN 0-8130-0202-8). U Presses Fla.
Tarica, Ralph. Imagery in the Novels of Andre Malraux. LC 78-75189. 192p. 1980. 17.50 (ISBN 0-8386-2269-0). Fairleigh Dickinson.
Wilkinson, David O. Malraux: An Essay in Political Criticism. LC 67-22875. 1967. 12.50x (ISBN 0-674-54400-5). Harvard U Pr.

MALRAUX, ANDRE, 1901-1976–DICTIONARIES, INDEXES, ETC.

Juilland, Ileana. Dictionnaire Des Idees Dans L'oeuvre D'andre Malraux. 325p. (Fr.). 1968. 29.95 (ISBN 0-686-56887-7, F-111080). French & Eur.
Julland, Ileana. Dictionnaire Des Idees Dans L'oeuvre D'Andre Malraux: Collection Dictionaries Des Idees Dans le Litteratures Occidentales, Litterature Francaise: Dictionnnaires D'auteurs. (No. 2). 1968. 21.25x (ISBN 0-686-21240-1). Mouton.

MALT

Breweries & Malsters in Europe, 1980. 69th ed. LC 46-33153. Orig. Title: Brauereien und Malzereien in Europa 1980. 610p. (Orig., Eng, Fr. & Ger.). 1980. 92.50x (ISBN 3-8203-0034-1). Intl Pubns Serv.
Despain, R. O. The Malt-Ease Flagon: Your Complete Guide to Homebrewing. LC 78-24695. 1978. 8.95 (ISBN 0-913668-88-5); pap. 4.95 (ISBN 0-913668-87-7). Ten Speed Pr.
Hough, J. S., et al. Malting & Brewing Science, Vol. 1. 2nd ed. 1981. 39.95x (ISBN 0-412-16580-5, Pub. by Chapman & Hall). Methuen Inc.

MALTA

Austin, Dennis. Malta & the End of the Empire. (Illus.). 144p. 1971. 22.50x (ISBN 0-7146-2774-7, F Cass Co). Biblio Dist.
Blouet, Brian. The Story of Malta. (Story Ser.). (Illus., Orig.). 1972. pap. 6.95 (ISBN 0-571-09654-9, Pub. by Faber & Faber). Merrimack Bk Serv.
Blue Guide - Malta. 1979. 21.95 (ISBN 0-528-84636-1); pap. 12.95 (ISBN 0-528-84634-5). Rand.
Boissevain, Jeremy. Saints & Fireworks, Religion & Politics in Rural Malta. (Monographs on Social Anthropology Ser: No. 30). 1969. pap. text ed. 3.25x (ISBN 0-391-00756-4, Athlone Pr). Humanities.
--A Village in Malta. LC 79-21054. 136p. 1980. pap. text ed. 5.95 (ISBN 0-03-053411-9, HoltC). HR&W.
De Jaeger, Charles. Paul Is a Maltese Boy. LC 68-13444. (Children Everywhere Ser.: No. 6). (Illus.). (gr. 2-4). 1968. PLB 4.95 (ISBN 0-8038-5699-7). Hastings.
Dennis, Nigel. Malta. LC 73-83041. (Illus.). 64p. 1974. 6.95 (ISBN 0-8149-0732-6). Vanguard.
Elliott, Peter R. The Cross & the Ensign: A Naval History of Malta 1798-1978. LC 79-93365. (Illus.). 192p. 1980. 16.95 (ISBN 0-87021-926-X). Naval Inst Pr.
Evans, J. D. The Prehistoric Antiquities of the Maltese Island: A Survey. 1971. 83.25x (ISBN 0-485-11093-8, Athlone Pr). Humanities.
Kininmonth, Christopher. The Travellers' Guide to Malta & Gozo. 3rd. ed. (Travellers' Guide Ser.). (Illus.). 230p. 1979. 7.95 (ISBN 0-224-01656-3, Pub. by Chatto Bodley Jonathan). Merrimack Bk Serv.
Lewis, Harrison. Ancient Malta & Its Antiquities. 1977. pap. text ed. 10.50x (ISBN 0-901072-25-7). Humanities.
Nagel Travel Guide to Malta. (Nagel Encyclopedia Guide). 1978. 26.00 (ISBN 2-8263-0711-8). Hippocrene Bks.
Nagel's Encyclopedia Guide: Malta. (Illus.). 224p. 1978. 26.00 (ISBN 2-8263-0711-8). Masson Pub.
Nelson, Nina. Malta. 1978. 22.50 (ISBN 0-7134-0941-X). David & Charles.
--Your Guide to Malta. LC 78-461225. (Your Guide Ser). (Illus.). 1969. 6.25x (ISBN 0-8002-0782-3). Intl Pubns Serv.
Pratt, L. R. East of Malta West of Suez. LC 75-23534. (Illus.). 224p. 1975. 31.95 (ISBN 0-521-20869-6). Cambridge U Pr.
Price, Charles A. Malta & the Maltese: A Study in Nineteenth Century Migration. LC 77-87724. Repr. of 1954 ed. 22.50 (ISBN 0-404-16516-8). AMS Pr.
Severin, Inge. See Malta (& Gozo) (Format's Complete Guides). (Illus.). 144p. 1979. 7.95 (ISBN 0-903372-03-7, Pub by Format Bks England). Hippocrene Bks.
Trump, D. H. Malta: An Archaeological Guide. (Illus.). 172p. 1972. 10.95 (ISBN 0-571-09802-9, Pub. by Faber & Faber). Merrimack Bk Serv.
U. S. Department of State. The Conferences at Malta & Yalta, 1945. LC 76-125. (U.S. Dept. of State Publication: No. 6199). 1032p. 1976. Repr. of 1955 ed. lib. bdg. 72.75 (ISBN 0-8371-8778-8, USCO). Greenwood.
Vassallo, Mario. From Lordship to Stewardship: Religion & Social Change in Malta. 1979. text ed. 32.50x (ISBN 90-279-7967-7). Mouton.

MALTA–SIEGE, 1565

Hoppen, Alison. The Fortification of Malta by the Order of St. John, 1530-1798. (Illus.). 215p. 1979. 15.00x (ISBN 0-7073-0241-2, Pub. by Scottish Academic Pr Scotland). Columbia U Pr.
Sultana, Donald E. Seige of Malta Rediscovered. 1977. 17.50x (ISBN 0-7073-0131-9, Pub. by Scottish Academic Pr Scotland). Columbia U Pr.

MALTA, KNIGHTS OF

see Knights of Malta

MALTA FEVER

see Brucellosis

MALTESE DOGS

see Dogs–Breeds–Maltese Dogs

MALTHUS, THOMAS ROBERT, 1766-1834

Bonar, James. Letters of David Ricardo to Thomas Robert Malthus. Repr. of 1887 ed. lib. bdg. 30.00 (ISBN 0-8414-2533-7). Folcroft.
--Malthus & His Work. 438p. 1966. 26.00x (ISBN 0-7146-1273-1, F Cass Co). Biblio Dist.
Bonar, James, ed. Letters of David Ricardo to Thomas Robert Malthus: 1810-1823. 1978. Repr. of 1887 ed. lib. bdg. 40.00 (ISBN 0-8492-2272-9). R West.
Bradlaugh, Charles. Jesus, Shelley, & Malthus. 1978. Repr. of 1877 ed. lib. bdg. 10.00 (ISBN 0-8495-0441-4). Arden Lib.
--Jesus, Shelley & Malthus, or Pious Poverty & Heterodox Happiness. LC 74-180509. 1972. lib. bdg. 5.50 (ISBN 0-8414-3271-6). Folcroft.
Byres, Terence. Adam Smith, Malthus & Marx. Yapp, Malcolm, et al, eds. (World History Ser.). (Illus.). 32p. (gr. 10). 1980. Repr. of 1977 ed. lib. bdg. 5.95 (ISBN 0-89908-046-4); pap. text ed. 1.95 (ISBN 0-89908-021-9). Greenhaven.
Gamon, Richard Louis. The Thoughts of Thomas Robert Malthus As They Apply to the Economic Complexities of Our Present Age. (The Living Thoughts of the Great Economists Ser.). (Illus.). 127p. 1981. 37.545 (ISBN 0-918968-87-9). Inst Econ Finan.
Glass, D. V., ed. Introduction to Malthus. 205p. 1966. 24.00x (ISBN 0-7146-1579-X, F Cass Co). Biblio Dist.
Greg, William R. Enigmas of Life. LC 72-323. (Essay Index Reprint Ser.). Repr. of 1879 ed. 19.00 (ISBN 0-8369-2794-X). Arno.
James, Patricia. Population Malthus: His Life & Times. (Illus.). 1979. 45.00x (ISBN 0-7100-0266-1). Routledge & Kegan.
Nickerson, Jane S. Homage to Malthus. 1975. 12.95 (ISBN 0-8046-9105-3, Natl U). Kennikat.
Paglin, Morton. Malthus & Lauderdale: The Anti-Ricardian Tradition. LC 62-409. Repr. of 1961 ed. 13.50x (ISBN 0-678-00859-0). Kelley.
Petersen, William. Malthus. LC 78-31479. 1979. text ed. 17.50x (ISBN 0-674-54425-0). Harvard U Pr.
Ricardo, David. Works & Correspondence, 11 vols. Sraffa, P., ed. 1951. Vols. 1-2, 4, 6 & 8-11. 49.50 ea.; Vols. 3, 5 & 7. 50.50 ea. Cambridge U Pr.
Smith, Kenneth. The Malthusian Controversy. 1978. Repr. of 1951 ed. lib. bdg. 18.00x (ISBN 0-374-97510-8). Octagon.

MALTHUSIANISM

see also Population

Albrecht, William P. William Hazlitt & the Malthusian Controversy. LC 70-85980. 1969. Repr. of 1950 ed. 12.50 (ISBN 0-8046-0597-1). Kennikat.
Birth Control & Morality in Nineteenth Century America. Incl. Fruits of Philosophy. Knowlton, Charles; Moral Physiology. Owen, Robert D. LC 78-169362. (Family in America Ser). 150p. 1972. 10.00 (ISBN 0-405-03883-6). Arno.
Bonar, James. Malthus & His Work. 438p. 1966. 26.00x (ISBN 0-7146-1273-1, F Cass Co). Biblio Dist.
Ensor, George. Inquiry Concerning the Population of Nations. LC 67-16339. Repr. of 1818 ed. 19.50x (ISBN 0-678-00209-6). Kelley.
Glass, D. V., ed. Introduction to Malthus. 205p. 1966. 24.00x (ISBN 0-7146-1579-X, F Cass Co). Biblio Dist.
Godwin, William. Of Population. LC 63-23523. Repr. of 1820 ed. 22.50x (ISBN 0-678-00030-1). Kelley.
Hazlitt, William. Reply to the Essay on Population by the Rev. T. R. Malthus. LC 66-21678. Repr. of 1807 ed. 17.50x (ISBN 0-678-00203-7). Kelley.
Knibbs, George H. The Shadow of the World's Future: Or, the Earth's Population Possibilities & the Consequences of the Present Rate of Increase of the Earth's Inhabitants. LC 75-38133. (Demography Ser.). 1976. Repr. of 1928 ed. 10.00x (ISBN 0-405-07986-9). Arno.
Ledbetter, Rosanna. A History of the Malthusian League, 1877-1927. LC 76-10822. (Illus.). 1976. 12.50x (ISBN 0-8142-0257-8). Ohio St U Pr.
Nitti, Francesco S. Population & the Social System. LC 75-38140. (Demography Ser.). (Illus.). 1976. Repr. of 1894 ed. 12.00x (ISBN 0-405-07993-1). Arno.
Place, Francis. Illustrations & Proofs of the Principle of Population. LC 67-16338. Repr. of 1930 ed. 19.50x (ISBN 0-678-00210-X). Kelley.
Sadler, M. T. The Law of Population: A Treatise in Six Books, 2 vols. 138p. 1971. Repr. of 1830 ed. Set. 72.00x (ISBN 0-7165-1579-2, Pub. by Irish Academic Pr Ireland). Biblio Dist.
Senior, Nassau W. Two Lectures on Population: Delivered Before the University of Oxford. LC 75-38143. (Demography Ser.). 1976. Repr. of 1828 ed. 10.00x (ISBN 0-405-07996-6). Arno.
Thompson, Warren S. Population: A Study in Malthusianism. LC 74-76699. (Columbia University Studies in the Social Sciences: No. 153). Repr. of 1915 ed. 18.50 (ISBN 0-404-51153-8). AMS Pr.
Weyland, J. The Principles of Population & Production. (The Development of Industrial Society Ser.). 493p. 1971. Repr. of 1816 ed. 38.00x (ISBN 0-7165-1777-9, Pub. by Irish Academic Pr Ireland). Biblio Dist.
Weyland, John. Principles of Population & Production. LC 68-58665. Repr. of 1816 ed. 19.50x (ISBN 0-678-00485-4). Kelley.

MALTHUSIANISM–BIBLIOGRAPHY

Boner, Harold A. Hungry Generations: The Nineteenth-Century Case Against Malthusianism. LC 79-139905. 1971. Repr. of 1955 ed. 13.00 (ISBN 0-8462-1553-5). Russell.

MALVERN, ENGLAND

Smith, Brian S. History of Malvern. 1964. text ed. 6.75x (ISBN 0-7185-1041-0, Leicester). Humanities.

MALWA, INDIA–HISTORY

Day, Upendra N. Medieval Malwa: A Political & Cultural History, 1401-1562. 1965. 10.00x (ISBN 0-8426-0239-9). Verry.
Jain, Kailash C. Malwa Through the Ages. (Illus.). 1972. text ed. 18.00x (ISBN 0-8426-0400-6). Verry.
--Malwa Through the Ages (from the Earliest Times to 1305 A.D.) (Illus.). 1972. 15.00 (ISBN 0-89684-275-4). Orient Bk Dist.
Sircar, D. C. Ancient Malwa & the Vikramaditya Tradition. 1969. 7.25x (ISBN 0-8426-1544-X). Verry.

MAMBUTI

see Bambute

MAMELUKES

Ayalon, David. Gunpowder & Firearms in the Mamluk Kingdom: A Challenge to Mediaeval Society. 2nd ed. 154p. 1978. 22.50x (ISBN 0-7146-3090-X, F Cass Co). Biblio Dist.
--The Mamluk Military Society. 364p. 1980. 69.00x (ISBN 0-686-69887-8, Pub. by Variorum England). State Mutual Bk.
--Studies on the Mamluks of Egypt. 360p. 1980. 60.00x (ISBN 0-86078-006-6, Pub. by Variorum England). State Mutual Bk.
Haldane, Duncan. Mamluk Painting. 1979. 44.00x (ISBN 0-85668-118-0, Pub. by Aris & Phillips). Intl Schol Bk Serv.
Muir, William. The Mameluke, or, Slave Dynasty of Egypt, 1260-1517. LC 71-180367. Repr. of 1896 ed. 16.00 (ISBN 0-404-56307-4). AMS Pr.
Poliak, Abraham N. Feudalism in Egypt, Syria, Palestine & Lebanon 1250-1900: With Two Additional Articles. LC 77-10729. (Studies in Islamic History: No. 13). 125p. Repr. of 1939 ed. lib. bdg. 12.50x (ISBN 0-87991-462-9). Porcupine Pr.

Ziadeh, Nicola A. Urban Life in Syria Under the Early Mamluks. Repr. of 1953 ed. lib. bdg. 14.25x (ISBN 0-8371-3162-6, ZILS). Greenwood.

MAMIYA SEKOR CAMERA

see Cameras–Types–Mamiya Sekor

MAMMALS

see also Carnivora; Cetaceae; Edentata; Fur-Bearing Animals; Marine Mammals; Marsupialia; Primates; Rodentia; Ruminants; Ungulata; also names of families, genera, species, etc.

Anderson, Sydney & Jones, J. Knox, Jr., eds. Recent Mammals of the World: A Synopsis of Families. (Illus.). 453p. 1967. 26.00 (ISBN 0-8260-0440-7, Pub. by Wiley-Interscience). Wiley.

Asdell, S. A. Patterns of Mammalian Reproduction. 2nd ed. (Illus.). 1964. 38.50x (ISBN 0-8014-0021-X). Comstock.

Barbour, Roger W. & Davis, Wayne H. Mammals of Kentucky. LC 74-7870. (Illus.). 368p. 1974. 18.00 (ISBN 0-8131-1314-8). U Pr of Ky.

Barret-Hamilton, Gerald E. & Hinton, Martin A. A History of British Mammals, 2 vols. Sterling, Keir B., ed. LC 77-81081. (Biologists & Their World Ser.). (Illus.). 1978. Repr. of 1921 ed. Set. lib. bdg. 69.00x (ISBN 0-405-10648-3); lib. bdg. 34.50x ea. Vol. 1 (ISBN 0-405-10649-1). Vol. 2 (ISBN 0-405-10650-5). Arno.

Bell, Richard Q. & Harper, Lawrence V. Child Effects on Adults. LC 77-24115. 1977. 16.50 (ISBN 0-470-99267-0). Halsted Pr.

Bertram, G. L. Conservation of Sirenia: Current Status & Perspectives for Action. 1974. pap. 7.50x (ISBN 2-88032-023-2, IUCN35, IUCN). Unipub.

Booth, Ernest S. How to Know the Mammals. 3rd ed. (Pictured Key Nature Ser.). 214p. 1971. wire coil avail. (ISBN 0-697-04871-3). Wm C Brown.

Boy Scouts of America. Mammals. LC 19-600. (Illus.). 48p. (gr. 6-12). 1972. pap. 0.70x (ISBN 0-8395-3271-7, 3271). BSA.

Buchanan, James W., et al. Dogs & Other Large Mammals in Aging Research, Vol. 2. LC 74-8039. 194p. 1974. text ed. 29.50x (ISBN 0-8422-7227-5). Irvington.

Charles-Dominique, Pierre. Ecology & Behavior of Nocturnal Primates. Martin, R. D., tr. LC 77-1227. (Illus.). 277p. 1977. 20.00x (ISBN 0-231-04362-7). Columbia U Pr.

Clegg, A. G. & Clegg, P. C. Biology of the Mammal. 4th ed. (Illus.). 1975. pap. 23.50x (ISBN 0-433-06122-7). Intl Ideas.

Cole, Joanna. Saber-Toothed Tiger & Other Ice-Age Mammals. (Illus.). (gr. 1-5). 1977. o.p. 8.25 (ISBN 0-688-22120-3); PLB 7.92 (ISBN 0-688-32120-8). Morrow.

Corbet, G. B. The Mammals of the Palearctic Region: A Taxonomic Review. LC 77-90899. (Illus.). 1978. 48.50x (ISBN 0-8014-1171-8). Cornell U Pr.

Corbet, G. B. & Hill, J. E. A World List of Mammalian Species. LC 79-53396. 1980. 35.00x (ISBN 0-8014-1260-9). Cornell U Pr.

Crandall, Lee S. Management of Wild Mammals in Captivity. LC 64-10498. (Illus.). 1964. 35.00x (ISBN 0-226-11758-8). U of Chicago Pr.

Crandall, Lee S. & Bridges, William. Zoo Man's Notebook. LC 66-13863. (Illus.). 1966. 7.95 (ISBN 0-226-11762-6). U of Chicago Pr.

Cuvier, Georges. The Class Mammalia: The Animal Kingdom Arranged in Conformity with Its Organization by the Baron Cuvier, Vols. 1-5. Sterling, Keir B., ed. LC 77-81117. (Biologists & Their World Ser.). (Illus.). 1978. Repr. of 1827 ed. Set. lib. bdg. 162.00x (ISBN 0-405-10746-3); lib. bdg. 32.40x ea. Vol. 1 (ISBN 0-405-10765-X). Vol. 2 (ISBN 0-405-10766-8). Vol. 3 (ISBN 0-405-10767-6). Vol. 4 (ISBN 0-405-10768-4). Vol. 5 (ISBN 0-405-10769-2). Arno.

DeBlase, Anthony F. & Martin, Robert E. A Manual of Mammalogy: With Keys to Families of the World. 2nd ed. 400p. 1980. wire coil avail. (ISBN 0-697-04591-9). Wm C Brown.

Degerbol, Magnus. Zoology I: Mammals. LC 74-20244. (Thule Expedition, 5th, 1921-24: Vol. 2, Pts. 4-5). (Illus.). 1976. Repr. of 1935 ed. 57.50 (ISBN 0-404-58309-1). AMS Pr.

Desmond, Adrian J. The Ape's Reflexion. 1979. 10.95 (ISBN 0-8037-0674-X, J Wade). Dial.

Duplaix, Nicole & Simon, Noel. World Guide to Mammals. 1977. 15.95 (ISBN 0-517-52920-3). Crown.

Eisenberg, John F. The Mammalian Radiations: An Analysis of Trends in Evolution, Adaption, and Behavior. LC 80-27940. (Illus.). 640p. 1981. 45.00 (ISBN 0-226-19537-6). U of Chicago Pr.

Elman, Robert. The Living World of Audubon Mammals. (Illus.). 272p. 1976. 12.95 (ISBN 0-448-12459-9, MSP). G&D.

Ewer, R. F. Ethology of Mammals. LC 68-21946. 416p. 1969. 37.50 (ISBN 0-306-30382-5, Plenum Pr). Plenum Pub.

Finerty, James P. The Population Ecology of Cycles in Small Mammals: Mathematical Theory & Biological Fact. LC 79-23774. (Illus.). 1981. text ed. 18.50x (ISBN 0-300-02382-0). Yale U Pr.

Fleischer, G. Evolutionary Principles of the Mammalian Middle Ear. (Advances in Anatomy, Embriology & Cell Biology: Vol. 55, Pt. 5). (Illus.). 1979. pap. 25.20 (ISBN 0-387-09140-8). Springer-Verlag.

Flower, William H. & Lydekker, Richard. An Introduction to the Study of Mammals, Living & Extinct. Sterling, Keir B., ed. LC 77-81075. (Biologists & Their World Ser.). (Illus.). 1978. Repr. of 1891 ed. lib. bdg. 45.00x (ISBN 0-405-10644-0). Arno.

Fowler, Charles W. & Smith, Tim D. Dynamics of Large Mammal Populations. LC 81-115. 525p. 1981. 40.00 (ISBN 0-471-05160-8, Pub. by Wiley-Interscience). Wiley.

Fox, Michael. The Dog: Its Domestication & Behavior. LC 76-57852. 1978. 27.50x (ISBN 0-8240-9858-7). Garland Pub.

Gambaryan, P. R. How Mammals Run: Anatomical Adaptations. Hardin, H., tr. from Rus. LC 74-16190. 367p. 1974. 43.95 (ISBN 0-470-29059-5). Halsted Pr.

Gilmore, Desmond. Environmental Factors in Mammal Reproduction. Cook, Brian, ed. 340p. 1981. pap. text ed. 44.50 (ISBN 0-8391-1656-X). Univ Park.

Godin, Alfred J. Wild Mammals of New England: Field Guide Edition. rev. ed. Vanderweide, Harry, ed. (Illus.). 200p. 1981. pap. 7.95 (ISBN 0-89933-012-6). DeLorme Pub.

Golley, F. B., et al, eds. Small Mammals. LC 74-25658. (International Biological Programme Ser.: No. 5). (Illus.). 448p. 1975. 65.00 (ISBN 0-521-20601-4). Cambridge U Pr.

Gotch, A. F. Mammals: Their Latin Names Explained. (Illus.). 1979. 18.95 (ISBN 0-7137-0939-1, Pub. by Blandford Pr England). Sterling.

Gregory, William K. The Orders of Mammals. LC 78-72718. Repr. of 1910 ed. 67.50 (ISBN 0-404-18293-3). AMS Pr.

Grollman, Sigmund. A Laboratory Manual of Mammalian Anatomy & Physiology. 4th ed. (Illus.). 266p. 1978. pap. text ed. 9.95 (ISBN 0-02-348090-4, 34809). Macmillan.

Grzimek, Bernhard, ed. Grzimek's Animal Life Encyclopedia, Vol. 11: Mammals 2. 1975. 39.50x (ISBN 0-442-22931-3). Van Nos Reinhold.

--Grzimek's Animal Life Encyclopedia, Vol. 12: Mammals 3. 1975. 39.50x (ISBN 0-442-22932-1). Van Nos Reinhold.

Gubernick, David J. & Klopfer, Peter H., eds. Parental Care in Mammals. 460p. 1981. 39.50 (ISBN 0-306-40533-4, Plenum Pr). Plenum Pub.

Gunderson, Harvey L. Mammalogy. 1976. text ed. 19.95 (ISBN 0-07-025190-8, C). McGraw.

Hafez, E. S., ed. Scanning Electron Microscope Atlas of Mammalian Reproduction. LC 73-33562. 1975. 99.00 (ISBN 0-387-91129-4). Springer-Verlag.

Hafez, E. S. & Blandau, R. J., eds. Mammalian Oviduct: Comparative Biology & Methodology. LC 68-29936. (Illus.). 1969. 27.50x (ISBN 0-226-31201-1). U of Chicago Pr.

Halstead, L. B. Evolution of Mammals. (Illus.). 124p. 1981. 12.95 (ISBN 0-8467-0561-3, Pub. by Euro Bks England). Hippocrene Bks.

Hamburg, David A. & McGown, Elizabeth R. The Great Apes. 1979. text ed. 23.95 (ISBN 0-8053-3669-9). Benjamin-Cummings.

Hamilton, W. R. The History of Mammals. (Illus.). 1972. pap. text ed. 2.00x (ISBN 0-565-00714-9, Pub. by Brit Mus Nat Hist). Sabbot-Natural Hist Bks.

Hamilton, William J., Jr. & Whitaker, John O., Jr. Mammals of the Eastern United States. 2nd ed. LC 79-12920. (HANH Ser.). (Illus.). 368p. 1979. 22.50x (ISBN 0-8014-1254-4). Comstock.

Hanzak, Jan & Veselovský, Zdenek. Encyclopedia of Animals. Stephen, David & McCormack, Tom, eds. LC 78-24833. (Illus.). 1979. 15.95 (ISBN 0-312-24571-8). St Martin.

Haug, F. M. Sulphide Silver Pattern & Cytoarchitectonics of Parahippocampal Areas in the Rat. (Advances in Anatomy, Embryology & Cell Biology: Vol. 52, Pt. 4). (Illus.). 1976. soft cover 21.30 (ISBN 0-387-07850-9). Springer-Verlag.

Henderson, Junius & Craig, Elberta L. Economic Mammalogy. 398p. 1932. photocopy ed. spiral 34.50 (ISBN 0-398-04276-4). C C Thomas.

Hockman, C. Chemical Transmission in the Mammalian Central Nervous System. (Illus.). 1976. 44.50 (ISBN 0-8391-0863-X). Univ Park.

Hoffmeister, Donald F. & Mohr, Carl D. Fieldbook of Illinois Mammals. (Illus.). 6.50 (ISBN 0-8446-4556-7). Peter Smith.

Hoffmeister, Donald F. & Mohr, Carl O. Fieldbook of Illinois Mammals. (Illus.). 256p. 1972. pap. 4.00 (ISBN 0-486-20220-8). Dover.

Hsu, T. C. & Benirschke, K. Atlas of Mammalian Chromosomes, Vols. 1-6. LC 67-19307. (Illus.). 1968-71. Vol. 1. loose-leaf boxed 21.70 (ISBN 0-387-03878-7); Vol. 3. loose-leaf boxed 21.70 (ISBN 0-387-04563-5); Vol. 4. loose-leaf boxed 31.20 (ISBN 0-387-04882-0); Vol. 5. loose-leaf boxed 31.20 (ISBN 0-387-05280-1); Vol. 6. 29.00 (ISBN 0-387-05590-8). ring binder for indiv. vols. 7.50 ea. (ISBN 0-387-90005-5); ring binder for indiv. vols. 6.80 ea. (ISBN 0-387-90005-5). Springer-Verlag.

International Conference on Comparative Mammalian Cytogenetics, Dartmouth Medical School, 1968. Proceedings. Benirschke, K., ed. (Illus.). 1969. 59.80 (ISBN 0-387-04442-6). Springer-Verlag.

Jenkins, Thomas W. Functional Mammalian Neuroanatomy: With Emphasis on the Dog and Cat, Including an Atlas of the Central Nervous System of the Dog. 2nd ed. LC 77-17308. (Illus.). 480p. 1978. text ed. 24.50 (ISBN 0-8121-0627-X). Lea & Febiger.

Jones, J. Knox, Jr., et al, eds. Selected Readings in Mammalogy. 2nd ed. (Monographs & Special Publications: No. 5). 1976. pap. 10.00 (ISBN 0-89338-001-6). U of KS Mus Nat Hist.

Kalter, Harold. Teratology of the Central Nervous System: Induced & Spontaneous Malformations of Laboratory, Agricultural, & Domestic Mammals. LC 68-14628. (Illus.). 1968. 20.00x (ISBN 0-226-42268-2). U of Chicago Pr.

Lawlor, Timothy E. Handbook to the Families & Orders of Living Mammals. 2nd ed. (Illus.). 327p. 1979. pap. 9.40x (ISBN 0-916422-16-X). Mad River.

Leuthold, W. African Ungulates: A Comparative Review of Their Ethology & Behavioral Ecology. Farner, D. S., ed. LC 76-44535. (Zoophysiology & Ecology Ser.: Vol. 8). (Illus.). 1977. 40.30 (ISBN 0-387-07951-3). Springer-Verlag.

Lillegraven, Jason A., et al, eds. Mesozoic Mammals: The First Two-Thirds of Mammalian History. 1980. 42.50x (ISBN 0-520-03582-8); pap. 11.95x (ISBN 0-520-03951-3, CAMPUS NO. 234). U of Cal Pr.

Line, Les & Ricciuti, Edward R. The Audubon Society Book of Wild Animals. LC 77-9159. (Illus.). 1977. 50.00 (ISBN 0-8109-0670-8). Abrams.

Loates, G. & Peterson, R. Mammals of the Eastern Region. 1980. 29.95 (ISBN 0-13-548081-7). P-H.

Loates, Martin G. & Peterson, Randolph. Mammals in Profile, Vol. I. (Illus.). 1978. pap. 3.95 (ISBN 0-684-15353-X, ScribT). Scribner.

--Mammals in Profile, Vol. II. (Illus.). 1978. pap. 3.95 (ISBN 0-684-15354-8, ScribT). Scribner.

Lodge, G. A. & Lamming, G. E., eds. Growth & Development of Mammals. LC 68-28665. 528p. 1968. 49.50 (ISBN 0-306-30690-5, Plenum Pr). Plenum Pub.

Lowery, George H., Jr. The Mammals of Louisiana & Its Adjacent Waters. LC 73-89662. (Illus.). 568p. 1974. 27.50 (ISBN 0-8071-0609-7). La State U Pr.

Lucas, J. Wild Animals. (Source Book Ser.). (Illus.). 1971. 5.00x (ISBN 0-7063-1175-2). Intl Pubns Serv.

Lyneborg, Leif. Mammals in Color. (European Ecology Ser.). (Illus.). 1971. 9.95 (ISBN 0-7137-0548-5, Pub by Blandford Pr England). Sterling.

McCullough, Dale R. The George Reserve Deer Herd: Population Ecology of a K-Selected Species. (Illus.). 1979. lib. bdg. 16.00x (ISBN 0-472-08611-1, 08611). U of Mich Pr.

McLaren, Anne. Mammalian Chimaeras. LC 75-40988. (Developmental and Cell Biology Ser.: No. 4). (Illus.). 160p. 1976. 35.50 (ISBN 0-521-21183-2). Cambridge U Pr.

McLoughlin, John C. Synapsida: A New Look into the Origin of Mammals. LC 79-56270. (Illus.). 160p. 1980. 14.95 (ISBN 0-670-68922-X). Viking Pr.

Mammals in the Seas, Vol. II: Pinniped Species Summaries & Report on Sirenians. (FAO Fisheries Ser.: No. 5, Vol. II). 151p. 1979. 24.50 (ISBN 92-5-100512-5, F2102, FAO). Unipub.

Maple, Terry L. Orang-Utan Behavior. (Van Nostrand Reinhold Primate Behavior & Development Ser.). 272p. 1980. text ed. 25.00 (ISBN 0-442-25154-8). Van Nos Reinhold.

Miller, Gerrit S. Catalogue of the Mammals of Western Europe in the British Museum. (Illus.). Repr. of 1912 ed. 61.50 (ISBN 0-384-38940-6). Johnson Repr.

Miller, Linus W. Notes of an Exile to Van Dieman's Land. Repr. of 1846 ed. 23.00 (ISBN 0-384-38970-8). Johnson Repr.

Murray, Andrew. The Geographical Distribution of Mammals. Sterling, Keir B., ed. LC 77-81073. (Biologists & Their World Ser.). (Illus.). 1978. Repr. of 1866 ed. lib. bdg. 41.00x (ISBN 0-405-10642-4). Arno.

Nelson, Dick & Nelson, Sharon. Easy Field Guide to Common Mammals of New Mexico. (Illus.). 32p. (Orig.). (gr. 1-12). 1977. pap. 1.00 (ISBN 0-915030-12-8). Tecolote Pr.

Orci, L. & Perrelet, A. Freeze-Etch Histology: A Comparison Between Thin Sections & Freeze-Etch Replicas. LC 74-22379. (Illus.). 184p. 1975. 79.20 (ISBN 0-387-07043-5). Springer-Verlag.

Osman, William C. Evolutionary Biology of the Primates. 1973. 31.00 (ISBN 0-12-528750-X). Acad Pr.

Palmer, T. S. Index Generum Mammalium: A List of the Genera & Families of Mammals. 1968. Repr. of 1904 ed. 100.00 (ISBN 3-7682-0535-5). Lubrecht & Cramer.

Ray, John. Synopsis Methodica Animalium Quadrupedum et Serpentini Generis. Sterling, Keir B., ed. LC 77-81111. (Biologists & Their World Ser.). (Latin.). 1978. Repr. of 1693 ed. lib. bdg. 21.00x (ISBN 0-405-10694-7). Arno.

Russell, L. B. Genetic Mosaics & Chimeras in Mammals. LC 78-23172. (Basic Life Sciences Ser.: Vol. 12). 499p. 1978. 39.50 (ISBN 0-306-40065-0, Plenum Pr). Plenum Pub.

Ryall, R. W. & Kelly, J. S., eds. Iontophoresis & Transmitter Mechanisms in the Mammalian Central Nervous System: Proceedings of a Satellite Symposium. 1978. 70.75 (ISBN 0-444-80012-3, Biomedical Pr). Elsevier.

Sanderson, Ivan I. Living Mammals of the World. LC 55-10515. 1955. 19.95 (ISBN 0-385-01445-7). Doubleday.

Schad, Wolfgang. Man & Mammals: Toward a Biology of Form. new ed. Scherer, Carroll, tr. from Ger. LC 76-52049. Orig. Title: Saugetiere und Mensch: Zur Gestaltbiologie Vom Gesichtspunkt der Dreigliederung. (Illus.). 1978. 14.95 (ISBN 0-914614-10-X). Waldorf Pr.

Schaller, George B. Mountain Monarchs: Wild Sheep & Goats of the Himalaya. LC 77-1336. (Wildlife Behavior & Ecology Ser.). 1977. lib. bdg. 27.50x (ISBN 0-226-73641-5). U of Chicago Pr.

Sclater, William L. & Sclater, Philip L. The Geography of Mammals. Sterling, Keir B., ed. LC 77-81080. (Biologists & Their World Ser.). (Illus.). 1978. Repr. of 1899 ed. lib. bdg. 24.00x (ISBN 0-405-10647-5). Arno.

Searle, Anthony G. Comparative Genetics of Coat Colour in Mammals. 1968. 46.50 (ISBN 0-12-633450-1). Acad Pr.

Segal, Sheldon J., et al. The Regulation of Mammalian Reproduction. (Illus.). 614p. 1973. photocopy ed. spiral 59.75 (ISBN 0-398-02405-7). C C Thomas.

Seton, Ernest S. Life-Histories of the Northern Animals: An Account of the Mammals of Manitoba, 2. LC 73-17845. (Natural Sciences in America Ser.). (Illus.). 1514p. 1974. Repr. Set. 79.00x (ISBN 0-405-05767-9); Vol. 1. 41.00x (ISBN 0-405-05768-7); Vol. 2. 38.00x (ISBN 0-405-05769-5). Arno.

Simpson, George G. Mammals around the Pacific. (Thomas Burke Memorial Lecture Ser.: No. 2). 1966. pap. 4.00 (ISBN 0-295-74056-6). U of Wash Pr.

Spero, James, ed. North American Mammals: A Photographic Album for Artists & Designers. LC 77-88736. (Pictorial Archive Ser.). (Illus.). 1978. pap. 4.00 (ISBN 0-486-23601-3). Dover.

Stehlin, Hans G. Die Saugethiere des schweizerischen Eocaens. LC 78-72723. Repr. of 1912 ed. 67.50 (ISBN 0-404-18300-X). AMS Pr.

Stoddart, D. M., ed. Ecology of Small Mammals. LC 79-8. 386p. 1979. 39.95x (ISBN 0-412-14790-4, Pub. by Chapman & Hall England). Methuen Inc.

Taglianti, Augusto V. The World of Mammals. Gilbert, John, tr. LC 80-69173. (Abbeville Press Encyclopedia of Natural Science). (Illus.). 256p. 1980. 13.95 (ISBN 0-89659-183-2); pap. 7.95 (ISBN 0-89659-184-0). Abbeville Pr.

Time-Life Television Editors. Rabbits & Other Small Mammals. new ed. (The Wild, Wild World of Animals). (Illus.). 1979. 10.95 (ISBN 0-913948-22-5). Time-Life.

Topsell, Edward. The Historie of Foure-Footed Beastes, Collected Out of All Volumes of C. Gesner, & All Other Writers to This Present Day. LC 72-6034. (English Experience Ser.: No. 561). 816p. 1973. Repr. of 1607 ed. 104.00 (ISBN 90-221-0561-X). Walter J Johnson.

Turner, Dennis C. The Vampire Bat: A Field Study in Behavior & Ecology. LC 74-24396. (Illus.). 160p. 1975. 15.00x (ISBN 0-8018-1680-7). Johns Hopkins.

Vaughan, Terry A. Mammalogy. 2nd ed. LC 77-2111. 1978. text ed. 17.95 (ISBN 0-7216-9009-2). Saunders.

Walker, Ernest P., et al. Mammals of the World, 2 vols. 3rd ed. LC 74-23327. (Illus.). 1568p. 1975. boxed set 49.50 (ISBN 0-8018-1657-2). Johns Hopkins.

Walker, Warren F., Jr. A Study of the Cat: With Reference to Human Beings. 3rd ed. LC 76-27064. (Illus.). 1977. pap. text ed. 7.95 (ISBN 0-7216-9093-9). HR&W.

Waterhouse, George R. A Natural History of the Mammalia. Sterling, Keir B., ed. LC 77-83843. (Biologists & Their World Ser.). (Illus.). 1978. Repr. of 1848 ed. lib. bdg. 63.00x (ISBN 0-405-10739-0). Arno.

Weber, G. Metabolic Regulation of Mammalian Systems. 1978. write for info. (ISBN 0-08-017706-9). Pergamon.

Widdowson, E. M. Feeding the Newborn Mammal. Head, J. J., ed. LC 78-74135. (Carolina Biology Reader Ser.). 32p. (gr. 11 up). 1981. pap. 2.75 (ISBN 0-89278-312-5, 45-9712). Carolina Biological.

Young, John Z. & Hobbs, M. J. The Life of Mammals: Their Anatomy & Physiology. 2nd ed. (Illus.). 528p. 1975. text ed. 39.00x (ISBN 0-19-857156-9). Oxford U Pr.

Zim, Herbert S. & Hoffmeister, Donald F. Mammals. (Golden Guide Ser). 1955. PLB 10.38 (ISBN 0-307-63510-4, Golden Pr); pap. 1.95 (ISBN 0-307-24497-0, Golden Pr). Western Pub.

Zoological Society of London - 26th Symposium. Variation in Mammalian Populations. Berry, R. J. & Southern, H. N., eds. 63.50 (ISBN 0-12-613326-3). Acad Pr.

MAMMALS–EMBRYOLOGY

see Embryology–Mammals

MAMMALS–JUVENILE LITERATURE

see also Zoology–Juvenile Literature

Boorer, Michael. The Life of Strange Mammals. LC 78-56571. (Easy Reading Edition of Introduction to Nature Ser.). (Illus.). 1978. lib. bdg. 7.95 (ISBN 0-686-51147-6). Silver.

Caputo, Robert & Hsia, Miriam. Hyena Day. (Illus.). (gr. 2-6). 1978. 7.95 (ISBN 0-698-20428-X). Coward.

Caras, Roger. The Wonderful World of Mammals: Adventuring with Stamps. LC 73-5235. (Illus.). (gr. 4-6). 1973. 6.95 (ISBN 0-15-299300-2, HJ). HarBraceJ.

Carrington, Richard. The Mammals. (Young Readers Library). (Illus.). 1977. lib. bdg. 7.95 (ISBN 0-686-51091-7). Silver.

Colby, C. B. Big Game: Animals of the Americas, Africa & Asia. (Illus.). (gr. 4-7). 1967. PLB 5.29 (ISBN 0-698-30024-6). Coward.

--Small Game: Animals of the Americas. (Illus.). (gr. 4-7). 1968. PLB 5.29 (ISBN 0-698-30317-2). Coward.

Editions les Belles Images Staff, tr. Butterfly Book of Mammals. (Butterfly Bks). (Orig.). (ps-2). 1976. pap. 1.50 (ISBN 0-8467-0225-8, Pub. by Two Continents). Hippocrene Bks.

Hartman, Jane E. Armadillos, Anteaters, & Sloths: How They Live. LC 79-20699. (Illus.). 96p. (gr. 5-9). 1980. 7.95 (ISBN 0-8234-0400-5). Holiday.

Holman, J. Allan & Gringhuis, Dirk. Mystery Mammals of the Ice Age-Great Lakes Region. LC 72-90919. (Illus.). 45p. (Orig.). (gr. 5-8). 1972. pap. 1.75 (ISBN 0-910726-74-4). Hillsdale Educ.

Hylander, Clarence J. Animals in Fur. (Illus.). (gr. 7 up). 1956. 8.95g (ISBN 0-02-746200-5). Macmillan.

Kevles, Bettyann. Thinking Gorillas: Testing & Teaching the Greatest Ape. LC 79-12782. (gr. 7 up). 1980. 10.95 (ISBN 0-525-41074-0). Dutton.

Kritzman, Ellen. Little Mammals of the Pacific Northwest. LC 76-58249. (Illus.). 128p. 1977. 7.95 (ISBN 0-914718-18-5). Pacific Search.

McClung, Robert. Hunted Mammals of the Sea. (Illus.). (gr. 7 up). 1978. 8.95 (ISBN 0-688-22146-7); PLB 8.59 (ISBN 0-688-32146-1). Morrow.

McClung, Robert M. Mammals & How They Live. (Gateway Ser: No. 30). (Illus.). (gr. 5-6). 1963. PLB 5.99 (ISBN 0-394-90130-4, BYR). Random.

Mason, George F. Moose Group. LC 68-25625. (Famous Museum Ser). (Illus.). (gr. 6-9). 1968. PLB 5.95 (ISBN 0-8038-4634-7). Hastings.

May, Julian. Mammals We Know. LC 73-4371. (Illus.). (gr. 2-4). 1973. PLB 5.95 (ISBN 0-87191-242-2). Creative Ed.

Nelson, Dick & Nelson, Sharon. Easy Field Guide to Mammals of Glacier National Park. (Illus.). 32p. (Orig.). (gr. 1-12). 1978. pap. 1.00 (ISBN 0-915030-15-2). Tecolote Pr.

Rabbits & Other Small Mammals. LC 78-62754. (Wild, Wild World of Animals Ser.). (Illus.). 1978. lib. bdg. 11.97 (ISBN 0-686-51175-1). Silver.

Ricciuti, Edward. Older Than the Dinosaurs: The Origin & Rise of the Mammals. LC 77-26606. (Illus.). 96p. (gr. 5-12). 1980. 7.95 (ISBN 0-690-01328-0, TYC-J); PLB 7.89 (ISBN 0-690-03879-8). T Y Crowell.

Selsam & Hunt. A First Look at Mammals. (gr. k-3). 1976. pap. 1.50 (ISBN 0-590-10287-7). Schol Bk Serv.

Spizzirri Publishing Co. Staff. Mammals: An Educational Coloring Book. Spizzirri, Linda, ed. (Illus.). 32p. (gr. 1-8). 1981. pap. 1.25 (ISBN 0-86545-027-7). Spizzirri.

Tee-Van, Helen D. Small Mammals Are Where You Find Them. (Illus.). (gr. 3-7). 1966. PLB 5.99 (ISBN 0-394-91643-3). Knopf.

Teleki, Geza & Steffy, Karen. Goblin, a Wild Chimpanzee. (gr. 3-6). 1977. 9.95 (ISBN 0-525-30747-8). Dutton.

Teleki, Geza, et al. Aerial Apes: Gibbons of Asia. LC 78-10721. (Illus.). (gr. 1-3). 7.50 (ISBN 0-698-20477-8). Coward.

What Is a Mammal? (Learning Shelf Kits Ser.). (gr. 2-4). 1977. incl. cassette & tchrs. guide 14.95 (ISBN 0-686-74385-7, 04992). Natl Geog.

MAMMALS–PHYSIOLOGY

Anderson, Paul D. Laboratory Manual & Study Guide for Clinical Anatomy & Physiology for Allied Health Sciences. LC 75-21143. (Illus.). 218p. 1976. 10.00 (ISBN 0-7216-1236-9). Saunders.

Challice, C. E. & Viragh, S., eds. Ultrastructure of the Mammalian Heart. (Ultrastructure in Biological Systems Series). 1973. 38.00 (ISBN 0-12-170050-X). Acad Pr.

Doty, Richard L., ed. Mammalian Olfaction: Reproducive Processes, & Behavior. 1976. 44.00 (ISBN 0-12-221250-9). Acad Pr.

Gesellschaft Fuer Biologische Chemie, 21st Colloquium, Mossbach-Baden, 1970. Mammalian Reproduction: Proceedings. Gibian, H. & Plotz, J., eds. LC 77-140558. (Illus.). 1970. 40.70 (ISBN 0-387-05066-3). Springer-Verlag.

Gessaman, James A. Ecological Energetics of Homeotherms. 1973. pap. 7.00 (ISBN 0-87421-053-4). Utah St U Pr.

Grave, Gilman. Thyroid Hormones & Brain Development. LC 76-52899. 392p. 1977. 36.00 (ISBN 0-89004-146-6). Raven.

Gwatkin, Ralph B. Fertilization Mechanisms in Man & Mammals. LC 77-1189. (Illus.). 161p. 1977. 22.50 (ISBN 0-306-31009-0, Plenum Pr). Plenum Pub.

Jamieson, G. A. & Robinson, D. M., eds. Mammalian Cell Membranes, 5 vols. (Illus.). 1977. text ed. 159.95 set (ISBN 0-686-25573-9). Butterworth.

Kempczinski, R. F., et al. Organ & Tissue Regeneration in Mammals II. new ed. LC 72-13503. 157p. 1973. text ed. 25.50x (ISBN 0-8422-7059-0). Irvington.

Kerkut, G. A. & Wheal, H. V., eds. Electrophysiology of Isolated Mammalian CNS Preparations. 408p. 1981. 67.00 (ISBN 0-12-404680-0). Acad Pr.

Madge, David S. The Mammalian Alimentary System: A Functional Approach. LC 75-34543. (Special Topics in Biology Ser). 195p. 1976. pap. 14.50x (ISBN 0-8448-0850-4). Crane-Russak Co.

Marshall, P. T. & Hughes, G. M. Physiology of Mammals & Other Vertebrates. 2nd ed. LC 78-73810. (Illus.). 1981. 39.50 (ISBN 0-521-22633-3); pap. 16.95 (ISBN 0-521-29586-6). Cambridge U Pr.

Mayer, William V. & Van Gelder, R. G., eds. Physiological Mammalogy, 2 vols. Incl. Vol. 1 (ISBN 0-12-481001-2); Vol. 2 (ISBN 0-12-481002-0). 1964. 52.50 ea. Acad Pr.

Moore, W. J. The Mammalian Skull. (Biological Structure & Function Ser.: No. 8). (Illus.). 400p. 1981. 85.00 (ISBN 0-521-23318-6). Cambridge U Pr.

Motta, P. M. & Hafez, E. S., eds. Biology of the Ovary. (Developments in Obstetrics & Gynecology Ser.: No. 2). 345p. 1980. lib. bdg. 87.00 (ISBN 90-247-2316-7, Pub. by Martinus Nijhoff Netherlands). Kluwer Boston.

Nettesheim, P., et al. Organ & Tissue Regeneration in Mammals I. LC 72-13503. 167p. 1972. text ed. 27.50x (ISBN 0-8422-7048-5). Irvington.

Papageorgiou, Nikolaos. Population Energy Relationships of the Agrimi (Capra Aegagrus Cretica) on Theodorou Island, Greece. (Mammalia Depicta Ser.). (Illus.). 56p. (Orig.). pap. text ed. 14.10 (ISBN 3-490-21518-4). Parey Sci Pubs.

Peters, Hannah & McNatty, Kenneth P. The Ovary: A Correlation of Structure & Function in Mammals. LC 79-6741. 1980. 38.75x (ISBN 0-520-04124-0). U of Cal Pr.

Scheline, R. R. Mammalian Metabolism of Plant Xenobiotics. 1979. 82.00 (ISBN 0-12-623350-0). Acad Pr.

Shirley, Barbara A. Laboratory Manual of Mammalian Physiology. (Illus.). 256p. 1974. pap. text ed. 9.95 (ISBN 0-02-409760-8). Macmillan.

Smith, Michael H. & Joule, James, eds. Mammalian Population Genetics. LC 80-24667. 1981. 25.00 (ISBN 0-8203-0547-2). U of Ga Pr.

Sokolov, V. E. Mammal Skin. LC 75-46042. (Illus.). 704p. 1981. 40.00x (ISBN 0-520-03198-9). U of Cal Pr.

Stoddart, D. M. & Stoddart, D. M., eds. Olfaction in Mammals. (Symposia of the Zoological Society of London: No. 45). 1980. 66.00 (ISBN 0-12-613345-X). Acad Pr.

MAMMALS–AFRICA

Altmann, Jeanne. Baboon Mothers & Infants. LC 79-21568. (Illus.). 1980. text ed. 18.50x (ISBN 0-674-05856-9). Harvard U Pr.

Delany, M. J. & Happold, D. C. Ecology of African Mammals. (Tropical Ecology Ser.). (Illus.). 1979. text ed. 65.00x (ISBN 0-582-44176-5). Longman.

Dorst, Jean. Field Guide to the Larger Mammals of Africa. (Peterson Field Guide Ser). (Illus.). 1970. 8.50 (ISBN 0-395-10839-X). HM.

Eltringham, S. K. The Ecology & Conservation of Large African Mammals. 286p. text ed. 49.95 (ISBN 0-8391-1493-1). Univ Park.

Frame, George & Frame, Lory. Swift & Enduring: Cheetahs & Wild Dogs of the Serengeti. (Illus.). 1981. 16.50 (ISBN 0-525-93060-4). Dutton.

Happold, D. C. Large Mammals of West Africa. LC 74-169364. (West African Nature Handbooks). (Illus.). 105p. (Orig.). 1973. pap. 5.00 (ISBN 0-582-60428-1). Intl Pubns Serv.

Hufnagl, Ernst. Libyan Mammals. (Illus.). 16.00 (ISBN 0-902675-08-7). Oleander Pr.

Kingdon, Jonathan. East African Mammals: An Atlas of Evolution in Africa. Vol. 1, 1971. 70.50 (ISBN 0-12-408301-3); Vol. 2, 2 Pts. 70.50 ea. Pt. A (ISBN 0-12-408302-1). Pt. B. (ISBN 0-12-408342-0); Vol. 3; Pt. A, 1978. 100.50 (ISBN 0-12-408303-X); Vol. 3b. 132.00 (ISBN 0-12-408343-9). Acad Pr.

Leuthold, W. African Ungulates: A Comparative Review of Their Ethology & Behavioral Ecology. Farner, D. S., ed. LC 76-44535. (Zoophysiology & Ecology Ser.: Vol. 8). (Illus.). 1977. 40.30 (ISBN 0-387-07951-3). Springer-Verlag.

McBride, Chris. The White Lions of Timbavati. LC 77-4896. 1977. 10.95 (ISBN 0-448-22677-4). Paddington.

Maglio, Vincent J. & Cooke, H. B., eds. Evolution of African Mammals. LC 77-19318. (Illus.). 1978. 60.00x (ISBN 0-674-27075-4). Harvard U Pr.

Meester, J. & Setzer, H. W., eds. The Mammals of Africa: An Identification Manual. LC 70-169904. 1971. three-ring binder 40.00x (ISBN 0-87474-116-5). Smithsonian.

Richard, Alison F. Behavioral Variation: Case Study of a Malagasy Lemur. LC 76-19837. 213p. 1978. 25.00 (ISBN 0-8387-1965-1). Bucknell U Pr.

Sinclair, A. R. E. The African Buffalo: A Study of Resource Limitations of Populations. LC 76-22955. (Wildlife Behavior & Ecology Ser.). (Illus.). 1977. 20.00x (ISBN 0-226-76030-8). U of Chicago Pr.

MAMMALS–ARABIA

Harrison, David L. The Mammals of Arabia. Incl. Vol. 1. Insectivora, Chiroptera, Primates. 1964; Vol. 2. The Carnivora, Hyracoidea & Artiodactyla. 1968; Vol. 3. Lagomorpha & Rodentia. 40.00 (ISBN 0-934454-04-3). (Illus.). Lubrecht & Cramer.

--Mammals of the Arabian Gulf. (The Natural History of the Arabian Gulf Ser.). (Illus.). 88p. 1981. text ed. 19.50x (ISBN 0-04-599007-7). Allen Unwin.

MAMMALS–AUSTRALIA

Parry, Veronica A. Kookaburras. LC 71-183133. (Illus.). 110p. 1972. 6.50 (ISBN 0-8008-4490-4). Taplinger.

Ride, W. D. Guide to the Native Mammals of Australia. (Illus.). 1970. 32.00x (ISBN 0-19-550252-3). Oxford U Pr.

MAMMALS–EUROPE

Bokonyi. History of Domestic Mammals in Central & Eastern Europe. 1974. 41.00 (ISBN 0-9960001-0-0, Pub. by Kaido Hungary). Heyden.

Corbet, G. B. Terrestrial Mammals of Western Europe. (Illus.). 1966. 10.95 (ISBN 0-8023-1030-3). Dufour.

Haltenorth, Theodore. Mammals. (Nature Guides Ser.). (Illus.). 144p. 1979. pap. 5.95 (ISBN 0-7011-2364-8, Pub. by Chatto Bodley Jonathan). Merrimack Bk Serv.

MAMMALS–GREAT BRITAIN

Lawrence, M. J. & Brown, R. W. Mammals of Britain: Their Tracks, Trails & Signs. (Illus.). 320p. 1974. 8.95 (ISBN 0-7137-0588-4). Transatlantic.

MAMMALS–HAWAII

Tomich, P. Q. Mammals in Hawaii: A Synopsis & Notational Bibliography. LC 69-19920. (Special Publication Ser: No. 57). (Illus.). 238p. 1969. 5.00 (ISBN 0-910240-05-1). Bishop Mus.

MAMMALS–INDIA

Hrdy, Sarah B. The Langurs of Abu: Female & Male Strategies of Reproduction. (Illus.). 1977. 17.50x (ISBN 0-674-51057-7); pap. 7.95x (ISBN 0-674-51058-5). Harvard U Pr.

MAMMALS–MEXICO

Mearns, Edgar A. Mammals of the Mexican Boundary of the United States: Catalogue of the Species of Mammals Occuring in That Region, Part 1, Families Didelphiidae to Muridae. LC 73-18787. (Natural Sciences in America Ser.). 576p. 1974. Repr. 30.00x (ISBN 0-405-05777-6). Arno.

Wright, N. Pelham. A Guide to Mexican Mammals & Reptiles. 1970. pap. 4.00 (ISBN 0-912434-08-2). Ocelot Pr.

MAMMALS–NEW ZEALAND

Poole, A. L. Wild Animals in New Zealand. LC 76-597144. (Illus.). 1969. 16.50 (ISBN 0-589-00411-5, Pub. by Reed Books Australia). C E Tuttle.

MAMMALS–NORTH AMERICA

Alaska Geographic Staff, ed. Alaska Mammals. (Alaska Geographic Ser.: Vol. 8, No. 2). (Illus.). 184p. (Orig.). 1981. pap. 12.95 (ISBN 0-88240-155-6). Alaska Northwest.

Allen, Glover M. Extinct & Vanishing Mammals of the Western Hemisphere. LC 72-85661. xv, 620p. 1973. Repr. of 1942 ed. lib. bdg. 23.50x (ISBN 0-8154-0433-6). Cooper Sq.

Allen, Joel A. History of the North American Pinnipeds: A Monograph of the Walruses, Sea-Lions, Sea-Bears & Seals of North America. LC 73-17792. (Natural Sciences in America Ser.). (Illus.). 806p. 1974. Repr. 40.00x (ISBN 0-405-05702-4). Arno.

Angell, Tony & Balcomb, Kenneth. Mammals & Waterbirds of Puget Sound. 1981. write for info. U of Wash Pr.

Audubon, John J. The Art of Audubon: The Complete Birds & Mammals. LC 79-51434. (Illus.). 1979. 35.00 (ISBN 0-8129-0841-4, Dist. by Har-Row). Times Bks.

Audubon, John J. & Bachman, John. The Quadrupeds of North America, 3 vols. LC 73-17796. (Natural Sciences of America Ser.). (Illus.). 1406p. 1974. Repr. Set. 75.00x (ISBN 0-405-05706-7); Vol. 1. 26.00x (ISBN 0-405-05707-5); Vol. 2. 23.00x (ISBN 0-405-05708-3); Vol. 3. 26.00x (ISBN 0-405-05709-1). Arno.

Baird, Spencer F. Mammals of North America: The Descriptions of Species Based Chiefly on the Collections in the Museum of the Smithsonian Institution. LC 73-17797. (Natural Sciences in America Ser.). (Illus.). 844p. 1974. Repr. 44.00x (ISBN 0-405-05710-5). Arno.

Banfield, A. F. Mammals of Canada. LC 73-92298. (Illus.). 1974. 25.00 (ISBN 0-8020-2137-9). U of Toronto Pr.

Berry, William D. & Berry, Elizabeth. Mammals of the San Francisco Bay Region. (California Natural History Guides: No. 2). 1959. 14.95x (ISBN 0-520-03088-5); pap. 3.95 (ISBN 0-520-00116-8). U of Cal Pr.

Booth, Ernest S. How to Know the Mammals. 3rd ed. (Pictured Key Nature Ser.). 214p. 1971. wire coil avail. (ISBN 0-697-04871-3). Wm C Brown.

Bowles, John B. Distribution & Biogeography of Mammals of Iowa. (Special Publications: No. 9). (Illus., Orig.). 1975. pap. 8.00 (ISBN 0-89672-034-9). Tex Tech Pr.

Brown, Vinson. Sea Mammals & Reptiles of the Pacific Coast. 1976. pap. 6.95 (ISBN 0-02-062280-5, Collier). Macmillan.

Burt, William H. A Field Guide to the Mammals. 3rd ed. (Peterson Field Guide Ser.). 1976. 14.95 (ISBN 0-395-24082-4); pap. 7.95 (ISBN 0-395-24084-0). HM.

--Mammals of the Great Lakes Region. (Illus.). (gr. 10-12). 1972. pap. 5.95 (ISBN 0-472-06183-6, 183, AA). U of Mich Pr.

Carnegie Institution Of Washington. Studies of Tertiary & Quaternary Mammals of North America. Repr. of 1936 ed. pap. 15.50 (ISBN 0-685-02165-3). Johnson Repr.

Cockrum, E. Lendell. The Recent Mammals of Arizona: Their Taxonomy & Distribution. LC 60-15914. (Illus.). 1960. 6.50x (ISBN 0-8165-0076-2). U of Ariz Pr.

Fauna Americana. LC 73-17819. (Natural Sciences in America Ser.). 424p. 1974. Repr. 21.00x (ISBN 0-405-05735-0). Arno.

Godin, Alfred J. Wild Mammals of New England. LC 77-4785. (Illus.). 1977. 25.00 (ISBN 0-8018-1964-4). Johns Hopkins.

Godman, John D. American Natural History: Mastogogy & Rambles of a Naturalist, Part No. 1, 3 vols. in one. LC 73-17821. (Natural Sciences in America Ser.). (Illus.). 1079p. 1974. Repr. 56.00x (ISBN 0-405-05737-7). Arno.

Gottschang, Jack L. Guide to the Mammals of Ohio. LC 80-27661. (Illus.). 181p. 1981. 37.50 (ISBN 0-8142-0242-X). Ohio St U Pr.

Grinnell, Joseph. An Account of the Mammals & Birds of the Lower Colorado Valley, with Especial Reference to the Distributional Problems Presented. Sterling, Keir B., ed. LC 77-81116. (Biologists & Their World Ser.). (Illus.). 1978. Repr. of 1914 ed. lib. bdg. 16.00x (ISBN 0-405-10708-0). Arno.

Hall, E. Raymond. Mammals of North America, 2 vols. 2nd. ed. LC 79-4109. 1981. Set. 80.00x (ISBN 0-471-05595-6, Pub. by Wiley-Interscience); Vol. 1, 690 Pgs. 45.00x (ISBN 0-471-05443-7); Vol. 2, 668 Pgs. 45.00x (ISBN 0-471-05444-5). Wiley.
Hamilton, William J. Mammals of Eastern United States. (Illus.). 1963. Repr. of 1943 ed. 14.75 (ISBN 0-02-845680-7). Hafner.
Hoffmeister, Donald F. Mammals of Grand Canyon. LC 75-141517. (Illus.). 1971. 12.50 (ISBN 0-252-00154-0); pap. 3.95 (ISBN 0-252-00155-9). U of Ill Pr.
Hoffmeister, Donald F. & Durham, Floyd E. Mammals of the Arizona Strip Including Grand Canyon National Monument. (Mna Technical Ser.9: No. 11). 1971. pap. 1.75 (ISBN 0-685-76471-0). Mus Northern Ariz.
Hoffmeister, Donald F. & Mohr, Carl D. Fieldbook of Illinois Mammals. (Illus.). 6.50 (ISBN 0-8446-4556-7). Peter Smith.
Hoffmeister, Donald F. & Mohr, Carl O. Fieldbook of Illinois Mammals. (Illus.). 256p. 1972. pap. 4.00 (ISBN 0-486-20220-8). Dover.
Ingles, Lloyd G. Mammals of the Pacific States: California, Oregon, Washington. (Illus.). 1965. 14.95 (ISBN 0-8047-0297-7); text ed. 11.20 (ISBN 0-8047-0298-5). Stanford U Pr.
Jackson, Hartley H. Mammals of Wisconsin. (Illus.). 518p. 1961. 22.50x (ISBN 0-299-02150-5). U of Wis Pr.
Krishtalka, Leonard. Late Paleocene Mammals from the Cypress Hills, Alberta. (Special Publications: No. 2). (Illus., Orig.). 1973. pap. 4.00 (ISBN 0-89672-027-6). Tex Tech Pr.
Kurten, Bjorn & Anderson, Elaine. Pleistocene Mammals of North America. LC 79-26679. 1980. 42.50x (ISBN 0-231-03733-3). Columbia U Pr.
Larrison, Earl J. Mammals of the Northwest (Washington, Oregon, Idaho, & British Columbia) LC 73-94501. (Trailside Ser.). (Illus.). 1976. 12.50 (ISBN 0-685-65345-5); pap. 8.50 (ISBN 0-914516-04-3). Seattle Audubon Soc.
Larrison, Earl J. & Johnson, Donald R. Mammals of Idaho. LC 80-51876. (GEM Bks-Natural History Ser.). (Illus.). 200p. 1981. pap. 6.95 (ISBN 0-89301-070-7). U Pr of Idaho.
Leopold, A. Starker, et al. North American Game Birds & Mammals. (Illus.). 224p. 1981. 19.95 (ISBN 0-684-17270-4, ScribT). Scribner.
Linzey, Alicia V. & Linzey, Donald W. Mammals of Great Smoky Mountains National Park. LC 74-111048. (Illus.). 1971. pap. 4.95 (ISBN 0-87049-114-8). U of Tenn Pr.
--Mammals of Great Smoky Mountains National Park. LC 74-111048. (Illus.). 1971. pap. 4.95 (ISBN 0-87049-114-8). U of Tenn Pr.
--Mammals of Great Smoky Mountains National Park. LC 74-111048. (Illus.). 1971. pap. 4.95 (ISBN 0-87049-114-8). U of Tenn Pr.
Lyon, Marcus W., Jr. Mammals of Indiana. LC 73-17829. (Natural Sciences in America Ser.). (Illus.). 388p. 1974. Repr. 22.00x (ISBN 0-405-05747-4). Arno.
Mearns, Edgar A. Mammals of the Mexican Boundary of the United States: Catalogue of the Species of Mammals Occuring in That Region, Part 1, Families Didelphiidae to Muridae. LC 73-18787. (Natural Sciences in America Ser.). 576p. 1974. Repr. 30.00x (ISBN 0-405-05777-6). Arno.
Merriam, Clinton H. The Mammals of the Adirondack Region, Northwestern New York: Introductory Chapter Treating of the Location & Boundaries of the Region, Its Geological History, Topography, Climate, General Features, Botany & Faunal Position. LC 73-17832. (Natural Sciences of America Ser.). 320p. 1974. Repr. 16.00x (ISBN 0-405-05750-4). Arno.
Mumford, Russell E. & Whitaker, John O., Jr. Mammals of Indiana. LC 79-2175. (Illus.). 1981. 37.50x (ISBN 0-253-30387-7). Ind U Pr.
Nowak, Ronald, et al. Wild Animals of North America. Allen, Thomas B., ed. LC 79-18452. (Illus.). 406p. 1979. 14.95 (ISBN 0-87044-294-5); deluxe ed. 26.90 in deluxe slipcase with our continent (ISBN 0-686-66211-3). Natl Geog.
Olin, George & Bierly, Edward. Mammals of the Southwest Mountains & Mesas. 4th ed. LC 61-11291. (Popular Ser.: No. 9). 1961. pap. 3.00 (ISBN 0-911408-32-0). SW Pks Mnmts.
Olin, George & Cannon, Jerry. Mammals of the Southwest Deserts. 5th ed. LC 75-21161. (Popular Ser.: No. 8). (Illus.). 1975. pap. 3.00 (ISBN 0-911408-36-3). SW Pks Mnmts.
Orr, Robert T. Mammals of Lake Tahoe. (Illus.). 127p. 1949. 7.50 (ISBN 0-940228-07-6). Calif Acad Sci.
Rue, Leonard L. Furbearing Animals of North America. (Illus.). 352p. 1981. 19.95 (ISBN 0-517-53942-X, Michelman Books). Crown.
Rue, Leonard L., III. Pictorial Guide to the Mammals of North America. (Apollo Eds.). (Illus.). 1977. pap. 7.95 (ISBN 0-8152-0420-5). T Y Crowell.
Savage, Arthur & Savage, Candace. Wild Mammals of Northwest America. (Illus.). 208p. 1981. before January 1, 1982 25.00 (ISBN 0-8018-2627-6); 25.00until12/1981 (ISBN 0-686-75330-5). Johns Hopkins.
Scammon, Charles M. The Marine Mammals of the Northwestern Coast of North America: Together with an Account of the American Whale-Fishery. (Illus.). 11.00 (ISBN 0-8446-0243-4). Peter Smith.
Schmidly, David J. Mammals of Trans-Pecos Texas: Including Big Bend National Park & Guadalupe Mountains National Park. LC 77-89514. (W. L. Moody, Jr., Natural History Ser.: No. 2). (Illus.). 240p. 1977. 12.50 (ISBN 0-89096-035-6). Tex A&M Univ Pr.
Schwartz, Charles W. & Schwartz, Elizabeth R. Wild Mammals of Missouri. rev. ed. LC 80-24138. 368p. 1981. text ed. 24.00 (ISBN 0-8262-0324-8). U of Mo Pr.
Seton, Ernest S. Life-Histories of the Northern Animals: An Account of the Mammals of Manitoba, 2. LC 73-17845. (Natural Sciences in America Ser.). (Illus.). 1514p. 1974. Repr. Set. 79.00x (ISBN 0-405-05767-9); Vol. 1. 41.00x (ISBN 0-405-05768-7); Vol. 2. 38.00x (ISBN 0-405-05769-5). Arno.
Sterling, Keir B., ed. Contributions to the Bibliographical Literature of American Mammals. LC 73-17808. (Natural Sciences in America Ser.). 304p. 1974. Repr. 15.00x (ISBN 0-405-05725-3). Arno.
--Selected Works of Clinton Hart Merriam. LC 73-17842. (Natural Sciences in America Ser.). 893p. 1974. Repr. 47.00x (ISBN 0-405-05764-4). Arno.
Wallmo, Olof C., ed. Mule & Black-tailed Deer of North America. LC 80-20128. (Illus.). xviii, 650p. 1981. 29.95 (ISBN 0-8032-4715-X). U of Nebr Pr.
Webb, S. David, ed. Pleistocene Mammals of Florida. LC 74-3115. 270p. 1974. 12.00 (ISBN 0-8130-0361-X). U Presses Fla.
West, Robert M. Review of the North American Eocene & Oligocene Apatemyidae (Mammalia: Insectivora) (Special Publications: No. 3). (Illus.). 42p. 1973. pap. 2.00 (ISBN 0-89672-028-4). Tex Tech Pr.
Whitaker, John O., Jr. The Audubon Field Guide to North American Mammals. LC 79-3525. (Illus.). 752p. 1980. 11.95 (ISBN 0-394-50762-2). Knopf.

MAMMALS–SOUTH AMERICA

Audubon, John J. The Art of Audubon: The Complete Birds & Mammals. LC 79-51434. (Illus.). 1979. 35.00 (ISBN 0-8129-0841-4, Dist. by Har-Row). Times Bks.
Hershkovitz, Philip. Living New World Monkeys (Platyrrhini) With an Introduction to Primates, Vol. 1. LC 75-9059. (Illus.). 1978. 90.00x (ISBN 0-226-32788-4). U of Chicago Pr.
Myers, Philip. Patterns of Reproduction of Four Species of Vespertilionia Bats in Paraguay. (Publ. in Zoology Ser: Vol. 107). 1977. pap. 11.50x (ISBN 0-520-09554-5). U of Cal Pr.
Simpson, George G. Splendid Isolation: The Curious History of South American Mannals. LC 79-17630. (Illus.). 1980. 18.50x (ISBN 0-300-02434-7). Yale U Pr.

MAMMALS, FOSSIL

see also Vertebrates, Fossil

Kurten, Bjorn. The Age of Mammals. LC 79-177479. (Illus.). 250p. 1972. 17.50x (ISBN 0-231-03624-8); pap. 7.50x (ISBN 0-231-03647-7). Columbia U Pr.
Lawrence, Barbara. Mammals Found at the Awatovi Site. (Illus.). 1951. pap. 5.00 (ISBN 0-527-01290-4). Kraus Repr.
Leidy, Joseph. The Extinct Mammalian Fauna of Dakota & Nebraska, & a Account of Some Allied Forms from Other Localities: Synopsis of the Mammalian Remains of North America. 2nd ed. LC 73-17828. (Natural Sciences in America Ser.: Vol. 3). (Illus.). 536p. 1974. Repr. 28.00x (ISBN 0-405-05746-6). Arno.
Simpson, George G. A Catalogue of the Mesozoic Mammalia in the Geological Department of the British Museum & American Mesozoic Mammalia: Memoirs of the Peabody Museum of Yale University, Vol. Iii, Pt. 1, 2vols. In 1. Gould, Stephen J., ed. LC 79-8350. (History of Paleontology Ser.). (Illus.). 1980. Repr. of 1928 ed. lib. bdg. 58.00x (ISBN 0-405-12743-X). Arno.

MAMMARY GLANDS

see also Breast; Udder

Degrell, I. Atlas of the Diseases of the Mammary Gland: Atlas der Brustdruesenerkrankungen. (Illus.). 186p. 1976. 100.75 (ISBN 3-8055-2219-3). S Karger.
Egan, Robert L. Technologist Guide to Mammography. 133p. 1968. 9.75 (ISBN 0-683-02770-0). Krieger.
Gallager, H. Stephen, et al, eds. The Breast. LC 78-14811. (Illus.). 1978. text ed. 69.50 (ISBN 0-8016-1727-8). Mosby.
Huggins, Charles B. Experimental Leukemia & Mammary Cancer: Induction, Prevention, Cure. LC 78-25790. (Illus.). 1979. lib. bdg. 20.00x (ISBN 0-226-35860-7). U of Chicago Pr.
Kon, S. K. & Cowie, Alfred T., eds. Milk: The Mammary Gland & Its Secretion, 2 Vols. (Illus.). 1961. Vol. 1. 56.00 (ISBN 0-12-418701-3); Vol. 2. 56.00 (ISBN 0-12-418702-1); Set. 92.00 (ISBN 0-685-05135-8). Acad Pr.
Larson, Bruce L. & Smith, Vearl R., eds. Lactation: A Comprehensive Treatise. Incl. Vol. 1, 1974. Development, Lactogenesis. 63.50 (ISBN 0-12-436701-1); subscription 63.50 (ISBN 0-686-77185-0); Vol. 2. 1974. 48.75, by subscription 41.75 (ISBN 0-12-436702-X); Vol. 3. Milk, Nutrution & Maintenance. 1974. 56.00, by subscription 56.00 (ISBN 0-12-436703-8); Vol. 4. 1978. 66.50, by subscription 66.50 (ISBN 0-12-436704-6). Acad Pr.
Logan, Wende W. & Muntz, E. Phillip. Reduced Dose Mammography. LC 79-63202. (Illus.). 576p. 1979. 41.25x (ISBN 0-89352-060-8). Masson Pub.
New Frontiers in Mammary Pathology. 308p. 1981. 39.50 (ISBN 0-306-40655-1, Plenum Pr). Plenum Pub.
Willemin, A. Mammographic Appearances. (Illus.). 1972. 87.00 (ISBN 3-8055-1584-7). S Karger.
Yokoyama. Physiology of the Mammary Gland. 1978. 44.50 (ISBN 0-8391-1303-X). Univ Park.

MAMMILARIA

Craig, Robert T. The Mammillaria Handbook. (Illus.). 1945. 23.00 (ISBN 0-384-10090-2). Johnson Repr.
Pilbeam, John. Mammillaria: A Collector's Guide. (Illus.). 200p. 1981. text ed. 40.00x (ISBN 0-87663-360-2). Universe.

MAMMOTH

Aliki. Wild & Woolly Mammoths. LC 76-18082. (A Let's-Read-&-Find-Out Science Bk). (Illus.). (gr. k-3). 1977. PLB 8.79 (ISBN 0-690-01276-4, TYC-J). Har-Row.

MAMMOTH CAVE, KENTUCKY

Brucker, Roger W. & Watson, Richard A. The Longest Cave. 1976. 13.95 (ISBN 0-394-48793-1). Knopf.
Hovey, H. C. One Hundred Miles in Mammoth Cave Eighteen Eighty. Jones, William R., ed. (Illus.). 1980. Repr. pap. 2.00 (ISBN 0-89646-054-1). Outbooks.
Palmer, Arthur N. A Geological Guide to Mammoth Cave National Park. (Speleologia Ser.). (Illus.). 1981. write for info. (ISBN 0-914264-27-3); pap. write for info. (ISBN 0-914264-28-1). Zephyrus Pr.
Thompson, Ralph S. The Sucker's Visit to the Mammoth Cave. Repr. of 1870 ed. 7.00 (ISBN 0-914264-33-8). Zephyrus Pr.
Watson, Patty J. Archeology of the Mammoth Cave Area. 1974. 28.50 (ISBN 0-12-785927-6). Acad Pr.

MAN

see also Anthropology; Anthropometry; Color of Man; Craniology; Creation; Ethnology; Heredity; Human Biology; Men; Men in Literature; Philosophical Anthropology; Women

Abel, Reuben. Man Is the Measure: A Cordial Invitation to the Central Problems of Philosophy. LC 75-16646. (Illus.). 1976. 12.95 (ISBN 0-02-900140-4); pap. text ed. 8.95 (ISBN 0-02-900110-2). Free Pr.
Adams, Mary, ed. Science in the Changing World. facs. ed. LC 68-29188. (Essay Index Reprint Ser). 1968. Repr. of 1933 ed. 16.00 (ISBN 0-8369-0136-3). Arno.
Alexander, Jason. In Praise of the Common Man. LC 80-54489. 86p. (Orig.). 1981. pap. write for info. (ISBN 0-931826-02-0). Sitnalta Pr.
Alland, Alexander, Jr. The Human Imperative. LC 77-183227. 185p. 1972. 17.00x (ISBN 0-231-03228-5); pap. 6.00x (ISBN 0-231-08301-7). Columbia U Pr.
Barbotin, Edmond. The Humanity of Man. O'Connell, Matthew, tr. from Fr. LC 74-21108. 320p. 1975. 12.95x (ISBN 0-88344-183-7). Orbis Bks.
Barnes, Harry E. Can Man Be Civilized? 69.95 (ISBN 0-87700-028-X). Revisionist Pr.
Bates, Marston. Gluttons & Libertines: Human Problems of Being Natural. LC 66-11978. 1971. pap. 2.45 (ISBN 0-394-71267-6, V-267, Vin). Random.
Beck, Lewis W. The Actor & the Spectator. LC 75-2771. (Cassirer Lectures). 160p. 1975. 12.50x (ISBN 0-300-01899-1). Yale U Pr.
Becker, Ernest. Angel in Armor: A Post-Freudian Perspective on the Nature of Man. LC 69-12803. 1975. pap. 3.95 (ISBN 0-02-902280-0). Free Pr.
Bernstein, Richard J. Praxis & Action: Contemporary Philosophies of Human Activity. LC 77-157048. 1971. 26.00x (ISBN 0-8122-7640-X); pap. 8.50x (ISBN 0-8122-1016-6, Pa Paperbks). U of Pa Pr.
Bronowski, J. Identity of Man. rev. ed. LC 71-188042. 1971. 5.95 (ISBN 0-385-01197-0, AMS); pap. 1.95 (ISBN 0-385-00171-1, AMS). Natural Hist.
Bronowski, Jacob. The Ascent of Man: Students Guide. Miami-Dade Community College, ed. 8.95 (ISBN 0-316-56940-2). Little.
--The Ascent of Man: Students Guide. Regents of the State of California at San Diego, ed. pap. 8.95 (ISBN 0-316-88730-7). Little.
Brues, Alice M. People & Races. 1977. 11.95 (ISBN 0-02-315670-8, 31567). Macmillan.
Buber, Martin. Between Man & Man. 1965. pap. 2.95 (ISBN 0-02-084200-7). Macmillan.
Burr, Harold S. The Nature of Man & the Meaning of Existence. 108p. 1962. photocopy spiral ed. 10.75 (ISBN 0-398-04225-X). C C Thomas.
Capon, Robert Farrar. The Third Peacock. LC 73-147357. 120p. 1972. pap. 1.95 (ISBN 0-385-03627-2, Im). Doubleday.
Carroll, John. Break-Out from the Crystal Palace: The Anarcho-Psychological Critique-Stirner, Nietzsche, Dostoevsky. (International Library of Sociology). 1974. 18.00x (ISBN 0-7100-7750-5). Routledge & Kegan.
Cassirer, Ernst. Essay on Man: An Introduction to a Philosophy of Human Culture. 1962. pap. 5.45 (ISBN 0-300-00034-0, Y52). Yale U Pr.
Collins, Gary. Hombre En Transicion. Ingledew, Roberto, tr. from Eng. 220p. (Orig., Span.). 1978. pap. 4.50 (ISBN 0-89922-124-6). Edit Caribe.
Columbia College - Contemporary Civilization Staff. Man in Contemporary Society. student ed. LC 62-17503. (gr. 12 up). 1962. 22.50x (ISBN 0-231-02587-4). Columbia U Pr.
Constant, Benjamin. De la Perfectibilite de l'Espece Humaine. 1967. 7.95 (ISBN 0-686-54608-3). French & Eur.
Cook, Joan M. In Defense of Homo Sapiens. 222p. 1975. 8.95 (ISBN 0-374-17552-7). FS&G.
Corner, George W. Ourselves Unborn: An Embryologist's Essay on Man. LC 71-143884. 1972. Repr. of 1944 ed. 16.50 (ISBN 0-685-02973-5, Archon). Shoe String.
Crosson, Frederick J., ed. Human & Artificial Intelligence. LC 78-131431. (Orig.). 1970. pap. text ed. 6.95x (ISBN 0-89197-220-X). Irvington.
Daires, John L. Man & His Universe. 1937. 10.00 (ISBN 0-686-17421-6). Ridgeway Bks.
Darwin, Charles R. The Descent of Man. 1902. 30.00 (ISBN 0-8274-2165-6). R West.
Davenport, Russell W. The Dignity of Man. LC 72-10694. 338p. 1973. Repr. of 1955 ed. lib. bdg. 20.00x (ISBN 0-8371-6614-4, DADI). Greenwood.
Dawkins, Richard. The Selfish Gene. LC 76-29168. 1978. pap. 4.95 (ISBN 0-19-520000-4, GB500, GB). Oxford U Pr.
Desan, Wilfrid. The Planetary Man. Incl. A Noetic Prelude to a United World; An Ethical Prelude to a United World. LC 71-169233. 384p. 1972. 9.95 (ISBN 0-02-531080-1, 53108). Macmillan.
Doniger, Simon, ed. The Nature of Man in Theological & Psychological Perspective. LC 72-10819. (Essay Index Reprint Ser.). 1973. Repr. of 1962 ed. 18.00 (ISBN 0-8369-7213-9). Arno.
Earle, William. The Autobiographical Consciousness. 1972. 10.00 (ISBN 0-8129-0191-6); pap. 2.95 (ISBN 0-8129-6164-1). Times Bks.
Eichler, Lilian. The Customs of Mankind. 1937. 30.00 (ISBN 0-685-73523-0). Norwood Edns.
Elders, Fons, ed. Reflexive Water: The Basic Concerns of Mankind. 1977. pap. 5.95 (ISBN 0-285-64749-0, Pub. by Souvenir Pr). Intl Schol Bk Serv.
Farb, Peter. Humankind. LC 77-9083. 1978. 15.95 (ISBN 0-395-25710-7). HM.
Fichte, Johann G. The Vocation of Man. Smith, William, tr. LC 56-44104. 1956. pap. 3.95 (ISBN 0-672-60220-2, LLA50). Bobbs.
--Vocation of Man. Smith, William, tr. from Ger. xii, 178p. 1965. 12.95 (ISBN 0-87548-074-8); pap. 4.95 (ISBN 0-87548-075-6). Open Court.
Flew, Anthony. A Rational Animal: & Other Philosophical Essays on the Nature of Man. 1978. 29.50x (ISBN 0-19-824576-9). Oxford U Pr.
Forster, Robert & Ranum, Orest, eds. Biology of Man in History, Vol. 1: Selections from the Annales: Economies-Societies, Civilistions. LC 74-24382. 1975. text ed. 15.00x (ISBN 0-8018-1690-4); pap. 4.95x (ISBN 0-8018-1691-2). Johns Hopkins.
Frank, Lawrence K. Nature & Human Nature: Man's New Image of Himself. LC 72-94584. Repr. of 1951 ed. lib. bdg. 15.00x (ISBN 0-8371-2453-0, FRNH). Greenwood.
Frankel, Charles. Case for Modern Man. facsimile ed. LC 71-167342. (Essay Index Reprint Ser). Repr. of 1956 ed. 16.00 (ISBN 0-8369-2648-X). Arno.

Froman, Creel. Manuscript of Hugo Potts: An Inquiry into Meaning. LC 73-5915. 376p. 1973. 12.85x (ISBN 0-8093-0608-5). S Ill U Pr.

Godwin, William. Thoughts on Man, His Nature, Productions, & Discoveries. LC 68-55719. Repr. of 1831 ed. 19.50x (ISBN 0-678-00442-0). Kelley.

Gordon, Milton M. Human Nature, Class, & Ethnicity. (Illus.). 1978. 14.95 (ISBN 0-19-502236-X); pap. 4.95 (ISBN 0-19-502237-8). Oxford U Pr.

Graham, Gerald S. & Alexander, John. Secular Abyss: An Interpretation of History & the Human Situation. 1968. pap. 1.95 (ISBN 0-8356-0019-X, Quest). Theos Pub Hse.

Gregory, Robert L. Rays of Hope. LC 69-20332. 1969. 7.00 (ISBN 0-8022-2291-9). Philos Lib.

Hall, C. Margaret. Vital Life. LC 72-96976. 80p. 1973. 4.95 (ISBN 0-8158-0302-8). Chris Mass.

Hampshire, Stuart. Freedom of Mind & Other Essays. 1971. 17.00x (ISBN 0-691-07176-4). Princeton U Pr.

Harrington, Alan. The Immortalist. rev ed. LC 76-56899. 1977. pap. 5.95 (ISBN 0-89087-135-3). Celestial Arts.

Harrison, Richard & Montagna, William. Man. 2nd ed. (Illus., Orig.). 1973. pap. text ed. 10.95 (ISBN 0-13-548198-8). P-H.

Haughton, Rosemary. Transformation of Man. rev. ed. 1980. pap. 6.95 (ISBN 0-87243-127-4). Templegate.

Heard, Gerald. Five Ages of Man. LC 63-22142. 1960. 8.50 (ISBN 0-517-52775-8). Crown.

Hess, Wilford, et al. The Appearance of Man: Replenishment of the Earth, Vol. 2. 1979. perfect bdg. 8.95 (ISBN 0-88252-094-6). Paladin Hse.

Hocking, William E. Human Nature & Its Remaking. rev. ed. LC 75-3185. Repr. of 1929 ed. 37.00 (ISBN 0-404-59187-6). AMS Pr.

--What Man Can Make of Man. LC 75-3191. Repr. of 1942 ed. 18.00 (ISBN 0-404-59192-2). AMS Pr.

Hofstadter, Albert. Agony & Epitaph: Man, His Art & His Poetry. LC 75-104963. 1970. 7.50 (ISBN 0-8076-0544-1). Braziller.

Hollis, M. Models on Man. LC 76-49902. (Illus.). 1977. 32.95 (ISBN 0-521-21546-3); pap. 8.95x (ISBN 0-521-29181-X). Cambridge U Pr.

Horoscz, William. The Promise & Peril of Human Purpose. LC 71-93793. 350p. 1970. 15.00 (ISBN 0-87527-018-2). Fireside Bks.

Huxley, Julian S. The Individual in the Animal Kingdom. LC 13-6037. 1912. Repr. 19.00 (ISBN 0-403-01787-4). Scholarly.

--Man Stands Alone. LC 72-128265. (Essay Index Reprint Ser). 1941. 20.00 (ISBN 0-8369-1961-0). Arno.

Jacob, Stanley W., et al. Structure & Function in Man. 4th ed. LC 77-84673. (Illus.). 678p. 1978. text ed. 15.95 (ISBN 0-7216-5098-8); lab man. avail. (ISBN 0-7216-5099-6). Saunders.

Jantsch, Erich. Design for Evolution: Self-Organization & Planning in the Life of Human Systems. Laszlo, Ervin, ed. LC 74-77525. (International Library of Systems Theory & Philosophy Ser). 320p. 1975. 9.95 (ISBN 0-8076-0757-6); pap. 5.95 (ISBN 0-8076-0758-4). Braziller.

Johannes, Walter & Stein. Man & His Place in History. 1980. pap. 4.25x (ISBN 0-906492-35-1, Pub. by Kolisko Archives). St George Bk Serv.

Johnstone, Henry W., Jr. Problem of the Self. LC 71-84666. 1970. 9.95x (ISBN 0-271-00102-X). Pa St U Pr.

Kaelin, E. F. Man & Value: Essays in Honor of William H. Werkmeister. Florida State University, Dept. of Philosophy, ed. LC 80-27314. (A Florida State University Book). 1981. 19.25 (ISBN 0-686-31645-2, IS-00139, Pub. by U Pr of FL). Univ Microflims.

Kaelin, E. F., ed. Man & Value: Essays in Honor of William H. Werkmeister. (Imprint Ser). 1981. write for info. (ISBN 0-8130-0688-0). U Presses Fla.

Kainz, Howard P. The Philosophy of Man: A New Introduction to Some Perennial Issues. LC 79-14716. (Illus.). 206p. 1981. text ed. 18.95x (ISBN 0-8173-0019-8); pap. text ed. 8.95 (ISBN 0-8173-0066-X). U of Ala Pr.

Kaplan, Edward K. Michelet's Poetic Vision: A Romantic Philosophy of Nature, Man, & Woman. LC 76-45050. 1977. 12.50x (ISBN 0-87023-236-3). U of Mass Pr.

Kaufmann, Walter. Man's Lot. (Illus.). 1978. 60.00 (ISBN 0-07-033314-9, GB). McGraw.

Keller, Albert G. Man's Rough Road. 1932. 37.50x (ISBN 0-685-69831-9). Elliots Bks.

Kirkpatrick, Edwin A. Sciences of Man in the Making. facsimile ed. LC 75-156672. (Essay Index Reprints - International Library of Psychology, Philosophy, & Scientific Method). Repr. of 1932 ed. 20.00 (ISBN 0-8369-2282-4). Arno.

Klubertanz, George P. Philosophy of Human Nature. LC 53-6357. 1953. 38.50x (ISBN 0-89197-343-5). Irvington.

Knox, Malcolm. Action. LC 68-25993. (Muirhead Library of Philosophy). 1968. text ed. 8.25x (ISBN 0-04-170020-1). Humanities.

Korzybski, Alfred. Manhood of Humanity. 2nd ed. 326p. 1950. 9.00x (ISBN 0-937298-00-X). Inst Gen Semantics.

Kraus, Gerhard. Man in Decline. LC 76-23595. 1977. 14.95x (ISBN 0-312-51030-6). St Martin.

Krimsky, Joseph. The Wonder of Man. 1968. pap. 3.95 (ISBN 0-911336-21-4). Sci of Mind.

Kruger, Maximilian. The Maximal Problems of Philosophy. (Illus.). 137p. 1981. 43.45 (ISBN 0-89266-274-3). Am Classical Coll Pr.

Kurtz, Paul. Language & Human Nature. LC 73-108782. 264p. 1971. 17.50 (ISBN 0-87527-022-0). Fireside Bks.

La Barre, Weston. Human Animal. LC 54-12371. 1954. 12.00x (ISBN 0-226-46705-8). U of Chicago Pr.

--Human Animal. LC 54-12371. 1960. pap. 2.25 (ISBN 0-226-46706-6, P45, Phoen). U of Chicago Pr.

Langdon-Brown, Walter. Thus We Are Men. facs. ed. LC 79-86768. (Essay Index Reprint Ser). 1938. 18.00 (ISBN 0-8369-1148-2). Arno.

Laszlo, Ervin. The Inner Limits of Mankind: Heretical Reflections on Today's Values, Culture & Politics. LC 77-30732. 1978. text ed. 21.00 (ISBN 0-08-023013-X); pap. text ed. 9.75 (ISBN 0-08-023012-1). Pergamon.

Leary, Daniel J. Voices of Convergence. 1969. 4.95 (ISBN 0-685-07673-3, 80394). Glencoe.

Lewis, H. D. Elusive Mind. (Muirhead Library of Philosophy). 1969. text ed. 26.00x (ISBN 0-00-430013-0). Humanities.

Lewis, John. Uniqueness of Man. 1974. pap. 7.95x (ISBN 0-8464-0948-8). Beekman Pubs.

Lewis, John & Towers, Bernard. Naked Ape or Homo Sapiens: A Reply to Desmond Morris. 2nd ed. (Teilhard Study Library). 1972. text ed. 6.25x (ISBN 0-900391-21-9). Humanities.

Loos, Amandus W., ed. Nature of Man. facs. ed. LC 69-18930. (Essay Index Reprint Ser). 1950. 12.00 (ISBN 0-8369-1042-7). Arno.

McKern, Sharon S. The Many Faces of Man. (Illus.). 192p. (gr. 5-12). 1972. PLB 7.92 (ISBN 0-688-50062-5). Lothrop.

Marias, Julian. Metaphysical Anthropology: The Empirical Structure of Human Life. Lopez-Morillas, Frances M., tr. LC 78-127386. 1971. 15.75x (ISBN 0-271-01139-4). Pa St U Pr.

Maritain, Jacques. Person & the Common Good. 1966. pap. 2.45x (ISBN 0-268-00204-5). U of Notre Dame Pr.

Matson, Floyd W. The Idea of Man. 1976. 8.95 (ISBN 0-440-04038-8). Delacorte.

Mayer, Milton. The Nature of the Beast. Gustafson, W. Eric, ed. LC 74-21243. 376p. 1975. 12.50x (ISBN 0-87023-176-6). U of Mass Pr.

Mead, Margaret. Male & Female: A Study of the Sexes in a Changing World. LC 77-22027. 1977. Repr. of 1949 ed. lib. bdg. 30.75x (ISBN 0-8371-9781-3, MEMAF). Greenwood.

Miller, Benjamin F., et al. Masculinity & Femininity. LC 75-134861. (Illus.). 120p. (gr. 7 up). 1971. pap. text ed. 4.23 (ISBN 0-395-03243-1, 2-37390); instructor's manual 1.17 (ISBN 0-395-11210-9). HM.

Montagu, Ashley. The Biosocial Nature of Man. LC 72-11331. 123p. 1973. Repr. of 1956 ed. lib. bdg. 15.00 (ISBN 0-8371-6658-6, MOBN). Greenwood.

--Culture & the Evolution of Man. (Illus., Orig.). 1962. pap. 4.95 (ISBN 0-19-500701-8, GB88, GB). Oxford U Pr.

Mooney, Tom. The Early History of a Purpose Machine. 1976. 5.95 (ISBN 0-9601240-1-2); pap. 2.95 (ISBN 0-9601240-2-0). Mooney.

Morgan, George W. Human Predicament: Dissolution & Wholeness. LC 68-23791. 360p. 1971. Repr. of 1968 ed. text ed. 15.00x (ISBN 0-87057-111-7, Pub. by Brown U Pr). U Pr of New Eng.

Munro, Donald J. The Concept of Man in Early China. LC 68-21288. 1969. 12.50x (ISBN 0-8047-0682-4); pap. 3.95 (ISBN 0-8047-0829-0, SP130). Stanford U Pr.

Nasr, Seyyed H. Man & Nature. (Mandala Books). 1976. pap. 4.50 (ISBN 0-04-109013-6). Allen Unwin.

Neitzsche, Friedrich. The Gay Science. Kauffmann, Walter, tr. 1974. pap. 3.95 (ISBN 0-394-71985-9, Vin). Random.

Nero, Lee. Man & the Cycle of Prophecy. pap. 4.95 (ISBN 0-910122-50-4). Amherst Pr.

North, Gloria. Twentieth Century Man. 16p. 1979. pap. 1.00 (ISBN 0-686-27736-8). Samisdat.

Noyes, Charles R. Economic Man in Relation to His Natural Environment, 2 Vols. LC 48-7550. 1948. 27.50x (ISBN 0-231-01646-8). Columbia U Pr.

Ong, Walter J. Fighting for Life: Contest, Sexuality, & Consciousness. LC 80-66968. (Illus.). 240p. 1981. 14.95 (ISBN 0-8014-1342-7). Cornell U Pr.

Pearson, Harry. Livelihood of Man. Polany, Karl, ed. 1977. 27.50 (ISBN 0-12-548150-0). Acad Pr.

Percival, Harold W. Democracy Is Self-Government. LC 52-30629. 1952. 3.95 (ISBN 0-911650-05-9). Word Foun.

Petacchi, Donald. Work for Being in the Machine Age. LC 80-82646. 80p. 1980. 12.50 (ISBN 0-8022-2376-1). Philos Lib.

Peterson, Forrest H. Philosophy of Man & Society. LC 76-136014. 1970. 8.50 (ISBN 0-8022-2043-6). Philos Lib.

Pico Della Mirandola, Giovanni. On the Dignity of Man. Wallis, Charles G., et al, trs. Bd. with On Being & Unity; Heptaplus. LC 65-26540. 1965. pap. 5.50 (ISBN 0-672-60483-3, LLA227). Bobbs.

--Oration on the Dignity of Man. Caponigri, A. Robert, tr. 1956. pap. 1.95 (ISBN 0-89526-925-2). Regnery-Gateway.

Poh, Caroline & Country Beautiful Editors. The Life of Man. LC 73-79615. (Illus.). 192p. 1973. 12.95 (ISBN 0-87294-043-8). Country Beautiful.

Rauch, Friedrich. Psychology; or, a View of the Human Soul, Including Anthropology. LC 74-22335. (Hist. of Psych. Ser.). 1975. 42.00x (ISBN 0-8201-1142-2). Schol Facsimiles.

Reade, Winwood. The Martyrdom of Man. 1977. Repr. of 1926 ed. lib. bdg. 35.00 (ISBN 0-8492-2317-2). R West.

Rensch, Bernhard. Homo Sapiens: From Man to DemiGod. LC 72-80482. 1972. 17.50x (ISBN 0-231-03683-3). Columbia U Pr.

Rhinelander, Philip H. Is Man Incomprehensible to Man? (Illus.). 1974. text ed. 10.95x (ISBN 0-7167-0765-9); pap. text ed. 5.95x (ISBN 0-7167-0764-0). W H Freeman.

Riezler, Kurt. Man, Mutable & Immutable: The Fundamental Structure of Social Life. LC 74-33747. 365p. 1975. Repr. of 1950 ed. lib. bdg. 19.75x (ISBN 0-8371-7979-3, RIMM). Greenwood.

Robert, Charles, ed. Manipulated Man: The Power of Man Over Man, Its Risks & Its Limits. European Studies. Strasbourg, September 24-29, 1973. Frank, C. P., tr. LC 77-24330. (Pittsburgh Theological Monographs: No. 16). 1977. pap. 7.85 (ISBN 0-915138-21-2). Pickwick.

Robinson, Lytle W. Edward Cayce's Story of the Origin & Destiny of Man. 208p. 20.00x (ISBN 0-85435-311-9, Pub. by Spearman England). State Mutual Bk.

Romeo, Ligi. Ecce Homo! A Lexicon of Man. xv, 163p. 1979. 16.00 (ISBN 90-272-2006-9). Benjamins North Am.

Romero, Francisco. Theory of Man. Cooper, William F., tr. 1965. 28.00x (ISBN 0-520-01087-6). U of Cal Pr.

Roslansky, J. Uniqueness of Man. LC 69-18385. (Nobel Conference Lectures Ser.). 9.50x (ISBN 0-8303-0092-9, Acad Edns). Fleet.

Roubiczek, Paul. Misinterpretation of Man: A Study of European Thought in the 19th Century. LC 67-27641. Repr. of 1947 ed. 12.50 (ISBN 0-8046-0394-4). Kennikat.

Rousseau, Jean-Jacques. L' Hommes. Khodoss, Florence, ed. 160p. 1971. 14.95 (ISBN 0-686-55349-7). French & Eur.

Runes, Dagobert D. On the Nature of Man. 1956. 3.00 (ISBN 0-8022-1445-2). Philos Lib.

Russell, Bertrand. Diccionario del Hombre Contemporaneo. (Span.). pap. 17.50 (ISBN 0-686-56655-6). French & Eur.

Sands, Lionel. Natural Man 40,000 B.C. & 4,000 A.D. 1978. 6.95 (ISBN 0-533-03091-9). Vantage.

Scheler, Max. Man's Place in Nature. Meyerhoff, Hans, tr. 605p. 1962. pap. 4.25 (ISBN 0-374-50252-8, N231). FS&G.

Schreiner, Olive. From Man to Man: Or Perhaps Only. Repr. of 1927 ed. 34.50 (ISBN 0-384-54278-6). Johnson Repr.

Sears, Robert R. & Feldman, S. Shirley, eds. The Seven Ages of Man: A Survey of Human Development. LC 73-12029. 155p. 1973. pap. 5.50 (ISBN 0-913232-08-4). W Kaufmann.

Seligman, Herbert J. Race Against Man. Repr. of 1939 ed. 20.00 (ISBN 0-8492-9969-1). R West.

Sheldon, William. Atlas of Men: A Guide for Somatotyping the Adult Male of All Ages. 1970. Repr. of 1954 ed. 24.00 (ISBN 0-02-852160-9). Hafner.

Sherrington, Charles S. Man on His Nature. 1951. 39.95 (ISBN 0-521-06436-8); pap. 11.95x (ISBN 0-521-09203-5). Cambridge U Pr.

Sidi Ali Al-Jamal Of Fez. The Meaning of Man. Abd Al-Kabir Al Munawarra, ed. Aisha Abd Ar-Rahman At-Tarjumana, tr. from Arabic. Orig. Title: The Foundations of the Science of Knowledge. (Illus.). 455p. (Orig.). 1977. 20.00 (ISBN 0-9504446-6-9); pap. 12.00 (ISBN 0-9504446-5-0). Iqra.

Simmons, James R. Quest for Ethics. LC 62-15036. 1962. 2.75 (ISBN 0-8022-1573-4). Philos Lib.

Smith, Elva B. A Long Look at Man: Who Is He? What Is He? Where Is He Going? 1981. 3.50 (ISBN 0-8059-2693-3). Dorrance.

Smith, Grafton E. The Evolution of Man: Essays. 2nd ed. LC 77-86438. Repr. of 1927 ed. 18.50 (ISBN 0-404-16677-6). AMS Pr.

Snell, Sr. Roberta. The Nature of Man in St. Thomas Aquinas Compared with the Nature of Man in American Sociology. 35.00 (ISBN 0-8490-0715-1). Gordon Pr.

Spengler, Oswald. Man & Technics: A Contribution to a Philosophy of Life. Atkinson, Charles F., tr. from Ger. LC 76-7913. 1976. Repr. of 1932 ed. lib. bdg. 15.00 (ISBN 0-8371-8875-X, SPMT). Greenwood.

Spuhler, James N., ed. The Evolution of Man's Capacity for Culture. LC 59-10223. (Waynebooks Ser: No. 17). 1959. pap. text ed. 3.95x (ISBN 0-8143-1114-8). Wayne St U Pr.

Stevenson, Leslie. Seven Theories of Human Nature. 1974. text ed. 8.95 (ISBN 0-19-875033-1); pap. text ed. 3.95x (ISBN 0-19-875034-X). Oxford U Pr.

Stulman, J. & Laszlo, E. Emergent Man. new ed. LC 72-188124. (World Institute Creative Findings Ser.). 196p. 1973. 26.50x (ISBN 0-677-14930-1). Gordon.

Tarneja, Sukh R. Nature, Spirituality & Science. 240p. 1980. text ed. 27.50x (ISBN 0-7069-1203-9, Pub by Vikas India). Advent NY.

Tchurmin, Avrhum Y. Meditations from an Exploration of the Ultimate Mysteries. LC 72-85932. 110p. 1972. 3.95 (ISBN 0-8158-0295-1). Chris Mass.

Teilhard De Chardin, Pierre. Place De L'homme Dans la Nature. (Coll. le monde en 10-18). 1963. pap. 3.95 (ISBN 0-685-11497-X). French & Eur.

Twain, Mark. What Is Man? & Other Philosophical Writings. Baender, Paul, ed. & intro. by. LC 78-104109. (Mark Twain Papers Ser.: Vol. 1). 1973. 24.95 (ISBN 0-520-01621-1). U of Cal Pr.

Von Hildebrand, Dietrich. The Role of Human Love. 1978. 0.65 (ISBN 0-8199-0719-7). Franciscan Herald.

Wallimann, Isidor. Estrangement: Marx's Conception of Human Nature & the Division of Labor. LC 80-929. (Contributions in Philosophy: No. 16). xxiv, 195p. 1981. lib. bdg. 29.95 (ISBN 0-313-22096-4, WAE/). Greenwood.

Weiss, Paul. Beyond All Appearances. LC 74-5484. 413p. 1974. 18.95x (ISBN 0-8093-0617-4). S Ill U Pr.

Wells, Calvin. Man in His World. (Illus.). 187p. 1971. 9.50x (ISBN 0-8426-1589-X). Verry.

Wells, Herbert G. Fate of Man. LC 70-105049. (Essay Index Reprint Ser). 1939. 17.00 (ISBN 0-8369-1487-2). Arno.

White, Alan R., ed. Philosophy of Action. (Oxford Readings in Philosophy Ser). 1968. pap. text ed. 5.95x (ISBN 0-19-875006-4). Oxford U Pr.

Williams, Oliver P. & Adrian, Charles R. Four Cities: A Study in Comparative Policy Making. LC 63-7853. 1963. 10.00x (ISBN 0-8122-7381-8). U of Pa Pr.

Wilson, Edward O. On Human Nature. LC 78-17675. 1978. 12.50 (ISBN 0-674-63441-1). Harvard U Pr.

Wilson, Gordon A. The Drama of the Past. 1979. 15.00x (ISBN 0-87291-128-4). Coronado Pr.

Winkler, Franz E. Man: The Bridge Between Two Worlds. LC 60-5301. 268p. 1975. pap. 4.95 (ISBN 0-914614-07-X). Waldorf Pr.

The Works of Aristotle: The Famous Philosopher. LC 73-20613. (Sex, Marriage & Society Ser.). (Illus.). 268p. 1974. Repr. 14.00x (ISBN 0-405-05792-X). Arno.

Zdravomyslov, A. G., et al, eds. Man & His Work. Dunn, Stephen P., tr. LC 72-77457. 1970. 20.00 (ISBN 0-87332-026-3). M E Sharpe.

MAN-ATTITUDE AND MOVEMENT

see also Posture

Goldberg, Herb. The New Male: From Self-Destruction to Self Care. LC 79-13197. 1979. 10.95 (ISBN 0-688-03526-4). Morrow.

Gosnell, Jan. Shape Makes the Man. LC 78-6830. (Illus.). 1979. pap. 3.95 (ISBN 0-88289-195-2). Pelican.

Langworthy, Orthello R. The Sensory Control of Posture & Movement. LC 79-125297. 129p. 1970. 10.25 (ISBN 0-683-04872-4). Krieger.

Reynolds, Edward. Evolution of the Human Pelvis in Relation to the Mechanics of the Erect Posture. 1931. pap. 5.00 (ISBN 0-527-01222-X). Kraus Repr.

Scott, M. Gladys. Analysis of Human Motion: A Textbook in Kinesiology. 2nd ed. LC 63-13839. (Illus.). 1963. 18.95x (ISBN 0-89197-023-1); pap. text ed. 9.50x (ISBN 0-89197-024-X). Irvington.

Tel Ngandong Fossil Hominids: A Comparative Study of a Far Eastern Homo Erectus Group. LC 80-50035. (Publications in Anthropology: No. 78). 1980. pap. 13.50 (ISBN 0-686-29094-1). Yale U Anthro.

MAN-CONSTITUTION
see also Heredity, Human; Temperament
Brierley, John. A Natural History of Man. 184p. 1970. 10.00 (ISBN 0-8386-7819-X). Fairleigh Dickinson.
Goldenberg, Naomi R. Changing of the Gods: Feminism & the End of Traditional Religions. LC 78-19602. 1979. 9.95 (ISBN 0-8070-1110-X); pap. 5.95 (ISBN 0-8070-1111-8, BP600). Beacon Pr.
Kretschmer, Ernst. Physique & Character: An Investigation of the Nature of Constitution and of the Theory of Temperament. LC 73-119165. Repr. of 1936 ed. 16.50x (ISBN 0-8154-0332-1). Cooper Sq.
Lessa, W. A. Appraisal of Constitutional Typologies. LC 44-4905. 1943. pap. 6.00 (ISBN 0-527-00561-4). Kraus Repr.
Parnell, Richard W. Behavior & Physique: An Introduction to Practical & Applied Somatometry. LC 73-20503. (Illus.). 1978. Repr. of 1958 ed. lib. bdg. 17.25x (ISBN 0-8371-7327-2, PABE). Greenwood.

MAN-ECONOMIC VALUE
see Human Capital

MAN-FOOD HABITS
see Food Habits

MAN-INFLUENCE OF CLIMATE
see also Climatology, Medical
Auliciems, Andris. Atmospheric Environment: A Study of Thermal Comfort & Performance. LC 72-80647. (Illus.). 200p. 1972. pap. 6.50x (ISBN 0-8020-3291-5). U of Toronto Pr.
Brooks, Charles E. Climate in Everyday Life. LC 75-36507. (Illus.). 314p. 1976. Repr. of 1950 ed. lib. bdg. 17.50x (ISBN 0-8371-8647-1, BRCEL). Greenwood.
Hadlow, Leonard. Climate, Vegetation & Man. 6.00 (ISBN 0-685-28346-1). Philos Lib.
Halacy, D. S., Jr. Ice or Fire? Surviving Climatic Change. LC 78-2139. 1978. 10.95 (ISBN 0-06-011778-8, HarpT). Har-Row.
Huntington, Ellsworth. Civilization & Climate. 3rd ed. LC 78-143891. (Illus.). 1971. Repr. of 1925 ed. 27.50 (ISBN 0-208-01159-5, Archon). Shoe String.
--World-Power & Evolution. LC 73-14157. (Perspectives in Social Inquiry Ser.). 292p. 1974. Repr. 15.00x (ISBN 0-405-05503-X). Arno.
Kavanagh, P. J. People & Weather. 1980. pap. 5.95 (ISBN 0-7145-3666-0). Riverrun NY.
Petersen, William F. Man, Weather, Sun. (Illus.). 496p. 1948. photocopy ed. spiral 49.75 (ISBN 0-398-04392-2). C C Thomas.
Weather, Climate & Human Settlements. (Special Environmental Report: No. 7). (Illus.). 45p. 1977. pap. 12.00 (ISBN 92-63-10448-4, WMO). Unipub.

MAN-INFLUENCE OF ENVIRONMENT
see also Altitude, Influence of; Anthropo-Geography; Color of Man; Environmental Health; Genetic Psychology; Regionalism; Religion and Geography; Weather-Mental and Physiological Effects; Weightlessness
Adler, Cy A. Ecological Fantasies. 352p. 1974. pap. 2.95 (ISBN 0-440-53209-4, Delta). Dell.
Alexander, Theron. Human Development in an Urban Age. (Illus.). 384p. 1973. ref. ed. 16.95 (ISBN 0-13-444786-7). P-H.
Altman, Ifrwin, et al, eds. Human Behavior & Environment - Advances in Theory & Research, Vol. 4: Environment & Culture. (Illus.). 368p. 1980. 25.00 (ISBN 0-306-40367-6, Plenum Pr). Plenum Pub.
Altman, Irwin. The Environment & Social Behavior. LC 75-14724. (Illus.). 1975. text ed. 14.95 (ISBN 0-8185-0168-5). Brooks-Cole.
Altman, Irwin & Wehlwill, J. F., eds. Human Behavior & Environment: Advances in Theory & Research, Vol. 1. (Illus.). 1976. 25.00 (ISBN 0-306-33301-5, Plenum Pr). Plenum Pub.
Altman, Irwin & Wohlwill, J. F., eds. Human Behavior & Environment: Advances in Theory & Research, Vol. 2. (Illus.). 358p. 1977. 18.95 (ISBN 0-306-33302-3, Plenum Pr). Plenum Pub.
Altman, Irwin, et al, eds. Transportation & Behavior. (Human Behavior & Environment - Advances in Theory & Research Ser.: Vol. 5). 290p. 1981. text ed. price not set (ISBN 0-306-40773-6, Plenum Pr). Plenum Pub.
American Academy of Political & Social Science, Annual Meeting, 83rd. The Environment & the Quality of Life: A World View: Proceedings. Wolfgang, Marvin E. & Ginsberg, Ralph B., eds. LC 79-50266. (Annals: No. 444). 1979. 7.50 (ISBN 0-87761-240-4); pap. 6.00 (ISBN 0-87761-241-2). Am Acad Pol Soc Sci.
American Environmental Studies, 42 Vols. 1971. Repr. Set. 725.00 (ISBN 0-405-02650-1). Arno.
Ashley Montague. Man, His First Two Million Years. pap. 2.95 (ISBN 0-440-55144-7, Delta). Dell.
Baker, P. T., ed. The Biology of High-Altitude Peoples. LC 76-50311. (International Biological Programme Ser.: No. 14). (Illus.). 1978. 68.00 (ISBN 0-521-21523-4). Cambridge U Pr.
Bamborough, J. B. Little World of Man: Elizabethan Psychological Theory. LC 72-191665. Repr. of 1952 ed. lib. bdg. 12.50 (ISBN 0-8414-0791-6). Folcroft.
Barker, Roger G. Ecological Psychology: Concepts & Methods for Studying the Environment of Human Behavior. LC 68-21287. 1968. 10.00x (ISBN 0-8047-0658-1). Stanford U Pr.
Barker, Roger G., et al. Habitats, Enviroments, & Human Behavior: Studies in Ecological Psychology & Eco-Behavioral Science. LC 77-82912. (Social & Behavioral Science Ser). 1978. text ed. 17.95x (ISBN 0-87589-356-2). Jossey-Bass.
Bell, Paul A., et al. Environmental Psychology. LC 77-84684. (Illus.). 1978. text ed. 16.95 (ISBN 0-7216-1706-9). Saunders.
Blixt, Raymons & Provost, Norman. Environment: Lifeland or Wasteland. (Illus.). 114p. (Orig.). 1972. pap. 3.25 (ISBN 0-88489-043-0). St Marys.
Brody, Erness B. & Brody, Nathan, eds. Intelligence: Nature, Determinants, & Consequences. 1976. 24.00 (ISBN 0-12-134250-6). Acad Pr.
Buchanan, R. H., et al. Man & His Habitat: Essays Presented to Emyr Estyn Evans. 1971. 26.50 (ISBN 0-7100-6908-1). Routledge & Kegan.
Burnham, P. C. & Allen, R. F., eds. Social & Ecological Systems. (Social Anthropologists Monographs Ser.). 1979. 24.00 (ISBN 0-12-146050-9). Acad Pr.
Calabrese, Edward J. Pollutants & High Risk Groups: The Biological Basis of Increased Human Susceptibility to Environmental & Occupational Pollutants. LC 77-13957. (Environmental Science & Technology: Wiley-Interscience Series of Texts & Monographs). 1977. 27.00 (ISBN 0-471-02940-8, Pub. by Wiley-Inerscience). Wiley.
Capstick, Peter H. Maneaters. 200p. 1981. 17.95 (ISBN 0-8227-3023-5). Petersen Pub.
Carson, D. H., ed. Man-Environment Interactions: Evaluations & Applications, 3 vols. LC 75-17820. (Community Development Ser: Vol. 22). 1466p. 1975. Set. 70.00 (ISBN 0-87933-207-7). Hutchinson Ross.
Coelho, George V., et al, eds. Uprooting & Development--Dilemmas of Coping with Modernization. (Current Topics in Mental Health Ser.). 500p. 1980. 27.50 (ISBN 0-306-40509-1, Plenum Pr). Plenum Pub.
Conklin, Edwin G. Heredity & Environment in the Development of Men. 6th rev. ed. (Illus.). 1930. 23.00 (ISBN 0-384-09755-3). Johnson Repr.
Cooke, Roderic C. Fungi, Man & His Environment. LC 77-1460. (Illus.). 144p. 1978. text ed. 20.00x (ISBN 0-582-46034-4); pap. text ed. 7.50x (ISBN 0-582-44262-1). Longman.
Cravens, Hamilton. Triumph of Evolution: American Scientists & the Heredity-Environment Controversy, 1900-1941. LC 77-20570. (Illus.). 1978. 22.00x (ISBN 0-8122-7744-9). U of Pa Pr.
Cronin, Ned, ed. EIS Annual Review, Vol. 1. LC 78-73101. (Illus.). 1978. text ed. 25.00 (ISBN 0-87815-024-2). Info Resources.
Da Silva, Armando. Tai Yu Shan: Traditional Ecological Adoptation in a South Chinese Island, No. 32. (Asian Folklore & Social Life Monograph). 1972. 4.60 (ISBN 0-89986-032-X). E Langstaff.
Davey, Peter. Man & Environment in the Isle of Man. 1978. 60.00x (ISBN 0-86054-034-0, Pub. by BAR). State Mutual Bk.
Dubos, Rene. A God Within. LC 76-37224. 1972. text ed. 24.50x (ISBN 0-684-12768-7). Irvington.
--Man Adapting. enl. ed. LC 80-16492. (Silliman Lectures Ser.). (Illus.). 527p. 1980. pap. 7.95 (ISBN 0-300-02581-5, Y-197). Yale U Pr.
--So Human an Animal. LC 68-27794. 1968. pap. 3.95 (ISBN 0-684-71753-0, SL195, ScribT). Scribner.
Edholm, O. G. & Bacharach, A. L., eds. Physiology of Human Survival. 1966. 82.00 (ISBN 0-12-231550-2). Acad Pr.
Eisenbud, Merril. Environment, Technology & Health: Human Ecology in Historical Perspective. LC 78-55062. 1978. 25.00 (ISBN 0-8147-2154-0); pap. 12.50x (ISBN 0-8147-2160-5). NYU Pr.
Ekirch, Arthur A., Jr. Man & Nature in America. LC 63-14925. xvi, 231p. 1973. pap. 4.75 (ISBN 0-8032-5785-6, BB 574, Bison). U of Nebr Pr.
Environment & Art in Catholic Worship. 1978. pap. 3.95 (ISBN 0-686-11135-4, V563). US Catholic.
The Environment & You. (How & Why Wonder Books Ser.). (gr. 4-6). pap. 0.79 (ISBN 0-448-05071-4). Wonder.
Ewald, William R., Jr., ed. Environment & Policy: The Next Fifty Years. LC 68-27344. 476p. 1968. pap. 4.95x (ISBN 0-253-12266-X). Ind U Pr.
--Environment for Man: The Next Fifty Years. LC 67-14215. (Midland Bks.: No. 102). (Illus.). 320p. 1967. pap. 2.95x (ISBN 0-253-20102-0). Ind U Pr.
Farber, Seymour M. & Wilson, Roger H. The Air We Breathe: A Study of Man & His Environment. (Illus.). 432p. 1961. ed. spiral bdg. 35.50photocopy (ISBN 0-398-00544-3). C C Thomas.
Folinsbee, Lawrence J., et al, eds. Environmental Stress: Individual Human Adaptations. 1978. 23.00 (ISBN 0-12-261350-3). Acad Pr.
Geller, E. Scott, et al. Perserving the Environment: New Strategies for Behavior Change. (Pergamon General Psychology Ser.: No. 102). (Illus.). 300p. 1982. 30.00 (ISBN 0-08-024615-X); pap. 9.95 (ISBN 0-08-024614-1). Pergamon.
Gerasimov, I. P., ed. Man Society & the Environment. 340p. 1975. 4.10 (ISBN 0-686-74562-0, Pub. by Progress Pubs Russia). Imported Pubns.
Glass, David C., ed. Environmental Influences. LC 68-56103. (Illus.). 1969. 11.00 (ISBN 0-87470-012-4). Rockefeller.
Gould, Richard A., ed. Explorations in Ethnoarchaeology. LC 77-89438. (School of American Research Advanced Seminar Ser). (Illus.). 329p. 1978. 20.00x (ISBN 0-8263-0454-0); pap. 9.95x (ISBN 0-8263-0462-1). U of NM Pr.
Gove, Walter R. & Carpenter, G. Russell. The Fundamental Connection Between Nature & Nurture: A Review of the Evidence. LC 80-8961. 1981. price not set (ISBN 0-669-04483-0). Lexington Bks.
Grossin, William. Les Temps de la Vie Quotidienne. (Interaction, l'Homme et Son Environment Social Ser.: No. 3). 416p. (Fr.). 1975. pap. text ed. 41.25x (ISBN 90-2797-785-2). Mouton.
Guidelines for Field Studies in Environmental Perception. (MAB Technical Notes: No. 5). 1978. pap. 9.25 (ISBN 92-3-101483-8, U783, UNESCO). Unipub.
Hadlow, Leonard. Climate, Vegetation & Man. 6.00 (ISBN 0-685-28346-1). Philos Lib.
Halsey, A. H., ed. Heredity & Environment. LC 77-2530. 1977. 13.95 (ISBN 0-02-913670-9). Free Pr.
Harris, Marvin. Cannibals & Kings: The Origins of Cultures. 1977. 10.00 (ISBN 0-394-40765-2). Random.
Huntington, Ellsworth. Mainsprings of Civilization. LC 72-4278. (World Affairs Ser.: National & International Viewpoints). 660p. 1972. Repr. of 1945 ed. 30.00 (ISBN 0-405-04572-7). Arno.
Jennings, Burgess H. & Murphy, John E. Interactions of Man & His Environment. LC 66-16371. 150p. 1966. 19.50 (ISBN 0-306-30234-9, Plenum Pr). Plenum Pub.
Jones, Michael. Finland, Daughter of the Sea. (Studies in Historical Geography). (Illus.). 1977. 19.50 (ISBN 0-208-01623-6, Archon). Shoe String.
Kiely, Margaret. Comparisons of Students of Teachers Colleges & Students of Liberal Arts Colleges. LC 72-176961. (Columbia University. Teachers College. Contributions to Education: No. 440). Repr. of 1931 ed. 17.50 (ISBN 0-404-55440-7). AMS Pr.
Klineberg, Otto. Negro Intelligence & Selective Migration. LC 74-12884. 66p. 1975. Repr. of 1935 ed. lib. bdg. 15.00x (ISBN 0-8371-7771-5, KLNI). Greenwood.
Koshuk, Ruth P. Social Influences Affecting the Behavior of Young Children. 1941. pap. 5.00 (ISBN 0-527-01518-0). Kraus Repr.
LeBlanc, Jacques. Man in the Cold. (American Lectures in Environmental Studies Ser.). (Illus.). 208p. 1975. 21.75 (ISBN 0-398-03429-X). C C Thomas.
Lee, Terence. Psychology & the Environment. (Essential Psychology Ser.). 1976. pap. 4.50x (ISBN 0-416-81920-6). Methuen Inc.
Leyburn, James G. Frontier Folkways. LC 79-122402. 1970. Repr. of 1935 ed. 19.50 (ISBN 0-208-00961-2, Archon). Shoe String.
Loehlin, John C. & Nichols, Robert C. Heredity, Environment & Personality: A Study of 850 Sets of Twins. LC 75-33794. 214p. 1976. 15.00x (ISBN 0-292-73003-9). U of Tex Pr.
Lotze, Hermann. Microcosmus: An Essay Concerning Man & His Relation to the World, 2 vols. facsimile ed. Hamilton, Elizabeth & Jones, E. E., trs. LC 76-169769. (Select Bibliographies Reprint Ser). Repr. of 1885 ed. Set. 70.00 (ISBN 0-8369-5989-2). Arno.
Lowenthal, David, et al. Environmental Perception & Behavior. LC 66-29233. (Research Papers Ser.: No. 109). 88p. 1967. pap. 8.00 (ISBN 0-89065-018-7). U Chicago Dept Geog.
McEvoy, James & Dietz, Thomas. Handbook for Environmental Planning: The Social Consequences of Environmental Change. LC 76-57239. 354p. 1977. 32.00 (ISBN 0-471-58389-8). Krieger.
McKenna, Harold, Jr. We Are the Targets: Environmental Impacts. (Student Scientist Ser.). (Illus.). (gr. 7-12). 1980. PLB 7.97 (ISBN 0-8239-0474-1). Rosen Pr.
Mehrabian, Albert. Public Places & Private Spaces: The Psychology of Work, Play, & Living Environments. LC 76-9341. 354p. 1980. pap. 5.95 (ISBN 0-686-61970-6). Basic.
Mehrabian, Albert & Russsell, James A. An Approach to Environmental Psychology. 240p. 1974. pap. 8.95x (ISBN 0-262-63071-0). MIT Pr.
Michelson, William H. Man & His Urban Environment: A Sociological Approach. rev. ed. 1976. 8.95 (ISBN 0-201-04726-8). A-W.
Moser, Leo J. The Technology Trap. LC 78-26034. 1979. 17.95x (ISBN 0-88229-419-9); pap. 8.95 (ISBN 0-88229-669-8). Nelson-Hall.
Murrell, K. F. Ergonomics: Man in His Working Environment. 496p. 1980. text ed. 19.95x (ISBN 0-412-21990-5, Pub. by Chapman & Hall England). Methuen Inc.
National Academy of Sciences, National Academy of Engineering. Man, Materials, & Environment. 252p. 1974. 15.50x (ISBN 0-262-14019-5); pap. 5.95x (ISBN 0-262-64013-9). MIT Pr.
Netting, Robert M. Balancing on an Alp: Ecological Change & Continuity in a Swiss Mountain Community. LC 81-358. (Illus.). 436p. Date not set. price not set (ISBN 0-521-23743-2); pap. price not set (ISBN 0-521-28197-0). Cambridge U Pr.
Newman, Horatio H., et al. Twins: A Study of Heredity & Environment. LC 37-11639. (Illus.). 1966. 14.00x (ISBN 0-226-57706-6). U of Chicago Pr.
Norwood, Christopher. At Highest Risk: Environmental Hazards to Young & Unborn Children. LC 79-20053. 1980. 10.95 (ISBN 0-07-047453-2). McGraw.
Oliver, John E. Climate & Man's Environment: An Introduction to Applied Climatology. LC 73-5707. 517p. 1973. text ed. 24.95x (ISBN 0-471-65338-1). Wiley.
Organization for Economic Cooperation & Development. Environment Policies for the 1980's. 110p. (Orig.). 1980. pap. text ed. 9.00x (ISBN 92-64-12049-1, 9780021). OECD.
Parry, M. L. Climatic Change, Agriculture, & Settlement. (Studies in Historical Geography). 1978. 17.50 (ISBN 0-208-01722-4, Archon). Shoe String.
Peate, I. C., ed. Studies in Regional Consciousness & Environment: Essays Presented to H. J. Fleure. facs. ed. LC 68-26478. (Essay Index Reprint Ser). (Illus.). 1968. Repr. of 1930 ed. 18.00 (ISBN 0-8369-0917-8). Arno.
Poulton, E. C. Environment & Human Efficiency. (American Lectures in Living Chemistry Ser.). (Illus.). 336p. 1972. photocopy ed. spiral 21.75 (ISBN 0-398-01515-5). C C Thomas.
Prince Philip. The Environmental Revolution: Speeches on Conservation 1962-1977. LC 78-60776. 1979. 8.95 (ISBN 0-87951-088-9). Overlook Pr.
Reno, Edward A., Jr., ed. The New York Times Cumulative Subject & Personal Name Index: Environment Nineteen Sixty-Five to Nineteen Seventy-Five. 778p. 1978. 75.00 (ISBN 0-667-00606-0). Microfilming Corp.
Richardson, Norman W. & Stubbs, Thomas H. Evolution, Human Ecology, & Society. (Illus.). 256p. 1976. pap. 7.95 (ISBN 0-02-399660-9). Macmillan.
Ripley, William Z. The Races of Europe: A Sociological Study. (Illus.). Repr. of 1899 ed. 38.50 (ISBN 0-384-50930-4). Johnson Repr.
Rubin, Milton D., ed. Man in Systems. (Illus.). 508p. 1971. 72.75 (ISBN 0-677-14060-6). Gordon.
Saarinen, T. F. Perception of Environment. LC 72-94261. (CCG Resource Papers Ser.: No. 5). (Illus.). 1969. pap. text ed. 4.00 (ISBN 0-89291-052-6). Assn Am Geographers.
Scott, Adelin. Comparative Study of Responses of Children of Different Nationalities & Environments on Intelligence & Achievement Tests. LC 73-177807. (Columbia University. Teachers College. Contributions to Education: No. 367). Repr. of 1929 ed. 17.50 (ISBN 0-404-55367-2). AMS Pr.
Seamon, David. A Geography of the Life World: Movement, Rest & Encounter. 1979. 23.95x (ISBN 0-312-32257-7). St Martin.

Searles, Harold F. Nonhuman Environment in Normal Development & in Schizophrenia. LC 60-9579. (Monograph Ser. on Schizophrenia: No. 5). 1960. text ed. 22.50 (ISBN 0-8236-3660-7). Intl Univs Pr.
Semple, Ellen C. Influences of Geographic Environment on the Basis of Ratzel's System of Anthropo-Geography. LC 68-27087. (Illus.). 1968. Repr. of 1911 ed. 16.00 (ISBN 0-8462-1177-7). Russell.
Slater, E. C. Types, Levels-Irregularities of Response to a Nursery School Situation of 40 Children Observed with Special Reference to the Home Environment. 1939. pap. 9.00 (ISBN 0-527-01509-1). Kraus Repr.
Sloan, A. W. Man in Extreme Environments. (Environmental Studies Ser.). (Illus.). 144p. 1979. text ed. 13.75 (ISBN 0-398-03941-0). C C Thomas.
Snyder, Ernest E. Man and the Physical Universe. LC 75-30446. (Physical Science Ser.). 373p. 1976. text ed. 21.95 (ISBN 0-675-08631-0). Merrill.
Soyka, Fred & Edmonds, Alan. The Ion Effect. 1978. pap. 2.50 (ISBN 0-553-14388-3). Bantam.
Steyaert, Thomas A. Biology: A Contemporary View. (Illus.). 512p. 1975. text ed. 18.50 (ISBN 0-07-061346-X, C); instructor's manual 2.95 (ISBN 0-07-061375-3). McGraw.
Suedfeld, Peter, et al, eds. The Behavioral Basis of Design: Bk. 2, Session Summaries & Papers. LC 76-11594. (Community Development Ser.: Vol. 36). (Illus.). 1977. 33.00 (ISBN 0-87933-293-X). Hutchinson Ross.
Suefeld, Peter & Russell, James A., eds. The Behavioral Basis of Design: Selected Papers, Bk. 1. LC 76-11594. (Community Development Ser.: Vol. 28). 1976. 33.00 (ISBN 0-87933-248-4). Hutchinson Ross.
Sulman, Felix G. The Effect of Air Ionization, Electric Fields, Atmospherics & Other Electric Phenomena on Man & Animal. (Environmental Studies Ser.). (Illus.). 424p. 1980. text ed. 24.75 (ISBN 0-398-03929-1); pap. text ed. 18.75 (ISBN 0-398-03930-5). C C Thomas.
Sydenstricker, Edgar. Health & Environment. LC 75-180593. (Medicine & Society in America Ser). 234p. 1972. Repr. of 1933 ed. 15.00 (ISBN 0-405-03975-1). Arno.
Technical Meeting of the Institute of Environment Sciences, 25th Annual, Seattle, Washington, April 1979. Learning to Use Our Environment: Proceedings. (Illus.). 1979. pap. text ed. 25.00 (ISBN 0-915414-19-8). Inst Environ Sci.
Tharp, Roland & Wetzel, Ralph. Behavior Modification in the Natural Environment. LC 75-91418. 1969. 17.95 (ISBN 0-12-686050-5). Acad Pr.
Thirgood, J. V. Man & the Mediterranean Forest. 1981. write for info. (ISBN 0-12-687250-3). Acad Pr.
Thoday, J. M. & Parkes, A. S., eds. Genetic & Environmental Influences on Behavior. LC 68-54003. (Eugenics Society Symposia Ser.: Vol. 4). 210p. 1969. 29.50 (ISBN 0-306-38704-2, Plenum Pr). Plenum Pub.
Thomas, Franklin. The Environmental Basis of Society. Repr. of 1925 ed. 15.50 (ISBN 0-384-60170-7). Johnson Repr.
Ting, Irwin, ed. Man in the Natural World. 1973. 29.50x (ISBN 0-8422-5135-9); pap. text ed. 9.95x (ISBN 0-8422-0315-X). Irvington.
Toepfer, Caroline T., et al. Environmental Psychology: Selected Readings. LC 72-86362. 290p. 1972. 28.00x (ISBN 0-8422-5001-8); pap. text ed. 8.95x (ISBN 0-8422-0234-X). Irvington.
Tuan, Yi-Fu. Space & Place: The Perspective of Experience. (Illus., LC 77-072910). 1977. 17.50x (ISBN 0-8166-0808-3); pap. 8.95 (ISBN 0-8166-0884-9). U of Minn Pr.
Van Alstyne, Dorothy. The Environment of Three-Year Old Children: Factors Related to Intelligence & Vocabulary Tests. LC 77-177682. (Columbia University. Teachers College. Contributions to Education: No. 366). Repr. of 1929 ed. 17.50 (ISBN 0-404-55366-4). AMS Pr.
Vayda, Andrew P., ed. Environment & Cultural Behavior: Ecological Studies in Cultural Anthropology. (Texas Press Sourcebooks in Anthropology: No. 8). 503p. 1976. pap. 8.95x (ISBN 0-292-72019-X). U of Tex Pr.
Vickery, Robert L., Jr. Anthrophysical Form: Two Families & Their Neighborhood Environments. LC 73-183896. 1973. 9.95x (ISBN 0-8139-0393-9). U Pr of Va.
Viollet-Le-Duc, Eugene E. Habitations of Man in All Ages. Bucknall, Benjamin, tr. LC 74-146922. 1971. Repr. of 1876 ed. 39.00 (ISBN 0-8103-3787-8). Gale.
Ward, Robert D. Climate, Considered Especially in Relation to Man. 2nd rev. ed. LC 77-10242. Repr. of 1918 ed. 30.00 (ISBN 0-404-16220-7). AMS Pr.
Watts, Elizabeth, et al. Biosocial Interrelations in Population Adaptation. (Mouton World Anthropology Ser.). (Illus.). 432p. 1975. 33.50x (ISBN 0-202-90004-5). Beresford Bk Serv.
The Way Things Work Book of Nature. 1980. 17.50 (ISBN 0-671-22455-7). S&S.
Whitbeck, Ray H. & Thomas, Olive J. Geographic Factor. LC 73-113303. 1970. Repr. of 1932 ed. 16.50 (ISBN 0-8046-1331-1). Kennikat.
White, Gilbert F. & Haas, J. Eugene. Assessment of Research on Natural Hazards. LC 75-2058. (Environmental Studies Ser.). (Illus.). 487p. 1975. text ed. 26.50x (ISBN 0-262-23071-2). MIT Pr.
White, Willo P., ed. Resources in Environment & Behavior. LC 78-16100. 1979. pap. 10.00x (ISBN 0-912704-06-3). Am Psychol.
Wicker, Allen W. Introduction to Ecological Psychology. Altman, Robert & Wrightsman, Lawrence S., eds. LC 78-10402. (Psychology of Environment & Behavior). (Illus.). 1979. pap. text ed. 8.95 (ISBN 0-8185-0284-3). Brooks-Cole.
Winkler, Franz E. Man: The Bridge Between Two Worlds. LC 80-82064. 268p. 1980. pap. 4.95 (ISBN 0-913098-32-9). Myrin Institute.
Wohlwill, J. F. & Weisman, G. D. The Physical Environment & Behavior: An Annotated Bibliography & Guide to the Literature. 474p. 1981. 45.00 (ISBN 0-306-40739-6, Plenum Pr). Plenum Pub.
Woodworth, Robert S. Heredity & Environment: A Critical Survey of Recently Published Material on Twins & Foster Children. LC 41-23998. 1941. pap. 2.25 (ISBN 0-527-03279-4). Kraus Repr.

MAN–INFLUENCE ON NATURE

see also Environmental Policy; Pollution

American Environmental Studies, 42 Vols. 1971. Repr. Set. 725.00 (ISBN 0-405-02650-1). Arno.
Anon. The Nature of the World and of Man. Newman, H. H., ed. 562p. 1981. Repr. of 1926 ed. lib. bdg. 50.00 (ISBN 0-89984-004-3). Century Bookbindery.
Appleyard, R. T., ed. Man & His Environment. (Octagon Lectures, 1969). 1970. pap. 6.50x (ISBN 0-85564-042-1, Pub. by U of W Austral Pr). Intl Schol Bk Serv.
Arbib, Robert S., Jr. Lord's Woods. LC 73-139373. 1971. 6.95 (ISBN 0-393-08639-9). Norton.
Ashby, Eric. Reconciling Man with the Environment. LC 77-91909. 1978. 7.95x (ISBN 0-8047-0986-6); pap. 2.95 (ISBN 0-8047-1041-4, SP-155). Stanford U Pr.
Bach, W., ed. Man's Impact on Climate. Pankrath, J. & Kellogg, W. (Developments in Atmospheric Science Ser.: Vol. 10). 1979. 58.75 (ISBN 0-444-41766-4). Elsevier.
Benarde, Melvin. Our Precarious Habitat. rev. ed. (Illus.). 384p. 1973. 8.25 (ISBN 0-393-06360-7); pap. 6.95x (ISBN 0-393-09372-7). Norton.
Bennett, Charles F., Jr. Man & Earth's Ecosystems: An Introduction to the Geography of Human Modification of the Earth. LC 75-22330. 352p. 1975. text ed. 22.50 (ISBN 0-471-06638-9). Wiley.
Beyer, Jan Erik. Aquatic Ecosystems: An Operational Research Approach. LC 79-57217. (Illus.). 316p. 1981. 20.00 (ISBN 0-295-95719-0). U of Wash Pr.
Borland, Hal. The History of Wildlife in America. Bourne, Russell & MacConomy, Alma D., eds. LC 75-15494. (Illus.). 208p. 1975. 14.95 (ISBN 0-912186-20-8). Natl Wildlife.
Carson, D. H., ed. Man-Environment Interactions: Evaluations & Applications, 3 vols. LC 75-17820. (Community Development Ser: Vol. 22). 1466p. 1975. Set. 70.00 (ISBN 0-87933-207-7). Hutchinson Ross.
Chigier, Norman A. Energy, Combustion & Environment. (Illus.). 689p. 1980. text ed. 35.95 (ISBN 0-07-010766-1, C). McGraw.
Cloudesley-Thompson, J. L. Man & the Biology of Arid Zones. LC 77-20663. (Contemporary Biology Ser). 1978. pap. 17.95 (ISBN 0-8391-1192-4). Univ Park.
Coleman, William. Carl Ernst Von Baer on the Study of Man & Nature. Cohen, I. Bernard, ed. LC 80-2105. (Development of Science Ser.). (Illus.). 1981. lib. bdg. 55.00x (ISBN 0-405-13870-9). Arno.
Commoner, Barry. Closing Circle. 1971. 12.50 (ISBN 0-394-42350-X). Knopf.
Cordell, Benjamin. The World Truth Bible. 304p. 1981. 12.50 (ISBN 0-682-49758-4). Exposition.
Dasmann, Raymond F. No Further Retreat: The Fight to Save Florida. LC 79-143780. 1971. 6.95 (ISBN 0-02-529600-0). Macmillan.
Disch, Robert, ed. Ecological Conscience: Values for Survival. LC 71-130009. 1970. pap. 2.45 (ISBN 0-13-222810-6, Spec). P-H.
Dobyns, Henry F. From Fire to Flood: Historic Human Destruction of Sonoran Desert Riverine Oases. (Anthropological Papers Ser.: No. 20). (Illus.). 222p. (Orig.). 1981. pap. 11.95 (ISBN 0-87919-092-2). Ballena Pr.
Eckholm, Erik P. Losing Ground: Environmental Stress & World Food Prospects. 223p. 1976. 7.95 (ISBN 0-393-06410-7); pap. text ed. 5.95x (ISBN 0-393-09167-8). Norton.
The Ecology of Man in the Tropical Environment. (Illus.). 1964. pap. 18.50x (ISBN 2-88032-054-2, IUCN36, IUCN). Unipub.
Effects of Human Activities on Global Climate. (Technical Note Ser: No. 156). 1978. pap. 10.00 (ISBN 92-63-10486-7, WMO 486, WMO). Unipub.
Ewald, William R., Jr., ed. Environment & Policy: The Next Fifty Years. LC 68-27344. 476p. 1968. pap. 4.95x (ISBN 0-253-12266-X). Ind U Pr.
Fleagle, Robert G., ed. Weather Modification: Science & Public Policy. LC 68-8511. (Public Policy Issues in Resource Management Ser.: Vol. 3). (Illus.). 158p. 1968. 11.50 (ISBN 0-295-78551-9). U of Wash Pr.
Fuller, R. Buckminster, et al. Approaching the Benign Environment. Littleton, Taylor, ed. LC 70-97770. (Franklin Lectures in the Sciences & Humanities I). 134p. 1970. 8.95x (ISBN 0-8173-6641-5). U of Ala Pr.
Gribbin, John. Future Worlds. 224p. 1981. 14.95 (ISBN 0-306-40780-9). Da Capo.
Group for Environmental Education, Inc. Our Man-Made Environment, Book 7. 1973. pap. 5.95 (ISBN 0-262-07050-2); french lang. ed. 5.95 (ISBN 0-262-57037-8). MIT Pr.
Hall, Gus. Ecology: Can We Survive Under Capitalism? LC 72-184673. (Illus.). 96p. (Orig.). 1972. pap. 1.50 (ISBN 0-7178-0347-3). Intl Pub Co.
Hancock, William K. Discovering Monaro: A Study of Man's Impact on His Environment. LC 78-178280. (Illus.). 256p. 1972. 27.50 (ISBN 0-521-08439-3). Cambridge U Pr.
Hilton, Suzanne. How Do They Cope with It? (Illus.). (gr. 5 up). 1970. 5.25 (ISBN 0-664-32481-9). Westminster.
Holdgate, Martin W. & White, Gilbert F., eds. Environmental Issues - Scope Report 10. LC 77-2667. 1977. 30.25 (ISBN 0-471-99503-7, Pub. by Wiley-Interscience). Wiley.
Human Activity & the Environment. 1979. pap. 5.25 (ISBN 0-685-90714-7, SSC 113, SSC). Unipub.
Human Influences in African Pastureland Environments. 89p. 1981. pap. 7.50 (ISBN 92-5-100874-4, F2076, FAO). Unipub.
Huxley, Julian S. The Individual in the Animal Kingdom. LC 72-78632. 185p. 1912. Repr. 21.00 (ISBN 0-403-04116-3). Somerset Pub.
Jackson, Wes. Man & the Environment. 3rd ed. 450p. 1979. pap. text ed. write for info. (ISBN 0-697-04704-0). Wm C Brown.
Jennings, Gary. The Shrinking Outdoors. LC 75-151483. (gr. 7 up). 1972. 6.95 (ISBN 0-397-31178-8, JBL-J). Har-Row.
Johnson, C. Natural World: Chaos & Conservation. 1971. text ed. 11.50 (ISBN 0-07-032591-X, C); pap. text ed. 8.50 (ISBN 0-07-032590-1). McGraw.
Jones, Claire, et al. Pollution: The Balance of Nature. LC 78-178674. (Real World of Pollution Ser). (Illus.). (gr. 5-11). 1972. PLB 4.95 (ISBN 0-8225-0632-7). Lerner Pubns.
Kabir, Humayun. Men & Rivers. 1981. 2.75x (ISBN 0-8364-0702-4, Pub. by Sargam India). South Asia Bks.
Lamb, Robert. World Without Trees. LC 78-21868. (Illus.). 1979. 9.95 (ISBN 0-448-22619-7). Paddington.
Leiss, William. The Domination of Nature. LC 75-188358. 1972. 6.95 (ISBN 0-8076-0646-4). Braziller.
--The Domination of Nature. LC 74-6090. 252p. 1974. pap. 4.95x (ISBN 0-8070-4161-0, BP492). Beacon Pr.
McGraw-Hill Editors. McGraw-Hill Encyclopedia of Environmental Science. (Illus.). 750p. 1974. 26.95 (ISBN 0-07-045260-1, P&RB). McGraw.
McHarg, Ian L. Design with Nature. LC 76-77344. 1971. 17.95 (ISBN 0-385-02142-9); pap. 6.95 (ISBN 0-385-05509-9). Natural Hist.
McKain, David W., ed. Whole Earth: Essays in Appreciation, Anger, & Hope. 384p. 1971. pap. text ed. 6.95 (ISBN 0-312-87045-0). St Martin.
Manners, I. A. & Mikesell, M. W., eds. Perspectives on Environment. LC 73-88849. (General Ser.: No. 13). 1974. pap. 3.95 (ISBN 0-89291-044-5). Assn Am Geographers.
Manshard, W. & Fischnich, O. E. Man & Environment. 108p. 1975. pap. text ed. 24.00 (ISBN 0-08-019673-X). Pergamon.
Marsh, George P. Earth As Modified by Human Action. LC 74-106906. 1970. Repr. of 1878 ed. 24.00 (ISBN 0-403-00198-6). Scholarly.
--Man & Nature. Lowenthal, David, ed. LC 65-11591. (The John Harvard Library). pap. 7.95x (ISBN 0-674-54400-5). Harvard U Pr.
Matthews, L. Harrison. Man & Wildlife. LC 75-4336. 250p. 1975. 18.95 (ISBN 0-312-51240-6). St Martin.
Matthews, William H., ed. Man's Impact on the Global Environment: Assessment & Recommendations for Action. (Study of Critical Environmental Problems). 1970. 17.50x (ISBN 0-262-19086-9); pap. 4.95 (ISBN 0-262-69027-6). MIT Pr.
Matthews, William H., et al, eds. Man's Impact on the Climate. (Study of Critical Environmental Problems). 1971. 37.00x (ISBN 0-262-13075-0). MIT Pr.
Mediterranean Forest & Maquis: Ecology, Conservation & Management. (MAB Technical Notes: No. 2). (Illus.). 1977. pap. 5.25 (ISBN 92-3-101388-2, U370, UNESCO). Unipub.
Le Monde de la nature. (Illus.). 1978. text ed. 26.95x (ISBN 2-03-019112-4). Larousse.
Moscovici, Serge. Society Against Nature. Rabinowitz, Sacha, tr. from Fr. (European Ideas Ser.). 1976. text ed. 17.00x (ISBN 0-391-00523-5). Humanities.
Moser, Leo J. The Technology Trap. LC 78-26034. 1979. 17.95x (ISBN 0-88229-419-9); pap. 8.95 (ISBN 0-88229-669-8). Nelson-Hall.
Mulvaney, D. Discovering Man's Place in Nature. (Australian Humanities Research Council Monograph: No. 11). 12p. 1971. pap. 2.00x (ISBN 0-424-06370-0, Pub. by Sydney U. Pr). Intl Schol Bk Serv.
National Geographic Society, ed. As We Live & Breathe: The Challenge of Our Environment. LC 74-151945. (Special Publications Ser.). (Illus.). 1971. 5.75, avail. only from Natl Geog (ISBN 0-87044-097-7). Natl Geog.
Phillips, A. D. & Turton, B. J., eds. Environment, Man & Economic Change: Essays Presented to S.H. Beaver. (Illus.). 500p. 1975. text ed. 42.00x (ISBN 0-582-50114-8). Longman.
Piburne, Michael. The Environment: A Human Crisis. (American Values Ser). 160p. (gr. 9-12). 1974. pap. text ed. 4.00x (ISBN 0-8104-5905-1). Hayden.
Prince Philip. The Environmental Revolution: Speeches on Conservation 1962-1977. LC 78-60776. 1979. 8.95 (ISBN 0-87951-088-9). Overlook Pr.
Property & Environment: The Social Obligation Inherent in Ownership, (EPLP 12) 1976. pap. 8.50x (ISBN 2-88032-082-8, IUCN41, IUCN). Unipub.
Reno, Edward A., Jr., ed. The New York Times Cumulative Subject & Personal Name Index: Environment Nineteen Sixty-Five to Nineteen Seventy-Five. 778p. 1978. 75.00 (ISBN 0-667-00606-0). Microfilming Corp.
Robinson, J. P. The Effects of Weapons on Ecosystems. LC 79-41226. (Illus.). 76p. 1979. 11.50 (ISBN 0-08-025656-2). Pergamon.
Rose, J., ed. Technological Injury: The Effect of Technology Advances on Environment Life & Society. 1969. pap. 29.25 (ISBN 0-677-13645-5). Gordon.
Russwurm, Lorne & Sommerville, Edward. Man's Natural Environments: A Systems Approach. LC 74-75715. 1974. pap. 6.95x (ISBN 0-87872-070-7). Duxbury Pr.
Salanki, J. & Biro, P., eds. Human Impacts on Life in Fresh Waters. (Sumposia Biologica Hungarica: Vol. 19). (Illus.). 223p. 1979. 25.00x (ISBN 963-05-1732-9). Intl Pubns Serv.
Sasson, Albert. Developpement et Environment: Fait et Perspectives dans les Pays Industrialises et en Voie de Developpement. LC 74-78190. 423p. (Fr.). 1975. pap. text ed. 41.25x (ISBN 90-2797-596-5). Mouton.
Schneider, Stephen H. & Morton, Lynne. The Primordial Bond. (Illus.). 336p. 15.95 (ISBN 0-306-40519-9). Da Capo.
--The Primordial Bond: Exploring Connections Between Man & Nature Through the Humanities & Sciences. (Illus.). 200p. 1981. 15.95 (ISBN 0-306-40519-9, Plenum Pr). Plenum Pub.
Schneider, Steven & Mestrow, L. E. Genesis Strategy. 1977. pap. 4.95 (ISBN 0-440-52792-9, Delta). Dell.
Schueler, Donald G. Incident at Eagle Ranch: Man & Predator in the American West. LC 80-13588. 320p. 1980. 12.95 (ISBN 0-87156-230-8). Sierra.
Sherman, Anthony C. Land & Trash: Our Wounded Land. new ed. Eblen, William, ed. LC 72-79107. (Illus.). 64p. (Orig.). (gr. 7-12). 1972. pap. 1.45 (ISBN 0-88301-043-7). Pendulum Pr.
Shostrom, Everett. Man, the Manipulator. 1968. pap. 2.75 (ISBN 0-553-13642-9). Bantam.
Singh, Indera P. & Tiwari, S. C., eds. Man & His Environment. (International Conference of Anthropological & Ethnological Sciences Ser.: No. 10). 299p. 1980. text ed. 18.00x (ISBN 0-391-02140-0). Humanities.
Spiro, Thomas G. & Stigliani, William. Environmental Issues in Chemical Perspective. 1980. 21.00 (ISBN 0-87395-427-0). State U NY Pr.

Stumm, Werner, ed. Global Chemical Cycles & Their Alterations by Man. (Physical & Chemical Sciences Research Reports: No. 2). 1977. lib. bdg. 22.00 (ISBN 0-910000-06-9). Dahlem.

Thomas, William L., Jr., ed. Man's Role in Changing the Face of the Earth, 2 Vols. LC 56-5865. (Illus.). 1971. Vol. 1. pap. 10.00x (ISBN 0-226-79604-3, P390, Phoen); Vol. 2. pap. 6.95 (ISBN 0-226-79605-1, P391). U of Chicago Pr.

Transport & the Environment. 1978. 43.00 (ISBN 0-258-97086-3, CLS3, CLS). Unipub.

Undercurrents Editors. Radical Technology: Viable Ways to Live in Harmony with Man & Nature. LC 75-10367. 288p. (YA) 1976. pap. 5.95 (ISBN 0-394-73093-3). Pantheon.

Volpe, Peter E. Man, Nature, & Society: An Introduction to Biology. 2nd ed. 650p. 1979. text ed. write for info. (ISBN 0-697-04568-4); instr's manual avail. (ISBN 0-685-91873-4); lab. manual avail. (ISBN 0-697-04569-2); study guide avail. (ISBN 0-697-04571-4). Wm C Brown.

Walker, D. & West, R. G., eds. Studies in the Vegetation History of the British Isles. 79.00 (ISBN 0-521-07565-3). Cambridge U Pr.

Wilkinson, Paul F. Environmental Impact of Outdoor Recreation & Tourism: A Bibliography. (Public Administration Ser.: P 57). 1978. pap. 9.00 (ISBN 0-686-24282-3). Vance Biblios.

Winkler, Franz E. Man: The Bridge Between Two Worlds. LC 80-82064. 268p. 1980. pap. 4.95 (ISBN 0-913098-32-9). Myrin Institute.

Witters, Weldon L. & Jones-Witters, Patricia. Environmental Biology: The Human Factor. 2nd ed. LC 75-35412. 1978. perfect bdg. 7.95 (ISBN 0-8403-8000-3). Kendall Hunt.

Yapp, W. B. & Smith, M. I. Production, Pollution, Protection. (Wykeham Science Ser.: No. 19). 1972. 9.95x (ISBN 0-8448-1121-1). Crane-Russak Co.

MAN–JUVENILE LITERATURE

see also Man–Origin–Juvenile Literature

Edwards, Gabrielle. Man & Woman: Inside Homo Sapiens. (Student Scientist Ser.). (gr. 7-12). 1979. PLB 7.97 (ISBN 0-8239-0445-8). Rosen Pr.

MAN–MIGRATIONS

see also Jews–Diaspora; Migration, Internal; Migrations of Nations

Baker, Robin, ed. The Mystery of Migration. LC 80-16839. (Illus.). 256p. 1981. 29.95 (ISBN 0-670-50286-3, Studio). Viking Pr.

Deichert, Jerome A., et al. Migration Patterns of Young Adults in Nebaska. (Nebraska Economic & Business Report: No. 25). 1978. 5.00 (ISBN 0-686-28413-5). Bur Busn Res U Nebr.

Du Toit, Brian M. & Safa, Helen I., eds. Migration & Urbanization. (World Anthropology Ser.). 320p. 1975. 23.00x (ISBN 0-202-90010-X). Beresford Bk Serv.

Haddon, Alfred C. The Wanderings of Peoples. LC 76-44730. (Illus.). Repr. of 1911 ed. 23.00 (ISBN 0-404-15931-1). AMS Pr.

Hammond, Nicholas G. Migrations & Invasions in Greece & Adjacent Areas. LC 76-17379. (Illus.). 1977. 28.00 (ISBN 0-8155-5047-2, NP). Noyes.

Heyerdahl, Thor. Early Man & the Ocean: A Search for the Beginnings of Navigation & Seaborne Civilizations. LC 79-23287. (Illus.). 1980. pap. 4.95 (ISBN 0-394-74218-4, Vin). Random.

Jansen, C. J. Readings in the Sociology of Migration. LC 72-105954. 1970. 21.00 (ISBN 0-08-006915-0); pap. 11.25 (ISBN 0-08-006914-2). Pergamon.

Jenness, Diamond, ed. The American Aborigines: Their Origin & Antiquity; a Collection of Papers by Ten Authors Published for Presentation at the 5th Pacific Science Congress, Canada. LC 78-180611. (Illus.). iv, 396p. 1972. Repr. of 1933 ed. 19.00 (ISBN 0-8462-1616-7). Russell.

Kiste, R. C. The Bikinians: A Study in Forced Migration. LC 79-224. 1974. pap. 5.95 (ISBN 0-8465-3752-4). Benjamin-Cummings.

Lanning, James W. The Old Colony Mennonites of Bolivia. (Illus.). 130p. 1972. pap. 9.75x (ISBN 0-8361-1189-3). Herald Pr.

Maamarv, Samir. Human Migration: Stages & Factors Involved in the Decision to Migrate. LC 75-36559. 1976. softbound 9.00 (ISBN 0-88247-402-2). R & E Res Assoc.

Mangalam, J. J. Human Migration: A Guide to Migration Literature in English, 1955-1962. LC 67-23777. (Illus.). 200p. 1968. 18.50x (ISBN 0-8131-1170-6). U Pr of Ky.

May, Charles P. The Uprooted. LC 75-42255. (gr. 6 up). 1976. 7.95 (ISBN 0-664-32591-2). Westminster.

Safa, Helen I. & Du Toit, Brian M., eds. Migration & Development. (World Anthropology Ser.). 232p. 1975. 21.50x (ISBN 0-202-90009-6). Beresford Bk Serv.

Smith, Grafton E. The Migrations of Early Culture. 1977. lib. bdg. 75.00 (ISBN 0-8490-2258-4). Gordon Pr.

Taylor, Griffith. Environment, Race & Migration: Fundamentals of Human Distribution, with Special Sections on Racial Classification, & Settlement in Canada & Australia. LC 38-9816. (Illus.). 1937. 45.00x (ISBN 0-8020-7043-4). U of Toronto Pr.

Webster, J. B., ed. Chronology, Migration & Drought in Interlacustrine Africa. LC 78-7050. (Dalhousie African Studies). 1979. text ed. 44.50x (ISBN 0-8419-0377-8, Africana); pap. text ed. 27.50x (ISBN 0-8419-0388-3, Africana). Holmes & Meier.

MAN–ORIGIN

see also Anatomy, Comparative; Evolution; Human Evolution; Life–Origin; Monogenism and Polygenism

Ardrey, Robert. African Genesis. LC 61-15889. (Illus.). 1961. 9.95 (ISBN 0-689-10013-2). Atheneum.

Black, Davidson, ed. Fossil Man in China. LC 73-38049. Repr. of 1933 ed. 32.00 (ISBN 0-404-56903-X). AMS pr.

Bonin, Gerhardt Von. The Evolution of the Human Brain. LC 63-13062. (Midway Reprint Ser.). 1963. pap. 6.95x (ISBN 0-226-06436-0). U of Chicago Pr.

Brodrick, Alan H. Early Man: A Survey of Human Origins. 1976. lib. bdg. 59.95 (ISBN 0-8490-1741-6). Gordon Pr.

Burgess, Robert F. Man: Twelve Thousand Years Under the Sea. LC 80-186. (Illus.). 448p. 1980. 12.95 (ISBN 0-396-07801-X). Dodd.

Casson, Stanly. The Discovery of Man: The Story of the Inquiry into Human Origins. (Historiography: Interdisciplinary Studies: No. 2). Repr. of 1939 ed. lib. bdg. 17.50x (ISBN 0-87991-105-0). Porcupine Pr.

Chatelain, Maurice. Our Ancestors Came from Outer Space. 1979. pap. 2.25 (ISBN 0-440-16654-3). Dell.

Cold Spring Harbor Symposia on Quantitative Biology: Origin & Evolution of Man, Vol. 15. LC 34-8174. (Illus.). 437p. 1951. 30.00 (ISBN 0-87969-014-3). Cold Spring Harbor.

Coon, Carleton S. Origin of Races. (Illus.). 1962. 17.50 (ISBN 0-394-43944-9). Knopf.

Criswell, W. A. Did Man Just Happen? (Orig.). 1980. pap. text ed. 2.25 (ISBN 0-8024-2212-8). Moody.

Dobzhansky, Theodosius. Mankind Evolving: The Evolution of the Human Species. (Silliman Memorial Lectures Ser.). (Illus.). 1962. 25.00x (ISBN 0-300-00427-3); pap. 6.95x 1964 (ISBN 0-300-00070-7, Y116). Yale U Pr.

Edwards, Gabrielle. Man & Woman: Inside Homo Sapiens. (Student Scientist Ser.). (gr. 7-12). 1979. PLB 7.97 (ISBN 0-8239-0445-8). Rosen Pr.

Eiseley, Loren. Immense Journey. 1957. pap. 1.95 (ISBN 0-394-70157-7, Vin). Random.

Emergence of Man, 10 vols. Spanish Version. 12.50 ea.; French Version. 19.95 ea. French & Eur.

Garn, Stanley M., ed. Culture & the Direction of Human Evolution. LC 64-16088. (Publications on Human Evolution Ser). 1964. 5.95x (ISBN 0-8143-1230-6). Wayne St U Pr.

Hill, Harold & Harrell, Irene. How Did It All Begin? LC 75-20898. 1976. pap. 1.95 (ISBN 0-88270-140-1). Logos.

Hooton, Earnest A. Apes, Men & Morons. LC 76-134095. (Essay Index Reprint Ser). 1937. 19.50 (ISBN 0-8369-1956-4). Arno.

Hoover, Arlie J. Fallacies of Evolution: The Case for Creationism. 1977. pap. 3.45 (ISBN 0-8010-4182-1). Baker Bk.

Howells, William, ed. Ideas on Human Evolution: Selected Essays, 1949-1961. LC 62-11399. (Illus.). 1967. pap. text ed. 3.95x (ISBN 0-689-70101-2, 98). Atheneum.

Huxley, Thomas H. Evolution & Ethics, & Other Essays. LC 70-8391. 334p. 1897. Repr. 24.00 (ISBN 0-403-00041-6). Scholarly.

James, E. O. The Beginnings of Man. 1929. 17.50 (ISBN 0-685-73526-5). Norwood Edns.

Jastrow, Robert. The Enchanted Loom: The Mind in the Universe. (Illus.). 1981. 13.95 (ISBN 0-671-43308-3). S&S.

Keith, Arthur. The Antiquity of Man, 2 vols. Set. 250.00 (ISBN 0-87968-159-4). Gordon Pr.

Leakey, L. S. Adam's Ancestors: The Evolution of Man & His Culture. pap. 2.95x (ISBN 0-06-131019-0, TB1019, Torch). Har-Row.

Leakey, Richard & Lewin, Roger. Origins: What New Discoveries Reveal About the Emergence of Our Species & Its Possible Future. 1977. 17.95 (ISBN 0-525-17194-0); pap. 8.95 (ISBN 0-525-47572-9). Dutton.

Lugenbeal, Edward. Who Killed Adam? A Look at the Major Types of Fossil Man. LC 78-8513. (Flame Ser.). 1978. pap. 0.95 (ISBN 0-8127-0186-0). Review & Herald.

Lyell, Charles. Geological Evidence of the Antiquity of Man. 4th ed. LC 72-1728. (Illus.). Repr. of 1873 ed. 35.00 (ISBN 0-404-08138-X). AMS Pr.

MacCurdy, George G., ed. Early Man. facs. ed. LC 77-86770. (Essay Index Reprint Ser). 1937. 25.00 (ISBN 0-8369-1184-9). Arno.

Morton, Newton, et al. Source Book for Linkage in Man. LC 78-21207. 1979. 22.50x (ISBN 0-8018-2188-6). Johns Hopkins.

Niesturi, M. F. El Origen Del Hombre. 402p. (Span.). 1979. 8.00 (ISBN 0-8285-1466-6, Pub. by Mir Pubs Russia). Imported Pubns.

Oakley, Kenneth P. Problem of Man's Antiquity. (Illus.). 1964. 8.50 (ISBN 0-384-42700-6); pap. 5.50 (ISBN 0-384-42701-4). Johnson Repr.

The Origin of Homo Sapiens. (Ecology & Conservation Ser.). (Illus.). 321p. 1972. 24.75 (ISBN 92-3-000948-2, U443, UNESCO). Unipub.

Overton, Basil. Evolution or Creation. 2.50 (ISBN 0-89225-088-7). Gospel Advocate.

Robinson, Lytle W. Edward Cayce's Story of the Origin & Destiny of Man. 208p. 20.00x (ISBN 0-85435-311-9, Pub. by Spearman England). State Mutual Bk.

Shaftesbury, Edmund & Edgerly, Webster. Origin of Man: A Shaftsbury Classic. 1977. Repr. 19.00 (ISBN 0-403-08598-5). Scholarly.

Singer, Andre, ed. Atlas of Man. LC 78-4364. (Illus.). 1978. 25.00 (ISBN 0-312-05991-4). St Martin.

Smith, Grafton E., et al. Early Man: His Origin, Development & Culture. facs. ed. LC 67-28750. (Essay Index Reprint Ser). 1931. 16.00 (ISBN 0-8369-0398-6). Arno.

Strickland, Glenn G. Genesis Revisited: A Revolutionary New Solution to the Mystery of Man's Origins. 1979. 8.95 (ISBN 0-8037-2828-X). Dial.

Teilhard De Chardin, Pierre. Place De L'homme Dans la Nature. (Coll. le monde en 10-18). 1963. pap. 3.95 (ISBN 0-685-11497-X). French & Eur.

Thorpe, William H. Science, Man, & Morals. LC 76-14962. (Illus.). 1976. Repr. of 1965 ed. lib. bdg. 14.50x (ISBN 0-8371-8143-7, THSMM). Greenwood.

Van Pelt, G. Man's Divine Parentage & Destiny: The Great Rounds & Races. Small, W. Emmett & Todd, Helen, eds. (Theosophical Manual: No. 7). 64p. 1975. pap. 1.75 (ISBN 0-685-53992-X, 913004-24). Point Loma Pub.

Von Koenigswald, G. H. The Evolution of Man. rev. ed. Pomerans, Arnold J., tr. from Ger. LC 73-80572. (Ann Arbor Science Library). (Illus.). 160p. 1976. 6.95 (ISBN 0-472-00120-5); pap. 2.95 (ISBN 0-472-05020-6). U of Mich Pr.

--The Evolution of Man. rev. ed. Pomerans, Arnold J., tr. from Ger. (Ann Arbor Science Library). (Illus.). 1976. pap. 2.95 (ISBN 0-472-05020-6, AA). U of Mich Pr.

Weidenreich, Franz. Apes, Giants & Man. (Illus.). 1946. 5.75x (ISBN 0-226-88147-4). U of Chicago Pr.

Wilder-Smith, A. W. Man's Origin, Man's Destiny. LC 74-28508. 320p. 1975. pap. 6.95 (ISBN 0-87123-356-8, 210356). Bethany Hse.

Yereance, Robert A. Strangers, All Strangers. 1981. 10.95 (ISBN 0-87949-151-5). Ashley Bks.

MAN–ORIGIN–JUVENILE LITERATURE

Asimov, Isaac. How Did We Find Out About Our Human Roots? (How Did We Find Out Ser.). (Illus.). (gr. 4-8). 1979. 6.95 (ISBN 0-8027-6360-X); PLB 6.85 (ISBN 0-8027-6361-8). Walker & Co.

Edwards, Gabrielle. Man & Woman: Inside Homo Sapiens. (Student Scientist Ser.). (gr. 7-12). 1979. PLB 7.97 (ISBN 0-8239-0445-8). Rosen Pr.

MAN–PARASITES

see Medical Parasitology

MAN (PHILOSOPHY)

see Philosophical Anthropology

MAN (THEOLOGY)

see also Fall of Man; Humanism, Religious; Identification (Religion); Pelagianism; Sex (Theology); Sin; Soul; Work (Theology)

Astley, H. J. Biblical Anthropology. 1977. Repr. of 1929 ed. 30.00 (ISBN 0-685-82796-8). Sharon Hill.

Axum, Donna. The Outer You...the Inner You. LC 77-83345. 1978. 5.95 (ISBN 0-8499-0055-7). Word Bks.

Bawa Muhaiyaddeen, M. R. Wisdom of Man: Selected Discourses. LC 80-20541. (Illus.). 168p. 1980. 7.95 (ISBN 0-914390-16-3). Fellowship Pr PA.

Bockle, Franz, ed. Man in a New Society. (Concilium Ser.: Religion in the Seventies: Vol. 75). 1972. pap. 4.95 (ISBN 0-8164-2531-0). Crossroad NY.

--Manipulated Man. (Concilium Ser.: Religion in the Seventies: Vol. 65). 1971. pap. 4.95 (ISBN 0-8245-0224-8). Crossroad NY.

Bucher, Glenn R., ed. Straight-White-Male. LC 75-13039. 160p. 1976. pap. 3.95 (ISBN 0-8006-1209-4, 1-1209). Fortress.

Carus, Paul. The Soul of Man. 59.95 (ISBN 0-8490-1090-X). Gordon Pr.

De Silva, Lynn A. The Problem of the Self in Buddhism & Christianity. LC 76-19860. (Library of Philosophy & Religion Ser). 1979. Repr. of 1975 ed. text ed. 23.50x (ISBN 0-06-491667-7). B&N.

D'Holbach, Paul H. Ecce Home Leucippe. 69.95 (ISBN 0-87968-077-6). Gordon Pr.

Doniger, Simon, ed. The Nature of Man in Theological & Psychological Perspective. LC 72-10819. (Essay Index Reprint Ser.). 1973. Repr. of 1962 ed. 18.00 (ISBN 0-8369-7213-9). Arno.

Fichtner, Joseph. Man: The Image of God. LC 77-15613. 1978. pap. 5.95 (ISBN 0-8189-0364-3). Alba.

Fisk, Samuel. Divine Sovereignty & Human Freedom. LC 73-81550. 1973. pap. 3.75 (ISBN 0-87213-166-1). Loizeaux.

Flynn, Leslie B. Man: Ruined & Restored. 1978. pap. 3.95 (ISBN 0-88207-762-7). Victor Bks.

Forizs, Loran. Loops and Interfaces of Man. LC 76-24283. 1977. 7.95 (ISBN 0-87212-072-4). Libra.

Getz, Gene, tr. Vers la Stature Parfaite De Jesus-Christ. (French Bks.). (Fr.). 1979. 1.95 (ISBN 0-8297-0820-0). Life Pubs Intl.

Hamilton, William. Christian Man. (Layman's Theological Library). 1956. pap. 1.00 (ISBN 0-664-24003-8). Westminster.

Haughton, Rosemary. On Trying to Be Human. 1966. 6.95 (ISBN 0-87243-011-1). Templegate.

Heline, Theodore. Archetype Unveiled. 1972. pap. 1.50 (ISBN 0-87613-032-5). New Age.

Howes, Elizabeth B. & Moon, Sheila. The Choicemaker. LC 76-54534. Orig. Title: Man, the Choicemaker. 1977. pap. 3.95 (ISBN 0-8356-0492-6, Quest). Theos Pub Hse.

Hunter, John E. World in Rebellion. 1978. pap. 2.95 (ISBN 0-89293-055-1). Beta Bk.

Jabay, Earl. God-Players. LC 69-11637. 1970. pap. 4.95 (ISBN 0-310-26541-X). Zondervan.

--Kingdom of Self. LC 73-89494. 1974. pap. 3.95 (ISBN 0-88270-062-6). Logos.

Kantonen, T. A. Man in the Eyes of God. 1973. pap. 2.35 (ISBN 0-89536-421-2). CSS Pub.

Lee, Jung Y. I: A Christian Concept of Men. LC 70-150100. 1971. 5.95 (ISBN 0-8022-2052-5). Philos Lib.

Littlefield, Charles. Man, Minerals & Masters. 172p. 1981. pap. 5.50 (ISBN 0-686-75085-3). Sun Pub.

McGinn, Bernard. The Golden Chain: A Study in the Theological Anthropology of Isaac of Stella. LC 70-152487. (Cistercian Studies: No. 15). 280p. 1972. 7.50 (ISBN 0-87907-815-4). Cistercian Pubns.

McGinn, Bernard, ed. Three Treatises on Man: A Cistercian Anthropology. LC 77-184906. (Cistercian Fathers Ser.: No. 24). 1977. 13.95 (ISBN 0-87907-024-2). Cistercian Pubns.

Mackey, J. P. Church: Its Credibility Today. 1970. pap. 3.50 (ISBN 0-02-804200-X). Glencoe.

Man & God. (Miniature Series). 0.50 (ISBN 0-685-61383-6). Aum Pubns.

Mascall, Eric L. Importance of Being Human. LC 74-12849. 118p. 1974. Repr. of 1958 ed. lib. bdg. 15.00 (ISBN 0-8371-7761-8, MABH). Greenwood.

Massey, Craig. Adjust or Self Destruct. pap. 1.50 (ISBN 0-8024-0136-8). Moody.

Miles, Margaret R. Fullness of Life: Historical Foundations for a New Asceticism. 1981. pap. price not set (ISBN 0-664-24389-4). Westminster.

Moltmann, Jurgen. Man: Christian Anthropology in the Conflicts of the Present. Sturdy, John, tr. from Ger. LC 73-88350. 136p. (Orig.). 1974. pap. 3.50 (ISBN 0-8006-1066-0, 1-1066). Fortress.

Muschell, Helen. Wells of Inner Space. 1970. 6.95 (ISBN 0-8158-0233-1). Chris Mass.

Nicoll, Maurice. New Man. (Metaphysical Lib.). 1972. pap. 3.95 (ISBN 0-14-003412-9). Penguin.

O'Connell, Robert J. Saint Augustine's Early Theory of Man, A. D. 386-391. LC 68-21981. 1968. text ed. 16.50x (ISBN 0-674-78520-7, Belknap Pr). Harvard U Pr.

Pannenberg, Wolfhart. What Is Man: Contemporary Anthropology in Theological Perepective. Priebe, Duane A., tr. from Ger. LC 74-101429. 168p. 1972. pap. 3.75 (ISBN 0-8006-1252-3, 1-1252). Fortress.

Paul, Pope John, II. The Whole Truth About Man. 1981. 7.95 (ISBN 0-686-73822-5); pap. 6.95 (ISBN 0-8198-8202-X). Dghtrs St Paul.

Purchas, Samuel. Purchas His Pilgrim. Microcosmus or, the Historie of Man. LC 76-25513. (English Experience Ser.: No. 146). 820p. 1969. Repr. of 1619 ed. 69.00 (ISBN 90-221-0146-0). Walter J Johnson.

Richards, Sr. Innocentia, tr. A Christian Anthropology. LC 73-94171. (Religious Experience Ser: Vol. 2). 1974. pap. 3.95 (ISBN 0-87029-026-6, 20093). Abbey.

Schwarz, Hans. Our Cosmic Journey: Christian Anthropology in the Light of Current Trends in the Sciences, Philosophy,& Theology. LC 77-72460. 1977. 12.95 (ISBN 0-8066-1551-6, 10-4861); pap. 8.95 (ISBN 0-8066-1592-3, 10-4860). Augsburg.

Segundo, Jean L. Grace & the Human Condition. Drury, John, tr. from Span. LC 72-85794. (A Theology for Artisans of a New Humanity Ser: Vol. 2). 196p. 1973. 7.95x (ISBN 0-88344-482-8); pap. 4.95x (ISBN 0-88344-488-7). Orbis Bks.

Shinn, Roger L. New Directions in Theology Today. (Vol. 6). 1968. pap. 2.85 (ISBN 0-664-24812-8). Westminster.

Stagg, Frank. Polarities of Man's Existence in Biblical Perspective. LC 73-8812. 1973. 7.50 (ISBN 0-664-20976-9). Westminster.

Stedman, Ray C. Understanding Man. LC 75-18257. (Discovery Bks.). 1975. pap. 3.25 (ISBN 0-87680-984-0, 98044). Word Bks.

Torrance, Thomas F. Calvin's Doctrine of Man. LC 77-5615. 1977. Repr. lib. bdg. 15.75x (ISBN 0-8371-9639-6, TOCD). Greenwood.

Tournier, Paul, et al. Are You Nobody? LC 66-21649. (Orig.). 1966. pap. 2.45 (ISBN 0-8042-3356-X). John Knox.

Tozer, Aiden W. Man, the Dwelling Place of God. 4.95 (ISBN 0-87509-188-1); pap. 2.75 (ISBN 0-87509-165-2); mass market 1.95 (ISBN 0-87509-166-0). Chr Pubns.

Vagaggini, Cipriano. Flesh: Instrument of Salvation. LC 59-15856. 1969. 3.95 (ISBN 0-8189-0049-0). Alba.

Vernon, Percy L. Man, the Creature of Three Worlds. 3.00 (ISBN 0-8338-0063-9). M Jones.

Vickers, Douglas. Man in the Maelstrom of Modern Thought. 1975. kivar 4.95 (ISBN 0-87552-501-6). Presby & Reformed.

Vinoi, Lawrence. God & Man: The Essential Knowledge Which Everyone, but Absolutely Everyone Ought to Possess About Human Nature & the Nature of God & How the Two Are Related. (Essential Knowledge Ser. Books). (Illus.). 1978. plastic spiral bdg. 24.75 (ISBN 0-89266-118-6). Am Classical Coll Pr.

What, Then, Is Man? A Symposium. 356p. 1971. 8.95 (ISBN 0-570-03125-7, 12-2361). Concordia.

Wolf, Arnold J. What Is Man. 102p. 1968. 3.50 (ISBN 0-8197-0193-9). Bloch.

MAN (THEOLOGY)–BIBLICAL TEACHING

Hicks, Robert & Bewes, Richard. Man. (Understanding Bible Truth Ser.). (Orig.). 1981. pap. 1.50 (ISBN 0-89840-025-2). Heres Life.

Mork, D. Wulstan. Biblical Meaning of Man. 1967. 4.95 (ISBN 0-685-07612-1, 80554). Glencoe.

Rogerson, J. W. Anthropology & the Old Testament. LC 78-71043. 1979. 8.95 (ISBN 0-8042-0083-1). John Knox.

Wolff, Hans W. Anthropology of the Old Testament. Kohl, Margaret, tr. from Ger. LC 74-21591. 304p. 1974. 14.95x (ISBN 0-8006-0298-6, 1-298). Fortress.

MAN, ANTIQUITY OF

see Man–Origin

MAN, DOCTRINE OF

see Man (Theology)

MAN, ERECT POSITION OF

see Man–Attitude and Movement; Posture

MAN, FALL OF

see Fall of Man

MAN, FOSSIL

see Fossil Man

MAN, PREHISTORIC

see also Bronze Age; Fossil Man; Glacial Epoch; Lake-Dwellers and Lake-Dwellings; Man–Origin; Megalithic Monuments; Paleo-Indians;
also subdivision Antiquities under names of countries, cities, etc., e.g. Rome (City)–Antiquities

Andrews, Roy C. On the Trail of Ancient Man. 1926. 25.00 (ISBN 0-685-73479-X). Norwood Edns.

Avebury. Prehistoric Times As Illustrated by Ancient Remains & the Manners & Customs of Modern Savages. 7th ed. 1969. Repr. of 1913 ed. text ed. 24.75x (ISBN 90-6234-001-6). Humanities.

Berenguer, Magin. Prehistoric Man & His Art: The Caves of Ribadesella. LC 74-81541. (Illus.). 168p. 1975. 8.95 (ISBN 0-8155-5031-6, NP). Noyes.

Bergier, Jacques. Extraterrestrial Visitations from Prehistoric Times to the Present. 1974. pap. 1.50 (ISBN 0-451-05942-5, W5942, Sig). NAL.

Berlitz, Charles. Mysteries from Forgotten Worlds. LC 79-175360. 288p. 8.95 (ISBN 0-385-02965-9). Doubleday.

Black, Davidson. Selected Paleoanthropological Papers: 1915-1934, 2 vols. LC 78-72689. Repr. 78.50 set (ISBN 0-404-18261-5); Vol. 1. (ISBN 0-404-18303-4); Vol. 2. (ISBN 0-404-18304-2). AMS Pr.

Borer, Mary C. Background to Archeology. 172p. 1975. 12.00 (ISBN 0-7207-0744-7). Transatlantic.

Brace, C. The Stages of Human Evolution. 2nd ed. 1979. 9.95 (ISBN 0-13-840157-8); pap. 6.95 (ISBN 0-13-840140-3). P-H.

Braidwood, Robert J. Prehistoric Men. 8th ed. 213p. 1975. pap. 7.95x (ISBN 0-673-07851-5). Scott F.

Breuil, Henri & Lantier, Raymond. The Men of the Old Stone Age: Palaeolithic & Mesolithic. Rafter, B. B., tr. LC 79-16777. (Illus.). 1980. Repr. of 1965 ed. lib. bdg. 28.25x (ISBN 0-313-21289-9, BRMO). Greenwood.

Butzer, Karl. Environment & Archeology: An Ecological Approach to Prehistory. 2nd ed. LC 74-115938. (Illus.). 1971. 29.95x (ISBN 0-202-33023-0). Aldine Pub.

Chard, Chester S. Man in Prehistory. 2nd ed. (Illus.). 416p. 1974. text ed. 15.95 (ISBN 0-07-010653-3, C). McGraw.

--Man in Prehistory. 2nd ed. (Illus.). 416p. 1974. text ed. 15.95 (ISBN 0-07-010653-3, C). McGraw.

Childe, V. Gordon. Man Makes Himself. 1952. pap. 1.50 (ISBN 0-451-61508-5, MW1508, Ment). NAL.

--New Light on the Most Ancient East. 4th ed. (Library Ser). (Illus.). 1969. pap. 4.95x (ISBN 0-393-00469-4, Norton Lib). Norton.

Clark, John Grahame Douglas. World Prehistory in New Perspective. 3rd ed. LC 76-51318. (Illus.). 1977. 57.00 (ISBN 0-521-21506-4); pap. 12.95 (ISBN 0-521-29178-X). Cambridge U Pr.

Cleland, Herdman F. Our Prehistoric Ancestors. 1979. Repr. of 1929 ed. lib. bdg. 50.00 (ISBN 0-8495-0922-X). Arden Lib.

Coates, Adrian. Prelude to History. 1952. 4.75 (ISBN 0-8022-0269-1). Philos Lib.

Constable, George. The Neanderthals. (Emergence of Man Ser.). (Illus.). 1973. 9.95 (ISBN 0-8094-1263-2); lib. bdg. avail. (ISBN 0-685-30024-2). Time-Life.

Coon, Carleton S. Origin of Races. (Illus.). 1962. 17.50 (ISBN 0-394-43944-9). Knopf.

Coppens, Yves, et al, eds. Earliest Man & Environments in the Lake Rudolf Basin: Stratigraphy, Paleoecology, & Evolution. LC 75-5075. (Prehistoric Archeology & Ecology Ser). (Illus.). 656p. 1976. 20.00x (ISBN 0-226-11577-1); pap. 11.50x (ISBN 0-226-11579-8). U of Chicago Pr.

Corliss, William R. Strange Artifacts: A Sourcebook on Ancient Man, Vol. M2. LC 74-75256. (Illus.). 275p. 1976. 8.95x (ISBN 0-9600712-6-1). Sourcebook.

--Strange Phenomena: A Sourcebook of Unusual Natural Phenomena, Vol. G2. LC 73-9148. 1974. 8.95x (ISBN 0-9600712-5-3). Sourcebook.

Cornwall, I. W. Prehistoric Animals & Their Hunters. (Illus.). 216p. 1968. 6.95 (ISBN 0-571-08340-4, Pub. by Faber & Faber). Merrimack Bk Serv.

Dawson, Christopher. The Age of the Gods. LC 68-9653. (Illus., Maps, Tabs). 1971. Repr. of 1928 ed. 27.50 (ISBN 0-86527-001-5). Fertig.

Day, Michael H. Guide to Fossil Man. 3rd rev. ed. LC 77-10517. 1978. Repr. of 1965 ed. lib. bdg. 17.50x (ISBN 0-226-13888-7). U of Chicago Pr.

De Morgan, Jacques. Prehistoric Man: A General Outline of Prehistory. 1924. 20.00 (ISBN 0-685-73486-2). Norwood Edns.

--Prehistoric Man: A General Outline of Prehistory. 1977. Repr. of 1924 ed. lib. bdg. 40.00 (ISBN 0-8492-0609-X). R West.

Fitzhugh, William, ed. Prehistoric Maritime Adaptations of the Circumpolar Zone. (World Anthropology Ser.). 416p. 1975. text ed. 40.50x (ISBN 0-202-90015-0). Beresford Bk Serv.

Forde-Johnston, J. Prehistoric Britain & Ireland. 1976. 11.50 (ISBN 0-393-05605-8). Norton.

Gooch, S. Neanderthal Question. 1977. 15.00 (ISBN 0-7045-0260-7). State Mutual Bk.

Gorjanovic-Kramberger, Dragutin. Der Diluviale Mensch Von Krapina in Kroatien. LC 78-72695. Repr. of 1906 ed. 76.50 (ISBN 0-404-18266-6). AMS Pr.

Gross, Ruth B. A Book About Your Skeleton. (Illus.). (gr. k-4). 1979. 7.95g (ISBN 0-8038-0794-5). Hastings.

Haviland, William A. Human Evolution & Prehistory. LC 78-14737. 1979. pap. text ed. 14.95 (ISBN 0-03-044761-5, HoltC); inst. manual avail. (ISBN 0-03-044766-6). HR&W.

Hawkes, J. Atlas of Ancient Archaeology. 1974. 25.95 (ISBN 0-07-027293-X, P&RB). McGraw.

Hawkes, Jacquetta. The Atlas of Early Man. LC 75-43424. (Illus.). 1976. 20.00 (ISBN 0-312-05985-X). St Martin.

Heyerdahl, Thor. Early Man & the Ocean: A Search for the Beginnings of Navigation & Seaborne Civilizations. LC 79-23287. (Illus.). 1980. pap. 4.95 (ISBN 0-394-74218-4, Vin). Random.

Hill, James N., ed. Explanation of Prehistoric Change. LC 76-57541. (School of American Research Advanced Seminar Ser). 356p. 1977. 25.00x (ISBN 0-8263-0451-6). U of NM Pr.

Hill, James N. & Gunn, Joel, eds. The Individual in Prehistory: Studies of Variability in Style in Prehistoric Technologies. 1977. 32.50 (ISBN 0-12-348150-3). Acad Pr.

Hill, Jane H. & Nolasquez, Rosinda. Mulu' Wetam: The First People. 1973. pap. 7.50 (ISBN 0-686-11773-5). Malki Mus Pr.

Howells, W. W. Cranial Variation in Man: A Study by Multivariate Analysis. LC 73-77203. (Peabody Museum Papers: Vol. 67). 1973. pap. text ed. 17.00 (ISBN 0-87365-189-8). Peabody Harvard.

Howells, W. W. & Crichton, J. M. Craniometry & Multivariate Analysis. LC 66-4603. (Peabody Museum Papers Ser.: Vol. 57, No. 1). 1966. pap. text ed. 8.00 (ISBN 0-87365-167-7). Peabody Harvard.

Hrdlicka, Ales. The Skeletal Remains of Early Man. 1930. 42.50 (ISBN 0-384-24710-5). Johnson Repr.

James, E. O. The Beginnings of Man. 1929. 17.50 (ISBN 0-685-73526-5). Norwood Edns.

Konigsson, Lars-Konig & Sundstrom, Stephan, eds. Current Argument on Early Man: Nobel Symposium "Current Argument on Early Man" Royal Swedish Academy of Sciences & the Nobel Foundation, Karlskoga, Sweden, May 21-27, 1978. (Illus.). 1980. 69.00 (ISBN 0-08-024956-6). Pergamon.

Leakey, L. S. Adam's Ancestors: The Evolution of Man & His Culture. pap. 2.95x (ISBN 0-06-131019-0, TB1019, Torch). Har-Row.

Leakey, Richard E. & Lewin, Roger. People of the Lake. 1979. pap. 2.75 (ISBN 0-380-45575-7, 45575). Avon.

MacCurdy, George G. Human Origins: A Manual of Prehistory, 2 Vols. (Illus.). Repr. of 1924 ed. Set. 54.00 (ISBN 0-384-34770-3). Johnson Repr.

MacCurdy, George G., ed. Early Man. facs. ed. LC 77-86770. (Essay Index Reprint Ser). 1937. 25.00 (ISBN 0-8369-1184-9). Arno.

Matiegka, Jindrich. Homo Predmostensis, fosilni Clovek z Predmosti na Morave, 2 vols. LC 78-72704. Repr. of 1938 ed. Set. 72.50 (ISBN 0-404-18273-9). Vol. 1 (ISBN 0-404-18274-7). Vol. 3 (ISBN 0-404-18275-5). AMS Pr.

Megaw, J. V., ed. Hunters, Gatherers & First Farmers Beyond Europe: An Archaeological Survey. (Illus.). 250p. 1976. pap. text ed. 15.00x (ISBN 0-7185-1136-0, Leicester). Humanities.

Mellersh, H. E. From Ape Man to Homer. LC 73-8567. (Illus.). 222p. 1974. Repr. of 1962 ed. lib. bdg. 15.00 (ISBN 0-8371-6962-3, MEAM). Greenwood.

Mooney, Richard E. Gods of Air & Darkness. LC 75-8926. 192p. 1975. 25.00 (ISBN 0-8128-1815-6). Stein & Day.

Moorehead, Warren K., et al. Prehistoric Implements. LC 76-43785. (Illus.). Repr. of 1900 ed. 74.50 (ISBN 0-404-15641-X). AMS Pr.

Moret, A. & Davy, G. From Tribe to Empire: Social Organization Among the Primitives & in the Ancient East. Childe, V. Gordon, tr. from Fr. LC 71-139997. (Illus.). 339p. 1971. Repr. of 1926 ed. lib. bdg. 17.50x (ISBN 0-8154-0368-2). Cooper Sq.

Movius, Hallam L., Jr., et al. The Analysis of Certain Major Classes of Upper Palaeolitic Tools. LC 68-55995. (ASPR Bulletin: No. 26). 1969. pap. text ed. 10.00 (ISBN 0-87365-527-3). Peabody Harvard.

Noorbergen, Rene. Secrets of the Lost Races. LC 77-76883. (Illus.). 1977. 12.95 (ISBN 0-672-52289-6). Bobbs.

Osborn, Henry. Men of the Old Stone Age, Their Environment, Life & Art. LC 78-72705. (Illus.). Repr. of 1918 ed. 47.00 (ISBN 0-404-18276-3). AMS Pr.

Pfeiffer, John. The Emergence of Society: A Prehistory of the Establishment. new ed. LC 76-27308. (Illus.). 528p. 1977. 15.00 (ISBN 0-07-049759-1, C); pap. text ed. 10.95 (ISBN 0-07-049758-3). McGraw.

Pfeiffer, John E. The Emergence of Man. 3rd ed. (Illus.). 1978. pap. text ed. 14.95 scp (ISBN 0-06-045196-3, HarpC); inst. manual free (ISBN 0-06-365188-2). Har-Row.

Pietrusewsky, Michael. Prehistoric Human Skeletal Remains from Papua New Guinea & the Marquesas. LC 76-521. (Asian & Pacific Archeology Ser.: No. 7). 1976. pap. 6.00x (ISBN 0-8248-0525-9). U Pr of Hawaii.

Prideaux, Tom. Cro-Magnon Man. (Emergence of Man Ser.). (Illus.). 1973. 9.95 (ISBN 0-8094-1271-3); lib. bdg. avail. (ISBN 0-685-41617-8). Time-Life.

Reader, John. Missing Links & the Men Who Found Them. (Illus.). 181p. 1981. 19.95 (ISBN 0-316-73590-6). Little.

Renfrew, Jane. Paleoethnobotany: The Prehistoric Food Plants of the Near East & Europe. 300p. 1973. 22.50x (ISBN 0-231-03745-7). Columbia U Pr.

Roe, Derek. Prehistory: An Introduction. LC 70-81799. 1970. 21.50x (ISBN 0-520-01406-5); pap. 3.25 (ISBN 0-520-02252-1). U of Cal Pr.

Sahlins, Marshall. Stone Age Economics. LC 75-169506. 1972. text ed. 21.95x (ISBN 0-202-01098-8); pap. text ed. 9.95x (ISBN 0-202-01099-6). Aldine Pub.

Saul, Frank P. The Human Skeletal Remains of Altar De Sacrificios: An Osteobiographic Analysis. LC 72-91442. (Peabody Museum Papers: Vol. 63, No. 2). 1972. pap. text ed. 15.00 (ISBN 0-87365-181-2). Peabody Harvard.

Schoetensack, Otto. Der Unterkiefer des homo heidelbergensis, aus den sanden von mauer bei Heidelberg: Ein Beitrag Zur Palaontologie Des Menschen. LC 78-72706. Repr. of 1908 ed. 47.50 (ISBN 0-404-18277-1). AMS Pr.

Scott, James. Palaentology & Introduction. 160p. 1980. 15.00x (ISBN 0-89771-000-2). State Mutual Bk.

Shackley, Myra. Neanderthal Man. (Illus.). 149p. 1980. 19.50 (ISBN 0-208-01850-6). Shoe String.

Shutler, Richard, Jr. & Shutler, M. E. Oceanic Prehistory. 1975. pap. text ed. 5.95 (ISBN 0-8465-1938-0). Benjamin-Cummings.

Smith, Grafton E., et al. Early Man: His Origin, Development & Culture. facs. ed. LC 67-28750. (Essay Index Reprint Ser). 1931. 16.00 (ISBN 0-8369-0398-6). Arno.

Steel, Rodney & Harvey, Anthony. The Encyclopedia of Pre-Historic Life. (Illus.). 1979. 24.95 (ISBN 0-07-060920-9). McGraw.

Stigler, Robert, ed. The Old World: Early Man to the Development of Agriculture. (Pre History Ser.). (Illus.). 192p. (Orig.). 1974. 15.95 (ISBN 0-312-58380-X); pap. text ed. 6.95 (ISBN 0-312-58415-6). St Martin.

Teilhard De Chardin, Pierre. Vision Du Passe. 1957. 13.50 (ISBN 0-685-11622-0). French & Eur.

Tylor, Edward B. Researches into the Early History of Mankind & the Development of Civilization. abr. ed. Bohannan, Paul, ed. LC 64-23416. 1964. 12.50x (ISBN 0-226-82121-8). U of Chicago Pr.

--Researches into the Early History of Mankind & the Development of Civilization. abr. ed. LC 64-23416. (Classics in Anthropology Ser.). (Orig.). 1964. pap. 2.95 (ISBN 0-226-82122-6, P175, Phoen). U of Chicago Pr.

Von Koenigswald, G. H. The Evolution of Man. rev. ed. Pomerans, Arnold J., tr. from Ger. LC 73-80572. (Ann Arbor Science Library). (Illus.). 160p. 1976. 6.95 (ISBN 0-472-00120-5); pap. 2.95 (ISBN 0-472-05020-6). U of Mich Pr.

--The Evolution of Man. rev. ed. Pomerans, Arnold J., tr. from Ger. (Ann Arbor Science Library). (Illus.). 1976. pap. 2.95 (ISBN 0-472-05020-6, AA). U of Mich Pr.

Vulliamy, C. E. Our Prehistoric Forerunners. 1925. 30.00 (ISBN 0-685-73537-0). Norwood Edns.

Watson, Virginia D. & Cole, J. David. Prehistory of the Eastern Highlands of New Guinea. LC 76-49166. (Anthropological Studies in the Eastern Highlands of New Guinea: No. 3). (Illus.). 243p. 1978. 35.00 (ISBN 0-295-95541-4). U of Wash Pr.

Weidenreich, Franz. Morphology of Solo Man. LC 76-44799. (American Museum of Natural History. Anthropological Papers: Vol. 43, Pt. 3). Repr. of 1951 ed. 14.50 (ISBN 0-404-15979-6). AMS Pr.

--Der Schadelfund von Weimar-Ehringsdorf. LC 78-72709. Repr. of 1928 ed. 45.00 (ISBN 0-404-18280-1). AMS Pr.

Wendt, Herbert. In Search of Adam. Cleugh, James, tr. LC 72-14091. (Illus.). 540p. 1973. Repr. of 1956 ed. lib. bdg. 25.75x (ISBN 0-8371-6755-8, WEIS). Greenwood.

Wilson, Gordon A. The Drama of the Past. 1979. 15.00x (ISBN 0-87291-128-4). Coronado Pr.

Wolpoff, Milford H. Introduction to Paleoanthopology. 1980. text ed. 21.95x (ISBN 0-394-32197-9). Random.

--Paleoanthropology. 416p. 1980. text ed. 21.95 (ISBN 0-394-32197-9). Knopf.

Wood, W. Raymond & McMillan, R. Bruce, eds. Prehistoric Man & His Environment: A Case Study in the Ozark Highland. (Studies in Archaeology Ser.). 1976. 35.00 (ISBN 0-12-762950-5). Acad Pr.

MAN, PREHISTORIC–JUVENILE LITERATURE

Baldwin, Gordon C. Inventors & Inventions of the Ancient World. LC 73-76461. (Illus.). 256p. (gr. 7-11). 1973. 7.95 (ISBN 0-590-07164-5, Four Winds). Schol Bk Serv.

Barr, Donald. Primitive Man. (How & Why Wonder Books Ser.). (Illus.). (gr. 4-6). pap. 1.00 (ISBN 0-448-05024-2). Wonder.

Goode, Ruth. People of the Ice Age. LC 72-85191. (Illus.). 144p. (gr. 5-8). 1973. 8.95 (ISBN 0-02-736420-8, CCPr). Macmillan.

Howell, F. Clark. Early Man. (Young Readers Library). (Illus.). 1977. lib. bdg. 7.95 (ISBN 0-686-51087-9). Silver.

Jones, Frederic W. Arboreal Man. LC 78-72698. Repr. of 1916 ed. 28.00 (ISBN 0-404-18269-0). AMS Pr.

McGowen, Tom. Album of Prehistoric Man. (Illus.). (gr. 5 up). 1979. pap. 2.95 (ISBN 0-528-87051-3). Rand.
Pfeiffer, John E. The Search for Early Man. LC 63-16371. (Horizon Caravel Bks.). 154p. (YA) (gr. 7 up). 1963. PLB 12.89 (ISBN 0-06-024696-0, HarpJ). Har-Row.
Ronen, Avraham. Introducing Prehistory: Digging up the Past. LC 72-10803. (Lerner Archaeology Ser.: Digging up the Past). (Illus.). (gr. 5 up). 1976. PLB 7.95 (ISBN 0-8225-0833-8). Lerner Pubns.
White, Anne T. Prehistoric America. (Landmark Ser: No. 38). (Illus.). (gr. 4-6). 1951. PLB 5.99 (ISBN 0-394-90311-0, BYR). Random.

MAN, PREHISTORIC–AFRICA

British Museum, et al. Rhodesian Man & Associated Remains. LC 77-86422. (Illus.). Repr. of 1928 ed. 17.00 (ISBN 0-404-16624-5). AMS Pr.
Broom, Robert. Finding the Missing Link. LC 75-11916. 104p. 1975. Repr. of 1951 ed. lib. bdg. 15.00x (ISBN 0-8371-8141-0, BRFM). Greenwood.
Clark, John D. The Prehistoric Cultures of the Horn of Africa. LC 70-159173. xix, 385p. 1971. Repr. of 1954 ed. lib. bdg. 20.00x (ISBN 0-374-91657-8). Octagon.
Clark, W. E. Man-Apes or Ape-Men? The Stories of Discoveries in Africa. LC 76-774. 160p. 1976. Repr. of 1967 ed. 6.50 (ISBN 0-88275-390-8). Krieger.
Derricourt, R. M. Prehistoric Man in the Ciskei & Transkei. (Illus.). 1977. text ed. 35.00x (ISBN 0-86977-077-2). Verry.
Hester, James J. & Hobler, Philip M. Prehistoric Settlement Patterns in the Libyan Desert. (Nubian Ser.: No. 4). Repr. of 1969 ed. 44.00 (ISBN 0-404-60692-X, UAP NO. 92). AMS Pr.
Leakey, Louis S. Stone Age Africa: An Outline of Prehistory in Africa. LC 73-91262. Repr. of 1936 ed. 15.25x (ISBN 0-8371-2022-5, Pub. by Negro U Pr). Greenwood.
Leakey, Richard E. & Lewin, Roger. People of the Lake: Mankind & Its Beginnings. LC 77-92219. 1978. 10.95 (ISBN 0-385-13025-2, Anchor Pr). Doubleday.
Senyuerek, M. S. Fossil Man in Tangier. 1940. pap. 4.00 (ISBN 0-527-01238-6). Kraus Repr.
Wulsin, Frederick R. Prehistoric Archaeology of Northwest Africa. (Illus.). 1941. pap. 10.00 (ISBN 0-527-01247-5). Kraus Repr.

MAN, PREHISTORIC–AMERICA

see also Indians

Amsden, Charles A. Prehistoric Southwesterners from Basketmaker to Pueblo. 5.00 (ISBN 0-686-20683-5). Southwest Mus.
Brose, David S. & Greber, N'omi, eds. Hopewell Archaeology: The Chillicothe Conference. LC 79-88607. (MCJA Special Paper: No. 3). (Illus.). 1980. 22.50x (ISBN 0-87338-235-8); pap. 12.50x (ISBN 0-87338-236-6). Kent St U Pr.
Fitting, James E., ed. The Schultz Site at Green Point: A Stratified Occupation Area in the Saginaw Valley of Michigan. (Memoirs Ser: No. 4). (Illus.). 1972. pap. 8.00x (ISBN 0-932206-66-2). U Mich Mus Anthro.
Greenman, Emerson F. The Younge Site: An Archaeological Record from Michigan. (Occasional Contributions Ser.: No. 6). (Illus.). 1967. pap. 3.00x (ISBN 0-932206-01-8). U Mich Mus Anthro.
Herold, Joyce. Prehistoric Settlement & Physical Environment in the Mesa Verde Area. (Utah Anthropological Papers: No. 53). Repr. of 1961 ed. 38.00 (ISBN 0-404-60653-9). AMS Pr.
Hibben, Frank C. Lost Americans. (Apollo Eds.). pap. 2.95 (ISBN 0-8152-0003-X, A3). T Y Crowell.
Jennings, Jesse D. & Norbeck, Edward, eds. Prehistoric Man in the New World. LC 63-18852. 1971. pap. 5.45 (ISBN 0-226-39739-4, P432, Phoen). U of Chicago Pr.
--Prehistoric Man in the New World. LC 63-18852. 1964. 17.50x (ISBN 0-226-39738-6). U of Chicago Pr.
Lyttle, Richard B. People of the Dawn. LC 79-22766. (Illus.). (gr. 6 up). 1980. 10.95 (ISBN 0-689-30750-0). Atheneum.
Morse, Dan F. The Steuben Village & Mounds: A Multicomponent Late Hopewell Site in Illinois. (Anthropological Papers Ser.: No. 21). (Illus.). 1963. pap. 2.50x (ISBN 0-932206-24-7). U Mich Mus Anthro.
Perceval, Don. From Ice Mountain: Indian Settlement of the Americas. LC 79-53088. (Illus.). 1979. 16.00 (ISBN 0-87358-204-7). Northland.
Rogers, David B. Prehistoric Man of the Santa Barbara Coast. LC 76-43812. Repr. of 1929 ed. 38.50 (ISBN 0-404-15667-3). AMS Pr.
Sharrock, Floyd W. Prehistoric Occupation Patterns in Southwest Wyoming & Cultural Relationships with the Great Basin & Plains Culture Areas. (Utah Anthropological Papers: No. 77). Repr. of 1966 ed. 24.00 (ISBN 0-404-60677-6). AMS Pr.
--Prehistoric Occupational Patterns in Southwest Wyoming & Cultural Relationships with the Great Basin & Plains Cultural Areas. (University of Utah Anthropological Papers: No. 77). 1966. pap. 15.00x (ISBN 0-87480-144-3). U of Utah Pr.
Stephenson, Robert L. & Ferguson, Alice L. The Accokeek Creek Site: A Middle Atlantic Seaboard Culture Sequence. (Anthropological Papers Ser.: No. 20). (Illus.). 1963. pap. 3.00x (ISBN 0-932206-23-9). U Mich Mus Anthro.
Willey, Gordon R. & Phillips, Philip. Method & Theory in American Archaeology. LC 57-11215. 1962. pap. 5.00x (ISBN 0-226-89888-1, P88, Phoen). U of Chicago Pr.

MAN, PREHISTORIC–ASIA

Allchin, F. R. Neolithic Cattle-Keepers of Southern India. (University of Cambridge Oriental Pubs). 1963. 38.50 (ISBN 0-521-04018-3). Cambridge U Pr.
American Association of Physical Anthropologists & American Anthropological Association. Early Man in the Far East: A Symposium, Dec. 28, 1946. Howells, W. W., ed. (Studies in Physical Anthropology: No. 1). (Illus.). 1969. pap. text ed. 9.75x (ISBN 90-6234-044-X). Humanities.
Black, Davidson. The Human Skeletal Remains from the Sha Kuo T'un Cave Deposits: In Comparison with Those from Yang Shao Tsun & Recent North China Skeletal Material. LC 77-86441. (China. Geological Survey. Palaeontologia Sinica. Ser. D.: Vol. 1, Fasc. 3). Repr. of 1925 ed. 24.00 (ISBN 0-404-16684-9). AMS Pr.
--On a Lower Molar Hominid Tooth from the Chou Kou Tien Deposit. LC 77-86443. (China. Geological Survey. Palaeontologia Sinica. Ser. D.: Vol. 7, Fasc. 1). 1977. 12.50 (ISBN 0-404-16686-5). AMS Pr.
--On an Adolescent Skull of Sinanthropus Pekinensis: In Comparison with an Adult Skull of the Same Species & with Other Hominid Skulls, Recent & Fossil. LC 77-86442. (China. Geological Survey. Palaeontologia Sinica. Ser. D.: Vol. 7, Fasc. 2). Repr. of 1930 ed. 23.00 (ISBN 0-404-16685-7). AMS Pr.
--A Study of Kansu & Honan Aeneolithic Skulls & Specimens from Later Kansu Prehistoric Sites in Comparison with North China & Other Recent Crania. LC 77-86444. (China. Geological Survey. Palaeontologia Sinica. Ser. D.: Vol. 6., Fasc. 1). Repr. of 1928 ed. 21.00 (ISBN 0-404-16687-3). AMS Pr.
Dupree, Louis, et al. Prehistoric Research in Afghanistan. LC 75-184166. (Transactions Ser.: Vol. 62, Pt. 4). (Illus.). 1972. pap. 2.50 (ISBN 0-87169-624-X). Am Philos.
Gordon, Douglas H. The Pre-Historic Background of Indian Culture. Barrett, D. & Madhuri, Desai, eds. LC 75-31825. (Illus.). 199p. 1976. lib. bdg. 20.00x (ISBN 0-8371-8440-1, GOIC). Greenwood.
Groot, Gerard J. The Prehistory of Japan. facsimile ed. Kraus, Bertram S., ed. LC 79-37884. (Select Bibliographies Reprint Ser). Repr. of 1951 ed. 36.00 (ISBN 0-8369-6721-6). Arno.
Institute of Vertebrate Paleontology & Paleoanthropology of the Chinese Academy of Sciences. Atlas of Primitive Man in China. (Illus.). 200p. 1980. text ed. 52.50 (ISBN 0-442-20013-7, Pub. by Sci Pr China). Van Nos Reinhold.
Movius, Hallam L. Early Man & Pleistocene Stratigraphy in Southern & Eastern Asia. (Illus.). 1944. pap. 14.00 (ISBN 0-527-01249-1). Kraus Repr.
Teilhard De Chardin, Pierre. Early Man in China. LC 77-86445. (Peking Institut de Geo-Biologie). Repr. of 1941 ed. 22.00 (ISBN 0-404-16688-1). AMS Pr.
Weidenreich, Franz. The Dentition of "Sinanthropus Pekinensis". A Comparative Odontography of the Hominids. LC 77-86446. (China. Geological Survey. Palaeontologia Sinica. New Ser. D.: No. 1, Whole Ser. No. 101). (Illus.). Repr. of 1937 ed. 35.00 (ISBN 0-404-16689-X). AMS Pr.
--The Extremity Bones of "Sinanthropus Pekinensis". LC 77-86447. (China. Geological Survey. Palaeontologia Sinica. New Ser. D.: No. 5. Whole Ser. No. 116). (Illus.). Repr. of 1941 ed. 27.50 (ISBN 0-404-16690-3). AMS Pr.
--The Mandibles of "Sinanthropus Pekinensis". A Comparative Study. LC 77-86448. (China. Geological Survey. Palaeontologia Sinica. Ser. D.: Vol. 7, Fasc. 3). (Illus.). Repr. of 1938 ed. 25.50 (ISBN 0-404-16691-1). AMS Pr.
--Observations on the Form & Proportions of the Endocranial Casts of "Sinanthropus Pekinensis". Other Hominids & the Great Apes: a Comparative Study of Brain Size. LC 77-86449. (China. Geological Survey. Palaeontologia Sinica, Ser. D.: Vol. 7, Fasc. 4). (Illus.). Repr. of 1936 ed. 13.50 (ISBN 0-404-16692-X). AMS Pr.
--The Skull of "Sinanthropus Pekinensis". A Comparative Study on a Primitive Hominid Skull. LC 77-86450. (China. Geological Survey. Palaeontologia Sinica. New Ser. D.: No. 10. Whole Ser. No. 127). (Illus.). Repr. of 1943 ed. 59.00 (ISBN 0-404-16693-8). AMS Pr.
--The Torus Occipitus & Related Structures: Their Transformations in the Course of Human Evolution. LC 77-86451. (China. Geological Survey. Bulletin of the Geological Survey of China). 1977. Repr. of 1940 ed. 18.00 (ISBN 0-404-16694-6). AMS Pr.
Woo, Ju-Kang. The Mandibles & Dentition of Gigantopithecus. LC 78-72727. (Illus., Chin. & Eng.). Repr. of 1962 ed. 48.00 (ISBN 0-404-18302-6). AMS Pr.

MAN, PREHISTORIC–DENMARK

Glob, P. V. The Mound People: Danish Bronze-Age Man Preserved. Bulman, Joan, tr. from Danish. LC 73-2602. (Illus.). 180p. 1974. 19.95x (ISBN 0-8014-0800-8). Cornell U Pr.

MAN, PREHISTORIC–EGYPT

Conroy, G. C. Primate Postcranial Remains from the Oligocene of Egypt. (Contributions to Primatology: Vol.8). 140p. 1976. 37.75 (ISBN 3-8055-2333-5). S Karger.
Sandford, Kenneth S. & Arkell, W. J. Paleolithic Man & the Nile-Faiyum Divide, Vol. 1. LC 30-8240. (Illus.). 1930. 20.00 (ISBN 0-226-62104-9, OIP10). U of Chicago Pr.

MAN, PREHISTORIC–EUROPE

Broste, Kurt, ed. Prehistoric Man in Denmark, 2 Vols. 1957. pap. text ed. 47.50x (ISBN 0-391-02029-3). Humanities.
Burkitt, Miles. Old Stone Age. rev. ed. LC 56-10678. (Illus.). 1963. pap. 1.45 (ISBN 0-689-70028-8, 26). Atheneum.
Childe, V. Gordon. Prehistoric Communities of the British Isles. LC 72-82207. (Illus.). Repr. of 1940 ed. 19.00 (ISBN 0-405-08358-0, Blom Pubns). Arno.
--Prehistoric Migrations in Europe. 1976. lib. bdg. 69.95 (ISBN 0-8490-2467-6). Gordon Pr.
Clark, John G. Mesolithic Settlement of Northern Europe. LC 75-95090. Repr. of 1936 ed. lib. bdg. 16.75x (ISBN 0-8371-2579-0, CLMS). Greenwood.
Coon, Carleton S. The Races of Europe. LC 76-184840. (Illus.). 739p. 1972. Repr. of 1939 ed. lib. bdg. 37.00x (ISBN 0-8371-6328-5, CORE). Greenwood.
Early Homo Sapiens in France. LC 78-72694. Repr. of 1912 ed. 32.50 (ISBN 0-404-18265-8). AMS Pr.
Glob, P. V. The Bog People: Iron-Age Man Preserved. Bruce-Mitford, R. L., tr. LC 69-20391. (Illus.). 200p. 1969. 19.95 (ISBN 0-8014-0492-4). Cornell U Pr.
Hibben, Frank C. Prehistoric Man in Europe. (Illus.). 1958. 14.95x (ISBN 0-8061-0415-5). U of Okla Pr.
Obermaier, Hugo. Fossil Man in Spain. LC 24-25757. (Illus.). 1969. Repr. of 1924 ed. lib. bdg. 33.50x (ISBN 0-8371-1504-3, OBFM). Greenwood.
Renfrew, Colin. Before Civilization. 1973. 12.95 (ISBN 0-394-48193-3). Knopf.
Sawtell, Ruth O. Azilian Skeletal Remains from Montardit, France. 1931. pap. 3.00 (ISBN 0-527-01221-1). Kraus Repr.
Sergi, Giuseppe. Mediterranean Race: A Study of the Origin of European Peoples. LC 68-112231. (Illus.). 1967. pap. text ed. 11.00x (ISBN 90-6234-038-5). Humanities.
Smith, Fred H. The Neandertal Remains from Krapina: A Descriptive & Comparative Study. 1976. pap. 9.00x (ISBN 0-87049-226-8). U of Tenn Pr.

MAN, PREHISTORIC–GREAT BRITAIN

Bord, Janet & Bord, Colin. The Secret Country. 1977. 9.95 (ISBN 0-8027-0559-6). Walker & Co.
Childe, Vere G. Prehistoric Communities of the British Isles. 2nd ed. LC 76-114498. (Illus.). 1971. Repr. of 1947 ed. lib. bdg. 15.75x (ISBN 0-8371-4732-8, CHPC). Greenwood.
Fleure, H. & Davies, M. Natural History of Man in Britain. 1971. pap. 2.75 (ISBN 0-531-06015-2, Fontana Pap). Watts.
Forde-Johnston, J. Prehistoric Britain & Ireland. 1976. 11.50 (ISBN 0-393-05605-8). Norton.
Renfrew, Colin, ed. British Prehistory: A New Outline. LC 74-83800. (Illus.). 1975. 20.00 (ISBN 0-8155-5032-4, NP). Noyes.

MAN, PREHISTORIC–INDIA

Sankalia, H. D. Prehistory of India. LC 77-906557. (Illus.). 1977. 12.50x (ISBN 0-8002-0239-2). Intl Pubns Serv.

MAN, PREHISTORIC–MEXICO

De Terra, Helmut, et al. Tepexpan Man. Linton, Ralph, ed. (Illus.). 1949. pap. 15.50 (ISBN 0-384-11525-X). Johnson Repr.
Kirkby, Ann. The Use of Land & Water Resources in the Past & Present Valley of Oaxaca. Flannery, Kent V., ed. (Memoirs No. 5, Prehistory & Human Ecology of the Valley of Caxaca Ser.: Vol. 1). (Illus.). 1973. pap. 6.00x (ISBN 0-932206-67-0). U Mich Mus Anthro.
Lees, Susan. Sociopolitical Aspects of Canal Irrigation in the Valley of Oaxaca. Flannery, Kent V., ed. (Memoirs No. 6, Prehistory & Human Ecology of the Valley of Caxaca Ser.: Vol. 2). (Illus.). 1973. pap. 6.00x (ISBN 0-932206-68-9). U Mich Mus Anthro.
Parsons, Jeffrey R. Prehistoric Settlement Patterns in the Southern Valley of Mexico: The Chalco-Xochimilco Region. (Memoir Ser.: No. 14). (Orig.). 1981. pap. write for info. (ISBN 0-932206-88-3). U Mich Mus Anthro.

MAN, PREHISTORIC–POLYNESIA

Jennings, Jessie D., ed. The Prehistory of Polynesia. LC 79-1055. (Illus.). 1979. text ed. 35.00x (ISBN 0-674-70060-0). Harvard U Pr.

MAN, PREHISTORIC–SOUTH AMERICA

Rick, John W. Prehistoric Hunters of the High Andes. LC 79-28090. (Studies in Archaeology Ser.). 1980. 27.50 (ISBN 0-12-587760-9). Acad Pr.

MAN, PRIMITIVE

see also Ethnology; Ethnopsychology; Society, Primitive

Avebury. Prehistoric Times As Illustrated by Ancient Remains & the Manners & Customs of Modern Savages. 7th ed. 1969. Repr. of 1913 ed. text ed. 24.75x (ISBN 90-6234-001-6). Humanities.
Avebury, John L. Origin of Civilisation & the Primitive Condition of Man. LC 72-1280. (Select Bibliographies Reprint Ser.). 1972. Repr. of 1912 ed. 29.00 (ISBN 0-8369-6819-0). Arno.
Blackburn, Julia. The White Men: The First Responses of Aboriginal Peoples to the White Man. LC 79-9859. (Illus.). 1979. 14.95 (ISBN 0-8129-0826-0, Dist. by Har-Row). Times Bks.
Bodley, John H. Victims of Progress. LC 74-84817. 1975. pap. text ed. 8.95 (ISBN 0-8465-0540-1). Benjamin-Cummings.
Clodd, Edward. The Story of "Primitive" Man. 1979. Repr. of 1904 ed. lib. bdg. 7.50 (ISBN 0-8482-7578-0). Norwood Edns.
--The Story of "Primitive" Man. 1979. Repr. of 1910 ed. lib. bdg. 20.00 (ISBN 0-8492-4032-8). R West.
Crawley, Alfred E. Studies of Savages & Sex. Besterman, Theodore, ed. (Landmarks in Anthropology Ser). 1969. Repr. of 1929 ed. 14.00 (ISBN 0-384-10140-2). Johnson Repr.
Fairchild, Hoxie N. Noble Savage: A Study in Romantic Naturalism. LC 61-12130. 1961. Repr. of 1928 ed. 15.00 (ISBN 0-8462-0180-1). Russell.
Hewitt, J. F. Primitive Traditional History: The Primitive History & Chronology of India, Southeastern & Southwestern Asia, Egypt, & Europe, 2 vols. 1977. lib. bdg. 200.00 (ISBN 0-8490-2477-3). Gordon Pr.
Hoernes, M. Primitive Man. 59.95 (ISBN 0-8490-0890-5). Gordon Pr.
Lubbock, John. The Origin of Civilization & the Primitive Condition of Man. Riviere, Peter, ed. LC 77-77486. (Classics in Anthrology Ser.). (Illus.). 1978. lib. bdg. 25.00x (ISBN 0-226-49637-6). U of Chicago Pr.
Lumholtz, Carl. Among Cannibals. 1979. Repr. of 1888 ed. text ed. 26.00x (ISBN 0-904573-13-3). Humanities.
Sahlins, Marshall D. Tribesmen. (Illus., Orig.). 1968. pap. 6.95 ref. ed. (ISBN 0-13-930925-X). P-H.
Schmidt, Max. Primitive Races of Mankind. Dallas, Alexander K., tr. LC 27-3949. Repr. of 1926 ed. 22.00 (ISBN 0-527-80250-6). Kraus Repr.
Service, Elman R. The Hunters. 2nd ed. (Foundations of Modern Anthropology Ser.). (Illus.). 1979. pap. 5.95 ref. (ISBN 0-13-448100-3). P-H.

MAN AND WIFE

see Husband and Wife

MAN IN SPACE PROGRAM

see Project Mercury

MAN-MACHINE CONTROL SYSTEMS

see Man-Machine Systems

MAN-MACHINE SYSTEMS

Chapanis, Alphonse. Man-Machine Engineering. LC 65-15099. (Behavioral Science in Industry Ser). (Orig.). 1966. pap. text ed. 6.95x (ISBN 0-8185-0306-8). Brooks-Cole.
Ledgard, H., et al. Directions in Human Factors for Interactive Systems. (Lecture Notes in Computer Science Ser.: Vol. 103). 190p. 1981. pap. 11.80 (ISBN 0-387-10574-3). Springer-Verlag.
Lilly, John C. Programming & Metaprogramming in the Human Biocomputer. LC 73-79777. 190p. 1972. 8.00 (ISBN 0-517-52757-X); pap. 4.95 (ISBN 0-517-52758-8). Crown.
Martin, James. Design of Man-Computer Dialogues. (Illus.). 496p. 1973. ref. ed. 30.95 (ISBN 0-13-201251-0). P-H.
Parsons, Henry McILvaine. Man-Machine System Experiments. LC 71-166483. (Illus.). 632p. 1972. 35.00x (ISBN 0-8018-1322-0). Johns Hopkins.
Petacchi, Donald. Work for Being in the Machine Age. LC 80-82646. 80p. 1980. 12.50 (ISBN 0-8022-2376-1). Philos Lib.

Sheridan, T. B. & Johannsen, G., eds. Monitoring Behavior & Supervisory Control. LC 76-41687. (NATO Conference Series No. III: Volume 1, Human Factors). 527p. 1976. 47.50 (ISBN 0-306-32881-X, Plenum Pr). Plenum Pub.
Sheridan, Thomas B. & Ferrell, William R. Man-Machine Systems: Information, Control & Decision Models of Human Performance. 472p. 1974. pap. text ed. 12.50x (ISBN 0-262-69072-1). MIT Pr.
--Man-Machine Systems: Information, Control, & Decision Models of Human Performance. LC 73-19777. (Illus.). 707p. 1974. 27.50x (ISBN 0-262-19118-0). MIT Pr.
Whitt, Frank R. & Wilson, David G. Bicycling Science: Ergonomics & Mechanics. 1975. pap. 6.95 (ISBN 0-262-73046-4). MIT Pr.

MAN-MADE LAKES
see Reservoirs

MAN ON OTHER PLANETS
see Life on Other Planets

MAN POWER
see Manpower

MAN SINGH, RAJA OF AMBER, 1550-1614
Prasad, Rajiva N. Raja Man Singh of Amber. 1966. 8.25x (ISBN 0-8426-1473-7). Verry.

MAN-TO-MAN COMBAT
see Hand-To-Hand Fighting

MANA
see also Animism
Clodd, Edward. Magic in Names, & in Other Things. LC 67-23906. 1968. Repr. of 1920 ed. 19.00 (ISBN 0-8103-3024-5). Gale.
Morris, Madeleine C. Miracle of MANA Force: Secret of Wealth,Love & Power. 1975. 10.95 (ISBN 0-13-585760-0). P-H.

MANAGEMENT
see also Business; Campaign Management; Computer Programming Management; Credit Management; Delegation of Authority; Executive Ability; Executives; Factory Management; Farm Management; Hospitals-Administration; Housing Management; Industrial Management; Office Management; Organization; Organizational Change; Personnel Management; Planning; Scheduling (Management); School Management and Organization; Theater Management; Work Measurement
also subdivision management under specific subjects, e.g. Railroads-Management
Academy of Management, Annual Meeting, 39th, 1979. Proceedings. Huseman, Richard C., ed. LC 40-2886. (Illus.). 1979. pap. text ed. 11.00 (ISBN 0-915350-18-1). Acad of Mgmt.
Academy of Management, 40th Annual Meeting, 1980. Proceedings. Huseman, Richard C., ed. LC 40-2886. 436p. (Orig.). 1980. pap. text ed. 11.00 (ISBN 0-915350-19-X). Acad of Mgmt.
Ackoff, Russell L. The Art of Problem Solving: Accompanied by Ackoff's Fables. LC 78-5627. 214p. 1978. 17.95 (ISBN 0-471-04289-7, Pub. by Wiley-Interscience). Wiley.
Adam, Everett E., Jr. & Ebert, Ronald J. Production & Operations Management: Concepts, Models & Behavior. 2nd ed. (Illus.). 736p. 1982. ref. ed. 24.95 (ISBN 0-13-724971-3). P-H.
Adizes, Ichak. How to Solve the Mismanagement Crisis: Diagnosis & Treatment of Management Problems. 300p. 1981. Repr. of 1979 ed. 16.00 (ISBN 0-686-77592-9). Irvington.
Administrative Management for Development. 1978. pap. 13.25 (ISBN 92-3-101176-6, U800, UNESCO). Unipub.
Adrian, James. Business Practices for Construction Management. LC 75-14999. 352p. 1975. 19.95 (ISBN 0-444-00169-7, North Holland). Elsevier.
Aggarwal, Raj & Khera, Inder. Management Science: Cases & Applications. 1979. pap. text ed. 12.95x (ISBN 0-8162-0096-3). Holden-Day.
Albanese, Robert. Managing: Toward Accountability for Performance. 3rd ed. 1981. text ed. 21.00x (ISBN 0-256-02505-3). Irwin.
Albers, Henry H. Management: The Basic Concepts. rev. ed. 336p. 1981. lib. bdg. write for info. (ISBN 0-89874-312-5). Krieger.
--Management: The Basic Concepts. LC 73-172949. 1979. text ed. 16.50 Arabic ed. (ISBN 0-471-06348-7); pap. 9.90 (ISBN 0-471-05142-X). Wiley.
--Principles of Management: A Modern Approach. 4th ed. LC 73-12217. (Management & Administration Ser.). 560p. 1974. text ed. 22.50 (ISBN 0-471-01916-X); tchrs'. manual 3.95 (ISBN 0-471-01915-1). Wiley.
Albert, Michael. Effective Management: Readings, Cases & Experiences. 220p. Date not set. pap. text ed. 8.50 scp (ISBN 0-06-166407-3, HarpC). Har-Row.
Albrecht, Karl. Executive Tune-Up: Personal Effectiveness Skills for Business & Professional People. (Illus.). 224p. 1981. text ed. 13.95 (ISBN 0-13-294215-1, Spec); pap. text ed. 6.95 (ISBN 0-13-294207-0, Spec). P-H.
--Stress & the Manager: Making It Work for You. (Illus.). 1978. 14.95 (ISBN 0-13-852681-8, Spec); pap. 6.95 (ISBN 0-13-852673-7). P-H.
--Successful Management by Objectives: An Action Manual. LC 77-14971. (Illus.). 1978. 14.95 (ISBN 0-13-863266-9, Spec); pap. 5.95 (ISBN 0-13-863258-8, Spec). P-H.
Alden, Thomas. Scientific Management: The Essential Knowledge Which Everyone, but Absolutely Everyone Ought to Possess of the Main Guiding Principles Which Intelligent Men Follow in the Management of Their Business & Personal Affairs. (The Essential Knowledge Ser.). 1978. 28.45 (ISBN 0-89266-120-8). Am Classical Coll Pr.
Alexander Hamilton Institute, Inc. Administracion Por Objectivos: Sistema Moderno Para Lograr Resultados. Jenks, James M., ed. (Illus.). 71p. (Orig., Span.). 1978. pap. 48.65 (ISBN 0-86604-033-1). Hamilton Inst.
Alexander Hamilton Institute, Inc. Administracao Por Objectivos: Sistema Moderno Para Obter Resultados. Jenks, James M., ed. (Illus.). 68p. (Orig., Portuguese.). 1978. pap. 53.25 (ISBN 0-86604-034-X). Hamilton Inst.
--La Gestion Par Objectifs: Un Systeme Moderne Pour Obtenir Des Resultats. Jenks, James M., ed. (Illus.). 74p. (Orig., Fr.). 1978. pap. 48.50 (ISBN 0-86604-035-8). Hamilton Inst.
--Management by Objectives: A Modern System for Getting Results. Jenks, James M., ed. (Illus.). 66p. (Orig.). 1978. pap. 53.15 (ISBN 0-86604-032-3). Hamilton Inst.
Alexander, John W. Managing Our Work. rev. ed. LC 72-186572. (Illus.). 104p. 1975. pap. 3.50 (ISBN 0-87784-352-X). Inter-Varsity.
Alexander, K. C. Participative Management: The India Experience. LC 72-906846. 132p. 1972. 7.50x (ISBN 0-8002-0945-1). Intl Pubns Serv.
Allen, L. A. Making Managerial Planning More Effective. 320p. 1981. 24.95 (ISBN 0-07-001078-1, P&RB). McGraw.
Allen, Louis A. Management & Organization. LC 57-13329. 353p. 1958. 17.50 (ISBN 0-686-65356-4). McGraw.
--Management Profession. (Management Ser.). 1964. 18.95 (ISBN 0-07-001375-6, P&RB). McGraw.
--Professional Management. 256p. 1973. 17.95 (ISBN 0-07-001110-9, P&RB). McGraw.
Allsopp, Michael. Management in the Professions: Guidelines to Improved Professional Performance. 201p. 1979. text ed. 29.50x (ISBN 0-220-67011-0, Pub. by Busn Bks England). Renouf.
Alter, Steven L. Decision Support Systems - Current Practice & Continuing Challenges: Current Practice & Continuing Challenges. LC 78-67960. 1979. text ed. 17.95 (ISBN 0-201-00193-4). A-W.
Altfelder, Klaus. Lexikon der Unternehmensfuehrung. (Ger.). 1973. 47.00 (ISBN 3-470-56191-5, M-7219). French & Eur.
Altman & Weil. How to Manage Your Law Office. 1973. 38.50 (ISBN 0-685-40615-6). Bender.
Anderson, Carl R. & Gannon, Martin J. Readings in Management: An Organizational Perspective. 1977. write for info. (CPCU 7). IIA.
Anderson, David, et al. Essentials of Management Science: Applications to Decision Making. (Illus.). 1978. text ed. 21.50 (ISBN 0-8299-0147-7); study guide 7.95 (ISBN 0-8299-0202-3); test bank avail. (ISBN 0-8299-0455-7); instrs.' manual avail. (ISBN 0-8299-0453-0); transparency masters avail. (ISBN 0-8299-0454-9). West Pub.
Anderson, I. G. Marketing & Management: A World Register of Organizations. 1969. 12.00x (ISBN 0-900246-03-0). Intl Pubns Serv.
Anderson, Richard C. Business Systems: The Fabric of Management. LC 73-17244. (Illus.). 124p. Date not set. 7.95 (ISBN 0-913842-06-0). Correlan Pubns.
--The Manager: A Profile. LC 72-7667. (Illus.). 71p. Date not set. 7.95 (ISBN 0-913842-00-1). Correlan Pubns.
--Thought Starters. (Illus.). 105p. Date not set. 12.95 (ISBN 0-913842-04-4). Correlan Pubns.
Anderson, Richard C. & Dobyns, L. R. Time: The Irretrievable Asset. LC 73-12755. (Illus.). 75p. Date not set. 7.95 (ISBN 0-913842-05-2). Correlan Pubns.
Ansoff, H. Igor. Strategic Management. LC 78-23402. 1979. 27.95 (ISBN 0-470-26585-X). Halsted Pr.
Ansoff, Igor, et al, eds. From Strategic Planning to Strategic Management. LC 74-20598. 259p. 1976. 40.25 (ISBN 0-471-03223-9, Pub. by Wiley-Interscience). Wiley.
Anthony, P. D. The Ideology of Work. 1979. 25.00x (ISBN 0-422-74310-0, Pub. by Tavistock England); pap. 9.95x (ISBN 0-422-76650-X). Methuen Inc.
Anthony, Robert N. & Dearden, John. Management Control Systems. 4th ed. 1980. 21.95x (ISBN 0-256-02325-5). Irwin.
Anthony, Willam P. Managing Incompetence. 256p. 1982. 15.95 (ISBN 0-8144-5672-3). Am Mgmt.
Anthony, William P. Management: Competencies & Incompetencies. LC 79-25171. 604p. 1981. text ed. write for info. (ISBN 0-201-00085-7). A-W.
--Participative Management. LC 77-83035. 1978. pap. text ed. 8.95 (ISBN 0-201-00253-1); instr's guide 1.25 (ISBN 0-201-00219-1). A-W.
Antolinez, Crescencio. Fachworterbuch Fur Recht und Verwaltung. (Span. & Ger.). 1970. leatherette 25.00 (ISBN 3-452-17065-9, M-7398, Pub. by Carl Heymanns Verlag KG). French & Eur.
Appleby, Robert C. & Burstiner, Irving. The Essential Guide to Management. 192p. 1981. 16.95 (ISBN 0-13-286211-5); pap. 7.95 (ISBN 0-13-286203-4). P-H.
Appley, Lawrence A. Formula for Success: A Core Concept of Management. LC 73-87546. 1974. 12.95 (ISBN 0-8144-5339-2). Am Mgmt.
Arabinda, Ray. The Manager Beyond the Organization. 1980. 9.50x (ISBN 0-8364-0636-2, Pub. by Macmillan India). South Asia Bks.
Aram, John D. Dilemmas of Administrative Behavior. 144p. 1976. Ref. Ed. 9.95 (ISBN 0-13-214247-3). P-H.
Archibald, Russell D. Managing High-Technology Programs & Projects. LC 76-3789. 288p. 1976. 32.50 (ISBN 0-471-03308-1, Pub. by Wiley-Interscience). Wiley.
Argenti, John. A Management System for the Seventies. 1972. text ed. 16.50x (ISBN 0-04-658044-1). Allen Unwin.
Argyris, C. Management & Organizational Development: The Paths from XA to YB. 1971. 18.50 (ISBN 0-07-002219-4, P&RB). McGraw.
Argyris, Chris. Intervention Theory & Method: A Behavioral Science View. LC 79-114331. (Business Ser). 1970. text ed. 18.95 (ISBN 0-201-00342-2). A-W.
Armerding, Hudson T. Leadership. 1978. 6.95 (ISBN 0-8423-2126-8); pap. 3.95 (ISBN 0-8423-2125-X). Tyndale.
Armstrong, Frank. Memos to Management. LC 73-92188. 228p. 1974. 25.00x (ISBN 0-8128-1691-9). Stein & Day.
Armstrong, Michael, ed. Personnel & Training Management Yearbook & Directory 1980. 8th ed. LC 73-643112. (Illus.). 365p. 1979. 30.00x (ISBN 0-85038-242-4). Intl Pubns Serv.
Arnold, John. Shooting the Executive Rapids: The First Year in a New Assignment. Newton, William R., ed. (Illus.). 288p. 1981. 17.95 (ISBN 0-07-002312-3, P&RB). McGraw.
Aronofsky, J. S., et al. Managerial Planning with Linear Programming: In Process Industry Operations. 379p. 1978. 46.50 (ISBN 0-471-03360-X, Pub. by Wiley-Interscience). Wiley.
Arthur, Henry B. Commodity Futures As a Business Management Tool. LC 71-162634. (Illus.). 1971. 17.50x (ISBN 0-87584-092-2). Harvard Busn.
Atchison, Thomas J. & Hill, Winston W. Management Today: Managing Work in Organizations. 575p. 1978. text ed. 18.95 (ISBN 0-15-554780-1, HC); instructor's manual avail. (ISBN 0-15-554781-X). HarBraceJ.
Atwater, Eastwood. I Hear You; Listening Skills to Make You a Better Manager. 224p. 1981. 12.95 (ISBN 0-13-450684-7); pap. 4.95 (ISBN 0-13-450676-6). P-H.
Auby, J. M., et al. Traite De Science Administrative: Anatomie et Physiologie De L'administration Publique. 1966. 61.75x (ISBN 90-2796-376-2). Mouton.
Aukee, Waino E., et al, eds. Inside the Management Team. 1973. pap. text ed. 2.00x (ISBN 0-8134-1571-3, 1571). Interstate.
Auxiliary Gift & Coffee Shop Management. 2nd ed. 136p. 1976. 16.25 (ISBN 0-686-68589-X, 1122). Hospital Finan.
Baehler, James R. The New Manager's Guide to Success. 160p. 1980. 19.95 (ISBN 0-03-058014-5). Praeger.
Baker, Alan J. Investment, Valuation & the Managerial Theory of the Firm. 336p. 1978. text ed. 30.25x (ISBN 0-566-00192-6, Pub. by Gower Pub Co England). Renouf.
Bard, Ray & Davis, Larry. Winning Ways. LC 79-20395. 1979. 3-ring notebk. 99.50 (ISBN 0-89384-043-2). Learning Concepts.
Barnard, Chester I. Functions of the Executive. 30th anniversary ed. LC 68-28690. 1968. 16.50x (ISBN 0-674-32800-0); pap. 5.95x (ISBN 0-674-32803-5). Harvard U Pr.
Barton, Richard F. The Imaginative Management Game. Date not set. pap. 12.50 (ISBN 0-914460-00-5). Active Learning.
--The Imaginit Management Game: 1978 Edition. 3rd ed. Date not set. 9.95 (ISBN 0-685-49689-9). Active Learning.
Bass, B. Stogdill's Handbook of Leadership. 587p. 1981. text ed. 29.95 (ISBN 0-02-901820-X). Macmillan.
Bass, Lawrence W. Management by Task Forces: A Manual on the Operation of Interdisciplinary Teams. LC 74-82702. 1975. 12.50 (ISBN 0-912338-09-1); microfiche 9.50 (ISBN 0-912338-10-5). Lomond.
Basu, K. S. Management Similarities & Differences Under Different Cultures. 1970. pap. 29.75x (ISBN 0-677-61500-0). Gordon.
Basu, P. K., ed. The New Managerial Order in Asia. 1981. 20.00x (ISBN 0-8364-0740-7, Pub. by Macmillan India). South Asia Bks.
Bates, Donald L. & Eldredge, David L. Strategy & Policy: Analysis, Formulation, & Implementation. 1980. text ed. write for info. (ISBN 0-697-08036-6); instr. man. avail. (ISBN 0-697-08038-2). Wm C Brown.
Batten, J. D. Tough-Minded Management. 3rd rev. ed. 1978. 14.95 (ISBN 0-8144-5477-1). Am Mgmt.
Batten, Joseph D. Beyond Management by Objectives. rev. ed. 112p. 11.95 (ISBN 0-8144-5614-6). Am Mgmt.
Batty, J. The Board & the Presentation of Financial Information to Management. 340p. 1978. text ed. 39.25x (ISBN 0-220-66352-1, Pub. by Busn Bks England). Renouf.
Baughman, James P., et al. Environmental Analysis for Management. 1974. 20.50x (ISBN 0-256-01561-9). Irwin.
Baumgartner, J. S. Systems Management. 64p. 1979. 17.50 (ISBN 0-87179-297-4). BNA.
Beach, Dale S. Managing People at Work: Readings in Personnel. 3rd ed. (Illus.). 1980. pap. text ed. 11.95 (ISBN 0-02-307030-7). Macmillan.
Beck, Arthur C. & Hillmar, Ellis D. Making MBO-R Work. LC 75-18151. 239p. 1975. text ed. 8.95 (ISBN 0-201-00469-0). A-W.
Beck, Arthur C., Jr. & Hillmar, Ellis D. A Practical Approach to Organization Development Through MBO: Selected Readings. LC 71-183665. (Illus.). 280p. 1972. pap. text ed. 8.95 (ISBN 0-201-00447-X). A-W.
Beck, John & Cox, Charles. Advances in Management Education. LC 80-40117. 360p. 1980. 47.50 (ISBN 0-471-27775-4, Pub. by Wiley-Interscience). Wiley.
Becker, Selwyn W. & Neuhauser, Duncan. The Efficient Organization. LC 75-8269. 256p. 1975. 14.95 (ISBN 0-444-99004-6). Elsevier.
Beckett, J. Management Dynamics: The New Synthesis. (Management Ser). 1971. text ed. 16.95 (ISBN 0-07-004255-1, C); instructor's manual 4.95 (ISBN 0-07-004257-8). McGraw.
Beckhard, Richard. Organization Development: Strategies & Models. Schein, Edgar, et al, eds. (Ser. in Organization Development). 1969. pap. text ed. 6.50 (ISBN 0-201-00448-8). A-W.
Beer, Michael. Organizational Change & Development: A Systems View. 1980. pap. text ed. 19.95 (ISBN 0-8302-6416-7). Goodyear.
Belasco, James A. & Hampton, David R. Managemant Today. 2nd ed. LC 80-28981. 460p. 1981. text ed. 19.95 (ISBN 0-471-08579-0). Wiley.
Belin, R. M. Management Teams Why They Succeed or Fail. 200p. 1981. 29.95 (ISBN 0-470-27172-8). Halsted Pr.
Belker, Loren B. The First-Time Manager. LC 78-12993. 1979. 13.95 (ISBN 0-8144-5492-5). Am Mgmt.
Bellaschi, Jules. To Lead & Manage. LC 80-83869. 70p. (Orig.). 1980. pap. 4.95 (ISBN 0-9605144-0-6). MJ Pubns.
Bendix, Reinhard. Work & Authority in Industry: Ideologies of Management in the Course of Industrialization. LC 73-78553. 1974. pap. 7.95x (ISBN 0-520-02628-4). U of Cal Pr.
Benge, Eugene. Elements of Modern Management. LC 76-25179. 1976. 12.95 (ISBN 0-8144-5428-3). Am Mgmt.
Bennett, Dudley. Successful Team Building Through TA. 1980. 14.95 (ISBN 0-8144-5607-3). Am Mgmt.
--TA & the Manager. (AMACOM Executive Bks). 1978. pap. 5.95 (ISBN 0-8144-7511-6). Am Mgmt.
--TA & the Manager. (Illus.). 1976. 13.95 (ISBN 0-8144-5422-4). Am Mgmt.
Bennis, Warren. The Unconscious Conspiracy: Why Leaders Can't Lead. (AMACOM Executive Bks). 1978. pap. 5.95 (ISBN 0-8144-7507-8). Am Mgmt.
Benton, Lewis, ed. Management for the Future. LC 77-22862. 1978. 19.95 (ISBN 0-07-004818-5). McGraw.
Berg, Ivar, et al. Managers & Work Reform: A Limited Engagement. LC 77-83165. (Illus.). 1978. 15.95 (ISBN 0-02-902900-7). Free Pr.
Berkeley, G. The Administrative Revolution: Notes on the Passing of the Organization Man. 1971. 2.95 (ISBN 0-13-008532-4, S244, Spec). P-H.
Berkman, Harold W. The Human Relations of Management. 1974. text ed. 14.95x (ISBN 0-685-70780-6). Dickenson.

Berliner, William M. Managerial & Supervisory Practice. 7th ed. 1979. 18.95x (ISBN 0-256-02040-X). Irwin.
Berry, William L., et al. Management Decision Sciences: Cases & Readings. 1980. 20.95x (ISBN 0-256-02219-4). Irwin.
Best of Management Today, Vol. 4. 17.50 (ISBN 0-686-22953-3). Hippocrene Bks.
Betts, Peter W. The Board & Administrative Management: Management for the Board. 192p. 1977. text ed. 23.50x (ISBN 0-220-66338-6, Pub. by Busn Bks England). Renouf.
Biggs, Charles L., et al. Managing the Systems Development Process. 1980. text ed. 26.95 (ISBN 0-13-550830-4). P-H.
Bingham, Robert E. Traps to Avoid in Good Administration. LC 78-67265. 1979. pap. 3.95 (ISBN 0-8054-2535-7). Broadman.
Birchall, D. W. & Hammond, V. Tomorrow's Office Today Managing Technological Change. 216p. 1981. 29.95 (ISBN 0-470-27236-8). Halsted Pr.
Biskirk, Richard A. Modern Management & Machiavelli. 1975. pap. 2.25 (ISBN 0-451-61703-7, ME1703, Ment). NAL.
Bittel, Lester R. Encyclopedia of Professional Management. (Illus.). 1979. 29.50 (ISBN 0-07-005478-9, P&RB). McGraw.
--Essentials of Supervisory Management. LC 80-13784. (Illus.). 288p. 1980. softcover 12.95 (ISBN 0-07-005571-8, G); instrs'. manual & key 4.50 (ISBN 0-07-005572-6). McGraw.
--Skills Development Portfolio for What Every Supervisor Should Know, The Basics of Supervisory Management. 4th ed. 1979. 5.30 (ISBN 0-07-005562-9). McGraw.
--What Every Supervisor Should Know, the Basics of Supervisory Management. 4th ed. LC 79-16387. 1980. 18.95x (ISBN 0-07-005573-4); text ed. 16.75x (ISBN 0-07-005561-0); Skills Development portfolio 5.95 (ISBN 0-07-005562-9); Course & Management key 4.50 (ISBN 0-07-005563-7). McGraw.
Blackler, F. H. & Brown, C. A. Whatever Happened to Shell's New Philosophy of Management? 184p. 1980. text ed. 27.00x (ISBN 0-566-00306-6, Pub. by Gower Pub Co England). Renouf.
Blagrove, Luanna C. Management for Proprietors & Partnerships. LC 80-70035. (Illus.). 165p. 1981. text ed. 24.95 (ISBN 0-9604466-7-2). Blagrove Pubns.
Blake, Claire. Greenhouse Gardening for Fun. (Illus.). 1967. pap. 3.95 (ISBN 0-688-06737-9). Morrow.
Blake, Robert R. & Mouton, Jane S. The Versatile Manager: A Grid Profile. LC 80-68466. 233p. 1981. 13.95 (ISBN 0-87094-222-0). Dow Jones-Irwin.
Blake, Robert R., et al. The Academic Administrator Grid: A Guide to Developing Effective Management Teams. LC 80-8908. (Higher Education Ser.). 1981. text ed. 17.95x (ISBN 0-87589-492-5). Jossey-Bass.
Blake, Stewart P. Managing for Responsive Research & Development. LC 77-26120. (Illus.). 1978. text ed. 21.95x (ISBN 0-7167-0036-0). W H Freeman.
Blanchard, Kenneth. The One Minute Manager. 1981. 15.00 (ISBN 0-686-30549-3). Blanchard-Johnson.
Bliss, Edwin C. Getting Things Done: The ABC's of Time Management. LC 76-1363. (Illus.). 128p. 1976. 9.95 (ISBN 0-684-14644-4, ScribT). Scribner.
Block, Peter. Flawless Consulting: A Guide to Getting Your Expertise Used. (Illus.). 245p. 1981. text ed. 18.95 (ISBN 0-89384-052-1). Learning Concepts.
Blumenfeld, Warren S. The Effectiveness of Management Three Hundred & Fifty. (Research Monograph: No. 54). 1974. spiral bdg. 5.00 (ISBN 0-88406-020-9). Ga St U Busn Pub.
Bobrow, Jerry & Covino, William A. GMAT (Graduate Management Admissions Test) 1980. pap. text ed. 5.25 (ISBN 0-8220-2006-8). Cliffs.
Boling, T. Edwin. Managemet: Making Organizations Perform, Study Guide. (Illus.). 1980. pap. text ed. 7.95 (ISBN 0-02-311870-9). Macmillan.
Bonoma, Thomas V. & Zaltman, Gerald. Psychology for Management. (Business Ser.). 337p. 1981. text ed. 11.95x (ISBN 0-686-73726-1). Kent Pub Co.
Boone, Louis E. & Bowen, Donald. Great Writings in Management & Organizational Behavior. 475p. 1980. pap. text ed. 13.90 (ISBN 0-87814-097-2). Pennwell Pub.
Boot, R. L., et al. Behavioural Sciences for Managers. 1977. 27.50x (ISBN 0-7131-3382-1); pap. 14.95x (ISBN 0-7131-3383-X). Intl Ideas.
Borsenik, Frank D. Property Management. (Illus.). 210p. (Orig.). 1974. 11.95x (ISBN 0-86612-003-3). Educ Inst Am Hotel.
Bowers, David. Systems of Organization: Management of the Human Resource. LC 75-31052. 1977. pap. text ed. 5.95x (ISBN 0-472-08173-X). U of Mich Pr.
Bowey, Angela. Guide to Manpower Planning. 1977. text ed. 13.50x (ISBN 0-333-15555-6). Verry.
Boyd, Bradford B. Management-Minded Supervision: A Self-Study Training Program. (Illus.). 1979. 32.95 (ISBN 0-07-006943-3, G); manager's guide 42.95 (ISBN 0-07-006944-1). McGraw.
Bozeman, Barry. Public Management & Policy Analysis. LC 78-65247. 1979. text ed. 13.95x (ISBN 0-312-65471-5). St Martin.
Bracey, Hyler J., et al. Basic Management: An Experience Based Approach. rev. ed. 1981. pap. 13.95x (ISBN 0-256-02572-X). Business Pubns.
Braverman, Jerome D. Management Decision-Making: A Formal-Intuitive Approach. 240p. 1980. 15.95 (ISBN 0-8144-5623-5). Am Mgmt.
Bray, Douglas W., et al. Formative Years in Business: A Long Term AT&T Study of Managerial Lives. LC 78-25609. 256p. 1979. Repr. of 1974 ed. text ed. 17.50 (ISBN 0-88275-824-1). Krieger.
Brech, E. F. The Principles & Practice of Management. 3rd ed. LC 73-88699. 1080p. 1976. text ed. 38.00x (ISBN 0-582-45039-X). Longman.
Bridge, John & Dodds, J. C. Planning & the Growth of the Firm. 211p. 1978. 28.00x (ISBN 0-85664-362-9, Pub by Croom Helm Ltd England). Biblio Dist.
Brightman, Harvey J. Problem-Solving: A Logical & Creative Approach. LC 80-25078. 1980. 14.95 (ISBN 0-88406-131-0). Ga St U Busn Pub.
Brinckloe, William D. & Coughlin, Mary T. Managing Organizations. 1977. text ed. 14.95x (ISBN 0-02-471200-0). Macmillan.
Brink, Victor Z. Understanding Management Policy--& Making It Work. new ed. (Illus.). 1978. 19.95 (ISBN 0-8144-5455-0). Am Mgmt.
Broadwell, Martin M. Supervising Today: A Guide for Positive Leadership. LC 79-12751. 1979. pap. 10.95 (ISBN 0-8436-0775-0). CBI Pub.
Bronner, Rolf. Decision Making Under Time Pressure: An Experimental Study of Stress Behavior in Business Management. LC 81-47626. 1981. price not set (ISBN 0-669-04696-5). Lexington Bks.
Bronson, C. & Bronson, R. Mathemathics for Management. 1977. text ed. 22.95 scp (ISBN 0-7002-2503-X, HarpC). Har-Row.
Broom, Halsey N. & Longenecker, J. G. Small Business Management. 3rd ed. 1971. text ed. 12.95 (ISBN 0-538-07220-2). SW Pub.
Brown, C. L., et al. Audit Committee Conference October 18, 19, 1978, Tarrytown, Ny: Proceedings. LC 79-87782. 1979. pap. text ed. 25.00 (ISBN 0-89413-076-5). Inst Inter Aud.
Brown, Courtney C. Putting the Corporate Board to Work. LC 75-14918. (Studies of the Modern Corporation). 1976. 10.95 (ISBN 0-02-904760-9). Free Pr.
Brown, Fred R., ed. Management: Concepts & Practice. LC 77-84858. 1977. 8.95 (ISBN 0-912338-15-6); microfiche 7.95 (ISBN 0-912338-16-4). Lomond.
Brown, J. Lewis. Principles & Practice of Management Accountancy. 3rd ed. 756p. 1975. 15.00x (ISBN 0-7121-1654-0). Intl Pubns Serv.
Brown, Ronald D. From Selling to Managing. (AMACOM Executive Books). 1978. pap. 5.95 (ISBN 0-8144-7500-0). Am Mgmt.
Brown, Warrren B. & Moberg, Dennis G. Organization Management: A Macro Approach. LC 79-18709. (Wiley Ser. in Management). 1980. text ed. 23.95 (ISBN 0-471-02023-0). Wiley.
Brown, Wilfred. Organization. 1971. text ed. 19.50x (ISBN 0-435-85103-9). Heinemann Ed.
Brown, Wilfred & Jaques, Elliot. Glacier Project Papers: Some Essays on Organization & Management from the Glacier Project Research. (Glacier Project Ser.). 285p. 1965. 7.95x (ISBN 0-8093-0373-6). S Ill U Pr.
Brownrigg, William. The Human Enterprise Process. LC 54-8520. 1954. 15.95x (ISBN 0-8173-4805-0). U of Ala Pr.
Brownstone, D. L. How to Run a Successful Specialty Food Store. 124p. 1978. pap. 5.95 (ISBN 0-471-04031-2). Wiley.
Buchele, Robert B. The Management of Business & Public Organizations. new ed. (Management Ser.). (Illus.). 1976. text ed. 15.95 (ISBN 0-07-008697-4, C); instructor's manual 5.95 (ISBN 0-07-008698-2). McGraw.
Buchholz, Rogene A. Business Environment & Public Policy: Implications for Management. (Illus.). 560p. 1982. text ed. 22.95 (ISBN 0-13-095554-X). P-H.
Budde, James F. Measuring Performance in Human Service Systems: Planning, Organization & Control. (Illus.). 1980. 14.95 (ISBN 0-8144-5551-4). Am Mgmt.
Buffa, Elwood S. Elements of Production-Operations Management. LC 80-26666. 250p. 1981. pap. text ed. 13.95 (ISBN 0-471-08532-4). Wiley.
--Operations Management: The Management of Productive Systems. LC 75-33179. (Management & Administration Ser.). 640p. 1976. text ed. 27.95 (ISBN 0-471-11890-7). Wiley.
Buffa, Elwood S. & Dyer, James S. Essentials of Management Science-Operations Research. LC 77-23799. (Manangement & Administration Ser.). 1978. text ed. 25.95 (ISBN 0-471-02003-6). Wiley.
--Management Science-Operations Research: Formulation & Solution Methods. 2nd ed. LC 80-18082. 718p. 1981. text ed. 25.95 (ISBN 0-471-05851-3). Wiley.
Bullock, G. William, Jr. & Conrad, Clifton F. Management: Perspectives from the Social Sciences. LC 80-6097. 343p. 1981. lib. bdg. 19.75 (ISBN 0-8191-1466-9); pap. text ed. 11.00 (ISBN 0-8191-1467-7). U Pr of Amer.
Burack, Elmer H. & Torda, Florence. The Manager's Guide to Change. LC 79-15537. 236p. pap. 9.95 (ISBN 0-534-97995-5). CBI Pub.
--The Manager's Guide to Change. LC 79-15537. 1979. pap. 9.95 (ISBN 0-534-97995-5). Lifetime Learn.
Burger, Chester. Survival in the Executive Jungle. 1964. 5.95 (ISBN 0-02-518140-8). Macmillan.
Burghes, D. N. Mathematical Models in the Social, Management & Life Sciences. LC 79-40989. (Mathematics & Its Applications Ser.). 287p. 1980. pap. 21.95 (ISBN 0-470-27073-X). Halsted Pr.
Burghes, D. N. & Wood, A. D. Mathematical Models in the Social, Management & Life Sciences. LC 79-40989. (Mathematics & Its Applications Ser.). 287p. 1980. 39.95x (ISBN 0-470-26862-X); pap. text ed. 19.95 (ISBN 0-470-27073-X). Halsted Pr.
Burgoyne, J. & Stuart, R., eds. Management Development: Context & Strategies. text ed. 29.00x (ISBN 0-566-02101-3, Pub. by Gower Pub England). Renouf.
Burke, Ronald S. & Bittel, Lester R. Introduction to Management Practice. LC 80-19088. (Illus.). 608p. 1981. text ed. 16.95x (ISBN 0-07-009042-4); course management guide & key 4.50 (ISBN 0-07-009042-4); self study guide 5.50 (ISBN 0-07-009044-0). McGraw.
Burns, A. F. The Management of Prosperity. LC 66-15365. (Benjamin Fairless Memorial Lectures). 69p. 1966. 7.50x (ISBN 0-231-02959-4). Columbia U Pr.
Business & Management Career Package, 7 vols. Set. 42.45 set (ISBN 0-686-64872-2). Bowker.
Buskirk, Richard H. Handbook of Management Tactics: Aggressive Strategies for Getting Things Done Your Way! LC 77-70138. (Orig.). 1978. pap. 5.95 (ISBN 0-8015-3489-5, Hawthorn). Dutton.
--Handbook of Managerial Tactics. LC 76-991. 1976. 13.95 (ISBN 0-8436-0745-9). CBI Pub.
--Modern Management & Machiavelli. LC 74-11194. 291p. 1974. 13.95 (ISBN 0-8436-0734-3). CBI Pub.
Butteriss, Margaret. New Management Tools: Ideas & Techniques to Help You As a Manager. LC 78-11826. (Illus.). 1978. 10.95 (ISBN 0-13-615195-7, Spec); pap. 4.95 (ISBN 0-13-615187-6). P-H.
--Techniques & Developments in Management. LC 76-354466. 184p. 1976. 8.50x (ISBN 0-85292-118-7). Intl Pubns Serv.
Buzzotta, V. R., et al. Effective Motivation Through Performance Appraisal. 1980. Repr. of 1977 ed. 18.50 (ISBN 0-88410-499-0). Ballinger Pub.
Canada, John R. & White, John A., Jr. Capital Investment Decision Analysis for Management & Engineering. 1980. text ed. 26.95 (ISBN 0-13-113555-4). P-H.
Cangemi, Joseph P. & Guttschaik, George E., eds. Effective Management: A Humanistic Perspective. LC 78-61106. 1980. 8.50 (ISBN 0-8022-2229-3). Philos Lib.
Cannie, Joan K. The Woman's Guide to Management Success: How to Win Power in the Real Organizational World. (Illus.). 1979. 12.95 (ISBN 0-13-961771-X, Spec); pap. 4.95 (ISBN 0-13-961763-9). P-H.
Cannie, John K. Take Charge: Success Tactics for Business & Life. (Illus.). 1980. 12.95 (ISBN 0-13-882621-8, Spec); pap. 4.95 (ISBN 0-13-882613-7, Spec). P-H.
Carlisle, Howard M. Management: Concepts & Situations. LC 75-29382. (Illus.). 608p. 1976. text ed. 19.95 (ISBN 0-574-19230-1, 13-2230); instr's guide avail. (ISBN 0-574-19231-X, 13-2231). SRA.
--Management Essentials: Concepts & Applications. LC 78-16303. 1979. text ed. 17.95 (ISBN 0-574-19370-7, 13-2370); instr's guide avail. (ISBN 0-574-19371-5, 13-2371); study guide 6.95 (ISBN 0-574-19372-3, 13-2372); lecture suppl. 2.95 (ISBN 0-574-19373-1, 13-2373). SRA.
Carnarius, Stanley E. Management Problems & Solution: A Guide to Problem Solving. LC 76-1741. 128p. 1976. pap. 8.95 (ISBN 0-201-00881-5). A-W.
Carney, Edward M., et al. The American Business Manual, 3 vols. Chandler, Alfred D., ed. LC 79-7536. (History of Management Thought & Practice Ser.). 1980. Repr. of 1914 ed. Set. lib. bdg. 90.00x (ISBN 0-405-12318-3); lib. bdg. 30.00x ea. Vol. 1 (ISBN 0-405-12319-1). Vol. 2 (ISBN 0-405-12320-5). Vol. 3 (ISBN 0-405-12321-3). Arno.
Carroll, Stephen J & Tosi, Henry L. Organizational Behavior. (Illus.). 1977. 23.95 (ISBN 0-914292-08-0). Wiley.
Carroll, Stephen J., Jr. & Paine, Frank T. Management Process: Cases & Readings. 2nd ed. 448p. 1977. pap. text ed. 11.95 (ISBN 0-02-319520-7, 31952). Macmillan.
Case Method in Management Development. (Management Development Ser.: No. 17). 264p. 1981. pap. 12.75 (ISBN 92-2-102363-X, ILO 160, ILO). Unipub.
Casey, David & Pearce, David, eds. More Than Management Development: Action Learning at GEC. LC 77-70350. 1977. 12.50 (ISBN 0-8144-5446-1). Am Mgmt.
Caskey, Clark. Balance in Management. LC 68-57174. 1968. 9.95 (ISBN 0-685-79073-8). Masterco Pr.
Cecchettini, Philip A. CLEP: Introduction to Business Management. (Illus.). 1979. pap. 5.95 (ISBN 0-07-010308-9, C). McGraw.
Certo, Samuel & Brenenstuhl, Daniel L. Fundamental Readings in Modern Management: Functions & Systems. 351p. 1980. pap. write for info. (ISBN 0-697-08035-8). Wm C Brown.
Certo, Samuel C. Principles of Modern Management: Functions & Systems. 600p. 1980. text ed. write for info. (ISBN 0-697-08033-1); instr. manual avail. (ISBN 0-697-08043-9); printed tests avail. (ISBN 0-697-08045-5); experiential wkbk. avail. (ISBN 0-697-08041-2); reader avail. (ISBN 0-697-08035-8). Wm C Brown.
Certo, Samuel C. & Graf, Lee. Experiencing Modern Management: Workbook of Study Activities. 368p. 1980. write for info. wkbk (ISBN 0-697-08041-2). Wm C Brown.
Chakraborty, S. K. Management by Objectives. rev. ed. 1981. 12.50x (ISBN 0-8364-0739-3, Pub. by Macmillan India). South Asia Bks.
Chambers, Harry T. The Management of Small Offset Print Departments. 2nd ed. 217p. 1979. text ed. 22.00x (ISBN 0-220-67007-2, Pub. by Busn Bks England). Renouf.
Champion, John M. & James, John H. Critical Incidents in Management. 4th ed. 1980. pap. 11.95x (ISBN 0-256-02269-0). Irwin.
Chandler, Alfred D., ed. The Application of Modern Systematic Management: An Original Anthology. LC 79-7522. (History of Management Thought & Practice Ser.). (Illus.). 1980. lib. bdg. 15.00x (ISBN 0-405-12307-8). Arno.
--History of Management Thought & Practice, 32 bks. (Ser.). (Illus.). 1980. Set. lib. bdg. 1025.00x (ISBN 0-405-12306-X). Arno.
--Management Thought in Great Britain: An Original Anthology. LC 79-7523. (History of Management Thought & Practice Ser.). 1980. lib. bdg. 22.00x (ISBN 0-405-12308-6). Arno.
--Managerial Innovation at General Motors: An Original Anthology. LC 79-7524. (History of Management Thought & Practice Ser.). 1980. lib. bdg. 14.00x (ISBN 0-405-12309-4). Arno.
--Precursors of Modern Management: An Original Anthology. LC 79-7527. (History of Management Thought & Practice Ser.). 1980. lib. bdg. 25.00x (ISBN 0-405-12311-6). Arno.
Chao, Lincoln & Rodich, G. Statistics for Management: Study Guide. 272p. 1980. pap. text ed. 6.95 (ISBN 0-8185-0409-9). Brooks-Cole.
Chao, Lincoln L. Statistics for Management. LC 79-22706. 1980. text ed. 20.95 (ISBN 0-8185-0367-X); study guide 6.95 (ISBN 0-8185-0409-9). Brooks-Cole.
Chapman, Margaret. Directing the Work of Others. (Illus.). 1972. pap. 0.35, 10 for 2.00 (ISBN 0-88441-023-4, 19-981). GS.
Chase, Lawrence, et al. Practicing Management: A Guide to Accompany Tansik, Chase, & Aquilano's Management: a Life Cycle Approach. 1980. pap. 6.50x (ISBN 0-256-02354-9). Irwin.
Chemical Engineering Magazine. Skills Vital to Successful Managers. 1979. 24.50 (ISBN 0-07-010737-8, P&RB). McGraw.

Chetuerikov, V. N. Data Processing for Control & Management. 374p. 1977. 6.00 (ISBN 0-8285-0675-2, Pub. by Mir Pubs Russia). Imported Pubns.
Chilver, J. W. The Human Aspects of Management: A Case Study Approach. text ed. 16.50 (ISBN 0-08-021048-1); pap. text ed. 7.75 (ISBN 0-08-021047-3). Pergamon.
Chironis, Nicholas P., ed. Management Guide for Engineers & Technical Administrators. LC 68-8661. 1969. 29.50 (ISBN 0-07-010794-7, P&RB). McGraw.
Choosing the Options. (Executive Ser.: No. 2). 76p. 1981. pap. 7.50 (ISBN 0-686-72098-9, UNEP 049, UNEP). Unipub.
Christensen, Roland C. Management Succesion in Small & Growing Enterpises. Bruchey, Stuart & Carosso, Vincent P., eds. LC 78-18957. (Small Business Enterprise in America Ser.). 1979. Repr. of 1953 ed. lib. bdg. 15.00x (ISBN 0-405-11516-4). Arno.
Christopher, Edward E. Behavioral Theory for Managers. 1977. pap. text ed. 9.75 (ISBN 0-8191-0352-7). U Pr of Amer.
Christopher, W. Management for the Nineteen Eighties. 1979. pap. 6.95 (ISBN 0-13-549154-1, Spec). P-H.
Christopher, William F. Management for the Nineteen Eighties. rev. ed. (Illus.). 1980. 15.95 (ISBN 0-8144-5600-6). Am Mgmt.
Chung, Kae H., ed. Academy of Management 1981: Proceedings. 1981. 12.00 (ISBN 0-686-73305-3). Acad of Mgmt.
Church, Alexander H. The Science & Practice of Management. LC 77-17901. (Management History Ser.: No. 24). 555p. Repr. of 1914 ed. 32.50 (ISBN 0-87960-037-3). Hive Pub.
Churchman, C. W. & Mason, R. O. World Modeling: A Dialogue. (North-Holland - TIMS Studies in the Management Sciences: Vol. 2). 1976. 17.00 (ISBN 0-444-11029-1, North-Holland). Elsevier.
Cios. Management & Growth Proceedings. 1969. 96.75x (ISBN 0-677-61575-2). Gordon.
Cissley, Charles H. Management Science: Study Guide. 1973. pap. 4.50 (ISBN 0-915322-06-4). LOMA.
Clark, John J., et al. Capital Budgeting: Planning & Control of Capital Expenditures. (Illus.). 1979. text ed. 21.95 (ISBN 0-13-113464-7). P-H.
Clarke. Executive Power: How to Use It Effectively. 1979. 18.95 (ISBN 0-13-294108-2, Busn). P-H.
Cohen, William A. Principles of Technical Management. (Illus.). 1980. 19.95 (ISBN 0-8144-5580-8). Am Mgmt.
Cohn, Theodore & Lindberg, Roy. Survival & Growth: Management Strategies for the Small Firm. 1978. pap. 2.50 (ISBN 0-451-61624-3, ME1624, Ment). NAL.
Cole, G. Management Principles & Practice. 1980. 10.00x (ISBN 0-905435-10-9, Pub. by DP Pubns). State Mutual Bk.
Coleman, David. Management of the Firm. LC 77-86276. 1979. 13.95 (ISBN 0-930726-03-0); pap. 9.95 (ISBN 0-930726-02-2). Concept Pub.
Coleman, Thomas E. Retail Drug Store Management & Control. LC 78-70424. 1978. 18.95 (ISBN 0-912016-76-0). Lebhar Friedman.
Company Administration Handbook. 4th ed. 832p. 1980. text ed. 69.75x (ISBN 0-566-02154-4, Pub. by Gower Pub Co England). Renouf.
Compton, H. K. Storehouse Management. 472p. 1980. 45.00x (ISBN 0-7121-1965-5, Pub. by Macdonald & Evans). State Mutual Bk.
Computer Application in Management: The Asian Scene. 1978. pap. 10.00 (ISBN 92-833-1405-0, APO 69, APO). Unipub.
Conducting Lawful Interviews. 69p. 1980. course manual 125.00 (ISBN 0-89290-138-1, SWB-129); participant's manual 45.00 (ISBN 0-89290-139-X). Soc for Visual.
Conference Board. Challenge to Leadership: Managing in a Changing World. LC 73-1861. (Orig.). 1973. pap. 5.95 (ISBN 0-02-906570-4). Free Pr.
Connor, Patrick E. Dimensions in Modern Management. 2nd ed. LC 77-75692. (Illus.). 1977. pap. text ed. 10.95 (ISBN 0-395-25515-5). HM.
Cook, Thomas M. & Russell, Robert A. Contemporary Operations Management: Texts & Cases. 1980. text ed. 23.95 (ISBN 0-13-170407-9). P-H.
--Introduction to Management Science. 2nd ed. (Illus.). 640p. 1981. text ed. 23.95 (ISBN 0-13-486092-6). P-H.
--Introduction to Management Science. 1977. text ed. 19.95 (ISBN 0-13-486084-5). P-H.
Cooper, Cary. Developing Managers for the Nineteen Eighties. LC 80-15212. 160p. 1981. text ed. 39.50x (ISBN 0-8419-0649-1). Holmes & Meier.
Cooper, J. Microprocessor Background for Management Personnel. 208p. 1981. 14.95 (ISBN 0-13-580829-4). P-H.
Cooperative Management & Administration. 7th rev ed. iv, 222p. 1978. 8.55 (ISBN 9-2210-1281-6). Intl Labour Office.
Corrado, Frank M. Media for Managers. 200p. 1982. 19.95 (ISBN 0-86569-081-2). Auburn Hse.
Cotton, Donald B. Company-Wide Planning. (Illus.). 1970. 8.95 (ISBN 0-02-896040-8). Macmillan.
Cowan, John. The Self-Reliant Manager. new ed. LC 77-12145. 1977. 13.95 (ISBN 0-8144-5447-X). Am Mgmt.
Coyle, John J. & Bardi, Edward. The Management of Business Logistics. 2nd ed. 500p. 1980. text ed. 19.95 (ISBN 0-8299-0325-9); instrs.' manual avail. (ISBN 0-8299-0472-7). West Pub.
--The Management of Business Logistics. LC 75-37998. (Illus.). 450p. 1976. text ed. 17.95 (ISBN 0-8299-0074-8). West Pub.
Crecine, John P., ed. Research in Public Policy & Management, Vol. 1. 1981. lib. bdg. 34.50 (ISBN 0-89232-044-3). Jai Pr.
Cribbin, James J. Effective Managerial Leadership. LC 71-166554. 264p. 1972. 13.95 (ISBN 0-8144-5277-9). Am Mgmt.
--Effective Managerial Leadership. (AMACOM Executive Books). 1978. pap. 4.95 (ISBN 0-8144-7504-3). Am Mgmt.
Crix, Frederick C. Reprographic Management Handbook. 2nd ed. 332p. 1979. text ed. 30.75x (ISBN 0-220-67010-2, Pub. by Busn Bks England). Renouf.
Croft, David. Applied Statistics for Management Studies. 2nd ed. (Illus.). 304p. (Orig.). 1976. pap. text ed. 15.95x (ISBN 0-7121-0136-5, Pub. by Macdonald & Evans England). Intl Ideas.
Crosby, Philip. Quality Is Free: The Art of Making Quality Free. 1979. 13.50 (ISBN 0-07-014512-1, P&RB). McGraw.
Cuming, Pamela. The Power Handbook: A Strategic Guide to Personal & Organizational Effectiveness. LC 80-14039. 340p. 1980. pap. 12.95 (ISBN 0-8436-0778-5). CBI Pub.
Cummings, Paul W. Open Management: Guides to Successful Practice. 240p. 1980. 14.95 (ISBN 0-8144-5522-0). Am Mgmt.
Curtis, W. Robert & Yessian, Mark. Effective Management of Human Services: An Analytic Framework, Pt. I. (Organizational Development of State Human Services Ser.). (Orig.). 1979. pap. 1.95 (ISBN 0-89995-001-9). Social Matrix.
Daft, R. L. & Becker, S. W. The Innovative Organization: Innovation Adoption in High Schools. 1978. pap. 10.95 (ISBN 0-444-99039-9). Elsevier.
Dailey, Charles A. & Madsen, Ann M. Good Judgement About People. new ed. LC 78-31339. (Illus.). 1979. 12.95 (ISBN 0-07-015086-9, P&RB). McGraw.
Dale, E. Management: Theory & Practice. (Management Ser.). (Illus.). 1978. text ed. 17.95 (ISBN 0-07-015188-1, C); instructors manual 6.95 (ISBN 0-07-015189-X). McGraw.
Dannebring, David D. & Starr, Martin K. Management Science: An Introduction. (Quantitative Methods in Management Ser.). 1981. 23.50 (ISBN 0-07-015352-3, C); write for info study guide (ISBN 0-07-015353-1); instr's. manual 15.00 (ISBN 0-07-015354-X). McGraw.
Danner, Jack. People-Empathy: Key to Painless Supervision. 1976. 10.95 (ISBN 0-13-655738-4, Parker). P-H.
D'Aprix, Roger M. In Search of a Corporate Soul. new ed. LC 75-33364. (Illus.). 244p. 1976. 12.95 (ISBN 0-8144-5409-7). Am Mgmt.
Das, Ranjan. Managing Diversification: The General Management Process. 1981. 14.00x (ISBN 0-8364-0710-5, Pub. by Macmillan India). South Asia Bks.
Davar, Rustom S. & Davar, Dhun R. The Art of Damaging: A Sequel. (Illus.). 1979. 15.00x (ISBN 0-7069-0783-3, Pub. by Vikas India). Advent NY.
--The Art of Managing-Damaging: Games People Play to Get Their Way. (Illus.). 1979. 12.00x (ISBN 0-7069-0691-8, Pub. by Vikas India). Advent NY.
Davar, Rustom S., ed. Human Side of Management. LC 70-908454. (Progressive Management Ser). (Illus.). 1969. 7.50x (ISBN 0-8002-0643-6). Intl Pubns Serv.
Davar, Sohrab R. Business Organisation & Management. 14th ed. LC 73-216265. (Illus.). 1977. 12.50x (ISBN 0-8002-0403-4). Intl Pubns Serv.
Davidson, James. Effective Time Management: A Practical Workbook. LC 78-6126. 1978. 9.95 (ISBN 0-87705-332-4). Human Sci Pr.
Davis, Gordon B. & Everest, Gordon. Readings in Management Information Systems. 1976. pap. 10.50 (ISBN 0-07-015835-5, C). McGraw.
Davis, K. Roscoe & McKeown, Patrick G. Quantitative Models for Management. (Business Ser.). 735p. 1981. text ed. 23.95x (ISBN 0-534-00935-2). Kent Pub Co.
Davis, Keith. Human Behavior at Work. 6th ed. (Management Ser.). (Illus.). 576p. 1981. text ed. 18.95x (ISBN 0-07-015516-X, C); instr's. manual & test file 15.00 (ISBN 0-07-015517-8); study guide avail. (ISBN 0-07-015535-6). McGraw.
Davis, Ralph C. Fundamentals of Top Management. Chandler, Alfred D., ed. LC 79-7539. (History of Management Thought & Practice Ser.). 1980. Repr. of 1951 ed. lib. bdg. 60.00x (ISBN 0-405-12324-8). Arno.
--Principles of Business Organization & Operation. 4th ed. LC 72-9522. (Management History Ser.: No. 16). (Illus.). 150p. 1973. Repr. of 1937 ed. 20.00 (ISBN 0-87960-019-5). Hive Pub.
De, Nitish, et al. Managing & Developing New Forms of Work Organization. (Management Development Ser.: No. 16). (Illus.). 158p. (Orig.). 1980. pap. 11.40 (ISBN 92-2-102145-9). Intl Labour Office.
Dealership Business Management. LC 75-9416. 10.00 (ISBN 0-87359-007-4). Northwood Inst.
Dealership Organization & Management. LC 73-88867. 10.00 (ISBN 0-87359-002-3). Northwood Inst.
De Bono, E. Lateral Thinking for Management. LC 79-157307. 1971. 12.50 (ISBN 0-8144-5257-4). Am Mgmt.
Deegan, Arthur X., 2nd. Coaching: A Management Skill for Improving Individual Performance. LC 79-619. 1979. pap. text ed. 8.95 (ISBN 0-201-01266-9). A-W.
--Management by Objectives for Hospitals. LC 76-45523. 1977. 24.95 (ISBN 0-912862-33-5). Aspen Systems.
Deep, Samuel D. Human Relations in Management. 1978. text ed. 14.95 (ISBN 0-02-472180-8). Glencoe.
DeGreene, K. B. The Adaptive Organization: Anticipation & Management of Crisis. 550p. 1982. 29.95 (ISBN 0-471-08296-1, Pub. by Wiley-Interscience). Wiley.
Deitzer, Bernard A., et al. Contemporary Management Concepts. LC 79-11974. 1979. text ed. 20.95 (ISBN 0-88244-187-6). Grid Pub.
Dejon, William L. Principles of Management: Text & Cases. LC 77-75123. 1978. 18.95 (ISBN 0-8053-2336-8); instr's man. 8.95 (ISBN 0-8053-2337-6). Benjamin-Cummings.
Delaney, William A. Micromanagement: How to Solve the Problems of Growing Companies. 176p. 1981. 14.95 (ISBN 0-8144-5642-1). Am Mgmt.
Del Mar, Donald. Classics in Scientific Management. Collons, Roger D., ed. LC 75-20471. 464p. 1976. 25.25 (ISBN 0-8173-8701-3). U of Ala Pr.
Demone, Harold W., Jr. & Harshbarger, Dwight. The Planning & Administration of Human Services. LC 73-6870. (Developments in Human Services Ser.: Vol. 1, No. 2). 127p. 1973. pap. text ed. 7.95 (ISBN 0-87705-077-5). Human Sci Pr.
Denyer, J. C. Office Management. 5th ed. (Illus.). 528p. 1980. pap. text ed. 17.95x (ISBN 0-7121-1525-0). Intl Ideas.
Derbyshire, A. Leslie. Mastering Management. LC 80-83028. 300p. 1981. 12.95 (ISBN 0-88290-159-1, 2046). Horizon Utah.
Derkinderen, Frans G. & Crum, Roy L. Project Set Strategies. (Nijenrode Studies in Business: Vol. 4). 1979. lib. bdg. 20.75 (ISBN 0-89838-014-6, Pub. by Martinus Nijhoff Netherlands). Kluwer Boston.
Dermer, Jerry. Management Planning & Control Systems: Advanced Concepts & Cases. 1977. 19.95x (ISBN 0-256-01874-X). Irwin.
Derossi, Flavia. The Technocratic Illusion: A Study of Managerial Power in Italy. Lobello, Susan, tr. from Italian. 225p. 1981. 25.00 (ISBN 0-87332-185-5). M E Sharpe.
Dessler, Gary. Management Fundamentala: A Framework. 2nd ed. (Illus.). 1979. text ed. 18.95 (ISBN 0-8359-4211-2); instrs'. manual avail. (ISBN 0-8359-4212-0); study guide 6.95 (ISBN 0-8359-4213-9). Reston.
--Organization & Management: A Contingency Approach. ref. ed. (Illus.). 1976. 21.00 (ISBN 0-13-641225-4). P-H.
Dews, Jule N. Decision Structure of Organization. LC 78-53774. (Illus.). 120p. 1978. pap. 11.00 (ISBN 0-937300-00-4). Stoneridge Inst.
Diamond, Susan Z. Preparing Administrative Manuals. 199p. 1981. 17.95 (ISBN 0-8144-5631-6). Am Mgmt.
Didactic Systems. Management for Supervisors. 1970. pap. 24.90 (ISBN 0-89401-056-5); pap. 21.50 per set for 2 or more sets (ISBN 0-685-73201-0); pap. 24.90 french ed. (ISBN 0-89401-057-3); pap. 24.90 portuguese ed. (ISBN 0-89401-058-1); pap. 0.50 leader guide (ISBN 0-685-73202-9). Didactic Syst.
Dill, William R. Running the American Corporation. LC 78-16922. (American Assembly Ser.). 1978. 10.95 (ISBN 0-13-783894-8, Spec); pap. 4.95 (ISBN 0-13-783886-7). P-H.
Dilworth, James. Production & Operations Management: Manufacturing & Nonmanufacturing. 1979. 21.95x (ISBN 0-394-32204-5). Random.
Dinkel, John J. & Kochenberger, Gary A. Using Management Science: A Workbook, Vol. 1. LC 79-67422. (Illus.). 234p. (Orig.). 1980. 10.95x (ISBN 0-931920-15-9). Dame Pubns.
Dinkel, John J., et al. Management Science: Text & Applications. 1978. 21.95x (ISBN 0-256-02037-X). Irwin.
Dinsmore, Francis W. Developing Tomorrow's Managers Today. LC 75-9785. 144p. 1975. 10.95 (ISBN 0-8144-5387-2). Am Mgmt.
Doctoroff, Michael. Synergistic Management: Creating the Climate for Superior Performance. (Illus.). 1978. 12.95 (ISBN 0-8144-5445-3). Am Mgmt.
Doctors, Samuel, et al. Educating the Innovative Public Manager. LC 80-39481. 160p. 1981. text ed. 20.00 (ISBN 0-89946-079-8). Oelgeschlager.
Doktar, R., et al, eds. The Implementation of Management Science. (TIMS Studies in Management Science: Vol. 13). 246p. 1979. 80.50 (ISBN 0-444-85224-7, North Holland). Elsevier.
Donaldson, Hamish. A Guide to the Successful Management of Computer Projects. LC 78-16180. 1978. 38.95 (ISBN 0-470-26472-1). Halsted Pr.
Donnelly, James, et al. Fundamentals of Management: Functions, Behavior, Models. 3rd ed. 1978. 18.50x (ISBN 0-256-02073-6). Business Pubns.
--Fundamentals of Management: Selected Readings. 3rd ed. 1978. pap. 9.95x (ISBN 0-256-02075-2). Business Pubns.
Donnelly, James H., Jr., et al. Fundamentals of Management: Functions, Behavior, Models. 4th ed. 1981. 19.50 (ISBN 0-256-02424-3); pap. 10.95 (ISBN 0-256-02426-X). Dorsey.
Donnelly, James H., Jr., et al, eds. Fundamentals of Management: Selected Readings. 4th ed. pap. 10.95 (ISBN 0-256-02426-X). Business Pubns.
Douglass, Merrill E. & Douglass, Donna N. Manage Your Time, Manage Your Work, Manage Yourself. 1980. 15.95 (ISBN 0-8144-5597-2). Am Mgmt.
--Mangage Your Time, Manage Your Work, Manage Yourself. 304p. 1980. 15.95 (ISBN 0-8144-5597-2). Am Mgmt.
Douglass, Steve, et al. Ministry of Management Workbook. rev. ed. 1981. pap. text ed. 12.95 (ISBN 0-686-73039-9). Campus Crusade.
Drucker, Peter. People & Performance: The Best of Peter Drucker on Management. 1977. pap. text ed. 10.95 scp (ISBN 0-06-166400-6, HarpC). Har-Row.
Drucker, Peter F. Adventures of a Bystander. LC 78-2120. 344p. 1980. pap. 4.95 (ISBN 0-06-090774-6, CN 774, CN). Har-Row.
--An Introductory View of Management. 1978. text ed. 21.50 scp (ISBN 0-06-166402-2, HarpC); scp casebk 10.50 (ISBN 0-06-166403-0); inst. manual avail. (ISBN 0-685-88069-9). Har-Row.
--Management: Tasks, Practices, Responsibilities. LC 72-79655. 854p. 1974. 23.95 (ISBN 0-06-011092-9, HarpT). Har-Row.
--Managing in Turbulent Times. LC 79-33389. 1980. 9.95 (ISBN 0-06-011094-5, HarpT). Har-Row.
--Technology, Management & Society. 1977. pap. 3.95 (ISBN 0-06-090569-7, CN569, CN). Har-Row.
--Toward the Next Economics & Other Essays. LC 80-8370. 256p. 1981. 11.95 (ISBN 0-06-014828-4, HarpT). Har-Row.
DuBrin, Andrew J. Managerial Deviance: How to Deal with Problem People in Key Jobs. 288p. 1976. 8.95 (ISBN 0-442-80134-3). Van Nos Reinhold.
--The Practice of Supervision: Achieving Results Through People. 1980. 16.95x (ISBN 0-256-02272-0). Business Pubns.
Duerr, Michael & Roach, John M. Organization & Control of International Operations. (Report Ser.: No. 597). 1973. text ed. 15.00 (ISBN 0-8237-0182-4). Conference Bd.
Duerr, Michael G. Problems Facing International Management. (Report Ser: No. 634). 1974. pap. 5.00 (ISBN 0-8237-0046-1). Conference Bd.
Duffendack, Stanley D. Effective Management Through Work Planning. 1971. 28.95 (ISBN 0-932078-00-1). GE Tech Prom & Train.
Duncan, W. Jack. Essentials of Management. LC 77-81236. 1978. text ed. 20.95 (ISBN 0-03-039826-6). Dryden Pr.
Dunn, J. D., et al. Management Essentials: Resource. (Illus.). 384p. 1973. 16.30 (ISBN 0-07-018307-4, G); Practicium 5.90 (ISBN 0-07-018308-2); instructor's manual & key 6.40 (ISBN 0-07-018309-0). McGraw.

Dunn, William N. & Obradovic, Josip, eds. Worker's Self-Management & Organizational Power in Yugoslavia. LC 78-16307. 1978. pap. text ed. 9.95 (ISBN 0-916002-30-6, Pub. by U Ctr Intl St). U of Pittsburgh Pr.

Dunsing, Richard J. You & I Have Got to Stop Meeting This Way. (Illus.). 1978. 10.95 (ISBN 0-8144-5472-0). Am Mgmt.

Durst, Gary M. Management by Responsibility. (Illus.). 100p. 1980. pap. write for info. (ISBN 0-9602552-1-4). Ctr Art Living.

Duties & Responsibilities of New Zealand Company Directors. 100p. 1973. 18.00 (ISBN 0-909720-54-1). Commerce.

E R C Editorial Staff. Executive's Desk Manual for Profitable Employee Handling. 1972. 79.50 (ISBN 0-685-27765-8). P-H.

Easley, G. M. Primer for Small Systems Management. (Illus.). 1978. 20.95 (ISBN 0-87626-716-9). Winthrop.

Easton, Allan. Complex Managerial Decisions Involving Multiple Objectives. LC 79-25513. 446p. 1980. Repr. of 1973 ed. lib. bdg. 22.50 (ISBN 0-89874-079-7). Krieger.

--Managing for Negative Growth: A Handbook for Practitioners. 272p. 1976. 15.95 (ISBN 0-87909-479-6). Reston.

Eddy, William B. & Burke, W. Warner, eds. Behavioral Science & the Manager's Role. 2nd rev. & enl. 2nd ed. LC 79-67692. 376p. 1980. pap. 18.50 (ISBN 0-88390-123-4). Univ Assocs.

Edge, Alfred G., et al. The Multinational Management Game. 1980. pap. 7.95x (ISBN 0-256-02362-X). Business Pubns.

Edmunds, Stahrl W. Basics of Private & Public Management. LC 77-9147. 1978. 22.95 (ISBN 0-669-01679-9). Lexington Bks.

Efficiency Society. Transactions, Vol. 1, 1912. (Management History Ser.: No. 44). 450p. Repr. of 1913 ed. 23.75 (ISBN 0-87960-068-3). Hive Pub.

Eglash, Albert. Beyond Assertive Management: Humanistic Communication Skills for Supervisors. LC 79-54752. (Beyond Assertion Training Ser.: No. 6). (Illus.). 100p. (Orig.). 1982. 30.00 (ISBN 0-935320-15-6). Quest Pr.

Eilon, Samuel. Aspects of Management. 2nd ed. 1979. text ed. 26.00 (ISBN 0-08-022480-6); pap. text ed. 11.25 (ISBN 0-08-022479-2). Pergamon.

--Management Control. 2nd ed. 1979. text ed. 19.00 (ISBN 0-08-022482-2); pap. text ed. 9.75 (ISBN 0-08-022481-4). Pergamon.

Eliasson, Gunnar. Business Economic Planning: Theory, Practice & Comparison. LC 76-5895. 1977. 28.00 (ISBN 0-471-01813-9, Pub. by Wiley-Interscience). Wiley.

Elkins, A. Management: Structures, Functions, & Practices. 1980. 17.95 (ISBN 0-201-01517-X). A-W.

Elkins, Arthur. Managing Organizations: Structure, Functions & Practices. LC 79-5371. 1980. text ed. cancelled (ISBN 0-201-01517-X). A-W.

Elkins, Arthur & Callaghan, Dennis W. Managerial Odyssey: Problems in Business & Its Enviroment. 600p. 1981. text ed. 17.50 (ISBN 0-201-03962-1). A-W.

Ellis, Dean S. Management & Administrative Communication: Workbook with Supporting Text Material. (Illus.). 1978. pap. 10.95 (ISBN 0-02-332510-0). Macmillan.

Ellis, Susan J. & Noyes, Katherine H. No Excuses: The Team Approach to Volunteer Management. (Volunteer Energy Ser.: No. 2). (Illus.). 65p. 1981. pap. 7.50 (ISBN 0-940576-04-X). Energize.

Emery, D. A. The Compleat Manager: Combining the Humanistic & Scientific Approaches to the Management Job. 1970. 17.50 (ISBN 0-07-019336-3). McGraw.

Emshoff, James R. Managerial Breakthroughs. 1980. 15.95 (ISBN 0-8144-5612-X). Am Mgmt.

--Managerial Breakthroughs: Action Techniques for Strategic Change. (Illus.). 1980. 15.95 (ISBN 0-8144-5612-X). Am Mgmt.

Engel, James F., et al. Promotional Strategy. 4th ed. 1979. 20.95x (ISBN 0-256-02156-2). Irwin.

England, George W. The Manager & His Values: An International Perspective. LC 75-31833. 1976. 17.50 (ISBN 0-88410-288-2). Ballinger Pub.

England, George W., et al. The Manager & the Man: A Cross-Cultural Study of Personal Values. LC 74-11582. 120p. 1974. 9.50x (ISBN 0-87338-161-0, Pub. by Comp. Adm. Research Inst.). Kent St U Pr.

--Organizational Functioning in Cross-Cultural Perspective. LC 78-31169. 1979. 17.50x (ISBN 0-87338-225-0). Kent St U Pr.

Engstrom, Ted W. & MacKenzie, Alex. Managing Your Time. LC 67-17239. (Orig.). (YA) 1968. pap. 2.95 (ISBN 0-310-24262-2). Zondervan.

Enrick, N. L. Management Planning. 1967. 19.50 (ISBN 0-87245-097-X). Textile Bk.

Enrick, Norbert L. Management Control Manual for the Textile Industry. 2nd rev. ed. LC 79-13534. 356p. 1980. lib. bdg. 17.50 (ISBN 0-88275-994-9). Krieger.

--Management Handbook of Decision-Oriented Statistics. LC 79-13206. 250p. 1980. lib. bdg. 12.75 (ISBN 0-88275-984-1). Krieger.

--Management Planning: A Systems Approach. LC 67-27823. 240p. 1967. 24.95 (ISBN 0-686-74219-2). Krieger.

Erickson, Steve M. Management Tools for Everyone. (Illus.). 160p. 1981. 17.50 (ISBN 0-89433-131-0). Petrocelli.

Erlich, et al. Business Administration for the Medical Assistant. 2nd ed. LC 81-67045. (Illus.). 1981. 8.95 (ISBN 0-940012-01-4). Colwell Co.

Ettinger, Karl E. Management Primer. Hook, Ralph C., Jr. & Overton, John R., eds. LC 72-86485. 353p. 1973. 18.25 (ISBN 92-833-1023-3, APO48, APO). Unipub.

Evan, William M. Frontiers in Organization & Management. LC 79-20512. (Praeger Special Studies). 192p. 1980. 19.95 (ISBN 0-03-048441-3). Praeger.

Evered, James F. Shirt-Sleeves Management. 273p. 1981. 12.95 (ISBN 0-8144-5636-7). Am Mgmt.

Ewing, David W., ed. Technological Change & Management. LC 78-125645. 1970. 7.95x (ISBN 0-674-87230-4, Pub. by Harvard Busn. School). Harvard U Pr.

Executive Checklist for Finance & Administration. 70.00 (ISBN 0-686-51437-8). Auerbach.

Executive Compensation Survey of the Retailing Industry. 120p. 1981. 60.00 (ISBN 0-686-77797-2, P53680). Natl Ret Merch.

Exton, William. Motivational Leverage: a New Approach to Managing People. 1974. 10.95 (ISBN 0-13-604082-9). P-H.

Farmer, David & Taylor, Bernard, eds. Corporate Planning & Procurement. LC 74-19369. 1975. 30.95 (ISBN 0-470-25499-8). Halsted Pr.

Federico, Pat A., et al. Management Information Systems & Organizational Behavior. Brun, Kim & McCalla, Douglas B., eds. LC 80-15174. 204p. 1980. 20.95 (ISBN 0-03-057021-2). Praeger.

Feinberg, Mortimer R. Effective Psychology for Managers. 1965. 14.95 (ISBN 0-13-244855-6, Reward); pap. 3.95 (ISBN 0-13-244848-3). P-H.

Feinberg, Samuel. Management's Challenge: The People Problem. 336p. 1976. 12.50 (ISBN 0-87005-141-5). Fairchild.

Fenn, Margaret. Making It in Management: A Behavioral Approach for Women Executives. LC 78-17005. (Illus.). 1978. 10.95 (ISBN 0-13-547638-0, Spec); pap. 5.95 (ISBN 0-13-547620-8). P-H.

Fiedler, F. Theory of Leadership Effectiveness. 1967. text ed. 22.50 (ISBN 0-07-020675-9, C). McGraw.

Filley, Alan C. The Compleat Manager: What Works When. LC 78-62907. (Illus., Orig.). 1978. pap. text ed. 9.95 (ISBN 0-87822-184-0). Res Press.

Finch, F. E., et al. Managing for Organizational Effectiveness: An Experiential Approach. (Management Ser). 1975. text ed. 13.95 (ISBN 0-07-020899-9, C); instructors' manual 5.95 (ISBN 0-07-020900-6). McGraw.

Finch, Frank. A Concise Encyclopedia of Management Techniques. LC 76-5913. 1976. 24.50x (ISBN 0-8448-0963-2). Crane-Russak Co.

Firth, Michael. Forecasting Methods in Business & Management. 1977. pap. 17.95x (ISBN 0-7131-3372-4). Intl Ideas.

Flaherty, John E. Managing Change: Today's Challenge to Management. LC 78-4179. 1978. 9.95 (ISBN 0-8424-0115-6). Nellen Pub.

Flanders, Allan. The Fawley Productivity Agreements. (Illus.). 268p. (Orig.). 1966. pap. 3.95 (ISBN 0-571-06756-5, Pub. by Faber & Faber). Merrimack Bk Serv.

Fletcher, A. & Clark, G. Management & Mathematics. (Illus.). 1972. 29.95x (ISBN 0-8464-0589-X). Beekman Pubs.

Flippo, Edwin B. & Munsinger, Gary M. Management. 4th ed. 1978. text ed. 19.95 (ISBN 0-205-05978-3, 0859788); instr's man. avail. (ISBN 0-205-05979-1, 0859796). Allyn.

Flory, Charles, ed. Managers for Tomorrow. 1971. pap. 2.75 (ISBN 0-451-61732-0, ME1938, Ment). NAL.

Ford, Robert C. & Heaton, Cherrill P. Principles of Management: A Decision-Making Approach. (Illus.). 1980. text ed. 17.95 (ISBN 0-8359-5593-1); instr's manual avail. Reston.

Forrester, Jay W. Principles of Systems. 2nd ed. 1968. pap. 12.00x (ISBN 0-262-56017-8). MIT Pr.

Forshee, Kenneth J. The Eternal Triangle. 272p. 1975. 8.00 (ISBN 0-934914-10-9). NACM.

Fournies, Ferdinand F. Management Performance Appraisal: A National Study. 1977. 12.00 (ISBN 0-917472-03-9). F Fournies.

Fox, Samuel. Management & the Law. LC 66-20469. (Orig.). 1980. pap. text ed. 6.95x (ISBN 0-89197-288-9). Irvington.

Frank, Michael R. The Effective EDP Manager. 323p. 1981. 17.95 (ISBN 0-8144-5635-9). Am Mgmt.

Frankenberg, Paul. Management Information Systems. 54p. 1968. 3.00 (ISBN 0-685-44054-0, RR3468). Natl Ret Merch.

Franklin, Jerome L., ed. Human Resource Development in the Organization: A Guide to Information Sources. LC 76-28289. (Management Information Guide Ser.: No. 35). 1978. 36.00 (ISBN 0-8103-0835-5). Gale.

Franks, J. R. & Broyles, J. E. Modern Managerial Finance. LC 79-83955. 1979. 43.50 (ISBN 0-471-99751-X); pap. 20.50 (ISBN 0-471-27563-8, Pub. by Wiley-Interscience). Wiley.

Frean, D. Board & Management Development. 1977. 22.50x (ISBN 0-8464-0201-7). Beekman Pubs.

Frean, David. The Board & Management Development. 188p. 1980. text ed. 30.75x (ISBN 0-220-66304-1, Pub. by Busn Bks England). Renouf.

Friday, William. Successful Management for One to Ten Employee Businesses. LC 78-111544. (Illus.). 1979. 14.50 (ISBN 0-934432-04-X). Prudent Pub Co.

Frith, Stan W. The Expatriate Dilemma: How to Relocate & Compensate U. S. Employees Assigned Overseas. LC 81-2740. 192p. 1981. text ed. 18.95 (ISBN 0-88229-701-5). Nelson-Hall.

Fulmer, Robert M. Management & Organization. LC 78-15830. 1980. pap. 4.95 (ISBN 0-06-460176-5, CO 176, COS). Har-Row.

--The New Management. 3rd ed. 1982. text ed. 19.95 (ISBN 0-686-75041-1). Macmillan.

--The New Management. 2nd ed. (Illus.). 480p. 1978. text ed. 20.95 (ISBN 0-02-339860-4, 33986). Macmillan.

--Supervision: Principles of Management. 1976. text ed. 17.95x (ISBN 0-02-473070-X). Macmillan.

Fulmer, Robert M. & Franklin, Steven C. Supervision: Principles of Professional Management. 2nd ed. 1982. text ed. price not set. Macmillan.

Fulmer, Robert M. & Herbert, Theodore T. Exploring the New Management. (Illus.). 256p. 1978. pap. text ed. 6.50 (ISBN 0-02-339840-X, 33984). Macmillan.

Galley, J. N. The Board & Computer Management. 185p. 1978. text ed. 23.50x (ISBN 0-220-67000-5, Pub. by Busn Bks England). Renouf.

Gannon, Martin J. Management: An Organizational Perspective. 1977. write for info. (CPCU 7). IIA.

--Management: Organizational Perspective. 1977. text ed. 18.95 (ISBN 0-316-30326-7); tchr's manual free (ISBN 0-316-30328-3). Little.

Gantt, H. L., et al. How Scientific Management Is Applied. LC 72-9521. (Management History Ser.: No. 26). (Illus.). 128p. 1973. Repr. of 1911 ed. 15.00 (ISBN 0-87960-033-0). Hive Pub.

--Organizing for Production & Other Papers on Management, 1912-1924. (Management History Ser.: No. 71). (Illus.). 400p. 1974. Repr. of 1923 ed. 22.50 (ISBN 0-87960-102-7). Hive Pub.

Gautschi, Theodore F. Management Forum. (Illus.). 271p. 1979. pap. 16.00 (ISBN 0-536-03096-0). Herman Pub.

Gelb, Gabriel M. & Gelb, Betsy D. Research at the Top: Better Data for Organizational Policy Making. LC 75-37588. (AMA Monographs Ser.: No. 2). 1975. pap. 3.00 (ISBN 0-87757-069-8). Am Mktg.

Gellerman. Manager & Subordinates. 1976. 13.95 (ISBN 0-03-089928-1). Dryden Pr.

Gellerman, S. W. Managers & Subordinates. LC 76-385. (Dryden Press). 1976. text ed. 13.95 (ISBN 0-03-089928-1, HoltC). HR&W.

George, Claude S. Action Guide for Supervisors. 370p. 1981. 14.95 (ISBN 0-8359-0122-X). Reston.

George, Claude S., Jr. The History of Management Thought. 2nd ed. 256p. 1972. pap. text ed. 12.95 (ISBN 0-13-390187-4). P-H.

--Supervision in Action: The Art of Managing Others. 2nd ed. (Illus.). 1979. ref. 16.95 (ISBN 0-8359-7152-X); instrs' manual free. Reston.

Gibson, James L., et al. Readings in Organizations: Behavior, Structure, Processes. 3rd ed. 1979. pap. 9.95x (ISBN 0-256-02247-X). Business Pubns.

Giegold, William C. Practical Management Skills for Engineers & Scientists. (Engineering Ser.). (Illus.). 350p. 1982. text ed. 30.00 (ISBN 0-686-73122-0). Lifetime Learn.

Glaser, Rollin & Glaser, Christine. Managing by Design. LC 80-22455. 192p. 1981. text ed. 9.95 (ISBN 0-201-02717-8). A-W.

Glass, Dick. Service Shop Management Handbook. LC 79-62999. 1979. pap. 9.95 (ISBN 0-672-21602-7). Sams.

Glos, R. E. & Baker, Harold. Business: Its Nature & Environment, an Introduction. 7th ed. 1972. 10.00 (ISBN 0-538-07710-7). SW Pub.

Glover, John D. & Simon, Gerald A., eds. The Chief Executives Handbook. LC 75-11387. (Illus.). 1129p. 1976. 37.50 (ISBN 0-87094-104-6). Dow Jones-Irwin.

Glover, John D., et al. The Administrator: Cases on Human Aspects in Management. 5th ed. 1973. text ed. 20.50x (ISBN 0-256-00170-7). Irwin.

Glueck. Management Essentials. 1979. 14.95 (ISBN 0-03-045416-6). Dryden Pr.

Glueck, William F. Business Policy & Strategic Management. 3rd ed. (Management Ser.). (Illus.). 1980. text ed. 19.95x (ISBN 0-07-023519-8, C). McGraw.

--Strategic Management & Business Policy. (Management Ser.). (Illus.). 288p. 1980. text ed. 10.95 (ISBN 0-07-023506-6, C). McGraw.

Glueck, William G. Management. 2nd ed. 640p. 1980. text ed. 21.95 (ISBN 0-03-050906-8). Dryden Pr.

Glueck, William G., et al. The Managerial Experience. 2nd ed. 317p. 1980. 8.95 (ISBN 0-03-050916-5). Dryden Pr.

Godfrey, Eleanor P. & Fiedler, Fred E. Boards, Management, & Company Success. (Illus.). pap. text ed. 3.00x (ISBN 0-8134-0491-6, 491). Interstate.

Godiwalla, Yezdi M., et al. Corporate Strategy & Functional Management. LC 79-65182. 1979. 20.95 (ISBN 0-03-049781-7). Praeger.

Golde, Roger A. Muddling Through: The Art of Properly Unbusinesslike Management. LC 76-888. 1976. 12.95 (ISBN 0-8144-5411-9). Am Mgmt.

Goldhaber, C. Information Strategies: New Pathways to Corporate Power. 1979. 18.95 (ISBN 0-13-464651-7). P-H.

Goldschmidt, Yaaqov. Information for Management Decisions: A System for Economics, Analysis & Accounting Procedures. (Illus.). 329p. 1970. 27.50x (ISBN 0-8014-0541-6). Cornell U Pr.

Golembiewski, Robert, et al, eds. Managerial Behavior & Organization Demands: Management As a Linking of Levels of Interaction. Gibson, Frank & Miller, Gerald J. LC 77-95395. 1978. pap. text ed. 14.95 (ISBN 0-87581-233-3). Peacock Pubs.

Golightly, Henry O. Managing with Style: And Making It Work for You. new ed. LC 76-51445. 1977. 11.95 (ISBN 0-8144-5435-6). Am Mgmt.

Gordon, George G. & Cummins, Walter. Managing Management Climate. (Illus.). 1979. 19.95 (ISBN 0-669-02545-3). Lexington Bks.

Goslin, Lewis N. & Rethans, Arno J. Basic Systems for Decision Making. 2nd ed. 208p. 1980. pap. text ed. 9.95 (ISBN 0-8403-2191-0). Kendall-Hunt.

Gowler, Dan & Legge, Karen, eds. Managerial Stress. LC 74-20107. 236p. 1975. 16.95 (ISBN 0-470-31985-2). Halsted Pr.

Grad, Burton, et al. Management Systems. 2nd ed. 504p. 1979. text ed. 24.95 (ISBN 0-03-047541-4). Dryden Pr.

Granick, David. The Red Executive: A Study of the Organization Man in Russian Industry. Coser, Lewis A. & Powell, Walter W., eds. LC 79-6993. (Perennial Works in Sociology Ser.). (Illus.). 1979. Repr. of 1960 ed. lib. bdg. 23.00x (ISBN 0-405-12094-X). Arno.

Grawoig, Dennis E. & Hubbard, Charles L. Strategic Financial Planning with Simulation. (Illus.). 1981. 35.00 (ISBN 0-89433-115-9). Petrocelli.

Gray, Jerry & Starke, Frederick. Readings in Organizational Behavior: Concepts and Applications. (Business Ser.). 1976. pap. text ed. 12.95 (ISBN 0-675-08522-5). Merrill.

Gray, Jerry L., ed. The Glacier Project: Concepts & Critiques-Selected Readings on the Glacier Theories of Organization & Management. LC 75-27252. (Illus.). 452p. 1976. 27.50x (ISBN 0-8448-0716-8). Crane-Russak Co.

Gray, Jim, et al. Interpersonal Conflict Management: A Trainer's Manual. 106p. (Orig.). 1980. pap. 19.95 (ISBN 0-937636-00-2). Gray Assoc.

Grear, A. C. & Oxborough, J. Company Property Management in Great Britain. 1970. 24.00x (ISBN 0-8464-0264-5). Beekman Pubs.

Green, Mark R. & Serbein, Oscar N. Risk Management: Text & Cases. (Illus.). 1978. text ed. 17.95 (ISBN 0-87909-730-2); instrs'. manual avail. Reston.

Greene, Richard M., Jr. The Management Game. 1973. pap. 4.95 (ISBN 0-8015-4866-7, Hawthorn). Dutton.

Greiner, John M., et al. Monetary Incentives & Work Standards in Five Cities: Impacts & Implications for Management & Labor. 94p. 1977. pap. 3.95 (ISBN 0-87766-187-1, 17300). Urban Inst.

Groder, Martin G. & Von Hartz, John. Business Games. LC 80-19095. 250p. 1980. 50.00 (ISBN 0-932648-14-2). Boardroom.

Gross, Bertram M. Organizations & Their Managing. LC 68-22642. 1968. text ed. 19.95 (ISBN 0-02-913140-5). Free Pr.
Gross, Paul & Smith, Robert D. Systems Analysis & Design for Management. 1976. 15.00 (ISBN 0-685-65300-5). Tech Pub.
Grossman, Lee. Fat Paper: Diets for Trimming Paperwork. 1978. pap. 3.95 (ISBN 0-07-024983-0, SP). McGraw.
Gruber, William H. & Niles, John S. The New Management: Line Executive & Staff Professional in the Future Firm. 1976. 21.00 (ISBN 0-07-025073-1, P&RB). McGraw.
Gulick, L. & Urwick, L., eds. Papers on the Science of Administration. LC 37-25327. 8.00x (ISBN 0-913824-02-X). Inst Public Adm.
Gulland, John A. The Management of Marine Fisheries. LC 74-2473. (Illus.). 206p. 1974. 18.50 (ISBN 0-295-95335-7). U of Wash Pr.
Hague, Hawdon. The Organic Organization & How to Manage It. LC 78-23272. 1979. 27.95x (ISBN 0-470-26563-9). Halsted Pr.
Hailes & Hubbard. Small Business Management. LC 76-3945. 1977. pap. 8.80 (ISBN 0-8273-1400-0); instructor's guide 1.60 (ISBN 0-8273-1401-9). Delmar.
Haimann, Theo, et al. Managing the Modern Organization. 3rd ed. LC 77-75879. (Illus.). 1977. text ed. 18.95 (ISBN 0-395-25512-0); inst. manual 0.95 (ISBN 0-395-25513-9); study guide 6.95 (ISBN 0-395-25514-7). HM.
Hall, Douglas T., et al. Experiences in Management & Organizational Behavior. LC 75-1991. (Illus.). 1975. pap. text ed. 9.95 (ISBN 0-914292-03-X). Wiley.
Hall, Jay. The Competence Process. LC 80-51211. (Illus.). 1980. text ed. 22.95 (ISBN 0-937932-01-9). Teleometrics.
Hamilton, Walton H. Industrial Policy & Institutionalism: Selected Essays. LC 74-1361. 1974. lib. bdg. 15.00x (ISBN 0-678-00879-5). Kelley.
Hamner, W. Clay. Organizational Shock. LC 80-11910. (St. Clair Series in Management & Organizational Behavior). 1980. pap. text ed. 15.50 (ISBN 0-471-06251-0). Wiley.
Hampton, David. Behavioral Concepts in Management. 3rd ed. (Contemporary Thought in Mngt. Ser.). 1978. pap. text ed. 10.95x (ISBN 0-534-00576-4). Wadsworth Pub.
Hampton, David R. Contemporary Management. 2nd ed. (Management Ser.). (Illus.). 528p. 1981. text ed. 19.95x (ISBN 0-07-025935-6); instructor's manual 7.95 (ISBN 0-07-025936-4); write for info study guide (ISBN 0-07-025937-2); test file 15.00 (ISBN 0-07-025938-0). McGraw.
--Contemporary Management. (Management Ser.). (Illus.). 1977. text ed. 16.95 (ISBN 0-07-025930-5, C); instructor's manual 4.95 (ISBN 0-07-025931-3); study guide 5.95 (ISBN 0-07-025932-1); transparency masters 15.00 (ISBN 0-07-025933-X). McGraw.
Hampton, David R., et al. Organizational Behavior & the Practice of Management. 3rd ed. 1978. text ed. 20.95x (ISBN 0-673-15119-0). Scott F.
Hanan, Mack. Fast-Growth Management: How to Improve Profits with Entrepreneurial Stategies. (Illus.). 1980. 14.95 (ISBN 0-8144-5559-X). Am Mgmt.
--Venture Management: A Game Plan for Corporate Growth & Diversification. new ed. (Illus.). 1976. 21.50 (ISBN 0-07-025970-4, P&RB). McGraw.
Handern, Geoff. Business Organisation & Management. 1978. 22.50x (ISBN 0-86003-023-7, Pub. by Allan Pubs England); pap. 11.25x (ISBN 0-86003-124-1). State Mutual Bk.
Hanford, Lloyd D., Sr. The Property Management Process. 100p. 1972. pap. 4.95 (ISBN 0-912104-11-2). Inst Real Estate.
Harris, Roy D. & Gonzalez, Richard F. The Operations Manager. (Illus.). 490p. 1981. text ed. 22.95 (ISBN 0-8299-0332-1). West Pub.
Harrison, E. Frank. Management & Organizations. LC 77-75476. (Illus.). 1977. text ed. 18.95 (ISBN 0-395-25481-7); inst. manual 0.50 (ISBN 0-395-25482-5). HM.
Harrison, F. L. Advanced Project Management. 340p. 1981. 34.95 (ISBN 0-470-27213-9). Halsted Pr.
Harrison, Frank. The Managerial Decision-Making Process. 2nd ed. LC 80-82459. (Illus.). 496p. 1981. text ed. 21.95 (ISBN 0-395-30073-8); instr's manual 1.00 (ISBN 0-395-30074-6). HM.
Harrison, Jared F. Improving Performance & Productivity: Why Won't They Do What I Want Them to Do? (Illus.). 1978. pap. text ed. 8.95 (ISBN 0-201-02956-1). A-W.
Hartmann, Heinz. Authority & Organization in German Management. Repr. of 1959 ed. lib. bdg. 15.00 (ISBN 0-8371-3104-9, HAGM). Greenwood.
Harvard Business Review Editors, ed. Harvard Business Review - on Management. LC 75-6339. (Illus.). 448p. 1976. 19.95 (ISBN 0-06-011769-9, HarpT). Har-Row.
Harwell, Edward M. & Kinslow, William E. New Horizons in Checkout Management. LC 78-61790. 1978. 20.00 (ISBN 0-912016-64-7). Lebhar Friedman.
Hayes, Harold P. Realism in EEO. LC 79-2295. 1980. 27.95 (ISBN 0-471-05796-7, Pub. by Wiley-Interscience). Wiley.
Hayes, Stephan R. & Howell, John C. How to Finance Your Small Business with Government Money: SBA Loans. LC 80-12015. (Small Business Management Ser.). 1980. pap. 14.95 (ISBN 0-471-05689-8, Pub. by Wiley Interscience). Wiley.
Hayhurst, G. Mathematical Programming for Management & Business. 1976. pap. 13.50x (ISBN 0-7131-3355-4). Intl Ideas.
Hecht, Maurice R. What Happens in Management: Principles & Practices. 240p. 1980. 15.95 (ISBN 0-8144-5586-7); pap. 7.95 (ISBN 0-8144-7004-1). Am Mgmt.
Hefner, Robert L. & Seifert, Edward H., eds. Studies in Administrative Theory. 466p. (Orig.). 1980. pap. text ed. 14.95x (ISBN 0-89641-046-3). American Pr.
Heller, Frank A. Competence & Power in Management Decision-Making. Wilpert, Bernhard, ed. LC 80-49978. 242p. 1981. 39.95 (ISBN 0-471-27837-8, Pub. by Wiley-Interscience). Wiley.
Heller, Robert. The Business of Business: Management Strategies for the 1980's. 250p. 1981. 14.95 (ISBN 0-686-72888-2). HarBraceJ.
Hellriegel, Don & Slocum, John W., Jr. Management: Contingency Approaches. 2nd ed. LC 77-76177. 1978. text ed. 17.95 (ISBN 0-201-02854-9). A-W.
--Management in the World Today: A Book of Readings. 400p. 1975. pap. text ed. 8.95 (ISBN 0-201-02833-6). A-W.
Henderson & Bracker. Performance Workbook to Compensation Management. 224p. (Orig.). pap. 7.95 (ISBN 0-8359-0909-3). Reston.
Henderson, Richard I. Compensation Management: Rewarding Performance. 2nd ed. (Illus.). 1979. text ed. 18.95 (ISBN 0-8359-0907-7); instrs'. manual avail. (ISBN 0-8359-0908-5). Reston.
Hendrix, Olan. Management for the Christian Worker. LC 76-3510. (Illus.). 196p. 1976. 6.95 (ISBN 0-916608-01-8). Quill Pubns.
Heneman, Herbert G., III, et al. Managing Personnel & Human Resources: Strategies & Programs. LC 80-69960. 420p. 1981. 19.95 (ISBN 0-87094-234-4). Dow Jones-Irwin.
Hennessey, J. E., Jr. Financial Manager's Handbook. 1976. 34.95 (ISBN 0-13-316224-9, Busn). P-H.
Henrici, Stanley B. Salary Management for the Nonspecialist. 240p. 1980. 15.95 (ISBN 0-8144-5565-4). Am Mgmt.
Henshaw, Richard C. & Jackson, James R. Executive Game. 3rd ed. 1978. 10.95x (ISBN 0-256-02034-5). Irwin.
Herbert, Leo. Auditing the Performance of Management. LC 79-4551. 1979. 26.95 (ISBN 0-534-97998-X); ans. bk. 4.95 (ISBN 0-534-97997-1). Lifetime Learn.
Herman, Stanley & Korenich, Michael. Authentic Management: A Gestalt Orientation to Organizations & Their Development. 1977. 10.95 (ISBN 0-201-02886-7). A-W.
Hersey, Paul & Blanchard, Kenneth H. Management of Organizational Behavior: Utilizing Human Resources. 4th ed. (Illus.). 368p. 1982. 16.95 (ISBN 0-13-549618-7); pap. text ed. 11.95 (ISBN 0-13-549600-4). P-H.
Hersey, Paul & Stinson, John E., eds. Perspectives in Leader Effectiveness. LC 79-14646. (Illus.). vii, 175p. 1980. 11.95x (ISBN 0-8214-0411-3). Ohio U Pr.
Herzberg, Frederick. The Managerial Choice: To Be Efficient & to Be Human. 1976. pap. 12.95x (ISBN 0-256-01882-0). Irwin.
Heydebrand, Wolf. Comparative Organizations. (General Sociology Ser.). (Illus.). 608p. 1973. text ed. 24.95 (ISBN 0-13-153932-9). P-H.
Heyel, Carl. The Manager's Bible: How to Resolve One Hundred Twenty-Seven Classic Management Dilemmas. LC 81-66434. (Illus.). 1981. 12.95 (ISBN 0-02-914680-1). Free Pr.
Heyel, Carl, ed. The Van Nostrand Reinhold Concise Guide to Business Logistics: Concise Management. 1979. pap. 7.95 (ISBN 0-442-23402-3). Van Nos Reinhold.
--VNR Concise Guide to Management Decision Making. (VNR Concise Management Ser.). 227p. 1980. pap. text ed. 7.95 (ISBN 0-442-23400-7). Van Nos Reinhold.
Hicks, Herbert G. & Gullett, C. Ray. The Management of Organizations. 4th ed. (Illus.). 656p. 1981. text ed. 19.95 (ISBN 0-07-028773-2, C); instr's. manual 15.00 (ISBN 0-07-028774-0); study guide 5.95 (ISBN 0-07-028777-5). McGraw.
--The Management of Organizations. 3rd ed. (Management Ser.). (Illus.). 1976. text ed. 16.95 (ISBN 0-07-028721-X, C); instructor's manual 4.95 (ISBN 0-07-028722-8). McGraw.
--Organizations: Theory & Behavior. (Management Ser.). (Illus.). 448p. 1975. text ed. 16.95 (ISBN 0-07-028730-9, C); instructors' manual by Slaughter 2.95 (ISBN 0-07-058160-6). McGraw.
Hicks, Herbert G. & Powell, James D. Management, Organizations & Human Resources: Selected Readings. 2nd ed. 1975. text ed. 9.95 (ISBN 0-07-028733-3, C). McGraw.
Hill, Norman C. Increasing Managerial Effectiveness: Keys to Management & Motivation. LC 78-62547. 1979. pap. text ed. 8.95 (ISBN 0-201-02888-3). A-W.
Himes, Joseph S. Conflict & Conflict Management. LC 78-32164. 342p. 1980. 23.00x (ISBN 0-8203-0473-5); pap. 9.00 (ISBN 0-8203-0509-X). U of Ga Pr.
Hines, George H. The New Zealand Manager. LC 74-167425. 77p. 1973. pap. 7.00x (ISBN 0-8002-0094-2). Intl Pubns Serv.
Hines, William W. & Montgomery, Douglas C. Probability & Statistics in Engineering & Management Science. 2nd ed. LC 79-26257. 634p. 1980. text ed. 25.95 (ISBN 0-471-04759-7); solutions manual avail. (ISBN 0-471-05006-7). Wiley.
Hitt, Michael A., et al. Effective Management. (Management Ser). (Illus.). 1979. text ed. 19.50 (ISBN 0-8299-0196-5); pap. study guide 7.95 (ISBN 0-8299-0246-5); instrs.' manual avail. (ISBN 0-8299-0489-1); transparency masters avail. (ISBN 0-8299-0490-5). West Pub.
Hodge, Billy J. & Johnson, Herbert J. Management & Organizational Behavior: A Multidimensional Approach. (Management & Administration Ser.). 552p. 1981. Repr. of 1970 ed. lib. bdg. 21.50 (ISBN 0-89874-086-X). Krieger.
Hodgetts, Richard M. Management Fundamentals. LC 80-65800. 464p. 1981. text ed. 19.95 (ISBN 0-03-058104-4). Dryden Pr.
--Management: Theory, Process, & Practice. LC 74-6687. (Illus.). 603p. 1975. 14.95x (ISBN 0-7216-4708-1). HR&W.
Hodgkinson, Christopher. Towards a Philosophy of Administration. LC 78-676. 1978. 18.50x (ISBN 0-312-81036-9). St Martin.
Hofer, Charles W., et al. Strategic Management: Cases in Business Policy & Planning. 1980. text ed. 21.95 (ISBN 0-8299-0331-3). West Pub.
Hofstede, G. Futures for Work. 1979. lib. bdg. 19.50 (ISBN 0-89838-015-4, Pub. by Martinus Nijhoff Netherlands). Kluwer Boston.
Hollingsworth. Readings in Basic Management. 2nd ed. 1979. pap. 10.95 (ISBN 0-7216-4753-7). Dryden Pr.
Holtz, Herman R. Profit-Line Management: Managing a Growing Business Successfully. 320p. 1981. 17.95 (ISBN 0-8144-5690-1). Am Mgmt.
Holzer, Marc, et al. Literature in Bureaucracy: Readings in Administrative Fiction. 1979. pap. text ed. 7.95 (ISBN 0-89529-092-8). Avery Pub.
Hopf, Harry A. Papers on Management, 2 vols. LC 72-9524. (Management History Ser.: No. 17). 648p. 1973. Repr. Set. 38.50 (ISBN 0-87960-020-9). Hive Pub.
Horn, Maurice. The World Encyclopedia of Comics, 1 vol. ed. LC 75-22322. (Illus.). 785p. 1976. text ed. 30.00 (ISBN 0-87754-030-6). Chelsea Hse.
Horovitz, Jacques H. Top Management Control in Europe. 210p. 1980. 28.50x (ISBN 0-312-80908-5). St Martin.
Hoslett, Schuyler D. Human Factors in Management. rev. ed. Repr. of 1951 ed. lib. bdg. 15.00x (ISBN 0-8371-3833-7, HOMA). Greenwood.
Hosmer, La Rue T. Strategic Management: Text & Cases on Business Policy. (Illus.). 736p. 1982. 21.95 (ISBN 0-13-851063-6). P-H.
Houck, Lewis D., Jr. A Practical Guide to Budgetary & Management Control Systems. LC 78-14716. 272p. 1979. 22.95 (ISBN 0-669-02705-7). Lexington Bks.
How to Delegate Effectively. pap. 10.00 (ISBN 0-686-02520-2). Preston.
How to Manage Through Leadership. 1975. pap. 10.00 (ISBN 0-686-10813-2). Preston.
Howells, G. W. Executive Aspects of Man Management. (Times Management Library). 1972. 16.95x (ISBN 0-8464-0392-7). Beekman Pubs.
Hsiao, James C. & Cleaver, David S. Management Science: Quantitative Approaches to Resource Allocation & Decision Making. LC 80-80960. (Illus.). 584p. 1981. text ed. 19.95 (ISBN 0-395-29488-6); write for info. (ISBN 0-395-29489-4). HM.
Hubbard, L. Ron. How to Live Through an Executive. 13.00 (ISBN 0-686-30786-0). Church Scient NY.
--The Management Series. 47.00 (ISBN 0-686-30799-2). Church Scient NY.
--Modern Management Technology Defined. 43.00 (ISBN 0-686-30806-9). Church Scient NY.
--The Organization Executive Course. 338.00 (ISBN 0-686-30798-4). Church Scient NY.
Hughes & De Maria. Managing to Stay Non-Union. 1979. pap. 6.95 (ISBN 0-917386-26-4). Exec Ent.
Hull, John, et al. Model Building Techniques for Management. (Illus.). 1977. 19.95 (ISBN 0-566-00149-7, 00719-6, Pub. by Saxon Hse). Lexington Bks.
Hultman, Kenneth E. The Path of Least Resistance. LC 79-11178. 1979. text ed. 15.95 (ISBN 0-89384-046-7). Learning Concepts.
Human Values in Management. 5.95 (ISBN 0-686-02554-7); pap. 1.95x (ISBN 0-686-02555-5). Dun.
Humble, John. Management by Objectives in Action. 1971. 12.95 (ISBN 0-07-094217-X, P&RB). McGraw.
Humble, John W. How to Manage by Objectives. (AMACOM Executive Bks). 1978. pap. 5.95 (ISBN 0-8144-7508-6). Am Mgmt.
Hunsacker, Philip & Alessandra, Anthony. The Art of Managing People. (Illus.). 1980. 15.95 (ISBN 0-13-047472-X, Spec); pap. 6.95 (ISBN 0-13-047464-9, Spec). P-H.
Hunt, Alfred L. Corporate Cash Management: Including Electronic Funds Transfer. LC 78-16648. 1978. 19.95 (ISBN 0-8144-5464-X). Am Mgmt.
Hunter, David M. Supervisory Management: Skill Building Techniques. 300p. 1981. text ed. 16.95 (ISBN 0-8359-7155-4); pap. text ed. 12.95 (ISBN 0-8359-7156-2); instr's. manual free (ISBN 0-8359-7157-0). Reston.
Huntsman, Ann & Binger, Jane. Communicating Effectively. LC 80-83694. (Nursing Magnagement Anthologies). 220p. 1981. pap. text ed. 10.95 (ISBN 0-913654-67-1). Nursing Res.
Huse, Edgar F. The Modern Manager. (Illus.). 1979. text ed. 19.95 (ISBN 0-8299-0197-3); pap. study guide 7.95 (ISBN 0-686-67406-5); study guide 7.50 (ISBN 0-8299-0253-8). instrs.' manual avail. (ISBN 0-8299-0492-1); transparency masters avail. (ISBN 0-8299-0493-X). West Pub.
Hutzler, Laurie H. The Regulatory & Paperwork Maze. Incl. A Guide for Association Executives. pap. (ISBN 0-937542-03-2); A Guide for Government Personnel. pap. (ISBN 0-937542-04-0); A Guide for Small Business. pap. (ISBN 0-937542-02-4). (Illus.). 1980. pap. 10.00 ea. Legal Mgmt Serv.
Hutzler, Laurie H., ed. Small Business - Big Government: Getting What You Need from Uncle Sam. (Illus.). 504p. 1981. pap. 89.95 (ISBN 0-937542-06-7). Legal Mgmt Serv.
Hyman, Stanley. The Management of Associations. 160p. 1979. 30.00x (ISBN 0-900246-27-8). Intl Pubns Serv.
IBP Research & Editorial Staff. Successful Techniques That Multiply Profits & Personal Payoff in the Closely - Held Corporation. 4th ed. LC 80-16143. (Illus.). 500p. 1980. 49.50 (ISBN 0-87624-532-7). Inst Busn Plan.
Imboden, N. A Management Approach to Project Appraisal & Evaluation: With Special Reference to Non-Directly Productive Projects. 172p. (Orig.). 1977. pap. 8.50x (ISBN 92-64-11721-0). OECD.
Indian Council of Social Science Research, New Delhi. A Survey of Research in Management, Vol. I. (ICSSR Research Survey Ser). 502p. 1974. 15.00x (ISBN 0-8002-2043-9). Intl Pubns Serv.
Indian Council of Social Science Research. Survey of Research in Management, Vol. 1. 1973. 15.00 (ISBN 0-686-20313-5). Intl Bk Dist.
--Survey of Research in Management, Vol. 2. 1977. 27.00 (ISBN 0-686-21733-0). Intl Bk Dist.
Interfutures: Facing the Future: Mastering the Probable & Managing the Unpredictible. 1979. 20.00x (ISBN 92-64-11967-1). OECD.
International Business & Management Institute. Little Known Business Secrets & Shortcuts for Entrepreneurs & Managers. (Illus.). 110p. (Orig.). pap. 25.00 (ISBN 0-935402-03-9). Intl Comm Serv.
Itami, Hiroyuki. Adaptive Behavior: Management Control & Information Analysis, Vol. 15. (Studies in Accounting Research). 164p. 1977. 6.00 (ISBN 0-686-31108-6); nonmembers 6.00 (ISBN 0-686-31109-4). Am Accounting.
Ivancevich, John M., et al. Managing for Perfomance. 1980. 18.95x (ISBN 0-256-02274-7); wkbk. 5.50x (ISBN 0-256-02356-5). Business Pubns.
Jaffee, Cabot. Assessing & Developing Management Skills: Perception, Vol. 1. 204p. 1981. 3-ring special binder 24.95 (ISBN 0-8436-0791-2). CBI Pub.

Jaffee, Cabot L. & Frank, Fredric D. Interviews Conducted at Assessment Centers: A Guide for Training Managers. 1977. pap. text ed. 7.95 (ISBN 0-8403-1414-0). Kendall-Hunt.
Jaques, Elliott. General Theory Bureaucracy. 1981. pap. text ed. 10.00x (ISBN 0-435-82478-3). Heinemann Ed.
Jelinek, Mariann. Institutionalizing Innovation: A Study of Organizational Learning Systems. (Praeger Special Studies). 1979. 23.95 (ISBN 0-03-047031-5). Praeger.
Johnson, Edie F. & O'Neill, John J. The Essentials of Management. 1978. pap. 1.25 (ISBN 0-686-11136-2, V572). US Catholic.
--The Essentials of Organization. 1977. pap. 0.95 (ISBN 0-686-11137-0, V537). US Catholic.
Johnson, Ross H. & Winn, Paul R. Quantitative Methods for Management. LC 75-25239. (Illus.). 448p. 1976. text ed. 19.95 (ISBN 0-395-20633-2); inst. manual with solutions 2.00 (ISBN 0-395-20634-0). HM.
Johnson, Thomas W. & Stinson, John E. Managing Today & Tomorrow. LC 77-76123. (Illus.). 1978. text ed. 15.95 (ISBN 0-201-03487-5); instr's man. 3.95 (ISBN 0-201-03488-3). A-W.
Jones, G. L. Financial Measurement for Managers. 1976. pap. text ed. 13.95x (ISBN 0-7131-3367-8). Intl Ideas.
Jones, James. Meeting Management: A Professional Approach. Schott, Connie, ed. LC 78-74192. 1978. text ed. 17.95 (ISBN 0-933268-00-9). Bayard Pubns.
Jones, William M. Survival: A Manual on Manipulating. 261p. 1979. 14.95 (ISBN 0-13-879114-7, Busn). P-H.
Juran, Joseph M. Managerial Breakthrough: A New Concept of the Manager's Job. (Illus.). 1964. 19.50 (ISBN 0-07-033172-3, P&RB). McGraw.
Kafka, Vincent W. & Shaefer, John H. Open Management: How to Improve the Quality of Work Life. 2nd ed. LC 79-55384. 1979. pap. 7.95 (ISBN 0-931290-22-8). Alchemy Bks.
Kanter, Rosabeth M. & Stein, Barry. A Tale of "O". On Being Different in an Organization. LC 79-2625. (Illus., Orig.). 1980. pap. 4.95 (ISBN 0-06-090729-0, CN 729, HarpT). Har-Row.
Karrell, Robert J. How to Improve Your Managerial Skills. (The International Council for Excellence in Management Library). (Illus.). 117p. 1980. plastic spiral bdg. 28.95 (ISBN 0-89266-249-2). Am Classical Coll Pr.
Kast, Fremont & Rosenzweig, James. Experiential Exercises & Cases in Management. (Illus.). 1976. text ed. 11.95 (ISBN 0-07-033343-2); instructor's manual 4.95 (ISBN 0-07-033344-0). McGraw.
--Organization & Management: A Systems & Contingency Approach. 3rd rev. ed. (Management Ser.). (Illus.). 1979. text ed. 22.50x (ISBN 0-07-033346-7, C); instructor's manual 7.50 (ISBN 0-07-033347-5). McGraw.
Kast, Fremont E. & Rosenzweig, James. Organization & Management: Experiential Exercises. 1976. text ed. 12.95x (ISBN 0-07-033346-7, C); instructor's manual 4.95 (ISBN 0-07-033347-5). McGraw.
Kast, Fremont E. & Rosenzweig, James E. Contingency Views of Organization & Management. LC 73-75421. (Illus.). 355p. 1973. pap. text ed. 10.95 (ISBN 0-574-17135-5, 13-0135). SRA.
Kastens, Merritt. Redefining the Manager's Job: The Proactive Manager in a Reactive World. 256p. 1980. 14.95 (ISBN 0-8144-5619-7). Am Mgmt.
Katz, Ralph. Career Issues in Human Resource Management. (Applied Management Ser.). (Illus.). 224p. 1982. 17.95 (ISBN 0-13-114819-2). P-H.
Katz, Robert L. Cases & Concepts in Corporate Strategy. 1970. ref. ed 22.95 (ISBN 0-13-118422-9). P-H.
Kavanagh, Thomas C., et al. Construction Management: A Professional Approach. (Modern Structures Ser.). (Illus.). 1978. 18.50 (ISBN 0-07-033386-6, P&RB). McGraw.
Kazmier, Leonard J. Principles of Management: A Programmed-Instructional Approach. (Illus.). 480p. 1974. text ed. 15.95 (ISBN 0-07-033450-1, C); pap. text ed. 10.95 (ISBN 0-07-033451-X); instructors' manual 4.95 (ISBN 0-07-033452-8). McGraw.
Keller, A. Z., ed. Uncertainty in Risk & Reliability Appraisal in Management. 1975. 29.50 (ISBN 0-9960018-5-9, Pub. by A Hilger England). Heyden.
Kelley, Joe. How Managers Manage. (Illus.). 1980. 14.95 (ISBN 0-13-423756-0, Spec); pap. 7.95 (ISBN 0-686-59488-6, Spec); study guide 5.95 (ISBN 0-13-423731-5). P-H.
Kellogg, Marion S. Putting Management Theories to Work. rev. ed. 1980. pap. text ed. 6.95 (ISBN 0-13-744490-7, Spec). P-H.
Kempner, Thomas, ed. A Handbook of Management. 442p. 1971. 27.50x (ISBN 0-8448-0043-0). Crane-Russak Co.
Keys, Bernard & Leftwich, Howard. The Executive Simulation. 2nd ed. 1977. pap. text ed. 6.95 (ISBN 0-8403-1657-7). Kendall-Hunt.
Khandwalla, Pradip N. The Design of Organizations. 1977. text ed. 23.95 (ISBN 0-15-517366-9, HC). HarBraceJ.
Killen, Kenneth H. Management: A Middle Management Approach. LC 76-13088. (Illus.). 1977. text ed. 15.95 (ISBN 0-395-16980-1); inst. manual 1.25 (ISBN 0-395-19860-7). HM.
Killian, Ray A. Managers Must Lead! rev. ed. 1979. 14.95 (ISBN 0-8144-5482-8). Am Mgmt.
Kilmann, Ralph H, et al. The Management of Organization Design, 2 vols. LC 76-23404. 1976. 22.95 ea. (North Holland). Vol. 1 (ISBN 0-444-00188-3). Vol. 2 (ISBN 0-444-00189-1). Elsevier.
Kim, Chaiho. Quantitative Analysis for Managerial Decisions. LC 75-372. (Illus.). 448p. 1975. text ed. 16.95 (ISBN 0-201-03739-4). A-W.
Kimball, Patrick. Managing: The Art of Making Things Happen. 1979. pap. text ed. 9.95 (ISBN 0-89669-020-2). Collegium Bk Pubs.
Kivenko. Managing Work in Process. (Industrial Engineering; a Series of Reference Books & Textbooks: Vol. 5). 1981. 29.75 (ISBN 0-8247-1268-4). Dekker.
Kleinschrod, Walter. Management's Guide to Word Processing. 1980. 65.50 (ISBN 0-85013-070-0). Dartnell Corp.
Knezevich, Stephen. Management by Objectives & Results. 76p. 1973. 4.00 (ISBN 0-686-08745-3, 021-00396). Am Assn Sch Admin.
Knoeppel, C. E. Organization & Administration. LC 72-9516. (Management History Ser.: No. 48). 464p. Repr. of 1917 ed. 23.50 (ISBN 0-686-76978-3). Hive Pub.
Knotts, Ulysses S. & Swift, Ernest W. Management Science for Management Decisions. 1978. text ed. 19.95 (ISBN 0-205-06039-0, 1060392); instr's man. avail. (ISBN 0-205-06040-4, 1060406); sol. man. avail. (ISBN 0-205-06041-2, 1060414). Allyn.
Knudson, Harry R. Organizational Behavior: Cases for Developing Nations. 1967. 8.25 (ISBN 0-201-03799-8). A-W.
Knudson, Harry R. & Woodworth, Robert T. Management: An Experiential Approach. 2nd ed. (Management Ser.). (Illus.). 1978. pap. text ed. 11.95 (ISBN 0-07-035243-7, C); instructor's manual 5.95 (ISBN 0-07-035244-5). McGraw.
Kobert, Norman. The Aggressive Management Style. 270p. 1980. 18.95 (ISBN 0-13-018762-3). P-H.
Kohn, Mervin. Dynamic Managing: Principles, Process, Practice. LC 76-14002. 1977. pap. text ed. 18.95 (ISBN 0-8465-3676-5); instr's guide 3.50 (ISBN 0-8465-3677-3). Benjamin-Cummings.
Kolb, David A. & McIntyre, James M. Organizational Psychology: A Book of Readings. (Ser. in Behavior Sciences in Business). 1979. text ed. 14.95 (ISBN 0-13-641274-2). P-H.
Koontz, Harold. Board of Directors & Effective Management. 2nd ed. 286p. 1981. lib. bdg. write for info. (ISBN 0-89874-188-2). Krieger.
Koontz, Harold & O'Donnell, Cyril. Essentials of Management. 2nd ed. Davis, Keith, ed. (Management Ser.). (Illus.). 1977. pap. text ed. 12.95 (ISBN 0-07-035372-7, C); instructor's manual 5.50 (ISBN 0-07-035373-5). McGraw.
Koontz, Harold, et al. Management. 7th, rev. ed. (Illus.). 1980. text ed. 18.95 (ISBN 0-07-035377-8); instructor's manual 9.95 (ISBN 0-07-035378-6); study guide 6.95 (ISBN 0-07-035379-4). McGraw.
Koontz, Harold D. & O'Donnell, Cyril. Management: A Book of Readings. 4th ed. 1976. text ed. 15.50 (ISBN 0-07-035353-0, C); pap. text ed. 10.95 (ISBN 0-07-035352-2). McGraw.
Korman, Abraham & Korman, Rhoda. Career Success - Personal Failure. 150p. 1980. text ed. 13.95 (ISBN 0-13-114777-3). P-H.
Korman, Abraham K. Managerial Alienation. (Illus.). 160p. 1980. text ed. 12.95 (ISBN 0-13-549782-5). P-H.
Kossen, Stan. Supervision: A Guide to Practical First-Line Management. 436p. 1981. text ed. 17.50 scp (ISBN 0-06-384723-X, HarpC); instr's. manual avail. (ISBN 0-06-373620-9). Har-Row.
Kotter, John P. Power in Management. 1979. 10.95 (ISBN 0-8144-5507-7). Am Mgmt.
Krajewski, Lee J. & Thompson, Howard E., eds. Management Science: Quantitative Methods in Context. LC 80-17103. (Management Ser.). 544p. 1981. text ed. 24.95 (ISBN 0-471-06109-3). Wiley.
Kreitner, Robert. Management: A Problem-Solving Process. LC 79-88719. (Illus.). 1980. text ed. 18.75 (ISBN 0-395-28490-2); inst. manual 1.75 (ISBN 0-395-28491-0) (ISBN 0-395-31768-1). HM.
Kreitner, Robert & Sova, Margaret. Understanding Management: Study Guide to Management: A Problem-Solving Process. LC 79-88719. (Illus.). pap. 6.95 (ISBN 0-395-28492-9). HM.
Krentzman, Harvey C. Successful Management Strategies for Small Business. (Illus.). 208p. 1981. text ed. 13.95 (ISBN 0-13-863126-3, Spec); pap. text ed. 6.95 (ISBN 0-13-863118-2, Spec). P-H.
Kuhn, Jim. Management by Hassling. 1978. pap. 3.95 (ISBN 0-425-03927-7, Medallion). Berkley Pub.
Kuntz, Walter N. Modern Corporate Management: New Approaches to Financial Control, Operations, Customer Development & Equity Sources. (Illus.). 1978. 32.95 (ISBN 0-13-589754-8, Busn). P-H.
Kuttner, Monroe S. Managing the Paperwork Pipeline. LC 77-15041. 244p. 1978. 28.95 (ISBN 0-471-03154-2, Pub. by Wiley-Interscience). Wiley.
LaFlair, Roy M. Managerial Psychology: Business Success Through the Power of Scientific Psychology. (The Library of Scientific Psychology). (Illus.). 1979. 39.75 (ISBN 0-89266-184-4). Am Classical Coll Pr.
Lanford, H. W. System Management: Planning & Control. (National University Publications Ser.). 200p. 1981. 15.00 (ISBN 0-8046-9223-8). Kennikat.
Lapin, Lawrence L. Management Science for Business Decisions. 613p. 1980. text ed. 19.95 (ISBN 0-15-554690-2, HC); instructor's manual avail. HarBraceJ.
Lasser, Jacob K. Business Management Handbook. 3rd ed. 1968. 34.95 (ISBN 0-07-036555-5, P&RB). McGraw.
Latham, Fred W. & Sanders, George S. Urwick, Orr on Management. 272p. 1981. 17.95 (ISBN 0-8144-5689-8). Am Mgmt.
Lawler, Edward E. & Rhode, John G. Information & Control in Organizations. LC 75-20582. (Goodyear Series in Management & Organizations). (Illus.). 208p. 1976. text ed. 13.95 (ISBN 0-87620-424-8); pap. text ed. 9.95x (ISBN 0-87620-425-6). Goodyear.
Lawless, David J. Organizational Behavior: The Psychology of Effective Management. 2nd ed. (Illus.). 1979. text ed. 21.00 (ISBN 0-13-640706-4). P-H.
Lazarsfeld, P. F., et al. Contributions to Scientific Research in Management. (Illus.). 1959. 2.50 (ISBN 0-911798-11-0). UCLA Mgmt.
Lazer, Robert I. & Wikstrom, Walter S. Appraising Managerial Performance: Current Practices & Future Directions. LC 77-87101. (Report Ser.: No. 723). (Illus.). 1977. pap. 30.00 (ISBN 0-8237-0157-3). Conference Bd.
Leavitt, Harold, et al, eds. Organizations of the Future: Interaction with the External Environment. LC 74-1733. (Special Studies). (Illus.). 220p. 1974. text ed. 25.95 (ISBN 0-275-28864-1). Praeger.
Leavitt, Harold J. & Pondy, Louis R. Readings in Managerial Psychology. 3rd ed. LC 79-21587. xii, 732p. 1980. lib. bdg. 25.00x (ISBN 0-226-46986-7); pap. text ed. 12.95x (ISBN 0-226-46987-5). U of Chicago Pr.
Leavitt, Harold J., et al. The Organizational World. 1973. pap. text ed. 10.95 (ISBN 0-15-567562-1, HC). HarBraceJ.
Lee, David E. The Motivating Administrator. 112p. 1981. 6.95 (ISBN 0-88289-255-X). Pelican.
Lee, James A. The Gold & the Garbage in Management Theories & Prescriptions. LC 80-12758. (Illus.). x, 480p. 1980. 22.95x (ISBN 0-8214-0436-9); pap. 10.95x (ISBN 0-8214-0578-0). Ohio U Pr.
Lee, Sang M. Management by Multiple Objective. (Illus.). 240p. 1981. 20.00 (ISBN 0-89433-083-7). Petrocelli.
Lee, Sang M., ed. Personnel Management: A Computer Based System. Thorp, Cary. 1979. text ed. 17.50 (ISBN 0-89433-052-7); pap. 14.00 (ISBN 0-89433-053-5). Petrocelli.
Lee, Sang M., et al. Management Science. 1050p. 1981. text ed. write for info. (ISBN 0-697-08046-3); solutions manual avail. (ISBN 0-697-08052-8). Wm C Brown.
Leeds, C. A. Management & Business Studies. 430p. 1974. pap. 7.00x (ISBN 0-7121-1366-5). Intl Pubns Serv.
Leenders, Michael R., et al. Purchasing & Materials Management. 7th ed. 1980. 22.95x (ISBN 0-256-02374-3). Irwin.
Lefton, Robert, et al. Improving Productivity Through People Skills. 1980. 22.50 (ISBN 0-88410-498-2). Ballinger Pub.
Legge, K. & Mugford, E. Designing Organisations for Satisfaction & Efficiency. 160p. 1978. text ed. 29.00x (ISBN 0-566-02102-1, Pub. by Gower Pub Co England). Renouf.
Lehmann, Cara & Glenn, Dolores. The Intriguing World of Modern Management. 1977. 6.95 (ISBN 0-533-02437-4). Vantage.
Leontiades, Milton. Management Policy: Strategies & Plans. 680p. 1981. text ed. 18.95 (ISBN 0-316-52104-3); tchrs'. manual free (ISBN 0-316-52105-1). Little.
Lerbinger, Otto & Sperber, Nathaniel H. Key to the Executive Head. LC 74-10352. (Illus.). 111p. 1975. 9.95 (ISBN 0-201-04258-4). A-W.
LeTourneau, Richard. Management Plus: Getting Things Done Through People. 128p. 1976. pap. 1.95 (ISBN 0-310-27562-8). Zondervan.
Levin, Richard I. Statistics for Management. 2nd ed. (Illus.). 800p. 1981. text ed. 21.95 (ISBN 0-13-845255-5). P-H.
Lewis, C. D. Operations Management in Practice. 304p. 1980. 36.00x (ISBN 0-86003-511-5, Pub. by Allan Pubs England); pap. 18.00x (ISBN 0-86003-611-1). State Mutual Bk.
Life Office Management Association, ed. Readings for the Administrative Management Specialty. (FLMI Ins. Ed. Prog. Ser.). 1981. pap. text ed. price not set (ISBN 0-915322-44-7). Loma.
Likert, Rensis. Human Organization: Its Management & Value. (Illus.). 1967. 16.50 (ISBN 0-07-037851-7, C). McGraw.
Likert, Rensis & Likert, Jane G. New Ways of Managing Conflict. 1976. 19.95 (ISBN 0-07-037842-8, P&RB). McGraw.
Likert's System 4. rev. ed. (AMACOM Reprint Collections). 52p. 1975. pap. 6.50 (ISBN 0-8144-6508-0). Am Mgmt.
Lilienthal, David E. Management: A Humanist Art. LC 67-20667. (Benjamin Fairless Memorial Lectures Ser.). 67p. 1967. 9.00x (ISBN 0-231-03064-9). Columbia U Pr.
Lindberg, Roy A. What You Should Know About the Foundations of Management. LC 73-3319. (Business Almanac Ser: No. 21). 128p. 1973. lib. bdg. 5.95 (ISBN 0-379-11221-3). Oceana.
Lindenberg, Marc & Crosby, Benjamin. Managing Development: The Political Dimension. LC 80-83345. 200p. 1981. text ed. 19.95 (ISBN 0-931816-49-1); pap. text ed. 9.95 (ISBN 0-931816-27-0). Transaction Bk.
Lindo, David K. Supervision Can Be Easy. (Illus.). 1979. 14.95 (ISBN 0-8144-5548-4). Am Mgmt.
Lines, James. The Role of the Chief Executive. 172p. 1978. text ed. 24.50x (ISBN 0-220-66355-6, Pub. by Busn Bks England). Renouf.
Linowes, David F. Strategies for Survival. LC 73-75673. 1973. 10.95 (ISBN 0-8144-5326-0). Am Mgmt.
Litterer, J. Organizations: Structure & Behavior. 3rd ed. LC 80-15645. (Wiley Series in Management). 625p. 1980. pap. 15.95 (ISBN 0-471-07786-0). Wiley.
Litterer, Joseph A. The Analysis of Organizations. 2nd ed. LC 72-8586. (Management & Administration Ser.). (Illus.). 640p. 1973. text ed. 26.95x (ISBN 0-471-54106-0). Wiley.
--An Introduction to Management. LC 77-23820. (Ser. in Management & Administration). 1978. text ed. 22.95 (ISBN 0-471-54100-1). Wiley.
--Management: Concepts & Controversies. LC 77-20031. 1978. pap. text ed. 13.95 (ISBN 0-471-03611-0). Wiley.
Littlechild, S. C. Operational Research for Managers. 256p. 1977. 33.00x (ISBN 0-86003-504-2, Pub. by Allan Pubs England); pap. 16.50 (ISBN 0-86003-604-9). State Mutual Bk.
Lohmann, Roger. Breaking Even: Financial Management in Human Service Organizations. 1980. 25.00 (ISBN 0-87722-166-9). Temple U Pr.
Longenecker, Justin G. Essentials of Management: A Behavioral Approach. 1977. text ed. 15.95 (ISBN 0-675-08552-7); instructor's manual 3.95 (ISBN 0-686-67520-7). Merrill.
--Principles of Management & Organizational Behavior. 4th ed. 1977. text ed. 19.95 (ISBN 0-675-08556-X); instructor's manual 3.95 (ISBN 0-686-67528-2). Merrill.
Longenecker, Justin G. & Pringle, Charles D. Management. 5th ed. (Illus.). 544p. 1981. text ed. 20.95 (ISBN 0-675-08061-4); tchrs' manual 3.95 (ISBN 0-686-77724-7); study guide 3.95 (ISBN 0-675-09995-1). Merrill.
--Principles of Management & Organizational Behavior: Selected Readings. 1973. pap. text ed. 11.50x (ISBN 0-675-08950-6). Merrill.
Longest, Beafort B., Jr. Management Practices for the Health Professional. 2nd ed. (Illus.). 1980. text ed. 15.95 (ISBN 0-8359-4224-4). Reston.
Loomba, N. Paul & Holsinger, Alden O., Jr. Management: A Quantative Perspective. (Illus.). 1978. text ed. 21.95 (ISBN 0-02-371640-1); study guide 2.95 (ISBN 0-02-371670-3). Macmillan.
Lorentzen, John F. The Manager's Personal Problem Solver: A Handbook of Creative Solutions to Human Relations Problems in Your Organization. 1980. 15.95 (ISBN 0-13-549915-1, Spec); pap. 7.95 (ISBN 0-13-549907-0, Spec). P-H.
Lorsch, Jay W. & Barnes, Louis B. Managers & Their Careers. 1972. 9.95x (ISBN 0-256-01296-2). Irwin.

Love, Barbara, ed. Handbook of Circulation Management. 1980. 49.95 (ISBN 0-918110-02-5). Folio.
Love, Sydney F. Mastery & Management of Time. (Illus.). 1978. 14.95 (ISBN 0-13-559971-7, Busn). P-H.
Lucey, T. Management Information Systems. 1980. 10.00x (ISBN 0-905435-11-7, Pub. by DP Pubns). State Mutual Bk.
--Management Information Systems: An Instructional Manual. 112p. 1981. pap. text ed. 6.00x (ISBN 0-905435-01-X). Verry.
Lumsden, George J. Impact Management: Personal Power Strategies for Success. LC 79-11632. 1979. 12.95 (ISBN 0-8144-5519-0). Am Mgmt.
Lurie, Adolph. Business Segments: A Guide for Managers & Accountants. (Illus.). 1979. 15.95 (ISBN 0-07-039113-0). McGraw.
Luthans, Fred. Introduction to Management: A Contingency Approach. 1975. text ed. 18.95x (ISBN 0-07-039125-4, C); instructors' manual 4.95 (ISBN 0-07-039126-2). McGraw.
--Organizational Behavior. 2nd ed. Davis, Keith, ed. (Management Ser.). (Illus.). 1976. text ed. 16.95 (ISBN 0-07-039130-0, C); instrs manual 4.95 (ISBN 0-07-039133-5); study guide 6.95 (ISBN 0-07-039131-9). McGraw.
Lynch, Edith M. The Woman's Guide to Management. 1978. pap. 3.95 (ISBN 0-346-12324-0). Cornerstone.
Lyon, Herbert L., et al. Management Science in Organizations. LC 75-20807. 580p. 1976. text ed. 16.95 (ISBN 0-87620-561-9); tchrs manual free (ISBN 0-87620-562-7). Goodyear.
McAlpine, T. S. The Process of Management. 1973. 16.50x (ISBN 0-8464-0765-5). Beekman Pubs.
--Profit Planning & Control. (Illus.). 164p. 1969. 14.95x (ISBN 0-8464-1122-9). Beekman Pubs.
McCafferty, Donald N. Successful Field Service Management. (Illus.). 1980. 16.95 (ISBN 0-8144-5583-2). Am Mgmt.
McCarthy, Daniel J., et al. Business Policy & Strategy: Concepts & Readings. rev ed. 1979. pap. 13.95x (ISBN 0-256-02168-6). Irwin.
McCarthy, John J. Why Managers Fail. 1978. 10.95 (ISBN 0-07-044316-5, SP); pap. 4.95 (ISBN 0-07-044315-7). McGraw.
McCaslin, Barbara S. & McNamara, Patricia P. Be Your Own Boss: A Woman's Guide to Planning & Running Her Own Business. (Illus.). 352p. 1980. 16.95 (ISBN 0-13-072215-4, Spec); pap. 8.95 (ISBN 0-13-072207-3). P-H.
Maccoby, Michael. The Leader: Managing the Work Place. 1981. 12.95 (ISBN 0-671-24123-0). S&S.
McConkey, Dale D. How to Manage by Results. 3rd ed. LC 76-41332. 1976. 14.95 (ISBN 0-8144-5393-7). Am Mgmt.
--No-Nonsense Delegation. (Illus.). 1979. pap. 5.95 (ISBN 0-8144-7517-5). Am Mgmt.
McConkey, Dale D. & Vanderweele, Ray. Financial Management by Objectives. 1976. 27.95 (ISBN 0-13-315937-X). P-H.
Macdonald, Charles R. MBO Can Work! How to Manage by Contract. (Illus.). 224p. 1981. 16.95 (ISBN 0-07-044331-9, P&RB). McGraw.
McDonald, James O. Management Without Tears. 160p. 1981. pap. price not set (ISBN 0-87251-068-9). Crain Bks.
McDonald, T. Marll. Mathematical Methods for Social & Management Scientists. 544p. 1974. text ed. 19.95 (ISBN 0-395-17089-3); instructor's manual pap. 2.25 (ISBN 0-395-17858-4). HM.
McDonough, Adrian M. & Garrett, Leonard J. Management Systems. 1965. 19.50x (ISBN 0-256-00321-1). Irwin.
McFarlan, F. Warren, et al. The Management Game. rev. ed. 153p. 1980. pap. 14.98 (ISBN 0-933836-11-2). Simtek.
McFarland, D. E. Management: Principles & Practices. 4th ed. 1974. 14.50 (ISBN 0-02-378900-X). Macmillan.
McFarland, Dalton. Managerial Achievement: Action Strategies. 1979. pap. text ed. 5.95 (ISBN 0-13-549741-8, Spec). P-H.
McFarland, Dalton E. Management: Foundations & Practices. 5th ed. 1979. text ed. 20.95 (ISBN 0-02-378890-9); instrs'. manual avail. Macmillan.
McGovney, Warren C. Selecting the Right Supervisor: Guidelines for Non Discriminatory Hiring Practices. Reilly, Harry A., ed. 85p. 1981. course manual 175.00 (ISBN 0-89290-140-3, NB-136); participant's manual 18.00 (ISBN 0-89290-141-1). Soc for Visual.
McGraw-Hill Management Awareness Program Editors. McGraw-Hill Management Awareness Program No. 8. 1976. 8.00 (ISBN 0-07-045188-5, P&RB). McGraw.
--McGraw-Hill Management Awareness Program No. 7. 1976. 8.00 (ISBN 0-07-045187-7, P&RB). McGraw.
Mack, Ruth P. Planning on Uncertainty: Decision Making in Business & Government Administration. LC 79-155905. 233p. 1971. 20.25 (ISBN 0-471-56280-7, Pub. by Wiley). Krieger.
McKain, Robert J., Jr. Realize Your Potential. 1979. pap. 5.95 (ISBN 0-8144-7515-9). Am Mgmt.
Mackenzie, R. Alec. New Time Management Methods for You & Your Staff. 1975. 65.50 (ISBN 0-85013-064-6). Dartnell Corp.
--The Time Trap. LC 72-82874. 208p. 1972. 11.95 (ISBN 0-8144-5308-2). Am Mgmt.
Mackintosh, Donald P. Management by Exception. (Illus.). 1978. 32.95 (ISBN 0-13-548917-2, Busn). P-H.
McLagan, Patricia A. Helping Others Learn: Designing Programs for Adults. 1978. pap. text ed. 7.95 (ISBN 0-201-04617-2). A-W.
McLaughlin, Frank S. & Pickhardt, Robert C. Quantitative Techniques for Management Decisions. LC 78-69586. (Illus.). 1978. text ed. 19.50 (ISBN 0-395-26669-6); inst. manual 2.90 (ISBN 0-395-26668-8). HM.
McMaster, John B. Optimum Management. (Illus.). 1981. 17.50 (ISBN 0-89433-120-5). Petrocelli.
McMurry, Robert N. The Maverick Executive. LC 73-85189. (Illus.). 1974. 12.95 (ISBN 0-8144-5345-7). Am Mgmt.
Magnusen, Karl O. Organizational Design, Development, & Behavior. 1977. pap. 8.95x (ISBN 0-673-15042-9). Scott F.
Maheshwari, B. L. Decision Styles & Organizational Effectiveness. 240p. 1980. text ed. 22.50 (ISBN 0-7069-1032-X, Pub. by Vikas India). Advent NY.
Maidment, Robert. Robert's Rules of Disorder: A Guide to Mismanagement. new ed. LC 76-3580. 104p. 1976. pap. 3.95 (ISBN 0-88289-111-1). Pelican.
Making Leaders More Effective. (AMACOM Reprint Collections). 34p. 1975. 10.50 (ISBN 0-8144-6510-2); pap. 4.50 (ISBN 0-8144-6504-8). Am Mgmt.
Mali, Paul. How to Manage by Objectives: A Short Course for Managers. LC 75-27387. (Wiley Professional Development Programs, Business Administration Ser.). 288p. 1975. text ed. 45.95 (ISBN 0-471-56574-1, Pub. by Wiley-Interscience). Wiley.
--Management Handbook Operating Guidelines & Techniques & Practices. LC 80-20514. 1522p. 1981. 49.95 (ISBN 0-471-05263-9). Wiley.
--Managing by Objectives: An Operating Guide to Faster & More Profitable Results. LC 72-1803. (Illus.). 314p. 1972. 27.50 (ISBN 0-471-56575-X, Pub. by Wiley-Interscience). Wiley.
Maloney, Clifford J. Tequilap: Illusions of Administrative Practice. (Illus.). 1968. pap. 3.00 (ISBN 0-87164-009-0). William-F.
Management by Objectives. (Management Ser.). 1972. 4.00 (ISBN 0-934356-08-4); member 3.00 (ISBN 0-686-00283-0). Assn Syst Mgmt.
Management Control of Fire Emergencies. (Zero Ser). 1974. pap. 2.00 (ISBN 0-685-58136-5, 7). Natl Fire Prot.
The Management of the Family Company. 19p. 1973. 2.75 (ISBN 0-686-70983-7, APO43, APO). Unipub.
Management Principles. (Learning Guide (CEBS): Course IV). 1977. spiral bdg. 13.00 (ISBN 0-89154-070-9). Intl Found Employ.
Management Principles. (Answers to the Questions on Subject Matter for the Learning Guide (CEBS): Course IV). 1978. pap. text ed. 10.00 (ISBN 0-89154-077-6). Intl Found Employ.
Managing & Developing New Forms of Work Organization. 158p. 1981. pap. 12.75 (ISBN 92-2-102145-9, ILO 166, ILO). Unipub.
Managing for Productivity: Handling "Problem Employees". 1980. write for info. binder (ISBN 0-89290-063-6); write for info. participant (ISBN 0-89290-062-8). Soc for Visual.
Managing the External Relations of Multinational Corporations. 1978. pap. 8.25 (ISBN 0-915814-18-8, COA 18, CoA). Unipub.
Mancuso, Joseph, ed. The Entrepreneur's Handbook, 2 vols. LC 74-82601. 300p. 1974. Vol. 1. 22.95 (ISBN 0-89006-040-1); Vol. 2. 22.95 (ISBN 0-89006-041-X); Set. 35.50 (ISBN 0-89006-042-8). Artech Hse.
Mandelstam, Dorothy. Incontinence: A Guide to Understanding & Management. (Illus.). 1977. pap. 9.95x (ISBN 0-433-20260-2). Intl Ideas.
Manning, Frank V. Managerial Dilemmas & Executive Growth. 1981. text ed. 17.95 (ISBN 0-8359-4231-7). Reston.
Margerison, C. J. Managerial Problem Solving. 1975. 19.50 (ISBN 0-07-084445-3, P&RB). McGraw.
Margolis, Diane R. The Managers: Corporate Life in America. 312p. 1981. pap. 5.95 (ISBN 0-688-00351-6, Quill). Morrow.
Marinaccio, Anthony & Marinaccio, M. Maxine. Human Relations & Cooperative Planning in Education & Management. 1978. pap. text ed. 7.95 (ISBN 0-8403-0921-X). Kendall-Hunt.
Maris, Terry. Assessment Centers. 1981. text ed. cancelled (ISBN 0-89832-014-3). Brighton Pub Co.
Markham, Jesse W. Conglomerate Enterprise & Public Policy. LC 73-75882. (Illus.). 218p. 1973. 10.00x (ISBN 0-87584-104-X). Harvard Busn.
Markland, Robert E. Topics in Management Science. LC 78-17932. (Management & Administration Ser.). 1979. text ed. 28.95 (ISBN 0-471-01745-0). Wiley.
Martin & Shell. What Every Engineer Should Know About Human Resources Management. (What Every Engineer Should Know Ser.: Vol. 5). 264p. 1980. 12.75 (ISBN 0-8247-1130-0). Dekker.
Martin, Thomas L., Jr. Malice in Blunderland. LC 73-4376. 156p. 1973. 7.95 (ISBN 0-07-040617-0, GB). McGraw.
MAS Guidelines Series, 7 vols. Set. 25.50 (ISBN 0-685-27239-7). Am Inst CPA.
Maslow, Abraham H. Eupsychian Management. 1965. 11.50x (ISBN 0-256-00353-X). Irwin.
Mason, Joseph G. How to Build Your Management Skills. LC 64-8730. 1971. pap. 3.95 (ISBN 0-07-040686-3, SP). McGraw.
Mason, Richard H. & Swanson, E. Burton. Measurement for Management Decision. (Computer Science: Decision Support). (Illus.). 448p. 1981. text ed. 15.95 (ISBN 0-201-04646-6). A-W.
Massie, Joseph L. Blazer & Ashland Oil: A Study in Management. LC 60-8519. (Illus.). 272p. 1960. 17.00x (ISBN 0-8131-1051-3). U Pr of Ky.
--Essentials of Management. 3rd ed. (Essentials of Management Ser.). (Illus.). 1979. ref. 15.95 (ISBN 0-13-286351-0); pap. 9.95 ref. (ISBN 0-13-286344-8). P-H.
Massie, Joseph L. & Douglas, John. Managing: A Contemporary Introduction. 3rd ed. (Illus.). 544p. 1981. text ed. 18.95 (ISBN 0-13-550327-2); pap. 8.95 student manual (ISBN 0-13-550368-X). P-H.
Matteson, Michael & Ivancevich, John. Management Classics. 2nd ed. 1981. pap. text ed. 13.95 (ISBN 0-8302-5469-2). Goodyear.
Matteson, Michael T., ed. Management Classics. Ivancevich, John M. LC 76-42891. (Illus.). 1977. pap. text ed. 11.95 (ISBN 0-87620-587-2); objective tests free (ISBN 0-87620-581-3). Goodyear.
Matthews, Don Q. The Design of the Management Information System. 2nd ed. 238p. 1981. 18.95 (ISBN 0-86670-002-1). Moffat Pub.
Matthies, Leslie H. The Management System: Systems Are for People. LC 76-4572. (Wiley Series on Systems & Controls for Financial Management). 240p. 1976. 29.50 (ISBN 0-471-57697-2, Pub. by Wiley-Interscience). Wiley.
Maude, Barry. Leadership in Management. 240p. 1978. text ed. 29.50x (ISBN 0-220-66361-0, Pub. by Busn Bks England). Renouf.
Mayer, Raymond. Production & Operations Management. 4th ed. (Illus.). 688p. 1982. text ed. 23.95x (ISBN 0-07-041025-9, C); instructors manual 5.95x (ISBN 0-07-041026-7). McGraw.
MBO: What's in It for You? 1974. 8.00 (ISBN 0-8144-6951-5). Am Mgmt.
Medical Group Management Assocation. The Best of MGM: Nineteen Fifty to Nineteen Eighty. 1981. pap. cancelled (ISBN 0-686-30453-5). Med Group Mgmt.
Medical Group Management Association. MGMA Digest of Bylaws & Buy-Sell Agreements. (Illus.). 162p. 1976. 25.00 (ISBN 0-933948-04-2). Med Group Mgmt.
--MGMA Digest of Medical Group Employment Contracts & Income Distribution Plans. 2nd ed. (Illus.). 179p. 1978. 30.00 (ISBN 0-933948-06-9). Med Group Mgmt.
--The Superbill: Guide to a Uniform Billing & or Claims System. (Illus.). 51p. 1974. 10.00 (ISBN 0-933948-02-6). Med Group Mgmt.
Melcher, Arlyn J. Structure & Process of Organization: A Systems Approach. (Illus.). 480p. 1976. 21.00 (ISBN 0-13-855254-1). P-H.
Meltzer, H. & Nord, Walter R. Making Organizations Humane & Productive: A Handbook for Practitioners. 512p. 1981. 27.95 (ISBN 0-471-07813-1, Pub. by Wiley-Interscience). Wiley.
Meltzer, Morton F. Information--the Ultimate Management Resource: How to Find, Use, & Manage It. 224p. 1981. 14.95 (ISBN 0-8144-5700-2). Am Mgmt.
Mencher, A. G., ed. Management & Technology: An Anglo-American Exchange of Views. 96p. 1972. 23.00 (ISBN 0-08-018748-X). Pergamon.
Mendenhall & Reinmuth. Statistics for Management & Economics. 3rd ed. LC 77-22411. 1978. 15.95 (ISBN 0-87872-142-8). Duxbury Pr.
Mercer, James L., et al. Managing Urban Government Services: Strategies, Tools, & Techniques for the Eighties. 240p. 1981. 21.95 (ISBN 0-8144-5725-8). Am Mgmt.
Meredith, Jack R. & Gibbs, T. E. Management of Operations. LC 79-24512. (Wiley Series in Management). 1980. text ed. 24.95 (ISBN 0-471-02574-7). Wiley.
Merrell, V. Dallas. Huddling: The Informal Way to Management Success. LC 78-31941. 1979. 11.95 (ISBN 0-8144-5506-9). Am Mgmt.
Merry, Uri & Allerhand, Melvin E. Developing Teams & Organizations: A Practical Handbook for Managers & Consultants. LC 76-17719. (Illus.). 1977. text ed. 18.95 (ISBN 0-201-04531-1). A-W.
Mescon, Michael H., et al. Management. 714p. 1981. text ed. 21.50 scp (ISBN 0-06-166401-4, HarpC). Har-Row.
--The Management of Enterprise. Khedouri, Frank, ed. 242p. 1973. pap. text ed. 7.95 (ISBN 0-02-380600-1). Macmillan.
Metcalf, Henry C., ed. Business Management As a Profession. LC 79-12318. (Management History Ser.: No. 54). 223p. Repr. of 1927 ed. 20.00 (ISBN 0-87960-056-X). Hive Pub.
Meyer, J. & Farrar, D. Managerial Economics. 1970. pap. 9.95 ref. ed. (ISBN 0-13-549980-1). P-H.
Miles, Raymond E. Theories of Management: Implications for Organizational Behavior & Development. Davis, Keith, ed. (Management Ser.). (Illus.). 256p. 1975. text ed. 14.95 (ISBN 0-07-041927-2, C). McGraw.
Milgliore, R. Henry. MBO: Blue Collar to Top Executive. LC 77-8538. 198p. 1977. 15.00 (ISBN 0-87179-262-1). BNA.
Millar, Jean A. British Management German Management. text ed. 20.75x (ISBN 0-566-00289-2, Pub. by Gower Pub Co England). Renouf.
Miller, Harry. Management & the Working Environment. 1975. 9.95 (ISBN 0-09-122390-3, Pub. by Hutchinson). Merrimack Bk Serv.
Miller, Martin R. Climbing the Corporate Pyramid. LC 72-86427. 1973. 9.95 (ISBN 0-8144-5314-7). Am Mgmt.
Miner, John B. Case Analyses & Description of Managerial Role-Motivation Training to Accompany: The Challenge of Managing. LC 75-5054. 149p. 1975. pap. 6.95 (ISBN 0-7216-6414-8). HR&W.
--The Challenge of Managing. LC 74-24516. 330p. 1975. text ed. 11.00 (ISBN 0-7216-6410-5); pap. text ed. 8.50 (ISBN 0-7216-6411-3). HR&W.
--The Management Process: Theory, Research, & Practice. 2nd ed. (Illus.). 1978. text ed. 19.95 (ISBN 0-02-381650-3). Macmillan.
--Management Theory. 1971. pap. text ed. 6.95x (ISBN 0-02-381720-8). Macmillan.
--Motivation to Manage: A Ten Year Update on the "Studies in Management Education" Research. (Illus.). 1977. text ed. 13.95 (ISBN 0-917926-00-5). Organizat Meas.
Mintzberg, H. Nature of Managerial Work. 1980. 12.95 (ISBN 0-13-610402-9). P-H.
Mintzberg, Henry. The Nature of Managerial Work. (Illus.). 1973. pap. text ed. 17.50 scp (ISBN 0-06-044556-4, HarpC). Har-Row.
--Structuring of Organizations. (Theory of Management Policy Ser.). (Illus.). 1979. ref. ed. 22.95 (ISBN 0-13-855270-3). P-H.
Mintzberg, Henry. Impediments to the Use of Management Information. 3.50 (ISBN 0-686-11622-4, 7474). Natl Assn Accts.
Misshauk, Michael. Management: Theory & Practice. 1979. text ed. 16.95 (ISBN 0-316-57482-1); tchrs' manual free (ISBN 0-316-57484-8). Little.
Mitchell, Terence R. People in Organizations. (Illus.). 1978. text ed. 16.50 (ISBN 0-07-042530-2, C); instructor's manual 5.95 (ISBN 0-07-042531-0). McGraw.
Mitton, Daryl G. & Lilligren-Mitton, Betty, eds. Managerial Clout: Getting It & Keeping It. (Illus.). 240p. 1980. 15.95 (ISBN 0-13-549816-3, Spec); pap. 7.95 (ISBN 0-13-549808-2). P-H.
Mohan, Raj P., ed. Management & Complex Organizations in Comparative Perspective. LC 78-22133. (Contributions in Sociology: No. 36). (Illus.). 1979. lib. bdg. 22.95 (ISBN 0-313-20752-6, MMA/). Greenwood.
Mohanty, Brajaraj. Management Control Systems. 1979. 12.00x (ISBN 0-8364-0375-4). South Asia Bks.
Mondy, et al. Management: Concepts & Practices. 704p. 1980. text ed. 19.95 (ISBN 0-205-06859-6, 0868590); study guide 7.95 (ISBN 0-205-06861-8, 0868612). Allyn.
Montgomery, Robert M., ed. The Best Critical Studies Issued by the American Institute for Management & Inventiveness, 2 vols. 1979. Set. deluxe ed. 97.45 (ISBN 0-918968-25-9). Inst Econ Finan.

Moore, Franklin G. Management of Organizations. LC 81-4665. 550p. 1982. text ed. 24.95 (ISBN 0-88244-234-1). Grid Pub.
Moore, George. Managing Corporate Relations. 1980. text ed. 29.50x (ISBN 0-566-02158-7, Pub. by Gower Pub Co England). Renouf.
Moore, Russell F., ed. AMA Management Handbook. LC 77-135671. 1970. 44.95 (ISBN 0-8144-5212-4). Am Mgmt.
Moran, Robert T. & Harris, Philip R. Managing Cultural Synergy: Positive Interaction for Multinational Leadership. (Illus.). 380p. 1981. 18.95 (ISBN 0-87201-827-X). Gulf Pub.
Morell, R. W. & Henry, M. Daniel. The Practice of Management. LC 80-8136. 510p. 1981. lib. bdg. 26.00 (ISBN 0-8191-1489-8); pap. text ed. 16.75 (ISBN 0-8191-1490-1). U Pr of Amer.
Morgan, James E. Administrative & Supervisory Management. 2nd ed. (Illus.). 336p. 1982. reference 14.95 (ISBN 0-13-008508-1). P-H.
Morgan, James E., Jr. Principles of Administrative & Supervisory Management. (Illus.). 336p. 1973. ref. ed. 16.95 (ISBN 0-13-709386-1). P-H.
Morita, Edward K., et al. Group Practice Administration: Current & Future Roles. (Illus.). 96p. (Orig.). 1977. 8.50 (ISBN 0-933948-50-6). Med Group Mgmt.
Morris, Ralph. Computer Basics for Managers. 241p. 1980. text ed. 30.75x (ISBN 0-09-141570-5, Pub. by Busn Bks England). Renouf.
Morris, William T. Decentralization in Management Systems: An Introduction to Design. LC 67-22736. (Illus.). 1968. 7.50 (ISBN 0-8142-0097-4). Ohio St U Pr.
Morrisey, George L. Management by Objectives & Results for Business & Industry. 2nd ed. (Illus.). 260p. 1977. pap. text ed. 8.95 (ISBN 0-201-04906-6); inst. guide 1.00 (ISBN 0-201-04907-4). A-W.
Morrison, James H. The Human Side of Management. (Business Ser). (Illus.). 1971. pap. text ed. 8.95 (ISBN 0-201-04839-6). A-W.
Moskowitz, H. & Wright, G. Operations Research Techniques for Management. 1979. 21.95 (ISBN 0-13-637389-5). P-H.
Mueller, Robert K. Board Compass: What It Means to Be a Director in a Changing World. (Arthur D. Little Books). (Illus.). 1979. 21.95 (ISBN 0-669-02903-3). Lexington Bks.
--Career Conflict: Management's Inelegant Dysfunction. LC 78-19240. (Arthur D. Little Books). 1978. 15.95 (ISBN 0-669-02471-6). Lexington Bks.
Mumford, Alan. Making Experience Pay: Management Success Through Effective Learning. 184p. 1981. 19.95 (ISBN 0-07-084536-0, P&RB). McGraw.
Murdick, Robert G. MIS: Concepts & Design. 1980. text ed. 21.95 (ISBN 0-13-585331-1). P-H.
Murdick, Robert G., et al. Business Policy: A Framework for Analysis. 3rd ed. LC 79-20129. (Management Ser.). 1980. pap. text ed. 11.95 (ISBN 0-88244-204-X). Grid Pub.
Murphy, Thomas P., et al. Contemporary Public Administration: A Study in Emerging Realities. LC 80-83377. 572p. 1981. text ed. 15.95 (ISBN 0-87581-269-4). Peacock Pubs.
Murray, William. Management by Objectives. 1981. 19.95 (ISBN 0-686-76196-0). CBI Pub.
Myers, M. Scott. Managing with Unions. LC 77-88060. 1978. text ed. 9.95 (ISBN 0-201-04922-8). A-W.
Myers, Scott. Managing Without Unions. LC 75-18153. (Illus.). 208p. 1976. text ed. 9.95 (ISBN 0-201-04916-3). A-W.
Nadler, David A., et al. Managing Organizational Behavior. 1979. pap. text ed. 9.95 (ISBN 0-316-59679-5); tchrs' manual free (ISBN 0-316-59680-9). Little.
Nadler, Leonard. Management Tool: A Management Tool. (American Society for Training &Development Ser.). 224p. 1980. text ed. 16.95 (ISBN 0-442-25624-8). Van Nos Reinhold.
Nagashima, Soichiro. One Hundred Management Charts. LC 73-77686. (Illus.). 346p. 1973. 18.75 (ISBN 92-833-1043-8, APO41, APO). Unipub.
Nash, Allan. Management Compensation, Vol. 15. (Studies in Productivity-Highlights of the Literature). (Orig.). 1980. pap. 25.00 (ISBN 0-89361-022-4). Work in Amer.
National Retail Merchants Assn. Organization Survival & Growth Including Management by Objectives. 1976. 16.25 (ISBN 0-685-68875-5, P52776). Natl Ret Merch.
Negandhi, Anant R. & Prasad, S. Benjamin. Comparative Management. LC 72-139504. (Orig.). 1971. 18.50x (ISBN 0-89197-098-3); pap. text ed. 7.95x (ISBN 0-89197-099-1). Irvington.
Negoita, Constantin. Management Applications of System Theory. (Interdisciplinary Systems Research: No. 57). 155p. 1979. 19.50 (ISBN 3-7643-1032-4). Birkhauser.
Neuschel, Richard F. Management Systems for Profit & Growth. 1976. text ed. 16.95 (ISBN 0-07-046323-9, P&RB). McGraw.
Newbould, Gerald D. & Luffman, George A. Successful Business Policies. LC 78-70561. 1979. 25.95 (ISBN 0-03-049386-2). Praeger.
Newman, W. H. Management of Expanding Enterprise: Report of Round Table Discussions by Leading Business & Professional Men. LC 55-7927. 125p. 1955. 20.00x (ISBN 0-231-02102-X). Columbia U Pr.
Newman, William H. Administrative Action: The Techniques of Organization & Management. 2nd ed. 1963. ref. ed. 21.95x (ISBN 0-13-007195-1). P-H.
--Managers for the Year Two Thousand. (Illus.). 1978. ref. ed. 16.95 (ISBN 0-13-549378-1). P-H.
Newman, William H. & Logan, James P. Strategy, Policy & Central Management. 6th ed. 1971. text ed. 14.35 (ISBN 0-538-07470-1). SW Pub.
Newport, M. Gene. The Tools of Managing: Functions, Techniques & Skills. (Illus.). 1972. pap. text ed. 8.95 (ISBN 0-201-05271-7). A-W.
Newson, E. F. Management Science & the Manager: A Casebook. (Illus.). 1980. pap. text ed. 12.95 (ISBN 0-13-549444-3). P-H.
Newstrom, John, et al. Contingency Approach to Management Readings. (Illus.). 592p. 1974. pap. text ed. 10.95 (ISBN 0-07-046415-4, C). McGraw.
Nichols, Theodore. Ownership, Control & Ideology. (Studies in Management). 1969. pap. 9.95x (ISBN 0-8464-0699-3). Beekman Pubs.
Nicolson, Miklos S. Director's & Officers' Encyclopedic Manual. 2nd ed. 1975. 32.95 (ISBN 0-13-215442-0). P-H.
Nissman, Albert & Lutz, Jack. Organizing & Developing a Summer Professional Workshop. LC 75-145804. (Illus.). 1971. pap. 10.00 (ISBN 0-208-01168-4, Linnet). Shoe String.
Nord, Walter R., ed. Concepts & Controversy in Organizational Behavior. 2nd ed. LC 75-10424. 700p. 1976. pap. text ed. 14.95 (ISBN 0-87620-164-8). Goodyear.
Normann, Richard. Management for Growth. LC 77-2839. 210p. 1977. 40.00 (ISBN 0-471-99513-4, Pub by Wiley-Interscience). Wiley.
O'Connor, Rochelle. Managing Corporate Development. LC 80-65310. (Report Ser.: No. 771). (Illus.). ix, 62p. (Orig.). 1980. pap. text ed. 22.50 (ISBN 0-8237-0207-3). Conference Bd.
--Preparing Managers for Planning. (Report No. 781). (Illus.). 555p. (Orig.). 1980. pap. text ed. 7.50 (ISBN 0-8237-0217-0); pap. text ed. 22.50 non-members (ISBN 0-686-64376-3). Conference Bd.
Odiorne, George, et al. Executive Skills: A Management by Objectives Approach. 225p. 1980. pap. text ed. write for info. (ISBN 0-697-08037-4). Wm C Brown.
Odiorne, George S. MBO II: A System of Managerial Leadership for the 80's. LC 78-72336. 1979. 17.95 (ISBN 0-8224-0977-1). Pitman Learning.
O'Donnell, Harold K. & Weihrich, Heinz. Management: A Book of Readings. 5th ed. (Illus.). 736p. text ed. 18.95x (ISBN 0-07-035418-9); pap. 14.95x (ISBN 0-07-035417-0). McGraw.
Ogden, Richard W. Manage Your Plant for Profit & Your Promotion. 1978. 14.95 (ISBN 0-8144-5466-6). Am Mgmt.
Ogden, Roland. Imaginative Management Control. (British Library of Business Studies). (Orig.). 1969. text ed. 12.75x (ISBN 0-7100-6584-1). Humanities.
Oliver, Stanley. O & M for First Line Managers. 1975. pap. 14.95x (ISBN 0-7131-3350-3). Intl Ideas.
Olm, et al. Management Decisions & Organizational Policy. 3rd ed. 560p. 1981. text ed. 21.95 (ISBN 0-205-07215-1, 0872156); free tchr's ed. (ISBN 0-205-07216-X). Allyn.
Olsson, David E. Management by Objectives. LC 67-21207. (Illus.). 1968. 7.95x (ISBN 0-87015-168-1). Pacific Bks.
Organization & Management of the Wholesaler. 10.00 (ISBN 0-87359-004-X). Northwood Inst.
Organizational Development: A Closer Look. (AMACOM Reprint Collections). 33p. 1974. pap. 4.50 (ISBN 0-8144-6506-4). Am Mgmt.
Osgood, William R. Basics of Successful Business Management. 304p. 1981. 19.95 (ISBN 0-8144-5641-3). Am Mgmt.
Pansini, Anthony J. Maximizing Management Effectiveness. LC 77-85653. (Illus.). 1977. pap. 15.00 (ISBN 0-685-87014-6, 0-911876-04). Greenvale.
Papageorgiou, J. C. Management Science & Environmental Problems. (Illus.). 160p. 1980. 16.75 (ISBN 0-398-03995-X). C C Thomas.
Parker, B. V. Dynamics of Supervision. (Management Ser.). 1971. 7.95 (ISBN 0-07-048490-2, G); instructor's manual 3.00 (ISBN 0-07-048491-0). McGraw.
Pascale, Richard T. & Althos, Anthony G. The Art of Japanese Management. 1981. 11.95 (ISBN 0-671-22539-1). S&S.
Pascarella, Perry. Industry Week's Guide to Tomorrow's Executive: Humanagement in the Future Corporation. 320p. 1980. text ed. 16.95 (ISBN 0-442-23122-9). Van Nos Reinhold.
Paterson, Lee T. & Liebert, John. Management Strike Handbook, No. 47. new ed. 72p. 1974. pap. 6.00 (ISBN 0-87373-147-6). Intl Personnel Mgmt.
Patterns for Success in Managing a Business. pap. 1.95x (ISBN 0-686-02550-4). Dun.
Patton, Eugene. Managerial Secrets Executives Follow in Their Search for Greatness. (Illus.). 1978. deluxe ed. 39.75 (ISBN 0-918968-03-8). Inst Econ Finan.
Patz, Alan L. & Rowe, A. J. Management Control & Decision Systems: Text, Cases, & Readings. (Ser. on Management, Accounting & Information Systems). 1977. 27.50 (ISBN 0-471-67195-9). Wiley.
Pearse, Robert F. Manager to Manager II: What Managers Think of Their Managerial Careers. LC 77-16522. 1977. 10.00 (ISBN 0-8144-3131-3). Am Mgmt.
Peebles, Marvin L. Directory of Consultants & Management Training Programs: 1981. 100p. 1981. 12.00x (ISBN 0-939020-25-4). MLP Ent.
Pell, Arthur. Managing Through People. 2nd ed. 1978. 10.95 (ISBN 0-671-24547-3). S&S.
Perret, Gene. Hit or Miss Management: The World's First Organic, Natural, Holistic, Environmentally Sound Management Technique. 1980. 8.95 (ISBN 0-87477-123-4). HM.
Perry, William E. How to Manage Management. LC 78-57259. 1979. 12.50 (ISBN 0-8149-0804-7). Vanguard.
Peskin, Dean B. The Corporate Casino: How Managers Win & Lose at the Biggest Game in Town. LC 78-12779. 1979. 12.95 (ISBN 0-8144-5485-2). Am Mgmt.
Peter, Laurence & Hull, Raymond. Peter Principle. 1970. pap. 2.95 (ISBN 0-553-14527-4). Bantam.
Peter, Laurence J. The Peter Plan. 1977. pap. 2.95 (ISBN 0-553-20251-0). Bantam.
--Peter's People & Their Marvelous Ideas. 1981. pap. 2.25 (ISBN 0-505-51751-5, T51751). Tower Bks.
Petit, Thomas A. Fundamentals of Management Coordination: Supervisors, Middle Managers, & Executives. LC 74-19474. (Management & Administration Ser). 528p. 1975. text ed. 24.95 (ISBN 0-471-68443-0). Wiley.
Phillips, Richard. Managing for Greater Returns. 1962. 11.95 (ISBN 0-686-00369-1). AG Pr.
Piercy, B. & Jandrell, R. Coordinated Work Measurement. (Illus.). 1975. 16.95x (ISBN 0-7131-3345-7). Intl Ideas.
Pinder, Craig C. & Moore, Larry F., eds. Middle Range Theory & the Study of Organizatons. 1980. lib. bdg. 30.00 (ISBN 0-89838-021-9, Pub. by Martinus Nijhoff Netherlands). Kluwer Boston.
Pinkstaff, Dick & Pinkstaff, Marlene A. Personal Skill Building for the Emerging Manager. LC 79-16920. 1979. pap. 10.95 (ISBN 0-8436-0785-8). CBI Pub.
Pinney, William E. & Mc Williams, Donald B. Introduction to Quantitative Analysis for Management. 592p. 1981. text ed. write for info. (ISBN 0-06-045222-6, HarpC). Har-Row.
Place, Irene & Armstrong, Alice. Management Careers for Women. LC 75-18015. (Illus.). 219p. (gr. 10 up). 1975. text ed. 6.60 (ISBN 0-8442-6434-2); pap. text ed. 4.95 (ISBN 0-8442-6433-4). Natl Textbk.
Plachy, Roger. When I Lead, Why Don't They Follow? 2nd ed. LC 78-58718. 1978. pap. text ed. 9.95 (ISBN 0-931028-07-8). Teach'em.
Planning a Performance Improvement Project: A Practical Guide. 2nd rev. ed. LC 80-8175. (Guideline Ser.). 60p. (Orig.). 1981. pap. write for info. (ISBN 0-931816-26-2); wkbk. avail.; tapes 5.45x (ISBN 0-686-77545-7). Kumarian Pr.
PoKempner, Stanley J. Management Science in Business. LC 77-90989. (Report Ser.: No. 732). (Illus.). 1977. pap. 30.00 (ISBN 0-8237-0166-2). Conference Bd.
Pokempner, Stanley J. & O'Connor, Rochelle, eds. Senior Management & the Data Processing Function. (Report Ser: No. 636). 1974. pap. 25.00 (ISBN 0-8237-0051-8). Conference Bd.
Pollard, Harold R. Developments in Management Thought. LC 72-84394. 277p. 1975. pap. 14.50x (ISBN 0-8448-0772-9). Crane-Russak Co.
--Trends in Management Thinking, 1960-1970. 331p. 1978. 14.95 (ISBN 0-87201-880-6). Gulf Pub.
Pollock, Ted. Managing Creatively. 2nd ed. 300p. 1981. 16.95 (ISBN 0-8436-0861-7). CBI Pub.
--Managing Others Creatively. 1974. pap. 4.50 (ISBN 0-8015-4854-3, Hawthorn). Dutton.
--Managing Yourself Creatively. 1974. pap. 3.95 (ISBN 0-8015-4860-8, Hawthorn). Dutton.
Porter, Lyman W., et al. Behavior in Organizations. (Psychology & Management Ser.). (Illus.). 561p. 1974. text ed. 17.95 (ISBN 0-07-050527-6, C); exam questions 2.95 (ISBN 0-07-050528-4). McGraw.
Porter, Michael E. Competitive Strategy: Techniques for Analyzing Industries & Competitors. (Illus.). 1980. 15.95 (ISBN 0-02-925360-8). Macmillan.
Potter, Beverly A. Turning Around: The Behavioral Approach to Managing People. (Illus.). 1980. 15.95 (ISBN 0-8144-5533-6). Am Mgmt.
Powelson, John P. Institutions of Economic Growth: A Theory of Conflict Management in Developing Countries. 1972. 18.00x (ISBN 0-691-04164-4). Princeton U Pr.
Prabhu, V. V. A Manager at Large. 1979. 9.00x (ISBN 0-7069-0767-1, Pub. by Vikas India). Advent NY.
Pray, Thomas & Strong, Daniel. Decide: A Managerial Decision Game to Accompany Principles of Management by Kurtz & Boone. 120p. 1981. pap. text ed. 8.95 (ISBN 0-394-32698-9). Random.
Preston, P. Communication for Managers. 1979. 17.95 (ISBN 0-13-153957-4). P-H.
Preston, Paul & Zimmerer, Thomas. Management for Supervisors. (Illus.). 1978. ref. ed. 17.95x (ISBN 0-13-549220-3); pap. text ed. 12.95x (ISBN 0-13-549212-2). P-H.
Pritchard, Robert E. & Hindelang, Thomas J. The Strategic Evaluation & Management of Capital Expenditures. 304p. 1981. 29.95 (ISBN 0-8144-5656-1). Am Mgmt.
Public Management Institute Staff. How to Be an Effective Board Member. LC 80-80201. 400p. 1980. 47.50 (ISBN 0-916664-20-1). Public Management.
--Managing Staff for Results. LC 80-65012. 400p. 1980. 47.50 (ISBN 0-916664-16-3). Public Management.
--Nonprofit Management Skills for Women. LC 80-80200. 400p. 1980. 47.50 (ISBN 0-916664-21-X). Public Management.
Pugh, D. S., ed. Organization Theory. (Education Ser). 1972. pap. 3.95 (ISBN 0-14-080601-6). Penguin.
Pugh, Eric. Third Dictionary of Acronyms & Abbreviations: More Abbreviations in Management, Technology, & Information Science. 1977. 17.50 (ISBN 0-208-01535-3, Linnet). Shoe String.
Quick, Thomas L. Person to Person Managing. 1977. 10.00 (ISBN 0-312-60217-0). St Martin.
--The Quick Motivation Method. 1980. 9.95 (ISBN 0-312-66062-6). St Martin.
Quinn, James B. Strategies for Change, Logical Incrementalism. 1980. pap. 7.50x (ISBN 0-256-02543-6). Irwin.
--Strategies for Change: Logical Incrementalism. LC 80-82098. 222p. 1980. 15.95 (ISBN 0-87094-220-4). Dow Jones-Irwin.
Rabin, Robert. Perspectives on the Administrative Process. 1979. pap. 6.95 (ISBN 0-316-73001-7). Little.
Rachman, David J. & Mescon, Michael M. Business Today. 2nd ed. LC 78-20701. 1979. text ed. 18.95x (ISBN 0-394-32092-1); pap. text ed. 6.95 Student Course Mastery Guide by Dennis Guseman et al (ISBN 0-686-77209-1). Random.
Radde, Paul O. The Supervision Decision! (Illus.). 150p. 1981. vinyl binder 24.95 (ISBN 0-89384-060-2); write for info. wkbk. 8.00 (ISBN 0-89384-061-0). Learning Concepts.
Radford, K. J. Managerial Decision Making. (Illus.). 256p. 1975. 14.95 (ISBN 0-87909-473-7). Reston.
--Modern Managerial Decision Making. 1981. text ed. 19.95 (ISBN 0-8359-4571-5); instr's. manual avail. (ISBN 0-8359-4229-5). Reston.
Raia, Anthony P. Managing by Objectives. 1974. pap. 8.95x (ISBN 0-673-07757-8). Scott F.
Ramo, Simon. The Management of Innovative Technological Corporations. LC 79-19460. 1980. 24.95 (ISBN 0-471-04436-9, Pub. by Wiley-Interscience). Wiley.
Randolph, Robert M. Planagement: Moving Concept into Reality. LC 79-17075. 1979. Repr. of 1975 ed. 16.95 (ISBN 0-89384-056-4). Learning Concepts.
Rausch, Erwin. Balancing Needs of People & Organizations: The Linking Elements Concept. LC 78-62297. 344p. 1978. 17.50 (ISBN 0-87179-274-5). BNA.
Readings in Management. rev. ed. (Annual Editions Ser.). (Illus., Orig.). (gr. 12). 1979. pap. text ed. 6.95 (ISBN 0-87967-246-3). Dushkin Pub.
Ready, R. K. Administrator's Job: Issues & Dilemmas. 1967. pap. text ed. 7.50 (ISBN 0-07-051300-7, C). McGraw.
Reber, Jan & Shaw, Paul. Executive Protection Manual. 1976. 39.95 (ISBN 0-916070-02-6); soft cover 29.95 (ISBN 0-686-70710-9). MTI Tele.

Reddin, W. J. Effective Management by Objectives: The 3-D Method of MBO. 1971. 18.00 (ISBN 0-07-051360-0, P&RB). McGraw.
--Managerial Effectiveness. 1970. 15.95 (ISBN 0-07-051358-9, C). McGraw.
Reece, B. & Manning, G. Wilson RV: An in-Basket Simulation. 1976. soft bdg. 5.32 (ISBN 0-07-051485-2, G); instructor's manual & key 4.00 (ISBN 0-07-051486-0). McGraw.
Reekie, W. Duncan. Macroeconomics for Managers. 160p. 1980. 18.00x (ISBN 0-86003-510-7, Pub. by Allan Pubs England); pap. 9.00x (ISBN 0-86003-610-3). State Mutual Bk.
--Managerial Economics. 440p. 1975. 45.00x (ISBN 0-86003-007-5, Pub. by Allan Pubs England); pap. 22.50x (ISBN 0-86003-108-X). State Mutual Bk.
Reeser, Clayton & Loper, Marvin. Management: The Key to Organizational Effectiveness. 1978. pap. 13.95x (ISBN 0-673-15077-1). Scott F.
Reinfeld, Nyles. Survival Management for Industry. 1981. text ed. 17.95 (ISBN 0-8359-7410-3); instr's. manual free (ISBN 0-8359-7411-1). Reston.
Render, Barry & Stair, Ralph M., Jr. Management Science: A Self-Correcting Approach. 1978. pap. text ed. 13.95 (ISBN 0-205-06079-X, 1060791). Allyn.
Revans, R. W. Action Learning. 256p. 40.00x (ISBN 0-85634-101-0, Pub. by Muller Ltd). State Mutual Bk.
Reynolds, John. Case Method in Management Development: Guide for Effective Use. (Management Development Ser.: No. 17). vi, 264p. 1980. 11.40 (ISBN 92-2-102363-X). Intl Labour Office.
Reynolds, R. K. & Luckham, W. R. Business Management Techniques for Nurserymen. LC 89-62604. 1980. pap. 19.50 (ISBN 0-918436-10-9). Environ Des VA.
Richards, Max D. & Greenlaw, Paul S. Management: Decisions & Behavior. rev. ed. 1972. 19.95x (ISBN 0-256-00474-9). Irwin.
Richman, Eugene & Brara, Arvinder. Practical Guide to Managing People. 1975. 10.95 (ISBN 0-13-690958-2). P-H.
Riggs, James L. & Inoue, Michael S. Introduction to Operations Research & Management Science: A General Systems Approach. (Industrial Engineering & Management Ser.). (Illus.). 384p. 1975. text ed. 22.00 (ISBN 0-07-052870-5, C). McGraw.
Ritter, Paul M. The Business Manager in the Independent School. 1980. pap. 6.50 (ISBN 0-934338-40-X). NAIS.
Robbins, Stephen P. Organizational Behavior: Concepts & Controversies. (Illus.). 1979. ref. 21.00 (ISBN 0-13-641464-8). P-H.
Roberts, Tom. Developing Effective Managers. LC 75-318208. (Management in Perspective Ser.). 168p. 1974. pap. 7.50x (ISBN 0-85292-100-4). Intl Pubns Serv.
Robillard, James H. Abortion, Divorce, Vasectomy, Extra-Marital Affairs, Concubinage, Promiscuity, Sexuality & Their Impact Upon the Management of the Firm. (Illus.). 1979. deluxe ed. 41.60 (ISBN 0-918968-42-9). Inst Econ Finan.
Robinson, James C. Behavior Modeling. 200p. 1981. text ed. price not set (ISBN 0-89384-064-5). Learning Concepts.
Robinson, R. International Business Management. 2nd ed. 1978. 22.95 (ISBN 0-03-040181-X). Dryden Pr.
Robinson, Shepard D. How to Turn-Around a Troubled Company. (Illus., Orig.). 1979. pap. 15.00 (ISBN 0-9603502-0-9). Ingleside.
Roethlisberger, Fritz J. Man-In-Organization: Essays of F. J. Roethlisberger. LC 68-28695. (Illus.). 1968. 16.50x (ISBN 0-674-54500-1, Belknap Pr). Harvard U Pr.
Rogers, David C. Business Policy & Planning: Text & Cases. (Illus.). 1977. 22.95 (ISBN 0-13-107409-1). P-H.
Rohrer, Hibler & Replogle, Inc. The Changing World of Management. (Orig.). 1981. pap. 3.50 (ISBN 0-451-62021-6, M E 2021, Ment). NAL.
Rolichek. Management Fin. Inst. 2nd ed. 1976. 22.95 (ISBN 0-03-089912-5). Dryden Pr.
Ronstadt, Robert. Art of Case Analysis: A Guide to the Diagnosis of Business Situations. 2nd ed. 1980. pap. 7.95 (ISBN 0-686-60647-7). Lord Pub.
Roseman, Edward. Confronting Nonpromotability. 1980. pap. 5.95 (ISBN 0-8144-7530-2). Am Mgmt.
Rosenberg, Seymour L. Self-Analysis of Your Organization. LC 74-75170. 200p. 1974. 12.95 (ISBN 0-8144-5362-7). Am Mgmt.
Rosenstein, Jack. Independent Stores EDP Specification. 1979. pap. text ed. 24.50 (ISBN 0-685-95728-4, R6479). Natl Ret Merch.
Ross, Joel E. Modern Management & Information Systems. (Illus.). 288p. 1976. 15.95 (ISBN 0-87909-499-0). Reston.
Rothery, Brian. How to Organize Your Time & Resources. 1972. 12.50x (ISBN 0-8464-0492-3). Beekman Pubs.
Rothschild, William E. Putting It All Together: A Guide to Strategic Thinking. LC 76-10535. (Illus.). 224p. 1976. 17.95 (ISBN 0-8144-5405-4). Am Mgmt.
--Strategic Alternatives: Selection, Development & Implementation. 1979. 15.95 (ISBN 0-8144-5514-X). Am Mgmt.
Roy, Robert H. The Cultures of Management. LC 76-47385. (Illus.). 512p. 1977. 21.50x (ISBN 0-8018-1875-3); pap. text ed. 9.95 (ISBN 0-8018-2524-5). Johns Hopkins.
Roy, S. K. Management in India: New Perspectives. LC 74-902072. 187p. 1974. 11.25x (ISBN 0-8002-0922-2). Intl Pubns Serv.
Rudman, Jack. Administrative Analyst. (Career Examination Ser.: C-2144). (Cloth bdg. avail. on request). 1977. pap. 10.00 (ISBN 0-8373-2144-1). Natl Learning.
--Administrative Consultant. (Career Examination Ser.: C-2089). (Cloth bdg. avail. on request). 1977. pap. 10.00 (ISBN 0-8373-2089-5). Natl Learning.
--Administrative Manager. (Career Examination Ser.: C-1754). (Cloth bdg. avail on request). 1977. pap. 10.00 (ISBN 0-8373-1754-1). Natl Learning.
--Administrator, One. (Career Examination Ser.: C-1769). (Cloth bdg. avail. on request). 1977. pap. 10.00 (ISBN 0-8373-1769-X). Natl Learning.
--Assistant General Superintendent. (Career Examination Ser.: C-2109). (Cloth bdg. avail. on request). 1977. pap. 10.00 (ISBN 0-8373-2109-3). Natl Learning.
--Assistant Management Analyst. (Career Examination Ser.: C-2094). (Cloth bdg. avail. on request). 1977. pap. 10.00 (ISBN 0-8373-2094-1). Natl Learning.
--Assistant Program Manager. (Career Examination Ser.: C-934). (Cloth bdg. avail. on request). pap. 8.00 (ISBN 0-8373-0934-4). Natl Learning.
--Assistant Public Buildings Manager. (Career Examination Ser.: C-2718). (Cloth bdg. avail. on request). 1980. pap. 12.00 (ISBN 0-8373-2718-0). Natl Learning.
--Chief Executive Officer. (Career Examination Ser.: C-2828). (Cloth bdg. avail. on request). 1980. pap. 16.00 (ISBN 0-8373-2828-4). Natl Learning.
--Director of Administrative Services. (Career Examination Ser.: C-1865). (Cloth bdg. avail. on request). pap. 10.00 (ISBN 0-8373-1865-3). Natl Learning.
--Management Analysis Trainee. (Career Examination Ser.: C-470). (Cloth bdg. avail. on request). pap. 8.00 (ISBN 0-8373-0470-9). Natl Learning.
--Management Analyst. (Career Examination Ser.: C-1061). (Cloth bdg. avail. on request). pap. 10.00 (ISBN 0-8373-1061-X). Natl Learning.
--Management Analyst Aide. (Career Examination Ser.: C-1721). (Cloth bdg. avail. on request). 1977. pap. 8.00 (ISBN 0-8373-1721-5). Natl Learning.
--Management Intern. (Career Examination Ser.: C-1927). (Cloth bdg. avail. on request). 1977. pap. 8.00 (ISBN 0-8373-1927-7). Natl Learning.
--Management Technician. (Career Examination Ser.: C-2751). (Cloth bdg. avail. on request). 1980. pap. 10.00 (ISBN 0-8373-2751-2). Natl Learning.
--Operations Management, Level 1. (ACT Proficiency Examination Program: PEP-24). (Cloth bdg. avail. on request). pap. 9.95 (ISBN 0-8373-5524-9). Natl Learning.
--Operations Management, Level 2. (ACT Proficiency Examination Program: PEP-25). (Cloth bdg. avail. on request). pap. 9.95 (ISBN 0-8373-5525-7). Natl Learning.
--Operations Management, Level 3. (ACT Proficiency Examination Program: PEP-26). (Cloth bdg. avail. on request). pap. 9.95 (ISBN 0-8373-5526-5). Natl Learning.
--Operations Management 1. (Regents External Degree Ser.: REDP-13). (Cloth bdg. avail. on request). pap. 9.95 (ISBN 0-8373-5613-X). Natl Learning.
--Operations Management 2. (Regents External Degree Ser.: REDP-14). (Cloth bdg. avail. on request). pap. 9.95 (ISBN 0-8373-5614-8). Natl Learning.
--Operations Management 3. (Regents External Degree Ser.: REDP-15). (Cloth bdg. avail. on request). pap. 9.95 (ISBN 0-8373-5615-6). Natl Learning.
--Principal Administrative Associate. (Career Examination Ser.: C-2394). (Cloth bdg. avail. on request). pap. 12.00 (ISBN 0-8373-2394-0). Natl Learning.
--Principal Management Technician. (Career Examination Ser.: C-2753). (Cloth bdg. avail. on request). 1980. pap. 14.00 (ISBN 0-8373-2753-9). Natl Learning.
--Professional & Administrative Career Examination (PACE) (Career Examination Ser.: CS-26). (Cloth bdg. avail. on request). pap. 7.50 (ISBN 0-8373-5026-3). Natl Learning.
--Public Buildings Manager. (Career Examination Ser.: C-2719). (Cloth bdg. avail. on request). 1980. pap. 14.00 (ISBN 0-8373-2719-9). Natl Learning.
--Repair Shop Manager. (Career Examination Ser.: C-1801). (Cloth bdg. avail. on request). pap. 8.00 (ISBN 0-8373-1801-7). Natl Learning.
--Senior Business Manager. (Career Examination Ser.: C-2359). (Cloth bdg. avail. on request). pap. 10.00 (ISBN 0-8373-2359-2). Natl Learning.
--Senior Management Analyst. (Career Examination Ser.: C-1782). (Cloth bdg. avail. on request). pap. 10.00 (ISBN 0-8373-1782-7). Natl Learning.
--Senior Management Technician. (Career Examination Ser.: C-2752). (Cloth bdg. avail. on request). 1980. pap. 12.00 (ISBN 0-8373-2752-0). Natl Learning.
--Supervisor of Menagerie. (Career Examination Ser.: C-1792). (Cloth bdg. avail. on request). pap. 8.00 (ISBN 0-8373-1792-4). Natl Learning.
Rue, Leslie W. & Byars, Lloyd L. Management: Theory & Application. rev. ed. 1980. 19.95x (ISBN 0-256-02346-8). Irwin.
Rutenberg, Daniel P. Multinational Management. 450p. 1982. 19.95 (ISBN 0-686-76613-X). Winthrop.
Sampson, Robert C. Managing the Managers: A Realistic Approach to Applying the Behavioral Sciences. 1965. 19.95 (ISBN 0-07-054509-X, P&RB). McGraw.
Sanders, Derek A. Aural Rehabilitation: A Management Model. 2nd ed. (Illus.). 464p. 1982. 19.95 (ISBN 0-13-053215-0). P-H.
Sanderson, Michael. Sucessful Problem Management. LC 78-21050. 1978. 21.95 (ISBN 0-471-04871-2, Pub. by Wiley-Interscience). Wiley.
Sanford, Edward & Adelman, Harvey. Management Decisions: A Behavioral Approach. (Illus.). 1977. pap. text ed. 5.50 (ISBN 0-87626-548-4). Winthrop.
Sarabhai, Vikram. Management for Development. Kamha, Chowdhry, ed. LC 74-902587. 132p. 1974. 7.50x (ISBN 0-7069-0330-7). Intl Pubns Serv.
--Management for Development. 1974. 6.00 (ISBN 0-686-26301-4). Intl Bk Dist.
Sargent, Alice G. The Androgynous Manager. 240p. 1981. 12.95 (ISBN 0-8144-5568-9). Am Mgmt.
Sargent, Howard. Fishbowl Management: A Paricipative Approach to Systematic Management. LC 77-27924. 1978. 21.95 (ISBN 0-471-03574-2, Pub. by Wiley-Interscience). Wiley.
Sashkin, Marshall. Assessing Performance Appraisal. 150p. (Orig.). 1981. pap. write for info. Univ Assocs.
Savage, Christopher I. & Small, John R. Introduction to Managerial Economics. 1967. text ed. 6.50x (ISBN 0-09-084092-5, Hutchinson U Lib). Humanities.
Sawyer, Lawrence B. The Manager & the Modern Internal Auditor. (Illus.). 1979. 24.95 (ISBN 0-8144-5515-8). Am Mgmt.
Sayles, Leonard & Strauss, George. Strauss' & Sayles' Behavioral Stategies for Managers. 304p. 1980. text ed. 17.95 (ISBN 0-13-791459-8). P-H.
Sayles, Leonard R. Leadership, What Effective Managers Really Do & How They Do It: Effective Behavioral Skills. (Management Ser.). (Illus.). 1979. text ed. 12.95 (ISBN 0-07-055012-3, C); pap. text ed. 7.95 (ISBN 0-07-055011-5). McGraw.
--Managerial Behavior: Administration in Complex Organizations. 2nd ed. LC 78-31454. 312p. 1979. lib. bdg. 14.50 (ISBN 0-88275-854-3). Krieger.
Scanlan, B. K. Management Eighteen: Short Course for Managers. LC 74-9816. (Professional Development Programs, Business Administration Ser). 1974. 45.95 (ISBN 0-471-75633-4). Wiley.
Scanlan, Burt & Keys, J. Bernard. Management & Organizational Behavior. LC 78-15477. (Management Ser.). 1979. text ed. 23.95 (ISBN 0-471-02484-8); study guide (ISBN 0-471-04773-2). Wiley.
Schendel, Dan E. & Hofer, Charles W., eds. Strategic Management: A New View of Business Policy & Planning. 1979. 23.95 (ISBN 0-316-77312-3). Little.
Schnee, Jerome E., et al. The Progress of Management: Process & Behavior in a Changing Environment. 3rd ed. (Illus.). 1977. pap. text ed. 13.95 (ISBN 0-13-730622-9). P-H.
Schneider, Kenneth C. & Byers, C. Randall. Quantitative Management: A Self Teaching Guide. LC 78-21052. (Self Teaching Guides Ser.). 1979. pap. text ed. 7.95 (ISBN 0-471-02917-3). Wiley.
Schoderbek, Peter P., et al. Management Systems: Conceptual Considerations. rev. ed. 1980. pap. 11.95x (ISBN 0-256-02275-5). Business Pubns.
Schoemaker, Paul J. Experiments on Decisions Under Risk: The Expected Utility Hypothesis. 192p. 1980. lib. bdg. 18.95 (ISBN 0-89838-035-9, Pub. by Martinus Nijhoff Netherlands). Kluwer Boston.
Schoen, Sterling H. & Durand, Douglas E. Supervision: The Management of Organizational Resources. (Illus.). 1979. ref. 16.95 (ISBN 0-13-876235-X). P-H.
Schoenberg, Robert J. The Art of Being a Boss. 1980. pap. 3.50 (ISBN 0-451-61990-0, ME1990, Ment). NAL.
--Art of Being a Boss: Inside Intelligence from Top-Level Business Leaders & Young Executives on the Move. 1978. 11.95 (ISBN 0-397-01291-8). Har-Row.
Schoennauer, Alfred W. Problem Finding & Problem Solving. LC 81-9591. 208p. 1981. text ed. 18.95x (ISBN 0-88229-590-X); pap. text ed. 9.95x (ISBN 0-88229-792-9). Nelson-Hall.
Schultz, Randall L., ed. Applications of Management Science, Vol. 1. 350p. (Orig.). 1981. lib. bdg. 39.50 (ISBN 0-89232-023-0). Jai Pr.
Schuster, Fred E. Contemporary Issues in Human Resources Management. (Illus.). 496p. 1980. text ed. 22.95 (ISBN 0-8359-1005-9). Reston.
Schwartz, David. Introduction to Management: Principles, Practices, & Processes. 649p. 1980. text ed. 19.95 (ISBN 0-15-543423-3, HC); Instructor's resource manual avail. (ISBN 0-15-543424-1); study guide 6.95 (ISBN 0-15-543425-X). HarBraceJ.
Scott, Charles R., Jr. & Strickland, Alonzo J., III. Tempomatic IV: A Management Simulation. 2nd ed. LC 79-89182. (Illus.). 1980. pap. text ed. 9.50 (ISBN 0-395-28731-6); instrs'. manual 0.80 (ISBN 0-395-28732-4); computer centers manual 1.75 (ISBN 0-395-28733-2); punched card deck avail. (ISBN 0-395-28734-0). HM.
Scott, William C. & Hart, David K. Organizational America. 1979. 13.95 (ISBN 0-395-27599-7). HM.
Seashore, S. E. & McNeill, R. J. Management of Urban Crisis: Metropolitan Government & the Behavioral Sciences. LC 74-122275. 1971. 13.95 (ISBN 0-02-928240-3). Free Pr.
Seckler-Hudson, Catheryn. Organization & Management: Theory & Practice. LC 55-11617. 1955. 10.50 (ISBN 0-686-58000-1). Lomond.
Sethi, Kiran. Executive Training in India. (Illus.). 90p. 1979. 7.50x (ISBN 0-8002-0987-7). Intl Pubns Serv.
Sethi, S. P. & Thompson, G. L. Optimal Control Theory: Applications to Management Science. (International Series in Management Science - Operations Research: Vol. 1). 1981. lib. bdg. 25.00 (ISBN 0-89838-061-8). Kluwer Boston.
Shanahan, Donald T. Patrol Administration: Management by Objectives. 2nd ed. 1978. pap. text ed. 19.95 (ISBN 0-205-06036-6, 8260362). Allyn.
Shapiro, Steven L. Supervision: An Introduction to Business Management. 1978. 13.50 (ISBN 0-87005-213-6); instructor's guide 2.50 (ISBN 0-87005-306-X). Fairchild.
Shave, Gordon A. Nuts, Bolts & Gut-Level Management. 1974. 10.95 (ISBN 0-13-627844-2, Parker). P-H.
Shaw, John C. The Quality-Productivity Connection in Service-Sector Management. 1978. text ed. 13.95x (ISBN 0-442-27542-0). Van Nos Reinhold.
Shaw, Malcom E. Assertive Responsive Management: A Personal Handbook. LC 78-74691. 1979. pap. text ed. 7.95 (ISBN 0-201-06819-2). A-W.
Shay, Philip W. The Need for a Unified Discipline of Management. LC 77-22131. 1977. 7.50 (ISBN 0-8144-2211-X). Am Mgmt.
Shea, Gordon F. New Employee: Developing a Productive Human Resource. LC 80-16346. 1980. pap. text ed. 8.95 (ISBN 0-201-07137-1). A-W.
Sheldon, Oliver. The Philosophy of Management. Chandler, Alfred D., ed. LC 79-7555. (History of Management Thought & Practice Ser.). 1980. Repr. of 1923 ed. lib. bdg. 23.00x (ISBN 0-405-12341-8). Arno.
Sherman, T. D. O & M in Local Government. 1969. 22.00 (ISBN 0-08-013317-7); pap. 10.75 (ISBN 0-08-013309-6). Pergamon.
Shilt, Bernard A., et al. Business Principles & Management. 6th ed. (gr. 11 up). 1973. text ed. 8.48 (ISBN 0-538-07270-9, G27); study guide & problems 3.44 (ISBN 0-538-07271-7); tests 0.44 (ISBN 0-538-07273-3). SW Pub.

Shore, Barry. Operations Management. (Management Ser.). (Illus.). 544p. 1973. text ed. 21.00 (ISBN 0-07-057045-0, C); instructor's manual 7.95 (ISBN 0-07-057046-9). McGraw.
Shorris, Earl. The Oppressed Middle: The Politics of Middle Management. LC 80-717. 408p. 1981. 13.95 (ISBN 0-385-14564-0, Anchor Pr). Doubleday.
Shtogren, John A., ed. Models for Management: The Structure of Competence. LC 79-93291. (Illus.). 520p. 1981. pap. 17.95 (ISBN 0-937932-00-0). Teleometrics.
Shull, F. A., et al. Organizational Decision Making. 1970. 18.95 (ISBN 0-07-057182-1, C). McGraw.
Siemens, Nicolai, et al. Operations Research: Planning, Operating & Information Systems. LC 70-184529. 1973. text ed. 19.95 (ISBN 0-02-928740-5). Free Pr.
Sikula, Andrew F. Management & Administration. LC 72-95954. 1973. text ed. 15.95x (ISBN 0-675-09000-8). Merrill.
Silber, Mark B. & Sherman, V. Clayton. Managerial Performance & Promotability: The Making of an Executive. LC 73-75675. 192p. 1974. 12.95 (ISBN 0-8144-5325-2). Am Mgmt.
Silver, Gerald A. Introduction to Management. (Illus.). 530p. 1981. text ed. 20.50 (ISBN 0-8299-0415-8). West Pub.
Simmons, Richard E. Managing Behavioral Processes: Applications of Theory & Research. Mackenzie, Kenneth D., ed. LC 77-86007. (Organizational Behavior Ser.). (Illus.). 1978. pap. text ed. 9.95x (ISBN 0-88295-454-7). Harlan Davidson.
Simon, Herbert A. Administrative Behavior. 3rd ed. LC 75-18009. 1976. 17.95 (ISBN 0-02-928970-X); pap. text ed. 9.95 (ISBN 0-02-929000-7). Free Pr.
Singer, Edwin J. Effective Management Coaching. 2nd ed. (Management in Perspective Ser.). 212p. 1979. pap. 13.50x (ISBN 0-85292-248-5). Intl Pubns Serv.
Sisk, Henry L. Management & Organization. 2nd ed. 1973. text ed. 13.50 (ISBN 0-538-07410-8, G41). SW Pub.
Siu, R. G. The Master Manager. 1982. pap. 3.95 (ISBN 0-451-62032-1, ME2032, Ment). NAL.
--The Master Manager. LC 80-13390. 341p. 1980. 17.50 (ISBN 0-471-07961-8). Wiley.
Sloma, Richard S. How to Measure Managerial Performance. LC 79-55375. (Illus.). 1980. 10.95 (ISBN 0-02-929240-9). Free Pr.
--No-Nonsense Management. 176p. 1981. pap. 3.50 (ISBN 0-553-20035-6). Bantam.
Slyman, Raymond A. Why Managers Fail. LC 77-85762. 1979. 8.75 (ISBN 0-87218-005-0). Natl Underwriter.
Smith, H. R., et al. Readings in Management: Making Organization Peform. (Illus.). 1980. pap. text ed. 9.95 (ISBN 0-02-412520-2). Macmillan.
--Management: Making Organizations Perform. (Illus.). 1980. text ed. 19.95 (ISBN 0-02-412500-8). Macmillan.
Smith, Harold & Baker, William. The Administrative Manager. LC 78-6085. 1978. text ed. 17.95 (ISBN 0-574-20030-4, 13-3030); instr's guide avail. (ISBN 0-574-20031-2, 13-3031); study guide 6.95 (ISBN 0-574-20032-0, 13-3032). SRA.
Smith, Martin R. Qualitysense: Organizational Approaches to Improving Product Quality & Service. (Illus.). 1980. 16.95 (ISBN 0-8144-5534-4). Am Mgmt.
Soldofsky & Olive. Financial Management. 13.95 (ISBN 0-538-06150-2). SW Pub.
Solomon, Ezra & Pringle, John J. An Introduction to Financial Management. 2nd ed. 1980. text ed. 18.95 (ISBN 0-87620-475-2); inst. manual by john j. pringle free (ISBN 0-8302-4753-X); study guide by john a. holloran & howard p. lanser 7.95 (ISBN 0-8302-4754-8). Goodyear.
Sommerfeld, Ray M. Federal Taxes & Management Decisions. 3rd ed. 1981. 18.95 (ISBN 0-256-02575-4). Irwin.
Spaulding, Asa T. Opening Pandora's Box: A Management Dilemma. (Business Leadership Lecture, 1971). 1971. pap. 1.00 (ISBN 0-87712-154-0). U Mich Busn Div Res.
Spitz, John. Building Your Management Team: A Framework for Public Sector Labor Relations. (IPA Training Manual). 1976. 10.50 (ISBN 0-89215-070-X). U Cal LA Indus Rel.
Spray, S. Lee. Organizational Effectiveness: Theory, Research & Application. LC 75-36534. 1976. 15.95x (ISBN 0-87338-183-1, Pub. by Comp. Adm. Research Inst.). Kent St U Pr.
Spronck, Lambert H. The Financial Executive's Handbook for Managing Multinational Corporations. 1980. 27.95 (ISBN 0-471-05277-9, Pub. by Ronald Pr). Wiley.
Staff of Didactic Systems. Management by Objectives. 2nd ed. 1978. pap. 24.90 (ISBN 0-89401-142-1). Didactic Syst.
--Planning & Assigning Work. (Study Units Ser.). 1978. pap. 9.00 (ISBN 0-89401-121-9). Didactic Syst.
Stanford, Melvin J. Management Policy. (Illus.). 1979. ref. ed. 21.95 (ISBN 0-13-548974-1). P-H.
Stapleton, Richard C. Managing Creatively: Action Learning in Action. 1976. pap. text ed. 9.45 (ISBN 0-8191-0035-8). U Pr of Amer.
Starr, Martin K. Operations Management. LC 77-22692. (Illus.). 1978. ref. 23.95 (ISBN 0-13-637603-7). P-H.
Statements on Management Advisory Services. 1975. pap. 3.00 (ISBN 0-685-27241-9). Am Inst CPA.
Staw, Barry M. & Salancik, Gerald R., eds. New Directions in Organizational Behavior. LC 76-47795. (Illus.). 316p. 1976. pap. text ed. 11.95 (ISBN 0-914292-06-4). Wiley.
Steers, Richard M. Organizational Effectiveness: A Behavioral View. Porter, Lyman W., ed. LC 76-17203. (Goodyear Ser. in Management & Organizations). (Illus.). 1977. text ed. 13.95 (ISBN 0-87620-655-0); pap. text ed. 9.95 (ISBN 0-87620-639-9). Goodyear.
Steiner, George A. & Miner, John B. Management Policy & Strategy. 2nd ed. 1982. text ed. 14.95 (ISBN 0-02-416790-8). Macmillan.
--Management Policy & Strategy. 1977. 21.95 (ISBN 0-02-416740-1, 41674); pap. 19.95 (ISBN 0-02-416750-9, 41675). Macmillan.
Steinhoff, D. Small Business Management Fundamentals. 3rd ed. (Management Ser.). 1982. price not set (ISBN 0-07-061146-7); price not set instr's manual (ISBN 0-07-061147-5). McGraw.
Steinmetz, Lawrence L. & Todd, H. Ralph, Jr. First-Line Management: Approaching Supervision Effectively. rev. ed. 1979. pap. 10.50x (ISBN 0-256-02213-5). Business Pubns.
Stemp, Isay, ed. Corporate Growth Strategies. LC 75-103426. 1970. 12.00 (ISBN 0-8144-5196-9). Am Mgmt.
Stephanov, Stephen E. Management, Technology Innovation & Engineering. rev. ed. 391p. 1982. text ed. 18.00x (ISBN 0-936496-02-9). Spencer Pubs.
Stephens, James C. Managing Complexity: Work, Technology, Resources, & Human Relations. rev. ed. LC 77-124381. 1977. 16.50 (ISBN 0-912338-13-X); microfiche 9.50 (ISBN 0-912338-14-8). Lomond.
Stewart, Valerie & Stewart, Andrew. Managing the Manager's Growth. 1979. 25.95 (ISBN 0-470-26561-2). Halsted Pr.
Stogdill, Ralph M. Leadership Abstracts & Bibliography, 1904-1974. 1977. 29.50 (ISBN 0-87776-310-0, AA10). Ohio St U Admin Sci.
Stoner, J. A. Management. (Illus.). 1978. text ed. 21.95 (ISBN 0-13-549303-X); study guide & wkbk 8.95 (ISBN 0-13-549329-3). P-H.
Stoner, James A. Management. 2nd ed. 704p. 1982. text ed. 21.95 (ISBN 0-13-549667-5); study guide & wkbk. 8.95 (ISBN 0-13-549683-7). P-H.
Storey, John. Challenge to Management Control. 160p. 1980. 30.00x (ISBN 0-85038-187-8). Nichols Pub.
Straub, Joseph T. Applied Management. 1979. 18.95 (ISBN 0-87626-014-8); student involvement guide 7.95 (ISBN 0-87626-016-4). Winthrop.
Strickland, A. G. How to Get Action: Key to Successful Management. 1976. 10.95 (ISBN 0-13-407239-1, Parker). P-H.
Sturdivant, Frederick A. Business & Society: A Managerial Approach. rev. ed. 1981. 18.95x (ISBN 0-256-02516-9). Irwin.
Sudhalter. The Management Option. LC 80-12992. 256p. 1980. 19.95 (ISBN 0-87705-084-8). Human Sci Pr.
Sudhalter, David L. The Management Option: Nine Strategies for Leadership. 1980. pap. 8.95 (ISBN 0-87705-089-9). Human Sci Pr.
Sullivan, George. How Do They Run It? LC 73-121764. (Illus.). (gr. 5 up). 1971. 5.50 (ISBN 0-664-32480-0). Westminster.
Summer, Charles E., Jr., et al. The Managerial Mind: Science & Theory in Policy Decisions. 4th ed. 1977. 21.00x (ISBN 0-256-01922-3). Irwin.
Surboeck, Erich K. Management Von EDV-Projekten. 1978. 37.75x (ISBN 3-11-006981-4). De Gruyter.
Survey of Current Management Techniques in the Insurance Industry. 37p. 1981. 24.00x (ISBN 0-686-75459-X, Pub. by Insurance Inst England). State Mutual Bk.
Survey of Research in Management, Vol. 2. 1978. 22.50x (ISBN 0-8364-0165-4). South Asia Bks.
Survey of Research in Management, India, Vol. 1. 1973. 14.00x (ISBN 0-8364-0471-8). South Asia Bks.
Swanson, Carl A. Steps to Take to Save a Business Which Is on the Verge of Collaspe. (The International Council for Excellence in Management Library). (Illus.). 105p. 1980. plastic spiral bdg. 24.95 (ISBN 0-89266-243-3). Am Classical Coll Pr.
Sweeney, Neil R. Art of Managing Managers. 120p. 1981. text ed. price not set (ISBN 0-201-07644-6). A-W.
--Managing People: Techniques for Food Service Operators. new ed. LC 76-7286. 128p. 1976. pap. 13.95 (ISBN 0-912016-54-X). Lebhar Friedman.
Swieringa, Robert J. & Moncur, Robert H. Some Effects of Participative Budgeting on Managerial Behavior. 9.95 (ISBN 0-686-11621-6, 7475). Natl Assn Accts.
Swift, Eric. Managing Your Export Office. 150p. 1977. text ed. 22.00x (ISBN 0-220-66310-6, Pub. by Busn Bks England). Renouf.
Swingle, P. G. Management of Power. LC 75-45316. 1976. 12.95 (ISBN 0-470-15030-0). Halsted Pr.
Sylvester, Richard R. Management Decisions & Actions. Date not set. 29.95 (ISBN 0-932010-23-7). Phd Pub.
Szarejko, Francis W. How to Manage Yourself & Others. 1979. pap. 4.95 (ISBN 0-88270-358-7). Logos.
Szilagyi, Andrew. Management & Performance. 1981. text ed. 20.95 (ISBN 0-8302-5467-6). Goodyear.
Taetzsch, Lyn. Taking Charge on the Job: Techniques for Assertive Management. Benson, Eileen, ed. 1978. 8.95 (ISBN 0-917386-22-1). Exec Ent.
Tagliere, Daniel A. The Participative Prince: Techniques for Developing Your Organization & Improving Its Performance. LC 79-83886. (Illus.). 1979. 14.95 (ISBN 0-9602516-0-X). ODS Pubns.
Tansik, David A., et al. Management: A Life Cycle Approach. 1980. 19.95x (ISBN 0-256-02278-X). Irwin.
Tapiero, C. S. Managerial Planning: An Optimum & Stochistic Approach, 2 vols. 1977. 57.75 set (ISBN 0-677-05400-9). Gordon.
Taylor, Bernard & Hussey, David, eds. The Realities of Planning. (Illus.). 224p. 1981. 36.00 (ISBN 0-08-022226-9). Pergamon.
Taylor, Bernard W. Introduction to Management Science Techniques. 600p. 1981. text ed. price not set (ISBN 0-697-08059-5); study guide avail. (ISBN 0-697-08063-3); manual instrs.' avail. (ISBN 0-697-08067-6). Wm C Brown.
Taylor, W. J. & Watling, T. F. The Basic Arts of Management. 207p. 1977. text ed. 22.00x (ISBN 0-220-66812-4, Pub. by Busn Bks England). Renouf.
Taylor, W. J. & Watling, T. T. The Basic Arts of Management. 1972. 14.95x (ISBN 0-220-66812-4). Beekman Pubs.
Tead, Ordway. Administration: Its Purpose & Performance. 1968. Repr. of 1959 ed. 10.00 (ISBN 0-208-00622-2, Archon). Shoe String.
Tedeschi, James T., ed. Impression Management Theory & Social Psychological Research. 1981. 29.50 (ISBN 0-12-685180-8). Acad Pr.
Tellier, Richard. Operations Management: Fundamental Concepts & Methods. 1978. text ed. 24.50 scp (ISBN 0-06-388690-1, HarpC); instr's manual avail. (ISBN 0-06-377500-X). Har-Row.
Terence, Austen, ed. The Managerial Wisdom of Benjamin Franklin. (Illus.). 1978. 41.75 (ISBN 0-89266-106-2). Am Classical Coll Pr.
Terry. Plaid for Principles of Management. 3rd ed. 1978. 5.50 (ISBN 0-256-02134-1, 11-0757-03). Learning Syst.
Terry, George R. A Guide to Management, Bk. 265. (Irwin Publications for Professional Development Guides Ser.). 194p. Date not set. pap. 6.95 (ISBN 0-686-75005-5). Dow Jones-Irwin.
--Supervision. rev. ed. 1978. pap. 13.50x (ISBN 0-256-02047-7). Irwin.
Tersine, Richard J. & Davidson, Fredrick. Problems & Models in Operations Management. 2nd ed. LC 79-21810. (Management Ser.). 1980. pap. text ed. 11.95 (ISBN 0-88244-207-4). Grid Pub.
Thain, Richard J. The Managers: Career Alternatives for the College Educated. LC 78-61296. (Orig.). 1978. pap. 4.95 (ISBN 0-913936-11-1). Coll Placement.
Thierauf, Robert J., et al. Management Principles & Practices: A Contingency & Questionnaire Approach. LC 77-23297. (Management & Administration Ser.). 819p. 1977. text ed. 26.95x (ISBN 0-471-29504-3); tchr's manual avail. (ISBN 0-471-03728-1). Wiley.
This, Leslie E. A Guide to Effective Management: Practical Applications from Behavioral Science. (Illus.). 288p. 1974. pap. text ed. 8.95 (ISBN 0-201-07559-8). A-W.
Thomas, Adin B. Stock Control in Manufacturing Industries. 2nd ed. 240p. 1980. text ed. 29.50 (ISBN 0-566-02140-4, Pub. by Gower Pub Co England). Renouf.
Thompson, Ann M. & Wood, Marcia D. Management Strategies for Women: Or, Now That I'm Boss, How Do I Run This Place? 1981. 12.95 (ISBN 0-671-25476-6). S&S.
Thompson, Arthur A., Jr. & Strickland, A. J., III. Strategy & Policy. rev. ed. 1981. text ed. 20.95x (ISBN 0-256-02385-9). Business Pubns.
--Strategy & Policy: Concepts & Cases. rev. ed. 1981. 20.95 (ISBN 0-256-02385-9). Dorsey.
Thompson, Arthur A., Jr. & Strickland, A. J., 3rd. Strategy Formulation & Implementation: Tasks of the General Manager. 1980. pap. 10.50x (ISBN 0-256-02277-1). Business Pubns.
Thompson, David W. Managing People: Influencing Behavior. LC 77-15993. 1978. pap. text ed. 10.45 (ISBN 0-8016-4933-1). Mosby.
Thompson, Marilyn T. Management Information: Where to Find It. LC 81-2027. 280p. 1981. 15.00 (ISBN 0-8108-1424-2). Scarecrow.
Thornton, Charles B. Challenge to Business Management. (Annual Business Leadership Lecture, 1968). 1968. pap. 1.00 (ISBN 0-87712-151-6). U Mich Busn Div Res.
The Three Toughest on-the-Job Problems. 1974. pap. 2.25 (ISBN 0-917386-80-9). Exec Ent.
Timm, Paul R. Managerial Communication: A Finger on the Pulse. (Illus.). 1980. text ed. 15.95 (ISBN 0-13-549824-4). P-H.
Tipper, Harry, Jr. The System & What You Can Do With It. LC 73-80845. (Illus.). 260p. 1973. 6.95 (ISBN 0-87645-079-6). Gambit.
Tosi, Henry, et al, eds. Managerial Motivation & Compensation. LC 72-619500. 1972. 10.00 (ISBN 0-87744-101-4). Mich St U Busn.
Tosi, Henry L. Readings in Management: Contingencies, Structure & Process. LC 76-5292. (Illus.). 1976. pap. text ed. 11.50 (ISBN 0-914292-07-2). Wiley.
Tosi, Henry L. & Carroll, Stephen J. Management: Contingencies, Structure & Process. LC 75-43280. (Series in Critical Sociologies). (Illus.). 608p. 1976. text ed. 23.95 (ISBN 0-914292-04-8). Wiley.
Tosi, Henry L. & Hamner, W. Clay, eds. Organizational Behavior & Management: A Contingency Approach. rev. ed. LC 77-77475. (Series in Critical Sociologies). 1977. pap. text ed. 17.95 (ISBN 0-914292-09-9). Wiley.
Tourangeau, Kevin. Strategy Management: How to Plan, Execute & Control Strategic Plans for Your Business. 256p. 1980. 16.95 (ISBN 0-07-065043-8, P&RB). McGraw.
Townsend, Robert. Up the Organization. 240p. 1978. pap. 2.50 (ISBN 0-449-23368-5, Crest). Fawcett.
Townsend, Robert C. Up the Organization. LC 72-98654. 1970. 10.00 (ISBN 0-394-45034-5). Knopf.
Tregoe, Benjamin B. & Zimmerman, John W. Top Management Strategy. 1980. 9.95 (ISBN 0-671-25401-4). S&S.
Trewatha, Robert L. & Newport, M. Gene. Management: Functions & Behavior. rev. ed. 1979. text ed. 17.50x (ISBN 0-256-02214-3). Business Pubns.
Tricker, R. I., ed. The Individual, the Enterprise & the State. LC 77-78350. 1977. 20.95 (ISBN 0-470-99211-5). Halsted Pr.
Trugman, Leonard. Corporate Management in Action: Sixteen Critical Cases in Operations, Finance & Manufacturing. LC 80-15133. 180p. 1981. 29.95 (ISBN 0-13-174433-X). P-H.
Tsurumi, Yoshi. Multinational Management: Business Strategy & Government Policy. 622p. 1976. write for info. (ISBN 0-88410-297-1). Ballinger Pub.
Turban, Efraim & Meredith, Jack. Fundamentals of Management Science. rev. ed. 1981. 22.50x (ISBN 0-686-77310-1); wkbk. avail. Business Pubns.
Turban, Efraim & Loomba, N. Paul, eds. Readings in Management Science. 1976. pap. 10.95x (ISBN 0-256-01705-0). Business Pubns.
Turban, Efraum & Meredith, Jack. Fundamentals of Management Science. 1976. 22.50 (ISBN 0-256-02393-X); pap. 7.50 study guide (ISBN 0-256-02564-9). Business Pubns.
Turner, David R. Management Analyst - Assistant, Associate. LC 75-18904. 1976. pap. 8.00 (ISBN 0-668-03864-0). Arco.
Tweedy, D. B. Public Management Research. 1981. 21.75 (ISBN 0-398-04481-3). C C Thomas.
Tyson, John C. & Piele, Linda J. Materials & Methods for Business Research. LC 80-20332. (Bibliographic Instruction Ser.). 1980. lib. bdg. 14.95x (ISBN 0-918212-15-4); wkbk. 5 or more 4.95 (ISBN 0-918212-14-6). Neal-Schuman.
Ullrich, Robert. Motivation Methods That Work. 176p. 1981. 12.95 (ISBN 0-13-603860-3); pap. 5.95 (ISBN 0-13-603852-2). P-H.
Uris, Auren. The Executive Deskbook. 1979. pap. 8.95 (ISBN 0-442-26107-1). Van Nos Reinhold.
--Mastery of Management. 1975. pap. 2.25 (ISBN 0-87216-616-3). Playboy Pbks.
Urwick, Lyndall. The Golden Book of Management: A Historical Record of the Life & Work of Seventy Pioneers. Chandler, Alfred D., ed. LC 79-7557. (History of Management Thought & Practice Ser.). (Illus.). 1980. Repr. of 1956 ed. lib. bdg. 18.00x (ISBN 0-405-12343-4). Arno.

--Management of Tomorrow. Chandler, Alfred D., ed. LC 79-7558. (History of Management Thought & Practice Ser.). 1980. Repr. of 1933 ed. lib. bdg. 26.00x (ISBN 0-405-12344-2). Arno.

Vallen, Jerome J. Check in-Check Out: Principles of Effective Front Office Management. 2nd ed. 370p. 1980. text ed. write for info. (ISBN 0-697-08412-4); instrs' manual avail. (ISBN 0-697-08413-2). Wm C Brown.

Vancil, Richard F. Decentralization: Managerial Ambiguity by Design. LC 79-51782. 1979. 22.50 (ISBN 0-910586-32-2). Dow Jones-Irwin.

Van Fleet, James. Twenty-Two Biggest Mistakes Managers Make & How to Correct Them. 1973. 10.95 (ISBN 0-13-935031-4, Parker). P-H.

Van Fleet, James K. Van Fleet's Master Guide for Managers. 1978. 18.95 (ISBN 0-13-940452-X, Parker). P-H.

Van Gunsteren, Herman R. The Quest for Control: A Critique of the Rational-Central-Planning Approach in Public Affairs. LC 75-19228. 162p. 1976. 26.75 (ISBN 0-471-89920-8, Pub. by Wiley-Interscience). Wiley.

Varney, Glenn H. Management by Objectives Workbook. rev. ed. 1972. 4.95 (ISBN 0-686-05624-8). Mgmt Advisory.

--Organization Development Approach to Management Development. LC 75-9007. (Illus.). 192p. 1976. text ed. 10.94 (ISBN 0-201-07982-8). A-W.

--Organization Development for Managers. LC 77-73948. 1977. pap. text ed. 10.95 (ISBN 0-201-07983-6). A-W.

Vash, Carolyn L. The Burnt-Out Administrator. LC 79-14057. 1979. text ed. 10.95 (ISBN 0-8261-2910-2). Springer Pub.

Vatter, Paul A., et al. Quantitative Methods in Management: Text & Cases. 1978. 21.95x (ISBN 0-256-02006-X). Irwin.

Verma, Harish L. & Gross, Charles W. Introduction to Quantitative Methods: A Managerial Emphasis. LC 77-21089. 1978. text ed. 26.95 (ISBN 0-471-02610-7); tchrs. manual o.p. avail. (ISBN 0-471-02495-3, Pub. by Wiley-Hamilton). Wiley.

Vervalin, Charles H., ed. Management Handbook for the Hydrocarbon Processing Industries. 242p. 1981. pap. text ed. 16.95 (ISBN 0-87201-480-0). Gulf Pub.

Vested, I. M. The Unsent Letters of I. M. Vested: An Expose of Corporate Mismanagement in America. LC 81-47558. 192p. 1981. 9.95 (ISBN 0-15-193072-4). HarBraceJ.

Viola, Richard H. Organizations in a Changing Society: Administration & Human Values. 1977. text ed. 6.50 (ISBN 0-7216-9055-6). HR&W.

Vroom, Victor H. & Deci, Edward L., eds. Management & Motivation. (Education Ser). 1971. pap. 4.50 (ISBN 0-14-080144-8). Penguin.

Wachs, William. One Hundred One Managerial Situations & How to Handle Them. 1976. 10.95 (ISBN 0-13-635367-3). P-H.

Waddell, William C. Overcoming Murphy's Law. 618p. 1981. 14.95 (ISBN 0-8144-5628-6). Am Mgmt.

Walley, B. H. Management Services Handbook. (Illus.). 452p. 1973. 34.95x (ISBN 0-8464-1113-X). Beekman Pubs.

Walsh, John. Management Tactics: Short Cases in Operational Management. (Illus.). 1979. 7.95 (ISBN 0-07-067963-0); instructor's manual 9.95 (ISBN 0-07-067964-9). McGraw.

Wareham, John. Secrets of a Corporate Headhunter. LC 81-80780. 288p. 1981. pap. 3.50 (ISBN 0-87216-924-3). Playboy Pbks.

Wasson, Chester R. & Shreve, Richard R. Interpreting & Using Quantitative Aids to Business Decision. LC 75-44596. (Illus.). 447p. 1976. text ed. 10.00x (ISBN 0-914872-08-7). Austin Pr.

Watson, C. E. Results-Oriented Management: How to Effectively Get Things Done. 1981. pap. write for info. (ISBN 0-201-08355-8). A-W.

Watson, Charles E. Management Development Through Training. LC 78-52504. 1979. text ed. 11.95 (ISBN 0-201-08358-2). A-W.

--Managing for Results: How to Effecttively Get Things Done. LC 80-24047. 208p. 1981. pap. text ed. write for info. A-W.

Webber, Ross. Management Pragmatics. 1979. pap. 11.95x (ISBN 0-256-02232-1). Irwin.

Webber, Ross A. Time & Management. 167p. 1981. 14.95 (ISBN 0-86670-001-3). Moffat Pub.

Webber, Ross D. To Be a Manager. 1981. 18.95x (ISBN 0-256-02520-7). Irwin.

Weilbacher, William M. Marketing Management Cases: Planning & Executing Marketing Strategy. 3rd ed. (Illus.). 1980. pap. text ed. 9.95 (ISBN 0-02-425070-8). Macmillan.

Weinberg, Charles. Management. LC 78-59615. (Cases in Computer & Model Assisted Marketing Ser.). pap. cancelled (ISBN 0-685-85049-8); cancelled (ISBN 0-89426-009-X). Scientific Pr.

Weinstock, Irwin T. & Torgerson, Paul E. Management: An Integrated Approach. LC 71-162354. (Illus.). 1972. text ed. 24.00 (ISBN 0-13-548396-4). P-H.

Weiss, W. H. The Art & Skill of Managing People. 1975. 10.95 (ISBN 0-13-048736-8). P-H.

Welsh, A. N. The Skills of Management. 247p. 1981. 14.95 (ISBN 0-8144-5670-7). Am Mgmt.

Wenzel, William J. Wenzel on Management & Purchasing. 1981. 24.95 (ISBN 0-8436-2208-3). CBI Pub.

What Determines Organizational Performance? (AMACOM Reprint Collections). 79p. 1974. pap. 9.00 (ISBN 0-8144-6502-1). Am Mgmt.

What the Manager Should Know About the Computer. pap. 2.95x (ISBN 0-686-02556-3). Dun.

Wheelwright, Steven C. & Makridakis, Spyros. Forecasting Methods for Management. 3rd ed. LC 79-23476. (Systems & Controls for Financial Management Ser.). 300p. 1980. 29.95 (ISBN 0-471-05630-8, Pub by Ronald Pr). Wiley.

White, E. N. Maintenance Planning, Control & Documentation. 1979. text ed. 37.25x (ISBN 0-566-02144-7, Pub. by Gower Pub Co England). Renouf.

Whitmore, D. A. Managing Motivation & Remuneration. 1977. 34.50x (ISBN 0-8464-0597-0). Beekman Pubs.

Whitmore, D. A. & Ibbetson, J. The Management of Motivation & Renumeration. 230p. 1977. text ed. 29.50x (ISBN 0-220-66319-X, Pub. by Busn Bks England). Renouf.

Wieche, Vernon. Management by Objectives in Mental Health Services. 1974. 4.50 (ISBN 0-685-79081-9). Masterco Pr.

Wikstrom, Walter S. Managing By, & with Objectives. (Studies in Personnel Policy: No. 212). (Illus.). 1969. pap. 15.00 (ISBN 0-8237-0036-4). Conference Bd.

Wild, Ray. Operations Management: A Policy Framework. (Illus.). 1979. 35.00 (ISBN 0-08-022504-7); pap. 15.00 (ISBN 0-08-022505-5). Pergamon.

Wild, Rolf H. Management by Compulsion: The Corporate Urge to Grow. 1978. 10.00 (ISBN 0-395-26467-7). HM.

Wilings, David R. Understanding Management. 320p. 1979. text ed. 14.90x (ISBN 0-7715-5728-0); instr's. manual 7.45x (ISBN 0-7715-5730-2). Forkner.

Williams, Ervin, ed. Participative Management: Concepts, Theory, & Implementation. LC 76-13650. 1976. 14.95 (ISBN 0-88406-102-7). Ga St U Busn Pub.

Willings, D. Human Element in Management. 1969. 46.75 (ISBN 0-677-61420-9). Gordon.

Willsmer, R. Basic Arts of Management. 1977. 21.00x (ISBN 0-8464-0171-1). Beekman Pubs.

Willsmore, A. W. Managing Modern Man. (Illus.). 253p. 1973. 18.00x (ISBN 0-8464-1114-8). Beekman Pubs.

Wilson, Howard. Management & Supervisory Development Reading Program: Improving Supervisory Skills. 44p. 1968. pap. 2.50 (ISBN 0-910022-07-0). ARA.

--Management & Supervisory Development Reading Program: Understanding & Motivating Employees. 36p. 1968. pap. 2.50 (ISBN 0-910022-03-8). ARA.

--Utilizing Time Effectively Through Better Management Processes. 1973. pap. 1.50 (ISBN 0-910022-23-2). ARA.

Wilson, J. P. Inflation, Deflation, Reflation: Managemnent & Accounting in Economic Uncertainty. 345p. 1980. text ed. 36.75x (ISBN 0-220-67015-3, Pub. by Busn Bks England). Renouf.

Winger, Bernard J. Cases in Financial Management. LC 80-11532. (Finance Ser.). 211p. 1981. pap. 8.95 (ISBN 0-88244-224-4). Grid Pub.

Winter, M. Mind Your Own Business, Be Your Own Boss. 1980. 12.95 (ISBN 0-13-583468-6); pap. 6.95 (ISBN 0-13-583450-3). P-H.

Wise, Sheldon. Essentials of Management. LC 79-88238. (The ALA ESP Ser.). (Illus.). v, 110p. (Orig.). 1979. pap. text ed. 6.25x (ISBN 0-934270-06-6). Am Lang Acad.

Wiseman, A. J., et al. Arable Management Nineteen Eighty. 240p. 1981. 35.00x (ISBN 0-7198-2538-5, Pub. by Northwood Bks). State Mutual Bk.

Wofford, Jerry C., et al. Organizational Communication. (Management Ser.). (Illus.). 1977. text ed. 16.95 (ISBN 0-07-070230-6, C); instrs manual 4.95 (ISBN 0-07-070231-4). McGraw.

Wolf, Harvey J. & Frangia, George W. Behavioral Applications in Public Management: A Reader. LC 79-63852. (Illus.). 1979. pap. text ed. 7.75 (ISBN 0-8191-0744-1). U Pr of Amer.

Wolf, William B. The Basic Barnard: An Introduction to Chester I. Barnard & His Theories of Organization & Management. LC 73-620199. (ILR Paperback Ser.: No. 14). 1974. pap. 7.50 (ISBN 0-87546-054-2). NY Sch Indus Rel.

--Conversations with Chester I. Barnard. LC 72-619666. (ILR Paperback Ser.: No. 12). 1973. pap. 6.25 special bdg. (ISBN 0-87546-280-4); pap. 3.25 (ISBN 0-87546-047-X). NY Sch Indus Rel.

Wortman, Max & Sperling, Joann. Defining the Manager's Job. rev. ed. 1980. pap. 9.95 (ISBN 0-8144-7526-4). Am Mgmt.

Wortmen, Max S., Jr. & Luthans, Fred. Emerging Concepts in Management. 2nd ed. (Illus.). 480p. 1975. pap. text ed. 8.50 (ISBN 0-02-430040-3). Macmillan.

Wren, Daniel A. Evolution of Management Thought. 2nd ed. LC 78-10959. (Management & Administration Ser.). 1979. text ed. 25.95 (ISBN 0-471-04695-7). Wiley.

Wren, Daniel A. & Voich, Dan, Jr. Principles of Management: Process & Behavior. 2nd ed. LC 75-43472. 1976. 23.95x (ISBN 0-8260-9640-9, Pub. by Wiley-Hamilton). Wiley.

Wright, Robert G. Exploring Vital Elements of Organization & Management. 1978. pap. text ed. 6.50 (ISBN 0-8403-1384-5). Kendall-Hunt.

Wyckoff, D. Daryl & Sasser, W. Earl. The U. S. Lodging Industry. LC 78-24716. (The Lexington Industry Analysis Casebook). 1981. 25.95 (ISBN 0-669-02819-3). Lexington Bks.

Yessian, Mark & Curtis, W. Robert. Effective Management of Human Services, Pt. II. (Organizational Development of State Human Services Ser.). (Orig.). 1979. pap. 1.95 (ISBN 0-89995-002-7). Social Matrix.

Young, David W. The Managerial Process in Human Service Agencies. LC 78-19767. (Praeger Special Studies). 1979. 27.95 (ISBN 0-03-047081-1). Praeger.

--Managing Smaller Institutions: The Accounting & Control Process. 200p. 1981. 19.95 (ISBN 0-86569-092-8). Auburn Hse.

Young, George A. Effective Management: Basic Principles & Practices. 1977. 12.00 (ISBN 0-8059-2452-3). Dorrance.

Young, Jerrald F. Decision Making for Small Business Management. 256p. 1981. Repr. of 1977 ed. lib. bdg. 15.50 (ISBN 0-89874-346-X). Krieger.

Zaltman, Gerald, ed. Management Principles for Nonprofit Organizations & Agencies. (Illus.). 1979. 34.95 (ISBN 0-8144-5518-2). Am Mgmt.

Zand, Dale. Information, Organization, & Power: Effective Management in the Knowledge Society. LC 80-22160. (Illus.). 224p. 1981. 13.95 (ISBN 0-686-73412-2, P&RB). McGraw.

--Management in a Knowledge Society. Newton, William R., ed. (Illus.). 224p. Date not set. 12.95 (ISBN 0-07-072743-0, P&RB). McGraw.

Zeldman, Maurice. Keeping Technical Projects on Target. LC 78-13713. 1978. pap. 7.50 (ISBN 0-8144-2228-4). Am Mgmt.

Zimet, Melvin & Greenwood, Ronald G., eds. The Evolving Science of Management: The Collected Papers of Harold Smiddy & Papers by Others in His Honor. (Illus.). 1980. 24.95 (ISBN 0-8144-5552-2). Am Mgmt.

Zoll, Allen A., III. Explorations in Managing. (Illus.). 356p. 1974. pap. text ed. 9.95 (ISBN 0-201-08814-2). A-W.

Zuwaylif, Fadil H., et al. Management Science: An Introduction. LC 78-5827. (Management & Administration Ser.). 1979. text ed. 27.95 (ISBN 0-471-98675-5); sol. manual avail. (ISBN 0-471-03222-0). Wiley.

MANAGEMENT-BIBLIOGRAPHY

Bakewell, K. G., ed. Management Principles & Practice: A Guide to Information Sources. LC 76-16127. (Management Information Guide Series: No. 32). 1977. 36.00 (ISBN 0-8103-0832-0). Gale.

Bensoussan, A. & Keindorfer, P. Applied Optimal Control. (TIMS Studies in the Management Science Ser.: Vol. 9). 1978. pap. 27.00 (ISBN 0-444-85175-5, North Holland). Elsevier.

Bradley, Hugh E. The Operations Research & Management Science CumIndex, Vol. 10. 1979. 60.00 (ISBN 0-88274-009-1). R & D Pr.

Evered, Roger. Futures Planning in Management: Bibliography & Information Sources. (CPL Bibliographies: No. 5). 52p. 1979. pap. 7.00 (ISBN 0-86602-005-5). CPL Biblios.

Hills, William G., et al. Administration & Management: A Selected & Annotated Bibliography. 1975. pap. 5.95x (ISBN 0-8061-1285-9). U of Okla Pr.

Institute of Personnel Management. IPM Bibliography: Part Three, Education Training & Development. 114p. 1975. 10.00x (ISBN 0-85292-112-8). Intl Pubns Serv.

Leavitt, Judith A. Women in Management, Nineteen Seventy to Nineteen Eighty: An Annotated Sourcelist. 1982. lib. bdg. write for info. (ISBN 0-89774-010-6). Oryx Pr.

McKamy, K. Books for Businessmen: A Bibliography. LC 65-27747. (Business Almanac Ser: No. 1). 1967. 5.95 (ISBN 0-379-11201-9). Oceana.

Morrill, Chester, Jr., ed. Systems & Procedures Including Office Management Information Sources. LC 67-31261. (Management Information Ser.: No. 12). 1967. 36.00 (ISBN 0-8103-0812-6). Gale.

Rath, Frederick L. & O'Connell, Merrilyn R. Administration: A Bibliography on Historical Organization Practices, Vol. 5. 250p. 1980. text ed. 14.95x (ISBN 0-910050-44-9). AASLH.

Sandeau, Georges. Selective Management Bibliography. 250p. 1975. 35.00x (ISBN 0-85935-037-1). Herman Pub.

Tega, Vasile G., ed. Management & Economics Journals: An International Selection. LC 76-4578. (Management Information Guide Ser.: No. 33). 1977. 36.00 (ISBN 0-8103-0833-9). Gale.

Van Fleet, David D. An Historical Bibliography of Administration, Business & Management. (Public Administration Ser.: P 27). 1978. pap. 5.00 (ISBN 0-686-24283-1). Vance Biblios.

MANAGEMENT-CASE STUDIES

Berry, William L. & Whybark, D. Clay. Computer Augmented Cases in Operations & Logistics Management. 325p. 1972. pap. 5.10 (ISBN 0-538-07020-X). SW Pub.

Byars. Readings & Cases in Personnel Management. 1979. 11.95 (ISBN 0-7216-2252-6). Dryden Pr.

Carroll, Stephen J., Jr. & Paine, Frank T. Management Process: Cases & Readings. 2nd ed. 448p. 1977. pap. text ed. 11.95 (ISBN 0-02-319520-7, 31952). Macmillan.

Christensen, C. Roland, et al. Policy Formulation & Administration: A Casebook of Top-Management Problems in Business. 8th ed. 1980. 20.95x (ISBN 0-256-02345-X). Irwin.

French, Wendell L., et al. The Personnel Management Process: Cases on Human Resources Administration. LC 77-74422. (Illus.). 1977. pap. text ed. 9.25 (ISBN 0-395-25531-7); inst. manual 0.50 (ISBN 0-395-26087-6). HM.

Gitman, Larry & Moses, Edward A. Financial Management: Cases. 1978. text ed. 20.95 (ISBN 0-8299-0167-1); instrs.' manual avail. (ISBN 0-8299-0480-8). West Pub.

Glover, Randy & Talmey, Paul. Improved Modeling & Solution of Practical Management Science Problems Through Netforms: Inventory Systems, Pt. 1. 1977. 2.50 (ISBN 0-686-64188-4). U CO Busn Res Div.

Goodstein, Leonard D., et al, eds. Organizational Change Sourcebook II: Cases in Conflict Management. LC 79-63006. 236p. 1979. pap. 12.95 (ISBN 0-88390-151-X). Univ Assocs.

Hilgert, Raymond L., et al. Cases & Policies in Human Resources Management. 3rd ed. LC 77-72903. (Illus.). 1977. pap. text ed. 10.95 (ISBN 0-395-25070-6); inst. manual 0.75 (ISBN 0-395-25071-4). HM.

Hodgetts, Richard M. & Wortman, Max S. Administrative Policy: Text & Cases in Strategic Management. 2nd ed. LC 78-24528. (Management Ser.). 712p. 1979. text ed. 24.95 (ISBN 0-471-03605-6); case notes avail. (ISBN 0-471-05041-5). Wiley.

Huber, George. Managerial Decision Making. 1980. pap. text ed. 8.95x (ISBN 0-673-15141-7). Scott F.

Ivancevich, John M & Szilagyi, Andrew D. Organizational Behavior & Performance. LC 76-43427. (Illus.). 1977. 18.95 (ISBN 0-87620-635-6); instructors manual free (ISBN 0-87620-636-4). Goodyear.

Joyce, R. D. Encounters in Organizational Behavior: Problem Situations. 1972. text ed. 18.50 (ISBN 0-08-017013-7); pap. text ed. 9.25 (ISBN 0-08-017116-8). Pergamon.

Katz, Robert L. Cases & Concepts in Corporate Strategy. 1970. ref. ed 22.95 (ISBN 0-13-118422-9). P-H.

Kimball, Patrick. Planning Business Strategy. 190p. (Orig.). 1980. pap. text ed. 9.95 (ISBN 0-89669-055-5). Collegium Bk Pubs.

Let's Get Down to Cases, 2 pts. 1976. 4.50 set (ISBN 0-686-68031-6); Pt. 1 (ISBN 0-8144-6953-1). Am Mgmt.

McLennan, Roy. Cases in Organisational Behaviour. (Illus.). 282p. 1975. 29.50x (ISBN 0-8448-0761-3). Crane-Russak Co.

Marshall, Paul W., et al. Operations Management: Text & Cases. 1975. 21.95x (ISBN 0-256-01682-8). Irwin.

Menezes, Francis A. Cases in Management: India. 1977. 14.00x (ISBN 0-8364-0045-3). South Asia Bks.

Milgliore, R. Henry. MBO: Blue Collar to Top Executive. LC 77-8538. 198p. 1977. 15.00 (ISBN 0-87179-262-1). BNA.

Murray, John V. & Van Der Embse, Thomas J. Organizational Behavior: Incidents & Analysis. LC 72-95928. 1973. pap. text ed. 13.95 (ISBN 0-675-08963-8). Merrill.

Raymond, Corey E., et al. Problems in Marketing. 6th ed. (Marketing Ser.). (Illus.). 832p. 1981. 22.95 (ISBN 0-07-013141-4); instructor's manual 16.95 (ISBN 0-07-013142-2). McGraw.

Roethlisberger, F. J. & Dickson, William J. Management & the Worker: An Account of a Research Program Conducted by Western Electric Co. LC 39-25984. 1939. 30.00x (ISBN 0-674-54676-8). Harvard Busn.

Schuler, Randall S. & Huse, Edgar F. Case Problems in Management. (Management Ser.). (Illus.). 1979. pap. text ed. 9.95 (ISBN 0-8299-0242-2); instrs.' manual avail. (ISBN 0-8299-0604-5). West Pub.

Searle-Barnes, R. G. Pay & Productivity Bargaining. LC 71-94226. (Illus.). 1969. 12.50x (ISBN 0-678-06776-7). Kelley.

Stapleton, Richard C. Managing Creatively: Action Learning in Action. 1976. pap. text ed. 9.45 (ISBN 0-8191-0035-8). U Pr of Amer.

Steiner, George A., et al. Management Policy & Strategy: Cases & Readings. 2nd ed. 1982. 21.95 (ISBN 0-02-416800-9). Macmillan.

Thomas, William R. The Sterling Apparel Company: An Experimental Exercise. 160p. 1981. pap. text ed. 9.95 (ISBN 0-8403-2456-1). Kendall-Hunt.

Werther, William & Davis, Keith. Personnel Management. (Management Ser.). (Illus.). 528p. (Orig.). 1981. text ed. 19.95x (ISBN 0-07-069436-2); instructor's manual & test bank 15.00 (ISBN 0-07-069437-0). McGraw.

Wilson, C. Case Studies in Quantitative Management. 1972. text ed. 14.95x (ISBN 0-7002-0166-1). Intl Ideas.

Wilson, J. Holton, et al. Managerial Economics: Concepts, Applications, & Cases. 1979. text ed. 21.50 scp (ISBN 0-912212-08-X, HarpC); instr's manual avail. (ISBN 0-06-367153-0). Har-Row.

Zey-Ferrell, Mary. Dimensions of Organizations, 2 bks. LC 78-10271. (Illus.). 1979. Text. pap. 16.95 (ISBN 0-87620-217-2); Readings. pap. 12.95 (ISBN 0-87620-771-9). Goodyear.

MANAGEMENT–DICTIONARIES

Autorentaem. Management Enzyklopaedie, 7 vols, Vols. 1-7. (Ger.). 1973. Set. 995.00 (ISBN 0-686-56647-5, M-7091). French & Eur.

Autorenteam. Management Enzyklopaedie, 10 vols, Vols. 1-10. 3200p. (Ger.). 1975. Set. pap. 125.00 (ISBN 0-686-56648-3, M-7092). French & Eur.

Banki, Ivan S. Dictionary of Supervision & Management. LC 74-12933. 265p. 1976. 16.95 (ISBN 0-912352-03-5). Systems Res.

Bolado, Victor H. Management Terminology: English-Spanish & Spanish-English. 192p. 1981. 9.95 (ISBN 0-89962-034-5). Todd & Honeywell.

Colasse. Lexique de Comptabilite et de Gestion. (Fr.). 1975. pap. 14.95 (ISBN 0-686-56768-4, M-6079). French & Eur.

Conveney, James & Moore, Shiela J. Lexique De Termes Anglais-Francais De Gestion: Les Cycle Au Superieur, Ecoles Superieures De Gestion. 160p. (Eng.-Fr.). 1972. pap. 9.95 (ISBN 0-686-56963-6, M-6087). French & Eur.

Coveney, James & Amey, J. Glossary of Spanish & English Management Terms. (English for Special Purposes Bk.). 1978. pap. text ed. 6.00x (ISBN 0-582-55541-8). Longman.

Coveney, James & Moore, Shelia J., eds. Glossary of French & English Management Terms. (English for Special Purposes Bk.). 158p. 1972. pap. text ed. 6.00x (ISBN 0-582-55502-7). Longman.

Encyclopedie Du Management: Centre D'enseignement Superieur Des Affaires, 3 vols. 2000p. (Fr.). Set. 250.00 (ISBN 0-686-57151-7, M-6209). French & Eur.

Haas & Huelck. Management-Taschenlexikon. 200p. (Ger.). 1974. 15.95 (ISBN 3-478-32050-X, M-7547, Pub. by Vlg. Moderne Industrie). French & Eur.

Johannsen, H. Management Glossary: (English-Arabic) 16.00x (ISBN 0-86685-069-4). Intl Bk Ctr.

Johannsen, H. & Page, G. T., eds. International Dictionary of Management. 1977. pap. 11.50 (ISBN 0-85038-122-3, Pub by Kogan Pg). Nichols Pub.

Johannsen, H., et al. Diccionario de Management. 244p. (Espn.). 1972. 21.50 (ISBN 84-281-0220-1, S-31465). French & Eur.

Linnert, Peter. Lexikon Angloamerikanischer und Deutscher Managementbegriffe. (Ger.). 1972. 75.00 (ISBN 3-921099-00-5, M-7286). French & Eur.

Management Dictionary. 1978. Ger. - Eng., 4th Ed. 26.00 (ISBN 3-11-004863-9); Eng. - Ger., 5th Ed. 29.25x (ISBN 3-11-007708-6). De Gruyter.

Sommer-Schoenfeld, Management Dictionary, Deutsch-English: Fachwoerterbuch Fuer Betriebswirtschaft Wirtschafts-und Steuerrecht und Datenverarbeitung. 4th ed. 290p. 1978. 24.50x (ISBN 3-11-002663-5). De Gruyter.

Sommer, Werner & Schoenfeld, Hanns-Martin. Management Dictionary. 5th rev. enl. ed. 621p. 1979. text ed. 34.25x (ISBN 0-686-77467-1). De Gruyter.

Sommer, Werner & Schoenfeld, Hans-Martin. Management Dictionary: Fachwoerterbuch fuer Betriebswirtschaft, Wirtschafts- und Steuerrecht und Datenverarbeitung. 4th ed. LC 78-190431. (English-Deutsch). 328p. 1972. 17.75x (ISBN 3-11-001981-7). De Gruyter.

Spreutels, Marcel. Dictionnaire du Style et des Usages Administratifs. 484p. (Fr.). 19.95 (ISBN 0-686-57225-4, M-6523). French & Eur.

Wortman, Leon A. A Deskbook of Business Management Terms. LC 78-23257. 1979. 24.95 (ISBN 0-8144-5470-4). Am Mgmt.

MANAGEMENT–PROGRAMMED INSTRUCTION

Babb, Emerson M. Purdue Supermarket Chain Management Game: Includes Computer Service. rev. ed. (Illus., Prog. Bk.). 1979. pap. 50.00 (ISBN 0-933836-00-7); students' manual 4.95 (ISBN 0-933836-07-4). Simtek.

How to Set Objectives. pap. 10.00 (ISBN 0-686-02517-2). Preston.

Kazmier, Leonard J. Management: A Programmed Approach with Cases & Applications. 4th, rev. ed. (Illus.). 1980. pap. text ed. 12.95 (ISBN 0-07-033453-6); instrs'. manual 4.95x (ISBN 0-07-033454-4). McGraw.

Making the Computer Work for Management. (PRIME-PRIME 100 Ser). 1967. 35.00 (ISBN 0-8144-1100-2). Am Mgmt.

Schmidt, J. William. Mathematical Foundations for Management Science & Systems Analysis. (Operations Research & Industrial Engineering Ser.). 1974. text ed. 22.95 (ISBN 0-12-627050-3). Acad Pr.

MANAGEMENT–STUDY AND TEACHING

Association of Teachers of Management. Breaking Down Barriers. Garratt, Bob & Stopford, John, eds. 333p. text ed. 41.00x (ISBN 0-566-02122-6, Pub. by Gower Pub Co England). Renouf.

Broadwell, Martin M. Supervisor As an Instructor: A Guide for Classroom Training. 3rd ed. LC 77-81201. (Illus.). 1978. pap. text ed. 8.95 (ISBN 0-201-00329-5). A-W.

Filley, Alan C., et al. Managerial Process & Organizational Behavior. 2nd ed. 1976. text ed. 18.95x (ISBN 0-673-07857-4). Scott F.

Fussler, Herman H. & Jenck, John E., eds. Management Education: Implications for Libraries & Library Schools. LC 73-92600. vi, 116p. 1974. 10.00x (ISBN 0-226-27560-4). U of Chicago Pr.

Getting Results from Courses, Workshops, Seminars, & Conferences: Tips for Participants. 1980. pap. 9.95 cancelled (ISBN 0-89384-059-9). Learning Concepts.

Gruber, Gary. Professional & Administrative Career Examination. (Exam Prep Ser.). 1975. pap. 6.95 (ISBN 0-671-18090-8). Monarch Pr.

Herbert, Theodore T. & Yost, Edward. Management Education & Development: An Annotated Resource Book. LC 77-91110. 1978. lib. bdg. 17.50x (ISBN 0-313-20040-8, HME/). Greenwood.

Hilbert, Stephen & Jaffe, Eugene. Barron's How to Prepare for the Graduate Management Admission Test (GMAT) 4th ed. 576p. 1981. pap. text ed. 6.95 (ISBN 0-8120-2350-1). Barron.

Hill, Thomas M., et al. Institution Building in India: A Study of International Collaboration in Management Education. LC 73-75880. (Illus.). 381p. 1973. 16.50x (ISBN 0-87584-105-8). Harvard Busn.

Howe, Richard L. & Hodgetts, Richard M. Management: Theory, Process & Practice, Study Guide. LC 74-17756. 260p. 1975. pap. text ed. 6.50x (ISBN 0-7216-4790-1). HR&W.

Huber, George. Managerial Decision Making. 1980. pap. text ed. 8.95x (ISBN 0-673-15141-7). Scott F.

An Introductory Course in Teaching & Training Methods for Management Development. 6th ed. (Management Development Manual Ser.: No. 36). 1978. 19.95 (ISBN 92-2-101006-6). Intl Labour Office.

Jaffe & Hilbert. Barron's How to Prepare for the Graduate Management Admission Test(GMAT) 4th ed. LC 78-31875. 1981. pap. write for info. (ISBN 0-8120-2350-1). Barron.

LaFitte, Pat C. The MBA: How to Prepare for, Apply for, and Derive Maximum Advantage from Graduate Study in Management. 224p. 1981. pap. 4.95 (ISBN 0-06-460200-1). B&N.

La Fitte, Pat C. The MBA: How to Prepare for, Apply for, & Derive Maximum Advantage from Graduate Study in Management. (Illus.). 224p. (Orig.). 1981. pap. 5.95 (ISBN 0-06-460200-1, CO 200, BN). Har-Row.

Leeds, C. S., et al. Management & Business Studies. 2nd ed. 448p. 1978. pap. text ed. 16.95x (ISBN 0-7121-1298-7, Pub. by Macdonald & Evans England). Intl Ideas.

Lucas, Harold. Companion to Management Studies: A Survey of Ideas, Theories & Concepts Relevant to Management. 1978. pap. 14.95x (ISBN 0-434-91161-5). Intl Ideas.

Making the Computer Work for Management. (PRIME-PRIME 100 Ser). 1967. 35.00 (ISBN 0-8144-1100-2). Am Mgmt.

Mondy, et al. Management: Concepts & Practices. 704p. 1980. text ed. 19.95 (ISBN 0-205-06859-6, 0868590); study guide 7.95 (ISBN 0-205-06861-8, 0868612). Allyn.

Rogers, David C. Essentials of Business Policy. 128p. 1975. pap. text ed. 9.95 scp (ISBN 0-06-045544-6, HarpC). Har-Row.

Singleton, W. T. Management Skills. (The Study of Real Skills Ser.). 320p. 1981. text ed. 24.50 (ISBN 0-8391-1683-7). Univ Park.

Slyman, Raymond A. Why Managers Fail. LC 77-85762. 1979. 8.75 (ISBN 0-87218-005-0). Natl Underwriter.

Suessmuth, Patrick. Ideas for Training Managers & Supervisors. LC 77-93408. 328p. 1978. pap. 17.50 (ISBN 0-88390-143-9). Univ Assocs.

Tyson, John C. & Piele, Linda J. Materials & Methods for Business Research. LC 80-20332. (Bibliographic Instruction Ser.). 1980. lib. bdg. 14.95x (ISBN 0-918212-15-4); wkbk. 5 or more 4.95 (ISBN 0-918212-14-6). Neal-Schuman.

Vaughn, James A. & Deep, Samuel D. Program of Exercises for Management & Organizational Behavior. 1975. pap. text ed. 6.95x (ISBN 0-02-479440-6); tchrs' manual free (ISBN 0-02-479450-3). Macmillan.

Voss, Fred E., ed. Directory of Management Education Programs. LC 77-82267. (Annual). 1977. 175.00 (ISBN 0-8144-5525-5). Am Mgmt.

Wagner, Harvey M. Principles of Management Science: With Applications to Executive Decisions. 2nd ed. (Illus.). 576p. 1975. 22.95 (ISBN 0-13-709535-X). P-H.

Zoll, Allen A., 3rd. Dynamic Management Education. 2nd ed. 1969. 21.95 (ISBN 0-201-08800-2). A-W.

MANAGEMENT–STUDY AND TEACHING–DIRECTORIES

Drake, et al. Principles of Management: Study Guide. 176p. 1980. wkbk. 7.95 (ISBN 0-8359-5597-4). Reston.

MANAGEMENT, EMPLOYEES' REPRESENTATION IN

see Employees' Representation in Management

MANAGEMENT, GAME

see Wildlife Management

MANAGEMENT, INDUSTRIAL

see Industrial Management

MANAGEMENT, MARKETING

see Marketing Management

MANAGEMENT, PRODUCT

see Product Management

MANAGEMENT, SALES

see Sales Management

MANAGEMENT, WILDLIFE

see Wildlife Management

MANAGEMENT ACCOUNTING

see Managerial Accounting

MANAGEMENT AUDIT

Burstein, Herman. Sample Size Tables for Quality Control & Auditing. LC 72-11086. 1978. text ed. 38.00 (ISBN 0-910972-90-7). IHS PDS.

Elliott, Robert K. & Willingham, John J. Management Fraud: Detection & Deterrence. 300p. 1980. 25.00 (ISBN 0-07-091072-3). McGraw.

Flesher, Dale L. Operations Auditing in Hospitals. LC 75-29936. 128p. 1976. 16.95 (ISBN 0-669-00363-8). Lexington Bks.

Herbert, Leo. Auditing the Performance of Management. 400p. 1979. 24.95 (ISBN 0-534-97998-X). CBI Pub.

--Auditing the Performance of Management. LC 79-4551. 1979. 26.95 (ISBN 0-534-97998-X); ans. bk. 4.95 (ISBN 0-534-97997-1). Lifetime Learn.

Institute of Internal Auditors. Bibliography of Internal Auditing: Nineteen Fifty to Nineteen Sixty-Eight. LC 78-69925. 1978. pap. text ed. 8.00 (ISBN 0-89413-067-6, 202). Inst Inter Aud.

--One-Day Seminar on Contract Audits: Digest of Controls & Tests & Audit Questionnaire & Survey Guide, 3 bks. 1978. 15.00 set (ISBN 0-89413-060-9, 441). Inst Inter Aud.

McFarland, Walter B. Concepts for Management Accounting. 5.95 (ISBN 0-686-09788-2, 6640). Natl Assn Accts.

Multidisciplinary Audit. (QRB Special Edition). 1978. 25.00 (ISBN 0-86688-037-2, QRB-200). Joint Comm Hosp.

Mustafi, Chandan Kumar. Statistical Methods in Managerial Decisions. 1981. 24.00x (ISBN 0-8364-0722-9, Pub. by Macmillan India). South Asia Bks.

National Association of Accountants, ed. Management Accounting for Multinational Corporations, 2 vols. 12.95 ea. (7464); 22.95 set (ISBN 0-686-09767-X, 7466). Natl Assn Accts.

Smith, Billy E. Managing the Information Systems Audit: A Case Study-Policies, Procedures, & Guidelines. (Illus.). 65p. 1980. pap. text ed. 22.50 (ISBN 0-89413-086-2); avail. wkbk. (ISBN 0-89413-087-0). Inst Inter Aud.

Thierauf, Robert J. Management Auditing: A Questionnaire Approach. (Illus.). 1980. 19.95 (ISBN 0-8144-5535-2). Am Mgmt.

MANAGEMENT AUDITING

see Management Audit

MANAGEMENT CONSULTANTS

see Business Consultants

MANAGEMENT-EMPLOYEE RELATIONS IN GOVERNMENT

see Employee-Management Relations in Government

MANAGEMENT GAMES

Barton, Richard F. The Imaginit Management Game. (Illus.). 320p. 1974. pap. text ed. 9.95x (ISBN 0-685-40092-1). Active Learning.

Bowen, K. C. Research Games: An Approach to the Study of Decision Processes. (ORASA Text Ser.: No. 3). 1978. pap. 21.95 (ISBN 0-470-26535-3). Halsted Pr.

Brooks, Leroy D. Financial Management Decision Game (Fingame) 1975. pap. 10.95x (ISBN 0-256-01668-2). Irwin.

Broom, H. Business Policy & Strategic Action: Text, Cases, Management Game. 1969. text ed. 22.95 (ISBN 0-13-107540-3). P-H.

Cotter, R. Business Policy Game: A Player's Manual. 1973. 11.95 (ISBN 0-13-107433-4). P-H.

Crosby, Philip B. The Art of Getting Your Own Sweet Way. 2nd ed. (Illus.). 240p. 1981. 14.95 (ISBN 0-07-014515-6, P&RB). McGraw.

Didactic Systems Staff. Appraisal by Objectives: Coaching & Appraising. (Simulation Game Ser.). 1970. pap. 24.90 (ISBN 0-89401-003-4); pap. 21.50 two or more (ISBN 0-685-78131-3). Didactic Syst.

--Assigning Work. (Simulation Game Ser.). 1973. pap. 24.90 (ISBN 0-89401-006-9); pap. 21.50 two or more (ISBN 0-685-78097-X); pap. 24.90 french ed. (ISBN 0-89401-096-4); pap. 21.50 two or more (ISBN 0-685-78098-8). Didactic Syst.

--Effective Delegation. Euro-Training & Garcia De Leon, Luis, trs. (Simulation Game Ser.). 1971. pap. 24.90 (ISBN 0-89401-145-6); pap. 21.50 two or more (ISBN 0-686-77274-1); pap. 24.90 french ed. (ISBN 0-89401-017-4); pap. 21.50 ea. two or more; pap. 24.90 spanish ed. (ISBN 0-89401-018-2); pap. 21.50 ea. two or more spanish eds. Didactic Syst.

--The Instructor As Manager of Learning Experiences. (Simulation Game Ser.). 1975. pap. 24.90 (ISBN 0-89401-044-1); pap. 21.50 two or more (ISBN 0-685-78124-0). Didactic Syst.

--Long Range Planning. (Simulation Game Ser.). 1971. pap. 24.90 (ISBN 0-89401-049-2); pap. 21.50 two or more (ISBN 0-686-57893-7). Didactic Syst.

--Management by Objectives. (Simulation Game Ser.). 1970. pap. 24.90 (ISBN 0-89401-051-4); pap. 21.50 two or more (ISBN 0-685-78111-9); pap. 24.90 portuguese ed. (ISBN 0-89401-053-0); pap. 21.50 ea. two or more portuguese eds. Didactic Syst.

--Managing in a Foreign Culture. (Simulation Game Ser.). 1974. pap. 24.90 (ISBN 0-89401-062-X). pap. 21.50 ea. two or more. Didactic Syst.

--Optimum Delegation. (Simulation Game Ser.). 1973. pap. 24.90 (ISBN 0-89401-019-0); pap. 21.50 two or more (ISBN 0-685-78122-4). Didactic Syst.

--Planning for Growth. (Simulation Game Ser.). 1972. pap. 24.90 (ISBN 0-89401-074-3); pap. 21.50 two or more (ISBN 0-686-57895-3). Didactic Syst.

--Productivity - Improving Performance. (Simulation Game Ser.). 1975. pap. 24.90 (ISBN 0-89401-081-6); pap. 21.50 two or more (ISBN 0-685-78135-6). Didactic Syst.

--Selecting Effective People. (Simulation Game Ser.). 1970. pap. 24.90 (ISBN 0-89401-087-5); pap. 21.50 two or more (ISBN 0-685-78133-X); pap. 24.90 portuguese ed. (ISBN 0-89401-089-1). Didactic Syst.

Finn, Kenneth R. Time Management. (Simulation Game Ser.). 1975. pap. 24.90 (ISBN 0-89401-092-1); pap. 21.50 additional materials (ISBN 0-685-78118-6). Didactic Syst.

Frazer, J. Ronald. Business Decision Simulation: A Time Sharing Approach. LC 74-28036. 1975. pap. 7.95 (ISBN 0-87909-113-4); free instrs'. manual. Reston.

--Introduction to Business Simulation. 1977. pap. 6.95 (ISBN 0-87909-387-0); instrs'. manual avail. Reston.

Gray, Jack C., et al. Accounting Information & Business Decisions: A Simulation. 1964. text ed. 7.95 (ISBN 0-07-024210-0, C); instructor's manual 4.95 (ISBN 0-07-024211-9). McGraw.

Hausrath, A. H. Venture Simulation in War, Business & Politics. 1971. 29.50 (ISBN 0-07-027230-1, P&RB). McGraw.

Henderson, Thomas A. & Foster, John L. Urban Policy Game: A Simulation of Urban Politics. LC 78-17118. 1978. pap. text ed. 10.95 (ISBN 0-471-03398-7). Wiley.

Hinkle, Charles L. & Koza, Russell C. Marketing Dynamics: Decision & Control. (Illus.). 144p. 1975. pap. text ed. 7.95 (ISBN 0-07-028960-3, C); instructors' manual 2.95 (ISBN 0-07-028961-1). McGraw.

James, Francisco, ed. Business Adventures Series. 1979. pap. 150.00 (ISBN 0-933836-03-1). Simtek.

Lieberman, Harvey & Rausch, Erwin. Managing & Allocating Time (Non-Industrial) (Simulation Game Ser.). 1976. pap. 24.90 (ISBN 0-89401-061-1); pap. 21.50 two or more (ISBN 0-686-57894-5). Didactic Syst.

Macoby, Michael. The Gamesman. 1978. pap. 2.75 (ISBN 0-553-11450-6). Bantam.

Miles & Randolph. The Organization Game--Participants Manual. new ed. LC 78-25699. (Illus.). 1979. pap. text ed. 10.95 (ISBN 0-685-66462-7); inst. manual free (ISBN 0-685-66463-5). Goodyear.

Moore, B. Australian Management Games. LC 78-54876. 1979. text ed. 27.95 (ISBN 0-909465-74-6, 5028). Bks Australia.

Patz, Alan. Strategic Decision Analysis: A Managerial Approach to Policy. 1981. text ed. 18.95 (ISBN 0-316-69400-2); tchrs'. manual free (ISBN 0-316-69401-0). Little.

Rausch, Erwin. Financial Analysis. (Simulation Game Ser.). 1972. pap. 24.90 (ISBN 0-89401-026-3); pap. 21.50 two or more (ISBN 0-685-78119-4). Didactic Syst.

Rausch, Erwin & Wohlking, Wallace. Handling Conflict in Management: Conflict Among Peers-Game 1. (Simulation Game Ser.). 1969. pap. 24.90 (ISBN 0-89401-035-2); pap. 24.90 portuguese ed. (ISBN 0-685-78109-7); pap. 21.50 two or more (ISBN 0-685-78110-0). Didactic Syst.

--Handling Conflict in Management: Superior - Subordinate Conflict Game 111. (Simulation Game Ser.). 1969. pap. 24.90 french ed. (ISBN 0-89401-098-0); pap. 21.50 ea. two or more french eds.; pap. 24.90 spanish ed. (ISBN 0-89401-041-7); pap. 24.90 portuguese ed. (ISBN 0-89401-042-5). Didactic Syst.

Rubin, Irwin M., et al. Task-Oriented Team Development. (Illus.). 1978. 50.00 (ISBN 0-07-054197-3, T&D); 3-ring binder 75.00 (ISBN 0-07-054196-5); facilitator manual 15.00 (ISBN 0-07-054197-3). McGraw.

See, Trude. Looking Good Is Feeling Good. (Simulation Game Ser.). 1975. pap. 24.90 (ISBN 0-89401-050-6); pap. 21.50 two or more (ISBN 0-685-78127-5). Didactic Syst.

Shubik, Martin. Games for Society, Business and War: Towards a Theory of Gaming. LC 74-21867. 380p. 1975. 18.95 (ISBN 0-444-41285-9). Elsevier.

Simtek Inc. International Business Games Directory. (Orig.). 1981. pap. 3.95 (ISBN 0-933836-15-5). Simtek.

Smith, W. Nye, et al. Integrated Simulation. 2nd ed. 1974. text ed. 3.95 (ISBN 0-538-07790-5). SW Pub.

Thorelli, Hans B. & Graves, R. L. International Operations Simulation. LC 64-16969. 1964. 17.00 (ISBN 0-02-932540-4). Free Pr.

MANAGEMENT INFORMATION SYSTEMS

Baldridge, J. Victor & Tierney, Michael L. New Approaches to Management: Creating Practical Systems of Management Information & Management by Objectives. LC 79-88105. (Higher Education Ser.). 1979. text ed. 14.95x (ISBN 0-87589-420-8). Jossey-Bass.

Blumenthal, Sherman S. Management Information Systems: A Framework for Planning & Development. 1969. ref. ed. 18.95 (ISBN 0-13-548636-X). P-H.

Bocchino, William A. Management Information Systems: Tools & Techniques. LC 73-38416. (Illus.). 384p. 1972. ref. ed. 19.95 (ISBN 0-13-548693-9). P-H.

Bowers, David G. & Franklin, Jerome L. Survey-Guided Development I: Data-Based Organizational Change. rev. ed. LC 77-154461. 146p. 1977. pap. 11.50 (ISBN 0-88390-137-4). Univ Assocs.

Brightman, Richard W., et al. Data Processing for Decision Making. 2nd ed. 1971. 15.95 (ISBN 0-02-314970-1, 31497). Macmillan.

Buzzell, R. D., et al. Marketing Research & Information Systems: Text & Cases. 1969. text ed. 19.95 (ISBN 0-07-009475-6, C); instructor's manual 4.95 (ISBN 0-07-009476-4). tapes 325.00 (ISBN 0-07-097280-X). McGraw.

Caruth, Donald L. & Rachel, Frank M., eds. Business Systems: Articles, Analyses, & Cases. LC 70-172163. (Orig.). 1972. pap. text ed. 12.50 scp (ISBN 0-06-453703-X, HarpC); scp student guide 8.50 (ISBN 0-06-453706-4). Har-Row.

Chang, S. K. & Fu, K. S., eds. Pictorial Information Systems. (Lecture Notes in Computer Science: Vol. 80). 441p. 1980. pap. 24.50 (ISBN 0-387-09757-0). Springer-Verlag.

Christie, Bruce. Face to File Communication: A Psychological Approach to Information Systems. 1981. price not set (ISBN 0-471-27939-0, Pub. by Wiley-Interscience). Wiley.

Churchill, Neil C., et al. Computer-Based Information Systems for Management. 5.95 (ISBN 0-686-09781-5, 6947). Natl Assn Accts.

Churchman, C. West, et al, eds. Systems & Management Annual 1975. 1975. 24.95x (ISBN 0-442-80318-4). Van Nos Reinhold.

Dare, Gillian A. & Bakewell, K. G. The Manager's Guide to Getting the Answers. 69p. 1981. pap. text ed. 4.50x (ISBN 0-85365-843-9, Pub. by Lib Assn England). Oryx Pr.

Davis, Gordon B. Management Information Systems: Conceptual Foundations, Structure & Development. (Illus.). 480p. 1974. text ed. 20.95 (ISBN 0-07-015827-4, C); instructor's manual 4.95 (ISBN 0-07-015831-2). McGraw.

Dock, V. Thomas, et al, eds. MIS: A Managerial Perspective. LC 77-7063. 1977. pap. text ed. 12.95 (ISBN 0-574-21050-4, 13-4050). SRA.

Donald, A. G. Management, Information & Systems. 2nd ed. 1979. text ed. 37.00 (ISBN 0-08-021271-9); pap. text ed. 13.25 (ISBN 0-08-021270-0). Pergamon.

Donaldson, H., et al. Computer by the Tail: A User's Guide to Computer Management. 1976. text ed. 25.00x (ISBN 0-04-658220-7). Allen Unwin.

Ein-Dor, Phillip & Segev, Eli. A Paradigm for Management Information Systems. 232p. 1980. 27.50 (ISBN 0-03-058017-X). Praeger.

Elliot, C. Orville & Wasley, Robert S. Business Information Processing System. 4th ed. 1975. 19.95x (ISBN 0-256-01579-1). Irwin.

Enger, Norman L. Management Standards for Developing Information Systems. new ed. LC 76-41827. (Illus.). 1977. 15.95 (ISBN 0-8144-5425-9). Am Mgmt.

Fahey, Robert J., et al. Computers, Science & Management Dynamics. LC 72-102175. 1969. 11.25 (ISBN 0-910586-38-1). Finan Exec.

Federico, Pat A., et al. Management Information Systems & Organizational Behavior. Brun, Kim & McCalla, Douglas B., eds. LC 80-15174. 204p. 1980. 20.95 (ISBN 0-03-057021-2). Praeger.

Forkner, Irvine H. Computerized Business Systems: An Introduction to Data Processing. LC 73-19. 501p. 1973. text ed. 22.95 (ISBN 0-471-26620-5). Wiley.

Franklin, Jerome L., et al. Survey-Guided Development III: A Manual for Concepts Training. rev. ed. LC 77-75523. 118p. 1977. pap. 11.50 (ISBN 0-88390-139-0). Univ Assocs.

Harrison, William. Management Information Systems: An Introduction for CETA Personnel. (Papers in Manpower Studies & Education: No. 2). 1975. 2.00 (ISBN 0-87071-328-0). Oreg St U Pr.

Hausser, Doris L., et al. Survey-Guided Development II: A Manual for Consultants. rev. ed. LC 77-154460. 162p. 1977. pap. 11.50 (ISBN 0-88390-138-2). Univ Assocs.

Hobsley, M. Arbeitsdiagnose - Neve Wege der Chirurgischen Diagnose und Therapie. Seemann, Caroline, tr. from Eng. Orig. Title: Pathways in Surgical Management. 480p. (Ger.). 1981. pap. 58.75 (ISBN 3-8055-0747-X). S Karger.

Hodson, Bernard A. Modern Data Processing for Management: A Basic Systems Approach. LC 71-80541. 1973. 16.95 (ISBN 0-8436-0728-9). CBI Pub.

Hopeman, Richard. Systems Analysis & Operations Management. LC 69-19269. 1969. text ed. 15.95 (ISBN 0-675-09514-X). Merrill.

House, William C., Jr. Interactive Decision Oriented Data Base Systems. 1977. 21.95x (ISBN 0-442-80339-7). Van Nos Reinhold.

Industrial Relations Counselors Symposium, 1965. Computer Technology: Concepts for Management. pap. 3.50 (ISBN 0-87330-015-7). Indus Rel.

Jackson, Barbara B. Computer Models in Management. 1979. 20.95x (ISBN 0-256-02225-9). Irwin.

Johnson, Charles B. & Katzenmeyer, William G. Management Information Systems in Higher Education: The State of the Art. LC 74-109171. 1969. 14.75 (ISBN 0-8223-0233-0); pap. 7.75 (ISBN 0-686-66406-X). Duke.

Johnson, Margaret H. & Quible, Zane K. Introduction to Word Processing. (Illus.). 1980. text ed. 16.95 (ISBN 0-87626-446-1). Winthrop.

Jones, G. T. Data Capture in the Retail Environment. (Illus.). 1977. pap. 29.00x (ISBN 0-85012-168-X). Intl Pubns Serv.

Katzan, Harry, Jr. Multinational Computer Systems: An Introduction to Transnational Data Flow & Data Regulation. (Van Nostrand Reinhold International Series on Data Communications & Networks). 224p. 1980. text ed. 16.95 (ISBN 0-442-21573-8). Van Nos Reinhold.

Kelly, Joseph F. Computerized Management Information Systems. (Illus.). 1970. text ed. 18.95 (ISBN 0-02-362240-7). Macmillan.

Kirk, Francis G. Total System Development for Information Systems. LC 73-4359. (Business Data Processing: A Wiley Ser.). 284p. 1973. 32.95 (ISBN 0-471-48260-9, Pub. by Wiley-Interscience). Wiley.

Krauss, Leonard I. Computer-Based Management Information Systems. LC 73-119382. 1970. 21.95 (ISBN 0-8144-5223-X). Am Mgmt.

Li, David H. Design & Management of Information Systems. LC 72-75327. (Illus.). 312p. 1972. pap. text ed. 10.50 (ISBN 0-574-16134-1, 13-1570). SRA.

Llewellyn, Robert W. Information Systems. LC 75-40223. (Illus.). 368p. 1976. 17.95x (ISBN 0-13-464487-5). P-H.

Lucas, Henry & Gibson, Cyrusf. Casebook for Management Information Systems. 2nd ed. (Management Information Systems Ser.). (Illus.). 480p. 1980. pap. text ed. 10.95 (ISBN 0-07-038939-X, C); instructor's guide avail. (ISBN 0-07-038941-1). McGraw.

Lucas, Henry C. Computer-Based Information Systems in Organizations. LC 72-92561. (Illus.). 292p. 1973. text ed. 17.95 (ISBN 0-574-18590-9, 13-1590); instr's guide avail. (ISBN 0-574-18591-7, 13-1591). SRA.

--Toward Creative Systems Design. LC 74-4129. 147p. 1974. text ed. 15.00x (ISBN 0-231-03791-0). Columbia U Pr.

Lucas, Henry C., Jr. Why Information Systems Fail. LC 74-18395. 130p. 1975. 12.50x (ISBN 0-231-03792-9). Columbia U Pr.

McCosh, Andrew, et al. Developing Managerial Information Systems. 1980. 29.95x (ISBN 0-470-26913-8). Halsted Pr.

McLean, Ephraim R. & Soden, John V. Strategic Planning for MIS. LC 77-58483. 1977. 34.95 (ISBN 0-471-58562-9, Pub. by Wiley-Interscience). Wiley.

Martino, R. L. Information Management: The Dynamics of MIS. 1970. 19.95 (ISBN 0-07-040651-0, P&RB). McGraw.

Matthews, Don Q. The Design of the Management Information System. rev. ed. 221p. 1976. 13.95x (ISBN 0-442-80320-6). Van Nos Reinhold.

Morton, Michael S. Management Decision Systems: Computer-Based Support for Decision Making. LC 72-132152. (Illus.). 1971. 10.00x (ISBN 0-87584-090-6). Harvard Busn.

Murdick, Robert C. & Ross, Joel E. Introduction to Management Information Systems. (Illus.). 1977. 19.95 (ISBN 0-13-486233-3). P-H.

Murdick, Robert G. & Ross, Joel E. Information Systems for Modern Management. 2nd ed. (Illus.). 640p. 1975. ref. ed. 22.95 (ISBN 0-13-464602-9). P-H.

--M. I. S. in Action. 724p. 1975. pap. text ed. 15.50 (ISBN 0-8299-0031-4). West Pub.

--Mis: A Guide to Understanding. 1975. pap. 2.95 (ISBN 0-913878-06-5). T Horton & Dghts.

Paulson, R. Lee. The Computer Challenge in Retailing. LC 73-83984. (Illus.). 224p. 1978. 14.95 (ISBN 0-912016-32-9). Lebhar Friedman.

Payne, Eugene E., et al. The Scope of Management Information Systems. 1975. pap. text ed. 10.00 (ISBN 0-89806-014-1, 45). Am Inst Indus Eng.

Peart, Alan T. Design of Project Management Systems & Records. LC 71-185564. (Illus.). 1971. 16.95 (ISBN 0-8436-0719-X). CBI Pub.

Philippakis, Andreas S. & Kazmier, Leonard J. Information Systems Through COBOL. 2nd ed. (Illus.). 1978. text ed. 18.95 (ISBN 0-07-049791-5, C); instructor's manual 4.95 (ISBN 0-07-049792-3). McGraw.

Putnam, Arnold O., et al. Unified Operations Management: A Practical Approach to a Management Information System. rev. ed. LC 63-1546. (Illus.). 1969. 10.95 (ISBN 0-89047-024-3). Herman Pub.

Radford, K. J. Information Systems in Management. LC 73-80911. 1973. 15.95 (ISBN 0-87909-352-8). Reston.

Rappaport, Alfred. Information for Decision-Making: Quantitative & Behavioral Dimensions. 2nd ed. (Illus.). 384p. 1975. ref. ed. 19.95 (ISBN 0-13-464388-7). P-H.

Riley, M. J., ed. Management Information Systems: Selected Readings. 2nd ed. 400p. 1981. pap. text ed. 14.50x (ISBN 0-8162-7190-9). Holden-Day.

Rullo, Thomas A. The Manager's Standard Manual. LC 77-10033. (Illus.). 1977. text ed. 12.00 (ISBN 0-89433-000-4); pap. text ed. 10.00 (ISBN 0-89433-018-7). Petrocelli.

Sanders, Donald H. Computers & Management in a Changing Society. 2nd ed. (Illus.). 624p. 1974. pap. text ed. 11.95 (ISBN 0-07-054620-7, C). McGraw.

Senn, James A. Information Systems in Management. 1978. text ed. 24.95x (ISBN 0-534-00563-2). Wadsworth Pub.

Siegel, Paul. Strategic Planning of Management Information Systems. 1975. 19.95x (ISBN 0-442-80278-1). Van Nos Reinhold.

Sollenberger, Harold. Major Changes Caused by the Implementation of a Management Information System. 5.95 (ISBN 0-686-09783-1, 6845). Natl Assn Accts.

Sollenberger, Harold M. Management Control of Information Systems Development. 9.95 (ISBN 0-686-09778-5, 7150). Natl Assn Accts.

Stout, Russell, Jr. Organizations, Management, & Control: An Annotated Bibliography. LC 79-3639. 208p. 1980. 15.00x (ISBN 0-253-14448-5). Ind U Pr.

Taggart. Informations Systems: An Introduction to Computers in Organizations. 608p. 1980. text ed. 20.95 (ISBN 0-205-06908-8, 2069083). Allyn.

Taraboi, V. Organization, Functioning & Activities of National Documentary Information Systems in the Scientific, Technical & Economic Fields. LC 67-1784. 88p. 1973. pap. text ed. 35.00 (ISBN 0-08-017725-5). Pergamon.

Teglovic, Steve & Lynch, Robert, eds. Topics in Management Information Systems. LC 73-3315. 295p. 1973. text ed. 29.50x (ISBN 0-8422-5092-1); pap. text ed. 8.50x (ISBN 0-8422-0277-3). Irvington.

Thierauf, Robert J. Distributed Processing Systems. (Illus.). 1978. 23.95 (ISBN 0-13-216507-4). P-H.

--Systems Analysis & Design of Real-Time Management Information Systems. LC 74-28368. (Illus.). 624p. 1975. ref. ed. 22.95 (ISBN 0-13-881219-5). P-H.

Tou, Julius T., ed. Information Systems (COINS IV) LC 74-4403. (Illus.). 506p. 1974. 42.50 (ISBN 0-306-35134-X, Plenum Pr). Plenum Pub.

Tricker, R. I. Management Information & Control Systems. 1975. 61.50 (ISBN 0-471-88855-9). Wiley.

Verzijl, J. J. Production Planning & Information Systems. LC 76-7906. 1976. 32.95 (ISBN 0-470-90620-0). Halsted Pr.

WAMEX Scientific & Management Regional Committee, 2nd Session. Report, No. 33. (GARP Special Report Ser.). 66p. 1980. pap. 25.00 (ISBN 0-686-60084-3, W436, WMO). Unipub.

Westin, Alan F., ed. Information Technology in a Democracy. LC 72-143233. (Studies in Technology & Society). 1971. 20.00x (ISBN 0-674-45435-9). Harvard U Pr.

MANAGEMENT MARKETING

see Marketing Management

MANAGEMENT OF FACTORIES

see Factory Management

MANAGERIAL ACCOUNTING

see also Cost Accounting

Anderson, Donald L. & Raun, Donald L. Information Analysis in Management Accounting. LC 77-14938. (Wiley Ser. in Accounting & Information Systems). 706p. 1978. pap. text ed. 27.50 (ISBN 0-471-02815-0). Wiley.

Anthony. Plaid for Management Accounting. 3rd ed. Date not set. price not set (ISBN 0-256-02235-6, 01-0814-03). Learning Syst.

Anthony, Robert N. Plaid for Management Accounting. 1974. pap. 5.50 (ISBN 0-256-01277-6, 01-0814-00). Learning Syst.

Anthony, Robert N. & Reece, James S. Accounting Principles. 4th ed. 1979. 19.50x (ISBN 0-256-02147-3). Irwin.

Anthony, Robert N. & Welsch, Glenn A. Fundamentals of Management Accounting. 3rd ed. 1981. 21.95x (ISBN 0-256-02454-5); practice set 5.95x (ISBN 0-256-01610-0); study guide 6.50x (ISBN 0-256-02455-3). Irwin.

Anton, Hector R., et al. Contemporary Issues in Cost & Managerial Accounting: A Discipline in Transition. 3rd ed. LC 77-74383. (Illus.). 1977. text ed. 18.95 (ISBN 0-395-25435-3). HM.

Bailes, Jack C. Management Budgeting for CETA. (Papers in Manpower Studies & Education: No. 1). 1975. 2.00 (ISBN 0-87071-327-2). Oreg St U Pr.

Baron, Paul B. When the Company Is for Sale. LC 80-66938. 396p. 1980. three ring binder 85.00 (ISBN 0-936936-50-9). Ctr Busn Info.

Batty, J., ed. Cost & Management Accountancy for Students. 2nd ed. 1970. pap. text ed. 15.95x (ISBN 0-434-90112-1). Intl Ideas.

Belkaoui, Ahmed. Conceptual Foundations of Management Accounting. LC 80-16086. (A-W Paperback Series in Accounting). 125p. 1980. pap. 6.50 (ISBN 0-201-00097-0). A-W.

Black, Homer A. & Edwards, James D., eds. The Managerial & Cost Accountant's Handbook. LC 78-61201. 1979. 37.50 (ISBN 0-87094-173-9). Dow Jones-Irwin.

Brockington, R. B. Financial Management. 1980. 20.00x (ISBN 0-905435-07-9, Pub. by DP Pubns). State Mutual Bk.

Brown, J. Lewis. Principles & Practice of Management Accountancy. 3rd ed. 756p. 1975. 15.00x (ISBN 0-7121-1654-0). Intl Pubns Serv.

Caplan, E. H. Management Accounting & Behavioral Science. 2nd ed. 1981. pap. 6.50 (ISBN 0-201-00952-8). A-W.

Cashin, James & Polimeni, Ralph S. Cost Accounting. 1981. write for info. oHT's (ISBN 0-07-010213-9, C); write for info. instrs.' manual (ISBN 0-07-010214-7); study guide 5.95 (ISBN 0-07-010257-0); write for info. (ISBN 0-07-075018-1); job order costing practice set 6.95 (ISBN 0-07-010258-9); process costing practice set 6.95 (ISBN 0-07-010259-7); exam questions avail. (ISBN 0-07-010215-5). McGraw.

Chakraborty, S. K. New Perspectives in Management Accounting. 1979. 9.50x (ISBN 0-8364-0374-6). South Asia Bks.

Chenhall, Robert H., et al. The Organizational Context of Management Accounting. 398p. (Orig.). 1981. pap. text ed. 15.95 (ISBN 0-273-01644-X). Pitman Pub MA.

Copeland, Ronald M. & Dascher, Paul E. Managerial Accounting: An Introduction to Planning, Information Processing & Control. 2nd ed. LC 74-5147. 658p. 1978. text ed. 23.95 (ISBN 0-471-17171-9); study guide 7.95 (ISBN 0-471-02346-9). Wiley.

Cowan, T. K. Management Accounting: Objectives Systems Analysis of Relevant Costs. 554p. 1971. 26.00x (ISBN 0-457-01040-1). Intl Pubns Serv.

Davidson, et al. Managerial Accounting. 1978. 21.95 (ISBN 0-03-017416-3). Dryden Pr.

Decoster, D. T., et al. Accounting for Managerial Decision Making. 2nd ed. LC 77-15785. (Accounting & Information Systems Ser.). 1978. pap. text ed. 16.50 (ISBN 0-471-02204-7). Wiley.

Demski, Joel S. Information Analysis. 2nd ed. LC 80-15971. (A-W Paperback Series in Accounting). 200p. 1980. pap. text ed. 6.50 (ISBN 0-201-01231-6). A-W.

De Paula, F. Clive. Management Accounting in Practice. 4th ed. 1972. 15.95x (ISBN 0-8464-0587-3); pap. 11.50x (ISBN 0-686-77031-5). Beekman Pubs.

Drebin. Managerial Accounting. 3rd ed. 1978. 20.95 (ISBN 0-7216-3188-6). Dryden Pr.

Flesher, Dale L. & Flesher, Tonya K. Accounting for the Middle Manager. 462p. 1980. 16.95 (ISBN 0-442-23875-4). Van Nos Reinhold.

Flesher, Tonya K. & Flesher, Dale L. Accounting Principles for Midmanagement. LC 78-62620. (Accounting Ser.). 464p. 1980. text ed. 13.80 (ISBN 0-8273-1628-3); instructor's guide 3.00 (ISBN 0-8273-1629-1). Delmar.

Foley, Bernard & Maunders, Keith. Accounting Information Disclosure & Collective Bargaining. LC 78-31148. 1979. text ed. 36.00x (ISBN 0-8419-0481-2). Holmes & Meier.

Francia, Arthur J. & Strawser, Robert H. Managerial Accounting. 3rd ed. (Illus.). 565p. 1980. pap. text ed. 18.95 (ISBN 0-931920-20-5); practice problems 4.95x (ISBN 0-686-70444-4); study guide 5.95x (ISBN 0-686-70445-2); work papers 6.95x (ISBN 0-686-70446-0). Dame Pubns.

Frederiksen, Christian P. Money Management for Results: Accounting & Budgeting for Nonprofit Agencies. LC 79-89135. 1979. 57.50 (ISBN 0-916664-12-0). Public Management.

Garrison, Ray H. Managerial Accounting: Concepts for Planning, Control, Decision Making. rev. ed. 1979. 18.95x (ISBN 0-256-02209-7); study guide 5.95x (ISBN 0-256-02249-6). Business Pubns.

Geller, Louis & Shim, Jae K. Readings in Cost & Managerial Accounting. 448p. 1980. pap. text ed. 10.95 (ISBN 0-8403-2266-6). Kendall-Hunt.

Gibbs, John & McGee, Robert W. Let Accounting Help You Manage: A Managerial Accounting Primer. 272p. 1981. 17.95 (ISBN 0-13-531319-8); pap. 8.95 (ISBN 0-13-531301-5). P-H.

Goff, Walter. Management Accounting for Managers: Practical Management Ser. LC 76-353519. 1975. pap. 10.50x (ISBN 0-7121-1369-X). Intl Pubns Serv.

Goldschmidt, Yaaqov. Information for Management Decisions: A System for Economics, Analysis & Accounting Procedures. (Illus.). 329p. 1970. 27.50x (ISBN 0-8014-0541-6). Cornell U Pr.

Goosen, Kenneth R. Introduction to Managerial Accounting: A Business Game. 1976. pap. text ed. 12.95x (ISBN 0-673-15300-2). Scott F.

Gray, Jack C. & Johnston, Kenneth S. Accounting & Management Action. 2nd ed. (Illus.). 1977. text ed. 18.50 (ISBN 0-07-024216-X, C); wkbk avail. (ISBN 0-07-024212-7); instr's manual avail. (ISBN 0-07-024217-8). McGraw.

Grimsley, Bob. Management Accounting Systems & Records. 1972. 14.95x (ISBN 0-8464-0588-1). Beekman Pubs.

Hartley, W. C. An Introduction to Business Accounting for Managers. 3rd ed. 1980. 28.00 (ISBN 0-08-024061-5); pap. 12.00 (ISBN 0-08-024062-3). Pergamon.

Heitger, Lester E. & Matulich, Serge. Managerial Accounting. 1980. text ed. 18.95 (ISBN 0-07-027941-1); study guide 6.95 (ISBN 0-07-027942-X); job costing packet (ISBN 0-07-027943-8); profit planning packet (ISBN 0-07-027946-2); solutions manual 25.00 (ISBN 0-07-027944-6); examination questions 15.00 (ISBN 0-07-027945-4); overhead transparencies 325.00 (ISBN 0-07-074792-X). McGraw.

Henke, Emmerson O., et al. Managerial Use of Accounting Data. 291p. 1978. 15.00 (ISBN 0-87201-001-5); wkbk. 6.95x (ISBN 0-87201-003-1). Gulf Pub.

Horngren, Charles T. Introduction to Management Accounting. 5th ed. (Ser. in Accounting). (Illus.). 848p. 1981. text ed. 21.00 (ISBN 0-13-487652-0); wkbk. by Dudley W. Curry 8.95 (ISBN 0-13-487785-3). P-H.

Houlton, M. L. Introduction to Cost & Management Accounting. LC 73-331289. (Illus.). 261p. 1973. 13.00x (ISBN 0-434-90770-7). Intl Pubns Serv.

Howe, Richard L. Managerial Accounting: An Introduction, Study Guide. 3rd ed. 1978. pap. text ed. 6.95 (ISBN 0-7216-4792-8). HR&W.

Johnson, Thomas H. System & Profits: Early Management Accounting at Dupont & General Motors. original anthology ed. Brief, Richard P., ed. LC 80-1458. (Dimensions of Accounting Theory & Practice Ser.). 1981. lib. bdg. 25.00x (ISBN 0-405-13481-9). Arno.

Keith, Lyman. Accounting: A Management Perspective. (Illus.). 1980. text ed. 19.95 (ISBN 0-13-001214-9). P-H.

Korn, S. Winton & Boyd, Thomas. Managerial Accounting: A Short Course for Non-Financial Managers. LC 74-31816. (Business Administration Ser). 295p. 1975. text ed. 45.95 (ISBN 0-471-50390-8). Wiley.

Louderback, Joseph G., 3rd & Dominiak, Geraldine F. Managerial Accounting. 2nd ed. 1978. text ed. 21.95x (ISBN 0-534-00556-X); study guide 6.95x (ISBN 0-534-00603-5). Wadsworth Pub.

Lucking, Richard C. Mathematics for Management. LC 80-40127. 1980. 52.00 (ISBN 0-471-27779-7, Pub. by Wiley-Interscience); pap. write for info. (ISBN 0-471-27781-9). Wiley.

Luoma, Gary A. Accounting Information in Managerial Decision-Making for Small & Medium Manufacturers. 3.95 (ISBN 0-686-09786-6, 6742). Natl Assn Accts.

McFarland, Walter B. Concepts for Management Accounting. 5.95 (ISBN 0-686-09788-2, 6640). Natl Assn Accts.

McKinsey, James O. Managerial Accounting. Chandler, Alfred D., ed. LC 79-7551. (History of Management Thought & Practice Ser.). 1980. Repr. of 1924 ed. lib. bdg. 48.00x (ISBN 0-405-12335-3). Arno.

Madden, Donald L. Management Accounting. LC 80-17277. (Self Teaching Guides Ser.). 326p. 1980. 8.95 (ISBN 0-471-03135-6, Pub. by Wiley-Interscience). Wiley.

Management Accounting, Vols. 1-40. Orig. Title: Cost Accountant. 1921-62. Repr. Set. lib. bdg. 1042.00x (ISBN 0-8371-9196-3, CAP2). Greenwood.

Management Accounting Problems in Foreign Operations. 3.95 (ISBN 0-686-09804-8, 6024). Natl Assn Accts.

Management Institute Staff. Bookkeeping for Nonprofit Organizations. LC 79-90010. 1979. 42.50 (ISBN 0-916664-14-7). Public Management.

May, Robert, et al. A Brief Introduction to Managerial & Social Uses of Accounting. 1975. pap. text ed. 9.95 (ISBN 0-13-082008-3). P-H.

Moore, Carl L. & Jaedicke, Robert J. Managerial Accounting. 3rd ed. 1972. text ed. 13.50 (ISBN 0-538-01920-4). SW Pub.

Mustafi, Chandan Kumar. Statistical Methods in Managerial Decisions. 1981. 24.00x (ISBN 0-8364-0722-9, Pub. by Macmillan India). South Asia Bks.

Nelson & Miller. Modern Management Accounting. 2nd ed. 640p. 1981. 23.95 (ISBN 0-8302-5904-X). Goodyear.

Newton, Grant W. Certificate in Management Accounting Review, 6 vols. 1979. pap. text ed. 94.50 scp package set (ISBN 0-06-453735-8, HarpC). Har-Row.

--CMA, 6 vols. Incl. Vol. 1. Economics & Business. 177p. pap. text ed. 18.50 scp (ISBN 0-06-453723-4); Vol. 2. Organization & Behavior, Including Ethical Considerations. 123p. pap. text ed. 14.50 scp (ISBN 0-06-453729-3); Vol. 3. Public Reporting Standards & Auditing. 201p. pap. text ed. 18.95 scp (ISBN 0-06-453730-7); Vol. 4. Periodic Reporting for Internal & External Purposes. 260p. pap. text ed. 18.95 scp (ISBN 0-06-453731-5); Vol. 5. Decision Analysis, Including Modeling & Information Systems. 246p. pap. text ed. 18.50 scp (ISBN 0-06-453732-3); Vol. 6. Taxes Current Pronouncements, & Updated CMA Questions. 1980. pap. text ed. 18.95 scp (ISBN 0-06-453742-0). pap. (HarpC). Har-Row.

O'Connor, Dennis J. & Bueso, Alberto T. Managerial Finance: Theory & Techniques. (Illus.). 528p. 1981. text ed. 21.00 (ISBN 0-13-550269-1); pap. 9.95 study guide (ISBN 0-13-550293-4). P-H.

Rayburn, L. Gayle. Principles of Cost Accounting with Managerial Implications. 1979. 20.95x (ISBN 0-256-02144-9). Irwin.

Reekie, W. Duncan. Managerial Economics. 440p. 1975. 45.00x (ISBN 0-86003-007-5, Pub. by Allan Pubs England); pap. 22.50x (ISBN 0-86003-108-X). State Mutual Bk.

Rogers, David C. Accounting for Managers: The Non-Accountant's Guide to the Language of Business. 136p. 1971. 17.50x (ISBN 0-85227-003-8). Intl Pubns Serv.

Rotch, William, et al. The Executive's Guide to Management Accounting & Control Systems, Vol. 1. LC 78-67168. (Illus.). 169p. 1978. text ed. 16.95x (ISBN 0-931920-06-X). Dame Pubns.

Schattke, Rudolph W., et al. Managerial Accounting: Concepts & Uses. 2nd ed. 656p. 1981. text ed. 22.95 (ISBN 0-205-07319-0, 0573191); avail. tchrs guide (ISBN 0-205-06073-0); write for info. study guide (ISBN 0-205-07322-0). Allyn.

Shank, John K. Contemporary Managerial Accounting: A Casebook. (Illus.). 352p. 1981. 14.95 (ISBN 0-13-170357-9). P-H.

Simpson, L. Management Accounting: Techniques for Non-Financial Mangers. 246p. 1979. pap. 12.25x (ISBN 0-220-67023-4, Pub. by Busn Bks England). Renouf.

Sinn, Gerald R. Cash Operations Management: Profit from Within. 1980. 19.00 (ISBN 0-89433-116-7). Petrocelli.

Staples, Frederick. Management Accounting Fundamentals. LC 76-23725. 229p. 1976. 9.85 (ISBN 0-915026-21-X). Counting Hse.

Still, Jack W. A Guide to Managerial Accounting in Small Companies. Bruchey, Stuart & Carosso, Vincent P., eds. LC 78-18978. (Small Business Enterprise in America Ser.). (Illus.). 1979. Repr. of 1969 ed. lib. bdg. 18.00x (ISBN 0-405-11480-X). Arno.

Thacker, Ronald & Ellis, Loudell. Student Guide to Management Accounting: Concepts & Applications. 336p. 1980. pap. text ed. 8.95 (ISBN 0-8359-4196-5). Reston.

Thacker, Ronald J. & Smith, Richard L. Modern Management Accounting. (Illus.). 1977. 16.95 (ISBN 0-87909-504-0); student guide 6.50 (ISBN 0-87909-503-2); instrs'. manual avail. Reston.

Thornton, Norman. Management Accounting. 1978. pap. text ed. 21.00x (ISBN 0-434-91960-8). Intl Ideas.

Tracy, John A. Fundamentals of Management Accounting. LC 75-26988. 565p. 1976. text ed. 23.95 (ISBN 0-471-88151-1, Pub. by Wiley-Hamilton). Wiley.

Van Dam, Cees. Trends in Managerial & Financial Accounting: Income Determining & Financial Reporting. (Nijenrode Studies in Business: Vol. 1). 1978. lib. bdg. 22.00 (ISBN 90-207-0693-4, Pub. by Martinus Nijhoff Netherlands). Kluwer Boston.

Weston, J. Fred & Brigham, Eugene F. Managerial Finance. 7th ed. LC 80-65811. 1088p. 1981. text ed. 23.95 (ISBN 0-03-058186-9). Dryden Pr.

Wood, E. G. Costing Matters for Managers. 1977. Repr. 21.00x (ISBN 0-8464-0294-7). Beekman Pubs.

Wright, Wilmer. Management Accounting Simplified. (Illus.). 1979. 14.95 (ISBN 0-07-072080-0). McGraw.

MANAGERIAL ECONOMICS

Baron, Paul B. When the Company Is for Sale. LC 80-66938. 396p. 1980. three ring binder 85.00 (ISBN 0-936936-50-9). Ctr Busn Info.

Bell, Colin E. Quantitative Methods for Administration. 1977. 20.50x (ISBN 0-256-01875-8). Irwin.

Blair, R. D. & Kenny, L. W. Microeconomics for Managerial Decision Making. 1981. price not set (ISBN 0-07-005800-8); price not set instr's. manual (ISBN 0-07-005801-6). McGraw.

Bolten, Steven E. Managerial Finance: Principles & Practice. LC 75-31036. (Illus.). 896p. 1976. text ed. 20.95 (ISBN 0-395-20462-3); instr's. manual 2.00 (ISBN 0-395-20461-5). HM.

Bridge, J. & Dodds, J. C. Managerial Decision Making. LC 75-18977. 309p. 1975. 17.95 (ISBN 0-470-10365-5). Halsted Pr.

Brown, James K. This Business of Issues: Coping with the Company's Environments. LC 79-87756. (Report Ser.: No. 758). (Illus.). 1979. pap. 30.00 (ISBN 0-8237-0194-8). Conference Bd.

Bueso, Alberto T. & O'Connor, Dennis J. A Self-Correcting Approach to Managerial Finance: A Theory & Techniques. (Illus.). 320p. 1981. pap. text ed. 11.95 (ISBN 0-13-803189-4). P-H.

Business Borrowers Complete Success Kit, 7 bks. 1978. 99.50 (ISBN 0-685-83455-7). Intl Wealth.

Business Capital Sources. 1978. 15.00 (ISBN 0-685-83438-7). Intl Wealth.

Carrol, Frieda. Survival Handbook for Small Business. LC 80-70496. 73p. 1981. 16.95 (ISBN 0-9605246-4-9); pap. 12.95 (ISBN 0-9605246-4-9). Biblio Pr GA.

Casebier, Eleanor. Managerial Statistics. LC 77-70316. 1977. pap. text ed. 7.95x (ISBN 0-8134-1946-8, 1946). Interstate.

Christenson, Charles J., et al. Managerial Economics: Text & Cases. rev ed. 1973. 19.95x (ISBN 0-256-00089-1). Irwin.

Coates, C. Robert. The Demand for Money by Firms. (Business Economics & Finance Ser.: Vol. 7). 1976. 26.50 (ISBN 0-8247-6327-0). Dekker.

Colberg, Marshall R., et al. Business Economics: Principles & Cases. 6th ed. 1980. 19.50x (ISBN 0-256-02155-4). Irwin.

Coyne, Thomas J. Readings in Managerial Economics. 3rd ed. 1981. pap. 9.95x (ISBN 0-256-02422-7). Business Pubns.

Coyne, Thomas J., et al. Readings in Managerial Economics. rev. ed. 1977. pap. 9.95x (ISBN 0-256-01904-5). Business Pubns.

Curwen, Peter J. Managerial Economics. 249p. 1974. 26.00x (ISBN 0-8448-0372-3). Crane-Russak Co.

Deiner, Royce. How to Finance a Growing Business. 414p. 1974. 14.95x (ISBN 0-8464-1108-3). Beekman Pubs.

Delbecq, Andre & Filley, Alan. Program & Project Management in a Matrix Organization: A Case Study. (Wisconsin Business Monographs: No. 9). (Orig.). 1974. pap. 5.00 (ISBN 0-86603-001-8). Bureau Busn Res U Wis.

Douglas, Evan J. Managerial Economics: Theory, Practice & Problems. (Illus.). 1979. ref. ed. 21.95 (ISBN 0-13-550236-5). P-H.

Dwivedi, D. N. Managerial Economics. 1980. text ed. 20.00x (ISBN 0-7069-0794-9, Pub. by Vikas India). Advent NY.

Economic Information Systems, ed. Congressional District Business Patterns, 1981, 2 vols. LC 81-66161. 1981. Set. 125.00 (ISBN 0-86692-014-5). Vol. 1 (ISBN 0-86692-012-9). Vol. 2 (ISBN 0-86692-013-7). Econ Info Syst.

--The Second Fifteen Hundred Companies, 1981. LC 81-65901. 325p. 1981. 100.00 (ISBN 0-86692-009-9). Econ Info Syst.

--The Top Fifteen Hundred Companies, 1981. LC 81-65902. 350p. 1981. 100.00 (ISBN 0-86692-008-0). Econ Info Syst.

--The Top Fifteen Hundred Private Companies, 1981. LC 81-65900. 350p. 1981. 100.00 (ISBN 0-86692-010-2). Econ Info Syst.

--Zip Code Business Patterns, 1981. LC 81-65903. 546p. 1981. 125.00 (ISBN 0-86692-011-0). Econ Info Syst.

Eliasson, Gunnar. Business Economic Planning: Theory, Practice & Comparison. LC 76-5895. 1977. 28.00 (ISBN 0-471-01813-9, Pub. by Wiley-Interscience). Wiley.

Elton, E. J. & Gruber, M. J., eds. Portfolio Theory: Twenty Five Years After. (TIMS Studies in the Management Sciences Ser.: Vol. 11). 1979. 29.50 (ISBN 0-444-85279-4, North Holland). Elsevier.

Executive Reports Corporation Editorial Staff. The Treasurer's Guide. 1976. 97.50 (ISBN 0-13-930503-3). Exec Reports.

Federal Financial Management. 1976. 16.00 (ISBN 0-685-58506-9). Am Inst CPA.

Friedland, Seymour. Principles of Financial Management: Corporate Finance, Investments & Macrofinance. 1978. text ed. 16.95 (ISBN 0-87626-710-X); tchrs. manual free (ISBN 0-87626-711-8). Winthrop.

Gitman, Lawrence J. Principles of Managerial Finance. 2nd ed. 1979. text ed. 22.95 scp (ISBN 0-06-042339-0, HarpC); instructor's manual avail. (ISBN 0-06-362356-0); scp study guide 8.95 (ISBN 0-06-042337-4). Har-Row.

Godfrey, A. I. Quantitative Methods for Managers. 1977. pap. text ed. 15.95x (ISBN 0-7131-3349-X). Intl Ideas.

Goff, Walter S. Finance for Managers. LC 76-35239. (Practical Management Ser.). 1975. pap. 8.50x (ISBN 0-7121-0620-0). Intl Pubns Serv.

Gonder, Peggy. Cutting Cost. 1977. pap. 8.00 (ISBN 0-87545-008-3). Natl Sch Pr.

Grossack, Irvin M. & Martin, David D. Managerial Economics: Microtheory & the Firm's Decisions. (Ser. in Economics). 1973. 17.95 (ISBN 0-316-32960-6). Little.

Hailstones, Thomas J. & Rothwell, John C. Introduction to Managerial Economics. (Illus.). 1979. ref. 19.95 (ISBN 0-13-486290-2). P-H.

Halpern, et al. Essentials of Canadian Managerial Finance. 1978. text ed. 16.95 (ISBN 0-03-920002-7, Pub by HR&W Canada); tchr's guide & student wkbk. with purchase of text free (ISBN 0-685-86067-1). HR&W.

Hemingway, G. S. Introduction to Business Finance. 1975. 19.95x (ISBN 0-434-90730-8); pap. 12.95x (ISBN 0-434-90731-6). Intl Ideas.

Henry, William R. & Haynes, Warren W. Managerial Economics: Analysis and Cases. 4th ed. 1978. 19.95x (ISBN 0-256-02079-5). Business Pubns.

Ibrahim, I., et al. Readings in Managerial Economics. LC 75-4618. 1976. text ed. 41.00 (ISBN 0-08-019605-5); pap. text ed. 18.00 (ISBN 0-08-019604-7). Pergamon.

Kellar, Elizabeth K., ed. Managing with Less. LC 79-26163. 1979. pap. 12.00 (ISBN 0-87326-995-0). Intl City Mgt.

Kroncke, Charles, et al. Managerial Finance: Essentials. 2nd ed. (Illus.). 1978. text ed. 20.95 (ISBN 0-8299-0159-0); study guide 6.95 (ISBN 0-8299-0161-2); instrs.' manual avail. (ISBN 0-8299-0550-2). West Pub.

Kuniansky, Harry R. & Marsh, William H. New Cases in Managerial Finance. 2nd ed. 1979. pap. text ed. 10.50 scp (ISBN 0-06-043819-3, HarpC); inst. manual free (ISBN 0-06-362357-9). Har-Row.

Loasby, B. J. Choice, Complexity & Ignorance. LC 75-22558. 1976. 38.50 (ISBN 0-521-21065-8). Cambridge U Pr.

Lowes, Bryan. Modern Managerial Economics. LC 74-196298. 1974. 15.00x (ISBN 0-434-91150-X). Intl Pubns Serv.

McGuigan, James R. & Moyer, R. Charles. Managerial Economics. 2nd ed. 1979. text ed. 20.95 (ISBN 0-8299-0176-0); solutions manual avail. (ISBN 0-8299-0558-8); study guide 7.95 (ISBN 0-8299-0287-2); study guide 6.95 (ISBN 0-8299-0559-6). West Pub.

Mansfield, Edwin, ed. Managerial Economics & Operations Research. rev. ed. LC 70-95540. 1970. pap. text ed. 4.50x (ISBN 0-393-09919-9). Norton.

--Managerial Economics & Operations Research. 3rd ed. 1975. pap. 6.95x (ISBN 0-393-09297-6). Norton.

Maurice, S. Charles & Smithson, Charles W. Managerial Economics. 4th ed. 1981. 20.95x (ISBN 0-256-02495-2). Irwin.

Moyer, R. Charles, et al. Managerial Economics: Readings, Cases & Exercises. 1979. pap. text ed. 12.95 (ISBN 0-8299-0157-4); pap. text ed. solutions manual avail. (ISBN 0-8299-0632-0). West Pub.

National Association of Accounting Editorial Staff, ed. Management Reporting Under Inflation. 4.95 (ISBN 0-686-11625-9, 7580). Natl Assn Accts.

Pappas. Managerial Economics. 3rd ed. 1979. 22.95 (ISBN 0-03-045126-4). Dryden Pr.

Pappas, James L. & Brigham, Eugene F. Fundamentals of Managerial Economics. LC 79-51063. 560p. 1981. text ed. 22.95 (ISBN 0-03-040841-5). Dryden Pr.

Rousmaniere, Peter. The Public Money Managers Handbook. (Illus.). 320p. 1981. write for info. (ISBN 0-87251-064-6). Crain Bks.

Rowley, Charles K. Readings in Industrial Economics, 2 vols. LC 73-76642. 1973. Vol. 1. pap. 11.50x (ISBN 0-8448-0207-7); Vol. 2. pap. 11.50x (ISBN 0-8448-0208-5). Crane-Russak Co.

Seo, K. K. & Winger, Bernard J. Managerial Economics. 5th ed. 1979. 19.95x (ISBN 0-256-02177-5). Irwin.

Sharpe, William F. Introduction to Managerial Economics. LC 73-7950. 128p. 1973. 15.00x (ISBN 0-231-03693-0); pap. 6.00x (ISBN 0-231-03786-4). Columbia U Pr.

Sherman, Roger. The Economics of Industry. new ed. (Series in Economics). 1974. text ed. 15.95 (ISBN 0-316-78539-3). Little.

Simon, Julian. Applied Managerial Economics. (Illus.). 560p. 1975. ref. ed. 21.95 (ISBN 0-13-041194-9). P-H.

Steffy, Wilbert, et al. Financial Ratio Analysis: An Effective Management Tool. (Illus.). 100p. 1977. 12.00 (ISBN 0-686-72873-4, FRA). Indus Dev Inst Sci.

Taylor, George A. Managerial & Engineering Economy. 3rd ed. 1975. text ed. 19.95x (ISBN 0-442-24866-0); instructor's manual 2.00x (ISBN 0-442-25743-0). D Van Nostrand.

Theil, H. Statistical Decomposition Analysis. (Studies in Mathematical & Managerial Economics: Vol. 14). 1972. 34.25 (ISBN 0-444-10378-3, North-Holland). Elsevier.

Thompson, A. Economics of the Firm: Theory & Practice. 3rd ed. 1981. 21.95 (ISBN 0-13-231423-1). P-H.

Trower-Subira, George. Black Folks' Guide to Making Big Money in America. 184p. 1980. 11.00 (ISBN 0-9605304-0-1). VSBE.

Turner, P. H. Business Economics: A Comprehensive Course, 2 vols. 1974. Set. pap. text ed. 19.95x (ISBN 0-686-31745-9) (ISBN 0-245-52375-8). Vol. 1 (ISBN 0-245-52376-6). Vol. 2. Intl Ideas.

Watts, B. K. Elements of Finance for Managers. (Illus.). 256p. 1976. pap. 12.95x (ISBN 0-7121-0551-4, Pub. by Macdonald & Evans England). Intl Ideas.

Webb, Samuel C. Managerial Economics. LC 75-31039. (Illus.). 608p. 1976. text ed. 20.95 (ISBN 0-395-20589-1); solutions manual 2.75 (ISBN 0-395-20590-5). HM.

Wert, James E. & Henderson, Glenn V., Jr. Financing Business Firms: Private, Bk. 204. rev. ed. 633p. Date not set. 19.95 (ISBN 0-686-74989-8). Dow Jones-Irwin.

Weston & Brigham. Essentials of Managerial Finance. 5th ed. LC 78-56194. 1979. text ed. 22.95 (ISBN 0-03-045446-8). Dryden Pr.

Wildsmith, J. R. Managerial Theories of the Firm. LC 73-82263. 200p. 1973. 12.50 (ISBN 0-8046-7073-0). Kennikat.

Winger, Bernard J. Cases in Managerial Economics. LC 78-27382. (Grid Series in Economics). 1979. pap. text ed. 8.95 (ISBN 0-88244-183-3). Grid Pub.

Zill. Introductory Calculus for Business Economics & Social Science. 1977. pap. 20.95x (ISBN 0-534-00475-X); solutions manual 5.95x (ISBN 0-534-00531-4). Wadsworth Pub.

Zudak, Lawrence S. Managerial Economics. 1980. text ed. 18.95 scp (ISBN 0-06-047451-3, HarpC); inst. manual free (ISBN 0-06-367375-4). Har-Row.

MANAGERS

see Executives

MANAHEM MENDEL, OF KOCK, 1788-1859

Heschel, Abraham J. A Passion for Truth. 336p. 1973. 8.95 (ISBN 0-374-22992-9); pap. 5.95 (ISBN 0-374-51184-5). FS&G.

MANASSAS, BATTLES OF

see Bull Run, 1st Battle of, 1861

MANATEES

Bertram, G. L. Conservation of Sirenia: Current Status & Perspectives for Action. 1974. pap. 7.50x (ISBN 2-88032-023-2, IUCN35, IUCN). Unipub.

Biological Synopsis of the Manatee. 1979. pap. 8.50 (ISBN 0-88936-168-1, TS13, IDRC). Unipub.

Domning, Daryl. Sirenian Evolution in the North Pacific Ocean. (Publications in Geological Science Ser.: Vol. 118). 1978. 12.00x (ISBN 0-520-09581-2). U of Cal Pr.

Jacobs, Francine. Sewer Sam: The Sea Cow. (Illus.). (gr. k-3). 1979. 6.95 (ISBN 0-8027-6368-5); PLB 6.85 (ISBN 0-8027-6369-3). Walker & Co.

Kaiser, H. E. Morphology of the Sirenia. (Illus.). 1974. 56.50 (ISBN 3-8055-1609-6). S Karger.

Leatherwood, Stephen, et al. Marine Mammals of the World, Vol. 2: Seals, Sea Lions, Otters & Sea Cows. 200p. 1980. 45.00 (ISBN 0-525-10473-9). Dutton.

Mammals in the Seas, Vol. II: Pinniped Species Summaries & Report on Sirenians. (FAO Fisheries Ser.: No. 5, Vol. II). 151p. 1979. 24.50 (ISBN 92-5-100512-5, F2102, FAO). Unipub.

MANCHESTER, EDWARD MONTAGU, 2ND EARL OF, 1602-1671

Masson, David, ed. The Quarrel Between the Earl of Manchester & Oliver Cromwell: An Episode of the English Civil War. Repr. of 1875 ed. 22.50 (ISBN 0-384-35850-0). Johnson Repr.

MANCHESTER, ENGLAND

Aikin, J. A Description of the Country from Thirty to Forty Miles Round Manchester 1795. (Illus.). 12.50 (ISBN 0-7153-4237-1). David & Charles.

Bamford, Samuel. The Autobiography of Samuel Bamford, 2 vols. Chaloner, W. H., ed. & intro. by. Incl. Vol. 1. Early Days. Repr. of 1849 ed; Vol. 2. Passages in the Life of a Radical. Repr. of 1844 ed. LC 67-23461. 30.00x (ISBN 0-678-05025-2). Kelley.

Bradley, Helen. The Queen Who Came to Tea. LC 79-301613. (Illus.). 32p. (gr. 1-3). 1979. 9.95 (ISBN 0-224-01545-1, Pub. by Chatto Bodley Jonathan). Merrimack Bk Serv.

Chaloner, W. H. The Movement for the Extension of Owens College, Manchester, Eighteen Sixty-Three to Seventy-Three. 136p. 1973. 9.00x (ISBN 0-7190-0552-3, Pub by Mancherster U Pr England). State Mutual Bk.

Farnie, D. A. The Manchester Ship Canal. 128p. 1981. 35.00x (ISBN 0-686-73063-1, Pub. by Manchester U Pr England). State Mutual Bk.

Faucher, L. Manchester in 1844: It's Present Condition & Future Prospects. Culverwell, J. P., ed. 152p. 1969. 22.50x (ISBN 0-7146-1392-4, Pub by F Cass Co). Biblio Dist.

Hindle, G. B. Provision for the Relief of the Poor in Manchester, 1754-1826. (Chetham Society Remains Ser). 240p. 1974. text ed. 19.50x (ISBN 0-7190-1166-3). Humanities.

Jones, G. D. Roman Manchester. Grealey, S., ed. 198p. 1974. pap. 7.00 (ISBN 0-7190-0670-8, Pub. by Manchester U Pr England). State Mutual Bk.

Kennedy, Michael. Portrait of Manchester. LC 70-550611. (Portrait Bks.). 1970. 10.50x (ISBN 0-7091-1812-0). Intl Pubns Serv.

Manchester Old & New. 1975. pap. text ed. 10.50x (ISBN 0-8277-4162-6). British Bk Ctr.

O'Connor, Feargus. Trial of Feargus O'connor and Fifty-Eight Other Chartists. LC 71-109591. Repr. of 1843 ed. 19.50x (ISBN 0-678-00608-3). Kelley.

Prentice, Archibald. Historical Sketches & Personal Recollections of Manchester: Intended to Illustrate Progress of Public Opinion from 1792-1832. 3rd & rev. ed. 432p. 1970. 35.00x (ISBN 0-7146-1353-3, F Cass Co). Biblio Dist.

Redford, Arthur. Manchester Merchants & Foreign Trade, 2 vols. Incl. Vol. 1. 1794-1858. xii, 251p; Vol. 2. 1850-1939. 304p. Repr. of 1956 ed. LC 73-1675. 30.00x (ISBN 0-678-00750-0). Kelley.

Slugg, J. T. Reminiscences of Manchester Fifty Years Ago. (The Development of Industrial Society Ser.). 355p. 1971. Repr. of 1881 ed. 24.00x (ISBN 0-7165-1771-X, Pub. by Irish Academic Pr). Biblio Dist.

Vigier, Francois. Change & Apathy: Liverpool & Manchester During the Industrial Revolution. (Illus.). 1970. 15.00x (ISBN 0-262-22012-1). MIT Pr.

White, H. P. The Continuing Conurbation: Change & Development in Greater Manchester. 207p. 1980. text ed. 30.75x (ISBN 0-566-00248-5, Pub. by Gower Pub Co England). Renouf.

Willan, T. S. Elizabethan Manchester. (Chetham Society Third Ser.: Vol. 27). (Illus.). 163p. 1980. 30.00x (ISBN 0-8476-3235-0). Rowman.

Williams, Bill. The Making of Manchester Jewry: 1740-1875. LC 75-43635. (Illus.). 400p. 1976. text ed. 32.50x (ISBN 0-8419-0252-6). Holmes & Meier.

Wilson, H. & Womersley, L. A Manchester Education Precinct. 119p. 1975. 30.00x (ISBN 0-7190-1284-8, Pub. by Manchester U Pr England). State Mutual Bk.

MANCHESTER, ENGLAND–PETERLOO MASSACRE, 1819

Read, Donald. Peterloo. LC 72-7212. Repr. of 1958 ed. 13.50x (ISBN 0-678-06791-0). Kelley.

Walmsley, Robert. Peterloo: The Case Reopened. LC 73-81146. (Illus.). 1969. 19.50x (ISBN 0-678-06777-5). Kelley.

MANCHESTER GUARDIAN

Ayerst, David. Manchester Guardian: Biography of a Newspaper. (Illus.). 1971. 24.50x (ISBN 0-8014-0642-0). Cornell U Pr.

C. P. Scott, Eighteen Forty-Six to Nineteen Thirty-Two: The Making of the 'Manchester Guardian' LC 73-19220. (Illus.). 252p. 1974. Repr. of 1946 ed. lib. bdg. 15.75x (ISBN 0-8371-7312-4, SCMG). Greenwood.

MANCHESTER SCHOOL OF ECONOMICS

Grampp, William D. The Manchester School of Economics. 1960. 10.00x (ISBN 0-8047-0020-6). Stanford U Pr.

MANCHU LANGUAGE

Norman, Jerry. A Concise Manchu-English Lexicon. LC 77-14307. (Publications on Asia of the School for International Studies: No. 32). 336p. 1979. 22.50 (ISBN 0-295-95574-0). U of Wash Pr.

MANCHU LITERATURE

Poppe, Nicholas, et al. Catalogue of the Manchu-Mongol Section of Toyo Bunko. LC 65-63112. (Publications on Asia of the School of International Studies: No. 12). 391p. 1964. 20.00 (ISBN 0-295-73732-8). U of Wash Pr.

MANCHURIA

Clyde, Paul H. International Rivalries in Manchuria, 1689-1922. 1966. lib. bdg. 15.00x (ISBN 0-374-91786-8). Octagon.

Detwiler, Donald S. & Burdick, Charles B., eds. Japanese Military Studies 1937-1949: China, Manchuria, & Korea, Pt. 2. (War in Asia & the Pacific Ser., 1937 to 1949: Vol. 9). 650p. 1980. lib. bdg. 55.00 (ISBN 0-8240-3293-4); lib. bdg. 60.50 set of 15 vols. (ISBN 0-686-77791-3). Garland Pub.

Doenecke, Justus D., compiled by. The Diplomacy of Frustration: The Manchurian Crisis of 1931-1933 As Revealed in the Papers of Stanley K. Hornbeck. (Publication Ser.: No. 231). 1981. text ed. 22.95 (ISBN 0-8179-7311-7). Hoover Inst Pr.

Hosie, Alexander. Manchuria: Its People, Resources & Recent History, London, 1904. LC 78-74311. (The Modern Chinese Economy Ser.: Vol. 24). 326p. 1980. lib. bdg. 38.00 (ISBN 0-8240-4272-7). Garland Pub.

James, Henry E. Long White Mountain or a Journey in Manchuria, with Some Account of the History, People, Administration & Religion of That Country. LC 68-55199. (Illus.). 1968. Repr. of 1888 ed. lib. bdg. 18.25x (ISBN 0-8371-0497-1, JALW). Greenwood.

Kawakami, K. K. Manchoukuo: Child of Conflict. LC 79-94317. Repr. of 1933 ed. 10.50 (ISBN 0-404-03639-2). AMS Pr.

Lattimore, Owen. Manchuria: Cradle of Conflict. rev. ed. LC 72-4435. Repr. of 1935 ed. 26.75 (ISBN 0-404-10632-3). AMS Pr.

Lee, Robert H. Manchurian Frontier in Ch'ing History. LC 70-95926. (East Asian Ser: No. 43). 1970. text ed. 12.50x (ISBN 0-674-54775-6). Harvard U Pr.

Lensen, George A. The Damned Inheritance: The Soviet Union & the Manchurian Crises, 1924-1935. LC 74-186318. (Illus.). 533p. 1974. 19.80 (ISBN 0-910512-17-5). Diplomatic Fla.

Mangeot, Sylvain. Manchurian Adventure. LC 74-12173. 288p. 1975. 7.95 (ISBN 0-688-00224-2). Morrow.

Meng, Chih. China Speaks. LC 74-115205. 1971. Repr. of 1932 ed. 13.50 (ISBN 0-8046-1098-3). Kennikat.

Price, Ernest B. Russo-Japanese Treaties of 1907-1916. LC 76-101274. Repr. of 1933 ed. 17.50 (ISBN 0-404-05135-9). AMS Pr.

Romanov, B. A. Russia in Manchuria: 1892-1906. LC 74-4181. 559p. 1974. Repr. of 1952 ed. lib. bdg. 25.00x (ISBN 0-374-96903-5). Octagon.

Sakatani, Baron Y. Manchuria: A Survey of Its Economic Development. LC 78-74315. (The Modern Chinese Economy Ser.). 305p. 1980. lib. bdg. 33.00 (ISBN 0-8240-4279-4). Garland Pub.

Smith, Sara R. Manchurian Crisis Nineteen Thirty One to Nineteen Thirty Two: A Tragedy in International Relations. Repr. of 1948 ed. lib. bdg. 14.50x (ISBN 0-8371-3344-0, SMMC). Greenwood.

Sun, Kungtu C. Economic Development of Manchuria in the First Half of the Twentieth Century. LC 70-7023. (East Asian Monographs Ser: No. 28). 1969. pap. 9.00x (ISBN 0-674-22720-4). Harvard U Pr.

Tan, Chester C. Boxer Catastrophe. 1967. Repr. lib. bdg. 17.00x (ISBN 0-374-97752-6). Octagon.

Tang, Peter S. Russian & Soviet Policy in Manchuria & Outer Mongolia, 1911-1931. LC 59-7084. 1959. 19.75 (ISBN 0-8223-0170-9). Duke.

Willoughby, Westel W. Sino-Japanese Controversy & the League of Nations. LC 68-54995. (Illus.). 1968. Repr. of 1935 ed. lib. bdg. 26.25x (ISBN 0-8371-0755-5, WISJ). Greenwood.

Young, Carl W. International Relations of Manchuria. LC 74-158859. Repr. of 1929 ed. 14.45 (ISBN 0-404-07071-X). AMS Pr.

--International Relations of Manchuria: A Digest & Analysis of Treaties, Agreements, & Negotiations Concerning the Three Eastern Provinces of China. LC 30-3997. (Illus.). 1969. Repr. of 1929 ed. lib. bdg. 16.50x (ISBN 0-8371-0771-7, YOMA). Greenwood.

MANCHUS

see also China–History–Ch'Ing Dynasty, 1644-1912

Michael, Franz. Origin of Manchu Rule in China. 1965. lib. bdg. 14.00x (ISBN 0-374-95605-7). Octagon.

Shirokogorov, Sergei M. Social Organization of the Manchus: A Study of the Manchu Clan Organization. LC 77-38082. Repr. of 1924 ed. 15.00 (ISBN 0-404-56946-3). AMS Pr.

MANDAEAN LANGUAGE

Macuch, Rudolf. Handbook of Classical & Modern Mandaic. 1965. 123.55x (ISBN 3-11-000261-2). De Gruyter.

Yamauchi, Edwin M. Mandaic Incantation Texts. (American Oriental Ser.: Vol. 49). 1967. 9.00x (ISBN 0-940490-49-8). Am Orient Soc.

MANDAEANS

Harkins, Paul W., tr. from Gr. John Chrysostom Saint: Discourses Against Judaizing Christians. LC 77-8466. (Fathers of the Church Ser.: Vol. 68). Orig. Title: Logoi Kata Ioudaion. 366p. 1979. 24.00 (ISBN 0-8132-0068-7). Cath U Pr.

Kraeling, Carl H. Anthropos & Son of Man. LC 27-23162. (Columbia University. Oriental Studies: No. 25). Repr. of 1927 ed. 18.50 (ISBN 0-404-50515-5). AMS Pr.

Macuch, Rudolf. Zur Sprache und Literatur der Mandaer: Mit Beitraegen von Kurt Rudolph & Eric Segelberg. 1976. 99.75x (ISBN 3-11-004838-8). De Gruyter.

MANDALA

Arguelles, Jose & Arguelles, Miriam. Mandala. LC 70-189856. (Illus.). 144p. 1972. pap. 9.95 (ISBN 0-394-73000-3). Shambhala Pubns.

Guerin, Wilfred L., et al. Mandala: Literature for Critical Analysis. LC 72-103917. (Orig.). 1970. pap. text ed. 14.50 scp (ISBN 0-06-043825-8, HarpC); instructor's manual avail. (ISBN 0-06-363828-2). Har-Row.

Jung, Carl G. Mandala Symbolism. Hull, R. F., tr. (Bollingen Ser.: Vol. 20). (Illus.). 204p. 1972. pap. 3.95 (ISBN 0-691-01781-6). Princeton U Pr.

Pant, Apa. Mandala: An Awakening. 1978. 9.50x (ISBN 0-8364-0183-2, Orient Longman). South Asia Bks.

MANDAMUS

Henderson, Edith G. Foundations of English Administrative Law. 1963. 6.50x (ISBN 0-678-08033-X). Kelley.

--Foundations of English Administrative Law: Certiorari & Mandamus in the Seventeenth Century. LC 63-11421. (Ames Foundation Publications Ser). 1963. 10.00x (ISBN 0-674-31351-8). Harvard U Pr.

Moses, Halsey H. The Law of Mandamus & the Practice Connected with It, with an Appendix of Forms. iv, 268p. 1981. Repr. of 1878 ed. lib. bdg. 27.50x (ISBN 0-8377-0838-9). Rothman.

MANDAN INDIANS

see Indians of North America–The West

MANDARI (AFRICAN PEOPLE)

Buxton, Jean. Religion & Healing in Mandari. (Illus.). 446p. 1973. 45.00x (ISBN 0-19-823174-1). Oxford U Pr.

MANDATE (CONTRACT LAW, ROMAN)

Yanaihara, Tadao. Pacific Islands Under Japanese Mandate. LC 75-41304. (Institute of Pacific Relations). 1977. Repr. of 1940 ed. 27.50 (ISBN 0-404-14636-8). AMS Pr.

MANDATES

see also International Trusteeships; State Succession

Clyde, Paul H. Japan's Pacific Mandate. LC 67-27586. Repr. of 1935 ed. 11.50 (ISBN 0-8046-0081-3). Kennikat.

Cohen, Michael J. Palestine, Retreat from the Mandate: The Making of British Policy, 1936-45. LC 78-933. 1978. text ed. 29.50x (ISBN 0-8419-0373-5). Holmes & Meier.

Hall, H. D. Mandates, Dependencies, & Trusteeship. (Studies in the Administration of International Law & Organization). 1948. pap. 25.00 (ISBN 0-527-00887-7). Kraus Repr.

Halpern, Ben. The Jewish National Home in Palestine. 1970. 25.00x (ISBN 0-87068-050-1). Ktav.

Hidayatullah, M. South-West Africa Case. 1968. 7.25x (ISBN 0-210-27194-9). Asia.

Ireland, Philip W. Iraq: A Study in Political Development. LC 75-83852. (Illus.). 1970. Repr. of 1937 ed. 15.00 (ISBN 0-8462-1412-1). Russell.

Logan, Rayford W. The Senate & the Versailles Mandate System. LC 74-14357. 112p. 1975. Repr. of 1945 ed. lib. bdg. 15.00x (ISBN 0-8371-7798-7, LOVM). Greenwood.

Longrigg, Stephen H. Syria & Lebanon Under French Mandate. 1972. lib. bdg. 20.00x (ISBN 0-374-95088-1). Octagon.

Rathbone, Eleanor F. War Can Be Averted. LC 72-89269. 224p. 1973. Repr. of 1938 ed. 13.00 (ISBN 0-8046-1759-7). Kennikat.

Slonim, Solomon. South West Africa & the United Nations: An International Mandate in Dispute. LC 72-4020. 428p. 1973. 28.00x (ISBN 0-8018-1430-8). Johns Hopkins.

Wright, Quincy. Mandates Under the League of Nations. LC 68-57649. (Illus.). 1968. Repr. of 1930 ed. lib. bdg. 27.75x (ISBN 0-8371-0765-2, WRLN). Greenwood.

Yanaihara, Tadao. Pacific Islands Under Japanese Mandate. LC 76-18921. (Institute of Pacific Relations: International Research Ser). (Illus.). 312p. 1976. Repr. of 1940 ed. lib. bdg. 21.00x (ISBN 0-8371-8667-6, YAPI). Greenwood.

Ziff, William B. The Rape of Palestine. LC 73-97310. (Illus.). 612p. 1975. Repr. of 1938 ed. lib. bdg. 29.25x (ISBN 0-8371-2639-8, ZIRP). Greenwood.

MANDE LANGUAGES

see also Bambara Language; Vei Language

MANDEL, GEORGES, 1885-1944

Sherwood, John M. Georges Mandel & the Third Republic. LC 74-97916. (Illus.). 1970. 18.50x (ISBN 0-8047-0731-6). Stanford U Pr.

MANDELSHTAM, NADEZHDA, 1899-

Mandelstam, Nadezhda. Hope Abandoned, Vol. 2. Hayward, Max, tr. from Rus. LC 80-24491. 1973. 13.95 (ISBN 0-689-10549-5, 265); pap. 12.95 (ISBN 0-689-70608-1). Atheneum.

MANDEL'SHTAM, OSIP EMIL'EVICH, 1891-1938?

Baines, Jennifer. Mandelstam: The Later Poetry. LC 76-8515. 1977. 36.00 (ISBN 0-521-21273-1). Cambridge U Pr.

Brown, Clarence. Mandelstam. LC 72-90491. (Illus.). 400p. 1973. 38.50 (ISBN 0-521-20142-X); pap. 12.95 (ISBN 0-521-29347-2). Cambridge U Pr.

Broyde, Steven. Osip Mandelstam & His Age. LC 74-16801. (Slavic Monographs: No. 1). 264p. 1975. text ed. 12.50x (ISBN 0-674-64492-1). Harvard U Pr.

Koubourlis, Demetrius J. & Parrish, Stephen M., eds. A Concordance to the Poems of Osip Mandelstam. LC 73-8387. (Concordances Ser.). 704p. (Rus. & Eng.). 1974. 38.50x (ISBN 0-8014-0806-7). Cornell U pr.

Mandelstam, Nadezhda. Hope Abandoned, Vol. 2. Hayward, Max, tr. from Rus. LC 80-24491. 1973. 13.95 (ISBN 0-689-10549-5, 265); pap. 12.95 (ISBN 0-689-70608-1). Atheneum.

--Hope Against Hope. LC 77-124984. 1976. pap. 6.95 (ISBN 0-689-70530-1, 218). Atheneum.

Taranovsky, Kiril. Essays on Mandel'stam. (Slavic Studies: Vol. 6). 242p. 1976. 14.50x (ISBN 0-674-26705-2). Harvard U Pr.

MANDEVILLE, GEOFFREY DE, EARL OF ESSEX, d. 1144

Round, John H. Geoffrey De Mandeville: A Study of the Anarchy. (Illus.). 461p. 1972. Repr. of 1892 ed. 32.50 (ISBN 0-8337-3071-1). B Franklin.

MANDEVILLE, JOHN, SIR

Bennett, Josephine W. Rediscovery of Sir John Mandeville. 1954. pap. 20.00 (ISBN 0-527-06700-8). Kraus Repr.

Letts, Malcolm. Sir John Mandeville: The Man & His Book. LC 70-161957. 192p. 1949. Repr. 11.00 (ISBN 0-403-01318-6). Scholarly.

--Sir John Mandeville: The Man & His Book. 1949. Repr. lib. bdg. 30.00 (ISBN 0-8414-5856-1). Folcroft.

Pollard, A. W., intro. by. The Travels of Sir John Mandeville: The Version of the Cotton Manuscript in Modern Spelling. 1978. Repr. of 1900 ed. lib. bdg. 35.00 (ISBN 0-8495-3722-3). Arden Lib.

Swanton, M. J., ed. The Travels of Sir John Mandeville. 135p. 1980. pap. text ed. 5.00x (ISBN 0-686-75478-6, Pub. by U Exeter England). Humanities.

MANDIBULAR JOINT

see Temporomandibular Joint

MANDINGO LANGUAGE

see also Bambara Language

MANET, EDOUARD, 1832-1883

Courthion, Pierre. Manet. (Library of Great Painters Ser). (Illus.). 1963. 40.00 (ISBN 0-8109-0260-5). Abrams.

De Leiris, Alain. The Drawings of Edouard Manet. LC 68-13017. (Studies in the History of Art: No. 10). 1969. 58.50x (ISBN 0-520-01547-9). U of Cal Pr.

Duret, Theodore. Manet & the French Impressionists. facsimile ed. Crawford Flitch, J. E., tr. (Select Bibliographies Reprint Ser). Repr. of 1910 ed. 24.00 (ISBN 0-8369-6687-2). Arno.

Gay, Peter. Art & Act: On Causes in History - Manet, Gropius, Mondrian. LC 75-12291. (Icon Editions). (Illus.). 320p. 1976. 20.00 (ISBN 0-06-433248-9, HarpT). Har-Row.

Guerin, Marcel. L'Oeuvre Grave De Manet. (Graphic Art Ser). (Illus.). 1970. Repr. of 1944 ed. lib. bdg. 45.00 (ISBN 0-306-71920-7). Da Capo.

Hanson, Anne C. Manet & the Modern Tradition. LC 75-43319. 1977. 40.00x (ISBN 0-300-01954-8); pap. 14.95 (ISBN 0-300-02492-4). Yale U Pr.

Manet, Edouard. Manet. Orienti, Sandra, ed. (Art Library Ser.: Vol. 12). (Illus., Orig.). 1968. pap. 3.50 (ISBN 0-448-00461-5). G&D.

Mauner, George. Manet, Peintre-Philosophe: A Study of the Painter's Themes. LC 74-31056. 230p. 1975. 24.50x (ISBN 0-271-01187-4). Pa St U Pr.

Mortimer, Ray A. Edouard Manet & the Folies-Bergere. (Great Masters Art Book). (Illus.). 1979. deluxe ed. 31.25 (ISBN 0-930582-23-3). Gloucester Art.

Niess, Robert J. Zola, Cezanne, & Manet: A Study of l'Oeuvre. LC 68-16443. 1968. 7.50 (ISBN 0-472-67400-5). U of Mich Pr.

Schneider, Pierre. World of Manet. (Library of Art). (Illus.). 1968. 15.95 (ISBN 0-8094-0248-3). Time-Life.

--World of Manet. LC 68-58484. (Library of Art Ser.). (Illus.). (gr. 6 up). 1968. 12.96 (ISBN 0-8094-0277-7, Pub. by Time-Life). Silver.

Valery, Paul. Collected Works of Paul Valery, Vol. 12, Degas, Manet, Morisot. Matthews, Jackson, ed. Paul, David, tr. (Bollingen Ser.: Vol. 45). 1960. 15.00 (ISBN 0-691-09839-5). Princeton U Pr.

MANEUVERS, MILITARY

see Military Maneuvers

MANFRED, FREDERICK

Wright, Robert C. Frederick Manfred. (United States Authors Ser.: No. 336). 1979. lib. bdg. 13.50 (ISBN 0-8057-7247-2). Twayne.

MANGAIAN LANGUAGE

Christian, F. W. Vocabulary of the Mangaian Language. Repr. of 1924 ed. pap. 5.00 (ISBN 0-527-02114-8). Kraus Repr.

MANGAN, JAMES CLARENCE, 1803-1849

Donaghy, Henry J. James Clarence Mangan. (English Authors Ser.: No. 171). 1974. lib. bdg. 10.95 (ISBN 0-8057-1370-0). Twayne.

Kilroy, James. James Clarence Mangan. LC 78-124648. (Irish Writers Ser.). 74p. 1971. 4.50 (ISBN 0-8387-7749-X); pap. 1.95 (ISBN 0-8387-7617-5). Bucknell U Pr.

Mangan, James C. The Autobiography of James Clarence Mangan. Kilroy, James, ed. (New Dolmen Chapbooks: No. 9). 40p. 1968. pap. text ed. 2.50x (ISBN 0-85105-138-3, Dolmen Pr). Humanities.

O'Donoghue, David J. The Life & Writings of James Clarence Mangan. LC 12-3288. 1971. Repr. of 1897 ed. 17.50 (ISBN 0-384-42970-X, F448). Johnson Repr.

MANGANESE MINES AND MINING, SUBMARINE

see also Hydraulic Mining

Mero, J. L. The Mineral Resources of the Sea. (Oceanography Ser.: Vol. 1). 1965. 39.00 (ISBN 0-444-40394-9). Elsevier.

MANGANESE ORES

Arndt, Diether. Manganese Compounds As Oxidizing Agents in Organic Chemistry. Muller, Eugen, ed. Lee, Donald G., tr. from Ger. 1981. 55.00 (ISBN 0-87548-355-0). Open Court.

Brooks, David B. Low-Grade & Nonconventional Sources of Manganese. (Resources for the Future Ser). (Illus.). 160p. (Orig.). 1966. pap. 4.95x (ISBN 0-8018-0089-7). Johns Hopkins.

Glasby, G. P., ed. Marine Manganese Deposits. LC 76-48895. (Elsevier Oceanography Ser.). 1977. 68.50 (ISBN 0-444-41524-6). Elsevier.

Josephson, Emanuel M. The Thymus, Myasthenia Gravis & Manganese. 1979. write for info. (ISBN 0-685-96470-1). Revisionist Pr.

Max Planck Society for the Advancement of Science, Gmelin Institute for Inorganic Chemistry. Manganese, Pt. C, The Compounds: Section 2, Manganate Compounds with Metals, from Li to U. (Gmelin Handbuch der Anorganischen Chemie, 8th Ed.). (Illus.). 302p. 1975. 287.40 (ISBN 0-387-93287-9). Springer-Verlag.

Sorem & Fewkes. Manganese Nodules: Research Data & Methods of Investigation. 1979. 95.00 (ISBN 0-306-65186-6). IFI Plenum.

United Nations Ocean Economics & Technology Office. Manganese Nodules: Dimensions & Perspectives. (Natural Resources Forum Library). 1979. lib. bdg. 34.00 (ISBN 90-277-0500-3, Pub. by Reidel Holland); pap. 16.00 (ISBN 90-277-0902-5). Kluwer Boston.

MANG'ANJA LANGUAGE

see Nyanja Language

MANGER IN CHRISTIAN ART AND TRADITION

see Crib in Christian Art and Tradition

MANGGARESE PEOPLE

Verheijen, J. A. Het Hoogste Wezen Bij De Manggaraiers. Repr. of 1951 ed. 38.50 (ISBN 0-384-64290-X). Johnson Repr.

MANGROVE

Chapman, V. J. Mangrove Vegetation. (Illus.). 1976. 60.00x (ISBN 0-686-26286-7, Pub. by J. Cramer). Intl Schol Bk Serv.

--Mangrove Vegetation. 1976. 75.00 (ISBN 3-7682-0926-1). Lubrecht & Cramer.

Lear, Richard & Turner, Tom. Mangroves of Australia. (Illus.). 1977. pap. 5.95x (ISBN 0-7022-1420-5). U of Queensland Pr.

MANHATTAN (BOROUGH)

Ballard, F. R. Directory of Manhattan Office Space. (Illus.). 1978. 79.50 (ISBN 0-07-003485-0). McGraw.

DuBois, George. Anneke. LC 81-80149. 200p. 1981. 9.95 (ISBN 0-86666-010-0). GWP.

Harris, M. A. Negro History Tour of Manhattan. LC 68-54217. (Illus.). 1968. lib. bdg. 15.00 (ISBN 0-8371-1498-5, HAN/). Greenwood.

Koolhaas, Rem. Delirious New York. (Illus.). 1978. pap. 18.95 (ISBN 0-19-502733-7). Oxford U Pr.

Rippner, William. The New York Times Manhattan Coloring Book. LC 74-26012. (Illus.). 64p. (Orig.). 1975. pap. 3.95 (ISBN 0-8129-0546-6). Times Bks.

Smith, James R. Springs & Wells of Manhattan & the Bronx. LC 38-30365. (Illus.). 1938. 8.00x (ISBN 0-685-73927-9, New York Historical Society). U Pr of Va.

Suares, J. C. & Madden, Chris C., eds. Manhattan. (Illus.). 256p. 1981. 45.00 (ISBN 0-8109-1311-9). Abrams.

Tucker, Kerry. Greetings from New York: A Visit to Manhattan in Postcards. (Illus.). 112p. (Orig.). 1981. pap. 8.95 (ISBN 0-933328-04-4). Delilah Comm.

Watson, Edward B. New York Then & Now: Eightythree Manhattan Sites Photographed in the Past & Present. (Illus.). 192p. (Orig.). 1976. pap. 6.00 (ISBN 0-486-23361-8). Dover.

Weitenkampf, Frank. Manhattan Kaleidoscope. 1947. 35.00 (ISBN 0-685-72792-0). Norwood Edns.

MANHATTAN PROJECT

see United States–Army–Manhattan Engineering District

MANHATTANVILLE

Woolston, Howard B. Study of the Population of Manhattanville. LC 79-76684. (Columbia University. Studies in the Social Sciences: No. 93). Repr. of 1909 ed. 12.50 (ISBN 0-404-51093-0). AMS Pr.

MANIA

see Psychoses

MANIC-DEPRESSIVE PSYCHOSES

see also Depression, Mental; Psychology, Pathological

Fieve, Ronald. Moodswing: The Third Revolution in Psychiatry. 256p. 1976. pap. 3.25 (ISBN 0-553-20024-0). Bantam.

--Moodswing: The Third Revolution in Psychology. LC 75-15624. 1975. 8.95 (ISBN 0-688-02938-8). Morrow.

Flach, Frederic F. & Draghi, Suzanne C. The Nature & Treatment of Depression. LC 74-28265. 448p. 1975. 44.95 (ISBN 0-471-26271-4, Pub. by Wiley Medical). Wiley.

Fraser, Sarah. Living with Depression and Winning. 1975. pap. 1.45 (ISBN 0-8423-3680-X). Tyndale.

Gaylin, Willard, ed. Meaning of Despair: Psychoanalytic Contributions to the Understanding of Depression. LC 68-17262. 1968. 25.00x (ISBN 0-87668-028-7). Aronson.

Gilliam, Mary A. I Am As I Am. 1980. 5.95 (ISBN 0-533-04245-3). Vantage.

Himwich, Harold E. Biochemistry, Schizophrenias & Affective Illnesses. LC 77-2015. (Illus.). 514p. 1977. 24.50 (ISBN 0-88275-524-2). Krieger.

Kline, Nathan S., ed. Factors in Depression. LC 74-77571. 284p. 1974. 24.50 (ISBN 0-911216-79-0). Raven.

Kraepelin, Emil. Manic-Depressive Insanity & Paranoia. Barclay, R. Mary, tr. from Ger. LC 75-16712. (Classics in Psychiatry Ser.). (Illus.). 1976. Repr. of 1921 ed. 17.00x (ISBN 0-405-07441-7). Arno.

Kraines, Samuel H. & Thetford, Eloise S. Help for the Depressed. (Illus.). 272p. 1979. pap. 11.75 (ISBN 0-398-02335-2). C C Thomas.

Mendels, Joseph. Concepts of Depression. LC 72-5497. (Approaches to Behavior Pathology Ser). 1970. pap. text ed. 10.95x (ISBN 0-471-59351-6). Wiley.

Ross, Harvey. Fighting Depression. 221p. (Orig.). 1975. pap. 1.95 (ISBN 0-686-71005-3). Larchmont Bks.

Schou, M. Lithium Treatment of Manic-Depressive Illness. (Illus.). viii, 72p. 1980. pap. 14.50 (ISBN 3-8055-0392-X). S Karger.

Shopsin, Baron, ed. Manic Illness. LC 78-66347. 252p. 1979. text ed. 21.00 (ISBN 0-89004-211-X). Raven.

Usdin, Gene, ed. Depression: Clinical, Biological & Psychological Perspectives. LC 76-49429. 1977. 20.00 (ISBN 0-87630-137-5). Brunner-Mazel.

MANICHAEISM

Asmussen, Jes P., compiled by. Manichaean Literature: Representative Texts, Chiefly from Middle Persian & Parthian Writings. LC 74-22063. (Unesco Collection of Representative Works, Oriental Ser.). 155p. 1975. lib. bdg. 18.00x (ISBN 0-8201-1141-4). Schol Facsimiles.

Augustinus, Aurelius. Contra Felicem De Natura Boni Epistula Secundini, Contra Secundinum, Pt. 2. Bd. with De Natura Boni Epistula Secundini; Contra Secundinum. (Corpus Scriptorum Ecclesiasticorum Latinorum Ser: Vol. 25). (Lat.). Repr. of 1892 ed. unbound 41.50 (ISBN 0-384-02365-7). Johnson Repr.

--De Utilitate Credendi, Pt. 1. Bd. with De Duabus Animabus; Contra Fortunatem; Contra Adimantum. (Corpus Scriptorum Ecclesiasticorum Latinorum Ser: Vol. 25). Repr. of 1891 ed. pap. 41.50 (ISBN 0-384-02364-9). Johnson Repr.

Burkitt, Francis C. The Religion of the Manichees: Donnellan Lectures for 1924. LC 77-84698. Repr. of 1925 ed. 18.50 (ISBN 0-404-16105-7). AMS Pr.

Cameron, Ron & Dewey, Arthur J., trs. The Cologne Mani Codex. LC 79-14743. (Society of Biblical Literature Texts & Translations, 15. Early Christian Literature Ser.: No. 3). 1979. 10.50 (ISBN 0-89130-311-1, 060215); pap. 6.00 (ISBN 0-89130-312-X). Scholars Pr Ca.

Jackson, Abraham V. Researches in Manichaeism with Special Reference to the Turfan Fragments. LC 32-9567. (Columbia University. Indo-Iranian Ser.: No. 13). Repr. of 1932 ed. 31.00 (ISBN 0-404-50483-3). AMS Pr.

Kraeling, Carl H. Anthropos & Son of Man. LC 27-23162. (Columbia University. Oriental Studies: No. 25). Repr. of 1927 ed. 18.50 (ISBN 0-404-50515-5). AMS Pr.

Serapion, Saint Against the Manichees. Casey, Robert P., ed. 1931. pap. 5.00 (ISBN 0-527-01015-4). Kraus Repr.

Un Traite Neo-Manicheen du XIIIe siecle. LC 78-63185. (Heresies of the Early Christian & Medieval Era: Second Ser.). 1979. Repr. of 1939 ed. 23.00 (ISBN 0-404-16224-X). AMS Pr.

MANIFEST DESTINY (U. S.)
see Messianism, American; United States–Territories and Possessions

MANIFOLDING
see Copying Processes

MANIFOLDS (MATHEMATICS)

Aliprantis, Charalambos D. & Burkinshaw, Owen. Locally Solid Riesz Spaces. (Pure & Applied Mathematics Ser.). 1978. 29.50 (ISBN 0-12-050250-X). Acad Pr.

Allendoerfer, C. B. Calculus of Several Variables & Differential Manifolds. 1974. 16.95 (ISBN 0-02-301840-2, 30184). Macmillan.

Atiyah, M. F. Elliptic Operators & Compact Groups. (Lecture Notes in Mathematics Ser.: Vol. 401). v, 93p. 1974. pap. 9.90 (ISBN 3-540-06855-4). Springer-Verlag.

Auslander, L. & Tolimieri, R. Abelian Harmonic Analysis, Theta Functions & Functional Analysis on a Nilmanifold. (Lecture Notes in Mathematics Ser.: Vol. 436). v, 99p. 1975. pap. 10.00 (ISBN 0-387-07134-2). Springer-Verlag.

Besse, A. L. Manifolds All of Whose Geodesics Are Closed. (Ergebnisse der Mathmatik und Ihrer Grenzbebiete: Vol. 93). (Illus.). 1978. 45.10 (ISBN 0-387-08158-5). Springer-Verlag.

Bishop, Richard & Goldberg, Samuel. Tensor Analysis on Manifolds. (Illus.). 1980. pap. 5.50 (ISBN 0-486-64039-6). Dover.

Browder, W. Surgery on Simply-Connected Manifolds. LC 70-175907. (Ergebnisse der Mathematik und Ihrer Grenzgebiete: Vol. 65). 140p. 1972. 17.50 (ISBN 0-387-05629-7). Springer-Verlag.

Burghelea, D. & Lashof, R. Groups of Automarphisms of Manifolds. (Lecture Notes in Mathematics Ser.: Vol. 473). 156p. 1975. pap. 10.00 (ISBN 0-387-07182-2). Springer-Verlag.

Carr, J. Applications of Centre Manifold Theory. (Applied Mathematical Sciences Ser.: Vol. 35). 160p. pap. 14.00 (ISBN 0-387-90577-4). Springer-Verlag.

Chapman, T. A. Lectures on Hilbert Cube Manifolds. LC 76-48316. (Conference Board of the Mathematical Sciences Ser.: No. 28). 1976. 11.20 (ISBN 0-8218-1678-0, CBMS28). Am Math.

Chen, Bang-Yen. Geometry of Submanifolds. (Pure & Applied Mathematics Ser: Vol. 22). 310p. 1973. 29.75 (ISBN 0-8247-6075-1). Dekker.

Choquet-Bruhat, Y. C., et al. Analysis, Manifolds & Physics. 1977. 19.50 (ISBN 0-7204-0494-0, North-Holland). Elsevier.

Conference on Topological Methods in Algebraic Topology, SUNY, Binghamton, Oct. 1973. Algebraic & Geometrical Methods in Topology: Proceedings. McAuley, L. F., ed. (Lecture Notes in Mathematics Ser.: Vol. 428). xi, 280p. 1975. pap. 14.70 (ISBN 0-387-07019-2). Springer-Verlag.

De Medrano, Lopez. Involutions on Manifolds. LC 74-139952. (Ergebnisse der Mathematik und Ihrer Grenzgebiete: Vol. 59). (Illus.). 1971. 23.60 (ISBN 0-387-05092-2). Springer-Verlag.

Eberlein, Patrick. Surfaces of Nonpositive Curvature. LC 79-15112. 90p. 1979. 8.00 (ISBN 0-8218-2218-7). Am Math.

Fenn, R., ed. Topology of Low-Dimensional Manifolds: Proceedings. (Lecture Notes in Mathematics: Vol. 722). 1979. pap. 10.30 (ISBN 0-387-09506-3). Springer-Verlag.

Hamilton, R. S. Harmonic Maps of Manifolds with Boundary. (Lecture Notes in Mathematics Ser.: Vol. 471). 168p. 1975. pap. 10.90 (ISBN 0-387-07185-7). Springer-Verlag.

Hempel, John. Three-Manifolds. LC 76-3027. (Annals of Mathematics Studies: No. 86). 204p. 1976. 16.00 (ISBN 0-686-75221-X); pap. 8.50 (ISBN 0-691-08183-2). Princeton U Pr.

Hermann, Robert. Geometry, Physics & Systems. (Pure & Applied Mathematics Ser: Vol. 18). 320p. 1973. 34.75 (ISBN 0-8247-6052-2). Dekker.

Hirsch, Morris W. & Mazur, Barry. Smoothings of Piecewise Linear Manifolds. LC 74-2967. (Annals of Mathematics Studies: No. 80). 165p. 1974. 11.00x (ISBN 0-691-08145-X). Princeton U Pr.

Iberkleid, W. & Petrie, T. Smooth S-One Manifolds. (Lecture Notes in Mathematics: Vol. 557). 1976. soft cover 9.50 (ISBN 0-387-08002-3). Springer-Verlag.

Jackson, R. J. Canonical Differential Operators & Lower-Order Symbols. LC 73-8760. (Memoirs: No. 135). 1973. 9.60 (ISBN 0-8218-1835-X, MEMO-135). Am Math.

James, I. M. The Topology of Stiefel Manifolds. LC 76-9646. (London Mathematical Society Lecture Notes Ser.: No. 24). 1977. 14.50x (ISBN 0-521-21334-7). Cambridge U Pr.

Jensen, G. Higher Order Contact of Submanifolds of Homogeneous Spaces. LC 77-14394. (Lecture Notes in Mathematics: Vol. 610). 1977. pap. text ed. 10.70 (ISBN 0-387-08433-9). Springer-Verlag.

Johannson, K. Homotopy Equivalence of Three-Manifolds with Boundaries. (Lecture Notes in Mathematics: Vol. 761). 303p. 1979. pap. 18.90 (ISBN 0-387-09714-7). Springer-Verlag.

Karras, U., et al. Cutting and Pasting of Manifolds: SK-Groups. LC 73-76374. (Mathematics Lecture Ser: No. 1). 70p. 1973. pap. 3.00 (ISBN 0-914098-10-1). Publish or Perish.

Kirby, Robion C. & Siebenmann, Laurence C. Foundational Essays on Topological Manifolds, Smoothing & Triangulations. LC 76-45918. (Annals of Mathematical Studies: No. 88). 352p. 1977. 22.00x (ISBN 0-691-08190-5); pap. 9.95x (ISBN 0-691-08191-3). Princeton U Pr.

Lu, Y. C. Singularity Theory & Introduction to Catastrophe Theory. LC 76-48307. (Illus.). 1976. soft cover 16.80 (ISBN 0-387-90221-X). Springer-Verlag.

Madsen, Ib & Milgram, R. James. The Classified Spaces for Surger & Cobordism of Manifolds. LC 78-70311. (Annals of Mathematics Studies: No. 92). 1979. 25.00x (ISBN 0-691-08225-1); pap. text ed. 8.50 (ISBN 0-691-08226-X). Princeton U Pr.

Matsushima, Y. Differentiable Manifolds. (Pure & Applied Mathematics Ser.: Vol. 9). 1972. 29.50 (ISBN 0-8247-1445-8). Dekker.

Matsushima, Yozo. Holomorphic Vector Fields on Compact Kaehler Manifolds. LC 77-145641. (CBMS Regional Conference Series in Mathematics: No. 7). 1971. 7.40 (ISBN 0-8218-1656-X, CBMS-7). Am Math.

Millett, K. C., ed. Algebraic & Geometric Topology: Proceedings of a Symposium Held at Santa Barbara in Honor of Raymond L. Wilder, July 25-29, 1977. LC 78-15091. (Lecture Notes in Mathematics: Vol. 664). 1978. pap. 12.80 (ISBN 0-387-08920-9). Springer-Verlag.

Moishezon, B. Complex Surfaces & Connected Sums of Complex Projective Plans. LC 77-22136. (Lecture Notes in Mathematics: Vol. 603). (Illus.). 1977. pap. text ed. 14.60 (ISBN 0-387-08355-3). Springer-Verlag.

Neuwirth, L. P., ed. Knots, Groups, & 3-Manifolds: Papers Dedicated to the Memory of R. H. Fox. LC 75-5619. (Annals of Mathematics Studies: No. 84). 345p. 1975. 24.00 (ISBN 0-691-08170-0); pap. 9.50 (ISBN 0-691-08167-0). Princeton U Pr.

Orlik, P. Seifert Manifolds. LC 72-90184. (Lecture Notes in Mathematics: Vol. 291). 155p. 1972. pap. 6.30 (ISBN 0-387-06014-6). Springer-Verlag.

Poston, T. & Woodcock, A. E. A Geometrical Study of the Elementary Catastrophes. LC 73-22575. (Lectures Notes in Mathematics: Vol. 373). (Illus.). v, 257p. 1974. pap. 14.60 (ISBN 0-387-06681-0). Springer-Verlag.

Stone, D. A. Stratified Polyhedra. LC 77-187427. (Lecture Notes in Mathematics: Vol. 252). 193p. 1972. pap. 7.00 (ISBN 0-387-05726-9). Springer-Verlag.

Sundararaman, D. Moduli, Deformations & Classifications of Compact, Complex Manifolds. (Research Notes in Mathematics Ser.: No. 45). 240p. 1980. pap. text ed. 22.95 (ISBN 0-273-08458-5). Pitman Pub MA.

Wall, C. T. Surgery on Compact Manifolds. (London Mathematical Society Monograph Ser). 1971. 45.00 (ISBN 0-12-732750-9). Acad Pr.

Weinstein, Alan. Lectures on Symplectic Manifolds. LC 77-3399. (Conference Board of the Mathematical Sciences Ser.: No. 29). 1979. Repr. of 1977 ed. with corrections 8.40 (ISBN 0-8218-1679-9, CBMS29). Am Math.

Yano, Kentaro & Kon, Masahiro. Anti-Inavariant Submanifolds. (Lecture Notes in Pure & Applied Math Ser.: Vol. 21). 1976. 23.75 (ISBN 0-8247-6555-9). Dekker.

Zagier, D. B. Equivariant Pontrjagin Classes & Applications to Orbit Spaces. LC 72-90185. (Lecture Notes in Mathematics: Vol. 290). 130p. 1972. pap. 6.30 (ISBN 0-387-06013-8). Springer-Verlag.

MANIFOLDS, ALMOST COMPLEX
see Almost Complex Manifolds

MANIFOLDS, DIFFERENTIABLE
see Differential Topology

MANIFOLDS, RIEMANNIAN
see Riemannian Manifolds

MANIKINS
see Anatomy, Human–Charts, Diagrams, etc.; Models, Fashion

MANILA

McHale, Thomas R. & McHale, Mary C. Early American-Philippine Trade: The Journal of Nathaniel Bowditch in Manila, 1796. (Monograph Ser.: No. 2). viii, 63p. 1962. 3.25 (ISBN 0-686-30905-7). Yale U SE Asia.

Reed, Robert R. Colonial Manila: The Context of Hispanic Urbanism & Process of Morphogenesis. (Publications in Geography Ser.: Vol. 22). 1978. pap. 13.50x (ISBN 0-520-09579-0). U of Cal Pr.

Torrevillas-Suarez, Domini. Vendors of Manila. 1972. wrps. 2.50x (ISBN 0-686-18712-1). Cellar.

MANILA BAY, BATTLE OF, 1898

Conroy, Robert. Battle of Manila Bay. (Battle Book Series). (Illus.). (gr. 5-8). 1968. 3.50g (ISBN 0-02-724270-6). Macmillan.

Dewey, George. Autobiography. LC 74-108813. (BCL Ser. I). (Illus.). Repr. of 1913 ed. 17.50 (ISBN 0-404-02121-2). AMS Pr.

MANILA ROPE
see Rope

MANIN, DANIELE, 1804-1857

Ginsborg, Paul. Daniele Manin & the Venetian Revolution of 1848-49. LC 78-56180. (Illus.). 1979. 41.50 (ISBN 0-521-22077-7). Cambridge U Pr.

Trevelyan, George M. Manin & the Venetian Revolution of 1848. LC 75-80597. xvi, 284p. 1974. Repr. of 1923 ed. 22.50 (ISBN 0-86527-122-4). Fertig.

MANIPULATION (THERAPEUTICS)

Bradbury, Parnell. Mechanics of Healing: Spinology. 7.50x (ISBN 0-87556-038-5). Saifer.

Buerger, Alfred A. & Tobis, Jerome S. Approaches to the Validation of Manipulation Therapy. (Illus.). 352p. 1977. 34.50 (ISBN 0-398-03565-2). C C Thomas.

Fisk, James W. A Practical Guide to Management of the Painful Neck & Back: Diagnosis, Manipulation, Exercises, Prevention. (Illus.). 248p. 1977. 22.50 (ISBN 0-398-03640-3). C C Thomas.

Ghista, Dhanjoo N. & Roaf, R., eds. Orthopaedic Mechanics, Procedures & Devices. 1981. Vol. II August, 1981. write for info. (ISBN 0-12-281602-1); Vol. III, September, 1981. write for info. (ISBN 0-12-281603-X). Acad Pr.

Grieve, Gregory P. Mobilisation of the Spine. 3rd ed. LC 78-40947. (Illus.). 1979. pap. text ed. 11.25 (ISBN 0-443-01865-0). Churchill.

Korr, I. M., ed. The Neurobiologic Mechanisms in Manipulative Therapy. LC 78-4667. 488p. 1978. 25.00 (ISBN 0-306-31150-X, Plenum Pr). Plenum Pub.

Lawrence, Paul A. Manipulative Therapy Style Massage. LC 81-80701. (Positive Health Ser.). (Illus.). 80p. (Orig.). 1981. pap. 6.95 (ISBN 0-938034-04-9). PAL Pr.

Maitland, G. D. Vertebral Manipulation. 4th ed. 1977. pap. 24.95 (ISBN 0-407-43505-0). Butterworth.

Mennell, John M. Back Pain: Diagnosis & Treatment Using Manipulative Techniques. 226p. 1960. 14.95 (ISBN 0-316-56667-5). Little.

--Joint Pain: Diagnosis & Treatment Using Manipulative Techniques. 178p. 1964. 14.95 (ISBN 0-316-56668-3). Little.

Nwuga, Vincent C. Manipulation of the Spine. (Illus.). 124p. 1976. pap. 9.95 (ISBN 0-683-06600-5). Williams & Wilkins.

Rogoff, Joseph K. Manipulation, Traction & Massage. 2nd ed. (Rehabilitation Medicine Library Ser.). (Illus.). 225p. 1980. lib. bdg. 25.50 (ISBN 0-683-07324-9). Williams & Wilkins.

Schiotz, Eiler H. & Cyriax, James. Manipulation: Past & Present. (Illus.). 1975. 18.95x (ISBN 0-433-07010-2). Intl Ideas.

MANITOBA

Begg, Alexander. Red River Journal & Other Papers Relative to the Red River Resistance of 1869-1870. Morton, W. L., ed. LC 69-14506. 1969. Repr. of 1956 ed. lib. bdg. 36.75x (ISBN 0-8371-5074-4, BERR). Greenwood.

Dawson, Simon J. Report on the Exploration of the Country Between Lake Superior & the Red River Settlement, & Between the Latter Place & the Assiniboine & Saskatchewan. LC 68-55184. 1968. Repr. of 1859 ed. lib. bdg. 40.00x (ISBN 0-8371-5031-0, DALS). Greenwood.

Hind, Henry Y. Narrative of the Canadian Red River Exploring Expedition of 1857, 2 vols. in 1. LC 70-133868. (Illus.). 1971. 23.10 (ISBN 0-8048-1009-5). C E Tuttle.

--Narrative of the Canadian Red River Exploring Expedition of 1857, & of the Assiniboine & Saskatchewan Exploring Expedition of 1858, 2 Vols. LC 68-55195. (Illus.). 1968. Repr. of 1860 ed. Set. lib. bdg. 35.00x (ISBN 0-8371-3896-5, HIRR). Greenwood.

--North-West Territory: Reports of Progress. Bd. with Report on the Exploration. LC 68-55184. 1968. Repr. of 1859 ed. lib. bdg. 40.00x (ISBN 0-8371-5031-0, DALS). Greenwood.

Keating, William H. Narrative of the Expedition to the Source of St. Peter's River. facsimile ed. (Illus.). 1825. 12.50 (ISBN 0-87018-036-3). Ross.

MacMillan, James A., et al. Manitoba Interlake Area: A Regional Development Evaluation. (Illus.). 1975. pap. text ed. 4.95x (ISBN 0-8138-1045-0). Iowa St U Pr.

Morton, William L. Manitoba: A History. 2nd ed. LC 67-4598. (Illus.). 1967. 27.50x (ISBN 0-8020-1711-8); pap. 10.00 (ISBN 0-8020-6070-6). U of Toronto Pr.

Powell & Van Dyke. Minnesota & Manitoba One Hundred Years Ago. (Illus.). pap. 3.50 (ISBN 0-89540-056-1). Sun Pub.

West, John. Substance of a Journal During a Residence at the Red River Colony. 14.00 (ISBN 0-384-66930-1). Johnson Repr.

MANJU LANGUAGE
see Manchu Language

MANN, ANTHONY, 1906-1967

Basinger, Jeanine. Anthony Mann. (Theatrical Arts Ser.). 1979. lib. bdg. 12.50 (ISBN 0-8057-9263-5). Twayne.

MANN, HEINRICH, 1871-1950

Gross, David. The Writer & Society: Heinrich Mann & Literary Politics in Germany Eighteen Ninety to Nineteen Forty. LC 79-11707. 1980. text ed. 15.00x (ISBN 0-391-00972-9). Humanities.

Hamilton, Nigel. The Brother Mann: The Lives of Heinrich & Thomas Mann, 1871-1950, 1875-1955. LC 78-15114. 1979. 30.00 (ISBN 0-300-02348-0); pap. 9.95 (ISBN 0-300-02668-4). Yale U Pr.

Trapp, Frithjof. Kunst als Gesellschaftanalyse bei Heinrich Mann. (Quellen und Forschungen Zur Sprach und Kulturgeschichte der Germanischen Voelker NF 64-188). vi, 328p. 1975. text ed. 50.60x (ISBN 3-11-005968-1). De Gruyter.

Winter, Lorenz. Heinrich Mann & His Public: A Socioliterary Study of the Relationship Between an Author & His Public. Gorman, John, tr. LC 72-81616. 1970. 7.95x (ISBN 0-87024-123-0). U of Miami Pr.

MANN, HORACE, 1796-1859

Culver, Raymond B. Horace Mann & Religion in the Massachusetts Public Schools. LC 72-89168. (American Education: Its Men, Institutions & Ideas, Ser. 1). 1969. Repr. of 1929 ed. 17.00 (ISBN 0-405-01406-6). Arno.

Downs, Robert B. Horace Mann. (World Leaders Ser: No. 29). 1974. lib. bdg. 9.95 (ISBN 0-8057-3544-5). Twayne.

Filler, Louis, ed. Horace Mann on the Crisis in Education. LC 65-18902. 1965. 9.00x (ISBN 0-87338-071-1). Kent St U Pr.

Hinsdale, Burke A. Horace Mann & the Common School Revival in the U. S. LC 72-78748. 1898. Repr. 21.00 (ISBN 0-403-08928-X). Somerset Pub.

King, C. S. Bibliography of Horace Mann: Seventeen Ninety-Six to Eighteen Fifty-Nine. LC 66-11926. 1966. 17.50 (ISBN 0-379-00258-2). Oceana.

McCluskey, Neil Gerard. Public Schools & Moral Education. LC 74-12848. 315p. 1975. Repr. of 1958 ed. lib. bdg. 17.50x (ISBN 0-8371-7762-6, MCPS). Greenwood.

Mann, Horace. Letters of Horace Walpole, Earl of Oxford, to Sir Horace Mann, 2 vols. 1979. Repr. of 1843 ed. lib. bdg. 75.00 (ISBN 0-8495-3848-3). Arden Lib.

Mann, Mary. Life of Horace Mann. facs. ed. LC 73-89396. (Black Heritage Library Collection Ser). 1865. 20.00 (ISBN 0-8369-8624-5). Arno.

Mann, Mary P. Life of Horace Mann. (Educational Ser.). 1937. Repr. 30.00 (ISBN 0-685-43649-7). Norwood Edns.

Morgan, Joy E. Horace Mann: His Ideas & Ideals. (Educational Ser.). 1936. Repr. 10.00 (ISBN 0-685-43135-5). Norwood Edns.

Pierce, Edith G. Horace Mann: Our Nation's First Educator. LC 78-128805. (Real Life Bks). (Illus.). (gr. 5-11). 1972. PLB 3.95 (ISBN 0-8225-0703-X). Lerner Pubns.

Tharp, Louise H. Until Victory: Horace Mann & Mary Peabody. LC 77-6360. (Illus.). 1977. Repr. of 1953 ed. lib. bdg. 24.50x (ISBN 0-8371-9653-1, THUV). Greenwood.

MANN, THOMAS, 1875-1955

Apter, T. E. Thomas Mann: The Devil's Advocate. LC 78-61134. 1979. 17.50x (ISBN 0-8147-0566-9). NYU Pr.

Bauer, Arnold. Thomas Mann. Henderson, Alexander & Henderson, Elizabeth, trs. from Ger. LC 71-139221. (Modern Literature Ser.). 1971. 10.95 (ISBN 0-8044-2023-8); pap. 4.95 (ISBN 0-8044-6018-3). Ungar.

Berendsohn, Walter A. Thomas Mann: Artist & Partisan in Troubled Times. Buck, George C., tr. LC 77-104934. 1973. 19.95x (ISBN 0-8173-8062-0). U of Ala Pr.

Bergsten, Gunilla. Thomas Mann's Doctor Faustus: The Sources & Structure of the Novel. Winston, Krishna, tr. LC 69-14483. 1969. 12.00x (ISBN 0-226-04365-7). U of Chicago Pr.

Block, Haskell M. Naturalistic Triptych: The Fictive & the Real in Zola, Mann & Dreiser. 1970. pap. text ed. 2.95 (ISBN 0-685-19749-2). Phila Bk Co.

Brennan, J. G. Three Philosophical Novelists. 1964. 9.95 (ISBN 0-02-514930-X). Macmillan.
Bulhof, Francis. Wortindex Zu Thomas Mann: Der Zauberberg. LC 75-42984. 614p. (Sponsored by The College of Humanities, The University of Texas at Austin). 1976. 39.00 (ISBN 0-8357-0159-X, SS-00006). Univ Microfilms.
Burgin, Hans & Mayer, Hans-Otto. Thomas Mann: A Chronicle of His Life. rev. ed. Dobson, Eugene, tr. LC 68-10989. (Illus.). 320p. 1969. pap. 6.95 (ISBN 0-8173-8064-7). U of Ala Pr.
Cleugh, James. Thomas Mann: A Study. LC 66-27054. (Illus.). 1968. Repr. of 1933 ed. 7.50 (ISBN 0-8462-1038-X). Russell.
Corngold, Stanley, et al. Thomas Mann, 1875-1955. (Illus.). 1975. pap. 3.00 (ISBN 0-87811-021-6). Princeton Lib.
Czermak, Herberth. Magic Mountain Notes. (Orig.). 1969. pap. 1.95 (ISBN 0-8220-0789-4). Cliffs.
Feuerlicht, Ignace. Thomas Mann. LC 68-24312. (World Authors Ser.: Germany: No. 47). 1969. lib. bdg. 12.50 (ISBN 0-8057-2584-9). Twayne.
Gray, Ronald D. German Tradition in Literature. LC 65-17206. 1966. 48.00 (ISBN 0-521-05133-9); pap. 17.50 (ISBN 0-521-29278-6). Cambridge U Pr.
Hamilton, Nigel. The Brother Mann: The Lives of Heinrich & Thomas Mann, 1871-1950, 1875-1955. LC 78-15114. 1979. 30.00 (ISBN 0-300-02348-0); pap. 9.95 (ISBN 0-300-02668-4). Yale U Pr.
Hatfield, Henry. From "The Magic Mountain". Mann's Later Masterpieces. LC 78-74213. (Illus.). 1979. 17.50 (ISBN 0-8014-1204-8). Cornell U Pr.
Heiney, Donald. Barron's Simplified Approach to Mann's Magic Mountain & Other Works. 1966. pap. text ed. 1.50 (ISBN 0-8120-0177-X). Barron.
Heller, Erich. The Poet's Self & the Poem: Essays on Goethe, Nietzsche & Thomas Mann. 1976. text ed. 13.00x (ISBN 0-485-11164-0, Athlone Pr). Humanities.
--Thomas Mann: The Ironic German. LC 79-63046. 1979. pap. 5.95 (ISBN 0-89526-906-6). Regnery-Gateway.
--Thomas Mann: The Ironic German, a Study. 1958. 12.00 (ISBN 0-911858-29-6). Appel.
Heller, Peter. Dialectics & Nihilism: Essays on Lessing, Nietzsche, Mann & Kafka. LC 65-26240. 1969. Repr. of 1966 ed. 15.00x (ISBN 0-87023-019-0). U of Mass Pr.
Hollingdale, R. J. Thomas Mann: a Critical Study. LC 79-161509. 204p. 1971. 12.00 (ISBN 0-8387-1004-2). Bucknell U Pr.
Hughes, Kenneth, ed. Thomas Mann in Context: Papers of the Clark University Centennial Colloquim. LC 77-26366. 1978. 15.00 (ISBN 0-914206-11-7, IS-00043, Pub. by Clark Univ. Press). Univ Microfilms.
Jonas, Ilsedore B. Thomas Mann & Italy. Crouse, Betty, tr. LC 79-9779. 208p. 1979. 14.95 (ISBN 0-8173-8063-9). U of Ala Pr.
Juhasz, Leslie. Monarch Notes on Mann's Major Works. (Orig.). pap. 1.95 (ISBN 0-671-00566-9). Monarch Pr.
Kaufmann, Fritz. Thomas Mann: The World As Will & Representation. LC 73-75847. xiii, 322p. 1973. Repr. of 1957 ed. lib. bdg. 12.50x (ISBN 0-8154-0480-8). Cooper Sq.
Lukacs, Georg. Essays on Thomas Mann. Mitchell, S., tr. from Ger. 1964. text ed. write for info. (ISBN 0-85036-070-6); pap. text ed. write for info. (ISBN 0-685-19578-3). Humanities.
--Essays on Thomas Mann. Mitchell, Stanley, tr. from Ger. 1979. Repr. of 1965 ed. 19.50 (ISBN 0-86527-245-X). Fertig.
Mann, Erika. Last Year of Thomas Mann. facs. ed. Graves, Richard, tr. LC 72-126323. (Biography Index Reprint Ser.). 1958. 12.00 (ISBN 0-8369-8029-8). Arno.
Neider, Charles, ed. Stature of Thomas Mann. facs. ed. LC 68-16961. (Essay Index Reprint Ser). 1947. 24.75 (ISBN 0-8369-0737-X). Arno.
Nelson, Donald F. Portrait of the Artist As Hermes: A Study of Myth & Psychology in Thomas Mann's Felix-Krull. (Studies in the Germanic Languages & Literatures Ser.: No. 70). 158p. 1971. 11.00x (ISBN 0-8078-8070-1). U of NC Pr.
Nicholls, Roger A. Nietzsche in the Early Work of Thomas Mann. LC 73-89426. 119p. 1976. Repr. of 1955 ed. 12.00 (ISBN 0-8462-1770-8). Russell.
Reed, T. J. Thomas Mann: The Uses of Tradition. 442p. 1974. 36.00x (ISBN 0-19-815742-8); pap. 8.25x (ISBN 0-19-815747-9). Oxford U Pr.
Slochower, Harry. Three Ways of Modern Man. LC 37-17328. 1968. Repr. of 1937 ed. 12.00 (ISBN 0-527-83656-7). Kraus Repr.
Stern, Joseph P. Thomas Mann. LC 67-16891. (Columbia Essays on Modern Writers Ser.: No. 24). 1967. pap. 2.00 (ISBN 0-231-02847-4, MW24). Columbia U Pr.
Swales, Martin. Thomas Mann: A Study. 117p. 1980. 11.50x (ISBN 0-8476-6270-5). Rowman.
Tollinchi, Esteban. Las Visiones De Thomas Mann. (UPREX, E. Literarios: No. 16). pap. 1.85 (ISBN 0-8477-0016-X): U of PR Pr.
Universidad De Puerto Rico.(Rio Piedras Campus) Rectoria. Cuatro Conferencias Conmemorativas: Miguel Angel, Thomas Mann, Rainer Maria Rilke, Carlos Gustavo Jung. LC 77-4452. 1977. pap. 2.50 (ISBN 0-8477-3180-4). U of PR Pr.
Von Gronicka, Andre. Thomas Mann: Profile & Perspectives. (Orig.). 1971. pap. text ed. 3.95x (ISBN 0-685-04770-9). Phila Bk Co.
Weigand, Herman J. The Magic Mountain. LC 78-27850. (North Carolina, University. Studies in the Germanic Languages & Literatures: No. 49). Repr. of 1965 ed. 18.50 (ISBN 0-404-50949-5). AMS Pr.
Weigand, Hermann J. Thomas Mann's Novel, "Der Zauberberg". A Study. LC 78-149678. Repr. of 1933 ed. 18.50 (ISBN 0-404-06889-8). AMS Pr.
Winston, Richard. Thomas Mann: The Making of an Artist, 1875-1911. LC 81-47515. 1981. 17.95 (ISBN 0-394-47171-7). Knopf.
Winston, Richard & Winston, Clara, eds. Letters of Thomas Mann, 1889-1955. LC 68-23967. (Illus.). 1971. 17.50 (ISBN 0-394-43304-1). Knopf.

MANN, THOMAS, 1875-1955–BIBLIOGRAPHY

Jonas, Klaus W. Fifty Years of Thomas Mann Studies: A Bibliography of Criticism. LC 55-6013. 1969. Repr. of 1955 ed. 12.00 (ISBN 0-527-46650-6). Kraus Repr.
Porter, Robert G. Preparation of Computerized Index to Nonfiction of Thomas Mann. (Rice University Studies: Vol. 55, No. 2). 118p. 1969. pap. 3.25x (ISBN 0-89263-200-3). Rice Univ.

MANNED ORBITAL LABORATORIES

see Space Stations

MANNED SPACE FLIGHT

see also Astronauts; Outer Space; Project Mercury; Space Medicine; Space Ships; X-Fifteen (Rocket Aircraft)

Bergaust, Erik. Colonizing the Planets: The Factual Story of Manned Interplanetary Flight into the 21st Century. (Illus.). 96p. (gr. 6-8). 1975. PLB 5.49 (ISBN 0-399-60961-X). Putnam.
Florkin, M. & Dollfus, A., eds. Life Sciences & Space Research, Vol. 2. (Cospar Ser). 1964. 44.00 (ISBN 0-444-10198-5, North-Holland). Elsevier.
Gatland, Kenneth. Manned Spacecraft. rev. ed. LC 76-1994. 1976. 9.95 (ISBN 0-02-542820-9, 54282). Macmillan.
Soviet Writings on Earth Satellites & Space Travel. LC 78-117846. (Essay Index Reprint Ser). 1958. 14.50 (ISBN 0-8369-1719-7). Arno.
Symposium on Manned Lunar Flight, Denver, 1961. Manned Lunar Flight. Morgenthaler, G. W. & Jacobs, H., eds. (Advances in the Astronautical Sciences Ser.: Vol. 10). 1963. 35.00 (ISBN 0-87703-011-1). Am Astronaut.

MANNED SPACE FLIGHT–PHYSIOLOGICAL EFFECT

see Space Flight–Physiological Effect

MANNED SPACE FLIGHT–RESCUE WORK

see Space Rescue Operations

MANNED UNDERSEA RESEARCH STATIONS

Ross, Frank, Jr. Undersea Vechicles & Habitats: The Peaceful Uses of the Ocean. LC 76-106577. (Illus.). (gr. 5-8). 1970. 10.95 (ISBN 0-690-84416-6, TYC-J). Har-Row.
Talkington. Undersea Work Systems. (Ocean Engineering Ser.: Vol. 1). 240p. 1981. 27.50 (ISBN 0-8247-1226-9). Dekker.

MANNEQUINS

see Models, Fashion

MANNERISM (ART)

Forster, Kurt. Mannerist Painting: Sixteenth Century. (Color Slide Program of Art Enjoyment Ser). (Illus.). 1966. 17.95 (ISBN 0-07-021617-7, P&RB). McGraw.
Friedlaender, Walter. Mannerism & Anti-Mannerism in Italian Painting. LC 57-8295. (Illus.). 1965. pap. 3.45 (ISBN 0-8052-0094-0). Schocken.
Haraszti-Takacs, Marianne & Racz, Eva. The Masters of Mannerism. 2nd & rev. ed. (Illus.). 1977. 25.00 (ISBN 0-8283-1724-0). Branden.
Harhszti-Takacs, M. The Masters of Mannerism. 13.00 (ISBN 0-912728-99-X). Newbury Bks Inc.
Hayward, J. F. Virtuoso Goldsmiths & the Triumph of Mannerism, 1540-1620. (Illus.). 796p. 1976. 145.00x (ISBN 0-85667-005-7, Pub. by Sotheby Parke Bernet England). Biblio Dist.
Murray, Linda. The High Renaissance & Mannerism: Italy, the North, & Spain, 1500-1600. (World of Art Ser.). (Illus.). 1978. pap. text ed. 9.95 (ISBN 0-19-519990-1). Oxford U Pr.
Robinson, Franklin W. & Nichols, Stephen G., Jr., eds. The Meaning of Mannerism. LC 71-189512. (Illus.). 142p. 1972. text ed. 9.00x (ISBN 0-87451-068-6). U Pr of New England.
Rowland, Daniel B. Mannerism - Style & Mood. 1964. 29.50x (ISBN 0-685-69860-2). Elliots Bks.
Shearman, John. Mannerism. (Illus.). 1978. pap. 5.95 (ISBN 0-14-020808-9, Pelican). Penguin.
Smart, Alastair. Renaissance & Mannerism in Italy. (History of Art Ser.). (Illus.). 1971. pap. text ed. 8.95 (ISBN 0-15-576595-7, HC). HarBraceJ.
Studing, Richard & Kruz, Elizabeth. Mannerism in Art, Literature, & Music: A Bibliography. LC 79-63612. (Checklists in the Humanities & Education Ser.). 79p. 1979. 7.50 (ISBN 0-911536-79-5). Trinity U Pr.

MANNERS AND CUSTOMS

see also Birth (In Religion, Folk-Lore, etc.); Bohemianism; Caste; Chivalry; Clothing and Dress; Costume; Courts and Courtiers; Cries; Drinking Customs; Dueling; Etiquette; Fairs; Festivals; Funeral Rites and Ceremonies; Gifts; Halloween; Holidays; Kissing; Marriage Customs and Rites; Minstrels; Mourning Customs; Oaths; Popular Culture; Rings; Rites and Ceremonies; Sports; Students; Taboo; Tattooing; Toasts; Tournaments; Travel; Wayfaring Life; Women–History

Ajisafa, Ajawi K. The Laws & Customs of the Yoruba People. 1976. lib. bdg. 59.95 (ISBN 0-8490-2135-9). Gordon Pr.
Baring-Gould, Sabine. Strange Survivals, Some Chapters in the History of Man. LC 67-23909. (Illus.). 1968. Repr. of 1892 ed. 19.00 (ISBN 0-8103-3422-4). Gale.
Boehn, Max Von & Fischel, Oskar. Modes & Manners of the Ninteenth Century, 4 Vols in 2. rev. & enl. ed. LC 68-56493. (Illus.). Repr. of 1927 ed. Set. 50.00 (ISBN 0-405-08283-5, Blom Pubns); 25.00 ea. Vol. 1 (ISBN 0-405-08281-9). Vol. 2 (ISBN 0-405-08282-7). Arno.
Burton, Richard F. The Sotadic Zone. LC 77-90796. 1977. Repr. lib. bdg. 12.50 (ISBN 0-89341-466-2). Longwood Pr.
Donald, Elsie B., ed. Debrett's Etiquette & Modern Manners. (Illus.). 400p. 1981. 25.00 (ISBN 0-670-26231-5). Viking Pr.
Eadie, John W. Classical Traditions in Early America. LC 76-51864. 265p. (Orig.). 1976. pap. 10.00 (ISBN 0-915932-02-4). Trillium Pr.
Eckenstein, Lina. Spell of Words: Studies in Language Bearing on Custom. LC 68-23153. 1969. Repr. of 1932 ed. 19.00 (ISBN 0-8103-3892-0). Gale.
Etkin, William. Social Behavior from Fish to Man. abr. ed. LC 67-28654. 1967. pap. 2.45 (ISBN 0-226-22037-0, P533, Phoen). U of Chicago Pr.
Frazer, James G. Garnered Sheaves: Essays, Addresses, Reviews. facs. ed. LC 67-30212. (Essay Index Reprint Ser). 1931. 19.50 (ISBN 0-8369-0457-5). Arno.
Freedman, Warren. Societal Behavior: New & Unique Rights of the Person. 356p. 1965. ed. spiral bdg. 27.50photocopy (ISBN 0-398-00609-1). C C Thomas.
Griswold, William H. Descriptive Lists of American, International, Romantic & British Novels, 2 Vols. (Bibliography & Reference Ser.: No. 134). 1968. Repr. of 1964 ed. 48.00 (ISBN 0-8337-1463-5). B Franklin.
Hammerton, J. A., ed. Manners & Customs of Mankind, 2 vols. 1977. Set. lib. bdg. 250.00 (ISBN 0-8490-2202-9). Gordon Pr.
Jones, T. Gwynn. Welsh Folklore & Folk-Custom. rev. ed. 1979. Repr. of 1930 ed. 17.50x (ISBN 0-8476-6185-7). Rowman.
Keller, Irene. Thingumajig Book of Manners. (Illus.). (gr. k-4). 1981. PLB 8.65 (ISBN 0-516-09155-7). Childrens.
Knowlson, Thomas S. Origins of Popular Superstitions & Customs. LC 68-30946. 1968. Repr. of 1910 ed. 20.00 (ISBN 0-8103-3357-0). Gale.
Odor, Ruth S. Thanks. LC 79-23926. (What Does It Mean? Ser.). (Illus.). (ps-2). 1980. PLB 5.50 (ISBN 0-89565-113-0). Childs World.
Peters, Charles C. Motion Pictures & Standards of Morality. LC 72-124030. (Literature of Cinema Ser.: Payne Fund Studies). Repr. of 1933 ed. 9.00 (ISBN 0-405-01648-4). Arno.
Prevo, Helen. Manners. 1970. pap. 2.50x (ISBN 0-88323-055-0, 153); tchr's. key 2.50x (ISBN 0-88323-056-9, 154). Richards Pub.
Prevot, Floriane. Dictionnaire du Savoir-Vivre Moderne. 336p. (Fr.). 1970. 10.95 (ISBN 0-686-56871-0, M-6649). French & Eur.
Scudder, H. E. Men & Manners in America One Hundred Years Ago. 1876. Repr. 15.00 (ISBN 0-685-43300-5). Norwood Edns.
Smith, T. Lynn & Das, Man S., eds. Sociocultural Change Since 1950. 380p. 1978. 34.00x (ISBN 0-7069-0659-4, Pub. by Croom Helm Ltd England). Biblio Dist.
Tonnies, Ferdinand. Custom: An Essay on Social Codes. LC 61-9175. 1971. pap. 2.95 (ISBN 0-89526-990-2). Regnery-Gateway.
Verrill, Alpheus H. Strange Customs, Manners & Beliefs. facs. ed. LC 75-86791. (Essay Index Reprint Ser). 1946. 18.00 (ISBN 0-8369-1199-7). Arno.
Wagner, Leopold. Manners, Customs & Observances. LC 68-22059. 1968. Repr. of 1894 ed. 19.00 (ISBN 0-8103-3097-0). Gale.
Walsh, William S. Curiosities of Popular Customs. LC 66-23951. 1966. Repr. of 1898 ed. 44.00 (ISBN 0-8103-3008-3). Gale.
Watson, Lillian E. Customs of Mankind, with Notes on Modern Etiquette & the Newest Trend in Entertainment. LC 72-111590. (Illus.). Repr. of 1924 ed. 32.00x (ISBN 0-8371-4620-8). Greenwood.
Wernecke, Herbert H. Christmas Customs Around the World. LC 59-9581. 1979. pap. 3.95 (ISBN 0-664-24258-8). Westminster.
Wolff, Christian. Vernunfitige Gedanken Von Dem Gesellschaftlichen Leben der Menschen. 338p. Repr. of 1756 ed. 27.00 (ISBN 0-384-69055-6). Johnson Repr.
Wolff, Edwin D. Why We Do It. facs. ed. LC 68-16990. (Essay Index Reprint Ser). 1929. 15.00 (ISBN 0-8369-1006-0). Arno.

MANNHEIM, KARL, 1893-1947

Baum, Gregory. Truth Beyond Relativism: Karl Mannheim's Sociology of Knowledge. LC 77-76605. (Pere Marquette Ser.). 1977. 6.95 (ISBN 0-87462-509-2). Marquette.
Maquet, J. P. The Sociology of Knowledge. Locke, John F., tr. from Fr. LC 70-168963. 318p. 1973. Repr. of 1951 ed. lib. bdg. 17.75x (ISBN 0-8371-6236-X, MASK). Greenwood.
Simonds, A. P. Karl Mannheim's Sociology of Knowledge. 1978. text ed. 22.00x (ISBN 0-19-827238-3). Oxford U Pr.

MANNHEIM SLIDE RULE

see Slide-Rule

MANNING, HENRY EDWARD, CARDINAL, 1808-1892

Donald, Gertrude. Men Who Left the Movement. facs. ed. LC 67-23207. (Essay Index Reprint Ser). 1933. 18.00 (ISBN 0-8369-0385-4). Arno.
Drexler, Charles H. The Authority to Teach: A Study in the Ecclesiology of Henry Edward Manning. LC 77-18567. 1978. pap. text ed. 9.00 (ISBN 0-8191-0410-8). U Pr of Amer.
Fitzsimmons, John, ed. Manning: Anglican & Catholic. LC 78-11571. 1979. Repr. of 1951 ed. lib. bdg. 15.00x (ISBN 0-313-21005-5, FIMA). Greenwood.
Leslie, Shane. Henry Edward Manning, His Life & Labours. Repr. of 1921 ed. lib. bdg. 21.25x (ISBN 0-8371-4257-1, LEHM). Greenwood.
Newsome, David H. Wilberforces & Henry Manning: The Parting of Friends. LC 67-2. (Illus.). 1966. 25.00x (ISBN 0-674-95280-4, Belknap Pr). Harvard U Pr.
Purcell, Edmund S. Life of Cardinal Manning, Archbishop of Westminster, 2 vols. 1973. Repr. of 1896 ed. 50.00 set (ISBN 0-8274-1075-1). R West.
--Life of Cardinal Mannings, Archbishop of Westminster, 2 vols. LC 70-126605. (Europe 1815-1945 Ser.). 1534p. 1974. Repr. of 1896 ed. Set. lib. bdg. 85.00 (ISBN 0-306-70050-6). Da Capo.
Strachey, Lytton. Eminent Victorians. 1969. pap. 4.50 (ISBN 0-15-628697-1, HPL40, HPL). HarBraceJ.

MANNIX, DANIEL, ABP., 1864-1963

Santamaria, B. A. Archbishop Mannix: His Contribution to the Art of Public Leadership. 1978. pap. 3.95 (ISBN 0-522-84155-4, Pub. by Melbourne U Pr). Intl Schol Bk Serv.

MANOBO LANGUAGE–DICTIONARIES–ENGLISH

Elkins, Richard E. Manobo-English Dictionary. LC 68-63364. (Oceanic Linguistics Special Publications: No. 3). 1968. pap. text ed. 7.50x (ISBN 0-87022-225-2). U Pr of Hawaii.

MANOMETER

Weihrauch. Esophageal Manometry: Methods & Clinical Practice. 1981. text ed. price not set (ISBN 0-8067-2151-0). Urban & S.

MANORS

see also Copyhold

Addy, Sidney O. Church & Manor: A Study in English Economic History. LC 70-107902. (Illus.). Repr. of 1913 ed. 19.50x (ISBN 0-678-00632-6). Kelley.
Bennett, Henry S. Life on the English Manor. (Cambridge Studies in Medieval Life & Thought). 1960. 32.95 (ISBN 0-521-04154-6); pap. 8.95x (ISBN 0-521-09105-5). Cambridge U Pr.
Calthorpe, Charles. The Relation Betweene the Lord of a Mannor & the Coppy-Holder His Tenent, Etc. LC 74-38163. (English Experience Ser.: No. 440). 100p. 1972. Repr. of 1635 ed. 15.00 (ISBN 90-221-0440-0). Walter J Johnson.
Davenport, Frances G. A Classified List of Printed Original Materials for English Manorial & Agrarian History During the Middle Ages. (Radcliffe College Monographs: No. 6). 1964. Repr. of 1894 ed. 20.00 (ISBN 0-8337-0774-4). B Franklin.

Fedden, Katharine. Manor Life in Old France: From the Journal of the Sire De Gouberville for the Years 1549-1562. LC 70-168013. Repr. of 1933 ed. 21.00 (ISBN 0-404-02374-6). AMS Pr.

Hatcher, John. Rural Economy & Society in the Duchy of Cornwall, 1300-1500. LC 74-105495. (Illus.). 1970. 44.50 (ISBN 0-521-07660-9). Cambridge U Pr.

Hone, Nathaniel J. Manor & Manorial Records. LC 73-137947. (Economic Thought, History & Challenge Ser). 1971. Repr. of 1906 ed. 17.00 (ISBN 0-8046-1449-0). Kennikat.

Johnson, J. H. Old Maryland Manors with the Records of a Court Leet & a Court Baron. 1973. Repr. of 1883 ed. pap. 7.00 (ISBN 0-685-30635-6). Johnson Repr.

Kim, Sung B. Landlord & Tenant in Colonial New York: Manorial Society, 1664-1775. LC 77-24423. (Institute of Early American History & Culture Ser.). (Illus.). 1978. 22.50x (ISBN 0-8078-1290-0). U of NC Pr.

Lockley, Ronald. Orielton-the Human & Natural History of a Welsh Manor. (Illus.). 1978. 15.00 (ISBN 0-233-96928-4). Transatlantic.

London-St. Paul'S Cathedral. Domesday of Saint Paul of the Year Twelve Twenty-Two. Repr. of 1858 ed. 31.00 (ISBN 0-384-33475-X). Johnson Repr.

Moore, Margaret F. Two Select Bibliographies of Medieval Historical Study. 1912. 21.00 (ISBN 0-8337-2452-5). B Franklin.

Muhlfeld, Helen E., ed. A Survey of the Manor of Wye. LC 74-5047. 256p. 1974. Repr. of 1933 ed. lib. bdg. 14.00x (ISBN 0-374-95991-9). Octagon.

Vinogradoff, Paul. Growth of the Manor. 2nd ed. LC 65-5962. Repr. of 1911 ed. 17.50x (ISBN 0-678-00413-7). Kelley.

MANPOWER

see also Labor Supply; Military Service, Compulsory;

also such headings as Agricultural Laborers, Chemists, etc.

Adams, Leonard P. Public Employment Service in Transition, 1933-1968: Evolution of a Placement Service into a Manpower Agency. LC 68-66941. (Cornell Studies Ser: No. 16). 1969. pap. 3.50 (ISBN 0-87546-037-2); pap. 6.50 special hard bdg. (ISBN 0-87546-274-X). NY Sch Indus Rel.

Agarwal, S. P. Manpower Demand. 1970. 13.25x (ISBN 0-8426-0238-0). Verry.

Bartholomew, David J. & Forbes, Andrew F. Statistical Techniques for Manpower Planning. LC 78-8604. (Probability & Mathematical Statistics: Applied Section Ser.). 288p. 1979. 51.75 (ISBN 0-471-99670-X, Pub. by Wiley-Interscience). Wiley.

Bowey, Angela. Guide to Manpower Planning. 1977. text ed. 13.50x (ISBN 0-333-15555-6). Verry.

Bramham, John. Practical Manpower Planning. (Management in Perspective Ser.). 1975. 9.50x (ISBN 0-85292-119-5). Intl Pubns Serv.

Brinker, Paul A., et al. Poverty, Manpower & Social Security. rev. ed. (Illus.). 600p. 1982. text ed. 19.95 (ISBN 0-914872-19-2). Lone Star Pubs.

Bryant, D. & Niehaus, R., eds. Manpower Planning & Organization Design. LC 78-4623. (NATO Conference Ser.: Series II,Systems Science, Vol. 7). 803p. 1978. 65.00 (ISBN 0-306-40006-5, Plenum Pr). Plenum Pub.

Cassell, Frank H. Public Employment Service: Organization in Change. LC 68-27448. (Orig.). 1968. pap. 4.50x (ISBN 0-87736-310-2). U of Mich Inst Labor.

Coffey, Kenneth J. Manpower for Military Mobilization. 1978. pap. 4.25 (ISBN 0-8447-3291-5). Am Enterprise.

Council, Jon D. Profitable People Planning: A Guide to Effective Human Resource Management. (Illus.). 1978. 12.50 (ISBN 0-682-49104-7). Exposition.

Demone, Harold W., Jr. & Harshbarger, Dwight. The Planning & Administration of Human Services. LC 73-6870. (Developments in Human Services Ser.: Vol. 1, No. 2). 127p. 1973. pap. text ed. 7.95 (ISBN 0-87705-077-5). Human Sci Pr.

Doeringer, Peter B. & Piore, Michael J. Internal Labor Markets & Manpower Analysis. 1971. 13.95 (ISBN 0-669-63529-4). Lexington Bks.

Dyer, Lee, ed. Careers in Organizations: Individual Planning & Organizational Development. LC 76-49471. (Miscellaneous Ser). (Illus.). 1976. pap. 3.25 (ISBN 0-87546-061-5); pap. 6.25 special hard bdg. (ISBN 0-87546-288-X). NY Sch Indus Rel.

Freedman, Marcia & Maclachlan, Gretchen. Labor Markets: Segments & Shelters. LC 76-470. (Conservation of Human Resources Ser: No. 1). 224p. 1976. 18.50 (ISBN 0-916672-00-X). Allanheld.

Ginzberg, Eli. The Ineffective Soldier: The Lost Divisions. LC 75-29042. (Illus.). 225p. 1975. Repr. of 1959 ed. lib. bdg. 15.00x (ISBN 0-8371-8467-3, GIIT). Greenwood.

Ginzberg, Eli, et al. The Ineffective Soldier: Patterns of Performance. LC 75-29042. (Illus.). 340p. 1975. Repr. of 1959 ed. lib. bdg. 18.50x (ISBN 0-8371-8469-X, GIIV). Greenwood.

Grinold, Richard C & Marshall, Kneale T. Manpower Planning Models. LC 76-40243. (Publications in Operations Research Ser.). (Illus.). 1977. 24.95 (ISBN 0-444-00190-5, North Holland). Elsevier.

Jenkins, David. Job Power: Blue & White Collar Democracy. 1974. pap. 2.95 (ISBN 0-14-003811-6). Penguin.

Kaumeyer, Richard A. Planning & Using Skills Inventory Systems. LC 78-25959. 1979. text ed. 15.95x (ISBN 0-442-24240-9). Van Nos Reinhold.

Kleinfeld, Judith, et al. Land Claims & Native Manpower: Staffing Regional & Village Corporations Under Alaska Native Claims Settlement Act of 1971. LC 73-620103. (Illus.). 52p. 1973. pap. 2.00 (ISBN 0-88353-009-0). U Alaska Inst Res.

Meier, Gretl S. Job Sharing: A New Pattern for Quality of Work & Life. LC 79-4145. 1979. pap. 4.50 (ISBN 0-911558-59-4). Upjohn Inst.

Mesics, Emil A. Education & Training for Effective Manpower Utilization: An Annotated Bibliography. (Bibliography Ser.: No. 9). 1969. pap. 2.50 (ISBN 0-87546-023-2). NY Sch Indus Rel.

Mills, Daniel Q. Industrial Relations & Manpower in Construction. 1972. 20.00x (ISBN 0-262-13078-5). MIT Pr.

Ross, Joe. Productivity, People & Profits. 150p. 1981. text ed. 17.95 (ISBN 0-8359-5473-0); pap. 10.95 (ISBN 0-8359-5472-2). Reston.

Rudman, Jack. Supervising Manpower Counselor. (Career Examination Ser.: C-2437). (Cloth bdg. avail. on request). pap. 12.00 (ISBN 0-8373-2437-8). Natl Learning.

Smith, A. R. Models of Manpower Systems. 1971. 24.00 (ISBN 0-444-19634-X). Elsevier.

Stahel, Walter R. The Potential for Substituting Manpower for Energy. 1981. 12.50 (ISBN 0-533-04799-4). Vantage.

Stainer, Gareth. Manpower Planning: The Management of Human Resources. (Illus.). 1971. 15.00x (ISBN 0-434-91850-4). Intl Pubns Serv.

Technological Change & Manpower in a Centrally Planned Economy: A Study Dealing with the Metal-Working Industry in the USSR. (Labour & Automation, Bulletin: No. 3). 1966. 2.30 (ISBN 92-2-100973-4). Intl Labour Office.

U. S. Bureau Of The Census. Population & Manpower of China: An Annotated Bibliography. LC 68-55103. (Illus.). 1968. Repr. of 1958 ed. lib. bdg. 14.50x (ISBN 0-8371-0691-5, POMA). Greenwood.

Vajda, S. Mathematics of Manpower Planning. LC 77-26104. 1978. 43.75 (ISBN 0-471-99627-0, Pub. by Wiley-Interscience). Wiley.

Walker, James W. & Gutteridge, Thomas G. Career Planning Practices. LC 78-31340. 1979. pap. 10.00 (ISBN 0-8144-3136-4). Am Mgmt.

Zook, Paul D., ed. Foreign Trade & Human Capital. LC 62-13276. 1962. 4.00 (ISBN 0-87074-130-6). SMU Press.

MANPOWER DEVELOPMENT AND TRAINING

see Occupational Training

MANPOWER POLICY

see also Full Employment Policies; Labor Supply; Occupational Retraining

American Chamber of Commerce in Japan. Manual of Employment Practices in Japan. 1979. 45.00 (ISBN 0-686-16957-3). A M Newman.

Annual Research Conference, 14th, UCLA, 1972. National Incomes Policy & Manpower Problems: Proceedings. 2.00 (ISBN 0-89215-032-7). U Cal LA Indus Rel.

Aronson, Robert L., ed. The Localization of Federal Manpower Planning. LC 73-620149. 1973. pap. 4.50 (ISBN 0-87546-053-4); pap. 7.50 special hard bdg. (ISBN 0-87546-283-9). NY Sch Indus Rel.

Assembly of Behavioral & Social Sciences, National Research Council. Knowledge & Policy in Manpower: A Study of the Manpower, Research & Development Program in the Department of Labor. LC 75-37384. xi, 171p. 1975. pap. 6.25 (ISBN 0-309-02439-0). Natl Acad Pr.

Bailes, Jack C. Management Budgeting for CETA. (Papers in Manpower Studies & Education: No. 1). 1975. 2.00 (ISBN 0-87071-327-2). Oreg St U Pr.

Ball, Geraldine. Magic Circle: An Overview of the Human Development Program. 1974. 4.95 (ISBN 0-86584-007-5). Human Dev Train.

Bartholomew, D. J. & Morris, B. R. Aspects of Manpower Planning. (NATO Ser). 1971. 18.00 (ISBN 0-444-19603-X). Elsevier.

Berg, Ivar E., Jr., ed. Human Resources & Economic Welfare: Essays in Honor of Eli Ginzberg. LC 72-8331. 366p. 1972. 17.00x (ISBN 0-231-03710-4). Columbia U Pr.

Biles, Steven & Holmberg, George, eds. Human Resource Strategic Planning: Readings & Comments. 1980. pap. text ed. 10.95x cancelled (ISBN 0-89832-007-0). Brighton Pub Co.

Borus, Michael E. & Tash, William R. Measuring the Impact of Manpower Programs: A Primer. LC 73-633548. (Policy Papers in Human Resources & Industrial Relations Ser.: No. 17). (Orig.). 1970. pap. 2.50x (ISBN 0-87736-117-7). U of Mich Inst Labor.

Caddy, Douglas. The Hundred Million Dollar Payoff: How Big Labor Buys Its Democrats. LC 74-5348. 420p. 1976. pap. 2.95 (ISBN 0-916054-30-6, Caroline Hse Inc). Green Hill.

Cascio, Wayne F. & Awad, Elias M. Human Resources Management: An Information Systems Approach. 450p. 1981. text ed. 22.95 (ISBN 0-8359-3008-4); student activities guide 7.95 (ISBN 0-8359-3010-6); instr's. manual avail. (ISBN 0-8359-3009-2). Reston.

Childers, Victor E. Human Resources Development: Venezula. (Illus.). 1974. pap. text ed. 4.00 (ISBN 0-89249-003-9). Intl Development.

Christopher, Edward E. Behavioral Theory for Managers. 1977. pap. text ed. 9.75 (ISBN 0-8191-0352-7). U Pr of Amer.

Davidson, Roger H. The Politics of Comprehensive Manpower Legislation. LC 72-10874. (Policy Studies in Employment & Welfare: No. 15). 123p. 1973. 8.50x (ISBN 0-8018-1471-5); pap. 3.95x (ISBN 0-8018-1470-7). Johns Hopkins.

Donaldson, Les & Scannell, Edward. Human Resource Development: The New Trainer's Guide. 1978. pap. text ed. 8.95 (ISBN 0-201-03081-0). A-W.

Editorial Research Reports on Jobs for Americans. LC 77-18994. 1978. pap. text ed. 6.95 (ISBN 0-87187-120-3). Congr Quarterly.

Employment After CETA: Outcomes of Recent Research. 1980. 4.00 (ISBN 0-86671-067-1). Comm Coun Great NY.

Fellner, William. Employment Policy at the Crossroads: An Interim Look at Pressures to Be Resisted. 1972. 3.25 (ISBN 0-8447-3091-2). Am Enterprise.

Ferman, Louis A. & Manela, Roger. Agency Company Relationships in Manpower Operations for the Hard to Employ. 1973. pap. 6.50x (ISBN 0-87736-329-3). U of Mich Inst Labor.

Ferman, Louis A., et al. Agency & Company: Partners in Human Resource Development. LC 80-23246. (Sage Human Services Guides Ser.: Vol. 18). 136p. 1981. 7.50 (ISBN 0-8039-1558-6). Sage.

Frank, H. Eric. Human Resource Development: The European Approach. (Building Blocks of Human Potential Ser.). 1974. 14.95 (ISBN 0-87201-370-7). Gulf Pub.

Franklin, Paul L. The Comprehensive Employment & Training Act: A Guide for Educators. 1979. pap. 6.50 (ISBN 0-87447-112-5, 219011). College Bd.

Gartner, Alan, et al, eds. Public Service Employment: An Analysis of Its History, Problems & Prospects. LC 72-93186. (Special Studies in U.S. Economics, Social, & Political Issues). 1973. 29.50x (ISBN 0-275-06630-4). Irvington.

Gellerman. Management of Human Resources. 1976. 10.95 (ISBN 0-03-080485-X). Dryden Pr.

Gellerman, S. W. The Management of Human Resources. LC 76-386. (Dryden Press). 1976. pap. text ed. 10.95 (ISBN 0-03-080485-X, HoltC). HR&W.

Ginzberg, Eli. Good Jobs, Bad Jobs, No Jobs. LC 79-10706. 1979. 15.00x (ISBN 0-674-35710-8). Harvard U Pr.

--The Human Economy. 1976. 13.95 (ISBN 0-07-023283-0). McGraw.

--Human Resources: The Wealth of a Nation. LC 73-9263. 183p. 1973. Repr. of 1958 ed. lib. bdg. 15.00x (ISBN 0-8371-6999-2, GIHR). Greenwood.

--The Manpower Connection: Education & Work. 288p. 1975. 15.00x (ISBN 0-674-54810-8). Harvard U Pr.

Ginzberg, Eli & Conservation of Human Resources Staff. Manpower Strategy for the Metropolis. LC 68-27290. 321p. 1968. 18.50x (ISBN 0-231-03161-0). Columbia U Pr.

Ginzberg, Eli, ed. Employing the Unemployed. LC 79-5352. 250p. 1980. 15.00 (ISBN 0-465-01957-9). Basic.

--Jobs for Americans. 1976. 9.95 (ISBN 0-13-510024-0); pap. 3.95 (ISBN 0-13-510016-X). Am Assembly.

Globerson, Arye. Higher Education & Employment: A Case Study of Israel. LC 78-60131. (Praeger Special Studies). 1979. 22.95 (ISBN 0-03-046226-6). Praeger.

Guha, Sunil. Rural Manpower & Capital Formation in India. 1969. 7.75x (ISBN 0-8426-1285-8). Verry.

Hallman, Howard W. Community-Based Employment Programs. LC 79-3718. (Policy Studies in Employment & Welfare: 36). 128p. 1980. text ed. 10.00x (ISBN 0-8018-2391-9). Johns Hopkins.

Hansen, Niles M. Improving Access to Economic Opportunity: Nonmetropolitan Labor Markets in an Urban Society. LC 75-38800. 280p. 1976. text ed. 16.50 (ISBN 0-88410-289-0). Ballinger Pub.

Hasenfeld, Yeheskel. Manpower Placement: Service Delivery for the Hard-to-Employ. LC 73-620092. (Policy Papers in Human Resources & Industrial Relations Ser.: No. 21). 95p. 1973. 7.95x (ISBN 0-87736-124-X); pap. 2.95 (ISBN 0-87736-125-8). U of Mich Inst Labor.

Heenan, David A. Multinational Management of Human Resources: A Systems Approach. (Studies in International Business: No. 2). 1975. pap. 4.00 (ISBN 0-87755-213-4). U of Tex Busn Res.

Heyel, Carl, ed. The VNR Concise Guide to Human Resources Development. (VNR Concise Management Ser.). 213p. 1980. pap. text ed. 7.95 (ISBN 0-442-23401-5). Van Nos Reinhold.

Hopwood, A. G., ed. Human Resource Accounting. 1976. pap. text ed. 29.00 (ISBN 0-08-021419-3). Pergamon.

Horowitz, Morris A. Manpower & Education in Franco's Spain. 164p. 1974. 15.00 (ISBN 0-208-01382-2, Archon). Shoe String.

Human Resources for Industrial Development. 2nd ed. (Studies & Reports, New Ser.: No. 71). vi, 237p. 1971. 6.85 (ISBN 92-2-100145-8). Intl Labour Office.

Human Resources Management: The Past Is Prologue. (A Personnel Reprint Collection). 1979. pap. 10.50 (ISBN 0-8144-6802-0). Am Mgmt.

Ingalls, John D. Human Energy: The Critical Factor for Individuals & Organizations. 285p. 1979. Repr. of 1976 ed. text ed. 18.95 (ISBN 0-89384-055-6). Learning Concepts.

International Labour Office, Geneva. Guidelines for the Development of Employment & Manpower Information Programmes in Developing Countries: A Practical Manual. (Illus.). 87p. (Orig.). 1979. pap. 7.15 (ISBN 9-22-102176-9). Intl Labour Office.

Karlins, Marvin. The Human Use of Human Resources. (Illus.). 208p. (Orig.). 1981. 11.95 (ISBN 0-07-033298-3); pap. text ed. 6.95 (ISBN 0-07-033297-5). McGraw.

Katz, Ralph. Career Issues in Human Resource Management. (Applied Management Ser.). (Illus.). 224p. 1982. 17.95 (ISBN 0-13-114819-2). P-H.

Keil, E. C. Assessment Centers: A Guide for Human Resource Management. 1981. write for info. (ISBN 0-201-03782-3). A-W.

Kiefer, Nicholas M. The Economic Benefits from Four Employment & Training Programs. LC 78-75061. (Outstanding Dissertations in Economics Ser.). 1979. lib. bdg. 15.00 (ISBN 0-8240-4138-0). Garland Pub.

Kinlaw, Dennis C. Helping Skills for Human Resource Development: A Facilitator's Package. LC 80-54159. 131p. (Orig.). 1981. looseleaf 49.95 (ISBN 0-88390-163-3). Univ Assocs.

Kreps, Juanita & Clark, Robert. Sex, Age & Work: The Changing Composition of the Labor Force. LC 75-34452. (Policy Studies in Employment & Welfare: No. 23). (Illus.). 108p. 1976. 7.50x (ISBN 0-8018-1806-0); pap. 3.65x (ISBN 0-8018-1807-9). Johns Hopkins.

Lathrop, Richard. The Job Market--What Ails It & What Needs to Be Done About It to Reduce Unemployment. (Illus., Orig.). 1978. pap. 4.85 (ISBN 0-935234-00-4). Natl Ctr Job Mkt.

LBJ School of Public Affairs. Manpower & Vocational Education Planning Processes: Four Regional Case Studies. LC 75-62008. (Policy Research Project Report Ser.: No. 9). 1975. 3.00 (ISBN 0-89940-605-X). LBJ Sch Public Affairs.

Lecht, Leonard A. Occupational Choices & Training Needs. LC 76-24356. (Special Studies). 1977. text ed. 23.95 (ISBN 0-275-23960-8). Praeger.

Levine, Charles H., ed. Managing Human Resources: A Challenge to Urban Governments. LC 77-79869. (Urban Affairs Annual Reviews Ser.: Vol. 13). (Illus.). 319p. 1977. 22.50 (ISBN 0-8039-0741-9); pap. 9.95 (ISBN 0-8039-0938-1). Sage.

Levitan, Sar A. & Mangum, Garth L. Making Sense of Federal Manpower Policy. 2nd ed. (Policy Papers in Human Resources & Industrial Relations Ser.: No. 2). (Orig.). 1973. pap. 2.50x (ISBN 0-87736-102-9). U of Mich Inst Labor.

Levitan, Sar A. & Taggart, Robert, 3rd. Social Experimentation & Manpower Policy: The Rhetoric & the Reality. LC 78-153557. (Policy Studies in Employment & Welfare: No. 9). 111p. 1971. 8.50x (ISBN 0-8018-1276-3). Johns Hopkins.

Levitan, Sar A. & Zickler, Joyce K. The Quest for Federal Manpower Partnership. LC 74-16541. 144p. 1974. text ed. 7.95x (ISBN 0-674-74125-0). Harvard U Pr.

Levitan, Sar A., et al. Human Resources & Labor Markets: Labor & Manpower in the American Economy. 2nd ed. 631p. 1976. text ed. 24.50 scp (ISBN 0-06-043999-8, HarpC). Har-Row.

McBeath, Gordon. Manpower Planning & Control. 218p. 1978. text ed. 24.50x (ISBN 0-220-66348-3, Pub. by Busn Bks England). Renouf.

Manpower & Employment: Problems & Prospects. (Document Ser.). 1979. 8.00x (ISBN 92-64-11807-1). OECD.

Manpower Policy in Finland. 1977. 8.00x (ISBN 92-64-11598-6). OECD.

Market Efficiency & Inflation: Two Documents from the Cabinet Committee on Price Stability of the Johnson Administration. LC 70-83785. 1969. 6.95 (ISBN 0-405-00055-3, Pub. by Ind. Pubns.). Arno.

Marshall, Ray, et al. Human Resource Development in Rural Texas. LC 74-12528. (Studies in Human Resource Development: No. 6). (Illus.). 150p. 1974. pap. 5.00 (ISBN 0-87755-198-7). U of Tex Busn Res.

Matheson, R. People Development in Developing Countries. LC 77-28208. 246p. 1978. 32.95x (ISBN 0-470-99382-0). Halsted Pr.

Meeting of the Manpower & Social Affairs Committee at Ministerial Level, 1st, Paris, Mar. 4-5, 1976. Ministers of Labour & the Problems of Employment: Papers, Introductory & Concluding Statements, Vol. 1. 1976. 6.00x (ISBN 92-64-11533-1). OECD.

Megginson, Leon C. Personnel & Human Resources Administration. 4th ed. 1981. 20.95x (ISBN 0-256-02511-8). Irwin.

Meyers, Frederic. Ownership of Jobs: A Comparative Study. (Monograph Ser.: No. 11). 1964. 5.00 (ISBN 0-89215-012-2). U Cal LA Indus Rel.

Midwest Council Association For Latin America - 1967. Human Resources in Latin America, an International Focus: Proceedings. Bachmura, Frank T., ed. (Business Paper Ser: No. 16). (Illus.). 1968. pap. 4.50 (ISBN 0-685-12534-3). Ind U Busn Res.

Miller, Donald B. Working with People: Human Resource Management in Action. LC 79-16914. 1979. pap. 13.50 (ISBN 0-8436-0776-9). CBI Pub.

Miller, Edwin, et al. Management of Human Resources: Newer Approaches. (Illus.). 1980. pap. text ed. 14.95 (ISBN 0-13-549410-9). P-H.

Mirengoff, William & Rindler, Lester. CETA: Manpower Programs Under Local Control. 1978. pap. text ed. 10.50x (ISBN 0-309-02792-6). Natl Acad Pr.

--The Comprehensive Employment & Training Act: Impact on People, Places, & Programs: an Interim Report. LC 75-42971. 175p. 1976. pap. 6.00 (ISBN 0-309-02443-9). Natl Acad Pr.

Nadler, Leonard. Developing Human Resources. 2nd ed. LC 79-4147. 1979. text ed. 17.95 (ISBN 0-89384-044-0). Learning Concepts.

Needham, Barrie. Guidelines for a Local Employment Study. 1978. text ed. 28.00x (ISBN 0-566-00241-8, Pub. by Gower Pub Co England). Renouf.

Niehaus, Richard J. Computer-Assisted Human Resources Planning. LC 78-27708. 338p. 1979. 33.50 (ISBN 0-471-04081-9, Pub. by Wiley-Interscience). Wiley.

O'Neill, Dave M. The Federal Government & Manpower: A Critical Look at the MDTA-Institutional & Job Corps Program. 1973. pap. 4.25 (ISBN 0-8447-3109-9). Am Enterprise.

Orr, David B., ed. New Directions in Employability: Reducing Barriers to Full Employment. LC 73-6094. (Special Studies in U.S. Economic, Social & Political Issues). 1973. 28.50x (ISBN 0-275-28838-2). Irvington.

Peterson, Richard B. & Tracy, Lane. Systematic Management of Human Resources. LC 78-55826. 1979. text ed. 17.95 (ISBN 0-201-05814-6); readings book avail. 10.95 (ISBN 0-201-05815-4). A-W.

Reubens, Beatrice G. The Hard-to-Employ: European Programs. (Illus.). 1970. 20.00x (ISBN 0-231-03388-5). Columbia U Pr.

Ripley, Randall B. The Politics of Economic & Human Resource Development. LC 79-173977. (Policy Analysis Ser). 1972. 8.95 (ISBN 0-672-51479-6). Bobbs.

--The Politics of Economic & Human Resource Development. LC 79-173977. (Policy Analysis Ser). 1972. 8.95 (ISBN 0-672-51479-6). Bobbs.

Ritterbush, Philip C., ed. Talent Waste: How Institutions of Learning Misdirect Human Resources. LC 72-3816. (Prometheus Original Paperbacks Ser.). (Illus.). 1972. pap. 3.95 (ISBN 0-87491-502-3). Acropolis.

Roberts, Paul A., et al. Manpower Planning for the Public Service. 1971. 3.00 (ISBN 0-87373-285-5). Intl Personnel Mgmt.

Rogers, D. & Ruchlin, H. Economics & Education: Principles & Applications. LC 74-143519. 1971. text ed. 14.95 (ISBN 0-02-926690-4). Free Pr.

Rudman, Jack. Human Resources Technician. (Career Examination Ser.: C-2071). (Cloth bdg. avail. on request). 1977. pap. 8.00 (ISBN 0-685-78620-X). Natl Learning.

--Management of Human Resources, Level 1. (ACT Proficiency Examination Program: PEP-18). (Cloth bdg. avail. on request). pap. 9.95 (ISBN 0-8373-5518-4). Natl Learning.

--Management of Human Resources, Level 2. (ACT Proficiency Examination Program: PEP-19). (Cloth bdg. avail. on request). pap. 9.95 (ISBN 0-8373-5519-2). Natl Learning.

--Management of Human Resources, Level 3. (ACT Proficiency Examination Program: PEP-20). (Cloth bdg. avail. on request). pap. 9.95 (ISBN 0-8373-5520-6). Natl Learning.

--Management of Human Resources 1. (Regents External Degree Ser.: REDP-7). (Cloth bdg. avail. on request). pap. 9.95 (ISBN 0-8373-5607-5). Natl Learning.

--Management of Human Resources 2. (Regents External Degree Ser.: REDP-8). (Cloth bdg. avail. on request). pap. 9.95 (ISBN 0-8373-5608-3). Natl Learning.

--Management of Human Resources 3. (Regents External Degree Ser.: REDP-9). (Cloth bdg. avail. on request). pap. 9.95 (ISBN 0-8373-5609-1). Natl Learning.

--Manpower Counselor. (Career Examination Ser.: C-2435). (Cloth bdg. avail. on request). pap. 10.00 (ISBN 0-8373-2435-1). Natl Learning.

--Principal Planner (Manpower) (Career Examination Ser.: C-1599). (Cloth bdg. avail. on request). pap. 10.00 (ISBN 0-8373-1599-9). Natl Learning.

--Senior Manpower Counselor. (Career Examination Ser.: C-2436). (Cloth bdg. avail. on request). pap. 10.00 (ISBN 0-8373-2436-X). Natl Learning.

Sarri, Rosemary & Hasenfeld, Yeheskel. The Management of Human Services. (Illus.). 1978. 20.00x (ISBN 0-231-04628-6). Columbia U Pr.

Schuler, Randall S. Personnel & Human Resource Management. (Management Ser.). (Illus.). 572p. 1981. text ed. 21.50 (ISBN 0-8299-0406-9). West Pub.

Schuler, Randall S., et al. Applied Readings in Personnel & Human Resource Management. (Management Ser.). (Illus.). 328p. 1981. pap. text ed. 9.95 (ISBN 0-8299-0408-5). West Pub.

Schultz, Theodore W. Investing in People: The Economics of Population Quality. LC 80-6062. 200p. 1981. 12.95 (ISBN 0-520-04437-1). U of Cal Pr.

Shaeffer, Ruth G. Monitoring the Human Resource System. (Report Ser.: No. 717). (Illus.). 1977. pap. 15.00 (ISBN 0-8237-0151-4). Conference Bd.

Showler, Brian. The Public Employment Service. LC 76-8923. 1976. text ed. 13.00x (ISBN 0-582-48541-X); pap. text ed. 9.00x (ISBN 0-582-48542-8). Longman.

Siegel, Irving H., ed. Manpower Tomorrow: Prospects & Priorities. LC 67-29747. 1968. 11.50x (ISBN 0-678-00343-2). Kelley.

Smith, A. R. Models of Manpower Systems. 1971. 24.00 (ISBN 0-444-19634-X). Elsevier.

Snider, Patricia J., ed. Human Resources Planning: A Guide to Data. 2nd ed. LC 80-67468. 392p. 1980. pap. 21.00 (ISBN 0-937856-00-2). Equal Employ.

Stahel, Walter R. & Reday-Mulvey, Genevieve. Jobs for Tomorrow. 120p. 1981. 12.50 (ISBN 0-533-04799-4). Vantage.

Stanback, Thomas M. & Knight, Richard V. Metropolitan Economy. LC 77-133492. 1970. 20.00x (ISBN 0-231-03426-1). Columbia U Pr.

Stewart, Charles T., Jr. Low-Wage Workers in an Affluent Society. LC 73-78912. 1974. 17.95x (ISBN 0-88229-101-7). Nelson-Hall.

Swanson, Gordon I. & Michaelson, Jon, eds. Manpower Research & Labor Economics. LC 79-11162. 332p. 1979. 22.50 (ISBN 0-8039-1268-4); pap. 12.50 (ISBN 0-8039-1269-2). Sage.

Towards Full Employment: A Programme for Colombia. 3rd ed. 1973. 13.70 (ISBN 92-2-100058-3). Intl Labour Office.

Tracey, William R. Human Resources Development Standards: A Self-Evaluation Manual for HRD Managers & Specialists. 576p. 1981. 39.95 (ISBN 0-8144-5633-2). Am Mgmt.

Ulman, Lloyd, ed. Manpower Programs in the Policy Mix. LC 72-11850. (Illus.). 173p. 1973. 12.50x (ISBN 0-8018-1452-9). Johns Hopkins.

U. S. Department of Health, Education, & Welfare. Work in America: Report of a Special Task Force to the Secretary of Health, Education, & Welfare. 262p. 1973. pap. 4.95 (ISBN 0-262-58023-3). MIT Pr.

Vaughan, Roger J. Inflation & Unemployment: Surviving the Nineteen Eighties. Barker, Michael, ed. LC 79-67383. (Studies in State Development Policy: Vol. 5). 1979. pap. 8.95 (ISBN 0-934842-04-3). Coun State Plan.

Viaud, Gaston. Intelligence, Its Evolution & Forms. Pomerans, A. J., tr. LC 72-10983. (Illus.). 127p. 1973. Repr. of 1960 ed. lib. bdg. 15.00 (ISBN 0-8371-6640-3, VIIN). Greenwood.

Viscardi, Henry, Jr. A Man's Stature. LC 52-9615. 256p. 1972. 6.95 (ISBN 0-8397-5733-6). Eriksson.

Walker, James W. Human Resource Planning. (Management Ser.). (Illus.). 1980. text ed. 17.95x (ISBN 0-07-067840-5, C). McGraw.

Weeks, David A., ed. Human Resources: Toward Rational Policy Planning. LC 75-27307. (Report Ser: No. 669). 53p. 1975. pap. 15.00 (ISBN 0-8237-0103-4). Conference Bd.

Winpisinger, William W. Trade Union View of U. S. Manpower Policy. LC 80-81536. 52p. 1980. 3.00 (ISBN 0-89068-052-3). Natl Planning.

Wolfle, Dael. Uses of Talent. LC 71-143817. 1971. 15.00x (ISBN 0-691-08603-6). Princeton U Pr.

MANPOWER TRAINING PROGRAMS

see Occupational Training

MANPOWER UTILIZATION

see Manpower Policy

MANSFIELD, KATHERINE, 1888-1923

Alpers, Antony. The Life of Katherine Mansfield. (Illus.). 1980. 16.95 (ISBN 0-670-42805-1). Viking Pr.

Clarke, Isabel C. Katherine Mansfield: A Biography. LC 74-7387. 1944. lib. bdg. 10.00 (ISBN 0-8414-3579-0). Folcroft.

--Katherine Mansfield: A Biography. 1978. Repr. of 1944 ed. lib. bdg. 10.00 (ISBN 0-8495-0803-7). Arden Lib.

--Six Portraits. facs. ed. LC 67-26725. (Essay Index Reprint Ser). 1935. 18.00 (ISBN 0-8369-0309-9). Arno.

Daly, Saralyn R. Katherine Mansfield. (English Authors Ser.: No. 23). 1965. lib. bdg. 9.95 (ISBN 0-8057-1372-7). Twayne.

Eustace, Cecil J. Infinity of Questions. facs. ed. LC 70-84356. (Essay Index Reprint Ser). 1946. 14.50 (ISBN 0-8369-1080-X). Arno.

Friis, Anne. Katherine Mansfield: Life & Stories. LC 74-4423. 1946. lib. bdg. 20.00 (ISBN 0-8414-4181-2). Folcroft.

Gurr, Andrew & Hanson, Clare. Katherine Mansfield. 160p. 1981. 18.95 (ISBN 0-312-45093-1). St Martin.

Johnson, Elizabeth, compiled by. Katherine Mansfield: An Exhibition. LC 75-620027. (Illus.). 1975. pap. 5.00 (ISBN 0-87959-018-1). U of Tex Hum Res.

LM. Katherine Mansfield: The Memories of LM. (Illus.). 240p. 1972. 7.95 (ISBN 0-8008-4447-5). Taplinger.

Mantz, R. & Murry, John Middleton. Life of Katherine Mansfield. LC 75-42109. (English Literature Ser., No. 33). 1974. lib. bdg. 45.95 (ISBN 0-8383-1882-7). Haskell.

Mantz, R. E. Bibliography of Katherine Mansfield. 1979. lib. bdg. 42.50 (ISBN 0-685-94323-2). Porter.

Mantz, Ruth E. Critical Bibliography of Katherine Mansfield. LC 68-58430. (Bibliography & Reference Ser.: No. 241). 1969. Repr. of 1931 ed. 22.50 (ISBN 0-8337-2210-7). B Franklin.

--Critical Bibliography of Katherine Mansfield. LC 72-194084. 1931. lib. bdg. 16.25 (ISBN 0-8414-5973-8). Folcroft.

Mantz, Ruth E. & Murray, John M. The Life of Katherine Mansfield. LC 78-145163. 349p. 1933. Repr. 27.00 (ISBN 0-403-01091-8). Scholarly.

Meyers, Jeffrey. Katherine Mansfield: A Biography. LC 79-18885. (Illus.). 1980. 17.50 (ISBN 0-8112-0751-X). New Directions.

Moore, James. Gurdjieff & Mansfield. (Illus.). 304p. 1980. 25.00 (ISBN 0-7100-0488-5). Routledge & Kegan.

Morris, G. N. Mansfieldiana: A Brief Katherine Mansfield Bibliography. Repr. of 1948 ed. lib. bdg. 6.50 (ISBN 0-8414-6338-7). Folcroft.

Murry, J. Middleton. The Letters of Katherine Mansfield, 2 vols. 1979. Repr. of 1928 ed. Set. lib. bdg. 40.00 (ISBN 0-8492-6812-5). R West.

Murry, J. Middleton, ed. Journal of Katherine Mansfield. 1979. Repr. of 1927 ed. lib. bdg. 25.00 (ISBN 0-8492-6813-3). R West.

Rohrberger, Mary H. The Art of Katherine Mansfield. LC 77-70174. 1977. 16.00 (ISBN 0-8357-0195-6, SS-00025). Univ Microfilms.

Sewell, Arthur. Katherine Mansfield: A Critical Essay. 1973. lib. bdg. 6.50 (ISBN 0-8414-8119-9). Folcroft.

MANSFIELD, RICHARD, 1857-1907

Wilstach, Paul. Richard Mansfield, the Man & the Actor. facsimile ed. LC 79-107836. (Select Bibliographies Reprint Ser). 1908. 25.00 (ISBN 0-8369-5201-4). Arno.

Winter, William. Life & Art of Richard Mansfield, with Selections from His Letters, 2 Vols. facs. ed. LC 77-126264. (Select Bibliographies Reprint Ser). 1910. Set. 45.00 (ISBN 0-8369-5491-2). Arno.

--Life & Art of Richard Mansfield, with Selections from His Letters. Repr. of 1910 ed. lib. bdg. 36.00x (ISBN 0-8371-4084-6, WIRM). Greenwood.

MANSI LANGUAGE

see Vogul Language

MANSLAUGHTER

see Assassination; Homicide; Murder

MANSON, CHARLES 1934-

Atkins, Susan & Slosser, Bob. Child of Satan, Child of God. 1977. 7.95 (ISBN 0-88270-229-7); pap. 2.95 (ISBN 0-88270-276-9). Logos.

Bugliosi, Vincent & Gentry, Curt. Helter Skelter. (Illus.). 704p. 1975. pap. 2.50 (ISBN 0-553-13162-1). Bantam.

--Helter Skelter: The True Story of the Manson Murders. (Illus.). 502p. 1974. 15.00 (ISBN 0-393-08700-X). Norton.

Cooper, David & French, Peter, eds. The Manson Murders: A Philosophical Inquiry. LC 73-78119. 160p. 1974. pap. text ed. 5.95 (ISBN 0-87073-533-0). Schenkman.

Livsey, Clara. The Manson Women: A "Family" Portrait. LC 79-26454. 1980. 10.95 (ISBN 0-399-90073-X). Marek.

Manson, Charles. Your Children. 24p. 3.00 (ISBN 0-931106-13-3). TVRT.

Wizinski, Sy. Charles Manson: Love Letters to a Secret Disciple. LC 76-28869. 1977. 9.95 (ISBN 0-917918-01-0). Moonmad Pr.

MANTEGNA, ANDREA, 1431-1506

Lehmann, Phyllis & Lehman, Karl. Samothracian Reflections: Aspects of the Revival of the Antique. LC 71-163867. (Bollingen Ser.: No. 92). 216p. 1973. 35.00 (ISBN 0-691-09909-X). Princeton U Pr.

MANTLE, MICKEY, 1931-

Hasegawa, Sam. Mickey Mantle. LC 74-9807. (Creative Education Sports Superstars Ser.). (Illus.). 32p. (gr. 3-6). 1974. 5.95 (ISBN 0-87191-375-5). Creative Ed.

MANU

Ayyar, R. S. Manu's Land & Trade Laws. 1976. Repr. 12.50x (ISBN 0-88386-852-0). South Asia Bks.

MANUA

Mead, Margaret. Social Organization of Manua. (BMB Ser.: No. 76). Repr. of 1930 ed. pap. 6.00 (ISBN 0-527-02182-2). Kraus Repr.

--Social Organization of Manu'a. rev. ed. LC 76-92276. (Bulletin Ser: No. 76). 237p. 1969. 5.00 (ISBN 0-910240-08-6). Bishop Mus.

Patwardham, M. V. Manusmrti: Ideal Democratic Republic of Manu. 1968. 4.95 (ISBN 0-89684-276-2). Orient Bk Dist.

MANUAL ALPHABETS

see Deaf-Means of Communication

MANUAL SKILL

see Motor Ability

MANUAL TRAINING

see also Arts and Crafts Movement; Basket Making; Carpentry; Design; Drawing; Handicraft; Industrial Arts; Models and Modelmaking; Needlework; School Shops; Technical Education; Wood-Carving; Woodwork (Manual Training)

AIAA Conference, 31st Annual, 1969. Where the Action Is: Proceedings. 1969. pap. 4.50 (ISBN 0-686-00328-4). Am Indus Arts.

Barlow, Melvin L. History of Industrial Education in the United States. 1967. pap. text ed. 23.44 (ISBN 0-87002-241-5). Bennett IL.

Bennett, Charles A. History of Manual & Industrial Education, 2 Vols, Vol. 1. to 1870, Vol. 2. 1870-1917. Vol. 1. text ed. 18.00 (ISBN 0-87002-005-6); Vol. 2. text ed. 20.68 (ISBN 0-87002-006-4). Bennett IL.

Blake, James V. Manual Training in Education. 1976. Repr. of 1886 ed. 25.00 (ISBN 0-685-71162-5, Regency). Scholarly.

Drolet, Robert P. & Dowling, John R. Developing & Administering an Industrial Training Program. LC 79-10713. (Illus.). 1979. pap. 12.95 (ISBN 0-8436-0777-7). CBI Pub.

Groneman, Chris H. & Feirer, John L. General Industrial Education. 5th ed. LC 73-9827. Orig. Title: General Shop. (Illus.). 584p. (gr. 7-9). 1973. text ed. 14.64 (ISBN 0-07-024965-2, W); tchr's. resource guide 1.84 (ISBN 0-07-024976-8); study guide 4.60 (ISBN 0-07-024968-7). McGraw.

--General Industrial Education. 6th ed. (M-H Publications in Industrial Education). (gr. 7-9). 1979. text ed. 14.64 (ISBN 0-07-024991-1, W); study guide 4.60 (ISBN 0-07-024992-X); tchr's. guide 1.84 (ISBN 0-07-024993-8). McGraw.

Lindbeck, John R. & Lathrop, Irving T. General Industry. (Illus.). (gr. 7-9). 1977. 15.96 (ISBN 0-87002-185-0). student guide 4.64 (ISBN 0-87002-196-6). answer sheet free. Bennett IL.

Person, Harlow S. Industrial Education: A System of Training for Men Entering Upon Trade & Commerce. (Management History Ser.: No. 69). (Illus.). 93p. 1973. Repr. of 1907 ed. 10.00 (ISBN 0-87960-103-5). Hive Pub.

Romano, Louis A. Manual & Industrial Education at Girard College 1831-1965: An Era in American Educational Experimentation. Cordasco, Fransecso, ed. LC 80-1075. (American Ethnic Groups Ser.). 1981. lib. bdg. 39.00x (ISBN 0-405-13450-9). Arno.

Silvius, G. Harold & Bohn, Ralph C. Planning & Organizing Instruction. rev. ed. Orig. Title: Organizing Course Materials for Industrial Education. 1976. text ed. 16.09 (ISBN 0-87345-720-X). McKnight.

Stombaugh, Ray M. Survey of the Movements Culminating in Industrial Arts Education in Secondary Schools. LC 76-177821. (Columbia University. Teachers College. Contributions to Education: No. 670). Repr. of 1936 ed. 17.50 (ISBN 0-404-55670-1). AMS Pr.

Swierkos, et al. Industrial Arts for Elementary Classrooms. 1973. pap. text ed. 6.60 (ISBN 0-87002-116-8). Bennett IL.

Woodward, Calvin M. Manual Training School. LC 79-89254. (American Education: Its Men, Institutions & Ideas, Ser. 1). 1969. Repr. of 1887 ed. 15.00 (ISBN 0-405-01492-9). Arno.

Zaetz, Jay L. Occupational Activities Training Manual: For Severely Retarded Adults. (Illus.). 124p. 1969. photocopy ed. spiral 12.50 (ISBN 0-398-02138-4). C C Thomas.

MANUEL 1ST, KING OF PORTUGAL, 1469-1521

Sanceau, Elaine. Reign of the Fortunate King: Manuel First of Portugal. LC 70-105396. 1970. 14.00 (ISBN 0-208-00968-X, Archon). Shoe String.

MANUEL 1ST COMNENUS, 1120-1180

Kinnamos, John. Deeds of John & Manuel Comnenus. Brand, Charles M., tr. from Greek. LC 76-15317. (Records of Civilization, No. 85). 1976. 20.00x (ISBN 0-231-04080-6). Columbia U Pr.

Urbansky, Andrew B. Byzantium & the Danube Frontier. LC 68-17232. 174p. 1968. text ed. 24.50x (ISBN 0-8290-0158-1); pap. text ed. 9.95x (ISBN 0-8290-0159-X). Irvington.

MANUEL 2ND PALAEOLOGUS, 1391-1425

Barker, John W. Manuel Ii Palaeologus, 1391-1425: A Study in Late Byzantine Statesmanship. 1969. 40.00 (ISBN 0-8135-0582-8). Rutgers U Pr.

Dennis, George T., ed. & tr. The Letters of Manuel II Palaeologus. LC 77-14898. (Dumbarton Oaks Texts: Vol. 4). 315p. 1977. 35.00x (ISBN 0-88402-068-1, Ctr Byzantine). Dumbarton Oaks.

MANUFACTURERS

Here is entered inclusive material on manufacturers as individuals. Works dealing with manufacturing firms are entered under the heading Manufactures or, if restricted to a specific industry, under the name of the industry, e.g. Steel industry and trade.

Ansoff, H. Igor, et al. Acquisition Behavior of United States Manufacturing Firms, 1946-1965. LC 79-163771. (Illus.). 1971. 7.95 (ISBN 0-8265-1174-0). Vanderbilt U Pr.

Berry, Dick. Understanding & Motivating the Manufacturers' Agent. 176p. 1981. 19.95 (ISBN 0-8436-0773-4). CBI Pub.

Coates, J. B. Coates Brothers: A History, 1877-1977. (Illus.). 103p. 1980. 28.50 (ISBN 0-913720-12-7). Sandstone.

Edmonds, Peggy, ed. Harris Michigan Industrial Directory. rev. ed. (Illus., Annual). 1981. 63.95 (ISBN 0-916512-17-7). Harris Pub.

Kelly's Manufacturers & Merchants Directory, 1980-81. 94th ed. LC 12-34808. 2840p. 1980. 90.00x (ISBN 0-610-00527-8). Intl Pubns Serv.

Lebell, Frank. The Manufacturer's Representative. 192p. 1981. 17.50 (ISBN 0-89047-037-5). Herman Pub.

Roberts, Kenneth D., ed. Stanley Rule & Level Co. 1888 Price List of Tools. 1975. 4.50 (ISBN 0-913602-14-0). K Roberts.

--Stanley Rule & Level Co: 1898 Price List. 1975. 5.00 (ISBN 0-913602-15-9). K Roberts.

--Stanley Rule & Level Co.'s Combination Planes. 1975. 4.50 (ISBN 0-913602-09-4). K Roberts.

Smith, David C., ed. Ward's Who's Who Among U.S. Motor Vechicle Manufacturers. 1977. 29.75 (ISBN 0-686-18832-2). Wards Comm.

Tower Publishing Company. Maine Marketing Directory Nineteen Eighty. 1980. pap. 12.50 (ISBN 0-89442-020-8). Tower Pub Co.

Tyron, Rolla M. Household Manufacturers in the United States, 1640-1860. Repr. of 1917 ed. 18.50 (ISBN 0-384-61790-5). Johnson Repr.

Who's Who in Engine & Component Markets 1981 - Companies. 400p. 1981. lib. bdg. 89.95x (ISBN 0-906237-19-X, Pub. by Martin Pub England). Marlin.

MANUFACTURES

see also Catalogs, Commercial; Commerce; Factory System; Home Labor; Industrial Arts; Industrial Capacity; Machinery; Manufacturing Processes; Mills and Mill-Work; Patents; Prices; Production Engineering; Trade-Marks;
also names of articles manufactured, e.g. Boots and Shoes, Hosiery, Knit Goods; and names of industries, e.g. Automobile Industry and Trade, Paper Making and Trade; also subdivision Manufactures under names of countries, cities, etc. e.g. United States–Manufactures

Alexandersson, Gunnar. Geography of Manufacturing. 1967. pap. 7.95 ref. ed. (ISBN 0-13-351262-2). P-H.

Babbage, Charles. On the Economy of Machinery & Manufactures. 4th ed. LC 74-22019. Repr. of 1835 ed. 17.50x (ISBN 0-678-00001-8). Kelley.

Dean, H. Manufacturing: Industry & Careers. 1975. 7.20 (ISBN 0-13-555615-5); pap. text ed. 5.80 (ISBN 0-685-73756-X). P-H.

Delph, John & Delph, Shirley. Factory Decoys of Mason Stevens. (Illus.). 176p. 35.00 (ISBN 0-916838-33-1). Schiffer.

Ephraim, Asher. Relative Productivity, Factor Intensity & Technology in the Manufacturing Sectors of the U.S. & the U.K. During the Nineteenth Century. Bruchey, Stuart, ed. LC 76-39822. (Nineteen Seventy-Seven Dissertations Ser.). (Illus.). 1977. lib. bdg. 15.00x (ISBN 0-405-09902-9). Arno.

Guggenheim, S. Frederic. Problems for Materials & Processes in Manufacturing. 1969. text ed. 4.50 (ISBN 0-02-348420-9, 34842). Macmillan.

Hamilton, F. E. & Linge, G. J., eds. Spatial Analysis, Industry & the Industrial Environment-Progress in Research & Applications: Industrial Systems, Vol. 1. LC 78-10298. 1979. 48.95x (ISBN 0-471-99738-2, Pub. by Wiley-Interscience). Wiley.

Jellinek, J. Stephan. The Use of Fragrance in Consumer Products. LC 75-2106. 219p. 1975. 31.50 (ISBN 0-471-44151-1, Pub. by Wiley-Interscience). Wiley.

Lary, Hal B. Imports of Manufactures from Less Developed Countries. (Studies in International Economic Relations: No. 4). 1968. 12.50x (ISBN 0-87014-485-5, Dist. by Columbia U Pr). Natl Bur Econ Res.

Mancuso, Joseph, ed. Technology Products, 2 vols. LC 74-82598. 1975. Vol.1. 8.75x (ISBN 0-89006-045-2); Vol. 2. 8.75x (ISBN 0-89006-046-0); Set. 17.50x (ISBN 0-89006-047-9). Artech Hse.

Morrison, Robert S. Handbook for Manufacturing Entrepreneurs. LC 73-91212. (Illus.). 1973. 19.50 (ISBN 0-686-05578-0). Western Res Pr.

Ray, Willis. Introduction to Manufacturing Careers. (gr. 7-10). 1975. pap. text ed. 5.28 activity ed. (ISBN 0-87345-177-5). McKnight.

Samuelson, Lee. A New Model of World Trade. (Occasional Economic Studies Ser.). 1973. 2.50x (ISBN 92-64-11148-4). OECD.

Thompson, James M. The Handbook of Small Business Organization & Management-Including Information for the Small Manufacturer. LC 79-55346. (Illus.). 242p. (Orig.). 1980. pap. 19.95 (ISBN 0-686-27309-5). Akens-Morgan.

United States Market Profiles: Twenty Latin American Products Included in the U. S. General System of Preference, Series 1. 1977. 20.00 (ISBN 0-8270-3350-8). OAS.

Ure, Andrew. Philosophy of Manufactures. 3rd ed. 1969. 29.50 (ISBN 0-8337-3599-3). B Franklin.

--Philosophy of Manufactures. (Illus.). 480p. 1967. Repr. of 1835 ed. 32.50x (ISBN 0-7146-1048-8, F Cass Co). Biblio Dist.

Vaccara, Beatrice N. Employment & Output in Protected Manufacturing Industries. LC 79-27932. (Illus.). x, 107p. 1980. Repr. of 1960 ed. lib. bdg. 17.50x (ISBN 0-313-22302-5, VAEO). Greenwood.

Vernon, Ivan R., ed. Introduction to Manufacturing Management, Vol. 1. LC 79-81737. (Manufacturing Management Ser). (Illus., Orig.). 1969. 12.50 (ISBN 0-87263-016-1). SME.

Woodbury, Charles J. Bibliography of the Cotton Manufacture. 1910. 22.50 (ISBN 0-8337-3869-0). B Franklin.

The World of Manufacturing. (gr. 7-9). text ed. 15.96 (ISBN 0-87345-550-9); tchr's guide 32.00 (ISBN 0-87345-552-5); lab. manual 5.00 (ISBN 0-87345-551-7); game 15.00 (ISBN 0-686-31680-0); filmstrip set 306.00 (ISBN 0-686-31681-9); transparency set 390.00 (ISBN 0-686-31682-7). McKnight.

MANUFACTURES–ACCOUNTING

see also Factories–Accounting

MANUFACTURES–CATALOGS

Israel, Fred L., ed. Eighteen Ninety-Seven Sears Roebuck Catalogue. abr. ed. LC 80-69200. (Illus.). 256p. 1981. pap. 4.95 (ISBN 0-87754-138-8). Chelsea Hse.

Kresge's. Kresge's Katalog of 5 Cent & 10 Cent Merchandise. (YA) 1975. pap. 1.95 (ISBN 0-394-73151-4). Random.

Mirken, Alan, ed. Sears, Roebuck Catalogue: 1902 Edition. (Bounty Bks.). (Illus.). 1970. 7.98 (ISBN 0-517-00982-X); pap. 4.95 (ISBN 0-517-00922-6). Crown.

Schulz, Phillip S. Extravagant Things: A Catalog of Indulgences. (Illus.). 450p. (Orig.). 1980. pap. cancelled (ISBN 0-8092-7044-7). Contemp Bks.

The Sears Roebuck Catalog of the 1930's. (Illus.). 1978. pap. 4.95 (ISBN 0-517-53532-7, Dist. by Crown). Nostalgia Pr.

Sears Roebuck Catalogue - Reprint 1897. LC 76-19085. (Illus.). 1976. pap. 3.50 (ISBN 0-87754-045-4). Chelsea Hse.

Sears, Roebuck Catalogue: 1927 Edition. (Bounty Bks.). 1970. 7.98 (ISBN 0-517-01866-7); pap. 5.95 (ISBN 0-517-01865-9). Crown.

Stanley Rule & Level, Eighteen Ninety-Two Price List Revised to Eighteen Ninety-Seven, Abbrigment. 1980. pap. 3.00 (ISBN 0-913602-36-1). K Roberts.

Underhill Edge Tool Co., Eighteen Fifty-Nine Price List Axes & Mechanics' Tools. 1980. pap. 3.00 (ISBN 0-913602-37-X). K Roberts.

William Chapple: Eighteen Seventy-Six Revised Price List Planes. 1980. pap. 2.50 (ISBN 0-913602-35-3). K Roberts.

William Marples & Sons Price List of American Tools & Hardware, Nineteen Hundred Nine. 1980. pap. 4.50 (ISBN 0-913602-41-8). K Roberts.

MANUFACTURES–COSTS

Basche, James R., Jr. Production Cost Trends & Outlook. (Report Ser.: No. 724). (Illus.). 1977. pap. 15.00 (ISBN 0-8237-0158-1). Conference Bd.

Clugston, Richard. Estimating Manufacturing Costs. LC 78-185563. (Illus.). 214p. 1971. 15.95 (ISBN 0-8436-0811-0). CBI Pub.

Metcalfe, Henry. The Cost of Manufactures & the Administration of Workshops, Public & Private. (Management History Ser.: No. 53). 325p. Repr. of 1885 ed. 38.50 (ISBN 0-87960-057-8). Hive Pub.

Myers, John G. & Nakamura, Leonard. Saving Energy in Manufacturing: The Post-Embargo Record. LC 78-7586. 1978. 16.50 (ISBN 0-88410-082-0). Ballinger Pub.

Ostwald, Phillip F., ed. Manufacturing Cost Estimating. LC 79-67648. (Manufacturing Update Ser.). (Illus.). 1980. 29.00 (ISBN 0-87263-053-6). SME.

MANUFACTURES–DIRECTORIES

Annuario Politecnico Italiano, 1978-79: General Directory of Italian Manufacturers. 55th ed. LC 46-43840. 1979. 120.00x (ISBN 0-8002-1209-6). Intl Pubns Serv.

British Sulphur Corp. Ltd. World Directory of Fertilizer Manufacturers. 4th ed. Wahba, C., ed. LC 76-356341. 1977. 210.00x (ISBN 0-902777-28-9). Intl Pubns Serv.

Davis, John G. & Maynes, Terry, eds. Washington Manufacturers Register, 1980-81. 2nd ed. 1980. pap. 42.50 (ISBN 0-911510-81-8). Times-M Pr.

Davis, John G. & Newman, Phyllis, eds. California Manufacturers Register, 1981. 34th rev. ed. LC 48-3418. 880p. 1981. 85.00 (ISBN 0-911510-83-4). Times-M Pr.

--California Services Register, 1981. 2nd ed. 680p. 1981. 100.00 (ISBN 0-911510-84-2). Times-M Pr.

Directory of Colorado Manufacturers: 1980. 1980. 30.00 (ISBN 0-686-64746-7). U CO Busn Res Div.

Directory of Industrial Distributors. 750p. 1979. 27.50 (ISBN 0-686-65875-2). B Klein Pubns.

The Directory of Motor Component Manufacturers in Western Europe. 1981. 165.00x (ISBN 0-686-75442-5, Pub. by European Directories England). State Mutual Bk.

Directory of Pollution Control Equipment Companies in Western Europe. 3rd ed. 1981. 165.00x (ISBN 0-686-75443-3, Pub. by European Directories England). State Mutual Bk.

Directory of Premium, Incentive & Travel Buyers: 1980 Edition. rev. ed. 1979. pap. 110.00 (ISBN 0-87228-033-0). Salesmans.

The Directory of Pump, Valve & Compressor Manufacturers in Western Europe. 1981. 200.00x (ISBN 0-686-75444-1, Pub. by European Directories England). State Mutual Bk.

The Directory of Toiletry & Cosmetic Manufacturers in Western Europe. 1981. 150.00x (ISBN 0-686-75445-X, Pub. by European Directories England). State Mutual Bk.

European Paint Manufacturers, Nineteen Seventy-Seven to Nineteen Seventy-Nine. 3rd ed. 186p. (Orig.). 1977. pap. 55.00x (ISBN 90-6156-514-6). Intl Pubns Serv.

European Plastics Nineteen Seventy-Eight to Nineteen Eighty. 5th ed. 339p. (Orig.). 1978. pap. 55.00x (ISBN 90-6156-516-2). Intl Pubns Serv.

Harsey, Paula. Harris-Indiana Industrial Directory 1981. (Illus., Annual). 1981. 38.90 (ISBN 0-916512-26-6). Harris Pub.

Holtje, Herbert F. Directory of Manufacturers' Representatives. LC 77-14580. 1978. 54.00 (ISBN 0-07-029640-5, P&RB). McGraw.

Hong, Alfred. Marketing Economics Key Plants, Nineteen Seventy-Nine to Nineteen Eighty: The Guide to Industrial Purchasing Power. LC 73-642154. 1979. 90.00 (ISBN 0-914078-34-8). Marketing Econs.

Idaho Manufacturing Directory: 1982-83. rev. ed. 1982. 30.00x (ISBN 0-686-05494-6). Ctr Bus Devel.

Kemps Directory, 1978-79, 3 vols. 1979. Set. pap. 48.50 (ISBN 0-686-59757-5, KEMP001, Kemps). Vol. 1 (ISBN 0-905255-47-X). Vol. 2 (ISBN 0-905255-49-6). Vol. 3 (ISBN 0-905255-50-X). Unipub.

Kruzas, Anthony T. & Thomas, Robert C., eds. Business Organizations & Agencies Directory. LC 80-32. 1980. 110.00 (ISBN 0-8103-1135-6). Gale.

Lace, Vivian, ed. Ohio Industrial Directory: 1981. rev. ed. LC 75-42929. (Illus., Annual). 1981. 65.00 (ISBN 0-916512-56-8). Harris Pub.

Made in Austria. 312p. (Orig.). 1978. pap. 27.50x (ISBN 0-8002-2234-2). Intl Pubns Serv.

Mississippi Manufacturers Directory. 25.00 (ISBN 0-686-30809-3). MS Res & Dev Ctr.

State Industrial Directories Corp. Alabama State Industrial Directory, 1979. 1979. 30.00 (ISBN 0-686-77193-1). State Indus Dir.

--Connecticut State Industrial Directory, 1979. (State Industrial Directory Ser.). 1979. 45.00 (ISBN 0-916112-92-6). State Indus Dir.

--Delaware State Industrial Directory, 1979-1980. (State Industrial Directory Ser.). 1979. 15.00 (ISBN 0-916112-85-3). State Indus Dir.

--Florida State Industrial Directory, 1979. (State Industrial Directory Ser.). 1979. 35.00 (ISBN 0-916112-94-2). State Indus Dir.

--Florida State Industrial Directory 1980. 1980. pap. 65.00 (ISBN 0-89910-039-2). State Indus Dir.

--Georgia State Industrial Directory, 1978. (State Industrial Directory Ser.). 1979. 30.00 (ISBN 0-916112-98-5). State Indus Dir.

--Indiana State Industrial Directory, 1980. (State Industrial Directory Ser.). 1979. pap. 70.00 (ISBN 0-916112-84-5). State Indus Dir.

--Kentucky State Industrial Dirctory, 1979. (State Industrial Directory Ser.). 1979. write for info. (ISBN 0-916112-88-8). State Indus Dir.

--Louisiana State Industrial Directory, 1979. (State Industrial Directory Ser.). 1979. 20.00 (ISBN 0-916112-83-7). State Indus Dir.

--Maine State Industrial Directory 1977. (Maine State Industrial Directory Ser.). 1976. 20.00 (ISBN 0-916112-53-5). State Indus Dir.

--Maine State Industrial Directory, 1979. (State Industrial Directory Ser.). 1979. 20.00 (ISBN 0-916112-78-0). State Indus Dir.

--Maryland State Industrial Directory, 1979. (State Industrial Directory Ser.). 1979. 30.00 (ISBN 0-916112-79-9). State Indus Dir.

--Maryland State Industrial Directory 1980. 1980. pap. 35.00 (ISBN 0-89910-040-6). State Indus Dir.

--Michigan State Industrial Directory, 1980. (State Industrial Directory Ser.). 1979. pap. 70.00 (ISBN 0-916112-82-9). State Indus Dir.

--Mississippi State Industrial Directory, 1979. (State Industtrial Directory Ser.). 1979. write for info. (ISBN 0-916112-87-X). State Indus Dir.

--Montana State Industrial Directory, 1980. 1980. pap. 25.00 (ISBN 0-89910-026-0). State Indus Dir.

--New Jersey Industrial Directory 1980. 1980. pap. 90.00 (ISBN 0-89910-027-9). State Indus Dir.

--New Mexico State Industrial Directory 1980. 1980. pap. write for info. (ISBN 0-89910-037-6). State Indus Dir.

--New York State Industrial Directory, 1979. (State Industrial Directory Ser.). 1979. 90.00 (ISBN 0-916112-90-X). State Indus Dir.

--North Carolina State Industrial Directory, 1979. (North Carolina State Industrial Directory Ser.). 1979. 30.00 (ISBN 0-916112-99-3). State Indus Dir.

--Ohio State Manufacturer's Guide, 1981. 1981. pap. text ed. write for info. (ISBN 0-89910-055-4). State Indus Dir.

--Oklahoma State Industrial Directory 1981. 1980. pap. 35.00 (ISBN 0-89910-036-8). State Indus Dir.

--Pennsylvania State Industrial Directory, 1979. (State Industrial Directory Ser.). 1979. 87.50 (ISBN 0-916112-91-8). State Indus Dir.

--South Carolina State Industrial Directory, 1979. (State Industrial Directory Ser.). 1979. 30.00 (ISBN 0-916112-93-4). State Indus Dir.

--Tennessee State Industrial Directory, 1979. (State Industrial Directory Ser.). 1979. write for info. (ISBN 0-916112-86-1). State Indus Dir.

--Virginia State Industrial Directory, 1979. (State Industrial Directory Ser.). 1979. write for info. (ISBN 0-916112-89-6). State Indus Dir.

--Wisconsin State Industrial Directory, 1980. 1979. pap. 50.00 (ISBN 0-89910-010-4). State Indus Dir.

State Industrial Directories Corporation. New Hampshire State Industrial Directory, 1980-81. (State Industrial Directory Ser.). 1979. 20.00 (ISBN 0-89910-012-0). State Indus Dir.

--New Jersey State Industrial Directory, 1979. (State Industrial Directory Ser.). 1979. 87.00 (ISBN 0-916112-75-6). State Indus Dir.

--Ohio Manufacturers Guide, 1980. (State Industrial Directory Ser.). 1979. write for info. (ISBN 0-89910-009-0). State Indus Dir.

--Vermont State Industrial Directory, 1980-81. (State Industrial Directory Ser.). 1979. pap. 20.00 (ISBN 0-89910-013-9). State Indus Dir.

State Industrial Directory Corp. Alabama State Industrial Directory, 1978. 1979. 30.00 (ISBN 0-916112-95-0). State Indus Dir.

--Kansas State Industrial Directory, 1980. 1980. pap. 35.00 (ISBN 0-89910-002-3). State Indus Dir.

--North Carolina State Industrial Directory, 1978. (State Industrial Directory Ser.). 1979. 30.00 (ISBN 0-916112-99-3). State Indus Dir.

Swedish Export Council. Swedish Export Directory. 60th ed. LC 72-623267. 728p. 1979. 30.00x (ISBN 0-8002-2222-9). Intl Pubns Serv.

MANUFACTURES–JUVENILE LITERATURE

Gottlieb, Leonard. Factory Made: How Things Are Manufactured. (gr. 5 up). 1978. 7.95 (ISBN 0-395-26450-2). HM.

How Things Are Made. LC 79-3242. (Ser. Two). (Illus.). 104p. (gr. 3-8). 1981. 6.95 (ISBN 0-87044-334-8); PLB 8.50 (ISBN 0-87044-339-9). Natl Geog.

Lewis, Stephen. How's It Made? A Photo Tour of Seven Small Factories. LC 77-5485. (gr. 1-5). 1977. 8.25 (ISBN 0-688-80111-0); PLB 7.92 (ISBN 0-688-84111-2). Greenwillow.

Sullivan, George. More How Do They Make It. LC 79-79958. (Illus.). (gr. 5-8). 1969. 4.95 (ISBN 0-664-32454-1). Westminster.

MANUFACTURING ENGINEERING

see Production Engineering

MANUFACTURING MANAGEMENT

see Production Management

MANUFACTURING PLANNING

see Production Planning

MANUFACTURING PROCESSES

see also Assembly-Line Methods; Fasteners; Finishes and Finishing; Machine-Tools; Manufactures; Materials; Metal-Work; Mills and Mill-Work; Process Control; Turning; Woodwork

Amstead, B. H., et al. Manufacturing Processes. 7th ed. LC 76-26542. 739p. 1977. 29.95 (ISBN 0-471-06245-6). Wiley.

--Manufacturing Processes. 7th ed. LC 78-16185. 739p. 1979. text ed. 29.95 (ISBN 0-471-03575-0); solutions manual avail. (ISBN 0-471-03679-X). Wiley.

Andrew, William G. & Williams, H. B. Applied Instrumentation in the Process Industries, Vol. 2. 2nd ed. (Illus.). 312p. 1980. 32.95x (ISBN 0-87201-383-9). Gulf Pub.

Beebe, William, intro. by. Autofact West Proceedings, Vol. 1. LC 80-53423. (Illus.). 939p. 1980. pap. 55.00 (ISBN 0-87263-065-X). SME.

Black, Bruce J. Manufacturing Technology for Level-Three Technicians. 224p. 1981. pap. 13.95x (ISBN 0-7131-3430-5). Intl Ideas.

Branan, Carl R. Process Engineer's Pocket Handbook. LC 76-1680. 144p. 1976. pap. 6.95 (ISBN 0-87201-712-5). Gulf Pub.

Buckley, Page S. Techniques of Process Control. LC 78-27015. 316p. 1979. Repr. of 1964 ed. lib. bdg. 27.50 (ISBN 0-88275-777-6). Krieger.

Burnham, Don, intro. by. Manufacturing Productivity Solutions II. LC 80-54415. (Illus.). 161p. 1980. pap. text ed. 20.00 (ISBN 0-87263-106-0). SME.

Business Communications, ed. New Directions in Robots for Manufacturing, G-053. 1979. 750.00 (ISBN 0-89336-219-0). BCC.

Cheek, G. Manufacturing Processes: Woods. 1975. 7.20 (ISBN 0-13-555656-2); pap. text ed. 5.80 (ISBN 0-13-555649-X). P-H.

DeGarmo, E. Paul. Materials & Processes in Manufacturing. 5th ed. (Illus.). 1979. text ed. 22.95 (ISBN 0-02-328120-0); instrs'. manual avail. Macmillan.

Dodd, George. Days at the Factories; or, the Manufacturing Industry of Great Britain, Described & Illustrated by Numerous Engravings of Machines & Processes. (Illus.). 408p. 1975. Repr. of 1843 ed. 16.50x (ISBN 0-87471-620-9). Rowman.

Energy Policy for the Manufacturing Sector. 155p. 1980. pap. 13.25 (ISBN 92-833-1459-X, APO 90, APO). Unipub.

Enrick, Norbert L. Management Control Manual for the Textile Industry. 2nd rev. ed. LC 79-13534. 356p. 1980. lib. bdg. 17.50 (ISBN 0-88275-994-9). Krieger.

Fales, James, et al. Manufacturing: A Basic Text for Industrial Arts. (Illus.). 1980. 15.96 (ISBN 0-87345-586-X, B82088); instr's guide 5.28 (ISBN 0-87345-587-8); activities 5.28 (ISBN 0-87345-588-6). McKnight.

Gillespie, LaRoux K., ed. Advances in Deburring. LC 78-57204. (Illus.). 1978. text ed. 17.95x (ISBN 0-87263-044-7). SME.

Gregor, T. Manufacturing Processes: Ceramics. 1976. 7.20 (ISBN 0-13-555672-4); pap. text ed. 5.80 (ISBN 0-13-555664-3). P-H.

Groover, Mikell P. Automation, Production Systems & Computer-Aided Manufacturing. 1980. text ed. 24.95 (ISBN 0-13-054668-2). P-H.

H. B. Maynard & Company. Production: An International Appraisal of Contemporary Manufacturing Systems & the Changing Role of the Worker. Tiefenthal, R., ed. LC 75-16144. 224p. 1976. 22.95x (ISBN 0-470-58033-X). Halsted Pr.

Hales, Mike. Living Thinkwork: Where Do Labour Processes Come from? 1981. text ed. 26.00x (ISBN 0-906336-14-7, Pub. by CSE Bks England); pap. text ed. 9.25x (ISBN 0-906336-15-5, Pub. by CSE Bks England). Humanities.

Harrington, Joseph, Jr. Computer Integrated Manufacturing. LC 78-31268. 336p. 1979. Repr. of 1973 ed. lib. bdg. 18.50 (ISBN 0-88275-856-X). Krieger.

Harris. Manufacturing Technology, No. 3. 1981. text ed. 13.95 (ISBN 0-408-00493-2). Butterworth.

Hine, Charles R. Machine Tools & Processes for Engineers. 634p. Date not set. Repr. of 1971 ed. lib. bdg. price not set (ISBN 0-89874-354-0). Krieger.

International Conference on Programming Languages for Machine Tools, 3rd. Advances in Computer Aided Manufacture: Proceedings. McPherson, D., ed. 1978. 53.75 (ISBN 0-7204-0500-9, North-Holland). Elsevier.

Jambro, D. Manufacturing Processes: Plastics. 1976. 7.20 (ISBN 0-13-555631-7); pap. text ed. 5.80 (ISBN 0-13-555623-6). P-H.

Jambro, Donald. Introduction to Manufacturing. LC 80-51267. (Industrial Arts Ser.). (Illus.). 352p. (Orig.). 1981. text ed. 17.60 (ISBN 0-8273-1741-7); text ed. write for info. instr's. guide (ISBN 0-8273-1742-5). Delmar.

Jameson, E. C. Thermal Machining Processes. LC 79-62917. (Manufacturing Update Ser.). (Illus.). 29.00x (ISBN 0-87263-049-8). SME.

Johnson. Manufacturing Process. 1979. text ed. 23.72 (ISBN 0-87002-299-7); study guide 5.28 (ISBN 0-87002-044-7). Bennett IL.

Jones, R. F., Jr., et al, eds. Numerical Modeling of Manufacturing Processes, PVP-PB-025. 188p. 1977. pap. text ed. 20.00 (ISBN 0-685-86872-9, G00131). ASME.

Jowitt, R., ed. Hygenic Design & Operation of Food Plant. (Illus., American edition). 1980. pap. text ed. 27.50 (ISBN 0-87055-345-3). AVI.

Kazanas, H. Manufacturing Processes: Metals. 1976. 7.20 (ISBN 0-13-555698-8); pap. text ed. 5.80 (ISBN 0-13-555680-5). P-H.

Kazanas, H., et al. Manufacturing Processes. 1981. text ed. write for info.; instr's. manual 4.95 (ISBN 0-07-033466-8). McGraw.

Kenlay, G. & Harris, K. W. Manufacturing Technology, Vol. 1. (Illus.). 155p. 1979. pap. 12.95x (ISBN 0-7131-3401-1). Intl Ideas.

Koben, Shelly & Rose, Michael. Electronic Manufacturing Process. (Illus.). 320p. 1982. text ed. 25.95 (ISBN 0-8359-1642-1). Reston.

Lindberg, Roy A. Materials & Manufacturing Technology. (Illus.). 1968. text ed. 26.95x (ISBN 0-205-01947-1, 321947X). Allyn.

--Processes & Materials of Manufacture. 2nd ed. 1977. text ed. 27.95 (ISBN 0-205-05414-5, 32544143); a. b. avail. (ISBN 0-205-05492-7, 3254143). Allyn.

Link, Albert N. Research & Development in U.S. Manufacturing. 124p. 1981. 18.95 (ISBN 0-03-057677-6). Praeger.

McCarty, Frank, intro. by. Autofact West Proceedings, Vol. 2. LC 80-53423. (Illus.). 842p. 1980. pap. 55.00 (ISBN 0-87263-066-8). SME.

Major Loss Prevention in the Process Industries: Proceedings, No. 34, Newcastle Upon Tyne, 1971. 258p. 1981. 72.00x (ISBN 0-85295-078-0, Pub. by Inst Chem Eng England). State Mutual Bk.

Management's Guide to Computer Integrated Manufacturing. 117.00 (ISBN 0-686-31443-3). Prod Intl.

Mayr, Otto & Post, Robert C., eds. Yankee Enterprise: The Rise of the American System of Manufactures. LC 81-607315. (Illus.). 300p. (Orig.). 1981. text ed. 19.95x (ISBN 0-87474-634-5); pap. text ed. 9.95x (ISBN 0-87474-631-0). Smithsonian.

MiCon Seventy-Eight: Optimization of Processing, Properties & Service Performance Through Microstructural Control. (Special Technical Publications Ser.). 677p. 1979. 59.50x (ISBN 0-686-76058-1, 672, 04-672000-28). ASTM.

Moore, Harry D. & Kibbey, Donald R. Manufacturing: Materials & Processes. 3rd ed. LC 81-4261. 380p. 1982. text ed. 26.95 (ISBN 0-88244-236-8). Grid Pub.

Ouellette, Robert P., et al, eds. Applications in Manufacturing, Vol.2. LC 77-85093. (Electrotechnology Ser.). 1978. 39.95 (ISBN 0-250-40207-6). Ann Arbor Science.

Paul, A. Materials & Processes in Manufacturing: Lab Manual. 1969. 3.95x (ISBN 0-02-393200-7). Macmillan.

Plossi, George. Manufacturing Control: The Last Frontier for Profits. LC 73-8965. 1973. 16.95 (ISBN 0-87909-483-4). Reston.

Pressman, R. S. & Williams, J. E. Numerical Control & Computer-Aided Manufacturing. 310p. 1977. text ed. 28.95 (ISBN 0-471-01555-5). Wiley.

Rajbman, N. S. & Chadeev, V. M. Identification of Industrial Processes: The Application of Computers in Research & Production Control. 1978. 46.50 (ISBN 0-444-85181-X, North-Holland). Elsevier.

Rembold, U., ed. Information-Control Problems in Manufacturing Technology: Proceedings of the Second IFAC/IFIP Symposium, Stuttgart, Federal Republic of Germany, 22-24 October, 1979. LC 80-49945. (IFAC Proceedings Ser.). (Illus.). 330p. 1980. 75.00 (ISBN 0-08-024452-1). Pergamon.

Schey, John A. Introduction to Manufacturing Processes. (Illus.). 1977. text ed. 24.50 (ISBN 0-07-055274-6, C); solutions manual 3.95 (ISBN 0-07-055275-4). McGraw.

Schor, Stanley S. The Capital Product Ratio & Size of Establishment for Manufacturing Industries. new ed. Bruchey, Stuart & Carosso, Vincent P., eds. LC 78-18976. (Small Business Enterprise in America Ser.). (Illus.). 1979. lib. bdg. 12.00x (ISBN 0-405-11479-6). Arno.

Smith, Donald, et al. CAD-CAM International Delphi Forecast. LC 80-53001. (Illus.). 181p. 1980. pap. 29.00 (ISBN 0-87263-062-5). SME.

Strassmann, Wolfgang P. Risk & Technological Innovation: American Manufacturing Methods During the Nineteenth Century. LC 81-4252. x, 249p. 1981. Repr. lib. bdg. 25.00x (ISBN 0-313-23083-8, STRIT). Greenwood.

Symposium on Advanced Techniques for Material Investigation & Fabrication, Cocoa Beach, Florida. Nov. 5-7, 1968. Proceedings. (Science of Advanced Materials & Process Engineering Ser., Vol. 14). 10.00 (ISBN 0-938994-14-X). Soc Adv Material.

Symposium on Filament Winding, Pasedena, Ca. Mar. 28-30, 1961. Proceedings. (Science of Advanced Materials & Process Engineering Ser., Vol. 1). pap. 3.00 (ISBN 0-938994-07-7). Soc Adv Material.

Taraman, Khalil S., ed. CAD-CAM, Meeting Today's Productivity Challenge. LC 80-69006. (Manufacturing Update Ser.). (Illus.). 281p. 1980. 29.00 (ISBN 0-87263-063-3). SME.

Thode, Bradley. Materials Processing. LC 80-70702. (Industrial Arts Ser.). (Illus.). 350p. 1981. text ed. 17.60 (ISBN 0-8273-1767-0); text ed. write for info. instr's. guide (ISBN 0-8273-1768-9). Delmar.

Town, H. C. & Moore, H. Manufacturing Technology, Vol. 1. 1979. 27.00 (ISBN 0-7134-1094-9, Pub. by Batsford England); pap. 14.95 (ISBN 0-7134-1095-7). David & Charles.

Wilson, R. C. & Henry, Robert A. Introduction to Group Technology in Manufacturing & Engineering. (Illus.). 70p. 1977. 12.00 (ISBN 0-686-72876-9, GROUP). Indus Dev Inst Sci.

Wright, R. T. & Jensen, T. R. Manufacturing Material Processing, Management, Careers. 336p. 1981. 10.96 (ISBN 0-87006-203-4). Goodheart.

Yankee, Herbert W. Manufacturing Processes. LC 78-13059. (Illus.). 1979. 27.95 (ISBN 0-13-555557-4). P-H.

MANUKUTUBA LANGUAGE

see Congo Language

MANUMISSION OF SLAVES

see Slavery–Emancipation

MANURES

see Fertilizers and Manures

MANUS TRIBE

Buhler, G. The Laws of Manu. lib. bdg. 59.95 (ISBN 0-87968-492-5). Krishna Pr.

Mead, Margaret. Growing up in New Guinea. LC 75-21740. 400p. 1976. pap. 5.95 (ISBN 0-688-07989-X). Morrow.

--New Lives for Old. LC 75-21699. 576p. 1976. pap. 4.95 (ISBN 0-688-07169-4). Morrow.

--New Lives for Old: Cultural Transformation-Manus 1928-1953. LC 79-20771. (Illus.). 1980. Repr. of 1975 ed. lib. bdg. 39.75x (ISBN 0-313-22130-8, MENI). Greenwood.

MANUSCRIPT DEPOSITORIES

see Archives

MANUSCRIPT TRANSMISSION

see Transmission of Texts

MANUSCRIPTS

see also Autographs; Charters; Diplomatics; Genizah; Illumination of Books and Manuscripts; Incipits; Music–Manuscripts; Paleography; Transmission of Texts

Alexander, J. J., ed. The Decorated Letter. (Magnificent Paperback Ser.). 1978. 22.95 (ISBN 0-8076-0894-7); pap. 10.95 (ISBN 0-8076-0895-5). Braziller.

--Insular Manuscripts from the 6th Century to the 9th Century. (A Survey of Manuscripts Illuninated in the British Isles: Vol. 1). (Illus.). 95.00 (ISBN 0-905203-01-1, Pub. by H Miller England). Heyden.

American Literary Manuscripts in the Boston Public Library: A Checklist. 1973. 3.00 (ISBN 0-89073-021-0). Boston Public Lib.

Ash, Lee. Subject Collections. 5th ed. LC 74-19331. 1978. 72.50 (ISBN 0-8352-0924-5). Bowker.

Baikie, James. Egyptian Papyri & Papyrus-Hunting. facsimile ed. LC 76-152972. (Select Bibliographies Reprint Ser). (Illus.). Repr. of 1925 ed. 24.00 (ISBN 0-8369-5724-5). Arno.

Bergman, Floyd. Manuscript Diagnosis: The Text Ray. pap. 3.00 (ISBN 0-87506-053-6). Campus.

Berkeley, Edmund, Jr., ed. Autographs & Manuscripts: A Collector's Manual. (Illus.). 1978. 24.95 (ISBN 0-684-15622-9, ScribR). Scribner.

Birch, Walter De Goay. Catalogue of a Collection of Original Manuscripts, Formerly Belonging to the Holy Office of the Inquisition in the Canary Islands, 2 vols. LC 72-79200. 1903. Repr. 49.00 (ISBN 0-403-03347-0). Somerset Pub.

Blake, William. The Pickering Manuscript. (Illus.). 28p. 1972. pap. 3.00 (ISBN 0-87598-036-8). Pierpont Morgan.

Brown, John H. & Grant, Steven A. The Russian Empire & Soviet Union: A Guide to Manuscripts & Archival Materials in the United States. (Libary Catalogs Supplement). 1981. lib. bdg. 75.00 (ISBN 0-8161-1300-9). G K Hall.

Brown, Peter. The Book of Kells. abr. ed. (Illus.). 1981. 22.50 (ISBN 0-500-23326-8). Thames Hudson.

Brumbaugh, Robert S., ed. The Most Mysterious Manuscript: The Voynich "Roger Bacon" Cipher Manuscript. LC 77-15024. (Illus.). 189p. 1978. 12.50x (ISBN 0-8093-0808-8). S Ill U Pr.

Cahoon, Herbert. The Dannie & Hettie Heineman Collection. LC 78-65388. (Illus.). 109p. 1978. 25.00 (ISBN 0-87598-067-8). Pierpont Morgan.

Cardenas, Anthony, et al. Bibliography of Old Spanish Texts. 2nd, rev., enl. ed. (Literary texts). 1977. 9.50x (ISBN 0-686-16324-9); pap. 7.50x (ISBN 0-686-16325-7). Hispanic Seminary.

Cripe, Helen & Campbell, Diane. American Manuscripts, 1763-1815: An Index to Documents Described in Auction Records & Dealers' Catalogs. LC 77-2525. 1977. 99.00 (ISBN 0-8420-2122-1). Scholarly Res Inc.

Derolez, Albert. Library of Raphael De Marcetellis. 335p. 1980. text ed. 83.75x (ISBN 90-6439-191-2). Humanities.

Dibdin, Thomas F. Bibliographical, Antiquarian, & Picturesque Tour in France & Germany, 3 Vols. 2nd ed. LC 76-111768. Repr. of 1829 ed. Set. 80.00 (ISBN 0-404-02130-1). AMS Pr.

Earle, John. Gloucester Fragments. LC 74-18301. 1974. Repr. of 1861 ed. lib. bdg. 35.00 (ISBN 0-8414-3989-3). Folcroft.

Evans, Frank B., et al. A Basic Glossary for Archivists, Manuscript Curators, & Records Managers. 19p. 1974. pap. 2.00 (ISBN 0-931828-02-3). Soc Am Archivists.

Fleckner, John A. Archives & Manuscripts: Surveys. rev. ed. LC 77-14554. (Saa Basic Manual Ser.). 28p. 1977. pap. 5.00 (ISBN 0-931828-05-8). Soc Am Archivists.

Forstemann, E. Commentary on the Maya Manuscript in the Royal Public Library of Dresden. 1906. pap. 14.00 (ISBN 0-527-01202-5). Kraus Repr.

Forsythe, J. History of Ancient Manuscripts. lib. bdg. 59.95 (ISBN 0-8490-1967-2). Gordon Pr.

Fraser, James, ed. Childrens Authors & Illustrators: A Guide to Manuscript Collections in U. S. Libraries. 130p. 1980. pap. text ed. 14.80 (ISBN 0-89664-950-4). K G Saur.

Gordan, John D. Novels in Manuscript: An Exhibition from the Berg Collection. 1965. pap. 3.00 (ISBN 0-87104-134-0). NY Pub Lib.

Gracy, David B. An Introduction to Archives & Manuscripts. LC 81-5677. (Professional Development Ser.: Vol. 2). 1981. 7.25 (ISBN 0-87111-288-4). SLA.

Gracy, David B., II. Archives & Manuscripts: Arrangement & Description. rev. ed. LC 77-13527. (Saa Basic Manual Ser.). 49p. 1977. pap. 5.00 (ISBN 0-931828-07-4). Soc Am Archivists.

Greg, Walter W. Calculus of Variants. 1927. lib. bdg. 7.50 (ISBN 0-8414-4681-4). Folcroft.

Grimsted, Patricia K. Archives & Manuscript Repositories in the USSR: Estonia, Latvia & Belorussia. LC 79-15427. (Studies of the Russian Institute, Columbia University & Harvard Ser. in Ukrainian Studies). (Illus.). 1981. 60.00x (ISBN 0-691-05279-4). Princeton U Pr.

Gutmann, Joseph. Hebrew Manuscript Painting. (Magnificent Paperback Art Ser.). 1978. 22.95 (ISBN 0-8076-0890-4); pap. 10.95 (ISBN 0-8076-0891-2). Braziller.

Haenel, G. F. Dictionnaire des Manuscrits, Ou Recueil De Catalogues De Manuscrits Existants Dans les Pri Cipales Bibliotheques D'europe, 2 vols. Migne, J. P., ed. (Nouvelle Encyclopedie Theologique Ser.: Vols. 40-41). 1624p. (Fr.). Date not set. Repr. of 1853 ed. lib. bdg. 205.50x (ISBN 0-89241-280-1). Caratzas Bros.

Hamilton, Charles. Collecting Autographs & Manuscripts. 2nd ed. LC 61-9007. 1961. pap. 9.95 (ISBN 0-8061-1156-9). U of Okla Pr.

Harvard, Stephen. An Italic Copybook: The Cantaneo Manuscript. LC 81-50465. 64p. 1981. 20.00 (ISBN 0-8008-0410-4, Pentalic). Taplinger.

Hatch, William H. Greek & Syrian Miniatures in Jerusalem. (Illus.). 1931. 15.00 (ISBN 0-910956-04-9). Medieval Acad.

Higgins, L. James, Jr. A Guide to the Manuscript Collections at the Nevada Historical Society. rev. ed. 1975. pap. 7.50 spiral bd. (ISBN 0-686-10435-8). Nevada Hist Soc.

Holbert, Sue E. Archives & Manuscripts: Reference & Access. rev. ed. LC 77-21004. (Saa Basic Manual Ser.). 30p. 1977. pap. 5.00 (ISBN 0-931828-09-0). Soc Am Archivists.

Hughes, Andrew. Medieval Manuscripts for Mass & Office: A Guide to Their Organization & Terminology. 496p. 1981. 45.00x (ISBN 0-8020-5467-6). U of Toronto Pr.

Index of English Literary Manuscripts: Vol. 1, 1450-1625 Parts 1 & 2. 1159p. 1980. 300.00 set (ISBN 0-7201-0807-1, Co-Pub. by Mansell Pub Inc England). Bowker.

Inventories & Registers: A Handbook of Techniques & Examples. 36p. 1976. pap. 4.00 (ISBN 0-931828-10-4). Soc Am Archivists.

James, M. R. Medieval Manuscripts: Part 3 of Biblioteca Pepysiana, a Descriptive Catalogue of the Library of Samuel Pepys. 7.50x (ISBN 0-87556-471-2). Saifer.

Kasten, Lloyd & Nitti, John. Concordances & Texts of the Royal Scriptorium Manuscripts of Alfonso X, el Sabio, 2 vols. (Spanish Ser.: No. 2). 1978. 150.00 (ISBN 0-686-27739-2). Hispanic Seminary.

Kauffmann, C. M. Romanesque Manuscripts 1066-1190. (A Survey of Manuscripts Illuminated in the British Isles: Vol. 3). (Illus.). 95.00 (ISBN 0-85602-017-6, Pub. by H Miller England). Heyden.

Kenney, James F. Sources for the Early History of Ireland: Ecclesiastical. 1967. lib. bdg. 50.00x (ISBN 0-374-94560-8). Octagon.

Ker, Neil R., ed. Medieval Manuscripts in British Libraries, Vol. 1. 1969. 39.50x (ISBN 0-19-818219-8). Oxford U Pr.

Kienast, R. Johann Valentin Andreae und Die Vier Echten Rosenkreutzer-Schriften. (Ger). Repr. of 1926 ed. 21.50 (ISBN 0-384-29405-7); pap. 18.50 (ISBN 0-685-02276-5). Johnson Repr.

Kiernan, Kevin S. Beowulf & the Beowulf Manuscript. (Illus.). 280p. 1981. 19.50 (ISBN 0-8135-0925-4). Rutgers U Pr.

Klinkenborg, Verlyn, ed. British Literary Manuscripts: Series I. 1981. pap. 10.00 (ISBN 0-486-24124-6). Dover.

--British Literary Manuscripts: Series II. 1981. pap. 10.00 (ISBN 0-486-24125-4). Dover.

Knight, R. J. B., ed. Guide to the Manuscripts in the National Maritime Museum: Public Records,Business Records & Artificial Collections, Vol. 2. 304p. 1981. text ed. 40.00 (ISBN 0-7201-1591-4, Pub. by Mansell England). Merrimack Bk Serv.

Knorozov, Yuri V. & Proskouriakoff, Tatiana, eds. Selected Chapters from the Writings of the Maya Indians. Coe, Sophie, tr. LC 70-38502. (Harvard University. Peabody Museum of Archaeology & Ethnology. Russian Translation Ser.: No. 4). Repr. of 1967 ed. 17.50 (ISBN 0-404-52647-0). AMS Pr.

Lutz, Cora E. Essays on Manuscripts & Rare Books. (Illus.). 177p. (Orig.). 1975. 15.00 (ISBN 0-208-01513-2, Archon). Shoe String.

Lytle, Richard H., ed. Management of Archives & Manuscript Collections for Librarians. LC 79-92650. 124p. 1980. Repr. of 1975 ed. 7.00 (ISBN 0-931828-27-9). Soc Am Archivists.

Madan, Falconer. Books in Manuscript. LC 68-25315. (Reference Ser., No. 44). (Illus.). 1972. Repr. of 1893 ed. lib. bdg. 29.95 (ISBN 0-8383-0213-0). Haskell.

Martin, Thomas J., ed. North American Collections of Islamic Manuscripts. (Reference Publications Ser.). 1977. lib. bdg. 8.00 (ISBN 0-8161-8080-6). G K Hall.

Meiss, Millard. The De Levis Hours & the Bedford Workshop. 73p. 1981. text ed. 10.00x (ISBN 0-300-03507-1). Yale U Pr.

Meyer, Karl H. Altkirchenslavisch-Griechisches Woerterbuch Des Codex Supraliensis. 25.00 (ISBN 0-685-71713-5). J J Augustin.

Milligan, George, ed. & tr. Selections from the Greek Papyri. LC 76-103654. (Select Bibliographies Reprint Ser). 1910. 17.00 (ISBN 0-8369-5154-9). Arno.

Miniatures from Persian Manuscripts. 1981. 150.00x (ISBN 0-7141-0659-3, Pub. by Brit Lib England). State Mutual Bk.

Moorman, Charles. Editing the Middle English Manuscript. LC 74-17511. (Illus.). 1975. 7.95x (ISBN 0-87805-063-9). U Pr of Miss.

Munby, A. N. Essays & Papers. Barker, Nicolas, ed. (Illus.). 256p. 1978. 25.00x (ISBN 0-85967-349-9, Pub. by Scolar Pr England). Biblio Dist.

O'Callaghan, Edmund B., ed. Calandar of Historical Manuscripts in the Office of the Secretary of State, Albany, New York: Dutch Manuscripts 1630 - 1664, Pt. 1. 423p. 1968. Repr. of 1865 ed. 26.00 (ISBN 0-8398-1451-8). Parnassus Imprints.

--Calandar of Historical Manuscripts in the Office of the Secretary of State, Albany, New York: English Manuscripts 1664 - 1776, Pt. 2. 891p. 1968. Repr. of 1866 ed. 52.00 (ISBN 0-8398-1452-6). Parnassus Imprints.

Osborn, James. Neo-Philobiblon: Ruminations on Manuscript Collecting. LC 72-619565. (Bibliographical Monograph: No. 7). (Illus.). 1973. 5.95 (ISBN 0-87959-049-1). U of Tex Hum Res.

Parkes, M. B. & Watson, Andrew G., eds. Medieval Scribes, Manuscripts & Libraries: Essays Presented to N. R. Ker. (Illus.). 408p. 1978. 80.00x (ISBN 0-85967-450-9, Pub. by Scolar Pr England). Biblio Dist.

Putnam, George H. Books & Their Makers During the Middle Ages, 2 Vols. 1962. Set. text ed. 42.50x (ISBN 0-391-01060-3). Humanities.

Reeves, Arthur M. Finding of Wineland the Good, the History of the Icelandic Discovery of America. rev. ed. 1895. 24.00 (ISBN 0-8337-2918-7). B Franklin.

Reychman, Jan & Zajaczkowski, Ananiasz. Handbook of Ottoman-Turkish Diplomatics. rev ed. Ehrenkreutz, Andrew S., tr. (Publications in Near & Middle East Studies, Ser. A: No. 7). (Illus.). 1968. 56.50x (ISBN 90-2790-513-4). Mouton.

Richter-Bernburg, Lutz. Persian Medical Manuscripts at the University of California, Los Angeles. LC 77-94986. (Humana Civilitas Ser.: Vol. 4). (Illus.). xxi, 297p. 1978. 45.00 (ISBN 0-89003-026-X). Undena Pubns.

Rigg, George, ed. Editing Medieval Texts. LC 76-52722. (Conference on Editorial Problems Ser.: Vol. 12). 1977. lib. bdg. 16.50 (ISBN 0-8240-2426-5). Garland Pub.

Robb, David M. The Art of the Illuminated Manuscript. (Illus.). 356p. 1974. 45.00 (ISBN 0-87982-001-2). Art Alliance.

SAA State & Local Records Committee. Records Retention & Disposition Schedules: A Survey Report. 30p. 1977. pap. 4.00 (ISBN 0-931828-11-2). Soc Am Archivists.

Sanders, Henry A. New Testament Manuscripts in the Freer Collection. Repr. of 1918 ed. 31.00 (ISBN 0-384-38809-4). Johnson Repr.

--Old Testament Manuscripts in the Freer Collection. Repr. of 1917 ed. 31.00 (ISBN 0-384-38808-6). Johnson Repr.

Sandler, Lucy F. The Peterborough Psalter in Brussels & Other Fenland Manuscripts. (Illus.). 1981. 62.50 (ISBN 0-85602-009-5, Pub. by H Miller England). Heyden.

Schellhas, P. Representation of Deities of the Maya Manuscripts. (Illus.). 1904. pap. 4.00 (ISBN 0-527-01198-3). Kraus Repr.

Spalding, Frances. Mudejar Ornament in Manuscripts. 1953. 4.50 (ISBN 0-87535-078-X). Hispanic Soc.

Szewczyk, David M., ed. Peruvian & Other South American Manuscripts in the Rosenbach Foundation: 1536-1914. 1977. 10.00 (ISBN 0-939084-06-6). Rosenbach Mus and Lib.

Taylor, Robert H. & Liebert, Herman W. Authors at Work. (Illus.). 52p. 1957. 10.50x (ISBN 0-8139-0441-2, Grolier Club). U Pr of Va.

Temple, E. Anglo-Saxon Manuscripts 900-1066. Alexander, J. J., ed. (A Survey of Manuscripts Illuminated in the British Isles: Vol. 2). (Illus.). 95.00 (ISBN 0-85602-016-8, Pub. by H Miller England). Heyden.

Turyn, Alexander. Dated Greek Manuscripts of the Thirteenth & Fourteenth Centuries in the Libraries of Great Britian. LC 80-81547. (Dumbarton Oaks Studies: Vol. 17). (Illus.). 198p. 1980. 65.00x (ISBN 0-88402-077-0, Ctr Byzantine). Dumbarton Oaks.

--Dated Greek Manuscripts of the Thirteenth & Fourteenth Centuries in the Libraries of Italy, 2 Vols. LC 79-94402. 1972. 100.00 (ISBN 0-252-00083-8). U of Ill Pr.

Wade, Ira O. Clandestine Organization & Diffusion of Philosophic Ideas in France from 1700 to 1750. 1967. Repr. lib. bdg. 16.50x (ISBN 0-374-98094-2). Octagon.

Walch, Timothy. Archives & Manuscripts: Security. rev. ed. LC 77-15117. (Saa Basic Manual Ser.). 30p. 1977. pap. 5.00 (ISBN 0-931828-13-9). Soc Am Archivists.

Wells, Maria X. The Ranuzzi Manuscripts: An Exhibit. 1980. 9.50 (ISBN 0-87959-094-7). U of Tex Hum Res.

Worrell, William H. The Coptic Manuscripts in the Freer Collection. Repr. of 1923 ed. 31.00 (ISBN 0-384-38810-8). Johnson Repr.

MANUSCRIPTS–BIBLIOGRAPHY

Adler, Elkan N. About Hebrew Manuscripts. LC 78-136769. (Illus.). 1971. Repr. of 1905 ed. 12.50 (ISBN 0-87203-025-3). Hermon.

Akeroyd, Joanne V. & Butterick, George F. Where Are Their Papers? Locating the Papers of Forty-Two Contemporary American Poets & Writers. LC 77-3707. (Bibliography Ser.: No. 9). 1977. pap. 4.00 (ISBN 0-917590-02-3). Univ Conn Lib.

Crum, Margaret, ed. First-Line Index of English Poetry, 1500-1800, in Manuscripts of the Bodleian Library, Oxford, 2 vols. 1257p. Set. 55.00x (ISBN 0-87352-018-1). Modern Lang.

De Ricci, S. & Wilson, W. J. Census of Medievel and Renaissance Manuscripts in the United States and Canada, 2 vols. Incl. Supplement. Bond, W. H. & Faye, C. U. 1962. 35.00 (ISBN 0-685-23298-0). Repr. of 1940 ed. Set. 118.00 (ISBN 0-527-75200-2). Kraus Repr.

Edinburgh University Library. Index to Manuscripts, 2 Vols. 1964. Set. 165.00 (ISBN 0-8161-0706-8). G K Hall.

Evans, Frank B., compiled by. Modern Archives & Manuscripts: A Select Bibliography. LC 75-23058. 209p. 1975. pap. 11.00 (ISBN 0-931828-03-1). Soc Am Archivists.

Hardy, Thomas D. Descriptive Catalogue of Materials Relating to the History of Great Britain & Ireland, to the End of the Reign of Henry 7th, 3 Vols. in 4. 1862-71. Set. 187.00 (ISBN 0-8337-1576-3). B Franklin.

Hermannsson, Halldor. Icelandic Manuscripts. LC 29-14127. (Islandica Ser.: Vol. 19). 1929. pap. 10.00 (ISBN 0-527-00349-2). Kraus Repr.

Jeanroy, Alfred. Bibliographie Sommaire Des Chansonniers Provencaux. 1971. Repr. of 1916 ed. lib. bdg. 18.50 (ISBN 0-8337-1829-0). B Franklin.

Joyce, William L. Manuscript Collection of the American Antiquarian Society. 30p. 1980. pap. 3.00x (ISBN 0-912296-43-7, Dist. by U Pr of Va). Am Antiquarian.

Kane, Lucile M. & Johnson, Kathryn A.compiled by. Manuscripts Collections of the Minnesota Historical Society, Guide No. 2. LC 35-27911. 212p. 1955. pap. 3.75 (ISBN 0-87351-011-9). Minn Hist.

Kristeller, Paul O. Latin Manuscript Books Before 1600. 3rd ed. LC 60-7726. 1965. 35.00 (ISBN 0-8232-0380-8). Fordham.

Little, Andrew G. Initia Operum Latinorum, Quae Saeculis Treizieme Quatorzieme Quinzieme Attribuuntur, Secundum Ordinem Alphabeti Disposita. (Victoria Univ. of Manchester). 1904. 26.50 (ISBN 0-8337-2118-6). B Franklin.

National Union Catalogue of Manuscript Collections, 1962: Index 1959-62, 2 Vols. 1964. Set. 22.50 (ISBN 0-208-00209-X, Archon). Shoe String.

New York Public Library, Research Libraries. Dictionary Catalog & Shelf List of the Spencer Collection of Illustrated Books & Manuscripts & Fine Bindings, 2 vols. 1970. Set. lib. bdg. 170.00 (ISBN 0-8161-0862-5). G K Hall.

--Dictionary Catalog of the Manuscript Division, 2 Vols. 1967. Set. lib. bdg. 120.00 (ISBN 0-8161-0750-5). G K Hall.

Pack, Roger A. The Greek & Latin Literary Texts from Greco-Roman Egypt. LC 65-10786. 1967. 8.50 (ISBN 0-910294-22-4). Brown Bk.

Pillet, Alfred. Bibliographie Des Troubadours: Erganzt Weitergefuhrt und Hrsg. von Henry Carstens. (Research & Source Works Ser: No. 166). 1968. Repr. of 1933 ed. 33.50 (ISBN 0-8337-2771-0). B Franklin.

Plante, Julian G. Checklist of Manuscripts Microfilmed for the Hill Monastic Manuscript Library, Volume II Spain, Pt. 1. LC 78-27115. 1978. pap. 19.75 (ISBN 0-8357-0366-5, IS-00068, Hill Monastic Manuscript Library). Univ Microfilms.

Poleman, Horace I. Census of Indic Manuscripts in the United States & Canada. 1938. pap. 25.00 (ISBN 0-527-02686-7). Kraus Repr.

Raimo, John W., ed. A Guide to Manuscripts Relating to America in Great Britain & Ireland: Crick & Alman. LC 78-12672. 1979. lib. bdg. 99.50x (ISBN 0-930466-06-3). Meckler Bks.

Rand, E. K. & Jones, L. W. Earliest Book of Tours. 1934. 78.00 (ISBN 0-527-01692-6). Kraus Repr.

Revell, Peter. Fifteenth-Century English Prayers & Meditations: A Bibliography of Manuscripts Preserved at the British Museum Library. LC 75-6579. (Reference Library of Humanities: Vol. 19). 150p. 1975. lib. bdg. 21.00 (ISBN 0-8240-1098-1). Garland Pub.

Schmelzer, Menahem H. Bibliographical Studies & Notes Describing Rare Books & Manuscripts in the Library of the Jewish Theological Seminary of America. 1974. 100.00x (ISBN 0-87068-248-2). Ktav.

Swanson, Dorothy T. Guide to the Manuscript Collection of the Tamiment Library. LC 76-52595. (Reference Library of Social Science: Vol. 49). (Illus.). 1977. lib. bdg. 16.00 (ISBN 0-8240-9859-5). Garland Pub.

Thornidike, Lynn & Kibre, Pearl, eds. Catalogue of Incipits of Mediaeval Scientific Writings in Latin. rev. & enl. ed. 1963. 35.00 (ISBN 0-910956-11-1). Medieval Acad.

Washington, Mary. An Annotated Bibliography of Western Manuscripts in the Merrill Library at Utah State University, Logan, Utah. (Western Text Society Ser.: Vol. 1, No. 3). 157p. (Orig.). 1971. pap. 5.00 (ISBN 0-87421-046-1). Utah St U Pr.

Weathers, Shirley A. Bibliographic Guide to the Guatemalan Collection. (Finding Aids to the Microfilmed Manuscript Collection of the Genealogical Society of Utah Ser.: No. 7). 640p. (Orig.). 1981. pap. 35.00x (ISBN 0-87480-198-2). U of Utah Pr.

Zorzanello, Giulio, ed. Catalogo Dei Manoscritti Latini Della Biblioteca Nazionale Marciana Di Venezia, Vol. 1. (Illus.). 579p. (Latin & Ital.). 1981. lib. bdg. 200.00 (ISBN 0-88354-161-0, Pub. by Etimar Italy). Clearwater Pub.

MANUSCRIPTS–CATALOGS

American Jewish Archives, Cincinnati. Manuscript Catalog of the American Jewish Archives, 4 vols. 1971. Set. lib. bdg. 385.00 (ISBN 0-8161-0899-4). G K Hall.

--Manuscript Catalog of the American Jewish Archives, Cincinnati: First Supplement. 1978. lib. bdg. 100.00 (ISBN 0-8161-0934-6). G K Hall.

Andrews, C. M. & Davenport, F. G. Guide to the Manuscript Materials for the History of the United States to 1783. 1908. pap. 28.00 (ISBN 0-527-00685-8). Kraus Repr.

Athos Monasteries. Catalogue of the Greek Manuscripts in the Library of the Laura on Mt. Athos, with Notices from Other Libraries. 1925. pap. 35.00 (ISBN 0-527-01012-X). Kraus Repr.

--Catalogue of the Greek Manuscripts in the Library of the Monastery of Vatopedi on Mt. Athos. 1924. pap. 16.00 (ISBN 0-527-01011-1). Kraus Repr.

Batts, John S. British Manuscript Diaries of the 19th Century: An Annotated Listing. 345p. 1976. 29.50x (ISBN 0-87471-685-3). Rowman.

Bell, Whitfield J., Jr. & Smith, Murphy D. Guide to the Archives & Manuscript Collections of the American Philosophical Society. LC 66-30208. (Memoirs Ser.: Vol. 66). 1966. 4.50 (ISBN 0-87169-066-7). Am Philos.

Brichford, Maynard J., et al. Manuscripts Guide to Collections at the University of Illinois at Urbana-Champaign. LC 75-38797. 1976. 17.50 (ISBN 0-252-00599-6). U of Ill Pr.

The Card Catalog of the Manuscript Collections of the Archives of American Art, 10 vols. LC 80-53039. 5000p. 1980. lib. bdg. 595.00 set (ISBN 0-8420-2174-4). Scholarly Res Inc.

Catalogue of Additions to the Manuscripts in the British Museum (Now the British Library) 1946-1950, 3 vols. 1981. 300.00x (ISBN 0-904654-41-9, Pub. by Brit Lib England). State Mutual Bk.

Catalogue of Royal & Kings Manuscripts in the British Museum, 4 vols. (Illus.). 1212p. 1981. 275.00x set (ISBN 0-686-72039-3, Pub. by Brit Lib England). State Mutual Bk.

Commonwealth Relations Office, Great Britain. Index of Post-Nineteen Thirty Seven European Manuscript Accessions. India Office Library. 1964. 95.00 (ISBN 0-8161-0687-8). G K Hall.

Congress & Executive: A Checklist of American Political Manuscripts, Seventeen Seventy-Four to Nineteen Forty. 1971. 2.00 (ISBN 0-89073-022-9). Boston Public Lib.

Dee, John. Private Diary of Dr. John Dee & the Catalogue of His Library of Manuscripts. Halliwell, James O., ed. (Camden Society, London. Publications, First Ser.: No. 19). Repr. of 1842 ed. 14.00 (ISBN 0-404-50119-2). AMS Pr.

--Private Diary of Dr. John Dee & the Catalogue of His Library of Manuscripts. 1842. 15.50 (ISBN 0-384-11180-7). Johnson Repr.

De Gayangos, Don Pascual. Catalogue of the Manuscripts in the Spanish Language in the British Museum, 4 vols. 2821p. 1981. 275.00x set (ISBN 0-686-72038-5, Pub. by Brit Lib England). State Mutual Bk.

De Navarrete, Martin F. Biblioteca Maritima Espanola, 2 vols. LC 68-58225. (Bibliography & Reference Ser.: No. 244). (Span). 1969. Repr. of 1851 ed. 98.00 (ISBN 0-8337-1115-6). B Franklin.

Dillon, Myles. Catalogue of Irish Manuscripts, Vol. 111. 290p. 1981. 35.00x (ISBN 0-7141-0419-1, Pub. by Brit Lib England). State Mutual Bk.

Djaparidze, David, ed. Mediaeval Slavic Manuscripts: A Bibliography of Printed Catalogues. 1957. 7.50 (ISBN 0-910956-38-3). Medieval Acad.

Duke University Library. Dante Gabriel Rossetti. Baum, Paull F., ed. LC 31-11769. Repr. of 1931 ed. 9.00 (ISBN 0-404-05414-5). AMS Pr.

Edinburgh University Library. First Supplement to Manuscripts, Edinburgh University Library. (Library Catalogs-Supplements). lib. bdg. 190.00 (ISBN 0-8161-0319-4). G K Hall.

Edwards, A. S. & Pearsall, Derek, eds. Middle English Prose: Essays on Bibliographical Problems. LC 80-8595. 150p. 1981. lib. bdg. 25.00 (ISBN 0-8240-9453-0). Garland Pub.

Freeman, John F. & Smith, Murphy D. Guide to Manuscripts Relating to the American Indian in the Library of the American Philosophical Society. LC 65-23435. (Memoirs Ser.: Vol. 65). 1966. 12.00 (ISBN 0-87169-065-9). Am Philos.

Freimann, Aron. Union Catalog of Hebrew Manuscripts & Their Location, 2 vols. LC 66-7594. 1964-1973. Set. 100.00 (ISBN 0-527-02372-8). Kraus Repr.

Gordan, John D. Anniversary Exhibition: The Henry W. & Albert A. Berg Collection 1940-1965. 1965. pap. 3.00 (ISBN 0-87104-003-4). NY Pub Lib.

Guide to American Historical Manuscripts in the Huntington Library. LC 76-9350. 1979. 30.00 (ISBN 0-87328-100-4). Huntington Lib.

Guide to Literary Manuscripts in the Huntington Library. LC 79-84369. 1979. 35.00 (ISBN 0-87328-102-0). Huntington Lib.

Guide to the Catalogues & Indexes of the Department of Manuscripts. 1981. pap. 75.00x (ISBN 0-904654-15-X, Pub. by Brit Lib England). State Mutual Bk.

Haile, Getatchew. A Catalogue of Ethiopian Manuscripts, Vol. IV: Project Numbers 1101-1500. LC 79-365354. (Catalogue of the Ethiopian Manuscript Microfilm Library: No. 4). (Illus.). 776p. 1979. pap. 47.50 (ISBN 0-8357-0457-2, IS-00087, Pub. by Hill Monastic Manuscript Library). Univ Microfilms.

Harper, Josephine L., ed. Guide to the Manuscripts of the State Historical Society of Wisconsin. Incl. Supplement Number One. xii, 222p. 1957. 5.00x (ISBN 0-87020-041-0). LC 45-1974. State Hist Soc Wis.

Harrsen, Meta P., compiled by. Central European Manuscripts in the Pierpont Morgan Library. (Illus.). 1958. boxed 45.00 (ISBN 0-87598-014-7). Pierpont Morgan.

Hirsch, Rudolph, ed. Catalog of Manuscripts & Archives in F. Clark Wood Institute at College of Physicians in Philadelphia. 1981. write for info. U of Pa Pr.

Hughes-Hughes, A. Catalogue of Manuscript Music in the British Museum: Instrumental Music, Treatises Etc, Vol. 3. 568p. 1981. 40.00x (ISBN 0-7141-0427-2, Pub. by Brit Lib England). State Mutual Bk.

--Catalogue of Manuscript Music in the British Museum: Sacred Vocal Music, Vol. 1. 644p. 1981. 40.00x (ISBN 0-7141-0425-6, Pub. by Brit Lib England). State Mutual Bk.

--Catalogue of Manuscript Music in the British Museum: Secular Vocal Music, Vol. 2. 988p. 1981. 45.00x (ISBN 0-7141-0426-4, Pub. by Brit Lib England). State Mutual Bk.

Jackson, Abraham V. & Yohannan, Abraham, eds. Catalogue of the Collection of Persian Manuscripts. LC 14-4238. (Columbia University. Indo-Iranian Ser.: No. 1). Repr. of 1914 ed. 19.50 (ISBN 0-404-50471-X). AMS Pr.

Kamil, Murad. Catalogue of All Manuscripts in the Monastery of St. Catherine on Mount Sinai. LC 72-506949. 222p. 1970. 75.00x (ISBN 3-447-00496-7). Intl Pubns Serv.

Ker, Neil R., ed. Medieval Manuscripts in British Libraries: Abbotsford - Keele, Vol. II. (Illus.). 1977. pap. text ed. 89.00x (ISBN 0-19-818162-0). Oxford U Pr.

Kraft, Walter C. Codices Vindobonenses Hispanici. (Bibliographic Ser: No. 4). 1957. pap. 3.50 (ISBN 0-87071-124-5). Oreg St U Pr.

Loewinger, David S., ed. Catalogue of the Hebrew Manuscripts in the Library of the Juedisch-Theologisches Seminar in Breslan. LC 67-76903. 318p. 1965. 32.00x (ISBN 3-447-00565-3). Intl Pubns Serv.

Louisiana Historical Association, New Orleans. Calendar of the Jefferson Davis Post War Manuscripts in the Louisiana Historical Association Collection. (Bibliography & Reference Ser.: No. 314). 1970. Repr. of 1943 ed. 29.50 (ISBN 0-8337-0781-7). B Franklin.

Mach, Rudolph. Catalogue of Arabic Manuscripts (Yahuda Section) in the Garrett Collection, Princeton University Library. LC 75-2999. (Illus.). 1976. 130.00 (ISBN 0-691-03908-9). Princeton U Pr.

McKinlay, A. P., ed. Arator: The Codices. 1942. 8.00 (ISBN 0-910956-18-9). Medieval Acad.

Macomber, William F. A Catalogue of Ethiopian Manuscripts, Vol. III: Project Numbers 701-1100. LC 76-365354. 1978. pap. 34.50 (ISBN 0-8357-0303-7, IS00048, Hill Monastic Manuscript Library). Univ Microfilm.

Massachusetts Historical Society, Boston. Catalog of Manuscripts of the Massachusetts Historical Society, Boston, 7 Vols. 1969. Set. 700.00 (ISBN 0-8161-0822-6). G K Hall.

Matteson, D. M. List of Manuscripts Concerning American History Preserved in European Libraries. 1925. pap. 14.00 (ISBN 0-527-00690-4). Kraus Repr.

Moll, June, compiled by. Gothic & Renaissance Illuminated Manuscripts from Texas Collections. (Illus.). 1971. pap. 6.00 (ISBN 0-87959-010-6). U of Tex Hum Res.

Morgan Library Curators, compiled by. The Pierpont Morgan Library: A Review of Acquisitions, 1949-1968. (Illus.). 1969. 22.50 (ISBN 0-87598-022-8); pap. 10.00 (ISBN 0-87598-005-8). Pierpont Morgan.

Mukherjee, T. P. Catalogue of the Bengali Manuscripts of the Bridaban Research Institute. 1979. 13.50x (ISBN 0-7286-0053-6). South Asia Bks.

National Library Of Ireland - Dublin. Manuscript Sources for the History of Irish Civilisation, 11 Vols. 1965. Set. lib. bdg. 960.00 (ISBN 0-8161-0662-2). G K Hall.

Parkes, M. B., compiled by. Medieval Manuscripts of Keble College, Oxford: A Descriptive Catalogue with Summary Descriptions of the Greek & Oriental Manuscripts. (Illus.). 365p. 1979. 175.00x (ISBN 0-85967-504-1, Pub. by Scolar Pr England). Biblio Dist.

Pedley, A. J. The Manuscript Collections of the Maryland Historical Society. LC 68-23074. 1968. 15.00 (ISBN 0-938420-08-9). Md Hist.

Pierpont Morgan Library: Review of the Activities & Major Acquisitions, 1941-1948. (Illus.). 1949. pap. 3.00 (ISBN 0-87598-020-1). Pierpont Morgan.

Pigeaud, Theodore G. Literature of Java: Supplement Catalogue Raisonne of Javanese Manuscripts in the Library of the University of Leiden & Other Public Collections in the Netherlands. (Codices Manuscript Ser.: No. XX). (Illus.). 390p. 1980. pap. 64.00 (ISBN 90-6021-453-6, Pub. by Leiden Univ. Holland). Kluwer Boston.

Radcliffe College, the Arthur & Elizabeth Schlesinger Library on the History of Women in America. Manuscripts Inventory & the Catalogs of the Manuscripts, Books & Pictures, 3 vols. 1973. lib. bdg. 235.00 book catalog (ISBN 0-8161-1053-0). G K Hall.

Richardson, Ernest C. A Union World Catalog of Manuscript Books Vol. 3: A List of Printed Catalogs of Manuscript Books. American Library Association Committee on Bibliography, ed. LC 70-132686. v, 386p. 1972. Repr. of 1935 ed. 23.50 (ISBN 0-8337-2991-8). B Franklin.

Rodriguez-Monino, Antonio & Marino, Maria B., eds. Catalogo De los Manuscritos Poeticos Castellanos De The Hispanic Society of America, 3 Vols. (Illus.). 1966. 50.00 (ISBN 0-87535-103-4); lib. bdg. 60.00 (ISBN 0-87535-129-8); pap. 45.00 (ISBN 0-87535-130-1). Hispanic Soc.

Schmitt, Martin. Catalogue of Manuscripts in the University of Oregon Library. LC 72-30080. 1971. pap. text ed. 7.50 (ISBN 0-87114-054-3). U of Oreg Bks.

Sell, Donna & Walle, Dennis. A Guide to the Heinrich A. Rattermann Collection of German-American Manuscripts. LC 79-16018. (Robert B. Downs Publication Fund Ser.: No. 4). 215p. 1979. 15.00 (ISBN 0-87845-052-1). U of Ill Lib Info Sci.

Simsar, Muhammed A. Oriental Manuscripts of the John Frederick Lewis Collection: A Descriptive Catalogue. (Illus.). 1937. 15.00 (ISBN 0-911132-03-1). Phila Free Lib.

Sinclair, K. Descriptive Catalogue of Medieval & Renaissance Western Manuscripts in Australia. 1969. 37.50x (ISBN 0-424-05760-3, Pub by Sydney U Pr). Intl Schol Bk Serv.

Sinclair, Keith V., compiled by. French Devotional Texts of the Middle Ages: A Bibliographic Manuscript Guide. LC 79-7587. 1979. lib. bdg. 35.00 (ISBN 0-313-20649-X, SFT/). Greenwood.

Smith College, Women's History Archive, Northampton, Massachusetts. The Manuscript, Subject & Author Catalogs of the Sophia Smith Collection (Women's History Archive), Smith College, 7 vols. 1975. Set. lib. bdg. 535.00 (ISBN 0-8161-0001-2). G K Hall.

Smith, H. Daniel. The Smith Agama Collection: Sanskrit Books & Manuscripts Relating to Pancaratra Studies- a Descriptive Catalog. LC 78-9149. (Foreign & Comparative Studies-South Asian Special Publications Ser.: No. 2). 1978. pap. text ed. 6.50x (ISBN 0-915984-79-2). Syracuse U Foreign Comp.

Strelcyn, S. Catalogue of Ethiopian Manuscripts in the British Library Acquired Since the Year 1877. 232p. 1981. 125.00 (ISBN 0-7141-0649-6, Pub. by Brit Lib England). State Mutual Bk.

Thompson, David. A Descriptive Catalogue of Middle English Grammatical Texts. LC 78-68277. (Library of Humanities Ser.). 1979. lib. bdg. 35.00 (ISBN 0-8240-9765-3). Garland Pub.

Tilley, Nannie M. & Goodwin, Norma L. Guide to the Manuscript Collections in the Duke University Library. (Duke University. Trinity College Historical Society, Historical Papers: Nos. 27-28). 1947. 17.50 (ISBN 0-404-51777-3). AMS Pr.

U. S. Library Of Congress - Processing Department. British Manuscripts Project: A Checklist of the Microfilm Prepared in England & Wales for the American Council of Learned Societies 1941-1945. LC 68-55138. (Illus.). 1968. Repr. of 1955 ed. lib. bdg. 18.75x (ISBN 0-8371-0713-X, BRMP). Greenwood.

University of Illinois at Urbana-Champaign - Library. Mereness Calendar: Federal Documents on the Upper Mississippi Valley, 1780-1890, 13 vols. 1971. Set. 1470.00 (ISBN 0-8161-0915-X). G K Hall.

Walpole, Horace. Catalogue of the Classic Contents of Strawberry Hill: Sold by Auction of 25, April 1842. LC 70-149673. Repr. of 1842 ed. lib. bdg. 47.50 (ISBN 0-404-52336-6). AMS Pr.

Watson, Andrew G. Catalogue of Dated & Datable Manuscripts c. 700-1600 in the Department of Manuscripts, the British Library, 2 vols. 666p. 1981. 300.00 (ISBN 0-7141-0487-6, Pub. by Brit Lib England). State Mutual Bk.

Whipkey, Harry E. Guide to the Manuscript Groups in the Pennsylvania State Archives. 1976. 7.00 (ISBN 0-911124-84-5). Pa Hist & Mus.

Wolf, Edwin, 2nd, ed. Descriptive Catalogue of the John Frederick Lewis Collection of European Manuscripts. (Illus.). 1937. 15.00 (ISBN 0-911132-04-X). Phila Free Lib.

MANUSCRIPTS–CERTIFICATION

Malone, Edmond. Inquiry into the Authenticity of Certain Miscellaneous Papers & Legal Instruments Published 1795 & Attributed to Shakespeare, Queen Elizabeth & Henry, Earl of Southampton. 440p. 1970. Repr. of 1796 ed. 32.50x (ISBN 0-7146-2514-0, F Cass Co). Biblio Dist.

MANUSCRIPTS–CONSERVATION AND RESTORATION

see also Books–Conservation and Restoration; Engravings–Conservation and Restoration

Barrow, W. J. Manuscripts & Documents: Their Deterioration & Restoration. rev. ed. LC 72-89855. (Illus.). 86p. 1972. 8.95x (ISBN 0-8139-0408-0). U Pr of Va.

Fraser, James H. Children's Authors & Illustrators: A Guide to Manuscript Collections in United States Research Libraries. 130p. 1980. 14.80 (ISBN 3-598-40504-9, Pub. by K G Saur). Shoe String.

Guide to the Department of Oriental Manuscripts & Printed Books. 1981. pap. 6.00x (ISBN 0-7141-0658-5, Pub. by Brit Lib England). State Mutual Bk.

Haenel, G. F. Dictionnaire des Manuscrits, Ou Recueil De Catalogues De Manuscrits Existants Dans les Pri Cipales Bibliotheques D'europe, 2 vols. Migne, J. P., ed. (Nouvelle Encyclopedie Theologique Ser.: Vols. 40-41). 1624p. (Fr.). Date not set. Repr. of 1853 ed. lib. bdg. 205.50x (ISBN 0-89241-280-1). Caratzas Bros.

Kane, Lucile M. Guide to the Care & Administration of Manuscripts. 2nd ed. (Illus.). 1966. pap. 3.50 (ISBN 0-910050-02-3). AASLH.

MANUSCRIPTS–EXHIBITIONS

see also Bibliographical Exhibitions

Agrawal, O. P. Paintings & MS of Southeast Asia. 1982. text ed. write for info. (ISBN 0-408-10671-9). Butterworth.

MANUSCRIPTS–FACSIMILES

see also Diplomatics; Paleography

Anglo, Sydney, ed. Great Tournament Roll of Westminster. 1968. boxed 96.00x (ISBN 0-19-821340-9). Oxford U Pr.

Bannatyne Manuscript: National Library of Scotland Advocates' Ms 1.1.6. facsim. ed. 856p. 1980. Repr. of 1568 ed. 340.00x (ISBN 0-85967-540-8, Pub. by Scolar Pr England). Biblio Dist.

Browne, Edward G. Literary History of Persia, 4 Vols. 1928. 62.00 ea. Vol. 1 (ISBN 0-521-04344-1). Vol. 2 (ISBN 0-521-04345-X). Vol. 3 (ISBN 0-521-04346-8). Vol. 4. Cambridge U Pr.

Chansonnier D'Arras, Reproduction En Phototypie. 1925. 28.00 (ISBN 0-384-08465-6); pap. 23.00 (ISBN 0-384-08475-3). Johnson Repr.

Coryate, Thomas. Coryats Crudities Sixteen Eleven. facsim. ed. (Illus.). 1978. Repr. of 1611 ed. 110.00x (ISBN 0-85967-478-9, Pub. by Scolar Pr England). Biblio Dist.

Goodspeed, Edgar J., et al, eds. Rockefeller McCormick New Testament, 3 Vols. LC 32-30657. (Illus.). 1932. Set. 100.00x (ISBN 0-226-30379-9). U of Chicago Pr.

Hatch, William H. Greek & Syrian Miniatures in Jerusalem. (Illus.). 1931. 15.00 (ISBN 0-910956-04-9). Medieval Acad.

Jenkinson, Hilary. Later Court Hands in England from the Fifteenth to the Seventeenth Century. LC 68-8117. (Illus.). 1968. 95.00 (ISBN 0-8044-5523-6). Ungar.

Johnson, Charles & Jenkinson, Hilary. English Court Hand, AD 1066 to 1500, 2 pts. LC 66-28836. (Illus.). 95.00 (ISBN 0-8044-5532-5). Ungar.

Jones, L. W. Script of Cologne, from Hildebald to Hermann. 1932. 85.00 (ISBN 0-527-01684-5). Kraus Repr.

Kubler, George & Gibson, Charles. Tovar Calendar: An Illustrated Mexican Manuscript Circa 1585. (Connecticut Academy of Arts & Sciences Memoirs: Vol. 11). 1951. pap. 12.50 (ISBN 0-208-00617-6). Shoe String.

Lowe, E. A., ed. Codices Latini Antiquiores, Pt. 2: Great Britain - Ireland. 2nd ed. (Illus.). 74p. 1972. 58.00x (ISBN 0-19-818222-8). Oxford U Pr.

Norton-Smith, John, intro. by. Bodleian Library Ms Fairfax 16. facsim. ed. (Illus.). 680p. 1979. Repr. 190.00x (ISBN 0-85967-513-0, Pub. by Scolar Pr England). Biblio Dist.

O'Curry, Eugene. Lectures in the Manuscript Materials of Ancient Irish History, 2 vols in 1. Repr. of 1861 ed. 46.50 (ISBN 0-685-06758-0). B Franklin.

Paltsits, Victor H., ed. Washington's Farewell Address. LC 74-137706. (New York Public Library Publications in Reprint Ser). (Illus.). 1971. Repr. of 1935 ed. 35.00 (ISBN 0-405-01742-1). Arno.

Physiologus. Icelandic Physiologus. facsimile ed. Hermannsson, Halldor, ed. (Islandica Ser.: Vol. 27). 1938. pap. 9.00 (ISBN 0-527-00357-3). Kraus Repr.

Pickford, C. E., intro. by. L' Hystoire du Sainct Greaal. facsim. ed. (Fr.). 1978. Repr. 80.00x (ISBN 0-85967-477-0, Pub. by Scolar Pr England). Biblio Dist.

Plimpton, George A. Education of Chaucer. LC 74-160453. Repr. of 1935 ed. 17.50 (ISBN 0-404-05064-6). AMS Pr.

Rand, E. K. & Jones, L. W. Earliest Book of Tours. 1934. 78.00 (ISBN 0-527-01692-6). Kraus Repr.

Return from Parnassus, Pt 2. LC 72-133728. (Tudor Facsimile Texts. Old English Plays: No. 111). Repr. of 1912 ed. 31.50 (ISBN 0-404-53411-2). AMS Pr.

Stevens, B. F. Index to Facsimiles of Manuscripts in European Archives Relating to America 1773-1783. LC 74-114216. 1970. Repr. of 1898 ed. 40.00 (ISBN 0-404-07208-9). AMS Pr.

Thomas a Becket. Fragments D'une Vie De Saint Thomas De Cantorbery En Vers Accouples. Repr. of 1885 ed. 20.00 (ISBN 0-384-60189-8); pap. 15.50 (ISBN 0-384-60179-0). Johnson Repr.

Verey, Christopher D., et al, eds. Early English Manuscripts in Facsimile: The Durham Gospels, Vol. 20. 1981. 1040.00 (ISBN 0-8018-2315-3); pap. 975.00 (ISBN 0-8018-2316-1). Johns Hopkins.

Wilson, John D. Manuscript of Shakespeare's Hamlet, 2 Vols. 1934. Set. 60.00 (ISBN 0-521-06833-9). Cambridge U Pr.

MANUSCRIPTS–PRICES

see also Books–Prices

Brichford, Maynard J. Archives & Manuscripts: Appraisal & Accessioning. rev. ed. LC 77-14523. (Saa Basic Manual Ser.). 24p. 1977. pap. 5.00 (ISBN 0-931828-01-5). Soc Am Archivists.

Kirchhoff, Albrecht. Handschriftenhandler Des Mittelalters. 2nd ed. 1853. 22.50 (ISBN 0-8337-1929-7). B Franklin.

MANUSCRIPTS–REPRODUCTION

see also Photocopying Processes

MANUSCRIPTS–RESTORATION

see Manuscripts–Conservation and Restoration

MANUSCRIPTS (PAPYRI)

see also Egyptian Language–Papyri

Abbott, Nabia. Quaranic Commentary & Tradition: Studies in Arabic Literary Papyri, Vol. 2. LC 56-5027. (Oriental Inst. Pubns. Ser: No. 76). 1967. 35.00x (ISBN 0-226-62177-4, OIP76). U of Chicago Pr.
--Studies in Arabic Literary Papyri: Language & Literature, Vol. 3. LC 56-5027. (Oriental Institute Pubns. Ser: No. 77). (Illus.). xvi, 216p. 1974. lib. bdg. 40.00x (ISBN 0-226-62178-2). U of Chicago Pr.
Aland, Kurt, ed. Repertorium der Griechischen Christlichen Papyri, Pt.1: Biblische Papyri, Altes Testament, Neues Testament, Varia, Apokryphen. (Patristische Texte und Studien, Vol. 18). 473p. 1976. 93.00x (ISBN 3-11-004674-1). De Gruyter.
Austin, Colinus, ed. Comicorum Graecorum Fragmenta in papyris reperta (1838-1971) 1973. 197.00x (ISBN 3-11-004046-8). De Gruyter.
Bagnall, Roger & Lewis, Naphtali. Columbia Papyri Seven: Fourth Century Documents from Karanis. LC 78-31952. 1980. 45.00 (ISBN 0-89130-277-8, 31 00 20). Scholars Pr CA.
Bagnall, Roger S. & Worp, K. A. Regnal Formulas in Byzantine Egypt. LC 79-1316. (Supplements to the Bulletin of American Society of Papyrologists). 1979. pap. 9.00 (ISBN 0-89130-280-8, 311102). Scholars Pr Ca.
Bell, H. Idris & Skeat, T. C., eds. Fragments of an Unknown Gospel & Other Early Christian Papyri. 76p. 1981. 25.00x (ISBN 0-7141-0438-8, Pub. by Brit Lib England). State Mutual Bk.
Casson, L. & Hettich, E. L. The Literary Papyri. (Excavations at Nessana: Vol. 2). 1950. 22.00 (ISBN 0-691-03515-6). Princeton U Pr.
Davis, W. Hersey. Greek Papyri of the First Century. 84p. 1980. 6.00 (ISBN 0-89005-332-4). Ares.
Exler, F. J. The Form of the Ancient Greek Letter of the Epistolary Papyri. 1976. 10.00 (ISBN 0-89005-120-8). Ares.
Griffith, F. L. & Thompson, Herbert, eds. The Leyden Papyrus: An Egyptian Magical Book. LC 73-90639. 224p. 1974. pap. 2.75 (ISBN 0-486-22994-7). Dover.
Kapsomenakis, S. G. Voruntersuchungen Zu Einer Grammatik der Papyri der Nachchristlichen Zeit. 148p. 1980. 12.50 (ISBN 0-89005-294-8). Ares.
Laum, Bernhard. Das Alexandrinische Akzentuationssystem Unter Zugrundelegung der Theoretischen Lehren der Grammatik. Repr. of 1928 ed. pap. 34.00 (ISBN 0-384-31620-4). Johnson Repr.
McCarren, Vincent P. Michigan Papyri XIV. (American Studies in Papyrology: No. 22). 15.00x (ISBN 0-89130-295-6). Scholars Pr CA.
Meyer, Paul M. Juristische Papyri. 1980. 35.00 (ISBN 0-686-52196-X). Ares.
Milligan, George. Selections from Greek Papyri. 152p. 1980. 15.00 (ISBN 0-89005-335-9). Ares.
Oates, John F., et al. Checklist of Editions of Greek Papyri & Ostraca. LC 78-26003. (Bulletin of the American Society of Papyrologists Supplements: No. 1). 1978. pap. 6.00 (ISBN 0-89130-272-7, 311101). Scholars Pr Ca.
Reymond, E. A. Catalogue of Demotic Papyri in the Ashmolean Museum. (Embalmers' Archives from Hawara: Vol. 1). (Illus.). 170p. 1973. text ed. 78.00x (ISBN 0-686-72796-7, Pub. by Aris & Phillips England). Humanities.
Schuman, Verne B. Washington University Papyri I: Non-Literary Texts, Nos. 1-16. LC 79-14199. (American Society of Papyrologists Ser.: No. 17). 15.00 (ISBN 0-89130-286-7). Scholars Pr CA.
Skeat, T. C., ed. Greek Papyri in the British Museum (Now in the British Library) 356p. 1981. 125.00x (ISBN 0-7141-0486-8, Pub. by Brit Lib England). State Mutual Bk.
Tait, W. J. Papyri from Tebtunis in Egyptian & in Greek. (Texts from Excavations Ser.: Memoir 3). (Illus.). 1978. 53.00x (ISBN 0-85698-062-5, Pub. by Aris & Phillips). Intl Schol Bk Serv.
Turner, E. G. Greek Papyri: An Introduction. (Illus.). 242p. (Orig.). 1981. pap. text ed. 22.50 (ISBN 0-19-814841-0). Oxford U Pr.
White, John L. The Form & Structure of the Official Petition: A Study in Greek Epistolography. LC 72-87889. (Society of Biblical Literature. Dissertations Ser.: No. 5). (Illus.). 1972. pap. 9.00 (ISBN 0-89130-161-5, 060105). Scholars Pr Ca.
Winlock, Herbert E., et al. The Monastery of Epiphanius at Thebes: Metropolitan Museum of Art Egyptain Expedition Publications, Vols. 3 & 4, 2 vols. LC 72-168413. (The Metropolitan Museum of Art Publication in Reprint Ser.). 1926. 80.00 set (ISBN 0-405-02249-2). Arno.

MANUSCRIPTS, ILLUMINATED
see Illumination of Books and Manuscripts

MANUSCRIPTS ON MICROFILM-CATALOGS

U. S. Library Of Congress - Processing Department. British Manuscripts Project: A Checklist of the Microfilm Prepared in England & Wales for the American Council of Learned Societies 1941-1945. LC 68-55138. (Illus.). 1968. Repr. of 1955 ed. lib. bdg. 18.75x (ISBN 0-8371-0713-X, BRMP). Greenwood.

MANX FOLK-LORE
see Folk-Lore, Manx

MANX LANGUAGE

Fargher, Douglas C. Fargher's English Manx Dictionary. 1979. text ed. 6.75x (ISBN 0-904980-23-5). Humanities.
Gell, John. Conversational Manx. pap. 2.95 (ISBN 0-686-10838-8). British Am Bks.
Goodwin, E. First Lessons in Manx. pap. 3.95 (ISBN 0-686-10842-6). British Am Bks.
Kneen, J. J. Manx Idioms & Phrases. pap. 3.95 (ISBN 0-686-10854-X). British Am Bks.
Kneen, John J. A Grammar of the Manx Language. LC 78-72639. (Celtic Language & Literature: Goidelic & Brythonic). Repr. of 1931 ed. 21.50 (ISBN 0-404-17564-3). AMS Pr.
Manx Gaelic Society. Manx, a Course in the Spoken Language. pap. 4.95 (ISBN 0-686-10850-7). British Am Bks.

MANX TALES
see Tales, Manx

MANY-BODY PROBLEM
see Problem of Many Bodies

MANZONI, ALESSANDRO, 1785-1873

Barricelli, Gian P. Alessandro Manzoni. LC 76-16481. (World Authors Ser., Italy: No. 411). 1976. lib. bdg. 11.95 (ISBN 0-8057-6251-5). Twayne.
Chandler, S. B. Manzoni. 1974. 10.00x (ISBN 0-85224-247-6, Pub. by Edinburgh U Pr Scotland). Columbia U Pr.
Colquhoun, Archibald. Manzoni & His Times: A Biography of the Author of The Betrothed (I Promessi Sposi) LC 78-59013. (Illus.). 1979. Repr. of 1954 ed. 25.00 (ISBN 0-88355-688-X). Hyperion Conn.
Wall, Bernard. Alessandro Manzoni. 1954. 24.50 (ISBN 0-686-51343-6). Elliots Bks.

MAO TSE-TUNG, 1893-1976

Altaiski, M. & Gueorguiev, V. Critica De las Cocepciones Filosoficas De Mao Tse-Tung. 239p. (Span.). 1976. pap. 2.70 (ISBN 0-8285-1415-1, Pub. by Progress Pubs Russia). Imported Pubns.
Avakian, Bob. The Loss in China & the Revolutionary Legacy of Mao Tsetung. (Illus.). 1978. pap. 2.00 (ISBN 0-89851-017-1). RCP Pubns.
--Mao Tsetung's Immortal Contributions. 1978. 12.95 (ISBN 0-89851-020-1); pap. 4.95 (ISBN 0-89851-021-X). RCP Pubns.
Bandyopadhyaya, J. Mao Tse-Tung & Gandhi. 1973. 6.00x (ISBN 0-8188-1184-6). Paragon.
Bandyopadhyaya, Jayantanuja. Mao Tse-Tung & Gandhi: Perspectives on Social Transformation. 156p. 1973. 6.50x (ISBN 0-8002-1698-9). Intl Pubns Serv.
Barnett, A. Doak. China After Mao: With Selected Documents. 1967. 18.00 (ISBN 0-691-03008-1); pap. 6.95 (ISBN 0-691-00000-X). Princeton U Pr.
Bloodworth, Dennis & Ching Ping. Heirs Apparent: What Happens When Mao Dies? 272p. 1973. 7.95 (ISBN 0-374-16898-9). FS&G.
Boorman, Scott A. Protracted Game: A Wei-Ch'i Interpretation of Maoist Revolutionary Strategy. (Illus.). 1971. pap. 4.95 (ISBN 0-19-501493-6, GB). Oxford U Pr.
Bouc, Alain. Mao Tse-Tung: A Guide to His Thought. Auster, Paul & Davis, Lydia, trs. LC 76-62749. 1977. 10.00 (ISBN 0-312-51397-6). St Martin.
Burlatsky, F. Mao-Tse-Tung: An Ideological & Psychological Portrait. 396p. 1980. 8.00 (ISBN 0-8285-1712-6, Pub. by Progress Pubs Russia). Imported Pubns.
Carter, Peter. Mao. LC 78-26294. (gr. 7 up). 1979. 9.95 (ISBN 0-670-45425-7). Viking Pr.
Chairman Mao's Theory of the Differentiation of the Three Worlds. 1977. 0.95 (ISBN 0-8351-0469-9). China Bks.
Ch'En, Jerome. Mao & the Chinese Revolution. (Illus.). 1967. pap. 6.95 (ISBN 0-19-500270-9, GB). Oxford U Pr.
Chou, Eric. Mao Tse-Tung: The Man & the Myth. LC 80-22758. 304p. 1981. 16.95 (ISBN 0-8128-2769-4). Stein & Day.
Chu, Don-Chean. Chairman Mao: Education of the Proletariat. 1980. 19.95 (ISBN 0-8022-2236-6). Philos Lib.
Cohen, Arthur A. Communism of Mao Tse-Tung. LC 64-23420. 1964. 11.00x (ISBN 0-226-11281-0). U of Chicago Pr.
--Communism of Mao Tse-Tung. LC 64-23420. 1964. pap. 2.95 (ISBN 0-226-11282-9, P207, Phoen). U of Chicago Pr.
DeFrancis, John. Annotated Quotations from Chairman Mao. LC 74-20080. (Linguistic Ser). 336p. 1975. text ed. 25.00x (ISBN 0-300-01749-9); pap. text ed. 8.95x (ISBN 0-300-01870-3). Yale U Pr.
Dures, Alan & Dures, Katherine. Mao Tse-Tung. (Leaders Ser.). (Illus.). 96p. (gr. 9-12). 1980. 14.95 (ISBN 0-7134-1923-7, Pub. by Batsford England). David & Charles.
Edmonds, I. G. China's Red Rebel: The Story of Mao Tse-Tung. (Illus.). 176p. (gr. 7 up). 1973. 6.50 (ISBN 0-8255-3017-2). Macrae.
--Mao's Long March. LC 72-12337. (Illus.). 128p. (gr. 7 up). 1973. 6.50 (ISBN 0-8255-3004-0). Macrae.
Evans, Leslie, ed. China After Mao. LC 78-59264. (Illus.). 1978. lib. bdg. 16.00 (ISBN 0-913460-61-3); pap. 3.95 (ISBN 0-913460-64-8). Monad Pr.
Fitzgerald, C. P. Mao Tse-Tung & China. 1977. pap. 2.50 (ISBN 0-14-021947-1). Penguin.
Fitzgerald, Charles P. Mao Tse-Tung & China. LC 76-3700. (Illus.). 175p. 1976. text ed. 16.00x (ISBN 0-8419-0268-2). Holmes & Meier.
Gurley, John G. Challengers to Capitalism. LC 75-29749. (Portable Stanford Ser.). (Illus.). 1976. 8.95 (ISBN 0-913374-34-2); pap. 4.95 (ISBN 0-913374-35-0). SF Bk Co.
--Challengers to Capitalism, Marx, Lenin, Stalin & Mao. (Illus.). 224p. 1980. 12.95 (ISBN 0-393-01224-7); Portable Stanford Ser. pap. 4.95x (ISBN 0-393-95005-0). Norton.
Hammond, Ed. To Embrace the Moon: An Illustrated Biography of Mao Zedong. 196p. 1980. 14.95 (ISBN 0-89581-455-2); pap. 8.95 (ISBN 0-89581-502-8). Lancaster-Miller.
Han Suyin. Wind in the Tower: Mao Tse-Tung & the Chinese Revolution, 1949-1975. 1976. 14.95 (ISBN 0-316-34288-2). Little.
Harris, Nigel. The Mandate of Heaven: Marx & Mao in Modern China. 12.50 (ISBN 0-7043-2191-2, Pub. by Quartet England). Charles River Bks.
Hawkins, John N. Mao Tse Tung & Education: His Thoughts & Teachings. (Illus.). 1974. 17.50 (ISBN 0-208-01222-2, Linnet). Shoe String.
Howard, Roger. Mao Tse-tung & the China People. LC 77-70969. 1977. 16.50 (ISBN 0-85345-413-2, CL4132). Monthly Rev.
Karnow, Stanley. Mao & China: From Revolution to Revolution. LC 77-187967. 512p. 1972. 15.00 (ISBN 0-670-45427-3). Viking Pr.
Kerry, Tom. The Mao Myth: The Legacy of Stalinism in China. LC 77-81290. 1977. 14.00 (ISBN 0-87348-521-1); pap. 3.95 (ISBN 0-87348-461-4). Path Pr NY.
Konstantinov, F. & Sladkovski, M. Critica De los Concepciones Teoricas De Mao Tse-Tung. 303p. (Span.). 1973. 4.00 (ISBN 0-8285-1416-X, Pub. by Progress Pubs Russia). Imported Pubns.
Konstantinov, N. Maoism & Mao's Heirs. 187p. 1979. pap. 3.00 (ISBN 0-8285-1504-2, Pub. by Progress Pubs Russia). Imported Pubns.
Kuo-Sin, Chang. Mao Tse-Tung & His China. LC 79-112635. (Orig.). 1978. pap. text ed. 10.95x (ISBN 0-686-71778-3, 00125). Heinemann Ed.
Kurland, Gerald. Mao Tse-Tung: Founder of Communist China. Rahmas, D. Steve, ed. LC 75-190232. (Outstanding Personalities Ser: No. 14). 32p. (Orig.). (gr. 7-9). 1972. lib. bdg. 2.95 incl. catalog cards (ISBN 0-87157-514-0); pap. 1.50 vinyl laminated covers (ISBN 0-87157-014-9). SamHar Pr.
Li, Jui. The Early Revolutionary Activities of Comrade Mao Tse-Tung. Hsiung, James C., ed. Sariti, Anthony W., tr. from Chinese. LC 74-24422. (The China Book Project Ser.). 1977. 27.50 (ISBN 0-87332-070-0). M E Sharpe.
Lifton, Robert J. Revolutionary Immortality: Mao-Tse-Tung & the Chinese Cultural Revolution. new ed. 176p. 1976. pap. 2.95 (ISBN 0-393-00797-9, Norton Lib). Norton.
--Revolutionary Immortality: Mao Tse-Tung & the Chinese Revolution. 5.25 (ISBN 0-8446-4437-4). Peter Smith.
Lindquist, Harry M. & Meyer, Roger D., eds. Concordance of Proper Nouns in the Five Volume English Language, Selected Works of Mao Tse-Tung. LC 68-66895. (International Studies, East Asian Ser No. 2). (Orig.). 1968. pap. 3.00x (ISBN 0-685-19291-1). Paragon.
Lotta, Raymond. And Mao Makes Five: Mao Tsetung's Last Great Battle. LC 78-70431. (Illus.). 1978. 15.00 (ISBN 0-916650-09-X); pap. 5.95 (ISBN 0-916650-08-1). Banner Pr IL.
Mao. Carter, Peter. 1980. pap. 2.25 (ISBN 0-451-61845-9, ME 1845, Ment). NAL.
Mao Tse Tung on Literature & Art. 1967. 2.95 (ISBN 0-8351-0456-7). China Bks.
Mao Tse-Tung. Mao Tse-Tung on Revolution & War. Rejai, M., ed. 10.00 (ISBN 0-8446-5275-X). Peter Smith.
--Selected Works of Mao Tse-Tung, 5 vols. LC 77-30658. 1977. Set. text ed. 60.00 (ISBN 0-08-022262-5); text ed. 15.00 (ISBN 0-686-68045-6); Vol. I. text ed. 15.00 (ISBN 0-08-022980-8); Vol. II. text ed. 15.00 (ISBN 0-08-022981-6); Vol. III. text ed. 15.00 (ISBN 0-08-022982-4); Vol. IV. text ed. 15.00 (ISBN 0-08-022983-2). Vol. V (ISBN 0-08-022984-0). Pergamon.
Michael, Franz. Mao Tse-Tung & the Perpetual Revolution. Cadenhead, I. E., Jr., ed. LC 77-24400. 1977. pap. text ed. 10.95 (ISBN 0-8120-5132-7). Barron.
Ming, W. Mao's Betrayal. 278p. 1979. 7.20 (ISBN 0-8285-0404-0, Pub. by Progress Pubs Russia). Imported Pubns.
--Medio Siglo Del Partido Comunista De China y la Traicion De Mao Tse-Tung. 329p. 1979. 6.15 (ISBN 0-8285-1678-2, 001210, Pub. by Progress Pubs Russia). Imported Pubns.
Mohanty, Manoranjan. The Political Philosophy of Mao Tse-Tung. 1978. 14.00x (ISBN 0-8364-0266-9). South Asia Bks.
O'Malley, Martin J. The Tao of Mao Tse-Tung. 1977. pap. 1.00 (ISBN 0-9606610-1-8). M J O'Malley.
Painter, Desmond. Mao Tse-Tung. Yapp, Malcolm & Killingray, Margaret, eds. (World History Ser.). (Illus.). (gr. 10). 1980. lib. bdg. 5.95 (ISBN 0-89908-127-4); pap. write for info. (ISBN 0-89908-102-9). Greenhaven.
Paloczi-Horvath, Gyorgy. Mao Tse-Tung, Emperor of the Blue Ants. LC 73-434. 393p. 1973. Repr. of 1963 ed. lib. bdg. 19.25x (ISBN 0-8371-6775-2, PAMT). Greenwood.
Philosophy Is No Mystery: The Application of Mao Tse-Tung Thought in Solving Problems on the Communes. 1972. pap. 0.75 (ISBN 0-8351-0254-8). China Bks.
Purcell, Hugh. Mao Tse-Tung. LC 77-304. (History Makers Ser). (Illus.). 1977. 6.95 (ISBN 0-312-51399-2). St Martin.
Pye, Lucian W. Mao Tse-Tung: The Man in the Leader. LC 75-7272. (Illus.). 1976. 15.00x (ISBN 0-465-04396-8). Basic.
Rice, Edward E. Mao's Way. LC 70-186116. (Center for Chinese Studies, Uc Berkeley). 600p. 1972. 31.50x (ISBN 0-520-02199-1); pap. 4.95 (ISBN 0-520-02623-3). U of Cal Pr.
Rius. Mao for Beginners. (Illus.). 1980. 8.95 (ISBN 0-394-50589-1); pap. 2.95 (ISBN 0-394-73886-1). Pantheon.
Rue, John E. Mao Tse-tung in Opposition, 1927-1935. 1966. 20.00x (ISBN 0-8047-0222-5). Stanford U Pr.
Schram, Stuart, ed. Chairman Mao Talks to the People: Talks & Letters 1956-1971. LC 73-18731. 1975. pap. 4.95 (ISBN 0-394-70641-2). Pantheon.
Schram, Stuart R. Mao Tse-Tung. 1967. 9.95 (ISBN 0-671-44874-9). S&S.
Schwartz, Benjamin I. Chinese Communism & the Rise of Mao. LC 51-12067. (Russian Research Center Studies: No. 4). 1951. 14.00x (ISBN 0-674-12251-8); pap. 4.95 (ISBN 0-674-12260-7). Harvard U Pr.
Shih, Bernadette. Mao: A Young Man from the Yangtze Valley. Young, Billie, ed. LC 74-76433. 1974. 12.95 (ISBN 0-87949-026-8). Ashley Bks.
Siao-Yu. Mao Tse-Tung & I Were Beggars. LC 59-15411. (Illus.). 1959. deluxe ed. 12.95 (ISBN 0-8156-0015-1). Syracuse U Pr.
Starr, John B. Continuing the Revolution: The Political Thought of Mao. LC 78-63597. 1979. 25.00x (ISBN 0-691-07596-4); pap. 6.95 (ISBN 0-691-02189-9). Princeton U Pr.
Starr, John B. & Dyer, Nancy A. Post-Liberation Works of Mao Zedong: A Bibliography & Index. new ed. LC 67-65707. (China Research Monographs: Special). 1976. pap. 7.50 (ISBN 0-912966-16-5). IEAS Ctr Chinese Stud.
Suyin, Han. The Morning Deluge: Mao Tsetung & the Chinese Revolution, 1893-1954. 1972. 12.50 (ISBN 0-316-34289-0). Little.
Tarling, Nicholas. Mao & the Transformation of China 1921-49. 1977. pap. text ed. 4.50x (ISBN 0-435-31780-6). Heinemann Ed.
Terrill, Rose. Mao: A Biography. LC 79-1687. 1980. 17.50 (ISBN 0-06-014243-X, HarpT). Har-Row.
Terrill, Ross. Mao: A Biography. LC 79-1687. 481p. 1980. pap. 6.95 (ISBN 0-06-090859-9, CN859, CN). Har-Row.
Tsetung, Mao. A Critique of Soviet Economics. Roberts, Moss, tr. LC 77-70971. 1978. pap. 4.50 (ISBN 0-85345-459-0, PB4590). Monthly Rev.
Vladimirov, O. Mao-Tse-Tung: A Brief Political Biography. 96p. 1976. pap. 1.80 (ISBN 0-8285-0484-9, Pub. by Progress Pubs Russia). Imported Pubns.
Wakeman, Frederic. History & Will: Philosophical Perspectives of Mao Tse-Tung's Thought. 408p. 1976. pap. 8.95x (ISBN 0-520-02907-0). U of Cal Pr.

Waller, Derek J. Kiangsi Soviet Republic: Mao and the National Congresses of 1931 and 1934. (China Research Monographs: No. 10). 1973. pap. 5.00 (ISBN 0-912966-11-4). IEAS Ctr Chinese Stud.
Whitehead, Raymond. Love & Struggle in Mao's Thought. LC 76-41902. 1977. 8.95x (ISBN 0-88344-289-2); pap. 4.95x (ISBN 0-88344-290-6). Orbis Bks.
Wilson, D., ed. Mao Tse-Tung in the Scales of History. LC 76-57100. (Contemporary China Institute Publications Ser.). 1977. 36.50 (ISBN 0-521-21583-8); pap. 8.95 (ISBN 0-521-29190-9). Cambridge U Pr.
Wilson, Dick. The People's Emperor: A Biography of Mao-Tse-Tung. LC 77-15176. (Illus.). 552p. 1980. 17.50 (ISBN 0-385-11645-4). Doubleday.
Wylie, Raymond F. The Emergence of Maoism: Mao-Tse-Tung, Ch'en Po-Ta, & the Search for Chinese Theory, 1935-1945. LC 79-64221. 368p. 1980. 25.00x (ISBN 0-8047-1051-1). Stanford U Pr.

MAO TSE-TUNG, 1893-1976–DRAMA
Albee, Edward. Box. Bd. with Quotations from Chairman Mao Tse-Tung. LC 69-15501. 1969. 4.50 (ISBN 0-689-10007-8). Atheneum.

MAOISM
see Communism

MAORI BALLADS AND SONGS
see also Songs, Maori
Mitcalfe, Barry. Maori Poetry: The Singing Word. LC 74-183400. (Illus.). 209p. 1974. 11.00x (ISBN 0-8002-1701-2). Intl Pubns Serv.

MAORI FOLK-LORE
see Folk-Lore, Maori

MAORI LANGUAGE
see also Tahitian Language
Biggs, Bruce. Let's Learn Maori: A Guide to the Study of the Maori Language. 1969. 4.50 (ISBN 0-589-04242-4, Pub. by Reed Books Australia). C E Tuttle.
Harawira, K. T. Teach Yourself Maori. 1975. pap. 5.25 (ISBN 0-589-00907-9, Pub. by Reed Books Australia). C E Tuttle.
Ngata, Apirana N. Complete Manual of Maori Grammar & Conversation, with Vocabulary. 5th rev. enl. ed. LC 75-35261. Repr. of 1939 ed. 19.00 (ISBN 0-404-14433-0). AMS Pr.
Tregear, Edward. Maori-Polynesian Comparative Dictionary. 1969. Repr. of 1891 ed. text ed. 26.50x (ISBN 90-6234-045-8). Humanities.

MAORI LANGUAGE–DICTIONARIES
Armstrong, Alan. Say It in Maori. 60p. 1968. pap. 2.50x (ISBN 0-85467-010-6, Pub. by Viking New Zealand). Intl Schol Bk Serv.
Reed, A. W. Concise Maori Dictionary. 1974. pap. 5.25 (ISBN 0-589-00026-8, Pub. by Reed Books Australia). C E Tuttle.

MAORI LEGENDS
see Legends, Polynesian

MAORI MUSIC
see Music, Maori

MAORI MYTHOLOGY
see Mythology, Polynesian

MAORI PAINTINGS
see Paintings, Maori

MAORI SONGS
see Songs, Maori

MAORI TALES
see Tales, Maori

MAORI WARS, 1843-1870
see New Zealand–History

MAORIS
see also New Zealand–History
Archey, Gilbert. Maori Art & Artists. (Illus.). 1976. 30.00x (ISBN 0-00-216910-X). Intl Pubns Serv.
Armstrong, Alan. Maori Games & Hakas: Instructions, Words & Actions. (Illus.). 1964. pap. 5.95 (ISBN 0-589-00890-0, Pub. by Reed Books Australia). C E Tuttle.
Best, Elsdon. The Astronomical Knowledge of the Maori, Genuine & Empirical. Bd. with The Maori Division of Time. LC 75-35226. Repr. of 1922 ed. 12.50 (ISBN 0-404-14405-5). AMS Pr.
--Fishing Methods & Devices of the Maori. LC 75-35228. Repr. of 1929 ed. 27.50 (ISBN 0-404-14406-3). AMS Pr.
--The Maori, 2 vols. LC 75-35231. Repr. of 1924 ed. Set. 95.00 (ISBN 0-404-14310-5). AMS Pr.
--Maori Agriculture. (New Zealand - Dominion Museum Bulletin: No. 9). (Illus.). 1977. 20.00x (ISBN 0-8426-1002-2). Verry.
--The Maori As He Was: A Brief Account of Maori Life. 296p. 1974. Repr. text ed. 16.50x (ISBN 0-8426-0983-0). Verry.
--The Maori Canoe. Bd. with Polynesian Voyagers. LC 75-35234. Repr. of 1925 ed. 57.50 (ISBN 0-404-14411-X). AMS Pr.
--The Maori Canoe. (New Zealand - Dominion Museum Bulletin: No. 7). (Illus.). 1977. text ed. 23.00x (ISBN 0-8426-1158-4). Verry.
--Maori Religion & Mythology. LC 75-35236. Repr. of 1924 ed. 37.50 (ISBN 0-404-14412-8). AMS Pr.
Biggs, Bruce. Maori Marriage. (Illus.). 1960. 5.25 (ISBN 0-589-00473-5, Pub. by Reed Books Australia). C E Tuttle.
Brown, John M. Maori & Polynesian, Their Origin, History & Culture. LC 75-35240. Repr. of 1907 ed. 26.50 (ISBN 0-404-14415-2). AMS Pr.
Buddle, Thomas. The Maori King Movement in New Zealand. LC 75-35241. Repr. of 1860 ed. 12.50 (ISBN 0-404-14416-0). AMS Pr.
Buick, Thomas L. The Moa-Hunters of New Zealand: Sportsmen of the Stone Age. LC 75-35242. Repr. of 1937 ed. 22.50 (ISBN 0-404-14417-9). AMS Pr.
--The Mystery of the Moa, New Zealand's Avian Giant. LC 75-35244. (Illus.). Repr. of 1931 ed. 30.00 (ISBN 0-404-14418-7). AMS Pr.
Caselberg, John, ed. Maori Is My Name: Historical Maori Writings. LC 75-331658. 152p. 1975. 11.50x (ISBN 0-8002-0471-9). Intl Pubns Serv.
Cowan, James. The Caltex Book of Maori Lore. 1959. pap. 3.75 (ISBN 0-589-00014-4, Pub. by Reed Books Australia). C E Tuttle.
--The Maori Yesterday & to-Day. LC 75-35247. Repr. of 1930 ed. 22.50 (ISBN 0-404-14421-7). AMS Pr.
--New Zealand Wars, 2 Vols. LC 76-100514. (BCL Ser. II). Repr. of 1922 ed. 37.50 (ISBN 0-404-00600-0). AMS Pr.
Dansey, Harry. New Zealand Maori in Colour. LC 70-109418. (Illus.). 1970. 7.75 (ISBN 0-8048-0889-9). C E Tuttle.
De Bres, Pieter H. Religion in Atene: Religious Associations & the Urban Maori. 1971. text ed. 8.20x (ISBN 0-8248-0583-6). U Pr of Hawaii.
Firth, Raymond. Economics of the New Zealand Maori. 2nd ed. Orig. Title: Primitive Economics of the New Zealand Maori. 1959. text ed. 14.50x (ISBN 0-391-00494-8). Humanities.
Fox, Aileen. Prehistoric Maori Fortifications in the North Island of New Zealand. new ed. (New Zealand Archaeological Association Monographs: No. 6). (Illus.). 1976. text ed. 15.00x (ISBN 0-582-71746-9). Longman.
Grey, George. Ko Nga Whakapepeha: Proverbial & Popular Sayings of the Ancestors of the New Zealand Race. LC 75-35252. Repr. of 1857 ed. 10.75 (ISBN 0-404-14424-1). AMS Pr.
Hawthorn, H. D. Maori: A Study in Acculturation. LC 44-47267. (American Anthropological Association Memoirs). Repr. of 1944 ed. pap. 8.00 (ISBN 0-527-00563-0). Kraus Repr.
Higham, Charles. The Maoris. LC 77-88678. (Cambridge Introduction to the History of Mankind: Topic Book). (Illus.). Date not set. price not set (ISBN 0-521-21931-0). Cambridge U Pr.
Hopa, Ngapare. The Art of Piupiu Making. (Illus.). 46p. 1971. 7.50 (ISBN 0-589-00651-7, Pub. by Reed Books Australia). C E Tuttle.
Kawharu, I. H., ed. Orakei: A Ngati Whatua Community. (New Zealand Council for Educational Research Ser.: No. 54). 192p. 1975. text ed. 18.00x (ISBN 0-8426-0985-7). Verry.
Kawharu, Ian H. Maori Land Tenure: Studies of a Changing Institution. 1977. 59.00x (ISBN 0-19-823177-6). Oxford U Pr.
King, Michael. Te Puea; a Biography. (Illus.). 1977. 20.00x (ISBN 0-340-22482-7). Intl Pubns Serv.
King, Michael, ed. Te Ao Hurihuri: The World Moves on. LC 76-458024. (Illus.). 235p. 1975. pap. 10.50x (ISBN 0-456-01810-7). Intl Pubns Serv.
Linge, Gabriel. In Search of the Maori. (Illus.). 174p. 1974. 10.50x (ISBN 0-8002-0465-4). Intl Pubns Serv.
Main, William. Maori in Focus: A Selection of Photographs of the Maori from 1850-1914. LC 77-363159. (Illus.). 1976. 13.50x (ISBN 0-8002-1700-4). Intl Pubns Serv.
Metge, Joan. The Maoris of New Zealand. 1976. 26.00x (ISBN 0-7100-8352-1); pap. 12.50 (ISBN 0-7100-8381-5). Routledge & Kegan.
Mitcalfe, Barry. The Maori. (Illus.). 104p. 1972. pap. 5.30x (ISBN 0-7233-0327-4). Intl Pubns Serv.
Pearce, G. L. The Story of the Maori People. (Illus.). 164p. 1968. 9.15x (ISBN 0-8002-0066-7). Intl Pubns Serv.
Polack, Joel S. Manners & Customs of the New Zealanders. LC 75-35263. Repr. of 1840 ed. 52.50 (ISBN 0-404-14435-7). AMS Pr.
Pomare, Maui, et al. Legends of the Maori, 2 vols. LC 75-35265. (Illus.). 1976. Repr. of 1934 ed. Set. 62.50 (ISBN 0-404-14350-4). AMS Pr.
Pownall, Glen. New Zealand Maori Arts & Crafts. 160p. 1980. 21.00 (ISBN 0-85467-033-5, Pub. by Viking Sevenseas). Intl Schol Bk Serv.
--Primitive Art of the New Zealand Maori. 92p. 1980. 21.00 (ISBN 0-85467-013-0, Pub. by Viking Sevenseas). Intl Schol Bk Serv.
Reed, A. W. An Illustrated Encyclopedia of Maori Life. (Illus.). 1963. 10.50 (ISBN 0-589-00115-9, Pub. by Reed Books Australia). C E Tuttle.
Schwimmer, Eric. The World of the Maori. (Illus.). 1978. pap. 5.95 (ISBN 0-589-05085-0, Pub. by Reed Books Australia). C E Tuttle.
Scott, Dick. Ask That Mountain. LC 75-315794. (Illus.). 216p. 1975. 13.00x (ISBN 0-86863-375-5). Intl Pubns Serv.
Siers, James. The Maori People of New Zealand. 55p. 1967. pap. 1.50x (ISBN 0-85467-037-8, Pub. by Viking New Zealand). Intl Schol Bk Serv.
Siers, James & Ngata, W. T. The Maori People of New Zealand. LC 78-670037. (Illus.). 1976. pap. 6.50 (ISBN 0-85467-037-8). Intl Pubns Serv.
Smith, Jean. Tapu Removal in Maori Religion. 1974. text ed. 12.00x (ISBN 0-8248-0591-7). U Pr of Hawaii.
Sutherland, Ivan L. The Maori People Today: A General Survey. LC 75-30085. (Institute of Pacific Relations). Repr. of 1940 ed. 42.50 (ISBN 0-404-59563-4). AMS Pr.
Taylor, Alan. Maori Builds. 1967. 4.00x (ISBN 0-8426-1565-2). Verry.
Tregear, Edward. The Maori Race. LC 73-12314. (Illus.). Repr. of 1926 ed. 30.00 (ISBN 0-404-11222-6). AMS Pr.
White, John, 1826-1891. The Ancient History of the Maori, His Mythology & Traditions, 7 vols. LC 75-35274. (Illus.). Repr. of 1891 ed. Set. 195.00, incl. atlas (ISBN 0-404-14380-6). AMS Pr.

MAORIS–EDUCATION
Ausubel, David P. Maori Youth. 1978. pap. 5.95 (ISBN 0-8158-0358-3). Chris Mass.

MAP COLLECTIONS
Barley, M. W. A Guide to British Topographical Collections. 159p. 1974. pap. text ed. 17.95x (ISBN 0-686-74108-0, Pub. by Coun Brit Archaeological). Humanities.
Carrington, David K. & Stephenson, Richard W., eds. Map Collections in the United States & Canada: A Directory. 3rd ed. LC 77-26685. 1978. 19.75 (ISBN 0-87111-243-4). SLA.
Catalogue of Printed Maps, Charts & Plans: Ten-Year Supplement, 1965-1974. 1981. 150.00x (ISBN 0-7141-0366-7, Pub. by Brit Lib England). State Mutual Bk.
Drazniowsky, Roman. Map Librarianship: Readings. LC 74-19244. (Illus.). 1975. 22.00 (ISBN 0-8108-0739-4). Scarecrow.
Public Archives of Canada (Ottawa) Catalogue of the National Map Collection, 16 vols. 1976. Set. lib. bdg. 1250.00 (ISBN 0-8161-1215-0). G K Hall.
Ristow, Walter W. The Emergence of Maps in Libraries. 358p. 1980. 27.50 (ISBN 0-208-01841-7, Linnet). Shoe String.
Ristow, Walter W., ed. World Directory of Map Collections. 326p. 1976. 26.00 (ISBN 3-7940-4428-2, Pub by K G Saur). Shoe String.

MAP DRAWING
see also Cartography; Topographical Drawing
Ali, Jamil. Determination of the Coordinates of Positions for the Correction of Distances Between Cities. 1967. 24.95x (ISBN 0-8156-6007-3, Am U Beirut). Syracuse U Pr.
Anthony, Anne. Orienteering Handbook: Physical Education Ser. (Illus.). 64p. 1981. pap. 5.95 (ISBN 0-87663-618-0, Pub. by Hancock Hse). Universe.
Cartwright, Sally. What's in a Map? LC 76-10694. (Illus.). (gr. k-3). 1976. PLB 5.29 (ISBN 0-698-30635-X). Coward.
Crone, G. R. Maps & Their Makers: An Introduction to the History of Cartography. (Illus.). 1978. 22.50 (ISBN 0-208-01724-0, Archon). Shoe String.
Keates, J. S. Cartographic Design & Production. LC 72-9251. 240p. 1976. pap. 30.95 (ISBN 0-470-15106-4). Halsted Pr.
Larsgaard, Mary L. World Plainimetric & Contour Mapping. 550p. 1982. text ed. price not set (ISBN 0-87287-276-9). Libs Unl.
Slater, Leslie G. Compass Mapping. (Pocket Handbook: Vol. 2). (Illus.). Date not set. pap. 1.00 (ISBN 0-686-10126-X). Terry Pub.
Tannenbaum, Harold & Stillman, Nathan. Math Projects: Map-Making. (Illus., Orig.). (gr. 4-9). 1968. pap. 2.50 (ISBN 0-87594-013-7, 3010). Book-Lab.
Thrower, Norman J., ed. The Compleat Plattmaker: Essays on Chart, Map, & Globe-Making in England in the 17th & 18th Centuries. LC 77-78415. 1979. 22.75x (ISBN 0-520-03522-4). U of Cal Pr.

MAP PRINTING
Ringel, G. Map Color Theorem. LC 73-17986. (Die Grundlehren der mathematischen Wissenschaften: Vol. 209). (Illus.). 220p. 1974. 29.40 (ISBN 0-387-06548-2). Springer-Verlag.
Woodward, David. The All-American Map: Wax Engraving & Its Influence on Cartography. LC 76-8099. (Illus.). 1977. lib. bdg. 12.50x (ISBN 0-226-90725-2). U of Chicago Pr.
--Five Centuries of Map Printing. LC 74-11635. 1975. pap. 7.95 (ISBN 0-226-90726-0, P723, Phoen). U of Chicago Pr.
Woodward, David, ed. Five Centuries of Map Printing. LC 74-11635. (Nebenzahl Lectures in the History of Cartography Ser). xii, 177p. 1975. 20.00x (ISBN 0-226-90724-4). U of Chicago Pr.

MAP-PROJECTION
see also Cartography; Orthographic Projection; Surfaces, Representation Of
Deetz, Charles H. & Adams, Oscar S. Elements of Map Projection with Applications to Map & Chart Construction. 5th ed. LC 77-89015. Repr. of 1945 ed. lib. bdg. 32.25x (ISBN 0-8371-2268-6, DEMP). Greenwood.
McDonnel. Introduction to Map Projections. 1979. 14.75 (ISBN 0-8247-6830-2). Dekker.
Maling, D. H. Coordinate Systems & Map Projections. LC 73-330722. (Illus.). 255p. 1973. 22.50x (ISBN 0-540-00974-1). Intl Pubns Serv.
Richardus & Adler, R. Map Projections. LC 79-182493. 174p. 1975. pap. 22.00 (ISBN 0-444-10843-2, North-Holland). Elsevier.

MAP READING
see Maps; Maps, Military

MAPLE
Maple Tree Problems. 0.25 (ISBN 0-686-20731-9). SUNY Environ.
Selsam, Millicent E. Maple Tree. LC 68-25933. (Illus.). (gr. 2-5). 1968. PLB 7.92 (ISBN 0-688-31496-1). Morrow.
Vertrees, J. D. Japanese Maples. LC 77-18737. (Illus.). 1978. 40.00 (ISBN 0-917304-09-8, Pub. by Timber Pr). Intl Schol Bk Serv.

MAPLE SUGAR
Gemming, Elizabeth. Maple Harvest: The Story of Maple Sugaring. LC 75-45132. (Illus.). (gr. 3-5). 1976. 5.95 (ISBN 0-698-20360-7). Coward.
Nearing, Helen & Nearing, Scott. The Maple Sugar Book: Together with Remarks on Pioneering As a way of Living in the Twentieth Century. LC 73-148417. (Illus.). 1971. 8.95 (ISBN 0-8052-3400-4); pap. 4.95 (ISBN 0-8052-0308-7). Schocken.
Perrin, Noel. Amateur Sugar Maker. LC 78-175534. (Illus.). 104p. 1972. 7.50 (ISBN 0-87451-061-9). U Pr of New Eng.
Thompson, Bruce. Syrup Trees. Motsinger, Marilyn, ed. LC 78-63316. (Illus.). 1978. pap. 6.95 (ISBN 0-931318-00-9). Walnut AZ.

MAPPING, CONFORMAL
see Conformal Mapping

MAPS
see also Atlases; Automobile Touring–Road Guides; Nautical Charts; World Maps
Adams, John. Sketches Taken During Ten Voyages to Africa Between the Years 1786 & 1800. (Landmarks in Anthropology Ser). (Illus.). Repr. of 1822 ed. 11.50 (ISBN 0-384-00330-3). Johnson Repr.
American Geographical Society-Map Department-New York. Index to Maps in Books & Periodicals, First Supplement. 1971. lib. bdg. 105.00 (ISBN 0-8161-0806-4). G K Hall.
Atwood, Beth S. Building a Map Skills Program. LC 76-29234. (Learning Handbooks Ser.). 1976. pap. 4.95 (ISBN 0-8224-1971-8). Pitman Learning.
Baues, H. J. Obstruction Theory on the Homotopy Classification of Maps. (Lecture Notes in Mathematics Ser: Vol. 628). 1977. pap. 18.30 (ISBN 0-387-08534-3). Springer-Verlag.
Birch, T. W. Maps: Topographical & Statistical. (Illus.). 1964. pap. text ed. 10.95x (ISBN 0-19-831645-3). Oxford U Pr.
Bonacker, Wilhelm. Karten-Woerterbuch. (Ger.). 1970. 14.95 (ISBN 3-7812-0704-8, M-7493, Pub. by Kirschbaum). French & Eur.
Brown, Lloyd. The Story of Maps. (Illus.). 1979. pap. 6.00 (ISBN 0-486-23873-3). Dover.
Brown, Lloyd A. The Story of Maps. (Illus.). 12.00 (ISBN 0-8446-5739-5). Peter Smith.
--The Story of Maps. LC 79-52395. (Illus.). 417p. 1980. Repr. of 1949 ed. 11.95 (ISBN 0-938164-00-7). Vintage Bk Co.
Claussen, Martin P. & Friis, Herman R. American & Foreign Maps Published by the U.S. Congress, 1789-1861: Historical Catalog & Index. (Illus.). 400p. 1977. pap. 30.00 (ISBN 0-912680-00-8). Piedmont.
Coastal Zone '78: Coastal Mapping Papers Reprinted from American Society of Civil Engineers, 4 vols. 188p. 1978. pap. 5.00 (ISBN 0-937294-15-2). ASP.
Crone, G. R. Maps & Their Makers: An Introduction to the History of Cartography. (Illus.). 1978. 22.50 (ISBN 0-208-01724-0, Archon). Shoe String.
Dickinson, G. C. Maps & Air Photographs: Images of the Earth. 2nd ed. 348p. 1979. 21.95 (ISBN 0-470-26641-4). Halsted Pr.

Educational Challenges, Inc. Map Skills. Hayes, Heidi, ed. Incl. Book C (ISBN 0-8372-3505-7). tchr's ed.; Book D (ISBN 0-8372-3506-5). tchr's ed. (ISBN 0-8372-9196-8); Book E (ISBN 0-8372-3507-3). tchr's ed (ISBN 0-8372-9197-6); Book F (ISBN 0-8372-3508-1). tchr's ed (ISBN 0-8372-9198-4). (Elementary Skills Ser). 1977. 1.35 ea. Bowmar-Noble.
Geary, Don. Step in the Right Direction: A Basic Map & Compass Book. (Illus.). 224p. 1980. pap. 6.95 (ISBN 0-8117-2097-7). Stackpole.
Girl Scouts of the U.S.A. Compass & Maps. (Campcraft Skills Ser.). (Illus.). 1976. pap. text ed. 0.95 (ISBN 0-88441-420-5, 26-210). GS.
Greenhood, David. Mapping. rev. ed. LC 63-20905. 1964. 16.00x (ISBN 0-226-30696-8); pap. 5.50 (ISBN 0-226-30697-6, P521, Phoen). U of Chicago Pr.
Harley, J. B. Maps for the Local Historian: A Guide to the British Sources. (Illus.). 86p. 1972. pap. 5.00x (ISBN 0-7199-0834-5). Intl Pubns Serv.
Hodgkiss, A. G. Understanding Maps: A Systematic History of Their Use & Development. 208p. 1981. 40.00x (ISBN 0-7129-0940-0, Pub. by Dawson). State Mutual Bk.
Iooss, G. Bifurcation of Maps & Applications. (North-Holland Mathematics Studies: Vol. 36). 1979. 31.75 (ISBN 0-444-85304-9, North Holland). Elsevier.
Jennings, J. H. Elementary Map Interpretation. 1960. text ed. 5.95 (ISBN 0-521-20899-8). Cambridge U Pr.
Kjellstrom, Bjorn. Be Expert with Map & Compass: The Orienteering Handbook. rev. ed. LC 76-12550. (Illus.). 176p. 1976. pap. 7.95 (ISBN 0-684-14270-8, SL595, ScribT). Scribner.
Klinefelter, Walter. A Fourth Display of Old Maps & Plans. LC 77-94176. 1978. 6.00 (ISBN 0-911462-11-2). Sumac.
--A Third Display of Old Maps & Plans. LC 73-86565. 80p. 1973. 5.00 (ISBN 0-911462-10-4). Sumac.
Kranich, Robert E. & Messec, Jerry L. Learning to Use Maps. (Illus.). 1978. text ed. write for info. (ISBN 0-88323-149-2, 236); 2.50x (ISBN 0-88323-150-6); teacher's answer key free (239). Richards Pub.
Lenglet Dufresnoy, A. Catalogue Des Meillures Cartes Geographiques. 1742. text ed. 10.00x (ISBN 9-06041-039-4). Humanities.
Lewis, Peter. Maps & Statistics. LC 77-1184. 318p. 1977. text ed. 30.95x (ISBN 0-416-65370-7, Pub. by Chaman & Hall England); pap. text ed. 20.95x (ISBN 0-416-65380-4). Methuen Inc.
Lister, Raymond. Antique Maps & Cartographers. (Illus.). 1970. 16.50 (ISBN 0-208-01041-6, Archon). Shoe String.
McManis, Douglas R. European Impressions of the New England Coast, 1497-1620. LC 70-187026. (Research Papers Ser: No. 139). (Illus.). 147p. 1972. pap. 8.00 (ISBN 0-89065-046-2, 139). U Chicago Dept Geog.
Map Reading. 1976. pap. 2.50 (ISBN 0-8277-4887-6). British Bk Ctr.
Mariners Museum Library - Newport News - Virginia. Catalog of Maps, Ships' Papers & Logbooks. 1964. lib. bdg. 55.00 (ISBN 0-8161-0686-X). G K Hall.
Meyers Kontinente und Meere-Daten, Karten Die Enzyklopadie der Erde, 8 vols. (Ger.). 1973. 625.00 (ISBN 0-686-56633-5). French & Eur.
Monmonier, Mark S. Maps, Distortion, & Meaning. Natoli, Salvatore, ed. LC 76-44640. (Resource Papers for College Geography Ser). 48p. 1977. pap. text ed. 4.00 (ISBN 0-89291-120-4). Assn Am Geographers.
Muehrcke, Phillip C. Map Use: Reading, Analysis & Interpretation. rev. ed. LC 78-70573. (Illus.). xi, 469p. 1980. pap. text ed. 16.25 (ISBN 0-9602978-1-2). JP Pubns WI.
Numerology Map - Interstate System. 1978. 1.00 (ISBN 0-686-29465-3). AASHTO.
Post, J. B. An Atlas of Fantasy. (Illus.). 1979. pap. 8.95 (ISBN 0-345-27399-0). Ballantine.
Riffel, Paul. Reading Maps. LC 79-13628. (Illus.). (gr. 7 up). 1973. pap. 5.95 plastic comb bdg. (ISBN 0-8331-1300-3). Hubbard Sci.
Robinson, Arthur H. & Petchenik, Barbara B. The Nature of Maps: Essays Toward Understanding Maps & Mapping. LC 75-36401. (Illus.). 1976. lib. bdg. 8.95x (ISBN 0-226-72281-3). U of Chicago Pr.
Simonetti, Martha L. Descriptive List of the Map Collection in the Pennsylvania State Archives. Kent, Donald H. & Whipkey, Harry E., eds. 1976. 8.00 (ISBN 0-911124-83-7). Pa Hist & Mus.
Skelton, R. A. Maps: A Historical Survey of Their Study & Collecting. Woodward, David, ed. (Illus.). xvi, 138p. 1975. 7.95x (ISBN 0-226-76166-5); pap. 2.75 (ISBN 0-226-76165-7, P632, Phoen). U of Chicago Pr.
Soil Map of Europe. 31p. 1965. 41.75 (ISBN 0-685-02466-0, F425, FAO). Unipub.
Speak, P. & Carter, A. H. Map Reading & Interpretation. (Illus., New Edition with Metric Examples). 1974. pap. text ed. 6.50x (ISBN 0-582-31010-5). Longman.
Sumrall, Raymond O., et al. The Map Abstract of Trends in Calls for Police Service: Birmingham, Alabama, 1975-1976. LC 78-359. 104p. 1978. spiral bdg. 9.75 (ISBN 0-8173-9006-5). U of Ala Pr.
Tupper, F. & Ogle, M. B. Master Walter Map's Book: De Nugis Curialium. 1973. lib. bdg. 20.00x (ISBN 0-374-98030-6). Octagon.
Uzielle, G., et al. Mappamondi, Carte Nautiche, Portolani et Altre Monumenti Cartografici. 1882. text ed. 19.00x (ISBN 9-06041-068-8). Humanities.

MAPS–BIBLIOGRAPHY

American Geographical Society - Map Department, New York. Index to Maps in Books & Periodicals, 10 vols. 1968. Set. lib. bdg. 950.00 (ISBN 0-8161-0753-X). G K Hall.
American Geographical Society Map Department (New York) Index to Maps in Books & Periodicals, Second Suppl. 1976. lib. bdg. 105.00 (ISBN 0-8161-0995-8). G K Hall.
Bancroft Library, University of California, Berkeley. University of California, Berkeley, Bancroft Library: Index to Printed Maps, 1st Suppl. 1975. lib. bdg. 80.00 (ISBN 0-8161-1172-3). G K Hall.
Merrett, C. E. A Selected Bibliography of Natal Maps. 1979. lib. bdg. 42.50 (ISBN 0-8161-8276-0). G K Hall.
Monteiro, Palmyra V. Catalogue of Latin American Flat Maps, 1926-1964, 2 vols. Incl. Vol. 1. Mexico, Central America, West Indies. 411p. 1967 (ISBN 0-292-78371-X); Vol. 2. South America, Falkland(Malvinas) Islands & the Guianas. 442p. 1969 (ISBN 0-292-78429-5). (Institute of Latin American Studies Guides & Bibliographies Ser.: No. 2). 1967. 10.00x ea.; Set. 15.00x (ISBN 0-292-74612-1). U of Tex Pr.
New York Public Library, Research Libraries. Dictionary Catalog of the Map Division, 10 vols. 1971. Set. lib. bdg. 795.00 (ISBN 0-8161-0783-1). G K Hall.
Research Libraries of the New York Public Library & the Library of Congress. Bibliographic Guide to Maps & Atlases: Nineteen Seventy-Nine. (Library Catalogs-Bib. Guides). 1980. lib. bdg. 75.00 (ISBN 0-8161-6874-1). G K Hall.
--Bibliographic Guide to Maps & Atlases: 1980. (Library Catalogs-Bib. Guides Ser.). 1981. lib. bdg. 95.00 (ISBN 0-8161-6890-3). G K Hall.
Sobel. Maps on File. 1981. 125.00 (ISBN 0-87196-525-9). Facts on File.
U. S. Library of Congress Map Division. A List of Maps of America in the Library of Congress, 2 vols. in 1. 1967. Repr. of 1902 ed. 46.50 (ISBN 0-8337-2739-7). B Franklin.
University of California - Berkeley. Bancroft Library, Index to Printed Maps. 1964. lib. bdg. 60.00 (ISBN 0-8161-0704-1); First Suppl., 1975, 1 Vol. 105.00 (ISBN 0-8161-1172-3). G K Hall.
Wheat, James C. & Brun, Christian F. Maps & Charts Published in America Before Eighteen Hundred: A Bibliography, Vol. 3. rev. ed. (Illus.). 1979. 60.00x (ISBN 0-900470-89-5, Pub. by Holland Pr). W G Arader.
Winch, Kenneth, ed. International Maps & Atlases in Print. 2nd ed. LC 73-13336. 1976. 47.50 (ISBN 0-85935-036-3). Bowker.

MAPS–CATALOGING

see Cataloging of Maps

MAPS–JUVENILE LITERATURE

Hart, Tony. Fun with Map Making. (Learning with Fun Ser.). Date not set. 12.50x (ISBN 0-7182-0062-4, SpS). Sportshelf.
McCreary, Paul. Michigan Map Skills & Information Workbook. (Illus.). 32p. (Orig.). (gr. 6-10). 1978. wkbk. 4.50 (ISBN 0-910726-92-2). Hillsdale Educ.
Madden, James F. The Wonderful World of Maps. Hammond Incorporated Staff, ed. (Illus., Orig.). (gr. 7-11). 1977. 5.95 (ISBN 0-8437-3411-6). Hammond Inc.
Mahoney, Susan & Winston, Barbara. Map & Globe Skills Learning Module. (gr. 3-4). 1976. pap. 231.00 (ISBN 0-89290-144-6, CM-63). Soc for Visual.
Preksto, Peter W., Jr. Map Reading Skills. (Basic Skills Library). (Illus.). (gr. 4 up). 1979. PLB 5.95 (ISBN 0-87191-715-7). Creative Ed.

MAPS, EARLY

see also Geography, Ancient–Maps

Blundeville, Thomas. M. Blundeville, His Exercises Containing Sixe Treatises. LC 78-171736. (English Experience Ser.: No. 361). (Illus.). 718p. 1971. Repr. of 1594 ed. 64.00 (ISBN 90-221-0361-7). Walter J Johnson.
Campbell, Tony. Early Maps. Benjamin, Phyllis, ed. (Illus.). 148p. 1981. text ed. 39.95 (ISBN 0-89659-191-3). Abbeville Pr.
Dainville, F. Langage des Geographes Termes, Signes, Couleurs des Cartes Anciennes: 1500-1800. 404p. (Fr.). 1964. pap. 49.95 (ISBN 0-686-56973-3, M-6100). French & Eur.
Davis, John. Voyages & Works of John Davis the Navigator. Markham, Albert H., ed. & intro. by. LC 71-134714. (Hakluyt Society, First Ser.: No. 59). (Illus.). 1970. Repr. of 1880 ed. lib. bdg. 32.00 (ISBN 0-8337-2241-7). B Franklin.
Gilbert, Humphrey. A Discourse of a Discoverie for a New Passage to Cataia. Gascoigne, George, ed. LC 68-54645. (English Experience Ser.: No. 72). 88p. 1968. Repr. of 1576 ed. 11.50 (ISBN 90-221-0072-3). Walter J Johnson.
McMullen, Edwin W., Jr. English Topographic Terms in Florida, 1563-1874. LC 52-12531. 1953. pap. 5.50 (ISBN 0-8130-0160-9). U Presses Fla.
Nordenskiold, Nils A. Periplus: An Essay on the Early History of Charts & Sailing Directions. Bather, Francis A., tr. from Swed. (Illus.). 1897. 189.00 (ISBN 0-8337-2572-6). B Franklin.
Orr, Mary A. Dante & the Early Astronomers. LC 71-101029. 1969. Repr. of 1956 ed. 13.75 (ISBN 0-8046-0696-X). Kennikat.
Ptolemy, Claudius. Geography of Claudius Ptolemy. Stevenson, Edward L., ed. LC 70-174287. Repr. of 1932 ed. 245.00 (ISBN 0-404-05148-0). AMS Pr.
Skelton, R. A., et al. Vinland Map & the Tartar Relation. (Illus.). 1965. 35.00x (ISBN 0-300-00959-3). Yale U Pr.
Taylor, Eva G. Tudor Geography, 1485-1583. 1968. lib. bdg. 18.00x (ISBN 0-374-97847-6). Octagon.
Washburn, Wilcomb E., ed. Vinland Map Conference: Proceedings. LC 77-152380. 1971. 12.50x (ISBN 0-226-87394-3). U of Chicago Pr.

MAPS, EARLY–FACSIMILES

Black, Jeannette D., ed. Blathwayt Atlas, Vol. 1, The Maps. LC 78-654217. (Illus.). 1970. Set. text ed. 500.00x unbound boxed (ISBN 0-87057-125-7, Pub. by Brown U Pr). U Pr of New Eng.
Klemp, Egon, compiled by. Africa on Maps Dating from the Twelfth to the Eighteenth Century. LC 72-86086. (Illus.). 1972. text ed. 425.00x (ISBN 0-8419-0270-4). Holmes & Meier.
Paullin, Charles O. Atlas of the Historical Geography of the U. S. Wright, John K., ed. LC 75-14058. (Carnegie Institution of Washington Ser.: No. 4). (Illus.). 162p. 1975. Repr. of 1932 ed. lib. bdg. 135.25 (ISBN 0-8371-8208-5, PAHG). Greenwood.

MAPS, GEOLOGICAL

see Geology–Maps

MAPS, HISTORICAL

see Classical Geography; Geography, Ancient–Maps; Geography, Historical–Maps

MAPS, LINEAR

see Linear Operators

MAPS, METEOROLOGICAL

see Meteorology–Charts, Diagrams, etc.

MAPS, MILITARY

see also Military Reconnaissance

Banks, Arthur. A World Atlas of Military History: Up to 1485. LC 73-90857. 225p. 1973. 12.95 (ISBN 0-88254-177-3). Hippocrene Bks.

MAPS, PICTORIAL

George, Wilma. Animals & Maps. (Illus.). 1969. 30.00x (ISBN 0-520-01480-4). U of Cal Pr.

MAPS, WORLD

see World Maps

MAPS FOR THE VISUALLY HANDICAPPED

Kidwell, Ann M. & Greer, Peter S. Sites, Perception & the Nonvisual Experience: Making & Designing Mobility Maps. 1973. pap. 7.00 (ISBN 0-89128-055-3, PMR055). Am Foun Blind.

MAPUCHE LANGUAGE

see Araucanian Language

MAQUIS

see World War, 1939-1945–Underground Movements–France

MARANAO LANGUAGE

McKaughan, Howard P. & Macaraya, Batua A. Maranao Dictionary. LC 67-13668. 1967. pap. 15.00x (ISBN 0-87022-505-7). U Pr of Hawaii.

MARANAW LANGUAGE

see Maranao Language

MARANOS

see also Sephardim

Barnett, Richard. The Sephardi Heritage. 1971. 35.00x (ISBN 0-685-38387-3, 87068-170-21). Ktav.
Liebman, Seymour B. The Inquisitors & the Jews in the New World: Summaries of Procesos 1500-1810, & Bibliographical Guide. LC 72-85110. 160p. 1973. 12.95x (ISBN 0-87024-245-8). U of Miami Pr.
Yerushalmi, Yosef H. From Spanish Court to Italian Ghetto: Isaac Cardoso, a Study in Seventeenth-Century Marranism & Jewish Apologetics. LC 76-109544. (Illus.). 548p. 1981. pap. 15.00 (ISBN 0-295-95824-3). U of Wash Pr.

MARAT, JEAN PAUL, 1744-1793

Bax, E. Belfort. Jean-Paul Marat: The People's Friend. 59.95 (ISBN 0-8490-0439-X). Gordon Pr.
Gottschalk, Louis. Jean-Paul Marat. 59.95 (ISBN 0-8490-0438-1). Gordon Pr.
Gottschalk, Louis R. Jean Paul Marat: A Study in Radicalism. LC 66-29542. Repr. of 1927 ed. 15.00 (ISBN 0-405-08566-4, Blom Pubns). Arno.
--Jean Paul Marat: A Study in Radicalism. LC 67-16987. 1967. pap. 12.50x (ISBN 0-226-30532-5). U of Chicago Pr.
Roberts, W. Marat in England. 69.95 (ISBN 0-8490-0583-3). Gordon Pr.
Scherr, Marie. Charlotte Corday & Certain Men of the Revolutionary Torment. LC 79-100512. Repr. of 1929 ed. 22.50 (ISBN 0-404-05588-5). AMS Pr.

MARAT, JEAN PAUL, 1744-1793–DRAMA

Weiss, Peter. Persecution & Assassination of Jean-Paul Marat As Performed by the Inmates of the Asylum of Charenton Under the Direction of the Marquis De Sade. LC 65-15915. (Orig.). 1966. pap. text ed. 3.95x (ISBN 0-689-10288-7). Atheneum.

MARATHAS

Duff, James D. History of the Mahrattas, 2 vols. 1971. 65.00 set (ISBN 0-686-20243-0). Intl Bk Dist.
Kincaid, A. Charles & Parasnis, R. B. History of the Maratha People. 1968. Repr. of 1931 ed. 11.00x (ISBN 0-8426-1333-1). Verry.
Sharma, S. R. The Founding of Maratha Freedom. rev ed. 467p. 1964. 6.50x (ISBN 0-8426-1524-5). Verry.

MARATHI LANGUAGE

Bloch, J. The Formation of the Marathi Language. Chanana, D. R., tr. 1970. 7.95 (ISBN 0-89684-206-1). Orient Bk Dist.
Katre, S. M. The Formation of Konkani Language. 1966. pap. 3.95 (ISBN 0-89684-205-3). Orient Bk Dist.
Kavadi, Naresh B. & Southworth, Franklin C. Spoken Marathi: Book One. rev. ed. LC 64-23368. 1968. text ed. 9.50x (ISBN 0-8122-7457-1). U of Pa Pr.

MARATHON RUNNING

Aaseng, Nathan. Track's Marathon Masters. (Sports Heroes Library). (Illus.). 80p. (gr. 4 up). 1981. PLB 6.95 (ISBN 0-8225-1325-0). Lerner Pubns.
Barrett, Thomas & Morrissey, Robert, Jr. Marathon Runners. (Illus.). 160p. (gr. 7 up). 1981. PLB 9.79 (ISBN 0-671-34019-0). Messner.
Bloom, Marc. The Marathon: What It Takes to Go the Distance. LC 80-18859. (Illus.). 304p. 1981. 15.95 (ISBN 0-03-052476-8); pap. 8.95 (ISBN 0-686-69124-5). HR&W.
Brown, Skip & Graham, John. Target Twenty Six: A Practical Guide to the Marathon. 1979. pap. 5.95 (ISBN 0-02-028820-4, Collier). Macmillan.
Clayton, Derek. Running to the Top. LC 79-64297. (Illus.). 137p. 1980. pap. 5.95 (ISBN 0-89037-212-8). Anderson World.
D'Alton, Martina. The Runner's Guide to the U. S. A. LC 78-10315. (Illus.). 1979. 12.95 (ISBN 0-671-40070-3); pap. 6.95 (ISBN 0-671-40022-3). Summit Bks.
Falls, Joe. The Boston Marathon. 1979. pap. 3.95 (ISBN 0-02-028520-5, Collier). Macmillan.
Fogel, Julianna A. Wesley Paul, Marathon Runner. LC 78-23649. (Illus.). (gr. 1-5). 1979. 7.95 (ISBN 0-397-31845-6, JBL-J); PLB 8.89 (ISBN 0-397-31861-8). Har-Row.
Gordon, Jennie & Scaff, Jack H., Jr. Your First Marathon: Training with the Honolulu Marathon Clinic. (Illus.). 72p. 1979. pap. 4.95 (ISBN 0-939350-00-9). Running Wild.
Higdon, Hal. The Marathoners. (Illus.). (gr. 6-8). 1980. 8.95 (ISBN 0-399-20695-7). Putnam.
Hosler, Ray, ed. Boston: America's Oldest Marathon. LC 78-68621. (Illus.). 192p. 1980. pap. 4.95 (ISBN 0-89037-204-7, Anderson World. Inc.). Anderson World.
Kiemel, Ann. I'm Running to Win. 1980. 7.95 (ISBN 0-8423-1736-8). Tyndale.
Martin, David E. & Gynn, Roger W. The Marathon Footrace: Performers & Performances. (Illus.). 504p. 1979. 35.50 (ISBN 0-398-03883-X). C C Thomas.
Milvy, Paul, ed. Long Distance Runner: A Definitive Study. 1981. pap. 9.95 (ISBN 0-89396-048-9). Urizen Bks.
--The Marathon: Physiological, Medical, Epidemiological, & Psycological Studies, Vol. 301. (Annals of the New York Academy of Sciences). 1090p. 1977. 75.00x (ISBN 0-89072-047-9). NY Acad Sci.
Nentl, Jerolyn. Marathon Running. Schroeder, Howard, ed. LC 79-27799. (Funseekers Ser.). (Illus.). (gr. 3-5). 1980. lib. bdg. 6.95 (ISBN 0-89686-074-4); pap. 3.25 (ISBN 0-89686-078-7). Crestwood Hse.
Osler, Tom & Dodd, Ed. Ultramarathoning: The Next Challenge. LC 78-68612. (Illus.). 299p. 1980. 14.95 (ISBN 0-89037-169-5). Anderson World.

Osmun, Mark. The Honolulu Marathan. 1979. 12.95 (ISBN 0-397-01322-1). Har-Row.

Rodgers, Bill. One for the Road: The Marathon & Me. 1981. 10.95 (ISBN 0-671-25087-6). S&S.

Rodgers, Bill & Concannon, Joe. Marathoning. 1980. 11.95 (ISBN 0-671-25087-6). S&S.

Schreiber, Michael. Training to Run the Perfect Marathon. LC 80-82638. (Illus.). 181p. (Orig.). 1980. pap. 7.50 (ISBN 0-912528-19-2). John Muir.

Shapiro, Jim. On the Road: The Marathon. (Illus.). 1978. 10.00 (ISBN 0-517-53443-6). Crown.

--Ultramarathon. 1980. pap. 5.95 (ISBN 0-553-01275-4). Bantam.

Sullivan, George. Marathon: The Longest Race. LC 80-6776. (Illus.). (gr. 5-8). 1980. PLB 9.95 (ISBN 0-664-32671-4). Westminster.

MARAVI (AFRICAN TRIBE)

see Chewa (African Tribe)

MARAVICH, PETE, 1948-

Armstrong, Robert. Pete Maravich. (Sports Superstars Ser.). (Illus.). (gr. 3-9). 1978. PLB 5.95 (ISBN 0-87191-669-X); pap. 2.95 (ISBN 0-89812-183-3). Creative Ed.

Saladino, Tom. Pistol Pete Maravich: The Louisiana Purchase. LC 74-15507. 1974. 5.95 (ISBN 0-87397-056-X). Strode.

MARBLE, MANTON, 1834-1917

McJimsey, George T. Genteel Partisan: Manton Marble, 1834-1917. (Illus.). 1971. 10.75x (ISBN 0-8138-1105-8). Iowa St U Pr.

MARBLE

Baumann, Paul. Collecting Antique Marbles. softbound 8.95 (ISBN 0-87069-017-5). Wallace-Homestead.

Rinne, David. The Conservation of Ancient Marble. (J. Paul Getty Museum Publications). (Orig.). 1976. pap. 2.95x (ISBN 0-89236-003-8, Pub. by J. P. Getty Mus). Hennessey.

Torres, Louis. Tuckahoe Marble: The Rise & Fall of an Industry in Eastchester, N. Y., 1822-1930. LC 76-26126. (Illus.). 1976. pap. 6.95 (ISBN 0-916346-21-8). Harbor Hill Bks.

MARBLE-STAINING

see Stains and Staining

MARBLE CUTTERS

see Stone-Cutters

MARBLEHEAD, MASSACHUSETTS-DESCRIPTION-VIEWS

Chamberlain, Samuel. Old Marblehead: A Camera Impression. rev. ed. (Illus.). 96p. 1975. 6.95 (ISBN 0-8038-5378-5). Hastings.

MARBLES (GAME)

Ferretti, Fred. The Great American Marble Book. LC 74-156778. (Illus.). 128p. 1973. pap. 2.95 (ISBN 0-911104-27-5). Workman Pub.

MARBURG-POLITICS AND GOVERNMENT

Gimbel, John. A German Community Under American Occupation. 1961. 15.00x (ISBN 0-8047-0061-3). Stanford U Pr.

MARC, FRANZ, 1880-1916

Levine, Frederick S. The Apocalyptic Vision: The Art of Franz Marc As German Expressionism. LC 78-4736. (Icon Editions). (Illus.). 1979. 16.95 (ISBN 0-06-435275-7, HarpT). Har-Row.

MARC PROJECT

see Marc System

MARC SYSTEM

Bibliography, Machine-Readable Cataloguing & the ESTC. 1981. pap. 36.00x (ISBN 0-904654-17-6, Pub. by Brit Lib England). State Mutual Bk.

Clinic on Library Applications of Data Processing, Proceedings, 1975. The Use of Computers in Literature Searching & Related Reference Activities in Libraries. Lancaster, F. W., ed. LC 76-1790. 1976. 8.00 (ISBN 0-87845-043-2). U of Ill Lib Info Sci.

Gore, Daniel, et al, eds. Requiem for the Card Catalog: Management Issues in Automated Cataloging. LC 78-7129. (New Directions in Librarianship: No. 2). 1979. lib. bdg. 18.95 (ISBN 0-313-20608-2, GMI/). Greenwood.

Jeffreys, A. E. & Wilson, T. D., eds. U.K. Marc Project. 1970. pap. 10.50 (ISBN 0-85362-105-5, Oriel). Routledge & Kegan.

O A S General Secretariat. Marcal: Manual Para la Automatizacion De las Reglas Catalograficas Para America Latina. (Manuales Del Bibliotecario: No. 9). 131p. (Span.). 1980. pap. text ed. 15.00 (ISBN 0-8270-1280-2). OAS.

Williams, Martha E. & Rouse, Sandra H., eds. Computer-Readable Bibliographic Data Bases: A Directory & Data Sourcebook. LC 76-46249. 1976. 68.00 (ISBN 0-87715-114-8). Am Soc Info Sci.

MARCANTONIO, VITO, 1902-

Schaffer, Alan L. Vito Marcantonio, Radical in Congress. LC 66-29201. (Men & Movements Ser.). 1966. 12.95x (ISBN 0-8156-0053-4). Syracuse U Pr.

MARCEAU, MARCEL

Martin, Ben. Marcel Marceau: Master of Mime. LC 77-13090. (Illus.). 1978. 12.95 (ISBN 0-448-22680-4). Paddington.

MARCEL, GABRIEL, 1887-

Cain, Seymour. Gabriel Marcel. LC 79-50156. 1979. pap. 3.95 (ISBN 0-89526-905-8). Regnery-Gateway.

Gallagher, Kenneth T. Philosophy of Gabriel Marcel. rev. ed. LC 62-15666. 1975. pap. 8.00 (ISBN 0-8232-0471-5). Fordham.

Lapointe, Francois H. & Lapointe, Clarie C. Gabriel Marcel & His Critics: An International Bibliography (1935-1976) LC 76-24736. (Reference Library of the Humanities Ser.: Vol. 57). 1977. lib. bdg. 32.00 (ISBN 0-8240-9941-9). Garland Pub.

Lazaron, Hilda. Gabriel Marcel the Dramatist. 1978. text ed. 20.75x (ISBN 0-901072-77-X). Humanities.

McCown, Joe. Availability: Gabriel Marcel & the Phenomenology of Human Openness. LC 77-22358. (American Academy of Religion. Studies in Religion: No. 14). 1978. pap. 7.50 (ISBN 0-89130-144-5, 010014). Scholars Pr Ca.

MARCELLO, BENEDETTO, 1686-1739

Fruchtman, C. S. Checklist of Vocal Chamber Works by Benedetto Marcello. (Detroit Studies in Music Bibliography Ser.: No. 10). 1967. pap. 2.00 (ISBN 0-911772-30-8). Info Coord.

MARCH, FREDRIC, 1897-

Quirk, Lawrence J. Films of Fredric March. (Illus.). 1971. 9.95 (ISBN 0-8065-0259-2); pap. 6.95 (ISBN 0-8065-0413-7). Citadel Pr.

MARCH, PEYTON CONWAY, 1864-1955

Coffman, Edward M. Hilt of the Sword: The Career of Peyton C. March. (Illus.). 360p. 1966. 25.00 (ISBN 0-299-03910-2). U of Wis Pr.

MARCH ON WASHINGTON MOVEMENT

Garfinkel, Herbert. When Negroes March. LC 69-15522. (Studies in American Negro Life Ser). 1969. pap. 3.25x (ISBN 0-689-70078-4, NL13). Atheneum.

MARCHING

see Drill and Minor Tactics

MARCHING BANDS

see Bands (Music)

MARCION, OF SINOPE, 2ND CENTURY

Blackman, Edwin C. Marcion & His Influence. LC 77-84695. Repr. of 1948 ed. 18.50 (ISBN 0-404-16103-0). AMS Pr.

Knox, John. Marcion & the New Testament. LC 78-63168. (Heresies of the Early Christian & Medieval Era: Second Ser.). Repr. of 1942 ed. 21.50 (ISBN 0-404-16183-9). AMS Pr.

Wilson, Robert S. Marcion. LC 78-63176. (Heresies of the Early Christian & Medieval Era: Second Ser.). Repr. of 1933 ed. 23.00 (ISBN 0-404-16194-4). AMS Pr.

MARCO DA NIZZA, FATHER, ca. 1510-ca. 1570

Marco Da Nizza, tr. The Journey of Fray Marcos de Niza, by Cleve Hallenbeck. LC 73-11861. (Illus.). 115p. 1973. Repr. of 1949 ed. lib. bdg. 15.00 (ISBN 0-8371-7091-5, MAJO). Greenwood.

MARCONI, GUGLIELMO, MARCHESE, 1874-1937

Dunlap, Orrin E., Jr. Marconi: The Man & His Wireless. rev. ed. LC 72-161142. (History of Broadcasting: Radio to Television Ser). 1971. Repr. of 1937 ed. 24.00 (ISBN 0-405-03563-2). Arno.

Vyvyan, R. N. Marconi & Wireless. 1975. Repr. of 1933 ed. 12.50x (ISBN 0-8464-0606-3). Beekman Pubs.

MARCOS, FERDINAND EDRALIN, PRES. PHILIPPINE REPUBLIC, 1917-

Rosenberg, David A., ed. Marcos & Martial Law in the Philippines. LC 78-15145. 1979. 22.50x (ISBN 0-8014-1195-5). Cornell U Pr.

MARCUS, DAVID, 1901-1948

Berkman, Ted. Cast a Giant Shadow: The Story of Mickey Marcus, a Soldier for All Humanity. LC 67-16184. (Covenant Ser). (gr. 6-10). 1967. Repr. of 1962 ed. 3.50 (ISBN 0-8276-0034-8, 269). Jewish Pubn.

MARCUS, STANLEY, 1905-

Marcus, Stanley. Minding the Store. LC 74-10833. (Illus.). 1974. 10.95 (ISBN 0-316-54598-8). Little.

MARCUS AURELIUS

see Aurelius Antoninus, Marcus, Emperor of Rome, 121-180

MARCUSE, HERBERT, 1898-

Fry, John. Marcuse-Dilemma & Liberation: A Critical Analysis. 184p. 1974. pap. text ed. 10.00x (ISBN 0-391-00872-2). Humanities.

Lipshires, Sudney. Marcuse's Dilemma: The Case for a Non-Repressive Civilization. LC 73-82377. 188p. 1974. pap. text ed. 8.95 (ISBN 0-87073-677-9). Schenkman.

MacIntyre, Alasdair. Herbert Marcuse: An Exposition & a Polemic. Kermode, Frank, ed. LC 72-104145. (Modern Masters Ser). 1970. 4.95 (ISBN 0-670-36869-5). Viking Pr.

Mitchell, Arthur. Monarch Notes on Herbert Marcuse's Major Works. 1975. pap. 1.50 (ISBN 0-671-00945-1). Monarch Pr.

Schoolman, Morton. The Imaginary Witness: The Critical Theory of Herbert Marcuse. LC 80-640. 1980. 19.95 (ISBN 0-02-928040-0). Free Pr.

Steuernagel, Gertrude A. Political Philosophy As Therapy: Marcuse Reconsidered. LC 77-94747. (Contributions in Political Science: No. 11). 1979. lib. bdg. 15.95 (ISBN 0-313-20315-6, SPP/). Greenwood.

Woddis, Jack. New Theories of Revolution: A Commentary on the Views of Frantz Fanon, Regis Debray & Herbert Marcuse. LC 75-85923. 415p. 1972. 10.00 (ISBN 0-7178-0350-3); pap. 4.00 (ISBN 0-7178-0366-X). Intl Pub Co.

MARCY, WILLIAM LEARNED, 1786-1857

Spencer, Ivor D. Victor & the Spoils: A Life of William L. Marcy. LC 59-6898. (Illus.). 450p. 1959. text ed. 20.00x (ISBN 0-87057-056-0, Pub. by Brown U Pr). U Pr of New Eng.

MARENZIO, LUCA, 1553-1599

Chater, James. Luca Marenzio & the Italian Madrigal Fifteen Seventy-Seven to Fifteen Ninety-Three, 2 vols. Fortune, Nigel, ed. (British Studies in Musicology). 1981. Set. price not set (ISBN 0-8357-1242-7, Pub. by UMI Res Pr). Vol. 1 (ISBN 0-8357-1255-9). Vol. 2 (ISBN 0-8357-1256-7). Univ Microfilms.

Marenzio, Luca. Madrigali a Quatto Cinque E Sei Voc, Libro Primo 1588: Luca Marenzio, the Secular Works, No. 7. Ledbetter, Steven, ed. xxvi, 167p. 1977. pap. 25.00 (ISBN 0-8450-7107-6). Broude.

--Il Settimo Libro de'madrigali a Cinque Voci (1595) Luca Marenzio, the Secular Works, 14. Myers, Patricia, ed. xxxv, 224p. 1980. 35.00x (ISBN 0-8450-7114-9). Broude.

MARGARET, PRINCESS OF GREAT BRITAIN, 1930-

Brough, James. Margaret: The Tragic Princess. 1979. pap. 2.25 (ISBN 0-380-44206-X, 44206). Avon.

Frischauer, Willi. Margaret. (Illus.). 224p. 1978. 12.95 (ISBN 0-7181-1611-9, Pub. by Michael Joseph). Merrimack Bk Serv.

Marguerite D'Angouleme. Marguerites De la Marguerite Des Princesses: Queen of Navarre, 2 vols. xxv, 884p. 1970. Repr. of 1547 ed. Set. 38.50 (ISBN 0-384-35353-3). Johnson Repr.

MARGARET, SAINT, QUEEN OF SCOTLAND, d. 1093-JUVENILE LITERATURE

Johnson, Jan. Margaret, the Good Queen: A Story About Queen Margaret of Scotland. (Stories About Christian Heroes Ser). (gr. 1-5). 1977. pap. 1.95 (ISBN 0-03-022116-1). Winston Pr.

MARGARET MARY ALACOQUE, SAINT, 1647-1690

see Alacoque, Marguerite Marie, Saint, 1647-1690

MARGARETHA, OF AUSTRIA, REGENT OF THE NETHERLANDS, 1480-1530

Picker, Martin. The Chanson Albums of Marguerite of Austria. 1965. 62.50x (ISBN 0-520-01009-4). U of Cal Pr.

MARGARINE

see Oleomargarine

MARGARITA ISLAND

Dauxion-Lavaysse, Jean F. Statistical, Commercial & Political Description of Venezuela, Trinidad, Margarita, & Tobago. LC 70-97363. Repr. of 1820 ed. 21.50x (ISBN 0-8371-2445-X, Pub. by Negro U Pr). Greenwood.

MARGI LANGUAGE

Hoffman, Carl. Grammar of the Margi Language. LC 63-23583. 1963. 13.25x (ISBN 0-8002-0749-1). Intl Pubns Serv.

MARGIL DE JESUS, ANTONIO, FATHER, 1657-1726

Habig, Marion A., ed. Nothingness Itself: Selected Writings of Ven Fr. Antonio Margil. Leutenegger, Benedict, tr. (Illus.). 280p. 1976. 8.95 (ISBN 0-8199-0595-X). Franciscan Herald.

MARGINAL UTILITY

Black, R. Collison, et al, eds. The Marginal Revolution in Economics: Interpretation & Evaluation. LC 72-91850. 375p. 1973. 16.75 (ISBN 0-8223-0278-0). Duke.

Dickinson, Henry D. Institutional Revenue. LC 66-21368. Repr. of 1932 ed. 15.00x (ISBN 0-678-00160-X). Kelley.

Dmitriev, V. K. & Nuti, D. M. Economic Essays on Value: Competition & Utility. LC 73-77176. (Illus.). 280p. 1974. 42.50 (ISBN 0-521-20253-1). Cambridge U Pr.

Frisch, Ragnar. New Methods of Measuring Marginal Utility. LC 78-15136. (Illus.). Repr. of 1932 ed. lib. bdg. 13.50x (ISBN 0-87991-863-2). Porcupine Pr.

Page, A. N. Utility Theory: Book of Readings. 454p. 1968. text ed. 15.00 (ISBN 0-471-65754-9, Pub. by Wiley); pap. text ed. 9.50 (ISBN 0-471-65755-7). Krieger.

MARGINALIA

see also Autographs; Manuscripts

MARGINALIST SCHOOL OF ECONOMICS

see Austrian School of Economists

MARGINS (SECURITY TRADING)

Zerden, Sheldon. Margin - Key to a Stock Market Fortune. LC 68-55428. 1969. pap. 2.00 (ISBN 0-87576-017-1). Pilot Bks.

MARGOLIUS, RUDOLF, 1913-1952

Kovaly, Heda & Kohak, Erazim. The Victors & the Vanquished. 320p. 1973. 8.95 (ISBN 0-8180-1603-5). Horizon.

MARGUERITE D'ANGOULEME, QUEEN OF NAVARRE, 1492-1549

Davis, Betty J. The Storytellers in Marguerite de Navarre's Heptameron. LC 77-93406. (Monographs: No. 9). 203p. (Orig.). 1978. pap. 9.50x (ISBN 0-917058-08-9). French Forum.

Freer, M. The Life of Marguerite D'angouleme, Queen of Navarre, 2 vols. 1976. lib. bdg. 250.00 (ISBN 0-8490-2166-9). Gordon Pr.

Gelernt, Jules. World of Many Loves: The "Heptameron" of Marguerite De Navarre. (Studies in Comparative Literature Ser.: No. 38). (Orig.). 1966. pap. 12.00x (ISBN 0-8078-7038-2). U of NC Pr.

Hartley, K. Bandello & the Heptmaron: Study in Comparative Literature. (Australian Humanities Research Council Monograph: No. 5). 1960. pap. 2.00x (ISBN 0-424-05460-4, Pub. by Sydney U Pr). Intl Schol Bk Serv.

Tetel, Marcel. Marguerite de Navarre's Heptameron: Themes, Language, & Structure. LC 72-88735. 214p. 1973. 12.75 (ISBN 0-8223-0279-9). Duke.

MARI LANGUAGE

see Cheremissian Language

MARIA DE JESUS DE AGREDA, MOTHER, 1602-1665

Thekla, Sr., ed. Mother Maria: Her Life in Letters. LC 79-63455. 1979. 12.95 (ISBN 0-8091-0286-2). Paulist Pr.

MARIA THERESA, EMPRESS OF AUSTRIA, 1717-1780

Bright, James F. Maria Theresa. facsimile ed. LC 71-154145. (Select Bibliographies Reprint Ser.). Repr. of 1897 ed. 16.00 (ISBN 0-8369-5761-X). Arno.

Gooch, G. P. Maria Theresa & Other Studies. 1965. Repr. of 1951 ed. 19.50 (ISBN 0-208-00019-4, Archon). Shoe String.

MARIANNE, WIFE OF HEROD 1ST-DRAMA

Hebbel, Friedrich. Herod & Mariamne. Curts, Paul H., tr. LC 51-895. (North Carolina. University. Studies in the Germanic Languages & Literatures: No. 3). Repr. of 1950 ed. 18.50 (ISBN 0-404-50903-7). AMS Pr.

Valency, Maurice J. Tragedies of Herod & Mariamne. LC 70-8450. Repr. of 1940 ed. 19.50 (ISBN 0-404-06750-6). AMS Pr.

MARIATEQUI, JOSE CARLOS, 1894-1930

Baines, John M. Revolution in Peru: Mariategui & the Myth. LC 72-148690. 1972. 13.75x (ISBN 0-8173-4721-6). U of Ala Pr.

Chavarria, Jesus. Jose Carlos Mariategui & the Rise of Modern Peru, 1890-1930. LC 78-21426. 1979. 14.95 (ISBN 0-8263-0507-5). U of NM Pr.

MARICOPA INDIANS

see Indians of North America-Southwest, New

MARIE ANTOINETTE, CONSORT OF LOUIS 16TH, KING OF FRANCE, 1755-1793

Asquith, Annunziata. Marie Antoinette. LC 76-5195. (Illus.). (YA) (gr. 10 up). 1976. 13.95 (ISBN 0-8008-5119-6). Taplinger.

Belloc, Hilaire. Marie Antoinette. facsimile ed. LC 70-37871. (Select Bibliographies Reprint Ser). Repr. of 1909 ed. 34.00 (ISBN 0-8369-6708-9). Arno.

Gooch, G. P. Maria Theresa & Other Studies. 1965. Repr. of 1951 ed. 19.50 (ISBN 0-208-00019-4, Archon). Shoe String.

Gosselin, Louis L. Flight of Marie Antoinette. LC 73-168160. (Illus.). Repr. of 1906 ed. 27.50 (ISBN 0-404-07128-7). AMS Pr.

Gower, Ronald C. Last Days of Marie Antoinette: An Historical Sketch. LC 74-168163. Repr. of 1886 ed. 15.00 (ISBN 0-404-07129-5). AMS Pr.

MARIE ANTOINETTE, CONSORT OF LOUIS 16TH, KING OF FRANCE, 1755-1793-FICTION

Holt, Victoria. Queen's Confession: A Biography of Marie Antoinette. LC 68-10586. 1968. 8.95 (ISBN 0-385-08276-2). Doubleday.

MARIE DE FRANCE, 12TH CENTURY

Donovan, Mortimer J. Breton Lay: A Guide to Varieties. 1968. 9.95x (ISBN 0-268-00024-7). U of Notre Dame Pr.

Knapton, Antoinette. Mythe et Psychologie Chez Marie de France. (Studies in the Romance Languages & Literatures: No. 142). 1976. pap. 9.95x (ISBN 0-8078-9142-8). U of NC Pr.

Le Mee, Katherine W. A Metrical Study of Five Lais of Marie De France. (De Proprietatibus Litterarum, Series Practica: No. 85). 1978. pap. text ed. 34.50x (ISBN 0-686-27029-0). Mouton.

Marie De France. French Mediaeval Romances from the Lays of Marie De France. Mason, Eugene, tr. from Fr. LC 75-41188. Repr. of 1924 ed. 17.00 (ISBN 0-404-14571-X). AMS Pr.

Rothschild, Judith. Narrative Technique in the Lais of Marie de France: Themes & Variations. (Studies in the Romance Languages & Literature: No. 139). 1974. pap. 13.50 (ISBN 0-8078-9139-8). U of NC Pr.

MARIE DE L'INCARNATION, MOTHER, 1599-1672

L'Heureux, Mother Aloysius G. Mystical Vocabulary of Venerable Mere Marie De L'Incarnation & Its Problems. LC 72-94190. (Catholic University of America Studies in Romance Languages & Literatures Ser: No. 53). (Fr). Repr. of 1956 ed. 18.75 (ISBN 0-404-50353-5). AMS Pr.

Oury, Dom G. Marie De l'Incarnation, 2 vols. 1973. Set. 17.50x (ISBN 2-7637-6622-6, Pub. by Laval). Intl Schol Bk Serv.

Repplier, Agnes. Mere Marie of the Ursulines: A Study in Adventure. 1979. Repr. of 1931 ed. lib. bdg. 15.00 (ISBN 0-8495-4606-0). Arden Lib.

MARIE DE MEDICIS, CONSORT OF HENRY 4TH, KING OF FRANCE, 1573-1642

Batiffol, Louis. Marie De Medicis & the French Court in the Seventeenth Century. Davis, H. W., ed. King, Mary, tr. from Fr. LC 72-137368. (Select Bibliographies Reprint Ser.). 1972. Repr. of 1908 ed. 17.00 (ISBN 0-8369-5569-2). Arno.

MARIES COUNTY, MISSOURI

King, Everett M. History of Maries County, Missouri. rev. ed. (Illus.). 1967. 12.50 (ISBN 0-911208-05-4). Ramfre.

MARIHUANA

Aafen, Brent. Marijuana. 1980. 3.50 (ISBN 0-89486-073-9). Hazelden.

Abel, Ernest L. Marihuana: The First Twelve Thousand Years. 300p. 1980. 17.95 (ISBN 0-306-40496-6, Plenum Pr). Plenum Pub.

Abel, Ernest L., compiled by. A Comprehensive Guide to the Cannabis Literature. LC 78-20014. 1979. lib. bdg. 37.50 (ISBN 0-313-20721-6, ACG/). Greenwood.

Abel, Ernest L., ed. The Scientific Study of Marihuana. LC 76-4508. 288p. 1976. 20.95x (ISBN 0-88229-144-0). Nelson-Hall.

Abel, Ernest L., et al. Behavioral & Social Effects of Marijuana. (Illus.). 220p. 1973. text ed. 26.50x (ISBN 0-8422-7093-0). Irvington.

Analysis of Drugs & Metabolites by Gas Chromatography - Mass Spectometry: Natural, Pyrolytic & Metabolic Products of Tobacco & Marijuana, Vol. 7. 1980. 69.50 (ISBN 0-8247-6861-2). Dekker.

Anderson, Patrick. High in America: The True Story Behind NORML & the Politics of Marijuana. LC 80-51772. 360p. 1981. 13.95 (ISBN 0-670-11990-3). Viking Pr.

Auld, John. Marijuana Use a Social Control. 1981. write for info. (ISBN 0-12-068280-X). Acad Pr.

Barber, Theodore X. LSD, Marijuana, Yoga, & Hypnosis. LC 73-115935. 1970. 24.95x (ISBN 0-202-25004-0). Aldine Pub.

Bauman, Carl E. Predicting Adolescent Drug Use: Utility Structure & Marijuana. 192p. 1980. 22.95 (ISBN 0-03-050636-0). Praeger.

Berke, Joseph & Hernton, Calvin C. The Cannabis Experience: An Interpretative Study of the Effects of Marijuana & Hashish. 288p. 1974. text ed. 17.00x (ISBN 0-7206-0073-1). Humanities.

Bonnie, Richard J. Marijuana Use & Criminal Sanctions: Essays on the Theory & Practice of Law Reform. 264p. 1980. 20.00 (ISBN 0-87215-244-8). Michie-Bobbs.

Bonnie, Richard J. & Whitebread, Charles H. The Marihuana Conviction: A History of Marihuana Prohibition in the United States. LC 73-89907. 395p. 1974. 17.50x (ISBN 0-8139-0417-X). U Pr of Va.

Braude, Monique C. & Szara, Stephen, eds. Pharmacology of Marihuana, 2 vols. LC 75-14562. (National Institute on Drug Abuse Monograph). 901p. 1976. Set. 68.50 (ISBN 0-89004-067-2). Raven.

Carter, William E., ed. Cannabis in Costa Rica: A Study of Chronic Marihuana Use. LC 80-14726. (Illus.). 1980. text ed. 17.50x (ISBN 0-89727-008-8). Inst Study Human.

Clarke, Robert C. Marijuana Botany. LC 81-2478. (Illus.). 220p. 1981. pap. 7.95 (ISBN 0-915904-45-4). And-or Pr.

Cohen, Sidney & Stillman, Richard C., eds. The Therapeutic Potential of Marihuana. LC 76-17106. 515p. 1976. 29.50 (ISBN 0-306-30955-6, Plenum Pr). Plenum Pub.

Croes, Martin & McNicoll, Andre. Marijuana Reappraised: Two Personal Accounts. LC 77-15695. 28p. 1977. pap. 1.00 (ISBN 0-913098-08-6). Myrin Institute.

Danaceau, Paul. Pot Luck in Texas: Changing a Marijuana Law. LC 74-20154. (Special Studies Ser). 1974. 1.25 (ISBN 0-686-09381-X). Drug Abuse.

Daniels, Patrick. How to Grow Marijuana Hydroponically. (Illus.). 1978. perfect bdg. 5.95 (ISBN 0-686-25126-1). Pacific Pipeline.

Dennis, Paul & Barry, Carolyn. The Marijuana Catalogue. LC 77-93132. (Orig.). 1978. pap. 1.95 (ISBN 0-87216-457-8). Playboy Pbks.

Dews, Peter B., et al. Marijuana: Biochemical, Physiological, & Pathological Effects. (Illus.). 220p. 1973. text ed. 32.50x (ISBN 0-8422-7094-9). Irvington.

Drake, Bill. Cultivators Handbook of Marijuana. rev ed. (Illus.). 224p. (Orig.). pap. 8.95 (ISBN 0-914728-31-8). Wingbow Pr.

Dreher, Melanie C. Working Men & Ganja: Marihuana Use in Rural Jamaica. (Illus.). 256p. 1981. text ed. 18.50x (ISBN 0-89727-025-8). Inst Study Human.

Faber, Stuart J. If the Cops Come, Eat This Book. rev. ed. 100p. 1975. pap. 2.95 (ISBN 0-89074-014-3). Good Life.

--Marijuana: If the Cops Come, Eat This Book. new ed. 70p. (Orig.). 1974. pap. 1.95 (ISBN 0-89074-003-8). Good Life.

Frank, Mel & Rosenthal, Ed. The Indoor-Outdoor Highest Quality Marijuana Grower's Guide. rev. ed. 1981. pap. 4.95 (ISBN 0-915904-59-4). And-or Pr.

--The Indoor-Outdoor Highest Quality Marijuana Grower's Guide. LC 78-54344. 1974. pap. 4.95 (ISBN 0-915904-05-5). And-or Pr.

--Marijuana Grower's Guide. LC 77-82452. 1978. deluxe ed. 10.95 (ISBN 0-915904-26-8); spiral bdg. 14.95 (ISBN 0-686-77226-1). And-or Pr.

Frazier, J. The Marijuana Farmers: Hemp Cults & Cultures. (Illus.). 1973. pap. 4.95 (ISBN 0-914304-00-3). Solar Age Pr.

Gamage, J. R. & Zerkin, E. L. A Comprehensive Guide to the English-Language Literature on Cannabis (Marihuana) 1969. pap. 10.00x (ISBN 0-932204-00-7). Stash.

Goldman, Albert. Grass Roots: Marijuana in America Today. LC 77-11806. (Illus.). 1979. 12.95 (ISBN 0-06-011554-8, HarpT). Har-Row.

Grinspoon, Lester. Marihuana Reconsidered. rev. ed. LC 77-76767. 1977. 20.00x (ISBN 0-674-54833-7); pap. 8.95 (ISBN 0-674-54834-5). Harvard U Pr.

Grupp, Stanley. Marijuana. LC 72-157698. 1971. pap. text ed. 5.95x (ISBN 0-675-09834-3). Merrill.

Hart, Roy H. Bitter Grass: The Cruel Truth About Marijuana. LC 79-91582. (Illus.). 1980. pap. 3.95 (ISBN 0-935688-00-5). Psychoneurologia.

Hellman, Arthur D. Laws Against Marijuana: The Price We Pay. LC 74-34150. 224p. 1975. 14.50 (ISBN 0-252-00438-8). U of Ill Pr.

International Congress of Pharmacology, 7th, Reims, 1978. Satellite Symposium. Marihuana - Biological Effects, Analysis, Metabolism, Cellular Responses, Reproduction & Brain: Proceedings. Nahas, Gabriel G. & Paton, William D., eds. (Illus.). 1979. text ed. 80.00 (ISBN 0-08-023759-2). Pergamon.

Isyurhash, Mahash & Rusoff, Garry. The Gourmet Guide to Grass. (Illus.). 224p. (Orig.). 1974. pap. 1.95 (ISBN 0-523-40324-0). Pinnacle Bks.

Lall, Bernard & Lall, Geeta. Marijuana-Friend or Foe? LC 78-23656. (Better Living Ser.). 1979. pap. 0.95 (ISBN 0-8127-0222-0). Review & Herald.

Lewin, Brenda. The New Truth About Pot. 1977. pap. 1.75 (ISBN 0-89041-167-0, 3167). Major Bks.

Lewis, M. F., ed. Current Research in Marijuana. 1972. 24.00 (ISBN 0-12-447050-5). Acad Pr.

Margolis, Jack S. & Clorfene, Richard. A Child's Garden of Grass. (Illus.). 1978. pap. 2.25 (ISBN 0-345-29530-7). Ballantine.

Mechoulam, Raphael, ed. Marijuana: Chemistry, Pharmacology, Metabolism & Clinical Effects. 1973. 56.00 (ISBN 0-12-487450-9). Acad Pr.

Mendelson, Jack H., et al, eds. The Use of Marihuana: A Psychological & Physiological Inquiry. LC 74-17169. (Illus.). 210p. 1974. 27.50 (ISBN 0-306-30805-3, Plenum Pr). Plenum Pub.

Mercer, Frank L. Thinking About Marijuana. 1977. pap. 0.75 (ISBN 0-89422-004-7). Clarion.

Merlin, Mark D. Man & Marijuana: Some Aspects of Their Relationship. LC 73-150239. (Illus.). 120p. 1973. pap. 3.95 (ISBN 0-498-04095-X). A S Barnes.

Mikuriya, Tod H., ed. Marijuana: Medical Papers, 1839-1972. LC 72-87736. 23.50 (ISBN 0-9600704-1-9); pap. 12.00 (ISBN 0-685-48562-5). Medi-Comp.

Miller, L. L. Marijuana: Effects on Human Behavior. 1974. 56.00 (ISBN 0-12-497050-8). Acad Pr.

--Marijuana: Effects on Human Behavior. 1974. 56.00 (ISBN 0-12-497050-8). Acad Pr.

Moller, Richard. Marijuana: Your Legal Rights. (Illus.). 256p. 1981. 11.95 (ISBN 0-201-04777-2); pap. 6.95 (ISBN 0-201-04769-1). A-W.

Mountain Girl. The Primo Plant: Growing Sinsemilla Marijuana. 1977. pap. 4.50 (ISBN 0-915070-04-9, Co-Pub. by Wingbow Pr). Leaves of Grass.

Nahas, G. G., ed. Marihuana: Chemistry, Biochemistry, & Cellular Efffects. 400p. 26.40 (ISBN 0-387-07554-2). Springer-Verlag.

Nahas, Gabriel G. Keep off the Grass: A Scientific Enquiry into the Biological Effects of Marijuana. (Illus.). 1979. 16.50 (ISBN 0-08-023779-7); pap. 6.95 (ISBN 0-08-023780-0). Pergamon.

--Marijuana-Deceptive Weed. rev. ed. LC 72-76743. 352p. 1975. 19.00 (ISBN 0-911216-39-1). Raven.

Novak, William. High Culture: Marijuana in the Lives of Americans. LC 79-2229. 1980. 12.95 (ISBN 0-394-50395-3); pap. 6.95 (ISBN 0-394-73828-4). Knopf.

Oakum, Peter. Growing Marijuana in New England. rev. ed. (Illus.). 1977. pap. 2.95 (ISBN 0-89166-008-9). Cobblesmith.

Ochsner, et al. Tobacco & Marijuana. 1976. perfect bdg. 6.95 (ISBN 0-88252-048-2). Paladin Hse.

Pascal, Harold J. The Marijuana Maze. LC 76-21591. (Illus., Orig.). 1977. pap. 1.75 (ISBN 0-8189-1138-7, Pub. by Alba Bks). Alba.

Paton, W. D. & Crown, June, eds. Cannabis & Its Derivatives: Pharmacology & Experimental Psychology. (Illus.). 200p. 1972. text ed. 18.00x (ISBN 0-19-261115-1). Oxford U Pr.

Peck, David G. Belief, Deterrence & Marijuana Use. LC 79-65263. 125p. 1980. 9.00 (ISBN 0-86548-018-4). Century Twenty One.

Peters, Jackson. Bong! How to Make & Use Waterpipes. (Illus.). 96p. (Orig.). 1980. pap. 2.95 (ISBN 0-935232-00-1). Deep River Pr.

Richardson, Jim & Woods, Arik. Sinsemilla: Marijuana Flowers. LC 77-365518. 1976. pap. 12.95 (ISBN 0-915904-23-3). And-or Pr.

Roffman, Roger. Marijuana As Medicine. (Illus.). 120p. 1981. 10.95 (ISBN 0-914842-71-4); pap. 5.95 (ISBN 0-914842-72-2). Madrona Pubs.

Rosevear, John. Pot-a Handbook of Marijuana. 2.25 (ISBN 0-8065-0204-5). Citadel Pr.

Rubin, Vera & Comitas, Lambros. Ganja in Jamaica. (New Babylon, Studies in the Social Sciences: No.26). 206p. 1975. text ed. 20.00x (ISBN 90-2797-731-3). Mouton.

Rubin, Vera, ed. Cannabis & Culture. (World Anthropology Ser.). (Illus.). 568p. 1975. 34.50 (ISBN 0-202-90005-3). Beresford Bk Serv.

Russell, G. K. Marihuana Today: A Compilation of Medical Findings for the Layman. 3rd, rev. ed. LC 77-79477. (Illus.). 80p. 1979. pap. 3.45 (ISBN 0-08-025509-4). Pergamon.

Russell, George K. Marihuana Today: A Compilation of Medical Findings for the Layman. LC 77-79477. (Illus.). 86p. 1980. pap. 3.00 (ISBN 0-913098-33-7). Myrin Institute.

Schmevelyn, Evelyn. Cooking with Marijuana. (Illus.). 1976. perfect bdg 4.95 (ISBN 0-686-25124-5). Pacific Pipeline.

Smith, David E., ed. New Social Drug: Cultural, Medical & Legal Perspectives on Marijuana. 1970. pap. 1.95 (ISBN 0-13-615757-2, Spec). P-H.

Smith, Malcolm E. The Real Marijuana Danger. 256p. 1981. 9.95 (ISBN 0-936066-02-4). Suffolk Hse.

Snyder, Solomon H. Uses of Marijuana. (Illus.). 1971. pap. 3.95x (ISBN 0-19-501576-2). Oxford U Pr.

Starks, Michael. Marijuana Potency. LC 77-82454. 1977. pap. 6.95 (ISBN 0-915904-27-6). And-or Pr.

Stevens & Perillo. Growing Marijuana for Home Medical Use. (Illus.). Date not set. perfect bdg. 5.95 (ISBN 0-686-26920-9). Pacific Pipeline.

Stevens, Murphy. Grow the Finest Marijuana Indoors. (Illus.). 1979. perfect bdg. 9.95 (ISBN 0-686-25125-3). Pacific Pipeline.

--How to Grow Marijuana Indoors Under Lights. rev. ed. (Illus.). 1977. perfect bdg. 4.95 (ISBN 0-686-25127-X). Pacific Pipeline.

--Indoor Marijuana Cultivation. (Illus.). 1977. perfect bdg. 3.95 (ISBN 0-686-25128-8). Pacific Pipeline.

Stwertka, Eve & Stwertka, Albert. Marijuana. (First Bks.). (Illus.). (gr. 4 up). 1979. PLB 6.90 s&l (ISBN 0-531-02944-1). Watts.

Tart, Charles T. On Being Stoned: A Psychological Study of Marijuana Intoxication. LC 79-153848. 1971. 7.95 (ISBN 0-8314-0027-7). Sci & Behavior.

Tobias, Ann. Pot -- What It Is, What It Does. LC 78-10817. (Greenwillow Read-Alone Bk.). (Illus.). 48p. (gr. 1-3). 1981. pap. 2.95 (ISBN 0-688-00463-6). Greenwillow.

--Pot--What It Is, What It Does. LC 78-10817. (Greenwillow Read-Alone Bks.). (Illus.). 48p. (gr. 3-4). 1979. 5.95 (ISBN 0-688-80200-1); PLB 5.71 (ISBN 0-688-84200-3). Greenwillow.

Vinson, Joseph A., ed. Cannabinoid Analysis in Physiological Fluids. LC 79-10934. (ACS Symposium Ser.: No. 98). 1979. 25.00 (ISBN 0-8412-0488-8). Am Chemical.

Vye, George & Grossman, Stewart. Cooking with Grass. LC 75-39089. (Illus.). 128p. (Orig.). 1976. pap. 3.95 (ISBN 0-8467-0151-0, Pub. by Two Continents). Hippocrene Bks.

Waller, Coy W., et al. Marihuana: An Annotated Bibliography. LC 76-20635. 1976. 14.95 (ISBN 0-02-699800-9). Macmillan Info.

Walton, Robert P. Marihuana, America's New Drug Problem: A Sociologic Question with Its Basic Explanation Dependent on Biologic & Medical Principles. LC 75-17248. (Social Problems & Social Policy Ser.). 1976. 14.00x (ISBN 0-405-07523-5). Arno.

Wilkerson, Don. Marijuana. (Spire Bks.). 128p. 1980. pap. 1.95 (ISBN 0-8007-8384-0). Revell.

MARII LANGUAGE

see Cheremissian Language

MARIIA, MOTHER, 1891-1945

Smith, T. Stratton. Rebel Nun. 1965. 6.95 (ISBN 0-87243-024-3). Templegate.

MARIJUANA

see Marihuana

MARIN, FRANCISCO DE PAULA, 1774?-1837

Gast, Ross H. & Conrad, Agnes C. Don Francisco De Paula Marin: A Biography with Letters & Journal. LC 77-188980. 300p. 1973. 10.95 (ISBN 0-8248-0220-9). U Pr of Hawaii.

MARIN, JOHN, 1872-1953

Helm, Mackinley. John Marin. LC 75-87484. (Library of American Art Ser.). (Illus.). 1970. Repr. of 1948 ed. lib. bdg. 29.50 (ISBN 0-306-71489-2). Da Capo.

McBride, Henry, et al. John Marin. LC 66-26650. (Museum of Modern Art Publications in Repr. Ser). Repr. of 1936 ed. 14.00 (ISBN 0-405-01520-8). Arno.

Reich, Sheldon, ed. John Marin Drawings, 1886-1951. LC 79-83660. (Illus.). 1969. 10.00 (ISBN 0-87480-015-3). U of Utah Pr.

MARINAS

see also Docks; Piers; Shore Protection

Adie, Donald W. Marinas: A Working Guide to Their Development & Design. 2nd ed. (Illus.). 1977. 50.00 (ISBN 0-89397-018-2). Nichols Pub.

Ecology of Small Boat Marinas. (Marine Technical Report: No. 5). 1973. pap. 1.00 (ISBN 0-938412-17-5). URI MAS.

Fire Protection Standard for Marinas & Boatyards. (Three Hundred Ser). 1969. pap. 2.00 (ISBN 0-685-58056-3, 303). Natl Fire Prot.

Head, Derek. Marinas: Harbor Design, Vol. 2. (Viewpoint Marina Ser.). (Illus.). 1976. pap. 9.50 (ISBN 0-7210-1022-9). Scholium Intl.

--Marinas: Water Recreation, Vol. 1. (Viewpoint Marina Ser.). (Illus.). 1974. pap. 10.50 (ISBN 0-685-82987-1). Scholium Intl.

--Residential Marinas & Yachting Amenities. (Marinas Ser.: No. 3). (Illus.). 84p. (Orig.). 1980. pap. text ed. 15.00 (ISBN 0-7210-1135-7, Pub. by C & CA London). Scholium Intl.

Operation of Marine Terminals. (Three Hundred Ser). 1967. pap. 2.00 (ISBN 0-685-58058-X, 307). Natl Fire Prot.

MARINDINESE LANGUAGE

Drabbe, P. Spraakkunst Van Het Marind. 1955. 23.00 (ISBN 0-384-12595-6). Johnson Repr.

MARINE ACCIDENTS

see also Ships-Fires and Fire Prevention; Shipwrecks

Rattray, Jeannette E. The Perils of the Port of New York: Maritime Disasters from Sandy Hook to Execution Rocks. LC 72-12441. 256p. 1973. 12.50 (ISBN 0-396-06790-5). Dodd.

MARINE AIDS

see Aids to Navigation

MARINE ALGAE

Abbott, Isabella A. & Dawson, E. Yale. How to Know the Seaweeds. 2nd ed. (Pictured Key Nature Ser.). 1978. Wire Coil. wire coil avail. (ISBN 0-697-04892-6); text ed. write for info. (ISBN 0-697-04895-0). Wm C Brown.

Abbott, Isabella A. & Hollenberg, George J. Marine Algae of California. LC 74-82774. (Illus.). 1976. 22.50x (ISBN 0-8047-0867-3). Stanford U Pr.

Chapman, V. J., ed. The Marine Algae of New Zealand: Phaeophyceae, Vol.2. 1961. pap. 20.00 (ISBN 3-7682-0077-9). Lubrecht & Cramer.

Dawes, Clinton J. Marine Algae of the West Coast of Florida. LC 73-22107. (Illus.). 272p. 1974. 15.00x (ISBN 0-87024-258-X). U of Miami Pr.

Dawson, E. Y. Marine Red Algae of Pacific Mexico: Ceramiales, Dasyaceae, Rhodomelaceae, Part 8. (Illus.). 1963. pap. 10.00 (ISBN 3-7682-0209-7). Lubrecht & Cramer.

Farlow, W. C. The Marine Algae of New England & Adjacent Coast. (Illus.). 1969. Repr. of 1881 ed. 50.00 (ISBN 3-7682-0582-7). Lubrecht & Cramer.

Funk, Georg. Die Algenvegetation Des Golfes Von Neapel. (Pubbl. d. Stazione Zool. di Napoli). (Illus., Ger.). Repr. of 1927 ed. lib. bdg. 90.00 (ISBN 3-87429-142-1). Lubrecht & Cramer.

Harvey, W. H. Nereis Australis, or Algae of the Southern Ocean: 1847-49. (Illus.). 1965. 80.00 (ISBN 3-7682-0261-5). Lubrecht & Cramer.

--Nereis Boreali-Americana: 1852-1858, 3 parts in 1. (Illus.). 1976. 125.00 (ISBN 3-7682-1063-4). Lubrecht & Cramer.
Hillson, Charles J. Seaweeds: A Color-Coded, Illustrated Guide to Common Marine Plants of the East Coast of the United States. LC 76-42192. (Keystone Books). 1977. lib. bdg. 10.00 (ISBN 0-271-01239-0); pap. 6.95 (ISBN 0-271-01247-1). Pa St U Pr.
Hoppe, ed. Marine Algae in Pharmaceutical Science. 1979. 107.00 (ISBN 3-11-007375-7). De Gruyter.
Humm, Harold J. The Marine Algae of Virginia. LC 78-16319. (Virginia Institute of Marine Science, Special Papers in Marine Science Ser.: No. 3). (Illus.). 1979. 13.95x (ISBN 0-8139-0701-2). U Pr of Va.
International Seaweed Symposium, 7th, Sappora, Japan, Aug. 1971. Proceedings. Science Council of Japan, ed. 607p. 1973. 53.95 (ISBN 0-470-77090-2). Halsted Pr.
Johnson, H. H. & Ferris, B. J. Tertiary & Pleistocene Coralline Algae from Lau, Fiji. 1950. pap. 6.00 (ISBN 0-527-02309-4). Kraus Repr.
Kapraun, Donald F. An Illustrated Guide to Benthic Marine Algae of Coastal North Carolina: I. Rhodophyta. LC 79-21566. (Illus.). viii, 206p. 1980. pap. 15.00x (ISBN 0-8078-4063-7). U of NC Pr.
Kingsbury, John M. Seaweeds of Cape Cod & the Islands. LC 69-15903. (Illus.). 1969. 12.50 (ISBN 0-85699-009-4). Chatham Pr.
Kjellman, F. R. The Algae of the Arctic Sea. (Illus.). 1972. 120.00 (ISBN 3-87429-015-8). Lubrecht & Cramer.
Lamb, I. Mackenzie & Zimmerman, Martin H. Benthic Marine Algae of the Antarctic Peninsula: Paper 3 in Biology of the Antarctic Seas V. Pawson, David L., ed. (Antarctic Research Ser: Vol. 23). 1977. pap. 30.75 (ISBN 0-87590-127-1). Am Geophysical.
Levring, Tore, et al. Marine Algae: A Survey of Research & Utilization. (Botanica Marina Handbks, Vol. 1). (Illus.). 421p. 1969. 82.24x (ISBN 3-11-005621-6). De Gruyter.
Mathieson, A. C. Morphological Studies of the Marine Brown Alga Taonia Lennebackerae Farlow Ex. J. Agardh L. (Illus.). 1966. pap. 4.00 (ISBN 3-7682-0439-1). Lubrecht & Cramer.
Mshigeni, K. Biology & Ecology of Benthic Marine Algae with Special Reference to Hypnea (Rhodophyta, Gigartinales: A Review of the Literature. (Bibliotheca Phycologica Ser.: No. 36). 1978. pap. 20.00x (ISBN 3-7682-1166-5). Lubrecht & Cramer.
Neal, M. C. Hawaiian Marine Algae. Repr. of 1930 ed. pap. 7.00 (ISBN 0-527-02173-3). Kraus Repr.
North, W. J., ed. Biology of the Giant Kelp Beds (Macrocystis) in California. 1971. 100.00 (ISBN 3-7682-5432-1). Lubrecht & Cramer.
Percival, Elizabeth & McDowell, Richard H. Chemistry & Enzymology of Marine Algal Polysaccharides. 1967. 32.00 (ISBN 0-12-550650-3). Acad Pr.
Setchell, W. A: & Gardener, N. L. The Marine Algae of the Pacific Coast of North America: 1919-29, 3parts in 1, Vol.1. (Bibl. Phyco.). 1967. 90.00 (ISBN 3-7682-0454-5). Lubrecht & Cramer.
Stephenson, W. A. Seaweed in Agriculture & Horticulture. 3rd ed. Bargyla & Rateaver, Gylver, eds. LC 74-12812. (Conservation Gardening & Farming Ser: Ser. C). 1974. pap. 7.00 (ISBN 0-9600698-3-6). Rateavers.
Taylor, W. R. The Marine Algae of Florida: With Special Reference to Dry Tortugas. (Bibl. Phyco.: Vol.2). 1967. Repr. of 1928 ed. 60.00 (ISBN 3-7682-0504-5). Lubrecht & Cramer.
Taylor, William R. Marine Algae of the Eastern Tropical & Sub-Tropical Coasts of the Americas. LC 59-9736. (Illus.). 1960. 30.00x (ISBN 0-472-08841-6). U of Mich Pr.
--Marine Algae of the Northeastern Coast of North America. 2nd rev. ed. LC 57-7103. (Illus.). 1957. 27.50x (ISBN 0-472-08840-8). U of Mich Pr.

MARINE AQUARIUMS

Axelrod, Herbert R. Breeding Aquarium Fishes, Bk. 2. 1971. 12.95 (ISBN 0-87666-007-3, H-941). TFH Pubns.
Axelrod, Herbert R. & Burgess, Lourdes. Breeding Aquarium Fishes, Bk. 3. 1973. 12.95 (ISBN 0-87666-025-1, H-946). TFH Pubns.
Axelrod, Herbert R. & Burgess, Warren. Saltwater Aquarium Fishes. 9.95 (ISBN 0-87666-138-X, H914). TFH Pubns.
Axelrod, Herbert R., et al. Exotic Marine Fishes. (Illus.). 608p. 1973. 15.00 (ISBN 0-87666-102-9, H938); looseleaf bdg. 20.00 (ISBN 0-87666-103-7, H-938L). Tfh Pubns.
Barker, Craig. Starting a Marine Aquarium. 1972. 2.95 (ISBN 0-87666-751-5, PS-305). TFH Pubns.
Burgess, Warren E. Marine Aquaria. (Illus.). 96p. text ed. 2.95 (ISBN 0-87666-533-4, KW-088). TFH Pubns.
Campbell, Gail. Salt-Water Tropical Fish in Your Home. LC 76-1175. (Illus.). 160p. (YA) 1976. 10.95 (ISBN 0-8069-3730-0); PLB 9.29 (ISBN 0-8069-3731-9). Sterling.
Emmens, Cliff W. The Marine Aquarium in Theory & Practice. (Illus.). 208p. 1975. 12.95 (ISBN 0-87666-446-X, PS-735). TFH Pubns.
Friese, U. Erich. Marine Invertebrates in the Home Aquarium. (Illus.). 240p. (Orig.). 1973. pap. 9.95 (ISBN 0-87666-105-3, PS-658). TFH Pubns.
Kingsford, Edward. Marine Aquarium Compatibility Guide. LC 78-25989. (Illus.). 1979. 8.95 (ISBN 0-684-16220-2, ScribT). Scribner.
Moe, Martin A., Jr. The Marine Aquarium Handbook: Beginner to Breeder. 200p. (Orig.). 1981. 15.95 (ISBN 0-939960-01-X); pap. 8.95 (ISBN 0-939960-02-8). Norns Pub Co.
O'Connell, R. F. The Marine Aquarium for the Home Aquarist. 1975. pap. 5.95 (ISBN 0-686-77058-7). Great Outdoors.
Ostermoeller, Wolfgang. Aquarium Science & Technique. 1973. pap. 5.95 (ISBN 0-87666-027-8, PS-308). TFH Pubns.
Reichenbach-Klinke, Heinz-Hermann. All About Marine Aquarium Fish Diseases. (Illus.). 1977. pap. 2.95 (ISBN 0-87666-467-2, PS-747). TFH Pubns.
Spotte, Stephen. Marine Aquarium Keeping: The Science, Animals & Art. LC 73-4425. (Illus.). 176p. 1973. 16.00 (ISBN 0-471-81759-7, Pub. by Wiley-Interscience). Wiley.
Steene, Roger C. Butterfly & Angelfishes of the World: Australia, Vol. 1. LC 78-17351. 144p. 1977. 27.00 (ISBN 0-471-04737-6, Pub. by Wiley-Interscience). Wiley.
Stevenson, Robert A. The Complete Book of Salt-Water Aquariums: How to Equip & Maintain Your Marine Aquarium & Understand Its Ecology. (Funk & W Bk.). 224p. 1974. 9.95 (ISBN 0-308-10090-5). T Y Crowell.
--The Complete Book of Saltwater Aquariums. LC 73-21528. (Funk & W Bk.). (Illus.). 1976. pap. 3.95 (ISBN 0-308-10232-0). T Y Crowell.
Straughan, Robert P. The Salt-Water Aquarium in the Home. 4th rev. ed. LC 73-22603. (Illus.). 384p. 1976. 17.50 (ISBN 0-498-01531-9). A S Barnes.
Straughan, Robert P. L. Keeping Live Corals & Invertebrates. LC 74-9311. (Illus.). 300p. 1975. 17.50 (ISBN 0-498-01635-8). A S Barnes.
Wickler, Wolfgang. Breeding Behavior of Aquarium Fishes. (Illus.). 1973. pap. 7.95 (ISBN 0-87666-029-4, PS-306). TFH Pubns.
--The Marine Aquarium. Vevers, Gwynne, tr. from Ger. (Illus.). 178p. (Orig.). 1973. pap. 6.95 (ISBN 0-87666-098-7, PS-695). TFH Pubns.

MARINE ARCHAEOLOGY
see Underwater Archaeology

MARINE ARCHITECTURE
see Naval Architecture; Ship-Building

MARINE BIOLOGY
see also Marine Aquariums; Marine Ecology; Marine Fauna; Marine Flora; Marine Microbiology; Marine Resources; Marine Sediments; Nets; Ocean Bottom; Photography, Submarine; Seashore Biology; Sedimentation and Deposition; Shells

Agassiz, Elizabeth & Agassiz, Alexander. Seaside Studies in Natural History: Marine Animals of Massachusetts Bay. LC 75-125726. (American Environmental Studies). (Illus.). 1970. Repr. of 1865 ed. 17.00 (ISBN 0-405-02651-X). Arno.
Andersen, Neil R. & Zahuranec, Bernard J., eds. Oceanic Sound Scattering Prediction. LC 77-3445. (Marine Science Ser.: Vol. 5). 859p. 1977. 65.00 (ISBN 0-306-35505-1, Plenum Pr). Plenum Pub.
Angel, Heather. The World of a Stream. (Illus.). 128p. 1976. 8.95 (ISBN 0-571-10450-9, Pub. by Faber & Faber). Merrimack Bk Serv.
Armour, Richard. Strange Monsters of the Sea. LC 78-11263. (Illus.). (gr. 5-9). 1979. 7.95 (ISBN 0-07-002294-1). McGraw.
Baiardi, John C. & Ruggieri, George D., eds. Aquatic Sciences. (Annals of the New York Academy of Sciences: Vol. 245). 70p. 1974. 15.00x (ISBN 0-89072-759-7). NY Acad Sci.
Barhes, Harold, ed. Proceedings of the Ninth European Marine Biology Symposium, Oban 1974. 1976. 55.00x (ISBN 0-900015-34-9). Taylor-Carlisle.
Barica, J. & Mur, L., eds. Hypertrophic Ecosystems. (Developments in Hydrobiology Ser.: No. 2). 330p. 1981. PLB 87.00 (ISBN 90-6193-752-3, Pub. by Junk Pubs. Netherlands). Kluwer Boston.
Barnes, Harold, ed. Oceanography & Marine Biology: An Annual Review, Vol. 15. 1977. 70.00 (ISBN 0-900015-39-X). Taylor-Carlisle.
--Oceanography & Marine Biology: An Annual Review, Vol. 16. 1978. 75.00 (ISBN 0-900015-44-6). Taylor-Carlisle.
--Oceanography & Marine Biology: Annual Review, Vol. 14. 1976. 70.00 (ISBN 0-900015-37-3). Taylor-Carlisle.
Barnes, John A. & Von Bodungen, Bodo. The Bermuda Marine Environment, Vol. II. (Bermuda Biological Station Special Pubn Ser.: No. 17). (Illus.). 1978. pap. 6.00 (ISBN 0-917642-17-1). Bermuda Bio.
Barnes, Margaret & Barnes, Harold, eds. Oceanography & Marine Biology: An Annual Review, Vol. 18. (Illus.). 528p. 1980. 84.00 (ISBN 0-08-025732-1). Pergamon.
Battaglia, Bruno & Beardmore, John A., eds. Marine Organisms: Genetics, Ecology, & Evolution. LC 78-9715. (NATO Conference Ser.: IV, Marine Science, Vol. 2). 767p. 1978. 49.50 (ISBN 0-306-40020-0, Plenum Pr). Plenum Pub.
The Bay Bib: Rhode Island Marine Bibliography, 2 vols. (Marine Technical Report: Nos 70 & 71). 5.00 ea.; keyword in context index 2.00 (ISBN 0-938412-02-7). URI MAS.
Berrill, N. J. Life of the Ocean. (Our Living World of Nature Ser). 1967. 9.95 (ISBN 0-07-005025-2, P&RB); by subscription 3.95 (ISBN 0-07-046007-8). McGraw.
Blaxter, J. H. S., et al, eds. Advances in Marine Biology, Vol. 17. LC 63-14040. (Serial Publication). 1980. 79.50 (ISBN 0-12-026117-0). Acad Pr.
Boehme, Eckart, ed. From the Law of the Sea Towards an Ocean Space Regime: Practical & Legal Implications of the Marine Revolution. 174p. 1972. pap. 25.00x (ISBN 3-7875-2119-4). Intl Pubns Serv.
Borgese, Elisabeth M. Drama of the Oceans. LC 74-16165. (Illus.). 300p. 1976. 25.00 (ISBN 0-8109-0337-7). Abrams.
Brusca, Gary J. & Brusca, Richard C. A Naturalist's Seashore Guide: Common Marine Life Along the Northern California Coast & Adjacent Shores. 215p. 1978. pap. 8.50x (ISBN 0-916422-12-7). Mad River.
Carson, Rachel. Under the Sea Wind: A Naturalist's Picture of Ocean Life. 1952. 15.95 (ISBN 0-19-500501-5). Oxford U Pr.
Cavanaugh, G. M., et al. Formulae & Methods. 1964. 6.00 (ISBN 0-685-52858-8). Marine Bio.
Coker, Robert E. This Great & Wide Sea: An Introduction to Oceanography & Marine Biology. (Illus.). pap. 4.95x (ISBN 0-06-130551-0, TB551, Torch). Har-Row.
Colin, Patrick I. Caribbean Reef Invertebrates & Plants. (Illus.). 1978. 20.00 (ISBN 0-87666-460-5, H-971). TFH Pubns.
Cousteau, Jacques. Guide to the Sea. LC 74-23072. (Ocean World of Jacques Cousteau Ser.: Vol. 20). (Illus.). 144p. 1975. 9.95 (ISBN 0-8109-0594-9). Abrams.
Cousteau, Jacques Y. Oasis in Space. new ed. LC 74-23053. (Ocean World of Jacques Cousteau: Vol. 1). (Illus.). 144p. 1972. 9.95 (ISBN 0-8109-0575-2). Abrams.
Craig, Janet. What's Under the Ocean. LC 81-11425. (Now I Know Ser.). (Illus.). 32p. (gr. k-2). 1982. PLB 7.95 (ISBN 0-89375-652-0); pap. 1.25 (ISBN 0-89375-653-9). Troll Assocs.
Crane, Jules M. Introduction to Marine Biology (a Laboratory Text) LC 73-76466. 1973. pap. text ed. 11.95 (ISBN 0-675-08954-9); instructor's manual 3.95 (ISBN 0-686-66860-X). Merrill.
Crisp, D. J., ed. European Marine Biology Symposium, Fourth. (Illus.). 1971. 97.50 (ISBN 0-521-08101-7). Cambridge U Pr.
Crowder, William. Seashore Life Between the Tides. LC 75-16036. Orig. Title: Between the Tides. (Illus.). 512p. 1975. pap. 6.00 (ISBN 0-486-23221-2). Dover.
Cushing, D. H. Productivity of the Sea. rev ed. Head, J. J., ed. LC 78-53754. (Carolina Biology Readers Ser.). 1978. pap. 1.65 (ISBN 0-89278-278-1, 45-9678). Carolina Biological.
Dawes, Clinton J. Marine Botany. 600p. 1981. 45.00 (ISBN 0-471-07844-1, Pub. by Wiley-Interscience). Wiley.
Diole, Philippe & Falco, Albert. Falco, Chief Diver of the Calypso. LC 77-376. Orig. Title: Falco, Chef Plongeur de la Calypso. 1977. 12.95 (ISBN 0-8120-5130-0). Barron.
Douglas, Philip A. & Stroud, Richard H., eds. A Symposium on the Biological Significance of Estuaries. 1971. 4.00 (ISBN 0-686-21854-X). Sport Fishing.
Drew, E. A., et al, eds. Underwater Research. 1976. 68.00 (ISBN 0-12-221950-3). Acad Pr.
Dumont, H. J. & Green, J., eds. Rotatoria. (Developments in Hydrobiology Ser.: No. 1). 268p. 1980. lib. bdg. 79.00 (ISBN 90-6193-754-X, Pub. Junk Pubs Netherlands). Kluwer Boston.
Eisler, ed. Trace Metal Concentrations in Marine Organisms. 3500p. text ed. 195.00 (ISBN 0-08-025975-8). Pergamon.
Falkowski, Paul G., ed. Primary Productivity in the Sea: Environmental Science Research Ser. (Vol. 19). 335p. 1980. 49.50 (ISBN 0-306-40623-3). Plenum Pub.
Forbes, Edward & Godwin-Austen, Robert. The Natural History of the European Seas. Egerton, Frank N., 3rd, ed. LC 77-74221. (History of Ecology Ser.). 1978. Repr. of 1859 ed. lib. bdg. 18.00x (ISBN 0-405-10392-1). Arno.
Freeland, Howard J., et al, eds. Fjord Oceanography. (NATO Conference Ser., Ser. IV: Marine Science: Vol. 4). 713p. 1980. 69.50 (ISBN 0-306-40439-7, Plenum Pr). Plenum Pub.
Friedrich, Hermann. Marine Biology: An Introduction to Its Problems & Results. LC 71-93028. (Biology Ser). (Illus.). 486p. 1970. 16.00 (ISBN 0-295-95011-0). U of Wash Pr.
Galbraith, Robert & Boehler, Ted. Subtidal Marine Biology of California. LC 74-11235. (Seashore Life Books: No. 4). (Illus., Orig.). 1974. 8.95 (ISBN 0-87961-027-1); pap. 4.95 (ISBN 0-87961-026-3). Naturegraph.
George, J. David & George, Jennifer. Marine Life: An Illustrated Encyclopedia of Invertebrates in the Sea. LC 79-10976. 1979. 49.00x (ISBN 0-471-05675-8, Pub. by Wiley-Interscience). Wiley.
Gery, Jacques. Characoids of the World. (Illus.). 1978. 20.00 (ISBN 0-87666-458-3, H-961). TFH Pubns.
Gotshall, Daniel W. & Laurent, Laurence L. Pacific Coast Subtidal Marine Invertebrates, a Fishwatchers' Guide. LC 79-64128. 112p. 1979. 14.50 (ISBN 0-930118-02-2); pap. 11.50 (ISBN 0-930118-03-0). Sea Chall.
Hardy, Alister. Open Sea: Its Natural History. 1971. 20.00 (ISBN 0-395-07777-X). HM.
Harvey, Hildebrande W. Chemistry & Fertility of Sea Waters. 2nd ed. 1957. 43.00 (ISBN 0-521-05225-4). Cambridge U Pr.
Hashimoto, Yoshiro. Marine Toxins & Other Bioactive Marine Metabolites. 1979. 46.00x (ISBN 0-89955-131-9, Pub. by Japan Sci Soc). Intl Schol Bk Serv.
Hedgpeth, Joel W., ed. Outer Shores One: Ed Ricketts & John Steinbeck Explore the Pacific Coast. 128p. 1978. pap. 7.95x (ISBN 0-916422-13-5). Mad River.
Hickson, Sydney J. The Story of Life in the Seas. 1978. Repr. of 1904 ed. lib. bdg. 20.00 (ISBN 0-8495-2324-9). Arden Lib.
Idyll, C. P. Abyss: The Deep Sea & the Creatures That Live in It. 3rd rev. ed. (Apollo Eds.). (Illus.). pap. 6.95 (ISBN 0-8152-0400-0, A400). T Y Crowell.
Jacques Cousteau: The Ocean World. (Illus.). 1979. 55.00 (ISBN 0-8109-0777-1). Abrams.
Jensen, Albert C. Wildlife of the Oceans. (Wldlife Habitat Ser.). (Illus.). 1979. 18.95 (ISBN 0-8109-1758-0). Abrams.
Johnson, Alexander B. Deep Sea Soundings & Explorations of the Bottom. LC 68-19282. 1970. Repr. lib. bdg. 15.00x (ISBN 0-8371-0499-8, JOSE). Greenwood.
Johnstone, James. Conditions of Life in the Sea: Short Account of Quantitative Marine Biological Research. Egerton, Frank N., 3rd, ed. LC 77-74232. (History of Ecology Ser.). (Illus.). 1978. Repr. of 1908 ed. lib. bdg. 20.00x (ISBN 0-405-10401-4). Arno.
Jones, O. A. & Endean, R., eds. Biology & Geology of Coral Reefs, 4 vols. Incl. Vol. 1. Geology. 1973. 55.50 (ISBN 0-12-389601-0); Vol. 2. Biology - One. 1974. 67.50 (ISBN 0-12-389602-9); Vol. 3. Biology - Two. 1975. 76.50 (ISBN 0-12-389603-7); Vol. 4. 1977. 59.00 (ISBN 0-12-389604-5). Set. 258.00 (ISBN 0-686-77183-4). Acad Pr.
Ketchum, Bostwick H. The Water's Edge: Critical Problems of the Coastal Zone. 1972. 17.50x (ISBN 0-262-11048-2). MIT Pr.
Kirsch, Catherine A. Things That Stings. (Illus.). 1978. 20.00 (ISBN 0-916750-66-3). Dayton Labs.
Kohlmeyer, Jan & Kohlmeyer, Ericka. Marine Mycology: The Higher Fungi. LC 79-14703. 1979. 65.00 (ISBN 0-12-418350-6). Acad Pr.
McConnaughey, Bayard H. Introduction to Marine Biology. 3rd ed. LC 77-25826. (Illus.). 1978. text ed. 23.50 (ISBN 0-8016-3258-7). Mosby.
Macdonald, A. G. Physiological Aspects of Deep Sea Biology. LC 73-90652. (Physiological Society Monographs: No. 31). (Illus.). 440p. 1975. 78.00 (ISBN 0-521-20397-X). Cambridge U Pr.
McGovern, Ann. The Underwater World of the Coral Reef. LC 75-44305. (Illus.). 40p. (gr. k-3). 1977. 6.95 (ISBN 0-590-07467-9, Four Winds). Schol Bk Serv.
McLusky, Donald S. Ecology of Estuaries. (Scholarship Ser. in Biology). 1971. text ed. 9.50x (ISBN 0-435-61600-5). Heinemann Ed.
--Estuarine Ecosystem. LC 80-28199. (Tertiary Level Biology Ser.). 150p. 1981. 29.95 (ISBN 0-470-27127-2). Halsted Pr.
Malins, D. C. & Sargent, J. R. Biochemical & Biophysical Perspectives in Marine Biology. Vol. 1 1975. 54.50 (ISBN 0-12-466601-9); Vol. 2 1975. 57.00 (ISBN 0-12-466602-7); Vol. 3 1976. 73.00 (ISBN 0-12-466603-5). Acad Pr.

Malins, D. C. & Sargent, J. R., eds. Biochemical & Biophysical Perspectives in Marine Biology, Vol. 4. 1979. 50.00 (ISBN 0-12-466604-3). Acad Pr.
Marine Biological Laboratory. Serial Publications. 1975. 6.00 (ISBN 0-685-52862-6). Marine Bio.
Marine Biological Laboratory & Woods Hole Oceanographic Institution, Woods Hole, Massachusetts. Catalog of the Library of the Marine Biological Laboratory & the Woods Hole Oceanographic Institution, 12 vols. 1971. lib. bdg. 1060.00 set (ISBN 0-8161-0937-0); journal catalog 55.00 (ISBN 0-8161-0115-9). G K Hall.
Marine Biology. Incl. Vol. 2. Phytoplanviton. International Interdisciplinary Conference, 2nd. Oppenheimer, C. H., ed. 359p. 1966. 59.50 (ISBN 0-677-65090-6); Vol. 3. Ecology of Invertebrates. International Interdisciplinary Conference, 3rd. Edmondson, W. T., ed. 311p. 1966. 52.25 (ISBN 0-677-65100-7); Vol. 4. Unresolved Problems in Marine Microbiology. International Interdisciplinary Conference, 4th. Oppenheimer, C. H., ed. 485p. 1968. 78.75 (ISBN 0-677-65110-4); Vol. 5. International Interdisciplinary Conference, 5th. Costlow, John D., Jr., ed. 1969. 101.25 (ISBN 0-677-13310-3). Gordon.
Marine Science Instrumentation. Proceedings, Vol. 5. Murdock, L. C., ed. LC 68-27860. 1973. 9.00 (ISBN 0-87664-216-4). Instru Soc.
Mariscal, R. N. Experimental Marine Biology. 1974. 37.50 (ISBN 0-12-472450-7). Acad Pr.
Marshall, N. B. Aspects of Deep Sea Biology. 1977. lib. bdg. 105.00 (ISBN 0-8490-1458-1). Gordon Pr.
--Developments in Deep-Sea Biology. LC 79-25526. 576p. 1980. lib. bdg. 40.00 (ISBN 0-686-64346-1). Garland Pub.
Meadows, P. S. & Campbell, J. I. An Introduction to Marine Science. LC 78-6738. (Tertiary Level Biology Ser.). 179p. 1978. pap. text ed. 21.95x (ISBN 0-470-26379-2). Halsted Pr.
Moe, Martin A., Jr. The Marine Aquarium Handbook: Beginner to Breeder. 200p. (Orig.). 1981. 15.95 (ISBN 0-939960-01-X); pap. 8.95 (ISBN 0-939960-02-8). Norns Pub Co.
Mordukhai-Boltovskoi, D., ed. The River Volga & Its Life. (Monographiae Biologicae: No. 33). 1979. lib. bdg. 74.00 (ISBN 90-6193-084-7, Pub. by Junk Pubs Netherlands). Kluwer Boston.
North, Wheeler. Underwater California. LC 75-13153. (Natural History Guide Ser). (Illus.). 1976. 14.95x (ISBN 0-520-03025-7); pap. 5.95 (ISBN 0-520-03039-7). U of Cal Pr.
Oceanography & Marine Biology: An Annual Review, Vol. 17. 1979. 80.00 (ISBN 0-08-023849-1). Taylor-Carlisle.
Oceanography & Marine Biology: An Annual Review, Vol. 18. 1980. 95.00 (ISBN 0-686-29371-1). Taylor Carlisle.
Olausson, Eric & Cato, Ingemar. Chemistry & Biochemistry of Estuaries. LC 79-41211. 452p. 1980. 80.00 (ISBN 0-471-27679-0, Pub. by Wiley-Interscience). Wiley.
Perkins, E. J. The Biology of Estuaries & Coastal Waters. 1974. 102.00 (ISBN 0-12-550750-X). Acad Pr.
Phillips, Ronald C. & McRoy, C. Peter. Handbook of Seagrass Biology. new ed. LC 77-90470. 1979. text ed. 42.50x (ISBN 0-8240-7025-9, Garland STPM Pr). Garland Pub.
Pickering, A. D., ed. Stress & Fish. 1981. price not set (ISBN 0-12-554550-9). Acad Pr.
Polikarpov, G. G. Radio-Ecology of Aquatic Organisms. 1966. 19.95x (ISBN 0-442-15100-4). Van Nos Reinhold.
A Preliminary Classification of Coastal & Marine Environments. 1975. pap. 7.50x (ISBN 0-686-53042-X, IUCN44, IUCN). Unipub.
Reay. The Biology of Aquaculture. (Studies in Biology: No. 106). 1979. 5.95 (ISBN 0-8391-0256-9). Univ Park.
Reseck, John, Jr. Marine Biology. (Illus.). 1979. text ed. 16.95 (ISBN 0-8359-4276-7); instrs'. manual avail. Reston.
Rheinheimer, G., ed. Microbial Ecology of a Brackish Water Environment. (Ecological Studies: Vol. 25). (Illus.). 1977. 48.20 (ISBN 0-387-08492-4). Springer-Verlag.
Russell, F. S., ed. Advances in Marine Biology. Incl. Vol. 1. 1963. 64.50 (ISBN 0-12-026101-4); Vol. 2. 1964. 44.00 (ISBN 0-12-026102-2); Vol. 3. 1966; Vol. 4. 1966. 51.50 (ISBN 0-12-026104-9); Vol. 5. 1968. 66.00 (ISBN 0-12-026105-7); Vol. 6. Yonge, Maurice, ed. 1969. 64.00 (ISBN 0-12-026106-5); Vol. 7. 1969. 60.00 (ISBN 0-12-026107-3); Vol. 8. 1970. 55.00 (ISBN 0-12-026108-1); Vol. 9. 1971. 88.50 (ISBN 0-12-026109-X); Vol. 10. 1972. 81.00 (ISBN 0-12-026110-3); Vol. 11. 1973. 49.50 (ISBN 0-12-026111-1); Vol. 15. 1978. 91.00 (ISBN 0-12-026115-4). Acad Pr.
--Advances in Marine Biology. Incl. Vol. 12. 1974. 71.50 (ISBN 0-12-026112-X); Vol. 13. 1976. 71.50 (ISBN 0-12-026113-8); Vol. 14. Cushing, D. H., ed. 1976. 79.00 (ISBN 0-12-026114-6). (Serial Publication). Acad Pr.
--Advances in Marine Biology, Vol. 16. (Serial Publication). 1979. 103.00 (ISBN 0-12-026116-2). Acad Pr.
Russell, Findlay E. Poisonous Marine Animals. (Illus.). 1972. 8.95 (ISBN 0-87666-134-7, PS-686). TFH Pubns.
Russell, H. D. Notes on Methods for the Narcotization, Killing, Fixation, & Preservation of Marine Organisms. 1963. 6.00 (ISBN 0-685-52861-8). Marine Bio.
Russell-Hunter, W. D. Aquatic Productivity: An Introduction to Some Basic Aspects of Biological Oceanography & Limnology. (Illus.). 1970. text ed. 9.95x (ISBN 0-685-04258-8); pap. 8.95 (ISBN 0-02-404920-4). Macmillan.
Shilling, Charles W. & Werts, Margaret, eds. The Underwater Handbook: A Guide to Physiology & Performance for the Engineer. (Illus.). 912p. 1977. 75.00 (ISBN 0-306-30843-6, Plenum Pr). Plenum Pub.
The Southern Ocean: The Living Resources of the Southern Ocean. 1978. pap. 10.50 (ISBN 92-5-100428-5, F1321, FAO). Unipub.
The Southern Ocean: The Utilization of Krill. 1978. pap. 7.50 (ISBN 92-5-100416-1, F1314, FAO). Unipub.
Stickney, Robert R. Principles of Warmwater Aquaculture. LC 78-25642. 375p. 1979. 30.00 (ISBN 0-471-03388-X, Pub. by Wiley-Interscience). Wiley.
Storr, John F. Ecology & Oceanography of the Coral-Reef Tract, Abaco Island, Bahamas. LC 64-66221. (Special Paper: No. 79). (Illus., Orig.). 1964. pap. 5.50x (ISBN 0-8137-2079-6). Geol Soc.
Sumich, James L. & Dudley, Gordon H. Laboratory & Field Investigations in Marine Biology. 208p. 1980. write for info. wire coil (ISBN 0-697-04594-3). Wm C Brown.
Torchio, Menico. The World Beneath the Sea. (The World of Nature Ser.). (Illus.). 128p. 1973. 4.98 (ISBN 0-517-12041-0). Crown.
Vermeij, Geerat J. Biogeography & Adaptation: Of Marine Life. LC 78-3722. (Illus.). 1978. 25.00x (ISBN 0-674-07375-4). Harvard U Pr.
Vernberg, F. John & Vernberg, Winona B., eds. Pollution & Physiology of Marine Organisms. 1974. 38.50 (ISBN 0-12-718250-0). Acad Pr.
Wilber, Charles G. Biological Aspects of Water Pollution. (Illus.). 308p. 1971. text ed. 31.75 (ISBN 0-398-02062-0). C C Thomas.
Yentsch, A., et al. Marine & Estuarine Environments Organisms & Geology of the Cape Cod Region 1665-1965. 1966. 6.00 (ISBN 0-912544-02-3). Marine Bio.
Zann, Leon P. Living Together in the Sea. (Illus.). 416p. 1980. 20.00 (ISBN 0-87666-500-8, H-990). TFH Pubns.
Zeitzschel, B., ed. The Biology of the Indian Ocean. LC 72-90196. (Ecological Studies: Vol. 3). (Illus.). 650p. 1973. 62.80 (ISBN 0-387-06004-9). Springer-Verlag.
Zottoli, Robert A. Introduction of Marine Environments. 2nd ed. LC 78-6938. 1978. pap. text ed. 11.50 (ISBN 0-8016-5694-X). Mosby.

MARINE BIOLOGY-JUVENILE LITERATURE

Cadbury, B. Bartram. Fresh & Salt Water. LC 60-6114. (Community of Living Things Ser). (Illus.). (gr. 4-8). 1967. PLB 7.45 (ISBN 0-87191-017-9). Creative Ed.
Clarke, Arthur C. Boy Beneath the Sea. LC 58-9782. (Illus.). (gr. 5 up). 1958. PLB 9.89 (ISBN 0-06-021266-7, HarpJ). Har-Row.
Goldin, Augusta. Sunlit Sea. LC 68-17075. (A Let's-Read- & Find-Out Science Bk). (Illus.). (gr. k-3). 1968. bds. 8.95 (ISBN 0-690-79411-8, TYC-J). Har-Row.
Morris, Dean. Underwater Life: The Oceans. LC 77-23051. (Read About Animals Ser.). (Illus.). (gr. k-3). 1977. PLB 11.15 (ISBN 0-8393-0009-3). Raintree Child.
Paige, David. A Day in the Life of a Marine Biologist. LC 80-54097. (Illus.). 32p. (gr. 4 up). 1981. PLB 6.89 (ISBN 0-89375-446-3); pap. 2.50 (ISBN 0-89375-447-1). Troll Assocs.
Thompson, Brenda & Overbeck, Cynthia. Under the Sea. LC 76-22470. (First Fact Books Ser). (Illus.). (gr. k-3). 1977. PLB 4.95g (ISBN 0-8225-1363-3). Lerner Pubns.

MARINE BIOLOGY-RESEARCH

Kinne, O. Diseases of Marine Animals: Bivalvia to Arthopoda, Vol. 2. 1980. write for info. (ISBN 0-471-99585-1, Pub. by Wiley-Interscience). Wiley.
Kinne, O. & Bulnheim, H. P. Cultivation of Marine Organisms & Its Importance for Marine Biology. (International Symposium Helgoland 1969 Ser.). (Illus.). 722p. 1973. pap. text ed. 90.00x (ISBN 3-87429-059-X). Lubrecht & Cramer.
Schlieper, Carl, ed. Research Methods in Marine Biology. LC 72-6089. (Biology Ser.). (Illus.). 300p. 1972. 16.00 (ISBN 0-295-95234-2). U of Wash Pr.
Symposium on Progress in Marine Research in the Caribbean & Adjacent Regions. (FAO Fisheries Report Ser: No. 200). 1978. pap. 26.75 (ISBN 92-5-000533-4, F1428, FAO). Unipub.

MARINE BIOLOGY-ANTARCTIC REGIONS

Llano, George A., ed. Biology of the Antarctic Seas Two. LC 64-60030. (Antarctic Research Ser.: Vol. 5). 1965. 12.00 (ISBN 0-87590-105-0). Am Geophysical.
Llano, George A. & Schmitt, Waldo L., eds. Biology of the Antarctic Seas Three. LC 64-60030. (Antarctic Research Ser.: Vol. 11). 1967. 13.50 (ISBN 0-87590-111-5). Am Geophysical.
Llano, George A. & Wallen, I. Eugene, eds. Biology of the Antarctic Seas Four. LC 64-60030. (Antarctic Research Ser.: Vol. 17). (Illus.). 1971. 30.00 (ISBN 0-87590-117-4). Am Geophysical.
Newman, William A. & Ross, Arnold, eds. Antarctic Cirripedia. LC 74-129339. (Antarctic Research Ser.: Vol. 14). (Illus.). 1971. 25.00 (ISBN 0-87590-114-X). Am Geophysical.
Park, Taisoo. Biology of the Antarctic Seas Nine Paper 2: Calanoid Copepods of the Genus Scolecithricella from Antarctic & Subantarctic Waters. Kornicker, Louis S., ed. (Antarctic Research Ser.: Vol. 31). 79p. 1980. 17.60 (ISBN 0-87590-151-4). Am Geophysical.

MARINE BIOLOGY-ATLANTIC OCEAN

Butler, James N., et al. Pelagic Tar from Bermuda & the Sargasso Sea. LC 73-175455. (Bermuda Biological Station Special Pubn.: No. 10). (Illus.). vi, 346p. pap. 6.00 (ISBN 0-917642-10-4). Bermuda Bio.
Chesher, Richard H. The Systematics of Sympatric Species in West Indian Spatangoids: A Revision of the Genera Brissopsis, Plethotaenia, Paleopneustes, & Saviniaster. LC 68-30264. (Studies in Tropical Oceanography Ser: No. 7). 1968. 12.00x (ISBN 0-87024-088-9). U Miami Marine.
Morris, Byron, et al. The Bermuda Marine Environment. (BBS Special Publication Ser.: No. 15). (Illus.). 1977. pap. 6.00 (ISBN 0-917642-15-5). Bermuda Bio.
Morris, Byron F. & Mogelberg, Deborah D. Identification Manual to the Pelagic Sargassum Fauna. (Bermuda Biological Station Special Pubn.: No. 11). ii, 63p. 1973. pap. 3.00 (ISBN 0-917642-11-2). Bermuda Bio.
Morris, Byron F. & Schroeder, Elizabeth. Hydrographic Observations in the Sargasso Sea off Bermuda: 1967-1973. (Bermuda Biological Station Special Pubn.: No. 12). 105p. 1973. pap. 3.00 (ISBN 0-917642-12-0). Bermuda Bio.
Pocklington, Roger. Variability in the Ocean off Bermuda. (Bermuda Biological Station Special Pubn.: No. 8). ii, 45p. 1972. 2.00 (ISBN 0-917642-08-2). Bermuda Bio.
Taylor, William R. & Bernatowicz, Albert J. Distribution of Marine Algae About Bermuda. LC 70-54248. (Bermuda Biological Station Special Pubn.: No. 1). (Illus.). ii, 42p. 1969. pap. 3.00 (ISBN 0-917642-01-5). Bermuda Bio.

MARINE BIOLOGY-AUSTRALIA

Veron, J. E. & Pichon, Michel. Scleractinia of Eastern Australia: Pt. III: Families Agaricidae, Siderastreidae, Fungiidae, Oculinidae, Merulinidae, Mussidae, Pectinidae, Caryophylliidae, Dendrophylliidae. LC 78-304433. (Australian Institute of Marine Science Monograph: No. 4). (Illus.). 450p. 1981. pap. text ed. 39.95 (ISBN 0-7081-0768-0, 0085, Pub. by ANUP Australia). Bks Australia.

MARINE BIOLOGY-PACIFIC AREA

Biology Colloquium, 33rd, Oregon St. U., 1972. The Biology of the Oceanic Pacific: Proceedings. Miller, Charles, ed. (Illus.). 1974. 8.95 (ISBN 0-87071-172-5). Oreg St U Pr.
Committee On Oceanography. Scientific Exploration of the South Pacific. LC 72-603750. (Orig.). 1970. 11.50 (ISBN 0-309-01755-6). Natl Acad Pr.
Devaney, D. M. & Eldredge, L. G., eds. Reef & Shore Fauna of Hawaii: Protoza Through Ctenophora. LC 77-89747. (Special Publication Ser: No. 64 (1)). (Illus.). 1977. pap. 15.00 (ISBN 0-910240-22-1). Bishop Mus.
Galtsoff, P. S. Pearl & Hermes Reef, Hawaii, Hydrographical & Biographical Observations. Repr. of 1933 ed. pap. 6.00 (ISBN 0-527-02213-6). Kraus Repr.
Johannes, R. E. Words of the Lagoon: Fishing & Marine Lore in the Palau District of Micronesia. (Illus.). 320p. 1981. 24.95x (ISBN 0-520-03929-7). U of Cal Pr.
Johnson, Myrtle E. & Snook, Harry J. Seashore Animals of the Pacific Coast. (Illus.). pap. 6.95 (ISBN 0-486-21819-8). Dover.
Krauss, Robert W., ed. The Marine Plant Biomass of the Pacific Northwest Coast: A Potential Economic Resource. (Illus.). 1978. text ed. 16.95 (ISBN 0-87071-447-3). Oreg St U Pr.
McDonald, Gary R. & Nybakken, James W. Guide to the Nudibranchs of California. Abbott, R. T., ed. LC 80-70748. (Illus.). 72p. (Orig.). 1981. pap. 13.50 (ISBN 0-915826-08-9). Am Malacologists.
Mori, S. & Yamamoto, G., eds. Productivity of Communities in Japanese Inland Waters. (Japan International Biological Program Synthetics Ser.: Vol. 10). 1975. pap. 46.50x (ISBN 0-86008-220-2, Pub. by U of Tokyo Pr). Intl Schol Bk Serv.
Pillay, T. V., ed. Coastal Aquaculture in the Indo-Pacific Region. (Illus.). 497p. (Orig.). 1974. 27.50 (ISBN 0-85238-023-2, FAO). Unipub.
Towle, Albert. A Paguran Adventure. 1978. 7.50 (ISBN 0-533-03635-6). Vantage.

MARINE BOILERS

see Steam-Boilers

MARINE BORERS

Edmondson, C. H. Resistance of Woods to Marine Borers in Hawaiian Waters. Repr. of 1955 ed. pap. 7.00 (ISBN 0-527-02325-6). Kraus Repr.
Ray, Dixy L., ed. Marine Boring & Fouling Organisms. LC 59-14772. (Illus.). 548p. 1959. 12.50 (ISBN 0-295-73840-5). U of Wash Pr.

MARINE CHEMISTRY

see Chemical Oceanography

MARINE COOKERY

see Cookery, Marine

MARINE CORROSION

see Ships-Corrosion

MARINE DEPOSITION

see Sedimentation and Deposition

MARINE DIESEL MOTORS

Burghardt, M. & Kingsley, G. Marine Diesels. 1981. 15.95 (ISBN 0-13-556985-0). P-H.
Christensen, Stanley G. Lamb's Questions & Answers on the Marine Diesel Engine. 7th. ed. 466p. 1978. text ed. 29.75x (ISBN 0-85264-248-2, Pub. by Charles Griffin & Co Ltd England). Lubrecht & Cramer.
Europort Conference, 1973. Marine Diesel Engines: Proceedings. 40p. 1974. limp bdg. 9.00 (ISBN 0-900976-37-3, Pub. by Inst Marine Eng). Intl Schol Bk Serv.
Ford, Louis R. Practical Marine Diesel Engineering. 4th ed. LC 43-4152. (Illus.). 1948. 7.00 (ISBN 0-911090-11-8). Pacific Bk Supply.
Henshall, S. H. Medium & High Speed Diesel Engines for Marine Use. 418p. 1972. 27.00 (ISBN 0-900976-01-2, Pub. by Inst Marine Eng). Intl Schol Bk Serv.
Henshall, S. H. & Jackson, G. G. Slow Speed Diesel Engines. (Marine Engineering Practice Ser.: Vol. 2, Pt. 17). 1979. pap. 9.00x (ISBN 0-900976-60-8, Pub. by Inst Marine Eng). Intl Schol Bk Serv.
Lamb, John. The Running & Maintenance of the Marine Diesel Engine. 6th ed. (Illus.). 722p. 1976. text ed. 29.75x (ISBN 0-85264-105-2, Pub. by Charles Griffin & Co Ltd England). Lubrecht & Cramer.
--Running & Maintenance of the Marine Diesel Engine. 722p. 1977. 57.95x (ISBN 0-85264-105-2, Pub. by Griffin England). State Mutual Bk.
Lamb's Questions & Answers on the Marine Diesel Engine. 466p. 1978. 35.95x (ISBN 0-85264-248-2, Pub. by Griffin England). State Mutual Bk.
Woodward, John B. Low Speed Marine Diesel Engines. LC 80-39635. (Ocean Engineering: a Wiley Ser.). 271p. 1981. 42.50 (ISBN 0-471-06335-5, Pub.by Wiley-Interscience). Wiley.

MARINE DISASTERS

see Shipwrecks

MARINE ECOLOGY

Bartlett, Jonathan, ed. The Ocean Environment. (Reference Shelf Ser.). 1977. 6.25 (ISBN 0-8242-0600-2). Wilson.
Bayer, Frederick M. & Weinheimer, Alfred J., eds. Prostaglandins from Plexaura Homomalla: Ecology, Utilization & Conservation of a Major Medical Marine Resource, a Symposium. LC 74-3562. (Studies in Tropical Oceanography Ser: No. 12). 1974. 15.00x (ISBN 0-87024-275-X). U Miami Marine.
Bougis, P., ed. Marine Plankton Ecology. 1976. 75.75 (ISBN 0-444-11033-X, North-Holland). Elsevier.
Brusca, Gary J. & Brusca, Richard C. A Naturalist's Seashore Guide: Common Marine Life Along the Northern California Coast & Adjacent Shores. 215p. 1978. pap. 8.50x (ISBN 0-916422-12-7). Mad River.
Burrell, D. C., et al. Marine Environmental Studies in Boca de Quadra & Smeaton Bay: Physical & Chemical, Nineteen Seventy-Nine. (Science Technical Report Ser.: No. R80-1). (Illus.). 144p. pap. 10.50 (ISBN 0-914500-10-4). U of AK Inst Marine.
Carefoot, Thomas. Pacific Seashores: A Guide to Intertidal Ecology. LC 76-7782. (Illus.). 192p. 1977. pap. 14.95 (ISBN 0-295-95522-8). U of Wash Pr.
Cobb & Harlin. Marine Ecology: Selected Readings. (Illus.). 1976. 19.95 (ISBN 0-8391-0959-8). Univ Park.
Commission for Marine Meteorology. (WMO Ser: No. 462). 1977. pap. 25.00 (ISBN 92-63-10462-X, WMO). Unipub.

Costlow, John D., ed. Fertility of the Sea, 2 vols. LC 74-132383. (Illus.). 646p. 1971. Set. 95.25x (ISBN 0-677-14730-9). Gordon.
Cushing, D. H. Marine Ecology & Fisheries. LC 74-82218. (Illus.). 228p. 1975. 52.50 (ISBN 0-521-20501-8); pap. 17.50x (ISBN 0-521-09911-0). Cambridge U Pr.
Dunbar, M. J., ed. Marine Production Mechanisms. LC 77-88675. (International Biological Programme Ser: No. 20). (Illus.). 1979. 72.00 (ISBN 0-521-21937-X). Cambridge U Pr.
Egerton, Frank N., ed. Early Marine Ecology: An Original Anthology. LC 77-74216. (History of Ecology Ser.). 1978. lib. bdg. 28.00x (ISBN 0-405-10370-0). Arno.
Fay, Rimmon C. Southern California's Deteriorating Marine Environment: An Evaluation of the Health of the Benthic Marine Biota of Ventura, los Angeles & Orange Counties. LC 72-83453. (Environmental Studies Ser: No. 2). (Illus.). 76p. 1972. pap. 4.50x (ISBN 0-912102-06-3). Cal Inst Public.
Flint, R. Warren & Rabalais, Nancy N., eds. Environmental Studies of a Marine Ecosystem: South Texas Outer Continental Shelf. 268p. 1981. text ed. 35.00x (ISBN 0-292-72030-0). U of Tex Pr.
Flint, Warren R. & Rabalais, Nancy N., eds. Enviornmental Studies of a Marine Ecosystem: South Texas Outer Continental Shelf. 272p. 1981. 35.00 (ISBN 0-292-74015-8). U of Tex Pr.
Galtsoff, Paul S., ed. Bibliography of Oysters & Other Marine Organisms Associated with Oyster Bottoms & Estuarine Ecology. 1972. lib. bdg. 74.00 (ISBN 0-8161-0945-1). G K Hall.
Green, J. Biology of Estuarine Animals. LC 68-21828. (Biology Ser.). (Illus.). 404p. 1968. 16.00 (ISBN 0-295-95122-2). U of Wash Pr.
Hart, Paul & Pitcher, Tony. Fisheries Ecology. 224p. 1980. 35.00x (ISBN 0-85664-894-9, Pub. by Croom Helm England). State Mutual Bk.
Hedgpeth, Joel W., ed. Outer Shores One: Ed Ricketts & John Steinbeck Explore the Pacific Coast. 128p. 1978. pap. 7.95x (ISBN 0-916422-13-5). Mad River.
Hedgpeth, Joel W. & Ladd, Harry S., eds. Treatise on Marine Ecology & Paleoecology, 2 vols. (Memoir: No. 67). 1957. Vol. 1. 32.50x (ISBN 0-8137-1167-3); Vol. 2. 30.00x (ISBN 0-8137-1267-X); Set. 55.00x (ISBN 0-8137-1067-7). Geol Soc.
Kinne, O. Marine Ecology: A Comprehensive Integrated Treatise on Life in Oceans & Coastal Waters, Vols. 1-4. Incl. Vol. 1, 3 pts. 1970. Pt. 1. 69.95 (ISBN 0-471-48001-0); Pt. 2. 64.50 (ISBN 0-471-48002-9); Pt. 3. 69.95 (ISBN 0-471-48003-7); Vol. 2, 2 pts. 1975. Pt. 1. 68.25 (ISBN 0-471-48004-5); Pt. 2. 83.95 (ISBN 0-471-48006-1); Vol. 3, 3 pts. 1976. Pt. 1. 87.25 (ISBN 0-471-48005-3); Pt. 2. 113.50 (ISBN 0-471-01577-6); Pt. 3. 52.50 (ISBN 0-471-48007-X); Vol. 4. 1978. Pt. 1. 111.00 (ISBN 0-471-48008-8). LC 79-221779 (Pub. by Wiley-Interscience). Wiley.
Kremer, J. & Nixon, S. W. A Coastal Marine Ecosystem: Simulation & Analysis. LC 77-22785. (Ecological Studies: Vol. 24). (Illus.). 1977. 39.40 (ISBN 0-387-08365-0). Springer-Verlag.
Laevastu, Taivo & Hayes, Murray L. Fisheries Oceanography & Ecology. 1981. 75.00x (ISBN 0-686-75649-5, Pub. by Fishing News England). State Mutual Bk.
Laevastu, Taivo & Larkins, Herbert A. Marine Fisheries Ecosystem: Its Quantitative Evaluation & Management. 1981. 65.00x (ISBN 0-85238-116-6, Pub. by Fishing News England). State Mutual Bk.
L'association Europeenne Oceanique. Metallic Effluents of Industrial Origin in the Marine Environment. 204p. 1977. 33.00x (ISBN 0-86010-063-4, Pub. by Graham & Trotman England). State Mutual Bk.
Livingston, R. J., ed. Ecological Processes in Coastal & Marine Systems. LC 79-12388. (Marine Science Ser.: Vol. 10). 560p. 1979. 49.50 (ISBN 0-306-40318-8, Plenum Pr). Plenum Pub.
Longhurst, A. R., ed. Analysis of Marine Ecosystems. 1981. 125.00 (ISBN 0-12-455560-8). Acad Pr.
McRoy, C. Peter & Helfferich, eds. Seagrass Ecosystems. (Marine Science Ser.: Vol. 4). 1977. 37.75 (ISBN 0-8247-6459-5). Dekker.
Menzies, Robert J., et al. Abyssal Environment & Ecology of the World Oceans. LC 72-8780. 488p. 1973. 35.00 (ISBN 0-686-65289-4, Pub. by Wiley). Krieger.
Nichols, David, ed. Monitoring the Marine Environment. LC 78-71806. 220p. 1979. 27.95 (ISBN 0-03-050746-4). Praeger.
North, W. J., ed. Biology of the Giant Kelp Beds (Macrocystis) in California. 1971. 100.00 (ISBN 3-7682-5432-1). Lubrecht & Cramer.
Olausson, Eric & Cato, Ingemar. Chemistry & Biochemistry of Estuaries. LC 79-41211. 452p. 1980. 80.00 (ISBN 0-471-27679-0, Pub. by Wiley-Interscience). Wiley.
Organism-Substrate Relationships in Lowland Streams. 211p. 1981. pap. 34.25 (ISBN 90-220-0759-6, PDC 222, Pudoc). Unipub.
Paasch, H. Illustrated Marine Encyclopedia. facsimile ed. (Illus.). 1977. 25.00x (ISBN 0-85242-539-2). Intl Pubns Serv.
Por, F. D. Lessepsian Migration: The Influx of Red Sea Biota into the Mediterranaen by Way of the Suez Canal. LC 77-24546. (Ecological Studies: Vol. 23). (Illus.). 1978. 35.20 (ISBN 0-387-08381-2). Springer-Verlag.
Steele, J. H., ed. Marine Food Chains: Proceedings of a Symposium Held at the University of Aarhus, Denmark, from 23rd to 26th July 1968. (Illus.). 1973. Repr. of 1970 ed. lib. bdg. 67.50x (ISBN 3-87429-047-6). Lubrecht & Cramer.
Steele, John H. The Structure of Marine Ecosystems. LC 73-82350. 144p. 1974. text ed. 7.95x (ISBN 0-674-84420-3); pap. 3.95x (ISBN 0-674-84421-1). Harvard U Pr.
Steeman, Nielson E. Marine Photosynthesis. LC 74-29691. (Oceanography Ser: Vol. 13). 141p. 1975. 41.50 (ISBN 0-444-41320-0). Elsevier.
Storr, John F. Ecology & Oceanography of the Coral-Reef Tract, Abaco Island, Bahamas. LC 64-66221. (Special Paper: No. 79). (Illus., Orig.). 1964. pap. 5.50x (ISBN 0-8137-2079-6). Geol Soc.
Tait, R. V. Elements of Marine Ecology. 3rd ed. (Illus.). 304p. 1981. pap. write for info. (ISBN 0-408-71054-3). Butterworth.
Thomas Telford Ltd. Editorial Staff. The Marine Environment & Oil Facilities. 168p. 1980. 69.00x (ISBN 0-7277-0075-8, Pub. by Telford England). State Mutual Bk.
Thorson, Gunner. Life in the Sea. LC 73-118405. (World University Library). (Illus., Orig.). 1971. pap. 3.95 (ISBN 0-07-064543-4, SP). McGraw.
Vernberg, F. J. & Vernberg, W. B., eds. Functional Adaptations of Marine Organisms. (Physiological Ecology Ser.). 1981. 39.50 (ISBN 0-12-718280-2). Acad Pr.
Vernberg, W. B. & Vernberg, F. J. Environmental Physiology of Marine Animals. LC 70-183485. (Illus.). 346p. 1972. 27.30 (ISBN 0-387-05721-8). Springer-Verlag.
Ward, C. H., et al, eds. Offshore Ecology Investigation. (Rice University Studies: Vol. 65, Nos. 4 & 5). (Illus.). 600p. (Orig.). 1980. pap. 11.00x (ISBN 0-89263-243-7). Rice Univ.
Wolfe, Douglas A., ed. Fate & Effects of Petroleum Hydrocarbons in Marine Organisms & Ecosystems. LC 77-76464. 1977. text ed. 67.00 (ISBN 0-08-021613-7). Pergamon.
Yentsch, A., et al. Marine & Estuarine Environments Organisms & Geology of the Cape Cod Region 1665-1965. 1966. 6.00 (ISBN 0-912544-02-3). Marine Bio.

MARINE ENGINEERING

see also Electricity on Ships; Marine Engines; Nautical Instruments; Ship Propulsion; Steam-Boilers

Beeching, L. J. Engineering Science: Questions & Answers. (Marine Engineering Ser.). 116p. 1975. pap. 9.50x (ISBN 0-540-07341-5). Sheridan.
Bennett, J. V. Heat Engines: Questions & Answers. (Marine Engineering Ser.). 116p. 1975. pap. 9.50x (ISBN 0-540-07340-7). Sheridan.
Bhattacharya, Rameswar. Dynamics of Marine Vehicles. LC 78-950. (Ocean Engineering Ser.). 498p. 1978. text ed. 54.00 (ISBN 0-471-07206-0, Pub. by Wiley-Interscience). Wiley.
Brockett, W. A., et al. Elements of Applied Thermodynamics. 4th ed. LC 77-73341. 1978. text ed. 23.95x (ISBN 0-87021-169-2). Naval Inst Pr.
Business Opportunities in Ocean Engineering, GB-024. rev. ed. 1978. 550.00 (ISBN 0-89336-131-3). BCC.
Claviez, Wolfram. Seemaennisches Woerterbuch. (Ger.). 1973. 38.50 (ISBN 3-7688-0166-7, M-7620, Pub. by Delius, Klaving & Co.). French & Eur.
Coastal Lagoon Survey. (UNESCO Technical Papers in Marine Science: No. 31). 280p. 1980. pap. 17.75 (ISBN 0-686-74026-2, U1085, UNESCO). Unipub.
Commission for Marine Meteorology. (WMO Ser: No. 462). 1977. pap. 25.00 (ISBN 92-63-10462-X, WMO). Unipub.
Curling, B. C. The History of the Institute of Marine Engineers. 242p. 1961. 3.00x (ISBN 0-900976-92-6, Pub. by Inst Marine Eng). Intl Schol Bk Serv.
Duffett, John. Modern Marine Maintenance. 256p. 1973. 9.95 (ISBN 0-910990-15-8). Hearst Bks.
Educational Research Council of America. Marine Engineer. Ferris, Theodore N., ed. (Real People at Work Ser: K). (Illus.). 1975. pap. text ed. 2.25 (ISBN 0-89247-086-0). Changing Times.
--Ship's Engineer. Kunze, Linda J. & Marchak, John P., eds. (Real People at Work Ser: J). (Illus.). 1975. pap. text ed. 2.25 (ISBN 0-89247-076-3). Changing Times.
Europort Conference, 1973. Wear, Lubrication & Repair: Proceedings. 40p. 1973. limp bdg. 9.00 (ISBN 0-900976-36-5, Pub. by Inst Marine Eng). Intl Schol Bk Serv.
Felger, Dan. Engineering for the OOD. LC 78-70964. (Illus.). 1979. 16.95x (ISBN 0-87021-172-2). Naval Inst Pr.
Flanagan, G. T. Feed Water Systems & Treatment. (Marine Engineering Ser.). 144p. 1978. pap. 9.50x (ISBN 0-540-07343-1). Sheridan.
--Marine Boilers: Questions & Answers. 2nd ed. (Marine Engineering Ser.). 102p. 1980. pap. 9.50x (ISBN 0-540-07348-2). Sheridan.
Ford, Louis R. Practical Marine Diesel Engineering. 4th ed. LC 43-4152. (Illus.). 1948. 7.00 (ISBN 0-911090-11-8). Pacific Bk Supply.
Frederick, S. H. & Capper, H., eds. Materials for Marine Machinery. 1977. 45.00 (ISBN 0-900976-42-X, Pub. by Inst Marine Eng). Intl Schol Bk Serv.
Gritzen, Edward F. Introduction to Naval Engineering. LC 79-90773. 448p. 1980. text ed. 14.95x (ISBN 0-87021-319-9). Naval Inst Pr.
Institute of Marine Engineers. Factors in the Selection of Marine Machinery & Plant with Particular Reference to Reliability, Maintenance & Cost. (Illus.). 104p. 1972. limp bdg. 15.00x (ISBN 0-900976-91-8, Pub. by Inst Marine Eng). Intl Schol Bk Serv.
Institute of Marine Engineers, compiled by. Business Management, One. Incl. The Functions of Management. Kenrick, K. G; An Introduction of Management Techniques. Boyes, J; Communication. Casson, J; Financial Aspects of Management. Turner, J. B; Financial Accounting. Philips, J; Some Aspects of Planning Control. Nelson, R. G. (Topics in Marine Engineering Ser.). 56p. 1973. pap. 3.50x (ISBN 0-900976-10-1, Pub. by Inst Marine Eng). Intl Schol Bk Serv.
Institute of Marine Engineers, International Marine & Shipping Conference, 1973. IMAS Seventy-Three: Proceedings. Incl. Boilers, Main Steam Turbines & Gearing. 76p. Group 1. 9.00 (ISBN 0-900976-16-0); Ship Operation & Management: Ship & Propulsion Systems. 60p. Group 2. 9.00 (ISBN 0-900976-17-9); Fuel, Lubrication & Fire. 22p. Group 3. 6.00 (ISBN 0-900976-18-7); Marine Pollution - Noise, Sewage & Oil. 66p. Group 4. 9.00 (ISBN 0-686-11943-6); Training & Manning. 30p. Group 5. 6.00 (ISBN 0-900976-20-9); Radio Communications & Navigational Aids. 34p. Group 6. 6.00 (ISBN 0-900976-21-7); Ocean Engineering. 16p. Group 7. 6.00 (ISBN 0-900976-22-5); Marine Diesel Engines. 66p. Group 8. 9.00 (ISBN 0-900976-23-3); Stern Gear, Shafting & Propellers. 70p. Group 9. 9.00 (ISBN 0-900976-24-1). 434p. 1973. Set Of Parts. 89.00 (ISBN 0-900976-25-X, Pub. by Inst Marine Eng); Bound Volume. 36.00 (ISBN 0-686-11942-8). Intl Schol Bk Serv.
International Conference on Port & Ocean Engineering Under Arctic Conditions, Third, Fairbanks, Alaska, 11-15 August 1975. Assessment of the Arctic Marine Environment: Selected Topics. Hood, D. W. & Burrell, D. C., eds. LC 75-43209. (Occasional Publications: No. 4). (Illus.). 468p. 1976. 25.00 (ISBN 0-914500-07-4). U. of AK Inst Marine.
Jolliff, James V. & Robertson, H. E. Naval Engineer's Guide. LC 78-188009. 1972. 8.50x (ISBN 0-87021-415-2). Naval Inst Pr.
Laws, W. Electricity Applied to Marine Engineering. 4th ed. Tyrell, R., rev. by. 454p. 1966. pap. 12.00x (ISBN 0-900976-31-4, Pub. by Inst Marine Eng). Intl Schol Bk Serv.
McCormick, Michael E., ed. Anchoring Systems. 1979. pap. text ed. 40.00 (ISBN 0-08-022694-9). Pergamon.
McGeorge, H. D. General Engineering Knowledge. (Marine Engineering Ser.). 96p. pap. 9.50x (ISBN 0-540-07345-8). Sheridan.
Norris, A. Commissioning & Sea Trials of Machinery in Ships. (Marine Engineering Practice Ser.: Vol. 2, Pt. 12). 1979. pap. 12.00x (ISBN 0-900976-60-8, Pub. by Inst Marine Eng). Intl Schol Bk Serv.
--Operation of Machinery in Ships: Steam Turbines Boilers & Auxiliary Plant. (Practice Ser.: Vol. 2, Pt. 15). 1979. 9.00x (ISBN 0-900976-80-2, Pub. by Inst Marine Eng). Intl Schol Bk Serv.
Osbourne, Alan A. & Neild, A. B., eds. Modern Marine Engineer's Manual, 2 Vols. LC 65-18208. (Illus.). 1965. Vol. 1. 25.00x (ISBN 0-87033-063-2); Vol. 2. 25.00x (ISBN 0-87033-064-0). Cornell Maritime.
Practical Experience with Shipboard Automation: A Joint Conference Held on 6 March 1974. (Illus.). 58p. 1975. pap. 15.00 (ISBN 0-900976-40-3, Pub. by Inst Marine Eng). Intl Schol Bk Serv.
Roy, G. J. Notes on Instrumentation & Control. (Marine Engineering Ser.). 144p. 1978. pap. 9.50x (ISBN 0-540-07344-X). Sheridan.
Running and Maintenance of Marine Machinery. 5th ed. (Illus.). 286p. 1975. pap. 15.00 (ISBN 0-900976-02-0, Pub. by Inst Marine Eng). Intl Schol Bk Serv.
Shannon, J. F. Marine Gearing. (Marine Engineering Design & Installation Ser.). (Illus.). 1978. pap. 19.50 (ISBN 0-900976-67-5, Pub. by Inst Marine Eng). Intl Schol Bk Serv.
Smith, I. & Mulroney, R. A. Parallel Indexing Techniques. 1979. pap. 6.50x (ISBN 0-540-07353-9). Sheridan.
The Society of Naval Architects & Marine Engineers: Transactions, Vol. 87. 412p. 1980. text ed. 35.00 (ISBN 0-9603048-1-9). Soc Naval Archh.
Timm, Simon, ed. Directory of Shipowners, Shipbuilders & Marine Engineers 1980. 78th ed. LC 25-4199. 1514p. 1980. 55.00x (ISBN 0-617-00301-7). Intl Pubns Serv.
Ward, Robert J. Workboat Engineer & Oiler. Block, Richard A., ed. (Illus.). 420p. (Orig.). 1981. pap. 27.00 (ISBN 0-934114-31-5). Marine Educ.
Watson. Marine Electrical Practice. 5th ed. 1981. text ed. 44.95 (ISBN 0-408-00498-3). Butterworth.
Weddle, A. J. Marine Engineering Systems: An Introduction for Merchant Navy Officers. (Illus.). 1976. text ed. 16.50x (ISBN 0-434-92233-1). Sheridan.
Yeandle, P. T. Mathematics: Questions & Answers. (Marine Engineering Ser.). 144p. 1979. pap. 9.50x (ISBN 0-540-07337-7). Sheridan.

MARINE ENGINEERING–BIBLIOGRAPHY

Institute of Marine Engineers. Glossary of Marine Technology Terms. 178p. 1980. pap. 15.00 (ISBN 0-434-90840-1). Sheridan.

MARINE ENGINEERING–EXAMINATIONS, QUESTIONS, ETC.

Paterson, William B. Red Book of Marine Engineering Questions & Answers, Vol. 1: Third & Second Assistant Engineers. 4th ed. LC 76-153141. (Illus.). 1972. pap. 9.00x (ISBN 0-87033-088-8). Cornell Maritime.
--Red Book of Marine Engineering Questions & Answers, Vol. 2: First Assistant & Chief Engineer. 2nd ed. LC 65-13. (Illus.). 1973. pap. 9.00x (ISBN 0-87033-089-6). Cornell Maritime.
Rudman, Jack. Chief Marine Engineer. (Career Examination Ser.: C-1794). (Cloth bdg. avail. on request). pap. 10.00 (ISBN 0-8373-1794-0). Natl Learning.
--Marine Engineer. (Career Examination Ser.: C-1363). (Cloth bdg. avail. on request). pap. 10.00 (ISBN 0-8373-1363-5). Natl Learning.

MARINE ENGINES

see also Diesel Motor; Marine Diesel Motors; Marine Nuclear Reactor Plants; Steam-Boilers; Steam-Turbines

Bowyer, P. J. Boat Engines: A Manual for Work & Pleasure Boats. LC 79-5369. (Illus.). 1979. 22.50 (ISBN 0-7153-7776-0). David & Charles.
Clymer Publications. Stern Drive Service-Repair Handbook: OMC, MerCruiser, Volvo, Stern-Powr, Berkeley, Jacuzzi. (Illus.). pap. 9.00 (ISBN 0-89287-186-5, B641). Clymer Pubns.
Donat, Hans. Practical Points on Boat Engines. 204p. 1980. 8.00x (ISBN 0-245-53333-8, Pub. by Nautical England). State Mutual Bk.
McBirnie, S. C. & Fox, W. J. Marine Steam Engines & Turbines. 4th ed. (Illus.). 627p. 1980. text ed. 39.95 (ISBN 0-408-00387-1). Butterworth.
Paterson, William B. Marine Engine Room Blue Book. LC 65-25382. (Illus.). 1966. pap. 8.50x (ISBN 0-87033-044-6). Cornell Maritime.
Rayman, A. A. High Speed Marine Steam Engine. rev. ed. (Illus.). 60p. 1978. pap. 5.00 (ISBN 0-85242-540-6). Intl Pubns Serv.
Warren, Nigel. Marine Conversions: Car Engine Conversions for Boats. 1979. 14.95x (ISBN 0-8464-0074-X). Beekman Pubs.
Witt, Glen L. & Hankinson, Ken. Inboard Motor Installations. 2nd rev. ed. (Illus.). 1978. text ed. 13.95 (ISBN 0-686-08739-9). Glen-L Marine.
Wright, Dermot. Marine Engines & Boating Mechanics. 1977. 19.95 (ISBN 0-7153-5988-6). David & Charles.

MARINE FAUNA

see also Fishes; Marine Aquariums; Marine Mammals; Sea Monsters

Aleyev, Yu G. Nekton. (Illus.). 1977. lib. bdg. 63.00 (ISBN 90-6193-560-1, Pub. by Junk Pubs Netherlands). Kluwer Boston.
Arnold, Augusta F. Sea-Beach at Ebb-Tide. LC 68-20554. (Illus.). 1968. pap. 5.00 (ISBN 0-486-21949-6). Dover.
Aspects of Brackish Water Fish & Crustacean Culture in the Mediterranean. 135p. 1981. pap. 8.75 (ISBN 92-5-000964-X, F2103, FAO). Unipub.

Baker, Joseph T. & Murphy, Vreni. Compounds from Marine Organisms, Vol. 2. (Section B, Handbook of Marine Science). 240p. 1981. 49.95 (ISBN 0-8493-0214-5). CRC Pr.
Baslow, Morris H. Marine Pharmacology. rev. ed. LC 76-57213. (Illus.). 342p. 1977. pap. text ed. 11.50 (ISBN 0-88275-470-X). Krieger.
Behrens, David W. Pacific Coast Nudibranchs. LC 80-51439. (Illus.). 112p. 1980. pap. 14.95 (ISBN 0-930118-05-7). Western Marine Ent.
Briggs, John C. Marine Zoogeography. new ed. (Population Biology Ser.). (Illus.). 496p. 1974. text ed. 30.50 (ISBN 0-07-007800-9, C). McGraw.
Bullen, Frank T. Creatures of the Sea: Sea Birds, Beasts, & Fishes. 1977. lib. bdg. 69.95 (ISBN 0-8490-1682-7). Gordon Pr.
Burger, Joanna, et al, eds. Behavior of Marine Animals: Marine Birds, Vol. 4. 545p. 1980. 45.00 (ISBN 0-306-37574-5, Plenum Pr). Plenum Pub.
Clark, A. H. Ophiuroidea of the Hawaiian Islands. Repr. of 1949 ed. pap. 13.00 (ISBN 0-527-02303-5). Kraus Repr.
Costello, D. P. & Henley, Catherine. Methods for Obtaining & Handling Marine Eggs & Embryos. LC 76-171320. 1971. 10.00 (ISBN 0-685-52860-X). Marine Bio.
Dangerous Sea Creatures. (Wild, Wild World of Animal Ser.). (Illus.). 1976. 10.95 (ISBN 0-913948-04-7). Time-Life.
Edmondson, C. H., et al. Marine Zoology of Tropical Central Pacific. Repr. of 1925 ed. pap. 13.00 (ISBN 0-527-02130-X). Kraus Repr.
Ely, C. A. Shallow-Water Asteroidea & Ophiuroidea of Hawaii. Repr. of 1942 ed. pap. 8.00 (ISBN 0-527-02284-5). Kraus Repr.
European Symposium on Marine Biology, 12th. Physiology & Behaviour of Marine Organisms: Proceedings. McLusky, D. S. & Berry, A. J., eds. LC 77-30559. 1978. text ed. 60.00 (ISBN 0-08-021548-3). Pergamon.
FAO-UNEP Expert Consultation on Contaminent Monitoring, Rome, 1974. Data on Contaminants in Aquatic Organisms. (FAO Fisheries Reports: No. 161). 30p. 1976. pap. 6.00 (ISBN 0-685-67380-4, FAO). Unipub.
Fotheringham, Nick & Brunenmeister, Susan L. Beachcomber's Guide to Gulf Coast Marine Life. LC 80-10607. (Illus.). 176p. 1980. pap. 6.95 (ISBN 0-88415-062-3). Pacesetter Pr.
Fowler, H. W. & Ball, S. C. Fishes of Hawaii, Johnston Island, & Wake Island. Repr. of 1925 ed. pap. 5.00 (ISBN 0-527-02129-6). Kraus Repr.
Grant, P. T. & Mackie, A. M., eds. Chemoreception in Marine Organisms. 1974. 48.00 (ISBN 0-12-295650-8). Acad Pr.
Great Britain Challenger Office. Report on the Scientific Results of the Voyage of H. M. S. Challenger During the Years 1873-1876, 50 Vols. (Illus.). 1880-1895. Set. 3500.00 (ISBN 0-384-19750-7). Johnson Repr.
Green, J. Biology of Estuarine Animals. LC 68-21828. (Biology Ser.). (Illus.). 404p. 1968. 16.00 (ISBN 0-295-95122-2). U of Wash Pr.
Greenberg, Idaz & Greenberg, Jerry. Sharks & Other Dangerous Sea Creatures. (Illus.). 64p. 1981. pap. 4.95 (ISBN 0-686-75091-8, G-095). Banyan Bks.
--Sharks & Other Dangerous Sea Creatures. (Illus.). 1981. saddlestiched 4.95 (ISBN 0-913008-09-5). Seahawk Pr.
Gulland, John A. The Management of Marine Fisheries. LC 74-2473. (Illus.). 206p. 1974. 18.50 (ISBN 0-295-95335-7). U of Wash Pr.
Helm, Thomas. Dangerous Sea Creatures: A Complete Guide to Hazardous Marine Life. LC 75-25960. (Funk & W Bk.). (Illus.). 288p. 1976. pap. 4.95 (ISBN 0-308-10238-X). T Y Crowell.
Hobson, Edmund & Chave, Edith H. Hawaiian Reef Animals. LC 72-84060. (Illus.). 1979. pap. 12.95 (ISBN 0-8248-0653-0). U Pr of Hawaii.
Hogner, Dorothy C. Sea Mammals. LC 78-22503. (Illus.). (gr. 4 up). 1979. 7.95 (ISBN 0-690-03949-2, TYC-J); PLB 7.89 (ISBN 0-690-03950-6). Har-Row.
Holly, M. Polychaeta from Hawaii. Repr. of 1935 ed. pap. 5.00 (ISBN 0-527-02235-7). Kraus Repr.
Illies, Joachim, ed. Limnofauna Europaea: A Checklist of the Animals Inhabiting European Inland Waters, with Accounts of Their Distribution & Ecology (Except Protozoa) 532p. 1978. text ed. 120.00 (ISBN 90-265-0275-3, Pub. by Swets Pub Serv Holland). Swets North Am.
Iversen, Edwin S. & Skinner, Renate. How to Cope with Dangerous Sea Life. LC 77-81166. (Illus.). 1977. pap. 3.25 (ISBN 0-89317-017-8). Windward Pub.
Khan, M. A., et al, eds. Pesticide & Xenobiotic Metabolism in Aquatic Organisms. LC 79-4598. (ACS Symposium Ser.: No. 99). 1979. 22.25 (ISBN 0-8412-0489-6). Am Chemical.
Krogh, August. Osmotic Regulation in Aquatic Animals. 7.50 (ISBN 0-8446-2408-X). Peter Smith.
Line, Les & Reiger, George. The Audubon Society Book of Marine Wildlife. (Audubon Society Bks.). (Illus.). 1980. 45.00 (ISBN 0-8109-0672-4). Abrams.
The Living Marine Resources of the Southeast Atlantic. (Fisheries Technical Paper: No. 178). 1978. pap. 7.50 (ISBN 92-5-100446-3, F1310, FAO). Unipub.
McEwan, Graham J. Sea Serpents, Sailors & Sceptics. (Illus.). 1978. 12.50 (ISBN 0-7100-8931-7). Routledge & Kegan.
Malins, D. C. & Sargent, J. R., eds. Biochemical & Biophysical Perspectives in Marine Biology, Vol. 4. 1979. 50.00 (ISBN 0-12-466604-3). Acad Pr.
Millar, R. H. British Ascidians. (Synopses of British Fauna: No. 1). 1970. 6.50 (ISBN 0-12-496650-0). Acad Pr.
Miner, Roy W. Field Book of Seashore Life. (Putnam's Nature Field Bks.). (Illus.). 1950. 9.75 (ISBN 0-399-10293-0). Putnam.
Murray, John. Selections from the Report on the Scientific Results of the Voyage of H.M.S. Challenger During the Years 1872-76. Egerton, Frank N., 3rd, ed. LC 77-74242. (History of Ecology Ser.). (Illus.). 1978. Repr. of 1895 ed. lib. bdg. 14.00x (ISBN 0-405-10411-1). Arno.
Naylor, E. & Hartnoll, E. G., eds. Cyclic Phenomena in Marine Plants & Animals. 1979. 68.00 (ISBN 0-08-023217-5). Pergamon.
Newell, R. C. Biology of Intertidal Animals. 1970. 25.00x (ISBN 0-236-17733-8, Pub. by Paul Elek). Merrimack Bk Serv.
Paasch, H. Illustrated Marine Encyclopedia. facsimile ed. (Illus.). 1977. 25.00x (ISBN 0-85242-539-2). Intl Pubns Serv.
Pequegnat, Willis E. & Chace, Fenner A., Jr., eds. Contributions on the Biology of the Gulf of Mexico. LC 71-135998. (Texas A&M University Oceanographic Studies: Vol. 1). (Illus.). 270p. 1970. 19.95x (ISBN 0-87201-346-4). Gulf Pub.
Plough, Harold H. Sea Squirts of the Atlantic Continental Shelf from Maine to Texas. LC 76-47388. (Illus.). 1978. text ed. 20.00x (ISBN 0-8018-1687-4). Johns Hopkins.
Reichenbach-Klinke, Heinz-Hermann. All About Marine Aquarium Fish Diseases. (Illus.). 1977. pap. 2.95 (ISBN 0-87666-467-2, PS-747). TFH Pubns.
Ricketts, Edward F. & Calvin, Jack. Between Pacific Tides. 4th rev. ed. LC 68-17140. (Illus.). 1968. 12.50 (ISBN 0-8047-0641-7); text ed. 9.50x (ISBN 0-8047-0642-5). Stanford U Pr.
Roessler, Carl. Underwater Wilderness: Life Around the Great Reefs. (Illus.). 1977. 35.00 (ISBN 0-918810-00-0). Chanticleer.
Ruivo, Mario, ed. Marine Pollution & Sea Life. 1978. 59.00 (ISBN 0-685-63432-9). State Mutual Bk.
Scheffer, Victor B. A Natural History of Marine Animals. 1981. pap. 5.95 (ISBN 0-684-16952-5, ScribT). Scribner.
Scilla, Agostino. De Corporibus Marinis Lapidescentibus Quae Defossa Reperuntur Addita Dissertatione FABII Columnae Glossopetris: On Petrified Marine Bodies Discovered Buried, to Which Is Appended a Dissertation by Fabio Colonna on Tongue Stones. Gould, Stephen J., ed. LC 79-8349. (History of Paleontology Ser.). (Illus., Latin.). 1980. Repr. of 1747 ed. lib. bdg. 10.00x (ISBN 0-405-12742-1). Arno.
Smith, R. I., et al. Keys to Marine Invertebrates of the Woods Hole Region. (Illus.). 1964. 5.00 (ISBN 0-912544-01-5). Marine Bio.
Stancyk, Stephen E., ed. Reproductive Ecology of Marine Invertebrates. (Belle W. Baruch Library in Marine Science Ser.). 1979. lib. bdg. 27.50 (ISBN 0-87249-379-2). U of SC Pr.
Steene, Roger C. Butterfly & Angelfishes of the World: Australia, Vol. 1. LC 78-17351. 144p. 1977. 27.00 (ISBN 0-471-04737-6, Pub. by Wiley-Interscience). Wiley.
Sumich, James L. An Introduction to the Biology of Marine Life. 2nd ed. 384p. 1980. pap. write for info. (ISBN 0-697-04574-9); tchrs'. manual avail. (ISBN 0-697-04592-7); lab manual avail. (ISBN 0-697-04594-3). Wm C Brown.
Sweeney, James B. A Pictorial History of Sea Monsters & Other Dangerous Marine Life. 1972. 12.95 (ISBN 0-517-50112-0). Crown.
Thomson, Donald A., et al. Reef Fishes of the Sea of Cortez: The Rocky Shore Fishes of the Gulf of California. LC 78-18835. 302p. 1979. 43.50 (ISBN 0-471-86162-6, Pub. by Wiley-Interscience). Wiley.
Time Life Books Editors. Life in the Coral Reef. (Wild, Wild World of Animals Ser.). (Illus.). 1977. 10.95 (ISBN 0-913948-15-2). Time-Life.
Time-Life Television, ed. Whales & Other Sea Animals. (Wild Wild World of Animal Ser.). 1977. 10.95 (ISBN 0-913948-10-1). Time-Life.
Vernberg, F. J. & Vernberg, W. B., eds. Functional Adaptations of Marine Organisms. (Physiological Ecology Ser.). 1981. 39.50 (ISBN 0-12-718280-2). Acad Pr.
Vernberg, W. B. & Vernberg, F. J. Environmental Physiology of Marine Animals. LC 70-183485. (Illus.). 346p. 1972. 27.30 (ISBN 0-387-05721-8). Springer-Verlag.
Whyte, Mal. North American Sealife Coloring Album. (Wildlife Ser.). (Illus.). 1973. pap. 3.50 (ISBN 0-912300-27-2, 27-2). Troubador Pr.
Winberg, G. G. Methods for the Estimation of Production of Aquatic Animals. 1971. 29.00 (ISBN 0-12-758350-5). Acad Pr.
Winn, H. E. & Olla, B. L. Behavior of Marine Animals, Vols. 1-3. Incl. Vol. 1. Invertebres. 244p. 1972. 27.50 (ISBN 0-306-37571-0); Vol. 2. Vertebrates. 259p. 1972. 27.50 (ISBN 0-306-37572-9); Vol. 3. Cetaceans. 460p. 1978. 37.50 (ISBN 0-306-37573-7). LC 79-16775 (Plenum Pr). Plenum Pub.

MARINE FAUNA–JUVENILE LITERATURE

Chester, Michael. Water Monster. LC 72-92925. (Illus.). (gr. 4-7). 1978. pap. 3.95 (ISBN 0-448-14674-6). G&D.
Dangerous Sea Creatures. LC 75-45283. (Wild, Wild World of Animals). (Illus.). (gr. 5 up). 1976. lib. bdg. 11.97 (ISBN 0-685-73291-6, Pub. by Time-Life Television). Silver.
Gambell, Ray. The Life of Sea Mammals. LC 78-56582. (Easy Reading Edition of Introduction to Nature Ser.). (Illus.). 1978. lib. bdg. 7.95 (ISBN 0-686-51146-8). Silver.
Hylander, Clarence J. Sea & Shore. (Illus.). (gr. 7 up). 1950. 9.95 (ISBN 0-02-747110-1). Macmillan.
Ipcar, Dahlov. Deep Sea Farm. (gr. 1-4). 1961. PLB 5.99 (ISBN 0-394-90709-4). Knopf.
Jacobs, Francine. Sounds in the Sea. LC 77-345. (Illus.). (gr. 3-7). 1977. 6.25 (ISBN 0-688-22113-0); PLB 6.00 (ISBN 0-688-32113-5). Morrow.
McClung, Robert. Hunted Mammals of the Sea. (Illus.). (gr. 7 up). 1978. 8.95 (ISBN 0-688-22146-7); PLB 8.59 (ISBN 0-688-32146-1). Morrow.
Maidoff, Ilka. Let's Explore the Shore. (Illus.). (gr. 5 up). 1962. 4.50 (ISBN 0-8392-3017-6). Astor-Honor.
Myers, Arthur. Sea Creatures Do Amazing Things. LC 80-20089. (Step-Up Bks.: No. 34). (Illus.). 72p. (gr. 2-5). 1981. 3.95 (ISBN 0-394-84487-4); PLB 4.99 (ISBN 0-394-94487-9). Random.
Reed, W. Maxwell & Bronson, Wilfrid S. Sea for Sam. rev. ed. Brandwein, Paul F., ed. LC 59-12826. (gr. 7 up). 1960. 7.95 (ISBN 0-15-271380-8, HJ). HarBraceJ.
Rinard, Judy & O'Neill, Catherine. Amazing Animals of the Sea. LC 80-8796. (Illus.). 100p. (gr. 3-8). 1981. write for info. (ISBN 0-87044-382-8); PLB write for info. (ISBN 0-87044-387-9). Natl Geog.
Sajarnov, Sviatoslav. Habitantes Del Mar Templado. (Illus.). 16p. 1975. pap. 1.00 (ISBN 0-8285-1295-7, Pub. by Progress Pubs Russia). Imported Pubns.
Sakharnov, S. Who Lives in the Warm Sea? 15p. 1975. pap. 0.755 (ISBN 0-8285-1269-8, Pub. by Progress Pubs Russia). Imported Pubns.
Scheffer, Victor. Natural History of Marine Mammals. LC 76-14820. (Illus.). 170p. (gr. 8 up). 1976. 7.95 (ISBN 0-684-14576-6, ScribJ). Scribner.
Selsam, Millicent. Animals of the Sea. LC 75-27447. (Illus.). 40p. (gr. k-3). 1976. 6.95 (ISBN 0-590-07458-X, Four Winds). Schol Bk Serv.
Spizzirri Publishing Co. Staff. Prehistoric Sea Life: An Educational Coloring Book. Spizzirri, Linda, ed. (Illus.). 32p. (gr. 1-8). 1981. pap. 1.25 (ISBN 0-86545-020-X). Spizzirri.
Waters, John F. Marine Animal Collectors: How Creatures of the Sea Contribute to Science & Our Knowledge of Man. LC 69-15053. (Illus.). (gr. 6-9). 1969. PLB 6.95 (ISBN 0-8038-4648-7). Hastings.
Wise, William A. Monsters of the Deep. LC 72-97316. (See & Read Science). (Illus.). (gr. 1-4). 1975. PLB 6.29 (ISBN 0-399-60844-3). Putnam.

MARINE FAUNA–ATLANTIC COAST

The Living Marine Resources of the Southeast Atlantic. (Fisheries Technical Paper: No. 178). 1978. pap. 7.50 (ISBN 92-5-100446-3, F1310, FAO). Unipub.
Rudloe, Jack. The Living Dock at Panacea. 1977. 10.00 (ISBN 0-394-48855-5). Knopf.

MARINE FAUNA–PACIFIC COAST

Braun, Earnest & Brown, Vinson. Exploring Pacific Coast Tide Pools. (Illus.). (gr. 4 up). 1966. 7.95 (ISBN 0-911010-67-X); pap. 3.95 (ISBN 0-911010-66-1). Naturegraph.
Burgess, Warren E. & Axelrod, Herbert R. Pacific Marine Fishes, Bk. 3. (Illus.). 272p. 1973. 20.00 (ISBN 0-87666-125-8, PS-719). TFH Pubns.
Harbo, Richard. Tidepool & Reef: Marine Life Guide to the Pacific Northwest Coast. (Natural History Ser.). (Illus.). 64p. (Orig.). 1980. pap. 5.95 (ISBN 0-87663-603-2, Pub. by Hancock Hse). Universe.
Hewlett, S. I. & Gilbey, K. Sea Life of the Pacific Northwest. (Illus.). 176p. 1976. 14.95 (ISBN 0-07-082336-7, GB). McGraw.
Kozloff, Eugene. Seashore Life of the Northern Pacific Coast: An Illustrated Guide to the Common Marine Organisms of Northern California, Oregon, Washington & British Columbia. 1981. write for info. U of Wash Pr.
Ricketts, Edward F. & Calvin, Jack. Between Pacific Tides. 4th rev. ed. LC 68-17140. (Illus.). 1968. 12.50 (ISBN 0-8047-0641-7); text ed. 9.50x (ISBN 0-8047-0642-5). Stanford U Pr.
Smith, Lynwood. Common Seashore Life of the Pacific Northwest. (Illus.). 1962. 7.25 (ISBN 0-911010-65-3). pap. 3.25 (ISBN 0-911010-64-5). Naturegraph.

MARINE FLORA

see also Coastal Flora; Marine Algae; Marine Aquariums; Phytoplankton; Primary Productivity (Biology)

Arnold, Augusta F. Sea-Beach at Ebb-Tide. LC 68-20554. (Illus.). 1968. pap. 5.00 (ISBN 0-486-21949-6). Dover.
Baker, Joseph T. & Murphy, Vreni. Compounds from Marine Organisms, Vol. 2. (Section B, Handbook of Marine Science). 240p. 1981. 49.95 (ISBN 0-8493-0214-5). CRC Pr.
Baslow, Morris H. Marine Pharmacology. rev. ed. LC 76-57213. (Illus.). 342p. 1977. pap. text ed. 11.50 (ISBN 0-88275-470-X). Krieger.
Church, Arthur H. Thalassiophyta & the Subaerial Transmigration. 1968. Repr. of 1919 ed. 10.75 (ISBN 0-02-842890-0). Hafner.
Cyclopaedia of Aquatic Plants. 1981. 40.00x (ISBN 0-686-72779-7, Pub. by Saiga Pub). State Mutual Bk.
Dawes, Clinton J. Marine Botany. 600p. 1981. 45.00 (ISBN 0-471-07844-1, Pub. by Wiley-Interscience). Wiley.
Dawson, E. Yale. Seashore Plants of Northern California. (California Natural History Guides: No. 20). 1966. 14.95x (ISBN 0-520-03089-3); pap. 3.25 (ISBN 0-520-00301-2). U of Cal Pr.
--Seashore Plants of Southern California. (California Natural History Guides: No. 19). 1966. 14.95x (ISBN 0-520-02991-7); pap. 2.95 (ISBN 0-520-00300-4). U of Cal Pr.
Dawson, Elmer Y. Marine Botany: An Introduction. LC 66-16952. 1966. text ed. 22.95 (ISBN 0-03-055590-6, HoltC). HR&W.
European Symposium on Marine Biology, 12th. Physiology & Behaviour of Marine Organisms: Proceedings. McLusky, D. S. & Berry, A. J., eds. LC 77-30559. 1978. text ed. 60.00 (ISBN 0-08-021548-3). Pergamon.
Hartley, L. P. Shrimp & Anemone. 140p. 1963. pap. 2.95 (ISBN 0-571-07061-2, Pub. by Faber & Faber). Merrimack Bk Serv.
Hillson, Charles J. Seaweeds: A Color-Coded, Illustrated Guide to Common Marine Plants of the East Coast of the United States. LC 76-42192. (Keystone Books). 1977. lib. bdg. 10.00 (ISBN 0-271-01239-0); pap. 6.95 (ISBN 0-271-01247-1). Pa St U Pr.
Krauss, Robert W., ed. The Marine Plant Biomass of the Pacific Northwest Coast: A Potential Economic Resource. (Illus.). 1978. text ed. 16.95 (ISBN 0-87071-447-3). Oreg St U Pr.
Kuznetsov, S. I. The Microflora of Lakes & Its Geochemical Activity. Oppenheimer, Carl, ed. LC 73-21215. (Illus.). 503p. 1975. 27.50x (ISBN 0-292-75010-2). U of Tex Pr.
McRoy, C. Peter & Helfferich, eds. Seagrass Ecosystems. (Marine Science Ser.: Vol. 4). 1977. 37.75 (ISBN 0-8247-6459-5). Dekker.
Naylor, E. & Hartnoll, E. G., eds. Cyclic Phenomena in Marine Plants & Animals. 1979. 68.00 (ISBN 0-08-023217-5). Pergamon.
Sculthorpe, C. Duncan. Biology of Aquatic Vascular Plants. (Illus.). 1967. 39.95 (ISBN 0-312-07945-1). St Martin.
Steeman, Nielson E. Marine Photosynthesis. LC 74-29691. (Oceanography Ser: Vol. 13). 141p. 1975. 41.50 (ISBN 0-444-41320-0). Elsevier.
Zaneveld, J. S. Iconography of Antartic & Sub-Antarctic Benthie Marine Algae: Chlorophycophyto & Chrysophycophyta, Part 1. 1969. pap. 20.00 (ISBN 3-7682-0631-9). Lubrecht & Cramer.

MARINE FUNGI

Anastasiou, C. J. Ascomycetes & Fungi Imperfecti from the Salton Sea. 1963. 8.00 (ISBN 3-7682-0210-0). Lubrecht & Cramer.
Ingold, C. T. An Illustrated Guide to Aquatic & Water Borne Hyphomycetes (Fungi Imperfecti) 1975. 11.00x (ISBN 0-900386-22-3, Pub. by Freshwater Bio). State Mutual Bk.
Johnson, T. W., Jr. & Sparrow, F. K., Jr. Fungi in Oceans & Estuaries. (Illus.). 1970. pap. 50.00 (ISBN 3-7682-0076-0). Lubrecht & Cramer.
Kirk, P. W. Morphogenesis & Microscopic Cytochemistry of Marine Pyrenomycete Ascospores. (Illus.). 1966. pap. 20.00 (ISBN 3-7682-5422-4). Lubrecht & Cramer.

Kohlmeyer, J. & Kohlmeyer, E. Synoptic Plates of Higher Marine Fungi. 3rd rev. ed. 1971. 14.00 (ISBN 3-7682-0218-6). Lubrecht & Cramer.

MARINE GEOLOGY

see Submarine Geology

MARINE GEOTECHNIQUE

Richards, Adrian, ed. Marine Geotechnology: Marine Slope Stability Conference, Vol. 2. 1977. 45.00x (ISBN 0-8448-1352-4). Crane-Russak Co.

Richards, Adrian F., ed. Marine Geotechnique. LC 67-27773. (Illus.). 1967. 20.00 (ISBN 0-252-72670-7). U of Ill Pr.

MARINE INSTRUMENTS

see Nautical Instruments

MARINE INSURANCE

see Insurance, Marine

MARINE INVERTEBRATES

Brusca, Richard C. Handbook to the Common Intertidal Invertebrates of the Gulf of California. LC 72-76901. (Illus.). 1973. pap. 10.95x (ISBN 0-8165-0356-7). U of Ariz Pr.

Chia, F. & Rice, M. E. Settlement & Metamorphosis of Marine Invertebrate Larvae: Proceedings of a Symposium Held at Toronto, Canada, Dec. 27-28, 1977. 1978. 25.00 (ISBN 0-444-00277-4, North Holland). Elsevier.

DeLuca, Charles J. & DeLuca, Diana M. Pacific Marine Life: A Survey of Pacific Ocean Invertebrates. LC 76-12228. 1976. pap. 2.75 (ISBN 0-8048-1212-8). C E Tuttle.

Giese, Arthur C. & Pearse, John S., eds. Reproduction of Marine Invertebrates: Acoelomate & Psuedocollomate Metazoans, Vol. 1. 1974. 60.50 (ISBN 0-12-282501-2); by subscription 52.00 (ISBN 0-12-282607-8). Acad Pr.

--Reproduction of Marine Invertebrates: Molluscs: Pelecypods & Lesser Classes, Vol. 5. LC 72-84365. 1979. 48.50 (ISBN 0-12-282505-5). Acad Pr.

Giese, Pearse. Reproduction of Marine Invertebrates: Entoprocts: Lesser Callomates. 1975. Vol. 2. 51.00, by subscription 50.50 (ISBN 0-12-282502-0). Acad Pr.

Gosner, Kenneth L. A Field Guide to the Atlantic Seashore from the Bay of Fundy to Cape Hatteras. (Peterson Field Guide Ser.). 1979. 16.95 (ISBN 0-395-24379-3). HM.

Gotshall, Daniel W. & Laurent, Laurence L. Pacific Coast Subtidal Marine Invertebrates. (Illus.). 112p. pap. 11.50 (ISBN 0-686-62677-X). Western Marine Ent.

Hammen, Carl S. Marine Invertebrates: Comparative Physiology. LC 80-51505. (Illus.). 141p. 1980. text ed. 12.00x (ISBN 0-87451-188-7). U Pr of New Eng.

Kozloff, Eugene N., et al. Keys to the Marine Invertebrates of Puget Sound, the San Juan Archipelago, & Adjacent Regions. LC 74-12027. (Illus.). 236p. 1974. text ed. 13.00 (ISBN 0-295-95347-0). U of Wash Pr.

Lowry, James K. Soft Bottom Macrobenthic Community of Arthur Harbor, Antarctica: Paper 1 in Biology of the Antarctic Seas V. Pawson, David L., ed. LC 75-22056. (Antarctic Research Ser: Vol. 23). (Illus.). 1975. pap. 4.00 (ISBN 0-87590-123-9). Am Geophysical.

Smith, Walter L. & Chanley, Matoira H., eds. Culture of Marine Invertebrate Animals. LC 74-11367. 338p. 1974. 32.50 (ISBN 0-306-30804-5, Plenum Pr). Plenum Pub.

Stancyk, Stephen E., ed. Reproductive Ecology of Marine Invertebrates. (Belle W. Baruch Library in Marine Science Ser.). 1979. lib. bdg. 27.50 (ISBN 0-87249-379-2). U of SC Pr.

Straughan, Robert P. L. Keeping Live Corals & Invertebrates. LC 74-9311. (Illus.). 300p. 1975. 17.50 (ISBN 0-498-01635-8). A S Barnes.

Walls, Jerry G. Starting with Marine Invertebrates. (Illus.). 160p. (Orig.). 1974. 7.95 (ISBN 0-87666-767-1, PS-729). TFH Pubns.

MARINE LAW

see Maritime Law

MARINE MAMMALS

Allen, Glover M. Extinct & Vanishing Mammals of the Western Hemisphere. LC 72-85661. xv, 620p. 1973. Repr. of 1942 ed. lib. bdg. 23.50x (ISBN 0-8154-0433-6). Cooper Sq.

Brown, Vinson. Sea Mammals & Reptiles of the Pacific Coast. 1976. pap. 6.95 (ISBN 0-02-062280-5, Collier). Macmillan.

Carnegie Institution Of Washington. Marine Mammals. Repr. of 1934 ed. pap. 15.50 (ISBN 0-685-02195-5). Johnson Repr.

Cousteau, Jacques. Mammals in the Sea. LC 74-23070. (The Ocean World of Jacques Cousteau Ser.: Vol. 10). (Illus.). 144p. 1975. 9.95 (ISBN 0-8109-0584-1). Abrams.

Fay, F. H., et al, eds. A Field Manual of Procedures for Postmortem Examination of Alaskan Marine Mammals. write for info. (ISBN 0-914500-09-0). U of AK Inst Marine.

Haley, Delphine. Marine Mammals. LC 78-16859. (Illus.). 272p. 1979. 26.50 (ISBN 0-914718-35-5); pap. text ed. 16.95 (ISBN 0-914718-48-7). Pacific Search.

Harrison, R. J. Functional Anatomy of Marine Mammals. 60.00 (ISBN 0-12-328002-8). Vol. 2, 1975. Vol. 3, 1978. 59.00 (ISBN 0-12-328003-6). Acad Pr.

Harrison, R. J. & Kooyman, G. L. Diving in Marine Mammals. rev. ed. Head, J. J., ed. LC 77-94952. (Carolina Biology Readers Ser.). 16p. (gr. 11 up). 1981. pap. 1.65 (ISBN 0-89278-206-4, 45-9606). Carolina Biological.

Harrison, R. J., ed. Functional Anatomy of Marine Mammals, Vol. 1. 1973. 72.00 (ISBN 0-12-328001-X). Acad Pr.

Harrison, Richard J. & King, Judith E. Marine Mammals. (Repr. of 1965 ed.). 1968. pap. text ed. 10.50x (ISBN 0-09-074342-3, Hutchinson U Lib). Humanities.

Kooyman, Gerald L. Weddell Seal: Consummate Diver. LC 80-18794. (Illus.). 176p. 1981. 39.95 (ISBN 0-521-23657-6). Cambridge U Pr.

Leatherwood, Stephen, et al. Marine Mammals of the World, 2 vols. 1980. 90.00 set (ISBN 0-525-10474-7). Dutton.

--Marine Mammals of the World, Vol. 1: Whales, Dophins, & Porpoises. 200p. 1980. 45.00 (ISBN 0-525-10472-0). Dutton.

--Marine Mammals of the World, Vol. 2: Seals, Sea Lions, Otters & Sea Cows. 200p. 1980. 45.00 (ISBN 0-525-10473-9). Dutton.

Mammals in the Seas. 1979. 20.50 (ISBN 92-5-100511-7, F1538, FAO). Unipub.

Orr, Robert T. Marine Mammals of California. LC 78-165233. (California Natural History Guides Ser.: No. 29). 88p. 1972. pap. 5.95 (ISBN 0-520-02077-4). U of Cal Pr.

Report of the Advisory Committee of Marine Resources Research Working Party on Marine Mammals. (Fisheries Report: No. 194). 1978. pap. 7.50 (ISBN 0-685-09221-6, F1313, FAO). Unipub.

Ridgeway, Sam H. & Harrison, Richard, eds. Handbook of Marine Mammals: Seals, Vol. 2. 1981. price not set (ISBN 0-12-588502-4). Acad Pr.

--Handbook of Marine Mammals: The Walrus, Sea Lions, Fur Seals & Sea Otter, Vol. 1. 1981. write for info. (ISBN 0-12-588501-6). Acad Pr.

Ridgway, Sam H., ed. Mammals of the Sea: Biology & Medicine. (Illus.). 830p. 1972. 57.00 (ISBN 0-398-02389-1). C C Thomas.

Scammon, Charles M. Marine Mammals & the American Whale Fishery. LC 68-56382. (Illus.). 1969. Repr. of 1874 ed. lib. bdg. 75.00x (ISBN 0-910950-02-4). Manessier.

--Marine Mammals of the Northwestern Coast of North America. LC 68-54705. (Illus.). 1968. pap. 6.00 (ISBN 0-486-21976-3). Dover.

--The Marine Mammals of the Northwestern Coast of North America: Together with an Account of the American Whale-Fishery. (Illus.). 11.00 (ISBN 0-8446-0243-4). Peter Smith.

Time Life Books Editors. Life in the Coral Reef. (Wild, Wild World of Animals Ser.). (Illus.). 1977. 10.95 (ISBN 0-913948-15-2). Time-Life.

Waters, John F. Some Mammals Live in the Sea. LC 75-180936. (Illus.). 96p. (gr. 3-7). 1972. PLB 5.95 (ISBN 0-396-06490-6). Dodd.

MARINE METEOROLOGY

see Meteorology, Maritime

MARINE MICROBIOLOGY

Colwell, R. Marine & Estuarine Microbiology Laboratory Manual. 1975. 9.50 (ISBN 0-8391-0684-X). Univ Park.

Droop, M. & Wood, F., eds. Advances in Microbiology of the Sea, Vol. 1. 1968. 40.00 (ISBN 0-12-027801-4). Acad Pr.

Droop, M. R. & Jannasch, H. W., eds. Advances in Aquatic Microbiology, Vol. 2. LC 76-5988. 1980. 52.50 (ISBN 0-12-003002-0). Acad Pr.

Haq, B. U. & Boersma, A. Introduction to Marine Micropaleontology. 1978. 24.50 (ISBN 0-444-00267-7, North Holland). Elsevier.

Litchfield, C. D. Marine Microbiology. (Benchmark Papers in Microbiology: Vol. 11). 1976. 53.50 (ISBN 0-12-786975-1). Acad Pr.

McWhinnie, M. A., et al. Euphausiacea Bibliography: A World Literature Survey. 1981. 100.00 (ISBN 0-08-024649-4). Pergamon.

Rheinheimer, G. Aquatic Microbiology. 2nd ed. LC 79-40645. 235p. 1981. 28.00 (ISBN 0-471-27643-X, Pub. by Wiley-Interscience). Wiley.

Rodina, A. G. Methods in Aquatic Microbiology. (Illus.). 1976. 24.50 (ISBN 0-8391-0071-X). Univ Park.

Sieburth, John M. Microbial Seascapes: A Pictorial Essay on Marine Microorganisms & Their Environments. (Illus.). 190p. 1975. 12.50 (ISBN 0-8391-0802-8). Univ Park.

--Sea Microbes. (Illus.). 1979. text ed. 59.95x (ISBN 0-19-502419-2). Oxford U Pr.

Wood, E. F. The Living Ocean. LC 75-15138. (Biology & Environment Ser.). 200p. 1975. 18.95 (ISBN 0-312-49000-3). St Martin.

Wood, E. J. The Living Ocean. 250p. 1980. 29.00x (ISBN 0-85664-026-3, Pub. by Croom Helm England). State Mutual Bk.

MARINE NUCLEAR REACTOR PLANTS

Crouch, Holmes F. Nuclear Ship Propulsion. LC 59-13449. (Illus.). 1960. 20.00x (ISBN 0-87033-071-3). Cornell Maritime.

Stever, Donald W., Jr. Seabrook & the Nuclear Regulatory Commission: The Licensing of a Nuclear Power Plant. LC 79-56160. (Illus.). 264p. 1980. 15.00 (ISBN 0-87451-181-X). U Pr of New En.

MARINE PAINTING

American Neptune Pictorial Supplements: Marine Paintings of John Faunce Leavitt, Vol. 18. 1976. pap. 3.50 (ISBN 0-87577-105-X). Peabody Mus Salem.

American Neptune Pictorial Supplements, Vol. 2. Antoine Roux. 1960. pap. 2.50 (ISBN 0-87577-091-6). Peabody Mus Salem.

American Neptune Pictorial Supplements, Vol. 3. Civil War Blockade Runners. 1961. pap. 2.50 (ISBN 0-87577-092-4). Peabody Mus Salem.

American Neptune Pictorial Supplements, Vol. 6. Steamships. 1964. pap. 2.50 (ISBN 0-87577-093-2). Peabody Mus Salem.

American Neptune Pictorial Supplements, Vol. 7. Fitz Hugh Lane. 1965. pap. 2.50 (ISBN 0-87577-094-0). Peabody Mus Salem.

American Neptune Pictorial Supplements, Vol. 8. American & Canadian Fishing Schooners. 1966. pap. 2.50 (ISBN 0-87577-095-9). Peabody Mus Salem.

American Neptune Pictorial Supplements, Vol. 10. Penobscot Maine Museum Searsport, Maine. 1968. pap. 2.50 (ISBN 0-87577-097-5). Peabody Mus Salem.

American Neptune Pictorial Supplements, Vol. 16 Antonio N. G. Jacobsen. 1974. pap. 2.50 (ISBN 0-87577-103-3). Peabody Mus Salem.

Archibald, E. H. Dictionary of Sea Painters. (Illus.). 453p. 1980. 79.50 (ISBN 0-902028-84-7). Antique Collect.

Betts, Edward. Creative Seascrape Painting. 160p. 1981. 19.95 (ISBN 0-8230-1113-5). Watson-Guptill.

Blake, Wendon. Seascapes in Acrylic. (The Artist's Painting Library). (Illus.). 1979. pap. 5.95 (ISBN 0-8230-4728-8). Watson-Guptill.

Brandt, Frederick R. American Marine Painting. LC 76-28711. (Illus.). 152p. 1976. pap. 8.95x (ISBN 0-917046-01-3). VA Mus Fine Arts.

Brewington, M. V. Special Exhibition of the Irving S. Olds Collection of American Naval Prints & Paintings. 1959. pap. 1.00 (ISBN 0-87577-024-X). Peabody Mus Salem.

Brook-Hart, Denys. British Nineteenth Century Marine Painting. (Illus.). 370p. 1976. 49.50 (ISBN 0-902028-32-4). Antique Collect.

Carter, John S., ed. Contemporary Marine Art. (Illus.). 80p. (Orig.). 1981. pap. 9.95 (ISBN 0-87577-065-7). Peabody Mus Salem.

Cordingly, David. Marine Painting in England, 1700-1900. (Illus.). 1974. 17.95 (ISBN 0-517-51229-7). Potter.

--Painters of the Sea. (Illus.). 1980. pap. 14.95 (ISBN 0-85331-425-X). Eastview.

Corne, Michele F. American Neptune Pictorial Supplements, Vol. 14. pap. 2.50 (ISBN 0-87577-101-7). Peabody Mus Salem.

Curtis, Roger W. How to Paint Successful Seascapes. Movalli, Charles, ed. (Illus.). 176p. 1975. 19.95 (ISBN 0-8230-2467-9). Watson-Guptill.

Fischer, Katrina S. Anton Otto Fischer His Life Work: Marine Artist. (Illus.). 1978. 49.50 (ISBN 0-8390-0217-3). Allanheld & Schram.

Fitzgerald, Edmond J. Marine Painting in Watercolor. (Illus.). 176p. 1972. 19.50 (ISBN 0-8230-3008-3). Watson-Guptill.

Khanbegian. Painting Sea & Sky. (Pitman Art Ser.: Vol. 57). pap. 1.95 (ISBN 0-448-00566-2). G&D.

Olsen, Herb. Painting the Marine Scene in Watercolor. 1981. pap. 10.95 (ISBN 0-442-26198-5). Van Nos Reinhold.

Robinson, E. John. Marine Painting in Oil. (Illus.). 176p. 1973. 19.95 (ISBN 0-8230-3007-5). Watson-Guptill.

--The Seascape Painter's Problem Book. (Illus., Orig.). 1976. 18.50 (ISBN 0-8230-4737-7). Watson-Guptill.

Schaefer, Rudolph J. J. E. Buttersworth, 19th-Century Marine Painter. LC 74-82666. (Illus.). 276p. 1975. 75.00 (ISBN 0-913372-12-9). Mystic Seaport.

Serres, Dominick & Serres, John T. Liber Nauticus & Instructor in the Art of Marine Drawing. (Scolar Maritime Library). (Illus.). 100p. 1979. Repr. of 1805 ed. 110.00x (ISBN 0-85967-567-X, Pub. by Scolar Pr England). Biblio Dist.

Smart, Borlase. Seascape Painting Step-By-Step. LC 70-82748. (Illus.). 1969. pap. 9.95 (ISBN 0-8230-4741-5). Watson-Guptill.

Smith, Philip C. More Marine & Drawings in the Peabody Museum. (Illus.). 192p. 1979. 35.00 (ISBN 0-87577-064-9); boxed numbered 50.00 (ISBN 0-686-68319-6). Peabody Mus Salem.

Spectre, Peter H. & Putz, George. Marine Art Clipbook. 160p. 1980. pap. 8.95 (ISBN 0-442-25190-4). Van Nos Reinhold.

Whitehall, Walter M. & Jenkins, Lawrence W. Restoration of East India Marine Hall. 1948. pap. 0.50 (ISBN 0-87577-033-9). Peabody Mus Salem.

Wilmerding, John. History of American Marine Painting. 1968. 25.00 (ISBN 0-87577-001-0). Peabody Mus Salem.

--A History of American Marine Painting. LC 68-22210. (Illus.). 1968. 25.00 (ISBN 0-316-94123-9). Little.

Woodward, Stanley. The Sea. (Illus.). 7.50 (ISBN 0-87482-006-5). Wake-Brook.

MARINE PARKS AND RESERVES

An International Conference on Marine Parks & Reserves. 1976. pap. 10.50x (ISBN 2-88032-029-1, IUCN45, IUCN). Unipub.

Maritime Transportation Research Board, National Research Council. Public Involvement in Maritime Facility Development. 1979. pap. text ed. 7.00 (ISBN 0-309-02868-X). Natl Acad Pr.

Promotion of the Establishment of Marine Parks & Reserves in the Northern Indian Ocean Including the Red Sea & Persian Gulf. 1976. pap. 12.50x (ISBN 2-88032-032-1, IUCN39, IUCN). Unipub.

MARINE POLLUTION

see also Marine Resources Conservation; Oil Pollution of Rivers, Harbors, etc.

Barros, James & Johnston, Douglas M. International Law of Pollution. LC 73-6491. 1974. text ed. 19.95 (ISBN 0-02-901910-9). Free Pr.

Bioassays & Toxicity Testing. 1979. pap. 13.50 (ISBN 0-685-96671-2, F1576, FAO). Unipub.

Center for Ocean Management Studies. Impact of Marine Pollution on Society. (Illus.). 320p. 1981. 29.95 (ISBN 0-89789-019-1). J F Bergin.

Charney, Jonathan I., ed. The New Nationalism & the Use of Common Spaces: Issues in Marine Pollution & the Exploitation of Antarctica. 420p. 1981. text ed. 39.50 (ISBN 0-86598-012-8). Allanheld.

A Comprehensive Plan for the Global Investigation in the Marine Environment & Baseline Study Problems. (Intergovernmental Oceanographic Commission Technical Ser: No. 14). (Illus.). pap. 2.25 (ISBN 92-3-101430-7, UNESCO). Unipub.

Cousteau, Jacques. The Sea in Danger. LC 74-23100. (Ocean World of Jacques Cousteau Ser: Vol. 19). (Illus.). 144p. 1975. 9.95 (ISBN 0-8109-0593-0). Abrams.

Cusine, Douglas J. & Grant, John P., eds. The Impact of Marine Pollution. LC 80-670. 336p. 1980. text ed. 32.50 (ISBN 0-916672-54-9). Allanheld.

Directory of Mediterranean Marine Research Centres. 1979. pap. 40.00 (ISBN 0-686-59759-1, UNEP 028, UNEP). Unipub.

Giam, C. S. Pollutant Effects on Marine Organisms. LC 77-2475. (Illus.). 1977. 19.95 (ISBN 0-669-01518-0). Lexington Bks.

Global Marine Pollution: An Overview. (Intergovernmental Oceanographic Commission Technical Ser: No. 18). 1979. pap. 4.75 (ISBN 92-3-101551-6, U863, UNESCO). Unipub.

Goldberg, Edward D. The Health of the Oceans. (Orig.). 1976. pap. 10.50 (ISBN 92-3-101356-4, U281, UNESCO). Unipub.

International Conference on Marine Pollution, 1973 - 1977 Edition. 168p. 1977. 13.75 (ISBN 0-686-70791-5, IMCO). Unipub.

International Experts Discussion on Lead Occurrence, Fate & Pollution in the Marine Environment, Rovinj, Yugoslavia, 18-22 October 1977. Lead in the Marine Environment: Proceedings. Konrad, Z. & Branica, M., eds. LC 80-40023. (Illus.). 364p. 1980. pap. 69.00 (ISBN 0-08-022960-3). Pergamon.

Johnston, R., ed. Marine Pollution. 1977. 111.00 (ISBN 0-12-387650-8). Acad Pr.

McNulty, J. Kneeland. Effects of Abatement of Domestic Sewage Pollution on the Benthos, Volumes of Zooplankton, & the Fouling Organisms of Biscayne Bay, Florida. LC 69-19867. (Studies in Tropical Oceanography Ser: No. 9). 1970. 6.95x (ISBN 0-87024-113-3). U Miami Marine.

Manual of Methods in Aquatic Environment Research: Bases for Selecting Biological Tests to Evaluate Marine Pollution, Pt. 4. (FAO Fisheries Technical Paper: No. 164). 31p. 1977. pap. 7.50 (ISBN 92-5-100300-9, F896, FAO). Unipub.

Moorcraft, Colin. Must the Seas Die? LC 72-91818. (Illus.). 219p. 1973. 7.95 (ISBN 0-87645-069-9). Gambit.

Nash, A. E., et al. Oil Pollution & the Public Interest: A Study of the Santa Barbara Oil Spill. LC 72-5116. (Illus.). 157p. (Orig.). 1972. pap. 3.75x (ISBN 0-87772-085-1). Inst Gov Stud Berk.

Ocean Affairs Board. Assessing Potential Ocean Pollutants. 1975. pap. 9.25 (ISBN 0-309-02325-4). Natl Acad Pr.

Reed, Alexander W. Ocean Waste Disposal Practices. LC 75-15205. (Pollution Technology Review No. 23; Ocean Technology Review No. 4). (Illus.). 336p. 1976. 24.00 (ISBN 0-8155-0591-4). Noyes.
Report of the Symposium on Prevention of Marine Pollution from Ships: Acapulco-1976. 90p. 1976. 12.50 (ISBN 0-686-70793-1, IMCO). Unipub.
Royal Society. Assessment of Sublethal Effects of Pollutants in the Sea. Cole, H. A., ed. (Illus.). 1979. text ed. 53.60 (ISBN 0-85403-112-X, Pub. by Royal Soc. London). Scholium Intl.
Skinner, Brian J. & Turekian, Karl K. Man & the Ocean. (Foundations of Earth Science Ser). (Illus.). 160p. 1973. pap. 8.95 (ISBN 0-13-550970-X). P-H.
Timagenis. International Control of Marine Pollution, Vols. 1-2. 1980. 37.50 ea. Vol. 1 (ISBN 0-379-20685-4). Vol. 2 (ISBN 0-379-20686-2). Oceana.
Vernberg, John, et al, eds. Biological Monitoring of Marine Pollutants. 1981. 34.00 (ISBN 0-12-718450-3). Acad Pr.
Windom, H. L. & Duce, R. A. Marine Pollutant Transfer. (Illus.). 1976. 25.95 (ISBN 0-669-00855-9). Lexington Bks.

MARINE RESOURCES

see also Amber; Continental Shelf; Fisheries; Fishery Products; Ocean Engineering; Salt; Sea-Water

Advisory Committee of Experts on Marine Resources Research, 9th Session. Report, Supplement One. 1979. pap. 7.50 (ISBN 92-5-100646-6, F1523, FAO). Unipub.
Advisory Committee on Marine Resources Research, 8th Session, Sesimbra, Portugal, 1975. Report, Supplement One. (FAO Fisheries Reports: No. 171, Suppl. 1). 136p. 1976. pap. 9.50 (ISBN 0-685-67379-0, F821, FAO). Unipub.
Andrassy, Juraj. International Law & the Resources of the Sea. LC 76-130960. (International Legal Studies). (Illus.). 191p. 1970. 16.00x (ISBN 0-231-03409-1). Columbia U Pr.
Bartlett, Jonathan, ed. The Ocean Environment. (Reference Shelf Ser.). 1977. 6.25 (ISBN 0-8242-0600-2). Wilson.
Barton, Robert. Atlas of the Sea. LC 73-18541. (John Day Bk.). (Illus.). 128p. 1974. 10.95 (ISBN 0-381-98267-X). T Y Crowell.
Bibliography of Living Marine Resources. (Regional Fishery Survey & Development Project Ser). 47p. 1977. pap. 7.50 (ISBN 92-5-100200-2, F727, FAO). Unipub.
Brin, Andre. Energy & the Oceans. 1981. pap. text ed. 29.95 (ISBN 0-86103-024-9, Westbury Hse). Butterworth.
Bunich, P. C. & Kharchev, K. Ocean & Its Resources. 149p. 1977. pap. 3.60 (ISBN 0-8285-1513-1, Pub. by Mir Pubs Russia). Imported Pubns.
Cousteau, Jacques, intro. by. Riches of the Sea. LC 74-23068. (Ocean World of Jacques Cousteau Ser: Vol. 17). (Illus.). 144p. 1975. 9.95 (ISBN 0-8109-0591-4). Abrams.
Cronan, David S. Underwater Minerals. (Ocean Science Resources & Technology Ser.). 1980. 57.50 (ISBN 0-12-197480-4). Acad Pr.
Firth, Frank E. Encyclopedia of Marine Resources. (Illus.). 1969. 29.50 (ISBN 0-442-15610-3); pap. 15.95 (ISBN 0-442-22399-4). Van Nos Reinhold.
The Fish Resources of the Eastern Central Atlantic: Part 1, The Resources of the Gulf of Guinea from Angola to Mauritania. (Fisheries Technical Paper: No. 186). 171p. 1981. pap. 11.00 (ISBN 92-5-100851-5, F2028, FAO). Unipub.
Fishing News Bks. Ltd. Staff, ed. Study of the Sea: The Development of Marine Research Under the Auspices of the International Council for the Exploration of the Sea. 272p. 1981. 75.00x (ISBN 0-85238-112-3, Pub. by Fishing News England). State Mutual Bk.
Flemming, N. C., ed. The Undersea. LC 76-56827. 1977. 12.98 (ISBN 0-02-538740-5). Macmillan.
Friedheim, Robert L. Understanding the Debate on Ocean Resources. (Monograph Ser. in World Affairs, Vol. 6: 1968-69 Ser., Pt. C). 4.00 (ISBN 0-87940-020-X). U of Denver Intl.
Heikoff, Joseph M. Marine & Shoreland Resources Management. LC 79-89720. (Illus.). 1980. 28.95 (ISBN 0-250-40338-2). Ann Arbor Science.
Jones, Erin B. Law of the Sea: Oceanic Resources. LC 72-96510. xiv, 162p. 1972. 7.95 (ISBN 0-87074-134-9). SMU Press.
Judson, Vincent. The AQUA Declaration. LC 75-32591. (Illus., Mailing charge - 1.00). 1976. perfect bdg. 15.00 (ISBN 0-916146-02-2). Apex U Pr.
Ketchum, Bostwick H. The Water's Edge: Critical Problems of the Coastal Zone. 1972. 17.50x (ISBN 0-262-11048-2). MIT Pr.
Kolde, Endel. The Pacific Quest: The Concept & Scope of an Oceanic Community. LC 76-41117. (Pacific Rim Research Series: No. 1). 1976. 17.95 (ISBN 0-669-00978-4). Lexington Bks.
Lee, William W. L. Decisions in Marine Mining: The Role of Preferences & Tradeoffs. LC 79-648. 1979. reference 18.50 (ISBN 0-88410-369-2). Ballinger Pub.
Ling, Shao-Wen. Aquaculture in Southeast Asia: A Historical Overview. Mumaw, Laura, ed. LC 77-3828. (Washington Sea Hgrant Ser.). (Illus.). 108p. 1977. 19.50 (ISBN 0-295-95560-0); pap. 8.50 (ISBN 0-295-95563-5). U of Wash Pr.
Mangone, Gerard J. Marine Policy for America: The United States at Sea. LC 77-243. 1977. 26.95 (ISBN 0-669-01432-X). Lexington Bks.
Mero, J. L. The Mineral Resources of the Sea. (Oceanography Ser.: Vol. 1). 1965. 39.00 (ISBN 0-444-40394-9). Elsevier.
Monney, N. T., ed. Ocean Energy Resources, OED-1977, Vol. 4. 1977. pap. text ed. 15.00 (ISBN 0-685-86873-7, G00120). ASME.
Neumeyer, Ken. Sailing the Farm: Independence on 30 Feet - a Survival Guide to Homesteading the Ocean. 192p. (Orig.). 1981. pap. 7.95 (ISBN 0-89815-051-5). Ten Speed Pr.
An Overview: Marine Living Resources. (UNEP Report Ser.: No. 7). 73p. 1980. pap. 8.50 (ISBN 0-686-70042-2, UNEP 035, UNEP). Unipub.
Report of the Second Joint Meeting of the Working Party on Assessment of Fish Resources & the Working Party on Stock Assessment of Shrimp & Lobster Resources (WECAF) (FAO Fisheries Report Ser.: No. 235). 41p. 1981. pap. 7.50 (ISBN 92-5-101049-8, F2143, FAO). Unipub.
Report of the Third Session of the Committee on Resource Management of the General Fisheries Council for the Mediterranean. (FAO Fisheries Report: No. 240). 20p. 1981. pap. 7.50 (ISBN 92-5-100966-X, F2087, FAO). Unipub.
Scheuer, Paul J., ed. Marine Natural Products: Chemical & Biological Perspectives, Vol. III. LC 77-10960. 1980. 28.00 (ISBN 0-12-624003-5). Acad Pr.
--Marine Natural Products: Chemical & Biological Perspectives, Vol. 2. (Marine Natural Products: Chemical & Biological Perspectives Ser.). 1978. 49.50 (ISBN 0-12-624002-7). Acad Pr.
The Sea: A Select Bibliography on the Legal, Political, Economic & Technological Aspects, 1978-1979. 46p. 1980. pap. 5.00 (ISBN 0-686-68970-4, UN80/16, UN). Unipub.
Skinner, Brian J. & Turekian, Karl K. Man & the Ocean. (Foundations of Earth Science Ser). (Illus.). 160p. 1973. pap. 8.95 (ISBN 0-13-550970-X). P-H.
Thomson, R. H., ed. Marine Natural Products. 1977. text ed. 13.25 (ISBN 0-08-021242-5). Pergamon.
Thorson, Gunner. Life in the Sea. LC 73-118405. (World University Library). (Illus., Orig.). 1971. pap. 3.95 (ISBN 0-07-064543-4, SP). McGraw.
Working Party on Biological Accumulators of the Advisory Commitee on Marine Resources Research, Rome, 1975. Report. (FAO Fish Report: No. 165). 9p. 1976. pap. 7.50 (ISBN 0-685-66349-3, F807, FAO). Unipub.
World List of Aquatic Sciences & Fisheries Serial Titles. (FAO Fisheries Technical Paper: No. 147). 128p. 1980. pap. 8.50 (ISBN 92-5-100904-X, F1946, FAO). Unipub.
World List of Aquatic Sciences & Fisheries Serial Titles. (FAO Fisheries Technical Paper: No. 148). 128p. 1980. pap. 7.50 (ISBN 92-5-000882-1, F1947, FAO). Unipub.

MARINE RESOURCES–JUVENILE LITERATURE

Bergaust, Erik. Colonizing the Sea. LC 76-21355. (Illus.). (gr. 6 up). 1976. PLB 4.96 (ISBN 0-399-61035-9). Putnam.
Brown, Joseph E. The Sea's Harvest: The Story of Aquaculture. LC 75-9646. (Illus.). 96p. (gr. 5 up). 1975. PLB 5.95 (ISBN 0-396-07153-8). Dodd.
Foster, John. The Sea Miners. (Illus.). 128p. (gr. 7 up). 1977. reinforced bdg. 8.50 (ISBN 0-8038-6723-9). Hastings.
McCoy, J. J. A Sea of Troubles. LC 74-22474. (Illus.). 192p. (gr. 6 up). 1975. 7.95 (ISBN 0-8164-3140-X, Clarion). HM.

MARINE RESOURCES AND STATE

Armstrong, John M. & Ryner, Peter C. Ocean Management: Seeking a New Perspective. 180p. 1981. text ed. 22.50 (ISBN 0-250-40470-2). Ann Arbor Science.
Eckert, Ross D. The Enclosure of Ocean Resources: Economics & the Law of the Sea. LC 78-70388. (Publications Ser.: No. 210). (Illus.). 1979. 16.95 (ISBN 0-8179-7101-7). Hoover Inst Pr.
Hollick, Ann L. & Osgood, Robert E. New Era of Ocean Politics. LC 74-6833. (Studies in International Affairs: No. 22). (Illus.). 142p. 1974. 9.50x (ISBN 0-8018-1633-5); pap. 3.45x (ISBN 0-8018-1634-3). Johns Hopkins.
Johnston, Douglas M., ed. Marine Policy & the Coastal Community: Studies in the Social Sciences. 320p. 1976. 19.95x (ISBN 0-312-51520-0). St Martin.
Sibthorp, M. M., ed. Oceanic Management: Conflicting Uses of the Celtic Sea & Other Western U.K. Waters. (Illus.). 1977. 25.00x (ISBN 0-905118-05-7). Intl Pubns Serv.

MARINE RESOURCES CONSERVATION

see also Marine Parks and Reserves

Cousteau, Jacques. Challenge of the Sea. LC 74-23066. (Ocean World of Jacques Cousteau Ser.: Vol. 18). (Illus.). 144p. 1975. 9.95 (ISBN 0-8109-0592-2). Abrams.
--The Sea in Danger. LC 74-23100. (Ocean World of Jacques Cousteau Ser: Vol. 19). (Illus.). 144p. 1975. 9.95 (ISBN 0-8109-0593-0). Abrams.
Lewis, Tracy R. Stochastic Modeling of Ocean Fisheries Resource Management. LC 81-51282. (Illus.). 160p. 1981. 25.00 (ISBN 0-295-95838-3). U of Wash Pr.
Padelford, Norman J. Public Policy for the Use of the Seas. rev. ed. 1970. pap. 13.00x (ISBN 0-262-66001-6). MIT Pr.
Tomasevich, J. International Agreements on Conservation of Marine Resources, with Special Reference to the North Pacific. Repr. of 1943 ed. 17.00 (ISBN 0-527-90450-3). Kraus Repr.
Walsh, Don, ed. The Law of the Sea: Issues in Ocean Resource Management. LC 77-7823. (Praeger Special Studies). 1977. 29.95 (ISBN 0-03-022666-X). Praeger.

MARINE SAFETY

see Navigation–Safety Measures

MARINE SANCTUARIES

see Marine Parks and Reserves

MARINE SEDIMENTS

Cline, R. M. & Hays, J. D., eds. Investigation of Late Quaternary Paleoceanography & Paleoclimatology. LC 75-40899. (Memoir: No. 145). (Illus.). 1976. 30.00x (ISBN 0-8137-1145-2). Geol Soc.
Coleman, James M. Recent Coastal Sedimentation: Central Louisiana Coast. LC 67-63069. (Coastal Studies, Vol. 17). (Illus.). 1967. pap. 4.00x (ISBN 0-8071-0403-5). La State U Pr.
Fabricius, H. Frank & Fuechtbauer, H. Origins of Marine Ooids & Grapestones. (Contributions to Sedimentology: Vol. 7). (Illus.). 113p. (Orig.). 1977. pap. 42.50x (ISBN 3-510-57007-3). Intl Pubns Serv.
Gray, J. S. The Ecology of Marine Sediments. (Cambridge Studies in Modern Biology: No. 2). (Illus.). 170p. Date not set. 16.50 (ISBN 0-521-23553-7); pap. 34.50 (ISBN 0-521-28027-3). Cambridge U Pr.
Hampton, Lloyd. Physics of Sound in Marine Sediments. LC 74-8022. (Marine Science Ser.: Vol. 1). 569p. 1974. 45.00 (ISBN 0-306-35501-9, Plenum Pr). Plenum Pub.
Hardie, Lawrence A. Sedimentation of the Modern Carbonate Tidal Flats of Northwest Andros Island, Bahamas. LC 76-47389. (No. 22). (Illus.). 232p. 1977. 22.50x (ISBN 0-8018-1895-8). Johns Hopkins.
Heezen, B. C. Influence of Abyssal Circulation on Sedimentary Accumulations in Space & Time. (Developments in Sedimentology: 23). 1977. 39.00 (ISBN 0-444-41569-6). Elsevier.
Inderbitzen, Anton L., ed. Deep-Sea Sediments: Physical and Mechanical Properties. LC 74-7140. (Marine Science Ser.: Vol. 2). 497p. 1974. 45.00 (ISBN 0-306-35502-7, Plenum Pr). Plenum Pub.
Influence of Denitrification in Aquatic Sediments on the Nitrogen Content of Natural Waters. (Agricultural Research Reports Ser.: 858). 1976. pap. 10.00 (ISBN 90-220-0620-4, PUDOC). Unipub.
Kaplan, Isaac R., ed. Natural Gases in Marine Sediments. LC 74-11492. (Marine Science Ser.: Vol. 3). 324p. 1974. 42.50 (ISBN 0-306-35503-5, Plenum Pr). Plenum Pub.
Klein, G. deVries, ed. Holocene Tidal Sedimentation. (Benchmark Papers in Geology Ser.: Vol. 30). 432p. 1976. 53.50 (ISBN 0-12-786859-3). Acad Pr.
Komar, Paul D. Beach Processes & Sedimentation. (Illus.). 464p. 1976. 32.95 (ISBN 0-13-072595-1). P-H.
Kwon, H. J. Barrier Islands of the Northern Gulf of Mexico Coast: Sediment Sources & Development. (Coastal Studies, Vol. 25). (Illus.). viii, 52p. 1970. pap. 4.00x (ISBN 0-8071-0034-X). La State U Pr.
Merriam, D. F., ed. Quantitative Techniques for the Analysis of Sediments. 1976. text ed. 32.00 (ISBN 0-08-020613-1). Pergamon.
Schopf, Thomas J. Paleoceanography. LC 79-12546. (Illus.). 1980. 25.00x (ISBN 0-674-65215-0). Harvard U Pr.
Silvester, R. Coastal Engineering Two: Sedimentation, Estuaries, Tides, Effluents, Modelling. LC 72-97435. (Developments in Geotechnical Engineering: Vol. 4B). 232p. 1974. 58.75 (ISBN 0-444-41102-X). Elsevier.
Van Der Lingen, Gerrit J., ed. Diagenesis of Deep-Sea Biogenic Sediments. LC 77-7496. (Benchmark Papers in Geology: Vol. 40). 1977. 46.50 (ISBN 0-12-787646-4). Acad Pr.
Weaver, C. E. & Beck, K. C. Miocene of the South East United States: A Model for Chemical Sedimentation in a Peri-Marine Environment. (Developments in Sedimentology: 22). 1977. 44.00 (ISBN 0-444-41568-8). Elsevier.

MARINE SERVICE

see also Aids to Navigation; Lighthouses; Merchant Marine; Navigation; Shipping; Signals and Signaling

Putz, George & Spectre, Peter H., eds. The Mariner's Catalog, Vol. 3. LC 73-88647. (Illus.). 192p. 1975. pap. 5.95 (ISBN 0-87742-058-0). Intl Marine.
Sell's Publications Ltd. Staff, ed. Sell's Marine Market. 656p. 1981. 50.00x (ISBN 0-85499-988-4, Pub. by Sells Pubns England). State Mutual Bk.
Voskuil, C. A. & Wade, J. A., eds. Hague-Zagreb Essays-Three. 329p. 1980. 32.50 (ISBN 90-286-0749-8). Sijthoff & Noordhoff.

MARINE SHIPPING

see Shipping

MARINE SIGNALS

see Aids to Navigation

MARINE SOIL MECHANICS

see Marine Geotechnique

MARINE STRUCTURES

see Offshore Structures

MARINE SURVEYING

see Hydrographic Surveying

MARINE TECHNOLOGY

see Marine Engineering

MARINE TRANSPORTATION

see Shipping

MARINE ZOOLOGY

see Marine Fauna

MARINERS

see Seamen

MARINER'S COMPASS

see Compass

MARINIDES

see Beni Marin Dynasty

MARIO, JESSE WHITE

Daniels, Elizabeth A. Jessie White Mario: Risorgimento Revolutionary. LC 78-158178. (Illus.). vii, 199p. 1972. 13.95 (ISBN 0-8214-0103-3). Ohio U Pr.
Pearse, Cecilia M. & Hird, Frank. The Romance of a Great Singer: Memoir of Mario. Farkas, Andrew, ed. LC 76-29961. (Opera Biographies). (Illus.). 1977. Repr. of 1910 ed. lib. bdg. 19.00x (ISBN 0-405-09701-8). Arno.

MARIOLATRY

see Mary, Virgin–Cultus

MARIOLOGY

see Mary, Virgin–Theology

MARION, FRANCIS, 1732-1795

Gerson, Noel. The Swamp Fox, Francis Marion. 1980. pap. 2.25 (ISBN 0-89176-001-6, 6001). Mockingbird Bks.
Grant, Matthew G. Francis Marion. LC 73-10061. 1974. PLB 5.95 (ISBN 0-87191-257-0). Creative Ed.
Horry, Peter. Parson Weem's Life of Francis Marion. LC 76-21439. 1976. 10.00 (ISBN 0-937684-04-X). Tradd St Pr.
Simms, William G. The Life of Francis Marion. facsimile ed. LC 75-153130. (Select Bibliographies Reprint Ser.). Repr. of 1844 ed. 21.00 (ISBN 0-8369-5740-7). Arno.

MARIONETTES

see Puppets and Puppet-Plays

MARIPOSA COUNTY, CALIFORNIA

Phillips, Catherine C. Coulterville Chronicle: The Annals of a Mother Lode Mining Town. 1978. 17.95 (ISBN 0-913548-56-1, Valley Calif); pap. 7.95 (ISBN 0-913548-57-X, Valley Calif). Western Tanager.

MARIPOSAN LANGUAGE

see Yokuts Language

MARITAIN, JACQUES, 1882-1973

Dunaway, John M. Jacques Maritain. (World Authors Ser.: France: No. 474). 1978. lib. bdg. 12.50 (ISBN 0-8057-6315-5). Twayne.
Griffin, John H. & Simon, Yves R. Jacques Maritain: Homage in Words & Pictures. LC 73-85056. (Illus.). 1974. 12.95x (ISBN 0-87343-046-8). Magi Bks.
Jung, Hwa Yol. Foundation of Jacques Maritain's Political Philosophy. LC 60-53589. (U of Fla. Social Sciences Monograph Ser.: No. 7). 1960. pap. 3.00 (ISBN 0-8130-0124-2). U Presses Fla.
Maritain, Jacques. The Social & Political Philosophy of Jacques Maritain. Evans, Joseph W. & Ward, Leo R., trs. 1976. pap. 5.95x (ISBN 0-268-01674-7). U of Notre Dame Pr.

Rasco, Jose I. Jacques Maritain y la Democracia Cristiana. LC 80-68468. 63p. (Orig., Span.). 1980. pap. 4.95 (ISBN 0-89729-274-X). Ediciones.

Sampaio. L' Intuition dans la Philosophie de Jacques Maritain. (Coll. Problemes et Controverses). 13.25 (ISBN 0-685-34275-1). French & Eur.

Smith, B. W. Jacques Maritain, Antimodern or Ultramodern? 1976. 22.50 (ISBN 0-444-99013-5, Pub. by Elsevier). Greenwood.

MARITAL COUNSELING

see Marriage Counseling

MARITIME DISCOVERIES

see Discoveries (In Geography)

MARITIME HISTORY

see subdivisions Navy or History, Naval under names of countries, e.g. United States–History, Naval and Great Britain–Navy

MARITIME LAW

see also Admiralty; Carriers; Charter-Parties; Commercial Law; Free Ports and Zones; Freedom of the Seas; Freight and Freightage; Insurance, Marine; Neutrality; Pirates; Privateering; Prize Law; Rule of the Road at Sea; Salvage; Search, Right of; Shipmasters; Ships Papers; Slave-Trade; Submarine Warfare; Territorial Waters; War, Maritime (International Law)

Amendment Number One to the Fourth Edition of Ship's Routing. 36p. 1979. 11.00 (ISBN 0-686-70775-3, IMCO). Unipub.

Basic Documents, Vol. 1. 92p. 1979. 16.50 (ISBN 0-686-70811-3, IMCO). Unipub.

Bes, J. Chartering & Shipping Terms: Time-Sheet Supplements, Vols. 2 & 3. Set. 70.00 (ISBN 0-685-11999-8). Heinman.

Bowett, Derek. The Legal Regime of Islands in International Law. 1978. lib. bdg. 32.50 (ISBN 0-379-20346-4). Oceana.

Brittin, Burdick H. International Law for Seagoing Officers. 4th ed. LC 80-81095. (Illus.). 624p. 1981. 21.95x (ISBN 0-87021-304-0). Naval Inst Pr.

Buglass, Leslie J. General Average & the York-Antwerp Rules. 1974. 2nd ed. LC 59-12835. 10.00x (ISBN 0-87033-027-6). Cornell Maritime.

Burke, William T. Ocean Sciences, Technology, & the Future International Law of the Sea. LC 66-63004. (Orig.). 1966. pap. 1.50 (ISBN 0-8142-0031-1). Ohio St U Pr.

Burke, William T., et al. National & International Law Enforcement in the Ocean. LC 75-38847. (Washington Sea Grant). 256p. 1976. pap. 8.50 (ISBN 0-295-95489-2). U of Wash Pr.

Center for Ocean Management Studies, ed. Comparative Marine Policy. 336p. 1980. 26.95 (ISBN 0-03-058307-1). Praeger.

Christy, Francis T., Jr., et al, eds. Law of the Sea: Caracas & Beyond. LC 75-12540. (Law of the Sea Institute Ser). 416p. 1975. text ed. 20.00 (ISBN 0-88410-029-4). Ballinger Pub.

Churchill, Robin & Nordquist, Myron, eds. New Directions in the Law of the Sea: Documents, 2 vols, Vol. 3 & 4. LC 72-12713. 1975. Vol. 3. lib. bdg. 35.00 (ISBN 0-379-00496-8); Vol.4. lib. bdg. 45.00 (ISBN 0-379-00497-6). Oceana.

Clingan, Thomas A. & Alexander, Lewis M., Jr., eds. Hazards of Maritime Transit. LC 73-14617. (Law of the Sea Institute Ser). 1973. 18.50 (ISBN 0-88410-007-3). Ballinger Pub.

Code for the Construction & Equipment of Ships Carrying Dangerous Chemicals in Bulk. 86p. 1977. 11.00 (ISBN 0-686-70781-8, IMCO). Unipub.

Code of Safe Practice for Bulk Cargoes. (Illus.). 137p. 1977. 15.25 (ISBN 0-686-70783-4, IMCO). Unipub.

Code of Safe Practice for Ships Carrying Timber Deck Cargoes. 31p. 1974. 7.00 (ISBN 0-686-70785-0, IMCO). Unipub.

Conference Speakers. First National Maritime Preservation Conference: Proceedings. LC 77-94300. 1978. 3.50 (ISBN 0-89133-067-4). Preservation Pr.

Convention on the Inter-Governmental Maritime Consultative Organization. 24p. 1979. 8.25 (ISBN 0-686-70810-5, IMCO). Unipub.

Crecraft, Earl W. Freedom of the Seas. facsimile ed. LC 70-102232. (Select Bibliographies Reprint Ser). 1935. 24.00 (ISBN 0-8369-5117-4). Arno.

Dubner. The Law of Territorial Waters of Midocean Archipelagos & Archipelagic States. 1977. pap. 24.00 (ISBN 90-247-1893-7, Pub. by Martinus Nijhoff Netherlands). Kluwer Boston.

Dubner, Barry H. The Law of International Sea Piracy. (Developments in International Law Ser.: No. 2). lib. bdg. 34.00 (ISBN 90-247-2191-1, Pub. by Martinus Nijhoff Netherlands). Kluwer Boston.

Dupuy, Rene-Jean. The Law of the Sea: Current Problems. LC 74-79800. 200p. 1974. lib. bdg. 25.00 (ISBN 0-379-00217-5). Oceana.

Durante, F. Western Europe & the Development of the Law of the Sea: Release 2. 1980. 75.00 (ISBN 0-379-20288-3). Oceana.

Durante, Francesco & Rodino, Walter. Western Europe & the Development of the Law of the Sea, Binder 1. LC 79-55008. 1979. looseleaf 75.00 (ISBN 0-379-20287-5). Set. Oceana.

El-Hakim, Ali A. The Middle Eastern States & the Law of the Sea. (Illus.). 310p. 1979. 30.00x (ISBN 0-8156-2217-1). Syracuse U Pr.

Fincham, Charles & Van Rensburg, William. Bread Upon the Waters. 1980. 22.00x (ISBN 965-20-0009-4, Pub. by Turtledove Pub Ltd Israel). Intl Schol Bk Serv.

Fulton, Thomas W. The Sovereignity of the Sea. LC 11-7247. 1976. Repr. of 1911 ed. 36.00 (ISBN 0-527-31860-4). Kraus Repr.

Garoche, Pierre. Dictionary of Commodities Carried by Ship. 1952. pap. 10.00x (ISBN 0-87033-019-5). Cornell Maritime.

Goldenberg, Samuel, ed. Local Impacts of the Law of the Sea. (Washington Sea Grant). 141p. 1973. pap. 6.50 (ISBN 0-295-95312-8). U of Wash Pr.

Grotius, Hugo. The Freedom of the Seas. LC 71-38252. (The Evolution of Capitalism Ser.). 184p. 1972. Repr. of 1916 ed. 20.00 (ISBN 0-405-04123-3). Arno.

Hagberg, Lennart, ed. Enforced Sales of Vessels. (Maritime Law Ser.: No. 2). 1977. lib. bdg. 21.00 (ISBN 90-2680-939-5, Pub. by Kluwer Law Netherlands). Kluwer Boston.

--Maritime Law, Vol. 1: Arrest of Vessels. xvi, 92p. 1976. text ed. 12.00x (ISBN 90-268-0894-1). Rothman.

Hill, C. J. Introduction to the Law of Carriage of Goods by Sea. 88p. 1974. 7.50x (ISBN 0-540-07374-1). Sheridan.

--Introduction to the Law of Carriage of Goods by Sea. 80p. 1974. 14.00x (ISBN 0-8464-0526-1). Beekman Pubs.

Hollick, Ann L. U.S. Foreign Policy & the Law of the Sea. LC 80-8554. 456p. 1981. 32.50 (ISBN 0-691-09387-3); pap. 15.00 (ISBN 0-691-10114-0). Princeton U Pr.

Hollick, Ann L. & Osgood, Robert E. New Era of Ocean Politics. LC 74-6833. (Studies in International Affairs: No. 22). (Illus.). 142p. 1974. 9.50x (ISBN 0-8018-1633-5); pap. 3.45x (ISBN 0-8018-1634-3). Johns Hopkins.

Inter-Governmental Maritime Consultative Organization. International Maritime Dangerous Goods Code: Supplement, 4 vols. 3rd ed. (Illus.). 1977. Set. 150.00x (ISBN 92-801-1055-1). Intl Pubns Serv.

International Conference on Limitation of Liability for Maritime Claims. 46p. 1977. 8.25 (ISBN 0-686-70805-9, IMCO). Unipub.

International Maritime Dangerous Goods Code. 1977. Vol. 1, 509. pap. 184.25 set (ISBN 0-686-64012-8, IMCO). Vol. 2, 499. Vol. 3, 412. Vol. 4, 425. Unipub.

Jackson, David C., et al, eds. World Shipping Laws, Binder 1. LC 79-18789. 1979. looseleaf 75.00 (ISBN 0-686-59751-6). Oceana.

Janis, Mark W. Sea Power & the Law of the Sea. LC 76-11973. (Lexington Books Studies of Marine Affairs). (Illus.). 1976. 15.95 (ISBN 0-669-00717-X). Lexington Bks.

Jones, Erin B. Law of the Sea: Oceanic Resources. LC 72-96510. xiv, 162p. 1972. 7.95 (ISBN 0-87074-134-9). SMU Press.

Law of the Sea Institute, 10th Annual Conference. Law of the Sea: Conference Outcomes & Problems of Implementation: Proceedings. Miles, Edward L., ed. Gamble, John K., Jr. LC 77-1544. 1977. 20.00 (ISBN 0-88410-051-0). Ballinger Pub.

Law of the Sea 11th, Annual Conference, Law of the Sea Institute 1977. Regionalization in the Law of the Sea: Proceedings. Johnston, Douglas, ed. LC 78-15357. 1978. 20.00 (ISBN 0-88410-075-8). Ballinger Pub.

Lay, Houston, et al, eds. New Directions in the Law of the Sea, 2 vols. LC 72-12713. 911p. 1973. 45.00 ea. Oceana.

MacDonald, Charles G. Iran, Saudi Arabia, & the Law of the Sea: Political Interaction & Legal Development in the Persian Gulf. LC 79-6186. (Contributions in Political Science: No. 48). xv, 226p. 1980. lib. bdg. 28.50 (ISBN 0-313-20768-2, MLS/). Greenwood.

McDougal, Myers S. The Public Order of the Oceans: A Contemporary International Law of the Sea. 1962. 55.00x (ISBN 0-300-00741-8). Yale U Pr.

Markow, Herbert L. Small Boat Law Nineteen Seventy-Eight Supplement. LC 79-88475. 1979. pap. 18.00x (ISBN 0-934108-01-3). H L Markow.

--Small Boat Law: Nineteen Seventy-Nine to Nineteen Eighty Supplement. LC 77-154289. 1981. pap. 21.00x (ISBN 0-934108-02-1). H L Markow.

Nordquist, M. New Directions in the Law of the Sea, Vol. 10. 1980. 45.00 (ISBN 0-379-00535-2). Oceana.

Oda, S. International Law of the Resources of the Sea. 144p. 1979. Repr. 17.50 (ISBN 90-286-0399-9). Sijthoff & Noordhoff.

OECD. Maritime Transport Nineteen Seventy-Nine. (Illus.). 151p. (Orig.). 1980. pap. text ed. 10.50x (ISBN 92-64-12122-6). OECD.

Papadakis, N. International Law of the Sea: A Bibliography. 432p. 1980. 85.00x (ISBN 90-286-0269-0). Sijthoff & Noordhoff.

Procedures for the Control of Ships & Discharges. 22p. 1978. 7.00 (ISBN 0-686-70792-3, IMCO). Unipub.

Rao, P. Sreenivasa. The Public Order of Ocean Resources: A Critique of the Contemporary Law of the Sea. LC 75-12741. 336p. 1975. text ed. 26.00x (ISBN 0-262-18072-3). MIT Pr.

Rembe, N. S. Africa & the International Law of the Sea: A Study of the Contribution of the African States to the Third United Nations Conference on the Law of the Sea. (Series on Ocean Development: No. 6). 272p. 1980. 42.50 (ISBN 90-286-0639-4). Sijthoff & Noordhoff.

Report on the CIDA - FAO - CEDAF Seminar on the Cnanging Law of the Sea & the Fisheries of West Africa. 1979. pap. 10.75 (ISBN 92-5-100634-2, F 1500, FAO). Unipub.

Sebek, Viktor. The Eastern European States & the Development of the Law of the Sea: Regional Documents, National Legislation, 2 vols. LC 77-7734. 1977. looseleaf 75.00 ea. (ISBN 0-379-10186-6). Oceana.

Selden, John. Of the Dominion; or, Ownership of the Sea. Nedham, Marchamont, tr. from Lat. LC 76-38256. (The Evolution of Capitalism Ser.). Orig. Title: Mare Clasum. 548p. 1972. Repr. of 1652 ed. 30.00 (ISBN 0-405-04137-3). Arno.

Seminar Held at Bermuda Biological Station. Implications to Western North Atlantic Countries of the New Law of the Sea: Proceedings. Seaton, E. A., et al, eds. LC 78-104507. (BBS Special Publication Ser.: No. 14). (Illus.). 1977. pap. 6.00 (ISBN 0-917642-14-7). Bermuda Bio.

Simmonds, K. R., ed. Cases on Law of the Sea, 10 vols. 1976 ed. LC 76-27559. 1977. 42.50 ea. (ISBN 0-379-00886-6). Oceana.

Smith, George P., 2nd. Restricting the Concept of Free Seas: Modern Maritime Law Re-Evaluated. LC 79-10502. 260p. 1980. lib. bdg. 15.50 (ISBN 0-88275-998-1). Krieger.

Symmons, C. R. The Maritime Zones of Islands in International Law. (Developments in International Law Ser.: No. 1). 1979. lib. bdg. 40.00 (ISBN 90-247-2171-7, Pub. by Martinus Nijhoff Netherlands). Kluwer Boston.

Szekely, A. Latin America & the Law of the Sea, Release 1. 1980. 32.50 (ISBN 0-379-10180-7). Oceana.

Szekely, Alberto. Latin America & the Development of Law of the Sea: Regional Documents & National Legislation, Vol. 2. LC 76-40510. 1978. lib. bdg. 25.00x (ISBN 0-685-86999-7). Oceana.

Third U. N. Conference on the Law of the Sea: Summary Records of Meetings, Documents Resumed Eighth Session, Vol.12. 115p. 1980. pap. 9.00 (ISBN 0-686-29387-8, UN80-5-12, UN). Unipub.

Turpin, Edward A. & MacEwen, William A. Merchant Marine Officer's Handbook. 4th ed. LC 60-14988. (Illus.). 1965. 20.00x (ISBN 0-87033-056-X). Cornell Maritime.

United Nations Conference on the Law of the Sea, 3rd, Geneva, 1975. Proceedings. Platzoder, Renata, ed. xiv, 322p. 1975. pap. text ed. 17.95x (ISBN 3-7875-2127-5). Rothman.

University of Southampton. World Shipping Law, Release 2. 1980. 80.00 (ISBN 0-379-10168-8). Oceana.

University of Southampton Faculty Committee. Digest of World Shipping Law, Vol. 1. 1979. looseleaf 80.00 (ISBN 0-379-10166-1). Oceana.

Vitanyi, B. The International Regime of River Navigation. 406p. 1979. 57.50x (ISBN 90-286-0529-0). Sijthoff & Noordhoff.

Walsh, Don, ed. The Law of the Sea: Issues in Ocean Resource Management. LC 77-7823. (Praeger Special Studies). 1977. 29.95 (ISBN 0-03-022666-X). Praeger.

Warren, Gordon H. Fountain of Discontent: The Trent Affair & Freedom of the Seas. LC 80-24499. (Illus.). 366p. 1981. 18.95 (ISBN 0-930350-12-X). NE U Pr.

Welwood, William. An Abridgement of All Sea-Lawes. LC 72-6039. (English Experience Ser.: No. 565). 88p. 1973. Repr. of 1613 ed. 11.50 (ISBN 90-221-0565-2). Walter J Johnson.

--The Sea-Law of Scotland. LC 75-6890. (English Experience Ser.: No. 96). 36p. 1969. Repr. of 1590 ed. 7.00 (ISBN 90-221-0096-0). Walter J Johnson.

White, Irvin L. Decision-Making for Space: Law & Politics in Air, Sea, & Outer Space. LC 77-109153. 1970. 6.50 (ISBN 0-911198-24-5). Purdue.

Zacklin, Ralph, ed. The Changing Law of the Sea. LC 73-91982. 272p. 1974. 32.50x (ISBN 90-286-0084-1). Intl Pubns Serv.

--Changing Law of the Sea. 1974. 40.00 (ISBN 9-0286-0084-1). Heinman.

MARITIME LAW–AUSTRALIA

Lumb, R. D. The Law of the Sea & Australian off-Shore Areas. 2nd ed. 1978. 22.50x (ISBN 0-7022-1147-8). U of Queensland Pr.

MARITIME LAW–GREAT BRITAIN

Hill, C. J. Introduction to the Law of Carriage of Goods by Sea. 1974. 6.50 (ISBN 0-540-07374-1). Heinman.

MARITIME LAW–RUSSIA

Butler, William E. & Quigley, John B., Jr., eds. The Merchant Shipping Code of the USSR, 1968. Butler, William E. & Quigley, John B., Jr., trs. LC 73-101643. (Illus.). 181p. 1970. 14.00x (ISBN 0-8018-1127-9). Johns Hopkins.

MARITIME LAW–UNITED STATES

Gould Editorial Staff. Navigation Law of New York. 1978. looseleaf 5.00 (ISBN 0-87526-234-1). Gould.

Knauth, A. W. American Law of Ocean Bills of Lading. 4th rev. enl ed. 556p. 1953. 40.00 (ISBN 0-379-00014-8). Oceana.

Macveagh, Rogers. The Transportation Act 1920. Bruchey, Stuart, ed. LC 80-1330. (Railroads Ser.). 1981. Repr. of 1923 ed. lib. bdg. 85.00x (ISBN 0-405-13804-0). Arno.

Padelford, Norman J. Public Policy for the Use of the Seas. rev. ed. 1970. pap. 13.00x (ISBN 0-262-66001-6). MIT Pr.

Von Pfeil, Helena P., ed. Oceans, Coasts & Law: Holdings of 18 Libraries, with Union List & Suggested Subject Categories Plus Selected Additional Books, Papers, Foreign & U.S. Articles, 2 vols. LC 76-28310. 1976. 70.00x (ISBN 0-379-00586-7). Oceana.

MARITIME METEOROLOGY

see Meteorology, Maritime

MARITIME MUSEUMS

see Naval Museums

MARITIME PROVINCES, CANADA

Kerr, J. Ernest. Imprint of the Maritimes. (Illus.). 1959. 4.00 (ISBN 0-8158-0122-X). Chris Mass.

Kerr, Wilfred B. Maritime Provinces of British North America & the American Revolution. LC 73-83849. 1970. Repr. of 1941 ed. 8.50 (ISBN 0-8462-1393-1). Russell.

MacGregor, John. Historical & Descriptive Sketches of the Maritime Colonies of British America. Repr. of 1828 ed. 16.00 (ISBN 0-384-34800-9). Johnson Repr.

Pratson, Frederick J. A Guide to Atlantic Canada. new ed. LC 72-93258. (Illus., Orig.). 1973. pap. 3.95 (ISBN 0-85699-073-6). Chatham Pr.

Spicer, Stanley. Maritimes' Age of Sail. (Canadian Jackdaw Ser: No. C20). 1970. 6.95 (ISBN 0-670-45813-9, Grossman). Viking Pr.

MARITIME SHIPPING

see Shipping

MARITIME SURVEYING

see Hydrographic Surveying

MARITIME WAR

see War, Maritime (International Law)

MARIUS, GAIUS, ca. 155 B.C.-86 B.C.

Marius the Epicurean: His Sensations & Ideas. 1979. Repr. of 1896 ed. lib. bdg. 20.00- (ISBN 0-8482-2135-4). Norwood Edns.

MARIVAUX PIERRE CARLET DE CHAMBLAIN DE, 1688-1763

Cismaru, Alfred. Marivaux & Moliere: A Comparison. 1977. 12.95 (ISBN 0-89672-055-1). Tex Tech Pr.

Desvignes-Parent. Marivaux et l'Angleterre: Essai sur une Creation Dramatique Originale. 52.50 (ISBN 0-685-34043-0). French & Eur.

Haac, Oscar A. Marivaux. (World Authors Ser.: France: No. 294). 1974. lib. bdg. 10.95 (ISBN 0-8057-2593-8). Twayne.

Jamieson, Ruth K. Marivaux: A Study in Sensibility. LC 75-86278. 1969. Repr. of 1941 ed. lib. bdg. 14.00x (ISBN 0-374-94180-7). Octagon.

Kars, H. Le Portrait Chez Marivaux. (Degre' Second Ser.: No. 4). 259p. (Fr.). 1981. pap. text ed. 28.50x (ISBN 90-6203-653-8, Pub. by Rodopi Holland). Humanities.

McKee, Kenneth N. The Theater of Marivaux. LC 58-6823. (Illus.). 1958. 10.00x (ISBN 0-8147-0274-0). NYU Pr.

Rosbottom, Ronald C. Marivaux's Novels: Theme & Function in Early Eighteenth-Century Narrative. LC 73-8296. 240p. 1975. 14.50 (ISBN 0-8386-1419-1). Fairleigh Dickinson.

Spinelli, Donald C., ed. A Concordance to Marivaux's Comedies in Prose, 4 vols. LC 79-22708. (North Carolina Studies in the Romance Languages & Literatures: No. 218). 2794p. 1979. Set. 154.00 (ISBN 0-8078-9218-1, IS-00095, Pub. by NC Stud Romance Lang & Lit). Univ Microfilms.

Tilley, Arthur A. Three French Dramatists: Racine, Marivaux, Musset. LC 66-27169. 1967. Repr. of 1933 ed. 8.50 (ISBN 0-8462-0964-0). Russell.

MARK, SAINT

Hiebert, D. Edmond. Mark: A Portrait of the Servant. 400p. 1974. 12.95 (ISBN 0-8024-5182-9). Moody.

Vos, Howard F. Mark: A Study Guide Commentary. pap. 2.50 (ISBN 0-310-33873-5). Zondervan.

MARKEL, BART., 1935-

Scalzo, Joe. The Bart Markel Story. (Illus.). 1972. 5.95 (ISBN 0-87880-010-7). Norton.

MARKERS, HISTORICAL

see Historical Markers

MARKET GARDENING

see Truck Farming

MARKET SURVEYS

see also Advertising Research; Public Opinion Polls; Store Location

Barton, Leslie M. A Study of Eighty-One Principal American Markets. LC 75-22800. (America in Two Centuries Ser). (Illus.). 1976. Repr. of 1925 ed. 25.00x (ISBN 0-405-07672-X). Arno.

Blankenship, A. B. Professional Telephone Surveys. LC 77-7023. (Illus.). 1977. 19.50 (ISBN 0-07-005862-8, P&RB). McGraw.

Clover, Vernon T. & Balsley, Howard L. Business Research Methods. LC 78-50046. (Management Ser.). 1979. text ed. 24.95 (ISBN 0-88244-164-7). Grid Pub.

European Society for Opinion & Marketing Research. Fieldwork, Sampling & Questionnaire Design, Parts 1 & 2. (Seminars Ser.). 1973. 50.00x (ISBN 0-8002-1419-6). Intl Pubns Serv.

European Society for Opinion & Marketing Research, ed. Papers on Analysis of Data. 1978. pap. 55.00x (ISBN 0-8002-1781-0). Intl Pubns Serv.

Ferber, Robert, ed. Readings in the Analysis of Survey Data. LC 80-12975. 249p. (Orig.). 1980. pap. text ed. 24.00 (ISBN 0-87757-140-6). Am Mktg.

Goldstucker, Jac L., et al. New Developments in Retail Trading Area Analysis & Site Selection. LC 78-8033. (Research Monograph: No. 78). 1978. pap. 9.95 (ISBN 0-88406-115-9). Ga St U Busn Pub.

Golembiewski, Robert T. & Hilles, Richard J. Toward the Responsive Organization: The Theory & Practice of Survey Feed. 1979. pap. text ed. 12.95 (ISBN 0-89832-001-1). Brighton Pub Co.

Harder, T. Introduction to Mathematical Models in Market & Opinion Research: With Practical Applications,Computing Procedures, & Estimates of Computing Requirements. Friedlander, P. H. & Friedlander, E. H., trs. from Ger. 194p. 1969. lib. bdg. 29.00 (ISBN 90-277-0096-6, Pub. by Reidel Holland). Kluwer Boston.

Harvey, Joan M., ed. Statistics-Europe: Sources for Social, Economic & Market Research. 3rd ed. 1976. 62.00 (ISBN 0-900246-18-9, Pub. by CBD Research Ltd.). Gale.

Huber, Joan E., ed. Directory of U.S. & Canadian Marketing Surveys & Services. 3rd ed. 1979. loose-leaf 125.00 (ISBN 0-917148-75-4). Kline.

Hyman, Henry A. Where to Sell It. 400p. 1981. pap. 7.95 (ISBN 0-911818-21-9). World Almanac.

Institute of Internal Auditors. Marketing: One-Day Seminar, 3 books. Incl. Bk. 1. Digest of Controls & Tests. pap. text ed. 5.00 (ISBN 0-89413-025-0); Bk. 2. Notes. pap. text ed. 5.00 (ISBN 0-89413-026-9); Bk. 3. Seminar Leader's Discussion Notes. pap. text ed. 5.00 (ISBN 0-89413-027-7). 1974. Inst Inter Aud.

International Marketing Data & Statistics 1979-80. 1980. 115.00x (ISBN 0-686-60664-7, Euromonitor). Nichols Pub.

International Research Directory of Market Research Organizations 1977-78. 4th ed. 1977. 37.50x (ISBN 0-8002-1578-8). Intl Pubns Serv.

Magazine Marketing Service. M. M. S. County Buying Power Index. LC 75-22826. (America in Two Centuries Ser). 1976. Repr. of 1942 ed. 13.00x (ISBN 0-405-07698-3). Arno.

Pearce, Esmond. Marketing & Higher Management. (Professional Management Library). (Illus.). 1970. 17.50x (ISBN 0-04-658032-8). Intl Pubns Serv.

Robbins, Peter & Edwards, John. Guide to Non-Ferrous Metals & Their Markets. 1979. 32.50 (ISBN 0-89397-050-6). Nichols Pub.

Roth, Robert A. How to Conduct Surveys, Follow-up Studies, & Basic Data Collection in Evaluation Studies. (Illus.). 132p. (Orig.). 1981. pap. text ed. 8.75 (ISBN 0-8191-1650-5). U Pr of Amer.

Tower Publishing Company. New Hampshire Marketing Directory Nineteen Eighty. 1980. pap. 12.50 (ISBN 0-89442-021-6). Tower Pub Co.

Wilson, A. Marketing of Professional Services. 1972. 24.95 (ISBN 0-07-094239-0, P&RB). McGraw.

MARKETING

see also Bank Marketing; Commodity Exchanges; Customer Service; Distributive Education; Export Marketing; Merchandising; New Products; Physical Distribution of Goods; Price Discrimination; Price Maintenance; Price Policy; Retail Trade; Sales Management; Sales Promotion also Subdivision Marketing under Names of Commodities, E.g. Farm Produce–Marketing; Fruit–Marketing

Aaker, David A. Multivariate Analysis in Marketing. 2nd ed. 1980. pap. text ed. 13.50x (ISBN 0-89426-029-4). Scientific Pr.

Abell, Derek F. & Hammond, John. Strategic Market Planning: Problems & Analytical Approaches. 1979. text ed. 23.00 (ISBN 0-13-851089-X). P-H.

Alderson, Wroe. Marketing Behavior & Executive Action. Assael, Henry, ed. LC 78-222. (Century of Marketing Ser.). 1978. Repr. of 1957 ed. lib. bdg. 30.00x (ISBN 0-405-11162-2). Arno.

Allvine, Fred C. & Patterson, James M. Competition, Ltd.: The Marketing of Gasoline. LC 70-180491. (Illus.). 352p. 1972. 15.00x (ISBN 0-253-31390-2). Ind U Pr.

Allvine, Fred C., ed. Public Policy & Marketing Practices. 1973. 16.00 (ISBN 0-87757-044-2). Am Mktg.

Amarchand, D. & Varadharajan, B. An Introduction to Marketing. 1980. text ed. 15.00x (ISBN 0-7069-0699-3, Pub. by Vikas India). Advent NY.

Andersen, Clifton R. & Cateora, Philip R., eds. Marketing Insights: Selected Readings. 3rd ed. LC 74-82804. (Illus.). 561p. 1974. pap. 7.95x (ISBN 0-914872-01-X). Austin Pr.

Andersen, R. Clifton & Dommermuth, William P., eds. Distribution Systems: Firms, Functions, & Efficiencies. LC 70-184265. (Illus.). 1972. pap. text ed. 12.95x (ISBN 0-89197-127-0). Irvington.

Anderson, I. G. Marketing & Management: A World Register of Organizations. 1969. 12.00x (ISBN 0-900246-03-0). Intl Pubns Serv.

Anderson, W. Thomas, Jr., et al. Multidimensional Marketing: Managerial, Societal & Philosophical. LC 75-13358. (Illus.). 323p. (Orig.). 1976. pap. text ed. 6.95x (ISBN 0-914872-06-0). Austin Pr.

Andreasen, A. & Gardner, D., eds. Diffusing Marketing Theory & Research: The Contributions of Bauer, Green, Kotler & Levitt. LC 78-1544. (Proceedings Ser.). 1979. 13.00 (ISBN 0-87757-116-3). Am Mktg.

Annual Educators Conference Chicago, Illinois, August, 1980. Marketing in the Eighties, Changes & Challenges: Proceedings. Bagozzi, Richard P., et al, eds. LC 80-15934. (No. 46). (Illus., Orig.). 1980. pap. text ed. 30.00 (ISBN 0-87757-141-4). Am Mktg.

Assael, Henry, ed. A Century of Marketing Series, 33 bks. (Illus.). 1978. lib. bdg. 864.00x set (ISBN 0-405-11156-8). Arno.

--The Collected Works of C. C. Parlin: An Original Anthology. LC 78-260. (Century of Marketing Ser.). (Illus.). 1978. lib. bdg. 16.00x (ISBN 0-405-11159-2). Arno.

--Early Development & Conceptualization of the Field of Marketing: An Original Anthology. LC 78-278. (Century of Marketing Ser.). 1978. lib. bdg. 15.00x (ISBN 0-405-11188-6). Arno.

--A Pioneer in Marketing: L. D. H. Weld. an orginal anthology ed. LC 78-283. (Century of Marketing Ser.). 1978. lib. bdg. 40.00x (ISBN 0-405-11157-6). Arno.

Axel, Helen, ed. A Guide to Consumer Markets 1976-1977. LC 74-640154. (Report: No. 703). (Illus., Orig.). 1976. pap. 22.50 (ISBN 0-8237-0137-9). Conference Bd.

Axelrod, Nathan. Selected Cases in Fashion Marketing, 2 vols. 3rd ed. 1968. pap. 11.00 ea.; Vol. 1. pap. (ISBN 0-672-96037-0); Vol. 2. pap. (ISBN 0-672-96038-9). Bobbs.

Bachner, John P. & Khosla, Naresh K. Marketing & Promotion for Design Professionals. 368p. 1981. Repr. of 1977 ed. lib. bdg. price not set (ISBN 0-89874-362-1). Krieger.

Bagozzi, Richard P. Casual Models in Marketing. LC 79-11622. (Theories in Marketing Ser.). 303p. 1980. text ed. 24.95 (ISBN 0-471-01516-4). Wiley.

Bailey, Earl L. Formulating the Company's Marketing Policies. (Experience in Marketing Management Ser: No. 19). 1968. pap. 5.00 (ISBN 0-8237-0028-3). Conference Bd.

Bailey, Earl L., ed. Tomorrow's Marketing: A Symposium. (Report Ser: No. 623). 65p. (Orig.). 1974. pap. 5.00 (ISBN 0-8237-0053-4). Conference Bd.

Bair, Frank E., ed. International Marketing Handbook, 1981, 2 vols. LC 80-28549. (Illus.). 2380p. 1981. Set. 125.00 (ISBN 0-8103-0544-5). Gale.

Ballon, Robert J., ed. Marketing in Japan. LC 73-79771. (Illus.). 200p. 1973. 14.50x (ISBN 0-87011-200-7). Kodansha.

Bartels, Robert. Global Development & Marketing. LC 80-11542. (Marketing Ser.). 117p. 1981. pap. text ed. 8.95 (ISBN 0-88244-223-6). Grid Pub.

--Marketing Literature. Assael, Henry, ed. LC 78-228. (Century of Marketing Ser.). 1978. lib. bdg. 32.00x (ISBN 0-405-11165-7). Arno.

--Marketing Theory & Metatheory. LC 72-105536. 300p. 1970. 16.00 (ISBN 0-87757-030-2). Am Mktg.

Batzer & Greipl. Marketing-Lexikon. 330p. (Ger.). 1971. 38.00 (ISBN 3-478-22530-2, M-7548, Pub. by Vlg. Moderne Industrie). French & Eur.

Beaujeu-Garnier, J. & Delobez, A. Geography of Marketing. (Geographies for Advanced Study Ser.). (Illus.). 1979. pap. text ed. 19.95x (ISBN 0-582-48991-1). Longman.

Beaumont, John A., et al. Your Career in Marketing. 2nd ed. 1976. text ed. 11.96 (ISBN 0-07-004245-4, G); tchr's manual & key 3.00 (ISBN 0-07-004248-9); job activity guide 5.60 (ISBN 0-07-004246-2). McGraw.

Beckwith, Neil, et al, eds. Nineteen Seventy-Nine Educators Conference, Proceedings. LC 79-14547. (Proceedings Ser.: No. 44). (Illus.). pap. 24.00 (ISBN 0-87757-121-X). Am Mktg.

Bell, Chip R. The Marketing of Change. 1982. text ed. price not set (ISBN 0-89384-051-3). Learning Concepts.

Bell, Martin L. Marketing: Concepts & Strategy. 3rd ed. LC 78-69572. (Illus.). 1979. text ed. 19.95 (ISBN 0-395-26503-7); inst. manual 1.50 (ISBN 0-395-26504-5). HM.

Bennett, Peter D., et al. Marketing Management Student Learning Package. 1979. pap. text ed. 5.95 (ISBN 0-8403-2028-0). Kendall-Hunt.

Berry, Richard C. Industrial Marketing for Results. LC 80-18222. (Illus.). 144p. 1981. text ed. 19.95 (ISBN 0-201-00075-X). A-W.

Bettman, James R. Information Processing Theory of Consumer Choice. LC 78-52496. (Advances in Marketing). 1979. text ed. 16.95 (ISBN 0-201-00834-3). A-W.

Bikkie, J. A. General Business & Economic Foundations: Careers in Marketing. 1971. 5.96 (ISBN 0-07-005264-6, G); tchr's manual & key 3.00 (ISBN 0-07-005265-4). McGraw.

Bikkie, James A. Careers in Marketing. 2d ed. Dorr, Eugene, ed. LC 77-3865. (Occupational Manuals and Projects in Marketing). 1978. pap. text ed. 5.48 (ISBN 0-07-005236-0, G); teacher's manual & key 3.00 (ISBN 0-07-005237-9). McGraw.

Blokland, J. Continuous Consumer Equivalence Scales. 1976. pap. 17.00 (ISBN 90-247-1847-3, Pub. by Martinus Nijhoff Netherlands). Kluwer Boston.

Bobrow, Edwin E. Marketing Through Manufacturers Agents. 1978. 27.50 (ISBN 0-89846-003-4). Sales & Mktg.

Boone & Johnson. Marketing Channels. 2nd ed. 578p. 1977. 14.95 (ISBN 0-87814-026-3). Pennwell Pub.

Boone, Louis E. & Kurtz, David L. Contemporary Marketing. 3rd ed. 640p. 1980. 22.95 (ISBN 0-03-051391-X). Dryden Pr.

Borsodi, Ralph. The Distribution Age: A Study of the Economy of Modern Distribution. LC 75-39235. (Getting & Spending: the Consumer's Dilemma). (Illus.). 1976. Repr. of 1927 ed. 20.00x (ISBN 0-405-08011-5). Arno.

Brannen, William H. Practical Marketing for Your Small Retail Business. (Illus.). 272p. 1981. 16.95 (ISBN 0-13-692764-5, Spec); pap. 7.95 (ISBN 0-13-692756-4). P-H.

--Successful Marketing for Your Small Business. LC 78-1116. (Illus.). 1978. 16.95 (ISBN 0-13-863399-1, Spec); pap. 8.95 (ISBN 0-13-863381-9, Spec). P-H.

Brannen, William H., ed. Small Business Marketing: A Selected & Annotated Bibliography. LC 78-15082. (Bibliography Ser.: No. 31). 1978. 8.00 (ISBN 0-87757-112-0). Am Mktg.

Brennan, Michael J., ed. Patterns of Market Behavior: Essays in Honor of Philip Taft. LC 65-12932. (Illus.). viii, 258p. 1965. 15.00x (ISBN 0-87057-087-0, Pub. by Brown U Pr). U Pr of New Eng.

Breyer, Ralph F. The Marketing Institution. Assael, Henry, ed. LC 78-245. (Century of Marketing Ser.). 1978. Repr. of 1934 ed. lib. bdg. 21.00x (ISBN 0-405-11160-6). Arno.

Britt, Stewart H. Psychological Principles of Marketing & Consumer Behavior. LC 77-75658. 1978. 29.95 (ISBN 0-669-01513-X). Lexington Bks.

Brown, Robert W., ed. New Directions in Utility Marketing. (Michigan Business Papers: No. 53). 1970. pap. 2.00 (ISBN 0-87712-102-8). U Mich Busn Div Res.

Bucklin, Louis P. Productivity in Marketing. 1978. 10.00 (ISBN 0-87757-120-1). Am Mktg.

Buell, Victor P. & Heyel, Carl, eds. Handbook of Modern Marketing. LC 78-96238. (Illus.). 1504p. Date not set. 59.95 (ISBN 0-07-008838-1). McGraw.

Bush, Ronald F. & Brobst, Bob. Marketing Simulation: Analysis for Decision Making. 1979. pap. text ed. 8.95 scp (ISBN 0-06-040944-4, HarpC); scp computer deck write for info. (ISBN 0-06-040939-8); scp magnetic tape write for info. (ISBN 0-06-041103-1). Har-Row.

Business Communications Co. Direct Marketing Business, GB-060: New Perspectives. 1980. cancelled (ISBN 0-89336-276-X). BCC.

Buskirk, Richard H. Principles of Marketing. LC 74-29144. 1975. text ed. 19.20 (ISBN 0-913310-46-8). Par Inc.

Buxton, Graham. Effective Marketing Logistics: The Analysis Planning & Control of Distribution Operations. 1975. 37.50x (ISBN 0-8419-5007-5). Holmes & Meier.

Cafarelli, Eugene J. Developing New Products & Repositing Mature Brands: A Risk-Reduction System That Produces Investment Alternatives. (Marketing Management Ser.). 1980. 21.95 (ISBN 0-471-04634-5, Pub by Ronald Pr). Wiley.

Carlsen, Robert D. & McHugh, James F. Handbook of Sales & Marketing Forms & Formats. (Illus.). 1978. 45.00 (ISBN 0-13-380857-2, Busn). P-H.

Cassady, Ralph. Exchange by Private Treaty. LC 73-20659. (Studies in Marketing: No. 19). 1974. pap. 8.00 (ISBN 0-87755-183-9). U of Tex Busn Res.

Cateora, Philip R. & Richardson, Lee, eds. Readings in Marketing: The Qualitative & Quantitative Areas. LC 67-10928. (Illus., Orig.). 1967. pap. text ed. 5.95x (ISBN 0-89197-373-7). Irvington.

Chapman, R. W. Marketing Today. 2nd ed. 1973. 17.50x (ISBN 0-7002-0202-1). Intl Ideas.

Chase, Cochrane & Barasch, Kenneth L. Marketing Problem Solver. LC 76-57697. 1976. 34.95x (ISBN 0-8019-6496-2); pap. 18.95x (ISBN 0-8019-6495-4). Chilton.

Chisnall, Peter M. Effective Industrial Marketing. LC 76-54987. (Illus.). 1977. text ed. 20.00x (ISBN 0-582-45067-5). Longman.

Clark, Fred E. Principles of Marketing. Assael, Henry, ed. LC 78-255. (Century of Marketing Ser.). 1978. Repr. of 1922 ed. lib. bdg. 35.00x (ISBN 0-405-11158-4). Arno.

Cohen, William A. & Reddick, Marshall E. Successful Marketing for Small Business. 364p. 1981. 17.95 (ISBN 0-8144-5611-1). Am Mgmt.

Collins, Virgil D. World Marketing. Assael, Henry, ed. LC 78-271. (Century of Marketing Ser.). 1978. Repr. of 1935 ed. lib. bdg. 20.00x (ISBN 0-405-11186-X). Arno.

Constantin, James A., et al. Marketing Strategy & Management. 1976. text ed. 13.95x (ISBN 0-256-01694-1). Business Pubns.

Converse, Paul D. The Beginning of Marketing Thought in the United States, 2 vols. in one. Assael, Henry, ed. LC 78-282. (Century of Marketing Ser.). 1978. Repr. of 1959 ed. lib. bdg. 14.00x (ISBN 0-405-11161-4). Arno.

Corey, E. Raymond, ed. Industrial Marketing: Cases & Concepts. 2nd ed. (Illus.). 432p. 1976. 21.95 (ISBN 0-13-464248-1). P-H.

Cort, Stanton G. Perspectives on Retail Strategic Decision Making. 112p. 1979. pap. text ed. 30.00 (ISBN 0-686-60195-5, G28679). Natl Ret Merch.

Coxe, Weld. Marketing Architectural & Engineering Services. LC 78-31440. 214p. 1979. Repr. of 1971 ed. lib. bdg. 13.50 (ISBN 0-88275-861-6). Krieger.

Cravens, David W. & Hills, Gerald E. Marketing Decision Making. rev. ed. 1980. 21.95x (ISBN 0-256-02348-4). Irwin.

Crissy, W. J., et al. Selling: The Personal Force in Marketing. LC 76-45848. (Marketing Ser.). 1977. text ed. 24.95 (ISBN 0-471-18757-7). Wiley.

Cristol, Steven M., et al. Essentials of Media Planning: A Marketing Viewpoint. LC 75-21743. (Illus.). 96p. (Orig.). 1976. pap. text ed. 6.95x (ISBN 0-87251-019-0). Crain Bks.

Cundiff, Edward W. & Still, Richard R. Basic Marketing: Concepts, Decisions & Strategies. 2nd ed. LC 79-138478. 1971. ref. ed. 19.95 (ISBN 0-13-062638-4); study guide 4.95 (ISBN 0-13-062620-1). P-H.

Cundiff, Edward W., ed. Marketing Doctoral Dissertation Abstracts, 1978. (AMA Bibliography Ser.). 1979. pap. 14.00 (ISBN 0-686-59658-7). Am Mktg.

Cundiff, Edward W., et al. Fundamentals of Modern Marketing. 3rd ed. 1980. text ed. 19.95 (ISBN 0-13-341388-8). P-H.

Czepiel, John & Backman, Jules. Changing Marketing Strategies in a New Economy. LC 77-11109. (Key Issues Lecture Ser). 1977. pap. 5.50 (ISBN 0-672-97199-2). Bobbs.

Dalrymple, Douglas J. & Parsons, Leonard J. Marketing Mangement: Text & Cases. 2nd ed. LC 79-24833. (Wiley Ser. in Marketing). 1980. text ed. 24.95 (ISBN 0-471-03606-4). Wiley.

Davies, Ross L. Marketing Geography with Special Reference to Retailing. 300p. 1977. pap. text ed. 14.95x (ISBN 0-416-70700-9, Pub. by Chapman & Hall England). Methuen Inc.

Davis, Harry L. & Silk, Alvin J. Behavioral & Management Science in Marketing. LC 77-18878. 1978. 32.95 (ISBN 0-471-07179-X). Ronald Pr.

Dawson, John A., ed. The Marketing Environment. LC 78-31680. 1979. 32.00x (ISBN 0-312-51530-8). St Martin.

Delozier, M. Wayne, et al. Experiential Learning Exercises in Marketing. 1977. pap. text ed. 10.95 (ISBN 0-87620-285-7); instructor's manual on adoption of text free (ISBN 0-87620-280-6). Goodyear.
Delson, Donn. The Dictionary of Marketing & Related Terms in the Motion Picture Industry. LC 79-67865. 70p. (Orig.). 1979. pap. text ed. 7.95 (ISBN 0-9603574-0-8). Bradson.
DePaula, H. & Mueller, C. Marketing Today's Fashion. 1980. 15.95 (ISBN 0-13-558155-9). P-H.
De Torres, Juan. Metropolitan America: the Development of Its Major Markets. LC 76-20381. (Report Ser.: No. 692). (Illus.). 1976. pap. 15.00 (ISBN 0-8237-0126-3). Conference Bd.
Diamond, Jay & Pintel, Gerald. Principles of Marketing. 2nd ed. (Illus.). 1980. 15.95 (ISBN 0-13-701417-1); pap. text ed. 6.95 study guide (ISBN 0-13-701425-2). P-H.
Diamond, William M. Distribution Channels for Industrial Goods. 1963. 4.50x (ISBN 0-87776-114-0, R114). Ohio St U Admin Sci.
Didactic Systems Staff. Market Planning. (Simulation Game Ser.). 1972. pap. 24.90 (ISBN 0-89401-068-9); pap. 21.50 two or more (ISBN 0-685-78137-2). Didactic Syst.
--Market Strategy. (Simulation Game Ser.). 1970. pap. 24.90 (ISBN 0-89401-069-7); pap. 21.50 two or more (ISBN 0-685-78138-0); pap. 24.90 portuguese ed. (ISBN 0-89401-118-9). Didactic Syst.
Direct Marketing. LC 80-67813. (Marketing Ser.). 1980. pap. 4.95 (ISBN 0-87251-052-2). Crain Bks.
Dominguez, G. S. Marketing in Regulated Environment. (Marketing Management Ser.). 341p. 1978. 29.95 (ISBN 0-471-02402-3). Wiley.
Dominguez, George S. Marketing in a Regulated Environment. LC 77-22099. (Marketing Management Ser.). 1978. 29.95 (ISBN 0-471-02402-3). Ronald Pr.
Dorr, Eugene, et al. Merchandising. 2nd ed. (Occupational Manuals & Projects in Marketing Ser.). 1977. pap. text ed. 5.48 (ISBN 0-07-017615-9, G); tchr's manual & key 3.00 (ISBN 0-07-017616-7). McGraw.
Dow, R. Marketing & Work Study. 1969. 27.00 (ISBN 0-08-006430-2); pap. 14.00 (ISBN 0-08-006429-9). Pergamon.
Downing, George D. Basic Marketing. LC 79-142984. 448p. 1971. 17.95x (ISBN 0-675-09233-7); instructor's manual 3.95 (ISBN 0-686-66708-5). Merrill.
Educators' Conference of the American Marketing Association, Hartford, Aug. 7-10, 1977. Contemporary Marketing Thought - 1977: Educators' Proceedings. Greenberg, Barnett A. & Bellenger, Danny N., eds. LC 77-24923. (Series No. 41). 1977. pap. text ed. 12.00 (ISBN 0-87757-098-1). Am Mktg.
Eggert, Jim. Investigating Microeconomics. LC 79-16480. (Illus.). 136p. 1979. 8.95 (ISBN 0-913232-62-9); pap. 4.95 (ISBN 0-913232-61-0). W Kaufmann.
Eid, Nimr. Legal Aspects of Marketing Behavior in Lebanon & Kuwait. 142p. 1972. 5.00x (ISBN 0-8426-1251-3). Verry.
Eilenberg, Howard. What You Should Know About Research Techniques for Retailers. LC 67-28901. (Business Almanac Series No. 14). 1968. 5.95 (ISBN 0-379-11214-0). Oceana.
Eison, Irving L. Strategic Marketing in Food Service: Planning for Change. LC 80-16264. 1980. 18.95 (ISBN 0-912016-89-2). Lebhar Friedman.
Elsby, F. H. Marketing & the Sales Manager. 1969. 25.00 (ISBN 0-08-006537-6); pap. 13.25 (ISBN 0-08-006536-8). Pergamon.
--Marketing Cases. LC 70-122006. 1970. 25.00 (ISBN 0-08-015784-X); pap. text ed. 13.25 (ISBN 0-08-015783-1). Pergamon.
Ely, V. K. Organization for Marketing. (Occupational Manuals & Projects in Marketing). 1971. 5.96 (ISBN 0-07-019305-3, G); teacher's manual 3.00 (ISBN 0-07-019306-1). McGraw.
Enis, Ben. Marketing Principles. 3rd ed. 1980. write for info. (ISBN 0-8302-5484-6); instructor's manual by Gerald Albaum 18.95 (ISBN 0-8302-5485-4); study guide 8.95 (ISBN 0-8302-5486-2). Goodyear.
Enis, Ben M. & Cox, Keith M. Marketing Classics: A Selection of Influential Articles. 4th ed. 528p. 1981. text ed. 13.95 (ISBN 0-205-07325-5); tchr's guide free (ISBN 0-205-07326-3). Allyn.
Erickson, Gustav. Balanced Distribution. LC 64-13322. 1964. 5.00 (ISBN 0-8022-0457-0). Philos Lib.
European Marketing Data & Statistics 1981. 17th ed. (Illus.). 1980. 150.00 (ISBN 0-8103-0542-9). Gale.
Executive Checklist for Sales & Marketing. 50.00 (ISBN 0-686-51438-6). Auerbach.
Faria, Anthony J., et al. Compete: A Dynamic Marketing Simulation. rev. ed. 1979. pap. 8.50x (ISBN 0-256-02077-9). Business Pubns.
Financial & Operating Results of Department & Speciality Stores. 75p. 1980. pap. 50.00 (ISBN 0-686-60190-4, C134). Natl Ret Merch.
Financial Marketing. LC 80-67814. (Marketing Ser.). 1980. pap. 4.95 (ISBN 0-87251-051-4). Crain Bks.
Fisher, Lawrence. Industrial Marketing: An Analytical Approach to Planning & Execution. 2nd ed. 270p. 1976. text ed. 29.50x (ISBN 0-220-66292-4, Pub. by Busn Bks England). Renouf.
Fisk, George & Nason, Robert W., eds. Macromarketing, Vol. III: New Steps on the Learning Curve. 421p. 1979. 12.00 (ISBN 0-686-69387-6). U CO Busn Res Div.
Fisk, George, et al, eds. Macromarketng: Evolution of Thought, Vol. 4. 1980. 12.00 (ISBN 0-686-64748-3). U CO Busn Res Div.
Foster, Douglas. Marketing Imperative. 1974. 16.95x (ISBN 0-8464-0609-8). Beekman Pubs.
Fox, Edward J. & Wheatley, Edward W. Modern Marketing: Principles & Practice. 1978. text ed. 16.95x (ISBN 0-673-15045-3). Scott F.
Fram, E. H. What You Should Know About Small Business Marketing. LC 67-28902. (Business Almanac Ser: No. 11). 1968. 5.95 (ISBN 0-379-11211-6). Oceana.
Fraser, Richard G. Marketing One & Two. 1977. No. 1, 224p. text ed. 14.56x (ISBN 0-7715-0870-0); No. 2, 208p. text ed. 14.56x (ISBN 0-7715-0872-7); tchr's. guide 6.60x (ISBN 0-7715-0871-9). Forkner.
Frederick, John H. Industrial Marketing. Assael, Henry, ed. LC 78-223. (Century of Marketing Ser.). (Illus.). 1978. Repr. of 1934 ed. lib. bdg. 24.00x (ISBN 0-405-11187-8). Arno.
French, Warren A., et al. Views of Marketing: A Reader. (Illus.). 1979. pap. text ed. 10.50 scp (ISBN 0-06-042187-8, HarpC). Har-Row.
Frey, Cynthia J., et al, eds. Public Policy Issues in Marketing. Kinnear, Thomas C. & Reece, Bonnie B. (Illus.). 160p. (Orig.). 1980. pap. 6.00 (ISBN 0-87712-202-4). U Mich Busn Div Res.
Friday, William. How to Sell Your Product Through (Not to) Wholesalers. LC 79-90315. (Illus.). 1980. 14.50 (ISBN 0-934432-05-8). Prudent Pub Co.
Fuji Conference, Third, 1976. Marketing & Finance in the Course of Industrialization: Proceedings. Nakagawa, Keiichiro, ed. 1979. 29.50x (ISBN 0-86008-203-2, Pub. by U of Tokyo Pr). Intl Schol Bk Serv.
Fulmer, Robert M. The New Marketing. (Illus.). 1976. text ed. 19.95 (ISBN 0-02-339980-5). Macmillan.
Fulton, Sue, ed. Handbook of Independent Advertising & Marketing Services. annual 1978. pap. 35.00 (ISBN 0-917168-02-X). Executive Comm.
Fundamentals of Marketing. 5th ed. (Illus.). 1977. text ed. 17.50 (ISBN 0-07-060881-4, C); instructor's manual 6.95 (ISBN 0-07-060882-2); study 5.95 (ISBN 0-07-060883-0). McGraw.
Gaedeke, Ralph M., ed. Marketing in Private & Public Nonprofit Organizations: Perspectives & Illustrations. LC 76-23034. 1977. text ed. 13.95 (ISBN 0-87620-575-9). Goodyear.
Garfunkle, Stanley. Developing the Marketing Plan: A Practical Guide. 126p. 1980. pap. text ed. 4.95 (ISBN 0-394-32579-6). Random.
Gelb, Betsy & Gelb, Gabriel. Marketing Is Everybody's Business. 1980. pap. text ed. 8.95 (ISBN 0-8302-5492-7). Goodyear.
Gelb, Betsy D. & Enis, Ben M. Marketing Is Everybody's Business. 2d ed. LC 76-53774. 1977. pap. 8.95 (ISBN 0-87620-560-0). Goodyear.
Gelb, Betsy D., ed. Marketing Expansion in a Shrinking World-1978 Business Proceedings. new ed. LC 78-16711. (Proceedings Ser.: No. 42). (Illus.). 1978. pap. text ed. 7.00 (ISBN 0-87757-110-4). Am Mktg.
Gibson, Parke D. Seventy Billion in the Black: America's Black Consumers. 1978. 12.95 (ISBN 0-02-543160-9). Macmillan.
Gielnik, S. J. & Gossling, W. F., eds. Input, Output & Marketing: Proceedings of the 1977 London Conference & the 1979 Toledo Ohio Workshop. (I.-O.P.C. Conference Ser.: No. 4). (Illus.). 400p. 1980. 50.00x (ISBN 0-904870-14-6, Pub. by Input-Output England). Kelley.
Goble, Ross & Shaw, Roy. Controversy & Dialogue in Marketing. (Illus.). 480p. 1975. pap. text ed. 11.95 (ISBN 0-13-172320-0). P-H.
Goetsch, H. W. How to Prepare & Use Marketing Plans for Profit. LC 79-91046. 1979. pap. text ed. 20.00 (ISBN 0-686-63539-6). Am Mktg.
Goldstucker, Jac L., ed. Marketing Information: A Professional Reference Guide. 1981. 29.95 (ISBN 0-88406-132-9). Ga St U Busn Pub.
Gonzalez-Arce, Jorge F. Market Segmentation by Consumer Perception. LC 74-620059. 134p. 1974. pap. 6.00 (ISBN 0-87744-124-3). Mich St U Busn.
Good, Charles M. Market Development in Traditionally Marketless Societies. LC 73-713883. (Papers in International Studies: Africa: No. 12). (Illus.). 1971. pap. 4.00x (ISBN 0-89680-045-8). Ohio U Ctr Intl.
Gould, James. Marketing Anthology. (Illus.). 1979. pap. text ed. 10.50 (ISBN 0-8299-0255-4). West Pub.
Greenberg, Barnett & Bellenger, Danny. The Classification of Consumer Goods: An Empirical Study. LC 74-621745. (Research Monograph: No. 56). 82p. 1974. spiral bdg. 7.00 (ISBN 0-88406-022-5). Ga St U Busn Pub.
Greenhut, Melvin L. & Ohta, Hiroshi. Theory of Spatial Prices & Market Areas. LC 74-83786. x, 265p. 1975. 17.50 (ISBN 0-8223-0333-7). Duke.
Greensted, C. S., et al. Essentials of Statistics in Marketing. 1974. 19.95 (ISBN 0-470-32630-1). Halsted Pr.
Greer, Douglas F. Cases in Marketing: Orientation, Analysis, & Problems. 2nd ed. 1979. pap. text ed. 9.95 (ISBN 0-02-347030-5); instrs'. manual avail. Macmillan.
Griggs, John E. Evaluating Marketing Change: An Application of Systems Theory. LC 75-628281. 1970. 8.00 (ISBN 0-87744-097-2). Mich St U Busn.
Gruber, Clemens. Dictionary of Advertising & Marketing. (Eng. & Ger.). 1977. pap. 14.50 (ISBN 3-1900-6312-5). Adler.
--Woerterbuch der Werbung und des Marketing. (Eng. -Ger., Dictionary of Advertising & Marketing). 1977. pap. 15.00 (ISBN 3-19-006312-5, M-6942). French & Eur.
Guseman, Dennis & Dahringer, Lee. A Primer on Marketing Decision Making. 416p. 1980. pap. text ed. 6.95 (ISBN 0-394-32493-5). Random.
Gwinner, Robert F., et al. Marketing: An Environmental Perspective. (Illus.). 1977. text ed. 20.95 (ISBN 0-8299-0119-1); instrs.' manual avail. (ISBN 0-8299-0484-0). West Pub.
Haas, Kenneth. Opportunities in Sales & Marketing Careers. LC 76-14056. (Illus.). (gr. 9 up). 1976. PLB 6.60 (ISBN 0-8442-6407-5); pap. text ed. 4.95 (ISBN 0-685-67325-1). Natl Textbk.
Hafer, George B., ed. A Look Back, a Look Ahead. LC 80-10370. (Proceedings Ser.). (Illus.). 207p. (Orig.). 1980. pap. text ed. 10.00 (ISBN 0-87757-134-1). Am Mktg.
Hall, Elvajean. Jobs in Marketing & Distribution. LC 73-17711. (Exploring Careers Ser.). (Illus.). 96p. (gr. 5 up). 1974. 7.25 (ISBN 0-688-75009-5). Lothrop.
Hanna, Nessim. Marketing Opportunities in Egypt: A Business Guide. LC 77-78894. 10.00 (ISBN 0-88247-468-5). R & E Res Assoc.
Hansen, Harry L. Marketing: Text, Techniques, & Cases. 4th ed. 1977. 20.95x (ISBN 0-256-01642-9). Irwin.
Hasty, Ronald W. & Will, R. Ted. Marketing. LC 74-23166. 400p. 1975. text ed. 21.50 scp (ISBN 0-06-389407-6, HarpC); scp study guide 6.95 (ISBN 0-06-389408-4). Har-Row.
Head, Victor. Sponsorship: The Newest Marketing Skill. 160p. 1980. 39.00x (ISBN 0-85941-151-6, Pub. by Woodhead-Faulkner England). State Mutual Bk.
Healy, Denis F. Strategic Marketing Management in a Dynamic Environment. LC 77-70998. (Monograph Ser.). 1977. pap. text ed. 7.50 (ISBN 0-8046-9207-6). Kennikat.
Heidingsfield, Myron S. & Blankenship, Albert B. Marketing. 3rd ed. 1974. pap. 4.95 (ISBN 0-06-460157-9, CO 157, COS). Har-Row.
Henry, Harry. Perspectives in Management Marketing & Research. 400p. 1971. 19.00x (ISBN 0-8464-0711-6). Beekman Pubs.
Heskett, James L. Marketing. (Illus.). 640p. 1976. text ed. 20.95 (ISBN 0-02-353940-2). Macmillan.
Hill, Richard M., et al. Industrial Marketing. 4th ed. 1975. 20.50x (ISBN 0-256-00010-7). Irwin.
Hill, S. R. The Distributive System. 1966. 15.00 (ISBN 0-08-011738-4); pap. 7.00 (ISBN 0-08-011737-6). Pergamon.
Hise, et al. Basic Marketing: Concepts & Decisions. 1979. text ed. 18.95 (ISBN 0-87626-056-3); pap. 6.95 study guide (ISBN 0-87626-057-1). Winthrop.
Hiserodt, Donald. Human Relations in Marketing. 2nd ed. Dorr, Eugene, ed. (Occupational Manuals & Projects in Marketing Ser.). (Illus.). 1978. pap. text ed. 5.48 (ISBN 0-07-029052-0, G); tchr's manual & key 3.00 (ISBN 0-07-029053-9). McGraw.
Hoel, Robert F. Marketing Now! 192p. 1973. pap. 5.95x (ISBN 0-673-07875-2). Scott F.
Holbert, Neil. Careers in Marketing. LC 76-20704. (Monograph Ser.: No. 4). 1976. pap. 1.50 (ISBN 0-87757-077-9). Am Mktg.
Holtje, Herbert F. Schaum's Outline of Marketing. (Schaum's Outline Ser.). (Illus.). 176p. 1980. pap. 4.95 (ISBN 0-07-029661-8). McGraw.
Hong, Alfred. Marketing Economics Guide 1976-77: Current Market Dimensions for 1500 Cities, All 3100 Countie S, All Metro Areas. new ed. LC 76-647896. (Illus.). 280p. 1976. 20.00 (ISBN 0-914078-21-6). Marketing Econs.
Hong, Alfred, ed. Marketing Economics Guide Nineteen Seventy-Nine to Nineteen Eighty: Current Market Dimensions for 1500 Cities, All 3100 Counties All Metro Areas. LC 73-647896. (Illus.). 1979. 20.00 (ISBN 0-914078-33-X). Marketing Econs.
--Marketing Economics Guide 1973-74: Current Market Dimensions for 1500 Cities, All 3100 Counties, All Metro Areas. new ed. (Illus.). 264p. 1973. 20.00 (ISBN 0-914078-09-7). Marketing Econs.
--Marketing Economics Guide 1974-75: Current Market Dimensions for 1500 Cities, All 3100 Counties, All Metro Areas. (Illus.). 280p. 1974. 20.00 (ISBN 0-914078-10-0). Marketing Econs.
--Marketing Economics Guide 1975-76: Current Market Dimensions for 1500 Cities, All 3100 Counties, All Metro Areas. LC 73-647896. (Illus.). 280p. 1975. 20.00 (ISBN 0-914078-11-9). Marketing Econs.
--Marketing Economics Guide 1977-78: Current Market Dimensions for 1500 Cities, All 3100 Counties, All Metro Areas. LC 73-647896. (Illus.). 1977. 20.00 (ISBN 0-914078-22-4). Marketing Econs.
--Marketing Economics Guide 1978-79: Current Market Dimensions for 1500 Cities, All 3100 Counties All Metro Areas. LC 73-647896. (Illus.). 1978. 20.00 (ISBN 0-914078-32-1). Marketing Econs.
--Marketing Economics Guide, 1980-81: Current Market Dimensions for 1500 Cities, All 3100 Counties, All Metro Areas. LC 73-647896. (Illus.). 264p. 1980. 20.00 (ISBN 0-914078-43-7). Marketing Econs.
--Marketing Economics Key Plants, 1973: The Guide to Industrial Purchasing Power (National Edition) new ed. LC 73-642154. 600p. 1973. 90.00 (ISBN 0-914078-00-3). Marketing Econ.
--Marketing Economics Key Plants, 1975-76. Incl. The Guide to Industrial Purchasing Power (New England Regional Edition) 43p (ISBN 0-914078-13-5); The Guide to Industrial Purchasing Power (Middle Atlantic Regional Edition) 72p (ISBN 0-914078-14-3); The Guide to Industrial Purchasing Power (North Central Regional Edition) 79p (ISBN 0-914078-15-1); The Guide to Industrial Purchasing Power (West North Central Regional Edition) 37p (ISBN 0-914078-16-X); The Guide to Industrial Purchasing Power (South Atlantic Regional Edition) 63p (ISBN 0-914078-17-8); The Guide to Industrial Purchasing Power (East South Central Regional Edition) 43p (ISBN 0-914078-18-6); The Guide to Industrial Purchasing Power (West South Central Regional Edition) 39p (ISBN 0-914078-19-4); The Guide to Industrial Purchasing Power (Mountain & Pacific Regional Edition) 65p (ISBN 0-914078-20-8). LC 73-642154. 1975. 13.00 ea.; Set. 70.00 (ISBN 0-914078-12-7). Marketing Econs.
Horn, Maurice. The World Encyclopedia of Comics, 1 vol. ed. LC 75-22322. (Illus.). 785p. 1976. text ed. 30.00 (ISBN 0-87754-030-6). Chelsea Hse.
Howard, John A. Marketing: Executive & Buyer Behavior. LC 63-10525. 1963. 20.00x (ISBN 0-231-01979-3). Columbia U Pr.
Humbert, Jack & Williams, Larry. Petroleum Marketing. (Career Competencies in Marketing Ser.). (Illus.). (YA) (gr. 11-12). 1979. pap. 5.36 (ISBN 0-07-031206-0, G); tchr's manual & key 3.00 (ISBN 0-07-031207-9). McGraw.
International Marketing Data & Statistics 1981. 6th ed. (Illus.). 400p. 1980. 150.00 (ISBN 0-8103-0543-7). Gale.
International Marketing Data & Statistics 1979-80. 1980. 115.00x (ISBN 0-686-60664-7, Euromonitor). Nichols Pub.
Issel, Carl K. How to Promote Your Territory & Yourself. LC 81-80588. (Illus.). 178p. 1981. 22.95x (ISBN 0-939554-00-3). Indus Bk Pub.
Izraeli, D. & Zif, J. Societal Marketing Boards. LC 77-10606. 1978. 50.95 (ISBN 0-470-99308-1). Halsted Pr.
Jain, Chaman L. & Migliaro, Al. An Introduction to Direct Marketing. LC 78-4184. 1978. 7.50 (ISBN 0-8144-2218-7). Am Mgmt.
Jefkins, F. W. Marketing & PR Media Planning. LC 74-618347. 1974. text ed. 28.00 (ISBN 0-08-018086-8); pap. text ed. 13.25 (ISBN 0-08-018085-X). Pergamon.
Jefkins, Frank. Dictionary of Marketing & Communication. 1973. text ed. 17.95x (ISBN 0-7002-0218-8). Intl Ideas.
Kangun, Norman & Richardson, Lee, eds. Consumerism: New Challenges for Marketing. LC 77-7370. 1978. pap. text ed. 16.00 (ISBN 0-87757-097-3). Am Mktg.

Karp, Robert E. & Gorlick, Allan. Cross Cultural Considerations of Marketing & Consumer Behavior. 150p. 1974. pap. text ed. 7.95x (ISBN 0-8422-0407-5). Irvington.
Keay, F. Marketing & Sales Forecasting. 132p. 1972. pap. text ed. 12.75 (ISBN 0-08-016738-1). Pergamon.
Keay, F. & Wensley, G. F. Marketing Through Measurement. 1970. text ed. 27.00 (ISBN 0-08-015765-3); pap. 14.00 (ISBN 0-08-015764-5). Pergamon.
Keiser & Lupul. Marketing Interaction. (Orig.). 1977. pap. 11.95 (ISBN 0-87814-029-8). Pennwell Pub.
Kerin & Peterson. Perspectives on Strategic Marketing Management. 100p. 1980. text ed. 18.95 (ISBN 0-205-06722-0, 0867225). Allyn.
Kerin, Roger A. & Peterson, Robert A. Strategic Marketing Problems: Cases & Comments. 2nd ed. 1980. pap. text ed. 21.95 (ISBN 0-205-07329-8, 085980X). Allyn.
Kernan, Jerome B. & Sommers, Montrose S., eds. Perspectives in Marketing Theory. LC 68-19476. 1968. 24.50x (ISBN 0-89197-333-8); pap. text ed. 7.95x (ISBN 0-89197-334-6). Irvington.
Kerr, John R. & Littlefield, James E. Marketing: An Environmental Approach. (Illus.). 672p. 1974. ref. ed. 20.95 (ISBN 0-13-557330-0). P-H.
Kincaid, William M. Promotion: Products, Services & Ideas. (Illus.). 360p. 1981. text ed. 19.95 (ISBN 0-675-08082-7). Merrill.
King, Francis S. & Doukas, Peter T. Advertising Compendium. 1979. pap. text ed. 9.95 (ISBN 0-89669-015-6). Collegium Bk Pubs.
King, William R. & Zaltman, Gerald, eds. Marketing Scientific & Technical Information. (Special Studies in Science & Technology). 1979. lib. bdg. 25.75x (ISBN 0-89158-397-1). Westview.
Kirpalani, V. & Shapiro, S., eds. Marketing Effectiveness: Insights from Accounting & Finance: An Annotated Bibliography. LC 78-11534. (Bibliography Ser.: No. 33). 1978. 10.00 (ISBN 0-87757-118-X). Am Mktg.
Klaurens, M. K. Economics of Marketing. (Occupational Manuals & Projects in Marketing). 1971. text ed. 5.96 (ISBN 0-07-035018-3, G); tchr's manual & key 3.50 (ISBN 0-07-035019-1). McGraw.
Klaurens, Mary. The Economics of Marketing. 2nd ed. Dorr, Eugene L., ed. (Occupational Manuals & Projects in Marketing). (gr. 11-12). 1978. pap. text ed. 5.48 (ISBN 0-07-035020-5, G); tchr's manual & key 3.00 (ISBN 0-07-035021-3). McGraw.
Kobs, Jim. Profitable Direct Marketing. LC 79-53509. 1979. 22.95 (ISBN 0-87251-037-9). Crain Bks.
Kollat, D. T. & Blackwell, R. D. Strategic Marketing. LC 76-184299. 1972. text ed. 18.95 (ISBN 0-03-078770-X, HoltC). HR&W.
Kotler, Phillip. Marketing for Non-Profit Organizations. (Illus.). 448p. 1975. ref. ed. 20.95 (ISBN 0-13-556084-5). P-H.
Krieger, Murray. Student's Workbook for the Buyer's Manual. 300p. 1980. pap. text ed. 13.50 (ISBN 0-686-60198-X, M47579). Natl Ret Merch.
Kurtz, David L. & Boone, Louis E. Marketing. LC 80-65788. 736p. 1981. text ed. 22.95 (ISBN 0-03-057431-5). Dryden Pr.
Labys, Walter C. Market Structure, Bargaining Power, & Resource Price Formation. LC 78-19541. 256p. 1980. 23.95 (ISBN 0-669-02511-9). Lexington Bks.
LaPlaca, Peter J. & Frank, Newton, eds. Marketing Strategies for a Tough Environment. LC 79-15967. (Proceedings Ser.: No. 45). 211p. (Orig.). 1980. pap. text ed. 15.00 (ISBN 0-87757-125-2). Am Mktg.
Larrabee, Carroll B. How to Package for Profit: A Manual of Packaging. LC 75-39257. (Getting & Spending: the Consumer's Dilemma). (Illus.). 1976. Repr. of 1935 ed. 15.00x (ISBN 0-405-08030-1). Arno.
Larreche, Jean-C & Gatignon, Hubert. Markstrat: A Marketing Strategy Game. LC 77-89287. 1977. pap. 10.50x (ISBN 0-89426-010-3); teaching notes 10.00x (ISBN 0-89426-011-1). Scientific Pr.
Larreche, Jean-Claude & Strong, Edward C. Readings in Marketing Strategy. 1981. pap. text ed. 14.50x (ISBN 0-89426-030-8). Scientific Pr.
Lazer, William & Kelley, Eugene J. Social Marketing: Perspectives & Viewpoints. 1973. pap. 13.50x (ISBN 0-256-00284-3). Irwin.
Lebell, Frank. Independent Marketing-Selling. 288p. 1977. 19.95 (ISBN 0-9600762-3-9). Herman Pub.
Leeflang, P. S. Mathematical Models in Marketing. lib. bdg. 24.00 (ISBN 90-207-0436-2, Pub. by Martinus Nijhoff Netherlands). Kluwer Boston.
Leighton, David & Simmonds, Kenneth. Case Problems in Marketing. 1973. pap. text ed. 12.95 (ISBN 0-17-771026-8). Intl Ideas.
Lerner, Abba & Colander, David. MAP: A Market Anti-Inflation Plan. 128p. 1980. pap. text ed. 5.95 (ISBN 0-15-555060-8, HC). HarBraceJ.
Levitt, Theodore. Innovation in Marketing: New Perspectives for Profit & Growth. (Marketing & Advertising Ser.). 1962. text ed. 18.95 (ISBN 0-07-037377-9, P&RB); pap. text ed. 7.95 (ISBN 0-07-037378-7). McGraw.
--Marketing for Business Growth. Orig. Title: The Marketing Mode. (Illus.). 288p. 1974. 19.95 (ISBN 0-07-037415-5, P&RB). McGraw.
Levy, Leon, et al. Basic Retailing & Distribution. 3rd ed. LC 76-27635. 1977. text ed. 11.68 (ISBN 0-8224-2118-6); wkbk 5.00 (ISBN 0-8224-2119-4); tchrs'. manual 2.60 (ISBN 0-8224-2120-8). Pitman Learning.
Levy, Sidney J. Marketplace Behavior: Its Meaning for Management. (Illus.). 1979. 16.95 (ISBN 0-8144-5476-3). Am Mgmt.
Lewis, Edwin H. Marketing Channels: Structure & Strategy. 1968. pap. text ed. 6.95 (ISBN 0-07-037520-8, C). McGraw.
Lipson, Harry A. & Darling, John R. Marketing Fundamentals: Text & Cases. LC 80-12441. 590p. 1980. Repr. of 1974 ed. lib. bdg. 22.50 (ISBN 0-89874-166-1). Krieger.
Locander, William B. & Cocanougher, A. Benton. Problem Definition in Marketing. LC 75-8868. 20p. 1975. pap. 3.00 (ISBN 0-87757-066-3). Am Mktg.
Lovelock, Christopher & Weinberg, Charles. Cases in Public & Nonprofit Marketing. LC 77-87274. 1977. pap. 13.50x (ISBN 0-89426-015-4); teaching notes 12.50 (ISBN 0-89426-016-2). Scientific Pr.
Lovelock, Christopher H. & Weinberg, Charles B. Readings in Public & Nonprofit Marketing. LC 78-59621. 1978. pap. 14.50x (ISBN 0-89426-019-7). Scientific Pr.
Luck, David J. & Ferrell, O. C. Marketing Strategy & Plans. (Illus.). 1979. ref. ed. 20.95 (ISBN 0-13-558254-7). P-H.
Lund, Daulatram, et al. Marketing Distribution: A Selected & Annotated Bibliography. LC 79-18523. (AMA Bibliography Ser.). 1979. pap. 8.00 (ISBN 0-87757-130-9). Am Mktg.
Lusch, Robert F. & Zinszer, Paul H., eds. Contemporary Issues in Marketing Channels. 187p. 1979. 10.00 (ISBN 0-931880-00-9). U OK Ctr Econ.
Lynch, R. L. & Lunch, Richard L., eds. Food Marketing. (Career Competencies in Marketing Ser.). (Illus.). 1979. pap. text ed. 5.36 (ISBN 0-07-051483-6, G); teacher's manual & key 3.00 (ISBN 0-07-051484-4). McGraw.
Lyon, Leverett S. Salesman in Marketing Strategy. Assael, Henry, ed. LC 78-240. (Century of Marketing Ser.). 1978. Repr. of 1926 ed. lib. bdg. 25.00x (ISBN 0-405-11183-5). Arno.
McCarthy, E. Jerome. Essentials of Marketing. 1979. 19.95 (ISBN 0-256-02142-2); pap. 7.50x student aid (ISBN 0-256-02242-9). Irwin.
McCarthy, E. Jerome & Brogowicz, Andrew A. Learning Aid to Accompany Basic Marketing. 7th ed. 1981. pap. write for info. (ISBN 0-256-02534-7). Irwin.
McCarthy, E. Jerome & Shapiro, Stanley J. Basic Marketing: A Managerial Approach. Canadian ed. 2nd ed. 1979. text ed. 18.50x (ISBN 0-256-02138-4). Irwin.
McCarthy, E. Jerome, et al. Readings in Basic Marketing. 3rd ed. 1981. write for info. (ISBN 0-256-02535-5). Irwin.
McCarthy, Jerome E. & Brogowicz, Andrew A. Learning Aid to Accompany Basic Marketing. 7th ed. 1981. pap. write for info. (ISBN 0-256-02534-7). Irwin.
McCarthy, Jerome E., et al, eds. Readings in Basic Marketing. 3rd ed. 1981. pap. write for info. (ISBN 0-256-02535-5). Irwin.
Mc Daniel, Carl, Jr. Marketing: An Integrated Approach. 2nd ed. 736p. 1981. text ed, price not set (ISBN 0-06-044359-6, HarpC). Har-Row.
McDaniel, Carl, Jr. Marketing: An Integrated Approach. 1979. text ed. 21.50 scp (ISBN 0-06-044355-3, HarpC); inst. manual avail. (ISBN 0-06-364106-2); scp study guide 7.50 (ISBN 0-06-044356-1); test bank avail. (ISBN 0-06-364236-0); tapes o.p. 30.00 (ISBN 0-686-67347-6). Har-Row.
McKay, E. S. Marketing Mystique. LC 72-166557. 1972. 16.00 (ISBN 0-8144-5279-5). Am Mgmt.
Magee, John F. Physical Distribution Systems. (Illus.). 1967. pap. 7.50 (ISBN 0-07-039483-0, C). McGraw.
Mallen, Bruce. Principles of Marketing Channel Management. LC 76-27923. (Illus.). 1977. 23.95 (ISBN 0-669-00985-7). Lexington Bks.
Mallen, Bruce E. The Marketing Channel: A Conceptual Viewpoint. LC 67-17344. 308p. 1967. 12.50 (ISBN 0-471-56580-6, Pub. by Wiley). Krieger.
Mancuso, Joseph. Marketing Technology Products. 1975. Vol. 2. 8.75x (ISBN 0-89006-046-0). Artech Hse.
Mandell, M. & Rosenberg, L. Marketing. 2nd ed. 1981. 21.00 (ISBN 0-13-556225-2); pap. 7.95 study guide (ISBN 0-13-556233-3). P-H.
Marcus, Burton H. & Tauber, Edward M. Marketing Analysis & Decision Making. 1979. text ed. 18.95 (ISBN 0-316-54599-6); tchrs' manual free (ISBN 0-316-54600-3). Little.
Marketing for Bankers. 1975. 11.00 (ISBN 0-89982-071-9, 056600). Am Bankers.
Marketing Fruit & Vegetables. (FAO Marketing Guides: No. 2). (Orig.). 1974. pap. 12.25 (ISBN 0-685-02917-4, F271, FAO). Unipub.
The Marketing of Fish & Fishery Products in Europe: No. 2, Spain. (Fisheries Economics Research Unit Occasional Paper Ser.: No. 3). 56p. 1980. pap. 6.00 (ISBN 0-686-60080-0, WFA 041, WFA). Unipub.
Marketing, Sales Promotion, Advertising Planbook (S600) 65p. 1980. pap. 8.25 (ISBN 0-686-61528-X). Natl Ret Merch.
Markin, Rom. Marketing. 2nd ed. 768p. 1982. 20.95 (ISBN 0-471-08522-7); price not set tchr.'s ed. (ISBN 0-471-09466-8); price not set study guide (ISBN 0-471-09465-X); price not set tests (ISBN 0-471-08522-7). Wiley.
Markin, Rom J. Marketing. LC 78-11242. (Wiley Series in Marketing). 1979. text ed. 22.95 (ISBN 0-471-01999-2); study guide avail. (ISBN 0-471-02000-1). Wiley.
Martin, Warren S. Personality & Product Symbolism. LC 73-13395. (Studies in Marketing: No. 18). 1973. pap. 4.00 (ISBN 0-87755-182-0). U of Tex Busn Res.
Mason, R., et al. Marketing Practices & Principles. 3rd ed. (Illus.). 1980. text ed. 12.52 (ISBN 0-07-040693-6, G); activity guide 5.32 (ISBN 0-07-040694-4); tchr's manual & key 4.50 (ISBN 0-07-040695-2). McGraw.
Mathisen, Marilyn. Apparel & Accessories. Lynch, Richard, ed. (Career Competencies in Marketing). (Illus.). 1979. pap. text ed. 5.36 (ISBN 0-07-040905-6, G); teachers' manual & key 3.00 (ISBN 0-07-040906-4). McGraw.
Mazze, Edward. Personal Selling: Choice Against Chance. LC 75-35859. (Illus.). 350p. 1976. pap. text ed. 14.95 (ISBN 0-8299-0067-5); pap. text ed. 9.95 (ISBN 0-8299-0114-0). West Pub.
Mellott, Douglas W., Jr. Marketing: Principles & Practices. (Illus.). 1978. ref. ed. 16.95 (ISBN 0-87909-455-9); instrs'. manual avail. Reston.
Merchandising & Operating Results of Department & Specialty Stores (MOR) 200p. 1980. pap. 50.00 (ISBN 0-686-60192-0, C139). Natl Ret Merch.
Middle East Market Research Bureau Ltd. Marketing to Middle East Consumers. 220p. 1980. 55.00x (ISBN 0-86010-198-3, Pub. by Graham & Trotman England). State Mutual Bk.
Miller, Jody G., et al, eds. Penjerdel Location & Market Guide. LC 77-78304. (Illus.). 1981. pap. 20.00 (ISBN 0-918964-00-8). Greater Phila.
Minority Marketing. LC 80-67815. (Marketing Ser.). 1980. pap. 4.95 (ISBN 0-87251-054-9). Crain Bks.
Mitchell, Andrew A., ed. The Effect of Information on Consumer & Market Behavior. LC 77-15505. (Proceedings Ser.). (Illus.). 1978. pap. text ed. 7.00 (ISBN 0-87757-103-1). Am Mktg.
Mokwa, Michael P. & Dawson, William M. Marketing the Arts: Praeger Series in Public & Nonprofit Sector Marketing. Permut, S., ed. LC 79-26603. (Praeger Special Studies Ser.). 304p. 1980. 22.95 (ISBN 0-03-052141-6). Praeger.
Monroe, Wilbur F. Theory of Exchange Market Intervention. LC 70-111384. (Research Monograph: No. 51). 1970. spiral bdg. 5.00 (ISBN 0-88406-063-2). Ga St U Busn Pub.
Montana, Patrick J., ed. Marketing in Nonprofit Organizations. new ed. 1978. 13.95 (ISBN 0-8144-5494-1). Am Mgmt.
Mortenson, William P. Modern Marketing of Farm Products. 3rd ed. LC 76-14650. (Illus.). (gr. 9-12). 1977. 15.35 (ISBN 0-8134-1816-X). Interstate.
Moyer, Reed & Hutt, Michael D. Macro Marketing: A Social Perspective. 2nd ed. LC 77-26816. (Wiley Ser. in Marketing). 1978. text ed. 10.95 (ISBN 0-471-02699-9). Wiley.
Multinational Marketing & Employment Directory. 8th ed. 1981. 100.00 (ISBN 0-8360-0023-4). World Trade.
Murphy, Patrick E. & Laczniak, Eugene R. Marketing Education: Current Status & a View for the Nineteen Eighties. LC 80-10146. (Monograph: No. 11). 106p. (Orig.). 1980. pap. text ed. 7.00 (ISBN 0-87757-133-3). Am Mktg.
Naert, P. A. & Leeflang, P. S. Building Implementable Marketing Models. 1978. pap. 27.50 (ISBN 9-0207-0436-2, Pub. by Martinus Nijhoff Netherlands); lib. bdg. 43.00 (ISBN 90-207-0865-1, Martinus Nijhoff Pubs). Kluwer Boston.
Napier, Briggs & Hovelsrud, Joyce. How to Show & Tell to up the Sell. (Illus.). 160p. 1979. pap. 12.95 (ISBN 0-935814-00-0). Shepherd Pubns.
Nash, E. L. Direct Marketing: Strategy, Planning, Execution. 1981. price not set (ISBN 0-07-046019-1). McGraw.
Naylor, John & Wood, Alan. Practical Marketing Audits: A Guide to Increased Profitability. LC 78-2948. 1978. 27.95x (ISBN 0-470-26327-X). Halsted Pr.
Ness, Thomas E. Marketing in Action: A Decision Game Student's Manual. 4th ed. Day, Ralph L., tr. 1978. pap. 9.95x (ISBN 0-256-01924-X). Irwin.
Nickels, William G. Marketing Communications & Promotion. 2nd ed. LC 79-17114. (Grid Ser. in Marketing). 1980. text ed. 23.00 (ISBN 0-88244-197-3). Grid Pub.
Nickels, Williams G. Marketing Principles: A Broadened Concept of Marketing. LC 77-24308. 1978. text ed. 19.95 (ISBN 0-13-558205-9); study guide 5.95 (ISBN 0-13-558213-X). P-H.
Nyssen, Hubert. Lexique Du Marketing. 86p. (Fr.). 1971. pap. 7.50 (ISBN 0-686-57064-2, M-6435). French & Eur.
OECD. Bargain Price Offers & Similar Marketing Practices. (Illus., Orig.). 1980. pap. text ed. 6.00 (ISBN 92-64-12033-5, 24-80-01-1). OECD.
Otteson, Schuyler F., et al. Marketing Firms Viewpoint. (Illus.). 1964. text ed. 11.95x (ISBN 0-02-389980-8). Macmillan.
Padolecchia, S. P. Marketing in the Developing World. 190p. 1979. 14.00x (ISBN 0-7069-0667-5, Pub. by Croom Helm Ltd England). Biblio Dist.
Palamountain, Joseph C. Politics of Distribution. LC 68-8070. (Illus.). 1968. Repr. of 1955 ed. lib. bdg. 15.75x (ISBN 0-8371-0186-7, PAPD). Greenwood.
Paranka, Stephen. Marketing Implications of Inter-Urban Development. LC 58-63833. (Research Monograph: No. 11). 1958. spiral bdg. 5.00 (ISBN 0-88406-028-4). Ga St U Busn Pub.
Parsons, Leonard J. & Schultz, Randall L. Marketing Models & Econometric Research. LC 76-476. 1976. text ed. 28.50 (ISBN 0-7204-8601-7, North Holland). Elsevier.
Pearce, Colin. Prediction Techniques for Marketing Planners: The Practical Application of Forecasting Methods to Business Problems. 254p. 1971. 17.50x (ISBN 0-304-93885-8). Intl Pubns Serv.
Peterson, Robin, et al. Marketing in Action: An Experiential Approach. (Illus.). 1978. pap. text ed. 10.95 (ISBN 0-8299-0204-X); instrs.' manual avail. (ISBN 0-8299-0565-0). West Pub.
Peterson, Robin T. Personal Selling: An Introduction. LC 77-10979. (Marketing Ser.). 1978. text ed. 23.50 (ISBN 0-471-01743-4). Wiley.
Picard, Jacques L. Marketing Decisions for European Operations in the U.S. LC 78-24322. (Research for Business Decisions Ser.: No. 4). 1978. 20.50 (ISBN 0-8357-0956-6). Univ Microfilms.
Pride, William M. & Perrell, O. C. Marketing: Basic Concepts & Decisions. 2nd ed. LC 79-88040. 1980. text ed. 18.50 (ISBN 0-395-28059-1); study guide pap. 7.25 (ISBN 0-395-28163-6); instr's manual 3.25 (ISBN 0-395-28161-X). HM.
Progressive Grocer's Marketing Guidebook Staff. New Idea Book. 2nd ed. (Illus.). 1982. 18.95 (ISBN 0-911790-59-4). Prog Grocer.
Rabassa Asenjo, Bernardo & Garcia Tous, M. R. Diccionario De Marketing. 168p. (Espn.). 1978. 14.95 (ISBN 84-368-0075-3, S-50176). French & Eur.
Rachman, David. Marketing Strategy & Structure. LC 73-17352. (Illus.). 448p. 1974. text ed. 18.95 (ISBN 0-13-558338-1). P-H.
Rachman, David J. Modern Marketing. 704p. 1980. text ed. 19.95 (ISBN 0-03-054726-1). Dryden Pr.
Rachman, David J. & Berman, Barry. Marketing Strategy & Structure: Study Guide. (Illus.). 160p. 1975. pap. 4.95 (ISBN 0-13-558320-9). P-H.
Ramond, Charles. The Art of Using Science in Marketing. (Sheth Ser.). 1974. pap. text ed. 15.50 scp (ISBN 0-06-045321-4, HarpC). Har-Row.
Ranganadha, S. Economic Expansion & Marketing Motivation. 1975. 10.00x (ISBN 0-8002-0592-8). Intl Pubns Serv.
Rath, Patricia M., et al. Case Studies in Marketing & Distribution. (Illus.). 180p. (gr. 9-12). 1965. pap. text ed. 2.95x (ISBN 0-8134-0835-0, 835). Interstate.
Rathmell, J. Marketing in the Service Sector. 1974. text ed. 9.95 (ISBN 0-87626-561-1). Winthrop.
Readings in Marketing 1979-1980. rev. ed. LC 73-78578. (Illus., Orig.). 1979. pap. text ed. 6.95 (ISBN 0-686-51242-1). Dushkin Pub.

Readings in Marketing 77-78. rev. ed. LC 73-78578. (Annual Editions Ser.). 256p. (Orig.). 1976. pap. text ed. 5.95 (ISBN 0-685-61368-2). Dushkin Pub.
Readings in Marketing 78-79. LC 73-78578. (Annual Editions Ser.). (Illus.). 1978. pap. text ed. 6.25 (ISBN 0-87967-143-2). Dushkin Pub.
Reid, Margaret G. Consumers & the Market. 3rd ed. LC 75-39270. (Getting & Spending: a Consumer's Dilemma). (Illus.). 1976. Repr. of 1947 ed. 35.00x (ISBN 0-405-08042-5). Arno.
Reilly, William J. Marketing Investigations. Assael, Henry, ed. LC 78-251. (Century of Marketing Ser.). 1978. Repr. of 1929 ed. lib. bdg. 15.00x (ISBN 0-405-11176-2). Arno.
Revzan, David A. Wholesaling in Marketing Organization. Assael, Henry, ed. LC 78-256. (Century in Marketing Ser.). 1978. Repr. of 1961 ed. lib. bdg. 40.00x (ISBN 0-405-11181-9). Arno.
Rexroad, Robert A. Technical Marketing to the Government. 325p. 1981. 76.50 (ISBN 0-85013-122-7). Dartnell Corp.
Rice, William & Smith, Ted. The Marketing Experience. (Orig.). 1980. pap. text ed. 8.95 (ISBN 0-03-051401-0). Dryden Pr.
Robicheaux, Robert A. & Pride, William M. Marketing: Contemporary Dimensions. 2nd ed. LC 79-89125. 1980. pap. text ed. 9.50 (ISBN 0-395-28500-3). HM.
Robin, Donald. Marketing: Basic Concepts for Decision-Making. 1978. text ed. 20.50 scp (ISBN 0-06-387849-6, HarpC); tchr's ed. free (ISBN 0-06-376131-9); scp study guide 6.50 (ISBN 0-06-386805-9). Har-Row.
--Marketing: Basic Concepts for Decision-Making. 1978. text ed. 20.50 scp (ISBN 0-06-387849-6, HarpC); tchr's ed. free (ISBN 0-06-376131-9); scp study guide 6.50 (ISBN 0-06-386805-9). Har-Row.
Robinson, Richard K. & Lovelock, Christopher H., eds. Marketing Public Transportation. LC 80-12552. (Proceedings Ser.). (Illus.). 104p. (Orig.). 1981. pap. text ed. 7.00 (ISBN 0-87757-139-2). Am Mktg.
Rodger, L. W. Marketing in a Competitive Economy. 3rd ed. LC 73-3342. 253p. 1965. pap. 13.95 (ISBN 0-470-72928-7). Halsted Pr.
Rodger, Leslie W. Marketing in a Competitive Economy. 3rd ed. LC 66-871. 1971. 15.00x (ISBN 0-85227-006-2). Intl Pubns Serv.
Rodgers, Peggy. Marketing in the Textile Industry. 1979. 75.00x (ISBN 0-686-63774-7). State Mutual Bk.
Rogers, Robert S. & Chamberlain, V. B., 3rd, eds. National Account Marketing Handbook. 426p. 1981. 24.95 (ISBN 0-8144-5618-9). Am Mgmt.
Rosenberg, L. Marketing. (Illus.). 1977. 19.95 (ISBN 0-13-556100-0); wkbk. & study guide 4.95 (ISBN 0-13-556118-3). P-H.
Rosenberg, Larry J. & Assael, Henry, eds. The Roots of Marketing Strategy: An Original Anthology. LC 78-289. (Century of Marketing Ser.). 1978. lib. bdg. 32.00x (ISBN 0-405-11189-4). Arno.
Rosenbloom. Marketing Channels. 1978. 22.95 (ISBN 0-03-017831-2). Dryden Pr.
Rosenbloom, Bert. Retail Marketing. 470p. 1981. text ed. 20.95 (ISBN 0-394-32192-8). Random.
Rowe, K. L. & Jimerson, H. C. Communications in Marketing. 1971. 5.96 (ISBN 0-07-054156-6, G); tchr's manual & key 3.50 (ISBN 0-07-054157-4). McGraw.
Rudman, Jack. Introductory Marketing. (College Level Examination Ser.: CLEP-23). 14.95 (ISBN 0-8373-5373-4); pap. 9.95 (ISBN 0-8373-5323-8). Natl Learning.
--Marketing, Level 1. (ACT Proficiency Examination Program: PEP-21). (Cloth bdg. avail. on request). pap. 9.95 (ISBN 0-8373-5521-4). Natl Learning.
--Marketing, Level 2. (ACT Proficiency Examination Program: PEP-22). (Cloth bdg. avail. on request). pap. 9.95 (ISBN 0-8373-5522-2). Natl Learning.
--Marketing, Level 3. (ACT Proficiency Examination Program: PEP-23). (Cloth bdg. avail. on request). pap. 9.95 (ISBN 0-8373-5523-0). Natl Learning.
--Marketing One. (Regents External Degree Ser.: REDP-10). (Cloth bdg. avail. on request). pap. 9.95 (ISBN 0-8373-5610-5). Natl Learning.
--Marketing Representative. (Career Examination Ser.: C-2465). (Cloth bdg. avail. on request). pap. 8.00 (ISBN 0-8373-2465-3). Natl Learning.
--Marketing Three. (Regents External Degree Ser.: REDP-12). (Cloth bdg. avail. on request). pap. 9.95 (ISBN 0-8373-5612-1). Natl Learning.
--Marketing Two. (Regents External Degree Ser.: REDP-11). (Cloth bdg. avail. on request). pap. 9.95 (ISBN 0-8373-5611-3). Natl Learning.
--Senior Marketing Representative. (Career Examination Ser.: C-2053). (Cloth bdg. avail. on request). 1977. pap. 8.00 (ISBN 0-8373-2053-4). Natl Learning.
Runyon, Kenneth E. Advertising & the Practice of Marketing. (Marketing & Management Ser.). 1979. text ed. 22.95 (ISBN 0-675-08311-7); instructor's manual 3.95 (ISBN 0-686-67275-5); transparencies 3.95 (ISBN 0-686-67276-3). Merrill.
Ryan. Plaid for Principles of Marketing. 3rd ed. 1980. 6.95 (ISBN 0-256-02220-8, 09-0871-03). Learning Syst.
Ryan, William T. A Guide to Marketing, Bk. 264. (Irwin Publications for Professional Development Guides Ser.). 336p. Date not set. pap. 7.95 (ISBN 0-686-75004-7). Dow Jones-Irwin.
Ryans, John K., Jr., ed. Marketing Doctoral Dissertation Abstracts, 1979. (Bibliography Ser.: No. 38). 142p. 1980. 15.00 (ISBN 0-87757-146-5). Am Mktg.
Samli, A. Coskun. Marketing & Distribution Systems in Eastern Europe. LC 78-19754. 1978. 22.95 (ISBN 0-03-046486-2). Praeger.
Schewe, Charles D. & Smith, Rueben. Marketing: Concepts & Applications. (Marketing Ser.). (Illus.). 1979. text ed. 17.95 (ISBN 0-07-055272-X); instrs'. manual 5.95 (ISBN 0-07-055273-8); study guide 5.95 (ISBN 0-07-055278-9); test bank 11.95 (ISBN 0-07-055280-0). McGraw.
Schiller, R. Market & Media Evaluation. 1969. 15.00 (ISBN 0-02-896050-5). Macmillan.
Schwerin, Horace S. & Newell, Henry H. Persuasion in Marketing: The Dynamics of Marketing's Great Untapped Resource. LC 80-23133. (Ronald Series on Marketing Management). 259p. 1981. 24.95 (ISBN 0-471-04554-3, Pub. by Wiley-Interscience). Wiley.
Scotton, Donald W. & Zallocco, Ronald L. Readings in Market Segmentation. LC 80-478. 198p. 1980. pap. 22.00 (ISBN 0-87757-132-5). Am Mktg.
Seaton, Bruce. Modern Marketing: Study Guide. 1978. pap. 4.95x (ISBN 0-673-15128-X). Scott F.
Seltz, David. Food Service Marketing & Promotion. LC 76-566430. (Illus.). 1977. 16.95 (ISBN 0-912016-59-0). Lebhar Friedman.
Seltz, David D. Branchising: Proven Techniques for Rapid Company Expansion. LC 79-19549. (Illus.). 288p. 1980. 19.95 (ISBN 0-07-056215-6, P&RB). McGraw.
--Handbook of Innovative Marketing Techniques. LC 79-27415. 320p. 1981. text ed. 19.95 (ISBN 0-201-07617-9). A-W.
Sethi, S. Prakash. Promises of the Good Life. 1979. pap. 12.95x (ISBN 0-256-02230-5). Irwin.
Shapiro, Irving J. Dictionary of Marketing Terms. 4th ed. (Littlefield, Adams Quality Paperback Ser.: No. 363). 280p. (Orig.). 1981. pap. 7.95 (ISBN 0-8226-0363-2). Littlefield.
--Dictionary of Marketing Terms. 4th ed. 280p. 1981. 16.50x (ISBN 0-8476-6967-X). Rowman.
Shaw, Arch W. Some Problems in Market Distribution: Illustrating the Application of a Basic Philosophy of Business. LC 15-19535. (Illus.). 1915. 6.95x (ISBN 0-674-81960-8). Harvard U Pr.
Sheth, Jagdish N., ed. Research in Marketing, Vol. 3. (Orig.). 1979. lib. bdg. 34.50 (ISBN 0-89232-060-5). Jai Pr.
Shimaguchi, Mitsuaki. Marketing Channels in Japan. Dufey, Gunter, ed. LC 78-24373. (Research for Business Decisions Ser.: No. 7). 1978. 31.95 (ISBN 0-8357-0960-4, Pub. by UMI Res Pr). Univ Microfilms.
Skinner, R. N. Launching New Products in Competitive Markets. 190p. 1972. 11.00x (ISBN 0-304-29082-3). Intl Pubns Serv.
Slater, Charles C. & White, Phillip D., eds. Macromarketing, Vol. II: Distributive Processes from a Societal Perspective, an Elaboration of Issues. 477p. 1978. 10.00 (ISBN 0-686-69388-4). U CO Busn Res Div.
Spence, A. C. Cycle of Marketing. 18.50x (ISBN 0-392-02626-0, SpS). Sportshelf.
--Cycle of Marketing. 1967. 9.95x (ISBN 0-8464-0311-0). Beekman Pubs.
Stacey, Nicholas A. & Aubrey, Wilson. The Changing Pattern of Distribution. 1965. 16.50 (ISBN 0-08-010654-4); pap. 7.75 (ISBN 0-08-010653-6). Pergamon.
Stanton, William J. Fundamentals of Marketing. 6th ed. (Illus.). 704p. 1981. text ed. 19.95 (ISBN 0-07-060891-1, C); instrs. manual 10.95 (ISBN 0-07-060892-X); study guide 6.95 (ISBN 0-07-060893-8); test file 15.95 (ISBN 0-07-060894-6); transparency masters 15.00 (ISBN 0-07-060895-4). McGraw.
Stapleton, John, ed. Marketing Handbook. 400p. 1974. 25.00 (ISBN 0-7161-0161-0). Herman Pub.
Stasch, Stanley F. Systems Analysis for Marketing Planning & Control. 552p. 1971. pap. 10.95x (ISBN 0-673-07724-1). Scott F.
Stern, Edward. Direct Marketing Market Place 1981. 375p. 1981. pap. 40.00 (ISBN 0-934464-02-2). Hilary House Pubs.
Stern, Louis W. & El-Ansary, Adel I. Marketing Channels. 1977. ref. ed. 21.95x (ISBN 0-13-557124-3). P-H.
Stern, Mark E. Marketing Planning: A Systems Approach. 1966. pap. 7.95 (ISBN 0-07-061211-0, C). McGraw.
Still, Richard & Harris, Clyde E., Jr. Cases in Marketing: Decision, Policies, Strategies. (Illus.). 304p. 1972. pap. text ed. 10.95 (ISBN 0-13-118877-1). P-H.
Still, Richard R. & Cundiff, Edward W. Essentials of Marketing. 2nd ed. LC 79-170644. 1972. ref. ed. 10.95 (ISBN 0-13-286468-1). P-H.
Stone, Merlin. Marketing & Economics. LC 79-22206. 1980. 22.50 (ISBN 0-312-51527-8). St Martin.
Strang, Roger A. The Promotion Planning Process: Sales Promotion Vs. Advertising. 144p. 1980. 19.95 (ISBN 0-03-049101-0). Praeger.
Sturdivant, Frederick D., et al. Managerial Analysis in Marketing. 1970. text ed. 14.95x (ISBN 0-673-05938-3). Scott F.
Taylor, Jack L. Fundamentals of Marketing: Additional Dimensions, Selections from the Literatures. 2nd ed. 1975. 10.95 (ISBN 0-07-063116-6, C). McGraw.
Taylor, Weldon J. & Shaw, Roy T., Jr. Marketing: An Integrated, Analytical Approach. 2nd ed. LC 69-10883. 1969. text ed. 11.75 (ISBN 0-538-19710-2). SW Pub.
Taylor, Weldon L. & Shaw, Roy T., Jr. Marketing: An Integrated, Analytical Approach. 3rd ed. 1975. text ed. 8.10 (ISBN 0-538-19720-X). SW Pub.
Terpstra. International Marketing. 2nd ed. 1978. 22.95 (ISBN 0-03-039296-9). Dryden Pr.
Test Marketing. LC 80-60762. (Marketing Ser.). 1980. pap. 4.95 (ISBN 0-87251-053-0). Crain Bks.
Theory Conference, Phoenix, Arizona, February, 1980. Theoretical Developments in Marketing: Proceedings. Lamb, Charles W., Jr. & Dunne, Patrick M., eds. LC 80-12436. (Illus.). 269p. (Orig.). 1980. pap. text ed. 24.00 (ISBN 0-87757-138-4). Am Mktg.
Thompson, Donald N., et al, eds. Macromarketing: A Canadian Perspective. LC 79-16031. (Illus.). 318p. (Orig.). 1980. pap. text ed. 12.00 (ISBN 0-87757-124-4). Am Mktg.
Thompson, Howard A., ed. The Great Writings in Marketing. 2nd ed. LC 75-22965. (Illus.). 640p. 1981. pap. text ed. 13.95 (ISBN 0-916162-00-1); instructors' manual free. Pennwell Pub.
Thorelli, Hans & Becker, Helmut, eds. International Marketing Strategy. rev. ed. LC 80-14689. (Pergamon Policy Studies on Business). 400p. 1980. 40.00 (ISBN 0-08-025542-6); pap. 12.95 (ISBN 0-08-025543-4). Pergamon.
Tolman, Ruth. Fashion Marketing & Merchandising, Vol. 2. (Illus.). 372p. 1974. 19.95 (ISBN 0-87350-251-5). Milady.
Travers, David. Preparing Design Office Brochures: A Handbook. LC 78-54271. (Illus.). 1978. pap. 9.95 (ISBN 0-931228-00-X). Arts & Arch.
Udell, Jon G. & Laczniak, Gene R. Marketing in an Age of Change. LC 80-19923. (Marketing Ser.). 577p. 1981. text ed. 20.95 (ISBN 0-471-08169-8); tchrs.' ed. 11.00 (ISBN 0-471-08184-1); test file avail. (ISBN 0-471-08187-6). Wiley.
Walsh, L. A. & Dorr, E. L. Physical Distribution. (Occupational Manuals & Projects in Marketing). 1969. text ed. 5.96 (ISBN 0-07-067955-X, G); instructor's manual 3.50 (ISBN 0-07-067956-8). McGraw.
Walsh, L. S. International Marketing. 272p. 1978. pap. text ed. 11.95x (ISBN 0-7121-0943-9, Pub. by Macdonald & Evans England). Intl Ideas.
Walters, Glenn. Marketing Channels. LC 76-21545. 1955. text ed. 19.95 (ISBN 0-87620-571-6); inst. manual avail. (ISBN 0-87620-576-7). Goodyear.
Walters, Glenn & Robin, Donald. Classics in Marketing. LC 77-27511. 1978. pap. text ed. 11.95 (ISBN 0-87620-191-5). Goodyear.
Wasson, Chester R. & McConaughy, David H. Buying Behavior & Marketing Decisions. LC 69-11949. (Illus.). 1968. 23.50x (ISBN 0-89197-058-4). Irvington.
Webster, Frederick E. Industrial Marketing Strategy. LC 78-26599. (Marketing Management Ser.). 1979. 18.95 (ISBN 0-471-04879-8). Ronald Pr.
Webster, Frederick E., Jr. Curso de Mercadotecnica. (Span.). 1977. pap. text ed. 11.40 (ISBN 0-06-317070-1, IntlDept). Har-Row.
Weinrauch, J. Donald & Piland, William E. Applied Marketing Principles. (Illus.). 1979. ref. 16.95 (ISBN 0-13-041103-5). P-H.
Welch, Joe L. Marketing Law. 168p. 1980. 14.50 (ISBN 0-87814-107-3). Pennwell Pub.
Wendel, Richard, ed. Readings in Marketing 75-76. (Annual Editions Ser.). (Illus.). 288p. 1974. pap. text ed. 5.50 (ISBN 0-87967-079-7); tchr's guide free (ISBN 0-685-48970-1). Dushkin Pub.
Wentz, Walter B. Marketing. (Illus.). 1979. text ed. 19.95 (ISBN 0-8299-0227-9); study guide 7.95 (ISBN 0-8299-0263-5); instr.' manual avail. (ISBN 0-8299-0581-2). West Pub.
Westing, Howard J. & Albaum, Gerald. Modern Marketing Thought. 3rd ed. (Illus.). 544p. 1975. pap. text ed. 8.95 (ISBN 0-02-426590-X). Macmillan.
Whitehead, Harold. Administration of Marketing & Selling. 19.50x (ISBN 0-392-07566-0, SpS). Sportshelf.
Wiener, Solomon, et al. Marketing & Advertising Careers. (Career Concise Guides Ser). (Illus.). (gr. 7 up). 1977. PLB 6.90 (ISBN 0-531-01307-3). Watts.
Wills, Gordon. Contemporary Marketing. 1971. 18.00x (ISBN 0-8464-0279-3). Beekman Pubs.
--Strategic Issues in Marketing. LC 74-14910. 239p. 1974. 23.95 (ISBN 0-470-94958-9). Halsted Pr.
Wills, Gordon & Taylor, Bernard. Exploration in Marketing Thought. (Illus.). 416p. 1970. 19.95x (ISBN 0-8464-0395-1). Beekman Pubs.
Willsmer. Marketing Effort. 33.00x (ISBN 0-8464-0607-1). Beekman Pubs.
Willsmer, R. Basic Arts of Marketing. 1977. 19.95x (ISBN 0-8464-0172-X). Beekman Pubs.
Willsmer, Ray L. The Basic Arts of Marketing. 230p. 1976. text ed. 22.00x (ISBN 0-220-66307-6, Pub. by Busn Bks England). Renouf.
--Directing the Marketing Effort. 1971. 29.95x (ISBN 0-8464-0337-4). Beekman Pubs.
Wilson, A. Marketing of Professional Services. 1972. 24.95 (ISBN 0-07-094239-0, P&RB). McGraw.
Wilson, Bud. Principles of Merchandising: A Key to Profitable Marketing. LC 75-27405. (Illus.). 238p. 1976. pap. text ed. 6.95 (ISBN 0-87005-160-1). Fairchild.
Wind, Yoram J. Product Policy: Concepts, Methods & Strategies. 1981. text ed. 21.95 (ISBN 0-201-08343-4). A-W.
Winkler, John. Marketing for the Developing Company. 1969. 19.95x (ISBN 0-8464-0608-X). Beekman Pubs.
Winn, Charles S., et al. Exploring Marketing Occupations. (Careers in Focus Ser). (Illus.). 160p. (gr. 6-9). 1975. pap. text ed. 5.32 (ISBN 0-07-071039-2, G); tchr's manual & key 3.30 (ISBN 0-07-071040-6); wkshts. 6.08 (ISBN 0-07-071062-7). McGraw.
Woodside, Arch G., et al, eds. Foundations of Marketing Channels. LC 77-88040. (Illus.). 1978. pap. text ed. 9.95 (ISBN 0-914872-10-9). Austin Pr.
Wright, John S. & Dimsdale, Parks B. Pioneers in Marketing. LC 73-620235. 1974. pap. 8.95 (ISBN 0-88406-016-0). Ga St U Busn Pub.
Yarker, K. A. International Marketing. 178p. 1976. text ed. 23.50x (ISBN 0-220-66298-3, Pub. by Busn Bks England). Renouf.
Yoshino, M. Y. Japanese Marketing System: Adaptations & Innovations. 1971. 20.00x (ISBN 0-262-24012-2). MIT Pr.

MARKETING–BIBLIOGRAPHY

Filmrow Motion Picture Marketing Blackbook, 1981-82. (Combined Ser.). 600p. 1981. 74.95 (ISBN 0-937874-06-X). Filmrow Pubns.
Gardner, David M. & Belk, Russell W. A Basic Bibliography on Experimental Design in Marketing. LC 80-19563. (Bibliography Ser.: No. 37). 59p. 1980. pap. 6.00 (ISBN 0-87757-142-2). Am Mktg.
Hong, Alfred, ed. Marketing Economics Guide, 1980-81: Current Market Dimensions for 1500 Cities, All 3100 Counties, All Metro Areas. LC 73-647896. (Illus.). 264p. 1980. 20.00 (ISBN 0-914078-43-7). Marketing Econs.
Jackson, Donald W., Jr., et al, eds. Marketing Profitability Analysis: Bibliography. LC 77-11961. 1978. 8.00 (ISBN 0-87757-102-3). Am Mktg.
Michman, Ronald, et al. Marketing Channel Strategy: A Selected & Annotated Bibliography. LC 76-3693. (Bibliography Ser.: No. 21). 1976. pap. 5.50 (ISBN 0-87757-072-8). Am Mktg.
Michman, Ronald D, et al, eds. Market Segmentation: A Selected & Annotated Bibliography. LC 77-6726. (AMA Bibliography Ser.: No. 28). 1977. pap. text ed. 5.50 (ISBN 0-87757-094-9). Am Mktg.
Pingry, Jack R. & Bird, Monroe M., eds. Industrial Marketing: A Selected & Annotated Bibliography. LC 76-56237. (Bibliography Ser.: No. 25). 1977. pap. text ed. 5.50 (ISBN 0-87757-090-6). Am Mktg.
Raber, Nevin W. & Coachys, Richard, eds. Marketing: A Selected List of Current Titles. LC 72-619541. (Bibliographical Aids for Business Ser.: No. 1). 50p. (Orig.). 1972. pap. 2.95 (ISBN 0-87925-003-8). Ind U Busn Res.

Robinson, Larry M. & Adler, Roy D. Selected Contributions to Marketing Thought: An Annotated Bibliography. (Research Monograph: No. 91). 1981. pap. 9.95 (ISBN 0-88406-142-6). Ga St U Busn Pub.
Rothschild, Michael L. An Incomplete Bibliography of Works Relating to Marketing for Public Sector & Nonprofit Organizations. 3rd ed. (Monograph: No. 12). 178p. 1981. write for info. (ISBN 0-86603-011-5); pap. 7.50 (ISBN 0-86603-011-5). U Wis Grad Sch Busn.
Sandeau, Georges. Bibliographie Internationale du Marketing et de la Distribution: 1967-69. 384p. 1970. 47.50x (ISBN 0-8002-1235-5). Intl Pubns Serv.
Thompson, Ralph B. & Faricy, John H. A Selected & Annotated Bibliography of Marketing Theory. rev ed. (Bibliography Ser.: No. 18). 1976. pap. 4.00 (ISBN 0-87755-209-6). U of Tex Busn Res.
Zucker, Ralph. Filmrow Motion Picture Marketing Blackbook, 1981-82: Part II, New York. 150p. 1981. 50.00 (ISBN 0-937874-04-3). Filmrow Pubns.
--Filmrow Motion Picture Marketing Blackbook, 1981-82: Part III, Cross Country U. S. A.-Canada. 150p. 1981. write for info. (ISBN 0-937874-05-1). Filmrow Pubns.

MARKETING–CASE STUDIES

Adler, Roy D. Marketing & Society: Cases & Commentaries. (Illus.). 528p. 1981. text ed. 14.95 (ISBN 0-13-557074-3). P-H.
Ball, Terry T., et al. Marketing Readings: An Enrichment of Concepts. LC 78-59270. 1979. pap. text ed. 10.95x (ISBN 0-917974-16-6). Waveland Pr.
Fogelberg, Graeme. New Zealand Case Studies in Marketing. 2nd ed. 240p. 1976. pap. 16.50x (ISBN 0-456-02090-X). Intl Pubns Serv.
Foster, J. Robert, et al. Cases in Marketing Channel Strategy. LC 77-6436. 1977. pap. text ed. 9.50 scp (ISBN 0-06-046214-0, HarpC). Har-Row.
Gelb, Betsy D. & Enis, Ben M. Marketing Is Everybody's Business. 2d ed. LC 76-53774. 1977. pap. 8.95 (ISBN 0-87620-560-0). Goodyear.
Gostling, E. P. & Ambrose, K. Case Studies from the Distribution Trades. 1972. text ed. 14.95x (ISBN 0-07-002016-7). Intl Ideas.
Hartley, Robert F. Marketing Mistakes. 2nd ed. LC 80-13236. (Marketing Ser.). 229p. 1980. pap. text ed. 9.95 (ISBN 0-88244-225-2). Grid Pub.
Karp, Robert E., ed. Issues in Marketing. LC 74-4350. 1974. 29.75x (ISBN 0-8422-5165-0); pap. text ed. 12.95x (ISBN 0-8422-0393-1). Irvington.
MacStravic, Robin S. Marketing by Objectives for Hospitals. LC 80-10903. 280p. 1980. text ed. 26.95 (ISBN 0-89443-174-9). Aspen Systems.
Mellott, Douglas W., Jr. Marketing: Application & Cases. (Illus.). 1978. 8.95 (ISBN 0-8359-4253-8). Reston.
Rados, David L. & Gilmour, Peter. Australian Marketing Casebook. (Illus.). 236p. (Orig.). 1981. pap. text ed. 14.50x (ISBN 0-7022-1581-3). U of Queensland Pr.
Sood, James H. Situations in Marketing: A Collection of Marketing Cases & Questions. 1976. pap. 4.95x (ISBN 0-256-01856-1). Business Pubns.
Stanton, William J. Fundamentals of Marketing. 6th ed. (Illus.). 704p. 1981. text ed. 19.95 (ISBN 0-07-060891-1, C); instrs. manual 10.95 (ISBN 0-07-060892-X); study guide 6.95 (ISBN 0-07-060893-8); test file 15.95 (ISBN 0-07-060894-6); transparency masters 15.00 (ISBN 0-07-060895-4). McGraw.
Star, Steven H & Davis, Nancy. Problems in Marketing. 5th ed. LC 77-488. (Illus.). 1977. text ed. 18.95 (ISBN 0-07-060835-0, C); instructor's manual 7.95 (ISBN 0-07-060836-9). McGraw.
Stevens, J. & Grant, J. The Purchasing-Marketing Interface: Text & Cases. LC 75-9965. 1976. 21.95 (ISBN 0-470-82438-7). Halsted Pr.
Talarzyk. Contemporary Cases in Marketing. 2nd ed. 1979. 12.95 (ISBN 0-03-045436-0). Dryden Pr.
Talarzyk, W. Wayne. Cases for Analysis in Marketing. LC 76-24085. 220p. 1977. pap. text ed. 8.95 (ISBN 0-03-019016-9). Dryden Pr.
Talarzyk, Wayne. Cases for Analysis in Marketing. 2nd ed. LC 80-65809. 384p. 1981. pap. text ed. 9.95 (ISBN 0-03-058179-6). Dryden Pr.
Thompson, Howard. Cases in Marketing Including Interviews with Key Executives. 1979. pap. text ed. 8.95 scp (ISBN 0-06-046615-4, HarpC). Har-Row.

MARKETING–COSTS

Bailey, Earl L. Marketing-Cost Ratios of U. S. Manufacturers: A Technical Analysis. (Report Ser.: No. 662). (Illus.). 44p. (Orig.). 1975. pap. 75.00 (ISBN 0-8237-0081-X). Conference Bd.
Hardy, Leonard. Marketing for Profit: A Study in the Formulation of Commercial Policy Within the Business Organization. 2nd ed. (Management Studies Ser). 177p. 1971. 10.00x (ISBN 0-582-44575-2). Intl Pubns Serv.
Jackson, Donald W., Jr., et al, eds. Marketing Profitability Analysis: Bibliography. LC 77-11961. 1978. 8.00 (ISBN 0-87757-102-3). Am Mktg.
Johnson, A. S. Marketing & Financial Control. 1967. 23.00 (ISBN 0-08-012614-6); pap. text ed. 11.25 (ISBN 0-08-012613-8). Pergamon.
Stewart, Paul W. & Dewhurst, J. Frederic. Does Distribution Cost Too Much? LC 75-39276. (Getting & Spending: the Consumer's Dilemma). (Illus.). 1976. Repr. of 1939 ed. 23.00x (ISBN 0-405-08049-2). Arno.

MARKETING–DATA PROCESSING

Amstutz, Arnold E. Computer Simulation of Competitive Market Response. (Illus.). 1967. pap. 7.95 (ISBN 0-262-51009-X). MIT Pr.
Day, G., et al. Computer Models in Marketing: Planning. 128p. 1977. pap. 10.50 (ISBN 0-89426-004-9). Scientific Pr.
Eskin, Gerald & Montgomery, David. Computer Models in Marketing: Data Analysis. 128p. 1977. pap. 10.50 (ISBN 0-89426-002-2). Scientific Pr.
Hugo, I. S. Marketing & the Computer. 1967. 25.00 (ISBN 0-08-012606-5); pap. 13.25 (ISBN 0-08-012605-7). Pergamon.
Lewis, Richard J. Logistical Information System for Marketing Analysis. 1970. text ed. 4.00 (ISBN 0-538-07650-X). SW Pub.
Schewe, Charles D., ed. Marketing Information Systems: Selected Readings. LC 76-3791. 1976. pap. 13.00 (ISBN 0-87757-071-X). Am Mktg.
Wight, Oliver W. Production & Inventory Management in the Computer Age. LC 74-7127. 300p. 1974. 21.00 (ISBN 0-8436-0732-7). CBI Pub.

MARKETING–MATHEMATICAL MODELS

Bowersox, Donald J., et al. Dynamic Simulation of Physical Distribution Systems. LC 72-619501. 248p. 1972. 9.75 (ISBN 0-87744-112-X). Mich St U Busn.
Frank, Ronald E. & Massy, William F. An Economic Approach to a Marketing Decision Model. 1971. 21.00x (ISBN 0-262-06037-X). MIT Pr.
Funke, U. H., ed. Mathematical Models in Marketing: A Collection of Abstracts. 1976. soft cover 21.20 (ISBN 0-387-07869-X). Springer-Verlag.
Hinkle, Charles L. & Koza, Russell C. Marketing Dynamics: Decision & Control. (Illus.). 144p. 1975. pap. text ed. 7.95 (ISBN 0-07-028960-3, C); instructors' manual 2.95 (ISBN 0-07-028961-1). McGraw.
King, William R. Quantitative Analysis for Marketing Management. 1968. text ed. 18.95 (ISBN 0-07-034605-4, C). McGraw.
Metwally, M. M. Price & Non-Price Competition: Dynamics of Marketing. 1976. lib. bdg. 11.95 (ISBN 0-210-40568-6). Asia.
Wallace, J. P. & Sherret, A. Estimation of Product: Attributes & Their Importance. (Lecture Notes in Economics & Mathematical Systems: Vol. 89). v, 94p. 1974. pap. 9.10 (ISBN 0-387-06530-X). Springer-Verlag.

MARKETING–PROGRAMMED INSTRUCTION

Creating a Market. 6th ed. (An ILO Programmed Book). 180p. 1976. 4.55 (ISBN 92-2-100082-6). Intl Labour Office.
Physical Distribution Management: The Total Systems Route to New Profits. (PRIME-PRIME 100 Ser). 1967. 35.00 (ISBN 0-8144-1101-0). Am Mgmt.

MARKETING–RESEARCH

see Marketing Research

MARKETING–SOCIAL ASPECTS

Berry, Leonard L. & Hensel, James S., eds. Marketing & the Social Environment: A Reading Text. 412p. 1974. 14.95x (ISBN 0-442-80023-1); pap. 8.00x (ISBN 0-442-80068-1). Van Nos Reinhold.
Hartley, R. F. Marketing Fundamentals for Responsive Management. 2nd ed. 1976. text ed. 21.50 scp (ISBN 0-912212-05-5, HarpC). Har-Row.
Hasty, Ronald W. & Will, R. Ted. Marketing. LC 74-23166. 400p. 1975. text ed. 21.50 scp (ISBN 0-06-389407-6, HarpC); scp study guide 6.95 (ISBN 0-06-389408-4). Har-Row.
Kerr, John R. & Littlefield, James E. Marketing: An Environmental Approach. (Illus.). 672p. 1974. ref. ed. 20.95 (ISBN 0-13-557330-0). P-H.
Levy, Sidney J. & Zaltman, Gerald. Marketing, Society, & Conflict. (Economic Institutions & Social Systems Ser). (Illus.). 176p. 1975. text ed. 12.95 ref. ed. (ISBN 0-13-557819-1); pap. text ed. 9.95 (ISBN 0-13-557801-9). P-H.
Perry, Donald L. Social Marketing Strategies: Conservation Issues & Analysis. LC 75-13477. 200p. 1976. pap. text ed. 11.95 (ISBN 0-87620-865-0). Goodyear.
Reynolds, Fred D. & Barksdale, Hiram C., eds. Marketing & the Quality of Life: Papers. LC 78-17765. (Illus.). 1978. pap. text ed. 5.50 (ISBN 0-87757-111-2). Am Mktg.
Robertson, Andrew. Strategic Marketing: A Business Response to Consumerism. LC 78-3. 30.95 (ISBN 0-470-26313-X). Halsted Pr.
Sethi, S. Prakash. Promises of the Good Life. 1979. pap. 12.95x (ISBN 0-256-02230-5). Irwin.
Stengel, Mitchell. Racial Rent Differentials. LC 75-620096. 1976. pap. 5.00 (ISBN 0-87744-134-0). Mich St U Busn.
Uhr, Ernest B. & Jarvis, Lance P., eds. Social Responsibility in Marketing: A Selected & Annotated Bibliography. LC 77-5551. (AMA Bibliography Ser.: No. 27). 1977. pap. text ed. 5.50 (ISBN 0-87757-093-0). Am Mktg.
Webster, Frederick E., Jr. Social Aspects of Marketing. (Illus.). 128p. 1974. pap. 7.95 (ISBN 0-13-815449-X). P-H.

MARKETING (HOME ECONOMICS)

see also Consumers; Consumer Education; Shopping

Assael, Henry. Consumer Behavior & Marketing Action. (Business Ser.). 641p. 1981. text ed. 21.95x (ISBN 0-534-00958-1). Kent Pub Co.
Fornell, Claes. Consumer Input for Marketing Decisions: A Study of Corporate Departments for Consumer Affairs. LC 76-14397. 1976. text ed. 21.95 (ISBN 0-275-23480-0). Praeger.
Goldbeck, Nikki & Goldbeck, David. The Supermarket Handbook: Access to Whole Foods. 1974. pap. 4.95 (ISBN 0-452-25151-6, Z5151, Plume). NAL.
Hunt, Bernice & Hunt, Morton. Prime Time: A Guide to the Pleasures & Opportunities of the New Middleage. LC 74-79419. 1975. 25.00x (ISBN 0-8128-1713-3); pap. 1.95 (ISBN 0-8128-7010-7). Stein & Day.
Hunter, Beatrice T. Beatrice Trum Hunter's Favorite Natural Foods. 1974. 7.95 (ISBN 0-671-21820-4). S&S.
Kinder, Faye & Green, Nancy R. Meal Management. 5th ed. (Illus.). 576p. 1978. text ed. 18.95 (ISBN 0-02-364080-4, 36408). Macmillan.
Kotschevar, Lendal H. Quantity Food Purchasing. 2nd ed. LC 74-17407. 684p. 1975. text ed. 29.95 (ISBN 0-471-50524-2). Wiley.
Kratz, Carole & Lee, Albert. Coupons, Refunds, Rebates. new ed. LC 75-20064. (Illus.). 160p. pap. 2.95 (ISBN 0-911104-62-3). Workman Pub.
Miller, Erston V. & Munger, James I. Good Fruits & How to Buy Them. (Illus., Orig.). 1967. 4.50 (ISBN 0-910286-22-1); pap. 2.95 (ISBN 0-910286-04-3). Boxwood.
Sloane, Martin. Guide to Coupons & Refunds 1980. 224p. 1980. 2.95 (ISBN 0-553-14617-3). Bantam.
Woods, Mary. Turn Your Craft Hobbies into Cash. 2nd ed. 110p. 1981. pap. 12.95 (ISBN 0-939640-01-5). MWS Pubns.

MARKETING MANAGEMENT

see also Product Management

Aaker, David A. & Myers, John G. Advertising Management. (Illus.). 640p. 1975. 21.95 (ISBN 0-13-015974-3); pap. 8.95 (ISBN 0-13-015990-5). P-H.
Alderson, Wroe. Marketing Behavior & Executive Action. Assael, Henry, ed. LC 78-222. (Century of Marketing Ser.). 1978. Repr. of 1957 ed. lib. bdg. 30.00x (ISBN 0-405-11162-2). Arno.
Bernhardt, Kenneth L. & Kinnear, Thomas C. Cases in Marketing Management. rev. ed. 1981. 20.95x (ISBN 0-256-02419-7). Business Pubns.
Berry, Leonard L. & Hensel, James S., eds. Marketing & the Social Environment: A Reading Text. 412p. 1974. 14.95x (ISBN 0-442-80023-1); pap. 8.00x (ISBN 0-442-80068-1). Van Nos Reinhold.
Berry, Richard C. Industrial Marketing for Results. LC 80-18222. (Illus.). 144p. 1981. text ed. 19.95 (ISBN 0-201-00075-X). A-W.
Boone, Louis E. & Hackleman, Edwin C. Marketing Strategy: A Marketing Decision Game. 2nd ed. LC 74-27870. (Illus.). 224p. 1975. pap. text ed. 11.95 (ISBN 0-675-08713-9); manual 3.95 (ISBN 0-686-67124-4); card deck o. p. 3.95 (ISBN 0-686-67125-2). Merrill.
Bowersox, Donald J., et al. Management in Marketing Channels. (Illus.). 1979. text ed. 18.95 (ISBN 0-07-006740-6); instructor's manual 4.95 (ISBN 0-07-006741-4). McGraw.
Brion, John M. Corporate Marketing Planning. LC 67-19446. (Marketing Ser.). 1967. 31.50 (ISBN 0-471-10440-X). Wiley.
Britt, Steuart H. Marketing Manager's Handbook. 1973. 52.50 (ISBN 0-85013-034-4). Dartnell Corp.
Britt, Steuart H. & Boyd, Harper W. Marketing Management & Administrative Action. 4th ed. (Illus.). 1978. pap. text ed. 10.95 (ISBN 0-07-007923-4, C). McGraw.
Bursk, Edward C. & Grayser, Stephen A. Advanced Cases in Marketing Management. LC 68-24633. (Foundations of Marketing Ser). (Orig.). 1968. pap. 7.95x ref. ed. (ISBN 0-13-011320-4). P-H.
Buying Power: The Exercise of Market Power by Dominant Buyers. 178p. (Orig.). 1981. pap. 11.50x (ISBN 92-64-12168-4). OECD.
Buzzell, R. D., et al. Marketing Research & Information Systems: Text & Cases. 1969. text ed. 19.95 (ISBN 0-07-009475-6, C); instructor's manual 4.95 (ISBN 0-07-009476-4). tapes 325.00 (ISBN 0-07-097280-X). McGraw.
Choffray, Jean-Marie & Lilien, Gary L. Market Planning for New Industrial Products. LC 80-11347. (Ronald Ser. on Marketing Management). 264p. 1980. 21.95 (ISBN 0-471-04918-2, Ronald). Ronald Pr.
Constantin, James A., et al. Marketing Strategy & Management. 1976. text ed. 13.95x (ISBN 0-256-01694-1). Business Pubns.
Corey, E. Raymond & Star, Steven H. Organization Strategy: A Marketing Approach. LC 79-132151. 1971. 22.50x (ISBN 0-87584-088-4). Harvard Busn.
Crawford, Lucy. Supervisory Skills in Marketing. Dorr, Eugene, ed. (Occupational Manuals & Projects in Marketing Ser.). (Illus.). (gr. 9-10). 1977. pap. text ed. 5.48 (ISBN 0-07-013471-5, G); teacher's manual & key 3.00 (ISBN 0-07-013472-3). McGraw.
Davis, Kenneth R. Marketing Management. 4th ed. LC 80-19924. (Marketing Ser.). 778p. 1981. text ed. 24.95 (ISBN 0-471-05948-X). Wiley.
Davis, Robert T., et al. Marketing Management Casebook. 3rd ed. 1980. 21.95x (ISBN 0-256-02347-6). Irwin.
Dodge, H. Robert. Field Sales Management: Text & Cases. 1973. 13.50x (ISBN 0-256-01453-1). Business Pubns.
Doyle, Peter. Analytical Marketing Management. (European Marketing Ser.). 1975. 12.80 (ISBN 0-06-318018-9, IntlDept); pap. 6.60 (ISBN 0-06-318017-0, IntlDept). Har-Row.
Elam, Houston G. & Paley, Norton. Marketing for the Non-Marketing Executive. (Illus.). 1978. 15.95 (ISBN 0-8144-5465-8). Am Mgmt.
Ely, Vivian & Barnes, Michael. Starting Your Own Marketing Business. 2nd ed. Dorr, Eugene, ed. (Occupational Manuals & Projects Marketing Ser.). (Illus.). (gr. 11-12). 1978. pap. text ed. 5.48 (ISBN 0-07-019307-X, G); teacher's manual & key 3.00 (ISBN 0-07-019308-8). McGraw.
Farrell, Jack, et al, eds. Physical Distribution Forum. LC 72-91981. 1973. 15.95 (ISBN 0-8436-1403-X). CBI Pub.
Farrell, Jack W. Physical Distribution Case Studies. LC 72-91987. 1973. 15.95 (ISBN 0-8436-1404-8). CBI Pub.
Fitzroy, Peter T. Analytical Methods for Marketing Management. new ed. LC 75-31803. 1976. text ed. 17.95 (ISBN 0-07-084064-4, C). McGraw.
Foxall, Gordon R. Strategic Marketing Management. 272p. 1981. 22.95 (ISBN 0-470-27265-1). Halsted Pr.
Gaedeke, Ralph M. & Tootelian, Dennis, eds. Marketing Management Cases & Readings. 1980. pap. 18.95 (ISBN 0-87620-606-2). Goodyear.
Gelb, Gabriel M. & Gelb, Betsy D., eds. Insights for Marketing Management. 2d ed. LC 76-53773. (Illus.). 1977. pap. 9.95 (ISBN 0-87620-474-4). Goodyear.
Greenlaw, Paul S. & Kniffin, Fred W. Marksim: A Marketing Decision Simulation. 1964. pap. text ed. 10.95 scp (ISBN 0-7002-2040-2, HarpC); scp 1620 computer deck 19.50 (ISBN 0-352-05305-4); scp 700-7000 computer deck 18.50 (ISBN 0-686-67464-2); scp 360 computer deck 18.50 (ISBN 0-686-67465-0). Har-Row.
Guiltinan, J. P. & Paul, G. W. Marketing Management. (Marketing Ser.). 1981. price not set (ISBN 0-07-048920-3); price not set instr's manual (ISBN 0-07-048921-1). McGraw.
Haas, Robert F. Industrial Marketing Management. Berry, Leonard L., ed. (Priorities in Marketing Ser.). (Illus.). 1976. pap. text ed. 12.95x (ISBN 0-442-80333-8). Van Nos Reinhold.
Haedrich, Guenther, ed. Operationale Entscheidungshilfen fur die Marketingplanung. (Marketing Management: No. 3). 1977. 60.50x (ISBN 3-11-006882-6). De Gruyter.
Hartley, R. F. Marketing Fundamentals for Responsive Management. 2nd ed. 1976. text ed. 21.50 scp (ISBN 0-912212-05-5, HarpC). Har-Row.
Hartley, Robert. Marketing Fundamentals for Responsive Management. 2nd ed. 1976. 14.00 (ISBN 0-685-65299-8). Tech Pub.
Hawkins, Delbert I., et al. Consumer Behavior: Implications for Marketing Strategy. 1980. 18.50 (ISBN 0-256-02290-9). Business Pubns.

Hemple, Don & Hanaver, Joe F. Marketing Management Strategies. 400p. 1981. pap. price not set (ISBN 0-913652-30-X). Realtors Natl.
Hopkins, David S. The Marketing Plan. (Report Ser.: No. 801). (Illus.). vi, 138p. 1981. pap. text ed. 45.00 (ISBN 0-8237-0237-5). Conference Bd.
Hughes, G. David. Marketing Management: A Planning Approach. LC 77-83036. 1978. text ed. 17.95 (ISBN 0-201-03057-8); instr's resource manual o. p. 6.95 (ISBN 0-201-03056-X). A-W.
Hutt, Michael D. & Speh, Thomas W. Industrial Marketing Management. LC 80-65803. 576p. 1981. text ed. 22.95 (ISBN 0-03-052656-6). Dryden Pr.
Information for Marketing Management. 4.95 (ISBN 0-686-09777-7, 7151). Natl Assn Accts.
Jolson, Marvin A. Marketing Management: Integrated Text, Readings & Cases. (Illus.). 1978. text ed. 20.95 (ISBN 0-02-361180-4). Macmillan.
Jones, Fred M. Introduction to Marketing Management. LC 64-14409. (Illus.). 1964. 22.50x (ISBN 0-89197-242-0); pap. text ed. 14.95x (ISBN 0-89197-799-6). Irvington.
Kapoor, A. & McKay, Robert J. Managing International Markets: A Survey of Training Practices & Emerging Trends. LC 79-161052. 1971. pap. text ed. 2.95x (ISBN 0-87850-003-0). Darwin Pr.
Keagan, Warren J. Mulitnational Marketing Management. 2nd ed. (Illus.). 1980. text ed. 22.00 (ISBN 0-13-605055-7). P-H.
Keegan, Warren J. Multinational Marketing Management. (Illus.). 608p. 1974. ref. ed. 19.95 (ISBN 0-13-604793-9). P-H.
Kelley, Eugene J. Marketing Planning & Competitive Strategy. (Foundations of Marketing Ser). 1972. pap. 7.95 ref. ed. (ISBN 0-13-558304-7). P-H.
Kerby, Joe K. Essentials of Marketing Management. 1970. text ed. 10.75 (ISBN 0-538-19950-4). SW Pub.
Kerin & Peterson. Perspectives on Strategic Marketing Management. 100p. 1980. text ed. 18.95 (ISBN 0-205-06722-0, 0867225). Allyn.
King, William R. Quantitative Analysis for Marketing Management. 1968. text ed. 18.95 (ISBN 0-07-034605-4, C). McGraw.
Kotler, Philip. Marketing Management: Analysis, Planning & Control. 4th ed. 1980. text ed. 22.95 (ISBN 0-13-557975-9). P-H.
Kotler, Philip & Cox, Keith. Marketing Management & Strategy: A Reader. rev. ed. (Illus.). 1980. pap. text ed. 13.95 (ISBN 0-13-558122-2). P-H.
Kuhlmeijer, H. J. Managerial Marketing. pap. 29.00 (ISBN 90-207-0460-5, Pub. by Martinus Nijhoff Netherlands). Kluwer Boston.
Lambert, Clark. Field Sales Performance Appraisal. LC 79-18567. (Marketing Management Ser.). 313p. 1979. 24.95 (ISBN 0-471-04781-3, Pub by Ronald Pr). Wiley.
Langer, Steven. Income in Sales-Marketing Management. 1981. pap. 85.00 (ISBN 0-916506-58-4). Abbott Langer Assocs.
Lemon, Wayne A. The Owner's & Manager's Market Analysis Workbook for Small to Moderate Retail & Service Establishments. (Illus.). 240p. 1980. looseleaf bdg. 29.95 (ISBN 0-8144-5562-X). Am Mgmt.
Lewis, Richard J. Logistical Information System for Marketing Analysis. 1970. text ed. 4.00 (ISBN 0-538-07650-X). SW Pub.
Lipson, Harry A. & Darling, John R. Marketing Fundamentals: Text & Cases. LC 80-12441. 590p. 1980. Repr. of 1974 ed. lib. bdg. 22.50 (ISBN 0-89874-166-1). Krieger.
McCarthy, E. Jerome. Basic Marketing: A Managerial Approach. 7th ed. 1981. 20.95x (ISBN 0-256-02533-9). Irwin.
McKay, E. S. Marketing Mystique. LC 72-166557. 1972. 16.00 (ISBN 0-8144-5279-5). Am Mgmt.
Mallen, Bruce. Principles of Marketing Channel Management. LC 76-27923. (Illus.). 1977. 23.95 (ISBN 0-669-00985-7). Lexington Bks.
Marcus, Burton, et al. Modern Marketing Management. rev. ed. 709p. 1980. text ed. 19.95 (ISBN 0-394-32254-1); wkbk 5.95 (ISBN 0-394-32489-7). Random.
Michman, Ronald D. & Sibley, Stanley D. Marketing Channels & Strategies. 2nd ed. LC 78-4987. (Marketing Ser.). 1980. text ed. 24.00 (ISBN 0-88244-176-0). Grid Pub.
Moriarty, Rowland T. Industrial Buying Behavior: Concepts, Issues, & Marketing Implications. 200p. 1981. 19.95 (ISBN 0-86569-074-X). Auburn Hse.
Mossman, Frank H., et al. Financial Dimensions of Marketing Management. LC 77-14990. (Wiley Series on Marketing Management). 1978. 24.95 (ISBN 0-471-03376-6). Wiley.
Myers, John G., et al. Marketing Research & Knowledge Development: An Assessment for Marketing Management. (Illus.). 1980. text ed. 20.95 (ISBN 0-13-557686-5). P-H.
Myers, Kenneth H. Marketing Policy Determination by a Major Firm in a Capital Goods Industry. LC 75-41773. (Companies & Men: Business Enterprises in America). 1976. 32.00x (ISBN 0-405-08087-5). Arno.
Nystrom, Harry. Creativity & Innovation. LC 78-8594. 125p. 1979. 29.75 (ISBN 0-471-99682-3, Pub. by Wiley-Interscience). Wiley.
Orent, Norman B. Your Future in Marketing. (Careers in Depth Ser.). 1978. PLB 5.97 (ISBN 0-8239-0435-0). Rosen Pr.
Rausser, Gordon. Dynamic Agricultural Systems: Economic, Prediction & Control. (Dynamic Economics Ser.: Vol. 3). 1979. 25.00 (ISBN 0-444-00274-X, North Holland). Elsevier.
Ray, Michael L. Advertising & Commercial Management. (Illus.). 640p. 1982. 24.95 (ISBN 0-13-015230-7). P-H.
Rewoldt, Stewart H., et al. Introduction to Marketing Management. 4th ed. 1981. 23.95x (ISBN 0-256-02538-X). Irwin.
Rodger, L. W. Marketing in a Competitive Economy. 3rd ed. LC 73-3342. 253p. 1965. pap. 13.95 (ISBN 0-470-72928-7). Halsted Pr.
Rogers, L. A. Business Analysis for Marketing Managers. 1978. pap. 14.95x (ISBN 0-434-91738-9). Intl Ideas.
Rosenberg, L. Marketing. (Illus.). 1977. 19.95 (ISBN 0-13-556100-0); wkbk. & study guide 4.95 (ISBN 0-13-556118-3). P-H.
Rothberg, Robert R., ed. Corporate Strategy & Product Innovation. 2nd ed. LC 80-1857. (Illus.). 1981. text ed. 17.95 (ISBN 0-02-927520-2). Free Pr.
Rudman, Jack. Associate Marketing Representative. (Career Examination Ser.: C-2040). (Cloth bdg. avail. on request). pap. 10.00 (ISBN 0-8373-2040-2). Natl Learning.
--Chief Marketing Representative. (Career Examination Ser.: C-2041). (Cloth bdg. avail. on request). pap. 10.00 (ISBN 0-8373-2041-0). Natl Learning.
Shama, Avraham. Marketing in a Slow Growth Economy: The Impact of Stagflation on Consumer Psychology. LC 79-26312. (Praeger Special Studies). (Illus.). 184p. 1980. 19.95 (ISBN 0-03-052151-3). Praeger.
Sims, J. Taylor, et al. Marketing Channels: Systems & Strategies. 1977. pap. text ed. 20.50 scp (ISBN 0-06-046215-9, HarpC); scp cases bk. 9.50 (ISBN 0-06-046214-0). Har-Row.
Staudt, Thomas A. & Taylor, Donald. Managerial Introduction to Marketing. 3rd ed. (Illus.). 576p. 1976. 20.95x (ISBN 0-13-550186-5). P-H.
Tarpey, Lawrence X., et al. A Preface to Marketing Management. 1979. pap. 8.95x (ISBN 0-256-02207-0). Business Pubns.
Taylor, Bernard & Wills, Gordon. Longrange Planning for Marketing & Diversification. 464p. 1971. 22.00x (ISBN 0-8464-1112-1). Beekman Pubs.
Tolman, Ruth. Fashion Marketing & Merchandising, Vol. 2. 1974. soft cover 13.25 (ISBN 0-87350-254-X). Milady.
Udell, Jon G. & Laczniak, Gene R. Marketing in an Age of Change. LC 80-19923. (Marketing Ser.). 577p. 1981. text ed. 20.95 (ISBN 0-471-08169-8); tchrs.' ed. 11.00 (ISBN 0-471-08184-1); test file avail. (ISBN 0-471-08187-6). Wiley.
Varble, Dale. Cases in Marketing Management. (Business Ser.). 272p. 1976. pap. text ed. 12.50 (ISBN 0-675-08638-8); instructor's manual 3.95 (ISBN 0-686-67246-1). Merrill.
Walters, S. George. Marketing Management Viewpoints. 2nd ed. Swee, ed. Snider. 1970. pap. text ed. 5.90 (ISBN 0-538-19310-7). SW Pub.
White, Percival. Scientific Marketing Management. Assael, Henry, ed. LC 78-272. (Century of Marketing Ser.). 1978. Repr. of 1927 ed. lib. bdg. 20.00x (ISBN 0-405-11163-0). Arno.
Wiechmann, Ulrich E. Marketing Management in Multinational Firms: The Consumer Packaged Goods Industry. LC 75-19831. (Special Studies). 1976. text ed. 22.95 (ISBN 0-275-55850-9). Praeger.
Williams, L. A. Industrial Marketing Management & Controls. 1968. 22.50 (ISBN 0-444-19790-7). Elsevier.
Wilmshurst, John. Fundamentals & Practice of Marketing. 1978. pap. 14.95x (ISBN 0-434-92263-3). Intl Ideas.
Wilson, Aubrey, ed. Marketing of Industrial Products. 1966. text ed. 10.50x (ISBN 0-09-077310-1). Humanities.
Wilson, M. T. The Management of Marketing. LC 80-23617. 141p. 1981. 32.95 (ISBN 0-470-27074-8). Halsted Pr.
Wilson, R. M. Management Controls & Marketing Planning. 224p. 1979. 24.95x (ISBN 0-470-26673-2); pap. 21.95 (ISBN 0-470-27053-5). Halsted Pr.
Youdale, Peter J. Setting up an Effective Marketing Operation. (Illus.). 168p. 1972. 22.00x (ISBN 0-8464-0840-6). Beekman Pubs.
Zand, Dale. Management in a Knowledge Society. Newton, William R., ed. (Illus.). 224p. Date not set. 12.95 (ISBN 0-07-072743-0, P&RB). McGraw.
Zober, Martin. Marketing Management. 483p. 1964. text ed. 14.00 (ISBN 0-471-98385-3, Pub. by Wiley). Krieger.

MARKETING MANAGEMENT–CASE STUDIES

Blois, K. J. & Cowell, D. W. Short Cases in Marketing Management. 1973. text ed. 17.95x (ISBN 0-7002-0207-2). Intl Ideas.
Bursk, Edward C. & Greyset, Stephen A., eds. Cases in Marketing Management. 2nd ed. (Foundations of Marketing Ser.). (Illus.). 240p. 1975. pap. 7.95 ref. ed. (ISBN 0-13-118893-3). P-H.
DeLozier, M. Wayne & Woodside, Arch G. Marketing Management: Strategies & Cases. (Marketing & Management Ser.). 1978. text ed. 21.95 (ISBN 0-675-08417-2) (ISBN 0-686-67981-4). Merrill.
Raymond, Corey E., et al. Problems in Marketing. 6th ed. (Marketing Ser.). (Illus.). 832p. 1981. 22.95 (ISBN 0-07-013141-4); instructor's manual 16.95 (ISBN 0-07-013142-2). McGraw.
Star, Steven H & Davis, Nancy. Problems in Marketing. 5th ed. LC 77-488. (Illus.). 1977. text ed. 18.95 (ISBN 0-07-060835-0, C); instructor's manual 7.95 (ISBN 0-07-060836-9). McGraw.
Zikmund, William & Lundstrom, William J. A Collection of Outstanding Cases in Marketing Management. (Illus.). 1979. pap. text ed. 13.95 (ISBN 0-8299-0234-1); instrs.' manual avail. (ISBN 0-8299-0585-5). West Pub.

MARKETING MANAGEMENT–DATA PROCESSING

Kelleher, Robert F. Industrial Marketing & Sales Management in the Computer Age. 160p. 1981. text ed. 18.95 (ISBN 0-8436-0867-6). CBI Pub.

MARKETING MANAGEMENT–HISTORY

Gross, Edwin J. Personal Leadership in Marketing. 189p. 1968. pap. 4.50x (ISBN 0-912598-04-2). Florham.
Porter, Glenn & Livesay, Harold C. Merchants & Manufacturers: Studies in the Changing Structure of Nineteenth-Century Marketing. LC 72-156071. 272p. 1971. 19.00x (ISBN 0-8018-1251-8). Johns Hopkins.

MARKETING OF FARM PRODUCE

see Farm Produce–Marketing

MARKETING OF FRUIT

see Fruit–Marketing

MARKETING RESEARCH

see also Market Surveys; Motivation Research (Marketing); Sales Forecasting

Aaker, David A. & Day, George S. Marketing Research: Private & Public Sector Decisions. LC 79-18532. (Wiley Series in Marketing). 628p. 1980. text ed. 23.95 (ISBN 0-471-00059-0). Wiley.
Adler, Lee & Mayer, Charles S. Managing the Marketing Research Function. LC 76-46447. (Monograph Ser.: No. 5). 1977. 11.00 (ISBN 0-87757-082-5). Am Mktg.
--Readings in Managing the Marketing Research Function. LC 80-11092. 1980. pap. 22.00 (ISBN 0-87757-136-8). Am Mktg.
Andreasen, A. & Gardner, D., eds. Diffusing Marketing Theory & Research: The Contributions of Bauer, Green, Kotler & Levitt. LC 78-1544. (Proceedings Ser.). 1979. 13.00 (ISBN 0-87757-116-3). Am Mktg.
Bellenger, Danny N. & Greenberg, Barnett A. Marketing Research: A Management Information Approach. 1978. 19.95x (ISBN 0-256-01990-8). Irwin.
Bellenger, Danny N., et al. Qualitative Research in Marketing. LC 76-3765. (Monograph Ser.: No. 3). 1976. pap. 4.50 (ISBN 0-87757-070-1). Am Mktg.
Blankenship, A. B. Professional Telephone Surveys. LC 77-7023. (Illus.). 1977. 19.50 (ISBN 0-07-005862-8, P&RB). McGraw.
Boyd, Harper W., Jr., et al. Marketing Research: Text & Cases. 5th ed. 1981. 22.95 (ISBN 0-256-02530-4). Irwin.
Bradford's Directory of Marketing Research Agencies & Management Consultants in the U.S. & the World, 1971-72. 13th ed. 25.50 (ISBN 0-910290-02-4). Bradford's VA.
Bradford's Directory of Marketing Research & Management Consultants in the U.S. & the World: Addenda. 13th ed. LC 51-3505. 1978. 24.50 (ISBN 0-910290-03-2). Bradford's VA.
Breen, George E. Do-It-Yourself Marketing Research. (Illus.). 1977. 22.50 (ISBN 0-07-007445-3, P&RB). McGraw.
Brown, F. E. Marketing Research: A Structure for Decision Making. LC 79-25541. 1980. text ed. 18.95 (ISBN 0-201-00205-1). A-W.
Buzzell, R. D., et al. Marketing Research & Information Systems: Text & Cases. 1969. text ed. 19.95 (ISBN 0-07-009475-6, C); instructor's manual 4.95 (ISBN 0-07-009476-4). tapes 325.00 (ISBN 0-07-097280-X). McGraw.
Cannon, Tim. Distribution Research. 1973. pap. text ed. 11.00x (ISBN 0-7002-0232-3). Intl Ideas.
Cheskin, Louis. Secrets of Marketing Success. LC 67-16398. 1967. 5.95 (ISBN 0-671-64273-1). Trident.
Clifton, David S., Jr. & Fyffe, David E. Project Feasibility Analysis: A Guide to Profitable New Ventures. LC 76-51321. 1977. text ed. 29.95 (ISBN 0-471-01611-X, Pub. by Wiley-Interscience). Wiley.
Converse, Jean M. & Schuman, Howard. Conversations at Random: Survey Research As Interviewers See It. LC 73-15840. (Illus.). 121p. 1974. pap. text ed. 5.50 (ISBN 0-87944-248-4). Inst Soc Res.
Cox, Eli P., 3rd. Marketing Research: Information for Decision Making. 1979. text ed. 21.50 scp (ISBN 0-912212-14-4, HarpC); instr. manual avail. (ISBN 0-06-361361-1). Har-Row.
Cox, Keith K., ed. Readings in Market Research. LC 67-15866. (Illus., Orig.). 1967. pap. text ed. 11.95x (ISBN 0-89197-372-9). Irvington.
Cox, William E. Industrial Marketing Research. LC 78-11480. (Marketing Management Ser.). 1979. 29.95 (ISBN 0-471-03467-3, Pub. by Wiley-Interscience). Wiley.
Davies, Anthony H. Practice of Marketing Research. (Illus.). 1973. pap. text ed. 12.95x (ISBN 0-434-90296-9). Intl Ideas.
Davis, J. Ronnie & Hulett, Joe R. An Analysis of Market Failure: Externalities, Public Goods, & Mixed Goods. LC 77-12344. (University of Fla. Social Science Monograph: No. 61). (Illus.). 1977. pap. 3.00 (ISBN 0-8130-0587-6). U Presses Fla.
Dommermuth, William P. The Use of Sampling in Marketing Research. LC 75-8843. 40p. 1975. pap. 3.00 (ISBN 0-87757-065-5). Am Mktg.
Educational Research Council of America. Market Researcher. Kunze, Linda J. & Marchak, John P., eds. (Real People at Work Ser: J). (Illus.). 1975. pap. text ed. 2.25 (ISBN 0-89247-072-0). Changing Times.
Eighmey, J., ed. Attitude Research Under the Sun. LC 78-13992. (Proceedings Ser.). 1979. 12.00 (ISBN 0-87757-115-5). Am Mktg.
Enrick, Norbert L. Market & Sales Forecasting: A Quantitative Approach. rev. ed. LC 78-9090. 208p. 1979. 10.50 (ISBN 0-88275-690-7). Krieger.
European Society for Opinion & Marketing Research. From Market Research to Advertising Strategy & Vice Versa. (Seminars Ser.). 1973. 35.00x (ISBN 0-8002-1436-6). Intl Pubns Serv.
--Managing Market Research As a Business. (Seminars Ser.). 1975. 35.00x (ISBN 0-8002-1697-0). Intl Pubns Serv.
European Society for Opinion & Marketing Research Seminar on Research & the Travel & Tourism Market, Yugoslavia, 1972. Proceedings. 26.00x (ISBN 0-8002-1843-4). Intl Pubns Serv.
European Society for Opinion & Marketing Research Congress-24th-Helsinki, Aug. 22-26, 1971, ed. Proceedings: From Experience to Innovation, 2 vols. 1182p. 1973. Set. pap. 62.50x (ISBN 0-8002-1878-7). Intl Pubns Serv.
Ferber, Robert. Handbook of Marketing Research. (Illus.). 1344p. 1974. 52.95 (ISBN 0-07-020462-4, P&RB). McGraw.
Ferber, Robert, ed. Readings in Survey Research. LC 78-14428. 1978. 15.00 (ISBN 0-87757-113-9). Am Mktg.
--Readings in the Analysis of Survey Data. LC 80-12975. 249p. (Orig.). 1980. pap. text ed. 24.00 (ISBN 0-87757-140-6). Am Mktg.
Gelb, Gabriel M. & Gelb, Betsy D. Research at the Top: Better Data for Organizational Policy Making. LC 75-37588. (AMA Monographs Ser.: No. 2). 1975. pap. 3.00 (ISBN 0-87757-069-8). Am Mktg.
Green, Paul E. & Tull, Donald S. Research for Marketing Decisions. 4th ed. (Illus.). 1978. ref. 22.95 (ISBN 0-13-774158-8). P-H.
Handbook of Marketing Research in Europe 1976-77. LC 65-56398. 1976. pap. 80.00x (ISBN 92-831-1034-X). Intl Pubns Serv.
Harder, T. Introduction to Mathematical Models in Market & Opinion Research. 1970. 54.00x (ISBN 0-677-61820-4). Gordon.
Harris, E. Edward. Marketing Research. 2nd ed. Dorr, Eugene L., ed. (Occupational Manuals & Projects in Marketing Ser.). (Illus.). (gr. 7-12). 1978. pap. text ed. 5.48 (ISBN 0-07-026837-1, G); instructor's manual & key 3.00 (ISBN 0-07-026838-X). McGraw.
Harvey, Joan M. Statistics America: Sources for Social, Economic, & Marketing Research. 2nd ed. 300p. 1980. 160.00 (ISBN 0-900246-16-2). Gale.
Henry, Harry. Perspectives in Management Marketing & Research. 400p. 1971. 19.00x (ISBN 0-8464-0711-6). Beekman Pubs.
Home & Auto Do-It-Yourself Markets, GB-038. 1977. 500.00 (ISBN 0-89336-087-2). BCC.
Hughes, G. David. Demand Analysis for Marketing Decisions. 1973. 19.95x (ISBN 0-256-01479-5). Irwin.

Jain, Subhash C., ed. Research Frontiers in Marketing: Dialogues & Directions. LC 78-8596. (Proceedings Ser.: No. 43). 1978. pap. text ed. 12.00 (ISBN 0-87757-109-0). Am Mktg.

James, Don L. Youth, Media, & Advertising. LC 71-181494. (Studies in Marketing: No. 15). 1972. pap. 4.00 (ISBN 0-87755-149-9). U of Tex Busn Res.

King, William R. Marketing Management Information Systems. (Priorities in Marketing Ser). 1977. text ed. 16.95x (ISBN 0-442-80395-8); pap. text ed. 9.00x (ISBN 0-442-80448-2). Van Nos Reinhold.

Kinnear, Thomas C. & Taylor, James R. Marketing Research: An Applied Approach. (Marketing Ser.). 1979. text ed. 17.50 (ISBN 0-07-034741-7, C); instructor's manual 8.95 (ISBN 0-07-034742-5); exercises 5.50 (ISBN 0-07-034743-3); transparency masters avail. (ISBN 0-07-034744-1). McGraw.

Kress, George J. Marketing Research. (Illus.). 1979. text ed. 18.95 (ISBN 0-8359-4271-6); instrs'. manual avail. (ISBN 0-8359-4272-4). Reston.

Lee, Donald D. Industrial Marketing Research: Techniques & Practices. LC 77-95307. 1978. 12.50x (ISBN 0-87762-248-5). Technomic.

Lehmann, Donald R. Market Research & Analysis. 1979. 19.95x (ISBN 0-256-02140-6). Irwin.

Lipson, Harry A. & Darling, John R. Marketing Fundamentals: Text & Cases. LC 80-12441. 590p. 1980. Repr. of 1974 ed. lib. bdg. 22.50 (ISBN 0-89874-166-1). Krieger.

Luck, David J., et al. Experiential Exercises in Marketing Research. (Illus.). 192p. 1980. pap. text ed. 8.95 (ISBN 0-13-295220-3). P-H.

--Marketing Research. 5th ed. LC 77-17170. (Illus.). 1978. ref. ed. 19.95 (ISBN 0-13-557637-7). P-H.

Maloney, J. & Silverman, B., eds. Attitude Research Plays for High Stakes. LC 78-14033. (Proceedings Ser.). 1978. 12.00 (ISBN 0-87757-117-1). Am Mktg.

Market Research Handbook. 813p. 1980. pap. 46.50 (ISBN 0-686-68837-6, SSC146, SSC). Unipub.

Market Research Handbook. 1979. pap. 18.00 (ISBN 0-685-90715-5, SSC 115, SSC). Unipub.

Marketing Research in Europe ("Esomar") 1978. 136.00 (ISBN 0-685-58572-7). Heinman.

Miller, Thomas E. & Sher, Lisa, eds. Findex: The Directory of Market Research Reports, Studies & Surveys. 1981. 125.00 (ISBN 0-931634-07-5). Info Clearing House.

Myers, James H. & Tauber, Edward. Market Structure Analysis. LC 77-5773. 1977. pap. 13.00 (ISBN 0-87757-089-2). Am Mktg.

National Retail Merchants Assn. POS Update. 1978. pap. 35.00 (ISBN 0-685-41869-3). Natl Ret Merch.

Olshavsky, Richard W., ed. Attitude Research Enters the Eighties. LC 80-20621. (Proceedings Ser.). 196p. 1980. 12.00 (ISBN 0-87757-145-7). Am Mktg.

Padolecchia, Siro P. Marketing in the Developing World. 1979. text ed. 15.00x (ISBN 0-7069-0694-2, Pub. by Vikas India). Advent NY.

Peterson, Robert A. Trends in Consumer Behavior Research. LC 76-45657. (Monograph Ser.: No. 6). 1977. 5.50 (ISBN 0-87757-083-3). Am Mktg.

Petrof, John V. Comportement du Consommateur et Marketing. 2nd ed. (Illus.). 1978. pap. 14.50x (ISBN 2-7637-6854-7, Pub. by Laval). Intl Schol Bk Serv.

Pope, Jeffrey L. Practical Marketing Research. 304p. 1981. 24.95 (ISBN 0-8144-5651-0). Am Mgmt.

Powers, Mark J. & Vogel, David J. Inside the Financial Futures Markets. LC 80-23157. 320p. 1981. 19.95 (ISBN 0-471-08136-1). Ronald Pr.

Proctor, Tony & Stone, Marilyn A. Marketing Research. (Illus.). 192p. 1978. pap. text ed. 9.95x (ISBN 0-7121-1291-X, Pub. by Macdonald & Evans England). Intl Ideas.

Ramond, Charles. The Art of Using Science in Marketing. (Sheth Ser.). 1974. pap. text ed. 15.50 scp (ISBN 0-06-045321-4, HarpC). Har-Row.

Rath, Patricia M., et al. Case Studies in Marketing & Distribution. (Illus.). 180p. (gr. 9-12). 1965. pap. text ed. 2.95x (ISBN 0-8134-0835-0, 835). Interstate.

Reekie, W. Duncan. Industry, Prices & Markets. LC 79-14543. 166p. 1979. 20.95x (ISBN 0-470-26709-7). Halsted Pr.

Schoner, Bertram & Uhl, Kenneth P. Marketing Research: A Short Course for Professionals. (Wiley Professional Development Programs). 1976. 24.95 (ISBN 0-471-01701-9). Wiley.

Schoner, Bertran & Uhl, Kenneth P. Marketing Research: Information Systems & Decision Making. 2nd ed. LC 80-11127. 608p. 1980. Repr. of 1975 ed. 24.00 (ISBN 0-89874-184-X). Krieger.

Sheth, J. Multivariate Methods for Market & Survey Research. LC 76-39893. 388p. 1977. 20.00 (ISBN 0-87757-081-7). Am Mktg.

Sheth, Jagdish N., ed. Research in Marketing, Vol. 2. 357p. 1979. 34.50 (ISBN 0-89232-059-1). Jai Pr.

--Research in Marketing, Vol. 4. 300p. 1981. 34.50 (ISBN 0-89232-169-5). Jai Pr.

--Research in Marketing, Vol. 5. 325p. 1981. 34.50 (ISBN 0-89232-211-X). Jai Pr.

--Research in Marketing: An Annual Compilation of Research, Vol. 1. (Annual Ser.). (Orig.). 1978. lib. bdg. 34.50 (ISBN 0-89232-041-9). Jai Pr.

Staudt, Thomas A. & Taylor, Donald. Managerial Introduction to Marketing. 3rd ed. (Illus.). 576p. 1976. 20.95x (ISBN 0-13-550186-5). P-H.

Stone, Bob. Successful Direct Marketing Methods. 2nd, rev. ed. LC 78-74973. (Illus.). 1979. 24.95 (ISBN 0-87251-040-9). Crain Bks.

Theil, H. System-Wide Explorations in International Economics, Input-Output Analysis, & Marketing Research. (Lectures in Economics Ser.: Vol. 2). 139p. 1980. 29.50 (ISBN 0-444-85377-4). Elsevier.

Thompson, Stephanie. Shops & Markets. LC 78-64655. (Fact Finders Ser.). (Illus.). 1979. lib. bdg. 3.96 (ISBN 0-686-51131-X). Silver.

Tolley, B. Stuart. Advertising & Marketing Research: A New Methodology. LC 77-1120. 1977. 23.95x (ISBN 0-88229-179-3). Nelson-Hall.

Tull, Donald S. & Hawkins, Del I. Marketing Research: Measurement & Method. 2nd ed. (Illus.). 1980. text ed. 21.95 (ISBN 0-02-421760-3). Macmillan.

Twedt, Dik W. Survey of Marketing Research, 1978. 1978. 30.00 (ISBN 0-87757-119-8). Am Mktg.

Udell, Jon G. Successful Marketing Strategies in American Industry. Leslie, Gay, ed. (Illus.). 1972. 9.50x (ISBN 0-912084-07-3). Mimir.

Vega, Carole. Writing for the U. S. Astrology Market: Nineteen Eighty to Nineteen Eighty-One. 70p. 1979. pap. 4.95 (ISBN 0-930840-09-7). Ninth Sign.

Venkatesan, M. & Holloway, R. Introduction to Marketing Experimentation. LC 71-143510. 1971. pap. text ed. 6.95 (ISBN 0-02-933130-7). Free Pr.

Wasson, Chester R. Strategy of Marketing Research. LC 64-15387. (Illus.). 1964. 24.50x (ISBN 0-89197-426-1); pap. text ed. 14.95x (ISBN 0-89197-953-0). Irvington.

Wentz, Walter B. Marketing Research: Management, Materials, & Cases. 2nd ed. 784p. 1979. text ed. 25.50 scp (ISBN 0-06-047006-2, HarpC). Har-Row.

--Marketing Research: Management, Methods, & Cases. 2nd ed. 1979. text ed. 24.95 (ISBN 0-06-047006-2, CW); instr's manual avail. (ISBN 0-06-367032-1). Har-Row.

Williams, L. A. Industrial Marketing Management & Controls. 1968. 22.50 (ISBN 0-444-19790-7). Elsevier.

Wills, G. Marketing Through Research. 1967. 28.00 (ISBN 0-08-012620-0); pap. 14.50 (ISBN 0-08-012619-7). Pergamon.

Worcester, Robert M., ed. Consumer Market Research Handbook. 2nd ed. 1978. text ed. 34.50x (ISBN 0-442-30237-1). Van Nos Reinhold.

MARKETING RESEARCH–BIBLIOGRAPHY

Ferber, Robert, et al. A Basic Bibliography on Marketing Research. rev. ed. LC 74-81449. (Bibliography Ser.: No. 2). 1974. pap. 11.00 (ISBN 0-87757-000-0). Am Mktg.

Harvey, Joan M. Statistics-Europe: Guide for the Market Researcher to 34 Countries of Europe. 3rd ed. 1976. 55.00x (ISBN 0-900246-18-9). Intl Pubns Serv.

Twedt, Dik W., et al, eds. Personality Research in Marketing: A Bibliography. LC 76-45906. (Bibliographies Ser.: No. 23). 1977. pap. 5.50 (ISBN 0-87757-080-9). Am Mktg.

MARKETS

see also Commodity Exchanges; Fairs; also Retail Trade; Grocery Trade, and similar headings

Bathgate, M. A. The Structure of Rural Supply to the Honiara Market in the Solomon Islands. (The Australian National University Development Studies Centre Occasional Paper: No. 11). (Illus.). 1979. pap. text ed. 3.95 (ISBN 0-909150-62-1, Pub. by ANUP Australia). Bks Australia.

Berry, Brian. Geography of Market Centers & Retail Distribution. 1967. pap. 7.95 ref. ed. (ISBN 0-13-351304-1). P-H.

The Chicago Market 1972-1973. (Report Ser: No. 650). 24p. (Orig.). 1975. pap. 50.00 (ISBN 0-8237-0069-0). Conference Bd.

Darst, David M. The Handbook of the Bond & Money Markets. LC 80-36816. (Illus.). 461p. 1981. 29.95 (ISBN 0-07-015401-5, P&RB). McGraw.

The Detroit Market 1972-1973. (Report Ser.: No. 653). 24p. (Orig.). 1975. pap. 50.00 (ISBN 0-8237-0072-0). Conference Bd.

De Voe, Thomas F. Market Book Containing a Historical Account of the Public Markets in the Cities of New York, Boston, Philadelphia & Brooklyn: Vol. 1: A History of the Public Markets in the City of New York. LC 72-121319. Repr. of 1862 ed. lib. bdg. 25.00x (ISBN 0-678-00685-7). Kelley.

Good, Charles M. Rural Markets & Trade in East Africa. LC 72-128466. (Research Papers Ser.: No. 128). 252p. 1970. pap. 8.00 (ISBN 0-89065-035-7). U Chicago Dept Geog.

Hendershott, Patric H. Understanding Capital Markets, 2 vols. Sametz, Arnold W. & Wachtel, Paul, eds. Incl. Vol. 1. A Flow of Funds Financial Model. LC 76-55112 (ISBN 0-669-01006-5). 29.50 (ISBN 0-686-67901-6); Vol. 2. The Financial Environment & the Flow of Funds in the Next Decade. LC 76-55113. 22.00 (ISBN 0-669-01007-3). 1977. Lexington Bks.

Isogai, Hiroshi & Matsushima, Shunjiro. Marketplaces of the World. LC 72-184665. (This Beautiful World Ser.: Vol. 35). (Illus.). 130p. (Orig.). 1972. pap. 4.95 (ISBN 0-87011-165-5). Kodansha.

Kerblay, Basile H. Maches Paysans En U. R. S. S. (Etudes Sur L'histoire, L'economie et la Sociologie Des Pays Slaves: No. 10). 1968. pap. 57.75x (ISBN 90-2796-129-8). Mouton.

The Lawes of the Market. LC 74-80198. (English Experience Ser.: No. 676). 22p. 1974. Repr. of 1595 ed. 3.50 (ISBN 90-221-0676-4). Walter J Johnson.

Lenin, Vladimir I. On the So-Called Market Question. 50p. 1976. pap. 0.50 (ISBN 0-686-76787-X, Pub. by Progress Pubs Russia). Imported Pubns.

The Los Angeles Market 1972-1973. (Report Ser.: No. 651). 24p. (Orig.). 1975. pap. 50.00 (ISBN 0-8237-0070-4). Conference Bd.

Lubell, Winifred & Lubell, Cecil. Street Markets Around the World. LC 74-805. (Finding-Out Book). (Illus.). 64p. (gr. 2-4). 1974. PLB 6.95 (ISBN 0-8193-0732-7). Enslow Pubs.

Mossin, Jan. The Economic Efficiency of Financial Markets. 1977. 18.95 (ISBN 0-669-01004-9). Lexington Bks.

The New York Market 1972-1973. (Report Ser.: No. 649). 24p. (Orig.). 1975. pap. 50.00 (ISBN 0-8237-0068-2). Conference Bd.

The Philadelphia Market 1972-1973. (Report Ser.: No. 652). 24p. (Orig.). pap. 50.00 (ISBN 0-8237-0071-2). Conference Bd.

Rudman, Jack. Supervising Inspector of Markets, Weights & Measures. (Career Examination Ser.: C-1047). (Cloth bdg. avail. on request). pap. 10.00 (ISBN 0-8373-1047-4). Natl Learning.

Sametz, Arnold W. Prospects for Capital Formation & Capital Markets. LC 76-55113. (Illus.). 1978. 15.95 (ISBN 0-669-01505-9). Lexington Bks.

Szentes, Tamas. The Negative Impact of the Dualistic Socio-Economic Structure on Domestic Market, Capital Formation & Labour. LC 76-152096. (Studies on Developing Countries: No. 86). 1976. pap. 5.00x (ISBN 0-8002-2187-7). Intl Pubns Serv.

Vickers, Douglas. Financial Markets in the Capitalist Process. LC 77-20308. (Illus.). 1978. 16.00x (ISBN 0-8122-7739-2). U of Pa Pr.

Webster, Jonathan & Webster, Harriet. The Underground Marketplace: A Guide to New England & the Middle Atlantic States. 176p. 1981. 12.50 (ISBN 0-87663-348-3); pap. 6.95 (ISBN 0-87663-555-9). Universe.

White, Paul. Shops & Markets. (Junior Reference Ser.). (Illus.). 64p. (gr. 7 up). 1971. 7.95 (ISBN 0-7136-1155-3). Dufour.

MARKHAM, EDWIN, 1852-1940

Filler, Louis. Unknown Edwin Markham: His Mystery & Its Significance. LC 66-25696. (Illus.). 1966. 10.00x (ISBN 0-87338-087-8). Kent St U Pr.

Rather, Lois. The Man with the Hoe. (Illus.). 1977. ltd. ed. 20.00 (ISBN 0-686-20513-8). Rather Pr.

Stidger, William L. Edwin Markham. 1933. Repr. 40.00 (ISBN 0-8274-2231-8). R West.

MARKHAM, GERVASE, 1568-1637

Gittings, Robert. Shakespeare's Rival. LC 76-3689. (Illus.). 138p. 1976. Repr. of 1960 ed. lib. bdg. 15.00x (ISBN 0-8371-8814-8, GISR). Greenwood.

Lyon, John H. Study of the Newe Metamorphosis. LC 20-3786. Repr. of 1919 ed. 19.75 (ISBN 0-404-04087-X). AMS Pr.

MARKIEVICZ, CONSTANCE GEORGINA (GORE-BOOTH) DE, 1868-1927

Van Voris, Jacqueline. Constance de Markievicz: In the Cause of Ireland. LC 67-11245. (Illus.). 1967. 15.00x (ISBN 0-87023-025-5); pap. 7.50x (ISBN 0-87023-058-1). U of Mass Pr.

MARKING (STUDENTS)

see Grading and Marking (Students)

MARKO, PRINCE OF SERBIA, 1335-1394–POETRY

Low, David H., tr. Ballads of Marco Kraljevic. LC 69-10123. (Illus.). 1968. Repr. of 1922 ed. lib. bdg. 15.00 (ISBN 0-8371-0151-4, LOMK). Greenwood.

MARKOFF PROCESSES

see Markov Processes

MARKOV CHAINS

see Markov Processes

MARKOV PROCESSES

Bagchi, T. P. & Templeton, J. G. Numerical Methods in Markov Chains & Bulk Queues. LC 72-88380. (Lecture Notes in Economics & Mathematical Systems: Vol. 72). xi, 89p. 1972. pap. 6.30 (ISBN 0-387-05996-2). Springer-Verlag.

Bartos, Otomar J. Simple Models of Group Behavior. LC 67-21498. (Illus.). 345p. 1967. 22.50x (ISBN 0-231-02894-6); pap. 10.00x (ISBN 0-231-02893-8). Columbia U Pr.

Billingsley, Patrick. Statistical Inference for Markov Processes. LC 61-8646. (Midway Reprint Ser.). 84p. 1975. pap. text ed. 5.50x (ISBN 0-226-05077-7). U of Chicago Pr.

Blumenthal, Robert M. Markov Processes & Potential Theory. LC 68-18659. (Pure & Applied Mathematics Ser.: Vol. 29). 1968. 50.00 (ISBN 0-12-107850-7). Acad Pr.

Chover, Joshua, ed. Markov Processes & Potential Theory. LC 67-30083. 235p. 1967. 11.00 (ISBN 0-471-15603-5, Pub. by Wiley-Interscience). Krieger.

Chung, K. L. Lectures on Boundary Theory for Markov Chains. (Annals of Mathematics Studies: No. 65). 1970. 10.50 (ISBN 0-691-08075-5). Princeton U Pr.

Chung Kai Lai. Markov Chains with Stationary Transition Probabilities. 2nd ed. (Die Grundlehren der Mathematischen Wissenschaten: Vol. 104). 1967. 34.90 (ISBN 0-387-03822-1). Springer-Verlag.

CISM (International Center for Mechanical Sciences), Dept. of Automation & Information, University of Trieste, 1971. Coding for Markov Sources. Longo, G., ed. (CISM Pubns. Ser.: No. 110). (Illus.). 99p. 1972. pap. 13.90 (ISBN 0-387-81154-0). Springer-Verlag.

Derman, Cyrus. Finite State Markovian Decision Processes. (Mathematics in Science & Engineering Ser.: Vol. 67). 1970. 29.00 (ISBN 0-12-209250-3). Acad Pr.

Dobryshin, R. L., et al, eds. Locally Interacting Systems & Their Application in Biology: Proceedings of the School - Seminar on Markov Interaction Processes in Biology, Held in Pushchino, Moscow Region, March, 1976. (Lecture Notes in Mathematics Ser.: Vol. 653). 1978. pap. 12.80 (ISBN 0-387-08450-9). Springer-Verlag.

Dynkin, E. B. Markov Processes, 2 vols. Fabius, J., et al, trs. (Grundlehren der Mathematischen Wissenschaften: Vols. 121 & 122). 1965. Set. 77.90 (ISBN 0-387-03301-7). Springer-Verlag.

Dynkin, E. B. & Yushkevich, A. A. Markov Processes: Theorems & Problems. LC 69-12529. 237p. 1969. 27.50 (ISBN 0-306-30378-7, Plenum Pr). Plenum Pub.

Fleming, W. H. & Rishel, R. W. Deterministic & Stochastic Optimal Control. LC 75-28391. (Applications of Mathematics: Vol. 1). (Illus.). xi, 222p. 1975. 31.30 (ISBN 0-387-90155-8). Springer-Verlag.

Freedman, David A. Approximating Countable Markov Chains. LC 76-142943. 1972. 18.95x (ISBN 0-8162-3034-X). Holden-Day.

Getoor, R. K. Markov Processes: Ray Processes & Right Processes, Vol. 440. (Lecture Notes in Mathematics Ser). v, 118p. 1975. pap. 10.00 (ISBN 0-387-07140-7). Springer-Verlag.

Hartley, R. Recent Developments in Markow Decision Process. (IMA Conference Ser.). 1981. 36.00 (ISBN 0-12-328460-0). Acad Pr.

Howard, Ronald A. Dynamic Probabilistic Systems, 2 vols. LC 74-112593. (Decision & Control Ser). 1971. Vol. 1, Markovian Models. 41.50 (ISBN 0-471-41665-7); Vol. 2, Semi-markovian & Decision Models. 45.00 (ISBN 0-471-41666-5). Wiley.

Iosifescu, Marius. Finite Markov Processes & Applications. LC 79-42726. 250p. 1980. 32.50 (ISBN 0-471-27677-4). Wiley.

Isaacson, Dean L. & Madsen, Richard W. Markov Chains: Theory & Applications. LC 75-30646. (Probability & Mathematical Statistics Ser.). 1976. 35.95 (ISBN 0-471-42862-0, Pub. by Wiley-Interscience). Wiley.

Keilson, J. Markov Chain Models - Rarity & Exponentiality. (Applied Mathematical Sciences: Vol. 28). 1979. pap. 12.60 (ISBN 0-387-90405-0). Springer-Verlag.

Kemeny, J. G. & Snell, J. L. Finite Markov Chains. LC 76-11776. (Undergraduate Texts in Mathematics). 1976. 17.90 (ISBN 0-387-90192-2). Springer-Verlag.

Kemeny, J. G., et al. Denumerable Markov Chains. 2nd ed. LC 76-3535. (Graduate Texts in Mathematics Ser.: Vol. 40). Repr. 20.80 (ISBN 0-387-90177-9). Springer-Verlag.

Kindermann, Ross & Snell, J. Laurie. Markov Random Fields & Their Applications. (Contemporary Mathematics Ser.: Vol. 1). 1980. 10.00 (ISBN 0-8218-5001-6, CONM 1). Am Math.
Krein, M. G. & Nudel'Man, A. A. The Markov Moment Problem & Extremal Problems. LC 77-11716. (Translations of Mathematical Monographs: Vol. 50). 1977. 68.40 (ISBN 0-8218-4500-4, MMONO50). Am Math.
Kushner, Harold J. Stochastic Stability & Control. (Mathematics in Science & Engineering Ser.: Vol. 33). 1967. 29.50 (ISBN 0-12-430150-9). Acad Pr.
Lamperti, J. Stochastic Processes: A Survey of the Mathematical Theory. LC 77-24321. (Applied Mathematical Sciences: Vol. 23). 1977. pap. 13.80 (ISBN 0-387-90275-9). Springer-Verlag.
Mandl, P. Analytical Treatment of One-Dimensional Markov Processes. LC 68-59694. (Die Grundlehren der Mathematischen Wissenschaften: Vol. 151). 1968. 26.30 (ISBN 0-387-04142-7). Springer-Verlag.
Martin, J. J. Bayesian Decision Problems & Makrov Chains. LC 74-32489. 216p. 1975. Repr. of 1967 ed. 13.50 (ISBN 0-88275-277-4). Krieger.
Mine, H. & Osaki, S. Markovian Decision Processes. (Modern Analytic & Computational Methods in Science & Mathematics: No. 25). 1970. 22.95 (ISBN 0-444-00079-8, North Holland). Elsevier.
Norman, M. Frank. Markov Processes & Learning Models. (Mathematics in Science & Engineering Ser.: Vol. 84). 1972. 37.50 (ISBN 0-12-521450-2). Acad Pr.
Paz, Azaria. Introduction to Probabilistic Automata. LC 74-137627. (Computer Science & Applied Mathematics Ser). 1971. 38.50 (ISBN 0-12-547650-7). Acad Pr.
Rapoport, Amnon, et al. Response Models for Detection of Change. (Theory & Decision Library: No. 18). 1979. lib. bdg. 30.00 (ISBN 90-277-0934-3, Pub. by Reidel Holland). Kluwer Boston.
Revuz, D. Markov Chains. LC 74-80112. (Mathematical Library: Vol. 11). 336p. 1975. 41.50 (ISBN 0-444-10752-5, North-Holland). Elsevier.
Silverstein, M. L. Boundary Theory for Symmetric Markov Processes. (Lecture Notes in Mathematics Ser.: Vol. 516). 1976. pap. 16.40 (ISBN 0-387-07688-3). Springer-Verlag.
--Symmetric Markov Processes. LC 74-22376. (Lecture Notes in Mathematics Ser.: Vol. 426). 1975. pap. 14.70 (ISBN 0-387-07012-5). Springer-Verlag.
Stoica, L. Local Operator & Markow Processes. (Lecture Notes in Mathematics: Vol. 816). 104p. 1980. pap. 9.80 (ISBN 0-387-10028-8). Springer-Verlag.
Suppes, Patrick & Atkinson, Richard C. Markov Learning Models for Multiperson Interactions. 1960. 15.00x (ISBN 0-8047-0038-9). Stanford U Pr.
Wallace, Victor L. On the Representation of Markovian Systems by Network Models. LC 70-137674. 121p. 1969. 19.50 (ISBN 0-686-01952-0). Mgmt Info Serv.
White, D. J. Finite Dynamic Programming: An Approach to Finite Markov Decision Processes. LC 77-26333. 1978. 50.95 (ISBN 0-471-99629-7, Pub. by Wiley-Interscience). Wiley.
Williams, David. Diffusions, Markov Processes & Martingales: Volume 1: Foundation. LC 78-16634. (Probability & Mathematical Statistics Ser.: Applied Section). 1979. 47.25 (ISBN 0-471-99705-6, Pub. by Wiley-Interscience). Wiley.
Yushkevich, A. A. & Dykin, E. B. Controlled Markov Processes. Danskin, J. M., tr. from Rus. (Grundlehren der Mathematischen Wissenschaften: Vol. 235). (Illus.). 1979. 39.80 (ISBN 0-387-90387-9). Springer-Verlag.

MARKOVIC, SVETOZAR, 1846-1875

McClellan, W. D. Svetozar Markovic & the Origins of Balkan Socialism. 1964. 22.50x (ISBN 0-691-05158-5). Princeton U Pr.

MARKS, ARTISTS'

see Artists' Marks

MARKS, COLLECTORS'

see Collectors' Marks

MARKS, POTTERS'

see Pottery–Marks

MARKS, PRINTERS

see Printers' Marks

MARKS IN PAPER

see Water-Marks

MARKS OF ORIGIN

see also Trade-Marks

MacDonald-Taylor, Margaret. Dictionary of Marks. (Illus.). 1962. pap. 4.95 (ISBN 0-8015-2089-4, Hawthorn). Dutton.

MARKS ON PLATE

see Hall-Marks

MARKSMANSHIP

see Shooting

MARLBOROUGH, JOHN CHURCHILL, 1ST DUKE OF, 1650-1722

Chandler, David. Marlborough As Military Commander. LC 72-12160. (Illus.). 1975. 14.95 (ISBN 0-684-13314-8). Hippocrene Bks.
--Marlbouough As Military Commander. 1979. 30.00 (ISBN 0-7134-2075-8, Pub. by Batsford England). David & Charles.
Horn, Robert D. Marlborough: A Survey of Panegyrics, Satires & Biographical Writings, 1688-1788. LC 74-14647. (Reference Library of the Humanities: No. 2). (Illus.). 612p. 1974. lib. bdg. 65.00 (ISBN 0-8240-1054-X). Garland Pub.
Parker, Robert & De Merode-Westerloo, Comte. Marlborough Wars. (Military Memoirs Ser). 1968. 16.50 (ISBN 0-208-00707-5, Archon). Shoe String.
Saintsbury, George E. Marlborough. LC 76-22738. 1976. Repr. of 1888 ed. lib. bdg. 25.00 (ISBN 0-8414-7733-7). Folcroft.

MARLBOROUGH, SARAH (JENNINGS), DUCHESS OF, 1660-1744

Marlborough, Sarah. Letters of Sarah, Duchess of Marlborough. LC 77-37708. Repr. of 1875 ed. 12.00 (ISBN 0-404-56766-5). AMS Pr.

MARLIANI, GIOVANNI, d. 1483

Clagett, Marshall. Giovanni Marliani & Late Medieval Physics. LC 70-181929. (Columbia University Studies in the Social Sciences: No. 483). Repr. of 1941 ed. 12.50 (ISBN 0-404-51483-9). AMS Pr.

MARLOWE, CHRISTOPHER, 1564-1593

Ando, Sadao. A Descriptive Syntax of Christopher Marlowe's Language. 1976. 60.00x (ISBN 0-86008-162-1, Pub. by U of Tokyo Pr). Intl Schol Bk Serv.
Bakeless, John. Christopher Marlowe. LC 75-42103. (English Literature Ser., No. 33). 1974. lib. bdg. 49.95 (ISBN 0-8383-1881-9). Haskell.
Bakeless, John E. The Tragicall History of Christopher Marlowe, 2 vols. LC 70-106681. (Illus.). Repr. of 1942 ed. lib. bdg. 34.50x (ISBN 0-8371-3352-1, BACM). Greenwood.
--Tragicall History of Christopher Marlowe, 2 vols. Repr. of 1942 ed. 33.00 (ISBN 0-403-04315-8). Somerset Pub.
Benaquist, Lawrence M. Tripartite Structure of Christopher Marlowe's Tamburlaine Plays & Edward II. (Salzburg Studies in English Literature; Elizabethan & Renaissance Studies: No. 43). 223p. (Orig.). 1975. pap. text ed. 25.00x (ISBN 0-391-01324-6). Humanities.
Chan, Lois M., ed. Marlowe Criticism: A Bibliography. (Reference Publications). 1978. lib. bdg. 24.00 (ISBN 0-8161-7835-6). G K Hall.
Clark, Eleanor G. Raleigh & Marlowe: A Study in Elizabethan Fustian. LC 65-13956. (Illus.). 1965. Repr. of 1941 ed. 11.50 (ISBN 0-8462-0529-7). Russell.
Cole, Douglas. Suffering & Evil in the Plays of Christopher Marlowe. LC 70-148617. 1971. Repr. of 1962 ed. text ed. 10.00 (ISBN 0-87752-134-4). Gordian.
Dave, Smita. Christopher Marlowe. 118p. 1974. text ed. 3.75x (ISBN 0-391-00367-4). Humanities.
Eccles, Mark. Christopher Marlowe in London. 1967. Repr. lib. bdg. 14.50x (ISBN 0-374-92470-8). Octagon.
Fanta. Christopher G. Marlowe's Agonists: An Approach to the Ambiguity of His Plays. LC 74-143220. (LeBaron Russell Briggs Prize Honors Essays in English Ser: 1970). 1970. pap. 2.50x (ISBN 0-674-55060-9). Harvard U Pr.
Fehrenbach, Robert J., et al, eds. A Concordance to the Plays, Poems, & Translations of Christopher Marlowe. LC 81-67175. 1710p. 1981. 75.00x (ISBN 0-8014-1420-2). Cornell U Pr.
Fieler, Frank B. Tamburlaine, Part One, & Its Audience. LC 62-62580. (U of Fla. Humanities Monographs: No. 8). 1962. pap. 3.50 (ISBN 0-8130-0077-7). U Presses Fla.
Fitzwater, Eva. Doctor Faustus Notes. (Orig.). pap. 2.25 (ISBN 0-8220-0406-2). Cliffs.
Friedenreich, Kenneth. Christopher Marlowe: An Annotated Bibliography of Criticism Since 1950. LC 79-17646. (Scarecrow Author Bibliographies Ser.: No. 43). 1979. 10.00 (ISBN 0-8108-1239-8). Scarecrow.
Godshalk, W. L. The Marlovian World Picture. (Studies in English Literature: No. 93). 224p. 1974. pap. text ed. 40.00x (ISBN 90-2793-252-2). Mouton.
Heller, Otto. Faust & Faustus: A Study of Goethe's Relation to Marlowe. LC 72-187841. 174p. 1972. Repr. of 1931 ed. lib. bdg. 11.00x (ISBN 0-8154-0412-3). Cooper Sq.
Henderson, Philip. And Morning in His Eyes. LC 75-39861. (English Literature Ser., No. 33). 1972. Repr. of 1937 ed. lib. bdg. 42.95 (ISBN 0-8383-1406-6). Haskell.
Hilton, Della. Who Was Kit Marlow? The Story of the Poet & Playwright. LC 76-53911. (Illus.). 1977. 8.50 (ISBN 0-8008-8291-1). Taplinger.
Hosken, James D. Christopher Marlowe & Belphegor. 1896. Repr. 30.00 (ISBN 0-8274-2058-7). R West.
Hotson, J. Leslie. Death of Christopher Marlowe. LC 67-18292. (Illus.). 1967. Repr. of 1925 ed. 7.50 (ISBN 0-8462-0938-1). Russell.
Hotson, Leslie. Shakespeare Versus Shallow. LC 74-95430. (Studies in Shakespeare, No. 24). 1970. Repr. of 1931 ed. lib. bdg. 39.95 (ISBN 0-8383-0981-X). Haskell.
Howe, James R. Marlowe, Tamburlaine, & Magic. LC 75-36978. x, 220p. 1976. 12.95x (ISBN 0-8214-0200-5). Ohio U Pr.
Ingram, John H. Christopher Marlowe & His Associates. LC 70-116374. (Illus.). 1970. Repr. of 1904 ed. lib. bdg. 15.00x (ISBN 0-8154-0326-7). Cooper Sq.
--Marlowe & His Poetry. LC 72-120965. (Poetry & Life Ser.). Repr. of 1914 ed. 7.25 (ISBN 0-404-52522-9). AMS Pr.
--Marlowe & His Poetry. LC 72-187940. 1972. lib. bdg. 7.50 (ISBN 0-8414-5063-3). Folcroft.
--Marlowe & His Poetry. 1978. Repr. of 1914 ed. lib. bdg. 8.50 (ISBN 0-8495-2608-6). Arden Lib.
Kernan, Alvin B, ed. Two Renaissance Mythmakers, Christopher Marlowe & Ben Jonson. LC 77-3518. (Selected Papers from the English Institute Ser., 1975-76). 1977. text ed. 7.50x (ISBN 0-8018-1971-7). Johns Hopkins.
Knoll, Robert E. Christopher Marlowe. LC 68-17237. (English Authors Ser.: No. 74). 1969. lib. bdg. 10.95 (ISBN 0-8057-1376-X). Twayne.
Kocher, Paul H. Christopher Marlowe: A Study of His Thought, Learning & Character. LC 61-13761. 1962. Repr. of 1946 ed. 19.00 (ISBN 0-8462-0218-2). Russell.
Leech, C., ed. Marlowe: A Collection of Critical Essays. 1964. 10.95 (ISBN 0-13-558353-5, Spec). P-H.
Levin, Harry. Overreacher: A Study of Christopher Marlowe. 8.50 (ISBN 0-8446-2458-6). Peter Smith.
Lewis, J. G. Christopher Marlowe: Outlines of His Life & Works. LC 74-22125. 1974. Repr. of 1891 ed. lib. bdg. 5.50 (ISBN 0-8414-5684-4). Folcroft.
Lom, Herbert. Enter a Spy: The Double Life of Christopher Marlowe. (Illus.). 112p. 1978. 9.00x (ISBN 0-8476-6258-6). Rowman.
MacLure, Millar, ed. Marlowe: The Critical Heritage, Fifteen Eighty-Eight to Eighteen Ninety-Six. 1979. 24.00x (ISBN 0-7100-0245-9). Routledge & Kegan.
Marlowe, Christopher. Doctor Faustus: Text & Major Criticism. Ribner, Irving, ed. LC 65-26778. 1966. pap. 5.95 (ISBN 0-672-63058-3). Odyssey Pr.
--The Life of Marlowe. Tucker Brooke, C. F., ed. Bd. with The Tragedy of Dido Queen of Carthage. (Works & Life of Christopher Marlowe Ser.: Vol. 1). 238p. 1966. Repr. of 1930 ed. 10.00 (ISBN 0-87752-194-8). Gordian.
--Plays of Christopher Marlowe. Gill, Roma, ed. (Oxford Paperbacks Ser). 1971. pap. 8.95x (ISBN 0-19-281062-6). Oxford U Pr.
--Works & Life of Christopher Marlowe, 6 Vols. Case, R. H., ed. 1966. Repr. of 1933 ed. Set. 60.00 (ISBN 0-87752-067-4). Gordian.
Masinton, Charles G. Christopher Marlowe's Tragic Vision: A Study in Damnation. LC 77-181683. x, 168p. 1972. 10.95x (ISBN 0-8214-0101-7). Ohio U Pr.
Meehan, Virginia M. Christopher Marlowe Poet & Playwright Studies in Poetical Method. LC 74-79321. (De Proprietatibus Litterarum, Ser. Practica: No. 81). 100p. 1974. pap. text ed. 20.75x (ISBN 90-2793-382-0). Mouton.
Mullany, Peter. Monarch Notes on Marlowe's Dr. Faustus & Other Writings. (Orig.). pap. 1.95 (ISBN 0-671-00717-3). Monarch Pr.
O'Neill, Judith, ed. Critics on Marlowe. LC 69-15927. (Readings in Literary Criticism Ser: No. 4). 1970. 5.95x (ISBN 0-87024-121-4). U of Miami Pr.
Pearce, T. M. Christopher Marlowe, Figure of the Renaissance. 1934. lib. bdg. 10.00 (ISBN 0-8414-9210-7). Folcroft.
Pinciss, Gerald M. Christopher Marlowe. LC 72-79934. (World Dramatists Ser). (Illus.). 144p. 1975. 10.95 (ISBN 0-8044-2694-5). Ungar.
Poirier, Michel. Christopher Marlowe. 1968. Repr. of 1951 ed. 15.00 (ISBN 0-208-00715-6, Archon). Shoe String.
Robertson, John M. Marlowe: A Conspectus. 1931. Repr. lib. bdg. 30.00 (ISBN 0-8414-7465-6). Folcroft.
Roehrman, Hendrik. The Way of Life. LC 70-144677. Orig. Title: Marlow & Shakespeare. Repr. of 1952 ed. 5.00 (ISBN 0-404-05386-6). AMS Pr.
Rohrman, Hendrick. Marlowe & Shakespeare. LC 75-12770. 1952. lib. bdg. 4.95 (ISBN 0-8414-7372-2). Folcroft.
Sims, James H. Dramatic Uses of Biblical Allusions in Marlowe & Shakespeare. LC 66-64917. (U of Fla. Humanities Monographs: No. 24). 1966. pap. 3.50 (ISBN 0-8130-0206-0). U Presses Fla.
Smith, Marion B. Marlowe's Imagery & the Marlowe Canon. 1940. 25.00 (ISBN 0-8414-7620-9). Folcroft.
--Marlowe's Imagery & the Marlowe Canon. 1978. Repr. of 1939 ed. lib. bdg. 30.00 (ISBN 0-8495-4850-0). Arden Lib.
Smith, Mary E. Love Kindling Fire: A Study Christopher Marlowe's the Tragedy of Dido Queen of Carthage. (Salzburg Studies in English Literature: Elizabethan & Renaissance: No.63). 1977. pap. text ed. 25.00x (ISBN 0-391-01529-X). Humanities.
Steane, J. B. Marlowe: A Critical Study. 1964. 54.00 (ISBN 0-521-06545-3); pap. 13.95x (ISBN 0-521-09624-3). Cambridge U Pr.
Summers, Claude J. Christopher Marlowe & the Politics of Power. (Salzburg Studies in English Literature, Elizabethan & Renaissance Studies: No. 22). 208p. 1974. pap. text ed. 25.00x (ISBN 0-391-01542-7). Humanities.
Verity, A. W. Influence of Christopher Marlowe on Shakespeare's Earlier Style. 1886. lib. bdg. 8.50 (ISBN 0-8414-9194-1). Folcroft.
Weil, Judith. Christopher Marlowe. LC 76-26586. 1977. 34.00 (ISBN 0-521-21554-4). Cambridge U Pr.
Williams, David R. Shakespeare, Thy Name Is Marlow. LC 66-16173. 1966. 3.00 (ISBN 0-8022-1884-9). Philos Lib.
Wraight, A. D. & Stern, Virginia. In Search of Christopher Marlowe: A Pictorial Biography. LC 65-20820. (Illus.). 1965. 15.00 (ISBN 0-8149-0213-8). Vanguard.
Zucker, David H. Stage & Image in the Plays of Christopher Marlowe. (Salzburg Studies in English Literature, Elizabethan & Renaissance Studies: No. 7). 188p. 1972. pap. text ed. 25.00x (ISBN 0-391-01578-8). Humanities.

MARMOTS

Harris, Mark. Saul Bellow, Drumlin Woodchuck. LC 80-14390. 192p. 1980. 10.95 (ISBN 0-8203-0529-4). U of Ga Pr.
Liers, Emil E. A Groundhog's Story. LC 76-25629. (Crown Ser.). (primer). 1976. pap. 4.50 (ISBN 0-8127-0130-5). Review & Herald.
McNulty, Faith. Woodchuck. LC 74-3585. (A Science I Can Read Bk.). (Illus.). 64p. (gr. k-3). 1974. 6.95 (ISBN 0-06-024166-7, HarpJ); PLB 7.89 (ISBN 0-06-024167-5). Har-Row.
Stephan, H., et al. The Brain of the Common Marmoset (Callithrix Jacchus) (Illus.). 1980. 92.40 (ISBN 0-387-09782-1). Springer-Verlag.

MARNE, BATTLE OF THE, 1914

Asprey, Robert B. The First Battle of the Marne. LC 78-10667. 1979. Repr. of 1962 ed. lib. bdg. 17.00x (ISBN 0-313-21229-5, ASFB). Greenwood.

MAROONS

see also Jamaica–History

Dallas, R. C. History of the Maroons, 2 vols. 1968. Repr. of 1803 ed. 75.00x set (ISBN 0-7146-1934-5, F Cass Co). Biblio Dist.
Fouchard, Jean. The Haitian Maroons: Liberty or Death. Watts, A. Faulkner, tr. from Fr. 500p. 1981. write for info. (ISBN 0-914110-11-X). Blyden Pr.
Higginson, Thomas W. Black Rebellion. LC 69-18539. (American Negro: His History & Literature, Ser. No. 2). Orig. Title: Travelers & Outlaws. 1969. Repr. of 1889 ed. 10.00 (ISBN 0-405-01870-3). Arno.
Price, Richard. The Guiana Maroons: A Historical & Bibliographical Introduction. LC 76-8498. (Studies in Atlantic History & Culture: No. 1). (Illus.). 208p. 1976. 18.50x (ISBN 0-8018-1840-0). Johns Hopkins.
Price, Richard, ed. Maroon Societies: Rebel Slave Communities in the Americas. LC 73-83603. 1979. pap. 5.95x (ISBN 0-8018-2247-5). Johns Hopkins.
--Maroon Societies: Rebel Slave Communities in the Americas. 6.75 (ISBN 0-8446-5075-7). Peter Smith.
Price, Sally & Price, Richard. Afro-American Arts of the Suriname Rain Forest. LC 80-54013. (Illus.). 240p. 1981. 37.50 (ISBN 0-520-04345-6); pap. 14.95 (ISBN 0-520-04412-6, CAL 516). U of Cal Pr.
Roth, Cecil. A History of the Marranos. facsimile ed. LC 74-29516. (Modern Jewish Experience Ser.). (Illus.). 1975. Repr. of 1932 ed. 26.00x (ISBN 0-405-06742-9). Arno.

MAROT, CLEMENT, 1497-1544

Griffin, Robert. Clement Marot & the Inflections of Poetic Voice. LC 73-84394. 1976. 25.00x (ISBN 0-520-02586-5). U of Cal Pr.
Hanisch, Gertrude S. Love Elegies of the Renaissance: Marot, Louise Labe & Ronsard. (Stanford French & Italian Studies: No. 15). 1979. pap. 20.00 (ISBN 0-915838-24-9). Anma Libri.

Harvitt, Helene. Eustorg De Beaulieu: A Disciple of Marot. LC 19-15144. (Columbia University. Studies in Romance Philology & Literature: No. 25). Repr. of 1918 ed. 17.50 (ISBN 0-404-50625-9). AMS Pr.

MAROTSE

see Lozi (African Tribe)

MARPRELATE CONTROVERSY

Arber, Edward. An Introductory Sketch to the Martin Marprelate Controversy, 1558-90. 2nd ed. 1964. Repr. of 1895 ed. 19.50 (ISBN 0-8337-0077-4). B Franklin.

McGinn, Donald J. John Penry & the Marprelate Controversy. 1966. 17.50 (ISBN 0-8135-0513-5). Rutgers U Pr.

Wilson, John D. Martin Marprelate & Shakespeare's Fluellen. LC 72-194068. 1912. lib. bdg. 10.00 (ISBN 0-8414-1065-8). Folcroft.

MARQUAND, JOHN PHILLIPS, 1893-1960

Bell, Millicent. Marquand: An American Life. LC 79-12818. 1979. 17.95 (ISBN 0-316-08828-5, Pub. by Atlantic-Little Brown). Little.

Gross, John. John P. Marquand. (Twayne's United States Authors Ser). 1963. pap. 3.45 (ISBN 0-8084-0188-2, T33, Twayne). Coll & U Pr.

Gross, John J. John P. Marquand. (U. S. Authors Ser.: No. 33). 1962. lib. bdg. 10.95 (ISBN 0-8057-0476-0). Twayne.

MARQUE, LETTERS OF

see Privateering

MARQUESADO DEL VALLE DE OAZACA

Barrett, Ward J. Sugar Hacienda of the Marqueses Del Valle. LC 74-110146. (Illus.). 1970. 12.50x (ISBN 0-8166-0565-3). U of Minn Pr.

MARQUESAS ISLANDS

Adamson, A. M. Marquesan Insects: Environment. Repr. of 1936 ed. pap. 9.00 (ISBN 0-527-02245-4). Kraus Repr.

Christian, Frederick W. Eastern Pacific Lands: Tahiti & the Marquesas Islands. LC 75-35185. (Illus.). Repr. of 1910 ed. 28.00 (ISBN 0-404-14212-5). AMS Pr.

Chubb, L. J. Geology of the Marquesas Islands. Repr. of 1930 ed. pap. 8.00 (ISBN 0-527-02174-1). Kraus Repr.

Dening, Greg. Islands & Beaches: Discourse on a Silent Land, Marquesas, 1774-1880. (Illus.). 350p. 1980. text ed. 27.50 (ISBN 0-8248-0721-9). U Pr of Hawaii.

Handy, E. S. Native Culture in the Marquesas. Repr. of 1923 ed. pap. 28.00 (ISBN 0-527-02112-1). Kraus Repr.

Handy, E. S. & Winne, J. L. Music in the Marquesas Islands. Repr. of 1925 ed. pap. 6.00 (ISBN 0-527-02120-2). Kraus Repr.

Linton, R. Archaeology of the Marquesas Islands. Repr. of 1925 ed. pap. 17.00 (ISBN 0-527-02126-1). Kraus Repr.

Pietrusewsky, Michael. Prehistoric Human Skeletal Remains from Papua New Guinea & the Marquesas. LC 76-521. (Asian & Pacific Archeology Ser.: No. 7). 1976. pap. 6.00x (ISBN 0-8248-0525-9). U Pr of Hawaii.

MARQUESAS ISLANDS–FICTION

Melville, Herman. Typee. (Classics Ser). (gr. 10 up). pap. 1.50 (ISBN 0-8049-0053-1, CL-53). Airmont.

--Typee. pap. 1.95 (ISBN 0-451-51258-8, CJ1258, Sig Classics). NAL.

--Typee. Center for Editions of American Authors, ed. LC 67-11990. (The Writings of Herman Melville Ser.). (Illus.). 1968. 23.95x (ISBN 0-8101-0161-0); pap. 6.95x (ISBN 0-8101-0159-9). Northwestern U Pr.

MARQUETRY

Hobbs, Harry J., ed. Modern Marquetry Handbook. Fitchett, Allan E. 1981. 11.95 (ISBN 0-684-16762-X, ScribT). Scribner.

Zlinszky-Sternegg, Maria. Renaissance Inlay in Old Hungary. LC 66-81797. (Illus.). 1966. 3.75x (ISBN 0-8002-1919-8). Intl Pubns Serv.

MARQUETTE, JACQUES, 1637-1675

Donnelly, Joseph P. Jacques Marquette, S. J., Sixteen Thirty-Seven to Sixteen Seventy-Five. LC 68-9498. 1968. 8.00 (ISBN 0-8294-0024-9). Loyola.

Hamilton, Raphael. Marquette's Explorations: The Narratives Reexamined. (Illus.). 292p. 1970. 19.50 (ISBN 0-299-05570-1). U of Wis Pr.

Kjelgaard, Jim A. Explorations of Pere Marquette. (Landmark Ser.: No. 17). (Illus.). (gr. 4-6). 1951. PLB 5.99 (ISBN 0-394-90317-X). Random.

Repplier, Agnes & Cimino, Harry. Pere Marquette: Priest, Pioneer & Adventurer. 1978. Repr. of 1929 ed. lib. bdg. 20.00 (ISBN 0-8482-5856-8). Norwood Edns.

Steck, Frances B. The Joliet-Marquette Expedition, 1673. rev. ed. LC 73-5360. (Catholic University of America. Studies in American Church History: No. 6). (Illus.). Repr. of 1928 ed. 27.00 (ISBN 0-404-57756-3). AMS Pr.

Stein, R. Conrad. The Story of Marquette & Jolliet. (Cornerstones of Freedom Ser.). (Illus.). (gr. 3-6). 1981. PLB 7.95 (ISBN 0-516-04630-6); pap. 2.50 (ISBN 0-516-44630-4). Childrens.

MARRANOS

see Maroons

MARRIAGE

see also Betrothal; Celibacy; Child Marriage; Courtship; Divorce; Domestic Relations; Family; Family Life Education; Free Love; Home; Marriage Counseling; Polyandry; Remarriage; Sex; Sex in Marriage; Sexual Ethics; Teen-Age Marriage; Weddings; Wives

Achtemeier, Elizabeth. The Committed Marriage. LC 76-7611. (Biblical Perspectives on Current Issues). 1976. pap. 5.95 (ISBN 0-664-24754-7). Westminster.

Adams, Jay E. Marriage, Divorce & Remarriage. 120p. 1981. pap. 3.50 (ISBN 0-8010-0168-4). Baker Bk.

--Marriage, Divorce & Remarriage. 1980. pap. 3.50 (ISBN 0-87552-068-5). Presby & Reformed.

Aginsky, Bernard W. Kinship Systems & the Forms of Marriage. LC 36-6759. 1935. pap. 7.00 (ISBN 0-527-00544-4). Kraus Repr.

Ainsworth, Charles H., ed. Selected Readings for Marriage & the Family. LC 72-11042. 1973. 34.50x (ISBN 0-8422-5123-5). Irvington.

Alcott, William A. The Physiology of Marriage. LC 79-180551. (Medicine & Society in America Ser). 266p. 1972. Repr. of 1866 ed. 13.00 (ISBN 0-405-03931-X). Arno.

--The Young Husband or, Duties of Man in the Marriage Relation. LC 70-169368. (Family in America Ser). (Illus.). 392p. 1972. Repr. of 1841 ed. 19.00 (ISBN 0-405-03844-5). Arno.

Aldous, Joan & Dahl, Nancy, eds. International Bibliography of Research in Marriage & the Family, Vol. 2: 1965-1972. LC 67-63014. 1519p. 1974. 35.00x (ISBN 0-8166-0726-5). U of Minn Pr.

Amstutz, H. Clair. Marriage in Today's World. LC 78-955. 1978. pap. 4.95 (ISBN 0-8361-1849-9). Herald Pr.

--So You're Going to Be Married. rev. ed. 1971. pap. 0.95 (ISBN 0-8361-1427-2). Herald Pr.

Andrews, Stephen P., ed. Love, Marriage, & Divorce, & the Sovereignty of the Individual. LC 78-67573. (Free Love in America). Repr. of 1853 ed. 14.50 (ISBN 0-404-60962-7). AMS Pr.

Andrews, Stephen P., Sr., et al. Love, Marriage, & Divorce. Shively, Charles, ed. 1975. 12.50x (ISBN 0-87730-010-0). M&S Pr.

Anobile, Richard & Anobile, Ulla. Beyond Open Marriage. LC 78-58769. (Illus.). 1979. 12.50 (ISBN 0-89479-029-3). A & W Pubs.

--Freeform Marriage. 288p. 1981. pap. 2.95 (ISBN 0-523-41627-X). Pinnacle Bks.

Anobile, Richard J. & Anobile, Ulla. Beyond Open Marriage. Date not set. pap. price not set. Pinnacle Bks.

Arnold, Heini. In the Image of God: Marriage & Chastity in Christian Life. LC 76-53542. 1977. pap. 3.95 (ISBN 0-87486-169-1). Plough.

Augsburger, David. Caring Enough to Confort. rev. ed. 160p. 1980. pap. 3.95 (ISBN 0-8361-1928-2). Herald Pr.

--Cherishable: Love & Marriage. LC 71-171536. 4.95 (ISBN 0-8361-1707-7). Herald Pr.

--Cherishable: Love & Marriage. LC 71-171536. 4.95 (ISBN 0-8361-1707-7). Herald Pr.

--Cherishable: Love & Marriage. 1975. pap. 1.25 (ISBN 0-89129-065-6, PV065). Jove Pubns.

Bach, George R. & Wyden, Peter. Intimate Enemy: How to Fight Fair in Love & Marriage. LC 69-14232. 1969. 12.95 (ISBN 0-688-01884-X). Morrow.

Bailey, Derrick S. The Mystery of Love & Marriage: A Study in the Theology of Sexual Relation. LC 77-3313. 1977. Repr. of 1952 ed. lib. bdg. 15.00 (ISBN 0-8371-9577-2, BAML). Greenwood.

Ballonoff, Paul A. Mathematical Foundations of Social Anthropology. (Publications of the Maison Des Sciences De L'homme). (Illus.). 131p. 1976. pap. text ed. 16.25x (ISBN 90-2797-934-0). Mouton.

Balzac, Honore de. Physiologie du Mariage. Regard, Maurice, ed. 320p. 1968. 3.95 (ISBN 0-686-53923-0). French & Eur.

Beardsley, Lou & Spry, Toni. The Fulfilled Woman. LC 74-29206. 1977. 2.50 (ISBN 0-89081-072-9, 0729). Harvest Hse.

Bell, Robert R. Marriage & Family Interaction. 5th ed. 1979. text ed. 19.50x (ISBN 0-256-02110-4); pap. study guide 6.50x (ISBN 0-256-02243-7). Dorsey.

Bellamy, Charles. Experiment in Marriage. LC 77-16040. 320p. 1977. Repr. of 1889 ed. 32.00 (ISBN 0-8201-1304-2). Schol Facsimiles.

Benton, Josephine M. The Pace of a Hen. 103p. 1961. 2.95 (ISBN 0-8298-0100-6). Pilgrim NY.

Bertrams, Wilhelmus, et al. De Matrimonio Coniectanea. (Lat.). 1970. pap. 17.50 (ISBN 0-8294-0318-3, Pub. by Gregorian U Pr). Loyola.

Berven, Ken. I Love Being Married to a Grandma. LC 78-530. 1978. 6.95 (ISBN 0-8407-5132-X). Nelson.

Betzold, Michael J. Sexual Scarcity: The Marital Mistake & the Communal Alternative. 1978. pap. 2.50 (ISBN 0-686-10620-2). Betzold.

Biddle, Perry H., Jr. Abingdon Marriage Manual. LC 73-21799. 256p. 1974. 6.95 (ISBN 0-687-00484-5). Abingdon.

Bier, William C., ed. Marriage: A Psychological & Moral Approach. LC 64-25381. (Pastoral Psychology Ser: No. 4). 1965. 15.00 (ISBN 0-8232-0605-X). Fordham.

Billnitzer, Harold. Chances for a Happy Marriage. 1978. pap. 0.75 (ISBN 0-933350-00-7). Morse Pr.

Bird, Joseph W. & Bird, Lois F. Marriage Is for Grownups. LC 79-78725. 1971. pap. 2.95 (ISBN 0-385-04256-6, Im). Doubleday.

Birdsong, Robert E. Soul Mates: The Facts & the Fallacies. (Aquarian Academy Supplementary Lecture Ser.: No. 9). 22p. (Orig.). 1980. pap. 1.25 (ISBN 0-917108-32-9). Sirius Bks.

Birner, Herbert A. Marriage Should Be Honored by All. 5.95 (ISBN 0-686-76769-1). Northwest Pub.

Bishop, Sharon & Weinzweig, Marjorie. Philosophy & Women. 1979. pap. text ed. 13.95x (ISBN 0-534-00609-4). Wadsworth Pub.

Blankenship, Judy. Scenes from Life: Views of Family, Marriage & Intimacy. 1976. pap. 12.95 (ISBN 0-316-09945-7). Little.

Bloem, Diane B. & Bloem, Robert C. A Women's Workshop on Bible Marriages. (Woman's Workshop Series of Study Books). 128p. (Orig.). 1980. pap. 1.95 (ISBN 0-310-21391-6); pap. 2.50 leader's manual (ISBN 0-310-21401-7). Zondervan.

Blood, Bob & Blood, Margaret. Marriage. 3rd ed. LC 77-3847. 1978. text ed. 15.95 (ISBN 0-02-904180-5). Free Pr.

Blood, Robert O. & Wolfe, Donald M. Husbands & Wives: The Dynamics of Married Living. LC 78-5734. 293p. 1978. Repr. of 1960 ed. lib. bdg. 25.75x (ISBN 0-313-20453-5, BLHW). Greenwood.

Blood, Robert O., Jr. & Wolfe, D. M. Husbands & Wives: The Dynamics of Married Living. LC 59-6824. 1965. pap. text ed. 5.95 (ISBN 0-02-904070-1). Free Pr.

Blum, Leon. Marriage. Wells, Warre B., tr. from Fr. LC 72-9703. (Illus.). Repr. of 1937 ed. 20.00 (ISBN 0-404-57416-5). AMS Pr.

Boll, Eleanor. Man That You Marry. (gr. 9 up). 1963. 6.25 (ISBN 0-8255-1700-1). Macrae.

Boone, Shirley & Boone, Pat. The Honeymoon Is Over. 192p. 1980. pap. 4.95 (ISBN 0-8407-5721-2). Nelson.

Bowman, Henry A. Marriage for Moderns. 7th ed. (Illus.). 576p. 1974. text ed. 13.94 (ISBN 0-07-006800-3, C); 5.95 (ISBN 0-07-006801-1). McGraw.

--Marriage for Moderns. 1948. 20.00 (ISBN 0-8482-7397-4). Norwood Edns.

Bowman, Henry A. & Spanier, Graham B. Modern Marriage. 8th ed. 1977. text ed. 16.50 (ISBN 0-07-006802-X, C); instructor's manual 5.95 (ISBN 0-07-006803-8). McGraw.

Brandt, Henry & Landrum, Phil. I Want My Marriage to Be Better. 1976. pap. 3.95 (ISBN 0-310-21621-4). Zondervan.

Brant, Henry. Quero Melhorar Meu Casamento. Lamdrum, Phil, tr. (Portuguese Bks.). 1979. 1.25 (ISBN 0-8297-0790-5). Life Pubs Intl.

Brenneman, Helen G. Marriage: Agony & Ecstasy. LC 74-25490. 88p. (Orig.). 1975. pap. 1.50 (ISBN 0-8361-1762-X). Herald Pr.

Brenton, Myron. Lasting Relationships: How to Recognize the Man or Woman Who's Right for You. 204p. 1981. 10.95 (ISBN 0-89479-078-1). A & W Pubs.

Briffault, Robert. The Mothers. abr. ed. Taylor, Gordon R., ed. & intro. by. LC 76-28642. (Illus.). 1977. pap. text ed. 5.95x (ISBN 0-689-70541-7, 232). Atheneum.

--The Mothers: A Study of the Origins of Sentiments & Institutions, 3 vols. (Anthropology Ser). Repr. of 1927 ed. Set. 115.50 (ISBN 0-384-05800-0). Johnson Repr.

Briffault, Robert & Malinowski, Bronislaw. Marriage-Past & Present. (Extending Horizons Ser). 1956. 3.95 (ISBN 0-87558-027-0); pap. 2.45 (ISBN 0-87558-028-9). Porter Sargent.

Brody, Jean & Osborne, Gail B. The Twenty Year Phenomenon. 1980. 11.95 (ISBN 0-671-25042-6). S&S.

Bryson, Jeff B. & Bryson, Rebecca B., eds. Dual-Career Couples. LC 77-89983. 120p. 1978. 9.95x (ISBN 0-87705-371-5). Human Sci Pr.

Bullinger, Heinrich. The Christian State of Matrimonye. Coverdale, Myles, tr. LC 74-80167. (English Experience Ser.: No. 646). 168p. 1974. Repr. of 1541 ed. 11.50 (ISBN 90-221-0646-2). Walter J Johnson.

Burgess, Jack, tr. from Eng. Los Recien Casados. rev. ed. 128p. (Span.). 1980. pap. 1.50 (ISBN 0-87067-921-X, Melrose Sq). Holloway.

Burghardt, W. J., et al, eds. Tertullian, Treatise on Marriage & Remarriage: To His Wife, an Exhortation to Chastity Monogamy. LC 78-62462. (Ancient Christian Writers Ser.: No. 13). 103p. 1951. 9.95 (ISBN 0-8091-0149-1). Paulist Pr.

Burtchaell, James T., et al. Marriage Among Christians: A Curious Tradition. LC 77-81396. (Illus.). 192p. 1977. pap. 3.50 (ISBN 0-87793-139-9). Ave Maria.

Butler, Edgar W. Traditional Marriage & Emerging Alternatives. LC 78-26026. 1979. text ed. 18.95 scp (ISBN 0-06-041114-7, HarpC). Har-Row.

Butterfield, Oliver M. Sex Life in Marriage. (Illus.). 7.95 (ISBN 0-87523-035-0). Emerson.

--Sexual Harmony in Marriage. (Illus.). pap. 1.95 (ISBN 0-87523-092-X). Emerson.

Calverton, V. F. Bankruptcy of Marriage. LC 76-169403. (Family in America Ser). 344p. 1972. Repr. of 1928 ed. 20.00 (ISBN 0-405-03852-6). Arno.

Cana Conference of Chicago. Marriage: Discoveries & Encounters. 1978. pap. 1.25 (ISBN 0-915388-10-3). Buckley Pubns.

--Marriage: Discoveries and Encounters. 1973. pap. 1.25 (ISBN 0-915388-10-3, Pub. by Delaney). Buckley Pubns.

Capon, Robert F. Bed & Board: Plain Talk About Marriage. pap. 1.95 (ISBN 0-671-07051-7, Fireside). S&S.

Carr, Gwen B., ed. Marriage & Family in a Decade of Change: A Humanistic Reader. 1972. pap. text ed. 6.50 (ISBN 0-201-00899-8). A-W.

--Marriage & Family in a Decade of Change: A Humanistic Reader. 1972. pap. text ed. 6.50 (ISBN 0-201-00899-8). A-W.

Carson, Mary. Como Hacer Que el Matrimonio Dure Toda una Vida. Velasco, Amparo & Velasco, Asterio, trs. from Sp. 64p. 1980. pap. 1.50 (ISBN 0-89570-193-6). Claretian Pubns.

Carter, Hugh & Glick, Paul C. Marriage & Divorce: A Social & Economic Study. rev. ed. LC 79-105369. (Vital & Health Statistics Monographs, American Public Health Association). 1970. 20.00x (ISBN 0-674-55075-7). Harvard U Pr.

Carter, Stephen J. & McKinney, Charles. Keeping a Good Thing Going. 1979. pap. 2.95 (ISBN 0-570-03787-5, 12-2745). Concordia.

Cartland, Barbara. Romantic Royal Marriages. (Illus.). 128p. 1981. pap. 9.95 (ISBN 0-8253-0076-2). Beaufort Bks NY.

Casler, Lawrence. Is Marriage Necessary? LC 73-18236. 249p. 1974. text ed. 19.95 (ISBN 0-87705-132-1). Human Sci Pr.

Chafin, Kenneth. Is There a Family in the House? A Realistic & Hopeful Look at Marriage & the Family. 1978. 6.95 (ISBN 0-8499-0109-X); pap. 3.95 (ISBN 0-8499-2839-7). Word Bks.

Champlin, Joseph M. Alone No Longer. LC 77-77817. 128p. 1977. pap. 2.45 (ISBN 0-87793-134-8). Ave Maria.

--Together for Life: Regular Edition. rev. ed. (Illus.). 96p. 1970. pap. 1.25 (ISBN 0-87793-018-X). Ave Maria.

--Together for Life: Special Edition for Marriage Outside Mass. rev. ed. (Illus.). 96p. 1972. pap. 1.25 (ISBN 0-87793-118-6). Ave Maria.

Cherlin, Andrew J. Marriage, Divorce, Remarriage. (Social Trends in the United States Ser.). (Illus.). 160p. 1981. text ed. 14.00x (ISBN 0-674-55080-3). Harvard U Pr.

Chimbos, Peter D. Marital Violence: A Study of Interspouse Homicide. LC 77-94287. 1978. pap. 12.00 perfect bdg. (ISBN 0-88247-507-X). R & E Res Assoc.

Christensen, James L. The Minister's Marriage Handbook. rev. ed. 1974. Repr. 7.95 (ISBN 0-8007-0205-0). Revell.

Christenson, Larry & Christenson, Nordis. The Christian Couple. LC 77-24085. 1977. pap. 1.25 (ISBN 0-87123-051-8); 0.95 (ISBN 0-87123-046-1, 210046). Bethany Hse.

Clayton, Richard R. Family Marriage & Social Change. 2nd ed. 1979. text ed. 17.95x (ISBN 0-669-01957-7); instr's manual 1.95 (ISBN 0-669-01956-9). Heath.

Clear, Val & Greenberg, Martin H., eds. Marriage & the Family Through Science Fiction. LC 75-38023. 400p. 1976. text ed. 15.95 (ISBN 0-312-51555-3); pap. text ed. 7.95 (ISBN 0-312-51590-1). St Martin.

Cline, Victor, et al. Between Ring & Temple: A Book for Engaged L.D.S. Couples. 1981. 6.95 (ISBN 0-913420-87-5). Olympus Pub Co.

Clinebell, Charlotte H. Meet Me in the Middle: On Becoming Human Together. LC 72-11353. 160p. 1973. pap. 2.95 (ISBN 0-06-061502-8, RD 193, HarpR). Har-Row.

Clinebell, Charlotte H. & Clinebell, Howard J., Jr. Intimate Marriage. LC 72-109062. 1970. 9.95 (ISBN 0-06-061499-4, HarpR). Har-Row.

Coleman, John D. A Study for Do Yourself a Favor: Love Your Wife. 1976. wkbk. 1.25 (ISBN 0-88270-162-2). Logos.

Collins, Sam, Jr. A Survival Kit for a Happier Marriage. LC 77-76534. Orig. Title: A Marriage Worth Having. 1977. pap. 1.75 (ISBN 0-89516-002-1). Condor Pub Co.
Comaroff, J., ed. The Meaning of Marriage Payments. (Studies in Anthropolgy: No. 7). 1980. 34.00 (ISBN 0-12-183450-6). Acad Pr.
Conn, Charles P. The Meaning of Marriage. LC 76-26408. (Illus.). (gr. 10-12). pap. 1.35 (ISBN 0-87148-569-9). Pathway Pr.
Cooper, Darien & Carroll, Anne K. Darien Cooper's Happy Husband Book. 1980. text ed. 8.95 (ISBN 0-88207-785-6). Victor Bks.
Cooper, Jilly. How to Stay Married. LC 72-121666. 1970. 3.95 (ISBN 0-8008-3981-1). Taplinger.
Corbin, Marie, ed. The Couple. 1978. pap. 2.95 (ISBN 0-14-021969-2, Pelican). Penguin.
Corin, James. Mating, Marriage & the Status of Women. LC 72-9633. Repr. of 1910 ed. 17.25 (ISBN 0-404-57432-7). AMS Pr.
Cornell, Dale D. & Erickson, Frances G. Marriage: The Phoenix Contract. 1982. price not set (ISBN 0-87527-264-9). Green.
Corwin, Sheila. Marriage & the Family & Child-Rearing Practices. Zak, Therese A., ed. (Lifeworks Ser.). (Illus.). 160p. 1981. text ed. 4.56 (ISBN 0-07-013198-8). McGraw.
Cox, Frank D. Human Intimacy: Marriage, the Family & Its Meaning. 2nd ed. (Illus.). 560p. 1981. 19.50 (ISBN 0-8299-0367-4). West Pub.
--Human Intimacy: Marriage, the Family & Its Meaning. (Illus.). 1978. text ed. 16.95 (ISBN 0-8299-0152-3); instrs.' manual avail. (ISBN 0-8299-0473-5). West Pub.
Crawley, Alfred E. Studies of Savages & Sex. Besterman, Theodore, ed. (Landmarks in Anthropology Ser). 1969. Repr. of 1929 ed. 14.00 (ISBN 0-384-10140-2). Johnson Repr.
Crawley, Ernest. Studies of Savages & Sex. facs. ed. Besterman, Theodore, ed. LC 77-102231. (Select Bibliographies Reprint Ser). 1929. 24.00 (ISBN 0-8369-5116-6). Arno.
Critcher, Harold & Critcher, June, eds. Why We Are Happily Married. 1979. pap. 3.95 (ISBN 0-89265-054-0). Randall Hse.
Croly, David G. The Truth About Love. 2nd ed. LC 78-22167. (Free Love in America). Repr. of 1872 ed. 24.50 (ISBN 0-404-60971-6). AMS Pr.
Crosby, John. Illusion & Disillusion: The Serf in Love & Marriage. 2nd ed. 1976. pap. text ed. 10.95x (ISBN 0-534-00450-4). Wadsworth Pub.
Curtis, Donald. Love & Marriage. 2nd ed. 20p. (Orig.). 1975. pap. 1.00 (ISBN 0-87707-049-0). CSA Pr.
Dahl, Gerald L. Why Christian Marriages Are Breaking up. 1981. pap. 3.95 (ISBN 0-686-73557-9). Nelson.
Daniels, Elam J. Como Ser Feliz En el Matrimonio. Orig. Title: How to Be Happily Married. 96p. 1979. pap. 1.80 (ISBN 0-311-46066-6). Casa Bautista.
Darrow, Frank M. Wifestyles & Lifestyles. new ed. 34p. 1974. 2.50 (ISBN 0-912630-02-7). Darrow.
Daughters of St. Paul Editorial Staff. Looking Ahead to Marriage. (Divine Master Ser.). (Illus.). 1969. 5.25 (ISBN 0-8198-0259-X); pap. 4.25 (ISBN 0-8198-0260-3); discussion & projects manual 0.50 (ISBN 0-8198-0261-1). Dghtrs St Paul.
Davitz, Joel & Davitz, Lois. Love & Understanding. (Emmaus Book). 1978. pap. 1.95 (ISBN 0-8091-2072-0). Paulist Pr.
Deaton, John. Love & Sex in Marriage: Doctor's Guide to the Sensual Union. 1978. 12.95 (ISBN 0-13-540856-3, Parker). P-H.
De Balzac, Honore. Conjugal Life. 1958. 3.75 (ISBN 0-685-06549-9). Assoc Bk.
--Physiology of Marriage. (Black & Gold Lib). 1943. 6.95 (ISBN 0-87140-983-6, Co-Pub with Tudor). Liveright.
De Burger, James E., ed. Marriage Today: Problems, Issues & Alternatives. 750p. 1981. pap. 9.95 (ISBN 0-87073-169-6). Schenkman.
Dechant, Emerald. How to Be Happily Married. LC 74-38983. 120p. 1972. pap. 1.65 (ISBN 0-8189-0236-1). Alba.
Defoe, Daniel. Conjugal Lewdness, or Matrimonial Whoredom. LC 67-10178. 1967. Repr. of 1727 ed. 43.00x (ISBN 0-8201-1013-2). Schol Facsimiles.
Del Buono, John & Del Buono, Barbara. When Two Become One: The Miracle in Marriage. 1976. 10.00 (ISBN 0-9605698-0-4); soft cover 6.40 (ISBN 0-9605698-1-2). Ellingsworth Pr.
Demarest, Don, et al. Marriage Encounter. LC 77-88195. 1978. 8.95 (ISBN 0-89310-051-X); pap. 3.95 (ISBN 0-89310-052-8). Carillon Bks.
Demarest, Gary. Christian Alternatives Within Marriage. LC 77-83322. 1977. 5.95 (ISBN 0-8499-0021-2). Word Bks.
De Santo, Charles P. Love & Sex Are Not Enough. LC 76-45731. 1977. pap. 3.95 (ISBN 0-8361-1809-X); student activity bk. 1.25 (ISBN 0-8361-1865-0). Herald Pr.
DeYonker, John F. & Tobin, Thomas E. Your Marriage. rev. ed. LC 68-57211. 1976. pap. 1.95 (ISBN 0-89243-059-1, 38850). Liguori Pubns.
Ditzion, Sidney. Marriage, Morals & Sex in America: A History of Ideas. LC 72-96179. 1970. Repr. of 1953 ed. lib. bdg. 22.50x (ISBN 0-374-92204-7). Octagon.
Dobson, James. What Wives Wish Their Husbands Knew About Women. 1975. 5.95 (ISBN 0-8423-7890-1). Tyndale.
Dohr, Donald A. Camino Hacia el Amor. Orig. Title: Beginning Your Marriage. 92p. (Span.). 1972. pap. 1.15 (ISBN 0-915388-02-2). Buckley Pubns.
Dominian, J. Marital Breakdown. 1969. 5.95 (ISBN 0-8199-0151-2, L38436). Franciscan Herald.
Doty, Betty. Marriage Insurance. cancelled (ISBN 0-930822-01-3). Green Hill.
--Marriage Insurance. LC 77-92285. (Illus.). 1978. pap. 8.95 (ISBN 0-930822-01-3). Bookery.
Drakeford, John W. Games Husbands & Wives Play. LC 76-132922. 1971. 4.95 (ISBN 0-8054-5604-X). Broadman.
--Marriage: How to Keep a Good Thing Growing. LC 79-52767. 1979. pap. 3.95 (ISBN 0-914850-64-4). Impact Tenn.
Dreikurs, Rudolf. Challenge of Marriage. 1978. pap. 5.95 (ISBN 0-8015-1177-1, Hawthorn). Dutton.
Drescher, John M. When Opposites Attract. LC 79-53272. (When Bks.). (Illus., Orig.). 1979. pap. 2.45 (ISBN 0-87029-153-X, 20239). Abbey.
Drury, Michael. Advice to a Young Wife from an Old Mistress. LC 68-22668. 1968. 6.95 (ISBN 0-385-03632-9). Doubleday.
Duberman, Lucile. Marriage & Other Alternatives. 2nd ed. LC 75-36200. 239p. 1977. pap. text ed. 9.95 (ISBN 0-03-038336-6, HoltC). HR&W.
Duff, Bill. Getting Married. LC 73-331250. (New Citizen Books). (Illus.). 80p. 1973. 7.50x (ISBN 0-85340-238-8). Intl Pubns Serv.
Dufresne, Edward R. Partnership: Marriage & the Committed Life. LC 74-27423. 141p. 1975. pap. 5.95 (ISBN 0-8091-1866-1). Paulist Pr.
Dumont, Louis. Dravidien et Kariera: L'Alliance De Marriage Dans L'Inde Du Sud et En Australie. (Texts de Sciences Sociales Ser.: No. 14). 148p. 1975. pap. text ed. 21.25x (ISBN 90-2797-715-1). Mouton.
--Introduction a Deux Theories D'anthropologie Sociale: Groupes De Filiation et Alliance De Mariage. (Les Textes Sociologiques: No. 6). 139p. (Orig.). 1976. pap. text ed. 9.45x (ISBN 90-2796-896-9). Mouton.
Earnshaw, George L. Serving Each Other in Love. (Orig.). (YA) 1967. pap. text ed. 2.95 (ISBN 0-8170-0371-1). Judson.
Edens, David. Marriage: How to Have It the Way You Want It. 160p. 1981. 9.95 (ISBN 0-13-558510-4); pap. 4.95 (ISBN 0-13-558502-3). P-H.
Edgell, Stephen. Middle Class Couples: A Study of Segregation, Domination & Inequality in Marriage. 160p. 1980. text ed. 18.50x (ISBN 0-04-301109-8). Allen Unwin.
Edwards, Cliff. Biblical Christian Marriage. LC 76-44973. 1977. 6.95 (ISBN 0-8042-1100-0). John Knox.
Ellis, Albert & Harper, Robert. Creative Marriage. 1961. 5.00 (ISBN 0-8184-0022-6). Lyle Stuart.
--Guide to Successful Marriage. pap. 4.00 (ISBN 0-87980-044-5). Wilshire.
Ellis, Havelock. Sex & Marriage: Eros in Contemporary Life. LC 77-7264. 1977. Repr. of 1952 ed. lib. bdg. 20.25 (ISBN 0-8371-9667-1, ELSM). Greenwood.
Elwood, J. Murray. Growing Together in Marriage. LC 76-51468. 176p. 1977. pap. 2.95 (ISBN 0-87793-128-3). Ave Maria.
Elwood, Roger. Blessed by God: The Christian Marriage of Pat & Shirley Boone. (Illus., Orig.). 1979. pap. 1.75 (ISBN 0-451-08467-5, E8467, Sig). NAL.
Erdahl, Lowell & Erdahl, Carol. Be Good to Each Other-An Open Letter on Marriage. 1976. 5.95 (ISBN 0-8015-0584-4, Hawthorn). Dutton.
Eshleman, J. Ross & Clarke, Juanne N. Intimacy, Commitments & Marriage: Development of Relationships. 1978. pap. text ed. 15.95 (ISBN 0-205-05932-5); instr's manual (ISBN 0-205-05934-1). Allyn.
Evans, Colleen & Evans, Louis, Jr. My Lover, My Friend. 1975. 7.95 (ISBN 0-8007-0751-6). Revell.
Evans, David. Living Together in Marriage. (Christian Living Ser). 16p. 1976. pap. 0.30 (ISBN 0-8170-0731-8). Judson.
Exel, G. W. Live Happily with the Woman You Love. 1977. pap. 2.95 (ISBN 0-8024-4900-X). Moody.
Faber, Stuart J. How to Get Rid of Your Wife: And No Court Will Ever Convict You. 200p. 1974. 7.95 (ISBN 0-685-50674-6). Good Life.
Fairfield, James G. T. When You Don't Agree. LC 77-3133. 1977. pap. text ed. 3.95 (ISBN 0-8361-1819-7). Herald Pr.
Fanti, Silvio. Against Marriage. LC 77-9218. 1978. 7.95 (ISBN 0-8022-2215-3). Philos Lib.
Fields, Wilbert J. Unity in Marriage. LC 61-18222. 1962. 4.95 (ISBN 0-570-03191-5, 12-2593). Concordia.
Flannery, Harry. Love Marriage Divorce or Happiness. 1979. pap. 4.00 (ISBN 0-89502-042-4). FEB.
Florio, Anthony. Two to Get Ready. 1978. pap. 3.95 (ISBN 0-88207-635-3). Victor Bks.
Ford, Edward. Why Marriage: A Reality Therapist Looks at Married Life. LC 73-93668. 175p. 1974. pap. 2.95 (ISBN 0-913592-25-0). Argus Comm.
Forell, George W. & Lazareth, William H., eds. Crisis in Marriage. LC 77-20538. (Justice Bks). 64p. (Orig.). 1978. pap. 1.95 (ISBN 0-8006-1552-2, 1-1552). Fortress.
Foreman, Kenneth J. From This Day Forward: Thoughts About a Christian Marriage. pap. 2.95x (ISBN 0-685-02584-5). Outlook.
A Fortress for Well-Being: Bahai Teachings on Marriage. (Comprehensive Deepening Program Ser.: Gift Ed.). 1974. 14.95 (ISBN 0-87743-093-4, 364-010-10); pap. 5.00 o.s.i (ISBN 0-87743-153-1, 364-011-10). Bahai.
Friermood, Elisabeth H. Frier & Elisabeth. 1979. 10.00 (ISBN 0-533-03711-5). Vantage.
Gagnon, John H. & Greenblat, Cathy S. Life Designs: Individuals, Marriages, & Families. 1978. text ed. 16.95x (ISBN 0-673-07911-2). Scott F.
Garrett, Yvonne. The Newlywed Handbook. 160p. 1981. text ed. 8.95 (ISBN 0-8499-0276-2). Word Bks.
Gathorne-Hardy, Jonathan. Marriage, Love, Sex & Divorce: What Brings Us Together, What Drives Us Apart. 384p. 1981. 13.95 (ISBN 0-671-40103-3). Summit Bks.
Georg, I. E. Truth About Rhythm. 1962. 4.95 (ISBN 0-02-833720-4, 83372). Kenedy.
Gerl, George & Lane, George. Two Called Together. 1978. pap. text ed. 4.00 (ISBN 0-8294-0274-8); tchr's ed. 4.00 (ISBN 0-8294-0277-2). Loyola.
Getz, Gene A. The Measure of a Marriage. LC 78-53356. 144p. 1980. pap. 2.50 (ISBN 0-8307-0638-0, 5017203). Regal.
--The Measure of a Marriage Workbook. 96p. 1980. lab manual 5.95 (ISBN 0-8307-0756-5). Regal.
God, Phyllis. God. Date not set. 7.95 (ISBN 0-533-04754-4). Vantage.
Godard, James M. Blue Light. (Orig.). 1964. pap. 1.95 (ISBN 0-8042-9614-6). John Knox.
Golanty, Eric & Kephart, William M. Marriage & the Family. LC 81-82013. (Illus.). 480p. 1981. text ed. 15.95 (ISBN 0-686-73126-3); write for info. HM.
Goldstine, Daniel. The Dance-Away Lover. 1978. pap. 2.50 (ISBN 0-345-29763-6). Ballantine.
Goode, William J. World Revolution & Family Patterns. LC 63-13538. 1970. pap. text ed. 9.95 (ISBN 0-02-912460-3). Free Pr.
Gottman, John M. Marital Interaction: Experimental Investigations. LC 78-22527. 1979. 28.00 (ISBN 0-12-293150-5). Acad Pr.
Gould, Roger L. Transformations. 1979. 5.95 (ISBN 0-671-25066-3, Touchstone Bks). S&S.
Grammer, Grethe. How to Have a Happy Marriage. 1977. pap. 6.50 (ISBN 0-89351-012-2). Western Her Texas.
Green, Ernest J. Marriage & Family. LC 76-30848. (McGraw-Hill Basic Self-Instructional Guide Ser.). 1977. pap. text ed. 7.95 (ISBN 0-07-024261-5, C); instructor's guide 2.95 (ISBN 0-07-024262-3). McGraw.
Greenblat, Cathy & Cottle, Thomas J. Getting Married. LC 80-16369. 276p. 1980. 11.95 (ISBN 0-07-024330-1). McGraw.
Greenblat, Cathy S., et al. The Marital Game: Personal Growth & Fulfillment. 2nd ed. 1977. pap. text ed. 6.95x (ISBN 0-685-86656-4). Random.
Greenwald, Dorothy & Greenwald, Robert. Learning to Live with the Love of Your Life. LC 79-1825. 1979. 7.95 (ISBN 0-15-149482-7). HarBraceJ.
Griffin, G. G. The Silent Misery-Why Marriages Fail. (American Lecture in Social & Rehabilitation Psychology). 296p. 1974. 13.75 (ISBN 0-398-03214-9); pap. 8.75 (ISBN 0-398-03237-8). C C Thomas.
Groves, Ernest R., et al. Sex Fulfillment in Marriage. (Illus.). 8.95 (ISBN 0-87523-065-2). Emerson.
Grunebaum, Henry & Christ, Jacob. Contemporary Marriage: Structure, Dynamics, & Therapy. 1976. pap. text ed. 14.95 (ISBN 0-316-33042-6, Little Med Div). Little.
Guerin, Philip J. Recien Casados O Por Casarse. Nodarse, Connie, tr. (Illus.). 1977. pap. 0.95 (ISBN 0-89570-145-6). Claretian Pubns.
Guernsey, Dennis. Thoroughly Married. LC 75-19903. 1975. 4.95 (ISBN 0-87680-410-5). Word Bks.
Guggenbuhl-Craig, A. Marriage - Dead or Alive? 1981. pap. 6.00 (ISBN 0-686-31752-1). Spring Pubns.
Guthrie, Lorna & Mattinson, Janet. Brief Casework with a Marital Problem. 62p. 1971. 5.00x (ISBN 0-901882-03-8, CBO-901-I). Natl Assn Soc Wkrs.
Haire, Norman. Hymen, or the Future of Marriage. 1928. 7.50 (ISBN 0-686-17700-2). Quality Lib.
Hamilton, Cicely M. Marriage As a Trade. LC 71-149782. 1971. Repr. of 1909 ed. 19.00 (ISBN 0-8103-3394-5). Gale.
Hamilton, Eleanor. Partners in Love. 3rd rev. ed. LC 79-51018. 1981. Repr. 9.95 (ISBN 0-498-02431-8). A S Barnes.
Hancock, Maxine. Love, Honor & Be Free. study ed. 5.95 (ISBN 0-8024-5015-6). Moody.
--Love, Honor & Be Free. 1976. pap. 1.50 (ISBN 0-8024-5017-2). Moody.
Hannon, Robert J. & Slattery, Anastasia S. Marriage & Family: A Complete Course. 172p. (Orig.). 1978. tchrs. ed. 30.00 (ISBN 0-9606040-0-6). Patio Pubns.
Harakas, S. Guidelines for Marriage in the Orthodox Church. 1980. pap. 1.25 (ISBN 0-937032-21-2). Light&Life Pub Co MN.
Hardisty, Margaret. How to Get Your Husband to Fulfill Your Emotional Needs. (Orig.). 1980. pap. 4.95 (ISBN 0-89081-249-7). Harvest Hse.
Harnik, Bernard. Risk & Chance in Marriage. LC 70-144365. 1975. pap. 3.50 (ISBN 0-87680-899-2, 98041). Word Bks.
Hart, Thomas. Living Happily Everafter: Toward a Theology of Christian Marriage. LC 79-89475. 1979. pap. 3.95 (ISBN 0-8091-2213-8). Paulist Pr.
Hasegawa, Seikan. Essays on Marriage. LC 76-24974. (Companions of Zen Training: No. 2). 96p. 1977. pap. 2.95 (ISBN 0-915556-02-2). Great Ocean.
Haspel, Eleanor C. Marriage in Trouble: A Time of Decision. LC 76-4780. 308p. 1976. 13.95 (ISBN 0-88229-222-6); pap. 7.95 (ISBN 0-88229-428-8). Nelson-Hall.
Hastings, Donald W. A Doctor Speaks on Sexual Expression in Marriage. 2nd ed. 190p. 1971. 12.95 (ISBN 0-316-35017-6). Little.
Hauck, Paul A. Marriage Is a Loving Business. 1977. pap. 3.95 (ISBN 0-664-24137-9). Westminster.
Haughton, Rosemary. Problems of Christian Marriage. (Orig.). 1968. pap. 1.45 (ISBN 0-8091-1665-0). Paulist Pr.
Henslin, James M., ed. Marriage & Family in a Changing Society. LC 79-7853. (Illus.). 1980. pap. text ed. 10.95 (ISBN 0-02-914580-5). Free Pr.
Hess, Newton T. Before-After All Alone. new ed. 80p. 1980. looseleaf bdg. 7.50x (ISBN 0-9605232-0-0). Bala Pub Div.
Heywood, John. The Proverbs & Epigrams of John Heywood, A.D. 1562. 1966. Repr. of 1562 ed. 32.00 (ISBN 0-8337-1689-1). B Franklin.
Hine, James R. Grounds for Marriage. 6th ed. 1977. pap. text ed. 4.95 (ISBN 0-8134-1976-X, 1976). Interstate.
--Will You Make a Wise Marriage Choice? pk of 12 7.50 (ISBN 0-8134-2002-4, 2002). Interstate.
--Your Marriage: Analysis & Renewal. 1976. pap. 4.95x (ISBN 0-8134-1900-X, 1900). Interstate.
Hocking, David L. Love & Marriage. LC 81-413. (Orig.). 1981. pap. 4.95 (ISBN 0-89081-291-8). Harvest Hse.
Hollick, Frederick. The Marriage Guide, or Natural History of Generation. LC 73-20628. (Sex, Marriage & Society Ser.). (Illus.). 438p. 1974. Repr. of 1850 ed. 24.00x (ISBN 0-405-05804-7). Arno.
Hopson, Barrie & Hopson, Charlotte. Intimate Feedback: Lover's Guide to Getting in Touch with Each Other. 1976. pap. 1.50 (ISBN 0-451-06894-7, W6894, Sig). NAL.
How to Be Happy Though Married: Discussion Guide. 0.75 (ISBN 0-8423-1502-0). Tyndale.
Hulme, William E. Building a Christian Marriage. LC 65-22192. 1968. pap. 2.95 (ISBN 0-8066-0813-7, 10-0940). Augsburg.
--When Two Become One: Reflections for the Newly Married. LC 76-176481. 1974. pap. 2.95 (ISBN 0-8066-1438-2, 10-7061). Augsburg.
Hunt, Bernice K. Marriage. LC 75-32253. 128p. (gr. 6-12). 1976. 6.50 (ISBN 0-03-014776-X). HR&W.
Hunt, Joan & Hunt, Richard. Growing Love in Christian Marriage: Couple's Manual. 1981. pap. 2.25 (ISBN 0-687-15931-8). Aberigdow.
Hunt, Richard A. & Rydman, Edward J. Creative Marriage. 2nd ed. LC 78-32004. 1979. pap. text ed. 13.95 (ISBN 0-205-06597-X); tchr's man. avail. (ISBN 0-205-06605-4). Allyn.
Hunter, Charles & Hunter, Frances. How to Make Your Marriage Exciting. 1971. pap. 2.50 (ISBN 0-8307-0147-8). Hunter Bks.

Hutchinson, Henry N. Marriage Customs in Many Lands. LC 73-5520. (Illus.). xii, 348p. 1975. Repr. of 1897 ed. 32.00 (ISBN 0-8103-3971-4). Gale.
Hutton, Isabel E. Sex Technique in Marriage. rev. enl. ed. (Illus.). 1961. 7.95 (ISBN 0-87523-001-6). Emerson.
Irving, John. The One Hundred Fifty-Eight-Pound Marriage. 1974. 7.95 (ISBN 0-394-48414-2). Random.
James, Muriel. Marriage Is for Loving. (Illus.). 1979. 10.95 (ISBN 0-201-03454-9); pap. 5.95 (ISBN 0-201-03455-7). A-W.
Jenkins, Ray. Taking Time for Marriage. 1977. pap. 1.75 (ISBN 0-89225-182-4). Gospel Advocate.
Jenner, Heather. Marriages Are Made on Earth. 1979. 14.95 (ISBN 0-7153-7662-4). David & Charles.
Johnson, Caesar, compiled by. Today, Tomorrow & Always. (Illus.). 1977. boxed 4.95 (ISBN 0-8378-1729-3). Gibson.
Jones, William M. & Jones, Ruth A. Two Careers: One Marriage. 1980. 12.95 (ISBN 0-8144-5589-1). Am Mgmt.
Jordan, Helen M., ed. You & Marriage. LC 70-177960. (Essay Index Reprint Ser.). Repr. of 1942 ed. 21.00 (ISBN 0-8369-2911-X). Arno.
--You & Marriage. 1977. Repr. of 1942 ed. lib. bdg. 17.50 (ISBN 0-8414-2173-0). Folcroft.
Kalellis, Peter M. Wedded or Wedlocked? LC 78-73624. (Illus., Orig.). 1979. pap. 2.75 (ISBN 0-8189-1157-3, 157, Pub. by Alba Bks). Alba.
Kammeyer, Kenneth. Confronting the Issues: Sex Roles, Marriage & the Family. 2nd ed. 372p. 1980. pap. text ed. 10.95 (ISBN 0-205-06996-7, 816996-9). Allyn.
Kassorla, Irene. Putting It All Together. 224p. 1976. pap. 2.50 (ISBN 0-446-91802-4). Warner Bks.
Kelley, Robert K. Courtship, Marriage, & the Family. 3rd ed. 650p. 1979. text ed. 17.95 (ISBN 0-15-515338-2, HC); student guidebk. 5.95 (ISBN 0-15-516120-2); instructor's manual avail. (ISBN 0-15-516121-0). HarBraceJ.
Key, Ellen. Love & Marriage. Chater, Arthur G., tr. 1970. Repr. 16.00 (ISBN 0-685-55673-5). Hacker.
Keyes, Margaret F. Staying Married. LC 75-9443. 1977. pap. 4.95 (ISBN 0-89087-902-8). Les Femmes Pub.
Kilgore, James E. Try Marriage Before Divorce. 1978. 6.95 (ISBN 0-8499-0056-5). Word Bks.
Kimball, Spencer W. Marriage. LC 78-4132. (Illus.). 1978. 4.95 (ISBN 0-87747-675-6). Deseret Bk.
Kindregan, Charles P. Theology of Marriage. (Contemporary Theology Series). 1967. pap. 2.95x (ISBN 0-02-819720-8). Glencoe.
Kirby, Jonell. Second Marriage. new ed. LC 78-74004. (Orig.). 1979. pap. text ed. 8.95x (ISBN 0-915202-18-2). Accel Devel.
Kirkendall, Lester A. & Adams, Wesley J. Student's Guide to Marriage-Family Life Literature: An Aid to Individualized Study & Instruction. 8th ed. 200p. 1980. pap. text ed. write for info. (ISBN 0-697-07559-1). Wm C Brown.
Klemer, Richard H., ed. Counseling in Marital & Sexual Problems: A Physician's Handbook. LC 75-31593. 320p. 1976. Repr. of 1965 ed. 14.50 (ISBN 0-88275-362-2). Krieger.
Knox, D. Marriage: Who, When & Why? 1974. pap. 9.95 (ISBN 0-13-559336-0). P-H.
Knox, David. Exploring Marriage & the Family. 1979. text ed. 16.95x (ISBN 0-673-15046-1). Scott F.
Kohn, Barry & Matusow, Alice. Barry & Alice: Portrait of a Bisexual Marriage. LC 79-24551. 1980. 10.95 (ISBN 0-13-056150-9). P-H.
Kohut, Nester C. Therapeutic Family Law. LC 68-16525. 1968. 7.00 (ISBN 0-910574-09-X). Am Family.
Komarovsky, Mirra. Blue-Collar Marriage. 1964. pap. 2.95 (ISBN 0-394-70361-8, Vin). Random.
Kostyu, Frank A. How to Spark a Marriage When the Kids Leave Home. LC 72-75098. (Illus.). 1972. 4.95 (ISBN 0-8298-0231-2). Pilgrim NY.
Kristy, Norton F. Staying in Love: Reinventing Marriage & Other Realationships. (Orig.). pap. 2.75 (ISBN 0-515-05089-X). Jove Pubns.
Kroll, Una. Flesh of My Flesh. 1975. pap. 6.50 (ISBN 0-232-51336-8). Attic Pr.
Krutza, William J. Twenty-Five Keys to a Happy Marriage. (Contempo Ser). pap. 0.95 (ISBN 0-8010-5345-5). Baker Bk.
La Follette, Suzanne. Concerning Women. LC 72-2610. (American Women Ser: Images & Realities). 320p. 1972. Repr. of 1926 ed. 16.00 (ISBN 0-405-04464-X). Arno.
LaHaye, Tim. How to Be Happy Though Married. 5.95 (ISBN 0-8423-1500-4); pap. 2.95 (ISBN 0-8423-1501-2). Tyndale.
--Six Keys to a Happy Marriage. 1978. pap. 0.95 (ISBN 0-8423-5895-1). Tyndale.
LaHaye, Tim & LaHaye, Beverly. The Act of Marriage. 1976. o. p. 7.95 (ISBN 0-310-27060-X); pap. 5.95 (ISBN 0-310-27061-8); pap. 2.95 (ISBN 0-310-27062-6). Zondervan.
--The Act of Marriage. 1978. pap. 2.95 (ISBN 0-553-20237-5). Bantam.
Lamanna, Mary A. & Riedmann, Agnes. Marriages & Families. 640p. 1981. text ed. 18.95x (ISBN 0-534-00953-0); wkbk. 6.95x (ISBN 0-534-00956-5). Wadsworth Pub.
Landis. Building a Successful Marriage. 7th ed. 1977. 18.95 (ISBN 0-13-087007-2). P-H.
Landis, Judson T., et al. Personal Adjustment, Marriage & Family Living. 6th ed. 1975. text ed. 15.96 (ISBN 0-13-657338-X). P-H.
Landis, Paul H. Making the Most of Marriage. 5th ed. 624p. 1975. text ed. 19.95 (ISBN 0-13-547968-1). P-H.
--Your Marriage & Family Living. 3rd ed. (American Home & Family Ser.). 1969. text ed. 14.00 (ISBN 0-07-036185-1, W); tchrs' manual 1.32 (ISBN 0-07-036186-X). McGraw.
--Your Marriage & Family Living. 4th ed. (Illus.). (gr. 10-12). 1976. text ed. 14.00 (ISBN 0-07-036187-8, W). McGraw.
Landorf, Joyce. Tough & Tender. 1975. 7.95 (ISBN 0-8007-0753-2). Revell.
Lane, Lee & Gleaves, Suzanne. I Gathered the Bright Days: A Courageous Woman's Story of Her Family, Struggles, & Triumphs. LC 72-6591. 256p. 1973. 6.95 (ISBN 0-8037-4119-7). Dial.
Laney, J. Carl. The Divorce Myth. 160p. 1981. 7.95 (ISBN 0-87123-144-1). Bethany Hse.
La Roe, Marlene S. & Herrick, Lee. How Not to Ruin a Perfectly Good Marriage. 208p. 1980. pap. 2.50 (ISBN 0-553-13818-9). Bantam.
--How Not to Ruin a Perfectly Good Marriage. 1979. 10.95 (ISBN 0-695-81303-X). New Century.
Lasswell, Marcia & Lobsenz, Norman. Styles of Loving: Why You Love the Way You Do. 192p. 1981. pap. 2.50 (ISBN 0-345-29228-6). Ballantine.
Lasswell, Thomas E. & Lasswell, Marcia E. Love - Marriage - Family: A Developmental Approach. 544p. 1973. pap. 8.95x (ISBN 0-673-07523-0). Scott F.
Lasswell, Thomas E. & Lasswell, Marcia. Marriage & the Family. 544p. 1982. text ed. 16.95 (ISBN 0-669-04373-7). Heath.
Laverack, Elizabeth. With This Ring... One Hundred Years of Marriage. (Illus.). 138p. 1980. pap. 17.95 (ISBN 0-241-89895-1, Pub. by Hamish Hamilton England). David & Charles.
Lawrence, Lynda. The Un-Marriage Manual: How to Live Together Without a License. LC 74-81772. 160p. (Orig.). 1975. pap. 1.25 (ISBN 0-89041-005-4, 3005). Major Bks.
Laz, Medard. Six Levels of a Happy Marriage. 1978. pap. 1.50 (ISBN 0-89243-079-6). Liguori Pubns.
Lederach, John & Lederach, Naomi. Marriage in Today's World: Student Activity Book. 56p. 1980. pap. 2.50 (ISBN 0-8361-1946-0). Herald Pr.
Lederer, William J. Marital Choices: Forecasting, Assesing & Improving a Relationship. 1981. 12.95 (ISBN 0-393-01412-6). Norton.
Lederer, William J. & Jackson, Don D. Mirages of Marriage. LC 67-16608. 1968. 14.95 (ISBN 0-393-08400-0). Norton.
Lee, Albert & Lee, Carol A. The Total Couple. 1978. pap. 2.95 (ISBN 0-346-12346-1). Cornerstone.
Lee, Essie E. Marriage & Families. LC 77-26962. 224p. (gr. 7 up). 1978. PLB 7.79 (ISBN 0-671-32854-9). Messner.
Lee, Mark. Creative Christian Marriage. LC 77-74535. 1977. pap. 3.95 (ISBN 0-8307-0539-2, 54-061-02). Regal.
Leedy, G. Frank. Check List for Marriage. LC 72-181367. 1971. 5.00 (ISBN 0-87212-023-6). Libra.
LeShan, Eda. The Wonderful Crisis of Middle Age. 320p. 1974. pap. 2.95 (ISBN 0-446-93746-0). Warner Bks.
Leslie, Gerald R. & Leslie, Elizabeth M. Marriage in a Changing World. 2nd ed. LC 79-16195. 1980. text ed. 17.95x (ISBN 0-471-05593-X). study guide avail. (ISBN 0-471-06104-2). Wiley.
Leslie, Robert C. & Alter, Margaret G. Sustaining Intimacy: Christian Faith & Wholeness in Marriage. LC 78-7247. 1978. pap. 3.95 (ISBN 0-687-40769-9). Abingdon.
Lester, Gordon. Living & Loving. 1976. pap. 1.75 (ISBN 0-89243-063-X, 41470). Liguori Pubns.
Levi-Strauss, Claude. Elementary Structures of Kinship. Needham, Rodney, ed. LC 68-12840. (Illus.). 1969. pap. 8.95x (ISBN 0-8070-4669-8, BP340). Beacon Pr.
--Structures Elementaires De la Parente. 2nd ed. (Reeditions: No. 2). 1968. text ed. 33.50x (ISBN 90-2797-293-1). Mouton.
Libby, Roger W. & Whitehurst, Robert N. Marriage & Alternatives: Exploring Intimate Relationships. 1977. pap. 9.95x (ISBN 0-673-15050-X). Scott F.
Lichtenberger, J. P. Divorce: A Social Interpretation. LC 70-169392. (Family in America Ser). 488p. 1972. Repr. of 1931 ed. 23.00 (ISBN 0-405-03869-0). Arno.
Lindsay, Gordon. Marriage, Divorce & Remarriage. 1.25 (ISBN 0-89985-004-9). Christ Nations.
Lindsey, Ben B. & Evans, Wainwright. The Companionate Marriage. LC 73-169393. (Family in America Ser). 400p. 1972. Repr. of 1927 ed. 17.00 (ISBN 0-405-03870-4). Arno.
Linthorst, Ann T. A Gift of Love: Marriage As a Spiritual Journey. LC 79-53953. 1979. 9.95 (ISBN 0-8091-0302-8). Paulist Pr.
Lipetz, Marcia. Studying Life Designs. 1978. pap. 4.95x (ISBN 0-673-15121-2). Scott F.
Lipke, Jean. Marriage. LC 70-104896. (Being Together Books). Orig. Title: Sex Outside of Marriage. (gr. 5-11). 1971. PLB 4.95 (ISBN 0-8225-0598-3). Lerner Pubns.
Littauer, Florence. After Every Wedding Comes a Marriage. LC 81-80023. 208p. (Orig.). 1981. pap. 4.95 (ISBN 0-89081-289-6). Harvest Hse.
Locke, Harvey J. Predicting Adjustment in Marriage: A Comparison of a Divorced & a Happily Married Group. LC 68-54424. (Illus.). 1968. Repr. of 1951 ed. lib. bdg. 17.50x (ISBN 0-8371-0541-2, LOMA). Greenwood.
Loeb, Robert H., Jr. Marriage: For Better or for Worse? (gr. 9 up). 1980. PLB 8.90 (ISBN 0-686-65254-1, G25). Watts.
Loomis, Mildred J. Go Ahead & Live. LC 65-10659. 1965. 4.00 (ISBN 0-8022-0996-3). Philos Lib.
Lopata, Helena. Marriages & Families. (Transaction Ser.). 1973. pap. text ed. 9.95x (ISBN 0-442-24888-1). D Van Nostrand.
Loudin, Jo. The Hoax of Romance. (Transformation Ser.). 320p. 1981. 12.95 (ISBN 0-13-392456-4, Spec); pap. 6.95 (ISBN 0-13-392449-1). P-H.
Love & Marriage. 1967. 2.95 (ISBN 0-442-82323-1). Peter Pauper.
The Love Test Book: Rate Your Compatibility, Romantic Style, Honesty, Assertiveness, Sexual Satisfaction, & Much More. LC 78-15730. 1978. lib. bdg. 12.90 (ISBN 0-89471-053-2); pap. 3.95 (ISBN 0-89471-052-4). Running Pr.
Lowrie, Joyce & King, Sally. Marriage Book. 15.00 (ISBN 0-392-03906-0, SpS). Sportshelf.
Ludwig, David. The Spirit of Your Marriage. LC 79-50088. 1979. pap. 3.95 (ISBN 0-8066-1721-7, 10-5890). Augsburg.
Lunan-Ferguson, Ira. Don't Marry That Woman: Or, How to Get & Hold a Husband. LC 73-92689. 456p. 1973. 9.95 (ISBN 0-911724-14-1). Lunan-Ferguson.
--Twenty-Five Good Reasons Why Men Should Marry: With a Marriage Manual for Husbands on How to Treat a Wife. LC 76-2990. 1976. 7.95 (ISBN 0-911724-11-7). Lunan-Ferguson.
Lyon, William. Let Me Live! rev. ed. 192p. 1975. 8.95 (ISBN 0-8158-0243-9); pap. 5.95 (ISBN 0-686-67119-8). Chris Mass.
McCary, James L. Freedom & Growth in Marriage. 2nd ed. LC 79-17199. 1980. text ed. 16.95 (ISBN 0-471-05341-4); tchrs' manual (ISBN 0-471-07845-X). Wiley.
McCray, Walter A. Solid: Nine Vital Lessons on Settling, Saving & Solidifying the Black Marriage. 72p. (Orig.). 1981. pap. 2.50 (ISBN 0-933176-05-8). Black Light Fellow.
McCune, George. Blessings of Temple Marriage. 1974. pap. 4.95 (ISBN 0-89036-040-5). Hawkes Pub Inc.
McDonald, Cleveland. Creating a Successful Christian Marriage. LC 74-20202. 1975. 13.95 (ISBN 0-8010-5957-7). Baker Bk.
--Creating a Successful Christian Marriage. LC 74-20202. 1975. 10.95 (ISBN 0-87227-038-6). Reg Baptist.
MacDonald, Gordon. Magnificent Marriage. 1976. pap. 3.95 (ISBN 0-8423-3890-X). Tyndale.
Mace, David & Mace, Vera. How to Have a Happy Marriage. LC 77-7575. 1977. 6.95 (ISBN 0-687-17830-4). Abingdon.
--We Can Have Better Marriages If We Really Want Them. LC 73-17468. (Illus.). 176p. 1974. 7.95 (ISBN 0-687-44282-6). Abingdon.
Mace, David R. Success in Marriage. (Festival Ser.). 160p. 1980. pap. 1.95 (ISBN 0-687-40555-6). Abingdon.
--Whom God Hath Joined. rev. ed. 1973. 4.50 (ISBN 0-664-20988-2). Westminster.
McGinnis, Tom. Your First Year of Marriage. pap. 3.00 (ISBN 0-87980-256-1). Wilshire.
McRae, William J. Preparing for Your Marriage. 160p. (Orig.). 1980. pap. 5.95 (ISBN 0-310-42761-4, 9366P). Zondervan.
McRoberts, Darlene. Second Marriage: The Promise & the Challenge. LC 77-84087. 1978. pap. 3.50 (ISBN 0-8066-1612-1, 10-5635). Augsburg.
Mair, Lucy. Marriage. rev. ed. (Illus.). 222p. 1977. 9.95 (ISBN 0-85967-363-4, Pub. by Scolar Pr England); pap. 4.95 (ISBN 0-85967-360-X). Biblio Dist.
Makins, Peggy. Evelyn Home's New Handbook of Marriage. 1977. pap. 1.95 (ISBN 0-09-914140-X, Pub. by Hutchinson). Merrimack Bk Serv.
Marriage & Sex. (Faith & Life Ser.). 2.10 (ISBN 0-02-803600-X). Benziger Pub Co.
Marriage: Pro & Con. 1968. 2.95 (ISBN 0-442-82336-3). Peter Pauper.
Marryshow, Lester. The Other Woman: & How to Break Her Spell! LC 79-84218. Date not set. 12.95 (ISBN 0-9602562-0-2). Annandale-Intl.
Martin, John R. Divorce & Remarriage. 144p. 1974. pap. 4.95 (ISBN 0-8361-1328-4). Herald Pr.
Masters, William H., et al. The Pleasure Bond. 304p. 1976. pap. 3.50 (ISBN 0-553-14486-3). Bantam.
--The Pleasure Bond: A New Look at Sexuality & Commitment. LC 74-18390. 1975. 9.95 (ISBN 0-316-54981-9). Little.
El Matrimonio En Perspectiva: Perspectives on Marriage. spanish ed. LC 81-65505. 64p. Date not set. pap. 2.25 (ISBN 0-915388-12-X). Buckley Pubns.
Mattinson, Janet. Marriage & Mental Handicap: A Study of Subnormality in Marriage. LC 70-137335. (Contemporary Community Health Ser). 1971. 9.95 (ISBN 0-686-31671-1). U of Pittsburgh Pr.
Maupin, Richard H. The Confidential Message to a Couple Who Are Considering Marriage. (The Intimate Life of Man Library). (Illus.). 101p. 1980. 19.45 (ISBN 0-930582-73-X). Gloucester Art.
Mayfield, James L. Up with Marriage. LC 79-16194. 1979. pap. 6.00 (ISBN 0-8309-0246-5). Herald Hse.
Mazur, Ronald M. The New Intimacy: Open-Ended Marriage & Alternative Lifestyles. LC 73-5928. 144p. 1974. pap. 3.50 (ISBN 0-8070-2767-7, BP497). Beacon Pr.
Meier, Paul & Harris, Jan. Formula for a Happy Marriage. LC 77-78462. (Lifeline Ser.). 1977. pap. 0.95 (ISBN 0-88419-138-9). Creation Hse.
Melville, Keith. Marriage & Family Today. 2nd ed. 491p. 1980. text ed. 18.95 (ISBN 0-394-32346-7). Random.
Melville, Keith & Melville, Charles. Exploring Marriage & Family Today. (Illus.). 280p. 1980. pap. text ed. 5.95 (ISBN 0-394-32183-9). Random.
Messer, Judy. To Know Him Is to Love Him. LC 77-7835. 1977. pap. 1.95 (ISBN 0-06-065559-3, HJ 36, HarpR). Har-Row.
Meyendorff, John. Marriage: An Orthodox Perspective. LC 75-14241. 184p. 1975. pap. 4.95 (ISBN 0-913836-05-2). St Vladimirs.
Miles, Herbert J. Sexual Happiness in Marriage. 1967. pap. 2.95 (ISBN 0-310-29202-6). Zondervan.
Miller, Sherod, ed. Marriage & Families: Enrichment Through Communication. LC 75-27012. (Sage Contemporary Social Science Issues Ser.: Vol. 20). 125p. 1975. 5.95 (ISBN 0-8039-0569-6). Sage.
Mitchelson, Marvin. Made in Heaven, Settled in Court. 1979. pap. 2.25 (ISBN 0-446-92224-2). Warner Bks.
Monks Of Solesmes, ed. Matrimony: One Hundred & Thirty-Eight Pronouncements from Benedict Fourteenth to John Twenty-Third. 5.50 (ISBN 0-8198-0098-8); pap. 4.50 (ISBN 0-8198-0099-6). Dghtrs St Paul.
Montgomery, Herb & Montgomery, Mary. The Two of Us: Reflections on Shared Growth in Marriage. LC 77-78256. (Books to Encourage & Inspire). 1977. pap. text ed. 5.95 (ISBN 0-03-042296-5). Winston Pr.
Morgan, Marabel. Total Joy. 1978. pap. 2.25 (ISBN 0-425-04342-8, Medallion). Berkley Pub.
--Total Joy. 1977. 6.95 (ISBN 0-8007-0816-4). Revell.
--The Total Woman. 192p. 1973. 8.95 (ISBN 0-8007-0608-0). Revell.
--The Total Woman. (Spire Bks.). 1975. pap. 2.25 (ISBN 0-8007-8218-6). Revell.
--The Total Woman. 1976. pap. 2.50 (ISBN 0-671-41664-2). PB.
Mornell, Pierre. Passive Men, Wild Women. 1979. 8.95 (ISBN 0-671-24579-1). S&S.
Morrison, Eleanor S. & Borosage, Vera, eds. Human Sexuality: Contemporary Perspectives. 2nd ed. LC 76-56509. 504p. 1977. pap. text ed. 11.95 (ISBN 0-87484-381-2). Mayfield Pub.
Mow, Anna B. The Secret of Married Love. (Trumpet Bks). 1976. pap. 1.50 (ISBN 0-87981-054-8). Holman.
--Secret of Married Love. 1976. pap. 1.50 (ISBN 0-89129-190-3). Jove Pubns.
Mullenders, Joannes. Le Mariage Presume. (Analecta Gregoriana: Vol. 181). (Fr.). 1971. pap. 5.25 (ISBN 0-8294-0327-2, Pub. by Gregorian U Pr). Loyola.
Mumford, Bob. Living Happily Ever After. 1974. pap. 1.25 (ISBN 0-8007-8151-1, Spire Bks). Revell.

Murdock, George P. Social Structure. 1965. pap. text ed. 8.95 (ISBN 0-02-922290-7). Free Pr.
Murstein, Bernard I. Exploring Intimate Life Styles. LC 77-27272. 1978. text ed. 18.95 (ISBN 0-8261-2380-5); pap. text ed. 11.95 (ISBN 0-8261-2381-3). Springer Pub.
--Love, Sex, & Marriage Through the Ages. LC 73-92201. 1974. text ed. 18.95 (ISBN 0-8261-1460-1); pap. text ed. 10.95 (ISBN 0-8261-1461-X). Springer Pub.
--Who Will Marry Whom. LC 75-46588. 400p. 1976. text ed. 17.95 (ISBN 0-8261-2030-X). Springer Pub.
Nass, Gilbert D. Marriage & the Family. (Illus.). 1978. text ed. 16.95 (ISBN 0-201-02500-0); instr's man 3.00 (ISBN 0-201-02502-7); study guide 4.95 (ISBN 0-201-02501-9); tests 2.00 (ISBN 0-201-02503-5). A-W.
Nichols, Thomas L. Marriage: Its History, Character, & Results. LC 78-22161. (Free Love in America). Repr. of 1854 ed. 36.50 (ISBN 0-404-60955-4). AMS Pr.
Nordau, Max S. The Matrimonial Lies of Our Contemporary Civilization. 1979. Repr. of 1884 ed. 37.75 (ISBN 0-89266-148-8). Am Classical Coll Pr.
Oda, Stephanie C., compiled by. I Thee Wed. (Illus.). 1980. 3.00 (ISBN 0-8378-2021-9). Gibson.
Ogden, Dunbar H. Wedding Bells. (Orig.). 1945. pap. 1.25 (ISBN 0-8042-1884-6). John Knox.
Olsen, Martin G. & Von Kaenel, George E. Two As One: A Christian Marriage Preparation Manual. 1977. pap. 3.95 (ISBN 0-8091-1994-3). Paulist Pr.
--Two As One: A Christian Marriage Preparation Workbook. 1977. pap. 2.50 (ISBN 0-8091-1995-1). Paulist Pr.
Olson, David H., ed. Inventory of Marriage & Family Literature, Vol. 5. LC 67-63014. 485p. 1979. 60.00x (ISBN 0-8039-1232-3); pap. 29.95 (ISBN 0-8039-1233-1). Sage.
O'Neill, Nena. The Marriage Premise. LC 77-22389. 230p. 1977. 8.95 (ISBN 0-87131-241-7). M Evans.
Orthmer, D. K. Intimate Relationships: An Introduction to Marriage & the Family. 1981. 17.95 (ISBN 0-201-05519-8); instr.'s man. 2.50 (ISBN 0-201-05520-1); student resource guide 5.95 (ISBN 0-201-05521-X). A-W.
Osborne, Cecil. Art of Understanding Your Mate. pap. 2.95 (ISBN 0-310-30602-7). Zondervan.
Otto, Herbert A., ed. Marriage & Family Enrichment: New Perspectives & Programs. LC 75-30743. 1976. 14.95 (ISBN 0-687-23621-5); pap. 8.95 (ISBN 0-687-23620-7). Abingdon.
Parker, D. Coffey. The Divinity of Marriage. 1980. 2.50x (ISBN 0-686-28978-1). D C Parker.
Paul, Norman L. & Paul, Betty B. A Marital Puzzle. 302p. 1975. 12.95 (ISBN 0-393-01116-X). Norton.
Penrose, Maryly B., ed. & compiled by. Philadelphia Marriages & Obituaries, 1857-1860 Philadelphia Saturday Bulletin. LC 74-84453. 294p. 1974. 35.00 (ISBN 0-918940-03-6); softcover 30.00 (ISBN 0-918940-04-4). Libty Bell Assoc.
Perspectives on Marriage. LC 80-67039. 68p. 1980. pap. 2.25 (ISBN 0-915388-08-1). Buckley Pubns.
Peterkiewicz, Jerzy. The Third Adam: The Mariavite Experiment in Mystical Marriage. (Illus.). 256p. 1975. 27.50x (ISBN 0-19-212198-7). Oxford U Pr.
Petersen, J. Allan. Before You Marry. 1974. pap. 1.75 (ISBN 0-8423-0104-6). Tyndale.
Petersen, J. Allan, compiled by. The Marriage Affair. pap. 5.95 (ISBN 0-8423-4171-4). Tyndale.
Peterson, Yen. Marital Adjustment in Couples of Which One Spouse Is Physically Handicapped. LC 78-68447. 1979. perfect bdg. 10.00 (ISBN 0-88247-572-X). R & E Res Assoc.
Polenz, Joanna M. In Defense of Marriage. 226p. 1981. text ed. 17.50 (ISBN 0-89876-013-5). Gardner Pr.
Pope John Paul II. Love & Responsibility. Willetts, H. T., tr. 1981. 15.00 (ISBN 0-374-19247-2). FS&G.
Posin, S. Elihu. Marriage. 1980. 5.95 (ISBN 0-533-04491-X). Vantage.
Powers, Edward A. & Lees, Mary W. Encounter with Family Realities. (Illus.). 1977. pap. 9.95 (ISBN 0-8299-0051-9). West Pub.
--Process in Relationship: Marriage & Family. 2nd ed. (Illus.). 300p. 1976. pap. text ed. 8.95 (ISBN 0-8299-0082-9). West Pub.
Prescod, Suzanne. Current Research on Marriage, Families, & Divorce. 1979. looseleaf bdg. 25.50 (ISBN 0-915260-09-3). Atcom.
Priests in the Christian Community. Marriage: A Collection of Three Articles. 1972. pap. 1.25 (ISBN 0-900285-12-5, Floris Books). St George Bk Serv.
Rama, Swami. Marriage, Parenthood & Enlightenment. (Orig.). 1977. pap. 1.95 (ISBN 0-89389-021-9). Himalayan Intl Inst.
Rayner, Claire. Related to Sex: Understanding Sexual Tensions in Your Family. LC 78-26728. 1979. pap. 8.95 (ISBN 0-448-22918-8). Paddington.
Readings in Marriage & Family 77-78. new ed. LC 74-84596. (Annual Editions Ser.). (Illus., Orig.). 1977. write for info. (ISBN 0-87967-174-2). Dushkin Pub.
Readings in Marriage & Family 78-79. LC 74-884596. (Annual Editions Ser.). (Illus.). 1978. pap. text ed. 5.75 (ISBN 0-87967-226-9). Dushkin Pub.
Reid, William D. Marriage Notices of Ontario. 1980. lib. bdg. 25.00 (ISBN 0-912606-05-3). Hunterdon Hse.
Reul, Myrtle R. Practical Approach to Marriage. 180p. 1965. text ed. 3.50x (ISBN 0-87013-092-7). Mich St U Pr.
Rheinstein, Max. Marriage Stability, Divorce, & the Law. LC 79-169582. 496p. 1972. 19.50x (ISBN 0-226-71773-9). U of Chicago Pr.
Rice, David G. Dual-Career Marriage: Conflict & Treatment. LC 79-7179. 1979. 12.95 (ISBN 0-02-926380-8). Free Pr.
Rice, F. Philip. Marriage & Parenthood. 1979. text ed. 19.95 (ISBN 0-205-06517-1, 8165173); instr's man. avail. (ISBN 0-205-06539-2, 8165394). Allyn.
Rice, Mac M. & Rice, Vivian B. When Can I Say, "I Love You"? 1977. pap. 1.95 (ISBN 0-8024-9436-6). Moody.
Riker, Audrey, et al. Married Life. rev. ed. (gr. 10-12). 1976. text ed. 15.60 (ISBN 0-87002-071-4); student guide 3.08 (ISBN 0-87002-208-3). tchr's guide free. Bennett IL.
Rivers, Caryl & Lupo, Alan. For Better! for Worse! 256p. 1981. 12.95 (ISBN 0-671-25446-4). Summit Bks.
Robb, Dale. Love & Living Together. LC 77-15242. 112p. (Orig.). 1978. pap. 3.50 (ISBN 0-8006-1326-0, 1-1326). Fortress.
Roberts, Doug. To Adam with Love. pap. 1.95 (ISBN 0-89728-059-8, 533232). Omega Pubns OR.
Roddick, Ellen. Together. LC 78-21362. 1979. 8.95 (ISBN 0-312-80768-6). St Martin.
Rodman, Hyman, ed. Marriage, Family & Society: A Reader. 1965. pap. text ed. 4.95x (ISBN 0-685-69597-2). Phila Bk Co.
Rogers, Carl R. Becoming Partners. 1973. pap. 4.95 (ISBN 0-440-50597-6, Delta). Dell.
Roleder, George. Marriage Means Encounter. 2nd ed. 281p. 1979. pap. text ed. write for info. (ISBN 0-697-07590-7). Wm C Brown.
Rolfe, David J. Marriage Preparation Manual. 1976. pap. 5.95 (ISBN 0-8091-1908-0). Paulist Pr.
Romanov, Panteleimon S. Diary of a Soviet Marriage. Furnivall, J. & Parmenter, R., trs. from Rus. LC 74-10090. (Soviet Literature in English Translation Ser). 143p. 1974. Repr. of 1936 ed. 13.00 (ISBN 0-88355-176-4). Hyperion Conn.
Rosner, Stanley & Hobe, Laura. The Marriage Gap. 1978. pap. 3.95 (ISBN 0-07-053808-5, SP). McGraw.
Ross, Lewis. Extra-Marital Relationships. (Topics in Human Behavior Ser.). 1978. pap. text ed. 5.95 (ISBN 0-8403-1853-7). Kendall-Hunt.
Rothberg, R. I. & Rabb, T. K. Marriage & Fertility. (Studies in Interdisciplinary History Ser.). 1980. 20.00 (ISBN 0-691-05319-7); pap. 5.95 (ISBN 0-691-00781-0). Princeton U Pr.
Rowland, Beatrice & Rowland, Howard. In Celebration of Marriage. (Illus.). 1981. 15.95 (ISBN 0-698-11066-8); pap. 8.95 (ISBN 0-698-11065-X). Coward.
Rueschemeyer, Marilyn. Professional Work & Marriage. 1981. 22.50x (ISBN 0-312-64782-4). St Martin.
Runnels, Rachel. Marriage & the Home. 72p. (Orig.). 1973. pap. 2.50 (ISBN 0-87604-069-5). ARE Pr.
Russell, Bertrand. Marriage & Morals. new ed. LC 70-114377. 1970. pap. 5.95 (ISBN 0-87140-011-1). Liveright.
Rutherford, Robert & Rutherford, Jean. Doctor Discusses Family Problems. (Illus.). 1969. pap. 2.50 (ISBN 0-910304-17-3). Budlong.
Ryan, Michael. The Philosophy of Marriage, in Its Social Moral, & Physical Relations. LC 73-20638. (Sex, Marriage & Society Ser.). 400p. 1974. Repr. 22.00x (ISBN 0-405-05815-2). Arno.
Salley, Alexander S., Jr. Marriage Notices in Charleston Courier 1803-1808. LC 76-16889. 1976. Repr. of 1919 ed. 5.00 (ISBN 0-8063-0727-7). Genealog Pub.
Sammons, David. The Marriage Option. LC 76-48531. 1977. 9.95 (ISBN 0-8070-2746-4); pap. 3.95 (ISBN 0-8070-2747-2, BP586). Beacon Pr.
Samuel, Dorothy T. Fun & Games in Marriage. LC 72-84171. 1976. pap. 1.50 (ISBN 0-87680-825-9, Key-Word Bks). Word Bks.
Saul, Leon J. The Childhood Emotional Pattern in Marriage. LC 78-17400. 1979. text ed. 15.95x (ISBN 0-442-27359-2). Van Nos Reinhold.
Saxton, Lloyd. Individual, Marriage & the Family. 4th ed. 672p. 1980. text ed. 18.95x (ISBN 0-534-00799-6); study guide 6.95x (ISBN 0-534-00800-3). Wadsworth Pub.
Scanzoni, John. Love & Negotiate: Creative Conflict in Marriage. 1979. 6.95 (ISBN 0-8499-0100-6). Word Bks.
Scanzoni, Letha & Scanzoni, John. Men, Women, & Change: A Sociology of Marriage & Family. (Illus.). 512p. 1975. text ed. 17.00 (ISBN 0-07-055040-9, C); instructor's manual 2.95 (ISBN 0-07-055041-7). McGraw.
Schnepp, A. F. & Schnepp, G. J. To God Through Marriage. rev. ed. (Orig.). 1967. pap. 3.96 (ISBN 0-02-827860-7). Glencoe.
Schulz, David A. The Changing Family: Its Function & Future. 3rd ed. (Illus.). 368p. 1982. reference 19.95 (ISBN 0-13-127910-6). P-H.
Schulz, David A. & Rogers, Stanley F. Marriage, the Family & Personal Fulfillment. 2nd ed. (P-H Ser. in Sociology). (Illus.). 1980. text ed. 19.95 (ISBN 0-13-559385-9). P-H.
Scorseby, Lynn A. Marriage Dialogue. LC 76-45150. 1977. text ed. 6.95 (ISBN 0-201-06789-7). A-W.
Seagren, Daniel R. Togetherness. (Contempo Ser.). 32p. 1978. pap. 0.95 (ISBN 0-8010-8114-9). Baker Bk.
Seidenberg, Robert. Marriage in Life & Literature. LC 70-97939. 1970. 5.95 (ISBN 0-8022-2331-1). Philos Lib.
Self, Carolyn S. & Self, William L. A Survival Kit for Marriage. 1981. pap. 4.95 (ISBN 0-8054-5643-0). Broadman.
Shapiro, David S. & Shapiro, Elaine S. The Search for Love & Achievement: Marriage & the Family in a Changing World. 2nd ed. 1980. pap. text ed. 10.95x (ISBN 0-917974-48-4). Waveland Pr.
Shedd, Charlie & Shedd, Martha. How to Stay in Love. 1980. 7.95 (ISBN 0-8362-2900-2). Andrews & McMeel.
Shedd, Charlie W. Letters to Karen. (Festival Books). 1977. pap. 1.25 (ISBN 0-687-21566-8). Abingdon.
--Letters to Karen: On Keeping Love in Marriage. LC 66-15726. (YA) (gr. 9 up). 1966. 7.95 (ISBN 0-687-21568-4). Abingdon.
--Letters to Karen: On Keeping Love in Marriage. 1968. pap. 1.75 (ISBN 0-380-00207-8, 55277). Avon.
--Letters to Philip. (YA) 1969. pap. 1.95 (ISBN 0-8007-8025-6, Spire Bks). Revell.
--Letters to Philip: On How to Treat a Woman. LC 68-11400. 1968. 6.95 (ISBN 0-385-01210-1). Doubleday.
--Talk to Me. 1976. pap. 1.50 (ISBN 0-89129-112-1). Jove Pubns.
Shimek, Michael. Dating & Marriage: A Christian Approach to Intimacy. (Illus.). 1978. pap. text ed. 4.25 (ISBN 0-03-022136-6); tchr's. guide 2.25 (ISBN 0-03-042786-X). Winston Pr.
Shoulson, Abraham B., ed. Marriage & Family Life: A Jewish View. 7.50 (ISBN 0-8084-0378-8). Coll & U Pr.
Siegel, Eli. Furious Aesthetics of Marriage. 1964. pap. 1.00x (ISBN 0-911492-03-8). Aesthetic Realism.
Silverstone, Harry. Adventure of Marriage. 1967. 7.50 (ISBN 0-87948-006-8). Beatty.
Skala, John. Marriage Maze. (Orig.). 1965. 2.25 (ISBN 0-8198-0086-4). Dghtrs St Paul.
Skidmore, Rex A. Marriage: Much More Than a Dream. LC 79-26375. 96p. 1979. 5.95 (ISBN 0-87747-783-3). Deseret Bk.
Small, Dwight H. After You've Said I Do. 1976. pap. 1.75 (ISBN 0-89129-213-6). Jove Pubns.
Smith, James R. & Smith, Lynn G., eds. Beyond Monogamy: Recent Studies of Sexual Alternatives in Marriage. LC 73-19345. (Illus.). 374p. 1974. 20.00x (ISBN 0-8018-1577-0). Johns Hopkins.
Smith, Nancy C. The Marriage Connection. 1979. pap. 4.05 (ISBN 0-89536-399-2). CSS Pub.
Smith, Rebecca M. Klemer's Marriage & Family Relationships. 2nd ed. 424p. 1975. text ed. 20.95 scp (ISBN 0-06-046311-2, HarpC); instructor's manual free (ISBN 0-06-366303-1). Har-Row.
Snawsel, Robert. A Looking-Glasse for Married Folkes. LC 74-28886. (English Experience Ser.: No. 763). 1975. Repr. of 1631 ed. 7.00 (ISBN 90-221-0763-9). Walter J Johnson.
Sommers, Helen. The Married Single. 1981. 4.95 (ISBN 0-8062-1548-8). Carlton.
Sondashi, Ludwig S. Marriage Is Not for Weaklings. 1977. pap. 4.00 (ISBN 0-682-48859-3). Exposition.
A Special Kind of Marrying. LC 80-67686. 120p. 1980. pap. 3.50 (ISBN 0-915388-09-X). Buckley Pubns.
Sperry, Len. The Together Experience. 1978. pap. 3.95 (ISBN 0-89293-005-5). Beta Bk.
Sproul, R. C. Discovering the Intimate Marriage. 160p. 1981. pap. 2.95 (ISBN 0-87123-118-2, 200118). Bethany Hse.
Stapleton, Jean & Bright, Richard. Equal Marriage. LC 76-19048. 1976. 5.95 (ISBN 0-687-11993-6). Abingdon.
Stein, Peter, et al. The Marital Game: Understanding Marital Decision Making. 2nd ed. 1977. pap. text ed. 7.95x (ISBN 0-394-31136-1). Random.
Steinmetz, Urban G. I Will. LC 71-84816. (Illus.). 136p. 1969. pap. 1.50 (ISBN 0-87793-010-4). Ave Maria.
--Strangers, Lovers, Friends. LC 80-69479. (Illus.). 176p. (Orig.). 1981. pap. 3.95 (ISBN 0-87793-217-4). Ave Maria.
Stevens, Barbara C. Marriage & Fertility of Women Suffering from Schizophrenia or Affective Disorders. (Maudsley Monographs). 1969. 9.75x (ISBN 0-19-712141-1). Oxford U Pr.
Stinnett, Nick & Walters, James. Relationships in Marriage & Family. 1977. 13.95 (ISBN 0-02-417530-7). Macmillan.
Stockham, Alice B. Karezza: Ethics of Marriage. LC 78-72363. (Free Love in America). Repr. of 1903 ed. 17.00 (ISBN 0-404-60993-7). AMS Pr.
Stone, Hannah & Stone, Abraham. Marriage Manual. rev. & enl. ed. Aitken, Gloria S. & Sobrero, Acquiles, eds. (Illus.). 1968. 8.95 (ISBN 0-671-45101-4). S&S.
Strauss, Richard. Living in Love. 1978. pap. 3.95 (ISBN 0-8423-2488-7). Tyndale.
Strauss, Richard L. Marriage Is for Love. pap. 2.95 (ISBN 0-8423-4181-1). Tyndale.
Strean, Herbert S. The Extramarital Affair: A Psychoanalytic View. LC 79-55937. 1980. 12.95 (ISBN 0-02-932180-8). Free Pr.
Strong, F. Bryan, et al. The Marriage & Family Experience: A Text with Readings. (Illus.). 1979. pap. text ed. 17.95 (ISBN 0-8299-0278-3); instrs.' manual avail. (ISBN 0-8299-0577-4). West Pub.
Sussman, Marvin B. Marriage & the Family: Current Critical Issues. LC 79-53232. (Collected Essay Ser.). 1979. pap. 6.95 (ISBN 0-917724-08-9). Haworth Pr.
Sussman, Marvin B., ed. Sourcebook in Marriage & the Family. 4th ed. 432p. 1974. pap. text ed. 11.50 (ISBN 0-395-17538-0). HM.
Swedenborg, Emanuel. Conjugal Love. LC 79-93407. student ed. 6.50 (ISBN 0-87785-054-2); 8.25 (ISBN 0-87785-117-4). Swedenborg.
Sweeney, Karen O. Improve Your Love Life. 1976. pap. 1.50 (ISBN 0-89041-120-4, 3120). Major Bks.
Swift, Morrison I. Marriage & Race Death. 1977. lib. bdg. 59.95 (ISBN 0-8490-2211-8). Gordon Pr.
Taylor, Jack R. What Every Husband Should Know. 1981. 6.95 (ISBN 0-8054-5642-2). Broadman.
Tegg, William. The Knot Tied: Marriage Ceremonies of All Nations. 59.95 (ISBN 0-8490-0474-8). Gordon Pr.
Telford, Dr. Andrew. Miscarriage of Marriage. pap. 1.45 (ISBN 0-686-12750-1). Grace Pub Co.
Thatcher, Floyd & Thatcher, Harriett. Long Term Marriage. 1980. 8.95 (ISBN 0-8499-0096-4). Word Bks.
Thomas, David M., ed. Marital Spirituality. LC 78-69753. (Marriage & Family Living in Depth Ser.: Vol. 3). 1978. pap. 2.45 (ISBN 0-87029-139-4, 20222). Abbey.
Thomas, Edwin J. Marital Communication & Decision Making: Analysis, Assessment, & Change. LC 75-41551. 1977. 12.95 (ISBN 0-02-932570-6). Free Pr.
Thomas, Terry C. Adios, Amor Mio. Bautista, Sara, tr. from Eng. LC 77-79933. 202p. (Orig., Span.). 1977. pap. 2.50 (ISBN 0-89922-089-4). Edit Caribe.
Timmons, Tim. Maximum Marriage. 1977. pap. 4.95 (ISBN 0-8007-5003-9, Power Bks). Revell.
Tingle, Dolli, compiled by. Going to Be a Bride. LC 75-98695. (Illus.). 1970. 3.00 (ISBN 0-8378-1991-1). Gibson.
Tippit, Sammy & Jenkins, Jerry. You Me He. 1978. pap. 2.95 (ISBN 0-88207-766-X). Victor Bks.
Tizard, Leslie J. Guide to Marriage. (Unwin Books). 1960. pap. 2.95 (ISBN 0-04-173004-6). Allen Unwin.
Tournier, Paul. To Understand Each Other. Gilmour, John S., tr. LC 67-15298. (Illus.). 1967. 4.25 (ISBN 0-8042-2235-5). John Knox.
Trobisch, Ingrid. The Joy of Being a Woman. LC 75-9324. 144p. 1975. pap. 3.95 (ISBN 0-06-068453-4, RD 353, HarpR). Har-Row.
Trobisch, Walter. I Married You. LC 78-148437. 144p. 1975. pap. 3.95 (ISBN 0-06-068452-6, RD 351, HarpR). Har-Row.
Tseng, Wen-Shing, et al, eds. Adjustment in Intercultural Marriage. 1977. pap. text ed. 5.00x (ISBN 0-8248-0579-8). U Pr of Hawaii.
Tyrer, Alfred H. Sex Satisfaction & Happy Marriage. (Illus.). 1951. 6.95 (ISBN 0-87523-039-3). Emerson.
Udry, J. Richard. The Social Context of Marriage. 3rd ed. LC 73-20059. 525p. 1974. pap. text ed. 14.50 scp (ISBN 0-397-47305-2, HarpC); instructor's manual free (ISBN 0-397-47251-X). Har-Row.

Urlin, E. L. A History of Marriage. 59.95 (ISBN 0-8490-0334-2). Gordon Pr.
Van De Velde, T. A. Ideal Marriage: Its Physiology & Technique. 400p. 1975. pap. 2.25 (ISBN 0-345-25841-X). Ballantine.
Van De Velde, Theodoor H. Ideal Marriage: Its Physiology & Technique. 2nd ed. Smyth, Margaret, ed. LC 80-13454. (Illus.). xxi, 257p. 1980. Repr. of 1965 ed. lib. bdg. 25.00x (ISBN 0-313-22442-0, VEIM). Greenwood.
Vanton, Monte. Marriage: Grounds for Divorce. 1979. 10.00 (ISBN 0-671-24803-0). S&S.
Vernon, Bob & Carlson, Carole. The Married Man. 1980. 6.95 (ISBN 0-8007-1117-3). Revell.
Viorst, Judith. It's Hard to Be Hip Over Thirty & Other Tragedies of Married Life. 1980. 4.95 (ISBN 0-453-00276-5, H276). NAL.
Von Hildebrand, D. Man & Woman. 1981. pap. 3.95 (ISBN 0-89526-883-3). Regnery-Gateway.
Voshell, Dorothy. Whom Shall I Marry. 1979. pap. 2.95 (ISBN 0-87552-509-1). Presby & Reformed.
Wake, Charles S. The Development of Marriage & Kinship. Needham, Rodney, ed. LC 66-20596. (Midway Reprint Ser). 566p. 1974. pap. 19.00x (ISBN 0-226-87019-7). U of Chicago Pr.
Walker, E. Jerry. Til Business Do Us Part. LC 77-6823. 1977. pap. 3.00 (ISBN 0-918734-01-0). Reymont.
Ward, Ruth. Encouragement: A Wife's Special Gift. 1979. pap. 1.95 (ISBN 0-8010-9634-0). Baker Bk.
Ward, William B. When You're Married. (Orig.). 1947. pap. 1.50 (ISBN 0-8042-2604-0). John Knox.
The Wedded Life. 1979. 2.50 (ISBN 0-686-30767-4). Rod & Staff.
Weed, James A. National Estimates of Marriage Dissolution & Suvivorship. Cox, Klaudia, ed. (Ser. 3, No. 19). 50p. 1980. pap. text ed. 1.75 (ISBN 0-8406-0196-4). Natl Ctr Health Stats.
Weil, Mildred W. Marriage, the Family, & Society: Toward a Sociology of Marriage & the Family. 2nd ed. LC 76-50685. 1977. pap. 6.95x (ISBN 0-8134-1897-6, 1897). Interstate.
Weil, Mildred W., ed. Sociological Perspectives in Marriage & the Family. 2nd ed. LC 78-54230. 1979. pap. text ed. 8.95x (ISBN 0-8134-2033-4, 2033). Interstate.
Weiss, Robert S. Marital Separation: Managing After a Marriage Ends. LC 74-78307. 1977. pap. 4.95 (ISBN 0-465-09723-5, CN-5023). Basic.
Wells, J. Gipson. Current Issues in Marriage & the Family. 2nd ed. 1979. pap. text ed. 9.95 (ISBN 0-02-425440-1). Macmillan.
Wells, J. Gipson & Hampe, Gary D. Contemporary Marriage: A Realistic Approach. (Illus.). 1978. 12.95 (ISBN 0-02-425460-6). Macmillan.
Wessel, Helen. Under the Apple Tree: Marrying - Birthing - Parenting. LC 79-52050. 325p. (Orig.). 1981. pap. 5.95 (ISBN 0-933082-02-9). Bookmates Intl.
Westermarck, Edward. Future of Marriage in Western Civilization. facsimile ed. LC 72-114900. (Select Bibliographies Reprint Ser). 1936. 17.00 (ISBN 0-8369-5304-5). Arno.
Wheat, E. Love Life for Every Married Couple. 288p. 1980. pap. 5.95 (ISBN 0-310-42511-5). Zondervan.
Wheat, Ed & Wheat, Gaye. Intended for Pleasure. (Illus.). 1977. 8.95 (ISBN 0-8007-0824-5). Revell.
Whitehead, James D. Marrying Well: Possibilities in Christian Marriage Today. LC 81-43046. 480p. 1981. 15.95 (ISBN 0-385-17130-7). Doubleday.
Wiese, Bennard R. & Steinmetz, Urban G. Everything You Need to Know to Stay Married & Like It. 256p. 1975. pap. 3.95 (ISBN 0-310-34422-0). Zondervan.
Wilczak, Paul F., ed. Marriage Enrichment. LC 79-53514. (Marriage & Family Living in Depth: Vol. V). (Orig.). 1979. pap. 2.45 (ISBN 0-87029-155-6, 20241). Abbey.
Wilke, Richard B. Tell Me Again, I'm Listening: How to Make Your Marriage Work. LC 73-3051. (Festival Books). 1977. pap. 1.25 (ISBN 0-687-41227-7). Abingdon.
Williams, Carl E. & Crosby, John F. Choice-Challenge: Contemporary Readings in Marriage. 2nd ed. 240p. 1979. pap. text ed. write for info. (ISBN 0-697-07556-7); instrs.' manual avail. (ISBN 0-686-60833-X). Wm C Brown.
Williams, H. Page. Do Yourself a Favor: Love Your Wife. 131p. 1973. pap. 2.50 (ISBN 0-88270-204-1). Logos.
Williamson, Robert C. Marriage & Family Relations. 2nd ed. LC 70-37027. 1972. text ed. 19.95 (ISBN 0-471-94905-1). Wiley.
Willimon, William H. Saying Yes to Marriage. 1979. pap. 4.95 (ISBN 0-8170-0812-8). Judson.
Willke, J. C. & Wilke, Mrs. Marriage. 1979. pap. 2.95 (ISBN 0-910728-13-5). Hayes.
Winch, Robert F. Mate Selection: A Study of Complementary Needs. (Reprints in Sociology Ser). lib. bdg. 26.50x (ISBN 0-697-00215-2); pap. text ed. 8.95x (ISBN 0-89197-842-9). Irvington.
Woman & Marriage, 5 vols. Incl. Some Reflections Upon Marriage. Astell, Mary. Repr. 9.50 (ISBN 0-442-81056-3); Home: Its Work & Influence. Gilman, Charlotte P. Repr. of 1903 ed. 13.00 (ISBN 0-442-81992-7); Women & Economics. Gilman, Charlotte P. Repr. 15.00 (ISBN 0-442-81081-4); Two Vols. In One. Love, Marriage, & Divorce, & the Sovereignity of the Individual: Bound with Divorce. Greeley, Horace, et al. Repr; Divorce. Greeley, Horace & Owen, Robert D. Repr. 10.50 (ISBN 0-685-37112-3); Law of Baron & Femme, of Parent & Child, Guardian & Ward, Master & Servant, & of the Powers of the Courts of Chancery. 3rd ed. Reeve, Tapping. Repr. 32.50 (ISBN 0-442-81067-9). (Source Library of the Women's Movement). 1970. 80.50 set (ISBN 0-442-81250-7). Hacker.
Women's Co-Operative Guild. Maternity: Letters from Working-Women, Collected by the Women's Co-Operative Guild with a Preface by the Right Hon. Herbert Samuel, M.P., London 1915. LC 79-56940. (The English Working Class Ser.). 1980. lib. bdg. 20.00 (ISBN 0-8240-0127-3). Garland Pub.
Wood, Leland Foster. Harmony in Marriage. 1979. 4.95 (ISBN 0-8007-1087-8). Revell.
Wright, H. Norman. Communication: Key to Your Marriage. rev. ed. LC 73-88317. 208p. 1979. pap. 4.95 (ISBN 0-8307-0726-3, 5415004). Regal.
--The Living Marriage. (Illus.). 1975. 9.95 (ISBN 0-8007-0722-2). Revell.
Wright, Norm. After You Say I Do. LC 79-66960. 80p. (Orig.). 1979. pap. 3.95 (ISBN 0-89081-205-5, 2055). Harvest Hse.
Wright, Norman. Fulfilled Marriage. LC 76-21981. (Answer Ser.). 1976. pap. 1.25 (ISBN 0-89081-060-5, 0605). Harvest Hse.
Wright, Rusty & Wright, Linda. How to Unlock the Secrets of Love, Sex, & Marriage. LC 81-80373. 128p. 1981. pap. 3.95 (ISBN 0-89081-288-8). Harvest Hse.
Wunsch, William F. Marriage (Ideals & Realizations) 155p. 1973. 1.75 (ISBN 0-87785-122-0). Swedenborg.
Yancy, Philip. After the Wedding: Nine Couples Tell How They Survived the Most Dangerous Years of Marriage. LC 76-195317. 1976. 5.95 (ISBN 0-87680-456-3, 80456). Word Bks.
Zola, Marion. All the Good Ones Are Married. Kane, Susan N., ed. LC 80-5776. 256p. 1981. 12.95 (ISBN 0-8129-0967-4). Times Bks.
Zouras, Nicholas L. & Zouras, Mary A. America, Who Shall We Be? (Illus.). 1979. 8.37 (ISBN 0-934176-00-0). Family World Pub Hse.

MARRIAGE–ANNULMENT

see also Divorce

Gould Editorial Staff, ed. Uncontested Divorces & Annulments in New York. 2nd ed. 175p. 1980. text ed. 12.50 (ISBN 0-87526-251-1). Gould.
Marshner, William H. Annulment or Divorce? 96p. (Orig.). 1978. pap. 2.95 (ISBN 0-931888-00-X, Chris. Coll. Pr.). Christendom Pubns.
Noonan, John T., Jr. Power to Dissolve: Lawyers & Marriages in the Courts of the Roman Curia. LC 75-176044. (Illus.). 464p. 1972. 25.00x (ISBN 0-674-69575-5, Belknap Pr). Harvard U Pr.
Weinberg, Meyer. Illinois Divorce, Separate Maintenance & Annulment, with Forms. 2nd ed. 1969. with suppl. 25.00 (ISBN 0-672-82919-3, Bobbs-Merrill Law); 1976 suppl. 10.00 (ISBN 0-672-82804-9). Michie-Bobbs.

MARRIAGE–ANNULMENT (CANON LAW)

Castelli, James. Que esta haciendo la Iglesia por los catolicos divorciados y casados de nuevo. Hechavarria, Juan C., tr. Orig. Title: What the Church Is Doing for Divorced & Remarried Catholics. (Illus., Orig., Span.). 1979. pap. 1.50 (ISBN 0-89570-188-X). Claretian Pubns.
Tierney, Terence E. Annulment: Do You Have a Case? LC 78-6790. 1978. pap. 3.95 (ISBN 0-8189-0372-4). Alba.

MARRIAGE–BIBLICAL TEACHING

Augustine, St. Treatises on Marriage & Other Subjects. (Fathers of the Church Ser.: Vol. 27). 23.00 (ISBN 0-8132-0027-X). Cath U Pr.
Bailey, Derrick S. The Mystery of Love & Marriage: A Study in the Theology of Sexual Relation. LC 77-3313. 1977. Repr. of 1952 ed. lib. bdg. 15.00 (ISBN 0-8371-9577-2, BAML). Greenwood.
Bryant, Al. Love Songs: Daily Meditations for Married Couples. 1978. 7.95 (ISBN 0-8499-0080-8). Word Bks.
Geromel, Gene, Jr. How You Can Help Your Engaged Child Prepare for Christian Marriage. (Illus.). 40p. 1981. pap. 1.95 (ISBN 0-89570-203-7). Claretian Pubns.
Gundry, Patricia. Heirs Together: Biblical Equality in Marriage. 192p. 1980. 7.95 (ISBN 0-310-25370-5). Zondervan.
Hubbard, David A. Is the Family Here to Stay? LC 74-170912. 1971. pap. 0.95 (ISBN 0-87680-928-X, 90028). Word Bks.
Mace, David R. Getting Ready for Marriage. LC 75-175280. 1972. 6.95 (ISBN 0-687-14135-4). Abingdon.
Mack, Wayne. Homework Manual for Biblical Counseling: Family & Marital Problems, Vol. 2. pap. 3.50 (ISBN 0-87552-357-9). Presby & Reformed.
Seagren, Daniel R. Couples in the Bible. (Contemporary Discussion Ser). 1972. pap. 2.50 (ISBN 0-8010-7971-3). Baker Bk.
Small, Dwight H. Marriage As Equal Partnership. 1980. pap. 2.95 (ISBN 0-8010-8177-7). Baker Bk.
Swindoll, Charles R. Strike the Original Match. LC 80-15639. 1980. 7.95 (ISBN 0-930014-36-7); pap. 4.95 (ISBN 0-930014-37-5); study guide 2.95 (ISBN 0-930014-49-9). Multnomah.
A Theology of Marriage. 2nd ed. 3.95 (ISBN 0-02-659500-1, 65950). Benziger Pub Co.
Timmons, Tim. God's Plan for Your Marriage: An Important Book for Newlyweds & Engaged Couples. 1978. 4.50 (ISBN 0-8010-8839-9). Baker Bk.
--Maximum Marriage. 1976. 4.95 (ISBN 0-8007-0801-6). Revell.
Warren, Thomas B. Marriage Is for Those Who Love God & One Another. 1976. 5.95 (ISBN 0-934916-37-3). Natl Christian Pr.
Warren, Thomas B., ed. Your Marriage Can Be Great. 1978. pap. 13.95 (ISBN 0-934916-44-6). Natl Christian Pr.
Wright, H. Norman. The Living Marriage. (Illus.). 1975. 9.95 (ISBN 0-8007-0722-2). Revell.

MARRIAGE–BRUDERHOF COMMUNITIES

Arnold, Eberhard. Love & Marriage in the Spirit. LC 64-24321. 1965. 7.95 (ISBN 0-87486-103-9). Plough.

MARRIAGE–CATHOLIC CHURCH

see also Marriage (Canon Law)

Bassett, William W., ed. Bond of Marriage. 1968. 8.95x (ISBN 0-268-00023-9). U of Notre Dame Pr.
Bockle, Franz, ed. Future of Marriage As an Institution. LC 70-113057. (Concilium Ser.: Religion in the Seventies: Vol. 55). 1970. pap. 4.95 (ISBN 0-8245-0215-9). Crossroad NY.
Bosler, Raymond T. What They Ask About Marriage. LC 75-11019. 288p. 1975. pap. 3.50 (ISBN 0-87793-096-1). Ave Maria.
Castelli, James. Que esta haciendo la Iglesia por los catolicos divorciados y casados de nuevo. Hechavarria, Juan C., tr. Orig. Title: What the Church Is Doing for Divorced & Remarried Catholics. (Illus., Orig., Span.). 1979. pap. 1.50 (ISBN 0-89570-188-X). Claretian Pubns.
--What the Church Is Doing for Divorced & Remarried Catholics. (Illus.). 1978. pap. 1.95 (ISBN 0-89570-155-3). Claretian Pubns.
Catoir, John. Catholics & Broken Marriage. LC 78-74434. 72p. 1979. pap. 1.95 (ISBN 0-87793-176-3). Ave Maria.
Coleman, William & Coleman, Patricia. Sexuality & Marriage. rev. ed. (Mine Is the Morning Ser.). 160p. (gr. 9-12). 1978. tchrs. manual & duplicator masters 16.95 (ISBN 0-89622-064-8). Twenty-Third.
Dominian, J. Christian Marriage. pap. 3.50 (ISBN 0-8199-0010-9, L38105). Franciscan Herald.
Hiesberger, Jean M., ed. Marriage Enrichment Manual. (Paths of Life Ser.). 1980. cancelled (ISBN 0-8091-9187-3). Paulist Pr.
--Marriage Preparation & Single Adult Living Manual. (Paths of Life Ser.). 1980. 5.95 (ISBN 0-8091-9186-5). Paulist Pr.
--Preparing for Marriage Handbook. (Paths of Life Ser.). 1980. 2.45 (ISBN 0-8091-2260-X). Paulist Pr.
Kennedy, Eugene. What a Modern Catholic Believes About Sex & Marriage. 1975. pap. 6.95 (ISBN 0-88347-059-4). Thomas More.
Langer, Thomas E. Christian Marriage: A Guide for Young People. rev. ed. 1967. pap. 2.96 (ISBN 0-02-820180-9). Glencoe.
LeMaire, H. Paul. Marrying Takes a Lifetime. 185p. 1981. pap. 5.95 (ISBN 0-686-75464-6). Twenty-Third.
Lynch, William A. Marriage Manual for Catholics. 1964. 4.95 (ISBN 0-671-45110-3). Trident.
Rite of Marriage. (Large Type, Two Colors, Homiletic Notes). red cloth 5.75 (ISBN 0-686-14316-7, 238/22). Catholic Bk Pub.
Rue, James J. & Shanahan, Louise. A Catechism for Divorced Catholics. rev. ed. 1978. pap. 2.95 (ISBN 0-8199-0754-5). Franciscan Herald.
Wojtyla, Karol. Fruitful & Responsible Love. (Orig.). 1979. pap. 2.95 (ISBN 0-8245-0310-4). Crossroad NY.
Wrenn, Lawrence G., ed. Divorce & Remarriage in the Catholic Church. LC 73-75744. 1973. pap. 4.95 (ISBN 0-8091-1769-X). Paulist Pr.

MARRIAGE–HISTORY

Cole, Margaret I. Marriage: Past & Present. LC 72-9632. Repr. of 1939 ed. 24.50 (ISBN 0-404-57431-9). AMS Pr.
Crawley, Ernest. The Mystic Rose: A Study of Primitive & Primitive Thought in Its Bearing on Marriage. 1932. 35.00 (ISBN 0-685-73522-2). Norwood Edns.
--Mystic Rose: A Study of Primitive Marriage & of Primitive Thought in Its Bearing on Marriage, 2 Vols. rev. & enl. ed. Besterman, Theodore, ed. LC 72-164193. 1971. Repr. of 1927 ed. 32.00 (ISBN 0-8103-3781-9). Gale.
--The Mystic Rose: A Study of Primitive Marriage and of Primitive Thought in Its Bearing on Marriage, 2 vols. Besterman, Theodore, ed. 1978. Repr. of 1927 ed. lib. bdg. 50.00 (ISBN 0-8495-0718-9). Arden Lib.
Ditzion, Sidney. Marriage, Morals, & Sex in America: A History of Ideas. 1978. pap. 6.95 (ISBN 0-393-00890-8, Norton Lib). Norton.
Duby, Georges. Medieval Marriage: Two Models from Twelfth-Century France. Forster, Elborg, tr. from Fr. LC 77-17255. (Johns Hopkins Symposia in Comparative History: No. 11). (Illus.). 1978. text ed. 12.00x (ISBN 0-8018-2049-9). Johns Hopkins.
Dupquier, J., et al, eds. Marriage & Remarriage in Populations of the Past. (Population & Social Structure Ser.). 1981. 72.00 (ISBN 0-12-224660-8). Acad Pr.
Goodsell, Willystine. A History of Marriage & the Family. rev. ed. LC 72-9641. Repr. of 1934 ed. 34.50 (ISBN 0-404-57446-7). AMS Pr.
Kohler, Josef. On the Prehistory of Marriage. Barnes, R. H., ed. LC 74-11626. (Classics in Anthropology Ser). x, 298p. 1975. pap. text ed. 12.50x (ISBN 0-226-45025-2, Midway Reprint). U of Chicago Pr.
McLennan, John F. Primitive Marriage. Riviere, Peter, ed. LC 72-111602. 1970. Repr. 9.50x (ISBN 0-226-56080-5). U of Chicago Pr.
--Primitive Marriage: An Inquiry into the Origin of the Form of Capture in Marriage Ceremonies. LC 72-9662. Repr. of 1865 ed. 17.00 (ISBN 0-404-57473-4). AMS Pr.
May, Elaine T. Great Expectations: Marriage & Divorce in Post-Victorian America. LC 80-10590. (Illus.). 1980. 15.00 (ISBN 0-226-51166-9). U of Chicago Pr.
Tegg, William. Knot Tied: Marriage Ceremonies of All Nations. LC 75-99073. 1970. Repr. of 1877 ed. 28.00 (ISBN 0-8103-3585-9). Gale.
Westermarck, Edward A. The History of Human Marriage, 3 vols. 5th ed. 1795p. Repr. of 1921 ed. 107.00 (ISBN 0-384-66954-9). Johnson Repr.

MARRIAGE–ISLAM

see also Marriage (Islamic Law)

Abdul-Rauf, Muhammed. Marriage in Islam: A Manual. LC 75-186483. 1972. 6.50 (ISBN 0-682-47431-2, Banner). Exposition.
Rauf, Dr. M. Marriage in Islam. 6.95 (ISBN 0-686-18461-0). Kazi Pubns.

MARRIAGE–JEWS

see also Marriage, Mixed

Abramowitz, Bernard. Marriage & Family Life Code of the Jewish Faith. (Heb., Heb, & Eng). 12.50 (ISBN 0-87559-098-5). Shalom.
Breur, Joseph. The Jewish Marriage. 3.00 (ISBN 0-87306-097-0). Feldheim.
Davidovitch, David. The Ketuba: Jewish Marriage Contracts Through the Ages. 2nd ed. (Illus.). 1974. 26.50 (ISBN 0-87203-054-7). Hermon.
Epstein, Louis M. The Jewish Marriage Contract: A Study in the Status of the Woman in Jewish Law. LC 73-2195. (The Jewish People; History, Religion, Literature Ser.). Repr. of 1927 ed. 25.00 (ISBN 0-405-05261-8). Arno.
--Marriage Laws in the Bible & the Talmud. 1942. 19.50 (ISBN 0-384-14535-3). Johnson Repr.
Feldman, David M. Birth Control in Jewish Law: Marital Relations, Contraception, & Abortion As Set Forth in the Classic Texts of Jewish Law. LC 79-16712. 1980. Repr. of 1968 ed. lib. bdg. 25.00x (ISBN 0-313-21297-X, FEBC). Greenwood.
Gaster, Moses. The Ketubah. new ed. LC 68-9532. (Illus.). 90p. 1974. 7.95 (ISBN 0-87203-029-6). Hermon.
Gittelsohn, Roland B. Love, Sex & Marriage: A Jewish View. (Illus.). (gr. 10-12). 1980. pap. 7.95x (ISBN 0-8074-0046-7, 142683). UAHC.
Goodman, Philip, ed. Jewish Marriage Anthology. Goodman, Hanna. LC 65-17045. (Illus.). 1965. 7.50 (ISBN 0-8276-0145-X, 236). Jewish Pubn.
How to Stop an Intermarriage. Date not set. 7.95 (ISBN 0-686-76518-4). Feldheim.
Kahane, Meir. Why Be Jewish? Intermarriage, Assimilation & Alienation. LC 77-8774. 1977. 8.95 (ISBN 0-8128-2239-0). Stein & Day.
Lamm, Maurice. The Jewish Way in Love & Marriage. LC 79-1760. 1980. 14.95 (ISBN 0-06-064916-X, HarpR). Har-Row.
Lamm, Norman. A Hedge of Roses: Jewish Insights into Marriage. LC 66-19539. 1977. pap. 2.50 (ISBN 0-87306-095-4). Feldheim.
Luka, Ronald & Zlotowitz, Bernard. When a Christian & a Jew Marry. LC 73-77393. 96p. (Orig.). 1973. pap. 1.95 (ISBN 0-8091-1748-7). Paulist Pr.

Man-Woman. Date not set. pap. 1.50 (ISBN 0-686-76542-7). Feldheim.
Rosenblatt. Under the Nuptial Canopy. 1975. 6.00 (ISBN 0-87306-109-8). Feldheim.
Routtenberg, Lilly S. & Seldin, Ruth R. The Jewish Wedding Book: A Practical Guide to the Traditions & Social Customs of the Jewish Wedding. LC 67-13723. (Illus.). 1969. pap. 4.50 (ISBN 0-8052-0186-6). Schocken.

MARRIAGE–ORTHODOX EASTERN CHURCH

Basaroff, F. The Sacrament of Matrimony According to the Doctrine & Ritual of the Eastern Orthodox Church. Bjerring, N., tr. from Russian. pap. 1.50 (ISBN 0-686-16370-2). Eastern Orthodox.
Coniaris, Anthony M. Getting Ready for Marriage in the Orthodox Church. 1972. pap. 1.00 (ISBN 0-937032-11-5). Light & Life Pub Co MN.
Constantelos, D. J. Marriage, Sexuality & Celibacy: A Greek Orthodox Perspective. 1975. pap. 3.95 (ISBN 0-937032-15-8). Light&Life Pub Co MN.

MARRIAGE–POETRY

Schaffer, Ulrich. A Growing Love: Meditations on Marriage and Commitment. LC 76-62951. (Illus.). 1977. pap. 3.95 (ISBN 0-06-067079-7, HarpR). Har-Row.
Webster, David E. To Love & to Cherish. LC 67-29308. (Illus.). 1968. boxed 4.95 (ISBN 0-8378-1714-5). Gibson.

MARRIAGE–PROHIBITED DEGREES

see Consanguinity; Marriage Law

MARRIAGE–SERMONS

see also Wedding Sermons

MARRIAGE–AFRICA

Bernard, Guy. Ville Africaine, Famille Urbaine: Les Enseignants De Kinshasa. (Recherches Africaines: No. 6). 1968. pap. 23.50x (ISBN 90-2797-543-4). Mouton.
Brain, Robert. Bangwa Kinship & Marriage. LC 70-166945. (Illus.). 1972. 24.95 (ISBN 0-521-08311-7). Cambridge U Pr.
Harrell-Bond, Barbara E. Modern Marriage in Sierra Leone: A Study of the Professional Group. (Change & Continuity in Africa Ser.). (Illus.). 1975. pap. text ed. 16.75x (ISBN 90-2797-871-9). Mouton.
Mair, Lucy P. African Marriage & Social Change. 2nd & rev. ed. 171p. 1969. 24.00x (ISBN 0-7146-1908-6, F Cass Co). Biblio Dist.
Nukunya, G. K. Kinship & Marriage Among the Anlo Ewe. LC 68-18054. (Monographs on Social Anthropology Ser: No. 37). 1969. text ed. 23.50x (ISBN 0-485-19537-2, Athlone Pr). Humanities.
Phillips, Arthur, ed. Survey of African Marriage & Family Life. LC 74-15079. Repr. of 1953 ed. 47.50 (ISBN 0-404-12128-4). AMS Pr.
Shropshire, D. W. Primitive Marriage & European Law: A South African Investigation. 186p. 1970. Repr. 25.00x (ISBN 0-7146-1913-2, F Cass Co). Biblio Dist.

MARRIAGE–ARABIA

Smith, William R. Kinship & Marriage in Early Arabia. new ed. Cook, Stanley A., ed. LC 76-44789. Repr. of 1903 ed. 22.00 (ISBN 0-404-15971-0). AMS Pr.

MARRIAGE–ASIA

Foon, Chew S. & MacDougall, John A. Forever Plural: The Perception & Practice of Inter-Communal Marriage in Singapore. LC 77-620031. (Papers in International Studies: Southeast Asia: No. 45). (Illus.). 1977. pap. 6.00 (ISBN 0-89680-030-X). Ohio U Ctr Int.
Lapuz, Lourdes V. Filipino Marriages in Crisis. 1977. wrps. 7.50x (ISBN 0-686-09466-2). Cellar.

MARRIAGE–BARBADOES

Greenfield, Sidney M. English Rustics in Black Skin: A Study of Modern Family Forms in a Pre-Industrialized Society. 1966. 5.00x (ISBN 0-8084-0121-1); pap. 1.95 (ISBN 0-8084-0122-X, B40). Coll & U Pr.

MARRIAGE–CHINA

Freedman, Maurice. Chinese Family & Marriage in Singapore. (Colonial Research Studies). pap. 23.00 (ISBN 0-384-16760-8). Johnson Repr.
Ku Chieh-Kang. Marriage & Funerals of Su-Chow. Bd. with Marriage & Funerals of Canton. Liu Wan-Chang. (Folklore Series of National Sun Yat-Sen University: No. 21). (Chinese.). 5.50 (ISBN 0-89986-065-6). E Langstaff.
Schak, David C. Dating & Mate-Selection in Modern Taiwan, No. 55. (Asian Folklore & Social Life Monograph). 264p. 1974. 6.60 (ISBN 0-89986-052-4). E Langstaff.
Wolf, Arthur P. & Huang, Chieh-Shan. Marriage & Adoption in China, 1845-1945. LC 78-66182. 1980. 18.95x (ISBN 0-8047-1027-9). Stanford U Pr.
Wu Man-Sha. Marriage Customs of the Chinese. (National Pekinguniversity & Chinese Assn. for Folklore, Folklore & Folkliterature Ser.: No. 30). (Chinese.). 6.00 (ISBN 0-89986-125-3). E Langstaff.

MARRIAGE–GREAT BRITAIN

Dickson, Lance E., intro. by. Treatise of Femme Coverts: Or the Lady's Law. LC 74-79267. 264p. 1974. Repr. of 1732 ed. text ed. 22.50x (ISBN 0-8377-2129-6). Rothman.
Gorer, Geoffrey. Sex & Marriage in England Today: A Study of the Views & Experience of the Under 45's. 318p. 1971. text ed. 10.00x (ISBN 0-391-00236-8). Humanities.
Helmholz, R. H. Marriage Litigation in Medieval England. LC 73-93395. (Studies in English Legal History). 272p. 1975. 36.00 (ISBN 0-521-20411-9). Cambridge U Pr.
Mattinson, Janet & Sinclair, Ian. Mate & Stalemate: Working with Marital Problems in a Social Services Dept. (The Practice of Social Work: Vol. 1). 318p. 1979. 21.95x (ISBN 0-631-11821-7, Pub. by Basil Blackwell England). Biblio Dist.
Orford, Jim & Edwards, Griffith. Alcoholism: A Comparison of Treatment & Advice, with a Study of the Influence of Marriage. (Maudsley Monographs: No. 26). (Illus.). 1978. text ed. 19.50x (ISBN 0-19-712148-9). Oxford U Pr.
Powell, Chilton L. English Domestic Relations, 1487-1653: A Study of Matrimony & Family Life in Theory & Practice As Revealed by the Literature, Law & History of the Period. LC 77-184232. (Illus.). xii, 274p. 1972. Repr. of 1917 ed. 17.00 (ISBN 0-8462-1662-0). Russell.
Ratcliff, Rosemary. Dear Worried Brown Eyes. 1969. 10.00 (ISBN 0-08-007041-8). Pergamon.
Walschap, Gerald. Marriage: Bibliotheca Neerlandica Ser. Incl. Ordeal. 1963. 10.00 (ISBN 0-8277-0261-2). British Bk Ctr.

MARRIAGE–GREECE

Licht, Hans, pseud. Sexual Life in Ancient Greece. Dawson, Lawrence, ed. Freese, J. H., tr. from Gr. LC 75-27675. (Illus.). 556p. 1976. Repr. of 1953 ed. lib. bdg. 31.50x (ISBN 0-8371-8464-9, BRSLG). Greenwood.

MARRIAGE–HAWAII

Adams, Romanzo. Interracial Marriage in Hawaii: A Study of Mutually Conditioned Processes of Acculturation & Amalgamation. LC 69-14907. (Criminology, Law Enforcement, & Social Problems Ser.: No. 65). (Illus.). 1969. Repr. of 1937 ed. 12.50 (ISBN 0-87585-065-0). Patterson Smith.
--Interracial Marriage in Hawaii: A Study of the Mutually Conditioned Processes of Acculturation & Amalgamation. LC 75-96473. (BCL Ser.: No. I). Repr. of 1937 ed. 12.00 (ISBN 0-404-00293-5). AMS Pr.

MARRIAGE–INDIA

Ahmad, Imtiaz, ed. Family, Kinship, & Marriage Among the Muslims. LC 77-74484. 1977. 17.50x (ISBN 0-88386-757-5). South Asia Bks.
Puthenkalam, J. Marriage & Family in Kerala. 1981. 16.00x (ISBN 0-8364-0687-7, Pub. by U Calgary India). South Asia Bks.
Reddy, V. N. Marriages in India. 1978. 13.50x (ISBN 0-8364-0300-2). South Asia Bks.
Srinvas, Mysore N. Marriage & Family in Mysore. LC 76-44794. Repr. of 1942 ed. 20.00 (ISBN 0-404-15975-3). AMS Pr.
Sur, A. K. Sex & Marriage in India. 1973. 6.00x (ISBN 0-8188-1194-3). Paragon.

MARRIAGE–NORWAY

Sundt, Eilert. On Marriage in Norway. Drake, M., tr. from Norwegian. LC 79-42648. 1980. 29.50 (ISBN 0-521-23199-X). Cambridge U Pr.

MARRIAGE–PALESTINE

Granqvist, H. Marriage Conditions in a Palestinian Village. (Societas Scientiarum Fennica, Commentationes Humaniarum Litterarum III: V. 1-8). (Illus.). 1980. Repr. of 1935 ed. text ed. 36.25x (ISBN 0-391-00955-9). Humanities.
Granqvist, Hilma N. Marriage Conditions in a Palestinian Village, 2 vols. LC 72-9644. Repr. of 1935 ed. Set. 52.50 (ISBN 0-404-57450-5). AMS Pr.

MARRIAGE–UNITED STATES

Arnold, William V., et al. Divorce: Prevention or Survival. LC 77-22066. 1977. pap. 4.95 (ISBN 0-664-24142-5). Westminster.
Baker, Russell P. Marriages & Obituaries from the Tennessee Baptist, Eighteen Forty-Four to Eighteen Sixty-Two. 137p. 1979. 18.50 (ISBN 0-89308-127-2). Southern Hist Pr.
Cahen, Alfred. Statistical Analysis of American Divorce. LC 68-58553. (Columbia University Studies in the Social Sciences: No. 360). Repr. of 1932 ed. 14.50 (ISBN 0-404-51360-3). AMS Pr.
Carlier, Auguste. Marriage in the United States. LC 70-169376. (Family in America Ser). 200p. 1972. Repr. of 1867 ed. 15.00 (ISBN 0-405-03853-4). Arno.
Chapman, Jane R. & Gates, Margaret, eds. Women into Wives: The Legal & Economic Impact of Marriage. LC 76-47070. (Sage Yearbooks in Women's Policy Studies: Vol. 2). 320p. 1977. 22.50 (ISBN 0-8039-0700-1); pap. 9.95 (ISBN 0-8039-0701-X). Sage.
Drachsler, Julius. Intermarriage in New York City: A Statistical Study of the Amalgamation of European Peoples. (Columbia University. Studies in the Social Sciences: No. 213). 7.50 (ISBN 0-404-51213-5). AMS Pr.
--Intermarriage in New York City: A Statistical Study of the Amalgamation of European Peoples. LC 74-145477. (The American Immigration Library). 204p. 1971. Repr. of 1921 ed. lib. bdg. 10.95x (ISBN 0-89198-009-1). Ozer.
Durkin, Henry P. Forty Four Hours to Change Your Life. LC 74-80349. 96p. (Orig.). 1974. pap. 1.75 (ISBN 0-8091-1849-1). Paulist Pr.
Francoeur, Robert T. Eve's New Rib. 1973. pap. 2.65 (ISBN 0-440-52340-0, Delta). Dell.
--Eve's New Rib: Twenty Faces of Sex, Marriage, & Family. LC 78-182328. 256p. 1972. 6.50 (ISBN 0-15-129384-8). HarBraceJ.
Freedman, Hy. Sex Link: The Three-Billion-Year-Old Urge & What the Animals Do About It. LC 77-8546. 224p. 1977. 8.95 (ISBN 0-87131-242-5). M Evans.
Groves, Ernest R. & Ogburn, William F. American Marriage & Family Relationships. LC 75-38129. (Demography Ser.). (Illus.). 1976. Repr. of 1928 ed. 30.00x (ISBN 0-405-07983-4). Arno.
Haven, Susan & Klein, Daniel. Seven Perfect Marriages That Failed. LC 74-28077. 280p. 1975. 25.00x (ISBN 0-8128-1777-X). Stein & Day.
Johnson, Robert A. Religious Assortative Mariage in the United States. LC 80-978. (Studies in Population). 1980. 25.00 (ISBN 0-12-386580-8). Acad Pr.
Kobrin, Frances E. & Goldscheider, Calvin. The Ethnic Factor in Family Structure & Mobility. LC 77-25838. 1978. 16.50 (ISBN 0-88410-358-7). Ballinger Pub.
L'Abate, Luciano & L'Abate, Bess. How to Avoid Divorce. LC 76-12389. 1976. pap. 4.95 (ISBN 0-8042-1118-3). John Knox.
Lafollette, Cecile T. Study of the Problems of Six Hundred-Fifty Two Gainfully Employed Married Women Homemakers. LC 71-176969. (Columbia University. Teachers College. Contributions to Education: No. 619). Repr. of 1934 ed. 17.50 (ISBN 0-404-55619-1). AMS Pr.
Lucas, S. Emmett, Jr., ed. Old Ninety-Six & Abbeville District, S. C. Marriages Seventeen Seventy-Seven to Eighteen Fifty-Two. 80p. 1979. 12.50 (ISBN 0-89308-173-6). Southern Hist Pr.
McGinnis, Tom. More Than Just a Friend: The Joys & Disappointments of Extramarital Affairs. 228p. 1981. 9.95 (ISBN 0-13-600973-5). P-H.
McKenney, Mary. Divorce: A Selected Annotated Bibliography. LC 74-22423. 1974. 10.00 (ISBN 0-8108-0777-7). Scarecrow.
May, Elaine T. Great Expectations: Marriage & Divorce in Post-Victorian America. LC 80-10590. (Illus.). 1980. 15.00 (ISBN 0-226-51166-9). U of Chicago Pr.
Morgan, Marabel. Total Joy. 224p. 1981. pap. 2.75 (ISBN 0-425-04913-2). Berkley Pub.
--The Total Woman Cookbook. 304p. 1981. pap. 2.95 (ISBN 0-425-05045-9). Berkley Pub.
Oliver, Bernard J., Jr. Marriage & You. 1964. 7.00 (ISBN 0-8084-0211-0); pap. 3.45 (ISBN 0-8084-0212-9, B48). Coll & U Pr.
Perry, John & Perry, Erna. Pairing & Parenthood. (Illus.). 1976. text ed. 18.95 scp (ISBN 0-06-386751-6, HarpC); tchrs ed. free (ISBN 0-06-375931-4). Har-Row.
Pietropinto, Anthony & Simenauer, Jacqueline. Husbands & Wives: A Nationwide Survey of Marriage. LC 78-58174. 1979. 12.50 (ISBN 0-8129-0792-2). Times Bks.
Scanzoni, John. Sexual Bargaining: Power Politics in the American Marriage. 1972. pap. 2.95 (ISBN 0-13-807453-4, Spec). P-H.
Schreiber, Angela M., ed. Marriage & Family in a World of Change. LC 75-14740. (Know Your Faith Ser.). (Illus.). 184p. 1975. pap. 2.25 (ISBN 0-87793-097-X). Ave Maria.
Schultz, David A. & Rodgers, Stanley F. Marriage, Family & Personal Fulfillment. (Illus.). 432p. 1975. text ed. 19.95 (ISBN 0-13-559377-8). P-H.
Shipp, Audrey, ed. First Marriages: United States Nineteen Sixty-Eight to Nineteen Seventy-Six. (Ser. 21: No. 35). 1979. pap. text ed. 1.75 (ISBN 0-8406-0168-9). Natl Ctr Health Stats.
Skolnick, Arlene. The Intimate Environment: Exploring Marriage & Family. 2nd ed. 1978. 17.95 (ISBN 0-316-79700-6); instructor's manual free, by dale harrentsian (ISBN 0-316-79701-4). Little.
Snyder, William L. The Geography of Marriage or Legal Perplexities of Wedlock in the United States. Repr. of 1889 ed. lib. bdg. 35.00 (ISBN 0-8495-5012-2). Arden Lib.
Stouffer, Samuel A. & Lazarsfeld, Paul F. Research Memorandum on the Family in the Depression. LC 76-162839. (Studies in the Social Aspects of the Depression). 1971. Repr. of 1937 ed. 12.00 (ISBN 0-405-00842-2). Arno.
United States. Bureau of the Census. Marriage & Divorce, Nineteen Sixteen, Nineteen Twenty-Two to Thirty-Two, 12 vols. in one. LC 78-24170. 1979. Repr. of 1919 ed. lib. bdg. 62.50x (ISBN 0-313-20694-5, USMA). Greenwood.
Viscott, David. How to Live with Another Person. LC 74-80711. 148p. 1974. 6.95 (ISBN 0-87795-092-X). Arbor Hse.
--How to Live with Another Person. 1976. pap. 2.25 (ISBN 0-671-83566-1, 80272). PB.
Warner, Ralph & Ihara, Toni. California Marriage & Divorce Law. 4th ed. 1981. pap. 7.95 (ISBN 0-917316-16-9). Nolo Pr.
Weiss, Robert S. Marital Separation. LC 74-78307. 1975. 12.50x (ISBN 0-465-04388-7). Basic.
Wright, Carroll D. Marriage & Divorce in the United States: 1867-1886. LC 75-38146. (Demography Ser.). (Illus.). 1976. Repr. of 1897 ed. 59.00x (ISBN 0-405-07999-0). Arno.
Young, Donald, ed. The Modern American Family. LC 72-169402. (Family in America Ser). 232p. 1972. Repr. of 1932 ed. 14.00 (ISBN 0-405-03879-8). Arno.

MARRIAGE (CANON LAW)

see also Marriage–Annulment (Canon Law)

Bontrager, G. Edwin. Divorce & the Faithful Church. LC 78-4671. 1978. 7.95 (ISBN 0-8361-1850-2); pap. 5.95 (ISBN 0-8361-1851-0). Herald Pr.
Castelli, James. Que esta haciendo la Iglesia por los catolicos divorciados y casados de nuevo. Hechavarria, Juan C., tr. Orig. Title: What the Church Is Doing for Divorced & Remarried Catholics. (Illus., Orig., Span.). 1979. pap. 1.50 (ISBN 0-89570-188-X). Claretian Pubns.
Esmein, Adhemar. Mariage En Droit Canonique, 2 Vols. (Fr). 1969. Repr. of 1891 ed. Set. 47.00 (ISBN 0-8337-1072-9). B Franklin.
Mace, David R. Modern Marriage & the Clergy. LC 74-19593. 1977. 7.95 (ISBN 0-87705-368-5). Human Sci Pr.
Marshner, William H. Annulment or Divorce? 96p. (Orig.). 1978. pap. 2.95 (ISBN 0-931888-00-X, Chris. Coll. Pr.). Christendom Pubns.
Muggeridge, Malcolm, et al. Christian Married Love: Five Contributions. Dennehy, Raymond, ed. Englund, Sergia & Leiva, Erasmo, trs. 150p. (Orig.). 1981. pap. price not set (ISBN 0-89870-008-6). Ignatius Pr.
Richards, Larry. Remarriage. 1981. 7.95 (ISBN 0-686-72231-0). Word Bks.
Siegle, Bernard. Marriage Today: A Commentary on the Code of Canon Law. 3rd ed. LC 79-18786. 1979. pap. 10.95 (ISBN 0-8189-0384-8). Alba.
West, Morris L. & Francis, Robert. Scandal in the Assembly: A Bill of Complaints & a Proposal for Reform in the Matrimonial Laws & Tribunals of the Roman Catholic Church. 1970. 4.95 (ISBN 0-688-02432-7). Morrow.
Young, James J., ed. Ministering to the Divorced Catholic. LC 78-61731. 1978. pap. 6.95 (ISBN 0-8091-2142-5). Paulist Pr.

MARRIAGE (ISLAMIC LAW)

Shukri, Ahmed. Muhammedan Law of Marriage & Divorce. (Columbia University. Contributions to Oriental History & Philology: No. 7). Repr. of 1917 ed. 15.25 (ISBN 0-404-50537-6). AMS Pr.

MARRIAGE (JEWISH LAW)

see Marriage–Jews

MARRIAGE, CHILD

see Child Marriage

MARRIAGE, INTERRACIAL

see Interracial Marriage

MARRIAGE, MIXED

Here are entered works on marriage between persons of different religions, or person of different denominations within christianity. Works on marriage between persons of different races are entered under the heading Miscegenation.

see also Interracial Marriage

Berry, Jo. Beloved Unbeliever: Loving Your Husband into the Faith. 176p. (Orig.). 1981. pap. 4.95 (ISBN 0-310-42621-9). Zondervan.
Besanceney, Paul H. Interfaith Marriages: Who & Why. 1970. 6.50 (ISBN 0-8084-0164-5); pap. 2.95 (ISBN 0-8084-0165-3, B53). Coll & U Pr.
Billnitzer, Harold. Chances in a Mixed Marriage. 1978. pap. 1.30 (ISBN 0-933350-11-2). Morse Pr.
Day, Caroline. Study of Some Negro-White Families in the U. S. LC 76-106857. (Illus.). Repr. of 1932 ed. 27.00x (ISBN 0-8371-3479-X, Pub. by Negro U Pr). Greenwood.
Deal, William. God's Answer for the Unequally Yoked. LC 80-67387. 96p. 1980. pap. 2.95 (ISBN 0-89107-182-2). Good News.
DeGrave, Louise. From This Day Forward: Staying Married When No One Else Is & Other Reckless Acts. 228p. 1981. 10.95 (ISBN 0-316-17930-2). Little.

Gordis, Robert. Love & Sex: A Modern Jewish Perspective. 290p. 1978. 8.95 (ISBN 0-374-19252-9). FS&G.
Gordon, Albert I. Intermarriage: Interfaith, Interracial, Interethnic. LC 80-19279. (Illus.). xiii, 420p. 1980. Repr. of 1966 ed. lib. bdg. 29.75x (ISBN 0-313-22711-X, GOIN). Greenwood.
Kahane, Meir. Why Be Jewish? Intermarriage, Assimilation & Alienation. LC 77-8774. 1977. 8.95 (ISBN 0-8128-2239-0). Stein & Day.
Kannan, C. T. Inter-Racial Marriages in London: A Comparative Study. 1972. 10.00 (ISBN 0-685-79107-6). Heinman.
Kirshenbaum, David. Mixed Marriage & the Jewish Future. LC 58-10451. 1958. 4.95 (ISBN 0-8197-0098-3). Bloch.
Larsson, Clotye M., ed. Marriage Across the Color Line. 1965. 4.95 (ISBN 0-87485-014-2). Johnson Chi.
Luka, Ronald & Zlotowitz, Bernard. When a Christian & a Jew Marry. LC 73-77393. 96p. (Orig.). 1973. pap. 1.95 (ISBN 0-8091-1748-7). Paulist Pr.
Lunday, Berneice. Unblessed. LC 78-15244. (Orion Ser). 1979. pap. 1.95 (ISBN 0-8127-0200-X). Review & Herald.
Mayer, John E. Jewish-Gentile Courtships: An Exploratory Study of a Social Process. LC 80-16130. x, 240p. 1980. Repr. of 1961 ed. lib. bdg. 22.50x (ISBN 0-313-22465-X, MAJG). Greenwood.
Sandmel, Samuel. When a Jew & Christian Marry. LC 77-78639. 132p. (Orig.). 1977. pap. 3.25 (ISBN 0-8006-1311-2, 1-1311). Fortress.
Thomas, John L. Beginning Your Marriage, 2 vols. 1980. pap. 1.75 standard ed., lc 80-65486 (ISBN 0-915388-06-5); pap. 1.95 interfaith ed., LC 80-65487 (ISBN 0-915388-07-3). Buckley Pubns.
Walker, Alexander. Intermarriage. 75.00 (ISBN 0-87968-356-2). Gordon Pr.

MARRIAGE, PROMISE OF
see Betrothal

MARRIAGE COUNSELING

Ables, Billie S. & Brandsma, Jeffrey M. Therapy for Couples: A Clinician's Guide for Effective Treatment. LC 76-50698. (Social & Behavioral Science Ser.). 1977. text ed. 16.95x (ISBN 0-87589-312-0). Jossey-Bass.
Abse, D. Wilfred, et al. Marital & Sexual Counseling in Medical Practice. 2nd ed. 1974. text ed. 22.00x (ISBN 0-06-140045-9, Harper Medical). Har-Row.
Ard, Ben N., Jr. & Ard, Constance C., eds. Handbook of Marriage Counseling. LC 69-20467. 1976. 15.95x (ISBN 0-8314-0054-4). Sci & Behavior.
Arnold, William V., et al. Divorce: Prevention or Survival. LC 77-22066. 1977. pap. 4.95 (ISBN 0-664-24142-5). Westminster.
Bagarozzi, Dennis & Jackson, Robert W. Marital & Family Therapy: New Perspectives in Theory, Research & Practice. 1982. in prep. (ISBN 0-89885-069-X). Human Sci Pr.
Barbeau, Clayton C. Joy of Marriage. Orig. Title: Creative Marriage: the Middle Years. 132p. 1980. pap. 4.95 (ISBN 0-03-057841-8). Winston Pr.
Barber, Aldyth & Barber, Cyril. Your Marriage Has Real Possibilities. 200p. (Orig.). 1981. pap. 4.95 (ISBN 0-89840-015-5). Heres Life.
Beck, Dorothy F. Research Findings on the Outcomes of Marital Counseling. 1975. pap. 1.00 (ISBN 0-87304-138-0). Family Serv.
Berkey, Barry R. Save Your Marriage. LC 75-45338. 224p. 1976. 16.95x (ISBN 0-88229-235-8). Nelson-Hall.
Billnitzer, Harold. Before You Divorce. 1978. pap. 0.75 (ISBN 0-933350-12-0). Morse Pr.
Blanck, Rubin & Blanck, Gertrude. Marriage & Personal Development. LC 68-9577. 191p. 1968. 17.50x (ISBN 0-231-03150-5). Columbia U Pr.
Bockus, Frank. Couple Therapy. LC 80-66923. 300p. 1980. 27.50 (ISBN 0-87668-412-6). Aronson.
Bowlby, John. Separation: Anxiety & Anger. LC 70-78464. (Attachment & Loss Ser.: Vol. 2). 429p. 1973. text ed. 20.00x (ISBN 0-465-07691-2); pap. 4.95x (ISBN 0-465-09716-2, CN-5016). Basic.
Brand, Henry & Landrum, Phil. Como Mejorao Mi Matrimonio. (Span.). Date not set. pap. 2.00 (ISBN 0-686-75326-7). Life Pubs Intl.
Broderick, Carlfred. Couples: How to Confront Problems & Maintain Loving Relationships. 1979. 13.95 (ISBN 0-671-24246-6). S&S.
Brown, Joan W. & Brown, Bill. Together Each Day. 1980. 9.95 (ISBN 0-8007-1127-0). Revell.
Bustanoby, Andre & Bustanoby, Fay. Just Talk to Me. 192p. (Orig.). 1981. pap. text ed. 5.95 (ISBN 0-310-22181-1). Zondervan.
Carson, Mary. How to Make Marriage Last a Lifetime. (Illus., Orig.). 1979. pap. 1.95 (ISBN 0-89570-185-5, CP-325). Claretian Pubns.
Chapman, Gary. Toward a Growing Marriage. 1979. 7.95 (ISBN 0-8024-8787-4); pap. 4.95 (ISBN 0-8024-8789-0). Moody.
Chesser, Barbara J. & Gray, Ava A. Marriage: Creating a Partnership, an Experiential Approach to the Study of Marriage & the Family. 2nd ed. (Orig.). 1979. pap. text ed. 17.95 (ISBN 0-8403-2101-5). Kendall-Hunt.
Chick, Jack T., illus. The Marriage Mess. (Illus.). 224p. pap. 2.95 (ISBN 0-937958-05-0). Chick Pubns.
Clinebell, Howard J. Growth Counseling for Marriage Enrichment: Pre-Marriage & the Early Years. Stone, Howard W., ed. LC 74-26335. (Creative Pastoral Care & Counseling Ser.). 96p. 1975. pap. 3.25 (ISBN 0-8006-0551-9, 1-551). Fortress.
--Growth Counseling for Mid-Years Couples. Stone, Howard W., ed. LC 76-7863. (Creative Pastoral Care & Counseling Ser.). 1977. pap. 3.25 (ISBN 0-8006-0558-6, 1-558). Fortress.
Cook, et al. Family Mediation Workbook. Polk, Donice, ed. 90p. (Orig.). 1980. pap. 10.00 (ISBN 0-686-29084-4). D Polk.
Dale, Robert D. & Dale, Carrie Kondy. Making Good Marriages Better. LC 78-60052. 1978. 4.95 (ISBN 0-8054-5631-7). Broadman.
Deal, William S. Happiness & Harmony in Marriage. pap. 1.95 (ISBN 0-686-13723-X). Deal Pubns.
--Picking a Partner. 1.50 (ISBN 0-686-13716-7). Deal Pubns.
DeJong, Peter & Wilson, Donald R. Husband & Wife: The Sexes in Scripture & Society. 1979. 6.95 (ISBN 0-310-37760-9). Zondervan.
Del Vecchio, Anthony & Del Vecchio, Mary. Preparing for the Sacrament of Marriage. LC 80-67721. (Illus.). 144p. (Orig.). 1980. pap. 3.95 (ISBN 0-87793-208-5). Ave Maria.
DeVille, Roberta & DeVille, Jard. Lovers for Life: The Key to a Loving & Lasting Marriage. LC 80-10652. 224p. 1980. 8.95 (ISBN 0-688-03618-X). Morrow.
Dicks, Henry V. Marital Tensions. 1967 ed. LC 67-24965. 12.50x (ISBN 0-465-04390-9). Basic.
Dillow, Linda. Creative Counterpart Bible Study & Project Guide. LC 78-675. 1978. pap. 1.95 (ISBN 0-8407-5648-8). Nelson.
Dobbert, John. First Aid for Marriage. LC 78-56106. (Orig.). 1979. pap. 3.95 (ISBN 0-88449-036-X). Vision Hse.
Dobson, James C. Straight Talk to Men & Their Wives. 1980. 8.95 (ISBN 0-8499-0260-6). Word Bks.
Dominiam, Jack. Marital Pathology. 1980. 11.00x (ISBN 0-686-75609-6, Pub. by Darton-Longman-Todd England). State Mutual Bk.
Dominian, J. Marital Breakdown. 1969. 5.95 (ISBN 0-8199-0151-2, L38436). Franciscan Herald.
Durkin, Mary G. & Anzia, Joan M. Marital Intimacy. 92p. 1980. pap. 6.95 (ISBN 0-8362-3601-7). Andrews & McMeel.
Edelman, Alice & Stuzin, Roz. How to Survive a Second Marriage. 1980. 11.95 (ISBN 0-8184-0307-1). Lyle Stuart.
Erdahl, Lowell & Erdahl, Carol. Be Good to Each Other: An Open Letter on Marriage. LC 80-8893. 96p. 1981. pap. 3.95 (ISBN 0-06-062248-2, RD358, HarpR). Har-Row.
Eyrich, Howard A. Three to Get Ready. 1979. pap. 3.95 (ISBN 0-8010-3350-0). Baker Bk.
--Three to Get Ready: A Christian Premarital Counselor's Manual. 1978. pap. 3.95 (ISBN 0-87552-259-9). Presby & Refomed.
Fanshel, David & Moss, Freda. Playback: A Marriage in Jeopardy Examined. LC 72-170925. 1972. 17.50x (ISBN 0-231-03573-X); pap. 6.00x (ISBN 0-231-03574-8); 6 cassettes o.p. 100.00 (ISBN 0-685-00288-8). Columbia U Pr.
Filsinger, Erik E. & Lewis, Robert A. Marital Observation & Behavioral Assessment. (Sage Focus Editions: Vol. 34). 320p. 1981. 20.00 (ISBN 0-8039-1570-5); pap. 9.95 (ISBN 0-8039-1571-3). Sage.
Fitzgerald, R. V. Conjoint Marital Therapy. LC 73-81208. 256p. 1973. 25.00x (ISBN 0-87668-091-0). Aronson.
Florio, Anthony. You Can Make Your Marriage Stronger. (Christian Counseling Aids Ser). 1978. pap. 0.75 (ISBN 0-8010-3484-1). Baker Bk.
Framo, James L. Explorations in Marital & Family Therapy: Selected Papers of James L. Framo. Date not set. price not set (ISBN 0-8261-3400-9). Springer Pub.
Gallagher, Chuck. Marriage Encounter: As I Have Loved You. LC 75-12224. 168p. 1975. 6.95 (ISBN 0-385-00991-7). Doubleday.
Glick, Ira D. & Kessler, David, eds. Marital & Family Therapy: An Introductory Text. 2nd ed. 352p. 1980. 23.50 (ISBN 0-8089-1232-1). Grune.
Grace, Chester G. The Confidential Message to a Couple Who Are on the Verge of Divorce. (The Intimate Life of Man Library). (Illus.). 97p. 1980. 19.45 (ISBN 0-930582-75-6). Gloucester Art.
Greene, Bernard L. A Clinical Approach to Marital Problems: Diagnosis, Prevention & Treatment. 2nd ed. (Illus.). 556p. 1981. text ed. 53.75 (ISBN 0-398-04138-5). C C Thomas.
Gurman, Alan S. & Rice, David G., eds. Couples in Conflict. LC 74-6951. 372p. 1975. 30.00x (ISBN 0-87668-150-X). Aronson.
Hardy, Richard E. & Cull, John G., eds. Creative Divorce Through Social & Psychological Approaches. (American Lectures in Social & Rehabilitation Psychology Ser.). 192p. 1975. text ed. 16.50 (ISBN 0-398-03101-0). C C Thomas.
--Techniques & Approaches in Marital & Family Counseling. (American Lectures in Social & Rehabilitation Psychology Ser.). 240p. 1974. text ed. 18.75 (ISBN 0-398-03093-6). C C Thomas.
Hauck, Paul A. Marriage Is a Loving Business. 1977. pap. 3.95 (ISBN 0-664-24137-9). Westminster.
Hawkins, Robert L. A Pastor's Primer for Premarital Guidance. 1978. pap. 3.95 (ISBN 0-686-24647-0). R L Hawkins.
Haynes, John M. Divorce Mediation: A Practical Guide for Therapists & Counselors. LC 80-25065. 193p. 1981. 17.95 (ISBN 0-8261-2590-5); pap. write for info. (ISBN 0-8261-2591-3). Springer Pub.
Herbert, W. L. & Jarvis, F. J. Marriage Counselling in the Community. 1970. 8.25 (ISBN 0-08-006911-8); pap. 5.75 (ISBN 0-08-006910-X). Pergamon.
Herbert, W. L. & Jarvis, F. V. Art of Marriage Counseling. 1959. 6.95 (ISBN 0-87523-120-9). Emerson.
Hinchcliffe, Mary K., et al. The Melancholy Marriage: Depression in Marriage & Psychosocial Approaches to Therapy. LC 78-4526. 1978. 26.25 (ISBN 0-471-99650-5, Pub. by Wiley-Interscience). Wiley.
Hine, James R. Alternative to Divorce. 3rd ed. 1978. pap. 4.95 (ISBN 0-8134-2008-3, 2008). Interstate.
--Marriage Counseling Kit. 14.75 (ISBN 0-8134-2096-2, 2096). Interstate.
Hof, Larry & Miller, William. Marriage Enrichment: Philosophy Process & Program. (Illus.). 192p. 1980. text ed. 14.95 (ISBN 0-87619-717-9). R J Brady.
How to Do Creative Marriage Counseling. 8.05 (ISBN 0-686-31579-0). Ministers Life.
Jackins, Harvey. Co-Counseling for Married Couples. 1965. pap. 0.50 (ISBN 0-911214-13-5). Rational Isl.
Jacobson, Neil S. & Margolin, Gayla. Marital Therapy: Strategies Based on Social Learning & Behavior Exchange Principles. LC 79-728. 1979. 17.50 (ISBN 0-87630-199-5). Brunner Mazel.
Kenny, James & Kenny, Mary. When Your Marriage Goes Stale. LC 79-51277. (When Bks). (Illus.). 1979. pap. 2.45 (ISBN 0-87029-150-5, 20236). Abbey.
Klemer, Richard H., ed. Counseling in Marital & Sexual Problems: A Physician's Handbook. LC 75-31593. 320p. 1976. Repr. of 1965 ed. 14.50 (ISBN 0-88275-362-2). Krieger.
Knight, John F. What a Married Couple Should Know About Sex. LC 78-71469. 1979. pap. 5.95 (ISBN 0-8163-0388-6, 23104-3). Pacific Pr Pub Assn.
Kohut, Nester C. Therapeutic Family Law. LC 68-16525. 1968. 7.00 (ISBN 0-910574-09-X). Am Family.
Kreitler, Peter, et al. Affair Prevention. 256p. 1981. 10.95 (ISBN 0-02-566710-6). Macmillan.
Kuhn, Jerold R. Marriage Counseling: Fact or Fallacy? LC 80-22269. 146p. 1980. Repr. of 1973 ed. lib. bdg. 9.95x (ISBN 0-89370-622-1). Borgo Pr.
--Marriage Counseling: Fact or Fallacy? 160p. (Orig.). 1973. pap. 2.95 (ISBN 0-87877-022-4, W-22). Newcastle Pub.
L'Abate, Luciano & L'Abate, Bess. How to Avoid Divorce. LC 76-12389. 1976. pap. 4.95 (ISBN 0-8042-1118-3). John Knox.
Lantz, James E. Family & Marital Therapy: A Transactional Approach. (Illus.). 224p. 1978. pap. 13.50 (ISBN 0-8385-2521-0). ACC.
Lasswell, Marcia & Lobsenz, Norman M. No-Fault Marriage. 1977. pap. 1.95 (ISBN 0-345-27085-1). Ballantine.
Laz, Medard. Six Levels of a Happy Marriage. 1978. pap. 1.50 (ISBN 0-89243-079-6). Liguori Pubns.
Leaman, David R. Making Decisions: A Guide for Couples. LC 78-27153. 1979. pap. 2.95 (ISBN 0-8361-1882-0). Herald Pr.
Lee, Mark W. How to Have a Good Marriage. LC 78-56794. 1981. pap. 5.95 (ISBN 0-915684-89-6). Christian Herald.
--Time Bombs in Marriage. LC 81-65727. 192p. 1981. pap. 5.95 (ISBN 0-915684-92-6). Christian Herald.
Le Peau, Phyllis J. & Le Peau, Andrew T. One Plus One Equals One. 96p. (Orig.). 1981. pap. 3.95 (ISBN 0-87784-803-3). Inter-Varsity.
Liberman, R. P., et al. The Handbook of Marital Therapy: A Positive Approach to Helping Troubled Relationships. (Applied Clinical Psychology Ser.). (Illus.). 250p. 1980. 19.50 (ISBN 0-306-40235-1, Plenum Pr). Plenum Pub.
Lovett, Gene. All Bliss & Heaven Too: Sex & the Bible. new ed. (Illus.). 1979. 9.95 (ISBN 0-930054-02-4); pap. 5.95 (ISBN 0-930054-01-6). Titan Pr.
Mace, David & Mace, Vera. How to Have a Happy Marriage. (Festival Bks). 1979. pap. 1.95 (ISBN 0-687-17831-2). Abingdon.
--Marriage Enrichment in the Church. LC 76-49710. 1977. pap. 3.25 (ISBN 0-8054-5621-X). Broadman.
Mace, Vera & Mace, David. How to Have a Happy Marriage. 176p. 1979. pap. 1.95 (ISBN 0-441-34503-4, Pub. by Charter Bks). Ace Bks.
Mack, Wayne. How to Develop Deep Unity in the Marriage Relationship. (Christian Growth Ser.). 1977. pap. 4.50 (ISBN 0-87552-333-1). Presby & Reformed.
McMillin, Barbara. No Credentials, but Credible Counseling. 61p. (Orig.). 1981. pap. 10.50 (ISBN 0-912178-05-1). Mor Mac.
Marshall, Bill & Marshall, Christina M. The Marriage Secret. 1980. 8.95 (ISBN 0-8437-3349-7). Hammond Inc.
Martin, Peter A. A Marital Therapy Manual. LC 76-2587. 1976. 15.00 (ISBN 0-87630-120-0). Brunner-Mazel.
Mason, Robert L. & Jacobs, Carrie. How to Choose the Wrong Marriage Partner & Live Unhappily Ever After. LC 78-52452. 1979. pap. 5.50 (ISBN 0-8042-2093-X). John Knox.
Massey, Craig. I Love You, I Hear You. 160p. 1980. text ed. 6.95 (ISBN 0-8024-3957-8). Moody.
Mayhall, Jack & Mayhall, Carole. Marriage Takes More Than Love. LC 77-85736. 1978. pap. 4.50 (ISBN 0-89109-426-1, 14266). NavPress.
Meier, Paul D. You Can Avoid Divorce. (Christian Counseling Aids Ser). 1978. pap. 0.75 (ISBN 0-8010-6052-4). Baker Bk.
Merrill, Dean. How to Really Love Your Wife. 196p. 1980. pap. 4.95 (ISBN 0-310-35321-1, 10685). Zondervan.
Miller, Andrew S. Marital Expectations: What to Do When They Go Unmet. 125p. (Orig.). 1980. pap. 3.50 (ISBN 0-937442-00-3). Bibl Based Develop.
Mitchell, Ann K. Someone to Turn To: Experiences of Help Before Divorce. 136p. 1981. 20.00 (ISBN 0-08-025741-0). Pergamon.
Mitman, John L. C. Premarital Counseling: A Manual for Clergy & Counselors. 144p. 1980. 9.95 (ISBN 0-8164-0467-4). Seabury.
Morin, David & Warnock, Jeanine. I in the Sky. 1979. 5.95 (ISBN 0-533-03696-8). Vantage.
Oates, Wayne E. & Rowatt, Wade. Before You Marry Them: Guidebook for Pastors. LC 74-80340. 144p. 1976. bds. 5.95 (ISBN 0-8054-2408-3). Broadman.
Ohlsen, Merle M. Marriage Counseling in Groups. LC 79-66180. (Illus., Orig.). 1979. pap. text ed. 8.95 (ISBN 0-87822-201-4). Res Press.
Paolino, Thomas J. & McCrady, Barbara S., eds. Marriage & Marital Therapy: Psychoanalytic, Behavioral & Systems Theory Perspectives. LC 78-17398. 1978. 25.00 (ISBN 0-87630-171-5). Brunner-Mazel.
Petranek, Charles & Petranek, Diana. Inside Marriage; You, Me & Us. new ed. Jankowski, Michael, ed. (Orig.). 1978. pap. 4.95 (ISBN 0-686-00806-5). Helm Pub.
Phillips, Bob. How Can I Be Sure: A Pre-Marriage Inventory. LC 77-94448. (Orig.). 1978. pap. 3.95 (ISBN 0-89081-073-7, 0737). Harvest Hse.
Ranieri, Ralph. When & How to Choose a Marriage Counselor. 24p. 1977. pap. 0.25 (ISBN 0-89570-103-0). Claretian Pubns.
Ripple, Paula. The Pain & the Possibility. LC 78-67745. 144p. 1978. pap. 2.95 (ISBN 0-87793-162-3). Ave Maria.
Rock, Stanley A. This Time Together: A Guide for Premarital Counseling. 1980. pap. 3.95 (ISBN 0-310-39171-7). Zondervan.
Rosenbaum, Jean & Rosenbaum, Veryl. How to Avoid Divorce. LC 79-2999. 160p. (Orig.). 1980. pap. 3.95 (ISBN 0-06-250740-0, BN 3001). Har-Row.
Rouner, Arthur A., Jr. You Can Restore Love to Your Marriage. (Christian Counseling Aids Ser.). pap. 0.75 (ISBN 0-8010-7661-7). Baker Bk.
Rudhyar, Dane. We Can Begin Again Together. 1974. pap. 5.00 (ISBN 0-916108-50-3). Seed Center.
Rue, James J. The Nine Most Common Marriage Problems & How to Overcome Them. (Orig.). 1976. pap. 1.50 (ISBN 0-89243-058-3, 29055). Liguori Pubns.

Ruhnke, Robert. For Better & for Ever: Sponsor Couple Program for Christian Marriage Preparation. 1981. pap. 3.95 (ISBN 0-89243-143-1); dialogue packet wkbk. 3.75 (ISBN 0-89243-144-X). Liguori Pubns.
Sager, Clifford J. Marriage Contracts & Couple Therapy. LC 76-21842. 1976. 17.50 (ISBN 0-87630-130-8). Brunner-Mazel.
Seidenberg, Robert. Marriage in Life & Literature. LC 70-97939. 1970. 5.95 (ISBN 0-8022-2331-1). Philos Lib.
Seifert, Anne. His, Mine, & Ours: A Guide to Keeping Marriage from Ruining a Perfectly Good Relationship. 1979. 8.95 (ISBN 0-02-609030-9). Macmillan.
Sholerar, G. P. The Handbook of Marriage & Marital Therapy. 600p. Date not set. text ed. 40.00 (ISBN 0-89335-120-2). Spectrum Pub.
Silverman, Hirsch L., ed. Marital Therapy: Moral, Sociological, & Psychological Factors. (Illus.). 576p. 1972. 32.75 (ISBN 0-398-02415-4); pap. 19.75 (ISBN 0-398-03065-0). C C Thomas.
Skynner, A. C. Systems of Family & Marital Psychotherapy. LC 76-2577. 1976. 20.00 (ISBN 0-87630-117-0). Brunner-Mazel.
Smith, Gerald W. & Phillips, Alice I. Couple Therapy. 160p. 1973. pap. 1.95 (ISBN 0-02-078000-1, Collier). Macmillan.
Smith, Leon. Pastors Manual for Growing Love in Christian Marriage. LC 80-28001. 1981. pap. 4.50 (ISBN 0-687-15930-X). Abingdon.
Smith, Riley K. & Tessina, Tina B. How to Be a Couple & Still Be Free. 1980. pap. 4.95 (ISBN 0-87877-051-8). Newcastle Pub.
Stahmann, Robert F. & Hiebert, William. Premarital Counseling: Education for Marriage. LC 78-19727. 192p. 1980. 19.95 (ISBN 0-669-02726-X). Lexington Bks.
Stahmann, Robert F. & Hiebert, William J., eds. Klemer's Counseling in Marital & Sexual Problems: A Clinical Handbook. 2nd ed. 1977. pap. 19.95 (ISBN 0-683-07911-5). Williams & Wilkins.
Stewart, Charles W. Minister As Marriage Counselor. rev. ed. LC 61-5559. 1970. 8.95 (ISBN 0-687-26957-1). Abingdon.
Stuart, Richard B. Helping Couples Change: A Social Learning Approach to Marital Therapy. (Guilford Family Therapy Ser.). 464p. 1980. 22.50 (ISBN 0-89862-604-8). Guilford Pr.
Swain, Clark. A Tuneup for Partners in Love. LC 80-84568. 250p. 1981. 7.95 (ISBN 0-88290-171-0, 2015). Horizon Utah.
Thomas, Edwin J. Marital Communication & Decision Making: Analysis, Assessment, & Change. LC 75-41551. 1979. pap. text ed. 7.95 (ISBN 0-02-932440-8). Free Pr.
Thompson, David A. Five Steps Toward a Better Marriage. 96p. (Orig.). 1980. pap. 3.95 (ISBN 0-87123-164-6, 210164). Bethany Hse.
--A Premarital Guide for Couples & Their Counselors. 1979. pap. 3.95 (ISBN 0-87123-465-3, 210465). Bethany Hse.
Timmons, Tim. Game Plan for Marriage. LC 77-80377. 1977. pap. 1.25 (ISBN 0-88449-067-X). Vision Hse.
Travis, Patricia Y. & Travis, Robert P. Vitalizing Intimacy in Marriage. LC 79-4374. 1979. 13.95 (ISBN 0-88229-398-2). Nelson-Hall.
Trimble, J. Thomas. Intimacy in Marriage. LC 77-73452. 1978. 4.95 (ISBN 0-8054-5624-4). Broadman.
Twombly, Gerald H. A Superman for a Total Woman. 1978. pap. 3.95 (ISBN 0-89293-029-2). Beta Bk.
Van Pelt, Nancy. The Complete Marriage. LC 78-20770. (Orion Ser). 1979. pap. 2.95 (ISBN 0-8127-0218-2). Review & Herald.
Vath, Raymond E. & O'Neill, Daniel W. Marrying for Life. (Illus., Orig.). 1981. pap. 8.00 (ISBN 0-939336-00-6). Messenger Comm.
Vayhinger, John M. Before Divorce. Hulme, William E., ed. LC 72-171512. (Pocket Counsel Bks). 56p. 1972. pap. 1.75 (ISBN 0-8006-1106-3, 1-1106). Fortress.
Venditti, Michael C. How to Be Your Own Marriage Counselor: A Commonsense Guide to Marital Happiness. 256p. 1980. 12.95 (ISBN 0-8264-0013-2). Continuum.
Vincent, Clark E. Sexual & Marital Health: The Physician As a Consultant. (Illus.). 192p. 1973. text ed. 13.95 (ISBN 0-07-067487-6, HP); pap. text ed. 10.95 (ISBN 0-07-067488-4). McGraw.
Wallis, Booker. Marriage Counselling. 17.95x (ISBN 0-392-08121-0, SpS). Sportshelf.
Warren, Thomas B. Keeping the Lock in Wedlock. 1980. pap. 10.95 (ISBN 0-934916-26-8). Natl Christian Pr.
Willi, Jurg. Couples in Collusion. Tchorek, Mariusz & Inayat-Khan, Waltraud, trs. from Ger. LC 78-70619. 1980. 14.95 (ISBN 0-89793-022-3); pap. 7.95 (ISBN 0-89793-004-5). Hunter Hse.
--Couples Therapy. Simon, Anita & Oliver, David, trs. from Ger. LC 79-89946. Orig. Title: Therapie der Zweierbeziehung. (Orig.). Date not set. 12.95 (ISBN 0-89793-029-0). Hunter Hse.
Woolfolk, Joanna. Honeymoon for Life. LC 77-15966. 1979. 8.95 (ISBN 0-8128-2443-1). Stein & Day.
--Honeymoon for Life: How to Live Happily Ever After. LC 77-15966. 252p. 1981. pap. 6.95 (ISBN 0-8128-6102-7). Stein & Day.
Wright, H. Norman. Communication: Key to Your Marriage, Manual. (Illus.). 1979. 9.95 (ISBN 0-8307-0718-2, 5202507). Regal.
--Marital Counseling: A Biblical Behavioral Cognitive Approach. 370p. 1981. 16.95 (ISBN 0-938786-00-8). Chr Marriage.
--The Pillars of Marriage. LC 78-68849. 1979. pap. 4.95 (ISBN 0-8307-0698-4, 5412501); leader's guide 9.95 (ISBN 0-8307-0699-2, 5202418). Regal.
--Premarital Counseling. rev. ed. 1981. 9.95 (ISBN 0-8024-6812-8). Moody.
Wright, Norman & Roberts, Wes. Before You Say I Do: Study Manual. LC 77-94133. 1978. 3.95 (ISBN 0-89081-119-9). Harvest Hse.

MARRIAGE CUSTOMS AND RITES
see also Wedding Etiquette
Ahmad, Imtiaz, ed. Family, Kinship, & Marriage Among the Muslims. LC 77-74484. 1977. 17.50x (ISBN 0-88386-757-5). South Asia Bks.
Baker, Margaret. Wedding Customs & Folklore. (Illus.). 144p. 1977. 13.50x (ISBN 0-87471-821-X). Rowman.
Ch'en Kou-Chun. Studies in Marriage & Funerals of Taiwan Aborigines, No. 4. (Asian Folklore & Social Life Monograph). (Chinese.). 1970. 6.60 (ISBN 0-89986-007-9). E Langstaff.
Constantine, Larry L. & Constantine, Joan M. Group Marriage: A Study of Contemporary Multilateral Marriage. LC 74-10607. 299p. 1974. pap. 2.95 (ISBN 0-02-075910-X, 07591, Collier). Macmillan.
Daniels, Elam J. Como Ser Feliz En el Matrimonio. Orig. Title: How to Be Happily Married. 96p. 1979. pap. 1.80 (ISBN 0-311-46066-6). Casa Bautista.
Evans-Pritchard, Edward E. Kinship & Marriage Among the Nuer. (Illus.). 1951. 24.00x (ISBN 0-19-823104-0). Oxford U Pr.
Fielding, William J. Strange Customs of Courtship & Marriage. 315p. 1980. Repr. of 1942 ed. lib. bdg. 25.00 (ISBN 0-89987-259-X). Darby Bks.
Fison, Lorimer & Howitt, Alfred W. Kamilaroi & Kurnai: Group Marriage & Relationship, & Marriage by Elopement, the Kurnai Tribe: Their Customs in Peace & War. (Maps). 1967. pap. text ed. 15.50x (ISBN 90-6234-053-9). Humanities.
Freeman, Ruth & Freeman, Larry G. O Promise Me Picture Album. 1954. 10.00 (ISBN 0-87282-067-X). Century Hse.
Granqvist, Hilma N. Marriage Conditions in a Palestinian Village, 2 vols. LC 72-9644. Repr. of 1935 ed. Set. 52.50 (ISBN 0-404-57450-5). AMS Pr.
Lasker, Joe. Merry Ever After: The Story of Two Medieval Weddings. (Illus.). (gr. k-3). 1976. 7.95 (ISBN 0-670-47257-3). Viking Pr.
Luzbetak, Louis J. Marriage & the Family in Caucasia. Repr. of 1951 ed. 38.50 (ISBN 0-384-34300-7). Johnson Repr.
Mogey, John, ed. Sociology of Marriage & Family Behavior 1957-1968: A Trend Report & Bibliography. 364p. 1971. text ed. 38.50x (ISBN 0-686-22483-3). Mouton.
Monsarrat, Ann. And the Bride Wore... The Story of the White Wedding. LC 74-6958. 252p. 1974. 15.00 (ISBN 0-396-07007-8). Dodd.
Nordtvedt, Matilda & Steinkuehler, Pearl. Something Old, Something New. (Orig.). 1981. pap. 1.95 (ISBN 0-8024-0927-X). Moody.
Pearce, Elizabeth C. Outline of Duties of Members of the Bridal Party. text ed. 1.50x pk. of 10 (ISBN 0-8134-0274-3, 274). Interstate.
Radcliff-Brown, Alfred R., ed. African Systems of Kinship & Marriage. 1950. pap. 14.95x (ISBN 0-19-724147-6). Oxford U Pr.
Scher, Paula. The Honeymoon Book: A Tribute to the Last Ritual of Sexual Innocence. Graver, Fred, ed. LC 80-27900. (Illus.). 192p. (Orig.). 1981. pap. 9.95 (ISBN 0-87131-339-1). M Evans.
Stannard, Una. Married Women v. Husbands' Names. LC 73-87334. 1973. 4.95 (ISBN 0-914142-00-3). Germainbooks.
Sutton, Joan L. & Watson de Barros, Leda. Novia Hoy-Esposa Manana: Guia Para Novias. S. D. de Lerin, Olivia, tr. Orig. Title: Manual das Noivas. 1980. pap. 1.85 (ISBN 0-311-46056-9, Edit Mundo). Casa Bautista.
Tegg, William. Knot Tied: Marriage Ceremonies of All Nations. LC 75-99073. 1970. Repr. of 1877 ed. 28.00 (ISBN 0-8103-3585-9). Gale.
Tung Tso-Pin. Wedding Songs & Customs of China. (National Peking University & Chinese Assn. for Folklore, Folklore & Folkliterature Ser.: No. 93). (Chinese.). 6.50 (ISBN 0-89986-173-3). E Langstaff.
Urlin, Ethel L. Short History of Marriage: Marriage Rites, Customs, & Folklore in Many Countries in All Ages. LC 69-16071. 1969. Repr. of 1913 ed. 22.00 (ISBN 0-8103-3569-7). Gale.
Van Der Veen, K. W. I Give Thee My Daughter: A Study on Marriage & Hierarchy Among the Anvil Brahmans of South Gujarat. (Studies in Developing Countries: No. 13). 336p. 1972. text ed. 24.50x (ISBN 9-0232-0914-1). Humanities.
Worlton, Lois F. & Jasinski, Opal D. Planning LDS Weddings & Receptions. LC 72-88908. (Illus.). 1972. pap. 4.95 (ISBN 0-88290-014-5). Horizon Utah.

MARRIAGE GUIDANCE
see Marriage Counseling

MARRIAGE IN ART
Carter, C. F. The Wedding Day in Literature & Art. 59.95 (ISBN 0-8490-1280-5). Gordon Pr.
Carter, Charles F. The Wedding Day in Literature & Art: A Collection of the Best Descriptions of Wedding from the Works of the World's Leading Novelists & Poets. LC 74-86598. 1969. Repr. of 1900 ed. 19.00 (ISBN 0-8103-0154-7). Gale.
Little, Alan. Roman Bridal Drama. 1978. 6.50 (ISBN 0-89679-009-6). Moretus Pr.

MARRIAGE IN LITERATURE
see also Family in Literature
Carter, C. F. The Wedding Day in Literature & Art. 59.95 (ISBN 0-8490-1280-5). Gordon Pr.
Carter, Charles F. The Wedding Day in Literature & Art: A Collection of the Best Descriptions of Wedding from the Works of the World's Leading Novelists & Poets. LC 74-86598. 1969. Repr. of 1900 ed. 19.00 (ISBN 0-8103-0154-7). Gale.
Fehrenbach, C. G. Marriage in Wittenwiler's Ring. LC 70-140019. (Catholic University Studies in German Ser.: No. 15). Repr. of 1941 ed. 18.50 (ISBN 0-404-50235-0). AMS Pr.
Johnson, Wendell S. Sex & Marriage in Victorian Poetry. LC 74-25370. 288p. 1975. 19.50x (ISBN 0-8014-0845-8). Cornell U Pr.
Lerner, Laurence. Love & Marriage: Literature & Its Social Context. 1979. 25.00x (ISBN 0-312-49938-8). St Martin.
McGhee, Richard D. Marriage, Duty, & Desire in Victorian Poetry & Drama. LC 80-11962. 336p. 1980. 22.50x (ISBN 0-7006-0203-8). Regents Pr KS.
Miller, Leo. John Milton Among the Polygamophiles. LC 73-89792. 378p. 1974. lib. bdg. 15.00 (ISBN 0-914382-00-4). Loewenthal Pr.
Olson, David H. Inventory of Marriage & Family Literature. (Inventory of Family & Marriage Literature Ser.: Vol. 7). 520p. 1981. 75.00 (ISBN 0-8039-1661-2); pap. 35.00 (ISBN 0-8039-1662-0). Sage.
Seidenberg, Robert. Marriage in Life & Literature. LC 70-97939. 1970. 5.95 (ISBN 0-8022-2331-1). Philos Lib.
Voort, D. Van De. Love & Marriage in the English Medieval Romance. 59.95 (ISBN 0-8490-0562-0). Gordon Pr.

MARRIAGE LAW
see also Adultery; Community Property; Divorce; Husband and Wife; Marriage–Annulment; Marriage–Jews; Marriage (Canon Law); Matrimonial Actions; Remarriage; Separation (Law)
Cahen, Alfred. Statistical Analysis of American Divorce. LC 68-58553. (Columbia University Studies in the Social Sciences: No. 360). Repr. of 1932 ed. 14.50 (ISBN 0-404-51360-3). AMS Pr.
Canudo, Eugene R. Marriage, Divorce & Adoption: New York. 1979. pap. 5.50x (ISBN 0-87526-222-8). Gould.
--Marriage Divorce & Adoption (NY) 134p. 1979. 5.50 (ISBN 0-87526-222-8). Gould.
Chotiner, Renee D. Marriage & the Supreme Court: A Study of the Judicial Attitudes & Woman's Legal Status. LC 73-10873. (Law & Women Ser.). 32p. 1974. pap. 2.00 (ISBN 0-87999-003-1). Today News.
Derrett, J. Duncan. The Death of a Marriage Law. LC 77-93389. 1978. 13.95 (ISBN 0-89089-056-0). Carolina Acad Pr.
Editorial Staff of Family Law Reporter. Desk Guide to the Uniform Marriage & Divorce Act. 106p. 1974. pap. text ed. 4.00 (ISBN 0-87179-219-2). BNA.
Forrester, Ian S., ed. Introductory Act to the German Civil Code & Marriage Law of the Federal Republic of Germany. Goren, Simon L., tr. from Ger. LC 76-17384. x, 54p. 1976. pap. text ed. 12.50x (ISBN 0-8377-0604-1). Rothman.
Honea, Sterling R. Love, Sex, Marriage, & Divorce. 5.95 (ISBN 0-686-31323-2). Cal Lawyers Pr.
Kuchler, Frances W. Law of Engagement & Marriage. 2nd ed. LC 78-3470. (Legal Almanac Ser.). 1978. 5.95 (ISBN 0-379-11107-1). Oceana.
Mariage et divorce. (Collection que faire?). 1978. pap. text ed. 5.75x (ISBN 2-03-001204-1). Larousse.
Marital Property Rights. (Co-Op East Law Outline Ser.). 1974. pap. text ed. 6.00 (ISBN 0-88408-065-X). Sterling Swift.
Marriage, Divorce & Adoption Laws (U.S.) 160p. (Supplemented annually). looseleaf 6.50 (ISBN 0-87526-182-5). Gould.
Marsh, Harold, Jr. Marital Property in Conflict of Laws. LC 51-12274. 277p. 1952. 11.00 (ISBN 0-295-73841-3). U of Wash Pr.
Palsson, L. Marriage & Divorce in Comparative Conflict of Laws. write for info. (ISBN 90-286-0423-5). Heinman.
Shropshire, D. W. Primitive Marriage & European Law: A South African Investigation. 186p. 1970. Repr. 25.00x (ISBN 0-7146-1913-2, F Cass Co). Biblio Dist.
Statsky, William P. Domestic Relations: Law & Skills. LC 78-7303. (Paralegal Ser.). 537p. 1978. text ed. 20.50 (ISBN 0-8299-2007-2). West Pub.
Traer, James F. Marriage & the Family in Eighteenth-Century France. LC 80-11121. 240p. 1980. 17.50x (ISBN 0-8014-1298-6). Cornell U Pr.
Weitzman, Lenore J. The Marriage Contract: Couples, Lovers & the Law. 1980. 14.95 (ISBN 0-13-558403-5, Spec); pap. 6.95 (ISBN 0-13-558395-0). P-H.
--The Marriage Contract: Spouses, Lovers, & the Law. LC 80-69645. 600p. 1981. 14.95 (ISBN 0-02-934630-4). Free Pr.

MARRIAGE LAW (ISLAMIC LAW)
see Marriage (Islamic Law)

MARRIAGE LICENSES
see Registers of Births, Deaths, Marriages, etc.

MARRIAGE REGISTERS
see Registers of Births, Deaths, Marriages, Etc.

MARRIAGE SERVICE
Arisian, Khoren. The New Wedding: Creating Your Own Marriage Ceremony. 1973. 8.95 (ISBN 0-394-48334-0). Knopf.
--The New Wedding: Creating Your Own Marriage Ceremony. 160p. 1973. pap. 5.95 (ISBN 0-394-71919-0, Vin). Random.
Hickman, Hoyt, ed. A Service of Christian Marriage: With Introduction, Commentary, & Additional Resources. 1979. pap. 2.95 (ISBN 0-687-38073-1). Abingdon.
Hodsdon, Nick. The Joyful Wedding: New Songs & Ideas for Celebration. LC 73-8421. 80p. (Orig.). 1973. pap. 3.50 (ISBN 0-687-20651-0). Abingdon.
Hutton, Samuel W. Minister's Marriage Manual. 1968. 4.95 (ISBN 0-8010-4031-0). Baker Bk.
Lamont, Corliss. A Humanist Wedding Service. 32p. pap. 2.95 saddle bdg. (ISBN 0-87975-000-6). Prometheus Bks.
Marriage Service. boxed 3.50 (ISBN 0-664-21050-3); moire boxed 4.95 (ISBN 0-664-21075-9); pap. 12.50 pkg. of 10 (ISBN 0-664-29035-3). Westminster.
Peterson, Robert J. A Marriage Service for You. (Orig.). 1977. pap. 4.55 (ISBN 0-89536-160-4). CSS Pub.
Reid, John C. Marriage Covenant. LC 67-11305. (Orig.). 1967. pap. 1.25 (ISBN 0-8042-1710-6). John Knox.
Vaporis, Nomikos M. The Orthodox Marriage Service. LC 77-14992. 30p. 1977. pap. 1.50 (ISBN 0-916586-12-X). Holy Cross Orthodox.
Wall, Wendy. The Creative Wedding Handbook. LC 72-93983. 1973. 5.95 (ISBN 0-8091-0177-7); pap. 2.45 (ISBN 0-8091-1831-9). Paulist Pr.

MARRIAGE STATISTICS
see Vital Statistics

MARRIAGES, INTERNATIONAL
Atherton, Gertrude. American Wives & English Husbands. Repr. of 1901 ed. lib. bdg. 17.50 (ISBN 0-8414-3078-0). Folcroft.
Eliot, Elizabeth. Heiresses & Coronets. (Illus.). 1959. 7.95 (ISBN 0-8392-1061-2). Astor-Honor.

MARRIED PEOPLE–PRAYER-BOOKS AND DEVOTIONS
Bjorge, James R. Forty Ways to Say I Love You. LC 78-52179. 1978. pap. 2.95 (ISBN 0-8066-1654-7, 10-2360). Augsburg.
Deal, William S. Happiness & Harmony in Marriage. pap. 1.95 (ISBN 0-686-13723-X). Deal Pubns.
Drescher, John M. Meditations for the Newly Married. LC 69-10835. 1969. gift-boxed 7.95 (ISBN 0-8361-1571-6). Herald Pr.
Durkin, Henry P. Forty-Four Hours to Change Your Life: Marriage Encounter. (Orig.). pap. 1.25 (ISBN 0-89129-139-3). Jove Pubns.
Krutza, William J. & Krutza, Vilma. His-Hers Devotionals. (Ultra Bks Ser.). 1971. 3.95 (ISBN 0-8010-5309-9). Baker Bk.

MARRIED WOMEN

Here are entered works on the legal status of women during marriage, especially on the effect of marriage on their legal capacity. Works on legal relations between husband and wife are entered under Husband and wife. For works on the legal conditions of women in general, see the heading Women–Legal Status, Laws, etc.

Chotiner, Renee D. Marriage & the Supreme Court: A Study of the Judicial Attitudes & Woman's Legal Status. LC 73-10873. (Law & Women Ser.). 32p. 1974. pap. 2.00 (ISBN 0-87999-003-1). Today News.

Epstein, Louis M. The Jewish Marriage Contract: A Study in the Status of the Woman in Jewish Law. LC 73-2195. (The Jewish People; History, Religion, Literature Ser.). Repr. of 1927 ed. 25.00 (ISBN 0-405-05261-8). Arno.

Stannard, Una. Married Women v. Husbands' Names. LC 73-87334. 1973. 4.95 (ISBN 0-914142-00-3). Germainbooks.

Woman & Marriage, 5 vols. Incl. Some Reflections Upon Marriage. Astell, Mary. Repr. 9.50 (ISBN 0-442-81056-3); Home: Its Work & Influence. Gilman, Charlotte P. Repr. of 1903 ed. 13.00 (ISBN 0-442-81992-7); Women & Economics. Gilman, Charlotte P. Repr. 15.00 (ISBN 0-442-81081-4); Two Vols. In One. Love, Marriage, & Divorce, & the Sovereignity of the Individual: Bound with Divorce. Greeley, Horace, et al. Repr; Divorce. Greeley, Horace & Owen, Robert D. Repr. 10.50 (ISBN 0-685-37112-3); Law of Baron & Femme, of Parent & Child, Guardian & Ward, Master & Servant, & of the Powers of the Courts of Chancery. 3rd ed. Reeve, Tapping. Repr. 32.50 (ISBN 0-442-81067-9). (Source Library of the Women's Movement). 1970. 80.50 set (ISBN 0-442-81250-7). Hacker.

MARROW

Balner, H. Bone Marrow Transplantation & Other Treatment After Radiation Injury. 1977. pap. 21.00 (ISBN 90-247-2056-7, Pub. by Martinus Nijhoff Netherlands). Kluwer Boston.

Bone-Marrow Conservation, Culture & Transplantation. (Illus., Orig.). 1969. pap. 13.00 (ISBN 92-0-111269-6, ISP219, IAEA). Unipub.

Burkhardt, R. Bone Marrow & Bone Tissue: Color Atlas of Clinical Histopathology. LC 79-126889. (Illus.). xii, 115p. 1971. 108.80 (ISBN 0-387-05059-0). Springer-Verlag.

Custer, R. Philip, ed. Atlas of the Blood & Bone Marrow. 2nd ed. LC 78-165276. (Illus.). 562p. 1974. text ed. 45.00 (ISBN 0-7216-2815-X). Saunders.

Dupont, Bo & Good, Robert A., eds. Immunobiology of Bone Marrow Transplantation. (Transplantation Proceedings Reprint). 352p. 1977. 49.75 (ISBN 0-8089-0982-7). Grune.

Gale, R. P. & Opelz, Gerhard, eds. Immunobiology of Bone Marrow Transplantation, Vol. 2. (Transplantation Proceedings). 288p. 1978. 39.00 (ISBN 0-8089-1116-3). Grune.

Gale, Robert P. & Fox, C. Fred, eds. Biology of Bone Marrow Transplantation. (ICN-UCLA Symposia on Molecular & Cellular Biology Ser.: Vol. 17). 1980. 40.00 (ISBN 0-12-273960-4). Acad Pr.

Huhn, Dieter & Stich, Walter, eds. Fine Structure of Blood & Bone Marrow: An Introduction to Electron Microscopic Hematology. 1969. 27.50 (ISBN 0-02-846130-4). Hafner.

Israels, M. C. An Atlas of Bone-Marrow Pathology. 4th ed. (Illus.). 82p. 1971. 29.75 (ISBN 0-8089-0572-4). Grune.

Kass, Lawrence. Bone Marrow Interpretation. 1979. text ed. 45.00 (ISBN 0-397-50414-4, JBL-Med-Nursing). Har-Row.

Krause, John R., et al. Bone Marrow Biopsy. (Illus.). 288p. 1981. text ed. write for info. (ISBN 0-443-08099-2). Churchill.

O'Kunewick, James P. & Meredith, Ruby F., eds. Graft vs. Leukemia in Man & Animal Models. 304p. 1981. 74.95 (ISBN 0-8493-5745-4). CRC Pr.

Rywlin, Arkadi M. Histopathology of the Bone Marrow. LC 75-41570. (Series in Laboratory Medicine). 229p. 1976. text ed. 22.50 (ISBN 0-316-76369-1). Little.

Schleicher, E. M. Bone Marrow Morphology & Mechanics of Biopsy. (Illus.). 210p. 1974. 22.75 (ISBN 0-398-02838-9). C C Thomas.

Silver, Richard T. Morphology of the Blood & Marrow in Clinical Practice. LC 75-75146. (Illus.). 160p. 1970. 54.50 (ISBN 0-8089-0429-9). Grune.

Snapper, Isidore & Kahn, Alvin. Myelomatosis: Fundamentals & Clinical Features. (Illus.). 1971. 24.50 (ISBN 0-8391-0588-6, Pub. by Karger). Univ Park.

Thierfelder, S., et al, eds. Immunobiology of Bone Marrow Transplantation. (Illus.). 380p. 1980. pap. 57.90 (ISBN 0-387-09405-9). Springer-Verlag.

Waldenstrom, Jan. Diagnosis & Treatment of Multiple Myeloma. LC 76-82109. 240p. 1970. 48.75 (ISBN 0-8089-0518-X). Grune.

Wright, Richard K. & Cooper, Edwin L., eds. Phylogeny of Thymus & Bone Marrow-Bursa Cells: Proceedings of an International Symposium on Cells, 1976. 1976. 44.00 (ISBN 0-7204-0603-X, North-Holland). Elsevier.

MARRYAT, FREDERICK, 1792-1848

Hannay, D. Life of Frederick Marryat. LC 73-6945. (English Biography Ser., No. 31). 1973. Repr. of 1880 ed. lib. bdg. 32.95 (ISBN 0-8383-1695-6). Haskell.

MARS (PLANET)

see also Space Flight to Mars

Blunck, Jurgen. Mars & Its Satellites: A Detailed Commentary on the Nomenclature. 1977. 10.00 (ISBN 0-682-48676-0, University). Exposition.

Brandt, J. C. & McElroy, M. E. Atmosphere of Venus & Mars. (Orig.). 1968. 63.75x (ISBN 0-677-11590-3). Gordon.

Carr, Michael H. The Surface of Mars. LC 81-3425. (Illus.). 1981. 45.00x (ISBN 0-300-02750-8). Yale U Pr.

Chapman, Clark R. Inner Planets. LC 76-58914. (Illus.). 1977. 9.95 (ISBN 0-684-14898-6, ScribT). Scribner.

Conference on Origins of Life, 3rd, California, 1970. Planetary Astronomy: Proceedings. Margulis, L., ed. LC 72-91514. (Illus.). 268p. 1973. 24.90 (ISBN 0-387-06065-0). Springer-Verlag.

Firsoff, Axel. The New Face of Mars. 1978. 9.95 (ISBN 0-86025-818-1). State Mutual Bk.

Grossinger, Richard. Mars: A Science Fiction Vision. (Illus.). 230p. (Orig.). 1971. pap. 3.50 (ISBN 0-913028-00-2). North Atlantic.

Moore, Patrick. Guide to Mars. (Illus.). 1978. 14.95 (ISBN 0-393-06432-8). Norton.

Moore, Patrick & Cross, Charles A. Mars. 1973. 8.50 (ISBN 0-517-50527-4). Crown.

Moore, Patrick & Jackson, Francis. Life on Mars. (Illus.). 1966. 4.50 (ISBN 0-393-05225-7). Norton.

Morgenthaler, G. W., ed. Exploration of Mars. (Advances in the Astronautical Sciences Ser.: Vol. 15). 1963. 45.00 (ISBN 0-87703-016-2). Am Astronaut.

Mutch, Thomas A., et al. The Geology of Mars. LC 75-30199. (Illus.). 436p. 1976. 45.00 (ISBN 0-691-08173-5). Princeton U Pr.

Rovin, Jeff. Mars! LC 77-15949. (Illus.). 1978. 15.00 (ISBN 0-89474-011-3). Corwin.

Rukl, Antonin. Moon, Mars & Venus. (Concise Guides Ser.). (Illus.). 1979. 7.95 (ISBN 0-600-36219-1). Transatlantic.

Schiaparelli, G. V. Le Opere Publicate per Cura Della Reale Specola Di Brera, Vols. 1-11. (Sources of Science Ser). (It). Repr. of 1930 ed. Set. 339.00 (ISBN 0-384-53780-4). Johnson Repr.

Space Science Board. Biology & the Exploration of Mars. 1966. 8.75 (ISBN 0-309-01296-1). Natl Acad Pr.

Wells, R. A. Geophysics of Mars. (Developments in Solar System & Space Science Ser.: Vol. 4). 1979. 88.00 (ISBN 0-444-41802-4). Elsevier.

MARS (PLANET)–JUVENILE LITERATURE

Asimov, Isaac. Mars, the Red Planet. LC 77-24151. (Illus.). (gr. 7 up). 1977. 9.25 (ISBN 0-688-41812-0); PLB 8.88 (ISBN 0-688-51812-5). Lothrop.

Branley, Franklyn M. Book of Mars for You. LC 68-11058. (Illus.). (gr. 3-6). 1968. (TYC-J); PLB 9.89 (ISBN 0-690-15296-5). Har-Row.

Gemme, Leila Boyle. True Book of the Mars Landing. (True Books). (Illus.). 48p. (gr. 2-5). 1977. PLB 9.25 (ISBN 0-516-01145-6). Childrens.

Moche, Dinah. Mars. LC 78-2762. (Easy-Read-Fact Bks.). (Illus.). (gr. 2-4). 1978. PLB 6.90 s&l (ISBN 0-531-01374-X). Watts.

MARS PROBES

Flinn, E., ed. Scientific Results of Viking Project. 1977. 30.00 (ISBN 0-87590-207-3). Am Geophysical.

MARSH, OTHNIEL CHARLES, 1831-1899

Cohen, I. Bernard, ed. The Life & Scientific Work of Othniel Charles Marsh: An Original Anthology. LC 79-7973. (Three Centuries of Science in America Ser.). (Illus.). 1980. lib. bdg. 50.00x (ISBN 0-405-12555-0). Arno.

Lanham, Url N. The Bone Hunters. LC 73-5596. (Illus.). 285p. 1973. 20.00x (ISBN 0-231-03152-1). Columbia U Pr.

Schuchert, Charles & Levene, Clara M. O. C. Marsh: Pioneer in Paleontology. Sterling, Keir B., ed. LC 77-81133. (Biologists & Their World Ser.). (Illus.). 1978. Repr. of 1940 ed. lib. bdg. 35.00x (ISBN 0-405-10733-1). Arno.

MARSH ECOLOGY

Carr, Archie. The Everglades. (The American Wilderness Ser). (Illus.). 1973. 12.95 (ISBN 0-8094-1172-5). Time-Life.

Chapman, Valentine J., ed. Wet Coastal Ecosystems. LC 77-342. (Ecosystems of the World Ser.: NO. 1). 1977. 66.00 (ISBN 0-444-41560-2). Elsevier.

Coverdale, Joan. I Share This Marsh. LC 73-80407. (Illus.). 1973. 3.95 (ISBN 0-686-23658-0). Whale & Eagle.

Gard, Robert E. & Mueller, Edgar G. Wild Goose Marsh. LC 72-89568. (Illus.). 1972. 12.95 (ISBN 0-88361-000-0). Stanton & Lee.

Higman, Harry W. & Larrison, Earl J. Union Bay: The Life of a City Marsh. LC 51-13089. (Illus.). 325p. 1951. 8.50 (ISBN 0-295-73976-2). U of Wash Pr.

Mason, Herbert L. A Flora of the Marshes of California. LC 57-7960. (Illus.). 1957. 35.00x (ISBN 0-520-01433-2). U of Cal Pr.

Meanley, Brooke. Birds & Marshes of the Chesapeake Bay Country: Including the Chincoteague Salt Marshes. LC 75-17558. (Illus.). 168p. 1975. pap. 6.50 (ISBN 0-87033-207-4, Pub. by Tidewater). Cornell Maritime.

Niering, W. A. Life of the Marsh. 1966. 9.95 (ISBN 0-07-046555-X, P&RB); by subscription 3.95 (ISBN 0-07-046006-X). McGraw.

Pomeroy, L. R. & Wiegert, R. G., eds. The Ecology of a Salt Marsh. (Ecological Studies Ser.: Vol. 38). (Illus.). 288p. 1981. 29.80 (ISBN 0-387-90555-3). Springer-Verlag.

Ursin, Michael J. Life in & Around the Freshwater Wetlands. LC 74-13632. (Apollo Eds.). (Illus.). 192p. 1975. pap. 2.95 (ISBN 0-8152-0378-0, 0-378). T Y Crowell.

MARSHALL, ALFRED, 1842-1924

Davenport, Herbert J. Economics of Alfred Marshall. LC 65-19648. Repr. of 1935 ed. 19.50x (ISBN 0-678-00095-6). Kelley.

Homan, Paul T. Contemporary Economic Thought. facs. ed. LC 68-20310. (Essay Index Reprint Ser). 1928. 19.50 (ISBN 0-8369-0546-6). Arno.

Jha, Narmedeshwar. Age of Marshall: Aspects of British Economic Thought. 220p. 1973. 25.00x (ISBN 0-7146-2954-5, F Cass Co). Biblio Dist.

Souter, Ralph W. Prolegomena to Relativity Economics. LC 68-58623. (Columbia University. Studies in the Social Sciences: No. 391). 16.50 (ISBN 0-404-51391-3). AMS Pr.

MARSHALL, D. N.

Gidwani, N. N., ed. Comparative Librarianship. 1973. 10.50 (ISBN 0-686-20202-3). Intl Bk Dist.

MARSHALL, GEORGE CATLETT, 1880-1959

Bland, Larry I. & Hadsel, Fred L., eds. The Papers of George Catlett Moushall, "the Soldierly Spirit". Vol. I, 1880-1939. LC 81-47593. (Illus.). 750p. 1981. text ed. 30.00x (ISBN 0-8018-2552-0). Johns Hopkins.

Ferrell, Robert H. George C. Marshall Nineteen Forty-Seven to Nineteen Forty-Nine. LC 72-197304. (American Secretaries of State & Their Diplomacy, New Ser.: Vol. 15). 1966. 12.00x (ISBN 0-8154-0070-5). Cooper Sq.

Hobbs, Joseph P. Dear General: Eisenhower's Wartime Letters to Marshall. LC 72-123573. (Illus.). 263p. 1971. 18.00x (ISBN 0-8018-1205-4). Johns Hopkins.

McCarthy, Joseph. America's Retreat from Victory. 1955. 4.95 (ISBN 0-8159-5004-7). Devin.

Marshall, George C. Marshall's Mission to China: The Report & Appended Documents. 1976. Set. 60.00 (ISBN 0-89093-115-1). U Pubns Amer.

Pogue, Forrest C. George C. Marshall: Education of a General 1889-1939. Harrison, Gordon, ed. 1963. 15.00 (ISBN 0-670-33685-8). Viking Pr.

--George C. Marshall: Organizer of Victory 1943-1945. LC 63-18373. (Illus.). 512p. 1973. 15.00 (ISBN 0-670-33694-7). Viking Pr.

MARSHALL, HUMPHRY, 1722-1801

Darlington, William. Memorials of John Bartram & Humphry Marshall. (Classica Botanica Americana Ser: Suppl. 1). 1967. Repr. of 1849 ed. 31.25 (ISBN 0-02-843620-2). Hafner.

MARSHALL, JOHN, 1755-1835

Baker, Leonard. John Marshall: A Life in Law. 864p. 1981. pap. 12.95 (ISBN 0-02-001700-6, Collier). Macmillan.

Beveridge, Albert J. John Marshall, 4 vols. LC 80-24550. (American Statesmen Ser.). 2400p. 1981. Set. pap. 30.00 (ISBN 0-87754-178-7). Chelsea Hse.

--Life of John Marshall: Unabridged, 4 vols. in 2. new ed. LC 34-7756. (Illus.). 2496p. 1974. lib. bdg. 100.00 set (ISBN 0-910220-65-4). Larlin Corp.

Faulkner, Robert K. The Jurisprudence of John Marshall. LC 80-14281. xii, 307p. 1980. Repr. of 1968 ed. lib. bdg. 25.50x (ISBN 0-313-22508-7, FAJU). Greenwood.

Gunther, Gerald, ed. John Marshall's Defense of "McCulloch Vs Maryland". 1969. 10.00x (ISBN 0-8047-0698-0); pap. 2.95 (ISBN 0-8047-0699-9, SP108). Stanford U Pr.

Haskins, George L. The Foundations of Power: John Marshall, 1801-1815. (History of the Supreme Court of the United States: Vol. II). (Illus.). 900p. 1981. 60.00 (ISBN 0-02-541360-0). Macmillan.

Johnson, Herbert A., et al, eds. The Papers of John Marshall, Vol. 1: Correspondence & Papers, November 10, 1775-June 23, 1788, & Account Book, September 1783-June 1788. LC 74-9575. (Institute of Early American History & Culture Ser.). (Illus.). 1974. 22.50x (ISBN 0-8078-1233-1). U of NC Pr.

Jones, W. M., ed. Chief Justice John Marshall: A Reappraisal. LC 70-152688. (American Constitutional & Legal History Ser). 1971. Repr. of 1956 ed. lib. bdg. 22.50 (ISBN 0-306-70132-4). Da Capo.

Loth, David G. Chief Justice: John Marshall & the Growth of the Republic. Repr. of 1949 ed. lib. bdg. 18.75x (ISBN 0-8371-2450-6, LOJM). Greenwood.

Magruder, Allan B. John Marshall. Morse, John T., Jr., ed. LC 73-128974. (American Statesmen: No. 10). Repr. of 1898 ed. 18.00 (ISBN 0-404-50860-X). AMS Pr.

--John Marshall. 1888. 10.00 (ISBN 0-8414-6447-2). Folcroft.

Marshall, John. An Autobiographical Sketch by John Marshall. Adams, John S., ed. LC 71-160849. (American Constitutional Legal History Ser.). (Illus.). 74p. 1973. Repr. of 1937 ed. lib. bdg. 15.00 (ISBN 0-306-70216-9). Da Capo.

Marshall, John & Oster, John E. The Political & Economic Doctrines of John Marshall. 1914. 22.50 (ISBN 0-8337-2636-6). B Franklin.

Martini, Teri. John Marshall. LC 73-11430. (Illus.). (gr. 4-7). 1974. 5.25 (ISBN 0-664-32540-8). Westminster.

Newmyer, R. Kent. Supreme Court Under Marshall & Taney. LC 68-29540. (AHM American History Ser.). (Orig.). 1969. pap. 4.95x (ISBN 0-88295-746-5). Harlan Davidson.

Oliver, Andrew. The Portraits of John Marshall. LC 76-13648. (Illus.). 1977. 12.50x (ISBN 0-8139-0633-4, Institute of Early American History & Culture). U Pr of Va.

Palmer, Benjamin W. Marshall & Taney, Statesmen of the Law. LC 66-24745. 1966. Repr. of 1939 ed. 7.50 (ISBN 0-8462-0794-X). Russell.

Stinchcombe, William C. & Cullen, Charles T., eds. Papers of John Marshall, Vol. III: Correspondence & Papers January 1796-December 1798. LC 74-9575. (Illus.). 1979. 27.50x (ISBN 0-8078-1337-0). U of NC Pr.

Stites, Frances N. John Marshall: Defender of the Constitution. (Library of American Biography). (Orig.). 1981. 11.95 (ISBN 0-316-81669-8); pap. text ed. 4.95 (ISBN 0-316-81667-1). Little.

Surrency, Erwin C., ed. The Marshall Reader. LC 55-11500. (Orig.). 1955. 7.50 (ISBN 0-379-11303-1); pap. 2.50 (ISBN 0-685-19007-2). Oceana.

Thayer, James B. John Marshall. LC 76-155923. (American Constitutional & Legal History Ser.). 157p. 1974. Repr. of 1901 ed. lib. bdg. 19.50 (ISBN 0-306-70287-8). Da Capo.

Thayer, James B., et al. John Marshall. LC 67-25514. 1967. pap. 1.95 (ISBN 0-226-79408-3, P260, Phoen). U of Chicago Pr.

MARSHALL, PETER, 1902-1949

Marshall, Catherine. Man Called Peter. 1971. pap. 2.50 (ISBN 0-380-00894-7, 48256). Avon.

MARSHALL, THURGOOD, 1908-

Bland, Randall W. Private Pressure on Public Law: Legal Career of Justice Thurgood Marshall. LC 72-91170. 1973. 15.00 (ISBN 0-8046-9035-9, Natl U). Kennikat.

--Private Pressure on Public Law: The Legal Career of Justice Thurgood Marshall. LC 72-91170. (Illus.). 220p. 1973. pap. 7.50 (ISBN 0-8046-9048-0, Natl U). Kennikat.

Swindler, William F. The Constitution & Chief Justice Marshall. (Illus.). 1979. 17.95 (ISBN 0-396-07500-2). Dodd.

MARSHALL FIELD AND COMPANY

Twyman, Robert W. History of Marshall Field & Co., 1852-1906. LC 75-41784. (Companies & Men: Business Enterprises in America). (Illus.). 1976. Repr. of 1954 ed. 18.00x (ISBN 0-405-08099-9). Arno.

Wendt, Lloyd & Kogan, Herman. Give the Lady What She Wants: The Story of Marshall Fields & Company. LC 52-7501. (Illus.). 1979. pap. 3.95 (ISBN 0-89708-020-3). And Bks.

MARSHALL LANGUAGE

Abo, Takaji, et al. Marshallese-English Dictionary. LC 76-26156. (PALI Language Texts-Micronesia). 600p. 1976. pap. text ed. 11.50x (ISBN 0-8248-0457-0). U Pr of Hawaii.

Bender, Byron W. Spoken Marshallese. (PALI Language Texts: Micronesian). (Orig., Marshallese & Eng.). 1969. pap. text ed. 10.00x (ISBN 0-87022-070-5). U Pr of Hawaii.

MARSHALL PLAN

see Economic Assistance, American

MARSHALLIAN ECONOMICS

see Neoclassical School of Economics

MARSHALS

Arizona's Angry Man: U. S. Marshal Milton B. Duffield. 1970. pap. 3.00 (ISBN 0-910152-03-9). AZ Hist Foun.

O'Neal, William. Henry Brown: Outlaw Marshal. LC 80-65457. 165p. 1981. 12.95 (ISBN 0-932702-09-0); collector's edtion 75.00 (ISBN 0-932702-10-4). Creative Texas.

Shirley, Glenn. Heck Thomas: Frontier Marshal. LC 81-40293. (Illus.). 320p. 1981. 15.95 (ISBN 0-8061-1664-1). U of Okla Pr.

MARSHALS (COURT OFFICIALS)

see United States Marshals

MARSHALS, COURT

see United States Marshals

MARSHES

see also Drainage; Fens; Marsh Ecology; Moors and Heaths; Reclamation of Land

Buck, Lewis A. Wetlands: Bogs, Marshes & Swamps. LC 73-5711. (Finding-Out Book). 64p. (gr. 2-4). 1974. PLB 7.95 (ISBN 0-8193-0702-5, Pub. by Parents). Enslow Pubs.

Cavanaugh, Cam. Saving the Great Swamp: The People, the Power Brokers & an Urban Wilderness. LC 78-8132. (Illus.). 1978. 11.95 (ISBN 0-914366-11-4). Columbia Pub.

Chapman, V. J. Salt Marshes & Salt Deserts of the World. suppl'd, 2nd ed. (Illus.). 1976. pap. 60.00x (ISBN 3-7682-0927-X, Pub. by J. Cramer). Intl Schol Bk Serv.

--Salt Marshes & Salt Deserts of the World. 2nd ed. 1974. 75.00 (ISBN 3-7682-0927-X). Lubrecht & Cramer.

Coleman, James M. Recent Coastal Sedimentation: Central Louisiana Coast. LC 67-63069. (Coastal Studies, Vol. 17). (Illus.). 1967. pap. 4.00x (ISBN 0-8071-0403-5). La State U Pr.

Cowgill, Ursula M. & Hutchinson, G. E. Bajo De Santa Fe. LC 63-22635. (Transactions Ser.: Vol. 53, Pt. 7). (Illus.). 1963. pap. 1.00 (ISBN 0-87169-537-5). Am Philos.

Daiber, Franklin C. Animals of the Tidal Marsh. 432p. 1981. text ed. 19.95 (ISBN 0-442-24854-7). Van Nos Reinhold.

Dame, Richard F., ed. Marsh-Estuarine Systems Simulation. LC 78-31554. (Belle W. Baruch Library in Marine Science Ser.). 1979. lib. bdg. 27.50x (ISBN 0-87249-375-X). U of SC Pr.

Errington, Paul L. Of Men & Marshes. fasc. ed. (Illus.). 1957. pap. 9.45x (ISBN 0-8138-2350-1). Iowa St U Pr.

Gates, David A. Seasons of the Salt Marsh. LC 74-27956. 128p. 1975. 8.95 (ISBN 0-85699-121-X). Chatham Pr.

Hydrology of Marsh-Ridden Areas. (Studies and Reports in Hydrology: No. 19). (Illus.). 562p. 1975. pap. 37.50 (ISBN 0-685-65018-9, 92-3-101264-9, UNESCO). Unipub.

Poinssot, Bernard. The Stinson Beach Salt Marsh: The Form of Its Growth. LC 77-70990. (Illus.). 1977. pap. 12.00 (ISBN 0-918540-01-1). Stinson Beach.

Ranwell, D. S. Ecology of Salt Marshes & Sand Dunes. (Illus.). 258p. 1972. text ed. 26.00x (ISBN 0-412-10500-4, Pub. by Chapman & Hall England). Methuen Inc.

Roberts, Mervin F. The Tide Marsh Guide. (Illus.). 1979. pap. 7.95 (ISBN 0-525-93080-9). Dutton.

Snow, John. Secrets of a Salt Marsh. 64p. (Orig.). (gr. 4-10). pap. 5.95 (ISBN 0-930096-09-6). G Gannett.

MARSILIUS OF PADUA, d. 1342

D'Entreves, Alexander P. Medieval Contribution to Political Thought: Thomas Aquinas, Marsilius of Padua, Richard Hooker. 1959. Repr. of 1939 ed. text ed. 8.50x (ISBN 0-391-00513-8). Humanities.

Gewirth, Alan. Marsilius of Padua, 2 vols. in one. Mayer, J. P., ed. LC 78-67352. (European Political Thought Ser.). 1979. Repr. of 1956 ed. Set. lib. bdg. 54.00x (ISBN 0-405-11699-3). Arno.

MARSTON, JOHN, 1575-1634

Allen, Morse S. Satire of John Marston. LC 65-26460. (Studies in Drama, No. 39). 1969. Repr. of 1920 ed. lib. bdg. 45.95 (ISBN 0-8383-0500-8). Haskell.

Caputi, Anthony. John Marston, Satirist. 289p. 1976. Repr. of 1961 ed. lib. bdg. 18.00x (ISBN 0-374-91286-6). Octagon.

Colley, John S. John Marston's Theatrical Drama. (Salzburg Studies in English Literature, Jacobean Drama Studies: No. 33). 202p. 1974. pap. text ed. 25.00x (ISBN 0-391-01347-5). Humanities.

Finkelpearl, Philip J. John Marston of the Middle Temple: An Elizabethan Dramatist in His Social Setting. LC 69-12722. (Illus.). 1969. 15.00x (ISBN 0-674-47860-6). Harvard U Pr.

Geckle, George L. John Marston's Plays: Themes, Images, Sources. LC 77-89777. 224p. 1979. 18.50 (ISBN 0-8386-2157-0). Fairleigh Dickinson.

Ingram, R. W. John Marston. (English Authors Ser.: No. 216). 1978. 12.50 (ISBN 0-8057-6725-8). Twayne.

Jensen, Ejner J. John Marston, Dramtist. (Salzburg Institute for English Literature Jacobean Drama Studies). (Orig.). 1980. pap. text ed. 25.00x (ISBN 0-391-01717-9). Humanities.

Lyon, John H. Study of the Newe Metamorphosis. LC 20-3786. Repr. of 1919 ed. 19.75 (ISBN 0-404-04087-X). AMS Pr.

Scott, Michael. John Marston Plays: Theme, Structure & Performance. LC 76-56045. 1978. text ed. 23.50x (ISBN 0-06-496128-1). B&N.

MARSUPIALIA

Gardner, Alfred L. The Systematics of the Genus Didelphis (Marsupialia: Didelphidae) in North & Middle America. (Special Publications: No. 4). (Illus., Orig.). 1973. pap. 4.00 (ISBN 0-89672-029-2). Tex Tech Pr.

Lauber, Patricia. Surprising Kangaroos & Other Pouched Mammals. (Gateway Ser.: No. 37). (Illus.). (gr. 3-6). 1965. PLB 5.99 (ISBN 0-394-90137-1, BYR). Random.

Lavine, Sigmund A. Wonders of Marsupials. (Wonders Ser.). (Illus.). (gr. 4 up). 1979. 5.95 (ISBN 0-396-07619-X). Dodd.

Lyne, Gordon. Marsupials & Monotremes of Australia. LC 67-12697. 1968. 9.95 (ISBN 0-8008-5125-0). Taplinger.

Marshall, Larry G. Evolution of the Borhyaenidae, Extinct South American Predaceous Marsupials. (Publications in Geological Sciences: Vol. 117). 1978. pap. 12.50x (ISBN 0-520-09571-5). U of Cal Pr.

Rabinowich, Ellen. Kangaroos, Koalas, & Other Marsupials. LC 78-5805. (First Bks). (Illus.). (gr. 4-6). 1978. PLB 6.45 s&l (ISBN 0-531-01489-4). Watts.

Sherman, Geraldine. Animals with Pouches: The Marsupials. LC 77-27592. (Illus.). (gr. 1-4). 1978. reinforced bdg. 7.95 (ISBN 0-8234-0324-6). Holiday.

Smith, Ivan. Death of a Wombat. 1972. 14.95 (ISBN 0-85885-009-5). David & Charles.

Stonehouse, B., ed. Biology of Marsupials. 1977. 39.50 (ISBN 0-8391-0852-4). Univ Park.

Tyndale-Biscoe, Hugh. Life of Marsupials. LC 73-2310. (Contemporary Biology Ser.). 262p. 1973. 24.50 (ISBN 0-444-19558-0). Univ Park.

MARTENS, CONRAD

Lindsay, Lionel. Conrad Martens - the Man & His Art. rev. & enl. ed. (Illus.). 1968. 30.00x (ISBN 0-8426-1354-4). Verry.

Steele, J. G. Conrad Martens in Queensland: The Frontier Travels of a Colonial Artist. (Illus.). 1979. 25.00x (ISBN 0-7022-1065-X). U of Queensland Pr.

MARTENSITE

Nishiyama, Zenji. Martensitic Transformation. Fine, M. & Meshii, M., trs. (Materials Science & Technology Ser.). 1978. 60.00 (ISBN 0-12-519850-7). Acad Pr.

MARTHA (COMPUTER PROGRAM LANGUAGE)

Penfield, Paul, Jr. MARTHA User's Manual. 1971. pap. 7.95x (ISBN 0-262-66015-6). MIT Pr.

MARTHA'S VINEYARD, MASSACHUSETTS

Burroughs, Polly. Exploring Martha's Vineyard. LC 72-93259. (Illustrated Guide Ser.). 1973. pap. 3.95 (ISBN 0-85699-064-7). Chatham Pr.

--Guide to Martha's Vineyard. LC 79-50695. (Illus.). 1979. pap. 4.95 (ISBN 0-87106-030-2). Globe Pequot.

Byers, D. & Johnson, F. Two Sites on Martha's Vineyard, Vol. 1. LC 40-3078. 1940. 4.00 (ISBN 0-939312-00-X). Peabody Found.

Chamberlain, Barbara B. These Fragile Outposts. 352p. 1981. pap. 9.95 (ISBN 0-940160-12-9). Parnassus Imprints.

Gillespie, Mabel. Where the Birds Are. LC 76-55062. (Illus., Orig.). 1976. pap. 4.95 (ISBN 0-932384-03-X). Tashmoo.

Hare, Lloyd C. Thomas Mayhew, Patriarch to the Indians, 1593-1682. LC 76-104347. (Illus.). Repr. of 1932 ed. 20.00 (ISBN 0-404-03108-0). AMS Pr.

Hough, Henry B. Martha's Vineyard - Summer Resort After One Hundred Years. 2nd ed. (Illus.). 278p. 1966. 9.95 (ISBN 0-914960-33-4, Pub. by Academy Bks); pap. write for info. (ISBN 0-914960-32-6). C E Tuttle.

--Soundings at Sea Level. 1980. 10.95 (ISBN 0-395-29165-8). HM.

Simon, Peter, ed. On the Vineyard. LC 79-7878. (Illus., Orig.). 1980. pap. 10.95 (ISBN 0-385-15052-0, Anch). Doubleday.

Sterling, Dorothy. The Outer Lands: A Natural History Guide to Cape Cod, Martha's Vineyard, Nantucket, Block Island, & Long Island. (Illus.). 1978. 10.95 (ISBN 0-393-06438-7); pap. 5.95 (ISBN 0-393-06441-7). Norton.

MARTHA'S VINEYARD, MASSACHUSETTS-POETRY

Riggs, Lineaweaver, et al. Martha's Vineyard: Poems & Prints. 1973. pap. 2.95 (ISBN 0-87233-839-8). Bauhan.

MARTI, JOSE, 1853-1895

Agramonte, Roberto. Marti y Su Concepcion De la Sociedad. LC 81-10377. (Illus.). 307p. 1981. pap. price not set (ISBN 0-8477-3500-1). U of PR Pr.

--Marti y su Concepcion Del Mundo. 9.35 (ISBN 0-8477-3102-2); pap. 7.50 (ISBN 0-8477-3103-0). U of PR Pr.

De Zendegui, Guillermo. Marti's Circle. Johnson, Scott, tr. from Span. 1980. lib. bdg. 59.95 (ISBN 0-8490-3061-7). Gordon Pr.

Garcia, Cisneros F. Jose Marti y las Artes Plasticas. 1972. 9.95 (ISBN 0-88303-996-6); pap. 7.95 (ISBN 0-685-73207-X). E Torres & Sons.

Gray, Richard B. Jose Marti: Cuban Patriot. LC 62-20772. 1962. 9.50 (ISBN 0-8130-0090-4). U Presses Fla.

Lizaso, Felix. Marti, Martyr of Cuban Independence. LC 73-20502. (Illus.). 260p. 1974. Repr. of 1953 ed. lib. bdg. 15.00x (ISBN 0-8371-7329-9, LIMA). Greenwood.

Magdaleno, Mauricio. Jose Marti. 1976. lib. bdg. 59.95 (ISBN 0-8490-2108-1). Gordon Pr.

Manach, Jorge. Marti, Apostle of Freedom. (Illus.). 7.50 (ISBN 0-8159-6201-0). Devin.

Ripoll, Carlos. Archivo Jose Marti: Repertorio Critico, Medio Siglo De Estudios Martianos. 1971. 14.50 (ISBN 0-88303-010-1); pap. 11.50 (ISBN 0-685-73214-2). E Torres & Sons.

--Indice Universal De la Obra De Jose Marti. 1971. 15.00 (ISBN 0-88303-009-8); pap. 10.95 (ISBN 0-685-73213-4). E Torres & Sons.

Vitier, Cintio & Garcia, Fina. Temas martianos. LC 81-68709. (La Nave y el Puerto Ser.). 345p. (Span.). 1982. pap. 8.95 (ISBN 0-940238-44-6). Ediciones Huracan.

MARTIAL (MARTIALUS, MARCUS VALERIUS)

Nixon, Paul. Martial & the Modern Epigram. LC 63-10304. (Our Debt to Greece & Rome Ser). Repr. of 1930 ed. 7.50x (ISBN 0-8154-0165-5). Cooper Sq.

Pott, J. A. & Wright, F. A., trs. Martial, the Twelve Books Epigrams. 402p. 1981. Repr. lib. bdg. 65.00 (ISBN 0-89987-566-1). Darby Bks.

Whipple, Thomas K. Martial & English Epigram from Sir Thomas Wyatt to Ben Jonson. LC 70-90362. 1970. Repr. of 1925 ed. 7.50 (ISBN 0-87753-043-2). Phaeton.

MARTIAL LAW

see also Courts-Martial and Courts of Inquiry; Habeas Corpus; Military Law

Anthony, J. Garner. Hawaii Under Army Rule. 213p. 1975. pap. 3.95 (ISBN 0-8248-0377-9). U Pr of Hawaii.

Bhatia, H. S. Martial Law: Theory & Practice. 1979. text ed. 11.00x (ISBN 0-391-01039-5). Humanities.

Elliott. Thailand: Origins of Military Rule. 190p. 1978. 11.95 (ISBN 0-905762-10-X); pap. 5.95 (ISBN 0-905762-11-8). Lawrence Hill.

Finlason, W. F. Commentaries Upon Martial Law, with Special Reference to Its Regulation & Restraint: With an Introduction, Containing Comments Upon the Charge of the Lord Chief Justice in the Jamaica Case. 287p. 1980. Repr. of 1867 ed. lib. bdg. 28.50x (ISBN 0-8377-0536-3). Rothman.

Glenn, Garrard. Army & the Law. LC 72-168168. Repr. of 1943 ed. 18.00 (ISBN 0-404-02819-5). AMS Pr.

Klaus, Samuel, ed. Milligan Case. LC 78-118031. (Civil Liberties in American History Ser). 1970. Repr. of 1929 ed. lib. bdg. 42.50 (ISBN 0-306-71945-2). Da Capo.

Marshall, John A. American Bastille. LC 71-121115. (Civil Liberties in American History Ser). 1970. Repr. of 1869 ed. lib. bdg. 69.50 (ISBN 0-306-71963-0). Da Capo.

Rankin, Robert S. When Civil Law Fails. LC 39-16186. Repr. of 1939 ed. 16.50 (ISBN 0-404-05224-X). AMS Pr.

Rosenberg, David A., ed. Marcos & Martial Law in the Philippines. LC 78-15145. 1979. 22.50x (ISBN 0-8014-1195-5). Cornell U Pr.

Whiting, William. War Powers Under the Constitution of the United States. LC 70-169640. (American Constitutional & Legal History Ser). 1972. Repr. of 1871 ed. lib. bdg. 59.50 (ISBN 0-306-70361-0). Da Capo.

MARTIALL, JOHN, 1534-1597

Calfhill, James. An Answer to John Martiall's Treatise of the Cross. 1846. 25.50 (ISBN 0-384-07020-5). Johnson Repr.

Fulke, William. Stapleton's Fortress Overthrown: A Rejoinder to Martiall's Reply. Repr. of 1848 ed. 25.50 (ISBN 0-384-17240-7). Johnson Repr.

MARTIN, SAINT, BISHOP OF TOURS, 4TH CENT.

Donaldson, Christopher. Martin of Tours. (Illus.). 1980. 20.00 (ISBN 0-7100-0422-2). Routledge & Kegan.

Freeman, Margaret B. The St. Martin Embroideries. LC 68-21564. (Illus.). 1968. 2.95 (ISBN 0-87099-071-3). Metro Mus Art.

Severus, Sulpicius. The Life of Saint Martin of Tours. pap. 1.50 (ISBN 0-686-05653-1). Eastern Orthodox.

MARTIN, GREGORY, d. 1582

Fulke, William. Defence of the Sincere & True Translations of the Holy Scriptures into the English Tongue. Repr. of 1843 ed. 42.50 (ISBN 0-384-17230-X). Johnson Repr.

MARTIN, JOHN, 1789-1854

Feaver, William. The Art of John Martin. (Illus.). 360p. 1975. 36.00x (ISBN 0-19-817334-2). Oxford U Pr.

MARTIN, KINGSLEY

Rolph, C. H. Kingsley: The Life, Letters & Diaries of Kingsley Martin. LC 73-164111. 1974. 14.00x (ISBN 0-575-01636-1). Intl Pubns Serv.

MARTIN, LUTHER

Clarkson, Paul S. & Jett, R. Samuel. Luther Martin of Maryland. LC 76-94392. 352p. 1970. 22.50x (ISBN 0-8018-1067-1). Johns Hopkins.

Goddard, Henry P. Luther Martin: The "Federal Bulldog". Bd. with A Sketch of the Life & Character of Nathaniel Ramsey. Brand, W. F. LC 72-14408. (Maryland Historical Society. Fund-Publications: No. 24). Repr. of 1887 ed. 7.50 (ISBN 0-404-57624-9). AMS Pr.

MARTIN, PAUL ELLIOT, 1897-

Vernon, Walter N. Forever Building: The Life & Ministry of Paul E. Martin. LC 73-88016. (Illus.). 192p. 1973. 6.95 (ISBN 0-87074-142-X). SMU Press.

MARTIN, VICTORIA (CLAFLIN) WOODHULL, 1838-1927

Arling, Emanie S. The Terrible Siren: Victoria Woodhull (1838-1927) LC 72-2587. (American Women Ser: Images & Realities). (Illus.). 478p. 1972. Repr. of 1928 ed. 20.00 (ISBN 0-405-04474-7). Arno.

MARTIN, ZELIE MARIE (GUERIN), 1831-1877

Foley, Barbara. Zelie Martin. (Illus.). 1960. 1.00 (ISBN 0-8198-0181-X). Dghtrs St Paul.

MARTIN DE PORRES, SAINT, 1579-1639

Bishop, Claire H. Martin De Porres, Hero. (Illus.). (gr. 4-6). 1954. 4.25 (ISBN 0-395-06634-4). HM.

MARTIN FAMILY

Haslam, Malcolm. The Martin Brothers, Potters. (Illus.). 174p. 1978. 75.00x (ISBN 0-903685-06-X). Wittenborn.

MARTINEAU, HARRIET, 1802-1876

Bosanquet, Theodora. Harriet Martineau. 1971. Repr. of 1927 ed. 19.00 (ISBN 0-403-00526-4). Scholarly.

--Harriet Martineau. 1973. Repr. of 1927 ed. 25.00 (ISBN 0-8274-1332-7). R West.

--Harriet Martineau: An Essay in Comprehension. LC 74-16320. Repr. of 1927 ed. lib. bdg. 25.00 (ISBN 0-8414-9940-3). Folcroft.

Colson, Percy. Victorian Portraits. facs. ed. LC 68-16921. (Essay Index Reprint Ser). 1932. 15.00 (ISBN 0-8369-0328-5). Arno.

Miller, F. Fenwick. Harriet Martineau. LC 70-160772. 1971. Repr. of 1884 ed. 12.00 (ISBN 0-8046-1604-3). Kennikat.

--Harriet Martineau. 1973. Repr. of 1889 ed. 9.00 (ISBN 0-8274-1333-5). R West.

Miller, Mrs. F. Fenwick. Harriet Martineau. 1979. Repr. of 1890 ed. lib. bdg. 25.00 (ISBN 0-8495-3840-8). Arden Lib.

Nevill, John C. Harriet Martineau. LC 73-11354. 1943. Repr. lib. bdg. 15.00 (ISBN 0-8414-2368-7). Folcroft.

Neville, John C. Harriet Martineau. 1978. Repr. of 1943 ed. lib. bdg. 17.50 (ISBN 0-8495-4012-7). Arden Lib.

Pichanick, Valerie. Harriet Martineau: The Woman & Her Work, Eighteen Hundred & Two to Eighteen Seventy-Six. (Women & Culture Ser.). 336p. 1980. 15.00x (ISBN 0-472-10002-5). U of Mich Pr.

Von Petzold, Gertrud. Harriet Martineau und Ihre Sittlich Religiose Weltschau. 1941. pap. 5.00 (ISBN 0-384-46100-X). Johnson Repr.

Webb, R. K. Harriet Martineau: A Radical Victorian. 385p. 1980. Repr. of 1960 ed. lib. bdg. 27.50x (ISBN 0-374-98288-0). Octagon.

Wheatley, Vera. The Life & Work of Harriet Martineau. 1957. Repr. 40.00 (ISBN 0-8274-2915-0). R West.

MARTINEAU, JAMES, 1805-1900

Hertz, Joseph H. Ethical System of James Martineau. LC 3-12373. Repr. of 1894 ed. 16.00 (ISBN 0-404-03258-3). AMS Pr.

Sidgwick, Henry. Lectures on the Ethics of T. H. Green, Herbert Spencer, & J. Martineau. LC 3-865. 1968. Repr. of 1902 ed. 22.00 (ISBN 0-527-82812-2). Kraus Repr.

MARTINEZ, MARIA (MONTOYA)

Marriott, Alice. Maria: The Potter of San Ildefonso. rev. ed. (CAI Ser.: Vol. 27). (Illus.). 1976. Repr. of 1948 ed. 11.95 (ISBN 0-8061-0176-8). U of Okla Pr.

Nelson, Mary C. Maria Martinez. 2nd ed. LC 74-12323. (Story of an American Indian Ser.). (Illus.). (gr. 5 up). 1974. PLB 6.95 (ISBN 0-87518-098-1). Dillon.

Peterson, Susan. The Living Tradition of Maria Martinez. LC 77-75373. (Illus.). 300p. 1977. 39.95 (ISBN 0-87011-319-4). Kodansha.

MARTINEZ MONTANES, JUAN, 1568-1648

Proske, Beatrice G. Juan Martinez Montanes, Sevillian Sculptor. (Illus.). 1967. 35.00 (ISBN 0-87535-107-7). Hispanic Soc.

MARTINEZ RUIZ, JOSE, 1873-
Glenn, Kathleen M. Azorin (Jose Martinez Ruiz) (World Authors Ser.: No. 604). 1981. lib. bdg. 14.95 (ISBN 0-8057-6446-1). Twayne.
MARTINGALES (MATHEMATICS)
Cornea, A. & Licea, G. Order & Potential Resolvent Familiers of Kernels. (Lecture Notes in Mathematics: Vol. 494). iv, 154p. 1976. pap. 9.90 (ISBN 0-387-07531-3). Springer-Verlag.
Garsia, Adriano M. Martingale Inequalities. (Mathematics Lecture Note: Vol. 53). 1973. pap. 9.50 (ISBN 0-8053-3103-4, Adv Bk Prog). Benjamin-Cummings.
Hall, P. G. & Hayde, C. C. Martingale Limit Theory & Its Application. LC 80-536. (Probability & Mathematical Statistics Ser.). 1980. 36.00 (ISBN 0-12-319350-8). Acad Pr.
Hayes, C. A. & Pauc, C. Y. Derivation & Martingales. (Ergebnisse der Mathematik und Ihrer Grenzgebiete: Vol. 49). 1970. 31.20 (ISBN 0-387-04807-3). Springer-Verlag.
Meyer, P. A. Martingales & Stochastic Integrals I. LC 72-88111. (Lecture Notes in Mathematics: Vol. 284). vi, 89p. 1972. pap. 6.30 (ISBN 0-387-05983-0). Springer-Verlag.
Neveu, J. Discrete-Parameter Martingales. LC 74-79241. (Mathematical Library: Vol. 10). 236p. 1975. pap. 36.75 (ISBN 0-444-10708-8, North-Holland). Elsevier.
Williams, David. Diffusions, Markov Processes & Martingales: Volume 1: Foundation. LC 78-16634. (Probability & Mathematical Statistics Ser.: Applied Section). 1979. 47.25 (ISBN 0-471-99705-6, Pub. by Wiley-Interscience). Wiley.
MARTINIQUE
Anderson, Susan H. Cosimo Brunetti: Three Relations of the West Indies in 1659-60. LC 72-93501. (Transactions Ser.: Vol. 59, Pt. 6). (Illus.). 1969. pap. 1.00 (ISBN 0-87169-596-0). Am Philos.
Hearn, Lafcadio. Two Years in the French West Indies. LC 73-104479. (Illus.). Repr. of 1890 ed. lib. bdg. 17.50x (ISBN 0-8398-0775-9). Irvington.
Horowitz, Michael M. Morne-Paysan: Peasant Village in Martinique. Spindler, George & Spindler, Louise, eds. (Case Studies in Cultural Anthropology). 128p. pap. text ed. 6.95x (ISBN 0-8290-0309-6). Irvington.
Kennan, George. Tragedy of Pelee: A Narrative of Personal Experience & Observation in Martinique. LC 69-18984. (Illus.). Repr. of 1902 ed. 14.25x (ISBN 0-8371-0932-9). Greenwood.
MARTINS
see Purple Martin
MARTIN'S BANK, LIMITED, LONDON
Martin, John B. Grasshopper in Lombard Street. LC 68-56788. (Research & Source Works Ser.: No. 277). (Illus.). 1969. Repr. of 1892 ed. 24.00 (ISBN 0-8337-2266-2). B Franklin.
MARTINU, BOHUSLAV, 1890-1959
Large, Brian. Martinu. LC 75-45082. (Illus.). 198p. 1976. text ed. 32.50x (ISBN 0-8419-0256-9). Holmes & Meier.
MARTORELL, JOANNET-TIRANT LO BLANCH
Vaeth, Joseph A. Tirant Lo Blanch: A Study of Its Authorship, Principal Sources & Historical Setting. LC 18-11455. (Columbia University. Studies in Romance Philology & Literature). Repr. of 1918 ed. 18.00 (ISBN 0-404-50623-2). AMS Pr.
MARTYN, EDWARD, 1859-1923
Davis, Thomas. Essays Literary & Historical. O'Donoghue, D. J., ed. 456p. 1973. Repr. of 1914 ed. 19.50 (ISBN 0-685-26065-8). Lemma.
Gwynn, Denis R. Edward Martyn & the Irish Revival. (Illus.). 349p. 1973. Repr. of 1930 ed. 19.50 (ISBN 0-685-26069-0). Lemma.
Setterquist, Jan. Ibsen & the Beginnings of Anglo-Irish Drama. Liljegren, S. B., ed. Incl. John Millington Synge. (Irish Language & Literature Institute). 92p. Repr. of 1952 ed (ISBN 0-88211-045-4); Edward Martyn. (Upsala Irish Studies). 116p. Repr. of 1960 ed (ISBN 0-88211-048-9). LC 73-80308. 1973. Repr. 7.50 ea. S A Russell.
MARTYRDOM
see also Martyrs
Frend, W. H. Martydom & Persecution in the Early Church. (Twin Brooks Ser.). 645p. 1981. pap. 12.95 (ISBN 0-8010-3502-3). Baker Bk.
Horbury, W. & McNeil, B., eds. Suffering & Martyrdom in the New Testament. LC 80-40706. 240p. Date not set. 39.95 (ISBN 0-521-23482-4). Cambridge U Pr.
Reade, Winwood. The Martyrdom of Man. 1981. lib. bdg. 69.95 (ISBN 0-686-71630-2). Revisionist Pr.
Weinrich, William C. Spirit & Martyrdom: A Study of the Work of the Holy Spirit in Contexts of Persecution & Martyrdom in the New Testament & Early Christian Literature. LC 80-5597. 334p. (Orig.). 1981. lib. bdg. 20.75 (ISBN 0-8191-1655-6); pap. text ed. 11.75 (ISBN 0-8191-1656-4). U Pr of Amer.
Williams, Sam K. Jesus' Death As Saving Event the Background & Origin of a Concept. LC 75-28341. (Harvard Dissertations in Religion). 1975. pap. 9.00 (ISBN 0-89130-029-5, 020102). Scholars Pr Ca.
Wurmbrand, Richard. Tortured for Christ. 1973. pap. 1.75 (ISBN 0-88264-001-1). Diane Bks.
MARTYROLOGIES
Aengus, Saint Martyrology of St. Aengus. pap. 12.50 (ISBN 0-686-25554-2). Eastern Orthodox.
Budge, Ernest A., ed. Coptic Martyrdoms, Etc. in the Dialect of Upper Egypt. LC 77-3588. (Coptic Texts: Vol. 4). (Illus.). Repr. of 1914 ed. 50.00 (ISBN 0-404-11554-3). AMS Pr.
Catholic Church. The Roman & British Martyrology. 1980. lib. bdg. 79.95 (ISBN 0-8490-3128-1). Gordon Pr.
Herzfeld, G., ed. Martyrologium: An Old English Martyrology. (EETS, OS Ser.: No. 116). Repr. of 1900 ed. 15.00 (ISBN 0-527-00115-5). Kraus Repr.
Wilson, John. The English Martyrologe. LC 78-25578. (English Experience Ser.: No. 495). 356p. 1970. Repr. of 1608 ed. 42.00 (ISBN 90-221-0254-8). Walter J Johnson.
MARTYRS
see also Martyrdom
Acts of the Christian Martyrs. pap. 3.95 (ISBN 0-686-19380-6). Eastern Orthodox.
Augsburger, Myron. Faithful Unto Death: Fifteen Young People Who Were Not Afraid to Die for Their Faith. LC 77-92462. (Illus.). 1978. 5.95 (ISBN 0-8499-0067-0). Word Bks.
Delehaye, Hippolyte. Les Origines du Culte des martyrs. 2nd, rev. ed. LC 78-63459. (The Crusades & Military Orders: Second Ser.). Repr. of 1933 ed. 40.00 (ISBN 0-404-16518-4). AMS Pr.
Dreyer, Peter. Martyrs & Fanatics. 1980. 11.95 (ISBN 0-671-24428-0). S&S.
Elliot, Elisabeth. Through Gates of Splendor. 1981. 2.95 (ISBN 0-8423-7151-6). Tyndale.
Fink, Leo G. Martyrs of the Sacred Heart. 1934. 10.00 (ISBN 0-8414-4255-X). Folcroft.
Forbush, W. B., ed. Fox's Book of Martyrs. 7.95 (ISBN 0-310-24390-4); pap. 4.95 (ISBN 0-310-24391-2). Zondervan.
Foxe. Foxe's Book of Martyrs. Repr. 8.00 (ISBN 0-686-12388-3). Church History.
Foxe, John. Acts & Monuments, 8 Vols. Cattley, S. R. & Townsend, George, eds. LC 79-168132. Repr. of 1849 ed. Set. 320.00 (ISBN 0-404-02590-0); 40.00 ea. AMS Pr.
--Foxe's Book of Martyrs. 400p. 1981. pap. 2.95 (ISBN 0-88368-095-5). Whitaker Hse.
--Foxe's Book of Martyrs. pap. 2.50 (ISBN 0-8007-8013-2, Spire Bks). Revell.
--Foxe's Book of Martyrs. Berry, W. Grinton, ed. (Giant Summit Bks). 1978. pap. 5.95 (ISBN 0-8010-3483-3). Baker Bk.
--Foxe's Christian Martyrs of the World. 11.95 (ISBN 0-8024-2872-X). Moody.
Gillies, John. The Martyrs of Guanabara. 1976. 5.95 (ISBN 0-8024-5187-X). Moody.
Gregorius, Saint Les Livres Des Miracles et Autres Opuscules, 4 Vols. 1863. Set. 126.00 (ISBN 0-384-19888-0); 31.50 ea.; pap. 27.00 ea.; Set. pap. 108.00 (ISBN 0-384-19889-9). Johnson Repr.
Hefley, James & Hefley, Marti. By Their Blood: Christian Martyrs of the Twentieth Century. LC 78-6187. 1979. 13.95 (ISBN 0-915134-28-4); pap. 7.95 (ISBN 0-915134-24-1). Mott Media.
Homan, Helen. Letters to the Martyrs. facs. ed. LC 79-148220. (Biography Index Reprint Ser.). 1951. 18.00 (ISBN 0-8369-8067-0). Arno.
Life of John Kline. 7.95 (ISBN 0-87178-118-2). Brethren.
Lowry, James W. In the Whale's Belly & Other Martyr Stories. (Illus.). Date not set. price not set (ISBN 0-87813-513-8). Christian Light.
McKee, John. A Martyr Bishop: The Life of St. Oliver Plunkett. 181p. 1975. 7.95 (ISBN 0-912414-21-9). Lumen Christi.
Marmorstein, Emil. The Murder of Jacob De Haan by the Zionists: A Martyr's Message. 1980. lib. bdg. 59.95 (ISBN 0-686-68747-7). Revisionist Pr.
Moiseyev, Ivan V. A Russian Martyr. 0.95 (ISBN 0-89985-107-X). Christ Nations.
Musurillo, Herbert. The Acts of the Christian Martyrs: Text & Translations. (Oxford Early English Texts Ser). 416p. 1972. 52.00x (ISBN 0-19-826806-8). Oxford U Pr.
Peterson, Reona. Tomorrow You Die. pap. 2.95 (ISBN 0-89728-060-1, 659262). Omega Pubns OR.
Ridley, Jasper G. Nicholas Ridley: A Biography. 1978. Repr. of 1957 ed. lib. bdg. 35.00 (ISBN 0-8492-2273-7). R West.
Russo-Alesi, Anthony I. Martyrology Pronouncing Dictionary. LC 79-167151. 1973. Repr. of 1939 ed. 19.00 (ISBN 0-8103-3272-8). Gale.
Saloff-Astakhoff, N. I. Judith. pap. 2.50 (ISBN 0-310-32462-9). Zondervan.
Schroetter, Hilda N. Foxe's Book of English Martyrs. 360p. 1981. 10.95 (ISBN 0-8499-0152-9). Word Bks.
Thomas, D. Aneurin, ed. Welsh Elizabethan Catholic Martyrs: Trial Documents of Saint Richard Gwyn & of the Venerable William Davies. new ed. 331p. 1972. 12.50x (ISBN 0-900768-97-5). Verry.
Van Braght, Thieleman J. Martyrs' Mirror. (Illus.). 1938. 22.50 (ISBN 0-8361-1390-X). Herald Pr.
Van Braught. Martyr's Mirror. Repr. 22.50 (ISBN 0-686-12366-2). Church History.
MARVELL, ANDREW, 1621-1678
Bagguley, William H., ed. Andrew Mavell, Sixteen Twenty-One to Sixteen Seventy-Eight: Tercentenary Tributes. LC 65-18787. (Illus.). 1965. Repr. of 1922 ed. 7.00 (ISBN 0-8462-0587-4). Russell.
Bennett, Joan. Five Metaphysical Poets: Donne, Herbert, Vaughan, Crashaw, Marvell. 1964. 27.50 (ISBN 0-521-04156-2); pap. 8.95x (ISBN 0-521-09238-8). Cambridge U Pr.
Birrell, Augustine. Andrew Marvell. LC 78-14755. 1905. lib. bdg. 15.00 (ISBN 0-8414-1730-X). Folcroft.
Brett, R. I. & Grant, G. F., eds. Andrew Marvell: Essays on the Tercentenary of His Death. 1979. 19.95x (ISBN 0-19-713435-1). Oxford U Pr.
Collins, Dan S. Andrew Marvell: A Reference Guide. (Reference Bks). 1981. lib. bdg. 32.00 (ISBN 0-8161-8017-2). G K Hall.
Craze, Michael. The Life & Lyrics of Andrew Marvell. 1979. text ed. 24.50x (ISBN 0-06-491309-0). B&N.
Cullen, Patrick. Spenser, Marvell, & Renaissance Pastoral. LC 76-123566. 1970. 10.00x (ISBN 0-674-83195-0). Harvard U Pr.
Donno, Elizabeth S., ed. Andrew Marvell: The Critical Heritage. (The Critical Heritage Ser.). 1978. 21.50x (ISBN 0-7100-8791-8). Routledge & Kegan.
Friedenreich, Kenneth. Tercentenary Essays in Honor of Andrew Marvell. (Illus.). 1977. 22.50 (ISBN 0-208-01567-1, Archon). Shoe String.
Guffey, George R., ed. A Concordance to the English Poems of Andrew Marvell. LC 73-21550. xiv, 623p. 1974. text ed. 32.00x (ISBN 0-8078-1230-7). U of NC Pr.
Hall, Marie. Andrew Marvell & His Friends. 1895. Repr. 45.00 (ISBN 0-8274-1867-1). R West.
Hodge, R. I. Foreshortened Time: Andrew Marvell & Seventeenth Century Revolutions. (Illus.). 170p. 1978. 15.00x (ISBN 0-8476-6089-3). Rowman.
Kelliher, Hilton. Andrew Marvell: Poet & Politician 1621-78. 128p. 1981. 40.00x (ISBN 0-7141-0395-0, Pub. by Brit Lib England); pap. 25.00x (ISBN 0-7141-0395-0). State Mutual Bk.
King, Bruce. Marvell's Allegorical Poetry. (Oleander Language & Literature Ser.: Vol. 8). 1977. 8.95 (ISBN 0-902675-60-5). Oleander Pr.
Legouis, Pierre. Andre Marvell, Poete, Puritain, Patriote, 1621-1678. LC 65-18816. (Orig., Fr). 1965. Repr. of 1929 ed. 16.50 (ISBN 0-8462-0648-X). Russell.
McQueen, William A. & Rockwell, Kiffin A. Latin Poetry of Andrew Marvell. (University of North Carolina Studies in Comparative Literature: No. 34). Repr. of 1964 ed. 13.00 (ISBN 0-384-34916-1). Johnson Repr.
Patrides, C. A., ed. Approaches to Marvell: The York Tercentenary Lectures. (Illus.). 1978. 28.00x (ISBN 0-7100-8818-3). Routledge & Kegan.
Patterson, Annabel M. Marvell & the Civic Crown. LC 77-85555. 1979. 19.50 (ISBN 0-691-06356-7). Princeton U Pr.
Poscher, Robert. Andrew Marvells Poetische Werke. 1908. pap. 21.00 (ISBN 0-384-47290-7). Johnson Repr.
Sackville-West, V. Andrew Marvell. 64p. 1980. Repr. of 1929 ed. lib. bdg. 10.00 (ISBN 0-8495-5036-X). Arden Lib.
Wallace, John M. Destiny His Choice: The Loyalism of Andrew Marvell. 266p. 1981. pap. 13.50 (ISBN 0-521-28042-7). Cambridge U Pr.
--Destiny His Choice: The Loyalism of Andrew Marvell. LC 68-10334. 1968. 44.00 (ISBN 0-521-06725-1). Cambridge U Pr.
Wallerstein, Ruth C. Studies in Seventeenth-Century Poetic. (Illus.). 432p. 1950. pap. 7.50 (ISBN 0-299-00654-9). U of Wis Pr.
Wilding, Michael, ed. Marvell. LC 70-127558. (Modern Judgement Ser). 1970. pap. text ed. 2.50 (ISBN 0-87695-089-6). Aurora Pubs.
MARX, ELEANOR
see Aveling, Eleanor (Marx), 1856-1898
MARX, GROUCHO, 1891-1977
Anobile, Richard J. Hooray for Captain Spaulding. (Illus.). 1975. pap. 4.95 (ISBN 0-380-00458-5, 25882). Avon.
Arce, Hector. Groucho. 1980. pap. 6.95 (ISBN 0-686-63014-9, Perigee). Putnam.
--Groucho: The Authorized Biography. LC 78-16019. (Illus.). 1979. 14.95 (ISBN 0-399-12046-7). Putnam.
Chandler, Charlotte. Hello, I Must Be Going--Groucho & His Friends. LC 77-89876. 1978. 10.95 (ISBN 0-385-12444-9). Doubleday.
--Hello, I Must Be Going: Groucho & His Friends. (Illus.). 1979. pap. 4.95 (ISBN 0-14-005222-4). Penguin.
Marx, Groucho. Groucho & Me. 1978. pap. 1.95 (ISBN 0-532-19165-X). Woodhill.
--The Groucho Letters. 1978. pap. 1.95 (ISBN 0-532-19163-3). Woodhill.
--Memoirs of a Mangy Lover. 1978. pap. 1.95 (ISBN 0-532-19164-1). Woodhill.
Marx, Groucho & Arce, Hector. The Secret Word Is Groucho. 1977. pap. 1.75 (ISBN 0-425-03747-9, Medallion). Berkley Pub.
MARX, KARL, 1818-1883
Adams, H. P. Karl Marx in His Earlier Writings. LC 65-18180. 1972. pap. 2.95 (ISBN 0-689-70291-4, 185). Atheneum.
Adams, H. Packwood. Karl Marx in His Earlier Writings. 221p. 1965. 24.00x (ISBN 0-7146-1545-5, F Cass Co). Biblio Dist.
Adams, Henry P. Karl Marx in His Earlier Writings. LC 65-18180. 1965. Repr. of 1940 ed. 8.00 (ISBN 0-8462-0573-4). Russell.
Afanasyev, V. G. Marxist Philosophy. 1980. 8.00 (ISBN 0-8285-1848-3, Pub. by Progress Pubs Russia). Imported Pubns.
Althusser, Louis. For Marx. Brewster, Ben, tr. from Ger. 1979. pap. 9.50 (ISBN 0-902308-79-3, Pub. by Verso). Schocken.
--Politics & History: Montesquieu, Rousseau, Hegel, Marx. 1978. pap. 5.50 (ISBN 0-902308-96-3, Pub by NLB). Schocken.
Avineri. Varieties of Marxism. (Van Leer Jerusalem Foundation Ser.). 1977. lib. bdg. 30.00 (ISBN 90-247-2024-9, Pub by Martinus Nijhoff Netherland). Kluwer Boston.
Avineri, Shlomo. Social & Political Thought of Karl Marx. LC 68-12055. (Studies in the History & Theory of Politics). 1971. 32.50 (ISBN 0-521-04071-X); pap. 8.95x (ISBN 0-521-09619-7). Cambridge U Pr.
Avineri, Shlomo, ed. Marx's Socialism. (Controversy Ser). 236p. 1973. 9.95x (ISBN 0-88311-004-0); pap. 3.95 (ISBN 0-88311-005-9). Lieber-Atherton.
Axelos, Kostas. Alienation, Praxis, & Techne in the Thought of Karl Marx. Bruzina, Ronald, tr. from Fr. LC 76-5429. 434p. 1976. text ed. 17.50x (ISBN 0-292-78013-3). U of Tex Pr.
Balz, Albert. The Value Doctrine of Karl Marx. 1972. lib. bdg. 10.00x (ISBN 0-374-90372-7). Octagon.
Barth, Hans. Truth & Ideology. LC 74-81430. Orig. Title: Wahrheit und Ideologie. 1977. 21.75x (ISBN 0-520-02820-1). U of Cal Pr.
--Wahrheit und Ideologie: Truth & Ideology. LC 74-25738. (European Sociology Ser.). 352p. 1975. Repr. 19.00x (ISBN 0-405-06494-2). Arno.
Bender, Frederick L., ed. The Betrayal of Marx. 12.50 (ISBN 0-8446-5158-3). Peter Smith.
Berlin, Isiah. Karl Marx: His Life & Environment. 4th ed. 1978. 12.95 (ISBN 0-19-219122-5). Oxford U Pr.
Bernstein, Samuel. Beginnings of Marxian Socialism in France. LC 65-25426. (With a new preface). 1965. Repr. of 1933 ed. 8.50 (ISBN 0-8462-0654-4). Russell.
Bevan, Ruth A. Marx & Burke: A Revisionist View. LC 73-79625. 208p. 1973. 12.95 (ISBN 0-87548-144-2). Open Court.
Bloom, Solomon F. World of Nations: A Study of the National Implications in the Work of Karl Marx. Repr. of 1941 ed. 16.50 (ISBN 0-404-00899-2). AMS Pr.
Bober, Mandell M. Karl Marx's Interpretation of History. 2nd rev. ed. LC 48-8857. (Economic Studies: No. 31). 1948. 18.50x (ISBN 0-674-50150-0). Harvard U Pr.
--Karl Marx's Interpretation of History. 1965. pap. 7.45x (ISBN 0-393-00270-5, Norton Lib). Norton.
Bohm Von Bawerk, Eugen. Karl Marx & the Close of His System. Sweezy, Paul M., ed. LC 73-8804. Repr. of 1949 ed. lib. bdg. 12.50x (ISBN 0-678-00140-5). Kelley.
Bologh, Roslyn W. Dialectical Phenomenology: Marx's Method. (International Library of Phenomenology & Moral Sciences). 1979. 23.50x (ISBN 0-7100-0335-8). Routledge & Kegan.
Bottomore, Tom. Modern Interpretations of Marx. 1981. 15.00x (ISBN 0-631-18040-0, Pub. by Basil Blackwell England); pap. 7.95x (ISBN 0-631-12708-9). Biblio Dist.
Bottomore, Tom, ed. Karl Marx. 194p. 1979. 29.00x (ISBN 0-631-10961-7, Pub. by Basil Blackwell); pap. 10.50x (ISBN 0-631-11061-5). Biblio Dist.
Browder, Earl. Marx & America. LC 73-16734. 146p. 1974. Repr. of 1958 ed. lib. bdg. 15.00x (ISBN 0-8371-7218-7, BRMA). Greenwood.

Bukharin, Nikolai I., et al. Marxism & Modern Thought. Fox, Ralph, tr. from Rus. LC 73-835. (Russian Studies: Perspectives on the Revolution Ser). 1973. Repr. of 1935 ed. 25.00 (ISBN 0-88355-031-8). Hyperion Conn.
Bulgakov, Sergei. Karl Marx: As a Religious Type. Lang, Virgil, ed. Barna, Luba, tr. from Rus. LC 78-78117. 116p. 1980. 12.50 (ISBN 0-913124-34-6). Nordland Pub.
Byres, Terence. Adam Smith, Malthus & Marx. Yapp, Malcolm, et al, eds. (World History Ser.). (Illus.). 32p. (gr. 10). 1980. Repr. of 1977 ed. lib. bdg. 5.95 (ISBN 0-89908-046-4); pap. text ed. 1.95 (ISBN 0-89908-021-9). Greenhaven.
Cain, Maureen & Hunt, Alan. Marx & Engels on Law. (Law, State & Society Ser.). 1979. 29.00 (ISBN 0-12-154850-3); pap. 15.00 (ISBN 0-12-154852-X). Acad Pr.
Cameron, Kenneth N. Marx & Engels Today: A Modern Dialogue on Philosophy & History. LC 76-5098. 1976. 5.00 (ISBN 0-682-48512-8, University). Exposition.
Carlsnaes, Walter. The Concept of Ideology & Political Analysis: A Critical Examination of Its Usage by Marx, Lenin, & Mannheim. LC 80-1202. (Contributions in Philosophy Ser.: No. 17). xii, 274p. 1981. lib. bdg. 32.50 (ISBN 0-313-22267-3, CCI/). Greenwood.
Childs, David. Marx & the Marxists: An Outline of Practice & Theory. 1973. text ed. 6.25x (ISBN 0-510-26260-0). Humanities.
Chiodi, Pietro. Sartre & Marxism. Soper, Kate, tr. from It. (European Philosophy & the Human Sciences Ser.). 1976. text ed. 26.25x (ISBN 0-391-00590-1); pap. text ed. 10.50x (ISBN 0-391-00886-2). Humanities.
Cleaver, Harry. Reading CAPITAL Politically. 1979. text ed. 14.95x (ISBN 0-292-77014-6); pap. 5.95x (ISBN 0-292-77015-4). U of Tex Pr.
Coe, Samuel. Marxism & Psychology: A Bibliography. (Bibliographical Ser.: No. 14). (Orig.). 1980. pap. 2.75 (ISBN 0-89977-031-2). Am Inst Marxist.
Coe, Samuel P. Contemporary Psychology in Marx & Engels. (Occasional Papers: No. 26). 1978. 1.25 (ISBN 0-89977-033-9). Am Inst Marxist.
Cohen, G. A. Karl Marx's Theory of History: A Defence. LC 78-51206. 392p. 1980. 22.50 (ISBN 0-691-07175-6); pap. 8.95 (ISBN 0-691-02008-6). Princeton U Pr.
Cooper, Rebecca. The Logical Influence of Hegel on Marx. 1974. lib. bdg. 75.00 (ISBN 0-8490-0550-7). Gordon Pr.
Croce, Benedetto. Essays on Marx & Russia. DeGennaro, Angelo A., tr. LC 66-17538. (Milestones of Thought Ser.). 1966. pap. 3.95 (ISBN 0-8044-6098-1). Ungar.
Cummings, Ian. Marx, Engels & National Movements. LC 80-10283. 224p. 1980. 25.00 (ISBN 0-312-51792-0). St Martin.
Dandavate, M. Marx & Gandhi. 1979. text ed. 6.00x (ISBN 0-8426-1627-6). Verry.
Della Volpe, Galvano. Rousseau & Marx & Other Writings. Fraser, John, tr. from Ital. 1979. text ed. 17.50 (ISBN 0-391-01211-8). Humanities.
Dematteis, Phillip. Max Stirner Versus Karl Marx: Individuality & the Social Organism. 1975. lib. bdg. 69.95 (ISBN 0-87700-239-8). Revisionist Pr.
Djilas, Milovan. Unperfect Society: Beyond the New Class. Cooke, Dorian, tr. LC 70-76568. 1969. 5.75 (ISBN 0-15-193056-2). HarBraceJ.
Drennen, D. A. Karl Marx's Communist Manifesto: A Full Textual Explication. LC 73-184893. 202p. (Orig.). 1972. pap. text ed. 2.75 (ISBN 0-8120-0437-X). Barron.
Duncan, G. Marx & Mill: Two Views of Social Conflict & Social Harmony. 416p. 1973. 32.50 (ISBN 0-521-20257-4); pap. 9.95x (ISBN 0-521-29130-5). Cambridge U Pr.
Eastman, Max F. Marx, Lenin & the Science of Revolution. LC 73-838. (Russian Studies: Perspectives on the Revolution Ser). 267p. 1973. Repr. of 1926 ed. 19.75 (ISBN 0-88355-034-2). Hyperion Conn.
Engels, Friedrich, et al. Marx & Engels Through the Eyes of Their Contemporaries. 206p. 1972. 2.60 (ISBN 0-8285-0064-9, Pub. by Progress Pubs Russia). Imported Pubns.
Eubanks, Cecil L. Karl Marx & Friedrich Engels, an Analytical Bibliography. LC 75-24779. (Reference Library of Social Science: Vol. 23). 1978. lib. bdg. 23.50 (ISBN 0-8240-9957-5). Garland Pub.
Evans, Michael. Karl Marx. (Political Thinkers). 1975. text ed. 17.95x (ISBN 0-04-921020-3). Allen Unwin.
Federn, Karl. Materialist Conception of History: A Critical Analysis. LC 75-114523. 1971. Repr. of 1939 ed. lib. bdg. 15.00x (ISBN 0-8371-4789-1, FECH). Greenwood.
Fedoseyev, P. N., et al. Karl Marx-a Biography. 635p. 1973. 7.00 (ISBN 0-8285-0063-0, Pub. by Progress Pubs Russia). Imported Pubns.
Ferguson, A. Thomas & O'Neill, Stephen, eds. Karl Marx, Friedrich Engels: The Collected Writings of the New York Daily Tribune, Vol. 1. 80.00x (ISBN 0-916354-36-9). Urizen Bks.
Fetscher, Iring. Marx & Marxism. LC 77-150299. 1971. 12.50 (ISBN 0-8164-9127-5). Continuum.
Fine, Ben. Marx's Capital. (Macmillan Studies in Economics Ser.). 71p. 1975. pap. text ed. 3.75x (ISBN 0-333-17845-9). Humanities.
Fulton, Robert B. Original Marxism - Estranged Offspring. 1960. 4.50 (ISBN 0-8158-0097-5). Chris Mass.
Gandy, D. Ross. Marx & History: From Primitive Society to the Communist Future. (Illus.). 1979. text ed. 14.95x (ISBN 0-292-74302-5). U of Tex Pr.
Garaudy, Roger. Karl Marx, Evolution of His Thought. Apotheker, Nan, tr. from French. LC 76-43305. 1976. Repr. of 1967 ed. lib. bdg. 16.50x (ISBN 0-8371-9044-4, GAKM). Greenwood.
Giddens, Anthony. Capitalism & Modern Social Theory: An Analysis of the Writings of Marx, Durkheim & Max Weber. LC 70-161291. 1971. 29.95 (ISBN 0-521-08293-5); pap. 8.95x (ISBN 0-521-09785-1). Cambridge U Pr.
Gilbert, Alan. Marx's Politics: Communists & Citizens. 320p. 1981. 21.00 (ISBN 0-8135-0903-3). Rutgers U Pr.
Gould, Carol C. Marx's Social Ontology. 1978. pap. 5.95 (ISBN 0-262-57056-4). MIT Pr.
Gurley, John G. Challengers to Capitalism. LC 75-29749. (Portable Stanford Ser.). (Illus.). 1976. 8.95 (ISBN 0-913374-34-2); pap. 4.95 (ISBN 0-913374-35-0). SF Bk Co.
--Challengers to Capitalism, Marx, Lenin, Stalin & Mao. (Illus.). 224p. 1980. 12.95 (ISBN 0-393-01224-7); Portable Stanford Ser. pap. 4.95x (ISBN 0-393-95005-0). Norton.
Haldane, John B. Marxist Philosophy & the Sciences. LC 78-86757. (Essay Index Reprint Ser). 1939. 15.00 (ISBN 0-8369-1137-7). Arno.
Hazelkorn, Ellen. Marx & Engels: On Ireland - an Annotated Checklist. (Bibliographical Ser.: No. 15). 1981. 2.00 (ISBN 0-89977-031-2). Am Inst Marxist.
Herod. The Nation in the History of Marxian Thought. 1976. pap. 24.00 (ISBN 90-247-1749-3, Pub. by Martinus Nijhoff Netherlands). Kluwer Boston.
Hodges, Donald C. Socialist Humanism. LC 73-96983. 384p. 1974. 19.75 (ISBN 0-87527-042-5). Fireside Bks.
Hoeven, Johan Van Der. Karl Marx: The Roots of His Thought. (Bidragen Tot De Filosophie: No. 8). (Orig.). 1976. pap. text ed. 14.00x (ISBN 90-232-1388-2). Humanities.
Hook, Sidney. From Hegel to Marx: Studies in the Intellectual Development of Karl Marx. 1962. pap. 4.95 (ISBN 0-472-06066-X, 66, AA). U of Mich Pr.
Howard, Dick. The Development of the Marxian Dialectic. LC 75-181984. 222p. 1972. 9.95x (ISBN 0-8093-0559-3). S Ill U Pr.
--The Marxian Legacy. 1978. 15.00 (ISBN 0-916354-95-4); pap. 6.95 (ISBN 0-916354-96-2). Urizen Bks.
Hunt, Richard N. The Political Ideas of Marx & Engels, Vol. 1: Marxism & Totalitarian Democracy, 1818-1850. LC 74-13536. 1974. 17.95x (ISBN 0-8229-3285-7). U of Pittsburgh Pr.
Hyppolite, Jean. Studies on Marx & Hegel. O'Neill, John, tr. LC 70-77231. 1969. 7.50x (ISBN 0-465-08284-X). Basic.
International Council For Philosophy And Humanistic Studies & International Social Science Council. Marx & Contemporary Scientific Thought. LC 70-101066. (International Social Science Council Publications Ser: No. 13). (Fr). 1969. text ed. 45.50x (ISBN 0-686-22417-5). Mouton.
Jackson, Thomas A. Dialectics: The Logic of Marxism & Its Critics. LC 78-159699. (Research & Source Works Ser.: No. 734). 1971. lib. bdg. 32.00 (ISBN 0-8337-1814-2). B Franklin.
Janke, Wolfgang. Historische Dialektik: Destruktion Dialektrischer Grundformen Von Kant Bis Marx. 1977. 84.00x (ISBN 3-11-007286-6). De Gruyter.
Jordan, Z. A., ed. Karl Marx: Economy, Class & Social Revolution. LC 74-3770. 332p. 1975. 10.00 (ISBN 0-684-13947-2, ScribT). Scribner.
Kalin, Martin G. The Utopian Flight from Unhappiness: Freud Against Marx on Social Progress. (Quality Paperback: No. 314). 231p. 1975. pap. 3.50 (ISBN 0-8226-0314-4). Littlefield.
Karl Marx-Frederick Engels. (Collected Works: Vol. 13). 1980. 8.50 (ISBN 0-7178-0513-1). Intl Pub Co.
Karl Marx-Frederick Engels. (Colected Works: Vol. 12). (Illus.). 1979. 8.50 (ISBN 0-7178-0512-3). Intl Pub Co.
Karl Marx-Frederick Engels: Collected Works, Vol. 16. (Illus.). 8.50 (ISBN 0-7178-0516-6). Intl Pub Co.
Karl Marx-Frederick Engels Collected Works: Vol. 38, The Correspondence of Marx & Engels. (Illus.). 1981. 8.50 (ISBN 0-7178-0538-7). Intl Pub Co.
Korsch, Karl. Karl Marx. LC 63-15166. (Illus.). 1963. Repr. of 1938 ed. 15.00 (ISBN 0-8462-0383-9). Russell.
Krader, Lawrence. The Asiatic Mode of Production: Sources Development & Critique in the Writings of Karl Marx. 454p. 1975. text ed. 58.25x (ISBN 90-232-1289-4). Humanities.
Lafargue, Paul. Karl Marx, the Man. 4th ed. 1972. pap. 0.50 (ISBN 0-935534-36-9). NY Labor News.
Lenin on Marx & Engels. 1975. pap. 1.50 (ISBN 0-8351-0183-5). China Bks.
Lenin, V. I. Karl Marx. 1976. pap. 0.75 (ISBN 0-8351-0123-1). China Bks.
--Marx-Engels-Marxism. 511p. 1973. pap. 2.75 (ISBN 0-8285-0139-4, Pub. by Progress Pubs Russia). Imported Pubns.
--Marx, Engels, Marxism. 1978. 7.95 (ISBN 0-8351-0553-9); pap. 4.95 (ISBN 0-8351-0545-8). China Bks.
Lenin, Vladimir I. State & Revolution. 1965. pap. 1.95 (ISBN 0-8351-0372-2). China Bks.
--State & Revolution. 1932. pap. 1.25 (ISBN 0-7178-0196-9). Intl Pub Co.
--State & Revolution: Marxist Teachings About the Theory of the State & the Tasks of the Proletariat in the Revolution. LC 78-2228. 1978. Repr. of 1935 ed. lib. bdg. 15.00x (ISBN 0-313-20351-2, LESTR). Greenwood.
--Teachings of Karl Marx. rev. ed. 1964. pap. 1.00 (ISBN 0-7178-0199-3). Intl Pub Co.
Lichtheim, George. From Marx to Hegel. LC 70-167871. 1971. pap. 3.95 (ISBN 0-8164-9188-7); (Continuum). Continuum.
Liebknecht, Wilhelm. Karl Marx: Biographical Memoirs. 1975. pap. 4.00 (ISBN 0-904526-05-4, Journeyman Press). Carrier Pigeon.
Liebknecht, Wilhelm P. Karl Marx: Biographical Memoirs. Untermann, E., tr. LC 69-10119. 1969. Repr. of 1901 ed. lib. bdg. 15.00x (ISBN 0-8371-0536-6, LIKM). Greenwood.
--Karl Marx, Biographical Memoirs. 1901. 12.00 (ISBN 0-403-00200-1). Scholarly.
Lindsay, Alexander D. Karl Marx's 'Capital' LC 73-7456. (Illus.). 128p. 1973. Repr. of 1925 ed. lib. bdg. 15.00x (ISBN 0-8371-6935-6, LIMC). Greenwood.
Lippi, Marco. Value & Naturalism in Marx. 160p. 1980. 12.50 (ISBN 0-8052-7076-0, Pub. by NLB). Schocken.
Loria, Achille. Karl Marx. 69.95 (ISBN 0-87968-304-X). Gordon Pr.
Lyon, David. Karl Marx: A Christian Assessment of His Life & Thought. 192p. (Orig.). 1981. pap. 5.95 (ISBN 0-87784-879-3). Inter-Varsity.
McBride, William L. The Philosophy of Marx. LC 77-74774. 1977. 12.95x (ISBN 0-312-60675-3). St Martin.
McClellan, David. Young Hegelians & Karl Marx. 1918. Repr. of 1964 ed. text ed. 9.95x (ISBN 0-333-08788-7). Humanities.
McLellan, David. Karl Marx. (Modern Masters Ser). 1976. pap. 2.95 (ISBN 0-14-004320-9). Penguin.
--Karl Marx: His Life & Thought. 1977. pap. 5.95 (ISBN 0-06-090585-9, CN585, CN). Har-Row.
McLellan, David, ed. Karl Marx: Interviews & Recollections. (Interviews & Recollections Ser.). 176p. 1981. 26.50x (ISBN 0-389-20114-6). B&N.
McMurty, John. The Structure of Marx's World-View. LC 77-85552. 1978. 18.50 (ISBN 0-691-07229-9); pap. 5.95 (ISBN 0-691-01998-3). Princeton U Pr.
Maguire, J. M. Marx's Theory of Politics. LC 77-90214. 1979. 29.95 (ISBN 0-521-21955-8). Cambridge U Pr.
Martin, Joseph. A Guide to Marxism. LC 79-20376. 1980. 14.95 (ISBN 0-312-35297-2). St Martin.
Marx & Engels Through the Eyes of Their Contemporaries. (Illus.). 12.95x (ISBN 0-8464-0611-X). Beekman Pubs.
Marx, Karl. Communist Manifesto. Sweezy, Paul M. & Huberman, Leo, eds. Bd. with Principles of Communism. Friedrich, Engels. LC 64-21175. 1964. 5.50 (ISBN 0-85345-019-6, CL0196); pap. 3.50 (ISBN 0-85345-062-5, PB0625). Monthly Rev.
--The Ethnological Notebooks of Karl Marx: Studies of Morgan, Phear, Maine, Lubbock. Krader, Lawrence, ed. 448p. 1972. text ed. 52.00x (ISBN 9-0232-0924-9). Humanities.
--Marx on China. 1973. lib. bdg. 69.95 (ISBN 0-87968-352-X). Gordon Pr.
Marx, Karl & Engels, Frederick. Karl Marx-Frederick Engels: Collected Works, 9 vols. Incl. Vol. 1. Marx 1835-1843. 1975 (ISBN 0-7178-0407-0); Vol. 2. Engels 1838-1842. 1975 (ISBN 0-7178-0413-5); Vol. 3. Marx & Engels 1843-1844. 1975 (ISBN 0-7178-0414-3); Vol. 4. Marx & Engels 1844-1845. 1975 (ISBN 0-7178-0455-0); Vol. 5. Marx & Engels 1845-1847. 1976 (ISBN 0-7178-0505-0); Vol. 6. Marx & Engels 1845-1848. 1976 (ISBN 0-7178-0506-9); Vol. 7. Marx & Engels 1848. 1977 (ISBN 0-7178-0507-7); Vol. 8. Marx & Engels 1848-1849. 1977 (ISBN 0-7178-0508-5); Vol. 9. Marx & Engels 1849. 1977 (ISBN 0-7178-0509-3). (Illus.). 8.50 ea. Intl Pub Co.
--Marx & Engels on the Means of Communication. De La Haye, Yves, ed. 176p. (Orig.). 1980. pap. 5.00 (ISBN 0-88477-013-3). Intl General.
--Selected Correspondence: 1846-1895. LC 75-25261. 551p. 1976. Repr. of 1942 ed. lib. bdg. 29.50x (ISBN 0-8371-8385-5, MAKMF). Greenwood.
Marx, Karl & Engels, Friedrich. Marx & Engels on the United States. 1979. 5.50 (ISBN 0-8285-1763-0, Pub. by Progress Pubs Russia). Imported Pubns.
--Selected Correspondence. 552p. 1975. 3.00 (ISBN 0-8285-0048-7, Pub. by Progress Pubs Russia). Imported Pubns.
Mattick, Paul. Marx & Keynes: The Limits of the Mixed Economy. LC 69-15526. (Extending Horizons Ser.). 1973. pap. 3.45 (ISBN 0-87558-069-6). Porter Sargent.
Mehring, Franz. Karl Marx: The Story of His Life. 1962. pap. 6.95 (ISBN 0-472-06073-2, 73, AA). U of Mich Pr.
Meszaros, I. Marx's Theory of Alienation. 356p. 1973. text ed. 13.00x (ISBN 0-85036-144-3). Humanities.
Meszaros, Istvan. Marx's Theory of Alienation. 352p. 12.50x (ISBN 0-87556-438-0). Saifer.
Meynell, Hugo. Freud, Marx & Morals. (New Studies in Practical Philosophy). 222p. 1981. 23.00 (ISBN 0-389-20045-X). B&N.
Miller, James. History & Human Existence: From Marx to Merleau-Ponty. LC 78-51747. 1979. 24.00x (ISBN 0-520-03667-0). U of Cal Pr.
Miranda, Jose P. Marx Against the Marxists. Drury, John, tr. LC 80-14415. 336p. 1980. pap. 12.95 (ISBN 0-88344-322-8). Orbis Bks.
Monarch Notes on Marxist & Utopian Socialists. (gr. 7-12). pap. 1.95 (ISBN 0-671-00544-8). Monarch Pr.
Moride, Pierre. Produit Net Des Physiocrates et la Plus-Value De Karl Marx. LC 78-156820. (Research & Source Works Ser.: No. 708). (Selected Essays in History, Economics & Social Science Ser., No. 252). 1971. Repr. of 1908 ed. lib. bdg. 20.50 (ISBN 0-8337-2466-5). B Franklin.
Novack, George. Humanism & Socialism. LC 73-77559. 160p. 1973. 12.00- (ISBN 0-87348-308-1); pap. 3.45 (ISBN 0-87348-309-X). Path Pr NY.
Ollman, Bertell. Social & Sexual Revolution: Essays on Marx & Reich. LC 78-71204. (Orig.). 1979. 15.00 (ISBN 0-89608-081-1); pap. 5.50 (ISBN 0-89608-080-3). South End Pr.
Olsen, Richard. Karl Marx. (World Leaders Ser.: No. 70). 1978. lib. bdg. 11.95 (ISBN 0-8057-7678-8). Twayne.
Paci, Enzo. The Function of the Sciences & the Meaning of Man. Piccone, Paul & Hansen, James, trs. (Studies in Phenomenology & Existential Philosophy). 1972. 21.95x (ISBN 0-8101-0378-8); pap. 10.95 (ISBN 0-8101-0618-3). Northwestern U Pr.
Padover, S. Letters of Karl Marx. 1979. 19.95 (ISBN 0-13-531533-6). P-H.
Padover, Saul. Karl Marx: An Intimate Biography. 1978. 18.95 (ISBN 0-07-048072-9, GB). McGraw.
Padover, Saul K. The Essential Marx. (Orig.). 1979. pap. 2.50 (ISBN 0-451-61709-6, ME1709, Ment). NAL.
--Karl Marx: An Intimate Biography. abr. ed. (Illus.). 1980. pap. 3.50 (ISBN 0-451-61897-1, ME1897, Ment). NAL.
--Karl Marx on History & People. (Karl Marx Library: Vol. 7). 360p. 1977. 15.00 (ISBN 0-07-048100-8); pap. 7.95 (ISBN 0-07-048101-6). McGraw.
Padover, Saul K., ed. Karl Marx on Religion. LC 78-172260. (Karl Marx Library: Vol. 5). 312p. 1974. 10.00 (ISBN 0-07-048095-8, GB). McGraw.
--Karl Marx on the First International, Vol. 3. LC 78-172260. (Karl Marx Library). (Illus.). 720p. 1973. 20.00 (ISBN 0-07-048076-1, GB); pap. 4.95 (ISBN 0-07-048081-8). McGraw.
Payne, Robert, ed. The Unknown Karl Marx: Documents Concerning Karl Marx. LC 78-179986. 1971. 15.00x (ISBN 0-8147-6554-8). NYU Pr.
Petersen, Arnold. Karl Marx & Marxian Science. 1967. 3.00 (ISBN 0-935534-17-2); pap. 1.00 (ISBN 0-935534-18-0). NY Labor News.

Phillips, Paul. Marx & Engels on Law & Laws. 238p. 1980. 27.50x (ISBN 0-389-20120-0). B&N.

Plamenatz, John. Karl Marx's Philosophy of Man. 292p. 1975. 48.00x (ISBN 0-19-824551-3); pap. 14.95x (ISBN 0-19-824649-8). Oxford U Pr.

Plekhanov, G. V. Essays in the History of Materialism. 1968. 25.00 (ISBN 0-86527-061-9). Fertig.

Poggi, Gianfranco. Images of Society: Essays on the Sociological Theories of Tocqueville, Marx & Durkheim. LC 79-183892. 272p. 1972. 12.50x (ISBN 0-8047-0811-8). Stanford U Pr.

Prawer, S. S. Karl Marx & World Literature. 1978. pap. 5.95 (ISBN 0-19-281248-3, GB 554, GB). Oxford U Pr.

--Karl Marx & World Literature. 1976. 39.95x (ISBN 0-19-815745-2). Oxford U Pr.

Price, Ronald F. Marx & Education in Russia & China. 376p. 1977. 21.50x (ISBN 0-87471-873-2). Rowman.

Raddatz, Fritz J. Karl Marx: A Political Biography. Barry, Richard, tr. LC 78-23341. 1979. 16.95 (ISBN 0-316-73210-9). Little.

Rader, Melvin. Marx's Interpretation of History. 1979. 14.95x (ISBN 0-19-502474-5); pap. text ed. 5.95x (ISBN 0-19-502475-3). Oxford U Pr.

Rahmas, D. Steve. Karl Marx: Philosophical Father of Communism. new ed. (Outstanding Personalities Ser.). 32p. 1975. lib. bdg. 2.95 incl. catalog cards (ISBN 0-686-11247-4); pap. 1.50 vinyl laminated covers (ISBN 0-686-11248-2). SamHar Pr.

Raphael, Max, ed. Proudhon, Marx, Picasso: Three Studies in the Sociology of Art. LC 79-14017. 174p. 1980. text ed. 10.00x (ISBN 0-391-00596-0). Humanities.

Riazanov, D. Karl Marx & Friedrich Engels. 1979. Repr. of 1927 ed. lib. bdg. 30.00 (ISBN 0-8495-4601-X). Arden Lib.

Riazanov, David. Karl Marx & Friedrich Engels. Kunitz, Joshua, tr. from Rus. LC 73-8055. 240p. 1974. Repr. of 1927 ed. 8.95 (ISBN 0-85345-297-0, CL-2970). Monthly Rev.

--Karl Marx & Friedrich Engels. Kunitz, Joshua, tr. from Rus. LC 73-8055. (Modern Reader Paperbacks). 240p. 1974. pap. 5.50 (ISBN 0-85345-328-4, PB-3284). Monthly Rev.

Riis, S. M. Karl Marx: Master of Fraud. 1962. 3.00 (ISBN 0-8315-0042-5). Speller.

Rius. Marx for Beginners. LC 78-20422. (Illus.). 1979. pap. 2.95 (ISBN 0-394-73716-4). Pantheon.

Rosdolsky, Roman. The Making of Marx's "Capital". 1977. text ed. 45.00x (ISBN 0-904383-37-7). Humanities.

Rose, Margaret A. Reading the Young Marx & Engels: Poetry, Parody & the Censor. 165p. 1978. 15.75x (ISBN 0-8476-6087-7). Rowman.

Rosen. Bruno Bauer & Karl Marx. (Studies in Social History: No. 2). 1977. lib. bdg. 45.00 (ISBN 90-247-1948-8, Pub. by Martinus Nijhoff Netherlands). Kluwer Boston.

Rotenstreich, Nathan. Basic Problems of Marx's Philosophy. LC 64-66073. 168p. 1963. text ed. 24.00x (ISBN 0-8290-0154-9); pap. text ed. 8.95x (ISBN 0-8290-0155-7). Irvington.

Rubel, Macmillan. Marx: Life & Works. (Chronology Ser.). 226p. 1981. lib. bdg. 22.50 (ISBN 0-87196-516-X). Facts on File.

Rubel, Maximilien. Rubel on Karl Marx: Five Essays. O'Malley, Joseph & Algozin, Keith, eds. LC 80-21734. 272p. Date not set. price not set (ISBN 0-521-23839-0); pap. price not set (ISBN 0-521-28251-9). Cambridge U Pr.

Rubel, Maximilien & Manale, Margaret. Marx Without Myth. 1976. pap. 5.95x (ISBN 0-06-131860-4, TB1860, Torch). Har-Row.

--Marx Without Myth: A Chronological Study of His Life & Work. 10.00 (ISBN 0-8446-5859-6). Peter Smith.

Rubenstein, David. Marx & Wittgenstein: Social Praxis & Social Explanation. 240p. 1981. 25.00 (ISBN 0-7100-0688-8). Routledge & Kegan.

Ruhle, Otto. Karl Marx: His Life & Work. Paul, Eden & Cedar, Paul, trs. 419p. 1981. Repr. of 1929 ed. lib. bdg. 35.00 (ISBN 0-8495-4639-7). Arden Lib.

Schrader, Wiebke. Die Selbstkritik der Theorie: Philosophische Untersuchungen Zur Ersten Innermarxistischen Grundlagendiskussion. (Elementa Schriften Zur Philosophie und Ihrer Problemgeschichte: No. 8). 1978. pap. text ed. 19.25x (ISBN 90-6203-460-8). Humanities.

See, Henri. Economic Interpretation of History. Knight, Melvin M., tr. LC 67-30863. Repr. of 1929 ed. 11.00x (ISBN 0-678-00354-8). Kelley.

Seigel, Jerrold. Marx's Fate: The Shape of a Life. LC 77-25536. 1978. 27.50 (ISBN 0-691-05259-X). Princeton U Pr.

Shaw, George Bernard. Bernard Shaw & Karl Marx: A Symposium, 1884-1889. LC 77-1355. 1977. lib. bdg. 35.00 (ISBN 0-8414-3959-1). Folcroft.

Shaw, William H. Marx's Theory of History. LC 77-76154. 1978. 12.50x (ISBN 0-8047-0960-2); pap. 3.95 (ISBN 0-8047-1059-7, SP-160). Stanford U Pr.

Singer, Peter. Marx. 92p. 1980. 7.95 (ISBN 0-8090-7550-4); pap. 2.95 (ISBN 0-8090-1412-2). Hill & Wang.

Sprigge, C. Karl Marx. 1962. pap. 0.95 (ISBN 0-02-007140-X, Collier). Macmillan.

Stepanova, E. Carlos Marx: Esbozo Biografico. 119p. (Span.). 1979. pap. 1.90 (ISBN 0-8285-1358-9, Pub. by Progress Pubs Russia). Imported Pubns.

Struik, Dirk J., ed. Birth of the Communist Manifesto, Student's Edition. LC 77-148513. (Illus., Incl. the text of The Communist Manifesto by Marx & Engels). 1971. 7.50 (ISBN 0-7178-0288-4); pap. 3.25 (ISBN 0-7178-0243-4). Intl Pub Co.

Sweezy, Paul M. Theory of Capitalist Development. LC 64-21234. (Illus.). 1968. pap. 6.50 (ISBN 0-85345-079-X, PB-079X). Monthly Rev.

Symposium on the Role of Karl Marx in the Development of Contemporary Scientific Thought. Marx & Contemporary Scientific Thought: Proceedings. (Publications of the International Social Science Council: No. 13). 1970. 45.50 (ISBN 90-2796-276-6). Mouton.

Telford, Shirley. Economic & Political Peace, Vol. 1. 3rd ed. LC 75-31615. 254p. 1975. 8.95 (ISBN 0-9600202-9-2). William & Rich.

--Economic & Political Peace, Vol. 2. LC 76-51755. 1977. 6.95 (ISBN 0-9600202-5-X). William & Rich.

Thomas, Paul. Karl Marx & the Anarchists. 448p. 1980. 40.00x (ISBN 0-7100-0427-3). Routledge & Kegan.

Tonnies, Ferdinand. Karl Marx: His Life & Teachings. Loomis, Charles P. & Ingeborg, Paulus, trs. xvi, 169p. 1974. 8.50x (ISBN 0-87013-181-8). Mich St U Pr.

Tucker, Robert C. Marxian Revolutionary Idea. 1969. pap. 4.95 (ISBN 0-393-00539-9, Norton Lib). Norton.

--Philosophy & Myth in Karl Marx. 2nd ed. LC 70-180022. 250p. 1972. 32.95 (ISBN 0-521-08455-5); pap. 8.95x (ISBN 0-521-09701-0). Cambridge U Pr.

Turner, Denys. On the Philosophy of Karl Marx. 1968. pap. text ed. 1.75x (ISBN 0-85415-000-5). Humanities.

Turner, John K. Challenge to Karl Marx. 1976. lib. bdg. 48.00 (ISBN 0-8490-1593-6). Gordon Pr.

Van Der Hoeven, Johan. Karl Marx: The Roots of His Thought. 1976. 6.95x (ISBN 0-88906-001-0). Wedge Pub.

Varga, E. The Great Crisis & Its Political Consequences. 18.75 (ISBN 0-86527-089-9). Fertig.

Volkov, G. Birth of a Genius. 243p. 1978. 4.20 (ISBN 0-8285-1602-2, Pub. by Progress Pubs Russia). Imported Pubns.

Walker, Angus. Marx: His Theory & Its Context. (Illus.). 1978. pap. text ed. 10.95x (ISBN 0-582-44196-X). Longman.

Wallimann, Isidor. Estrangement: Marx's Conception of Human Nature & the Division of Labor. LC 80-929. (Contributions in Philosophy: No. 16). xxiv, 195p. 1981. lib. bdg. 29.95 (ISBN 0-313-22096-4, WAE/). Greenwood.

Wessell, Leonard P. Karl Marx, Romantic Irony & the Proletariat: Studies in the Mythopoetic Origins of Marxism. LC 79-12386. 1979. text ed. 25.00x (ISBN 0-8071-0587-2). La State U Pr.

Weyl, Nathaniel. Karl Marx: Racist. 1979. 11.95 (ISBN 0-87000-448-4). Arlington Hse.

Wolfson, Murray. Karl Marx. 1969. pap. 3.00 (ISBN 0-231-03146-7). Columbia U Pr.

Wood, Allen. Karl Marx. (The Arguments of the Philosophers Ser.). 280p. 1981. 25.00 (ISBN 0-7100-0672-1). Routledge & Kegan.

Zeitlin, Irving M. Marxism: A Re-Examination. (New Perspectives in Political Science Ser: No. 13). (Orig.). 1967. pap. 4.95x (ISBN 0-442-09561-9, NP13). Van Nos Reinhold.

Zeleny, Jindrich. The Logic of Marx. Carver, Terrell, ed. & tr. 251p. 1980. 27.50x (ISBN 0-8476-6767-7). Rowman.

MARX, KARL, 1818-1883–JUVENILE LITERATURE

Fromm, Erich. Marx's Concept of Man. LC 61-11935. (Milestones of Thought Ser.). xii, 263p. (With translations from Marx's Economic & Philosophical Manuscripts by T. B. Bottomore). 10.00 (ISBN 0-8044-5391-8); pap. 4.95 (ISBN 0-8044-6161-9). Ungar.

Rice, Edward. Marx, Engels & the Workers of the World. LC 76-56183. (Illus.). 192p. (gr. 7 up). 1977. 8.95 (ISBN 0-590-07407-5, Four Winds). Schol Bk Serv.

MARX BROTHERS

Adamson, Joe. Groucho, Harpo, Chico & Sometimes Zeppo: A Celebration of the Marx Brothers. (Illus.). 1974. pap. 3.95 (ISBN 0-671-21910-3, Touchstone Bks). S&S.

Anobile, Richard, ed. Why a Duck? (Illus.). 288p. 1974. pap. 5.95 large-format (ISBN 0-380-00452-6, 40774). Avon.

Chandler, Charlotte. Hello, I Must Be Going--Groucho & His Friends. LC 77-89876. 1978. 10.95 (ISBN 0-385-12444-9). Doubleday.

Eyles, Allen. The Marx Brothers: Their World of Comedy. (Illus., Orig.). 1966. pap. 4.95 (ISBN 0-498-07420-X). A S Barnes.

Jordan, Thomas. The Anatomy of Cinematic Humor, with an Analytic Essay on the Marx Brothers. (Cinema Ser). 1974. write for info. (ISBN 0-87700-205-3); lib. bdg. 69.95 (ISBN 0-685-50723-8). Revisionist Pr.

Marx, Groucho & Anobile, Richard. The Marx Brothers Scrapbook. 1974. 13.95 (ISBN 0-517-51546-6, Darien Hse). Crown.

Marx, Maxine. Growing up with Chico. LC 80-15387. 1980. 9.95 (ISBN 0-13-367821-0). P-H.

MARXIAN ECONOMICS

Abalkin, L. I. The Economic System of Socialism. 139p. 1980. 4.40 (ISBN 0-8285-1705-3, Pub. by Progress Pubs Russia). Imported Pubns.

Ahluwalia, Jasbir Singh. Marxism & Contempory Reality. 60p. 1973. lib. bdg. 5.25x (ISBN 0-210-40548-1). Asia.

Aranowitz, Stanley. The Crisis in Historical Materialism: Class, Politics & Culture in Marxist Theory. 272p. 1981. 24.95x (ISBN 0-686-76469-2); pap. 12.95x (ISBN 0-686-76470-6). J F Bergin.

Becker, J. Marxian Political Economy. LC 76-9172. (Illus.). 1977. 26.50x (ISBN 0-521-21349-5). Cambridge U Pr.

Bellis, Paul. Marxism & the USSR: The Theory of Proletarian Dictatorship & the Marxist Analysis of Soviet Society. 1979. text ed. 31.25x (ISBN 0-391-01007-7). Humanities.

Bettelheim, Charles. Economic Calculation & Forms of Property. Taylor, John, tr. from Fr. LC 74-21473. 192p. 1976. 11.50 (ISBN 0-85345-360-8, CL3608). Monthly Rev.

--The Transition to Socialist Economy. Mepham, John, ed. Pearce, Brian, tr. from Fr. (Marxist Theory & Contemporary Capitalism Ser). 248p. 1975. text ed. 18.50x (ISBN 0-391-00396-8); pap. text ed. 10.50x (ISBN 0-391-00884-6). Humanities.

Biro, Lajos & Cohen, Marc J., eds. The United States in Crisis: Marxist Analyses. LC 78-61686. (Studies in Marxism: Vol. 4). 256p. 1979. 12.50 (ISBN 0-930656-08-3); pap. 6.00 (ISBN 0-930656-07-5). Marxist Educ.

Bohm Von Bawerk, Eugen. Karl Marx & the Close of His System. Sweezy, Paul M., ed. LC 73-8804. Repr. of 1949 ed. lib. bdg. 12.50x (ISBN 0-678-00140-5). Kelley.

Bose, Arun. Marx on Exploitation & Inequality: An Essay in Marxian Analytical Economics. 364p. 1980. text ed. 14.50x (ISBN 0-19-561149-7). Oxford U Pr.

Brus, Wlodzimierz. The Economics & Politics of Socialism: Collected Essays. 1973. 15.00x (ISBN 0-7100-7474-3). Routledge & Kegan.

--The Market in a Socialist Economy. 1972. 19.00x (ISBN 0-7100-7276-7). Routledge & Kegan.

Bukharin, Nikolai I. Economic Theory of the Leisure Class. LC 71-120560. Repr. of 1927 ed. 7.00 (ISBN 0-404-01149-7). AMS Pr.

--Economic Theory of the Leisure Class. LC 68-30819. Repr. of 1927 ed. lib. bdg. 15.00x (ISBN 0-8371-0032-1, BUEC). Greenwood.

--Economic Theory of the Leisure Class. LC 73-10163. Repr. of 1927 ed. 6.50x (ISBN 0-678-00580-X). Kelley.

--Economic Theory of the Leisure Class. LC 72-81775. 224p. 1972. pap. 4.50 (ISBN 0-85345-261-X, PB-261X). Monthly Rev.

Burger, et al. Marxism, Science & the Movement of History. (Philosophical Currents Ser.: No. 27). 1981. pap. text ed. 34.25x (ISBN 90-6032-186-3). Humanities.

Caldwell, Malcolm. Wealth of Some Nations. 192p. 1977. 10.00 (ISBN 0-905762-01-0); pap. 6.00 (ISBN 0-686-71044-4). Lawrence Hill.

Campbell, Robert W. Soviet-Type Economies: Performance & Evolution. 3rd ed. 272p. 1974. pap. text ed. 9.95 (ISBN 0-395-17231-4). HM.

Carchedi, Guglielmo. On the Economic Identification of Social Classes. (Direct Editions Ser.). 1977. pap. 14.00 (ISBN 0-7100-8648-2). Routledge & Kegan.

Cole, George D. What Marx Really Meant. LC 79-90489. Repr. of 1934 ed. lib. bdg. 17.50x (ISBN 0-8371-3082-4, COWM). Greenwood.

Corrigan, Phillip, ed. Capitalism, State Formation & Marxist Theory. 9.95 (ISBN 0-7043-3311-2, Pub. by Quartet England). Charles River Bks.

Croce, Benedetto. Historical Materialism & the Economics of Karl Marx. LC 78-66239. (Social Science Classics). 225p. 1981. 19.95 (ISBN 0-87855-313-4); pap. text ed. 6.95 (ISBN 0-87855-695-8). Transaction Bks.

--Historical Materialism of the Economics of Karl Marx. 188p. 1966. 24.00x (ISBN 0-7146-1218-9, F Cass Co). Biblio Dist.

Cutler, Antony, et al. Marx's Capital & Capitalism Today, Vol. 1. 1977. 22.00x (ISBN 0-7100-8745-4); pap. 10.50 (ISBN 0-7100-8746-2). Routledge & Kegan.

De Brunhoff, Suzanne. Marx on Money. 1976. 10.00 (ISBN 0-916354-43-1); pap. 4.95 (ISBN 0-916354-44-X). Urizen Bks.

Desai, Meghnad. Marxian Economics. 265p. 1979. 27.50x (ISBN 0-8476-6204-7). Rowman.

--Marxian Economics. (Littlefield, Adams Quality Paperbacks: No. 348). (Orig.). 1979. pap. 8.95 (ISBN 0-8226-0348-9). Littlefield.

De Ste. Croix, G. E. M. The Class Struggle in the Ancient Greek World: From the Archaic Age to the Arab Conquests. 672p. 1981. 49.50x (ISBN 0-8014-1442-3). Cornell U Pr.

Dobb, Maurice. On Economic Theory & Socialism: Collected Papers. 1965. Repr. of 1955 ed. 26.00x (ISBN 0-7100-1283-7). Routledge & Kegan.

Draper, Hal. Karl Marx's Theory of Revolution, Part One: The State & Bureaucracy, 2 vols. in 1. LC 76-26319. 1978. pap. 9.50 (ISBN 0-85345-461-2, PB-4612). Monthly Rev.

Ellman, M. Socialist Planning. LC 78-57757. (Modern Cambridge Economics Ser.). 1979. 44.50 (ISBN 0-521-22229-X); pap. 11.95x (ISBN 0-521-29409-6). Cambridge U Pr.

Engels, Friedrich. On Marx's Capital. 126p. 1979. pap. 0.50 (ISBN 0-8285-0039-8, Pub. by Progress Pubs Russia). Imported Pubns.

--Origin of the Family, Private Property & the State. 181p. 1977. 2.00 (ISBN 0-8285-0043-6, Pub. by Progress Pubs Russia). Imported Pubns.

Faris, Ralph M. Revisionist Marxism: The Opposition Within. (Philosophical Currents Ser: No. 7). 90p. 1974. pap. text ed. 14.50x (ISBN 90-6032-017-4). Humanities.

Fedorenko, N. P. Optimal Functioning System for a Socialist Economy. 189p. 1974. 3.60 (ISBN 0-8285-0370-2, Pub. by Progress Pubs Russia). Imported Pubns.

--Optimal Functioning System for a Socialist Economy: A Look at Soviet Economic Planning. 189p. 1975. 12.00x (ISBN 0-8464-0688-8). Beekman Pubs.

Friedman, Andrew L. Industry & Labour: Class Struggle at Work & Monopoly Capitalism. 1977. text ed. 26.00x (ISBN 0-333-23031-0); pap. text ed. 12.50x (ISBN 0-333-23032-9). Humanities.

Gottheil, Fred M. Marx's Economic Predictions. 1967. 12.95x (ISBN 0-8101-0105-X). Northwestern U Pr.

Hardach, Gerd, et al. A Short History of Socialist Economic Thought. LC 78-21053. 1979. 10.95x (ISBN 0-312-72146-3); pap. 3.95 (ISBN 0-312-72147-1). St Martin.

Harris, Laurence & Fine, Ben. Rereading Capital. LC 78-20912. 1979. 17.50x (ISBN 0-231-04792-4). Columbia U Pr.

Harrision, John. Marxist Economics for Socialists. 176p. 1980. text ed. 14.00 (ISBN 0-86104-016-3); pap. 5.95 (ISBN 0-86104-015-5). Pluto Pr.

Hayek, Friedrich A., ed. Collectivist Economic Planning. LC 74-7272. Repr. of 1938 ed. 17.50x (ISBN 0-678-00782-9). Kelley.

Heller, Agnes. The Theory of Need in Marx. (Allison & Busby Motive Ser.). 136p. 1981. pap. 7.95 (ISBN 0-8052-8075-8, Pub. by Allison & Busby England). Schocken.

--The Theory of Need in Marx. LC 76-19162. 1976. 14.95x (ISBN 0-312-79800-8). St Martin.

Hindess, Barry & Hirst, Paul. Pre-Capitalist Modes of Production. 1975. 28.00x (ISBN 0-7100-8168-5). Routledge & Kegan.

Holloway, John & Picciotto, Sol, eds. State & Capital: A Marxist Debate. LC 78-65361. 226p. 1979. text ed. 13.50x (ISBN 0-292-77551-2). U of Tex Pr.

Horowitz, David. The Fate of Midas & Other Essays. LC 72-85903. 1973. 7.95 (ISBN 0-87867-032-7); pap. 4.50 (ISBN 0-87867-033-5). Ramparts.

Horowitz, David, ed. Marx & Modern Economics. LC 68-24053. 1968. pap. 6.95 (ISBN 0-85345-072-2, PB-0722). Monthly Rev.

Horvat, Branko. The Political Economy of Socialism: A Marxist Social Theory. 660p. 1981. 35.00 (ISBN 0-87332-184-7). M E Sharpe.

Jalee, Pierre. How Capitalism Works: An Introductory Marxist Analysis. Klopper, Mary, tr. LC 77-80313. 1977. pap. 3.95 (ISBN 0-85345-416-7, PB4167). Monthly Rev.

John, P. M. Marx on Alienation. 1976. 12.50x (ISBN 0-88386-801-6). South Asia Bks.

Kautsky, Karl. The Economic Doctrines of Karl Marx. Stenning, H. J., tr. from Ger. LC 79-1583. 1980. Repr. of 1936 ed. 19.75 (ISBN 0-88355-888-2). Hyperion Conn.

Kirichenko, V. N. Socialist Long Term Economic Planning. 1980. 4.50 (ISBN 0-8285-1787-8, Pub. by Progress Pubs Russia). Imported Pubns.

Kitching, Gavin. Class & Economic Change in Kenya: The Making of an African Petite Bourgeoisie, 1905-1970. LC 79-21804. 448p. 1980. text ed. 39.50x (ISBN 0-300-02385-5). Yale U Pr.

Kuhne, Karl. Economics & Marxism, 2 vols. Shaw, Robert, tr. Incl. Vol. 1. The Renaissance of the Marxian System (ISBN 0-312-23436-8); Vol. 2. The Dynamics of the Marxian System (ISBN 0-312-23437-6). 1979. Set. 27.50x (ISBN 0-686-52171-4). St Martin.

Kuruma, S. Marx-Lexikon zur Politischen Oekonomie, 3 vols. 1110p. (Ger.). 1973. pap. 54.00 (ISBN 3-87628-080-X, M-7549, Pub. by Oberbaum). French & Eur.

Lenin. Las Tres Fuentes y las Tres Partes Integrantes Del Marxismo. 68p. (Span.). 1977. pap. 0.60 (ISBN 0-8285-1409-7, Pub. by Progress Pubs Russia). Imported Pubns.

Lenin, V. I. A Characterization of Economic Romanticism. 144p. 1971. pap. 0.90 (ISBN 0-8285-0078-9, Pub. by Progress Pubs Russia). Imported Pubns.

Lowy, Michael. Revolution Without Frontiers. 256p. 1982. 19.50 (ISBN 0-8052-7105-8, Pub. by NLB England); pap. 8.50 (ISBN 0-8052-7106-6, Pub. by NLB England). Schocken.

Maarek, Gerard. Introduction to Karl Marx's 'Das Kapital' A Study in Formalisation. Evans, Mansel, ed. 1979. 22.00x (ISBN 0-19-520156-6). Oxford U Pr.

McQuarie, Donald. Marx: Sociology-Social Change Capitalism. 6.95 (ISBN 0-7043-3221-3, Pub. by Quartet England). Charles River Bks.

Mandel, Ernest. Formation of the Economic Thought of Karl Marx. Pearce, Brian, tr. from Fr. LC 71-142990. 1971. 7.95 (ISBN 0-85345-151-6, CL-1516); pap. 4.50 (ISBN 0-85345-187-7, PB-1877). Monthly Rev.

--Introduction to Marxist Economic Theory. new, 2nd ed. Pathfinder Press Staff, ed. LC 73-82169. 80p. 1974. 8.00 (ISBN 0-87348-314-6); pap. 2.25 (ISBN 0-87348-315-4). Path Pr NY.

--Marxist Economic Theory, 2 Vols. Pearce, Brian, tr. LC 68-13658. 1969. Set. pap. 13.00 (ISBN 0-85345-166-4, PB-1664). Monthly Rev.

Marx, Karl. Capital, 3 vols. 1979. Set. 19.00 (ISBN 0-8285-0014-2, Pub. by Progress Pubs Russia); Vol. 1, 767pp. 8.00 (ISBN 0-8285-0015-0); Vol. 2, 551pp. 6.00 (ISBN 0-8285-0016-9); Vol. 3, 947pp. 6.00 (ISBN 0-8285-0017-7). Imported Pubns.

--Contribution to the Critique of Political Economy. Dobb, Maurice, ed. LC 69-20357. 1971. pap. 3.25 (ISBN 0-7178-0041-5). Intl Pub Co.

--Economic & Philosophical Manuscripts of Eighteen Forty-Four. 199p. 1974. 2.10 (ISBN 0-8285-0024-X, Pub. by Progress Pubs Russia). Imported Pubns.

--Wage, Labour & Capital. 1978. pap. 1.25 (ISBN 0-8351-0547-4). China Bks.

--Wage-Labour & Capital & Value, Price & Profit. LC 76-10456. 1976. pap. 1.25 (ISBN 0-7178-0470-4). Intl Pub Co.

Marx, Karl & Engels, Frederick. Karl Marx-Frederick Engels: Collected Works, 2 vols. Incl. Vol. 10. Marx & Engels 1849-1851. 1978 (ISBN 0-7178-0510-7); Vol. 11. 1851-1853. 1978 (ISBN 0-7178-0511-5). 8.50 ea. Intl Pub Co.

Mashruwala, K. G. Gandhi & Marx. 119p. (Orig.). 1981. pap. 1.50 (ISBN 0-934676-30-5). Greenlf Bks.

Mattick, Paul. Marx & Keynes: The Limits of the Mixed Economy. LC 69-15526. (Extending Horizons Ser). 1969. 6.95 (ISBN 0-87558-045-9). Porter Sargent.

Medvedev, Roy. Leninism & Western Socialism. 1982. 12.95 (ISBN 0-8052-7109-0, Pub. by NLB England); pap. 5.50 (ISBN 0-8052-7110-4, Pub. by NLB England). Schocken.

Meek, Ronald L. Smith, Marx & After: Ten Essays in the Development of Economic Thought. LC 77-5345. 192p. 1977. text ed. 25.00x (ISBN 0-412-14360-7, Pub. by Chapman & Hall England). Methuen Inc.

--Studies in the Labour Theory of Value. LC 74-7792. 384p. 1976. 17.50 (ISBN 0-85345-344-6, CL-3446). Monthly Rev.

Morishima, M. Marx's Economics: A Dual Theory of Value & Growth. LC 72-83591. (Illus.). 224p. 1973. 32.95 (ISBN 0-521-08747-3); pap. 14.95x (ISBN 0-521-29303-0). Cambridge U Pr.

Napoleoni, Claudio. Smith, Ricardo, Marx. Gee, J. M., tr. from It. LC 75-15962. 198p. 1975. lib. bdg. 21.95 (ISBN 0-470-63011-6). Halsted Pr.

Negri, Antonio. Marx Beyond Marx: Notebooks on the Grundrisse. Orig. Title: Marx Oltre Marx. 232p. 1982. 21.95x (ISBN 0-89789-018-3). J F Bergin.

Nowak, Leszek. The Structure of Idealization: Towards a Systematic Interpretation of the Marxian Idea of Science. (Synthese Library: No. 139). 1980. lib. bdg. 34.00 (ISBN 90-277-1014-7, Pub. by Reidel Holland). Kluwer Boston.

Pilling, Geoffrey. Marx's Capital. 208p. 1980. 27.50x (ISBN 0-7100-0516-4). Routledge & Kegan.

Prybyla, Jan S. Issues in Socialist Economic Modernization. 140p. 1980. 19.95 (ISBN 0-03-057962-7). Praeger.

Rinkel, L. I. Money: A Labor Theory of Value. 202p. 1980. pap. text ed. 15.75x (ISBN 90-232-1744-6). Humanities.

Roberts, Dick. Capitalism in Crisis. LC 75-16886. 128p. 1975. 7.00 (ISBN 0-87348-408-8). Path Pr NY.

Roberts, Paul C. & Stephenson, Matthew A. Marx's Theory of Exchange, Alienation & Crisis. LC 79-91039. (Studies: No. 36). (Illus.). 127p. 1973. 7.50 (ISBN 0-8179-3361-1). Hoover Inst Pr.

Robinson, Joan. Essay on Marxian Economics. 2nd ed. 1966. 12.95 (ISBN 0-312-26180-2); pap. 4.95 (ISBN 0-312-26215-9, E55805). St Martin.

Robinson, Maxine. Marxism & the Modern World. LC 81-81695. 1981. 8.50 (ISBN 0-686-31610-X); pap. 4.75 (ISBN 0-686-31611-8). Monthly Rev.

Roemer, John. Analytical Foundations of Marxian Economic Theory. LC 80-22646. (Illus.). 224p. Date not set. price not set (ISBN 0-521-23047-0). Cambridge U Pr.

Roth, Mike & Eldred, Michael. Guide to Marx's "Capital". 1978. pap. text ed. 5.25x (ISBN 0-906336-11-2). Humanities.

Rousseas, S. Capitalism & Catastrophe. LC 78-11996. (Illus.). 1979. 18.95 (ISBN 0-521-22333-4). Cambridge U Pr.

Rowe, William E., ed. Studies in Labor Theory & Practice: Papers from the Fifth Midwst Marxist Scholars Conference. (Studies in Marxism: Vol. 12). 100p. (Orig.). 1981. 10.50 (ISBN 0-930656-23-7); pap. 3.95 (ISBN 0-930656-24-5). Marxist Educ.

Ruben, David. Marxism & Materialism. rev. ed. (Marxist Theory & Contemporary Capitalism Ser.). 1978. text ed. 27.50x (ISBN 0-391-00966-4); pap. text ed. 11.00x (ISBN 0-391-00965-6). Humanities.

Schwartz, Jesse G, ed. A Subtle Anatomy of Capitalism: Selected Readings. LC 76-26192. (Illus.). 1977. pap. 13.95 (ISBN 0-87620-871-5). Goodyear.

See, Henri E. Economic Interpretation of History. Knight, Melvin M., tr. LC 68-56744. (Research & Source Works Ser: No. 225). 1968. Repr. of 1929 ed. 11.50 (ISBN 0-8337-3219-6). B Franklin.

Sherman, Howard. Radical Political Economy: Capitalism & Socialism from a Marxist Humanist Perspective. LC 72-174829. 1972. text ed. 13.50x (ISBN 0-465-06823-5). Basic.

Silverman, Bertram, ed. Man & Socialism in Cuba: The Great Debate. LC 71-139327. 1971. pap. text ed. 3.75x (ISBN 0-689-70339-2, 195). Atheneum.

Smart, Barry. Sociology, Phenomenology & Marxian Analysis: A Critical Discussion of the Theory & Practice of a Science of Society. (International Library of Sociology). 1976. 16.50x (ISBN 0-7100-8372-6); pap. 12.50 (ISBN 0-7100-8373-4). Routledge & Kegan.

Sohn-Rethel, Alfred. Intellectual & Manual Labour: A Critique of Epistemology. LC 77-12975. (Critical Social Studies). 1978. text ed. 26.00x (ISBN 0-391-00774-2); pap. text ed. 10.25x (ISBN 0-333-23046-9). Humanities.

Steedman, Ian. Marx After Sraffa. 1978. 17.50 (ISBN 0-902308-49-1, Pub by NLB). Schocken.

Steedman, Ian, et al. The Value Controversy. 1982. 19.50 (ISBN 0-8052-7107-4, Pub. by NLB England); pap. 8.50 (ISBN 0-8052-7108-2, Pub. by NLB England). Schocken.

Sweezy, Paul M. & Bettelheim, Charles. On the Transition to Socialism. LC 72-158924. 1972. pap. 3.25 (ISBN 0-85345-191-5, PB-1915). Monthly Rev.

Tabb, William K. & Sawers, Larry, eds. Marxism & the Metropolis: New Perspectives in Urban Political Economy. 1978. pap. text ed. 6.95x (ISBN 0-19-502262-9). Oxford U Pr.

Telford, Shirley. Economic & Political Peace, Vol. 1. 3rd ed. LC 75-31615. 254p. 1975. 8.95 (ISBN 0-9600202-9-2). William & Rich.

--Economic & Political Peace, Vol. 2. LC 76-51755. 1977. 6.95 (ISBN 0-9600202-5-X). William & Rich.

Trotsky, Leon. The Living Thoughts of Karl Marx. 189p. 1980. Repr. lib. bdg. 17.50 (ISBN 0-89984-452-9). Century Bookbindery.

Urry, John. The Anatomy of Capitalist Societies: The Economy, Civil Society & the State. 178p. 1981. pap. text ed. 32.50x (ISBN 0-333-29430-0, Pub. by Macmillan England); pap. text ed. 17.50x (ISBN 0-391-02255-5). Humanities.

Weeks, John. Capital & Exploitation. LC 81-47163. 224p. 1981. 17.50x (ISBN 0-691-04228-4); pap. 5.95x (ISBN 0-691-00366-1). Princeton U Pr.

Wolfson, Murray. Karl Marx. 1969. pap. 3.00 (ISBN 0-231-03146-7). Columbia U Pr.

--Reappraisal of Marxian Economics. LC 66-14790. 1966. 17.50x (ISBN 0-231-02880-6). Columbia U Pr.

Yanowitch, Murray, ed. Contemporary Soviet Economics: A Collection of Readings from Soviet Sources. LC 68-14426. 1969. Set. (ISBN 0-87332-011-5); 17.50 ea. Vol. 1 (ISBN 0-87332-030-1). Vol.2 (ISBN 0-87332-031-X). M E Sharpe.

MARXISM

see Communism; Socialism

MARY 1ST, QUEEN OF ENGLAND, 1516-1558

Elder, John. The Copie of a Letter Sent in to Scotlande, or the Arivall of Prynce of Spaine. LC 72-193. (English Experience Ser.: No. 308). 96p. 1971. Repr. of 1555 ed. 9.50 (ISBN 90-221-0308-0). Walter J Johnson.

Erickson, Carolly. Bloody Mary. LC 77-75868. 1978. 12.95 (ISBN 0-385-11663-2). Doubleday.

Giles, John A., ed. Revolte Du Conte De Warwick Contre le Roi Edward 4e. (Fr). 1849. 24.00 (ISBN 0-8337-1347-7). B Franklin.

Harbison, E. Harris. Rival Ambassadors at the Court of Queen Mary. LC 73-107805. (Select Bibliographies Reprint Ser). 1940. 26.00 (ISBN 0-8369-5182-4). Arno.

Loades, D. M. The Reign of Mary Tudor: Politics, Government & Religions in England Fifteen Fifty-Three to Fifteen Fifty-Eight. LC 79-16479. 1979. 25.00x (ISBN 0-312-67029-X). St Martin.

Prescott, H. F. Spanish Tudor: The Life of Bloody Mary. LC 77-112942. Repr. of 1940 ed. 32.50 (ISBN 0-404-05133-2). AMS Pr.

Roll, Winifred. Mary I: The History of an Unhappy Tudor Queen. (Illus.). 1979. 9.95g (ISBN 0-13-559096-5). P-H.

MARY 2ND, QUEEN OF GREAT BRITAIN, 1662-1694

Chapman, Hester W. Mary Second: Queen of England. LC 75-17197. 1976. Repr. of 1953 ed. lib. bdg. 19.50x (ISBN 0-8371-8302-2, CHMQ). Greenwood.

Hamilton, Elizabeth. William's Mary. LC 78-164583. (Illus.). 1972. 12.95 (ISBN 0-8008-8248-2). Taplinger.

MARY, VIRGIN

Blunt, J. H., ed. The Myroure of Oure Lady. (EETS, ES Ser.: No. 19). Repr. of 1873 ed. 23.00 (ISBN 0-527-00232-1). Kraus Repr.

Breig, James. Hail Mary: Woman, Wife, Mother of God. (Today Paperback Ser.). (Illus.). 40p. (Orig.). 1980. pap. 1.95 (ISBN 0-89570-197-9). Claretian Pubns.

Brown, Raymond, et al, eds. Mary in the New Testament. LC 78-8797. 1978. pap. 3.95 (ISBN 0-8091-2168-9). Paulist Pr.

Brown, Raymond E., et al, eds. Mary in the New Testament: A Collaborative Assessment by Protestant & Roman Catholic Scholars. LC 78-8797. 336p. 1978. pap. 3.95 (ISBN 0-8006-1345-7, 1-1345). Fortress.

Cadoux, T., pref. by. The Sorrowful & Immaculate Heart of Mary. 1974. pap. 3.00 (ISBN 0-913382-02-7, 101-2). Prow Bks-Franciscan.

Carberry, Cardinal Mary Queen & Mother. 1979. 5.50 (ISBN 0-8198-0584-X); pap. 3.95 (ISBN 0-8198-0585-8). Dghtrs St Paul.

Carroll, Eamon R. & Carm, O. Understanding the Mother of Jesus. 1979. pap. 2.95 (ISBN 0-89453-100-X). M Glazier.

Constant, Alphonse L. La Mere de Dieu: Epopee religieuse et humanitaire. 389p. (Fr.). 1981. Repr. lib. bdg. 150.00 (ISBN 0-8287-1509-2). Clearwater Pub.

Daughters of St. Paul. Mary, Queen of Apostles. (gr. 4-8). plastic bdg. 2.00 (ISBN 0-8198-0215-8); pap. 1.25 (ISBN 0-8198-0216-6). Dghtrs St Paul.

De Santis, Zerlina. Journeys with Mary. 1981. 3.00 (ISBN 0-8198-3900-0). Dghtrs St Paul.

Giordani, Igino. Mary of Nazareth. (Orig.). 1965. 6.00 (ISBN 0-8198-0092-9); pap. 5.00 (ISBN 0-8198-0093-7). Dghtrs St Paul.

Habig, Marian A., ed. Marian Era, Vol. 9. 1959-1965. 4.95 (ISBN 0-8199-0209-8). Franciscan Herald.

Habig, Marion A. Marian Era, Vol. 10. 1970. 6.95 (ISBN 0-8199-0210-1). Franciscan Herald.

Haring, Bernard. Mary & Your Everyday Life. 1978. 6.95 (ISBN 0-89243-077-X); pap. 2.95 (ISBN 0-89243-075-3). Liguori Pubns.

Helme, Corinne. Life & Mission of the Blessed Virgin. 5.95 (ISBN 0-87613-011-2). New Age.

Helm-Pirgo, M. Virgin Mary, Queen of Poland: Historical Essay. 33p. 1966. pap. 2.50 (ISBN 0-686-09119-1). Polish Inst Arts.

Hinnebusch, Paul. The Mother of Jesus: Present with Us. pap. 5.95 (ISBN 0-686-74588-4, 101-27). Prow Bks-Franciscan.

Jameson, Anna B. Legends of the Madonna, As Represented in the Fine Arts. LC 70-89273. (Tower Bks). (Illus.). lxxvi, 344p. 1972. Repr. of 1890 ed. 28.00 (ISBN 0-8103-3114-4). Gale.

Lacy, Donald C. Mary & Jesus. 1979. pap. 1.95 (ISBN 0-89536-422-0). CSS Pub.

Lavasik, Lawrence. Mary My Hope. rev. ed. (Illus., LargeType). blue bdg., colored edges 3.50 (ISBN 0-686-14287-X, 365/00). Catholic Bk Pub.

Liguori, St. Alphonsus. Love Is Prayer - Prayer Is Love. LC 72-97592. 1973. pap. 2.50 (ISBN 0-89243-047-8, 41500). Liguori Pubns.

Long, Valentine. The Mother of God. 1977. 7.95 (ISBN 0-8199-0619-0). Franciscan Herald.

Lovasik, Lawrence G. Mary My Mother. rev. ed. (Saint Joseph Picture Bks). (Illus., LargeType). flexible bdg. 0.95 (ISBN 0-686-14288-8, 280). Catholic Bk Pub.

Maloney, George. Mary, the Womb of God. 5.95 (ISBN 0-87193-057-9). Dimension Bks.

Mary & the Fathers of the Church. Date not set. cancelled (ISBN 0-8198-0626-9). Dghtrs St Paul.

Mary in the Seraphic Order. (Franciscan Educational Conferences). 1954. pap. 6.00 (ISBN 0-685-77541-0). Franciscan Herald.

Meilach, Michael. Mary Immaculate & the Divine Plan. (The Mary Library). 120p. (Orig.). 1981. pap. 3.95 (ISBN 0-89453-258-8). M Glazier.

Miguens, M. Mary, Servant of the Lord. 1978. 3.75 (ISBN 0-8198-0538-6); pap. 2.25 (ISBN 0-8198-0539-4). Dghtrs St Paul.

Oberman, Heiko A. The Virgin Mary in Evangelical Perspective. LC 70-157546. (Facet Bks.). 56p. (Orig.). 1971. pap. 1.00 (ISBN 0-8006-3067-X, 1-3067). Fortress.

Pope Paul VI. Mary God's Mother & Ours. 1979. 4.75 (ISBN 0-8198-0571-8); pap. 3.50 (ISBN 0-8198-0572-6). Dghtrs St Paul.

Prophet, Mark & Prophet, Elizabeth. My Soul Doth Magnify the Lord! rev. ed. (Illus.). 350p. 1980. pap. 4.95 (ISBN 0-916766-35-7). Summit Univ.

Randall, John, et al. Mary: Pathway to Fruitfulness. (Orig.). 1978. pap. 1.95 (ISBN 0-914544-28-4). Living Flame Pr.

Ripley, Francis J. Mary, Mother of the Church: What Recent Popes Have Said About the Blessed Mother's Role in the Church. 1973. pap. 1.50 (ISBN 0-89555-094-6). TAN Bks Pubs.

Ruether, Rosemary R. Mary--the Feminine Face of the Church. LC 77-7652. (Illus.). 1977. pap. 3.65 (ISBN 0-664-24759-8). Westminster.

St. Alphonsus de Liguori. The Glories of Mary. LC 79-112485. 1977. pap. 10.00 (ISBN 0-89555-021-0, 187). TAN Bks Pubs.

Savoie, Sr. M. Alberta. Plantaire - in Honor of the Blessed Virgin Mary Taken from a French Manuscript of the Fourteenth Century. LC 73-94205. (Catholic University of America Studies in Romance Languages & Literatures Ser: No. 9). Repr. of 1933 ed. 18.00 (ISBN 0-404-50309-8). AMS Pr.

Suarez, F. Mary of Nazareth. 259p. 1979. pap. 4.95 (ISBN 0-933932-42-1). Scepter Pubs.

Warner, Marina. Alone of All Her Sex: The Myth & the Cult of the Virgin Mary. 1978. pap. 8.95 (ISBN 0-671-79011-0, Wallaby). PB.

--Alone of All Her Sex: The Myth & the Cult of the Virgin Mary. 1976. 15.00 (ISBN 0-394-49913-1). Knopf.

Worrell, William H. The Coptic Manuscripts in the Freer Collection. Repr. of 1923 ed. 31.00 (ISBN 0-384-38810-8). Johnson Repr.

MARY, VIRGIN–APPARITIONS AND MIRACLES

see also Shrines

Claudel, Paul. Le Symbolisme de la Salette. 64p. 1952. 2.95 (ISBN 0-686-54437-4). French & Eur.

Delaney, John J., ed. Woman Clothed with the Sun. LC 60-5922. pap. 3.50 (ISBN 0-385-08019-0, D118, Im). Doubleday.

Le Blanc, Sr. M. Francis. Cause of Our Joy. 1976. 4.00 (ISBN 0-8198-0391-X). Dghtrs St Paul.

Long, Valentine. The Mother of God. 1977. 7.95 (ISBN 0-8199-0619-0). Franciscan Herald.

Osee, Johan. Call of the Virgin at San Damiano. (Illus.). 1977. pap. 4.95 (ISBN 0-8158-0354-0). Chris Mass.

Sharkey, Don. The Woman Shall Conquer. 1976. pap. 4.95 (ISBN 0-913382-01-9, 101-1). Prow Bks-Franciscan.

Walne, Damien & Flory, Joan. Oh, What a Beautiful Lady. (Illus.). 1978. pap. 5.50 (ISBN 0-8199-0752-9). Franciscan Herald.

MARY, VIRGIN–ART

see also Icons; Jesus Christ–Art

Belvianes, Marcel. The Madonna in the Paintings of the Great Masters. (Illus.). 1980. Repr. 37.50 (ISBN 0-89901-010-5). Found Class Reprints.

Denny, Don. The Annunciation from the Right: From Early Christian Times to the Sixteenth Century. LC 76-23611. (Outstanding Dissertations in the Fine Arts - 2nd Ser. - Fifteenth Century). (Illus.). 1978. Repr. of 1965 ed. lib. bdg. 41.00 (ISBN 0-8240-2683-7). Garland Pub.

Hurlington, Vincent J. Great Art Madonnas Classed According to Their Significance As Types of Impressive Motherhood. (The Great Art Masters Library Bk.). (Illus.). 143p. 1981. 59.85 (ISBN 0-930582-97-7). Gloucester Art.

MARY, VIRGIN–BIOGRAPHY

Emmerich, Anne C. The Life of the Blessed Virgin Mary. Palairet, Michael, tr. from Ger. 1970. pap. 6.00 (ISBN 0-89555-048-2, 107). TAN Bks Pubs.

Emmerick, A. C. Life of the Blessed Virgin Mary. (Roman Catholic Ser.). 1979. lib. bdg. 69.95 (ISBN 0-8490-2959-7). Gordon Pr.

Heline, Corinne. The Blessed Virgin Mary: Her Life & Mission. 5.95 (ISBN 0-685-61613-4). New Age.

Mary Of Agreda. The Mystical City of God: A Popular Abridgement. Marison, Fiscar & Blatter, George J., trs. from Sp. LC 78-62255. 1978. pap. 10.00 (ISBN 0-89555-070-9, 126). TAN Bks Pubs.

MARY, VIRGIN–COREDEMPTION

see also Mary, Virgin–Meditation

MARY, VIRGIN–CULTUS

see also Mary, Virgin–Feasts; Sorrows of the Blessed Virgin Mary, Devotion To

Alberione, Rev. James. Glories & Virtues of Mary. 1970. 3.50 (ISBN 0-8198-3017-8); pap. write for info. (ISBN 0-8198-3018-6). Dghtrs St Paul.

Ashe, Geoffrey. The Virgin. (Illus.). 1976. 15.00x (ISBN 0-7100-8342-4). Routledge & Kegan.

Grimes, Ronald L. Symbol & Conquest: Public Ritual & Drama in Santa Fe, New Mexico. LC 76-13657. (Symbol, Myth, & Ritual Ser.). (Illus.). 1976. 25.00x (ISBN 0-8014-1037-1). Cornell U Pr.

MARY, VIRGIN–DOLORS

see Sorrows of the Blessed Virgin Mary, Devotion To

MARY, VIRGIN–FEASTS

Alberione, James. Mary, Mother & Model. 1958. 4.00 (ISBN 0-8198-0091-0). Dghtrs St Paul.

MARY, VIRGIN–ICONOGRAPHY

see Mary, Virgin–Art

MARY, VIRGIN–JUVENILE LITERATURE

Brem, M. M. Mary's Story. (Arch Bks: Set 4). 1967. laminated bdg. 0.79 (ISBN 0-570-06029-X, 59-1140). Concordia.

Dooley, Kate. Mary Book: The Story of Jesus' Mother with Creative Activities for Young Readers. LC 78-65128. 60p. 1979. pap. 1.95 (ISBN 0-8091-2181-6). Paulist Pr.

Hintze, Barbara. Mary: Mother of Jesus. (Illus.). (gr. 1-6). 1977. bds. 5.50 (ISBN 0-8054-4232-4). Broadman.

MARY, VIRGIN–LEGENDS

De Coinci, Gautier. Tumbler of Our Lady & Other Miracles. Kemp-Welch, A., tr. (Medieval Library). (Illus.). Repr. of 1926 ed. 7.50x (ISBN 0-8154-0076-4). Cooper Sq.

Gripkey, Sr. M. Vincentine. Blessed Virgin Mary As Mediatrix in the Latin & Old French Legend Prior to the Fourteenth Century. LC 72-94166. (Catholic University of America Studies in Romance Languages & Literatures Ser: No. 17). 1969. Repr. of 1938 ed. 20.50 (ISBN 0-404-50317-9). Ams Pr.

John Of Garland. The Stella Maris of John of Garland. Wilson, E. Faye, ed. 1946. 9.00 (ISBN 0-910956-19-7). Medieval Acad.

MARY, VIRGIN–MEDITATION

Gripkey, Sr. M. Vincentine. Blessed Virgin Mary As Mediatrix in the Latin & Old French Legend Prior to the Fourteenth Century. LC 72-94166. (Catholic University of America Studies in Romance Languages & Literatures Ser: No. 17). 1969. Repr. of 1938 ed. 20.50 (ISBN 0-404-50317-9). Ams Pr.

MARY, VIRGIN–MEDITATIONS

Barbieri, Albert. Mary, Star of the Sea. 1962. 3.50 (ISBN 0-8198-0094-5); pap. 2.50 (ISBN 0-8198-0095-3). Dghtrs St Paul.

Collins, John. Hail Holy Queen. 1963. 4.00 (ISBN 0-8198-3314-2); pap. 3.00 (ISBN 0-8198-3315-0). Dghtrs St Paul.

Dunn, James A. Mustard Meditations: Seeds for Christian Growth. 1974. pap. 2.45 (ISBN 0-89570-090-5). Claretian Pubns.

Hinnebusch, Paul. Sword of Sorrow. 1964. pap. 1.50 (ISBN 0-8199-0135-0, L38845). Franciscan Herald.

O'Driscoll, Herbert. Portrait of a Woman. 96p. (Orig.). 1981. pap. 5.95 (ISBN 0-686-74763-1). Seabury.

MARY, VIRGIN–POETRY

Goenner, M. E. Mary Verse of the Teutonic Knights. LC 72-140022. (Catholic University of America Studies in German: No. 19). Repr. of 1943 ed. 20.00 (ISBN 0-404-50239-3). AMS Pr.

Heyden, A. B. The Blessed Virgin Mary in Early Christian Latin Poetry. 59.95 (ISBN 0-87968-755-X). Gordon Pr.

Laube, Clifford J. Their Music Is Mary. 3.50 (ISBN 0-910984-11-5). Montfort Pubns.

Lydgate, John. Here Endeth the Book of the Lyf of Our Lady. LC 73-38207. (English Experience Ser.: No. 473). 192p. 1972. Repr. of 1484 ed. 63.00 (ISBN 90-221-0473-7). Walter J Johnson.

Lynch, John W. A Woman Wrapped in Silence. 288p. 1976. pap. 3.95 (ISBN 0-8091-1905-6). Paulist Pr.

Ostrander, Frederick C. Romans Dou Lis. Repr. of 1915 ed. 16.50 (ISBN 0-404-50616-X). AMS Pr.

Rilke, Rainer M. The Life of the Virgin Mary. Macintyre, C. F., tr. LC 74-138178. 55p. 1972. Repr. of 1947 ed. lib. bdg. 15.00x (ISBN 0-8371-5635-1, RIVM). Greenwood.

MARY, VIRGIN–PRAYER-BOOKS AND DEVOTIONS

Amatora, Mary. The Queen's Way. pap. 2.00 (ISBN 0-910984-16-6). Montfort Pubns.

Balskus, Pat. Mary's Pilgrim. LC 68-58160. (Encounter Ser.). 3.00 (ISBN 0-8198-0279-4). Dghtrs St Paul.

Carol, Juniper. De Corredemptione Beatae Virginis Mariae. (Theology Ser). 1950. 7.00 (ISBN 0-686-11586-4). Franciscan Inst.

De Montfort, St. Louis Marie. True Devotion to the Blessed Virgin. 4.95 (ISBN 0-910984-49-2); pap. 2.95 (ISBN 0-910984-50-6). Montfort Pubns.

Denis, Gabriel. Reign of Jesus Thru Mary. 5.00 (ISBN 0-910984-03-4). Montfort Pubns.

Doherty, Eddie. True Devotion to Mary. pap. 2.00 (ISBN 0-910984-02-6). Montfort Pubns.

Gaffney, Patrick. Mary's Spiritual Maternity. 4.95 (ISBN 0-910984-18-2); pap. 2.95 (ISBN 0-910984-19-0). Montfort Pubns.

Lelia, Mary. Leading the Little Ones to Mary. pap. 1.00 (ISBN 0-910984-13-1). Montfort Pubns.

Miguens, M. Mary, Servant of the Lord. 1978. 3.75 (ISBN 0-8198-0538-6); pap. 2.25 (ISBN 0-8198-0539-4). Dghtrs St Paul.

Paul The Sixth, Pope Devotion to the Blessed Virgin Mary. 1974. pap. 0.35 (ISBN 0-8198-0295-6). Dghtrs St Paul.

MARY, VIRGIN–SERMONS

Bernard Of Clairvaux & Amadeus Of Lausanne. Magnificat: Homilies in Praise of the Blessed Virgin Mary. LC 78-6249. (Cistercian Fathers Ser.: No. 18). 1979. 15.95 (ISBN 0-87907-118-4). Cistercian Pubns.

MARY, VIRGIN–SHRINES

see Shrines

MARY, VIRGIN–SORROWS

see Sorrows of the Blessed Virgin Mary, Devotion To

MARY, VIRGIN–THEOLOGY

Bojorge, Horacio. The Image of Mary: According to the Evangelists. Owen, Aloysius, tr. from Span. LC 77-15516. (Illus.). 1978. pap. 2.75 (ISBN 0-8189-0362-7). Alba.

De Simoni, Felix. Mary Magdalene & the Theory of Sin, 2 vols. LC 72-84832. (Illus.). 35p. 1972. 77.50 (ISBN 0-913314-04-8). Am Classical Coll Pr.

Perrin, Joseph-Marie. Mary Mother of Christ & of Christians. Finley, Jean D., tr. from Fr. LC 77-26608. (Illus.). 1978. pap. 3.50 (ISBN 0-8189-0367-8). Alba.

MARY, VIRGIN, IN LITERATURE

Goenner, M. E. Mary Verse of the Teutonic Knights. LC 72-140022. (Catholic University of America Studies in German: No. 19). Repr. of 1943 ed. 20.00 (ISBN 0-404-50239-3). AMS Pr.

Gripkey, Sr. M. Vincentine. Blessed Virgin Mary As Mediatrix in the Latin & Old French Legend Prior to the Fourteenth Century. LC 72-94166. (Catholic University of America Studies in Romance Languages & Literatures Ser: No. 17). 1969. Repr. of 1938 ed. 20.50 (ISBN 0-404-50317-9). Ams Pr.

Schroeder, M. J. Mary-Verse in "Meistergesang". (Catholic University Studies in German: No. 16). 1970. Repr. of 1942 ed. 23.50 (ISBN 0-404-50236-9). AMS Pr.

Vriend, Joannes. The Blessed Virgin Mary in Medieval Drama of England. 69.95 (ISBN 0-87968-756-8). Gordon Pr.

MARY MAGDALENE, SAINT

Branick, Vincent P. Mary, the Spirit & the Church. LC 80-82856. 128p. (Orig.). 1981. pap. 4.95 (ISBN 0-8091-2343-6). Paulist Pr.

Garth, Helen M. Saint Mary Magdalene in Medieval Literature. LC 78-64210. (Johns Hopkins University. Studies in the Social Sciences. Sixty-Seventh Ser. 1949: 3). Repr. of 1950 ed. 15.50 (ISBN 0-404-61315-2). AMS Pr.

Kelly, Edward T. Saga of the Shroud. 126p. (Orig.). pap. 2.95 (ISBN 0-933656-03-3). Trinity Pub Hse.

Neilson, Frances. Mary Called Magdalene. 176p. 1981. pap. 2.25 (ISBN 0-553-13918-5). Bantam.

Saba, Bonaventura. The Sinful, the Intimate, & the Mysterious Life of Mary Magdalene, 2 vols. (Illus.). 1978. Set. 79.75 (ISBN 0-89266-133-X). Am Classical Coll Pr.

Southwell, Robert. Marie Magdalens Funeral Teares. LC 74-22099. 180p. 1975. 20.00x (ISBN 0-8201-1144-9). Schol Facsimiles.

Wager, Lewis. Repentance of Mary Magdalene. LC 70-133754. (Tudor Facsimile Texts. Old English Plays: No. 36). Repr. of 1908 ed. 24.50 (ISBN 0-404-53336-1). AMS Pr.

MARY MAGDALENE, SAINT–ART

De Jong, Ralph. The Life of Mary Magdalene in the Paintings of the Great Masters, 2 vols. (Illus.). 1979. deluxe ed. 69.75 (ISBN 0-930582-30-6). Gloucester Art.

MARY MAGDALENE, SAINT–FICTION

Saltus, Edgar. Mary Magdalen. LC 78-116002. Repr. of 1891 ed. 17.50 (ISBN 0-404-05517-6). AMS Pr.

MARY OF THE APOSTLES, MOTHER, 1833-1907

Alberione, James. Mary, Queen of Apostles. rev. ed. 1976. 4.00 (ISBN 0-8198-0438-X); pap. 3.00 (ISBN 0-8198-0439-8). Dghtrs St Paul.

MARY STUART, QUEEN OF THE SCOTS, 1542-1587

Bingham, Caroline. James Fifth: King of Scots. 224p. 1971. 12.50x (ISBN 0-8448-0038-4). Crane-Russak Co.

Blackwood, Adam. History of Mary Queen of Scots. MacDonald, Alexander, ed. LC 73-39448. (Maitland Club, Glasgow. Publications: No. 31). Repr. of 1834 ed. 21.50 (ISBN 0-404-52991-7). AMS Pr.

Buchanan, George. The Tyrannous Reign of Mary Stewart. Gatherer, W. A., tr. from Latin. LC 78-3556. (Edinburgh University Publication: History, Philosophy, & Economics: No. 10). 1978. Repr. of 1958 ed. lib. bdg. 24.00x (ISBN 0-313-20343-1, BUTR). Greenwood.

Crosby, Allan J. & Bruce, John, eds. Accounts & Papers Relating to Mary Queen of Scots. (Camden Society, London. Publications. First Ser.: No. 93). Repr. of 1867 ed. 14.00 (ISBN 0-404-50193-1). AMS Pr.

Crosby, Allen J., ed. Accounts & Papers Relating to Mary Queen of Scots. 1967. Repr. of 1867 ed. 15.50 (ISBN 0-384-10235-2). Johnson Repr.

Elizabeth, Queen. The True Copie of a Letter from the Queens Maiesty to the Lord Mayor of London. LC 70-25636. (English Experience Ser.: No. 167). 8p. 1969. Repr. of 1586 ed. 7.00 (ISBN 90-221-0167-3). Walter J Johnson.

Fraser, Antonia. Mary Queen of Scots. 1978. 17.95 (ISBN 0-440-05261-0). Delacorte.

Henderson, Thomas F. Mary Queen of Scots: Her Environment & Tragedy, 2 Vols. LC 68-25241. (English Biography Ser., No. 31). 1969. Repr. of 1905 ed. Set. lib. bdg. 79.95 (ISBN 0-8383-0163-0). Haskell.

Hicks, Leo. Elizabethan Problem: Some Aspects of the Careers of Two Exile-Adventurers. LC 64-24786. 1965. 22.50 (ISBN 0-8232-0625-4). Fordham.

Laing, Malcolm. Preliminary Dissertation on the Participation of Mary Queen of Scots, in the Murder of Darnley, 2 vols. Repr. 150.00 (ISBN 0-8274-3201-1). R West.

Lang, Andrew. Mystery of Mary Stuart. LC 78-111771. Repr. of 1901 ed. 12.50 (ISBN 0-404-03858-1). AMS Pr.

Langdon-Davies, John. Mary Queen of Scots. (Jackdaw Ser: No. 26). (Illus.). 1970. 6.95 (ISBN 0-670-45962-3, Grossman). Viking Pr.

Linklater, Eric. Mary Queen of Scots. 162p. 1980. Repr. of 1933 ed. lib. bdg. 25.00 (ISBN 0-89984-318-2). Century Bookbindery.

Phillips, James E. Images of a Queen: Mary Stuart in Sixteenth-Century Literature. 1964. 25.00x (ISBN 0-520-01007-8). U of Cal Pr.

Plaidy, Jean. Mary Queen of Scots: The Fair Devil of Scotland. LC 75-7904. (Illus.). 272p. 1975. 15.95 (ISBN 0-399-11581-1). Putnam.

Skae, Hilda T. Mary, Queen of Scots. 1912. Repr. 30.00 (ISBN 0-8274-2681-X). R West.

Strong, Roy & Oman, Julia T. Elizabeth R. & Mary, Queen of Scots, 2 vols. 1980. Boxed Set. 14.95 (ISBN 0-686-65214-2). HM.

--Mary, Queen of Scots. LC 72-90026. (Illus.). 88p. 1973. 25.00x (ISBN 0-8128-1533-5). Stein & Day.

Tytler, William. Historical & Critical Inquiry into the Evidence Produced by the Earls of Murray & Morton Against Mary, Queen of Scots, 2vols. LC 78-67547. Repr. of 1790 ed. 75.00 set (ISBN 0-404-17686-0). AMS Pr.

Winstantley, Lilian. Macbeth, King Lear, & Contemporary History. LC 76-26068. 1922. lib. bdg. 20.00 (ISBN 0-8414-9540-8). Folcroft.

MARY STUART, QUEEN OF THE SCOTS, 1542-1587–DRAMA

Von Schiller, Friedrich. Maria Stuart. 1965. 5.95 (ISBN 0-312-51450-6). St Martin.

--Mary Stuart. Wilkins, Sophie, tr. from Ger. 1959. o. p. 5.25 (ISBN 0-8120-5060-6); pap. text ed. 3.50 (ISBN 0-8120-0132-X). Barron.

MARY STUART, QUEEN OF THE SCOTS, 1542-1587–FICTION

Hewlett, Maurice. Queen's Quair. LC 78-145084. 1971. Repr. of 1904 ed. 49.00 (ISBN 0-403-01023-3). Scholarly.

MARY WASHINGTON COLLEGE

Alvey, Edward, Jr. History of Mary Washington College, 1908-1972. LC 73-92624. (Illus.). 500p. 1974. 10.00x (ISBN 0-8139-0528-1). U Pr of Va.

MARYKNOLL SISTERS OF ST. DOMINIC

Cogan, Sr. Mary De Paul. Sisters of Maryknoll: Through Troubled Waters. LC 72-167329. (Essay Index Reprint Ser.). Repr. of 1947 ed. 16.00 (ISBN 0-8369-2764-8). Arno.

MARYLAND

Artes, Dorothy B. Bits & Pieces About Maryland. 120p. pap. text ed. 5.00 (ISBN 0-686-73104-2). Maryland Hist.

Baker Chapter, Captain Jeremiah D. A. R. Cecil County, Maryland, Marriage Licenses. LC 73-16489. 1976. pap. 5.00 (ISBN 0-8063-0596-7). Genealog Pub.

Blandi, Joseph G. Maryland Business Corporations, 1783-1852. LC 78-64155. (Johns Hopkins University. Studies in the Social Sciences. Fifty-Second Ser. 1934: 3). Repr. of 1934 ed. 15.00 (ISBN 0-404-61265-2). AMS Pr.

Bode, Carl. Maryland. (States & the Nation Ser.). (Illus.). 1978. 12.95 (ISBN 0-393-05672-4, Co-Pub by AASLH). Norton.

Carey, George C. Maryland Folk Legends & Folk Songs. LC 75-180857. 1971. pap. 4.00 (ISBN 0-87033-158-2, Pub. by Tidewater). Cornell Maritime.

Doud, Richard K., ed. Winterthur Portfolio: Thematic Issue on Maryland, No. 5. (Winterthur Bk.). (Illus.). 1969. 15.00 (ISBN 0-226-92126-3). U of Chicago Pr.

Federal Writers' Project. Maryland: A Guide to the Old Line State. 1940. Repr. 49.00 (ISBN 0-403-02171-5). Somerset Pub.

Hartzler, Daniel D. Arms Makers of Maryland. LC 74-24434. (Longrifle Ser.). (Illus.). 312p. 1977. 35.00 (ISBN 0-87387-054-9). Shumway.

Helmes, Winifred G., ed. Notable Maryland Women. LC 77-966. 1977. 12.50 (ISBN 0-87033-236-8, Pub. by Tidewater); pap. 8.00 (ISBN 0-685-80908-0). Cornell Maritime.

Ingle, Edward. Parish Institutions of Maryland. LC 78-63736. (Johns Hopkins University. Studies in Social Sciences. First Ser. 1882-1883: 6). Repr. of 1883 ed. 11.50 (ISBN 0-404-61006-4). AMS Pr.

Kaessman, et al. My Maryland. (Illus.). 1971. 4.50x (ISBN 0-938420-12-7). Md Hist.

Maryland. 28.00 (ISBN 0-89770-096-1). Curriculum Info Ctr.

Maryland Appellate Reports-Bound Volumes. cancelled. Michie-Bobbs.

Papenfuse, Edward C. & Stiverson, Gregory A., Jr., eds. Maryland Manual: 1979-1980. (Illus.). 1979. 8.00 (ISBN 0-686-21209-6). MD Hall Records.

Rollo, Vera F. & Henry, Harford. Last Proprietor of Maryland. 1976. lib. bdg. 9.75 (ISBN 0-917882-06-7). Maryland Hist Pr.

State Industrial Directories Corp. Maryland State Industrial Directory 1980. 1980. pap. 35.00 (ISBN 0-89910-040-6). State Indus Dir.

Stiverson, Gregory A. & Papenfuse, Edward C., eds. Maryland Manual: 1981-1982. (Illus.). 1981. 8.00 (ISBN 0-686-30564-7). MD Hall Records.

Wilhem, Lewis W. Local Institutions of Maryland. LC 78-63754. (Johns Hopkins University. Studies in the Social Sciences. Third Ser. 1885: 5-7). Repr. of 1885 ed. 11.50 (ISBN 0-404-61022-6). AMS Pr.

Wilstach, Paul. Tidewater Maryland. LC 76-92686. (Illus.). 1969. 10.00 (ISBN 0-87033-137-X, Pub. by Tidewater). Cornell Maritime.

MARYLAND–BIBLIOGRAPHY

Cox, Richard J. & Sullivan, Larry E., eds. Guide to the Research Collections of the Maryland Historical Society. LC 80-83821. x, 338p. 1981. write for info. (ISBN 0-938420-01-1). Maryland Hist Pr.

Enoch Pratt Free Library. Eastern Shore of Maryland: An Annotated Bibliography. Pritchett, Morgan H., ed. LC 80-50399. (Illus.). 233p. 1980. 29.95 (ISBN 0-937692-00-X). Queen Anne Pr.

MARYLAND–BIOGRAPHY

Anderson, George M. The Work of Adalbert Johann Volck, 1828-1912: Who Chose for His Name the Anagram, V. Blada, 1861-1865. (Illus.). 1970. 35.00 (ISBN 0-938420-19-4). Md Hist.

Donnelly, Mary L. & McFadden, Charles V. Craycroft Family: Colonial Maryland & Kentucky Kin. (Illus.). 300p. 1982. price not set (ISBN 0-939142-06-6). Donnelly.

Haw, James, et al. Stormy Patriot: The Life of Samuel Chase. LC 80-83807. (Illus.). 305p. 1980. 14.95 (ISBN 0-938420-00-3). Md Hist.

McKinney, J. Evans. Decoys of the Susquehanna Flats & Their Makers. LC 78-70722. (Illus.). 96p. 1979. pap. 12.95 (ISBN 0-935968-04-0). Holly Pr.

Papenfuse, Edward C., et al, eds. A Biographical Dictionary of the Maryland Legislature, 1635-1789, Vol. 1, A-H. 1979. text ed. 19.50 (ISBN 0-8018-1995-4). Johns Hopkins.

Stiverson, Gregory A. & Jacobsen, Phebe R. William Paca: A Biography. LC 76-17519. (Illus.). 1976. 7.95 (ISBN 0-938420-18-6); pap. 4.95 (ISBN 0-686-23680-7). Md Hist.

MARYLAND–DESCRIPTION AND TRAVEL

Alsop, George. Character of the Province of Maryland. LC 74-39491. (Select Bibliographies Reprint Series). 1972. Repr. of 1902 ed. 10.00 (ISBN 0-8369-9900-2). Arno.

Artes, Dorothy B. Bits & Pieces About Maryland. (Illus.). 150p. (gr. 3). 1974. pap. 5.00 (ISBN 0-917882-02-4). Maryland Hist Pr.

Bodine, A. Aubrey. Chesapeake Bay & Tidewater. LC 67-70707. (Illus.). 1969. 22.50 (ISBN 0-910254-02-8). Bodine.

Cannon, Timothy L. & Whitmore, Nancy F. Ghosts & Legends of Fredrick County. LC 79-64285. (Illus., Orig.). 1979. pap. 2.95 (ISBN 0-9602816-0-6). T L Cannon & N F Whitmore.

Federal Writers' Project. Maryland: A Guide to the Old Line State. 1940. Repr. 49.00 (ISBN 0-403-02171-5). Somerset Pub.

Footner, Hulbert. Maryland Main & the Eastern Shore. LC 67-1719. 1967. Repr. of 1942 ed. 19.00 (ISBN 0-8103-5034-3). Gale.

Gertler, Edward. Maryland & Delaware Canoe Trails. (Illus.). 180p. (Orig.). 1979. pap. 7.95 (ISBN 0-9605908-0-3). Seneca Pr MD.

Joynes, St. Leger M., et al. Insiders' Guide to Ocean City Maryland. rev. ed. (Insiders' Guides Ser.). (Illus., Orig.). 1981. pap. 3.95 (ISBN 0-932338-02-X). Insiders Pub.

Meanley, Brooke. Blackwater: National Wildlife Refuge Dorchester County Maryland. LC 78-35. (Illus.). 1978. pap. 6.00 (ISBN 0-87033-245-7, Tidewater). Cornell Maritime.

Morrison, Charles. The Western Boundary of Maryland. 1976. 5.00 (ISBN 0-87012-224-X). McClain.

Newell, Dianne. The Failure to Preserve the Queen City Hotel, Cumberland, Maryland. (Case Studies in Preservation). (Illus.). 36p. 1975. pap. 4.50 (ISBN 0-89133-023-2). Preservation Pr.

Papenfuse, Edward C., et al. Maryland: A New Guide to the Old Line State. LC 76-17224. (Illus.). 488p. 1976. 18.95x (ISBN 0-8018-1874-5); pap. 5.95 (ISBN 0-8018-1871-0). Johns Hopkins.

Rukert, Norman G. The Fells Point Story. LC 75-40655. (Illus.). 1976. 8.95 (ISBN 0-910254-11-7). Bodine.

Shosteck, Robert. Weekender's Guide: Places of Historic, Scenic, Cultural & Recreational Interest Within 200 Miles of the Washington-Baltimore Area. 7th rev. ed. LC 71-85813. (Illus.). 416p. 1979. pap. 4.95 (ISBN 0-87107-040-5). Potomac.

Shultz, Edward T. First Settlements of Germans in Md. Gross, Ruth T., ed. LC 76-151613. 1976. pap. 5.00 (ISBN 0-9606946-0-9). R T Gross.

Steiner, Bernard C. Descriptions of Maryland. LC 78-63904. (Johns Hopkins University. Studies in the Social Sciences. Twenty-Second Ser. 1904: 11-12). Repr. of 1904 ed. 14.50 (ISBN 0-404-61157-5). AMS Pr.

Torrence, Clayton. Old Somerset on the Eastern Shore of Maryland. LC 66-30004. 583p. 1979. Repr. of 1935 ed. 22.50 (ISBN 0-8063-7970-7). Regional.

Waesche, James F. Beautiful Maryland. Shangle, Robert D., ed. LC 79-22530. (Illus.). 72p. 1980. 14.95 (ISBN 0-915796-65-1); pap. 7.95 (ISBN 0-915796-64-3). Beautiful Am.

Whitehead, John H., III. Watermen of the Chesapeake Bay. (Illus.). 1979. 19.95 (ISBN 0-9603486-0-3). Whitehead Photo.

MARYLAND–ECONOMIC CONDITIONS

Bryan, Alfred C. History of State Banking in Maryland. LC 78-63868. (Johns Hopkins University. Studies in the Social Sciences. Seventeenth Ser. 1899: 1-3). Repr. of 1899 ed. 11.50 (ISBN 0-404-61124-9). AMS Pr.

Clemens, Paul G. The Atlantic Economy & Colonial Maryland's Eastern Shore: From Tobacco to Grain. LC 79-26181. (Illus.). 256p. 1980. 16.50x (ISBN 0-8014-1251-X). Cornell U Pr.

Deupree, Robert G. The Wholesale Marketing of Fruits & Vegetables in Baltimore. LC 78-64175. (Johns Hopkins University. Studies in the Social Sciences. Fifty-Seventh Ser. 1939: 2). Repr. of 1939 ed. 16.00 (ISBN 0-404-61284-9). AMS Pr.

Earle, Carville V. The Evolution of a Tidewater Settlement System: All Hallow's Parish, Maryland, 1650-1783. LC 75-11554. (Research Papers Ser.: No. 170). (Illus.). 1975. pap. 8.00 (ISBN 0-89065-077-2). U Chicago Dept Geog.

Gould, Clarence P. Money & Transportation in Maryland, 1720-1765. LC 78-63951. (Johns Hopkins University. Studies in the Social Sciences. Thirty-Third Ser. 1915: 1). Repr. of 1915 ed. 18.50 (ISBN 0-404-61199-0). AMS Pr.

Hanna, Hugh S. A Financial History of Maryland. LC 78-69923. (Johns Hopkins University. Studies in the Social Sciences. Twenty-Fifth Ser. 1907: 8-10). Repr. of 1907 ed. 16.50 (ISBN 0-404-61173-7). AMS Pr.

Hoffman, Ronald. A Spirit of Dissension: Economics, Politics, & the Revolution in Maryland. LC 73-8127. (Maryland Bicentennial Studies). (Illus.). 294p. 1974. 18.50x (ISBN 0-8018-1521-5). Johns Hopkins.

Hollander, Jacob H. The Financial History of Baltimore. LC 78-64266. (Johns Hopkins University. Studies in the Social Sciences. Extra Volumes: 20). Repr. of 1899 ed. 31.50 (ISBN 0-404-61368-3). AMS Pr.

Land, Aubrey G., et al, eds. Law, Society, & Politics in Early Maryland. LC 76-47374. (Illus.). 400p. 1977. 22.50x (ISBN 0-8018-1872-9). Johns Hopkins.

Res, Leonard O. The Financial History of Baltimore, 1900-1926. LC 78-64132. (Johns Hopkins University. Studies in the Social Sciences. Forty-Seventh Ser. 1929: 3). Repr. of 1929 ed. 16.00 (ISBN 0-404-61245-8). AMS Pr.

Rollo, Vera F. A Geography of Maryland: Ask Me! (About Maryland) 200p. (gr. k-6). 1981. casebnd. 8.50 (ISBN 0-917882-10-5); tchrs. handbk. 5.00 (ISBN 0-686-77442-6). Maryland Hist Pr.

Singleton, Evelyn E. Workmen's Compensation in Maryland. LC 78-64158. (Johns Hopkins University. Studies in the Social Sciences. Fifty-Third Ser. 1935: 2). Repr. of 1935 ed. 16.50 (ISBN 0-404-61268-7). AMS Pr.

Sioussant, St. George L. Economics & Politics in Maryland 1720-1750, & the Public Services of Daniel Dulany the Elder. LC 78-63897. (Johns Hopkins University. Studies in the Social Sciences, Twenty-First Ser. 1903: -7). Repr. of 1903 ed. 13.50 (ISBN 0-404-61150-8). AMS Pr.

Thon, Robert W. Mutual Savings Banks in Baltimore. LC 78-64159. (Johns Hopkins University. Studies in the Social Sciences. Fifty-Third Ser. 1935: 3). Repr. of 1935 ed. 15.00 (ISBN 0-404-61269-5). AMS Pr.

MARYLAND–GENEALOGY

Barnes, Robert. Marriages & Deaths from Baltimore Newspapers, 1796-1816. LC 78-61144. 1978. 17.50 (ISBN 0-8063-0826-5). Genealog Pub.

--Maryland Marriages: 1634-1777. LC 75-27355. 1978. 12.50 (ISBN 0-8063-0700-5). Genealog Pub.

--Maryland Marriages: 1778-1800. LC 77-88843. 1979. 15.00 (ISBN 0-8063-0791-9). Genealog Pub.

Bowie, Effie G. Across the Years in Prince George's County (Maryland) LC 74-18310. (Illus.). 904p. 1975. Repr. of 1947 ed. 35.00 (ISBN 0-8063-0643-2). Genealog Pub.

Brumbaugh, Gaius M. & Hodges, Margaret R. Revolutionary Records of Maryland. LC 67-28608. 1978. pap. 6.00 (ISBN 0-8063-0061-2). Genealog Pub.

Chamberlain, Samuel, compiled by. Genealogical Notes of the Chamberlain Family of Maryland. LC 70-175217. 1973. Repr. 20.00 (ISBN 0-686-26999-3). Polyanthos.

Cox, Richard J. & Sullivan, Larry E., eds. Guide to the Research Collections of the Maryland Historical Society. LC 80-83821. x, 338p. 1981. write for info. (ISBN 0-938420-01-1). Maryland Hist Pr.

Donnelly, Sr. Mary L. Arnold Livers Family in America (Lyvers, Lievers) LC 77-852223. (Illus.). 362p. 1977. 21.00 (ISBN 0-939142-02-3). Donnelly.

--The Buckman Family of Maryland & Kentucky. LC 79-90465. (Illus.). 530p. 1979. 32.00 (ISBN 0-939142-04-X). Donnelly.

--Genealogy of Thomas Hill & Rebecca Miles. LC 79-31237. (Illus.). 380p. 1971. 25.00 (ISBN 0-939142-00-7). Donnelly.

--Maryland Elder Family & Kin. LC 76-351164. 330p. 1975. 15.00 (ISBN 0-939142-01-5). Donnelly.

--Rapier, Hayden & Allied Families: Colonial Maryland & Kentucky. LC 78-656670. (Illus.). 595p. 1978. 30.00 (ISBN 0-939142-03-1). Donnelly.

Donnelly, Sr. Mary Louise. Imprints Sixteen Hundred Eight to Nineteen Eighty, Hamilton, Allied Families. LC 80-84574. (Illus.). 660p. 1980. 38.00 (ISBN 0-939142-05-8). Donnelly.

Gahn, Bessie W. Original Patentees of Land at Washington Prior to 1700. LC 77-77982. 1969. Repr. of 1936 ed. 8.50 (ISBN 0-8063-0155-4). Genealog Pub.

Gannett, Henry. A Gazetteer of Maryland & Delaware, 2 vols. in 1. LC 75-37016. 1979. Repr. of 1904 ed. 8.50 (ISBN 0-8063-0703-X). Genealog Pub.

Hollowak, Thomas L. Index to Marriages & Deaths in the (Baltimore) Sun 1837-1850. LC 77-16735. 1978. 25.00 (ISBN 0-8063-0796-X). Genealog Pub.

--Index to Marriages in the (Baltimore) Sun, 1851-1860. LC 77-16735. 1978. 15.00 (ISBN 0-8063-0827-3). Genealog Pub.

Jackson, Ronald V. & Teeples, Gary R. Maryland Census Index 1800. LC 77-85953. (Illus.). lib. bdg. 25.00 (ISBN 0-89593-060-9). Accelerated Index.

--Maryland Census Index 1810. LC 77-85954. (Illus.). lib. bdg. 26.00 (ISBN 0-89593-061-7). Accelerated Index.

--Maryland Census Index 1820. LC 77-85955. (Illus.). lib. bdg. 35.00 (ISBN 0-89593-062-5). Accelerated Index.

--Maryland Census Index 1830. LC 77-85956. (Illus.). lib. bdg. 35.00 (ISBN 0-89593-063-3). Accelerated Index.

--Maryland Census Index 1840. LC 77-85957. (Illus.). lib. bdg. 43.00 (ISBN 0-89593-064-1). Accelerated Index.

--Maryland Census Index 1850. LC 77-85959. (Illus.). lib. bdg. 57.00 (ISBN 0-89593-065-X). Accelerated Index.

Marine, William M. Brisith Invasion of Maryland, Eighteen Twelve to Eighteen Fifteen. Dielman, Louis H., ed. LC 77-70368. 1977. 18.50 (ISBN 0-8063-0760-9). Genealog Pub.

Marks, Lillian B. Reister's Desire: The Origin of Reisterstown... with a Genealigical History of the Reister Family. LC 75-18893. (Illus.). 1976. 15.00 (ISBN 0-938420-16-X). Md Hist.

Maryland Rent Rolls: Baltimore & Anne Arundel Counties, 1700-1707, 1705-1724. LC 76-1421. 1976. Repr. of 1924 ed. 15.00 (ISBN 0-8063-0716-1). Genealog Pub.

Meyer, Mary K., ed. Genealogical Research in Maryland: A Guide. 2nd ed. LC 72-91197. 1976. 6.00 (ISBN 0-938420-05-4). Md Hist.

Passano, Eleanor P. An Index to the Source Records of Maryland: Genealogical, Biographical, Historical. LC 67-17943. 1974. Repr. of 1940 ed. 20.00 (ISBN 0-8063-0271-2). Genealog Pub.

Rice, Millard M. William Rice of Frederick County, Maryland, & Some of His Descendants. (Illus.). 1979. pap. 4.00 (ISBN 0-913186-09-0). Monocacy.

Scott, Kenneth, ed. Abstracts from Ben Franklin's Pennsylvania Gazette, 1728-1748. LC 74-29164. 720p. 1975. 25.00 (ISBN 0-8063-0661-0). Genealog Pub.

Skordas, Gust. The Early Settlers of Maryland: An Index of Names of Immigrants Compiled from Records of Land Patents 1633-1680, in the Hall of Records, Annapolis, Maryland. LC 68-23457. 525p. 1979. Repr. of 1968 ed. 18.50 (ISBN 0-8063-0616-5). Genealog Pub.

U. S. Bureau of the Census. Heads of Families at the First Census of the United States Taken in the Year 1790: Maryland. LC 73-186488. 1977. Repr. of 1907 ed. 17.50 (ISBN 0-8063-0491-X). Genealog Pub.

--Heads of Families, First Census of the United States, 1790: Maryland. LC 64-61300. 1961-64. Repr. of 1908 ed. 17.50 (ISBN 0-87152-017-6). Reprint.

Wyand, Jeffrey & Wyand, Florence L. Colonial Maryland Naturalizations. LC 75-10681. 1975. 10.00 (ISBN 0-8063-0680-7). Genealog Pub.

MARYLAND–HISTORIC BUILDINGS

Coffin, Lewis A., Jr. & Holden, Arthur C. Brick Architecture of the Colonial Period in Maryland & Virginia. (Illus.). 10.00 (ISBN 0-8446-0062-8). Peter Smith.

Johnson, John H. Old Maryland Manors. LC 78-63737. (Johns Hopkins University. Studies in the Social Sciences. First Ser. 1882-1883: 7). Repr. of 1883 ed. 11.50 (ISBN 0-404-61007-2). AMS Pr.

Swann, Don, Jr. Colonial & Historic Homes of Maryland: With Text by Don Swann Jr. LC 75-9722. (Illus.). 224p. 1975. 35.00 (ISBN 0-8018-1727-7). Johns Hopkins.

MARYLAND–HISTORY

Adams, Herbert B. Maryland's Influence in Founding a National Commonwealth; or, the History of the Accession of Public Lands by the Old Confederation. LC 72-14393. (Maryland Historical Society. Fund-Publications: No. 11). Repr. of 1877 ed. 10.00 (ISBN 0-404-57611-7). AMS Pr.

--Maryland's Influence Upon Land Cessions to the United States. LC 4-8520. 1885. 1.00 (ISBN 0-403-00136-6). Scholarly.

Alsop, George. A Character of the Province of Maryland. LC 72-14398. (Maryland Historical Society. Fund-Publications: No. 15). Repr. of 1880 ed. 10.00 (ISBN 0-404-57615-X). AMS Pr.

Archer, George W. The Dismemberment of Maryland: An Historical & Critical Essay. Bd. with A Maryland Manor. Wilson, James G. LC 72-14414. (Maryland Historical Society, Fund-Publications Ser.: No. 30). Repr. of 1890 ed. 14.50 (ISBN 0-404-57630-3). AMS Pr.

Army of the Potomac: Part 1. LC 76-41427. (Civil War Monographs). 1977. lib. bdg. 41.00 (ISBN 0-527-17550-1); pap. 35.00 (ISBN 0-527-17548-X). Kraus Repr.

Baltimore, George C. The Calvert Papers, 3 vols. in 1. LC 72-14412. (Maryland Historical Society. Fund-Publications: Nos. 28, 34, 35). Repr. of 1899 ed. 45.00 (ISBN 0-404-57628-1). AMS Pr.

Barker, Charles A. Background of the Revolution in Maryland. 1967. Repr. of 1940 ed. 25.00 (ISBN 0-208-00470-X, Archon). Shoe String.

Black, J. W. Maryland's Attitude in the Struggle for Canada. pap. 7.00 (ISBN 0-384-04605-3). Johnson Repr.

Black, James W. Maryland's Attitude in the Struggle for Canada. LC 78-63812. (Johns Hopkins University. Studies in the Social Sciences. Tenth Ser. 1892: 7). Repr. of 1892 ed. 11.50 (ISBN 0-404-61075-7). AMS Pr.

Blandi, Joseph G. Maryland Business Corporations, 1783-1852. LC 78-64155. (Johns Hopkins University. Studies in the Social Sciences. Fifty-Second Ser. 1934: 3). Repr. of 1934 ed. 15.00 (ISBN 0-404-61265-2). AMS Pr.

Bond, Beverly W. State Government in Maryland, 1777-1781. LC 78-63907. (Johns Hopkins University. Studies in the Social Sciences. Twenty-Third Ser. 1905: 3-4). Repr. of 1905 ed. 15.50 (ISBN 0-404-61159-1). AMS Pr.

Boyd, Thomas H. History of Montgomery County, Maryland, from Its Earliest Settlement in 1650-1879. LC 68-31727. 1972. Repr. of 1879 ed. 12.50 (ISBN 0-8063-7954-5). Regional.

Bozman, John L. The History of Maryland: Its First Settlement, in 1633, to the Restoration, in 1660, 2 vols. Incl. Vol. 1. LC 68-30883. 314p. 15.00 (ISBN 0-87152-048-6); Vol. 2. LC 68-30883. 728p. 25.00 (ISBN 0-87152-049-4). (Illus.). 1968. Repr. of 1837 ed. Set. 40.00 (ISBN 0-87152-324-8). Reprint.

Brooks, Neal A., et al. A History of Baltimore County. LC 78-31598. (Illus.). 1979. 15.95 (ISBN 0-9602326-1-3). Friends Towson Lib.

Browne, William H. Maryland, the History of a Palatinate. rev. & enl. ed. LC 72-3758. (American Commonwealths: No. 3). Repr. of 1904 ed. 26.50 (ISBN 0-404-57203-0). AMS Pr.

Brumbaugh, Gaius M. Maryland Records, 2 vols. LC 67-24374. (Illus.). 1975. Repr. of 1915 ed. Set. 50.00 (ISBN 0-8063-0059-0). Genealog Pub.

Burdett, Harold N. Yesteryear in Annapolis. LC 74-26773. (Illus.). 1974. pap. 4.00 (ISBN 0-87033-197-3, Pub. by Tidewater). Cornell Maritime.

Calvert, Cecil & Baron Baltimore. A Relation of the Successefull Beginnings of the Lord Baltimore's Plantation in Mary-Land. LC 77-6864. (English Experience Ser.: No. 857). 1977. Repr. of 1634 ed. lib. bdg. 3.50 (ISBN 90-221-0857-0). Walter J Johnson.

Caper, Janice M. Between the Bays: Somerset, Wicomico & Worcester Counties Maryland. LC 78-71245. (Illus.). 86p. 1979. pap. 13.00 (ISBN 0-935968-05-9). Holly Pr.

Carroll, Kenneth. Quakerism on the Eastern Shore. LC 70-112986. (Illus.). 1970. 12.50x (ISBN 0-938420-15-1). Md Hist.

Clemens, Paul G. The Atlantic Economy & Colonial Maryland's Eastern Shore: From Tobacco to Grain. LC 79-26181. (Illus.). 256p. 1980. 16.50x (ISBN 0-8014-1251-X). Cornell U Pr.

Colwill, Stiles T. Francis Guy: Seventeen-Sixty to Eighteen-Twenty. LC 81-81085. (Illus.). 140p. (Orig.). 1981. pap. 15.00 (ISBN 0-938420-20-8). Md Hist.

Cook, Ebenezer, et al. Early Maryland Poetry. 1900. Repr. 19.00 (ISBN 0-403-08914-X). Somerset Pub.

Cox, Richard J. & Sullivan, Larry E., eds. Guide to the Research Collections of the Maryland Historical Society. LC 80-83821. x, 338p. 1981. write for info. (ISBN 0-938420-01-1). Maryland Hist Pr.

Crowl, Phillip A. Maryland During & After the Revolution: A Political & Economic Study. LC 78-64189. (Johns Hopkins University. Studies in the Social Sciences. Sixty-First Ser. 1943: 1). Repr. of 1943 ed. 18.50 (ISBN 0-404-61296-2). AMS Pr.

Davis, Edward G. Maryland & North Carolina in the Campaign of 1780-1781, with a Preliminary Notice of the Revolution, in Which the Troops of the Two States Won Distinction. LC 72-14418. (Maryland Historical Society. Fund-Publications: No. 33). Repr. of 1893 ed. 10.00 (ISBN 0-404-57633-8). AMS Pr.

Dozer, Donald M. Portrait of the Free State. LC 76-47023. (Illus.). 1976. 17.50 (ISBN 0-87033-226-0, Pub. by Tidewater). Cornell Maritime.

Four Generations of Commissions: The Peale Collection of the Maryland Historical Society. LC 75-1729. (Illus.). 1975. 7.50 (ISBN 0-686-11974-6). Md. Hist.

Gifford, George E., Jr. Cecil County, Maryland, 1608-1850. LC 74-84769. (Illus.). 241p. 1974. 7.50 (ISBN 0-686-11977-0). G E Gifford Memorial.
Gould, Clarence P. The Land System in Maryland, 1720-1765. LC 78-63943. (Johns Hopkins University. Studies in the Social Sciences. Thirty-First Ser. 1913: 1). Repr. of 1913 ed. 17.50 (ISBN 0-404-61192-3). AMS Pr.
--Land System in Maryland, 1720-1765. Bruchey, Stuart, ed. LC 78-53540. (Development of Public Land in the U. S. Ser.). 1979. Repr. of 1913 ed. lib. bdg. 10.00x (ISBN 0-405-11376-5). Arno.
--Money & Transportation in Maryland, 1720-1765. LC 78-63951. (Johns Hopkins University. Studies in the Social Sciences. Thirty-Third Ser. 1915: 1). Repr. of 1915 ed. 18.50 (ISBN 0-404-61199-0). AMS Pr.
Governors of Maryland,1777-1970. (Illus.). 1970. 12.00 (ISBN 0-686-21413-7); text ed. 12.00 (ISBN 0-686-21414-5). MD Hall Records.
Green Spring Valley: Its History & Heritage, 2 vols. Incl. Vol. 1. A History & Historic Houses. Thomas, Dawn F; Vol. 2. Genealogies. Barnes, Robert. LC 78-53033. (Illus.). 1978. 35.00 set (ISBN 0-938420-06-2). Md Hist.
Hahn, H. George & Behm, Carl. Towson: A Pictorial History of a Maryland Town. LC 77-20052. (Illus.). 1977. 15.95 (ISBN 0-915442-36-1). Donning Co.
Hall, Clayton C. The Great Seal of Maryland. LC 72-14406. (Maryland Historical Society. Fund-Publications). Repr. of 1886 ed. 10.00 (ISBN 0-404-57623-0). AMS Pr.
--Narratives of Early Maryland: Sixteen Thirty-Three to Sixteen Eighty-Four. LC 70-145066. 460p. 1925. Repr. 30.00 (ISBN 0-403-01009-8). Scholarly.
Hall, Clayton C., ed. Narratives of Early Maryland, Sixteen Thirty-Three to Sixteen Eighty-Four. (Original Narratives). 1967. Repr. of 1910 ed. 18.50x (ISBN 0-06-480346-5). B&N.
Hanley, Thomas. The American Revolution & Religion. 1972. 13.95 (ISBN 0-8132-0524-7). Cath U Pr.
Harrison, Samuel A. A Memoir of John Leeds Bozman, the First Historian of Maryland. LC 72-14410. (Maryland Historical Society. Fund-Publications: No. 26). Repr. of 1888 ed. 10.00 (ISBN 0-404-57626-5). AMS Pr.
--Wenlock Christison, & the Early Friends in Talbot County, Maryland. LC 72-14394. (Maryland Historical Society. Fund-Publications: No. 12). Repr. of 1878 ed. 7.50 (ISBN 0-404-57612-5). AMS Pr.
Harry, James W. The Maryland Constitution of 1851. LC 78-63890. (Johns Hopkins University. Studies in the Social Sciences. Twentieth Ser. 1902: 7-8). Repr. of 1902 ed. 13.50 (ISBN 0-404-61144-3). AMS Pr.
Hattery, Thomas H. Western Maryland: A Profile. LC 79-65634. 208p. 1980. 9.75 (ISBN 0-912338-21-0). Lomond.
Heyl, Edgar. I Didn't Know That: An Exhibition of First Happenings in Maryland. LC 73-85764. (Illus.). 1973. 3.00 (ISBN 0-938420-07-0). Md Hist.
Hienton, Louise J. Prince George's Heritage. LC 72-86376. (Illus.). 1972. 12.50 (ISBN 0-938420-13-5). Md Hist.
Holland, Celia M. Ellicott City, Maryland: Mill Town, U.S.A. 273p. bound 14.95case (ISBN 0-686-72726-6). Maryland Hist Pr.
Hull, William I. Maryland, Independence, & the Confederation. LC 72-14416. (Maryland Historical Society. Fund Publications: No. 31). Repr. of 1891 ed. 7.50 (ISBN 0-404-57631-1). AMS Pr.
Hurley, George & Hurley, Suzanne. Ocean City: A Pictorial History. LC 79-15873. (Illus.). 1979. ltd. ed. 29.95 (ISBN 0-89865-002-X); pap. 12.95 (ISBN 0-915442-98-1). Donning Co.
Ingle, Edward. Captain Richard Ingle, the Maryland "Pirate & Rebel," 1642-1653. LC 72-14402. (Maryland Historical Society. Fund-Publications: No. 19). Repr. of 1884 ed. 7.50 (ISBN 0-404-57619-2). AMS Pr.
Ives, J. Moss. Ark & the Dove: The Beginnings of Civil & Religious Liberties in America. LC 76-79200. (Illus.). 1969. Repr. of 1936 ed. 32.50x (ISBN 0-8154-0293-7). Cooper Sq.
Johnson, Bardley T. The Foundation of Maryland & the Origin of the Act Concerning Religion of April 21, 1649. LC 72-14401. (Maryland Historical Society, Fund Publications: No. 18). Repr. of 1883 ed. 14.00 (ISBN 0-404-57618-4). AMS Pr.
Johnson, Janet B. Robert Alexander, Maryland Loyalist. LC 72-8735. (American Revolutionary Ser.). 1979. Repr. of 1942 ed. text ed. 18.00x (ISBN 0-8398-0960-3). Irvington.
Johnston, George. History of Cecil County, Maryland. LC 67-23815. (Illus.). 1972. Repr. of 1881 ed. 25.00 (ISBN 0-8063-7988-X). Regional.
Jones, Carleton. Maryland, a Picture History (1632-1976) LC 75-36657. (Illus.). 192p. 1976. 19.95 (ISBN 0-910254-09-5). Bodine.
Key, Betty M. Maryland Manual of Oral History. 1979. 4.00 (ISBN 0-938420-11-9). Md Hist.
Krugler, John D. To Live Like Princes: A Short Treatise from the Young Collection of Early Maryland Manuscripts. 1976. pap. 2.50 (ISBN 0-910556-12-1). Enoch Pratt.
Land, Aubrey C. Colonial Maryland: A History. LC 80-21732. (A History of the American Colonies Ser.). 1981. lib. bdg. 25.00 (ISBN 0-527-18713-5). Kraus Intl.
Latane, John H. Early Relations Between Maryland & Virginia. 1973. Repr. of 1895 ed. pap. 7.00 (ISBN 0-384-31476-7). Johnson Repr.
--The Early Relations Between Maryland & Virginia. Bd. with Is History Past Politics? Adams, Herbert B., ed. LC 78-63837. (Johns Hopkins University. Studies in the Social Sciences. Thirteenth Ser. 1895: 3-4). Repr. of 1895 ed. 11.50 (ISBN 0-404-61096-X). AMS Pr.
Latrobe, John H. Maryland in Liberia: A History of the Colony Planted by the Maryland State Colonization Society Under the Auspices of the State of Maryland, U. S. at Cape Palmas on the Southwest Coast of Africa, 1833-1853. LC 72-14404. (Maryland Historical Society. Fund-Publications: No. 21). Repr. of 1885 ed. 10.00 (ISBN 0-404-57621-4). AMS Pr.
Lowdermilk, Will H. History of Cumberland, Maryland. LC 79-173260. (Illus.). 1976. Repr. of 1878 ed. 20.00 (ISBN 0-8063-7903-0). Regional.
McCormac, Eugene I. White Servitude in Maryland, 1634-1820. LC 78-63901. (Johns Hopkins University. Studies in the Social Sciences. Twenty-Second Ser. 1904: 3-4). Repr. of 1904 ed. 15.00 (ISBN 0-404-61154-0). AMS Pr.
McMahon, John V. An Historical View of the Government of Maryland: From Its Colonization to the Present Day. LC 68-30882. (Illus.). 1968. Repr. of 1831 ed. 25.00 (ISBN 0-87152-046-X). Reprint.
MacMaster, Richard K. & Hiebert, Ray E. A Grateful Remembrance: The Story of Montgomery County, Maryland. 1976. 6.95 (ISBN 0-686-63842-5). Montgomery Co Govt.
McSherry, James. History of Maryland. James, Bartlett B., ed. LC 68-30881. (Illus.). 1968. Repr. of 1904 ed. 20.00 (ISBN 0-87152-047-8). Reprint.
McSherry, William, compiled by. Relatio Itineris in Marylandiam. Declaratio Coloniae Domini Baronis De Baltimoro. Excerpta ex Diversis Litteris Missionariorum ab Anno 1635, ad Annum 1638. Dalrymple, E. A., tr. from Lat. LC 72-14389. (Maryland Historical Society. Fund Publications: No. 7). Repr. of 1874 ed. 14.00 (ISBN 0-404-57607-9). AMS Pr.
Magruder, James M. Index of Maryland Colonial Wills: 1634-1777. LC 67-28095. 1975. Repr. of 1933 ed. 20.00 (ISBN 0-8063-0233-X). Genealog Pub.
Manakee, Harold. Maryland. LC 68-9183. 1968. pap. 2.95 (ISBN 0-8077-1723-1). Tchrs Coll.
Marine, William M. British Invasion of Maryland, Eighteen Twelve to Eighteen Fifteen. Dielman, Louis H., ed. LC 66-128. (Illus.). xx, 519p. Repr. of 1913 ed. 22.00 (ISBN 0-8103-5036-X). Gale.
Maryland Genealogies. A Consolidation of Articles from the Maryland Historical Magazine, 2 vols. LC 80-80064. 1980. Set. 50.00 (ISBN 0-8063-0887-7); Vol. 1 P.549. Vol. 2 P.548. Genealog Pub.
Maryland Hall of Records. Calendar of Maryland State Papers, No. 1: The Black Books. LC 67-31020. (Hall of Records Commission Publications Ser: No. 1). 1967. Repr. of 1943 ed. 17.50 (ISBN 0-8063-0237-2). Genealog Pub.
Maryland Historical Society. Fund-Publications, 37 vols. in 35. Repr. of 1901 ed. 365.00 (ISBN 0-404-57600-1). AMS Pr.
--Muster Rolls & Other Records of Service of Maryland Troops in the American Revolution 1775-1783. LC 72-5687. (Archives of Maryland Ser: Vol. 18). 1972. Repr. of 1900 ed. 38.50 (ISBN 0-8063-0519-3). Genealog Pub.
Maryland Historical Society Committee on the Western Boundary of Maryland. Report. Maryland Historical Society, ed. LC 72-14413. (Maryland Historical Society. Fund-Publications: No. 29). Repr. of 1890 ed. 7.50 (ISBN 0-404-57629-X). AMS Pr.
Maryland Rent Rolls: Baltimore & Anne Arundel Counties, 1700-1707, 1705-1724. LC 76-1421. 1976. Repr. of 1924 ed. 15.00 (ISBN 0-8063-0716-1). Genealog Pub.
Mayer, Brantz. History, Possessions & Prospects of the Maryland Historical Society: Inaugural Discourse. LC 72-14382. (Maryland Historical Society. Fund-Publications). Repr. of 1867 ed. 7.50 (ISBN 0-404-57601-X). AMS Pr.
Morrison, Charles. Maryland Boundary Disputes. 1974. 3.75 (ISBN 0-87012-153-7). McClain.
Morriss, Margaret S. Colonial Trade of Maryland 1689-1715. LC 76-49477. (Perspectives in American History Ser.: No. 46). viii, 157p. Repr. of 1914 ed. lib. bdg. 15.00x (ISBN 0-87991-370-3). Porcupine Pr.
Myers, William S. The Maryland Constitution of 1864. LC 78-63882. (Johns Hopkins University. Studies in the Social Sciences. Nineteenth Ser. 1901: 8-9). Repr. of 1901 ed. 14.50 (ISBN 0-404-61137-0). AMS Pr.
--The Self-Reconstruction of Maryland: 1864-1867. LC 78-63931. (Johns Hopkins University. Studies in the Social Sciences. Twenty-Eighth Ser. 1910: 1-2). Repr. of 1909 ed. 16.00 (ISBN 0-404-61180-X). AMS Pr.
Nead, Daniel W. The Pennsylvania-German in the Settlement of Maryland. LC 75-7961. (Illus.). 304p. 1980. Repr. of 1914 ed. 18.50 (ISBN 0-8063-0678-5). Genealog Pub.
Papenfuse, Edward C., illus. The Decisive Blow Is Struck. 1977. pap. 2.00 (ISBN 0-686-21415-3). MD Hall Records.
Papenfuse, Edward C., et al. A Guide to the Maryland Hall of Records: Local Judicial & Administrative Records on Microform, Vol. 1. 231p. 1978. 9.00 (ISBN 0-686-27482-2). MD Hall Records.
Papenfuse, Edward C., et al, eds. A Biographical Dictionary of the Maryland Legislature, 1635-1789, Vol. 1, A-H. 1979. text ed. 19.50 (ISBN 0-8018-1995-4). Johns Hopkins.
--An Inventory to the Maryland State Papers: The Revolutionary War Era 1775-1789, Pt. 1. 1977. 16.00 (ISBN 0-686-21410-2). MD Hall Records.
Passano, Eleanor P. An Index to the Source Records of Maryland: Genealogical, Biographical, Historical. LC 67-17943. 1974. Repr. of 1940 ed. 20.00 (ISBN 0-8063-0271-2). Genealog Pub.
Pedley, A. J. The Manuscript Collections of the Maryland Historical Society. LC 68-23074. 1968. 15.00 (ISBN 0-938420-08-9). Md Hist.
Petrie, George. Church & State in Early Maryland. 1973. Repr. of 1892 ed. pap. 7.00 (ISBN 0-384-45970-6). Johnson Repr.
--Church & State in Early Maryland. LC 78-63810. (Johns Hopkins University. Studies in the Social Sciences. Tenth Ser. 1892: 4). Repr. of 1892 ed. 11.50 (ISBN 0-404-61073-0). AMS Pr.
A Pictorial History of Pikesville, Maryland. (Baltimore County Heritage Publications). (Illus.). 80p. 1981. 15.00x (ISBN 0-937076-02-3). Baltimore Co Pub Lib.
Preston, Dickson J. Wye Oak: The History of a Great Tree. LC 72-12911. (Illus.). 1972. pap. 3.50 (ISBN 0-87033-180-9, Pub by Tidewater). Cornell Maritime.
Preston, Walter W. History of Harford County, Maryland from 1608 to the Close of the War of 1812. LC 76-39470. (Illus.). 1972. Repr. of 1901 ed. 17.50 (ISBN 0-8063-7987-1). Regional.
Radcliffe, George L. Governor Thomas H. Hicks of Maryland & the Civil War. LC 78-63884. (Johns Hopkins University. Studies in the Social Sciences. Nineteenth Ser. 1901: 11-12). Repr. of 1901 ed. 17.00 (ISBN 0-404-61139-7). AMS Pr.
Radoff, Morris L., et al. The Old Line State, a History of Maryland. 1971. 5.00 (ISBN 0-686-21411-0); text ed. 5.00 (ISBN 0-686-21412-9). MD Hall Records.
Randall, Daniel R. Cooperation in Maryland & the South. LC 78-63785. (Johns Hopkins University. Studies in the Social Sciences. Sixth Ser. 1888: 11-12). Repr. of 1888 ed. 11.50 (ISBN 0-404-61051-X). AMS Pr.
--A Puritan Colony in Maryland. 1973. Repr. of 1886 ed. pap. 7.00 (ISBN 0-384-49568-0). Johnson Repr.
--A Puritan Colony in Maryland. LC 78-63763. (Johns Hopkins University. Studies in the Social Sciences. Fourth Ser. 1886: 6). Repr. of 1886 ed. 11.50 (ISBN 0-404-61031-5). AMS Pr.
A Relation of Maryland, 2 pts. LC 76-57399. (English Experience Ser.: No. 815). 1977. Repr. of 1635 ed. lib. bdg. 11.50 (ISBN 90-221-0815-5). Walter J Johnson.
Rice, Millard M. This Was the Life - Excerpts from the Judgment Records of Frederick County, Maryland, 1748-1765. LC 79-84276. 1979. 9.00 (ISBN 0-913186-08-2). Monocacy.
Richardson, H. D. Side-Lights on Maryland History: With Sketches of Early Maryland Families. LC 67-30497. (Illus.). 1967. 15.00 (ISBN 0-87033-108-6, Pub. by Tidewater). Cornell Maritime.
Rollo, Vera F. Henry Harford. (Maryland's Last Proprietor). 236p. 1976. lib. bdg. 9.75 (ISBN 0-686-73105-0). Maryland Hist.
--Your Maryland. 3rd ed. 417p. 1976. lib. bdg. 9.75 (ISBN 0-917882-05-9). Maryland Hist Pr.
St. Mary's County (Md.) in the American Revolution: Calendar of Events. 1975. 8.00 (ISBN 0-686-26992-6). E W Beitzel.
Scharf, Thomas J. History of Maryland from the Earliest Period to the Present Day, 3 vols. LC 67-5141. (Illus.). 1967. Repr. of 1879 ed. incl. index 82.00 (ISBN 0-8103-5037-8); index only 19.00 (ISBN 0-8103-5038-6). Gale.
Schaun, George & Schaun, Virginia. Everyday Life in Colonial Maryland. 130p. (gr. k-12). 1981. casebnd. 10.00 (ISBN 0-917882-11-3). Maryland Hist Pr.
Schwartz, Lee, et al. Allegany County: A Pictorial History. LC 79-25955. (Illus.). 1980. 16.95 (ISBN 0-89865-017-8). Donning Co.
Semmes, Raphael. Crime & Punishment in Early Maryland. LC 77-108227. (Criminology, Law Enforcement, & Social Problems Ser.: No. 110). 1970. Repr. of 1938 ed. 16.00 (ISBN 0-87585-110-X). Patterson Smith.
Silver, John A. The Provisional Government of Maryland (1774-1777) LC 78-63844. (Johns Hopkins University. Studies in the Social Sciences. Thirteenth Ser. 1895: 10). Repr. of 1895 ed. 11.50 (ISBN 0-404-61101-X). AMS Pr.
Sioussant, St. George L. Economics & Politics in Maryland 1720-1750, & the Public Services of Daniel Dulany the Elder. LC 78-63897. (Johns Hopkins University. Studies in the Social Sciences, Twenty-First Ser. 1903: -7). Repr. of 1903 ed. 13.50 (ISBN 0-404-61150-8). AMS Pr.
Smeal, Lee. Maryland Historical & Biographical Index. LC 78-53702. (Illus.). Date not set. lib. bdg. price not set (ISBN 0-89593-185-0). Accelerated Index.
Sparks, F. E. Causes of the Maryland Revolution of 1689. Repr. of 1896 ed. pap. 9.50 (ISBN 0-384-56903-X). Johnson Repr.
Sparks, Francis E. Causes of the Maryland Revolution of 1689. LC 78-63854. (Johns Hopkins University. Studies in the Social Sciences. Fourteenth Ser. 1896: 11-12). Repr. of 1896 ed. 11.50 (ISBN 0-404-61110-9). AMS Pr.
Steiner, Bernard C. Beginnings of Maryland, Sixteen Thirty-One to Sixteen Thirty-Nine. LC 78-63898. (Johns Hopkins University. Studies in the Social Sciences. Twenty-First Ser. 1903: 8-10). Repr. of 1903 ed. 15.00 (ISBN 0-404-61151-6). AMS Pr.
--Maryland During the English Civil Wars, 2 vols. in 1. LC 78-63918. (Johns Hopkins University. Studies in the Social Sciences. Twenty-Fourth Ser. 1906: 11-12). Repr. of 1906 ed. 19.50 (ISBN 0-404-61169-9). AMS Pr.
--Western Maryland in the Revolution. LC 78-63885. (Johns Hopkins University. Studies in the Social Sciences. Twentieth Ser. 1902: 1). Repr. of 1902 ed. 11.50 (ISBN 0-404-61140-0). AMS Pr.
Steiner, Bernard C., ed. Rev. Thomas Bray: His Life & Selected Works Relating to Maryland. LC 79-39862. (Religion in America, Ser. 2). 256p. 1972. Repr. of 1901 ed. 15.00 (ISBN 0-405-04088-1). Arno.
Stiverson, Gregory A. Poverty in a Land of Plenty: Tenancy in Eighteenth-Century Maryland. LC 77-4554. (Maryland Bicentennial Studies). (Illus.). 1978. text ed. 14.00x (ISBN 0-8018-1966-0). Johns Hopkins.
Streeter, Sebastian F. Papers Relating to the Early History of Maryland. LC 72-4224. (Select Bibliographies Reprint Ser.). 1972. Repr. of 1876 ed. 18.00 (ISBN 0-8369-6893-X). Arno.
--Papers Relating to the Early History of Maryland. LC 72-14391. (Maryland Historical Socity. Fund-Publications: No. 9). Repr. of 1876 ed. 18.50 (ISBN 0-404-57609-5). AMS Pr.
Sullivan, Larry E. Oral History in Maryland: A Directory. iv, 44p. (Orig.). 1981. pap. 3.00 (ISBN 0-938420-21-6). Maryland Hist Pr.
Tate, Thad W. & Ammerman, David L., eds. The Chesapeake in the Seventeenth Century: Essays on Anglo-American Society. LC 78-31720. (Institute of Early American History & Culture Ser.). 1979. 26.00x (ISBN 0-8078-1360-5). U of NC Pr.
--The Chesapeake in the Seventeenth Century: Essays on Anglo-American Society & Politics. 1980. pap. 5.95 (ISBN 0-393-00956-4). Norton.
Terranova, Elaine. Toward Morning-Swimmers. (Hollow Spring Poetry Ser.). 44p. (Orig.). 1980. pap. text ed. 4.00 (ISBN 0-936198-02-8). Hollow Spring Pr.
Torrence, Clayton. Old Somerset on the Eastern Shore of Maryland. LC 66-30004. 583p. 1979. Repr. of 1935 ed. 22.50 (ISBN 0-8063-7970-7). Regional.
Van Devanter, Ann C., et al. Anywhere So Long As There Be Freedom: Charles Carroll of Carrollton, His Family & His Maryland. LC 75-27470. (Illus.). 1975. pap. 15.00 (ISBN 0-912298-38-3). Baltimore Mus.

Vexler, R. I. Maryland Chronology & Factbook, Vol. 20. 1978. 8.50 (ISBN 0-379-16145-1). Oceana.
Walsh, Richard & Fox, William L. Maryland: A History, 1632-1974. LC 74-11875. (Illus.). 1974. 12.50 (ISBN 0-938420-09-7). Md Hist.
Walters, Stephen. Maryland: The Beginning. LC 81-81680. 62p. 1981. 7.50 (ISBN 0-917882-12-1). Maryland Hist Pr.
Walters, Stephen T. Maryland: The Beginning. 64p. 1981. 7.50 (ISBN 0-917882-12-1). Maryland Hist Pr.
Whitson, Skip, compiled by. Old Maryland. (Sun Historical Ser). (Illus., Orig.). 1976. pap. 3.50 (ISBN 0-89540-022-7, SB022). Sun Pub.
Wilson, Richard & Bridner, E. L., Jr. Maryland: Its Past & Present. LC 81-81874. 250p. 1981. 8.75 (ISBN 0-917882-13-X). Maryland Hist Pr.
Wroth, Lawrence C. A History of Printing in Colonial Maryland, 1686-1776. LC 75-31142. 1976. Repr. of 1922 ed. 28.50 (ISBN 0-404-13614-1). AMS Pr.

MARYLAND–HISTORY–FICTION

Carey, George G. Maryland Folklore & Folklife. LC 71-142189. (Illus.). 1971. pap. 5.00 (ISBN 0-87033-154-X, Pub. by Tidewater). Cornell Maritime.
Churchill, Winston. Richard Carvel. (Illus.). 1914. 12.95 (ISBN 0-02-525660-2). Macmillan.
Kennedy, John P. Rob of the Bowl. Osborne, William S., ed. (Masterworks of Literature Ser). 1965. 7.50x (ISBN 0-8084-0263-3); pap. 4.45x (ISBN 0-8084-0264-1, M12). Coll & U Pr.

MARYLAND–JUVENILE LITERATURE

Bailey, Bernadine. Picture Book of Maryland. rev. ed. LC 55-8829. (Illus.). (gr. 3-5). 1970. 5.50g (ISBN 0-8075-9522-5). A Whitman.
Carpenter, Allan. Maryland. LC 78-14892. (New Enchantment of America State Bks). (Illus.). (gr. 4 up). 1979. PLB 10.60 (ISBN 0-516-04120-7). Childrens.
Fradin, Dennis. Maryland: In Words & Pictures. LC 80-15185. (Young People's Stories of Our States Ser.). (Illus.). (gr. 2-5). 1980. PLB 9.25 (ISBN 0-516-03920-2). Childrens.
Mason, F. Van Wyck. Maryland Colony. LC 69-10782. (Forge of Freedom Ser). (Illus.). (gr. 5 up). 1969. 8.95 (ISBN 0-02-762870-1, CCPr). Macmillan.
Rollo, Vera F. Ask Me: About Maryland Geography. new ed. (Illus., With time line chart of Maryland history). (gr. 4-5). 1980. pap. 4.50 ea. (ISBN 0-917882-04-0); pap. 39.75 for 10 bks with chart (ISBN 0-686-67403-0). Maryland Hist Pr.

MARYLAND–POLITICS AND GOVERNMENT

Adams, Herbert B. Maryland's Influence Upon Land Cessions to the U. S. LC 77-97563. Repr. of 1885 ed. 11.50 (ISBN 0-404-00286-2). AMS Pr.
Baker, Jean H. The Politics of Continuity: Maryland Political Parties from 1858 to 1870. LC 72-12354. (Goucher College Ser.). (Illus.). 254p. 1973. 16.50x (ISBN 0-8018-1418-9). Johns Hopkins.
Bond, Beverly W. State Government in Maryland, 1777-1781. LC 78-63907. (Johns Hopkins University. Studies in the Social Sciences. Twenty-Third Ser. 1905: 3-4). Repr. of 1905 ed. 15.50 (ISBN 0-404-61159-1). AMS Pr.
Callcott, Margaret Law. The Negro in Maryland Politics, 1870-1912. LC 69-15395. (Historical & Political Science: Eighty-Seventh Series No. 1 (1969)). (Illus.). 358p. 1969. 22.50x (ISBN 0-8018-1023-X); pap. 5.95x (ISBN 0-8018-1556-8). Johns Hopkins.
Carr, Lois G. & Jordan, David W. Maryland's Revolution of Government, 1689-1692. (Illus.). 344p. 1974. 25.00x (ISBN 0-8014-0793-1). Cornell U Pr.
Cushing, John D., compiled by. The First Laws of the State of Maryland. (Earliest Laws of the Original Thirteen States Ser.). 1981. 49.00 (ISBN 0-89453-213-8). M Glazier.
Donaldson, John. State Administration in Maryland. LC 78-63959. (Johns Hopkins University. Studies in the Social Sciences. Thirty-Fourth Ser. 1916: 4). Repr. of 1916 ed. 19.50 (ISBN 0-404-61206-7). AMS Pr.
Everstine, Carl N. The General Assembly of Maryland: 1634-1776. 550p. 1980. 12.00 (ISBN 0-87215-312-6). Michie-Bobbs.
Evitts, William J. A Matter of Allegiances: Maryland from 1850 T0 1861. LC 73-19336. (Studies in Historical & Political Science, 92nd Ser). (Illus.). 224p. 1974. 14.50x (ISBN 0-8018-1520-7). Johns Hopkins.
Gibbons, Boyd. Wye Island. 1979. pap. 4.95 (ISBN 0-14-005230-5). Penguin.
Green, Harry J. A Study of the Legislature of the State of Maryland, with Special Reference to the Sessions of 1927 & 1929. LC 78-64137. (Johns Hopkins University. Studies in the Social Sciences. Forty-Eighth Ser. 1930: 3). Repr. of 1930 ed. 15.00 (ISBN 0-404-61249-0). AMS Pr.
Harry, James W. The Maryland Constitution of 1851. LC 78-63890. (Johns Hopkins University. Studies in the Social Sciences. Twentieth Ser. 1902: 7-8). Repr. of 1902 ed. 13.50 (ISBN 0-404-61144-3). AMS Pr.
Hoffman, Ronald. A Spirit of Dissension: Economics, Politics, & the Revolution in Maryland. LC 73-8127. (Maryland Bicentennial Studies). (Illus.). 294p. 1974. 18.50x (ISBN 0-8018-1521-5). Johns Hopkins.
Ives, J. Moss. Ark & the Dove: The Beginnings of Civil & Religious Liberties in America. LC 76-79200. (Illus.). 1969. Repr. of 1936 ed. 32.50x (ISBN 0-8154-0293-7). Cooper Sq.
Kent, Frank R. The Story of Maryland Politics: An Outline History of the Big Political Battles of the State from 1864 to 1910, with Sketches & Incidents of the Men & Measures That Figured As Factors, & the Names of Most of Those Who Held Office in That Period. LC 68-31444. xiv, 439p. Repr. of 1911 ed. 22.00 (ISBN 0-8103-5035-1). Gale.
Land, Aubrey G., et al, eds. Law, Society, & Politics in Early Maryland. LC 76-47374. (Illus.). 400p. 1977. 22.50x (ISBN 0-8018-1872-9). Johns Hopkins.
Lauchheimer, Malcolm H. The Labor Law of Maryland. LC 78-63969. (Johns Hopkins University. Studies in the Social Sciences. Thirty-Seventh Ser. 1919: 2). Repr. of 1919 ed. 18.00 (ISBN 0-404-61215-6). AMS Pr.
McMahon, John V. An Historical View of the Government of Maryland: From Its Colonization to the Present Day. LC 68-30882. (Illus.). 1968. Repr. of 1831 ed. 25.00 (ISBN 0-87152-046-X). Reprint.
Marley, D. Maryland Plan. 1973. 9.96 (ISBN 0-02-821100-6). Glencoe.
Michie Staff, ed. Maryland Rules of Procedure: 1980 Edition, 2 vols. 1500p. 1980. pap. 35.00 (ISBN 0-87215-337-1). Michie-Bobbs.
Myers, William S. The Maryland Constitution of 1864. LC 78-63882. (Johns Hopkins University. Studies in the Social Sciences. Nineteenth Ser. 1901: 8-9). Repr. of 1901 ed. 14.50 (ISBN 0-404-61137-0). AMS Pr.
O'Connell, Donald W., ed. Public Sector Labor Relations in Maryland: Issues & Prospects. LC 72-92069. (PSLRCB Publication No. 1). (Illus., Orig.). 1972. pap. 5.00 (ISBN 0-913400-00-9). Pub Sect Lab Rel.
Reiblich, George K. A Study of Judicial Administration in the State of Maryland. LC 78-64131. (Johns Hopkins University. Studies in the Social Sciences. Forty-Seventh Ser. 1929: 2). Repr. of 1929 ed. 18.00 (ISBN 0-404-61244-X). AMS Pr.
Renzulli, L. Marx. Maryland: The Federalist Years. LC 70-149405. 354p. 1972. 18.00 (ISBN 0-8386-7903-X). Fairleigh Dickinson.
Rohr, Charles J. The Governor of Maryland, a Constitutional Study. LC 78-64147. (Johns Hopkins University. Studies in the Social Sciences. Fiftieth Ser. 1932: 3). Repr. of 1932 ed. 21.00 (ISBN 0-404-61258-X). AMS Pr.
Schmeckebier, Laurence F. History of the Know-Nothing Party in Maryland. LC 78-63869. (Johns Hopkins University. Studies in the Social Sciences. Seventeenth Ser. 1899: 4-5). Repr. of 1899 ed. 11.50 (ISBN 0-404-61125-7). AMS Pr.
Silver, J. A. Provisional Government of Maryland: 1774-1777. 1973. Repr. of 1895 ed. pap. 7.00 (ISBN 0-384-55380-X). Johnson Repr.
Silver, John A. The Provisional Government of Maryland (1774-1777) LC 78-63844. (Johns Hopkins University. Studies in the Social Sciences. Thirteenth Ser. 1895: 10). Repr. of 1895 ed. 11.50 (ISBN 0-404-61101-X). AMS Pr.
Sioussant, St. George L. Economics & Politics in Maryland 1720-1750, & the Public Services of Daniel Dulany the Elder. LC 78-63897. (Johns Hopkins University. Studies in the Social Sciences, Twenty-First Ser. 1903: -7). Repr. of 1903 ed. 13.50 (ISBN 0-404-61150-8). AMS Pr.
--The English Statutes in Maryland. LC 78-63899. (Johns Hopkins University. Studies in the Social Sciences. Twenty-First Ser. 1903: 11-12). Repr. of 1903 ed. 18.00 (ISBN 0-404-61152-4). AMS Pr.
Skaggs, David C. Roots of Maryland Democracy, 1753-1776. LC 72-833. (Contributions in American History: No. 30). (Illus.). 253p. 1973. lib. bdg. 14.50 (ISBN 0-8371-6402-8, SMD/). Greenwood.
Steiner, Bernard C. Maryland Under the Commonwealth: A Chronicle of the Years 1649-1658. LC 79-158209. Repr. of 1911 ed. 12.50 (ISBN 0-404-06248-2). AMS Pr.
Steiner, Bernhard C. Life & Administration of Sir Robert Eden. Repr. of 1898 ed. pap. 11.50 (ISBN 0-384-57827-6). Johnson Repr.

MARYLAND–SOCIAL CONDITIONS

Bell, Howard M. Youth Tell Their Story: A Study of the Conditions & Attitudes of Young People in Maryland Between the Ages of 16 & 24. facsimile ed. LC 74-1665. (Children & Youth Ser.: Social Problems & Social Policy). 290p. 1974. Repr. of 1938 ed. 18.00x (ISBN 0-405-05946-9). Arno.
Clemens, Paul G. The Atlantic Economy & Colonial Maryland's Eastern Shore: From Tobacco to Grain. LC 79-26181. (Illus.). 256p. 1980. 16.50x (ISBN 0-8014-1251-X). Cornell U Pr.
Harvey, Katherine A. Best Dressed Miners: Life & Labor in the Maryland Coal Region, 1835-1910. LC 71-78924. 1969. 32.50x (ISBN 0-8014-0494-0). Cornell U Pr.
Semmes, Raphael. Crime & Punishment in Early Maryland. LC 77-108227. (Criminology, Law Enforcement, & Social Problems Ser.: No. 110). 1970. Repr. of 1938 ed. 16.00 (ISBN 0-87585-110-X). Patterson Smith.

MARYLAND AND PENNSYLVANIA RAILROAD COMPANY

Hilton, George W. The Ma & Pa. LC 63-17444. (Illus.). 1963. 6.00 (ISBN 0-8310-7036-6). Howell-North.
Mahan, Charles. Fifty Best of Maryland & Pennsylvania Railroad, Bk. 1. (Illus.). 1979. 12.00 (ISBN 0-934118-14-0). Barnard Robert.

MARYLAND CAMPAIGN, 1862

McClellan, George B. Report of the Organization & Campaigns of the Army of the Potomac: To Which Is Added an Account of the Campaign in Western Virginia, with Plans of Battle-Fields. LC 78-109629. (Select Bibliographies Reprint Ser). 1864. 29.00 (ISBN 0-8369-5238-3). Arno.
Murfin, James V. The Gleam of Bayonets. LC 65-11502. (Illus.). 320p. 1976. pap. 1.95 (ISBN 0-89176-007-5, 6007). Mockingbird Bks.

MARYLAND CAMPAIGN, 1863

see Gettysburg Campaign, 1863

MARYLAND, UNIVERSITY OF

Callcott, George H. A History of the University of Maryland. 422p. casebnd. 9.75 (ISBN 0-686-72727-4). Maryland Hist Pr.

MASACCIO, TOMMASO GUIDI, 1401-1428

Cole, Bruce. Masaccio & the Art of Early Renaissance Florence. LC 79-2601. (Illus.). 270p. 1980. 22.50x (ISBN 0-253-12298-8). Ind U Pr.

MASAI

see also Arusha (African Tribe); Meru (African Tribe); Turkana (African People)

Baumann, Oscar. Durch Massailand Zur Nilquelle: Reisen & Forschungen der Massai Expedition Des Deutschen Antisklaverei-Komitee in Den Jahren 1891-1893. (Landmarks in Anthropology Ser). (Illus., Ger). 1968. Repr. of 1894 ed. 31.00 (ISBN 0-384-03560-4). Johnson Repr.
Bleeker, Sonia. The Masai: Herders of East Africa. (Illus.). (gr. 3-6). 1963. PLB 6.67 (ISBN 0-688-31460-0). Morrow.
Bothwell, Jean. African Herdboy: A Story of the Masai. LC 76-117615. (Illus.). (gr. 4-6). 1970. 5.25 (ISBN 0-15-201630-9, HJ). HarBraceJ.
Hayne, Joseph E. Black Man or the Natural History of the Hamitic Race. LC 78-155393. Repr. of 1894 ed. 9.00x (ISBN 0-8371-6083-9, Pub. by Negro U Pr). Greenwood.
Hollis, Alfred C. Masai: Their Language & Folklore. facs. ed. LC 71-157372. (Black Heritage Library Collection Ser). 1905. 31.00 (ISBN 0-8369-8810-8). Arno.
--Masai: Their Language & Folklore. LC 77-132645. Repr. of 1905 ed. 23.25x (ISBN 0-8371-5156-2, Pub. by Negro U Pr). Greenwood.
Merker, M. Die Masai: Ethnographische Monographie Eines Ostafrikanischen Semitenvolkes. (Landmarks in Anthropology Ser). (Ger). 1968. Repr. of 1910 ed. 38.50 (ISBN 0-384-38185-5). Johnson Repr.
Shachtman, Tom. Growing up Masai. LC 80-25017. (Illus.). 56p. (gr. 3-7). 1981. PLB 8.95 (ISBN 0-02-782550-7). Macmillan.
Thompson, Joseph. Through Masai Land. 1885. 33.00 (ISBN 0-403-00272-9). Scholarly.
Thomson, Joseph. Through Masai Land. 3rd rev ed. 364p. 1968. 32.50x (ISBN 0-7146-1856-X, F Cass Co). Biblio Dist.
Young, Roland, ed. Through Masailand with Joseph Thomson. 218p. 1962. 5.95x (ISBN 0-89771-010-X). State Mutual Bk.

MASARYK, TOMAS GARRIGUE, PRES. CZECHOSLOVAK REPUBLIC, 1850-1937

Benes, Edvard. Masaryk's Path & Legacy: Funeral Oration at the Burial of the President-Liberator, 21 September 1937. LC 77-135793. (Eastern Europe Collection Ser). (Illus.). 1970. Repr. of 1937 ed. 8.00 (ISBN 0-405-02735-4). Arno.
Capek, Karel. President Masaryk Tells His Story. LC 71-135797. (Eastern Europe Collection Ser). 1970. Repr. of 1935 ed. 19.00 (ISBN 0-405-02739-7). Arno.
Ludwig, Emil. Defender of Democracy: Masaryk of Czechoslovakia. LC 70-135814. (Eastern Europe Collection Ser). 1970. Repr. of 1936 ed. 13.00 (ISBN 0-405-02756-7). Arno.
Selver, Paul. Masaryk, a Biography. LC 74-33506. (Illus.). 326p. 1975. Repr. of 1940 ed. lib. bdg. 21.00x (ISBN 0-8371-7972-6, SEMA). Greenwood.
Street, Cecil J. President Masaryk. facs. ed. LC 74-119945. (Select Bibliographies Reprint Ser). 1930. 17.00 (ISBN 0-8369-5388-6). Arno.
Szporluk, Roman. The Political Thought of Thomas G. Masaryk. (East European Monograph: No. 85). 256p. 1981. 17.50x (ISBN 0-914710-79-6). East Eur Quarterly.
Van Den Beld, Antonie. Humanity: The Political & Social Philosophy of Thomas Masaryk. (Issues in Contemporary Politics Ser: No. 1). 162p. 1975. text ed. 16.75x (ISBN 90-2797-981-2). Mouton.

MASCOT PICTURES CORPORATION, HOLLYWOOD, CALIFORNIA

Tuska, Jon. The Vanishing Legion: A History of Mascot Pictures, 1927-1935. LC 81-6014. (Illus.). 230p. 1982. lib. bdg. price not set (ISBN 0-89950-030-7). McFarland & Co.

MASCULINITY (PSYCHOLOGY)

Andelin, Aubrey P. Man of Steel & Velvet. 10.95 (ISBN 0-911094-03-2). Pacific Santa Barbara.
Bertels, Frank. The First Book on Male Liberation & Sex Equality. (Illus.). 415p. 1981. luxury hardcover 25.00 (ISBN 0-932574-05-X); pap. 15.00 (ISBN 0-932574-06-8). Brun Pr.
Bishop, Beata & McNeill, Pat. The Eggshell Ego: An Irreverent Look at Today's Male. LC 77-8249. 1978. pap. 3.95 (ISBN 0-89490-021-8). Enslow Pubs.
Conway, Sally. You & Your Husband's Mid-Life Crisis. (Orig.). 1980. pap. 4.95 (ISBN 0-89191-318-1). Cook.
Farrell, Warren. The Liberated Man. 384p. 1975. pap. 2.95 (ISBN 0-553-02275-X, G13599-6). Bantam.
Fasteau, Marc. The Male Machine. 1976. pap. 4.95 (ISBN 0-440-55356-3, Delta). Dell.
Fasteau, Marc F. The Male Machine. LC 74-9858. (Illus.). 240p. 1974. 8.95 (ISBN 0-07-019985-X, GB). McGraw.
Fike, Robert V. Sexual Hangups of the American Male. LC 77-90520. 1978. 8.95 (ISBN 0-89543-007-X). Grossmont Pr.
Firestone, Ross. A Book of Men: Visions of the Male Experience. rev. ed. (Illus.). 1978. 11.95 (ISBN 0-88373-040-5); pap. 6.95 (ISBN 0-88373-026-X). Stonehill Pub Co.
Gittelson, Natalie. Dominus: A Woman Looks at Men's Lives. 304p. 1978. 10.00 (ISBN 0-374-14177-0). FS&G.
Henry, George W. Masculinity & Femininity. Orig. Title: All the Sexes. 320p. 1973. pap. 1.95 (ISBN 0-02-076840-0, Collier). Macmillan.
Herdt, Gilbert H. Guardians of the Flutes: Idioms of Masculinity. (Illus.). 1980. 17.95 (ISBN 0-07-028315-X). McGraw.
Hughes, Joseph H., Jr. Sex - Love - Marriage & Divorce: A Male Primer. 1977. pap. 2.95 (ISBN 0-686-22750-6); pap. 3.25 signed (ISBN 0-686-28626-X). Aaron Jenkins.
Johnson, James L. What Every Woman Should Know About a Man. 1979. pap. 4.95 (ISBN 0-310-26621-1). Zondervan.
Johnson, Robert A. He: Understanding Masculine Psychology. 1977. pap. 1.95 (ISBN 0-06-080415-7, P415, PL). Har-Row.
Kasirsky, Gilbert. Vasectomy, Manhood & Sex. LC 76-189307. (Illus.). 128p. 1972. text ed. 8.50 (ISBN 0-8261-1390-7). Springer Pub.
Komarovsky, Mirra. Dilemmas of Masculinity: A Study of College Youth. 1976. pap. 6.95x (ISBN 0-393-09169-4). Norton.
Lasky, Ella, ed. Humanness: An Exploration into the Mythologies About Men & Women. 543p. 1975. 39.50x (ISBN 0-8422-5221-5); pap. text ed. 18.75x (ISBN 0-685-55478-3). Irvington.
Lewis, Robert A., ed. Men in Difficult Times: Masculinity Today & Tomorrow. (Illus.). 352p. 1981. 14.95 (ISBN 0-13-574418-0, Spec); pap. 7.95 (ISBN 0-13-574400-8). P-H.
Mitzel, John. Sports & the Macho Male. 2nd ed. 1976. pap. 2.50 (ISBN 0-915480-06-9). Fag Rag.
Nichols, Jack. Men's Liberation: A New Definition of Masculinity. (Orig.). 1975. pap. 3.95 (ISBN 0-14-004036-6). Penguin.
Pleck, Elizabeth H. & Pleck, Joseph H. The American Man. 1980. 14.95 (ISBN 0-13-028159-X, Spec); pap. 4.95 (ISBN 0-13-028142-5, Spec). P-H.
Pleck, Joseph H. The Myth of Masculinity. 204p. 1981. 17.50 (ISBN 0-262-16081-1). MIT Pr.
Rochlin, Gregory. The Masculine Dilemma. 288p. 1980. 12.95 (ISBN 0-316-75335-1). Little.
Ruitenbeek, Hendrik M., ed. Psychoanalysis & Male Sexuality. 1966. 6.50 (ISBN 0-8084-0255-2); pap. 2.95 (ISBN 0-8084-0256-0, B33). Coll & U Pr.

Skovholt, Thomas M., et al, eds. Counseling Men. LC 79-29722. (Counseling Psychology Ser.). (Orig.). 1980. pap. text ed. 9.95 (ISBN 0-8185-0372-6). Brooks-Cole.
Snodgrass, Jon, ed. For Men Against Sexism: A Book of Readings. LC 77-77388. (Orig.). 1977. pap. 6.00 (ISBN 0-87810-031-8). Times Change.
Spence, Janet T. & Helmreich, Robert L. Masculinity & Femininity: Their Psychological Dimensions, Correlates, & Antecedents. (Illus.). 309p. 1979. pap. text ed. 8.95x (ISBN 0-292-75052-8). U of Tex Pr.
Terman, Lewis M. & Miles, Catherine C. Sex & Personality. 600p. 1980. Repr. of 1936 ed. lib. bdg. 50.00 (ISBN 0-89987-811-3). Darby Bks.
Thornburg, Hershel D. Punt, Pop (a Male Sex Role Manual) (Psychologi Ser.). (Illus.). 1978. pap. 4.95 (ISBN 0-918500-77-X). HELP Bks.
Tolson, Andrew. The Limits of Masculinity. LC 78-69630. 1979. 8.95 (ISBN 0-06-014333-9, HarpT). Har-Row.
--The Limits of Masculinity. LC 78-69630. 1979. pap. 3.95 (ISBN 0-06-090673-1, CN-673, CN). Har-Row.
Unbecoming Men: A Men's Consciousness-Raising Group Writes on Oppression & Themselves. 64p. pap. 2.50 (ISBN 0-87810-015-6). Crossing Pr.
Ursin, Holger, et al, eds. Psychobiology of Stress: A Study of Coping Men. (Behavioral Biology Ser.). 1978. 26.00 (ISBN 0-12-709250-1). Acad Pr.
Vincent, P. Dictionnaire de la Virilite. 370p. (Fr.). 1973. 12.50 (ISBN 0-686-57247-5, M-6553). French & Eur.
Zolla, Elemire. The Androgyne: The Creative Tension of Male & Female. Purce, Jill, ed. LC 81-67701. (The Illustrated Library of Sacred Imagination Ser.). (Illus.). 96p. 1981. 19.95 (ISBN 0-8245-0060-1); pap. 9.95 (ISBN 0-8245-0065-2). Crossroad NY.

MASEFIELD, JOHN, 1878-1967

Biggane, Cecil. John Masefield: A Study. LC 73-15663. 1924. lib. bdg. 8.50 (ISBN 0-8414-3320-8). Folcroft.
The Centenary of John Masefield's Birth: An Exhibition of First Editions, Letters, Manuscripts, Photographs, Drawings & Portraits. (Illus.). 1978. 7.50 (ISBN 0-686-22960-6). Columbia U Libs.
Drew, Fraser. John Masefield's England: A Study of the National Themes in His Work. LC 72-415. (Illus.). 261p. 1973. 15.00 (ISBN 0-8386-1020-X). Fairleigh Dickinson.
Gautrey, R. Moffat. The Burning Cataracts of Christ: An Evangelical Interpretation of John Mosefield's "the Ever-Lasting Mercy". LC 78-23716. 1933. lib. bdg. 15.00 (ISBN 0-8414-4483-8). Folcroft.
Gfollner, S. Adelheid. John Masefield's Stellung Zum Religion. (SSEL Poetic Drama Ser.: No. 47). (Orig.). 1979. pap. text ed. 22.75x (ISBN 0-391-01613-X). Humanities.
Gordan, John D. John Masefields 'Salt-Water Ballads' An Exhibition from the Berg Collection on the Fiftieth Anniversary of Its Publication. 1952. pap. 3.00 (ISBN 0-87104-102-2). NY Pub Lib.
Hamilton, William. John Masefield: A Critical Study. LC 70-86022. (Illus.). 1969. Repr. of 1922 ed. 12.00 (ISBN 0-8046-0613-7). Kennikat.
Lamont, Corliss. Remembering John Masefield. LC 73-139992. 119p. 1971. 10.00 (ISBN 0-8386-7836-X). Fairleigh Dickinson.
Lamont, Corliss & Lamont, Lansing, eds. Letters of John Masefield to Florence Lamont. LC 78-27134. 416p. 1979. 20.00x (ISBN 0-231-04706-1). Columbia U Pr.
Smith, Babington C. John Masefield: A Life. 1978. 14.95 (ISBN 0-02-504600-4). Macmillan.
Sternlicht, Sanford. John Masefield. (English Authors Ser.: No. 209). 1977. lib. bdg. 10.95 (ISBN 0-8057-6678-2). Twayne.
Thomas, Gilbert O. John Masefield. 261p. 1980. Repr. of 1932 ed. lib. bdg. 25.00 (ISBN 0-8495-5151-X). Arden Lib.
--John Masefield. LC 75-19091. 1975. Repr. of 1932 ed. lib. bdg. 17.50 (ISBN 0-8414-8537-2). Folcroft.
Williams, I. A. John Masefield. LC 72-13893. 1973. Repr. of 1921 ed. lib. bdg. 8.50 (ISBN 0-8414-1253-7). Folcroft.

MASEFIELD, JOHN, 1878-1967–BIBLIOGRAPHY

Simmons, Charles H. Bibliography of John Masefield. LC 30-33082. Repr. of 1930 ed. 11.50 (ISBN 0-404-06005-6). AMS Pr.
Williams, I. A. Bibliography of John Masefield. 1979. 28.50 (ISBN 0-685-94322-4). Porter.
--The Elements of Book-Collecting. LC 75-43858. 1973. Repr. of 1927 ed. lib. bdg. 20.00 (ISBN 0-8414-9421-5). Folcroft.

MASERS

Atwater, Harry A. Introduction to Microwave Theory. rev. ed. LC 80-28674. 1981. Repr. of 1962 ed. lib. bdg. write for info. (ISBN 0-89874-192-0). Krieger.
Cook, A. H. Celestial Masers. LC 76-14028. (Cambridge Monographs on Physics). (Illus.). 1977. 28.95 (ISBN 0-521-21344-4). Cambridge U Pr.
Ishii, T. Koryu. Maser & Laser Engineering. LC 78-10694. 412p. 1980. lib. bdg. 22.50 (ISBN 0-88275-776-8). Krieger.
Klein, H. Arthur. Masers & Lasers. LC 63-18676. (Introducing Modern Science Books Ser). (Illus.). (gr. 7-9). 1963. 7.95 (ISBN 0-397-30696-2, JBL-J). Har-Row.
Orton, D. H., et al. The Solid State Maser. LC 74-101374. 1970. 35.00 (ISBN 0-08-006819-7); pap. 14.50 (ISBN 0-08-006818-9). Pergamon.
Siegman, A. E. Introduction to Lasers & Masers. 1971. text ed. 29.50 (ISBN 0-07-057362-X, C); solutions manual 2.50 (ISBN 0-07-057368-9). McGraw.
Skolbel'tsyn, D. V., ed. Soviet Maser Research. LC 64-16546. (P. N. Lebedev Physics Institute Ser.: Vol. 21). 186p. 1964. 32.50 (ISBN 0-306-10668-X, Consultants). Plenum Pub.
Stepin, L. D. Quantum Radio Frequency Physics. 1965. 17.50x (ISBN 0-262-19016-8). MIT Pr.
Unger, H. G. Introduction to Quantum Electronics. LC 76-86534. 1970. 19.50 (ISBN 0-08-006368-3). Pergamon.
Weber, Joseph, ed. Masers. (International Science Review Ser). 1967. 117.25 (ISBN 0-677-00870-8). Gordon.

MASERS, OPTICAL

see Lasers

MASHONA

Beach, D. N. The Shona & Zimbabwe Nine Hundred to Eighteen Fifty: An Outline of Shona History. LC 80-14116. 424p. 1980. text ed. 45.00x (ISBN 0-8419-0624-6, Africana). Holmes & Meier.
Berliner, Paul F. The Soul of Mbira: Music & Tradition of the Shona People of Zimbabwe. LC 76-24578. (Perspectives on Southern Africa Ser.: No. 26). 1978. 23.75x (ISBN 0-520-03315-9); pap. 4.95 (ISBN 0-520-04268-9). U of Cal Pr.
Bucher, Hubert. Spirits & Power: An Analysis of Shona Cosmology. (Illus.). 240p. 1981. 19.95 (ISBN 0-19-570176-3). Oxford U Pr.
Bullock, Charles. Mashona. LC 79-107469. Repr. of 1928 ed. 20.50x (ISBN 0-8371-3748-9, Pub. by Negro U Pr). Greenwood.
Daneel, M. L. God of the Matopo Hills: An Essay on the Mwari Cult in Rhodesia. (Communications Ser.: No. 1). (Illus.). 1970. pap. text ed. 8.90x (ISBN 90-2796-277-4). Mouton.
--Old & New in Southern Shona Independent Churches: Church Growth-Causative Factors & Recruitment Techniques, Vol. 2. new ed. LC 79-171101. (Change & Continuity in Africa Ser.). (Illus.). 373p. 1975. text ed. 29.00x (ISBN 90-2797-701-1). Mouton.
Murphree, M. W. Christianity & the Shona. LC 68-18053. (Monographs on Social Anthropology Ser: No. 36). 1969. text ed. 12.50x (ISBN 0-485-19536-4, Athlone Pr). Humanities.
Vambe, Lawrence. An Ill-Fated People: Zimbabwe Before & After Rhodes. LC 72-87477. 1973. 9.95 (ISBN 0-8229-3256-3). U of Pittsburgh Pr.

MASHONALAND

Finlason, C. E. Nobody in Mashonaland. (Rhodesiana Reprint Library Ser.: Vol. 9). 1970. Repr. of 1893 ed. 16.50x (ISBN 0-8426-1259-9). Verry.

MASHUKULUMBWE

see Ila (Bantu Tribe)

MASKS

see also Indians of North America–Masks; Mumming

Alkema, Chester J. Mask-Making. LC 80-54343. (Illus.). 96p. 8.95 (ISBN 0-8069-7038-3); lib. bdg. 8.29 (ISBN 0-8069-7039-1). Sterling.
Appel, Libby. Mask Characterization: An Acting Process. 128p. (Orig.). 1982. pap. price not set (ISBN 0-8093-1039-2). S Ill U Pr.
Bleakley, Robert. African Masks. LC 77-95303. (Art for All Ser.). 1978. pap. 5.95 (ISBN 0-312-00970-4). St Martin.
Boekholt, Albert. Puppets & Masks. LC 81-8572. (Illus.). 112p. (gr. 4 up). 1981. 9.95 (ISBN 0-8069-7042-1); PLB 9.29 (ISBN 0-8069-7043-X). Sterling.
Bruun-Rasmussen, Ole & Petersen, Grete. Make up, Costumes & Masks for the Stage. LC 76-19803. (Illus.). (gr. 5 up). 1976. 10.95 (ISBN 0-8069-7024-3); PLB 9.87 (ISBN 0-8069-7025-1). Sterling.
Cordry, Donald. Mexican Masks. (Illus.). 304p. 1980. 49.95 (ISBN 0-292-75050-1). U of Tex Pr.
Emerson, Ellen R. Masks, Heads, & Faces with Some Considerations Respecting the Rise & Development of Art. (Illus.). 1979. Repr. of 1891 ed. lib. bdg. 45.00 (ISBN 0-8495-1324-3). Arden Lib.
Grater, Michael. Cut & Color Paper Masks. (Dover Coloring Book Ser.). 32p. (Orig.). 1975. pap. 1.75 (ISBN 0-486-23171-2). Dover.
--Cut & Make Monster Masks in Full Color. LC 77-87448. (Illus.). 1978. pap. 2.00 (ISBN 0-486-23576-9). Dover.
Green, M. C. & Targett, B. R. Space Age Puppets & Masks. LC 77-89957. (Illus.). (gr. 4 up). 1969. 8.95 (ISBN 0-8238-0070-9). Plays.
Gregor, Josef. Masks of the World. LC 68-18150. (Illus.). 1968. Repr. of 1930 ed. 30.00 (ISBN 0-405-08579-6, Blom Pubns). Arno.
Harley, George W. Masks As Agents of Social Control in Northeast Liberia. (Illus.). 1950. pap. 8.00 (ISBN 0-527-01283-1). Kraus Repr.
Horner, Deborah. Masks of the World: To Cut Out & Wear. (gr. 2 up). 1977. pap. 7.95 (ISBN 0-684-14929-X, ScribJ). Scribner.
Horner, Deborah R. Creature Paws & Jaws: A Book of Animal Masks for Face & Hands...to Cut Out & Wear. (Illus.). (gr. k-3). 1979. 6.95 (ISBN 0-684-16102-8). Scribner.
Levi-Strauss, Claude & Modelski, Sylvia, eds. The Way of the Masks. 1982. price not set. U of Wash Pr.
Loehrer, Robert. Mienenspiel und Maske in der Griechischen Tragodie. Repr. of 1927 ed. 12.50 (ISBN 0-384-33370-2). Johnson Repr.
Masquerade. (Illus.). 84p. 1980. pap. 6.50 (ISBN 0-905171-26-8, Pub. by Welsh Art Council Wales). Intl Schol Bk Serv.
Meyer, Carolyn. Mask Magic. LC 77-14080. (Illus.). (gr. 4-7). 1978. 7.95 (ISBN 0-15-253107-6, HJ). HarBraceJ.
Nishikawa, Kyotaro. Bugaku Masks. Bethe, Monica, tr. LC 77-75971. (Japanese Arts Library: Vol. 5). (Illus.). 1978. 16.75 (ISBN 0-87011-312-7). Kodansha.
Price, Christine. Dancing Masks of Africa. LC 75-4028. (Illus.). 48p. (gr. 2-6). 1975. reinforced bdg. 6.95 (ISBN 0-684-14332-1, ScribJ). Scribner.
--The Mystery of Masks. LC 77-27558. (gr. 3 up). 1978. reinforced bdg. 7.95 (ISBN 0-684-15653-9, ScribJ). Scribner.
Rolfe, Bari. Behind the Mask. LC 77-76975. (Illus.). 66p. 1977. pap. 3.50 (ISBN 0-932456-01-4). Personabks.
Ross, Laura. Mask-Making with Pantomime & Stories from American History. LC 75-11960. (Illus.). 128p. (gr. 3 up). 1975. PLB 6.96 (ISBN 0-688-51721-8). Lothrop.
Segy, Ladislas. Masks of Black Africa. LC 74-15005. (Illus.). 246p. 1975. pap. 6.50 (ISBN 0-486-23181-X). Dover.
--Masks of Black Africa. 11.50 (ISBN 0-8446-5455-8). Peter Smith.
Snook, Barbara. Making Masks for School Plays. LC 76-180545. (Illus.). (gr. 3-12). 1972. 8.95 (ISBN 0-8238-0131-4). Plays.
Supraner, Robyn. Great Masks to Make. LC 80-24077. (Illus.). 48p. (gr. 1-5). 1981. PLB 6.92 (ISBN 0-89375-436-6); pap. 1.95 (ISBN 0-89375-437-4). Troll Assocs.

MASKS (PLAYS)

see Masques

MASKS (SCULPTURE)

Cook, William J., Jr. Masks, Modes, & Morals: The Art of Evelyn Waugh. LC 73-118125. 352p. 1971. 18.00 (ISBN 0-8386-7707-X). Fairleigh Dickinson.
Hunt, Kari & Carlson, Bernice W. Masks & Mask Makers. (Illus.). (gr. 4 up). 1961. 5.95 (ISBN 0-687-23705-X). Abingdon.

MASLOW, ABRAHAM H.

International Study Project Inc. Abraham H. Maslow: A Memorial Volume. LC 74-178890. (Illus.). 136p. 1972. 14.95 (ISBN 0-8185-0033-6). Brooks-Cole.
Lowry, Richard J. A. H. Maslow: An Intellectual Portrait. LC 72-95177. 1973. text ed. 10.95 (ISBN 0-8185-0083-2). Brooks-Cole.
Maslow, Abraham H. The Journals of A. H. Maslow, 2 vols. Lowrey, Richard J., ed. LC 74-81816. 1979. Set. 59.95 (ISBN 0-8185-0078-6). Brooks-Cole.

MASOCHISM

Braun, Walter. Cruel & the Meek. Meyer, N., tr. (Illus.). 1968. 6.00 (ISBN 0-8184-0024-2). Lyle Stuart.
Eisler, Robert. Man into Wolf, an Anthropological Interpretation of Sadism, Masochism & Lycanthropy. LC 77-88984. Repr. of 1951 ed. lib. bdg. 15.00x (ISBN 0-8371-2090-X, EIMW). Greenwood.
--Man into Wolf: An Anthropological Study of Sadism, Masochism, & Lycanthropy. LC 77-2497. 264p. 1978. text ed. 11.95 (ISBN 0-915520-16-8); pap. text ed. 5.95 (ISBN 0-915520-06-0). Ross-Erikson.
Greene, Gerald & Greene, Caroline. S-M: The Last Taboo. LC 74-7680. 1973. pap. 2.95 (ISBN 0-394-17832-7, B376, BC). Grove.
Leites, Nathan. Depression & Masochism: An Account of Mechanisms. 1979. 19.95x (ISBN 0-393-01247-6). Norton.
Linden, Robin R., et al, eds. Against Sadomasochism: A Radical Feminist Analysis. 240p. (Orig.). 1981. pap. 7.95 (ISBN 0-9603628-3-5). Frog in Well.
Panken, Shirley. The Joy of Suffering: The Psychoanalytic Understanding of Masochism. LC 73-96532. 320p. 1973. 25.00x (ISBN 0-87668-065-1). Aronson.
Roberts, Albert R. Self-Destructive Behavior. (Illus.). 232p. 1975. 22.75 (ISBN 0-398-03290-4). C C Thomas.
Schad-Somers, Susanne. Sadomasochism: Etiology & Treatment. 1981. 26.95 (ISBN 0-89885-059-2). Human Sci Pr.
Shapiro, David. Autonomy & Rigid Character. LC 80-68953. 167p. 1981. 12.95x (ISBN 0-465-00567-5). Basic.
Stekel, Wilhelm. Sadism & Masochism, 2 Vols. rev. ed. 1953. 15.95x (ISBN 0-87140-838-4). Liveright.

MASON, GEORGE, 1725-1792

Copeland, Pamela C. & MacMaster, Richard K. The Five George Masons: Patriots & Planters of Virginia & Maryland. LC 75-8565. (Illus.). 332p. 1975. 17.50x (ISBN 0-8139-0590-7). U Pr of Va.
Henri, Florette. George Mason of Virginia. Tragger, Carolyn, ed. LC 70-12760. (Illus.). (gr. 7 up). 1971. 4.50 (ISBN 0-02-743560-1, CCPr). Macmillan.
Miller, Helen H. George Mason, Gentleman Revolutionary. LC 75-1377. (Illus.). 416p. 1975. 19.95 (ISBN 0-8078-1250-1). U of NC Pr.

MASON, JOHN, 1586-1635

Dean, John W., ed. Captain John Mason Fifteen Eighty-Six to Sixteen Thirty-Five. LC 3-24569. (Prince Society Pubns.: No. 17). 1966. Repr. of 1887 ed. 32.00 (ISBN 0-8337-0810-4). B Franklin.

MASON, JOHN, 1927-

Haskell, Barbara, ed. John Mason Ceramic Sculpture. (Pasedena Art Museum Publications). (Illus.). 1974. 4.95x (ISBN 0-912158-74-3). Hennessey.

MASON, LOWELL, 1792-1872

Mason, H. Lowell. Hymn-Tunes of Lowell Mason. LC 74-24144. Repr. of 1944 ed. 15.00 (ISBN 0-404-13035-6). AMS Pr.

MASON, WILLIAM, 1810-1897

Gray, Thomas. The Correspondence of Thomas Gray & William Mason. (Illus.). 1853. Repr. lib. bdg. 50.00 (ISBN 0-8414-4670-9). Folcroft.

MASON AND DIXON'S LINE, 1763-1768

Mason, A. H. Journal of Charles Mason & Jeremiah Dixon. LC 69-17273. (Memoirs Ser.: Vol. 76). (Illus.). 1969. 6.50 (ISBN 0-87169-076-4). Am Philos.

MASON FAMILY

Copeland, Pamela C. & MacMaster, Richard K. The Five George Masons: Patriots & Planters of Virginia & Maryland. LC 75-8565. (Illus.). 332p. 1975. 17.50x (ISBN 0-8139-0590-7). U Pr of Va.
Dean, John W., ed. Captain John Mason Fifteen Eighty-Six to Sixteen Thirty-Five. LC 3-24569. (Prince Society Pubns.: No. 17). 1966. Repr. of 1887 ed. 32.00 (ISBN 0-8337-0810-4). B Franklin.

MASONIC ORDERS

see Freemasons

MASONRY

see also Arches; Bricklaying; Building, Brick; Cement; Concrete; Foundations; Grouting; Plastering; Scaffolding; Stone-Cutting; Walls

Adams, J. T. The Complete Concrete, Masonry, & Brick Handbook. LC 77-14003. (Illus.). 1979. lib. bdg. 19.95 (ISBN 0-668-04340-7, 4340). Arco.
Ball, John E. Practical Problems in Mathematics for Masons. LC 78-74431. (Mathematics - Construction Ser.). 112p. 1980. 6.60 (ISBN 0-8273-1283-0); instructor's guide 1.75 (ISBN 0-8273-1284-9). Delmar.
Blake, Marion E. Ancient Roman Construction in Italy from the Prehistoric Period to Augustus. (Carnegie Institution Publication Ser: No. 570). (Illus.). 1968. Repr. of 1947 ed. 36.00 (ISBN 0-527-08850-1). Kraus Repr.
Burch, Monte. Masonry & Concrete. Kummings, Gail, ed. LC 81-317. (Illus.). 144p. (Orig.). 1981. 17.95 (ISBN 0-932944-29-9); pap. 6.95 (ISBN 0-932944-30-2). Creative Homeowner.
Complete Book of Masonry, Cement & Brickwork. LC 80-52324. (Illus.). 192p. 1980. pap. 6.95 (ISBN 0-8069-8232-2). Sterling.
Concrete Masonry Units. 38p. 1979. 5.75 (ISBN 0-686-76030-1, 06-315079-07). ASTM.
Council on Tall Buildings & Urban Habitats of Fritz Engineering Lab., Lehigh Univ. Structural Design of Tall Concrete & Masonry Buildings. LC 78-60643. 960p. 1978. text ed. 50.00 (ISBN 0-87262-152-9). Am Soc Civil Eng.
Dalzell, J. Ralph. Simplified Concrete Masonry Planning & Building. 2nd, rev. ed. Merritt, Frederick S., rev. by. LC 81-385. 398p. 1981. Repr. of 1972 ed. lib. bdg. 17.50 (ISBN 0-89874-278-1). Krieger.
Dalzell, Ralph & Townsend, Gilbert. Masonry Simplified: Tools, Materials, Practices, Vol. 1. 3rd ed. (Illus.). 1972. 13.33 (ISBN 0-8269-0627-3). Am Technical.

DeCristoforo, R. J. Concrete & Masonry: Techniques & Design. (Illus.). 384p. 1975. 15.95 (ISBN 0-87909-149-5). Reston.
--Handyman's Concrete & Masonry. LC 60-13052. 1972. 3.95 (ISBN 0-668-00729-X). Arco.
--Handyman's Guide to Concrete & Masonry. (Illus.). 1978. pap. 6.95 (ISBN 0-8359-2752-0). Reston.
Dezettel, Louis M. Masons & Builders Library, 2 vols. 2nd ed. LC 78-186134. (Illus.). 1972. 9.95 ea. Vol. 1 (ISBN 0-672-23182-4, 23182). Vol. 2 (ISBN 0-672-23183-2, 23183). Set. 17.95 (ISBN 0-672-23185-9, 23185). Audel.
Duncan, Stuart B. The Complete Book of Outdoor Masonry. (Illus.). 1978. 11.95 (ISBN 0-8306-9904-X); pap. 6.95 (ISBN 0-8306-1080-4, 1080). TAB Bks.
Gage, Michael & Kirkbridge, T., eds. Design in Blockwork. 3rd ed. (Illus.). 1980. 25.00 (ISBN 0-686-60663-9, Pub. by Architectural Pr). Nichols Pub.
Huff, Darrell. How to Work with Concrete & Masonry. 2nd ed. LC 68-31231. (Popular Science Skill Books Ser.). (Illus.). 192p. 1977. pap. 3.95 (ISBN 0-06-012002-9, TD-267, HarpT). Har-Row.
International Masonry Institute. Masonry Glossary. 1981. 10.95 (ISBN 0-8436-0134-5). CBI Pub.
Kenny, Michael F. Masonry Estimating Handbook. LC 72-97069. (Illus.). 144p. 1973. 19.95 (ISBN 0-442-12162-8). Van Nos Reinhold.
Kern, et al. Stone Masonry. 192p. 10.95 (ISBN 0-686-31221-X). Owner-Builder.
Kern, Ken, et al. Stone Masonry. (Illus.). 1977. pap. 10.95 (ISBN 0-684-15288-6, SL747, ScribT). Scribner.
Kinklighter, Clois E. Modern Masonry. (Illus.). 256p. 1980. text ed. 12.00 (ISBN 0-87006-296-4). Goodheart.
Kreh, Richard. Masonry Skills. 2nd ed. LC 80-70701. (Masonry Trades Ser.). 336p. 1981. pap. text ed. 11.00 (ISBN 0-8273-1958-4); price not set instructor's guide (ISBN 0-8273-1957-6). Delmar.
Kreh, Richard T. Advanced Masonry Skills. LC 77-78176. 1978. pap. text ed. 11.44 (ISBN 0-8273-1636-4); instructor's guide 1.60 (ISBN 0-8273-1637-2). Delmar.
--Masonry Skills. 500p. 1976. 13.95 (ISBN 0-442-24548-3). Van Nos Reinhold.
--Masonry Skills. LC 75-27994. 1976. pap. 10.80 (ISBN 0-8273-1090-0); instructor's guide 1.60 (ISBN 0-8273-1091-9). Delmar.
--Safety for Masons. LC 78-53663. 1979. pap. text ed. 3.60 (ISBN 0-8273-1668-2); instructor's guide 0.75 (ISBN 0-8273-1669-0). Delmar.
Kreh, Richard T., Sr. Advanced Masonry Skills. 1978. 12.95 (ISBN 0-442-24289-1). Van Nos Reinhold.
Lavicka, William L., ed. Masonry, Carpentry, Joinery. 280p. (Orig.). 1980. pap. 15.00 (ISBN 0-914090-92-5). Chicago Review.
McKee, Harley J. Introduction to Early American Masonry: Stone, Brick, Mortar & Plaster. LC 73-84522. (Illus.). 92p. 1973. pap. 6.95 (ISBN 0-89133-006-2). Preservation Pr.
McRaven, Charles. Building with Stone. (Illus.). 1980. 14.95 (ISBN 0-690-01879-7); pap. 8.95 (ISBN 0-690-01912-2). Har-Row.
Maguire, Byron W. Masonry & Concrete. (Illus.). 1978. ref. ed. 18.95 (ISBN 0-87909-521-0). Reston.
Maldon, Leo D. How to Build with Stone, Brick, Concrete & Tile. (Illus.). 1977. pap. 6.95x (ISBN 0-8306-6980-9, 980). TAB Bks.
Masonry. (Illus.). 64p. (gr. 6-12). 1980. pap. 0.70x (ISBN 0-686-70358-8, 3339). BSA.
Masonry. (Home Repair & Improvement Ser.). (Illus.). 1976. 10.95 (ISBN 0-8094-2362-6). Time-Life.
Masonry: Past & Present. 1975. 30.00 (ISBN 0-686-52054-8, 04-589000-07). ASTM.
National Association of Home Builders. Incentive Apprenticeship Training for Cement Masons. (Illus.). 371p. 3-ring binder (slide tapes avail.) 63.00 (ISBN 0-86718-079-X). Natl Assn Home Builders.
--Incentive Apprenticeship Training for Plasterers. (Illus.). 345p. (slide tapes avail.) 63.00 (ISBN 0-86718-078-1). Natl Assn Home Builders.
Nickey, J. M. The Stoneworker's Bible. (Illus.). 1980. 12.95 (ISBN 0-8306-9714-4); pap. 7.95 (ISBN 0-8306-1226-2, 1226). TAB Bks.
Nolan, Kenneth. Masonry Contractors Handbook. (Orig.). 1981. pap. 13.50 (ISBN 0-910460-81-7). Craftsman.
Randall, Frank A., Jr. & Panarese, William C. Concrete Masonry Handbook. Portland Cement Association, ed. (Illus.). 1976. text ed. 11.00 (ISBN 0-89312-000-6, EB080M); pap. 9.75 (ISBN 0-89312-001-4, EB008M). Portland Cement.
Research & Education Association. Handbook of Concrete Technology & Masonry Construction. LC 81-50761. (Illus.). 832p. 1981. 26.85c (ISBN 0-87891-528-1). Res & Educ.
Roberts. The Complete Handbook of Stone Masonry...with Projects. 416p. 1981. 16.95 (ISBN 0-8306-9642-3); pap. 10.95 (ISBN 0-8306-1264-5, 1264). TAB Bks.
Rudman, Jack. Cement Mason. (Career Examination Ser.: C-132). (Cloth bdg. avail. on request). pap. 8.00 (ISBN 0-8373-0132-7). Natl Learning.
--Masonry. (Occupational Competency Examination Ser.: OCE-23). (Cloth bdg. avail. on request). pap. 9.95 (ISBN 0-8373-5723-3). Natl Learning.
Scharff, Robert. Successful & Masonry. Case, Virginia A., ed. (Successful Ser.). 144p. Date not set. cancelled (ISBN 0-89999-023-1); pap. 8.95 (ISBN 0-89999-024-X). Structures Pub.
--Successful Masonry. Date not set. cancelled (ISBN 0-686-71398-2); pap. 7.95 (ISBN 0-686-71399-0). Structures Pub.
Sementsov, S. A. & Kameiko, V. A. Designer's Manual: Masonry. 236p. 1971. 25.00x (ISBN 0-7065-1167-0, Pub. by IPST). Intl Schol Bk Serv.
Sheppard, Walter L., Jr. A Handbook of Chemically Resistant Masonry. (Illus.). 260p. 1977. 40.00 (ISBN 0-686-31229-5). W L Sheppard.
Sunset Editors. Basic Masonry Illustrated. LC 80-53484. (Illus.). 96p. (Orig.). 1981. pap. 4.95 (ISBN 0-376-01360-5, Sunset Bks.). Sunset-Lane.
--Walks, Walls, & Patio Floors: Wall Systems & Shelving. 3rd ed. LC 72-92521. (Illus.). 96p. 1973. pap. 3.95 (ISBN 0-376-01705-8, Sunset Bks.). Sunset-Lane.
Tab Editional Staff. Concrete & Masonry. LC 76-1553. 392p. 1976. pap. 5.95 (ISBN 0-8306-5902-1, 902). TAB Bks.
Time Life Books, ed. Masonry. LC 76-25711. (Home Repair & Improvement). (Illus.). (gr. 7 up). 1976. PLB 11.97 (ISBN 0-8094-2363-4, Pub. by Time-Life). Silver.
U. S. Army. Concrete, Masonry & Brickwork: A Practical Handbook for the Homeowner & Small Builder. LC 75-12130. Orig. Title: Concrete & Masonry. (Illus.). 204p. 1975. pap. 5.00 (ISBN 0-486-23203-4). Dover.
U. S. Department of the Army. Concrete, Masonry & Brickwork. LC 75-12130. (Illus.). 1975. lib. bdg. 12.50x (ISBN 0-88307-588-1). Gannon.

MASONS (SECRET ORDER)
see Freemasons

MASONS (TRADE)
see Stone-Masons

MASORAH

Butin, Romain. Ten Nequdoth of the Torah. rev. ed. (Library of Biblical Studies). 1969. 15.00x (ISBN 0-87068-043-9). Ktav.
Frensdorff, Salomon. Massora Magna. rev. ed. LC 67-11896. (Library of Biblical Studies). (Heb). 1968. 35.00x (ISBN 0-87068-052-8). Ktav.
Jacob, Ben Chayyim. Introduction to the Rabbinic Bible of 1525. rev. ed. (Library of Biblical Studies Ser). 1969. 25.00x (ISBN 0-87068-067-6). Ktav.
Orlinsky, Harry M., ed. Masoretic Studies. 10.00x (ISBN 0-685-56221-2). Ktav.
Revell, E. J. Biblical Texts with Palestinian Pointing. LC 77-8893. (Society of Biblical Literature. Masoretic Studies). 1977. pap. 9.00 (ISBN 0-89130-141-0, 060504). Scholars Pr Ca.
Yeivin, Israel. Introduction to the Tiberian Masorah. LC 79-24755. (Society of Biblical Literature Masoretic Studies: No. 5). pap. 10.50x (ISBN 0-89130-374-X, 06 05 05). Scholars Pr Ca.

MASQUES

Arkwright, G. E. P., ed. Old English Edition, 25 vols. Incl. Vol. 1. Masque in Honor of the Marriage of Lord Hayes, 1607. Campion, Thomas, et al. (ISBN 0-8450-1601-6); Vol. 2. Six Songs. Arne, Thomas A (ISBN 0-8450-1602-4); Vol. 3. Six Madrigals to Four Voices, 1597. Kirbye, George (ISBN 0-8450-1603-2); Vol. 4. Twelve Madrigals to Five Voices, 1597. Kirbye, George (ISBN 0-8450-1604-0); Vol. 5. Six Madrigals to Six Voices, 1597. Kirbye, George (ISBN 0-8450-1605-9); Vol. 6. Songs of Sundry Natures, 1589: Fourteen Songs to Three Voices. Byrd, William (ISBN 0-8450-1606-7); Vol. 7. Songs of Sundry Natures, 1589: Nine Songs to Four Voices. Byrd, William (ISBN 0-8450-1607-5); Vol. 8. Songs of Sundry Natures, 1589: Twelve Songs to Five Voices. Byrd, William (ISBN 0-8450-1608-3); Vol. 9. Songs of Sundry Natures, 1589: Ten Songs to Six Voices. Byrd, William (ISBN 0-8450-1609-1); Vol. 10. Mass to Six Voices, Euge Bone. Tye, Christopher (ISBN 0-8450-1610-5); Vol. 11. Nine Madrigals to Five Voices from Musica Transalpina, 1588. Ferrabosco, Alfonso. only as part of set avail. (ISBN 0-8450-1611-3); Vol. 12. Five Madrigals to Six Voices from Musica Transalpina, 1588. Ferrabosco, Alfonso (ISBN 0-8450-1612-1); Vol. 13. Eight Ballets & Madrigals, 1598. Weelkes, Thomas (ISBN 0-8450-1613-X); Vol. 14. Eight Ballets & Madrigals, 1598. Weelkes, Thomas (ISBN 0-8450-1614-8); Vol. 15. Eight Ballets & Madrigals, 1598. Weelkes, Thomas. only as part of set avail. (ISBN 0-8450-1615-6); Vol. 16. Airs or Fantastic Spirits, 1608. Weelkes, Thomas (ISBN 0-8450-1616-4); Vol. 17. Airs or Fantastic Spirits, 1608. Weelkes, Thomas (ISBN 0-8450-1617-2); Vol. 18. The First Book of Songs or Airs of Four Parts, 1605. Pilkington, Francis (ISBN 0-8450-1618-0); Vol. 19. The First Book of Songs or Airs of Four Parts, 1605. Pilkington, Francis (ISBN 0-8450-1619-9); Vol. 20. The First Book of Songs or Airs of Four Parts, 1605. Pilkington, Francis (ISBN 0-8450-1620-2); Vol. 21. Anthems & Motets. White, Robert, et al. (ISBN 0-8450-1621-0); Vol. 22. Six Anthems. Milton, John (ISBN 0-8450-1622-9); Vol. 23. Six Songs from Amphion Anglicus, 1700. Blow, John (ISBN 0-8450-1623-7); Vol. 24. Six Songs from the Orpheus Britannicus. Purcell, Henry (ISBN 0-8450-1624-5); Vol. 25. Venus & Adonis. Blow, John (ISBN 0-8450-1625-3). 1970. pap. 475.00 (ISBN 0-8450-1600-8); pap. 20.00x ea. Broude.
Bergeron, David M. Twentieth-Century Criticism of English Masques, Pageants, & Entertainments: 1558-1642. (Checklists in the Humanities & Education Ser.). 1972. 6.00 (ISBN 0-911536-46-9). Trinity U Pr.
Boas, Frederick, ed. Songs & Lyrics from the English Masques & Light Operas. 175p. 1949. Repr. 19.00 (ISBN 0-403-03693-3). Scholarly.
Brotanek, Rudolf. Die Englischen Maskenspiele. 1902. pap. 21.00 (ISBN 0-384-05945-7). Johnson Repr.
Cornelia, Marie. The Function of the Masque in Jacobean Tragedy & Tragicomedy. (Salzburg Studies in English Literature, Jacobean Drama Studies: No. 77). 1978. pap. text ed. 25.00x (ISBN 0-391-01350-5). Humanities.
Evans, Herbert A. English Masques. LC 72-10413. 1897. lib. bdg. 12.75 (ISBN 0-8414-0712-6). Folcroft.
Evans, Herbert A, ed. English Masques. facsimile ed. LC 71-169757. (Select Bibliographies Reprint Ser). Repr. of 1897 ed. 18.00 (ISBN 0-8369-5977-9). Arno.
Fletcher, Angus. Transcendental Masque: An Essay on Milton's Comus. LC 78-148019. (Illus.). 278p. 1972. 22.50x (ISBN 0-8014-0620-X). Cornell U Pr.
Greg, Walter W. List of Masques, Pageants, Etc. Supplementary to a List of English Plays. LC 68-25312. (Studies in Drama, No. 39). 1969. Repr. of 1902 ed. lib. bdg. 32.95 (ISBN 0-8383-0942-9). Haskell.
Jones, Inigo. Designs by Inigo Jones for Masques & Plays at Court. LC 66-13236. (Illus.). 1966. Repr. of 1924 ed. 35.00 (ISBN 0-8462-0732-X). Russell.
Jonson, Ben. Score for Lovers Made Men, a Masque by Ben Jonson. Sabol, Andrew J., ed. LC 63-8400. 117p. 1963. pap. 8.00 (ISBN 0-87057-073-0, Pub. by Brown U Pr). U Pr of New Eng.
Jonson, Ben, et al. A Book of Masques. Spencer, T. J. & Wells, S., eds. (Illus.). 448p. 1981. pap. 19.95 (ISBN 0-521-29758-3). Cambridge U Pr.
--Book of Masques. 1967. 68.00 (ISBN 0-521-05455-9). Cambridge U Pr.
Nicoll, Allardyce. Stuart Masques & the Renaissance Stage. LC 63-23186. (Illus.). 1938. 34.00 (ISBN 0-405-08817-5, Pub. by Blom). Arno.
Peters, Joan & Sutcliffe, Anna. Creative Masks for Stage & School. 1975. 8.95 (ISBN 0-8238-0186-1). Plays.
Reyher, Paul. Masques Anglais. LC 64-14712. 1909. 25.00 (ISBN 0-405-08880-9, Blom Pubns). Arno.
Sabol, Andrew J., ed. Four Hundred Songs & Dances from the Stuart Masque. LC 77-6686. 679p. 1978. text ed. 100.00x (ISBN 0-87057-146-X, Pub. by Brown U Pr). U Pr of New Eng.
Steele, Mary S. Plays & Masques at Court During the Reigns of Elizabeth, James & Charles, 1558-1642. LC 67-18296. 1968. Repr. of 1926 ed. 9.00 (ISBN 0-8462-1113-0). Russell.
Storey, Robert F. Pierrot: A Critical History of a Mask. LC 78-51194. (Illus.). 1978. 17.50 (ISBN 0-691-06374-5). Princeton U Pr.
Welsford, Enid. Court Masque: A Study in the Relationship Between Poetry & the Revels. LC 62-13854. (Illus.). 1962. Repr. of 1927 ed. 22.00 (ISBN 0-8462-0294-8). Russell.

MASS
see also Altar Boys; Catholic Church–Liturgy and Ritual–Missal; Lord's Supper; Transubstantiation

Becon, Thomas. Prayers & Others Pieces of Thomas Becon, Chaplain to Archbishop Cranmer. Repr. of 1844 ed. 46.00 (ISBN 0-384-03730-5). Johnson Repr.
Champlin, Joseph M. The New Yet Old Mass. LC 77-72286. (Illus.). 112p. 1977. pap. 2.25 (ISBN 0-87793-132-1). Ave Maria.
Coleman, William & Coleman, Patricia. The Mass & Prayer. rev. ed. (Mine Is the Morning Ser.). 160p. (gr. 9-12). 1978. tchrs. manual & duplicator masters 16.95 (ISBN 0-89622-067-2). Twenty-Third.
Cooper, Thomas. An Answer in Defence of the Truth Against the Apology of Private Mass. 1850. 17.00 (ISBN 0-384-09790-1). Johnson Repr.
Corless, Roger. I Am Food: The Mass in Planetary Perspective. LC 81-7836. 112p. 1981. 8.95 (ISBN 0-8245-0077-6). Crossroad NY.
Cronin, Gaynell & Cronin, Jim. The Mass: Great Common Prayer. 1977. pap. 7.55 (ISBN 0-88479-006-1). Arena Lettres.
Franciscan Educational Conference - 43rd. Holy Eucharist & Christian Unity. 1962. pap. 4.50 (ISBN 0-8199-0300-0, L38270). Franciscan Herald.
Goode, Teresa C. Gonzalo De Berceo. (Carl Ser.: No. 7). Repr. of 1933 ed. 16.00 (ISBN 0-404-50307-1). AMS Pr.
Hamman, Adelbert. Mass: Ancient Liturgies & Patristic Texts. Halton, Thomas, ed. LC 67-15202. 1967. 4.95 (ISBN 0-8189-0086-5). Alba.
Jungmann, Joseph. The Mass of the Roman Rite. 25.00 (ISBN 0-87061-054-6). Chr Classics.
Lanz, Kerry J. The Complete Server. (Illus.). 1978. 1.95 (ISBN 0-8192-1245-8). Morehouse.
McGloin, Joseph T. How to Get More Out of the Mass. LC 74-80938. 1974. pap. 2.50 (ISBN 0-89243-011-7, 41230). Liguori Pubns.
McMahon, Thomas. The Mass Explained. LC 78-59320. 1978. 8.95 (ISBN 0-89310-041-2); pap. 3.95 (ISBN 0-89310-042-0). Carillon Bks.
St. Leonard. The Hidden Treasure: Holy Mass. 1971. pap. 2.00 (ISBN 0-89555-036-9, 111). TAN Bks Pubs.
Schlitzer, Albert L. Prayerlife of the Church. 1962. 4.95x (ISBN 0-268-00214-2). U of Notre Dame Pr.
Schmitz, Walter J. Learning the Mass. rev. ed. 1966. pap. 2.50 (ISBN 0-685-07648-2, 80673). Glencoe.
Three Tudor Dialogues. LC 78-14887. 1979. 20.00x (ISBN 0-8201-1319-0). Schol Facsimiles.

MASS–CELEBRATION

Hileman, Louis G. The Celebration of Holy Mass. 154p. 1976. pap. 2.95 (ISBN 0-912414-23-5). Lumen Christi.
Kershaw, Jack. Christ's Mass. LC 74-28633. 1975. 9.95 (ISBN 0-87695-178-7). Aurora Pubs.
Our Eucharist Celebration: A Guide to the New Order of the Mass. (gr. 6-10). 1.98 (ISBN 0-02-648770-5). Benziger Pub Co.
Remember. (Liturgy Activity Book Ser.). (gr. 6). 1.80 (ISBN 0-02-642110-0); tchr's ed 2.22 (ISBN 0-02-642120-8). Benziger Pub Co.
Sign. (Liturgy Activity Book Ser.). (gr. 7). 1.80 (ISBN 0-02-642130-5); tchr's ed. 2.22 (ISBN 0-02-642140-2). Benziger Pub Co.
Sister Jean Daniel. Our Family Prepares for Mass. Orig. Title: Tomorrow Is Sunday. (Illus.). 216p. 1980. pap. 6.95 (ISBN 0-03-057842-6). Winston Pr.

MASS–JUVENILE LITERATURE

Daughters of St. Paul. St. Paul Mass Book for Children. (Illus.). 1973. plastic bdg. 1.50 (ISBN 0-8198-0336-7); pap. 0.95 (ISBN 0-8198-0337-5). Dghtrs St Paul.
Leichner, J. Joy Joy, the Mass: Our Family Celebration. (Illus.). (gr. k-3). 1978. pap. 1.50 (ISBN 0-87973-350-0). Our Sunday Visitor.

MASS (CHEMISTRY)
see Atomic Mass

MASS (MUSIC)
see also Masses

MASS (PHYSICS)
see also Atomic Mass; Inertia (Mechanics); Mass Spectrometry; Mass Transfer

Cherimisinoff, et al. Biomass: Applications, Technology & Production, Vol. 5. (Energy Power & Environment Ser.). 232p. 1980. 29.50 (ISBN 0-8247-6933-3). Dekker.

Measurement of Force & Mass. 181p. 1978. pap. 57.00x (ISBN 0-686-71870-4, Pub. by VDI Verlag Germany). Renouf.

Woolard, Frank G. Principles of Mass & Flow Production. 1955. 7.50 (ISBN 0-8022-1931-4). Philos Lib.

MASS-BOOKS
see Catholic Church–Liturgy and Ritual–Missal

MASS CASUALTIES–TREATMENT
see Emergency Medical Services

MASS COMMUNICATION
see Communication; Communication and Traffic; Mass Media; Telecommunication

Lent, John A. Caribbean Mass Communications: A Comprehensive Bibliography. (Archival & Bibliographic Ser.). 152p. 1981. pap. 20.00 (ISBN 0-918456-39-8). African Studies Assn.

MASS CULTURE
see Popular Culture

MASS FEEDING
see Food Service

MASS HYSTERIA
see Hysteria (Social Psychology)

MASS MEDIA
see also Moving-Pictures; Newspapers; Radio Broadcasting; Television Broadcasting; Violence in Mass Media

Agee, Warren K., ed. Mass Media in a Free Society. LC 69-16934. 1969. pap. 1.95x (ISBN 0-7006-0056-6). Regents Pr KS.

Agee, Warren K., et al. Introduction to Mass Communications. 6th ed. 1979. pap. text ed. 12.95 scp (ISBN 0-06-040172-9, HarpC); inst. manual free (ISBN 0-06-360176-1). Har-Row.

Altman, Sig. Comic Image of the Jew: Explorations of a Pop Culture Phenomenon. LC 71-146161. 234p. 1971. 15.00 (ISBN 0-8386-7869-6). Fairleigh Dickinson.

Aronoff, Craig. Business & the Media. LC 78-10394. 1979. text ed. 16.95 case ed. (ISBN 0-87620-104-4). Goodyear.

Aronson, James. Deadline for the Media. LC 72-179640. 1972. 8.95 (ISBN 0-672-51428-1). Bobbs.

--Deadline for the Media: Today's Challenges to Press, TV & Radio. LC 72-179640. 348p. 1975. pap. 2.95 (ISBN 0-672-52115-6). Bobbs.

Ashford, Gerald. Everyday Publicity. LC 73-132372. 90p. 1970. 6.95x (ISBN 0-88238-051-6). Law-Arts.

Atwan, Robert, et al. American Mass Media: Industries & Issues. 1978. pap. text ed. 11.95x (ISBN 0-394-32029-8). Random.

Bittner, John R. Mass Communication. 2nd ed. (Ser. in Speech Communication). (Illus.). 1980. pap. text ed. 15.95 (ISBN 0-13-559278-X). P-H.

Blumler, Jay G. & Katz, Elihu. The Uses of Mass Communications: Current Perspectives on Gratifications Research. LC 73-90713. (Sage Annual Reviess of Communication Research: Vol. 3). 320p. 1975. 22.50 (ISBN 0-8039-0340-5); pap. 9.95 (ISBN 0-8039-0494-0). Sage.

Bohn, Hiebert & Ungurait. Mass Media: An Introduction to Modern Communication. 2nd ed. LC 77-17721. (Illus.). 1979. pap. text ed. 13.95x (ISBN 0-582-28070-2). Longman.

Bornoff, Jack, ed. Music Theatre in a Changing Society: The Influence of the Technical Media. 1968. pap. 6.00 (ISBN 92-3-100709-2, U397, UNESCO). Unipub.

Bowman, Kathleen. New Women in Media. LC 76-6061. (New Women Ser.). (Illus.). (gr. 4-12). 1976. PLB 6.95 (ISBN 0-87191-511-1). Creative Ed.

Brown, Charlene, et al. The Media & the People. LC 78-8375. 480p. 1978. Repr. lib. bdg. 16.50 (ISBN 0-88275-689-3). Krieger.

Brown, Charlene J., et al. The Media & the People. LC 77-27977. 1978. pap. 14.95 (ISBN 0-03-019056-8, HoltC). HR&W.

Caso, Adolph. Mass Media vs. the Italian Americans. LC 80-66885. (Illus.). 278p. 1980. 12.00 (ISBN 0-8283-1737-2). Branden.

Cavert, C. Edward. Procedural Guidelines for the Design of Mediated Instruction. 1974. pap. 6.95 (ISBN 0-89240-021-8, 207). Assn Ed Comm Tech.

Center for Understanding Media. Doing the Media. (Illus.). 1978. pap. 6.95 (ISBN 0-07-010336-4, SP). McGraw.

Clark, David G., et al, eds. Mass Media & the Law. 478p. 1970. 22.50 (ISBN 0-471-15851-8, Pub. by Wiley). Krieger.

Communication Policies in the Federal Republic of Germany. 86p. (Orig.). 1975. pap. 6.00 (ISBN 92-3-101184-7, U81, UNESCO). Unipub.

Communication Policies in the Republic of Korea. (Communication Policy Studies). 1978. pap. 4.00 (ISBN 92-3-101582-6, U853, UNESCO). Unipub.

Compaine, Benjamin M., ed. Who Owns the Media? Concentration of Ownership in the Mass Communication Industry. (Illus.). 300p. 1980. 15.95 (ISBN 0-517-54058-4, Harmony); pap. 8.95 (ISBN 0-517-54059-2). Crown.

--Who Owns the Media? Concentration of Ownership in the Mass Communications Industry. LC 79-15891. (Communications Library). 1979. 24.95x (ISBN 0-914236-36-9). Knowledge Indus.

Davis, Dennis K. & Baran, Stanley J. Mass Communication & Everyday Life: A Perspective on Theory & Effects. 240p. 1980. pap. text ed. 8.95x (ISBN 0-534-00883-6). Wadsworth Pub.

Davis, Robert E. Response to Innovation: A Study of Popular Argument About New Mass Media. Loweth, Garth S., ed. LC 75-21430. (Dissertations on Film Ser.). 1976. lib. bdg. 35.00x (ISBN 0-405-07533-2). Arno.

Davison, Peter, et al, eds. Mass Media & Mass Communication. LC 77-90610. (Literary Taste, Culture & Mass Communication: Vol. 2). 1978. lib. bdg. 49.00x (ISBN 0-914146-45-9). Somerset Hse.

Davison, W. Phillips & Boylan, James. Mass Media: Systems & Effects. LC 74-31000. 245p. 1976. pap. text ed. 10.95x (ISBN 0-03-038896-1). Praeger.

DeFleur, Melvin & Ball-Rokeach, Sandra J. Theories of Mass Communication. 4th ed. (Illus.). 288p. 1981. text ed. 17.50x (ISBN 0-582-28278-0); pap. text ed. 9.95 (ISBN 0-582-28277-2). Longman.

Dennis, Everette, et al. Enduring Issues in Mass Communication. (Mass Communication Ser.). (Illus.). 1978. pap. text ed. 14.95 (ISBN 0-8299-0173-6). West Pub.

Dennis, Everette E. The Media Society: Evidence About Mass Communication in America. 275p. 1978. pap. text ed. write for info. (ISBN 0-697-04304-5). Wm C Brown.

Draves, Pamela, ed. Citizens Media Directory. 1977. pap. 3.50 (ISBN 0-9603466-3-5); 1980 update avail. NCCB.

Ephron, Nora. Scribble Scribble. LC 77-90927. 1978. 8.95 (ISBN 0-394-50125-X). Knopf.

Escarpit, Robert & Bouazis, Charles, eds. Systemes Partiels De Communication: Publications De la Maison Des Sciences De L'homme De Bordeaux - Travaux & Recherches De L'institut De Litterature & De Technique Artistiques De Masse. 1972. pap. 14.50x (ISBN 90-2797-039-4). Mouton.

Eysenck, H. J. & Nias, D. K. Sex, Violence & the Media. LC 78-24699. 1979. pap. 5.95 (ISBN 0-06-090684-7, CN 684, CN). Har-Row.

Fages, Jean Baptiste & Pagano, Christian. Dictionnaire des Media. 364p. (Fr.). 1971. pap. 22.50 (ISBN 0-686-56848-6, M-6626). French & Eur.

Fedler, Fred. An Introduction to the Mass Media. (Illus.). 1978. pap. text ed. 12.95 (ISBN 0-15-543470-5, HC); instructor's manual avail. (ISBN 0-685-87937-2). HarBraceJ.

Fischer, Heinz-Dietrich & Melnik, Stefan R., eds. Entertainment: A Cross-Cultural Examination. 1979. 20.50 (ISBN 0-8038-1945-5); pap. text ed. 12.50x (ISBN 0-8038-8047-2). Hastings.

Fischer, Heinz-Dietrich & Merrill, John C., eds. International & Intercultural Communication. (Humanistic Studies in the Communication Arts). 1976. 24.95 (ISBN 0-8038-3402-0); pap. text ed. 12.50x (ISBN 0-8038-3403-9). Hastings.

Fixx, James F., ed. The Mass Media & Politics. LC 76-183137. (Great Contemporary Issues Ser). (Illus.). 600p. 1971. 35.00 (ISBN 0-405-01291-8, New York Times) (ISBN 0-685-27572-8). Arno.

Francois, William E. Mass Media Law & Regulation. 2nd ed. LC 77-92582. (Law Ser.). 1978. 24.00 (ISBN 0-88244-168-X). Grid Pub.

Frank, Ronald E. & Greenberg, Marshall G. The Public's Use of Television: Who Watches & Why. LC 79-27067. (People & Communication: Vol. 9). (Illus.). 368p. 1980. 24.00 (ISBN 0-8039-1389-3). Sage.

Gamble, Teri K., ed. Intermedia: Communication & Society. LC 79-63912. (Illus.). 1979. pap. text ed. 8.95 (ISBN 0-87716-103-8, Pub. by Moore Pub Co). F Apple.

Gans, Herbert J. Deciding What's News: A Study of CBS Evening News, NBC Nightly News, Newsweek & Time. LC 79-22849. 1980. pap. 5.95 (ISBN 0-394-74354-7, Vin). Random.

Gardner, Carl, ed. Media, Politics, & Culture: A Socialist View. (Communications & Culture). 1979. text ed. 23.00x (ISBN 0-333-23588-6); pap. text ed. 10.50x (ISBN 0-333-23589-4). Humanities.

Gerbner, George, ed. Mass Media Policies in Changing Cultures. LC 77-2399. 1977. 29.50x (ISBN 0-471-01514-8, Pub. by Wiley-Interscience). Wiley.

Gitlin, Todd. The Whole World Is Watching: Mass Media in the Making & Unmaking of the New Left. LC 78-68835. 1980. 14.95 (ISBN 0-520-03889-4). U of Cal Pr.

Glessing, Robert & White, William. Mass Media: The Invisible Environment Revisited. rev. ed. LC 75-44488. (Illus.). 352p. 1976. pap. text ed. 10.95 (ISBN 0-574-22700-8, 13-5700). SRA.

Gordon, George N. The Communications Revolution: A History of Mass Media in the United States. LC 77-3037. (Humanistic Studies in the Communication Arts). 1977. 16.95 (ISBN 0-8038-1218-3); pap. 9.95x (ISBN 0-8038-1219-1). Hastings.

Gordon, Thomas F. & Verna, Mary E. Mass Communication Effects & Processes: A Comprehensive Bibliography, 1950-1975. LC 77-26094. 1978. 22.50x (ISBN 0-8039-0903-9). Sage.

Greenberg, Bradley S. & Parker, Edwin B., eds. Kennedy Assassination & the American Public: Social Communication in Crisis. 1965. 18.75x (ISBN 0-8047-0257-8). Stanford U Pr.

Grunig, James, ed. Decline of the Global Village: How Specialization Is Changing the Mass Media. LC 76-9295. (Illus.). 1976. lib. bdg. 18.95x (ISBN 0-930390-05-9); pap. text ed. 6.95x (ISBN 0-930390-04-0). Gen Hall.

Grupenhoff, John T., ed. National News Media Directory: Medicine-Health, 1980-1981. 222p. Date not set. text ed. 35.00 (ISBN 0-89443-350-4). Aspen Systems.

Gumpert, Gary & Cathcart, Robert, eds. Inter-Media: Interpersonal Communication in a Media World. LC 78-12227. 1979. 9.95x (ISBN 0-19-502505-9). Oxford U Pr.

Hachten, William A. The World News Prism: Changing Media, Clashing Ideologies. 120p. 1981. pap. text ed. 6.50 (ISBN 0-8138-1580-0). Iowa St U Pr.

Hancock, Alan. Planning for Educational Mass Media. LC 76-22496. (Illus.). 1977. text ed. 28.00x (ISBN 0-582-41055-X). Longman.

Hawes, William. The Performer in Mass Media: In Media Professions & in the Community. 1978. 17.50 (ISBN 0-8038-5824-8); pap. text ed. 10.50x (ISBN 0-8038-5825-6). Hastings.

Heintz, Anne C., et al. Mass Media. LC 72-5314. (Communication Education Ser). (Illus.). 240p. (gr. 9-12). 1975. pap. text ed. 3.50 (ISBN 0-8294-0215-2); news input tape, 5 inch reel 6.25 (ISBN 0-685-25012-1). Loyola.

Henderson, Gregory, et al. Public Diplomacy & Political Change: Four Case Studies: Okinawa, Peru, Czechoslovakia, Guinea. LC 72-14204. (Special Studies in International Politics & Government). 1973. 24.50x (ISBN 0-275-28710-6). Irvington.

Herschensohn, Bruce. The Gods of Antenna. 1976. 7.95 (ISBN 0-87000-346-1). Arlington Hse.

Hicks, Ronald G. A Survey of Mass Communication. LC 77-8438. 1977. pap. text ed. 7.95x (ISBN 0-88289-164-2). Pelican.

Holmgren, Rod & Norton, William. The Mass Media Book. 416p. 1972. pap. text ed. 10.95 (ISBN 0-13-559781-1). P-H.

Hood, Stuart. The Mass Media. (Studies in Contemporary Europe). (Orig.). 1973. pap. text ed. 3.00x (ISBN 0-333-12704-8). Humanities.

Hulteng, John L. The News Media: What Makes Them Tick? (Topics in Mass Communications Ser.). 1979. ref. 9.95 (ISBN 0-13-621094-5); pap. 8.95 (ISBN 0-13-621086-4). P-H.

Hulteng, John L. & Nelson, Roy P. Fourth Estate: An Informal Appraisal of the News & Opinion Media. (Illus.). 1971. pap. text ed. 10.95 scp (ISBN 0-06-042988-7, HarpC); instructor's manual avail. (ISBN 0-06-362990-9). Har-Row.

Intl. Mass Media Research Ctr., ed. Marxism & the Mass Media: Towards a Basic Bibliography, Nos. 1-2-3. rev. ed. International Mass Media Research Center. (Illus.). 106p. (Orig.). 1978. pap. 6.00 (ISBN 0-88477-009-5). Intl General.

Jacobson, Howard B., ed. Mass Communications Dictionary: A Reference Work of Common Terminologies for Press, Print, Broadcast, Film, Advertising & Communications Research. Repr. of 1961 ed. lib. bdg. 25.00x (ISBN 0-8371-2124-8, JAMC). Greenwood.

Jaeger, Peter. Mass Media: Our Moving Fingers. (Orig.). 1974. pap. text ed. 4.95 (ISBN 0-89076-000-4); pap. text ed. 3.00 5 or more (ISBN 0-685-51255-X). Educ Impact.

Jensen, Richard J., et al. Rhetorical Perspectives on Communication and Mass Madia. 176p. 1980. pap. text ed. 9.95 (ISBN 0-8403-2258-5, 40225801). Kendall-Hunt.

Jowett, Garth & Linton, James M. Movies As Mass Communication. LC 80-13508. (The Sage Comtext Ser.: Vol. 4). (Illus.). 149p. 1980. 14.00 (ISBN 0-8039-1090-8); pap. 6.95 (ISBN 0-8039-1091-6). Sage.

Kato, Hidetoshi. Japanese Research on Mass Communication: Selected Abstracts. LC 74-81141. (Orig.). 1974. pap. 3.50x (ISBN 0-8248-0345-0, Eastwest Ctr). U Pr of Hawaii.

Katz, Elihu, ed. Mass Media & Social Change. (Sage Studies in International Sociology: Vol. 22). 271p. 1981. 22.50 (ISBN 0-8039-9806-6); pap. 9.95 (ISBN 0-8039-9807-4). Sage.

Kirby, Jack T. Media-Made Dixie: The South in the American Imagination. LC 77-14551. 1978. 15.00 (ISBN 0-8071-0375-6). La State U Pr.

Kirschner, Allen. Film: Readings in the Mass Media. LC 70-158977. 1971. pap. 7.50 (ISBN 0-672-73221-1). Odyssey Pr.

Kraus, Sidney & Davis, Dennis. The Effects of Mass Communication on Political Behavior. LC 76-3480. (Illus.). 1976. 17.95x (ISBN 0-271-01226-9); pap. 8.95x (ISBN 0-271-00501-7). Pa St U Pr.

Labunski, Richard E., ed. The First Amendment Under Siege: The Politics of Broadcast Regulation. LC 80-39675. (Contributions in Political Science Ser.: No. 62). 224p. 1981. lib. bdg. 27.50 (ISBN 0-313-22756-X, LFA/). Greenwood.

Lakshmana Rao, Y. V. The Practice of Mass Communication: Some Lessons from Research. LC 72-79892. (Reports & Papers on Mass Communication, No. 65). 52p. (Orig.). 1973. pap. 3.25 (ISBN 92-3-100946-X, U476, UNESCO). Unipub.

Landes, Burton R. A Study of the International Press & Other Media in the Shaping of Public Opinion: The Sarah Churchill Cause. Bd. with The Making of a Senator, 1974: The Biography of Richard S. Schweiker. pap. 2.50 (ISBN 0-915568-06-3). LC 75-7003. 1979. pap. 2.50 (ISBN 0-915568-05-5). B R Landes.

Laybonrne, Kit & Cianciolo, Pauline, eds. Doing the Media: A Portfolio of Activities, Ideas, & Resources. rev. ed. LC 78-9076. 1978. 15.00 (ISBN 0-89560-027-7); pap. 6.95 (ISBN 0-89560-009-9). Dantree Pr.

Lazarsfeld, Paul F., et al, eds. Communications Research, Nineteen Forty-Eight to Nineteen Forty-Nine. LC 79-7005. (Perennial Works in Sociology Ser.). (Illus.). 1979. Repr. of 1949 ed. lib. bdg. 23.00x (ISBN 0-405-12103-2). Arno.

Lent, John A. Third World Mass Media & Their Search for Modernity: The Case of Commonwealth Caribbean, 1717-1976. LC 75-39110. 405p. 1978. 22.50 (ISBN 0-8387-1896-5). Bucknell U Pr.

Levy, Milton L. Media Awards Handbook. LC 68-24272. 190p. 1980. pap. 20.00 (ISBN 0-910744-03-3). Media Awards.

Lewell, John. Multivision. (Illus.). 251p. 1980. 24.95 (ISBN 0-240-51026-7). Focal Pr.

Lineberry, William P., ed. Mass Communications. (Reference Shelf Ser: Vol. 41, No. 3). 1969. 6.25 (ISBN 0-8242-0108-6). Wilson.

Littell, Joseph F., ed. Coping with the Mass Media. (Illus., Orig.). 1976. pap. text ed. 11.95 scp (ISBN 0-06-384900-3, HarpC). Har-Row.

Lois, George & Pitts, Bill. Art of Advertising: George Lois on Mass Communication. (Illus.). 1977. 55.00 (ISBN 0-8109-0373-3). Abrams.

McAnany, Emile, et al, eds. Structure & Communication: Critical Studies in Mass Media Research. 260p. 1981. 20.95 (ISBN 0-03-057954-6). Praeger.

McCombs, Maxwell E. & Becker, Lee. Using Mass Communication Theory. (Topics in Mass Communications). 1979. pap. 8.95 ref. ed. (ISBN 0-13-939702-7). P-H.

McGarry, K. J., ed. Mass Communications: Selected Readings for Librarians. 243p. 1972. 17.50 (ISBN 0-208-01188-9, Linnet). Shoe String.

McMahon, Michael, ed. Nineteen Hundred Eighty National Media Conference Report. 1980. pap. text ed. 49.95 (ISBN 0-935224-02-5). Larimi Comm.

Martin, L. John & Lambert, Richard D., eds. Role of the Mass Media in American Politics. LC 76-11898. (Annals Ser: No. 427). 200p. 1976. pap. 6.00 (ISBN 0-87761-205-6). Am Acad Pol Soc Sci.

Mattelart, Armand & Siegelaub, Seth, eds. Communications & Class Struggle: Capitalism, Imperialism, Vol. 1. 448p. 1979. pap. 16.95 (ISBN 0-88477-011-7). Intl General.

Media Guide International: Consummer Publications. 1981. 30.00 (ISBN 0-685-76911-9). Directories Intl.

Merrill, John C. & Lowenstein, Ralph L. Media, Messages & Men: New Perspectives in Communication. 2nd ed. 1979. pap. text ed. 10.95x (ISBN 0-582-29008-2). Longman.

Monaco, James. Celebrity: The Media As Image Maker. 1978. pap. 4.95 (ISBN 0-440-50991-2, Delta). Dell.

--Media Culture: TV, Radio, Records, Magazines, Newspaper, & Movies. 1978. pap. 4.95 (ISBN 0-440-59305-0, Delta). Dell.

Murphy, Robert D. Mass Communication & Human Interaction. LC 76-19906. (Illus.). 1976. pap. text ed. 13.95 (ISBN 0-395-24433-1); inst. manual 1.50 (ISBN 0-395-24434-X). HM.

Nair, Basskaran. Mass Media & the Transnational Corporation: A Study of Media-Corporate Relationship & Its Consequencees on the Third World. 180p. 1981. 18.00 (ISBN 9971-69-005-5, Pub. by Singapore U Pr); pap. 9.50 (ISBN 9971-69-022-5, Pub. by Singapore U Pr). Ohio U Pr.

Ohlgren, Thomas H. & Berk, Lynn M. The New Language: A Rhetorical Approach to the Mass Media & Popular Culture. (Series on English Composition). (Illus.). 1977. pap. text ed. 10.95 (ISBN 0-13-615104-3). P-H.

Ohliger, J. The Mass Media in Adult Education. LC 73-80717. (Occasional Papers Ser: No. 18). 1968. pap. text ed. 2.00 (ISBN 0-685-76689-6). Syracuse U Cont Ed.

Olson, David R., ed. Media & Symbols: The Forms of Expression, Communication, & Education. LC 6-16938. (NSSE 73rd Yearbook: Part 1). 560p. 1974. lib. bdg. 10.00 (ISBN 0-226-60114-5). U of Chicago Pr.

Overbeck, Wayne & Pullen, Rick D. Mass Media Law in California. 232p. 1981. pap. text ed. 9.95 (ISBN 0-8403-2373-5, 40237301). Kendall-Hunt.

Owen, Bruce M. Economics & Freedom of Expression: Media Structure & the First Amendment. LC 75-26645. 1975. text ed. 17.50 (ISBN 0-88410-044-8). Ballinger Pub.

Patterson, Thomas E. The Mass Media: How Americans Choose Their President. 220p. 1980. 21.95 (ISBN 0-03-057728-4); pap. 8.95 (ISBN 0-03-057729-2). Praeger.

Pei, Mario. Weasel Words: The Art of Saying What You Don't Mean. LC 76-5524. 1978. 11.95 (ISBN 0-06-013342-2, HarpT). Har-Row.

Pember, Don. Mass Media in America. 3rd ed. 416p. 1981. pap. text ed. 13.95 (ISBN 0-574-22715-6, 13-5715); instr's. guide avail. (ISBN 0-574-22716-4, 13-5716). SRA.

--Mass Media in America. 2nd ed. LC 76-50018. (Illus.). 1977. pap. text ed. 11.95 (ISBN 0-574-22705-9, 13-5705); instr's guide avail. (ISBN 0-574-22706-7, 13-5706). SRA.

Phelan, John M. Disenchantment: Meaning & Morality in the Media. new ed. (Humanistic Studies in the Communication Arts). 178p. 1980. 13.95 (ISBN 0-8038-1572-7, Communication Arts); pap. 8.95x (ISBN 0-8038-1573-5). Hastings.

--Mediaworld: Programming the Public. LC 76-56780. 1977. 8.95 (ISBN 0-8164-9317-0). Continuum.

Race As News. 173p. (Orig.). 1974. pap. 9.25 (ISBN 92-3-101191-X, U508, UNESCO). Unipub.

Read, William H. America's Mass Media Merchants. LC 76-17231. (Illus.). 224p. 1977. 14.00x (ISBN 0-8018-1851-6). Johns Hopkins.

Redd, Lawrence N. Rock Is Rhythm & Blues: The Impact of Mass Media. xviii, 167p. 1974. 7.50 (ISBN 0-87013-180-X). Mich St U Pr.

Reddick, De Witt C. The Mass Media & the School Newspaper. 1976. text ed. 13.95x (ISBN 0-534-00436-9). Wadsworth Pub.

Richstad, Jim & McMillan, Michael, eds. Mass Communication & Journalism in the Pacific Islands: A Bibliography. LC 77-20795. 1978. text ed. 15.00x (ISBN 0-8248-0497-X, Eastwest Ctr). U Pr of Hawaii.

Rissover, F. & Birch, D. Mass Media & the Popular Arts. 12.95x (ISBN 0-07-052950-7, C); pap. 8.95 (ISBN 0-07-052944-2); instructor's manual 5.50 (ISBN 0-07-052944-2). McGraw.

Rivera De Otero, Consuelo. Mass Communication Services: An Analysis (Puerto Rican Government: Radio, Television, & Community Education) LC 76-2025. 206p. (Orig.). 1978. pap. 6.25 (ISBN 0-8477-2731-9). U of PR Pr.

Rivers, William, et al, eds. Aspen Handbook on the Media, 1977-1979 Edition. 6.95 (ISBN 0-686-25999-8). Aspen Inst Human.

Rivers, William L. The Mass Media: Reporting, Writing, Editing. 2nd ed. 644p. 1975. text ed. 20.95 scp (ISBN 0-06-045421-0, HarpC). Har-Row.

Rivers, William L., et al. Responsibility in Mass Communication. 3rd ed. LC 79-3400. 384p. 1981. pap. 5.95 (ISBN 0-06-090832-7, CN 832, CN). Har-Row.

Rivers, William L., et al, eds. Aspen Handbook on the Media: 1977-1979 Edition, a Selective Guide to Research, Organizations, & Publications in Communications. LC 77-14556. (Praeger Special Studies). 1977. 32.50 (ISBN 0-03-023141-8). Praeger.

Rodman, George. Mass Media Issues: Analysis & Debate. 320p. 1981. pap. text ed. 12.95 (ISBN 0-574-22570-6, 13-5570). SRA.

Rubin, Bernard. Media, Politics, & Democracy. (Reconstruction of Society Ser.). (Illus.). 1977. pap. text ed. 5.95x (ISBN 0-19-502008-1). Oxford U Pr.

Rucker, Bryce W. First Freedom. LC 68-11651. (New Horizons in Journalism Ser.). 340p. 1968. 15.00x (ISBN 0-8093-0297-7). S Ill U Pr.

--First Freedom. LC 68-11651. (Arcturus Books Paperbacks). 340p. 1971. pap. 9.95 (ISBN 0-8093-0498-8). S Ill U Pr.

The SACI-EXERN Project in Brazil: An Analytical Case Study. (Reports & Papers on Mass Communication: No. 89). 46p. 1981. pap. 4.00 (ISBN 92-3-101770-5, U1081, UNESCO). Unipub.

Sandford, John. The Mass Media of the German Speaking Countries. 1976. pap. text ed. 6.00x (ISBN 0-8138-0085-4). Iowa St U Pr.

Sandman, Peter M., et al. Media: An Introductory Analysis of American Mass Communication. 2nd ed. 1976. 16.95x (ISBN 0-13-572586-0); pap. text ed. 13.95x (ISBN 0-13-572578-X). P-H.

--Media: An Introductory Analysis of American Masscommunication. 3rd ed. 520p. 1982. 15.95 (ISBN 0-686-76599-0). P-H.

Sandman, Peter S., et al. Media Casebook: An Introductory Reader in American Mass Communications. 2nd ed. 1977. pap. text ed. 10.95 (ISBN 0-13-572453-8). P-H.

Schiller, Herbert I. The Mind Managers. LC 73-6248. 224p. 1973. 9.95 (ISBN 0-8070-0506-1); pap. 4.95 (ISBN 0-8070-0507-X, BP499). Beacon Pr.

Schramm, Wilbur. Mass Media & National Development: The Role of Information in the Developing Countries. LC 64-17003. 1964. 15.00x (ISBN 0-8047-0227-6); pap. 4.95 (ISBN 0-8047-0228-4, SP117). Stanford U Pr.

--Men, Messages & Media: A Look at Human Communication. 1973. pap. text ed. 10.50 scp (ISBN 0-06-045797-X, HarpC). Har-Row.

Schramm, Wilbur & Rivers, William L. Responsibility in Mass Communication. 3rd ed. LC 68-28216. 1969. 14.95x (ISBN 0-06-013594-8, HarpT). Har-Row.

Schramm, Wilbur, ed. Mass Communications. 2nd ed. LC 60-8343. 1960. pap. 12.95 (ISBN 0-252-00015-3). U of Ill Pr.

Schramm, Wilbur & Roberts, Donald F., eds. Process & Effects of Mass Communications. rev. ed. LC 74-152000. 1971. 20.00x (ISBN 0-252-00197-4). U of Ill Pr.

Schrank, Jeffrey. Understanding Mass Media. LC 75-20876. (Illus.). 260p. 1976. pap. 10.00 (ISBN 0-8174-2902-6). Amphoto.

Seldes, Gilbert. New Mass Media. 1968. pap. 2.50 (ISBN 0-8183-0185-6). Pub Aff Pr.

Sellers, Leonard & Rivers, William R. Mass Media Issues: Articles & Commentaries. (Illus.). 432p. 1977. pap. text ed. 13.95 (ISBN 0-13-559500-2). P-H.

Servan-Schreiber, Jean-Jacques. The Power to Inform. LC 73-15822. 444p. 1974. 9.95 (ISBN 0-07-056317-9, GB). McGraw.

Severin, Werner J. & Tankard, James W. Communication Theories: Origins, Methods, Uses. (Humanistic Studies in the Communication Arts). (Illus.). 1979. 15.95 (ISBN 0-8038-1274-4); pap. text ed. 8.95 (ISBN 0-8038-1275-2). Hastings.

Silbermann, Alphons. La Sociologie Des Communications De Masse: Tendences Actuelles De la Recherche et Bibliographie. (Current Sociology-la Sociologie Contemporaine: No. 18-3). 1973. pap. 14.00x (ISBN 90-2797-175-7). Mouton.

Simmons, Steven J. The Fairness Doctrine & the Media. LC 77-85740. 1978. 18.95 (ISBN 0-520-03585-2). U of Cal Pr.

Smith, Howard K., et al. News Media: A Service & a Force. Viser, Festus J., ed. LC 78-113701. (M. L. Seidman Town Hall Lecture Ser.). 1970. 5.00 (ISBN 0-87870-003-X). Memphis St Univ.

Sobel, Lester A., ed. Media Controversies. 1980. 17.50 (ISBN 0-87196-242-X, Checkmark). Facts on File.

Spragens, William C. The Presidency & the Mass Media in the Age of Television. LC 78-51149. 1978. pap. text ed. 11.75 (ISBN 0-8191-0476-0). U Pr of Amer.

Stein, Robert. Media Power: Who Is Shaping Your Picture of the World? Orig. Title: Overexposed Society. 1972. 9.95 (ISBN 0-395-14006-4). HM.

Steinberg, Charles S. The Information Establishment: Our Government & the Media. 1980. 15.95 (ISBN 0-8038-3424-1); pap. text ed. 8.95x (ISBN 0-8038-3426-8). Hastings.

Steinberg, Charles S., ed. Mass Media & Communication. 2nd rev. & enl. ed. (Studies in Public Communication). 650p. 1972. pap. text ed. 8.50x (ISBN 0-8038-4663-0). Hastings.

Stephenson, William. Play Theory of Mass Communication. LC 66-23700. 1967. 12.00x (ISBN 0-226-77274-8). U of Chicago Pr.

Sterling, Christopher & Haight, T. The Mass Media: Aspen Institute Guide to Communication Industry Trends. 11.95 (ISBN 0-686-26000-7). Aspen Inst Human.

Sterling, Christopher H. & Haight, Timothy. The Mass Media: Aspen Guide to Communication Industry Trends. LC 76-24370. (Special Studies). 1978. text ed. 34.95 (ISBN 0-275-24020-7). Praeger.

Stevens, John D. & Porter, William E. The Rest of the Elephant: Perspectives on the Mass Media. 224p. 1973. pap. 8.95 (ISBN 0-13-774588-5). P-H.

Stonecipher, Harry W. & Trager, Robert. The Mass Media & the Law in Illinois. LC 76-25463. (New Horizons in Journalism Ser.). 256p. 1976. 14.95x (ISBN 0-8093-0788-X). S Ill U Pr.

Stott, William. Documentary Expression & Thirties America. (Illus.). 275p. 1973. 16.95 (ISBN 0-19-501717-X). Oxford U Pr.

--Documentary Expression & Thirties America. LC 73-82676. (Illus.). 441p. 1976. pap. 6.95 (ISBN 0-19-502099-5, 474, GB). Oxford U Pr.

Summers, Harrison B., et al. Broadcasting & the Public. 2nd ed. 1978. text ed. 19.95x (ISBN 0-534-00532-2). Wadsworth Pub.

Tebbel, John. The Media in America. 1976. pap. 2.50 (ISBN 0-451-61451-8, ME1451, Ment). NAL.

Thompson, Denys, ed. Discrimination & Popular Culture. 1973. text ed. 9.00x (ISBN 0-435-18883-6). Heinemann Ed.

Tunstall, Jeremy. The Media Are American. LC 77-2581. 1977. 17.50x (ISBN 0-231-04292-2); pap. 8.00x (ISBN 0-231-04293-0). Columbia U Pr.

Valdes, Joan & Crow, Jeanne, eds. The Media Works. vi, 282p. 1973. pap. text ed. 7.90 (ISBN 0-8278-0219-6); tchrs. manual 1.35x (ISBN 0-8278-0221-8); student logbook 2.85x (ISBN 0-8278-0218-8). Pflaum-Standard.

Voelker, Francis & Voelker, Ludmila. Mass Media: Forces in Our Society. 3rd ed. (Illus.). 1978. pap. text ed. 10.95 (ISBN 0-15-555122-1, HC); instructor's manual avail. (ISBN 0-15-555123-X). HarBraceJ.

Vogel, R. A. & Krabbe, M. Mass Communications. LC 76-44136. (Ser. in Speech Communication). 1977. pap. text ed. 5.95 (ISBN 0-8465-7601-5); instr's. guide 3.95 (ISBN 0-8465-7607-4). Benjamin-Cummings.

Volgyes, Ivan, ed. Political Socialization in Eastern Europe: A Comparative Framework. LC 72-83575. (Special Studies). 202p. 1975. text ed. 24.95 (ISBN 0-275-09550-9). Praeger.

Wall, C. Edward. Media Review Digest, Vol. 6. 1975-76. 150.00 set (ISBN 0-685-70577-3). Vol. 1 (ISBN 0-87650-076-9). Vol. 2 (ISBN 0-87650-079-3). Pierian.

Wall, C. Edward, et al, eds. Media Review Digest, Vol. 7. 1977. 150.00 (ISBN 0-87650-085-8). Pierian.

--Media Review Digest, Vol. 8. 1978. 150.00 (ISBN 0-87650-095-5). Pierian.

--Media Review Digest, Vol. 5. 1974-75. 150.00 set (ISBN 0-685-57150-5). Vol. 1 (ISBN 0-87650-065-3). Vol. 2 (ISBN 0-87650-066-1). Pierian.

--Media Review Digest, 1973-74, Vol. 2. 1974. 50.00 (ISBN 0-87650-053-X). Pierian.

Wall, Edward C., et al, eds. Media Review Digest, Vol. 9. 1979. 150.00 (ISBN 0-87650-101-3). Pierian.

Wells, Alan, ed. Mass Media & Society. 3rd ed. LC 78-71609. 515p. 1979. pap. text ed. 11.95 (ISBN 0-87484-430-4). Mayfield Pub.

Whale, John. Politics of the Media. LC 77-88395. (Political Issues of Modern Britain). 1977. text ed. 13.00x (ISBN 0-391-00550-2). Humanities.

Whetmore, Edward J. Mediamerica: Form, Content & Consequence of Mass Communication. 1979. pap. text ed. 12.95x (ISBN 0-534-00604-3). Wadsworth Pub.

White, Llewellyn & Leigh, Robert D. Peoples Speaking to Peoples: A Report on International Mass Communication from the Commission on Freedom of the Press. LC 72-4685. (International Propaganda & Communications Ser.). 131p. 1972. Repr. of 1946 ed. 13.00 (ISBN 0-405-04769-X). Arno.

Whitney, Frederick C. Mass Media & Mass Communications in Society. 488p. 1975. pap. text ed. write for info. (ISBN 0-697-04302-9); instr's manual avail. (ISBN 0-686-67138-4). Wm C Brown.

Wicklander, Dale R. Ethical Survey of Culture Media. 268p. 1978. 10.95x (ISBN 0-89459-041-3). Hunter NC.

Winick, Charles, ed. Deviance & Mass Media. LC 78-16024. (Sage Annual Reviews of Studies in Deviance: Vol. 2). 1978. 20.00x (ISBN 0-8039-1040-1); pap. 9.95x (ISBN 0-8039-1041-X). Sage.

World Communications: A 200 Country Survey of Press, Radio, Television, Film. 533p. 1975. 23.25 (ISBN 92-3-101180-4, UNESCO). Unipub.

Wright, Charles R. Mass Communication: A Sociological Perspective. 2nd ed. 1975. pap. text ed. 4.95x (ISBN 0-394-31883-8). Random.

Yu, Frederick T., ed. Behavioral Sciences & the Mass Media. LC 68-25421. 1968. 9.95 (ISBN 0-87154-983-2). Russell Sage.

Zelmer, A. C. Community Media Handbook. 2nd ed. LC 79-12989. (Illus.). 430p. 1979. 16.50 (ISBN 0-8108-1223-1). Scarecrow.

Zimmerman, Caroline. How to Break into the Media Professions. 216p. 1981. 11.95 (ISBN 0-385-15933-1). Doubleday.

--How to Break into the Media Professions. LC 79-6665. 1981. pap. 5.95 (ISBN 0-385-15934-X, Dolp). Doubleday.

MASS MEDIA–BIBLIOGRAPHY

Blum, Eleanor. Basic Books in the Mass Media: An Annotated, Selected Booklist Covering General Communications, Book Publishing, Broadcasting, Film, Editorial Journalism, & Advertising. 2nd ed. LC 80-11289. 430p. 1980. 22.50 (ISBN 0-252-00814-6). U of Ill Pr.

International Mass Media Research Center. Marxism & the Mass Media: Towards a Basic Bibliography, No. 4-5. (Illus.). 96p. (Orig.). 1976. pap. 6.00 (ISBN 0-88477-007-9). Intl General.

Wall, C. Edward & Northern, Penny B., eds. Multi-Media Reviews Index: 1970. LC 73-173772. 1971. 35.00 ea.; Set. 35.00 (ISBN 0-686-76830-2). Vol. 1 (ISBN 0-87650-023-8). Vol. 2, 1971 (ISBN 0-87650-042-4). Vol. 3, 1972 (ISBN 0-87650-051-3). Pierian.

MASS MEDIA–LAW AND LEGISLATION

Cass, Ronald. Revolution in the Wasteland. 1981. price not set (ISBN 0-8139-0900-7). U Pr of Va.

Cullen, Maurice R., Jr. The Mass Media & the First Amendment: An Introduction to the Issues, Problems, & Practices. 480p. 1981. pap. text ed. price not set (ISBN 0-697-04344-4); write for info. instr's. manual (ISBN 0-697-04346-0). Wm C Brown.

Gillmor, Donald M. & Barron, Jerome A. Mass Communications Law, Cases & Comment. 3rd ed. LC 79-15306. (American Casebook Ser.). 1008p. 1979. text ed. 21.95 (ISBN 0-8299-2050-1). West Pub.

Goodale, James C. Communications Law Nineteen Eighty Course Handbook, 2 vols. LC 80-83536. (Nineteen Eighty-Nineteen Eighty-One Patents, Copyrights, Trademarks, & Literary Property Course Handbook Ser. Subscription). 1402p. 1980. pap. text ed. 40.00 (ISBN 0-686-75084-5, G6-3680). PLI.

Lawrence, John S. & Timberg, Bernard, eds. Fair Use & Free Inquiry: Copyright Law & the New Media. (Communication & Information Science Ser.). 1980. 32.50 (ISBN 0-89391-028-7). Ablex Pub.

Pember, Don R. Mass Media Law. 2nd ed. 500p. 1981. text ed. write for info. (ISBN 0-697-04347-9). Wm C Brown.

Smith, Jo Anne, ed. Mass Communications Law Casebook. 302p. (Orig.). 1979. pap. text ed. 7.00 (ISBN 0-89894-033-8). Advocate Pub Group.

MASS MEDIA–MORAL AND RELIGIOUS ASPECTS

Daughters of St. Paul. Media Impact & You. 1981. 2.95 (ISBN 0-8198-4702-X); pap. 1.95 (ISBN 0-686-73820-9). Dghtrs St Paul.

Key, Wilson B. Media Sexploitation. (Illus.). (RL 10). 1977. pap. 2.50 (ISBN 0-451-08453-5, E8453, Sig). NAL.

Mass Media Codes of Ethics & Councils. (Reports & Papers on Mass Communication: Special Issue). 80p. 1980. pap. 4.75 (ISBN 92-3-101715-2, U 1017, UNESCO). Unipub.

Rivers, William L., et al. Responsibility in Mass Communication. 3rd ed. LC 79-3400. 320p. 1980. 14.95 (ISBN 0-06-013594-8, HarpT). Har-Row.

Rubin, Bernard, ed. Questioning Media Ethics. 1978. 25.95 (ISBN 0-03-046131-6); pap. 10.95 student ed. (ISBN 0-03-046126-X). Praeger.

Schwantes, Dave. Taming Your TV & Other Media. LC 79-16848. (Orion Ser.). 1979. pap. 2.95 (ISBN 0-8127-0246-8). Review & Herald.

Thayer, Lee, compiled by. Ethics, Morality & the Media: Reflections of American Culture. new ed. (Humanistic Studies in the Communication Arts). 320p. 1980. 21.50 (ISBN 0-8038-1957-9, Communication Arts); pap. text ed. 11.95 (ISBN 0-8038-1958-7). Hastings.

MASS MEDIA–SOCIAL ASPECTS

Altheide, David L. & Snow, Robert P. Media Logic. LC 78-19646. (SAGE Library of Social Research: No. 89). (Illus.). 256p. 1979. 20.00x (ISBN 0-8039-1296-X); pap. 9.95x (ISBN 0-8039-1297-8). Sage.

Baeher, Helen, ed. Women & Media. LC 80-41424. (Illus.). 150p. 1980. 14.25 (ISBN 0-08-026061-6). Pergamon.

Brown, Charlene J., et al. The Media & the People. LC 77-27977. 1978. pap. 14.95 (ISBN 0-03-019056-8, HoltC). HR&W.

Brown, Ray. Characteristics of Local Media Audiences. 1978. text ed. 28.00x (ISBN 0-566-00218-3, Pub. by Gower Pr England). Renouf.

Casebier, Allen & Casebier, Janet J., eds. Social Responsibilities of the Mass Media. LC 78-58603. 1978. pap. text ed. 10.25 (ISBN 0-8191-0539-2). U Pr of Amer.

Caso, Adolph. Mass Media Vs. the Italian Americans. 262p. 1980. 12.00 (ISBN 0-8283-1737-2). Dante U Am.

Cline, Victor B., ed. Where Do You Draw the Line? An Exploration into Media Violence, Pornography, & Censorship. LC 74-9670. 1974. 1.90 (ISBN 0-8425-0986-0); pap. 1.30 (ISBN 0-8425-0974-7). Brigham.

Cohen, Stanley, ed. The Manufacture of News: Deviance, Social Problem & the Mass Media. rev. ed. LC 81-50585. (Communication & Society: Vol. 3). 506p. 1981. 30.00 (ISBN 0-8039-1636-1); pap. 14.95 (ISBN 0-8039-1637-X). Sage.

Combs, James E. & Mansfield, Michael. Drama in Life: The Uses of Communication in Society. (Humanistic Studies in the Communication Arts). 1976. 19.95 (ISBN 0-8038-1555-7); pap. 10.50x (ISBN 0-8038-1556-5). Hastings.

Curran, James, et al, eds. Mass Communication & Society. LC 78-68700. 478p. 1979. pap. 12.50 (ISBN 0-8039-1193-9). Sage.

Czarra, Fred R. & Heaps, Joseph F. Censorship & the Media: Mixed Blessing or Dangerous Threat. Fraenkel, Jack R., ed. (Crucial Issues in American Government Ser.). (gr. 9-12). 1977. pap. text ed. 4.96 (ISBN 0-205-04910-9, 764910X). Allyn.

Gordon, George N. The Communications Revolution: A History of Mass Media in the United States. LC 77-3037. (Humanistic Studies in the Communication Arts). 1977. 16.95 (ISBN 0-8038-1218-3); pap. 9.95x (ISBN 0-8038-1219-1). Hastings.

Gordon, Robbie. We Interrupt This Program... A Citizen's Guide to Using the Media for Social Change. LC 79-624735. (Illus., Orig.). 1978. pap. 6.00x (ISBN 0-934210-03-9). Citizen Involve.

Gordon, Thomas F. & Verna, Mary E. Mass Communication Effects & Processes: A Comprehensive Bibliography, 1950-1975. LC 77-26094. 1978. 22.50x (ISBN 0-8039-0903-9). Sage.

Grunig, James, ed. Decline of the Global Village: How Specialization Is Changing the Mass Media. LC 76-9295. (Illus.). 1976. lib. bdg. 18.95x (ISBN 0-930390-05-9); pap. text ed. 6.95x (ISBN 0-930390-04-0). Gen Hall.

Hollander, Gayle D. Soviet Political Indoctrination: Developments in Mass Media & Propaganda Since Stalin. LC 70-163927. (Special Studies in International Politics & Government). 1972. 34.50x (ISBN 0-275-28202-3). Irvington.

Kato, Hidetoshi. Japanese Research on Mass Communication: Selected Abstracts. LC 74-81141. (Orig.). 1974. pap. 3.50x (ISBN 0-8248-0345-0, Eastwest Ctr). U Pr of Hawaii.

Kaufmann, Walter. Without Guilt & Justice. 288p. 1975. pap. 3.25 (ISBN 0-440-56128-0, Delta). Dell.

Klapper, Joseph T. Effects of Mass Communication. LC 60-14402. 1960. text ed. 14.95 (ISBN 0-02-917380-9). Free Pr.

Kline, F. Gerald & Tichenor, Phillip J., eds. Current Perspectives in Mass Communication Research. LC 72-84051. (Sage Annual Reviews of Communication Research Ser.: Vol. 1). 320p. 1974. 22.50 (ISBN 0-8039-0171-2); pap. 9.95 (ISBN 0-8039-0493-2). Sage.

Koppett, Leonard. Sports Illusion, Sports Reality: A Reporter's View of Sports, Journalism, & Society. 288p. 1981. 12.95 (ISBN 0-395-31297-3). HM.

Lee, Chin-Chuan. Media Imperialism Reconsidered: The Homogenizing of Television Culture. LC 80-16763. (People & Communication Ser.: Vol. 10). (Illus.). 276p. 1980. 22.00 (ISBN 0-8039-1495-4). Sage.

--Media Imperialism Reconsidered: The Homogenizing of Television Culture. LC 80-16763. (People & Communication Ser.: Vol. 10). (Illus.). 276p. 1980. pap. 9.95 (ISBN 0-8039-1496-2). Sage.

Lineberry, William P., ed. Mass Communications. (Reference Shelf Ser: Vol. 41, No. 3). 1969. 6.25 (ISBN 0-8242-0108-6). Wilson.

MacKuen, Michael B. & Coombs, Steven L. More Than News: Media Power in Public Affairs. LC 81-183. (People & Communication Ser.: Vol. 12). 232p. 1981. 20.00 (ISBN 0-8039-1575-6); pap. 9.95 (ISBN 0-8039-1576-4). Sage.

McQuail, D. Towards a Sociology of Mass Communications. 1969 (97480). pap. text ed. 2.45x (ISBN 0-686-66487-6). Macmillan.

A Manual on Mass Media in Population & Development. (Illus.). 1978. pap. 7.00 (ISBN 92-3-101439-0, U820, UNESCO). Unipub.

Marnell. The Right to Know: Media & the Common Good. 1973. 6.95 (ISBN 0-8164-9139-9). Continuum.

Mass Media in Society: The Need of Research. (Reports & Papers on Mass Communication Ser). (Orig.). 1970. pap. 2.50 (ISBN 92-3-100953-2, U372, UNESCO). Unipub.

Mattelart, Armand. Mass Media, Ideologies & the Revolutionary Movement. (Marxist Theory & Contemporary Capitalism Ser.: No. 30). 288p. 1980. text ed. 32.50x (ISBN 0-391-01777-2). Humanities.

Mendelsohn, Harold. Mass Entertainment. 1966. pap. 3.45 (ISBN 0-8084-0218-8, B38). Coll & U Pr.

Merrill, John C. & Lowenstein, Ralph L. Media, Messages & Men: New Perspectives in Communication. 2nd ed. 1979. pap. text ed. 10.95x (ISBN 0-582-29008-2). Longman.

Midura, Edmund M., ed. Blacks & Whites: The Urban Communication Crisis. LC 70-148676. Orig. Title: Why Aren't We Getting Through? (Illus.). 12.50 (ISBN 0-87491-312-8); pap. 6.95 (ISBN 0-87491-316-0). Acropolis.

Morin, Violette. L' Ecriture De Presse: A Propos Du Voyage De N. Khrouchtchev En France. 1969. pap. 12.75x (ISBN 0-686-21817-5). Mouton.

Nord, David P. Newspapers & New Politics: Midwestern Municipal Reform. Berkhofer, Robert, ed. (Studies in American History & Culture: No. 27). 1981. 31.95 (ISBN 0-8357-1168-4, Pub. by UMI Res Pr). Univ Microfilms.

Packard, Vance. Hidden Persuaders. rev. ed. 1981. pap. 3.95 (ISBN 0-671-83572-6). PB.

Paletz, David L. & Entman, Robert M. Media Power Politics. 304p. 1981. 15.00 (ISBN 0-02-923650-9). Macmillan.

Peterson, Theodore, et al. What's News: The Media in American Society. Abel, Elie, ed. LC 81-81414. (Orig.). 1981. pap. 7.95 (ISBN 0-917616-41-3). Inst Contemporary.

Piepe, Anthony, et al. Mass Media & Cultural Relationships. 184p. 1977. text ed. 28.00x (ISBN 0-566-00161-6, Pub. by Gower Pub Co England). Renouf.

Rein, Irving J. Rudy's Red Wagon: Communication Strategies in Contemporary Society. 160p. 1972. pap. 5.95x (ISBN 0-673-07623-7). Scott F.

Rohrer, Daniel M. Mass Media, Freedom of Speech, & Advertising: A Study in Communication Law. 1979. text ed. 24.95 (ISBN 0-8403-1988-6, 40198801). Kendall-Hunt.

Rubin, Bernard. Media, Politics, & Democracy. (Reconstruction of Society Ser.). (Illus.). 1977. pap. text ed. 5.95x (ISBN 0-19-502008-1). Oxford U Pr.

Rubin, Bernard, ed. Small Voices & Great Trumpets: Minorities & the Media. 295p. 1980. 24.95 (ISBN 0-03-056973-7); pap. 9.95 (ISBN 0-03-056972-9). Praeger.

Seiden. Who Controls the Mass Media. LC 73-90128. 1975. text ed. 10.00x (ISBN 0-465-09181-4). Basic.

Stein, Jay W. Mass Media, Education, & a Better Society. LC 79-11517. 1979. 17.95x (ISBN 0-88229-310-9). Nelson-Hall.

Strouse, James C. The Mass Media, Public Opinion & Public Policy Analysis. (Political Science Ser). 320p. 1975. text ed. 12.95 (ISBN 0-675-08701-5). Merrill.

Thayer, Lee, compiled by. Ethics, Morality & the Media: Reflections of American Culture. new ed. (Humanistic Studies in the Communication Arts). 320p. 1980. 21.50 (ISBN 0-8038-1957-9, Communication Arts); pap. text ed. 11.95 (ISBN 0-8038-1958-7). Hastings.

Tuchman, Gaye, et al, eds. Hearth & Home: Images of Women in the Mass Media. 1978. text ed. 16.95x (ISBN 0-19-502351-X); pap. text ed. 5.95x (ISBN 0-19-502352-8). Oxford U Pr.

Tunstall, Jeremy & Walker, David. Media Made in California: Hollywood, Politics, & the News. (Illus.). 224p. 1981. 15.95 (ISBN 0-19-502922-4). Oxford U Pr.

Tunstall, Jeremy, ed. Media Sociology: A Reader. LC 77-125598. 1970. 15.00 (ISBN 0-252-00126-5). U of Ill Pr.

MASS MEDIA–STUDY AND TEACHING

Katzen, May. Mass Communication: Teaching & Studies at University. 278p. 1975. pap. text ed. 17.00 (ISBN 92-3-101158-8, U369, UNESCO). Unipub.

Media Studies in Education. (Reports & Papers on Mass Communication: No. 80). (Illus.). 1978. pap. 4.00 (ISBN 92-3-101446-3, U775, UNESCO). Unipub.

Mercer, John. The Informational Film. LC 80-54273. (Illus.). 200p. Date not set. pap. text ed. 6.00x (ISBN 0-87563-197-5). Stipes.

Training for Mass Communication. (Reports & Papers on Mass Communication: No. 73). 44p. 1975. pap. 2.50 (ISBN 92-3-101234-7, U684, UNESCO). Unipub.

Yarrington, Roger, ed. Using Mass Media for Learning. 1979. 7.50 (ISBN 0-87117-087-6). Am Assn Comm Jr Coll.

MASS MEDIA–AFRICA

Mass Media in an African Context: An Evaluation of Senegal's Pilot Project. (Reports & Papers on Mass Communication, No. 69). 53p. (Orig.). 1974. pap. 2.50 (ISBN 92-3-101138-3, U370, UNESCO). Unipub.

Reporting Southern Africa. 168p. 1981. pap. 10.50 (ISBN 92-3-101700-4, U1097, UNESCO). Unipub.

Sussman, Leonard D. Mass News Media & the Third World Challenge. LC 77-93880. (The Washington Papers, No. 46). 80p. 1977. 4.00x (ISBN 0-8039-0951-9). Sage.

Vandi, Abdulai. A Model of Mass Communications & National Development: A Liberian Perspective. LC 79-89253. 1979. pap. text ed. 9.00 (ISBN 0-8191-0812-X). U Pr of Amer.

MASS MEDIA–CHINA

Whiting, Allen S. Chinese Domestic Politics & Foreign Policy in the 1970s. LC 78-31865. (Michigan Papers in Chinese Studies: No. 36). (Orig.). 1979. pap. text ed. 4.00 (ISBN 0-89264-036-7). U of Mich Ctr Chinese.

MASS MEDIA–INDIA

Malik, Amita. India Watching: The Media Game. 1978. 9.50x (ISBN 0-8364-0167-0). South Asia Bks.

Mullick, K. S. Tangled Tapes: The Inside Story of Indian Broadcasting. LC 74-901171. 1974. 7.50x (ISBN 0-88386-496-7). South Asia Bks.

Vajpeyi, Dhirenda K. Modernization & Social Change in India. 1979. 20.00x (ISBN 0-8364-0565-X, Pub. by Manohar India). South Asia Bks.

MASS MEDIA–RUSSIA

Harasymiw, Bohdan, ed. Education & the Mass Media in the Soviet Union & Eastern Europe. LC 75-19789. (Special Studies). 1976. text ed. 24.95 (ISBN 0-275-56170-4). Praeger.

Hollander, Gayle D. Soviet Political Indoctrination: Developments in Mass Media & Propaganda Since Stalin. LC 70-163927. (Special Studies in International Politics & Government). 1972. 34.50x (ISBN 0-275-28202-3). Irvington.

Mickiewicz, Ellen. Media & the Russian Public. 170p. 1981. 19.95 (ISBN 0-03-057681-4); pap. 8.95 (ISBN 0-03-057679-2). Praeger.

MASS MEDIA AND CHILDREN

see also Moving-Pictures and Children; Television and Children

Cohen, Monroe D. & Rice, Susan, eds. Children Are Centers for Understanding Media. LC 72-92022. (Illus., Orig.). 1978. Repr. of 1973 ed. 3.95x (ISBN 0-87173-017-0). ACEI.

MASS MEDIA IN RELIGION

see also Radio in Religion; Television in Religion

Jackson, B. F., Jr., compiled by. You & Communication in the Church. LC 74-78042. 1974. 5.95 (ISBN 0-87680-350-8). Word Bks.

Robertson, Pat & Buckingham, Jamie. Shout It from the Housetops: The Story of the Founder of the Christian Broadcasting Network. LC 72-76591. 248p. 1972. pap. 2.95 (ISBN 0-88270-097-9). Logos.

MASS MEDICAL SCREENING

see Medical Screening

MASS PSYCHOLOGY

see Social Psychology

MASS SCREENING, MEDICAL

see Medical Screening

MASS SOCIETY

see also Mass Media; Popular Culture

Arato, Andrew, et al. The Essential Frankfurt School Reader. 1978. 17.50 (ISBN 0-916354-30-X); pap. 7.95 (ISBN 0-916354-31-8). Urizen Bks.

Fontenay, Charles L. Epistle to the Babylonians: An Essay on the Natural Inequality of Man. LC 68-9778. 1969. 12.50x (ISBN 0-87049-088-5). U of Tenn Pr.

Halebsky, S. Mass Society & Political Conflict. LC 75-18118. (Illus.). 320p. 1976. 29.95 (ISBN 0-521-20541-7); pap. 9.95x (ISBN 0-521-09884-X). Cambridge U Pr.

Krooth, Richard, ed. The Dimensions of Mass Society. 1978. pap. 8.50 (ISBN 0-939074-03-6). Harvest Pubns.

Millas, Jorge. The Intellectual & Moral Challenge of Mass Society. Parent, David J., tr. from Span. LC 77-71315. (Illinois Language & Culture Ser: Vol. 3). 1977. 16.50 (ISBN 0-8357-0199-9, IS-00021, Pub. by Applied Literature Press). Univ Microfilms.

Schiffer, Irvine. Charisma: A Psychoanalytic Look at Mass Society. LC 72-95816. 192p. 1974. pap. 3.95 (ISBN 0-02-927890-2). Free Pr.

MASS SPECTROMETRY

see also Calutron; Molecular Spectra; Time-Of-Flight Mass Spectrometry

Ahearn, Arthur J., ed. Trace Analysis by Mass Spectrometry. 1972. 60.00 (ISBN 0-12-044650-2). Acad Pr.

American Society for Hospital Engineering. Mass Spectrometer Respiratory Monitoring Systems. LC 79-26957. (Illus., Orig.). 1980. pap. 8.75 (ISBN 0-87258-279-5, 1167). Am Hospital.

Analysis of Drugs & Metabolites by Gas Chromatography - Mass Spectometry: Natural, Pyrolytic & Metabolic Products of Tobacco & Marijuana, Vol. 7. 1980. 69.50 (ISBN 0-8247-6861-2). Dekker.

Ausloos, Pierre J., ed. Ion-Molecule Reactions in the Gas Phase. LC 66-28609. (Advances in Chemistry Ser: No. 58). 1966. 26.00 (ISBN 0-8412-0059-9). Am Chemical.

Beckey, H. D. Field Ionization & Field Desorption Mass Spectroscopy. 1978. text ed. 53.00 (ISBN 0-08-020612-3). Pergamon.

--Field Ionization Mass Spectrometry. LC 79-146601. 1971. 52.00 (ISBN 0-08-017557-0). Pergamon.

--Principles of Field Ionization & Field Desorption Mass Spectrometry. LC 77-33014. 1978. text ed. 52.00 (ISBN 0-686-67953-9). Pergamon.

Benninghoven, A., et al, eds. Secondary Ion Mass Spectrometry SIMS-II: Proceedings of the International Conference on Secondary Ion Mass Spectrometry. LC 79-23997. (Springer Ser. in Chemical Physics: Vol. 9). (Illus.). 298p. 1980. 30.00 (ISBN 3-540-09843-7). Springer-Verlag.

Beynon, J. H. & Williams, A. E. Mass & Abundance Tables for Use in Mass Spectrometry. 1963. 78.00 (ISBN 0-444-40044-3). Elsevier.

Beynon, J. H., et al. The Mass Spectra of Organic Molecules. (Illus.). 1968. 73.25 (ISBN 0-444-40046-X). Elsevier.

Binks, R., et al. Tables for Use in High Resolution Mass Spectrometry: Incorporating Chemical Formulae from Mass Determinations. (Eng., Fr., & Ger.). 97.00 (ISBN 0-85501-026-6). Heyden.

Budde, William L. & Eichelberger, James W., eds. Organics Analysis Using Gas Chromatography-Mass Spectrometry: A Techniques & Procedures Manual. LC 79-88484. (Illus.). 1979. 24.00 (ISBN 0-250-40318-8). Ann Arbor Science.

Chapman, J. R. Computers in Mass Spectroscopy. 1978. 40.50 (ISBN 0-12-168750-3). Acad Pr.

Charalambous, J. Mass Spectrometry of Metal Compounds. 320p. 1975. 34.95 (ISBN 0-408-70678-3). Butterworth.

Cooks, R. G., et al. Metastable Ions. LC 72-97419. 312p. 1973. 49.00 (ISBN 0-444-41119-4). Elsevier.

Cornu, A. Compilation of Mass Spectral Data, 2 vols. Massot, R., ed. 1975. Vol. 1. 73.00 (ISBN 0-85501-086-X); Vol. 2. 135.00 (ISBN 0-85501-087-8); Set. 187.00 (ISBN 0-85501-088-6). Heyden.

Daly, N. R., ed. Advances in Mass Spectrometry, Vol. 7 In 2 Parts. 1977. 339.00 (ISBN 0-85501-305-2). Heyden.

Das, K. G. Organic Mass Spectrometry. 1981. 25.00x (ISBN 0-686-72958-7, Pub. by Oxford & IBH India). State Mutual Bk.

Dawson, P. H. Quadrupole Mass Spectrometry & Its Applications. 1976. 66.00 (ISBN 0-444-41345-6). Elsevier.

De Galan, L. Analytical Spectrometry. (Illus.). 1981. text ed. 29.50 (ISBN 0-9960017-1-9, Pub. by A Hilger England). Heyden.

Derrick. Field Ionization & Field Desorption Mass Spectrometry. 1978. write for info. (ISBN 0-685-84731-4). Elsevier.

Drewes, S. E. Chroman & Related Compounds. LC 73-84458. (Progress in Mass Spectrometry: Vol. 2). (Illus.). 1974. 34.20 (ISBN 3-527-25494-3). Verlag Chemie.

Frigerio, Alberto & Ghisalberti, Emilio L. Mass Spectrometry in Drug Metabolism. LC 76-53013. 532p. 1977. 49.50 (ISBN 0-306-31018-X, Plenum Pr). Plenum Pub.

Gross, Michael L., ed. High Performance Mass Spectrometry: Chemical Applications. LC 78-789. (ACS Symposium Ser.: No. 70). 1978. 28.00 (ISBN 0-8412-0422-5). Am Chemical.

Gudzinowicz, B. J. Analysis of Drugs & Metabolites by Gas Chromatography - Mass Spectometry: Antipsychotic, Antiemetic & Antidepressant Drugs, Vol. 3. 1977. 37.75 (ISBN 0-8247-6586-9). Dekker.

Gudzinowicz, B. J., et al. Fundamentals of Integrated Gc-Ms, Pt.1: Gas Chromatograpghy. (Chromatographic Ser: Vol. 7). Orig. Title: Fundamentals of Integrated Gc-Ms-Gas Chromatography. 1976. 52.50 (ISBN 0-8247-6365-3). Dekker.

Gudzinowicz, Michael J. & Gudzinowicz, Benjamin J. The Analysis of Drugs & Related Compounds by GC-MS: Vol. 1; Respiratory Gases, Volatile Anesthetics, Ethyl Alcohol, & Related Toxicological Materials. 1977. 32.50 (ISBN 0-8247-6576-1). Dekker.

Hamming, Mynard C. & Foster, Norman G. Interpretation of Mass Spectra of Organic Compounds. 1972. 85.50 (ISBN 0-12-322150-1). Acad Pr.

Haque, Rizwanel & Biros, Francis J., eds. Mass Spectrometry & NMR Spectroscopy in Pesticide Chemistry. LC 73-20005. (Environmental Science Research Ser.: Vol. 4). 348p. 1974. 35.00 (ISBN 0-306-36304-6, Plenum Pr). Plenum Pub.

Hill, H. C. Introduction to Mass Spectrometry. 2nd ed. 31.50 (ISBN 0-85501-039-8); soft cover 1973 17.50 (ISBN 0-85501-038-X). Heyden.

Index on Mass Spectral Data. 1969. 50.00 (ISBN 0-686-50147-0, 10-011000-39). ASTM.

International Symposium on Quantitative Mass Spectrometry in Life Sciences, 1st, State University of Ghent Belgium June 16-18 1976. Quantitative Mass Spectrometry in Life Sciences: Proceedings. DeLeenheer, A. P. & Roncucci, Romeo R, eds. LC 77-3404. 1977. 44.00 (ISBN 0-444-41557-2). Elsevier.
International Symposium, 3rd, Amsterdam, Sept. 1976. Analytical Pryolysis: Proceedings. Jones, C. E. & Cramers, C. A., eds. 1977. 53.75 (ISBN 0-444-41558-0). Elsevier.
Jayaram, R. Mass Spectrometry: Theory & Applications. LC 65-25239. 225p. 1966. 29.50 (ISBN 0-306-30237-3, Plenum Pr). Plenum Pub.
Johnstone, R. A. Mass Spectrometry, Vols. 1-4. Incl. Vol. 1. 1968-70 Literature. 1971. 35.00 (ISBN 0-85186-258-6); Vol. 2. 1970-72 Literature. 1973. 37.50 (ISBN 0-85186-268-3); Vol. 3. 1972-74 Literature. 1975. 42.50 (ISBN 0-85186-278-0); Vol. 4. 1974-76 Literature. 1977. 56.25 (ISBN 0-85186-288-8). Am Chemical.
--Mass Spectrometry for Organic Chemists. (Illus.). 1972. 32.50 (ISBN 0-521-08381-8); pap. 11.95x (ISBN 0-521-09685-5). Cambridge U Pr.
Kennett, B. H., et al. Mass Spectra of Organic Compounds: Pt. 1. 158p. 1981. 60.00x (ISBN 0-643-00272-3, Pub. by CSIRO Australia). State Mutual Bk.
--Mass Spectra of Organic Compounds: Pt. 2. 158p. 1981. 60.00x (ISBN 0-643-00273-1, Pub. by CSIRO Australia). State Mutual Bk.
--Mass Spectra of Organic Compounds: Pt. 3. 158p. 1981. 60.00x (ISBN 0-686-73075-5, Pub. by CSIRO Australia). State Mutual Bk.
--Mass Spectra of Organic Compounds: Pt. 4. 158p. 1981. 60.00x (ISBN 0-686-73076-3, Pub. by CSIRO Australia). State Mutual Bk.
--Mass Spectra of Organic Compounds: Pt. 5. 158p. 1981. 60.00x (ISBN 0-643-00276-6, Pub. by CSIRO Australia). State Mutual Bk.
--Mass Spectra of Organic Compounds: Pt. 6. 158p. 1981. 60.00x (ISBN 0-643-00277-4, Pub. by CSIRO Australia). State Mutual Bk.
--Mass Spectra of Organic Compounds: Pt. 7. 158p. 1981. 60.00x (ISBN 0-643-02588-X, Pub. by CSIRO Australia). State Mutual Bk.
--Mass Spectra of Organic Compounds: Pt. 8. 158p. 1981. 60.00x (ISBN 0-643-02589-8, Pub. by CSIRO Australia). State Mutual Bk.
Knewstubb, P. F. Mass Spectrometry & Ion-Molecule Reactions. LC 69-16282. (Cambridge Chemistry Textbooks Ser). (Illus.). 1969. 27.50 (ISBN 0-521-07489-4); pap. 11.50x (ISBN 0-521-09563-8). Cambridge U Pr.
Levsen, K. Fundamental Aspects of Organic Mass Spectrometry. (Progress in Mass Spectroscopy Ser.: Vol. 4). (Illus.). 1978. 51.80 (ISBN 0-89573-009-X). Verlag Chemie.
Litzow, M. R. & Spalding, T. R. Mass Spectrometry of Inorganic & Organometallic Compounds. (Physical Inorganic Chemistry Monographs: No. 2). 1973. 90.25 (ISBN 0-444-41047-3). Elsevier.
McDowell, Charles A., ed. Mass Spectrometry. 1963. text ed. 33.50 (ISBN 0-07-044940-6, P&RB). McGraw.
--Mass Spectrometry. LC 78-12265. 652p. 1979. Repr. of 1963 ed. lib. bdg. 36.50 (ISBN 0-88275-761-X). Krieger.
McFadden, W. H. Techniques of Combined Gas Chromatography - Mass Spectrometry: Applications in Organic Analysis. LC 73-6916. 463p. 1973. 34.00 (ISBN 0-471-58388-X, Pub. by Wiley-Interscience). Wiley.
McLafferty, F. W., ed. Mass Spectrometry of Organic Ions. 1963. 71.50 (ISBN 0-12-483650-X). Acad Pr.
McLafferty, Fred W. Interpretation of Mass Spectra. Turro, Nicholas J., ed. LC 80-51179. (Organic Chemistry Ser.). 303p. 1980. text ed. 14.00x (ISBN 0-935702-04-0). Univ Sci Bks.
--Interpretation of Mass Spectra. 2nd corr. ed. 1977. text ed. 23.50 (ISBN 0-8053-7048-X, Adv Bk Prog); pap. text ed. 11.50 (ISBN 0-8053-7047-1). Benjamin-Cummings.
--Mass Spectral Correlations. LC 63-17704. (Advances in Chemistry Ser: No. 40). 1963. pap. 11.00 (ISBN 0-8412-0041-6). Am Chemical.
Majer, J. R. & Berry, M. The Mass Spectrometer. LC 77-15307. (Wykeham Science Ser.: No. 44). 1977. 16.95x (ISBN 0-8448-1171-8). Crane-Russak Co.
Margrave, J. L., ed. Mass Spectrometry in Inorganic Chemistry. LC 68-25995. (Advances in Chemistry Ser: No. 72). 1968. 26.00 (ISBN 0-8412-0073-4). Am Chemical.
Merritt & McEwen. Mass Spectronomy, Pt. A. (Practical Spectroscopy Ser.: Vol. 3). 1979. 38.50 (ISBN 0-8247-6749-7). Dekker.
Ogata, K. & Hayakawa, T., eds. Recent Developments in Mass Spectroscopy. (Illus.). 1970. 57.50 (ISBN 0-8391-0054-X). Univ Park.
Payne, J. P., et al. The Medical & Biological Applications of Mass Spectroscopy. 1979. 31.50 (ISBN 0-12-547950-6). Acad Pr.
Porter, Q. N. & Baides, J. Mass Spectrometry of Heterocyclic Compounds. (General Heterocyclic Chemistry Ser.). 582p. (Orig.). 1971. 39.50 (ISBN 0-471-69504-1). Krieger.
Price, D., ed. Dynamic Mass Spectrometry, Vol. 2. 1971. 73.00 (ISBN 0-85501-054-1). Heyden.
--Dynamic Mass Spectrometry, Vol. 3. 1974. 73.00 (ISBN 0-85501-061-4). Heyden.
Price, D. & Todd, J. F., eds. Dynamic Mass Spectrometry, Vol. 4. 1976. 73.00 (ISBN 0-85501-090-8). Heyden.
--Dynamic Mass Spectrometry, Vol. 5. 1978. 73.00 (ISBN 0-85501-143-2). Heyden.
Price, D. & Williams, J. E., eds. Dynamic Mass Spectrometry, Vol. 1. 1970. 73.00 (ISBN 0-85501-033-9). Heyden.
Quantitative Mass Spectroscopy. 160p. Date not set. 15.00 (ISBN 0-686-76121-9, 13-114000-39). ASTM.
Reed, R. I. Recent Topics in Mass Spectrometry. 366p. 1971. 76.00 (ISBN 0-677-14800-3). Gordon.
Reed, R. I., ed. Modern Aspects of Mass Spectroscopy. LC 68-16994. 389p. 1968. 42.50 (ISBN 0-306-30313-2, Plenum Pr). Plenum Pub.
Reed, Rowland I. Applications of Mass Spectrometry to Organic Chemistry. 1966. 40.50 (ISBN 0-12-585256-8). Acad Pr.
--Ion Production by Electron Impact. 1962. 37.00 (ISBN 0-12-585250-9). Acad Pr.
Roncucci, R. & Van Peteghem, C. Quantitative Mass Spectrometry in Life Sciences, Vol. II. 1979. 53.25 (ISBN 0-444-41760-5). Elsevier.
Schlunegger, U. P. Advanced Mass Spectrometry: Applications in Organic & Analytical Chemistry. (Illus.). 150p. 1980. 32.00 (ISBN 0-08-023842-4). Pergamon.
Sunshine, Irving, ed. Handbook of Mass Spectra of Drugs. 336p. 1981. 59.95 (ISBN 0-8493-3572-8). CRC Pr.
Waller, George R. & Dermer, Otis C. Biochemical Applications of Mass Spectrometry: First Supplementary Volume. 1980. 177.50 (ISBN 0-471-03810-5, Pub. by Wiley-Interscience). Wiley.
Waller, George R., ed. Biochemical Applications of Mass Spectrometry. LC 78-158529. 1972. 107.50 (ISBN 0-471-91900-4, Pub. by Wiley-Interscience). Wiley.
Watson, J. Throck. Introduction to Mass Spectrometry: Biomedical, Environmental & Forensic Applications. LC 74-21989. 249p. 1976. 27.00 (ISBN 0-89004-056-7). Raven.
Wilson, Robert G. Ion Nass Spectra. 442p. (Orig.). 1974. 29.75 (ISBN 0-471-94965-5). Krieger.
Zaretskei, Ze'Ev V. Mass Spectrometry of Steroids. LC 75-38916. 1976. 34.95 (ISBN 0-470-15225-7). Halsted Pr.

MASS TRANSFER

Conductivity - Heat & Mass Transfer - Refrigerants. 1964. pap. 10.75 (ISBN 0-685-99130-X, IIR58, IIR). Unipub.
Cussler, E. L. Multicomponent Diffusion. (Chemical Engineering Monographs: Vol. 3). 1976. 36.75 (ISBN 0-444-41326-X). Elsevier.
DeVries, D. A. & Afgan, N. H., eds. Heat & Mass Transfer in the Biosphere: Pt. 1, Transfer Processes in the Plant Environment. LC 74-28072. (Advances in Thermal Engineering Ser.). 594p. 1975. 28.50 (ISBN 0-470-20985-2). Halsted Pr.
Durst, Franz, et al, eds. Two-Phase Momentum, Heat & Mass Transfer in Chemical, Process, & Energy Engineering Systems, 2 vols. LC 79-12405. (Thermal & Fluid Engineering, Proceedings of the International Centre for Heat & Mass Transfer). (Illus.). 1079p. 1979. text ed. 105.00 set (ISBN 0-89116-154-6, Co-Pub by McGraw International). Hemisphere Pub.
Eckert, E. R. Heat & Mass Transfer. 2nd ed. LC 81-359. 344p. 1981. Repr. lib. bdg. 29.50 (ISBN 0-89874-332-X). Krieger.
Eckert, Ernest R. & Drake, R. M. Analysis of Heat & Mass Transfer. LC 73-159305. (Mechanical Engineering Ser). (Illus.). 832p. 1971. text ed. 26.95 (ISBN 0-07-018925-0, C). McGraw.
Edwards, D. K., et al. Transfer Processes. (Illus.). 1976. Repr. of 1973 ed. text ed. 18.00 (ISBN 0-07-019040-2, C). McGraw.
--Transfer Processes. 2nd ed. LC 78-7883. (Series in Thermal and Fluids Engineering). (Illus.). 1979. text ed. 28.95 (ISBN 0-07-019041-0, C). McGraw.
Geankoplis, Christie J. Mass Transport Phenomena. LC 79-154348. 1980. Repr. of 1972 ed. 26.95 (ISBN 0-9603070-0-1). Geankoplis.
Ghose, T. K., et al, eds. Mass Transfer & Process Control. LC 72-152360. (Advances in Biochemical Engineering Ser.: Vol. 13). (Illus.). 1979. 50.80 (ISBN 0-387-09468-7). Springer-Verlag.
Heat & Mass Transfer During Cooling & Storage of Agricultural Products As Influenced by Natural Convection. 158p. 1980. pap. 32.50 (ISBN 90-220-0728-6, PDC 208, Pudoc). Unipub.
Heat & Mass Transfer in Porous Structures. 1976. pap. 14.50 (ISBN 0-685-99143-1, IIR49, IIR). Unipub.
Heat & Mass Transfer in Refrigeration Systems & in Air Conditioning. 1972. pap. 41.25 (ISBN 0-685-99145-8, IIR52, IIR). Unipub.
International Symposium on Solar Terrestrial Physics. Physics of Solar Planetary Environments: Proceedings, 2 vols. Williams, Donald J., ed. LC 76-29443. (Illus.). 1976. pap. 20.00 (ISBN 0-87590-204-9). Am Geophysical.
Kays, William M. Convective Heat & Mass Transfer. (Mechanical Engineering Ser.). 1966. text ed. 25.50 (ISBN 0-07-033393-9, C). McGraw.
Kays, William M. & Crawford, Michael. Convective Heat & Mass Transfer. 2nd ed. (Mechanical Engineering Ser.). (Illus.). 1980. text ed. 31.50 (ISBN 0-07-033457-9); solutions manual 8.95 (ISBN 0-07-033458-7). McGraw.
Kothandaraman, C. P. & Subramanyan, S. Heat & Mass Transfer Data Book. 3rd ed. 149p. 1977. 13.95 (ISBN 0-470-99078-3). Halsted Pr.
Modern Research Laboratories for Heat & Mass Transfer. (Engineering Laboratories: No. 5). (Illus.). 148p. 1975. pap. 12.25 (ISBN 92-3-101103-0, U389, UNESCO). Unipub.
Quester, George H. The Politics of Nuclear Proliferation. LC 73-8119. 260p. 1973. 18.00x (ISBN 0-8018-1477-4). Johns Hopkins.
Rohsenow, Warren M. & Choi, H. Heat, Mass & Momentum Transfer. (Illus.). 1961. text ed. 27.95 (ISBN 0-13-385187-7). P-H.
Satterfield, Charles N. Mass Transfer in Heterogeneous Catalysis. LC 80-23432. 288p. 1981. Repr. of 1970 ed. text ed. 14.50 (ISBN 0-89874-198-X). Krieger.
Seagrave, Richard C. Biomedical Applications of Heat & Mass Transfer. LC 71-146930. (Illus.). 1971. 8.95 (ISBN 0-8138-0195-8). Iowa St U Pr.
Sherwood, T. K., et al. Mass Transfer. 1975. 25.95 (ISBN 0-07-056692-5, C). McGraw.
Shipes, R. F. Statistical Mechanical Theory of the Electrolytic Transport of Non-Electrolytes. (Lecture Notes in Physics: Vol. 24). 210p. 1974. pap. 14.70 (ISBN 0-387-06566-0). Springer-Verlag.
Spalding, D. Brian & Afgan, Naim H., eds. Heat & Mass Transfer in Metallurgical Systems. LC 80-27193. (International Center for Heat & Mass Transfer Ser.). (Illus.). 758p. 1981. text ed. 85.50 (ISBN 0-89116-169-4). Hemisphere Pub.
Spalding, Dudley B., ed. Progress in Heat & Mass Transfer, Vol. 19, No. 10 - Alan Ede Memorial Issue: Developments in Heat & Mass Transfer. 1977. pap. 32.00 (ISBN 0-08-021285-9). Pergamon.
Styrikovich, M. A., et al. Heat & Mass Transfer Source Book: Fifth All-Union Conference, Minsk, 1976. LC 77-22337. 1977. 42.95 (ISBN 0-470-99234-4). Halsted Pr.
Treybal, Robert E. Mass Transfer Operations. 3rd ed. (Chemical Engineering Ser.). (Illus.). 1979. text ed. 32.50x (ISBN 0-07-065176-0, C). McGraw.
Welty, James R., et al. Fundamentals of Momentum, Heat & Mass Transfer. 2nd ed. LC 76-16813. 897p. 1976. text ed. 36.95 (ISBN 0-471-93354-6). Wiley.
Wilcox, W. R., ed. Chemical Vapor Transport Secondary Nucleation & Mass Transfer in Crystal Growth. (Preparation & Properties of Solid State Materials Ser.: Vol. 2). 192p. 1976. 35.00 (ISBN 0-8247-6330-0). Dekker.
Zaric, Z., ed. Heat & Mass Transfers in Flows with Separated Regions. LC 72-85858. 232p. 1975. pap. text ed. 29.00 (ISBN 0-08-017156-7). Pergamon.

MASS TRANSIT

see Local Transit

MASSACHUSET LANGUAGE

Trumbull, James H. Natick Dictionary. Repr. of 1903 ed. 29.00 (ISBN 0-403-03656-9). Scholarly.
Wood, William. New Englands Prospect. LC 68-54670. (English Experience Ser.: No. 68). 104p. 1968. Repr. of 1634 ed. 16.00 (ISBN 90-221-0068-5). Walter J Johnson.
--New England's Prospect. Vaughan, Alden T., ed. LC 76-45051. (Commonwealth Ser: Vol. 3). (Illus.). 1977. 12.50x (ISBN 0-87023-226-6). U of Mass Pr.
--Wood's New England Prospect. Colburn, Jeremiah, ed. 1966. 19.00 (ISBN 0-8337-3864-X). B Franklin.

MASSACHUSETTS

see also names of cities, counties, towns, etc. in Massachusetts

Bacon, E. M., ed. Acts & Laws, of the Commonwealth of Massachusetts, 1780-1797: With Supplements 1780-1784, 13 vols. LC 74-19617. Repr. of 1896 ed. Set. 790.00 (ISBN 0-404-12439-9). AMS Pr.
Conuel, Thomas. Accidental Wilderness. (Orig.). 1981. pap. write for info. Greene.
Jennison, Keith. To Massachusetts with Love. 1970. pap. 4.95 (ISBN 0-911764-07-0). Durrell.
Koehler, Margaret. Recipes from the Portuguese of Provincetown. LC 72-93260. (Illus.). 128p. (Orig.). 1973. pap. 4.95 (ISBN 0-85699-060-4). Chatham Pr.
Massachusetts. 33.00 (ISBN 0-89770-097-X). Curriculum Info Ctr.
Sherman, Robert M. & Sherman, Ruth W. Vital Records of Marshfield, Massachusetts to the Year 1850. LC 73-85851. 491p. 1969. Repr. of 1969 ed. 13.00x (ISBN 0-930272-04-8). RI Mayflower.

MASSACHUSETTS–CHURCH HISTORY

Andrews, S. M. Daniel Hix & the First Christian Church of Dartmouth Mass. 1780-1880. Smith, Leonard H., Jr., ed. LC 78-69710. 1978. Repr. of 1880 ed. 25.00 (ISBN 0-932022-12-X). L H Smith.
Meyer, Jacob C. Church & State in Massachusetts from 1740 to 1833. LC 68-25043. 1968. Repr. of 1930 ed. 8.50 (ISBN 0-8462-1169-6). Russell.
Stoever, William K. A Faire & Easie Way to Heaven: Covenant Theology & Antinomianism in Early Massachusetts. LC 77-14851. 1978. 20.00x (ISBN 0-8195-5024-8, Pub. by Wesleyan U Pr). Columbia U Pr.

MASSACHUSETTS–DESCRIPTION AND TRAVEL

Drake, Samuel A. Historic Mansions & Highways Around Boston. LC 73-157256. (Illus.). 1971. pap. 3.75 (ISBN 0-8048-0992-5). C E Tuttle.
Dunton, John. Letters Written from New England Sixteen Eighty-Six. (Prince Soc: No. 4). 1966. 22.50 (ISBN 0-8337-0971-2). B Franklin.
Federal Writers' Project. Massachusetts: A Guide to Its Places & People. 675p. 1937. Repr. 49.00 (ISBN 0-403-02150-2). Somerset Pub.
Frado, John, et al. Twenty-Five Ski Tours in Western Massachusetts: Cross Country Trails from Worcester to the New York Border. LC 78-59804. (Illus.). 1978. pap. 4.95 (ISBN 0-912274-94-8). NH Pub Co.
From Our Cabinet. (Massachusetts Historical Society Picture Books Ser.). 1979. 2.00 (ISBN 0-686-28426-7). Mass Hist Soc.
Garland, Joseph E. Eastern Point, 1606-1950. 1971. 14.95 (ISBN 0-87233-019-2). Bauhan.
--The Gloucester Guide, a Retrospective Ramble. LC 72-97361. (Illus.). 1973. 2.95 (ISBN 0-930352-00-9). Nelson B Robinson.
Harris, Stuart K., et al. Flora of Essex County, Massachusetts. Snyder, Dorothy E., ed. 269p. 1975. 12.50 (ISBN 0-87577-049-5). Peabody Mus Salem.
Here We Have Lived. (Massachusetts Historical Society Picture Books Ser.). 1967. 2.00 (ISBN 0-686-21447-1). Mass Hist Soc.
Jane, Nancy. Bicycle Touring in the Pioneer Valley. LC 77-22677. (Illus.). 1978. pap. 3.95 (ISBN 0-87023-248-7). U of Mass Pr.
Lewis, Paul M. Beautiful Massachusetts. 72p. 1980. 14.95 (ISBN 0-915796-57-0); pap. 7.95 (ISBN 0-915796-56-2). Beautiful Am.
More Early Massachusetts Broadsides. (Massachusetts Historical Society Picture Book Ser.). 1981. 3.50 (ISBN 0-686-31819-6). Mass Hist Soc.
Morton, Thomas. New English Canaan or New Canaan. Cantaining an Abstract of New England. LC 76-25966. (English Experience Ser.: No. 140). 192p. 1969. Repr. of 1637 ed. 28.00 (ISBN 90-221-0140-1). Walter J Johnson.
Perry, E. G. A Trip Around Buzzards Bay Shores. LC 76-3145. (Illus.). 1976. Repr. 15.00 (ISBN 0-88492-013-5). W S Sullwold.
Rubin, Cynthia & Rubin, Jerome. Guide to Massachusetts Museums, Historic Houses & Points of Interest. new ed. 126p. (Orig.). 1972. pap. 1.95 (ISBN 0-88278-004-2). Emporium Pubns.
Sadlier, Paul & Sadlier, Ruth. Fifty Hikes in Massachusetts. LC 74-33817. (Illus.). 160p. 1975. pap. 7.95 (ISBN 0-912274-47-6). NH Pub Co.
Sandrof, Ivan. Yesterday's Massachusetts. (Seamann's Historic States Ser.: No. 7). (Illus.). 9.95 (ISBN 0-89530-000-1). E A Seemann.
Tree, Christina. Massachusetts: An Explorer's Guide. rev. ed. (Illus.). 1981. pap. 9.95 (ISBN 0-914378-70-8). Countryman.
Wood, William. New Englands Prospect. LC 68-54670. (English Experience Ser.: No. 68). 104p. 1968. Repr. of 1634 ed. 16.00 (ISBN 90-221-0068-5). Walter J Johnson.

--New England's Prospect. Vaughan, Alden T., ed. LC 76-45051. (Commonwealth Ser: Vol. 3). (Illus.). 1977. 12.50x (ISBN 0-87023-226-6). U of Mass Pr.
--Wood's New England Prospect. Colburn, Jeremiah, ed. 1966. 19.00 (ISBN 0-8337-3864-X). B Franklin.

MASSACHUSETTS-ECONOMIC CONDITIONS

Commerce Clearing House. Guidebook to Massachusettes Taxes: 1982. 1982. 10.00 (ISBN 0-686-76127-8). Commerce.
Douglas, Charles H. The Financial History of Massachusetts. 59.95 (ISBN 0-8490-0167-6). Gordon Pr.
Handlin, Oscar & Handlin, Mary F. Commonwealth: A Study of the Role of Government in the American Economy, Massachusetts, 1774-1861. rev. ed. LC 69-18032. 1969. 16.50x (ISBN 0-674-14690-5, Belknap Pr). Harvard U Pr.
Hannay, Agnes. A Chronicle of Industry on the Mill River. Stein, Leon, ed. LC 77-70501. (Work Ser.). 1977. Repr. of 1936 ed. lib. bdg. 12.00x (ISBN 0-405-10172-4). Arno.
Lincoln, Jonathan T. The City of the Dinner-Pail. Stein, Leon, ed. LC 77-70511. (Work Ser.). 1977. Repr. of 1909 ed. lib. bdg. 15.00x (ISBN 0-405-10181-3). Arno.
Prager, Audrey & Gettleman, Barry. Job Creation in the Community: An Evaluation of Locally Initiated Employment Projects in Massachusetts. 1977. 17.50 (ISBN 0-89011-506-0, EMT 114). Abt Assoc.
State Industrial Directories Corp. Massachusetts State Industrial Directory, 1978. LC 77-94030. (Massachusetts State Industrial Directory Ser.). 1978. 75.00 (ISBN 0-916112-67-5). State Indus Dir.

MASSACHUSETTS-GENEALOGY

The Ancestry of Lydia Foster, Wife of Stephen Lincoln of Oakham, Ma. 3.00 (ISBN 0-940748-01-0). Conn Hist Soc.
Appleton, William S., ed. Boston Births, Baptisms, Marriages & Deaths, 1630-1699 (and) Boston Births, 1700-1800, 2 vols. in 1. LC 78-55591. (Repr. of 1883, 1894 eds.). 1978. 25.00 (ISBN 0-8063-0810-9). Genealog Pub.
Bailey, Frederic W. Early Massachusetts Marriages Prior to 1800, 3 vols. in 1. Bd. with Plymouth County Marriages, 1692-1746. LC 68-28249. 1979. Repr. of 1897 ed. 25.00 (ISBN 0-8063-0008-6). Genealog Pub.
Bentley, Elizabeth P. Index to the Eighteen Hundred Census of Massachusetts. LC 78-58855. 1978. 20.00 (ISBN 0-8063-0817-6). Genealog Pub.
Boltwood, Lucius M. Genealogies of Hadley Families Embracing the Early Settlers of the Towns of Hatfield, South Hadley, Amherst & Granby. LC 79-52942. 1979. Repr. of 1905 ed. 12.50 (ISBN 0-8063-0848-6). Genealog Pub.
Boyer, Carl, 3rd, et al. Brown Families of Bristol Counties, Massachusetts & Rhode Island & Descendants of Jared Talbot. LC 80-68755. (New England Colonial Families: Vol. 1). 219p. 1981. 18.35 (ISBN 0-936124-04-0). C Boyer.
Cook, Lurana H., et al. Provincetown Massachusetts Cemetery Inscriptions. 255p. 1980. 15.00 (ISBN 0-917890-18-3). Heritage Bk.
Davis, William. Bench & Bar of the Commonwealth of Massachusetts, 2 vols. (American Constitutional & Legal History Ser). 1299p. 1974. Repr. of 1895 ed. Set. lib. bdg. 115.00 (ISBN 0-306-70612-1). Da Capo.
Davis, William T. Genealogical Register of Plymouth Families. LC 74-18071. 363p. 1977. Repr. of 1899 ed. 15.00 (ISBN 0-8063-0655-6). Genealog Pub.
Gannett, Henry. A Geographic Dictionary of Massachusetts. LC 78-59121. 1978. Repr. of 1894 ed. 8.50 (ISBN 0-8063-0818-4). Genealog Pub.
Goodwin, Nathaniel. Genealogical Notes, or Contributions to Family History of Some of the First Settlers of Connecticut& Massachusetts. LC 75-76817. 1978. Repr. of 1856 ed. 17.50 (ISBN 0-8063-0159-7). Genealog Pub.
Hammatt, Abraham. The Hammatt Papers: Early Inhabitants of Ipswich, Massachusetts, 1633 to 1700. LC 80-65361. 448p. 1980. Repr. of 1880 ed. 20.00 (ISBN 0-8063-0889-3). Genealog Pub.
Haxtun, Annie A. Signers of the Mayflower Compact. LC 67-28609. 1968. Repr. of 1897 ed. 12.50 (ISBN 0-8063-0173-2). Genealog Pub.
Hills, Leon C. History & Genealogy of the Mayflower Planters & First Comers to Ye Olde Colonie, 2 vols in 1. LC 72-10914. (Illus.). 284p. 1977. Repr. of 1941 ed. 15.00 (ISBN 0-8063-0775-7). Genealog Pub.
Holbrook, Jay M. Southbridge, Massachusetts Vital Records to 1850. LC 80-83873. 316p. 1981. lib. bdg. 55.00 (ISBN 0-931248-09-4). Holbrook Res.
Jackson, Ronald V. & Teeples, Gary R. Massachusetts Census Index 1800. LC 77-85960. (Illus.). lib. bdg. 35.00 (ISBN 0-89593-066-8). Accelerated Index.
--Massachusetts Census Index 1810. LC 77-85961. (Illus.). lib. bdg. 40.00 (ISBN 0-89593-067-6). Accelerated Index.
--Massachusetts Census Index 1820. LC 77-85967. (Illus.). lib. bdg. 46.00 (ISBN 0-89593-068-4). Accelerated Index.
--Massachusetts Census Index 1830. LC 77-85965. (Illus.). lib. bdg. 59.00 (ISBN 0-89593-069-2). Accelerated Index.
--Massachusetts Census Index 1840. LC 77-85964. (Illus.). lib. bdg. 68.00 (ISBN 0-89593-070-6). Accelerated Index.
--Massachusetts Census Index 1850. LC 77-85963. (Illus.). lib. bdg. 80.00 (ISBN 0-89593-071-4). Accelerated Index.
Jackson, Russell A., compiled by. Additions to the Catalogue of Portraits in the Essex Institute, Received Since 1936. (Illus.). 82p. 1950. pap. 7.50 (ISBN 0-88389-022-4). Essex Inst.
McGlenen, Edward W. Boston Marriages from 1700 to 1809, 2 vols. LC 77-82701. 1977. 40.00 (ISBN 0-8063-0784-6). Genealog Pub.
Massachusetts, Secretary of the Commonwealth. List of Persons Whose Names Have Been Changed in Massachusetts, 1780-1892. 2nd ed. LC 75-39364. 522p. 1972. Repr. of 1893 ed. 20.00 (ISBN 0-8063-0498-7). Genealog Pub.
Otis, Amos. Genealogical Notes of Barnstable Families, 2 vols. in 1. LC 79-52085. (With new index). 1979. Repr. of 1890 ed. 25.00 (ISBN 0-8063-0844-3). Genealog Pub.
Peirce, Ebenezer W. Peirce's Colonial Lists: Civil, Military & Professional Lists of Plymouth & Rhode Island Colonies. LC 68-24684. 1968. Repr. of 1881 ed. 12.00 (ISBN 0-8063-0274-7). Genealog Pub.
Pope, Charles H. Pioneers of Massachusetts. LC 65-22478. 1977. Repr. of 1900 ed. 18.50 (ISBN 0-8063-0774-9). Genealog Pub.
A Pride of Quincys. (Massachusetts Historical Society Picture Books Ser.). 1969. 2.50 (ISBN 0-686-21439-0). Mass Hist Soc.
Pro Bono Publico: The Shattucks of Boston. (Massachusetts Historical Society Picture Books Ser.). 1971. 2.50 (ISBN 0-686-21441-2). Mass Hist Soc.
Rider, Raymond A. The Fearings & the Fearing Tavern with the Bumpus Family. (Illus.). 1977. 10.00 (ISBN 0-88492-021-6). W S Sullwold.
Sherman, Robert M., et al, eds. Mayflower Families Through Five Generations--Descendants of the Pilgrims Who Landed at Plymouth, Mass. December 1620: Families James Chilton, Richard More, Thomas Rogers, Vol. 2. LC 75-30145. 1978. 15.00x (ISBN 0-930270-01-0). Mayflower.
Shurtleff, Nathaniel B. Records of Plymouth Colony: Births, Marriages, Deaths, Burials, & Other Records 1633-1689. LC 75-34715. 1979. Repr. of 1857 ed. 15.000 (ISBN 0-8063-0701-3). Genealog Pub.
Smith, Leonard H., Jr., ed. Index to Vital Records of Barnstable Mass. pap. 10.00 (ISBN 0-932022-04-9). L H Smith.
--Index to Vital Records of Chatham, Mass. & Harwich, Mass. pap. 10.00 (ISBN 0-932022-03-0). L H Smith.
Stevens, Cj. The Massachusetts Magazine, Marriages & Death Notices, 1789-1796. LC 71-85631. 1978. 17.50 (ISBN 0-686-27000-2). Polyanthos.
U. S. Bureau of the Census. Heads of Families at the First Census of the United States Taken in the Year 1790: Massachusetts. LC 73-8205. 1973. Repr. of 1908 ed. 25.00 (ISBN 0-8063-0570-3). Genealog Pub.
--Heads of Families, First Census of the United States, 1790: Massachusetts. LC 64-62657. (Illus.). 1961-64. Repr. of 1908 ed. 25.00 (ISBN 0-87152-021-4). Reprint.
Vital Records of Carlisle, Mass. to 1850. Repr. of 1918 ed. 7.50 (ISBN 0-88389-072-0). Essex Inst.
Vital Records of Hamilton, Massachusetts to 1850. Repr. of 1908 ed. 7.50 (ISBN 0-88389-075-5). Essex Inst.
Vital Records of Lynnfield, Massachusetts to 1850. Repr. of 1907 ed. 7.50 (ISBN 0-88389-077-1). Essex Inst.
Vital Records of Saugus, Massachusetts to 1850. Repr. of 1907 ed. 7.50 (ISBN 0-88389-078-X). Essex Inst.
Whitmore, William H. Massachusetts Civil List for the Colonial & Provincial Periods, 1630-1774. LC 68-57949. 1969. Repr. of 1870 ed. 13.50 (ISBN 0-8063-0377-8). Genealog Pub.
Whitney, Charles C. Brown Genealogy. 32p. pap. 3.50 (ISBN 0-685-48638-9). J-B Pubs.

MASSACHUSETTS-HISTORY

Adams, Charles F. Massachusetts, Its Historians & Its History: An Object Lesson. facsimile ed. LC 73-146849. (Select Bibliographies Reprint Ser). Repr. of 1893 ed. 11.00 (ISBN 0-8369-5616-8). Arno.
Babson, John J. History of the Town of Gloucester, (Mass.) Cape Ann: Including the Town of Rockport. (Illus.). 15.00 (ISBN 0-8446-0014-8). Peter Smith.
Ballou, Adin. History of the Hopedale Community, from Its Inception to Its Virtual Submergence in the Hopedale Parish. Heywood, William S., ed. LC 72-2935. (Communal Societies in America Ser.). Repr. of 1897 ed. 14.00 (ISBN 0-404-10701-X). AMS Pr.
Barnes, Thomas G., ed. The Book of the General Lawes & Libertyes Concerning the Inhabitants of the Massachusetts. LC 75-12004. 1975. pap. 5.00 (ISBN 0-87328-066-0). Huntington Lib.
Bradford, Alden. History of Massachusetts, for Two Hundred Years; from the Year 1620 to 1820. 1976. Repr. 61.00 (ISBN 0-685-71967-7, Regency). Scholarly.
Bullen, R. Excavations in Northeastern Massachusetts, Vol. 1, No. 3. LC 49-48491. 1949. 7.00 (ISBN 0-939312-02-6). Peabody Found.
Clap, Roger. Memoirs of Roger Clap: Collections of the Dorchester Antiquarian & Historical Society, No. 1. facsimile ed. LC 73-150176. (Select Bibliographies Reprint Ser.). 1972. Repr. of 1843 ed. 10.00 (ISBN 0-8369-5689-3). Arno.
Collections of the Massachusetts Historical Society, Vols. 2, 4-5, 8. (Fourth Ser.). 25.00 ea. Mass Hist Soc.
Collections of the Massachusetts Historical Society, Vols. 3-4, 8. (Sixth Ser.). 25.00 (ISBN 0-686-27106-8). Mass Hist Soc.
Collections of the Massachusetts Historical Society, Vols. 73-74, 78, 80-83. 35.00 ea. Mass Hist Soc.
The Demographic History of Massachusetts: An Original Anthology. LC 75-37311. (Demography Ser.). (Illus.). 1976. Repr. 25.00x (ISBN 0-405-07981-8). Arno.
Dexter, Lincoln A., ed. Maps of Early Massachusetts. LC 79-51535. (Illus.). 1979. text ed. 11.00 (ISBN 0-9601210-7-2); pap. text ed. 6.50 (ISBN 0-9601210-6-4). L A Dexter.
Drake, Samuel A. Historic Mansions & Highways Around Boston. LC 73-157256. (Illus.). 1971. pap. 3.75 (ISBN 0-8048-0992-5). C E Tuttle.
Emery, Helen F. The Puritan Village Evolves: A History of Wayland, Massachusetts. LC 81-5185. (Illus.). 384p. 1981. 15.00x (ISBN 0-914016-78-4). Phoenix Pub.
Federal Writers' Project, Massachusetts. The Armenians in Massachusetts. LC 73-3624. (American Guide Ser). Repr. of 1937 ed. 17.00 (ISBN 0-404-57926-4). AMS Pr.
Flagg, Charles A. An Index of Pioneers from Massachusetts to the West, Especially the State of Michigan. LC 74-29148. 86p. 1980. Repr. of 1915 ed. 8.50 (ISBN 0-8063-0660-2). Genealog Pub.
Forbes, Crosby & Lee, Henry. Massachusetts Help to Ireland During the Great Famine. LC 67-24085. (Illus.). 1967. 6.00x (ISBN 0-937650-00-5). Mus Am China.
Freiberg, Malcolm, ed. Stephen Thomas Riley: The Years of Stewardship. (Illus.). 1976. pap. 10.00 (ISBN 0-686-10136-7). Mass Hist Soc.
Frisch, Michael H. Town into City: Springfield, Massachusetts & the Meaning of Community, 1840-1880. LC 72-178075. (Studies in Urban History). (Illus.). 464p. 1972. 16.50x (ISBN 0-674-89820-6); pap. 6.95x (ISBN 0-674-89826-5). Harvard U Pr.
Gillon, Edmond V. A New England Town in Early Photographs: 149 Illus. of Southbridge, Massachusetts,1878-1930. 8.00 (ISBN 0-8446-5491-4). Peter Smith.
Hannay, Agnes. A Chronicle of Industry on the Mill River. Stein, Leon, ed. LC 77-70501. (Work Ser.). 1977. Repr. of 1936 ed. lib. bdg. 12.00x (ISBN 0-405-10172-4). Arno.
Hart, Albert B., ed. Commonwealth History of Massachusetts, Colony, Province & State, 5 Vols. LC 66-27095. (Illus., 1967 repr. of 1927-30 ed). Set. 125.00 (ISBN 0-8462-0766-4). Russell.
Hawthorne, Nathaniel. True Stories from History & Biography. Charvat, William, et al, eds. LC 73-150220. (Centenary Edition of the Works of Nathaniel Hawthorne: Vol. 6). (gr. 5 up). 1972. 12.50 (ISBN 0-8142-0157-1). Ohio St U Pr.
Here We Have Lived. (Massachusetts Historical Society Picture Books Ser.). 1967. 2.00 (ISBN 0-686-21447-1). Mass Hist Soc.
Hurd, John L. Weathersfield: Century Two. LC 75-22317. (Illus.). 1978. 15.00x (ISBN 0-914016-55-5). Phoenix Pub.
Jones, Douglas L. Village & Seaport: Migration & Society in Eighteenth-Century Massachusetts. LC 80-54469. (Illus.). 240p. 1981. text ed. 15.00x (ISBN 0-87451-200-X). U Pr of New Eng.
Kaestle, C. F. & Vinovskis, M. A. Education & Social Change in Nineteenth Century Massachusetts. LC 78-32130. (Illus.). 1980. 27.50 (ISBN 0-521-22191-9). Cambridge U Pr.
Keene, Betsey D. History of Bourne, 1622-1937. LC 75-5093. (Illus.). 288p. 1975. Repr. of 1937 ed. 10.00x (ISBN 0-88492-006-2). W S Sullwold.
Levitan, David, et al. The Massachusetts Constitution: A Citizens Edition. rev. 3rd ed. 1981. pap. 10.00 (ISBN 0-931684-02-1). Gov Res Pubns.
Levy, Leonard. Blasphemy in Massachusetts. LC 70-16634. 592p. 1974. lib. bdg. 55.00 (ISBN 0-306-70221-5). Da Capo.
The Massachusetts Historical Society,1791-1959. (Massachusetts Historical Society Picture Books Ser.). 1959. 2.00 (ISBN 0-686-21430-7). Mass Hist Soc.
Mofford, Juliet H., ed. Greater Lawrence: A Bibliography. LC 78-71920. 1978. 15.00 (ISBN 0-686-24231-9). Merrimack Vall Textile.
Molloy, Peter M. The Lower Merrimack River Valley: An Inventory of Historic Engineering & Industrial Sites. 2nd ed. 1978. 3.50 (ISBN 0-686-24230-0). Merrimack Vall Textile.
Moody, Robert E., ed. Papers of Leverett Saltonstall, 1816-1845. (Collections of the Massachusetts Historical Society Ser.). (Illus.). Vol. 1, 1978. 35.00 ea. Vol. 2, 1981. Mass Hist Soc.
Morison, Samuel E. The Maritime History of Massachusetts: Seventeen Eighty-Three to Eighteen Sixty. LC 79-5422. 421p. 1979. 19.95 (ISBN 0-930350-06-5); pap. text ed. 9.95 (ISBN 0-930350-04-9). NE U Pr.
Nichols, George. George Nichols, Salem Shipmaster & Merchant. facsimile ed. LC 74-124245. (Select Bibliographies Reprint Ser). Repr. of 1913 ed. 12.00 (ISBN 0-8369-5433-5). Arno.
Pencak, William. War, Politics, & Revolution in Provincial Massachusetts. LC 80-39487. (Illus.). 276p. 1981. 18.95 (ISBN 0-930350-10-3). NE U Pr.
Peters, Ronald M., Jr. The Massachusetts Constitution of 1780: A Social Compact. LC 77-90730. 1978. 15.00x (ISBN 0-87023-143-X). U of Mass Pr.
Pierce, Richard D., ed. Records of the First Church in Salem, Massachusetts, 1629-1736. LC 73-93302. 1974. 30.00 (ISBN 0-88389-050-X). Essex Inst.
Powell, Richard R. Compromises of Conflicting Claims: A History of California Law in the Period 1760-1860. LC 77-54938. (Orig.). 1977. lib. bdg. 22.50 (ISBN 0-379-00655-3). Oceana.
Prints, Maps & Drawings,1677-1822. 3rd ed. (Massachusetts Historical Society Picture Books Ser.). 1957. 2.00 (ISBN 0-686-21428-5). Mass Hist Soc.
Proceedings of the Massachusetts Historical Society, Vol. 92. 1981. price not set. Mass Hist Soc.
Reid, William J. Massachusetts. LC 64-7874. (Orig.). 1965. pap. 2.95 (ISBN 0-8077-2030-5). Tchrs Coll.
Sandrof, Ivan. Yesterday's Massachusetts. (Seamann's Historic States Ser.: No. 7). (Illus.). 9.95 (ISBN 0-89530-000-1). E A Seemann.
Seventeen Ninety-One to Nineteen Eighty, Vols. 71-92. Vols. 71-92. 20.00 ea.; Vols. 73-92. pap. 15.00 ea. Mass Hist Soc.
Siracusa, Carl. A Mechanical People: Perceptions of the Industrial Order in Massachusetts, 1815-1880. LC 78-26715. 1979. 22.50x (ISBN 0-8195-5029-9, Pub. by Wesleyan U Pr). Columbia U Pr.
Smeal, Lee. Massachusetts Historical & Biographical Index. LC 78-53703. (Illus.). Date not set. lib. bdg. price not set (ISBN 0-89593-186-9). Accelerated Index.
Smith, Philip C. Captain Samuel Tucker: Continental Navy 1747-1833. LC 76-17150. 1976. 10.00t (ISBN 0-88389-058-5). Essex Inst.
Taylor, Robert J. Construction of the Massachusetts Constitution. 29p. 1981. pap. 6.00 (ISBN 0-912296-49-6, Dist. by U Pr of Va). Am Antiquarian.
Thresher, Mary G., ed. Records & Files of the Quarterly Courts of Essex County, Massachusetts, Vol. 9, Sept. 25, 1683-April 20, 1686. LC 12-951. 1975. 30.00 (ISBN 0-88389-051-8). Essex Inst.
Todd, Charles B. In Olde Massachusetts: Sketches of Old Times & Places During the Early Days of the Commonwealth. LC 77-99060. 1971. Repr. of 1907 ed. 19.00 (ISBN 0-8103-3775-4). Gale.
Town Records of Salem, Massachusetts. Incl. Vol. 2, 1659-1680. 356p. 1913; Vol. 3, 1680-1691. 288p. 1934. LC 15-2612. 15.00 ea. (ISBN 0-88389-040-2). Essex Inst.
Vance, Mary. Historical Society Architectural Publications: Massachusetts, Michigan,Minnesota, Mississippi, Missouri. (Architecture Ser.: Bibliography A-159). 75p. 1980. pap. 8.00 (ISBN 0-686-26907-1). Vance Biblios.

Vital Records of Lowell, Massachusetts, to the End of the Year 1849, 4 vols. Incl. Vol. 1, Births. 404p. 1930; Vol. 2, Marriages. 543p. 1930; Vol. 3, Marriages. 427p. 1930; Vol. 4, Deaths. 324p. 1930. LC 30-17085. Set. 40.00 (ISBN 0-88389-032-1); 15.00 ea. Essex Inst.

Vital Records of Marblehead, Massachusetts, to the End of the Year 1849, 2 vols. Incl. Vol. 1, Births. 564p. 1903; Vol. 2, Marriages & Deaths. 708p. 1904. LC 5-14241. 15.00 ea. (ISBN 0-88389-036-4). Essex Inst.

Vital Records of Stoneham, Massachusetts, to the End of the Year 1849. LC 18-27123. 191p. 1918. 10.00 (ISBN 0-88389-042-9). Essex Inst.

Vital Records of Wenham, Massachusetts, to the End of the Year 1849. LC 6-13929. 227p. 1904. 7.50 (ISBN 0-88389-045-3). Essex Inst.

Watkins, Lura W. Middleton, Massachusetts: A Cultural History. 341p. 1970. 12.50 (ISBN 0-88389-048-8). Essex Inst.

Wellman, Thomas B. History of the Town of Lynnfield Mass: 1635-1895, 2 vols. Incl. Lynnfield, a Heritage Preserved: 1895-1977. Wiswell, Marcia W., ed. LC 76-56496. 15.00x (ISBN 0-914016-41-5). LC 76-56495. (Illus.). 1977. 30.00x set (ISBN 0-914016-40-7). Phoenix Pub.

Whitehill, Walter M. & Kotker, Norman. Massachusetts: A Pictorial History. LC 76-28586. (Encore Edition). (Illus.). 356p. 1976. 9.95 (ISBN 0-684-15962-7, ScribT). Scribner.

Whitson, Skip, compiled by. Massachusetts One Hundred Years Ago: The Northeast. (Sun Historical Ser). (Illus., Orig.). 1976. pap. 3.50 (ISBN 0-89540-017-0, SB017). Sun Pub.

--Massachusetts One Hundred Years Ago: The Southeast. (Sun Historical Ser). (Illus., Orig.). 1976. pap. 3.50 (ISBN 0-89540-018-9, SB018). Sun Pub.

Wroth, L. Kinvin, et al, eds. Province in Rebellion: A Documentary History of the Founding of the Commonwealth of Massachusetts, 1774-1775. 350p. (Incl. microfiche cards). 1975. paper covers 95.00 (ISBN 0-674-71955-7). Harvard U Pr.

Young, Alexander. Chronicles of the First Planters of the Colony of Massachusetts Bay, 1623-1636. LC 78-87667. (Law, Politics & History Ser.). 1970. Repr. of 1846 ed. lib. bdg. 55.00 (ISBN 0-306-71759-X). Da Capo.

MASSACHUSETTS–HISTORY–COLONIAL PERIOD, ca. 1600-1775

see also Pilgrims (New Plymouth Colony)

Abbot, W. W. The Colonial Origins of the United States, 1607-1763. LC 74-28127. (American Republic Ser). 160p. 1975. pap. text ed. 9.95 (ISBN 0-471-00140-6). Wiley.

Adams, Charles F. Three Episodes of Massachusetts History: The Settlement of Boston Bay; The Antinomian Controversy; A Study of Church & Town Government, 2 Vols. LC 65-18782. 1965. Repr. of 1892 ed. Set. 25.00 (ISBN 0-8462-0524-6). Russell.

Adams, Charles F., ed. Antionomianism in the Colony of Massachusetts Bay, 1636-38, Including the Short Story & Documents. 1966. 26.00 (ISBN 0-8337-0010-3). B Franklin.

Allen, David G. In English Ways: The Movement of Societies & the Transferal of English Local Law & Custom to Massachusetts Bay in the Seventeenth Century. LC 80-13198. (Institute of Early American History & Culture Ser.). xxi, 312p. 1981. 27.00x (ISBN 0-8078-1448-2). U of NC Pr.

Arber, E., ed. Story of the Pilgrim Fathers, 1606-1623. LC 1-12054. 1897. 30.00 (ISBN 0-527-02910-6). Kraus Repr.

Bacon, Leonard. The Genesis of the New England Churches. LC 74-38435. (Religion in America, Ser. 2). 510p. 1972. Repr. of 1874 ed. 25.00 (ISBN 0-405-04056-3). Arno.

Boyer, Paul & Nissenbaum, Stephen, eds. The Salem Witchcraft Papers: Verbatim Transcripts, 3 vols. 1977. lib. bdg. 125.00 (ISBN 0-306-70655-5). Da Capo.

Bradford, William. Of Plymouth Plantation: The Pilgrims in America. 8.75 (ISBN 0-8446-1718-0). Peter Smith.

--Of Plymouth Plantation: 1620-1647. Morison, Samuel E., ed. (The American Past Ser). (Illus.). (YA) 1952. 15.00 (ISBN 0-394-43895-7). Knopf.

Bradford, William & Winslow, Edward. Mourt's Relation. LC 72-78652. 1865. Repr. 25.00 (ISBN 0-686-01725-0). Somerset Pub.

Brown, E. Francis. Joseph Hawley: Colonial Radical. LC 31-29646. Repr. of 1931 ed. 15.00 (ISBN 0-404-01128-4). AMS Pr.

Brown, Richard D. Revolutionary Politics in Massachusetts: The Boston Committee of Correspondence & the Towns, 1772-1774. (Illus.). 304p. 1976. pap. 4.95x (ISBN 0-393-00810-X, Norton Lib). Norton.

Caffrey, Kate. The Mayflower. LC 73-91855. (Illus.). 304p. 1974. 10.00 (ISBN 0-8128-1679-X). Stein & Day.

Chamberlain, Nathan H. Samuel Sewall & the World He Lived In. LC 66-24679. (Illus.). 1967. Repr. of 1897 ed. 9.00 (ISBN 0-8462-0987-X). Russell.

Cushing, John D., intro. by. The Laws & Liberties of Massachusetts 1641-1691, 3 vol. facsimile ed. LC 75-24575. 1976. Set. 195.00 (ISBN 0-8420-2074-8). Scholarly Res Inc.

Ellis, George E. Puritan Age & Rule in the Colony of the Massachusetts Bay, 1629-1685. LC 75-122838. (Research & Source Ser.: No. 522). 1970. Repr. of 1888 ed. lib. bdg. 32.00 (ISBN 0-8337-1054-0). B Franklin.

Emerson, Everett, ed. Letters from New England: The Massachusetts Bay Colony, 1629-1638. LC 75-32484. (The Commonwealth Ser.: Vol. 2). 1976. 15.00x (ISBN 0-87023-209-6). U of Mass Pr.

Geller, Lawrence D. & Gomes, Peter J. The Books of the Pilgrims. LC 74-30056. (Reference Library of the Humanities: No. 13). (Illus.). 100p. 1975. lib. bdg. 21.00 (ISBN 0-8240-1065-5). Garland Pub.

Goodwin, J. A. Pilgrim Republic. LC 20-1346. (Illus.). Repr. of 1888 ed. 39.00 (ISBN 0-527-34500-8). Kraus Repr.

Haskins, George L. Law & Authority in Early Massachusetts: A Study in Tradition & Design. 1968. Repr. of 1960 ed. 18.50 (ISBN 0-208-00685-0, Archon). Shoe String.

Haxtun, Annie A. Signers of the Mayflower Compact. LC 67-28609. 1968. Repr. of 1897 ed. 12.50 (ISBN 0-8063-0173-2). Genealog Pub.

Haynes, George H. Representation & Suffrage in Massachusetts; 1620-1691. LC 78-63832. (Johns Hopkins University. Studies in the Social Sciences. Twelfth Ser. 1894: 8-9). Repr. of 1894 ed. 11.50 (ISBN 0-404-61092-7). AMS Pr.

Hubbard, William. General History of New England, 1620-1680, Vols. 5-6. 1815. Vol. 5. 26.00 (ISBN 0-384-24800-4); Vol. 6. 32.00 (ISBN 0-384-24801-2). Johnson Repr.

Hutchinson, T. History of the Colony & Province of Massachusetts Bay, 3 Vols. Repr. of 1936 ed. Set. 60.00 (ISBN 0-527-43610-0). Kraus Repr.

Hutchinson, Thomas. Additions to Thomas Hutchinson's History of Massachusetts Bay. Mayo, Catherine B., ed. 1949. pap. 4.00 (ISBN 0-527-43600-3). Kraus Repr.

--Diary & Letters of Thomas Hutchinson, 2 vols. Hutchinson, Peter O., compiled by. 1971. Repr. of 1883 ed. Set. lib. bdg. 55.50 (ISBN 0-8337-1783-9). B Franklin.

--History of the Colony of Massachusetts Bay, 3 vols. LC 77-141090. (Research Library of Colonial Americana). 1971. Repr. of 1764 ed. Set. 100.00 (ISBN 0-405-03289-7); 34.00 (ISBN 0-405-03290-0); 33.00 (ISBN 0-405-03291-9); 33.00 (ISBN 0-405-03292-7). Arno.

Johnson, Edward. Johnson's Wonder-Working Providence, 1638-1651. Jameson, J. Franklin, ed. (Original Narratives). 1967. Repr. of 1910 ed. 18.50x (ISBN 0-06-480428-3). B&N.

Labaree, Benjamin W. Colonial Massachusetts: A History. LC 79-33. (A History of the American Colonies Ser.). 1979. lib. bdg. 25.00 (ISBN 0-527-18714-3). Kraus Intl.

Langdon, George D., Jr. Pilgrim Colony: A History of New Plymouth, 1620-1691. (Publications in American Studies: No. 12). (Illus.). 1966. 20.00x (ISBN 0-300-00671-3). Yale U Pr.

Massachusetts Constitutional Convention - 1820-21. Journal of Debates & Proceedings. LC 76-133169. (Law, Politics, & History Ser). 1970. Repr. of 1853 ed. lib. bdg. 69.50 (ISBN 0-306-70068-9). Da Capo.

Mayo, Laurence S. John Endecott: A Biography. (Illus.). 1971. Repr. of 1936 ed. 25.00 (ISBN 0-403-01099-3). Scholarly.

Miller, Perry. Orthodoxy in Massachusetts 1630-1650. 8.00 (ISBN 0-8446-1312-6). Peter Smith.

Moore, George H. Notes on the History of Slavery in Massachusetts. LC 68-55901. Repr. of 1866 ed. 13.00x (ISBN 0-8371-0574-9, Pub. by Negro U Pr). Greenwood.

Morison, Samuel E. Builders of the Bay Colony. 2nd ed. (Illus.). 405p. 1981. 21.95x (ISBN 0-930350-23-5); pap. text ed. 9.95x (ISBN 0-930350-22-7). NE U Pr.

--Builders of the Bay Colony. LC 75-41198. Repr. of 1930 ed. 26.45 (ISBN 0-404-14741-0). AMS Pr.

Morton, Thomas. New English Canaan or New Canaan. Cantaining an Abstract of New England. LC 76-25966. (English Experience Ser.: No. 140). 192p. 1969. Repr. of 1637 ed. 28.00 (ISBN 90-221-0140-1). Walter J Johnson.

Mourt, George. Journal of the Pilgrims at Plymouth: Mourt's Relation. Heath, Dwight B., intro. by. 1962. 3.95 (ISBN 0-87091-019-1, AE); pap. 2.50 (ISBN 0-87091-018-3). Corinth Bks.

Pencak, William. War, Politics & Revolution in Provincial Massachusetts. (Illus.). 276p. 1981. write for info. (ISBN 0-930350-10-3). NE U Pr.

Randolph, Edward. Edward Randolph Including His Letters & Official Papers, 7 Vols. Toppan, R. N., ed. 1966. 183.00 (ISBN 0-685-06751-3). B Franklin.

Reid, John G. Maine, Charles II & Massachusetts: Governmental Relationships in Early Northern New England. LC 77-18562. (Maine Historical Society Research Ser.: No. 1). 1977. 28.00 (ISBN 0-915592-28-2, IS-00041, Pub. by Maine Historical Soc.). Univ Microfilms.

Reid, John P. In a Rebellious Spirit: The Argument of Facts, the Liberty Riot, & the Coming of the American Revolution. LC 78-50065. 1979. 15.95x (ISBN 0-271-00202-6). Pa St U Pr.

A Relation or Journall of the Beginning of the English Plantation at Plimouth. LC 74-80210. (English Experience Ser.: No. 683). 1974. Repr. of 1622 ed. 8.00 (ISBN 90-221-0683-7). Walter J Johnson.

Rose-Troup, Frances. Massachusetts Bay Company & Its Predecessors. LC 68-56574. Repr. of 1930 ed. 13.50x (ISBN 0-678-00871-X). Kelley.

Sewall, Samuel. Diary of Samuel Sewall, 1674-1729, 3 Vols. LC 77-141102. (Research Library of Colonial Americana). (Illus.). 1972. Repr. of 1878 ed. Set. 100.00 (ISBN 0-405-03311-7); Vol. 1. 34.00 (ISBN 0-405-03312-5); Vol. 2. 33.00 (ISBN 0-405-03313-3); Vol. 3. 33.00 (ISBN 0-405-03314-1). Arno.

Smith, John. Advertisements for the Unexperienced Planters of New England. LC 77-171792. (English Experience Ser.: No. 356). 40p. 1971. Repr. of 1631 ed. 8.00 (ISBN 90-221-0356-0). Walter J Johnson.

Smith, Philip C., ed. Seafaring in Colonial Massachusetts. LC 80-51256. (Illus.). xvii, 240p. 1981. 25.00x (ISBN 0-8139-0897-3, Colonial Soc MA). U Pr of Va.

Smith, Robert. Massachusetts Colony. LC 69-19575. (Forge of Freedom Ser). (Illus.). (gr. 5-8). 1969. 8.95 (ISBN 0-02-785880-4, CCPr). Macmillan.

Steele, Ashbel. Chief of the Pilgrims: Or, the Life & Time of William Brewster. facs. ed. LC 72-133535. (Select Bibliographies Reprint Ser). (Illus.). 1857. 21.00 (ISBN 0-8369-5567-6). Arno.

Talpalar, Morris. Sociology of the Bay Colony. LC 75-27960. 388p. 1976. 15.00 (ISBN 0-8022-2176-9). Philos Lib.

Tapley, Harriet S. St. Peter's Church in Salem: Massachusetts Before the Revolution. (Illus.). 92p. 1944. 5.00 (ISBN 0-88389-020-8). Essex Inst.

Washburn, Emory. Sketches of the Judicial History of Massachusetts from 1630 to the Revolution in 1775. LC 74-6427. (American Constitutional & Legal History Ser.). 407p. 1974. Repr. of 1840 ed. lib. bdg. 42.50 (ISBN 0-306-70616-4). Da Capo.

White, John, 1575-1648. The Planters Plea. LC 68-54669. (English Experience Ser.: No. 60). 84p. 1968. Repr. of 1630 ed. 11.50 (ISBN 90-221-0060-X). Walter J Johnson.

Winslow, Edward. Hypocrisie Unmasked by the True Relation of the Proceedings of the Governour & Company of Massachusetts Against Samuel Gorton. LC 68-57130. (Research & Source Works Ser.: No. 312). 1969. Repr. of 1916 ed. 19.00 (ISBN 0-8337-3820-8). B Franklin.

Winthrop, John. Winthrop's Journal, History of New England: Sixteen Thirty to Sixteen Forty-Nine, 2 Vols. Hosmer, James K., ed. (Original Narratives). 1959. Repr. of 1908 ed. Set. 37.00x (ISBN 0-06-480384-8). B&N.

Wood, George A. William Shirley, Governor of Massachusetts, 1741-1756. LC 72-78001. (Columbia University. Studies in the Social Sciences: No. 209). Repr. of 1920 ed. 17.50 (ISBN 0-404-51209-7). AMS Pr.

Wood, William. New Englands Prospect. LC 68-54670. (English Experience Ser.: No. 68). 104p. 1968. Repr. of 1634 ed. 16.00 (ISBN 90-221-0068-5). Walter J Johnson.

--New England's Prospect. Vaughan, Alden T., ed. LC 76-45051. (Commonwealth Ser.: Vol. 3). (Illus.). 1977. 12.50x (ISBN 0-87023-226-6). U of Mass Pr.

--Wood's New England Prospect. Colburn, Jeremiah, ed. 1966. 19.00 (ISBN 0-8337-3864-X). B Franklin.

Young, Alexander. Chronicles of the Pilgrim Fathers of the Colony of Plymouth, 1602-1625. LC 78-87667. (Law, Politics & History Ser). 1971. Repr. of 1841 ed. lib. bdg. 37.50 (ISBN 0-306-71760-3). Da Capo.

MASSACHUSETTS–HISTORY–COLONIAL PERIOD, ca. 1600-1775–SOURCES

Andros Tracts, 3 Vols. (Prince Society Publications: 5-7). 1966. 63.50 (ISBN 0-8337-0067-7). B Franklin.

Channing, Edward & Coolidge, Archibald C. The Barrington-Bernard Correspondence, & Illustrative Matter, 1760-1770. LC 75-109612. (Era of the American Revolution Ser). 1970. Repr. of 1912 ed. lib. bdg. 32.50 (ISBN 0-306-71909-6). Da Capo.

Hutchinson, Thomas & Whitmore, W. H., eds. The Thomas Hutchinson Papers, 2 vols. (Prince Soc.: Nos. 1 & 2). 1967. 47.50 (ISBN 0-8337-1779-0). B Franklin.

Massachusetts Colony Court Of Assistants. Records of the Court of Assistants of the Colony of the Massachusetts Bay, 1630-1692, 3 Vols. LC 70-172853. Repr. of 1928 ed. Set. 97.50 (ISBN 0-404-07350-6); 32.50 ea. Vol. 1 (ISBN 0-404-07351-4). Vol. 2 (ISBN 0-404-07352-2). Vol. 3 (ISBN 0-404-07353-0). AMS Pr.

Morison, Samuel E., et al, eds. Winthrop Papers, Prepared for the Massachusetts Historical Society, 2 vols. Incl. Vol. 1. 1498-1628. (Illus.). Repr. of 1929 ed. 15.00 (ISBN 0-8462-1089-4); Vol. 2. 1623-1630. Mitchell, Stewart, ed. (Illus.). Repr. of 1931 ed. 12.50 (ISBN 0-8462-1132-7). LC 68-10956. 1968. Russell.

Pope, Charles H. Pioneers of Massachusetts. LC 65-22478. 1977. Repr. of 1900 ed. 18.50 (ISBN 0-8063-0774-9). Genealog Pub.

Quincy, Josiah, Jr. Reports of Cases Argued & Adjudged in the Superior Court of Judicature of the Province of Massachusetts Bay Between 1761 & 1772. Quincy, Samuel M., ed. LC 69-17843. 1969. Repr. of 1865 ed. 15.75 (ISBN 0-8462-1327-3). Russell.

Sewall, Samuel. Samuel Sewall's Diary. Van Doren, Mark, ed. LC 62-16693. (With a new introduction). 1963. Repr. of 1927 ed. 8.00 (ISBN 0-8462-0386-3). Russell.

Shurtleff, Nathaniel B., ed. Records of the Governor & Company of Massachusetts Bay in New England, 1628-1686, 5 Vols in 6. LC 72-1721. Repr. of 1854 ed. Set. lib. bdg. 390.00 (ISBN 0-404-06020-X). AMS Pr.

Shurtleff, Nathaniel B. & Pulsifer, David, eds. Records of the Colony of New Plymouth in New England, 12 Vols in 6. LC 1-12098. Repr. of 1861 ed. Set. 437.50 (ISBN 0-404-06040-4). AMS Pr.

Weeks, Lyman H. & Bacon, Edwin M., eds. Historical Digest of the Provincial Press: Massachusetts Series 1689-1707. LC 73-177858. Repr. of 1911 ed. 20.00 (ISBN 0-404-06888-X). AMS Pr.

Wheelwright, John. John Wheelwright: His Writings, Including His Fast-Day Sermon, 1637. 1966. 24.00 (ISBN 0-8337-3763-5). B Franklin.

--John Wheelwright's Writings, Including His Fast-Day Sermon, 1637, & His Mercurius Americanus, 1645. facs. ed. LC 70-128897. (Select Bibliographies Reprint Ser). 1876. 16.00 (ISBN 0-8369-5517-X). Arno.

Young, Alexander. Chronicles of the First Planters of the Colony of Massachusetts Bay, from 1623-1636. LC 74-18329. 1975. Repr. of 1846 ed. 22.50 (ISBN 0-8063-0637-8). Genealog Pub.

MASSACHUSETTS–HISTORY–REVOLUTION, 1775-1783

Gross, Robert A. The Minutemen & Their World. 1976. 8.95 (ISBN 0-8090-6933-4, AmCen); pap. 4.95 (ISBN 0-8090-0120-9). Hill & Wang.

Hoerder, Dirk. Crowd Action in Revolutionary Massachusetts, 1765-1780. 1977. 32.00 (ISBN 0-12-351650-1). Acad Pr.

Jones, Edward A. Loyalists of Massachusetts: Their Memorials, Petitions & Claims. LC 71-86810. (Illus.). 1969. Repr. of 1930 ed. 17.50 (ISBN 0-8063-0196-1). Genealog Pub.

Leonard, Daniel. Massachusettensis. LC 72-10246. (American Revolutionary Ser.). 1979. Repr. of 1776 ed. lib. bdg. 14.50x (ISBN 0-8398-1180-2). Irvington.

Lowance, Mason I. & Bumgardner, Georgia B., eds. Massachusetts Broadsides of the American Revolution. LC 75-32488. (Illus.). 1976. 15.00x (ISBN 0-87023-208-8). U of Mass Pr.

Martyn, Charles. Life of Artemas Ward. LC 71-120883. (American Bicentennial Ser). 1970. Repr. of 1921 ed. 15.50 (ISBN 0-8046-1276-5). Kennikat.

Newcomer, Lee N. Embattled Farmers: A Massachusetts Countryside in the American Revolution. LC 78-151552. 1971. Repr. of 1953 ed. 14.00 (ISBN 0-8462-1598-5). Russell.

Oliver, Peter. Peter Oliver's "Origin & Progress of the American Rebellion". A Tory View. Adair, Douglass & Schutz, John A., eds. 1961. 10.00x (ISBN 0-8047-0599-2); pap. 2.95 (ISBN 0-8047-0601-8, SP59). Stanford U Pr.

Pencak, William. War, Politics & Revolution in Provincial Massachusetts. (Illus.). 276p. 1981. write for info. (ISBN 0-930350-10-3). NE U Pr.

Reid, John P. In a Defiant Stance: The Conditions of Law in Massachusetts Bay, the Irish Comparison, & the Coming of the American Revolution. LC 76-42453. 1977. 16.75x (ISBN 0-271-01240-4). Pa St U Pr.

Snape, Sue E. Mighty Liberty Men. LC 75-23916. (Illus.). 1976. 8.00 (ISBN 0-88492-016-X). W S Sullwold.

Taylor, R. J. Western Massachusetts in the Revolution. 1954. 16.00 (ISBN 0-527-89075-8). Kraus Repr.

Taylor, Robert J., ed. Massachusetts, Colony to Commonwealth: Documents on the Formation of Its Constitution, 1775-1780. (Documentary Problems in Early American History Ser). 1972. pap. text ed. 3.95x (ISBN 0-393-09396-4). Norton.

MASSACHUSETTS–HISTORY, JUVENILE

Daugherty, James. Landing of the Pilgrims. (Landmark Ser). (Illus.). (gr. 4-6). 1950. PLB 5.99 (ISBN 0-394-90302-1, BYR). Random.

Fradin, Dennis. Massachusetts: In Words & Pictures. LC 80-26161. (Young People's Stories of Our States Ser.). (Illus.). 48p. (gr. 2-5). 1981. PLB 9.25 (ISBN 0-516-03921-0). Childrens.

Gruenbaum, Thelma. Before Seventeen Seventy-Six: The Massachusetts Bay Colony from Founding to Revolution. (Illus.). 38p. (gr. 4-10). 1974. pap. 3.75 (ISBN 0-936190-01-9); study guide 1.75 (ISBN 0-936190-02-7). ExPressAll.

Smith, E. Brooks & Meredith, Robert. Pilgrim Courage. (Illus.). (gr. 5 up). 1962. 6.95 (ISBN 0-316-80045-7). Little.

Wood, James P. Colonial Massachusetts. LC 71-82917. (Colonial History Ser.). (Illus.). (gr. 5 up). 1969. 7.75 (ISBN 0-525-67101-3). Elsevier-Nelson.

MASSACHUSETTS–HISTORY, LOCAL

Barnard, Charles N. It Was a Wonderful Summer for Running Away. LC 78-17282. 1978. 8.95 (ISBN 0-396-07574-6). Dodd.

Barnard, John. Ashton's Memorial: A History of the Strange Adeventure, & Signal Deliverances of Mr. Philip Ashton, Sun of Marblehead. Knight, Russell W., ed. 1976. 12.50 (ISBN 0-87577-051-7). Peabody Mus Salem.

Braddock, Ellsworth C. Memories of North Carver Village. Snow, E. J., ed. LC 76-51098. (Illus.). 1977. pap. text ed. 6.50 (ISBN 0-9600496-6-5). Channing Bks.

Chesbro, Paul L. & Crosby, Chester A. Osterville, a Walk Through the Past, Five Hundred Photos, Eighteen Sixty to Nineteen Thirty. (Illus.). 1979. 30.00x (ISBN 0-88492-026-7). W S Sullwold.

Dincauze, Dena F. Cremation Cemeteries in Eastern Massachusetts. LC 68-2247. (Peabody Museum Papers Ser.: Vol. 59, No.1). 1968. pap. text ed. 10.00 (ISBN 0-87365-171-5). Peabody Harvard.

Doherty, Katherine M., ed. History Highlights: Bridgewater, Massachusetts, a Commemorative Journal. LC 76-2972. (Illus.). 1976. 12.00 (ISBN 0-88492-014-3). W S Sullwold.

Emery, Sarah A. Reminiscences of a Newburyport Nonagenarian. LC 78-5010. (Illus.). 1978. Repr. of 1879 ed. 20.50 (ISBN 0-917890-09-4). Heritage Bk.

Garland, Joseph E. The Gloucester Guide, a Retrospective Ramble. LC 72-97361. (Illus.). 1973. 2.95 (ISBN 0-930352-00-9). Nelson B Robinson.

Gillon, Edmund V., ed. A New England Town in Early Photographs: Illustrations of Southbridge, Massachusetts 1878 - 1930. LC 75-463. (Illus.). 176p. (Orig.). 1976. pap. 6.00 (ISBN 0-486-23286-7). Dover.

Gitelman, Howard M. Workingmen of Waltham: Mobility in American Urban Industrial Development, 1850-1890. LC 74-6822. (Illus.). 208p. 1974. 14.00x (ISBN 0-8018-1570-3). Johns Hopkins.

Gloucester 350th Anniversary Celebration, Inc. Gloucester 350th Anniversary Program. 1973. 1.00 (ISBN 0-930352-04-1). Nelson B Robinson.

Hodges, Maud. Crossroads on the Charles: A History of Watertown, Massachusetts. Reddy, Sigrid, ed. LC 80-13753. (Illus.). 248p. 1980. 15.00x (ISBN 0-914016-68-7). Phoenix Pub.

Jedrey, Christopher M. The World of John Cleaveland: Family & Community in Eighteenth-Century New England. (Illus.). 1979. 15.95 (ISBN 0-393-01270-0). Norton.

Merrill, Joseph. The History of Amesbury & Merrimac, Massachusetts. LC 78-5866. (Illus.). 1978. Repr. of 1880 ed. 27.50 (ISBN 0-917890-08-6). Heritage Bk.

O'Gorman, James F., intro. by. Portrait of a Place, Some American Landscape Painters in Gloucester. (Illus.). 1973. 7.50 (ISBN 0-930352-03-3). Nelson B Robinson.

Paine, Josiah. A History of Harwich, Barnstable County, Massachusetts Sixteen Twenty to Eighteen Hundred. 503p. 1971. Repr. of 1937 ed. 15.00 (ISBN 0-940160-03-X). Parnassus Imprints.

Parsons, Peter & Anastes, Peter. When Gloucester Was Gloucester, Toward an Oral History of the City. LC 73-76939. (Illus.). 1973. 3.95 (ISBN 0-930352-02-5). Nelson B Robinson.

Russell, Clifford, et al. Drought & Water Supply: Implications of the Massachusetts Experience for Municipal Planning. LC 72-123861. (Resources for the Future Ser). (Illus.). 350p. 1970. 16.00x (ISBN 0-8018-1183-X). Johns Hopkins.

Scribners. Historic Buildings of Massachusetts. LC 76-12600. 1976. 14.95 (ISBN 0-684-14567-7, ScribT). Scribner.

Smith, Leonard H., Jr. Index to Vital Records of Eastham, Mass. & Orleans, Mass. pap. 12.50 (ISBN 0-932022-09-X). L H Smith.

--Index to Vital Records of Sandwich, Mass. & Wareham, Mass. pap. 7.50 (ISBN 0-932022-05-7). L H Smith.

Smith, Leonard H., Jr., ed. Index to Vital Records of Barnstable Mass. pap. 10.00 (ISBN 0-932022-04-9). L H Smith.

--Index to Vital Records of Chatham, Mass. & Harwich, Mass. pap. 10.00 (ISBN 0-932022-03-0). L H Smith.

--Index to Vital Records of Dennis, Mass. & Yarmouth, Mass. pap. 8.00 (ISBN 0-932022-06-5). L H Smith.

--Index to Vital Records of Middleboro, Mass. pap. 10.00 (ISBN 0-932022-02-2). L H Smith.

--Records of the First Church of Wareham, Mass., 1739-1891. pap. 15.00 (ISBN 0-932022-01-4). L H Smith.

--St. Mary's Bay, 1818-1829: Catalog of Families. pap. 15.00 (ISBN 0-932022-07-3). L H Smith.

--St. Mary's Bay, 1840-1844: Catalog of Families. pap. 15.00 (ISBN 0-932022-08-1). L H Smith.

Smith, William C. A History of Chatham, Massachusetts: Formerly the Constablewick or Village of Monomoit. 3rd ed. (Illus.). 431p. 1981. 15.00 (ISBN 0-940160-06-4). Parnassus Imprints.

Snape, Sue E. In Old Rehoboth. LC 79-88068. (Illus.). 1979. 12.00x (ISBN 0-88492-030-5); pap. 6.00x (ISBN 0-88492-031-3). W S Sullwold.

Swan, Marshall W. Town on Sandy Bay: A History of Rockport Massachusetts. LC 80-15578. (Illus.). 456p. 1980. 15.00x (ISBN 0-914016-72-5). Phoenix Pub.

Thomas, Gordon W. Fast & Able, Life Stories of Great Gloucester Fishing Schooners. new ed. Kenyon, Paul B., ed. LC 72-97362. (Illus.). 1973. 4.95 (ISBN 0-930352-01-7). Nelson B Robinson.

Vital Records of Danvers, Massachusetts, to the End of the Year 1849: Marriages & Deaths, Vol. 2. LC 9-7227. 1910. 12.50 (ISBN 0-88389-028-3). Essex Inst.

MASSACHUSETTS–IMPRINTS

Historical Records Survey: Check List of Massachusetts Imprints, 1801. 1942. pap. 17.00 (ISBN 0-527-01927-5). Kraus Repr.

Historical Records Survey: Check List of Massachusetts Imprints, 1802. 1942. pap. 17.00 (ISBN 0-527-01931-3). Kraus Repr.

MASSACHUSETTS–JUVENILE LITERATURE

see also Massachusetts–History, Juvenile

Bailey, Bernadine. Picture Book of Massachusetts. rev. ed. LC 65-5509. (Illus.). (gr. 3-5). 1969. 5.50g (ISBN 0-8075-9523-3). A Whitman.

Carpenter, Allan. Massachusetts. new ed. LC 78-3785. (New Enchantment of America State Bks.). (Illus.). (gr. 4 up). 1978. PLB 10.60 (ISBN 0-516-04121-5). Childrens.

MASSACHUSETTS–METROPOLITAN STATE HOSPITAL, WALTHAM

Umbarger, Carter C., et al. College Students in a Mental Hospital. LC 62-14136. 192p. 1962. pap. 19.75 (ISBN 0-8089-0513-9). Grune.

MASSACHUSETTS–POLITICS AND GOVERNMENT

Adams, John & Sewall, Jonathan. Novanglus, & Massachusettensis: Or, Political Essays, Published in the Years 1774 & 1775 on the Principal Points of Controversy Between Great Britain & Her Colonies. LC 68-17641. 1968. Repr. of 1819 ed. 10.00 (ISBN 0-8462-1068-1). Russell.

Bacon, E. M., ed. Acts & Laws, of the Commonwealth of Massachusetts, 1780-1797: With Supplements 1780-1784, 13 vols. LC 74-19617. Repr. of 1896 ed. Set. 790.00 (ISBN 0-404-12439-9). AMS Pr.

Bedford, Henry F. Socialism & the Workers in Massachusetts, 1886-1912. LC 66-15794. (Illus.). 1966. 12.50x (ISBN 0-87023-010-7). U of Mass Pr.

Cary, Thomas G. Memoir of Thomas Handasyd Perkins. LC 77-164040. (Research & Source Works Ser.: No. 591). 1971. Repr. of 1856 ed. lib. bdg. 21.00 (ISBN 0-8337-0491-5). B Franklin.

Channing, Edward & Coolidge, Archibald C. The Barrington-Bernard Correspondence, & Illustrative Matter, 1760-1770. LC 75-109612. (Era of the American Revolution Ser). 1970. Repr. of 1912 ed. lib. bdg. 32.50 (ISBN 0-306-71909-6). Da Capo.

Gould Editorial Staff. Criminal Laws of Massachusetts. (Supplemented annually). looseleaf 13.50 (ISBN 0-87526-135-3). Gould.

Hennessy, Michael E. Four Decades of Massachusetts Politics, 1890-1935. facsimile ed. LC 76-150187. (Select Bibliographies Reprint Ser). Repr. of 1935 ed. 32.00 (ISBN 0-8369-5700-8). Arno.

Higginson, Thomas W. Cheerful Yesterdays. LC 68-29000. (American Negro: His History & Literature, Ser. No. 1). 1968. Repr. of 1899 ed. 13.00 (ISBN 0-405-01819-3). Arno.

Hindus, Michael S., et al. The Files of the Massachusetts Superior Court, 1859-1959: An Analysis & a Plan for Action. (Reference Publications Ser.). 1980. lib. bdg. 50.00 (ISBN 0-8161-9037-2). G K Hall.

Howland, Gerald. You're in the Driver's Seat. 128p. (Orig.). 1981. pap. 4.95 (ISBN 0-8289-0418-9). Greene.

Huthmacher, J. Joseph. Massachusetts People & Politics, 1919-1933. LC 59-9276. (Illus.). 1969. pap. text ed. 3.95x (ISBN 0-689-70103-9, 140). Atheneum.

Journals of the House of Representatives of Massachusetts, Vol. 50. 1981. 25.00 (ISBN 0-686-31626-6). Mass Hist Soc.

Levin, Murray B. & Blackwood, George. The Compleat Politician: Political Strategy in Massachusetts. LC 62-18204. 1962. 24.50x (ISBN 0-672-51133-9); pap. text ed. 12.95x (ISBN 0-8290-0138-7). Irvington.

Levitan, Donald & Mariner, E. E. Your Massachusetts Government. rev, 9th ed. (Illus.). 260p. 1980. pap. 13.90 (ISBN 0-686-64694-0). Gov Res Pubns.

Levitan, Donald & Mariner, Elwyn E. Your Massachusetts Government. 9th ed. LC 77-95280. (Illus.). 1980. pap. 12.90 (ISBN 0-931684-01-3). Gov Res Pubns.

Litt, Edgar. Political Cultures of Massachusetts. 1965. 16.50x (ISBN 0-262-12021-6). MIT Pr.

Mariner, Elwyn E. The Massachusetts Constitution: A Citizen's Edition. 2nd ed. LC 72-166478. 1977. pap. 3.75 (ISBN 0-685-58338-4). Mariner.

Massachusetts Constitutional Convention - 1820-21. Journal of Debates & Proceedings. LC 76-133169. (Law, Politics, & History Ser). 1970. Repr. of 1853 ed. lib. bdg. 69.50 (ISBN 0-306-70068-9). Da Capo.

Mileur, Jerome M. & Sulzner, George T. Campaigning for the Massachusetts Senate: Electioneering Outside the Political Limelight. LC 73-85898. (University of Massachusetts Government Ser: Vol. 1). 208p. 1974. pap. 5.00x (ISBN 0-87023-140-5). U of Mass Pr.

Quincy, Josiah. Memoir of the Life of Josiah Quincy. LC 78-146274. (Era of American Revolution Ser.). 1971. Repr. of 1825 ed. lib. bdg. 49.50 (ISBN 0-306-70098-0). Da Capo.

Siracusa, Carl. A Mechanical People: Perceptions of the Industrial Order in Massachusetts, 1815-1880. LC 78-26715. 1979. 22.50x (ISBN 0-8195-5029-9, Pub. by Wesleyan U Pr). Columbia U Pr.

Special Commission on Investigation of the Judicial System, Commonwealth of Massachusetts. Report: Under Chapter Sixty-Two of the Resolves of 1935. facsimile ed. LC 74-3833. (Criminal Justice in America Ser.). 1974. Repr. of 1936 ed. 10.00x (ISBN 0-405-06153-6). Arno.

Taylor, Robert J., et al, eds. Papers of John Adams: September 1755-April 1775, Vols. 1 & 2. (The Adams Papers Ser.). 1977. 50.00x set (ISBN 0-674-65441-2). Harvard U Pr.

Weeden, William B. War Government, Federal & State, 1861-65. LC 75-87685. (Law, Politics & History Ser.). 1972. Repr. of 1906 ed. lib. bdg. 39.50 (ISBN 0-306-71707-7). Da Capo.

Weinberg, Martha. Managing the State. 1977. text ed. 16.00x (ISBN 0-262-23077-1); pap. text ed. 5.95x (ISBN 0-262-73048-0). MIT Pr.

Whitten, Robert H. Public Administration in Massachusetts: The Relation of Central to Local Activity. LC 73-82249. (Columbia University. Studies in the Social Sciences: No. 22). Repr. of 1898 ed. 16.50 (ISBN 0-404-51022-1). AMS Pr.

MASSACHUSETTS–POLITICS AND GOVERNMENT–COLONIAL PERIOD, ca. 1600-1775

Bradford, Alden. Speeches of the Governors of Massachusetts from 1765 to 1775. LC 71-119048. (Era of the American Revolution Ser). 1971. Repr. of 1818 ed. 45.00 (ISBN 0-306-71947-9). Da Capo.

Brown, Richard D. Revolutionary Politics in Massachusetts: The Boston Committee of Correspondence & the Towns, 1772-1774. LC 71-119072. (Illus.). 1970. 15.00x (ISBN 0-674-76781-0). Harvard U Pr.

Brown, Robert E. Middle-Class Democracy & the Revolution in Massachusetts, 1691-1780. LC 68-10906. (Illus.). 1968. Repr. of 1955 ed. 28.00 (ISBN 0-8462-1073-8). Russell.

Cushing, Harry A. History of the Transition from Provincial to Commonwealth Government in Massachusetts. LC 78-120212. (Columbia University. Studies in the Social Sciences: No. 17). Repr. of 1896 ed. 21.50 (ISBN 0-404-51017-5). AMS Pr.

Cushing, John D., compiled by. The First Laws of the Commonwealth of Massachusetts. (Earliest Laws of the Original Thirteen States Ser.). 1981. 48.00 (ISBN 0-89453-212-X). M Glazier.

Handlin, Oscar & Handlin, Mary F., eds. Popular Sources of Political Authority: Documents on the Massachusetts Constitution of 1780. LC 66-18247. (Center for the Study of the History of Liberty in America Ser). 1966. 35.00x (ISBN 0-674-69000-1, Belknap Pr). Harvard U Pr.

Haynes, G. H. Representation & Suffrage in Massachusetts: 1620-1691. 1973. Repr. of 1894 ed. pap. 8.50 (ISBN 0-384-21865-2). Johnson Repr.

Patterson, Stephen E. Political Parties in Revolutionary Massachusetts. LC 72-7991. 312p. 1973. 25.00 (ISBN 0-299-06260-0). U of Wis Pr.

Ryerson, A. E. Loyalists of America and Their Times, 1620-1816, 2 Vols. LC 68-31273. (American History & Americana Ser., No. 47). 1969. Repr. lib. bdg. 89.95 (ISBN 0-8383-0195-9). Haskell.

Seventeen Fifteen to Seventeen Seventy-Four, Vols. 1-50. 1919-1981. 20.00 (ISBN 0-686-21424-2). Mass Hist Soc.

Ware, Edith E. Political Opinion in Massachusetts During Civil War & Reconstruction. LC 77-76697. (Columbia University. Studies in the Social Sciences: No. 175). Repr. of 1916 ed. 18.00 (ISBN 0-404-51175-9). AMS Pr.

Zemsky, Robert. Merchants, Farmers & River Gods: An Essay on Eighteenth-Century American Politics. LC 70-116559. 1971. 10.00 (ISBN 0-87645-035-4). Gambit.

MASSACHUSETTS–POPULATION

Chickering, Jesse. Statistical View of the Population of Massachusetts from 1765 to 1840. LC 68-55505. Repr. of 1846 ed. 13.50x (ISBN 0-678-01034-X). Kelley.

The Demographic History of Massachusetts: An Original Anthology. LC 75-37311. (Demography Ser.). (Illus.). 1976. Repr. 25.00x (ISBN 0-405-07981-8). Arno.

Huthmacher, J. Joseph. Massachusetts People & Politics, 1919-1933. LC 59-9276. (Illus.). 1969. pap. text ed. 3.95x (ISBN 0-689-70103-9, 140). Atheneum.

U. S. Bureau of the Census. Heads of Families at the First Census of the United States Taken in the Year 1790: Massachusetts. LC 73-8205. 1973. Repr. of 1908 ed. 25.00 (ISBN 0-8063-0570-3). Genealog Pub.

Vinovskis, Maris A. Fertility Decline in Antebellum Massachusetts. (Studies in Social Discontinuity). 1981. price not set (ISBN 0-12-722040-2). Acad Pr.

MASSACHUSETTS–SOCIAL LIFE AND CUSTOMS

Behrens, June & Brower, Pauline. Pilgrims Plantation. LC 77-2852. (Living Heritage Ser.). (Illus.). (gr. 1-4). 1977. PLB 9.25 (ISBN 0-516-08736-3, Golden Gate). Childrens.

Blue, Rose. My Mother the Witch. LC 79-23950. (gr. 6-8). 1980. 8.95 (ISBN 0-07-006169-6). McGraw.

Chamberlain, Nathan H. Samuel Sewall & the World He Lived In. LC 66-24679. (Illus.). 1967. Repr. of 1897 ed. 9.00 (ISBN 0-8462-0987-X). Russell.

Dow, George F. Everyday Life in the Massachusetts Bay Colony. LC 67-13326. (Illus.). Repr. of 1935 ed. 20.00 (ISBN 0-405-08463-3, Blom Pubns). Arno.

Fradin, Dennis. Massachusetts: In Words & Pictures. LC 80-26161. (Young People's Stories of Our States Ser.). (Illus.). 48p. (gr. 2-5). 1981. PLB 9.25 (ISBN 0-516-03921-0). Childrens.

Lincoln, Jonathan T. The City of the Dinner-Pail. Stein, Leon, ed. LC 77-70511. (Work Ser.). 1977. Repr. of 1909 ed. lib. bdg. 15.00x (ISBN 0-405-10181-3). Arno.

Massachusetts Historical Society. Catalog of Manuscripts of the Massachusetts Historical Society: First Supplement. (Supplements Ser.). 1980. lib. bdg. 220.00 (ISBN 0-8161-0850-1). G K Hall.

Walett, Francis G., ed. The Diary of Ebenezer Parkman 1703-1782: 1719-1755, Pt. 1. LC 68-30686. 316p. 1974. 22.50x (ISBN 0-912296-04-6, Dist. by U. Pr. of Va.). Am Antiquarian.

MASSACHUSETTS ANTI-SLAVERY SOCIETY

Chapman, Maria. Right & Wrong in Massachusetts. LC 70-90110. Repr. of 1839 ed. 10.50x (ISBN 0-8371-2024-1). Greenwood.

MASSACHUSETTS BAY COMPANY

Rose-Troup, Frances. Massachusetts Bay Company & Its Predecessors. LC 68-56574. Repr. of 1930 ed. 13.50x (ISBN 0-678-00871-X). Kelley.

Young, Alexander. Chronicles of the First Planters of the Colony of Massachusetts Bay, from 1623-1636. LC 74-18329. 1975. Repr. of 1846 ed. 22.50 (ISBN 0-8063-0637-8). Genealog Pub.

MASSACHUSETTS GENERAL HOSPITAL, BOSTON

Bowditch, Nathaniel I. A History of the Massachusetts General Hospital to August 5, 1851. 2nd ed. LC 74-180558. (Medicine & Society in America Ser). (Illus.). 768p. 1972. Repr. of 1872 ed. 34.00 (ISBN 0-405-03938-7). Arno.

Faxon, Nathaniel W. Massachusetts General Hospital, 1935-1955. LC 59-12968. (Illus.). 1959. 22.50x (ISBN 0-674-55150-8). Harvard U Pr.

MASSACHUSETTS INFANTRY-20TH REGT. 1861-1865

Howe, Mark D. Touched with Fire Civil War Letters & Diary of Oliver Wendell Holmes. LC 73-96218. (American Scene Ser). 1967. Repr. of 1947 ed. lib. bdg. 32.50 (ISBN 0-306-71825-1). Da Capo.

MASSACHUSETTS INFANTRY-54TH REGT., 1863-1865

Emilio, Louis F. History of the Fifty-Fourth Regiment of Massachusetts Volunteer Infantry, 1863 - 1865. (Basic Afro-American Reprint Library). 1969. Repr. of 1891 ed. 23.00 (ISBN 0-384-14330-X). Johnson Repr.

Emilio, Luis F. History of the Fifty-Fourth Regiment of Massachusetts Volunteer Infantry, 1863-1865. LC 69-18538. (American Negro: His History & Literature Ser., No. 2). 1969. Repr. of 1894 ed. 17.00 (ISBN 0-405-01861-4). Arno.

MASSACHUSETTS INSTITUTE OF TECHNOLOGY

Raffel, Jeffrey A. & Shisko, Robert. Systematic Analysis of University Libraries: Application of Cost-Benefit Analysis to the M. I. T. Libraries. 1969. 14.50x (ISBN 0-262-18037-5). MIT Pr.

Shrock, Robert. Geology at MIT: 1865-1965. LC 77-71235. (Illus.). 1977. 25.00x (ISBN 0-262-19161-X). MIT Pr.

Wylie, Francis E. M.I.T. in Perspective. 1976. 15.00 (ISBN 0-316-96200-7). Little.

MASSACHUSETTS MENTAL HEALTH CENTER, BOSTON

Kramer, B. M. Day Hospital. LC 62-12473. (Illus.). 120p. 1962. pap. 12.00 (ISBN 0-8089-0245-8). Grune.

MASSACHUSETTS REFORMATORY, CONCORD

Glueck, Sheldon S. & Glueck, Eleanor T. Five Hundred Criminal Careers. 1930. 14.00 (ISBN 0-527-34076-6). Kraus Repr.

--Later Criminal Careers. 1937. 14.00 (ISBN 0-527-34088-X). Kraus Repr.

MASSADA, ISRAEL

Greenspan, Sophie. Masada Will Not Fall Again. LC 72-12179. (Covenant Ser). (Illus.). (gr. 5-9). 1973. 4.25 (ISBN 0-8276-0007-0, 164). Jewish Pubn.

Rosenfield, Geraldine. The Heroes of Masada. (Illus.). 38p. (gr. 6-10). pap. 1.50 (ISBN 0-8381-0733-8, 10-732). United Syn Bk.

Yadin, Yigael. Masada, Herod's Fortress & the Zealots Last Stand. 1966. 20.00 (ISBN 0-394-43542-7). Random.

MASSAGE

see also Chiropractic; Electrotherapeutics; Mechanotherapy; Osteopathy; Shiatsu

Bean, Roy E. Helping Your Health with Pointed Pressure Therapy. 1975. 12.95 (ISBN 0-13-386466-9); pap. 3.95 (ISBN 0-13-386391-3). P-H.

Becker, Paul & Wood, Elizabeth C. Beard's Massage. 1981. pap. write for info. (ISBN 0-7216-9592-2). Saunders.

De Langre, Jacques. Do-in Primer. (Illus.). 128p. (Orig.). 1981. 10.00 (ISBN 0-916508-26-9); pap. 8.00 (ISBN 0-916508-27-7). Happiness Pr.

Do-in Two: A Most Complete Work on the Ancient Art of Self-Massage. 4th rev. ed. 156p. 1981. 10.50 (ISBN 0-916508-02-1); lib. bdg. 13.50 (ISBN 0-916508-00-5). Happiness Pr.

Downing, George. Massage Book. 1972. pap. 6.95 (ISBN 0-394-70770-2, Co-Pub by Random). Bookworks.

Ebner, Maria. Connective Tissue Massage: Theory & Therapeutic Application. LC 74-23523. 230p. 1977. Repr. of 1962 ed. 11.50 (ISBN 0-88275-243-X). Krieger.

Inkeles, Gordon. The New Massage: Total Body Conditioning for People Who Exercise. 1980. 14.95 (ISBN 0-399-12455-1, Perigee); pap. 6.95 (ISBN 0-399-50453-2). Putnam.

Inkles, Gordon. The New Massage. 1980. pap. 6.95 (ISBN 0-686-63019-X, Perigee). Putnam.

Jackson, Richard. Holistic Massage. rev. ed. LC 77-72393. (Illus.). 128p. 1980. pap. 5.95 (ISBN 0-8069-8382-5). Sterling.

Lawrence, Paul A. Lomi-Lomi Hawaiian Massage. LC 80-83756. (Positive Health Ser.). (Illus.). 80p. 1981. 12.95 (ISBN 0-938034-01-4); pap. 5.95 (ISBN 0-938034-02-2). PAL Pr.

Lawson-Wood, D. & Lawson-Wood, J. Five Elements of Acupuncture & Chinese Massage. 1980. 20.00x (ISBN 0-85032-167-0, Pub. by Daniel Co England). State Mutual Bk.

--Five Elements of Acupuncture & Chinese Massage. 96p. 1976. 8.95x (ISBN 0-8464-1010-9). Beekman Pubs.

Lee, Hor Ming, tr. from Chinese. Chinese Massage Therapy. (Illus.). Date not set. cancelled (ISBN 0-88930-048-8, Pub. by Cloudburst Canada); pap. cancelled (ISBN 0-88930-047-X). Madrona Pubs.

Licht, Sidney, ed. Massage, Manipulation & Traction. LC 76-7959. 292p. 1976. Repr. of 1960 ed. 14.50 (ISBN 0-88275-415-7). Krieger.

Lust, Benedict. Zone Therapy: Relieving Pain & Sickness by Nerve Pressure. (Illus.). 1980. pap. 3.95 (ISBN 0-87904-038-6). Lust.

Lust, John B. The Complete Massage Book. (Illus.). 1981. 14.95 (ISBN 0-87904-021-1). Lust.

Miller, Roberta D. Psychic Massage. (Illus.). 224p. (Orig.). 1975. pap. 7.95 (ISBN 0-06-090353-8, CN353, CN). Har-Row.

Moor, Fred B., et al. Manual of Hydrotherapy & Massage. LC 64-23214. 169p. 1964. 4.95 (ISBN 0-8163-0023-2, 13160-7). Pacific Pr Pub Assn.

Nichols, Frank. Theory & Practice of Body Massage. 1973. 9.95 (ISBN 0-87350-088-1). Milady.

Rogoff, Joseph K. Manipulation, Traction & Massage. 2nd ed. (Rehabilitation Medicine Library Ser.). (Illus.). 225p. 1980. lib. bdg. 25.50 (ISBN 0-683-07324-9). Williams & Wilkins.

Strange de Jim. The Strange Experience: How to Become the World's Second Greatest Lover. LC 80-69868. (Illus.). 192p. (Orig.). 1980. perfect bdg. 6.95 (ISBN 0-9605308-1-9). Ash-Kar Pr.

Tappan, Frances. Healing Massage Techniques: A Study of Eastern & Western Methods. (Illus.). 1978. ref. ed. 15.95 (ISBN 0-8359-2821-7); pap. 6.95 (ISBN 0-8359-2819-5). Reston.

Whelan, Stanley. Art of Erotic Massage. 1979. pap. 1.75 (ISBN 0-451-08824-7, E8824, Sig). NAL.

Wood, Elizabeth C. Beard's Massage: Principles & Techniques. 2nd ed. LC 73-86389. (Illus.). 190p. 1974. text ed. 14.00 (ISBN 0-7216-9591-4). Saunders.

Woody, Robert H. The Use of Massage in Facilitating Holistic Health. (Illus.). 136p. 1980. text ed. 12.50 (ISBN 0-398-03954-2). C C Thomas.

MASSAI

see Masai

MASSENET, JULES EMILE FREDERIC, 1842-1912

Finck, Henry T. Massenet & His Operas. 1976. Repr. of 1910 ed. 21.50 (ISBN 0-404-12912-9). AMS Pr.

Harding, James. Massenet. LC 70-132189. (Illus.). 1971. 8.95 (ISBN 0-312-51940-0, M18100). St Martin.

MASSES

see also Requiems

Hassler, Hans L. Mass Dixit Maria. Gano, Peter, ed. LC 66-18195. (Penn State Music Series, No. 11). 39p. 1966. pap. 3.25x (ISBN 0-271-73123-0). Pa St U Pr.

Miles, Cassian. The Masses of Advent. 48p. (Orig.). 1979. pap. 0.95 (ISBN 0-912228-59-8). St Anthony Mess Pr.

--The Masses of Lent. 48p. (Orig.). 1980. pap. 0.95 (ISBN 0-912228-67-9). St Anthony Mess Pr.

Order of the Mass. 1970. 8.75 (ISBN 0-02-640420-6, 64042); pap. 5.00 (ISBN 0-02-640430-3, 64043). Benziger Pub. Co.

Palestrina, Giovani Pierluigi da. Pope Marcellus Mass. new ed. Lockwood, Lewis, ed. (Critical Scores Ser.). 1975. 8.95x (ISBN 0-393-02185-8); pap. 3.95x (ISBN 0-393-09242-9). Norton.

Robertson, Alec. Requiem: Music of Mourning & Consolation. LC 75-32462. 1976. Repr. of 1968 ed. lib. bdg. 22.75x (ISBN 0-8371-8552-1, RORE). Greenwood.

Van Den Borren, Charles, ed. Polyphonia Sacra: A Continental Miscellany of the Fifteenth Century. LC 63-18891. 1963. 27.50x (ISBN 0-271-73092-7). Pa St U Pr.

MASSINGER, PHILIP, 1583-1640

Ball, Robert H. Amazing Career of Sir Giles Overreach. 1967. lib. bdg. 18.00x (ISBN 0-374-90361-1). Octagon.

Cruickshank, Alfred H. Philip Massinger. LC 72-139914. (Illus.). 1971. Repr. of 1920 ed. 13.00 (ISBN 0-8462-1555-1). Russell.

Evenhuis, Francis D. Massinger's Imagery. (Salzburg Studies in English Literature, Jacobean Drama Studies: No. 14). 176p. 1973. pap. text ed. 25.00x (ISBN 0-391-01373-4). Humanities.

Hensman, Bertha. The Shares of Fletcher, Field & Massinger in Twelve Plays of the Beaumont & Fletcher Canon, 2 vols. (Salzburg Studies in English Literature, Jacobean Drama Studies: No.6). 1974. Set. pap. text ed. 50.25x (ISBN 0-391-01406-4). Humanities.

McMamaway, James G. Philip Massinger & the Restoration Drama. 1978. Repr. of 1931 ed. lib. bdg. 7.50 (ISBN 0-8495-3503-4). Arden Lib.

Mc Manaway, James G. Philip Massinger & the Restoration Drama. LC 74-635. 1934. Repr. lib. bdg. 5.00 (ISBN 0-8414-6111-2). Folcroft.

Makkink, Henri J. Philip Massinger & John Fletcher: A Comparison. LC 68-1145. (Studies in Drama, No. 39). 1969. Repr. of 1927 ed. lib. bdg. 32.95 (ISBN 0-8383-0669-1). Haskell.

--Philip Massinger & John Fletcher: A Comparison. 1927. 12.50 (ISBN 0-8274-3129-5). R West.

Massinger, Philip. Philip Massinger: The Roman Actor. Repr. of 1912 ed. 22.00 (ISBN 0-403-04204-6). Somerset Pub.

Maxwell, Baldwin. Studies in Beaumont, Fletcher & Massinger. 1966. lib. bdg. 16.00x (ISBN 0-374-95396-1). Octagon.

MASSON, ANDRE, 1896-

Hahn, Otto. Masson. (Modern Artists Ser). 1965. 12.50 (ISBN 0-8109-4413-8). Abrams.

Rubin, William & Lanchner, Carolyn. Andre Masson. (Illus.). 1976. 20.00 (ISBN 0-87070-465-6); pap. 8.95 (ISBN 0-87070-464-8). Museum Mod Art.

MAST CELLS

Pepys, J. The Mast Cell. 873p. pap. text ed. 29.95 (ISBN 0-272-79582-8). Univ Park.

MASTABAS

see Tombs

MASTER AND SERVANT

see also Agency (Law); Apprentices; Employees, Dismissal Of; Employers' Liability; Negligence; Servants; Trade Secrets

McBride, Theresa. The Domestic Revolution: The Modernization of Household Service in England & France 1820-1920. LC 75-35720. (Illus.). 250p. 1976. text ed. 25.75x (ISBN 0-8419-0248-8). Holmes & Meier.

MASTERMAN, CHARLES FREDERICK GURNEY, 1873-1927

Masterman, Lucy B. C. F. G. Masterman: A Biography. LC 68-88329. (Illus.). Repr. of 1939 ed. 18.00x (ISBN 0-678-05187-9). Kelley.

MASTERS, EDGAR LEE, 1869-1950

Blout, Harry L. Spoon River Legacy. (Illus.). 1969. 4.65 (ISBN 0-685-02601-9). RSVP Pub & Dist.

Derleth, August. Three Literary Men: A Memoir of Sinclair Lewis, Sherwood Anderson & Edgar Lee Masters. LC 78-11518. Repr. of 1963 ed. lib. bdg. 10.00 (ISBN 0-8414-3686-X). Folcroft.

Flanagan, John T. Edgar Lee Masters: The Spoon River Poet & His Critics. LC 74-20530. 1974. 10.00 (ISBN 0-8108-0741-6). Scarecrow.

Hallwas, John E. & Reader, Dennis J., eds. The Vision of This Land: Studies of Vachel Lindsay, Edgar Lee Masters, & Carl Sandburg. LC 76-4350. 1976. pap. 5.00 (ISBN 0-934312-00-1). Essays in Lit W Ill U.

Masters, Hardin W. Edgar Lee Masters: A Biographical Sketchbook About a Great American Author. LC 76-20337. 1978. 12.50 (ISBN 0-8386-2031-0). Fairleigh Dickinson.

Primeau, Ronald. Beyond "Spoon River". The Legacy of Edgar Lee Masters. 230p. 1981. text ed. 22.50x (ISBN 0-292-70731-2). U of Tex Pr.

--Beyond the Spoon River: The Legacy of Edgar Lee Master. 230p. 1981. 22.50x (ISBN 0-292-70731-2). U of Tex Pr.

Robinson, Frank K., compiled by. Edgar Lee Masters: An Exhibition in Commemoration of the Centenary of His Birth. LC 71-31042. (Illus.). 1970. pap. 5.00 (ISBN 0-87959-015-7). U of Tex Hum Res.

MASTERS, WILLIAM H.-HUMAN SEXUAL RESPONSE

Brecher, Ruth & Brecher, Edward, eds. Analysis of Human Sexual Response. 1974. pap. 1.95 (ISBN 0-451-08440-3, J8440, Sig). NAL.

MASTERS GOLF TOURNAMENT

Taylor, Dawson. The Masters: Profiles of a Tournament. 3rd rev. ed. (Illus.). 192p. 1981. 19.95 (ISBN 0-498-01661-7). A S Barnes.

MASTERS OF SHIPS

see Shipmasters

MASTERSON, WILLIAM BARCLAY, 1853-1921

Churchill, E. Richard. Doc Holliday, Bat Masterson, Wyatt Earp: Their Colorado Careers. 1978. 2.00 (ISBN 0-913488-05-4). Timberline Bks.

DeArment, Robert K. Bat Masterson: The Man & the Legend. LC 78-21383. (Illus.). 1979. 15.95 (ISBN 0-8061-1522-X). U of Okla Pr.

MASTICATION

Anderson, D. J. Mastication. (Illus.). 1976. 29.50 (ISBN 0-8151-0188-0). Year Bk Med.

Griffin, C. J., et al, eds. The Temporomandibular Joint Syndrome: Masticatory Apparatus of Man in Normal & Abnormal Function. (Monographs in Oral Science: Vol. 4). (Illus.). 200p. 1975. 55.75 (ISBN 3-8055-2106-5). S Karger.

Kawamura, Y., ed. Physiology of Mastication. (Frontiers of Oral Physiology: Vol. 1). 1974. 104.25 (ISBN 3-8055-1281-3). S Karger.

Sessle, Barry J. & Hannam, Alan G., eds. Mastication & Swallowing: Biological & Clinical Correlates. LC 75-38957. (Illus.). 1975. 30.00x (ISBN 0-8020-2207-3). U of Toronto Pr.

MASTIFF

see Dogs-Breeds-Mastiff

MASTURBATION

Barbach, Lonnie G. For Yourself: Fulfillment of Female Sexuality - a Guide to Orgasmic Response. 1976. pap. 1.95 (ISBN 0-451-08969-3, J8969, Sig). NAL.

--For Yourself: The Fulfillment of Female Sexuality. 240p. 1976. pap. 3.95 (ISBN 0-385-11245-9, Anchor Pr). Doubleday.

Blank, Joani & Cottrell, Honey L. I Am My Lover. (Illus.). 1978. pap. 4.50 (ISBN 0-9602324-3-5). Down There Pr.

DeMartino, Manfred. Human Autoerotic Practices. LC 78-8766. 1978. 29.95 (ISBN 0-87705-373-1). Human Sci Pr.

Marcus, Irwin M. & Francis, John J., eds. Masturbation: From Infancy to Senescene. LC 73-16855. 634p. 1975. text ed. 27.50 (ISBN 0-8236-3150-8). Intl Univs Pr.

Sarnoff, Suzanne & Sarnoff, Irving. Sexual Excitement - Sexual Peace. LC 78-23755. 336p. 1979. 12.50 (ISBN 0-87131-281-6). M Evans.

The Secret Vice Exposed. LC 73-20648. (Sex, Marriage & Society Ser.). 470p. 1974. Repr. of 1839 ed. 26.00x (ISBN 0-405-05816-0). Arno.

Trobisch, Walter & Trobisch, Ingrid. My Beautiful Feeling: Letters to Ilona. LC 76-21459. 128p. 1976. pap. 2.95 (ISBN 0-87784-577-8). Inter-Varsity.

MAT

see Miller Analogies Test

MATA HARI

see Zelle, Margaretha Geertrudia, 1876-1917

MATABELE

Carnegie, David. Among the Matabele. LC 74-97399. (Illus.). Repr. of 1894 ed. 10.00x (ISBN 0-8371-5094-9, Pub. by Negro U Pr). Greenwood.

Rasmussen, R. A. Mzilikazi of the Ndebele. (African Historical Biographies Ser.). (Illus.). 48p. 1977. pap. text ed. 2.75x (ISBN 0-435-94475-4). Heinemann Ed.

MATABELE-HISTORY-FICTION

Plaatje, Solomon T. Mhudi: An Epic of South African Native Life a Hundred Years Ago. LC 74-100298. Repr. of 1930 ed. 12.25x (ISBN 0-8371-2930-3, Pub. by Negro U Pr). Greenwood.

MATABELE WAR, 1896

Baden-Powell, Robert S. Matabele Campaign, 1896. LC 79-109309. (Illus.). Repr. of 1897 ed. 24.75x (ISBN 0-8371-3566-4, Pub. by Negro U Pr). Greenwood.

Selous, Frederick C. Sunshine & Storm in Rhodesia. 2nd ed. LC 69-18660. (Illus.). Repr. of 1896 ed. 17.25x (ISBN 0-8371-4947-9, Pub. by Negro U Pr). Greenwood.

Sykes, Frank W. With Plumer in Matabeleland. LC 72-82471. (Illus.). Repr. of 1897 ed. 22.00x (ISBN 0-8371-1640-6). Greenwood.

Wills, William A. & Collingridge, L. T. Downfall of Lobengula: The Cause, History & Effect of the Matabeli War. LC 79-82324. (Illus.). Repr. of 1894 ed. 27.00x (ISBN 0-8371-1653-8, Pub. by Negro U Pr). Greenwood.

MATABELELAND

Selous, Frederick C. Sunshine & Storm in Rhodesia. 2nd ed. LC 69-18660. (Illus.). Repr. of 1896 ed. 17.25x (ISBN 0-8371-4947-9, Pub. by Negro U Pr). Greenwood.

MATADOR LAND AND CATTLE COMPANY, LTD.

Pearce, W. M. The Matador & Cattle Company. (Illus.). 288p. 1981. 14.95 (ISBN 0-8061-0595-X). U of Okla Pr.

MATADORS

see Bull-Fighters

MATCHES

Stephens, Kent. Matches, Flames & Rails: The Diamond Match Co. in the High Sierra. rev., 2nd ed. LC 80-51156. 1980. 17.95 (ISBN 0-87046-056-0). Trans-Anglo.

MATERIA MEDICA

see also Anesthetics; Aphrodisiacs; Drugs; Drugs-Dosage; Materia Medica, Dental; Materia Medica, Vegetable; Medicine-Formulae, Receipts, Prescriptions; Pharmacognosy; Pharmacology; Pharmacy; Poisons; Therapeutics; Veterinary Materia Medica and Pharmacy; also names of drugs

Allen, H. C. Keynotes & Characteristics with Comparisons. 319p. 1980. Repr. of 1959 ed. lib. bdg. 40.00 (ISBN 0-89987-005-8). Darby Bks.

Blair, Thomas S. Botanic Drugs: Their Materia Medica, Pharmacology & Therapeutics. 1976. lib. bdg. 134.75 (ISBN 0-8490-1539-1). Gordon Pr.

Boretos, John W. Concise Guide to Biomedical Polymers: Their Design, Fabrication & Molding. (Illus.). 208p. 1973. 18.75 (ISBN 0-398-02674-2). C C Thomas.
Buchman, Dian D. Herbal Medicine: The Natural Way to Get Well & Stay Well. (Illus.). 1979. pap. 7.95 (ISBN 0-679-51081-8). McKay.
Challem, Jack & Lewin-Challem, Renate. What Herbs Are All About. LC 80-82913. 150p. (Orig.). 1980. pap. 2.95 (ISBN 0-87983-204-5). Keats.
Clarke, John H. A Clinical Repertory to the Dictionary of Materia Medica. 1971. 15.95 (ISBN 0-85032-061-5, Pub. by C. W. Daniels). Formur Intl.
--A Dictionary of Practical Materia Medica. 1980. 125.00x (ISBN 0-85032-139-5, Pub. by Daniel Co England). State Mutual Bk.
Emboden, William. Narcotic Plants. LC 80-10900. 224p. 1980. pap. 7.95 (ISBN 0-02-062840-4, Collier). Macmillan.
Falconer, Mary W. Patient Studies in Pharmacology: A Guidebook. LC 75-44608. 160p. 1976. pap. text ed. 7.00 (ISBN 0-7216-3545-8). Saunders.
Goodrich, Jennie, et al. Kashaya Pomo Plants. 168p. 1980. softcover 8.95 (ISBN 0-935626-01-8). U Cal AISC.
Hinman. Advanced Medical Systems: An Assessment of the Contributions. 1979. 23.75 (ISBN 0-8151-4461-X). Year Bk Med.
Kent, J. T. Repertory of Homoeopathic Materia Medica. 1975. 30.00 (ISBN 0-685-76570-9, Pub. by Harjeet). Formur Intl.
Leonard, C. Henri & Christy, Thomas. Dictionary of Materia Medica & Therapeutics. 1980. lib. bdg. 75.00 (ISBN 0-8490-3120-6). Gordon Pr.
Le Rossignol, J. N. An Encyclopedia of Materia Medica & Therapeutics for Chiropodists. 184p. 1980. 12.95 (ISBN 0-571-11483-0, Pub. by Faber & Faber). Merrimack Bk Serv.
Marchetti, Albert. Common Cures for Common Ailments: A Doctor's Guide to Nonprescription, Over-the-Counter Medicines & His Recommendations for Their Use. LC 77-16114. 368p. 1981. pap. 8.95 (ISBN 0-8128-6107-8). Stein & Day.
Meyer, Clarence. Vegetarian Medicines. Meyer, David C., ed. (Illus.). 96p. (Orig.). 1981. pap. 5.95 (ISBN 0-916638-06-5). Meyerbooks.
Meyer, Joseph E. The Herbalist. (Illus.). 304p. 1981. 11.95 (ISBN 0-8069-3902-8); lib. bdg. 10.79 (ISBN 0-8069-3903-6). Sterling.
Morton, Julia F. Atlas of Medicinal Plants of Middle America: Bahamas to Yucatan. (Illus.). 1472p. 1981. 147.50 (ISBN 0-398-04036-2). C C Thomas.
The Old Herb Doctor. 1981. pap. 6.95 (ISBN 0-87877-052-6). Newcastle Pub.
Patient Medication Profiles. 1975. 9.00 (ISBN 0-917330-02-1). Am Pharm Assn.
Perry, Lily M. & Metzger, Judith. Medicinal Plants of East & Southeast Asia: Attributed Properties & Uses. 632p. 1980. 45.00x (ISBN 0-262-16076-5). MIT Pr.
Powell, Eric F. Kelp the Health Giver. 1980. 15.00x (ISBN 0-85032-195-6, Pub. by Daniel Co England). State Mutual Bk.
Research Staff of F&S Press with Duane Gingerich, ed. Medical Products Liability: A Comprehensive Guide & Sourcebook. 500p. 1981. prof. ref. 59.50 (ISBN 0-86621-001-6). Ballinger Pub.
Rosauer, Elmer A. Instruments for Material Analysis. (Illus.). 198p. 1981. text ed. 16.25 (ISBN 0-8138-1750-1). Iowa St U Pr.
Schubert, Jack. Copper & Peroxides in Radiobiology & Medicine. (Illus.). 228p. 1964. photocopy ed. spiral 22.50 (ISBN 0-398-01689-5). C C Thomas.
Smith, William. Wonders in Weeds. 187p. 1977. 13.00x (ISBN 0-8464-1062-1). Beekman Pubs.
Stebbing, L. Honey As Healer. 1973. lib. bdg. 59.95 (ISBN 0-87968-554-9). Krishna Pr.
Swazey, Judith P. Chlorpromazine in Psychiatry: A Study of Therapeutic Innovation. 519p. 1974. 27.50x (ISBN 0-262-19130-X). MIT Pr.
U. K. Health Markets. 100p. 1981. 120.00x (ISBN 0-686-71959-X, Pub. by Euromonitor). State Mutual Bk.
Windholz, Martha, ed. The Merck Index. 9th ed. LC 76-27231. 1976. 18.00 (ISBN 0-911910-26-3). Merck.

MATERIA MEDICA-EARLY WORKS TO 1800

Culpeper, Nicholas. Culpeper's Complete Herbal. (Illus.). 1959. 12.95 (ISBN 0-8069-3900-1); lib. bdg. 10.79 (ISBN 0-8069-3901-X). Sterling.
Dioscorides, Pedanius. Greek Herbal. Gunther, Robert T., ed. Goodyear, J., tr. (Illus.). 1968. Repr. of 1933 ed. 23.00 (ISBN 0-02-843930-9). Hafner.
Hester, John. The Key of Philosphie, in Two Bookes, 2 bks. LC 73-6141. (English Experience Ser.: No. 605). 116p. 1973. Repr. of 1596 ed. Set. 9.50 (ISBN 90-221-0605-5). Walter J Johnson.
Monardes, Nicolas. Joyfull Newes Out of the Newe Founde Worlde, 2 Vols. Frampton, John, tr. LC 25-20529. (Tudor Translations, Second Series: Nos. 9, 10). Repr. of 1925 ed. Set. 70.00 (ISBN 0-404-51990-3); 35.00 ea. Vol. 1 (ISBN 0-404-51991-1). Vol. 2 (ISBN 0-404-51992-X). AMS Pr.
--Joyfull Newes Out of the Newe Founde Worlde. Frampton, J., tr. LC 74-25786. (English Experience Ser.: No. 251). 110p. 1970. Repr. of 1577 ed. 22.00 (ISBN 90-221-0251-3). Walter J Johnson.

MATERIA MEDICA, ARABIC

see Medicine, Arabic

MATERIA MEDICA, DENTAL

Neidle, Enid A. Pharmacology & Therapeutics for Dentistry. LC 80-10522. (Illus.). 736p. 1980. text ed. 29.50 (ISBN 0-8016-3635-3). Mosby.
Requa-Clark, Barbara & Holroyd, Sam V. Applied Pharmacology for the Dental Hygienists. 384p. 1981. pap. 17.50 (ISBN 0-8016-2239-5). Mosby.

MATERIA MEDICA, VEGETABLE

see also Botany, Medical; Herbs; Medicine, Medieval

Bishop, Carol. Book of Home Remedies & Herbal Cures. (Octopus Bk.). (Illus.). 1979. 12.50 (ISBN 0-7064-1069-6, Mayfower Bks); pap. 6.95 (ISBN 0-7064-1088-2). Smith Pubs.
Bullein, William. Bulleins Bulwarke of Defence Againste All Sickness, Sorness & Woundes. LC 73-37139. (English Experience Ser.: No. 350). (Illus.). 488p. 1971. Repr. of 1562 ed. 83.00 (ISBN 90-221-0350-1). Walter J Johnson.
Diers Rau, Henrietta A. Healing with Herbs: Nature's Way to Better Health. LC 75-23579. 240p. 1976. pap. 1.95 (ISBN 0-668-03878-0). Arco.
Dymock, William, et al. Pharmacographia Indica: A History of Principal Drugs of Vegetable Origin Met with in British India, 3 vols. 1978. Repr. of 1890 ed. Set. 220.00 (ISBN 0-89955-296-X, Pub. by Intl Bk Dist). Intl Schol Bk Serv.
Grieve, M. A Modern Herbal. Leyel, Mrs. C. F., ed. LC 72-169784. (Illus.). 1971. pap. 6.50 ea.; Vol. 1. pap. (ISBN 0-486-22798-7); Vol. 2. pap. (ISBN 0-486-22799-5). Dover.
Griffin, LaDean. No Side Effects: Return to Herbal Medicine. 7.95 (ISBN 0-686-29931-0). Cancer Bk Hse.
Harris, Ben C., ed. The Compleat Herbal. LC 77-185615. 243p. (Orig.). 1972. pap. 1.75 (ISBN 0-915962-15-2). Larchmont Bks.
Henslow, George. Medical Works of the Fourteenth Century, Together with a List of Plants Recorded in Contemporary Writings, with Their Identifications. LC 72-82036. 278p. 1972. Repr. of 1899 ed. lib. bdg. 21.00 (ISBN 0-8337-1666-2). B Franklin.
International Congress on Pharmacognosy & Phytochemistry, Munich, 1970. Proceedings. Wagner, H. & Hoerhammer, L., eds. LC 79-149122. (Illus.). 1971. pap. 46.10 (ISBN 0-387-05316-6). Springer-Verlag.
Jackson, Betty & Snowden, Derek. Powdered Vegetable Drugs. 1968. 19.50 (ISBN 0-444-19903-9). Elsevier.
Kaaiakamanu, D. M. & Akina, J. K. Hawaiian Herbs of Medicinal Value. Akana, Akaiko, tr. LC 76-177367. 1972. pap. 4.75 (ISBN 0-8048-1019-2). C E Tuttle.
Kloss, Jethro. Back to Eden: The Authentic Kloss Family Edition. 5th ed. LC 75-585. (Lifeline Bks.). (Illus.). 1975. 9.95 (ISBN 0-912800-33-X); pap. 2.95 (ISBN 0-912800-12-7); pap. 5.95 large format (ISBN 0-912800-61-5). Woodbridge Pr.
Lewis, Walter H. & Elvin-Lewis, P. F. Medical Botany: Plants Affecting Man's Health. LC 76-44376. 1977. 38.50 (ISBN 0-471-53320-3, Pub by Wiley-Interscience). Wiley.
Lucas, Richard. Common & Uncommon Uses of Herbs for Healthful Living. LC 74-128898. 1970. pap. 1.95 (ISBN 0-668-02396-1). Arco.
--Secrets of the Chinese Herbalists. 1977. 8.95 (ISBN 0-13-797639-9, Parker). P-H.
Lust, Benedict. About Herbs: Nature's Medicine. 1980. pap. 1.95 (ISBN 0-87904-045-9). Lust.
Lust, John, ed. The Herb Book. 672p. 1974. pap. 3.95 (ISBN 0-553-20148-4). Bantam.
Meyer, Joseph E. Herbalist. 6.95 (ISBN 0-685-85699-2, Pub. by Meyerbooks). Formur Intl.
Millspaugh, Charles F. American Medicinal Plants. 1974. 10.00 (ISBN 0-486-23034-1, Pub. by Dover). Formur Intl.
--American Medicinal Plants: An Illustrated & Descriptive Guide to Plants Indigenous to & Naturalized in the United States Which Are Used in Medicine, Vol. 1. LC 73-91487. (Illus.). 450p. 1974. pap. 10.00 (ISBN 0-486-23034-1). Dover.
Morton, Julia F. Major Medicinal Plants: Botany, Culture & Uses. (Illus.). 448p. 1978. 62.75 (ISBN 0-398-03673-X). C C Thomas.
Null, Gary, et al. Herbs for the Seventies. LC 72-187998. (The Health Library: Vol. 2). 168p. 1972. 5.95 (ISBN 0-8315-0129-4). Speller.
Powell, Eric. Kelp, the Health Giver. 1980. pap. 1.95 (ISBN 0-87904-041-6). Lust.
Ramalingam, Vimala, et al. Medicinal Plants, 3 vols, Vol. 1. Singh, N. & Mital, H. C., eds. 161p. 1974. text ed. 22.50x (ISBN 0-8422-7240-2). Irvington.
Rose, Jeanne. Herbs & Things: Jeanne Rose's Herbal. 1972. 5.95 (ISBN 0-448-01139-5). G&D.
--Jeanne Rose's Herbal Guide to Inner Health. (Illus.). 1978. pap. 6.95 1980 (ISBN 0-448-14522-7). G&D.
Swain, Tony. Plants in the Development of Modern Medicine. LC 79-169862. (Illus.). 548p. 1972. 18.50x (ISBN 0-674-67330-1). Harvard U Pr.
Twitchell, Paul. Herbs, the Magic Healers. 1971. pap. 2.95 (ISBN 0-914766-10-4). IWP Pub.
Wheelwright, Edith G. Medicinal Plants & Their History. LC 74-78815. (Illus.). 288p. 1974. pap. 3.50 (ISBN 0-486-23103-8). Dover.
--Medicinal Plants & Their History. (Illus.). 6.50 (ISBN 0-8446-5258-X). Peter Smith.

MATERIAL HANDLING

see Materials Handling

MATERIAL SCIENCE

see Materials

MATERIALISM

see also Dualism; Idealism; Mechanism (Philosophy); Monism; Naturalism; Realism

Armstrong, D. M. Materialist Theory of the Mind. (International Library of Philosophy & Scientific Method). 1968. text ed. 24.50x (ISBN 0-7100-3634-5). Humanities.
Aronowitz, Stanley. The Crisis in Historical Materialism: Class, Politics, & Culture in Marxist Theory. 256p. 1981. 25.95 (ISBN 0-03-059031-0). Praeger.
Bennett, John G. Material Objects. 1977. 2.50 (ISBN 0-900306-35-1, Pub. by Coombe Springs Pr). Claymont Comm.
Berkeley, George. Three Dialogues Between Hylas & Philonous. Adams, Robert M., ed. LC 79-65276. 1979. lib. bdg. 12.50 (ISBN 0-915144-62-X); pap. text ed. 2.75 (ISBN 0-915144-61-1). Hackett Pub.
Broussais, Francois J. On Irritation & Insanity. Cooper, Thomas, tr. LC 75-3091. Repr. of 1831 ed. 31.50 (ISBN 0-404-59089-6). AMS Pr.
Colman, Morris. On Consciousness, Language, & Cognition: Three Studies in Materialism. (Occasional Papers: No. 31). 1978. 1.50 (ISBN 0-89977-027-4). Am Inst Marxist.
Cornman, James W. Materialism & Sensations. LC 75-151570. 1971. 25.00x (ISBN 0-300-01250-0). Yale U Pr.
Douglas, Mary & Isherwood, Baron. The World of Goods: An Anthropologist's Perspective. LC 78-54498. 1979. 12.95 (ISBN 0-465-09228-4). Basic.
Engels, Friedrich. On Historical Materialism. LC 76-42699. (BCL Ser.: II). Repr. of 1940 ed. 11.50 (ISBN 0-404-15370-4). AMS Pr.
Giddens, Anthony. A Contemporary Critique of Historical Materialism. LC 81-+009. 250p. 1981. 29.50x (ISBN 0-520-04535-1, CAL 288); pap. 10.95x (ISBN 0-520-04490-8). U of Cal Pr.
Haldane, J. S. Materialism. 1979. Repr. of 1932 ed. lib. bdg. 30.00 (ISBN 0-8495-2262-5). Arden Lib.
Hearn, Roy J. Handbook on Materialism. 1950. pap. 2.00 (ISBN 0-686-21479-X). Firm Foun Pub.
Krishan Mittal, Kewal. Materialism in Indian Thought. LC 74-901145. 344p. 1974. 18.75x (ISBN 0-8002-0045-4). Intl Pubns Serv.
La Mettrie, Julien O. Man a Machine. 216p. (Fr. & Eng.). 12.95 (ISBN 0-87548-041-1); pap. 4.95 (ISBN 0-87548-041-1). Open Court.
--Man a Machine. 216p. (Fr. & Eng.). 12.95 (ISBN 0-87548-041-1); pap. 4.95 (ISBN 0-87548-041-1). Open Court.
Lange, Frederick A. The History of Materialism: Criticism of Its Present Importance. LC 73-14163. (Perspectives in Social Inquiry Ser.). 380p. 1974. Repr. 25.00x (ISBN 0-405-05508-0). Arno.
Lenin, V. I. Materialism & Empirio-Criticism. 397p. 1977. 2.75 (ISBN 0-8285-0140-8, Pub. by Progress Pubs Russia). Imported Pubns.
Margolis, Joseph. Persons & Minds: The Prospects of Nonreductive Materialism. (Synthese Library: No. 121). 1977. lib. bdg. 34.00 (ISBN 90-277-0854-1, Pub. by Reidel Holland); pap. 16.00 (ISBN 90-277-0863-0, Pub. by Reidel Holland). Kluwer Boston.
Marx, Karl, et al. On Historical Materialism. 751p. 1972. 18.00x (ISBN 0-8464-0683-7). Beekman Pubs.
Novack, George. Origins of Materialism. LC 76-160511. (Orig.). 1965. 14.00 (ISBN 0-87348-023-6); pap. 4.95 (ISBN 0-87348-022-8). Path Pr NY.
Plekhanov, G. Materialismus Militans. 128p. pap. 1.75 (ISBN 0-8285-0201-3, Pub. by Progress Pubs Russia). Imported Pubns.
Plekhanov, G. V. Essays in the History of Materialism. 1968. 25.00 (ISBN 0-86527-061-9). Fertig.
Price, Richard. A Free Discussion of the Doctrine of Materialism and Philosophical Necessity, 1778. Wellek, Rene, ed. LC 75-11247. (British Philosophers & Theologians of the 17th & 18th Centuries Ser.). 1978. lib. bdg. 42.00 (ISBN 0-8240-1798-6). Garland Pub.
Rosenfield, Leonora. From Beast Machine to Man Machine: Animal Soul in French Letters from Descartes to La Mettrie. 1968. lib. bdg. 25.00x (ISBN 0-374-96955-8). Octagon.
Rosenthal, David. Materialism & the Mind-Body Problem. LC 77-157186. (Central Issues in Philosophy Ser). (Illus.). 1971. pap. 9.50 ref. ed. (ISBN 0-13-560177-0). P-H.
--Materialism & the Mind-Body Problem. LC 77-157186. (Central Issues in Philosophy Ser). (Illus.). 1971. pap. 9.50 ref. ed. (ISBN 0-13-560177-0). P-H.
Ross, Eric B., ed. Beyond the Myths of Culture: Essays in Cultural Materialism. LC 79-6772. (Studies in Anthropology Ser.). 1980. 31.00 (ISBN 0-12-598180-5). Acad Pr.
Ruben, David. Marxism & Materialism. rev. ed. (Marxist Theory & Contemporary Capitalism Ser.). 1978. text ed. 27.50x (ISBN 0-391-00966-4); pap. text ed. 11.00x (ISBN 0-391-00965-6). Humanities.
Schofield, Robert E. Mechanism & Materialism: British Natural Philosophy in the Age of Reason. LC 72-90960. 1969. 21.00x (ISBN 0-691-08072-0). Princeton U Pr.
Seely, Charles. Essentials of Modern Materialism. LC 69-14359. 1969. 3.50 (ISBN 0-8022-2276-5). Philos Lib.
Seely, Charles S. Philosophy of Science. LC 64-13327. 1964. 3.75 (ISBN 0-8022-1531-9). Philos Lib.
Sollers, Philippe. Sur le Materialisme: De l'Atomisme a la Dialectique Revolutionnaire. 192p. 1974. 11.95 (ISBN 0-686-55017-X). French & Eur.
Timpanaro, Sebastiano. On Materialism. 1976. 14.00x (ISBN 0-902308-03-3, Pub. by NLB). Schocken.
Vartanian, Aram. Diderot & Descartes: A Study of Scientific Naturalism in the Enlightment. LC 75-18406. (History of Ideas Series: No. 6). 336p. 1975. Repr. of 1953 ed. lib. bdg. 17.50x (ISBN 0-8371-8337-5, VADD). Greenwood.
White, John. The Golden Cow: Materialism in the 20th Century Church. LC 78-13884. 1979. pap. 3.95 (ISBN 0-87784-490-9). Inter-Varsity.
Williams, Raymond. Problems in Materialism & Culture: Selected Essays. 288p. 1981. 19.50x (ISBN 0-8052-7093-0, Pub. by NLB England); pap. 8.75 (ISBN 0-8052-7092-2). Schocken.

MATERIALISM, DIALECTICAL

see Dialectical Materialism

MATERIALS

see also Biomedical Materials; Building Materials; Composite Materials; Finishes and Finishing; Granular Materials; Heat Resistant Materials; Manufacturing Processes; Materials at High Temperatures; Materials at Low Temperatures; Materials Management; Raw Materials; Slurry; Strategic Materials

Abelson, Philip H. & Dorfman, Mary, eds. Advanced Technology. LC 80-67368. (Science Compendia Ser.: Vol. 8). (Illus.). 168p. 1980. text ed. 14.00x (ISBN 0-686-72329-5); pap. text ed. 6.00x (ISBN 0-87168-249-4). AAAS.
Abelson, Philip H. & Hammond, Allen L., eds. Materials: Renewable & Nonrenewable Resources. LC 76-7295. (Science Compendium Ser.: Vol. 4). 1976. casebound 12.00 (ISBN 0-87168-216-8); pap. 4.50 (ISBN 0-87168-227-3). AAAS.
Abraham, F. & Tiller, W. A., eds. An Introduction to Computer Simulation in Applied Science. LC 72-83047. 220p. 1972. 25.00 (ISBN 0-306-30579-8, Plenum Pr). Plenum Pub.
Amelinckx, S., et al. Diffraction & Imaging Techniques in Material Science, 2 vol. set. 2nd rev. ed. 1978. 109.75 (ISBN 0-444-85130-5, North-Holland). Elsevier.
American Physical Society Conference, New York City, Feb. 2-5, 1976. Materials Technology: Proceedings. Chynoweth, A. G. & Walsh, W. M., eds. LC 76-27967. (AIP Conference Proceedings: No. 32). 1976. 18.00 (ISBN 0-88318-131-2). Am Inst Physics.
Ashby, M. F. & Jones, D. R. Engineering Materials: An Introduction to Their Properties & Applications. (International Ser. on Materials Science & Technology: Vol. 34). (Illus.). 120p. 1980. 36.00 (ISBN 0-08-026139-6); pap. 11.50 (ISBN 0-08-026138-8). Pergamon.
Barrett, C., et al. The Principles of Engineering Materials. 1973. 26.95 (ISBN 0-13-709394-2). P-H.
Beer, Ferdinand P. & Johnston, E. Russell, Jr. Mechanics of Materials. (Illus.). 672p. 1981. text ed. 26.95x (ISBN 0-07-004284-5, C); write for info solutions manual (ISBN 0-07-004291-8). McGraw.

Biggs, W. D. The Mechanical Behaviour of Engineering Materials. 1978. text ed. 11.75 (ISBN 0-08-011415-6); pap. text ed. 8.50 (ISBN 0-08-011414-8). Pergamon.
Bolton. Materials Technology for Technicians, No. 2. 1982. text ed. price not set (ISBN 0-408-01117-3). Butterworth.
--Materials Technology for Technicians 3, No. 3. 1982. price not set (ISBN 0-408-01117-3). Butterworth.
Borland, D. W., et al. Physics of Materials. 338p. 1981. 75.00x (ISBN 0-643-02449-2, Pub. by CSIRO Australia). State Mutual Bk.
Borland, D. W., et al, eds. Physics of Materials. LC 79-67059. 1980. 42.00x (ISBN 0-643-02449-2, Pub by CSIRO). Intl Schol Bk Serv.
Breitschuh, K. Triangular Plates & Slabs. (Illus.). 199p. (Eng. & Ger.). 1974. 31.25 (ISBN 3-4330-0647-4). Adler.
Brick, R. M., et al. Structure & Properties of Engineering Materials. 4th ed. (McGraw-Hill Ser. in Materials Science & Engineering). Orig. Title: Structure & Properties of Alloys. (Illus.). 1977. text ed. 25.00 (ISBN 0-07-007721-5, C). McGraw.
Brostow, Witold. Science of Materials. LC 78-5983. 1979. 39.50 (ISBN 0-471-01885-6, Pub. by Wiley-Interscience). Wiley.
Budinski, Kenneth G. Engineering Materials: Properties & Selection. (Illus.). 1979. ref. 20.95 (ISBN 0-8359-1693-6); students manual avail. (ISBN 0-8359-1694-4). Reston.
Bunge, Hans. Texture Analysis in Materials Science: Mathematical Methods. 2nd ed. Morris, Peter, tr. from Ger. LC 79-40054. 1981. text ed. 79.95 (ISBN 0-408-10642-5). Butterworth.
Chalmers, B., ed. Progress in Materials Science, Vol. 23. 280p. 1980. 93.75 (ISBN 0-08-024846-2). Pergamon.
Chalmers, B., et al, eds. Progress in Materials Science, Vols. 15-21. Incl. Vol. 15, Pt. 1. 1971. pap. 15.50 (ISBN 0-08-015869-2); Vol. 15, Pt. 2. 1972. pap. 15.50 (ISBN 0-08-016824-8); Vol. 15, Pt. 3. 1972. pap. 15.50 (ISBN 0-08-016877-9); Vol. 15, Pt. 4. 1973. pap. 15.50 (ISBN 0-08-017132-X); Vol. 15, Complete. 85.00 (ISBN 0-08-017154-0); Vol. 16. 1972. 85.00 (ISBN 0-08-016866-3); Vol. 17. 1972. 31.00 (ISBN 0-08-017011-0); Vol. 18. 1974. 85.00 (ISBN 0-08-017155-9); Vol. 19. 1974. 85.00 (ISBN 0-08-017964-9); Vol. 20. 1977. 300.00 (ISBN 0-08-021143-7); Vol. 21, Pt. 1. 1975. pap. 12.00 (ISBN 0-08-018172-4); Vol. 21, Pt. 2. 1976. pap. 15.50 (ISBN 0-08-019831-7); Vol. 21, Pts. 3 & 4. pap. 33.00 (ISBN 0-08-019987-9); Vol. 21, Complete. 1977. 85.00 (ISBN 0-08-018171-6). Pergamon.
--Progress in Materials Science, Vols. 6-10, 12-13. Incl. Vol. 6. 1956. 85.00 (ISBN 0-08-009035-4); Vol. 7. 1958. 85.00 (ISBN 0-08-009177-6); Vol. 8. 1959. 60.00 (ISBN 0-08-009294-2); Vol. 9, Pt. 1. 1961; Vol. 9, Pt. 2. 1962; Vol. 9, Pt. 3. Effects of Environment on Mechanical Properties of Metals. 1962; Vol. 9, Pt. 4. 1962; Vol. 9, Pt. 5. 1962; Vol. 10, Pt. 1. Alloy Phases of the Noble Metals. 1963. pap. 15.50 (ISBN 0-08-009618-2); Vol. 10, Complete. 1963. 67.50 (ISBN 0-08-010981-0); Vol. 12, Pt. 1. 1963; Vol. 12, Pt. 2. 1964. pap. 12.50 (ISBN 0-08-010035-X); Vol. 13, Pt. 1. Pergamon.
Christian, J. W., et al, eds. Chalmers Anniversary Volume: Supplement to Progress in Materials Science. (Illus.). 330p. 1981. 50.00 (ISBN 0-08-027147-2). Pergamon.
Clauser, H. R. Encyclopedia Handbook of Materials, Parts & Finishes. new rev. ed. LC 75-43010. 1976. 35.00 (ISBN 0-87762-189-6). Technomic.
Clauser, Henry. Industrial & Manufacturing Materials. (Illus.). 416p. 1975. text ed. 18.50 (ISBN 0-07-011285-1, G). McGraw.
Collieu, A. & Powney, Derek J. The Mechanical & Thermal Properties of Materials. LC 72-85498. 294p. 1973. 19.50x (ISBN 0-8448-0074-0). Crane-Russak Co.
Committee on Materials Specifications, Testing Methods & Standards, National Research Council. Materials & Process Specifications & Standards. LC 77-92433. (Illus.). 1977. pap. text ed. 8.50 (ISBN 0-309-02731-4). Natl Acad Pr.
Conference on Surface Properties of Materials, Held at the University of Missouri, Rolla, June 24-27, 1974. Surface Properties of Materials: Proceedings. Levenson, L. L., ed. (Journal of Surface Science: Vol. 48). 294p. 1975. Repr. of 1975 ed. 44.00 (ISBN 0-444-10846-7, North-Holland). Elsevier.
Cordon, William A. Properies, Evaluation & Control of Engineering Materials. 1979. text ed. 19.50 (ISBN 0-07-013123-6, C); solution manual 3.95 (ISBN 0-07-013124-4). McGraw.
Crilly, Eugene R. Material & Process Applications: Land, Sea, Air, Space. (The Science of Advanced Materials & Process Engineering Ser.). 1981. 60.00 (ISBN 0-938994-18-2). Soc Adv Material.
Davis, H., et al. The Testing of Engineering Materials. 4th ed. 480p. 1981. text ed. 27.95 (ISBN 0-07-015656-5, C). McGraw.
Derucher, Kenneth & Heins, Conrad. Materials for Civil & Highway Engineers. (Illus.). 416p. 1981. text ed. 26.95 (ISBN 0-13-560490-7). P-H.
Eisenstadt, Melvin M. Introduction to Mechanical Properties of Materials: An Ecological Approach. 1971. text ed. 23.95 (ISBN 0-02-332140-7, 33214). Macmillan.
Electronic Properties of Materials: A Guide to the Literature, 3 vols. Incl. Vol. 1. Johnson, H. Thayne. 1681p. 1965. 195.00 (ISBN 0-306-68221-4); Vol. 2. Grigsby, Donald L., et al. 1800p. 1967. 195.00 (ISBN 0-306-68222-2); Vol. 3. Grigsby, Donald L. LC 65-12176. 1895p. 1971. 195.00 (ISBN 0-306-68223-0). IFI Plenum.
Ericsson, T., ed. Computers in Materials Technology: Proceedings of the Conference Held in Linkoping, June 1980. 200p. 1981. 30.00 (ISBN 0-08-027570-2). Pergamon.
Evans, L. S. Chemical & Process Plant: A Guide to the Selection of Engineering Materials. 2nd ed. LC 80-20355. 190p. 1980. 38.95 (ISBN 0-470-27064-0). Halsted Pr.
Farag, M. M. Materials & Process Selection in Engineering. (Illus.). 1979. 59.50x (ISBN 0-85334-824-3). Intl Ideas.
Feltham, P. Deformation & Strength of Materials. 142p. 1966. 25.00 (ISBN 0-306-30648-4, Plenum Pr). Plenum Pub.
Finniston, H. M., ed. Structural Characteristics of Materials. (Illus.). 1971. 48.50x (ISBN 0-444-20045-2, Pub. by Applied Science). Burgess-Intl Ideas.
Fitzgerald, R. W. Mechanics of Materials. 2nd ed. 1982. price not set (ISBN 0-201-04073-5). A-W.
Flinn, Richard & Trojan, Paul K. Engineering Materials & Their Applications. 1975. 22.95 (ISBN 0-395-18916-0); instructor's manual 2.50 (ISBN 0-395-19378-8). HM.
Flinn, Richard A. & Trojan, Paul K. Engineering Materials & Their Applications. 2nd ed. (Illus.). 753p. 1981. text ed. 22.95 (ISBN 0-395-29645-5); instr's manual 3.50 (ISBN 0-395-29646-3). HM.
Francis, Philip H. & Lindholm, Ulric S. Advanced Experimental Techniques in the Mechanics of Materials. 1973. 83.75x (ISBN 0-677-12570-4). Gordon.
Frandin, Herman F. Treatise on Materials Science & Technology: Vol. 21, Electronic Structure & Properties. LC 81-2457. 1981. 51.00 (ISBN 0-12-341821-6). Acad Pr.
Geller, Yu. A. & Rakhshtadt, A. G. Science of Materials. 519p. 1977. 6.90 (ISBN 0-8285-0693-0, Pub. by Mir Pubs Russia). Imported Pubns.
Gentry, George. Hardening & Tempering Engineers' Tools. 6.50x (ISBN 0-85344-054-9). Intl Pubns Serv.
Gillies, M. T. Nonwoven Materials-Recent Developments. LC 79-5445. (Chemical Technology Review: No. 141). (Illus.). 1980. 45.00 (ISBN 0-8155-0776-3). Noyes.
Granet, Irving. Modern Materials Science. (Illus.). 1980. text ed. 21.95 (ISBN 0-8359-4569-3); instrs' manual avail. Reston.
Guy, A. G. Essentials of Materials Science. 1976. text ed. 21.95 (ISBN 0-07-025351-X, C); solutions manual 4.50 (ISBN 0-07-025352-8). McGraw.
Handbook of Industrial Materials: Ferrous & Non-Ferrous Metals, Non-Metallic Materials, Plastics, Adhesives. 1978. 105.00x (ISBN 0-85461-068-5). Intl Ideas.
Harris, Bryan & Bunsell, A. R. Structure & Properties of Engineering Materials. LC 76-41771. (Introductory Engineering Ser.). 1977. text ed. 26.00x (ISBN 0-582-44000-9); pap. text ed. 17.95x (ISBN 0-582-44001-7). Longman.
Hausner, Henry, ed. Modern Materials: Advances in Development & Applications. Incl. Vol. 1. 1958; Vol. 2. 1960. 56.00 (ISBN 0-12-462202-X); Vol. 3. 1963. 56.00 (ISBN 0-12-462203-8); Vol. 4. Gonser, B. W. & Hausner, Henry H., eds. 1964. 56.00 (ISBN 0-12-462204-6); Vol. 5. Gonser, B. W., ed. 1965; Vol. 6. 1968. 49.50 (ISBN 0-12-462206-2); Vol. 7. 1970. 49.00 (ISBN 0-12-462207-0). Acad Pr.
Henisch, H. K., et al, eds. Phase Transitions & Their Applications in Materials Science. LC 73-14411. 300p. 1974. text ed. 38.00 (ISBN 0-08-017955-X). Pergamon.
Herbst, John A. & Sastry, K. V., eds. On-Stream Characterization & Control of Particulate Processes. 308p. 1981. pap. 15.00 (ISBN 0-939204-02-9, 78-19). Eng Found.
Herman, Herbert. Treatise on Materials Science & Technology: Vol. 19 Experimental Methods, Pt. a. LC 77-182672. 1980. 32.00 (ISBN 0-12-341819-4). Acad Pr.
Herman, Herbert, ed. Treatise on Materials Science, Vols. 1-14. Incl. Vol. 1. 1972. 46.50 (ISBN 0-12-341801-1); Vol. 2. 1973. 60.00 (ISBN 0-12-341802-X); Vol. 3. Ultrasonic Investigation of Mechanical Properties. Green, Robert E., Jr. 1973. 30.00 (ISBN 0-12-341803-8); Vol. 4, 1974. 55.00 (ISBN 0-12-341804-6); Vol. 5. 1974. 55.00 (ISBN 0-12-341805-4); Vol. 6. Plastic Deformation of Materials. 71.50 (ISBN 0-12-341806-2); Vol. 7. Microstructure of Irradiated Materials. 1975. 38.00 (ISBN 0-12-341807-0); Vol. 8. 1975. 46.50 (ISBN 0-12-341808-9); Vol. 9. Ceramic Fabrication Processes. Wang, F. F., ed. 1976. 63.00 (ISBN 0-12-341809-7); Vol. 10. Properties of Solid Polymeric Materials: Part A. Schulz, J. M., ed. 1977. 64.00 (ISBN 0-12-341810-0); Vol. 10. Properties of Solid Polymeric Materials: Part B. Schultz, J. M., ed. 1977. 58.50 (ISBN 0-12-341841-0); Vol. 11. Properties & Microstructure. MacCrone, R. K., ed. 1977. 68.50 (ISBN 0-12-341811-9); Vol. 12. Glass I: Interaction with Electromagnetic Radiation. Tomozawa, Minoru, ed. 1977. 59.00 (ISBN 0-12-341812-7). LC 78-27077. Acad Pr.
--Treatise on Materials Science & Technology Vol. 15: Neutron Scattering in Materials Science. (Treatise on Materials Science & Technology Ser.). 1979. 66.50 (ISBN 0-12-341815-1). Acad Pr.
Higgins, R. A. Properties of Engineering Materials. rev. ed. LC 77-22284. 448p. 1979. pap. 19.50 (ISBN 0-88275-575-7). Krieger.
Hornsey, et al. Mechanics of Materials: An Individualized Approach. LC 76-18470. (Illus.). 1977. pap. 18.95 incl. ref. manual & study guide (ISBN 0-395-24993-7); solutions manual 2.15 (ISBN 0-395-24994-5). HM.
Huggins, R. A., et al, eds. Annual Review of Materials Science, Vol. 7. LC 75-172108. (Illus.). 1977. text ed. 17.00 (ISBN 0-8243-1707-6). Annual Reviews.
Huggins, Robert A., et al, eds. Annual Review of Materials Science, Vol. 8. LC 75-172108. (Illus.). 1978. text ed. 17.00 (ISBN 0-8243-1708-4). Annual Reviews.
--Annual Review of Materials Science, Vol. 9. LC 75-172108. (Illus.). 1979. text ed. 17.00 (ISBN 0-8243-1709-2). Annual Reviews.
--Annual Review of Materials Science, Vol. 10. LC 75-172108. (Illus.). 1980. text ed. 20.00 (ISBN 0-8243-1710-6). Annual Reviews.
--Annual Review of Materials Science, Vol. 11. LC 75-172108. (Illus.). 1981. text ed. 20.00 (ISBN 0-8243-1711-4). Annual Reviews.
Institute for Power System. Handbook of Industrial Materials. 600p. 1979. 99.00x (ISBN 0-686-65620-2). State Mutual Bks.
Institution of Chemical Engineers, Research Committee Working Party. Materials & Energy Resources. 68p. 1981. 42.00x (ISBN 0-85295-012-8, Pub. by Inst Chem Eng England). State Mutual Bk.
Interim Specifications - Materials. 1980. 6.00 (ISBN 0-686-29455-6). AASHTO.
Jackson, Neil. Civil Engineering Materials. LC 76-381536. (Illus.). 1977. pap. 19.50x (ISBN 0-333-19310-5). Scholium Intl.
Jastrzebski, Zbigniew D. The Nature & Properties of Engineering Materials. 2nd ed. LC 75-20431. 656p. 1975. text ed. 31.95x (ISBN 0-471-44089-2). Wiley.
--The Nature & Properties of Engineering Materials: SI Version. 2nd ed. LC 77-83735. 1977. text ed. 30.95 (ISBN 0-471-02859-2); solns. manual avail. (ISBN 0-471-03671-4). Wiley.
Jones, S. W. Materials Science: Selection of Materials. (Illus.). 1971. 13.50x (ISBN 0-408-70110-2). Transatlantic.
Kaldis, E., ed. Current Topics in Material Science, Vol. 1. 1978. 127.00 (ISBN 0-7204-0708-7, North-Holland). Elsevier.
--Current Topics in Materials Science, Vol. 3. 700p. 1979. 112.25 (ISBN 0-444-85245-X, North Holland). Elsevier.
Kazanas & Klein. Technology of Industrial Materials. 1981. pap. 14.28 (ISBN 0-87002-301-2); lab manual 5.28 (ISBN 0-87002-170-2). Bennett IL.
Kenney, George B. An Analysis of the Energy Efficiency & Economic Viability of Expanded Magnesium Utilization. LC 78-75004. (Outstanding Dissertations on Energy Ser.). 1979. lib. bdg. 20.00 (ISBN 0-8240-3975-0). Garland Pub.
Krebs, R. D. & Walker, R. D. Highway Materials. 1971. text ed. 24.50 (ISBN 0-07-035465-0, C). McGraw.
Lee, P. A., ed. Optical & Electrical Properties. (Physics & Chemistry of Materials with Layered Structures Ser: No. 4). 1976. lib. bdg. 71.00 (ISBN 90-277-0676-X, Pub. by Reidel Hollad). Kluwer Boston.
Lefax Pub. Co. Editors. Mechanics of Materials. (Lefax Data Bks.: No. 635). (Illus.). looseleaf bdg. 3.00 (ISBN 0-685-14156-X). Lefax.
Levy, Francis A., ed. Intercalated Layered Materials. (Physics & Chemistry of Materials with Layered Structures: No. 6). 1979. lib. bdg. 78.95 (ISBN 90-277-0967-X, Pub. by Reidel Holland). Kluwer Boston.
Libowitz, G. G. & Whittingham, M. S., eds. Materials Science in Energy Technology. LC 78-51235. (Materials Science & Technology Ser.). 1979. 58.00 (ISBN 0-12-447550-7). Acad Pr.
Lindberg, Roy A. Materials & Manufacturing Technology. (Illus.). 1968. text ed. 26.95x (ISBN 0-205-01947-1, 321947X). Allyn.
--Processes & Materials of Manufacture. 2nd ed. 1977. text ed. 27.95 (ISBN 0-205-05414-5, 32544143); a. b. avail. (ISBN 0-205-05492-7, 3254143). Allyn.
Lovell, M. C. & Avery, A. J. Physical Properties of Materials. LC 75-35836. (Modern University Physics Series). 1976. text ed. 29.50x (ISBN 0-442-30096-4); pap. 13.10x (ISBN 0-442-30097-2). Van Nos Reinhold.
Lynch, Charles T., ed. Handbook of Materials Science, CRC, Vols. 1-3. Incl. Vol. 1. General Properties, 1974. 760p. 69.95 (ISBN 0-87819-231-X); Vol. 2. Metals, Composites & Refractory Materials. 448p. 1975. 49.95 (ISBN 0-87819-232-8); Vol. 3. Nonmetallic Materials & Applications. 642p. 1975. 64.95 (ISBN 0-87819-233-6). LC 73-90240. (Handbook Ser.). CRC Pr.
McClintock, F. A. & Argon, A. S. Mechanical Behavior of Materials. 1966. 27.95 (ISBN 0-201-04545-1). A-W.
Maslow, Philip. Chemical Materials for Construction. LC 73-85217. (Illus.). 570p. 1974. 32.50 (ISBN 0-912336-07-2). Structures Pub.
Materials & Processes-in Service Performance. (National SAMPE Technical Conference Ser.). (Illus.). 1977. 40.00 (ISBN 0-938994-04-2). Soc Adv Material.
Matthews, J. W., ed. Epitaxial Growth, Pts. A & B. (Materials Science & Technology Ser). 1975. Pt. A. 60.50 (ISBN 0-12-480901-4); Pt. B. deluxe ed. 56.00 (ISBN 0-12-480902-2). Acad Pr.
Mattiat, Oskar E., ed. Ultrasonic Transducer Materials. LC 71-131885. (Ultrasonic Technology Monographs Ser.). 185p. 1971. 25.00 (ISBN 0-306-30501-1, Plenum Pr). Plenum Pub.
May, Luke C. The Nineteen Eighties--Payoff Decade for Advanced Materials. (The Science of Advanced Materials & Process Engineering Ser.). (Illus.). 1980. 55.00 (ISBN 0-938994-17-4). Soc Adv Material.
Merchant, Harish D. Problems in Material Science. 1972. 101.75x (ISBN 0-677-13450-9). Gordon.
Moore, Harry D. & Kibbey, Donald R. Manufacturing: Materials & Processes. 3rd ed. LC 81-4261. 380p. 1982. text ed. 26.95 (ISBN 0-88244-236-8). Grid Pub.
Mulvey, T. & Webster, R. K., eds. Modern Physical Techniques in Materials Technology. (Harwell Ser.). (Illus.). 336p. 1974. text ed. 59.00x (ISBN 0-19-851708-4). Oxford U Pr.
Neely, John. Practical Metallurgy & Materials of Industry. LC 78-19166. 1979. text ed. 23.95 (ISBN 0-471-02962-9); tchrs. manual o.p. avail. (ISBN 0-471-05121-7). Wiley.
Nielsen, J. Merle. Material Safety Data Sheets Collection. 980p. 1981. 260.00 (ISBN 0-931690-06-4). GE Tech Marketing.
Niku-Lari, A. & Al-Hassani, S. T., eds. Shot Peening: Proceedings of the 1st International Conference, Paris, 14-17 September 1981. 528p. 1982. 75.00 (ISBN 0-08-027599-0). Pergamon.
Olsen, G. Elements of Mechanics of Materials. 4th ed. 1982. 24.95 (ISBN 0-13-267013-5). P-H.
Patton, W. Materials in Industry. 2nd ed. 1976. text ed. 24.95 (ISBN 0-13-560722-1). P-H.
Pettit, T. Appreciation of Materials & Design. (Illus.). 192p. (gr. 6-12). 1981. pap. 9.95x (ISBN 0-7131-0356-6). Intl Ideas.
Physics of Modern Materials, Vol. 1. 530p. 1980. pap. 66.75 (ISBN 92-0-130080-8, ISP 538, IAEA). Unipub.
Polakowski, N. H. & Ripling, E. Strength & Structure of Engineering Materials. 1965. text ed. 26.95 (ISBN 0-13-851790-8). P-H.
Pollack. Material Science & Metallurgy. 3rd ed. (Illus.). 416p. 1980. text ed. 21.95 (ISBN 0-8359-4280-5). Reston.
--Materials Science & Metallurgy. 2nd ed. 1977. text ed. 18.95 (ISBN 0-87909-480-X); students manual avail. Reston.
Pollock, Daniel D., ed. Physical Properties of Materials for Engineers, Vol. I. 224p. 1981. price not set (ISBN 0-8493-6201-6). CRC Pr.
--Physical Properties of Materials for Engineers, Vol. III. 256p. 1982. price not set (ISBN 0-8493-6203-2). CRC Pr.
Popov, Egor O. Mechanics of Materials: SI Version. 2nd ed. (Illus.). 1978. 24.95 (ISBN 0-13-571299-8). P-H.

Pugh, H. L., ed. Mechanical Behaviour of Materials Under Pressure. (Illus.). 1970. 90.80x (ISBN 0-444-20043-6). Intl Ideas.
Ralls, Kenneth, et al. Introduction to Materials Science & Engineering. LC 76-10813. 608p. 1976. text ed. 29.95 (ISBN 0-471-70665-5). Wiley.
Reid, C. N. Deformation Geometry for Material Scientists. LC 73-4716. 220p. 1973. text ed. 25.00 (ISBN 0-08-017237-7); pap. text ed. 13.25 (ISBN 0-08-017745-X). Pergamon.
Richardson & Peterson. Systematic Materials Analysis. 1974. Vol. 2. 43.00, by subscription 37.00 (ISBN 0-12-587802-8); Vol. 3. 51.50, by subscription 44.00 (ISBN 0-12-587803-6). Acad Pr.
Rose, R. M., et al. Electronic Properties. LC 66-16132. (Structure & Properties of Materials, Vol. 4). 1966. pap. text ed. 14.95 (ISBN 0-471-73548-5). Wiley.
Rosen, Stephen L. Fundamental Principles of Polymeric Materials for Practicing Engineers. LC 76-146260. 1971. pap. 8.95 (ISBN 0-8436-0319-4). CBI Pub.
Rosenthal, Daniel & Asimow, Robert M. Introduction to Properties of Materials. 2nd ed. 1971. text ed. 15.95x (ISBN 0-442-07037-3); instructors' manual 1.00x (ISBN 0-442-27038-0). Van Nos Reinhold.
Roy, Rustum, ed. Materials Science & Engineering in the United States. LC 77-84670. (Illus.). 1970. 16.50x (ISBN 0-271-00101-1). Pa St U Pr.
Ruoff, Arthur L. Introduction to Materials Science. LC 79-4668. 718p. 1979. Repr. of 1972 ed. lib. bdg. 31.50 (ISBN 0-88275-960-4). Krieger.
Sax, N. Irving. Dangerous Properties of Industrial Materials. 5th ed. 1979. text ed. 57.50x (ISBN 0-442-27373-8). Van Nos Reinhold.
Schlenker, B. R. An Introduction to Materials Science: S. I. Edition. LC 73-16682. 364p. 1974. 24.95 (ISBN 0-471-76177-X). Wiley.
Schroder, K., ed. Electronic, Magnetic & Thermal Properties of Solid Materials. (Materials Science Ser.: Vol. 5). 1978. 55.00 (ISBN 0-8247-6487-0). Dekker.
Schultz, Jerold M. Diffraction for Materials Scientists. (Illus.). 336p. 1982. 34.95 (ISBN 0-13-211920-X). P-H.
Science & Public Policy Comm., Comm. on the Survey of Materials Science & Engineering. Materials & Man's Needs. LC 74-2118. (Illus.). 246p. 1974. pap. 8.00 (ISBN 0-309-02220-7). Natl Acad Pr.
Sensory Evaluation of Appearance of Materials. 1973. 19.75 (ISBN 0-686-52092-0, 04-545000-36). ASTM.
Singh, Surendra. Engineering Materials. 2nd rev. ed. 1980. text ed. 12.50x (ISBN 0-7069-0789-2, Pub. by Vikas India). Advent NY.
Sittig, Marshall. Metal & Inorganic Waste Reclaiming Encyclopedia. LC 80-21669. (Pollution Tech. Rev. 70; Chem. Tech. Rev. 175). (Illus.). 591p. (Orig.). 1981. 54.00 (ISBN 0-8155-0823-9). Noyes.
Skalimierski, B. & Bogdan. Mechanics & Strength of Materials. LC 78-10900. (Studies in Applied Mechanics Ser.: Vol. 1). 432p. 1979. 72.75 (ISBN 0-444-99793-8). Elsevier.
Sloane, A. Mechanics of Materials. (Illus.). 8.75 (ISBN 0-8446-2954-5). Peter Smith.
Smit, J. Magnetic Properties of Materials. (Inter-University Electronics Ser.). 1971. 33.00 (ISBN 0-07-058445-1, C). McGraw.
Smith, Charles O. Science of Engineering Materials. 2nd ed. (Illus.). 1977. text ed. 25.95 (ISBN 0-13-794990-1). P-H.
Smith, M. J. Materials & Structures. 2nd ed. (Illus.). 180p. 1980. pap. text ed. 13.95x (ISBN 0-7114-5639-9). Intl Ideas.
Society of Automotive Engineers. Materials Availability for the Automotive Industries. 1980. 15.00 (ISBN 0-89883-233-0). SAE.
Solymar, L. & Walsh, D. Lectures on the Electrical Properties of Materials. 2nd ed. (Illus.). 1980. 36.50x (ISBN 0-19-851144-2); pap. 18.95x (ISBN 0-19-851145-0). Oxford U Pr.
Source Book on Materials Selection, 2 vols. (TA 403.s62 (vol. 1) tA 403.s62 (vol. 2)). 1977. 38.00 ea. Vol. 1 (ISBN 0-87170-031-X). Vol. 2 (ISBN 0-87170-032-8). ASM.
Stein, Charles, ed. Critical Materials Problems in Energy Production. 1976. 49.50 (ISBN 0-12-665050-0). Acad Pr.
Stokes, Vernon L. Manufacturing Materials. (Electronics Technology Ser.). 1977. text ed. 20.95 (ISBN 0-675-08493-8); instructor's manual 3.95 (ISBN 0-685-74285-7). Merrill.
Symposium on Energistic Materials, Chicago, Ill. May 7-9, 1968. Proceedings. (Science of Advanced Materials & Process Engineering Ser., Vol. 13). 8.00 (ISBN 0-938994-13-1). Soc Adv Material.
Symposium on Materials Review for 1972. los Angeles, Ca. April 11-13, 1972. Proceedings. (Science of Advanced Materials & Process Engineering Ser., Vol. 17). 10.00 (ISBN 0-686-09874-9). Soc Adv Material.
Symposium on Materials 1971, Anaheim, Ca. April 20-23, 1971. Proceedings. (Science of Advanced Materials & Process Engineering Ser., Vol. 16). 10.00 (ISBN 0-938994-15-8). Soc Adv Material.
Tennissen, A. Nature of Earth Materials. 1974. ref. ed. 18.95 (ISBN 0-13-610501-7). P-H.
Thomas, Gareth, et al, eds. Electron Microscopy & Structure of Materials: Proceedings of the Fifth Annual Symposium on the Structure & Properties of Materials, Berkeley, September, 1971. 1972. 60.00x (ISBN 0-520-02114-2). U of Cal Pr.
Tottle, C. R. Encyclopedia of Metallurgy & Materials. 512p. 1980. 54.00x (ISBN 0-686-71794-5, Pub. by Macdonald & Evans). State Mutual Bk.
Trade & Technical Press Editors. Handbook of Industrial Materials. 600p. 1977. 98.00x (ISBN 0-85461-060-X, Pub by Trade & Tech England). Renouf.
Tulloch, D. S. Physical Fundamentals of Materials Science. 193p. 1971. 9.95 (ISBN 0-408-70097-1). Butterworth.
Van Vlack, Lawrence H. Elements of Materials Science & Engineering. 4th ed. LC 79-19352. (Metallurgy & Materials Ser.). 1980. text ed. 22.95 (ISBN 0-201-08090-7). A-W.
--Materials Science for Engineers. LC 74-91151. (Metallurgy & Materials Ser). 1970. text ed. 24.95 (ISBN 0-201-08074-5). A-W.
--A Textbook of Materials Technology. LC 70-190614. 1973. text ed. 20.95 (ISBN 0-201-08066-4); instructor's manual 3.95 (ISBN 0-201-08067-2). A-W.
Waseda, Yoshio. The Structure of Non-Crystalline Materials. (Illus.). 304p. 1980. text ed. 44.50 (ISBN 0-07-068426-X, C). McGraw.
Wulff, J., ed. Structure & Properties of Materials, 4 vols. Incl. Vol. 1. Structures. Moffatt, G. W., et al. 236p (ISBN 0-471-61265-0); Vol. 3. Mechanical Behavior. Hayden, H. W., et al. 247p (ISBN 0-471-36469-X); Vol. 4. Electronic Properties. Rose, R. M., et al. 306p (ISBN 0-471-73548-5). 1964-66. Set. pap. 31.50 (ISBN 0-471-96495-6). Wiley.
Wyatt, L. M. Materials of Construction for Steam Power Plant. (Illus.). 1976. 44.00x (ISBN 0-85334-661-5). Intl Ideas.
Wyskida, Richard M. & McDaniel, Don M. Modeling of Cushioning Systems. 334p. 1980. 46.25 (ISBN 0-677-05480-7). Gordon.
Zimmerman, O. T. & Lavine, Irvin. Handbook of Material Trade Names, with Supplements 1, 2, 3, & 4. 1953-65. 175.00 (ISBN 0-940770-01-6). Indus Res Serv.

MATERIALS–BIBLIOGRAPHY

Design News, ed. Design News Materials Directory. (Design News Directories Ser.). 164p. 1981. pap. 12.00x (ISBN 0-686-73568-4, DNM). Herman Pub.

MATERIALS–BRITTLENESS

see Brittleness

MATERIALS–CREEP

see also Concrete–Creep; Metals–Creep

Bernasconi, G. & Piatti, G., eds. Creep of Engineering Materials & Structures. (Illus.). xii, 420p. 1980. 65.00x (ISBN 0-85334-878-2, Pub. by Applied Science). Burgess-Intl Ideas.
Bressers, J., ed. Creep & Fatigue in High Temperature Alloys. (Illus.). xii, 192p. 1981. 50.00x (ISBN 0-85334-947-9). Intl Ideas.
CISM (International Center for Mechanical Sciences), Dept. for Mechanics of Deformable Bodies. Creep Transition in Cylinders. Seth, B. R., ed. (CISM Pubns. Ser.: No. 149). 29p. 1973. pap. 5.90 (ISBN 0-387-81170-2). Springer-Verlag.
Conway, J. B. Numerical Methods for Creep & Rupture Analysis. 1967. 45.25 (ISBN 0-677-01090-7). Gordon.
Conway, J. B. & Flagella, P. N. Creep-Rupture Data for the Refractory Metals to High Temperatures. 1971. 161.75x (ISBN 0-677-02660-9). Gordon.
Cundy, M. R., ed. Measurement of Irradiation-Enhanced Creep in Nuclear Materials. (Journal of Nuclear Materials: Vol. 65). 1977. 122.00 (ISBN 0-7204-0572-6, North-Holland). Elsevier.
International Union of Theoretical & Applied Mechanics Colloquium, Stanford Univ, 1960. Creep in Structures. Hoff, N. J., ed. (Illus.). 1962. 74.40 (ISBN 0-387-02796-3). Springer-Verlag.
International Union of Theoretical & Applied Mechanics Symposium, 2nd, Gothenburg, Sweden, 1970. Creep in Structures, Nineteen Seventy. Holt, J., ed. LC 75-182441. (Illus.). 440p. 1972. 82.60 (ISBN 0-387-05601-7). Springer-Verlag.
Kraus, Harry. Creep Analysis. LC 80-15242. 250p. 1980. 29.95 (ISBN 0-471-06255-3, Pub. by Wiley-Interscience). Wiley.
Lucas, Glenn E. Effects of Anisotrophy & Irradiation on the Creep Behavior of Zircaloy-2. LC 78-75012. (Outstanding Dissertations on Energy Ser.). 1979. lib. bdg. 35.00 (ISBN 0-8240-3987-4). Garland Pub.
Odquist, Folke K. Mathematical Theory of Creep & Creep Rupture. 2nd ed. (Oxford Mathematical Monographs). (Illus.). 210p. 1974. 39.50x (ISBN 0-19-853522-8). Oxford U Pr.
Rabotnov, Y. N. Creep Problems in Structural Members. (Applied Mathematics & Mechanics Ser.: Vol. 7). 1969. 97.75 (ISBN 0-444-10259-0, North-Holland). Elsevier.

MATERIALS–DETERIORATION

see also Corrosion and Anti-Corrosives

Applied Science Publishers Ltd London, ed. Materials Deterioration & Mechanisms of Deterioration. (Illus.). 1976. 50.40x (ISBN 0-85334-705-0). Intl Ideas.
Corrosion & Degradation of Implant Materials. (Special Technical Publications Ser.). 369p. 1979. 37.75x (ISBN 0-686-76092-1, 684, 04-684000-27). ASTM.
Erosion, Wear & Interfaces with Corrosion. 1974. 35.00 (ISBN 0-686-52022-X, 04-567000-29). ASTM.
Glaeser, W. A., et al, eds. Wear of Materials. 1977. pap. text ed. 50.00 (ISBN 0-685-81976-0, H00100). ASME.
Ludema, K. C., et al, eds. Wear of Materials, Nineteen Seventy-Nine: Bk. No. H00143. 1979. 60.00 (ISBN 0-685-95762-4). ASME.

MATERIALS–DYNAMIC TESTING

see also Impact; Structural Dynamics

Burke & Weiss, eds. Nondestructive Evaluation of Materials. (Sagamore Army Materials Research Conference: Vol. 23). 1979. 49.50 (ISBN 0-306-40185-1, Plenum Pr). Plenum Pub.
Engel, Peter A. Impact Wear of Materials. 1976. 61.00 (ISBN 0-444-41533-5). Elsevier.
Instrumented Impacted Testing. 1974. 21.75 (ISBN 0-686-52049-1, 04-563000-23). ASTM.

MATERIALS–FATIGUE

see also Fracture Mechanics;
also subdivision Fatigue under specific subjects, e.g. Metals–Fatigue

Bressers, J., ed. Creep & Fatigue in High Temperature Alloys. (Illus.). xii, 192p. 1981. 50.00x (ISBN 0-85334-947-9). Intl Ideas.
Burke, John J., et al, eds. Fatigue: An Interdisciplinary Approach. LC 64-21083. (Sagamore Army Materials Research Conference Proceedings Ser.: Vol. 10). 414p. 1964. 35.00 (ISBN 0-306-34510-2, Plenum Pr). Plenum Pub.
Cruse, T. A., ed. Fatigue Life Technology, Bk No. H00096. Gallagher, J. P. pap. text ed. 18.00 (ISBN 0-685-79860-7). ASME.
Cyclic Stress-Strain Behavior: Analysis, Experimentation & Failure Prediction. 1973. 28.00 (ISBN 0-8031-0078-7, STP519). ASTM.
Durability of Building Materials & Components. (Special Technical Publications Ser.). 1034p. 1980. 74.95x (ISBN 0-686-76026-3, 691, 04-691000-10). ASTM.
Effects of Environment & Complex Load History on Fatigue Life. 1970. 22.00 (ISBN 0-8031-0032-9, 04-462000-30). ASTM.
Fatigue Mechanisms. (Special Technical Publications Ser.). 922p. 1979. 65.00x (ISBN 0-686-76042-5, 675, 04-675000-30). ASTM.
Hertzberg, Richard W. & Manson, John A. Fatigue of Engineering Plastics. LC 79-6786. 1980. 35.50 (ISBN 0-12-343550-1). Acad Pr.
Liebowitz, H., ed. Progress in Fatigue & Fracture, Vol. 8 No. 1. 1976. text ed. 60.00 (ISBN 0-08-020866-5). Pergamon.
Little, R. E. & Jebe, E. H. Statistical Design of Fatigue Experiments. LC 74-14802. 280p. 1975. 49.95 (ISBN 0-470-54115-6). Halsted Pr.
Manson, S. S. Thermal Stress & Low-Cycle Fatigue. 416p. 1981. Repr. of 1966 ed. write for info. (ISBN 0-89874-279-X). Krieger.
--Thermal Stress & Low-Cycle Fatigue. 416p. 1981. lib. bdg. 39.50 (ISBN 0-89874-279-X). Krieger.
--Thermal Stress & Low-Cycle Fatigue. 1966. 39.50 (ISBN 0-07-039930-1, P&RB). McGraw.
Osgood, Carl C. Fatigue Design. 2nd ed. (International Ser. on the Strength & Fracture of Materials & Structures). 500p. 1981. 65.00 (ISBN 0-08-026167-1); pap. 33.00 (ISBN 0-08-026166-3). Pergamon.
Parker, A. P. Mechanics of Fracture & Fatigue: An Introduction. 1981. 29.95x (ISBN 0-419-11460-2, Pub. by E & FN Spon); pap. 14.95x (ISBN 0-419-11470-X). Methuen Inc.
Part-Through Crack Fatigue Life Prediction. (Special Technical Publications Ser.). 226p. 1979. 26.25x (ISBN 0-686-76041-7, 687, 04-687000-30). ASTM.
Probalistic Aspects of Fatigue. 203p. 1972. 19.75 (ISBN 0-8031-0103-1, STP511). ASTM.
Sandor, Bela I. Fundamentals of Cyclic Stress & Strain. LC 70-176415. (Illus.). 184p. 1972. text ed. 17.50x (ISBN 0-299-06100-0). U of Wis Pr.
Service Fatigue Loads Monitoring, Simulation, Analysis. (Special Technical Publications Ser.). 298p. 1979. 29.50x (ISBN 0-686-76043-3, 671, 04-671000-30). ASTM.
Society of Automotive Engineers. Fatigue Resistance: Testing & Forecasting. 1979. 13.50 (ISBN 0-89883-219-5). SAE.

MATERIALS–HANDLING AND TRANSPORTATION

see Materials Handling

MATERIALS–RADIOGRAPHY

see Radiography, Industrial

MATERIALS–RESEARCH

see Materials Research

MATERIALS–STRENGTHENING MECHANISMS

see Strengthening Mechanisms in Solids

MATERIALS–TESTING

see also Brittleness; Materials–Fatigue; Mechanical Wear; Moire Method

Adjuncts to ASTM Standards: Metric Practice Guide. 42p. 1979. softcover 5.00x (ISBN 0-686-76017-4, E 380-79, 06-503807-41). ASTM.
Adjuncts to ASTM Standards: Positive Displacement Meter Prover Tanks, ASTM Tables for Volume Reduction of Contents of. 46p. 1961. pap. 7.50 spiral bdg. (ISBN 0-686-76018-2, D 1750, 12-417500-00). ASTM.
Annual Book of ASTM Standards, Pts. Thirty to Forty-Eight. Incl. Pt. 10. Metals - Mechanical, Fracture & Corrosion Testing; Fatigue; Erosion; Effect of Temperature (109 Standards) 41.00 (ISBN 0-8031-0170-8, 01-010080-23); Pt. 11. Metallography; Nondestructive Tests (91 Standards) 36.00 (ISBN 0-8031-0171-6, 01-011080-22); Pt. 13. Cement; Line; Ceilings & Walls, Including Manual of Cement Testing (115 Standards) 27.00 (ISBN 0-8031-0172-4, 01-013079-07); Pt. 14. Concrete & Mineral Aggregates, Including Manual of Concrete Testing (152 Standards) 33.00 (ISBN 0-8031-0173-2, 01-014080-07); Pt. 18. Thermal & Cryogenic Insulating Materials; Building Seals & Sealants; Fire Tests; Building Constructions; Environmental Acoustics (230 Standards) 47.00 (ISBN 0-8031-0174-0, 01-018080-10); Pt. 22. Wood; Adhesive(193 Standards) 42.00 (ISBN 0-8031-0175-9, 01-022080-45); Pt. 23. Petroleum Products & Lubricants, Two (140 Standards) 44.00 (ISBN 0-8031-0176-7, 01-023080-12); Pt. 24. Petroleum Products & Lubricants, Two (143 Standards) 29.00 (ISBN 0-8031-0177-5, 01-024080-12); Pt. 25. Petroleum Products & Lubricants, Three; Aerospace Materials; Cataclysm (185 Standards) 49.00 (ISBN 0-8031-0178-3, 01-025080-12); Pt. 26. Gaseous Fuels; Coal & Coke; Atmospheric Analysis (148 Standards) 39.00 (ISBN 0-8031-0179-1, 01-026080-13); Pt. 30. Soap; Engine Coolants; Polishes; Halogenated Organic Solvents; Activated Carbon; Industrial Chemicals (234 Standards) 44.00 (ISBN 0-8031-0180-5, 01-030080-15); Pt. 31. Water (170 Standards) 47.00 (ISBN 0-8031-0181-3, 01-031080-16); Pt. 32. Textile Materials - Yarns, Fabrics & General Methods (119 Standards) 37.00 (ISBN 0-8031-0182-1, 01-032080-18); Pt. 43. Electronics (221 Standards) 49.00 (ISBN 0-8031-0183-X, 01-043080-46); Pt. 44. Magnetic Properties & Magnetic Materials; Metallic Materials for Thermostats & for Electrical Resistance, Heating & Contacts; Temperature Measurement (106 Standards) 49.00 (ISBN 0-8031-0184-8, 01-044080-40); Pt. 45. Nuclear Standards (156 Standards) 49.00 (ISBN 0-8031-0185-6, 01-045080-35); Pt. 46. End Use & Consumer Products (238 Standards) 52.00 (ISBN 0-8031-0186-4, 01-046080-47); Pt. 47. Test Methods for Rating Motor, Diesel & Aviation Fuels (7 Standards) 29.00 (ISBN 0-8031-0187-2, 01-047080-12); Pt. 48. Index. 11.50 (ISBN 0-8031-0188-0, 01-048080-42). 1980. of 48 vols. 1826.00 set, if paid in full in advance 1600.00 (ISBN 0-8031-0169-4). ASTM.
Annual Book of ASTM Standards, 1981: Electrical Insulation - Specifications: Solids, Liquids & Gases; Test Methods: Liquids & Gases; Protective Equipment, Pt. 40. 1152p. 1981. 46.00 (ISBN 0-686-76008-5, 01-040081-21). ASTM.
Annual Book of ASTM Standards, 1981: Electrical Isulation - Test Methods: Solids & Solidifying Fluids, Pt. 39. 1020p. 1981. 42.00 (ISBN 0-686-76007-7, 01-039081-21). ASTM.
Annual Book of ASTM Standards, 1981: Electronics, Pt. 43. 1400p. 1981. 54.00 (ISBN 0-686-76011-5, 01-043081-46). ASTM.
Annual Book of ASTM Standards, 1981: Emission, Molecular & Mass Spectroscopy; Chromatography; Resinography; Microscopy; Computerized Systems, Pt. 42. 672p. 1981. 30.00 (ISBN 0-686-76010-7, 01-042081-39). ASTM.
Annual Book of ASTM Standards, 1981: End Use & Consumer Products, Pt. 46. 1546p. 1981. 54.00 (ISBN 0-686-76014-X, 01-046081-47). ASTM.

Annual Book of ASTM Standards, 1981: General Test Methods, Nonmetal; Statistical Methods; Space Simulation; Particle Size Measurement; Laboratory Apparatus; Durability of Nonmetallic Materials; Metric Practice, Pt. 41. 1348p. 1981. 52.00 (ISBN 0-686-76009-3, 01-041081-41). ASTM.
Annual Book of ASTM Standards, 1981: Index, Subject & Alphanumeric, Pt. 48. 630p. 1981. 12.00 (ISBN 0-686-76016-6, 01-048081-42). ASTM.
Annual Book of ASTM Standards, 1981: Magnetic Properties & Magnetic Materials; Metallic Materials for Thermostats & for Electrical Resistance, Heating & Contacts; Temperature Measurement, Pt. 44. 1026p. 1981. 45.00 (ISBN 0-686-76012-3, 01-044081-40). ASTM.
Annual Book of ASTM Standards, 1981: Nuclear Standards, Pt. 45. 1448p. 1981. 53.00 (ISBN 0-686-76013-1, 01-046081-35). ASTM.
Annual Book of ASTM Standards, 1981: Plastics-General Test Methods, Nonmenclature, Pt. 35. 1194p. 1981. 48.00 (ISBN 0-686-76003-4, 01-035081-19). ASTM.
Annual Book of ASTM Standards, 1981: Plastics-Materials, Film, Reinforced & Cellular Plastics, High Modulus Fibers & Their Composites, Pt. 36. 1156p. 1981. 46.00 (ISBN 0-686-76004-2, 01-036081-19). ASTM.
Annual Book of ASTM Standards, 1981: Plastic Pipe & Building Products, Pt. 34. 1014p. 1981. 42.00 (ISBN 0-686-76002-6, 01-034081-19). ASTM.
Annual Book of ASTM Standards, 1981: Rubber, Natural & Synthetic-General Test Methods, Carbon Black, Pt. 37. 1000p. 1981. 42.00 (ISBN 0-686-76005-0, 01-037081-20). ASTM.
Annual Book of ASTM Standards, 1981: Rubber Products, Idustrial - Specifications & Related Test Methods, Gaskets, Tires, Pt. 38. 848p. 1981. 36.00 (ISBN 0-686-76006-9, 01-038081-20). ASTM.
Annual Book of ASTM Standards, 1981: Soap, Engine Coolants, Polishes, Halogenated Organic Solvents, Activated Carbon, Industrial Chemicals, Pt. 30. 1210p. 1981. 47.00 (ISBN 0-686-75998-2, 01-030081-5). ASTM.
Annual Book of ASTM Standards, 1981: Textiles-Fibers, Zippers, Pt. 33. 882p. 1981. 38.00 (ISBN 0-686-76001-8, 01-033081-18). ASTM.
Annual Book of ASTM Standards, 1981: Test Methods for Rating Motor, Diesel & Aviation Fuels, Pt. 47. 510p. 1981. 32.00 (ISBN 0-686-76015-8, 01-047081-12). ASTM.
Annual Book of ASTM Standards, 1981: Water, Pt. 31. 1512p. 1981. 53.00 (ISBN 0-686-75999-0, 01-031081-16). ASTM.
Berger, Harold, ed. Non Destructive Testing Standards: A Review. (ASTM Special Technical Publication Ser.: No. 624). 1977. 33.75 (ISBN 0-8031-0196-1, 04-624009-22). ASTM.
Burke & Weiss, eds. Nondestructive Evaluation of Materials. (Sagamore Army Materials Research Conference: Vol. 23). 1979. 49.50 (ISBN 0-306-40185-1, Plenum Pr). Plenum Pub.
Composite Materials: Testing & Design (Fifth Conference) (Special Technical Publications Ser.). 697p. 1979. 52.50x (ISBN 0-686-76025-5, 674, 04-674000-33). ASTM.
Computer Automation of Materials Testing. (Special Technical Publications Ser.). 235p. 1980. 21.75x (ISBN 0-686-76028-X, 710, 04-710000-32). ASTM.
Conference on Dimensioning & Strength Calculations, Fifth & Congress on Material Testing, Sixth, Budapest, Oct.-Nov. 1974. Proceedings, 2 vols. (Illus.). 1974. Set. 57.50x (ISBN 963-05-0472-3). Intl Pubns Serv.
Current Status of Plane Strain Crack Toughness Testing of High Strength Metallic Materials. 1967. 5.50 (ISBN 0-8031-0094-9, STP410). ASTM.
Davis, Harmer E., et al. Testing & Inspection of Engineering Materials. 3rd ed. (Civil Engineering Ser.). 1964. text ed. 21.50 (ISBN 0-07-015655-7, C). McGraw.
Dictionary of Material Testing: English - German - French, Vol. II. 486p. 1980. pap. 74.00x (ISBN 3-18-400435-X, Pub. by VDI Verlag Germany). Renouf.
Dictionary of Material Testing: French - German - English, Vol. III. 490p. 1980. pap. 74.00x (ISBN 0-686-71876-3, Pub. by VDI Verlag Germany). Renouf.
Dictionary of Material Testing: German - English - French, Vol. I. 382p. 1980. pap. 62.00x (ISBN 0-686-71877-1, Pub. by VDI Verlag Germany). Renouf.
Effect of Automotive Emission Requirements on Gasoline Characteristics. 1971. pap. 9.50 (ISBN 0-8031-0004-3, 04-487000-12). ASTM.
Elevated Temperature Testing Problem Areas. 1971. pap. 5.50 (ISBN 0-8031-0062-0, 04-488000-40). ASTM.
Fairbanks, Jesse R. Observable Materials Testing Text & Workbook. 1978. pap. text ed. 7.50 (ISBN 0-8191-0386-1). U Pr of Amer.
Five-Year Index to ASTM Technical Papers & Reports, 1951-55. 1957. 3.50 (ISBN 0-8031-0040-X, 13-002550-00). ASTM.
Five-Year Index to ASTM Technical Papers & Reports, 1956-60. 1962. 3.50 (ISBN 0-8031-0041-8, 13-002600-00). ASTM.
Five-Year Index to ASTM Technical Papers & Reports, 1961-65. 1966. 6.50 (ISBN 0-8031-0042-6, 13-002650-00). ASTM.
Five-Year Index to ASTM Technical Papers & Reports, 1966-70. 1971. 9.50 (ISBN 0-8031-0043-4, 13-002700-00). ASTM.
Five Year Index (1971-1975) 282p. Date not set. 16.25x (ISBN 0-686-76053-0, 13-002750-00). ASTM.
Fracture Toughness Testing at Cryogenic Temperatures. 1971. pap. 5.00 (ISBN 0-8031-0034-5, 04-496000-30). ASTM.
Gillemot, L. F. Material Testing Laboratories. 1970. pap. 2.50 (ISBN 92-3-100826-9, U373, UNESCO). Unipub.
Ignition, Heat Release, & Noncombustibility of Material. 165p. 1972. 10.00 (ISBN 0-8031-0111-2, STP502). ASTM.
Kobayashi, Albert S., ed. Experimental Techniques in Fracture Mechanics. LC 72-13967. (Society for Experimental Stress Analysis Ser.: No. 1). (Illus.). 160p. 1973. 7.50x (ISBN 0-8138-0710-7). Iowa St U Pr.
--Experimental Techniques in Fracture Mechanics, No. 2. (Society for Experimental Stress Analysis Ser.: No.2). (Illus.). 216p. 1975. text ed. 8.95x (ISBN 0-8138-0735-2). Iowa St U Pr.
Krautkramer, J. & Krautkramer, H. Ultrasonic Testing of Materials. LC 76-12561. 1977. 78.90 (ISBN 0-387-07716-2). Springer-Verlag.
Manual on Test Sieving Methods. 1972. pap. 3.00 (ISBN 0-8031-0015-9, 04-447010-23). ASTM.
Materials World Standards Mutual Speedy Finder. 800p. Date not set. 95.00 (ISBN 0-686-76110-3, 13-103000-00). ASTM.
Pao, Y. H., ed. Elastic Waves & Non-Destructive Testing of Materials: AMD, Vol. 29. 112p. 1978. 24.00 (ISBN 0-685-66796-0, H00112). ASME.
Richardson, J. H. & Peterson, R. V., eds. Systematic Materials Analysis, Vol. 4. (Materials Science & Technology Ser). 1978. 52.50 (ISBN 0-12-587804-4); subscription 45.00 (ISBN 0-686-67866-4). Acad Pr.
Significance of Tests & Properties of Concrete & Concrete-Making Materials. (Special Technical Publications Ser.). 882p. 1978. 65.00x (ISBN 0-686-76029-8, 169*B, 04-169020-07). ASTM.
Society for the Advancement of Materials and Process Engineering. Bicentennial of Materials. (National SAMPE Technical Conference Ser.). (Illus.). 1976. 40.00 (ISBN 0-938994-03-4). Soc Adv Material.
Spath, Wilhelm. Impact Testing of Materials. rev. ed. Rosner, M. E., ed. (Illus.). 1962. 47.25x (ISBN 0-677-00910-0). Gordon.
Symposium on Mechanical Behavior of Materials Under Dynamic Loads, San Antonio, 1967. Proceedings. Lindholm, U. S., ed. (Illus.). 1968. 43.10 (ISBN 0-387-04263-6). Springer-Verlag.
Testing for Prediction of Material Performance in Structures & Components. 313p. 1972. 28.50 (ISBN 0-8031-0117-1, STP515). ASTM.
Theocaris, P. S. Moire Fringes in Strain Analysis. 1969. text ed. 32.00 (ISBN 0-08-012974-9); pap. text ed. 15.00 (ISBN 0-08-012973-0). Pergamon.

MATERIALS-THERMAL PROPERTIES

CISM (International Center for Mechanical Sciences), Dept. of Mechanics of Solids, 1971. Entropy, Absolute Temperature & Coldness in Thermodynamics Boundary Conditions in Porous Material. Muller, I., ed. (CISM Pubns. Ser.: No. 76). (Illus.). 53p. 1973. pap. text ed. 8.20 (ISBN 0-387-81126-5). Springer-Verlag.
Collieu, A. & Powney, Derek J. The Mechanical & Thermal Properties of Materials. LC 72-85498. 294p. 1973. 19.50x (ISBN 0-8448-0074-0). Crane-Russak Co.
Heller, Gerhardt B. Thermophysics of Spacecraft & Planetary Bodies. (Progress in Astronautics & Aeronautics Ser.: Vol. 20). 1968. 30.00 (ISBN 0-12-535120-8). Acad Pr.
Heller, Gerhardt B., ed. Thermophysics & Temperature Control of Spacecraft & Entry Vehicles. (Progress in Astronautics & Aeronautics: Vol. 18). 1966. 27.00 (ISBN 0-12-535118-6). Acad Pr.
Heschong, Lisa. Thermal Delight in Architecture. 1979. 12.50x (ISBN 0-262-08101-6); pap. 5.95 (ISBN 0-262-58039-X). MIT Pr.
Siegel, R. & Howell, J. R. Thermal Radiation Heat Transfer. 1971. text ed. 26.50 (ISBN 0-07-057318-2, C); solution manual 5.00 (ISBN 0-07-057319-0). McGraw.
Svet, Darii Y. Thermal Radiation: Metals, Semiconductors, Ceramics, Partly Transparent Bodies, & Films. LC 65-25260. 93p. 1965. 25.00 (ISBN 0-306-10737-6, Consultants). Plenum Pub.
Thermodynamics of Nuclear Materials - 1962. 1962. 33.50 (ISBN 92-0-040062-0, ISP58, IAEA). Unipub.

MATERIALS, EFFECT OF RADIATION ON

Effects of Radiation on Structual Materials. (Special Technical Publications Ser.). 696p. 1979. 58.50x (ISBN 0-686-76081-6, 683, 04-683000-35). ASTM.
Fridman, Ya. B., ed. Strength & Deformation in Nonuniform Temperature Fields. LC 63-17641. 169p. 1964. 30.00 (ISBN 0-306-10688-4, Consultants). Plenum Pub.
Interaction of Radiation with Condensed Matter. (ICTP Ser: Vol. 2). (Illus.). 1978. pap. 48.00 (ISBN 92-0-130477-3, 1SP-443-2, IAEA). Unipub.
Kircher, John F. & Bowman, Richard E. Effects of Radiation on Materials. (Illus.). 1964. 27.50x (ISBN 0-442-15527-1). Van Nos Reinhold.
Silverman, Joseph, ed. Advances in Radiation Processing: Transactions of the Second International Meeting on Radiation Processing Held at Miami, Florida 22-26 Oct. 1978, 2 vols, Vol. 14, No. 1-3 & 4-6. 948p. 1980. Set. 130.00 (ISBN 0-08-025025-4). Pergamon.

MATERIALS, MAGNETIC

see Magnetic Materials

MATERIALS, RADIOACTIVE

see Radioactive Substances

MATERIALS, STRENGTH OF

see Strength of Materials

MATERIALS AT HIGH TEMPERATURES

see also Heat Resistant Materials; Metals at High Temperatures

Bahn, Gilbert S. Kinetics, Equilibria, & Performance of High Temperature Systems. 1963. 83.75 (ISBN 0-677-10030-2). Gordon.
Belton, G. R. & Worrell, W. L., eds. Heterogeneous Kinetics at Elevated Temperatures. LC 70-128401. 532p. 1970. 45.00 (ISBN 0-306-30500-3, Plenum Pr). Plenum Pub.
British Ceramic Research Association Symposium. Special Ceramics: Proceedings, 3 vols. Popper, P., ed. Incl. Vol. 1. 1961. 38.50 (ISBN 0-12-561650-3); Vol. 2. 1963. 72.00 (ISBN 0-12-561662-7); Vol. 3. 1966. 44.00 (ISBN 0-12-561664-3). Acad Pr.
Chu, C. W. & Woolam, J. A., eds. High Pressure & Low-Temperature Physics. 594p. 1978. 49.50 (ISBN 0-306-40014-6, Plenum Pr). Plenum Pub.
International Union of Theoretical & Applied Mechanics Symposium, Glasgow, 1968. Thermoinelasticity: Proceedings. Boley, B. A., ed. LC 75-94050. (Illus.). 1970. 79.70 (ISBN 0-387-80961-9). Springer-Verlag.
Plansee Seminar De Re Metallica - 6th - Reutte - 1968. High Temperature Materials: Papers presented at the Sixth Plansee Seminar. Benesovsky, F., ed. (Illus.). 1969. 82.60 (ISBN 0-387-80916-3). Springer-Verlag.
Toropov, N. A. Structural Transformations in Glasses at High Temperatures. LC 58-44503. (The Structure of Glass Ser.: Vol. 5). 223p. 1965. 37.50 (ISBN 0-306-18305-6, Consultants). Plenum Pub.
Toropov, N. A., ed. Chemistry of High Temperature Materials. LC 74-79891. (Illus.). 237p. 1969. 35.00 (ISBN 0-306-10820-8, Consultants). Plenum Pub.

MATERIALS AT LOW TEMPERATURES

Chu, C. W. & Woolam, J. A., eds. High Pressure & Low-Temperature Physics. 594p. 1978. 49.50 (ISBN 0-306-40014-6, Plenum Pr). Plenum Pub.
Clark, et al, eds. Nonmetallic Materials & Composites at Low Temperatures. (Cryogenic Materials Ser.). 1979. 39.50 (ISBN 0-306-40077-4, Plenum Pr). Plenum Pub.
Fracture Toughness Testing at Cryogenic Temperatures. 1971. pap. 5.00 (ISBN 0-8031-0034-5, 04-496000-30). ASTM.
Ives, M. B., ed. Materials Engineering in the Arctic. (Illus., TA 407.m36). 1977. 42.00 (ISBN 0-87170-050-6). ASM.
Perepechko, I. I. Low-Temperature Properties of Polymers. 272p. 1981. 40.00 (ISBN 0-08-025301-6). Pergamon.
Scurlock, R. G. Low Temperature Behaviour of Solids. (Solid-State Physics Ser). 1966. pap. 3.75 (ISBN 0-7100-4383-X). Routledge & Kegan.
White, Guy K. Experimental Techniques in Low-Temperature Physics. 3rd ed. (Monographs on the Physics & Chemistry of Materials). (Illus.). 1979. 29.50x (ISBN 0-19-851359-3). Oxford U Pr.
Wigley, D. A. Mechanical Properties of Materials at Low Temperatures. LC 72-159030. (International Cryogenics Monographs Ser.). 326p. 1971. 32.50 (ISBN 0-306-30514-3, Plenum Pr). Plenum Pub.

MATERIALS HANDLING

see also Bulk Solids Handling; Cargo Handling; Conveying Machinery; Freight and Freightage; Hydraulic Conveying; Motor-Trucks; Pallets (Shipping, Storage, etc.)

Apple, J. M. Plant Layout & Materials Handling. 3rd ed. LC 77-75127. (Illus.). 600p. 1977. 24.95 (ISBN 0-8260-0501-2). Wiley.
Apple, James M. Material Handling Systems Design. (Illus.). 656p. 1972. 36.00 (ISBN 0-8260-0485-7, Pub. by Wiley-Interscience). Wiley.
Bolz, Harold A., et al, eds. Materials Handling Handbook. LC 57-11291. 1958. 65.50 (ISBN 0-8260-1175-6, Pub. by Wiley-Interscience). Wiley.
Boresi, Arthur P., et al. Advanced Mechanics of Materials. 3rd ed. LC 77-28283. 1978. text ed. 35.50 (ISBN 0-471-08892-7). Wiley.
Bowman, Daniel. Lift Trucks: A Practical Guide for Buyers & Users. LC 72-83304. (Illus.). 1973. 19.95 (ISBN 0-8436-1007-7). CBI Pub.
Chemical Engineering Magazine. Solids Handling. McNaughton, Kenneth, ed. (Illus.). 263p. 1981. 29.50 (ISBN 0-07-010781-5). McGraw.
Colijn, Hendrik. Weighing & Proportioning of Bulk Solids. new ed. LC 74-77792. (Bulk Materials Handling Ser). (Illus.). 450p. 1975. 60.00 (ISBN 0-87849-011-6). Trans Tech.
Conference on Materials on the Move, NSTC 6, Dayton, Ohio, Oct. 8-10, 1974. Proceedings. (National Society for the Advancement of Material & Process Engineering Technical Conference Ser.). 30.00 (ISBN 0-938994-01-8). Soc Adv Material.
Ericsson, Dag. Materials Administration. 1974. 21.50 (ISBN 0-07-084441-0, P&RB). McGraw.
Johnston, John E. Site Control of Materials: Handling, Storage, & Security. (Illus.). 1981. text ed. price not set (ISBN 0-408-00377-4). Butterworth.
Kay, E. A Mathematical Model for Handling in a Warehouse. LC 68-21104. 1968. pap. 10.75 (ISBN 0-08-012831-9). Pergamon.
Leenders, Michael R., et al. Purchasing & Materials Management. 7th ed. 1980. 22.95x (ISBN 0-256-02374-3). Irwin.
Material Handling Equipment. (Machinery Studies). 1981. 350.00 (ISBN 0-686-31530-8). Busn Trend.
Murphy, G. J. Transport & Distribution. 2nd ed. 300p. 1978. text ed. 24.50x (ISBN 0-220-66321-1, Pub. by Busn Bks England). Renouf.
--The Transport Operators Guide to Professional Competence. 314p. 1980. pap. 21.00x (ISBN 0-09-141591-8, Pub. by Busn Bks England). Renouf.
Muther, Richard & Haganas, Knut. Systematic Handling Analysis. LC 73-90920. 1969. spiral bdg. 24.95 (ISBN 0-8436-1002-6). CBI Pub.
Rasper, Ludwig. The Bucket Wheel Excavator: Bulk Materials Handling Ser. LC 74-77790. Orig. Title: Der Schaufelradbagger. (Illus.). 450p. 1975. text ed. 65.00x (ISBN 0-87849-012-4). Trans Tech.
Reisner, W. & Rothe, M. Eisenhart. Bins & Bunkers for Handling Bulk Materials. new ed. (Ser. on Rock & Soil Mechanics). (Illus.). 1976. pap. 24.00x (ISBN 0-87849-001-9). Trans Tech.
Wasp, Edward J., et al. Slurry Pipeline Transportation. new ed. (Bulk Materials Handling Ser.). (Illus.). 300p. 1977. text ed. 60.00 (ISBN 0-87849-016-7). Trans Tech.
Williams, Ivor. Using Industrial Trucks for Materials Handling. 1973. 7.95 (ISBN 0-09-114140-0, Pub. by Hutchinson). Merrimack Bk Serv.
Zajic, J. E. & Himmelman, W. A. Highly Hazardous Material Spills & Emergency Planning. (Hazardous & Toxic Substances Ser.: Vol. 1). 1978. 29.75 (ISBN 0-8247-6622-9). Dekker.

MATERIALS MANAGEMENT

see also Purchasing

Amann, Dick. How to Make the Purchased Part Cycle Work to Your Company's Advantage. LC 76-52041. (Illus.). 250p. 1977. 19.95 (ISBN 0-917194-03-9); looseleaf 29.95 (ISBN 0-917194-05-5). Prog Studies.
Ammer, Dean S. Materials Management & Purchasing. 4th ed. 1980. 21.95x (ISBN 0-256-02146-5). Irwin.
Baily, Peter & Farmer, David. Managing Materials in Industry. (Illus.). 341p. 1972. text ed. 39.50x (ISBN 0-7161-0113-0, Pub. by Gower Pub Co England). Renouf.
Beekman-Love, Gilian & Neiger, L. Materials Management. (Applied Business Logistics Ser: Vol. 1). 1978. pap. 16.00 (ISBN 90-207-0748-5, Pub. by Martinus Nijhoff Netherlands). Kluwer Boston.
Bowersox, Donald J. Logistical Management: A System Integration of Physical Distribution Management, & Materials Management. (Illus.). 512p. 1978. text ed. 23.95x (ISBN 0-02-313110-1, 31311). Macmillan.
Brown, Robert G. Materials Management Systems: A Modular Library. LC 77-8281. 436p. 1977. 34.50 (ISBN 0-471-11182-1). Ronald Pr.
Bruce, Harry J. & Burke, Frederick J. How to Apply Statistics to Physical Distribution. 1967. 13.95 (ISBN 0-8436-1402-1). CBI Pub.

Compton, H. K. Supplies & Materials Management. 2nd ed. (Illus.). 512p. 1979. text ed. 62.50x (ISBN 0-7121-1964-7, Pub. by Macdonald & Evans England). Intl Ideas.
Gilchrist, Jack. Hidden Profits in Stamping: A Creative Materials Management Guide. LC 77-2145. 1977. 21.50 (ISBN 0-8436-0818-8). CBI Pub.
Heskett, J. L., et al. Case Problems in Business Logistics. 1973. 17.50x (ISBN 0-471-06599-4). Wiley.
Johnston, John E. Site Control of Materials: Handling, Storage, & Security. (Illus.). 1981. text ed. price not set (ISBN 0-408-00377-4). Butterworth.
Lee, Lamar, Jr. & Dobler, Donald W. Purchasing & Materials Management. 3rd ed. 1976. 19.50 (ISBN 0-07-037027-3, C); instructor's manual 5.50 (ISBN 0-07-037028-1). McGraw.
Leenders, Michael R., et al. Purchasing & Materials Management. 7th ed. 1980. 22.95x (ISBN 0-256-02374-3). Irwin.
Mossman, Frank. Logistics Systems Analysis. rev. ed. 375p. 1977. pap. text ed. 13.50 (ISBN 0-8191-0360-8). U Pr of Amer.
National Materials Advisory Board. National Materials Policy. LC 74-23549. 1975. pap. 11.50 (ISBN 0-309-02247-9). Natl Acad Pr.
Niku-Lari, A. & Al-Hassani, S. T., eds. Shot Peening: Proceedings of the 1st International Conference, Paris, 14-17 September 1981. 528p. 1982. 75.00 (ISBN 0-08-027599-0). Pergamon.
Tersine, R. J. & Campbell, J. H. Modern Materials Management. 1977. text ed. 18.95 (ISBN 0-444-00228-6, North Holland). Elsevier.
Tersine, Richard J. Materials Management & Inventory Systems. LC 76-477. 1976. text ed. 21.50 (ISBN 0-444-00186-7, North Holland). Elsevier.
Williams, Cicely D. & Jelliffe, Derrick B. Mother & Child Health: Delivering the Servicea. 1972. pap. 18.95x (ISBN 0-19-264153-0). Oxford U Pr.
Zenz, Gary L. Purchasing & the Management of Materials in Motion. 5th ed. LC 80-21649. (Marketing Ser.). 514p. 1981. text ed. 24.95 (ISBN 0-471-06091-7); tchrs.' ed. avail. (ISBN 0-471-08935-4). Wiley.

MATERIALS RESEARCH

Altenpohl, D. G., et al. Materials in World Perspective. (Materials Research & Engineering Ser.: Vol. 1). (Illus.). 208p. 1980. pap. 34.80 (ISBN 0-387-10037-7). Springer-Verlag.
Anderson, J. C., et al. Materials Science. 2nd ed. LC 74-9620. 1975. 24.95 (ISBN 0-470-02830-0). Halsted Pr.
Bewersdorff, A., ed. Materials Science in Space. (Advances in Space Research: Vol. 1, No. 5). (Illus.). 171p. 1981. pap. 21.25 (ISBN 0-08-027161-8). Pergamon.
Braun, J. D., et al. Microstructural Science, Vol. 5. 1977. 70.00 (ISBN 0-444-00204-9, North Holland). Elsevier.
Burke, John J. & Weiss, Volker, eds. Risk & Failure Analysis for Improved Performance & Reliability. (Sagamore Army Materials Research Conference Ser.: Vol. 24). 365p. 1980. 42.50 (ISBN 0-306-40446-X, Plenum Pr). Plenum Pub.
Fontana, M. G. & Staehle, R. W. Advances in Corrosion Sciences & Technology, Vol. 7. (Illus.). 375p. 1980. 39.50 (ISBN 0-306-39507-X, Plenum Pr). Plenum Pub.
Francis, Philip H. & Lindholm, Ulric S. Advanced Experimental Techniques in the Mechanics of Materials. 1973. 83.75x (ISBN 0-677-12570-4). Gordon.
Huggins, R. A., et al, eds. Annual Review of Materials Science, Vol. 2. LC 75-172108. (Illus.). 1972. text ed. 17.00 (ISBN 0-8243-1702-5). Annual Reviews.
--Annual Review of Materials Science, Vol. 3. LC 75-172108. (Illus.). 1973. text ed. 17.00 (ISBN 0-8243-1703-3). Annual Reviews.
--Annual Review of Materials Science, Vol. 6. LC 75-172108. (Illus.). 1976. text ed. 17.00 (ISBN 0-8243-1706-8). Annual Reviews.
Huggins, Robert A., et al, eds. Annual Review of Materials Science, Vol. 4. LC 75-172108. (Illus.). 1974. text ed. 17.00 (ISBN 0-8243-1704-1). Annual Reviews.
--Annual Review of Materials Science, Vol. 10. LC 75-172108. (Illus.). 1980. text ed. 20.00 (ISBN 0-8243-1710-6). Annual Reviews.
--Annual Review of Materials Science, Vol. 5. LC 75-172108. (Illus.). 1975. text ed. 17.00 (ISBN 0-8243-1705-X). Annual Reviews.
International Conference on Mechanical Behavior of Materials, Kyoto, Aug., 1971. Mechanical Behavior of Materials: Proceedings, 6 vols. Society of Materials Science, Japan, ed. (Illus.). 3500p. 1974. Set. 175.00x (ISBN 0-8002-1713-6). Intl Pubns Serv.
Kanert, O. & Mehring, M. Static Quadrupole Effects in Disordered Cubic Solids. Diehl, P., ed. Bd. with Nuclear Magnetic Relaxation Spectroscopy. Noack, F. (NMR-Basic Principles & Progress: Vol. 3). (Illus.). 130p. 1971. 26.30 (ISBN 0-387-05392-1). Springer-Verlag.
Keyser. Materials Science in Engineering. 3rd ed. (Engineering Ser.). 488p. 1980. text ed. 22.95 (ISBN 0-675-08182-3). Merrill.
Kriegel, W. W. & Palmour, H., 3rd, eds. Ceramics in Severe Environments. LC 63-17645. (Materials Science Research Ser.: Vol. 5). 610p. 1971. 55.00 (ISBN 0-306-38505-8, Plenum Pr). Plenum Pub.
Materials Performance & the Deep Sea. 1969. pap. 9.50 (ISBN 0-8031-0001-9, 04-445000-41). ASTM.
National Research Council, Commission on Sociotechnical Systems. Materials Technology in the Near-Term Energy Program. xiii, 122p. 1974. pap. 7.00 (ISBN 0-309-02322-X). Natl Acad Pr.
Research Needs Report: Design, Materials, & Manufacturing Research. 1976. pap. text ed. 5.00 (ISBN 0-685-72347-X, H00089). ASME.
Roy, Rustum, ed. Materials Science & Engineering in the United States. LC 77-84670. (Illus.). 1970. 16.50x (ISBN 0-271-00101-1). Pa St U Pr.
Solymar, L. & Walsh, D. Lectures on the Electrical Properties of Materials. 2nd ed. (Illus.). 1980. 36.50x (ISBN 0-19-851144-2); pap. 18.95x (ISBN 0-19-851145-0). Oxford U Pr.
Thomas, J. P. & Cachard, A., eds. Material Characterization Using Ion Beams. LC 77-13269. (NATO Advanced Study Institutes Ser. B: Physics, Vol. 28). 535p. 1977. 49.50 (ISBN 0-686-64758-0, Plenum Pr). Plenum Pub.
Wert, Charles. Opportunities in Materials Science & Engineering. LC 78-58666. 1973. lib. bdg. 6.60 (ISBN 0-8442-6464-4); pap. 4.95 (ISBN 0-685-92971-X). Natl Textbk.

MATERNAL AND INFANT WELFARE

see also Unmarried Mothers

Action Guide for Maternal & Child Care Committees. pap. 1.00 (ISBN 0-89970-021-7, OP-438). AMA.
Aladjem, Silvio & Brown, Audrey K., eds. Perinatal Intensive Care. LC 76-57754. (Illus.). 1977. 35.50 (ISBN 0-8016-0105-3). Mosby.
Anderson, Kathleen. Have Your Baby You're Own Way: Alternative Birth. (Orig.). 1981. pap. write for info. (ISBN 0-917982-14-2). Cougar Bks.
Barnes, Florence E., ed. Ambulatory Maternal Health Care & Family Planning Services. 1978. 12.00 (ISBN 0-87553-089-3, 029); pap. 8.00x (ISBN 0-87553-085-0, 033). Am Pub Health.
Bowlby, J. Maternal Care & Mental Health. 2nd ed. (Monograph Ser: No. 2). 194p. (Eng, Fr, & Span.). 1952. 7.20 (ISBN 92-4-140002-1). World Health.
Bremner, Robert H., ed. Security & Services for Children: An Original Anthology, Vol. 24. LC 74-1703. (Children & Youth Ser.). 1974. 12.00x (ISBN 0-405-05980-9). Arno.
Brennan, Barbara & Heilman, Joan R. The Complete Book of Midwifery. 1977. pap. 4.95 (ISBN 0-525-03180-4). Dutton.
Buss, Fran L. La Partera: Story of a Midwife. 1980. 10.95x (ISBN 0-472-09322-3); pap. 6.95 (ISBN 0-472-06322-7). U of Mich Pr.
Dancis, J. & Hwang, J. C., eds. Perinatal Pharmacology: Problems & Priorities. LC 73-91163. 240p. 1974. 27.00 (ISBN 0-911216-70-7). Raven.
Health Services Research Study, Institute of Medicine. Infant Death: An Analysis by Maternal Risk & Health Care. Orig. Title: Maternal & Infant Health Services. (Illus.). 192p. 1973. pap. 8.50 (ISBN 0-309-02119-7). Natl Acad Pr.
Klerman, Lorraine V. & Jekel, James F. School-Age Mothers: Problems, Programs & Policy. 256p. (Orig.). 1973. (Linnet); pap. 2.95 (ISBN 0-208-01413-6, Linnet). Shoe String.
Preparation for Childbearing. 4th ed. (Illus.). 1972. Repr. of 1969 ed. pap. 1.00, 10-99 copies 0.80 ea. 100 copies or more 0.60 ea. (ISBN 0-912758-01-5). Maternity Ctr.
Proceedings: Health Care for Mothers & Infants in Rural & Isolated Areas. 2.75 (ISBN 0-686-24131-2). Am Coll Obstetric.
Rosenkrantz, Barbara G., ed. The Health of Women & Children: An Original Anthology. LC 76-43205. (Public Health in America Ser.). (Illus.). 1977. Repr. of 1977 ed. lib. bdg. 18.00x (ISBN 0-405-09876-6). Arno.
Rudman, Jack. Maternal & Child Nursing - Associate. (College Proficiency Examination Ser.: CPEP-22). (Cloth bdg. avail. on request). 9.95 (ISBN 0-8373-5422-6). Natl Learning.
--Maternal & Child Nursing: Associate Degree. (ACT Proficiency Examination Program: PEP-37). (Cloth bdg. avail. on request). pap. 9.95 (ISBN 0-8373-5537-0). Natl Learning.
--Maternal & Child Nursing-Baccalaureate. (College Proficiency Examination Ser.: CPEP-23). (Cloth bdg. avail. on request). pap. 9.95 (ISBN 0-8373-5423-4). Natl Learning.
--Maternal & Child Nursing: Baccalaureate Degree. (ACT Proficiency Examination Program: PEP-38). (Cloth bdg. avail. on request). pap. 9.95 (ISBN 0-8373-5538-9). Natl Learning.
Shaw, Nancy S. Forced Labor: Maternity Care in the United States. 1974. 18.50 (ISBN 0-08-017835-9); pap. text ed. 9.75 (ISBN 0-08-017834-0). Pergamon.
Sidel, Ruth. Women & Child Care in China. 1973. pap. 2.95 (ISBN 0-14-003718-7). Penguin.
Sinai, Nathan & Anderson, Odin W. EMIC (Emergency Maternity & Infant Care) A Study of Administrative Experience. LC 74-1704. (Children & Youth Ser.: Vol. 23). 234p. 1974. Repr. of 1948 ed. 16.00x (ISBN 0-405-05981-7). Arno.
Slesinger, Doris P. Mothercraft & Infant Health: A Sociodemographic & Sociocultural Approach. LC 81-47181. (Illus.). 224p. 1981. 21.95x (ISBN 0-669-04562-4). Lexington Bks.
Wallace, Helen M. Health Care of Mothers & Children in National Health Services: Implications for the United States. LC 75-19162. 364p. 1975. text ed. 18.50 (ISBN 0-88410-130-4). Ballinger Pub.

MATERNAL AND INFANT WELFARE-GREAT BRITAIN

Lewis, Jane. The Politics of Motherhood: Child & Maternal Welfare in England, 1900-1939. 240p. 1980. 27.95 (ISBN 0-7735-0521-0). McGill-Queens U Pr.

MATERNAL AND INFANT WELFARE-INDIA

De Coulanges, Fustel. Ancient City. 10.00 (ISBN 0-8446-1960-4). Peter Smith.
Srya, Subhash C. Infant & Child Care for the Indian Mother. 195p. 1972. 9.50x (ISBN 0-8002-1566-4). Intl Pubns Serv.

MATERNAL DEPRIVATION

Bowlby, John. Attachment. LC 70-78464. (Attachment & Loss Ser., Vol. 1). 1969. text ed. 20.00x (ISBN 0-465-00539-X); pap. 4.95x (ISBN 0-465-09715-4, CN-5015). Basic.
George, Victor & Wilding, Paul. Motherless Families. (International Library of Sociology). 1972. 20.00x (ISBN 0-7100-7305-4). Routledge & Kegan.
Heinicke, Christoph M. & Westheimer, Ilse. Brief Separations. LC 65-25911. 1966. text ed. 22.50 (ISBN 0-8236-0600-7). Intl Univs Pr.
Rutter, Michael. Maternal Deprivation Reassessed. rev. ed. 1981. pap. 3.95 (ISBN 0-14-080561-3). Penguin.
Van Den Berg, J. H. Dubious Maternal Affection. 110p. 1972. pap. text ed. 2.50x (ISBN 0-8207-0140-8). Duquesne.

MATERNAL-FETAL EXCHANGE

Beard, R. W. & Nathanielsz, P. W. Fetal Physiology & Medicine. LC 76-20126. (Illus.). 1976. text ed. 32.00 (ISBN 0-7216-1600-3). Saunders.
Chamberlain, Geoffrey. Placental Transfer. 212p. text ed. 44.50 (ISBN 0-272-79531-3). Univ Park.
Grundmann, E. & Kirsten, W. H., eds. Perinatal Pathology. LC 79-450. (Current Topics in Pathology: Vol. 66). (Illus.). 1979. 55.40 (ISBN 0-387-09207-2). Springer-Verlag.
Hayashi, T., ed. Symposium on Nucleic Acid Metabolism of Placenta & Fetus. (Gynecologic Investigation: Vol. 8, No. 3). (Illus.). 1977. 18.00 (ISBN 3-8055-2771-3). S Karger.
Hemmings, W. A., ed. Materno Foetal Transmission of Immunoglobulins. LC 75-2721. (Clinical & Experimental Immunoreproduction: No. 2). (Illus.). 400p. 1975. 57.50 (ISBN 0-521-20747-9). Cambridge U Pr.
Josimovich, John B., et al, eds. Lactogenic Hormones, Fetal Nutrition, & Lactation. LC 73-12542. 483p. 1974. 34.50 (ISBN 0-471-45091-X, Pub. by Wiley). Krieger.
Loke, Y. W. Immunology & Immunopathology of the Human Foetal-Maternal Interaction. 1978. 70.75 (ISBN 0-444-80055-7, Biomedical Pr). Elsevier.
Medizinische Hochschule Meeting. Hannover, Federal Republic of Germany. Oct. 6-7, 1971. Transplacental Carcinogenesis: Proceedings. Tomatis, L., et al, eds. (IARC Scientific Pub.: No. 4). 1973. 16.00 (ISBN 0-686-16794-5). World Health.
Newth, D. R. & Balls, M., eds. Maternal Effects in Development. LC 78-73812. (British Society for Developmental Biology Symposium: No. 4). (Illus.). 1980. 92.00 (ISBN 0-521-22685-6). Cambridge U Pr.
Notake, Y. & Suzuki, S. Biological & Clinical Aspects of the Fetus. (Illus.). 1977. 65.00 (ISBN 0-8391-0986-5). Univ Park.
Shanklin, Douglas R. & Hodin, Jay. Maternal Nutrition & Child Health. (Illus.). 224p. 1979. 16.25 (ISBN 0-398-03813-9). C C Thomas.
Visser, H. K., ed. Nutrition & Metabolism of the Fetus & Infant. (Nutricia Symposium: No. 5). 1979. lib. bdg. 56.50 (ISBN 90-247-2202-0, Pub. by Martinus Nijhoff Netherlands). Kluwer Boston.

MATERNAL LOVE

see Love, Maternal

MATERNAL REJECTION

see also Maternal Deprivation

MATERNITY NURSING

see Obstetrical Nursing

MATHEMATICAL ABILITY

Everett, John P. Fundamental Skills of Algebra. LC 78-176759. (Columbia University. Teachers College. Contributions to Education: No. 324). Repr. of 1928 ed. 17.50 (ISBN 0-404-55324-9). AMS Pr.
Geromme, B. D. Forty-Eight Games to Make & Play for the Primary School. 1976. 14.00x (ISBN 0-8002-0807-2). Intl Pubns Serv.
Howett, Jerry. Number Power 2: Fractions, Decimals, Percents. 1977. wkbk. 3.45 (ISBN 0-8092-8010-8). Contemp Bks.
Krutetskii, V. A. The Psychology of Mathematical Abilities in School Children. Kilpatrick, Jeremy & Wirszup, Izaak, eds. Teller, Joan, tr. LC 74-33520. 1978. pap. text ed. 6.00x (ISBN 0-226-45485-1). U of Chicago Pr.
Mallory, Virgil S. The Relative Difficulty of Certain Topics in Mathematics for Slow-Moving Ninth Grade Pupils. LC 79-177050. (Columbia University. Teachers College. Contributions to Education: No. 769). Repr. of 1939 ed. 17.50 (ISBN 0-404-55769-4). AMS Pr.
Miklos, Mary O. Preparation for Criterion-Referenced Tests: A Brief Review of Mathamatical Competencies for Teachers of Early Childhood. LC 80-5430. 88p. 1980. pap. text ed. 6.25 (ISBN 0-8191-1092-2). U Pr of Amer.

MATHEMATICAL ABILITY-TESTING

Bitter, Gary G., et al. One Step at a Time. LC 77-82666. 1977. pap. text ed. 15.00 (ISBN 0-88436-419-4). EMC.
Daily, Benjamin W. Ability of High School Pupils to Select Essential Data in Solving Problems. LC 73-176704. (Columbia University. Teachers College. Contributions to Education: No. 190). Repr. of 1925 ed. 17.50 (ISBN 0-404-55190-4). AMS Pr.
Hotz, Henry G. First Year Algebra Scales. LC 79-176881. (Columbia University. Teachers College. Contributions to Education: No. 90). Repr. of 1918 ed. 17.50 (ISBN 0-404-55090-8). AMS Pr.
Howett, Jerry. The Cambridge Program for the GED Mathematic's Test. (GED Preparation Ser.). (Illus.). 352p. (Orig.). 1981. pap. text ed. price not set (ISBN 0-8428-9386-5). Cambridge Bk.
Kirby, Thomas J. Practice in the Case of School Children. LC 70-176955. (Columbia University. Teachers College. Contributions to Education: No. 58). Repr. of 1913 ed. 17.50 (ISBN 0-404-55058-4). AMS Pr.
Rizzuto, James J. Barron's How to Prepare for the College Board Achievement Tests - Mathematics Level I. 3rd rev. ed. 240p. (gr. 11-12). 1981. pap. text ed. 5.50 (ISBN 0-8120-2344-7). Barron.
Rogers, Agnes L. Experimental Tests of Mathematical Ability & Their Prognostic Value. LC 72-177201. (Columbia University. Teachers College. Contributions to Education: No. 89). Repr. of 1918 ed. 17.50 (ISBN 0-404-55089-4). AMS Pr.
Stone, Cliff W. Arithmetical Abilities & Some Factors Determining Them. LC 70-177822. (Columbia University. Teachers College. Contributions to Education: No. 19). Repr. of 1908 ed. 17.50 (ISBN 0-404-55019-3). AMS Pr.
--Standardized Reasoning Tests in Arithmetic & How to Utilize Them. 2nd, rev. & enl. ed. LC 70-177817. (Columbia University. Teachers College. Contributions to Education: No. 83). Repr. of 1921 ed. 17.50 (ISBN 0-404-55083-5). AMS Pr.
Sumner, Ray. Tests of Attainment in Mathematics in Schools: Vol. 1, Monitoring Feasability Study. (NFER Occasional Reports: Second Ser.). 200p. (Orig.). 1975. pap. text ed. 15.25x (ISBN 0-85633-084-1, NFER). Humanities.
Symonds, Percival M. Special Disability in Algebra. LC 73-177728. (Columbia University. Teachers College. Contributions to Education: No. 132). Repr. of 1923 ed. 17.50 (ISBN 0-404-55132-7). AMS Pr.
Williams, Edward. Getting Ready for the High School Equivalency Examination--Beginning Preparation in Mathematics. 200p. (gr. 9-12). 1982. pap. text ed. 5.95 (ISBN 0-8120-2398-6). Barron.
Woody, Clifford. Measurements of Some Achievements in Arithmetic. LC 73-177622. (Columbia University. Teachers College. Contributions to Education: No. 80). Repr. of 1920 ed. 17.50 (ISBN 0-404-55080-0). AMS Pr.

MATHEMATICAL ANALYSIS

see also Algebra; Algebras, Linear; Calculus; Combinatorial Analysis; Engineering Mathematics; Fourier Analysis; Functions; Functions, Special; Harmonic Analysis; Mathematical Optimization; Nonlinear Theories; Numerical Analysis; Programming (Electronic Computers); Random Walks (Mathematics)

Adamjan, V. M., et al. Eleven Papers in Analysis. LC 51-5559. (Translations, Ser.: No. 2, Vol. 95). 1970. 26.00 (ISBN 0-8218-1795-7, TRANS 2-95). Am Math.

Aheizer, N. I., et al. Nine Papers on Analysis. LC 51-5559. (Translations Ser.: No. 2, Vol. 22). 1962. 26.00 (ISBN 0-8218-1722-1, TRANS 2-22). Am Math.

Ahlfors, Lars. Complex Analysis. 3rd ed. (Illus.). 1979. text ed. 21.50 (ISBN 0-07-000657-1, C). McGraw.

Ahlfors, Lars V., et al, eds. Contributions to Analysis: A Collection of Papers Dedicated to Lipman Bers. 1974. 60.00 (ISBN 0-12-044850-5). Acad Pr.

Aizerman, M. A., et al. Seventeen Papers on Analysis. LC 51-5559. (Translations Ser.: No. 2, Vol. 26). 1963. 24.80 (ISBN 0-8218-1726-4, TRANS 2-26). Am Math.

Akopjan, S. A., et al. Fifteen Papers on Analysis. LC 51-5559. (Translations Ser.: No. 2, Vol. 72). 1968. 29.60 (ISBN 0-8218-1772-8, TRANS 2-72). Am Math.

Al'ber, S. I., et al. Eleven Papers on Analysis. LC 51-5559. (Translations, Ser: No. 2, Vol. 14). 1964. Repr. of 1960 ed. 23.60 (ISBN 0-8218-1714-0, TRANS 2-14). Am Math.

Albert, Abraham A. Structure of Algebras. LC 41-9. (Colloquium Pbns. Ser.: Vol. 24). 1980. Repr. of 1939 ed. 28.40 (ISBN 0-8218-1024-3, COLL-24). Am Math.

Allen, Roy G. Mathematical Analysis for Economists. rev. ed. 1962. pap. 8.50 (ISBN 0-312-52185-5). St Martin.

Amick, Daniel J. & Walberg, Herbert, eds. Introductory Multivariate Analysis (for Educational Psychological and Social Research) LC 74-30754. (Illus.). 275p. 1975. 18.80 (ISBN 0-8211-0013-0); text ed. 17.00 in ten or more copies (ISBN 0-685-52138-9). McCutchan.

Andreotti, A. & Stoll, W. Analytic & Algebraic Dependence of Meromorphic Functions. (Lecture Notes in Mathematics: Vol. 234). iii, 390p. 1971. pap. 10.20 (ISBN 0-387-05670-X). Springer-Verlag.

Apostol, T. M. Calculus: Multi-Variable Calculus & Linear Algebra with Application, Vol. 2. 2nd ed. LC 67-14605. 673p. 1969. text ed. 27.95 (ISBN 0-471-00007-8). Wiley.

--Calculus: One-Variable Calculus with an Introduction to Linear Algebra, Vol. 1. 2nd ed. LC 73-20899. 666p. 1967. text ed. 27.95 (ISBN 0-471-00005-1). Wiley.

Apostol, Tom M. Mathematical Analysis: A Modern Approach to Advanced Calculus. 2nd ed. LC 72-11473. 1974. text ed. 21.95 (ISBN 0-201-00288-4). A-W.

Armore, Sidney J. Introduction to Statistical Analysis & Inference for Psychology & Education. 546p. 1966. text ed. 22.50 (ISBN 0-471-03343-X). Wiley.

Arnol'd, V. I., et al. Eleven Papers on Analysis. LC 51-5559. (Translations, Ser.: No. 2, Vol. 53). 1966. 31.20 (ISBN 0-8218-1753-1, TRANS 2-53). Am Math.

--Seventeen Papers on Analysis. LC 51-5559. (Translations Ser.: No. 2, Vol. 28). 1963. 24.40 (ISBN 0-8218-1728-0, TRANS 2-28). Am Math.

Arya, Jagdish C. & Lardner, Robin W. Mathematical Analysis for Business & Economics. (Illus.). 768p. 1981. text ed. 21.95 (ISBN 0-13-561019-2). P-H.

Ash, Robert B. Real Analysis & Probability. (Probability & Mathematical Statistics Ser.). 476p. 1972. 23.95 (ISBN 0-12-065201-3); solutions to problems 3.00 (ISBN 0-12-065240-4). Acad Pr.

Azar, Edward E. & Ben-Dak, Joseph. Theory & Practice of Events Research. 1975. 51.25x (ISBN 0-677-15550-6). Gordon.

Barbasin, E. A., et al. Twelve Papers on Analysis, Applied Mathematics & Algebraic Topology. LC 51-5559. (Translations Ser.: No. 2, Vol. 25). 1963. 24.40 (ISBN 0-8218-1725-6, TRANS 2-25). Am Math.

Bartle, Robert G. The Elements of Real Analysis. 2nd ed. LC 75-15979. 480p. 1975. text ed. 27.95 (ISBN 0-471-05464-X); arabic translation avail. Wiley.

Baumol, W. Economic Theory & Operations Analysis. 4th ed. 1977. 21.95 (ISBN 0-13-227132-X). P-H.

Beals, R. Advanced Mathematical Analysis. LC 73-6884. (Graduate Texts in Mathematics Ser.: Vol. 12). 288p. 1973. 16.80 (ISBN 0-387-90065-9); pap. 11.50 (ISBN 0-387-90066-7). Springer-Verlag.

Beckenbach, F., ed. General Inequalities I. (International Ser. of Numerical Mathematics: No. 41). 332p. 1978. 38.50 (ISBN 3-7643-0972-5). Birkhauser.

Berezanskii, Ju. M., et al. Twelve Papers on Analysis & Applied Mathematics. LC 51-5559. (Translations Ser.: No. 2, Vol. 35). 1964. 25.60 (ISBN 0-8218-1735-3, TRANS 2-35). Am Math.

Bermant, A. F. & Aramanovich, I. G. Mathematical Analyis. 781p. 1975. 10.80 (ISBN 0-8285-0730-9, Pub. by Mir Pubs Russia). Imported Pubns.

Binmore, K. G. Foundations of Analysis: A Straightforward Introduction: Bk. 1 Logic, Sets & Numbers. LC 79-41790. (Illus.). 200p. 1981. 24.95 (ISBN 0-521-23322-4); pap. 12.95 (ISBN 0-521-29915-2). Cambridge U Pr.

--Foundations of Analysis: A Straightforward Introduction: Bk. 2 Topological Ideas. LC 79-41790. (Illus.). 350p. Date not set. 39.50 (ISBN 0-521-23350-X); pap. 16.95 (ISBN 0-521-29930-6). Cambridge U Pr.

--Mathematical Analysis. LC 76-28006. (Illus.). 1977. 47.00 (ISBN 0-521-21480-7); pap. 13.95x (ISBN 0-521-29167-4). Cambridge U Pr.

Birkhoff, Garrett. A Source Book in Classical Analysis. LC 72-85144. (Source Books in the History of the Sciences Ser). 488p. 1973. text ed. 25.00x (ISBN 0-674-82245-5). Harvard U Pr.

Birman, M. S., et al. Fifteen Papers on Analysis. LC 51-5559. (Translations Ser.: No. 2, Vol. 54). 1966. 30.80 (ISBN 0-8218-1754-X, TRANS 2-54). Am Math.

Blanc, C. Equations Aux Derivees Partielles. (International Ser. of Numerical Mathematics: No. 34). 136p. (Fr.). 1976. pap. 20.50 (ISBN 3-7643-0869-9). Birkhauser.

Boyd, Lawrence H. & Iversen, Gudmund R. Contextual Analysis: Concepts & Statistical Techniques. 1979. text ed. 29.95x (ISBN 0-534-00693-0). Wadsworth Pub.

Brodsky, M. S., et al. Nine Papers in Analysis. LC 51-5559. (Translations Ser.: No. 2, Vol. 103). 208p. 1974. 34.40 (ISBN 0-685-41045-5, TRANS 2-103). Am Math.

Bronstein, I. U., et al. Eleven Papers on Logic, Algebra, Analysis & Topology. LC 51-5559. (Translations, Ser.: No. 2, Vol. 97). 1970. 28.00 (ISBN 0-8218-1797-3, TRANS 2-97). Am Math.

Buck, R. C., ed. Studies in Modern Analysis. LC 62-11884. (MAA Studies: No. 1). 182p. 1962. 12.50 (ISBN 0-88385-101-6). Math Assn.

Buck, R. Creighton. Advanced Calculus. 3rd ed. LC 77-2859. (McGraw-Hill Intl. Ser. in Pure & Applied Mathematics). (Illus.). 1978. text ed. 18.95 (ISBN 0-07-008728-8, C); instructor's manual 4.50 (ISBN 0-07-008729-6). McGraw.

Buckholtz, J. D., ed. Complex Analysis, Kentuckt 1976. (Lecture Notes in Mathematics: Vol. 599). 1977. 10.70 (ISBN 0-387-08343-X). Springer-Verlag.

Budjanu, M. S., et al. Ten Papers in Analysis. LC 73-16013. (Translations Ser.: No. 2, Vol. 102). 1973. 36.00 (ISBN 0-8218-3052-X, TRANS 2-102). Am Math.

Burckel, Robert B. An Introduction to Classical Complex Analysis, Vol. 1. LC 78-67403. (Pure and Applied Mathematics Ser.). 1980. 51.50 (ISBN 0-12-141701-8). Acad Pr.

Burkhill, J. C. & Burkhill, H. Second Course in Mathematical Analysis. LC 69-16278. (Illus.). 1970. text ed. 35.50x (ISBN 0-521-07519-X); pap. 23.50 (ISBN 0-521-28061-3). Cambridge U Pr.

Burkill, John C. First Course in Mathematical Analysis. 1962. 23.95x (ISBN 0-521-04381-6); pap. 13.95x (ISBN 0-521-29468-1). Cambridge U Pr.

Butzer, P. L. & Szokefalvi-Nagy, B., eds. Abstract Spaces & Approximation. (International Series of Numerical Mathematics: No. 10). 423p. 1969. 59.50 (ISBN 3-7643-0194-5). Birkhauser.

Bylov, B. F., et al. Ten Papers on Analysis. LC 51-5559. (Translations Ser.: No. 2, Vol. 74). 1968. 29.60 (ISBN 0-8218-1774-4, TRANS 2-74). Am Math.

Caratheodory, C. Funktionentheorie, 2 vols. rev. 2nd ed. (Mathematische Reihe: Nos. 8 & 9). (Ger.). 1961. Vol 1, 288p. 28.00 (ISBN 3-7643-0064-7); Vol. 2, 194p. 21.50 (ISBN 3-7643-0065-5). Birkhauser.

--Mass und Integral und Ihre Alebraisierung. Finsler, P., et al, eds. (Mathematische Reihe Ser.: No. 10). (Illus.). 337p. (Ger.). 1956. 36.00 (ISBN 3-7643-0066-3). Birkhauser.

Cazacu, A. Theorie der Funktionen Mehrerer Komplexer Veranderlicher. (Mathematische Reihe Ser.: No. 51). 360p. (Ger.). 1975. 64.50 (ISBN 3-7643-0770-6). Birkhauser.

Cesari, Lamberto & Kannan, Rangacesari, eds. Nonlinear Analysis: A Collection of Papers in Honor or Eric Rothe. 1978. 36.00 (ISBN 0-12-165550-4). Acad Pr.

Chambers, John M. Computational Methods for Data Analysis. LC 77-9493. (Wiley Ser. in Probability & Mathematical Statistics: Applied Section). 1977. 22.50 (ISBN 0-471-02772-3, Pub. by Wiley-Interscience). Wiley.

Choquet, Gustave. Lectures on Analysis, 3 vols. Marsden, J., et al, eds. Incl. Vol. 1. Integration & Topological Vector Spaces. pap. (ISBN 0-8053-6955-4); Vol. 2. Representation Theory (ISBN 0-8053-6957-0); Vol. 3. Infinite Dimensional Measures & Problem Solutions (ISBN 0-8053-6959-7). (Math Lecture Notes Ser.: Nos. 24, 25, & 26). 1969. pap. 11.50 ea. (Adv Bk Prog). Benjamin-Cummings.

Clapham, C. R. Introduction to Mathematical Analysis. (Library of Mathematics). (Illus.). 92p. 1973. pap. 5.00 (ISBN 0-7100-7529-4). Routledge & Kegan.

Clarke, D. A., et al. Foundations of Analysis: With an Introduction to Logic & Set Theory. LC 73-136217. (Century Mathematics Ser.). (Illus., Orig.). 1971. text ed. 18.95x (ISBN 0-89197-171-8). Irvington.

Collatz, L., et al, eds. Iterationsverfahren-Numerische Mathematik-Approximationstheorie. (International Ser. of Numerical Mathematics: No. 15). 257p. (Ger.). 1970. 32.50 (ISBN 3-7643-0547-9). Birkhauser.

Colloquium on Mathematical Analysis, Jyvaskyla, 1970, et al. Topics in Analysis: Proceedings. Louhivaara, I. S., et al, eds. LC 74-20555. (Lecture Notes in Mathematics Ser.: Vol. 419). xiii, 392p. 1975. pap. 19.10 (ISBN 0-387-06965-8). Springer-Verlag.

Complex Analysis & Its Applications, 3 vols. 1977. Set. pap. 80.25 (ISBN 0-685-79710-4, ISP428-1-2-3, IAEA). Unipub.

Conference on Graph Theory - Western Michigan University - Kalamazoo - 1972. Graph Theory & Applications: Proceedings. Alavi, Y., et al, eds. LC 72-95978. (Lecture Notes in Mathematics: Vol. 303). 329p. 1973. pap. 12.30 (ISBN 0-387-06096-0). Springer-Verlag.

Cushing, James T. Applied Analytical Mathematics for Physical Scientists. LC 75-9611. 672p. 1975. text ed. 32.50 (ISBN 0-471-18997-9). Wiley.

Daus, Paul H. & Whyburn, William M. Introduction to Mathematical Analysis with Applications to Problems of Economics. 1958. 13.95 (ISBN 0-201-01445-9). A-W.

Davis, Martin. Applied Nonstandard Analysis. LC 76-28484. (Pure & Applied Mathematics Ser.). 1977. text ed. 30.00 (ISBN 0-471-19897-8, Pub. by Wiley-Interscience). Wiley.

De Bruijn, N. G. Asymptotic Methods in Analysis. 3rd ed. (Bibliotheca Mathematica Ser.: Vol. 4). 1958. 24.50 (ISBN 0-444-10330-9, North-Holland). Elsevier.

Demidovich, B., ed. Problems in Mathematical Analysis. (Russian Monographs Ser.). 1969. 83.75 (ISBN 0-677-20840-5). Gordon.

Dieudonne, J. A. Treatise on Analysis, 6 vols. Incl. Vol. 1. 1960. 22.95 (ISBN 0-12-215550-5); Vol. 2. rev. ed. 1970. 51.00 (ISBN 0-12-215502-5); Vol. 3. 1972. 55.50 (ISBN 0-12-215503-3); Vol. 4. 1974. 56.00 (ISBN 0-12-215504-1); Vol. 5. 1977. 39.50 (ISBN 0-12-215505-X); Vol. 6. 1978. 36.50 (ISBN 0-12-215506-8). (Pure & Applied Mathematics Ser.). Acad Pr.

Dobbins, Robert R. If & Only If in Analysis. 1977. pap. text ed. 9.50 (ISBN 0-8191-0344-6. U Pr of Amer.

Doetsch, G. Einfuhrung in Theorie und Anwendung der Laplace-Transformation. rev. 3rd ed. (Mathematische Reihe Ser.: No. 24). 351p. (Ger.). 1976. 60.00 (ISBN 3-7643-0784-6). Birkhauser.

--Handbuch der Laplace Transformation, 3 vols. Incl. Vol. 1. Theorie der Laplace Transformation. 581p. 80.50 (ISBN 3-7643-0083-3); Vol. 2. Anwendungen der Laplace Transformation, 1, Abteilung. 436p. 62.50 (ISBN 3-7643-0653-X); Vol. 3. Anwendungen der Laplace Transformation, 2, Abteilung. 2nd ed. 299p. 42.50 (ISBN 3-7643-0674-2). (Mathematische Reihe Ser.: Nos. 14, 15 & 19). (Ger.). 1971-73. Birkhauser.

Dolciani, Mary P., et al. Modern Introductory Analysis. 2nd ed. (gr. 11-12). 1977. text ed. 16.28 (ISBN 0-395-25157-5); tchr's ed. 17.20 (ISBN 0-395-25158-3). HM.

Dudley, R. M. Lectures in Modern Analysis & Applications - Three. Taam, C. T., ed. LC 64-54683. (Lecture Notes in Mathematics: Vol. 170). 1970. pap. 11.20 (ISBN 0-387-05284-4). Springer-Verlag.

Dynkin, E. B., et al. Eleven Papers on Analysis, Probability & Topology. LC 51-5559. (Translations, Ser.: No. 2, Vol. 12). 1966. Repr. of 1959 ed. 24.40 (ISBN 0-8218-1712-4, TRANS 2-12). Am Math.

Eaves, Edgar D. & Carruth, J. H. Introductory Mathematical Analysis. 5th ed. 1978. text ed. 24.95 (ISBN 0-205-05991-0, 5659914); instr's man. avail. (ISBN 0-205-05992-9); student study guide avail. (ISBN 0-205-05993-7). Allyn.

El'sgol'c, L. E. Qualitative Methods in Mathematical Analysis. LC 64-16170. (Translations of Mathematical Monographs: Vol. 12). 1980. Repr. of 1968 ed. 30.80 (ISBN 0-8218-1562-8, MMONO-12). Am Math.

Engel'son, Ja. L., et al. Seven Papers on Analysis. LC 51-5559. (Translations Ser.: No. 2, Vol. 60). 1967. 31.20 (ISBN 0-8218-1760-4, TRANS 2-60). Am Math.

Fedorjuk, M. V., et al. Eleven Papers on Analysis. LC 51-5559. (Translations, Ser.: No. 2, Vol. 34). 1963. 28.00 (ISBN 0-8218-1734-5, TRANS 2-34). Am Math.

Fikhtengol'ts, G. M. Fundamentals of Mathematical Analysis, 2 Vols. 1965. Vol. 1. 25.00 (ISBN 0-08-010059-7); Vol. 2. 25.00 (ISBN 0-08-010060-0); Vol. 1. pap. 18.75 (ISBN 0-08-013473-4); Vol. 2. pap. 21.00 (ISBN 0-08-013474-2). Pergamon.

Fomin, S., et al. Nine Papers on Foundations, Measure Theory, & Analysis. (Translations Ser.: No. 2, Vol. 57). 1966. 32.40 (ISBN 0-8218-1757-4, TRANS 2-57). Am Math.

Freud, G. Orthogonale Polynome. (Mathematische Eihe Ser.: No. 33). (Illus.). 294p. (Ger.). 1969. 42.50 (ISBN 3-7643-0127-9). Birkhauser.

Gagaev, B. M., et al. Thirteen Papers on Analysis. LC 51-5559. (Translations Ser.: No. 2, Vol. 10). 1963. Repr. of 1958 ed. 27.20 (ISBN 0-8218-1710-8, TRANS 2-10). Am Math.

Gahler, W. Grundstrukturen der Analysis, 2 vols. (Mathematische Reihe Ser.: Nos. 58 & 61). (Ger.). 1978. Vol. 1, 396p. 47.50 (ISBN 3-7643-0901-6); Vol. 2, 496p. prepub. 61.50 (ISBN 3-7643-0966-0). Birkhauser.

Garnir, H. G. Les Problemes aux Limites de la Physique Mathematique. (Mathematische Reihe Ser.: No. 23). (Illus.). 234p. (Fr.). 1958. 31.50 (ISBN 3-7643-0134-1). Birkhauser.

Garnir, H. G., et al. Analyse Fonctionnelle. 2nd ed. Incl. Vol. 1. Theorie Generale. 562p. 1968. 88.00 (ISBN 3-7643-0135-X); Vol. 2. Mesure et Integration dans l'Espace Euclidien. 288p. 1972. 53.50 (ISBN 3-7643-0545-2); Vol. 3. Espaces Fonctionnels Usuels. 375p. 1973. 70.50 (ISBN 3-7643-0546-0). (Mathematische Reihe Ser.: Vols. 36, 37 & 45). (Fr.). Birkhauser.

Gaughan, Edward D. Introduction to Analysis. 2nd ed. LC 75-16601. (Contemporary Undergraduate Mathematics Ser.). 1975. text ed. 18.95 (ISBN 0-8185-0172-3); instructor's manual avail. (ISBN 0-685-55262-4). Brooks-Cole.

Glimm, J., et al. Lectures in Modern Analysis & Applications - Two. Taam, C. T., ed. LC 76-94096. (Lecture Notes in Mathematics: Vol. 140). 1970. pap. 10.70 (ISBN 0-387-04929-0). Springer-Verlag.

Gohagan, John K. Quantitative Analysis for Public Policy. (Quantitative Methods for Management). (Illus.). 1980. text ed. 25.00x (ISBN 0-07-023570-8); instructor's manual 8.95 (ISBN 0-07-023571-6); solutions manual 8.95 (ISBN 0-07-023571-6). McGraw.

Gohberg, I. Z. & Feldman, I. A. Faltungsgleichungen und Projektionsverfahren Zu Ihrer Losung. Prossdorf, S., ed. (Mathematische Reihe Ser.: No. 49). 288p. (Ger.). 1974. 34.50 (ISBN 3-7643-0722-6). Birkhauser.

Goldberg, Richard R. Methods of Real Analysis. 2nd ed. LC 75-30615. 1976. text ed. 25.95 (ISBN 0-471-31065-4). Wiley.

Goldstein, M. & Dillon, W. R. Discrete Discriminant Analysis. 190p. 1978. 23.95 (ISBN 0-471-04167-X, Pub. by Wiley-Interscience). Wiley.

Golinskii, B. L., et al. Thirteen Papers on Algebra & Analysis. LC 51-5559. (Translations Ser.: No. 2, Vol. 76). 1968. 29.60 (ISBN 0-8218-1776-0, TRANS 2-76). Am Math.

Greenberg, Harvey & Maybee, John, eds. Computer-Assisted Analysis & Model Simplification. LC 80-28509. 1981. 29.50 (ISBN 0-12-299680-1). Acad Pr.

Greub, Werner, et al. Connections, Curvature, & Cohomology, 2 vols. Incl. Vol. 1. De Rham Cohomology of Manifold & Vector Bundles. 1972. 55.50 (ISBN 0-12-302701-2); Vol. 2. Lie Groups, Principal Bundles & Characteristic Classes. 1973. 63.00 (ISBN 0-12-302702-0); Vol. 3. Cohomology of Principle Bundles & Homogeneous Spaces. 1976. 78.00 (ISBN 0-12-302703-9). (Pure & Applied Mathematics Ser.). Acad Pr.

Gunning, R. C. Problems in Analysis: A Symposium in Honor of Salomon Bochner. (Mathematical Series, No. 31). 1970. 26.00x (ISBN 0-691-08076-3). Princeton U Pr.

Haack, W. & Wendland, W. Vorlesungen uber Partielle und pfaffsche Diggerentialgleichungen. (Mathematische Reihe Ser.: No. 39). (Illus.). 555p. (Ger.). 1969. 80.50 (ISBN 3-7643-0159-7). Birkhauser.

Hayes, Charles A., Jr. Concepts of Real Analysis. (Illus.). 190p. 1964. 9.25 (ISBN 0-471-36472-X, Pub by Wiley). Krieger.

Henrici, Henry. Applied & Computational Complex Analysis: Power Series, Integration-Conformal Mapping-Location of Zeroes. LC 73-19723. (Pure & Applied Mathematics Ser.: Vol. 1). 704p. 1974. 48.95 (ISBN 0-471-37244-7, Pub. by Wiley-Interscience). Wiley.
Hille, Einar. Einar Hille: Classical Analysis & Functional Analysis: Selected Papers. Kallman, Robert R., ed. LC 74-18465. (Mit Press Mathematicians of Our Time Ser.: Vol. 2). 752p. 1975. 40.00x (ISBN 0-262-08080-X). MIT Pr.
Hirsch, M. W., et al. Invariant Manifolds. (Lecture Notes in Mathematics: Vol. 583). 1977. soft cover 10.10 (ISBN 0-387-08148-8). Springer-Verlag.
Hirschmann, I. I., Jr., ed. Studies in Real & Complex Analysis. LC 65-22403. (MAA Studies: No. 3). 213p. 1965. 12.50 (ISBN 0-88385-103-2). Math Assn.
Hope, K. Methods of Multivariate Analysis. 1970. 44.00 (ISBN 0-677-61360-1). Gordon.
Hubbard, John H. Sur les sections analytiques de la courbe universelle de Techmuller. LC 75-41604. (Memoirs: No. 166). 137p. 1976. pap. 12.00 (ISBN 0-8218-1866-X, MEMO-166). Am Math.
Iverson, K. E. Elementary Analysis. (Illus., Orig.). 1976. pap. text ed. 6.25 (ISBN 0-917326-01-6). APL Pr.
Johnsonbaugh & Pfaffenberger, eds. Foundations of Mathematical Analysis. (Lecture Notes in Pure & Applied Mathematics Ser.: Vol. 62). 1981. 24.50 (ISBN 0-8247-6919-8). Dekker.
Khinchin, A. I. A Course of Mathematical Analysis. 1960. 104.00 (ISBN 0-677-20130-3). Gordon.
Klambauer. Problems & Propositions in Analysis. (Lecture Notes in Pure & Applied Mathematics Ser.: Vol. 49). 1979. 27.50 (ISBN 0-8247-6887-6). Dekker.
Klambauer, G. Mathematical Analysis. (Pure & Applied Mathematics Ser.: Vol. 31). 1975. 28.25 (ISBN 0-8247-6329-7). Dekker.
--Real Analysis. LC 72-93078. 416p. 1973. 22.95 (ISBN 0-444-00133-6, North Holland). Elsevier.
Klotzler, R. Mehrdimensionale Variationsrechnung. (Mathematische Reihe Ser.: No. 44). (Illus.). 299p. (Ger.). 1970. 42.50 (ISBN 3-7643-0223-2). Birkhauser.
Krall, A. M. Linear Methods of Applied Analysis. 1973. 19.50 (ISBN 0-201-03902-8); pap. 9.50 (ISBN 0-201-03903-6). A-W.
Krasnoselskiy, M. A., et al. Plane Vector Fields. 1966. 36.00 (ISBN 0-12-425950-2). Acad Pr.
Kurth, Rudolf. Elements of Analytical Dynamics. 200p. 1976. text ed. 28.00 (ISBN 0-08-019848-1). Pergamon.
Labarre, Anthony E. Elementary Mathematical Analysis. 1961. 15.95 (ISBN 0-201-04110-3). A-W.
Lachenbruch, Peter A. Discriminant Analysis. LC 74-11057. 1975. 13.00 (ISBN 0-02-848250-6). Hafner.
Lakshmikanthan, V., ed. Applied Nonlinear Analysis. LC 79-10237. 1979. 47.50 (ISBN 0-12-434180-2). Acad Pr.
Lang, Serge A. Analysis One. 1968. 20.95 (ISBN 0-201-04172-3). A-W.
--Analysis Two. 1969. text ed. 22.95 (ISBN 0-201-04179-0). A-W.
Lang, Serge R. Complex Analysis. LC 76-15463. (Illus.). 1977. text ed. 19.95 (ISBN 0-201-04137-5). A-W.
Laufer, Henry B. Normal Two-Dimensional Singularities. LC 78-160261. (Annals of Mathematics Studies: No. 71). 1971. 14.00 (ISBN 0-691-08100-X). Princeton U Pr.
Lawrynowicz, J., ed. Analytic Functions Kozubnik 1979: Proceedings. (Lecture Notes in Mathematics: Vol. 798). 476p. 1980. pap. 27.00 (ISBN 0-387-09985-9). Springer-Verlag.
Le Corbeiller, Philippe. Dimensional Analysis. (Program bk). 1966. pap. text ed. 12.95x (ISBN 0-89197-126-2). Irvington.
Levitan, B. M., et al. Six Papers in Analysis. LC 73-15614. (Translations Ser.: No. 2, Vol. 101). 1973. 36.80 (ISBN 0-8218-3051-1, TRANS 2-101). Am Math.
Li, Ching C. Path Analysis: A Primer. 1975. pap. text ed. 7.75x (ISBN 0-910286-40-X). Boxwood.
Loxton, John. Practical Map Production. LC 80-40118. 137p. 1980. 24.95 (ISBN 0-471-27782-7, Pub. by Wiley-Interscience); pap. 14.50 (ISBN 0-471-27783-5). Wiley.
McAdams, Alan K. Mathematical Analysis for Management Decisions: Introduction to Calculus & Linear Algebra. (Illus.). 1970. text ed. 15.95 (ISBN 0-02-378370-2). Macmillan.
McBrien, Vincent O. Introductory Analysis. LC 61-6044. (Century Mathematics Ser.). (Illus.). 1969. 32.00x (ISBN 0-89197-248-X); pap. text ed. 18.50x (ISBN 0-89197-804-6). Irvington.
McClain, Ernest G. The Pythagorean Plato: Prelude to the Song Itself. LC 77-13355. (Illus.). 1977. 12.95 (ISBN 0-89254-008-7). Nicolas-Hays.
McCullough, Thomas A. & Phillips, Keith. Foundations of Analysis in the Complex Plane. LC 72-87153. 1973. text ed. 18.50x (ISBN 0-03-009105-5). Irvington.
Mackie, R. K., et al. Mathematical Methods for Chemists. LC 72-4758. (Illus.). 154p. 1972. text ed. 15.95 (ISBN 0-470-56295-1). Halsted Pr.
Marsden, Jerrold E. Elementary Classical Analysis. LC 74-5764. (Illus.). 1974. text ed. 24.95x (ISBN 0-7167-0452-8). W H Freeman.
Marti, J. Konvexe Analysis. (Mathematische Reihe Ser.: No. 54). 286p. (Ger.). 1977. 50.00 (ISBN 3-7643-0839-7). Birkhauser.
Matalon, Benjamin. L'analyse Hierarchique. (Mathematiques et Sciences De L'homme: No. 1). pap. 10.50x (ISBN 90-2796-311-8). Mouton.
Maurin, Krzysztof. Analysis, Part 1: Elements. Lepa, Eugene, tr. from Polish. LC 74-80525. 672p. 1976. lib. bdg. 55.00 (ISBN 90-277-0484-8, Pub. by Reidel Holland). Kluwer Boston.
Mendelson, Elliot. Number Systems & the Foundations of Analysis. 1973. text ed. 19.95 (ISBN 0-12-490850-0). Acad Pr.
Michlin, S. G. Approximation Auf Dem Kubischen Gitter. Lehmann, R., tr. from Rus. (Mathematische Reihe Ser.: No. 59). 204p. (Ger.). 1976. 28.00 (ISBN 3-7643-0873-7). Birkhauser.
Mickley, Harold S., et al. Applied Mathematics in Chemical Engineering. 2nd ed. (Chemical Engineering Ser.). (Illus.). 1957. text ed. 23.50 (ISBN 0-07-041800-4, C). McGraw.
Milnor, John. Introduction to Algebraic K-Theory. LC 74-161197. (Annals of Mathematics Studies: No. 72). 220p. 1972. 10.50x (ISBN 0-691-08101-8). Princeton U Pr.
Mitrinovic, D. S. & Vasic, P. M. Analytic Inequalities. LC 76-116492. (Grundlehren der Mathematischen Wissenschaften: Vol. 165). (Illus.). 1970. 44.70 (ISBN 0-387-04837-5). Springer-Verlag.
Mozzochi, C. J. Foundations of Analysis: Landau Revisited. LC 75-46243. 1976. text ed. 7.50 (ISBN 0-682-48511-X, University). Exposition.
Munroe, Marshall E. Introductory Real Analysis. 1965. 17.95 (ISBN 0-201-04905-8). A-W.
Musielak, Julian, ed. Commentationes Mathematicae: Tomus Specialis in Honorem Ladislai Orlicz, 2 vols, Vol. I & Vol. II. LC 78-326639. 1979. 27.50x ea. Vol. 1, 384 P (ISBN 0-8002-2271-7). Vol. 2, 347 P (ISBN 0-8002-2272-5). Intl Pubns Serv.
Nachbin, Leopoldo, ed. Mathematical Analysis & Applications. (Advances in Mathematics Supplementary Studies: Vol. 7). 1981. Pt. A. 51.00 (ISBN 0-12-512801-0); Pt. B. 49.00 (ISBN 0-12-512802-9). Acad Pr.
Nevanlinna, F. & Nevanlinna, R. Absolute Analysis. Emig, P., tr. from Ger. LC 73-75652. (Die Grundlehren der Mathematischen Wissenschaften: Vol. 102). (Illus.). 280p. 1973. 51.60 (ISBN 0-387-05917-2). Springer-Verlag.
Nikolsky, S. M. Course of Mathematical Analysis, 2 vols. 901p. 1977. Set. 16.50 (ISBN 0-8285-0706-6, Pub. by Mir Pubs Russia); Vol. 1; 460 Pp. 8.50 (ISBN 0-8285-0709-0); Vol. 2; 441 Pp. 8.50 (ISBN 0-686-74525-6). Imported Pubns.
Nine Papers on Analysis. LC 78-5442. (Translation Ser.: No. 2, Vol. 111). 1978. 34.80 (ISBN 0-8218-3061-9, TRANS2-111). Am Math.
Nishisato, Shizuhiko. Analysis of Categorical Data: Dual Scaling & Its Applications. (Mathematical Expositions Ser.). 148p. 1980. 27.50x (ISBN 0-8020-5489-7). U of Toronto Pr.
Ostrowski, A. Aufgabensammling zur Infinitesimalrechnung. Incl. Vol. 1. Funktionen Einer Variablen. 341p. 1967. 32.00 (ISBN 3-7643-0290-9); Vol. 2A. Differentialrechnung Auf Dem Gebiete Mehrerer Variblen. Aufgaben und Hinweise. 300p. 1972. 35.50 (ISBN 3-7643-0534-7); Vol. 2B. Differentialrechnung Auf Dem Gebiete Mehrerer Variablen, Losungen. 233p. 1972. 35.50 (ISBN 3-7643-0572-X). (Mathematische Reihe Ser.: Vols. 28, 38, 47 & 56). (Ger.). Birkhauser.
Page, A. Mathematical Analysis & Techniques, Vols. 1 & 2. (Oxford Mathematical Handbooks Ser). (Illus.). 568p. 1974. pap. text ed. 8.00x ea.; Vol. 1. pap. text ed. (ISBN 0-19-859612-X); Vol. 2. pap. text ed. (ISBN 0-19-859613-8). Oxford U Pr.
Polya, G. & Szego, G. Problems & Theorems in Analysis, No. 1: Series, Integral Calculus, Theory of Functions. (Illus.). 1977. Repr. soft cover 16.90 (ISBN 0-387-90224-4). Springer-Verlag.
--Problems & Theorems in Analysis, Vol. 2: Theory of Functions, Zeros, Polynomials, Determinants, Number Theory, Geometry. rev. ed. Billigheimer, C. E., tr. from Ger. LC 75-189312. (Die Grundlehren der Mathematischen Wissenschaften Ser.: Vol. 216). Orig. Title: Aufgaben und Lehrsatze Aus der Analysis. 400p. 1975. 60.10 (ISBN 0-387-06972-0). Springer-Verlag.
Pothoven, K. & Mukherjea, A., eds. Real & Functional Analysis. (Mathematical Concepts & Methods in Science & Engineering Ser: Vol. 6). (Illus.). 539p. 1977. 32.50 (ISBN 0-306-31015-5, Plenum Pr). Plenum Pub.
Proceedings of the Symposium Held at the Univ. of Alberta, Edmonton, May 29-June 1, 1972 & Sharma, A. Spline Functions & Approximation Theory. Meir, A., ed. (International Series of Numerical Mathematics: No. 21). 386p. 1973. 47.50 (ISBN 3-7643-0670-X). Birkhauser.
Prossdorf, S. Einige Klassen Singularer Gleichungen. (Mathematische Reihe Ser.: No. 46). 366p. (Ger.). 1974. 56.00 (ISBN 3-7643-0724-2). Birkhauser.
Protter, M. H. & Morrey, C. B. A First Course in Real Analysis. LC 76-43978. (Undergraduate Texts in Mathematics Ser.). 1977. 21.80 (ISBN 0-387-90215-5). Springer-Verlag.
Pungor. Coulometric Analysis. 1979. 31.00 (ISBN 0-9960015-6-5, Pub. by Kaido Hungary). Heyden.
Reid, William H., ed. Mathematical Problems in the Gephysical Sciences II: Inverse Problems, Dynamo Theory & Tides. LC 62-21481. (Lectures in Applied Mathematics Ser.: Vol. 14). 1971. 39.60 (ISBN 0-8218-1114-2, LAM-14). Am Math.
Reimann, H. M. & Rychener, T. Funktionen Beschrankter Mittlerer Oszillation. (Lecture Notes in Mathematics: Vol. 487). 141p. 1975. pap. 10.70 (ISBN 0-387-07404-X). Springer-Verlag.
Rice, B. J. Applied Analysis for Physicists & Engineers. 1972. write for info. (ISBN 0-87150-137-6, PWS 1051). Prindle.
Riley, K. F. Mathematical Methods for the Physical Sciences. LC 73-89765. 512p. (Orig.). 1974. 57.50 (ISBN 0-521-20390-2); pap. 22.95x (ISBN 0-521-09839-4). Cambridge U Pr.
Rockafellar, R. Tyrrell. Convex Analysis. LC 68-56318. (Mathematical Ser.: No. 28). 1970. 28.00x (ISBN 0-691-08069-0). Princeton U Pr.
Rota, Gian-Carlo, ed. Studies in Analysis. (Advances in Mathematics Supplementary Studies Ser.: Vol. 4). 1979. 46.00 (ISBN 0-12-599150-9). Acad Pr.
Rudin, Walter. Lectures on the Edge-of-the-Wedge Theorem. LC 73-145640. (CBMS Regional Conference Series in Mathematics: No. 6). vi, 30p. 1971. 7.00 (ISBN 0-8218-1655-1, CBMS-6). Am Math.
--Principles of Mathematical Analysis. (International Series in Pure & Applied Mathematics). 1976. text ed. 21.00 (ISBN 0-07-054235-X). McGraw.
--Real & Complex Analysis. 2nd ed. (Higher Mathematics Ser.). 416p. 1973. text ed. 24.00 (ISBN 0-07-054233-3, C). McGraw.
Samoilenko, A. M. & Ronto, N. I. Numerical-Analytic Methods of Investigating Periodic Solutions. 183p. 1979. pap. 3.50 (ISBN 0-8285-1514-X, Pub. by Mir Pubs Russia). Imported Pubns.
Sanin, Nikolai A. Constructive Real Numbers & Function Spaces. LC 68-19437. (Translations of Mathematical Monographs: Vol. 21). 1968. 36.00 (ISBN 0-8218-1571-7, MMONO-21). Am Math.
Schulze, B. W. & Wildenhain, G. Methoden der Potential Theorie Fur Elliptische Differentialgleichungen Beliebiger Ordnung. (Mathematische Reihe Ser.: No. 60). 424p. (Ger.). 1977. 79.50 (ISBN 3-7643-0944-X). Birkhauser.
Seminaire Pierre Lelong (Analyse) Annee 1973-4. Proceedings. (Lecture Notes in Mathematics: Vol. 474). 182p. 1975. pap. 10.70 (ISBN 0-387-07189-X). Springer-Verlag.
Shilov, G. Y. Mathematical Analysis: A Special Course. 1965. 37.00 (ISBN 0-08-010796-6); pap. 21.00 (ISBN 0-08-013616-8). Pergamon.
Shilov, Georgi E. Mathematical Analysis, 2 vols. Incl. Vol. 1. Elementary Real & Complex Analysis. 1973 (ISBN 0-262-19109-1); Vol. 2. Elementary Functional Analysis. 1974 (ISBN 0-262-19122-9). 1974. 23.00x ea. MIT Pr.
Simmons, George F. Introduction to Topology & Modern Analysis. (International Series in Pure & Applied Mathematics). 1963. text ed. 21.00 (ISBN 0-07-057389-1, C). McGraw.
Singh, Jagjit. Great Ideas of Modern Mathematics. (Illus.). 1959. pap. text ed. 4.00 (ISBN 0-486-20587-8). Dover.
Sirovich, Lawrence. Techniques of Asymptotic Analysis. LC 70-149141. (Applied Mathematical Sciences Ser.: Vol. 2). (Illus.). 1971. pap. 16.00 (ISBN 0-387-90022-5). Springer-Verlag.
Smirnov, V. I. A Course of Higher Mathematics, 5 vols. Incl. Vol. 1. Elementary Calculus. text ed. 21.00 (ISBN 0-08-010206-9); Vol. 2. Advanced Calculus. text ed. 21.00 (ISBN 0-08-010207-7); Vol. 3, Pt. 1. Linear Algebra. text ed. 14.50 (ISBN 0-08-010208-5); pap. text ed. 7.50 (ISBN 0-08-013717-2); Vol. 3, Pt. 2. Complex Variables. text ed. 28.00 (ISBN 0-08-010209-3); pap. text ed. 14.50 (ISBN 0-08-013622-2); Vol. 4. Integral Functions & Partial Differential Equations. text ed. 28.00 (ISBN 0-08-010210-7); pap. text ed. 14.50 (ISBN 0-08-013718-0); Vol. 5. Integration & Functional Analysis. text ed. 28.00 (ISBN 0-08-010211-5); pap. text ed. 14.50 (ISBN 0-08-013719-9). 1964. Set. Pergamon.
Smith, W. Allen. Elementary Numerical Analysis. 1979. text ed. 22.95 scp (ISBN 0-06-046312-0, HarpC). Har-Row.
Snell, K. S. & Morgan, J. B. Elementary Analysis, Vol. 2. 1966. 22.00 (ISBN 0-08-011777-5); pap. 10.75 (ISBN 0-08-011776-7). Pergamon.
Soff, Edward B. & Snider, Arthur D. Fundamentals of Complex Analysis for Mathematics, Science & Engineering. (Illus.). 1976. 26.95 (ISBN 0-13-332148-7). P-H.
Stoll, W. Value Distribution on Parabolic Spaces. (Lecture Notes in Mathematics: Vol. 600). 1977. 14.60 (ISBN 0-387-08341-3). Springer-Verlag.
Stone, M. H. Linear Transformations in Hilbert Space & Their Applications to Analysis. LC 33-2746. (Colloquium Pbns. Ser: Vol. 15). 1979. Repr. of 1974 ed. 45.20 (ISBN 0-8218-1015-4, COLL-15). Am Math.
Stromberg, Karl. Introduction to Classical Real Analysis. (Wadsworth International Mathematics Ser.). 576p. 1981. text ed. 29.95x (ISBN 0-534-98012-0). Wadsworth Pub.
S.U.N.Y. Brockport Conference. Complex Analysis: Proceedings. Miller, Sanford, ed. (Lecture Notes in Pure & Applied Math: Vol. 36). 1978. 20.75 (ISBN 0-8247-6725-X). Dekker.
Symposium in Pure Mathematics - Berkeley - 1968. Global Analysis, Pt. 1. Smale, S. & Chern, S. S., eds. LC 70-95271. 1970. 33.60 (ISBN 0-8218-1414-1, PSPUM-14). Am Math.
--Global Analysis, Pt. 2. Smale, S. & Chern, S. S., eds. LC 70-95271. 1970. 30.80 (ISBN 0-8218-1415-X, PSPUM-15). Am Math.
--Global Analysis, Pt. 3. LC 70-95271. 1970. 28.40 (ISBN 0-8218-1416-8, PSPUM-16). Am Math.
Symposium On Probability Methods In Analysis - Loutraki - Greece - 1966. Proceedings. (Lecture Notes in Mathematics: Vol. 31). 1967. pap. 18.30 (ISBN 0-387-03902-3). Springer-Verlag.
Theory of Numbers, Mathematical Analysis & Their Applications. LC 79-20552. (Proceedings of the Steklov Institute). 1979. 73.20 (ISBN 0-8218-3042-2, STEKLO 142). Am Math.
Traub, J. F., ed. Analytic Computational Complexity. 1976. 23.00 (ISBN 0-12-697560-4). Acad Pr.
Victoria Symposium on Nonstandard Analysis. Proceedings. Loeb, P. & Hurd, A., eds. LC 73-22552. (Lecture Notes in Mathematics: Vol. 369). xviii, 339p. 1974. pap. 13.40 (ISBN 0-387-06656-X). Springer-Verlag.
Voelker, D. & Doetsch, G. Zweidimensionale Laplace-Transformation. (Mathematische Reihe Ser.: No. 12). (Illus.). 260p. (Ger.). 1950. 48.50 (ISBN 3-7643-0394-8). Birkhauser.
Walker, P. L. An Introduction to Complex Analysis. LC 74-24686. 141p. 1974. 20.95 (ISBN 0-470-91807-1). Halsted Pr.
Wall, H. S. Creative Mathematics. 201p. 1963. pap. 4.95x (ISBN 0-292-71039-9). U of Tex Pr.
Weber, Jean E. Draper & Klingman's Mathematical Analysis: Business & Economic Applications. 3rd ed. (Illus.). 688p. 1976. text ed. 26.95 scp (ISBN 0-06-041762-5, HarpC); scp solutions manual o.p. 8.50 (ISBN 0-06-041763-3). Har-Row.
Whitney, Hassler. Complex Analytic Varieties. 1972. 20.95 (ISBN 0-201-08653-0). A-W.
Whyburn, Gordon T. Analytic Topology. LC 63-21794. (Colloquium Pbns. Ser.: Vol. 28). 1980. Repr. of 1971 ed. 29.20 (ISBN 0-8218-1028-6, COLL-28). Am Math.
--Topological Analysis. rev ed. (Mathematical Ser.: Vol. 23). 1964. 14.50x (ISBN 0-691-08054-2). Princeton U Pr.
Yosida, K. Functional Analysis. 6th ed. (Grundlehren der Mathematischen Wissenschaften Ser.: Vol. 123). 501p. 1980. 39.00 (ISBN 0-387-10210-8). Springer-Verlag.
Zamansky, Mark W. Linear Algebra & Analysis. (New University Mathematics Ser). (Illus.). 1969. text ed. 16.95x (ISBN 0-442-09573-2). Van Nos Reinhold.

MATHEMATICAL ANALYSIS–BIBLIOGRAPHY

Dunford, Nelson & Schwartz, Jacob T. Linear Operators, 3 pts. Incl. Pt. 1. General Theory. 1958. 59.00 (ISBN 0-470-22605-6); Pt. 2. Spectral Theory, Self Adjoint Operators in Hilbert Space. 79.50 (ISBN 0-470-22638-2); Pt. 3. Spectral Operators. 1971. 67.50 (ISBN 0-471-22639-4). LC 57-10545. (Pure & Applied Mathematics Ser, Pub. by Wiley-Interscience). Wiley.

MATHEMATICAL ANALYSIS–PROBLEMS, EXERCISES, ETC.

Bass, Jean. Exercises in Mathematics. Scripta Technica, tr. 1966. 55.00 (ISBN 0-12-080750-5). Acad Pr.

Christensen, R. Mathematical Analysis of Bluffing in Poker. 60p. 1981. 9.50 (ISBN 0-686-28920-X). Entropy Ltd.

Demidovich, Boris, ed. Problems in Mathematical Analysis. MIR Publishers, tr. from Rus. 496p. 1975. text ed. 18.00x (ISBN 0-8464-0761-2). Beekman Pubs.

Polya, G. & Szegoe, G. Problems & Theorems in Analysis I: Series, Integral Calculus, Theory of Functions. (Grundlehren der Mathematischen Wissenschaften: Vol. 193). 1978. 56.70 (ISBN 0-387-05672-6). Springer-Verlag.

MATHEMATICAL ANTHROPOLOGY

Ballonoff, Paul A. Mathematical Foundations of Social Anthropology. (Publications of the Maison Des Sciences De L'homme). (Illus.). 131p. 1976. pap. text ed. 16.25x (ISBN 90-2797-934-0). Mouton.

Mathematical Paths in the Study of Human Needs. 82p. 1981. pap. 5.00 (ISBN 92-808-0160-0, W492, UNU). Unipub.

MATHEMATICAL CRYSTALLOGRAPHY

see Crystallography, Mathematical

MATHEMATICAL DRAWING

see Geometrical Drawing; Mechanical Drawing

MATHEMATICAL ECONOMICS

see Economics, Mathematical

MATHEMATICAL FORMULAE

see Mathematics–Formulae

MATHEMATICAL GEOGRAPHY

see Geography, Mathematical

MATHEMATICAL INDUCTION

see Induction (Mathematics)

MATHEMATICAL INSTRUMENTS

see also Abacus; Calculating-Machines; Planimeter

Bion, M. Construction & Principle Use of Mathematical Instruments, 1758. Stone, Edmund, tr. from Lat. (Illus.). 75.00 (ISBN 0-87556-159-4). Saifer.

Gunter, Edmund. The Description & Use of the Sector, the Crosse-Staffe & Other Instruments, 2 pts. LC 70-38418. (English Experience Ser.: No. 422). 500p. 1971. Repr. of 1624 ed. 53.00 (ISBN 90-221-0422-2). Walter J Johnson.

MATHEMATICAL LINGUISTICS

see also Linguistics–Data Processing

Akhmanova, O. S., et al. Exact Methods in Linguistic Research. Haynes, David G. & Mohr, Dolores V., trs. LC 63-19957. 1963. 24.50x (ISBN 0-520-00542-2). U of Cal Pr.

Anshen, Frank. Statistics for Linguists. LC 78-7216. 1978. pap. text ed. 4.95 (ISBN 0-88377-113-6). Newbury Hse.

Arbib, Michael A. Algebraic Theory of Machines, Languages & Semigroups. LC 68-18654. 1968. 55.00 (ISBN 0-12-059050-6). Acad Pr.

Dolezel, L., et al, eds. Prague Studies in Mathematical Linguistics, 3 Vols. LC 66-16432. 1966-71. Vol. 1. 25.00x (ISBN 0-8173-0100-3); Vol. 2. 25.00x (ISBN 0-8173-0101-1); Vol. 3. 25.00x (ISBN 0-8173-0102-X). U of Ala Pr.

Harris, Zellig S. Mathematical Structures of Language. LC 79-4568. 240p. 1979. Repr. of 1968 ed. lib. bdg. 12.50 (ISBN 0-88275-958-2). Krieger.

Heller, Louis G. & Macris, James. Parametric Linguistics. (Janua Linguarum, Ser. Minor: No. 58). (Orig.). 1967. pap. text ed. 7.80x (ISBN 0-686-22451-5). Mouton.

Hemphill, George. A Mathematical Grammar of English. (Janua Linguarum, Ser. Practica: No. 153). 1973. text ed. 20.75x (ISBN 90-2792-433-3). Mouton.

Herdan, G. Quantitative Linguistics. 1964. 18.50 (ISBN 0-208-00196-4, Archon). Shoe String.

Herdan, Gustav. Calculus of Linguistic Observations. (Janua Linguarum, Ser. Major: No. 9). 1962. text ed. 53.50x (ISBN 90-2790-604-1). Mouton.

Hockett, Charles F. Language, Mathematics, & Linguistics. (Janua Linguarum, Ser. Minor: No. 60). (Illus.). 1967. pap. text ed. 28.75x (ISBN 0-686-22442-6). Mouton.

Horecky, J., et al. Prague Studies in Mathematical Linguistics, Vol. 6. 1977. 46.50 (ISBN 0-7204-0439-8, North-Holland). Elsevier.

Horecky, J. P. & Testitelova, M. Prague Studies in Mathematical Linguistics, Vol. 5. 1977. 46.50 (ISBN 0-7204-8034-5, North-Holland). Elsevier.

Horecky, Jan, et al. Prague Studies in Mathematical Linguistics, Vol. 4. LC 66-16432. 256p. 1973. 25.00x (ISBN 0-8173-0103-8). U of Ala Pr.

Johnson, David E. & Postal, Paul M. Arc Pair Grammar. LC 80-7533. (Illus.). 700p. 1980. 35.00x (ISBN 0-691-08270-7). Princeton U Pr.

Kortlandt, F. H. Modelling the Phoneme: The Trends in East European Phonemic Theory. (Janua Linguarum, Ser. Major: No. 68). 177p. 1972. text ed. 31.25x (ISBN 90-2792-109-1). Mouton.

Levelt, W. J. Formal Grammars in Linguistics & Psycholinguistics: Applications in Linguistic Theory, Vol. 2. (Janua Linguarum, Ser. Minor: No. 192-2). (Illus.). viii, 194p. (Orig.). 1974. pap. text ed. 21.25x (ISBN 90-2792-708-1). Mouton.

--Formal Grammars in Linguistics & Psycholinguistics: Psycholinguistics Applications, Vol. 3. (Janua Linguarum, Ser. Minor: No. 192-3). 206p. 1974. pap. text ed. 26.25x (ISBN 90-2793-352-9). Mouton.

Manna, Zohar. Introduction to Mathematical Theory of Computation. (Computer Science Ser). (Illus.). 360p. 1974. text ed. 27.95 (ISBN 0-07-039910-7, C). McGraw.

Nowakowska, Maria. Language of Motivation & Language of Actions. LC 72-94491. (Janua Linguarum, Ser. Major: No. 67). (Illus.). 272p. 1973. text ed. 55.00x (ISBN 0-686-22550-3). Mouton.

Papp, Ferenc. Mathematical Linguistics in the Soviet Union. (Janua Linguarum, Ser. Minor: No. 40). (Orig.). 1966. pap. text ed. 15.00x (ISBN 0-686-22446-9). Mouton.

Partee, Barbara H. Mathematical Fundamentals of Linguistics. 1976. text ed. 15.95x (ISBN 0-89223-012-6). Greylock Pubs.

Shaw, Bryce R. Personalized Computational Skills Program. LC 79-90570. 544p. 1980. Set. pap. text ed. 14.75 (ISBN 0-395-29032-5); Mod. A. pap. text ed. 5.75 (ISBN 0-395-29033-3); Mod. B. pap. text ed. 5.75 (ISBN 0-395-29034-1); Mod. C. pap. text ed. 5.50 (ISBN 0-395-29035-X); pap. 1.00 inst. manual (ISBN 0-395-29036-8). HM.

Symposia in Applied Mathematics - New York - 1960. Structure of Language & Its Mathematical Aspects: Proceedings, Vol. 12. Jakobson, R., ed. LC 50-1183. 1980. Repr. of 1961 ed. 22.00 (ISBN 0-8218-1312-9, PSAPM-12). Am Math.

Wall, Robert. Introduction to Mathematical Linguistics. LC 75-38044. (Illus.). 304p. 1972. ref. ed. 16.95 (ISBN 0-13-487496-X). P-H.

Wilkins, D. A. Notional Syllabuses. 1977. pap. text ed. 6.50x (ISBN 0-19-437071-2). Oxford U Pr.

Zampolli, A., ed. Linguistic Structures Processing: Studies in Linguistics, Computational Linguistics & Artificial Intelligence. 1977. 53.75 (ISBN 0-444-85017-1, North-Holland). Elsevier.

MATHEMATICAL LOGIC

see Logic, Symbolic and Mathematical

MATHEMATICAL MACHINE THEORY

see Machine Theory

MATHEMATICAL MEASUREMENTS

see also Slide-Rule

Budlong, John P. Sky & Sextant. 232p. 1981. pap. text ed. 10.95 (ISBN 0-442-20460-4). Van Nos Reinhold.

Franks, Margaret L. & Graves, Joy D. Mathematical Concepts in Pharmacology. (A Skills Work Book for the Health Sciences). 1973. 3.95x (ISBN 0-88236-600-9). Anaheim Pub Co.

Math House Proficiency Review Tapes: Applications Involving Measurement, Unit C. (YA) (gr. 7 up). 1980. manual & cassettes 179.50 (ISBN 0-917792-05-X). Math Hse.

MATHEMATICAL MODELS

see also Digital Computer Simulation; Game Theory; Machine Theory; Monte Carlo Method; Programming (Electronic Computers); System Analysis;
also subdivision Mathematical Models under specific subjects, e.g. Human Behavior–Mathematical Models

Ackerman, Eugene & Gatewood, Lael C. Mathematical Models in the Health Sciences: A Computer-Aided Approach. 1979. 23.50x (ISBN 0-8166-0864-4). U of Minn Pr.

Andrews, J. G. & McLone, R. R., eds. Mathematical Modeling. 1976. 13.95 (ISBN 0-408-10601-8). Butterworth.

Bender, Edward A. An Introduction to Mathematical Modeling. LC 77-23840. 256p. 1978. 23.95 (ISBN 0-471-02951-3, Pub. by Wiley-Interscience); solutions manual 4.50 (ISBN 0-471-03407-X). Wiley.

Bittinger, Marvin L. & Crown, J. Conrad. Mathematics: A Modeling Approach. 1981. write for info. (ISBN 0-201-03116-7). A-W.

Boyce, W. E., ed. Case Studies in Mathematical Modelling. (Applicable Mathematics Ser.). 432p. 1981. text ed. 39.95 (ISBN 0-273-08486-0). Pitman Pub MA.

Bradley, R., et al. Case Studies in Mathematical Modelling. 250p. 1981. 44.95 (ISBN 0-470-27235-X). Halsted Pr.

Brebbia, C. A., ed. Applied Numerical Modeling: Proceedings of the International Conference, University of Southampton, 11-15 July, 1977. LC 77-11141. 1978. 54.95 (ISBN 0-470-99271-9). Halsted Pr.

Burghes, D. N. & Wood, A. D. Mathematical Models in the Social, Management & Life Sciences. LC 79-40989. (Mathematics & Its Applications Ser.). 287p. 1980. 39.95x (ISBN 0-470-26862-X); pap. text ed. 19.95 (ISBN 0-470-27073-X). Halsted Pr.

Cea, J., ed. Optimization Techniques Modeling & Optimization in the Service of Man: Pt. 2. LC 76-9857. (Lecture Notes in Computer Science: Vol. 41). 1976. pap. 33.90 (ISBN 0-387-07623-9). Springer-Verlag.

--Optimization Techniques: Modeling & Optimization in the Service of Man, Pt. 1. LC 76-9857. (Lecture Notes in Computer Science Ser.: Vol. 40.). 1976. pap. 33.90 (ISBN 0-387-07622-0). Springer-Verlag.

Chang, C. C. & Keisler, H. J. Model Theory. 2nd ed. (Studies in Logic & the Foundations of Mathematics Ser.: Vol. 73). 552p. 1977. 44.00 (ISBN 0-685-48940-X, North-Holland); pap. 25.00 (ISBN 0-7204-0692-7). Elsevier.

Ciriani, Tito A., ed. Mathematical Models for Surface Water Hydrology: Proceedings of the Workshop Held at the IBM Scientific Center, Pisa Italy. LC 76-13457. 1977. 80.25 (ISBN 0-471-99400-6, Pub. by Wiley-Interscience). Wiley.

Coffman, C. V. & Fix, G. J. Constructive Approaches to Mathematical Models. LC 79-51673. 1979. 55.00 (ISBN 0-12-178150-X). Acad Pr.

Cundy, Henry M. & Rollett, A. P. Mathematical Models. 2nd ed. (Illus.). 1961. 11.95 (ISBN 0-19-832504-5). Oxford U Pr.

Dantzig, George B. Linear Programming & Extensions. (Rand Corporation Research Studies). 1963. 30.00 (ISBN 0-691-08000-3). Princeton U Pr.

DiPrima, Richard O., ed. Modern Modeling of Continuum Phenomena. LC 77-9041. (Lectures in Applied Mathematics Ser.: Vol. 16). 1977. 44.40 (ISBN 0-8218-1116-9, LAM-16). Am Math.

Ditlevsen, Ove. Uncertainty Modeling: With Applications to Multidimensional Civil Engineering. (Illus.). 448p. 1980. text ed. 69.50 (ISBN 0-07-017046-0, C). McGraw.

Dorny, C. Nelson. A Vector Space Approach to Models & Optimization. LC 80-12423. 620p. 1980. lib. bdg. 34.50 (ISBN 0-89874-210-2). Krieger.

Dym, Clive L. & Ivey, Elizabeth. Principles of Mathematical Modeling. LC 79-65441. (Computer Science & Applied Mathematics Ser.). 261p. 1980. tchrs' ed. 18.95 (ISBN 0-12-226550-5); solutions manual 3.00 (ISBN 0-12-226560-2). Acad Pr.

Frauenthal, J. C. Mathematical Modeling in Epidemiology. (Universitexts Ser.). 118p. 1980. pap. 14.80 (ISBN 0-387-10328-7). Springer-Verlag.

Gaver, Donald P. & Thompson, Gerald L. Programming & Probability Models in Operations Research. LC 72-90938. 1973. text ed. 29.95 (ISBN 0-8185-0057-3). Brooks-Cole.

Gillispie, John V. & Zinnes, Dina A., eds. Mathematical Systems in International Relations Research. LC 75-23964. 1977. text ed. 45.95 (ISBN 0-275-55620-4). Praeger.

Goodwin, G. C. & Payne, R. L., eds. Dynamic System Identification: Experimental Design & Data Analysis. 1977. 43.00 (ISBN 0-12-289750-1). Acad Pr.

Greenberg, Harvey & Maybee, John, eds. Computer-Assisted Analysis & Model Simplification. LC 80-28509. 1981. 29.50 (ISBN 0-12-299680-1). Acad Pr.

Haberman, R. Mathematical Models: Mechanical Vibrations, Population, Dynamics & Traffic Flow, An Introduction to Applied Mathematics. 1977. 26.95 (ISBN 0-13-561738-3). P-H.

Harris, C. J. Mathematical Modelling of Turbulent Diffusion in the Environment. LC 79-50301. (Athe Institute of Mathematics & Its Applications Conference Ser.). 1980. 48.00 (ISBN 0-12-328350-7). Acad Pr.

Hayes, Patrick. Mathematical Methods in the Social & Managerial Sciences. LC 74-22361. 448p. 1975. 35.50 (ISBN 0-471-36490-8, Pub. by Wiley-Interscience). Wiley.

Jacoby, Samuel L. & Kowalik, Janusz S. Mathematical Modeling with Computers. (Illus.). 1980. text ed. 24.95 (ISBN 0-13-561555-0). P-H.

James, D. J. & McDonald, J. J. Case Studies in Mathematical Modelling. 224p. 1981. 17.95 (ISBN 0-470-27177-9). Halsted Pr.

Jones, A. J. Game Theory: Mathematical Models of Conflict. LC 79-40972. (Mathematics & Its Applications Ser.). 309p. 1980. pap. text ed. 24.95x (ISBN 0-470-26892-1). Halsted Pr.

Louden, Louise & Church, John. Mathematical Modeling. LC 77-88450. (Bibliographic Ser.: No. 278). 1977. pap. 45.00 (ISBN 0-87010-029-7). Inst Paper Chem.

Maki, Daniel & Thompson, Maynard. Mathematical Models & Applications: With Emphasis on the Social, Life, & Management Sciences. (Illus.). 464p. 1973. ref. ed. 25.95 (ISBN 0-13-561670-0). P-H.

Malita, Mircea & Zidaroiu, Corneliu. Mathematics of Organization. Hammel, John, ed. Zidaroiu, Corneliu, tr. from Romanian. (Illus.). 1976. 32.50x (ISBN 0-85626-019-3, Pub. by Abacus Pr). Intl Schol Bk Serv.

Mischke, Charles R. Mathematical Model Building. 2nd rev. ed. (Illus.). 1980. text ed. 18.50 (ISBN 0-8138-1005-1). Iowa St U Pr.

Modules for Mathematical Concepts in Pharmacology. pap. text ed. 1.95 (ISBN 0-88236-111-2). Anaheim Pub Co.

Nicholson, H., ed. Modelling of Dynamic Systems, Vol. 2, Vol. 2. (IEE Control Engineering Ser.). (Illus.). 256p. 1981. 67.50 (ISBN 0-906048-45-1, Pub. by Peregrinus England). Inst Elect Eng.

Pollard, J. H. Mathematical Models for the Growth of Human Populations. LC 72-91957. 204p. 1973. 29.50 (ISBN 0-521-20111-X); pap. 9.95x (ISBN 0-521-29442-8). Cambridge U Pr.

Reason, Peter & Rowan, John. Human Inquiry: A Sourcebook of New Paradigm Research. LC 80-41585. 1981. write for info. (ISBN 0-471-27936-6, Pub. by Wiley Interscience). Wiley.

Reismann, Herbert & Pawlik, Peter S. Elastokinetics. LC 74-4510. 512p. 1974. text ed. 40.00 (ISBN 0-8299-0016-0). West Pub.

Roberts, Peter C. Modelling Large Systems: Limits to Growth Revisited. LC 78-13339. (Orasa Text). 1978. pap. 21.95 (ISBN 0-470-26528-0). Halsted Pr.

Rose, L. M. The Application of Mathematical Modelling to Process Development & Design. LC 74-14543. 364p. 1974. 54.95 (ISBN 0-470-73351-9). Halsted Pr.

Rubinstein, Mashe F. Patterns of Problem Solving. LC 74-20721. (Illus.). 640p. 1975. text ed. 22.95 ref. ed. (ISBN 0-13-654251-4). P-H.

Saaty, Thomas L. & Alexander, Joyce M. Thinking with Models: Mathematical Models in the Physical, Biological & Social Sciences. (I S Modern Applied Mathematics & Computer Science: Vol. 2). (Illus.). 208p. 1981. 35.00 (ISBN 0-08-026475-1); pap. 20.00 (ISBN 0-08-026474-3). Pergamon.

Smith, J. M. Mathematical Modeling & Digital Simulation for Engineers & Scientists. LC 76-52419. 1977. 30.00 (ISBN 0-471-80344-8, Pub. by Wiley-Interscience). Wiley.

Tikhonov, A. N., et al, eds. Mathematical Models & Numerical Methods. (Banach Center Publications: Vol. III). 391p. 1978. 60.00 (ISBN 0-8002-2268-7). Intl Pubns Serv.

Waite, Thomas D. & Freeman, Neil J. Mathematics of Environmental Processes. LC 76-25770. 1977. 21.00x (ISBN 0-669-00979-2). Lexington Bks.

West, Bruce J. Mathematical Models As a Tool for Social Sciences. 120p. 1980. 29.25 (ISBN 0-677-10390-5). Gordon.

Wheeler, Ruric E. & Peeples, W. D. Finite Mathematics: An Introduction to Mathematical Models. LC 73-89593. (Contemporary Undergrad Math Ser). 1974. text ed. 18.95 (ISBN 0-8185-0117-0). Brooks-Cole.

Williams, H. P. Model Building in Mathematical Programming. LC 77-7380. 1978. 55.50 (ISBN 0-471-99526-6); pap. 24.50 (ISBN 0-471-99541-X, Pub. by Wiley-Interscience). Wiley.

MATHEMATICAL NOTATION

see also Quaternions; Vector Analysis

Cajori, Florian. History of Mathematical Notations, 2 vols. Incl. Vol. 1. Notations in Elementary Mathematics. xvi, 451p. 1951. pap. 7.95 (ISBN 0-87548-171-X); Vol. 2. Notations Mainly in Higher Mathematics. xviii, 367p. 1952. 19.95 (ISBN 0-87548-172-8). (Illus.). Open Court.

MATHEMATICAL OPTIMIZATION

see also Decision-Making–Mathematical Models; Dynamic Programming; Experimental Design; Games of Strategy (Mathematics); Programming (Mathematics); System Analysis

Albrecht, F. Topics in Control Theory. (Lecture Notes in Mathematics: Vol. 63). 1968. pap. 10.70 (ISBN 0-387-04233-4). Springer-Verlag.

Anderssen, R. S., et al, eds. Optimization. 246p. 1972. 9.95x (ISBN 0-7022-0805-1). U of Queensland Pr.

Arrow, K. J. & Hurwicz, L., eds. Studies in Resource Allocation Process. LC 76-9171. (Illus.). 1977. 47.50 (ISBN 0-521-21522-6). Cambridge U Pr.

Aubin, Jean-Pierre. Applied Abstract Analysis. LC 77-2382. (Pure & Applied Mathematics, a W-I Ser. of Texts, Monographs & Tracts). 263p. 1977. 38.50 (ISBN 0-471-02146-6, Pub. by Wiley-Interscience). Wiley.

Auslender, A., et al, eds. Optimization & Optimal Control: Proceedings. (Lecture Notes in Control & Information Sciences Ser.: Vol. 30). 254p. 1981. pap. 15.50 (ISBN 0-387-10627-8). Springer-Verlag.
Balakrishnan, A. V. Applied Functional Analysis. LC 75-25932. (Applications of Mathematics: Vol. 3). 605p. 1976. 26.00 (ISBN 0-387-90157-4). Springer-Verlag.
Balakrishnan, A. V. & Neustadt, L. W., eds. Techniques of Optimization. 1972. 43.00 (ISBN 0-12-076960-3). Acad Pr.
Balakrishnan, A. V. & Neustadt, Lucien W., eds. Computing Methods in Optimization Problems: Proceedings. 1964. 36.00 (ISBN 0-12-076950-6). Acad Pr.
Balinski, M. L. & Wolfe, P. Nondifferentiable Optimization. (Mathematical Programming Study: Vol. 3). 1976. 23.50 (ISBN 0-444-11008-9, North-Holland). Elsevier.
Bazaraa, M. S. & Shetty, C. M. Foundations of Optimization. (Lecture Notes in Economics & Mathematical Systems Ser.: Vol. 122). 1976. pap. 9.50 (ISBN 0-387-07680-8). Springer-Verlag.
Bell, D. J. & Jacobson, D. H. Singular Optimal Control Problems. (Mathematics in Science & Engineering Ser.). 1975. 32.00 (ISBN 0-12-085060-5). Acad Pr.
Beltrami, E. J. Algorithmic Approach to Nonlinear Analysis & Optimization. (Mathematics in Science & Engineering Ser.: Vol. 63). 1970. 40.50 (ISBN 0-12-085560-7). Acad Pr.
Bensoussan, A. & Lions, J. L., eds. International Symposium on Systems Optimization & Analysis. (Lecture Notes in Control & Information Sciences: Vol. 14). (Illus.). 1979. pap. 16.80 (ISBN 0-387-09447-4). Springer-Verlag.
Bertsekas, Dimitri P. & Shreve, Steven E. Stochastic Optimal Control: The Discrete Time Case. (Mathematics in Science & Engineering Ser.). 1978. 46.00 (ISBN 0-12-093260-1). Acad Pr.
Beveridge, S. G. & Schechter, Robert S. Optimization Theory & Practice. 1970. pap. text ed. 26.50 (ISBN 0-07-005128-3, C). McGraw.
Biennial Seminar of the Canadian Mathematical Congress, 14th Univ. of Western Ontario, August 1973. Optimal Control Theory & Its Applications: Proceedings, 2 pts. Kirby, B. J., ed. (Lecture Notes in Economics & Mathematical Systems Ser.). 1975. pap. 18.30 ea.; Pt. 1. pap. (ISBN 0-387-07018-4); Pt. 2. pap. (ISBN 0-387-07026-5). Springer-Verlag.
Burley, D. M. Studies in Optimization. LC 74-8454. 1974. text ed. 19.95 (ISBN 0-470-12410-5). Halsted Pr.
Cea, J. & Murthy, M. K. Lectures on Optimization: Theory & Algorithms. (Tata Institute Lectures on Mathematics Ser.). 1979. pap. 10.40 (ISBN 0-387-08850-4). Springer-Verlag.
Cea, J., ed. Optimization Techniques Modeling & Optimization in the Service of Man: Pt. 2. LC 76-9857. (Lecture Notes in Computer Science: Vol. 41). 1976. pap. 33.90 (ISBN 0-387-07623-9). Springer-Verlag.
--Optimization Techniques: Modeling & Optimization in the Service of Man, Pt. 1. LC 76-9857. (Lecture Notes in Computer Science Ser.: Vol. 40.). 1976. pap. 33.90 (ISBN 0-387-07622-0). Springer-Verlag.
Christofides, Nicos, et al, eds. Combinatorial Optimization. LC 78-11131. 1979. 64.50 (ISBN 0-471-99749-8, Pub. by Wiley-Interscience). Wiley.
CISM (International Center for Mechanical Sciences), Dept. of Automation & Information, 1972. Periodic Optimization, 2 vols. Marzollo, A., ed. (CISM Pubns. Ser.: No. 135). (Illus.). 532p. 1973. Set. pap. 50.70 (ISBN 0-387-81135-4). Springer-Verlag.
Clements, D. J. & Anderson, B. D. Singular Optimal Control: The Linear-Quadratic Problem. (Lecture Notes in Control & Information Science: Vol. 5). 1978. pap. 9.20 (ISBN 0-387-08694-3). Springer-Verlag.
Collatz, L. & Wetterling, W. Optimization Problems. Hadsack, P. R., tr. from Ger. (Applied Mathematical Sciences Ser.: Vol. 17). (Illus.). 370p. (Orig.). 1975. pap. text ed. 18.40 (ISBN 0-387-90143-4). Springer-Verlag.
Collatz, L. & Meinardus, G., eds. Numerische Methoden bei Graphentheoretischen und Kombinatorischen Problemen, Vol. 1. (International Series of Numerical Mathematics: No. 29). (Illus.). 159p. (Ger.). 1975. 24.00 (ISBN 3-7643-0786-2). Birkhauser.
Collatz, L., et al, eds. Numerische Methoden bei Graphentheoretischen und Kombinatorishen Problemen: Vol. II. (International Series of Numerical Mathematics: No. 46). (Illus.). 255p. (Ger. & Eng.). 1979. pap. 32.50 (ISBN 3-7643-1078-2). Birkhauser.
Colloquium on Methods of Optimization, Novosibirsk USSR, 1968. Proceedings. Moiseev, N. N., ed. LC 77-106194. (Lecture Notes in Mathematics: Vol. 112). (Eng. & Fr.). 1970. pap. 14.70 (ISBN 0-387-04901-0). Springer-Verlag.
Conference Held at Oberwolfach, Nov. 17-23, 1974, et al. Optimization & Optimal Control: Proceedings. Bulirsch, R. & Oettli, W., eds. LC 75-23372. (Lecture Notes in Mathematics: Vol. 477). vii, 294p. 1975. pap. 14.70 (ISBN 0-387-07393-0). Springer-Verlag.
Conference on Optimization in Action, Institute of Mathematics & Its Applications, University of Bristol, England, January 1975. Optimization in Action: Proceedings. Dixon, L. W., ed. 1977. 70.50 (ISBN 0-12-218550-1). Acad Pr.
Conference on Optimization Techniques, 5th. Proceedings, Pt. 1. Ruberti, A., ed. (Lecture Notes in Computer Science: Vol. 3). (Illus.). 565p. 1974. pap. 19.50 (ISBN 0-387-06583-0). Springer-Verlag.
--Proceedings, Pt. 2. Ruberti, A., ed. (Lecture Notes in Computer Science: Vol. 4). (Illus.). 389p. 1974. pap. 17.00 (ISBN 0-387-06600-4). Springer-Verlag.
Conley, William. Computer Optimization Techniques. (Illus.). 266p. 1980. 24.00 (ISBN 0-07-091059-6). McGraw.
--Computer Optimization Techniques. 1980. 25.00 (ISBN 0-89433-111-6). Petrocelli.
--Optimization: A Report. 40p. 1980. text ed. 10.00 (ISBN 0-89433-145-0). Petrocelli.
--Optimization: A Simplified Approach. (Illus.). 272p. 1981. 20.00 (ISBN 0-89433-121-3). Petrocelli.
Converse, A. O. Optimization. LC 74-22103. 308p. 1975. Repr. of 1970 ed. 14.50 (ISBN 0-88275-236-7). Krieger.
Dantzig, G. B. & Eaves, B. C., eds. Studies in Optimization. LC 74-21481. (MAA Studies: No. 10). 1977. 12.50 (ISBN 0-88385-110-5). Math Assn.
Denn, Morton M. Optimization by Variational Methods. LC 77-24739. 440p. 1978. Repr. of 1969 ed. lib. bdg. 22.50 (ISBN 0-88275-595-1). Krieger.
De Veubeke, B. F. Advanced Problems & Methods for Space Flight Optimization. 1969. 46.00 (ISBN 0-08-013290-1). Pergamon.
Dixit, A. K. Optimization in Economic Theory. (Illus.). 1977. pap. 8.95x (ISBN 0-19-877103-7). Oxford U Pr.
Dixon, L. C. & Szego, G. P., eds. Towards Global Optimisation, Vols. I & II. LC 74-28195. 1975. Vol. I. 53.75 (ISBN 0-444-10955-2, North-Holland); Vol. II. 49.00 (ISBN 0-444-85171-2). Elsevier.
Dixon, L. C., et al, eds. Nonlinear Optimization, Theory & Algorithms. 492p. 1980. 29.80 (ISBN 3-7643-3020-1). Birkhauser.
Dorny, C. Nelson. A Vector Space Approach to Models & Optimization. LC 80-12423. 620p. 1980. lib. bdg. 34.50 (ISBN 0-89874-210-2). Krieger.
Egardt, B. Stability of Adaptive Controllers. Balakrishnan, A. V. & Thoma, M., eds. (Lecture Notes in Control & Information Sciences: Vol. 20). (Illus.). 1979. pap. 10.30 (ISBN 0-387-09646-9). Springer-Verlag.
El-Hodiri, M. A. Constrained Extrema: Introduction to the Differentiable Case with Economic Applications. LC 72-177567. (Lecture Notes in Operations Research: Vol. 56). 130p. 1971. Springer-Verlag.
Fedorov, V. V. Theory of Optimal Experiments. (Probability & Mathematical Statistics Ser.). 1972. 44.50 (ISBN 0-12-250750-9). Acad Pr.
Fleming, W. H. & Rishel, R. W. Deterministic & Stochastic Optimal Control. LC 75-28391. (Applications of Mathematics: Vol. 1). (Illus.). xi, 222p. 1975. 31.30 (ISBN 0-387-90155-8). Springer-Verlag.
Fletcher, R. Practical Methods of Optimization: Constrained Optimization. 224p. 1981. 32.50 (ISBN 0-471-27828-9, Pub. by Wiley Interscience). Wiley.
--Practical Methods of Optimization: Unconstrained Optimization, Vol. 1. LC 79-41486. 120p. 1980. 24.50 (ISBN 0-471-27711-8, Pub. by Wiley-Interscience). Wiley.
Fletcher, R., ed. Optimization. 1970. 56.50 (ISBN 0-12-260650-7). Acad Pr.
Friedman, B. Economic Stabilization Policy: Methods in Optimization. LC 73-86080. (Studies in Mathematical & Managerial Economics: Vol. 15). 375p. 1975. 39.00 (ISBN 0-444-10566-2, North-Holland). Elsevier.
Gabasov, R. & Kirillova, F. The Qualitative Theory of Optimal Processes. Casti, John L., tr. (Control & Systems Theory: Vol. 3). 1976. 74.50 (ISBN 0-8247-6545-1). Dekker.
Gabasov, R. & Kirillova, F. M., eds. Singular Optimal Controls. (Mathematical Concepts & Methods in Science & Engineering: Vol. 10). (Illus.). 300p. 1978. 29.50 (ISBN 0-306-39250-X, Plenum Pr). Plenum Pub.
Gamkrelidze, R. V. Principles of Optimal Control Theory. (Mathematical Concepts & Methods in Science & Engineering Ser.: Vol. 7). 185p. 1977. 24.50 (ISBN 0-306-30977-7, Plenum Pr). Plenum Pub.
Girsanov, I. V. Lectures on Mathematical Theory of Extremum Problems. Louvish, D., tr. from Rus. LC 72-80360. (Lecture Notes in Economics & Mathematical Systems: Vol. 67). (Illus.). 139p. 1972. pap. 7.30 (ISBN 0-387-05857-5). Springer-Verlag.
Gottfried, Byron S. & Weisman, Joel. Introduction to Optimization Theory. (Illus.). 592p. 1973. ref. ed. 23.95 (ISBN 0-13-491472-4). P-H.
Greig, D. M. Optimisation. LC 79-42892. (Longman Mathematical Texts). (Illus.). 179p. 1980. pap. text ed. 14.50x (ISBN 0-582-44186-2). Longman.
Gumowski, Igor & Mira, C. Optimization in Control Theory & Practice. LC 68-12059. (Illus.). 1968. 40.75 (ISBN 0-521-05158-4). Cambridge U Pr.
Hasdorff, Lawrence. Gradient Optimization & Nonlinear Control. LC 75-40187. 1976. text ed. 32.50- (ISBN 0-471-35870-3, Pub. by Wiley-Interscience). Wiley.
Henn, R., et al, eds. Optimization & Operations Research: Proceedings of a Workshop Held at the University of Bonn, October 2-8, 1977. (Lecture Notes in Econometrics & Operations Research Ser.: Vol. 157). 1978. pap. 13.90 (ISBN 0-387-08842-3). Springer-Verlag.
Hestenes, M. Conjugate Direction Methods in Optimization. (Applications of Mathematics Ser.: Vol. 12). (Illus.). 325p. 1980. 29.80 (ISBN 0-387-90455-7). Springer-Verlag.
Hestenes, Magnus R. Calculus of Variations & Optimal Control Theory. LC 79-25451. 418p. 1980. Repr. of 1966 ed. lib. bdg. 32.50 (ISBN 0-89874-092-4). Krieger.
--Optimization Theory: The Finite Dimensional Case. LC 80-11516. 464p. 1981. Repr. of 1975 ed. lib. bdg. 32.50 (ISBN 0-89874-143-2). Krieger.
Holmes, R. B. A Course on Optimization & Best Approximation. (Lecture Notes in Mathematics: Vol. 257). 233p. 1972. pap. 7.50 (ISBN 0-387-05764-1). Springer-Verlag.
Hull, T. E., ed. Studies in Optimization One. (Illus.). 1970. text ed. 9.75 (ISBN 0-686-24730-2). Soc Indus-Appl Math.
Husain, Asghar & Gangiah, Kota. Optimization Techniques for Chemical Engineers. 1976. 8.00x (ISBN 0-333-90127-4). South Asia Bks.
IFIP Technical Conference, Novosibirsk, 1974. Optimization Techniques: IFIP Technical Conference. Marchuk, G. I., ed. (Lecture Notes in Computer Science Ser: Vol. 27). 515p. 1975. pap. 21.40 (ISBN 0-387-07165-2). Springer-Verlag.
Intriligator, Michael D. Mathematical Optimization & Economic Theory. (Mathematical Economics Ser.). 1971. text ed. 23.95 (ISBN 0-13-561753-7). P-H.
Iracki, K., et al, eds. Optimization Techniques Part One: Proceedings. (Lecture Notes in Control & Information Sciences: Vol. 22). (Illus.). 569p. 1980. pap. 34.90 (ISBN 0-387-10080-6). Springer-Verlag.
--Optimization Techniques Part Two: Proceedings, Vol. 23. (Lecture Notes in Control & Information Sciences). 621p. 1980. pap. 34.90 (ISBN 0-387-10081-4). Springer-Verlag.
Jacobson, D. H. Extensions of Linear-Quadratic Control, Optimization & Matrix Theory. 1977. 34.50 (ISBN 0-12-378750-5). Acad Pr.
Jamieson, T. H. Optimization of Techniques in Lens Design. (Applied Optics Monographs: No. 5). 1971. 25.00 (ISBN 0-444-19590-4). Elsevier.
Jorgenson, D. W., et al. Optimal Replacement Policy. 1971. 24.50 (ISBN 0-444-10219-1, North-Holland). Elsevier.
Knowles, Greg. An Introduction to Applied Optimal Control. (Mathematics in Science & Engineering Ser.). 1981. write for info. (ISBN 0-12-416960-0). Acad Pr.
Komkov, V. Optimal Control Theory for the Damping of Vibrations of Simple Elastic Systems. (Lecture Notes in Mathematics: Vol. 253). 240p. 1972. pap. 7.90 (ISBN 0-387-05734-X). Springer-Verlag.
Koo, D. D. Elements of Optimization. (Heidelberg Science Library). 1977. pap. 11.90 (ISBN 0-387-90263-5). Springer-Verlag.
Kowalik, J. & Osborne, M. R. Methods for Unconstrained Optimization Problems. (Modern Analytic & Computational Methods in Science & Mathematics). (Bellman ser. Vol. 13). 1966. 15.00 (ISBN 0-444-00041-0, North Holland). Elsevier.
Krabs, W. Optimization & Approximation. LC 78-10448. 220p. 1979. 40.25 (ISBN 0-471-99741-2, Pub. by Wiley-Interscience). Wiley.
Kunzi, Hans P., et al. Numerical Methods of Mathematical Optimization with Algol & Fortran Programs. LC 68-18673. (Computer Science & Applied Mathematics Ser). 1968. 29.50 (ISBN 0-12-428850-2). Acad Pr.
Ladany, S. P. & Machol, R. E., eds. Optimal Strategies in Sports. (Studies in Management Science & Systems: Vol. 5). 1977. 24.50 (ISBN 0-7204-0528-9, North-Holland). Elsevier.
Lasdon, Leon S. Optimization Theory for Large Systems. (Illus.). 1970. 20.95 (ISBN 0-02-367800-3). Macmillan.
Lawden, Derek F. Analytic Methods of Optimization. LC 74-11450. 1975. 16.25 (ISBN 0-02-848380-4). Hafner.
Lawler, Eugene L. Combinatorial Optimization Networks & Matroids. LC 76-13516. 1976. text ed. 30.95 (ISBN 0-03-084866-0, HoltC). HR&W.
Lazarevic, B. & Lazarevic, B., eds. Global & Large Scale System Models: Proceedings. (Lecture Notes in Control & Information Sciences: Vol. 19). 1979. pap. 13.10 (ISBN 0-387-09637-X). Springer-Verlag.
Liu & Sutinen. Control Theory & Mathematical Economics, Pt. B. (Lecture Notes in Pure & Applied Mathematics Ser.: Vol. 47). 1979. 26.50 (ISBN 0-8247-6852-3). Dekker.
Liu, Pon-Tai, ed. Dynamic Optimization & Mathematical Economics. (Mathematical Concepts & Methods in Science & Engineering Ser.: Vol. 19). (Illus.). 280p. 1980. 29.50 (ISBN 0-306-40245-9, Plenum Pr). Plenum Pub.
Lommatzsch, Klaus. Anwendngen der Linearen Parametrischen Optimierung. (Mathematische Reihe: No. 69). 200p. (Ger.). 1979. Repr. 31.50 (ISBN 3-7643-1058-8). Birkhauser.
Luenberger, D. G. Optimization by Vector Space Methods. (Series in Decision & Control). 1969. 33.00 (ISBN 0-471-55359-X, Pub. by Wiley-Interscience). Wiley.
McCausland, Ian. Introduction to Optimal Control. rev. ed. LC 76-55807. 272p. 1979. Repr. of 1977 ed. 19.50 (ISBN 0-88275-707-5). Krieger.
Marlow, W. H. Mathematics for Operations Research. LC 78-534. 1978. 33.95 (ISBN 0-471-57233-0, Pub. by Wiley-Interscience). Wiley.
Minieka, Edward. Optimization Algorithms for Networks & Graphs. (Industrial Engineering--a Ser. of Reference Books & Textbooks: Vol. 1). 1978. 23.50 (ISBN 0-8247-6642-3). Dekker.
Mirkin, Boris G. Group Choice. Fishburn, Peter C., ed. Oliker, Yelena, tr. LC 79-999. (Scripta Series in Mathematics). 1979. 22.50x (ISBN 0-470-26702-X). Halsted Pr.
Mital, K. V. Optimization Methods in Operations Research & Systems Analysis. 259p. 1980. pap. 8.95 (ISBN 0-470-27081-0). Halsted Pr.
--Optimization Methods in Operations Research & Systems Analysis. LC 76-56846. 1977. 16.95 (ISBN 0-470-99056-2). Halsted Pr.
Mohler, R. R. & Shen, C. N. Optimal Control of Nuclear Reactors. (Nuclear Science & Technology Ser.: Vol. 6). 1970. 55.00 (ISBN 0-12-504150-0). Acad Pr.
Murray, W., ed. Numerical Methods for Unconstrained Optimization. (Institute of Mathematics & Its Applications Conference Ser.). 1972. 25.00 (ISBN 0-12-512250-0). Acad Pr.
Neustadt, L. W. Optimization: A Theory of Necessary Conditions. 1976. 30.00 (ISBN 0-691-08141-7). Princeton U Pr.
Noton, M. Modern Control Engineering. LC 72-181056. 288p. 1972. text ed. 28.00 (ISBN 0-08-016820-5). Pergamon.
Oettli, W. K. & Ritter, K. G., eds. Optimization & Operations Research. (Lecture Notes in Economies & Math Systems: Vol. 117). 316p. 1976. pap. 15.30 (ISBN 0-387-07616-6). Springer-Verlag.
Pallu De La Barriere, R. Optimal Control Theory: A Course in Automatic Control Theory. Gelbaum, Bernard R., ed. Scripta Technica, tr. from Fr. (Illus.). 1980. pap. text ed. 7.00 (ISBN 0-486-63925-8). Dover.
Panik, M. J. Classical Optimization. (Studies in Mathematical & Managerial Economics: Vol. 16). 1976. text ed. 34.25 (ISBN 0-444-10568-9, North-Holland); pap. 22.00 (ISBN 0-444-10691-X). Elsevier.
Parthasarathy, T. Selection Theorems & Their Applications. LC 72-78192. (Lecture Notes in Mathematics: Vol. 263). 108p. 1972. pap. 6.30 (ISBN 0-387-05818-4). Springer-Verlag.
Polak, E. Computational Methods in Optimization. (Mathematics in Science & Engineering Ser.: Vol. 77). 1971. 48.50 (ISBN 0-12-559350-3). Acad Pr.
Ponstein, J. Approaches to the Theory of Optimization. LC 79-41419. (Cambridge Tracts in Mathematics: No. 77). (Illus.). 140p. 1980. 36.50 (ISBN 0-521-23155-8). Cambridge U Pr.

Rao, S. S. Optimization: Theory & Applications. LC 77-28171. 1980. 21.95 (ISBN 0-470-26784-4). Halsted Pr.
Rapoport, Amnon, et al. Response Models for Detection of Change. (Theory & Decision Library: No. 18). 1979. lib. bdg. 30.00 (ISBN 90-277-0934-3, Pub. by Reidel Holland). Kluwer Boston.
Ray, Willis H. & Szekely, Julian. Process Optimization with Applications in Metallurgy & Chemical Engineering. LC 73-936. 400p. 1973. 40.50 (ISBN 0-471-71070-9, Pub. by Wiley-Interscience). Wiley.
Rinaldi, S., ed. Topics in Combinatorial Optimization. (International Centre for Mechanical Sciences: No. 17). 1975. soft cover 19.40 (ISBN 0-387-81339-X). Springer-Verlag.
Rockafellar, R. Tyrrell. Conjugate Duality & Optimization. (CBMS Regional Conference Ser.: Vol. 16). (Orig.). 1974. pap. text ed. 6.50 (ISBN 0-89871-013-8). Soc Indus-Appl Math.
Ross, Sheldon M. Applied Probability Models with Optimization Applications. LC 73-111376. 1970. text ed. 19.95x (ISBN 0-8162-7336-7). Holden-Day.
Russell, David L. Optimization Theory. (Math Lecture Notes Ser.: No. 47). 1970. 17.50 (ISBN 0-8053-8364-6, Adv Bk Prog). Benjamin-Cummings.
Rustagi, Jagdish S., ed. Optimizing Methods in Statistics: Proceedings of an International Conference. LC 79-10487. 1979. 48.50 (ISBN 0-12-604580-1). Acad Pr.
Rustagi, Jaggish S., ed. Optimizing Methods in Statistics: Proceedings. 1971. 55.00 (ISBN 0-12-604550-X). Acad Pr.
Rusten, B. Projection Methods in Constrained Optimization & Applications to Optimal Policy Decisions. (Lecture Notes in Control & Information Sciences Ser.: Vol. 31). 315p. 1981. pap. 17.40 (ISBN 0-387-10646-4). Springer-Verlag.
Sage, Andrew P. & White, Chelsea C. Optimum Systems Control. 2nd ed. (Illus.). 1977. ref. ed. 27.95 (ISBN 0-13-638296-7). P-H.
Schwarzkopf, A. B., et al, eds. Optimal Control & Differential Equation. 1978. 26.50 (ISBN 0-12-632250-3). Acad Pr.
Schwefel, Hans-Paul. Numerical Optimization of Computer Models. 389p. 1981. 32.95 (ISBN 0-471-09988-0, Pub. by Wiley-Interscience). Wiley.
Sherali, H. D. & Shetty, C. M. Optimization with Disjunctive Constraints. (Lecture Notes in Economics & Mathematical Systems: Vol. 181). (Illus.). 156p. 1980. pap. 15.00 (ISBN 0-387-10228-0). Springer-Verlag.
Siddall, James. Analytical Decision Making in Engineering Design. (Illus.). 1972. ref. ed. 24.95 (ISBN 0-13-034538-5). P-H.
Smith, Donald R. Variational Methods in Optimization. (Illus.). 464p. 1974. 23.95 (ISBN 0-13-940627-1). P-H.
Smolinski, Leon, intro. by. Leonid V. Kantorovich: Essays in Optimal Planning. LC 75-46110. 1976. 22.50 (ISBN 0-87332-076-X). M E Sharpe.
Stoer, J. & Witzgall, C. Convexity & Optimization in Finite Dimensions One. LC 75-92789. (Die Grundlehren der Mathematischen Wissenschaften: Vol. 163). 1970. 34.40 (ISBN 0-387-04835-9). Springer-Verlag.
Stoer, J., ed. Optimization Techniques, Part 1: Proceedings of the 8th IFIP Conference on Optimization Techniques, Wuerzburg, Sept 5-9, 1977. (Lecture Notes in Control & Information Sciences: Vol. 6). (Illus.). 1978. pap. 24.30 (ISBN 0-387-08707-9). Springer-Verlag.
--Optimization Techniques, Part 2: Proceedings of the 8th IFIP Conference & Optimization Techniques, Wuerzburg, Sept. 5-9, 1977. (Lecture Notes in Control & Information Sciences: Vol. 7). (Illus.). 1978. pap. 24.30 (ISBN 0-387-08708-7). Springer-Verlag.
--Optimization Techniques, Part 2: Proceedings of the 8th IFIP Conference & Optimization Techniques, Wuerzburg, Sept. 5-9, 1977. (Lecture Notes in Control & Information Sciences: Vol. 7). (Illus.). 1978. pap. 24.30 (ISBN 0-387-08708-7). Springer-Verlag.
Stol, P. T. A Contribution to Theory & Practice of Non-Linear Parameter Optimization. (Agricultural Research Reports Ser.: No. 835). (Illus.). 160p. 1975. pap. 38.00 (ISBN 90-220-0562-3, Pub. by PUDOC). Unipub.
Striebel, C. Optimal Control of Discrete Time Stochastic Systems. (Lecture Notes in Economics & Mathematical Systems Ser.: Vol. 110). 208p. 1975. pap. 12.60 (ISBN 0-387-07181-4). Springer-Verlag.
Symposium on Optimization & Stability Problems in Continuum Mechanics, los Angeles, 1971. Proceedings. Wang, P. K., ed. (Lecture Notes in Physics: Vol. 21). vi, 94p. 1973. pap. 10.70 (ISBN 0-387-06214-9). Springer-Verlag.
Symposium on Optimization, Nice, 1969. Proceedings. Balakrishman, A. V., et al, eds. LC 70-120380. (Lecture Notes in Mathematics: Vol. 132). (Illus.). 1970. pap. 18.30 (ISBN 0-387-04921-5). Springer-Verlag.
Tabak, Daniel & Kuo, Benjamin C. Optimal Control by Mathematical Programming. LC 75-137985. 1971. 24.00 (ISBN 0-13-638106-5). SRL Pub Co.
Tolle, H. Optimization Methods. Sirk, W. U., tr. from Ger. LC 75-1313. (Universitext Ser.). (Illus.). xiv, 226p. 1975. pap. 25.10 (ISBN 0-387-07194-6). Springer-Verlag.
Walsh, G. R. Methods of Optimization. LC 74-20714. 200p. 1975. 43.75 (ISBN 0-471-91922-5); pap. 16.75 (ISBN 0-471-91924-1, Pub. by Wiley-Interscience). Wiley.
Warga, J. Optimal Control of Differential & Functional Equations. 1972. 56.00 (ISBN 0-12-735150-7). Acad Pr.
Whittle, Peter. Optimization Under Constraint: Theory & Applications of Nonlinear Programming. LC 75-149574. (Ser. on Probability & Mathematical Statistics: Applied Section). 1971. 40.25 (ISBN 0-471-94130-1, Pub. by Wiley-Interscience). Wiley.
Wismer. Introduction to Nonlinear Optimization. (System Science & Engineering Ser.). 1977. 21.95 (ISBN 0-444-00234-0, North-Holland). Elsevier.
Wismer, D. A. Optimization Methods for Large-Scale Systems with Applications. 1971. 37.50 (ISBN 0-07-071154-2, P&RB). McGraw.
Zadeh, L. A., et al, eds. Computing Methods in Optimization Problems Two. 1969. 47.00 (ISBN 0-12-775250-1). Acad Pr.
Zahradnik, Raymond L. Theory & Techniques of Optimization for Practicing Engineers. LC 70-146261. 1971. pap. 9.95 (ISBN 0-8436-0311-9). CBI Pub.
Ziemba, W. T. Stochastic Optimization Models in Finance. 1975. 47.50 (ISBN 0-12-780850-7). Acad Pr.

MATHEMATICAL PHYSICS

see also Boundary Value Problems; Dimensional Analysis; Elasticity; Electricity; Electronics-Mathematics; Engineering Mathematics; Ergodic Theory; Existence Theorems; Gases, Kinetic Theory of; Hydrodynamics; Invariant Imbedding; Magnetism; Nonlinear Theories; Optics, Physical; Perturbation (Mathematics); Potential, Theory of; Random Walks (Mathematics); Sound; Switching Theory; System Analysis; Thermodynamics; Transport Theory

Aigner, Martin, ed. Higher Combinatorics. (Advanced Study Institutes Math & Physical Sciences: No. 31). 1977. lib. bdg. 31.50 (ISBN 90-277-0795-2, Pub. by Reidel Holland). Kluwer Boston.
Alonso, Marcelo & Finn, Edward J. Fundamental University Physics, 2 vols. 2nd ed. Incl. Vol. 1. Mechanics. 1979. text ed. 17.95 (ISBN 0-201-00161-6); Vol. 2. Fields & Waves. 1979 (ISBN 0-201-00162-4). 1979. text ed. write for info. A-W.
Ames, Joseph S. & Murnaghan, Francis D. Theoretical Mechanics: An Introduction to Mathematical Physics. LC 58-11269. lib. bdg. 12.50x (ISBN 0-88307-003-0). Gannon.
Arfken, George. Mathematical Methods for Physicists. 2nd ed. 1970. text ed. 25.95 (ISBN 0-12-059851-5). Acad Pr.
Aseltine, J. A. Transform Method in Linear System Analysis. (Electrical & Electronic Eng. Ser). 1958. 24.50 (ISBN 0-07-002389-1, C). McGraw.
Avery, J. H. & Nelkon, M. Mathematics of Physics. 1973. text ed. 14.50x (ISBN 0-435-68045-5). Heinemann Ed.
Azcarraga, J. A., ed. Topics in Quantum Field Theory & Gauge Theories: Proceedings of the VIII International Seminar on Theoretical Physics, Held by GIFT in Salamanca, June 13-19, 1977. (Lecture Notes in Physics Ser.: Vol. 77). 1978. pap. 16.50 (ISBN 0-387-08841-5). Springer-Verlag.
Bailey, W. N. Generalized Hypergeometric Series. (Cambridge Tracts in Mathematics & Mathematical Physics Ser.: No. 32). 1972. Repr. of 1935 ed. 8.75 (ISBN 0-02-840760-1). Hafner.
Baker, George A., Jr. & Gammel, John L., eds. Pade Approximant in Theoretical Physics. (Mathematics in Science & Engineering Ser.: Vol. 71). 1970. 54.00 (ISBN 0-12-074850-9). Acad Pr.
Beiglbeeck, W., et al, eds. Feynman Path Integrals: Proceedings, International Colloquium, Marseilles May 1978. (Lecture Notes in Physics: Vol. 106). 1979. pap. 22.40 (ISBN 0-387-09532-2). Springer-Verlag.
Belinfante, F. J. Survey of Hidden Variables Theories. 376p. 1973. text ed. 50.00 (ISBN 0-08-017032-3). Pergamon.
Berezin, F. A. Method of Second Quantization. (Pure and Applied Physics Ser.: Vol. 24). 1966. 38.00 (ISBN 0-12-089450-5). Acad Pr.
Bhagavantam, S. & Venkatarayudu, T. Theory of Groups & Its Application to Physical Problems. 1969. 26.50 (ISBN 0-12-095460-5). Acad Pr.
Birman, M. S., ed. Topics in Mathematical Physics, 5 vols. Incl. Vol. 1. Spectral Theory & Wave Processes. LC 67-16365. 114p. 1967 (ISBN 0-306-18401-X); Vol. 2. Spectral Theory & Problems in Diffraction. LC 68-28089. 134p. 1968 (ISBN 0-306-18402-8); Vol. 3. Spectral Theory. LC 78-93768. 93p. 1969 (ISBN 0-306-18403-6); Vol. 4. Spectral Theory & Wave Processes. LC 68-28089. 121p. 1971 (ISBN 0-306-18404-4); Vol. 5. Spectral Theory. LC 68-28089. 112p. 1972 (ISBN 0-306-18405-2). 25.00 ea. (Consultants). Plenum Pub.
Bitsadze, A. V. Equations of Mathematical Physics. 1980. 8.00 (ISBN 0-8285-1809-2, Pub. by Mir Pubs Russia). Imported Pubns.
Bleuler, K. & Reetz, A., eds. Differential Geometrical Methods in Mathematical Physics. LC 76-30859. (Lecture Notes in Mathematics Ser: Vol. 570). 1977. pap. 24.60 (ISBN 0-387-08068-6). Springer-Verlag.
Bleuler, K., et al, eds. Differential Geometrical Methods in Mathematical Physics II: Proceedings, University of Bonn, July 13-16, 1977. (Lecture Notes in Mathematics Ser.: Vol. 676). 1979. pap. 31.80 (ISBN 0-387-08935-7). Springer-Verlag.
Bloom, C. O. & Kazarinoff, N. D. Short Wave Radiation Problems in Homogeneous Media: Asymptotic Solutions. (Lecture Notes in Mathematics: Vol. 522). 1976. 9.90 (ISBN 0-387-07698-0). Springer-Verlag.
Bowcock, J. E., ed. Methods & Problems of Theoretical Physics in Honor of R. E. Peierls. 1971. 53.75 (ISBN 0-444-10040-7, North-Holland). Elsevier.
Brittin, Wesley E., et al, eds. Boulder Lecture Notes in Theoretical Physics, 1968: Vol. 11-D, Mathematical Methods. 1969. 111.75 (ISBN 0-677-13140-2). Gordon.
Bromwich, T. J. Quadratic Forms & Their Classification by Means of Invariant Factors. (Cambridge Tracts in Mathematics & Mathematical Physics Ser.: No. 3). 1971. Repr. of 1906 ed. 8.75 (ISBN 0-02-842000-4). Hafner.
Burghes, David N. & Downs, A. M. Modern Introduction to Classical Mechanics & Control Series: Mathematics & Its Applications. LC 75-16463. 300p. 1975. 48.95 (ISBN 0-470-12362-1); pap. 38.95 (ISBN 0-470-26949-9). Halsted Pr.
Butkov, E. Mathematical Physics. 1968. 27.95 (ISBN 0-201-00727-4). A-W.
Byron, F. W. & Fuller, R. W. Mathematics of Classical & Quantum Physics, 2 pts. (Physics Ser.). 1969. 16.95 (ISBN 0-686-77033-1); Pt. 1. (ISBN 0-201-00745-2); Pt. 2. (ISBN 0-201-00746-0). A-W.
Cahen, M. & Flato, M., eds. Differential Geometry & Relativity. new ed. (Mathematical Physics & Applied Mathematics Ser: No. 3). 1976. lib. bdg. 42.00 (ISBN 90-277-0745-6, Pub. by Reidel Holland). Kluwer Boston.
Chaillou, Jacques. Hyperbolic Differential Polynomials & Their Singular Perturbations. Nienhuys, J. W., tr. from Fr. (Mathematics & Its Applications: No. 3). 1980. lib. bdg. 31.50 (ISBN 90-277-1032-5, Pub. by Reidel Holland). Kluwer Boston.
Choquet-Bruhat, Y. C., et al. Analysis, Manifolds & Physics. 1977. 19.50 (ISBN 0-7204-0494-0, North-Holland). Elsevier.
CISM (International Center for Mechanical Sciences), Dept. of Automation & Information. Mathematical Structure of Finite Random Cybernetic Systems. Quiasu, S., ed. (CISM Pubns. Ser.: No. 86). (Illus.). 215p. 1973. pap. 21.00 (ISBN 0-387-81174-5). Springer-Verlag.
Courant, R. & Hilbert, D. Methods of Mathematical Physics, 2 Vols. Set. 68.50 (ISBN 0-471-17990-6, Pub. by Wiley-Interscience); Vol. 1, 1953. 36.50 (ISBN 0-470-17952-X); Vol. 2, 1962. 49.00 (ISBN 0-470-17985-6). Wiley.
Crandall, Stephen H. Engineering Analysis: A Survey of Numerical Procedures. (Engineering Societies Monographs Ser). 1956. text ed. 23.95 (ISBN 0-07-013430-8, C). McGraw.
Dell'Antonio, G., et al, eds. Mathematical Problems in Theoretical Physics: International Conference, Held in Rome, June 6-15, 1977. (Lecture Notes in Physics: Vol. 80). 1978. pap. 19.00 (ISBN 0-387-08853-9). Springer-Verlag.
Diaz, J. G. & Pai, S. I., eds. Fluid Dynamics & Applied Mathematics. (Illus.). 1962. 45.25x (ISBN 0-677-10110-4). Gordon.
Dyachenko, V. F. Basic Computational Math. 125p. 1979. pap. 3.40 (ISBN 0-8285-1593-X, Pub. by Mir Pubs Russia). Imported Pubns.
Eisberg, Robert M. Applied Mathematical Physics with Programmable Pocket Calculators. (Illus.). 1976. pap. text ed. 9.95 (ISBN 0-07-019109-3, C). McGraw.
Enz, C. P. & Mehra, J., eds. Physical Reality & Mathematical Description: Dedicated to Josef Maria Jauch on the Occasion of His Sixtieth Birthday. LC 74-81937. xxiii, 552p. 1974. lib. bdg. 66.00 (ISBN 90-277-0513-5, Pub. by Reidel Holland). Kluwer Boston.
Falicov, L. M. Group Theory & Its Physical Applications. Luehrmann, A., ed. LC 66-13867. (Chicago Lectures in Physics Ser). (Orig.). 1966. 7.00x (ISBN 0-226-23540-8). U of Chicago Pr.
Fluegge, S. Practical Quantum Mechanics. LC 74-23732. (Illus.). xiv, 623p. 1975. pap. 20.80 (ISBN 0-387-07050-8). Springer-Verlag.
--Practical Quantum Mechanics One. rev. ed. (Die Grundlehren der Mathematischen Wissenschaften: Vol. 177). 1971. 52.00 (ISBN 0-387-05276-3). Springer-Verlag.
--Practical Quantum Mechanics Two. rev. ed. (Grundlehren der Mathematischen Wissenschaften: Vol. 178). 1971. 49.60 (ISBN 0-387-05277-1). Springer-Verlag.
Garcia, P. L., et al, eds. Differential Geometrical Methods in Mathematical Physics: Proceedings. (Lecture Notes in Mathematics: Vol. 836). 538p. 1981. 29.50 (ISBN 0-387-10275-2). Springer-Verlag.
Gilbert, Robert P. & Newton, Roger G. Analytic Methods in Mathematical Physics. 1970. 87.50 (ISBN 0-677-13560-2). Gordon.
Greenspan, Donald. Arithmetic Applied Mathematics. LC 80-40295. (Illus.). 172p. 1980. 29.00 (ISBN 0-08-025047-5); pap. 12.00 (ISBN 0-08-025046-7). Pergamon.
--Discrete Numerical Methods in Physics & Engineering. (Mathematics in Science & Engineering Ser.). 1974. 34.00 (ISBN 0-12-300350-4). Acad Pr.
Grodins, Fred S. Control Theory & Biological Systems. LC 63-10521. 205p. 1963. 15.00x (ISBN 0-231-02517-3). Columbia U Pr.
Guettinger, W. & Eikemeier, H., eds. Structural Stability in Physics: Proceedings of Two International Symposia. (Springer Ser. in Synergetics). (Illus.). 1979. 36.70 (ISBN 0-387-09463-6). Springer-Verlag.
Gunter, N. M. Potential Theory & Its Applications to Basic Problems of Mathematical Physics. Schulenberger, John R., tr. LC 67-13616. 1967. 15.00 (ISBN 0-8044-4357-2). Ungar.
Gurel, Okan, ed. Bifurcation Theory & Applications in Scientific Disciplines, Vol. 316. Rossler, Otto E. (Annals of the New York Academy of Sciences). 708p. (Orig.). 1979. pap. 85.00x (ISBN 0-89766-000-5). NY Acad Sci.
Hardy, G. H. Integration of Functions of a Single Variable. 2nd ed. (Cambridge Tracts in Mathematics & Mathematical Physics Ser: No. 2). 1971. Repr. of 1958 ed. 7.50 (ISBN 0-02-845720-X). Hafner.
--Orders of Infinity. (Cambridge Tracts in Mathematics & Mathematical Physics Ser: No. 12). 1971. Repr. of 1910 ed. 7.50 (ISBN 0-02-845730-7). Hafner.
Harper, Charlie. Introduction to Mathematical Physics. (Physics Ser.). 352p. 1976. ref. ed. 25.95 (ISBN 0-13-487538-9). P-H.
Harris, Edward G. Introduction to Modern Theoretical Physics, 2 vols. Incl. Vol. 1. Classical Physics & Relativity. 392p. 34.95 (ISBN 0-471-35325-6); Vol. 2. Quantum Theory & Statistical Physics. 402p. 36.95 (ISBN 0-471-35326-4). LC 75-14497. 1975 (Pub. by Wiley-Interscience). Wiley.
Havelock, T. H. The Propagation of Disturbances in Dispersive Media. (Cambridge Tracts in Mathematics & Mathematical Physics Ser.: No. 17). 1964. Repr. of 1914 ed. 7.50 (ISBN 0-02-845840-0). Hafner.
Hellwig, G. Differential Operators of Mathematical Physics: An Introduction. 1967. 15.50 (ISBN 0-201-02811-5, Adv Bk Prog). A-W.
Hermann, Robert. Energy Momentum Tensors. (Interdisciplinary Mathematics Ser: No. 4). 153p. 1973. 11.00 (ISBN 0-915692-03-1). Math Sci Pr.
--Lectures in Mathematical Physics, Vol. 2. (Math Lecture Notes Ser.: No. 50). 1972. text ed. 19.50 (ISBN 0-8053-3952-3, Adv Bk Prog). Benjamin-Cummings.
--Topics in General Relativity. (Interdisciplinary Mathematics Ser: No. 5). 171p. 1973. 12.00 (ISBN 0-915692-04-X). Math Sci Pr.
--Topics in the Mathematics of Quantum Mechanics. (Interdisciplinary Mathematics Ser: No. 6). 250p. 1973. 16.00 (ISBN 0-915692-05-8). Math Sci Pr.
--Vector Bundles in Mathematical Physics, Vol. 1. (Mathematical Physics Monographs: No. 14). 1970. pap. text ed. 9.50 (ISBN 0-8053-3945-0, Adv Bk Prog). Benjamin-Cummings.
--Vector Bundles in Mathematical Physics, Vol. 2. (Mathematical Physics Monographs: No. 16). 1970. text ed. 19.50 (ISBN 0-8053-3948-5, Adv Bk Prog); pap. 9.50 (ISBN 0-8053-3949-3, Adv Bk Prog). Benjamin-Cummings.

Hestenes, David. Space-Time Algebra. (Documents on Modern Physics Ser). (Orig.). 1966. 22.50x (ISBN 0-677-01390-6). Gordon.
Hochstadt, Harry. Functions of Mathematical Physics. LC 78-141199. (Pure & Applied Mathematics Ser.: Vol. 28). 1971. 37.50 (ISBN 0-471-40170-6, Pub. by Wiley-Interscience). Wiley.
Hughston, L. Twistors & Particles. (Lecture Notes in Physics Ser.: Vol. 97). 1979. pap. 10.30 (ISBN 0-387-09244-7). Springer-Verlag.
Iachello, ed. Interacting Bosons in Nuclear Physics. (Ettore Majorana International Science Ser.--Physical Sciences: Vol. 1). 1979. 29.50 (ISBN 0-306-40190-8, Plenum Pr). Plenum Pub.
Il'in, V. P., ed. Boundary Value Problems of Mathematical Physics & Related Aspects of Function Theory, Pt. 1. LC 69-12506. (Seminars in Mathematics Ser.: Vol. 5). 96p. 1969. 29.50 (ISBN 0-306-18805-8, Consultants). Plenum Pub.
International School Of Nonlinear Mathematics And Physics - Munich - 1966. Topics in Nonlinear Physics: Proceedings of the Physics Session. Zabusky, N. J. & Kruskal, M. D., eds. LC 67-20647. 1968. 23.30 (ISBN 0-387-04363-2). Springer-Verlag.
International Symposium "Fifty Years Schroedinger Equation", Vienna, June 10-12, 1976. The Schroedinger Equation: Proceedings. Thirring, W. & Urban, P., eds. (Acta Physica Austriaca Supplementum: 17). (Illus.). 1977. 39.00 (ISBN 0-387-81437-X). Springer-Verlag.
International Symposium on Mathematical Problems, Kyoto University, Kyoto, Japan, Jan. 23-29, 1975. Proceedings. (Lecture Notes in Physics Ser.). 562p. 1975. pap. 24.20 (ISBN 0-387-07174-1). Springer-Verlag.
International University Courses on Nuclear Physics, 12th, Schladming, Austria, 1973. Recent Developments in Mathematical Physics: Proceedings. Urban, P., ed. LC 73-13322. (Acta Physica Austriaca: Suppl. 2). (Illus.). vi, 610p. 1974. 87.40 (ISBN 0-387-81190-7). Springer-Verlag.
Jeffreys, H. Operational Methods in Mathematical Physics. 2nd ed. (Cambridge Tracts in Mathematics & Mathematical Physics Ser.: No. 23). 1964. Repr. of 1931 ed. 7.50 (ISBN 0-02-847190-3). Hafner.
Jeffreys, Harold & Jeffreys, Bertha S. Methods of Mathematical Physics. 3rd ed. (Illus.). 1956. pap. 22.95x (ISBN 0-521-09723-1). Cambridge U Pr.
Jones, Lorella M. An Introduction to Mathematical Methods of Physics. LC 78-57377. 1979. text ed. 21.95 (ISBN 0-8053-5130-2). Benjamin-Cummings.
Joshi, A. W. Matrices & Tensors in Physics. LC 75-26772. 251p. 1976. 9.95 (ISBN 0-470-45086-X). Halsted Pr.
Jost, R. Local Quantum Theory. (Italian Physical Society: Course 45). 1970. 47.00 (ISBN 0-12-368845-0). Acad Pr.
Kaiser, G. & Marsden, J. E., eds. Geometric Methods in Mathematical Physics: Proceedings. (Lecture Notes in Mathematics Ser.: Vol. 775). 257p. 1980. pap. 16.80 (ISBN 0-387-09742-2). Springer-Verlag.
Kemmer, N. Vector Analysis. LC 75-36025. (Illus.). 230p. 1977. 49.50 (ISBN 0-521-21158-1); pap. 15.95x (ISBN 0-521-29064-3). Cambridge U Pr.
Killingbeck, J. & Cole, G. H. Mathematical Techniques & Physical Applications. (Pure & Applied Physics Ser). 1971. text ed. 22.95 (ISBN 0-12-406850-2); solutions manual 3.00 (ISBN 0-12-406856-1). Acad Pr.
Kompaneyets, Alexander. Theoretical Physics. (Russian Monographs). (Illus.). 1964. 97.50x (ISBN 0-677-20150-8). Gordon.
Koshlyakov, N. S., et al. Differential Equations of Mathematical Physics. 1964. 58.75 (ISBN 0-444-10333-3, North-Holland). Elsevier.
Kraut, Edgar A. Fundamentals of Mathematical Physics. LC 79-4467. 480p. 1979. Repr. of 1967 ed. lib. bdg. 19.50 (ISBN 0-88275-918-3). Krieger.
Ladyzhenskaya, O. A., ed. Boundary Value Problems of Mathematical Physics & Related Aspects of Function Theory, Part 3. LC 69-12506. (Seminars in Mathematics Ser.: Vol. 11). 79p. 1970. 25.00 (ISBN 0-306-18811-2, Consultants). Plenum Pub.
Langer, Rudolph E., ed. Partial Differential Equations & Continuum Mechanics. (Mathematics Research Center Pubns., No. 5). (Illus.). 414p. 1961. 17.00x (ISBN 0-299-02350-8). U of Wis Pr.
Lattes, Robert. Methods of Resolution for Selected Boundary Problems in Mathematical Physics. (Documents on Modern Physics Ser). 1969. 45.25x (ISBN 0-677-30060-3). Gordon.
--Quelques Methodes De Resolutions De Problemes Aux Limites De la Physique Mathematiques. (Cours & Documents De Mathematiques & De Physique Ser). (Orig.). 1967. 44.25x (ISBN 0-677-50060-2). Gordon.
Lavrentiev, M. M. Some Improperly Posed Problems of Mathematical Physics. Sacker, R. J., tr. (Springer Tracts in Natural Philosophy: Vol. 11). (Illus.). 1967. 16.30 (ISBN 0-387-03984-8). Springer-Verlag.
Lebedev, N. N. Special Functions & Their Applications. rev. ed. Silverman, Richard A., tr. from Rus. LC 72-86228. 320p. 1972. pap. 5.00 (ISBN 0-486-60624-4). Dover.
Lerner, D. E. & Sommers, P. D., eds. Complex Manifold Techniques in Theoretical Physics. new ed. (Research Notes in Mathematics Ser.). (Illus.). text ed. cancelled (ISBN 0-8224-8437-4). Pitman Learning.
Levy, M. & Lurcat, F., eds. Cargese Lecture Notes, 1965: Application of Mathematics to Problems in Theoretical Physics. 1967. 94.50x (ISBN 0-677-11660-8). Gordon.
Liboff, Richard L. & Rostoker, Norman, eds. Kinetic Equations. LC 72-122848. (Illus.). 362p. 1971. 54.00x (ISBN 0-677-14080-0). Gordon.
Lieb, E. H., et al, eds. Studies in Mathematical Physics: Essays in Honor of Valentine Bargmenn. LC 76-4057. (Princeton Series in Physics). (Illus.). 472p. 1976. 34.50x (ISBN 0-691-08180-8); pap. 12.50x (ISBN 0-691-08185-9). Princeton U Pr.
Loebl, Ernest M., ed. Group Theory & Its Applications, 3 vols. LC 67-23166. Vol. 1 1968. 63.00 (ISBN 0-12-455150-5); Vol. 2 1971. 55.00 (ISBN 0-12-455152-1); 76.00 (ISBN 0-12-455153-X). Vol. 3, 1975. Acad Pr.
Lomont, John S. Applications of Finite Groups. 1959. 38.50 (ISBN 0-12-455550-0). Acad Pr.
Mackey, George W. Mathematical Foundations of Quantum Mechanics. (Mathematical Physics Monographs: No. 1). 1963. 14.50 (ISBN 0-8053-6701-2, Adv Bk Prog). Benjamin-Cummings.
Mahanthappa, K. T. & Randa, James, eds. Quantum Flavordynamics, Quantum Chromodynamics & Unified Theories. (NATO Advanced Study Institute Ser., Ser. B: Physics: Vol. 54). 505p. 1980. 59.50 (ISBN 0-306-40436-2, Plenum Pr). Plenum Pub.
Marcus, Paul M., et al, eds. Computational Methods in Band Theory. LC 77-142039. (IBM Research Symposia Ser). 578p. 1971. 52.50 (ISBN 0-306-30520-8, Plenum Pr). Plenum Pub.
Margenau, Henry. The Mathematics of Physics & Chemistry, Vol. 2. 1964. text ed. 14.95x (ISBN 0-442-05121-2). Van Nos Reinhold.
Margenau, Henry & Murphy, George M. The Mathematics of Physics & Chemistry. 2nd ed. LC 76-18724. 618p. 1976. Repr. of 1956 ed. text ed. 26.00 (ISBN 0-88275-423-8). Krieger.
Marsden, Jerry. Applications of Global Analysis in Mathematical Physics. LC 74-75308. (Mathematics Lecture Ser., No. 2). 273p. 1974. pap. 10.00x (ISBN 0-914098-11-X). Publish or Perish.
Martin-Loef, A. Statistical Mechanics & the Foundations of Thermodynamics. (Lecture Notes in Physics Ser.: Vol. 101). 1979. pap. 9.50 (ISBN 0-387-09255-2). Springer-Verlag.
Mathews, Jon & Walker, Robert L. Mathematical Methods of Physics. 2nd ed. 1970. text ed. 24.95 (ISBN 0-8053-7002-1). Benjamin-Cummings.
Maurin, K. & Raczka, R., eds. Mathematical Physics & Physical Mathematics. LC 74-34289. (Mathematical Physics & Applied Mathematics Ser.: No. 2). 1976. lib. bdg. 55.00 (ISBN 90-277-0537-2, Pub. by Reidel Holland). Kluwer Boston.
Menzel, Donald H. Fundamental Formulas of Physics, 2 Vols. 2nd ed. (Illus.). 1960. Vol. 1. pap. text ed. 5.00 (ISBN 0-486-60595-7); Vol. 2. pap. text ed. 5.00 (ISBN 0-486-60596-5). Dover.
--Mathematical Physics. Orig. Title: Theoretical Physics. 1953. pap. text ed. 6.00 (ISBN 0-486-60056-4). Dover.
Mersenne, Marin. Cogitata Physico-Mathematica, in Quibus Tam Naturae Quam Artis Effectus Admirandi Certissimis Demonstrationibus Explicantur. Repr. of 1644 ed. 164.00 (ISBN 0-8287-0603-4). Clearwater Pub.
--Novaum Observationum Physico-Mathematicarum F. Marini Mersenni Minimi Tomus III, Quibus Accessit Aristarchus Samius De Mundi Systemate. Repr. of 1647 ed. 74.00 (ISBN 0-8287-0604-2). Clearwater Pub.
Mickley, Harold S., et al. Applied Mathematics in Chemical Engineering. 2nd ed. (Chemical Engineering Ser.). (Illus.). 1957. text ed. 23.50 (ISBN 0-07-041800-4, C). McGraw.
Miller, Willard, Jr. On Lie Algebras & Some Special Functions of Mathematical Physics. LC 52-42389. (Memoirs: No. 50). 1969. pap. 7.20 (ISBN 0-8218-1250-5, MEMO-50). Am Math.
Moon, P. & Spencer, D. E. Field Theory Handbook: Including Coordinate Systems, Differential Equations & Their Solutions. 2nd ed. LC 77-178288. (Illus.). viii, 236p. 1971. 57.90 (ISBN 0-387-02732-7). Springer-Verlag.
Morse, Philip M. & Feshbach, H. Methods of Theoretical Physics, 2 Pts. (International Ser. in Pure & Applied Physics). (Illus.). 1953. text ed. 33.95 ea. (C). Pt. 1 (ISBN 0-07-043316-X). Pt. 2 (ISBN 0-07-043317-8). McGraw.
Naimpally, S. A. & Warrack, B. D. Proximity Spaces. LC 73-118858. (Tracts in Mathematics & Mathematical Physics: No. 59). 1971. 20.50 (ISBN 0-521-07935-7). Cambridge U Pr.
NATO Advanced Study Institute, Cargese, Corsica, June 24 - July, 1979. Bifurcation Phenomena in Mathematical Physics & Related Topics: Proceedings. Bardos, Claude & Bessis, Daniel, eds. (NATO Advanced Study Institute Series C. Mathematical & Physical Sciences: No. 54). 608p. 1980. lib. bdg. 59.50 (ISBN 90-277-1086-4). Kluwer Boston.
NATO Advanced Study Institute, Istanbul, Turkey, Aug, 1972. Group Theory in Non-Linear Problems: Lectures in Mathematical Physics. Barut, A. O., ed. LC 73-91202. (NATO Advanced Study Institutes: No. C-7). 1974. lib. bdg. 37.00 (ISBN 90-277-0412-0, Pub. by Reidel Holland). Kluwer Boston.
NATO Advanced Study Institute, Istanbul, Turkey, Aug., 1970. Studies in Mathematical Physics: Lectures in Mathematical Physics, Vol. 1. Barut, A. O., ed. LC 73-88587. (NATO Advanced Study Institutes: No. C-1). 1973. lib. bdg. 39.50 (ISBN 90-277-0405-8, Pub. by Reidel Holland). Kluwer Boston.
Novikov, S. P., ed. Mathematical Physics Review, Vol. I, Section C. (Soviet Scietific Reviews Ser.). 222p. 1980. 49.00 (ISBN 3-7186-0019-6). Harwood Academic.
--Soviet Scientific Reviews: Mathematical Physics, Vol. 2, Section C. 300p. 1981. 95.00 (ISBN 3-7186-0069-2). Harwood Academic.
Odabasi, Halis & Akyuz, O. Topics in Mathematical Physics. LC 77-84853. (Illus.). 1977. text ed. 15.00x (ISBN 0-87081-072-3). Colo Assoc.
Oppenheim, Irwin, et al. Stochastic Processes in Chemical Physics: The Master Equation. LC 76-27843. 1977. text ed. 25.00x (ISBN 0-262-15017-4). MIT Pr.
Peierls, Rudolf. Surprises in Theoretical Physics. LC 79-84009. (Princeton Ser. in Physics). 1979. 16.50x (ISBN 0-691-08241-3); pap. 5.50x (ISBN 0-691-08242-1). Princeton U Pr.
Phariseau, P., et al, eds. Electrons in Disordered Metals & at Metallic Surfaces: NATO Advanced Study Institutes Ser. (Series B, Physics, Vol. 42). 1979. 59.50 (ISBN 0-306-40170-3, Plenum Pr). Plenum Pub.
Pipes, L. A. & Harvill, L. R. Applied Mathematics for Engineers & Physicists. 3rd ed. 1970. text ed. 24.95 (ISBN 0-07-050060-6, C). McGraw.
Pirani, Felix A., et al. Local Jet Bundle Formulation of Backlund Transformations. (Mathematical Physics Studies: No. 1). 1979. pap. 12.00 (ISBN 90-277-1036-8, Pub. by Reidel Holland). Kluwer Boston.
Polya, G. & Szego, G. Isoperimetric Inequalities in Mathematical Physics. 1951. pap. 16.00 (ISBN 0-527-02743-X). Kraus Repr.
Potter, D. E. Computational Physics. LC 72-8613. 304p. 1973. 50.50 (ISBN 0-471-69555-6, Pub. by Wiley-Interscience). Wiley.
Reed, Michael & Simon, Barry. Methods of Modern Mathematical Physics, 4 vols. Incl. Vol. 1. Functional Analysis. 1972. 24.95 (ISBN 0-12-585001-8); Vol. 2. Fourier Analysis Self-Adjointness. 1975. 34.50 (ISBN 0-12-585002-6); Vol. 3. Scattering Theory. 1979. 42.00 (ISBN 0-12-585003-4); Vol. 4. 1978. 34.00 (ISBN 0-12-585004-2). Acad Pr.
Renner, B. Current Algebras & Their Applications. 1968. 34.00 (ISBN 0-08-012504-2). Pergamon.
Richtmyer, R. D. Principles of Advanced Mathematical Physics: Vol. 1. (Texts & Monographs in Physics Ser.). (Illus.). 1979. 20.80 (ISBN 0-387-08873-3). Springer-Verlag.
Richtmyer, Robert D. & Morton, K. W. Difference Methods for Initial-Value Problems. 2nd ed. LC 67-13959. (Pure & Applied Mathematics Ser.). (Illus.). 1967. 41.50 (ISBN 0-470-72040-9, Pub. by Wiley-Interscience). Wiley.
Roos, Bernard W. Analytic Functions & Distributions in Physics & Engineering. 521p. 1969. text ed. 26.00 (ISBN 0-471-73334-2, Pub. by Wiley). Krieger.
Roubine, E., et al, eds. Mathematics Applied to Physics. (Illus.). 1970. 35.30 (ISBN 0-387-04965-7). Springer-Verlag.
Rutherford, D. E. Modular Invariants. (Cambridge Tracts in Mathematics & Mathematical Physics Ser: No. 27). 1964. Repr. of 1932 ed. 7.50 (ISBN 0-02-851230-8). Hafner.
Schwartz, Laurent. Mathematics for the Physical Sciences. 1967. 17.50 (ISBN 0-201-06780-3, Adv Bk Prog). A-W.
Schwinger, Julian. Quantum Kinematics & Dynamics. (Frontiers in Physics Ser: No. 35). 1970. pap. text ed. 9.50 (ISBN 0-8053-8511-8, Adv Bk Prog). Benjamin-Cummings.
Segal, I. E. & Mackey, G. W. Mathematical Problems of Relativistic Physics. (Lectures in Applied Mathematics Ser.: Vol. 2). 1967. Repr. of 1963 ed. 13.20 (ISBN 0-8218-1102-9, LAM-2). Am Math.
Shannon, Claude E. & Weaver, Warren. The Mathematical Theory of Communication. LC 49-11922. 1949. 10.00 (ISBN 0-252-72548-4); pap. 4.95 (ISBN 0-252-72548-4). U of Ill Pr.
Simms, D. J. Lectures on Geometric Quantization. Ehlers, J., et al, eds. (Lecture Notes in Physics: Vol. 53). 1976. soft cover 11.00 (ISBN 0-387-07860-6). Springer-Verlag.
Sneed, Joseph D. The Logical Structure of Mathematical Physics. 2nd rev. ed. (Synthese Library, 35 - Pallas Paperbacks, 14). 1980. lib. bdg. 37.00 (ISBN 90-277-1056-2); pap. 15.00 (ISBN 90-277-1059-7, Pub. by Reidel Holland). Kluwer Boston.
Sniatycki, J. Geometric Quantization & Quantum Mechanics. John, F., et al, eds. LC 79-26090. (Applied Mathematical Sciences Ser.: Vol. 30). 230p. 1980. pap. 14.00 (ISBN 3-540-90469-7). Springer-Verlag.
Sobolev, Sergei L., tr. Applications of Functional Analysis in Mathematical Physics. LC 63-15658. (Translations of Mathematical Monographs: Vol. 7). 1969. Repr. of 1963 ed. 22.40 (ISBN 0-8218-1557-1, MMONO-7). Am Math.
Sokolnikoff, Ivan S. & Redheffer, R. M. Mathematics of Physics & Modern Engineering. 2nd ed. 1966. text ed. 24.00 (ISBN 0-07-059625-5, C). McGraw.
Sommerfeld, Arnold. Lectures on Theoretical Physics. Incl. Vol. 1. Mechanics. 1952. text ed. 19.95 (ISBN 0-12-654668-1); pap. 9.95 (ISBN 0-12-654670-3); Vol. 2. Mechanics of Deformable Bodies. 1950. text ed. 19.95 (ISBN 0-12-654650-9); pap. text ed. 9.95 (ISBN 0-12-654652-5); Vol. 3. Electrodynamics. 1952. text ed. 19.95 (ISBN 0-12-654662-2); pap. 9.95 (ISBN 0-12-654664-9); Vol. 4. Optics. 1954. text ed. 19.95 (ISBN 0-12-654674-6); pap. 9.95 (ISBN 0-12-654676-2); Vol. 5. Thermodynamics & Statistical Mechanics. 1956. text ed. 19.95 (ISBN 0-12-654680-0); pap. 9.95 (ISBN 0-12-654682-7); Vol. 6. Partial Differential Equations in Physics. 1949. 19.95 (ISBN 0-12-654656-8); pap. text ed. 9.95 (ISBN 0-12-654658-4). Acad Pr.
Spain, Barry & Smith, M. C. Functions of Mathematical Physics. (New University Mathematics Ser). 1970. 13.95x (ISBN 0-442-27877-2). Van Nos Reinhold.
Speer, Eugene E. Generalized Feynman Amplitudes. (Annals of Mathematics Studies: No. 62). 1970. 9.50x (ISBN 0-691-08066-6). Princeton U Pr.
Spiegel, Murray R. Statistics. 1961. pap. text ed. 5.95 (ISBN 0-07-060227-1, SP). McGraw.
Stakgold, Ivar. Green's Functions & Boundary Value Problems. LC 78-27259. (Pure & Applied Mathematics: Texts, Monographs & Tracts). 638p. 1979. 39.50 (ISBN 0-471-81967-0, Pub. by Wiley-Interscience). Wiley.
Steklov Institute of Mathematics, Academy of Sciences, U S S R, No. 110. Boundary Value Problems of Mathematical Physics VI: Proceedings. Ladyzenskaja, O. A., ed. 210p. 1971. 36.00 (ISBN 0-8218-3010-4, STEKLO-110). Am Math.
Steklov Institute of Mathematics, Academy of Sciences, U S S R, No. 74. Difference Methods of Solution of Problems of Mathematical Physics I: Proceedings. Janenko, N. N., ed. 1967. 37.20 (ISBN 0-8218-1874-0, STEKLO-74). Am Math.
Streater, R. F., ed. Mathematics of Contemporary Physics. (London Mathematical Society Symposia Ser.). 1973. 44.00 (ISBN 0-12-673150-0). Acad Pr.
Streater, Raymond F. & Wrightman, Arthur S. PCT, Spin & Statistics, & All That. (Mathematical Physics Monographs: No. 3). 1964. 17.50 (ISBN 0-8053-9252-1, Adv Bk Prog). Benjamin-Cummings.
Symposia in Applied Mathematics-New York-1959. Nuclear Reactor Theory: Proceedings, Vol. 11. Birkhoff, G. & Wigner, E. P., eds. LC 50-1183. 1961. 23.20 (ISBN 0-8218-1311-0, PSAPM-11). Am Math.
Symposia in Applied Mathematics-New York-1963. Stochastic Processes in Mathematical Physics & Engineering: Proceedings, Vol. 16. Bellman, R., ed. LC 64-18128. 1980. Repr. of 1964 ed. 28.80 (ISBN 0-8218-1316-1, PSAPM-16). Am Math.
Telling, H. G. The Rational Quadratic Curve in Space of Three or Four Dimensions. (Cambridge Tracts in Mathematics & Mathematical Physics Ser: No. 34). 1971. Repr. of 1936 ed. 7.50 (ISBN 0-02-853390-9). Hafner.
Thirring, W. A Course in Mathematical Physics: Classical Dynamical System, Vol. 1. LC 78-16172. (Illus.). 1978. 22.90 (ISBN 0-387-81496-5). Springer-Verlag.

--A Course in Mathematical Physics: Classical Field Theory, Vol II. 1980. 23.10 (ISBN 0-387-81532-5). Springer-Verlag.
Titchmarsh, E. C. The Zeta-Function of Riemann. (Cambridge Tracts in Mathematics & Mathematical Physics Ser: No. 26). 1964. Repr. of 1930 ed. 7.50 (ISBN 0-02-853600-2). Hafner.
Trainor, Lynn & Wise, Mark B. From Physical Concept to Mathematical Structure: An Introduction to Theoretical Physics. LC 78-11616. (Mathematical Expositions Ser.). 1979. 25.00x (ISBN 0-8020-5432-3); pap. 10.00x (ISBN 0-8020-6432-9). U of Toronto Pr.
Tranter, C. J. Integral Transforms in Mathematical Physics. 3rd ed. 150p. 1971. pap. text ed. 9.95x (ISBN 0-412-20860-1, Pub. by Chapman & Hall England). Methuen Inc.
Urban, P., ed. Current Problems in Elementary Particle & Mathematical Physics. (Acta Physica Austriaca: Supplementum 15). (Illus.). 1976. 87.40 (ISBN 0-387-81401-9). Springer-Verlag.
Verhulst, F., ed. Asymptotic Analysis: From Theory to Application. (Lecture Notes in Mathematics Ser.: Vol. 711). 1979. pap. 13.10 (ISBN 0-387-09245-5). Springer-Verlag.
Vladimirov, V. S. Equations of Mathematical Physics. (Pure & Applied Mathematics Ser.: Vol. 3). 1971. 35.75 (ISBN 0-8247-1713-9). Dekker.
--Generalized Functions in Mathematical Physics. 362p. 1979. 10.75 (ISBN 0-8285-0001-0, Pub. by Mir Pubs Russia). Imported Pubns.
Voelkel, A. H. Fields, Particles & Currents. LC 77-23001. (Lecture Notes in Physics: Vol. 66). 1977. pap. text ed. 18.30 (ISBN 0-387-08347-2). Springer-Verlag.
Volta Memorial Conference, Como, Italy, 1977. Stochastic Behavior in Classical & Quantum Hamiltonian Systems: Proceedings. Casati, G. & Ford, J., eds. (Lecture Notes in Physics: Vol. 93). Date not set. pap. 18.70 (ISBN 0-387-09120-3). Springer-Verlag.
Von Ignatowsky, W. Physikalisch-Mathematische Monographien, 3 vols. in 1. (Ger). 9.95 (ISBN 0-8284-0201-9). Chelsea Pub.
Von Westenholz, V. Differential Forms in Mathematical Physics. 1978. 73.25 (ISBN 0-7204-0537-8, North-Holland). Elsevier.
Watson, William H. Understanding Physics Today. 1963. 27.50 (ISBN 0-521-06745-6). Cambridge U Pr.
Whittaker, Edmund T. A Course of Modern Analysis. LC 75-41296. Repr. of 1944 ed. 52.00 (ISBN 0-404-14736-4). AMS Pr.
Wilf, Herbert S. Mathematics for the Physical Sciences. 1978. pap. text ed. 5.00 (ISBN 0-486-63635-6). Dover.
Wright, J. E. Invariants of Quadratic Differential Forms. (Cambridge Tracts in Mathematics & Mathematical Physics Ser.: No. 9). 1969. Repr. of 1908 ed. 7.50 (ISBN 0-02-855010-2). Hafner.
Wyld, H. W. Mathematical Methods for Physics. (Lecture Notes and Supplements in Physics: Vol. 15). 1976. 29.50 (ISBN 0-8053-9856-2, Adv Bk Prog); pap. 17.50 (ISBN 0-8053-9857-0). Benjamin-Cummings.
Yanenko, N. N. Method of Fractional Steps: The Solution of Problems of Mathematical Physics in Several Variables. Holt, M., ed. LC 78-139953. (Illus.). 1971. 31.20 (ISBN 0-387-05272-0). Springer-Verlag.
Zeldovich, Y. B.. Higher Mathematics for Beginners & Its Applications to Physics. 494p. 1974. 7.50 (ISBN 0-8285-0725-2, Pub. by Mir Pubs Russia). Imported Pubns.

MATHEMATICAL PHYSICS–PROBLEMS EXERCISES, ETC

Bitsadze, A. V. & Kalinichenko, D. F. A Collection of Problems on the Equations of Mathematical Physics. 1980. 8.50 (ISBN 0-8285-1779-7, Pub. by Mir Pubs Russia). Imported Pubns.
Dalton, B. J., et al, eds. Theory & Application of Moment Methods in Many-Fermion Systems. 504p. 1980. 59.50 (ISBN 0-306-40463-X, Plenum Pr). Plenum Pub.
Hopf, F. Mathematical Problems of Radiative Equilibrium. (Cambridge Tracts in Mathematics & Mathematical Physics Ser.: No. 31). 1964. Repr. of 1934 ed. 8.75 (ISBN 0-02-846070-7). Hafner.
Smirnov, M. M. Problems on the Equations of Mathematical Physics. 1968. 24.75x (ISBN 0-677-61310-5). Gordon.

MATHEMATICAL PROGRAMMING (MANAGEMENT)

see Scheduling (Management)

MATHEMATICAL RECREATIONS

see also Chess; Magic Squares

Adler, David A. Calculator Fun. (Easy-Read Activity Bks.). (Illus.). 32p. (gr. 1-3). 1981. PLB 8.90 (ISBN 0-531-04306-1). Watts.
Adler, Irving. Magic House of Numbers. LC 73-19471. (Illus.). 144p. (gr. 5-9). 1974. PLB 8.79 (ISBN 0-381-99986-6, JD-J). Har-Row.
Adler, Peggy & Adler, Irving. Math Puzzles. LC 78-2833. (Illus.). (gr. 4-6). 1978. PLB 6.90 s&l (ISBN 0-531-02216-1). Watts.
Andrews, W. S., et al. Magic Squares & Cubes. 1917. pap. 5.00 (ISBN 0-486-20658-0). Dover.
Aumann, R. J. & Shapley, L. S. Values of Non-Atomic Games. (A Rand Corporation Research Study). 300p. 1972. 24.00 (ISBN 0-691-08103-4). Princeton U Pr.
Balka, Don. Polyhedra Dice Games for Grades K to 6. Savage, Lyn, ed. (Illus.). (gr. k-6). 1978. 5.75 (ISBN 0-88488-102-4). Creative Pubns.
Ball, W. Rouse. Mathematical Recreations & Essays. rev. ed. 1960. 12.95 (ISBN 0-02-506430-4); pap. 1.95 (ISBN 0-02-091480-6). Macmillan.
Ball, Walter W. & Coxeter, H. S. Mathematical Recreations & Essays. 12th ed. LC 72-186276. 446p. 1974. pap. 7.50 (ISBN 0-8020-6138-9). U of Toronto Pr.
Barns, Robert E. Tangle Table. 1973. pap. 7.95 wkbk. (ISBN 0-88488-022-2). Creative Pubns.
Barr, George. Entertaining with Number Tricks. (Illus.). (gr. 4-6). 1971. PLB 6.95 (ISBN 0-07-003842-2, GB). McGraw.
Barr, Stephen. Miscellany of Puzzles: Mathematical & Otherwise. LC 65-14905. (Illus.). (gr. 6 up). 1965. 8.95 (ISBN 0-690-54419-7, TYC-J). Har-Row.
Beiler, Albert H. Recreations in the Theory of Numbers. (Orig.). 1964. pap. 5.50 (ISBN 0-486-21096-0). Dover.
Benson, William H. & Oswald, Jacoby. Magic Cubes: New Recreations, 2 pts. (Illus.). 96p. (Orig.). 1981. pap. 4.00 (ISBN 0-486-24140-8). Dover.
Bezuszka, Stanley, et al. Designs from Mathematical Patterns. Savage, Lyn, ed. (Illus.). (gr. 6-12). 1978. 7.95 (ISBN 0-88488-105-9). Creative Pubns.
Boyle, Pat. Palatable Plotting. 1972. pap. 4.95 wkbk. (ISBN 0-88488-021-4). Creative Pubns.
Brooke, Maxey. Tricks, Games & Puzzles with Matches. (Illus.). 64p. 1973. pap. 1.25 (ISBN 0-486-20178-3). Dover.
Bureloff, Morris & Johnson, Connie. Calculators, Number Patterns, & Magic. (Illus.). (gr. 4-12). 1977. pap. text ed. 4.95 (ISBN 0-918932-49-1). Activity Resources.
Burns, Marilyn. The I Hate Mathematics! Book. (Brown Paper School Book Ser.). (Illus.). 128p. (gr. 5 up). 1975. 8.95 (ISBN 0-316-11740-4); pap. 5.95 (ISBN 0-316-11741-2). Little.
Cadwell, James H. Topics in Recreational Mathematics. 1966. 17.95 (ISBN 0-521-04409-X). Cambridge U Pr.
Cameron, A. J. Mathematical Enterprises for Schools. 1966. 7.50 (ISBN 0-08-011833-X). Pergamon.
Carroll, Lewis. A Tangled Tale. LC 74-82735. 1975. 4.95 (ISBN 0-89388-181-3). Okpaku Communications.
Charosh, Mannis. Mathematical Games for One or Two. LC 74-187934. (Young Math Ser.). (Illus.). (gr. 1-5). 1972. 7.95 (ISBN 0-690-52324-6, TYC-J); PLB 8.79 (ISBN 0-690-52325-4). Har-Row.
Christensen, R. Mathematical Analysis of Bluffing in Poker. 60p. 1981. 9.50 (ISBN 0-686-28920-X). Entropy Ltd.
Clack, Alice & Leitch, Carol. Amusements Developing Algebra Skills, Vol. 1 & 2. 1975. pap. 6.95ea. (ISBN 0-686-57841-4). Vol. 1 (ISBN 0-910974-76-4). Vol. 2 (ISBN 0-910974-77-2). dittomasters for ea. vol 12.95 (ISBN 0-686-57842-2). Midwest Pubns.
--Math Amusements in Developing Skills, Vol.2. pap. text ed. 5.95 (ISBN 0-910974-44-6); duplicating masters 13.95 (ISBN 0-685-33492-9). Midwest Pubns.
Crescimbeni, Joseph. Arithmetic Enrichment Activities for Elementary School Children. 1965. 10.95 (ISBN 0-13-046177-6, Parker). P-H.
Crouch. Coordinated Cross Number Puzzle Books, 8 bks. Incl. Bks. A1 & A2. (gr. 1-2). pap. 1.64 ea. worktexts; Bk. A1, Gr. 1. pap. (ISBN 0-8009-0722-1); Bk. A2, Gr. 2. pap. (ISBN 0-8009-0725-6); spirit masters 15.32 ea. Bk. A1 (ISBN 0-8009-0746-9). Bk. A2 (ISBN 0-8009-0748-5). ans. keys. Bk. A1 (ISBN 0-8009-0764-7). Bk. A2 (ISBN 0-8009-0766-3); Bks. A-F. (gr. 3-8). Bk. A, Gr. 3. pap. (ISBN 0-8009-0727-2); Bk. B, Gr. 4. pap. (ISBN 0-8009-0729-9); Bk. C, Gr. 5. pap. (ISBN 0-8009-0735-3); Bk. D, Gr. 6. pap. (ISBN 0-8009-0739-6); Bk. E, Gr. 7. pap. (ISBN 0-8009-0742-6); Bk. F, Gr. 8. pap. (ISBN 0-8009-0744-2). (gr. 1-8). 1979. Bks. A-F. pap. 1.76 ea. worktexts; spiritmasters for Bks. A-F 16.68 ea.; ans. keys for Bks. A1, A2, A-F 3.32 ea. McCormick-Mathers.
Degrazia, Joseph. Math Is Fun. (Illus.). (gr. 9 up). 8.95 (ISBN 0-87523-094-6). Emerson.
Devi, Sahkuntala. Figuring. LC 78-4731. 160p. 1981. pap. 3.95 (ISBN 0-06-463530-9, HarpT). Har-Row.
Dudeney, Henry E. Amusements in Mathematics. 1917. pap. 3.25 (ISBN 0-486-20473-1). Dover.
Dunn, Angela. Mathematical Bafflers. rev. ed. (Illus.). 217p. 1980. pap. 3.00 (ISBN 0-486-23961-6). Dover.
Emmet, Eric E. Puzzles for Pleasure. LC 71-189618. (Illus.). 256p. 1972. 9.95 (ISBN 0-87523-178-0). Emerson.
Emmet, Eric R. Brain Puzzler's Delight. LC 68-31403. (Illus.). (gr. 9 up). 1968. 9.95 (ISBN 0-87523-166-7). Emerson.
Friedland, Aaron J. Puzzles in Math & Logic: 100 New Recreations. (Orig.). 1971. pap. 2.00 (ISBN 0-486-22256-X). Dover.
Friend, J. Newton. Numbers: Fun & Facts. 1972. 5.95 (ISBN 0-684-10186-6, ScribT); (ScribT). Scribner.
--Numbers: Fun & Facts. 1972. 5.95 (ISBN 0-684-10186-6, ScribT); (ScribT). Scribner.
Frohlichstein, Jack. Mathematical Fun, Games & Puzzles. 7.25 (ISBN 0-8446-2103-X). Peter Smith.
--Mathematical Fun, Games & Puzzles. (Illus., Orig.). 1962. pap. 3.50 (ISBN 0-486-20789-7). Dover.
Fuller, Robert. Amazement 1. (gr. 3-6). 1978. 5.00 (ISBN 0-88488-106-7). Creative Pubns.
--Amazement 2. (gr. 4-9). 1978. 5.00 (ISBN 0-88488-107-5). Creative Pubns.
Games & Puzzles for Elementary & Middle School Mathematics: Readings from the Arithmetic Teacher. LC 75-16349. 1975. pap. 7.30 (ISBN 0-87353-054-3). NCTM.
Gardner, Martin. Aha! Insight. LC 78-51259. (Illus.). 1978. pap. text ed. 7.95x (ISBN 0-89454-001-7). W H Freeman.
--Martin Gardner's New Mathematical Diversions from Scientific American. 1966. pap. 5.95 (ISBN 0-671-20913-2). S&S.
--Mathematical Carnival. 1975. 9.95 (ISBN 0-394-49406-7). Knopf.
--Mathematical Magic Show: More Puzzles, Games, Diversions, Illusions & Other Mathematical Sleight-of-Mind from Scientific American. (Giant Ser.). (Illus.). pap. 3.95 (ISBN 0-394-72623-5, V-623, Vin). Random.
--Mathematical Puzzles. LC 61-6142. (Illus.). (gr. 7 up). 1961. 7.95 (ISBN 0-690-52360-2, TYC-J). Har-Row.
--Mathematics, Magic, & Mystery. 1956. pap. 2.50 (ISBN 0-486-20335-2). Dover.
--New Mathematical Diversions from Scientific American. 1971. pap. 5.95 (ISBN 0-671-20913-2, Fireside). S&S.
--Unexpected Hanging & Other Mathematical Diversions. 1972. pap. 4.95 (ISBN 0-671-21425-X, Fireside). S&S.
Gardner, Martin, ed. Scientific American Book of Mathematical Puzzles & Diversions. 1963. pap. 3.95 (ISBN 0-671-63652-9, Fireside). S&S.
--Second Scientific American Book of Mathematical Puzzles & Diversions. 1965. pap. 3.95 (ISBN 0-671-63653-7, Fireside). S&S.
Gilbert, Jack. Numbers: Shortcuts & Pastimes. LC 75-1700. (Illus.). 294p. 1976. 9.95 (ISBN 0-8306-6675-3); pap. 6.95 (ISBN 0-8306-5675-8, 675). TAB Bks.
Graham, Lloyd A. Ingenious Mathematical Problems & Methods. 1959. pap. 3.50 (ISBN 0-486-20545-2). Dover.
--Surprise Attack in Mathematical Problems. (Illus., Orig.). 1968. pap. 3.00 (ISBN 0-486-21846-5). Dover.
Gregory, John & Seymour, Dale. I'm a Number Game. (gr. 5-9). 1978. 4.25 (ISBN 0-88488-100-8). Creative Pubns.
--Limerick Number Puzzles. (gr. 5-9). 1978. 4.25 (ISBN 0-88488-101-6). Creative Pubns.
Hallamore, Eliz. El Libro Metrico Cosas Divertidas Para Hacer. Wald, Heywood, tr. from Eng. Orig. Title: The Metric Book of Amusing Things to Do. (Span.). Date not set. pap. 1.95 (ISBN 0-8120-0741-7). Barron.
Harvey, Linda & Roper, Ann. Dots Math. (Illus.). (gr. k-4). 1978. 4.95 (ISBN 0-88488-104-0). Creative Pubns.
Heafford, Philip. Math Entertainer. (Illus.). (gr. 9 up). 1958. 8.95 (ISBN 0-87523-109-8). Emerson.
Heath, Royal V. Mathemagic: Magic, Puzzles & Games with Numbers. 1953. pap. 1.75 (ISBN 0-486-20110-4). Dover.
Hestwood, Diana & Huseby, Edward. Crossnumber Puzzle Books, 2 bks. 1972. Bk. 1. pap. 5.50 wkbk. (ISBN 0-88488-013-3); Bk. 2. pap. 5.50 wkbk. (ISBN 0-88488-014-1). Creative Pubns.
Holt, Michael. More Math Puzzles & Games. LC 77-75319. 1978. pap. 3.95 (ISBN 0-8027-7114-9). Walker & Co.
Hunter, J. A. Challenging Mathematical Teasers. LC 79-51888. 1980. pap. 2.75 (ISBN 0-486-23852-0). Dover.
--Fun with Figures. 1956. pap. 2.00 (ISBN 0-486-21364-1). Dover.
--Mathematical Brain-Teasers. 1976. pap. 2.00 (ISBN 0-486-23347-2). Dover.
--More Fun with Figures. Orig. Title: Figurets: More Fun with Figures. 1966. pap. 2.00 (ISBN 0-486-21670-5). Dover.
Hunter, J. A. & Madachy, Joseph S. Mathematical Diversions. LC 74-83619. (Illus.). 192p. (YA) 1975. pap. 2.75 (ISBN 0-486-23110-0). Dover.
Kadesch, Robert R. Math Menagerie. LC 66-11498. (Illus.). (gr. 7 up). 1970. PLB 7.89 (ISBN 0-06-023069-X, HarpJ). Har-Row.
Kordemsky, Boris A. Moscow Puzzles: Three Hundred Fifty-Nine Mathematical Recreations. Parry, Albert, tr. LC 74-162770. 1972. pap. 5.95 (ISBN 0-684-14870-6, SL692, ScribT). Scribner.
Kraitchik, Maurice. Mathematical Recreations. 2nd ed. LC 53-9354. (Illus.). 1953. pap. 5.00 (ISBN 0-486-20163-5). Dover.
Kremer, Ron & McNichols, Joan. Multiplication & Division Games. new ed. Laycock, Mary, ed. (Illus.). (gr. 3-6). 1977. pap. text ed. 4.95 (ISBN 0-918932-48-3). Activity Resources.
Lamb, Sidney. Mathematical Games, Puzzles & Fallacies. LC 76-27759. 1977. pap. 1.95 (ISBN 0-668-04092-0). Arco.
Lindgren, Harry. Recreational Problems in Geometric Dissections & How to Solve Them. Orig. Title: Geometric Dissections with Puzzles & Solutions. (Illus.). 184p. 1972. pap. 3.50 (ISBN 0-486-22878-9). Dover.
Longley-Cook, L. H. New Math Puzzle Book. (Illus.). 1970. 6.95 (ISBN 0-442-04873-4). Van Nos Reinhold.
Loyd, Sam. Best Mathematical Puzzles of Sam Loyd. Gardner, Martin, ed. 1959. pap. 2.75 (ISBN 0-486-20498-7). Dover.
--More Mathematical Puzzles of Sam Loyd. pap. 2.50 (ISBN 0-486-20709-9). Dover.
McLaughlin, Jack. People Piece Puzzles. (Illus.). (gr. 2-8). 1973. pap. 4.95 (ISBN 0-918932-38-6). Activity Resources.
Madachy, Joseph S. Madachy's Mathematical Recreations. LC 78-74116. (Illus.). 1979. pap. 3.25 (ISBN 0-486-23762-1). Dover.
Madachy, Joseph S., ed. Ten-Year Cumulative Index to the Journal of Recreational Mathematics. 160p. pap. 10.00x (ISBN 0-89503-020-9). Baywood Pub.
Maloney, Mary L. Mathematricks. (Pocketful of Puzzles Ser.). (Illus., Orig.). 1977. pap. 5.95x (ISBN 0-87628-646-5, C-6465-3). Ctr Appl Res.
Maltby, Richard, Jr. & Fulbrook, Edward. Cross Sums. (Illus.). 1977. pap. 1.95 (ISBN 0-911104-68-2). Workman Pub.
Maltby, Richard, Jr. & Fulbrook, Edward, eds. Geometric Cross Sums. (Illus.). 120p. 1977. pap. 1.95 (ISBN 0-911104-69-0, 0000965). Workman Pub.
Maxwell, Edwin A. Fallacies in Mathematics. 1959. 12.95 (ISBN 0-521-05700-0). Cambridge U Pr.
Mira, Julio A. Mathematical Teasers. LC 74-101122. (Orig.). 1970. pap. 3.95 (ISBN 0-06-463230-X, EH 230, EH). Har-Row.
Mott-Smith, Geoffrey. Mathematical Puzzles for Beginners & Enthusiasts. 2nd ed. 1954. pap. 2.95 (ISBN 0-486-20198-8). Dover.
--Mathematical Puzzles for Beginners & Enthusiasts. LC 55-3389. 1954. lib. bdg. 9.50x (ISBN 0-88307-570-9). Gannon.
Nourse, James G. The Simple Solution to Rubik's Cube. 1981. pap. 1.95 (ISBN 0-686-76182-0). Bantam.
Olney, Ross & Olney, Pat. Pocket Calculator Fun & Games. (Illus.). (gr. 4 up). 1977. PLB 6.45 s&l (ISBN 0-531-00387-6). Watts.
Pask, Gordon, et al. Calculator Saturnalia. LC 80-5489. 256p. 1981. pap. 5.95 (ISBN 0-394-74528-0, Vin). Random.
Pedoe, Dan. The Gentle Art of Mathematics. 143p. 1973. pap. 2.50 (ISBN 0-486-22949-1). Dover.
Perelman, Yakov. Figures for Fun: Stories & Conundrums. LC 65-23369. (Illus.). pap. 2.95 (ISBN 0-8044-6632-7). Ungar.
Phillips, Hubert C. My Best Puzzles in Mathematics. (Orig.). 1961. pap. 2.25 (ISBN 0-486-20091-4). Dover.
Rademacher, Hans & Toeplitz, Otto. Enjoyment of Mathematics: Selections from Mathematics for the Amateur. 14.00 (ISBN 0-691-07958-7); pap. 5.95 (ISBN 0-691-02351-4). Princeton U Pr.
Rapoport, Anatol. N-Person Game Theory: Concepts & Applications. (Ann Arbor Science Library). (Illus.). 348p. 1970. pap. 5.95 (ISBN 0-472-05017-6). U of Mich Pr.
Reinfeld, Don & Rice, David. One-Hundred One Mathematical Puzzles & How to Solve Them. 1977. pap. 1.95 (ISBN 0-346-12256-2). Cornerstone.
Rice, Trevor. Mathematical Games & Puzzles. LC 74-79958. (Illus.). 96p. 1974. 5.95 (ISBN 0-312-52290-8). St Martin.
Rogers, James T. The Calculating Book: Fun & Games with Your Pocket Calculator. LC 74-29606. 1975. pap. 3.95 (ISBN 0-394-73033-X, BYR). Random.
Schiro, Michael. Another Thirty-Three Arithmetic Skill Development Games. 1978. pap. 4.95 (ISBN 0-8224-0327-7). Pitman Learning.

Schlossberg, Edwin & Brockman, John. The Kids' Pocket Calculator Game Book. (Illus.). 1977. pap. 3.95 (ISBN 0-688-08233-5). Morrow.
--The Pocket Calculator Game Book. LC 75-26562. (Illus.). 1975. pap. 3.95 (ISBN 0-688-07983-0). Morrow.
--Pocket Calculator Game Book, No. 2. LC 77-7054. (Illus.). 1977. 6.95 (ISBN 0-688-03234-6); pap. 3.95 (ISBN 0-688-08234-3). Morrow.
Schuh, Fred. The Master Book of Mathematical Puzzles & Recreations. O'Beirne, T. H., ed. Gobel, F., tr. LC 68-28064. Orig. Title: Wonderlijke Problemen Leerzaam Tijoverdrijf Door Puzzle En Spel. (Illus.). 430p. 1969. pap. 4.95 (ISBN 0-486-22134-2). Dover.
--The Master Book of Mathematical Recreations. O'Beirne, T. H., ed. Gobel, F., tr. (Illus.). 7.50 (ISBN 0-8446-2888-3). Peter Smith.
Schwartz, Benjamin L., ed. Mathematical Solitaires & Games. LC 79-55714. (Excursions in Recreational Mathematics Ser.). (Illus.). 160p. (Orig.). 1980. pap. text ed. 6.00x (ISBN 0-89503-017-9). Baywood Pub.
Silvey, Linda. Polyhedra Dice Games for Grades 5 to 10. (Illus.). (gr. 5-10). 1978. 5.75 (ISBN 0-88488-103-2). Creative Pubns.
Simon, William. Mathematical Magic. LC 65-14727. 1969. pap. 3.45 (ISBN 0-684-71890-1, SL190, ScribT). Scribner.
Steig, William. C D B. LC 80-12376. (Illus.). 44p. (gr. 1 up). pap. 1.50 (ISBN 0-671-96030-X). Windmill Bks.
Steinhaus, Hugo. Mathematical Snapshots. 3rd ed. (Illus.). 1969. 15.95 (ISBN 0-19-500117-6). Oxford U Pr.
Stokes, William T. & Laycock, Mary. Math Activity Worksheet Masters. 1974. pap. text ed. 5.50 (ISBN 0-88488-012-5). Creative Pubns.
Summers, George J. New Puzzles in Logical Deduction. 1968. pap. 2.00 (ISBN 0-486-22089-3). Dover.
Taylor, Don. Mastering Rubik's Cube. 1981. 1.95 (ISBN 0-686-31076-4, Owl Bks). HR & W.
Taylor, L. P. Numbers. (Illus.). 1970. 9.75 (ISBN 0-571-09322-1). Transatlantic.
Thayer, Jane. The Little House: A New Math Story-Game. (Illus.). (ps-1). 1972. PLB 6.48 (ISBN 0-688-30051-0). Morrow.
Vine, James. Boggle. 1975. pap. 2.50 (ISBN 0-8431-0372-8). Price Stern.
Wyler, Rose & Baird, Eva-Lee. Nutty Number Riddles. LC 74-33695. (gr. 3-5). 1977. PLB 5.95 (ISBN 0-385-00685-3). Doubleday.

MATHEMATICAL RECREATIONS-BIBLIOGRAPHY

Schaaf, William L. A Bibliography of Recreational Mathematics. Vol. 1, 1970. pap. 9.00 (ISBN 0-87353-021-7); Vol. 2, 1970. pap. 9.00 (ISBN 0-87353-022-5); Vol. 3, 1973. pap. 9.00 (ISBN 0-87353-023-3); Vol. 4, 1978. pap. 9.00 (ISBN 0-87353-020-9). NCTM.
Wyler, Rose & Ames, Gerald. It's All Done with Numbers: Astounding & Confounding Feats of Mathematical Magic. LC 76-42416. (Illus.). (gr. 4-5). 1979. 7.95a (ISBN 0-385-03059-2); PLB (ISBN 0-385-09003-X). Doubleday.

MATHEMATICAL RECREATIONS-DATA PROCESSING

Clarke, M. R. Advances in Computer Chess Three: Proceedings of the Third Computer Chess Conference, London, 1981. 200p. 1982. 28.00 (ISBN 0-08-026898-6). Pergamon.
Clarke, M. R., ed. Advances in Computer Chess 3: Proceedings of the International Conference, London, April, 1981. 170p. 1981. 27.50 (ISBN 0-08-026898-6). Pergamon.
Judd, Wallace. Games, Tricks, & Puzzles for a Hand Calculator. 1976. pap. 4.95 (ISBN 0-918398-19-3). Dilithium Pr.
Sage, Edwin R. Fun & Games with the Computer. 250p. 1975. pap. text ed. 9.95 (ISBN 0-87567-075-X). Entelek.
--Fun & Games with the Computer. 250p. 1975. pap. text ed. 9.95 (ISBN 0-87567-075-X). Entelek.

MATHEMATICAL RESEARCH

Ashlock, Robert B. & Herman, Wayne L., Jr. Current Research in Elementary School Mathematics. (Illus.). 480p. 1970. pap. text ed. 10.95 (ISBN 0-02-304240-0, 30424). Macmillan.
El Tom, M. E. Developing Mathematics in Third World Countries. (North Holland Mathematics Studies: Vol. 33). 1979. 29.50 (ISBN 0-444-85260-3, North Holland). Elsevier.
Lie, Sophus. Vorlesungen Uber Continuierliche Gruppen Mit Geometrischen und Anderen Anwendungen. 2nd ed. LC 66-12879. (Ger). 1971. text ed. 35.00 (ISBN 0-8284-0199-3). Chelsea Pub.
Mehrtens, H., ed. Social History of Mathematics. 800p. 1981. write for info. Birkhauser.
Petrie, Chris J. Enlongational Flows. (Research Notes in Mathematics Ser.: No. 29). 254p. (Orig.). 1979. pap. text ed. 21.95 (ISBN 0-273-08406-2). Pitman Pub MA.
Sylvester, James J. Collected Mathematical Papers, 4 Vols. LC 76-250188. 1973. Repr. of 1904 ed. text ed. 125.00 (ISBN 0-8284-0253-1). Chelsea Pub.
Symposia in Applied Mathematics. The Influence of Computing on Mathematical Research & Education, Vol. 20. La Salle, Joseph P., ed. LC 74-5166. 1974. 33.20 (ISBN 0-8218-1326-9, PSAPM-20). Am Math.

MATHEMATICAL SEQUENCES

see Sequences (Mathematics)

MATHEMATICAL SETS

see Set Theory

MATHEMATICAL STATISTICS

see also Biometry; Correlation (Statistics); Errors, Theory Of; Estimation Theory; Law of Large Numbers; Least Squares; Mathematical Linguistics; Multivariate Analysis; Nonparametric Statistics; Probabilities; Regression Analysis; Sampling (Statistics); Sequential Analysis; Statistical Astronomy; Statistical Hypothesis Testing; Statistics; Time-Series Analysis

Aitchison, John & Brown, J. A. Lognormal Distribution. (Cambridge Department of Applied Economic Monographs). 1957. 29.50 (ISBN 0-521-04011-6). Cambridge U Pr.
Aivazjan, S. A., et al. Twenty-Two Papers on Statistics & Probability. LC 61-9803. (Selected Translations in Mathematical Statistics & Probability Ser.: Vol. 6). 1966. 30.40 (ISBN 0-8218-1456-7, STAPRO-6). Am Math.
Aleskjavicene, A., et al. Twenty-Two Papers on Statistics & Probability. (Selected Translations in Mathematical Statistics & Probability: Vol. 11). 1973. 28.00 (ISBN 0-8218-1461-3, STAPRO-11). Am Math.
Ambarcumjan, G. A., et al. Thirty-Five Papers on Statistics & Probability. LC 61-9803. (Selected Translations in Mathematical Statistics & Probability Ser.: Vol. 4). 1963. 27.20 (ISBN 0-8218-1454-0, STAPRO-4). Am Math.
Amstadter, Bertram L. Reliability Mathematics Fundamental Practical Procedures. 1971. 31.50 (ISBN 0-07-001598-8, P&RB). McGraw.
Anderson, Theodore W. Introduction to Multivariate Statistical Analysis. LC 58-6068. (Probability & Mathematical Statistics Ser.). 374p. 1958. 31.00 (ISBN 0-471-02640-9). Wiley.
Arato, M., et al. Thirty-Two Papers on Statistics & Probability. LC 61-9803. (Selected Translations in Mathematical Statistics & Probability Ser.: Vol. 10). 1972. 31.20 (ISBN 0-8218-1460-5, STAPRO-10). Am Math.
--Twenty Papers on Statistics & Probability. (Selected Transactions in Mathematics Statistics & Probability Ser.: Vol. 13). 1973. 47.20 (ISBN 0-8218-1463-X, STAPRO 13). Am Math.
Arthanari, Subramanvam & Dodge, Yadolah. Mathematical Programming in Statistics. LC 80-21637. (Probability & Math Statistics Ser.: Applied Probability & Statistics). 413p. 1981. 28.95 (ISBN 0-471-08073-X, Pub. by Wiley-Interscience). Wiley.
Bancroft, T. A. Topics in Intermediate Statistical Methods, Vol. 1. 1968. 7.50x (ISBN 0-8138-0842-1). Iowa St U Pr.
Bancroft, T. A. & Brown, Susan A., eds. Statistical Papers in Honor of George W. Snedecor. LC 79-106603. (Illus.). 1972. 13.50x (ISBN 0-8138-1585-1). Iowa St U Pr.
Barnett, V. Comparative Statistical Inference. LC 73-1833. (Probability & Mathematical Statistics Ser.: Probability Section). 287p. 1973. 40.25 (ISBN 0-471-05401-1, Pub. by Wiley-Interscience). Wiley.
Bauer, Edward L. Statistical Manual for Chemists. 2nd ed. 1971. 29.50 (ISBN 0-12-082756-5). Acad Pr.
Benjamin, J. & Cornell, C. A. Probability, Statistics, & Decisions for Civil Engineers. 1970. 25.00 (ISBN 0-07-004549-6, C). McGraw.
Berman, D. L., et al. Nineteen Papers on Statistics & Probability. LC 61-9803. (Selected Translations on Mathematical Statistics & Probability Ser: Vol. 5). 1965. 26.00 (ISBN 0-8218-1455-9, STAPRO-5). Am Math.
Bevan, John. Introduction to Statistics. 1968. 6.00 (ISBN 0-8022-0122-9). Philos Lib.
Bickel, P. J. & Doksum, K. A. Mathematical Statistics: Basic Ideas & Selected Topics. LC 76-8724. 1977. 28.95x (ISBN 0-8162-0784-4). Holden-Day.
Borovkov, A. A., et al. Nineteen Papers on Statistics & Probability. LC 61-9803. (Selected Translations on Mathematical Statistics & Probability Ser.: Vol. 2). 1962. 20.00 (ISBN 0-8218-1452-4, STAPRO-2). Am Math.
Bowley, Arthur L. F. Y. Edgeworth's Contributions to Mathematical Statistics. LC 68-24161. Repr. of 1928 ed. 11.50x (ISBN 0-678-00889-2). Kelley.
Box, George E. & Tiao, George C. Bayesian Inference in Statistical Analysis. LC 78-172804. 1973. text ed. 24.95 (ISBN 0-201-00622-7). A-W.
Brandt, Siegmund. Statistical & Computational Methods in Data Analysis. 2nd ed. 1976. 44.00 (ISBN 0-444-10893-9, North-Holland). Elsevier.
Breiman, Leo. Statistics: With a View Toward Applications. LC 72-3131. 480p. 1973. text ed. 22.50 (ISBN 0-395-04232-1, 3-05972). HM.
Brookes. Sequences, Series, Probability & Statistics. 1974. 4.95x (ISBN 0-534-00353-2). Wadsworth Pub.
Brooks, Charles E. & Carruthers, N. Handbook of Statistical Methods in Meteorology. LC 77-10222. Repr. of 1953 ed. 30.50 (ISBN 0-404-16202-9). AMS Pr.
Brownlee, Kenneth A. Statistical Theory & Methodology in Science & Engineering. 2nd ed. 1965. 39.95 (ISBN 0-471-11355-7). Wiley.
Brunk, H. D. Introduction to Mathematical Statistics. 3rd ed. LC 74-82348. 1975. text ed. 24.95 (ISBN 0-471-00834-6). Wiley.
Burr, Irving W. Applied Statistical Methods. (Operations Research & Industrial Engineering Ser.). 1973. 21.95 (ISBN 0-12-146150-5). Acad Pr.
Cerkasov, I. D., et al. Eighteen Papers on Statistics & Probability. LC 61-9803. (Selected Translations on Mathematical Statistics & Probability Ser.: Vol. 3). 1963. 24.80 (ISBN 0-8218-1453-2, STAPRO-3). Am Math.
Ch'En Hsi-Ju, et al. Twenty Papers on Statistics & Probability. LC 61-9803. (Selected Translations in Mathematical Statistics & Probability Ser.: Vol. 12). 1973. 40.00 (ISBN 0-8218-1462-1, STAPRO-12). Am Math.
Choi, Sung C. Introductory Applied Statistics in Science. (Illus.). 1978. ref. ed. 22.95 (ISBN 0-13-501619-3). P-H.
Cramer, H. Mathematical Methods of Statistics. (Mathematical Ser.: Vol. 9). 1946. 28.00 (ISBN 0-691-08004-6). Princeton U Pr.
Culanovski, I. V., et al. Twenty-Five Papers on Statistics & Probability. LC 61-9803. (Selected Translations in Mathematical Statistics & Probability Ser.: Vol. 1). 1961. 32.00 (ISBN 0-8218-1451-6, STAPRO-1). Am Math.
Daniel, Cuthbert & Wood, Fred S. Fitting Equations to Data: Computer Analysis of Multifactor Data. 2nd ed. LC 79-11110. (Probability & Mathematical Statistics Ser.: Applied Section). 1980. 26.00 (ISBN 0-471-05370-8, Pub. by Wiley-Interscience). Wiley.
Daniel, Wayne W. Introductory Statistics with Applications. LC 76-10897. (Illus.). 1977. text ed. 17.95 (ISBN 0-395-24430-7); inst. guide with solutions 3.00 (ISBN 0-395-24431-5); study guide 7.75 (ISBN 0-395-24843-4). HM.
Defrancesco, Henry F. Quantitative Analysis Methods for Substantive Analysts. LC 80-11355. 448p. 1981. Repr. of 1975 ed. lib. bdg. write for info. (ISBN 0-89874-139-4). Krieger.
Degroot, Morris. Probability & Statistics. LC 74-19691. (Behavioral Science Quantitative Methods Ser). (Illus.). 624p. 1975. text ed. 20.95 (ISBN 0-201-01503-X); sol. manual 7.95 (ISBN 0-201-01509-9). A-W.
Durran, J. H. Statistics & Probability. LC 70-96086. (School Mathematics Project Handbks). 1970. text ed. 24.95 (ISBN 0-521-06933-5). Cambridge U Pr.
Edwards, A. W. Likelihood: An Account of the Statistical Concept of Likelihood & Its Application to Scientific Inference. LC 70-163060. (Illus.). 1972. 31.95 (ISBN 0-521-08299-4). Cambridge U Pr.
Ehrenberg, A. S. Data Reduction: Analyzing & Interpreting Statistical Data. LC 74-3724. 391p. 1975. 47.25 (ISBN 0-471-23399-4, Pub. by Wiley-Interscience); pap. 19.25 (ISBN 0-471-23398-6). Wiley.
Ellis, L. E. Statistics & Probability (Draft Edition) (School Mathematics Project Further Mathematics Ser). (Illus.). 1971. text ed. 8.50 (ISBN 0-521-08026-6). Cambridge U Pr.
European Meeting of Statisticians, Sept. 6-11 1976, Grenoble, France, et al. Recent Developments in Statistics: Proceedings. 1977. 88.00 (ISBN 0-7204-0751-6, North-Holland). Elsevier.
Everitt, B. S. The Analysis of Contingency Tables. 128p. 1977. text ed. 12.95x (ISBN 0-412-14970-2, Pub. by Chapman & Hall England). Methuen Inc.
Finney, D. J. Probit Analysis. 3rd ed. LC 78-134618. (Illus.). 1971. 57.50 (ISBN 0-521-08041-X). Cambridge U Pr.
--Statistics for Mathematicians: An Introduction. 1968. 8.85 (ISBN 0-934454-74-4). Lubrecht & Cramer.
Fischer, Frederic E. Fundamental Statistical Concepts. LC 72-3309. 1973. text ed. 20.50 scp (ISBN 0-06-382662-3, HarpC). Har-Row.
Fisher, Ronald A. Statistical Methods & Scientific Inference. rev. ed. 1973. 13.00 (ISBN 0-02-844740-9). Hafner.
Fisz, Marek. Probability Theory & Mathematical Statistics. 3rd ed. LC 80-12455. 704p. 1980. lib. bdg. 34.50 (ISBN 0-89874-179-3). Krieger.
Fong, Peter. Statistical Theory of Nuclear Fission. (Documents on Modern Physics Ser.). (Orig.). 1969. 54.50x (ISBN 0-677-01850-9). Gordon.
Fraser, D. Structure of Inference. 346p. 1968. 19.00 (ISBN 0-471-27548-4, Pub. by Wiley). Krieger.
Freund, John E. & Walpole, Ronald E. Mathematical Statistics. 3rd ed. 1980. text ed. 23.95 (ISBN 0-13-562066-X). P-H.
Furstenberg, H. Stationary Processes & Prediction Theory. (Annals of Mathematics Studies, Vol. 44). (Orig.). 1960. pap. 21.00x (ISBN 0-691-08041-0). Princeton U Pr.
Galambos, Janos. The Asymptotic Theory of Extreme Order Statistics. LC 78-1916. (Series in Probability & Mathematical Staistics: Applied Probability & Statistics). 1978. 38.00x (ISBN 0-471-02148-2, Pub. by Wiley-Interscience). Wiley.
Georgii, H. O. Canonical Gibbs Measures. (Lecture Notes in Mathematics: Vol. 760). 190p. 1980. pap. text ed. 12.40 (ISBN 0-387-09712-0). Springer-Verlag.
Gilbert, Norma. Statistics. LC 75-22732. 350p. 1976. text ed. 13.75 (ISBN 0-7216-4127-X); tapes 125.00 (ISBN 0-7216-9918-9). HR&W.
Glass, Gene V., et al. Design & Analysis of Time-Series Experiments. Willson, Victor L. & Gottman, John M., eds. LC 74-84779. (Illus.). 200p. 1975. text ed. 13.50x (ISBN 0-87081-063-4). Colo Assoc.
Godambe, V. P. & Sprott, D. A. The Foundations of Statistical Inference. (Winston Mine Editions). 1972. text ed. 32.20 (ISBN 0-685-26946-9, HoltC). HR&W.
Goodman, L. A. & Kruskal, W. H. Measures of Association for Cross Classifications. (Springer Series in Statistics: Vol. 1). 1980. 12.60 (ISBN 0-387-90443-3). Springer-Verlag.
Gottinger, Hans W. Elements of Statistical Analysis. 248p. 1980. text ed. 37.50x (ISBN 3-11-007169-X). De Gruyter.
Grenander, Ulf. Abstract Inference. LC 80-22016. (Probability & Mathematical Statistics Ser.). 526p. 1981. 35.00 (ISBN 0-471-08267-8, Pub. by Wiley Interscience). Wiley.
Guenther, William C. Concepts of Statistical Inference. 2nd ed. (Illus.). 512p. 1973. text ed. 16.95 (ISBN 0-07-025098-7, C); instructors' manual 1.50 (ISBN 0-07-025099-5). McGraw.
Gumbel, Emil J. Statistics of Extremes. LC 57-10160. 1958. 20.50x (ISBN 0-231-02190-9). Columbia U Pr.
Hacking, Ian M. Logic of Statistical Inference. 1966. 35.50 (ISBN 0-521-05165-7); pap. 11.50x (ISBN 0-521-29059-7). Cambridge U Pr.
Hajek, P. & Havranek, T. Mechanizing Hypothesis Formation: Mathematical Foundations for a General Theory. 1978. pap. 27.70 (ISBN 0-387-08738-9). Springer-Verlag.
Hald, Anders. Statistical Theory with Engineering Applications. (Wiley Series in Probability & Mathematical Statistics-Applied Probability & Statistics Section). 1952. 40.50 (ISBN 0-471-34056-1, Pub. by Wiley-Interscience). Wiley.
Harper, W. L. & Hooker, C. A., eds. Foundations of Probability Theory Statistical Inference & Statistical Theories of Science: Proceedings, 3 vols. Incl. Vol. 1. Foundations & Philosophy of Epistemic Applications of Probability Theory. LC 75-34354. lib. bdg. 55.00 (ISBN 90-277-0616-6); pap. 28.95 (ISBN 90-277-0617-4); Vol. 2. Foundations & Philosophy of Statistical Inference. LC 75-38667. lib. bdg. 68.50 (ISBN 90-277-0618-2); pap. 37.00 (ISBN 90-277-0619-0); Vol. 3. Foundations & Philosophy of Statistical Theories in the Physical Sciences. LC 75-33879. lib. bdg. 39.50 (ISBN 90-277-0620-4); pap. 24.00 (ISBN 90-277-0621-2). (Western Ontatio Ser.: No. 6). 1976. 147.50 set (ISBN 90-277-0614-X, Pub. by Reidel Holland); pap. 79.00 set (ISBN 90-277-0615-8). Kluwer Boston.
Heyde, C. C. & Seneta, E. I. J. Bienayme: Statistical Theory Anticipated. LC 77-7367. (Studies in the History of Mathematics & Physical Sciences: Vol. 3). (Illus.). 1977. 25.20 (ISBN 0-387-90261-9). Springer-Verlag.
Hodge, S. E. & Seed, M. L. Statistics & Probability. 2nd ed. (Illus.). 1977. pap. text ed. 12.95x (ISBN 0-216-90450-1). Intl Ideas.
Hodges, J. L., Jr. & Lehmann, E. L. Basic Concepts of Probability & Statistics. rev. ed. 2nd ed. LC 72-104973. 1970. text ed. 17.95x (ISBN 0-8162-4004-3); ans. bk. 1.50x (ISBN 0-8162-4024-8). Holden-Day.
Hoel, Paul, et al. Introduction to Statistical Theory. LC 70-136172. 1971. text ed. 19.75 (ISBN 0-395-04637-8, 3-25652). HM.
Hoel, Paul G. Introduction to Mathematical Statistics. 4th ed. LC 70-139277. (Ser. in Probability & Mathematical Statistics). 1971. text ed. 25.95 (ISBN 0-471-40365-2). Wiley.
Hoel, Paul G. & Jessen, Raymond J. Basic Statistics for Business & Economics. 2nd ed. LC 76-54504. (Management & Administration Ser.). 1977. 23.95x (ISBN 0-471-40268-0); study guide 6.95 (ISBN 0-471-01697-7). Wiley.
Hogben, Lancelot. Statistical Theory. rev. ed. (Illus.). 1968. 15.00x (ISBN 0-393-06305-4). Norton.

Hogg, Robert V. & Craig, Allen T. Introduction to Mathematical Statistics. 4th ed. (Illus.). 1978. text ed. 19.95x (ISBN 0-02-355710-9, 35571). Macmillan.
Hogg, Robert V. & Tanis, Elliot A. Probability & Statistical Inference. (Illus.). 1977. text ed. 18.95 (ISBN 0-02-355650-1). Macmillan.
Hooke, Robert. Introduction to Scientific Inference. LC 75-28676. (Illus.). 101p. 1976. Repr. of 1963 ed. lib. bdg. 15.00 (ISBN 0-8371-8470-3, HOIS). Greenwood.
Huber, Peter J. Robust Statistical Procedures. (CBMS-NSF Regional Conference Ser.: Vol. 27). (Illus., Orig.). 1977. pap. text ed. 6.75 (ISBN 0-89871-024-3). Soc Indus-Appl Math.
--Robust Statistics. LC 80-18627. (Wiley Ser. on Probability & Math Statistics). 308p. 1981. 28.95 (ISBN 0-471-41805-6, Pub. by Wiley-Interscience). Wiley.
Huitema, Bradley E. The Analysis of Convariance & Alternatives. LC 80-11319. 445p. 1980. 27.50 (ISBN 0-471-42044-1, Pub. by Wiley-Interscience). Wiley.
Huitson, Alan. Analysis of Variance. (Griffin's Statistical Monographs & Courses Ser.: Vol. 18). 1973. pap. 9.95 (ISBN 0-02-846140-1). Hafner.
Hume, Beryl. An Introduction to Probability & Statistics. 3rd ed. 1969. pap. 11.00x (ISBN 0-85564-030-8, Pub. by U of W Austral Pr). Intl Schol Bk Serv.
Huntsberger & Billingsley. Elements of Statistical Inference. 5th ed. 416p. 1981. text ed. 20.50 (ISBN 0-205-07305-0, 5673054); tchr's ed. 4.95 (ISBN 0-205-07306-9); student's guide 6.95 (ISBN 0-205-07307-7). Allyn.
Index to Translations Selected by the American Mathematical Society, Vol. 2. 1973. 20.80 (ISBN 0-8218-0059-0, TRAN2I-51). Am Math.
Ipsen, Johannes & Feigl, Polly. Bancroft's Introduction to Biostatistics. 2nd ed. (Illus.). 1970. 14.95x (ISBN 0-06-141332-1, Harper Medical). Har-Row.
Jacobs, Konrad. Measure & Integral. (Probability & Mathematical Statistics). 1978. 55.00 (ISBN 0-12-378550-2). Acad Pr.
Johnson, Norman L. & Leone, Fred C. Statistics & Experimental Design in Engineering & the Physical Sciences, 2 vols. 2nd ed. LC 76-28337. (Wiley Series in Probability & Mathematical Statistics). 1977. Vol 1. write for info. (ISBN 0-471-01756-6, Pub. by Wiley-Interscience). Vol 2 (ISBN 0-471-01757-4). Wiley.
Johnston, John. Econometric Methods. 2nd ed. 1971. text ed. 19.00 (ISBN 0-07-032679-7, C). McGraw.
Kac, Mark. Mark Kac: Probability, Number Theory, & Statistical Physics: Selected Papers. Baclawski, K. & Donsker, M. D., eds. (Mathematicians of Our Time Ser.). 1979. 45.00x (ISBN 0-262-11067-9). MIT Pr.
Kagan, A. M., et al. Characterization Problems in Mathematical Statistics. Ramachandran, B., tr. LC 73-9643. (Ser. in Probability & Mathematical Statistics Ser.). 499p. 1973. 41.00 (ISBN 0-471-45421-4). Wiley.
Kalbfleisch, J. G. Probability & Statistical Inference I. (Universitexts). (Illus.). 342p. 1980. pap. 15.80 (ISBN 0-387-90457-3). Springer-Verlag.
--Probability & Statistical Inference II. (Universitexts). (Illus.). 316p. 1980. pap. 15.80 (ISBN 0-387-90458-1). Springer-Verlag.
Kempthorne, Oscar & Folks, Leroy. Probability, Statistics & Data Analysis. 1971. 24.00x (ISBN 0-8138-2470-2). Iowa St U Pr.
Klonecki, W., et al, eds. Mathematical Statistics & Probability Theory: Proceedings. (Lecture Notes in Statistics: Vol. 2). 373p. 1980. pap. 20.00 (ISBN 0-387-90493-X). Springer-Verlag.
Kozesnik, Jaroslav, ed. Information Theory, Statistical Decision Functions, Random Processes, 2 vols. 1978. Vol. A. lib. bdg. 68.45 (ISBN 90-277-0852-5, Pub. by Reidel Holland); Vol. B. lib. bdg. 68.45 (ISBN 90-277-0894-0). Kluwer Boston.
Kreyszig, Erwin. Introductory Mathematical Statistics: Principles & Methods. LC 70-107583. 470p. 1970. 29.95 (ISBN 0-471-50730-X). Wiley.
Krishnaiah, P., ed. Multivariate Analysis. 1966. 63.00 (ISBN 0-12-426650-9). Acad Pr.
Kyburg, Henry E., Jr. The Logical Foundations of Statistical Inference. LC 72-92530. (Synthese Library: No. 65). 420p. 1974. lib. bdg. 60.50 (ISBN 90-277-0330-2, Pub. by Reidel Holland); pap. 25.00 (ISBN 90-277-0430-9). Kluwer Boston.
Larsen, R. & Marx, M. Introduction to Mathematical Statistics & Its Applications. 1981. 24.95 (ISBN 0-13-487744-6). P-H.
Larson, Harold J. Introduction to Probability Theory & Statistical Inference. 2nd ed. LC 73-19852. (Ser. in Probability & Mathematical Statistics). 430p. 1974. 24.95 (ISBN 0-471-51781-X). Wiley.
--Introduction to the Theory of Statistics. LC 72-5321. (Probability & Mathematical Statistics Ser.). 242p. 1973. 21.95 (ISBN 0-471-51775-5). Wiley.
Lawless, J. F. Statistical Models & Methods for Lifetime Data. (Wiley Ser. in Probability & Mathematical Statistics). 736p. 1981. 36.95 (ISBN 0-471-08544-8, Pub. by Wiley Interscience). Wiley.
Lehmann, Erich L. Testing Statistical Hypotheses. LC 59-11803. (Illus.). 1959. 30.95 (ISBN 0-471-52470-0). Wiley.
Li, C. Introduction to Experimental Statistics. (Probibility & Statistics Ser.). 1964. text ed. 18.95 (ISBN 0-07-037706-5, C). McGraw.
Lindgren, Bernard W. Statistical Theory. 3rd ed. (Illus.). 576p. 1976. text ed. 23.95 (ISBN 0-02-370830-1). Macmillan.
Longley-Cook, Laurence H. Statistical Problems. LC 76-126340. (Illus., Orig.). 1971. pap. 4.50 (ISBN 0-06-460009-2, CO 9, COS). Har-Row.
Loveday, Robert. Statistical Mathematics. 1973. text ed. 5.95x (ISBN 0-521-08643-4). Cambridge U Pr.
Lukacs, Eugene. Probability & Mathematical Statistics: An Introduction. 1972. text ed. 19.95 (ISBN 0-12-459850-1). Acad Pr.
Lukacs, Eugene & Laha, R. G. Applications of Characteristic Functions. (Griffin's Statistical Monographs & Courses Ser: Vol. 14). 1964. pap. 12.95 (ISBN 0-02-848540-8). Hafner.
Mack, C. Essentials of Statistics for Scientists & Technologists. LC 67-17769. 174p. 1967. 22.50 (ISBN 0-306-30303-5, Plenum Pr). Plenum Pub.
McNeil, Donald R. Interactive Data Analysis: A Practical Primer. LC 76-46571. 1977. text ed. 17.00 (ISBN 0-471-02631-X, Pub. by Wiley-Interscience). Wiley.
Malik, Henrick J. & Mullen, Kenneth. A First Course in Probability & Statistics. LC 72-1941. 1973. text ed. 16.95 (ISBN 0-201-04413-7). A-W.
Mardia, K. V. Statistics & Directional Data. (Probability & Mathematical Statistics Ser.: Vol. 13). 1972. 60.50 (ISBN 0-12-471150-2). Acad Pr.
Mathematics for Fishery Statisticians. (FAO Fisheries Technical Paper: No. 169). 1978. pap. 12.25 (ISBN 92-5-100314-9, F1241, FAO). Unipub.
Mather, K. Statistical Analysis in Biology. 5th ed. 267p. 1972. text ed. 11.95x (ISBN 0-412-21020-7, Pub. by Chapman & Hall England). Methuen Inc.
Medhi, J. P. An Introduction to Stochastic Processes. LC 81-1607. 320p. 1981. 17.95 (ISBN 0-470-27000-4). Halsted Pr.
Mendenhall, William. Introduction to Probability & Statistics. 5th ed. LC 78-15037. (Illus.). 1979. 15.95 (ISBN 0-87872-189-4). Duxbury Pr.
Mendenhall, William & Schaeffer, Richard L. Mathematical Statistics with Applications. LC 72-90584. 1973. pap. text ed. 15.95x (ISBN 0-87872-047-2). Duxbury Pr.
Meyer, Paul L. Introductory Probability & Statistical Applications. 2nd ed. 1970. 17.95 (ISBN 0-201-04710-1). A-W.
Meyer, Stuart L. Data Analysis for Scientists & Engineers. LC 74-8873. (Illus.). 448p. 1975. text ed. 32.95 (ISBN 0-471-59995-6). Wiley.
Miller, Rupert, Jr. Simultaneous Statistical Inference. (Springer Ser. in Statistics). (Illus.). 299p. 1981. 22.00 (ISBN 0-387-90548-0). Springer-Verlag.
Moore, Richard W. Introduction to the Use of Computer Packages for Statistical Analyses. (Illus.). 1978. pap. text ed. 12.95 (ISBN 0-13-480970-X). P-H.
Morris, Carl & Rolph, John. Introduction to Data Analysis & Statistical Inference. (Illus.). 416p. 1981. pap. text ed. 13.95 (ISBN 0-686-69777-4). P-H.
Neff, Norman D. & Naus, Joseph I. The Distribution of the Size of the Maximum Cluster of Points on a Line. LC 74-6283. (Selected Tables in Mathematical Statistics: Vol. 6). 1980. 14.40 (ISBN 0-8218-1906-2). Am Math.
Neyman, Jerzy & Pearson, E. S. The Selected Papers of Jerzy Neyman & E. S. Pearson, 3 vols. Incl. Vol. 1. The Selected Papers of E. S. Pearson. 1966; Vol. 2. Joint Statistical Papers. 1967. 30.00x (ISBN 0-520-00991-6); Vol. 3. A Selection of Early Statistical Papers of J. Neyman. 1967. 32.50x (ISBN 0-520-00992-4). U of Cal Pr.
Norcliffe, G. B. Inferential Statistics for Geographers: An Introduction. LC 77-9427. 272p. 1981. pap. 14.95 (ISBN 0-470-27146-9). Halsted Pr.
Odeh, R., et al, eds. Pocketbook of Statistical Distribution. (Statistics: Textbooks and Monographs Ser.). 1977. 9.95 (ISBN 0-8247-6515-X). Dekker.
Olkin, Ingram, et al, eds. Contributions to Probability & Statistics: Essays in Honor of Harold Hotelling. 1960. 15.00x (ISBN 0-8047-0596-8). Stanford U Pr.
O'Meara, Timothy. Symplectic Groups. (Mathematical Surveys Ser.). 1978. 30.40 (ISBN 0-686-65397-1, SURV 16). Am Math.
Orkin, Michael & Drogin, Richard. Vital Statistics. Orig. Title: Introductory Probability & Statistics. (Illus.). 352p. 1974. text ed. 15.95 (ISBN 0-07-047720-5, C); instructor's manual 3.50 (ISBN 0-07-047721-3). McGraw.
Ott. Introduction to Statistical Methods & Data Analysis. LC 77-4722. 1977. text ed. 15.95 (ISBN 0-87872-134-7). Duxbury Pr.
Pearson, E. S. & Kendall, M. G. Studies in the History of Statistics & Probability. (Illus.). 1970. 18.95 (ISBN 0-02-850110-1). Hafner.
Pennsylvania University Bicentennial Conference. Fluid Mechanics & Statistical Methods in Engineering. Dryden, Hugh & Von Karman, Theodore, eds. LC 68-26203. Repr. of 1941 ed. 11.50 (ISBN 0-8046-0359-6). Kennikat.
Peterson, R. Exercises in Statistical Inference. pap. 7.95x (ISBN 0-88246-085-4). Oreg St U Bkstrs.
Phillips, David S. Basic Statistics for Health Science Students. LC 77-13865. (Psychology Ser.). (Illus.). 1978. text ed. 14.95x (ISBN 0-7167-0051-4); pap. text ed. 7.95x (ISBN 0-7167-0050-6). W H Freeman.
Pitman, E. J. Some Basic Theory for Statistical Inference. LC 78-11921. (Monographs on Applied Probability & Statistics). 105p. 1979. text ed. 14.50x (ISBN 0-412-21720-1, Pub. by Chapman & Hall England). Methuen Inc.
Polish Academy of Sciences-Institute of Mathematics, ed. Mathematical Statistics. (Banach Center Publications: Vol. 6). (Illus.). 376p. 1980. 52.50x (ISBN 83-01-01493-8). Intl Pubns Serv.
Raktoe & Hubert. Basic Applied Statistics. (Statistics; Textbook & Monograph Ser.: Vol. 27). 1979. 14.50 (ISBN 0-8247-6537-0). Dekker.
Rao, C. Radhakrishna. Linear Statistical Inference & Its Applications. 2nd ed. LC 72-13093. (Ser. in Probability & Mathematical Statistics). 608p. 1973. 40.50 (ISBN 0-471-70823-2). Wiley.
Reason, Peter & Rowan, John. Human Inquiry: A Sourcebook of New Paradigm Research. LC 80-41585. 1981. write for info. (ISBN 0-471-27936-6, Pub. by Wiley Interscience). Wiley.
Reinhardt, Howard E. & Loftsgaarden, Don O. Elementary Probability & Statistical Reasoning. 1976. text ed. 16.95x (ISBN 0-669-08300-3). Heath.
Revesz, P., et al, eds. First Pannonian Symposium on Mathematical Statistics: Proceedings. (Lecture Notes in Statistics Ser.: Vol. 8). 308p. 1981. pap. 19.80 (ISBN 0-387-90583-9). Springer-Verlag.
Rickmers, A. D. & Todd, H. N. Statistics: An Introduction. 1967. 16.95 (ISBN 0-07-052616-8, C); ans. 3.95 (ISBN 0-07-052622-2). McGraw.
Rietz, Henry L. Mathematical Statistics. (Carus Monograph: No. 3). 181p. 1927. 12.50 (ISBN 0-88385-003-6). Math Assn.
Rohatgi, Vijay K. An Introduction to Probability Theory & Mathematical Statistics. LC 75-14378. (Series in Probability & Mathematical Statistics: Probability & Mathematical Statistics Section). 704p. 1976. 36.00 (ISBN 0-471-73135-8, Pub by Wiley-Interscience). Wiley.
Roussas, G. G. Contiguity of Probability Measures: Some Applications in Statistics. LC 71-171682. (Cambridge Tracts in Mathematics & Mathematical Physics: No. 63). 1972. 44.50 (ISBN 0-521-08354-0). Cambridge U Pr.
Roussas, George G. A First Course in Mathematical Statistics. LC 71-183673. 1973. text ed. 24.95 (ISBN 0-201-06522-3). A-W.
Rustagi, Jaggish S., ed. Optimizing Methods in Statistics: Proceedings. 1971. 55.00 (ISBN 0-12-604550-X). Acad Pr.
Salmon, Wesley C., et al. Statistical Explanation & Statistical Relevance. LC 77-158191. 1971. pap. 3.95x (ISBN 0-8229-5225-4). U of Pittsburgh Pr.
Scheffe, Henry. Analysis of Variance. LC 59-14994. (Wiley Series in Probability & Mathematical Statistics). (Illus.). 1959. 34.00 (ISBN 0-471-75834-5). Wiley.
Schmetterer, L. Introduction to Mathematical Statistics. Wickwire, K., tr. from Ger. LC 73-15290. (Grundlehren der Mathematischen Wissenschaften: Vol. 202). (Illus.). 540p. 1974. 64.60 (ISBN 0-387-06154-1). Springer-Verlag.
Seidenfeld, Teddy. Philosophical Problems of Statistical Inference. (Theory & Decision Library: No. 22). 1979. lib. bdg. 37.00 (ISBN 90-277-0965-3, Pub. by Reidel Holland). Kluwer Boston.
Selected Tables in Mathematical Statistics, Vol. 1. rev. ed. LC 71-111981. 1973. 20.80 (ISBN 0-8218-1901-1, TABLES-1). Am Math.
Selected Tables in Mathematical Statistics, Vol. 5. LC 74-6283. 1977. 24.40 (ISBN 0-8218-1905-4, TABLES-5). Am Math.
Selected Translations in Mathematical Statistics & Probability, Vol. 14. LC 61-9803. 1978. 50.80 (ISBN 0-8218-1464-8, STAPRO-14). Am Math.
Sen, P. K. Sequential Nonparametrics: Invariance Principles & Statistical Inference. LC 81-4432. (Probability & Mathematical Statistics Ser.). 350p. 1981. 30.00 (ISBN 0-471-06013-5, Pub. by Wiley-Interscience). Wiley.
Serfling, Robert J. Approximation Theorems of Mathematical Statistics. LC 80-13493. (Wiley Ser. in Probability & Mathematical Statistics). 371p. 1980. 34.95 (ISBN 0-471-02403-1). Wiley.
Spiegel, Murray R. Probability & Statistics. 304p. (Orig.). 1975. pap. text ed. 6.95 (ISBN 0-07-060220-4, SP). McGraw.
Steel, Robert G. & Torrie, James H. Principles & Procedures of Statistics: With Special Reference to the Biological Sciences. 1960. text ed. 19.95 (ISBN 0-07-060925-X, C); ans. bk. 3.50 (ISBN 0-07-060923-3). McGraw.
Steklov Institute of Mathematics, Academy of Sciences, U S S R, No. 104. Studies in Mathematical Statistics: Proceedings. Linnick, J. V., ed. 1971. 35.60 (ISBN 0-8218-3004-X, STEKLO-104). Am Math.
Steklov Institute of Mathematics, Academy of Sciences, U S S R, No. 111. Theoretical Problems of Mathematical Statistics: Proceedings. Linnik, Ju V., ed. LC 72-5245. 320p. 1971. 46.80 (ISBN 0-8218-3011-2, STEKLO-111). Am Math.
Stigler, Stephen M. & Cohen, I. Bernard, eds. American Contributions to Mathematical Statistics in the Nineteenth Century: An Original Anthology, 2 vols. LC 79-8002. (Three Centuries of Science in America Ser.). (Illus.). 1980. Set. lib. bdg. 55.00x (ISBN 0-405-12590-9). Arno.
Thompson, Colin J. Mathematical Statistical Mechanics. LC 78-70319. 1979. 17.50x (ISBN 0-691-08219-7); pap. 7.50 (ISBN 0-691-08220-0). Princeton U Pr.
Upton, Graham J. The Analysis of Cross-Tabulated Data. LC 78-4210. (Probability & Mathematical Statistics: Applied Section Ser.). 1978. 40.25 (ISBN 0-471-99659-9, Pub. by Wiley-Interscience). Wiley.
Van Der Waerden, B. L. Mathematical Statistics. LC 72-84145. (Grundlehren der Mathematischen Wissenschaften: Vol. 156). (Illus.). 1969. 35.70 (ISBN 0-387-04507-4). Springer-Verlag.
Van Dobben De Bruyn, C. S. Cumulative Sum Tests. (Griffin's Statistical Monographs & Courses: Vol. 24). 1968. pap. 8.25 (ISBN 0-02-843830-2). Hafner.
Wald, Abraham. Selected Papers in Statistics & Probability. 1955. 25.00x (ISBN 0-8047-0493-7). Stanford U Pr.
--Statistical Decision Functions. LC 77-113154. 1971. Repr. of 1950 ed. text ed. 7.50 (ISBN 0-8284-0243-4). Chelsea Pub.
Wiener, Norbert. Cybernetics: Or Control & Communication in the Animal & the Machine. 2nd ed. (Illus., Orig.). 1961. 17.50x (ISBN 0-262-23007-0); pap. 5.95 (ISBN 0-262-73009-X). MIT Pr.
Wolfowitz, J. Selected Papers. 642p. 1980. 35.00 (ISBN 0-387-90463-8). Springer-Verlag.
Wonnacott, Thomas H. & Wonnacott, Ronald J. Introductory Statistics. 3rd ed. (Wiley Ser. in Probability & Mathematical Statistics). 1977. text ed. 26.95 (ISBN 0-471-95982-0). Wiley.
Zacks, Shelemyahu. Theory of Statistical Inference. LC 77-132227. (Ser. in Probability & Mathematical Statistics). 1971. 56.00 (ISBN 0-471-98103-6, Pub. by Wiley-Interscience). Wiley.
Zubrzycki, Stefan. Lectures in Probability Theory & Mathematical Statistics. 1973. 22.50 (ISBN 0-444-00120-4, North Holland). Elsevier.

MATHEMATICAL STATISTICS–BIBLIOGRAPHY

Savage, I. Richard. Bibliography of Nonparametric Statistics. LC 62-11403. 1962. pap. 6.50x (ISBN 0-674-07101-8). Harvard U Pr.

MATHEMATICAL STATISTICS–PROGRAMMED INSTRUCTION

Brown, Foster F., et al. Statistical Concepts: A Basic Program. 2nd ed. 160p. 1975. pap. text ed. 8.95 scp (ISBN 0-06-040988-6, HarpC). Har-Row.

MATHEMATICAL STATISTICS–TABLES, ETC.

see also Numbers, Random

Mardia, K. V. Families of Bivariate Distributions. Stuart, Alan, ed. (Griffin's Statistical Monographs & Courses Ser: No. 27). 1970. pap. 9.75 (ISBN 0-02-848810-5). Hafner.
Newman, T. G. & Odell, P. L. Generation of Random Variates. Stuart, Alan, ed. (Griffin's Statistical Monographs & Courses Ser: No. 29). 1971. pap. 7.50 (ISBN 0-02-849680-9). Hafner.

Rohlf, F. James & Sokal, Robert R. Statistical Tables. LC 68-54121. (Biology Ser.). (Illus.). 1969. text ed. 19.95x (ISBN 0-7167-0673-3); pap. text ed. 9.95x (ISBN 0-7167-0664-4). W H Freeman.

MATHEMATICAL SYMBOLS
see Abbreviations

MATHEMATICAL WEATHER FORECASTING
see Numerical Weather Forecasting

MATHEMATICIANS
see also Mathematics As a Profession

Al-Daffa, A. A. Great Arab & Muslim Mathematicians: Arabic Edition. 1978. 13.95 (ISBN 0-471-04611-6); pap. write for info. (ISBN 0-471-06327-4). Wiley.
Bell, Eric T. Men of Mathematics. (Illus.). 1937. 12.95 (ISBN 0-671-46400-0); pap. 6.95 (ISBN 0-671-46401-9). S&S.
Butzer, P. L. & Feher, F., eds. E. B. Christoffel: The Influence of His Work in Mathematics & the Physical Sciences. (Illus.). 656p. 1981. 65.00 (ISBN 3-7643-1162-2). Birkhauser.
Chern, S. S. Complex Manifolds Without Potential Theory. (Universitext Ser.). 1979. 12.60 (ISBN 0-387-90422-0). Springer-Verlag.
Christoffel-Symposium. (WK Ser.: No. 36). 650p. 1980. write for info. (ISBN 3-7643-1162-2). Birkhauser.
Cohen, I. Bernard, ed. Benjamin Peirce: Father of Pure Mathematics in America. An Original Anthology. LC 79-7981. (Three Centuries of Science in America Ser.). (Illus.). 1980. lib. bdg. 28.00x (ISBN 0-405-12563-1). Arno.
Dick, A. Emmy Noether: 1882-1935. (Supplement Ser.: No. 13). 72p. (Ger.). 1970. pap. 12.00 (ISBN 3-7643-0519-3). Birkhauser.
Dick, Auguste. Emmy Noether (1882-1935) 192p. 1980. pap. 12.95 (ISBN 3-7643-3019-8). Birkhauser.
Ferrante, J. & Rackoff, C. W. The Computational Complexity of Logical Theories. (Lecture Notes in Mathematics Ser.: Vol. 718). 1979. pap. 15.00 (ISBN 0-387-09501-2). Springer-Verlag.
Hardy, Godfrey H. Ramanujan. 3rd ed. LC 59-10268. 1978. 9.95 (ISBN 0-8284-0136-5). Chelsea Pub.
Hofmann, Joseph E. History of Mathematics to Eighteen Hundred. (Quality Paperback: No. 144). 1967. pap. 2.95 (ISBN 0-8226-0144-3). Littlefield.
Husen, Torsten, ed. International Study of Achievement in Mathematics, 2 vols. (Orig.). 1967. Vol. 1. 10.95 (ISBN 0-686-74170-6); Vol. 2. 10.95 (ISBN 0-686-74171-4). Krieger.
Infeld, Leopold. Whom the Gods Love: The Story of Evariste Galois, Vol. 7. LC 78-3709. (Classics in Mathematics Education Ser.). (Illus.). 1978. Repr. of 1948 ed. 11.00 (ISBN 0-87353-125-6). NCTM.
Kennedy, Hubert. Peano: Life & Works of Giuseppe Peano. (Studies in the History of Modern Science: No. 4). 227p. 1980. lib. bdg. 34.00 (ISBN 90-277-1067-8, Pub. by Reidel Holland); pap. 14.95 (ISBN 90-277-1068-6, Pub. by Reidel Holland). Kluwer Boston.
Klarner, David A., ed. The Mathematical Gardiner. 382p. 1980. 22.45x (ISBN 0-534-98015-5). Wadsworth Pub.
Kovalevskaya, S. A Russian Childhood. (Illus.). 1979. 17.10 (ISBN 0-387-90348-8). Springer-Verlag.
Lazar, A. L. & Taylor, D. C. Multipliers of Pedersen's Ideal. LC 75-44302. (Memoirs: No. 169). 1976. pap. 12.00 (ISBN 0-8218-1869-4, MEMO-169). Am Math.
Morgan, Bryan. Men & Discoveries in Mathematics. 235p. 1980. 15.00x (ISBN 0-7195-2587-X, Pub. by Murray Pubs England). State Mutual Bk.
--Men & Discoveries in Mathematics. 1972. 10.95 (ISBN 0-7195-2587-X). Transatlantic.
National Council of Teachers of Mathematics. Directory of NCTM Individual Members. 1980. 20.00 (ISBN 0-87353-168-X). NCTM.
Newell, Virginia K., et al, eds. Black Mathematicians & Their Works. 1980. 18.00 (ISBN 0-8059-2556-2); pap. 12.50 (ISBN 0-8059-2677-1). Dorrance.
Osen, Lynn M. Women in Mathematics. 224p. 1974. 15.00x (ISBN 0-262-15014-X); pap. 4.95 (ISBN 0-262-65009-6). MIT Pr.
Oxtoby, J. C., et al, eds. John von Neuman, 1903-1957. 130p. 1978. pap. 8.40 soft cover (ISBN 0-8218-0021-3). Am Math.
Perl, Teri. Math Equals: Biography of Women Mathematicians & Related Activities. (gr. 7-12). 1978. 10.75 (ISBN 0-201-05709-3, Sch Div). A-W.
Rapport, Samuel & Wright, Helen, eds. Mathematics. LC 62-17998. (N Y U Lib. of Science Ser). 1963. 7.95x (ISBN 0-8147-0356-9). NYU Pr.
Rudman, Jack. Mathematician. (Career Examination Ser.: C-479). (Cloth bdg. avail. on request). pap. 10.00 (ISBN 0-8373-0479-2). Natl Learning.
Scott, Joseph F. The Mathematical Work of John Wallis. abr. ed. LC 80-85524. (Illus.). xii, 240p. 1981. text ed. 12.95 (ISBN 0-8284-0314-7). Chelsea Pub.
Singh, Jagjit. Memoirs of a Mathematician Manque. 176p. 1980. text ed. 15.00x (ISBN 0-7069-1128-8, Pub. by Vikas India). Advent NY.
Stonaker, Frances B. Famous Mathematicians. LC 66-15159. (gr. 4-9). 1966. 8.95 (ISBN 0-397-30866-3). Lippincott.
Tarwater, J. Dalton, et al. Men & Institutions in American Mathematics. (Graduate Studies: No. 13). (Orig.). 1976. pap. 6.00 (ISBN 0-89672-023-3). Tex Tech Pr.
Turnbull, Herbert Westren. The Great Mathematicians. LC 61-16934. (Illus.). 1961. usa 10.00x (ISBN 0-8147-0419-0). NYU Pr.
Ulam, S. M. Adventures of a Mathematician. LC 75-20133. 1976. pap. 4.95 (ISBN 0-684-15064-6, SL728, ScribT). Scribner.

MATHEMATICS
see also Algebra; Arithmetic; Ausdehnungslehre; Axioms; Binary System (Mathematics); Biomathematics; Business Mathematics; Calculus; Combinations; Congruences (Geometry); Conic Sections; Coordinates; Curves; Determinants; Dynamics; Economics, Mathematical; Engineering Mathematics; Equations; Errors, Theory of; Forms (Mathematics); Fourth Dimension; Fractions; Functions; Game Theory; Geography, Mathematical; Geometry; Graphic Methods; Groups, Theory of; Harmonic Analysis; Hyperspace; Induction (Mathematics); Kinematics; Least Squares; Logic, Symbolic and Mathematical; Maxima and Minima; Mensuration; Metric System; Numbers, Theory of; Numerals; Numeration; Permutations; Potential, Theory of; Probabilities; Projection; Quaternions; Sequences (Mathematics); Series; Set Theory; Shop Mathematics; Statics; Transformations (Mathematics); Trigonometry; Vector Analysis; also headings beginning with the word Mathematical

Ablon, L. J., et al. Series in Mathematics Modules, Pts. 7, 8, 9, 10, 11. Incl. Module 7. Trigonometry with Applications. LC 75-262499 (ISBN 0-8465-0261-5); Module 8. Exponents & Logarithms. LC 75-35281 (ISBN 0-8465-0262-3); Module 9. Advanced Algebraic Techniques (ISBN 0-8465-0263-1). 1976. pap. 3.95 (ISBN 0-686-67410-3). Benjamin-Cummings.
Ablon, Leon, et al. Series in Mathematics Modules, 5 modules. 1981. softbound 3.95 ea. Module 1 (ISBN 0-8053-0131-3). Module 2 (ISBN 0-8053-0132-1). Module 3 (ISBN 0-8053-0133-X). Module 4 (ISBN 0-8053-0134-8). Module 5 (ISBN 0-8053-0135-6). Benjamin-Cummings.
--The Steps in Mathematics Modules One Thru Five. 1981. pap. 19.75 (ISBN 0-8053-0140-2). Benjamin-Cummings.
Ablon, Leon J., ed. Series in Mathematics Modules. Incl. Module 2A. Practical Mathematics. Siner, Helen B. LC 75-12083. 1975. pap. text ed. 3.25 (ISBN 0-8465-6714-8). Benjamin-Cummings.
Abramowitz, Milton & Stegun, Irene A., eds. Handbook of Mathematical Functions. LC 65-12253. 1965. lib. bdg. 24.50x (ISBN 0-88307-589-X). Gannon.
Acosta, Antonio A. & Calvo, Joraida. Matematicas: Repaso Para el Examen De Equivalencia De la Escuela Superior En Espanol. rev. ed. LC 80-25182. 256p. (Orig.). 1981. pap. 5.00 (ISBN 0-668-04821-2, 4821-2). Arco.
Adams, W. Fundamentals of Mathematics for Business, Social, & Life Sciences. 1979. 21.95 (ISBN 0-13-341073-0). P-H.
Adler, Irving. The Impossible in Mathematics. LC 77-33757. 1957. pap. 1.70 (ISBN 0-87353-062-4). NCTM.
Adler, R. L. & Weiss, B. Similarity of Automorphisms of the Torus. LC 52-42839. (Memoirs: No. 98). 1970. pap. 6.40 (ISBN 0-8218-1298-X, MEMO-98). Am Math.
Administrative Directory, 1981. LC 80-17018. 12.60 (ISBN 0-8218-0075-2). Am Math.
Afraimovic, V. S., et al. Transactions of the Moscow Mathematical Society, Vol. 28 (1973) LC 65-7413. 1975. 64.80 (ISBN 0-8218-1628-4, MOSCOW-28). Am Math.
Ahlfors, Lars. Conformal Invariants. (Higher Mathematics Ser.). (Illus.). 168p. 1973. 22.00 (ISBN 0-07-000659-8, C). McGraw.
Airey, Dennis D. Basic Mathematics. 1976. coil bdg. 7.50 (ISBN 0-88252-021-0). Paladin Hse.
Al-Daffa, A. A. Modern Mathematics & Intellect: Arabic Edition. 1979. pap. text ed. 5.50 (ISBN 0-471-05139-X). Wiley.
Aleksandrov, A. D., et al, eds. Mathematics: Its Content, Methods, & Meaning, 3 Vols. 2nd ed. Gould, S. H., tr. 1969. pap. 8.95 ea.; Vol. 1. pap. (ISBN 0-262-51005-7); Vol. 2. pap. (ISBN 0-262-51004-9); Vol. 3. pap. (ISBN 0-262-51003-0); pap. 25.00 set (ISBN 0-262-51014-6). MIT Pr.
Alger, Philip L. Mathematics for Science & Engineering. 2nd ed. LC 69-11937. (Illus.). 1969. 19.50 (ISBN 0-07-001050-1, P&RB). McGraw.
Ali, N., et al. Transactions of the Moscow Mathematical Society, 1975. LC 65-4713. 1977. 54.00 (ISBN 0-8218-1632-2, MOSCOW-32). Am Math.
Allard, S. Metals: Thermal & Mechanical Data. 1969. text ed. 105.00 (ISBN 0-08-006588-0). Pergamon.
Allendoerfer, Carl B. & Oakley, Cletus O. Fundamentals of Freshman Mathematics. 3rd ed. (Illus.). 1972. text ed. 15.95 (ISBN 0-07-001366-7, C); instructor's manual 3.50 (ISBN 0-07-001367-5). McGraw.
--Principles of Mathematics. 3rd ed. LC 69-12258. (Illus.). 1969. text ed. 15.50 (ISBN 0-07-001390-X, C); instructor's manual 3.95 (ISBN 0-07-001386-1). McGraw.
Allendoerfer, Carl B., et al, eds. Fiftieth Anniversary Issue. 109p. 1967. pap. 2.00 (ISBN 0-88385-402-3). Math Assn.
Anderson, Paul, et al. Addison Wesley General Mathematics: Level One. 1980. text ed. 13.40 (ISBN 0-201-03825-0, Sch Div); tchr's. manual 15.28 (ISBN 0-201-03826-9, Sch Div); tests & d.m. avail. A-W.
Andree, Josephine & Andree, Richard. Cryptarithms. 1978. pap. 2.95 (ISBN 0-686-23790-0); instructor's manual 2.00 (ISBN 0-686-28564-6). Mu Alpha Theta.
Andree, Josephine & Andree, Richard V. Cryptarithms. (gr. 9-12). 1978. pap. 3.60 (ISBN 0-686-65435-8); tchr's. manual 2.50 (ISBN 0-686-65436-6). NCTM.
Andree, Josephine P. Lines from the O. U. Mathematics Letter, Vol. 2: Theory of Games. pap. 1.00 (ISBN 0-686-01239-9). Mu Alpha Theta.
Andree, Josephine P., ed. Chips from the Mathematical Log. (YA) 1966. pap. 2.00 (ISBN 0-686-00750-6). Mu Alpha Theta.
--Lines from the O. U. Mathematics Letter, Vol. 1: Number Extensions. pap. 1.25 (ISBN 0-686-01238-0). Mu Alpha Theta.
--Lines from the O. U. Mathematics Letter, Vol. 3: Geometric Extensions. pap. 1.25 (ISBN 0-686-01240-2). Mu Alpha Theta.
Andree, Josephine P, ed. More Chips from the Mathematical Log. pap. 1.25 (ISBN 0-686-00324-1). Mu Alpha Theta.
Andres, P. G., et al. Basic Mathematics for Engineers. LC 55-8369. 776p. 1944. text ed. 27.50x (ISBN 0-471-02937-8). Wiley.
--Basic Mathematics for Science & Engineering. LC 55-8369. 846p. 1955. text ed. 29.95 (ISBN 0-471-02970-X). Wiley.
Andrews, F. Emerson. Numbers, Please. 2nd enlarged ed. LC 77-20492. 1977. pap. 5.25x (ISBN 0-8077-2545-5). Tchrs Coll.
Angel, Allen R. & Porter, Stuart R. Survey of Mathematics: With Applications. LC 80-19471. (Mathematics Ser.). (Illus.). 576p. 1981. text ed. write for info. (ISBN 0-201-00045-8). A-W.
Anton, Howard & Kolman, Bernard. Applied Finite Mathematics. 2nd ed. 558p. 1978. 16.95 (ISBN 0-12-059565-6); instr's manual 3.00 (ISBN 0-12-059564-8). Acad Pr.
--Applied Finite Mathematics with Calculus. 760p. 1978. 17.95 (ISBN 0-12-059560-5); instrs'. manual 3.00 (ISBN 0-12-059567-2). Acad Pr.
Applications in School Mathematics. (National Council of Teachers of Mathematics Yearbook). 1979. 13.95 (ISBN 0-87353-139-6). NCTM.
Arco Editorial Board. Mathematics, Simplified & Self Taught. 5th ed. LC 65-21203. (Orig.). 1968. pap. 5.95 (ISBN 0-668-00567-X); lib. bdg. 10.00 (ISBN 0-668-01399-0). Arco.
Arendsen, Carl. Business Mathematics. 450p. 1980. write for info. (ISBN 0-87150-293-3, 2312). Prindle.
Arfken, George. Mathematical Methods for Physicists. 2nd ed. 1970. text ed. 25.95 (ISBN 0-12-059851-5). Acad Pr.
Armstrong, James W. Elements of Mathematics. 2nd ed. 1976. text ed. 16.95 (ISBN 0-02-303910-8, 30391). Macmillan.
Ashlock, Robert B. & Humphrey, James H. Teaching Elementary School Mathematics Through Motor Learning. 168p. 1976. 16.25 (ISBN 0-398-03578-4). C C Thomas.
Athreya, K. B. & Ney, P. E. Branching Processes. LC 72-75819. (Die Grundlehren der Mathematischen Wissenshaften: Vol. 196). 300p. 1972. 31.00 (ISBN 0-387-05790-0). Springer-Verlag.
Auslander, Louis, et al. Mathematics Through Statistics. 1973. pap. 6.95 (ISBN 0-683-00281-3, Pub. by W & W). Krieger.
--Mathematics Through Statistics. LC 79-9749. 224p. 1979. pap. 8.50 (ISBN 0-88275-949-3). Krieger.
Author Index of Zentralblatt fuer Mathematik, und Ihre Grenzgebiete, 1931-1939, 2 pts. 126.00 (ISBN 0-685-64497-9, MREVIN 131-40). Am Math.
Author Index to Soviet Mathematics-Doklady, 1960-69. 12.40 (ISBN 0-8218-0050-7, DOKLIN-1). Am Math.
Averbhh, V. I., et al. Transactions of the Moscow Mathematical Society, Vol. 27 (1972) LC 65-7413. 1974. 54.40 (ISBN 0-8218-1627-6, MOSCOW-27). Am Math.
Averbuh, V. I., et al. Transactions of the Moscow Mathematical Society, Vol. 24 (1971) LC 65-7413. 1974. 61.60 (ISBN 0-8218-1624-1, MOSCOW-24). Am Math.
Ayres, Frank, Jr. First Year College Mathematics. (Schaum's Outline Ser). (Orig.). 1958. pap. 5.95 (ISBN 0-07-002650-5, SP). McGraw.
Bachmann, F. & Schmidt, E. N-Gons. Garner, C. W., tr. LC 70-185699. 208p. 1975. 20.00x (ISBN 0-8020-1843-2). U of Toronto Pr.
Bailey, Frank A. Basic Mathematics. 1977. pap. 10.95x (ISBN 0-673-15064-X). Scott F.
Bak, Thor A. & Lichtenberg, J. Mathematics for Scientists, 3 vols. Incl. Vol. 1. Vectors, Tensors, & Groups (ISBN 0-8053-0431-2); Vol. 2. Functions of One & Several Real Variables (ISBN 0-8053-0432-0); Vol. 3. Series, Differential Equations, & Complex Functions (ISBN 0-8053-0433-9). 1967. pap. 5.00 ea. (Adv Bk Prog). Benjamin-Cummings.
Baker, C. C. Introduction to Mathematics. LC 66-20198. (Illus.). 1966. pap. 1.65 (ISBN 0-668-01479-2). Arco.
Baratta-Lorton, Mary. Mathematics: A Way of Thinking. new ed. (gr. 1-8). 1977. tchr's. ed. 19.75 (ISBN 0-201-04322-X, Sch Div). A-W.
--Mathematics Their Way. (gr. k-2). 1976. tchr's ed 20.00 (ISBN 0-201-04320-3, Sch Div). A-W.
Barbasin, E. A., et al. Twelve Papers on Analysis, Applied Mathematics & Algebraic Topology. LC 51-5559. (Translations Ser.: No. 2, Vol. 25). 1963. 24.40 (ISBN 0-8218-1725-6, TRANS 2-25). Am Math.
Barron, Linda. Mathematics Experiences for the Early Childhood Years. 1979. pap. text ed. 12.95 (ISBN 0-675-08284-6). Merrill.
Barrow, Isaac. Usefulness of Mathematical Learning. Kirby, J., tr. (Illus.). 458p. 1970. Repr. of 1734 ed. 29.00x (ISBN 0-7146-1591-9, F Cass Co). Biblio Dist.
Bashaw, W. L. Mathematics for Statistics. LC 69-16123. 326p. 1969. pap. 15.95 (ISBN 0-471-05531-X). Wiley.
Basic Mathematics Simplified. 4th ed. LC 76-3941. (Illus.). 368p. 1977. 15.00 (ISBN 0-8273-1270-9); pap. 11.20 (ISBN 0-8273-1269-5); instructor's guide 3.00 (ISBN 0-8273-1271-7). Delmar.
Bear, H. S. Lectures on Gleason Parts. (Lecture Notes in Mathematics: Vol. 121). 1970. 10.70 (ISBN 0-387-04910-X). Springer-Verlag.
Beck, Anatole, et al. Excursions into Mathematics. LC 68-57963. (Illus.). 1969. text ed. 17.95x (ISBN 0-87901-004-5). H S Worth.
Begel, E. G. Critical Variables in Mathematics Education: Findings from a Survey of the Empirical Literature. 1979. 8.00 (ISBN 0-88385-430-9). NCTM.
Behnke, H., et al, eds. Fundamentals of Mathematics, 3 vols. Gould, S. H., tr. Incl. Vol. 1. Foundations of Mathematics: The Real Number System & Algebra. (ISBN 0-262-02048-3); Vol. 2. Geometry. (ISBN 0-262-02069-6); Vol. 3. Analysis. (ISBN 0-262-02049-1). 1974. Set. 55.00x (ISBN 0-262-02143-9); 20.00x ea. MIT Pr.
Bell, K. W. & Parrish, R. G. Computational Skills with Applications. 448p. 1975. pap. text ed. 14.95x (ISBN 0-669-91082-1); instructor's manual 1.95 (ISBN 0-669-93237-X). Heath.
Bellman, Richard & Cooke, Kenneth. Modern Elementary Differential Equations. 2nd ed. (Mathematics Ser). 1971. text ed. 19.95 (ISBN 0-201-00511-5). A-W.
Bello, Ignacio. Contemporary Basic Mathematical Skills. (Illus.). 1978. pap. text ed. 17.50 scp (ISBN 0-06-040613-5, HarpC); solution & test manual free (ISBN 0-06-360610-0). Har-Row.
Benedetto, John J. Real Variable & Integration. (Illus.). 1976. pap. 32.50 (ISBN 3-5190-2209-5). Adler.
Benice, Daniel D. Mathematics: Ideas & Applications. 1978. 14.95 (ISBN 0-12-088250-7); instrs'. ed. 3.00 (ISBN 0-12-088252-3). Acad Pr.
Bennett, Albert B & Nelson, Leonard T. Mathematics: An Activity Approach. 1979. text ed. 12.50 (ISBN 0-205-06518-X, 5665183); instr's man. 5.95 (ISBN 0-205-06540-6, 566540X). Allyn.
Berezanskii, Ju. M., et al. Twelve Papers on Analysis & Applied Mathematics. LC 51-5559. (Translations Ser.: No. 2, Vol. 35). 1964. 25.60 (ISBN 0-8218-1735-3, TRANS 2-35). Am Math.
Berkeley, Edmund C. Guide to Mathematics for the Intelligent Non-Mathematician. 1967. pap. 2.45 (ISBN 0-671-20027-5, Fireside). S&S.
Berlinghoff, William P., et al. A Mathematical Panorama: Topics for the Liberal Arts. 1980. text ed. 16.95 (ISBN 0-669-02423-6). Heath.

Berman, Elizabeth. Mathematics Revealed. 546p. 1979. 12.95 (ISBN 0-12-092450-1); instrs'. manual 3.00 (ISBN 0-12-092452-8). Acad Pr.

Bernstein, A. L. & Wells, D. W. Trouble-Shooting Mathematics Skills. rev. ed. (gr. 7-12). 1969. text ed. 11.56 (ISBN 0-03-068735-7, HoltC); tchrs' annot. ed. 13.12 (ISBN 0-03-068740-3). HR&W.

Biggs, J. B. Mathematics & the Conditions of Learning: A Study of Arithmetic in the Primary School. (General Ser.). 1970. Repr. of 1967 ed. text ed. 24.75x (ISBN 0-901225-24-X, NFER). Humanities.

Bila, Dennis, et al. Mathematics for Technical Occupations. (Illus.). 1978. pap. text ed. 17.95 (ISBN 0-87626-572-7); pap. 2.95 study guide (ISBN 0-87626-143-8). Winthrop.

Billingsley, Patrick. Ergodic Theory & Information. LC 78-2442. 210p. 1978. Repr. of 1965 ed. lib. bdg. 15.00 (ISBN 0-88275-666-4). Krieger.

--Ergodic Theory & Information. LC 78-2442. 210p. 1978. Repr. of 1965 ed. lib. bdg. 15.00 (ISBN 0-88275-666-4). Krieger.

Bird & May. Mathematics Three Checkbook. 1981. text ed. price not set (ISBN 0-408-00634-X); price not set limp bdg. (ISBN 0-408-00611-0). Butterworth.

--Mathematics Two: Checkbook. 1981. limp bdg. 8.95 (ISBN 0-408-00610-2). Butterworth.

Bitter, et al. Classroom Management Guide, Grade 1. (McGraw-Hill Mathematics Ser.). 1981. 1.28 (ISBN 0-07-006091-6). McGraw.

--Classroom Management Guide, Grade 3. (McGraw-Hill Mathematics Ser.). 1981. 1.28 (ISBN 0-686-75985-0); of 4 desktop duplicators 26.37 set (ISBN 0-07-079023-X); duplicator 3A 6.72 (ISBN 0-07-006043-6); duplicator 3B 6.72 (ISBN 0-07-006053-3); duplicator 3C 6.72 (ISBN 0-07-006063-0); duplicator 3D 6.72 (ISBN 0-07-006073-8). McGraw.

--Classroom Management Guide, Grade 5. (McGraw-Hill Mathematics Ser.). 1981. 1.28 (ISBN 0-07-006095-9); of 5 desktop duplicators 32.94 set (ISBN 0-07-079025-6); duplicator 5A 6.72 (ISBN 0-07-006045-2); duplicator 5B 6.72 (ISBN 0-07-006055-X); duplicator 5C 6.72 (ISBN 0-07-006065-7); duplicator 5D 6.72 (ISBN 0-07-006075-4); duplicator 5E 6.72 (ISBN 0-07-006085-1). McGraw.

--Classroom Management Guide, Grade 7. (McGraw-Hill Mathematics Ser.). 1981. 1.28 (ISBN 0-07-006097-5); Extra Practics Kwebster masters, level 7 25.68 (ISBN 0-07-005747-8); of 5 desktop duplicators 32.94 set (ISBN 0-07-079027-2); duplicator 7A 6.72 (ISBN 0-07-006047-9); duplicator 7B 6.72 (ISBN 0-07-006057-6); duplicator 7C 6.72 (ISBN 0-07-006067-3); duplicator 7D 6.72 (ISBN 0-07-006077-0); duplicator 7E 6.72 (ISBN 0-07-006087-8). McGraw.

--Classroom Management Guide, Grade 8. (McGraw-Hill Mathematics Ser.). 1981. 1.28 (ISBN 0-07-006098-3); Extra Practice Webstermasters, level 8 25.68 (ISBN 0-07-005748-6); of 5 desktop duplicators 32.94 set (ISBN 0-07-079027-2); duplicator 8A 6.72 (ISBN 0-07-006048-7); duplicator 8B 6.72 (ISBN 0-07-006058-4); duplicator 8C 6.72 (ISBN 0-07-006068-1); duplicator 8D 6.72 (ISBN 0-07-006078-9); duplicator 8E 6.72 (ISBN 0-07-006088-6). McGraw.

--Classroom Mangement Guide, Grade 6. (McGraw-Hill Mathematics Ser.). 1981. 1.28 (ISBN 0-686-75986-9); Extra Practice Webstermasters, level 6 25.68 (ISBN 0-07-005746-X); of 5 desktop duplicators 32.94 set (ISBN 0-07-079026-4); duplicator 6A 6.72 (ISBN 0-07-006046-0); duplicator 6B 6.72 (ISBN 0-07-006056-8); duplicator 6C 6.72 (ISBN 0-07-006066-5); duplicator 6D 6.72 (ISBN 0-07-006076-2); duplicator 6E 6.72 (ISBN 0-07-006086-X). McGraw.

--Extra Practice Webstermasters, Level 4. (McGraw-Hill Mathematics Ser.). 1981. 25.68 (ISBN 0-07-005744-3); of 4 desktop duplicators 26.37 set (ISBN 0-07-079024-8); duplicator 4A 6.72 (ISBN 0-07-006044-4); duplicator 4B 6.72 (ISBN 0-07-006054-1); duplicator 4C 6.72 (ISBN 0-07-006064-9); duplicator 4D 6.72 (ISBN 0-07-006074-6). McGraw.

Bitter, Gary, et al. McGraw-Hill Mathematics, 8 levels. Jillson, Katherine, ed. Incl. Level K. 112p. pap. text ed. 3.92 (ISBN 0-07-005760-5); tchrs. ed., 160 pgs. 7.00 (ISBN 0-07-005770-2); Level 2. 416p. pap. text ed. 6.00 (ISBN 0-07-005762-1); tchrs. ed., 416 pgs. 17.20 (ISBN 0-07-005772-9); Level 3. 382p. text ed. 9.72 (ISBN 0-07-005763-X); tchrs. ed., 512pgs. 18.00 (ISBN 0-07-005773-7); dupl. masters sets A-D 6.72 ea.; 4 sets 26.37 (ISBN 0-686-77512-0); Level 4. 384p. text ed. 9.72 (ISBN 0-07-005764-8); tchrs. ed., 600 pgs. 18.00 (ISBN 0-07-005774-5); dupl. masters sets A-D 6.72 ea.; 4 sets 26.37 (ISBN 0-686-77513-9); Level 5. 384p. text ed. 9.72 (ISBN 0-07-005765-6); tchrs. ed., 512 pgs. 18.00 (ISBN 0-07-005775-3); dupl. masters sets A-D 6.72 ea.; 4 sets 26.37 (ISBN 0-686-77514-7); Level 6. 384p. text ed. 9.72 (ISBN 0-07-005776-1); tchrs. ed., 512 pgs. 18.00 (ISBN 0-686-62503-X); dupl. masters sets A-E 6.72 ea.; 5 sets 32.94 (ISBN 0-686-77515-5); Level 7. 416p. text ed. 11.88 (ISBN 0-07-005767-2); tchrs. ed., 544 pgs. 19.16 (ISBN 0-07-005777-X); dupl. masters sets A-E 6.72 ea.; 5 sets 32.94 (ISBN 0-686-77516-3); Level 8. 416p. text ed. 11.88 (ISBN 0-686-62504-8); tchrs. ed., 544 pgs. 19.16 (ISBN 0-07-005778-8); dupl. masters sets A-E 6.72 ea.; 5 sets 32.94 (ISBN 0-686-77517-1). (McGraw-Hill Elementary Mathematics Ser.). (Illus.). 1980. Extra Practice Webstemasters, levels 1-8 25.68 ea. McGraw.

Bjerhammar, A. Theory of Errors & Generalized Matrix Inverses. LC 72-179998. 440p. 1973. 75.75 (ISBN 0-444-40981-5). Elsevier.

Black, J. & Bradley, J. F. Essential Mathematics for Economists. 2nd ed. LC 79-40826. 316p. 1980. 53.25 (ISBN 0-471-27659-6, Pub. by Wiley-Interscience). Wiley.

Black, Max. The Nature of Mathematics: A Critical Survey. 1979. Repr. of 1933 ed. lib. bdg. 35.00 (ISBN 0-8414-9838-5). Folcroft.

Blackadder, D. A. & Nedderman, R. M. Handbook of Unit Operations. 1971. 44.00 (ISBN 0-12-102950-6). Acad Pr.

Boas, Mary L. Mathematical Methods in Physical Sciences. LC 66-17646. 1966. 28.50 (ISBN 0-471-08417-4). Wiley.

Boivin, Alberic. Theorie et Calcul Des Figures De Diffraction De Revolution. 1965. 16.20x (ISBN 2-7637-6513-0, Pub. by Laval). Intl Schol Bk Serv.

Boliver, David E. Basic Mathematical Skills for College Students. 224p. 1981. pap. text ed. 10.95 (ISBN 0-8403-2470-7). Kendall-Hunt.

Bolza, Oskar, et al. Festschrift Schwarz. LC 73-20209. Orig. Title: Mathematische Abhandlungen. viii, 451p. 1974. Repr. text ed. 19.50 (ISBN 0-8284-0275-2). Chelsea Pub.

Borel, Emile. Elemente der Mathematik, 2 vols. in 1. Staeckel, Paul, ed. (Bibliotheca Mathematica Teubneriana Ser: No. 42). Repr. of 1920 ed. 54.00 (ISBN 0-384-05115-4). Johnson Repr.

Borho, W., et al. Lebendige Zahlen - Fuenf Exkhursionen. (Mathematical Miniatures Ser.: Vol. 1). 116p. 1981. 9.80 (ISBN 3-7643-1203-3). Birkhauser.

Boss, Bernhelm & Niss, Mogens. Mathematics & the Real World: Proceedings of an International Workshop, Dennmark. (Interdisciplinary Systems Research: No. 68). 136p. 1979. pap. 22.00 (ISBN 3-7643-1079-0). Birkhauser.

Bosstick, Maurice & Cable, John L. Patterns in the Sand: An Exploration in Mathematics. 2nd ed. (Illus.). 1975. text ed. 13.95x (ISBN 0-02-471960-9); ans. bk free (ISBN 0-02-471970-6). Macmillan.

Boutet De Monvel, Louis B. & Guillemin, Victor. The Spectral Theory of Toeplitz Operators. LC 80-8538. (Annals of Mathematics Studies: No. 99). 222p. 1981. 17.50x (ISBN 0-691-08284-7); pap. 7.00x (ISBN 0-691-08279-0). Princeton U Pr.

Bowen, Earl K. Mathematics: With Applications in Management & Economics. 5th ed. 1980. 20.95x (ISBN 0-256-02349-2). Irwin.

Bradford, Robert. Mathematics for Carpenters. LC 75-19525. 1975. pap. 9.40 (ISBN 0-8273-1116-8); instructor's guide 1.60 (ISBN 0-8273-1117-6). Delmar.

Bramson, Morris. Mathematics: Level 1. 4th ed. LC 81 3540. 128p. (Orig.). 1981. pap. 3.95 (ISBN 0-668-05319-4, 5319). Arco.

Branch, James E., Sr. Basic Mathematics: Clear & Simple. 1979. pap. text ed. 11.50 (ISBN 0-8403-1979-7, 40197901). Kendall-Hunt.

Braverman, H. Precalculus Mathematics: Algebra, Trigonometry & Analytical Geometry. 533p. 1975. 14.50 (ISBN 0-683-01013-1, Pub. by W & W). Krieger.

Breneman, John W. Mathematics. 2nd ed. (Illus.). 1944. text ed. 15.95 (ISBN 0-07-007480-1, G). McGraw.

Brjuno, A. D., et al. Transactions of the Moscow Mathematical Society, Vol. 26 (1972) LC 65-4713. 239p. 1974. 61.60 (ISBN 0-8218-1626-8, MOSCOW-26). Am Math.

Brodetsky, S. The Meaning of Mathematics. 1979. Repr. of 1929 ed. lib. bdg. 15.00 (ISBN 0-8492-3745-9). R West.

Bronson, C. & Bronson, R. Mathemathics for Management. 1977. text ed. 22.95 scp (ISBN 0-7002-2503-X, HarpC). Har-Row.

Brown, Kenneth E. General Mathematics in American Colleges. LC 73-176692. (Columbia University. Teachers College. Contributions to Education: No. 893). Repr. of 1943 ed. 17.50 (ISBN 0-404-55893-3). AMS Pr.

Brown, Richard & Robbins, David. Advanced Mathematics: An Introductory Course. (gr. 11-12). 1978. text ed. 16.28 (ISBN 0-395-25553-8); instrs'. guide & solns. 9.40 (ISBN 0-395-25554-6). HM.

Brown, Walter C. Basic Mathematics. rev. ed. 128p. 1981. pap. text ed. 4.80 (ISBN 0-87006-315-4). Goodheart.

Broyles, Robert & Lay, Colin. Mathematics in Health Administration. LC 80-19451. 542p. 1980. text ed. 45.00 (ISBN 0-89443-297-4). Aspen Systems.

Bryant, John & Lacher, Chris. College Math. 500p. 1981. text ed. write for info. (33L 2551). Prindle.

Buechi, J. R. & Siefkes, D. Decidable Theories Two: The Monadic Second Order Theory of All Countable Ordinals. (Lecture Notes in Mathematics: Vol. 328). 217p. 1973. pap. 12.20 (ISBN 0-387-06345-5). Springer-Verlag.

Bunday, B. D. & Mulholland, H. Pure Mathematics for Advanced Level. 538p. 1967. 9.95 (ISBN 0-408-70032-7). Butterworth.

Burleson, Donald R. Topics in Mathematics. LC 76-27301. (Illus.). 1977. 19.95 (ISBN 0-13-925305-X). P-H.

Burris, Joanna. Basic Mathematics: An Individualized Approach, 6, Modules 1-6. 1974. write for info. (ISBN 0-87150-172-4, PWS 1381-6). Prindle.

Bush, Grace A. & Young, John E. Foundations of Mathematics. 2nd ed. (Illus.). 512p. 1973. text ed. 17.95 (ISBN 0-07-009275-3); instructor's manual 3.50 (ISBN 0-07-009276-1). McGraw.

Butcher, M. V. & Nesbitt, C. J. Mathematics of Compound Interest. LC 70-157152. 1971. 12.00x (ISBN 0-9603000-1-5). Ulrich.

Bye, M. P., et al. Holt Mathematics 3. (Holt Mathematics Ser.). (YA) (gr. 9). 1978. text ed. 10.00 (ISBN 0-03-920014-0, Pub. by HR&W Canada); Tchr's Ed. 14.44 (ISBN 0-03-920015-9). HR&W.

Cabarga, Leslie. The Fleischer Story. 1976. 12.50 (ISBN 0-517-52580-1). Crown.

Cahiers Mathematiques, 4 tomes. Incl. Tome 1. Exercises Corriges Sur Des Structures Elementaires. Bentz, J., et al. (No. 7). 1966. pap. 6.15x (ISBN 90-2796-317-7); Tome 2. Exercises Corriges Sur Des Structures Elementaires. Decaillot, A. M. (No. 9). 1969. pap. 6.15x (ISBN 90-2796-321-5); Tome 3. Morceaux Choisis D'algebre et De Combinatiore Pour les Sciences Humaines. (No. 13). 1970. pap. 7.80x (ISBN 90-2797-008-4); Tome 4. Distributions Statistiques et Lois De Probabilite. Leclerc, Bruno (No. 15). 1972. pap. 12.75x (ISBN 0-686-22161-3). (Mathematiques et Sciences De L'homme). Mouton.

Camden, K. R. A Revision Course in School Certificate Mathematics. Date not set. pap. 4.50x (ISBN 0-392-08359-0, SpS). Sportshelf.

Camm, Frederick J. Mathematical Tables & Formulae. pap. 0.95 (ISBN 0-685-19408-6, 21, WL). Citadel Pr.

Campbell, Hugh G. & Spencer, Robert E. Finite Mathematics & Calculus. 1977. 18.95 (ISBN 0-02-318600-3, 31860). Macmillan.

Carico, Charles C. Exponential & Logarithmic Functions. pap. 4.95x (ISBN 0-534-00314-1). Wadsworth Pub.

Carlo & Murphy. Merchandising Mathmatics. 136p. 1981. pap. 6.60 (ISBN 0-8273-1416-7); instructor's guide 2.10 (ISBN 0-8273-1417-5). Delmar.

Carman, Robert A. & Carman, Marilyn J. Basic Mathematical Skills: A Guided Approach. 2nd ed. LC 80-19121. 576p. 1981. pap. text ed. 18.95 (ISBN 0-471-03608-0). Wiley.

Carman, Robert A. & Saunders, Hal M. Mathematics for the Trades: A Guided Approach. LC 79-11491. 580p. 1981. pap. text ed. 16.95 (ISBN 0-471-13481-3); tchr's manual avail. (ISBN 0-471-07791-7). Wiley.

Carpenter, Thomas, et al. Results from the First Mathematics Assessment of the National Assessment of Educational Progress. LC 78-2345. 1978. pap. 6.00x (ISBN 0-87353-123-X). NCTM.

Carrell, Mary J. Learning Math Skills. 1978. pap. text ed. 2.50x (ISBN 0-88323-139-5, 228). Richards Pub.

Carter, Hobart C. Modern Basic Mathematics. LC 63-19876. (Illus.). 1964. 24.00x (ISBN 0-89197-305-2). Irvington.

Case, D. H. Modern Mathematical Topics. 1968. 4.75 (ISBN 0-8022-0217-9). Philos Lib.

Castellano, Carmine C. & Seitz, Clifford P. Basic Mathematics. LC 81-2210. 192p. (Orig.). 1981. pap. 5.00 (ISBN 0-668-05126-4, 5126). Arco.

Cerreto, Frank. The Mathematics Test. (Illus.). 1979. pap. 4.95 (ISBN 0-07-010337-2, SP). McGraw.

--Power Skills in Mathematics II. (Illus.). 1979. pap. 4.95 (ISBN 0-07-010338-0, SP). McGraw.

Chandrasekharan, K. Arithmetical Functions. LC 72-102384. (Die Grundlehren der Mathematischen Wissenschaften: Vol. 167). (Illus.). 1970. 34.40 (ISBN 0-387-05114-7). Springer-Verlag.

Chern, S. S. Selected Papers. (Illus.). 1979. 27.30 (ISBN 0-387-90339-9). Springer-Verlag.

Chew, Al H., et al. Technical Mathematics. LC 75-25011. (Illus.). 576p. 1976. text ed. 17.50 (ISBN 0-395-24009-3); inst. manual 2.75 (ISBN 0-395-24010-7). HM.

Chirgwin, B. & Plumpton, C. A. Course of Mathematics for Engineers & Scientists. 2nd ed. Vol. 1, 1970. text ed. 34.00 (ISBN 0-08-006388-8); pap. text ed. 18.00 (ISBN 0-08-021678-1); Vol. 2, 1972. text ed. 16.50 (ISBN 0-08-015970-2); Vol. 3, 1978. text ed. 34.00 (ISBN 0-08-023042-3); Vol. 4. text ed. 12.00 (ISBN 0-08-021634-X). Pergamon.

Chisanbop Finger Calculation Method Home Study: Addition. 1978. pap. 10.00 (ISBN 0-442-24802-4). Van Nos Reinhold.

Chisanbop Finger Calculation Method Home Study Work Stage One. 1978. pap. 3.00 (ISBN 0-442-24776-1). Van Nos Reinhold.

Churchill, Ruel V. Operational Mathematics. 3rd ed. 1971. text ed. 21.50 (ISBN 0-07-010870-6, C). McGraw.

Clark, Alice & Leitch, Carol. Math Amusements in Developing Skills, Vol. 1. (Illus.). (gr. 4-9). pap. 5.95 (ISBN 0-910974-68-3); 57 duplicating masters 13.95 (ISBN 0-685-40576-1). Midwest Pubns.

Clark, Colin W. Mathematical Bioeconomics: The Optimal Management of Renewable Resources. LC 76-16473. (Pure & Applied Mathematics Ser.). 1976. 31.00 (ISBN 0-471-15856-9, Pub. by Wiiley-Interscience). Wiley.

Clifford, Martin. Modern Electronics Math. LC 73-86767. (Illus.). 602p. 1976. pap. 11.95 (ISBN 0-8306-5655-3, 655). TAB Bks.

Cobb, Loren & Thrall, Robert M., eds. Mathematical Frontiers of the Social & Policy Sciences. (AAAS Selected Symposium Ser.: No. 54). 186p. 1980. lib. bdg. 23.25x (ISBN 0-89158-953-8). Westview.

Colerus, Egmont. Mathematics for Everyman: From Simple Numbers to the Calculus. (Illus.). (gr. 9 up). 1957. 8.95 (ISBN 0-87523-104-7). Emerson.

Combinatoire, Graphes & Algebre. (Par le Centre De Mathematique Sociale Mathematiques et Sciences De L'homme: No. 19). 1973. pap. 14.50x (ISBN 90-2797-511-6). Mouton.

A Compendium of CUPM Recommendations, 2 vols. 756p. 1975. Set. 12.00 (ISBN 0-685-58339-2). Vol. 1 (ISBN 0-88385-419-8). Vol. 2 (ISBN 0-88385-420-1). Math Assn.

Comtet, L. Advanced Combinatorics: The Art of Finite & Infinite Expansions. enl. & rev. ed. Nienhuys, J., tr. LC 73-86091. 1974. lib. bdg. 60.50 (ISBN 90-277-0380-9, Pub. by Reidel Holland); pap. text ed. 34.00 (ISBN 90-277-0441-4, Pub. by Reidel Holland). Kluwer Boston.

Conference on Analytical Theory of Differential Equations, Kalamazoo, Mich, 1970. Analytic Theory of Differential Equations: Proceedings. Hsieh, P. F. & Stoddart, A. W., eds. LC 77-153467. (Lecture Notes in Mathematics: Vol. 183). (Illus.). 1971. 11.20 (ISBN 0-387-05369-7). Springer-Verlag.

Conference on Martingales, Oberwolfach Germany, 1970. Proceedings. Dinges, H., ed. (Lecture Notes in Mathematics: Vol. 190). 1971. pap. 8.20 (ISBN 0-387-05396-4). Springer-Verlag.

Connelly, James F. & Fratangelo, Robert A. Elementary Technical Mathematics. (Illus.). 1978. text ed. 18.95 (ISBN 0-02-324430-5). Macmillan.

--Elementary Technical Mathematics with Calculus. 1979. 17.95 (ISBN 0-02-324440-2). Macmillan.

--Precalculus Mathematics: A Functional Approach. 2nd ed. (Illus.). 1979. text ed. 18.95 (ISBN 0-02-324400-3). Macmillan.

--Precalculus Mathematics: A Functional Approach, Study Guide. 2nd ed. (Illus.). 1980. pap. text ed. 7.95 (ISBN 0-02-324420-8). Macmillan.

Cooley, James & Mansfield, Ralph. Basic Mathematics Review: Text & Workbook, Arithmetic & Elementary Algebra. 3rd ed. (Illus.). 448p. 1976. pap. text ed. 16.95x (ISBN 0-02-324480-1, 32448). Macmillan.

Cooperstein, Bruce & Mason, Geoffrey, eds. Proceedings of Symposia in Pure Mathematics, Vol. 37. LC 80-26879. 1981. 44.00 (ISBN 0-8218-1440-0). Am Math.

Copeland, Richard W. Math Activities for Children: A Diagnostic Approach. (Elementary Curriculum Ser.). 1979. pap. text ed. 9.95 (ISBN 0-675-08316-8). Merrill.

Corbitt, Mary K., ed. Results from the Second Mathematics Assessment of the NAEP. 1981. 12.50 (ISBN 0-686-76214-2). NCTM.

Corcoran, Eileen. Meeting Basic Competencies in Math. 1978. pap. text ed. 2.50x (ISBN 0-88323-138-7, 227); tchrs answer key free (ISBN 0-88323-141-7, 230). Richards Pub.

Cornish-Bowden, A. Basic Mathematics for Biochemists. 1981. 23.00x (ISBN 0-412-23000-3, Pub. by Chapman & Hall); pap. 12.95x (ISBN 0-412-23010-0). Methuen Inc.

Cotzin, Sumner B. A Quick Guide to the New Math. 171p. 1977. pap. text ed. 9.00 (ISBN 0-8191-0253-9). U Pr of Amer.

Courant, Richard & Robbins, Herbert. What Is Mathematics? An Elementary Approach to Ideas & Methods. (Illus.). 1979. pap. 9.95 (ISBN 0-19-502517-2, GB576, GB). Oxford U Pr.

Crooks, Thomas C. & Hancock, Harry L. Basic Technical Mathematics. 1969. text ed. 17.95 (ISBN 0-02-325640-0, 32564). Macmillan.

Crowdis, David G. & Wheeler, Brandon W. Introduction to Mathematical Ideas. LC 68-27505. (Illus.). 1969. text ed. 13.95 (ISBN 0-07-014705-1, C). McGraw.

--Precalculus Mathematics. 1976. text ed. 13.95x (ISBN 0-02-472030-5). Macmillan.

Crowhurst, Norman. Basic Mathematics, 2 vols. (Illus., Orig.). (gr. 9 up). 1961. Vol. 1 Arithmetic. pap. 7.65 (ISBN 0-8104-0447-8); Vol. 2 Integrated Algebra, Geometry & Calculus. pap. 7.65 (ISBN 0-8104-0448-6); Vol. 1. exam set 0.50 (ISBN 0-8104-0567-9); Vol. 2. exam set 0.50 (ISBN 0-8104-0568-7). Hayden.

Crowhurst, Norman H. Taking the Mysticism from Mathematics. 2nd ed. 178p. (Orig.). 1981. pap. 6.95 (ISBN 0-89420-223-5, 297020). Natl Book.

Cruikshank, Douglas E., et al. Young Children Learning Mathematics. 1980. text ed. 16.95 (ISBN 0-205-06752-2, 236752-1). Allyn.

Curtiss, David R. Analytic Functions of a Complex Variable. (Carus Monograph: No. 2). 173p. 1926. 12.50 (ISBN 0-88385-002-8). Math Assn.

Dalton, Leroy C. & Snyder, Henry D., eds. Topics for Mathematics Clubs. pap. 2.80 (ISBN 0-686-05576-4). Mu Alpha Theta.

Daniels, Farrington. Mathematical Preparation for Elementary Physical Chemistry. 1958. pap. 3.95 (ISBN 0-07-015301-9, SP). McGraw.

D'Arcangelo, et al. Mathematics for Plumbers & Pipefitters. LC 73-2166. 199p. 1973. 6.80 (ISBN 0-8273-0291-6); instr's manual 1.60 (ISBN 0-8273-0292-4). Delmar.

Davidson, J. New Mathematics. (Teach Yourself Ser.). 1974. pap. 4.95 (ISBN 0-679-12326-1). McKay.

Davis, Martin. Lectures on Modern Mathematics. (Notes on Mathematics & Its Applications Ser). 1967. 45.25x (ISBN 0-677-00200-9). Gordon.

Davis, Morton. Mathematically Speaking. 484p. 1980. text ed. 17.95 (ISBN 0-15-555190-6, HC); instr's manual avail. (ISBN 0-15-555191-4). HarBraceJ.

Davis, Philip J. Schwarz Function & Its Applications. LC 74-77258. (Carus Monograph: No. 17). 1973. 12.50 (ISBN 0-88385-017-6). Math Assn.

DeFelice, Gerald T. Introduction to Mathematics. 400p. (Orig.). 1981. pap. text ed. 29.95 (ISBN 0-686-30239-7). Une Pub.

De Finetti, Bruno. Die Kunst Des Sehens in der Mathematik. Bechtolsheim, Lulu, tr. from It. (Science & Civilization Ser.: No. 28). 92p. (Ger.). 1974. 20.50 (ISBN 3-7643-0677-7). Birkhauser.

DeGonzalez, Fe Acosta & DeMatos, Isabel Freire. Matematicas Modernas En el Nivel Elemental: Guia Metodologica. (Illus.). 6.25 (ISBN 0-8477-2700-9); pap. 5.00 (ISBN 0-8477-2701-7). U of PR Pr.

Delaney, G. Harwood. Comprehensive Review & Analysis of Mathematics & Physics. (Illus.). 192p. (gr. 10-12). 1981. 10.95 (ISBN 0-89962-210-0). Todd & Honeywell.

Demillo, Richard A., et al, eds. Foundations of Secure Computation. 1978. 29.50 (ISBN 0-12-210350-5). Acad Pr.

Denholm, Richard. Basic Math with Applications. 1981. pap. text ed. 12.95x (ISBN 0-673-15233-2). Scott F.

Derrick, William R. & Derrick, Judith L. Finite Mathematics with Calculus for the Management, Life & Social Sciences. LC 78-18639. (Illus.). 1979. text ed. 18.95 (ISBN 0-201-01400-9). A-W.

Dettman, John W. Mathematical Methods in Physics & Engineering. 2nd ed. LC 68-28412. (International Pure & Applied Mathematics Ser). 1969. text ed. 18.95 (ISBN 0-07-016597-1, C). McGraw.

Devi, Shakuntala. Figuring: The Joy of Numbers. LC 78-4731. 1978. 8.95 (ISBN 0-06-011069-4, HarpT). Har-Row.

--Mathematical Merry-Go-Round. 150p. 1978. 14.95 (ISBN 0-306-31031-7, Plenum Pr). Plenum Pub.

Dienes, Z. P. The Six Stages in the Process of Learning Mathematics. Seabourne, P. L., tr. (NFER General Ser). 64p. 1973. pap. text ed. 6.25x (ISBN 0-85633-022-1, NFER). Humanities.

Dieudonne, J. A. Treatise on Analysis, 6 vols. Incl. Vol. 1. 1960. 22.95 (ISBN 0-12-215550-5); Vol. 2. rev. ed. 1970. 51.00 (ISBN 0-12-215502-5); Vol. 3. 1972. 55.50 (ISBN 0-12-215503-3); Vol. 4. 1974. 56.00 (ISBN 0-12-215504-1); Vol. 5. 1977. 39.50 (ISBN 0-12-215505-X); Vol. 6. 1978. 36.50 (ISBN 0-12-215506-8). (Pure & Applied Mathematics Ser.). Acad Pr.

Dieudonne, Jean. A Panorama of Pure Mathematics: As Seen by N. Bourbaki. Macdonald, I., tr. LC 80-2330. (Pure & Applied Mathematics Ser.). 1981. write for info. (ISBN 0-12-215560-2). Acad Pr.

Doan, Robert L. Number Readiness Achievement Activities. (Early Childhood Achievement Units Ser.). 1979. pap. 5.95x (ISBN 0-87628-283-4). Ctr Appl Res.

Dodes, I. A. Finite Mathematics. 1970. text ed. 15.50 (ISBN 0-07-017250-1, C); instructor's manual 3.50 (ISBN 0-07-017251-X). McGraw.

Dodes, Irving A. Finite Mathematics with Basic: A Liberal Arts Approach. LC 78-31505. (Illus.). 372p. 1981. Repr. lib. bdg. 21.00 (ISBN 0-88275-862-4). Krieger.

--Mathematics with BASIC: A Liberal Arts Approach. rev. ed. LC 79-131. 464p. 1980. Repr. of 1974 ed. lib. bdg. 18.50 (ISBN 0-88275-892-6). Krieger.

Doman, Glenn. Teach Your Baby Math. 1980. 8.95 (ISBN 0-671-25128-7). S&S.

Dorling. Use of Mathematical Literature. 1977. 34.95 (ISBN 0-408-70913-8). Butterworth.

Dorofeyev, G., et al. Elementary Mathematics. 488p. 1973. 6.90 (ISBN 0-8285-0718-X, Pub. by Mir Pubs Russia). Imported Pubns.

Dottori, D. Mathematics for Today & Tomorrow. 2nd ed. 1975. 8.76 (ISBN 0-07-082244-1, W). McGraw.

Douglas, A. H. An Approach to Engineering Mathematics. 1971. pap. 10.75 (ISBN 0-08-016016-6). Pergamon.

Dow Education Systems. Basic Industrial Mathematics: A Text Workbook. 1972. text ed. 10.95 (ISBN 0-07-017660-4, G); ans. key 2.00 (ISBN 0-07-017661-2). McGraw.

Draper, Jean. Mathematics Para Administration y Economia. new ed. 1976. text ed. 14.50x (ISBN 0-06-310100-9, IntlDept). Har-Row.

Dressler, Isidore. Preliminary Mathematics. (gr. 8). 1981. text ed. 17.92 (ISBN 0-87720-243-5). AMSCO Sch.

--Preliminary Mathematics Review Guide. (Illus.). (gr. 8-10). 1965. pap. text ed. 5.00 (ISBN 0-87720-205-2). AMSCO Sch.

--Review Text in Preliminary Mathematics. (Illus.). (gr. 7-9). 1962. text ed. 9.83 (ISBN 0-87720-203-6); pap. text ed. 6.25 (ISBN 0-87720-202-8). AMSCO Sch.

Dressler, Isidore & Keenan, Edward P. Integrated Mathematics: Course I. (Orig.). (gr. 9). 1980. text ed. 19.17 (ISBN 0-87720-249-4); pap. text ed. 12.09 (ISBN 0-87720-248-6). AMSCO Sch.

Driscoll, P., et al. Whole Numbers. West, K. & Johnston, D., eds. (Math Skills for Daily Living Ser.). (Illus.). 32p. (gr. 7-12). 1979. pap. text ed. 3.95x (ISBN 0-87453-091-1, 82091). Denoyer.

Drooyan, Irving & Wooten, William. Intermediate Mathematics. 1971. 19.95x (ISBN 0-534-00095-9). Wadsworth Pub.

Dryjanski, Deborah A. Conquering Word Problems in Mathematics. (gr. 6-8). 1979. incl. manual & cassettes 167.50 (ISBN 0-917792-02-5). Math Hse.

Dubbey, J. M. Development of Modern Mathematics. LC 72-88125. 153p. 1975. pap. 9.50x (ISBN 0-8448-0656-0). Crane-Russak Co.

Dubinsky, Ed & Ramanujan, M. S. On Lambda Nuclearity. LC 72-4515. (Memoirs: No. 128). 1972. pap. 7.60 (ISBN 0-8218-1828-7, MEMO-128). Am Math.

Dyachenko, V. F. Basic Computational Math. 125p. 1979. pap. 3.40 (ISBN 0-8285-1593-X, Pub. by Mir Pubs Russia). Imported Pubns.

Dydak, J. & Segal, J. Shape Theory: An Introduction. (Lecture Notes in Mathematics: Vol. 688). 1979. pap. 11.30 (ISBN 0-387-08955-1). Springer-Verlag.

Edwards, Barry. The Readable Maths & Statistics Book. (Illus.). 336p. (Orig.). 1980. text ed. 34.95x (ISBN 0-04-310007-4); pap. text ed. 13.50x (ISBN 0-04-310008-2). Allen Unwin.

Edwards, R. A Formal Background to Mathematics: Pt. II, A & B. (Universitext). 1170p. 1980. pap. 39.80 (ISBN 0-387-90513-8). Springer-Verlag.

Edwards, R., ed. A Formal Background to Mathematics Ia Ib Logic, Sets & Numbers, 2 pts. LC 79-15045. 1979. pap. 31.30 (ISBN 0-387-90431-X). Springer-Verlag.

Edwards, R. E. & Gaudry, G. I. Littlewood-Paley & Multiplier Theory. (Ergebnisse der Mathematik und ihrer Grenzgebiete: Vol. 90). 1976. 32.60 (ISBN 0-387-07726-X). Springer-Verlag.

Eggan, Lawrence C. & Vanden Eynden, Charles. Mathematics: Models & Applications. 1979. text ed. 16.95x (ISBN 0-669-01051-0); instr's manual 1.95 (ISBN 0-669-01052-9). Heath.

Eicholz, Robert, et al. Mathematics in Our World Primer. (Mathematics in Our World Ser.). 1978. pap. text ed. 3.92 (ISBN 0-201-09800-8, Sch Div); tchr's ed. 11.76 (ISBN 0-201-09801-6). A-W.

Eicholz, Robert E., et al. Mathematics in Our World. Incl. Bk. 1. (gr. 1). text ed. 3.92 kindergarten (ISBN 0-201-09800-8); text ed. 6.08 (ISBN 0-201-09810-5); tchr's. ed. 14.12 (ISBN 0-201-09811-3); wkbk. 2.76 (ISBN 0-201-09813-X); wkbk. tchr's. ed. 3.00 (ISBN 0-201-09814-8); duplicator masters 38.88 (ISBN 0-201-09812-1); enrichment wkbk. 2.76 (ISBN 0-201-09815-6); tchr's. enrichment wkbk. 3.00 (ISBN 0-201-09816-4); Bk. 2. (gr. 2). text ed. 6.08 (ISBN 0-201-09820-2); tchr's ed. 14.12 (ISBN 0-201-09821-0); wkbk. 2.76 (ISBN 0-201-09823-7); wkbk. tchr's ed. 3.00 (ISBN 0-201-09824-5); duplicator masters 38.88 (ISBN 0-201-09822-9); enrichment wkbk. 2.76 (ISBN 0-201-09825-3); tchr's enrichment wkbk 3.00 (ISBN 0-201-09826-1); Bk. 3. (gr. 3). text ed. 10.24 (ISBN 0-201-09830-X); tchr's ed. 16.00 (ISBN 0-201-09831-8); duplicator masters 38.88 (ISBN 0-201-09832-6); wkbk 3.52 (ISBN 0-201-09833-4); wkbk 3.68 (ISBN 0-201-09835-0); wkbk tchr's ed. 3.80 (ISBN 0-201-09836-9); Bk. 4. (gr. 4). text ed. 10.24 (ISBN 0-201-09840-7); tchr's ed. 16.00 (ISBN 0-201-09841-5); duplicator masters 38.88 (ISBN 0-201-09842-3); wkbk 3.52 (ISBN 0-201-09843-1); wkbk tchr's ed. 4.16 (ISBN 0-201-09844-X); Bk. 5. (gr. 5). text ed. 10.24 (ISBN 0-201-09850-4); tchr's ed. 16.00 (ISBN 0-201-09851-2); duplicator masters 38.88 (ISBN 0-201-09852-0); wkbk 3.52 (ISBN 0-201-09853-9); wkbk tchr's ed. 4.16 (ISBN 0-201-09854-7); Bk. 6. (gr. 6). text ed. 10.24 (ISBN 0-201-09860-1); tchr's ed. 16.00 (ISBN 0-201-09861-X); duplicator masters 38.88 (ISBN 0-201-09862-8); wkbk 3.52 (ISBN 0-201-09863-6); wkbk. tchr's ed. 4.16 (ISBN 0-201-09864-4); Bk. 7. (gr. 7). 1980. text ed. 12.32 (ISBN 0-201-09870-9); tchr's ed. 16.00 (ISBN 0-201-09871-7); Bk. 8. (gr. 8). 1978. text ed. 12.32 (ISBN 0-201-09880-6); tchr's ed. 16.00 (ISBN 0-201-09881-4); wkbk 3.52 (ISBN 0-201-09883-0); tchr's ed. wkbk 3.52 (ISBN 0-201-09884-9). (gr. 1-6). 1978. duplicator masters 43.40 ea. (ISBN 0-201-09882-2, Sch Div). A-W.

--Mathematics in Our World. 2nd ed. Incl. Bk. 1. (gr. k). student ed. 3.92 (ISBN 0-201-16000-5); tchr's ed. 11.76 (ISBN 0-201-16001-3); (gr. 1). pap. 6.08 student ed. (ISBN 0-201-16010-2); tchr's ed. 16.00 (ISBN 0-201-16011-0); wkbk. 2.76 (ISBN 0-201-16013-7); tchr's ed. wkbk. 3.00 (ISBN 0-201-16014-5); (gr. 2). student ed. 6.08 (ISBN 0-201-16020-X); tchr's ed. 16.00 (ISBN 0-201-16021-8); wkbk. 2.76 (ISBN 0-201-16023-4); tchr's ed. wkbk. 3.00 (ISBN 0-201-16024-2); (gr. 3). student ed. 10.24 (ISBN 0-201-16030-7); tchr's ed. 16.00 (ISBN 0-201-16031-5); wkbk. 3.52 (ISBN 0-201-16033-1); tchr's ed. wkbk. 4.16 (ISBN 0-201-16034-X); consumable ed. 7.20 (ISBN 0-201-16009-9); (gr. 4). student ed. 10.24 (ISBN 0-201-16040-4); tchr's ed. 16.00 (ISBN 0-201-16041-2); wkbk. 3.52 (ISBN 0-201-16043-9); tchr's ed. wkbk. 4.16 (ISBN 0-201-16044-7); (gr. 5). student ed. 10.24 (ISBN 0-201-16050-1); tchr's ed. 16.00 (ISBN 0-201-16051-X); wkbk. 3.52 (ISBN 0-201-16053-6); tchr's ed. wkbk. 4.16 (ISBN 0-201-16054-4); (gr. 6). student ed. 10.24 (ISBN 0-201-16060-9); tchr's ed. 16.00 (ISBN 0-201-16064-1); wkbk. 3.52 (ISBN 0-201-16063-3); tchr's ed. wkbk. 4.16 (ISBN 0-201-16064-1); (gr. 7). student ed. 12.32 (ISBN 0-201-16070-6); tchr's ed. 16.00 (ISBN 0-201-16071-4); wkbk. 3.52 (ISBN 0-201-16073-0); tchr's ed. wkbk. 4.16 (ISBN 0-201-16074-9); (gr. 8). student ed. 12.32 (ISBN 0-201-16080-3); tchr's ed. 16.00 (ISBN 0-201-16081-1); wkbk. 3.52 (ISBN 0-201-16083-8); tchr's ed. wkbk. 4.16 (ISBN 0-201-16084-6). (gr. 1-8). 1981 (Sch Div). A-W.

--Mathematics in Our World: Spanish Edition. 2nd ed. (gr. 1-6). 1981. Bk. 1. text ed. 6.08 (ISBN 0-201-09700-1, Sch Div); Bk. 2. text ed. 6.08 (ISBN 0-201-09701-X); Bk. 3. text ed. 6.76 (ISBN 0-201-09702-8). A-W.

Eisen, Martin & Eisen, Carole. Finite Mathematics. 1978. text ed. 19.95x (ISBN 0-02-472450-5). Macmillan.

Elliott, J. S., et al. Project Mathematics, 16 bks. Incl. Bks. 1-5. 1969. Bk.1. text ed. 1.32 (ISBN 0-685-33358-2); Bks.2&3. text ed. 1.48 (ISBN 0-685-33359-0); Bk.4. text ed. 1.60 (ISBN 0-685-33360-4); Bk.5. text ed. 1.72 (ISBN 0-685-33361-2); tchr's guidebk. 8.28 (ISBN 0-685-33362-0); Bks. 6 & 7. 1971. text ed. 2.56ea (ISBN 0-685-33363-9); tchr's, guidebk. 11.00 (ISBN 0-685-33364-7); activity cards 40.00 (ISBN 0-685-33365-5); Bks. 8-10. 1971. text ed. 1.76 ea; tchr's. guidebk 11.00 (ISBN 0-685-33367-1); Bks. 11-13. 1972-73. Bk.11. text ed. 2.16 (ISBN 0-685-33368-X); Bks.12 & 13. text ed. 1.76 ea; tchr's.guidebk. 11.00 (ISBN 0-685-33370-1); Bks. 14-16. 1973. Bks. 14 & 15. text ed. 2.16 ea; Bk. 16. text ed. 1.76 (ISBN 0-685-33372-8); tchr's guidebk. 11.00 (ISBN 0-685-33373-6). (Winston Mine Editions, HoltC). HR&W.

Emerson, Lloyd & Paquette, Laurence. Fundamental Mathematics for the Management & Social Sciences. alt. ed. 688p. 1981. text ed. 21.95 (ISBN 0-205-07166-X, 567166-3); tchrs. ed. avail. (ISBN 0-205-07169-4). Allyn.

Eremin, I. I., et al. Twelve Papers on Real & Complex Function Theory. LC 51-5559. (Translations Ser.: No. 2, Vol. 88). 1970. 32.40 (ISBN 0-8218-1788-4, TRANS 2-88). Am Math.

Ernst Edward Kummer: Selected Papers. LC 74-23838. 900p. 1975. 57.90 (ISBN 0-387-06836-8). Springer-Verlag.

Eves, Howard W. Mathematical Circles Adieu. 1977. write for info. (ISBN 0-87150-240-2, PWS 1941). Prindle.

--Mathematical Circles Squared. 186p. 1972. text ed. write for info. (ISBN 0-87150-154-6, PWS 1201). Prindle.

Evyatar, A. & Rosenbloom, P. Motivated Mathematics. LC 80-40491. (Illus.). 250p. Date not set. price not set (ISBN 0-521-23308-9). Cambridge U Pr.

Ewen, Dale & Topper, Michael A. Mathematics for Technical Education. (Technical Mathematics Ser.). (Illus.). 384p. 1976. 17.95x (ISBN 0-13-565150-6); study guide 2.95 (ISBN 0-13-565143-3). P-H.

Experiences in Mathematical Discovery. Incl. Bk. 1. Formulas, Graphs & Patterns (ISBN 0-87353-042-X); Bk. 2. Properties of Operations with Numbers (ISBN 0-87353-043-8); Bk. 3. Mathematical Sentences (ISBN 0-87353-044-6); Bk. 4-o.p. Geometry (ISBN 0-87353-045-4); Bk. 5. Arrangements & Selections, Answers for Units 1-5 (ISBN 0-87353-046-2); Bk. 6. Mathematical Thinking (ISBN 0-87353-048-9); Bk. 7. Rational Numbers (ISBN 0-87353-049-7); Bk. 9. Positive & Negative Numbers (ISBN 0-87353-050-0). LC 66-25000. 1971. pap. 2.25 ea. NCTM.

Fadiman, Clifton, ed. Fantasia Mathematica. pap. 2.95 (ISBN 0-671-24451-5, Fireside). S&S.

--Mathematical Magpie. 1964. pap. 1.95 (ISBN 0-671-45511-7, Fireside). S&S.

Farmer, Evelyn. Second Math Helper. (Classroom Pairing Ser). 64p. (gr. k-1). 1975. 2.25 (ISBN 0-87594-141-9, 3112). Book-Lab.

Fehr, Howard F., et al. Unified Mathematics Series, 4 levels. (gr. 7-9). 1971-74. Level 1. text ed. 11.84 (ISBN 0-201-01833-0, Sch Div); Level 2. text ed. 12.20 (ISBN 0-201-01836-5); Level 3. text ed. 12.44 (ISBN 0-201-01838-1); tchrs' commentaries for levels 1-3 7.04 ea.; Level 4. tchr's ed. 7.04 (ISBN 0-201-02252-4). A-W.

Feldman, W. M. Rabbinical Mathematics & Astronomy. rev. ed. LC 78-60816. 1978. 8.75 (ISBN 0-87203-026-1). Hermon.

Felix, Lucienne. Modern Mathematics & the Teacher. (Orig.). 1966. 17.95 (ISBN 0-521-04989-X); pap. 6.95x (ISBN 0-521-09385-6). Cambridge U Pr.

Felker, Charles A. & Bradley, John G. Shop Mathematics. 5th ed. 1976. 8.96 (ISBN 0-02-816280-3); tchrs' ed. 11.96 (ISBN 0-02-816300-1). Glencoe.

Fennell, Francis M. Elementary Mathematics Diagnosis & Correction Kit. 1981. pap. 24.95x comb-bound (ISBN 0-87628-295-8). Ctr Appl Res.

--Elementary Mathematics: Priorities for the 1980s. LC 81-80015. (Fastback Ser.: No. 157). 1981. pap. 0.75 (ISBN 0-87367-157-0). Phi Delta Kappa.

Fenyo, S. Modern Mathematical Methods in Technology, Vol. 2. LC 69-16400. (Applied Mathematics & Mechanics Ser.: Vol. 17). 326p. 1975. 46.50 (ISBN 0-444-10565-4, North-Holland). Elsevier.

Fenyo, S. & Frey, T. Modern Mathematical Methods in Technology, Vol. 1. (Series in Applied Mathematics & Mechanics: Vol. 9). 1969. 44.00 (ISBN 0-444-10193-4, North-Holland). Elsevier.

--Moderne Mathematische Methoden in de Technik, Vol. III. (International Series of Numerical Mathematics: No. 18). 348p. (Ger.). 1980. pap. 56.00 (ISBN 3-7643-1097-9). Birkhauser.

Ferrar, William L. Advanced Mathematics for Science: A Sequel to Mathematics for Science. 1969. 10.25x (ISBN 0-19-853143-5); pap. 5.00x (ISBN 0-19-853144-3). Oxford U Pr.

Ferrara, S., et al, eds. Conformal Algebra in Space - Time & Operator Product Expansion. LC 25-9130. (Springer Tracts in Modern Physics: Vol. 67). iv, 69p. 1973. 22.50 (ISBN 0-387-06216-5). Springer-Verlag.

Filippone, Samuel R. & Williams, Michael Z. Elementary Mathematics: A Fundamentals & Techniques Approach. LC 75-19539. (Illus.). 448p. 1976. text ed. 17.50 (ISBN 0-395-20028-8); inst. manual 3.25 (ISBN 0-395-20029-6). HM.

Fineberg, Marjorie. Everyday Math: Tables, Graphs, & Scale. LC 79-730692. (Illus.). 1979. pap. text ed. 135.00 (ISBN 0-89290-129-2, A514-SATC). Soc for Visual.

Foley, et al. Building Math Skills. Incl. Level 1. text ed. 8.32 (ISBN 0-201-13350-4); tchr's manual with ans. 6.00 (ISBN 0-686-69676-X, 13359); test & practice dupl. masters avail.; Level 2. text ed. 8.32 (ISBN 0-686-69677-8); tchr's manual with ans. 6.00 (ISBN 0-686-69678-6, 13379); test & practice dupl. masters avail.. (Gr. 7-12 Basal, Gr. 9-12 Remedial, Gr. 7-12 Supplemental). 1981. A-W.

Folkman, Jon. Equivariant Maps of Spheres into the Classical Groups. LC 52-42839. (Memoirs: No. 95). 1971. pap. 7.20 (ISBN 0-8218-1295-5, MEMO-95). Am Math.

Forman, William & Gavurin, Lester L. Elements of Arithmetic, Algebra, & Geometry. LC 78-159159. 1972. text ed. 19.95 (ISBN 0-471-00654-8). Wiley.

Forte, Imogene & MacKenzie, Joy. Creative Math Experiences for the Young Child. LC 77-670122. (Illus.). 1973. pap. text ed. 6.95 (ISBN 0-913916-04-8, IP 04-8); avail. dup masters 5.95 ea. Incentive Pubns.

Fowler, Frank P. & Sandberg, E. W. Basic Mathematics for Administration. LC 62-15189. 1962. text ed. 22.50 (ISBN 0-471-26976-X). Wiley.

Francis, Philip. Mathematics of the Universe: The Universe of the Mind. (Illus.). 1977. pap. 13.50 (ISBN 0-902675-75-3). Oleander Pr.

Francis, Philip H. Cartesian & Argand Values. (Mathematics Ser.: Vol. 3). (Illus.). 1978. pap. 13.50 (ISBN 0-900891-47-5). Oleander Pr.

Frand, Jason & Granville, Evelyn B. Theory & Application of Mathematics for Teachers. 2nd ed. 1978. text ed. 19.95 (ISBN 0-534-00535-7). Wadsworth Pub.

Freedman. Deterministic Mathematical Models in Population Ecology. (Pure & Applied Math. Ser.: Vol. 57). 264p. 1980. 29.75 (ISBN 0-8247-6653-9). Dekker.

Freudenthal, Hans. Weeding & Sowing: Preface to a Science of Mathematical Education. ix, 314p. 1980. lib. bdg. 47.50 (ISBN 90-277-0789-8, Pub. by Reidel Holland); pap. 15.00 (ISBN 90-277-1072-4). Kluwer Boston.

Friedland, Joyce & Gross, Irene. Reading for Mathematics. 1977. pap. 2.50x (ISBN 0-88323-129-8, 218); tchrs answer key 3.00 (ISBN 0-88323-142-5, 231). Richards Pub.

Friedman, Avner. Differential Games. LC 75-155119. (Pure & Applied Mathematics Ser.). 1971. 44.00 (ISBN 0-471-28049-6, Pub. by Wiley-Interscience). Wiley.

Friedrichs, K. O. From Pythagoras to Einstein. LC 65-24963. (New Mathematics Library: No. 16). 1975. pap. 5.50 (ISBN 0-88385-616-6). Math Assn.

Gabbay, S. M. Elementary Mathematics for Basic Chemistry & Physics. 128p. (Orig.). 1980. pap. 9.95 (ISBN 0-9604722-0-7). Basic Science Prep Ctr.

Gafney, Leo & Beers, John C. Essential Math Skills. Devine, Peter, ed. 224p. 1980. pap. text ed. 5.20 (ISBN 0-07-010260-0, W); tchr's ed. 6.08 (ISBN 0-07-010261-9); Webstermasters tests 4.52 (ISBN 0-07-010262-7). McGraw.

Gagliardi, R. & Valenza, S. W., Jr., eds. The Mathematics of the Energy Crises. LC 78-53592. 96p. (gr. 7-12). 1978. 6.96 (ISBN 0-936918-01-2). Intergalactic NJ.

Galerstein, David H. Mastering Fundamental Mathematics. (Orig.). (gr. 7). 1976. pap. text ed. 5.83 (ISBN 0-87720-226-5). AMSCO Sch.

Gandz, Solomon. Studies in Hebrew Astronomy & Mathematics. 1970. 35.00x (ISBN 0-87068-078-1). Ktav.

Garcia, C. B. & Zangwill, Willard I. Pathways to Solutions, Fixed Points, & Equilibria. (Computational Math Ser.). 336p. 1981. text ed. 29.95 (ISBN 0-686-76579-6). P-H.

Garding, L. Encounter with Mathematics. LC 76-54765. 1977. 15.50 (ISBN 0-387-90229-5). Springer-Verlag.

Gardner, Martin. Mathematical Circus. 1981. pap. 4.95 (ISBN 0-394-74712-7, V-712, Vin). Random.

--Mathematics, Magic & Mystery. LC 57-1546. lib. bdg. 9.50x (ISBN 0-88307-104-5). Gannon.

--Mathematics, Magic & Mystery. (Illus.). 6.75 (ISBN 0-8446-4742-X). Peter Smith.

Garrido, L., et al, eds. Stochastic Processes in Nonequilibrium Systems: Proceedings, Sitges International School of Statistical Mechanics, June 1978, Sitges, Barcelona, Spain. (Lecture Notes in Physics: Vol. 84). 1978. pap. 20.60 (ISBN 0-387-08942-X). Springer-Verlag.

Gauss, Karl. Briefwechsel Zwischen Carl Friedrich Gauss und W. Bolyai. 1971. Repr. of 1899 ed. 18.50 (ISBN 0-384-17765-4); 12.00 (ISBN 0-686-66286-5). Johnson Repr.

--Untersuchungen ueber Hoehere Arithmetik. 2nd ed. Maser, H., tr. LC 65-17614. 695p. (Ger.). 1981. text ed. 30.00 (ISBN 0-8284-0191-8, 191). Chelsea Pub.

Geier, Alvin E. & Lamm, Nathaniel. Mathematics & Your Career. (gr. 10-12). 1978. pap. text ed. 6.58 (ISBN 0-87720-241-9). AMSCO Sch.

General Mathematics. (Lefax Data Bks.: No. 613). (Illus.). Date not set. pap. 3.00 (ISBN 0-685-52845-6). LeFax.

Gerrish, F. Pure Mathematics, a University & College Course: Calculus. 1960. text ed. 28.95 (ISBN 0-521-05069-3). Cambridge U Pr.

Gersting, Judith L. & Kuczkowski. Yes-No, Stop-Go: Some Patterns in Mathematic Logic. LC 76-46376. (Young Math Ser.). (Illus.). (gr. k-3). 1977. PLB 8.79 (ISBN 0-690-01130-X, TYC-J). Har-Row.

Gewirtz, Allan & Quintas, Louis V., eds. Second International Conference on Combinatorial Mathematics. (Annals of the New York Academy of Sciences: Vol. 319). 602p. (Orig.). 1979. pap. 110.00x (ISBN 0-89766-010-2). NY Acad Sci.

Gibbons. Basic Math, 9 bks. Incl. Gr. K. pap. text ed. 2.92 (ISBN 0-8009-1401-5); tchr's. ed. 4.40 (ISBN 0-8009-1403-1); Gr. 1 & 2. pap. text ed. 4.64 ea.; Gr. 1. pap. text ed. (ISBN 0-8009-1406-6); Gr. 2. pap. text ed. (ISBN 0-8009-1410-4); tchr's. eds, 6.16 ea. Gr. 1 (ISBN 0-8009-1408-2). Gr. 2 (ISBN 0-8009-1412-0); Gr. 3-6. Gr. 3. pap. text ed. 4.64 (ISBN 0-8009-1414-7); Gr. 4. pap. text ed. 4.64 (ISBN 0-8009-1425-2); Gr. 5. 4.64 (ISBN 0-8009-1433-3); Gr. 6. tchr's. eds. 6.16 ea. (ISBN 0-8009-1443-0); tchr's. ed. gr. 3 6.16 (ISBN 0-8009-1416-3); tchr's. ed. gr. 4 6.16 (ISBN 0-8009-1427-9); tchr's. ed. gr. 5 6.16 (ISBN 0-8009-1437-6); tchr's. ed. gr. 6 6.16 (ISBN 0-8009-1445-7); tests for gr. 3-6 1.12 ea.; Gr. 7 & 8. pap. text ed. 5.08 ea.; Gr. 7. pap. text ed. (ISBN 0-8009-1462-7); Gr. 8. pap. text ed. (ISBN 0-8009-1472-4); tchr's. eds. 6.60 ea. Gr. 7 (ISBN 0-8009-1464-3). Gr. 8 (ISBN 0-8009-1474-0). tests for gr. 7-8 1.12 ea. Gr. 7 (ISBN 0-8009-1468-6). Gr. 8 (ISBN 0-8009-1476-7). (gr. k-8). 1977-78. McCormick-Mathers.

Gibson, Carol, ed. The Facts on File Dictionary of Mathematics. 224p. 1981. prepub. 14.95 (ISBN 0-87196-512-7). Facts on File.

Gilligan, Lawrence & Nenno, Bob. Finite Mathematics: An Elementary Approach. 2nd ed. 1979. text ed. 16.95 (ISBN 0-87620-314-4); instructor's man. free (ISBN 0-87620-315-2). Goodyear.

Glenn, William H. & Johnson, Donovan A. Invitation to Mathematics. LC 72-81535. (Illus.). 384p. 1973. pap. 4.00 (ISBN 0-486-22906-8). Dover.

Goff, Gerald K. & Berg, Milton E. Basic Mathematics. 1968. pap. 17.95 (ISBN 0-13-063438-7, Appleton-Century-Crofts). P-H.

Goldstein, Larry. Finite Mathematics & Its Applications. (Illus.). 1980. text ed. 18.95 (ISBN 0-13-317263-5). P-H.

Goldstein, Larry, et al. Modern Mathematics & Its Applications. (Illus.). 816p. 1980. pap. text ed. 23.95 (ISBN 0-13-595173-9). P-H.

Golos, Ellery B. Patterns in Mathematics. LC 80-25883. 456p. 1981. text ed. write for info. (ISBN 0-87150-301-8). Prindle.

Gonis, Antonios & Strnad, Wayne. Mastering Mathematical Skills. LC 80-19989. (Illus.). 432p. 1981. pap. text ed. 13.95 (ISBN 0-201-03062-4). A-W.

Good, R. A. Introduction to Mathematics. 1966. text ed. 15.95 (ISBN 0-15-543480-2, HC); solutions manual avail. (ISBN 0-15-543481-0, HC). HarBraceJ.

Goodman, A. W. & Ratti, J. S. Finite Mathematics with Applications. 1979. text ed. 18.95 (ISBN 0-02-344760-5); instrs'. manual avail. Macmillan.

Goozner, Calman. Computational Skills for College Students. 1976. pap. text ed. 7.58 (ISBN 0-87720-976-6). AMSCO Sch.

Gordon, David. Living Method Course in Speed Mathematics. 14.95, with 4 lp records & manual (ISBN 0-517-50825-7). Crown.

Gossage & Briggs. Basic Mathematics Review. (Adult & Continuing Education Ser.). 168p. 1969. 2.64 (ISBN 0-538-14200-6). SW Pub.

Gould, S. H. & Liu, P. H. Kinship, Marriage & Mathematics. (Pure & Applied Mathematics Ser.). 1981. write for info. (ISBN 0-12-293720-1). Acad Pr.

Gowar, Norman. An Invitation to Mathematics. (Illus.). 214p. 1979. text ed. 29.50x (ISBN 0-19-853002-1); pap. 11.50x (ISBN 0-19-853001-3). Oxford U Pr.

Graham, Lloyd A. Surprise Attack in Mathematical Problems. (Illus., Orig.). 1968. pap. 3.00 (ISBN 0-486-21846-5). Dover.

Graham, Malcolm. Modern Elementary Mathematics. 3rd ed. 470p. 1979. text ed. 16.95 (ISBN 0-15-561041-4, HC); instructor's manual avail. (ISBN 0-15-561042-2). HarBraceJ.

Graham, Ronald, et al. Ramsey Theory. LC 80-14110. (Wiley Interscience Ser. in Discrete Mathematics). 174p. 1980. 22.95 (ISBN 0-471-05997-8, Pub. by Wiley Interscience). Wiley.

Granville, Henry C., Jr. Logos: Mathmatics & Christian Theology. LC 74-25529. 361p. 1976. 18.00 (ISBN 0-8387-1653-9). Bucknell U Pr.

Grassmann, Hermann. Gesammelte Mathematische und Physikalische Werke, 3 vols in 6 pts. (Ger). Repr. of 1911 ed. Set. 146.00 (ISBN 0-384-09730-8). Johnson Repr.

Grawoig, Dennis E. Decision Mathematics. (Accounting Ser.). 1967. text ed. 18.95 (ISBN 0-07-024177-5, C); solutions manual 3.00 (ISBN 0-07-024178-3). McGraw.

Grawoig, Dennis E., et al. Mathematics: A Foundation for Decisions. LC 75-12097. (Illus.). 542p. 1976. text ed. 18.95 (ISBN 0-201-02598-1); instr's guide 4.50 (ISBN 0-201-02595-7). A-W.

Gray, A. William & Ulm, Otis M. Applications of College Mathematics. 1970. text ed. 11.95x (ISBN 0-02-474540-5, 47454). Macmillan.

Graybill, Franklin A. Theory & Applications of the Linear Model. LC 75-41970. 1976. text ed. 22.95x (ISBN 0-87872-108-8). Duxbury Pr.

Green, Robert T. & Laxon, Veronica J. Entering the World of Number. (Illus.). 1978. 12.95 (ISBN 0-500-01196-6). Thames Hudson.

Greene, R. E. & Wu, H. H. Function Theory on Manifolds Which Possess a Pole. (Lecture Notes in Mathematics: Vol. 699). 1979. pap. 13.10 (ISBN 0-387-09108-4). Springer-Verlag.

Gregson, M. J., ed. Recent Theoretical Developments in Control. (Institute of Mathematics & Applications Conference Ser.). 1978. 62.50 (ISBN 0-12-301650-9). Acad Pr.

Greitzer, Samuel L., compiled by. International Mathematical Olympiads Nineteen Fifty-Nine to Nineteen Seventy-Seven. 1979. pap. 2.95 (ISBN 0-88385-600-X). NCTM.

Grossnickle, Foster E. Fundamental Mathematics. (Adult Basic Education Ser.) (RL 7-8). 1971. text ed. 7.77 (ISBN 0-03-085393-1, HoltC). HR&W.

Grosswald, Emil & Rademacher, Hans. Dedekind Sums. LC 72-88698. (Carus Monograph: No. 16). 102p. 1972. 12.50 (ISBN 0-88385-016-8). Math Assn.

Guha, Ushri. An Introduction to Modern Mathematics. 364p. 1981. 15.00x (ISBN 0-86125-503-8, Pub. by Orient Longman India). State Mutual Bk.

Guillelmin, Victor, et al. Seminar on Micro-Local Analysis. LC 78-70609. (Annals of Mathematics Studies: No. 93). 1979. 18.00x (ISBN 0-691-08228-6); pap. 6.50 (ISBN 0-691-08232-4). Princeton U Pr.

Gulati, Bodh R. Finite Mathematics: An Introduction. 389p. 1975. text ed. 23.50 scp (ISBN 0-06-042537-7, HarpC); answers to even numbered problems free (ISBN 0-06-362550-4). Har-Row.

Hackworth, Robert D. & Howland, Joseph. Introductory College Mathematics: Consumer Mathematics. LC 75-23617. 67p. 1976. pap. text ed. 2.95 (ISBN 0-7216-4410-4). HR&W.

Hadamard, Jacques. An Essay on the Psychology of Invention in the Mathematical Field. LC 54-4731. lib. bdg. 9.50x (ISBN 0-88307-121-5). Gannon.

Hadley, G. & Kemp, M. C. Finite Mathematics in Business & Economics. 1972. text ed. 24.50 (ISBN 0-444-10356-2, North-Holland). Elsevier.

Halberg, Leland R. & Zink, Howard E. Mathematics for Technicians with an Introduction to Calculus. 1972. 17.95x (ISBN 0-534-00144-0). Wadsworth Pub.

Haldi, John F. Basic Mathematics: Skills & Structure. (Illus., LC 77-073943). 1978. pap. text ed. 14.25 (ISBN 0-395-25117-6); inst. manual 2.00 (ISBN 0-395-25114-1). HM.

Hall. Computational Structures. (Computer Monographs: Vol. 23). 1975. 19.95 (ISBN 0-444-19522-X). Elsevier.

Halmos, P. R. & Sunder, V. S. Bounded Integral Operatores on L Two Spaces. (Ergebnisse der Mathematik und Ihrer Grenzgebiete: Vol. 96). 1979. 21.00 (ISBN 0-387-08894-6). Springer-Verlag.

Hamming, Richard W. Numerical Methods for Scientists & Engineers. rev. ed. (Illus.). 612p. 1973. text ed. 22.50 (ISBN 0-07-025887-2, C). McGraw.

Hannon, Ralph H. Mathematics for Technical Careers. new ed. (Mathematics Ser.). 304p. 1976. text ed. 17.95 (ISBN 0-675-08656-6); instructor's manual 3.95 (ISBN 0-686-67254-2). Merrill.

Hansberger, Ross. Ingenuity in Mathematics. LC 77-134351. (New Mathematical Library: No. 23). 1975. pap. 6.50 (ISBN 0-88385-623-9). Math Assn.

Hardy, Godfrey H. Mathematician's Apology. rev. ed. LC 67-21958. 1969. 18.95 (ISBN 0-521-05207-6); pap. 5.50x (ISBN 0-521-09577-8). Cambridge U Pr.

Harris, Z. A Grammar of English on Mathematical Principles. 480p. 1981. 35.00 (ISBN 0-471-02958-0, Pub. by Wiley-Interscience). Wiley.

Hartkopf, Roy. Math Without Tears. (Illus.). 1970. 10.95 (ISBN 0-87523-173-X). Emerson.

Hatcher, William S. The Logical Foundations of Mathematics. LC 80-41253. (Foundations & Philosophy of Science & Technology Ser.). 400p. Date not set. 48.00 (ISBN 0-08-025800-X). Pergamon.

Heading, J. Mathematical Methods in Science & Engineering. 1970. 19.00 (ISBN 0-444-19680-3). Elsevier.

Hemmerling, Edwin M. Elementary Mathematics for the Technician. 1974. text ed. 16.95 (ISBN 0-07-028074-6, G); answers to even-numbered problems 2.00 (ISBN 0-07-028075-4). McGraw.

Hermann, Robert. Yang-Mills, Kaluza-Klein & the Einstein Program. (Interdisciplinary Mathematics Ser.: No. 19). 1978. 20.00 (ISBN 0-915692-25-2). Math Sci Pr.

Herstein, I. N. Notes from Ring-Theory Conference. LC 72-165202. (CBMS Regional Conference Series in Mathematics: No. 9). 1971. 7.40 (ISBN 0-8218-1658-6, CBMS-9). Am Math.

Heywood, Arthur. A First Program in Mathematics. 3rd ed. 1977. 16.95x (ISBN 0-8221-0185-8). Dickenson.

Hildebrand, Francis B. Methods of Applied Mathematics. 2nd ed. 1965. ref. ed. 27.95 (ISBN 0-13-579201-0). P-H.

Hinchey, Fred A. Introduction to Applicable Mathematics: Elementary Analysis, Vol. 1. LC 80-18569. (Ser. of Introduction to Applicable Mathematics). 288p. 1981. 19.95 (ISBN 0-470-27041-1). Halsted Pr.

Hirzebruch, F. E., et al. Prospects in Mathematics. LC 72-155007. (Annals of Mathematics Studies: No. 70). 1971. 14.00x (ISBN 0-691-08094-1). Princeton U Pr.

Hobbs, Glenn M. & McKinney, James. Practical Mathematics. 3rd ed. (Illus.). 1973. 13.33 (ISBN 0-8269-2242-2). Am Technical.

Hockett, Shirley. Basic Mathematics: What Every College Student Should Know. (Illus.). 1977. pap. 15.95 (ISBN 0-13-063446-8). P-H.

Hoffman, Laurence D. & Orkin, Michael. Mathematics with Applications. (Illus.). 1979. text ed. 15.95 (ISBN 0-07-029301-5, C); 3.95 (ISBN 0-07-029302-3); study guide 4.95 (ISBN 0-07-029303-1). McGraw.

Hoffman, Laurence D. & Orkin, Micheal. Finite Mathematics with Applications. (Illus.). 1979. text ed. 14.95 (ISBN 0-07-029310-4, C); instructor's manual 2.95 (ISBN 0-07-029311-2); study guide 3.95 (ISBN 0-07-029312-0). McGraw.

Hofmann, K. H. & Mislove, M. The Pontryagin Duality of Compact O-Dimensional Semilattices & Its Applications. (Lecture Notes in Mathematics: Vol. 396). xvi, 122p. 1974. pap. 9.90 (ISBN 0-387-06807-4). Springer-Verlag.

Hogben, Lancelot. Mathematics for the Million. 4th ed. 1968. 22.50 (ISBN 0-393-06361-5). Norton.

Honsberger, Ross. Mathematical Gems I. LC 73-89661. 1974. 11.00 (ISBN 0-88385-301-9). Math Assn.

Honsberger, Ross, ed. Mathematical Plums. LC 79-65513. (Dolciani Mathematical Expositions: Vol. IV). 14.00 (ISBN 0-88385-304-3). Math Assn.

Horadam, A. F. Outline Course of Pure Mathematics. 1969. 23.00 (ISBN 0-08-012593-X). Pergamon.

Hornof, John A. Traditional Math, Restored, Simplified, Condensed, Brought up to Date, Made Relevant, Programmed & All Those Good Things. (Illus.). 1977. pap. 8.95 (ISBN 0-918094-01-1); answer bk 1.00 (ISBN 0-918094-02-X). Bedous.

Horrobin, Peter. Constructional Mathematics, Vol. 1. 1969. pap. 7.00 (ISBN 0-08-006890-1). Pergamon.

Horton, Holbrook L. Mathematics at Work. 2nd ed. (Illus.). 728p. 1957. 16.00 (ISBN 0-8311-1047-3). Indus Pr.

Howett, J. Basic Skills with Math: A General Review. 192p. 1980. pap. text ed. 3.78 (ISBN 0-8428-2119-8). Cambridge Bk.

Howson, A. G., ed. Developments in Mathematical Education. (Illus.). 250p. 1973. pap. 13.95 (ISBN 0-521-09803-3). Cambridge U Pr.

Hughston, L. P., ed. Advances in Twister Theory. Ward, R. S. (Research Notes in Mathematics Ser.: No. 37). 352p. (Orig.). 1979. pap. text ed. 21.95 (ISBN 0-273-08448-8). Pitman Pub MA.

Huntley, H. E. The Divine Proportion: A Study in Mathematical Beauty. LC 70-93195. lib. bdg. 10.50x (ISBN 0-88307-152-5). Gannon.

Immerzeel, George & Wills, Bob, eds. Ideas from the Arithmetic Teacher. 1979. pap. 5.40 (ISBN 0-87353-143-4). NCTM.

Index to Translations Selected by the American Mathematical Society, Vol. 2. 1973. 20.80 (ISBN 0-8218-0059-0, TRAN2I-51). Am Math.

International Conference on Functional Analysis & Related Topics, 1969. Proceedings. Mathematical Society of Japan, ed. 460p. 1970. 26.50x (ISBN 0-86008-026-9, Pub by U of Tokyo Pr). Intl Schol Bk Serv.

International Congress of Mathematicians, 1978, Helsinki. Proceedings. 1980. 70.00 (ISBN 951-41-0352-1). Am Math.

International Summer School, University of Antwerp, 1972. Modular Functions of One Variable 2: Proceedings. Kuyk, W. & Deligne, P., eds. (Lecture Notes in Mathematics: Vol. 349). v, 598p. 1974. pap. 21.50 (ISBN 0-387-06558-X). Springer-Verlag.

Introduction to Mathematics, 2 bks. 1980. Bk. 1. pap. text ed. 2.50 (ISBN 0-8428-9341-5). Bk. 2 (ISBN 0-8428-9341-5). Cambridge Bk.

Italian National Institute of Higher Mathematics Conventions. Symposia Mathematica: Proceedings. Incl. Vol. 1. Group Theory. 1970. 65.00 (ISBN 0-12-612201-6); Vol. 2. Functional Analysis & Geometry. 1970. 79.00 (ISBN 0-12-612202-4); Vol. 3. Problems in the Evolution of the Solar System. 1970. 70.00 (ISBN 0-12-612203-2); Vol. 4. 1971. 73.50 (ISBN 0-12-612204-0); Vol. 5. 1971. 62.50 (ISBN 0-12-612205-9); Vol. 6. 1971. 78.00 (ISBN 0-12-612206-7); Vol. 7. 1972. 44.50 (ISBN 0-12-612207-5); Vol. 8. 1972. 82.50 (ISBN 0-12-612208-3); Vol. 9. 1972. 64.50 (ISBN 0-12-612209-1); Vol. 10. 1973. 78.00 (ISBN 0-12-612210-5); Vol. 18. 1977. 68.00 (ISBN 0-12-612218-0); Vol. 19. 1977. 52.50 (ISBN 0-12-612219-9). Acad Pr.

Jacobs, Harold R. Mathematics, a Human Endeavor: A Textbook for Those Who Think They Don't Like the Subject. LC 70-116898. (Illus.). 1970. text ed. 11.95x (ISBN 0-7167-0439-0); tchr's guide 6.95x (ISBN 0-7167-0446-3). W H Freeman.

Jaffe, Philip M. & Maglio, Rodolfo. Technical Mathematics. 1979. text ed. 17.95x (ISBN 0-673-15111-5). Scott F.

James, Elizabeth & Barkin, Carol. What Do You Mean by "Average"? Means, Medians, & Modes. LC 78-7227. (Illus.). (gr. 3-8). 1978. 6.95 (ISBN 0-688-41854-6); PLB 6.67 (ISBN 0-688-51854-0). Lothrop.

James, G. D. The Representation Theory of the Symmetric Groups. (Lecture Notes in Mathematics Ser.: Vol. 682). 1979. pap. 11.30 (ISBN 0-387-08948-9). Springer-Verlag.

Jeffreys, Harold & Jeffreys, Bertha S. Methods of Mathematical Physics. 3rd ed. (Illus.). 1956. pap. 22.95x (ISBN 0-521-09723-1). Cambridge U Pr.

Jenkins, Lee & McLean, Peggy. Set & Think. (Illus.). 08p. 1972. 2.50 (ISBN 0-912990-05-8). Ed Sci.

Jenkins, Lee, et al. It's a Tangram World. (Illus.). 94p. 1971. tchrs. ed. 4.25 (ISBN 0-912990-00-7). Ed Sci.

Johnson, Grace G. Mathematics for Nursing. 208p. 1981. pap. text ed. 7.95 (ISBN 0-8385-6174-8). ACC.

Johnson, James F., et al. Applied Mathematics. 4th ed. 1975. text ed. 8.96 (ISBN 0-02-819070-X); tchr's ed. 11.40 (ISBN 0-02-819080-7). Glencoe.

Johnson, Robert M. & Tibbits, Patricia. Basic Industrial Mathematics, Metric Edition. (Illus.). 1979. pap. text ed. 9.95 (ISBN 0-07-032671-1, G); answers to even numbered problems 4.95 (ISBN 0-07-032672-X). McGraw.

Jumde, A. G., et al. A New Course in Mathematics, Vol. I. 334p. 1981. 15.00x (ISBN 0-86125-413-9, Pub. by Orient Longman India). State Mutual Bk.

--A New Course in Mathematics, Vol. II. 378p. 1981. 15.00x (ISBN 0-86131-061-6, Pub. by Orient Longman India). State Mutual Bk.

Juszli, Frank L. & Rodgers, Charles A. Elementary Technical Mathematics. 3rd ed. (Illus.). 1980. text ed. 17.95 (ISBN 0-13-260869-3). P-H.

Kahn, Donald W. Topology: An Introduction to the Point-Set & Algebraic Areas. 211p. 1980. Repr. of 1975 ed. 14.50 (ISBN 0-683-04500-8). Krieger.

Kalmanson, Kenneth & Kenschaft, Patricia C. Mathematics: A Practical Approach. LC 77-81755. (Illus.). 1978. text ed. 18.95x (ISBN 0-87901-085-1). H S Worth.

Kami, Constance & De Vries, Rheta. Piaget, Children & Numbers. 1979. pap. 3.10 (ISBN 0-912674-49-0). NCTM.

Kamke, Erich. Differentialgleichungen: Loesungsmethoden und Loesungen, Vol. 2: Partielle Differentialgleichungen Erster Ordnung Fuer eine Gesuchte Funktion. LC 49-5862. 243p. 1974. Repr. of 1967 ed. text ed. 11.95 (ISBN 0-8284-0277-9). Chelsea Pub.

Kaplansky, Irving. Fields & Rings. rev. 2nd ed. LC 72-78251. (Chicago Lectures in Mathematics Ser). 224p. 1972. text ed. 10.00x (ISBN 0-226-42450-2); pap. text ed. 8.00x (ISBN 0-226-42451-0). U of Chicago Pr.

Kaufmann, Jerome E. Mathematics Is... 2nd ed. LC 80-39984. 504p. 1981. text ed. write for info. (ISBN 0-87150-313-1, 33L 2501). Prindle.

Keedy, M. L. Exploring Modern Mathematics, Bks. 1 & 2. 3rd ed. (gr. 7-8). 1971. text ed. 11.80 ea. Bk. 1. Bk. 2 (ISBN 0-03-084094-5). tchrs' annot. eds. 10.80 ea. Tchrs' Ed. For Bk. 1 (ISBN 0-03-084088-0). Tchrs' Ed. For Bk. 2 (ISBN 0-03-084095-3). HR&W.

--Nongraded Approach to Exploring Elementary Mathematics. 1972. pap. text ed. 2.64 (ISBN 0-03-091923-1). HR&W.

Keedy, M. L., et al. Exploring Modern Mathematics, Bks. 1 & 2. 4th ed. (gr. 7-8). 1976. Bk. 1 - Gr. 7. text ed. 10.64 (ISBN 0-03-089766-1, HoltC); Bk. 2, Gr. 8. text ed. 10.64 (ISBN 0-03-089774-2); Bk. 1. tchr's ed. 17.28 (ISBN 0-03-089767-X); Bk. 2. tchr's ed. 17.28 (ISBN 0-03-089775-0). HR&W.

--Exploring Modern Mathematics: An Individual Approach. 1976. 3.00 (ISBN 0-03-089764-5, HoltC). HR&W.

Keedy, Mervin L. & Bittinger, Marvin L. Essential Mathematics. 3rd ed. 1980. pap. text ed. 16.95 (ISBN 0-201-03837-4). A-W.

Keenan, Edward P. & Dressler, Isidore. Integrated Mathematics: Course II. (Orig.). (gr. 10). 1981. text ed. 19.17 (ISBN 0-87720-251-6); pap. text ed. 12.08 (ISBN 0-87720-250-8). AMSCO Sch.

Keeves, J. P. & Radford, W. C. Some Aspects of Performance in Mathematics in Australian Schools. (Australian Council for Educational Research). 1969. pap. 4.50x (ISBN 0-8426-1330-7). Verry.

Keiffer, Mildred & Smith, Harold. Pathways in Mathematics. Incl. Level One. rev. ed. (gr. 7). 1977. pap. text ed. 6.64 (ISBN 0-913688-31-2); tchr's guide 6.00 (ISBN 0-913688-33-9); Level Two. rev. ed. (gr. 8). 1977 (ISBN 0-913688-32-0). tchr's guide (ISBN 0-913688-34-7). pap. text ed. 6.64x ea.; tchr's guide 6.00x (ISBN 0-685-77480-5). Pawnee Pub.

Keller, M. Wiles & Zant, James H. Basic Mathematics. 3rd ed. LC 78-69602. (Illus.). 1979. pap. text ed. 14.95 (ISBN 0-395-27050-2); inst. annot. ed. 15.95 (ISBN 0-395-27051-0). HM.

Kempf, Albert F. New Math Made Simple. LC 66-12224. pap. 3.50 (ISBN 0-385-04174-8, Made). Doubleday.

Kempf, G., et al. Toroidal Embeddings 1. LC 73-11598. (Lecture Notes in Mathematics: Vol. 339). 209p. 1973. pap. 12.20 (ISBN 0-387-06432-X). Springer-Verlag.

Kendall, P. G., et al. Mathematics in the Archeological & Historical Sciences. 1972. 31.50 (ISBN 0-85224-213-1, Pub. by Edinburgh U Pr Scotland). Columbia U Pr.

Kennedy, Leonard M. Guiding Children to Mathematical Discovery. 3rd ed. 544p. 1979. text ed. 19.95x (ISBN 0-534-00757-0). Wadsworth Pub.

Kenschaft, Patricia C. Linear Mathematics: A Practical Approach. LC 77-81757. (Illus.). 1978. text ed. 13.95x (ISBN 0-87901-084-3). H S Worth.

Kerr, Donald R. Basic Mathematics: Arithmetic with an Introduction to Algebra. (Illus.). 1979. pap. text ed. 11.95 (ISBN 0-07-034230-X, C); instructors manual 4.95 (ISBN 0-07-034231-8). McGraw.

Kertz, George J. The Nature & Application of Mathematics. LC 78-20979. (Illus.). 1979. pap. 17.95 (ISBN 0-87620-614-3); answer book avail. (ISBN 0-685-65098-7). Goodyear.

Keyser, Cassius J. Human Worth of Rigorous Thinking. facs. ed. LC 71-142651. (Essay Index Reprint Ser). 1925. 16.00 (ISBN 0-8369-2169-0). Arno.

Keystrokes Series, 4 bks. 1981. Set. 22.00 (ISBN 0-88488-215-2, 10560). Creative Pubns.

Kim & Roush. Introduction to Mathematical Theories of Social Consensus. (Lecture Notes in Pure & Applied Mathematics Ser.: Vol. 59). 192p. 1980. 25.00 (ISBN 0-8247-1001-0). Dekker.

Kim, K. A. & Roush, F. W. Mathematics for Social Scientists. LC 79-19336. 304p. 1979. 18.95 (ISBN 0-444-99066-6, Pub. by Elsevier). Greenwood.

Kingston, J. M. Mathematics for Teachers of the Middle Grades. 322p. 1966. text ed. 12.50 (ISBN 0-471-47960-8, Pub. by Wiley). Krieger.

Klarner, David A., ed. Mathematical Gardner. 1980. write for info. (ISBN 0-87150-294-1, 2321). Prindle.

Kleene, S. C. Introduction to Metamathematics. 1971. text ed. 39.00 (ISBN 0-444-10088-1, North-Holland). Elsevier.

Kline, Morris. Mathematics: A Cultural Approach. 1962. text ed. 19.95 (ISBN 0-201-03770-X). A-W.

--Mathematics for Liberal Arts. 1967. text ed. 18.95 (ISBN 0-201-03771-8); instr's manual 2.50 (ISBN 0-201-03772-6). A-W.

--Why Johnny Can't Add: The Failure of the New Math. 1961. pap. 1.95 (ISBN 0-394-71981-6, Vin). Random.

Kline, Morris, intro. by. Mathematics: An Introduction to Its Spirit & Use: Readings from Scientific American. LC 78-7878. (Illus.). 1979. text ed. 19.95x (ISBN 0-7167-0370-X); pap. text ed. 9.95x (ISBN 0-7167-0369-6). W H Freeman.

Klinger, Fred. Mathematics for Everyone. 1967. pap. 1.95 (ISBN 0-8065-0097-2, C253). Citadel Pr.

Knight, Frank B., ed. Essentials of Brownian Motion & Diffusion. LC 80-29504. (Mathematical Surveys: Vol. 18). 1981. 34.40 (ISBN 0-8218-1518-0, SURV 18). Am Math.

Knuth, Donald E. Surreal Numbers. LC 74-5998. 1974. pap. text ed. 5.95 (ISBN 0-201-03812-9). A-W.

Kogbetliantz, E. G. Fundamentals of Mathematics from an Advanced Viewpoint, 4 vols. in 2. Incl. Vols. 1 & 2. Algebra & Analysis: Evolution of the Number Concept & Determinants-Equations-Logarithms-Limits. 592p. 1968. 87.50x (ISBN 0-677-02000-7); Vols. 3 & 4. Geometry & Geometric Analysis & Solid Geometry & Spherical Trigonometry. 498p. 1969. 87.50x (ISBN 0-677-02010-4). complete set 158.00x (ISBN 0-677-00470-2); pap. 104.00 (ISBN 0-677-00475-3). Gordon.

Kogelman, Stanley & Warren, Joseph. Mind Over Math: Put Yourself on the Road to Success by Freeing Yourself from Math Anxiety. 1979. pap. 3.95 (ISBN 0-07-035281-X). McGraw.

Kopochenova, N. V. & Maron, I. A. Computational Mathematics. 395p. 1975. 5.60 (ISBN 0-8285-0705-8, Pub. by Mir Pubs Russia). Imported Pubns.

Korn, Granino A. & Korn, Theresa M. Mathematical Handbook for Scientists & Engineers. 2nd ed. 1968. 46.50 (ISBN 0-07-035370-0, P&RB). McGraw.

Korn, Henry J. Exact Change. (Orig.). 1974. pap. 2.00 (ISBN 0-915066-05-X). Assembling Pr.

Koza, Russell C. Mathematical & Operations Research Techniques in Health Administration. LC 72-96158. (Illus.). 319p. 1973. text ed. 13.50x (ISBN 0-87081-051-0). Colo Assoc.

Kramer, A. D. Fundamentals of Technical Mathematics. 1982. price not set (ISBN 0-07-035427-8); price not set instr's manual (ISBN 0-07-035428-6). McGraw.

Krantz, David H., et al, eds. Contemporary Developments in Mathematical Psychology: Measurement, Psychophysics, & Neural Information Processing, Vol. 2. LC 73-21887. (Illus.). 1974. text ed. 14.00x (ISBN 0-7167-0849-3). W H Freeman.

Kruglak, Haym & Moore, J. T. Basic Mathematics with Applications. (Schaum Outline Ser.). 1973. text ed. 4.95 (ISBN 0-07-035551-7, SP). McGraw.

Krylov, N. V. Controlled Diffusion Processes. (Applications of Mathematics Ser.: Vol. 14). 448p. 1980. 40.00 (ISBN 0-387-90461-1). Springer-Verlag.

Krzyzanski, Miroslaw. Partial Differential Equations of Second Order, 2 vols. 1971. Vol. 1. 20.75 (ISBN 0-02-848100-3); Vol. 2. 15.25 (ISBN 0-02-848120-8). Hafner.

Kudrjavcev, L. D. Direct & Inverse Imbedding Theorem. LC 73-22139. (Translations of Mathematical Monographs: Vol. 42). 1974. 41.20 (ISBN 0-8218-1592-X, MMONO-42). Am Math.

Kudryavtsev, V. A. & Demidovich, B. P. A Brief Course in Higher Mathematics. 1981. 16.00 (ISBN 0-686-74550-7, Pub. by Mir Pubs Russia). Imported Pubns.

Kuehn, Martin H. Mathematics for Electricians. 3rd ed. 1949. text ed. 16.95 (ISBN 0-07-035599-1, G). McGraw.

Kuipers, L. & Niederreiter, H. Uniform Distribution of Sequences. LC 73-20497. (Pure & Applied Mathematics Ser.). 390p. 1974. 42.50 (ISBN 0-471-51045-9, Pub. by Wiley-Interscience). Wiley.

Kuipers, L. & Timman, R. Handbook of Mathematics. 1969. 60.00 (ISBN 0-08-011857-7); pap. 29.00 (ISBN 0-08-018996-2). Pergamon.

Kuratowski, K. A Half Century of Polish Mathematics: Remembrances & Reflections. (International Series in Pure & Applied Mathematics: Vol. 108). (Illus.). 212p. 1980. 26.00 (ISBN 0-08-023046-6). Pergamon.

Kuzawa, Sr. M. Grace. Modern Mathematics: The Genesis of a School in Poland. 1968. 4.50x (ISBN 0-8084-0222-6); pap. 2.25x (ISBN 0-8084-0223-4, P14). Coll & U Pr.

Lallement, Gerard. Semigroups & Combinatorial Applications. LC 78-23561. (Pure & Applied Mathematics Ser.). 400p. 1979. 37.00 (ISBN 0-471-04379-6, Pub. by Wiley-Interscience). Wiley.

Lalor, et al. Mathematics: Back to Basics. 1977. 7.50x (ISBN 0-916060-03-9). Math Alternatives.

Lamb, George L. Elements of Solition Theory. LC 80-13373. (Pure & Applied Mathematics: Texts & Monographs). 289p. 1980. 29.95 (ISBN 0-471-04559-4, Pub. by Wiley-Interscience). Wiley.

Lang, Serge A. SL-Two(R) 1975. text ed. 26.50 (ISBN 0-201-04248-7). A-W.

Lapwood, E. R. & Usami, T. Free Oscillations of the Earth. (Cambridge Monographs on Mechanics & Applied Mathematics). (Illus.). 168p. 1981. 49.95 (ISBN 0-521-23536-7). Cambridge U Pr.

Larue, Alexandre & Decelles, Pierre. Initiation Aux Mathematiques Contemporaines. (Fr). 1966. pap. 3.00x (ISBN 2-7637-6301-4, Pub. by Laval). Intl Schol Bk Serv.

Larue, Alexandre & Gaulin, Claude. Mathematiques Generales: Ensembles, Systemes, Induction, Variable, Relations, Fonctions. (Fr). 1962. 3.50x (ISBN 2-7637-6025-2, Pub. by Laval). Intl Schol Bk Serv.

Larue, Alexandre & Risi, Marcel. Mathematiques Intermediaires. (Fr). 1960. 4.50x (ISBN 2-7637-6017-1, Pub. by Laval). Intl Schol Bk Serv.

Laughlin, Blanche. Guidebook to Mathematics. (Remedial). (gr. 7 up). 1967. pap. text ed. 2.19 (ISBN 0-87892-611-9); tchrs' handbook 2.19 (ISBN 0-87892-612-7). Economy Co.

Lawrence, E. T. Mathematics & the Universe: An Interpretation Based on the Theory of Relativity. 1977. 8.95 (ISBN 0-533-02537-0). Vantage.

Lax, Peter D., ed. Mathematical Aspects of Production & Distribution of Energy. LC 77-7174. (Proceedings of Symposia in Applied Mathematics: No. 21). 1979. Repr. of 1977 ed. with corrections 15.20 (ISBN 0-8218-0121-X, PSAPM-21). Am Math.

Lebesgue, Henri. Lecons sur L'integration et la Recherche des Fonctions Primitives. 3rd ed. LC 73-921. 340p. (Fr.). (gr. 12 up). 1973. text ed. 9.95 (ISBN 0-8284-0267-1). Chelsea Pub.

LeBlanc, John F., et al. Mathematics-Methods Program: Analysis of Shapes. (Mathematics Ser.). (Illus.). 112p. 1976. pap. text ed. 3.25 (ISBN 0-201-14618-5); instr's man. 1.50 (ISBN 0-201-14619-3). A-W.

--Mathematics-Methods Program: Graphs, the Picturing of Information. (Mathematics Ser.). (Illus.). 160p. 1976. pap. text ed. 3.95 (ISBN 0-201-14622-3); instr's man. 1.50 (ISBN 0-201-14623-1). A-W.

--Mathematics-Methods Program: Measurement. (Mathematics Ser.). (Illus.). 144p. 1976. pap. text ed. 3.50 (ISBN 0-201-14620-7); instr's man. 1.50 (ISBN 0-201-14621-5). A-W.

LeCuyer, E. J. College Mathematics with a Programming Language. (Undergraduate Texts in Mathematics). 1978. 17.10 (ISBN 0-387-90280-5). Springer-Verlag.

Ledermann, Walter. Handbook of Applicable Mathematics, Vol. 1: Algebra. LC 79-42724. (Handbook of Applicable Mathematics Ser.). 524p. 1980. text ed. 85.00 (ISBN 0-471-27704-5, Pub. by Wiley-Interscience). Wiley.

Lee, Virginia. Basic Mathematics. 1976. pap. text ed. 16.95 scp (ISBN 0-06-384820-1, HarpC); tchr's manual free (ISBN 0-06-373851-1). Har-Row.

Leffin, et al. Basic Technical Mathematics. LC 80-23384. 402p. 1981. text ed. write for info. (ISBN 0-87150-298-4, 2341). Prindle.

Leitmann, G. & Marzollo, A., eds. Multicriteria Decision Making. (International Centre for Mechanical Sciences. Courses & Lectures: No. 211). 1977. soft cover 28.70 (ISBN 0-387-81340-3). Springer-Verlag.

Leonard, John & Warner, Blaine. Beginning Mathematics for College Students. (Illus.). 416p. 1971. text ed. 15.95 (ISBN 0-13-074013-6). P-H.

Leonhardy, Adele. Introductory College Mathematics. 2nd ed. LC 63-12284. 1963. text ed. 23.95 (ISBN 0-471-52736-X). Wiley.

Lerro, Joseph. Basic Mathematics. 1976. 14.95 (ISBN 0-8436-0336-4); student ed. o.p. 9.95 (ISBN 0-8436-0337-2). CBI Pub.

Leslie, John F., et al. Core Mathematics. 2nd ed. 1980. pap. text ed. 11.95x (ISBN 0-673-15320-7). Scott F.

Levin, Simon. Some Mathematical Questions in Biology. (Lectures in Mathematics in the Life Sciences Ser.: Vol. 12). 1979. 15.40 (ISBN 0-8218-1162-2). Am Math.

Levine, Samuel. Vocational & Technical Mathematics in Action. (Illus., Orig.). 1969. pap. 12.95x (ISBN 0-8104-5717-2); inst. guide & ans. bk. 1.95x (ISBN 0-8104-5719-9); transparencies 102.15 (ISBN 0-8104-8851-5). Hayden.

Lewis, J. Parry. Introduction to Mathematics for Students of Economics. 2nd ed. LC 77-76382. 1969. pap. text ed. 9.95 (ISBN 0-312-42945-2). St Martin.

Liebeck, Pamela. Vectors & Matrices. 192p. 1971. 25.00 (ISBN 0-08-015823-4); pap. 12.75 (ISBN 0-08-015822-6). Pergamon.

Lions, J. L. Some Aspects of the Optimal Control of Distributed Parameter Systems: Proceedings. (CBMS Regional Conference Ser.: Vol. 6). (Illus., Orig.). 1972. pap. text ed. 7.25 (ISBN 0-686-24258-0). Soc Indus-Appl Math.

Lipschutz, Seymour. Outline of Discrete Mathematics. (Schaum's Outline Ser.). (Illus.). 1976. pap. 4.95 (ISBN 0-07-037981-5, SP). McGraw.

Lipsman, R. L. Group Representations: A Survey of Some Current Topics. (Lecture Notes in Mathematics: Vol. 388). 166p. 1974. pap. 10.90 (ISBN 0-387-06790-6). Springer-Verlag.

Liu, Chung L. Elements of Discrete Mathematics. (Computer Science Ser.). 1977. text ed. 20.50 (ISBN 0-07-038131-3, C); instructor's manual 4.95 (ISBN 0-07-038132-1). McGraw.

Logsdon, Mayme I. Mathematician Explains. (Midway Reprint Ser). 208p. 1975. pap. 8.00x (ISBN 0-226-49185-4). U of Chicago Pr.

Long, John, Jr., et al. Tune in to Early Math: Picture Workbook. (Illus.). 1978. pap. 2.90x (ISBN 0-87076-321-0). Stanwix.

--Tune in to Early Math: Songs You Can Count on. 1976. pap. 5.00x (ISBN 0-87076-323-7). Stanwix.

Lovelock, David & Rund, Hanno. Tensors, Differential Forms, & Variational Principles. LC 75-2261. (Pure & Applied Mathematics Ser). 364p. 1975. 38.00 (ISBN 0-471-54840-5, Pub. by Wiley-Interscience). Wiley.

Luke, Y. L., et al. Index to Mathematics of Computation, 1943-1969. 1972. 28.80 (ISBN 0-8218-4000-2, MCOMIN-1). Am Math.

Lusin, Nicolas. Lecons Sur les Ensembles Analytiques. LC 74-144043. xv, 328p. (Fr.). 1972. Repr. of 1930 ed. text ed. 12.95 (ISBN 0-8284-0250-7). Chelsea Pub.

Luxemburg & Zaanen. Riesz Spaces. 63.50 (ISBN 0-444-10129-2, North-Holland). Elsevier.

Luxenburg, Walter J. Mathematics for Technical Education. LC 75-41974. 1977. pap. text ed. 8.95x (ISBN 0-87872-111-8). Duxbury Pr.

Lyng, Merwin J., et al. Applied Technical Mathematics. LC 77-76423. (Illus.). 1978. text ed. 16.75 (ISBN 0-395-25429-9); inst. manual 0.80 (ISBN 0-395-25428-0). HM.

McCoy, Neal H. Rings & Ideals. (Carus Monograph: No. 8). 216p. 1948. 11.00 (ISBN 0-88385-008-7). Math Assn.

McCully, Ron. Up with Math: Basic Skills Step by Step. Jacobs, Russell F., ed. (Illus.). (gr. 5-12). 1979. pap. text ed. 4.90 (ISBN 0-918272-03-3); tchr's ed. 5.85 (ISBN 0-918272-04-1). Jacobs.

MacDonald, Peter. Mathematics & Statistics for Scientists & Engineers. (Illus.). 1966. 13.95x (ISBN 0-442-05067-4). Van Nos Reinhold.

McElroy, Norman L. & Carr, Joseph J. Simplified Mathematics for Nurses. LC 76-53017. (Arco Nursing Ser.). (Illus.). 1977. lib. bdg. 9.00 (ISBN 0-668-04464-0, 4464); pap. text ed. 5.00 (ISBN 0-668-04197-8, 4197). Arco.

McFadden, F. Lee, ed. Consumer Math Cassettes. (Illus.). (gr. 8-10). 1979. manual & cassettes 187.50 (ISBN 0-917792-01-7). Math Hse.

McGuinness, Brian, ed. The Infinite in Mathematics. (Vienna Circle Collection: No. 9). 1978. lib. bdg. 45.00 (ISBN 90-277-0847-9, Pub. by Reidel Holland); pap. 24.00 (ISBN 90-277-0848-7). Kluwer Boston.

Machol, Robert E. Elementary Systems Mathematics. (Industrial Engineering & Management Ser.). 1976. text ed. 17.95 (ISBN 0-07-039373-7, C); solutions manual 2.50 (ISBN 0-07-039374-5). McGraw.

McKeague, Pat. Basic Mathematics. 608p. 1981. pap. text ed. 17.95x (ISBN 0-534-00905-0). Wadsworth Pub.

McMackin, et al. Mathematics of the Shop. 4th ed. LC 76-6726. 1978. 13.60 (ISBN 0-8273-1297-0); tchr's ed. 1.60 (ISBN 0-8273-1298-9). Delmar.

McMullen, John R. Extensions of Positive-Definite Functions. LC 52-42893. (Memoirs: No. 117). 1972. pap. 6.40 (ISBN 0-8218-1817-1, MEMO-117). Am Math.

Maeki, S. The Determination of Units in Real Cyclic Sextic Fields. (Lecture Notes in Mathematics: Vol. 797). 1980. pap. 14.00 (ISBN 0-387-09984-0). Springer-Verlag.

Maffei, Anthony C. & Buckley, Patricia. Teaching Preschool Math: Foundations & Activities. LC 79-27448. 176p. 1980. text ed. 14.95 (ISBN 0-87705-492-4). Human Sci Pr.

Maher, Carolyn A., et al. Math, No. 1. Gafney, Leo, ed. (General Math Ser.). (Illus.). (gr. 7-9). 1981. text ed. write for info pupil's ed. (ISBN 0-07-039591-8, W); tchr's ed., 448 p. 13.20 (ISBN 0-07-039592-6); wkbk. to pupils ed. 4.80 (ISBN 0-07-039593-4); wkbk. to tchrs. ed. 5.20 (ISBN 0-07-039594-2). McGraw.

--General Math. Gafney, Leo, ed. 160p. 1980. pupil's ed. 4.80 (ISBN 0-07-039593-4, W); tchrs. ed. 5.20 (ISBN 0-07-039594-2). McGraw.

Mahoney, Susan & Gregorvich, Barbara. Math Word Problems. LC 79-730247. (Illus.). 1979. pap. text ed. 135.00 (ISBN 0-89290-130-6, A515-SATC). Soc for Visual.

Malkevitch, Joseph. Properties of Planar Graphs with Uniform Vertex & Face Structure. LC 52-42839. (Memoirs: No. 99). 1970. pap. 7.20 (ISBN 0-8218-1299-8, MEMO-99). Am Math.

Manin, Y. I. Mathematics & Physics. (Progress in Physics Ser.). 112p. 1981. 10.00 (ISBN 3-7643-3027-9). Birkhauser.

Marano, Joseph & Kaufman, Kenneth. Fundamentals of Mathematics. (Illus.). 480p. 1973. text ed. 17.95 (ISBN 0-13-341081-1). P-H.

Marcy, Steve & Marcy, Janis. Mathimagination. Incl. Bk. A. Beginning Multiplication & Division (ISBN 0-88488-029-X); Bk. B. Operations with Whole Numbers (ISBN 0-88488-030-3); Bk. C. Number Theory, Sets, & Number Bases (ISBN 0-88488-031-1); Bk. D. Fractions (ISBN 0-88488-025-7); Bk. E. Decimals & Per Cent (ISBN 0-88488-026-5); Bk. F. Geometry, Measurement, & Cartesian Coordinates (ISBN 0-88488-032-X). (Illus.). (gr. 4-9). 1973. wkbk. 5.50 ea. Creative Pubns.

--Pre-Algebra with Pizzazz! AA. (YA) 1978. wkbk. 6.50 (ISBN 0-88488-096-6). Creative Pubns.

--Pre-Algebra with Pizzazz! BB. (YA) 1978. wkbk. 6.50 (ISBN 0-88488-097-4). Creative Pubns.

--Pre-Algebra with Pizzazz! CC. (YA) 1978. wkbk. 6.50 (ISBN 0-88488-098-2). Creative Pubns.

--Pre-Algebra with Pizzazz! DD. (YA) 1978. wkbk. 6.50 (ISBN 0-88488-099-0). Creative Pubns.

Margenau, Henry. The Mathematics of Physics & Chemistry, Vol. 2. 1964. text ed. 14.95x (ISBN 0-442-05121-2). Van Nos Reinhold.

Margenau, Henry & Murphy, George M. The Mathematics of Physics & Chemistry. 2nd ed. LC 76-18724. 618p. 1976. Repr. of 1956 ed. text ed. 26.00 (ISBN 0-88275-423-8). Krieger.

Marion, Jerry B. & Davidson, Ronald C. Mathematical Preparation for General Physics. LC 72-176212. (Illus., Orig.). 1972. pap. 6.95 (ISBN 0-7216-6070-3). HR&W.

Marjoram, D. T. Exercises in Modern Mathematics. 1965. text ed. 6.95 (ISBN 0-08-011004-5); pap. 5.40 (ISBN 0-08-011003-7). Pergamon.

--Modern Mathematics in Secondary Schools. 1964. text ed. 6.95 (ISBN 0-08-010719-2); pap. 5.40 (ISBN 0-08-010718-4). Pergamon.

Markus, L. Lectures in Differntiable Dynamics. LC 80-16847. 47p. 1971. 7.40 (ISBN 0-8218-1695-0). Am Math.

Markus, L. & Meyer, K. R. Generic Hamiltonian Dynamical Systems Are Neither Integrable nor Ergodic. LC 74-8095. (Memoirs: No. 144). 1974. pap. 7.60 (ISBN 0-8218-1844-9, MEMO-144). Am Math.

Marriott, F. H. Basic Mathematics for the Biological & Social Sciences. LC 73-99863. 1970. text ed. 17.25 (ISBN 0-08-006663-1); pap. 9.25 (ISBN 0-08-006664-X). Pergamon.

Marsh, L. G. Let's Explore Mathematics, 4 bks. Incl. Bk. 1. (Illus.). 96p. (gr. 6). 1964. pap. text ed. 2.45 (ISBN 0-668-01511-X); Bk. 2. (Illus.). 112p. (gr. 7). 1964. pap. text ed. 2.45 (ISBN 0-668-01512-8); Bk. 3. (Illus.). 112p. (gr. 8). 1964. pap. text ed. 2.45 (ISBN 0-668-01513-6); Bk. 4. (Illus.). 96p. (gr. 9). 1968. pap. 2.45 (ISBN 0-668-01825-9); Teacher's Guide: Children Explore Mathematics. 152p. 1967. 3.00 (ISBN 0-668-02077-6). LC 66-22887. (YA) Arco.

Mathematical Association of America & National Council of Teachers of Mathematics. A Sourcebook for Applications of School Mathematics. 1980. 15.00 (ISBN 0-87353-164-7). NCTM.

Mathematical Exposition Ser. Incl. Mathematical Gems. Honsberger, Ross. LC 73-89661. 1974. 11.00 (ISBN 0-88385-301-9). (ISBN 0-685-40276-2). Math Assn.

Mathematical Ideas. 4th ed. 1981. text ed. 17.95x (ISBN 0-673-15524-2). Scott F.

Mathematics for Christian Living Ser. (gr. 1-2). 1972. write for info (ISBN 0-686-05605-1). Rod & Staff.

Mathematics International, Vol. 1. LC 78-122860. 286p. 1973. 72.75x (ISBN 0-677-30410-2). Gordon.

The Mathematics of Choice. LC 65-17470. (New Mathematical Library: No. 15). 1975. pap. 6.50 (ISBN 0-88385-615-8). Math Assn.

Matthias, Margaret & Thiessen, Diane. Children's Mathematics Books: A Critical Bibliography. LC 79-11896. 1979. pap. 5.00 (ISBN 0-8389-0285-5). ALA.

Mavrommatis, P. D. & Reichmeider, P. F. Precalculus Mathematics for Technical Students. (Technical Mathematics Ser.). (Illus.). 416p. 1976. 18.95 (ISBN 0-13-695163-5). P-H.

Maxwell, Patricia. Mathematics 104. 1972. text ed. 3.95 (ISBN 0-685-48768-7). Collegiate Pub.

Menger, Karl. Selected Papers in Logic & Foundations, Didactics, & Economics. (Vienna Circle Collection: No. 10). 1978. lib. bdg. 58.00 (ISBN 90-277-0320-5, Pub. by Reidel Holland); pap. 29.00 (ISBN 90-277-0321-3, Pub. by Reidel Holland). Kluwer Boston.

Merritt, F. S. Applied Mathematics in Engineering Practice. 1970. 28.50 (ISBN 0-07-041511-0, P&RB). McGraw.

Merserve, Bruce E. & Sobel, Max A. Introduction to Mathematics. 4th ed. (Illus.). 1978. text ed. 19.95 (ISBN 0-13-487553-2). P-H.

Meserve, Bruce E. An Introduction to Finite Mathematics. LC 77-168764. (Mathematics Ser). 1972. text ed. 11.95 (ISBN 0-201-04717-9); instructor's manual 2.00 (ISBN 0-201-04718-7). A-W.

Meserve, Bruce E. & Sobel, Max A. Contemporary Mathematics. 3rd ed. (Illus.). 688p. 1981. text ed. 19.95 (ISBN 0-13-170076-6). P-H.

Meyer, Richard, ed. Transition & Turbulence. LC 81-7903. (Mathematics Research Center Symposium & Advances Seminar Ser.). 1981. 15.50 (ISBN 0-12-493240-1). Acad Pr.

Midwest Category Seminar, 2nd. Reports. MacLane, S., ed. (Lecture Notes in Mathematics: Vol. 61). (Orig.). 1968. pap. 10.70 (ISBN 0-387-04231-8). Springer-Verlag.

Midwestern Conference on Ergodic Theory, 1st, Ohio State Univ, 1970. Contributions to Ergodic Theory & Probability: Proceedings. LC 79-137785. (Lecture Notes in Mathematics: Vol. 160). (Illus.). 1970. pap. 11.20 (ISBN 0-387-05188-0). Springer-Verlag.

Miller, Charles D. & Heeren, Vern E. Mathematical Ideas. 3rd ed. 1978. text ed. 17.95x (ISBN 0-673-15090-9). Scott F.

--Mathematics: An Everyday Experience. 2nd ed. 1980. text ed. 17.95x (ISBN 0-673-15279-0). Scott F.

Miller, Charles D. & Lial, Margaret L. Mathematics & Calculus with Applications. 1980. text ed. 21.95x (ISBN 0-673-15352-5). Scott F.

Miller, Mary K. Mathematics for Nurses with Clinical Applications. LC 80-26040. 385p. (Orig.). 1981. pap. text ed. 14.95 (ISBN 0-8185-0429-3). Brooks-Cole.

Minc, Henryk. Permanents. (Encyclopedia of Mathematics & Its Applications: Vol. 6). 1978. text ed. 21.50 (ISBN 0-201-13505-1, Adv Bk Prog). A-W.

Mirsky, L., ed. Studies in Pure Mathematics. 1971. 33.00 (ISBN 0-12-498450-9). Acad Pr.

Mirsky, Leon, ed. Transversal Theory. (Mathematics in Science & Engineering Ser.: Vol. 75). 1971. 32.50 (ISBN 0-12-498550-5). Acad Pr.

Mitchell, Merle. Mathematical History: Activities, Puzzles, Stories & Games. 1978. pap. 5.00 (ISBN 0-87353-138-8). NCTM.

Monin, J. P., et al. Initiation to the Mathematics of the Processes of Diffusion, Contagion & Propagation. Brandon, M., tr. (Methods & Models in the Social Sciences: No. 4). 1976. pap. text ed. 14.00x (ISBN 90-2797-611-2). Mouton.

Montel, Paul. Familles Normales. LC 73-14649. xiii, 301p. 1974. text ed. 12.00 (ISBN 0-8284-0271-X). Chelsea Pub.

Moon, Robert. Applied Mathematics for Technical Programs: Arithmetic & Geometry. LC 72-96904. 1973. pap. text ed. 19.95 (ISBN 0-675-08983-2); media: audiocassettes 140.00, 2-5 sets, 95.00 ea., 6 or more sets, 70.00 ea. (ISBN 0-675-08918-2); instructor's manual 3.95 (ISBN 0-686-66869-3); test 3.95 (ISBN 0-686-66870-7). Merrill.

Moon, Robert G. Applied Mathematics for Technical Programs: Trigonometry. LC 73-77913. 1973. pap. text ed. 18.95 (ISBN 0-675-08923-9); media: audiocassettes 140.00, 2-5 sets, 95.00 ea., 6 or more sets, 70.00 ea. (ISBN 0-675-08900-X); instructor's manual 3.95 (ISBN 0-686-66871-5). Merrill.

Moore, Claude, et al. Applied Math for Technicians. 2nd ed. 384p. 1982. 17.95 (ISBN 0-13-041178-7). P-H.

Moore, Hal G. Pre-Calculus Mathematics. 2nd ed. LC 76-18678. 1977. text ed. 22.95x (ISBN 0-471-61454-8). Wiley.

Morgan, Bryan. Men & Discoveries in Mathematics. 1972. 10.95 (ISBN 0-7195-2587-X). Transatlantic.

Morgan, Michael, et al. Core Mathematics for Occupational Students. 1976. text ed. 16.95 scp (ISBN 0-06-453301-8, HarpC); instr. manual avail. (ISBN 0-06-453302-6). Harper-Row.

Morris, Victoria S. String Along with Me: The Math Way. (gr. 4 up). 1976. pap. 3.00 (ISBN 0-914318-05-5). V S Morris.

Morrison, Peter. Basic Math Skills. 1972. text ed. 6.64 (ISBN 0-07-043197-3, G). McGraw.

Mueller, Francis J. General Mathematics for College Students. LC 75-140690. 1972. pap. text ed. 13.95 (ISBN 0-13-350512-X). P-H.

Mukherjee, Kanai L. Introductory Mathematics for the Clinical Laboratory. LC 78-10915. (Illus.). 1979. pap. text ed. 20.00 (ISBN 0-89189-069-6, 45-9-006-00). Am Soc Clinical.

Mulholland, H. & Phillips, J. H. Applied Mathematics for Advanced Level. 6.95 (ISBN 0-408-70449-7). Butterworth.

Murakami, S. On Automorphisms of Siegel Domains. LC 72-88927. (Lecture Notes in Mathematics: Vol. 286). 95p. 1972. pap. 6.30 (ISBN 0-387-05985-7). Springer-Verlag.

Murray, F. J. Applied Mathematics: An Intellectual Orientation. (Mathematical Concepts & Methods in Science & Engineering Ser.: Vol. 12). (Illus.). 290p. 1978. 29.50 (ISBN 0-306-39252-6, Plenum Pr). Plenum Pub.

Murthy, V. K. The General Point Process. LC 74-16382. (Applied Mathematics & Computation Ser.: No. 5). 624p. 1974. text ed. 27.50 (ISBN 0-201-04892-2, Adv Bk Prog); pap. text ed. 15.50 (ISBN 0-201-04893-0, Adv Bk Prog). A-W.

Myer, Russell. Let's Talk Math. (Illus.). 100p. 1980. pap. 8.00 (ISBN 0-686-27825-9). RCM Pubns.

Nachbin, L., ed. Functional Analysis & Applications. LC 74-4653. (Lecture Notes in Mathematics: Vol. 384). 270p. (12 contributions in Eng., 2 in Fr.). 1974. pap. 12.50 (ISBN 0-387-06752-3). Springer-Verlag.

Nahikian, H. M. Topics in Modern Mathematics. 1966. text ed. 12.95 (ISBN 0-02-385880-X). Macmillan.

NAIS Task Force on Secondary Mathematics. Signed Numbers, Linear Functions, Surface Area Blocks. (Occasional Papers Ser.: No. 1). (Illus.). 21p. 1977. pap. 3.25 (ISBN 0-934338-13-2). NAIS.

National Council of Teachers of Mathematics. Cumulative Index: The Mathematics Teacher, 1908-1965. LC 42-24844. 1967. pap. 9.00 (ISBN 0-87353-028-4). NCTM.

--Evaluation in Mathematics, 26th Yearbk. Johnson, Donovan A., ed. LC 61-11906. 1961. 12.40 (ISBN 0-87353-004-7). NCTM.

--Organizing Data & Dealing with Uncertainty. 1979. pap. 6.25 (ISBN 0-87353-141-8). NCTM.

--The Rhind Mathematical Papyrus. 1979. Repr. 15.00 (ISBN 0-87353-133-7). NCTM.

Nevanlinna, R. Le Theoreme de Picard-Borel. LC 73-14779. 179p. 1974. Repr. of 1970 ed. text ed. 9.95 (ISBN 0-8284-0272-8). Chelsea Pub.

Newby, J. C. Mathematics for the Biological Sciences: From Graph Through Calculus to Differential Equations. (Illus.). 250p. 1980. 59.00x (ISBN 0-19-859623-5); pap. 27.00x (ISBN 0-19-859624-3). Oxford U Pr.

Nichols, E. D. Pre-Algebra Mathematics. (gr. 7-12). 1970. text ed. 11.96 (ISBN 0-03-082844-9, HoltE); annot. tchrs' ed. 8.20 (ISBN 0-03-082845-7); exercises & tchrs' ed. 3.32 ea. HR&W.

Nickel, Karl L. Interval Mathematics: 1980. LC 80-25009. 1980. 29.50 (ISBN 0-12-518850-1). Acad Pr.

Nikol'skii, S. M. Approximation of Functions of Several Variables & Embedding Theorems. Danskin, J., tr. from Rus. LC 74-4652. (Die Grundlehren der Mathematischen Wissenschaften Ser.: Vol. 205). 450p. 1974. 59.00 (ISBN 0-387-06442-7). Springer-Verlag.

Northrop, Eugene P. Riddles in Mathematics: A Book of Paradoxes. LC 74-32267. 270p. 1975. pap. 11.50 (ISBN 0-88275-273-1). Krieger.

Norton, Karl K. Numbers with Small Prime Factors & the Least Kth Power Non-Residue. LC 52-42839. (Memoirs: No. 106). 1971. pap. 7.20 (ISBN 0-8218-1806-6, MEMO-106). Am Math.

Oberhettinger, F. Tables of Mellin Transforms. vii, 275p. 1975. pap. 20.30 (ISBN 0-387-06942-9). Springer-Verlag.

Oden, J. T. Finite Elements of Nonlinear Continua. 1972. text ed. 26.50 (ISBN 0-07-047604-7, C). McGraw.

Ohmer, M. M. Mathematics for a Liberal Education. LC 79-119669. (Mathematics Ser). (Illus.). 1971. text ed. 13.95x (ISBN 0-201-05435-3); instructor's manual 2.75 (ISBN 0-201-05436-1). A-W.

Okikiolu, G. O. Aspects of the Theory of Bounded Integral Operators in LSRP-Spaces. 1971. 86.00 (ISBN 0-12-525150-5). Acad Pr.
Oliva, Ralph A. & LaMont, M. Dean. The Great International Math on Keys. rev. ed. (Illus.). 1976. pap. text ed. 4.95 (ISBN 0-89512-002-X, LCB-2050). Tex Instr Inc.
Olmsted, John M. Prelude to Calculus & Linear Algebra. LC 68-14040. (Century Mathematics Ser.). (Illus.). 1968. 28.00x (ISBN 0-89197-355-9). Irvington.
Orekov, V. P. & Sanin, N. A., eds. Problems in the Constructive Trend in Mathematics: VI 1973. LC 75-11951. (Proceedings of the Steklov Institute of Mathematics: Vol. 129). 1976. 86.00 (ISBN 0-8218-3029-5, STEKLO 129). Am Math.
Orlick, Gloria. First Math Helper. (Classroom Pairing Ser). 48p. 1975. wkbk 2.20 (ISBN 0-87594-140-0, 3111). Book-Lab.
Osborne, M. Scott & Warner, Garth. The Theory of Eisenstein Systems. (Pure & Applied Mathematics Ser.). 1981. price not set. Acad Pr.
Owen, George E. Fundamentals of Scientific Mathematics. 274p. 1961. 18.50x (ISBN 0-8018-0512-0). Johns Hopkins.
Owen, Guillermo. Finite Mathematics. LC 71-92142. (Illus.). 1970. 12.95 (ISBN 0-7216-7033-4). HR&W.
Oxtoby, J. C. Measure & Category. 2nd ed. (Graduate Texts in Mathematics: Vol. 2). 106p. 1980. 19.80 (ISBN 0-387-90508-1). Springer-Verlag.
P-H Learning Systems. Mathematics Resource Center: Level a, Boxed Kit. 1976. 120.00 set (ISBN 0-13-565291-X); replacement pkg. 84.00 (ISBN 0-685-93531-0). P-H.
--Mathematics Resource Center: Level B, Boxed Kit. 1976. 120.00set (ISBN 0-685-73768-3). P-H.
Palmer, Claude I., et al. Practical Mathematics. 6th ed. (Illus.). (gr. 10 up). 1977. text ed. 15.50 (ISBN 0-07-048253-5, G); instructor's manual 5.95 (ISBN 0-07-048252-7). McGraw.
Pappin, Charlene. Arithmetic, Complete Course. Maier, Eugene, ed. 1970. pap. text ed. 10.95x (ISBN 0-02-476650-X, 47665); progress tests 9.95x (ISBN 0-02-476640-2, 47664). Macmillan.
Papy, G. Modern Mathematics, 2 vols. 1969. Vol. 1. text ed. 6.96 (ISBN 0-02-974980-8); Vol. 2. text ed. 6.96 (ISBN 0-02-974990-5). Macmillan.
Parsons, Judith N. Math-a-Dot Series, Math Learning Games. Incl. Level I. Addition & Subtraction. (gr. 1-2). 1975 (ISBN 0-8224-4415-1); Level II. Addition & Subtraction. (gr. 1-3). 1975 (ISBN 0-8224-4416-X); Level III. Addition & Subtraction. (gr. 2-4). 1974 (ISBN 0-8224-4417-8); Level IV. Multiplication. (gr. 3-4). 1979 (ISBN 0-8224-4418-6); Level V. Division. (gr. 4-5). 1979 (ISBN 0-8224-4419-4). (Makemaster Bk.). pap. 5.95 ea. Pitman Learning.
--Math-a-Riddle Secret-Message Challenges to Build Basic Skills. Incl. Bk. I. Subtraction. (gr. 2-4) (ISBN 0-8224-4433-X); Bk. II. Multiplication. (gr. 3-5) (ISBN 0-8224-4434-8). (Makemaster Bk.). 1979. pap. 5.95 ea. Pitman Learning.
Parsonson, S. L. Pure Mathematics, 2 vols. LC 70-100026. (Illus.). 1971. Vol. 1. text ed. 14.50x (ISBN 0-521-07683-8); Vol. 2. text ed. 16.95x (ISBN 0-521-08032-0). Cambridge U Pr.
Pedoe, Dan. The Gentle Art of Mathematics. LC 73-77445. 1973. lib. bdg. 9.50 (ISBN 0-88307-625-X). Gannon.
Peirce, Charles S. The New Elements of Mathematics, 4 vols. Eisele, Carolyn, ed. Incl. Vol. 1. Arithmetic. 256p. text ed. 46.25x (ISBN 90-2793-174-7); Vol. 2. Elements of Algebra & Geometry. 608p. text ed. 111.75x (ISBN 90-2793-025-2); Vol. 3. Mathematical Miscellanea, 2 pts. 1030p. text ed. 187.75x (ISBN 0-686-22602-X); Vol. 4. Mathematical Philosophy. 480p. text ed. 70.50x (ISBN 90-2793-045-7). 1976. Mouton.
Person, Russell V. Essentials of Mathematics. 4th ed. LC 79-10708. 1980. text ed. 21.95 (ISBN 0-471-05184-5); study guide avail. (ISBN 0-471-06288-X). Wiley.
Peterson, Daniel R. & Peter, Gilbert M. Introduction to Industrial Mathematics. 1972. text ed. 13.95x (ISBN 0-673-07785-3). Scott F.
--Introduction to Technical Mathematics. 416p. 1974. text ed. 12.95x (ISBN 0-673-07784-5). Scott F.
Peterson, John M. Basic Concepts of Elementary Mathematics. 3rd ed. 1978. text ed. write for info. (ISBN 0-87150-247-X, PWS 2011). Prindle.
Pettofrezzo, Anthony J. & Hight, Donald W. Elementary Mathematics: Number Systems & Algebra. 1970. text ed. 13.95x (ISBN 0-673-05997-9). Scott F.
Piersel. Photomath. (gr. 3-9). pap. 1.99 (ISBN 0-87783-076-2); tchrs. guide 0.29 (ISBN 0-685-19020-X). Oddo.
Pink, Heinz-Guenther. Magic of Simplified Mathematics: Selfteaching Course in 30 Easy Lessons. (Illus.). 36p. (Orig., Prog. Bk.). (gr. 5 up). 1970. pap. 4.95 (ISBN 0-915946-01-7, A226535). Pink Hse Pub.
--Mathpower U. S. A. Thirty Subject Volume. 1980. write for info. (ISBN 0-915946-08-4). Pink Hse Pub.
Plumpton, C. & MacIlwaine, P. S. New Tertiary Mathematics: Applied Mathematics, Vol. 1, Pt. 2: Basic Applied Mathematics. (Illus.). 42.00 (ISBN 0-08-025035-1); pap. 16.75 (ISBN 0-08-021645-5). Pergamon.
--New Tertiary Mathematics: Further Applied Mathematics, Vol. 2, Pt. 2. (Illus.). 1981. 42.00 (ISBN 0-08-025037-8); pap. 16.75 (ISBN 0-08-025026-2). Pergamon.
--New Tertiary Mathematics: Further Pure Mathematics, Vol. 2, Pt. 1. LC 79-41454. (Illus.). 408p. 1981. 42.00 (ISBN 0-08-025033-5); pap. 16.75 (ISBN 0-08-021644-7). Pergamon.
--New Tertiary Mathematics: The Core. (Pure Mathematics: Vol. 1). (Illus.). 1980. 42.00 (ISBN 0-08-025031-9); pap. 16.75 (ISBN 0-08-021643-9). Pergamon.
Plumpton, C. & Tomkys, W. H. Sixth Form Pure Mathematics, Vols. 1-2. 1968. Vol. 1. pap. 9.50 (ISBN 0-686-57456-7); Vol. 2. pap. 11.00 (ISBN 0-08-009383-3). Pergamon.
Pollack, Eva. Third Math Helper. (Classroom Pairing Ser). 64p. (gr. k-1). 1975. 2.55 (ISBN 0-87594-142-7, 3113). Book-Lab.
Polley, Joseph H. Applied Real Estate Math. (Illus.). 272p. 1976. pap. 9.95 (ISBN 0-87909-040-5). Reston.
Polya, G. Mathematik und Plausibles Schliessen, 2 vols. Incl. Vol. 1. Induktion und Analogie in der Mathematik. 2nd ed. 404p. 1969 (ISBN 3-7643-0295-X); Vol. 2. Typen und Strukturen Plausibler Folgerung. 326p. 1975 (ISBN 3-7643-0715-3). (Science & Civilization Ser.: Nos. 14 & 15). 32.00 ea. Birkhauser.
--Vom Losen Mathematischer Aufgaben-Einsicht und Entdeckung, Lernen und Lehren, Vol. I. 2nd ed. (Science & Civilization Ser.: No. 20). (Illus.). 315p. (Ger.). 1979. 35.50 (ISBN 3-7643-1101-0). Birkhauser.
--Vom Losen Mathematischer Aufgaben-Einsicht und Entdeckung, Lernen und Lehren, Vol. II. (Science & Civilization Ser.: No. 21). (Illus.). 286p. 1967. 35.50 (ISBN 3-7643-0298-4). Birkhauser.
Powell, Michael H. Compactly Covered Reflections, Extension of Uniform Dualities & Generalized Almost Periodicity. LC 52-42839. (Memoirs: No. 105). 1970. pap. 7.60 (ISBN 0-8218-1805-8, MEMO-105). Am Math.
Power Skills in Mathematics. 1979. pap. 4.95 (ISBN 0-07-055225-8, SP). McGraw.
Practical Problems in Math Automotive Technicians. LC 77-82372. 1979. pap. 4.40 (ISBN 0-8273-1273-3); instructor's guide 1.60 (ISBN 0-8273-1274-1). Delmar.
Practical Problems in Mathematics for Consumers. LC 74-24811. 1975. pap. 6.00 (ISBN 0-8273-0266-5); instructor's guide 1.60 (ISBN 0-8273-0267-3). Delmar.
The Principal Works of Simon Stevin, 5 vols. Incl. Vol. 1. General Introduction-Mechanism. Dijksterhuis, E. J., ed. 1955 (ISBN 90-265-0070-X); Vols. 2 A & B. Mathematics. Struik, D. J., ed. 973p. 1958 (ISBN 90-265-0071-8); Vol. 3. Astronomy & Navigation. Pannekoek, A. & Croone, E., eds. 632p. 1961 (ISBN 90-265-0073-4); Vol. 4. Art of War. Schukking, W. H., ed. 525p. 1964 (ISBN 90-265-0074-2); Vol. 5. Engineering-Music-Civic Life. Forbes, R. J., et al. 609p. 1967 (ISBN 90-265-0075-0). (Dutch & Eng.). text ed. 95.00 ea. (Pub. by Swets Pub Serv Holland). Swets North Am.
Pshenichnyi, B. N. Necessary Conditions for an Extremum. (Pure & Applied Mathematics Ser.: Vol. 4). 1971. 24.50 (ISBN 0-8247-1556-X). Dekker.
Radlow, James. Understanding Finite Math. 640p. 1981. text ed. write for info. (ISBN 0-87150-328-X, 33L 2621). Prindle.
Rallis, Stephen & Schiffmann, Gerard. Weil Representation I: Intertwining Distributions & Discrete Spectrum. LC 80-12191. (Memoirs of the American Mathematical Society Ser.). 1980. 7.60 (ISBN 0-8218-2231-4, MEMO-231). Am Math.
Reband, P. Related Mathematics for Carpenters. 2nd ed. (Illus.). 1972. 7.00 (ISBN 0-8269-2332-1). Am Technical.
Reichmann, W. J. The Spell of Mathematics. 272p. 1967. text ed. 7.95x (ISBN 0-416-46440-8, Pub. by Chapman & Hall England). Methuen Inc.
Rektorys, Karel. Variational Methods in Mathematics, Science & Engineering. Basch, Michael, tr. from Czech. 572p. 1980. lib. bdg. 34.00 (ISBN 90-277-0561-5, Pub. by Reidel Holland). Kluwer Boston.
Renyi, A. Briefe Uber Die Wahrscheinlichkeit. (Science & Civilization Ser.: No. 25). 94p. (Ger.). 1969. 16.50 (ISBN 3-7643-0307-7). Birkhauser.
--Dialoge Uber Mathematik. (Science & Civilization Ser.: No. 22). 123p. (Ger.). 1967. 19.50 (ISBN 3-7643-0308-5). Birkhauser.
Research Institute for Mathematical Sciences Symposium, Kyoto, 1965. Kuramochi Boundaries of Riemann Surfaces: Proceedings. (Lecture Notes in Mathematics: Vol. 58). 1968. pap. 10.70 (ISBN 0-387-04228-8). Springer-Verlag.
Rice, Harold S. & Knight, Raymond M. Technical Mathematics. 3rd ed. 1972. text ed. 16.95 (ISBN 0-07-052200-6, G); instructor's manual 2.00 (ISBN 0-07-052201-4); answer key 2.00 (ISBN 0-07-052202-2). McGraw.
Rice, John R., ed. Mathematical Software. (ACM Monograph Ser). 1971. 49.75 (ISBN 0-12-587250-X). Acad Pr.
Richardson, M. & Richardson, L. F. Fundamentals of Mathematics. 4th ed. 1973. 16.95 (ISBN 0-02-399690-0). Macmillan.
Rider, Paul R. First-Year Mathematics for Colleges. 2nd ed. 1962. text ed. 12.95x (ISBN 0-02-400480-4). Macmillan.
Riedesel, C. Alan. Teaching Elementary School Mathematics. 3rd ed. (Illus.). 1980. text ed. 20.95 (ISBN 0-13-892549-6). P-H.
Roberts, A. Wayne & Varberg, Dale E. Faces of Mathematics: An Introductory Course for College Students. 1978. text ed. 21.50 scp (ISBN 0-7002-2507-2, HarpC); answer manual & prob. avail. (ISBN 0-06-365511-X). Har-Row.
Roberts, Blaine & Schulze, David L. Modern Mathematics & Economic Analysis. 1973. 16.95x (ISBN 0-393-09392-1); study guide 4.95x (ISBN 0-393-09374-3). Norton.
Robinson, J. E., et al. Fundamentals for Mathematics: A Foundation for Decisions. 1976. 4.50 (ISBN 0-201-06507-X). A-W.
Robinson, R. W., et al. Combinatorial Mathematics VII: Proceedings. (Lecture Notes in Mathematics Ser.: Vol. 829). (Illus.). 256p. 1981. pap. 16.80 (ISBN 0-387-10254-X). Springer-Verlag.
Rockafellar, R. Tyrrell. Conjugate Duality & Optimization. (CBMS Regional Conference Ser.: Vol. 16). (Orig.). 1974. pap. text ed. 6.50 (ISBN 0-89871-013-8). Soc Indus-Appl Math.
Rogers, James, et al. Basic Mathematics: A Review. LC 77-77107. (Illus.). 1978. pap. text ed. 12.95 (ISBN 0-7216-7633-2). HR&W.
Rota, Gian-Carlo, ed. Encyclopedia of Mathematics & Its Applications, Vols. 3-4. Incl. Vol. 3. The Theory of Information & Coding, Section-Probability. McEliece, Robert J., ed. LC 77-21837 (ISBN 0-201-13502-7); Vol. 4. Symmetry & Separation of Variables, Section-Special Functions. Miller, Willard, Jr. Askey, Richard, ed. LC 77-12572 (ISBN 0-201-13503-5). 1977. 21.50 ea. (Adv Bk Prog). A-W.
Rothenberg, Ronald I. Finite Mathematics. LC 79-22637. (Wiley Self-Teaching Guide Ser.). 1980. pap. text ed. 7.95 (ISBN 0-471-04320-6). Wiley.
Rothman, M. An Introduction to Industrial Mathematics. 370p. 1970. 19.50 (ISBN 0-442-27054-2, Pub. by Van Nos Reinhold). Krieger.
Roueche, N. E. & Mink, B. Washburn. The Language of Mathematics: An Individualized Introduction. LC 78-13397. 1979. 19.95 (ISBN 0-13-522920-0). P-H.
Rubenstein, L. I. Stefan Problem. LC 75-168253. (Translations of Mathematical Monographs: Vol. 27). 1971. 48.00 (ISBN 0-8218-1577-6, MMONO-27). Am Math.
Ruberti, A., ed. Realization Theory. LC 76-21964. 1977. pap. text ed. 19.50 (ISBN 0-08-021276-X). Pergamon.
Rudman, Jack. Mathematics. (Undergraduate Program Field Test Ser.: UPFT-15). (Cloth bdg. avail. on request). pap. 9.95 (ISBN 0-8373-6015-3). Natl Learning.
--Mathematics Aide. (Career Examination Ser.: C-480). (Cloth bdg. avail. on request). pap. 8.00 (ISBN 0-8373-0480-6). Natl Learning.
Rusinoff, S. E. Mathematics for Industry. 3rd ed. (Illus.). 1968. 13.33 (ISBN 0-8269-2200-7). Am Technical.
Ryser, Herbert J. Combinatorial Mathematics. LC 65-12288. (Carus Monograph: No. 14). 154p. 1963. 12.50 (ISBN 0-88385-014-1). Math Assn.
Saaty, T. L. Topics in Behavioral Mathematics. 1973. pap. 3.50 (ISBN 0-88385-416-3). Math Assn.
Sachs, R. K. General Relativity for Mathematicians. LC 76-47697. (Graduate Texts in Mathematics: Vol. 48). 1977. 26.20 (ISBN 0-387-90218-X). Springer-Verlag.
Saigal, J. C. Choice of Sectors & Regions. 1969. pap. 26.50x (ISBN 0-677-61610-4). Gordon.
St. John, Michael. From Arithmetic to Algebra. 132p. (Orig.). 1980. pap. text ed. 4.50 (ISBN 0-937354-00-7, TX-334-207). Delta Systems.
Saint Paul Technical Vocational Institute Curriculum Committee. Mathematics for Careers: Adding & Subtracting Whole Numbers. LC 80-70486. (General Mathematics Ser.). 128p. (Orig.). 1981. pap. text ed. 5.80 (ISBN 0-8273-1590-2); instr's. guide 2.70 (ISBN 0-8273-1595-3). Delmar.
--Mathematics for Careers: Consumer Applications. LC 80-67550. (Trade Mathematics Ser.). 176p. (Orig.). 1981. pap. text ed. 5.80 (ISBN 0-8273-2056-6); instr's. guide 1.70 (ISBN 0-8273-1881-2). Delmar.
--Mathematics for Careers: Decimals. LC 80-70487. (General Mathematics Ser.). 112p. (Orig.). 1981. pap. text ed. 5.80 (ISBN 0-8273-1592-9); instr's. guide 2.70 (ISBN 0-8273-1595-3). Delmar.
--Mathematics for Careers: Fractions. LC 80-70485. (General Mathematics Ser.). 176p. (Orig.). 1981. pap. text ed. 5.80 (ISBN 0-8273-1593-7); instr's. guide 2.70 (ISBN 0-8273-1595-3). Delmar.
St. Paul Technical Vocational Institute Curriculum Commitee. Mathematics for Careers: Measurement & Geometry. LC 80-67549. (General Mathematics Ser.). 176p. 1981. pap. text ed. 5.80 (ISBN 0-8273-2058-2); instr's. guide 1.70 (ISBN 0-8273-1881-2). Delmar.
Saint Paul Technical Vocational Institute Curriculum Committee. Mathematics for Careers: Mixed Numbers. LC 80-70488. (General Mathematics Ser.). 112p. Date not set. pap. text ed. 5.80 (ISBN 0-8273-1594-5); instr's. guide 2.70 (ISBN 0-8273-1595-3). Delmar.
--Mathematics for Careers: Multiplying & Dividing Whole Numbers. LC 80-70489. (General Mathematics Ser.). 192p. (Orig.). 1981. pap. text ed. 5.80 (ISBN 0-8273-1591-0); instr's. guide 2.70 (ISBN 0-8273-1595-3). Delmar.
Sanchez, David A. Ordinary & Differential Equations & Stability Theory: An Introduction. 1979. pap. text ed. 3.00 (ISBN 0-486-63828-6). Dover.
Saunders, P. T. An Introduction to Catastrophe Theory. LC 79-54172. (Illus.). 1980. 27.50 (ISBN 0-521-23042-X); pap. 8.95 (ISBN 0-521-29782-6). Cambridge U Pr.
Sawyer, W. W. Mathematicians Delight. lib. bdg. 10.50x (ISBN 0-88307-446-X). Gannon.
Scalzo, Frank & Hughes, Rowland. A Computer Approach to Introductory College Mathematics. 1977. pap. text ed. 13.95x (ISBN 0-442-80434-2). Van Nos Reinhold.
Scandinavian Congress - 15th - Oslo - 1968. Proceedings. Aubert, K. E. & Ljunggren, W., eds. LC 70-112305. (Lecture Notes in Mathematics: Vol. 118). 1970. pap. 10.70 (ISBN 0-387-04907-X). Springer-Verlag.
Schaaf, William L. Mathematics & Science: An Adventure in Postage Stamps. LC 78-1680. (Illus.). 1978. pap. 7.90x (ISBN 0-87353-122-1). NCTM.
Schaaf, William L., ed. High School Mathematics Library. rev. ed. LC 76-24798. 1976. pap. 3.40 (ISBN 0-87353-057-8). NCTM.
Schechter, M. Spectra of Partial Differential Operators. LC 76-157010. (Applied Mathematics & Mechanics Ser.: Vol. 14). 281p. 1972. 39.00 (ISBN 0-444-10109-8, North-Holland). Elsevier.
Schillinger, Joseph. Mathematical Basis of the Arts. LC 76-8189. (Music Reprint Ser.). 696p. 1976. Repr. of 1948 ed. 45.00 (ISBN 0-306-70781-0). Da Capo.
Schoenstadt, A. L., et al, eds. Information Linkage Between Applied Mathematics & Industry II. LC 80-17975. 1980. 20.00 (ISBN 0-12-628750-3). Acad Pr.
Schofield, C. W. Basic Mathematics for Technicians. (Illus.). 1977. pap. text ed. 11.00x (ISBN 0-7131-3379-1). Intl Ideas.
--Mathematics for Construction Students. 3rd ed. (Illus.). 1975. pap. text ed. 11.00x (ISBN 0-7131-3333-3). Intl Ideas.
Schofield, C. W. & Smethurst, D. Mathematics for Level-2 Technicians. (Illus.). 1979. pap. text ed. 12.95x (ISBN 0-7131-3385-6). Intl Ideas.
Schools Council Sixth Form Mathematics Project. Mathematics Applicable: Understanding Indices. 1975. pap. text ed. 5.95x (ISBN 0-435-51696-5). Heinemann Ed.
Schuh, J. F. Mathematical Tools for Modern Physics. 1968. 93.00x (ISBN 0-677-61090-4). Gordon.
Schwarz, Hermann A. Gesammelte Mathematische Abhandlungen, 2 vols. in 1. 2nd ed. LC 70-113147. (Ger). text ed. 39.50 (ISBN 0-8284-0260-4). Chelsea Pub.
Scott, John B. & Hutton, E. L. Mathematics for the Health Sciences. 1978. pap. text ed. 13.95x (ISBN 0-89641-009-9). American Pr.
Segel, Lee A. Mathematics Applied to Continuum Machanics. 1977. 25.95 (ISBN 0-02-408700-9, 40870). Macmillan.

Seifert, Herbert & Threlfall, W. Variationsrechnung Im Grossen. LC 77-160837. (Ger.). 6.95 (ISBN 0-8284-0049-0). Chelsea Pub.

Selby, Henry A. Notes of Lectures on Mathematics in the Behavioral Sciences. 1973. pap. 3.00 (ISBN 0-88385-417-1). Math Assn.

Sellers, Gene. Understanding Algebra & Trigonometry. 1979. text ed. 19.95 (ISBN 0-675-08306-0); instructor's manual 3.95 (ISBN 0-685-96157-5); test 3.95 (ISBN 0-686-67369-7). Merrill.

Setek, William M., Jr. Fundamentals of Mathematics. 1976. text ed. 18.95x (ISBN 0-02-478370-6). Macmillan.

Sewoster, Edward. Eight Place Tables of Arc Lengths. text ed. 15.00 (ISBN 0-8284-0240-X). Chelsea Pub.

Shanks, M., et al. Pre-Calculus Mathematics. 3rd ed. (gr. 10-12). 1976. text ed. 17.24 (ISBN 0-201-00768-1, Sch Div). A-W.

Shanks, Merrill, et al. Pre-Calculus Mathematics. 4th ed. (gr. 11-12). 1981. text ed. 15.24 (ISBN 0-201-07684-5, Sch Div); tchr's ed. 7.12 (ISBN 0-201-07685-3); solution manual 13.08 (ISBN 0-201-07686-1). A-W.

Shapes to Color, Cut Out & Make. (Coloring Book Ser.). (Illus.). 1979. 2.50 (ISBN 0-8431-0626-3). Price Stern.

Shields, Paul. Theory of Bernouilli Shifts. (Chicago Lectures in Mathematics Ser). 1973. pap. 6.00x (ISBN 0-226-75297-6). U of Chicago Pr.

Shoemaker, Terry. Performance Activities in Mathematics, 6 bks. Incl. Bk. 1 (ISBN 0-913688-10-X); Bk. 2 (ISBN 0-913688-11-8); Bk. 3 (ISBN 0-913688-12-6); Bk. 4 (ISBN 0-913688-13-4); Bk. 5 (ISBN 0-913688-14-2); Bk. 6 (ISBN 0-913688-15-0). 1974. pap. 6.64x ea. Pawnee Pub.

Silver, Edith & Cornelius, Betty. Unraveling Mathematical Concepts. 1978. wire coil bdg. 18.75 (ISBN 0-88252-084-9). Paladin Hse.

Silver, Howard A. Mathematics: Contemporary Topics & Applications. (Illus.). 1979. text ed. 19.95 (ISBN 0-13-563304-4). P-H.

Simmons, George. Precalculus Math in a Nut Shell. (Illus.). 176p. pap. 7.95 (ISBN 0-86576-009-8). W Kaufmann.

Slade, B. A. Complete Course in Short-Cut Mathematics: Combined with Simplified Mechanics for the Practical Man. 1953. 12.95 (ISBN 0-911012-11-7). Nelson-Hall.

Slisenko, A. O., ed. Studies in Constructive Mathematics & Mathematical Logic, Part 2. LC 69-12507. (Seminars in Mathematics Ser.: Vol. 8). 136p. 1970. 25.00 (ISBN 0-306-18808-2, Consultants). Plenum Pub.

Slook, Thomas H. & Wurster, Marie A. Elementary Modern Mathematics: With Calculus & Computer Programing. 1972. text ed. 13.95x (ISBN 0-673-07708-X). Scott F.

Smale, S. The Mathematics of Time. (Illus.). 151p. 1981. pap. 16.00 (ISBN 0-387-90519-7). Springer-Verlag.

Smart, D. R. Fixed Point Theorems. (Cambridge Tracts in Mathematics: No. 66). (Illus.). 100p. 1980. pap. 13.95x (ISBN 0-521-29833-4). Cambridge U Pr.

Smith, Harold & Keiffer, Mildred. Pathways in Mathematics: Level II. 3rd ed. Sharpe, Glyn, ed. (Illus.). (gr. 8). 1980. pap. text ed. 6.64x (ISBN 0-913688-37-1); tchr's guide 6.00x (ISBN 0-913688-34-7). Pawnee Pub.

Smith, Julius & Burton, David. Basic Mathematics with Electronic Applications. (Illus.). 620p. 1972. text ed. 15.95 (ISBN 0-685-26685-0). Macmillan.

Smith, Karl J. Arithmetic for College Students. 400p. 1981. text ed. 16.95 (ISBN 0-8185-0422-6). Brooks-Cole.

--Basic Mathematics for College Students. LC 80-20492. 400p. (Orig.). 1981. pap. text ed. 16.95 (ISBN 0-8185-0419-6). Brooks-Cole.

--Finite Mathematics: A Discrete Approach. 378p. 1975. text ed. 14.95x (ISBN 0-673-07921-X). Scott F.

Smith, Robert. Applied General Mathematics. LC 79-51586. (General Mathematics Ser.). (Illus.). 360p. 1981. text ed. 18.20 (ISBN 0-8273-1674-7); write for info. instr's. guide (ISBN 0-8273-1675-5). Delmar.

Smithsi, T. Basic Mathematical Skills. 1974. pap. 14.95 (ISBN 0-13-063420-4). P-H.

Society for Industrial & Applied Mathematics - American Mathematical Society Symposia - New York - April, 1973. Complexity of Computation: Proceedings, Vol. 7. Karp, R. M., ed. LC 74-22062. 1974. 28.80 (ISBN 0-8218-1327-7, SIAMS-7). Am Math.

Spargo, Edward & Harris, Raymond. Reading the Content Fields: Mathematics. (Content Skills Ser-Advanced Level). (Illus.). (gr. 9-12). 1978. pap. text ed. 2.40x (ISBN 0-89061-139-4, 553A). Jamestown Pubs.

--Reading the Content Fields: Mathematics. (Content Skills Ser.-Middle Level). (Illus.). (gr. 6-8). 1978. pap. text ed. 2.40x (ISBN 0-89061-129-7, 553M). Jamestown Pubs.

Sparks, Fred W. Survey of Basic Mathematics. 3rd ed. 1971. text ed. 13.50 (ISBN 0-07-059900-9, C); instructor's manual 2.95 (ISBN 0-07-059901-7). McGraw.

Sparks, Fred W. & Rees, Charles S. A Survey of Basic Mathematics. 4th ed. (Illus.). 1979. pap. text ed. 13.95 (ISBN 0-07-059902-5, C); answer manual 2.95 (ISBN 0-07-059903-3). McGraw.

Speiser, A. Die Geistige Arbeit. (Science & Civilization Ser.: No. 9). 207p. (Ger.). 1955. 20.50 (ISBN 3-7643-0343-3). Birkhauser.

Spence, Lawrence E. Finite Mathematics. 544p. 1981. text ed. 18.95 scp (ISBN 0-06-046369-4, HarpC). Har-Row.

Sperling, A. P. & Stuart, Monroe. Mathematics Made Simple. rev. ed. LC 62-16025. pap. 3.50 (ISBN 0-385-02088-0, Made). Doubleday.

Sperling, Abraham & Stuart, Monroe. Mathematics Made Simple. LC 80-2627. (Made Simple Bk.). (Illus.). 192p. 1981. pap. 3.95 (ISBN 0-385-17481-0). Doubleday.

Spiegel, Murray R. Advanced Mathematics for Engineers & Scientists. (Schaum Outline Ser). 1970. pap. 6.95 (ISBN 0-07-060216-6, SP). McGraw.

Srivastava, J. N., et al. A Survey of Combinatorial Theory. LC 72-88578. 470p. 1973. 58.75 (ISBN 0-444-10425-9, North-Holland). Elsevier.

Staszkow, Ronald. Developmental Mathematics: Basic Arithmetic with a Brief Introduction to Algebra. 384p. 1980. pap. text ed. 14.95 (ISBN 0-8403-2213-5). Kendall-Hunt.

Steele, J. H., ed. Fisheries Mathematics. 1978. 32.00 (ISBN 0-12-665250-3). Acad Pr.

Steen, Lynn A. Mathematics Today. LC 80-10888. (Illus.). 384p. 1980. pap. 4.95 (ISBN 0-394-74503-5, Vin). Random.

Stefani, S. & Hubbard, Lincoln B. Mathematics for Technologists in Radiology, Nuclear Medicine & Radiation Therapy. LC 78-32110. (Illus.). 1979. pap. text ed. 13.95 (ISBN 0-8016-4762-2). Mosby.

Stein. Basic Mathematics for College Students. 6th ed. 1980. text ed. 18.95 (ISBN 0-205-06814-6). Allyn.

Stein, Edwin I. First Course in Fundamentals of Mathematics. (gr. 7-12). 1978. text ed. 13.96 (ISBN 0-205-05540-0, 5655404); tchr's guide 2.00 (ISBN 0-205-05541-9, 5655412). Allyn.

--Fundamentals of Mathematics. (gr. 7-12). 1980. text ed. 15.80 (ISBN 0-205-06895-2, 5668956); tchrs'. guide 4.20 (ISBN 0-205-06896-0). Allyn.

--Fundamentals of Mathematics. (gr. 7-12). 1976. text ed. 15.80 (ISBN 0-205-05003-4, 5650038); tchrs'. ed. 4.20 (ISBN 0-205-05004-2, 5650046). Allyn.

--Practical Applications in Mathematics. (gr. 7-12). 1981. pap. text ed. 4.80 (ISBN 0-205-07161-9, 5671612). Allyn.

--Refresher Mathematics. (gr. 7-12). 1980. text ed. 13.56 (ISBN 0-205-06160-5, 5661609); tchrs'. guide 5.12 (ISBN 0-205-06161-3, 5661617). Allyn.

--Second Course in Fundamentals of Mathematics. (gr. 7-12). 1978. text ed. 14.20 (ISBN 0-205-05538-9, 5655382); tchr's guide 2.40 (ISBN 0-205-05539-7, 5655390). Allyn.

Stein, Sherman K. Mathematics, the Man-Made Universe: An Introduction to the Spirit of Mathematics. 3rd ed. LC 75-25950. (Mathematics Ser.). (Illus.). 1976. text ed. 19.95x (ISBN 0-7167-0465-X); tchrs manual avail. W H Freeman.

Steinfeld, Otto. Quasi-Ideals in Rings & Semi-Groups. LC 79-308570. (Illus.). 154p. 1978. 17.50x (ISBN 963-05-1696-9). Intl Pubns Serv.

Steinhoff, Richard. Basic Mathematics. 224p. 1972. 13.95 (ISBN 0-07-061123-8, G); instructor's manual 2.00 (ISBN 0-07-061124-6). McGraw.

Steklov Institute of Mathematics, Academy of Sciences, U S S R, No. 115. Mathematical Questions in the Theory of Wave Diffraction & Propagation: Proceedings. Babic, V. M., ed. LC 74-2363. 1974. 52.00 (ISBN 0-8218-3015-5, STEKLO-115). Am Math.

Steklov Institute of Mathematics, Academy of Sciences, U.S.S.R., No. 114. Some Questions in Constructive Functional Analysis: Proceedings. LC 73-21929. 238p. 1974. 59.20 (ISBN 0-8218-3014-7, STEKLO-114). Am Math.

Stern, David P. Math Squared: Graph Paper Activities for Fun & Fundamentals. LC 80-15932. 115p. 1981. pap. text ed. 6.50x (ISBN 0-8077-2585-4). Tchrs Coll.

Stewart, Ian & Tall, David. The Foundations of Mathematics. (Illus.). 1977. 26.00x (ISBN 0-19-853164-8); pap. 13.50x (ISBN 0-19-853165-6). Oxford U Pr.

Stewart, William C. Mathematics: With Applications. 1979. 16.95x (ISBN 0-256-02114-7). Business Pubns.

Stockton, Doris S. Essential Mathematics. 400p. 1972. pap. 11.95x (ISBN 0-673-07825-6). Scott F.

Stromberg, Karl. Introduction to Classical Real Analysis. (Wadsworth International Mathematics Ser.). 576p. 1981. text ed. 29.95x (ISBN 0-534-98012-0). Wadsworth Pub.

Sullivan Assoc. Sullivan Basal Mathematics Program, 37 bks. pap. text ed. 3.00 ea. (ISBN 0-8449-0304-3). Learning Line.

Suter, Heinrich. Die Mathematiker und Astronomen der Araber und Ihre Werke: Einschliesslich Nachtrage und Berichtungen. Repr. of 1900 ed. 23.00 (ISBN 0-384-58855-7). Johnson Repr.

Suydam, Marilyn, ed. Developing Computational Skills: 1978 Yearbook. LC 77-28831. (Illus.). 1978. 12.00x (ISBN 0-87353-121-3). NCTM.

Symposia in Pure Mathematics-Northern Illinois Univ., May 1974. Mathematical Developments Arising from the Hilbert Problems: Proceedings, 2 pts, Vol. 28. Browder, F. E., ed. LC 76-20437. 1976. soft cover 20.40 (ISBN 0-8218-1428-1, PSPUM-28). Am Math.

Symposia in Pure Mathematics, University of Calif. Berkeley June 1971. Tarski Symposium: Proceedings, Vol. 25. Henkin, L., ed. LC 74-8666. 1979. Repr. of 1974 ed. with additions 39.20 (ISBN 0-8218-1425-7, PSPUM-25). Am Math.

Symposia on Applied Probability & Monte Carlo Methods & Modern Aspects of Dynamics. Studies in Applied Mathematics, Three: Proceedings. Agins, B. R. & Kalos, M. H., eds. (Illus.). 1969. text ed. 9.75 (ISBN 0-686-24259-9). Soc Indus-Appl Math.

Symposium on Automatic Demonstration, Versailles, 1968. Proceedings. Laudet, M., ed. LC 79-117526. (Lecture Notes in Mathematics: Vol. 125). (Illus.). 1970. pap. 18.30 (ISBN 0-387-04914-2). Springer-Verlag.

Symposium on Special Topics in Applied Mathematics. Proceedings. (Slaught Memorial Paper: No. 3). 73p. 1954. pap. 2.00 (ISBN 0-88385-412-0). Math Assn.

Szel, Karoly. Magic-Mystic-Logic-Mathematics. 1979. 4.95 (ISBN 0-533-03840-5). Vantage.

Tabberer, Frank. Mathematics for Technicians, Vol. 1. (TEC Techicians Ser.). (Illus.). 1978. pap. 6.95 (ISBN 0-408-00326-X). Butterworth.

Tarwater, J. Dalton, et al. Men & Institutions in American Mathematics. (Graduate Studies: No. 13). (Orig.). 1976. pap. 6.00 (ISBN 0-89672-023-3). Tex Tech Pr.

Taub, A. H., ed. Studies in Applied Mathematics. LC 74-168565. (MAA Studies: No. 7). 217p. 1971. 12.50 (ISBN 0-88385-107-5). Math Assn.

Taylor, Clarence E. Mathematics for Nursing. 1978. pap. text ed. 7.95 (ISBN 0-316-83304-5). Little.

Taylor, R. L. Stochastic Convergence of Weighted Sums of Random Elements in Linear Spaces. LC 78-13024. (Lecture Notes in Mathematics: Vol. 672). 1978. pap. 14.40 (ISBN 0-387-08929-2). Springer-Verlag.

Taylor, S. J. Introduction to Measure & Integration. LC 73-84325. 272p. 1975. pap. text ed. 15.50x (ISBN 0-521-09804-1). Cambridge U Pr.

Thompson, L. General Mathematics with Applications. Vorndran, Richard A., ed. 1976. 8.96 (ISBN 0-02-829390-8); tchr's ed. 15.98 (ISBN 0-02-829400-9); solns. manual avail. Glencoe.

Three Papers on Dynamical Systems. LC 81-4981. (Translations Series Two: Vol. 116). 1981. 32.40 (ISBN 0-8218-3066-X). Am Math.

Tobias, Sheila. Overcoming Math Anxiety. (Illus.). 288p. 1980. pap. 5.95 (ISBN 0-395-29088-0). HM.

Tocquet. Magic of Numbers. pap. 2.00 (ISBN 0-87980-091-7). Wilshire.

Topping, J. Errors of Observation & Their Treatment, S.I. 4th ed. 119p. 1972. pap. text ed. 6.95x (ISBN 0-412-21040-1, Pub. by Chapman & Hall England). Methuen Inc.

Transactions of the Moscow Mathematical Society, Vol. 23 (1970, Vol. 23. LC 65-7413. 316p. 1972. text ed. 59.60 (ISBN 0-8218-1623-3, MOSCOW-23). Am Math.

Triola, Mario F. Mathematics & the Modern World. 2nd ed. LC 77-99264. 1978. 18.95 (ISBN 0-8053-9301-3); instr's guide 5.95 (ISBN 0-8053-9303-X). Benjamin-Cummings.

Tronaas, Edward M. Mathematics for Technicians. (Illus.). 1971. text ed. 17.95 (ISBN 0-13-562546-7). P-H.

Tsokos, Chris P. Mainstreams of Finite Mathematics with Applications. (Mathematics Ser.). 1978. text ed. 20.95 (ISBN 0-675-08436-9); instructor's manual 3.95 (ISBN 0-685-86838-9). Merrill.

Tuchinsky, P. M. Man in Competition with the Spruce Budworm. 60p. 1981. pap. text ed. 7.95 (ISBN 3-7643-3047-3). Birkhauser.

University of California. Publications in Mathematical & Physical Sciences, Vol. 1-3. (Partly in the original edition). pap. 43.00 (ISBN 0-685-23290-5). Johnson Repr.

University of Oregon. Mathematics in Science & Society. 1977. 28.50 (ISBN 0-88488-092-3). Creative Pubns.

Usher, Michael & Bormuth, Robert. Experiencing Life Through Mathematics, Vol. 2. (Illus.). (gr. 9-12). 1980. pap. text ed. 4.92 (ISBN 0-913688-68-1); tchr's ed. 6.00x (ISBN 0-913688-69-X). Pawnee Pub.

Valenza, Samuel W., Jr. Conceptual Mathematics. (Illus.). (gr. 9-12). 1976. 9.50 (ISBN 0-936918-02-0). Intergalactic NJ.

Vance, Elbridge P. Introduction to Modern Mathematics. 2nd ed. 1968. text ed. 17.95 (ISBN 0-201-08015-X). A-W.

Van der Waerden, B. L. Erwachende Wissenschaft, Vol. I: Agyptische, Babylonische und Griechische Mathematik. enl. 2nd ed. (Science & Civilization Ser.: No. 8). 488p. (Ger.). 1966. 39.50 (ISBN 3-7643-0399-9). Birkhauser.

Van Leuven, Edwin P. General Trade Mathematics. 2nd ed. 1952. text ed. 13.20 (ISBN 0-07-067079-X, W). McGraw.

Van Oystaeyen & Verschoren. Reflectors & Localization. (Lecture Notes in Pure & Applied Math.: Vol. 41). 1979. 23.50 (ISBN 0-8247-6844-2). Dekker.

Veech, W. A. Second Course in Complex Analysis. 1967. 14.00 (ISBN 0-8053-9470-2, Adv Bk Prog). Benjamin-Cummings.

Vidal, P. Systems Echantillonnes Nonlineaires - Exercises et Problemes: Exercises et Problemes. (Theorie des Systemes Ser.). (Fr.). 1970. 32.00 (ISBN 0-677-50500-0). Gordon.

Vinik, Aggie, et al. Mathematics & Humor. 1978. pap. 4.00 (ISBN 0-87353-137-X). NCTM.

Vitkovitch, D. Experimental Methods of Field Analysis. 1966. 19.95x (ISBN 0-442-09032-3). Van Nos Reinhold.

Vogan, D. Representation Theory. 1981. text ed. 20.00 (ISBN 3-7643-3037-6). Birkhauser.

Vorobyov, N. N. Criteria for Divisibility. Levine, Daniel A. & McLarnan, Timothy, trs. from Rus. LC 74-11634. (Popular Lectures in Mathematics). 1980. pap. text ed. 6.00x (ISBN 0-226-86516-9). U of Chicago Pr.

Wain. Mathematics & Education. 1978. 21.00x (ISBN 0-442-30141-3). Van Nos Reinhold.

Washington, Allyn J. Basic Technical Mathematics. 3rd ed. LC 77-71469. 1978. pap. text ed. 21.95 (ISBN 0-8053-9520-2); instr's guide 8.95 (ISBN 0-8053-9522-9). Benjamin-Cummings.

--Introduction to Geometry. LC 75-27737. (Modules in Technical Mathematics: No. 4). 1976. pap. 5.95 (ISBN 0-8465-8616-9). Benjamin-Cummings.

--Introduction to Technical Mathematics. 2nd ed. LC 77-85502. 1978. 19.95 (ISBN 0-8053-9525-3). Benjamin-Cummings.

--Mathematics: A Developmental Approach. LC 78-65558. 1979. 13.95 (ISBN 0-8053-9527-X); instr's guide 3.95 (ISBN 0-8053-9528-8). Benjamin-Cummings.

Washington, Allyn J., et al. Essentials of Basic Mathematics. 3rd ed. 1981. 16.95 (ISBN 0-8053-9529-6). Benjamin-Cummings.

Weber, H. R., et al. Festschrift Heinrich Weber. LC 71-125926. 1971. Repr. of 1912 ed. text ed. 25.00 (ISBN 0-8284-0246-9). Chelsea Pub.

Weil, A. Dirichlet Series & Automorphic Forms. LC 72-151320. (Lecture Notes in Mathematics: Vol. 189). 1971. pap. 11.80 (ISBN 0-387-05382-4). Springer-Verlag.

Weiland, R. G. & Woytek, S. J. Mathematics in Living, 4 bks. Incl. Bk. I. Buying. 1979 (ISBN 0-87108-152-0); Bk. II. Wages & Budgets. 1979 (ISBN 0-87108-153-9); Bk. III. Banking & Loans. 1970 (ISBN 0-87108-154-7); Bk. IV. Credit, Loans & Taxes. 1974 (ISBN 0-87108-179-2). (Illus.). 1970. pap. text ed. 2.95x ea.; ans. bk. 4.95x (ISBN 0-87108-156-3). Pruett.

Weiss, N. A. & Yoseloff, M. L. Finite Mathematics. LC 74-20001. (Illus.). ix, 628p. 1975. text ed. 18.95x (ISBN 0-87901-039-8). H S Worth.

Weiss, Sol. Elementary College Mathematics. 1977. text ed. write for info. (ISBN 0-87150-217-8, PWS 1771). Prindle.

Weissglass, Julian. Exploring Elementary Mathematics: A Small-Group Approach for Teaching. LC 79-14931. (Mathematical Sciences Ser.). (Illus.). 1979. text ed. 15.95x (ISBN 0-7167-1027-7); instr's manual 3.95x (ISBN 0-7167-1223-7). W H Freeman.

Wheeler, Margariete M. & Hardgrove, Clarence E. Mathematics Library: Elementary & Junior High School. 4th ed. LC 78-57526. 1978. pap. 4.00x (ISBN 0-87353-126-4). NCTM.

Wheeler, R. E. & Wheeler, E. R. Mathematics: An Everyday Language. LC 78-13072. 1979. text ed. 21.95x (ISBN 0-471-03423-1); student supplement 7.50 (ISBN 0-471-04924-7); tchrs. manual o.p. 2.85 (ISBN 0-471-05409-7). Wiley.

Wheeler, Ruric. Modern Mathematics: An Elementary Approach, Alternative Edition. 585p. 1981. text ed. 18.95 (ISBN 0-8185-0413-7). Brooks-Cole.

Wheeler, Ruric E. Fundamental College Mathematics: From Patterns to Applications. 2nd ed. LC 75-23857. (Contemporary Undergraduate Mathematics Ser.). 1976. text ed. 16.95 (ISBN 0-8185-0178-2). Brooks-Cole.
--Modern Mathematics: An Elementary Approach. 5th ed. 625p. 1981. text ed. 19.95 (ISBN 0-8185-0430-7). Brooks-Cole.
Whipkey, Kenneth L., et al. The Power of Mathematics: Applications to the Management & the Social Sciences. 2nd ed. LC 80-19576. 622p. 1981. text ed. 21.95 (ISBN 0-471-07709-7). Wiley.
Whitehead, Alfred N. Introduction to Mathematics. rev. ed. 1959. pap. 4.95 (ISBN 0-19-500211-3, GB). Oxford U Pr.
Whitehead, Alfred N. & Russell, Bertrand. Principia Mathematica, 3 Vols. Set. 270.00 (ISBN 0-521-06791-X). Cambridge U Pr.
--Principia Mathematica to Fifty-Six. 2nd ed. 1925-27. pap. 19.95x (ISBN 0-521-09187-X). Cambridge U Pr.
Whitson, M. E. & Elston, C. A. Basic Agricultural Mathematics. rev. ed. 61p. 1966. pap. text ed. 6.95 (ISBN 0-87484-043-0). Mayfield Pub.
Willerding, Margaret F. & Engelsohn, H. S. Mathematics: The Alphabet of Science. 3rd ed. LC 76-48913. 376p. 1977. 22.95 (ISBN 0-471-94653-2); o.p. instructor's manual (ISBN 0-471-02388-4). Wiley.
Williams, Edward & Cohen, Jacob. Survival Math. (gr. 9-12). 1981. pap. 4.95 (ISBN 0-8120-2012-X). Barron.
Williams, Elizabeth & Shuard, Hilary. Elementary Mathematics Today-Metric: Student. 2nd ed. 1976. Resource Book. 19.25 (ISBN 0-201-08616-6, Sch Div). A-W.
Williams, Gareth. Mathematics with Applications in the Management, Natural, & Social Sciences. 656p. 1981. text ed. 22.95 (ISBN 0-205-07188-0, 567188-4); tchrs'. ed. 4.95 (ISBN 0-205-07189-9). Allyn.
Williamson, Richard & Trotter, Hale. Multivariable Mathematics: Linear Algebra, Calculus, Differential Equations. 2nd ed. (Illus.). 1979. ref. 26.95 (ISBN 0-13-604850-1). P-H.
Wittenberg, A. I. Vom Denken in Begriffen. (Science & Civilization Ser.: No. 12). 360p. (Ger.). 1968. 24.50 (ISBN 3-7643-0417-0). Birkhauser.
Wiznitzer, Martine R. Basic Mathematic Skills. 1979. pap. 4.95 (ISBN 0-07-055226-6, Trafalgar Hse Pub). McGraw.
Wohlfort, F. & Sheridan, A. Investigating Mathematical Ideas, Levels A-D. (gr. 7-8). 1969. pap. text ed. 1.92 ea. skillbk. (HoltC); tchrs' eds. 1.92 ea. HR&W.
Wolf, Enid G. Beginning Mathematics Concepts. pap. 2.50x (ISBN 0-88323-116-6, 143); tchr's manual 1.00 (ISBN 0-88323-117-4, 144). Richards Pub.
--More Mathematics Concepts. 1975. pap. 2.50x (ISBN 0-88323-126-3, 214). Richards Pub.
Wood, Martha, et al. Developmental Mathematics. 2nd ed. 1980. write for info. (ISBN 0-87150-287-9, 2272). Prindle.
Wright, Crispin. Wittgenstein on the Foundations of Mathematics. 500p. 1980. text ed. 30.00x (ISBN 0-674-95385-1). Harvard U Pr.
Yamada, T. The Schur Subgroup of the Brauer Group. (Lecture Notes in Mathematics: Vol. 397). v, 159p. 1974. pap. 9.90 (ISBN 0-387-06806-6). Springer Verlag.
Yamane, Taro. Mathematics for Economists: An Elementary Survey. 2nd ed. 1968. text ed. 24.95 (ISBN 0-13-562496-7). P-H.
Young, Frederick H. Nature of Mathematics. 1967. text ed. 11.25 (ISBN 0-471-97980-5, Pub. by Wiley). Krieger.
Young, Hugh D. Statistical Treatment of Experimental Data. 1962. pap. 3.50 (ISBN 0-07-072646-9, SP). McGraw.
Yum - Ton Siu. Techniques of Extension of Analytic Objects. (Lecture Notes in Pure & Applied Mathematics Ser.: Vol.8). Orig. Title: Techniques of Extension in Pure & Applied Mathmatics. 272p. 1974. 20.50 (ISBN 0-8247-6168-5). Dekker.
Zaitsev, V., et al. Elementary Mathematics. 590p. 1978. 10.00 (ISBN 0-8285-0719-8, Pub. by Mir Pubs Russia). Imported Pubns.
Zameeruddin, Qazi, et al. Elementary Mathematics. 1975. 10.50 (ISBN 0-7069-0388-9, Pub. by Vikas India). Advent NY.
Zaslavsky, Claudia. Preparing Young Children for Math: A Book of Games. LC 79-12552. (Illus.). 1979. 10.95 (ISBN 0-8052-3723-2). Schocken.
Zawadski, Wladyslaw. Les Mathematiques Appliques a l'Economie Politique. 1965. Repr. of 1914 ed. 23.50 (ISBN 0-8337-3916-6). B Franklin.
Zeldovich, Y. & Myskis, A. Elements of Applied Mathematics. 656p. 1976. 12.00 (ISBN 0-8285-0720-1, Pub. by Mir Pubs Russia). Imported Pubns.
Zill, Dennis G., et al. The Basic Math for Calculus. 1978. text ed. 20.95x (ISBN 0-534-00568-3). Wadsworth Pub.
--College Mathematics for Students of Business & the Social Sciences. 1977. text ed. 21.95x (ISBN 0-534-00467-9). Wadsworth Pub.
Zippin, Leo. Uses of Infinity. LC 61-12187. (New Mathematical Library: No. 7). 1975. pap. 5.50 (ISBN 0-88385-607-X). Math Assn.
Zuckerman, Martin M. Basic Mathematics. 520p. 1980. text ed. 16.95 (ISBN 0-442-21911-3); instr's. manual 2.50 (ISBN 0-442-23264-0). Van Nos Reinhold.
Zurflieh, Thomas. Basic Technical Mathematics Explained. (Illus.). 640p. 1974. text ed. 17.95 (ISBN 0-07-073595-6, G); inst. guide & answer key 2.00 (ISBN 0-07-073599-9). McGraw.

MATHEMATICS–ABILITY TESTING

see also Mathematical Ability–Testing

Kyles, I. & Sumner, R. Tests of Attainment Mathematics in Schools: Vol. 2, Continuation of Monitoring Feasibility Study, Vol. 1. (Occasional Reports Ser.: No. 2). (Illus.). 1977. pap. text ed. 9.00x (ISBN 0-85633-135-X, NFER). Humanities.

MATHEMATICS–ADDRESSES, ESSAYS, LECTURES

Abikoff, W. The Real Analytic Theory of Teichmueller Space. (Lecture Notes in Mathematics Ser.: Vol. 820). (Illus.). 144p. 1981. pap. 11.80 (ISBN 0-387-10237-X). Springer-Verlag.
Adams, J. Frank. Stable Homotopy & Generalized Homology. LC 74-5735. (Chicago Lectures in Mathematics Ser.). x, 374p. 1980. pap. text ed. 10.00x (ISBN 0-226-00524-0). U of Chicago Pr.
Ahlfors, L. V., et al. Some Problems of Mathematics & Physics. LC 76-4884. (Translations Ser.: No. 2, Vol. 104). 1976. 46.80 (ISBN 0-8218-3054-6, TRANS 2-104). Am Math.
Aizerman, M. A., et al. Thirty-One Invited Addresses at the International Congress of Mathematicians in Moscow 1966. LC 51-5559. (Translations Ser.: No. 2, Vol. 70). 1968. 30.00 (ISBN 0-8218-1770-1, TRANS 2-70). Am Math.
Aleksandrov, P. S., et al. Transactions of the Moscow Mathematical Society, Vol. 31 (1974) LC 65-4713. 1976. 60.40 (ISBN 0-8218-1631-4, MOSCOW-31). Am Math.
Andrunakievic, V. A., et al. Transactions of the Moscow Mathematical Society, Vol. 29 (1973) 1976. 57.20 (ISBN 0-8218-1629-2, MOSCOW-29). Am Math.
Balslev, E., ed. Eighteenth Scandinavian Congress of Mathematicians. (Progress in Mathematics Ser.). 528p. 1981. 26.00 (ISBN 0-686-77403-5). Birkhauser.
Baum, Robert J., ed. Philosophy & Mathematics: From Plato to the Present. LC 73-84704. 320p. 1974. text ed. 11.00x (ISBN 0-87735-513-4). Freeman C.
Brjuno, A. D., et al. Transactions of the Moscow Mathematical Society for the Year 1971, Vol. 25. LC 65-7413. 1973. text ed. 54.40 (ISBN 0-8218-1625-X, MOSCOW-25). Am Math.
Ceitin, G. S., et al. Fourteen Papers on Logic, Geometry, Topology, & Algebra. LC 72-2350. (Translations Ser.: No. 2, Vol. 100). 1972. 42.00 (ISBN 0-8218-3050-3, TRANS 2-100). Am Math.
Choquet, Gustave. What Is Modern Mathematics. 46p. 1963. pap. 2.75 (ISBN 0-685-46930-1). Ed Solutions.
Christoffel-Symposium. (WK Ser.: No. 36). 650p. 1980. write for info. (ISBN 3-7643-1162-2). Birkhauser.
CISM (International Center for Mechanical Sciences), Dept. of Automation & Information, Univ of Geneva, 1971. Controlled & Conditioned Invariance. Basile, G., ed. (CISM Pubns. Ser.: No. 109). (Illus.). 51p. 1972. pap. 7.50 (ISBN 0-387-81132-X). Springer-Verlag.
Clifford, William K. Mathematical Papers. LC 67-28488. 1968. Repr. 29.50 (ISBN 0-8284-0210-8). Chelsea Pub.
Clunie, J. G. & Hayman, W. K., eds. Symposium on Comples Analysis. LC 73-92787. (London Mathematical Society Lecture Note Ser.: No. 12). 200p. 1974. 21.50 (ISBN 0-521-20452-6). Cambridge U Pr.
Cohen, R. S., et al, eds. Essays in Memory of Imre Lakatos. new ed. LC 76-16770. (Synthese Library Ser.: No. 99). 1976. lib. bdg. 87.00 (ISBN 90-277-0654-9, Pub. by Reidel Holland); pap. 47.50 (ISBN 90-277-0655-7, Pub. by Reidel Holland). Kluwer Boston.
--Boston Studies in the Philosophy of Science, Vol. 15: Scientific,Historical & Political Essays in Honor of Dirk J. Struik. LC 73-83556. (Synthese Library: No.61). 652p. 1974. 76.00 (ISBN 90-277-0393-0, Pub. by Reidel Holland); pap. 47.50- (ISBN 90-277-0379-5). Kluwer Boston.
Conference, Murat-le-Quaire, March 1976. Convex Analysis & Its Applications: Proceedings. Auslender, A., ed. (Lecture Notes in Economics & Mathematical Systems: Vol. 144). 1977. soft cover 14.10 (ISBN 0-387-08149-6). Springer-Verlag.
Conference on Operator Theory, Dalhousie Univ., Halifax, 1973. Proceedings. Fillmore, P. A., ed. LC 73-14482. (Lecture Notes in Mathematics: Vol. 345). pap. 11.60 (ISBN 0-387-06496-6). Springer-Verlag.
Continuous Convergence on C (X) LC 75-16495. (Lecture Notes in Mathematics Ser.: Vol. 469). 140p. 1975. pap. 10.00 (ISBN 0-387-07179-2). Springer-Verlag.
Derrick Henry Lehmer Dedication: Dedication Issue on His 70th Birthday. (Mathematics of Computation Ser.: Vol. 29, No. 129). 1975. 20.80 (ISBN 0-8218-0061-2, MCOM 29-129, DHL). Am Math.
Diamond, Cora. Wittgenstein's Lectures on the Foundations of Mathematics, Cambridge, 1939: From the Notes of R. G. Bosanquet, Norman Malcolm, Rush Rhees, & Yorick Smythies. LC 75-17129. (Illus.). 320p. 1976. 27.50x (ISBN 0-8014-0959-4). Cornell U Pr.
Division of Mathematics - Committee on Support of Research in Mathematical Sciences. Mathematical Sciences: A Report. pap. 7.25 (ISBN 0-309-01681-9). Natl Acad Pr.
Dlab, V. & Gabriel, P., eds. Representation Theory I. (Lecture Notes in Mathematics Ser.: Vol. 831). 373p. 1981. pap. 22.00 (ISBN 0-387-10263-9). Springer-Verlag.
--Representation Theory II. (Lecture Notes in Mathematics: Vol. 832). 673p. 1981. pap. 40.20 (ISBN 0-387-10264-7). Springer-Verlag.
Dynkin, E. B., et al. Six Lectures Delivered at the International Congress of Mathematicians in Stockholm, 1962. LC 51-5559. (Translations Ser.: No. 2, Vol. 31). 1963. 13.20 (ISBN 0-8218-1731-0, TRANS 2-31). Am Math.
Equibbrium States & the Ergodic Theory of Anosov Diffeomorphisms. (Lecture Notes in Mathematics Ser.: Vol. 470). 108p. 1975. pap. 10.00 (ISBN 0-387-07187-3). Springer-Verlag.
Freiman, Grigori. It Seems I Am a Jew: A Samizdat Essay. Nathanson, Melvyn B., ed. & tr. from Russian. LC 80-404. (Science & International Affairs Ser.). 114p. 1980. 9.95 (ISBN 0-8093-0962-9). S Ill U Pr.
Gilkey, Peter B. The Index Theorem & the Heat Equation. LC 74-84575. (Mathematics Lecture Ser., No. 4). 130p. 1975. pap. 6.25x (ISBN 0-914098-13-6). Publish or Perish.
Goldschmidt, David M. Lectures on Character Theory. LC 80-81648. (Mathematics Lecture Ser.: No. 8). 245p. 1980. 12.00 (ISBN 0-686-62777-6). Publish or Perish.
Grassl, Wolfgang, ed. Friedrich Waismann: Lectures in the Philosophy of Mathematics. (Studien Zur Oesterreichischen Philosophie). 125p. 1981. pap. text ed. 25.00x (ISBN 90-6203-613-9, Pub. by Rodopi Holland). Humanities.
Grmela, M., ed. Global Analysis. (Lecture Notes in Mathematics: Vol. 755). 1980. pap. 21.00 (ISBN 0-387-09703-1). Springer-Verlag.
Hardiman, N. J. Exploring University Mathematics, 3 Vols. Vol. 1. 1967. text ed. 15.00 (ISBN 0-08-011990-5); Vol. 2. 1966. text ed. 16.50 (ISBN 0-08-012567-0); Vol. 3. 1969. text ed. 15.00 (ISBN 0-08-012903-X); Vol. 1. pap. 7.00 (ISBN 0-08-011991-3); Vol. 2 1968. pap. 7.75 (ISBN 0-08-012566-2); Vol. 3 1969. pap. 7.00 (ISBN 0-08-012902-1). Pergamon.
Hardy, Godfrey H. Ramanujan. 3rd ed. LC 59-10268. 1978. 9.95 (ISBN 0-8284-0136-5). Chelsea Pub.
Hermes, Hans. Term Logic with Choice Operator. rev. ed. LC 79-125498. (Lecture Notes in Mathematics: Vol. 6). 1970. pap. 10.70 (ISBN 0-387-04899-5). Springer-Verlag.
Hirzebruch, F. & Zagier, D. The Atiyah-Singer Theorem & Elementary Number Theory. LC 74-78679. (Mathematics Lecture Ser., No. 3). 287p. 1974. pap. 10.00x (ISBN 0-914098-12-8). Publish or Perish.
IFAC-FIP International Conference on Digit al Computer a75211. Proceedings, 2 pts. Mansour, M. & Schaufelberger, W., eds. LC 73-21003. (Lecture Notes in Economics & Mathematical Systems, Vol. 93 & 94). 1974. pap. 20.30 ea. (ISBN 0-685-40869-8). Pt. 1 (ISBN 0-387-06620-9). Pt. 2 (ISBN 0-387-06621-7). Springer-Verlag.
Index of Mathematical Papers. Incl. Vol. 1. July-December, 1970. 1972. 50.00 (ISBN 0-8218-4001-0, IMP-1); Vol. 2, 2 pts. 1972. Set. 90.80 (ISBN 0-686-70178-X, IMP-2); Jan-June, 1971 (ISBN 0-8218-4002-9); July-Dec., 1971 (ISBN 0-8218-4003-7); Vol. 3, 2 pts. 1973. Set. 124.00 (ISBN 0-686-70179-8, IMP-3); Jan.-June, 1972 (ISBN 0-8218-4004-5); July-Dec., 1972 (ISBN 0-8218-4005-3); Vol. 4, 2 pts. 1973-74. Set. 124.00 (ISBN 0-686-70180-1, IMP-4); Jan.-June, 1973 (ISBN 0-8218-4006-1); July-Dec., 1973 (ISBN 0-8218-4007-X); Vol. 5. Index to Mathematical Reviews for 1973. Date not set. 124.00 (ISBN 0-8218-4008-8, IMP-5); Vol. 6. Index to Mathematical Reviews for 1974. 124.00 (ISBN 0-8218-4009-6, IMP-6); Vol. 7. Index to Mathematical Reviews for 1975. 124.00 (ISBN 0-8218-4010-X, IMP-7); Vol. 8. Index to Mathematical Reviews for 1976. 186.00 (ISBN 0-8218-4011-8, IMP-8); Vol. 11. Index to Mathematical Reviews for 1979. 186.00 (ISBN 0-8218-4014-2, IMP-11); Cumulative Index (Author & Subject Index of Mathematical Reviews, 1973-1979) 1070.00 (ISBN 0-8218-0035-3, MREVIN-73-79). Am Math.
International Mathematical Conference, College Park, 1970. Several Complex Variables 1: Proceedings. Horvath, J., ed. (Lecture Notes in Mathematics: Vol. 155). 1970. pap. 11.20 (ISBN 0-387-05183-X). Springer-Verlag.
Jameson, G. J. Ordered Linear Spaces. LC 70-125282. (Lecture Notes in Mathematics: Vol. 141). 1970. pap. 14.70 (ISBN 0-387-04930-4). Springer-Verlag.
Kechris, A. S., et al, eds. Cabal Seminar Seventy-Seven to Seventy-Nine: Proceedings. (Lecture Notes in Mathematics Ser.: Vol. 839). 274p. 1981. pap. 16.80 (ISBN 0-387-10288-4). Springer-Verlag.
Kedem. Binary Time Series. (Lecture Notes in Pure & Applied Mathematics Ser.: Vol. 58). 160p. 1980. 23.50 (ISBN 0-686-77493-0). Dekker.
Lam, T. Y. Serre's Conjecture. (Lecture Notes in Mathematics: Vol. 635). 1978. pap. 14.30 (ISBN 0-387-08657-9). Springer-Verlag.
Lambeck, J. Torsion Theories, Additive Semantics & Rings of Quotients. LC 70-148538. (Lecture Notes in Mathematics: Vol. 177). 1971. pap. 8.20 (ISBN 0-387-05340-9). Springer-Verlag.
Lawson, H. Blaine, Jr. Lectures on Minimal Submanifolds, Vol. 1. LC 80-81649. (Mathematics Lecture Ser.: No. 9). 178p. 1980. 10.00 (ISBN 0-914098-18-7). Publish or Perish.
Lokken, Roy N. The Scientific Papers of James Logan. LC 72-76613. (Transactions Ser.: Vol. 62, Pt. 6). (Illus.). 1972. pap. 2.00 (ISBN 0-87169-626-6). Am Philos.
Malina, Frank J., ed. Visual Art, Mathematics & Computers: Selections from the Journal Leonardo. 1979. text ed. 64.00 (ISBN 0-08-021854-7); pap. cancelled. Pergamon.
Matthews, D. E., ed. Mathematics & the Life Sciences: Selected Lectures, Canadian Mathematical Congress, Aug.1975. LC 77-11151. (Lect. Notes in Biomathematics: Vol. 18). 1977. pap. text ed. 18.30 (ISBN 0-387-08351-0). Springer-Verlag.
Meyer, Paul R., ed. Papers in Mathematics. (Annals of the New York Academy of Sciences: Vol. 321). (Orig.). 1979. pap. 20.00x (ISBN 0-89766-026-9). NY Acad Sci.
Midwest Category Seminar, 4th. Reports. MacLane, S., ed. LC 78-126772. (Lecture Notes in Mathematics: Vol. 137). 1970. pap. 10.70 (ISBN 0-387-04926-6). Springer-Verlag.
Millet, Kenneth C. Piecewise Linear Concordances & Isotopies. LC 74-18328. (Memoirs: No. 153). 74p. 1974. pap. 8.40 (ISBN 0-8218-1853-8, MEMO-153). Am Math.
Moore, Eliakim H., et al. The New Haven Mathematical Colloquium. 1910. 75.00x (ISBN 0-686-51424-6). Elliots Bks.
Nagell, Trygve, et al, eds. Selected Mathematicae Papers of Axel Thue. 1977. 40.00x (ISBN 82-00-01649-8, Dist. by Columbia U Pr). Universitet.
Neyman, J. & Pearson, E. K. Joint Statistical Papers. 299p. 1967. lib. bdg. 17.50x (ISBN 0-521-05820-1, Pub. by Charles Griffin & Co Ltd England). Lubrecht & Cramer.
Papers in the Foundation of Mathematics: Supplement to June/July 1973 American Mathematical Monthly. (Slaught Paper: No, 13). 109p. 1975. pap. 2.00 (ISBN 0-88385-418-X). Math Assn.
Pearson, E. S. Selcted Papers. 327p. 1966. lib. bdg. 17.50x (ISBN 0-521-05926-7, Pub. by Charles Griffin & Co Lts England). Lubrecht & Cramer.
Peterson, F. P., ed. Steenrod Algebra & Its Applications: Proceedings. (Lecture Notes in Mathematics: Vol. 168). 1970. 14.10 (ISBN 0-387-05300-X). Springer-Verlag.

Power Computation Conference, 7th, Lausanne, Switzerland, July 12-17, 1980. Proceedings. 1981. text ed. write for info. (ISBN 0-86103-025-7). Butterworth.
Ramsey, F. P., intro. by. Foundations: Essays in Philosophy, Logic, Mathematics & Economics. (International Library of Psychology, Philosophy & Scientific Method). 1978. text ed. 24.75x (ISBN 0-391-00814-5). Humanities.
Rapport, Samuel & Wright, Helen, eds. Mathematics. LC 62-17998. (N Y U Lib. of Science Ser). 1963. 7.95x (ISBN 0-8147-0356-9). NYU Pr.
Rasevskii, P. K., et al. Transactions of the Moscow Mathematical Society, Vol. 30 (1974) 1976. 44.40 (ISBN 0-8218-1630-6, MOSCOW-30). Am Math.
Sierpinski, Waclaw, et al. Congruence of Sets, & Other Monographs, 4 vols. in 1. Incl. On the Congruence of Sets. Sierpinski, Waclaw; Mathematical Theory of the Top. Klein, Felix; Graphical Methods. Runge, Carl; Algebraic Equations. Dickson, Leonard E. LC 67-17000. 14.95 (ISBN 0-8284-0209-4). Chelsea Pub.
Smith, J. D. Mal'cev Varieties. (Lecture Notes in Mathematics: Vol. 554). 1976. soft cover 9.50 (ISBN 0-387-07999-8). Springer-Verlag.
Smith, L. Lectures on the Eilenberg-Moore Spectral Sequence. LC 71-121060. (Lecture Notes in Mathematics: Vol. 134). 1970. pap. 10.70 (ISBN 0-387-04923-1). Springer-Verlag.
Steen, L. A., ed. Mathematics Today - Twelve Informal Essays. LC 78-7594. (Illus.). 1978. 15.50 (ISBN 0-387-90305-4). Springer-Verlag.
Steen, Lynn A., ed. Mathematics Tomorrow. (Illus.). 288p. 1981. 18.00 (ISBN 0-387-90564-2). Springer-Verlag.
Steklov Institute of Mathematics, No. 112. Collection of Articles, I: Proceedings. Petrovsky, I. G. & Nikol'sky, S. M., eds. LC 73-6783. 1973. 67.20 (ISBN 0-8218-3012-0, STEKLO-112). Am Math.
Stelov Institute of Mathematics, Vol. 128. Collection of Articles, II: Dedicated to Acadamician I. M. Vinogradov on the Eightieth Anniversary of His Birth. Nikol'sky, S. M., ed. LC 73-6783. 303p. 1974. 58.00 (ISBN 0-8218-3028-7, STEKLO-128). Am Math.
Symposium On Several Complex Variables - Park City - Utah - 1970. Proceedings. Brooks, R. M., ed. LC 76-153464. (Lecture Notes in Mathematics: Vol. 184). (Illus.). 1971. pap. 11.20 (ISBN 0-387-05370-0). Springer-Verlag.
Symposium, Scandinavian Logic, 3rd. Proceedings. Kanger, S., ed. LC 74-80113. (Studies in Logic & the Foundation of Mathematics: Vol. 82). 214p. 1975. 29.50 (ISBN 0-444-10679-0, North-Holland). Elsevier.
Tarwooter, Dalton, ed. Bicentennial Tribute to American Mathematics. LC 77-14706. 1976. 15.00 (ISBN 0-88385-424-4). Math Assn.
Topology Symposium, Seigen, 1979. Proceedings. Neumann, W. B. & Neumann, W. D., eds. (Lecture Notes in Mathematics: Vol. 788). 495p. 1980. pap. 29.50 (ISBN 0-387-09968-9). Springer-Verlag.
Twenty Lectures Delivered at the International Congress of Mathematicians in Vancouver, 1974. LC 77-9042. (Translation Ser. No. 2: Vol. 109). 1977. 28.80 (ISBN 0-8218-3059-7, TRANS 2/109). Am Math.
Walters, P. Ergodic Theory: Introductory Lectures. LC 75-9853. (Lecture Notes in Mathematics Ser.: Vol. 458). 200p. 1975. pap. 11.40 (ISBN 0-387-07163-6). Springer-Verlag.
Weizsaecker, C. C. Barriers to Entry: A Theoretical Treatment. (Lecture Notes in Economics & Mathematical Systems Ser.: Vol. 185). (Illus.). 220p. 1981. pap. 19.00 (ISBN 0-387-10272-8). Springer-Verlag.
Zagier, D. B. Equivariant Pontrjagin Classes & Applications to Orbit Spaces. LC 72-90185. (Lecture Notes in Mathematics: Vol. 290). 130p. 1972. pap. 6.30 (ISBN 0-387-06013-8). Springer-Verlag.

MATHEMATICS–BIBLIOGRAPHY

American Mathematical Society. Mathematical Reviews Cumulative Author Indexes. Incl. Twenty Volume Author Index of Mathematical Reviews, 1940-59, 2 pts. 1977. 250.00 set (ISBN 0-685-22496-1, MREVIN 40-59); Author Index of Mathematical Reviews, 1960-64, 2 pts. 1966. 190.00 set (ISBN 0-8218-0026-4, MREVIN 60-64); Author Index of Mathematical Reviews, 1965-72. 1974. 356.00 (ISBN 0-8218-0027-2, MREVIN 65-72). Repr. Am Math.
Carr, George S. Formulas & Theorems in Pure Mathematics. LC 78-113122. Orig. Title: Synopsis of Pure Mathematics. 1970. text ed. 35.00 (ISBN 0-8284-0239-6). Chelsea Pub.
Frenchsem. Union List of French Mathematical Seminars. LC 78-10797. (Frenchsem Miscellaneous Publications). 1978. 16.80 (ISBN 0-8218-0063-9). Am Math.
Gaffney, M. P. & Steen, L. A., eds. Annotated Bibliography of Expository Writing in the Mathematical Sciences. 1976. 9.00 (ISBN 0-88385-422-8). Math Assn.
Index to Translations Selected by the American Mathematical Society, Vol. 1. 1966. 12.40 (ISBN 0-8218-0042-6, TRAN2I-1-50). Am Math.
Karpinski, Louis C. Bibliography of Mathematical Works Printed in America Through Eighteen Fifty: Reprinted with Supplement & Second Supplement to the Bibliography. Cohen, I. Bernard, ed. LC 79-7971. (Three Centuries of Science in America Ser.). (Illus.). 1980. Repr. of 1940 ed. lib. bdg. 52.00x (ISBN 0-405-12553-4). Arno.
Mathematical Reviews Cumulative Index: 1973-1979. 1981. 1070.00 (ISBN 0-8218-0035-3). Am Math.
Matthias, Margaret & Thiessen, Diane. Children's Mathematics Books: A Critical Bibliography. LC 79-11896. 1979. pap. 5.00 (ISBN 0-8389-0285-5). ALA.
May, K. O. Bibliography & Research Manual of the History of Mathematics. LC 71-151379. (Scholarly Reprint Ser.). 1973. 40.00x (ISBN 0-8020-7077-9). U of Toronto Pr.
National Council of Teachers of Mathematics. Cumulative Index: The Mathematics Teacher, 1908-1965. LC 42-24844. 1967. pap. 9.00 (ISBN 0-87353-028-4). NCTM.
Pemberton, J. E. How to Find Out in Mathematics. 2nd ed. 1970. 22.00 (ISBN 0-08-006824-3); pap. 10.75 (ISBN 0-08-006823-5). Pergamon.
Steen, Lynn & Seebach, J. A., eds. Fifty-Year Index of the Mathematics Magazine. 1979. pap. 8.80 (ISBN 0-88385-432-5). Math Assn.

MATHEMATICS–COLLECTED WORKS

Abbott, James, ed. The Chauvenet Papers, Vol. 1. 1979. 16.00 (ISBN 0-88385-425-2). Math Assn.
Abbott, James C., ed. The Chauvenet Papers, Vol. 2. 1979. 16.00 (ISBN 0-88385-427-9). Math Assn.
Abel, Niels H. Oeuvres Completes, 2 vols in 1. Sylow, L. & Lie, S., eds. Set. 54.00 (ISBN 0-384-00103-3). Johnson Repr.
Adolf Hurwitz: Mathematische Werke, Vol. I, Funktionentheorie. 2nd ed. 734p. (Ger.). 1962. 76.50 (ISBN 3-7643-0184-8). Birkhauser.
Adolf Hurwitz: Mathematische Werke, Vol. II, Zahlentheorie, Algebra & Geometrie. 2nd ed. 755p. (Ger.). 1963. 76.50 (ISBN 3-7643-0185-6). Birkhauser.
American Mathematical Monthly. To Lester R. Ford, on His Seventieth Birthday: Supplement to the American Mathematical Monthly October 1957. (Slaught Memorial Paper: No. 6). 106p. 1957. pap. 2.00 (ISBN 0-88385-413-9). Math Assn.
Andrews, George E., ed. Percy Alexander MacMahon: Collected Papers: Combinatorics, Vol. 1. LC 77-28962. (Mathematicians of Our Time Ser.). 1978. 75.00x (ISBN 0-262-13121-8). MIT Pr.
Barrow, Isaac. Mathematical Works. Whewell, W., ed. Repr. of 1860 ed. 128.00 (ISBN 3-4870-4788-8). Adler.
Birkhoff, George D. Collected Mathematical Papers, 3 Vols. LC 66-23748. 1968. Repr. of 1950 ed. 12.50 ea.; Vol. 1. (ISBN 0-486-61955-9); Vol. 2. (ISBN 0-486-61956-7); Vol. 3. (ISBN 0-486-61957-5). Dover.
Boas, R. P. Collected Works of Hidehiko Yamabe. (Notes on Mathematics & Its Applications Ser). 1967. 30.25x (ISBN 0-677-00610-1). Gordon.
Boltyanskii, Vladimir G. & Gokhberg, Izrail T. The Decomposition of Figures into Smaller Parts. Christoffers, Henry & Branson, Thomas P., trs. from Rus. LC 79-10382. (Popular Lectures in Mathematics). 1980. pap. text ed. 6.00x (ISBN 0-226-06357-7). U of Chicago Pr.
Brauer, Richard. Richard Brauer: Collected Papers, 3 vols. Wong, Warren J. & Fong, Paul, eds. 1980. Vol. 1. 55.00x (ISBN 0-262-02135-8); Vol. 2. 55.00x (ISBN 0-262-02148-X); Vol. 3. 55.00x (ISBN 0-262-02149-8). MIT Pr.
Brouwer, L. E. L. E. J. Brouwer-Collected Works, Vol. 2. Heyting, A., ed. LC 73-75529. 628p. 1976. 122.00 (ISBN 0-444-10643-X, North-Holland). Elsevier.
Cayley, Arthur. Collected Mathematical Papers, Vols. 1-13. 1889-1897. with index 554.50 (ISBN 0-384-07970-9); 42.50 ea.; Vol. suppl. 23.00 (ISBN 0-685-13389-3). Johnson Repr.
Chebyshev, Pafnuti L. Oeuvres: Collected Papers, 2 Vols. LC 61-17956. (Fr). 69.50 set (ISBN 0-8284-0157-8). Chelsea Pub.
Dickson, Leonard E. Collected Mathematical Papers, 5 vols. Albert, A. Adrian, ed. LC 69-19943. 3300p. 1975. Set. text ed. 160.00 set (ISBN 0-8284-0273-6). Chelsea Pub.
Fleckenstein, J. O. Jakob Bernoulli, Die Gesammelten Werke: Vol. I, Astronomia-Philosophia Naturalis. (Ger.). 1969. 65.50 (ISBN 3-7643-0028-0). Birkhauser.
Grosswald, Emil, ed. Collected Papers of Hans Rademacher, 2 vols. (Mathematicians of Our Time Ser.: Vols. 3 & 4). 1356p. 1974. text ed. 45.00x ea.; Vol. 1. text ed. (ISBN 0-262-07054-5); Vol. 2. text ed. (ISBN 0-262-07055-3); Set. text ed. 85.00x (ISBN 0-686-31697-5). MIT Pr.
Hamilton, William R. Mathematical Papers of Sir William Rowan Hamilton, Vol. 3. Halberstam, H. & Ingram, R. E., eds. 1967. 130.00 (ISBN 0-521-05183-5). Cambridge U Pr.
Hardy, G. H. Collected Papers of G. H. Hardy: Including Joint Papers with J. E. Lockwood & Others, Vol. 7. 1979. 89.00x (ISBN 0-19-853347-0). Oxford U Pr.
Herrtage, Sidney J., ed. The English Charlemagne Romances. Incl. Pt. 1. Sir Ferumbras. 1879. 14.95x (ISBN 0-19-722569-1); Pt. 6. The Tail of Rauf Coilyear, with the Fragments of Roland & Vernagu & Otuel. Herrtage, Sidney J., ed. 164p. 1882. 12.95x (ISBN 0-19-722513-6). Oxford U Pr.
Hilbert, David. Gesammelte Abhandlungen, 3 Vols. 3rd ed. LC 65-21834. (Ger). 1981. Set. 49.95 (ISBN 0-8284-0195-0). Chelsea Pub.
Hill, George W. The Collected Mathematical Works, 4 Vols. 1905-1907. Set. 192.50 (ISBN 0-384-23255-8). Johnson Repr.
Jacobi, Karl G. Gesammelte Werke, 8 vols. 2nd ed. LC 68-31427. (Illus., Ger., Includes Supplementband Vorlesugen Uber Dynamik). 1969. Vols. 1-7. 160.00 (ISBN 0-8284-0226-4); Vol. 8. 15.00 (ISBN 0-8284-0227-2). Chelsea Pub.
Kodaira, Kunihiko. Collected Works, 3 vols. 540p. 1975. Set. 95.00 (ISBN 0-685-51710-1). Vol. 1. 40.00 (ISBN 0-691-08158-1); Vol. 2. 35.00x (ISBN 0-691-08163-8); Vol. 3. 35.00x (ISBN 0-691-08164-6). Princeton U Pr.
Kozesnik, Jaroslav, ed. Information Theory, Statistical Decision Functions, Random Processes, Vol. C. 1979. lib. bdg. 42.15 (ISBN 90-277-0938-6, Pub. by Reidel Holland). Kluwer Boston.
Kronecker, Leopold. Werke, 5 vols. LC 66-20394. 1969. Repr. Set. 99.50 (ISBN 0-8284-0224-8). Chelsea Pub.
Lejeune-Dirichlet, P. G. Werke, 2 Vols. in 1. Kronecker, L., ed. LC 68-54716. (Ger) 1969. Repr. 39.50 (ISBN 0-8284-0225-6). Chelsea Pub.
Lorenz, Ludwig V. Oeuvres Scientifiques De L. Lorenz, 2 Vols. 1898-1904. Set. 38.50 (ISBN 0-384-33740-6). Johnson Repr.
Midonick, Henrietta O. Treasury of Mathematics. LC 62-20873. 1965. 15.00 (ISBN 0-8022-1114-3). Philos Lib.
Minkowski, Hermann. Gesammelte Abhandlungen, 2 Vols. in 1. LC 66-28570. (Ger). 35.00 (ISBN 0-8284-0208-6). Chelsea Pub.
Plucker, Jul. Gesammelte Wissenschaftliche Abhandlungen, 2 Vols. 1971. Repr. of 1895 ed. Set. 92.50 (ISBN 0-384-46890-X). Johnson Repr.
Ramanujan, S. Collected Papers. LC 62-8326. 1962. 13.95 (ISBN 0-8284-0159-4). Chelsea Pub.
Robinson. Selected Papers of Abraham Robinson, 2 vols. Korner, S., et al, eds. LC 77-92395. 1979. Vol. 2. text ed. 45.00x (ISBN 0-300-02072-4); Vol. 3. text ed. 35.00x (ISBN 0-300-02073-2). Yale U Pr.
Schafli, Ludwig. Gesammelte Mathematische Abhandlungen, Vol. 3. 402p. (Ger.). 1956. 53.50 (ISBN 3-7643-0330-1). Birkhauser.
Schlafli, Ludwig. Gesammelte Mathematische Abhandlungen, Vol. 1. 392p. (Ger.). 1953. 53.50 (ISBN 3-7643-0328-X). Birkhauser.
--Gesammelte Mathematische Abhandlungen, Vol. 2. 381p. (Ger.). 1953. 53.50 (ISBN 3-7643-0329-8). Birkhauser.
Selecta Hermann Weyl. 592p. (Ger.). 1965. 48.50 (ISBN 3-7643-0414-6). Birkhauser.
Smith, Henry J. Collected Mathematical Papers, 2 Vols. LC 65-11859. 60.00 (ISBN 0-8284-0187-X). Chelsea Pub.
Szego, Gabor, et al, eds. Studies in Mathematical Analysis & Related Topics: Essays in Honor of George Polya. 1962. 20.00x (ISBN 0-8047-0140-7). Stanford U Pr.
Transactions of the Moscow Mathematical Society. Incl. Vol. 12. 1963. 49.20 (ISBN 0-8218-1612-8, MOSCOW-12); Vol. 13. 1967. 40.80 (ISBN 0-8218-1613-6, MOSCOW-13); Vol. 14. 1967. 40.80 (ISBN 0-8218-1614-4, MOSCOW-14); Vol. 15. 1967. 49.20 (ISBN 0-8218-1615-2, MOSCOW-15); Vol. 16. 1968. 42.00 (ISBN 0-8218-1616-0, MOSCOW-16); Vol. 17. 1969. 43.60 (ISBN 0-8218-1617-9, MOSCOW-17); Vol. 18. 1969. 40.00 (ISBN 0-8218-1618-7, MOSCOW-18); Vol. 19. 1969. 34.80 (ISBN 0-8218-1619-5, MOSCOW-19); Vol. 20. 1971. 52.40 (ISBN 0-8218-1620-9, MOSCOW-20); Vol. 21. 1971. 45.60 (ISBN 0-8218-1621-7, MOSCOW-21); Vol. 22. 1972. 40.80 (ISBN 0-8218-1622-5). LC 65-7413. Am Math.
V. D. Waerden, B., et al. Jakob Bernoulli, Die Gesammelten Werke: Vol. III, Wahrscheinlichkeitsrechnung. 584p. (Ger.). 1975. 70.80 (ISBN 3-7643-0713-7). Birkhauser.
Von Neumann, John. Collected Works, 6 vols. Taub, A. W., ed. Incl. Vol. 1. Logic, Theory of Sets & Quantum Mechanics. 1961. 110.00 (ISBN 0-08-009567-4); Vol. 2. Operators, Ergodic Theory & Almost Periodic Functions in a Group. 1962. 110.00 (ISBN 0-08-009568-2); Vol. 3. Rings of Operators. 1962. 110.00 (ISBN 0-08-009569-0); Vol. 4. 1963. 110.00 (ISBN 0-08-009570-4); Vol. 5. 1963. 110.00 (ISBN 0-08-009571-2); Vol. 6. Theory of Games, Astrophysics, Hydrodynamics & Meteorology. 1963. 110.00 (ISBN 0-08-009572-0). 1963. Set. 660.00 (ISBN 0-08-009566-6). Pergamon.
Weierstrass, Karl T. Mathematische Werke, 7 Vols. LC 68-7407. (Illus.). Set. 134.00 (ISBN 0-384-66490-3). Johnson Repr.
Weil, A. Oeuvres Mathematiques: Collected Papers, 1926-1978, 3 vol. set. 1979. 120.00 (ISBN 0-387-90330-5). Springer-Verlag.
Weiner, Norbert. Norbert Wiener: Collected Work: Vol. 1 Mathematical Philosophy & Foundations, Potential Theory, Brownian Movement, Wiener Integrals, Ergodic & Chaos Theories, Turbulence & Statistical Mechanics. Masani, P., ed. LC 74-17362. (Mit Mathematicians of Our Time Ser.). 1975. text ed. 45.00x (ISBN 0-262-23070-4). MIT Pr.
--Norbert Wiener: Collected Work: Vol. 2 Generalized Harmonic Analysis & Tauberian Theory, Classical Harmonic & Complex Analysis. Masani, P., ed. (Mathematicians of Our Time Ser.). 1979. 50.00x (ISBN 0-262-23092-5). MIT Pr.
Weyl, Hermann, et al. Das Kontinuum und Andere Monographien, 4 vols. in 1. Incl. Kantinuum; Mathematische Analyse Des Raumproblems; Neuere Funktionentheorie. Landau; Hypothesen. Reimann. LC 72-81808. 14.95 (ISBN 0-8284-0134-9). Chelsea Pub.
Zariski, Oscar. Oscar Zariski: Collected Papers. Incl. Vol. 1. Foundations of Algebric Geometry & Resolution of Singularities. Hironaka & Mumford, eds. 1972. 32.50x (ISBN 0-262-08049-4); Vol. 2. Holomorphic Functions & Linear Systems. Artin & Mumford, eds. 1973. 32.50x (ISBN 0-262-01038-0); Vol. 3. Topology of Curves & Surfaces. Artin & Mazur, eds. LC 73-171558. 1978. 40.00x (ISBN 0-262-24021-1); Vol. 4. Equisingularity on Algebraic Varieties. 1979. 50.00x (ISBN 0-262-24022-X). (Mathematicians of Our Times Ser.). MIT Pr.

MATHEMATICS–COMPETITIONS

Gruver, Howell L. School Mathematics Contests: A Report. LC 68-21511. 1968. pap. 1.70 (ISBN 0-87353-089-6). NCTM.

MATHEMATICS–CURIOSA AND MISCELLANY

Adler, Irving. Magic House of Numbers. LC 73-19471. (Illus.). 144p. (gr. 5-9). 1974. PLB 8.79 (ISBN 0-381-99986-6, JD-J). Har-Row.
Eves, Howard W. In Mathematical Circles, 2 Vols. 1969. Set. write for info. (ISBN 0-685-19591-0, PWS0671); write for info. Prindle.
--Mathematical Circles Revisited. (Illus.). 1971. text ed. write for info. (ISBN 0-87150-121-X, PWS0951); text ed. write for info. (ISBN 0-685-04722-9). Prindle.
Honsberger, Ross. Mathematical Gems II. LC 76-15927. (Dolciani Mathematical Expositions). 1976. 12.50 (ISBN 0-88385-302-7). Math Assn.
Marmaduke, Multiply. Marmaduke Multiply's Merry Method of Making Minor Mathematicians. facsimile ed. Bleiler, E. F., ed. pap. 1.60 (ISBN 0-486-22773-1). Dover.
Mott-Smith, Geoffrey. Mathematical Puzzlers for Beginners & Enthusiasts. ind rev. ed. (Illus.). 6.75 (ISBN 0-8446-4785-3). Peter Smith.

MATHEMATICS–DATA PROCESSING

Ahl, David H. Computers in Mathematics: A Sourcebook of Ideas. LC 79-57487. (Illus.). 224p. 1980. pap. 15.95 (ISBN 0-916688-16-X). Creative Comp.
Andree, R., et al. Computer Programming: Techniques, Analyses & Mathematics. 1973. ref. ed. 23.95 (ISBN 0-13-166082-9). P-H.
Ashley, R. Background Math for a Computer World. 2nd ed. LC 80-11562. (Wiley Self-Teaching Guides). 308p. 1980. pap. text ed. 7.95 (ISBN 0-471-08086-1). Wiley.
Automated Education Center. Hybrid Computer Application to Mathematical Models of Physical Systems. LC 70-125998. 19.00 (ISBN 0-686-02005-7). Mgmt Info Serv.
Bellman, Richard E. Introduction to the Mathematical Theory of Control Processes. LC 76-127679. (Mathematics in Science & Engineering Ser.: Vol. 40). Vol. 1 1967. 42.50 (ISBN 0-12-084801-5); Vol. 2 1971. 50.00 (ISBN 0-12-084802-3). Acad Pr.

Calter, Paul. Problem Solving with Computers. 1972. pap. text ed. 11.95 (ISBN 0-07-009648-1, G); instructor's manual 2.50 (ISBN 0-07-009649-X). McGraw.

Carlile, R. E. & Gillett, B. E. Fortran & Computer Mathematics. LC 72-95446. 520p. 1974. 23.00 (ISBN 0-87814-016-6). Pennwell Pub.

Casti, John & Kalaba, Robert. Imbedding Methods in Applied Mathematics. LC 73-6977. (Applied Mathematics & Computation Ser: No. 2). (Illus.). 320p. 1973. pap. text ed. 8.50 (ISBN 0-201-00919-6, Adv Bk Prog). A-W.

Clark, Frank J. Mathematics for Data Processing. LC 73-8868. (Illus.). 432p. 1974. 17.95 (ISBN 0-87909-470-2); students manual avail. Reston.

Cottle, R. W., et al, eds. Variational Inequalities & Complementarity Problems: Theory & Applications. Giannessi, F. & Lions, J. L. LC 79-40108. 1980. 48.95 (ISBN 0-471-27610-3, Pub. by Wiley-Interscience). Wiley.

Dixon, W. J. & Nicholson, W. L. Exploring Data Analysis: The Computer Revolution in Statistics. LC 73-85786. 1974. 23.75x (ISBN 0-520-02470-2). U of Cal Pr.

Fiacco. Mathematical Programming with Data Perturbations. (Lecture Notes in Pure & Applied Mathematics Ser.). 320p. 1981. price not set (ISBN 0-8247-1543-8). Dekker.

Forsythe, George E. & Moler, C. Computer Solution of Linear Algebraic Systems. 1967. ref. ed. 19.95 (ISBN 0-13-165779-8). P-H.

Freiberger, W. & Grenander, U. A Course in Computational Probability & Statistics. LC 76-176272. (Applied Mathematical Sciences: Vol. 6). 168p. 1971. pap. 16.00 (ISBN 0-387-90029-2). Springer-Verlag.

Gear, C. W. Numerical Initial Value Problems in Ordinary Differential Equations. (Automatic Computation Ser). (Illus.). 1971. ref. ed. 22.95 (ISBN 0-13-626606-1). P-H.

Gonzalez, Richard F. & McMillan, Claude, Jr. Machine Computation: An Algorithmic Approach. (Irwin-Dorsey Information Processing Ser). 1971. text ed. 17.95x (ISBN 0-256-00234-7). Irwin.

Greenspan, Donald. Discrete Models. LC 73-7957. (Applied Mathematics & Computation Ser: No. 3). (Illus.). xvi, 165p. 1973. text ed. 16.00 (ISBN 0-201-02612-0, Adv Bk Prog); pap. text ed. 8.50 (ISBN 0-201-02613-9, Adv Bk Prog). A-W.

Immerzeel, George & Ockenga, Earl. Calculator Activities for the Classroom: Book 2. Preiss, Irene, ed. 1977. wkbk. 7.25 (ISBN 0-88488-109-1). Creative Pubns.

--Calculator Activities for the Classroom: Book 1. Preiss, Irene, ed. 1977. wkbk. 7.25 (ISBN 0-88488-108-3). Creative Pubns.

Klerer, Melvin & Reinfelds, Juris, eds. Interactive Systems for Experimental Applied Mathematics. 1968. 50.00 (ISBN 0-12-414650-3). Acad Pr.

Korfhage, Robert R. Discrete Computational Structures. 1974. 25.00 (ISBN 0-12-420850-9). Acad Pr.

Kousourou, Gabriel, et al. An Introduction to Technical Mathematics with Computing. (Illus.). 510p. text ed. 24.00x (ISBN 0-89433-038-1). Petrocelli.

Kuester & Mize. Optimization Techniques with Fortran. 256p. 1973. text ed. 16.95 (ISBN 0-07-035606-8, C). McGraw.

Leech, J. Computational Problems in Abstract Algebra. 1970. 60.00 (ISBN 0-08-012975-7). Pergamon.

Leinbach, L. Carl. Calculus with the Computer: A Laboratory Manual. (Illus.). 208p. 1974. pap. text ed. 10.95x (ISBN 0-13-111518-9). P-H.

Loeckx, J. Computability & Decidability. LC 72-82761. (Lecture Notes in Economics & Mathematical Systems: Vol. 68). (Illus.). 82p. 1972. pap. 6.30 (ISBN 0-387-05869-9). Springer-Verlag.

Miller, R. E. & Thatcher, J. W., eds. Complexity of Computer Computations. LC 72-85736. (IBM Research Symposia Ser.). 225p. 1972. 27.50 (ISBN 0-306-30707-3, Plenum Pr). Plenum Pub.

Nievergelt, Jurg, et al. Computer Approaches to Mathematical Problems. (Illus.). 272p. 1974. ref. ed. 19.95 (ISBN 0-13-164855-1). P-H.

Prekopa, A., ed. Survey of Mathematical Programming, 3 vols. in one. 1979. Set. 190.25 (ISBN 0-444-85033-3, North Holland). Elsevier.

Rau, Nicholas. Matrices & Mathematical Prgramming: An Introduction for Economists. 1980. 18.50 (ISBN 0-312-52299-1). St Martin.

Rodin, E. Y. Computers & Mathematics with Applications: A Memorial Dedicated to Cornelius Lanczos. 1976. text ed. 82.50 (ISBN 0-08-020521-6). Pergamon.

Sage, Edwin R. Problem Solving with the Computer. (Illus.). 244p. (Orig.). 1969. pap. 9.95 (ISBN 0-87567-030-X). Entelek.

Shampine, Lawrence F. & Allen, Richard C. Numerical Computing: An Introduction. LC 72-93122. 258p. 1973. text ed. 12.95 (ISBN 0-7216-8150-6). HR&W.

Society for Industrial & Applied Mathematics - American Mathematical Society Symposia - New York - March, 1971. Computers in Algebra & Number Theory: Proceedings, Vol. 4. Birkhoff, Garrett & Hall, Marshall, Jr., eds. LC 76-167685. 208p. 1980. Repr. of 1971 ed. 16.00 (ISBN 0-8218-1323-4, SIAMS-4). Am Math.

Stewart, G. W. Introduction to Matrix Computations. (Computer Science & Applied Mathematics Ser.). 1973. 21.95 (ISBN 0-12-670350-7). Acad Pr.

Symposia in Applied Mathematics. The Influence of Computing on Mathematical Research & Education, Vol. 20. La Salle, Joseph P., ed. LC 74-5166. 1974. 33.20 (ISBN 0-8218-1326-9, PSAPM-20). Am Math.

Tewarson, Reginald P. Sparse Matrices. (Mathematics in Science & Engineering Ser.: Vol. 99). 1973. 27.00 (ISBN 0-12-685650-8). Acad Pr.

Thompson, Linda L. Consumer Mathematics. Vorndran, Richard A., ed. LC 76-4003. 470p. 1978. text ed. 13.12 (ISBN 0-02-479280-2); tchrs. manual 4.40 (ISBN 0-02-479300-0); wkbk. 4.80 (ISBN 0-02-479290-X); solutions key 3.32 (ISBN 0-686-65782-9). Glencoe.

Tinsley, J. D. Computing in Mathematics: Some Experimental Ideas for Teachers. (School Mathematics Project Computing Ser.). (Illus.). 1971. 17.95 (ISBN 0-521-08150-5); pap. 7.95 (ISBN 0-521-09683-9). Cambridge U Pr.

Traub, J. F., ed. Algorithms & Complexity: New Directions & Recent Results. 1976. 36.00 (ISBN 0-12-697540-X). Acad Pr.

--Complexity of Sequential & Parallel Numerical Algorithms. 1973. 30.00 (ISBN 0-12-697550-7). Acad Pr.

Tucker, Allen B., Jr. Text Processing: Algorithms, Languages, & Applications. LC 79-23130. (Computer Science & Applied Mathematics Ser.). 1979. 16.50 (ISBN 0-12-702550-2). Acad Pr.

Wang, Peter C., et al, eds. Information Linkage Between Applied Mathematics & Industry. 1979. 43.50 (ISBN 0-12-734250-8). Acad Pr.

Williams, Gareth. Finite Mathematics with Models. 1976. text ed. 18.50x (ISBN 0-205-04913-3); instr's manual 4.95 (ISBN 0-205-04914-1). Allyn.

MATHEMATICS–DICTIONARIES

Alsina, Claudi. Vocabulari Catala De Matematica Basica. 48p. (Cata.). 1977. pap. 8.75 (ISBN 84-85008-06-5, S-50127). French & Eur.

Ballentyne, D. W. & Walker, L. E. Diccionario de Leyes y Efectos Cleentificos En Quimica-Fisicay Matematicas. 216p. (Span.). 14.95 (ISBN 0-686-56711-0, S-33054). French & Eur.

Bendick, Jeanne & Levin, Marcia. Mathematics Illustrated Dictionary: Facts, Figures & People, Including the New Math. (Illus.). (gr. 7 up). 1972. 6.95 (ISBN 0-07-004460-0, GB). McGraw.

Boursin, Jean-Louis. DEMO: Dictionnaire Elementaire de Mathematiques Modernes. 320p. (Fr.). 1972. 14.95 (ISBN 0-686-56927-X, M-6045). French & Eur.

Chambadal, Lucien. Diccionario De las Matematicas Modernas. 2nd ed. 264p. (Espn.). 1976. pap. 5.25 (ISBN 84-01-90307-6, S-12248). French & Eur.

--Dictionnaire des Mathematiques Modernes. rev. ed. 250p. (Fr.). 1972. pap. 6.95 (ISBN 0-686-56847-8, M-6625). French & Eur.

Costa, Vasco & Frances, Osvald. Diccionario De Unidadaes y Tablas De Conversion. 3rd ed. 168p. (Espn.). 1977. pap. 8.75 (ISBN 84-252-0214-0, S-50579). French & Eur.

Dictionary of Physics & Mathematics Abbreviations, Signs & Symbols. pap. 5.95 (ISBN 0-671-18912-3). Monarch Pr.

Encyclopedia of Math & Computer Terms. 1982. price not set (2519-9). Barron.

Fachlexikon ABC Mathematik. 624p. (Ger.). 1978. 30.95 (ISBN 3-87144-030-2, M-7381, Pub. by Verlag Harri Deutsch). French & Eur.

Fachlexikon ABC Mathematik. (Ger.). 1977. 30.95 (ISBN 3-87144-336-0, M-7382, Pub. by Harri Deutsch). French & Eur.

Gellert, W. Kleine Enzyklopaedie Mathematik. 2nd ed. 837p. (Ger.). 1972. 27.50 (ISBN 3-87144-104-X, M-7090). French & Eur.

Gellert, W., et al. Kleine Enzyklopadie Mathmetik. 820p. (Ger.). 1977-78. 28.95 (ISBN 3-87144-323-9, M-7498, Pub. by Verlag Harri Deutsch). French & Eur.

Herland, Leo. Dictionary of Mathematical Sciences, 2 vols. Incl. Vol. 1. German-English. 2nd ed. xii, 320p (ISBN 0-8044-4393-9); Vol. 2. English-German. 320p (ISBN 0-8044-4394-7). LC 65-16622. 18.50 ea. Ungar.

Iyanaga, Shokichi & Kawada, Yukiyosi, eds. Encyclopedic Dictionary of Mathematics, 2 vols. 1977. Set. text ed. 165.00 (ISBN 0-262-09016-3); pap. text ed. 40.00x (ISBN 0-262-59010-7). MIT Pr.

Klaften, Berthold. Mathematisches Vokabular. 4th ed. (Eng. -Ger., Vocabulary of Mathematics). 1971. 13.50 (ISBN 0-686-56630-0, M-7551, Pub. by Wila). French & Eur.

Lohwater, A. J. Russian-English Dictionary of the Mathematical Sciences. LC 61-15685. 267p. (Eng. & Rus.). 1979. Repr. of 1974 ed. 12.40 (ISBN 0-8218-0036-1, RED). Am Math.

Maravall Casesnoves, Dario. Diccionario De Matematica Moderna. 332p. (Espn.). 1975. pap. 9.95 (ISBN 0-686-57333-1, S-50009). French & Eur.

Millington, William & Millington, T. Alaric. Dictionary of Mathematics. 1971. pap. 3.95 (ISBN 0-06-463311-X, EH 311, EH). Har-Row.

Milne-Thomson, L. M. Russian-English Mathematical Dictionary. (Mathematical Research Center Pubns., No. 7). 206p. 1962. 40.00x (ISBN 0-299-02600-0). U of Wis Pr.

Reck, J. Herder - Lexikon Mathematik. 238p. (Ger.). 1974. 15.95 (ISBN 3-451-16458-2, M-7445, Pub. by Herder). French & Eur.

Reck, Jurgen. Diccionario Rioduero Matematica. 224p. (Espn.). 1977. leatherette 12.50 (ISBN 84-220-0832-7, S-50162). French & Eur.

Rota, Gian-Carlo, ed. Encyclopedia of Mathematics & Its Applications, 2 vols. Incl. Vol. 1. Integral Geometry & Geometric Probability, Section-Probability. Santalo, Luis A. Kac, Mark, ed. (Illus.). 21.50 (ISBN 0-201-13500-0); Vol. 2. The Theory of Partitions, Section-Number Theory. Andrews, George E. Turan, Paul, ed. 21.50 (ISBN 0-201-13501-9). 1976 (Adv Bk Prog). A-W.

Shanahan, William F. Essential Math, Science, & Computer Terms for College Freshmen. LC 79-3323. (Illus.). 1981. pap. 5.95 (ISBN 0-671-18435-0). Monarch Pr.

Shapiro, Max & Cadillac Publishing Company. Mathematics Encyclopedia: A Made Simple Book. LC 76-23817. 1977. pap. 5.95 (ISBN 0-385-12427-9, Made). Doubleday.

Silverman, Alan S. Handbook of Chinese for Mathematicians. new ed. (Current Chinese Language Project Ser.: No. 17). 1976. pap. 3.50 (ISBN 0-912966-17-3). IEAS Ctr Chinese Stud.

Sneddon, I. N., ed. Encyclopedic Dictionary of Mathematics for Engineers. LC 73-6800. 1976. 150.00 (ISBN 0-08-021149-6). Pergamon.

Sube, Ralf. Woerterbuch der Mathematik. 800p. (Eng., Ger., Fr. & Rus., Dictionary of Mathematics). 1979. 80.00 (ISBN 3-87144-445-6, M-6983). French & Eur.

Universal Encyclopedia of Mathematics. 1963. 12.95 (ISBN 0-671-77406-9); pap. 8.95 (ISBN 0-671-20348-7). S&S.

Universal Encyclopedia of Mathematics. 1969. pap. 6.95 (ISBN 0-671-20348-7, Fireside). S&S.

Warusfel, Andre. Dictionnaire Raisonne De Mathematiques. (Fr.). 1966. pap. 27.95 (ISBN 0-686-57257-2, M-6567). French & Eur.

MATHEMATICS–EARLY WORKS TO 1800

see also Mathematics, Greek

Abu Al-Hasan & Ahmed-Ibn Ibrahim. The Arithmetic of Al-Uqlidisi. Saidan, A. S., tr. 1978. lib. bdg. 103.00 (ISBN 90-277-0752-9, Pub. by Reidel Holland). Kluwer Boston.

Davis, Margaret D. Piero Della Francesca's Mathematical Treatises: The "Trattato d'Abaco" & "Libellus de Quinque Corporibus Regularibus". (Speculum Artium: No. 1). (Illus.). 165p. (It.). 1977. pap. 17.50x (ISBN 0-8150-0912-7). Wittenborn.

Dee, John. John Dee the Mathematical Praeface. Debus, Allen, intro. by. LC 74-31377. (Primary Sources from the Scientific Revolution Ser.). (Illus.). 96p. 1975. Repr. of 1570 ed. text ed. 17.00 (ISBN 0-88202-020-X, Sci Hist). N Watson.

De Moivre, Abraham. Doctrine of Chances: Including Treatise on Annuities. 3rd ed. LC 66-23756. 1967. 15.95 (ISBN 0-8284-0200-0). Chelsea Pub.

Descartes, Rene. Geometry. Smith & Latham, trs. 7.00 (ISBN 0-8446-1972-8). Peter Smith.

--Geometry. (Eng. & Fr.). 1925. pap. 3.50 (ISBN 0-486-60068-8). Dover.

Digges, Leonard & Digges, Thomas. An Arithmeticall Militarie Treatise, Named Stratioticos. LC 68-27478. (English Experience Ser.: No. 71). 192p. 1968. Repr. of 1579 ed. 21.00 (ISBN 90-221-0071-5). Walter J Johnson.

Hood, Thomas. A Copie of the Speeche Made by the Mathematicall Lecturer at the House of M. Thomas Smith, 4 November, 1588. LC 74-80189. (English Experience Ser.: No. 688). 16p. 1974. Repr. of 1588 ed. 3.50 (ISBN 90-221-0668-3). Walter J Johnson.

Napier, John. De Arte Logistica Joannis Naperi Merchistonii, Baronis Libri Qui Supersunt. LC 76-173010. (Maitland Club, Glasgow. Publications: No. 47). Repr. of 1839 ed. 27.50 (ISBN 0-404-52773-6). AMS Pr.

Newton, Isaac. Mathematical Papers of Isaac Newton, Vol. 5. Whiteside, D. T., et al, eds. LC 65-11203. (Illus.). 600p. 1972. 150.00 (ISBN 0-521-08262-5). Cambridge U Pr.

--Mathematical Papers of Isaac Newton, Vol. 1, 1664-1666. Whiteside, D. T. & Hoskin, M. A., eds. 150.00 (ISBN 0-521-05817-1). Cambridge U Pr.

--Mathematical Papers of Isaac Newton, Vol. 3, 1670-1673. Whiteside, D. T. & Hoskin, M. A., eds. LC 65-11203. (Illus.). 150.00 (ISBN 0-521-07119-4). Cambridge U Pr.

--Mathematical Papers of Isaac Newton, Vol. 6: 1684-1691. Whiteside, D. T. & Hoskin, M. A., eds. LC 73-86046. (Illus.). 6000p. 1975. 150.00 (ISBN 0-521-08719-8). Cambridge U Pr.

--Mathematical Works, 2 Vols. Whiteside, Derek T., ed. 1964. Vol. 1. 22.50 (ISBN 0-384-41230-0); Vol. 2. 27.00 (ISBN 0-384-41232-7). Johnson Repr.

North, J. D., ed. Richard of Wallingford: An Edition of His Writings with Introduction, English Translation & Commentary, 3 vols. (Illus.). 1976. 159.00x (ISBN 0-19-858139-4). Oxford U Pr.

Oresme, Nicole, ed. De Proportionibus Proportionum. Grant, Edward, tr. Bd. with Ad Pauca Respicientes. (Medieval Science Publications Ser). (Illus.). 488p. 1966. 50.00x (ISBN 0-299-04000-3). U of Wis Pr.

Roberval, Gilles. Divers Ouvrages De Mathematique et De Physique Par Messieurs De L'academie Royale Des Sciences. Repr. of 1693 ed. 72.00 (ISBN 0-8287-0735-9). Clearwater Pub.

Saccheri, Girolamo. Euclides Vindicatus. 2nd ed. Halstead, George B., tr. from Lat. 1980. text ed. 12.95 (ISBN 0-8284-0289-2). Chelsea Pub.

Struik, D. J., ed. Source Book in Mathematics: Twelve Hundred to Eighteen Hundred. LC 68-21980. (Source Books in the History of the Sciences Ser). (Illus.). 1969. 22.50x (ISBN 0-674-82355-9). Harvard U Pr.

Tapp, John. The Path-Way to Knowledge: Containing the Whole Art of Arithmeticke. LC 68-54667. (English Experience Ser.: No. 66). 1968. Repr. of 1613 ed. 49.00 (ISBN 90-221-0066-9). Walter J Johnson.

MATHEMATICS–EXAMINATIONS, QUESTIONS, ETC.

Allasid, John. Practice RCT Math Exams: No. 2, Spanish Version. 1981. of 20 6.50 set (ISBN 0-937820-13-X); set includes 20 westsea original practice rCT math exam booklets, 20 answer sheets, 1 answer key, 1 scoring conversion table. Westsea Pub.

Allasid, John, et al. Practice RCT Math Exams: No. 1, Spanish Version. 1981. of 20 6.50 set (ISBN 0-937820-12-1); set includes 20 westsea original practice rCT math exam booklets, 20 answer sheets, 1 answer key, 1 scoring conversion table. Westsea Pub.

Allasio, John, et al. Practice RCT Math Exam, No. 6. (gr. 9-12). 1981. Set Of 20. 5.50 (ISBN 0-937820-07-5). Westsea Pub.

--Practice RCT Math Exam, No. 7. (gr. 9-12). 1981. Set Of 20. 5.50 (ISBN 0-937820-08-3). Westsea Pub.

--Practice RCT Math Exam, No. 8. (gr. 9-12). 1981. Set Of 20. 5.50 (ISBN 0-937820-09-1). Westsea Pub.

--Practice RCT Math Exam, No. 9. (gr. 9-12). 1981. Set Of 20. 5.50 (ISBN 0-937820-21-0). Westsea Pub.

--RCT Mathematics: A Workbook. 168p. (gr. 9-12). 1980. pap. 5.95 (ISBN 0-937820-00-8); ans. key 1.00 (ISBN 0-937820-01-6). Westsea Pub.

Arco Editorial Board. College Level Examinations in Mathematics: Algebra, Algebra-Trigonometry, Trigonometry. LC 77-21106. (Illus.). 1978. pap. text ed. 5.95 (ISBN 0-668-04339-3, 4339). Arco.

Bird, May. Mathematics One Checkbook. 1981. text ed. 18.95 (ISBN 0-408-00632-3). Butterworth.

Bramson, Morris. CBAT-CLEP College Board Achievement Test: College Level Examinations in Mathematics Level 2. LC 77-14611. 1978. pap. text ed. 4.95 (ISBN 0-668-04284-2, 4284). Arco.

--Mathematics: Level I. 3d ed. LC 76-55817. 1977. pap. 3.00 (ISBN 0-668-03847-0). Arco.

--Mathematics: Level Two Achievement Test. (College Board Achievement Tests Ser.). 1966. 4.50 (ISBN 0-668-01455-5). Arco.

Brown, Walter C. Basic Mathematics Test Sheets. 1981. write for info. (ISBN 0-87006-317-0). Goodheart.

Buros, Oscar K., ed. Mathematics Tests & Reviews. LC 75-8113. xxv, 435p. 1975. 25.00x (ISBN 0-910674-18-3). U of Nebr Pr.

De Zayas, Zoila. Desarrollando Destrezas En Preparacion Para el Examen Equivalencia De Escuela Superior En Espanol: Mathematicas: Developing Skills in Math for High School Equivalency Test in Spanish. (gr. 10-12). 1982. pap. text ed. 3.75 (ISBN 0-8120-0560-0). Barron.
Dodge, Howard. Barron's How to Prepare for the College Board Achievement Tests - Mathematics Level II. LC 78-8655. 1979. pap. 5.95 (ISBN 0-8120-0325-X). Barron.
Eicholz, Robert E., et al. Mathematics in Our World: Test Duplicator Masters. (Mathematics in Our World Ser.). (gr. 7-8). 1979. Gr. 7. 34.48 (ISBN 0-201-09875-X, Sch Div); Gr. 8. 43.40 (ISBN 0-201-09882-2). A-W.
Gruber, Gary A. Preparation for the New Mathematics Test (GED) rev. ed. (Exam Preparation Ser.). (gr. 11). 1980. pap. text ed. 5.95 (ISBN 0-671-09240-5). Monarch Pr.
Guercio, E., et al. General Mathematical Ability: Preparation & Review for the Mathematics Part of the High School Equivalency Diploma Test. LC 74-19738. (GED Preparation Ser.). 160p. (Orig.). 1975. lib. bdg. 7.00 (ISBN 0-668-03841-1); pap. 6.00 (ISBN 0-668-03689-3). Arco.
Hockett, Shirley. Barron's How to Prepare for the Advanced Placement Examination - Mathematics. rev. ed. (gr. 10-12). 1981. pap. text ed. 9.95 (ISBN 0-8120-2071-5). Barron.
Hockett, Shirley O. Barron's How to Prepare for the Advanced Placement Examination - Mathematics: Mathematics. rev. ed. LC 77-149360. (gr. 11-12). 1977. pap. text ed. 8.50 (ISBN 0-8120-0354-3). Barron.
Kaplan, Stanley & Peters, Max, eds. Barron's Regents Exams & Answers 10th. Year Mathematics. rev ed. 300p. (gr. 9-12). 1981. pap. text ed. 3.95 (ISBN 0-8120-0204-0). Barron.
Kaplan, Stanley, et al, eds. Barron's Regents Exams & Answers - 11th. Year Mathematics. rev ed. 250p. 1981. pap. text ed. 3.95 (ISBN 0-8120-0112-5). Barron.
Koch, Harry W. Work & Compare Arithmetic. 1975. 4.00 (ISBN 0-913164-58-5). Ken-Bks.
Lees, Beatrice. How to Prepare for the Graduate Record Examination - Mathematics. 1979. pap. 5.95 (ISBN 0-07-037045-1, SP). McGraw.
Lockhart, William E. Mathematics Response Sheets & Prescription Sheets. (Michigan Prescriptive Program,High School Epuivalency-GED Ser.). (gr. 10). 1975. 2.00x (ISBN 0-89039-165-3). Ann Arbor Pubs.
--Mathematics Study Material: High School Equivalency-GED. (Michigan Prescriptive Program Ser.). (gr. 10). 1975. pap. text ed. 8.00x (ISBN 0-89039-120-3). Ann Arbor Pubs.
Luftig, Milton. Computer Programmer: Analyst Trainee. 4th ed. LC 74-82865. (Illus., Orig.). 1975. o. p. 10.00 (ISBN 0-668-01344-3); pap. 8.00 (ISBN 0-668-01232-3). Arco.
Math Refresher. LC 78-106209. (Test Preparation Guide Ser). 1971. pap. 5.95 (ISBN 0-8092-9425-7). Contemp Bks.
Moran, Deborah, et al. GED Mathematics Test Preparation Guide: High School Equivalency Examination. (Cliffs Test Preparation Ser.). 182p. (gr. 10 up). 1981. pap. 3.95 (ISBN 0-8220-2016-5). Cliffs.
National Council of Teachers of Mathematics. Evaluation in Mathematics, 26th Yearbk. Johnson, Donovan A., ed. LC 61-11906. 1961. 12.40 (ISBN 0-87353-004-7). NCTM.
Practice RCT Math Exam: No. 1. 1980. of twenty 5.50 set (ISBN 0-937820-02-4). Westsea Pub.
Practice RCT Math Exam: No. 2. 1980. of twenty 5.50 set (ISBN 0-937820-03-2). Westsea Pub.
Practice Rct Math Exam: No. 3. 1980. of twenty 5.50 set (ISBN 0-937820-04-0). Westsea Pub.
Practice RCT Math Exam: No. 5. 1980. of twenty 5.50 set (ISBN 0-937820-06-7). Westsea Pub.
Practice RCT Math Exams: No. 4. 1980. of twenty 5.50 set (ISBN 0-937820-05-9). Westsea Pub.
Prindle, Anthony. Barron's How to Prepare for the High School Equivalency Examination (Ged)-General Mathematics, 4 vols. Incl. Vol. 1. Arithmetic (ISBN 0-8120-0727-1); Vol. 2. Algebra (ISBN 0-8120-0728-X); Vol. 3. Geometry, Tables & Graphics, Word Problems (ISBN 0-8120-0729-8); Vol. 4. Model Examinations (ISBN 0-8120-0730-1). LC 78-14808. 1979. pap. 2.25 ea. Barron.
Rich, Barnett. Level One Mathematics: For the College Boards. (gr. 11-12). 1970. pap. text ed. 7.75 (ISBN 0-87720-231-1). AMSCO Sch.
Rizzuto, James J., et al. Barron's How to Prepare for the College Board Achievement Tests - Mathematics Level I. rev. ed. LC 76-45412. (gr. 11-12). 1976. pap. text ed. 5.50 (ISBN 0-8120-0673-9). Barron.
Rudman, Jack. General Mathematical Ability (G.E.D.) (Career Examination Ser.: CS-33). (Cloth bdg. avail. on request). pap. 6.00 (ISBN 0-8373-3733-X). Natl Learning.
--General Mathematics. (Teachers License Examination Ser.: G-4). (Cloth bdg. avail. on request). pap. 8.00 (ISBN 0-8373-8194-0). Natl Learning.
--Mathematics. (National Teachers Examination Ser.: NT-6). (Cloth bdg. avail. on request). pap. 9.95 (ISBN 0-8373-8416-8). Natl Learning.
--Mathematics. (Graduate Record Examination Ser.: GRE-12). (Cloth bdg. avail. on request). pap. 9.95 (ISBN 0-8373-5212-6). Natl Learning.
--Mathematics. (Admission Test Ser.: ATS-9C). (Cloth bdg. avail. on request). pap. 9.95 (ISBN 0-8373-5009-3). Natl Learning.
--Mathematics-Jr. H.S. (Teachers License Examination Ser.: T-40). (Cloth bdg. avail. on request). pap. 10.00 (ISBN 0-8373-8040-5). Natl Learning.
--Mathematics-Sr. H.S. (Teachers License Examination Ser.: T-41). (Cloth bdg. avail. on request). pap. 10.00 (ISBN 0-8373-8041-3). Natl Learning.
--Science & Mathematics. (National Teachers Examination Ser.: NC-5). (Cloth bdg. avail. on request). pap. 9.95 (ISBN 0-8373-8405-2). Natl Learning.
--Senior Mathematician. (Career Examination Ser.: C-2078). (Cloth. bdg. avail on request). 1977. pap. 10.00 (ISBN 0-8373-2078-X). Natl Learning.
Saunders, Brigitte. Mathematics Workbook for the SAT (College Entrance Examinations) 1980. pap. 6.00 (ISBN 0-668-04820-4). Arco.
Scholastic Testing Service. Practice for High School Minimum Educational Competency Tests in Reading & Mathematics. LC 78-78331. (Orig.). pap. 3.95 (ISBN 0-671-18447-4). Monarch Pr.
Wieland. Barron's How to Prepare for the Minimum Competency Examination in Mathematics. 1981. pap. 6.95 (ISBN 0-8120-2246-7). Barron.
Ziegler, Ann & Bazen, Frances. Student Solutions Manual for Basic Technical Mathematics. 3rd ed. 1981. pap. 5.95 (ISBN 0-8053-9534-2). Benjamin-Cummings.

MATHEMATICS–FORMULAE

Bartsch, Hans-Jochen. Handbook of Mathematical Formulas. 1974. 22.00 (ISBN 0-12-080050-0). Acad Pr.
Campbell, A. The Sinclair Book of Technical Calculations. 1977. 7.00 (ISBN 0-85941-037-4). State Mutual Bk.
Carmichael, Robert D. & Smith, Edwin R. Mathematical Tables & Formulas. 1931. pap. 3.25 (ISBN 0-486-60111-0). Dover.
Carr, George S. Formulas & Theorems in Pure Mathematics. LC 78-113122. Orig. Title: Synopsis of Pure Mathematics. 1970. text ed. 35.00 (ISBN 0-8284-0239-6). Chelsea Pub.
Eswaran, K. S. Mathematical Formulae & Tables. 84p. 1981. 10.00x (ISBN 0-86125-149-0, Pub. by Orient Longman India). State Mutual Bk.
Lewis, Harry R. Unsolvable Classes of Quantificational Formulas. LC 79-17573. 1979. pap. text ed. 13.50 (ISBN 0-201-04069-7). A-W.
Magnus, W., et al. Formulas & Theorems for the Special Functions of Mathematical Physics. 3rd ed. (Grundlehren der Mathematischen Wissenschaften: Vol. 52). 1966. 42.50 (ISBN 0-387-03518-4). Springer-Verlag.
Menzel, Donald H. Fundamental Formulas of Physics, 2 Vols. 2nd ed. (Illus.). 1960. Vol. 1. pap. text ed. 5.00 (ISBN 0-486-60595-7); Vol. 2. pap. text ed. 5.00 (ISBN 0-486-60596-5). Dover.
Spiegel, Murray R. Mathematical Handbook of Formulas & Tables. (Schaum's Outline Ser). 1968. pap. text ed. 5.95 (ISBN 0-07-060224-7, SP). McGraw.

MATHEMATICS–HANDBOOKS, MANUALS, ETC.

Assaf, Karen & Assaf, Said. Handbook of Mathematical Calculations: For Science Students & Researchers. (Illus.). 350p. 1974. text ed. 5.50x (ISBN 0-8138-1135-X). Iowa St U Pr.
Assistantships & Fellowships in Mathematics in 1980-1981. 3.20 (ISBN 0-685-47853-X, ASST). Am Math.
Bitter & Mikesell. Activities Handbook for Teaching with the Hand Held Calculator. 1979. text ed. 16.95 (ISBN 0-205-06713-1, 2367130). Allyn.
Bronshtein, I. N. & Semendyayev, K. A. A Guide-Book to Mathematics. Jaworowsky, J. & Bleicher, M. N., trs. from Rus. LC 60-16788. (Illus.). 783p. 1972. 12.20 (ISBN 0-387-91106-5). Springer-Verlag.
Buckeye, Donald A., et al. Cloudburst of Math Lab Experiments. Incl. Vol. 1, Elementary; Vol. 2, Upper Elementary. pap. 6.95 (ISBN 0-910974-30-6); Vol. 3, Junior High School. pap. 6.95 (ISBN 0-910974-61-6); Vol. 4, High School. pap. 3.95 (ISBN 0-910974-32-2); card form o.p. 16.00 (ISBN 0-910974-62-4); Vol. 5, Lower College. tchrs. manual 3.50 (ISBN 0-910974-33-0). Midwest Pubns.
Central State University Dept. of Mathematics. Essential Mathematics for College Freshmen. 1978. pap. text ed. 10.95 (ISBN 0-8403-1518-X). Kendall-Hunt.
Clark, Clara E. Nineteen Seventy-Five Teacher's Manual: 1975 Teacher's Manual. (The Basic Skills in Math). (Illus.). Date not set. cancelled (ISBN 0-89170-006-4); pap. 2.95 (ISBN 0-89170-001-3). Laurel Pub.
Davidson, Donald. Science for Physical Geographers. LC 78-11957. 1978. 18.95 (ISBN 0-470-26556-6). Halsted Pr.
Dewhurst, R. F. Mathematics for Accountants. (Illus.). 177p. 1968. 7.50x (ISBN 0-434-90300-0). Intl Pubns Serv.
Gattegno, Caleb. Mathware: A Math Workshop for Home Use Kit. 1973. 25.00 (ISBN 0-87825-010-7). Ed Solutions.
Gellert, W., et al, eds. VNR Concise Encyclopedia of Mathematics. 1977. 18.95 (ISBN 0-442-22646-2). Van Nos Reinhold.
Grazda, Edward E., et al. Handbook of Applied Mathematics. 4th ed. LC 77-10309. 1128p. 1977. Repr. of 1966 ed. 32.50 (ISBN 0-88275-615-X). Krieger.
Handy Math, 6 bks. 1981. Set Of 6. 32.00 (ISBN 0-88488-216-0, 10624); binder 35.00 (ISBN 0-88488-217-9, 10625). Creative Pubns.
Herold, P. J. Math Helper's Handbook. (Winston Mine Editions). 1974. write for info (ISBN 0-685-47260-4). HR&W.
Immerzeel, George & Ockenga, Earl. The Calculator Book. (Mathematics in Our World Ser.). (gr. 7-8). 1980. pap. text ed. 2.76 (ISBN 0-686-72377-5, 201-16075); Bk. 1, Gr. 7. tchr's ed. 2.79 (ISBN 0-686-72378-3, 201-16076); pap. text ed. 2.76 (ISBN 0-686-72379-1, 201-16085); Bk. 2, Gr. 8. tchr's ed. 2.79 (ISBN 0-686-72380-5, 201-16085). A-W.
Krenz, A. & Osterloh, H. Clothoid Design & Setting Out Manual. LC 68-43798. (Illus.). 1975. 15.00x (ISBN 3-7625-0576-4). Intl Pubns Serv.
Ledermann. Handbook of Applicable Mathematics: Probability, Vol. 2. LC 79-42724. (Handbook of Applicable Mathematics Ser.). 450p. 1981. 85.00 (ISBN 0-471-27821-1, Pub. by Wiley-Interscience). Wiley.
Ledermann, Walter. Handbook of Applicable Mathematics: Numerical Methods, Vol. 3. LC 79-42724. (Handbook of Applicable Mathematics Ser.). 592p. 1981. 85.00 (ISBN 0-471-27947-1, Pub. by Wiley-Interscience). Wiley.
Lefax Pub. Co. Editors. Manual of Mathematics. (Lefax Technical Manuals.: No. 781). (Illus.). looseleaf bdg. 9.50 (ISBN 0-685-14154-3). Lefax.
Levine, Sol. Mathematics Handbook. LC 76-116618. (Illus.). (gr. 7 up). 1972. PLB 9.66 (ISBN 0-8239-0207-2). Rosen Pr.
Livsic, M. S. Operators, Oscillations, Waves. LC 72-11580. (Translations of Mathematical Monographs: Vol. 34). 280p. (Orig.). 1973. 40.80 (ISBN 0-8218-1584-9, MMONO-34). Am Math.
Math in Stride: Teacher's Manual Book 2. (Illus.). 139p. (Orig.). 1981. write for info. (ISBN 0-934734-13-5). Construct Educ.
Meyer, Robert. Consumer & Business Math. rev. ed. (Illus.). 192p. (gr. 9-12). 1982. pap. 4.95 (ISBN 0-671-09216-2). Monarch Pr.
Pearson, Carl E. Handbook of Applied Mathematics. 1152p. 1974. text ed. 39.50x (ISBN 0-442-26493-3). Van Nos Reinhold.
Practical Problems in Mathematics for Mechanical Drafting. LC 77-78236. 1979. pap. 7.00 (ISBN 0-8273-1670-4); instructor's guide 1.60 (ISBN 0-8273-1671-2). Delmar.
Research & Education Association Staff. Handbook of Mathematical Formulas, Tables, Functions, Graphs, Transforms. LC 80-52490. (Illus.). 800p. (Orig.). pap. text ed. 17.85x (ISBN 0-87891-521-4). Res & Educ.
Shaffer. Using the Mathematical Literature. (Books in Library & Information Science Ser.: Vol. 25). 1979. 22.75 (ISBN 0-8247-6675-X). Dekker.
Shklyarsky & Chensov. Selected Problems & Theorems in Elementary Mathematics. 427p. 1979. 8.50 (ISBN 0-8285-1535-2, Pub. by Mir Pubs Russia). Imported Pubns.
Sumner, Graham N. Mathematics for Physical Geographers. LC 78-12156. 1979. 19.95x (ISBN 0-470-26557-4). Halsted Pr.
Svenconis, Daniel J. Preparation for the S. A. T. Mathematics Examination. 254p. (Orig.). (gr. 10-12). 1978. pap. 5.00 (ISBN 0-930124-02-2). Transemantics.
Swartz, Clifford E. Used Math for the First Two Years of College Science. (Illus.). 320p. 1973. pap. 11.95 ref. ed. (ISBN 0-13-939736-1). P-H.
Swezey, Kenneth. Formulas, Methods, Tips & Data for Home & Workshop. rev. ed. Scharff, Robert, rev. by. LC 68-54377. (Popular Science Bk.). (Illus.). 1979. 15.95 (ISBN 0-06-014164-6, HarpT). Har-Row.
Vygodsky, M. Mathematical Handbook: Elementary Math. 422p. 1979. 6.75 (ISBN 0-8285-1701-0, Pub. by Mir Pubs Russia). Imported Pubns.
--Mathematical Handbook: Higher Mathematics. 872p. 1975. 12.00 (ISBN 0-8285-1750-9, Pub. by Mir Pubs Russia). Imported Pubns.

MATHEMATICS–HISTORY

see also Mathematics, Chinese; Mathematics, Greek, and similar headings

Aaboe, A. Episodes from the Early History of Mathematics. LC 63-21916. (New Mathematical Library: No. 13). 1975. pap. 5.50 (ISBN 0-88385-613-1). Math Assn.
Archibald, Raymond C. Outline of the History of Mathematics. 6th ed. pap. 5.50 (ISBN 0-384-01880-7). Johnson Repr.
Ball, W. Rouse, et al, eds. String Figures & Other Monographs, 4 vols. in 1. Incl. String Figures. Ball, W. R; History of the Slide Rule. Cajori, F; Non Euclidean Geometry. Carslaw, Horatio S; Methods Geometrical Construction. Petersen, Julius. LC 59-11780. 12.95 (ISBN 0-8284-0130-6). Chelsea Pub.
Ball, W. W. A History of the Study of Mathematics. LC 74-166607. 1889. Repr. 16.50 (ISBN 0-403-03605-4). Scholarly.
--Short Account of the History of Mathematics. 4th ed. 1908. pap. 6.00 (ISBN 0-486-20630-0). Dover.
--A Short Account of the History of Mathematics. LC 60-3187. 1960. lib. bdg. 13.50x (ISBN 0-88307-009-X). Gannon.
Bell, E. T. Men of Mathematics. 1961. pap. 4.95 (ISBN 0-671-46401-9, Fireside). S&S.
Bell, Eric T. Development of Mathematics. 2nd ed. 1945. 18.95 (ISBN 0-07-004330-2, C). McGraw.
--Men of Mathematics. (Illus.). 1937. 12.95 (ISBN 0-671-46400-0); pap. 6.95 (ISBN 0-671-46401-9). S&S.
Bidwell, James K. & Clason, Robert G., eds. Readings in the History of Mathematics Education. LC 74-113172. 1970. 16.90 (ISBN 0-87353-087-X). NCTM.
Bloomfield, Derek. Arithmetic to Algebra. 2nd ed. (Illus.). 464p. 1982. pap. text ed. 14.95 (ISBN 0-8359-2110-7); instr's. manual free. Reston.
Bochner, Salomon. Role of Mathematics in the Rise of Science. 1966. 25.00 (ISBN 0-691-08028-3). Princeton U Pr.
Boyer, Carl B. History of Mathematics. LC 68-16506. 1968. 29.95 (ISBN 0-471-09374-2). Wiley.
--History of the Calculus & Its Conceptual Development. Orig. Title: Concepts of Calculus. 1959. pap. 4.50 (ISBN 0-486-60509-4). Dover.
Brett, William F., et al. An Introduction to the History of Mathematics, Number Theory, & Operations Research. 1974. 13.00 (ISBN 0-8422-5170-7); pap. text ed. 12.50x (ISBN 0-8422-0379-6). Irvington.
Bunt, Lucas N. H. & Jones, Phillip S. Historical Roots of Elementary Mathematics. (Illus.). 352p. 1976. Ref. Ed. 18.95 (ISBN 0-13-389015-5). P-H.
Cajori, Florian. A History of Mathematics. 3rd ed. Nim, A. G, ed. LC 70-113120. 1979. text ed. 18.50 (ISBN 0-8284-0303-1). Chelsea Pub.
Cantor, Moritz B. Vorlesungen Ueber Geschichte der Mathematik, 4 Vols. 1900-08. 154.00 (ISBN 0-384-07380-8). Johnson Repr.
Clagett, Marshall. Archimedes in the Middle Ages, Vol. 1. Arabo-Latin Tradition. (Medieval Science Pubns., No. 6). (Illus.). 752p. 1964. 50.00x (ISBN 0-299-03360-0). U of Wis Pr.
--Studies in Medieval Physics & Mathematics. 366p. 1980. 75.00x (ISBN 0-86078-048-1, Pub. by Variorum England). State Mutual Bk.
Crowley, Charles B. Universal Mathematics in Aristotelian-Thomistic Philosophy: The Hermeneutics of Aristotelian Texts Relative to Universal Mathematics. LC 79-48093. 239p. 1980. text ed. 18.50 (ISBN 0-8191-1009-4); pap. text ed. 9.50 (ISBN 0-8191-1010-8). U Pr of Amer.
Curtze, Maximilian. Urkunden Zur Geschichte der Mathematik Im Mittelalter & der Renaissance. (Bibliotheca Mathematica Teubneriana Ser: No. 45). (Ger). 1969. Repr. of 1902 ed. 38.50 (ISBN 0-384-10402-9). Johnson Repr.
Dauben, Joseph W., ed. Mathematical Perspectives: Essays on Mathematics & Its Historical Development. LC 80-1781. 1981. write for info. (ISBN 0-12-204050-3). Acad Pr.
Davis, Philip J. & Hersh, Reuben. The Mathematical Experience. 460p. 1981. 24.00 (ISBN 3-7643-3018-X). Birkhauser.
Dickson, Leonard E. History of the Theory of Numbers, 3 Vols. LC 66-26932. 49.50 (ISBN 0-8284-0086-5). Chelsea Pub.
Dubbey, J. M. The Mathematical Work of Charles Babbage. LC 77-71409. (Illus.). 1978. 47.50 (ISBN 0-521-21649-4). Cambridge U Pr.

Dyck, Martin. Novalis & Mathematics. LC 76-164817. (North Carolina. University. Studies in the Germanic Languages & Literatures: No. 27). Repr. of 1960 ed. 18.50 (ISBN 0-404-50927-4). AMS Pr.
Eves, H. An Introduction to the History of Mathematics. 4th ed. LC 75-23053. 1976. text ed. 23.95 (ISBN 0-03-089539-1, HoltC). HR&W.
Friedrichs, K. O. From Pythagoras to Einstein. LC 65-24963. (New Mathematics Library: No. 16). 1975. pap. 5.50 (ISBN 0-88385-616-6). Math Assn.
Gerhardt, Karl I. Geschichte Der Mathematik in Deutschland. Repr. of 1877 ed. 25.00 (ISBN 0-384-18150-3). Johnson Repr.
Gittleman, Arthur. History of Mathematics. new ed. 304p. 1975. text ed. 20.95x (ISBN 0-675-08784-8). Merrill.
Gow, James. Short History of Greek Mathematics. LC 68-21639. 1968. 11.95 (ISBN 0-8284-0218-3). Chelsea Pub.
Heath, Thomas. Mathematics in Aristotle. LC 78-66593. (Ancient Philosophy Ser.). 305p. 1980. lib. bdg. 30.00 (ISBN 0-8240-9595-2). Garland Pub.
Heath, Thomas L. A History of Greek Mathematics, 2 vols. (Illus.). 1058p. 1981. pap. 8.50 (ISBN 0-686-77392-6). Vol. I (ISBN 0-486-24073-8). Vol. II (ISBN 0-486-24074-6). Dover.
Historia De las Ideas Modernas En la Matematica. (Serie De Matematica: No. 4). (Span.). 1974. pap. 1.00 (ISBN 0-8270-6230-3). OAS.
Hofmann, Joseph E. History of Mathematics to Eighteen Hundred. (Quality Paperback: No. 144). 1967. pap. 2.95 (ISBN 0-8226-0144-3). Littlefield.
Husen, Torsten, ed. International Study of Achievement in Mathematics, 2 vols. (Orig.). 1967. Vol. 1. 10.95 (ISBN 0-686-74170-6); Vol. 2. 10.95 (ISBN 0-686-74171-4). Krieger.
Klein, Felix. Entwicklung Der Mathematik Im Neunzehnten Jahrhundert, 2 Vols. in 1. (Ger). 22.50 (ISBN 0-8284-0074-1). Chelsea Pub.
Klein, Felix, et al. Development of Mathematics in the Nineteenth Century. (LIE Groups Ser.: No. 9). 1979. 50.00 (ISBN 0-915692-28-7). Math Sci Pr.
Kline, Morris. Mathematical Thought from Ancient to Modern Times. 1300p. 1972. 60.00 (ISBN 0-19-501496-0). Oxford U Pr.
--Mathematics & the Physical World. (Illus.). 496p. 1981. pap. 6.50 (ISBN 0-486-24104-1). Dover.
--Mathematics in Western Culture. 1953. 19.95 (ISBN 0-19-500603-8). Oxford U Pr.
--Mathematics in Western Culture. (Illus.). 1964. pap. 8.95 (ISBN 0-19-500714-X, GB). Oxford U Pr.
Kreitner, John. Man's Mathematical Mind: From Thales to Weiner. 26p. 1976. Repr. of 1956 ed. pap. 1.50 (ISBN 0-913098-14-0). Myrin Institute.
Libri, Guglielmo. Histoire Des Sciences Mathematiques En Italie, 4 Vols. Repr. of 1841 ed. Set. 104.00 (ISBN 0-384-32615-3). Johnson Repr.
May, K. O. Bibliography & Research Manual of the History of Mathematics. LC 71-151379. (Scholarly Reprint Ser.). 1973. 40.00x (ISBN 0-8020-7077-9). U of Toronto Pr.
May, Kenneth O., ed. The Mathematical Association of America, Its First Fifty Years. 172p. 1972. 10.00 (ISBN 0-88385-401-5). Math Assn.
Mehrtens, H., ed. Social History of Mathematics. 800p. 1981. write for info. Birkhauser.
Midonick, Henrietta O. Treasury of Mathematics. LC 62-20873. 1965. 15.00 (ISBN 0-8022-1114-3). Philos Lib.
Morgan, Bryan. Men & Discoveries in Mathematics. 235p. 1980. 15.00x (ISBN 0-7195-2587-X, Pub. by Murray Pubs England). State Mutual Bk.
--Men & Discoveries in Mathematics. 1972. 10.95 (ISBN 0-7195-2587-X). Transatlantic.
National Council of Teachers of Mathematics. Historical Topics for the Mathematics Classroom, 31st Yearbk. LC 72-97787. 1969. 15.75 (ISBN 0-87353-011-X, 09380). NCTM.
Neugebauer, O. Exact Sciences in Antiquity. 2nd ed. LC 57-12342. (Illus.). 256p. 1970. Repr. of 1957 ed. text ed. 12.50x (ISBN 0-87057-044-7, Pub. by Brown U Pr). U Pr of New Eng.
Newton, Isaac. The Mathematical Papers of Isaac Newton: Vol. 8, 1697-1722. Whiteside, D. T., ed. LC 65-11203. (Illus.). 750p. Date not set. 195.00 (ISBN 0-521-20103-9). Cambridge U Pr.
Nidditch, P. H. The Development of Mathematical Logic. (Monographs in Modern Logic). 1971. Repr. of 1962 ed. 6.00 (ISBN 0-7100-3801-1). Routledge & Kegan.
Ore, Oystein. Number Theory & Its History. (Illus.). 1948. text ed. 15.95 (ISBN 0-07-047675-6, C). McGraw.
Paul, Richard S. & Shaevel, M. Leonard. Essentials of Technical Mathematics. 2nd ed. (Illus.). 704p. 1982. 21.95 (ISBN 0-13-288050-4). P-H.
Resnikoff, H. L. & Wells, R. O. Mathematics in Civilization. LC 72-83805. (Illus.). 24.50x (ISBN 0-03-085035-5); pap. text ed. 8.95x (ISBN 0-89197-843-7). Irvington.
Scott, J. F. History of Mathematics: From Antiquity to the Beginning of the Nineteenth Century. 2nd ed. 1975. Repr. of 1960 ed. 21.50x (ISBN 0-06-496130-3). B&N.
Smith, David. Mathematics. LC 63-10294. (Our Debt to Greece & Rome Ser). Repr. of 1930 ed. 7.50x (ISBN 0-8154-0207-4). Cooper Sq.
Smith, David E. History of Mathematics, 2 Vols. Set. 12.50 ea. (ISBN 0-8446-2955-3). Peter Smith.
--History of Mathematics, 2 vols. Incl. Vol. 1. General Survey of the History of Elementary Mathematics. Repr. of 1923 ed (ISBN 0-486-20429-4); Vol. 2. Special Topics of Elementary Mathematics. Repr. of 1925 ed (ISBN 0-486-20430-8). pap. text ed. 7.50 ea. Dover.
Smith, David E. & Ginsberg, Jekuthiel. A History of Mathematics in America Before Nineteen Hundred. Cohen, I. Bernard, ed. LC 79-7992. (Three Centuries of Science in America Ser.). (Illus.). 1980. Repr. of 1934 ed. lib. bdg. 16.00x (ISBN 0-405-12578-X). Arno.
Struik, Dirk J. A Concise History of Mathematics. LC 66-28622. 1967. lib. bdg. 10.50 (ISBN 0-88307-615-2). Gannon.
--Concise History of Mathematics. 3rd rev. ed. (Illus.). (YA) (gr. 7-12). 1967. pap. text ed. 3.00 (ISBN 0-486-60255-9). Dover.
Todhunter, Isaac. History of the Mathematical Theory of Probability. LC 51-146. 1949. 15.95 (ISBN 0-8284-0057-1). Chelsea Pub.
Turnbull, Herbert Westren. The Great Mathematicians. LC 61-16934. (Illus.). 1961. usa 10.00x (ISBN 0-8147-0419-0). NYU Pr.
Zaslavsky, Claudia. Africa Counts. LC 72-91248. (Illus.). 1979. pap. 6.95 (ISBN 0-88208-104-7). Lawrence Hill.
Zeuthen, H. G. Geschichte der Mathematik Im 1600 und 1700. 23.00 (ISBN 0-384-70890-0). Johnson Repr.
--Die Mathematik Im Altertum und Im Mittelalter. 10.00 (ISBN 0-384-70892-7). Johnson Repr.

MATHEMATICS–JUVENILE LITERATURE

Addition, Zero to Ten. (Michigan Arithmetic Program Ser.). 1976. wkbk. 7.00x (ISBN 0-89039-946-8). Ann Arbor Pubs.
Alberti, Delbert & Mason, George. Laboratory Laughter. (Math Is Everywhere Ser.). (Illus., Orig.). (gr. 2-9). 1974. pap. 4.95 (ISBN 0-918932-25-4). Activity Resources.
Arithmetic Fun. (Golden Fun at Home Workbooks). 64p. (ps). 1981. 0.99 (ISBN 0-307-01435-5, Golden Pr). Western Pub.
Barns, R. E. The Answer Is One-1st One. (Illus.). (gr. 2-12). 1977. wkbk. 5.95 (ISBN 0-88488-068-0). Creative Pubns.
--The Answer Is One-3rd One. (gr. 2-12). 1977. wkbk. 5.95 (ISBN 0-88488-070-2). Creative Pubns.
Barns, R. E. & Eral, Bill. The Answer Is One-2nd One. (gr. 2-12). 1977. wkbk. 5.95 (ISBN 0-88488-069-9). Creative Pubns.
Barson, Alan. Motivational Games for Mathematics. (Illus.). 40p. (gr. 3-7). 1981. pap. 6.95 (ISBN 0-937138-02-9). Fabmath.
Becker, Jan, et al. Enhance Chance. (Illus., Orig.). (gr. k-9). 1973. pap. 4.95 (ISBN 0-918932-10-6). Activity Resources.
Booth, Eugene. In the Garden. LC 77-7628. (A Raintree Spotlight Book). (Illus.). (gr. k-3). 1977. PLB 9.30 (ISBN 0-8393-0115-4). Raintree Child.
Buechner, Katy. File Folder Math, Bk. D. (gr. 4-6). 1978. pap. 15.95 (ISBN 0-88488-113-X). Creative Pubns.
--File Folder Math, Bk. E. (gr. 5-7). 1979. pap. 14.25 (ISBN 0-88488-114-8). Creative Pubns.
Charosh, Mannis. The Ellipse. LC 73-132293. (Young Math Ser). (Illus.). (gr. 1-4). 1971. 8.79 (ISBN 0-690-01120-2, TYC-J). Har-Row.
Chiamos, Mary, et al. Zoom. (Illus., Orig.). (gr. k-3). 1973. pap. 5.95 (ISBN 0-918932-46-7). Activity Resources.
Clark, Clara E. Beginning Addition & Subtraction: A. (The Basic Skills in Math Ser.). (Illus.). (gr. k-1). 1975. tchr's manual 3.25 (ISBN 0-89170-005-6); wkbk 2.95 (ISBN 0-89170-000-5). Laurel Pub.
--Beginning Fractions. (The Basic Skills in Math Ser.). (Illus.). 1975. wkbk 2.95 (ISBN 0-89170-004-8). Laurel Pub.
--Beginning Multiplication & Division. (The Basic Skills in Math Ser.). (Illus.). (gr. 2-3). 1975. wkbk 2.95 (ISBN 0-89170-002-1). Laurel Pub.
--A Tangram Diary. (Illus.). 64p. (Orig.). (gr. 3-6). 1980. pap. 4.95 (ISBN 0-934734-05-4). Construct Educ.
Clark, Clara E. & Sternberg, Betty J. Math in Stride, Bk. 1. (Illus.). 166p. (Orig.). (gr. k-2). 1980. pap. 5.65 (ISBN 0-934734-06-2). Construct Educ.
--Math in Stride, Bk. 2. (Illus.). 203p. (Orig.). (gr. 1-3). 1980. pap. 5.80 (ISBN 0-934734-07-0). Construct Educ.
--Math in Stride, Bk. 3. (Illus.). 219p. (Orig.). (gr. 2-4). 1980. pap. 5.95 (ISBN 0-934734-08-9). Construct Educ.
Cook, Peter D. The Ages of Mathematics: The Modern Ages, Vol. 4. LC 76-10336. (Illus.). (YA) (gr. 10 up). 1977. 5.95a (ISBN 0-385-11220-3); PLB (ISBN 0-385-11221-1). Doubleday.
Cornwall, Susan. Mathematical Manka. (Math Is Everywhere Ser.). (Illus.). (gr. 1-9). 1974. pap. 4.95 (ISBN 0-918932-29-7). Activity Resources.
Dawson, Dan T. & Mellott, M. Numbers for You & Me. (gr. k-1). pap. text ed. 4.80 (ISBN 0-13-625392-X); teachers' manual o.p. 1.95 (ISBN 0-685-04689-3, 62654-9). P-H.
Degrazia, Joseph. Math Is Fun. (Illus.). (gr. 9 up). 8.95 (ISBN 0-87523-094-6). Emerson.
Donatucci, Frederich J., et al. Motivational Activities for Child Involvement in Mathematics. (Illus.). 40p. (gr. 3-6). 1980. pap. 6.95 (ISBN 0-937138-00-2). Fabmath.
Earle, Vana. Numbers Workbook Four (with the Scarecrow from Oz) (Funny Face Activity Bks.). (Illus.). 48p. (ps-1). 1981. pap. 1.95 saddle-stitched (ISBN 0-394-84670-2). Random.
Eicholz, Robert, et al. Extending the Ideas Enrichment Workbook. (Mathematics in Our World Ser.). 1980. pap. text ed. 1.89 (ISBN 0-686-72381-3, 201-16015); Grade 1. tchr's ed. 2.01 (ISBN 0-686-72382-1, 201-16016); pap. text ed. 1.89 (ISBN 0-686-72383-X, 201-16025); Grade 2. tchr's ed. 2.01 (ISBN 0-686-72384-8, 201-16026). A-W.
--Extending the Ideas Enrichment Workbook. 2nd ed. (Mathematics in Our World Ser.). 1980. pap. text ed. 2.76 (ISBN 0-686-72385-6, 201-16035); Grade 3. tchr's ed. 2.85 (ISBN 0-686-72386-4, 201-16036); pap. text ed. 2.76 (ISBN 0-686-72387-2, 201-16045); Grade 4. tchr's ed. 2.85 (ISBN 0-686-72388-0, 20-16046). A-W.
--Extending the Ideas Enrichment Workbook. 2nd ed. (Mathematics in Our World Ser.). 1980. pap. text ed. 2.76 (ISBN 0-686-72389-9, 201-16055); Grade 5. tchr's ed. 2.85 (ISBN 0-686-72390-2); pap. text ed. 2.76 (ISBN 0-686-72391-0, 201-16065); Grade 6. tchr's ed. 2.85 (ISBN 0-686-72392-9, 201-16066). A-W.
Erdtmann, Greta. The Path to Math. (The Gentle Revolution Ser.). (Illus.). 60p. (ps). 1981. 6.95 (ISBN 0-936676-11-6). Better Baby.
Forte, Imogene & Mackenzie, Joy. Experiencias Matematicas Creativas Para los Ninos. LC 75-5346. (Illus.). 1975. pap. text ed. 6.95 (ISBN 0-913916-14-5, IP 14-5). Incentive Pubns.
Greenes, Carole, et al. The Mathworks. (gr. k-8). 1978. pap. 18.00 (ISBN 0-88488-117-2). Creative Pubns.
Grimm, Gary & Mitchell, Don. Good Apple Math Book. (gr. 3-8). 1975. 10.95 (ISBN 0-916456-00-5, GA59). Good Apple.
Hoban, Tana. Count & See. LC 72-175597. (Illus.). 40p. (ps-2). 1972. 8.95 (ISBN 0-02-744800-2). Macmillan.
Holmberg, Verda, et al. Metric Multibase Mathematics. (Illus., Orig.). (gr. 1-9). 1974. pap. 5.95 (ISBN 0-918932-33-5). Activity Resources.
Jenkins, Lee. The Balance Book. (Illus., Orig.). (gr. 2-8). 1974. pap. 4.50 (ISBN 0-918932-02-5). Activity Resources.
Johnson, Donovan A. Mathmagic with Flexagons. Kaz, Diane, ed. (Orig.). (gr. 4-12). 1974. pap. 4.50 (ISBN 0-918932-30-0). Activity Resources.
Joseph, Andre. The Psyche-Mathematical Basic Skills Learning Workbooklet. 67p. (gr. 6-7). 1980. write for info. (ISBN 0-936264-00-4); write for info. (ISBN 0-936264-01-2). Andre's & Co.
Laycock, Mary. Base Ten Mathematics. (gr. 1-9). 1976. pap. 4.95 (ISBN 0-918932-03-3). Activity Resources.
Laycock, Mary & Smart, Margaret. Solid Sense of Mathematics, 3 vols. (Illus.). 64p. (Orig., 64). (gr. 4-9). 1981. pap. text ed. 4.95 ea. (ISBN 0-918932-74-2). Activity Resources.
McLean, Peggy & Sternberg, Betty. People Piece Primer. (Orig.). (gr. k-3). 1975. pap. 4.95 (ISBN 0-918932-37-8). Activity Resources.
McLean, Peggy, et al. Let's Pattern Block H. (Illus., Orig.). (gr. k-8). 1973. pap. 7.50 (ISBN 0-918932-26-2). Activity Resources.
McNichols, Joan & Purkiss, Gerri. Word Ways. (Math Is Everywhere Ser.). (Illus., Orig.). (gr. 1-9). 1974. pap. 4.95 (ISBN 0-918932-44-0). Activity Resources.
Mahoney, Susan. Division Learning Module. May, Lola J., ed. 1976. pap. 302.50 (ISBN 0-89290-135-7, CM-56). Soc for Visual.
Matez, Beth & Fielden, Moreen. Math Story Problems: Level I. (Get Ahead for Kids). (Illus.). (gr. 1-4). 1978. pap. 2.95 (ISBN 0-933048-02-5). Matez Fielden.
Mathews, Louise. The Great Take-Away. LC 80-12961. (Illus.). 48p. (ps-3). 1980. PLB 7.95 (ISBN 0-396-07846-X). Dodd.
Moffatt, Michael. The Ages of Mathematics: The Origins, Vol. 1. LC 76-10336. (Illus.). (YA) (gr. 10 up). 1977. 5.95a (ISBN 0-385-11214-9); PLB (ISBN 0-385-11215-7). Doubleday.
Mult. Facts. (Mystery Story Problems). 1981. 10.95 (ISBN 0-88488-202-0, 10447 (5)); 55.00 (ISBN 0-88488-230-6, 10448 (30)). Creative Pubns.
Nichols, Joan & Nichols, Larry. Sports. (Math Is Everywhere Ser.). (Illus., Orig.). (gr. 1-9). 1974. pap. 4.95 (ISBN 0-918932-41-6). Activity Resources.
O'Connor, Vincent F. Mathematics at the Farm. LC 77-19169. (Raintree Mathematics Ser.). (Illus.). (gr. k-3). 1978. PLB 10.25 (ISBN 0-8393-0055-7). Raintree Child.
--Mathematics in Buildings. LC 77-19158. (Raintree Mathematics Ser.). (Illus.). (gr. k-3). 1978. PLB 10.28 (ISBN 0-8393-0053-0). Raintree Child.
--Mathematics in the Circus Ring. LC 77-19168. (Raintree Mathematics Ser.). (Illus.). (gr. k-3). 1978. PLB 10.25 (ISBN 0-8393-0056-5). Raintree Child.
--Mathematics in the Kitchen. LC 77-19160. (Raintree Mathematics Ser.). (Illus.). (gr. k-3). 1978. PLB 10.25 (ISBN 0-8393-0054-9). Raintree Child.
--Mathematics in the Toy Store. LC 77-19155. (Raintree Mathematics Ser.). (Illus.). (gr. k-3). 1978. PLB 10.25 (ISBN 0-8393-0052-2). Raintree Child.
--Mathematics on the Playground. LC 77-19180. (Raintree Mathematics Ser.). (Illus.). (gr. k-3). 1978. PLB 10.25 (ISBN 0-8393-0051-4). Raintree Child.
Overholt, James. Dr. Jim's Elementary Math Prescriptions. LC 78-2031. (Illus.). (gr. k-8). 1978. text ed. 11.95 (ISBN 0-87620-225-3); pap. text ed. 10.95 (ISBN 0-87620-224-5). Goodyear.
Parkis, Michael. Arithmetic Handbook. (gr. 4-8). 1971. 1.50x (ISBN 0-89039-068-1). Ann Arbor Pubs.
Pearson, James, et al. Cube-O-Gram Math Level A. (Cube-O-Gram Math Ser.). (Illus.). 37p. (gr. k-1). 1979. pap. 7.95 (ISBN 0-933358-54-7). Enrich.
--Cube-O-Gram Math Level B. (Cube-O-Gram Math Ser.). (Illus.). 37p. (gr. 1-2). 1979. pap. 7.95 (ISBN 0-933358-55-5). Enrich.
--Cube-O-Gram Math Level C. (Cube-O-Gram Math Ser.). (Illus.). 37p. (gr. 2-3). 1979. pap. 7.95 (ISBN 0-933358-56-3). Enrich.
Perry, Cheryl & Faulkner, Hal. Holiday Mathemagic. new ed. (Illus.). (gr. 4-10). 1977. pap. text ed. 4.95 (ISBN 0-918932-50-5). Activity Resources.
Plus Duplicating Masters: Elementary Math, 2 vols. (Spice Ser.). 1975. 5.95 ea. Vol. 1, Grades K-2 (ISBN 0-89273-533-3). Vol. 2, Grades 2-4 (ISBN 0-89273-534-1). Educ Serv.
Polis, A. Richard, et al. Magic Squares & Arrays. (Illus.). 40p. (gr. 4-8). 1980. pap. 6.95 (ISBN 0-937138-01-0). Fabmath.
Rice, Sharon, et al. Time Out for Math. LC 79-89160. (Illus.). 176p. (gr. 2-6). 1979. pap. text ed. 7.95 (ISBN 0-913916-82-X, IP-82X). Incentive Pubns.
Rohm, Robert. Guinness World Records Math Learning Module. LC 79-730909. (Illus.). (gr. 6-7). 1979. pap. text ed. 225.00 (ISBN 0-89290-091-1, CM-73). Soc for Visual.
Schurr, Sandra. Mainly Math. (Choose-a-Card Ser.). (Illus.). 32p. (gr. 2-6). 1980. pap. text ed. 5.95 (ISBN 0-913916-67-6, IP 67-6). Incentive Pubns.
Souviney & Keyser. Mathmatters: Developing Computational Skills with Developmental Sequences. LC 78-3535. (gr. 1-5). 1978. text ed. 12.95 (ISBN 0-87620-601-1); pap. text ed. 10.95 (ISBN 0-87620-600-3). Goodyear.
Srivastava, Jane J. Area. LC 73-18057. (Young Math Ser.). (Illus.). (gr. 1-5). 1974. 8.95 (ISBN 0-690-00404-4, TYC-J); PLB 8.79 (ISBN 0-690-00405-2). Har-Row.
Stein, Edwin I. Practical Applications in Mathematics. new ed. Orig. Title: Refresher Workbook in Arithmetic. (gr. 7-12). 1972. 4.80 (ISBN 0-205-03385-7, 5633850); answer bk 2.40 (ISBN 0-205-03386-5, 5633869). Allyn.
Sternberg, Betty. Attribute Acrobatics. (Illus., Orig.). (gr. 1-9). 1974. pap. 5.95 (ISBN 0-918932-01-7). Activity Resources.
--Colored Cubes Activity Cards. (Illus., Orig.). (gr. 2-8). 1973. pap. 2.95 (ISBN 0-918932-06-8). Activity Resources.
Sussman, Ellen. Now Cut That Out! Math Activities to Cut & Paste. (Illus.). (gr. k-2). 1979. pap. 4.95 (ISBN 0-933606-04-4). Monkey Sisters.

Svendson, May. Numbers Workbook Three (with Daring Dog) (Funny Face Activity Bks.). (Illus.). 48p. (ps-1). 1981. pap. 1.95 saddle-stitched (ISBN 0-394-84458-0). Random.

Taylor, Anne. Math in Art. (Math Is Everywhere Ser.). (Illus., Orig.). (gr. 1-9). 1974. pap. 4.95 (ISBN 0-918932-28-9). Activity Resources.

Trivett, John V. Building Tables on Tables: A Book About Multiplication. LC 74-11263. (Young Math Ser.). (Illus.). 40p. (gr. k-3). 1975. (TYC-J); PLB 8.79 (ISBN 0-690-00600-4). Har-Row.

University of Oregon. Statistics & Information Organization. (gr. 5-9). 1978. 36.95 (ISBN 0-88488-093-1). Creative Pubns.

Usher, Michael A. & Bormuth, Robert. Experiencing Life Through Mathematics, Vol. 1. rev. ed. (Illus.). 128p. (Orig.). (gr. 8-12). 1978. pap. text ed. 4.92x (ISBN 0-913688-66-5); tchrs. ed. 6.00x (ISBN 0-913688-67-3). Pawnee Pub.

Watson, Clyde. Binary Numbers. LC 75-29161. (Young Math Ser.). (Illus.). (gr. 1-4). 1977. PLB 8.79 (ISBN 0-690-00993-3, TYC-J). Har-Row.

Wehrli, K. Division. (Michigan Arithmetric Program Ser.). (gr. 4). 1976. wkbk. 7.00x (ISBN 0-89039-180-7). Ann Arbor Pubs.

Wehrli, Kitty. Addition, Ten to Twenty. (Michigan Arithmetic Program Ser.). (gr. 2). 1977. wkbk. 7.00x (ISBN 0-89039-105-X). Ann Arbor Pubs.

Wiebe, A. J. & Goodfellow. Explorations in Mathematics. (gr. 9-12). 1970. text ed. 10.72 (ISBN 0-03-062535-1); tchrs' ed. 12.96 (ISBN 0-03-062540-8). HR&W.

Young, Sharon. Mathematics in Children's Books: An Annotated Bibliography for Pre-School Thru Grade 3. (ps-3). 1978. pap. 2.95 (ISBN 0-88488-116-4). Creative Pubns.

Yunker, Mary Jo. Solving Word Problems Learning Module. May, Lola J., ed. (gr. 5-8). 1977. pap. write for info. (ISBN 0-89290-137-3, CM-58). Soc for Visual.

Yunker, Mary Jo & May, Lola J. Problem Learning Module. (Illus.). (gr. 3-4). 1977. pap. 129.80 (ISBN 0-89290-134-9, CM-55R). Soc for Visual.

Zaslavsky, Claudia. Count on Your Fingers African Style. LC 77-26586. (Illus.). 32p. (gr. k-3). 1980. 8.95 (ISBN 0-690-03864-X, TYC-J); PLB 8.79 (ISBN 0-690-03865-8). Har-Row.

MATHEMATICS–LABORATORIES

see Computation Laboratories

MATHEMATICS–METHODOLOGY

Davis, Philip J. & Hersh, Reuben. The Mathematical Experience. 460p. 1981. 24.00 (ISBN 3-7643-3018-X). Birkhauser.

Hill, Thomas, ed. Mathematical Challenges II-Plus Six. LC 74-9766. 128p. 1974. pap. 4.50 (ISBN 0-87353-067-5). NCTM.

Jerman, Max E. & Beardslee, Edward C. Elementary Mathematics Method. (Illus.). 1978. text ed. 16.50 (ISBN 0-07-032531-6, C); 3.95 (ISBN 0-07-032532-4). McGraw.

LeBlanc, John F., et al. Mathematics Methods Program: Rational Numbers with Integers & Reals. (Mathematics Ser). (Illus.). 240p. 1976. pap. text ed. 4.50 (ISBN 0-201-14612-6); instructor's manual 1.50 (ISBN 0-201-14613-4). A-W.

Rao, M. M. Stochastic Processes & Integration. 467p. 1979. 55.00x (ISBN 90-286-0438-3). Sijthoff & Noordhoff.

Scarpellini, Bruno. Proof Theory & Intuitionistic Systems. LC 78-169705. (Lecture Notes in Mathematics: Vol. 212). 1971. pap. 11.20 (ISBN 0-387-05541-X). Springer-Verlag.

Singh, Jagjit. Great Ideas on Modern Mathematics: Their Nature & Their Use. (Illus.). 7.50 (ISBN 0-8446-0911-0). Peter Smith.

Swetz, Frank, ed. Socialist Mathematics Education. LC 78-68025. 1979. pap. 14.00 (ISBN 0-917574-04-4). Burgundy Pr.

MATHEMATICS–OUTLINES, SYLLABI, ETC.

Clifford, William K. Mathematical Papers. LC 67-28488. 1968. Repr. 29.50 (ISBN 0-8284-0210-8). Chelsea Pub.

Gruber, Edward C. Graduate Record Examination Math Review. (Exam Prep. Ser.). pap. 5.95 (ISBN 0-671-18992-1). Monarch Pr.

Hockett, Shirley O. Barron's How to Prepare for the Advanced Placement Examination - Mathematics: Mathematics. rev. ed. LC 77-149360. (gr. 11-12). 1977. pap. text ed. 8.50 (ISBN 0-8120-0354-3). Barron.

Laycock, Mary & Johnson, Connie. The Tapestry of Mathematics. new ed. (Illus.). 1978. pap. text ed. 15.95 (ISBN 0-918932-51-3). Activity Resources.

Lipschutz, Seymour. Finite Mathematics. 1966. pap. 5.95 (ISBN 0-07-037987-4, SP). McGraw.

Nielsen, Kaj L. College Mathematics. (Orig.). 1958. pap. 3.95 (ISBN 0-06-460105-6, CO 105, COS). Har-Row.

Schaaf, William L. Course for Teachers of Junior High School Mathematics. LC 77-177808. (Columbia University. Teachers College. Contributions to Education: No. 313). Repr. of 1928 ed. 17.50 (ISBN 0-404-55313-3). AMS Pr.

Williams, Edward. Back to Basics Mathematics, 3 vols. Incl. Vol. 1. From Addition to Division. LC 78-21490 (ISBN 0-8120-0691-7); Vol. 2. Improving Skills with Fractions (ISBN 0-8120-0692-5); Vol. 3. Decimals, Percents & Other Matter (ISBN 0-8120-0693-3). LC 78-21490. (Math Ser.). 1979. pap. text ed. 4.75 ea. Barron.

MATHEMATICS–PERIODICALS

Abbreviations of Names of Journals. 1980. 3.20 (ISBN 0-8218-0000-0, ABBR). Am Math.

May, Kenneth O. Index of the American Mathematical Monthly, Vol. 1-80. LC 77-79281. 1973. 16.00 (ISBN 0-88385-426-0). Math Assn.

National Council of Teachers of Mathematics. Cumulative Index: The Mathematics Teacher, 1908-1965. LC 42-24844. 1967. pap. 9.00 (ISBN 0-87353-028-4). NCTM.

MATHEMATICS–PHILOSOPHY

see also Arithmetic–Foundations; Continuity; Metamathematics; Semantics (Philosophy)

Ambrose, Alice, ed. Wittgenstein's Lectures, Cambridge 1932-1935: From the Notes of Alice Ambrose & Margaret Macdonald. 225p. 1979. 19.50x (ISBN 0-8476-6151-2). Rowman.

Beller, A., et al. Coding the Universe. LC 81-2663. (London Mathematical Society Lecture Notes: No. 47). 300p. Date not set. price not set (ISBN 0-521-28040-0). Cambridge U Pr.

Beth, E. W. Mathematical Thought. 1965. 40.25x (ISBN 0-677-00600-4). Gordon.

--Mathematical Thought: An Introduction to the Philosophy of Mathematics. (Synthese Library: No. 11). 208p. 1965. lib. bdg. 22.00 (ISBN 90-277-0070-2, Pub. by Reidel Holland). Kluwer Boston.

Beth, E. W. & Piaget, J. Mathematical Epistemology & Psychology. 1966. 56.75x (ISBN 0-677-01290-X). Gordon.

--Mathematical Epistemology & Psychology. Mays, W., tr. from Fr. (Synthese Library: No. 12). 326p. 1966. lib. bdg. 39.50 (ISBN 90-277-0071-0, Pub. by Reidel Holland). Kluwer Boston.

Black, Max. Nature of Mathematics. (Quality Paperback: No. 201). 219p. 1965. pap. 2.95 (ISBN 0-8226-0201-6). Littlefield.

Bledsoe, Albert T. The Philosophy of Mathematics. LC 75-3004. Repr. of 1868 ed. 20.00 (ISBN 0-404-59048-9). AMS Pr.

Bostock, David. Logic & Arithmetic: Vol. II, Rational & Irrational Numbers. (Illus.). 1979. 49.50x (ISBN 0-19-824591-2). Oxford U Pr.

Boyer, Carl B. History of the Calculus & Its Conceptual Development. Orig. Title: Concepts of Calculus. 1959. pap. 4.50 (ISBN 0-486-60509-4). Dover.

Buchanan, Scott. Poetry & Mathematics. (Midway Reprint Ser). 156p. 1975. pap. text ed. 4.95x (ISBN 0-226-07821-3). U of Chicago Pr.

Bulloff, J. J., et al, eds. Foundations of Mathematics: Symposium Papers Commemorating the Sixtieth Birthday of Kurt Goedel. LC 68-28757. (Illus.). 1969. 27.10 (ISBN 0-387-04490-6). Springer-Verlag.

Carnap, Rudolf. Foundations of Logic & Mathematics. (Foundations of the Unity of Science Ser: Vol. 1, No. 3). 1937. pap. 3.00x (ISBN 0-226-57578-0, P402, Phoen). U of Chicago Pr.

Carus, Paul. The Foundations of Mathematics: A Contribution to the Philosophy of Geometry. LC 75-3104. Repr. of 1908 ed. 18.00 (ISBN 0-404-59101-9). AMS Pr.

Castonguay, C. Meaning & Existence in Mathematics. LC 72-96052. (Library of Exact Philosophy: Vol. 9). 159p. 1973. 22.30 (ISBN 0-387-81110-9). Springer-Verlag.

Ceitin, G. S., et al. Five Papers on Logic & Foundations. LC 51-5559. (Translations Ser.: No. 2, Vol. 98). 292p. 1971. text ed. 29.60 (ISBN 0-8218-1798-1, TRANS 2-98). Am Math.

Cohen, R. S., et al, eds. Essays in Memory of Imre Lakatos. new ed. LC 76-16770. (Synthese Library Ser.: No. 99). 1976. lib. bdg. 87.00 (ISBN 90-277-0654-9, Pub. by Reidel Holland); pap. 47.50 (ISBN 90-277-0655-7, Pub. by Reidel Holland). Kluwer Boston.

Curry, Haskell B. Outline of a Formalist Philosophy of Mathematics. (Studies in Logic & Foundation of Math). 1958. pap. text ed. 12.00x (ISBN 0-7204-2206-X, Pub. by North Holland). Humanities.

Davis, Philip J. & Hersh, Reuben. The Mathematical Experience. 460p. 1981. 24.00 (ISBN 3-7643-3018-X). Birkhauser.

Frege, Gottlob. The Philosophical & Mathematical Correspondence. McGuinness, Brian, ed. Kaal, Hans, tr. LC 79-23199. 1980. lib. bdg. 31.00x (ISBN 0-226-26197-2). U of Chicago Pr.

--Translations from the Philosophical Writings of Gottlob Frege. 3rd ed. Geach, Peter & Black, Max, eds. 228p. 1980. 25.00x (ISBN 0-8476-6286-1); pap. 10.95x (ISBN 0-8476-6287-X). Rowman.

Godel, Kurt. Consistency of the Continuum Hypothesis. (Annals of Mathematics Studies, Vol. 3). (Orig.). 1940. pap. 10.50x (ISBN 0-691-07927-7). Princeton U Pr.

Goodstein, R. L. Essays in the Philosophy of Mathematics. 1965. text ed. 12.50x (ISBN 0-7185-1044-5, Leicester). Humanities.

Grassl, Wolfgang, ed. Friedrich Waismann: Lectures in the Philosophy of Mathematics. (Studien Zur Oesterreichischen Philosophie). 125p. 1981. pap. text ed. 25.00x (ISBN 90-6203-613-9, Pub. by Rodopi Holland). Humanities.

Hadamard, Jacques. Psychology of Invention in the Mathematical Field. 1945. pap. text ed. 3.00 (ISBN 0-486-20107-4). Dover.

Haken, H., ed. Synergetics-A Workshop: Proceedings of the International Workshop on Synergetics at Schloss Elmau, Bavaria, Germany, May 2-7,1977. (Illus.). 1977. 34.30 (ISBN 0-387-08483-5). Springer-Verlag.

Howard, Homer. Mathematics Teachers' Views on Certain Issues in the Teaching of Mathematics. LC 76-176883. (Columbia University. Teachers College. Contributions to Education: No. 827). Repr. of 1941 ed. 17.50 (ISBN 0-404-55827-5). AMS Pr.

Kasner & Newman. Mathematics & the Imagination. 1962. pap. 4.95 (ISBN 0-671-20855-1, Touchstone Bks). S&S.

Kattsoff, Louis O. Philosophy of Mathematics. facs. ed. LC 73-84314. (Essay Index Reprint Ser). 1948. 16.50 (ISBN 0-8369-1086-9). Arno.

Kleene, Stephen. Mathematical Logic. LC 66-26747. 398p. 1967. 29.95 (ISBN 0-471-49033-4). Wiley.

Klenk. Wittgenstein's Philosophy of Mathematics. 1976. pap. 24.00 (ISBN 90-247-1842-2, Pub. by Martinus Nijhoff Netherlands). Kluwer Boston.

Kline, Morris. Mathematics: The Loss of Certainty. (Illus.). 400p. 1980. 19.95 (ISBN 0-19-502754-X). Oxford U Pr.

Korner, Stephen. The Philosophy of Mathematics: An Introductory Essay. 1979. pap. text ed. 5.75x (ISBN 0-09-056642-4, Hutchinson U Lib). Humanities.

Korzybski, Alfred. Science & Sanity: An Introduction to Non-Aristotelian Systems & General Semantics. 4th ed. LC 58-6260. 806p. 1958. 19.50x (ISBN 0-937298-01-8). Inst Gen Semantics.

Kuyk, Willem. Complimentarity in Mathematics. LC 77-8838. (Mathematics & Its Applications Ser.: No. 1). 1977. lib. bdg. 21.00 (ISBN 90-277-0814-2, Pub. by Reidel Holland). Kluwer Boston.

Lakatos, E. Proofs & Refutations. Worrall, J., ed. LC 75-32478. 160p. 1976. 32.50 (ISBN 0-521-21078-X); pap. 8.95 (ISBN 0-521-29038-4). Cambridge U Pr.

Lakatos, Imre. Philosophical Papers: Mathematics, Science & Epistemology, Vol. 2. Worrall, J. & Currie, G., eds. LC 77-14374. 295p. 1980. pap. 13.50 (ISBN 0-521-28030-3). Cambridge U Pr.

--Philosophical Papers: Mathematics, Science & Epistology, Vol. 2. Worrall, J. & Currie, G., eds. LC 77-71415. 1978. 32.50 (ISBN 0-521-21769-5). Cambridge U Pr.

Leach, M. Logic & Boolean Algebra. (Finite Math Text Ser.). write for info. (ISBN 0-685-84475-7). J W Wills.

Lehman, Hugh. Introduction to the Philosophy of Mathematics. (American Philosophical Quarterly Library of Philosophy). 1979. 18.00x (ISBN 0-8476-6109-1). Rowman.

Lieber, Hugh G. & Lieber, Lillian R. Human Values & Science, Art & Mathematics. (Illus.). 1961. 3.95 (ISBN 0-393-06339-9). Norton.

Mathematical Ideas. 4th ed. 1981. text ed. 17.95x (ISBN 0-673-15524-2). Scott F.

Mueller, Ian. Philosophy of Mathematics & Deductive Structure in Euclid's "Elements". (Illus.). 400p. 1981. 37.50x (ISBN 0-262-13163-3). MIT Pr.

Newton, Sir Isaac. Mathematical Principles of Natural Philosophy and His System of the World. (Principia) Cajori, Florian, rev. by. Motte, Andrew, tr. Incl. Vol. I. The Motions of Bodies. pap. 5.95x (ISBN 0-520-00928-2, CAMPUS70); Vol. II. The System of the World. pap. 5.95 (ISBN 0-520-00929-0, CAMPUS71). 1962. U of Cal Pr.

Poincare, Henri. Science & Hypothesis. 1905. pap. 4.00 (ISBN 0-486-60221-4). Dover.

Polya, Gyorgy. Mathematics & Plausible Reasoning, 2 vols. Incl. Vol. 1. Induction & Analogy in Mathematics. 1954 (ISBN 0-691-08005-4); Vol. 2. Patterns of Plausible Inference. rev. ed. 1969 (ISBN 0-691-08006-2). 15.00 ea.; Set. 25.50 (ISBN 0-685-23091-0). Princeton U Pr.

Putnam, H. Philosophical Papers: Mathematics, Matter & Methods, Vol. 1. 2nd ed. LC 75-8315. 1979. 38.50 (ISBN 0-521-22553-1); pap. 11.95 (ISBN 0-521-29550-5). Cambridge U Pr.

Renyi, Alfred. Dialogues on Mathematics. LC 67-13839. 1967. 8.95x (ISBN 0-8162-7124-0); pap. 3.95x (ISBN 0-8162-7134-8). Holden-Day.

Russell, Bertrand. Introduction to Mathematical Philosophy. (Muirhead Library of Philoaophy Ser.). Repr. of 1963 ed. text ed. 19.50x (ISBN 0-04-510020-9). Humanities.

--Principles of Mathematics. 2nd ed. 1964. pap. 7.95 (ISBN 0-393-00249-7, Norton Lib). Norton.

Sicha, Jeffrey. A Metaphysics of Elementary Mathematics. LC 73-79504. 456p. 1974. pap. 10.00x (ISBN 0-87023-149-9). U of Mass Pr.

Singh, Jagjit. Great Ideas of Modern Mathematics. (Illus.). 1959. pap. text ed. 4.00 (ISBN 0-486-20587-8). Dover.

Steiner, Mark. Mathematical Knowledge. LC 74-7639. (Contemporary Philosophy Ser.). 176p. 1975. 18.50x (ISBN 0-8014-0894-6). Cornell U Pr.

Swetz, Frank, ed. Socialist Mathematics Education. LC 78-68025. 1979. pap. 14.00 (ISBN 0-917574-04-4). Burgundy Pr.

Symposium, Oslo, Norway, Jun, 1972. Generalized Recursion Theory: Proceedings. Fenstad, J. E. & Hinman, P. G., eds. LC 73-81531. (Studies in Logic & the Foundation of Mathematics Ser: Vol. 79). 460p. 1974. 49.00 (ISBN 0-444-10545-X, North-Holland). Elsevier.

Takeuti, Gaisi. Two Applications of Logic to Mathematics. (Publications of the Mathematical Society of Japan: No. 13). 1978. 18.50x (ISBN 0-691-08212-X). Princeton U Pr.

Tarski, Alfred. Introduction to Logic & to the Methodology of Deductive Sciences. 3rd ed. pap. 5.95x (ISBN 0-19-501076-0). Oxford U Pr.

--Logic, Semantics, Metamathematics. Corcoran, John, ed. Woodger, J. H., tr. from Polish. 1981. lib. bdg. 40.00 (ISBN 0-915144-75-1); pap. text ed. 19.50 (ISBN 0-915144-76-X). Hackett Pub.

Tullock, Gordon. Toward a Mathematics of Politics. 1972. pap. 2.25 (ISBN 0-472-06187-9, 187, AA). U of Mich Pr.

Van Heijenoort, Jean, ed. From Frege to Godel: A Source Book in Mathematical Logic, 1879-1931. LC 67-10905. (Source Books in the History of the Sciences Ser). 1967. 30.00x (ISBN 0-674-32450-1); pap. 13.95x (ISBN 0-674-32449-8). Harvard U Pr.

Waismann, Friedrich. Introduction to Mathematical Thinking. Benac, T., tr. 1951. 12.00 (ISBN 0-8044-4984-8). Ungar.

Webb, Judson C. Mechanism, Mentalism, & Metamathematics. (Synthese Library: No. 137). xiii, 263p. 1980. lib. bdg. 29.00 (ISBN 90-277-1046-5, Pub. by Reidel Holland). Kluwer Boston.

Wedberg, Anders. Plato's Philosophy of Mathematics. LC 76-50071. 1977. Repr. of 1955 ed. lib. bdg. 15.00 (ISBN 0-8371-9405-9, WEPP). Greenwood.

Weyl, Hermann. Philosophy of Mathematics & Natural Science. LC 49-9797. 1963. pap. 1.65 (ISBN 0-689-70207-8, 31). Atheneum.

Whitehead, Alfred N. & Russell, Bertrand. Principia Mathematica, 3 Vols. Set. 270.00 (ISBN 0-521-06791-X). Cambridge U Pr.

--Principia Mathematica to Fifty-Six. 2nd ed. 1925-27. pap. 19.95x (ISBN 0-521-09187-X). Cambridge U Pr.

Wilder, Raymond I. Mathematics As a Cultural System. (Foundations & Philosophy of Science & Technology Ser.). 170p. 1981. 23.00 (ISBN 0-08-025796-8). Pergamon.

Wilder, Raymond L. Introduction to the Foundations of Mathematics. 2nd ed. LC 80-12446. 346p. 1980. Repr. of 1965 ed. pap. 19.50 (ISBN 0-89874-170-X). Krieger.

Wittgenstein, Ludwig. Remarks on the Foundations of Mathematics. 1967. pap. 6.95x (ISBN 0-262-73017-0, 74). MIT Pr.

--Remarks on the Foundations of Mathematics. rev ed Von Wright, G. H. & Rhees, R., eds. Anscombe, G. E., tr. from Ger. 1978. text ed. 30.00x (ISBN 0-262-23080-1). MIT Pr.

Young, Frederick H. Nature of Mathematics. 1967. text ed. 11.25 (ISBN 0-471-97980-5, Pub. by Wiley). Krieger.

MATHEMATICS–POPULAR WORKS

Adler, Irving. Readings in Mathematics. 1972. pap. 5.60 (ISBN 0-663-24123-5). NCTM.

Anderson, John G. Technical Shop Mathematics. 510p. 1974. 17.50 (ISBN 0-8311-1085-6); wkd.-out solutions 6.00 (ISBN 0-8311-1106-2). Indus Pr.

Ellis, Keith. Number Power. 1980. pap. 4.95 (ISBN 0-312-57989-6). St Martin.

Jurgin, Y. Bueno, y Que? 406p. (Span.). 1973. pap. 2.85 (ISBN 0-8285-1693-6, Pub. by Mir Pubs Russia). Imported Pubns.

Klinger, Fred. Math for Everyone. 1966. 4.75 (ISBN 0-8022-0869-X). Philos Lib.
Pedoe, Dan. The Gentle Art of Mathematics. 143p. 1973. pap. 2.50 (ISBN 0-486-22949-1). Dover.
Perelman, Y. Algebra Can Be Fun. 228p. 1979. pap. 3.75 (ISBN 0-8285-1523-9, Pub. by Mir Pubs Russia). Imported Pubns.
Perelman, Ya. Figures for Fun. 183p. 1979. pap. 3.40 (ISBN 0-8285-1512-3, Pub. by Mir Pubs Russia). Imported Pubns.
Peter, Rozsa. Playing with Infinity: Mathematical Explorations & Excursions. LC 75-26467. 288p. 1976. pap. text ed. 3.50 (ISBN 0-486-23265-4). Dover.

MATHEMATICS–PROBLEMS, EXERCISES, ETC.

Andrew, Larry D. & Andrew, Patricia. Math Exercises (in Addition) 1980. pap. 1.95 (ISBN 0-931992-36-2). Penns Valley.
--Math Exercises (in Division) 1980. pap. 1.95 (ISBN 0-931992-39-7). Penns Valley.
--Math Exercises (in Multiplication) 1980. pap. 1.95 (ISBN 0-931992-38-9). Penns Valley.
--Math Exercises (in Subtraction) 1980. pap. 1.95 (ISBN 0-931992-37-0). Penns Valley.
Averbach, Bonnie & Chein, Orin. Mathematics: Problem Solving Through Recreational Mathematics. LC 80-11989. (Mathematical Sciences Ser.). (Illus.). 1980. text ed. 16.95x (ISBN 0-7167-1124-9); instrs'. guide avail.; solutions manual avail. W H Freeman.
Barns, R. E. The Answer Is One-1st One. (Illus.). (gr. 2-12). 1977. wkbk. 5.95 (ISBN 0-88488-068-0). Creative Pubns.
--The Answer Is One-3rd One. (gr. 2-12). 1977. wkbk. 5.95 (ISBN 0-88488-070-2). Creative Pubns.
Barns, R. E. & Eral, Bill. The Answer Is One-2nd One. (gr. 2-12). 1977. wkbk. 5.95 (ISBN 0-88488-069-9). Creative Pubns.
Bezuszka, Stanley & Kenney, Margaret. Wonder-Full World of Numbers. (Contemporary Motivated Mathematics Ser.). 97p. (Orig.). (gr. 3-6). 1971. pap. text ed. 1.50 (ISBN 0-917916-05-0). Boston Coll Math.
Bezuszka, Stanley, et al. Finite Differences. (Motivated Math Project Activity Booklets). 108p. (Orig.). (gr. 10-12). 1976. pap. text ed. 2.50 (ISBN 0-917916-11-5). Boston Coll Math.
--Perfect Numbers. (Motivated Math Project Activity Booklets). 169p. (Orig.). (gr. 7-12). 1980. pap. text ed. 3.50 (ISBN 0-917916-19-0). Boston Coll Math.
--Wonder Square. (Motivated Math Project Activity Booklets). 30p. (Orig.). (gr. 6-12). 1976. pap. text ed. 1.25 (ISBN 0-917916-15-8). Boston Coll Math.
--Comtemporary Motivated Mathematics, Bk. 3. (Comtemporary Motivated Mathematics Ser.). 97p. (Orig.). (gr. 7-10). 1972. pap. text ed. 1.50 (ISBN 0-917916-04-2). Boston Coll Math.
--Contemporary Motivated Mathematics, Bk. 1. (Contemporary Motivated Mathematics Ser.). 97p. (Orig.). (gr. 5-8). 1972. pap. text ed. 1.50 (ISBN 0-917916-02-6). Boston Coll Math.
--Contemporary Motivated Mathematics, Bk. 2. (Comtemporary Motivated Mathematics Ser.). 97p. (Orig.). (gr. 6-9). 1973. pap. text ed. 1.50 (ISBN 0-917916-03-4). Boston Coll Math.
Bitter, et al. McGraw-Hill Mathematics Parents Guide to Problem Solving. (McGraw-Hill Mathematics, Ser.). 16p. 1981. 0.80 (ISBN 0-07-005749-4, W). McGraw.
Briggaman, Joan. Practical Problems in Mathematics for Office Workers. LC 76-54051. 1977. pap. text ed. 5.60 (ISBN 0-8273-1612-7); instructor's guide 1.60 (ISBN 0-8273-1613-5). Delmar.
Brownstein. Mathematics Workbook for College Entrance Examinations. rev. ed. (gr. 10-12). 1976. pap. text ed. 5.95 (ISBN 0-8120-0654-2). Barron.
Burns, Marilyn. The Good Time Math Event Book. (Illus.). (gr. 4-6). 1977. wkbk. 7.95 (ISBN 0-88488-059-1). Creative Pubns.
Charosh, Mannis, compiled by. Mathematical Challenges: Selected Problems from the Mathematics Student Journal. LC 65-19606. 1965. pap. 3.40 (ISBN 0-87353-066-7, 09210). NCTM.
Chowla, S. Riemann Hypothesis & Hilberts Tenth Problem. (Mathematics & Its Applications Ser.). 1965. 34.75x (ISBN 0-677-00140-1). Gordon.
Clifford, William K. Mathematical Papers. LC 67-28488. 1968. Repr. 29.50 (ISBN 0-8284-0210-8). Chelsea Pub.
Degrazia, Joseph. Math Is Fun. (Illus.). (gr. 9 up). 8.95 (ISBN 0-87523-094-6). Emerson.
DeVore, Russell B. Practical Problems in Mathematics for Heating & Cooling Technicians. LC 79-57141. (Practical Problems in Mathematics Ser.). 175p. 1981. pap. text ed. 6.60 (ISBN 0-8273-1682-8); instr's. guide 2.10 (ISBN 0-8273-1683-6). Delmar.
Dewar, Darrell. Fundamental Math Workbooks & Answer Key. (Illus.). (gr. 7-12). 1972. answer key o.p. 3.95 (ISBN 0-88499-045-1); wkbk. pt. 1 7.95 (ISBN 0-88499-043-5); wkbk. pt. 2 5.95 (ISBN 0-88499-044-3). Inst Mod Lang.
Disney Practice Workbooks. Incl. Phonics (ISBN 0-448-16120-6); Spelling & Dictionary Skills (ISBN 0-448-16121-4); Creative Writing (ISBN 0-448-16122-2); Reading Comprehension (ISBN 0-448-16123-0); Numbers: Addition & Subtraction (ISBN 0-448-16124-9); Number: Multiplication (ISBN 0-448-16125-7). (Mickey's Practice Workbooks Ser.). (Illus.). (gr. k-3). 1978. pap. 1.25 ea. G&D.
Dorrie, Heinrich. One Hundred Great Problems of Elementary Mathematics: Their History & Solution. Antin, David, tr. from Ger. 393p. 1965. pap. 4.50 (ISBN 0-486-61348-8). Dover.
Dressler, I Sidore. Current Mathematics: A Work-Text. (gr. 7 up). 1977. Bk. I. wkbk 8.67 (ISBN 0-87720-239-7). AMSCO Sch.
Dynkin, E. G., et al. Mathematical Problems: An Anthology. (Pocket Mathematical Library Ser). 1967. 18.75 (ISBN 0-677-20710-7). Gordon.
Fair, Jan & Rand, Ken. Handy Math: Focus on Purchasing. (gr. 7-9). 1979. 6.25 (ISBN 0-88488-126-1). Creative Pubns.
--Handy Math: Focus on Sports. (gr. 7-9). 1979. 6.25 (ISBN 0-88488-128-8). Creative Pubns.
--Handy Math: Focus on Travel. (gr. 7-9). 1979. 6.25 (ISBN 0-88488-127-X). Creative Pubns.
Garrard & Boyd. Practical Problems in Mathematics for Electricians. LC 79-56247. 1981. pap. text ed. 5.00 (ISBN 0-8273-1277-6); instructor's guide 2.00 (ISBN 0-8273-1278-4). Delmar.
Gattegno, Caleb. Algebricks Exercise Workbooks 1-6. 1970. pap. 1.10 (ISBN 0-87825-001-8). Ed Solutions.
GED - Mathematics Test 5. 1976. pap. 4.95 (ISBN 0-8092-8112-0). Contemp Bks.
Graham, Lloyd A. Ingenious Mathematical Problems & Methods. 1959. pap. 3.50 (ISBN 0-486-20545-2). Dover.
Greenes, Carole, et al. Successful Problem Solving Techniques. (gr. 6-12). 1977. tchrs. ed. 7.25 (ISBN 0-88488-086-9). Creative Pubns.
Greenes, Carole E., et al. Problem-Mathics. (gr. 7-12). 1977. tchrs. ed. 7.25 (ISBN 0-88488-085-0). Creative Pubns.
Greitzer, Samuel L., ed. International Mathematical Olympiads, Nineteen Fifty-Nine to Nineteen Seventy-Seven. LC 78-54027. (New Mathematical Library Ser.). 1979. pap. 6.50 (ISBN 0-88385-627-1). Math Assn.
Honsberger, Ross. Mathematical Morsels. LC 78-60731. (Dolciani Mathematical Exposition Ser.). 1979. 16.00 (ISBN 0-88385-303-5). Math Assn.
Hughes, Barnabas. Thinking Through Problems. (YA) 1977. wkbk 6.95 (ISBN 0-88488-056-7). Creative Pubns.
Hungarian Problem Book 1. LC 63-16149. (New Mathematical Library: No. 11). 1975. pap. 4.50 (ISBN 0-88385-611-5). Math Assn.
Iglewicz, B. & Stoyle, J. Introduction to Mathematical Reasoning. 1973. pap. 8.95 (ISBN 0-02-359600-7). Macmillan.
Kahan, Steven. Have Some Sums to Solve: The Compleat Alphamatics Book. LC 77-94008. 128p. (Orig.). 1978. pap. text ed. 4.95 (ISBN 0-89503-007-1). Baywood Pub.
Kenney, Margaret. Incredible Pascal Triangle. (Motivated Math Project Activity Booklets). 91p. (Orig.). (gr. 6-12). 1976. pap. text ed. 2.50 (ISBN 0-917916-16-6). Boston Coll Math.
--Mathematical Doodling. (Motivated Math Project Activity Booklets). 86p. (Orig.). (gr. 6-12). 1976. pap. text ed. 2.50 (ISBN 0-917916-17-4). Boston Coll Math.
--Super Sum. (Motivated Math Project Activity Booklets). 41p. (Orig.). (gr. 10-12). 1976. pap. text ed. 2.00 (ISBN 0-917916-18-2). Boston Coll Math.
Lebedev, N. N., et al. Worked Problems in Applied Mathematics. LC 78-67857. 1979. pap. text ed. 6.00 (ISBN 0-486-63730-1). Dover.
LeBlanc, John F., et al. Mathematics-Methods Program: Experiences in Problem Solving. (Mathematics Ser). 64p. 1976. pap. text ed. 2.95 (ISBN 0-201-14628-2); instr's man. 1.50 (ISBN 0-201-14629-0). A-W.
Marjoram, D. T. Further Exercises in Modern Mathematics. 1966. text ed. 6.95 (ISBN 0-08-011969-7); pap. 5.40 (ISBN 0-08-011968-9). Pergamon.
Mauldin, D., ed. The Scottish Book. 480p. 1981. write for info. (ISBN 3-7643-3045-7). Birkhauser.
National Council of Teachers of Mathematics. Problem Solving in School Mathematics, 1980 Yearbook. 1980. 13.75 (ISBN 0-87353-162-0). NCTM.
Ogilvy, Charles S. Tomorrow's Math: Unsolved Problems for the Amateur. 2nd ed. 1972. 12.95 (ISBN 0-19-501508-8). Oxford U Pr.
Park Lane Press. Inc. Eleventh Year Math. (Regents Review Ser.). pap. 2.50 (ISBN 0-671-18147-5). Monarch Pr.
Park Lane Press, Inc. Ninth Year Math. (Regents Review Ser.). pap. 2.50 (ISBN 0-671-18146-7). Monarch Pr.
--Tenth Year Math. (Regents Review Ser.). pap. 2.50 (ISBN 0-671-18144-0). Monarch Pr.
Polya, George. Mathematical Discovery: On Understanding, Learning, & Teaching Problem Solving. 448p. 1981. text ed. 18.95 (ISBN 0-471-08975-3). Wiley.
Polya, George & Kilpatrick, Jeremy. The Stanford Mathematics Problem Book: With Hints & Solutions. LC 73-86270. 1974. pap. text ed. 4.50x (ISBN 0-8077-2416-5). Tchrs Coll.
Polya, Gyorgy. How to Solve It. 1971. 15.50x (ISBN 0-691-08097-6); pap. 4.95 (ISBN 0-691-02356-5). Princeton U Pr.
--Mathematical Discovery on Understanding, Learning & Teaching Problem Solving, 2 Vols. LC 62-8784. 1962. Vol. 1. 19.95 (ISBN 0-471-69333-2). Wiley.
Practical Problems in Mathematics for Mechanical Drafting. LC 77-78236. 1979. pap. 7.00 (ISBN 0-8273-1670-4); instructor's guide 1.60 (ISBN 0-8273-1671-2). Delmar.
Practical Problems in Mathematics for Carpenters. LC 77-82373. 1979. pap. text ed. 5.72 (ISBN 0-685-30196-6); instructor's guide 1.60 (ISBN 0-8273-1276-8). Delmar.
Rabin, M. Automata on Infinite Objects & Church's Problem. LC 72-6749. (CBMS Regional Conference Series in Mathematics: No. 13). 1972. 8.80 (ISBN 0-8218-1663-2, CBMS-13). Am Math.
Rand, Ken. Point-Counterpoint. (gr. 3-8). 1979. 5.95 (ISBN 0-88488-125-3). Creative Pubns.
Rapaport, E., tr. Hungarian Problem Book 2: Based on the Eotvos Competition. LC 63-16149. (New Mathematical Library: No. 12). 1975. pap. 5.50 (ISBN 0-88385-612-3). Math Assn.
Reys, et al. Keystrokes: Calculator Activities for Young Students, Multiplication & Division. (gr. 2-6). 1979. 6.50 (ISBN 0-88488-130-X). Creative Pubns.
Rich, Barnett. Review of Elementary Mathematics. (Schaum's Outline Ser). (Orig.). 1977. pap. 4.95 (ISBN 0-07-052260-X, SP). McGraw.
Roper, Ann & Harvey, Linda. Dots Math Too! (gr. 3-6). 1979. 4.95 (ISBN 0-88488-118-0). Creative Pubns.
Ruderman, Harry, ed. Mathematical Buds. (Illus.). 1978. pap. text ed. 2.50 (ISBN 0-686-10172-3). Mu Alpha Theta.
Salkind, C. T., ed. The Contest Problem Book. LC 61-13843. (New Mathematical Library: No. 5). 1975. pap. 5.50 (ISBN 0-88385-605-0). Math Assn.
--The Problem Book 11: Annual High School Contests of the MAA. LC 66-15479. (New Mathematical Library: No. 17). 1975. pap. 5.50 (ISBN 0-88385-617-4). Math Assn.
Salkind, C. T. & Earl, J. M., eds. The Contest Problem Book III: Annual High School Contests of the MAA & Four Other Organizations. LC 66-15479. (New Mathematical Library: No. 25). 1975. pap. 6.50 (ISBN 0-88385-625-5). Math Assn.
Schell, F. Practical Problems in Mathematics--Metric System. LC 78-73133. 1975. pap. text ed. 5.00 (ISBN 0-8273-1418-3); instructor's guide 1.60 (ISBN 0-8273-1419-1). Delmar.
Schell, Frank R. & Matlock, Bill J. Practical Problems in Mathematics for Welders. LC 74-24810. 1975. pap. text ed. 6.60 (ISBN 0-8273-0262-2); instructor's guide 1.60 (ISBN 0-8273-0263-0). Delmar.
Schneider, Harold. Solving Math Word Problems for Students & Adults. 1965. 4.50 (ISBN 0-911642-01-3); pap. 1.95 (ISBN 0-911642-02-1). Word-Fraction.
Schulz, Martin, ed. Eiliptic Problem Solvers. 1981. write for info. (ISBN 0-12-632620-7). Acad Pr.
Schumacher, F. Practical Problems in Mathematics for Sheet Metal Technicians. LC 71-74885. 1973. pap. text ed. 5.20 (ISBN 0-8273-0287-8); instructor's guide 1.60 (ISBN 0-8273-0288-6). Delmar.
Smith, James A. Basic Mathematics, 12 bks. 2nd ed. Incl. Bk. 1. Numbers & Numerals. 1.95 (ISBN 0-916780-00-7); Bk. 2. Addition of Whole Numbers & Subtraction of Whole Numbers. 4.15 (ISBN 0-916780-01-5); Bk. 3. Multiplication of Whole Numbers. 3.25 (ISBN 0-916780-02-3); Bk. 4. Division of Whole Numbers. 3.70 (ISBN 0-916780-03-1); Bk. 5. Fractions & Fractional Numbers. 2.40 (ISBN 0-916780-04-X); Bk. 6. Addition & Subtraction of Fractional Numbers & Multiplication & Division of Fractional Numbers. 3.70 (ISBN 0-916780-05-8); Bk. 7. Decimal Numerals: Addition & Subtraction with Decimals & Multiplication & Division with Decimals. 4.15 (ISBN 0-916780-06-6); Bk. 8. Percents & Applications. 2.80 (ISBN 0-916780-07-4); Bk. 9. Formulas & Applications. 3.70 (ISBN 0-916780-08-2); Bk. 10. Measurement & Applications. 4.15 (ISBN 0-916780-09-0); Bk. 11. Measurement in Geometry. 4.15 (ISBN 0-916780-10-4); Bk. 12. Units of Measure & the Metric System. 3.25 (ISBN 0-916780-11-2). (Illus.). 1974. pap. text ed. 35.00 set (ISBN 0-916780-12-0); tchr's. manual 3.50 (ISBN 0-916780-14-7); student test booklet 4.00 (ISBN 0-916780-13-9). CES.
Steenburgen, Fran. Steenburgen Diagnostic-Prescriptive Math Program. 1978. complete program 12.00 (ISBN 0-87879-209-0). Acad Therapy.
Steinhaus, Hugo. One Hundred Problems in Elementary Mathematics. 1979. pap. 2.75 (ISBN 0-486-23875-X). Dover.
Steklov Institute of Mathematics, Academy of Sciences, U.S.S.R., No. 93. Problems in the Constructive Trend in Mathematics: Pt. IV Proceedings. Orevkov, V. P. & Sanin, N. A., eds. 1970. 43.20 (ISBN 0-8218-1893-7, STEKLO-93). Am Math.
Stokes, George G. Mathematical & Physical Papers, 5 Vols. 2nd ed. Repr. of 1905 ed. Set. 115.50 (ISBN 0-384-58370-9). Johnson Repr.
Sullivan Associates. Math Word Problems, 3 vols. (gr. 2-6). 1972. pap. text ed. 2.50 each ans. key 1, 2, 3 (ISBN 0-686-57755-8). Learning Line.
Tietze, Heinrich. Famous Problems of Mathematics. 2nd ed. LC 64-8910. (Illus.). 1965. 20.00x (ISBN 0-910670-11-0). Graylock.
Weston, J. D. & Godwin, Herbert J. Some Exercises in Pure Mathematics. (Orig.). pap. 6.95x (ISBN 0-521-09561-1). Cambridge U Pr.

MATHEMATICS–PROGRAMMED INSTRUCTION

Addition, Zero to Ten. (Michigan Arithmetic Program Ser.). 1976. wkbk. 7.00x (ISBN 0-89039-946-8). Ann Arbor Pubs.
Baggaley, Andrew R. Mathematics for Introductory Statistics: A Programmed Review. 203p. 1969. pap. 13.50 (ISBN 0-471-04008-8). Wiley.
Bajpai, A. C., et al. Mathematics for Engineers & Scientists, Vols. 1-2. LC 72-14009. (Programs on Mathematics for Scientist & Technologist Ser.). 800p. 1973. Vol. 1. 22.95 (ISBN 0-471-04373-7); Vol. 2. 19.50 (ISBN 0-471-04374-5, Pub. by Wiley-Interscience). Wiley.
Bila, Dennis, et al. Core Mathematics. LC 74-82696. (Illus.). ix, 603p. (Prog. Bk.). 1975. text ed. 14.95x (ISBN 0-87901-035-5). H S Worth.
Crowhurst, Norman H. Problem Solving Arts: Part One Syllabus. 1976. pap. text ed. 9.95 (ISBN 0-89420-085-2, 256040); cassette recordings 227.10 (ISBN 0-89420-175-1, 256000). Natl Book.
Dressler, Isidore. Preliminary Mathematics. (Orig.). 1980. pap. text ed. 10.83 (ISBN 0-87720-242-7). AMSCO Sch.
Gould, Lawrence D., et al. Essentials for College Mathematics: A Programmed Text. (Illus.). 1970. pap. text ed. 3.95x (ISBN 0-89197-152-1); access pen 0.65x (ISBN 0-686-66705-0). Irvington.
Gray, Al & Matousek, Clifford H. General Mathematics: Syllabus. 2nd ed. 1972. pap. text ed. 5.75 (ISBN 0-89420-019-4, 350899); cassette recordings 102.55 (ISBN 0-89420-148-4, 350900). Natl Book.
Heywood, Arthur. A First Program in Mathematics. 3rd ed. 1977. 16.95x (ISBN 0-8221-0185-8). Dickenson.
Howes, Vernon E. Essentials of Mathematics: Precalculus- a Programmed Text. LC 75-9733. 1975. Bk. 2: Algebra II. text ed. o.p. (ISBN 0-471-41737-8); Bk. 3: Trigonometric Functions & Applications. text ed. 18.95x (ISBN 0-471-41738-6); instr's manual avail. (ISBN 0-471-41739-4). Wiley.
Mathematics Research Center, Univ. of Wisconsin, Advanced Seminar. Mathematical Programming: Proceedings. Hu, T. C. & Robinson, Stephen M., eds. 1973. 18.00 (ISBN 0-12-358350-0). Acad Pr.

Sullivan Associates. Programmed Mathematics Series, Bks. 9-15. Incl. Bk. 9. Consumer Math (ISBN 0-07-062069-5); Bk. 10. Personal Math (ISBN 0-07-062070-9); Bk. 11. More Personal Math (ISBN 0-07-062071-7); Bk. 12. Understanding Algebra (ISBN 0-07-062072-5); Bk. 13. Using Algebra (ISBN 0-07-062073-3); Bk. 14. Using Geometry (ISBN 0-07-062074-1); Bk. 15. Using Trigonometry (ISBN 0-07-062075-X). 1975. 3.32 ea.; instructor's guide 7.32 (ISBN 0-07-062076-8); exam pak 24.00 (ISBN 0-07-079360-3). McGraw.

Suppes, Patrick C., et al. Computer-Assisted Instruction: Stanford's 1965-66 Arithmetic Program. (Illus.). 1968. 37.50 (ISBN 0-12-676850-1). Acad Pr.

Wehrli, Kitty. Addition, Ten to Twenty. (Michigan Arithmetic Program Ser.). (gr. 2). 1977. wkbk. 7.00x (ISBN 0-89039-105-X). Ann Arbor Pubs.

--Michigan Arithmetic Program,Multiplication, Level 2: Consuable Edition. (gr. 3). 1975. 7.00x (ISBN 0-89039-132-7). Ann Arbor Pubs.

--Multiplication,Level 1: Consumable Edition. (Michigan Arithmetic Program Ser.). (gr. 3). 1975. Repr. wkbk 7.00x (ISBN 0-89039-094-0). Ann Arbor Pubs.

Wheeler, Ruric E. & Wheeler, Ed. R. Programmed Study of Number Systems. (Contemporary Undergrad Math Ser). (Prog. Bk.). 1972. pap. text ed. 9.95 (ISBN 0-8185-0042-5). Brooks-Cole.

MATHEMATICS–STATISTICAL METHODS
see Mathematical Statistics

MATHEMATICS–STUDY AND TEACHING
see also Mathematical Models

Ablon, Leon J., et al. Series in Mathematics Modules: Six Modules. Incl. Module 1. Operations on Numbers. 2nd ed. 4.95 (ISBN 0-8465-0240-2); Module 1A. Arithmetic. 2nd ed. 3.95 (ISBN 0-8465-6713-X); Module 2. Operations on Numbers. 2nd ed. 4.95 (ISBN 0-8465-0241-0); Module 3. Linear Equations & Lines. 2nd ed. 4.95 (ISBN 0-8465-0242-9); Module 4. Factoring & Operations on Algebraic Functions. 2nd ed. 4.95 (ISBN 0-8465-0243-7); Module 5. Quadratic Equations & Curves. 2nd ed. 4.95 (ISBN 0-8465-0244-5); Module 6. Basic Trigonometry. 2nd ed. 3.75 (ISBN 0-8465-0260-7); Module M. Medical Dosage Calculations. 2nd ed. 6.95 (ISBN 0-8053-7570-8). LC 72-94408. 1973. instr's guide 3.95 (ISBN 0-8465-0245-3). Benjamin-Cummings.

Adams, Anne & Coble, Chas. Mainstreaming Science & Mathematics. LC 76-50042. (Goodyear Education Ser.). (Illus.). 1977. text ed. 12.95 (ISBN 0-87620-592-9). Goodyear.

Adler, David A. Base Five. LC 74-18325. (Young Math Ser.). (Illus.). (gr. k-3). 1975. 8.95 (ISBN 0-690-00668-3, TYC-J); PLB 8.79 (ISBN 0-690-00669-1). Har-Row.

An Agenda for Action: Recommendations for School Mathematics of the 1980's. 1980. pap. 1.00 (ISBN 0-87353-166-3). NCTM.

Albers, D. J. & Steen, L. A., eds. Teaching Teachers, Teaching Students. 152p. 1981. 12.95 (ISBN 3-7643-3043-0). Birkhauser.

Alberti, Del & Laycock, Mary. The Correlation of Activity-Centered Science & Mathematics. 1975. 8.50 (ISBN 0-918932-07-6). Activity Resources.

Allen, Layman E. & Ross, Joan. IMP (Instructional Math Play) Kits: Individual Solitare Kits. 15.00 (ISBN 0-911624-18-X). Wffn Proof.

Arco Editorial Board. Mathematics: Teaching Area Exam for the National Teacher Exam. 2nd ed. LC 76-3492. (National Teacher Examination Ser.). 1976. pap. 6.00 (ISBN 0-668-01639-6). Arco.

Association for Supervision & Curriculum Development. Changing Curriculum: Mathematics. LC 67-26128. 1967. pap. 2.00 (ISBN 0-87120-005-8, 611-17724). Assn Supervision.

Association Of Teachers Of Mathematics. Mathematical Reflections. (Illus.). 1970. 27.50 (ISBN 0-521-07260-3); pap. 11.50 (ISBN 0-521-09582-4, 582). Cambridge U Pr.

Ballou, Dalene L. & Dublin, Lewis. Easy Steps in Modern Math. pap. 2.95 (ISBN 0-671-17688-9). Monarch Pr.

Bartoo, Grover C., et al. Foundation Mathematics. 3rd ed. (gr. 9). 1968. text ed. 7.72 (ISBN 0-07-003989-5, W). McGraw.

Baur, G. R. & George, L. O. Helping Children Learn Mathematics: A Competency Based Laboratory Approach. LC 75-16772. 1976. 17.95 (ISBN 0-8465-0408-1); instr's guide 3.95 (ISBN 0-8465-0409-X). Benjamin-Cummings.

Begle, E. G. Critical Variables in Mathematics Education: Findings from a Survey of the Empirical Literature. 1979. 8.00 (ISBN 0-88385-430-9). Math Assn.

Bennett, Albert B. & Nelson, Leonard T. Mathematics: An Informal Approach. 1979. instr's man. 5.95 (ISBN 0-205-06519-8, 5665191); avail. instr's man. 5.95 (ISBN 0-205-06541-4, 5665418). Allyn.

Biggs, E. & MacLean, J. Freedom to Learn: An Active Learning Approach to Mathematics. 1969. text ed. 14.00 (ISBN 0-201-00572-7). A-W.

Bley, Nancy S. & Thornton, Carol A. Teaching Mathematics to the Learning Disabled. 350p. 1981. text ed. write for info. (ISBN 0-89443-357-1). Aspen Systems.

Boeker, M. Status of the Beginning Calculus Students in Pre-Calculus College Mathematics: Study Carried Out with Students in Brooklyn College & City College of New York. LC 76-176690. (Columbia University. Teachers College. Contributions to Education: No. 922). Repr. of 1947 ed. 17.50 (ISBN 0-404-55922-0). AMS Pr.

Bond, Elias A. The Professional Treatment of the Subject Matter of Arithmetic for Teacher-Training Institutions. LC 75-176576. (Columbia University. Teachers College. Contributions to Education: No. 525). Repr. of 1934 ed. 17.50 (ISBN 0-404-55525-X). AMS Pr.

Boyd, Elizabeth N. A Diagnostic Study of Student's Difficulties in General Mathematics in First Year College Work. LC 79-176585. (Columbia University. Teachers College. Contributions to Education: No. 798). Repr. of 1940 ed. 17.50 (ISBN 0-404-55798-8). AMS Pr.

Brett, William F., et al. Contemporary College Mathematics. 320p. 1975. text ed. 16.95 (ISBN 0-8299-0038-1). West Pub.

Brissenden, T. H. F. Mathematics Teaching. 1980. text ed. 21.00 (ISBN 0-06-318159-2, IntlDept); pap. text ed. 11.90 (ISBN 0-06-318160-6). Har-Row.

Brush, Lorelei R. Encouraging Girls in Mathematics: The Problems & the Solution. LC 79-55774. (Illus.). 1980. text ed. 16.00 (ISBN 0-89011-542-7). Abt Assoc.

Buechner, Katy & Lowell. File Folder Math: Books A-C, 3 bks. 1977. pap. 15.95 ea.; Set. pap. 36.75 (ISBN 0-88488-153-9); Bk. A. pap. (ISBN 0-88488-141-5); Bk. B. pap. (ISBN 0-88488-142-3); Bk. C. pap. (ISBN 0-88488-143-1). Creative Pubns.

Challenge: A Handbook of Classroom Ideas to Motivate the Teaching of Intermediate Math. (The Spice Ser.). 1975. 6.50 (ISBN 0-89273-116-8). Educ Serv.

Chapman, L. R. The Process of Learning Mathematics. LC 71-178683. 405p. 1972. text ed. 51.00 (ISBN 0-08-016623-7); pap. text ed. 21.00 (ISBN 0-08-017357-8). Pergamon.

Charlesworth, R. & Radeloff, D. J. Experiences in Math for Young Children. LC 77-80039. 1978. pap. text ed. 7.20 (ISBN 0-8273-1660-7); instructor's guide 1.60 (ISBN 0-8273-1661-5). Delmar.

Clack, Alice & Leitch, Carol. Mathamerica, Vols 1 & 2. 1975. pap. 4.95 ea. Vol. 1 (ISBN 0-910974-80-2). Vol. 2 (ISBN 0-910974-81-0). dittomasters ea. vol 10.95 (ISBN 0-686-67478-2). Midwest Pubns.

Cohen, Louis S. How to Teach Eureka! A Discovery Approach to the Basics in Math. new ed. 1976. manual & cassettes 179.50 (ISBN 0-917792-00-9). Math Hse.

Conference on Prospects in Mathematics Education in the 1980's, Virginia, 1978. Prime-Eighty: Proceedings. pap. 3.50 (ISBN 0-88385-429-5). Math Assn.

Corlett, P. N. Practical Programming. 2nd ed. LC 75-161295. (School Mathematics Project Handbooks). (Illus.). 1971. 23.95 (ISBN 0-521-08198-X); pap. 10.95x (ISBN 0-521-09740-1). Cambridge U Pr.

Curatalo, Charles. Teacher-Made Materials for Math. LC 75-17342. 1975. pap. 4.50 (ISBN 0-8224-6755-0). Pitman Learning.

Davis, Philip J. & Hersh, Reuben. The Mathematical Experience. 460p. 1981. 24.00 (ISBN 3-7643-3018-X). Birkhauser.

Dawes, Cynthia G. Early Maths. (Longman Early Childhood Education Ser.). (Illus.). 1977. text ed. 9.95x (ISBN 0-582-25013-7); pap. text ed. 5.50x (ISBN 0-582-25012-9). Longman.

Dean, Peter. Teaching & Learning Mathematics. (The Woburn Educational Ser.). Date not set. 18.50x (ISBN 0-7130-0168-2, Pub by Woburn Pr England). Biblio Dist.

Dubisch, Roy. Teaching of Mathematics from Intermediate Algebra Through First Year Calculus. LC 74-23520. 136p. 1975. Repr. of 1963 ed. 7.50 (ISBN 0-88275-198-0). Krieger.

Duker, Sam. Individualized Instruction in Mathematics. LC 72-5739. 1972. 13.50 (ISBN 0-8108-0533-2). Scarecrow.

Educational Systems Corp. Skills in Mathematics, Bks. 1-2. (Cambridge Skill Power Ser.). 192p. (gr. 10-12). Bk. 1. pap. text ed. 4.15 (ISBN 0-8428-2108-2); Bk. 2. pap. text ed. 4.15 (ISBN 0-8428-2110-4). Cambridge Bk.

Elsgolts, L. E. & Norkin, S. B. Introduction to the Theory & Application of Differential Equations with Deviating Arguments. 1973. 36.00 (ISBN 0-12-237750-8). Acad Pr.

El Tom, M. E. Developing Mathematics in Third World Countries. (North Holland Mathematics Studies: Vol. 33). 1979. 29.50 (ISBN 0-444-85260-3, North Holland). Elsevier.

Fagerstrom, William H. Mathematical Facts & Processes Prerequisite to the Study of Calculus. LC 76-176761. (Columbia University. Teachers College. Contributions to Education: No. 572). Repr. of 1933 ed. 17.50 (ISBN 0-404-55572-1). AMS Pr.

Fang, Joong. Numbers Racket: The Aftermath of New Math. LC 68-8247. 1968. 11.00 (ISBN 0-8046-0138-0). Kennikat.

Far West Laboratory for Educational Research & Development. Minicourse Five: Individualizing Instruction in Mathematics. 1971. pap. 3.80 coordinators' handbook (ISBN 0-02-273680-8); tchrs' handbook 2.55 (ISBN 0-02-273690-5); films & paperbound bks 1545.00 (ISBN 0-02-273650-6). Macmillan.

Fawcett, Harold & Cummins, Kenneth. Teaching of Mathematics: From Counting to Calculus. LC 69-19768. 1970. text ed. 13.95x (ISBN 0-675-09512-3). Merrill.

Feldman, L. Mathematical Learning. 224p. 1969. 25.25 (ISBN 0-677-13250-6). Gordon.

Feurzeig, W., et al. The LOGO Language: Learning Mathematics Through Programming. 1977. pap. text ed. 15.00x (ISBN 0-87567-105-5). Entelek.

Fey, James T. Patterns of Verbal Communication in Mathematics Classes. Bellack, Arno A., ed. LC 74-103135. (Illus.). 1970. text ed. 7.50x (ISBN 0-8077-1342-2). Tchrs Coll.

Fiala, F. Teaching of Mathematics at University Level. LC 77-868935. (Education in Europe Ser). (Orig.). 1970. pap. 7.50x (ISBN 0-245-50321-8). Intl Pubns Serv.

Finkle, Louis J. Math Lesson Plans for Teachers for Assisting Handicapped Children. 383p. 1977. pap. text ed. 10.50 (ISBN 0-8191-0026-9). U Pr of Amer.

For the Teaching of Mathematics, 3 vols. Incl. Vol. 1. Pedagogical Discussions. pap. 3.30 (ISBN 0-685-46932-8); Vol. 2. Psychological Studies, 2 pts. pap. 3.85 (ISBN 0-685-46933-6); Vol. 3. Elementary Mathematics. 133p. pap. 3.85 (ISBN 0-685-46934-4). 1963. Ed Solutions.

Frank, Marjorie. Kids' Stuff Math. LC 74-18907. (The Kids' Stuff Set). (gr. 2-6). 1974. 10.95 (ISBN 0-913916-12-9, IP 12-9). Incentive Pubns.

Freudenthal, H. Mathematics As an Educational Task. LC 72-77874. (Illus.). 680p. 1973. lib. bdg. 39.50 (ISBN 90-277-0235-7, Pub. by Reidel Holland); pap. text ed. 21.00 (ISBN 90-277-0322-1). Kluwer Boston.

Fujii, John N. Puzzles & Graphs. (Illus.). 1966. pap. 2.10 (ISBN 0-87353-085-3). NCTM.

Garritson, Jane. Childarts. (gr. k-4). 1979. 10.35 (ISBN 0-201-02874-3, Sch Div). A-W.

Gattegno, Caleb. Arithmetics. (Illus.). 28p. 1971. pap. 2.15 (ISBN 0-87825-019-0). Ed Solutions.

--The Common Sense of Teaching Mathematics. (Common Sense of Teaching Ser.). (Illus.). 144p. 1974. pap. 5.45 (ISBN 0-87825-024-7). Ed Solutions.

--Notes on the Gattegno Approach to Math. 31p. 1973. 1.65 (ISBN 0-87825-043-3). Ed Solutions.

Glenn, J. A. The Third R: Towards a Numerate Society. 1978. text ed. 11.95 (ISBN 0-06-318075-8, IntlDept); pap. text ed. 6.60 (ISBN 0-06-318076-6, IntlDept). Har-Row.

Gray, A. William & Ulm, Otis M. Mathematics for the College Student: Elementary Concepts. 2nd ed. LC 73-7359. 1975. text ed. 9.95x (ISBN 0-02-474700-9, 47470). Macmillan.

Griffiths, H. B. & Howson, A. G. Mathematics: Society & Curricula. (Illus.). 400p. 1974. 49.50 (ISBN 0-521-20287-6); pap. 17.50x (ISBN 0-521-09892-0). Cambridge U Pr.

Gruver, Howell L. School Mathematics Contests: A Report. LC 68-21511. 1968. pap. 1.70 (ISBN 0-87353-089-6). NCTM.

Guidelines for the Preparation of Teachers of Mathematics, No. 127. 2nd ed. 1981. 4.00 (ISBN 0-87353-177-9). NCTM.

Hailpern, Raoul. Guidebook to Departments in the Mathematical Sciences. 6th ed. 99p. 1975. pap. text ed. 3.00 (ISBN 0-88385-421-X). Math Assn.

Heddens, James. Today's Mathematics. 4th ed. 1980. pap. text ed. 15.95 (ISBN 0-574-23095-5, 13-6095); instr. guide 1.95 (ISBN 0-574-23096-3, 13-6096). SRA.

Heintz, Ruth. Mathematics for Elementary Teachers: A Content Approach. LC 79-18727. (Illus.). 512p. 1980. text ed. 17.95 (ISBN 0-201-03227-9); instructor's manual 2.50 (ISBN 0-201-03228-7). A-W.

Hellmich, Eugene W. The Mathematics in Certain Elementary Social Studies in Secondary Schools & Colleges. LC 12-32085. (Columbia University. Teachers College. Contributions to Education: No. 706). Repr. of 1937 ed. 17.50 (ISBN 0-404-55706-6). AMS Pr.

Henle, James M. Numerous Numerals. LC 75-19347. 1975. pap. 2.40 (ISBN 0-87353-079-9). NCTM.

Hess, Adrien L. Mathematics Project Handbook. LC 77-8611. 1977. pap. 2.25 (ISBN 0-87353-118-3). NCTM.

Hodges, Raymond W., et al. Understanding Mathematics. Smith, Barry M., ed. LC 73-80234. (Basic Studies Program). (Illus.). 166p. 1973. pap. text ed. 8.40 (ISBN 0-913310-30-1). PAR Inc.

Howard, Homer. Mathematics Teachers' Views on Certain Issues in the Teaching of Mathematics. LC 76-176883. (Columbia University. Teachers College. Contributions to Education: No. 827). Repr. of 1941 ed. 17.50 (ISBN 0-404-55827-5). AMS Pr.

Howell, Daisy, et al. Activities for Teaching Mathematics to Low Achievers. LC 73-93330. (Illus.). 1974. pap. 1.00 (ISBN 0-87805-052-3). U Pr of Miss.

Howes, Virgil M. Individualizing Instruction in Science & Mathematics: Selected Readings on Programs, Practices, & Uses of Technology. (Illus.). 1970. pap. text ed. 5.25x (ISBN 0-02-357480-1). Macmillan.

Howett, Jerry. Building Basic Skills in Mathematics. (Orig.). 1981. pap. 4.95 (ISBN 0-8092-5877-3). Contemp Bks.

Howson, A. G., et al. Curriculum Development in Mathematics. 200p. Date not set. 49.50 (ISBN 0-521-23767-X). Cambridge U Pr.

Hufendick, Lawrence H. Mathematics for the Liberal Arts Student. 163p. (Preliminary ed.). 1971. 5.00 (ISBN 0-910268-03-7); pap. 3.00 (ISBN 0-910268-04-5). Books.

Immerzeel, George & Ockenga, Earl. Calculator Activities for the Classroom: Book 2. Preiss, Irene, ed. 1977. wkbk. 7.25 (ISBN 0-88488-109-1). Creative Pubns.

--Calculator Activities for the Classroom: Book 1. Preiss, Irene, ed. 1977. wkbk. 7.25 (ISBN 0-88488-108-3). Creative Pubns.

Jacobs, Russell F. Problem Solving with the Calculator. (gr. 6-9). 1977. pap. text ed. 4.25 (ISBN 0-918272-00-9); tchr's guide with ans. key 0.75 (ISBN 0-918272-01-7); answer key 0.75 (ISBN 0-918272-02-5). Jacobs.

Jelks, Peggie A. Much Ado About Math: Ideas & Activities for Math. LC 81-65610. (Illus.). 250p. 1981. perfect bound 14.95 (ISBN 0-88247-596-7). R & E Res Assocs.

Johnson, Donovan A. & Rising, Gerald R. Guidelines for Teaching Mathematics. 2nd ed. 560p. 1972. 19.95x (ISBN 0-534-00189-0). Wadsworth Pub.

Johnson, Paul B. From Sticks & Stones: Personal Adventures in Mathematics. LC 74-23322. (Illus.). 552p. 1975. text ed. 17.95 (ISBN 0-574-19115-1, 13-6005); instr's guide avail. (ISBN 0-574-19116-X, 13-6006). SRA.

Kempe, A. B. How to Draw a Straight Line. LC 77-6669. 1977. 6.75 (ISBN 0-87353-120-5). NCTM.

Kepner, Henry S., Jr. & Johnson, David R. Guidelines for the Tutor of Mathematics. LC 77-6426. 1977. pap. 1.70 (ISBN 0-87353-030-6). NCTM.

Kidd, Kenneth P., et al. The Laboratory Approach to Mathematics. 1970. pap. text ed. 11.95 (ISBN 0-574-34790-9, 3-4790). SRA.

Kimball, Richard L. You...& Me. (Illus.). 62p. 1972. tchrs ed. 3.95 (ISBN 0-912990-06-6). Ed Sci.

Kline, Morris. Why the Professor Can't Teach: Mathematics & the Dilemma of American Undergraduate Education. LC 76-62777. (Illus.). 256p. 1977. 10.00 (ISBN 0-312-87867-2). St Martin.

Kogelman, Stanley & Warren, Joseph. Mind Over Math. 1978. 8.95 (ISBN 0-8037-5658-5). Dial.

Kristiensson, Margareta. Matematikkunskaper Lgr. Sixty-Two, Lgr. Sixty-Nine. (Goteborg Studies in Educational Sciences: No. 29). (Orig., Swedish.). 1979. pap. text ed. 11.25x (ISBN 91-7346-067-2). Humanities.

Lamon, William E., ed. Learning & the Nature of Mathematics. LC 75-183335. 236p. 1972. pap. text ed. 10.95 (ISBN 0-574-18420-1, 13-1420). SRA.

Laycock, Mary & Watson, Gene. The Fabric of Mathematics: A Resource Book for Teachers. (Illus.). 1975. 15.95 (ISBN 0-918932-11-4). Activity Resources.

Lieberman, Arthur. College Mathematics for Business & the Social Sciences. (Mathematics Ser.). 618p. 1982. text ed. 19.95 (ISBN 0-8185-0501-X). Brooks-Cole.

Lindquist, Mary M. Selected Issues in Mathematics Education. 1981. pap. 15.00 (ISBN 0-8211-1114-0). NCTM.

Lindquist, Mary M., ed. Selected Issues in Mathematics Education. LC 80-82903. (National Society for the Education Series on Contemporary Education Issues). 250p. 1981. text ed. 15.75 (ISBN 0-8211-1114-0); text ed. 15.75 (ISBN 0-686-77731-X). McCutchan.
Long, John J. & Morris, Morton M. Tune in to Early Math: Teacher Guide. 1978. ringbound 13.80x (ISBN 0-87076-325-3). Stanwix.
Lyon, Lorraine D. & Karplus, Elizabeth. Math in & Out of the Mainstream. 112p. (Orig.). 1980. pap. text ed. 7.00 (ISBN 0-87879-245-7). Acad Therapy.
McCormick, Clarence. The Teaching of General Mathematics in the Secondary Schools of the United States: A Study of the Development & Present Status of General Mathematics. LC 70-178806. (Columbia University. Teachers College. Contributions to Education: No. 386). Repr. of 1929 ed. 17.50 (ISBN 0-404-55386-9). AMS Pr.
Mahaffey, Michael L. & Perrodin, Alex F. Teaching Elementary School Mathematics. LC 76-138646. (Illus.). 375p. 1973. text ed. 13.50 (ISBN 0-87581-084-5). Peacock Pubs.
Marjoram, D. T. Teaching Mathematics. 1974. text ed. 17.50x (ISBN 0-435-50600-5). Heinemann Ed.
Marsh, L. G. Let's Explore Mathematics, 4 bks. Incl. Bk. 1. (Illus.). 96p. (gr. 6). 1964. pap. text ed. 2.45 (ISBN 0-668-01511-X); Bk. 2. (Illus.). 112p. (gr. 7). 1964. pap. text ed. 2.45 (ISBN 0-668-01512-8); Bk. 3. (Illus.). 112p. (gr. 8). 1964. pap. text ed. 2.45 (ISBN 0-668-01513-6); Bk. 4. (Illus.). 96p. (gr. 9). 1968. pap. 2.45 (ISBN 0-668-01825-9); Teacher's Guide: Children Explore Mathematics. 152p. 1967. 3.00 (ISBN 0-668-02077-6). LC 66-22887. (YA) Arco.
Mason, Robert D. Plaid for College Mathematics: With Applications in Business & Economics. 1976. pap. 5.50 (ISBN 0-256-01267-9, 15-0498-00). Learning Syst.
Math Made Easy. Date not set. 4.95 (ISBN 0-686-75976-1, 2503). Barron.
Mathematics Textbooks, 7 bks. Incl. Bk. 1. Study of Numbers up to 20. 102p. pap. text ed. 1.65 (ISBN 0-87825-011-5); Bk. 2. Study of Numbers up to 1,000. 147p. pap. text ed. 2.50 (ISBN 0-87825-012-3); Bk. 3. Applied Arithmetic. 53p. pap. text ed. 1.65 (ISBN 0-87825-013-1); Bk. 4. Fractions, Decimals, Percentages. 65p. pap. text ed. 1.65 (ISBN 0-87825-014-X); Bk. 5. Study of Numbers. 83p. pap. text ed. 1.65 (ISBN 0-87825-015-8); Bk. 6. Applied Mathematics. 104p; Bk. 7. Algebra & Geometry. 92p. pap. text ed. O.S.I (ISBN 0-87825-017-4). Ed Solutions.
Measurement in School Mathematics, 1976 Yearbook. LC 75-43533. 1976. 11.25 (ISBN 0-87353-018-7). NCTM.
Miklos, Mary O. Preparation for Criterion-Referenced Tests: A Brief Review of Mathematical Competencies for Teachers of Middle Grades. 110p. (Orig.). 1981. pap. text ed. 7.50 (ISBN 0-8191-1545-2). U Pr of Amer.
Milnor, John W. & Stasheff, James D. Characteristic Classes. LC 72-4050. (Annals of Mathematics Studies: No. 76). 250p. 1974. 20.00 (ISBN 0-691-08122-0). Princeton U Pr.
Moore, David S. & Yackel, James W. Applicable Finite Mathematics. 432p. 1974. text ed. 20.50 (ISBN 0-395-17771-5); instructors' manual 2.15 (ISBN 0-395-17813-4). HM.
Mueller, Francis J. Essential Mathematics for College Students. 3rd ed. (Illus.). 320p. 1976. pap. 16.95 (ISBN 0-13-286518-1). P-H.
National Academy Of Sciences - Division Of Mathematics Committee On Support Of Research In Mathematical Sciences. Mathematical Sciences: Undergraduate Education. 1968. pap. 5.50 (ISBN 0-309-01682-7). Natl Acad Pr.
National Council of Teachers of Mathematics. Enrichment Mathematics for the Grades, 27th Yearbk. LC 63-14060. 1963. 14.60 (ISBN 0-87353-005-5); pap. 10.70 (ISBN 0-87353-006-3). NCTM.
--Evaluation in Mathematics, 26th Yearbk. Johnson, Donovan A., ed. LC 61-11906. 1961. 12.40 (ISBN 0-87353-004-7). NCTM.
--Experiences in Mathematical Ideas, 2 vols. LC 71-135151. (Illus.). (gr. 5-8). 1970. incl. teaching pkgs. 15.75 ea. Vol. 1 (ISBN 0-87353-052-7). Vol. 2 (ISBN 0-87353-053-5). NCTM.
--A History of Mathematics Education in the United States & Canada, 32nd Yearbk. LC 71-105864. 1970. 16.90 (ISBN 0-87353-012-8). NCTM.
--Insights into Modern Mathematics, 23rd Yearbk. Wren, F. Lynwood, ed. 1957. 14.60 (ISBN 0-87353-001-2). NCTM.
--Learning of Mathematics, Its Theory & Practice, 21st Yearbk. 1953. 14.00 (ISBN 0-87353-000-4). NCTM.
--Problem Solving in School Mathematics, 1980 Yearbook. 1980. 13.75 (ISBN 0-87353-162-0). NCTM.
New Trends in Mathematics Teaching, Nineteen Seventy-Nine, Vol. 4. 1979. pap. 20.50 (ISBN 92-3-101546-X, U902, UNESCO). Unipub.
Noller, Ruth B., et al. Creative Problem Solving in Mathematics. (Illus.). 1978. tchr's idea bk. 1.75 (ISBN 0-914634-55-0). DOK Pubs.
Olgilvie, Eric & Wood, Anthony. Making Changes-Mathematics: Curriculum Enrichment Units for the Gifted & Academically Talented. (Special Education Ser.). (Illus.). 1980. 59.00 (ISBN 0-89568-229-X). Spec Learn Corp.
Olson, Alton T. Mathematics Through Paper Folding. LC 75-16115. 1975. pap. 2.25 (ISBN 0-87353-076-4). NCTM.
Organizing for Mathematics Instruction: 1977 Yearbook. LC 77-23294. 1977. 11.25 (ISBN 0-87353-019-5). NCTM.
Osborne, Alan, ed. An In-Service Handbook for Mathematics Education. LC 77-7287. 1977. pap. 6.20 (ISBN 0-87353-119-1). NCTM.
Overview & Analysis of School Mathematics. LC 75-34807. 1975. pap. 3.40 (ISBN 0-87353-146-9). NCTM.
Pascoe, L. C. Teach Yourself New Mathematics. (Orig.). 1979. pap. 4.95 (ISBN 0-679-12326-1). McKay.
Payne, Joseph N. & Goodman, F. L. Mathematics Education: Index & Bibliography, 2 Vols. 1965. Set. pap. 3.10 (ISBN 0-87506-017-X). Campus.
Philadelphia Suburban School Study Council. Improving Today's Curriculum for Tomorrow's Challenges. LC 64-20044. 1964. pap. text ed. 1.50x (ISBN 0-8134-0064-3, 64). Interstate.
Polya, Gyorgy. How to Solve It. 1971. 15.50x (ISBN 0-691-08097-6); pap. 4.95 (ISBN 0-691-02356-5). Princeton U Pr.
Priorities in School Mathematics: An Executive Summary. 1981. pap. 1.00 (ISBN 0-87353-174-4). NCTM.
Reisman, Fredericka K. & Kauffman, Samuel H. Teaching Mathematics to Children with Special Needs. (Special Education Ser.). 336p. 1980. text ed. 18.50x (ISBN 0-675-08175-0). Merrill.
Resnick, Lauren B. & Ford, Wendy W. The Psychology of Mathematics for Instruction. LC 80-29106. 272p. 1981. text ed. 24.95x (ISBN 0-89859-029-9). L Erlbaum Assocs.
A Rhythmic Approach to Mathematics. LC 75-10555. (Classics in Mathematics Education Ser: Vol. 5). 1975. 8.40 (ISBN 0-87353-040-3). NCTM.
Rich, Barnett. Mathematics for the College Boards: PSAT, SAT. (Illus., Orig.). (gr. 10-12). 1967. wkbk. 7.75 (ISBN 0-87720-201-X). AMSCO Sch.
Roberts, Keith & Michels, Leo. Mathematics for Allied Health Occupations. (Mathematics Ser.). 442p. 1982. pap. 15.95 (ISBN 0-8185-0478-1). Brooks-Cole.
Robinson, Arthur E. The Professional Education of Elementary Teachers in the Field of Arithmetic. LC 78-177196. (Columbia University. Teachers College. Contributions to Education: No. 672). Repr. of 1936 ed. 17.50 (ISBN 0-404-55672-8). AMS Pr.
Roper, Ann. Metric Recipes for the Classroom. 1977. 3.95 (ISBN 0-88488-084-2). Creative Pubns.
Rosenberg, R. Robert. College Mathematics for Accounting & Business Administration. 2nd ed. 240p. 1972. text ed. 13.50 (ISBN 0-07-053730-5, G); tchr's ed. 12.95 (ISBN 0-07-053731-3). McGraw.
Sage, Edwin R. Problem Solving with the Computer. (Illus.). 244p. (Orig.). 1969. pap. 9.95 (ISBN 0-87567-030-X). Entelek.
Santos, Mary G. Math Can Be Easy. 120p. (Orig.). 1980. pap. 8.00 (ISBN 0-914562-10-X). Merriam-Eddy.
Schaaf, William L. Course for Teachers of Junior High School Mathematics. LC 77-177808. (Columbia University. Teachers College. Contributions to Education: No. 313). Repr. of 1928 ed. 17.50 (ISBN 0-404-55313-3). AMS Pr.
Schall, William E. Activity-Oriented Mathematics. 1976. pap. text ed. write for info. (ISBN 0-87150-173-2, PWS 1392). Prindle.
Schreiner, Nikki B. Games & Aides for Teaching Math. (Illus., Orig.). (gr. k-8). 1972. pap. 5.95 (ISBN 0-918932-21-1). Activity Resources.
Seidlin, Joseph. Critical Study of the Teaching of Elementary College Mathematics. LC 77-177796. (Columbia University. Teachers College. Contributions to Education: No. 482). Repr. of 1931 ed. 17.50 (ISBN 0-404-55482-2). AMS Pr.
Sentlowitz, Michael & Trivisone, Margaret. Dice & Dots. (gr. 1-6). 1979. pap. text ed. 7.95 (ISBN 0-201-06982-2, Sch Div). A-W.
Servais, W. & Varga, T., eds. Teaching School Mathematics: A UNESCO Source Bk. (Illus.). 308p. (Orig.). 1972. pap. 7.50 (ISBN 92-3-100884-6, UNESCO). Unipub.
Shuard, H. & Quadling, D. Teachers of Math. 1980. text ed. 18.35 (ISBN 0-06-318174-6, IntlDept); pap. text ed. 9.25 (ISBN 0-06-318175-4). Har-Row.
Shumway, Richard, ed. Research in Mathematics Education. National Council of Teachers of Mathematics. 1980. 27.00 (ISBN 0-87353-163-9). NCTM.
Silbert, Jerry, et al. Direct Instruction Mathematics. (Illus., Orig.). 1981. pap. text ed. 19.95 (ISBN 0-675-08047-9). Merrill.
Smith, David E. The Teaching of Arithmetic. (Educational Ser.). 1909. Repr. 15.00 (ISBN 0-685-43645-4). Norwood Edns.
Smith, M. K. Professional Training in Mathematics. rev. ed. 1979. Repr. of 1976 ed. 2.20 (ISBN 0-685-91809-2, PT). Am Math.
Sobel, Max & Maletsky, Evan. Teaching Mathematics: A Source Book for Aids, Activities, & Strategies. (Illus.). 288p. 1975. pap. text ed. 12.95 (ISBN 0-13-894121-1). P-H.
Souviney, Randall. Solving Problems Kids Care About. (Illus.). 176p. (Orig.). 1981. pap. 9.95 (ISBN 0-8302-8653-5). Goodyear.
Soviet Studies in the Psychology of Learning & Teaching Mathematics. Incl. Bk. 1. The Learning of Mathematical Concepts (ISBN 0-87353-148-5); Bk. 2. The Structure of Mathematical Abilities (ISBN 0-87353-149-3); Bk. 3. Problem Solving in Arithmetic & Algebra (ISBN 0-87353-150-7); Bk. 4. Problem Solving in Geometry (ISBN 0-87353-151-5); Bk. 5. The Development of Spatial Abilities (ISBN 0-87353-152-3); Bk. 6. Instruction in Problem Solving (ISBN 0-87353-153-1); Bk. 7. Children's Capacity for Learning Mathematics (ISBN 0-87353-154-X); Bk. 8. Methods of Teaching Mathematics (ISBN 0-87353-155-8); Bk. 9. Problem-Solving Processes of Mentally Retarded Children (ISBN 0-87353-156-6); Bk. 10. Teaching Mathematics to Mentally Retarded Children (ISBN 0-87353-157-4); Bk. 11. Analysis & Synthesis As Problem-Solving Methods (ISBN 0-87353-158-2); Bk. 12. Problems of Instruction (ISBN 0-87353-159-0); Bk. 13. Analyses of Reasoning Processes (ISBN 0-87353-160-4); Bk. 14. Teaching Arithmetic in the Elementary School (ISBN 0-87353-161-2). 1969. pap. 4.00 ea; pap. 22.50 set, vol. 7-14 (ISBN 0-87353-147-7). NCTM.
Stanley, Julian C., et al, eds. Mathematical Talent, Discovery, Description, & Development. LC 73-19342. (Illus.). 234p. 1974. 15.00x (ISBN 0-8018-1585-1); pap. 4.45x (ISBN 0-8018-1592-4). Johns Hopkins.
Storms, Earl R. Math Made Easy. 1972. 2.50x (ISBN 0-88323-110-7, 198). Richards Pub.
Studies in Mathematics Education, Vol. 2. 179p. 1981. pap. 9.25 (ISBN 92-3-101905-8, U1101, UNESCO). Unipub.
Studies in Mathmematics Education. 129p. 1980. pap. 7.00 (ISBN 92-3-101779-9, U 1013, UNESCO). Unipub.
Success in Mathematics. (Success Studybooks Ser.). (Illus.). 609p. 1975. 6.95 (ISBN 0-7195-2901-8). Transatlantic.
Sund, Robert & Picard, Anthony J. Behavioral Objectives & Evaluation Measures: Science & Mathematics. LC 74-161434. pap. text ed. 4.95x (ISBN 0-675-09761-4, 9761). Merrill.
Swabb, Barbara S. & Thomason, Mary E. Mathematics Bulletin Boards. 1971. pap. 2.95 (ISBN 0-8224-4420-8). Pitman Learning.
Swetz, Frank, ed. Socialist Mathematics Education. LC 78-68025. 1979. pap. 14.00 (ISBN 0-917574-04-4). Burgundy Pr.
Tammadge, A. & Starr, P. A Parents' Guide to School Mathematics. LC 75-46135. (School Mathematics Project Handbooks Ser.). 1977. 21.50 (ISBN 0-521-21108-5); pap. 6.50 (ISBN 0-521-29169-0). Cambridge U Pr.
Thomason, Mary E. Modern Math Games, Activities & Puzzles. (Illus., Orig.). 1970. pap. 4.50 (ISBN 0-8224-4490-9). Pitman Learning.
Thyer, Maggs. Teaching Mathematics to Young Children. (Winston Mine Editions). 1971. text ed. 4.68 (ISBN 0-685-33349-3, HoltC). HR&W.
Tobias, Sheila. Overcoming Math Anxiety. (Illus.). 1978. 12.95 (ISBN 0-393-06439-5). Norton.
Travers, Kenneth J., et al. Mathematics Teaching. 1977. text ed. 20.95 scp (ISBN 0-06-045233-1, HarpC). Har-Row.
Triola, Mario F. A Survey of Mathematics. LC 74-27627. 1973. 18.95 (ISBN 0-8465-7555-8, 57555). Benjamin-Cummings.
Underhill, Robert G. Teaching Elementary School Mathematics. 3rd ed. 1981. text ed. 14.95 (ISBN 0-675-09998-6); instr's. manual 3.95 (ISBN 0-686-69502-X). Merrill.
University of Oregon. Didactics & Mathematics. 1978. 12.95 (ISBN 0-88488-088-5). Creative Pubns.
Wallace, Pearlena S., ed. Teaching Mathematics Through the Multisensory Approach: A Research Perspective in the Elementary School. 1977. 5.95 (ISBN 0-8059-2396-9). Dorrance.
Wardle, M. E., ed. From Problem to Program. (School Mathematics Project Computing Ser). (Illus.). (gr. 8-12). 1971. 16.95 (ISBN 0-521-08301-X); pap. 6.95 (ISBN 0-521-09684-7). Cambridge U Pr.
Washington, Allyn J. Introductory Topics from Arithmetic. LC 73-90823. (Modules in Technical Mathematics: No. 1). 1974. pap. 5.95 (ISBN 0-8465-8613-4, 58613). Benjamin-Cummings.
Weiss, Sol. Elementary Mathematics: Teaching Suggestions & Strategies. LC 77-28616. (Illus.). 1978. pap. text ed. write for info. (ISBN 0-87150-251-8, PWS 2062). Prindle.
Wenninger, Magnus J. Polyhedron Models for the Classroom. (Illus.). 1975. pap. 2.10 (ISBN 0-87353-083-7). NCTM.
Wittmann, E. Grundfragen Des Mathematikunterrichts. 202p. (Ger.). 1978. pap. 13.50 (ISBN 3-528-48332-6). Birkhauser.

MATHEMATICS–STUDY AND TEACHING–AUDIO-VISUAL AIDS

Blazek, Ron. Influencing Students Toward Media Center Use. LC 75-26769. (Studies in Librarianship Ser: No. 5). 238p. 1976. pap. text ed. 7.00 (ISBN 0-8389-0201-4). ALA.
Crowhurst, Norman E. Problem Solving Arts: Part Three Syllabus. 1978. pap. text ed. 10.45 (ISBN 0-89420-040-2, 256130); cassette recordings 196.20 (ISBN 0-89420-177-8, 256090). Natl Book.
Lenchner, George. The Overhead Projector in the Mathematics Classroom. LC 74-23237. 1974. pap. 2.00 (ISBN 0-87353-080-2). NCTM.
Math House Proficiency Review Tapes: Applications Involving Measurement, Unit C. (YA) (gr. 7 up). 1980. manual & cassettes 179.50 (ISBN 0-917792-05-X). Math Hse.
Smith, Seaton E., Jr. Bulletin Board Ideas for Elementary & Middle School Mathematics. LC 77-5567. 1977. pap. 4.00 (ISBN 0-87353-116-7). NCTM.
Soracco, Lionel J., Jr. Math House Proficiency Review Tapes: Applications Involving Money, Unit D. (YA) (gr. 7 up). 1980. manual & cassettes 179.50 (ISBN 0-917792-06-8). Math Hse.
--Math House Proficiency Review Tapes: Operations with Decimals & Percent, Unit B. (YA) (gr. 7 up). 1980. manual & cassettes 179.50 (ISBN 0-917792-04-1). Math Hse.
Sorracco, Lionel J., Jr. Math House Proficiency Review Tapes: Operations with Whole Numbers & Fractions, Unit A. (YA) (gr. 7 up). 1980. manual & cassettes 179.50 (ISBN 0-917792-03-3). Math Hse.

MATHEMATICS–STUDY AND TEACHING (ELEMENTARY)

Adams, Anne, et al, eds. Mainstreaming Science & Mathematics. Coble, Charles & Hounshell, Paul. LC 76-50042. (Goodyear Education Ser.). (Illus.). 1976. pap. text ed. 10.95 (ISBN 0-87620-599-6). Goodyear.
Adams, Sam, et al. Teaching Mathematics: With Emphasis on the Diagnostic Approach. (Illus.). 1977. pap. text ed. 13.50 scp (ISBN 0-06-040164-8, HarpC). Har-Row.
--Teaching Mathematics: With Emphasis on the Diagnostic Approach. (Illus.). 1977. pap. text ed. 13.50 scp (ISBN 0-06-040164-8, HarpC). Har-Row.
Aichele, Douglas B., ed. Mathematics Teacher Education. 64p. 1978. pap. 4.50 (ISBN 0-686-63708-9, 1618-1-06). NEA.
Ashlock, Robert B. & Herman, Wayne L., Jr. Current Research in Elementary School Mathematics. (Illus.). 480p. 1970. pap. text ed. 10.95 (ISBN 0-02-304240-0, 30424). Macmillan.
Association of Teachers of Mathematics. Notes on Mathematics for Children. LC 76-14026. (Illus.). 1977. 28.95 (ISBN 0-521-20970-6); pap. 10.50 (ISBN 0-521-29015-5). Cambridge U Pr.
--Notes on Mathematics in Primary Schools. 1967. pap. 9.95x (ISBN 0-521-09440-2). Cambridge U Pr.
Ballew, Hunter. Teaching Children Mathematics. LC 73-75000. 1973. text ed. 18.95 (ISBN 0-675-08982-4). Merrill.
Baratta-Lorton, Mary. Mathematics Their Way. (gr. k-2). 1976. tchr's ed 20.00 (ISBN 0-201-04320-3, Sch Div). A-W.
Bausell, R. Barker, et al. The Bausell Home Learning Guide: Teach Your Child Math. 356p. 1981. text ed. 12.95 (ISBN 0-7216-1597-X). Saunders.
Bell, Frederick. Teaching Elementary School Mathematics, Methods & Content for Grades K-8. 1980. pap. text ed. write for info. (ISBN 0-697-06018-7). Wm C Brown.

Bell, Max S., et al. Algebraic & Arithmetic Structures: A Concrete Approach for Elementary School Teachers. LC 75-2807. (Illus.). 1976. text ed. 16.95 (ISBN 0-02-902270-3). Free Pr.

Billstein, R., et al. A Problem Solving Approach to Mathematics for Elementary School Teachers. 1981. text ed. 19.95 (ISBN 0-8053-0851-2); instr.'s manual 3.95 (ISBN 0-8053-0852-0). A-W.

Billstein, Richard, et al. A Problem-Solving Approach to Mathematics for Elementary School Teachers. 1981. 19.95 (ISBN 0-8053-0851-2). Benjamin-Cummings.

Bitter, et al. Classroom Management Guide, Grade 2. (McGraw-Hill Mathematics Ser.). 1981. 1.28 (ISBN 0-07-006092-4). McGraw.

Bitter, Gary G., et al. One Step at a Time. LC 77-82666. 1977. pap. text ed. 15.00 (ISBN 0-88436-419-4). EMC.

Blum, Peter. Everybody Counts: A T. A. Self-Help Book for Math Aversion. LC 81-80247. 54p. (Orig.). 1981. pap. 6.95 (ISBN 0-9605756-0-X). Math Counsel Inst.

Bosstick, Maurice & Cable, John L. Patterns in the Sand: An Exploration in Mathematics. 2nd ed. (Illus.). 1975. text ed. 13.95x (ISBN 0-02-471960-9); ans. bk free (ISBN 0-02-471970-6). Macmillan.

Callahan, Leroy G. & Glennon, Vincent J. Elementary School Mathematics: Guide to Current Research. 4th ed. LC 75-29896. 152p. 1975. pap. 5.00 (ISBN 0-87120-076-7, 611-75056). Assn Supervision.

Cameron, A. J. Mathematical Enterprises for Schools. 1966. 7.50 (ISBN 0-08-011833-X). Pergamon.

Caravella, Joseph R. Minicalculators in the Classroom. 64p. 1977. pap. 3.50 (ISBN 0-686-63710-0, 1812-5-06). NEA.

Cathcart, W. George. The Mathematics Laboratory: Readings from the Arithmetic Teacher. LC 77-341. 1977. pap. 6.20 (ISBN 0-87353-073-X). NCTM.

Choat, E. Mathematics & the Primary School Curriculum. 128p. 1980. pap. text ed. 18.75x (ISBN 0-85633-206-2, NFER). Humanities.

Choat, Ernest. Children's Acquisition of Mathemathics. (General Ser.). (Illus.). 1978. pap. text ed. 14.50x (ISBN 0-685-90799-6, NFER). Humanities.

Condorcet, Jean A. Moyens D'apprendre a Compter Surement et Avec Facilite. 134p. 1981. Repr. of 1798 ed. lib. bdg. 65.00 (ISBN 0-8287-1458-4). Clearwater Pub.

Copeland, Richard W. How Children Learn Mathematics. 3rd ed. (Illus.). 1978. text ed. 16.95 (ISBN 0-02-324780-0). Macmillan.

--Mathematics & the Elementary Teacher. 3rd ed. LC 75-5044. (Illus.). 400p. 1976. text ed. 14.95 (ISBN 0-7216-2697-1). HR&W.

Crouch, R., et al. Preparatory Mathematics for Elementary Teachers. 595p. 1965. text ed. 13.50x (ISBN 0-471-18913-8, Pub. by Wiley). Krieger.

Cullen, C., et al. Fundamentals of Math, Vols. 1 & 2. (gr. 9-12). 1981. pap. text ed. 6.95 ea. Vol. 1 (ISBN 0-8120-2501-6). Vol. 2 (ISBN 0-8120-2508-3). Barron.

Cumulative Index: The Arithmetic Teacher, 1954-1973. LC 56-37587. 1974. pap. 8.40 (ISBN 0-87353-027-6). NCTM.

Dacey, John. Where the World Is, Teaching Basic Skills Outdoors. (Illus.). 192p. (Orig.). 1981. pap. 10.95 (ISBN 0-8302-9605-0). Goodyear.

D'Augustine, Charles H. Multiple Methods of Teaching Mathematics in the Elementary School. 2nd ed. (Illus.). 400p. 1973. pap. text ed. 17.50 scp (ISBN 0-06-041546-0, HarpC); instructor's manual free (ISBN 0-06-361544-4). Har-Row.

Devine, Donald F. & Kaufman, Jerome E. Mathematics for Elementary Education. LC 73-14692. 609p. 1973. 21.95 (ISBN 0-471-20969-4). Wiley.

Devine, Donald F. & Kaufmann, Jerome E. Elementary Mathematics. LC 76-24805. 1977. text ed. 22.95 (ISBN 0-471-20970-8). Wiley.

Dienes, Zoltan P. Experimental Study of Mathematics Learning. 1963. text ed. 9.25x (ISBN 0-09-068650-0). Humanities.

Dubisch, Roy. Basic Concepts of Mathematics for Elementary Teachers. 2nd ed. LC 80-19446. (Mathematics Ser.). (Illus.). 483p. 1981. write for info. (ISBN 0-201-03170-1). A-W.

Eicholz, Robert, et al. Answer Booklet. (Mathematics in Our World Ser.). 1981. Grade 3. pap. text ed. write for info. (201-15933); Grade 4. pap. text ed. write for info. (201-15934); Grade 5. pap. text ed. write for info. (201-15935); Grade 6. pap. text ed. write for info. (201-15936); Grade 7. pap. text ed. write for info. (201-15937); Grade 8. pap. text ed. write for info. (201-15938). A-W.

--Team Binder: Includes Teacher's Edition & Teacher's Resource Book. (Mathematics in Our World Ser.). 1981. Grade K. pap. text ed. write for info. (201-15970); Grade 1. pap. text ed. write for info. (201-15971); Grade 2. pap. text ed. write for info. (201-15972); Grade 3. pap. text ed. write for info. (201-15973). A-W.

--Team Binder: Includes Teacher's Edition & Teacher's Resource Book. (Mathematics in Our World Ser.). 1981. Grade 4. pap. text ed. write for info. (201-15974); Grade 5. pap. text ed. write for info. (201-15975); Grade 6. pap. text ed. write for info. (201-15976); Grade 7. pap. text ed. write for info. (201-15977); Grade 8. pap. text ed. write for info. (201-15978). A-W.

Eicholz, Robert E., et al. Investigating School Mathematics Primer. (Investigating School Math Ser.). (gr. 1-6). 1973. pap. text ed. 3.92 (ISBN 0-201-01290-1, Sch Div); tchr's. ed. 11.84 (ISBN 0-201-01291-X). A-W.

--Investigating School Mathematics, Bk. 8. (ISM Ser.). (gr. 8). 1974. text ed. 12.32 (ISBN 0-201-01280-4, Sch Div); tchr's ed. 16.00 (ISBN 0-201-01281-2); wkbk. 3.52 (ISBN 0-201-01282-0). A-W.

Evans, Dorothy. Mathematics: Friend or Foe? (Classroom Close-Ups Ser.). 1977. pap. text ed. 8.95x (ISBN 0-04-372023-4). Allen Unwin.

Fletcher, H. & Howell, A. A. Mathematics with Understanding. Vol. 1. 19.50 (ISBN 0-08-015657-6); Vol. 2. 18.75 (ISBN 0-08-016745-4); Vol. 1. pap. 9.75 (ISBN 0-08-015656-8). Pergamon.

Forbes, Jack E. & Eicholz, Robert E. Mathematics for Elementary Teachers. LC 75-137839. (Mathematics Ser.). 1971. text ed. 16.95 (ISBN 0-201-01853-5); instr's manual 2.50 (ISBN 0-201-01854-3). A-W.

Glenn, J. A. Teaching Primary Mathematics: Strategy & Evaluation. 1977. text ed. 9.50 (ISBN 0-06-318071-5, IntlDept); pap. text ed. 6.65 (ISBN 0-06-318072-3, IntlDept). Har-Row.

Glennon, Vincent J. & Callahan, Leroy G. Elementary School Mathematics: A Guide to Current Research. LC 75-29896. 1975. pap. 6.25 (ISBN 0-87120-076-7). NCTM.

Glennon, Vincent J., ed. The Mathematical Education of Exceptional Children & Youth: An Interdisciplinary Approach. 1981. 28.00 (ISBN 0-87353-171-X). NCTM.

Goodwin, Irene & Silvers, Ruth. Polka Dotted Pencil Pushers: Math. LC 79-63129. 156p. (Orig.). 1979. pap. 8.95 (ISBN 0-932970-08-7). Prinit Pr.

Grossnickle, F. E. & Brueckner, L. J. Discovering Meanings in Elementary School Mathematics. 6th ed. LC 72-84402. 1973. 18.95 (ISBN 0-03-003291-1, HoltC). HR&W.

Hannigan, Irene L. Math Centers You Can Make. LC 78-72075. (Makemaster Bk.). 1979. pap. 5.95 (ISBN 0-8224-4423-2). Pitman Learning.

Heimer, Ralph T. & Trueblood, Cecil R. Strategies for Teaching Children Mathematics. LC 76-20030. 1977. text ed. 16.95 (ISBN 0-201-02882-4). A-W.

Hollis, L. Y. & Houston, W. Robert. Acquiring Competencies to Teach Mathematics in Elementary Schools. LC 72-89057. (The Professional Education Ser). 80p. (Orig.). 1973. pap. 1.75 (ISBN 0-88224-032-3). Cliffs.

Jeffery, Peter, ed. Primary School Mathematics in Australia: Review & Forecast. (Illus.). 298p. 1976. pap. text ed. 16.50x (ISBN 0-85563-134-1). Verry.

Jensen, Rosalie. Exploring Mathematical Concepts & Skills in the Elementary School. LC 72-91083. (gr. 2-6). 1973. text ed. 16.95 (ISBN 0-675-09029-6). Merrill.

Judd, Wallace P. Patterns to Play on a Hundred Chart. (Illus.). 96p. (Orig.). (gr. 4-12). 1975. wkbk. 6.50 (ISBN 0-88488-040-0). Creative Pubns.

Kelley, John L. & Richert, Donald. Elementary Mathematics for Teachers. LC 70-11612. 1970. text ed. 18.95x (ISBN 0-8162-4654-8); sol. man 2.50x (ISBN 0-8162-4664-5). Holden-Day.

Kelley, S. Jeanne. Learning Math Through Activities: A Resource Book for Elementary Teachers. (Page-Ficklin Math Ser). 1973. pap. 5.95x (ISBN 0-8087-1150-4). Burgess.

Kelly, S. Jeanne. Learning Mathematics Through Activities: A Resource Book for Elementary Teachers. 1973. pap. 5.50 (ISBN 0-685-65369-2). Page-Ficklin.

Kennedy, Leonard & Michon, Ruth. Games for Individualizing Mathematics Learning. LC 73-75681. (gr. 2-7). 1973. text ed. 11.95x (ISBN 0-675-08899-2). Merrill.

Kennedy, Leonard M. Experiences for Teaching Children Mathematics. 1973. pap. text ed. 10.95x (ISBN 0-534-00217-X). Wadsworth Pub.

Kingston, J. M. Mathematics for Teachers of the Middle Grades. 322p. 1966. text ed. 12.50 (ISBN 0-471-47960-8, Pub. by Wiley). Krieger.

Kramer, Klaas. Teaching Elementary School Mathematics. 4th ed. 1978. text ed. 18.95 (ISBN 0-205-06054-4, 2360543); instr's man. o.p. avail. (ISBN 0-205-06055-2); performance based study guide 7.95 (ISBN 0-205-06056-0, 2360543). Allyn.

--Teaching Elementary School Mathematics. 4th ed. 1978. text ed. 18.95 (ISBN 0-205-06054-4, 2360543); instr's man. o.p. avail. (ISBN 0-205-06055-2); performance based study guide 7.95 (ISBN 0-205-06056-0, 2360543). Allyn.

Kurtz, V. Ray. Metrics for Elementary & Middle Schools. 120p. 1978. pap. 4.50 (ISBN 0-686-63709-7, 1714-5-06). NEA.

Larsen, Max D. & Fejfar, James L. Essentials of Elementary School Mathematics. 1974. text ed. 18.95 (ISBN 0-12-438640-7); solution manual 3.00 (ISBN 0-12-438642-3). Acad Pr.

Lerch, Harold H. Active Learning Experiences for Teaching Elementary School Mathematics. (Illus.). 592p. 1981. pap. text ed. 10.95 (ISBN 0-395-29764-8). HM.

--Teaching Elementary School Mathematics: An Active Learning Approach. (Illus.). 416p. 1981. text ed. 15.95 (ISBN 0-395-29762-1); 0.75 (ISBN 0-395-29763-X). HM.

Let's Play Games in Mathematics. Incl. Grade 1. Henderson & Oberlin. 1970 (ISBN 0-8442-3332-3); Grade 2. Henderson & Oberlin. 1970 (ISBN 0-8442-3333-1); Grade 3. Henderson & Glunn. 1970 (ISBN 0-8442-3336-6); Grade 4. Henderson & Glunn. 1971 (ISBN 0-8442-3337-4); Grade 5. Henderson & Glunn. 1971 (ISBN 0-8442-3338-2); Grade 6. Henderson & Glunn. 1971 (ISBN 0-8442-3339-0); Grades 7&8. Miller & Henderson. 1972 (ISBN 0-8442-3340-4). (gr. 1-8). pap. text ed. 5.00 ea. Natl Textbk.

Marks, John L. Teaching Elementary School Mathematics for Understanding. 4th ed. (Illus.). 512p. 1975. text ed. 16.95 (ISBN 0-07-040422-4, C). McGraw.

Mathematics Learning in Early Childhood: 37th Yearbook. LC 75-6631. 16.90 (ISBN 0-87353-017-9). NCTM.

Matthias, Margaret & Thiessen, Diane. Children's Mathematics Books: A Critical Bibliography. LC 79-11896. 1979. pap. 5.00 (ISBN 0-8389-0285-5). ALA.

May, Lola. Modern Math Grade by Grade, 9 bks. (gr. k-8). pap. 1.95 gr. k (ISBN 0-685-47095-4); pap. 2.50 ea. gr. 1-8. Macmillan.

May, Lola J. Teaching Mathematics in the Elementary School. 2nd ed. LC 73-11694. (Illus.). 1974. 16.95 (ISBN 0-02-920380-5); pap. text ed. 10.95 (ISBN 0-02-920370-8). Free Pr.

Mira Math Pub. Mira Math for Elementary Schools. 1973. pap. 4.75 wkbk. (ISBN 0-88488-023-0). Creative Pubns.

Mock, Valerie E. Laugh & Learn Math. (Makemaster Bk.). 1979. pap. 8.95 (ISBN 0-8224-4230-2). Pitman Learning.

Morton, Robert L. Teaching Arithmetic in the Primary Grades. (Educational Ser.). 1927. Repr. 10.00 (ISBN 0-685-43132-0). Norwood Edns.

Paige, Donald D., et al. Elementary Mathematical Methods. LC 77-2683. 1978. 20.95 (ISBN 0-471-65756-5); tchrs. manual avail. (ISBN 0-471-04057-6). Wiley.

Pasternack, Marian & Silvey, Linda. Pattern Blocks Activities, Bks. 8A & B. (Illus., Orig., Bk A grades 2-6; bk. B grades 4-8). (gr. 2-8). 1975. Bk. A. pap. 6.95 (ISBN 0-88488-041-9); Bk. B. pap. 6.95 (ISBN 0-88488-042-7). Creative Pubns.

Pearson, James, et al. Cube-O-Gram Math Teacher Lesson Plan & Activity Book. (Cube-O-Math Ser.). (Illus.). 194p. (gr. k-3). 1979. pap. 9.95 (ISBN 0-933358-57-1). Enrich.

Phibbs, Mollie. Making Math Meaningful: Using Beads for Pre-Math. (Illus.). 1977. 2.00 (ISBN 0-914634-40-2). DOK Pubs.

Pink, Heinz-Guenther. Multiplication Hula. (Illus.). 52p. (gr. 1-4). 1971. pap. 3.95 (ISBN 0-915946-03-3, A292208); cassettes 4.95tape (ISBN 0-685-28751-3). Pink Hse Pub.

Plus: A Handbook of Classroom Ideas to Motivate the Teaching of Elementary Mathematics. (The Spice Ser). 1975. 6.50 (ISBN 0-89273-103-6). Educ Serv.

Pratt, Edna M. Picture-Graphs. (Illus., Orig., Prog. Bk.). (gr. 6-10). 1970. pap. 0.95 (ISBN 0-87594-041-2, 4010). Book-Lab.

Price, S. & Price, M. The Primary Math Lab. LC 78-7984. (Illus.). 1978. text ed. 12.95 (ISBN 0-87620-680-1); pap. text ed. 10.95 (ISBN 0-87620-679-8). Goodyear.

Research on Mathematical Thinking of Young Children. LC 75-22461. 1975. pap. 6.00 (ISBN 0-87353-088-8). NCTM.

Richardson, Lloyd I., et al. A Mathematics Activity Curriculum for Early Childhood & Special Education. (Illus.). 1980. pap. text ed. 11.95 (ISBN 0-02-399710-9). Macmillan.

Riedesel, C. Alan. Guiding Discovery to Elementary School Math. 2nd ed. 1973. text ed. 21.95 (ISBN 0-13-371583-3). P-H.

Riedesel, C. Alan & Burns, Paul C. Handbook for Exploratory & Systematic Teaching of Elementary School Mathematics. 1977. write for info. (ISBN 0-06-045403-2, HarpC). Har-Row.

Rising, Gerald R. & Harkin, Joseph B. The Third "R". Mathematics Teaching for Grades K-8. 1978. text ed. 18.95x (ISBN 0-534-00567-5). Wadsworth Pub.

Rogers, Agnes L. Experimental Tests of Mathematical Ability & Their Prognostic Value. LC 72-177201. (Columbia University. Teachers College. Contributions to Education: No. 89). Repr. of 1918 ed. 17.50 (ISBN 0-404-55089-4). AMS Pr.

Romberg, Thomas A. Individually Guided Mathematics. LC 75-40905. (Leadership Ser in Indiv. Guided Ed.). 160p. 1976. pap. text ed. 7.95 (ISBN 0-201-19411-2); instr's guide 2.95 (ISBN 0-201-19421-X). A-W.

Rosskopf, Myron F., ed. Children's Mathematical Concepts: Six Piagetian Studies in Mathematical Education. LC 75-12872. 1975. text ed. 14.95x (ISBN 0-8077-2447-5). Tchrs Coll.

Schiro, Michael. Thirty-Three Arithmetic Skill Development Games. 1978. pap. 4.95 (ISBN 0-8224-2849-0). Pitman Learning.

Schminke, C. W. & Duman, Enoch. Math Activities for Child Involvement. 3rd ed. 288p. 1981. text ed. 18.95 (ISBN 0-205-07295-X); pap. text ed. 11.95 (ISBN 0-205-07302-6, 2373025). Allyn.

Schminke, C. W., et al. Teaching the Child Mathematics. 2nd ed. LC 77-18809. 1978. 19.95 (ISBN 0-03-020766-5, HoltC). HR&W.

Schultz, James E. Mathematics for Elemenatry School Teachers. (Mathematics Ser.). 1977. text ed. 18.95 (ISBN 0-675-08509-8); instructor's manual 3.95 (ISBN 0-685-74286-5). Merrill.

Scott, Louise B. & Garner, Jewell. Mathematical Experiences for Young Children. (Illus.). 1977. text ed. 13.60 (ISBN 0-07-055585-0, W). McGraw.

Seymour, Dale, et al. Aftermath One to Four. rev. ed. (Illus.). 122p. 1975. Bks. 1-4. wkbks. 6.95 ea. Bk. 1 (ISBN 0-88488-033-8). Bk. 2 (ISBN 0-88488-034-6). Bk. 3 (ISBN 0-88488-035-4). Bk. 4 (ISBN 0-88488-036-2). Creative Pubns.

Sharp, Richard M., et al. Thirty Math Games for the Elementary Grades. 1974. pap. 3.95 (ISBN 0-8224-6945-6). Pitman Learning.

Sherman, Helene. Common Elements in New Mathematics Programs: Their Origins & Evolution. LC 72-75560. (Illus.). 1972. pap. text ed. 7.25x (ISBN 0-8077-2151-4). Tchrs Coll.

The Slow Learner in Mathematics: 35th Yearbook. LC 72-8350. 1972. 16.90 (ISBN 0-87353-015-2). NCTM.

Smith, David E. The Teaching of Elementary Mathematics. (Educational Ser.). 1904. Repr. 15.00 (ISBN 0-685-43644-6). Norwood Edns.

Smith, Douglas B. & Topp, William R. Activity Approach to Elementary Concepts of Mathematics. (Mathematics Ser.). (Illus.). 150p. 1981. pap. text ed. price not set (ISBN 0-201-07694-2). A-W.

Smith, Seaton E., Jr. & Backman, Carl A., eds. Teacher-Made Aids for Elementary School Mathematics: Readings from the Arithmetic Teacher. LC 73-21581. 186p. 1974. pap. 5.60 (ISBN 0-87353-093-4). NCTM.

Suppes, Patrick C., et al. Computer-Assisted Instruction: Stanford's 1965-66 Arithmetic Program. (Illus.). 1968. 37.50 (ISBN 0-12-676850-1). Acad Pr.

Swenson, Esther J. Teaching Mathematics to Children. 2nd ed. Chilton, Lloyd C., ed. (Illus.). 558p. 1973. text ed. 15.95x (ISBN 0-02-418700-3). Macmillan.

Throop, Sara & Wick, Barbara H. Mathematics Readiness Program. (gr. k). 1975. pap. text ed. 3.84 (ISBN 0-87895-024-9); tchrs' ed. 2.00 (ISBN 0-87895-025-7). Modern Curr.

Tischler, Rosamond W. & Fuys, David J. Teaching Mathematics in the Elementary School. 1979. text ed. 14.95 (ISBN 0-316-29720-8); tchrs' manual free (ISBN 0-316-29721-6). Little.

Troutman, Andria & Lichtenberg, Betty K. Mathematics: A Good Beginning. LC 76-57694. (Contemporary Undergraduate Mathematics Ser.). 1977. pap. text ed. 17.95 (ISBN 0-8185-0222-3). Brooks-Cole.

Underhill, Richard G., et al. Diagnosing Mathematical Difficulties. (Elementary Education Ser.: No. C22). 408p. 1980. text ed. 15.95 (ISBN 0-675-08195-5). Merrill.

Underhill, Robert G. Teaching Elementary School Mathematics. 2nd ed. (Elementary Education Ser.). 1977. text ed. 19.95 (ISBN 0-675-08541-1); instructor's manual 3.95 (ISBN 0-686-67644-0). Merrill.

Underhill, Robert J. Methods of Teaching Elementary School Mathematics. new ed. (Elementary Education Ser). 224p. 1975. pap. text ed. 7.95x (ISBN 0-675-08780-5); media: audiocassettes & filmstrips 495.00 (ISBN 0-675-08781-3); 2-3 sets 395.00 (ISBN 0-686-77047-1); 4 or more set 315.00 (ISBN 0-686-77048-X). Merrill.

University of Maryland Mathematics Project. Unifying Concepts & Processes in Elementary Mathematics. 1978. pap. text ed. 23.50 (ISBN 0-205-05844-2, 5658446); instr's manual avail. (ISBN 0-205-05845-0). Allyn.

Virginia Council of Teachers of Mathematics. Practical Ways to Teach the Basic Mathematical Skills. 1979. pap. 7.50 (ISBN 0-686-65437-4). NCTM.

Vochko, Lee E., ed. Manipulative Activities & Games in the Mathematics Classroom. 112p. 1979. pap. 6.00 (ISBN 0-686-63707-0, 17706-4-06). NEA.

Watson, F. R. Developments in Mathematics Teaching. (Changing Classroom). 1976. text ed. 9.75x (ISBN 0-7291-0085-5); pap. text ed. 4.75x (ISBN 0-7291-0080-4). Humanities.

Westcott, Alvin M. & Smith, James A. Creative Teaching of Mathematics in the Elementary School. 2nd ed. 1978. pap. text ed. 11.95 (ISBN 0-205-06051-X). Allyn.

Whitcraft, Leslie H. Some Influences of the Requirements & Examinations of the College Entrance Examination Board on Mathematics in Secondary Schools in the United States. LC 70-177640. (Columbia University. Teachers College. Contributions to Education: No. 557). Repr. of 1933 ed. 17.50 (ISBN 0-404-55557-8). AMS Pr.

MATHEMATICS–STUDY AND TEACHING (SECONDARY)

Aichele, Douglas B. & Reys, Robert E. Readings in Secondary School Mathematics. 2nd ed. 1977. pap. text ed. write for info. (ISBN 0-87150-202-X, PWS 1742). Prindle.

Assistant Masters Association. Teaching of Mathematics in Secondary Schools. 2nd ed. (Illus.). 235p. 1974. text ed. 10.95x (ISBN 0-521-20181-0). Cambridge U Pr.

Bell, Frederick H. Teaching & Learning Math in Secondary Schools. 575p. 1978. pap. text ed. write for info. (ISBN 0-697-06017-9). Wm C Brown.

Blazek, Ron. Influencing Students Toward Media Center Use. LC 75-26769. (Studies in Librarianship Ser: No. 5). 238p. 1976. pap. text ed. 7.00 (ISBN 0-8389-0201-4). ALA.

Brumfiel, Charles & Krause, Eugene. Mathematics I & II: Grade 8 Mathematics, 2 bks. 1975. Bk. 1. text ed. 11.20 (ISBN 0-201-00603-0, Sch Div); Bk. 2. text ed. 11.20 (ISBN 0-201-00605-7); Bk. 1. tchr's. ed. 14.52 (ISBN 0-201-00604-9); Bk. 2. tchr's. ed. 14.52 (ISBN 0-201-00606-5). A-W.

Butler, D. H. & Wren, F. L. Teaching of Secondary Mathematics. 5th ed. (Curriculum & Methods in Education). 1970. text ed. 17.95 (ISBN 0-07-009330-X, C). McGraw.

Congdon, Allan R. Training in High-School Mathematics Essential for Success in Certain College Subjects. (Columbia University. Teachers College. Contributions to Education: No. 403). Repr. of 1930 ed. 17.50 (ISBN 0-404-55403-2). AMS Pr.

Cooney, Thomas J., et al. Dynamics of Teaching Secondary Mathematics. 1975. 17.95 (ISBN 0-395-18617-X). HM.

Crawford, Rudd, et al. Achievement in Mathematics, 2 vols. (Mathematics Program). (gr. 7-8). 1974. Vol. 1. text ed. 14.60 (ISBN 0-205-03976-6, 563976X); Vol. 2. text ed. 14.60 (ISBN 0-205-04225-2, 5642256); tchrs'. guide for vol. 1 10.96 (ISBN 0-205-03977-4, 5639778); tchrs'. guide for vol. 2 10.96 (ISBN 0-205-04226-0, 5642264). Allyn.

Del Santo, Louise. Mastering Mathematics. LC 75-2049. (High School Equivalency Prog. Ser.). 205p. (Orig.). (gr. 9-12). 1975. pap. text ed. 5.50 (ISBN 0-913310-38-7). Par Inc.

Dressler, Isidore. Algebra I. (gr. 9). 1966. text ed. 10.67 (ISBN 0-87720-208-7). AMSCO Sch.

--Algebra One Review Guide. (Illus., Orig.). (gr. 9). 1966. pap. text ed. 5.00 (ISBN 0-87720-207-9). AMSCO Sch.

Farrell, Margaret A. & Farmer, Walter A. Systematic Instruction in Mathematics for the Middle & High School Years. LC 79-4250. (Illus.). 1980. pap. text ed. 12.95 (ISBN 0-201-02436-5). A-W.

Glennon, Vincent J., ed. The Mathematical Education of Exceptional Children & Youth: An Interdisciplinary Approach. 1981. 28.00 (ISBN 0-87353-171-X). NCTM.

Greenes, Carole, et al. Successful Problem Solving Techniques. (gr. 6-12). 1977. tchrs. ed. 7.25 (ISBN 0-88488-086-9). Creative Pubns.

Greenes, Carole E., et al. Problem-Mathics. (gr. 7-12). 1977. tchrs. ed. 7.25 (ISBN 0-88488-085-0). Creative Pubns.

Guercio, E., et al. General Mathematical Ability: Preparation & Review for the Mathematics Part of the High School Equivalency Diploma Test. LC 74-19738. (GED Preparation Ser.). 160p. (Orig.). 1975. lib. bdg. 7.00 (ISBN 0-668-03841-1); pap. 6.00 (ISBN 0-668-03689-3). Arco.

Hassler, Jasper O. & Smith, Rolland R. The Teaching of Secondary Mathematics. Hedrick, Earle R., ed. 1979. Repr. of 1937 ed. lib. bdg. 25.00 (ISBN 0-8482-4499-0). Norwood Edns.

Hughes, Barnabas. Thinking Through Problems. (YA) 1977. wkbk 6.95 (ISBN 0-88488-056-7). Creative Pubns.

Johnson, D. C. & Tinsley, J. D., eds. Informatics & Mathematics in Secondary Schools: Proceedings of the IFIP TC3 Working Conference, Bulgaria. 1978. 22.00 (ISBN 0-444-85160-7, North-Holland). Elsevier.

Kastner, Bernice. Applications of Secondary School Mathematics. LC 78-8918. (Illus.). 1978. pap. 7.00 (ISBN 0-87353-127-2). NCTM.

Krulik, Stephen & Weise, Ingrid B. Teaching Secondary School Mathematics. LC 74-9435. 243p. 1975. text ed. 15.95 (ISBN 0-7216-5548-3). HR&W.

Larsen, M. D. & Shumway, R. J. Essentials of Precalculus Mathematics. (Mathematics Ser.). 1971. 12.95 (ISBN 0-201-04123-5); instructor's manual 4.00 (ISBN 0-201-04124-3). A-W.

Lewis, Harry. Mathematics for Daily Living. 2nd ed. (Illus.). (gr. 7-12). 1975. text ed. 12.40 (ISBN 0-8009-1720-0); tchr's. ed. 14.00 (ISBN 0-8009-1722-7); wkbk. 4.36 (ISBN 0-8009-1724-3); tchr's. ed. wkbk. 6.52 (ISBN 0-8009-1728-6); 1970 ed. of text also avail. write for further info. McCormick-Mathers.

McDonough, Martin. Mastering General Mathematics. LC 74-27437. 160p. 1976. pap. 5.00 (ISBN 0-668-03732-6). Arco.

Mallory, Virgil S. The Relative Difficulty of Certain Topics in Mathematics for Slow-Moving Ninth Grade Pupils. LC 79-177050. (Columbia University. Teachers College. Contributions to Education: No. 769). Repr. of 1939 ed. 17.50 (ISBN 0-404-55769-4). AMS Pr.

Margenau, James & Sentlowitz, Michael. How to Study Mathematics: A Handbook for Students. LC 77-5560. 1977. pap. 1.70 (ISBN 0-87353-115-9). NCTM.

Miklos, Mary O. Mathematical Ideas. LC 80-5871. 344p. 1980. pap. text ed. 11.50 (ISBN 0-8191-1099-X). U Pr of Amer.

Morton, Robert L. Teaching Arithmetic in the Intermediate Grades. (Educational Ser.). 1927. Repr. 10.00 (ISBN 0-685-43131-2). Norwood Edns.

Posamentier, Alfred. Teaching Mathematics in the Secondary School. 1981. pap. text ed. 16.95 (ISBN 0-675-08033-9). Merrill.

Prindle, Anthony. Barron's How to Prepare for the High School Equivalency Examination (Ged)-General Mathematics, 4 vols. Incl. Vol. 1. Arithmetic (ISBN 0-8120-0727-1); Vol. 2. Algebra (ISBN 0-8120-0728-X); Vol. 3. Geometry, Tables & Graphics, Word Problems (ISBN 0-8120-0729-8); Vol. 4. Model Examinations (ISBN 0-8120-0730-1). LC 78-14808. 1979. pap. 2.25 ea. Barron.

Rizzuto, James & Dodge, Howard. Barron's How to Prepare for the College Board Achievement Tests - Mathematics Level I. 3rd ed. (gr. 10-12). 1981. pap. text ed. 5.50 (ISBN 0-8120-0673-9). Barron.

Rosenberger, Noah B. The Place of the Elementary Calculus in the Senior High School Mathematics. LC 71-177209. (Columbia University. Teachers College. Contributions to Education: No. 117). Repr. of 1921 ed. 17.50 (ISBN 0-404-55117-3). AMS Pr.

Rosier, M. J. Changes in Secondary School Mathematics in Australia, 1964-1978. (ACER Research Monographs: No. 8). 1980. pap. 20.00 (ISBN 0-85563-208-9). Verry.

Schlumpf, Lester, ed. Barron's Three-Year Sequence for High School Mathematics - Course I. 250p. (gr. 9-12). 1981. pap. text ed. 3.95 (ISBN 0-8120-2401-X). Barron.

Schultze, Arthur. The Teaching of Mathematics in Secondary Schools. (Educational Ser.). 1926. Repr. 12.50 (ISBN 0-685-43547-4). Norwood Edns.

Scopes, P. G. Mathematics in Secondary Schools. LC 72-78894. (Illus.). 128p. 1973. pap. text ed. 6.95x (ISBN 0-521-09728-2). Cambridge U Pr.

Sinha, D. K. & Roy, A. B., eds. Higher Secondary Mathematics, Vol. 1. 252p. 1981. 20.00x (ISBN 0-86131-077-2, Pub. by Orient Longman India). State Mutual Bk.

--Higher Secondary Mathematics, Vol. 2. 224p. 1981. 20.00x (ISBN 0-86131-078-0, Pub. by Orient Longman India). State Mutual Bk.

Stein, Edwin I. Practical Applications in Mathematics. new ed. Orig. Title: Refresher Workbook in Arithmetic. (gr. 7-12). 1972. 4.80 (ISBN 0-205-03385-7, 5633850); answer bk 2.40 (ISBN 0-205-03386-5, 5633869). Allyn.

--Refresher Mathematics. rev. ed. (gr. 7-12). 1974. text ed. 13.56 (ISBN 0-205-04306-2, 5643066); tchrs'. guide 5.12 (ISBN 0-205-04307-0, 5643074). Allyn.

Vesselo, I. R., ed. Further Training of Mathematics Teachers at Secondary Level. (International Studies in Education, No. 22). (Orig.). 1970. pap. 6.25 (ISBN 0-685-04909-4, U260, UNESCO). Unipub.

Vogeli, Bruce R. Soviet Secondary Schools for the Mathematically Talented. LC 68-30961. 1968. pap. 3.40 (ISBN 0-87353-092-6). NCTM.

Williams, Edward. Barron's Getting Ready for the High School Equivaency Examination: Beginning Preparation in Mathematics. LC 76-3662. 1976. pap. 5.95 (ISBN 0-8120-0466-3). Barron.

MATHEMATICS–TABLES, ETC.

see also Integrals; Logarithms; Ready-Reckoners; Trigonometry–Tables, etc.

Abramowitz, Milton & Stegun, Irene A., eds. Handbook of Mathematical Functions with Formulas, Graphs & Mathematical Tables. (Illus.). 1964. pap. 14.95 (ISBN 0-486-61272-4). Dover.

Allen, Edward S. Six-Place Tables. 7th ed. LC 81-360. 256p. 1981. Repr. of 1947 ed. lib. bdg. 12.50 (ISBN 0-89874-287-0). Krieger.

--Six-Place Tables. 7th ed. 1947. 9.95 (ISBN 0-07-057751-X, P&RB). McGraw.

Barlows, Peter. Tables, Squares & Cubes. 1948. 5.95 (ISBN 0-685-19505-8). Powner.

Beyer, William H. Handbook of Mathematical Sciences, CRC. 5th ed. 1978. 49.95 (ISBN 0-8493-0655-8). CRC Pr.

Beyer, William H., ed. Standard Mathematical Tables. 26th ed. 614p. 1981. 24.95 (ISBN 0-8493-0625-6). CRC Pr.

--Standard Mathematical Tables, CRC. 25th ed. LC 30-4052. (Handbook Ser.). 1978. 19.95 (ISBN 0-8493-0624-8). CRC Pr.

Bigsbee, Earle M. Mathematics Tables with Explanations of Tables. (Quality Paperbacks: No. 8). (Orig.). 1977. pap. 3.50 (ISBN 0-8226-0008-0). Littlefield.

Bulgren, W. G., et al. Four Sets of Tables. Institute of Mathematical Statistics, ed. LC 74-6283. (Selected Tables in Mathematical Statistics Ser.: Vol. 2). 1974. 25.60 (ISBN 0-8218-1902-X, TABLES-2). Am Math.

Burington, Richard S. Handbook of Mathematical Tables & Formulas. 5th ed. LC 78-39634. (Illus.). 480p. 1973. text ed. 10.50 (ISBN 0-07-009015-7, C). McGraw.

Carmichael, Robert D. & Smith, Edwin R. Mathematical Tables & Formulas. 1931. pap. 3.25 (ISBN 0-486-60111-0). Dover.

Enrick, Norbert L. Handbook of Effective Graphic & Tabular Communication. LC 79-44833. 224p. 1980. 12.50 (ISBN 0-88275-914-0). Krieger.

Eswaran, K. S. Mathematical Formulae & Tables. 84p. 1981. 10.00x (ISBN 0-86125-149-0, Pub. by Orient Longman India). State Mutual Bk.

Godfrey, Charles & Siddons, A. W. Four-Figure Tables. text ed. 2.50x (ISBN 0-521-05097-9). Cambridge U Pr.

Hackworth, Robert D. & Howland, Joseph. Introductory College Mathematics: Tables & Graphs. LC 75-23628. (Illus.). 62p. 1976. pap. text ed. 2.95 (ISBN 0-7216-4421-X). HR&W.

Halberstam, H. & Richert, H. E. Sieve Methods. 1975. 60.00 (ISBN 0-12-318250-6). Acad Pr.

Harris, Bernard, et al. Five Sets of Tables: Tables of the 2 Factor & 3 Factor Generalized Incomplete Modified Bessel Distributions. Institute of Mathematical Statistics, ed. LC 74-6283. (Selected Tables in Mathematical Statistics: Vol. 3). 1975. 33.60 (ISBN 0-8218-1903-8, TABLES-3). Am Math.

Jahnke, Eugene & Emde, Fritz. Tables of Functions with Formulae & Curves. 4th ed. (Ger & Eng). 1945. pap. text ed. 5.00 (ISBN 0-486-60133-1). Dover.

Johnson, William W. Addition & Substraction Logarithms: Gaussian Tables. 1943. 3.00 (ISBN 0-685-19461-2). Powner.

Kuntsevich, I. M. & Sheleg, A. V. Tables of Trigonometric Functions for the Numerical Computation of Electron Density in Crystals. 1967. 25.95 (ISBN 0-470-51090-0). Halsted Pr.

LeFax Pub. Co. Editors. Mathematical Tables. (Lefax Data Bks.: No. 647). (Illus.). Date not set. looseleaf bdg. 3.00 (ISBN 0-685-52844-8). LeFax.

--Mathematical Tables. (Lefax Technical Manuals.: No. 785). (Illus.). looseleaf bdg. 8.50 (ISBN 0-685-14155-1). Lefax.

Shaw, A. M., ed. Handbook of Conversion Factors. 24p. 1978. 3.00x (ISBN 0-934366-01-2). Intl Research Serv.

Smoley, C. K. How to Use Smoley's Tables. Smoley, E. R. & Smoley, N. G., eds. 1976. pap. text ed. 3.00 (ISBN 0-911390-07-3). Smoley.

Spiegel, Murray R. Mathematical Handbook of Formulas & Tables. (Schaum's Outline Ser). 1968. pap. text ed. 5.95 (ISBN 0-07-060224-7, SP). McGraw.

Wuytack, L. Pade Approximation & Its Application. (Lecture Notes in Mathematics: Vol. 765). 392p. 1980. pap. 21.00 (ISBN 0-387-09717-1). Springer-Verlag.

MATHEMATICS–1961-

Althoen, Steven C. & Bumcrot, Robert J. Finite Mathematics. (Illus.). 1978. text ed. 16.95x (ISBN 0-393-09046-9). Norton.

Ash, Peter F. & Robinson, Edward E. Basic College Mathematics: A Calculator Approach. LC 80-15352. (Illus.). 544p. 1981. write for info. (ISBN 0-201-00091-1). A-W.

Austin, Jacqueline & Isern, Margarita S. Technical Mathematics. 2nd ed. LC 74-9427. (Illus.). 430p. 1979. text ed. 14.95x (ISBN 0-7216-1456-6). HR&W.

Bajpai, A. C., et al. Mathematics for Engineers & Scientists, Vols. 1-2. LC 72-14009. (Programms on Mathematics for Scientist & Technologist Ser.). 800p. 1973. Vol. 1. 22.95 (ISBN 0-471-04373-7); Vol. 2. 19.50 (ISBN 0-471-04374-5, Pub. by Wiley-Interscience). Wiley.

Barrata-Lorton, Mary. Math Their Way. (gr. k-2). 1976. 24.55 (ISBN 0-201-04320-3, Sch Div). A-W.

Begle, Edward G. The Mathematics of the Elementary School. (Illus.). 576p. 1975. text ed. 16.50 (ISBN 0-07-004325-6, C); instructor's manual 3.50 (ISBN 0-07-004327-2). McGraw.

Bender, Edward A. An Introduction to Mathematical Modeling. LC 77-23840. 256p. 1978. 23.95 (ISBN 0-471-02951-3, Pub. by Wiley-Interscience); solutions manual 4.50 (ISBN 0-471-03407-X). Wiley.

Benharbit, Abdelali & Al-Moajil, Abdullah H. Mathematics for Pre-Calculus Students. 240p. 1981. 44.25 (ISBN 0-471-27941-2, Pub. by Wiley Interscience); pap. price not set (ISBN 0-471-27942-0). Wiley.

Birtwistle, C. Mathematical Puzzles & Perplexities. 1971. 14.50x (ISBN 0-8448-0552-1). Crane-Russak Co.

Bohuslov, Ronald L. Basic Mathematics for Technical Occupations. (Illus.). 480p. 1976. 19.95 (ISBN 0-13-063396-8). P-H.

Britton, Jack R. & Bello, Ignacio. Topics in Contemporary Mathematics. 1979. text ed. 21.50 scp (ISBN 0-06-040953-3, HarpC); free instr. manual (ISBN 0-06-360921-5). Har-Row.

Burleson, Donald R. Topics in Precalculus Mathematics. (Illus.). 544p. 1974. text ed. 18.95 (ISBN 0-13-925461-7); study guide o.p. 1.95 (ISBN 0-13-925214-2). P-H.

Childress, R. L. Fundamentals of Finite Mathematics. (Illus.). 1976. ref. ed. 18.95 (ISBN 0-13-339325-9). P-H.

Childress, Robert L. Mathematics for Managerial Decisions. LC 73-17352. (Illus.). 656p. 1974. ref. ed. 21.00 (ISBN 0-13-562231-X). P-H.

Christy, Dennis T. Essentials of Precalculus Mathematics. 2nd ed. 598p. 1981. text ed. 19.50 (ISBN 0-06-041303-4, HarpC); answers to even-numbered exercises avail. (ISBN 0-06-361192-9). Har-Row.

Clar, Lawrence M. & Hart, James A. Mathematics for the Technologies. (Illus.). 1978. text ed. 19.95 (ISBN 0-13-565200-6). P-H.

Crown, J. Conrad & Bittinger, Marvin L. Finite Mathematics: A Modeling Approach. 2nd ed. LC 80-19472. (Mathematics Ser.). (Illus.). 480p. 1981. text ed. 15.95 (ISBN 0-201-03145-0). A-W.

Devine, Donald F. & Kaufmann, Jerome E. Elementary Mathematics. LC 76-24805. 1977. text ed. 22.95 (ISBN 0-471-20970-8). Wiley.

Dickenson, Harry & Kleinschmidt, Robert. Technical Mechanics. (Illus.). 736p. 1974. text ed. 17.95 (ISBN 0-07-016790-7, G); instructor's manual 1.95 (ISBN 0-07-016791-5). McGraw.

Dodge, Howard. Barron's How to Prepare for the College Board Achievement Tests - Mathematics Level II. LC 78-8655. 1979. pap. 5.95 (ISBN 0-8120-0325-X). Barron.

Ewen, Dale, et al. Elementary Technical Mathematics. 2nd ed. 1978. text ed. 17.95x (ISBN 0-534-00542-X). Wadsworth Pub.

Falbo. Finite Mathematics Applied. 1977. 20.95x (ISBN 0-534-00481-4). Wadsworth Pub.

Gill, Jack C. Mathematics & the Liberal Arts. LC 72-95501. 1973. pap. text ed. 16.95 (ISBN 0-675-08981-6); media: audiocassettes 89.50, 2-4 sets, 65.00 ea., 5 or more sets, 49.50 ea. (ISBN 0-675-08973-5); instructor's manual 3.95 (ISBN 0-686-66864-2). Merrill.

Gilligan, Lawrence G. & Nenno, Robert B. Finite Mathematics: An Elementary Approach. LC 74-11826. 448p. 1975. text ed. 16.95 (ISBN 0-87620-327-6); solutions manual free (ISBN 0-87620-328-4). Goodyear.

Goodstein, R. L. Fundamental Concepts of Mathematics. 2nd ed. 1978. text ed. 45.00 (ISBN 0-08-021665-X); pap. text ed. 19.25 (ISBN 0-08-021666-8). Pergamon.

Griffiths, H. B. & Hilton, P. J. A Comprehensive Textbook of Classical Mathematics: A Contemporary Interpretation. 1978. pap. 21.80 (ISBN 0-387-90342-9). Springer-Verlag.

Groza, Vivian & Shelley, Susanne. Precalculus Mathematics. LC 76-158479. 1972. text ed. 14.95x (ISBN 0-03-077670-8). Irvington.

Gudder, Stanley. A Mathematical Journey. 1976. text ed. 14.95 (ISBN 0-07-025105-3, C); instructor's manual 3.95 (ISBN 0-07-025106-1). McGraw.

Guggenheimer, Heinrich W. Mathematics for Engineering & Science. LC 76-28336. (Applied Math Ser.). 290p. 1976. pap. 11.50 (ISBN 0-88275-462-9). Krieger.

Gulati, Bodh R. College Mathematics with Applications to the Business & Social Sciences. (Illus.). 1978. text ed. 22.50 scp (ISBN 0-06-042538-5, HarpC); ans. bklt. free (ISBN 0-06-362551-2). Har-Row.

Hancock. Introduction to Modern Mathematics Series 1. (gr. 8-12). 1972. pap. text ed. 7.50 each incl. 5 texts, 1 tchrs' manual & test (ISBN 0-8449-0210-1). Learning Line.

--Introduction to Modern Mathematics Series 2. (gr. 8-12). 1972. pap. text ed. 7.50 each incl. 4 texts, 1 tchrs' manual & test (ISBN 0-8449-0220-9). Learning Line.

Hannon, Ralph H. Basic Technical Mathematics with Calculus. LC 76-20934. (Illus.). 1978. text ed. 15.95 (ISBN 0-7216-4497-X). HR&W.

Hardy, F. Lane. Finite Mathematics. 1977. text ed. 18.95 scp (ISBN 0-06-042642-X, HarpC). Har-Row.

Hayden, Seymour & Mineka, John. Algebra & Geometry: An Introduction with Applications. LC 74-23358. 400p. 1976. 12.50 (ISBN 0-683-03913-X). Krieger.

Herstein, I. N. & Kaplansky, Irving. Matters Mathematical. 2nd ed. LC 77-16091. 1978. 10.95 (ISBN 0-8284-0300-7). Chelsea Pub.

Hofstadter, Douglas R. Godel, Escher, Bach: An Eternal Golden Braid. LC 80-11354. (Illus.). 800p. 1980. pap. 8.95 (ISBN 0-394-74502-7, Vin). Random.

Holder, Leonard. Primer for Calculus. 1978. text ed. 19.95x (ISBN 0-534-00855-0); solutions manual 7.95x (ISBN 0-534-00981-6). Wadsworth Pub.

Howes, Vernon E. Essentials of Mathematics: Precalculus- a Programmed Text. LC 75-9733. 1975. Bk. 2: Algebra II. text ed. o.p. (ISBN 0-471-41737-8); Bk. 3: Trigonometric Functions & Applications. text ed. 18.95x (ISBN 0-471-41738-6); instr's manual avail. (ISBN 0-471-41739-4). Wiley.

Hunkins, Dalton R. & Pirnot, Thomas L. Mathematics: Tools & Models. LC 76-15462. (Illus.). 1977. text ed. 17.95 (ISBN 0-201-03046-2); instr's man 2.00 (ISBN 0-201-03047-0). A-W.

Hyatt, Herman R., et al. Introduction to Technical Mathematics: A Calculator Approach. LC 78-17016. 1979. text ed. 18.95x (ISBN 0-471-22240-2); tchrs. manual avail. (ISBN 0-471-04053-3). Wiley.

International Symposium, 3rd, December 5-9, 1977. Computing Methods in Applied Sciences & Engineering, 1977, I: Proceedings. Glowinski, R. & Lions, J. L., eds. (Lecture Notes in Mathematics: Vol. 704). 1979. pap. 18.70 (ISBN 0-387-09123-8). Springer-Verlag.

Kemeny, John G., et al. Introduction to Finite Mathematics. 3rd ed. 512p. 1974. ref. ed. 19.95 (ISBN 0-13-483834-3); answers 1.00 (ISBN 0-13-468835-X). P-H.

Khazanie & Saltz. Introduction to Mathematics. LC 74-11741. 448p. 1975. text ed. 19.95 (ISBN 0-87620-469-8); instructors' manual free (ISBN 0-87620-467-1). Goodyear.

Kim, K. A. & Roush, F. W. Mathematics for Social Scientists. LC 79-19336. 304p. 1979. 18.95 (ISBN 0-444-99066-6, Pub. by Elsevier). Greenwood.

Knaupp, Jonathan, et al. Patterns & Systems of Elementary Mathematics. LC 76-13087. (Illus.). 1977. pap. text ed. 17.75 (ISBN 0-395-20638-3); instructors' manual 3.25 (ISBN 0-395-20639-1). HM.

Koshy, Thomas. An Elementary Approach to Mathematics. LC 75-11271. 512p. 1976. text ed. 18.95 (ISBN 0-87620-274-1); instuctor's guide avail. (ISBN 0-87620-275-X). Goodyear.

Kra, I. & Maskit, B., eds. Riemann Surfaces & Related Topics: Proceedings of the 1978 Stony Brook Conference. LC 79-27923. (Annals of Mathematics Studies: No.97). 400p. 1981. 25.00x (ISBN 0-691-08264-2); pap. 9.50x (ISBN 0-691-08267-7). Princeton U Pr.

Krause, Eugene F. Mathematics for Elementary Teachers. (Illus.). 1978. text ed. 19.95 (ISBN 0-13-562702-8). P-H.

Kyle, James. Mathematics Unraveled - a New Commonsense Approach. LC 76-8609. (Illus.). 1976. 9.95 (ISBN 0-8306-6791-1); pap. 6.95 (ISBN 0-8306-5791-6, 791). TAB Bks.

Lake, Frances & Neiomark, Joseph. Mathematics As a Second Language. 2nd ed. LC 76-14659. (Illus.). 1977. text ed. 17.95 (ISBN 0-201-04099-9). A-W.

Lial, Margaret L. & Miller, Charles D. Finite Mathematics: With Applications in Business, Biology, & Behavioral Sciences. 1977. text ed. 17.95x (ISBN 0-673-15044-5). Scott F.

Lue, A. S. Basic Pure Mathematics Two. 1974. 9.95x (ISBN 0-442-30048-4). Van Nos Reinhold.

McDonald, T. Marll. Mathematical Methods for Social & Management Scientists. 544p. 1974. text ed. 19.95 (ISBN 0-395-17089-3); instructor's manual pap. 2.25 (ISBN 0-395-17858-4). HM.

Mahler, Kurt. P-adic Numbers & Their Functions. 2nd ed. LC 79-20103. (Cambridge Tracts in Mathematics Ser.: No. 76). 1981. 45.00 (ISBN 0-521-23102-7). Cambridge U Pr.

Maki, Daniel P. & Thompson, Maynard. Finite Mathematics. (Illus.). 1978. text ed. 14.95 (ISBN 0-07-039745-7, C); instr's manual 3.50 (ISBN 0-07-039746-5). McGraw.

Malkevitch, Joseph & Meyer, Walter. Graphs, Models & Finite Mathematics. (Illus.). 480p. 1974. ref. ed. 19.95 (ISBN 0-13-363465-5). P-H.

Mansfield, Ralph. Introduction to Technical Mathematics. 1979. text ed. 20.95 scp (ISBN 0-06-044185-2, HarpC); free solutions manual (ISBN 0-06-364150-X). Har-Row.

Meserve, Bruce E. & Sobel, Max A. Contemporary Mathematics. 2nd ed. (Illus.). 1977. text ed. 18.95 (ISBN 0-13-170092-8). P-H.

Mizrahi, Abe & Sullivan, Michael. Finite Mathematics with Applications for Business & Social Sciences. 3rd ed. LC 78-12522. 1979. text ed. 22.95 (ISBN 0-471-03336-7). study guide avail. (ISBN 0-471-05499-2). Wiley.

Mrachek, L. & Kromschlies, C. Technical-Vocational Mathematics. LC 76-48917. 1978. pap. 14.95 (ISBN 0-13-898569-3). P-H.

Myers, Nancy. The Math Book. LC 74-14806. (Illus.). 1975. text ed. 12.00 (ISBN 0-02-849400-8). Hafner.

Olive, Gloria. Mathematics for Liberal Arts Students. Smethurst, Everett W., ed. (Illus.). 320p. 1973. text ed. 12.95x (ISBN 0-02-389200-5). Macmillan.

Pachucki, Chester. Mathematics for Industrial Technicians. (Illus.). 448p. 1974. text ed. 17.95 (ISBN 0-13-563221-8). P-H.

Paul, Richard S. & Shaevel, M. Leonard. Essentials of Technical Mathematics. (Illus.). 656p. 1974. 19.95 (ISBN 0-13-288084-9). P-H.

Payne, Michael. Pre-Calculus Mathematics. LC 76-19608. (Illus.). 1977. text ed. 13.95 (ISBN 0-7216-7122-5). HR&W.

Pearson, John G., et al. Math Skills for the Sciences. LC 75-40065. (Wiley Self-Teaching Guides Ser). 1976. text ed. 5.95 (ISBN 0-471-67541-5). Wiley.

Person, Russell V. & Person, Vernon J. Practical Mathematics. LC 76-21732. 400p. 1977. 19.95 (ISBN 0-471-68216-0). Wiley.

Peterson, John. Finite Mathematics. LC 73-10457. 1974. 12.95x (ISBN 0-89197-559-4). Irvington.

Polhamus, Edward C., Jr., et al. Applied Math for Technicians. (Illus.). 512p. 1975. text ed. 16.95 (ISBN 0-13-041236-8). P-H.

Polis, A. Richard & Beard, Earl M. Fundamental Mathematics: A Cultural Approach. 1977. text ed. 21.50 scp (ISBN 0-06-045258-7, HarpC); ans. to odd-numbered probs. avail. (ISBN 0-06-365231-5). Har-Row.

Potter, Merle C. Mathematical Methods in the Physical Sciences. (Illus.). 1978. ref. ed. 25.95 (ISBN 0-13-561134-2). P-H.

Pulsinelli, Linda. Living Mathematics: A Survey. (Illus.). 576p. 1982. 19.95 (ISBN 0-13-538819-8). P-H.

Rees, Paul & Rees, Charles. Principles of Mathematics. 3rd ed. (Illus.). 1977. 18.95 (ISBN 0-13-709683-6). P-H.

Rich, Barnett. Review of Elementary Mathematics. (Schaum's Outline Ser). (Orig.). 1977. pap. 4.95 (ISBN 0-07-052260-X, SP). McGraw.

Schools Council Sixth Form Mathematics Project. Mathematics Applicable: Mathematics Changes Gear. 1975. pap. text ed. 2.95x (ISBN 0-435-51695-7). Heinemann Ed.

Schultz, James E. Mathematics for Elemenatry School Teachers. (Mathematics Ser.). 1977. text ed. 18.95 (ISBN 0-675-08509-8); instructor's manual 3.95 (ISBN 0-685-74286-5). Merrill.

Smith, Karl J. The Nature of Modern Mathematics. 3rd ed. LC 79-20064. 1980. text ed. 17.95 (ISBN 0-8185-0352-1). Brooks-Cole.

Spencer, Donald D. Computer Science Mathematics. (Mathematics Ser.). 320p. 1976. text ed. 19.95 (ISBN 0-675-08650-7). Merrill.

Stanat, Donald F. & McAllister, David F. Discrete Mathematics in Computer Science. (Illus.). 1977. 21.95 (ISBN 0-13-216150-8). P-H.

Stein, Robert G. Mathematics: An Exploratory Approach. (Illus.). 352p. 1975. text ed. 14.95 (ISBN 0-07-060993-4, C). McGraw.

Swift, William & Wilson, D. Principles of Finite Mathematics. (Illus.). 1977. ref. ed. 19.95 (ISBN 0-13-701359-0). P-H.

Taylor, Thomas J. Medical Mathematics. LC 74-79839. (Allied Health Ser). 1975. pap. 4.55 (ISBN 0-672-61393-X). Bobbs.

Tremblay, J. P. & Manohar, R. Discrete Mathematical Structures with Applications to Computer Science. (Computer Science Ser). (Illus.). 544p. 1975. text ed. 23.95 (ISBN 0-07-065142-6, C); instructor's manual 4.95 (ISBN 0-07-065144-2). McGraw.

University of Maryland Mathematics Project. Unifying Concepts & Processes in Elementary Mathematics. 1978. pap. text ed. 23.50 (ISBN 0-205-05844-2, 5658446); instr's manual avail. (ISBN 0-205-05845-0). Allyn.

Wade, Thomas L. & Taylor, Howard E. Fundamental Mathematics. 4th ed. (Illus.). 608p. 1974. text ed. 15.95 (ISBN 0-07-067652-6, C); instructor's manual 3.95 (ISBN 0-07-067657-7). McGraw.

Webber, Robert P. Precalculus: An Elementary Functions Approach. LC 78-10882. 1979. text ed. 18.95 (ISBN 0-8185-0292-4). Brooks-Cole.

Wheeler, Ruric E. Modern Mathematics: An Elementary Approach. 4th ed. LC 76-44423. (Contemporary Undergraduate Mathematics Ser.). 1977. text ed. 19.95 (ISBN 0-8185-0213-4). Brooks-Cole.

Wheeler, Ruric E. & Peeples, W. D., Jr. Finite Mathematics: With Applications to Business & the Social Sciences. LC 80-13916. 550p. 1980. text ed. 19.95 (ISBN 0-8185-0418-8). Brooks-Cole.

--Modern Mathematics with Applications to Business & the Social Sciences. 3rd ed. LC 79-18636. 1980. text ed. 19.95 (ISBN 0-8185-0366-1). Brooks-Cole.

Whipkey, Mary N., et al. The Power of Relevant Mathematics: The Basic Concept. (Illus.). 1977. text ed. 19.95 (ISBN 0-13-687202-6). P-H.

Willerding, Margaret. The Business of Mathematics. 1977. write for info. (ISBN 0-87150-210-0, PWS 1681). Prindle.

Williams, Bill R. & Crotts, Gwen. Man's Mathematical Models: Fundamental Concepts for the Nonmathematician. LC 73-93104. 1975. 16.95x (ISBN 0-88229-110-6). Nelson-Hall.

Williams, Donald R. Modern Mathematics for Business Decision-Making. 2nd ed. 1978. text ed. 19.95x (ISBN 0-534-00558-6). Wadsworth Pub.

Wylie, Clarence R., Jr. Advanced Engineering Mathematics. 4th ed. (Illus.). 864p. 1975. text ed. 22.50 (ISBN 0-07-072180-7, C); solns. manual 3.50 (ISBN 0-07-072183-1). McGraw.

MATHEMATICS, ANCIENT

Ascher, Marcia & Ascher, Robert. Code of the Quipu: A Study in Media, Mathematics & Culture. LC 80-25409. (Illus.). 176p. 1981. text ed. 18.95x (ISBN 0-472-09325-8); pap. 8.95 (ISBN 0-686-73279-0). U of Mich Pr.

Heggie, Dougles C. Megalithic Science: Ancient Mathematics & Astronomy in Northwest Europe. (Illus.). 27.50 (ISBN 0-686-76218-5). Thames Hudson.

Neugebauer, Otto. The Exact Sciences in Antiquity. 2nd ed. LC 69-20421. (Illus.). 1969. pap. 4.50 (ISBN 0-486-22332-9). Dover.

MATHEMATICS, ARABIC

Abu Al-Hasan & Ahmed-Ibn Ibrahim. The Arithmetic of Al-Uqlidisi. Saidan, A. S., tr. 1978. lib. bdg. 103.00 (ISBN 90-277-0752-9, Pub. by Reidel Holland). Kluwer Boston.

Al-Daffa, Ali A. The Muslim Contribution to Mathematics. 1977. text ed. 20.75x (ISBN 0-391-00714-9). Humanities.

Khayyam, Omar. The Algebra of Omar Khayyam. Kasir, Daoud S., ed. LC 70-177135. (Columbia University. Teachers College. Contributions to Education: No. 385). Repr. of 1931 ed. 17.50 (ISBN 0-404-55385-0). AMS Pr.

Kushyar ibn Labban. Principles of Hindu Reckoning. Levey, Martin, ed. Petruck, Marvin, tr. (Medieval Science Pubns., No. 8). 128p. 1965. 17.50x (ISBN 0-299-03610-3). U of Wis Pr.

Shuja Ibn Aslam, Abukamil. The Algebra of Abu Kamil, in a Commentary by Mordecai Finzi. Levey, Martin, tr. (Publications in Medieval Science No. 10). 240p. 1966. 24.50x (ISBN 0-299-03800-9). U of Wis Pr.

MATHEMATICS, BABYLONIAN

Van Der Waerden, B. L. Science Awakening. 1961. 45.00x (ISBN 0-19-519076-9). Oxford U Pr.

MATHEMATICS, BUSINESS

see Business Mathematics

MATHEMATICS, CHINESE

Committee on Scholarly Communications with the Peoples Republic of China National Research Council. Pure & Applied Mathematics in the Peoples Republic of China. 1977. pap. 12.50 (ISBN 0-686-25566-6, PB279 509); microfiche 3.50 (ISBN 0-686-25567-4). Natl Tech Info.

Fitzgerald, Anne & Lane, Saunders M., eds. Pure & Applied Math in People's Republic of China. LC 77-79329. (CSCPRC Report: No. 3). 1977. pap. 8.25 (ISBN 0-309-02609-1). Natl Acad Pr.

Gould, S. H. Contemporary Chinese Research Mathematics, Vol. 2: A Report on Chinese-English Mathematical Dictionaries. 1964. 3.20 (ISBN 0-8218-0016-7, CED). Am Math.

Mikami, Y. The Development of Mathematics in China & Japan. 2nd ed. LC 74-6716. 383p. 1974. text ed. 12.95 (ISBN 0-8284-0149-7). Chelsea Pub.

Swetz, Frank. Mathematics Education in China: Its Growth & Development. 350p. 1974. 17.50x (ISBN 0-262-19121-0). MIT Pr.

Swetz, Frank & Kao, T. I. Was Pythagoras Chinese? An Examination of Right Triangle Theory in Ancient China. LC 76-41806. (Penn State Studies: No. 40). (Illus.). 1977. pap. 3.95 (ISBN 0-271-01238-2). Pa St U Pr.

MATHEMATICS, CONSTRUCTIVE

see Constructive Mathematics

MATHEMATICS, EGYPTIAN

Van Der Waerden, B. L. Science Awakening. 1961. 45.00x (ISBN 0-19-519076-9). Oxford U Pr.

MATHEMATICS, GREEK

see also Geometry–Early Works to 1800

Allman, George J. Greek Geometry from Thales to Euclid. facsimile ed. LC 75-13250. (History of Ideas in Ancient Greece Ser.). 1976. Repr. of 1889 ed. 16.00x (ISBN 0-405-07287-2). Arno.

Brumbaugh, Robert S. Plato's Mathematical Imagination: The Mathematical Passages in the Dialogues & Their Interpretation. LC 55-62013. (Illus.). 1954. 16.00 (ISBN 0-527-12900-3). Kraus Repr.

Clagett, Marshall. Archimedes in the Middle Ages, Vol. 1. Arabo-Latin Tradition. (Medieval Science Pubns., No. 6). (Illus.). 752p. 1964. 50.00x (ISBN 0-299-03360-0). U of Wis Pr.

Euclid. The Elements, 3 Vols. Heath, Thomas L., ed. 1926. pap. 6.00 ea; Vol 1. pap. (ISBN 0-486-60088-2); Vol 2. pap. (ISBN 0-486-60089-0); Vol 3. pap. (ISBN 0-486-60090-4). Dover.

Gow, James. Short History of Greek Mathematics. LC 68-21639. 1968. 11.95 (ISBN 0-8284-0218-3). Chelsea Pub.

Heath, Thomas L. A History of Greek Mathematics, 2 vols. (Illus.). 1058p. 1981. pap. 8.50 (ISBN 0-686-77392-6). Vol. I (ISBN 0-486-24073-8). Vol. II (ISBN 0-486-24074-6). Dover.

Nicomachus, Gerasenus. Introduction to Arithmetic. D'Ooge, Martin L., tr. Repr. of 1926 ed. 31.00 (ISBN 0-384-38816-7). Johnson Repr.

Sachs, Eva. Die Funf Platonischen Korper: Zur Geschichte der Mathematik & der Elementenlehre Platons & der Pythagoreer. facsimile ed. LC 75-13292. (History of Ideas in Ancient Greece Ser.). (Ger.). 1976. Repr. of 1917 ed. 14.00x (ISBN 0-405-07336-4). Arno.

Szabo, Arprad. The Beginnings of Greek Mathematics. (Synthese Historical Library: No. 17). 1978. lib. bdg. 53.00 (ISBN 90-277-0819-3, Pub. by Reidel Holland). Kluwer Boston.

Tannery, Paul. La Geometrie Grecque: Comment Son Histoire Nous Est Parvenue & E Que Nous En Savons. facsimile ed. LC 75-13296. (History of Ideas in Ancient Greece Ser.). (Fr.). 1976. Repr. of 1887 ed. 11.00x (ISBN 0-405-07340-2). Arno.

Taran, Leonardo. Asclepius of Tralles: Commentary to Nicomachus' Introduction to Arithmetic. LC 69-18747. (Transactions Ser.: Vol. 59, Pt. 4). 1969. pap. 2.00 (ISBN 0-87169-594-4). Am Philos.

Theon Of Smyrna. Theon of Smyrna: Mathematics Useful for Understanding Plato or, Pythagorean Arithmetic, Music, Astronomy, Spiritual Disciplines. Lawlor, Robert, tr. from Greek. LC 77-73716. (Secret Doctrine Reference Ser.). (Illus.). 1979. 11.95 (ISBN 0-913510-24-6). Wizards.

Thomas, Ivor, tr. Greek Mathematical Works, 2 Vols. (Loeb Classical Library: No. 335, 362). 11.00x (ISBN 0-686-76873-6). Vol. 1 (ISBN 0-674-99369-1). Vol. 2 (ISBN 0-674-99399-3). Harvard U Pr.

Tod, M. N. Ancient Greek Numerical Systems. 128p. 1979. 20.00 (ISBN 0-89005-290-5). Ares.

Toomer, G. J., tr. & commentary by. Diocles on Burning Mirrors. (Sources in the History of Mathematics & the Physical Sciences Ser.: Vol. 1). (Illus.). 240p. 1976. 37.10 (ISBN 0-387-07478-3). Springer-Verlag.

Van Der Waerden, B. L. Science Awakening. 1961. 45.00x (ISBN 0-19-519076-9). Oxford U Pr.

MATHEMATICS, HINDU

Kushyar ibn Labban. Principles of Hindu Reckoning. Levey, Martin, ed. Petruck, Marvin, tr. (Medieval Science Pubns., No. 8). 128p. 1965. 17.50x (ISBN 0-299-03610-3). U of Wis Pr.

Tirthaji, Bharati K. Vedic Mathematics. 1978. 12.95 (ISBN 0-89684-036-0, Pub. by Motilal Banarsidass India). Orient Bk Dist.

MATHEMATICS, JAPANESE

Smith, David Eugene & Mikami, Yoshio. History of Japanese Mathematics. 280p. 1914. 15.00 (ISBN 0-87548-170-1). Open Court.

MATHEMATICS, LOGIC OF

see Mathematics–Philosophy

MATHEMATICS, GERMAN

Hasse, Helmut. Mathematische Abhandlungen, 3 vols. Leopoldt, Heinrich W. & Roquette, Peter, eds. xxxvi, 1592p. 1975. 300.00x (ISBN 3-11-005931-2). De Gruyter.

Hesse, Ludwig O. Gesammelte Werke. LC 72-78370. 741p. 1972. Repr. text ed. 29.50 (ISBN 0-8284-0261-2). Chelsea Pub.

Landau, Edmund. Ueber Einige Neuee Fortschritte der additiven Zahlentheorie. (Cambridge Tracts in Mathematics & Mathematical Physics Ser: No. 35). (Ger.). 1971. Repr. of 1937 ed. 7.50 (ISBN 0-02-848330-8). Hafner.

MATHEMATICS AS A PROFESSION

Combined Membership List. (Miscellaneous Publications). 1980. 21.00 (ISBN 0-8218-0071-X). Am Math.

Curriculum Committee of St. Paul Technical Vocational Institute. Mathematics for Careers: Percents. LC 79-51557. (Trade Mathematics). 176p. pap. 5.80 (ISBN 0-8273-1880-4); instrs' guide 1.70 (ISBN 0-8273-1881-2). Delmar.

MAA Committee on Advisement & Personnel. Professional Opportunities in Mathematics. 10th ed. 1978. pap. 1.50x (ISBN 0-88385-431-7). Math Assn.

Rock, Sidney & Miller, Samuel I. Career Mathematics: Practical Applications for Nonmechanical & Business Occupations. (gr. 10 up). 1978. text ed. 13.95x (ISBN 0-8104-5536-6); pap. text ed. 10.95x (ISBN 0-8104-5535-8); tchrs'. guide 1.95 (ISBN 0-8104-5625-7). Hayden.

MATHEMATICS OF FINANCE

see Business Mathematics

MATHER, COTTON 1663-1728

Boas, Ralph & Boas, Louise. Cotton Mather, Keeper of the Puritan Conscience. (Illus.). 1964. Repr. of 1928 ed. 18.50 (ISBN 0-208-00332-0, Archon). Shoe String.

Cohen, I. Bernard, ed. Cotton Mather & American Science & Medicine: With Studies & Documents Concerning the Introduction of Inoculation or Variolation, 2 vols. LC 79-7974. (Three Centuries of Science in America Ser.). (Illus.). 1980. lib. bdg. 65.00x (ISBN 0-405-12556-9). Arno.

Holmes, Thomas J. Cotton Mather: A Bibliography of His Works, 3 vols. 1395p. 1974. Repr. Set. 70.00x (ISBN 0-89020-000-9). Crofton Pub.

Holmes, Thomas S. Cotton Mather: A Bibliography of His Works. 1940. Set. 70.00 (ISBN 0-89020-000-9). Vol 1 (ISBN 0-89020-001-7). Vol. 2 (ISBN 0-89020-002-5). Vol. 3 (ISBN 0-89020-003-3). Brown Bk.

Levin, David. Cotton Mather: The Young Life of the Lord's Remembrancer, 1663-1703. LC 78-2355. (Illus.). 1978. 17.50x (ISBN 0-674-17507-7). Harvard U Pr.

Levy, Babette M. Cotton Mather. (United States Authors Ser.: No. 328). 1979. lib. bdg. 9.95 (ISBN 0-8057-7261-8). Twayne.

--Cotton Mather. (Twayne United States Authors Ser.). 1979. lib. bdg. 8.95 (ISBN 0-8057-7261-8). G K Hall.

Lovelace, Richard. American Pietism of Cotton Mather. 1979. pap. 9.95 (ISBN 0-8028-1750-5). Eerdmans.

Marvin, Abijah P. The Life & Times of Cotton Mather. LC 72-1979. (American Biography Ser., No. 32). 1972. Repr. of 1892 ed. lib. bdg. 52.95 (ISBN 0-8383-1454-6). Haskell.

Mather, Cotton. Magnalia Christi Americana, Bks. I & II In 1 Vol. Murdock, Kenneth B., ed. (The John Harvard Library). 512p. 1976. text ed. 30.00x (ISBN 0-674-54155-3, Belknap Pr). Harvard U Pr.

--Paterna: The Autobiography of Cotton Mather. Bosco, Ronald A., ed. LC 76-10595. (Center for Editions of American Authors). 450p. 1976. lib. bdg. 50.00x (ISBN 0-8201-1273-9). Schol Facsimiles.

--Selected Letters of Cotton Mather. Silverman, Kenneth, ed. LC 78-142338. (Illus.). 1971. 27.50x (ISBN 0-8071-0920-7). La State U Pr.

Mather, Increase. Life & Death of That Reverend Man of God, Mr. Richard Mather. 94p. 1975. pap. 2.95 (ISBN 0-913126-06-3). York Mail Print.

Mather, Samuel. Life of the Very Reverend & Learned Cotton Mather. LC 72-78779. 1729. Repr. 19.00 (ISBN 0-403-01946-X). Somerset Pub.

--The Life of the Very Reverend & Learned Cotton Mather, D.D. & F.F.S. 1972. Repr. of 1729 ed. lib. bdg. 18.00 (ISBN 0-8422-8167-3). Irvington.

Middlekauff, Robert. Mathers: Three Generations of Puritan Intellectuals, 1596-1728. 1971. 19.95x (ISBN 0-19-501305-0). Oxford U Pr.

--The Mathers: Three Generations of Puritan Intellectuals, 1596-1728. LC 79-140912. 1976. pap. 5.95 (ISBN 0-19-502115-0, 479, GB). Oxford U Pr.

Wendell, Barrett. Cotton Mather: The Puritan Priest. 1978. Repr. of 1891 ed. lib. bdg. 35.00 (ISBN 0-8495-5626-0). Arden Lib.

MATHER, INCREASE, 1639-1723

Andros Tracts, 3 Vols. (Prince Society Publications: 5-7). 1966. 63.50 (ISBN 0-8337-0067-7). B Franklin.

Increase Mather Vs. Solomon Stoddard: Two Puritan Tracts. LC 72-141117. (Research Library of Colonial Americana). 1971. Repr. of 1700 ed. 17.00 (ISBN 0-405-03328-1). Arno.

Mather, Cotton. Ratio Disciplinae Fratrum Novanglorum: A Faithful Account of the Discipline Professed & Practised, in the Churches of New-England. LC 71-141114. (Research Library of Colonial Americana). 1971. Repr. of 1726 ed. 17.00 (ISBN 0-405-03327-3). Arno.

Middlekauff, Robert. Mathers: Three Generations of Puritan Intellectuals, 1596-1728. 1971. 19.95x (ISBN 0-19-501305-0). Oxford U Pr.

--The Mathers: Three Generations of Puritan Intellectuals, 1596-1728. LC 79-140912. 1976. pap. 5.95 (ISBN 0-19-502115-0, 479, GB). Oxford U Pr.

Murdock, Kenneth B. Increase Mather: The Foremost American Puritan. LC 66-24736. (Illus.). 1966. Repr. of 1925 ed. 12.50 (ISBN 0-8462-0780-X). Russell.

MATHEWS, ARTHUR

Kuhn, Isobel S. Green Leaf in Drought Time. 1957. pap. 1.95 (ISBN 0-8024-0046-9). Moody.

MATHEWS, CORNELIUS, 1817-1889

Stein, Allen F. Cornelius Matthews. (U. S. Authors Ser.: No. 221). 1974. lib. bdg. 10.95 (ISBN 0-8057-0478-7). Twayne.

MATHEWS, WILDA

Kuhn, Isobel S. Green Leaf in Drought Time. 1957. pap. 1.95 (ISBN 0-8024-0046-9). Moody.

MATHEWSON, CHRISTOPHER, 1880-1925

Mathewson, Christy. Pitching in a Pinch. LC 76-55835. (Illus.). 1977. 10.00 (ISBN 0-8128-2196-3); pap. 5.95 (ISBN 0-8128-2207-2). Stein & Day.

MATHIEU FUNCTIONS

Meixner, J., et al. Mathieu Functions & Spheroidal Functions & Their Mathematical Foundations. (Lecture Notes in Mathematics: Vol. 837). 126p. 1981. pap. 9.80 (ISBN 0-387-10282-5). Springer-Verlag.

MATILDA, QUEEN OF ENGLAND, 1102-1167

Potter, K. R., ed. Gesta Stephani. (Oxford Medieval Texts). 1976. 67.50x (ISBN 0-19-822234-3). Oxford U Pr.

MATILDA OF TUSCANY, 1046-1115

Huddy, Mary E. Matilda, Countess of Tuscany. 1977. Repr. of 1906 ed. lib. bdg. 25.00 (ISBN 0-8274-4326-9). R West.

MATHURINS

see Trinitarians

MATISSE, HENRI, 1869-1954

Barr, Alfred H., Jr. Matisse: His Art & His Public. LC 66-26118. (Museum of Modern Art Publications in Reprint Ser). Repr. of 1951 ed. 30.00 (ISBN 0-405-01525-9). Arno.

--Matisse: His Art & His Public. rev. & enl. ed. LC 66-26118. (Illus.). 592p. 1974. pap. 10.95 (ISBN 0-87070-469-9, Pub. by Museum Mod Art). NYGS.

Bock, Catherine C. Henri Matisse & Neo-Impressionism, 1898-1908. Foster, Stephen, ed. (Studies in Fine Arts--the Avant-Garde: No. 13). 1981. 41.95 (ISBN 0-8357-1169-2, Pub. by UMI Res Pr). Univ Microfilms.

Cowart, J., et al. Henri Matisse Paper Cut-Outs. (Illus.). 1978. 25.00 (ISBN 0-8109-1301-1). Abrams.

Elderfield, John. Henri Matisse-Cut-Outs. 1978. 22.50 (ISBN 0-8076-0885-8); pap. 10.95 (ISBN 0-8076-0886-6). Braziller.

--Matisse in the Collection of the Museum of Modern Art. LC 78-56155. (Illus.). 1978. 25.00 (ISBN 0-87070-470-2); pap. 12.50 (ISBN 0-87070-471-0). Museum Mod Art.

Flam, Jack D., ed. Matisse on Art. 1978. pap. 6.95 (ISBN 0-525-47490-0). Dutton.

Flanner, Janet. Men & Monuments. facs. ed. LC 73-121468. (Essay Index Reprint Ser). 1957. 19.50 (ISBN 0-8369-1876-2). Arno.

Gowing, Lawrence. Matisse. (World of Art Ser.). (Illus.). 1979. 17.95 (ISBN 0-19-520157-4); pap. 9.95 (ISBN 0-19-520158-2). Oxford U Pr.

Izerghina, A., intro. by. Henri Matisse. Rosengrant, R. J., et al, trs. Date not set. 45.00 (ISBN 0-89893-031-6). CDP.

Jacobus, John. Matisse. LC 72-6633. (Library of Great Painters). (Illus.). 160p. 1973. 40.00 (ISBN 0-8109-0277-X). Abrams.

Kostenevich, Albert. Matisse. (Illus.). 44p. (Orig.). 1981. pap. 4.95 (ISBN 0-8109-2240-1). Abrams.

Legg, Alicia, ed. The Sculpture of Matisse. LC 73-188667. (Illus.). 1972. pap. 3.50 (ISBN 0-87070-448-6). Museum Mod Art.

Lieberman, William S. Matisse: Fifty Years of His Graphic Art. 150p. 1981. 30.00 (ISBN 0-8076-0037-7); pap. 12.95 (ISBN 0-8076-1022-4). Braziller.

Longstreet, Stephen, ed. The Drawings of Matisse. 48p. treasure trove bdg. 6.47x (ISBN 0-685-27799-2); pap. 2.95 (ISBN 0-685-27800-X). Borden.

Matisse, No. 46-47. (Derriere le Miroir Ser.). (Fr.). 1977. pap. 19.95 (ISBN 0-8120-0911-8). Barron.

Matisse, Herni. Matisse Line Drawings & Prints. (Illus.). 1980. pap. 2.00 (ISBN 0-486-23877-6). Dover.

Russell, John. World of Matisse. (Library of Art). (Illus.). 1969. 15.95 (ISBN 0-8094-0249-1). Time-Life.

--World of Matisse. LC 69-19503. (Library of Art Ser.). (Illus.). (gr. 6 up). 1969. 12.96 (ISBN 0-8094-0278-5, Pub. by Time-Life). Silver.

MATRIARCHY

see also Family; Matrilineal Kinship

De Moubray, George A. Matriarchy in the Malay Peninsula & Neighbouring Countries. LC 77-87025. Repr. of 1931 ed. 34.50 (ISBN 0-404-16810-8). AMS Pr.

Families Headed by Women in New York City: An Analysis of the 1970 Census Facts. 1975. pap. 2.00 (ISBN 0-86671-069-8). Comm Coun Great NY.

Farnsworth, William O. Uncle & Nephew in the Old French Chansons De Geste. LC 70-168008. (Columbia University. Studies in Romance Philology & Literature: No. 14). Repr. of 1913 ed. 22.00 (ISBN 0-404-50614-3). AMS Pr.

Malinowski, Bronislaw. Father in Primitive Psychology. 1966. pap. 2.95 (ISBN 0-393-00332-9, Norton Lib). Norton.

Potter, Murray A. Sohrab & Rustem, the Epic Theme of a Combat Between Father & Son: A Study of Its Genesis & Use in Literature & Popular Tradition. LC 75-144527. (Grimm Library: No. 14). Repr. of 1902 ed. 11.50 (ISBN 0-404-53557-7). AMS Pr.

Schmidt, Wilhelm. Das Mutterrecht. Repr. of 1955 ed. 23.00 (ISBN 0-384-54095-3). Johnson Repr.

MATRICES

see also Eigenvalues; Games of Strategy (Mathematics); Linear Programming; Matrix Groups; Multivariate Analysis

Almon, Clopper. Matrix Methods in Economics. 1967. 14.95 (ISBN 0-201-00224-8). A-W.

Althoen, Steven C. & Bumcrot, Robert J. Matrix Methods in Finite Mathematics: An Introduction with Applications to Business & Industry. new ed. 350p. 1976. text ed. 14.95x (ISBN 0-393-09192-9). Norton.

Amundson, Neal R. Mathematical Methods in Chemical Engineering: Matrices & Their Application. 1966. ref. ed. 25.95 (ISBN 0-13-561084-2). P-H.

Atkinson, F. V. Multiparameter Eignevalue Problems: Matrices & Compact Operators. (Mathematics in Science & Engineering Ser.). 1972. Vol. 1. 33.50 (ISBN 0-12-065801-1); Vol.2. write for info. (ISBN 0-12-065802-X). Acad Pr.

Ayres, Frank, Jr. Matrices. (Schaum's Outline Ser). (Orig.). 1968. pap. 4.95 (ISBN 0-07-002656-4, SP). McGraw.

Azar, J. J. Matrix Structural Analysis. 1972. text ed. 28.00 (ISBN 0-08-016781-0). Pergamon.

Bart, H., et al. Minimal Factorization of Matrix & Operator Functions. (Operator Theory: Advances & Applications Ser.: No. 1). 236p. 1979. pap. 17.50 (ISBN 3-7643-1139-8). Birkhauser.

Beer. Applied Calculus for Business & Economics: With an Introduction to Matrics. (Illus.). 1978. text ed. 18.95 (ISBN 0-87626-039-3). Winthrop.

Ben-Israel, Adi & Greville, Thomas N. Generalized Inverses: Theory & Applications. LC 79-13385. 410p. 1980. Repr. of 1974 ed. lib. bdg. 24.00 (ISBN 0-88275-991-4). Krieger.

Berman, A. Cones, Matrices & Mathematical Programming. LC 72-96725. (Lecture Notes in Economics & Mathematical Systems: Vol. 79). 96p. 1973. pap. 8.80 (ISBN 0-387-06123-1). Springer-Verlag.

Berman, Abraham & Plemmons, Robert J. Non-Negative Matrices in the Mathematical Sciences. (Computer Sciences & Applied Mathematics Ser.). 1979. 40.00 (ISBN 0-12-092250-9). Acad Pr.

Blaker, J. W. Geometric Optics: The Matrix Theory. 1971. 19.50 (ISBN 0-8247-1046-0). Dekker.

Bommer, C. M. & Symonds, D. A. Skeletal Structures: Matrix. 1968. 29.75x (ISBN 0-677-61120-X). Gordon.

Boullion, Thomas L. & Odell, Patrick L. Generalized Inverse Matrices. 116p. 1971. 15.00 (ISBN 0-471-09110-3, Pub. by Wiley). Krieger.

Braae, R. Matrix Algebra for Electrical Engineers. (Illus.). 1965. 6.50 (ISBN 0-201-00651-0, Adv Bk Prog). A-W.

Brickell, F. Matrices & Vector Spaces. (Problem Solvers). (Illus.). 1972. text ed. 10.95x (ISBN 0-04-512016-1); pap. text ed. 4.95x (ISBN 0-04-512017-X). Allen Unwin.

Bronson, R. Matrix Methods: An Introduction. 1970. text ed. 19.95 (ISBN 0-12-135250-1). Acad Pr.

Brown, Homer E. Solution of Large Networks by Matrix Methods. LC 74-34159. 256p. 1975. 29.00 (ISBN 0-471-11045-0, Pub. by Wiley-Interscience). Wiley.

Bunch, James R., ed. Sparse Matrix Computations. 1976. 31.50 (ISBN 0-12-141050-1). Acad Pr.

Campbell, Hugh G. Introduction to Matrices, Vectors & Linear Programming. 2nd ed. LC 76-22757. (Illus.). 1977. text ed. 18.95 (ISBN 0-13-487439-0). P-H.

--Matrices with Applications. (Illus.). 1968. pap. text ed. 10.95 (ISBN 0-13-565424-6). P-H.

Childress, Robert L. Sets, Matrices & Linear Programmings. LC 73-17313. (Illus.). 224p. 1974. ref. ed. 12.95 (ISBN 0-13-806737-6). P-H.

Chu-Kia, Wang. Introductory Structural Analysis with Matrix Methods. LC 72-667. 240p. 1973. ref. ed. 26.95 (ISBN 0-13-501650-9). P-H.

Cline, Randall E. Elements of the Theory of Generalized Inverses of Matrices. 94p. 1979. pap. text ed. 5.95 (ISBN 3-7643-3013-9). Birkhauser.

Cradock, S. & Hinchcliffe, A. J. Matrix Isolation. LC 74-31786. (Illus.). 140p. 1975. 29.95 (ISBN 0-521-20759-2). Cambridge U Pr.

Cunninghame-Green, R. A. Minimax Algebra. LC 79-1314. (Lecture Notes in Economics & Mathematical Systems: Vol. 166). 1979. pap. 15.00 (ISBN 0-387-09113-0). Springer-Verlag.

Davis, P. J. The Mathematics of Matrices: A First Book of Matrix Theory & Linear Algebra. 2nd ed. 1973. text ed. 22.95 (ISBN 0-471-00928-8). Wiley.

Davis, Philip J. Circulant Matrices. LC 79-10551. (Pure & Applied Mathematics: Texts, Monographs, & Tracts). 1979. 23.00 (ISBN 0-471-05771-1, Pub. by Wiley-Interscience). Wiley.

Davis, Stanley M., et al. Matrix. LC 77-81192. (An Organization Development Ser.). 1977. pap. text ed. 7.95 (ISBN 0-201-01115-8). A-W.

Donoghue, W. F., Jr. Monotone Matrix Functions & Analytic Continuation. LC 73-15293. (Grundlehren der Mathematischen Wissenschaften: Vol. 207). 210p. 1974. 27.80 (ISBN 0-387-06543-1). Springer-Verlag.

Duff, I., ed. Sparse Matrices & Thier Uses. 1981. write for info. (ISBN 0-12-223280-1). Acad Pr.

Eves, Howard. Elementary Matrix Theory. 1980. pap. 5.50 (ISBN 0-486-63946-0). Dover.

Faddeeva, V. N. Computational Methods of Linear Algebra. 1959. pap. 4.50 (ISBN 0-486-60424-1). Dover.

Finkbeiner, Daniel T., 2nd. Introduction to Matrices & Linear Transformations. 3rd ed. LC 78-18257. (Mathematical Sciences Ser.). (Illus.). 1978. text ed. 21.95x (ISBN 0-7167-0084-0). W H Freeman.

Forsythe, George E. & Moler, C. Computer Solution of Linear Algebraic Systems. 1967. ref. ed. 19.95 (ISBN 0-13-165779-8). P-H.

Franklin, Joel N. Matrix Theory. 1968. ref. ed. 22.95 (ISBN 0-13-565648-6). P-H.

Frazer, Robert A., et al. Elementary Matrices & Some Applications to Dynamics & Differential Equations. LC 76-29426. (BCL Ser.: II). Repr. of 1946 ed. 34.00 (ISBN 0-404-15334-8). AMS Pr.

Gantmacher, Felix R. Theory of Matrices, 2 Vols. LC 59-11779. Vol. 1. 15.95 (ISBN 0-8284-0131-4); Vol. 2. 12.95 (ISBN 0-8284-0133-0). Chelsea Pub.

Gelbart, Stephen S. Fourier Analysis on Matrix Space. LC 52-42839. (Memoirs: Vol. 108). 1971. pap. 6.40 (ISBN 0-8218-1808-2, MEMO-108). Am Math.

Gere, James M. Matrix Algebra for Engineers. (Orig.). 1965. pap. text ed. 9.95x (ISBN 0-442-02636-6). Van Nos Reinhold.

Ghali, A. & Neville, A. M. Structural Analysis: A Unified Classical & Matrix Approach. 2nd ed. LC 77-13954. 779p. 1978. pap. 24.95x (ISBN 0-412-14990-7, Pub. by Chapman & Hall). Methuen Inc.

Gourlay, A. R. & Watson, G. A. Computational Methods for Matrix Eigenproblems. LC 73-2783. 1979. pap. text ed. 13.25x (ISBN 0-471-27586-7, Pub. by Wiley-Interscience). Wiley.

Gregory, Robert & Karney, David L. A Collection of Matrices for Testing Computational Algorithms. LC 77-19262. 164p. 1978. Repr. of 1969 ed. lib. bdg. 15.00 (ISBN 0-88275-649-4). Krieger.

Hammer, A. G. Elementary Matrix Algebra for Psychologists & Social Scientists. LC 72-117464. 212p. 1971. 12.75 (ISBN 0-08-017502-3). Pergamon.

Hancock, Norman N. Matrix Analysis of Electrical Machinery. 2nd ed. LC 74-3286. 1974. text ed. 25.00 (ISBN 0-08-017898-7); pap. text ed. 13.25 (ISBN 0-08-017899-5). Pergamon.

Hill, Ray & White, B. Joseph, eds. Matrix Organization & Project Management: Theory & Practice. (Michigan Business Papers Ser.: No. 64). (Illus.). 1979. pap. 12.95 (ISBN 0-87712-196-6). U Mich Busn Div Res.

Hilton, Gordon. Intermediate Politometrics. LC 75-43733. 336p. 1976. 17.00x (ISBN 0-231-03783-X). Columbia U Pr.

Hohn, Franz E. Elementary Matrix Algebra. 3rd ed. 1973. text ed. 22.95 (ISBN 0-02-355950-0). Macmillan.

Iagolnitzer, D. The S-Matrix. 1978. 36.75 (ISBN 0-444-85060-0, North-Holland). Elsevier.

Joshi, A. W. Matrices & Tensors in Physics. LC 75-26772. 251p. 1976. 9.95 (ISBN 0-470-45086-X). Halsted Pr.

Kardestuncer, Hayrettin. Elementary Matrix Analysis of Structures. (Illus.). 448p. 1974. text ed. 25.50 (ISBN 0-07-033318-1, C); solutions manual 3.00 (ISBN 0-07-033319-X). McGraw.

Katz, M. B. Questions of Uniqueness & Resolution in Reconstruction of 2-D & 3-D Objects from Their Projections. (Lecture Notes in Biomathematics: Vol. 26). 1979. pap. 11.30 (ISBN 0-387-09087-8). Springer-Verlag.

Kowalewski, Gerhard. Determinantentheorie. 3rd ed. LC 49-22682. (Ger). 14.95 (ISBN 0-8284-0039-3). Chelsea Pub.

Lomont, John S. Applications of Finite Groups. 1959. 38.50 (ISBN 0-12-455550-0). Acad Pr.

MacDuffee, Cyrus C. Theory of Matrices. 2nd ed. LC 49-2197. 8.95 (ISBN 0-8284-0028-8). Chelsea Pub.

Maddox, I. J. Infinite Matrices of Operators. (Lecture Notes in Mathematics: Vol. 786). 122p. 1980. pap. 9.80 (ISBN 0-387-09764-3). Springer-Verlag.

Martin, Harold C. Introduction to Matrix Methods of Structural Analysis. 1966. text ed. 25.50 (ISBN 0-07-040633-2, C). McGraw.

Mehta, Madan L. Random Matrices. 1967. 44.50 (ISBN 0-12-488050-9). Acad Pr.

Moore, John T. Elementary Linear & Matrix Algebra: The Viewpoint of Geometry. (Illus.). 288p. 1972. text ed. 15.95 (ISBN 0-07-042910-3, C); solutions manual 4.50 (ISBN 0-07-042886-7). McGraw.

--Elements of Linear Algebra & Matrix Theory. (International Pure & Applied Mathematics Ser). 1968. text ed. 16.95 (ISBN 0-07-042885-9, C). McGraw.

Newman, Morris. Integral Matrices. (Pure & Applied Mathematics Ser.: Vol. 45). 1972. 38.00 (ISBN 0-12-517850-6). Acad Pr.

Painter, Richard J. & Yantis, Richard C. Elementary Matrix Algebra with Applications. 2nd ed. 1977. text ed. write for info. (ISBN 0-87150-227-5, PWS 1801). Prindle.

Peck, Lyman C. Secret Codes, Remainder Arithmetic, & Matrices. LC 61-12376. 1961. pap. 2.00 (ISBN 0-87353-090-X). NCTM.

Pettofrezzo, Anthony J. Matrices & Transformations. 1978. pap. text ed. 3.00 (ISBN 0-486-63634-8). Dover.

Pringle, R. M. & Rayner, A. A. Generalized Inverse Matrices with Applications to Statistics. Stuart, Alan, ed. (Griffin's Statistical Monographs & Courses Ser: No. 28). 1970. pap. 11.00 (ISBN 0-02-850360-0). Hafner.

Przemieniecki, J. S. Theory of Matrix Structural Analysis. 1968. text ed. 27.50 (ISBN 0-07-050904-2, C). McGraw.

Rao, C. R. & Mitra, Sujit K. Generalized Inverse of Matrices & Its Applications. LC 74-158528. (Ser. in Probability & Statistics Section). 1971. 31.00 (ISBN 0-471-70821-6, Pub. by Wiley-Interscience). Wiley.

Rau, Nicholas. Matrices & Mathematical Prgramming: An Introduction for Economists. 1980. 18.50 (ISBN 0-312-52299-1). St Martin.

Reiner, I. Introduction to Matrix Theory & Linear Algebra. LC 79-151082. 1971. pap. text ed. 8.95 (ISBN 0-03-085410-5, HoltC). HR&W.

Rose, D. J. & Willoughby, R. A., eds. Sparse Matrices & Their Applications. LC 71-188917. (IBM Research Symposia Ser). 210p. 1972. 25.00 (ISBN 0-306-30587-9, Plenum Pr). Plenum Pub.

Rubinstein, Moshe F. Matrix Computer Analysis of Structures. (Illus.). 1966. 26.95 (ISBN 0-13-565481-5). P-H.

Schneider, Hans, ed. Recent Advances in Matrix Theory. (Mathematics Research Center Pubns., No. 12). (Illus.). 1964. 17.50x (ISBN 0-299-03220-5). U of Wis Pr.

Searle, S. R. Matrix Algebra for the Biological Sciences: Including Applications in Statistics. LC 66-11528. (Quantitative Methods for Biologists & Medical Statistics Ser.). 1966. 30.00 (ISBN 0-471-76930-4, Pub. by Wiley-Interscience). Wiley.

Searle, S. R. & Hausman, W. H. Matrix Algebra for Business & Economics. LC 66-11528. 1970. 33.50 (ISBN 0-471-76941-X, Pub. by Wiley-Interscience). Wiley.

Shank, J. K. Matrix Methods in Accounting: An Introduction. 1972. pap. text ed. 6.50 (ISBN 0-201-07053-7). A-W.

Shipley, R. Bruce. Introduction to Matrices & Power Systems. LC 76-16482. 1976. 33.00 (ISBN 0-471-78642-X, Pub. by Wiley-Interscience). Wiley.

Silberger, A. J. P G L-2, Over the P-Adics: Its Representations, Spherical Functions, & Fourier Analysis. LC 70-139951. (Lecture Notes in Mathematics: Vol. 166). 1970. pap. 11.20 (ISBN 0-387-05193-7). Springer-Verlag.

Smythe, R. T. & Wierman, J. C. First-Passage Percolation on the Square Lattics. LC 78-13679. (Lecture Notes in Mathematics: Vol. 671). 1978. pap. 14.40 (ISBN 0-387-08928-4). Springer-Verlag.

Steinberg, David. Computational Matrix Algebra. (Illus.). 320p. 1974. text ed. 18.95 (ISBN 0-07-061110-6, C). McGraw.

Sullins, Walter L. Matrix Algebra for Statistical Applications. (Illus.). 1973. pap. 2.95x (ISBN 0-8134-1591-8, 1591). Interstate.

Suprunenko, Dmitri A. & Tyshkevich, R. I. Commutative Matrices. LC 68-18683. (Orig.). 1968. 25.50 (ISBN 0-12-677049-2); pap. 14.50 (ISBN 0-12-677050-6). Acad Pr.

Varga, Richard S. Matrix Iterative Analysis. 1962. ref. ed. 22.95 (ISBN 0-13-565507-2). P-H.

Venancio Filho, Fernando. Introduction to Matrix Structural Theory in Its Application to Civil & Aircraft Construction. LC 67-14507. 11.50 (ISBN 0-8044-4965-1). Ungar.

Wang, C. K. Matrix Methods of Structural Analysis. (Illus.). 1977. Repr. of 1966 ed. text ed. 18.50x (ISBN 0-89534-000-3). Am Pub Co WI.

Wang, Ping'Chun. Numerical & Matrix Methods in Structural Mechanics, with Applications to Computers. LC 66-11529. 1966. 41.50 (ISBN 0-471-91950-0, Pub. by Wiley-Interscience). Wiley.

Westlake, Joan R. Handbook of Numerical Matrix Inversion & Solution of Linear Equations. LC 74-26623. 182p. 1975. Repr. of 1968 ed. 13.50 (ISBN 0-88275-225-1). Krieger.

Wilkinson, James H. Algebraic Eigenvalue Problem. (Monographs on Numerical Analysis Ser). 1965. 89.00x (ISBN 0-19-853403-5). Oxford U Pr.

MATRICES–PROGRAMMED INSTRUCTION

Dorf, Richard C. Matrix Algebra: A Programmed Introduction. 1969. pap. 15.95 (ISBN 0-471-21909-6). Wiley.

MATRILINEAL KINSHIP

Hartland, Edwin S. Matrilineal Kinship & the Question of Its Priority. LC 18-15715. 1917. pap. 7.00 (ISBN 0-527-00516-9). Kraus Repr.

Nakane, Chie. Garo & Khasi: A Comparative Study in Matrilineal Systems. 1967. pap. text ed. 22.25x (ISBN 0-686-22433-7). Mouton.

Schneider, David M. & Gough, Kathleen, eds. Matrilineal Kinship. (California Library Reprint Ser.). 1974. 42.50x (ISBN 0-520-02587-3); pap. 10.95x (ISBN 0-520-02529-6, CAMPUS 103). U of Cal Pr.

MATRIMONIAL ACTIONS

see also Alimony; Marriage–Annulment

Djamour, Judith. Muslim Matrimonial Court in Singapore. (Monographs on Social Anthropology: No. 31). 1966. text ed. 20.75x (ISBN 0-485-19531-3, Athlone Pr). Humanities.

O'Gorman, Hubert J. Lawyers & Matrimonial Cases: Study of Informal Pressures in Private Professional Practices. Zuckerman, Harriet & Merton, Robert K., eds. LC 79-3754. (Dissertations on Sociology Ser.). 1980. Repr. of 1963 ed. lib. bdg. 18.00x (ISBN 0-405-12986-6). Arno.

Stone, Olive M. Family Law. xxxv, 277p. 1977. text ed. 25.00x (ISBN 0-333-19629-5). Rothman.

MATRIMONIAL REGIME

see Husband and Wife

MATRIMONIAL SUITS

see Matrimonial Actions

MATRIMONY

see Marriage

MATRIX GROUPS

Curtis, M. L. Matrix Groups. LC 79-23523. (Universitext Ser.). 191p. 1980. pap. 12.60 (ISBN 3-540-90462-X). Springer-Verlag.

Graham, Alexander. Matrix Theory & Applications for Engineers & Mathematicians. LC 79-40988. (Mathematics & Its Applications). 295p. 1980. pap. 27.95 (ISBN 0-470-27072-1). Halsted Pr.

Hinze, J., ed. The Unitary Group for the Evaluation of Electronic Energy: Matrix Elements. (Lecture Notes in Chemistry Ser.: Vol. 22). 371p. 1981. pap. 25.50 (ISBN 0-387-10287-6). Springer-Verlag.

Neuts, Marcel F. Matrix-Geometric Solutions in Stochastic Models. LC 80-8872. (Johns Hopkins Series in the Mathematical Sciences: No. 2). 352p. 1981. text ed. 32.50x (ISBN 0-8018-2560-1). Johns Hopkins.

Rogers. Matrix Derivatives. (Lecture Notes in Statistics Ser.: Vol. 2). 224p. 1980. 27.50 (ISBN 0-8247-1176-9). Dekker.

MATRIX MECHANICS

see also Quantum Statistics; Quantum Theory; S-Matrix Theory; Wave Mechanics

Barker, V. A., ed. Sparse Matrix Techniques. LC 77-1128. (Lecture Notes in Mathematics: Vol. 572). 1977. pap. 10.10 (ISBN 0-387-08130-5). Springer-Verlag.

Bhatt, P. Problems in Structural Analysis by Matrix Methods. (Illus.). 270p. (Orig.). 1981. pap. text ed. 22.50x (ISBN 0-86095-881-7). Longman.

Bray, K. H., et al. Matrix Analysis of Structures. 1978. pap. 8.95x (ISBN 0-7131-3373-2, Pub. by Edward Arnold). Intl Schol Bk Serv.

Chew, Geoffrey F. S-Matrix Theory of Strong Interactions. (Frontiers in Physics Ser.: No. 2). 1962. 10.00 (ISBN 0-8053-1950-6, Adv Bk Prog). Benjamin-Cummings.

Crouch, T. Matrix Methods Applied to Engineering Rigid Body Mechanics. LC 80-41186. 385p. 1980. 46.00 (ISBN 0-08-024245-6); pap. 18.00 (ISBN 0-08-024246-4). Pergamon.

Dirac, Paul A. Principles of Quantum Mechanics. 4th ed. (Int'l Series of Monographs on Physics). 1958. 29.50x (ISBN 0-19-851208-2). Oxford U Pr.

Ghadially, Feroze N. Ultrastructural Pathology of the Cell & Matrix. 2nd ed. 752p. 1981. text ed. price not set (ISBN 0-407-00166-2). Butterworth.

International Symposium on Recent Developments in Classical Wave Scattering, Ohio State Univ., Columbus, 1979. Recent Developments in Classical Wave Scattering: Focus on the T-Matrix Approach. Varadan, V. V. & Varadan, V. K., eds. (Illus.). 670p. 1980. 70.00 (ISBN 0-08-025096-3). Pergamon.

Jacobson, D. H. Extensions of Linear-Quadratic Control, Optimization & Matrix Theory. 1977. 34.50 (ISBN 0-12-378750-5). Acad Pr.

Jennings, Alan. Matrix Computation for Engineers & Scientists. LC 76-21079. 330p. 1980. pap. 16.50 (ISBN 0-471-27832-7, Pub. by Wiley Interscience). Wiley.

Meek, J. L. Matrix Structural Analysis. 1971. 24.50 (ISBN 0-07-041316-9, C). McGraw.

Smith, B. T., et al. Matrix Eigensystem Routines-Eispack Guide. (Lecture Notes in Computer Science: Vol. 6). 1976. pap. 19.10 (ISBN 0-387-07546-1). Springer-Verlag.

Von Neumann, John. Mathematical Foundations of Quantum Mechanics. (Investigations in Physics Ser.: Vol. 2). 1955. pap. 25.00x (ISBN 0-691-08003-8). Princeton U Pr.

Von Randow, R. Introduction to the Theory of Matroids. (Lecture Notes Economics & Mathematics System Ser.: Vol. 109). ix, 102p. 1975. pap. 10.00 (ISBN 0-387-07177-6). Springer-Verlag.

MATRONS OF DORMITORIES

see Housemothers

MATSOUKA, YOKO, 1916-

Matsuoka, Yoko. Daughter of the Pacific. LC 72-12634. 245p. 1973. Repr. of 1952 ed. lib. bdg. 15.00 (ISBN 0-8371-6683-7, MADP). Greenwood.

MATSUDA, KIYOKO

Danker, William. More Than Healing. LC 73-78105. 128p. 1973. pap. 2.50 (ISBN 0-570-03161-3, 12-2565). Concordia.

MATSUO, BASHO, 1664-1694

see Basho, Matsuo, 1644-1694

MATTER

see also Form (Philosophy); Hylomorphism; Interstellar Matter; Substance (Philosophy)

Balian, R., et al, eds. Ill-Condensed Matter. 550p. 1979. 97.50 (ISBN 0-444-85296-4, North Holland). Elsevier.

Blair, G. W. Measurement of Mind & Matter. 1956. 4.50 (ISBN 0-8022-0138-5). Philos Lib.

Booth, Verne H. & Bloom, Mortimer. Physical Science: A Study of Matter & Energy. 3rd ed. (Illus.). 800p. 1972. text ed. 19.95 (ISBN 0-02-312280-3, 31228). Macmillan.

Carington, Whately. Matter, Mind & Meaning. facsimile ed. LC 78-111818. (Essay Index Reprint Ser). 1949. 19.50 (ISBN 0-8369-1596-8). Arno.

Darwin, Charles G. The New Conceptions of Matter. facsimile ed. (Select Bibliographies Reprint Ser). Repr. of 1931 ed. 18.00 (ISBN 0-8369-6610-4). Arno.

Devreese, J. T., ed. Recent Developments in Condensed Matter Physics, Vol. 2. 470p. 1981. text ed. 59.50 (ISBN 0-306-40647-0, Plenum Pr). Plenum Pub.

--Recent Developments in Condensed Matter Physics, Vol. 3. 420p. 1981. text ed. 55.00 (ISBN 0-306-40648-9, Plenum Pr). Plenum Pub.

--Recent Developments in Condensed Matter Physics, Vol. 4. 448p. 1981. text ed. 57.50 (ISBN 0-306-40649-7, Plenum Pr). Plenum Pub.

Fujita, S. Science of Matter: Festschrift in Honor of Professor Ta You Wu. 1978. 71.00 (ISBN 0-677-13650-1). Gordon.

Graves, John C. Conceptual Foundations of Contemporary Relativity Theory. 1971. pap. text ed. 6.95x (ISBN 0-262-57049-1). MIT Pr.

Heisenberg, Werner. Natural Law & the Structure of Matter. 47p. 1981. pap. 5.00 (ISBN 0-900615-27-3, Pub. by Element Bks England). Hydra Bk.

Hinman, Frank. Impact of the New Physics. LC 60-15956. 1961. 4.50 (ISBN 0-8022-0725-1). Philos Lib.

Interaction of Radiation with Condensed Matter, Vol. I. (Illus.). 1977. pap. 48.00 (ISBN 92-0-130377-7, ISP443-1, IAEA). Unipub.

Joske, W. D. Material Objects. 1967. 17.95 (ISBN 0-312-52150-2). St Martin.

Leclerc, Ivor. The Nature of Physical Existence. (Muirhead Library of Philosophy). 300p. 1972. text ed. 16.50x (ISBN 0-04-100033-1). Humanities.

McMullin, Ernan. Newton on Matter & Activity. LC 77-82480. 1979. pap. text ed. 3.95x (ISBN 0-268-01343-8). U of Notre Dame Pr.

McMullin, Ernan, ed. Concept of Matter in Greek & Mediaeval Philosophy. 1965. pap. 4.95x (ISBN 0-268-00055-7). U of Notre Dame Pr.

--The Concept of Matter in Modern Philosophy. LC 74-27891. 370p. 1978. text ed. 14.95x (ISBN 0-268-00706-3); pap. text ed. 5.95x (ISBN 0-268-00707-1). U of Notre Dame Pr.

Marcinkowski, M. J. Unified Theory of Mechanical Behavior of Matter. LC 78-27799. 1979. 36.50 (ISBN 0-471-05434-8, Pub by Wiley-Interscience). Wiley.

Sanchez-Zarazua, J. R. The Theory of the Integration of Matter. 1978. 10.00 (ISBN 0-533-02685-7). Vantage.

Santayana, George. Realms of Being. LC 72-79638. xxxvi, 862p. 1972. Repr. of 1942 ed. lib. bdg. 24.00x (ISBN 0-8154-0425-5). Cooper Sq.

Savage, N. E. & Wood, R. S. Matter & Energy: General Science, Bk. 1. (Secondary Science Ser). (gr. 8-11). 1972. pap. text ed. 5.75 (ISBN 0-7100-7076-4). Routledge & Kegan.

Stewart, J. M. Non-Equilibrium Relativistic Kinetic Theory. LC 70-179436. (Lecture Notes in Physics: Vol. 10). iii, 113p. 1971. pap. 10.70 (ISBN 0-387-05652-1). Springer-Verlag.

Zichichi, A., ed. Understanding the Fundamental Constituents of Matter. (The Subnuclear Ser.). 980p. 1978. 75.00 (ISBN 0-306-38183-4, Plenum Pr). Plenum Pub.

MATTER–CONSTITUTION

see also Atoms; Chemical Structure; Dipole Moments; Electrons; Ether (Of Space); Molecular Theory; Nuclear Models; Nuclear Shell Theory; Neutrons; Protons

Beiser, Arthur. Concepts of Modern Physics. 2nd ed. (Fundamentals of Physics Ser.). (Illus.). 480p. 1973. text ed. 18.95 (ISBN 0-07-004363-9, C). McGraw.

Born, Max. Restless Universe. 2nd ed. (Illus.). 1951. pap. 4.50 (ISBN 0-486-20412-X). Dover.

Burstein, Elias & De Martini, Francesco, eds. Polaritons: Proceedings, Taormina Research Conference on the Structure of Matter, 1st, Taormina, Italy, Oct, 1972. LC 73-12845. 1974. text ed. 45.00 (ISBN 0-08-017825-1). Pergamon.

Eisberg, Robert M. Fundamentals of Modern Physics. LC 61-6770. (Illus.). 1961. 31.95 (ISBN 0-471-23463-X). Wiley.

Fano, U. & Fano, L. Physics of Atoms & Molecules: An Introduction to the Structure of Matter. LC 76-184808. 456p. 1973. text ed. 20.00x (ISBN 0-226-23782-6). U of Chicago Pr.

Gasiorowicz, Stephen. Structure of Matter: A Survey of Modern Physics. LC 78-18645. (Physics Ser.). (Illus.). 1979. text ed. 23.95 (ISBN 0-201-02511-6). A-W.

Karabetyants, M. & Drakin, S. The Structure of Matter. 335p. 1974. 4.10 (ISBN 0-8285-0804-6, Pub. by Mir Pubs Russia). Imported Pubns.

Kitaigorodsky, A. I. Order & Disorder in the World of Atoms. 165p. 1980. pap. 4.40 (ISBN 0-8285-1724-X, Pub. by Mir Pubs Russia). Imported Pubns.

Oldenberg, Otto & Holladay, Wendell G. Introduction to Atomic & Nuclear Physics. LC 77-5544. 424p. 1977. Repr. of 1949 ed. 19.50 (ISBN 0-88275-548-X). Krieger.

Polkinghorne, J. C. The Particle Play: An Account of the Ultimate Constituents of Matter. LC 79-17846. (Illus.). 1979. pap. text ed. 7.95x (ISBN 0-7167-1316-0). W H Freeman.

Samsonov, G. V., et al. A Configurational Model of Matter. LC 73-83893. (Studies in Soviet Science - Physical Sciences Ser.). (Illus.). 289p. 1973. 35.00 (ISBN 0-306-10890-9, Consultants). Plenum Pub.

Silverman, Sanford L. & Silverman, Martin G. Theory of Relationships. LC 63-13349. 1964. 6.00 (ISBN 0-8022-1571-8). Philos Lib.

Slater, John C. Quantum Theory of Molecules & Solids, Vol. 1, 3 & 4. Incl. Vol. 1. Electronic Structure of Molecules. 1963; Vol. 3. Insulators, Semiconductors & Solids. 1969; Vol. 4. The Self-Consistent Field for Molecules & Solids. 29.95 (ISBN 0-07-058038-3, C). C). McGraw.

Sommerfeld, Arnold. Atombau und Spektrallinien, 2 Vols. 1951. Set. 95.00 (ISBN 0-8044-4886-8); Vol. 1. 35.00 (ISBN 0-8044-4887-6); Vol. 2. 40.00 (ISBN 0-8044-4888-4). Ungar.

Symposium of the International Astronomical Union, 53rd, Boulder, 21-26 August, 1972. Physics of Dense Matter: Proceedings. Hansen, Carl J., ed. LC 73-91431. (IAU Symposium Ser: No. 53). 1974. lib. bdg. 53.00 (ISBN 90-277-0406-6, Pub. by Reidel Holland); pap. text ed. 37.50 (ISBN 90-277-0407-4, Pub. by Reidel Holland). Kluwer Boston.

Toulmin, Stephen & Goodfield, June. The Architecture of Matter. (Midway Reprint Ser). 1976. pap. text ed. 11.00x (ISBN 0-226-80839-4). U of Chicago Pr.

Trefil, James S. From Atoms to Quarks. (Illus.). 288p. 1980. 12.95 (ISBN 0-684-16484-1, ScribT). Scribner.

Wilson, William. Microphysical World. 1954. 3.75 (ISBN 0-8022-1898-9). Philos Lib.

MATTER-PROPERTIES

see also Anisotropy; Atomic Mass; Brownian Movements; Capillarity; Chemistry, Physical and Theoretical; Colloids; Compressibility; Diffusion; Elasticity; Flocculation; Gases; Gravitation; Ions; Mass (Physics); Solution (Chemistry); Torsion; Viscosity

Brophy, J. H., et al. Thermodynamics of Structure. (Structure & Properties of Materials Ser: Vol. 2). 1964. pap. text ed. 15.95x (ISBN 0-471-10610-0). Wiley.

Caspari, W. A. The Structure & Properties of Matter. 1979. Repr. of 1928 ed. lib. bdg. 12.50 (ISBN 0-8492-4021-2). R West.

Cottrell, A. H. The Mechanical Properties of Matter. LC 80-12439. 340p. 1981. Repr. of 1964 ed. lib. bdg. 23.50 (ISBN 0-89874-168-8). Krieger.

DeWitt, C. & DeWitt, eds. Les Houches Lectures: 1972, Black Holes. 564p. 1973. 104.00x (ISBN 0-677-15610-3). Gordon.

Enge, Harald A., et al. Introduction to Atomic Physics. LC 77-162464. 1972. text ed. 20.95 (ISBN 0-201-01871-3). A-W.

Flowers, B. H. & Mendoza, E. Properties of Matter. LC 70-11815. (Manchester Physics Ser.). 1970. 38.25 (ISBN 0-471-26497-0, Pub. by Wiley-Interscience). Wiley.

Goodstein, David L. States of Matter. 544p. 1975. 29.95 (ISBN 0-13-843557-X). P-H.

Gopal, E. S. Statistical Mechanics & Properities of Matter: Theory & Applications. LC 74-3382. 1976. pap. 27.95 (ISBN 0-470-15168-4). Halsted Pr.

Leighton, Robert B. Principles of Modern Physics. (International Ser. in Pure & Applied Physics). 1959. text ed. 22.95 (ISBN 0-07-037130-X, C). McGraw.

Levere, Trevor H. Affinity & Matter: Elements of Chemical Philosophy, 1800-1865. 248p. 1971. 37.50x (ISBN 0-19-858134-3). Oxford U Pr.

Lovesey, Stephen W. Condensed Matter Physics: Dynamic Correlations. LC 79-25794. (Frontiers of Physics Ser.: No. 49). 1980. text ed. 26.50 (ISBN 0-8053-6610-5); pap. text ed. 14.50 (ISBN 0-8053-6611-3). A-W.

Lundqvist, Bengt & Lundqvist, Stig, eds. Collective Properties of Physical Systems: Proceedings. 1974. 50.00 (ISBN 0-12-460350-5). Acad Pr.

McMullin, Ernan. Newton on Matter & Activity. LC 77-82480. 1978. text ed. 7.95x (ISBN 0-268-01342-X). U of Notre Dame Pr.

Marcinkowski, M. J. Unified Theory of Mechanical Behavior of Matter. LC 78-27799. 1979. 36.50 (ISBN 0-471-05434-8, Pub by Wiley-Interscience). Wiley.

Oparin, Alexander I. Origin of Life. 2nd ed. 1953. pap. 4.00 (ISBN 0-486-60213-3). Dover.

Pekalski, A. & Przystawa, J. A., eds. Modern Trends in the Theory of Condensed Matter: Proceedings. (Lecture Notes in Physics: Vol. 115). 587p. 1980. pap. 40.20 (ISBN 0-387-09752-X). Springer-Verlag.

Rickayzen, G. Green's Functions & Condensed Matter. 1981. 55.00 (ISBN 0-12-587950-4). Acad Pr.

Riste, T., ed. Fluctuations, Instabilities & Phase Transition. LC 75-32413. (NATO - Advanced Study Institute Ser.: (B: Physics), Vol. 11). 390p. 1975. 34.50 (ISBN 0-306-35711-9, Plenum Pr). Plenum Pub.

Touloukian, Y. S. & Ho, C. Y. Thermophysical Properties of Matter: Master Index to Materials & Properties. 1979. 75.00 (ISBN 0-306-67092-5). IFI Plenum.

MATTER AND FORM

see Hylomorphism

MATTERHORN

Rebuffat, Gaston. Between Heaven & Earth. Brockett, E., tr. (Illus.). 1965. 17.50 (ISBN 0-19-519058-0). Oxford U Pr.

--Men & the Matterhorn. Brockett, Eleanor, tr. (Illus.). 215p. 1973. 19.95 (ISBN 0-19-519059-9). Oxford U Pr.

Whymper, Edward. Scrambles Amongst the Alps in the Years Eighteen Sixty to Eighteen Sixty-Nine. (Illus.). 176p. 1981. pap. 12.95 (ISBN 0-89815-055-8). Ten Speed Pr.

Winnett, Thomas, ed. High Sierra Hiking Guide to Matterhorn Peak. 2nd ed. LC 75-10957. (High Sierra Hiking Guide Ser: Vol. 7). (Illus., Orig.). 1975. pap. 4.95 (ISBN 0-911824-44-8). Wilderness.

MATTHESON, JOHANN, 1681-1764

Cannon, Beekman C. Johann Mattheson, Spectator in Music. (Illus.). 1968. Repr. of 1947 ed. 16.50 (ISBN 0-208-00311-8, Archon). Shoe String.

MATTHEW, SAINT, APOSTLE

Dickson, David. Matthew. (Geneva Ser. Commentaries). Orig. Title: A Brief Exposition of the Evangel of Jesus Christ According to Matthew. 416p. 1981. 14.95 (ISBN 0-85151-319-0). Banner of Truth.

Johnson, Luke T. Some Hard Blessings: Meditations on the Beatitudes in Matthew. 96p. 1981. pap. 3.50 (ISBN 0-89505-058-7, 21053). Argus Comm.

MacDonald, William. Matthew: Behold Your King. pap. 4.95 (ISBN 0-937396-26-5). Walterick Pubs.

Tolbert, Malcolm O. Good News from Matthew. LC 75-2537. 256p. 1975. pap. 3.50 (ISBN 0-8054-1353-7). Broadman.

White, R. E. The Mind of Matthew. LC 79-23682. 1980. pap. 6.95 (ISBN 0-664-24310-X). Westminster.

MATUPI ISLAND

Epstein, A. L. Matupit: Land, Politics & Change Among the Tolai of New Britain. LC 70-92679. 1969. 24.50x (ISBN 0-520-01556-8). U of Cal Pr.

MATURATION (PSYCHOLOGY)

see also Adulthood; Emotional Maturity

Doll, Edgar A. Measurement of Social Competence. (Illus.). 1953. 15.00 (ISBN 0-913476-09-9). Am Guidance.

Hall, Manly P. A Vital Concept of Personal Growth. pap. 1.75 (ISBN 0-89314-367-7). Philos Res.

Heath, Douglas H. Explorations of Maturity: Studies of Mature & Immature College Men. LC 65-14792. (Century Psychology Ser.). (Illus.). 1965. text ed. 20.00x (ISBN 0-89197-160-2); pap. text ed. 6.95x (ISBN 0-89197-161-0). Irvington.

Johnston, F. E., et al, eds. Human Physical Growth & Maturation: Methodologies & Factors. (NATO Advanced Study Institute Series, Series A: Life Sciences: Vol. 30). 375p. 1980. 42.50 (ISBN 0-306-40420-6, Plenum Pr). Plenum Pub.

Kao, Charles C. Psychological & Religious Development: Maturity & Maturation. LC 80-5852. 382p. (Orig.). 1981. lib. bdg. 22.25 (ISBN 0-8191-1759-5); pap. text ed. 12.75 (ISBN 0-8191-1760-9). U Pr of Amer.

Katz, Richard. Preludes to Growth: An Experiential Approach. LC 72-94013. 1973. pap. text ed. 7.95 (ISBN 0-02-917190-3). Free Pr.

Kugelmass, I. Newton. Adolescent Immaturity: Prevention & Treatment. (American Lectures in Living Chemistry Ser.). (Illus.). 320p. 1973. text ed. 17.50 (ISBN 0-398-02707-2). C C Thomas.

Levinson, Daniel J., et al. The Seasons of a Man's Life. LC 77-20978. 1978. 12.95 (ISBN 0-394-40694-X). Knopf.

Loughary, John W. & Ripley, Theresa M. Career & Life Planning Guide: How to Choose Your Job, How to Change Your Career, How to Manage Your Life. (Illus.). 204p. 1976. pap. 5.95 (ISBN 0-695-80678-5). Follett.

Lyon, William. Let Me Live! rev. ed. 192p. 1975. 8.95 (ISBN 0-8158-0243-9); pap. 5.95 (ISBN 0-686-67119-8). Chris Mass.

McClelland, David C., ed. Development of Social Maturity. 1981. text ed. 18.50x (ISBN 0-8290-0089-5). Irvington.

Riley, Matilda W., ed. Aging from Birth to Death: Interdisciplinary Perspectives. (AAAS Selected Symposium: No. 30). (Illus.). 1979. lib. bdg. 20.00x (ISBN 0-89158-363-7). Westview.

Rosenfels, Paul. Love & Power: The Psychology of Interpersonal Creativity. LC 66-25081. 1966. 4.95 (ISBN 0-87212-009-0). Libra.

Rossi, Ernest L. Dreams & the Growth of Personality: Expanding Awareness in Psychotherapy. 232p. 1972. text ed. 19.00 (ISBN 0-08-016787-X). Pergamon.

Solomon, Joseph. A Synthesis of Human Behavior. LC 54-7258. (Illus.). 276p. 1954. 28.75 (ISBN 0-8089-0438-8). Grune.

MATURIN, BASIL WILLIAM, 1847-1915

Donald, Gertrude. Men Who Left the Movement. facs. ed. LC 67-23207. (Essay Index Reprint Ser). 1933. 18.00 (ISBN 0-8369-0385-4). Arno.

MATURIN, CHARLES ROBERT, 1780-1824

Harris, John B. Charles Robert Maturin: The Forgotten Imitator. Varma, Devendra P., ed. LC 79-8456. (Gothic Studies & Dissertations Ser.). 1980. lib. bdg. 33.00x (ISBN 0-405-12646-8). Arno.

Henderson, Peter M. A Nut Between Two Blades: The Novels of Charles Robert Maturin. Varma, Devendra P., ed. LC 79-8457. (Gothic Studies & Dissertations Ser.). 1980. lib. bdg. 25.00x (ISBN 0-405-12672-7). Arno.

Hinck, Henry W. Three Studies on Charles Robert Maturin. Varma, Devendra P., ed. LC 79-8458. (Gothic Studies & Dissertations Ser.). 1980. lib. bdg. 19.00x (ISBN 0-405-12647-6). Arno.

Kramer, Dale. Charles Robert Maturin. (English Authors Ser.: No. 156). 1973. lib. bdg. 10.95 (ISBN 0-8057-1382-4). Twayne.

Lougy, Robert E. Charles Robert Maturin. 89p. 1975. 4.50 (ISBN 0-8387-7941-7); pap. 1.95 (ISBN 0-8387-7986-7). Bucknell U Pr.

Monroe, Judson T. Tragedy in the Novels of the Reverend Charles Robert Maturin. Varma, Devendra P., ed. LC 79-8466. (Gothic Studies & Dissertation Ser.). 1980. lib. bdg. 22.00x (ISBN 0-405-12655-7). Arno.

Scott, Shirley C. Myths of Consciousness in the Novels of Charles Maturin. Varma, Devendra P., ed. LC 79-8479. (Gothic Studies & Dissertations Ser.). 1980. lib. bdg. 22.00x (ISBN 0-405-12661-1). Arno.

MATURITY, EMOTIONAL

see Emotional Maturity

MATUTE, ANA, MARIE

Diaz, Janet. Ana Maria Matute. LC 70-125268. (World Authors Ser.). 1971. lib. bdg. 12.95x (ISBN 0-8057-2600-4). Irvington.

Diaz, Janet W. Ana Maria Matute. (World Authors Ser.: No. 152). 10.95 (ISBN 0-686-75160-4). Twayne.

MAU MAU

Barnett, Donald L. & Njama, Karari. Mau Mau from Within. LC 65-24519. 1968. pap. 7.50 (ISBN 0-85345-135-4, PB-1354). Monthly Rev.

British Government. Handbook on Anti-Mau Mau Operations. 170p. 1977. pap. 8.00 (ISBN 0-87364-099-3). Paladin Ent.

Buijtenhuijs, Robert. Mau Mau: Twenty Years After, the Myth & the Survivors. (Publications of the Afrika-Studiecentrum, Leiden). (Illus.). 1973. pap. 27.25x (ISBN 90-2797-245-1). Mouton.

Clayton, Anthony. Counter-Insurgency in Kenya, 1952-1960: A Study of Military Operations Against the Mau Mau. (Transafrica Historical Papers: No. 4). (Illus.). 1976. pap. 5.00x (ISBN 0-8002-0203-1). Intl Pubns Serv.

Kariuki, Josiah M. Mau Mau Detainee: The Account by a Kenya African of His Experiences in Detention Camps 1953-1960. (Illus.). 214p. 1975. pap. 7.00x (ISBN 0-19-572381-3). Oxford U Pr.

Kinyatti, Maina W., ed. Thunder from the Mountain: Mau Mau Patriotic Songs. 128p. (Orig.). 1980. 10.95 (ISBN 0-905762-83-5, Pub. by Zed Pr); pap. cancelled (ISBN 0-905762-84-3). Lawrence Hill.

Leakey, Louis S. Defeating Mau Mau. LC 74-15061. Repr. of 1954 ed. 14.00 (ISBN 0-404-12102-0). AMS Pr.

Rosberg, Carl G., Jr. & Nottingham, John. The Myth of Mau Mau. LC 66-21793. (Publications Ser.: No. 49). 427p. 1966. 17.50 (ISBN 0-8179-1491-9). Hoover Inst Pr.

Rossberg, Carl, Jr. & Nottingham, John. Myth of the Mau Mau: Nationalism in Kenya. pap. 4.95 (ISBN 0-452-00297-4, F297, Mer). NAL.

Wamweya, Joram. Freedom Fighter. (Illus.). 201p. (Orig.). 1971. pap. 5.00x (ISBN 0-8002-0569-3). Intl Pubns Serv.

MAUA IRINEO EVANGELISTA DE SOUZA, VISCONDE DE, 1813-1889

Marchant, Anyda. Viscount Maua & the Empire of Brazil: A Biography of Irineu Evangelista De Sousa. 1965. 26.50x (ISBN 0-520-00807-3). U of Cal Pr.

MAUGHAM, FREDERIC HERBERT MAUGHAM, 1ST VISCOUNT, 1866-1958

Maugham, Robin. Somerset & All the Maughams. LC 75-22759. (Illus.). 1977. Repr. of 1966 ed. lib. bdg. 18.75x (ISBN 0-8371-8236-0, MASOM). Greenwood.

MAUGHAM, WILLIAM SOMERSET, 1874-1965

Aldington, Richard. W. Somerset Maugham: An Appreciation. LC 76-30814. 1977. lib. bdg. 7.50 (ISBN 0-8414-2953-7). Folcroft.

Bason, F. T. Bibliography of William Somerset Maugham. 1977. 22.50 (ISBN 0-685-81152-2). Porter.

Bason, Frederick T. Bibliography of the Writings of William Somerset Maugham. LC 73-16154. 1931. lib. bdg. 15.00 (ISBN 0-8414-9879-2). Folcroft.

--A Bibliography of the Writings of William Somerset Maugham. LC 74-6376. (Bibliography Ser., No. 59). 1974. lib. bdg. 49.95 (ISBN 0-8383-1880-0). Haskell.

--A Bibliography of the Writings of William Somerset Maugham. 1979. Repr. of 1931 ed. lib. bdg. 15.00 (ISBN 0-8495-0508-9). Arden Lib.

Cliff's Notes Editors. Of Human Bondage Notes. (Orig.). pap. 1.95 (ISBN 0-8220-0930-7). Cliffs.

Curtis, Anthony. The Pattern of Maugham: A Critical Portrait. 278p. 1974. 10.95 (ISBN 0-8008-6240-6). Taplinger.

--Somerset Maugham. (Illus.). 1977. 6.98 (ISBN 0-02-529280-3). Macmillan.

DuBose, Larocque. Barron's Simplified Approach to Maugham's Of Human Bondage. LC 67-31236. 1968. pap. text ed. 1.50 (ISBN 0-8120-0279-2). Barron.

Fisher, Richard B. Syrie Maugham. (Illus.). 104p. 1979. 22.00 (ISBN 0-7156-1307-3, Pub. by Duckworth England). Biblio Dist.

Hunt, Cecil. Author-Biography. 1979. Repr. of 1935 ed. lib. bdg. 30.00 (ISBN 0-8495-2257-9). Arden Lib.

Jensen, Sven A. William Somerset Maugham: Some Aspects of the Man & His Work. LC 72-194425. 1957. lib. bdg. 15.00 (ISBN 0-8414-5380-2). Folcroft.

Jonas, Klaus W., ed. The World of Somerset Maugham: An Anthology. LC 73-156196. 200p. 1972. Repr. of 1959 ed. lib. bdg. 18.75x (ISBN 0-8371-6147-9, JOSM). Greenwood.

MacCarthy, Desmond. William Somerset Maugham: An Appreciation. LC 73-3462. 1933. lib. bdg. 7.50 (ISBN 0-8414-2331-8). Folcroft.

McIver, Claude S. William Somerset Maugham: A Study of Technique & Literary Sources. LC 73-3463. 1936. lib. bdg. 15.00 (ISBN 0-8414-2346-6). Folcroft.

Maugham, Robin. Somerset & All the Maughams. LC 75-22759. (Illus.). 1977. Repr. of 1966 ed. lib. bdg. 18.75x (ISBN 0-8371-8236-0, MASOM). Greenwood.

Maugham, W. Somerset. Andalusia: The Land of the Blessed Virgin. LC 75-25381. (Works of W. Somerset Maugham Ser.). 1977. Repr. of 1920 ed. 15.00x (ISBN 0-405-07833-1). Arno.

--Don Fernando: Or Variations on Some Spanish Themes. LC 75-25382. (Works of W. Somerset Maugham Ser.). 1977. Repr. of 1935 ed. 15.00x (ISBN 0-405-07834-X). Arno.

--The Gentleman in the Parlour: A Record of a Journey from Rangoon to Haiphong. LC 75-25383. (Works of W. Somerset Maugham Ser.). 1977. Repr. of 1930 ed. 15.00x (ISBN 0-405-07836-6). Arno.

--Strictly Personal. LC 75-25376. (Works of W. Somerset Maugham Ser.). 1977. Repr. of 1941 ed. 15.00x (ISBN 0-405-07829-3). Arno.

--The Writer's Point of View. LC 73-16186. 1951. Repr. lib. bdg. 10.00 (ISBN 0-8414-6079-5). Folcroft.

Monarch Notes on Maugham's of Human Bondage. (Orig.). pap. 1.75 (ISBN 0-671-00622-3). Monarch Pr.

Morgan, Ted. Maugham. 1981. pap. 9.95 (ISBN 0-671-42811-X, Touchstone Bks). S&S.

--Maugham. 1980. 17.95 (ISBN 0-671-24077-3). S&S.

Raphael, Frederick. W. Somerset Maugham & His World. LC 76-19742. (Encore Edition). (Illus.). 1977. 3.95 (ISBN 0-684-16552-X, ScribT). Scribner.

Stirling, Nora. Who Wrote the Modern Classics. (John Day Bk.). (Illus.). 1970. 6.95 (ISBN 0-381-98184-3, A88500). T Y Crowell.

Toole-Scott, Raymond. A Bibliography of the Works of W. Somerset Maugham. rev., exp. ed. LC 73-175351. 320p. 1973. 25.00x (ISBN 0-575-01652-3). Intl Pubns Serv.

Towne, Charles H. W. Somersett Maugham, Novelist, Essayist, Dramatist. LC 76-13210. 1976. Repr. of 1925 ed. lib. bdg. 10.00 (ISBN 0-8414-8551-8). Folcroft.

Ward, Richard H. William Somerset Maugham. Repr. of 1937 ed. lib. bdg. 27.50 (ISBN 0-8414-9520-3). Folcroft.

MAUI
Clark, John R. The Beaches of Maui County. (Illus.). 1980. pap. 7.95 (ISBN 0-8248-0694-8). U Pr of Hawaii.
Gleasner, Bill & Gleasner, Diana. Maui Traveler's Guide. 1979. pap. 4.00 (ISBN 0-932596-08-8, Pub. by Oriental). Intl Schol Bk Serv.
Kyselka, Will & Lanterman, Ray. Maui: How It Came to Be. LC 80-10743. (Illus.). 128p. (gr. 5-10). 1980. pap. 5.95 (ISBN 0-8248-0530-5). U Pr of Hawaii.
Lewis, Paul M. Beautiful Maui. Shangle, Robert D., ed. (Illus.). 72p. 1981. 14.95 (ISBN 0-89802-277-0); pap. 7.95 (ISBN 0-89802-276-2). Beautiful Am.
Paitson, Hupi. Maui Booklet. (Illus.). 1970. pap. 0.50 (ISBN 0-686-12244-5). Aquarius.
Smith, Robert. Hiking Maui: The Valley Isle. 2nd ed. Winnett, Thomas, ed. LC 79-93159. (Wilderness Press Trail Guide Ser.). (Illus.). 144p. 1980. pap. 4.95 (ISBN 0-911824-99-5). Wilderness Pr.
Speakman, Cummins E., Jr., illus. Mowee, an Informal History of the Hawiian Island: An Internal History. (Illus.). 1978. 10.00 (ISBN 0-87577-056-8). Peabody Mus Salem.
Wenkam, Robert. Maui. LC 80-50364. (Illus.). 144p. 1980. 29.95 (ISBN 0-528-81537-7). Rand.

MAUI (POLYNESIAN DIETY)
Luomala, K. Maui-Of-A-Thousand-Tricks: His Oceanic & European Biographers. Repr. of 1949 ed. pap. 25.00 (ISBN 0-527-02306-X). Kraus Repr.
Lyons, Barbara. Maui, Mischievous Hero of Hawaii. (Illus.). 1969. pap. 2.95 (ISBN 0-912180-07-2). Petroglyph.

MAUNA LOA
Stone, Scott C. Volcano!! (Illus.). 1978. pap. 4.95 (ISBN 0-89610-064-2). Island Her.

MAUNOIR, JULIEN, 1606-1683
Harney, Martin P. Good Father in Brittany. (Illus.). 1964. pap. 4.00 (ISBN 0-8198-0049-X). Dghtrs St Paul.

MAUPASSANT, GUY DE, 1850-1893
Artinian, Artine. Maupassant Criticism in France, 1880-1940. LC 75-83844. 1969. Repr. of 1941 ed. 9.50 (ISBN 0-8462-1361-3). Russell.
Artinian, Robert Willard. La Technique Descriptive Chez Guy de Maupassant. 1973. lib. bdg. 12.95 (ISBN 0-916948-01-3). Augustan Lib.
Boyd, Ernest. Guy De Maupassant: A Biographical Study. 1973. Repr. of 1926 ed. 30.00 (ISBN 0-8274-0071-3). R West.
Butler. Les Parlers Dialectaux et Populaires dans l'Oeuvre de Guy de Maupassant. (Publ. Romanes et Franc.). 15.50 (ISBN 0-685-34943-8). French & Eur.
Dugan, John R. Illusion & Reality: A Study of Descriptive Techniques in the Works of Guy de Maupassant. (De Proprietatibus Litterarum Ser. Pratica: No. 59: No. 59). 1973. pap. text ed. 27.50x (ISBN 90-2792-445-7). Mouton.
Jackson, Stanley. Guy De Maupassant. LC 74-8739. 1938. lib. bdg. 20.00 (ISBN 0-8414-5299-7). Folcroft.
Lerner, Michael. Maupassant. LC 75-10912. (Illus.). 304p. 1975. 12.50 (ISBN 0-8076-0803-3). Braziller.
Los Angeles Public Library. Index to the Stories of Guy de Maupassant. 1960. lib. bdg. 15.00 (ISBN 0-8161-0513-8). G K Hall.
Maupassant, Guy de. Chroniques Inedites. (Illus.). 10.95 (ISBN 0-686-54797-7). French & Eur.
Sherard, Robert H. The Life, Work, & Evil Fate of Guy De Maupassant. LC 76-15985. 1976. Repr. of 1926 ed. lib. bdg. 25.00 (ISBN 0-8414-7621-7). Folcroft.
Steegmuller, Francis. Maupassant: A Lion in the Path. LC 76-39210. (Select Bibliographies Reprint Ser.). Repr. of 1949 ed. 21.00 (ISBN 0-8369-6812-3). Arno.
Sullivan, Edward D. Maupassant the Novelist. LC 78-6859. 1978. Repr. of 1954 ed. lib. bdg. 19.75x (ISBN 0-313-20497-7, SUMN). Greenwood.
Tolstoy, Leo. Guy De Maupassant. LC 74-7281. (Studies in French Literature, No. 45). 1974. lib. bdg. 39.95 (ISBN 0-8383-1898-3). Haskell.
Wallace, A. H. Guy de Maupassant. (World Authors Ser.: France: No. 265). 1973. lib. bdg. 9.95 (ISBN 0-8057-2602-0). Twayne.

MAURIAC, FRANCOIS, 1885-1970
Glenisson, ed. L' Amour dans les Romans de Francois Mauriac. 21.95 (ISBN 0-685-34310-3). French & Eur.
Heppenstall, Rayner. Double Image: Mutations of Christian Mythology in the Works of Four French Catholic Writers of Today & Yesterday. LC 72-93063. 1969. Repr. of 1947 ed. 12.00 (ISBN 0-8046-0676-5). Kennikat.
Jenkins, Cecil. Mauriac. 120p. 1980. Repr. text ed. 10.00 (ISBN 0-89760-406-7, Telegraph). Dynamic Learn Corp.
Landry, Sr. Anne G. Represented Discourse in the Novels of Francois Mauriac. LC 70-128933. (Carl Ser.: No. 44). Repr. of 1953 ed. 14.50 (ISBN 0-404-50344-6). AMS Pr.
Mauriac, Francois & Blanche, Jacques-Emile. Correspondance 1916-1942. Collet, Georges-Paul, ed. 256p. 1976. 16.50 (ISBN 0-686-55456-6). French & Eur.
Mauriac, Francois & Touzot, Jean. Mauriac Avant Mauriac 1913-1922: Recueil de Textes. 225p. 1977. 15.95 (ISBN 0-686-55467-1). French & Eur.
Paine, Ruth B. Thematic Analysis of Francois Mauriac's "Genitrix, le Desert De L'amour, & le Noeud De Viperes". LC 76-8024. (Romance Monographs: No. 20). 1976. 18.00x (ISBN 84-399-4950-2). Romance.
Scott, Malcolm. Mauriac's Politics. 165p. 1980. 16.00x (ISBN 0-7073-0262-5, Pub. by Scottish Academic Pr Scotland). Columbia U Pr.
Smith, Maxwell A. Francois Mauriac. LC 70-110710. (World Author Ser.). 1970. lib. bdg. 12.95x (ISBN 0-8057-2604-7). Irvington.
Stratford, Philip. Faith & Fiction: Creative Process in Greene & Mauriac. 1964. pap. 2.95x (ISBN 0-268-00379-3). U of Notre Dame Pr.

MAURICE, FREDERICK DENISON, 1805-1872
Brose, Olive J. Frederick Denison Maurice: Rebellious Conformist, 1805-1872. LC 74-141380. xxiii, 308p. 1971. 16.00x (ISBN 0-8214-0092-4). Ohio U Pr.
McClain, Frank M. Maurice: Man & Moralist, 1805-1872. 1972. text ed. 12.50x (ISBN 0-8401-1459-1). Allenson-Breckinridge.

MAURITANIA
Carpenter, Allan & Hughes, James. Mauritania. LC 76-53010. (Enchatment of Africa Ser.). (Illus.). (gr. 5 up). 1977. PLB 10.60 (ISBN 0-516-04576-8). Childrens.
Gerteing, Alfred. Mauritania. 12.50 (ISBN 0-686-22376-4). British Am Bks.
Gerteiny, Alfred G. Historical Dictionary of Mauritania. LC 81-5291. (African Historical Dictionaries Ser.: No. 31). 116p. 1981. 10.00 (ISBN 0-686-72784-3). Scarecrow.
Stewart, C. C. & Stewart, E. K. Islam & Social Order in Mauritania: A Case Study from the Nineteenth Century. (Oxford Studies in African Affairs Ser.). 1973. 24.00x (ISBN 0-19-821688-2). Oxford U Pr.

MAURITIUS
Beaton, Patrick. Creoles & Coolies. LC 77-118457. 1971. Repr. of 1859 ed. 12.50 (ISBN 0-8046-1207-2). Kennikat.
Keller, Konrad. Madagascar, Mauritius, & the Other East-African Islands. LC 70-89005. (Illus.). Repr. of 1901 ed. 20.50x (ISBN 0-8371-1766-6, Pub. by Negro U Pr). Greenwood.
Mathieson, William L. British Slave Emancipation, 1838-1849. 1967. lib. bdg. 13.50x (ISBN 0-374-95339-2). Octagon.
Meade, James Edward, et al. Economic & Social Structure of Mauritius. 246p. 1968. Repr. of 1961 ed. 25.00x (ISBN 0-7146-1233-2, F Cass Co). Biblio Dist.
Pike, Nicholas. Sub-Tropical Rambles in the Land of the Aphanapteryx: Personal Experiences, Adventures, & Wanderings in & Around the Island of Mauritus. LC 72-4081. (Black Heritage Library Collection Ser.). Repr. of 1873 ed. 40.25 (ISBN 0-8369-9103-6). Arno.
Ramdin, T. Mauritius: A Geographical Survey. (Illus., Orig.). 1969. pap. 5.00x (ISBN 0-7231-0620-7). Intl Pubns Serv.
Sinh, Ranbir. Mauritius, the Key to the Indian Ocean. 80p. 1980. text ed. 30.00x (ISBN 0-8426-1693-4). Verry.
Titmuss, Richard M. & Abel-Smith, Brian. Social Policies & Population Growth in Mauritius. 308p. 1968. Repr. of 1961 ed. 27.50x (ISBN 0-7146-1254-5, F Cass Co). Biblio Dist.

MAURITIUS–HISTORY
Jeremie, John. Recent Events at Mauritius. LC 70-93818. Repr. of 1835 ed. 15.50x (ISBN 0-8371-3230-4). Greenwood.

MAUROIS, ANDRE, 1885-1967
Keating, L. Clark. Andre Maurois. (World Authors Ser.: No. 53). 10.95 (ISBN 0-8057-2608-X). Twayne.
Suffel. Andre Maurois: Avec des Remarques d'Andre Maurois. pap. 4.95 (ISBN 0-685-36970-6). French & Eur.

MAURRAS, CHARLES, 1868-1952
Buthman, W. C. The Rise of Integral Nationalism in France with Special Reference to the Ideas & Activities of Charles Maurras. LC 78-120239. 1970. Repr. lib. bdg. 20.00x (ISBN 0-374-91128-2). Octagon.
Curtis, Michael. Three Against the Third Republic: Sorel, Barres & Maurras. LC 76-26140. 1976. Repr. of 1959 ed. lib. bdg. 22.50x (ISBN 0-8371-9048-7, CUTR). Greenwood.

MAURY, MATTHEW FONTAINE, 1806-1873
Lewis, Charles L. Matthew Fontaine Maury. LC 79-6116. (Navies & Men Ser.). (Illus.). 1980. Repr. of 1927 ed. lib. bdg. 25.00x (ISBN 0-405-13045-7). Arno.
--Matthew Fontaine Maury, the Pathfinder of the Seas. LC 72-98638. Repr. of 1927 ed. 16.00 (ISBN 0-404-03984-7). AMS Pr.
Williams, Frances L. Matthew Fontaine Maury, Scientist of the Sea. (Illus.). 1963. 32.50 (ISBN 0-8135-0433-3). Rutgers U Pr.

MAURYA DYNASTY
Paranavitana, Senarat. The Greeks & the Mauryas. (Illus.). 188p. 1975. pap. text ed. 18.00x (ISBN 0-8426-0793-5). Verry.

MAUSER PISTOL
Belford & Dunlap. Mauser Self Loading Pistol. 13.50 (ISBN 0-685-07376-9). Borden.
Holland, Claude V. The Military Four. 4.95 (ISBN 0-932092-05-5); pap. 2.98 (ISBN 0-932092-04-7). Hol-Land Bks.
Pender. Mauser Pocket Pistols: 1910-1946. 14.50 (ISBN 0-685-27808-5). Borden.

MAUSOLEUMS
see Sepulchral Monuments; Tombs

MAUTHNER, FRITZ, 1849-1923
Kuehn, Joachim. Gescheiterte Sprachkritik: Fritz Mauthners Leben und Werk. 379p. (Ger.). 1975. 73.50x (ISBN 3-11-005833-2). De Gruyter.

MAVAR (ELECTRONICS)
see Parametric Amplifiers

MAVERICK (AUTOMOBILE)
see Automobiles–Types–Maverick

MAVERICK, MAURY
Henderson, Richard B. Maury Maverick: A Political Biography. (Illus.). 410p. 1970. 17.95 (ISBN 0-292-70090-3). U of Tex Pr.

MAXIM, HIRAM STEVENS, SIR, 1840-1916
Maxim, Hiram P. Genius in the Family. (Illus.). 1936. pap. 1.50 (ISBN 0-486-20948-2). Dover.

MAXIMA AND MINIMA
see also Calculus of Variations; Mathematical Optimization
Cunninghame-Green, R. A. Minimax Algebra. LC 79-1314. (Lecture Notes in Economics & Mathematical Systems: Vol. 166). 1979. pap. 15.00 (ISBN 0-387-09113-0). Springer-Verlag.
Danskin, J. M. Theory of Max-Min, & Its Application to Weapons Allocation Problems. (Econometrics & Operation Research: Vol. 5). (Illus.). 1967. 24.10 (ISBN 0-387-03943-0). Springer-Verlag.
Demyanov, V. & Malozemov, V. N. Introduction to Minimax. Louvish, D., tr. from Rus. LC 74-8156. 1974. 36.95 (ISBN 0-470-20850-3). Halsted Pr.
Demyanov, V. F. & Rubinov, A. M. Approximate Methods in Optimization Problems. (Modern Analytical & Computational Methods in Sci. & Math. Ser.: No. 32). 1970. 28.95 (ISBN 0-444-00088-7, North Holland). Elsevier.
Elliott, Robert J. & Kalton, Nigel J. The Existence of Value in Differential Games. LC 72-4562. (Memoirs: No. 126). 67p. 1972. pap. 7.20 (ISBN 0-8218-1826-0, MEMO-126). Am Math.
Girsanov, I. V. Lectures on Mathematical Theory of Extremum Problems. Louvish, D., tr. from Rus. LC 72-80360. (Lecture Notes in Economics & Mathematical Systems: Vol. 67). (Illus.). 139p. 1972. pap. 7.30 (ISBN 0-387-05857-5). Springer-Verlag.
Gumbel, Emil J. Statistics of Extremes. LC 57-10160. 1958. 20.50x (ISBN 0-231-02190-9). Columbia U Pr.
Hight, Donald W. A Concept of Limits. 2nd ed. LC 77-80029. 1978. pap. text ed. 3.25 (ISBN 0-486-63543-0). Dover.
Kowalik, J. & Osborne, M. R. Methods for Unconstrained Optimization Problems. (Modern Analytic & Computational Methods in Science & Mathematics). (Bellman ser. Vol. 13). 1966. 15.00 (ISBN 0-444-00041-0, North Holland). Elsevier.
Morse, Marston. Variational Analysis: Critical Extremals & Sturmian Extensions. LC 72-8368. (Pure & Applied Mathematics Ser). 304p. 1973. 38.95 (ISBN 0-471-61700-8, Pub. by Wiley-Interscience). Wiley.
Sperb, Rene. Maximum Principles & Their Applications. LC 81-2436. (Mathematics in Science & Engineering). 1981. 29.50 (ISBN 0-12-656880-4). Acad Pr.

MAXIMILIAN 1ST, EMPEROR OF GERMANY, 1459-1519
Appelbaum, Stanley, tr. The Triumph of Maximilian the First: One Hundred & Thirty-Seven Woodcuts by Hans Burgkmsir & Others. 11.00 (ISBN 0-686-74246-X). Peter Smith.
Burgkmair, Hans. The Triumph of Maximilian the First: 137 Woodcuts. Appelbaum, Stanley, tr. (Illus., Orig.). 1883-1884. pap. 5.95 (ISBN 0-486-21207-6). Dover.
Howaert, J. B. Letters of Ogier Chislain De Busbecq to the Holy Roman Emperor Maximillian II. Jones, Robert E. & Weber, Bernerd C., eds. Jones, Robert E. & Weber, Bernerd C., trs. from Lat. LC 61-17940. 180p. 1980. Repr. of 1961 ed. text ed. 18.50x (ISBN 0-8290-0182-4). Irvington.
Maximilian One. Triumph of Maximilian One. Applebaum, ed. (Illus.). 8.00 (ISBN 0-8446-2550-7). Peter Smith.
Van Dyke, Paul. Renascence Portraits. facs. ed. LC 69-17593. (Essay Index Reprint Ser). 1905. 17.00 (ISBN 0-8369-0096-0). Arno.
Waas, Glenn E. Legendary Character of Kaiser Maximilian. (Columbia University. Germanic Studies, New Ser.: No. 14). Repr. of 1941 ed. 17.00 (ISBN 0-404-50464-7). AMS Pr.

MAXIMILIAN, EMPEROR OF MEXICO, 1832-1867
Basch, Samuel. Memories of Mexico: History of the Last Ten Months of the Empire. Oechler, Hugh M., tr. 235p. 1973. text ed. 9.00 (ISBN 0-911536-41-8). Trinity U Pr.
Burgkmair, Hans, et al. The Triumph of Maximilian First: One Hundred Thirty-Seven Woodcuts, Texts & Notes. Appelbaum, Stanley, tr. 11.00 (ISBN 0-8446-5690-9). Peter Smith.
Corti, Egon C. Maximilian & Charlotte of Mexico, 2 vols. 1976. lib. bdg. 250.00 (ISBN 0-8490-0595-7). Gordon Pr.
Dawson, Daniel. The Mexican Adventure. facsimile ed. (Select Bibliographies Reprint Ser). Repr. of 1935 ed. 24.00 (ISBN 0-8369-6682-1). Arno.
Musser, John M. The Establishment of Maximilian's Empire in Mexico. 1976. lib. bdg. 59.95 (ISBN 0-8490-1789-0). Gordon Pr.
Strauss, Walter L., ed. The Book of Hours of Emperor Maximilian the First. LC 73-81346. 345p. 1974. 49.50 (ISBN 0-913870-01-3). Abaris Bks.
Taylor, John M. Maximilian & Carlotta: A Story of Imperialism. 1976. lib. bdg. 69.95 (ISBN 0-8490-0594-9). Gordon Pr.
Trifilo, S. Samuel. Maximilian & Carlota in Mexican Drama. LC 80-12251. (Center Essay Ser.: No. 8). 1980. pap. 5.00 (ISBN 0-930450-14-0). Univ of Wis Latin Am.

MAXIMS
see also Aphorisms and Apothegms; Proverbs
Beirne, Piers & Sharlet, Robert, eds. Pashukanis: Selected Writings on Maxism & Law. LC 79-40895. (Law, State & Society Ser.). 1980. 48.00 (ISBN 0-12-086350-2). Acad Pr.
Carnegie, Dorothy, ed. Dale Carnegie's Scrapbook. 1959. 9.95 (ISBN 0-671-18950-6). S&S.
Christy, Robert. Proverbs Maxims & Phrases of All Ages: Classified Subjectively & Arranged Alphabetically, 2 vols. in one. 1977. Repr. of 1888 ed. lib. bdg. 100.00 (ISBN 0-8482-0476-X). Norwood Edns.
Davis, John F. Chinese Novels. LC 76-43332. 1976. Repr. of 1822 ed. 30.00x (ISBN 0-8201-1278-X). Schol Facsimiles.
Dobie, J. Frank, ed. Spur-Of-The-Cock. LC 34-1434. (Texas Folklore Society Publications: No. 11). 1965. Repr. of 1933 ed. 4.95 (ISBN 0-87074-043-1). SMU Press.
Erasmus. Adages (One to Five Hundred, Vol. 31. Phillips, Margaret M. & Mynors, R. A., trs. (Collected Works of Erasmus). 1981. 35.00x (ISBN 0-8020-2373-8). U of Toronto Pr.
Faber, Harold. The Book of Laws. LC 78-19608. 1979. 7.95 (ISBN 0-8129-0728-0). Times Bks.
Greenberg, Sidney. Treasury of the Art of Living. pap. 5.00 (ISBN 0-87980-168-9). Wilshire.
Greenberg, Sidney, ed. Treasury of the Art of Living. 1964. 6.95 (ISBN 0-87677-019-7). Hartmore.
Guicciardini, Francesco. Maxims & Reflections. LC 64-23752. 1972. pap. 4.95x (ISBN 0-8122-1037-9, Pa. Paperbacks). U of Pa Pr.
Jackson, Holbrook. Maxims of Books & Reading. 1973. lib. bdg. 5.00 (ISBN 0-8414-5355-1). Folcroft.
Kielkopf, Charles F. Formal Sentential Entailment. 1977. pap. text ed. 14.00 (ISBN 0-8191-0313-6). U Pr of Amer.
La Rochefoucauld, Francois de. Reflexions Ou Sentences et Maxims Morales: Reflexions Diverses. 286p. 1967. 7.95 (ISBN 0-686-54281-9). French & Eur.
La Rochefoucauld, Francois. Maximes. (Documentation thematique). (Illus., Fr.). pap. 2.95 (ISBN 0-685-13985-9, 123). Larousse.
Maloux, M. Dictionnaire des proverbes, sentences et maximes. (Fr). 23.50 (ISBN 2-03-020291-6, 3618). Larousse.
Penn, William. Some Fruits of Solitude in Reflections & Maxims. LC 76-14439. 1976. Repr. of 1903 ed. lib. bdg. 25.00 (ISBN 0-8414-6718-8). Folcroft.
Tancock, L. W. Maxims-la Rochefoucauld. (Penguin Classic Ser.). 1982. pap. 4.95 (ISBN 0-14-044095-X). Penguin.
Walten, Maximilian G., ed. Holy State & the Profane State, 2 Vols. LC 70-168072. Repr. of 1938 ed. 37.50 (ISBN 0-404-02637-0). AMS Pr.
Yoo, Young H. Wisdom of the Far East: A Dictionary of Proverbs, Maxims, & Famous Classical Phrases of the Chinese, Japanese, & Korean. LC 70-168691. (Dictionary Ser., No. 5). 1972. 11.00 (ISBN 0-912580-00-3). Far Eastern Res.
Zeller, Sr. M. Francine. New Aspects of Style in the Maxims of La Rochefoucauld. LC 77-94186. (Catholic University of America Studies in Romance Languages & Literatures Ser: No. 48). Repr. of 1954 ed. 18.50 (ISBN 0-404-50348-9). AMS Pr.

MAXIMUS, SAINT, BP. OF TURIN, d. ca. 420

Burghardt, W. J., et al, eds. St. Maximus the Confessor: The Ascetic Life, the Four Centuries on Charity. LC 55-8642. (ACW Ser.: No. 21). 293p. 1955. 11.95 (ISBN 0-8091-0258-7). Paulist Pr.

Thunberg, Lars. Microcosm & Mediator: The Theological Anthropology of Maximus the Confessor. Allchin, A. L., rev. by. LC 80-2368. 1981. Repr. of 1965 ed. 58.00 (ISBN 0-404-18917-2). AMS Pr.

MAXWELL, GAVIN

Frere, Richard. Maxwell's Ghost: An Epilogue to Gavin Maxwell's Camusfearna. 1976. text ed. 16.00x (ISBN 0-575-02044-X). Verry.

MAXWELL, JAMES CLERK, 1831-1879

Campbell, Lewis & Garnett, William. Life of James Clerk Maxwell. (Sources of Science, House Ser: No. 85). 1970. Repr. of 1882 ed. 42.50 (ISBN 0-384-07295-X). Johnson Repr.

Everitt, C. W. James Clerk Maxwell: Physicist & Natural Philosopher. LC 75-7594. 1976. pap. 2.95 (ISBN 0-684-14253-8, SL587, ScribT). Scribner.

Tricker, R. A. Contributions of Faraday & Maxwell to Electrical Science. 1966. 23.00 (ISBN 0-08-011977-8); pap. 11.25 (ISBN 0-08-011976-X). Pergamon.

MAXWELL EQUATIONS

Bevensee, Robert M. Handbook of Conical Antennas & Scatterers. LC 71-172793. (Illus.). 188p. 1973. 52.25x (ISBN 0-677-00480-X). Gordon.

MAY DAY

Potts, William. Banbury Cross & the Rhyme. LC 76-25535. 1976. Repr. of 1930 ed. lib. bdg. 10.00 (ISBN 0-8414-6737-4). Folcroft.

MAY-FLIES

see also Caddis-Flies

Britt, N. Wilson. Biology of Two Species of Lake Erie Mayflies. 1962. 2.50 (ISBN 0-686-30319-9). Ohio Bio Survey.

Burks, B. D. The Mayflies, or Ephemeroptera, of Illinois. LC 75-2296. (Illus.). viii, 216p. 1975. Repr. of 1953 ed. 15.00 (ISBN 0-911836-06-3). Entomological Repr.

Edmunds, George F., Jr., et al. The Mayflies of North & Central America. LC 75-39446. 1976. 30.00x (ISBN 0-8166-0759-1). U of Minn Pr.

Jennings, Preston. Book of Trout Flies. Lyons, Nick, ed. (Illus.). 1970. 7.50 (ISBN 0-517-50204-6). Crown.

Leonard, Justin W. & Leonard, Fannie A. Mayflies of Michigan Trout Streams. LC 62-9726. (Bulletin Ser.: No. 43). 139p. 1962. pap. 8.00x (ISBN 0-87737-020-6). Cranbrook.

MAY FOURTH MOVEMENT

Chow Tse-Tsung. May Fourth Movement: Intellectual Revolution in Modern China. LC 60-10034. (East Asian Ser: No. 6). 1960. 25.00x (ISBN 0-674-55750-6); pap. 8.95x (ISBN 0-674-76450-1). Harvard U Pr.

Schwartz, Benjamin I., ed. Reflections on the May Fourth Movement. LC 77-183976. (East Asian Monographs Ser: No. 44). 1972. pap. 9.00x (ISBN 0-674-75230-9). Harvard U Pr.

MAYA (HINDUISM)

Whitlock, Ralph. Everyday Life of the Maya. 1976. 19.95 (ISBN 0-7134-3232-2, Pub. by Batsford England). David & Charles.

MAYA ARCHITECTURE

see Architecture, Maya

MAYA ART

see Mayas–Art

MAYA CALENDAR

see Calendar, Maya

MAYA HIEROGLYPHICS

see Picture-Writing, Maya

MAYA LANGUAGE

see also Tzeltal Language

Berlin, Brent, et al. Principles of Tzeltal Plant Classification: An Introduction to the Botanical Ethnography of a Mayan Speaking People of Highland Chiapas. (Language, Thought & Culture: Advances in the Study of Cognition). 1974. 70.00 (ISBN 0-12-785047-3). Acad Pr.

Blair, Robert W. & Vermont-Salas, Refugio. Spoken (Yucatec) Maya, Bk. 1, Lessons 1-12. 1979. pap. text ed. 19.00x (ISBN 0-87543-147-X). Lucas.

Collard, Howard & Collard, Elizabeth. Vocabulario Mayo, Vol. 6. rev. ed. 1974. pap. 4.00x (ISBN 0-88312-657-5). Summer Inst Ling.

Kelley, David H. Deciphering the Maya Script. LC 75-17989. (Illus.). 352p. 1976. 45.00x (ISBN 0-292-71504-8). U of Tex Pr.

Knorozov, Yuri V. & Proskouriakoff, Tatiana, eds. Selected Chapters from the Writings of the Maya Indians. Coe, Sophie, tr. LC 70-38502. (Harvard University. Peabody Museum of Archaeology & Ethnology. Russian Translation Ser.: No. 4). Repr. of 1967 ed. 17.50 (ISBN 0-404-52647-0). AMS Pr.

Martin, Laura. Papers in Mayan Linguistics. 7.95 (ISBN 0-686-71052-5). Lucas.

Roys, Ralph L. The Ethno-Botany of the Maya. LC 76-29024. (ISHI Reprints on Latin America & the Caribbean). 416p. 1976. Repr. of 1931 ed. text ed. 28.95x (ISBN 0-915980-22-3). Inst Study Human.

Roys, Ralph L., ed. Book of Chilam Balam of Chumayel. (Civilization of the American Indian Ser.: No. 87). (Illus.). 1973. Repr. of 1967 ed. pap. 5.95x (ISBN 0-8061-0735-9). U of Okla Pr.

Straight, Stephen H. The Acquisition of Maya Phonology: Variation in Yucatec Child Language. LC 75-25123. (American Indian Linguistics Ser.). 1976. lib. bdg. 42.00 (ISBN 0-8240-1973-3). Garland Pub.

Tozzer, Alfred M. Maya Grammar. 1921. pap. 16.00 (ISBN 0-527-01215-7). Kraus Repr.

--A Maya Grammar. 8.75 (ISBN 0-8446-5659-3). Peter Smith.

--A Maya Grammar with Bibliography & Appraisement of the Works Noted. 1977. pap. 4.00 (ISBN 0-486-23465-7). Dover.

--A Maya Grammar with Bibliography & Appraisement of the Works Noted. 1977. pap. 4.00 (ISBN 0-486-23465-7). Dover.

Whorf, Benjamin. Maya Hieroglyphs. facs. ed. 24p. Repr. of 1941 ed. pap. 3.95 (ISBN 0-8466-0122-2, SJS122). Shorey.

MAYA LITERATURE

Brinton, Daniel G., ed. The Maya Chronicles. LC 70-83457. (Library of Aboriginal American Literature Ser.: No. 1). Repr. of 1882 ed. 22.50 (ISBN 0-404-52181-9). AMS Pr.

Fought, John G. Chorti (Mayan) Texts: I. LC 72-80380. (Folklore & Folklife Ser). 592p. 1973. 18.00x (ISBN 0-8122-7667-1). U of Pa Pr.

MAYA LITERATURE–HISTORY AND CRITICISM

Leon-Portilla, Miguel. Pre-Columbian Literatures of Mexico. Lobanov, Grace, tr. (Civilization of the American Indian Ser: Vol. 22). (Illus.). 1969. 9.95 (ISBN 0-8061-0818-5). U of Okla Pr.

Tozzer, Alfred M. A Maya Grammar with Bibliography & Appraisement of the Works Noted. 1977. pap. 4.00 (ISBN 0-486-23465-7). Dover.

MAYA MYTHOLOGY

see Mayas–Religion and Mythology

MAYAKOVSKY, VLADIMIR VLADIMIROVICH, 1893-1930

Baroolshian, Vahab D. Brik & Mayakovsky. (Slavistic Printings & Reprintings Ser.: No. 301). 1978. pap. text ed. 26.75x (ISBN 90-279-7826-3). Mouton.

Charters, Ann & Charters, Samuel. I Love: The Story of Vladimir Mayakovsky & Lili Brik. 432p. 1979. 17.50 (ISBN 0-374-17406-7). FS&G.

MAYAN LANGUAGES

see also Maya Language; Tzeltal Language

Edmonson, Munro S., ed. Meaning in Mayan Languages: Ethnolinguistic Studies. (Janua Linguarum Series Practica: No. 158). 1973. pap. text ed. 55.00x (ISBN 90-2792-489-9). Mouton.

England, Nora C., ed. Papers in Mayan Linguistics. (Miscellaneous Publications in Anthropology No. 6; Studies in Mayan Linguistics: No. 2). v, 310p. 1978. pap. 12.00 (ISBN 0-913134-87-2). Mus Anthro Mo.

Freeze, Ray A., ed. A Fragment of an Early K'EKCHI' Vocabulary. LC 76-365636. (Monographs in Anthropology: No.2). (Illus.). iv, 70p. 1975. pap. 4.00x (ISBN 0-913134-95-3). Mus Anthro Mo.

Furbee, Louanna, ed. Mayan Texts III. LC 76-15159. (International Journal of American Linguistics Native American Texts Ser.: No. 5). 122p. (Orig.). 1980. pap. 10.75 (ISBN 0-8357-0567-6, IS-00115, Pub. by U of Chicago Pr). Univ Microfilms.

Furbee-Losee, Louanna, ed. Mayan Texts II. LC 76-15194. (IJAL-NATS Monograph: No. 3). 1978. pap. 12.50 (ISBN 0-226-36715-0, IS-00073, Pub. by University of Chicago Press). Univ Microfilms.

Gates, William. An Outline Dictionary of Maya Glyphs. LC 77-92481. (Illus.). 1978. pap. 3.50 (ISBN 0-486-23618-8). Dover.

Martin, Laura. Papers in Mayan Linguistics. 7.95 (ISBN 0-686-71052-5). Lucas.

MAYAS

Adams, Richard W., ed. The Origins of Maya Civilization. LC 76-57537. (School of American Research Advanced Seminar Ser). (Illus.). 1978. pap. 9.50x (ISBN 0-8263-0474-5). U of NM Pr.

Bennett, Evan. The Maya Epic. 135p. 1974. 12.95 (ISBN 0-686-27297-8); pap. 5.95 (ISBN 0-686-27298-6). U Pr Wisc River Falls.

Benson, Elizabeth P., ed. Maya World. rev ed. LC 77-4955. (Apollo Eds.). 1977. pap. 4.95 (ISBN 0-8152-0423-X). T Y Crowell.

Brainerd, George W. The Maya Civilization. LC 76-43669. Repr. of 1954 ed. 12.50 (ISBN 0-404-15503-0). AMS Pr.

--The Maya Civilization. (Illus.). 3.00 (ISBN 0-686-20684-3). Southwest Mus.

Bunch, Roland & Bunch, Roger. The Highland Maya: Patterns of Life & Clothing in Indian Guatemala. LC 77-77864. 1977. 7.95 (ISBN 0-930740-01-7). Indigenous Pubns.

Carmack, Robert M. The Quiche Mayas of Utatlan: The Evolution of a Highland Guatemala Kingdom. LC 80-5241. (The Civilization of the American Indian Ser.: No. 155). (Illus.). 400p. 1981. 24.95 (ISBN 0-8061-1546-7). U of Okla Pr.

Coe, Michael D. Classic Maya Pottery at Dumbarton Oaks. LC 75-1727. (Illus.). 1975. 25.00x (ISBN 0-88402-063-0, Ctr Pre-Columbian). Dumbarton Oaks.

--The Maya. rev. ed. (Ancient People & Places Ser.). (Illus.). 180p. 1980. 19.95 (ISBN 0-500-02097-3); pap. 9.95 (ISBN 0-500-27195-X). Thames Hudson.

Culbert, T. Patrick. Lost Civilization: The Story of the Classic Maya. (Longacre Ser.). (Illus.). 1974. pap. text ed. 9.50 scp (ISBN 0-06-041448-0, HarpC). Har-Row.

Culbert, T. Patrick, ed. The Classic Maya Collapse. LC 72-94657. (School of American Research: Advanced Seminar Ser). (Illus.). 549p. 1977. pap. 12.50x (ISBN 0-8263-0463-X). U of NM Pr.

Diven, T. Aztecs & Mayas. 1976. lib. bdg. 59.95 (ISBN 0-8490-1465-4). Gordon Pr.

Gallenkamp, Charles. Maya: The Riddle & Rediscovery of a Lost Civilization. 288p. 1981. pap. 4.95 (ISBN 0-14-005367-0). Penguin.

Gann, T. History of the Mayas. 1976. lib. bdg. 59.95 (ISBN 0-8490-2002-6). Gordon Pr.

Gann, Thomas. Ancient Cities & Modern Tribes: The Maya Lands. 1977. lib. bdg. 39.95 (ISBN 0-8490-1424-7). Gordon Pr.

--In an Unknown Land. facs. ed. LC 76-150182. (Select Bibliographies Reprint Ser). 1924. 25.00 (ISBN 0-8369-5695-8). Arno.

Hammond, Norman, ed. Social Process in Maya Prehistory: Studies in Honor of Sir Eric Thompson. 1978. 95.00 (ISBN 0-12-322050-5). Acad Pr.

Hammond, Norman & Willey, Gordon R., eds. Maya Archaeology & Ethnohistory. (Texas Pan American Ser.). (Illus.). 310p. 1979. text ed. 23.50x (ISBN 0-292-75040-4). U of Tex Pr.

Harrison, Peter D. & Turner, B. L., II, eds. Pre-Hispanic Maya Agriculture. LC 78-55703. (Illus.). 414p. 1978. 20.00x (ISBN 0-8263-0483-4). U of NM Pr.

Hay, Clarence L., et al, eds. The Maya & Their Neighbors. LC 72-97753. (Illus.). xxiii, 606p. 1973. Repr. of 1940 ed. lib. bdg. 30.00x (ISBN 0-8154-0477-8). Cooper Sq.

--The Maya & Their Neighbors: Essays on Middle American Anthropology & Archaeology. LC 77-72861. (Illus.). 1977. pap. 7.50 (ISBN 0-486-23510-6). Dover.

Henderson, John S. The World of the Ancient Maya. LC 81-3148. (Illus.). 336p. 1981. 29.95 (ISBN 0-8014-1232-3). Cornell U Pr.

Highwater, Jamake. Journey to the Sky. LC 78-3324. (Illus.). 1978. 9.95 (ISBN 0-690-01758-8). T Y Crowell.

Jones, Grant D., ed. Anthropology & History in Yucatan. (Texas Pan American Ser.). 368p. 1977. text ed. 22.50x (ISBN 0-292-70314-7). U of Tex Pr.

Lister, Robert H. In Search of Maya Glyphs. (Illus.). 1970. 8.95 (ISBN 0-89013-044-2); pap. 4.95 (ISBN 0-89013-045-0). Museum NM Pr.

Means, Philip A. History of the Spanish Conquest of Yucatan & of the Itzas. (Illus.). 1917. pap. 16.00 (ISBN 0-527-01210-6). Kraus Repr.

Morales, Demetrio Sodi. The Maya World. (Illus.). 192p. 1976. pap. 5.00 (ISBN 0-912434-21-X). Ocelot Pr.

Morley, Sylvanus G. The Ancient Maya. 3rd rev. ed. Brainerd, George W., ed. LC 56-5580. (Illus.). 1956. 15.00 (ISBN 0-8047-0388-4); pap. 6.95 (ISBN 0-8047-0389-2, SP80). Stanford U Pr.

Pettersen, Carmen L. The Maya of Guatemala: Their Life & Dress. LC 76-42102. (Illus.). 276p. 1977. 45.00 (ISBN 0-295-95537-6). U of Wash Pr.

Pre-Columbian America: The Mayas. rev. ed. 1980. pap. 1.00 (ISBN 0-8270-4891-2). OAS.

Press, Irwin. Tradition & Adaptation: Life in a Modern Yucatan Maya Village. LC 75-71. (Illus.). 288p. 1975. lib. bdg. 16.00 (ISBN 0-8371-7954-8, PYM/). Greenwood.

Puxley, W. Lavallin. Magic Land of the Maya. 1977. lib. bdg. 59.95 (ISBN 0-8490-2194-4). Gordon Pr.

Redfield, Robert. Folk Culture of Yucatan. LC 41-15380. (Illus.). 1941. 20.00x (ISBN 0-226-70659-1). U of Chicago Pr.

Redfield, Robert & Rojas, Alfonso V. Chan Kom: A Maya Village. abr. ed. LC 62-2616. 1962. pap. 4.45 (ISBN 0-226-70661-3, P86, Phoen). U of Chicago Pr.

Reed, Nelson. The Caste War of Yucatan. (Illus.). 1964. 15.00x (ISBN 0-8047-0164-4); pap. 4.95 (ISBN 0-8047-0165-2, SP52). Stanford U Pr.

Rivet, Paul. Maya Cities. 1973. 24.95 (ISBN 0-236-30912-9, Pub. by Paul Elek). Merrimack Bk Serv.

Robicsek, Francis. A Study in Maya Art & History: The Mat Symbol. LC 75-18351. (Illus.). 1975. 22.00x (ISBN 0-934490-25-2); soft cover 15.00x (ISBN 0-934490-26-0). Mus Am Ind.

Schell, Rolfe. F., ed. Album Maya. new ed. Schell, Rolfe F. & Camus, Pierre-Albert, trs. from Span., Fr., Eng. LC 73-87109. (Illus.). 1973. 3.50 (ISBN 0-87208-020-X); pap. 1.50 (ISBN 0-87208-019-6). Island Pr.

Sexton, James D., ed. Son of Tecun Uman: A Maya Indian Tells His Life Story. 1981. 19.95x (ISBN 0-8165-0736-8); pap. 8.95 (ISBN 0-8165-0751-1). U of Ariz Pr.

Smith, Waldemar R. Fiesta System & Economic Change. LC 77-390. 1977. 16.00x (ISBN 0-231-04180-2). Columbia U Pr.

Steggerda, Morris. Maya Indians of Yucatan. LC 77-11524. (Carnegie Institution of Washington. Publication: No. 531). Repr. of 1941 ed. 34.00 (ISBN 0-404-16283-5). AMS Pr.

Stierlin, Henri. The Pre-Colombian Civilizations: The World of the Maya, Aztecs & Incas. (Illus.). Date not set. 7.98 (ISBN 0-8317-7116-X, Pub. by Mayflower Bks). Smith Pubs.

Stuart, George E. & Stuart, Gene S. The Mysterious Maya. LC 76-52648. (Special Publications Ser.: No. 12). (Illus.). 1977. avail. only from natl geog 6.95 (ISBN 0-87044-233-3). Natl Geog.

Thompson, J. Eric. Maya Archaeologist. (Illus.). 1975. 14.95 (ISBN 0-8061-0561-5); pap. 6.95 (ISBN 0-8061-1206-9). U of Okla Pr.

--Maya History & Religion. LC 72-88144. (Civilization of the American Indian Ser.: Vol. 99). 1976. Repr. of 1970 ed. 15.95 (ISBN 0-8061-0884-3). U of Okla Pr.

Thompson, Richard A. The Winds of Tomorrow: Social Change in a Maya Town. LC 73-90940. x, 182p. 1974. text ed. 12.50x (ISBN 0-226-79757-0). U of Chicago Pr.

Tozzer, Alfred M. A Comparative Study of the Mayas & the Lacandones. LC 76-43869. (Archaeological Institute of America. Report on the Fellow in American Archaeology: 1902-1905). Repr. of 1907 ed. 24.50 (ISBN 0-404-15728-9). AMS Pr.

Valle, Rafael H. Bibliografia Maya. LC 75-144831. (Bibliography & Reference Ser.: No. 436). 1971. Repr. of 1937 ed. lib. bdg. 29.00 (ISBN 0-8337-3611-6). B Franklin.

Villa Rojas, Alfonso. The Maya of East Central Quintana Roo. LC 77-11527. (Carnegie Institution of Washington. Publication: No. 559). Repr. of 1945 ed. 21.50 (ISBN 0-404-16286-X). AMS Pr.

Von Hagen, Victor W. World of the Maya. 1960. pap. 2.25 (ISBN 0-451-61826-2, ME1826, Ment). NAL.

Webster, Edna R. Early Exploring in Lands of the Maya. 1973. 7.50 (ISBN 0-686-21899-X); pap. 5.00 (ISBN 0-686-21900-7). Wilmar Pubs.

Wilson, Carter. Crazy February: Death & Life in the Mayan Highlands of Mexico. 1973. pap. 3.95 (ISBN 0-520-02399-4). U of Cal Pr.

MAYAS–ANTIQUITIES

see also Calendar, Maya; Guatemala–Antiquities

Aguiar, Walter R. Maya Land in Color. (Profiles of America Ser.). (Illus.). 1978. 7.95 (ISBN 0-8038-4703-3). Hastings.

Ashmore, Wendy, ed. Lowland Maya Settlement Patterns. (School of American Research Advanced Seminar Ser.). 464p. 1981. 30.00x (ISBN 0-8263-0556-3). U of NM Pr.

Aveni, Anthony F., ed. Native American Astronomy. LC 76-53569. (Illus.). 304p. 1977. text ed. 17.50x (ISBN 0-292-75511-2). U of Tex Pr.

Blom, Frans. Conquest of Yucatan. LC 77-164521. 1972. Repr. of 1937 ed. 15.00x (ISBN 0-8154-0390-9). Cooper Sq.

Brunhouse, Robert L. Frans Blom, Maya Explorer. LC 75-40833. (Illus.). 291p. 1976. 10.00x (ISBN 0-8263-0408-7). U of NM Pr.

--In Search of the Maya: The First Archaeologists. LC 73-75904. (Illus.). 243p. 1973. Repr. of 1974 ed. 8.95x (ISBN 0-8263-0276-9). U of NM Pr.

--Pursuit of the Ancient Maya: Some Archaeologists of Yesterday. LC 74-27443. (Illus.). 252p. 1975. 8.95x (ISBN 0-8263-0363-3). U of NM Pr.

Bullard, William R., Jr., ed. Monographs & Papers in Maya Archaeology. LC 72-105721. (Peabody Museum Papers: Vol. 61). 1970. pap. text ed. 40.00 (ISBN 0-87365-175-8). Peabody Harvard.

Coe, Michael D. Lords of the Underworld: Masterpieces of Classical Maya Ceramics. LC 77-72144. (Illus.). 1978. 50.00x (ISBN 0-691-03917-8). Princeton U Pr.

--The Maya Scribe & His World. LC 73-17731. (Illus.). 160p. 1978. Repr. of 1973 ed. 50.00x (ISBN 0-8139-0568-0, Dist. by U Pr of Va). Grolier Club.

Coe, William R. Piedras Negras Archaeology: Artifacts, Caches & Burials. (Museum Monographs). (Illus.). 245p. 1959. soft bound 10.00 (ISBN 0-934718-11-3). Univ Mus of U PA.

Culbert, T. Patrick. Lost Civilization: The Story of the Classic Maya. (Longacre Ser.). (Illus.). 1974. pap. text ed. 9.50 scp (ISBN 0-06-041448-0, HarpC). Har-Row.

Gallenkamp, Charles. Maya: The Riddle & Rediscovery of a Lost Civilization. (Illus.). 1981. pap. 4.95 (ISBN 0-14-005367-0). Penguin.

Gann, Thomas. Ancient Cities & Modern Tribes: Exploration & Adventure in Maya Lands. LC 72-83086. (Illus.). Repr. of 1926 ed. 15.00 (ISBN 0-405-08550-8, Blom Pubns). Arno.

Graham, Ian. Corpus of Maya Hieroglyphic Inscriptions, Vol. 2, Pt. 3: Ucanal, Ixkun, Ixtutz. pap. text ed. 12.00 (ISBN 0-87365-786-1). Peabody Harvard.

--Corpus of Maya Hieroglyphic Inscriptions, Vol. 3, Pt. 2: Yaxchilan. 1979. pap. text ed. 12.00 (ISBN 0-87365-789-6). Peabody Harvard.

--Corpus of Maya Hieroglyphic Inscriptions: Yaxchilan, Vol. 3, No. 3. Condon, Lorna, ed. (Peabody Museum Press Ser.). (Illus.). 60p. (Orig.). 1981. pap. text ed. 12.00 (ISBN 0-87365-799-3). Peabody Harvard.

Graham, Ian & Von Euw, Eric. Corpus of Maya Hieroglyphic Inscriptions, Vol. 2, Pt. 1: Naranjo. LC 75-39917. 1975. pap. 12.00 (ISBN 0-87365-780-2). Peabody Harvard.

Hammond, Norman. Lubaantum: A Classic Maya Realm. Flint, Emily, ed. LC 75-18219. (Peabody Museum Monographs Ser.: No. 2). (Illus.). 1975. pap. 25.00 (ISBN 0-87365-901-5). Peabody Harvard.

Hammond, Norman & Willey, Gordon R., eds. Maya Archaeology & Ethnohistory. (Texas Pan American Ser.). (Illus.). 310p. 1979. text ed. 23.50x (ISBN 0-292-75040-4). U of Tex Pr.

Hay, Clarence, et al. The Maya & Their Neighbors: Essays on Middle American Anthropology & Archaeology. 12.50 (ISBN 0-8446-5656-9). Peter Smith.

Hencken, Hugh. Mecklenburg Collection, Pt. II: The Iron Age Cemetary of Magdalenska. Condon, Lorna, ed. LC 78-52401. (American School of Prehistoric Research Bulletin Ser.: No. 32). 1978. pap. text ed. 30.00 (ISBN 0-87365-539-7). Peabody Harvard.

Hunter, C. Bruce. A Guide to Ancient Maya Ruins. LC 74-5956. (Illus.). 300p. 1974. 14.95 (ISBN 0-8061-1214-X); pap. 6.95 (ISBN 0-8061-1215-8). U of Okla Pr.

Kubler, George. Aspects of Classic Maya Rulership on Two Inscribed Vessels. LC 77-84830. (Studies in Pre-Columbian Art & Archaeology Ser.: No. 18). (Illus.). 60p. 1977. pap. 6.00x (ISBN 0-88402-070-3, Ctr Pre-Columbian). Dumbarton Oaks.

Lothrop, S. K. Metals from the Cenote of Sacrifice. (Harvard University Peabody Museum of Archaeology & Ethnology Memoirs). Repr. of 1952 ed. pap. 16.00 (ISBN 0-527-01177-0). Kraus Repr.

Mercer, Henry C. The Hill-Caves of Yucatan: A Search for Evidence of Man's Antiquity in the Caverns of Central America. LC 75-12599. (Speleologia Ser). (Illus.). 256p. 1975. 11.95 (ISBN 0-914264-04-4, Pub. by Zephyrus Pr). Cave Bks TN.

--The Hill-Caves of Yucatan: A Search for Evidence of Man's Antiquity in the Caverns of Central America. (Civilization of the American Indian Ser.: Vol. 135). (Illus.). 252p. 1975. Repr. of 1896 ed. 14.50x (ISBN 0-8061-1310-3). U of Okla Pr.

Michels, Joseph W. The Kaminaljuyu Chiefdom. LC 79-15181. (Monograph Ser. on Kaminaljuyu). (Illus.). 1979. text ed. 22.50x (ISBN 0-271-00224-7). Pa St U Pr.

Morris, Earl H. The Temple of the Warriors: The Adventure of Exploring & Restoring a Masterpiece of Native American Architecture in the Ruined City of Chichen Itza, Yucatan. LC 76-44764. (Illus.). Repr. of 1931 ed. 32.50 (ISBN 0-404-15871-4). AMS Pr.

Nuttall, Zelia. Fundamental Principles of Old & New World Civilization. 1901. pap. 35.00 (ISBN 0-527-01190-8). Kraus Repr.

Pollack. The Puuc: An Architectural Survey of the Hill Country of Yucatan & North Campeche, Mexico. LC 79-92051. (Peabody Museum Memoirs). (Illus.). 612p. 1980. pap. write for info. (ISBN 0-87365-693-8). Peabody Harvard.

Proskouriakoff, Tatiana A. A Study of Classic Maya Sculpture. LC 77-11515. (Carnegie Institution of Washington. Publication: No. 593). Repr. of 1950 ed. 62.50 (ISBN 0-404-16275-4). AMS Pr.

Ranney, Edward. Stonework of the Maya. LC 73-82769. (Illus.). 119p. 1974. pap. 9.95x (ISBN 0-8263-0277-7). U of NM Pr.

Reina, Ruben E. & Hill, Robert M., II. The Traditional Pottery of Guatemala. LC 77-17455. (Texas Pan American Ser.). (Illus.). 321p. 1978. 35.00 (ISBN 0-292-78024-9). U of Tex Pr.

Roys, Ralph L., ed. Book of Chilam Balam of Chumayel. (Civilization of the American Indian Ser.: No. 87). (Illus.). 1973. Repr. of 1967 ed. pap. 5.95x (ISBN 0-8061-0735-9). U of Okla Pr.

Spinden, Herbert J. Reduction of Mayan Dates. 1924. pap. 16.00 (ISBN 0-527-01209-2). Kraus Repr.

Thompson, J. Eric. The Rise & Fall of the Maya Civilization. 2nd enl. ed. (Civilization of the American Indian Ser.: No. 39). (Illus.). 328p. 1977. Repr. of 1954 ed. 15.95 (ISBN 0-8061-0301-9). U of Okla Pr.

Thompson, John E. Excavations at San Jose, British Honduras. LC 77-11525. (Carnegie Institution of Washington. Publication: No. 506). Repr. of 1939 ed. 34.00 (ISBN 0-404-16284-3). AMS Pr.

Totten, George O. Maya Architecture. LC 71-122845. (Research & Source Works Ser.: No. 513). 1971. Repr. of 1926 ed. lib. bdg. 76.50 (ISBN 0-8337-3560-8). B Franklin.

Tozzer, Alfred M. & Allen, G. M. Animal Figures in the Maya Codices. 1910. pap. 10.00 (ISBN 0-527-01203-3). Kraus Repr.

Weaver, Muriel P. The Aztecs, Maya, & Their Predecessors: Archaeology of MesoAmerica. LC 70-183477. (Studies in Archeology). 364p. 1972. 17.25 (ISBN 0-12-785935-7). Acad Pr.

Willson, R. W. Astronomical Notes on the Maya Codices. (Harvard University Peabody Museum of Archaeology & Ethnology Papers Ser). Repr. of 1924 ed. pap. 7.00 (ISBN 0-527-01208-4). Kraus Repr.

MAYAS–ART

Anton, Ferdinand. Art of the Maya. (Illus.). 1979. 29.95 (ISBN 0-500-23129-X). Thames Hudson.

Carnegie Institution of Washington. Ancient Maya Paintings of Bonampak Mexico. LC 55-12545. (Illus.). 1955. pap. 5.50 (ISBN 0-87279-945-X, S46). Carnegie Inst.

Charlot, Jean. Art from the Mayans to Disney. facsimile ed. LC 78-99623. (Essay Index Reprint Ser). 1939. 22.00 (ISBN 0-8369-1399-X). Arno.

Coe, Michael D. Lords of the Underworld: Masterpieces of Classical Maya Ceramics. LC 77-72144. (Illus.). 1978. 50.00x (ISBN 0-691-03917-8). Princeton U Pr.

--The Maya Scribe & His World. (Illus.). 1978. Repr. of 1973 ed. 50.00x (ISBN 0-8139-0568-0, Grolier Club). U Pr of Va.

Coe, Michael D. & Benson, Elizabeth P. Three Maya Relief Panels at Dumbarton Oaks. LC 66-30016. (Studies in Pre-Columbian Art & Archaeology: No. 2). (Illus.). 1966. pap. 3.00x (ISBN 0-88402-014-2, Ctr Pe-Columbian). Dumbarton Oaks.

Kubler, George. Studies in Classic Maya Iconography. (Connecticut Academy of Arts & Sciences - Memoirs: Vol. 18). (Illus.). 1969. 35.00 (ISBN 0-208-00833-0). Shoe String.

Maya Monuments: Sculptures of Unknown Provenance in Mexico & Guatemala. Date not set. price not set (ISBN 0-916552-23-3). Acoma Bks.

Mayer, Karl H. Classic Maya Relief Columns. 1981. smythe-sewn bdg. 9.95 (ISBN 0-916552-22-5). Acoma Bks.

--Maya Monuments: Sculptures of Unknown Provenance in Europe. Brizee, Sandra L., tr. from Ger. (Illus.). 1978. pap. 12.00 (ISBN 0-916552-11-X). Acoma Bks.

--Maya Monuments: Sculptures of Unknown Provenance in the U.S. (Illus.). 1980. pap. 19.95 (ISBN 0-916552-16-0). Acoma Bks.

Robicsek, Francis. The Smoking Gods: Tobacco in Maya Art, History, & Religion. LC 78-64904. (Illus.). 1978. 35.00 (ISBN 0-8061-1511-4). U of Okla Pr.

--A Study in Maya Art & History: The Mat Symbol. LC 75-18351. (Illus.). 1975. 22.00x (ISBN 0-934490-25-2); soft cover 15.00x (ISBN 0-934490-26-0). Mus Am Ind.

Spinden, H. J. A Study of Maya Art. 1976. lib. bdg. 39.95 (ISBN 0-8490-2711-X). Gordon Pr.

--Study of Maya Art: Its Subject Matter & Historical Development. Repr. of 1913 ed. 55.00 (ISBN 0-527-01168-1). Kraus Repr.

Spinden, Herbert J. A Study of Maya Art: Its Subject Matter & Historical Development. LC 74-20300. (Illus.). 352p. 1975. pap. text ed. 6.95 (ISBN 0-486-21235-1). Dover.

Stierlin, Henri. Art of the Maya: From the Olmecs to the Maya-Toltecs. (Illus.). 208p. 1981. 50.00 (ISBN 0-8478-0368-6). Rizzoli Intl.

MAYAS–JUVENILE LITERATURE

Beck, Barbara. First Book of the Ancient Maya. LC 65-11746. (First Bks). (Illus.). (gr. 4-6). 1965. PLB 7.40 (ISBN 0-531-00464-3). Watts.

Bleeker, Sonia. The Maya: Indians of Central America. (Illus.). (gr. 3-6). 1961. PLB 6.67 (ISBN 0-688-31461-9). Morrow.

O'Dell, Scott. The Feathered Serpent. (gr. 7 up). 1981. 10.95 (ISBN 0-395-30851-8). HM.

MAYAS–RELIGION AND MYTHOLOGY

Abreu-Gomez, Emilo. Canek: History & Legends of a Maya Hero. Davila, Mario L. & Wilson, Carter, trs. from Span. LC 75-32674. 1980. 14.50 (ISBN 0-520-03148-2); pap. 2.95 (ISBN 0-520-03982-3). U of Cal Pr.

Bolton, David. Kukulcan - Rainman: A Legend of the Maya. Platt, Deborah, ed. (Illus.). 240p. 1980. 12.95 (ISBN 0-934506-02-7). Westminster Co.

Bricker, Victoria R. The Indian Christ, the Indian King: The Historical Substrate of Maya Myth & Ritual. (Illus.). 368p. 1981. text ed. 45.00x (ISBN 0-292-73824-2). U of Tex Pr.

Brintnall, D. E. Revolt Against the Dead: The Modernization of a Mayan Community in the Highlands of Guatemala. 1979. 23.25x (ISBN 0-677-05170-0). Gordon.

Colby, Benjamin N. & Colby, Lore M. The Daykeeper: The Life & Discource of As Ixtil Dviner. (Illus.). 352p. 1981. text ed. 25.00x (ISBN 0-674-19409-8). Harvard U Pr.

Craven, Roy C., Jr. Ceremonial Centers of the Maya. LC 74-2016. (Illus.). viii, 152p. 1974. 20.00 (ISBN 0-8130-0447-0). U Presses Fla.

Crumrine, N. Ross. The Mayo Indians of Sonora: A People Who Refuse to Die. LC 76-8563. 1977. 12.50x (ISBN 0-8165-0605-1); pap. text ed. 5.95x (ISBN 0-8165-0473-3). U of Ariz Pr.

Gossen, Gary H. Chamulas in the World of the Sun: Time & Space in a Maya Oral Tradition. LC 73-83424. 384p. 1974. text ed. 18.50x (ISBN 0-674-10726-8). Harvard U Pr.

Goudriaan, Teun. Maya Divine & Human. 1978. 19.95 (ISBN 0-89684-040-9, Pub. by Motilal Banarsidass India). Orient Bk Dist.

Le Plongeon, Augustus. Sacred Mysteries Among the Mayas & the Quiches. LC 73-76094. (Secret Doctrine Reference Ser). (Illus.). 200p. 1973. Repr. of 1886 ed. 8.95 (ISBN 0-913510-02-5). Wizards.

Nelson, Ralph, tr. Popol Vuh: The Great Mythological Book of the Ancient Maya. 1976. 5.95 (ISBN 0-395-24302-5); pap. 4.95 (ISBN 0-395-25168-0). HM.

Redfield, Robert. Village That Chose Progress: Chan Kom Revisited. 1962. pap. 1.95 (ISBN 0-226-70668-0, P87, Phoen). U of Chicago Pr.

Redfield, Robert & Rojas, Alfonso V. Chan Kom: A Maya Village. abr. ed. LC 62-2616. 1962. pap. 4.45 (ISBN 0-226-70661-3, P86, Phoen). U of Chicago Pr.

Roys, Ralph L., ed. Book of Chilam Balam of Chumayel. (Civilization of the American Indian Ser.: No. 87). (Illus.). 1973. Repr. of 1967 ed. pap. 5.95x (ISBN 0-8061-0735-9). U of Okla Pr.

Spence, Lewis. The Myths of Mexico & Peru. LC 76-27516. (Illus.). 1976. Repr. of 1914 ed. lib. bdg. 45.00 (ISBN 0-89341-031-4). Longwood Pr.

MAYER, JULIUS ROBERT VON, 1814-1878

Lindsay, R. B. Julius Robert Mayer, Prophet of Energy. LC 72-8045. (Men of Physics Ser.). 1973. 22.00 (ISBN 0-08-016985-6). Pergamon.

MAYER, LOUIS B., 1885-1957

Carey, Gary. All the Stars in Heaven: The Story of Louis B. Mayer & Metro-Goldwyn-Mayer. (Illus.). 1980. 18.50 (ISBN 0-525-05245-3). Dutton.

Marx, Samuel. Mayer & Thalberg: The Make-Believe Saints. (Illus.). 336p. 1980. pap. 2.95 (ISBN 0-446-83987-6). Warner Bks.

MAYES, EDYTHE BEAM

Mayes, Edythe B. Washington - God's Workshop. LC 73-92388. 1973. 9.95 (ISBN 0-89002-021-3); pap. 2.95 (ISBN 0-89002-020-5). Northwoods Pr.

MAYFAIR, LONDON

Borer, Mary C. Mayfair: The Years of Grandeur. (Illus.). 308p. 1976. 15.00 (ISBN 0-491-01645-X). Transatlantic.

MAYFLIES

see May-Flies

MAYFLOWER (SHIP)

Caffrey, Kate. The Mayflower. LC 73-91855. (Illus.). 304p. 1974. 10.00 (ISBN 0-8128-1679-X). Stein & Day.

--Mayflower. LC 73-91855. 1975. pap. 5.95 (ISBN 0-8128-1857-1). Stein & Day.

Colloms, Brenda. The Mayflower Pilgrims. LC 77-310. (History Makers Ser). (Illus.). 1977. 6.95 (ISBN 0-312-52315-7). St Martin.

Haxtun, Annie A. Signers of the Mayflower Compact. LC 67-28609. 1968. Repr. of 1897 ed. 12.50 (ISBN 0-8063-0173-2). Genealog Pub.

Heaton, Vernon. The Mayflower. (Illus.). 200p. 1980. 19.95 (ISBN 0-8317-5745-0, Mayflower Bks). Smith Pubs.

Langdon-Davies, John. Mayflower & the Pilgrim Fathers. (Jackdaw Ser: No. 8). (Illus.). 1972. 6.95 (ISBN 0-670-46369-8, Grossman). Viking Pr.

Leynse, James P. Preceeding the Mayflower. 300p. 1972. 7.95 (ISBN 0-685-25215-9). Fountainhead.

McGovern, Ann. If You Sailed on the Mayflower. (Illus.). (gr. k-3). 1975. pap. 1.25 (ISBN 0-590-08738-X, Schol Pap). Schol Bk Serv.

Noyes, Ethel J. Women of the Mayflower & Women of Plymouth Colony. LC 73-12780. Repr. of 1921 ed. 20.00 (ISBN 0-8103-3668-5). Gale.

Simon, Philip J. Log of the Mayflower. LC 56-9513. 208p. 1980. Repr. of 1958 ed. 7.95 (ISBN 0-911180-02-8, Pub. by Priam Pr). Chicago Review.

--Log of the Mayflower. LC 56-9513. 208p. 1980. Repr. 7.95 (ISBN 0-911180-02-8). Priam Pr.

Vinton, Iris. Boy on the Mayflower. (gr. 3-7). 1970. pap. 1.25 (ISBN 0-590-00257-0, Schol Pap). Schol Bk Serv.

MAYFLOWER COMPACT, 1620

Richards, Norman. Story of the Mayflower Compact. LC 67-22901. (Cornerstones of Freedom Ser). (Illus.). (gr. 2-5). 1967. PLB 7.95 (ISBN 0-516-04625-X); pap. 2.50 (ISBN 0-516-44625-8). Childrens.

MAYHEW, THOMAS, 1593-1682

Hare, Lloyd C. Thomas Mayhew, Patriarch to the Indians, 1593-1682. LC 76-104347. (Illus.). Repr. of 1932 ed. 20.00 (ISBN 0-404-03108-0). AMS Pr.

--Thomas Mayhew, Patriarch to the Indians 1593 to 1682. LC 76-145070. 231p. 1932. Repr. 12.00 (ISBN 0-403-01012-8). Scholarly.

MAYO, KATHERINE (MOTHER INDIA), 1868-1940

Douglas, Norman. Good-Bye to Western Culture: Some Footnotes on East & West. LC 70-184841. 241p. 1930. Repr. lib. bdg. 15.00x (ISBN 0-8371-6330-7, DOWC). Greenwood.

Lajpat Rai, Lala. Unhappy India. rev. 2nd enl. ed. LC 72-171642. Repr. of 1928 ed. 36.45 (ISBN 0-404-03803-4). AMS Pr.

MAYO CLINIC, ROCHESTER, MINNESOTA

Braasch, William F. Early Days in the Mayo Clinic. (Illus.). 152p. 1969. ed. spiral bdg. 14.75photocopy (ISBN 0-398-00211-8). C C Thomas.

Mayo Clinic Dietetic Staff, et al. Mayo Clinic Diet Manual. Pemberton, Cecilia & Gastineau, Clifford, eds. LC 77-88298. (Illus.). 250p. 1981. text ed. write for info. (ISBN 0-7216-6212-9). Saunders.

Wilder, Lucy. The Mayo Clinic. 2nd ed. (Illus.). 80p. 1955. photocopy ed. spiral 9.75 (ISBN 0-398-02063-9). C C Thomas.

MAYO FAMILY

Clapesattle, Helen. Doctors Mayo. 2nd ed. (Illus.). 1954. 19.50x (ISBN 0-8166-0029-5). U of Minn Pr.

Hammontree, Marie. Will & Charlie Mayo: Boy Doctors. (Childhood of Famous Americans Ser). (Illus.). (gr. 3-7). 3.95 (ISBN 0-672-50185-6). Bobbs.

Johnson, Spencer. The Value of Sharing: The Story of the Mayo Brothers. LC 78-10578. (ValueTales Ser). (Illus.). (gr. k-6). 1978. PLB 6.95 (ISBN 0-916392-28-7, Dist. by Oak Tree Pubns). Value Comm.

Johnson, Spencer & Johnson, Ann D. Value of Sharing. (Value Tales Ser). (gr. 1-5). 1979. PLB 10.69 (ISBN 0-307-69953-6, Golden Pr). Western Pub.

MAYORS

Berry, Jason. Amazing Grace: With Charles Evers in Mississippi. 1978. pap. 4.95 (ISBN 0-918784-20-4). Legacy Pub Co.

Farkas, Suzanne. Urban Lobbying: Mayors in the Federal Arena. LC 77-124523. 1971. 12.50x (ISBN 0-8147-2550-3). NYU Pr.

FitzGerald, Kathleen W. Brass: Jane Byrne & the Pursuit of Power. 1981. 11.95 (ISBN 0-8092-7006-4). Contemp Bks.

Granger, Bill & Granger, Lori. Fighting Jane: Mayor Jane Byrne & the Chicago Machine. 1980. 12.95 (ISBN 0-8037-2470-5). Dial.

Holli, Melvin G. & Jones, Peter d'A, eds. Biographical Dictionary of American Mayors, 1820 to 1980. LC 80-1796. (Illus.). 576p. 1981. lib. bdg. 69.50 (ISBN 0-313-21134-5, HDA/). Greenwood.

Joint Center for Political Studies. Profiles of Black Negroes in America. 1976. pap. 10.00 (ISBN 0-87485-082-7). Johnson Chi.

Langford, Carl T. Hizzoner the Mayor. LC 75-40537. 1976. 8.95 (ISBN 0-88435-005-3). Chateau Pub.

Martin, Harold. William Berry Hartsfield, Mayor of Atlanta. LC 78-1550. 248p. 1978. 10.00 (ISBN 0-8203-0445-X). U of Ga Pr.

Orpe, Frank & McQuade, Jean P. Dare to Be Brave. (Illus.). 1977. casebd. 10.00 (ISBN 0-912404-06-X). Alpha Pubns.

Tarrow, Sidney. Between Center & Periphery: Grassroots Politicians in Italy & France. LC 76-26642. 1977. 20.00x (ISBN 0-300-02047-3). Yale U Pr.

Tremper, Bill. They Call Him Tommie. (Illus.). 50p. (Orig.). 1980. pap. 6.95 (ISBN 0-9604166-0-9). Tremper.

Waddy, Lawrence. Mayor's Race. LC 80-81489. 260p. pap. text ed. 3.95 (ISBN 0-89882-009-X). Lane & Assoc.

MAYS, WILLIE, 1931-
Einstein, Charles. Willie's Time. 1979. 12.95 (ISBN 0-397-01329-9). Har-Row.
Epstein, Sam & Epstein, Beryl. Willie Mays: Baseball Superstar. LC 74-20954. (Sports Library). (Illus.). 96p. (gr. 2-6). 1975. PLB 6.48 (ISBN 0-8116-6671-9). Garrard.
Mays, Willie & Berger, Maxine. Willie Mays, "Play Ball!". LC 80-13352. (Illus.). 160p. (gr. 7 up). 1980. PLB 8.29 (ISBN 0-671-41314-7). Messner.
--Willie Mays, "Play Ball". (Illus., Orig.). (gr. 4-8). 1980. text ed. cancelled (ISBN 0-671-95697-3); pap. 3.95 (ISBN 0-671-95578-0). Wanderer Bks.
Mays, Willie & Einstein, Charles. Born to Play Ball. (Putnam Sport Shelf). (Illus.). 1955. PLB 6.29 (ISBN 0-399-10900-5). Putnam.
Sullivan, George. Willie Mays. (Beginning Biography Ser.). (Illus.). 64p. (gr. 2-4). 1973. PLB 5.99 (ISBN 0-399-60824-9). Putnam.
MAZARIN, JULES, CARDINAL, 1602-1661
Dethan, Georges. The Young Mazarin. Hattan, Ragnhild, ed. (Men in Office Ser.). (Illus.). 1977. 16.95 (ISBN 0-500-87004-7). Thames Hudson.
Hassall, Arthur. Mazarin. facs. ed. LC 73-137379. (Select Bibliographies Reprint Ser). 1903. 15.00 (ISBN 0-8369-5580-3). Arno.
Moreau, Celestin. Bibliographie Des Mazarinades, 3 Vols. Set. 94.50 (ISBN 0-384-40060-4); Set. pap. 81.50 (ISBN 0-384-40061-2). Johnson Repr.
Moreau, Celestin, ed. Choix De Mazarinades, 2 Vols. 1853. Set. 77.00 (ISBN 0-384-40103-1); Set. pap. 67.50 (ISBN 0-685-13377-X). Johnson Repr.
MAZARINADES
Lindsay, Robert O. & Neu, John. Mazarinades: A Checklist of Copies in Major Collections in the United States. LC 74-150720. 1972. 20.50 (ISBN 0-8108-0369-0). Scarecrow.
Moreau, Celestin. Bibliographie Des Mazarinades, 4 vols. (Societe De L'histoire De France: Nos. 61, 63, & 67). Repr. of 1850 ed. Set. 79.50 (ISBN 0-8337-2454-1); 4 supplements in 1 vol. incl. (ISBN 0-685-06734-3). B Franklin.
--Bibliographie Des Mazarinades, 3 Vols. Set. 94.50 (ISBN 0-384-40060-4); Set. pap. 81.50 (ISBN 0-384-40061-2). Johnson Repr.
Moreau, Celestin, ed. Choix De Mazarinades, 2 Vols. 1853. Set. 77.00 (ISBN 0-384-40103-1); Set. pap. 67.50 (ISBN 0-685-13377-X). Johnson Repr.
Walsh, James E. Mazarinades: A Catalogue of the Collection of Seventeenth Century French Civil War Tracts in the Houghton Library, Harvard University. (Reference Bks.). 1976. lib. bdg. 23.00 (ISBN 0-8161-7871-2). G K Hall.
MAZATECO LANGUAGE
Cowan, George M. Some Aspects of the Lexical Structure of a Mazatec Historical Text. (Publications in Linguistics & Related Fields Ser.: No. 11). 145p. 1965. microfiche 1.60 (ISBN 0-88312-411-4). Summer Inst Ling.
Pike, Kenneth L. Tone Languages: A Technique for Determining the Number & Type of Pitch Contrasts in a Language, with Studies in Tonemic Substitution & Fusion. 1948. pap. 6.95x (ISBN 0-472-08734-7). U of Mich Pr.
MAZDA AUTOMOBILE
see Automobiles, Foreign-Types-Mazda
MAZDAISM
see Zoroastrianism
MAZE PUZZLES
Bright, Greg. The Great Maze Book: Extraordinary Puzzles for Extraordinary People. LC 74-26198. (Illus.). 1975. pap. 3.50 (ISBN 0-394-73054-2). Pantheon.
--The Hole Maze Book. LC 79-1882. 1979. pap. 3.50 (ISBN 0-394-73754-7). Pantheon.
Brightfield, Rick & Brightfield, Glory. Outer Space Mazes. (Orig.). 1978. pap. 2.95 (ISBN 0-06-090588-3, CN 588, CN). Har-Row.
Bullock, Waneta B. & Loveless, Ganelle. ABC Mazes. (Educational Ser.). (Illus.). (gr. k-1). 1979. pap. 3.50 (ISBN 0-89039-244-7). Ann Arbor FL.
Chazaud, Jacques. Mazes for Amuzement: No. 3. 1979. pap. 1.25 (ISBN 0-89559-161-8). Dale Books Inc.
Goodman, Judy. The Maze Book. (Orig.). (gr. 3-10). 1974. pap. 3.50 (ISBN 0-918932-31-9). Activity Resources.
Koziakin, Vladimir. A-Maze-Ing Universe Mazer. pap. write for info. Ace Bks.
--Cosmic Christmas Mazes. 128p. (Orig.). 1981. pap. 1.75 (ISBN 0-448-17292-5). Ace Bks.
--Haunted Mazes. pap. write for info. Ace Bks.
--Mazes, No. 3. (Illus.). 96p. 1973. pap. 2.50 (ISBN 0-448-02064-5). G&D.
--Mazes, No. 5. (Illus.). 96p. 1975. pap. 2.50 (ISBN 0-448-11877-7). G&D.
--Mazes for Fun, No. 5. (Elephant Bks.). (Illus.). 64p. (gr. 2-5). 1976. pap. 1.50 (ISBN 0-448-12515-3). G&D.
--Mazes: No. 7. 1977. pap. 2.50 (ISBN 0-448-12896-9). G&D.
--Mystery Mazes. 128p. (gr. 6 up). 1981. pap. 1.75 (ISBN 0-448-17289-5, Tempo). Ace Bks.
--Mythology Mazes. 128p. 1980. pap. 1.50 (ISBN 0-448-17221-6, Tempo). Ace Bks.
--Science Fiction Mazes. 128p. (gr. 6 up). 1981. pap. 1.50 (ISBN 0-448-17259-3, Tempo). Ace Bks.
--Science Fiction Mazes. 128p. (gr. 4 up). pap. 1.50 (ISBN 0-448-17259-3, Tempo). Ace Bks.
--Super Fantasy Mazes. (Illus.). 128p. 1980. pap. 1.25 (ISBN 0-448-17145-7, Tempo). Ace Bks.
--Super Horror Mazes. write for info. Ace Bks.
--Super Supernatural Mazes. (Illus.). 128p. 1980. pap. 1.50 (ISBN 0-448-17193-7, Tempo). Ace Bks.
--Zodiac Mazes. 128p. (Orig.). (gr. 4 up). 1981. pap. 1.50 (ISBN 0-448-17218-6, Tempo). Ace Bks.
McCreary, Paul. The Maze Book. (Educational Ser.). (Illus.). (gr. 2-4). 1979. pap. 4.50 (ISBN 0-89039-218-8). Ann Arbor FL.
Matthews, W. H. Mazes & Labyrinths: Their History & Development. (Illus.). 7.50 (ISBN 0-8446-0790-8). Peter Smith.
Myller, Rolf. Mazes: 60 Beautiful & Beastly Labyrinths with Solutions. (Illus.). 160p. (gr. 1 up). 1976. pap. 3.95 (ISBN 0-394-83254-X). Pantheon.
Phillips, Dave. Graphic & Op-Art Mazes. (Illus.). 1976. pap. 2.00 (ISBN 0-486-23373-1). Dover.
--Mind-Boggling Mazes: Forty Graphic & Three-D Labyrinths. (Illus.). 1979. pap. 1.95 (ISBN 0-486-23798-2). Dover.
--Storybook Mazes. (Illus.). 1978. pap. 1.75 (ISBN 0-486-23628-5). Dover.
--The World's Most Difficult Maze. 1981. pap. 2.95 (ISBN 0-486-23970-5). Dover.
Quinn, Lee D. Challenging Mazes. LC 75-2822. (Illus.). 64p. 1975. pap. 2.00 (ISBN 0-486-21177-0). Dover.
Reynolds, Patrick. Celebrity Mazes. (Illus.). 1979. pap. 1.50 (ISBN 0-89437-059-6). Baronet.
Shepherd, Walter. Big Book of Mazes & Labyrinths. (Illus.). 6.50 (ISBN 0-8446-4815-9). Peter Smith.
MAZE TESTS
Porteus, Stanley D. Porteus Maze Test: Fifty Years' Application. LC 65-18125. (Illus.). 1965. 18.95x (ISBN 0-87015-139-8). Pacific Bks.
MAZEPA, IVAN STEPANOVICH, HETMAN OF THE COSSACKS, 1614-1709
Babinski, Hubert F. The Mazeppa Legend in European Romanticism. LC 74-6152. 164p. 1974. 15.00x (ISBN 0-231-03825-9). Columbia U Pr.
Subtelny, Orest. The Mazepists: Ukrainian Separatism in the Eighteenth Century. (East European Monograph: No. 87). 300p. 1981. 20.00x (ISBN 0-914710-81-8). East Eur Quarterly.
MAZUT
see Petroleum As Fuel; Petroleum Products
MAZZEI, FILIPPO, 1730-1816
Garlick, Richard C., Jr., et al. Italy & Italians in Washington's Time. LC 74-17930. (Italian American Experience Ser.). 142p. 1975. Repr. 8.00x (ISBN 0-405-06402-0). Arno.
Marchione, Margherita, ed. Philip Mazzei: My Life & Wanderings. unabridged ed. Scalia, S. Eugene, tr. from It. 472p. (Orig.). 1980. 14.95 (ISBN 0-916322-03-3); pap. 9.95 (ISBN 0-916322-04-1). Am Inst Ital Stud.
MAZZINI, GIUSEPPE, 1805-1872
Barr, Stringfellow. Mazzini: Portrait of an Exile. 1971. lib. bdg. 17.50x (ISBN 0-374-90415-4). Octagon.
Delzell, Charles F., ed. The Unification of Italy, 1859-1861, Cavour, Mazzini, or Garibaldi? LC 76-15352. (European Problem Studies Ser.). 126p. 1976. pap. text ed. 5.50 (ISBN 0-88275-658-3). Krieger.
Griffith, Gwilym O. Mazzini: Prophet of Modern Europe. LC 78-80552. 1970. Repr. 27.50 (ISBN 0-86527-124-0). Fertig.
Hinkley, Edyth. Mazzini. LC 78-112807. 1970. Repr. of 1924 ed. 12.50 (ISBN 0-8046-1074-6). Kennikat.
--Mazzini: The Story of a Great Italian. LC 73-114883. (Select Bibliographies Reprint Ser). 1924. 19.50 (ISBN 0-8369-5287-1). Arno.
King, Bolton. The Life of Mazzini. 1977. Repr. of 1912 ed. lib. bdg. 17.50 (ISBN 0-8495-3002-4). Arden Lib.
MacCunn, John. Six Radical Thinkers: Bentham, J. S. Mill, Cobden, Carlyle, Mazzini, T. H. Green. LC 64-20669. 1964. Repr. of 1910 ed. 7.50 (ISBN 0-8462-0502-5). Russell.
Masson, David. Memories of London in the Forties. 1908. lib. bdg. 40.00 (ISBN 0-8414-6493-6). Folcroft.
Mazzini, Giuseppe. The Living Thoughts of Mazzini Presented by Ignazio Silone. LC 79-138163. (Illus.). 130p. 1972. Repr. of 1939 ed. lib. bdg. 15.00 (ISBN 0-8371-5620-3, MALI). Greenwood.
--Mazzini's Letters. Jervis, Alice D., tr. from Ital. LC 78-27617. 1979. Repr. of 1930 ed. lib. bdg. 17.00x (ISBN 0-313-20934-0, MALR). Greenwood.
Mazzini, Guiseppe. Mazzini's Letters. Jervis, Alice, tr. LC 78-59031. 1979. Repr. of 1930 ed. 18.00 (ISBN 0-88355-703-7). Hyperion Conn.
Rudman, Harry. Italian Nationalism & English Letters. LC 72-182707. Repr. of 1940 ed. 17.50 (ISBN 0-404-05450-1). AMS Pr.
Salvemini, Gaetano. Mazzini. 1957. 10.00x (ISBN 0-8047-0496-1). Stanford U Pr.
MAZZUOLI, FRANCESCO, CALLED IL PARMIGIANINO, 1503-1540
Freedberg, Sydney J. Parmigianino: His Works in Painting. LC 72-95120. (Illus.). 1971. Repr. of 1950 ed. lib. bdg. 45.00x (ISBN 0-8371-3717-9, FRPA). Greenwood.
Popham, A. E. Catalogue of the Drawings of Parmigianino, 3 vols. LC 76-104619. (Franklin Jasper Walls Lectures, 1968, at the Piepont Morgan Library). (Illus.). 1971. Set. 175.00x (ISBN 0-300-01300-0). Yale U Pr.
MBA-BIVI
see Tivi (African People)
MBALA LANGUAGE
see Congo Language
MBAYA LANGUAGE
see also Guaycuruan Languages
MBOCHI LANGUAGE
see Congo Language
MBOMA LANGUAGE
see Congo Language
MBOYA, TOM
Amin, Mohamed. Tom Mboya: A Photographic Tribute. (Illus.). 1969. 7.50x (ISBN 0-8002-0506-5). Intl Pubns Serv.
MBUNDU (BANTU TRIBE)
Miller, Joseph C. Kings & Kingsman: Early Mbundu States in Angola. (Oxford Studies in African Affairs Ser.). (Illus.). 1976. 45.00x (ISBN 0-19-822704-3). Oxford U Pr.
MBUTI
see Bambute
MEAD, GEORGE HERBERT, 1863-1931
Corti, Walter R. The Philosophy of George Herbert Mead. 1977. pap. 17.75 (ISBN 3-7873-0353-7). Adler.
Kang, W. G. H. Mead's Concept of Rationality: A Study of the Use of Symbols & Other Implements. (Approaches to Semiotics: No. 54). 1976. text ed. 40.00x (ISBN 90-2793-165-8). Mouton.
Miller, David L. George Herbert Mead: Self, Language & the World. LC 80-14725. 324p. 1980. pap. 7.95 (ISBN 0-226-52613-5, P910, Phoen). U of Chicago Pr.
Pfuetze, Paul. Self, Society, Existence: Human Nature & Dialogue in the Thought of George Herbert Mead & Martin Buber. 400p. 1973. Repr. of 1961 ed. lib. bdg. 19.75x (ISBN 0-8371-6708-6, PFSS). Greenwood.
Schellenberg, James A. Masters of Social Psychology: Freud, Mead, Lewin, & Skinner. 1979. pap. 3.95 (ISBN 0-19-502622-5, GB 590, GB). Oxford U Pr.
MEAD, MARGARET, 1901-1978
Church, Carol B. Margaret Mead: Student of the Global Village. Bender, David L. & McCuen, Gary E., eds. (Focus on Famous Women Ser). (Illus.). (gr. 3-9). 1976. 6.95 (ISBN 0-912616-46-6); read-along cassette 9.95 (ISBN 0-89908-245-9). Greenhaven.
Epstein, Sam & Epstein, Beryl. She Never Looked Back: Margaret Mead in Samoa. LC 78-31821. (Science Discovery Ser.). (Illus.). (gr. 3-7). 1980. PLB 5.99 (ISBN 0-698-30715-1). Coward.
Frevert, Patricia D. Margaret Mead Herself. Redpath, Ann, ed. (People to Remember Ser.). (Illus.). 32p. (gr. 5-9). 1981. PLB 5.95 (ISBN 0-87191-799-8). Creative Ed.
Gordan, Joan, ed. Margaret Mead: The Complete Bibliography 1925-1975. 1976. text ed. 23.50x (ISBN 90-2793-026-0). Mouton.
Morse, Ann & Morse, Charles. Margaret Mead. LC 75-1343. (People to Remember Ser.). (Illus.). 32p. (gr. 3-6). 1975. PLB 5.95 (ISBN 0-87191-425-5). Creative Ed.
Rice, Edward. Margaret Mead: A Portrait. LC 76-3827. (Illus.). 224p. (gr. 7 up). 1979. 10.00 (ISBN 0-06-025001-1, HarpJ); PLB 9.89 (ISBN 0-06-025002-X). Har-Row.
Schwartz, Theodore, ed. Socialization As Cultural Communication. LC 75-17282. 1976. 16.50x (ISBN 0-520-03061-3); pap. 7.95x (ISBN 0-520-03955-6). U of Cal Pr.
MEAD, RICHARD, 1673-1754
Mead, Richard. The Medical Works of Richard Mead. LC 75-23740. Repr. of 1775 ed. 48.50 (ISBN 0-404-13550-1). AMS Pr.
MEADOW LAKE, CALIFORNIA
Fatout, Paul. Meadow Lake: Gold Town. LC 69-15995. (Illus.). xiv, 178p. 1974. pap. 3.95 (ISBN 0-8032-5788-0, BB 576, Bison). U of Nebr Pr.
MEADOWS
see also Grasses; Pastures
Leimbach, Patricia P. All My Meadows. LC 77-24352. (Illus.). 1977. 9.95 (ISBN 0-13-022525-8). P-H.
Trost, Lucille W. Lives & Deaths of a Meadow. (Illus.). 96p. (gr. 5 up). 1973. PLB 4.69 (ISBN 0-399-60835-4). Putnam.
MEAGHER, THOMAS FRANCIS, 1823-1867
Athearn, Robert G. Thomas Francis Meagher: An Irish Revolutionary in America. LC 76-6321. (Irish Americans Ser.). (Illus.). 1976. Repr. of 1949 ed. 12.00 (ISBN 0-405-09318-7). Arno.
Lyons, W. F. Brigadier-General Thomas Francis Meagher: His Political & Military Career; with Selections from His Speeches & Writings. LC 4-24937. (Illus.). 1975. Repr. of 1870 ed. 17.50 (ISBN 0-89097-005-X). Archer Edns.
MEALS FOR SCHOOL CHILDREN
see School Children-Food
MEALY BUGS
McKenzie, Howard L. Mealybugs of California: With Taxonomy, Biology, & Control of North American Species. (Illus.). 1968. 65.00x (ISBN 0-520-00844-8). U of Cal Pr.
MEANING (PHILOSOPHY)
Brennecke, John H. & Amick, Robert G. The Struggle for Significance. 2nd ed. 1975. pap. text ed. 9.95x (ISBN 0-02-471000-8, 47100); tchrs' manual free (ISBN 0-02-471010-5). Macmillan.
Bulka, Reuven. The Quest for Ultimate Meaning: Applications of Logotherapy. LC 78-61105. 1979. 11.95 (ISBN 0-8022-2232-3). Philos Lib.
Cohen, Jonathan L. Spoken & Unspoken Meanings. (Philospical Semantics 1). 1975. pap. text ed. 11.00x (ISBN 90-3160-006-7). Humanities.
Coseriu, Eugenio. Sprache und Funktionalitat Bei Fernao De Oliverra. (No. 1). (Ger.). 1975. pap. text ed. 1.50x (ISBN 90-316-0007-5). Humanities.
Edlow, R. B. Galen on Language & Ambiguity "De Captionibus" (on Fallacies) An English Translation of Galen's. (Philosophia Antiqua: No. 31). 1977. pap. text ed. 25.25x (ISBN 90-04-04869-3). Humanities.
Froman, Creel. Manuscript of Hugo Potts: An Inquiry into Meaning. LC 73-5915. 376p. 1973. 12.85x (ISBN 0-8093-0608-5). S Ill U Pr.
Hardy, William G. Language, Thought & Experience: A Tapestry of the Dimensions of Meaning. 1978. 29.50 (ISBN 0-8391-1213-0). Univ Park.
Holdcroft, David. Words & Deeds: Problems of the Theory of Speech Acts. (Illus.). 1978. 24.95x (ISBN 0-19-824581-5). Oxford U Pr.
Kestenbaum, Victor. The Phenomenological Sense of John Dewey: Habit & Meaning. 1977. text ed. 8.50x (ISBN 0-391-00668-1). Humanities.
Lewy, C. Meaning & Modality. LC 76-11084. 1977. 23.50 (ISBN 0-521-21314-2). Cambridge U Pr.
Polanyi, Michael & Prosch, Harry. Meaning. LC 75-5067. xiv, 246p. 1975. lib. bdg. 14.00x (ISBN 0-226-67294-8). U of Chicago Pr.
--Meaning. LC 75-5067. 1977. pap. 4.50 (ISBN 0-226-67295-6, P740, Phoen). U of Chicago Pr.
Powell, Robert. Return to Meaningfulness. LC 80-54613. 176p. 1981. pap. text ed. 6.95 (ISBN 0-932238-07-6). Word Shop.
Putnam, Hilary. Meaning & the Moral Sciences. (International Library of Philosophy). 1979. pap. 6.95 (ISBN 0-7100-0437-0). Routledge & Kegan.
Rollin, Bernard E. Natural & Conventional Meaning: An Examination of the Distinction. (Approaches to Semiotics Ser: No. 45). 112p. (Orig.). 1976. pap. text ed. 20.75x (ISBN 90-2793-274-3). Mouton.
Schiffer, Stephen R. Meaning. 184p. 1973. text ed. 32.00x (ISBN 0-19-824367-7). Oxford U Pr.
Smith, Steven B. Meaning & Negation. (Janua Linguarum, Ser. Minor: No. 206). (Illus.). 91p. 1978. pap. text ed. 17.50x (ISBN 90-279-3277-8). Mouton.
Vendler, Zeno. Res Cogitans: An Essay in Rational Psychology. LC 72-3182. (Contemporary Philosophy Ser.). 273p. 1972. 18.50x (ISBN 0-8014-0743-5). Cornell U Pr.
MEANING (PSYCHOLOGY)
see also Definition (Logic); Language and Languages; Logical Positivism; Semantics; Semantics (Philosophy); Thought and Thinking
Barasch, Frances K. The Grotesque: A Study in Meanings. (De Proprietatibus Litterarum, Ser. Major: No. 20). 1971. text ed. 25.00x (ISBN 90-2791-788-4). Mouton.
Chambers, Ross. Meaning & Meaningfulness: Studies in the Analysis & Interpretation of Texts. LC 79-50280. (French Forum Monographs: No. 15). 199p. 1979. pap. 11.50x (ISBN 0-917058-14-3). French Forum.
Chase, Stuart. Tyranny of Words. LC 38-27108. 1959. pap. 4.95 (ISBN 0-15-692394-7, HB26, Harv). HarBraceJ.
Davitz, J. R. Language of Emotion. (Personality & Psychopathology: Vol. 6). 1969. 27.00 (ISBN 0-12-206450-X). Acad Pr.

Drange, Theodore. Type Crossings: Sentential Meaninglessness in the Border Area of Linguistics & Philosophy. (Janua Linguarum, Ser. Minor: No. 44). (Orig.). 1966. pap. text ed. 30.00x (ISBN 90-2790-578-9). Mouton.
Erwin, Edward. The Concept of Meaninglessness. LC 75-101456. 164p. 1970. 10.00x (ISBN 0-8018-1110-4). Johns Hopkins.
Gordon, Rosemary, ed. Dying & Creating: A Search for Meaning. (Library of Analytical Psychology: Vol. 4). 1981. 18.00 (ISBN 0-12-291450-3). Acad Pr.
Gula, Robert J. Nonsense: How to Overcome It. LC 79-65121. (Illus.). 200p. 1981. pap. 6.95 (ISBN 0-8128-6116-7). Stein & Day.
Hal, William H. The Perception of Meaning: From Alphabet to Standard English. pap. 5.00 (ISBN 0-930176-01-4). Perception.
Hayakawa, S. I. & Dresser, William, eds. Dimensions of Meaning. LC 68-24164. (Composition & Rhetoric Ser). (Orig.). 1970. pap. 2.95 (ISBN 0-672-60902-9, CR16). Bobbs.
Jaffe, Aniela. The Myth of Meaning. LC 73-120093. 1971. 8.00 (ISBN 0-913430-07-2). C G Jung Foun.
MacKaye, James. Logic of Language. LC 65-18821. 1965. Repr. of 1939 ed. 8.50 (ISBN 0-8462-0689-7). Russell.
Ogden, Charles K. & Richards, Ivor A. Meaning of Meaning. 1959. pap. 4.50 (ISBN 0-15-658446-8, HB29, Harv). HarBraceJ.
Ohlander, Solve. Phonology, Meaning, Morphology: On the Role of Semantic & Morphological Criteria in Phonological Analysis. (Gothenburg Studies in English: No. 33). 221p. 1976. pap. text ed. 13.50x (ISBN 0-685-72010-1). Humanities.
Osgood, Charles E., et al. The Measurement of Meaning. LC 56-5684. (Illus.). 1967. pap. 6.95 (ISBN 0-252-74539-6). U of Ill Pr.
Peckham, Morse. Explanation & Power: The Control of Human Behavior. 1978. 17.95 (ISBN 0-8164-9352-9). Continuum.
Russell, Bertrand. Inquiry into Meaning & Truth. 1940. text ed. 18.00x (ISBN 0-04-121007-7). Humanities.
Szalay, Lorand B. & Deese, James. Subjective Meaning & Culture: An Assessment Through Word Associations. LC 78-15561. 1978. 12.95 (ISBN 0-470-26486-1). Halsted Pr.
Upton, Albert. Design for Thinking: A First Book in Semantics. rev. ed. LC 61-14653. (Illus.). xii, 240p. 1973. pap. text ed. 5.95x (ISBN 0-87015-207-6). Pacific Bks.
Urban, Wilbur M. Language & Reality: The Philosophy of Language & the Principles of Symbolism. facsimile ed. LC 75-179543. (Select Bibliographies Reprint Ser.). Repr. of 1939 ed. 34.00 (ISBN 0-8369-6672-4). Arno.
Vastenhouw, Jan. Relationships Between Meanings: Specifically with Regard to Trait Concepts Used in Psychology. 1962. text ed. 12.75x (ISBN 0-686-22456-6). Mouton.
Werner, H. & Kaplan, Edith. Acquisition of Word Meanings. (SRCD Ser.: Vol. 15, No. 1). 1950. pap. 6.00 (ISBN 0-527-01550-4). Kraus Repr.

MEANY, GEORGE

Finke, Blythe F. George Meany: Modern Leader of the American Federation of Labor. Rahmas, D. Steve, ed. (Outstanding Personalities Ser.: No. 38). 32p. (Orig.). (gr. 7-12). 1972. lib. bdg. 2.95 incl. catalog cards (ISBN 0-87157-548-5); pap. 1.50 vinyl laminated covers (ISBN 0-87157-048-3). SamHar Pr.
Robinson, Archie. George Meany. 1982. 16.95 (ISBN 0-671-42163-8). S&S.

MEARS, HENRIETTA

Baldwin, Ethel M. & Benson, David V. Henrietta Mears & How She Did It. pap. 2.65 (ISBN 0-8307-0018-8, 5000505). Regal.

MEASLES

see also Rubella

Measles & Cholera. (Bulletin of WHO: Vol. 30, No. 6). 116p. (Eng.). 1964. pap. 3.60 (ISBN 0-686-09180-9). World Health.

MEASURABLE SETS

see Measure Theory

MEASURE, CARATHEODORY

see Caratheodory Measure

MEASURE ALGEBRAS

see also Measure Theory

MEASURE OF DAMAGES

see Damages

MEASURE OF INFORMATION

see Information Measurement

MEASURE THEORY

see also Caratheodory Measure; Ergodic Theory; Integrals, Haar; Spectral Theory (Mathematics)

Abramov, L. M., et al. Ten Papers in Functional Analysis & Measure Theory. LC 51-5559. (Translations Ser.: No. 2, Vol. 49). 1966. 21.20 (ISBN 0-8218-1749-3, TRANS 2-49). Am Math.
Argabright, Loren & De Lamadrid, Jesus G. Fourier Analysis of Unbounded Measures on Locally Compact Abelian Groups. LC 74-6499. (Memoirs: No. 145). 1974. pap. 7.60 (ISBN 0-8218-1845-7, MEMO-145). Am Math.
Bahtin, I. A., et al. Eleven Papers on Differential Equations, Functional Analysis & Measure Theory. LC 51-5559. (Translations, Ser: No. 2, Vol. 51). 1966. 34.00 (ISBN 0-8218-1751-5, TRANS 2-51). Am Math.
Bartle, Robert G. Elements of Integration. LC 75-15979. 129p. 1966. 20.95 (ISBN 0-471-05457-7). Wiley.
Bauer, H. Probability Theory & Elements of Measure Theory. (Probability & Mathematical Statistics Ser.). 1981. price not set (ISBN 0-12-082820-0). Acad Pr.
Bellow, A. & Kolzow, D., eds. Measure Theory: Proceedings of the Conference Held at Oberwolfach, 15-21 June, 1975. LC 76-26664. (Lecture Notes in Mathematics: Vol. 541). 1976. soft cover 19.20 (ISBN 0-387-07861-4). Springer-Verlag.
Berberian, Sterling K. Measure & Integration. LC 74-128871. 1970. Repr. of 1965 ed. text ed. 11.95 (ISBN 0-8284-0241-8). Chelsea Pub.
Bichteler, K. Integration Theory: With Special Attention to Vector Measures. LC 72-97636. (Lecture Notes in Mathematics: Vol. 315). 357p. 1973. pap. 14.30 (ISBN 0-387-06158-4). Springer-Verlag.
Billingsley, P. Convergence of Probability Measures. (Probability & Mathematical Statistics Tracts: Probability & Statistics Section). 253p. 1968. 31.00 (ISBN 0-471-07242-7, Pub. by Wiley-Interscience). Wiley.
Bishop, Errett & Cheng, Henry. Constructive Measure Theory. LC 52-42839. (Memoirs: No. 116). 1972. pap. 6.40 (ISBN 0-8218-1816-3, MEMO-116). Am Math.
Brakke, Kenneth A. The Motion of a Surface by Its Mean Curvature. (Mathematical Notes Ser.: No. 20). 1978. 13.00x (ISBN 0-691-08204-9). Princeton U Pr.
Chae. Lebesque Integration. (Lecture Notes in Pure & Applied Mathematics Ser.: Vol. 58). 328p. 1980. 35.00 (ISBN 0-8247-6983-X). Dekker.
Cohn, Donald. Measure Theory. 276p. 1980. 19.95 (ISBN 3-7643-3003-1). Birkhauser.
Conference, 5th, Oberwolfach, Germany, Jan. 29 - Feb. 4, 1978. Probability Measures on Groups: Proceedings. Heyer, H., ed. (Lecture Notes in Mathematics: Vol. 706). 1979. pap. 18.70 (ISBN 0-387-09124-6). Springer-Verlag.
Constantinescu, C. Duality in Measure Theory. (Lecture Notes in Mathematics: Vol. 796). 197p. 1980. pap. 14.00 (ISBN 0-387-09989-1). Springer-Verlag.
DeBarra, G. Measure Theory & Integration. (Mathematics & Its Applications). 260p. 1981. 69.95 (ISBN 0-470-27232-5). Halsted Pr.
De Lepinay, Mace & Antoine, Jules C. Franges D'interference et Leurs Applications Metrologiques. 101p. 1981. Repr. of 1901 ed. lib. bdg. 50.00 (ISBN 0-8287-1466-5). Clearwater Pub.
Din Standards for Technology & Measuring Lengths. 743.00 (ISBN 0-686-28166-7, 10051-4/11). Heyden.
Faden, Arnold M. Economics of Space & Time: The Measure Theoretic Foundations of Social Science. 1977. 39.95x (ISBN 0-8138-0500-7). Iowa St U Pr.
Farrell, R. H. Techniques of Multivariate Calculation. (Lecture Notes in Mathematics: Vol. 520). 1976. pap. 16.40 (ISBN 0-387-07695-6). Springer-Verlag.
Federer, H. Geometric Measure Theory. LC 69-16846. (Die Grundlehren der Mathematischen Wissenschaften: Vol. 153). 1969. 65.20 (ISBN 0-387-04505-8). Springer-Verlag.
Fomin, S., et al. Nine Papers on Foundations, Measure Theory, & Analysis. (Translations Ser.: No. 2, Vol. 57). 1966. 32.40 (ISBN 0-8218-1757-4, TRANS 2-57). Am Math.
Fremlin, D. H. Topologieal Riesz Spaces & Measure Theory. LC 72-95410. 300p. 1974. 42.00 (ISBN 0-521-20170-5). Cambridge U Pr.
Gamelin, T. W. Uniform Algebras & Jensen Measures. LC 78-16213. (London Mathematical Society Lecture Note Ser.: No. 32). 1979. pap. 17.95x (ISBN 0-521-22280-X). Cambridge U Pr.
Good, I. S. & Osteyee, D. B. Information Weight of Evidence, the Singularity Between Probability Measures & Signal Detection. LC 74-393. (Lecture Notes in Mathematics: Vol. 376). xi, 156p. 1974. pap. 8.80 (ISBN 0-387-06726-4). Springer-Verlag.
Guzman, M. De. Differentiation of Integrals in R to the nth Power. (Lecture Notes in Mathematics: Vol. 481). xii, 226p. 1975. pap. 12.20 (ISBN 0-387-07399-X). Springer-Verlag.
Halmos, P. R. Measure Theory. LC 74-10690. (Graduate Texts in Mathematics: Vol. 18). 305p. 1974. 19.60 (ISBN 0-387-90088-8). Springer-Verlag.
Hengartner, Walter & Theodoresco, Rado. Concentration Functions. 1973. 27.50 (ISBN 0-12-341050-9). Acad Pr.
Jacobs, Konrad. Measure & Integral. (Probability & Mathematical Statistics). 1978. 55.00 (ISBN 0-12-378550-2). Acad Pr.
Kenyon, Hewitt & Morse, Anthony P. Web Derivatives. LC 73-2858. (Memoirs: No. 132). 178p. 1973. pap. 8.80 (ISBN 0-8218-1832-5, MEMO-132). Am Math.
Kingman, John F. & Taylor, S. J. Introduction to Measure & Probability. 1966. 44.50 (ISBN 0-521-05888-0). Cambridge U Pr.
Koelzow, D., ed. Measure Theory 1979: Proceedings. (Lecture Notes in Mathematics: Vol. 794). 592p. 1980. pap. 34.60 (ISBN 0-387-09979-4). Springer-Verlag.
Konsler, Runelle & Mirabella, Lauren, eds. Cruising into Measurements. 1980. pap. text ed. 8.95 (ISBN 0-8302-2140-9). Goodyear.
Krieger, Henry A. Measure-Theoretic Probability. LC 80-1431. 394p. 1980. lib. bdg. 20.50 (ISBN 0-8191-1228-3); pap. text ed. 12.50 (ISBN 0-8191-1229-1). U Pr of Amer.
Mahoney, Susan. Metric Measurement Learning Module. Mills, Richard G., ed. May, Lola J. 1976. pap. 214.00 (ISBN 0-89290-136-5, CM-57). Soc for Visual.
Markley, N. G., et al, eds. The Structure of Attractors in Dynamical Systems: Proceedings, North Dakota, June 20-24, 1977. LC 78-13670. (Lecture Notes in Mathematics: Vol. 668). 1978. pap. 16.50 (ISBN 0-387-08925-X). Springer-Verlag.
Milton, J. Susan & Tsokos, Chris P. Probability Theory with the Essential Analysis. LC 76-27867. (Applied Mathematics & Computation Ser: No. 10). 1976. text ed. 24.50 (ISBN 0-201-07604-7, Adv Bk Prog); pap. text ed. 14.50 (ISBN 0-201-07605-5, Adv Bk Prog). A-W.
Nikodym, Otton M. Mathematical Apparatus for Quantum-Theories. (Grundlehren der Mathematischen Wissenschaften: Vol. 129). 1966. 85.50 (ISBN 0-387-03523-0). Springer-Verlag.
Parthasarathy, K. R. Probability Measures on Metric Spaces. 1967. 32.50 (ISBN 0-12-545950-5). Acad Pr.
Pfanzagl, J. & Pierlo, W. Compact Systems of Sets. (Lecture Notes in Mathematics: Vol. 16). (Orig.). 1966. pap. 11.10 (ISBN 0-387-03599-0). Springer-Verlag.
Pfanzagl, Johann. Theory of Measurement. 2nd ed. 235p. 1971. 37.50x (ISBN 3-7908-0016-3). Intl Pubns Serv.
Pfeffer, Washek F. Integrals & Measures. (Monographs in Pure & Applied Mathematics: Vol. 42). 1977. 24.50 (ISBN 0-8247-6530-3). Dekker.
Roberts, F. S. Measurement Theory. (Encyclopedia of Mathematics & Its Applications: Vol. 7). 1979. text ed. 24.50 (ISBN 0-201-13506-X, Adv Bk Prog). A-W.
Rogers, Claude A. Hausdorff Measures. (Illus.). 1970. 28.95 (ISBN 0-521-07970-5). Cambridge U Pr.
Roussas, G. G. Contiguity of Probability Measures: Some Applications in Statistics. LC 71-171682. (Cambridge Tracts in Mathematics & Mathematical Physics: No. 63). 1972. 44.50 (ISBN 0-521-08354-0). Cambridge U Pr.
Sion, M. A Theory of Semigroup Valued Measures. LC 73-17935. (Lecture Notes in Mathematics: Vol. 355). v, 140p. 1974. pap. 9.10 (ISBN 0-387-06542-3). Springer-Verlag.
Spiegel, Murray R. Real Variables. 1969. pap. 6.95 (ISBN 0-07-060221-2, SP). McGraw.
Steklov Institute of Mathematics, Academy of Sciences, U S S R, No. 99. Limits of Interdeterminacy in Measure of Trigonometric & Orthogonal Series: Proceedings. 1968. 19.60 (ISBN 0-8218-1899-6, STEKLO-99). Am Math.
Taylor, Joseph L. Measure Algebras. LC 73-5930. (CBMS Regional Conference Series in Mathematics: No. 16). 1979. pap. 9.00 (ISBN 0-8218-1666-7, CBMS-16). Am Math.
Weir, A. J. General Integration & Measure. LC 73-91620. (Illus.). 344p. 1974. 35.50 (ISBN 0-521-20407-0); pap. 13.95 (ISBN 0-521-29715-X). Cambridge U Pr.
--Lebesgue Integration & Measure. LC 72-83584. (Illus.). 220p. (Orig.). 1973. 37.95 (ISBN 0-521-08728-7); pap. 14.95x (ISBN 0-521-09751-7). Cambridge U Pr.
Wilcox, Howard & Myers, David L. An Introduction to Lebesgue Integration & Fourier Analysis. LC 77-12013. 168p. 1978. 13.50 (ISBN 0-88275-614-1). Krieger.

MEASUREMENT, MENTAL

see Psychometrics

MEASUREMENT OF AREA

see Area Measurement

MEASUREMENT OF DISTANCES

see Distances–Measurement

MEASUREMENT OF SOUND

see Sound–Measurement

MEASUREMENT OF STREAMS

see Stream Measurements

MEASUREMENTS, ELECTRIC

see Electric Measurements

MEASUREMENTS, ELECTRONIC

see Electronic Measurements

MEASUREMENTS, OPTICAL

see Optical Measurements

MEASUREMENTS, PHYSICAL

see Physical Measurements

MEASUREMENT, PSYCHOLOGICAL

see Psychometrics

MEASURES

see Weights and Measures

MEASURING

see Mensuration

MEASURING INSTRUMENTS

see also Digital Counters; Gages; Instrument Manufacture; Planimeter; Slide-Rule

Abernethy, R. B. Measurement Uncertainty Handbook, 1980. rev. ed. 174p. 1980. pap. text ed. 12.00x (ISBN 0-87664-483-3). Instru Soc.
Analysis Instrumentation, Newark, Delaware, Nineteen Seventy - Nine, Vol. 17. 251p. 1979. pap. text ed. 30.00x (ISBN 0-87664-439-6). Instru Soc.
Baldwin, Clifford T. Fundamentals of Electrical Measurements. 11.50 (ISBN 0-8044-4080-8). Ungar.
Beckwith, Thomas G. & Buck, N. Lewis. Mechanical Measurements. 2nd ed. (Mechanical Engineering Ser). 1969. text ed. 24.95 (ISBN 0-201-00454-2). A-W.
Bedwell, William. Mesolabium Architectionicum That Is a Most Rare Instrument of Measuring. LC 72-172. (English Experience Ser.: No. 224). 24p. Repr. of 1631 ed. 7.00 (ISBN 90-221-0224-6). Walter J Johnson.
Bottaccini, M. R. Instruments & Measurement. LC 73-85467. 384p. 1975. text ed. 23.95x (ISBN 0-675-08889-5). Merrill.
Conference on Instruments & Measurements. Proceedings, 2 vols. Von Koch, H. & Ljungberg, G., eds. Incl. Vol. 1. Chemical Analysis, Electric Quantities, Nucleonics & Process Control. 50.00 (ISBN 0-12-725701-2); Vol. 2. Nuclear Instrumentation, Measurement of Electric & Magnetic Quantities, Reactor Control. 59.50 (ISBN 0-12-725702-0). 1961. Acad Pr.
Doebelin, Ernest O. Measurement Systems: Application & Design. 2nd ed. (Illus.). 768p. 1971. text ed. 24.50 (ISBN 0-07-017336-2, C). McGraw.
Farago, Francis T. Handbook of Dimensional Measurement. LC 68-55069. (Illus.). 400p. 1968. 36.00 (ISBN 0-8311-1025-2). Indus Pr.
Fundamentals of Aerospace Instrumentation, Vol. 10. Incl. Vol. 5. Fundamentals of Test Measurement. LC 68-59468. 64p. 1978. pap. text ed. 12.00 (ISBN 0-87664-404-3). Instru Soc.
Gray, B. F. Measurements, Instrumentation & Data Transmission. LC 76-49922. (Illus.). 1977. text ed. 13.50x (ISBN 0-582-41065-7); pap. text ed. 9.50x (ISBN 0-582-41066-5). Longman.
Horne, D. F. Dividing, Ruling & Mask-Making. LC 74-7856. (Illus.). 315p. 1974. 62.50x (ISBN 0-8448-0359-6). Crane Russak Co.
IBM Education Department. Precision Measurement in the Metal Working Industry. rev. ed. (Illus.). 1952. pap. 8.50x (ISBN 0-8156-2194-9). Syracuse U Pr.
Instrumentation in the Aerospace Industry, Vol. 24. Incl. Vol. 15. Advances in Test Measurement. 1978. pap. text ed. 40.00 (ISBN 0-87664-403-5); Set. pap. text ed. 75.00 (ISBN 0-686-53137-X). Instru Soc.
International Measurement Confederation Congress, Sixth & Imeko. Measurement & Instrumentation: Proceedings, 3 vols. 1975. Set. 158.75 (ISBN 0-444-10685-5, North-Holland). Elsevier.
Liptak, Bela G., ed. Instrument Engineers' Handbook, 2 vols. & supplement one. LC 73-80445. (Illus.). 1969-72. Set. 80.00x (ISBN 0-8019-5947-0); Vol. 1, Process Measurement. 35.00x (ISBN 0-8019-5502-5); supplement one 24.95x (ISBN 0-8019-5658-7); Vol. 2, Process Control. 45.00x (ISBN 0-8019-5519-X). Chilton.
Roberts, Kenneth D., frwd. by. Stanley Rule & Level Eighteen Hundred Seventy-Seven Price List of Rules, Squares, Levels, Planes, Etc. 64p. 1980. pap. 4.00 (ISBN 0-913602-34-5). K Roberts.
Sydenham, P. H. Measuring Instruments - Tools of Knowledge. (History of Technology Ser.: No. 1). (Illus.). 1979. 61.50 (ISBN 0-906048-19-2). Inst Elect Eng.
Trylinski, W. Fine Mechanisms & Precision Instruments, Principles of Design. 1971. 75.00 (ISBN 0-08-006361-6). Pergamon.
Valentich, Joseph H. Tube Type Dilatometers: Applications from Cyrogenic to Elevated Temperatures. LC 80-82116. 224p. 1981. text ed. 35.00 (ISBN 0-87664-468-X). Instru Soc.

MEAT

see also Beef; Cookery (Meat); Ham

Ashbrook, Frank G. Butchering, Processing & Preservation of Meat. (Illus.). 336p. 1955. pap. 5.95 (ISBN 0-442-20377-2). Van Nos Reinhold.
Black, Maggie. Meat Preserving at Home. (Invest in Living Ser.). 1976. pap. 5.00x (ISBN 0-7158-0454-5). Intl Pubns Serv.

Briskey, Ernest J., et al, eds. Physiology & Biochemistry of Muscle As a Food: Proceedings, 1965, 2 vols. (Illus.). 1966. Vol. 1. 35.00x (ISBN 0-299-04110-7); Vol. 2. 50.00 (ISBN 0-299-05680-5). U of Wis Pr.
Ellis, Merle. Cutting up the Kitchen: The Butcher's Guide to Saving Money on Meat & Poultry. LC 75-26502. 216p. 1975. pap. 6.95 (ISBN 0-87701-071-4). Chronicle Bks.
Forrest, John C., et al. Principles of Meat Science. LC 75-8543. (Food & Nutrition Ser.). (Illus.). 1975. text ed. 26.95x (ISBN 0-7167-0743-8). W H Freeman.
Giammatti, Victor M. Raising Small Meat Animals. LC 75-21050. 1976. 12.35 (ISBN 0-8134-1741-4). Interstate.
Helser, M. D. Farm Meats. (Illus.). 1923. text ed. 4.75x (ISBN 0-911090-12-6). Pacific Bk Supply.
Koniecko, Edward S. Handbook for Meat Chemists. 1979. pap. text ed. 20.00 (ISBN 0-89529-097-9). Avery Pub.
Lawrie, R., ed. Developments in Meat Science, Vol. 1. (Illus.). 255p. 1980. 42.50x (ISBN 0-85334-866-9, Pub. by Applied Science). Burgess-Intl Ideas.
Levie, Albert. The Meat Handbook. 4th ed. (Illus.). 1979. text ed. 23.00 (ISBN 0-87055-315-1). AVI.
Lobel, Leon & Lobel, Stanley. All About Meat. Krech, Inez M., ed. LC 77-3322. (Illus.). 1977. pap. 6.95 (ISBN 0-15-604600-8, Harv). HarBraceJ.
Mutkoski, Stephen A. & Schurer, Marcia L. Meat & Fish Management. 1981. text ed. 19.95x (ISBN 0-534-00907-7, Breton Pubs). Wadsworth Pub.
Report of the Sixth Session of the Intergovernmental Group on Meat. 35p. 1977. pap. 7.50 (ISBN 92-5-100123-5, F1106, FAO). Unipub.
Romans, John R. & Ziegler, P. Thomas. The Meat We Eat. 11th ed. LC 77-70869. 1977. 23.35 (ISBN 0-8134-1945-X). Interstate.
Sanz Egana, Cesareo. Enciclopedia de la Carne. 2nd ed. 1086p. (Espn.). 1967. 59.95 (ISBN 84-239-6006-4, S-13609). French & Eur.
Scharffenberg, John A. Problems with Meat As Human Food. LC 79-13056. (Illus., Orig.). 1979. pap. 3.95 (ISBN 0-912800-65-8). Woodbridge Pr.
Sebranek, Joseph. Meat Science & Processing. 1978. wire coil bdg. 8.95 (ISBN 0-88252-087-3). Paladin Hse.
Simoons, Frederick J. Eat Not This Flesh: Food Avoidances in the Old World. LC 80-22232. (Illus.). xiii, 241p. 1981. Repr. of 1967 ed. lib. bdg. 29.75x (ISBN 0-313-22772-1, SIEN). Greenwood.
Smith, G. C., et al. Laboratory Manual for Meat Science. 1978. pap. text ed. 10.95x (ISBN 0-89641-015-3). American Pr.
Sudweeks, Deanna S. Gluten: The Economical Meat Substitute. (Orig.). 1978. pap. 4.50 (ISBN 0-89036-113-4). Hawkes Pub Inc.

MEAT-INSPECTION
see Meat Inspection

MEAT CONSUMPTION
see Meat Industry and Trade

MEAT CUTTING
see also Carving (Meat, etc.)

Fabbricante, Thomas. Training Manual for Meat Cutting & Merchandising. (Illus.). 1977. pap. text ed. 10.50 (ISBN 0-87055-243-0). AVI.
Fabbricante, Thomas & Sultan, William J. Practical Meat Cutting & Merchandising, Vol. 2: Pork, Lamb & Veal. (Illus.). 242p. 1975. pap. text ed. 15.50 (ISBN 0-87055-177-9). AVI.
Recommended International System for the Description of Carcases of Bovine & Porcine Species. (Joint FAO-WHO Food Standards Programme). (Illus.). 1977. pap. 4.50 (ISBN 0-685-80149-7, F670, FAO). Unipub.
Rudman, Jack. Meat Cutter. (Career Examination Ser.: C-516). (Cloth bdg. avail. on request). pap. 6.00 (ISBN 0-8373-0516-0). Natl Learning.
--Senior Meat Cutter. (Career Examination Ser.: C-1012). (Cloth bdg. avail. on request). pap. 8.00 (ISBN 0-8373-1012-1). Natl Learning.

MEAT INDUSTRY AND TRADE
see also Butchers; Cattle Trade; Cold Storage; Meat Inspection; Packing-House Workers; Pork Industry and Trade; Slaughtering and Slaughter-Houses

Arrangement Regarding Bovine Meat. (Illus.). 11p. 1980. pap. 2.00 (ISBN 0-686-63035-1, G138, GATT). Unipub.
Boss, Andrew. Meat on the Farm: Butchering, Keeping & Curing. facs. ed. Repr. of 1903 ed. pap. 5.50 (ISBN 0-8466-6040-7, SJU40). Shorey.
Bowman, J. C. & Susmel, P., eds. The Future of Beef Production in the European Community. (Current Topics in Veterinary Medicine & Animal Science: No. 5). 1979. lib. bdg. 79.00 (ISBN 90-247-2234-9, Pub. by Martinus Nijhoff Netherlands). Kluwer Boston.
Buehr, Walter. Meat, from Ranch to Table. (Illus.). (gr. 5-9). 1956. PLB 6.96 (ISBN 0-688-31557-7). Morrow.
Chapman, Margaret. When Steak Was a Shilling a Pound. 72p. 1981. 21.00x (ISBN 0-906379-02-4, Pub. by Jupiter England). State Mutual Bk.
Clemen, Rudolf A. The American Livestock & Meat Industry. abr. ed. (Illus.). 1923. 31.00 (ISBN 0-384-09305-1). Johnson Repr.
Commonwealth Secretariat. Meat. 131p. 1974. pap. 10.50x (ISBN 0-85092-071-X). Intl Pubns Serv.
Cover, John H. Neighborhood Distribution & Consumption of Meat in Pittsburgh: As Related to Other Social & Economic Factors. LC 75-39353. (Getting & Spending: the Consumer's Dilemma). 1976. Repr. of 1932 ed. 15.00x (ISBN 0-405-08017-4). Arno.
Fabbricante, Thomas. Training Manual for Meat Cutting & Merchandising. (Illus.). 1977. pap. text ed. 10.50 (ISBN 0-87055-243-0). AVI.
Gerrard, Frank. Meat Technology. 5th ed. 414p. 1981. 35.00x (ISBN 0-686-75446-8, Pub. by Northwood Bks). State Mutual Bk.
--Meat Technology: Practical Textbook for Student & Butcher. 5th ed. (Illus.). 1977. 27.50x (ISBN 0-7198-2607-1). Intl Ideas.
--Sausage & Small Goods Production. 266p. 1981. 25.00x (ISBN 0-7198-2587-3, Pub. by Northwood Bks). State Mutual Bk.
--Sausage & Small Goods Production: Practical Handbook on the Manufacture of Sausages & Other Meat-Based Products. 6th ed. (Illus.). 1976. 19.95x (ISBN 0-7198-2587-3). Intl Ideas.
Harwell, Edward M., et al. Meat Management & Operations. LC 74-21115. (Illus.). 285p. 1974. 18.95 (ISBN 0-912016-45-0). Lebhar Friedman.
Helser, M. D. Farm Meats. (Illus.). 1923. text ed. 4.75x (ISBN 0-911090-12-6). Pacific Bk Supply.
Institute of American Meat Packers & the School of Commerce & Administration of the University of Chicago. The Packing Industry. LC 75-22796. (America in Two Centuries Ser). (Illus.). 1976. Repr. of 1924 ed. 22.00x (ISBN 0-405-07667-3). Arno.
Karmas, E. Fresh Meat Technology. LC 75-10355. (Food Technology Review Ser.: No. 23). (Illus.). 283p. 1975. 36.00 (ISBN 0-8155-0581-7). Noyes.
--Sausage Casing Technology. LC 75-185163. (Food Technology Review Ser: No. 14). 367p. 1974. 36.00 (ISBN 0-8155-0534-5). Noyes.
Kinsman, Donald M. International Meat Science Dictionary. (Illus.). 282p. 1979. pap. 9.95x (ISBN 0-89641-029-3). American Pr.
Kramlich, W. E., et al. Processed Meats. (Illus.). 1973. 32.00 (ISBN 0-87055-141-8). AVI.
Krol, B. & Tinbergen, B. J., eds. Proceedings of the International Symposium on Nitrite in Meat Products. 266p. 1974. pap. 36.00 (ISBN 90-220-0463-5, Pub. by PUDOC). Unipub.
McCoy, John H. Livestock & Meat Marketing. 2nd ed. (Illus.). 1979. text ed. 28.50 (ISBN 0-87055-321-6). AVI.
MacGregor, Roderick. The Structure of the Meat Animals. 1980. 25.00x (ISBN 0-291-39620-8, Pub. by Tech Pr). State Mutual Bk.
Marketing Livestock & Meat. (FAO Animal Production & Health Ser.: No. 1). (FAO Marketing Guide No. 3). 1979. pap. 14.25 (ISBN 92-5-100168-5, F1529, FAO). Unipub.
Meat Balances in OECD Member Countries, Nineteen Sixty-Four to Nineteen Seventy-Seven. (Document Ser.). 1979. 15.00x (ISBN 92-64-01924-3). OECD.
Minish & Lidvall. Fundamentals of Meat Animal Evaluation. 1981. text ed. 16.95 (ISBN 0-8359-2137-9); instr's. manual free (ISBN 0-8359-2138-7). Reston.
OECD. Meat Balances in OECD Member Countries, 1974 to 1979. 85p. (Orig., Eng & Fr.). 1981. pap. 9.50x (ISBN 92-64-02181-7). OECD.
Organization for Economic Cooperation & Development. Meat Balances in OECD Member Countries: 1973 to 1978. (Illus.). 85p. (Orig.). 1980. pap. text ed. 7.50x (ISBN 92-64-02090-X, 5180053). OECD.
Perren, Richard. The Meat Trade in Britain, 1840-1914. (Studies in Economic History). 1978. 19.50x (ISBN 0-7100-8841-8). Routledge & Kegan.
Portsmouth, John. Commercial Rabbit Meat Production. 1981. 25.00x (ISBN 0-904558-31-2, Pub. by Saiga Pub). State Mutual Bk.
Price, David P. Beef Production, Science & Economics, Application & Reality. (Illus.). 358p. 1981. 32.00 (ISBN 0-9606246-0-0). SW Sci Pub.
Price Formation & Marging Behaviour of Meat in the Netherlands & the Federal Republic of Germany. (Agricultural Research Reports: No. 856). 1978. pap. 40.00 (ISBN 90-220-0610-7, PDC140, PUDOC). Unipub.
Processed Meat Products. (Food & Beverage Studies). 1980. 389.00 (ISBN 0-686-31521-9). Busn Trend.
Report of the Seventh Session of the Intergovernmental Group on Meat to the Committee on Commodity Problems. 25p. 1978. pap. 7.50 (ISBN 92-5-100481-1, F1382, FAO). Unipub.
Sebranek, Joseph. Meat Science & Processing. 1978. wire coil bdg. 8.95 (ISBN 0-88252-087-3). Paladin Hse.
Second International Symposium on Nitrite in Meat Products, Zeist, the Netherlands, 7-10 Sept. 1976. Proceedings. Tinbergen, B. J., ed. 1977. pap. 52.00 (ISBN 90-220-0607-7, Pub. by PUDOC). Unipub.
Swanson, Wayne. Prime Rip. Schultz, George, ed. 276p. 1981. 12.95 (ISBN 0-13-799351-X). P-H.
Swift, L. F. & Von Vlissingen, A. Yankee of the Yards: The Biography of Gustavus Franklin Swift. LC 78-112003. Repr. of 1927 ed. 21.00 (ISBN 0-404-06309-8). AMS Pr.
Symposium on Nephrology, 3rd, Hannover, June 1975. Glomerulonephritis: Proceedings. Sterzel, R. B., ed. (Contributions to Nephrology: Vol.2). (Illus.). 200p. 1976. 30.75 (ISBN 0-8055-2318-9). S Karger.
Taylor, Elizabeth W. Money on the Hoof-Sometimes. (Illus.). 1974. 8.95 (ISBN 0-88342-031-7). Old Army.
Wilson, N. R., et al, eds. Meat & Meat Products: Factors Affecting Quality Control. (Illus.). ix, 204p. 1981. 32.00x (ISBN 0-85334-951-7). Intl Ideas.
Wood, Charles L. The Kansas Beef Industry. LC 79-22730. (Illus.). 1980. 22.50x (ISBN 0-7006-0197-X). Regents Pr KS.
Yeager, Mary. Competition & Regulation: The Development of Oligopoly in the Meat Packing Industry, Vol. 2. Porter, Glenn, ed. LC 76-52011. (Industrial Development & the Social Fabric). 250p. 1981. 30.00 (ISBN 0-89232-058-3). Jai Pr.

MEAT INSPECTION

Bremner, A. S. Poultry Meat Hygiene & Inspection. 2nd ed. (Illus.). 191p. 1982. pap. price not set (ISBN 0-8121-0827-2). Lea & Febiger.
Gracey, J. E. Thornton's Meat Hygiene. 7th ed. (Illus.). 436p. 1981. text ed. write for info. (ISBN 0-8121-0825-6). Lea & Febiger.
Guide to Meat Inspection in the Tropics. 95p. 1981. pap. 22.50 (ISBN 0-85198-456-8, CAB 10, CAB). Unipub.
Koniecko, Edward S. Handbook for Meat Chemists. 1979. pap. text ed. 20.00 (ISBN 0-89529-097-9). Avery Pub.
Libby, James A., ed. Meat Hygiene. 4th ed. LC 73-14959. (Illus.). 658p. 1975. text ed. 25.50 (ISBN 0-8121-0466-8). Lea & Febiger.
MacGregor, Roderick. The Structure of the Meat Animals. 1980. 25.00x (ISBN 0-291-39620-8, Pub. by Tech Pr). State Mutual Bk.
Minish & Lidvall. Fundamentals of Meat Animal Evaluation. 1981. text ed. 16.95 (ISBN 0-8359-2137-9); instr's. manual free (ISBN 0-8359-2138-7). Reston.
Recommended International Codes of Hygenic Practice for Fresh Meat, for Ante-Mortem & Post-Mortem Inspection of Slaughter Animals & for Processed Meat Products. 38p. 1978. pap. 4.00 (ISBN 92-5-100396-3, F1430, FAO). Unipub.
Recommended International Standard for Cooked, Cured & Chopped Meat. 1979. pap. 4.50 (ISBN 92-5-100644-X, F1572, FAO). Unipub.
Recommended International Standard for Luncheon Meat. (Joint FAO-WHO Food Standards Programme Codex Alimentarius Commission). 6p. 1978. pap. 4.50 (ISBN 92-5-100293-2, F1399, FAO). Unipub.
Recommended International Standards for Cooked Ham & for Cooked Cured Pork Shoulder. 1979. pap. 4.50 (ISBN 92-5-100637-7, F1570, FAO). Unipub.
Rudman, Jack. Chief Meat Inspector. (Career Examination Ser.: C-2042). (Cloth bdg. avail. on request). pap. 10.00 (ISBN 0-8373-2042-9). Natl Learning.
--Meat Inspector. (Career Examination Ser.: C-517). (Cloth bdg. avail. on request). pap. 8.00 (ISBN 0-8373-0517-9). Natl Learning.
--Meat Inspector Trainee. (Career Examination Ser.: C-518). (Cloth bdg. avail. on request). pap. 6.00 (ISBN 0-8373-0518-7). Natl Learning.
--Senior Inspector - Meat & Poultry. (Career Examination Ser.: C-1771). (Cloth bdg. avail. on request). pap. 10.00 (ISBN 0-8373-1771-1). Natl Learning.
--Senior Meat Inspector. (Career Examination Ser.: C-2054). (Cloth bdg. avail. on request). pap. 8.00 (ISBN 0-8373-2054-2). Natl Learning.
--Supervising Meat Inspector. (Career Examination Ser.: C-2056). (Cloth bdg. avail. on request). pap. 10.00 (ISBN 0-8373-2056-9). Natl Learning.
Sheard, Barrie, et al. An Illustrated Guide to Meat Inspection. 300p. 1981. 90.00x (ISBN 0-7198-2507-5, Pub. by Northwood Bks). State Mutual Bk.
Wiggins, Geoffrey S. & Wilson, Andrew. Color Atlas of Meat & Poultry Inspection. 1976. 19.95x (ISBN 0-442-29433-6). Van Nos Reinhold.

MEAT INSPECTION–GREAT BRITAIN

Perren, Richard. The Meat Trade in Britain, 1840-1914. (Studies in Economic History). 1978. 19.50x (ISBN 0-7100-8841-8). Routledge & Kegan.

MEAT PACKING INDUSTRY
see Meat Industry and Trade

MEATLESS MEALS
see Vegetarianism

MECCA

Asad, Muhammad. The Road to Mecca. LC 80-1937. Repr. of 1954 ed. 42.00 (ISBN 0-404-18953-9). AMS Pr.
De Gaury, Gerald. Rulers of Mecca. LC 78-63458. (The Crusades & Military Orders: Second Ser.). Repr. of 1954 ed. 34.50 (ISBN 0-404-16517-6). AMS Pr.
Guellouz, Ezzedine & Frikha, Abdelaziz. MECCA: The Muslim Pilgrimage. LC 79-1125. (Illus.). 1979. 14.95 (ISBN 0-448-22302-3). Paddington.
Hureau, Jean. Mecca Today. (J. A. Editions: Today Ser.). (Illus.). 240p. 1980. cancelled (ISBN 0-88254-538-8, Pub. by J. A. Editions France). Hippocrene Bks.
Makky, Ghazy A. Mecca, Pilgrimage City: A Study of Pilgrimage Accomodation. (Illus.). 95p. 1978. 28.00x (ISBN 0-85664-591-5, Pub. by Croom Helm Ltd England). Biblio Dist.
Stewart, Desmond. Mecca. Bayrd, Edwin, ed. LC 79-3548. (Illus.). 1980. 19.95 (ISBN 0-88225-287-9); prepub. 16.95 (ISBN 0-686-59492-4). Newsweek.

MECHANIC ARTS
see Industrial Arts

MECHANICAL ABILITY
see also Motor Ability

Stanton, Mildred B. Mechanical Ability of Deaf Children. LC 74-177747. (Columbia University. Teachers College. Contributions to Education: No. 751). Repr. of 1938 ed. 17.50 (ISBN 0-404-55751-1). AMS Pr.

MECHANICAL ABILITY–TESTING

Pritchard, Miriam C. The Mechanical Ability of Subnormal Boys. LC 70-177167. (Columbia University. Teachers College. Contributions to Education: No. 699). Repr. of 1937 ed. 17.50 (ISBN 0-404-55699-X). AMS Pr.
Rudman, Jack. Civil Service Mechanical Aptitude. (Career Examination Ser.: CS-15). (Cloth bdg. avail. on request). pap. 6.00 (ISBN 0-8373-3765-8). Natl Learning.
Stenquist, John L. Measurements of Mechanical Ability. LC 73-177744. (Columbia University. Teachers College. Contributions to Education: No. 130). Repr. of 1923 ed. 17.50 (ISBN 0-404-55130-0). AMS Pr.
Toops, Herbert A. Tests for Vocational Guidance of Children Thirteen to Sixteen. LC 73-177701. (Columbia University. Teachers College. Contributions to Education: No. 136). Repr. of 1923 ed. 17.50 (ISBN 0-404-55136-X). AMS Pr.
Turner, David R. Mechanical Aptitude & Spatial Relations Test. 5th ed. LC 75-39130. 1976. pap. 6.00 (ISBN 0-668-00539-4). Arco.

MECHANICAL ANALOGIES IN ELECTRICITY
see Electromechanical Analogies

MECHANICAL ARITHMETIC
see Calculating-Machines

MECHANICAL BANKS
see Coin Banks

MECHANICAL BRAINS
see Conscious Automata; Cybernetics

MECHANICAL DRAWING
see also Architectural Drawing; Blue-Prints; Design, Industrial; Drawing-Room Practice; Electric Drafting; Electronic Drafting; Engineering Graphics; Geometrical Drawing; Graphic Methods; Graphic Statics; Lettering; Machinery-Drawings; Projection; Structural Drawing; Technical Illustration

Bailey, Frank A. Basic Mathematics for Drafting & Machine Shop. 1977. pap. 6.95x (ISBN 0-673-15066-6). Scott F.
Bartholomew, Roy A. & Orr, Francis S. Learning to Read Mechanical Drawings. rev. ed. (gr. 9-12). 1970. pap. text ed. 5.20 (ISBN 0-87002-040-4); tchr. guide free. Bennett IL.
Bethune, J. Essentials of Drafting. 416p. 1977. text ed. 17.95 (ISBN 0-13-284430-3). P-H.
Betterley, Melvin. Sheet Metal Drafting. 2nd ed. (Illus.). 1977. pap. text ed. 12.95 (ISBN 0-07-005126-7, G). McGraw.
Boxall, V. E. Drawing & Materials. 2nd ed. (Illus.). 1975. pap. 16.50x (ISBN 0-7131-3320-1). Intl Ideas.
Boy Scouts Of America. Drafting. LC 19-600. (Illus.). 32p. (gr. 6-12). 1965. pap. 0.70x (ISBN 0-8395-3273-3, 3273). BSA.
Brown, Walter C. Drafting for Industry. rev. ed. (Illus.). 616p. 1981. text ed. 16.96 (ISBN 0-686-73778-4). Goodheart.

--Drafting for Industry: 1978 Ed. LC 77-25196. (Illus.). 616p. 1980. 16.96 (ISBN 0-87006-247-6); wkbk. 4.80 (ISBN 0-87006-306-5). Goodheart.
Clifford, Martin. Basic Drafting. (Orig.). 1980. 12.95 (ISBN 0-8306-9945-7); pap. 7.95 (ISBN 0-8306-1202-5, 1202). TAB Bks.
Colletti, Jack J. & Colletti, Paul J. A Freehand Approach to Technical Drawing. 336p. 1974. pap. 15.95 ref. ed. (ISBN 0-13-330548-1). P-H.
Cousins, M. F. Engineering Drawing from the Beginning. 1964. Vol. 1. 1964. 28.00 (ISBN 0-08-010839-3); pap. 11.25 (ISBN 0-08-010840-7). Pergamon.
D'Campo, G. Basic Technical Drawing. 388p. 1981. 25.00x (ISBN 0-86125-432-5, Pub. by Orient Longman India). State Mutual Bk.
Deshpande, D. L., ed. Basic Drawing. 68p. 1981. 5.00x (ISBN 0-86125-690-5, Pub. by Orient Longman India). State Mutual Bk.
Donaldson, Stanley S. Test Papers in Technical Drawing. 2nd ed. (Illus.). 104p. 1981. pap. text ed. 11.95x (ISBN 0-291-39488-4). Intl Ideas.
Feirer & Lindbeck. Basic Drafting. (gr. 9-12). 1978. 6.00 (ISBN 0-87002-287-3); pap. 4.32 (ISBN 0-87002-273-3); activities for basic drafting 2.84 (ISBN 0-87002-306-3). Bennett IL.
Feirer, John L. & Lindbeck. Drawing & Planning for the Industrial Arts. new ed. (Illus.). (gr. 7-12). 1975. text ed. 13.16 (ISBN 0-87002-159-1); tchr's guide, charts & worksheets 5.60 (ISBN 0-87002-162-1). Bennett IL.
French, Thomas E. & Svensen, C. L. Familiar Problems in Mechanical Drawing. 1973. 5.72 (ISBN 0-07-022312-2, W). McGraw.
French, Thomas E. & Vierck, Charles J. Engineering Drawing & Graphic Technology. 11th ed. LC 70-38135. Orig. Title: Manual of Engineering Drawing for Students & Draftsmen. (Illus.). 984p. 1972. text ed. 19.00 (ISBN 0-07-022157-X, C); tchrs' manual & solutions 4.95 (ISBN 0-07-067427-2); problems 9.95 (ISBN 0-07-067435-3). McGraw.
--Engineering Drawing & Graphic Technology. 12th ed. (Illus.). 1978. lib. bdg. 19.95 (ISBN 0-07-022158-8, C); problems 10.50 (ISBN 0-07-022160-X); tchr. manual 3.95 (ISBN 0-07-022159-6). McGraw.
Fryklund, Verne C. & Kepler, Frank R. General Drafting. 4th ed. LC 78-81375. (Illus.). (gr. 9-10). 1969. text ed. 11.16 (ISBN 0-87345-095-7). McKnight.
Fuglsby, Glen O., et al. General Mechanical Drawing. rev. ed. (gr. 7-9). 1966. text ed. 6.60 (ISBN 0-02-820580-4). Glencoe.
Gerevas, Lawrence E. Basic Drafting Problems. 2nd ed. 240p. 1981. pap. text ed. 8.95 (ISBN 0-672-97866-0); tchrs.' ed. 6.67 (ISBN 0-672-97867-9). Bobbs.
--Drafting Technology Problems. 2nd ed. 1981. pap. 8.95 (ISBN 0-672-97701-X); answer bk. 3.33 (ISBN 0-672-97864-4). Bobbs.
Giachino, J. W. & Beukema, Henry J. Engineering - Technical Drafting. 4th ed. (Illus.). 1978. 23.00 (ISBN 0-8269-1154-4). Am Technical.
--Everyday Sketching & Drafting. 2nd ed. (Illus.). 1973. pap. 9.00 spiral bdg. (ISBN 0-8269-1162-5). Am Technical.
Giachino, J. W. & Beukema, Henry J., eds. Freehand Sketching. 2nd ed. (Illus.). 1973. 7.33 (ISBN 0-8269-1022-X). Am Technical.
--Freehand Sketching. 2nd ed. (Illus.). 1973. 7.33 (ISBN 0-8269-1022-X). Am Technical.
Giesecke, F. H., et al. Technical Drawing Problems. 6th ed. (Series I). 1981. pap. text ed. 9.95x (ISBN 0-02-342740-X). Macmillan.
Giesecke, Frederick E., et al. Technical Drawing. 7th ed. (Illus.). 1980. text ed. 25.95 (ISBN 0-02-342610-1). Macmillan.
Glegg, Gordon L. Making & Interpreting Mechanical Drawings. (Illus.). 1971. 5.25 (ISBN 0-521-09680-4). Cambridge U Pr.
Goetsch, David L. Structural Drafting. (Drafting Ser.). (Illus.). 384p. (Orig.). 1981. pap. text ed. 9.60 (ISBN 0-8273-1930-4); price not set instructor's guide (ISBN 0-8273-1931-2). Delmar.
Grant, Hiram E. Engineering Drawing with Creative Design. 2nd ed. 1968. text ed. 18.50 (ISBN 0-07-024104-X, C); instructor's solutions book 2.95 (ISBN 0-07-024101-5). McGraw.
Gutmann, Fredrick T. Metric Guide to Mechanical Design & Drafting. LC 78-8632. (Illus.). 76p. 1978. 12.00 (ISBN 0-8311-1122-4). Indus Pr.
Hale, E. M., et al. Introduction to Applied Drawing. rev. ed. (gr. 7 up). 1962. pap. 4.48 (ISBN 0-87345-051-5). McKnight.
Harman, Earl W. Introduction to Mechanical Drawing. new ed. (gr. 7-12). 1979. pap. text ed. 6.40 (ISBN 0-205-06580-5, 3265803). Allyn.
Helsel, Jay & Urbanick, Byron. Mechanical Drawing. 9th ed. Lindquist, Hal, ed. (Illus.). 1980. text ed. 16.80 (ISBN 0-07-022313-0). McGraw.
Hood, George J., et al. Geometry of Engineering Drawing. 5th ed. LC 78-12289. (Illus.). 482p. 1979. Repr. of 1969 ed. lib. bdg. 19.50 (ISBN 0-88275-756-3). Krieger.
Hoover, T. W. & Schumacher, H. G. Tool & Die Drafting. LC 57-12844. 1968. 5.25x (ISBN 0-911168-09-5). Prakken.
Jensen, C. & Viosinet, D. Advanced Design Problems: To Accompany Engineering Drawing & Designs. 2nd ed. 1981. write for info. (ISBN 0-07-032522-7); price not set solutions manual (ISBN 0-07-032530-8). McGraw.
Jensen, C. H. & Hines, R. D. Interpreting Engineering Drawings: Metric Edition. LC 77-78175. 1979. pap. text ed. 10.60 (ISBN 0-8273-1061-7); instructor's guide 1.60 (ISBN 0-8273-1062-5). Delmar.
Jensen, Cecil & Helsel, Jay. Worksheets for Fundamentals of Engineering Drawing. 2nd ed. (Illus.). 1979. text ed. 17.95x (ISBN 0-07-032516-2, G). McGraw.
Jensen, Cecil, et al. Worksheets for Engineering Drawing & Design: Chapters 1-18. 1979. 12.95x (ISBN 0-07-032518-9, G). McGraw.
Joens. Basic Drafting Skills. (Technical Drafting Ser.). 1977. 6.95 (ISBN 0-87618-888-9). R J Brady.
Joens, Clifford J. Technical Drafting, 4 bks. LC 77-12932. 686p. 1977. Set. pap. text ed. 19.95 (ISBN 0-87618-891-9). R J Brady.
Knowlton, K., et al. Technical Freehand Drawing & Sketching. 1976. 13.95 (ISBN 0-07-035207-0, G). McGraw.
Lawson, Philip J. Perspective Charts. 1940. 9.95 (ISBN 0-442-13053-8). Van Nos Reinhold.
LeFax Pub. Co. Editors. Mechanical Drawing. (Lefax Data Bks.: No. 617). (Illus.). Date not set. looseleaf bdg. 2.50 (ISBN 0-685-52841-3); pap. 3.00 (ISBN 0-685-52842-1). LeFax.
Lexikon der Graphischen Technik. 4th ed. (Ger.). 1977. 29.95 (ISBN 3-7940-4078-3, M-7253). French & Eur.
Lieblich, Jerome H., ed. Dimension & Tolerances (an Interpretation of ANSI y14.5) 1973. pap. 3.75x (ISBN 0-912702-05-2). Global Eng.
--Drawing Requirement Manual. 4th ed. 624p. 1981. lib. bdg. 21.95x perfect bdg (ISBN 0-912702-02-8); loose leaf 39.95x (ISBN 0-912702-09-5). Global Eng.
Lindbeck. Metric Practices in Drafting. 1979. pap. 2.64 (ISBN 0-87002-298-9). Bennett IL.
Los Angeles Unified School District. Drafting. Vorndran, Richard A., ed. LC 77-73291. 64p. (gr. 7-9). 1978. pap. text ed. 3.64 (ISBN 0-02-820410-7). Glencoe.
Luzadder, Warren J. Fundamentals of Engineering Drawing. 1981. 24.95 (ISBN 0-13-338350-4). P-H.
McCabe, Francis T., et al. Mechanical Drafting Essentials. 4th ed. (gr. 10-12). text ed. 18.00 (ISBN 0-13-568931-7). P-H.
Madsen, David A. Drafting: Syllabus. 1974. pap. text ed. 7.90 (ISBN 0-89420-070-4, 107015); cassette recordings 103.90 (ISBN 0-89420-140-9, 107000). Natl Book.
Manual of Mechanical Drawing: How to Draw & How to Comprehend Mechanical Drawing. 12.50 (ISBN 0-87559-087-X). Shalom.
Martin, C. Leslie. Design Graphics. 2nd ed. (Illus.). 1968. text ed. 22.95 (ISBN 0-02-376640-9). Macmillan.
Miller, Wilbur R. Drafting. LC 78-53388. (Basic Industrial Arts Ser.). (Illus.). 1978. 6.00 (ISBN 0-87345-793-5); softbound 4.48 (ISBN 0-87345-785-4). McKnight.
Morling, K. Geometric & Engineering Drawing. 2nd ed. (Illus.). 1974. pap. 15.95x (ISBN 0-7131-3319-8). Intl Ideas.
Mossman, Marshall & Baker, Kermit. Drafting: Basic Techniques. LC 70-93136. 1970. 9.65x (ISBN 0-911168-06-0); pap. 7.20x (ISBN 0-911168-07-9); tchrs.' guide 5.00x (ISBN 0-911168-08-7). Prakken.
Nee, John G. Mechanism Drafting & Design: A Workbook. LC 80-80861. (Illus.). 1980. pap. text ed. 14.95x (ISBN 0-911168-45-1); solutions manual 3.95x (ISBN 0-911168-46-X). Prakken.
Nelson, John. Drafting for Trades & Industry - Basic Skills. LC 77-91450. (Drafting Ser.). 472p. 1979. pap. text ed. 14.52 (ISBN 0-8273-1841-3); instructor's guide 2.25 (ISBN 0-8273-1641-0). Delmar.
--Drafting for Trades & Industry - Civil. LC 77-91450. (Drafting Ser.). 112p. 1979. pap. text ed. 4.20 (ISBN 0-8273-1844-8); instructor's guide 2.25 (ISBN 0-8273-1641-0). Delmar.
--Drafting for Trades & Industry - Mechanical. LC 77-91450. (Drafting Ser.). 328p. 1979. pap. text ed. 11.00 (ISBN 0-8273-1846-4); instructor's guide 2.25 (ISBN 0-8273-1641-0). Delmar.
Nelson, John A. Handbook of Drafting Technology. 368p. 1981. text ed. 22.95 (ISBN 0-442-28661-9); pap. text ed. 14.95 (ISBN 0-442-28662-7). Van Nos Reinhold.
Ostrowsky, O. Engineering Drawing for Technicians, Vol. 1. (Illus.). 94p. 1979. pap. 11.00x (ISBN 0-7131-3408-9). Intl Ideas.
--Engineering Drawing for Technicians, Vol. 2. 96p. 1981. pap. 11.50x (ISBN 0-7131-3429-1). Intl Ideas.
Parkinson & Ayres. Solid Geometry & Mechanical Drawing, Bk. 2. Date not set. 13.95x (ISBN 0-392-15179-0, SpS). Sportshelf.
Pawelek, S. & Otto, W. Introduction to Industrial Drafting. 1973. 7.96 (ISBN 0-02-824340-4). Glencoe.
Problems in Engineering Drawing for Design & Communications. 8th ed. pap. 8.95 ea. Vol. 1 (ISBN 0-13-716373-8). Vol. 2 (ISBN 0-13-716381-9). P-H.
Rhodes, R. S. & Cook, L. B. Basic Engineering Drawing. (Illus.). 192p. (Orig.). 1975. pap. text ed. 12.95x (ISBN 0-8464-0176-2). Beekman Pubs.
Rohlmeir, C. Drafting: Metric. 1980. 15.00 (ISBN 0-8269-1202-8). Am Technical.
Ross, Stan. World of Drafting. (gr. 7-9). 1971. text ed. 15.16 (ISBN 0-87345-078-7). McKnight.
Rotmans, Elmer A., et al. Basic Drafting Technology. 2nd ed. LC 78-50424. (gr. 8). 1980. pap. text ed. 18.00 (ISBN 0-8273-1293-8); instr's. guide 2.25 (ISBN 0-8273-1294-6). Delmar.
Rudman, Jack. Senior Draftsman. (Career Examination Ser.: C-1575). (Cloth bdg. avail. on request). pap. 10.00 (ISBN 0-8373-1575-1). Natl Learning.
Schaeffer, Glen N. & Spielman, Patrick E. Basic Mechanical Drawing. 1974. pap. 3.00 (ISBN 0-685-65903-8, 82795). Glencoe.
Segel, Yonny. Drafting Made Simple. LC 61-9550. pap. 3.50 (ISBN 0-385-01348-5, Made). Doubleday.
Shariff, Abdulla. Engineering Descriptive Geometry. 3rd rev. ed. (Illus.). 1979. pap. text ed. 12.95x (ISBN 0-210-22368-5). Asia.
Shawki, G. S. A. & Metwalli, S. M., eds. Current Advances in Mechanical Design & Production: Proceedings of the First International Conference, Cairo University, 27-29 December 1979. LC 80-41666. (Illus.). 500p. 1981. 75.00 (ISBN 0-08-027294-0). Pergamon.
Sliwa, Jan A. & Fairweather, Leslie. AJ Metric Handbook. 3rd ed. (Architects' Journal). (Illus.). 206p. (Orig.). 1970. pap. 10.00x (ISBN 0-85139-382-9). Intl Pubns Serv.
Spence. Basic Industrial Drafting. 1979. pap. text ed. 10.60 (ISBN 0-87002-297-0); worksheets 6.88 (ISBN 0-87002-142-7). Bennett IL.
--Drafting Technology & Practice. rev ed. (gr. 9-12). 1980. text ed. 23.92 (ISBN 0-87002-303-9); worksheets 11.20 (ISBN 0-87002-130-3). Bennett IL.
Spence & Atkins. Technical Drafting. (gr. 9-12). 1980. text ed. 19.00 (ISBN 0-87002-305-5). Bennett IL.
Spencer, Henry C., et al. Technical Drawing Problems: Series Two. 4th ed. (Illus.). 1980. pap. text ed. 10.95 (ISBN 0-02-414330-8). Macmillan.
Stirling, Norman. Introduction to Technical Drawing: Metric Edition. LC 79-56653. 370p. 1981. pap. text ed. 15.00 (ISBN 0-8273-1928-2). Delmar.
--Technical Drawing: An Introduction Metric. Edition. 370p. 1981. 18.95 (ISBN 0-442-23151-2). Van Nos Reinhold.
Thompson, Charles H. Fundamentals of Pipe Drafting. LC 58-13471. 66p. 1958. pap. 11.50 (ISBN 0-471-85998-2, Pub. by Wiley-Interscience). Wiley.
Traister, John. Practical Drafting for the HVAC Trades. LC 75-5404. (Illus.). 1975. pap. 12.95 (ISBN 0-672-21082-7). Sams.
Turner, David R. Draftsman: Civil & Mechanical Engineering (All Grades) 2nd ed. LC 70-111595. 256p. (Orig.). 1973. pap. 6.00 (ISBN 0-668-01225-0). Arco.
TYS Technical Drawing. 1980. pap. 4.95 (ISBN 0-679-12476-4). McKay.
Vezzani, A. A. & Salmonson, Donald. Reading & Detailing Assembly Drawings: Dies. LC 61-9841. 1972. 7.50x (ISBN 0-911168-10-9). Prakken.
Vogts, Raymond. Engineering Drawing & Blueprint Reading. (Illus.). 272p. 1981. pap. text ed. 8.00 (ISBN 0-668-05295-3, 5295). Arco.
Walker, John R. Exploring Drafting. LC 78-15883. (Illus.). 320p. 1978. text ed. 11.96 (ISBN 0-87006-262-X); wkbk. 4.80 (ISBN 0-87006-295-6); metric wkbk. 4.80 (ISBN 0-87006-242-5). Goodheart.
--Exploring Drafting Workbook-Metric Edition. 128p. 1981. 4.80 (ISBN 0-87006-242-5). Goodheart.
--Exploring Metric Drafting. LC 79-24019. (Illus.). 320p. 1980. text ed. 10.96 (ISBN 0-87006-289-1). Goodheart.
Wallach, Paul. Metric Drafting. Vorndran, Richard A., ed. 1979. text ed. 18.95 (ISBN 0-02-829690-7); instrs'. manual 6.20 (ISBN 0-02-829700-8); problems book 6.95 (ISBN 0-02-829710-5). Glencoe.
Wallach, Paul I. Basic Book of Drafting. (Illus.). 1979. 6.00 (ISBN 0-8269-1170-6). Am Technical.
Wyatt, Edwin M. Modern Drafting. (Illus., Orig.). 1962. pap. 3.00 (ISBN 0-02-829760-1). Glencoe.
Y-Fourteen Report, Digital Representation of Physical Object Shapes. 1976. pap. text ed. 4.00 (ISBN 0-685-75522-3, N00075). ASME.
Yankee, H. W. Machine Drafting & Related Technology. 2nd ed. 1981. 16.95 (ISBN 0-07-072252-8). McGraw.
Yaslow, Samuel. Elements of Mechanical Drafting. LC 78-67463. (Drafting Ser.). 375p. 1979. pap. text ed. 13.40 (ISBN 0-8273-1837-5); instructor's guide 1.60 (ISBN 0-8273-1838-3). Delmar.

MECHANICAL DRAWING–EXAMINATIONS, QUESTIONS ETC.

Rudman, Jack. Chief Draftsman. (Career Examination Ser.: C-1577). (Cloth bdg. avail. on request). pap. 10.00 (ISBN 0-8373-1577-8). Natl Learning.
--Civil Engineering Draftsman. (Career Examination Ser.: C-137). (Cloth bdg. avail. on request). pap. 10.00 (ISBN 0-8373-0137-8). Natl Learning.
--Drafting Aide. (Career Examination Ser.: C-202). (Cloth bdg. avail. on request). pap. 8.00 (ISBN 0-8373-0202-1). Natl Learning.
--Draftsman. (Career Examination Ser.: C-203). (Cloth bdg. avail. on request). pap. 8.00 (ISBN 0-8373-0203-X). Natl Learning.
--Engineering Draftsman. (Career Examination Ser.: C-247). (Cloth bdg. avail. on request). pap. 8.00 (ISBN 0-8373-0247-1). Natl Learning.
--Engineering Technician (Drafting) (Career Examination Ser.: C-991). (Cloth bdg. avail. on request). pap. 8.00 (ISBN 0-8373-0991-3). Natl Learning.
--Junior Draftsman. (Career Examination Ser.: C-396). (Cloth bdg. avail. on request). 14.00 (ISBN 0-8373-0396-6). Natl Learning.
--Machine Drafting. (Occupational Competency Examination Ser.: OCE-24). 14.95 (ISBN 0-8373-5774-8); pap. 9.95 (ISBN 0-8373-5724-1). Natl Learning.
--Mechanical Engineering Draftsman. (Career Examination Ser.: C-482). (Cloth bdg. avail. on request). pap. 10.00 (ISBN 0-8373-0482-2). Natl Learning.
--Senior Engineering Technician (Drafting) (Career Examination Ser.: C-1005). (Cloth bdg. avail. on request). pap. 10.00 (ISBN 0-8373-1005-9). Natl Learning.
Turner, David R. Draftsman: Civil & Mechanical Engineering (All Grades) 2nd ed. LC 70-111595. 256p. (Orig.). 1973. pap. 6.00 (ISBN 0-668-01225-0). Arco.

MECHANICAL DRAWING–PROBLEMS, EXERCISES, ETC.

Dobrovolny, J. S., et al. Problems in Engineering Drawing & Geometry, Series 12, 13, 15, 16, 21. 1964. pap. 5.20x ea. Stipes.
Hoelscher, Randolph P., et al. Problems in Engineering Drawing, Series A, B, C, D, & E. pap. 5.20x ea. Stipes.
Levens, A. S. & Edstrom, A. E. Problems in Mechanical Drawing. 4th ed. 1974. 10.15 (ISBN 0-07-037349-3, W); answer key 1.20 (ISBN 0-07-037355-8). McGraw.
Renton, Bruce A. Drafting Projects for Today. 1975. pap. 8.80 (ISBN 0-8273-1926-6). Delmar.
Spencer, Henry C., et al. Technical Drawing Problems: Series Three. 3rd ed. (Illus.). 1980. pap. text ed. 10.95 (ISBN 0-02-414360-X). Macmillan.
Weaver, Rip. Structural Drafting Workbook. (Illus.). 112p. 1980. pap. text ed. 9.95 (ISBN 0-686-70161-5). Gulf Pub.
Zozzora, Frank. Engineering Drawing Problems. 2nd ed. 1958. text ed. 11.95 (ISBN 0-07-073407-0, C). McGraw.

MECHANICAL DRAWING–STUDY AND TEACHING

Weaver, Rip. Modern Basic Drafting. 2nd ed. (Illus.). 392p. 1979. 16.95x (ISBN 0-87201-059-7); wkbks. 9.50x ea.; Wkbk. 1. (ISBN 0-87201-055-4); Wkbk 2. (ISBN 0-87201-056-2); Instructor's Manual. Gulf Pub.

MECHANICAL DRAWING–VOCATIONAL GUIDANCE

Delong, Fred J. Aim for a Job in Drafting. LC 68-10505. (Aim High Vocational Guidance Ser.). (gr. 7 up). 1976. PLB 5.97 (ISBN 0-8239-0365-6). Rosen Pr.
Stern, Benjamin J. Opportunities in Drafting Today. LC 75-5421. (Illus.). 100p. (gr. 7-12). 1975. PLB 6.60 (ISBN 0-685-53420-0); pap. text ed. 4.95 (ISBN 0-8442-6435-0). Natl Textbk.

MECHANICAL DRAWINGS

see Engineering Drawings

MECHANICAL ENGINEERING

Here are entered works relating to the application of the principles of mechanics to the design construction and operation of machinery.

see also Chemical Engineering; Diaphragms (Mechanical Devices); Electric Engineering; Electromechanical Devices; Heat Engineering; Horsepower (Mechanics); Machinery; Marine Engineering; Mechanical Movements; Mechanics, Applied; Power (Mechanics); Power Transmission; Production Engineering; Steam Engineering

Ahlstrand, Eric. Datsun F Ten & Three Hundred Ten: Nineteen Seventy-Six to Seventy-Nine Shop Manual. (Illus.). pap. text ed. 10.95 (ISBN 0-89287-318-3, A202). Clymer Pubns.

Alexander, J. M. Strength of Materials: Fundamentals, Vol. 1. LC 80-42009. (Mechanical Engineering Ser.). 267p. 1981. 72.95 (ISBN 0-470-27119-1). Halsted Pr.

American Society of Civil Engineers, compiled by. Engineering Mechanics Specialty Conference, 3rd. 952p. 1979. pap. text ed. 55.00 (ISBN 0-87262-192-8). Am Soc Civil Eng.

Armen, Harry, ed. Applications of Numerical Methods to Forming Processes: AMD, Vol. 28. Jones, R. F., Jr. 208p. 1978. 30.00 (ISBN 0-685-66790-1, H00111). ASME.

Artobolevsky, I. Mechanisms in Modern Engineering, Vol. V, Part 1. (Illus.). 637p. 1979. 7.75 (ISBN 0-8285-1540-9, Pub. by Mir Pubs Russia). Imported Pubns.

--Mechanisms in Modern Engineering Design, Vol. II. (Illus.). 1059p. 1979. 15.00 (ISBN 0-8285-0687-6, Pub. by Mir Pubs Russia). Imported Pubns.

--Mechanisms in Modern Engineering Design, Vol. III. (Illus.). 663p. 1977. 10.00 (ISBN 0-8285-0688-4, Pub. by Mir Pubs Russia). Imported Pubns.

--Mechanisms in Modern Engineering Design, Vol. IV. (Illus.). 663p. 1977. 9.00 (ISBN 0-8285-0689-2, Pub. by Mir Pubs Russia). Imported Pubns.

--Mechanisms of Modern Engineering, Vol. I. 631p. 1979. 6.00 (ISBN 0-8285-0686-8, Pub. by Mir Pubs Russia). Imported Pubns.

Artobolevsky, I. I. Mechanisms in Modern Engineering Design, Vol. V; Pt. 2. 1980. 9.20 (ISBN 0-8285-1791-6, Pub. by Mir Pubs Russia). Imported Pubns.

Ashworth & Bourbousson. Basic Engineering Craft Studies: Mechanical. 1977. text ed. 5.50 (ISBN 0-408-00057-0). Butterworth.

Bacon & Stephens. Mechanical Science for Higher Technicians, Nos. 4-5. 1981. text ed. 14.95 (ISBN 0-408-00570-X). Butterworth.

--Mechanical Technology. 1977. 19.95 (ISBN 0-408-00280-8). Butterworth.

Barnet, G., et al, eds. Mechanical Fitting, Vol. 2. 2nd ed. (Engineering Craftsmen: No. H25). (Illus.). 1973. spiral bdg. 17.95x (ISBN 0-85083-186-5). Intl Ideas.

Baugh, A., et al, eds. Mechanical Maintenance: Part One. (Engineering Craftsmen: No. J1). (Illus.). 1978. spiral bdg. 21.00x (ISBN 0-85083-016-8). Intl Ideas.

Baumeister, Theodore. Marks' Standard Handbook for Mechanical Engineers. 8th ed. (Illus.). 1978. 44.50 (ISBN 0-07-004123-7, P&RB). McGraw.

Beachley, Norman H. & Harrison, Howard L. Introduction to Dynamic System Analysis. (Illus.). 1978. text ed. 26.50 scp (ISBN 0-06-040557-0, HarpC). Har-Row.

Beer, Ferdinand P. & Johnston, E. R., Jr. Vector Mechanics for Engineers: Dynamics. 3rd ed. 1977. text ed. 18.50 (ISBN 0-07-004281-0, C); solutions manual 6.95 (ISBN 0-07-004282-9). McGraw.

Bennett, S. B., et al, eds. Failure Prevention & Reliability. 1977. pap. text ed. 30.00 (ISBN 0-685-86863-X, H00101). ASME.

Berger, T. & Davisson, L. D. Advances in Source Coding: Courses & Lectures. (CISM (International Centre for Mechanical Sciences) Ser.: Vol. 166). (Illus.). 71p. 1976. pap. 8.00 (ISBN 0-387-81302-0). Springer-Verlag.

Bishop, Mike. Kawasaki Snowmobiles Nineteen Seventy-Six to Nineteen Eighty: Service, Repair, Maintenance. Jorgensen, Eric, ed. (Illus.). 152p. (Orig.). 1980. pap. text ed. 8.95 (ISBN 0-89287-320-5, X995). Clymer Pubns.

Bolton, W. Mechanical Science for Technicians, No. 3. (Technician Ser.). (Illus.). 128p. 1980. pap. text ed. 12.50 (ISBN 0-686-29439-4). Butterworth.

Boothroyd. Automatic Assembly. (Mechanical Engineering Ser.). 352p. 1981. price not set (ISBN 0-8247-1531-4). Dekker.

Boresi, Arthur P., et al. Advanced Mechanics of Materials. 3rd ed. LC 77-28283. 1978. text ed. 35.50 (ISBN 0-471-08892-7). Wiley.

Bourbousson & Ashworth. Mechanical Engineering Craft Studies, Vol. I. 1974. 5.95 (ISBN 0-408-00120-8). Butterworth.

--Mechanical Engineering Craft Studies, Vol. 2. 1974. text ed. 9.95 (ISBN 0-408-00112-7). Butterworth.

Branson, Lane K. Engineering Mechanics. pap. 4.50 (ISBN 0-671-18902-6). Monarch Pr.

Briggs, T., et al, eds. Mechanical Fitting, Vol. 1. (Engineering Craftsmen: No. H3). 1968. spiral bdg. 13.50x (ISBN 0-85083-012-5). Intl Ideas.

British Mechanical Engineering Confederation in Association with 'Engineering' The European Economic Community & United Kingdom Engineering Companies. 57p. 1980. 78.75x (ISBN 0-89771-002-9). State Mutual Bk.

Byars, E. F. & Snyder, R. D. Engineering Mechanics of Deformable Bodies. 3rd ed. 1974. text ed. 29.50 scp (ISBN 0-7002-2460-2, HarpC). Har-Row.

Carvill, J. Student Engineer's Companion: A Handbook for Engineers, Draftsmen & Students. Orig. Title: Mechanical Engineering Components. (Illus.). 1980. pap. 12.50 (ISBN 0-408-00438-X). Butterworth.

Chung, T. J. Finite Element Analysis in Fluid Dynamics. 1978. text ed. 38.00 (ISBN 0-07-010830-7, C). McGraw.

Crouch, T. Matrix Methods Applied to Engineering Rigid Body Mechanics. LC 80-41186. 385p. 1980. 46.00 (ISBN 0-08-024245-6); pap. 18.00 (ISBN 0-08-024246-4). Pergamon.

Cumulative Index to Transactions of the ASME, 1971-1975. 495p. 1976. 59.00 (ISBN 0-685-25548-4, B00025). ASME.

Dean, D. L. Discrete Field Analysis of Structural Systems. (International Centre for Mechanical Sciences: No. 203). 1976. 18.90 (ISBN 0-387-81377-2). Springer-Verlag.

Dickie, D. E. & Short, Douglas. Lifting Tackle Manual. 1981. text ed. 48.95 (ISBN 0-408-00446-0, Newnes-Butterworth). Butterworth.

DIN Standards: Basic Standard for Mechanical Engineering. Date not set. price not set (10041-5/1, Pub. by DIN Germany). Heyden.

Din Standards for Mechanical Engineering for Study & Practice. 764.00 (ISBN 0-686-28161-6, 10043-6/03). Heyden.

Distandards: Basic Standards for Mechanical Engineering. 613.00 (ISBN 0-686-28159-4, 10041-2/01). Heyden.

Doebelin, Ernest O. System Modeling & Response: Theoretical & Experimental Approaches. LC 79-27609. 587p. 1980. text ed. 29.95 (ISBN 0-471-03211-5). Wiley.

Duffy, Joseph. Power: Prime Mover of Technology. rev. ed. (gr. 11-12). 1972. text ed. 17.16 (ISBN 0-87345-420-0). McKnight.

Engineering Industry Training Board, ed. Training for Riggers-Erectors, 15 vols. (Illus.). 1976. Set. 31.50x (ISBN 0-89563-030-3). Intl Ideas.

An Experiment in Synopsis Publishing in the Field of Mechanical Engineering. 1981. pap. 30.00x (ISBN 0-905984-41-2, Pub. by Brit Lib England). State Mutual Bk.

Fickett, Wildon & Davis, William C. Detonation. LC 77-85760. (Los Alamos Ser. in Basic & Applied Sciences). 1979. 35.00x (ISBN 0-520-03587-9). U of Cal Pr.

Gamlin, A. T., et al, eds. Mechanical Maintenance & Installation: Supplementary Training Manual. (Engineering Craftsmen: No. J21S). (Illus.). 1976. pap. 21.50x (ISBN 0-85083-332-9). Intl Ideas.

Ginoux, Jean J. Two Phase Flows & Heat Transfer with Application to Nuclear Reactor Design Problems. LC 77-2090. (McGraw-Hill - Hemisphere Thermal & Fluids Engineering Ser). (Illus.). 1978. text ed. 39.50x (ISBN 0-07-023305-5, C). McGraw.

Gladstone, J. Mechanical Estimating Guidebook. 4th ed. 1970. 39.50 (ISBN 0-07-023318-7, P&RB). McGraw.

Glenn, Harold T. Exploring Power Mechanics. (Illus.). (gr. 7-12). 1973. 13.00 (ISBN 0-87002-119-2); prog. wkbk. 3.32 (ISBN 0-87002-150-8). Bennett IL.

Gutman, I. Industrial Uses of Mechanical Vibrations. (Illus.). 332p. 1968. 20.00x (ISBN 0-8464-1110-5). Beekman Pubs.

Hadley, W. A. & Longobardo, G. Automatic Process Control. 1963. 15.00 (ISBN 0-201-02650-3, Adv Bk Prog). A-W.

Hall. The Language of Mechanical Engineering in English. (English for Careers Ser.). (gr. 10 up). 1977. pap. text ed. 3.50 (ISBN 0-88345-303-7). Regents Pub.

Hamilton, Douglas M. & Robb, William. Mechanical Engineering for Public Cleansing. (Illus.). 1969. 12.00x (ISBN 0-85334-121-4). Intl Ideas.

Hannah, John & Stephens, R. C. Mechanics of Machines: Elementary Theory & Examples. 3rd ed. (Illus.). 1970. 18.95x (ISBN 0-7131-3231-0); pap. text ed. 11.95x (ISBN 0-7131-3232-9). Intl Ideas.

Hardness Testing in Theory & Practice. 228p. 1978. pap. text ed. 66.00x (ISBN 3-18-090308-2, Pub. by VDI Verlag Germany). Renouf.

Harris, Norman C. & Hemmerling, E. M. Introductory Applied Physics. 3rd ed. 1972. text ed. 18.95 (ISBN 0-07-026805-3, G); instructor's manual 4.00 (ISBN 0-07-026810-X). McGraw.

Harrison, H. R. & Nettleton, T. Principles of Engineering Mechanics. 1978. pap. 19.95x (ISBN 0-7131-3378-3, Pub. by Edward Arnold). Intl Schol Bk Serv.

Hartenberg, R. S., ed. National Historic Mechanical Engineering Landmarks. (Illus., Orig.). 1979. 15.00 (ISBN 0-685-96308-X, H00140). ASME.

Helsdon, Harry. Mechanical Engineering Science. 1968. text ed. 6.50x (ISBN 0-442-03313-3). D Van Nostrand.

Hiscox, Gardner D. Mechanical Movements Powers & Devices. LC 78-18530. 1978. Repr. of 1907 ed. lib. bdg. 40.00 (ISBN 0-89341-512-X). Longwood Pr.

Horlock, J. H. Fluid Mechanics & Thermodynamics. LC 73-75588. 222p. 1973. Repr. of 1958 ed. 12.50 (ISBN 0-88275-096-8). Krieger.

Hosny, A. N. Propulsion Systems. rev. ed. LC 73-18277. 1974. 27.50x (ISBN 0-87249-310-5). U of SC Pr.

Houghton, Bernard. Mechanical Engineering: The Sources of Information. (Guides to Subject Literature Ser.). 1970. 19.50 (ISBN 0-208-01062-9, Archon). Shoe String.

Johnson, Ray C. Optimum Design of Mechanical Elements. 2nd ed. LC 79-14363. 519p. 1980. 37.50 (ISBN 0-471-03894-6, Pub. by Wiley-Interscience). Wiley.

Jorgensen, Eric, ed. BMW Three Hundred Twenty i: Nineteen Seventy-Seven to Nineteen Eighty Shop Manual. (Illus.). 248p. (Orig.). pap. text ed. 10.95 (ISBN 0-89287-326-4, A139). Clymer Pubns.

--Chevy Malibu Chevelle MonteCarlo: 1970-1980 Shop Manual. (Illus.). pap. text ed. 10.95 (ISBN 0-89287-319-1, A246). Clymer Pubns.

--Honda Twinstar Nineteen Seventy-Eight to Nineteen Eighty: Service, Repair, Maintenance. (Illus.). pap. text ed. 9.95 (ISBN 0-89287-325-6, M324). Clymer Pubns.

--Kawasaki Nine Hundred & 1000cc Four, 1973-1979: Includes Shaft Drive Service Repair Performance. (Illus., Orig.). pap. text ed. 9.95 (ISBN 0-89287-321-3, M359). Clymer Pubns.

--Oldsmobile Cutlass: Nineteen Seventy to Nineteen Eighty Shop Manual. (Illus.). 342p. (Orig.). pap. text ed. 10.95 (ISBN 0-89287-324-8, A285). Clymer Pubns.

--Suzuki SP-DR Three Hundred Seventy & Four Hundred Singles Nineteen Seventy-Eight to Nineteen Eighty: Service, Repair, Performance. (Illus.). 224p. (Orig.). pap. text ed. 9.95 (ISBN 0-89287-327-2, M374). Clymer Pubns.

--Yamaha Snowmobiles: Nineteen Seventy-Five to Nineteen Eighty Service, Repair & Maintenance. (Illus.). 180p. (Orig.). 1980. pap. text ed. 8.95 (ISBN 0-89287-323-X, X954). Clymer Pubns.

--Yamaha YZ One Hundred to Four Hundred Sixty-Five Monoshock Nineteen Seventy-Five to Nineteen Eighty: Service, Repair, Performance. (Illus.). 293p. (Orig.). pap. text ed. 9.95 (ISBN 0-89287-329-9, M413). Clymer Pubns.

Jorqgensen, Eric, ed. Datsun Two Hundred Ten: Nineteen Seventy-Nine to Nineteen Eighty Shop Manual. (Illus.). pap. text ed. 11.95 (ISBN 0-89287-322-1, A 203). Clymer Pubns.

Karafiath, L. L. & Nowatzki, E. A. Soil Mechanics for off-Road Vehicle Engineering. (Rock & Soil Mechanics Ser.). (Illus.). 1978. 58.00 (ISBN 0-87849-020-5). Trans Tech.

Konzo, Seichi & Bayne, James W. Opportunities in Mechanical Engineering. 2nd ed. LC 77-166404. 1978. lib. bdg. 6.60 (ISBN 0-685-59350-9); pap. 4.95 (ISBN 0-685-59351-7). Natl Textbk.

Kreith, Frank & Kreider, Jan F. Principles of Solar Engineering. LC 77-27861. (McGraw-Hill - Hemisphere Thermal & Fluids Engineering Ser). (Illus.). 1978. pap. 24.95 (ISBN 0-07-035476-6, C). McGraw.

Lieblich, Jerome H., ed. Dimension & Tolerances (an Interpretation of ANSI y14.5) 1973. pap. 3.75x (ISBN 0-912702-05-2). Global Eng.

Mabie, Hamilton H. & Ocvirk, Fred W. Mechanisms & Dynamics of Machinery, SI Version. 3rd ed. LC 78-1382. 1978. text ed. 30.95 (ISBN 0-471-02380-9). Wiley.

Mache, Ewald & Koziki, Igor. Random Signals Generation with Required Probability Density & Power Spectral Density Functions for Use in Life: Investigation of Materials & Mechanical Constructions. 52p. 1980. pap. 23.00x (ISBN 3-18-142309-2, Pub. by VDI Verlag Germany). Renouf.

McKelvey, John P. & Grotch, Howard. Fisica Paraciencias E Ingenieria, Vol. I. (Span.). 1980. pap. text ed. 13.00 (ISBN 0-06-315475-7, Pub. by HarLA Mexico). Har-Row.

--Fisica Paraciencias E Ingenieria, Vol. II. (Span.). 1981. pap. text ed. 14.00 (ISBN 0-06-315476-5, Pub. by HarLA Mexico). Har-Row.

McLean, W. G. & Nelson, E. W. Schaum's Outline of Engineering Mechanics. 3rd ed. (Schaum's Outline Ser.). 1978. pap. 6.95 (ISBN 0-07-044816-7, SP). McGraw.

Mechanical World Yearbook, 1979. 90th ed. (Illus.). 512p. (Orig.). 1979. pap. 12.50x (ISBN 0-85242-468-X). Intl Pubns Serv.

Meriam, J. L. Engineering Mechanics: Statics & Dynamics Combined. LC 78-518. 1978. text ed. 30.95x (ISBN 0-471-01979-8). Wiley.

Morlok, E. K. Introduction to Transportation System Engineering & Planning. (Illus.). 1978. text ed. 25.50 (ISBN 0-07-043132-9, C); solution man. 7.95 (ISBN 0-07-043133-7). McGraw.

Mueller, E. A., ed. Mechanics of Sound Generation in Flow. (IUTAM-Symposium Ser.). (Illus.). 302p. 1980. 43.70 (ISBN 0-387-09785-6). Springer-Verlag.

Nee, John G. Mechanism Drafting & Design: A Workbook. LC 80-80861. (Illus.). 1980. pap. text ed. 14.95x (ISBN 0-911168-45-1); solutions manual 3.95x (ISBN 0-911168-46-X). Prakken.

The Nineteen Seventy-Five Bound Transactions, 4 pts. Incl. Pt. 1. Power, Industry, & Pressure Vessel Technology (B00096); Pt. 2. Heat Transfer, Dynamic Systems, Measurement & Control Engineering Materials & Technology (B00097); Pt. 3. Applied Mechanics (B00098); Pt. 4. Lubrication & Fluids Engineering (B00099). 1976. 70.00 ea; 250.00 set (ISBN 0-685-68902-6). ASME.

Nogotov, E. F. Applications of Numerical Methods to Heat Transfer. (Illus.). 1978. pap. text ed. 28.50 (ISBN 0-07-046852-4, C). McGraw.

Paul, B., ed. Mechanics of Transportation Suspension Systems, AMD Vol. 15. 110p. 1975. pap. text ed. 12.00 (ISBN 0-685-62563-X, I00095). ASME.

Paul, Burton. Kinematics & Dynamics of Planar Machinery. (Illus.). 1979. text ed. 34.95 (ISBN 0-13-516062-6). P-H.

Peatfield, A. E. Teach Yourself Mechanical Engineering: Hand Tools, No. 1. (Teach Yourself Ser.). 1950. 1.00 (ISBN 0-486-21724-8). Dover.

Pefley, Richard & Newnan, Donald G. Mechanical Engineering License Review. 3rd ed. LC 79-11957. 378p. 1980. pap. 17.95 (ISBN 0-910554-28-5). Eng Pr.

Peterson, Rudolph E. Stress Concentration Factors. LC 53-11283. 336p. 1974. 36.95 (ISBN 0-471-68329-9, Pub. by Wiley-Interscience). Wiley.

Power Editors. Plant Energy System: Energy Systems Engineering. 1967. 39.50 (ISBN 0-07-050588-8, P&RB). McGraw.

Prentice, J. M. Dynamics of Mechanical Systems. 2nd ed. LC 79-41460. 486p. 1980. 64.95x (ISBN 0-470-26938-3). Halsted Pr.

Prentis, James M. Engineering Mechanics. (Oxford Engineering Science Texts Ser.). (Illus.). 272p. 1979. text ed. 39.00x (ISBN 0-19-856205-5); pap. text ed. 18.50x (ISBN 0-19-856206-3). Oxford U Pr.

Reliability & Safety of Air Separation Plant. 1973. pap. 10.75 (ISBN 0-685-99174-1, IIR44, IIR). Unipub.

Richards, C. J. Mechanical Engineering in Radar & Communications. 1970. 39.50x (ISBN 0-442-06913-8). Van Nos Reinhold.

Richmond, Nigel. Language of the Lines. 1978. 15.00 (ISBN 0-7045-0299-2). State Mutual Bk.

Rudman, Jack. Assistant Mechanical Construction Engineer. (Career Examination Ser.: C-2706). (Cloth bdg. avail. on request). 1980. pap. 12.00 (ISBN 0-8373-2706-7). Natl Learning.

--Mechanical Engineer. (Career Examination Ser.: C-481). (Cloth bdg. avail. on request). pap. 10.00 (ISBN 0-8373-0481-4). Natl Learning.

Schlichting, Hermann. Boundary Layer Theory. 7th ed. Kestin, J., tr. from Ger. (Mechanical Engineering Ser.). (Illus.). 1979. 29.50 (ISBN 0-07-055334-3, C). McGraw.

Sengupta, S., ed. Advances in Heat & Mass Transfer at Air Water Interfaces. 116p. 1978. 18.00 (ISBN 0-685-66789-8, H00127). ASME.

Simon, Refus. History of the Corps of Electrical & Mechanical Engineers, Vol. 1: Their Formative Years. 1977. 25.00 (ISBN 0-7069-0515-6, Pub. by Vikas India). Advent NY.

Sinclair, Bruce. A Centennial History of the American Society of Mechanical Engineers: 1880-1980. 256p. 1980. text ed. 15.00 (ISBN 0-686-69842-8, H0175H); pap. text ed. 10.00 (ISBN 0-686-69843-6, H0175P). ASME.

--A History of the American Society of Mechanical Engineers. 304p. 1980. 15.00x (ISBN 0-8020-2380-0). U of Toronto Pr.

Sirohi, R. S. Mechanical Measurements. LC 80-27233. 210p. 1981. 13.95 (ISBN 0-470-27107-8). Halsted Pr.

Sixth International Conference on Experimental Stress Analysis. 900p. 1978. pap. 232.00x (ISBN 0-686-71871-2, Pub. by VDI Verlag Germany). Renouf.

Staniar, William, ed. Plant Engineering Handbook. 2nd ed. 1959. 64.50 (ISBN 0-07-060824-5, P&RB). McGraw.

Stanley, P. Fracture Mechanics in Engineering Practice. (Illus.). 1977. 86.90x (ISBN 0-85334-723-9, Pub. by Applied Science). Burgess-Intl Ideas.
Stanley, R. C. Mechanical Properties of Solids & Fluids. (Illus.). 240p. 1972. 13.75 (ISBN 0-8088-7030-0). Davey.
Stoecker, W. F. Design of Thermal Systems. 2nd ed. (Illus.). 1980. 29.95 (ISBN 0-07-061618-3). McGraw.
Structural Optimization Symposium. AMD: Proceedings, Vol. 7. 162p. 1974. 18.00 (ISBN 0-685-48054-2, I00042). ASME.
Thirring, Hans. Energy for Man. 1976. pap. 7.50x (ISBN 0-06-131861-2, TB 1861, Torch). Har-Row.
Threlkeld, James L. Thermal Environmental Engineering. 2nd ed. 1970. ref. ed. 27.95 (ISBN 0-13-914721-7). P-H.
Trade & Technical Press Ltd, ed. Handbook of Mechanical Power Drives. 2nd ed. (Illus.). 1978. 105.00x (ISBN 0-85461-067-7). Intl Ideas.
U. S. Navy (Bureau of Naval Personnel) Basic Machines & How They Work. (Illus.). 1965. pap. 3.00 (ISBN 0-486-21709-4). Dover.
Veinott, Cyril G. Computer-Aided Design of Electric Machinery. (Monographs in Modern Electrical Technology). (Illus.). 168p. 1973. text ed. 17.50x (ISBN 0-262-22016-4). MIT Pr.
Waterhouse, R. B., ed. Fretting Fatigue. (Illus.). x, 246p. 1981. 40.00x (ISBN 0-85334-932-0). Intl Ideas.
The Way Things Work: An Encyclopedia of Modern Technology, Vol. 2. 1971. 16.95 (ISBN 0-671-21086-6). S&S.
Wilde, Douglass J. Globally Optimal Design. LC 78-2933. 1978. 29.95 (ISBN 0-471-03898-9, Pub. by Wiley-Interscience). Wiley.
Wirz, H. J. & Smolderen, J. J. Numerical Methods in Fluid Dynamics. (McGraw-Hill - Hemisphere Series in Thermal & Fluids Engineering). (Illus.). 1978. text ed. 37.50 (ISBN 0-07-071120-8, C). McGraw.
Wyskida, Richard M. & McDaniel, Don M. Modeling of Cushioning Systems. 334p. 1980. 46.25 (ISBN 0-677-05480-7). Gordon.

MECHANICAL ENGINEERING–BIBLIOGRAPHY

Auger, C. P., ed. Engineering Eponyms. 2nd rev. ed. 1975. 17.25x (ISBN 0-85365-437-9, Pub. by Lib Assn England). Oryx Pr.
Houghton, Bernard. Mechanical Engineering: The Sources of Information. (Guides to Subject Literature Ser.). 1970. 19.50 (ISBN 0-208-01062-9, Archon). Shoe String.

MECHANICAL ENGINEERING–CONTRACTS AND SPECIFICATIONS

Johnston, K. F. Electrical & Mechanical Engineering Contracts. LC 72-192195. 236p. 1971. 18.50x (ISBN 0-7161-0055-X). Intl Pubns Serv.
Towill, Denis R. Coefficient Plane Models for Control System Analysis & Design. LC 80-41695. (Mechanical Engineering Research Studies: Vol. 1). 271p. 1981. 45.00 (ISBN 0-471-27955-2, Pub. by Wiley-Interscience). Wiley.

MECHANICAL ENGINEERING–DICTIONARIES

European Committee of Associations of Gear & Transmission Element Manufacturers (EUROTRANS), ed. Glossary of Transmission Elements: Gears. (Illus., In 8 languages). 1976. lib. bdg. 30.00x (ISBN 3-7830-0104-8). Marlin.
Freeman, Henry G. Dictionary of Mechanical Engineering. 8th rev. ed. LC 72-347328. (Eng. Ger.). 1971. 45.00x (ISBN 3-7736-5031-0). Intl Pubns Serv.
--Spezialwoerterbuch Maschinenwesen. 207p. (Ger. -Eng., Dictionary of Mechanical Engineering). 1971. write for info (M-7625, Pub. by Verlag W. Girardet). French & Eur.
Horner, J. G. Dictionary of Mechanical Engineering Terms. 9th rev. & enl. ed. Grahame-White, G. K., ed. 27.50 (ISBN 0-685-29250-9). Heinman.
Lexikon der Graphischen Technik. 4th ed. (Ger.). 1977. 29.95 (ISBN 3-7940-4078-3, M-7253). French & Eur.
Nayler, J. L. & Nayler, G. H. Dictionary of Mechanical Engineering. 2nd ed. 1978. Repr. of 1975 ed. 19.95 (ISBN 0-408-00175-5). Butterworth.
Schulz, Ernst. Woerterbuch der Optik und Feinmechanik, Vol. 1. (Fr., Ger. & Eng., Dictionary of Optics & Mechanical Engineering). 1961. pap. 12.00 (ISBN 3-87097-036-7, M-6978). French & Eur.
--Woerterbuch der Optik und Feinmechanik, Vol. 2. (Fr., Ger. & Eng., Dictionary of Optics & Mechanical Engineering). 1961. pap. 12.00 (ISBN 3-87097-037-5, M-6977). French & Eur.
Shvarts, V. V. The Concise Illustrated Russian-English Dictionary of Mechanical Engineering. (Illus.). 224p. 1981. pap. 30.00 (ISBN 0-08-027574-5). Pergamon.
Stellhorn, Kurt. Woerterbuch Werkzeuge und Werkzeugmaschinen. (Ger. -Fr.). 1969. leatherette 56.00 (ISBN 3-7736-5260-7, M-6907). French & Eur.

MECHANICAL ENGINEERING–EXAMINATIONS, QUESTIONS, ETC.

Arco Editorial Board. Mechanical Engineer: Junior, Assistant & Senior Grades. 2nd ed. LC 71-140622. 1973. pap. 8.00 (ISBN 0-668-03314-2). Arco.
Constance, John D. Mechanical Engineering for Professional Engineers' Examinations. 2nd ed. 1969. 24.50 (ISBN 0-07-012443-4, P&RB). McGraw.
Coren, Gerald. Mechanical Engineering. rev. ed. LC 64-17862. (Orig.). 1978. pap. 12.00 (ISBN 0-668-01204-8). Arco.
--Mechanical Engineering: For State Board Examination Part B. (Illus.). 1979. pap. 12.00 (ISBN 0-668-01258-7, 1258-7). Arco.
Gladstone, John. Air Conditioning & Mechanical Trades: Preparing for the Contractor's License Examination. LC 74-18258. (Illus.). 425p. 1980. pap. 18.95 (ISBN 0-930644-04-2). Engineers Pr.
--Journeyman General Mechanical Examination: An Illustrated Review with Questions & Answers. LC 78-85357. 1973. 14.95 (ISBN 0-930644-00-X). Engineers Pr.
Koch, Harry W. Mechanical Work Examinations. 1967. 5.00 (ISBN 0-913164-23-2). Ken-Bks.
Morrison, James W. Mechanical Engineering Technician. LC 77-8518. (Illus.). 1978. pap. text ed. 10.00 (ISBN 0-668-04274-5, 4274). Arco.
Rudman, Jack. Assistant Mechanical Engineer. (Career Examination Ser.: C-44). (Cloth bdg. avail. on request). pap. 10.00 (ISBN 0-8373-0044-4). Natl Learning.
--Auto Machinist. (Career Examination Ser.: C-62). (Cloth bdg. avail. on request). pap. 8.00 (ISBN 0-8373-0062-2). Natl Learning.
--Chief Supervisor of Mechanical Installations. (Career Examination Ser.: C-2482). (Cloth bdg. avail. on request). pap. 10.00 (ISBN 0-8373-2482-3). Natl Learning.
--Junior Mechanical Engineer. (Career Examination Ser.: C-402). (Cloth bdg. avail. on research). pap. 10.00 (ISBN 0-8373-0402-4). Natl Learning.
--Mechanical Engineer. (Career Examination Ser.: C-481). (Cloth bdg. avail. on request). pap. 10.00 (ISBN 0-8373-0481-4). Natl Learning.
--Mechanical Engineering Trainee. (Career Examination Ser.: C-519). (Cloth bdg. avail. on request). pap. 8.00 (ISBN 0-8373-0519-5). Natl Learning.
--Mechanical Equipment Inspector. (Career Examination Ser.: C-2045). (Cloth bdg. avail. on request). pap. 10.00 (ISBN 0-8373-2045-3). Natl Learning.
--Senior Building Mechanical Engineer. (Career Examination Ser.: C-2572). (Cloth bdg. avail. on request). pap. 14.00 (ISBN 0-8373-2572-2). Natl Learning.
--Senior Mechanical Engineer. (Career Examination Ser.: C-1648). (Cloth bdg. avail on request). 1977. pap. 10.00 (ISBN 0-8373-1648-0). Natl Learning.

MECHANICAL ENGINEERING–HANDBOOKS, MANUALS, ETC.

American Society Of Mechanical Engineers. ASME Handbook: Engineering Tables. 1956. 44.50 (ISBN 0-07-001516-3, P&RB). McGraw.
--ASME Handbook: Metals Engineering-Design. 2nd ed. 1964. 53.50 (ISBN 0-07-001518-X, P&RB). McGraw.
--ASME Handbook: Metals Properties. (Illus.). 1956. 38.50 (ISBN 0-07-001513-9, P&RB). McGraw.
Atteberry, Pat H. Power Mechanics. LC 80-20581. (Illus.). 112p. 1980. text ed. 4.80 (ISBN 0-87006-307-3). Goodheart.
B-One.ThirteenM - 1979: Metric Screw Threads - M Profile. 40p. 1979. 10.00 (ISBN 0-685-25547-6, N00046). ASME.
Baumeister, E. T., ed. Standard Handbook for Mechanical Engineers. 8th ed. (Bk. No. E00028). 1978. pap. 50.00 (ISBN 0-685-99211-X). ASME.
Bovay, H. E., Jr., ed. Handbook of Mechanical & Electrical Systems for Buildings. (Illus.). 864p. 1981. 49.50 (ISBN 0-07-006718-X). McGraw.
Cruse, Thomas A. & Griffin, Donald S., eds. Three-Dimensional Continuum Computer Programs for Structural Analysis. 1972. pap. text ed. 6.00 (ISBN 0-685-30781-6, I00021). ASME.
Kent, R. T. Mechanical Engineers' Handbook, 2 pts. 12th ed. Incl. Pt. 1. Design & Production. Carmichael, C., ed. 1611p (ISBN 0-471-46959-9); Pt. 2. Power. Salisbury, J. K., ed. 1409p (ISBN 0-471-46992-0). 1950. (Pub. by Wiley-Interscience). Wiley.
Lindeburg, Michael R. Mechanical Engineering Review Manual. 5th ed. LC 80-83176. (Engineering Review Manual Ser.). (Illus.). 704p. 1980. pap. 26.50 (ISBN 0-932276-21-0); wkbk. 7.00 (ISBN 0-932276-23-7). Prof Engine.
Nelson, Carl A. Mechanical Trades Pocket Manual. LC 73-91639. 208p. (Orig.). 1974. pap. 8.95 (ISBN 0-672-23215-4). Audel.
--Millwrights & Mechanics Guide. 2nd ed. LC 72-75119. (Illus.). 800p. 1972. 14.95 (ISBN 0-672-23201-4). Audel.
Vogel, Werner. The Exact Overwire Measurement of Screws, Gears, Splines & Worms. LC 72-6682. 240p. 1973. 19.95x (ISBN 0-8143-1489-9). Wayne St U Pr.

MECHANICAL ENGINEERING–JUVENILE LITERATURE

Berry, Roland. Easy to Make Contraptions. LC 78-59249. (Easy to Make Ser.). (Illus.). (gr. 2-5). 1978. PLB 5.79 (ISBN 0-8178-5938-1). Harvey.
Dolan, Edward. Engines Work Like This. (Illus.). (gr. 4-6). 1972. 5.95 (ISBN 0-07-017401-6, GB). McGraw.
Would You Like to Be a Mechanical Engineer? 48p. (gr. 4-6). 1981. 2.95 (ISBN 0-686-31331-3). Unica Inc.

MECHANICAL ENGINEERING–PROBLEMS, EXERCISES, ETC.

Constance, John D. Mechanical Engineering for Professional Engineers' Examinations. 2nd ed. 1969. 24.50 (ISBN 0-07-012443-4, P&RB). McGraw.
Coren, Gerald. Mechanical Engineering. rev. ed. LC 64-17862. (Orig.). 1978. pap. 12.00 (ISBN 0-668-01204-8). Arco.
Kiseliov, V. A., et al. Mecanica De Construccion En Ejemplos y Problemas. (Illus.). 391p. (Span.). 1973. 7.00 (ISBN 0-8285-1457-7, Pub. by Mir Pubs Russia). Imported Pubns.
Rudman, Jack. Mechanical Engineer. (Career Examination Ser.: C-481). (Cloth bdg. avail. on request). pap. 10.00 (ISBN 0-8373-0481-4). Natl Learning.
Stamper, Eugene & Dublin, Stanley W. Mechanical Engineering & Economics & Ethics for Professional Engineering Examinations. Hollander, Lawrence J., ed. (Professional Engineering Examination Ser). (Illus.). 1971. 21.55 (ISBN 0-8104-5716-4). Hayden.
Szuladzinski, Gregory. Dynamics of Structures & Machinery: Problems & Solutions. 700p. 1981. 50.00 (ISBN 0-471-09027-1, Pub. by Wiley Interscience). Wiley.

MECHANICAL ENGINEERING–TABLES, CALCULATIONS, ETC.

American Society Of Mechanical Engineers. ASME Handbook: Engineering Tables. 1956. 44.50 (ISBN 0-07-001516-3, P&RB). McGraw.
Daryanani, Sital. Building Systems Design with Programmable Calculators. 1980. 27.50 (ISBN 0-07-015415-5, P&RB). McGraw.
Oberg, Erik, et al. Machinery's Handbook. 21st rev. ed. Schubert, Paul B., ed. LC 72-622276. (Illus.). 2482p. 1979. 34.00 (ISBN 0-8311-1129-1). Indus Pr.

MECHANICAL ENGINEERS

Calvert, Monte. The Mechanical Engineer in America, 1830-1910: Professional Cultures in Conflict. LC 66-26683. (Studies in the History of Technology Ser). 314p. 1967. 21.00x (ISBN 0-8018-0102-8). Johns Hopkins.
Franklin, George E. From Cotswolds to High Sierras. LC 66-20373. (Illus.). 167p. 1966. 4.00 (ISBN 0-87004-046-4). Caxton.
Mechanical Engineers in America Born Prior to 1861: A Biographical Dictionary. 330p. 1980. 20.00 (ISBN 0-686-69855-X, H00176). ASME.
Peterson, Aldor C. Applied Engineering Mechanics: Statics. 2nd ed. 260p. 1981. text ed. 21.95 (ISBN 0-205-07131-7, 3271315); write for info. solutions manual (ISBN 0-205-07183-X). Allyn.

MECHANICAL HANDLING

see Materials Handling

MECHANICAL HEART

see Heart, Mechanical

MECHANICAL MODELS

see Machinery–Models

MECHANICAL MOVEMENTS

see also Automata; Cams; Gearing; Links and Link-Motion; Machinery, Kinematics Of

Bickford, John H. Mechanisms for Intermittent Motion. LC 75-184639. 272p. 1972. write for info (ISBN 0-8311-1091-0). Krieger.
--Mechanisms for Internittent Motion. LC 75-184639. 272p. Date not set. Repr. of 1972 ed. price not set (ISBN 0-8311-1091-0). Krieger.
Brown, Henry T. Five Hundred & Seven Mechanical Movements. (Illus.). 102p. Repr. of 1896 ed. 13.95x (ISBN 0-935164-06-5). N T Smith.
Bucksch, H. Dictionary of Mechanisms. (Ger. - Eng.). 1976. leatherette 133.00 (ISBN 3-7625-0707-4, M-7111). French & Eur.
Chironis, Nicholas P. Mechanisms, Linkages, & Mechanical Controls. 1965. 30.00 (ISBN 0-07-010775-0, P&RB). McGraw.
Dijksman, E. A. Motion Geometry of Mechanism. LC 75-3977. (Illus.). 250p. 1976. 35.50 (ISBN 0-521-20841-6). Cambridge U Pr.
Duffy, J. Analysis of Mechanisms & Robot Manipulators. 419p. 1980. 126.95 (ISBN 0-470-27002-0). Halsted Pr.
Faires, Virgil M. & Keown, Robert M. Mechanism. 5th ed. 346p. 1980. Repr. of 1960 ed. lib. bdg. 17.50 (ISBN 0-89874-182-3). Krieger.
Frank, Adolph F. Animated Scale Models Handbook. LC 80-22858. (Illus.). 160p. 1981. lib. bdg. 15.95 (ISBN 0-668-05118-3, 5118). Arco.
Graf, Rudolph F., et al. How It Works, Illustrated Everyday Devices & Mechanisms. (Illus.). 192p. 1979. pap. 7.95 (ISBN 0-442-25158-0). Van Nos Reinhold.
Grafstein, Paul & Schwarz, Otto M. Pictorial Handbook of Technical Devices. (Illus.). 1971. 14.00 (ISBN 0-8206-0234-5). Chem Pub.
Jones, Franklin D., et al. Ingenious Mechanisms for Designers & Inventors, Vols. 1-4, 1930-67. LC 30-14992. (Illus.). Set. 80.00 (ISBN 0-685-12543-2); Vol. 1, 536 Pgs. 22.00 (ISBN 0-8311-1029-5); Vol. 2, 538 Pgs. 22.00 (ISBN 0-8311-1030-9); Vol. 3, 536 Pgs. 22.00 (ISBN 0-8311-1031-7); Vol. 4, 493 Pgs. 22.00 (ISBN 0-8311-1032-5). Indus Pr.
Kondratiev, V. N. & Nikitin, E. E. Gas-Phase Reactions: Kinetics & Mechanisms. (Illus.). 250p. 1980. 63.80 (ISBN 0-387-09956-5). Springer-Verlag.
Lent, Deane. Analysis & Design of Mechanisms. 2nd ed. (Technology Ser). 1970. text ed. 17.95 (ISBN 0-13-032797-2). P-H.
Mabie, Hamilton H. & Ocvirk, Fred W. Mechanisms & Dynamics of Machinery. 3rd ed. LC 74-30405. 616p. 1975. text ed. 30.95 (ISBN 0-471-55935-0). Wiley.
Martin, George H. Kinematics & Dynamics of Machines. 2nd ed. (Illus.). 544p. 1982. text ed. 28.95x (ISBN 0-07-040657-X, C); write for info. solutions manual (ISBN 0-07-040658-8). McGraw.
Shigley, Joseph E. & Uiker, John J. Theory of Machines & Mechanisms. (Mechanical Engineering Ser.). (Illus.). 576p. 1980. text ed. 27.95x (ISBN 0-07-056884-7); solutions manual 13.95 (ISBN 0-07-056885-5). McGraw.
Trylinski, W. Fine Mechanisms & Precision Instruments, Principles of Design. 1971. 75.00 (ISBN 0-08-006361-6). Pergamon.
Tuttle, S. B. Mechanisms for Engineering Design. 178p. 1967. text ed. 11.25 (ISBN 0-471-89458-3, Pub. by Wiley). Krieger.

MECHANICAL PAINTING

see Painting, Industrial

MECHANICAL PERSPECTIVE

see Perspective

MECHANICAL QUADRATURE

see Numerical Integration

MECHANICAL SHOCK

see Shock (Mechanics)

MECHANICAL SPEECH RECOGNIZER

see Automatic Speech Recognition

MECHANICAL TRANSLATING

see Machine Translating

MECHANICAL WEAR

Kragelsky, I. V. Methods of Calculating Friction & Wear. 100.00 (ISBN 0-08-027320-3). Pergamon.
Pronikov, A. S. Dependability & Durability of Engineering Products. 1973. text ed. 13.95 (ISBN 0-408-70383-0). Butterworth.
Pugh, B. Friction & Wear: A Trilogy Text for Students. 19.95 (ISBN 0-408-00097-X); pap. 6.95 (ISBN 0-408-00098-8). Butterworth.
Rabinowicz, Ernest. Friction & Wear of Materials. LC 65-12704. (Ser. on the Science & Technology of Materials). (Illus.). 1965. 33.00 (ISBN 0-471-70340-0). Wiley.

MECHANICS

see also Acceleration (Mechanics); Animal Mechanics; Biomechanics; Deformations (Mechanics); Dynamics; Elastic Solids; Elasticity; Electromechanical Analogies; Engineering; Fluids; Force and Energy; Friction; Gases; Hydraulics; Hydrodynamics; Hydrostatics; Inertia (Mechanics); Kinematics; Liquids; Machinery; Mass (Physics); Mathematical Physics; Matter–Properties; Mechanical Movements; Motion; Photoelasticity; Potential, Theory of; Power (Mechanics); Relativistic Mechanics; Rock Mechanics; Shock (Mechanics); Soil Mechanics; Stability; Statics; Statistical Mechanics; Steam-Engines; Strains and Stresses; Strength of Materials; Thermodynamics; Torque; Torsion; Vibration; Viscosity; Wave Mechanics; Wave-Motion, Theory of

Abir, David, ed. Contributions to Mechanics. 1969. 67.00 (ISBN 0-08-012822-X). Pergamon.
Ahmad, R. Fundamentals of Mechanics. 4.50x (ISBN 0-210-31233-5). Asia.

Alonso, Marcelo & Finn, Edward J. Fundamental University Physics, 2 vols. 2nd ed. Incl. Vol. 1. Mechanics. 1979. text ed. 17.95 (ISBN 0-201-00161-6); Vol. 2. Fields & Waves. 1979 (ISBN 0-201-00162-4). 1979. text ed. write for info. A-W.

Andronov, A. A., et al. Seven Papers on Equations Related to Mechanics & Heat. LC 51-5559. (Translations Ser.: No. 2, Vol. 75). 1968. 28.80 (ISBN 0-8218-1775-2, TRANS 2-75). Am Math.

Arnold, V. I. Mathematical Methods in Classical Mechanids. (Graduate Texts in Mathematics Ser.: Vol. 60). (Illus.). 1978. 24.80 (ISBN 0-387-90314-3). Springer-Verlag.

Au, Tung. Elementary Structural Mechanics. 1963. text ed. 28.95 (ISBN 0-13-260455-8). P-H.

Barger, Vernon D. & Olsson, Martin G. Classical Mechanics: A Modern Perspective. LC 72-5697. (Illus.). 352p. 1973. text ed. 19.95 (ISBN 0-07-003723-X, C); instructor's manual 3.95 (ISBN 0-07-003724-8). McGraw.

Bartlett, James H. Classical & Modern Mechanics. LC 74-5588. 489p. 1975. 20.00x (ISBN 0-8173-3100-X); pap. 6.50 (ISBN 0-8173-3101-8). U of Ala Pr.

Becker, Robert A. Introduction to Theoretical Mechanics. (International Pure & Applied Physics Ser). 1954. 21.95 (ISBN 0-07-004231-4, C). McGraw.

Bert, C. W., ed. Developments in Mechanics: Proceedings, Midwestern Mechanics Conference, Vol. 8. (Illus.). 626p. 35.00 (ISBN 0-8061-1291-3). U of Okla Pr.

Breneman, John W. Mechanics. 3rd ed. (Illus.). 1960. 14.95 (ISBN 0-07-007538-7, G); answers to odd-numbered problems 1.00 (ISBN 0-07-007543-3). McGraw.

Broad, C. D. Perception, Physics & Reality: An Enquiry into the Information That Physical Science Can Supply About the Real. LC 79-180606. 388p. 1972. Repr. of 1914 ed. 19.00 (ISBN 0-8462-1639-6). Russell.

Bullen, K. E. Introduction to the Theory of Mechanics. 8th ed. 1971. 35.50 (ISBN 0-521-08291-9). Cambridge U Pr.

Carpenter, Samuel T. Structural Mechanics. LC 75-31671. 550p. 1976. Repr. of 1966 ed. 26.50 (ISBN 0-88275-363-0). Krieger.

Chapple, M. A Level Physics: Mechanics & Heat, Vol. 1. 2nd ed. (Illus.). 336p. (Orig.). 1979. pap. text ed. 10.95x (ISBN 0-7121-0154-3, Pub. by Macdonald & Evans England). Intl Ideas.

Chester, W. Mechanics. (Illus.). 1980. text ed. 34.00x (ISBN 0-04-510058-6); pap. text ed. 18.95x (ISBN 0-04-510059-4). Allen Unwin.

CISM (International Center for Mechanical Sciences) Examples to Extremum & Variational Principles in Mechanics. Besdo, D., ed. (CISM International Centre for Mechanical Sciences Ser.: No. 65). (Illus.). 236p. 1974. pap. 23.80 (ISBN 0-387-81230-X). Springer-Verlag.

CISM (International Center for Mechanical Sciences), Dept. for General Mechanics, Technical Univ. of Brunswick, 1970. Extremum & Variational Principles in Mechanics. Lippmann, H., ed. (CISM Pubns. Ser.: No. 54). (Illus.). ii, 239p. 1972. pap. 33.10 (ISBN 0-387-81115-X). Springer-Verlag.

CISM (International Center for Mechanical Sciences) Fluidic Sensors & Some Large Scale Devices. Jacobs, B. E., ed. (CISM Intl. Centre for Mechanical Sciences, Courses & Lectures: No. 52). (Illus.). 41p. 1974. pap. 6.70 (ISBN 0-387-81228-8). Springer-Verlag.

CISM (International Center for Mechanical Sciences)-IFTOMM Symposium, 1st, 1973. On Theory & Practice of Robots & Manipulators: Proceedings. (CISM International Centre for Mechanical Sciences Ser.: No. 201). (Illus.). 668p. pap. 53.10 (ISBN 0-387-81252-0). Springer-Verlag.

CISM (International Center for Mechanical Sciences) Random Processes in Mechanical Sciences. Parkus, H., ed. (CISM Pubns. Ser.: No. 9). (Illus.). vi, 169p. 1973. pap. 19.80 (ISBN 0-387-81086-2). Springer-Verlag.

Clarke, Donald. The Encyclopedia of How It's Made. LC 78-58391. (Illus.). 1978. 16.95 (ISBN 0-89479-035-8). A & W Pubs.

Constant, F. Woodbridge. Theoretical Physics: Mechanics of Particles, Rigid & Elastic Bodies & Heat Flow. LC 78-14353. 296p. 1979. Repr. of 1954 ed. lib. bdg. 14.00 (ISBN 0-88275-738-5). Krieger.

Corben, H. C. & Stehle, Philip. Classical Mechanics. 2nd ed. LC 74-141. 402p. 1974. Repr. of 1960 ed. 21.50 (ISBN 0-88275-162-X). Krieger.

Darkov, A. & Kuznetsov, V. Structural Mechanics. Lachinov, B., tr. (Russian Monographs Ser.). 1969. 145.75x (ISBN 0-677-20830-8). Gordon.

Den Hartog, Jacob P. Mechanics. 1948. pap. 6.50 (ISBN 0-486-60754-2). Dover.

Desloge, Edward A. Classical Mechanics, Vol. 1. 592p. 1982. 40.00 (ISBN 0-471-09144-8, Pub. by Wiley-Interscience). Wiley.

--Classical Mechanics, Vol. 2. 544p. 1982. 40.00 (ISBN 0-471-09145-6, Pub. by Wiley-Interscience). Wiley.

Duvant, G. & Lions, J. L. Inequalities in Mechanics & Physics. John, C., tr. from Fr. (Die Grundlehren der Mathematischen Wissenschaften: Vol. 219). (Illus.). 400p. 1975. 53.60 (ISBN 0-387-07327-2). Springer-Verlag.

Dym, C. L. Stability Theory & Its Applications to Structural Mechanics. (Mechanics of Elastic Stability Ser.: No. 3). 200p. 1974. 22.50x (ISBN 90-286-0094-9). Sijthoff & Noordhoff.

Enciclopedia de la Tecnica y de la Mecanica, 8 vols. 5th ed. 2920p. (Espn.). 1975. Set. 360.00 (ISBN 84-278-0072-X, S-14237). French & Eur.

Fetter, Alexander L. & Walecka, J. Dirk. Theoretical Mechanics of Particles & Continua. (Illus.). 1980. text ed. 23.00 (ISBN 0-07-020658-9). McGraw.

Finkelstein, Robert J. Nonrelativistic Mechanics. (Modern Physics Monographs: No. 2). (Illus.). 394p. 1973. pap. text ed. 11.50 (ISBN 0-8053-2552-2, Adv Bk Prog). Benjamin-Cummings.

French, Anthony P. Newtonian Mechanics. (M.I.T. Introductory Physics Ser). (Illus.). 1971. pap. text ed. 12.95x (ISBN 0-393-09970-9). Norton.

Galilei, Galileo. Dialogues Concerning Two New Sciences. (Illus.). 1914. pap. text ed. 4.00 (ISBN 0-486-60099-8). Dover.

Generator-Motor: Physical Fundamentals & Basic Mechanical Forms. (Siemens Programmed Instruction "pi" Self-Study Bks.: No. 7). 1978. 2.90 (ISBN 0-85501-507-1). Heyden.

Geradin, M. B. M. Fraeijs De Veubeke Memorial Volume of Selected Papers. 791p. 1980. 57.50x (ISBN 90-286-0900-8). Sijthoff & Noordhoff.

Ghista, D. N., ed. Applied Physiological Mechanics. (Biomedical Engineering & Computation Ser.: Vol. 1). 936p. 1980. text ed. 129.25 (ISBN 3-7186-0013-7). Harwood Academic.

Goldstein, Herbert. Classical Mechanics. 2nd ed. LC 79-23456. (Illus.). 1980. text ed. 25.95 (ISBN 0-201-02918-9). A-W.

Gudehus, G. Finite Elements in Geomechanics. LC 77-792. (Wiley Series in Numerical Methods of Engineering). 464p. 1977. 78.75x (ISBN 0-471-99446-4, Pub. by Wiley-Interscience). Wiley.

Hamel, Georg. Elementare Mechanik. 2nd ed. (Illus.). 1912. 31.00 (ISBN 0-384-21140-2). Johnson Repr.

Hamlyn, W. T. Elementary Mechanics to Structure Design in Steel. pap. 6.00 (ISBN 0-89741-003-3). Roadrunner Tech.

Hannah, John & Stephens, R. C. Mechanics of Machines: Advanced Theory & Examples. 2nd ed. (Illus.). 456p. 1972. pap. 18.95x (ISBN 0-7131-3254-X). Intl Ideas.

Harr, Milton E. Mechanics of Particulate Media: A Probabilistic Approach. (Illus.). 1977. text ed. 24.50x (ISBN 0-07-026695-6, C); solutions manual 8.95 (ISBN 0-07-026696-4). McGraw.

Herman, George, ed. R. D. Mindlin & Applied Mechanics: A Collection of Studies in the Development of Applied Mechanics Dedicated to Prof. R. D. Mindlin by His Former Students. LC 73-22346. 1974. text ed. 46.00 (ISBN 0-08-017710-7). Pergamon.

Higdon, Archie, et al. Mechanics of Materials. 3rd ed. LC 75-28453. 1976. text ed. 28.95x (ISBN 0-471-38812-2); instr's manual avail. (ISBN 0-471-01679-9). Wiley.

Huggins, Elisha. Graphical Mechanics: Computer & Laboratory Assisted Introduction to Mechanics. (gr. 11-12). 1979. pap. text ed. 7.50x (ISBN 0-933694-02-4). COMPress.

Hunt, K. H. Kinematic Geometry of Mechanisms. (Engineering Science Ser.). (Illus.). 1979. 89.00x (ISBN 0-19-856124-5). Oxford U Pr.

Hunter, S. C. Mechanics of Continuous Media. LC 76-7923. (Mathematics & Its Applications Ser.). 567p. 1977. text ed. 73.95 (ISBN 0-470-15092-0); pap. 26.95 (ISBN 0-470-27015-2). Halsted Pr.

Irodov, I. E. Fundamental Laws of Mechanics. 1980. pap. 5.00 (ISBN 0-8285-1803-3, Pub. by Mir Pubs Russia). Imported Pubns.

IUTAM International Congress, 14th. Theoretical & Applied Mechanics: Proceedings. Koiter, W. T., ed. 1977. 58.75 (ISBN 0-7204-0549-1, North-Holland). Elsevier.

Ivey, D. G. & Hume, J. N. P. Physics: Classical Mechanics & Introductory Statistical Mechanics, Vol. 1. 1974. 28.50x (ISBN 0-471-06756-3). Wiley.

Japan National Committee for Theoretical & Applied Mechanics Science Council of Japan. Theoretical & Applied Mechanics, Vol. 26. 1978. 79.50x (ISBN 0-86008-200-8, Pub. by U of Tokyo Pr). Intl Schol Bk Serv.

Japan National Congress for Applied Mechanics, 23rd, 1973. Theoretical & Applied Mechanics, Vol. 23: Proceedings. Okumura, Toshie, ed. 510p. 1975. 47.50x (ISBN 0-86008-138-9, Pub. by U of Tokyo Pr). Intl Schol Bk Serv.

Japan National Congress for Applied Mechanics,1975. Theoretical & Applied Mechanics, Vol. 24: Proceedings. Tanaka, Hisashi, ed. (Theoretical & Applied Mechanics Ser.). 1976. 69.50x (ISBN 0-86008-158-3, Pub. by U of Tokyo Pr). Intl Schol Bk Serv.

Jensen, C. H. & Mason, F. H. Fundamentos De Dibujo Mecanico. 1970. text ed. 9.95 (ISBN 0-07-091605-5, G). McGraw.

Jouguet, E. Lectures De Mecanique, 2 vols. in 1. 1908-1909. 31.00 (ISBN 0-384-27940-6). Johnson Repr.

Kardestuncer, H. Discrete Mechanics: A Unified Approach. (International Centre for Mechanical Sciences Courses & Lectures: No. 221). (Illus.). 1976. soft cover 6.60 (ISBN 0-387-81379-9). Springer-Verlag.

Kerrod, Robin. The Way It Works. (Illus.). 224p. (Orig.). Date not set. 16.95 (ISBN 0-7064-1307-5, Pub. by Mayflower Bks); pap. 9.95 (ISBN 0-686-31072-1). Smith Pubs.

Kibble, T. W. Classical Mechanics. 2nd ed. LC 73-8910. 254p. 1973. text ed. 21.95 (ISBN 0-470-47395-9). Halsted Pr.

Kleppner, Daniel & Kolenkow, Robert J. An Introduction to Mechanics. (Illus.). 736p. 1973. text ed. 21.95 (ISBN 0-07-035048-5, C); solutions manual 4.95 (ISBN 0-07-035049-3). McGraw.

Knops, R. J., ed. Trends in Applications of Pure Mathematics to Mechanics, Vol. III. (Monographs & Studies: No. 11). 256p. 1981. text ed. 68.00 (ISBN 0-686-31381-X). Pitman Pub MA.

Kotkin, G. I. & Serbo, V. G. Collection of Problems in Classical Mechanics. 1971. 18.00 (ISBN 0-08-015843-9). Pergamon.

Krar, S. F., et al. Entrenamiento En el Taller Mecanico. 1974. 9.95 (ISBN 0-07-091612-8, G). McGraw.

LaGrange, Joseph-Louis. Mecanique Analytique. Repr. of 1788 ed. 140.00 (ISBN 0-8287-0486-4). Clearwater Pub.

Levinson, L. Fundamentals of Engineering Mechanics. (Russian Monographs & Texts on the Physical Sciences Ser). 1965. 63.75x (ISBN 0-677-20250-4). Gordon.

McDonagh, Ian. Mechanical Science for Technicians. (Illus.). 121p. 1979. pap. 11.95x (ISBN 0-7131-3411-9). Intl Ideas.

McKenzie, Arthur E. Physics. 4th ed. 1970. 17.95x (ISBN 0-521-07698-6). Cambridge U Pr.

MacKinnon, L. Mechanics & Motion. (Oxford Physics Ser.). (Illus.). 1978. 23.50x (ISBN 0-19-851825-0); pap. 9.95x (ISBN 0-19-851843-9). Oxford U Pr.

Maleh, Issac. Mechanics, Heat, & Sound. (Merrill Physical Science Library). pap. text ed. 3.75x (ISBN 0-675-09638-3). Merrill.

Mathur, D. S. Mechanics. 1978. 20.00 (ISBN 0-7069-0623-3, Pub. by Vikas India). Advent NY.

Midwestern Mechanics Conference, 12th. Developments in Mechanics: Proceedings, Vol. 6. Lee, L. H., et al, eds. 1971. 24.00x (ISBN 0-268-00455-2). U of Notre Dame Pr.

Millikan, Robert, et al. Mechanics, Molecular Physics, Heat, & Sound. (Illus.). 1965. pap. 4.95x (ISBN 0-262-63001-X). MIT Pr.

Movnin, M. Theoretical Mechanics. 324p. 1970. 4.80 (ISBN 0-8285-0805-4, Pub. by Mir Pubs Russia). Imported Pubns.

Nara, Harry R. Vector Mechanics for Engineers. LC 77-10175. 910p. 1977. Repr. lib. bdg. 27.50 (ISBN 0-88275-606-0). Krieger.

Nemat-Nasser, S. Mechanics Today, Vol. 5. (Mechanics Today Ser.). (Illus.). 500p. 1980. 68.00 (ISBN 0-08-024249-9). Pergamon.

Nemat-Nasser, S., ed. Mechanics Today, Vols. 1-3. Incl. Vol. 1. 1973. text ed. 36.00 (ISBN 0-08-017246-6); Vol. 2. 1976. text ed. 37.00 (ISBN 0-08-018113-9); Vol. 3. 1976. text ed. 37.00 (ISBN 0-08-019882-1); Vol. 4. 1978. text ed. 55.00 (ISBN 0-08-021792-3). Vols. 1-4. text ed. 121.00 (ISBN 0-08-022682-5). Pergamon.

--Mechanics Today, Vol. 6. LC 80-41699. (Illus.). 225p. 1981. prepub. 40.00 (ISBN 0-08-024749-0); pap. 40.00 (ISBN 0-686-77713-1). Pergamon.

Noll, W. The Foundations of Mechanics & Thermodynamics: Selected Papers. LC 74-1651. 340p. 1974. 30.70 (ISBN 0-387-06646-2). Springer-Verlag.

Norwood, Joseph, Jr. Intermediate Classical Mechanics. (Illus.). 1979. ref. 26.95 (ISBN 0-13-469635-2). P-H.

Oden, J. T. & Reddy, J. N. Variational Methods in Theoretical Mechanics. (Universitext Ser.). 310p. 1976. pap. 19.70 (ISBN 0-387-07600-X). Springer-Verlag.

Olsen, G. Elements of Mechanics of Materials. 4th ed. 1982. 24.95 (ISBN 0-13-267013-5). P-H.

Onicescu, O. Invariantive Mechanics. (International Centre for Mechanical Science Courses & Lectures Ser.: No. 218). 1975. soft cover 17.20 (ISBN 0-387-81349-7). Springer-Verlag.

Pashupati Singh & Prem Kumar Jha. Elementary Mechanics of Solids. 632p. 1981. 19.95 (ISBN 0-470-27149-3). Halsted Pr.

Perrone, Nicholas, et al, eds. Fracture Mechanics. LC 78-16063. 1978. 25.00x (ISBN 0-8139-0802-7). U Pr of Va.

Pilkey, Walter D. & Pilkey, Orrin H. Mechanics of Solids. (QPI Ser.). 1974. pap. 7.95 (ISBN 0-934644-11-X). Quantum Pubs.

Pletta, D. H. & Frederick, D. Engineering Mechanics: Statics & Dynamics. (Illus.). 1969. 28.95 (ISBN 0-8260-7190-2). Wiley.

Plumpton, C. & Tomkys, W. H. Theoretical Mechanics in SI Units: In SI Units, Vols. 1-2. 2nd ed. 1972. Vol. 1. pap. 9.25 (ISBN 0-08-016268-1); Vol. 2. pap. 11.25 (ISBN 0-08-016591-5). Pergamon.

Powerplant Mechanics' Manual. 2nd rev. & exp. ed. LC 74-84721. (Illus.). 1980. soft bdg. 17.95 (ISBN 0-87219-021-8). Pan Am Nav.

Proceedings: Symposium on Incremental Motion & Control Systems & Devices, 9th Annual. LC 73-647018. (Illus.). 1980. 41.50 (ISBN 0-931538-02-5). Incremental Motion.

Rabotnov, Yu. Elements of Hereditary Solid Mechanics. 387p. 1980. 9.50 (ISBN 0-8285-1537-9, Pub. by Mir Pubs Russia). Imported Pubns.

Research & Education Association Staff. The Mechanics Problem Solver: A Supplement to Any Class Text. LC 79-92403. (Illus.). 1088p. 1980. pap. text ed. 22.85x (ISBN 0-87891-519-2). Res & Educ.

Roberval, Gilles. Traite De Mecanique Des Poids Soutenus Par Des Puissances Sur les Plans Inclines. Repr. of 1636 ed. 20.00 (ISBN 0-8287-0736-7). Clearwater Pub.

Rudman, Jack. Assistant Supervisor of Mechanical Installations. (Career Examination Ser.: C1117). (Cloth bdg. avail. on request). pap. 10.00 (ISBN 0-8373-1117-9). Natl Learning.

--Mechanical Maintainer - Group A. (Career Examination Ser.: C-483). (Cloth bdg. avail. on request). pap. 8.00 (ISBN 0-8373-0483-0). Natl Learning.

--Mechanical Maintainer - Group B. (Career Examination Ser.: C-484). (Cloth bdg. avail. on request). pap. 8.00 (ISBN 0-8373-0484-9). Natl Learning.

--Mechanical Maintainer - Group C. (Career Examination Ser.: C-485). (Cloth bdg. avail. on request). pap. 8.00 (ISBN 0-8373-0485-7). Natl Learning.

--Mechanical Technology. (Occupational Competency Examination Ser.: OCE-25). (Cloth bdg. avail. on request). pap. 9.95 (ISBN 0-8373-5725-X). Natl Learning.

Santilli, R. M. Foundations of Theoretical Mechanics Part I: The Inverse Problem in Newtonian Mechanics. LC 78-9735. (Texts & Monographs in Physics). 1979. 34.30 (ISBN 0-387-08874-1). Springer-Verlag.

Sears, Francis W. Mechanics, Heat, & Sound. 2nd ed. (Illus.). 1950. 17.95 (ISBN 0-201-06905-9). A-W.

--Mechanics, Wave Motion & Heat. 1958. 15.95 (ISBN 0-201-06910-5). A-W.

Shawki, G. S. A. & Metwalli, S. M., eds. Current Advances in Mechanical Design & Production: Proceedings of the First International Conference, Cairo University, 27-29 December 1979. LC 80-41666. (Illus.). 500p. 1981. 75.00 (ISBN 0-08-027294-0). Pergamon.

Singer, Ferdinand L. Mecanica Para Ingenieros, Tomo Primero: Estatica. 1976. text ed. 11.00x (ISBN 0-06-316997-5, IntlDept). Har-Row.

Sloane, A. Mechanics of Materials. (Illus.). 8.75 (ISBN 0-8446-2954-5). Peter Smith.

Smith, Charles E. Applied Mechanics: Vol. I, Statics. 2nd ed. LC 81-4232. 320p. 1982. text ed. 19.95 (ISBN 0-471-02965-3). Wiley.

Strelkov, S. Mechanics. 560p. 1978. 12.50 (ISBN 0-8285-0791-0, Pub. by Mir Pubs Russia). Imported Pubns.

Symon, Keith R. Mechanics. 3rd ed. LC 75-128910. (Physics & Physical Science Ser). 1971. text ed. 24.95 (ISBN 0-201-07392-7). A-W.

Szabo, Istvan. Geschichte der Mechanischen Prinzipien: Und Ihre Wichtigsten Anwendungen. (Wissenschaft und Kultur: Band 32). (Illus.). 543p. (Ger.). 1979. 37.50 (ISBN 3-7643-1063-4). Birkhauser.

Targ, S. Curso Breve De Mecanica Teorica. 516p. (Span.). 1980. 9.00 (ISBN 0-8285-1346-5, Pub. by Mir Pubs Russia). Imported Pubns.

Targ, S. M. Theoretical Mechanics. (Russian Monographs). (Illus.). 1967. 57.75 (ISBN 0-677-20370-5). Gordon.

Tauchert, Theodore R. Energy Principles in Structural Mechanics. 394p. 1981. Repr. of 1974 ed. lib. bdg. write for info. (ISBN 0-89874-309-5). Krieger.

Taylor, Thomas T. Mechanics: Classical & Quantum. 1976. text ed. 42.00 (ISBN 0-08-018063-9); pap. text ed. 26.00 (ISBN 0-08-020522-4). Pergamon.

Ter Haar, D. Elements of Hamiltonian Mechanics. 2nd ed. 1971. 15.00 (ISBN 0-08-016726-8). Pergamon.

Townsend, A. A. The Structure of Turbulent Shear Flow. 2nd ed. LC 79-8526. (Cambridge Monographs on Mechanics & Applied Mathematics). (Illus.). 441p. 1980. pap. 19.95x (ISBN 0-521-29819-9). Cambridge U Pr.

Truesdell, C. A. Six Lectures on Modern Natural Philosophy. (Illus.). 1966. 11.80 (ISBN 0-387-03684-9). Springer-Verlag.

Truesdell, C. A., ed. Encyclopedia of Physics, 54 vols, Vol. 6a, Pt. 4. (Illus.). 430p. 1974. 109.20 (ISBN 0-387-06097-9). Springer-Verlag.

Vaughan, J., et al, eds. Mechanical Maintenance (and Installation) II, 2 vols. (Engineering Craftsmen Ser.: No. J21). (Illus.). 342p. 1970. Set. 28.95x (ISBN 0-85083-080-X). Intl Ideas.

Wang. Mathematical Principles in Mechanics & Electromagnetism, Pts A & B. Incl. Analytical & Continuum Mechanics; Electromagnetism & Gravitation (ISBN 0-306-40212-2). (Mathematical Concepts & Methods in Science & Engineering: Vol. 16). (Illus.). 1979. 29.50 ea. (Plenum Pr). 55.00 set (ISBN 0-686-52342-3). Plenum Pub.

Weiss, H. J., et al, eds. Developments in Mechanics, Vol. 5. LC 70-88000. (Illus.). 1969. 22.50x (ISBN 0-8138-1115-5). Iowa St U Pr.

Wicks, Harry, ed. Popular Mechanics Five Hundred Home & Shop Tips. (Illus.). 160p. 1981. pap. 12.95 (ISBN 0-910990-79-4). Hearst Bks.

Yamamoto, Toshiyuki, ed. Theoretical & Applied Mechanics, Vol. 27. 1979. 79.50 (ISBN 0-86008-245-8, Pub. by U of Tokyo Pr). Intl Schol Bk Serv.

Young, Donald F., et al. Essentials of Mechanics. (Illus.). 576p. 1974. text ed. 9.25 (ISBN 0-8138-1110-4). Iowa St U Pr.

Young, Hugh D. Fundamentals of Mechanics & Heat. 2nd ed. (Fundamentals of Physics Ser). (Illus.). 736p. 1973. text ed. 19.95 (ISBN 0-07-072638-8, C); instructo's manual 2.50 (ISBN 0-07-072639-6). McGraw.

--Fundamentals of Mechanics & Heat. 2nd ed. (Fundamentals of Physics Ser). (Illus.). 736p. 1973. text ed. 19.95 (ISBN 0-07-072638-8, C); instructo's manual 2.50 (ISBN 0-07-072639-6). McGraw.

Ziegler, H. Mechanics, Vols. 1 & 2. 1965. text ed. 12.00 ea. (Adv Bk Prog). Vol. 1 (ISBN 0-201-09000-7). Vol. 2 (ISBN 0-201-09001-5). A-W.

Zita, K. Lexikon der Schulphysik: Mechanik und Akustik, Vol. 1. (Ger.). 44.00 (ISBN 3-7614-0107-8, M-7222). French & Eur.

Zorski, H., ed. Trends in Applications of Pure Mathematics to Mechanics, Vol. II. new ed. (Monographs & Studies in Mathematics: No. 5). (Illus.). 1979. cancelled (ISBN 0-8224-8421-8). Pitman Learning.

MECHANICS–EARLY WORKS TO 1800

Clarke, John. Demonstration of Some of the Principal Sections of Sir Isaac Newton's Principles of Natural Philosophy. 1972. Repr. of 1730 ed. 23.00 (ISBN 0-384-09226-8). Johnson Repr.

Drake, Stillman & Drabkin, I. E., trs. Mechanics in Sixteenth-Century Italy: Selections from Tartaglia, Benedetti, Guido Ubaldo, & Galileo. (Medieval Science Pubns., No. 13). (Illus.). 442p. 1969. 25.00 (ISBN 0-299-05100-5). U of Wis Pr.

Gillispie, Charles C. Lazare Carnot Savant. LC 78-132238. 1971. 32.50x (ISBN 0-691-08082-8). Princeton U Pr.

Maclaurin, Colin. Account of Sir Isaac Newton's Philosophical Discoveries. 1968. Repr. of 1748 ed. 27.00 (ISBN 0-384-34900-5). Johnson Repr.

Newton, Isaac. Mathematical Principles of Natural Philosophy. LC 64-13310. 1964. 10.00 (ISBN 0-8022-1211-5). Philos Lib.

--Sir Isaac Newton's Mathematical Principles of Natural Philosophy & His System of the World. Motte, Andrew, tr. 1962. lib. bdg. 26.00x (ISBN 0-8371-2508-1, NEMP). Greenwood.

MECHANICS–ELECTRIC ANALOGIES

see Electromechanical Analogies

MECHANICS–HISTORY

Drachmann, A. G. The Mechanical Technology of Greek & Roman Antiquity. (Illus.). 1963. 7.50 (ISBN 0-934454-61-2). Lubrecht & Cramer.

Drake, Stillman & Drabkin, I. E., trs. Mechanics in Sixteenth-Century Italy: Selections from Tartaglia, Benedetti, Guido Ubaldo, & Galileo. (Medieval Science Pubns., No. 13). (Illus.). 442p. 1969. 25.00 (ISBN 0-299-05100-5). U of Wis Pr.

Hill, D. R. Al-Jazari: The Book of Knowledge of Ingenious Mechanical Devices. limited ed. LC 72-92529. 286p. 1974. 126.00 (ISBN 90-277-0329-9, Pub. by Reidel Holland). Kluwer Boston.

Mach, Ernst. The Science of Mechanics. McCormack, T. J., tr. from Ger. (Illus.). 634p. 1960. pap. 9.75 (ISBN 0-87548-202-3). Open Court.

Truesdell, C. A. Essays in the History of Mechanics. LC 68-17860. (Illus.). 1968. 44.30 (ISBN 0-387-04367-5). Springer-Verlag.

MECHANICS–JUVENILE LITERATURE

Cutts, David R. That's How It Works. 1978. 4.50 (ISBN 0-533-03127-3). Vantage.

Liebers, Arthur. You Can Be a Mechanic. LC 74-1398. (Illus.). 128p. (gr. 6 up). 1975. PLB 6.48 (ISBN 0-688-51700-5). Lothrop.

Pollard, Michael. How Things Work. LC 78-54638. (Illus.). (gr. 5-7). 1979. 8.95 (ISBN 0-88332-097-5, 8129). Larousse.

MECHANICS–PROBLEMS, EXERCISES, ETC.

Federal Aviation Administration. A&P Mechanics Powerplant Written Examination Questions. (Aviation Maintenance Training Course Ser.). (Illus.). 99p. 1979. pap. 3.75 (ISBN 0-89100-159-X, EA-AC65-22). Aviation Maintenance.

Habibi, Mohamad & Warisila, Robert. Mechanics: A Laboratory Manual. 2nd ed. (Illus.). 160p. 1980. pap. text ed. 8.50 (ISBN 0-89529-043-X). Avery Pub.

Saraf, B., ed. Physics Through Experiment: Mechanical Systems, Vol. II. 1980. text ed. 17.50x (ISBN 0-7069-0771-X, Pub. by Vikas India). Advent NY.

MECHANICS–TABLES, ETC.

Wolfe, John H. & Phelps, E. R. Mechanics' Vest Pocket Reference Book. 1945. 6.95 (ISBN 0-13-572024-9). P-H.

MECHANICS (PERSONS)

see also Automobile Mechanics; Aviation Mechanics (Persons)

Alpers, Byron J. & Afrow, Mitchell L. Metal & Machines. (Shoptalk - Vocational Reading Skills). (gr. 9-12). 1978. pap. text ed. 5.12 (ISBN 0-205-05823-X, 4958233); tchr's guide 5.40 (ISBN 0-205-05824-8, 4958241). Allyn.

Bernard, John. Every Man His Own Mechanic. 14.50x (ISBN 0-392-05395-0, LTB). Sportshelf.

Davis, Belfield & Everest. Spon's Mechanical & Electrical Services Price Book (Annual) 1981. 39.95x (ISBN 0-686-77447-7, Pub. by E & FN Spon). Methuen Inc.

Rudman, Jack. Foreman of Mechanics. (Career Examination Ser.: C-1605). (Cloth bdg. avail. on request). 1977. pap. 8.00 (ISBN 0-8373-1605-7). Natl Learning.

--Maintenance Mechanic (Automated Mail Processing Equipment) (A.M.P.E) (U.S.P.S.) (Career Examination Ser.: C-1606). (Cloth bdg. avail. on request). 1977. pap. 10.00 (ISBN 0-8373-1606-5). Natl Learning.

--Toll Equipment Mechanic. (Career Examination Ser.: C-2546). (Cloth bdg. avail. on request). pap. 10.00 (ISBN 0-8373-2546-3). Natl Learning.

MECHANICS, ANALYTIC

see also Continuum Mechanics; Dynamics; Elasticity; Hydrodynamics; Hydrostatics; Kinematics; Problem of Many Bodies; Statics; Statistical Mechanics

Abraham, Ralph & Marsden, Jerrold E. Foundations of Mechanics: A Mathematical Exposition of Classical Mechanics with an Introduction to the Qualitative Theory of Dynamical Systems & Applications to the Three-Body Problem. 2nd rev. & enl. ed. 1978. 46.50 (ISBN 0-8053-0102-X, Adv Bk Prog). Benjamin-Cummings.

Atteia, M., et al. Nonlinear Problems of Analysis in Geometry & Mechanics. (Research Notes in Mathematics: No. 46). 203p. (Orig.). 1981. pap. text ed. 21.95 (ISBN 0-273-08493-3). Pitman Pub MA.

Avery, H. E. Basic Reaction Kinetics & Mechanisms. 1974. pap. 11.50x (ISBN 0-8448-0897-0). Crane Russak Co.

Bernasconi, C. F. Relaxation Kinetics. 1976. 49.00 (ISBN 0-12-092950-3). Acad Pr.

Bleustein, Jeffrey L., ed. Mechanics & Sport AMD, Vol. 4. 318p. 1973. pap. text ed. 25.00 (ISBN 0-685-41497-3, H00007). ASME.

Cayley, Arthur. Collected Mathematical Papers, Vols. 1-13. 1889-1897. with index 554.50 (ISBN 0-384-07970-9); 42.50 ea.; Vol. suppl. 23.00 (ISBN 0-685-13389-3). Johnson Repr.

Cheng, D. G. Analysis of Linear Systems. 1959. 22.95 (ISBN 0-201-01020-8). A-W.

Dahl, W. & Lange, K. W., eds. Kinetics of Metallurgical Processes in Steelmaking: Proceedings. (Illus.). x, 584p. 1975. 100.30 (ISBN 0-387-07366-3). Springer-Verlag.

Developments in Theoretical & Applied Mechanics, Vols. 2-4. Vol. 3. 1968. 82.00 (ISBN 0-08-012211-6); Vol. 4, 1970. 75.00 (ISBN 0-08-006513-9). Pergamon.

Developments in Theoretical & Applied Mechanics: Proceedings. 1963. 52.50 (ISBN 0-306-30162-8, Plenum Pr). Plenum Pub.

Duhamel, Jean M. Lehrbuch der Analytischen Mechanik. Schloemilch, O., ed. (Bibliotheca Mathematica Teubneriana Ser: No. 37). (Ger). 1969. Repr. of 1861 ed. 46.00 (ISBN 0-384-13230-8). Johnson Repr.

Fowles, Grant. Analytical Mechanics. 3rd ed. LC 76-57839. 1977. text ed. 25.95 (ISBN 0-03-089725-4, HoltC). HR&W.

Fung, Y. C. Foundations of Solid Mechanics. 1965. ref. ed. 26.95 (ISBN 0-13-329912-0). P-H.

Gantmacher, F. Lectures in Analytical Mechanics. 264p. 1975. 5.40 (ISBN 0-8285-0790-2, Pub. by Mir Pubs Russia). Imported Pubns.

--Lectures in Analytical Mechanics. (Illus.). 286p. 1975. text ed. 15.00x (ISBN 0-8464-0551-2). Beekman Pubs.

Gantmacher, Felix R. Lectures on Analytical Mechanics. 2nd ed. write for info. (ISBN 0-685-07981-3). Chelsea Pub.

Hauser, Walter. Introduction to the Principles of Mechanics. 1965. 20.95 (ISBN 0-201-02806-9). A-W.

Lawden, D. F. Analytical Mechanics. (Problem Solvers). (Illus.). 1972. text ed. 9.50x (ISBN 0-04-531004-1); pap. text ed. 3.95x (ISBN 0-04-531005-X). Allen Unwin.

Moigno, F. Lecons De Mecanique Analytique. Repr. of 1868 ed. 42.50 (ISBN 0-384-39500-7). Johnson Repr.

Spiegel, Murray R. Theoretical Mechanics. (Schaum's Outline Ser). 1967. pap. 6.95 (ISBN 0-07-060232-8, SP). McGraw.

MECHANICS, APPLIED

see also Engineering Models; Mechanical Engineering

Aguilar, Rodolfo J. Systems Analysis & Design in Engineering, Architecture, Construction, & Planning. (Civil Engineering & Engineering Mechanics Ser). (Illus.). 448p. 1973. ref. ed. 25.95 (ISBN 0-13-881458-9). P-H.

Aseltine, J. A. Transform Method in Linear System Analysis. (Electrical & Electronic Eng. Ser). 1958. 24.50 (ISBN 0-07-002389-1, C). McGraw.

Beer, Ferdinand P. & Johnston, E. R. Vector Mechanics for Engineers: Statics. 3rd ed. 1977. text ed. 18.50 (ISBN 0-07-004278-0, C); instructor's manual 6.95 (ISBN 0-07-004279-9). McGraw.

Beer, Ferdinand P. & Johnston, E. R., Jr. Vector Mechanics for Engineers Combined. 3rd ed. 1977. text ed. 28.50 (ISBN 0-07-004277-2, C). McGraw.

Benham, P. P. Elementary Mechanics of Solids. (Illus.). 1965. 19.50 (ISBN 0-08-011216-1). Pergamon.

Bert, C. W., ed. Mechanics of Bimodulus Materials, Bk. No. G00150. LC 90-75422. (Applied Mechanics Division Ser.: Vol. 33). 96p. 1979. 18.00 (ISBN 0-686-62957-4). ASME.

Bradbury, Ted C. Theoretical Mechanics. 656p. 1981. Repr. of 1968 ed. text ed. write for info. (ISBN 0-89874-235-8). Krieger.

Broersma, G. Applied Mechanics of Machine Elements in Advanced Use. 182p. 1967. 50.00x (ISBN 0-85950-040-3, Pub. by Stam Pr England). State Mutual Bk.

Brown, G. Wayne. Applied Mechanics. LC 70-145957. 1971. text ed. 18.95 (ISBN 0-13-041301-1). P-H.

Bruch, Charles D. Mechanics for Technology. LC 75-31719. 400p. 1976. text ed. 22.95 (ISBN 0-471-11369-7). Wiley.

Chia-Shun, Yih, ed. Advances in Applied Mechanics, Vol. 22. (Serial Publication). 1981. price not set (ISBN 0-12-002022-X); price not set lib. ed. (ISBN 0-12-002055-6); price not set microfiche (ISBN 0-12-002056-4). Acad Pr.

Chia-Shun Yih, ed. Advances in Applied Mechanics, Vol. 19. LC 48-8503. 1979. 43.50 (ISBN 0-12-002019-X); lib ed. 52.00 (ISBN 0-12-002049-1); microfiche 28.00 (ISBN 0-12-002050-5). Acad Pr.

Chia Shun Yih, ed. Advances in Applied Mechanics, Vol. 21. (Serial Publication). 1981. price not set (ISBN 0-12-002021-1); price not set library ed. (ISBN 0-12-002053-X); price not set microfiche (ISBN 0-12-002054-8). Acad Pr.

Crandall, Stephen H., et al. An Introduction to the Mechanics of Solids. 3rd ed. (Illus.). 1978. text ed. 22.95 (ISBN 0-07-013441-3, C); solution manual 1.95 (ISBN 0-07-013442-1). McGraw.

Den Hartog, Jacob P. Mechanical Vibrations. 4th ed. 1956. text ed. 25.95 (ISBN 0-07-016389-8). McGraw.

Developments in Theoretical & Applied Mechanics. 519p. 1963. 52.50 (ISBN 0-306-30162-8, Plenum Pr). Plenum Pub.

Developments in Theoretical & Applied Mechanics, Vols. 2-4. Vol. 3. 1968. 82.00 (ISBN 0-08-012211-6); Vol. 4, 1970. 75.00 (ISBN 0-08-006513-9). Pergamon.

Developments in Theoretical & Applied Mechanics: Proceedings. 1963. 52.50 (ISBN 0-306-30162-8, Plenum Pr). Plenum Pub.

Dickenson, Harry & Kleinschmidt, Robert. Technical Mechanics. (Illus.). 736p. 1974. text ed. 17.95 (ISBN 0-07-016790-7, G); instructor's manual 1.95 (ISBN 0-07-016791-5). McGraw.

Edmunds, H. G. Mechanical Foundations of Engineering Science. 400p. 1981. 59.95 (ISBN 0-470-27253-8). Halsted Pr.

Eppler, R., ed. Laminar Turbulent Transitions. (International Union of Theoretical & Applied Mechanics). (Illus.). 432p. 1980. 43.70 (ISBN 0-387-10142-X). Springer-Verlag.

Francis, Philip H. & Lindholm, Ulric S. Advanced Experimental Techniques in the Mechanics of Materials. 1973. 83.75x (ISBN 0-677-12570-4). Gordon.

Geers, T. L. & Tong, P., eds. Survival of Mechanical Systems in Transient Environments, Bk. No. G00153. LC 79-954424. (Applied Mechanics Division Ser.: Vol. 36). 196p. 1979. 24.00 (ISBN 0-686-62963-9). ASME.

Ginsberg, Jerry H. & Genin, Joseph. Statics & Dynamics Combined Edition. LC 76-30664. 1016p. 1977. text ed. 31.95 (ISBN 0-471-01795-7). Wiley.

Ham, C. W., et al. Mechanics of Machinery. 4th ed. (Mechanical Engineering Ser.). 1958. text ed. 22.95 (ISBN 0-07-025688-5, C). McGraw.

Hartung, R. F., ed. Computing in Applied Mechanics AMD, Vol. 18. 179p. 1976. pap. text ed. 20.00 (ISBN 0-685-75515-0, I00108). ASME.

Heriman, J. L. ARA Engineering Mechanics, 2 vols. Incl. Vol. 1. SI Statics (ISBN 0-471-06312-6); Vol. 2. SI Dynamics (ISBN 0-471-06311-8). 1980. 18.95 ea. Wiley.

Herman, George, ed. R. D. Mindlin & Applied Mechanics: A Collection of Studies in the Development of Applied Mechanics Dedicated to Prof. R. D. Mindlin by His Former Students. LC 73-22346. 1974. text ed. 46.00 (ISBN 0-08-017710-7). Pergamon.

Higdon, A. & Stiles. Engineering Mechanics, 2 vols. 2nd ed. Incl. Vol. I. Statics (ISBN 0-13-279398-9); Vol. II. Dynamics (ISBN 0-13-279406-3). (Civil Engineering & Engineering Mechanic Ser.). (Illus.). 928p. 1976. 27.95x (ISBN 0-13-279380-6). P-H.

Higdon, A., et al. Engineering Mechanics. 3rd ed. Incl. Vol. 1. Statics. 21.95 (ISBN 0-13-279273-7); Vol. 2. Dynamics. 21.95 (ISBN 0-13-279281-8). 1968. 27.95 set (ISBN 0-13-279299-0). P-H.

Huang, T. C. Engineering Mechanics, 2 vols. Incl. Vol. 1. Statics (ISBN 0-201-03005-5); Vol. 2. Dynamics (ISBN 0-201-03006-3). 1967. 16.95 ea.; 24.95 set (ISBN 0-201-03007-1). A-W.

Hughes, T. J., ed. Finite Element Methods for Convection Dominated Flows, Bk. No. G00151. LC 90-75379. (Applied Mechanics Division Ser.: Vol. 34). 240p. 1979. 30.00 (ISBN 0-686-62956-6). ASME.

International Congress of Applied Mechanics, 12th, Stanford University, 1968. Proceedings. Hetenyi, M. & Vincenti, W. G., eds. (Illus.). 1969. 111.00 (ISBN 0-387-04420-5). Springer-Verlag.

International Congress of Applied Mechanics, 11th, Munich, 1964. Proceedings. Goertler, H., ed. (Eng, Fr, Ger & It.). 1966. 224.20 (ISBN 0-387-03462-5). Springer-Verlag.

International Congress of Applied Mechanics, 13th, Moscow. Proceedings. Becker, E. & Mikhailov, G. K., eds. LC 58-2749. (Illus.). 370p. 1974. 70.80 (ISBN 0-387-06244-0). Springer-Verlag.

IUTAM International Congress, 14th. Theoretical & Applied Mechanics: Proceedings. Koiter, W. T., ed. 1977. 58.75 (ISBN 0-7204-0549-1, North-Holland). Elsevier.

Japan National Committee for Theoretical & Applied Mechanics, ed. Theoretical & Applied Mechanics, Vol. 28. 579p. 1980. 89.50x (ISBN 0-86008-264-4, Pub. by Univ Tokyo Pr Japan). Intl Schol Bk Serv.

Japan National Committee for Theoretical & Applied Mechanics Science Council of Japan, ed. Theoretical & Applied Mechanics: Proceedings of the 21st Japan National Congress for Applied Mechanics 1971, Vol. 21. 528p. 1973. 47.50x (ISBN 0-86008-080-3, Pub. by U of Tokyo Pr). Intl Schol Bk Serv.

Japan National Congress for Applied Mechanics, 25th, 1975. Theoretical & Applied Mechanics, Vol. 25: Proceedings. (Illus.). 1977. 79.50x (ISBN 0-86008-181-8, Pub. by U of Tokyo Pr). Intl Schol Bk Serv.

Jensen, Alfred E. & Chenoweth, H. Applied Engineering Mechanics. 3rd ed. 1971. 16.95 (ISBN 0-07-032480-8, G); problem answers 1.50 (ISBN 0-07-032481-6). McGraw.

Juhasz, Stephen. The Applied Mechanics CumIndex, Vol. 14. 1979. 60.00 (ISBN 0-88274-013-X). R & D Pr.

Langhaar, Henry L. Energy Methods in Applied Mechanics. LC 62-10925. 350p. 1962. 30.95 (ISBN 0-471-51711-9, Pub. by Wiley-Interscience). Wiley.
Levinson, Irving J. Introduction to Mechanics. 2nd ed. 1968. text ed. 18.95 (ISBN 0-13-487660-1). P-H.
Levinson, L. Fundamentals of Engineering Mechanics. (Russian Monographs & Texts on the Physical Sciences Ser). 1965. 63.75x (ISBN 0-677-20250-4). Gordon.
Malvern, Lawrence E. Engineering Mechanics, 2 vols. Incl. Vol. 1. Statics. ref. ed. 19.95x (ISBN 0-13-278663-X); Vol. 2. Dynamics. ref. ed. 19.95x (ISBN 0-13-278671-0). (Illus.). 352p. 1976. P-H.
Meriam, J. L. Engineering Mechanics, 2 vols. Incl. Vol. 1. Statics: SI Version. text ed. 20.95 (ISBN 0-471-05558-1); Arabic ed. (ISBN 0-471-06312-6); Vol. 2. Dynamics: SI Version. text ed. 17.95 (ISBN 0-471-05559-X); Arabic ed. (ISBN 0-471-06311-8). LC 79-11173. 1980. Wiley.
--Engineering Mechanics, 2 vols. Incl. Vol. 1. Statics. text ed. 18.95x (ISBN 0-471-59460-1); Vol. 2. Dynamics. text ed. 20.95x (ISBN 0-471-59461-X). LC 77-24716. 1978. Wiley.
--Statics. 2nd ed. SI Version, ed. LC 74-11459. 381p. 1975. text ed. 21.95x (ISBN 0-471-59604-3). Wiley.
Meriam, James L. Statics. 2nd ed. LC 71-136719. (Illus.). 1971. text ed. 21.95x (ISBN 0-471-59595-0). Wiley.
Okumurs, Toshie, ed. Theoretical & Applied Mechanics, Vol. 22: Proceedings of the 22nd Japan National Congress for Applied Mechanics, 1972. 500p. 1974. 45.00x (ISBN 0-86008-117-6, Pub. by U of Tokyo Pr). Intl Schol Bk Serv.
Parker, Harry & Hauf, Harold D. Simplified Mechanics & Strength of Materials. 3rd ed. LC 76-56465. 304p. 1977. 25.50 (ISBN 0-471-66562-2, Pub. by Wiley-Interscience). Wiley.
Phelan, Richard M. Fundamentals of Mechanical Design. 3rd ed. LC 79-98487. 1970. text ed. 24.50 (ISBN 0-07-049776-1, C); solutions manual 2.50 (ISBN 0-07-049790-7). McGraw.
Pipes, L. A. & Harvill, L. R. Applied Mathematics for Engineers & Physicists. 3rd ed. 1970. text ed. 24.95 (ISBN 0-07-050060-6, C). McGraw.
Richards, T. H. Energy Methods in Stress Analysis: With an Introduction to Finite Element Techniques. (Ellis Horwood Series in Engineering Science). 1977. 58.95 (ISBN 0-470-98960-2). Halsted Pr.
Rossi, B. E., ed. Experimental Mechanics, Vol. 1: Proceedings, International Congress on Experimental Mechanics - 1st. 1963. 60.00 (ISBN 0-08-013346-0). Pergamon.
Schools Council-Project Technology. Project Technology Handbooks. Incl. Bk 1. Bernoulli's Principle & the Carburetor. pap. text ed. 1.50x (ISBN 0-435-75900-0); Bk 2. Simple Bridge Structures. pap. text ed. 8.50x (ISBN 0-435-75901-9); Bk 3. Simple Materials Testing Equipment. pap. text ed. 8.50x (ISBN 0-435-75902-7); Bk 4. Introducting Fluidics. pap. text ed. 1.50x (ISBN 0-435-75903-5); Bk 5. Engine Test Beds. pap. text ed. 1.50x (ISBN 0-435-75904-3); Bk 6. Gas-Fired Muffle Furnaces. pap. text ed. 1.50x (ISBN 0-435-75905-1); Bk 7. The Ship & Her Environment. pap. text ed. 2.00x (ISBN 0-435-75906-X); Bk 9. Simple Fluid Flow. pap. text ed. 5.00x (ISBN 0-435-75908-6); Bk 10. Industrial Archaeology for Schools. pap. text ed. 2.00x (ISBN 0-435-75909-4); Bk 11. Industrial Archaeology of Watermills & Waterpower. pap. text ed. 9.50x (ISBN 0-435-75910-8); Bk 12. Food Science & Technology. pap. text ed. 6.50x (ISBN 0-435-75911-6); Bk. 14. Simple Computer & Control Logic. pap. text ed. 12.50 (ISBN 0-435-75913-2). 1970. Heinemann Ed.
Seventh Proceedings U.S. National Congress of Applied Mechanics. 1974. 25.00 (ISBN 0-685-48055-0, G00085). ASME.
Shigley, Joseph E. Applied Mechanics of Materials. (Illus.). 1975. text ed. 23.95 (ISBN 0-07-056845-6); solutions manual 5.50 (ISBN 0-07-056846-4). McGraw.
Smith, Charles E. Applied Mechanics. Incl. Dynamics (ISBN 0-471-80178-X); Statics (ISBN 0-471-80460-6). 1976. text ed. 19.95x ea. Wiley.
Smith, M. E. & Martin, J. R., eds. Recommended Guide for the Prediction of the Dispersion of Airborne Effluents, Bk. No. H00037. 3rd ed. LC 90-75471. 87p. 1979. 10.00 (ISBN 0-686-62958-2). ASME.
Takami, Hideo. Theoretical & Applied Mechanics, Vol. 29. 500p. 1981. 89.50x (ISBN 0-86008-282-2, Pub. by U of Tokyo Japan). Columbia U Pr.
Targ, S. M. Theoretical Mechanics. (Russian Monographs). (Illus.). 1967. 57.75 (ISBN 0-677-20370-5). Gordon.
Von Mises, Richard & Von Karman, Theodore, eds. Advances in Applied Mechanics. Incl. Vol. 1. 1948. 50.50 (ISBN 0-12-002001-7); Vol. 2. 1951. 50.50 (ISBN 0-12-002002-5); Vol. 3. 1953. 50.50 (ISBN 0-12-002003-3); Vol. 4. Dryden, H. L., et al, eds. 1956. 50.50 (ISBN 0-12-002004-1); Vol. 5. 1958. 50.50 (ISBN 0-12-002005-X); Vol. 6. 1960. 50.50 (ISBN 0-12-002006-8); Vol. 7. 1962. 50.50 (ISBN 0-12-002007-6); Vol. 8. 1964. 50.50 (ISBN 0-12-002008-4); Vol. 9. Kuerti, G., ed. 1966. 50.50 (ISBN 0-12-002009-2); Vol. 10. Fascicle 1. 1967; Vol. 11. Chia-Sun Yih, ed. 1971. 50.50 (ISBN 0-12-002011-4); Vol. 12. 1972. 50.50 (ISBN 0-12-002012-2); Vol. 13. 1973. 50.50 (ISBN 0-12-002013-0); Vol. 16. Yih, Chia-Shun, ed. 1976. 55.50 (ISBN 0-12-002016-5); lib ed 76.00 (ISBN 0-12-002043-2); microfiche 342.50 (ISBN 0-686-66621-6); Vol. 17. Yih, Chia-Shun, ed. 1977. 59.00 (ISBN 0-12-002017-3); lib. ed 76.00 (ISBN 0-12-002045-9); microfiche 42.50 (ISBN 0-12-002046-7); Vol. 18. Yih, Chia-Shun, ed. 1979. 50.00 (ISBN 0-12-002018-1); lib. ed. 64.50 (ISBN 0-12-002047-5); 36.00 (ISBN 0-12-002048-3). LC 48-8503. Acad Pr.
--Advances in Applied Mechanics: Supplements. Incl. Suppl. 1. Rarefied Gas Dynamics: Proceedings. International Symposium on Rarefied Gas Dynamics - 2nd. Talbot, L., ed. 1961 (ISBN 0-12-002061-0); Suppl. 2. Rarefied Gas Dynamics: Proceedings. International Symposium on Rarefied Gas Dynamics - 3rd. Laurmann, John A., ed. 1963. Vol. 1-2. Vol. 1 (ISBN 0-12-002067-X). Vol. 2 (ISBN 0-12-002068-8); Suppl. 3. Rarefied Gas Dynamics: Proceedings. International Symposium on Rarefied Gas Dynamics - 4th. De Leeuw, J. H., ed. 1965-66. Vol. 1 (ISBN 0-12-002074-2). Vol. 2. 24.00 (ISBN 0-12-002075-0); Suppl. 4. Rarefied Gas Dynamics: Proceedings. International Symposium on Rarefied Gas Dynamics - 5th. Brundin, C. L., ed. 1967. Vol. 1-2. Vol. 1 (ISBN 0-12-002081-5). Vol. 2 (ISBN 0-12-002082-3); Suppl. 5. Rarefied Gas Dynamics: Proceedings. International Symposium on Rarefied Gas Dynamics - 6th. Trilling, L. & Wachman, H., eds. 1967-69. Vols. 1-2. Vol. 1 (ISBN 0-12-002085-8). Vol. 2 (ISBN 0-12-002086-6). Suppls. 1-5. 51.50 ea. Acad Pr.
Walker, Keith M. Applied Mechanics for Engineering Technology. 2nd ed. (Illus.). 1978. ref. 18.95 (ISBN 0-87909-025-1). Reston.
Yamamoto, Toshiyuki, ed. Theoretical & Applied Mechanics, Vol. 27. 1979. 79.50 (ISBN 0-86008-245-8, Pub. by U of Tokyo Pr). Intl Schol Bk Serv.
Yih, C. S., ed. Advances in Applied Mechanics, Vol. 20. (Serial Pub.). 1980. 31.50 (ISBN 0-12-002020-3); lib. ed. 42.00 (ISBN 0-12-002051-3); 22.00 (ISBN 0-12-002052-1). Acad Pr.
Yih, Chia-Shun, ed. Advances in Applied Mechanics, Vol. 14. (Serial Publication). 1974. 57.00 (ISBN 0-12-002014-9). Acad Pr.
--Advances in Applied Mechanics, Vol. 15. (Serial Publication). 1975. 55.00 (ISBN 0-12-002015-7); lib. ed. 70.50 (ISBN 0-12-002041-6); microfiche 40.00 (ISBN 0-12-002042-4). Acad Pr.
Young, Donald F. Introduction to Applied Mechanics: An Integrated Treatment for Students in Engineering, Life Science & Interdisciplinary Programs. LC 74-153162. (Illus.). 1972. 9.50x (ISBN 0-8138-1075-2). Iowa St U Pr.

MECHANICS, APPLIED–PROBLEMS, EXERCISES, ETC.

Beer, Ferdinand P. & Johnston, E. R. Vector Mechanics for Engineers: Statics. 3rd ed. 1977. text ed. 18.50 (ISBN 0-07-004278-0, C); instructor's manual 6.95 (ISBN 0-07-004279-9). McGraw.
Beer, Ferdinand P. & Johnston, E. R., Jr. Vector Mechanics for Engineers Combined. 3rd ed. 1977. text ed. 28.50 (ISBN 0-07-004277-2, C). McGraw.
Horton, Holbrook L. Mathematics at Work. 2nd ed. (Illus.). 728p. 1957. 16.00 (ISBN 0-8311-1047-3). Indus Pr.
Hunter, Thomas A. Engineering Mechanics. (Quality Paperback: No. 46). (Orig.). 1961. pap. 4.95 (ISBN 0-8226-0046-3). Littlefield.
Nara, Harry R. Vector Mechanics for Engineers. LC 77-10175. 910p. 1977. Repr. lib. bdg. 27.50 (ISBN 0-88275-606-0). Krieger.
Stoker, J. J. Nonlinear Vibrations in Mechanical & Electrical Systems Pure & Aplied Mechanics, Vol. 2. 294p. 1950. 35.50 (ISBN 0-470-82830-7). Wiley.

MECHANICS, CELESTIAL

see also Astrodynamics; Moon, Theory Of; Orbits; Perturbation (Astronomy); Planets, Theory Of; Problem of Many Bodies

Abraham, Ralph & Marsden, Jerrold E. Foundations of Mechanics: A Mathematical Exposition of Classical Mechanics with an Introduction to the Qualitative Theory of Dynamical Systems & Applications to the Three-Body Problem. 2nd rev. & enl. ed. 1978. 46.50 (ISBN 0-8053-0102-X, Adv Bk Prog). Benjamin-Cummings.
Aiton, E. J. The Vortex Theory of Planetary Motions. 1972. lib. bdg. 15.00 (ISBN 0-685-52456-6). N Watson.
Clagett, Marshall, tr. Nicole Oresme & the Medieval Geometry of Qualities & Motions. (Medieval Science Pubns., No. 12). (Illus.). 728p. 1968. 50.00x (ISBN 0-299-04880-2). U of Wis Pr.
Donahue, William H. & Cohen, I. Bernard, eds. The Dissolution of the Celestial Sphere. LC 80-2087. (Development of Science Ser.). (Illus.). 1981. lib. bdg. 28.00x (ISBN 0-405-13853-9). Arno.
Duncombe, Raynor L. & Szebehely, Victor G., eds. Methods in Astrodynamics & Celestial Mechanics. (Progress in Astronautics & Aeronautics: Vol. 17). 1966. 15.00 (ISBN 0-12-535117-8). Acad Pr.
Fitzpatrick, Philip M. Principles of Celestial Mechanics. 1970. text ed. 18.95 (ISBN 0-12-257950-X). Acad Pr.
Hagihara, Yusuke. Celestial Mechanics Vol. 1: Dynamical Principles & Transformation Theory. 1970. 40.00x (ISBN 0-262-08037-0). MIT Pr.
--Celestial Mechanics, Vol. 2: Perturbation Theory, 2 pts. 1972. 45.00x ea. Pt. 1 (ISBN 0-262-08048-6). Pt. 2 (ISBN 0-262-08053-2). MIT Pr.
Hill, R. Principles of Dynamics. 1964. 22.00 (ISBN 0-08-010571-8); pap. 9.75 (ISBN 0-08-013540-4). Pergamon.
Kopal, Zdenek. Figures of Equilibrium of Celestial Bodies: With Emphasis on Problems of Motion of Artificial Satellites. (Mathematics Research Center Pubns., No. 3). (Illus.). 142p. 1960. 17.50x (ISBN 0-299-02010-X). U of Wis Pr.
Kovalevsky, J. Introduction to Celestial Mechanics. (Astrophysics & Space Science Library: No.7). 126p. 1967. lib. bdg. 21.00 (ISBN 90-277-0126-1, Pub. by Reidel Holland). Kluwer Boston.
Laplace, Pierre S. Celestial Mechanics, Vols. 1-4. LC 69-11316. Set. text ed. 175.00 (ISBN 0-8284-0194-2). Chelsea Pub.
--Celestial Mechanics, Vol. 5. LC 63-11316. (Mecanique Celeste, Tome V, Fr). 1969. Repr. of 1832 ed. text ed. 20.00 (ISBN 0-8284-0214-0). Chelsea Pub.
Moser, Jurgen. Stable & Random Motions in Dynamical Systems: With Special Emphasis on Celestial Mechanics. LC 73-2481. (Annals of Mathematics Studies: No. 77). 1973. 14.00 (ISBN 0-691-08132-8). Princeton U Pr.
Newton, Isaac. Mathematical Principles of Natural Philosophy. LC 64-13310. 1964. 10.00 (ISBN 0-8022-1211-5). Philos Lib.
--Sir Isaac Newton's Mathematical Principles of Natural Philosophy & His System of the World. Motte, Andrew, tr. 1962. lib. bdg. 26.00x (ISBN 0-8371-2508-1, NEMP). Greenwood.
Opik, E. J. Interplanetary Encounters. (Developments in Solar Systems & Space Science: Vol. 2). 1976. 44.00 (ISBN 0-444-41371-5). Elsevier.
Orographic Effects in Planetary Flows. (GARP Publications Ser.: No. 23). 450p. 1980. pap. 40.00 (ISBN 0-686-71858-5, W470, WMO). Unipub.
Pollard, Harry. Celestial Mechanics. (Carus Monograph: No. 18). 1976. 12.50 (ISBN 0-88385-019-2). Math Assn.
Siegel, Carl L. & Moser, Juergen K. Lectures on Celestial Mechanics. rev. ed. Kalme, C. I., tr. from Ger. LC 71-155595. (Grundlehren der Mathematischen Wissenschaften: Vol. 187). 1971. 42.50 (ISBN 0-387-05419-7). Springer-Verlag.
--Lectures on Celestial Mechanics. rev. ed. Kalme, C. I., tr. from Ger. LC 71-155595. (Grundlehren der Mathematischen Wissenschaften: Vol. 187). 1971. 42.50 (ISBN 0-387-05419-7). Springer-Verlag.
Sternberg, Shlomo. Celestial Mechanics, Pt. 1. 1969. 17.50 (ISBN 0-8053-9100-2, Adv Bk Prog). Benjamin-Cummings.
--Celestial Mechanics: Pt. 2. 1969. 17.50 (ISBN 0-8053-9102-9, Adv Bk Prog). Benjamin-Cummings.
Stiefel, E. L. & Scheifele, G. Linear & Regular Celestial Mechanics: Perturbed Two-Body Motion, Numerical Methods, Canonical Theory. LC 72-133369. (Die Grundlehren der Mathematischen Wissenschaften: Vol. 174). 1971. 42.50 (ISBN 0-387-05119-8). Springer-Verlag.
Symposium on Planetary Cratering Mechanics, Flagstaff, Ariz., 1976. Impact & Explosion Cratering--Planetary & Terrestrial Implications: Proceedings. Roddy, D. J., et al, eds. LC 77-24753. 900p. 1978. 150.00 (ISBN 0-08-022050-9). Pergamon.
Szebehely, Victor G., ed. Instabilities in Dynamical Systems. (NATO Advanced Study Institutes Ser.). 1979. lib. bdg. 39.50 (ISBN 90-277-0973-4, Pub. by Reidel Holland). Kluwer Boston.
Thiry, Yves. Les Fondaments De la Mechanique Celeste. (Cours et Documents De Mathematiques et De Physique Ser.). 1970. 44.50x (ISBN 0-677-50270-2). Gordon.

MECHANICS, FRACTURE

see Fracture Mechanics

MECHANICS, NONLINEAR

see Nonlinear Mechanics

MECHANICS' LIENS

see also Foreclosure

How to Handle Mechanics Lien Claims. LC 80-65098. 1980. write for info. (ISBN 0-89648-076-3); pap. write for info. (ISBN 0-89648-077-1). Citizens Law.
Marks, Edward. Jensen on Mechanics' Liens: New York. 4th ed. LC 63-14740. 1963. with 1978 suppl. 42.50 (ISBN 0-87632-068-X). Boardman.
Marsh, Matthew E. California Mechanics' Lien Law Handbook. 3rd ed. LC 72-83952. 1979. 55.00 (ISBN 0-911110-30-5); 1980 suppl. incl. (ISBN 0-685-44105-9). Parker & Son.

MECHANICS OF CONTINUA

see Continuum Mechanics

MECHANISM (PHILOSOPHY)

see also Materialism; Naturalism

Anderson, Alan R., ed. Minds & Machines. (Orig.). 1964. pap. 7.95 ref. ed. (ISBN 0-13-583393-0). P-H.
Bailey, William. Man, Religion, & Science: A Functional View. LC 80-65860. (Illus.). 242p. (Orig.). 1981. pap. 9.95 (ISBN 0-9604196-0-8). W Bailey Pub.
Brown, Theodore & Cohen, I. Bernard, eds. The Mechanical Philosophy & the "Animal Oeconomy". LC 80-2085. (Development of Science Ser.). (Illus.). 1981. lib. bdg. 35.00x (ISBN 0-405-13851-2). Arno.
Hall, Marie B. & Cohen, I. Bernard, eds. The Mechanical Philosophy. LC 80-2108. (Development of Science Ser.). (Illus.). 1981. lib. bdg. 14.00x (ISBN 0-405-13874-1). Arno.
Schofield, Robert E. Mechanism & Materialism: British Natural Philosophy in the Age of Reason. LC 72-90960. 1969. 21.00x (ISBN 0-691-08072-0). Princeton U Pr.
Soni, Atmaram H. Mechanism Synthesis & Analysis. 512p. write for info. (ISBN 0-89874-380-X). Krieger.

MECHANISMS (MACHINERY)

see Mechanical Movements

MECHANISMS OF DEFENSE

see Defense Mechanisms (Psychology)

MECHANIZATION

see also Automation

Gandhi, Mohandas K. Man v. Machine. Hingorani, A. T., ed. 113p. (Orig.). 1980. pap. 2.00 (ISBN 0-934676-18-6). Greenlf Bks.
Giedion, Siegfried. Mechanization Takes Command. 1969. pap. 9.95 (ISBN 0-393-00489-9, Norton Lib.). Norton.

MECHANIZATION, AGRICULTURAL

see Farm Mechanization

MECHANIZATION, MILITARY

Here are entered works on the equipping of a military force with armed and armored motor vehicles in which the force travels and engages in combat.

see also Armored Vehicles, Military; Tanks (Military Science)

Gordon, Don E. Electronic Warfare: Element of Strategy & Multiplier of Combat Power. (Pergamon Policy Studies on Security Affairs). (Illus.). 200p. 1981. 20.01 (ISBN 0-08-027189-8). Pergamon.
Simpkin, Brigadier R. Mechanized Infantry. (Illus.). 144p. 1980. 26.00 (ISBN 0-08-027030-1). Pergamon.
Travers, Timothy & Archer, Christon, eds. Men at War: Politics, Technology & Innovation in the Twentieth Century. LC 81-80545. 300p. 1981. 19.95 (ISBN 0-913750-21-2); pap. text ed. 8.95 (ISBN 0-913750-46-8). Precedent Pub.

MECHANIZATION OF LIBRARY PROCESSES

see Libraries–Automation

MECHANIZED ACCOUNTING

see Machine Accounting

MECHANIZED FARMING

see Farm Mechanization

MECHANIZED FORCES

see Mechanization, Military

MECHANIZED INFORMATION STORAGE AND RETRIEVAL SYSTEMS

see Information Storage and Retrieval Systems

MECHANIZED WARFARE

see Mechanization, Military

MECHANOTHERAPY
see also Exercise Therapy; Massage
Nashelsky, Gunter M. Redaptor Guides for Rehabilitation. (Illus.). 1978. pap. text ed. 14.75x (ISBN 0-06-141807-2, Harper Medical). Har-Row.
Witkin, Kate & Philp, Richard. To Move, to Learn. LC 78-54395. (Illus.). 1978. pap. 4.95 (ISBN 0-8052-0602-7). Schocken.
MECHNIKOV, IL'IA IL'ICH, 1845-1916
Slosson, Edwin E. Major Prophets of To-Day. facs. ed. LC 68-8493. (Essay Index Reprint Ser). 1914. 18.00 (ISBN 0-8369-0882-1). Arno.
MECK, NADEZHDA FILARETOVNA (FROLOVSKAIA) VON, 1831-1894
Bowen, Catherine & Von Meck, Barbara. Beloved Friend: The Story of Tchaikowsky & Nadejda Von Meck. LC 73-3923. 1976. Repr. of 1961 ed. lib. bdg. 32.00x (ISBN 0-8371-6861-9, BOBF). Greenwood.
MECKLENBURG COUNTY, NORTH CAROLINA
Ray, Worth S. The Mecklenburg Signers & Their Neighbors. LC 67-8260. (Lost Tribes of North Carolina Ser: Pt. 3). (Illus.). 246p. 1975. Repr. of 1946 ed. 12.00 (ISBN 0-8063-0286-0). Genealog Pub.
MECKLENBURG DECLARATION OF INDEPENDENCE
Hoyt, William Henry. The Mecklenburg Declaration of Independence. LC 76-166330. (Era of the American Revolution Ser). 284p. 1972. Repr. of 1907 ed. lib. bdg. 32.50 (ISBN 0-306-70248-7). Da Capo.
Ray, Worth S. The Mecklenburg Signers & Their Neighbors. LC 67-8260. (Lost Tribes of North Carolina Ser: Pt. 3). (Illus.). 246p. 1975. Repr. of 1946 ed. 12.00 (ISBN 0-8063-0286-0). Genealog Pub.
MECOM, JANE (FRANKLIN) 1712-1794
Van Doren, Carl. Jane Mecom. LC 78-122067. (Illus.). Repr. of 1950 ed. 15.00x (ISBN 0-678-03174-6). Kelley.
MEDAL OF HONOR
Ross, Donald K. & Ross, Helen L. Men of Valor. 1979. 14.95 (ISBN 0-933992-04-1). Coffee Break.
Ross, Helen L. Touch of Smile. (Illus.). 1978. pap. 5.00 (ISBN 0-933992-01-7). Coffee Break.
MEDALISTS
Friedenberg, Daniel M. Jewish Minters & Medalists. LC 74-31721. (Illus.). 1976. 12.50 (ISBN 0-8276-0066-6, 368). Jewish Pubn.
Kienast, Gunter W. The Medals of Karl Goetz. LC 67-21457. (Illus.). 1980. Repr. of 1957 ed. 38.00 (ISBN 0-686-29666-4). Artus Co.
MEDALS
see also Medalists
Addison, Joseph. Dialogues on the Usefulness of Ancient Medals. LC 75-27883. (Renaissance & the Gods Ser.: Vol. 38). (Illus.). 1976. Repr. of 1726 ed. lib. bdg. 73.00 (ISBN 0-8240-2087-1). Garland Pub.
Arnold, Howard P. The Washington Medal. 1976. 3.00 (ISBN 0-89073-040-7). Boston Public Lib.
Belden, Bauman L. Indian Peace Medals Issued in the United States 1789-1889. LC 66-20865. (Illus.). 1966. 9.50 (ISBN 0-910598-04-5). Flayderman.
Betts, C. Wyllys. American Colonial History Illustrated by Contemporary Medals (1894) LC 72-85121. (Illus.). 356p. 1972. Repr. of 1894 ed. 15.00x (ISBN 0-88000-004-X). Quarterman.
Bolten, Johannes. Imago Clipeata, Ein Beitrag Zur Portrait Und Typengeschichte. pap. 9.50 (ISBN 0-384-04915-X). Johnson Repr.
Comstock, Mary & Vermeule, Cornelius. Roman Medallions. 2nd enl. ed. (Illus.). 1975. Repr. of 1962 ed. 5.00 (ISBN 0-87846-177-9). Mus Fine Arts Boston.
Connors, John J. Badges of Toledo & Lucas County, Ohio. 1973. 7.95 (ISBN 0-686-23927-X). J J Connors.
Dressell, H. Funf Gold Medaillons Aus Dem Funde Von Abukir Nineteen Hundred & Six. (Alexander the Great Ser.). (Illus.). 112p. 1981. 40.00 (ISBN 0-916710-90-4). Obol Intl.
Engstrom, J. Eric. The Medallic Portraits of Sir Winston Churchill. 1977. 9.00 (ISBN 0-685-51522-2, Pub by Spink & Son England). S J Durst.
Erbstein, Julius & Erbstein, Albert. Die Ritter Von Schulthess-Rechberg'sche Munz-U. Medaillen Sammlung. LC 73-92777. 1120p. 1974. Repr. 50.00x (ISBN 0-88000-029-5). Quarterman.
Gordon, L. L. British Battles & Medals. 1979. 42.00 (ISBN 0-685-51512-5, Pub by Spink & Son England). S J Durst.
Haffner, Sylvia. Judaic Tokens & Medals. Sobel, Nathan, ed. LC 78-54682. (Illus.). 1978. 25.00 (ISBN 0-9601658-1-9). Am Israel Numismatic.
Haffner, Sylvia, ed. Israel's Money & Medals. 2nd ed. LC 75-46129. 1976. with supplement 25.00 (ISBN 0-685-92169-7). Am Israel Numismatic.
Iverson, J. Medals & Coins of Peter the Great. 1979. 45.00 (ISBN 0-686-51596-X, Pub. by Spink & Son England). S J Durst.
Joslin, E. C. The Standard Catalogue of British Orders, Decorations & Medals, 2 vols. 1979. 30.00 (ISBN 0-685-51506-0, Pub by Spink & Son England). S J Durst.
--Standard Catalogue of British Orders, Decorations & Medals. 1978. Supplement. 3.50 (ISBN 0-686-52191-9, Pub by Spink & Son England). S J Durst.
Klobuchar, Jim. True Hearts & Purple Heads. pap. 2.95 (ISBN 0-87018-037-1). Ross.
Lawrence, Richard H. The Paduans, Medals by Giovanni Cavino. (Illus.). pap. 5.00 (ISBN 0-916710-74-2). Obol Intl.
Loubat, Joseph F. Medallic History of the U.S.A., 1776-1876. LC 67-28353. (Illus.). 1967. Repr. of 1878 ed. 19.50 (ISBN 0-910598-07-X). Flayderman.
Mackay, James A. Commemorative Medals. 137p. 1970. 6.00x (ISBN 0-213-00163-2). Intl Pubns Serv.
McSherry, Richard M. The National Medals of the United States. LC 72-14409. (Maryland Historical Society. Fund Publications: No. 25). Repr. of 1887 ed. 10.00 (ISBN 0-404-57625-7). AMS Pr.
Medina, Jose T. Medallas De Proclamaciones y Juras De Los Reyes De Espana En America. LC 72-85123. (Illus.). 356p. (Span.). 1973. Repr. of 1917 ed. 35.00x (ISBN 0-88000-017-1). Quarterman.
Norris, Andrea & Weber, Ingrid. Medals & Plaquettes from the Molinari Collection at Bowdoin College. LC 75-44691. (Illus.). 1976. 40.00x (ISBN 0-916606-00-7, Pub. by Wesleyan U Pr); pap. 17.50x (ISBN 0-8195-8039-2). Columbia U Pr.
Norton(R.W.) Art Gallery. Medallic Art of the United States, 1800-1972. LC 72-187912. (Illus.). 1972. pap. 3.00x (ISBN 0-9600182-9-8). Norton Art.
Prucha, Francis P. Indian Peace Medals in American History. LC 76-3772. (Illus.). 1976. 15.00 (ISBN 0-8032-0890-1). U of Nebr Pr.
Rosignoli, Guido. Air Force Badges & Insignia of World War Two. LC 77-1094. (Arco Color Ser.). 1977. 7.95 (ISBN 0-668-04249-4); pap. 5.95 (ISBN 0-668-04252-4). Arco.
--Ribbons of Orders, Decorations, and Medals. LC 76-28307. (Arco Color Books). 1977. 7.95 (ISBN 0-668-04104-8, 4104); pap. 5.95 (ISBN 0-668-04253-2, 4253). Arco.
Schembri, H. C. Coins & Medals of the Knights of Malta. 1966. 18.00 (ISBN 0-685-51537-0, Pub by Spink & Son England). S J Durst.
Tinson, A. R. Orders, Decorations & Medals of the Sultanate of Oman. 1979. 42.00 (ISBN 0-686-51597-8, Pub. by Spink & Son England). S J Durst.
Welter, G. & Schulman, H. Cleaning & Preservation of Coins & Medals. LC 76-3964. (Illus.). 1976. Repr. of 1970 ed. lib. bdg. 12.00 (ISBN 0-915262-03-7). S J Durst.
Werlich, R. Russian Orders, Decorations & Medals. 2nd ed. (Illus.). 1981. 36.00 (ISBN 0-685-90818-6). Quaker.
Weyl, Adolph, ed. Die Jules Fonrobert'che Sammlung Mittel & Sudamerikanischer Munzen & Medaillen. LC 73-93474. (Illus.). 608p. 1974. Repr. of 1878 ed. 25.00x (ISBN 0-88000-034-1). Quarterman.
MEDEA
Grillparzer, Franz. Medea. Burkhard, Arthur, tr. from Ger. pap. text ed. 5.00x (ISBN 0-685-48947-7). M S Rosenberg.
MEDIA CENTERS (EDUCATION)
see Instructional Materials Centers
MEDIA SERVICE PERSONNEL IN EDUCATION
see Instructional Materials Personnel
MEDIASTINUM
Leigh, Ted F. & Weens, H. Stephen. The Mediastinum. (Illus.). 256p. 1959. photocopy ed. spiral 24.74 (ISBN 0-398-01091-9). C C Thomas.
MEDIASTINUM–RADIOGRAPHY
Tricomi, G, et al, eds. Xeroradiography of the Lung & Mediastinum. 223p. 1979. 122.00 (ISBN 0-686-63099-8, Excerpta Medica). Elsevier.
MEDIATION, INTERNATIONAL
see also Arbitration, International
Rubin, Jeffrey Z., ed. Dynamics of Third-Party Intervention: Mediation in International Conflicts. 328p. 1981. 26.50 (ISBN 0-03-051061-9). Praeger.
Yarrow, C. H. Quaker Experiences in International Conciliation. LC 78-7415. 1978. 15.00x (ISBN 0-300-02260-3). Yale U Pr.
MEDIATION AND CONCILIATION, INDUSTRIAL
see also Arbitration, Industrial; Grievance Procedures
Barnett, George E. & McCabe, David A. Mediation, Investigation & Arbitration in Industrial Disputes. LC 75-156403. (American Labor Ser., No. 2). Repr. of 1916 ed. 14.00 (ISBN 0-405-02913-6). Arno.
Clark, R. Theodore, Jr. Coping with Mediation, Fact Finding, & Forms of Arbitration. (Public Employee Relations Library Ser.: No. 42). pap. 6.00 (ISBN 0-87373-142-5). Intl Personnel Mgmt.
Coffin, Royce A. The Negotiator: A Manual for Winners. LC 73-75768. (Illus.). 1973. 10.95 (ISBN 0-8144-5327-9). Am Mgmt.
Gilroy, Thomas P. & Russo, Anthony C. Bargaining Unit Issues: Problems Criteria, Tactics. (Public Employee Relations Library Ser.: No. 43). pap. 6.00 (ISBN 0-87373-143-3). Intl Personnel Mgmt.
Goldmann, Robert B., ed. Roundtable Justice: Case Studies in Conflict Resolution. (Westview Special Studies in Peace, Conflict, & Conflict Resolution). 231p. 1980. lib. bdg. 25.75x (ISBN 0-89158-962-7); pap. text ed. 9.00x (ISBN 0-86531-139-0). Westview.
Hoffman, Eileen B. Resolving Labor Management Disputes: A Nine-Country Comparison. (Report Ser: No. 600). (Illus.). 114p. (Orig.). 1973. pap. 17.50 (ISBN 0-8237-0049-6). Conference Bd.
Levin, Edward & De Santis, Daniel V. Mediation: An Annotated Bibliography. LC 78-18359. (Industrial & Labor Relations Bibliography Ser.: No. 15). 1978. pap. 3.25 (ISBN 0-87546-069-0). NY Sch Indus Rel.
Maggiolo, Walter A. Techniques of Mediation in Labor Disputes. LC 70-166000. 1971. lib. bdg. 15.00 (ISBN 0-379-00112-8). Oceana.
--Techniques of Mediation in Labor Disputes. LC 70-166000. 1971. lib. bdg. 15.00 (ISBN 0-379-00112-8). Oceana.
Newland, Chester A., ed. MBO & Productivity Bargaining in the Public Sector. (Public Employee Relations Library Ser.: No. 45). pap. 6.00 (ISBN 0-87373-145-X). Intl Personnel Mgmt.
MEDICAID
Cromwell, Jerry, et al. A Study of Administrative Costs in Physicians' Offices Under Medicaid. 1977. pap. 38.60 (ISBN 0-89011-508-7, HMD-144). Abt Assoc.
Davidson, Stephen M. Medicaid Decisions: Systematic Analysis of the Cost Problem. LC 80-10998. 1980. 23.50 (ISBN 0-88410-142-8). Ballinger Pub.
Feder, Judith & Holahan, John. Financing Health Care for the Elderly: Medicare, Medicaid & Private Health Insurance. (Health Policy & the Elderly Ser.). 106p. 1979. pap. 5.50 (ISBN 0-87766-244-4, 24900). Urban Inst.
Holahan, John. Financing Health Care for the Poor. LC 74-25273. (Illus.). 1975. 17.95 (ISBN 0-669-97634-2). Lexington Bks.
--Physician Supply, Peer Review, & Use of Health Services in Medicaid. (An Institute Paper). 70p. 1976. pap. 3.50 (ISBN 0-87766-159-6, 13800). Urban Inst.
Holahan, John & Scanlon, William. Price Controls, Physician Fees, & Physician Incomes from Medicare & Medicaid. (An Institute Paper). 110p. 1978. pap. 4.50 (ISBN 0-87766-219-3, 21800). Urban Inst.
Holahan, John & Stuart, Bruce. Controlling Medicaid Utilization Patterns. (Medicaid Cost Containment Ser.). 127p. 1977. pap. 4.00 (ISBN 0-87766-196-0, 17900). Urban Inst.
Holahan, John, et al. Restructuring Federal Medicaid Controls & Incentives. (Medicaid Cost Containment Ser.). 96p. 1977. pap. 2.00 (ISBN 0-87766-198-7, 18100). Urban Inst.
--Altering Medicaid Provider Reimbursement Methods. (Medicaid Cost Containment Ser.). 215p. 1977. pap. 8.50 (ISBN 0-87766-197-9, 17800). Urban Inst.
Rymer, Marilyn P., et al. Medicaid Eligibility: Problems & Solutions. (Westview Replica Edition: an Urban Systems Research Report). 1979. lib. bdg. 29.75x (ISBN 0-89158-478-1). Westview.
Spiegel, Allen D. The Medicaid Experience. LC 78-27669. (Illus.). 418p. 1979. text ed. 35.75 (ISBN 0-89443-088-2). Aspen Systems.
Spitz, Bruce & Holashan, John. Modifying Medicaid Eligibility & Benefits. (Medicaid Cost Containment Ser.). 93p. 1977. pap. 3.00 (ISBN 0-87766-195-2, 17700). Urban Inst.
MEDICAL ANTHROPOLOGY
see also Folk Medicine; Indians of North America–Health and Hygiene; Medicine, Primitive; Paleopathology
Aptekar, Herbert. Anjea; Infanticide, Abortion & Contraception in Savage Society. LC 79-2929. 192p. 1981. Repr. of 1931 ed. 17.50 (ISBN 0-8305-0097-9). Hyperion Conn.
Bletzer, Keith V. Selected References in Medical Anthropology. (Public Administration Ser.: Bibliography P-551). 59p. 1980. pap. 6.50 (ISBN 0-686-29068-2). Vance Biblios.
Brownlee, Ann T. Community, Culture & Care: A Cross-Cultural Guide for Health Workers. LC 77-16253. (Illus.). 1978. pap. text ed. 12.95 (ISBN 0-8016-0829-5). Mosby.
Jordan, Brigitte. Birth in Four Cultures: A Cross-Cultural Investigation of Childbirth in Yucatan, Holland, Sweden & the United States. 2nd ed. (Illus.). 128p. 1980. pap. 6.95 (ISBN 0-920792-05-7). EPWP.
Kleinman, Arthur. Patients & Healers in the Context of Culture: An Exploration of the Borderland Between Anthropology, Medicine, & Psychiatry. LC 78-57311. (Comparative Studies of Health Systems & Medical Care). 1979. 29.50x (ISBN 0-520-03706-5). U of Cal Pr.
Kleinman, Arthur, et al, eds. Culture & Healing in Asian Societies: Anthropological & Cross-Cultural Medical Studies. LC 77-2706. 480p. 1978. pap. text ed. 11.25x (ISBN 0-87073-573-X). Schenkman.
Landy, David. Culture, Disease, & Healing: Studies in Medical Anthropology. (Illus.). 1977. 20.95 (ISBN 0-02-367390-7). Macmillan.
Moore, Lorna G., et al. The Biocultural Basis of Health: Expanding Views of Medical Anthropology. LC 80-11554. (Illus.). 1980. pap. text ed. 12.95 (ISBN 0-8016-3481-4). Mosby.
Singer, Phillip, ed. Traditional Healing: New Science or New Colonialism? Essays in Critique of Medical Anthropology. LC 75-18490. (Traditional Healing Ser.: Vol. 1). 1977. 17.50 (ISBN 0-914970-36-4); pap. text ed. 10.00x (ISBN 0-914970-35-6). Trado-Medic.
Weaver, Thomas, ed. Essays on Medical Anthropology. (Southern Anthropological Society Proceedings Ser: No. 1). 98p. 1968. pap. 4.00x (ISBN 0-8203-0057-8). U of Ga Pr.
MEDICAL APPARATUS
see Medical Instruments and Apparatus
MEDICAL ASSISTANTS
see Medical Technologists
MEDICAL BOTANY
see Botany, Medical
MEDICAL CARE
see also Charities, Medical; Dental Care; Health Maintenance Organizations; Home Care Services; Hospital Care; Insurance, Health; Medical Social Work
Abels, Linda F. Mosby's Manual of Critical Care: 1979. LC 78-24358. (Illus.). 1979. pap. text ed. 16.95 (ISBN 0-8016-0055-3). Mosby.
Abernathy, William J., et al, eds. The Management of Health Care: A Technology Perspective. LC 74-14771. 192p. 1975. text ed. 22.50 (ISBN 0-88410-110-X). Ballinger Pub.
Advances in Patient, Care, Second Annual Conference, Feb. 15-22, 1975. Design & Use of Protocols: Proceedings. new ed. Kallstrom, Marta & Yarnall, Stephen, eds. (Illus.). 294p. 1975. 18.00 (ISBN 0-917054-02-4). Med Communications.
Ainsworth, Thomas H., Jr. Quality Assurance in Long Term Care. LC 77-70432. 200p. 1977. 27.50 (ISBN 0-912862-40-8). Aspen Systems.
Alford, Robert R. Health Care Politics: Idealogical & Interest Groups Barriers to Reform. LC 74-75611. xiv, 294p. 1975. 15.00x (ISBN 0-226-01379-0). U of Chicago Pr.
--Health Care Politics: Ideological & Interest Group Barriers to Reform. LC 74-75611. (Illus.). 1977. pap. 5.45 (ISBN 0-226-01380-4, P731, Phoen). U of Chicago Pr.
American Hospital Association. American Hospital Association Guide to the Health Care Field. 510p. 1980. pap. 50.00 (ISBN 0-87258-280-9, 2480). Am Hospital.
--American Hospital Association Guide to the Health Care Field. 1978 Ed. 692p. 1978. pap. 37.50 (ISBN 0-87258-215-9, 2478). Am Hospital.
--Delivery of Health Care in Rural America. LC 77-5097. 108p. 1977. pap. 9.50 (ISBN 0-87258-205-1, 2920). Am Hospital.
American Hospital Association Guide to the Health Care Field. 646p. 1979. pap. 43.75 (ISBN 0-87258-261-2, 2479). Am Hospital.
American Hospital Association Guide to the Health Care Field. Annual Ed. 630p. 1976. pap. 25.00 (ISBN 0-87258-184-5, 2476). Am Hospital.
American Medical Association. Distribution of Physicians, Hospitals, & Hospital Beds in the U. S., 1970. 329p. 1970. pap. 5.00 (ISBN 0-89970-035-7, OP-347). AMA.
American Public Health Association. Guide to Medical Care Administration, 2 vols. Incl. Vol. 1. Concepts & Principles. 112p. 1965. 6.50 (ISBN 0-87553-011-7, 056); Vol. 2. Medical Care Appraisal. 221p. 1969. 7.50 (ISBN 0-87553-012-5, 057). Am Pub Health.
Andersen, Ronald & Anderson, Odin W. Decade of Health Services: Social Survey Trends in Use & Expenditure. LC 67-30125. (Studies in Business & Society Ser.). (Midway reprint ser.). 1973. pap. 9.50x (ISBN 0-226-01761-3). U of Chicago Pr.
Andersen, Ronald, et al. Two Decades of Health Services: Social Survey Trends in Use & Expenditure. LC 76-14785. 1976. 22.50 (ISBN 0-88410-117-7). Ballinger Pub.

Andersen, Ronald, et al, eds. Equity in Health Services: Empirical Analyses in Social Policy. LC 75-22328. 1975. text ed. 18.00 (ISBN 0-88410-104-5). Ballinger Pub.

Anderson, Odin W. Health Care: Can There Be Equity? the United States, Sweden, & England. LC 72-7449. 273p. 1972. 25.50 (ISBN 0-471-02760-X, Pub. by Wiley-Interscience). Wiley.

Anthony, William A. The Art of Health Care. LC 75-40867. 104p. 1976. pap. text ed. 8.95x (ISBN 0-914234-25-0). Human Res Dev Pr.

Ashley, Benedict M. & O'Rourke, Kevin D. Health Care Ethics: A Theological Analysis. LC 77-88355. 1978. pap. 14.00 (ISBN 0-87125-044-6). Cath Health.

Assembly of Engineering, Institute of Medicine, National Research Council. Medical Technology & the Health Care System: A Study of the Diffusion of Equipment-Embodied Technology. 1979. pap. text ed. 10.75 (ISBN 0-309-02865-5). Natl Acad Pr.

Battistella, Roger M. & Rundall, Thomas G., eds. Health Care Policy in a Changing Environment. LC 78-57148. 1979. 24.70 (ISBN 0-8211-0131-5); text ed. 22.05 in ten or more copies (ISBN 0-686-67039-6). McCutchan.

Beatty, Sally R., ed. Continuity of Care. (Illus.). 253p. 1980. 17.50 (ISBN 0-8089-1304-2). Grune.

Becker, Marshall H. The Health Belief Model & Personal Health Behavior. 1976. pap. 9.00x (ISBN 0-913590-34-7). C B Slack.

Belsky, Marvin S. & Gross, Leonard. How to Choose Your Doctor. LC 75-11146. 1975. 7.95 (ISBN 0-87795-112-8). Arbor Hse.

Berk, James L., et al. Handbook of Critical Care. 1976. pap. text ed. 16.95- (ISBN 0-316-09170-7). Little.

Better Homes & Gardens Books Editors. Better Homes & Gardens After-40 Health & Medical Guide. (Illus.). 480p. 1980. 24.95 (ISBN 0-696-00810-6). Meredith Corp.

Blackwell, Deborah J. Telecommunications & Health Services. 1974. pap. 3.50x (ISBN 0-89011-466-8, TEC-104). Abt Assoc.

Blum, John. PSRO & the Law. LC 77-70436. 300p. 1977. 24.95 (ISBN 0-912862-39-4). Aspen Systems.

Blum, Richard, et al. Pharmaceuticals & Health Policy: International Perspectives on Provision & Control of Medicine. 1981. write for info. (ISBN 0-312-60402-5). St Martin.

Bowers, John Z. & Purcell, Elizabeth, eds. National Health Services: Their Impact on Medical Education & Their Role in Prevention. LC 73-77541. (Illus.). 168p. 1973. pap. 7.50 (ISBN 0-914362-03-8). J Macy Foun.

Braverman, Jordan. Crisis in Health Care. rev. ed. 1980. pap. 7.95 (ISBN 0-87491-299-7). Acropolis.

Brearley, P., et al. Admission to Residential Care. 1980. 25.00x (ISBN 0-422-76930-4, Pub. by Tavistock). Methuen Inc.

Breslow, Lori, ed. How to Get the Best Health Care for Your Money: A Family Guide to Whole Health Medical Services. 1979. pap. 7.95 (ISBN 0-87857-251-1). Rodale Pr Inc.

Brown, J. H. The Health Care Dilemma. LC 78-3891. 183p. 1978. 19.95 (ISBN 0-87705-360-X). Human Sci Pr.

Brown, J. H. U. The Politics of Health Care. LC 78-13755. 1978. 19.00 (ISBN 0-88410-531-8). Ballinger Pub.

Brown, Montague, ed. Health Care Management Review. LC 75-45767. annual subscription 44.50 (ISBN 0-912862-50-5). Aspen Systems.

Bullough, Bonnie, et al, eds. The Management of Common Human Miseries: A Text for Primary Health Care Practitioners. LC 78-24072. 1979. text ed. 26.50 (ISBN 0-8261-2190-X). Springer Pub.

Burrell, Craig D. & Sheps, Cecil G., eds. Primary Health Care in Industrialized Nations. (Annals of the New York Academy of Sciences: Vol. 310). 274p. 1978. pap. 40.00x professional (ISBN 0-89072-066-5). NY Acad Sci.

Burt, Marvin R. Policy Analysis: Introduction & Applications to Health Programs. LC 74-81587. (Illus.). 136p. 1974. text ed. 18.00 (ISBN 0-87815-013-7). Info Resources.

Caldwell, Esther & Hegner, Barbara. Health Assistant. 288p. 1981. text ed. 13.95 (ISBN 0-442-21850-8). Van Nos Reinhold.

Caliendo, Mary A. Nutrition & Preventative Health Care. (Illus.). 1981. text ed. 19.95 (ISBN 0-02-318330-6). Macmillan.

Callahan, James J., Jr. & Wallack, Stanley S., eds. Reforming the Long-Term-Care System: Financial & Organizational Options. LC 80-8366. (The University Health Policy Consortium Ser.). 272p. 1981. 24.95x (ISBN 0-669-04040-1). Lexington Bks.

Campbell, Alastair V. Medicine, Health, & Justice. 1978. pap. text ed. 8.95 (ISBN 0-443-01671-2). Churchill.

Careers in the Health Care Field, Nineteen Seventy-Nine. 1979. cancelled (ISBN 0-916524-10-8); pap. cancelled. US Direct Serv.

Carlson, Rick J. The End of Medicine. LC 75-6856. (Health, Medicine & Society Ser). 1975. pap. 25.50 (ISBN 0-471-13494-5, Pub. by Wiley-Interscience). Wiley.

Carlson, Rick J., ed. Future Directions in Health Care: A New Public Policy. LC 78-9568. 1978. 18.50 (ISBN 0-88410-519-9). Ballinger Pub.

CIBA Foundation. Medical Care of Prisoners & Detainees. (CIBA Foundation Symposium Ser.:No. 16). 244p. 1973. 18.00 (ISBN 0-444-15013-7, Excerpta Medica). Elsevier.

Citizens Board of Inquiry into Health Services for Americans. Heal Yourself. 2.95x (ISBN 0-685-31246-1, 086). Am Pub Health.

Clark, Ewen M. & Forbes, J. A. Evaluating Primary Care. 1981. 25.00x (ISBN 0-85664-856-6, Pub. by Croom Helm Ltd England). Biblio Dist.

C. McLaughlin, C. & Sheldon, A. The Future & Medical Care: A Health Manager's Guide to Forecasting. LC 74-14783. 1974. 16.50 (ISBN 0-88410-102-9). Ballinger Pub.

Coblentz, A. M. & Walter, J. R., eds. Systems Science in Health Care. LC 77-21046. 1978. text ed. 35.00 (ISBN 0-89433-067-5). Petrocelli.

Coe, Rodney M. & Brehm, Henry P. Preventive Health Care for Adults: A Study of Medical Practice. 1972. 6.00 (ISBN 0-8084-0040-1); pap. 2.45 (ISBN 0-8084-0041-X, B59). Coll & U Pr.

Cohen, Roberta G. & Lipkin, Gladys B. Therapeutic Group Work for Health Professionals. LC 79-12388. 1979. text ed. 16.95 (ISBN 0-8261-2310-4); pap. text ed. 10.95 (ISBN 0-8261-2311-2). Springer Pub.

Coleman, J. R. & Kaminsky, F. C. Ambulatory Care Systems, Vol. 5: Financial Design & Administration of Health Maintenance Organizations. LC 76-55865. 1977. 26.95 (ISBN 0-669-01328-5). Lexington Bks.

Comprehensive National Medical Care, Should the Federal Government Provide a Program of Comprehensive Medical Care for All U. S. Citizens? 1972. pap. 3.75 (ISBN 0-8447-1820-3). Am Enterprise.

Corey, Lawrence, et al. Medicine in a Changing Society. 2nd ed. LC 76-46313. (Illus.). 1977. pap. 10.00 (ISBN 0-8016-1044-3). Mosby.

Counte, Michael A. & Christman, Luther. Interpersonal Behavior & Health Care. (Behavioral Sciences for the Health Care Professional Ser.). 128p. (Orig.). 1981. lib. bdg. 15.00x (ISBN 0-86531-008-4); pap. text ed. 6.75x (ISBN 0-86531-009-2). Westview.

Crichton, Anne. Health Policy Making: The Fundamental Issues. (Illus.). 432p. 1981. text ed. 40.00 (ISBN 0-914904-44-2). Health Admin Pr.

Cullis, John G. & West, Peter A. The Economics of Health: An Introducton. LC 79-50451. 1979. 22.50x (ISBN 0-8147-1377-7). NYU Pr.

Cundy, et al. Infection Control in Health Care Facilities. (Illus.). 1977. 22.50 (ISBN 0-8391-1158-4). Univ Park.

Davidson, Sharon V. PSRO: Utilization & Audit in Patient Care. LC 75-43980. (Illus.). 380p. 1976. 18.95 (ISBN 0-8016-1209-8). Mosby.

Davies, Dean F. & Tchobanoff, James B., eds. Health Evaluation: An Entry to the Health Care System. LC 73-82039. (Illus.). 1973. 17.50 (ISBN 0-8151-2338-8, Pub. by Symposia Special). Year Bk Med.

Davis, Karen. National Health Insurance: Benefits, Costs, & Consequences. (Studies in Social Economics). 182p. 1975. 10.95 (ISBN 0-8157-1760-1); pap. 4.95 (ISBN 0-8157-1759-8). Brookings.

Dixon, Marlene & Bodenheimer, Thomas. Health Care in Crisis: Essays on Health Services Under Capitalism. LC 79-90213. (Orig.). 1980. pap. 5.00 (ISBN 0-89935-004-6). Synthesis Pubns.

Dixon, Samuel L. Working with People in Crisis: Theory & Practice. LC 78-31227. (Illus.). 1979. pap. text ed. 10.45 (ISBN 0-8016-1320-5). Mosby.

Donabedian, Avedis. Aspects of Medical Care Administration: Specifying Requirements for Health Care. LC 72-93948. (Commonwealth Fund Publications Ser). 800p. 1973. 40.00x (ISBN 0-674-04980-2). Harvard U Pr.

--Benefits in Medical Care Programs. 432p. 1976. 25.00x (ISBN 0-674-06580-8). Harvard U Pr.

--The Definition of Quality & Approaches to Its Assessment, Vol. 1. (Explorations in Quality Assessment & Monitoring Ser.). (Illus.). 180p. 1980. text ed. 17.95 (ISBN 0-914904-47-7); pap. text ed. 12.95 (ISBN 0-914904-48-5). Health Admin Pr.

Dowling, Michael J. Health Care & the Church. Koenig, Robert E., ed. LC 77-1242. (Doing the Word Resource Ser.). (Orig.). 1977. pap. text ed. 3.95 (ISBN 0-8298-0333-5). Pilgrim NY.

Drummond, M. F. Principles of Economic Appraisal in Health Care. (Illus.). 130p. 1980. pap. 12.95x (ISBN 0-19-261273-5). Oxford U Pr.

Dubos, Rene. Mirage of Health: Utopias, Progress, & Biological Change. LC 58-8825. 1979. pap. 4.95 (ISBN 0-06-090677-4, CN-677, CN). Har-Row.

Ducanis, Alex J. & Golin, Anne K. Interdisciplinary Health Care Team: A Handbook. LC 79-21028. (Illus.). 201p. 1979. text ed. 21.50 (ISBN 0-89443-167-6). Aspen Systems.

Egdahl, Richard H. & Gertman, Paul M., eds. Quality Health Care: The Role of Continuing Medical Education. LC 77-70434. 276p. 1977. 30.00 (ISBN 0-912862-37-8). Aspen Systems.

Elder, Jean. Transactional Analysis in Health Care. LC 78-57376. 1978. 10.95 (ISBN 0-201-01512-9, Med-Nurse). A-W.

Elliott, Katherine, ed. Auxiliaries in Primary Health Care: An Annotated Bibliography. 126p. (Orig.). 1979. pap. 8.25 (ISBN 0-903031-58-2, Pub. by Intermediate Tech England). Intermediate Tech.

Enos, Darryl & Sultan, Paul. The Sociology of Health Care: Social, Economic & Political Perspectives. LC 76-17250. 1977. 15.95 (ISBN 0-275-56970-5). Praeger.

Ezzati, Trena M. Ambulatory Care Utilization Patterns of Children & Young Adults: National Ambulatory Medican Care Survey United States, January-December 1975. Stevenson, Taloria, ed. (Ser. 13: No. 39). 1978. pap. text ed. 1.75 (ISBN 0-8406-0134-4). Natl Ctr Health Stats.

Falk, I. S., et al. The Costs of Medical Care: A Summary of Investigations on the Economic Aspects of the Prevention & Care of Illness, No. 27. LC 71-180568. (Medicine & Society in America Ser). 652p. 1972. Repr. of 1933 ed. 28.00 (ISBN 0-405-03950-6). Arno.

Falk, Isidore Sydney. Security Against Sickness. LC 79-38822. (FDR & the Era of the New Deal Ser). 424p. 1972. Repr. of 1936 ed. lib. bdg. 37.50 (ISBN 0-306-70447-1). Da Capo.

Findeiss, J. Clifford, ed. Emergency Medical Care, Vol. 1. LC 73-82042. 1974. 21.95 (ISBN 0-8151-3223-9, Pub. by Symposia Special). Year Bk Med.

Fish, Oscar & Walker, Godfrey. Mobile Health Services. 224p. 1981. 25.00x (ISBN 0-905402-03-0, Pub. by Tri-Med England). State Mutual Bk.

Flavell, John & Ross, Lee, eds. Social Cognitive Development: Frontiers & Possible Futures. (Cambridge Studies in Social & Emotional Development). (Illus.). 336p. 1981. 32.50 (ISBN 0-521-23687-8); pap. 12.95 (ISBN 0-521-28156-3). Cambridge U Pr.

Flint, Thomas, Jr. & Cain, Harvey D. Emergency Treatment & Management. 5th ed. LC 74-9433. (Illus.). 800p. 1975. text ed. 15.75 (ISBN 0-7216-3728-0). Saunders.

Ford, Amasa B. Urban Health in America. (Illus.). 275p. 1976. 13.95 (ISBN 0-19-502003-0); pap. 8.95x (ISBN 0-19-502002-2). Oxford U Pr.

Frank, Arthur & Frank, Stuart. The People's Handbook of Medical Care. pap. 2.95 (ISBN 0-394-71821-6, V-821, Vin). Random.

Freedman, Carol R. Teaching Patients: A Practical Handbook for the Health Care Professional. 178p. 1978. pap. text ed. 10.50x (ISBN 0-89805-000-6). Irvington.

Freese, Arthur S. Managing Your Doctor: How to Get Best Possible Medical Care. LC 74-78534. 1977. pap. 2.95 (ISBN 0-8128-2342-7). Stein & Day.

Freidson, Eliot. Professional Dominance: The Social Structure of Medical Care. LC 72-116538. 1970. 18.95x (ISBN 0-202-30203-2). Aldine Pub.

The French Health Care System. pap. 3.50 (ISBN 0-89970-044-6, OP-460). AMA.

French, Ruth. Dynamics of Health Care. 3rd ed. (Illus.). 1979. pap. text ed. 7.95 (ISBN 0-07-022143-X, HP). McGraw.

Frew, Mary A. & Frew, David R. Comprehensive Medical Assisting: Administrative & Clinical Procedures. 1982. 19.95 (ISBN 0-8036-3858-2). Davis Co.

Freymann, John G. The American Health Care System: Its Genesis & Trajectory. LC 80-15512. 432p. 1980. Repr. of 1974 ed. lib. bdg. 27.50 (ISBN 0-88275-627-3). Krieger.

Fries, B. E. Applications of Operations Research to Health Care Delivery Systems. (Lecture Notes in Medical Informatics: Vol. 10). 107p. 1981. pap. 11.90 (ISBN 0-387-10559-X). Springer-Verlag.

Fry, J. A New Approach to Medicine. 1978. 19.50 (ISBN 0-8391-1282-3). Univ Park.

Fry, J. & Farndale, W. A., eds. International Medical Care. 333p. 1973. 24.50 (ISBN 0-913086-01-0). Univ Park.

Fuchs, Victor. Who Shall Live? LC 74-79283. 1975. 9.95 (ISBN 0-465-09185-7). Basic.

Fuchs, Victor R., ed. Essays in the Economics of Health & Medical Care. (Human Resources & Social Institutions Ser.: No. 1). 250p. 1972. text ed. 10.00x (ISBN 0-87014-236-4, Dist. by Columbia U Pr). Natl Bur Econ Res.

Fuller, Benjamin J. & Fuller, B. Frank. Physician or Magician: The Myths & Realities of Patient Care. (Illus.). 1979. pap. text ed. 7.95 (ISBN 0-07-022617-2, HP). McGraw.

Gap Committee on Preventive Psychiatry. Mental Health & Primary Medical Care, Vol. 10. LC 80-19016. (Publication Ser.: No. 105). pap. 4.00 (ISBN 0-686-71039-8, 105, Mental Health Materials Center). Mental Health.

Gebert, Gordon, ed. Health-Care. 40p. 1981. pap. 33.00 (ISBN 0-08-028091-9). Pergamon.

Gentry, John T. Introduction to Health Services & Community Health Systems. new ed. LC 77-78899. 1978. text ed. 21.55 (ISBN 0-8211-0612-0); text ed. 19.45 in ten or more copies (ISBN 0-685-48956-6). McCutchan.

Ginzberg, Eli. The Limits of Health Reform. LC 77-75244. 1977. 12.50 (ISBN 0-465-04117-5). Basic.

--Urban Health Services: The Case of New York. LC 70-134987. 250p. 1970. 16.00x (ISBN 0-231-03515-2). Columbia U Pr.

Goen, Tex, Jr. Smile...or I'll Kick You Bed! LC 80-20223. (Illus.). 192p. 1981. 12.95 (ISBN 0-393-01433-9). Norton.

Golden, Archie S., et al. The Art of Teaching Primary Care. 1981. text ed. price not set (ISBN 0-8261-2960-9); pap. text ed. price not set (ISBN 0-8261-2961-7). Springer Pub.

Goldfarb, I. William & Yates, Anthony P. Critical Care Medicine. LC 77-151972. 1980. Repr. of 1977 ed. write for info. (ISBN 0-935170-01-4). Synapse Pubns.

Goldsmith, Seth B. Prison Health: Travesty of Justice. (Orig.). 1975. pap. text ed. 7.95 (ISBN 0-88202-101-X). N Watson.

Goodrich, Charles H., et al. Welfare Medical Care: An Experiment. LC 77-85075. (Illus.). 1970. 18.50x (ISBN 0-674-94895-5). Harvard U Pr.

Greenberg, Warren, ed. Competition in the Health Care Sector: Past, Present & Future. LC 78-24573. 420p. 1978. text ed. 35.00 (ISBN 0-89443-081-5). Aspen Systems.

Greene, Richard. Assuring Quality in Medical Care: The State of the Art. LC 75-37567. 320p. 1976. text ed. 22.50 (ISBN 0-88410-116-9). Ballinger Pub.

Grossman, Howard R. For Health's Sake: A Critical Analysis of Medical Care in the United States. LC 77-23828. 1977. 8.95 (ISBN 0-87015-222-X). Pacific Bks.

Haag, Jessie H. Consumer Health: Products & Services. LC 74-6033. (Illus.). 268p. 1976. pap. 10.00 (ISBN 0-8121-0562-1). Lea & Febiger.

Hadden, Wilbur C. Basic Data on Health Care Needs of Adults 25-74 Years of Age: United States, 1971-75. Cox, Klaudia, ed. (Ser. 11, No. 218). 150p. 1980. pap. text ed. 1.75 (ISBN 0-8406-0197-2). Natl Ctr Health Stats.

Hapgood, David. Diplomaism. LC 75-128665. 1971. 5.95 (ISBN 0-87975-053-7). Prometheus Bks.

Hardy, Robert C. Sick: How People Feel About Being Sick & What They Think of Those Who Care for Them. LC 77-90162. 1978. 18.95 (ISBN 0-931028-05-1); pap. 14.95 (ISBN 0-931028-04-3). Teach'em.

Harrison, Tinsley R. Your Future Health Care. LC 73-13222. 1974. 10.50 (ISBN 0-87527-132-4). Green.

Harwood, Alan. Ethnicity & Medical Care. LC 80-19339. (Commonwealth Fund Ser.). (Illus.). 544p. 1981. text ed. 25.00x (ISBN 0-674-26865-2). Harvard U Pr.

Havard, C. W. Current Medical Treatment. 4th ed. (Illus.). 1976. 39.95 (ISBN 0-8151-4200-5). Year Bk Med.

--Fundamentals of Current Medical Treatment. LC 67-27240. (Illus.). 876p. 1967. with 1968 supplement 15.00 (ISBN 0-87527-016-6). Green.

Havighurst, Clark C., ed. Health Care. LC 72-37739. (Library of Law & Contemporary Problems Ser). 458p. 1972. lib. bdg. 20.00 (ISBN 0-379-11515-8). Oceana.

Hawaii Conference, Third Annual Advances in Patient Care. The Changing Health Care Team-Improving Effectiveness: Proceedings. Yarnall, S. R. & Zoog, Spring, eds. 1976. 19.00 (ISBN 0-917054-11-3). Med Communications.

Haynes, Brian, et al. Compliance in Health Care. LC 78-20527. 1979. text ed. 25.00x (ISBN 0-8018-2162-2). Johns Hopkins.

Health Care at Home: An Essential Component of Nat'l Health Policy, Ch-9. 1978. pap. 1.50 (ISBN 0-686-11181-8). ANA.

Health Care Guidelines for Use in Developing Countries. pap. 4.50 (ISBN 0-912552-22-0). MARC.

Health Policy Advisory Committee, ed. American Health Empire: Power, Profits, Politics. 1971. pap. 2.45 (ISBN 0-394-71453-9, V-453, Vin). Random.

Health Status Indexes. LC 73-87778. 262p. 1973. 12.50 (ISBN 0-87914-025-9, 9190). Hosp Res & Educ.
Heidenheimer, Arnold J. & Elvander, Nile, eds. The Shaping of the Swedish Health System. LC 80-12410. 256p. 1980. write for info. (ISBN 0-312-71627-3). St Martin.
Heller, Tom. Restructuring the Health Service. 1978. lib. bdg. 14.00 (ISBN 0-85664-583-4). N Watson.
Hendricks, William S. America's Health Care Crisis. LC 80-66321. 1981. 10.95 (ISBN 0-9604698-0-X). Ducky Ent.
Hetzel, Basil S. Basic Health Care in Developing Countries: An Epidemiological Perspective. (IEA & WHO Handbooks Ser.). (Illus.). 1979. pap. text ed. 13.95x (ISBN 0-19-261223-9). Oxford U Pr.
Hicks, Dorothy J. Patient Care Techniques. LC 74-18673. (Allied Health Ser). 1975. pap. 7.05 (ISBN 0-672-61394-8). Bobbs.
Hill, E. Joy. General Health Occupations Practice. LC 71-176181. 320p. 1981. 24.50 (ISBN 0-87527-108-1). Green.
Hingson, Ralph, et al. In Sickness & in Health: Social Dimensions of Medical Care. LC 80-28794. 288p. 1981. pap. text ed. 14.95 (ISBN 0-8016-4411-9). Mosby.
Hin Man. Health Decision Systems. 1980. 32.50 (ISBN 0-8151-4461-X). Year Bk Med.
Hirschhorn, Norbert, et al. Quality of Care Assessment & Assurance: An Annotated Bibliography with a Point of View. (Medical Bks.). 1979. lib. bdg. 15.95 (ISBN 0-8161-2123-0, Hall Medical). G K Hall.
Hirschorn, Norbert, et al. Quality by Objectives. (Medical Publications). 1978. lib. bdg. 12.95 (ISBN 0-8161-2122-2). G K Hall.
Holahan, John. Financing Health Care for the Poor. LC 74-25273. (Illus.). 1975. 17.95 (ISBN 0-669-97634-2). Lexington Bks.
Holland, Walter & Karhauser, Lucien. Health Care & Epidemiology. (Medical Bks.). 1979. lib. bdg. 20.00 (ISBN 0-8161-2176-1, Hall Medical). G K Hall.
Howard, Jan & Strauss, Anselm, eds. Humanizing Health Care. LC 75-12874. (Health, Medicine & Society Ser). 326p. 1975. 25.50 (ISBN 0-471-41658-4, Pub. by Wiley-Interscience). Wiley.
Human Resources for Primary Health Care in the Middle East. 1981. 20.00x (ISBN 0-8156-6056-1). Syracuse U Pr.
Hyman, Andrew A. & Sainer, Elliot A., eds. Who's Who in Health Care. LC 77-79993. 764p. 1977. text ed. 60.00 (ISBN 0-89443-074-2). Aspen Systems.
Hyman, Herbert H. Health Planning: A Systematic Approach. LC 75-37405. 460p. 1976. text ed. 27.50 (ISBN 0-912862-17-3). Aspen Systems.
Illich, Ivan. Medical Nemesis: The Expropriation of Health. 1977. pap. 2.75 (ISBN 0-553-10596-5, 13371-3). Bantam.
Institute of Medicine. A Manpower Policy for Primary Health Care. LC 78-56907. 1978. 6.25 (ISBN 0-309-02764-0). Natl Acad Pr.
--A Strategy for Evaluating Health Services. (Contrasts in Health Status Ser. Vol. 2). (Illus.). 256p. 1973. pap. 8.50 (ISBN 0-309-02104-9). Natl Acad Pr.
International Symposium on Acute Care, Rio De Janeiro & Sao Paulo, 5th, November 1976. Physiology Monitor & Therapy of the Critically Ill Patient: Proceedings. Shoemaker, W. C. & Tavares, B. M., eds. (Current Topics in Critical Care Medicine: Vol. 3). (Illus.). 1977. 34.25 (ISBN 3-8055-2652-0). S Karger.
International Symposium on Acute Care, 4th, Rio de Janeiro, November 1975. Technical, Medical, & Educational Problems of Acute Care: Proceedings. Tavares, B. M., ed. (Current Topics in Critical Care Medicine: Vol 2). (Illus.). 200p. 1977. 29.50 (ISBN 3-8055-2374-2). S Karger.
International Symposium on Critical Care, 3rd, Rio de Janeiro, November, 1974. Current Topics in Critical Care Medicine: Proceedings. Shoemaker, W. C., et al, eds. (Current Topics in Critical Care Medicine: Vol. 1). (Illus.). 200p. 1976. 53.50 (ISBN 3-8055-2211-8). S Karger.
Jaco, E. Gartly, ed. Patients, Physicians, & Illness: A Sourcebook in Behavioral Science & Health. 3rd ed. LC 78-63407. 1979. text ed. 15.95 (ISBN 0-02-915850-8). Free Pr.
James, M. & Jongeward, D. Winning with People for Health Care Professionals. 1980. pap. cancelled (ISBN 0-201-00451-8). A-W.
Jarcho, Saul, ed. Medicine & Health Care. LC 76-29724. (Great Contemporary Issues Ser.). 1977. lib. bdg. 35.00x (ISBN 0-405-09850-2). Arno.
Johnson, T. C. Doctor! What You Should Know About Health Care Before You Call a Physician. 432p. 1975. 8.95 (ISBN 0-07-032664-9, GB). McGraw.
Jonas, Steven. Health Care Delivery in the United States. LC 77-3253. 1977. text ed. 23.00 (ISBN 0-8261-2070-9); pap. text ed. 15.95 (ISBN 0-8261-2071-7). Springer Pub.
Jones, David A. The Health Risks of Imprisonment. LC 76-5620. (Illus.). 1976. 21.50 (ISBN 0-669-00651-3). Lexington Bks.
Jones, Deborah, et al. A Guide to Assessing Ambulatory Health Care Needs in Your Community. 1974. pap. 8.60 (ISBN 0-89011-471-4, HMD-102). Abt Assoc.
Jospe, Michael, et al. Psychological Factors in Health Care: A Practitioner's Manual. Cohen, Barry D., et al. LC 77-11395. 496p. 1980. 29.95x (ISBN 0-669-02076-1). Lexington Bks.
Kane, Robert L., et al, eds. The Health Gap: Medical Services & the Poor. LC 75-30563. 1976. pap. text ed. 9.95 (ISBN 0-8261-1861-5). Springer Pub.
Kaur, Surjit. Wastage of Children: A Family Planning Foundation (India) Book. (Illus.). 1978. text ed. 18.00x (ISBN 0-8426-1104-5). Verry.
Kent, P. W., ed. International Aspects of the Provision of Medical Care. 1976. 25.00 (ISBN 0-85362-160-8, Oriel). Routledge & Kegan.
Kernaghan, Salvinija G., ed. Delivery of Health Care in Urban Underserved Areas. LC 79-21168. 128p. 1979. pap. 13.25 (ISBN 0-87258-278-7, 1165). Am Hospital.
Kime, Robert E. Health: A Consumer's Dilemma. 1970. pap. 5.95x (ISBN 0-534-00661-2). Wadsworth Pub.
Kinzer, David M. Health Controls Out of Control: Warnings to the Nation from Massachusetts. LC 77-75816. 1977. pap. 12.95 (ISBN 0-931028-03-5). Teach'em.
Kiple, Kenneth F. Another Dimension to the Black Diaspora: Diet, Disease, & Racism. LC 81-7696. (Illus.). 288p. Date not set. price not set (ISBN 0-521-23664-9). Cambridge U Pr.
Knopke, Harry J. & Diekelmann, Nancy L. Approaches to Teaching Primary Health Care. LC 81-1552. 322p. 1981. text ed. 18.95 (ISBN 0-8016-2732-X). Mosby.
Knowles, John H., ed. Doing Better & Feeling Worse. 1977. 9.95 (ISBN 0-393-06419-0); pap. text ed. 5.95 (ISBN 0-393-06423-9). Norton.
Kohn, Robert & White, Kerr L., eds. Health Care: An International Study. (Illus.). 557p. 1976. text ed. 42.50x (ISBN 0-19-264226-X). Oxford U Pr.
Kolesar, John. The Newark Experiment: A New Direction for Urban Health Care. 1975. 2.00 (ISBN 0-686-23338-7). Ctr Analysis Public Issues.
Kotelchuck, David, ed. Prognosis Negative: Crisis in the Health Care System. 1976. pap. 3.95 (ISBN 0-394-71757-0, Vin). Random.
Kron, Thora. The Management of Patient Care: Putting Leadership Skills to Work. (Illus.). 247p. 1981. pap. text ed. 9.95 (ISBN 0-7216-5529-7). Saunders.
Kunnes, Richard. Your Money or Your Life: An Indictment of the Medical Market Place. LC 72-169733. 1971. 5.95 (ISBN 0-396-06422-1). Dodd.
LaPatra, J. W. Health Care Delivery Systems: Evaluation Criteria. (Illus.). 368p. 1975. 27.25 (ISBN 0-398-03357-9). C C Thomas.
LaPorte, Valerie & Rubin, Jeffrey, eds. Reform & Regulation of Long Term Care. LC 79-9761. 230p. 1979. 22.95 (ISBN 0-03-049341-2). Praeger.
Lasagna, Louis, ed. Patient Compliance. LC 76-11720. (Principles & Techniques of Human Research Ser: Vol. 10). 1976. 14.50 (ISBN 0-87993-081-0). Futura Pub.
Lasdon, Gail S. Improving Ambulatory Health Care Delivery. LC 77-75659. (Ambulatory Care Systems Ser.). 1977. 19.95 (ISBN 0-669-01514-8). Lexington Bks.
Lee, Isaiah. Medical Care in a Mexican American Community. LC 76-4706. (Illus.). 186p. 1976. pap. text ed. 5.95 (ISBN 0-89260-024-1). Hwong Pub.
Lee, Phillip R., et al. Primary Care in a Specialized World. LC 76-10222. 1976. 20.00 (ISBN 0-88410-139-8). Ballinger Pub.
Lee, Ruth M. Orientation to Health Services. LC 77-15094. 1978. pap. 8.85 (ISBN 0-672-61434-0); tchr's manual 3.33 (ISBN 0-672-61435-9). Bobbs.
Levey, Samuel & McCarthy, Thomas, eds. Health Management for Tomorrow. (Illus.). 394p. 1980. text ed. 23.75 (ISBN 0-397-50442-X, JBL-Med-Nursing). Har-Row.
Levin, Lowell & Idler, Ellen. The Hidden Health Care System: Mediating Structures & Health. 1981. 19.00 (ISBN 0-88410-822-8). Ballinger Pub.
Lewis, Charles, et al. A Right to Health: The Problem of Access to Primary Medical Care. LC 76-18129. (Health, Medicine, & Society Ser.). 416p. 1976. 30.95 (ISBN 0-471-01494-X, Pub. by Wiley-Interscience). Wiley.
Lewis, Charles E. Health & Medical Care Services: Current Critical Issues. LC 80-17126. (Collected Essay Ser.). 64p. 1981. pap. text ed. 6.95 (ISBN 0-917724-17-8). Haworth Pr.
Lipp, Martin R. Respectful Treatment: The Human Side of Medical Care. 1977. pap. 14.50x (ISBN 0-06-141550-2, Harper Medical). Har-Row.
Long, Lynette, et al. Questioning: Skills for the Helping Process. LC 80-24385. (Orig.). 1980. pap. text ed. 8.95 (ISBN 0-87872-284-X). Brooks-Cole.
Low-Cost Rural Health Care & Health Manpower Training, Vol. 3. 1977. pap. 10.00 (ISBN 0-88936-138-X, IDRC 93, IDRC). Unipub.
Lusterman, Seymour. Industry Roles in Health Care. (Report Ser: No. 610). 130p. (Orig.). 1974. pap. 20.00 (ISBN 0-8237-0033-X). Conference Bd.
McEwan, Peter J., ed. International Conference on Social Science & Medicine, 6th, Amsterdam, 1979: Second Special Conference Issue. 80p. 1980. pap. 14.40 (ISBN 0-08-026763-7). Pergamon.
Mackichan, N. D. The GP & the Primary Health Care Team. (Illus.). 1976. text ed. 19.95x (ISBN 0-8464-0453-2). Beekman Pubs.
Mackie, Dustin & Decker, Douglas. Group & Ipa Hmo's. LC 81-2096. 492p. 1981. text ed. 34.50 (ISBN 0-89443-341-5). Aspen Systems.
MacKintosh, Douglas R. Systems of Health Care. LC 78-3134. (Illus.). 1978. lib. bdg. 28.75 (ISBN 0-89158-330-0); pap. text ed. 13.50x (ISBN 0-89158-818-3). Westview.
McLachlan, Gordon & McKeown, Thomas, eds. Medical History & Medical Care: A Symposium of Perspectives. (Nuffield Publications). 1971. 9.75x (ISBN 0-19-721362-6). Oxford U Pr.
MacStravic, Robin S. Marketing by Objectives for Hospitals. LC 80-10903. 280p. 1980. text ed. 26.95 (ISBN 0-89443-174-9). Aspen Systems.
McTaggart, Aubrey C. & McTaggart, Lorna M. The Health Care Dilemma. 2nd ed. 275p. 1976. pap. text ed. 14.95 (ISBN 0-205-05446-3, 7154461). Allyn.
Mahajan, Vijay & Pegels, C. Carl, eds. Systems Analysis in Health Care. 1979. 34.50 (ISBN 0-03-046656-3). Praeger.
Martinez, Ricardo A., et al, eds. Hispanic Culture & Health Care: Fact, Fiction, Folklore. LC 77-26985. 1978. pap. text ed. 11.50 (ISBN 0-8016-3143-2). Mosby.
Maxmen, Jerrold S. The Post-Physician Era: Medicine in the 21st Century. LC 76-2442. (Health, Medicine & Society Ser.). 1976. 26.95 (ISBN 0-471-57880-0, Pub. by Wiley-Interscience). Wiley.
Mayers, Marlene & El Camino Hospital. Standard Nursing Care Plans, Vols. 1-2. Incl. Vol. 1. Medical, Surgical, Orthopedic, & Gyn. 1974; Vol. 2. ICU, CCU, Emergency Room, Psychiatric Units, Hemodialysis. 1975. incl. 3 ring binder 25.00x ea. KP Med.
Mayfield, Peggy, et al. Health Assessment: A Modular Approach. Browning, Martha, ed. (Illus.). 1980. pap. text ed. 10.95 (ISBN 0-07-041027-5); ans. bklt. 2.95 (ISBN 0-07-041028-3). McGraw.
Mechanic, David. Politics, Medicine & Social Science. 306p. 1974. 23.50 (ISBN 0-471-59008-8, Pub. by Wiley-Interscience). Wiley.
Milio, Nancy. The Care of Health in Communities. (Illus.). 1975. text ed. 12.95 (ISBN 0-02-381130-7). Macmillan.
Miller, Alfred E. & Miller, Maria G. Options for Health & Health Care: The Coming of Post-Clinical Medicine. LC 80-27755. (Health Medicine & Society Ser.). 478p. 1981. 29.50 (ISBN 0-471-60409-7, Pub. by Wiley-Interscience). Wiley.
Miller, Lewis. The Life You Save. 272p. 1981. pap. 2.95 (ISBN 0-425-05047-5). Berkley Pub.
--The Life You Save: A Guide to Getting the Best Possible Care from Doctors, Hospitals, & Nursing Homes. LC 78-1728. 1979. 9.95 (ISBN 0-688-03461-6). Morrow.
Miller, M. Clinton & Knapp, Rebecca G. Evaluating Quality of Care: Analytic Procedures, Monitoring Techniques. LC 79-4482. 352p. 1979. 30.95 (ISBN 0-89443-091-2). Aspen Systems.
Mooney, G., et al. Choices for Health Care. 1981. pap. 17.00x (ISBN 0-333-26331-6). Verry.
Morgan, James. Checklist of OSHA Regulations for Health Care Institutions. (Illus., Orig.). 1974. pap. 3.00 (ISBN 0-87125-015-2). Cath Health.
Morreale, Joseph C., ed. The U. S. Medical Care Industry: The Economist's Point of View. (Michigan Business Papers: No. 60). 131p. 1974. pap. 5.50 (ISBN 0-87712-166-4). U Mich Busn Div Res.
Mushkin, Selma J., ed. Consumer Incentives for Health Care. 446p. 1974. pap. text ed. 14.00 (ISBN 0-88202-057-9, Prodist). N Watson.
National Center for Health Statistics. A Study of the Effect of Remuneration Upon Response in the Health & Nutrition Examination Survey. Knox, Kathleen, ed. LC 75-619184. (Data Evaluation & Methods Research Ser 2: No. 67). 52p. 1975. pap. text ed. 1.25 (ISBN 0-8406-0046-1). Natl Ctr Health Stats.
National Committee for Vital & Health Statistics. The Analytical Potential of Nchs Data for Health Care Systems. Shipp, Audrey M., ed. LC 75-619171. (Documents & Committee Reports Ser. 4: No. 17). 50p. 1976. pap. 1.25 (ISBN 0-8406-0044-5). Natl Ctr Health Stats.
Navarro, Vicente, ed. Health & Medical Care in the U.S. A Critical Analysis. LC 77-70380. (Policy, Politics, Health & Medicine Ser.: Vol. 1). 1977. pap. 6.00 (ISBN 0-89503-000-4). Baywood Pub.
Navarro, Vincent. Medicine Under Capitalism. 2nd ed. LC 76-28521. 1977. pap. 8.95 (ISBN 0-88202-116-8). N Watson.
NCHS. State Estimates of Disability and Utilization of Medical Services, 1969-1971 Derived from the United States Health Interview Survey. (Ser. 10: No. 108). 55p. 1976. pap. 1.50 (ISBN 0-8406-0076-3). Natl. Ctr Health Stats.
Neelon, Francis A. & Ellis, George. A Syllabus of Problem Oriented Patient Care. 1974. spiral binding 6.95 (ISBN 0-316-59980-8). Little.
Noble, John, ed. Primary Care & the Practice of Medicine. LC 75-41569. 1976. text ed. 19.95 (ISBN 0-316-61148-4). Little.
Oakes, Charles G. The Walking Patient & the Health Crisis. LC 73-6667. (Illus.). 1973. lib. bdg. 19.50x (ISBN 0-87249-272-9). U of SC Pr.
Oatman, Eric F., ed. Medical Care in the United States. (Reference Shelf Ser.: Vol. 50, No. 1). 1978. 6.25 (ISBN 0-8242-0622-3). Wilson.
Paringer, Lynn, et al. Health Status & Use of Medical Services: Evidence on the Poor, the Black, & the Rural Elderly. (An Institute Paper). 111p. 1979. pap. 7.50 (ISBN 0-87766-241-X, 24800). Urban Inst.
Payne, Beverly C. The Quality of Medical Care: Evaluation & Improvement. LC 75-27157. 1976. 8.00 (ISBN 0-87914-029-1, 9153). Hosp Res & Educ.
Pfeiffer, Carl C. Mental & Elemental Nutrients: A Physician's Guide to Nutrition & Health Care. LC 75-19543. 556p. 1976. 10.95 (ISBN 0-87983-114-6). Keats.
Plovnick, Mark S. & Fry, Ronald E. Managing Health Care Delivery: A Training Program for Primary Care Physicians. LC 77-21501. 1978. 15.00 (ISBN 0-88410-518-0). Ballinger Pub.
Powell, Francis D. Theory of Coping Systems: Change in Supportive Health Organizations. LC 75-24554. (Illus.). 244p. 1975. text ed. 13.25x (ISBN 0-87073-029-0). Schenkman.
The Practice of Planning in Health Care Institutions. LC 73-77589. 112p. 1973. pap. 15.00 (ISBN 0-87258-120-9, 2765). Am Hospital.
Proger, Samuel & Williams, Greer. A Career in Primary Care. LC 76-26685. 1976. professional ref. 16.00 (ISBN 0-88410-148-7). Ballinger Pub.
Raffel, Marshall. The U. S. Health System: Origins & Functions. LC 80-86. 1980. 19.95 (ISBN 0-471-04512-8, Pub. by Wiley Med). Wiley.
Rand, Royden N., et al, eds. Quality Assurance in Health Care: A Critical Appraisal of Clinical Chemistry. LC 80-66260. 460p. 1980. 26.50 (ISBN 0-915274-11-6). Am Assn Clinical Chem.
Rehr, Helen, ed. Ethical Dilemmas in Health Care: A Professional Search for Solutions. 1978. pap. text ed. 7.95 (ISBN 0-88202-124-9). N Watson.
Reisman, A. & Kiley, M. Health Care Delivery Planning. (Studies in Operations Research Ser.). 1973. 37.00x (ISBN 0-677-04570-0). Gordon.
Remen, Naomi. The Human Patient. LC 77-16941. 264p. 1980. 10.95 (ISBN 0-385-13251-4, Anchor Pr). Doubleday.
Richmond, Julius B. Currents in American Medicine: A Developmental View of Medical Care & Education. LC 69-12733. (Commonwealth Fund Publications Ser). 1969. 7.95x (ISBN 0-674-18015-1). Harvard U Pr.
Roemer. Healthcare Systems & Comparative Manpower Policies. (Health Policy Ser.: Vol. 1). 1981. 27.50 (ISBN 0-8247-1389-3). Dekker.
Roemer, Milton I. Health Care Systems in World Perspective. LC 75-36706. 600p. 1976. text ed. 25.00 (ISBN 0-914904-13-2). Health Admin Pr.
--Social Medicine: The Advance of Organized Health Services in America. LC 78-17621. (Health Care & Society Ser.: Vol. 3). 1978. text ed. 29.00 (ISBN 0-8261-2600-6). Springer Pub.
Roemer, Ruth, et al. Planning Urban Health Services - from Jungle to System. LC 73-92203. 384p. 1975. pap. text ed. 9.50 (ISBN 0-8261-1651-5). Springer Pub.
Rosen, Harry, et al, eds. The Consumer & the Health Care Systems: Social & Managerial Perspectives. (Health Systems Management Ser.: Vol. 9). 1977. 17.95 (ISBN 0-470-99112-7). Halsted Pr.

Rosoff, Arnold J. Informed Consent: A Guide for Health Care Providers. LC 80-23886. 520p. 1981. text ed. 37.50 (ISBN 0-89443-293-1). Aspen Systems.
Rosser, James M. & Mossberg, Howard E. An Analysis of Health Care Delivery. LC 80-11611. 188p. 1981. Repr. of 1977 ed. lib. bdg. write for info. (ISBN 0-89874-158-0). Krieger.
Rubenstein, E. Intensive Medical Care. 1971. 14.95 (ISBN 0-07-054185-X, HP). McGraw.
Rubin, Irwin, et al. Improving the Coordination of Care: A Program for Health Team Development. LC 75-22431. 96p. 1975. wkbk. 18.50 (ISBN 0-88410-120-7). Ballinger Pub.
Rubright, Bob & MacDonald, Dan. Marketing Health & Human Services. LC 81-737. 248p. 1981. text ed. 25.95 (ISBN 0-89443-338-5). Aspen Systems.
Rushmer, Robert F. Humanizing Health Care: Alternative Futures for Medicine. LC 75-1399. (Illus.). 211p. 1975. 15.50x (ISBN 0-262-18075-8); pap. 4.95x (ISBN 0-262-68032-7). MIT Pr.
Rutstein, David D. A Blueprint for Medical Care. 245p. 1974. 12.00x (ISBN 0-262-18065-0); pap. 5.95 (ISBN 0-262-68033-5). MIT Pr.
Salk, Lee. Ask Dr. Salk. 1981. 10.95 (ISBN 0-672-52677-8). Bobbs.
Sampson, Edward E. & Marthas, Marya S. Group Processes for the Health Professions. LC 77-23013. 1977. pap. 11.95 (ISBN 0-471-01987-9, Pub. by Wiley Medical). Wiley.
Savitt, Todd L. Medicine & Slavery: The Health Care of Blacks in Antebellum Virginia. LC 78-8520. (Blacks in the New World Ser.). (Illus.). 321p. 1981. pap. 7.95 (ISBN 0-252-00874-X). U of Ill Pr.
Schaller, Warren E. & Carroll, Charles R. Health, Quackery, & the Consumer. LC 75-5058. (Illus.). 425p. 1976. text ed. 14.95 (ISBN 0-7216-7949-8). Saunders.
Schwartz, Rosalind, ed. Health Care & Industrial Relations: Costs, Conflicts & Controversy. (Monograph Ser.: No. 28). 90p. 1981. 7.50 (ISBN 0-89215-112-9). U Cal LA Indus Rel.
Sheldon, Alan, et al, eds. Systems & Medical Care. 1970. 18.00x (ISBN 0-262-19077-X). MIT Pr.
Shindell, Sidney, et al. A Coursebook in Health Care Delivery. (Illus.). 602p. 1976. text ed. 26.50 (ISBN 0-8385-1270-4). ACC.
Sirrocco, Alvin. Inpatient Health Facilities As Reported in the 1973 MFI Survey. (Ser. 14: No. 16). 63p. 1976. pap. text ed. 1.50 (ISBN 0-8406-0058-5). Natl Ctr Health Stats.
Smith, David B. & Kaluzny, Arnold D. The White Labyrinth: Understanding the Organization of Health Care. LC 75-7012. 250p. 1975. 24.70x (ISBN 0-8211-1854-4); text ed. 22.05x (ISBN 0-685-53678-5). McCutchan.
Smith, Mickey C. & Knapp, David A. Pharmacy, Drugs & Medical Care. 3rd ed. (Illus.). 352p. 1980. soft cover 19.95 (ISBN 0-686-77763-8, 7761-9). Williams & Wilkins.
Sobel, Lester A., ed. Health Care: An American Crisis. 200p. 1976. lib. bdg. 17.50x (ISBN 0-87196-288-8). Facts on File.
Somers, Anne R. Health Care in Transition: Directions for the Future. LC 77-160033. 176p. 1971. 6.00 (ISBN 0-87914-005-4, 9070). Hosp Res & Educ.
Somers, Anne R. & Somers, Herman M. Health & Health Care: Policies in Perspective. LC 77-76921. 1977. 29.95 (ISBN 0-912862-45-9); pap. text ed. 15.95 (ISBN 0-912862-49-1). Aspen Systems.
Somers, Herman M. & Somers, Anne R. Doctors, Patients, & Health Insurance: The Organization & Financing of Medical Care. 1961. 15.95 (ISBN 0-8157-8036-2). Brookings.
Spiegel, Allen D. & Backhaut, Bernard. Curing & Caring: A Review of the Factors Affecting the Quality & Acceptability of Health Care. (Health Systems Management Ser.: Vol. 13). 205p. 1980. text ed. 30.00 (ISBN 0-89335-099-0). Spectrum Pub.
Squyres, Wendy. Patient Education-an Inquiry into the State of the Art. LC 79-27556. (Springer Ser. in Health Care & Society: Vol. 4). 1980. 26.50 (ISBN 0-8261-3120-4). Springer Pub.
Stamps, Paula L. Ambulatory Care Systems, Vol. 3: Evaluation of Outpatient Facilities. LC 76-55865. (Illus.). 1978. 21.50 (ISBN 0-669-01325-0). Lexington Bks.
Standard Medical Almanac. 2nd ed. LC 79-87624. 712p. 1980. 39.50 (ISBN 0-8379-4002-8, 031069). Marquis.
Staropoli, Charles J. & Waltz, Carolyn F. Developing & Evaluating Educational Programs for Health Care Providers. LC 77-15618. (Illus.). 210p. 1978. pap. text ed. 13.50 (ISBN 0-8036-8100-3). Davis Co.
Staum, M. & Larsen, Donald, eds. Doctors, Patients, & Society: Power & Authority in Medical Care. 347p. 1981. pap. text ed. 11.00x (ISBN 0-88920-111-0, Pub. by Laurier U Pr). Humanities.
Steinhaus, John E. Medical Care-Divided. 148p. 1981. 10.95 (ISBN 0-89313-053-2). G F Stickley.
Stevens, Rosemary. American Medicine & the Public Interest. LC 77-151592. 1971. pap. 7.95 (ISBN 0-300-01744-8, Y264). Yale U Pr.
Stimson, Gerry V. & Webb, Barbara. Going to See the Doctor. (Medicine, Illnes & Society Ser.). 1975. 18.00 (ISBN 0-7100-8075-1). Routledge & Kegan.
Tavares, B. M., ed. Acute Care: Based on the Proceedings of the Sixth International Symposium on Critical Care Medicine, Rio De Janeiro, 1977. (Anaesthesiologie und Intensivmedizin: Vol. 116). (Illus.). 1979. pap. 45.10 (ISBN 0-387-09210-2). Springer-Verlag.
Taylor, Carl E., et al. Doctors for the Villages. 1976. lib. bdg. 12.50x (ISBN 0-210-40583-X). Asia.
Thompson, Frank J. Health Policy & the Bureaucracy: Politics & Implementation. 252p. 1981. 25.00x (ISBN 0-262-20041-4). MIT Pr.
Thompson, John D. Applied Health Services Research. LC 75-12482. (Illus.). 1977. 19.95 (ISBN 0-669-00028-0). Lexington Bks.
Thypin, Marilyn & Glasner, Lynne. Health Care for the Wongs (Obtaining Medical Aid) LC 79-17188. (Consumer Education Ser.: No. 2). (Orig.). (gr. 9-12). 1980. pap. text ed. 3.50 (ISBN 0-88436-513-1). EMC.
Towell, D. & Harries, C. Innovations in Patient Care. 224p. 1980. 30.00x (ISBN 0-85664-692-X, Pub. by Croom Helm England). State Mutual Bk.
Towell, David & Harries, Clive, eds. Innovation in Patient Care. 1981. 25.00x (ISBN 0-85664-692-X, Pub. by Croom Helm Ltd England). Biblio Dist.
Tucker, Susan M., et al. Patient Care Standards. 2nd ed. LC 79-24410. (Illus.). 1980. pap. text ed. 17.95 (ISBN 0-8016-5122-0). Mosby.
Veldkamp, G. M. J. Social Security & Medical Care. 1978. pap. 27.50 (ISBN 90-312-0058-1, Pub. by Kluwer Law Netherlands). Kluwer Boston.
Verbrugge, Lois A. Medical Care of Acute Conditions United States, 1973-1974. Shipp, Audrey, ed. (Ser. 10: No. 129). 1979. pap. text ed. 1.75 (ISBN 0-8406-0155-7). Natl Ctr Health Stats.
Vickery, Donald M. & Fries, James F. Take Care of Yourself: A Consumer's Guide to Medical Care. LC 76-1378. (Illus.). 288p. 1976. 10.95 (ISBN 0-201-02401-2); pap. 6.95 (ISBN 0-201-02402-0). A-W.
Waisbren, Burton A. Critical Care Manual: A Systems Approach Method. 2nd ed. 1977. pap. 16.00 (ISBN 0-87488-983-9). Med Exam.
Waitzkin, Howard & Waterman, Barbara. Exploitation of Illness in Capitalist Society. LC 73-19706. (Studies in Sociology Ser). 1974. pap. text ed. 3.95 (ISBN 0-672-61327-1). Bobbs.
Wallis, Roy & Morley, Peter, eds. Marginal Medicine. LC 76-43129. 1977. 8.95 (ISBN 0-02-933740-2). Free Pr.
Walraven, Gail. Manual of Advanced Prehospital Care. (Illus.). 430p. 1978. pap. text ed. 14.95 (ISBN 0-87618-995-8). R J Brady.
Warner, Carmen G. Rape & Sexual Assault: Management & Intervention. LC 79-24643. (Illus.). 364p. 1980. text ed. 22.50 (ISBN 0-89443-172-2). Aspen Systems.
Watson, Annita & Mayers, Marlene. Care Planning: Chronic Problem - STAT Solution. 1976. soft cover 6.95x (ISBN 0-686-18879-9). KP Med.
Webb, Linda J., et al, eds. DSM-III Training Program for Health Professionals. 160p. 1981. pap. text ed. 9.95 A Guide to Clinical Use (ISBN 0-686-73216-2); price not set slides (ISBN 0-87630-281-9); price not set videotape (ISBN 0-87630-280-0); price not set complete pkg. (ISBN 0-87630-282-7). Brunner-Mazel.
Weller, Charles, ed. Computer Applications in Health Care Delivery. LC 76-10867. (Illus.). 192p. 1976. text ed. 22.00 (ISBN 0-8151-9214-2, Pub. by Symposia Special). Year Bk Med.
Werley, Harriet, et al, eds. Health Research: The Systems Approach. LC 73-92207. (Illus.). 330p. 1976. text ed. 17.95 (ISBN 0-8261-1710-4). Springer Pub.
Werther, William B. & Lockhart, Carol A. Labor Relations in the Health Professions. 1976. pap. 9.95 (ISBN 0-316-93100-4). Little.
WHO Expert Committee. Geneva, 1968, 2nd. WHO Expert Committee on Medical Rehabilitation: Report. (Technical Report Ser.: No. 419). (Also avail. in French). 1969. pap. 1.20 (ISBN 92-4-120419-2). World Health.
Williams, Kenneth & Donnelly, Paul. Medical Care Quality & the Public Trust. 1981. price not set (ISBN 0-931028-22-1); pap. price not set (ISBN 0-931028-23-X). Teach'em.
Williamson, John W. Assessing & Improving Health Care Outcomes: The Health Accounting Approach to Quality Assurance. LC 78-2367. 1978. 18.50 (ISBN 0-88410-706-X). Ballinger Pub.
Wilson, Florence & Neuhauser, Duncan. Health Services in the United States. LC 76-42472. 1976. 12.50 (ISBN 0-88410-700-0). Ballinger Pub.
World Organization of National College Physicians (WONCA) International Classification of Health Problems in Primary Care. 2nd ed. 1979. text ed. 16.95x (ISBN 0-19-261195-X); pap. text ed. 8.95x (ISBN 0-19-261186-0). Oxford U Pr.
Zimmerman, Clarence H. Techniques of Patient Care: A Manual of Bedside Procedures. 2nd ed. LC 75-41574. 1976. pap. text ed. 9.95 (ISBN 0-316-98868-5). Little.

MEDICAL CARE–ADMINISTRATION
see Public Health Administration

MEDICAL CARE–BIBLIOGRAPHY
American Hospital Association. American Hospital Association Guide to the Health Care Field: 1975 Ed. 612p. 1975. casebd. 25.00 (ISBN 0-87258-166-7, 2475). Am Hospital.
--Cumulative Index of Hospital Literature: 1975-1977. 564p. 1979. casebound 75.00 (ISBN 0-87258-260-4, 1386). Am Hospital.
Clark, Gary L. An Annotated Bibliography on Long-Term Care Administration 1974-1975. 5.00 (ISBN 0-686-24302-1). Assn Univ Progs Hlth.
Feierman, Steven, compiled by. Health & Society in Africa: A Working Bibliography. (Archival & Bibliographic Ser.). 1978. pap. 20.00 (ISBN 0-918456-16-9, Crossroads). African Studies Assn.
Health Care: A Bibliographic Guide to the 1979 Documents Update. 1981. pap. write for info. Microfilming Corp.
Health Care, Nineteen Seventy to Nineteen Seventy-Eight: A Bibliographic Guide to the Microfiche Collection. 262p. 1980. pap. 50.00 (ISBN 0-667-00549-8). Microfilming Corp.
Singer, Philip & Titus, Elizabeth A., eds. Resources for Third World Health Planners: A Selected Subject Bibliography. (Traditional Healing Ser.: No. 6). 168p. (Orig.). 1980. 17.50 (ISBN 0-932426-11-5); pap. 9.95 (ISBN 0-932426-12-3). Trado Medic.
Tichy, Monique K. Health Care Teams: An Annotated Bibliography. LC 74-14674. (Special Studies). 190p. 1974. text ed. 24.95 (ISBN 0-275-05750-X). Praeger.
Williamson, John W. Improving Medical Practice & Health Care: A Bibliographic Guide to Information Management in Quality Assurance & Continuing Education. LC 77-24711. 1977. 45.00 (ISBN 0-88410-702-7). Ballinger Pub.

MEDICAL CARE–DIRECTORIES
Abel-Smith, Brian. Value for Money in Health Services. 1976. pap. text ed. 16.50x (ISBN 0-435-82006-0). Heinemann Ed.
Alperin, Stanley & Alperin, Melvin, eds. U. S. Medical Directory. 5th ed. LC 72-92344. 1980-1981. 59.50 (ISBN 0-916524-05-1). US Direct Serv.
Grupenhoff, John T., ed. National Health Directory. rev. ed. 1981. text ed. 49.50 (ISBN 0-89443-368-7). Aspen Systems.
Kruzas, Anthony T., ed. Health Services Directory: A Guide to Clinics, Treatment Centers, Rehabilitation Facilities, Care Programs Counseling-Diagnostic Resources & Related Human Services Institutions, Agencies & Associations. 620p. 1981. 60.00 (ISBN 0-8103-0272-1). Gale.
--Medical & Health Information Directory: A Guide to Professional & Nonprofit Organizations, Government Agencies, Educational Institutons, Grant Award Sources, Health Care Insurers, Journals, Newsletters, Review Serials, Etc. 2nd ed. LC 77-82802. 1980. 110.00 (ISBN 0-8103-0267-5). Gale.
Ulene, Art & Feldman, Sandy. Help Yourself to Health: A Health Information & Services Directory. 1980. 19.95 (ISBN 0-399-12474-8, Perigee); pap. 10.00 (ISBN 0-399-50465-6). Putnam.

MEDICAL CARE–RESEARCH
see Medical Research

MEDICAL CARE–CANADA
Culyer, A. J. Measuring Health: Lessons for Ontario. (Ontario Economic Council Research Studies). 1978. pap. 12.50 (ISBN 0-8020-3354-7). U of Toronto Pr.

MEDICAL CARE–FRANCE
The French Health Care System. pap. 3.50 (ISBN 0-89970-044-6, OP-460). AMA.
Sandier, S. Comparison of Health Expenditures in France & the United States. Shipp, Audrey, ed. 60p. 1981. pap. text ed. 1.95 (ISBN 0-8406-0224-3). Natl Ctr Health Stats.

MEDICAL CARE–GREAT BRITAIN
Anderson, Odin W. Health Care: Can There Be Equity? the United States, Sweden, & England. LC 72-7449. 273p. 1972. 25.50 (ISBN 0-471-02760-X, Pub. by Wiley-Interscience). Wiley.
The British Health Care System. pap. 7.50 (ISBN 0-89970-025-X, OP-461). AMA.
Cule, John. A Doctor for the People: 2000 Years of General Practice in Britain. (Illus.). 1981. PLB 39.00 (ISBN 0-906141-29-X, Pub. by Update Pubns England). Kluwer Boston.
Davis, R. Harvard. General Practice for Students of Medicine. (Monographs for Students of Medicine Ser.). 1975. 16.50 (ISBN 0-12-328850-9). Acad Pr.
Forsyth, Gordon. Doctors & State Medicine in England. 224p. 1973. pap. text ed. 12.50x (ISBN 0-8464-0339-0). Beekman Pubs.
Honigsbaum, Frank. The Division in British Medicine: The Separation of General Practice from Hospital Care, Nineteen Eleven to Nineteen Sixty-Eight. LC 79-14789. 1979. 25.00x (ISBN 0-312-21431-6). St Martin.
Woodward, John. To Do the Sick No Harm: A Study of the British Voluntary Hospital System to 1875. (International Library of Social Policy Ser.). 1978. pap. 8.95 (ISBN 0-7100-8911-2). Routledge & Kegan.

MEDICAL CARE–LATIN AMERICA
Bordes, Ary & Couture, Andrea. For the People, for a Change: Bringing Health to the Families of Haiti. LC 77-88372. (Illus.). 1978. 11.95 (ISBN 0-8070-2166-0). Beacon Pr.
Navarro, Vincent. Medicine Under Capitalism. 2nd ed. LC 76-28521. 1977. pap. 8.95 (ISBN 0-88202-116-8). N Watson.
Young, James C. Medical Choice in a Mexican Village. 256p. 1981. 19.50 (ISBN 0-8135-0895-9). Rutgers U Pr.

MEDICAL CARE–NORWAY
Evang, Karl. Health Services in Norway. 1976. pap. 17.00x (ISBN 8-200-02373-7, Dist. by Columbia U Pr). Universitet.

MEDICAL CARE–RUSSIA
Ryan, Michael. The Organization of Soviet Medical Care. (Aspects of Social Policy). 168p. 1978. 24.50x (ISBN 0-631-18140-7, Pub. by Basil Blackwell). Biblio Dist.

MEDICAL CARE, AMBULATORY
see Ambulatory Medical Care

MEDICAL CARE, COST OF
see also Hospitals–Rates
Abel-Smith, B. International Study of Health Expenditure & Its Relevance for Health Planning. (Public Health Paper: No. 32). (Also avail. in French, Russian & Spanish). 1967. pap. 2.80 (ISBN 92-4-130032-9). World Health.
Aikman, Ralph & Schwartz, Rachel. Life Cycle Cost Analysis Handbook. 1977. pap. 18.00x (ISBN 0-89011-509-5, HMD-128). Abt Assoc.
American Medical Record Association. Glossary of Hospital Terms. 2nd rev. ed. 128p. 1974. 5.75 (ISBN 0-686-68577-6, 14911). Hospital Finan.
AUPHA Task Force on Financial Management. Financial Management of Health Care Organizations: A Referenced Outline & Annotated Bibliography. 237p. 1978. 8.00 (ISBN 0-686-68588-1, 14921). Hospital Finan.
Austin, Charles J. The Politics of National Health Insurance: An Interdisciplinary Research Study. LC 75-14975. (Trinity Univ. Health Services Research Ser.). 1975. 7.50 (ISBN 0-911536-60-4). Trinity U Pr.
Babson, J. H. Disease Costing. 104p. 1973. 21.00x (ISBN 0-7190-0524-8, Pub. by Manchester U Pr England). State Mutual Bk.
Berman, Howard W. & Weeks, Lewis E. The Financial Management of Hospitals. 3rd ed. (Illus.). 585p. 1976. 17.50 (ISBN 0-686-68573-3, 1496). Hospital Finan.
Birnbaum, Howard. The Cost of Catastrophic Illness. LC 77-9192. 1978. 14.95 (ISBN 0-669-01773-6). Lexington Bks.
Brandt, A., et al. Cost-Sharing in Health Care: Proceedings. (Illus.). 184p. 1981. pap. 20.00 (ISBN 0-387-10325-2). Springer-Verlag.
Braverman, Jordan. A Consumer's Book of Health: Advice on Stretching Your Health Care Dollar. 1981. 11.95 (ISBN 0-03-059079-5); pap. 6.95 (ISBN 0-03-059078-7). HR&
Buchanan, Robert J. Health-Care Finance: An Analysis of Cost & Utilization Issues. LC 80-8362. 1981. 19.95x (ISBN 0-669-04035-5). Lexington Bks.
Bureau of Business Research, ed. Health Care Cost Containment: The Managerial Approach. 1978. 7.50 (ISBN 0-686-28414-3). Bur Busn Res U Nebr.
Checkoway, Barry, ed. Condition Critical: Consumers & Health Care Planning. (Pergamon Policy Studies on Social Policy). (Illus.). 270p. 1981. 27.01 (ISBN 0-08-027192-8). Pergamon.
Choi, Jai. Out-of-Pocket Cost & Acquisition of Prescribed Medicines, U.S., 1973. Brown, Arlett, ed. (Ser 10: No. 108). 1977. pap. text ed. 1.75 (ISBN 0-8406-0091-7). Natl Ctr Health Stats.
Citizens Board of Inquiry into Health Services for Americans. Heal Yourself. 2.95x (ISBN 0-685-31246-1, 086). Am Pub Health.
Cleverley, William O. Financial Management of Health Care Facilities. 394p. 1976. 18.75 (ISBN 0-686-68581-4, 14915). Hospital Finan.

Cromwell, Jerry, et al. A Study of Administrative Costs in Physicians' Offices Under Medicaid. 1977. pap. 38.60 (ISBN 0-89011-508-7, HMD-144). Abt Assoc.
Dowling, William L. Prospective Rate Setting. LC 77-18700. 157p. 1977. text ed. 28.95 (ISBN 0-89443-028-9). Aspen Systems.
Drummond, M. F. Studies in Economic Appraisal in Health Care. 240p. 1981. text ed. 32.50x (ISBN 0-19-261274-3). Oxford U Pr.
Dublin, Louis I. & Lotka, Alfred J. The Money Value of a Man. Rosenkrantz, Barbara G., ed. LC 76-25659. (Public Health in America Ser.). (Illus.). 1977. Repr. of 1930 ed. lib. bdg. 18.00x (ISBN 0-405-09814-6). Arno.
Dye, Rex J. The Hospital Medical Racket & You. LC 74-34511. 1975. 6.50 (ISBN 0-682-48236-6, Banner). Exposition.
Eastaugh, Steven R. Medical Economics & Health Finance. LC 81-3450. 320p. 1981. 21.95 (ISBN 0-86569-065-0). Auburn Hse.
Egdahl, R. H. & Walsh, D. C., eds. Containing Health Benefit Costs: The Self-Insurance Option. (Springer Ser. on Industry & Health Care: Vol. 6). (Illus.). 1979. pap. 12.60 (ISBN 0-387-90385-2). Springer-Verlag.
Enthoven, Alain C. Health Plan: The Only Practical Solution to the Soaring Cost of Medical Care. LC 79-25583. (Illus.). 1980. text ed. 12.95 (ISBN 0-201-03143-4). A-W.
Erlich, David, ed. The Health Care Cost Explosion: Which Way Now? 250p. 1975. pap. 18.25 (ISBN 0-683-02789-1, Pub. by W & W). Krieger.
Falk, I. S., et al. The Costs of Medical Care: A Summary of Investigations on the Economic Aspects of the Prevention & Care of Illness, No. 27. LC 71-180568. (Medicine & Society in America Ser). 652p. 1972. Repr. of 1933 ed. 28.00 (ISBN 0-405-03950-6). Arno.
Falk, Isidore S., et al. The Incidence of Illness & the Receipt & Costs of Medical Care Among Representative Families: Experiences in Twelve Consecutive Months During 1928-1931. LC 75-17220. (Social Problems & Social Policy Ser.). (Illus.). 1976. Repr. of 1933 ed. 19.00x (ISBN 0-405-07491-3). Arno.
Feldstein, Paul J. Health Care Economics. LC 79-14268. (Health Services Ser.). 1979. 22.95 (ISBN 0-471-05361-9, Pub. by Wiley Medical). Wiley.
Fry, Phillip. Collecting Medical Debts, 1976. 1976. 25.00 (ISBN 0-686-15382-0). Tax Info Ctr.
GAP Committee on Governmental Agencies. Effect of the Method of Payment on Mental Health Care Practice, Vol. 9. LC 75-37988. (Report no. 95). 1975. pap. 4.00 (ISBN 0-87318-132-8, Pub. by Adv Psychiatry). Mental Health.
Hartunian, Nelson S., et al. The Incidence & Economic Costs of Major Health Impairments: A Comparative Analysis of Cancer, Motor-Vehicle Injuries, Coronary Heart Disease, & Stroke. LC 80-8189. 1981. 34.95 (ISBN 0-669-03975-6). Lexington Bks.
Hurtado, Arnold V., et al. Home Care & Extended Care in a Comprehensive Prepayment Plan. LC 72-85388. (Illus.). 127p. 1972. 6.00 (ISBN 0-87914-019-4, 9151). Hosp Res & Educ.
Keintz, Rita M., ed. Health Care Costs & Financing: A Guide to Information Sources. LC 80-23862. (Health Affairs Information Guide Ser.: Vol. 6). 400p. 1981. 36.00 (ISBN 0-8103-1482-7). Gale.
Kinzer, David M. Health Controls Out of Control. 194p. 9.75 (ISBN 0-686-68584-9, 14918). Hospital Finan.
Luke, Roice D. & Bauer, Jeffrey C. Readings in Health Economics. 600p. 1981. text ed. price not set (ISBN 0-89443-381-4). Aspen Systems.
Maxwell, Robert. Health & Wealth: An International Study of Health-Care Spending. LC 80-8472. 192p. 1981. 22.95 (ISBN 0-669-04109-2). Lexington Bks.
Monteiro, Lois A. Monitoring Health Status & Medical Care. LC 76-2483. 144p. 1976. text ed. 17.50 (ISBN 0-88410-106-1). Ballinger Pub.
Mumford, James G. How to Cut Your Children's Medical Costs. LC 79-67043. 54p. 1980. 5.95 (ISBN 0-533-04430-8). Vantage.
Murray, D. Stark. Blueprint for Health: A Multinational Portrait of the Costs & Administration of Medical Care in the Public Interest. LC 73-91343. 1974. 7.50x (ISBN 0-8052-3540-X). Schocken.
Musgrave, Frank W., ed. Health Economics & Health Care: Irreconcilable Gap? LC 78-59166. 1978. pap. text ed. 9.25 (ISBN 0-8191-0546-5). U Pr of Amer.
National Academy Of Engineering. Costs of Health Care Facilities. 1968. pap. 7.75 (ISBN 0-309-01592-8). Natl Acad Pr.
Pelton, Charles L. Doctor, My Bill Is Too High. 1978. 18.00 (ISBN 0-931470-01-3); pap. 14.95 (ISBN 0-931470-00-5). C L Pelton.
Personal Out-of-Pocket Health Expenses United States, 1975. (Ser. 10: No. 122). 1978. pap. text ed. 1.75 (ISBN 0-8406-0126-3). Natl Ctr Health Stats.
Rapoport, John, et al. Understanding Health Economics. 485p. 1981. text ed. price not set (ISBN 0-89443-380-6). Aspen Systems.
Salkever, David. Hospital Sector Inflation. (Illus.). 208p. 1979. 22.95 (ISBN 0-669-00704-8). Lexington Bks.
Silvers, John B. & Prahalad, C. K. Financial Management of Health Institutions. 339p. 1974. 17.95 (ISBN 0-686-68576-8, 14910). Hospital Finan.
Stakes, Mary E. & Chandler, R. Michael. Health Care Cost Containment. 62p. 1980. spiral bdg. 5.00 (ISBN 0-89854-061-5). U of GA Inst Govt.
Topics in Health Care Financing. Incl. Vol. 6, No. 2. Uniform Reporting (ISBN 0-912862-97-1); Vol. 6, No. 3. Employee Wage & Benefit Administration; Vol. 6, No. 4. Management Contracts (ISBN 0-912862-99-8); Vol. 7, No. 1. Financial Career Opportunities (ISBN 0-89443-175-7). 1979-80. write for info. Aspen Systems.
Turban, Ephraim, et al. Cost Containment in Hospitals. LC 80-13272. 648p. 1980. text ed. 39.75 (ISBN 0-89443-279-6). Aspen Systems.
Waller, Kal. How to Recover Your Medical Expenses. 96p. 1981. pap. 5.95 (ISBN 0-02-098940-7, Collier). Macmillan.
Ward, Richard A. The Economics of Health Resources. 150p. 1975. 10.25 (ISBN 0-686-68580-6, 14914). Hospital Finan.
Weeks, Lewis E. & Berman, Howard J., eds. Economics in Health Care. LC 77-10860. 402p. 1977. text ed. 25.00 (ISBN 0-89443-026-2). Aspen Systems.
Wilder, Charles S. Family Out-of-Pocket Health Expenses, U. S., 1970. Shipp, Audrey M., ed. LC 75-619266. (Ser. 10: No. 103). 51p. 1976. pap. 1.25 (ISBN 0-8406-0052-6). Natl Ctr Health Stats.
--Personal Out-of-Pocket Health Expenses U.S., 1970. LC 74-10911. (Data from the Health Interview Survey Ser. 10: No. 91). 53p. 1974. pap. text ed. 0.50 (ISBN 0-8406-0010-0). Natl Ctr Health Stats.
Wu, S. Y. & Zaidi, M. A., eds. Economic Issues Related to the Health Care Industry. (Journal: Health Communications & Informatics: Vol. 5, Nos. 5-6). (Illus.). 1980. pap. 22.75 (ISBN 3-8055-0473-X). S Karger.
Zubkoff, Michael. Health: A Victim or Cause of Inflation. (Orig.). 1976. pap. text ed. 10.95 (ISBN 0-88202-064-1). N Watson.

MEDICAL CARE, INDUSTRIAL
see Labor and Laboring Classes–Medical Care

MEDICAL CARE, PREPAID
see also Insurance, Health; Labor and Laboring Classes–Medical Care

Center for Information on America. Guide to Prepaid Group Health Care Programs. Keiser, A. Kay, ed. 1976. pap. 3.00 (ISBN 0-685-82750-X). Ctr Info Am.
Feder, Judith & Holahan, John. Financing Health Care for the Elderly: Medicare, Medicaid & Private Health Insurance. (Health Policy & the Elderly Ser.). 106p. 1979. pap. 5.50 (ISBN 0-87766-244-4, 24900). Urban Inst.
MacColl, William A. Group Practice & Prepayment of Medical Care. 1966. pap. 4.50 (ISBN 0-8183-0173-2). Pub Aff Pr.
Schoeck, Helmut, ed. Financing Medical Care: An Appraisal of Foreign Programs. LC 62-13033. 1966. 5.50 (ISBN 0-87004-148-7); pap. 2.50 (ISBN 0-87004-149-5). Caxton.
Shouldice, Robert G. & Shouldice, Katherine H. Medical Group Practice & Health Maintenance Organizations. LC 78-53824. (Illus.). 1978. text ed. 27.50 (ISBN 0-87815-020-X). Info Resources.

MEDICAL CARE, STATE
see Medicine, State

MEDICAL CARE FOR THE AGED
see Aged–Medical Care

MEDICAL CENTERS
see also Clinics; Hospitals; Medical Colleges; also names of medical centers, e.g. Mayo Clinic; Hunterdon Medical Center

American Hospital Association. Classification of Health Care Institutions. LC 74-19026. 32p. 1974. pap. 6.25 (ISBN 0-87258-159-4, 1700). Am Hospital.
Caruana, Russell A. A Guide to Organizing a Health Care Fiscal Services Division with Job Descriptions for Key Functions. 2nd ed. 94p. 1981. pap. 8.50 (ISBN 0-930228-13-8). Hospital Finan.
Gifford, James F. The Evolution of a Medical Center: A History of Medicine at Duke University to 1941. LC 73-185464. 1972. 14.75 (ISBN 0-8223-0290-X). Duke.
Ginzberg, Eli & Yohalem, Alice M., eds. The Medical Center & the Metropolis. LC 74-84413. (Illus.). 1974. 10.00 (ISBN 0-914362-12-7). J Macy Foun.
Harrell, George T. Planning Medical Center Facilities for Education, Research, & Public Service. LC 73-12293. 232p. 1974. 16.75x (ISBN 0-271-01163-7, Penn State). Pa St U Pr.
Holmgren, John H. Purchasing for the Health Care Facility. (Illus.). 288p. 1975. 28.75 (ISBN 0-398-03399-4). C C Thomas.
Hospitals, Clinics, & Health Centers. LC 70-142928. (An Architectural Record Book). (Illus.). viii, 264p. Repr. of 1960 ed. lib. bdg. 29.50x (ISBN 0-8371-5930-X, ARHC). Greenwood.
Lezer, Leon R. Community Medicine: Organization & Application of Principles. 1977. 8.95 (ISBN 0-533-02393-9). Vantage.
National Academy Of Engineering. Costs of Health Care Facilities. 1968. pap. 7.75 (ISBN 0-309-01592-8). Natl Acad Pr.
Schloen, Lloyd H. & Day, Stacey B., eds. Sloan-Kettering Institute Annual Report, 1973. LC 74-82707. (Illus.). 250p. 1974. 7.50 (ISBN 0-88485-000-5); pap. 5.00 (ISBN 0-685-50380-1). Sloan-Kettering.
Smith, David E. & Luce, John. Love Needs Care. LC 77-121434. (Illus.). 1971. 8.95 (ISBN 0-316-80143-7). Little.

MEDICAL CHARITIES
see Charities, Medical

MEDICAL CHEMISTRY
see Chemistry, Medical and Pharmaceutical

MEDICAL CLIMATOLOGY
see Climatology, Medical

MEDICAL CLINICS
see Clinics

MEDICAL COLLEGES
see also Medicine–Study and Teaching

Abse, Dannie, ed. My Medical School. (Illus.). 211p. 1978. 14.50x (ISBN 0-8476-3124-9). Rowman.
Alperin, Melvin & Alperin, Stanley. Worldwide Directory of Medical Schools. LC 79-3726. (Orig.). 1980. pap. 4.95 (ISBN 0-671-09184-0). Monarch Pr.
Alperin, Stanley, ed. Directory of Medical Schools Worldwide. 3rd ed. LC 77-93356. 1982. text ed. 24.95 (ISBN 0-916524-17-5). US Direct Serv.
Alperin, Stanley & Alperin, Melvin S., eds. Directory of Medical Schools Worldwide. 2nd ed. LC 77-93356. 1980. text ed. 19.95 (ISBN 0-916524-15-9). US Direct Serv.
American Medical Association. Foreign Medical Graduates in the U. S., 1970. pap. 5.00 (ISBN 0-89970-043-8, OP-376). AMA.
Barker, Wayne G. Medical Schools of the World Where Instruction Is Given in English. rev. ed. LC 76-47072. 1978. pap. 4.95 (ISBN 0-685-81945-0). Aegean Park Pr.
Beecher, Henry K. & Altschule, Mark D. Medicine at Harvard: The First Three Hundred Years. LC 75-40869. (Illus.). 603p. 1977. text ed. 30.00x (ISBN 0-87451-122-4). U Pr of New Eng.
Bowers, John Z. Western Medicine in a Chinese Palace: Peking Union Medical College, 1917-1951. LC 72-96069. (Illus.). 250p. 1973. 10.00 (ISBN 0-914362-06-2). J Macy Foun.
Bowers, John Z., ed. Medical Schools for the Modern World. LC 76-104059. (Josiah Macy Foundation Ser). (Illus.). 270p. 1970. 17.50x (ISBN 0-8018-1113-9). Johns Hopkins.
Bowers, John Z. & Purcell, Elizabeth F., eds. New Medical Schools at Home & Abroad. LC 78-54170. (Illus.). 552p. 1978. pap. 10.00 (ISBN 0-914362-26-7). J Macy Foun.
Bramson, Morris & Solomon, Lawrence. New MCAT. new ed. LC 78-2312. 1978. pap. 5.95 (ISBN 0-671-18990-5). Monarch Pr.
Bransford, Kent. The No-Nonsense Guide to Get You into Medical School. LC 78-11160. 1979. pap. 3.95 (ISBN 0-671-18353-2). Monarch Pr.
--The No-Nonsense Guide to Get You into Medical School. LC 78-11160. 1979. 8.95 (ISBN 0-671-18412-1); pap. write for info. Sovereign Bks.
Brown, Sanford J. Getting into Medical School. rev., upd. ed. LC 79-12544. 1979. pap. text ed. 3.95 (ISBN 0-8120-2157-6). Barron.
Bullock, Mary B. An American Transplant: The Rockefeller Foundation & Peking Union Medical College. LC 77-83098. 280p. 1981. 17.50x (ISBN 0-520-03559-3). U of Cal Pr.
Burn, Barbara B., ed. Admission to Medical Education in Ten Countries. (Access to Higher Education Ser.). 1978. pap. 6.00 (ISBN 0-89192-214-8). Interbk Inc.
Caplovitz, David. Student-Faculty Relations in Medical School: A Study of Professional Socialization. Zuckerman, Harriet & Merton, Robert K., eds. LC 79-8980. (Dissertations on Sociology Ser.). 1980. lib. bdg. 23.00x (ISBN 0-405-12956-4). Arno.
Council on Legal Education Opportunity. Bakke Versus Regents of the University of California, 6 vols. Slocum, Alfred A., ed. LC 78-3573. 1978. lib. bdg. 44.00 (ISBN 0-379-20297-2). Oceana.
Fine, Carla. Barron's Guide to Foreign Medical Schools. new ed. LC 78-15002. 1979. pap. 4.95 (ISBN 0-8120-0998-3). Barron.
Fogel, Marvin & Walker, Mort. How to Get into Medical School: A Comprehensive Guide. 196p. 1981. pap. 7.25 (ISBN 0-8015-3670-7, 0704-210, Hawthorn). Dutton.
Gottfried, Rosalie. Getting into American Medical-Veterinary Schools: A Practical "How to" Guide. LC 77-93397. (gr. 10 up). 1978. pap. text ed. 5.50x (ISBN 0-931084-01-6). Argee Pub.
Harrell, George T. Planning Medical Center Facilities for Education, Research, & Public Service. LC 73-12293. 232p. 1974. 16.75x (ISBN 0-271-01163-7, Penn State). Pa St U Pr.
Lerner, Marguerite. Medical School: The Interview & the Applicant. rev. ed. 175p. 1981. pap. text ed. 4.95 (ISBN 0-8120-2277-7). Barron.
--Medical School: The Interview & the Applicant. rev ed. LC 81-500. 175p. 1977. pap. 4.95 (ISBN 0-8120-0752-2, 3611-7). Barron.
Lewis, D. Sclater. The Royal College of Physicians & Surgeons of Canada, 1920-1960. (Illus.). 266p. 1962. 9.00 (ISBN 0-7735-9052-8). McGill-Queens U Pr.
Lief, Harold I. & Karlen, Arno, eds. Sex Education in Medicine. LC 76-44. 1976. 12.95 (ISBN 0-470-15023-8). Halsted Pr.
Lippard, Vernon W. & Purcell, Elizabeth F., eds. The Changing Medical Curriculum. LC 72-189355. (Illus.). 193p. 1974. pap. 4.50 (ISBN 0-914362-10-0). J Macy Foun.
Medical Branch of the University of Texas. The University of Texas Medical Branch at Galveston: A Seventy-Five Year History. (Illus.). 457p. 1967. 22.50x (ISBN 0-292-73697-5). U of Tex Pr.
Morgan, John. A Discourse Upon the Institution of Medical Schools in America. LC 74-26276. (History, Philosophy & Sociology of Science Ser). 1975. Repr. 9.00x (ISBN 0-405-06604-X). Arno.
Peterson, Shailer A. Preparing to Enter Medical School. 1979. text ed. 14.95 (ISBN 0-13-697342-6, Spec); pap. text ed. 6.95 (ISBN 0-13-697334-5). P-H.
--Preparing to Enter Pharmacy School. (His Health Career Ser.). (Illus.). 1979. 13.95 (ISBN 0-13-697367-1, Spec); pap. 6.95 (ISBN 0-13-697359-0). P-H.
Purcell, Elizabeth F., ed. The University & Medicine - the Past, Present & Tomorrow: Report of a Bicentennial Anglo-American Seminar. LC 77-73889. 1977. 7.50 (ISBN 0-914362-19-4). J Macy Foun.
Rudman, Jack. Medical College Admission Test (MCAT) (Admission Test Ser.: ATS-11). 300p. (Cloth bdg. avail. on request). pap. 9.95 (ISBN 0-8373-5011-5). Natl Learning.
Sandri-White, Alex & Pokress, E. New Directory of Medical Schools. 1981. 9.50 (ISBN 0-685-22749-9). Aurea.
Shugar, Gershon J., et al. How to Get into Medical & Dental School. 3rd ed. LC 80-23397. 192p. 1981. lib. bdg. 12.00 (ISBN 0-668-05105-1); pap. 6.95 (ISBN 0-668-05112-4). Arco.
--How to Get into Medical & Dental School. LC 77-169970. 1972. lib. bdg. 6.50 (ISBN 0-668-02524-7). Arco.
Shugar, Gershon L., et al. How to Get into Medical & Dental School. rev. ed. 1977. pap. 4.00 (ISBN 0-668-04095-5). Arco.
Stimson, Ruth H. Selection of Students for Admission to Graduate Programs in Health Administration, a Survey & Evaluation. 1974. 3.00 (ISBN 0-686-24310-2). Assn Univ Progs Hlth.
Tarlow, David M. Student Guide to the World's Medical Schools Where the Language of Instruction Is in English. 1981. pap. 9.00 (ISBN 0-931572-02-9). Datar Pub.
Waite, Frederick C. The Story of a Country Medical College: A History of the Clinical School of Medicine & the Vermont Medical College, Woodstock, Vermont, 1827-1856. (Illus.). 213p. 1945. 2.00x (ISBN 0-934720-12-6). VT Hist Soc.
Wechsler, Henry. A Guide to Medical Schools & Medical School Admission. 1981. 29.50 (ISBN 0-88410-723-X). Ballinger Pub.
WHO Study Group. Geneva, 1974. Planning of Schools of Medicine: Report. (Technical Report Ser.: No. 566). (Also avail. in French & Spanish). 1975. pap. 2.40 (ISBN 92-4-120566-0). World Health.
World Directory of Medical Schools. 4th ed. 348p. (Eng. & Fr.). 1970. 8.00 (ISBN 92-4-050000-6). World Health.

MEDICAL COMMUNICATION
see Communication in Medicine

MEDICAL COOPERATION
see Group Medical Practice; Medical Social Work

MEDICAL COSTS
see Medical Care, Cost of; Medical Economics

MEDICAL DELUSIONS
see also Medicine, Magic, Mystic, and Spagiric
Fishbein, Morris. The Medical Follies. LC 75-23710. Repr. of 1925 ed. 18.00 (ISBN 0-404-13261-8). AMS Pr.
Lasagna, Louis. Doctor's Dilemmas. LC 70-105025. (Essay Index Reprint Ser). 1962. 18.00 (ISBN 0-8369-1669-7). Arno.
MEDICAL DEVICES
see Medical Instruments and Apparatus
MEDICAL DIAGNOSIS
see Diagnosis
MEDICAL ECONOMICS
see also Group Medical Practice; Medical Care, Cost of; Medical Care, Prepaid; Medical Fees; Medical Office Management
Ackroyd, Ted J., ed. Health & Medical Economics: A Guide to Information Sources. LC 73-17567. (Economics Information Guide Ser.: Vol. 7). 1977. 36.00 (ISBN 0-8103-1390-1). Gale.
Birnbaum, Howard. The Cost of Catastrophic Illness. LC 77-9192. 1978. 14.95 (ISBN 0-669-01773-6). Lexington Bks.
Braverman, Jordan. Crisis in Health Care. rev. ed. 1980. pap. 7.95 (ISBN 0-87491-299-7). Acropolis.
Burrow, James G. Organized Medicine in the Progressive Era: The Move Toward Monopoly. LC 77-894. 1977. text ed. 14.50x (ISBN 0-8018-1918-0). Johns Hopkins.
Cleverley, William O. Financial Management of Health Care Facilities. LC 76-4034. 376p. 1976. 26.00 (ISBN 0-912862-20-3). Aspen Systems.
Committee on the Costs of Medical Care, October 1932. Medical Care for the American People: The Final Report of the Committee on the Costs of Medical Care. LC 75-180569. (Medicine & Society in America Ser). 242p. 1972. Repr. of 1932 ed. 12.00 (ISBN 0-405-03944-1). Arno.
Cooper, Philip D., et al, eds. Marketing & Preventive Health Care. LC 77-25849. 1978. 7.00 (ISBN 0-87757-105-8). Am Mktg.
Culyer, A. J. Need & the National Health Service: Economics & Social Choice. 163p. 1976. 13.50x (ISBN 0-87471-896-1). Rowman.
Culyer, A. J. & Wright, K. G. Economic Aspects of Health Services. 190p. 1978. 35.00x (ISBN 0-85520-227-0, Pub. by Martin Robertson England). Biblio Dist.
Culyer, A. J., et al, eds. An Annotated Bibliography of Health Economics. LC 77-79018. 1977. 29.95x (ISBN 0-312-03873-9). St Martin.
Davis, Michael M. Paying Your Sickness Bills. LC 77-180572. (Medicine & Society in America Ser). 292p. 1972. Repr. of 1931 ed. 14.00 (ISBN 0-405-03947-6). Arno.
Donabedian, Avedis. Benefits in Medical Care Programs. 432p. 1976. 25.00x (ISBN 0-674-06580-8). Harvard U Pr.
Dye, Rex J. The Hospital Medical Racket & You. LC 74-34511. 1975. 6.50 (ISBN 0-682-48236-6, Banner). Exposition.
Enos, Darryl & Sultan, Paul. The Sociology of Health Care: Social, Economic & Political Perspectives. LC 76-17250. 1977. 15.95 (ISBN 0-275-56970-5). Praeger.
Feldstein, Paul J. Health Associations & the Demand for Legislation: The Political Economy of Health. LC 76-53762. 1977. 18.00 (ISBN 0-88410-510-5). Ballinger Pub.
Fuchs, Victor. Who Shall Live? LC 74-79283. 1975. 9.95 (ISBN 0-465-09185-7). Basic.
Fuchs, Victor R., ed. Essays in the Economics of Health & Medical Care. (Human Resources & Social Institutions Ser.: No. 1). 250p. 1972. text ed. 10.00x (ISBN 0-87014-236-4, Dist. by Columbia U Pr). Natl Bur Econ Res.
Gorlick, S. Now That You've Incorporated. 1977. 14.95 (ISBN 0-87489-138-8). Med Economics.
--The Whys & Wherefores of Corporate Practice. 3rd ed. 1978. 14.50 (ISBN 0-87489-209-0). Med Economics.
Gottlieb, Manuel. Health Care Financing in Mainland Tanzania. (Foreign & Comparative Studies, Eastern African Ser.: No. 20). 104p. (Orig.). 1975. pap. text ed. 4.50 (ISBN 0-915984-17-2). Syracuse U Foreign Comp.
Griffiths, Adrian, et al. An Annotated Bibliography of Health Economics: Western European Sources. 1980. 37.50 (ISBN 0-312-03874-7). St Martin.
Hardy, C. Colburn. ABC's of Investing Your Retirement Funds. 1978. 22.50 (ISBN 0-87489-008-X). Med Economics.
Havighurst, Clark C., ed. Regulating Health Facilities Construction. 1974. 16.25 (ISBN 0-8447-2044-5); pap. 8.25 (ISBN 0-8447-2043-7). Am Enterprise.
Health Care: A Bibliographic Guide to the 1979 Documents Update. 1981. pap. write for info. Microfilming Corp.
Health Care, Nineteen Seventy to Nineteen Seventy-Eight: A Bibliographic Guide to the Microfiche Collection. 262p. 1980. pap. 50.00 (ISBN 0-667-00549-8). Microfilming Corp.
Institute of Medicine. Controlling the Supply of Hospital Beds. LC 77-74651. 1977. pap. 6.00 (ISBN 0-309-02610-5). Natl Acad Pr.
International Economic Association Conference, Tokyo. The Economics of Health & Medical Care: Proceedings. Perlman, Mark, ed. LC 73-20107. 1974. 39.95 (ISBN 0-470-68051-2). Halsted Pr.
Jacobs, Philip. Economics of Health: Medical Care. 309p. pap. text ed. 15.95 (ISBN 0-8391-1526-1). Univ Park.
Klarman, Herbert E. Economics of Health. LC 65-14323. 200p. 1965. 17.50x (ISBN 0-231-02797-4). Columbia U Pr.
Klarman, Herbert E. & Jaszi, Helen H., eds. Empirical Studies in Health Economics. LC 74-101646. (Illus.). 433p. 1970. 27.00x (ISBN 0-8018-1134-1). Johns Hopkins.
Klein, Elizabeth P. The Break-Even Point: A Guide to the Process of Management for the Medical Office. LC 79-90728. (Illus.). 237p. 1979. wkbk. 30.00 (ISBN 0-9604250-0-4). E P Klein.
LaDou, Joseph & Likens, James D. Medicine & Money: Physicians As Businessmen. LC 77-2332. 1977. 16.50 (ISBN 0-88410-145-2). Ballinger Pub.
Macleod, Gordon K. & Perlman, Mark, eds. Health Care Capital: Competition & Control. LC 77-22166. 1977. 25.00 (ISBN 0-88410-521-0). Ballinger Pub.
MacStravic, Robin E. Marketing Health Care. LC 76-58967. 250p. 1977. 25.75 (ISBN 0-912862-41-6). Aspen Systems.
Medical Economics: Medical-Surgical Tips-Techniques. (Medical Economics Books). 1975. 10.95 (ISBN 0-442-84043-8). Van Nos Reinhold.
Moya, Frank. Fundamentals of Management for the Physician. (Illus.). 208p. 1974. 14.75 (ISBN 0-398-02945-8). C C Thomas.
Navarro, Vicente. Class Struggle, the State & Medicine: An Historical & Contemporary Analysis of the Medical Sector in Great Britain. 1978. lib. bdg. 16.95 (ISBN 0-88202-122-2). N Watson.
Navarro, Vincent. Medicine Under Capitalism. 2nd ed. LC 76-28521. 1977. pap. 8.95 (ISBN 0-88202-116-8). N Watson.
Newhouse, Joseph P. Economics of Medical Care: A Policy Perspective. LC 78-52498. (Illus.). 1978. pap. text ed. 6.95 (ISBN 0-201-08369-8). A-W.
Phillips, C. I. & Wolfe, J. N. Clinical Practice & Economics. pap. 14.95x (ISBN 0-8464-0251-3). Beekman Pubs.
Rhodabarger, T. D. Personal Money Management for Physicians. 1973. 16.50 (ISBN 0-87489-027-6). Med Economics.
Rosett, Richard N., ed. The Role of Health Insurance in the Health Services Sector. LC 76-8856. (Universities-National Bureau Conference Ser.: No. 27). 1976. 20.00 (ISBN 0-87014-272-0). N Watson.
Rubright, Bob & MacDonald, Dan. Marketing Health & Human Services. LC 81-737. 248p. 1981. text ed. 25.95 (ISBN 0-89443-338-5). Aspen Systems.
Scheffler, Richard M., ed. Research in Health Economics: An Annual Compilation of Research, Vol. 1. 1979. lib. bdg. 34.50 (ISBN 0-89232-042-7). Jai Pr.
Somers, Herman M. & Somers, Anne R. Doctors, Patients, & Health Insurance: The Organization & Financing of Medical Care. 1961. 15.95 (ISBN 0-8157-8036-2). Brookings.
Sorkin, Alan. Health Economics: An Introduction. LC 73-11656. (Illus.). 160p. 1975. 16.95 (ISBN 0-669-93393-7). Lexington Bks.
Topics in Health Care Financing. Incl. Shared Services. 1976. Vol. 2, No. 4. 13.75 (ISBN 0-912862-83-1); Financial Management Under Third Party Reimbursement. 1976. Vol. 3, No. 1. 13.75 (ISBN 0-912862-84-X); Prospective Rate Setting. 1976. Vol. 3, No. 2. 13.75 (ISBN 0-912862-85-8); Pt. 1. Cost Containment. 1977. Vol. 3, No. 3. 13.75 (ISBN 0-912862-86-6); Pt. 2. Cost Containment. 1977. Vol. 3, No. 4. 13.75 (ISBN 0-912862-87-4). Aspen Systems.
Topics in Health Care Financing. Incl. Vol. 2, No. 2, 1975. Capital Projects. 13.75 (ISBN 0-912862-81-5); Vol. 2, No. 3, 1976. Medicare Reimbursement Controversies & Appeals. 13.75 (ISBN 0-912862-82-3); Vol. 1, No. 1, 1974. Financial Overview. 13.75 (ISBN 0-912862-76-9); Vol. 1, No. 3, 1975. Medicare Reimbursement. 13.75 (ISBN 0-912862-78-5); Vol. 2, No. 1, 1975. Private Third Party Reimbursement. 13.75 (ISBN 0-912862-80-7); Vol. 1, No. 2, 1974. Rate Setting. 13.75 (ISBN 0-912862-77-7); Vol. 1, No. 4, 1975. Risk Management. 13.75 (ISBN 0-912862-79-3). 1975-76. Aspen Systems.
Voluntary Health & Welfare Organizations. (Industry Audit Guides). 1974. pap. 5.00 (ISBN 0-685-58488-7). Am Inst CPA.
Ward, Richard A. Economics of Health Resources. LC 74-12804. 160p. 1975. text ed. 11.95 (ISBN 0-201-08522-4). A-W.
Weeks, Lewis E. & Berman, Howard J., eds. Economics in Health Care. LC 77-10860. 402p. 1977. text ed. 25.00 (ISBN 0-89443-026-2). Aspen Systems.
Williams, Pierce. The Purchase of Medical Care Through Fixed Periodic Payment. LC 75-17251. (National Bureau of Economic Research Ser.). 1975. Repr. 21.00x (ISBN 0-405-07525-1). Arno.
Zubkoff, Michael & Dunlop, David. The Economics of Health. LC 74-16937. Date not set. price not set (ISBN 0-669-95661-9). Lexington Bks.
MEDICAL EDUCATION
see also Medical Colleges; Medical Research; Medical Students; Medicine–Study and Teaching
Ali, D. S., et al. Aspects of Medical Education in Developing Countries: Selected Papers Presented at the 2nd WHO Conference on Medical Education in the Eastern Mediterranean Region. (Public Health Papers Ser: No. 47). 113p. 1972. pap. 3.20 (ISBN 92-4-130047-7, 545). World Health.
Baird, W. David. Medical Education in Arkansas, Eighteen Seventy Nine-Nineteen Seventy Eight. LC 79-126280. (Illus.). 1979. 21.95x (ISBN 0-87870-052-8). Memphis St Univ.
Barrows, Howard S. Simulated Patients (Programmed Patients) The Development & Use of a New Technique in Medical Education. (Illus.). 80p. 1971. spiral bdg. 9.75 (ISBN 0-398-02227-5). C C Thomas.
Barrows, Howard S. & Tamblyn, Robyn M. Problem Based Learning: An Approach to Medical Education. (Medical Education Ser.: Vol. 1). 1980. text ed. 19.95 (ISBN 0-8261-2840-8). Springer Pub.
Bergin, James J. & Holmes, Geraldine C. Continuing Medical Education in the Community Hospital. LC 79-55326. (Illus.). 1979. text ed. 22.00x (ISBN 0-935466-00-2); pap. text ed. 16.00x (ISBN 0-935466-01-0). Pierson Pubs.
Boissoneau, Robert. Continuing Education in the Health Professions. LC 80-19748. 322p. 1980. text ed. 27.50 (ISBN 0-89443-325-3). Aspen Systems.
Bowers, John Z. & Purcell, Elizabeth F., eds. The Impact of Health Services on Medical Education: A Global View. new ed. (Illus.). 497p. 1979. pap. 10.00 (ISBN 0-914362-27-5). J Macy Foun.
Brown, Sanford. Getting into Medical School. 5th ed. 1981. pap. text ed. 3.95 (ISBN 0-8120-2326-9). Barron.
Cadbury, William E., Jr., et al, eds. Medical Education: Response to a Challenge - Minorities & the Disadvantaged. LC 79-52754. (Illus.). 1979. pap. 13.50 (ISBN 0-87993-122-1). Futura Pub.
Campbell, Margaret A. Why Would a Girl Go into Medicine? Medical Education in the United States: A Guide for Women. 3rd ed. 128p. 1974. 4.95 (ISBN 0-912670-33-9). Feminist Pr.
Carnegie Council on Policy Studies in Higher Education. Progress & Problems in Medical & Dental Education: Federal Support Versus Federal Control. LC 76-11964. (Carnegie Council Series). (Illus.). 1976. 14.95x (ISBN 0-87589-295-7). Jossey-Bass.
Chapman, John S. The University of Texas Southwestern Medical School: Medical Education in Dallas, 1900-1975. LC 76-2593. 1976. 10.00 (ISBN 0-87074-154-3). SMU Press.
Coombs, Robert H. Mastering Medicine: Professional Socialization in Medical School. LC 77-85351. 1978. 17.95 (ISBN 0-02-906640-9). Free Pr.
Cordasco, Francesco & Alloway, David N., eds. Medical Education in the United States: A Guide to Information Sources. LC 79-24030. (Education Information Guide Ser.: Vol. 8). 1980. 36.00 (ISBN 0-8103-1458-4). Gale.
Curtis, James L. Blacks, Medical Schools, & Society. LC 76-184249. 1971. 7.95 (ISBN 0-472-26900-3). U of Mich Pr.
Daum, Susan L., ed. Guide to Audiovisual Resources for the Health Care Field, 1981. 200p. (Orig.). 1981. pap. 18.00 guidebook (ISBN 0-939450-00-3, AHPI 005). Med Media Pubs.
Death & Grief: Selected Readings for the Medical Student. LC 77-6195. (Journal Reprint Ser.). Orig. Title: Death & Medical Education: Selected Readings. 1977. pap. 6.95 (ISBN 0-88238-502-X). H S Pub Corp.
Egdahl, Richard H. & Gertman, Paul M., eds. Quality Health Care: The Role of Continuing Medical Education. LC 77-70434. 276p. 1977. 30.00 (ISBN 0-912862-37-8). Aspen Systems.
Everett, Mark R. Medical Education in Oklahoma: The University of Oklahoma School of Medicine & Medical Center, 1900-1931. LC 70-177333. (Illus.). 300p. 1972. 17.50x (ISBN 0-8061-0988-2); pap. 8.95 (ISBN 0-8061-1237-9). U of Okla Pr.
--Medical Education in Oklahoma: The University of Oklahoma School of Medicine & Medical Center, 1932-1964, Vol. 2. 1980. 25.00x (ISBN 0-8061-1541-6). U of Okla Pr.
Flexner, Abraham. The Flexner Report on Medical Education in the United States. 340p. 1910. text ed. 29.00 (ISBN 0-89443-354-7). Aspen Systems.
Ford, Charles W. & Morgan, Margaret K. Teaching in Health Professions. LC 75-37571. (Illus.). 250p. 1976. text ed. 16.95 (ISBN 0-8016-1622-0). Mosby.
Gerrard, Brian, et al. Interpersonal Skills for Health Professionals. (Illus.). 272p. 1980. text ed. 15.95 (ISBN 0-8359-3138-2); pap. text ed. 12.95 (ISBN 0-8359-3136-6). Reston.
Gifford, James F., Jr., ed. Undergraduate Medical Education & the Elective System: Experience with the Duke Curriculum, 1966-1975. LC 77-84615. 1978. 14.75 (ISBN 0-8223-0394-9). Duke.
Grob, Gerald N., ed. Psychiatry & Medical Education: Two Studies, 2 vols. in one. LC 78-22582. (Historical Issues in Mental Health Ser.). (Illus.). 1979. Repr. lib. bdg. 42.00x (ISBN 0-405-11934-8). Arno.
Hadley, Jack, ed. Medical Education Financing: Policy Analyses & Options for the Nineteen Eighties. (Illus.). 1980. 25.00 (ISBN 0-88202-129-X). N Watson.
Hammond, Kenneth. Teaching Comprehensive Medical Care: A Psychological Study of a Change in Medical Education. (Commonwealth Fund Ser.). 664p. 1959. text ed. 25.00x (ISBN 0-674-86910-9). Harvard U Pr.
Harrison, Tinsley R. Your Future Health Care. LC 73-13222. 1974. 10.50 (ISBN 0-87527-132-4). Green.
Jason, Hilliard & Westberg, Jane. Instructional Decision-Making: Clinical Supervision. (Instructional Decision-Making Ser.). (Orig.). 1980. pap. 5.00 (ISBN 0-938540-05-X). Natl Ctr Faculty.
--Instructional Decision-Making: Course Segment Design. (Instructional Decision-Making Ser.). (Orig.). 1980. pap. 5.00 (ISBN 0-938540-01-7). Natl Ctr Faculty.
--Instructional Decision-Making: Lecturing. (Instructional Decision-Making Ser.). 61p. (Orig.). 1980. pap. 5.00 (ISBN 0-938540-03-3). Natl Ctr Faculty.
--Instructional Decision-Making: Preview Package. (Instructional Decision-Making Preview Package Ser.). 297p. (Orig.). 1980. pap. 22.00 (ISBN 0-938540-00-9). Natl Ctr Faculty.
--Instructional Decision-Making: Research Supervision. (Instructional Decision-Making Ser.). 64p. (Orig.). 1980. pap. 5.00 (ISBN 0-938540-06-8). Natl Ctr Faculty.
--Instructional Decision-Making: Small Group Discussion. (Instructional Decision-Making Ser.). 64p. (Orig.). 1980. pap. 5.00 (ISBN 0-938540-04-1). Natl Ctr Faculty.
--Instructional Decision-Making: Test Construction. (Instructional Decision-Making Ser.). 64p. (Orig.). 1980. pap. 5.00 (ISBN 0-938540-02-5). Natl Ctr Faculty.
Jonas, Steven. Medical Mystery: The Training of Doctors in the United States. 1979. 15.00 (ISBN 0-393-06437-9). Norton.
Kaufman, Martin. American Medical Education: The Formative Years, 1765-1910. LC 75-35346. 224p. 1976. lib. bdg. 15.00x (ISBN 0-8371-8590-4, KME/). Greenwood.
Lazar, Stephen H. Barron's Guide to Financial Aid for Medical Students. 1979. pap. 5.95 (ISBN 0-8120-2151-7). Barron.
Lyden, Fremont J., et al. Training of Good Physicians: Critical Factors in Career Choices. LC 68-21977. (Commonwealth Fund Publications Ser). 1968. 12.50x (ISBN 0-674-90285-8). Harvard U Pr.
McDaniel, Lucy V., et al. Selected Medical Disabilities. LC 73-79322. 102p. 1973. text ed. 5.95x (ISBN 0-913590-10-X); plate 1.95x (ISBN 0-685-40632-6). C B Slack.
McLachlan, Gordon, ed. Medical Education & Medical Care: A Scottish American Symposium. (Nuffield Publications). 230p. 1977. text ed. 13.25x (ISBN 0-19-721394-4). Oxford U Pr.
Marxer, Webster L. & Cowgill, George R. The Art of Predictive Medicine: The Early Detection of Deteriortive Trends, Proceedings. (Illus.). 376p. photocopy ed. spiral 34.75 (ISBN 0-398-01230-X). C C Thomas.
Medical Education: Annotated Bibliography, 1946-1955. 391p. (Eng. & Fr.). 1958. 9.20 (ISBN 92-4-152003-5). World Health.
Medical Education in the U. S. 1.00 (ISBN 0-89970-059-4, OP-385). AMA.
Medical School Alumni 1967. 1967. pap. 2.50 (ISBN 0-89970-061-6, OP-229). AMA.
Melnick, V. L. & Hamilton, F. D. Minorities in Science: The Challenge for Change in Biomedicine. LC 77-9462. (Illus.). 296p. 1977. 19.50 (ISBN 0-306-31033-3). Plenum Pub.

Moore, Anthony R. The Missing Medical Text: Humane Patient Care. 1978. 25.95x (ISBN 0-522-84139-2, Pub. by Melbourne U Pr). Intl Schol Bk Serv.
Moore, Margaret L. Form & Function of Written Agreements in Clinical Education of Health Professionals. 1972. pap. 7.95 (ISBN 0-912452-25-0). Am Phys Therapy Assn.
Moore, Margaret L., et al. Form & Function of Written Agreements in the Clinical Education of Health Professionals. LC 72-84792. 81p. 1972. 9.00x (ISBN 0-913590-04-5). C B Slack.
National Academy Of Sciences. Reform of Medical Education. 1970. 8.75 (ISBN 0-309-01757-2). Natl Acad Pr.
Noack, Horst, ed. Medical Education & Primary Health Care. 351p. text ed. 32.50 (ISBN 0-8391-1475-3). Univ Park.
Norwood, William F. Medical Education in the U. S. Before the Civil War. LC 72-165726. (American Education, Ser. 2). 1972. Repr. of 1944 ed. 25.00 (ISBN 0-405-03714-7). Arno.
Numbers, Ronald L., ed. The Education of American Physicians: Historical Essays. LC 77-20326. 1980. 38.50x (ISBN 0-520-03611-5). U of Cal Pr.
O'Malley, C. D., ed. The History of Medical Education. LC 72-85449. (UCLA Forum in Medical Sciences: No. 12). (Illus.). 1970. 57.50x (ISBN 0-520-01578-9). U of Cal Pr.
Page, Robert G. & Littlemeyer, Mary H., eds. Preparation for the Study of Medicine. LC 69-19280. 1969. 7.00x (ISBN 0-226-64475-8). U of Chicago Pr.
Pickering, George. Quest for Excellence in Medical Education: A Personal Survey of Medical Education. 1978. 14.95x (ISBN 0-19-721399-5). Oxford U Pr.
Pinel, Philippe. The Clinical Training of Doctors: An Essay of 1793. Weiner, Dora B., ed. & tr. from Fr. LC 80-14500. (The Henry E. Sigerist Supplements to the Bulletin of the History of Medicine, New Ser.: No. 3). 108p. 1981. pap. text ed. 7.50x (ISBN 0-8018-2448-6). Johns Hopkins.
Poor, Russell S. Planning Florida's Health Leadership: A Summary. LC 54-9612. (Medical Center Study Ser: Vol. 1). 1954. pap. 1.50 (ISBN 0-8130-0187-0). U Presses Fla.
Popper, Hans P., ed. Trends in New Medical Schools. (Illus.). 184p. 1967. 28.50 (ISBN 0-8089-0366-7). Grune.
Postgraduate Education for Medical Personnel in the USSR: Report Prepared by the Participants in a Study Tour Organized by the World Health Organization. (Public Health Papers Ser: No. 39). 52p. 1970. pap. 2.00 (ISBN 92-4-130039-6, 558). World Health.
Probst, Gary & Levitt, Viola Y. Learning Skills for Health Careers. 240p. 1981. pap. text ed. 15.95 (ISBN 0-8403-2461-8). Kendall-Hunt.
Purcell, Elizabeth, ed. World Trends in Medical Education: Faculty, Students, & Curriculum. LC 79-144335. (Josiah Macy Foundation Ser). 256p. 1971. 16.50x (ISBN 0-8018-1270-4). Johns Hopkins.
Purcell, Elizabeth F., ed. Recent Trends in Medical Education: Report of a Conference. LC 76-40568. (Illus.). 1976. 7.50 (ISBN 0-914362-18-6). J Macy Foun.
Puschman, Theodor. A History of Medical Education. 69.95 (ISBN 0-8490-0335-0). Gordon Pr.
Puschmann, Theodor. A History of Medical Education: From the Most Remote to the Most Recent Times. Hare, Evan H., ed. (Historia Medicinae Ser.). xi, 650p. Repr. of 1891 ed. lib. bdg. 42.50x (ISBN 0-87991-077-1). Porcupine Pr.
Regensburg, Jeannette. Toward Education for Health Professions. 1978. text ed. 15.50 scp (ISBN 0-06-045357-5, HarpC). Har-Row.
Richards, Robert K. Continuing Medical Education: Perspectives, Problems, Prognosis. LC 77-91018. 1978. 17.50x (ISBN 0-300-02168-2). Yale U Pr.
Richmond, Julius B. Currents in American Medicine: A Developmental View of Medical Care & Education. LC 69-12733. (Commonwealth Fund Publications Ser). 1969. 7.95x (ISBN 0-674-18015-1). Harvard U Pr.
Rippey, Robert M. The Evaluation of Teaching in Medical Schools. LC 80-19891. (Medical Education Ser.). 1980. text ed. 19.95 (ISBN 0-8261-3440-8). Springer Pub.
Samph, Thomas & Templeton, Bryce, eds. Evaluation in Medical Education: Past, Present, Future. LC 79-1163. (Illus.). 1979. 22.50 (ISBN 0-88410-522-9). Ballinger Pub.
Schechter, Daniel S. Agenda for Continuing Education: A Challenge to Health Care Institutions. LC 74-83051. (Illus.). 96p. 1974. 8.00 (ISBN 0-87914-027-5, 9605). Hosp Res & Educ.
Schweitzer, George K. The Doctorate: A Handbook. (Illus.). 116p. 1965. photocopy ed. spiral 10.50 (ISBN 0-398-01701-8). C C Thomas.
Securis, John. A Detection & Querimonie of the Daily Enormities Comitted in Physick. LC 76-57415. (English Experience Ser.: No. 830). 1977. Repr. of 1566 ed. lib. bdg. 8.00 (ISBN 90-221-0830-9). Walter J Johnson.
Shortell, Stephen M., Jr. A Framework for Continuing Education for the Health Professions with Application to Mental Health & Mental Retardation-Developmental Disabilities Administration. LC 78-4100. (Illus., Orig.). 1978. pap. 8.50 (ISBN 0-914904-26-4). Health Admin Pr.
Simpson, M. A. Medical Education: A Critical Approach. 214p. 1972. 18.95 (ISBN 0-407-26495-7). Butterworth.
Staropoli, Charles J. & Waltz, Carolyn F. Developing & Evaluating Educational Programs for Health Care Providers. LC 77-15618. (Illus.). 210p. 1978. pap. text ed. 13.50 (ISBN 0-8036-8100-3). Davis Co.
Stewart, Charles T., Jr. & Siddayao, Corzaon M. Increasing the Supply of Medical Personnel: Needs & Alternatives. 1973. pap. 4.25 (ISBN 0-8447-3097-1). Am Enterprise.
Stookey, Byron. A History of Colonial Medical Education: In the Province of New York, with Its Subsequent Development (1767-1830) (Illus.). 312p. 1962. photocopy ed. spiral 29.50 (ISBN 0-398-01866-9). C C Thomas.
Stubbe, J. H. Medical Background. LC 79-76022. 1969. 11.00x (ISBN 0-85564-024-3, Pub. by U of W Austral Pr). Intl Schol Bk Serv.
Thompson & Hayden. Medical Science for Medical Record Personnel. 1974. 17.80 (ISBN 0-917036-00-X). Physicians Rec.
Training & Continuing Education: A Handbook for Health Care Institutions. LC 75-23733. (Illus.). 261p. 1970. 17.50 (ISBN 0-87914-006-2, 9600). Hosp Res & Educ.
Webb, Linda J., et al, eds. DSM-III Training Program for Health Professionals. 160p. 1981. pap. text ed. 9.95 A Guide to Clinical Use (ISBN 0-686-73216-2); price not set slides (ISBN 0-87630-281-9); price not set videotape (ISBN 0-87630-280-0); price not set complete pkg. (ISBN 0-87630-282-7). Brunner-Mazel.
Weed, Lawrence L. Medical Records, Medical Education & Patient Care. 1970. 25.00 (ISBN 0-8151-9188-X). Year Bk Med.
WHO Chronicle. Education & Training of Health Workers, Vol. 24, No. 10. (Also avail. in French, Russian & Spanish). 1970. pap. 1.20 (ISBN 0-686-16781-3). World Health.
WHO Expert Committee. Geneva, 1973. Continuing Education for Physicians: Report. (Technical Report Ser.: No. 534). (Also avail. in French & Spanish). 1973. pap. 1.60 (ISBN 92-4-120534-2). World Health.
--Planning of Medical Education Programmes: Report. (Technical Report Ser.: No. 547). (Also avail. in French & Spanish). 1974. pap. 1.60 (ISBN 92-4-120547-4). World Health.
WHO Meeting. Geneva, 1974. Education & Treatment in Human Sexuality; the Training of Health Professions: Report. (Technical Report Ser.: No. 572). (Also avail. in French & Spanish). 1975. pap. 2.40 (ISBN 92-4-120572-5). World Health.
WHO Study Group. Geneva, 1971. Implication of Individual & Small Group Learning Systems in Medical Education: Report. (Technical Report Ser.: No. 489). (Also avail. in French & Spanish). 1972. 2.40 (ISBN 92-4-120489-3). World Health.
WHO Study Group. Geneva, 1972. Training & Preparation of Teachers for Schools of Medicine & of Allied Health Sciences: Report. (Technical Report Ser.: No. 521). (Also avail. in French & Spanish). 1973. pap. 1.60 (ISBN 92-4-120521-0). World Health.
Williams, Greer. Western Reserve's Experiment in Medical Education & Its Outcome. 500p. 1980. 25.00x (ISBN 0-19-502679-9). Oxford U Pr.

MEDICAL ELECTRICITY

see Electrotherapeutics

MEDICAL ELECTRONICS

see also Electronics in Psychiatry; Radiotherapy; Telemeter (Physiological Apparatus)

Ackermann, Philip G. Electronic Instrumentation in the Clinical Laboratory. LC 72-155031. 349p. 1972. 28.50 (ISBN 0-316-00643-2). Little.
Bergveld, P. Electromedical Instrumentation: A Guide for Medical Personnel. LC 77-85711. (Techniques of Measurement in Medicine Ser.: No. 2). (Illus.). 1980. 29.50 (ISBN 0-521-21892-6); pap. 9.95 (ISBN 0-521-29305-7). Cambridge U Pr.
Buchsbaum, Walter H. & Goldsmith, Bonnie. Electrical Safety in the Hospital. 1975. 5.95 (ISBN 0-442-84047-0). Van Nos Reinhold.
Bukstein, Edward J. Introduction to Biomedical Electronics. LC 73-83370. (Orig.). 1973. pap. 7.50 (ISBN 0-672-21005-3). Sams.
Caceres, C. A., ed. Biomedical Telemetry. 1965. 55.50 (ISBN 0-12-153850-8). Acad Pr.
Carr, Joseph. Servicing Medical & Bio-Electronic Equipment. LC 77-73. (Illus.). 1977. 10.95 (ISBN 0-8306-7930-8); pap. 8.95 (ISBN 0-8306-6930-2, 930). TAB Bks.
Cromwell, Leslie, et al. Biomedical Instrumentation & Measurements. 2nd ed. (Illus.). 1980. text ed. 22.95 (ISBN 0-13-076448-5). P-H.
Dewhurst, D. J. An Introduction to Biomedical Instrumentation. 2nd ed. 288p. 1975. text ed. 50.00 (ISBN 0-08-018755-2); pap. text ed. 31.00 (ISBN 0-08-018884-2). Pergamon.
DuBovy, Joseph L. Introduction to Biomedical Electronics. (Illus.). 1978. text ed. 14.50 (ISBN 0-07-017895-X, G); instructor's manual 2.50 (ISBN 0-07-017896-8). McGraw.
Geddes, L. A. & Baker, L. E. Principles of Applied Biomedical Instrumentation. 2nd ed. LC 74-34390. (Biomedical Engineering & Health Systems Ser.). 616p. 1975. 34.95x (ISBN 0-471-29496-9, Pub. by Wiley-Interscience). Wiley.
Klein, Burton. Introduction to Medical Electronics: For Electronics & Medical Personnel. 2nd ed. 320p. 1975. 9.95 (ISBN 0-8306-5830-0); pap. 7.95 (ISBN 0-8306-4830-5, 830). TAB Bks.
Klemm, W. R. Applied Electronics for Veterinary Medicine & Animal Physiology. (Illus.). 484p. 1976. 41.50 (ISBN 0-398-03477-X). C C Thomas.
Miller, H. & Harrison, D. C. Biomedical Electrode Technology. 1974. 43.00 (ISBN 0-12-496850-3). Acad Pr.
Moir, John. Just in Case: Disaster Preparedness & Emergency Self-Help. LC 79-28435. (Orig.). 1980. pap. 4.95 (ISBN 0-87701-200-8). Chronicle Bks.
Neuman, Michael R., et al, eds. Physical Sensors for Biomedical Applications. 168p. 1980. 49.95 (ISBN 0-8493-5975-9). CRC Pr.
Ray, Charles D., ed. Medical Engineering. (Illus.). 1973. 132.50 (ISBN 0-8151-7113-7). Year Bk Med.
Roth, Herbert H., et al. Electrical Safety in Health Care Facilities. (Clinical Engineering Ser.). 1975. 39.50 (ISBN 0-12-599050-2). Acad Pr.
Rubin, Wallace & Norris, Charles. Electronystagmography: What Is ENG? 116p. 1974. photocopy ed. spiral 16.25 (ISBN 0-398-03098-7). C C Thomas.
Tammes, A. Electronics for Medical & Biology Laboratory Personnel. 1971. 12.25 (ISBN 0-685-83554-5, Pub by Williams & Wilkens). Krieger.
Watson, B. W., ed. IEE Medical Electronics Monographs. Incl. Vol. 1. Monographs 1-6. 1971. 20.00 (ISBN 0-901223-07-7); Vol. 2. Monographs 7-12. Hill, D. W., ed. 1974. 21.00 (ISBN 0-901223-51-4); Vol. 3. Monographs 13-17. Hill, D. W., ed. 1975. 27.50 (ISBN 0-901223-77-8); Vol. 4. Monographs 18-22. Hill, D. W., ed. 1976. 35.00 (ISBN 0-901223-84-0); Vol. 5. Monographs 23-27. Hill, D. W., ed. 1977. 35.00 (ISBN 0-901223-98-0). (Illus., Pub. by Peregrinus England). Inst Elect Eng.
Zucker, Mitchell H. Electronic Circuits for the Behavioral & Biomedical Sciences: A Reference Book of Useful Solid-State Circuits. LC 76-81921. (Illus.). 1969. text ed. 22.95x (ISBN 0-7167-0918-X). W H Freeman.

MEDICAL EMERGENCIES

see also Accidents; Emergency Medical Services; Emergency Nursing; First Aid in Illness and Injury

Abbott, Jean, et al. Protocols for Prehospital Emergency Medical Care. (Illus.). 200p. 1980. softcover 11.95 (ISBN 0-683-01563-X). Williams & Wilkins.
Aberman & Logan. Emergency Management of the Critically Ill. 1980. 47.50 (ISBN 0-8151-0003-5). Year Bk Med.
Aberman, Arnold, ed. Emergency Management of the Critically Ill. 1979. write for info. (ISBN 0-8151-0003-5). Symposia Special.
American College of Surgeons. Early Care of the Injured Patient. 2nd ed. LC 76-8566. (Illus.). 1976. text ed. 17.00 (ISBN 0-7216-1161-3). Saunders.
American Lung Assn. of Western N.Y. Emergency Manual Task Foce. Chemical Emergency Action Manual. 2nd ed. ALA-WNY, Technical Review Committee, ed. 1981. 12.25 (ISBN 0-686-71581-0). Am Lung Assn.
American National Red Cross. Advanced First Aid & Emergency Care. LC 73-76727. 320p. 1973. 3.95 (ISBN 0-385-05841-1). Doubleday.
Arnold, Peter & Pendagast, Edward L. Emergency Handbook: A First Aid Manual for Home & Travel. 1981. pap. 5.95 (ISBN 0-452-25288-1, Z5288, Plume). NAL.
Baderman, Howard, ed. Management of Medical Emergencies. (Illus.). 1978. text ed. 12.00 (ISBN 0-397-58245-5, JBL-Med-Nursing). Har-Row.
Barber, Janet M. & Budassi, Susan A. Mosby's Manual of Emergency Care: Practices & Procedures. LC 79-31708. (Illus.). 1979. pap. text ed. 20.95 (ISBN 0-8016-0447-8). Mosby.
Bodak-Gyovai, L. Z. & Manzione, J. V., Jr. Oral Medicine: Patient Evaluation & Management. (Illus.). 202p. 1980. soft cover 17.95 (ISBN 0-683-00901-X). Williams & Wilkins.
Bourne, Peter D., ed. Acute Drug Abuse Emergencies: A Treatment Manual. 1976. 34.00 (ISBN 0-12-119560-0). Acad Pr.
Cardiovascular Conference, 5th, Snowmass-at-Aspen, Colorado, Jan. 1974. Integrated Medical-Surgical Care in Acute Coronary Artery Disease: Proceedings. Vogel, J. H., ed. (Advances in Cardiology: Vol. 15). x, 199p. 1975. 64.75 (ISBN 3-8055-2098-0). S Karger.
Cavanagh, Denis, et al. Obstetric Emergencies. 2nd ed. (Illus.). 1978. pap. text ed. 22.50x (ISBN 0-06-140626-0, Harper Medical). Har-Row.
Clearfield, Harris R. & Dinoso, Vicente P., eds. Gastrointestinal Emergencies: Thirty-Fourth Hahnemann Symposium. LC 75-37629. (34th). (Illus.). 400p. 1976. 48.00 (ISBN 0-8089-0713-1). Grune.
Cohen, Alan S., et al, eds. Medical Emergencies: Diagnostic & Management Procedures from Boston City Hospital. LC 75-41566. 1977. text ed. 17.95 (ISBN 0-316-15009-6). Little.
D'Arcy, P. F. & Griffin, J. P. Drug-Induced Emergencies. (Illus.). 240p. 1980. 29.75 (ISBN 0-8151-2268-3). Year Bk Med.
Dealing with Emergencies. LC 80-11450. (Nursing Photobook). (Illus.). 160p. 1980. text ed. 12.95 (ISBN 0-916730-20-4). InterMed Comm.
Emergency Department - Handbook for Medical Staff. pap. 2.00 (ISBN 0-89970-040-3, OP-131). AMA.
Evans. Emergency Medicine. 1981. text ed. price not set (ISBN 0-407-00172-7). Butterworth.
Findeiss, J. Clifford, ed. Emergency Medical Care, Vol. 1. LC 73-82042. 1974. 21.95 (ISBN 0-8151-3223-9, Pub. by Symposia Special). Year Bk Med.
Frey, Charles F., ed. Initial Management of the Trauma Patient. LC 76-20773. (Illus.). 498p. 1976. text ed. 20.00 (ISBN 0-8121-0519-2). Lea & Febiger.
Friedmann, et al. Emergency Roentgen Diagnosis. 1980. 16.50 (ISBN 0-8151-3281-6). Year Bk Med.
Frimann-Dahl, J. Roentgen Examinations in Acute Abdominal Diseases. 3rd ed. (Illus.). 632p. 1974. text ed. 49.50 (ISBN 0-398-02939-3). C C Thomas.
Gazzaniga, Alan B., et al. Emergency Care: Principles & Practice for the EMT-Paramedic. (Illus.). 1979. 21.95 (ISBN 0-8359-1652-9); instrs'. manual avail. Reston.
Gill, William, et al. Shock Trauma Manual. (Illus.). 296p. 1979. pap. 24.00 (ISBN 0-683-03527-4). Williams & Wilkins.
Goldberger, Emanuel. Treatment of Cardiac Emergencies. 2nd ed. LC 77-5070. (Illus.). 1977. 25.95 (ISBN 0-8016-1854-1). Mosby.
Goldberger, Emanuel & Wheet, Myron W., Jr. Treatment of Cardiac Emergencies. 3rd ed. (Illus.). 392p. 1982. pap. text ed. 20.50 (ISBN 0-8016-1857-6). Mosby.
Grant, Harvey & Murray, Robert. Course Planning Guide for Emergency Care. 2nd ed. (Illus.). 336p. 1978. pap. text ed. 12.95 (ISBN 0-87618-961-3). R J Brady.
Greenberg, Michael I. & Roberts, James R. Emergency Medicine. LC 81-3182. 1981. 25.00 (ISBN 0-8036-4331-4). Davis Co.
Gupta, S. P. Medical Emergencies in General Practice. 311p. 1978. 14.00x (ISBN 0-7069-0614-4, Pub. by Croom Helm Ltd. England). Biblio Dist.
Hamilton, William P. & Lavin, Mary A. Decision Making in the Coronary Care Unit. 2nd ed. LC 75-30994. (Illus.). 184p. 1976. pap. text ed. 9.50 (ISBN 0-8016-2026-0). Mosby.
Hankoff, L. D. Emergency Psychiatric Treatment: A Handbook of Secondary Prevention. 100p. 1969. 8.75 (ISBN 0-398-00771-3). C C Thomas.
Hardy, R. H. Accidents & Emergencies: A Practical Handbook for Personal Use. 3rd ed. (Illus.). 240p. 1981. text ed. 15.95x (ISBN 0-19-261321-9). Oxford U Pr.
Heller. Emergencies in Gynecology & Obstetrics. 1981. 13.95 (ISBN 0-8151-4225-0). Year Bk Med.
Kaufman, William I. Help! 1978. pap. 1.50 (ISBN 0-89437-010-3). Baronet.
Kessler, Robert & Anderson, Rodney U. Handbook of Urologic Emergencies. 1976. spiral bdg. 11.00 (ISBN 0-87488-647-3). Med Exam.
Laskin, Daniel M. Management of Oral Emergencies. (Illus.). 128p. 1964. 7.25 (ISBN 0-398-01082-X). C C Thomas.
McClintock, James C. & Caroline, Nancy L. Workbook for Emergency Care in the Streets. 1979. pap. text ed. 8.95 (ISBN 0-316-54484-1). Little.

McRae, James T. Emergency Medicine Case Studies. LC 79-88721. 1979. pap. 15.50 (ISBN 0-87488-002-5). Med Exam.
Meislin, Harvey W. Priorities in Multiple Trauma. LC 80-11266. 159p. 1980. text ed. 21.95 (ISBN 0-89443-287-7). Aspen Systems.
Ming, Dennis & Siner, Elaine. Prehospital Emergency Drug Handbook. 160p. 1979. pap. text ed. 9.95 (ISBN 0-8359-1668-5). Reston.
Moore, Mary E. Medical Emergency Manual. 2nd ed. (Illus.). 196p. 1977. pap. 13.95 (ISBN 0-683-06129-1). Williams & Wilkins.
Oaks, Wilbur, et al, eds. Critical Care. (The Fortieth Hahnemann Symposium). 368p. 1978. 43.25 (ISBN 0-8089-1059-0). Grune.
Oaks, Wilbur W., et al, eds. Emergency Care. (The Forty-Ninth Hahnemann Symposium Ser.). 256p. 1979. 29.50 (ISBN 0-8089-1167-8). Grune.
O'Doherty, Desmond S. Handbook of Neurologic Emergencies. 1977. spiral bdg. 10.00 (ISBN 0-87488-643-0). Med Exam.
Parcel, Guy S. First Aid in Emergency Care. LC 77-322. (Illus.). 1977. 14.95 (ISBN 0-8016-3400-8); pap. 11.95 (ISBN 0-8016-3757-0). Mosby.
Pascoe, Delmer J. & Grossman, Moses, eds. Quick Reference to Pediatric Emergencies. 2nd ed. LC 78-10397. (Illus.). 1978. flexible cover 27.50 (ISBN 0-397-50403-9, JBL-Med-Nursing). Har-Row.
Platt, Frederic W. Case Studies in Emergency Medicine. LC 73-10611. 227p. 1974. pap. text ed. 10.95 (ISBN 0-316-70970-0). Little.
Reece, Robert M. Reece & Chamberlain's Manual of Emergency Pediatrics. 2nd ed. LC 77-11352. (Illus.). 1978. pap. text ed. 19.50 (ISBN 0-7216-7498-4). Saunders.
Rosen, Peter & Sternbach, George. Atlas of Emergency Medicine. (Illus.). 168p. 1979. 26.00 (ISBN 0-683-07363-X). Williams & Wilkins.
Rudman, Jack. Medical Emergency Dispatcher. (Career Examination Ser.: C-2331). (Cloth bdg. avail. on request). pap. 8.00 (ISBN 0-8373-2331-2). Natl Learning.
--Senior Medical Emergency Dispatcher. (Career Examination Ser.: C-2332). (Cloth bdg. avail. on request). pap. 8.00 (ISBN 0-8373-2332-0). Natl Learning.
Salter, R. H. Common Medical Emergencies. 1980. 12.50 (ISBN 0-8151-7527-2). Year Bk Med.
Sanders, Jay H. & Gardner, Laurence B. Handbook of Medical Emergencies. 2nd ed. LC 78-50127. 1978. pap. 12.75 (ISBN 0-87488-635-X). Med Exam.
Schneewind, John H. Medical & Surgical Emergencies. 3rd ed. (Illus.). 434p. 1973. pap. 13.95 (ISBN 0-8151-7559-0). Year Bk Med.
Schulzinger, Morris S. The Accident Syndrome: The Genesis of Accidental Injury--a Clinical Approach. 260p. 1956. photocopy ed. spiral 24.50 (ISBN 0-398-04411-2). C C Thomas.
Schwartz, George R. Principles & Practice of Emergency Medicine, 2 vols. Safar, Peter, et al, eds. LC 75-25277. (Illus.). 1978. text ed. 80.00 set (ISBN 0-7216-8034-8); Vol. I. text ed. 40.00 (ISBN 0-7216-8031-3); Vol. II. text ed. 40.00 (ISBN 0-7216-8033-X). Saunders.
Seager, Stephen. Breathe, Little Boy, Breathe: An Emergency Room Doctor's Story. 216p. 1981. 10.95 (ISBN 0-13-081729-5). P-H.
Shaftan, Gerald W. & Gardner, Bernard. Quick Reference to Surgical Emergencies. LC 74-1379. (Illus.). 650p. 1974. pap. text ed. 27.50 (ISBN 0-397-50307-5). Lippincott.
Sharpe, John C. & Marx, Fredrick. Management of Medical Emergencies. 2nd ed. (Illus.). 1969. 27.00 (ISBN 0-07-056484-1, HP). McGraw.
Shoemaker, William C. & Walker, William F. Fluid-Electrolyte Therapy in Acute Illness. (Illus.). 1970. 25.00 (ISBN 0-8151-7640-6). Year Bk Med.
Smith, Bradley & Stevens, Gus. The Emergency Book. 1980. pap. 4.95 (ISBN 0-686-61051-2, 25425, Fireside). S&S.
Spencer, James H., et al. The Hospital Emergency Department. (Illus.). 388p. 1972. 29.75 (ISBN 0-398-02482-0). C C Thomas.
Sternbach, George & Rosen, Peter. Emergency Medicine. (Illus.). 1977. 12.50x (ISBN 0-87762-220-5). Technomic.
Tavares, B. M., ed. Acute Care: Based on the Proceedings of the Sixth International Symposium on Critical Care Medicine, Rio De Janeiro, 1977. (Anaesthesiologie und Intensivmedizin: Vol. 116). (Illus.). 1979. pap. 45.10 (ISBN 0-387-09210-2). Springer-Verlag.
Thygerson, Alton L. Disaster Survival Handbook. LC 79-4242. (Illus.). 1979. pap. 7.95 (ISBN 0-8425-1629-8). Brigham.
Vakil, Rustom J. & Udwadia, Farokh E., eds. Diagnosis & Management of Medical Emergencies. 2nd ed. (Illus.). 1977. 24.00x (ISBN 0-19-261118-6). Oxford U Pr.
Wagner. Yearbook of Emergency Medicine, 1981. 1981. 35.00 (ISBN 0-8151-9052-2). Year Bk Med.
Warner, Carmen G., et al, eds. Emergency Care: Assessment & Intervention. 2nd ed. LC 77-18285. (Illus.). 1978. 19.95 (ISBN 0-8016-4744-4). Mosby.
Wasserberger, Jonathan & Eubanks, David H. Advanced Paramedic Procedures: A Practical Approach. LC 76-25886. (Illus.). 1977. pap. 11.95 (ISBN 0-8016-5351-7). Mosby.
Yates, Anthony P., et al. Emergency: A Practical Manual. 1980. pap. write for info. (ISBN 0-935170-03-0). Synapse Pubns.

MEDICAL ENGINEERING
see Biomedical Engineering

MEDICAL ENTOMOLOGY
see Insects As Carriers of Disease

MEDICAL ETHICS
see also Euthanasia; Human Experimentation in Medicine; Malpractice; Medicine and Religion; Nursing Ethics; Pastoral Medicine; Social Medicine

Abernethy, Virginia. Frontiers in Medical Ethics: Applications in a Medical Setting. LC 79-26566. 204p. 1980. 19.50 (ISBN 0-88410-710-8). Ballinger Pub.
Ashley, Benedict M. & O'Rourke, Kevin D. Health Care Ethics: A Theological Analysis. LC 77-88355. 1978. pap. 14.00 (ISBN 0-87125-044-6). Cath Health.
Augenstein, Leroy. Come, Let Us Play God. LC 68-29567. 160p. 1976. pap. 3.95x (ISBN 0-06-060396-8, RD133, HarpR). Har-Row.
Barber, Bernard & Lambert, Richard D., eds. Medical Ethics & Social Change. new ed. LC 77-26530. (Annals: No. 437). 1978. pap. 6.00 (ISBN 0-87761-227-7). Am Acad Pol Soc Sci.
Basson, Marc D., ed. Ethics, Humanism, & Medicine. LC 79-3650. (Progress in Clinical & Biological Research Ser.: Vol. 38). 1980. 55.00x (ISBN 0-8451-0038-6). A R Liss.
--Rights & Responsibilities in Modern Medicine: The Second Volume in a Series on Ethics, Humanism, & Medicine. LC 80-29391. (Progress in Clinical & Biological Research; Vol. 50). 272p. 1980. 22.00 (ISBN 0-8451-0050-5). A R Liss.
Beauchamp, Tom L. & Childress, James F. Principles of Biomedical Ethics. 1979. text ed. 15.95x (ISBN 0-19-502487-7); pap. text ed. 8.95x (ISBN 0-19-502488-5). Oxford U Pr.
Beauchamp, Tom L. & Walters, LeRoy. Contemporary Issues in Bioethics. 1978. 21.95x (ISBN 0-8221-0200-5). Dickenson.
Bergsma, Daniel, ed. Ethical Issues Arising in the Genetic Counseling Relationship. LC 78-70429. (National Foundation Ser.: Vol. 14, No. 9). 1978. write for info (ISBN 0-686-23952-0). March of Dimes.
Bleuler, Eugene. Autistic Undisciplined Thinking in Medicine & How to Overcome It. Harms, Ernest, tr. from Ger. 1970. 15.75 (ISBN 0-02-841500-0). Hafner.
Bliss, B. P. & Johnson, A. G. Aims & Motives in Clinical Medicine: A Practical Approach to Medical Ethics. 150p. 1975. pap. text ed. 12.50x (ISBN 0-8464-0123-1). Beekman Pubs.
--Aims & Motives in Clinical Medicine: A Practical Approach to Medical Ethics. 1975. pap. 11.00x (ISBN 0-685-83068-3). State Mutual Bk.
Brody, Howard. Ethical Decisions in Medicine. 2nd ed. 1981. pap. text ed. 15.95 (ISBN 0-316-10899-5). Little.
Bruckner. Medical Ethics. Date not set. price not set (ISBN 0-262-02171-4, Pub. by Bradford); pap. price not set (ISBN 0-262-52073-7). MIT Pr.
Buckner, Michael & Abrams, Natalie. Medical Ethics: A Clinical Textbook & Reference for the Health Care Professions. 1982. text ed. price not set (ISBN 0-262-02171-4, Pub. by Bradford); pap. text ed. price not set (ISBN 0-262-52073-7). MIT Pr.
Burns, Chester R., ed. Legacies in Ethics & Medicine. LC 76-44908. 1977. 15.00 (ISBN 0-88202-166-4). N Watson.
Campbell, Alastair V. Medicine, Health, & Justice. 1978. pap. text ed. 8.95 (ISBN 0-443-01671-2). Churchill.
--Moral Dilemmas in Medicine. 2nd ed. LC 75-7819. (Illus.). 210p. 1975. pap. text ed. 8.25 (ISBN 0-443-01286-5). Churchill.
Carlton, Wendy. In Our Professional Opinion... The Primacy of Clinical Judgment Over Moral Choice. LC 78-51524. 1978. text ed. 12.95x (ISBN 0-268-01143-5). U of Notre Dame Pr.
Cathell, D. W. The Physician Himself & What He Should Add to His Scientific Acquirements. 2nd ed. LC 70-180562. (Medicine & Society in America Ser). 216p. 1972. Repr. of 1882 ed. 11.00 (ISBN 0-405-03941-7). Arno.
Childress, James F. Priorities in Biomedical Ethics. LC 81-3. 1981. pap. 8.95 (ISBN 0-664-24368-1). Westminster.
Clark-Kennedy, A. E. Man, Medicine, & Morality. 1969. 17.50 (ISBN 0-208-00972-8, Archon). Shoe String.
Collier, Richard B. Pleneurethic: A World Class Philosophy. (Illus.). 368p. 1981. 20.00 (ISBN 0-682-49753-3). Exposition.
Curran, Charles E. Issues in Sexual & Medical Ethics. LC 77-89767. 1979. pap. 3.95 (ISBN 0-268-01142-7). U of Notre Dame Pr.
--Issues in Sexual & Medical Ethics. LC 77-89767. 1978. text ed. 9.95x (ISBN 0-268-01141-9). U of Notre Dame Pr.
Cutler, Donald R., ed. Updating Life & Death: Essays in Ethnics & Medicine. (Orig.). 1969. pap. 4.50x (ISBN 0-8070-1581-4, BP333). Beacon Pr.
Davis, et al, eds. Contemporary Issues in Biomedical Ethics. LC 78-71406. (Contemporary Issues in Biomedicine, Ethics, & Society Ser.). 1979. 25.00 (ISBN 0-89603-002-4). Humana.
Day, Stacey B., ed. Ethics in Medicine in a Changing Society. LC 73-85309. (Bell Symposia Ser.). (Orig.). 1973. pap. 2.50 (ISBN 0-912922-04-4). U of Minn Bell.
Dedek, John F. Contemporary Medical Ethics. 240p. 1975. text ed. 7.95 (ISBN 0-8362-0617-7). Andrews & McMeel.
Duncan, A. S., et al. Dictionary of Medical Ethics. 335p. 1980. 18.75x (ISBN 0-232-51302-3, Pub. by Darton-Longman-Todd England). State Mutual Bk.
Duncan, A. S., et al, eds. Dictionary of Medical Ethics. 496p. 1981. 24.50 (ISBN 0-8245-0038-5). Crossroad NY.
--Dictionary of Medical Ethics. 1977. pap. text ed. 15.50x (ISBN 0-232-51302-3). Humanities.
Ehrenreich, Barbara & English, Deirdre. Complaints & Disorders: The Sexual Politics of Sickness. (Illus.). 96p. 1974. pap. 2.95 (ISBN 0-912670-20-7). Feminist Pr.
Ehrlich, Ann. Ethics & Jurisprudence. 1978. 3.85 (ISBN 0-940012-07-3). Colwell Co.
Ellison, David L. The Bio-Medical Fix: Human Dimensions of Bio-Medical Technologies. LC 77-91104. 1978. lib. bdg. 15.95x (ISBN 0-313-20038-6, ELB/). Greenwood.
Fletcher, Joseph. Humanhood: Essays in Biomedical Ethics. LC 79-1756. (Impact Ser.). 204p. 1979. 14.95 (ISBN 0-87975-112-6); pap. 7.95 (ISBN 0-87975-123-1). Prometheus Bks.
--Morals & Medicine: The Moral Problems of the Patient's Right to Know the Truth. LC 54-9019. 1979. 17.50 (ISBN 0-691-07234-5); pap. 5.95 (ISBN 0-691-02004-3). Princeton U Pr.
Frazier, Claude A., ed. Is It Moral to Modify Man? 252p. 1973. 15.75 (ISBN 0-398-02632-7). C C Thomas.
Freund, Paul A., ed. Experimentation with Human Subjects. LC 70-107776. (Daedalus Library Ser). 1970. pap. 3.50 (ISBN 0-8076-0542-5). Braziller.
Fromer, Margot J. Ethical Issues in Health Care. LC 80-25058. 420p. 1981. pap. text ed. 14.95 (ISBN 0-8016-1728-6). Mosby.
Fundenberg, H. H. & Melnick, V. L., eds. Biomedical Scientists & Public Policy. LC 78-15052. 260p. 1978. 17.95 (ISBN 0-306-40085-5, Plenum Pr). Plenum Pub.
Gallant, Donald M. & Force, Robert, eds. Legal & Ethical Issues in Human Research & Treatment: Psychopharmacologic Considerations. 1978. 15.00 (ISBN 0-470-26354-7). Halsted Pr.
Goldstein, Doris M., ed. Bioethics: A Guide to Information Sources. (The Health Affairs Information Guide Ser.: Vol. 8). 375p. 1981. 36.00 (ISBN 0-8103-1502-5). Gale.
Gorovitz, Samuel. Moral Problem in Medicine. 500p. 1976. 19.95 (ISBN 0-13-600817-8). P-H.
Gosfield, Alice. PSRO's: The Law & the Health Consumer. LC 75-13340. 288p. 1975. text ed. 18.50 (ISBN 0-88410-123-1). Ballinger Pub.
Hayes, Donald M. Between Doctor & Patient. 1977. pap. 4.95 (ISBN 0-8170-0742-3). Judson.
Hiller, Marc D. Medical Ethics & the Law. 1981. 35.00 (ISBN 0-88410-707-8). Ballinger Pub.
Humber, James M. & Almeder, Robert E. Biomedical Ethics & the Law. 2nd ed. 1979. 39.50 (ISBN 0-306-40239-4, Plenum Pr); pap. 15.00 (ISBN 0-306-40242-4, Plenum Pr). Plenum Pub.
Hunt, Robert & Arras, John, eds. Ethical Issues in Modern Medicine. 524p. 1977. pap. text ed. 12.95 (ISBN 0-87484-396-0). Mayfield Pub.
Institute of Medicine. Ethics of Health Care. Tancredi, Laurence, ed. LC 74-28130. xi, 313p. 1974. pap. 8.25 (ISBN 0-309-02249-5). Natl Acad Pr.
Jacobs, William. The Pastor & the Patient: An Informal Guide to New Directions in Medical Ethics. LC 73-85727. 1974. pap. 2.25 (ISBN 0-8091-1789-4, Deus). Paulist Pr.
Jakobovits, Immanuel. Jewish Medical Ethics. rev. ed. LC 75-4125. 425p. 1975. 10.00x (ISBN 0-8197-0097-5); pap. 6.95x (ISBN 0-685-53492-8). Bloch.
Jones, James H. Bad Blood: The Tuskegee Syphilis Experiment. LC 80-69281. (Illus.). 1981. 14.95 (ISBN 0-02-916670-5). Free Pr.
Katz, Jay. Experimentation with Human Beings: The Authority of Investigator, Subject, Professions, & State in the Human Experimentation Process. LC 70-188394. 1200p. 1972. 22.50 (ISBN 0-87154-438-5). Russell Sage.
Kelly, David F. The Emergence of Roman Catholic Medical Ethics in North America: An Historical-Methodological-Bibliographical Study. LC 79-66372. (Texts & Studies in Religion: Vol. 3). xi, 520p. 1980. soft cover 39.95x (ISBN 0-88946-878-8). E Mellen.
Kepler, M. Oliver, ed. Medical Stewardship: Fulfilling the Hippocratic Legacy. LC 80-25457. 320p. 1981. lib. bdg. 29.95 (ISBN 0-313-22489-7, KMS/). Greenwood.
Kieffer, George H. Bioethics: A Textbook of Issues. LC 78-55822. (Life Sciences Ser.). (Illus.). 1979. text ed. 16.95 (ISBN 0-201-03891-9). A-W.
Kluge, Eike-Henner W. The Practice of Death. LC 74-14498. (Illus.). 256p. 1975. 20.00x (ISBN 0-300-01806-1); pap. 4.45x (ISBN 0-300-01987-4, 4286). Yale U Pr.
Kunnes, Richard. Your Money or Your Life: An Indictment of the Medical Market Place. LC 72-169733. 1971. 5.95 (ISBN 0-396-06422-1). Dodd.
Lander, Louise. Defective Medicine: Risk, Anger, & the Malpractice Crisis. LC 78-5577. 242p. 1978. 10.00 (ISBN 0-374-13627-0); pap. 4.95 (ISBN 0-374-51509-3). FS&G.
Lapp, Rhonda S. Devotionals for Nurses. (Ultra Bks.). 4.95 (ISBN 0-8010-5539-3). Baker Bk.
Lasko, Keith A. The Great Billion-Dollar Medical Swindle. LC 79-55443. 224p. 1980. 10.95 (ISBN 0-672-52625-5). Bobbs.
Leake, Chauncey D. Percival's Medical Ethics: With Supplemental Material. LC 76-8603. 352p. 1975. Repr. of 1927 ed. 15.50 (ISBN 0-88275-176-X). Krieger.
Lennard, Henry L. & Lennard, Suzanne H., eds. Ethics of Health Care: Dilemmas of Technology & Techniques in Health Care & Psychotherapy. LC 79-57022. 174p. (Orig.). 1980. pap. 16.00 (ISBN 0-935824-01-4). Gondolier.
Levey, Martin. Medical Ethics of Medieval Islam with Special Reference to Al Ruhawi's "Practical Ethics of the Phyician". LC 67-22797. (Transactions Ser.: Vol. 57, Pt. 3). 1967. pap. 1.00 (ISBN 0-87169-573-1). Am Philos.
Levy, Charlotte. The Human Body & the Law. LC 75-14041. (Legal Almanac Ser.). 128p. 1975. text ed. 5.95 (ISBN 0-379-11101-2). Oceana.
MacKay, William. Salesman Surgeon. 1978. 9.95 (ISBN 0-07-044390-4, GB). McGraw.
Mappes, Thomas & Zembaty, Jane. Biomedical Ethics. (Illus.). 640p. 1980. text ed. 17.95 (ISBN 0-07-040123-3). McGraw.
May, William E. Human Existence, Medicine, & Ethics. LC 77-8149. 1977. 5.25 (ISBN 0-8199-0677-8). Franciscan Herald.
Medical Ethics. Date not set. pap. 4.00 (ISBN 0-686-76544-3). Feldheim.
Mendelsohn, Everett, et al, eds. Human Aspects of Biomedical Innovation. LC 74-160027. (Studies in Technology & Society). 1971. 14.00x (ISBN 0-674-41331-8). Harvard U Pr.
Miller, George W. Moral & Ethical Implications of Human Organ Transplants. (Illus.). 164p. 1971. 12.75 (ISBN 0-398-01311-X). C C Thomas.
Munson, Ron. Intervention & Reflection: Basic Issues in Medical Ethics. 1979. text ed. 21.95x (ISBN 0-534-00608-6). Wadsworth Pub.
Nelson, James B. Human Medicine: Ethical Perspective on New Medical Issues. LC 73-78258. 1973. 5.95 (ISBN 0-8066-1323-8, 10-3183). Augsburg.
Oden, Thomas C. Should Treatment Be Terminated. LC 76-9970. 1977. pap. 2.95 (ISBN 0-06-066345-6, RD175, HarpR). Har-Row.
Pellegrino, Edmund D. Humanism & the Physician. LC 78-23174. 1979. 16.50x (ISBN 0-87049-218-7); pap. 7.50x (ISBN 0-87049-311-6). U of Tenn Pr.
Percival, Thomas. Percival's Medical Ethics. Leake, Chauncey D., ed. LC 75-23750. Repr. of 1927 ed. 24.50 (ISBN 0-404-13356-8). AMS Pr.
Petersen, William F. Hippocratic Wisdom: For Him Who Wishes to Pursue Properly the Science of Medicine: A Modern Appreciation of Ancient Scientific Wisdom. (Illus.). 286p. 1946. pap. write for info. (ISBN 0-398-04390-6). C C Thomas.
Purtilo, Ruth B. & Cassel, Christine K. Ethical Dimensions in the Health Professions. 200p. 1981. text ed. write for info. (ISBN 0-7216-7411-9). Saunders.
Ramsey, Paul. Ethics at the Edges of Life: Medical & Legal Intersections. LC 77-76308. 1980. pap. 7.95 (ISBN 0-300-02141-0). Yale U Pr.

--Ethics at the Edges of Life: Medical & Legal Intersections. LC 77-76308. 1978. 25.00x (ISBN 0-300-02137-2). Yale U Pr.
Reich, Warren T., ed. Encyclopedia of Bioethics, 4 vols. LC 78-8821. 1978. Set. 230.00 (ISBN 0-02-926060-4). Free Pr.
Reidy, Maurice. Foundations for a Medical Ethic. LC 79-65621. 104p. 1979. pap. 2.45 (ISBN 0-8091-2216-2). Paulist Pr.
Reiser, Stanley J. & Dyck, Arthur J., eds. Ethics in Medicine: Historical Perspectives and Contemporary Concerns. 1977. text ed. 45.00x (ISBN 0-262-18081-2); pap. 19.95x (ISBN 0-262-68029-7). MIT Pr.
Restak, Richard M. Premeditated Man: Bioethics & the Control of Future Human Life. 1977. pap. 1.95 (ISBN 0-14-004411-6). Penguin.
Robison, Wade L. & Pritchard, Michael S., eds. Medical Responsibility: Paternalism, Informed Consent, & Euthanasia. LC 79-87656. (Contemporary Issues in Biomedicine, Ethics & Society Ser.). 1979. 25.00 (ISBN 0-89603-007-5). Humana.
Rogers, William R. & Barnard, David, eds. Nourishing the Humanistic in Medicine: Interactions with the Social Sciences. LC 78-26222. (Contemporary Community Health Ser.). (Illus.). 1979. 10.95 (ISBN 0-8229-3395-0). U of Pittsburgh Pr.
Ryan, J. Corboy. Fail-Safe Human Research Protocols. LC 80-24690. 146p. 1981. 19.95 (ISBN 0-89874-292-7). Krieger.
Scorer, Gordon & Wing, Antony, eds. Decision Making in Medicine: The Practice of Its Ethics. (Illus.). 1979. 25.00 (ISBN 0-8151-7584-1). Year Bk Med.
Shapiro, Michael H. & Spece, Roy G., Jr. Cases, Materials & Problems on Bioethics & Law. LC 80-28699. (American Casebook Ser.). 915p. 1981. text ed. 23.95 (ISBN 0-8299-2134-6). West Pub.
Smith, Harmon L. Ethics & the New Medicine. LC 76-124756. (Orig.). 1970. pap. 3.50 (ISBN 0-687-12013-6). Abingdon.
Sobel, Lester A. Medical Science & the Law: The Life & Death Controversy. 1977. lib. bdg. 17.50x (ISBN 0-87196-286-1). Facts on File.
Spicker, Stuart F. & Englehardt, H. Tristam, eds. Philosophical Medical Ethics: Its Nature & Significance. (Philosophy & Medicine Ser.: No. 3). 1977. lib. bdg. 29.00 (ISBN 90-277-0772-3, Pub. by Reidel Holland). Kluwer Boston.
Steele, Shirley M. & Harmon, Vera M. Values Clarification in Nursing. (Illus.). 1979. 8.95 (ISBN 0-8385-9337-2). ACC.
Stein, Jane J. Making Medical Choices: Ethics & Medicine in a Technological Age. 1978. 10.95 (ISBN 0-395-27086-3). HM.
Stolz, Stephanie B., et al. Ethical Issues in Behavior Modification: Report of the American Psychological Association Commission. LC 78-52233. (Social & Behavioral Science Ser.). 1978. text ed. 15.95x (ISBN 0-87589-368-6). Jossey-Bass.
Stringer, Paul. Ethics & Judgment in Surgery & Medicine. 1970. pap. 9.95x (ISBN 0-433-31855-4). Intl Ideas.
Stroman, Duane F. The Medical Establishment & Social Responsibility. 1976. 15.00 (ISBN 0-8046-9136-3, Natl U). Kennikat.
Szasz, Thomas. The Theology of Medicine: The Political - Philosophical Foundations of Medical Ethics. LC 76-13332. 1977. 12.50x (ISBN 0-8071-0284-9). La State U Pr.
Tancredi, Lawrence P. & Slaby, Andrew E. Ethical Policy in Mental Health Care: The Goals of Psychiatric Intervention. LC 77-1996. 1977. 20.00 (ISBN 0-88202-102-8). N Watson.
Temkin, Owsei, et al. Respect for Life in Medicine, Philosophy, & the Law. LC 76-47366. (Thalheimer Lecture Ser.). 1977. text ed. 8.95x (ISBN 0-8018-1942-3). Johns Hopkins.
Thomas, John E. Matters of Life & Death: Crises in Bio-Medical Ethics. 1978. 15.95 (ISBN 0-89522-012-1); pap. text ed. 8.95 (ISBN 0-89522-013-X). Samuel Stevens.
Unschuld, Paul. Medical Ethics in Imperial China: A Study in Historical Anthropology. LC 78-80479. (Comparative Studies of Health Systems & Medical Care). 1979. 18.50x (ISBN 0-520-03543-7). U of Cal Pr.
Van Den Berg, Jan H. Medical Ethics & Medical Power. (Illus.). 1978. 7.95x (ISBN 0-393-06428-X). Norton.
VanHoose, William & Paradise, Louis V. Ethics in Counseling & Psychotherapy: Perspectives on Issues & Decision Making. LC 79-15429. 160p. 1979. pap. 10.00 (ISBN 0-686-60263-3). Carroll Pr.
Veatch, Robert M. Case Studies in Medical Ethics. 1977. 18.50x (ISBN 0-674-09931-1); pap. 7.95x (ISBN 0-674-09932-X). Harvard U Pr.
--A Theory of Medical Ethics. LC 81-66106. 448p. 1981. 20.00 (ISBN 0-465-08437-0). Basic.
--Value-Freedom in Science & Technology: A Study of the Importance of Religious, Ethical, & Other Socio-Cultural Factors in Selected Medical Decisions Regarding Birth Control. LC 76-28192. (Harvard Dissertations in Religion). 1976. pap. 9.00 (ISBN 0-89130-080-5, 020108). Scholars Pr Ca.
Veatch, Robert M. & Branson, Roy, eds. Ethics and Health Policy. LC 76-3741. 256p. 1976. text ed. 19.50 (ISBN 0-88410-137-1). Ballinger Pub.
Visscher, Maurice B. Ethical Constraints & Imperatives in Medical Research. (American Lectures in Behavioral Science & Law Ser.). 128p. 1975. 12.50 (ISBN 0-398-03404-4). C C Thomas.
Visscher, Maurice B., ed. Humanistic Perspectives in Medical Ethics. LC 72-90475. 312p. 1972. 11.95 (ISBN 0-87975-012-X). Prometheus Bks.
Wall, Thomas F. Medical Ethics: Basic Moral Issues. LC 80-5592. 180p. 1980. lib. bdg. 17.00 (ISBN 0-8191-1142-2); pap. text ed. 9.00 (ISBN 0-8191-1143-0). U Pr of Amer.
Walters, Leroy, ed. Bibliography of Bioethics, 6 vols. LC 75-4140. 44.00 ea.; Vol. 1 1975. (ISBN 0-8103-0978-5); Vol. 2 1976. (ISBN 0-8103-0980-7); Vol. 3 1977. (ISBN 0-8103-0982-3); Vol. 4 1978. (ISBN 0-8103-0983-1); Vol. 5 1979. Vol. 6 1980. (ISBN 0-8103-0987-4). Gale.
Warner, Richard. Morality in Medicine: An Introduction to Medical Ethics. LC 79-23049. 142p. 1980. pap. 8.95 (ISBN 0-88284-103-3). Alfred Pub.
Wertz, Richard W., ed. Readings on Ethical & Social Issues in Biomedicine. 320p. 1973. pap. 12.95 ref. ed. (ISBN 0-13-755884-8). P-H.
Wojcik, Jan. Muted Consent: A Casebook in Modern Medical Ethics. LC 77-89472. (Science & Society: a Purdue University Series in Science, Technology, & Human Values: Vol. 1). 176p. 1978. pap. 3.25 (ISBN 0-931682-02-9). Purdue Univ Bks.
Yezzi, Ronald. Medical Ethics. LC 79-25395. 238p. 1980. pap. text ed. 11.95 (ISBN 0-03-053256-6, HoltC). HR&W.

MEDICAL EXAMINATIONS

see Diagnosis; Insurance, Life-Medical Examinations; Medical Screening

MEDICAL EXAMINERS (LAW)

see also Coroners

Helpern, Milton & Knight, Bernard. Autopsy: The Memoirs of a Medical Detective. LC 77-76639. 1977. 10.00 (ISBN 0-312-06211-7). St Martin.
Rudman, Jack. Chief Medical Examiner. (Career Examination Ser.: C-1180). (Cloth bdg. avail. on request). pap. 17.95 (ISBN 0-8373-1180-2). Natl Learning.
--Deputy Chief Medical Examiner. (Career Examination Ser.: C-2723). (Cloth bdg. avail. on request). 1980. pap. 16.00 (ISBN 0-8373-2723-7). Natl Learning.
--Deputy Medical Examiner. (Career Examination Ser.: C-1245). (Cloth bdg. avail. on request). pap. 12.00 (ISBN 0-8373-1245-0). Natl Learning.
--Medical Examiner. (Career Examination Ser.: C-486). (Cloth bdg. avail. on request). pap. 14.00 (ISBN 0-8373-0486-5). Natl Learning.
--Medical Inspector. (Career Examination Ser.: C-487). (Cloth bdg. avail. on request). pap. 14.00 (ISBN 0-8373-0487-3). Natl Learning.

MEDICAL EXPERIMENTS ON HUMANS

see Human Experimentation in Medicine

MEDICAL FEES

see also Physicians-Salaries, Pensions, etc.

Carels, Edward, et al. The Physician & Cost Control. LC 79-21736. 196p. 1979. text ed. 22.50 (ISBN 0-89946-005-4). Oelgeschlager.
Gentile, Augustine. Physician Visits-Volume & Interval Since Last Visit: United States-1975. Stevenson, Taloria, ed. (Ser. 10: No. 128). 1978. pap. text ed. 1.75 (ISBN 0-8406-0150-6). Natl Ctr Health Stats.
Lewicki, Peter & Braly, George. Financial Planning for Physicians & Dentists. Wakefield, Jay S., ed. 1978. pap. 10.00 (ISBN 0-917054-16-4). Med Communications.
Pieroni, David. Physician Compensation. new ed. LC 78-59104. 142p. 1978. text ed. 26.00 (ISBN 0-89443-049-1). Aspen Systems.
Solomons, David, et al. The Cost of Physicians' & Certain Paramedical Services in New York Municipal Hospitals. 1973. pap. 4.00x (ISBN 0-256-01515-5). Irwin.
Topics in Health Care Financing. Incl. Vol. 4, No. 1. Improving Profitability. 1977 (ISBN 0-912862-88-2); Vol. 4, No. 2. Improving Productivity. 1977 (ISBN 0-912862-89-0); Vol. 4, No. 3. Physicians Compensation. 1978 (ISBN 0-912862-90-4); Vol. 4, No. 4. Hospital Information Systems. 1978 (ISBN 0-912862-91-2); Vol. 5, No. 1. Capital Financing. 1978 (ISBN 0-912862-92-0); Vol. 5, No. 2. Theft in the Health Care Industry. 1978 (ISBN 0-912862-93-9); Vol. 5, No. 3. Provider Reimbursement Review Board. 1979 (ISBN 0-912862-94-7); Vol. 5, No. 4. Flexible Budgeting. 1979 (ISBN 0-912862-95-5); Vol. 6, No. 1. Rate Regulation. 1979 (ISBN 0-912862-96-3). 13.75 ea. Aspen Systems.

MEDICAL FOLK-LORE

see Folk Medicine

MEDICAL FORMULARIES

see Medicine-Formulae, Receipts, Prescriptions

MEDICAL GENETICS

see also Cystic Fibrosis; Down'S Syndrome; Genetic Counseling; Metabolism, Inborn Errors of

Anderson, V. Elving, et al, eds. The Genetic Basis of the Epilepsies. 1981. text ed. price not set (ISBN 0-89004-676-X). Raven.
Berg, Kare, ed. Genetic Damage in Man Caused by Environmental Agents. LC 79-414. 1979. 27.00 (ISBN 0-12-089550-1). Acad Pr.
Bergsma, Daniel, ed. Congenital Malformations in Singletons: Epidemiologic Survey. LC 74-79906. (Symposia Spec. Ser.: Vol. 10, No. 11). 1976. 12.50 (ISBN 0-686-14567-4). March of Dimes.
--Genetic Forms of Hypogonadism. LC 75-8432. (Symposia Spec. Ser.: Vol. 11, No. 4). 1976. 13.95 (ISBN 0-686-14572-0). March of Dimes.
--Medical Genetics Today. LC 78-78434. (Johns Hopkins University Press Ser.: Vol. 10, No. 10). 1976. 20.00 (ISBN 0-686-14566-6). March of Dimes.
--New Chromosomal & Malformation Syndromes. LC 75-16885. (Symposia Spec. Ser.: Vol. 11, No.5). 1976. 16.95 (ISBN 0-686-14573-9). March of Dimes.
--Skeletal Dysplasias. LC 74-80734. (Excerpta Medica Ser.: Vol. 10, No. 12). 1976. 55.95 (ISBN 0-686-14568-2). March of Dimes.
Bergsma, Daniel, et al, eds. Medical Genetics Today. LC 78-78434. (National Foundation Ser: Birth Defects). 320p. 1974. 22.50x (ISBN 0-8018-1575-4). Johns Hopkins.
Birth Defects Conference-1975, Kansas City, Missouri. Cancer & Genetics: Proceedings. Bergsma, Daniel, ed. LC 75-43622. (Birth Defects-Original Article Ser.: Vol. 12, No. 1). 212p. 1976. 23.00x (ISBN 0-8451-1002-0). A R Liss.
Cohen, Bernice H., et al. Genetic Issues in Public Health & Medicine. (Illus.). 512p. 1978. 34.50 (ISBN 0-398-03659-4). C C Thomas.
Conference Held at Jackson Laboratory, Bar Harbor, Maine, Sept. 1976. Genetic Effects on Aging: Proceedings. Harrison, David E. & Bergsma, Daniel, eds. LC 77-20249. (Birth Defects Original Article Ser.: Vol. 14, No. 1). 550p. 1978. 58.00x (ISBN 0-8451-1016-0). A R Liss.
Crispens, Charles G., Jr. Essentials of Medical Genetics. (Illus.). 1971. text ed. 11.50x (ISBN 0-06-140669-4, Harper Medical). Har-Row.
Davenport, Charles B. Heredity in Relation to Eugenics. LC 73-180571. (Medicine & Society in America Ser). (Illus.). 320p. 1972. Repr. of 1911 ed. 16.00 (ISBN 0-405-03946-8). Arno.
De Grouchy, Jean & Turleau, Catherine. Clinical Atlas of Human Chromosomes. LC 77-2282. 1977. 57.50 (ISBN 0-471-01704-3, Pub. by Wiley Medical). Wiley.
Desnick, Robert J., ed. Enzyme Therapy in Genetic Diseases: Part 2. LC 79-48026. (Alan R. Liss Ser.: Vol. 16, No. 1). 1980. 64.00 (ISBN 0-686-29474-2). March of Dimes.
Dunlap, J. Diseases of Racial & Ethnic Groups. 1978. 10.00 (ISBN 0-686-00962-2). World Intl.
Dunlap, James. Intermarriage Prevents Disease. 1977. 8.95 (ISBN 0-686-17626-X). World Intl.
Emery, Alan. Methodology in Medical Genetics: An Introduction to Statistical Methods. LC 76-8946. (Illus.). 1976. text ed. 23.00 (ISBN 0-443-01438-8). Churchill.
Emery, Alan E. Elements of Medical Genetics. 5th ed. (Illus.). 1979. pap. text ed. 11.25 (ISBN 0-443-01832-4). Churchill.
--Elements of Medical Genetics. 250p. 1976. pap. 7.95x (ISBN 0-520-03018-4, CAMPUS 153). U of Cal Pr.
Evans, John, et al, eds. Human Gene Mapping Five. (S. Karger Ser.: Vol. 15, No. 11). 1979. 30.00 (ISBN 3-8055-0649-X). March of Dimes.
Goddard, Henry H. The Kallikak Family: A Study in the Heredity of Feeble-Mindedness. LC 73-2966. (Classics in Psychology Ser.). Repr. of 1931 ed. 9.00 (ISBN 0-405-05139-5). Arno.
Goodman, Richard M. Genetic Disorders Among the Jewish People. LC 78-21847. 1979. text ed. 32.50x (ISBN 0-8018-2120-7). Johns Hopkins.
Goodman, Richard M. & Gorlin, Robert J. Atlas of the Face in Genetic Disorders. 2nd ed. LC 76-40327. (Illus.). 1977. 69.50 (ISBN 0-8016-1895-9). Mosby.
Halcomb, Ruth. You Can Challenge Heredity. LC 75-13185. 192p. 1975. pap. 1.50 (ISBN 0-89041-029-1, 3029). Major Bks.
Holton, J. B. & Ireland, J. B., eds. Inborn Errors of Skin, Hair & Connective Tissue. (Illus.). 300p. 1975. 29.50 (ISBN 0-8391-0836-2). Univ Park.
Hutt, Frederick B. Genetic Resistance to Disease in Domestic Animals. (Illus.). 210p. 1958. 25.00x (ISBN 0-8014-0196-8). Comstock.
Jolly, Elizabeth. The Invisible Chain: Diseases Passed on by Inheritance. LC 72-80166. 1972. 15.95x (ISBN 0-911012-26-5). Nelson-Hall.
Kallmann, Franz J., ed. Expanding Goals of Genetics in Psychiatry. LC 62-15383. 288p. 1962. 41.25 (ISBN 0-8089-0224-5). Grune.
Kelly, Sally. Biochemical Methods in Medical Genetics. (Amer. Lec in Laboratory Medicine Ser.). (Illus.). 352p. 1977. 22.25 (ISBN 0-398-03630-6). C C Thomas.
Kerr, C. B., et al. The Etiology of Inherited Disorders. LC 73-11118. 196p. 1974. text ed. 19.00x (ISBN 0-8422-7151-1). Irvington.
Koller, Peo C. Chromosomes & Genes: The Biological Basis of Heredity. (Contemporary Science Library). (Illus.). 1971. pap. 1.95x (ISBN 0-393-00587-9). Norton.
Levin, Stefan & Knight, Connie H., eds. Genetic & Environmental Hearing Loss: Syndromic & Nonsyndromic. (Alan R. Liss Ser.: Vol. 16, No. 7). 1980. 16.00 (ISBN 0-8451-1040-3). March of Dimes.
Lipkin, Mack, Jr. & Rowley, Peter T. Genetic Responsibility: On Choosing Our Children's Genes. LC 74-12149. 176p. 1974. 22.50 (ISBN 0-306-30813-4, Plenum Pr). Plenum Pub.
Lynch, H. T. Hereditary Factors in Carcinoma, (Recent Results in Cancer Research: Vol. 12). (Illus.). 1967. 17.20 (ISBN 0-387-03960-0). Springer-Verlag.
McDevitt, Hugh O. & Landy, Maurice, eds. Genetic Control of Immune Responsiveness: Relationship to Disease Susceptibility. (Perspectives in Immunology Ser). 1973. 46.50 (ISBN 0-12-483250-4). Acad Pr.
Meier, Hans. Experimental Pharmacogenetics: Physiopathology of Heredity & Pharmacologic Responses. 1963. 38.50 (ISBN 0-12-488450-4). Acad Pr.
Mendlewicz, J. & Shopsin, Baron, eds. Genetic Aspects of Affective Illness: Current Concepts. LC 79-11827. 1979. text ed. 15.00 (ISBN 0-89335-088-5). Spectrum Pub.
Milunsky, Aubrey. Know Your Genes. 1977. 9.95 (ISBN 0-395-25374-8). HM.
--The Prenatal Diagnosis of Hereditary Disorders. (Illus.). 276p. 1973. text ed. 16.75 (ISBN 0-398-02747-1). C C Thomas.
--Prevention of Genetic Disease & Mental Retardation. LC 74-21015. (Illus.). 450p. 1975. 29.00 (ISBN 0-7216-6395-8). Saunders.
Milunsky, Aubrey, ed. Genetic Disorders & the Fetus: Diagnosis, Prevention, & Treatment. LC 79-14502. (Illus.). 730p. 1979. 49.50 (ISBN 0-306-40118-5, Plenum Pr). Plenum Pub.
Nora, James J. & Fraser, F. Clark. Medical Genetics: Principles & Practice. 2nd ed. LC 81-11808. (Illus.). 405p. 1981. text ed. price not set (ISBN 0-8121-0766-7). Lea & Febiger.
O'Donnell, James J. & Hall, Bryan D., eds. Penetrance & Variability in Malformation Syndromes. LC 79-5115. (Alan R. Liss Ser.: Vol. 15, No. 5b). 1979. 42.00 (ISBN 0-8451-1029-2). March of Dimes.
Okada, Shintaro, et al. Biochemical Basis of Inherited Human Disease. 1973. 29.50x (ISBN 0-8422-7087-6). Irvington.
Paul, Natalie W., ed. A Guide to Human Chromosome Defects. 2nd ed. LC 68-57287. (March of Dimes Birth Defects Foundation Ser.: Vol. 16, No. 6). 1980. 0.50 (ISBN 0-686-30821-2). March of Dimes.
Porter, Ian H. & Hook, Ernest B., eds. Service & Education in Medical Genetics. (Birth Defects Institute Symposium VIII Ser.). 1979. 27.00 (ISBN 0-12-562650-9). Acad Pr.
Priest, Jean H. Medical Cytogenetics & Cell Culture. 2nd ed. LC 76-7402. (Illus.). 344p. 1977. text ed. 19.50 (ISBN 0-8121-0556-7). Lea & Febiger.
Roberts, J. Fraser. Introduction to Medical Genetics. 7th ed. (Illus.). 320p. 1978. pap. text ed. 16.95x (ISBN 0-19-261214-X). Oxford U Pr.
Rosenthal, D. Genetic Theory & Abnormal Behavior. 1970. text ed. 22.00 (ISBN 0-07-053864-6, C). McGraw.
Roy, A. K. & Clark, J. H. Gene Regulation by Steroid Hormones. (Illus.). 400p. 1980. 42.50 (ISBN 0-387-90464-6). Springer-Verlag.

Salinas, Carlos F. & Jorgenson, Ronald J., eds. Dentistry in the Interdisciplinary Treatment of Genetic Diseases. (Alan R. Liss Ser.: Vol. 16, No. 5). 1980. 26.00 (ISBN 0-8451-1039-X). March of Dimes.

Sedano, H. O., et al. Oral Manifestations of Inherited Disorders. 1977. 22.95 (ISBN 0-409-95050-5). Butterworth.

Shine, I. Serendipity in St. Helena. 1970. 34.00 (ISBN 0-08-012794-0). Pergamon.

Smith, David W. Recognizable Patterns of Human Malformation: Genetic, Embryologic & Clinical Aspects, Vol. 7 2nd ed. LC 75-21150. (Illus.). 528p. 1976. text ed. 27.50 (ISBN 0-7216-8376-2). Saunders.

Steinberg, Arthur G. & Bearn, Alexander G., eds. Progress in Medical Genetics. Incl. Vol. II. (Illus.). 352p. 1962. 44.75 (ISBN 0-8089-0479-5); Vol. III. (Illus.). 272p. 1963. 47.75 (ISBN 0-8089-0480-9); Vol. V. (Illus.). 160p. 1967; Vol. VI. (Illus.). 296p. 1969. 59.50 (ISBN 0-8089-0482-5); Vol. VII. (Illus.). 256p. 1970. 54.75 (ISBN 0-8089-0483-3); Vol. VIII. 320p. 1972. 59.50 (ISBN 0-8089-0723-9); Vol. IX. 1973. 54.50 (ISBN 0-8089-0781-6); Vol. X. (Illus.). 1974. 54.50 (ISBN 0-8089-0841-3). LC 60-53514. (Vol. 1, 4, 5 o.p.). Grune.

Steinberg, Arthur G., et al. Progress in Medical Genetics, Vol. 1. LC 75-21151. (Illus.). 300p. 1976. text ed. 22.00 (ISBN 0-7216-8586-2). Saunders.

Steinberg, Arthur G., et al, eds. Progress in Medical Genetics, Vol. 2. Childs, Barton. LC 75-21151. 1977. text ed. 27.50 (ISBN 0-7216-8588-9). Saunders.

Steinberg, Authur G., et al, eds. Progress in Medical Genetics, Vol. 4. (Genetics of Gastrointestinal Disease Ser.). (Illus.). 320p. 1980. text ed. 39.50 (ISBN 0-7216-8604-4). Saunders.

Symposium of the Birth Defects Institute of the New York State Dept. of Health, Second, October, 1971. Heredity & Society. Porter, Ian H., et al, eds. 1973. 30.00 (ISBN 0-12-562850-1). Acad Pr.

Szabo, G. & Papp, Z., eds. Medical Genetics. (International Congress Ser: No. 428). 1978. 136.75 (ISBN 0-444-90002-0, Excerpta Medica). Elsevier.

Thorsby, E., et al. Genetics of Human Histocompatibility Antigens & Their Relation to Disease. (Illus.). 220p. 1973. text ed. 29.50x (ISBN 0-8422-7062-0). Irvington.

Tsuang, Ming T. & VanderMey, Randall. Genes & the Mind: Inheritance of Mental Illness. (Illus.). 158p. 1980. text ed. 12.95x (ISBN 0-19-261268-9). Oxford U Pr.

Vogel, H. G. & Schone, H. H., eds. Genes & Tumor Genes: Hoechst-Roussel Workshop. 1981. text ed. price not set (ISBN 0-89004-678-6). Raven.

Volpe, E. Peter. Human Heredity & Birth Defects. LC 75-124674. (Science & Society Ser). (Illus.). 1971. pap. 4.95 (ISBN 0-672-63549-6). Pegasus.

WHO Scientific Group, Geneva, 1968. Genetic Disorders-Prevention, Treatment & Rehabilitation: Report. (Technical Report Ser.: No. 497). (Also avail. in French, Russian & Spanish). 1972. pap. 1.40 (ISBN 92-4-120497-4). World Health.

Winick, Myron, ed. Nutritional Management of Genetic Disorders, Vol. 8. LC 79-16192. (Current Concepts in Nutrition Ser.). 1979. 32.50 (ISBN 0-471-05781-9, Pub. by Wiley-Interscience). Wiley.

MEDICAL GENETICS–BIBLIOGRAPHY

McKusick, Victor A. Mendelian Inheritance in Man: Catalogs of Autosomal Dominant, Autosomal Recessive, & X-Linked Phenotypes. 5th ed. LC 77-17248. (Illus.). 918p. 1975. 29.50x (ISBN 0-8018-2087-1). Johns Hopkins.

MEDICAL GEOGRAPHY

see also Climatology, Medical; Epidemics; Tropical Medicine

Bowditch, Henry I. Consumption in New England: Locality, One of Its Chief Causes & Is Consumption Contagious, or Communicated by One Person to Another in Any Manner, 2 vols. in 1. Rosenkrantz, Barbara G., ed. LC 76-25653. (Public Health in America Ser.). (Illus.). 1977. Repr. of 1864 ed. lib. bdg. 10.00x (ISBN 0-405-09806-5). Arno.

Currie, William. An Historical Account of the Climates & Diseases of the U. S. A. & of the Remedies & Methods of Treatment. LC 70-180570. (Medicine & Society in America Ser). 428p. 1972. Repr. of 1792 ed. 19.00 (ISBN 0-405-03945-X). Arno.

Diesfeld, H. J. & Hecklau, H. K. Kenya - A Geomedical Monograph. (Geomedical Monograph: Vol. 5). (Illus.). 1978. 46.10 (ISBN 0-387-08729-X). Springer-Verlag.

Drake, Daniel. Systematic Treastise, Historical, Etiological & Practical on the Principal Diseases of the Interior Valley of North America, 8 Pts. in 2 Vols. 1971. Repr. of 1850 ed. lib. bdg. 89.00 (ISBN 0-8337-0907-0). B Franklin.

Dutt, Ashok K., ed. Contemporary Perspectives on the Medical Geography of South & Southeast Asia. (Illus.). 78p. 1980. pap. 20.00 (ISBN 0-08-026762-9). Pergamon.

Ffrench, G. E. & Hill, A. G. Kuwait: Urban & Medical Ecology, a Geomedical Study. LC 71-156994. (Geomedical Monograph Ser.: Vol. 4). (Illus.). 1971. 34.30 (ISBN 0-387-05384-0). Springer-Verlag.

Fischer, L. Afghanistan. (Geomedical Monograph Ser.: Vol. 2). (Illus., Ger. & Eng.). 1968. 31.30 (ISBN 0-387-04266-0). Springer-Verlag.

Freedman, Jacob, ed. Trace Element Geochemistry in Health & Disease. LC 75-3801. (Special Paper: No. 155). (Illus.). 1975. pap. 15.00x (ISBN 0-8137-2155-5). Geol Soc.

Hartwig, Gerald W. & Patterson, K. David, eds. Disease in African History: An Introductory Survey & Case Studies. LC 78-52421. 1978. 13.75 (ISBN 0-8223-0410-4). Duke.

Howe, G. Melvyn, ed. A World Geography of Human Diseases. 1978. 97.00 (ISBN 0-12-357150-2). Acad Pr.

Jones, Billy M. Health-Seekers in the Southwest, 1817-1900. (Illus.). 1967. 15.95x (ISBN 0-8061-0739-1). U of Okla Pr.

Kanter, H. Libyan: Libya. (Geomedical Monograph Ser.: Vol. 1). (Illus., Eng. & Ger.). 1967. 31.30 (ISBN 0-387-03925-2). Springer-Verlag.

Learmonth, Andrew. Patterns of Disease & Hunger: A Study in Medical Geography. LC 77-91741. 27.00 (ISBN 0-7153-7538-5). David & Charles.

Maragos, G. D., ed. Seminar on Geographical Pediatrics. (Paediatrician: Vol. 6, No. 2). (Illus.). 1977. 18.75 (ISBN 3-8055-2795-0). S Karger.

May, Jacques M. & McLellan, Donna L., eds. Studies in Medical Geography, 14 vols. Incl. Vol. 2. Studies in Disease Ecology. (Illus.). 1961. 24.25 (ISBN 0-02-848980-2); Vol. 3. The Ecology of Malnutrition in the Far & Near East. (Illus.). 1961. 21.75 (ISBN 0-02-849010-X); Vol. 4. The Ecology of Malnutrition in Five Countries of Eastern & Central Europe: East Germany,Poland, Yugoslavia, Albania, Greece. (Illus.). 1964. 16.25 (ISBN 0-02-848970-5); Vol. 5. The Ecology of Malnutrition in Middle Africa: Ghana, Nigeria, Republic of the Congo, Rwanda & Burundi & the Former French Equatorial Africa. (Illus.). 1965. 14.25 (ISBN 0-02-848990-X); Vol. 6. The Ecology of Malnutrition in Central & Southern Europe: Austria, Hungary, Romania, Bulgaria & Czechoslovakia. (Illus.). 1966. 16.25 (ISBN 0-02-849000-2); Vol. 7. The Ecology of Malnutrition in Northern Africa: Libya, Tunisia, Algeria, Morocco, Spanish Sahara & Ifni, Mauretania. (Illus.). 1967. 16.25 (ISBN 0-02-848950-0); Vol. 8. The Ecology of Malnutrition in the French-Speaking Countries of West Africa & Madagascar: Senegal, Guinea, Ivory Coast, Togo, Dahomey, Cameroon, Niger, Mali, Upper Volta, & Madagascar. (Illus.). 1968. 18.50 (ISBN 0-02-848960-8); Vol. 9. The Ecology of Malnutrition in Eastern Africa: Equatorial Guinea, the Gambia, Liberia, Sierra Leone, Malawi, Rhodesia, Zambia, Kenya, Tanzania, Uganda, Ethiopia, the French Territory of the Atars & Issas, the Somali Republic & Sudan. 1970. 28.50 (ISBN 0-02-849020-7); Vol. 10. The Ecology of Malnutrition in Seven Countries of Southern Africa and in Portuguese Guinea: The/Republic of South Africa, South West Africa (Namibia), Botswana, Lesotho, Swaziland, Mozambique, Angola, Portuguese Guinea. 1971. 24.00 (ISBN 0-02-848940-3); Vol. 11. The Ecology of Malnutrition in Mexico & Central America. 1972. 21.75 (ISBN 0-02-848930-6); Vol. 12. The Ecology of Malnutrition in the Caribbean. 1973. 26.25 (ISBN 0-02-848920-9); Vol. 13. The Ecology of Malnutrition in Eastern South America. 1975. 36.25 (ISBN 0-02-849060-6); Vol. 14. The Ecology of Malnutrition in Western South America. 1975. 28.50 (ISBN 0-02-849070-3). Hafner.

Misra, R. P. Medical Geography of India. new ed. (India, the Land & People). (Illus.). 204p. 1972. 4.50x (ISBN 0-8426-0326-3). Verry.

Pyle, Gerald F. Applied Medical Geography. LC 78-27856. (Scripta Geography Ser.). 1979. 19.75x (ISBN 0-470-26643-0). Halsted Pr.

Pyle, Gerald F., ed. New Directions in Medical Geography: Medical Geography Papers from the 75th Anniversary Meeting of the Association of American Geographers, Philadelphia Pa., April 1979. (Illus.). 86p. 1980. 14.95 (ISBN 0-08-025817-4). Pergamon.

Rosenkrantz, Barbara G., ed. Health in the Southern United States: An Original Anthology. LC 76-40667. (Public Health in America Ser.). (Illus.). 1977. Repr. of 1977 ed. lib. bdg. 20.00x (ISBN 0-405-09875-8). Arno.

Sauer, Herbert I. Geographic Patterns in the Risk of Dying & Associated Factors United States, 1968-1972. Cox, Klaudia, ed. (Series 3: No. 18). 1980. pap. text ed. 1.70 (ISBN 0-8406-0184-0). Natl Ctr Health Stats.

Snapper, Isidore. Chinese Lessons to Western Medicine: A Contribution to Geographical Medicine from the Clinics of Peiping. 2nd ed. LC 64-7771. (Illus.). 416p. 1965. 53.25 (ISBN 0-8089-0435-3). Grune.

MEDICAL GROUP PRACTICE

see Group Medical Practice

MEDICAL GYMNASTICS

see Exercise Therapy

MEDICAL HELMINTHOLOGY

see also Worms, Intestinal and Parasitic

Marcial-Rojas, Raul A. Pathology of Protozoal & Helminthic Diseases with Clinical Correlation. LC 75-22106. 1028p. 1975. Repr. of 1971 ed. 65.00 (ISBN 0-88275-350-9). Krieger.

MEDICAL HISTORY TAKING

Alexander, Mary M. & Brown, Marie S. Pediatric History Taking & Physical Diagnosis for Nurses. 2nd ed. (Illus.). 1979. text ed. 14.95 (ISBN 0-07-001019-6, HP); pap. text ed. 9.95 (ISBN 0-07-001018-8). McGraw.

Bernstein, Lewis & Bernstein, Rosalyn S. Interviewing: A Guide for Health Professionals. 3rd ed. (Illus.). 224p. 1974. pap. 12.95 (ISBN 0-8385-4307-3). ACC.

Burdock, Eugene I. & Hardesty, Anne S. Structured Clinical Interview (SCI) (Illus.). 1969. 25 sets with scoring key & profile 12.00x (ISBN 0-8261-1001-0); manual pap. 4.50x (ISBN 0-8261-1002-9); special sample offer 4.95x (ISBN 0-8261-1004-5). Springer Pub.

Cannell, Charles F. & Marquis, Kent H. A Summary of Research Studies of Interviewing Methodology, 1959-1970. (Ser. 2: No. 69). 70p. 1976. pap. text ed. 2.00 (ISBN 0-8406-0062-3). Natl Ctr Health Stats.

DeGowin, Elmer L. & DeGowin, Richard L. Bedside Diagnostic Examination. 3rd ed. (Illus.). 1976. pap. text ed. 16.95 (ISBN 0-02-328050-6). Macmillan.

Del Guercio, Louis R. Multilingual Manual for Medical History-Taking. 1972. spiral bdg. 8.95 (ISBN 0-316-18025-4). Little.

Edinburg, Golda M., et al. Clinical Interviewing & Counseling: Principles & Techniques. (Illus.). 126p. 1975. pap. 12.75 (ISBN 0-8385-1139-2). ACC.

Froelich, Robert E. & Bishop, F. Marian. Clinical Interviewing Skills: A Programmed Manual for Data Gathering, Evaluation, & Patient Management. 3rd ed. LC 76-62992. (Illus.). 1977. pap. 17.50 (ISBN 0-8016-1702-2). Mosby.

GAP Committee on Family. Case History Method in the Study of Family Process, Vol. 7. LC 62-2872. (Report No. 76). 1970. pap. 5.00 (ISBN 0-87318-105-0, Pub. by Adv Psychiatry). Mental Health.

Lipkin, Mack. Care of Patients: Concepts & Tactics. 288p. 1974. text ed. 11.95x (ISBN 0-19-501809-5); pap. text ed. 6.95x (ISBN 0-19-501808-7). Oxford U Pr.

Mahoney, Elizabeth A., et al. How to Collect and Record a Health History. LC 76-8712. 1976. pap. text ed. 5.95x (ISBN 0-397-54185-6, JBL-Med-Nursing). Har-Row.

Malasanos, Lois, et al. Health Assessment. LC 77-2179. (Illus.). 1977. text ed. 22.95 (ISBN 0-8016-0478-8). Mosby.

Morgan, William L. & Engel, George L. Clinical Approach to the Patient. LC 69-12887. (Illus.). 1969. 14.95 (ISBN 0-7216-6550-0). Saunders.

Raus, Elmer E. & Raus, Madonna M. Manual of History Taking, Physical Examinations & Record Keeping. LC 73-37293. (Illus.). 584p. 1974. pap. text ed. 21.50 (ISBN 0-397-50306-7, JBL-Med-Nursing). Har-Row.

Reiser, David E., et al. Patient Interviewing: The Human Dimension. (Illus.). 299p. 1980. softcover 14.95 (ISBN 0-683-07226-9). Williams & Wilkins.

Sherman, Jacques L., Jr. & Fields, Sylvia K., eds. Guide to Patient Evaluation. 3rd ed. LC 78-50128. 1978. 17.50 (ISBN 0-87488-985-5); pap. 12.75 (ISBN 0-686-77010-2). Med Exam.

Szondi, L. Profile Blanks: Szondi Tableau. 15.25 (ISBN 0-8089-0602-X); answer sheet, pkg. of 50 8.75 (ISBN 0-686-76985-6); test pictures, set of 48 35.00 (ISBN 0-8089-0601-1). Grune.

Thompson, June M. & Bowers, Arden C. Clinical Manual of Health Assessment. LC 79-28832. (Illus.). 1980. pap. text ed. 17.95 (ISBN 0-8016-4935-8). Mosby.

Wolf, G. A. Collecting Data from Patients. (Illus.). 1977. 12.95 (ISBN 0-8391-0983-0). Univ Park.

MEDICAL ILLUSTRATION

see also Medicine and Art

Loechel, William E. Medical Illustration: A Guide for the Doctor-Author & Exhibitor. (Illus.). 360p. 1964. pap. 34.75 photocopy ed., spiral (ISBN 0-398-01139-7). C C Thomas.

Nakamura, Julia & Nakamura, Massy. Your Future in Medical Illustrating: Art & Photography. LC 78-140096. (Careers in Depth Ser). (Illus.). (gr. 7 up). 1971. PLB 5.97 (ISBN 0-8239-0236-6). Rosen Pr.

Netter, Frank H., illus. The C I B A Collection of Medical Illustrations, 7 vols. Incl. Vol. 1. Nervous System. 24.50x (ISBN 0-914168-01-0); Vol. 2. Reproductive System. 34.00x (ISBN 0-914168-02-9); Vol. 3, Pt. 1. Digestive System: Upper Digestive Tract. 27.00x (ISBN 0-914168-03-7); Vol. 3, Pt. 2. Digestive System: Lower Digestive Tract. 29.50x (ISBN 0-914168-04-5); Vol. 3, Pt. 3. Digestive System: Liver, Biliary Tract & Pancreas. 25.00x (ISBN 0-914168-05-3); Vol. 4. Endocrine System & Selected Metabolic Diseases. 34.00x (ISBN 0-914168-06-1); Vol. 5. Heart. 42.00x (ISBN 0-914168-07-X); Vol. 6. Kidneys, Ureters & Urinary Bladder. 44.00x (ISBN 0-914168-08-8). LC 53-2151. (Illus.). 1974. Set. 288.00x (ISBN 0-914168-00-2). C I B A Pharm.

Thornton, John L. Jan Van Rymsdyk: Medical Illustrator of the Eighteenth Century. (Illus.). 86p. 1981. 25.00 (ISBN 0-906672-02-3). Oleander Pr.

MEDICAL INSPECTION IN SCHOOLS

see School Health

MEDICAL INSTRUMENTS AND APPARATUS

see also Lasers in Medicine; Surgical Instruments and Apparatus

Advances in Instrumentation, Chicago, Nineteen Seventy - Nine, Vol. 34, Pts.1 & 2. LC 52-29277. 1979. Set. pap. text ed. 75.00x (ISBN 0-686-74251-6); Pt. 1, 475 Pp. pap. text ed. 40.00x (ISBN 0-87664-457-4); Pt. 2, 550. pap. text ed. 40.00x (ISBN 0-87664-458-2). Instru Soc.

Advances in Instrumentation, Houston, Nineteen Eighty, Vol. 35, Pts. 1 & 2. LC 52-29277. 1980. Set. pap. text ed. 75.00x (ISBN 0-686-74252-4); Pt. 1, 564 Pp. pap. text ed. 40.00x (ISBN 0-87664-491-4); Pt. 2 689 Pp. pap. text ed. 40.00x (ISBN 0-87664-492-2). Instru Soc.

American Society for Hospital Engineering of the American Hospital Association. Medical Equipment Management in Hospitals. 2nd ed. 1981. pap. text ed. price not set (ISBN 0-87258-360-0, 1273). Am Hospital.

Annual Rocky Mountain Bioengineering Symposium & the Annual International ISA Biomedical Sciences Instrumentation Symposium, 17th, Colorado Springs, Colorado, 1980. Biomedical Sciences Instrumentation: Proceedings, Vol. 16. LC 66-21220. 159p. 1980. pap. text ed. 20.00x (ISBN 0-87664-481-7). Instru Soc.

ASTM Standards for Medical & Surgical Materials & Devices. 122p. 1979. soft cover 7.50 (ISBN 0-686-76093-X, 06-604078-47). ASTM.

Bennion, Elizabeth. Antique Medical Instruments. LC 78-55189. 1979. 65.00 (ISBN 0-520-03832-0). U of Cal Pr.

Biloon, F. Medical Equipment Service Manual: Theory & Maintenance Procedures. LC 77-513. 1978. 23.95 (ISBN 0-13-572644-1). P-H.

Biomedical Sciences Instrumentation, Vol. 13. LC 66-21220. 153p. 1977. pap. text ed. 20.00 (ISBN 0-87664-360-8). Instru Soc.

Biomedical Sciences Instrumentation: Proceedings, Vol. 17. LC 66-21220. 128p. 1981. pap. text ed. 20.00x (ISBN 0-87664-522-8). Instru Soc.

Burri, C., ed. The Caval Catheter. LC 77-2784. 1978. pap. 16.20 (ISBN 0-387-08566-1). Springer-Verlag.

Carr, Joseph. Servicing Medical & Bio-Electronic Equipment. LC 77-73. (Illus.). 1977. 10.95 (ISBN 0-8306-7930-8); pap. 8.95 (ISBN 0-8306-6930-2, 930). TAB Bks.

Committee on Interplay of Engineering with Biology & Medicine. Study of Engineering in Medicine & Health Care. LC 74-7253. 80p. 1974. pap. 3.50 (ISBN 0-309-02148-0). Natl Acad Pr.

Critser, James R., Jr. Medical Diagnostic Apparatus-Systems. (Series 10 DAS-80). 1981. 80.00 (ISBN 0-914428-80-2). Lexington Data.

--Medical Technology: Advanced Medical Apparatus-Systems. (Ser. 10 AMA-78). 1980. 300.00 (ISBN 0-914428-59-4). Lexington Data.

--Medical Technology: Electrical-Electronic Apparatus 1976. (Ser. 10 - 76). 1977. 200.00 (ISBN 0-914428-41-1). Lexington Data.

Cromwell, Leslie & Arditti, M. Medical Instrumentation for Health Care. (Illus.). 1976. Ref. Ed. 22.95 (ISBN 0-13-572602-6). P-H.

Enlarged Type Reprint of the Nineteen Seventy-Six Medical Devices Act P. L. 94-295. 1976. pap. 3.80 ea 1-5 copies (ISBN 0-914176-08-0); pap. 3.50 ea. 6-15 copies; pap. 3.20 ea. 16-25 copies; pap. 2.90 ea. 26 or more copies. Wash Busn Info.

Ferris, Clifford D. Guide to Medical Laboratory Instruments. LC 80-80585. 260p. 1980. text ed. 14.95 (ISBN 0-316-28127-1). Little.

Hill, D. W. & Dolan, A. H. Instrumentation for Intensive Care. 320p. 1976. 44.00 (ISBN 0-8089-0886-3). Grune.

Hunt, Diana. The Doctor's Guide for Buying X-Ray Equipment & Accessories. (Illus.). 200p. 1981. text ed. price not set. Springtime.

Hyman, Stanley. Supplies Management for Health Services. 250p. 1981. 30.00x (ISBN 0-85664-707-1, Pub. by Croom Helm Ltd England). Biblio Dist.

Lerner, Marguerite R. Doctors' Tools. LC 59-15484. (Medical Bks. for Children). (Illus.). (gr. k-6). 1960. PLB 3.95 (ISBN 0-8225-0004-3). Lerner Pubns.

McPherson, Steven P. Respiratory Therapy Equipment. 2nd ed. LC 80-21627. (Illus.). 514p. 1980. text ed. 24.95 (ISBN 0-8016-3313-3). Mosby.

Mitchell, Silas W. Early History of Instrumental Precision in Medicine. LC 79-172192. (Research & Source Works Ser: No. 860). 1971. Repr. of 1892 ed. lib. bdg. 16.00 (ISBN 0-8337-2408-8). B Franklin.

Pacela, Allan F., ed. The Quest Guide to Essential Test Instrumentation for Medical Equipment. LC 78-66409. 1978. looseleaf 32.50x (ISBN 0-930844-05-X). Quest Pub.

Probst, Calvin, ed. Hospital Purchasing Guide: Nieteen Eighty Two. 6th ed. (Annual Ser.). 1982. pap. text ed. 95.00 (ISBN 0-933916-06-X). IMS Comm.

Ray, G. E. Precision Attachments. (Illus.). 1978. pap. 15.00 (ISBN 0-8151-7110-2). Year Bk Med.

Rocky Mountain Bioengineering Symposium, 12th & International ISA Biomedical Sciences Instrumentation Symposium, 12th, Denver, 1975. Biomedical Sciences Instrumentation: Proceedings, Vol. 11. Rock, K. C., ed. LC 66-21220. 192p. 1975. pap. 20.00 (ISBN 0-87664-263-6). Instru Soc.

Sequin, F. & Texhammar, R. AO-ASIF Instrumentation: Manual of Use & Care. (Illus.). 330p. 1981. 36.00 (ISBN 0-387-10337-6). Springer-Verlag.

Shoup, T. E. & Thacker, J. G., eds. International Conference on Medical Devices & Sports Equipment. 216p. 1980. 30.00 (ISBN 0-686-69853-3, H00166). ASME.

Society of Photo-Optical Instrumentation Engineers, Seminar. Application of Optical Instrumentation in Medicine: Proceedings, Vol. 35. 10.00 (ISBN 0-89252-046-9). Photo Optical.

Thomas, Harry E. Handbook of Biomedical Instrumentation Tasting & Measurement. LC 73-13804. 576p. 1974. 29.95 (ISBN 0-87909-323-4). Reston.

Tischler, Morris. Experiments in General & Biomedical Instrumentation. Haas, Mark, ed. (Illus.). 176p. 1980. pap. text ed. 8.95x (ISBN 0-07-064781-X, G). McGraw.

Tompkins, W. & Webster, J., eds. Design of Microcomputer-Based Medical Instrumentation. 1981. 27.95 (ISBN 0-13-201244-8). P-H.

Traister, Robert. Principles of Biomedical Instrumentation & Monitoring. 300p. 1981. text ed. 24.95 (ISBN 0-8359-5611-3). Reston.

Webster, John G. Medical Instrumentation: Application & Design. LC 77-76419. (Illus.). 1978. text ed. 29.95 (ISBN 0-395-25411-6); sol. manual 2.00 (ISBN 0-395-25412-4). HM.

Welkowitz, Walter & Deutsch, Sid. Biomedical Instrument: Theory & Design. 1976. 26.00 (ISBN 0-12-744150-6). Acad Pr.

Wirsching, Paul. Seibt Directory of Medical Appliances. 5th ed. 1976. pap. 40.00x (ISBN 0-8002-1963-5). Intl Pubns Serv.

MEDICAL INTERNATIONAL COOPERATION ORGANIZATION

Dooley, Thomas A. Night They Burned the Mountain. (RL 10). pap. 1.50 (ISBN 0-451-08681-3, W8681, Sig). NAL.

MEDICAL INTERNS

see Interns (Medicine)

MEDICAL INTERVIEWING

see Medical History Taking

MEDICAL JOURNALISM

see Journalism, Medical

MEDICAL JURISPRUDENCE

see also Autopsy; Chemistry, Forensic; Dental Jurisprudence; Forensic Hematology; Forensic Psychiatry; Gases, Asphyxiating and Poisonous; Medical Examiners (Law); Medical Laws and Legislation; Poisons; Psychology, Forensic; also subdivision Jurisprudence under subjects to which medical jurisprudence is applicable, e.g. Insanity–Jurisprudence

Adelson, Lester. The Pathology of Homicide: A Vade Mecum for Pathologist, Prosecutor & Defense Counsel. (Illus.). 992p. 1974. text ed. 67.50 (ISBN 0-398-03000-6). C C Thomas.

American Medical Association. Medicolegal Forms with Legal Analysis. 1973. pap. 2.50 (ISBN 0-89970-062-4, OP109). AMA.

Averbach, Albert. Handling Accident Cases: 1963-73, 7 vols. in 8 bks. LC 58-4149. 1973. Set. 320.00 (ISBN 0-686-14528-3); Vols. 1-2. 85.00 (ISBN 0-686-31708-4); Vols. 3a-3b. 42.50 ea.; Vols. 4-5. 85.00 (ISBN 0-686-31709-2); Vols. 6-7. 85.00 (ISBN 0-686-31710-6). Lawyers Co-Op.

Bander, Edward J. & Wallach, Jeffrey J. Medical Legal Dictionary. LC 73-83743. 1970. lib. bdg. 7.50 (ISBN 0-379-14101-9). Oceana.

Beck, Theodoric R. & Beck, John B. Elements of Medical Jurisprudence, 2 vols. LC 75-23681. Repr. of 1860 ed. Set. 73.50 (ISBN 0-404-13310-X). AMS Pr.

Beresford, H. Richard. Legal Aspects of Neurologic Practice. LC 75-16362. (Contemporary Neurology Ser.: No. 13). 150p. 1975. text ed. 22.00 (ISBN 0-8036-0730-X). Davis Co.

The Best of Law & Medicine, 1968-1970. 1970. pap. 2.00 (ISBN 0-89970-024-1, OP-179). AMA.

Blassingame, Wyatt. Science Catches the Criminal. LC 75-11979. (Illus.). 192p. (gr. 7 up). 1975. PLB 5.95 (ISBN 0-396-07152-X). Dodd.

Bridgman, R. F. & Roemer, M. I. Hospital Legislation & Hospital Systems. (Public Health Paper: No. 50). (Also avail. French & Spanish). 1973. pap. 4.80 (ISBN 92-4-130050-7). World Health.

Brooks, Stewart M. Our Murdered Presidents: The Medical Story. LC 65-23865. (Illus.). 234p. 1966. 8.95 (ISBN 0-686-70968-3). Fell.

Brown, Kent L. Medical Problems & the Law. (Illus.). 296p. 1971. 17.50 (ISBN 0-398-00239-8). C C Thomas.

Burges, S. H., ed. The New Police Surgeon: A Practical Guide to Clinical Forensic Medicine. (Illus.). 1978. 39.95 (ISBN 0-09-131640-5, Pub. by Hutchinson). Merrimack Bk Serv.

Burns, Chester R., ed. Legacies in Law & Medicine. LC 76-29641. 1977. 15.00 (ISBN 0-88202-164-8). N Watson.

Camps, F. E. Gradwohl's Legal Medicine. 3rd ed. (Illus.). 1976. 95.00 (ISBN 0-8151-1430-3). Year Bk Med.

Camps, Francis E., et al. Practical Forensic Medicine. 1971. 19.95 (ISBN 0-09-103610-0, Pub. by Hutchinson). Merrimack Bk Serv.

Christison, Robert. Treatise on Poisons in Relation to Medical Jurisprudence, Physiology, & the Practice of Physic. LC 79-156011. Repr. of 1845 ed. 45.00 (ISBN 0-404-09111-3). AMS Pr.

Clifford, Brian & Bull, Ray. The Psychology of Person Identification. 1978. 22.50 (ISBN 0-7100-8867-1). Routledge & Kegan.

Cravey, Robert H. & Baselt, Randall C., eds. Introduction to Forensic Toxicology. LC 79-56929. (Illus.). 350p. 1981. text ed. 62.50 (ISBN 0-931890-06-3). Biomed Pubns.

Curran, William J., et al. Modern Legal Medicine, Psychiatry & Forensic Science. LC 79-19477. (Illus.). 1310p. 1980. text ed. 89.50 (ISBN 0-8036-2292-9). Davis Co.

Douthwaite, Graham. Jury Instructions on Medical Issues. 2nd ed. 1980. text ed. 37.50 (ISBN 0-87473-129-1). A Smith Co.

East, William N. Medical Aspects of Crime. 1980. lib. bdg. 79.95 (ISBN 0-8490-3160-5). Gordon Pr.

Eckert, William G. Introduction to Forensic Sciences. LC 80-10864. (Illus.). 1980. pap. text ed. 10.45 (ISBN 0-8016-1489-9). Mosby.

Ehrlich, Ann. Ethics & Jurisprudence. 1978. 3.85 (ISBN 0-940012-07-3). Colwell Co.

Ewell, Marshall D. A Manual of Medical Jurisprudence for the Use of Students at Law & of Medicine. viii, 409p. 1981. Repr. of 1887 ed. lib. bdg. 30.00x (ISBN 0-8377-0542-8). Rothman.

Fatteh, Abdullah. Handbook of Forensic Pathology. LC 73-14529. 349p. 1973. 25.95 (ISBN 0-397-50328-8, JBL-Med-Nursing). Har-Row.

Fatteh, Adbullah. Medicolegal Investigation of Gunshot Wounds. LC 76-6957. (Illus.). 1976. 23.75 (ISBN 0-397-50356-3, JBL-Med-Nursing). Har-Row.

Fazekas, Gy & Kosa, F. Forensic Fetal Osteology. (Illus.). 1978. 42.50x (ISBN 963-05-1491-5). Intl Pubns Serv.

Fazekas, I. & Kosa, F. Forensic Fetal Osteology. 1978. 41.50 (ISBN 0-9960011-9-0, Pub. by Kiado Hungary). Heyden.

Fox, Sanford J. Science & Justice: The Massachusetts Witchcraft Trials. LC 68-18771. (Illus.). 140p. 1968. 10.00x (ISBN 0-8018-0203-2). Johns Hopkins.

Frumer, Louis R., ed. Personal Injury Annual. 32.50 (ISBN 0-685-02521-7). Bender.

Gallant, Donald M. & Force, Robert, eds. Legal & Ethical Issues in Human Research & Treatment: Psychopharmacologic Considerations. 1978. 15.00 (ISBN 0-470-26354-7). Halsted Pr.

Gibbens, T. C., et al. Medical Remands in the Criminal Court. (Maudaley Monographs). 1977. text ed. 45.00x (ISBN 0-19-712147-0). Oxford U Pr.

Gordon, Everett J. Practical Medico-Legal Guide for the Physician. (Illus.). 360p. 1973. 14.95 (ISBN 0-398-02688-2). C C Thomas.

Guy, William A. Principles of Forensic Medicine. 3rd rev. enl. ed. LC 75-23715. (Illus.). Repr. of 1868 ed. 54.00 (ISBN 0-404-13268-5). AMS Pr.

Harris, Raymond I. Outline of Death Investigation. (Illus.). 384p. 1973. photocopy ed. spiral 33.75 (ISBN 0-398-00784-5). C C Thomas.

Hayt, Emanuel & Hayt, Jonathan. Law of Hospital, Physician & Patient. 1972. 24.75 (ISBN 0-917036-03-4). Physicians Rec.

Heller, Marjorie K. Legal P's & Q's in the Doctor's Office. (Orig.). 1981. pap. cancelled (ISBN 0-686-59766-4). Monarch Pr.

Hemelt, M. & MacKert, M. Dynamics of Law in Nursing & Health Care. 1978. 15.95 (ISBN 0-87909-208-4). Reston.

Higgins, John J. & Stoneking, Gary E. Nebraska Legal Forms: Personal Injury 1981-82. 175p. 1981. 3-ring binder 19.95 (ISBN 0-86678-030-0). Mason Pub.

Hirsch, Charles P., et al. Handbook of Legal Medicine. 5th ed. LC 79-16053. (Illus.). 1979. pap. text ed. 20.95 (ISBN 0-8016-3509-8). Mosby.

Hollyhead, Robin. A Bibliography on Ethyl Alcohol in Forensic Science & Medicine & the Law. 230p. 1980. 60.00x (ISBN 0-9502425-6-X, Pub. by Scottish Academic Pr Scotland). Columbia U Pr.

Horsley & Carlova. Testifying in Court: The Advanced Course, A Comprehensive Guidebook Especially Written for Doctors. (Medical Economics Ser). 1972. 7.95 (ISBN 0-442-84012-8). Van Nos Reinhold.

Imperato, Pascal J. Medical Detective. LC 79-15315. 1979. 10.95 (ISBN 0-399-90058-6). Marek.

James, A. Everette, ed. Legal Medicine with Special Reference to Diagnostic Imaging. LC 79-19277. (Illus.). 412p. 1980. text ed. 32.50 (ISBN 0-8067-0951-0). Urban & S.

Jeffery, C. R., ed. Biology & Crime. LC 79-14490. (Sage Research Progress Ser. in Criminology: Vol. 10). (Illus.). 160p. 1979. 15.00 (ISBN 0-8039-1277-3); pap. 7.50 (ISBN 0-8039-1278-1). Sage.

Keiser-Nielsen, S. Person Identification by Means of the Teeth: A Practical Guide. (Illus.). 124p. 1980. pap. text ed. 27.50 (ISBN 0-7236-0557-2). Wright-PSG.

Kent, Arthur. Deadly Medicine: Doctors & True Crime. LC 74-20210. Orig. Title: The Death Doctors. 237p. 1975. 8.50 (ISBN 0-8008-2129-7). Taplinger.

Krogman, Wilton M. Human Skeleton in Forensic Medicine. (Illus.). 364p. 1978. 19.75 (ISBN 0-398-01054-4). C C Thomas.

Lawyers' Medical Cyclopedia of Personal Injuries & Allied Specialties, 7 vols. in 8. 1959-81. Set. text ed. 250.00 including 1980 service (ISBN 0-87473-005-8). A Smith Co.

Lifflander, Robert J. Final Treatment: The File on Dr. X. 1979. 11.95 (ISBN 0-393-08833-2). Norton.

Lowry, W. T. & Garriott, James C. Forensic Toxicology: Controlled Substances & Dangerous Drugs. LC 78-25439. (Illus.). 463p. 1979. 37.50 (ISBN 0-306-40124-X, Plenum Pr). Plenum Pub.

McCallum, John. The Crime Doctor. LC 78-16403. (Illus.). 272p. 1978. 9.95 (ISBN 0-916076-20-2). Writing.

Mason, J. K. Forensic Medicine for Lawyers. xv, 453p. 1978. 25.00x (ISBN 0-7236-0455-X, Pub by J Wright & Sons England). Rothman.

Mersky, Roy, et al. A Manual on Medical Literature for Law Librarians: A Handbook & Annotated Bibliography. LC 73-7475. 216p. 1974. 17.50x (ISBN 0-87802-101-9, Dist. by Oceana). Glanville.

Mersky, Roy M., et al. A Manual on Medical Literature for Law Librarians: A Handbook & Annotated Bibliography. LC 73-7475. 1974. 20.00 (ISBN 0-685-54237-8). Oceana.

Moritz, Alan R., et al. Handbook of Legal Medicine. 4th ed. LC 74-14826. 1975. 17.95 (ISBN 0-8016-3508-X). Mosby.

Nash, Donald J. Individual Identification & the Law Enforcement Officer. (Illus.). 176p. 1978. 16.75 (ISBN 0-398-03708-6). C C Thomas.

National Forensic Center. Forensic Services Directory, 1981. 800p. 1981. text ed. 52.50 (ISBN 0-686-72847-5). West Pub.

National Medicolegal Symposium 1971. Proceedings. 1972. 7.00 (ISBN 0-89970-071-3, OP381). AMA.

National Medicolegal Symposium 1973. Proceedings. 1974. 5.00 (ISBN 0-89970-072-1, OP-422). AMA.

Oliver, John S., ed. Forensic Toxicology. 320p. 1980. 50.00x (ISBN 0-686-69928-9, Pub. by Croom Helm England). State Mutual Bk.

--Forensic Toxicology. 320p. 1980. text ed. 32.50 (ISBN 0-8391-4117-3). Univ Park.

Ostheimer, Nancy C. & Ostheimer, John M., eds. Life or Death - Who Controls? LC 75-31522. 1976. text ed. 15.95 (ISBN 0-8261-2020-2); pap. text ed. 9.50 (ISBN 0-8261-2021-0). Springer Pub.

Parikh, C. K. Parikh's Textbook of Medical Jurisprudence & Toxicology. 3rd ed. (Illus.). 1092p. 1979. text ed. 35.00 (ISBN 0-910812-25-X). Johnny Reads.

--Parikh's Textbook of Medical Jurisprudence & Toxicology: For Classrooms & Courtrooms. (Illus.). 1108p. 1980. 91.00 (ISBN 0-08-025522-1). Pergamon.

Perper, Joshua A. Self-Assessment of Current Knowledge in Forensic Pathology & Legal Medicine. 1976. spiral bdg. 12.00 (ISBN 0-87488-178-1). Med Exam.

Perper, Joshua A. & Wecht, Cyril H. Microscopic Diagnosis in Forensic Pathology. (Illus.). 472p. 1980. 54.75 (ISBN 0-398-03969-0). C C Thomas.

Polsky, Samuel, ed. Medico-Legal Reader. LC 56-12250. 1956. o. p. 7.50 (ISBN 0-379-11306-6); pap. 2.50 (ISBN 0-379-11306-6). Oceana.

Polson, C. J. & Gee, D. J. Essentials of Forensic Medicine. 3rd rev. ed. LC 72-87949. 732p. 1973. 75.00 (ISBN 0-08-017023-4). Pergamon.

Ramsey, Paul. Ethics at the Edges of Life: Medical & Legal Intersections. LC 77-76308. 1978. 25.00x (ISBN 0-300-02137-2). Yale U Pr.

Saferstein, Richard. Forensic Science Handbook. (Illus.). 624p. 1982. reference 35.00 (ISBN 0-13-378034-1). P-H.

Sagall, Elliot L. & Reed, Barry C. Heart & the Law: A Practical Guide to Medicolegal Cardiology. (Illus.). 1968. 35.00 (ISBN 0-02-405260-4). Macmillan.

Sanazaro, Paul, ed. Final Report: Private Initiative in Professional Standards Review Organizations. (Illus.). 1978. pap. 17.50 (ISBN 0-914904-28-0). Health Admin Pr.

Siegal, Lewis J. Forensic Medicine: Courtroom Applications to Legal Principles. LC 61-17775. 368p. 1963. 42.00 (ISBN 0-8089-0427-2). Grune.

Smyth, Frank. Cause of Death: The Story of Forensic Science. (Illus.). 1980. 12.95 (ISBN 0-442-20041-2). Van Nos Reinhold.

Springer, Eric W., ed. Automated Medical Records & the Law. LC 70-110587. 178p. 1971. 25.00 (ISBN 0-912862-02-5). Aspen Systems.

Tedeschi, Cesare G., et al, eds. Forensic Medicine, 3 vols. LC 74-4593. (Illus.). 1680p. 1977. Vol. 1. 50.00 (ISBN 0-7216-8772-5); Vol. 2. 35.00 (ISBN 0-7216-8773-3); Vol. 3. 40.00 (ISBN 0-7216-8774-1); 125.00 set (ISBN 0-7216-8771-7). Saunders.

Tennenhouse, Dan J. Attorneys Medical Deskbook. LC 75-15123. 1975. 50.00 (ISBN 0-686-20645-2). Lawyers Co-Op.

University of Miami Law Center & School of Medicine. Medicine for Attorneys-Orthopedics. 225p. 1970. 10.00 (ISBN 0-913338-20-6). Trans-Media Pub.

Wadlington, Walter J., et al. Cases & Materials on Law & Medicine. LC 80-23725. (University Casebook Ser.). 1077p. 1980. text ed. write for info. (ISBN 0-88277-015-2). Foundation Pr.

Walls, H. J. Scotland Yard Scientist: My Thirty Years in Forensic Science. LC 73-1763. 1973. 6.95 (ISBN 0-8008-7010-7). Taplinger.

Waltz, J. R. & Inbau, F. E. Medical Jurisprudence. 1971. 15.95 (ISBN 0-02-424430-9). Macmillan.

Waters, John F. Crime Labs: The Science of Forensic Medicine. (Impact Ser.). (Illus.). (gr. 7 up). 1979. PLB 7.45 s&l (ISBN 0-531-02286-2). Watts.

Wecht, Cyril N. Legal Medicine Annual: 1976. (Illus.). 448p. 1976. 32.00 (ISBN 0-8385-5654-X). ACC.

Widmark, E. M. The Theoretical Foundations & the Practical Applications of Medicolegal Alcohol Determination. LC 81-66542. Orig. Title: Die theoretischen Grundlagen und die praktische Verwendbarkeit der gerichtlich-medizinischen Alkoholbestimmung (1932) (Illus.). 300p. 1981. text ed. 53.00 (ISBN 0-931890-07-1). Biomed Pubns.

Wood, Clive. The Influence of Litigation on Medical Practice. 228p. 1978. 27.50 (ISBN 0-8089-1076-0). Grune.

MEDICAL LABORATORIES

Bailey, Richard M. Clinical Laboratories & the Practice of Medicine: An Economic Perspective. LC 78-70545. (Health Care Ser.). 1979. 21.55 (ISBN 0-8211-0132-3); text ed. 19.45 in ten or more copies (ISBN 0-685-63680-1). McCutchan.

Baker, F. J. & Silverton, R. E. Introduction to Medical Laboratory Technology. 5th ed. 1976. 29.95 (ISBN 0-407-73251-9). Butterworth.

Bartlett, Raymond C. Medical Microbiology: Quality Cost & Clinical Relevance. LC 73-18482. (Quality Control Methods in the Clinical Laboratory Ser.). 272p. 1974. 37.50 (ISBN 0-471-05475-5, Pub. by Wiley Medical). Wiley.
Bennington, J. L., et al, eds. Management & Cost Control Techniques for the Clinical Laboratory. (Illus.). 350p. 1977. 24.50 (ISBN 0-8391-0767-6). Univ Park.
Benson, E. S. & Rubin, M., eds. Logic & Economics of Clinical Laboratory Use: Proceedings of Conference at Cancun, Mexico, March 1978. 1978. 37.50 (ISBN 0-444-00278-2, North-Holland). Elsevier.
Benson, E. S. & Strandjord, P. E., eds. Multiple Laboratory Screening. 1969. 39.50 (ISBN 0-12-089050-X). Acad Pr.
Berger, Melvin. Medical Center Lab. LC 76-12964. (Scientists at Work Seires). (Illus.). (gr. 3 up). 1976. PLB 9.89 (ISBN 0-381-99602-6, JD-J). Har-Row.
Blankenship, June & Campbell, Joe B. Laboratory Mathematics: Medical & Biological Applications. LC 75-15598. (Illus.). 288p. 1976. pap. text ed. 10.95 (ISBN 0-8016-0700-0). Mosby.
Byrne, Claire J., et al. Laboratory Tests: Implications for Nurses & Allied Health Professionals. 1981. 13.95 (ISBN 0-201-00088-1, Med-Nurse). A-W.
Cuviella, Patrick & Woosley, Hugh. Basic Medical Laboratory Subjects. LC 74-18675. (Allied Health Ser). 1975. pap. 5.10 (ISBN 0-672-61383-2). Bobbs.
Dharan, Murali. Total Quality Control in the Clinical Laboratory. LC 76-30688. (Illus.). 1977. pap. 16.95 (ISBN 0-8016-1290-X). Mosby.
Emmel, Victor E. & Cowdry, E. V. Laboratory Technique in Biology & Medicine. 4th ed. LC 64-13546. 1970. Repr. of 1964 ed. 19.50 (ISBN 0-88275-016-X). Krieger.
Enlander, Derek, ed. Computers in Laboratory Medicine. 1975. 23.00 (ISBN 0-12-239950-1). Acad Pr.
Faulkner, Willard R. & King, John W., eds. Handbook of Clinical Laboratory Data, CRC. 2nd ed. LC 68-54212. (Handbook Ser.). 1968. 28.00 (ISBN 0-87819-722-2). CRC Pr.
--Manual of Clinical Laboratory Procedures. 2nd ed. LC 78-108656. 1970. 18.95 (ISBN 0-87819-732-X). CRC Pr.
Ferris, Clifford D. Guide to Medical Laboratory Instruments. LC 80-80585. 260p. 1980. text ed. 14.95 (ISBN 0-316-28127-1). Little.
Flury, Patricia A. Environmental Health & Safety in the Hospital Laboratory. (Illus.). 200p. 1978. 23.75 (ISBN 0-398-03773-6). C C Thomas.
German, William M. Doctor's Anonymous: The Story of Laboratory Medicine. 1944. 20.00 (ISBN 0-8274-4204-1). R West.
Greenwalt, Tibor J., et al, eds. Blood Banking, Vol. 1. LC 76-27688. (Handbook Ser.). 616p. 1977. 69.95 (ISBN 0-8493-7011-6). CRC Pr.
Halper, H. Robert & Foster, Hope S. Laboratory Regulation Manual. LC 76-56666. 1977. 270.00 (ISBN 0-912862-29-7). Aspen Systems.
Halsted, James A., ed. The Laboratory in Clinical Medicine: Interpretation & Application. LC 74-12912. (Illus.). 1976. text ed. 45.00 (ISBN 0-7216-4478-3). Saunders.
Henry, John B. & Giegel, Joseph L. Quality Control in Laboratory Medicine. LC 77-78559. (Illus.). 250p. 1977. 35.00x (ISBN 0-89352-008-X). Masson Pub.
Hersh, Leroy, ed. New Developments in Clinical Instrumentation. 192p. 1981. 55.95 (ISBN 0-8493-5305-X). CRC Pr.
Hicks, M. Robert, et al, eds. Laboratory Instrumentation. (Illus.). 240p. 1980. pap. text ed. 19.00 (ISBN 0-06-141191-4). Har-Row.
Linne, Jean J. Basic Techniques for the Medical Laboratory. 2nd ed. (Illus.). 1979. text ed. 18.95 (ISBN 0-07-037948-3, HP). McGraw.
Loose Leaf References Services. Laboratory Medicine, 4 vols. Race, George J., ed. loose leaf bdg. 275.00 (ISBN 0-06-148009-6, Harper Medical); revision pages 50.00 (ISBN 0-685-57897-6). Har-Row.
Lundberg. Managing the Patient-Focused Laboratory. (Medical Economics Books). 1975. 19.95 (ISBN 0-442-84030-6). Van Nos Reinhold.
Lundberg, G. Managing the Patient-Focused Laboratory. 1975. 19.95 (ISBN 0-87489-065-9). Med Economics.
MacFate, Robert P. An Introduction to the Clinical Laboratory. 3rd ed. (Illus.). 1972. 22.50 (ISBN 0-8151-5712-6). Year Bk Med.
Newell, Jack E. Laboratory Management. LC 76-155040. (Series in Laboratory Medicine). 250p. 1972. 19.95 (ISBN 0-316-60451-8). Little.
Oppenheim, Irwin A. Textbook for Laboratory Assistants. 2nd ed. LC 75-31873. (Illus.). 168p. 1976. 11.95 (ISBN 0-8016-3721-X). Mosby.
Ottaviano, P. J. Quality Control in the Clinical Laboratory. (Illus.). 1977. 17.95 (ISBN 0-8391-1156-8). Univ Park.
Raphael, Stanley. Lynch's Medical Laboratory Technology: A Filmstrip Presentation. (Illus.). 1977. pap. text ed. 75.00 (ISBN 0-7216-9921-9). Saunders.
Raphael, Stanley S. Lynch's Medical Laboratory Technology, 2 vols. 3rd ed. LC 74-17761. (Illus.). 2080p. 1976. Vol. 1. text ed. 30.00 (ISBN 0-7216-7463-1); Vol. 2. text ed. 27.50 (ISBN 0-7216-7464-X). Saunders.
Remson, Susan T. & Ackermann, Phillip G. Calculations for the Medical Laboratory. 1977. 7.95 (ISBN 0-316-73999-5). Little.
Schweisinger, Dennis W., ed. Pulmonary & Blood Gas Laboratories: Laws, Regulations, Standards, & Safety. 276p. 1981. 27.95 (ISBN 0-939442-00-0). Brentwood Pub.
Siest, G., et al, eds. Interpretation Des Examens De Laboratoire. (Illus.). 500p. 1981. pap. 55.25 (ISBN 3-8055-2756-X). S Karger.
Spencer, Richard & Seligson, David, eds. Nuclear Medicine, Vol. 1. LC 76-27688. 632p. 1977. 69.95 (ISBN 0-8493-7071-X). CRC Pr.
Strike, P. W. Medical Laboratory Statistics. (Monographs in Medical Laboratory Science Ser.). 152p. 1981. pap. text ed. 15.00 (ISBN 0-7236-0582-3). Wright-PSG.
Triplett, Douglas A. Procedures for the Coagulation Laboratory. LC 81-10909. (Illus.). 137p. 1981. lab manual 19.00 (ISBN 0-89189-074-2, 45-5-008-00). Am Soc Clinical.
Von Graevenitz, Alexander & Seligson, David, eds. Microbiology, Vol. 1. LC 76-27688. 408p. 1977. 69.95 (ISBN 0-8493-7031-0). CRC Pr.

MEDICAL LABORATORY TECHNICIANS
see Medical Technologists

MEDICAL LABORATORY TECHNOLOGY
see Medical Technology

MEDICAL LAWS AND LEGISLATION
see also Medical Jurisprudence; Public Health Laws

Adriani, John & Eaton, Allen. The Law & Health Professionals: Fundamentals of the Law & Malpractice. 144p. 1981. 10.50x (ISBN 0-87527-189-8). Green.
Alton, Walter G., Jr. Malpractice: A Trial Lawyer's Advice for Physicians. 1977. 12.95 (ISBN 0-316-03500-9). Little.
American Society of Hospital Attorneys. Federal Regulation: Hospital Attorney's Desk Reference. 244p. (Orig.). 1980. pap. 35.00 (ISBN 0-87258-321-X, 1430). Am Hospital.
Amplification of Medical Certification of Cause of Death: Inquiries to Certifiers Concerning Incomplete or Vague Statements. 44p. (Eng. & Fr.). 1953. pap. 1.20 (ISBN 92-4-156008-8). World Health.
Annas, George J. The Rights of Doctors, Nurses, & Allied Health Professionals. 416p. 1981. pap. 3.95 (ISBN 0-380-77859-9, 77859, Discus). Avon.
Barber, Bernard. Informed Consent in Medical Therapy & Research. 1980. 14.50 (ISBN 0-8135-0889-4). Rutgers U Pr.
Bernstein, Arthur H. A Trustee's Guide to Hospital Law. 300p. 1981. 24.95 (ISBN 0-931028-14-0); pap. 19.95 (ISBN 0-931028-13-2). Teach'em.
Burns, Chester R., ed. Legacies in Law & Medicine. LC 76-29641. 1977. 15.00 (ISBN 0-88202-164-8). N Watson.
Chayet, Neil L. Emergency! Legal Implications of Emergency Care. 2nd ed. 360p. 1981. pap. 12.50 (ISBN 0-686-69605-0). ACC.
Curran, William J. & Shapiro, E. Donald. Law, Medicine & Forensic Science. 2nd ed. 1046p. 1970. 25.50 (ISBN 0-316-16512-3). Little.
Derbyshire, Robert C. Medical Licensure & Discipline in the United States. LC 78-17712. 1978. Repr. of 1969 ed. lib. bdg. 16.75x (ISBN 0-313-20528-0, DEML). Greenwood.
Faber, Samuel & Faber, Staurt. The Legal Stethoscope. (Illus.). 1976. pap. 19.50 (ISBN 0-89074-017-8, Lega Books). Good Life.
Gibson, J. Tyrone. Medication Law & Behavior. 429p. 1976. 19.50 (ISBN 0-471-29760-7). Krieger.
Gosfield, Alice. PSRO's: The Law & the Health Consumer. LC 75-13340. 288p. 1975. text ed. 18.50 (ISBN 0-88410-123-1). Ballinger Pub.
Grad, Frank P. & Marti, Noelia. Physicians' Licensure & Discipline. LC 79-21925. 471p. 1980. lib. bdg. 45.00 (ISBN 0-379-20463-0). Oceana.
Havighurst, Clark C., ed. Medical Progress & the Law. LC 69-19794. (Law & Contemporary Problems Ser.: No. 10). 1969. 10.00 (ISBN 0-379-11510-7). Oceana.
Health Law Center. Hospital Law Manual: Administrator's & Attorney's Set, 6 vols. LC 74-80713. 350.00 (ISBN 0-912862-05-X). Aspen Systems.
Hiller, Marc D. Medical Ethics & the Law. 1981. 35.00 (ISBN 0-88410-707-8). Ballinger Pub.
Holder, Angela R. Legal Issues in Pediatrics & Adolescent Medicine. LC 76-41385. 1977. 41.50 (ISBN 0-471-40612-0, Pub. by Wiley-Medical). Wiley.
Horsley, J. E. & Carlova, J. Testifying in Court. 1972. 8.95 (ISBN 0-87489-039-X). Med Economics.
--Testifying in Court. 1972. 8.95 (ISBN 0-87489-039-X). Med Economics.
--Your Family & the Law. 1975. 9.95 (ISBN 0-87489-096-9). Med Economics.
Horsley, Jack & Carlova, John. Your Family & the Law. 1975. 7.95 (ISBN 0-442-84033-0). Van Nos Reinhold.
Humber, James M. & Almeder, Robert E. Biomedical Ethics & the Law. 2nd ed. 1979. 39.50 (ISBN 0-306-40239-4, Plenum Pr); pap. 15.00 (ISBN 0-306-40242-4, Plenum Pr). Plenum Pub.
Huttmann, Barbara. The Patient's Advocate. (Handbook Ser.). 416p. (Orig.). 1981. pap. 8.95 (ISBN 0-14-046492-1). Penguin.
Kittrie, Nicholas N., et al, eds. Medicine, Law & Public Policy, Vol. 1. new ed. LC 75-793. (Medicine, Law & Public Policy Law Ser.). 30.00 (ISBN 0-404-10426-6). AMS Pr.
Knight, Bernard. Legal Aspects of Medical Practice. 2nd ed. (Illus.). 1976. pap. text ed. 15.75 (ISBN 0-443-01391-8). Churchill.
Lewis, Marti & Warden, Carol D. Law & Ethics. 1982. price not set. Davis Co.
Medical, Dental & Pharmaceutical Auxiliaries: A Survey of Existing Legislation. (International Digest of Health Legislation Ser: Vol. 19, No. 1). 143p. (Eng. & Fr.). 1968. pap. 3.60 (ISBN 92-4-169191-3). World Health.
Mersky, Roy M., et al. A Manual on Medical Literature for Law Librarians: A Handbook & Annotated Bibliography. LC 73-7475. 1974. 20.00 (ISBN 0-685-54237-8). Oceana.
Ordronaux, John. Jurisprudence in Medicine in Relation to the Law. LC 73-5158. (Mental Illness & Social Policy; the American Experience Ser.). Repr. of 1869 ed. 17.50 (ISBN 0-405-05239-1). Arno.
Pavalon, Eugene I. Human Rights & Health Care Law. LC 80-67574. 240p. 1980. pap. text ed. 10.95 (ISBN 0-937126-83-7). Am Journal Nurse.
Pearce, G. H. The Medical Report & Testimony. (Illus.). 1979. text ed. 17.95x (ISBN 0-04-610012-1). Allen Unwin.
Peters, J Douglas, et al. Law of Medical Practice in Michigan. (Illus.). 480p. 1981. text ed. price not set (ISBN 0-914904-71-X). Health Admin Pr.
Physician's Guide to Negotiations: An Introduction. pap. 5.00 (ISBN 0-89970-066-7, OP-111). AMA.
Pozgar, George D. Legal Aspects of Health Care Administration. LC 78-17276. 266p. 1979. text ed. 21.95 (ISBN 0-89443-044-0). Aspen Systems.
Protection Against Ionizing Radiations: A Survey of Current World Legislation. (International Digest of Health Legislation Ser: Vol. 22, No. 4). 328p. 1972. pap. 11.20 (ISBN 92-4-169224-3, 1024). World Health.
Quimby, Charles W., Jr. Law for the Medical Practitioner. 1979. text ed. 17.50 (ISBN 0-914904-39-6). Health Admin Pr.
Research Group & Gingerich, Duane, eds. Medical Products Liability: A Comprehensive Guide & Sourcebook. (Health Care Economics & Technology Ser.). 500p. 1981. 59.50x (ISBN 0-86621-001-6). F&S Pr.
Rettig, Richard. Cancer Crusade: The Story of the National Cancer Act of 1971. LC 77-72134. 1977. 20.00 (ISBN 0-691-07558-1). Princeton U Pr.
Rosenblatt, Stanley M., ed. Malpractice & Other Malfeasances. 1977. 10.00 (ISBN 0-8184-0234-2). Lyle Stuart.
Rosner, Fred. Modern Medicine & Jewish Law: Studies in Torah Judaism. 1972. 8.95x (ISBN 0-8197-0389-3). Bloch.
Rutherford, Margaret. The Model State Health Statistics Act: A Model State Law for the Collection, Sharing, & Confidentiality of Health Statistics. (Ser. 4: No. 21). 1979. pap. 1.75 (ISBN 0-8406-0168-9). Natl Ctr Health Stats.
Sharpe, David J., et al. Cases & Materials on Law & Medicine. LC 78-12529. (American Casebook Ser.). 882p. 1978. text ed. 19.95 (ISBN 0-8299-2015-3). West Pub.
Strickler, Matthew M. Representing Health Care Facilities. Ballard, Frederic L., Jr., ed. 300p. 1981. text ed. 35.00 (ISBN 0-686-76236-3, A1-1285). PLI.
Wadlington, Walter J., et al. Cases & Materials on Law & Medicine. LC 80-23725. (University Casebook Ser.). 1077p. 1980. text ed. write for info. (ISBN 0-88277-015-2). Foundation Pr.
Wasmuth & Wasmuth, C. E. Law & the Surgical Team. 424p. 1969. 17.50 (ISBN 0-683-08845-9, Pub. by W&W). Krieger.
Wecht, Cyril H. Legal Medicine 1980. (Illus.). 320p. 1980. text ed. 27.50 (ISBN 0-7216-9142-0). Saunders.
Wecht, Cyril H., ed. Legal Medicine Annual 1978. (Illus.). 352p. 1978. 38.00 (ISBN 0-8385-5656-6). ACC.
Weisstub, David N., ed. Law & Psychiatry III: Selected Papers Presented at the Fourth International Congress on Law & Psychiatry, Pembroke College, Oxford England, 19-22 July 1979. 100p. 1980. pap. 15.00 (ISBN 0-08-026113-2). Pergamon.
--Law & Psychiatry: Proceedings of an International Symposium Held at Clarke Institute of Psychiatry, Toronto, Canada, Feb. 1977. LC 78-9436. 125p. 1978. 19.00 (ISBN 0-08-023133-0). Pergamon.
Wood, Clive. The Influence of Litigation on Medical Practice. 228p. 1978. 27.50 (ISBN 0-8089-1076-0). Grune.
Ziegler, A. Doctor's Administrative Program, 6 vols. Incl. Dap 1. Patient Contract & Public Relations (ISBN 0-87489-150-7); Dap 2. Bookkeeping & Tax Reports (ISBN 0-87489-151-5); Dap 3. Insurance & Third-Party-Payable Claims (ISBN 0-87489-152-3); Dap 4. Correspondence (ISBN 0-87489-153-1); Billing & Collections; Dap 6. Patient Records Control (ISBN 0-87489-155-8). 1978. Set. write for info. (ISBN 0-87489-158-2); Ea. Vol. write for info.

MEDICAL LAWS AND LEGISLATION–GREAT BRITAIN

Dowd, D. W., et al, eds. Medical, Moral & Legal Implications of Recent Medical Advances: A Symposium. LC 71-152124. (Symposia on Law & Society Ser). 1971. Repr. of 1968 ed. lib. bdg. 14.50 (ISBN 0-306-70128-6). Da Capo.
James, A. Everette, ed. Legal Medicine with Special Reference to Diagnostic Imaging. LC 79-19277. (Illus.). 412p. 1980. text ed. 32.50 (ISBN 0-8067-0951-0). Urban & S.
Martin, C. R. Law Relating to Medical Practice. 1973. text ed. 25.00x (ISBN 0-272-76058-7). State Mutual Bk.

MEDICAL LIBRARIES
see also Information Storage and Retrieval Systems–Medicine

AACP Section of Librarians. Standards & Planning Guide for Pharmacy Library Service, 1975. 90p. 1975. 5.00 (ISBN 0-937526-09-6). Am Assn Coll Pharm.
Alperin, Melvin & Alperin, Stanley, eds. Directory of Major Medical Libraries Worldwide. 1978. 84.00x (ISBN 0-916524-07-8, 506). US Direct Serv.
Alperin, Stanley & Alperin, Melvin, eds. Directory of Major Medical Libraries in the United States. 1978. 29.00x (ISBN 0-916524-08-6, 507). US Direct Serv.
American Medical Association. Directory of Health Sciences Libraries, 1973. 1975. 15.00 (ISBN 0-686-15429-0, OP-424). AMA.
Basler, Beatrice K. & Basler, Thomas G., eds. Health Sciences Librarianship: A Guide to Information Sources. LC 74-11552. (Books, Publishing, & Libraries Information Guide Ser.: Vol. 1). 180p. 1977. 36.00 (ISBN 0-8103-1284-0). Gale.
Benson, E. S. & Rubin, M., eds. Logic & Economics of Clinical Laboratory Use: Proceedings of Conference at Cancun, Mexico, March 1978. 1978. 37.50 (ISBN 0-444-00278-2, North-Holland). Elsevier.
Books & Periodicals for Medical Libraries in Hospitals. 5th ed. (Library Association Bk.). 80p. 1978. 4.50x (ISBN 0-85365-500-6, Pub. by Lib Assn England). Oryx Pr.
Carmel, M., ed. Handbook on Medical Librarianship. 1981. 34.50x (ISBN 0-85365-502-2, Pub. by Lib Assn England); pap. 18.50x (ISBN 0-85365-703-3). Oryx Pr.
Chen, Ching-Chih. Sourcebook on Health Sciences Librarianship. LC 76-30263. 1977. 15.50 (ISBN 0-8108-1005-0). Scarecrow.
Cumming, E. E., ed. Hospital & Welfare Library Services: An International Bibliography. 1977. 32.00x (ISBN 0-85365-139-6, Pub. by Lib Assn England). Oryx Pr.
Directory of Medical Libraries in the British Isles. 4th ed. 1976. pap. 10.95x (ISBN 0-85365-049-7, Pub. by Lib Assn England). Oryx Pr.
Garland, Joseph E. Centennial History of the Boston Medical Library. (Illus.). 233p. 1975. 9.95 (ISBN 0-686-15546-7). F A Countway.
Gregorio, M. Pauline, ed. Medical Record Library Science Examination Review Book, Vol. 1. 3rd ed. 1976. spiral bdg. 10.00 (ISBN 0-87488-496-9). Med Exam.
Harvard Medical Library & Boston Medical Library. Author-Title Catalogue of the Francis A. Countway Library of Medicine for Imprints Through 1959, 10 vols. 8104p. 1973. Set. lib. bdg. 1530.00 (ISBN 0-8161-1024-7). G K Hall.
Key, Jack D. & Keys, Thomas E., eds. Classics & Other Selected Readings in Medical Librarianship. LC 78-9040. 768p. 1980. lib. bdg. 24.50 (ISBN 0-88275-691-5). Krieger.
Lea, J. Terminology & Communication Skills in the Health Sciences. 1975. pap. 7.95 (ISBN 0-87909-821-X). Reston.
Matthews, David & Picken, F. M. Medical Librarianship. 1980. 12.00 (ISBN 0-89664-416-2). K G Saur.

Morton, Leslie T. How to Use a Medical Library. 6th rev. ed. 1979. pap. 15.00 (ISBN 0-433-22451-7). Heinman.

Parkinson, E. M. Catalogue of Medical Books, Fourteen Eighty to Seventeen Hundred, in Manchester University Library. 406p. 1972. 111.50x (ISBN 0-7190-1246-5, Pub. by Manchester U Pr England). State Mutual Bk.

Rees, Alan M. & Crawford, Susan, eds. Directory of Health Sciences Libraries in the United States. LC 80-65893. 356p. 1980. 25.00 (ISBN 0-912176-10-5). Med Lib Assn.

Sewell, Winifred, ed. Reader in Medical Librarianship. LC 72-86634. (Reader Ser. in Library & Information Science: Vol. 8). 1973. 20.00 (ISBN 0-910972-27-3). IHS-PDS.

Strohlein, Alfred. Management of Thirty-Five Mm Medical Slides. LC 75-10487. (Illus.). 1975. pap. 11.00 (ISBN 0-915616-01-7). United Busn.

MEDICAL LITERATURE SEARCHING

see Information Storage and Retrieval Systems–Medicine

MEDICAL MANPOWER

see Medical Personnel; Public Health Personnel

MEDICAL MATHEMATICS

see Medicine–Mathematics

MEDICAL MICROBIOLOGY

see also Medical Mycology; Micro-Organisms, Pathogenic

Anderson, Theodore G. Exercises in Applied Microbiology. 1963. pap. 6.95x (ISBN 0-02-303390-8, 30339). Macmillan.

Audits of Antimicrobial Usage: JAMA. 1977. pap. 2.00 (ISBN 0-89970-023-3, OP-112). AMA.

Baker & Breach. Medical Microbiological Techniques. LC 80-40010. 1980. 49.00 (ISBN 0-407-00099-2). Butterworth.

Balows, Albert. Clinical Microbiology: How to Start & When to Stop. (American Lectures in Clinical Microbiology Ser.). (Illus.). 104p. 1975. 13.50 (ISBN 0-398-03389-7). C C Thomas.

Bartlett, Raymond C. Medical Microbiology: Quality Cost & Clinical Relevance. LC 73-18482. (Quality Control Methods in the Clinical Laboratory Ser.). 272p. 1974. 37.50 (ISBN 0-471-05475-5, Pub. by Wiley Medical). Wiley.

Behbehani, Abbas M. Laboratory Diagnosis of Viral, Bedsonial & Rickettsial Diseases: A Handbook for Laboratory Workers. (Illus.). 244p. 1972. 27.50 (ISBN 0-398-02229-1). C C Thomas.

Berg, Sheila R., ed. Microbiology for Medical Technologists: PreTest Self-Assessment & Review. LC 78-51703. (PreTest Self-Assessment & Review Ser.). (Illus.). 1979. pap. 10.95 (ISBN 0-07-051572-7). McGraw-Pretest.

Bergquist, Lois M. Microbiology for the Hospital Environment. (Illus.). 719p. 1981. text ed. 21.50 (ISBN 0-06-040646-1, HarpC); scp 10.95 (ISBN 0-686-77413-2); inst's manual avail. Har-Row.

Boyd, Robert F. & Hoerl, Bryan G. Basic Medical Microbiology. 2nd ed. 1980. text ed. 19.95 (ISBN 0-316-10433-7); lab manual 7.95 (ISBN 0-316-10434-5). Little.

--Laboratory Manual to Accompany Basic Medical Microbiology. 1980. 7.95 (ISBN 0-316-10434-5). Little.

Boyd, Robert F. & Marr, J. Joseph. Medical Microbiology. 1980. text ed. 24.95 (ISBN 0-316-10432-9). Little.

Braude, Abraham I. Medical Microbiology & Infectious Diseases. Samiy, A. H., et al, eds. (International System of Medicine Ser.: Vol. 2). 2000p. 1980. text ed. write for info. (ISBN 0-7216-1919-3). Saunders.

Center for Disease Control, U.S. Public Health Service. Microbial Diseases: Notes, Reports, Summaries, Trends. May, Carl W., ed. 334p. 1980. text ed. 14.00 (ISBN 0-913232-85-8); pap. text ed. 7.95 (ISBN 0-913232-87-4). W Kaufmann.

Collee, J. G. Applied Medical Microbiology. 1976. Vol. 3. 8.95 (ISBN 0-470-15001-7). Halsted Pr.

Davidson, Elizabeth W., ed. Pathogenesis of Invertebrate Microbial Diseases. 500p. 1981. text ed. 40.00 (ISBN 0-86598-014-4). Allanheld.

Deal, Samuel J., et al. Experimental Microbiology for the Health Sciences. 4th ed. 1976. spiral bdg. 9.95x (ISBN 0-8087-0436-2). Burgess.

Delaat, Adrian N. C. Microbiology for the Allied Health Professions. 2nd ed. LC 78-5731. (Illus.). 462p. 1979. pap. 14.50 (ISBN 0-8121-0612-1). Lea & Febiger.

DiLiello, Leo R. Clinical Microbiology. (Illus.). 1979. pap. text ed. 12.00 (ISBN 0-87055-325-9). AVI.

Duguid, J. P., et al, eds. Medical Microbiology, Vol. 1. 13th ed. (Illus.). 1979. text ed. 35.00 (ISBN 0-443-01787-5); pap. text ed. 29.75 (ISBN 0-443-01788-3). Churchill.

DuPont, Herbert L. Practical Antimicrobial Therapy. (Illus.). 192p. 1978. 11.50 (ISBN 0-8385-7869-1). ACC.

Ferris, E. B. Microbiology for Health Careers. (Illus.). 147p. 1974. pap. 7.00 (ISBN 0-8273-1326-8); instructor's guide 1.60 (ISBN 0-8273-1327-6). Delmar.

Gall, Lorraine S. & Curby, William A. Instrumented Systems for Microbiological Analysis of Body Fluids. 192p. 1980. 49.95 (ISBN 0-8493-5681-4). CRC Pr.

Gillies, R. F. Lecture Notes on Medical Microbiology. 2nd ed. (Illus.). 1978. softcover 13.00 (ISBN 0-632-00062-7, Blackwell). Mosby.

Graber, C. D. Rapid Diagnostic Methods in Medical Microbiology. 343p. 1970. 16.95 (ISBN 0-683-03741-2). Krieger.

Gruneberg, R. N. Microbiology for Clinicians. 200p. 1981. text ed. 19.95 (ISBN 0-8391-1682-9). Univ Park.

Jawetz, Ernest, et al. Review of Medical Microbiology. rev. 14th ed. LC 60-11336. (Illus.). 593p. 1980. lexotone cover 14.00 (ISBN 0-87041-053-9). Lange.

Lennette, E. H., et al, eds. Manual of Clinical Microbiology. 3rd ed. (Illus.). 1980. 25.00 (ISBN 0-914826-24-7); flexible 21.00 (ISBN 0-914826-26-3). Am Soc Microbio.

Lorian, Victor. Significance of Medical Microbiology in the Care of Patients. 2nd ed. (Illus.). 317p. 1981. lib. bdg. 35.00 (ISBN 0-683-05165-2). Williams & Wilkins.

Lorian, Victor, ed. Significance of Medical Microbiology in the Care of Patients. LC 76-21297. 274p. 1977. 27.00 (ISBN 0-683-05164-4). Krieger.

MacFaddin, Jean F. Biochemical Tests for Identification of Medical Bacteria. 2nd ed. (Illus.). 552p. 1980. softcover 26.50 (ISBN 0-683-05315-9). Williams & Wilkins.

Pelczar, Michael, Jr. & Chan, E. C. S. Elements of Microbiology. 1st ed. (Illus.). 704p. (Orig.). 1981. text ed. 22.95 (ISBN 0-07-049240-9, C); 10.95 (ISBN 0-07-049241-7); instrs'. manual 9.95 (ISBN 0-07-049230-1). McGraw.

Potter, C. W., et al. Introduction to Medical Microbiology. 1968. 8.95 (ISBN 0-407-56500-0). Butterworth.

Prier, J. Modern Methods in Medical Microbiology. (Illus.). 1976. 24.50 (ISBN 0-8391-0862-1). Univ Park.

--Opportunistic Pathogens. (Illus.). 1976. 19.50 (ISBN 0-8391-0710-2). Univ Park.

Rajam, R. V. & Rangiah, P. N. Donovanosis. (Monograph Ser.: No. 24). (Also avail. in French). 1954. 2.80 (ISBN 92-4-140024-2). World Health.

Rose, A. H. & Morris, J. G., eds. Advances in Microbial Physiology, Vol. 22. (Serial Publication). 1981. price not set (ISBN 0-12-027722-0). Acad Pr.

Schlessinger, David, ed. Microbiology 1975. LC 74-33538. (Annual Microbiology Ser.). 1975. 22.00 (ISBN 0-914826-05-0). Am Soc Microbio.

Schrader, B. & Meier, W., eds. Raman-IR Atlas of Organic Compounds. 1974-1976. Set. 467.70 (ISBN 0-686-71001-0). Vol. 1,345p (ISBN 3-527-25539-7). Vol. 2,386p (ISBN 3-527-25541-9). Vol. 3,507p (ISBN 3-527-25542-7). Verlag Chemie.

Schuhardt, Vernon T. Pathogenic Microbiology: The Biology & Prevention of Selected Bacterial, Fungal, Rickettsial, & Viral Diseases of Clinical Importance. 1978. (JBL-Med-Nursing); pap. text ed. 15.25x (ISBN 0-397-47370-2). Har-Row.

Schwebach, Gerhard H. A Practical Guide to Microbial & Parasitic Diseases. (Illus.). 256p. 1980. lexotone 19.75 (ISBN 0-398-03980-1). C C Thomas.

Skinner, Orten C. Introduction to Diagnostic Microbiology. LC 74-78591. (Allied Health Ser). 1975. pap. 12.05 (ISBN 0-672-61391-3). Bobbs.

Smith, Alice L. Microbiology & Pathology. 12th ed. LC 79-27338. (Illus.). 756p. 1980. text ed. 19.95 (ISBN 0-8016-4673-1). Mosby.

--Microbiology Laboratory Manual & Workbook. 5th ed. (Illus.). 199p. 1981. paper perfect 9.95 (ISBN 0-8016-4707-X). Mosby.

--Principles of Microbiology. 9th ed. LC 80-26593. (Illus.). 724p. 1981. text ed. 19.95 (ISBN 0-8016-4682-0). Mosby.

Thomas, C. G. Medical Microbiology: Concise Medical Textbook. 4th ed. (Illus.). 1979. pap. text ed. 14.95 (ISBN 0-02-859490-8). Macmillan.

Tischer, Robert G., et al. Problem Solving in Medical Technology & Microbiology. LC 79-11337. (Illus.). 1979. pap. text ed. 25.00 (ISBN 0-89189-068-8, 45-7-010-00). Am Soc Clinical.

Volk, Wesley. Essentials of Medical Microbiology. LC 77-17564. 1978. text ed. 28.00 (ISBN 0-397-47374-5); pap. text ed. 17.75x (ISBN 0-685-28807-2). Lippincott.

Washington, John A., ed. Laboratory Procedures in Clinical Microbiology. LC 74-127. (Ser. in Laboratory Medicine). 450p. 1975. text ed. 25.00 (ISBN 0-316-92406-7). Little.

Wistreich, George A. & Lechtman, Max D. Microbiology & Human Disease. 3rd ed. 1981. text ed. 21.95x (ISBN 0-02-470910-7). Macmillan.

Wu, William G. Medical Microbiology: A Laboratory Study. 250p. 1978. write for info. wire coil (ISBN 0-697-04683-4). Wm C Brown.

MEDICAL MICROSCOPY

see Microscopy, Medical

MEDICAL MISSIONS

see Missions, Medical

MEDICAL MYCOLOGY

see also Fungi, Pathogenic

Al-Doory, Yousef. The Epidemiology of Human Mycotic Diseases. (Illus.). 364p. 1976. 36.50 (ISBN 0-398-03380-3). C C Thomas.

--Laboratory Medical Mycology. LC 79-22500. (Illus.). 410p. 1980. text ed. 24.50 (ISBN 0-8121-0695-4). Lea & Febiger.

Baker, Roger D., et al. Human Infection with Fungi, Actinomycetes & Algae. LC 72-160588. (Illus.). 1971. 230.60 (ISBN 0-387-05378-6). Springer-Verlag.

Beneke, E. S. & Rogers, A. L. Medical Mycology Manual with Human Mycoses Monograph. 4th ed. 242p. Date not set. pap. 19.95x (ISBN 0-8087-4042-3). Burgess.

Bulmer, Glenn S. Introduction to Medical Mycology. (Illus.). 1979. pap. 19.95 (ISBN 0-8151-1320-X); slides 295.00 (ISBN 0-8151-1321-8). Year Bk Med.

Campbell, Mary C. & Stewart, Joyce L. The Medical Mycology Handbook. LC 80-11935. 436p. 1980. pap. 27.00 (ISBN 0-471-04728-7, Pub. by Wiley Med). Wiley.

Chick, Ernest, et al. Opportunistic Fungal Infections: Proceedings. (American Lectures in Clinical Microbiology Ser.). (Illus.). 376p. 1975. 28.50 (ISBN 0-398-03325-0). C C Thomas.

Delacretaz, J. E. Color Atlas of Medical Mycology. (Illus.). 1977. 67.50 (ISBN 0-8151-2422-8). Year Bk Med.

Emmons, Chester W., et al. Medical Mycology. 3rd ed. LC 76-15676. (Illus.). 592p. 1977. text ed. 19.50 (ISBN 0-8121-0566-4). Lea & Febiger.

Fetter, B., et al. Mycoses of the Central Nervous System. 219p. 1967. 14.25 (ISBN 0-683-03185-6, Pub. by Williams & Wilkins). Krieger.

Grigoriu, D., ed. Champignons "Opportunistes". (Dermatologica: Vol. 159, Supplement 1, 1979). (Illus.). 1979. pap. 46.25 (ISBN 3-8055-0084-X). S Karger.

Iwata, K. Recent Advances in Medical & Veterinary Mycology. 1977. 60.00 (ISBN 0-8391-1112-6). Univ Park.

Koneman, Elmer W., et al. Practical Laboratory Mycology. 2nd ed. (Illus.). 1978. pap. 16.95 (ISBN 0-683-04745-0). Williams & Wilkins.

McGinnis, Michael R. Laboratory Handbook of Medical Mycology. 1980. 55.00 (ISBN 0-12-482850-7). Acad Pr.

Moore, Gary S. & Jaciow, Douglas M. Mycology for the Clinical Laboratory. (Illus.). 1979. text ed. 22.95 (ISBN 0-8359-4771-8). Reston.

Moss, Emma & McQuown, Albert. Atlas of Medical Mycology. 3rd ed. 316p. (Orig.). 1969. 19.50 (ISBN 0-686-74176-5). Krieger.

Myrvik, Quentin N., et al. Fundamentals of Medical Bacteriology & Mycology: For Students of Medicine & Related Sciences. LC 74-2293. (Illus.). 510p. 1974. text ed. 14.50 (ISBN 0-8121-0423-4). Lea & Febiger.

Otcenasek, M. & Dvorak, J. Medical Mycology: Pictorial Dictionary. 75.00 (ISBN 9-0619-3022-7). Heinman.

Purchase, I. F., ed. Mycotoxins in Human Health: Symposium. LC 72-3778. 306p. 1971. 43.95 (ISBN 0-470-70232-X). Halsted Pr.

Robinson, Harry M., Jr. The Diagnosis & Treatment of Fungal Infections: A Symposium. (Illus.). 580p. 1974. 41.75 (ISBN 0-398-02789-7). C C Thomas.

Wilson, J. Walter & Plunkett, Orda A. The Fungous Diseases of Man. 1965. 42.75x (ISBN 0-520-01344-1). U of Cal Pr.

Wylie, Thomas & Morehouse, Lawrence, eds. Mycotoxic Fungi, Mycotoxins, Mycotoxicoses: An Encyclopedic Handbook, Vol. 2. 1978. 75.00 (ISBN 0-8247-6551-6). Dekker.

MEDICAL OFFICE MANAGEMENT

see also Medical Secretaries

Beck, Leif C. The Physician's Office. LC 77-87555. (Illus.). 1977. 14.95 (ISBN 0-444-90020-9). Excerpta-Princeton.

Bonito, Grace. Medical Office Management Workbook. rev. ed. McFadden, S. Michele, ed. 1981. 16.95x (ISBN 0-89262-049-8); guide 12.50 (ISBN 0-89262-050-1). Career Pub.

Bredow, Miriam, et al. Medical Office Procedures. 2nd ed. (Illus.). 480p. 1981. pap. text ed. 14.80 (ISBN 0-07-007441-0, G); simulation recordings, non-steno 115.00 (ISBN 0-07-087647-9); simulation recordings, steno 115.00 (ISBN 0-07-087646-0). McGraw.

Cotton. Medical Practice Management. (Medical Economics Books). 1977. 22.50 (ISBN 0-442-84006-3). Van Nos Reinhold.

Doble, Henry P., Jr. Medical Office Design, Territory & Conflict. 320p. 1981. 36.50 (ISBN 0-87527-243-6). Green.

Domer, Larry R., et al. Dental Practice Management: Concepts & Application. LC 80-15309. (Illus.). 376p. 1980. text ed. 33.50 (ISBN 0-8016-1422-8). Mosby.

Ehrlich, Ann. Medical Office Procedures Manual. (Illus.). 1977. 19.95 (ISBN 0-686-19657-0). Colwell Co.

Fordney, Marilyn T. Insurance Handbook for the Medical Office. LC 76-22293. (Illus.). 1977. soft cover 16.95 (ISBN 0-7216-3812-0); text ed. 19.95 (ISBN 0-7216-3811-2). Saunders.

Foster, Martha. Medical Office Practice. LC 75-4051. (Allied Health Ser). 1975. pap. 5.70 (ISBN 0-672-61381-6). Bobbs.

Frew, Mary A. & Frew, David R. Medical Office Administrative Procedures. (Illus.). 260p. Date not set. pap. 15.00 (ISBN 0-8036-3861-2). Davis Co.

Gorlick, S. The Whys & Wherefores of Corporate Practice. 3rd ed. 1978. 14.50 (ISBN 0-87489-209-0). Med Economics.

Goroll, Allan H., et al. Primary Care Medicine: Office Evaluation & Management of the Adult Patient. (Illus.). 855p. 1981. text ed. 37.50 (ISBN 0-397-58256-0, JBL-Med-Nursing). Har-Row.

Heller, Marjorie K. Legal P's & Q's in the Doctor's Office. (Orig.). 1981. pap. cancelled (ISBN 0-686-59766-4). Monarch Pr.

Lee, Leslie & Comte, Robert. Management Procedures. LC 74-18677. (Allied Health Ser). 1975. pap. 6.35 (ISBN 0-672-61397-2). Bobbs.

McCormick, John & Davis, W. Grayburn. The Management of Medical Practice. LC 78-2383. 1978. 20.00 (ISBN 0-88410-512-1). Ballinger Pub.

Malkin, Jain. The Design of Medical & Dental Facilities. 288p. 1981. text ed. price not set (ISBN 0-442-24493-2). Van Nos Reinhold.

Medical Accounting, Billing, & Office Management. 1976. 10.00 (ISBN 0-686-16905-0). Tax Info Ctr.

Merriam-Webster Editorial Staff. Webster's Medical Office Handbook. 1979. 10.95 (ISBN 0-87779-035-3). Merriam.

Morton, Judy C., et al. Building Assertive Skills: A Practical Guide to Professional Development for Allied Dental Health Providers. LC 80-19456. (Illus.). 283p. 1980. pap. text ed. 11.95 (ISBN 0-8016-3520-9). Mosby.

Moya, Frank. Fundamentals of Management for the Physician. (Illus.). 208p. 1974. 14.75 (ISBN 0-398-02945-8). C C Thomas.

Planning Guide for Physicians' Medical Facilities. 1975. pap. 4.50 (ISBN 0-89970-068-3, OP-439). AMA.

Reisman, Arnold. Systems Analysis in Health-Care Delivery. LC 79-3907. 336p. 1979. 24.95 (ISBN 0-669-02855-X). Lexington Bks.

Reschke, Elaine M. The Medical Office: Organization & Management. 2nd ed. (Illus.). 144p. 1980. pap. text ed. 12.95 (ISBN 0-06-142248-7). Har-Row.

Schwartz, Murray. Designing & Building Your Own Professional Office. (A Medical Economics Book). 1981. 22.50 (ISBN 0-686-71525-X). Van Nos Reinhold.

Sullivan, David J. Practice Made Perfect: How to Design, Establish, & Maintain Your Medical Office or Diagnose & Prescribe for Your Ailing One. rev. ed. Russo, Robert, ed. LC 78-65989. (Illus.). 304p. 1979. 39.95 (ISBN 0-9605606-0-2). Medi-Pub.

Toland, Drexel & Strong, Susan. Hospital-Based Medical Office Buildings. (Illus.). 260p. (Orig.). 1981. Repr. 45.00 (ISBN 0-87258-297-3, 1530). Am Hospital.

MEDICAL PARASITOLOGY

see also Blood–Parasites; Hookworm Disease; Lice; Medical Helminthology; Worms, Intestinal and Parasitic

Beck, J. Walter & Davies, John E. Medical Parasitology. 3rd ed. LC 80-25201. (Illus.). 355p. 1981. text ed. 21.95 (ISBN 0-8016-0552-0). Mosby.

--Medical Parasitology. 2nd ed. LC 77-42322. (Illus.). 1976. 18.95 (ISBN 0-8016-0551-2). Mosby.

Blecka, Lawernce J. Concise Medical Parasitology. LC 79-9452. 1980. pap. 17.95 (ISBN 0-201-00756-8, Med-Nurse). A-W.

Blecka, Lawrence J. Concise Medical Parasitology. 1980. cancelled (ISBN 0-201-00756-8). A-W.

Brown, Harold W. Basic Clinical Parasitology. 4th ed. 350p. 1975. 22.50 (ISBN 0-8385-0550-3). ACC.

Cameron, Thomas W. Parasites of Man in Temperate Climates. 2nd, rev. ed. LC 48-278. (Illus.). 1946. 10.00x (ISBN 0-8020-1014-8). U of Toronto Pr.

Chandler, Asa C. & Read, C. P. Introduction to Parasitology: With Special References to the Parasites of Man. 10th ed. LC 61-5670. 1961. 33.50 (ISBN 0-471-14487-8). Wiley.

Desowitz, Robert S. Ova & Parasites. (Illus.). 224p. 1980. pap. text ed. 22.50 (ISBN 0-06-140688-0, Harper Medical). Har-Row.

Faust, Ernest C., et al. Animal Agents & Vectors of Human Disease. 4th ed. LC 74-9689. (Illus.). 479p. 1975. text ed. 15.00 (ISBN 0-8121-0503-6). Lea & Febiger.

Houba, Vaclav, ed. Immunological Investigation of Tropical Parasitic Disease. (Practical Methods in Clinical Immunology Ser.: Vol. 2). (Illus.). 225p. 1980. text ed. 40.00x (ISBN 0-443-01900-2). Churchill.

Kean, B. H., et al, eds. Tropical Medicine & Parasitology: Classic Investigations, 2 vols. LC 76-12908. (Illus.). 1978. Set. 58.50x (ISBN 0-8014-0992-6). Cornell U Pr.

Koneman, Elmer W., et al. Practical Laboratory Parasitology. LC 78-21673. (Illus.). 142p. 1979. pap. text ed. 9.95 (ISBN 0-88275-804-7). Krieger.

Lapage, Geoffrey. Animals Parasitic in Man. rev. ed. (Illus.). 8.75 (ISBN 0-8446-2427-6). Peter Smith.

--Parasites. 1929. 15.00 (ISBN 0-8274-4228-9). R West.

Leventhal, Ruth & Cheadle, Russell. Medical Parasitology: A Self-Instructional Text. LC 79-10743. (Illus.). 1979. text ed. 19.95 (ISBN 0-8036-5596-7). Davis Co.

Majarian, Haig H. Patterns in Medical Parasitology. 2nd ed. 160p. 1980. Repr. of 1975 ed. lib. bdg. write for info. (U Pr of Pacific). Intl Schol Bk Serv.

Malek, Emile A. Snail Transmitted Parasitic Diseases, 2 vols. 1980. Vol. 1, 352p. 79.95 (ISBN 0-8493-5269-X); Vol. 2, 344 Pgs. 79.95 (ISBN 0-8493-5270-3). CRC Pr.

Mansfield. Advances in Parasitic Diseases, Vol. 1. 384p. 1981. write for info. Dekker.

Mansfield, John M., ed. Parasitic Diseases: The Immunology, Vol. 1. (Illus.). 336p. 1981. 45.75 (ISBN 0-8247-1409-1). Dekker.

Markell, Edward K. & Voge, Marietta. Medical Parasitology. 5th ed. (Illus.). 400p. 1981. text ed. write for info. (ISBN 0-7216-6082-7). Saunders.

--Medical Parasitology. 4th ed. LC 76-8580. (Illus.). 1976. text ed. 16.95 (ISBN 0-7216-6083-5); filmstrips 55.00 (ISBN 0-7216-9919-7); slides 165.00 (ISBN 0-7216-9920-0). Saunders.

Marois, M. Development of Chemotherapeutic Agents for Parasitic Diseases. 1976. 44.00 (ISBN 0-444-10996-X, North-Holland). Elsevier.

Miller, Louis H., et al, eds. Immunity to Blood Parasites of Animals & Man. (Advances in Experimental Medicine & Biology Ser.: Vol. 93). 321p. 1977. 29.50 (ISBN 0-306-32693-0, Plenum Pr). Plenum Pub.

Najarian, Haig H. Patterns in Medical Parasitology. 2nd ed. LC 80-10330. (Illus.). 1981. Repr. of 1967 ed. write for info. Krieger.

--Patterns in Medical Parasitology. 2nd ed. LC 80-10330. 168p. 1981. Repr. of 1967 ed. write for info. (ISBN 0-89874-031-2). Krieger.

Reifsnyder, David N. Parasitic Diseases Case Studies. LC 80-81733. 1980. pap. 18.50 (ISBN 0-87488-049-1). Med Exam.

Schwebach, Gerhard H. A Practical Guide to Microbial & Parasitic Diseases. (Illus.). 256p. 1980. lexotone 19.75 (ISBN 0-398-03980-1). C C Thomas.

Smith, James W., ed. Blood & Tissue Parasites. (Atlases of Diagnostic Medical Parasitology: 1). (Illus.). 1976. 76.50 (ISBN 0-89189-065-3, 15-7-006-00); microfiche ed. 22.00 (ISBN 0-89189-046-7, 17-7-006-00). Am Soc Clinical.

--Intestinal Helminths. LC 77-95410. (Atlases of Diagnostic Medical Parasitology: 3). (Illus.). 1976. slide atlas 76.50 (ISBN 0-89189-066-1, 15-7-008-00); microfiche ed. 22.00 (ISBN 0-89189-048-3, 17-7-008-00). Am Soc Clinical.

--Intestinal Protozoa. LC 77-95409. (Atlases of Diagnostic Medical Parasitology: 2). (Illus.). 1976. 76.50 (ISBN 0-89189-067-X, 15-007-00); microfiche ed. 22.00 (ISBN 0-89189-047-5, 17-7-007-00). Am Soc Clinical.

Soulsby, E. J., ed. Immunity to Animal Parasites. 1972. 56.00 (ISBN 0-12-655340-8). Acad Pr.

Weisbrod, Burton A., et al. Disease & Economic Development: The Impact of Parasitic Diseases in St. Lucia. LC 72-7997. 238p. 1973. 27.50x (ISBN 0-299-06340-2). U of Wis Pr.

Yamaguchi, Tomio, ed. Color Atlas of Clinical Parasitology. (Illus.). 296p. 1981. text ed. 98.00 (ISBN 0-8121-0820-5). Lea & Febiger.

Zaman, Viqar. Atlas of Medical Parasitology. (Illus.). 285p. 1979. text ed. 52.00 (ISBN 0-8121-0666-0). Lea & Febiger.

MEDICAL PERSONNEL

see also Dental Personnel; Dentists; Medicine–Specialties and Specialists; Medicine–Vocational Guidance; Pharmacists; Physicians; Public Health Personnel; Surgeons; also similar headings

Advances in Patient, Care, Second Annual Conference, Feb. 15-22, 1975. Design & Use of Protocols: Proceedings. new ed. Kallstrom, Marta & Yarnall, Stephen, eds. (Illus.). 294p. 1975. 18.00 (ISBN 0-917054-02-4). Med Communications.

American Hospital Association. Basic Personnel Policies & Programs for a Health Care Institution: Guidelines for Development. LC 74-11014. 48p. 1974. pap. 7.50 (ISBN 0-87258-156-X, 1105). Am Hospital.

--Medical Staff Cost Containment: Digest of Hospital Projects & Selected Bibliography. 72p. 1980. pap. 8.75 (ISBN 0-87258-314-7, 1538). Am Hospital.

Annas, George J., et al. The Rights of Doctors, Nurses, & Allied Health Professionals. 1981. 25.00 (ISBN 0-88410-727-2). Ballinger Pub.

Baker, Timothy D. & Perlman, Mark. Health Manpower in A Developing Economy: Taiwan, a Case Study in Planning. LC 67-22892. (Monographs in International Health). 224p. 1967. 16.00x (ISBN 0-8018-0050-1). Johns Hopkins.

Barnard, Martha U., et al. Human Sexuality for Health Professionals. LC 77-84663. (Illus.). 1978. pap. text ed. 10.95 (ISBN 0-7216-1544-9). Saunders.

Bohlander, George W. Impact of Third-Party Payors on Collective Bargaining in the Health Care Industry. (Monograph Ser.: No. 26). 130p. 1980. 6.50 (ISBN 0-89215-109-9). U Cal LA Indus Rel.

Boyer, John M., et al. Employee Relations & Collective Bargaining in Health Care Facilities. 2nd ed. LC 75-15677. (Illus.). 350p. 1975. text ed. 21.50 (ISBN 0-8016-0726-4). Mosby.

Boyles, Marcia V., et al. The Health Professions. LC 77-11331. (Illus.). 465p. Date not set. price not set (ISBN 0-7216-1904-5). Saunders.

Cooper, Marian & Bredow, Miriam. The Medical Assistant. 4th ed. (Illus.). 1978. text ed. 15.95 (ISBN 0-07-012751-4); instructor's manual 3.50 (ISBN 0-07-012753-0); wkbk. 7.95 (ISBN 0-07-012752-2). McGraw.

Daly, John C., et al. Medical Malpractice Dilemma. 1977. pap. 3.75 (ISBN 0-8447-2095-X). Am Enterprise.

Davis, Mary. Careers in a Medical Center. LC 72-7657. (Early Career Bks). (Illus.). 36p. (gr. 2-5). 1973. 4.95 (ISBN 0-8225-0310-7). Lerner Pubns.

Duke Law Journal. Medical Malpractice: The Duke Law Journal Symposium. LC 76-49822. 1977. 20.00 (ISBN 0-88410-701-9). Ballinger Pub.

Fottler, Myron D. Manpower Substitution in the Hospital Industry: A Study of New York City Voluntary & Municipal Hospital Systems. LC 73-173280. (Special Studies in U.S. Economic, Social & Political Issues). 1972. 32.50x (ISBN 0-275-06150-7). Irvington.

Golden, Archie S. An Inventory for Primary Health Care Practice. LC 76-5404. 208p. 1976. text ed. 17.50 (ISBN 0-88410-134-7). Ballinger Pub.

Goldstein, Harold M. & Horowitz, Morris Aaron. Entry-Level Health Occupations: Development & Future. LC 76-41270. (Policy Studies in Employment & Welfare: 27). 1977. 8.50x (ISBN 0-8018-1911-3); pap. 3.25x (ISBN 0-8018-1912-1). Johns Hopkins.

Grissum, Marlene & Spengler, Carol. Womanpower & Health Care. LC 75-41571. 1976. pap. 9.95 (ISBN 0-316-32895-2). Little.

Hardy, Margaret E., ed. Role Theory: Perspectives for Health Professionals. (Illus.). 354p. 1978. pap. 16.50 (ISBN 0-8385-8471-3). ACC.

Hiestand, Dale L. & Ostow, Miriam, eds. Health Manpower Information for Policy Guidance. LC 75-38687. 112p. 1976. text ed. 18.50 (ISBN 0-88410-135-5). Ballinger Pub.

Hill, E. Joy. Core Skills for the Health Occupations. LC 71-176181. 320p. 1981. 24.50 (ISBN 0-87527-108-1). Green.

Ilk, Craig R. Student's Career Guide to a Future in the Allied Health Professions. (Illus.). 160p. 1981. 9.95 (ISBN 0-668-04913-8); pap. 6.95 (ISBN 0-668-04921-9). Arco.

Keyes, Fenton. Aim for a Job in the Allied Health Field. LC 73-91273. (Aim High Vocational Guidance Ser.). (Illus.). 140p. (gr. 7-12). 1979. PLB 5.97 (ISBN 0-8239-0297-8). Rosen Pr.

Kirk. Your Future in Hospital & Health Services. (Careers in Depth Ser.). (Illus.). (gr. 7-12). 1975. PLB 5.97 (ISBN 0-8239-0339-7). Rosen Pr.

Krieghbaum, Hiller, compiled by. When Doctors Meet Reporters. LC 73-16949. 119p. 1974. Repr. of 1957 ed. lib. bdg. 15.00x (ISBN 0-8371-7249-7, JODR). Greenwood.

Laufman, Alan K. The Law of Medical Malpractice in Texas: A Primer for the Medical Community. LC 77-420. (Illus.). 136p. 1977. 10.00 (ISBN 0-292-74620-2). U of Tex Pr.

Lippard, Vernon W. & Purcell, Elizabeth F., eds. Intermediate-Level Health Practitioners. LC 73-82655. (Illus.). 232p. 1973. pap. 7.50 (ISBN 0-914362-05-4). J Macy Foun.

Lynch, L. Riddick. The Complete Guide to Selected Health & Health-Related Careers. Chatman, Urella, et al, eds. (Illus., Orig.). 1980. pap. 14.95 (ISBN 0-935872-01-9). R Bernard.

McLachlan, Gordon, et al, eds. Patterns for Uncertainty? Planning for the Greater Medical Profession. 1979. pap. 14.95x (ISBN 0-19-721223-9). Oxford U Pr.

Morgan, Margaret K. & Irby, David M. Evaluating Clinical Competence in the Health Profession. LC 77-26935. (Illus.). 1978. text ed. 19.95 (ISBN 0-8016-3493-8). Mosby.

Nassif, Janet Z. Handbook of Health Careers: A Guide to Employment Opportunities. LC 79-23027. 352p. 1980. 29.95 (ISBN 0-87705-489-4); pap. 12.95 (ISBN 0-87705-413-4). Human Sci Pr.

--Health Profession Careers in Medicine's New Technology. LC 80-22030. (Illus.). 240p. 1981. pap. 5.95 (ISBN 0-668-04436-5, 4436). Arco.

National Center for Health Statistics. Health Manpower, a County & Metropolitan Area Data Book, 1972-1973. 60p. 1976. pap. text ed. 1.25 (ISBN 0-8406-0066-6). Natl Ctr Health Stats.

Odegaard, Charles E. Minorities in Medicine - from Receptive Passivity to Positive Action 1966-76: Report of a Study. LC 77-75502. (Illus.). 1977. pap. 4.00 (ISBN 0-914362-20-8). J Macy Foun.

Patrick, Robert L. An Introduction to Health Careers. LC 78-2972. 1978. pap. 6.95 (ISBN 0-685-05983-9). D Armstrong.

Pitcairn, D. M. & Flahault, D., eds. Medical Assistant: An Intermediate Level of Health Care Personnel. (Public Health Paper: No. 60). (Also avail. in French, Russian & Spanish). 1974. pap. 4.00 (ISBN 92-4-130060-4). World Health.

Rudman, Jack. Medical Officer. (Career Examination Ser.: C-488). (Cloth bdg. avail. on request). pap. 14.00 (ISBN 0-8373-0488-1). Natl Learning.

--Medical Officer (Departmental) (Career Examination Ser.: C-489). (Cloth bdg. avail. on request). pap. 16.00 (ISBN 0-8373-0489-X). Natl Learning.

--Medical Specialist. (Career Examination Ser.: C-1965). (Cloth bdg. avail. on request). 1977. pap. 12.00 (ISBN 0-8373-1965-X). Natl Learning.

Sorkin, Alan. Health Manpower: An Economic Perspective. LC 75-17335. 1977. 17.95 (ISBN 0-669-00086-8). Lexington Bks.

Stewart, Charles T., Jr. & Siddayao, Corzaon M. Increasing the Supply of Medical Personnel: Needs & Alternatives. 1973. pap. 4.25 (ISBN 0-8447-3097-1). Am Enterprise.

Taylor, Carl E., et al. Health Manpower Planning in Turkey: An International Research Case Study. 300p. (MIH). 1968. 22.00x (ISBN 0-8018-0620-8). Johns Hopkins.

Training Programs for Health Care Workers: Ward Clerks. Incl. Being a Ward Clerk. 247p. student manual 9.95 (ISBN 0-87914-013-5, 9780); Training the Ward Clerk. 216p. instructor's guide 9.95 (ISBN 0-87914-014-3). 1967. Hosp Res & Educ.

WHO Scientific Group. Geneva, 1970. Development of Studies in Health Manpower: Report. (Technical Report Ser.: No. 481). (Also avail. in French & Spanish). 1971. pap. 2.00 (ISBN 92-4-120481-8). World Health.

Wolfe, Samuel, ed. Organization of Health Workers & Labor Conflict. LC 77-94410. (Policy, Politics, Health & Medicine Ser.: Vol. 2). 160p. 1978. pap. 6.00x (ISBN 0-89503-009-8). Baywood Pub.

MEDICAL PERSONNEL–EDUCATION

see Medical Education

MEDICAL PHOTOGRAPHY

see Photography, Medical

MEDICAL PHYSICS

Aird, Edwin A. Introduction to Medical Physics. (Illus.). 1975. 22.50x (ISBN 0-433-00350-2). Intl Ideas.

Benedek, G. B. & Villars, F. M. Physics with Illustrative Examples from Medicine & Biology, Vol. 3. 1979. pap. text ed. 15.95 (ISBN 0-201-00559-X). A-W.

Bergsma, Daniel, ed. Normal Values for Selected Physical Parameters: An Aid to Syndrome Delineation. LC 75-25485. (National Foundation Ser.: Vol 10, No. 13). 1974. write for info. (ISBN 0-686-18086-0). March of Dimes.

Black, M. & English, M., eds. Physical Science Techniques in Obstetrics & Gynecology. (Illus.). 1977. 39.50 (ISBN 0-8391-1145-2). Univ Park.

Cameron, John R. & Skofronick, James G. Medical Physics. LC 77-26909. 1978. 30.00 (ISBN 0-471-13131-8, Pub. by Wiley-Interscience). Wiley.

Damask, A. C. Medical Physics, 2 vols. 1978. Vol. 1 Physiological Physics, External Probes. 26.00 (ISBN 0-12-201201-1). Acad Pr.

Damask, Arthur. Medical Physics: External Senses, Vol. 2. 1981. 29.50 (ISBN 0-12-201202-X). Acad Pr.

International School of Physics "Enrico Fermi" Course 66 & Baarli. Health & Medical Physics: Proceedings. 1978. 97.75 (ISBN 0-7204-0728-1, North-Holland). Elsevier.

Klip, Willem. Theoretical Foundations of Medical Physics: An Introduction to Medical Physics, Vol. 2. LC 67-16145. 400p. 1969. 25.00x (ISBN 0-8173-1101-7). U of Ala Pr.

--Theoretical Foundations of Medical Physics: Mathematics for the Basic Sciences & Clinical Research, Vol. 1. LC 67-16145. 416p. 1969. 25.00x (ISBN 0-8173-1100-9). U of Ala Pr.

Laughlin, John S. Physical Aspects of Betatron Therapy. (American Lecture Medical Physics). (Illus.). 120p. 1954. photocopy ed. spiral 12.75 (ISBN 0-398-01086-2). C C Thomas.

Lawrence, John H. & Hamilton, J. G., eds. Advances in Biological & Medical Physics, 17 vols. Incl. Vol. 1. 1948 (ISBN 0-12-005201-6); Vol. 2. 1951 (ISBN 0-12-005202-4); Vol. 3. Lawrence, John H. & Tobias, Cornelius, eds. 1953 (ISBN 0-12-005203-2); Vol. 4. 1956 (ISBN 0-12-005204-0); Vol. 5. 1957 (ISBN 0-12-005205-9); Vol. 6. Tobias, Cornelius A. & Lawrence, John H., eds. 1958 (ISBN 0-12-005206-7); Vol. 7. 1960 (ISBN 0-12-005207-5); Vol. 8. 1962 (ISBN 0-12-005208-3); Vol. 9. Lawrence, John H. & Gofman, John W., eds. (ISBN 0-12-005209-1); Vol. 10. 1965 (ISBN 0-12-005210-5); Vol. 11. 1967. o.s.i (ISBN 0-12-005211-3); Vol. 12. 1968 (ISBN 0-12-005212-1); Vol. 13. 1971 (ISBN 0-12-005213-X); Vol. 14. 1973 (ISBN 0-12-005214-8); Vol. 15. 1974 (ISBN 0-12-005215-6); Vol. 16. 1978. 48.50 (ISBN 0-12-005216-4); lib. bdg. 59.50 (ISBN 0-12-005274-1); microfiche 35.00 (ISBN 0-12-005275-X); Vol. 17. 1980. 55.00 (ISBN 0-12-005217-2); lib. bdg. 71.50 (ISBN 0-12-005276-8); microfiche 38.50 (ISBN 0-12-005277-6). 49.00 ea. Acad Pr.

Molecular Aspects of Medicine, Vol. 3, No. 6. pap. 12.00 (ISBN 0-08-027978-3). Pergamon.

Nave, Carl R. & Nave, Brenda C. Physics for the Health Sciences. 2nd ed. LC 79-64599. (Illus.). 385p. 1980. pap. text ed. 11.95 (ISBN 0-7216-6666-3). Saunders.

Stanley, H. Eugene, ed. Biomedical Physics & Biomaterials Science. LC 72-8855. 1972. pap. 12.50x (ISBN 0-262-69038-1). MIT Pr.

Willis, C. A. & Handloser, J. S. Health Physics Operational Monitering, 3 vols. Incl. Vol. 1. 1972. 114.50 (ISBN 0-677-12320-5); Vol. 2. 1972. 67.25 (ISBN 0-677-12330-2); Vol. 3. 1972. 78.75 (ISBN 0-677-12340-X). 237.75 set (ISBN 0-677-13670-6). Gordon.

MEDICAL POLICY

see also Medicine, State; Medical Laws and Legislation

Berwick, Donald M., et al. Cholesterol, Children, & Heart Disease: An Analysis of Alternatives. (Illus.). 416p. 1980. 32.95x (ISBN 0-19-502669-1). Oxford U Pr.

Campbell, Alastair V. Medicine, Health, & Justice. 1978. pap. text ed. 8.95 (ISBN 0-443-01671-2). Churchill.

Culyer, A. J. Need & the National Health Service: Economics & Social Choice. 163p. 1976. 13.50x (ISBN 0-87471-896-1). Rowman.

Doty, Pamela. Guided Change of the American Health System: Where the Levers Are. (Center for Policy Research, Monograph Ser.: Vol. II). 272p. 1980. 24.95 (ISBN 0-87705-472-X). Human Sci Pr.

Dowling, Michael J. Health Care & the Church. Koenig, Robert E., ed. LC 77-1242. (Doing the Word Resource Ser.). (Orig.). 1977. pap. text ed. 3.95 (ISBN 0-8298-0333-5). Pilgrim NY.

Egdahl, Richard H. & Gertman, Paul M., eds. Quality Assurance in Health Care. LC 76-15770. 372p. 1976. 28.95 (ISBN 0-912862-23-8). Aspen Systems.

Elinson, Jack, et al, eds. Health Goals & Health Indicators: Policy, Planning & Evaluation. LC 77-14044. (AAAS Selected Symposium Ser.: No. 2). 1978. lib. bdg. 18.50x (ISBN 0-89158-429-3). Westview.

Ginzberg, Eli. The Limits of Health Reform. LC 77-75244. 1977. 12.50 (ISBN 0-465-04117-5). Basic.

Harvard Child Health Project. Harvard Child Health Project Report: Developing a Better Health Care System for Children. LC 77-3367. (Harvard Child Health Project Ser.: Vol. III). 1977. 16.50 (ISBN 0-88410-509-1). Ballinger Pub.

--Harvard Child Health Project Report: Toward a Primary Medical Care System Responsive to Children's Needs. LC 77-3387. (Harvard Child Health Project Ser.: Vol. 1). 1977. ref. ed 13.00 (ISBN 0-88410-507-5). Ballinger Pub.

Heidenheimer, Arnold J. & Elvander, Nile, eds. The Shaping of the Swedish Health System. LC 80-12410. 256p. 1980. write for info. (ISBN 0-312-71627-3). St Martin.

Krause, Elliot A. Power & Illness: The Political Sociology of Health & Medical Care. LC 77-317. 1977. text ed. 15.95 (ISBN 0-444-99037-2); pap. 8.95 (ISBN 0-444-99056-9). Elsevier.

Lewis, Charles, et al. A Right to Health: The Problem of Access to Primary Medical Care. LC 76-18129. (Health, Medicine, & Society Ser.). 416p. 1976. 30.95 (ISBN 0-471-01494-X, Pub. by Wiley-Interscience). Wiley.

Littrell, W. B. & Sjoberg, G. Current Issues in Social Policy. LC 76-21777. 1976. 18.00x (ISBN 0-8039-0609-9); pap. 8.95x (ISBN 0-8039-0610-2). Sage.

Merlis, S., ed. Non-Scientific Constraints on Medical Research. LC 72-133882. 114p. 1972. pap. 2.50 (ISBN 0-911216-17-0). Raven.

Roemer, Milton I. Comparative National Policies on Health Care. (Political Science & Public Administration Ser.: Vol. 2). 1977. 16.75 (ISBN 0-8247-6567-2). Dekker.

Veatch, Robert M. Death, Dying, & the Biological Revolution: Our Last Quest for Responsibility. LC 75-43337. 1976. 20.00x (ISBN 0-300-01949-1); pap. 6.95x (ISBN 0-300-02290-5). Yale U Pr.

Weaver, Jerry L. National Health Policy & the Underserved: Ethic Minorities, Women, & the Elderly. LC 76-6955. (Issues & Problems in Health Care). 176p. 1976. pap. 8.25 (ISBN 0-8016-5360-6). Mosby.

MEDICAL PROFESSION
see Medicine; Physicians

MEDICAL RADIOGRAPHY
see Radiography, Medical

MEDICAL RADIOLOGY
see Radiology, Medical

MEDICAL RECORDS
see also Medical History Taking

American Hospital Association. Hospital Medical Records: Guidelines for Their Use & the Release of Medical Information. LC 70-188799. 70p. 1972. pap. 7.50 (ISBN 0-87258-087-3, 1250). Am Hospital.

--ICD-Nine-CM Coding Handbook for Entry-Level Coders. 348p. 1979. 19.25 (ISBN 0-87258-263-9, 2062); with answers 23.75 (ISBN 0-87258-264-7, 2061). Am Hospital.

Benjamin, B. Medical Records. 2nd ed. 272p. 1981. 27.00x (ISBN 0-433-02451-8, Pub. by Heinemann England). State Mutual Bk.

Benjamin, Bernard. Medical Records. 1977. 24.60x (ISBN 0-433-02450-X). Intl Ideas.

Benjamin, Bernard, ed. Medical Records. 2nd ed. (Illus.). 257p. 1981. 26.95x (ISBN 0-433-02451-8). Intl Ideas.

Berni, Rosemarian & Readey, Helen. Problem-Oriented Medical Record Implementation: Allied Health Peer Review. 2nd ed. LC 77-18278. (Illus.). 1978. pap. text ed. 10.00 (ISBN 0-8016-0648-9). Mosby.

Blum, Richard H. & Ezekiel, Jonathan. Clinical Records for Mental Health Services: A Guide to the Study & Development of Clinical Records Systems Including a Manual of Model Forms & Procedures. 176p. 1962. ed. spiral bdg. 14.75photocopy (ISBN 0-398-00179-0). C C Thomas.

Conference on Confidentiality of Health Records, Key Biscayne, Fla., Nov. 6-9, 1974. Confidentiality: Report of the Conference on Confidentiality of Health Records. Springarn, Natalie D., ed. 58p. 1975. pap. 2.00 (ISBN 0-685-63944-4, P175-0). Am Psychiatric.

Confidentiality & Third Parties. (Task Force Report: No. 9). 59p. 1975. pap. 5.00 (ISBN 0-685-63945-2, P218-0). Am Psychiatric.

Corbus, Howard & Swanson, L. L. Adopting the Problem Oriented Medical Record in Nursing Homes. LC 78-53068. 98p. 1978. pap. text ed. 5.95 (ISBN 0-913654-44-2). Nursing Res.

Doyle, Owen, et al. Analysis Manual for Hospital Information Systems. (Illus.). 463p. (Orig.). 1980. pap. text ed. 42.50 (ISBN 0-914904-41-8). Health Admin Pr.

Gregorio, M. Pauline, ed. Medical Record Library Science Examination Review Book, Vol. 1. 3rd ed. 1976. spiral bdg. 10.00 (ISBN 0-87488-496-9). Med Exam.

Hirsch, Rudolph, ed. Catalog of Manuscripts & Archives in F. Clark Wood Institute at College of Physicians in Philadelphia. 1981. write for info. U of Pa Pr.

Huffman, Edna K. Medical Record Management. 1972. 16.75 (ISBN 0-917036-04-2). Physicians Rec.

--Medical Records in Nursing Homes. 1961. 5.00 (ISBN 0-917036-10-7). Physicians Rec.

IFIPtC4 Working Conference, Germany, 1976. Realization of Data Protection in Health Information Systems: Proceedings. Griesser, G, ed. LC 77-1802. 1977. 29.50 (ISBN 0-7204-0462-2, North-Holland). Elsevier.

Lang, Gerald S. & Dickie, Kenneth J. The Practice-Oriented Medical Record. LC 78-1931. (Illus.). 287p. 1978. text ed. 27.95 (ISBN 0-89443-032-7). Aspen Systems.

Laska, Eugene M. & Bank, Rheta, eds. Safeguarding Psychiatric Privacy: Computer Systems & Their Uses. LC 75-15570. 452p. (Orig.). 1975. 28.00 (ISBN 0-471-51831-X). Krieger.

Laumark, Eleanor & Christianson, Victoria. Keeping Track: A Personal Medical Record System. LC 80-22042. (Illus., Orig.). 1981. pap. 7.95 (ISBN 0-912800-79-8). Woodbridge Pr.

Liebler, Joan G. Managing Health Records: Administrative Principles. LC 79-22455. 306p. 1979. text ed. 26.50 (ISBN 0-89443-168-4). Aspen Systems.

Mosier, Alice & Pace, Frank J. Medical Records Technology. LC 74-18676. (Allied Health Ser). 1975. pap. 8.35 (ISBN 0-672-61396-4). Bobbs.

Patrikas, Elaine O., et al. Medical Records Administration Continuing Education Review. 1975. spiral bdg. 14.00 (ISBN 0-87488-369-5). Med Exam.

Petrie, J. C. & McIntyre, Neil, eds. The Problem-Orientated Medical Record in Clinical Practice. 1979. pap. text ed. 22.50 (ISBN 0-443-01405-1). Churchill.

Raus, Elmer E. & Raus, Madonna M. Manual of History Taking, Physical Examinations & Record Keeping. LC 73-37293. (Illus.). 584p. 1974. pap. text ed. 21.50 (ISBN 0-397-50306-7, JBL-Med-Nursing). Har-Row.

Record Controls, Inc., & H. F. M. A. Staff. A Guide to the Retention & Preservation of Records (with Destruction Schedules) 5th hospital ed. LC 77-94914. (Illus.). 1978. 15.00 (ISBN 0-930228-07-3). Hospital Finan.

Rudman, Jack. Medical Record Librarian. (Career Examination Ser.: C-491). (Cloth bdg. avail. on request). pap. 8.00 (ISBN 0-8373-0491-1). Natl Learning.

--Medical Record Technician. (Career Examination Ser.: C-2329). (Cloth bdg. avail. on request). pap. 8.00 (ISBN 0-8373-2329-0). Natl Learning.

--Medical Records Clerk. (Career Examination Ser.: C-2309). (Cloth bdg. avail. on request). 1977. pap. 8.00 (ISBN 0-8373-2309-6). Natl Learning.

--Senior Medical Records Clerk. (Career Examination Ser.: C-2310). (Cloth bdg. avail. on request). 1977. pap. 10.00 (ISBN 0-8373-2310-X). Natl Learning.

Self, Timothy H., et al. Systematic Patient Medication Record Review: A Manual for Nurses. LC 80-12481. 1980. pap. text ed. 9.45 (ISBN 0-8016-4479-8). Mosby.

Siegel, Carole & Fischer, Susan K. Psychiatric Records in Mental Health Care. LC 80-22564. (Illus.). 352p. (Orig.). 1981. pap. 29.95 (ISBN 0-87630-241-X). Brunner Mazel.

Society of Patient Representatives of the American Hospital Association. Essentials of Patient Representative Programs in Hospitals. LC 78-26889. 1978. pap. 8.75 (ISBN 0-87258-255-8, 1251). Am Hospital.

Sullivan, Robert J. Medical Record & Index Systems for Community Practice. LC 78-31817. (Rural Health Center Ser.). (Illus.). 1979. reference 14.50 (ISBN 0-88410-540-7); pap. 8.95 (ISBN 0-88410-546-6). Ballinger Pub.

Szondi, L. Profile Blanks: Szondi Tableau. 15.25 (ISBN 0-8089-0602-X); answer sheet, pkg. of 50 8.75 (ISBN 0-686-76985-6); test pictures, set of 48 35.00 (ISBN 0-8089-0601-1). Grune.

Ulisse, Gael C. POMR: How to Write Problem-Oriented Nurse's Progress Notes. LC 78-60718. 1978. 8.95 (ISBN 0-201-07880-5, 07880, Med-Nurse). A-W.

Van Egmond, J., et al, eds. Information Systems for Patient Care: Proceedings of the IFIP Working Conference on Information Systems for Patient Care Review, Analysis & Evaluation. 1976. 53.75 (ISBN 0-7204-0463-0, North-Holland). Elsevier.

Vorzimer, Jefferson J. Coordinated Ambulatory Care: the POMR. (Illus.). 128p. 1976. pap. text ed. 14.50 (ISBN 0-8385-1203-8). ACC.

Waters, Kathleen & Murphy, Gretchen. Medical Records in Health Information. LC 79-18793. 706p. 1979. text ed. 32.95 (ISBN 0-89443-157-9). Aspen Systems.

Weed, L. L., et al, eds. Implementing the Problem-Oriented Medical Record, Vol.2. 1976. 12.00 (ISBN 0-917054-00-8). Med Communications.

Weed, Lawrence L. Medical Records, Medical Education & Patient Care. 1970. 25.00 (ISBN 0-8151-9188-X). Year Bk Med.

Westin, Alan F. Computers, Health Records & Citizen Rights. 1977. text ed. 15.00 (ISBN 0-89433-014-4). Petrocelli.

Ziegler, A. Patient Records Control. (Illus.). 1979. pap. 12.00 (ISBN 0-87489-155-8). Med Economics.

MEDICAL REGISTRATION AND EXAMINATION
see Medical Laws and Legislation

MEDICAL RESEARCH
see also Cancer Research; Dental Research; Human Experimentation in Medicine; Laboratory Animals; Medicine, Experimental; Pharmaceutical Research; Psychosomatic Research; Space Medicine; Surgical Research

Academy Forum, National Academy of Science. Experiments & Research with Humans: Values in Conflicts. LC 75-13985. (Illus.). 224p. 1975. pap. 7.00 (ISBN 0-309-02347-5). Natl Acad Pr.

American Foundation. Medical Research: A Midcentury Survey, 2 vols. LC 77-13559. 1977. Repr. of 1955 ed. lib. bdg. 85.00x (ISBN 0-8371-9863-1, AMFO). Greenwood.

Assaykeen, Tatiana A., ed. Control of Renin Secretion. LC 76-185044. (Advances in Experimental Medicine & Biology Ser.: Vol. 17). 290p. 1972. 32.50 (ISBN 0-306-39017-5, Plenum Pr). Plenum Pub.

Barber, Bernard, et al. Research on Human Subjects: Problems of Social Control in Medical Experimentation. LC 78-55938. 263p. 1979. pap. text ed. 4.95 (ISBN 0-87855-649-4). Transaction Bks.

Beyond Tomorrow: Trends & Prospects in Medical Science. LC 77-24824. 1977. pap. 2.95 (ISBN 0-87470-023-X). Rockefeller.

Blanpain, Jan & Delesie, Luk. Community Health Investment: Health Services Research in Belgium, France, Federal German Republic & the Netherlands. McLachlan, Gordon, ed. (Nuffield Publications Ser). 1976. 24.50x (ISBN 0-19-721391-X). Oxford U Pr.

Bloom, Barry R. & David, John R., eds. In Vitro Methods in Cell-Mediated & Tumor Immunity. 1976. 54.00 (ISBN 0-12-107760-8). Acad Pr.

Bralow, S. Philip, ed. Basic Research & Clinical Medicine. (Illus.). 304p. 1981. text ed. 33.50 (ISBN 0-07-007150-0, Co-Pub by Hemisphere Pub). McGraw.

Burke, Abbot G. Magnetic Therapy: Healing in Your Hands. LC 80-22941. (Illus.). 86p. (Orig.). 1980. pap. text ed. 4.95 (ISBN 0-932104-04-5). St George Pr.

Ciba Foundation. Medical Research Systems in Europe: Proceedings. (Ciba Foundation Symposium: No. 21). 332p. 1974. 25.25 (ISBN 0-444-15018-8, Excerpta Medica). Elsevier.

Ciba Foundation, ed. Research & Medical Practice: Their Interaction. (Ciba Foundation Symposium: No. 44). 1976. 20.50 (ISBN 90-219-4049-3, Excerpta Medica). Elsevier.

CIOMS Round Table Conference, Geneva, 1970. Training of Research Workers in the Medical Sciences: Proceedings. 186p. 1972. pap. 9.60 (ISBN 92-4-156040-1, 566). World Health.

Coleman, Vernon. Paper Doctors: A Critical Assessment of Medical Research. 1977. 12.95 (ISBN 0-85117-109-5). Transatlantic.

Comroe, Julius H., Jr. Retrospectroscope: Insights into Medical Discovery. LC 77-88230. (Illus.). 1977. pap. 7.95 (ISBN 0-9601470-1-2). Von Gehr.

Cuschieri, A. & Baker, P. R. Introduction to Research in Medical Sciences. LC 76-22624. 1977. 13.25 (ISBN 0-443-01466-3). Churchill.

Dubos, Rene. The Professor, the Institute, & DNA. LC 76-26812. 1976. 14.50 (ISBN 0-87470-022-1). Rockefeller.

England, J. M. Medical Research: A Statistical & Epidemiological Approach. (Illus.). 128p. 1975. pap. text ed. 10.00 (ISBN 0-443-01139-7). Churchill.

Feinstein, Alvan R. Clinical Biostatistics. LC 77-3703. (Illus.). 1977. text ed. 22.50 (ISBN 0-8016-1563-1). Mosby.

Fisher, Ronald A. & Yates, Frank. Statistical Tables for Biological, Agricultural & Medical Research. 6th ed. 1978. text ed. 19.00x (ISBN 0-582-44525-6). Longman.

Forbes, Eric G. & Pacela, Allan F. A Source Book of Government-Owned Biomedical Inventions. LC 77-88370. (Illus.). 1978. looseleaf 82.50x (ISBN 0-930844-02-5). Quest Pub.

Fox, Renee C. Essays in Medical Sociology: Journeys into the Field. LC 79-10413. (Health, Medicine & Society: a Wiley Interscience Ser.). 1979. 25.50 (ISBN 0-471-27040-7, Pub. by Wiley-Interscience). Wiley.

Gaugas, Joseph M., ed. Polyamines in Biomedical Research. LC 79-40651. 474p. 1980. 85.00 (ISBN 0-471-27629-4, Pub. by Wiley-Interscience). Wiley.

Goldstein, Gerald. A Clinician's Guide to Research Design. LC 79-18818. 288p. 1981. text ed. 24.95x (ISBN 0-88229-340-0); pap. text ed. 11.95x (ISBN 0-88229-760-0). Nelson-Hall.

Gordon, R. A., et al, eds. International Symposium on Malignant Hyperthermia. (Illus.). 512p. 1973. 32.75 (ISBN 0-398-02549-5). C C Thomas.

Gregg, Alan. Furtherance of Medical Research. 1941. 17.50x (ISBN 0-685-89754-0). Elliots Bks.

Hamilton, Max. Lectures on the Methodology of Clinical Research. 2nd ed. LC 73-89665. (Illus.). 222p. 1974. text ed. 17.50x (ISBN 0-443-01080-3). Churchill.

Harvey, A. McGehee. Adventures in Medical Research: A Century of Discovery at Johns Hopkins. LC 75-36955. (Illus.). 480p. 1976. 22.50 (ISBN 0-8018-1785-4). Johns Hopkins.

--Research & Discovery in Medicine: Contributions from Johns Hopkins. LC 81-47647. (Illus.). 344p. 1981. text ed. 25.00x (ISBN 0-8018-2723-X). Johns Hopkins.

--Science at the Bedside: Clinical Research in American Medicine, 1905-1945. LC 80-28786. 496p. 1981. text ed. 17.50x (ISBN 0-8018-2562-8). Johns Hopkins.

Hill, D. W. Principles of Electronics in Medical Research. 2nd ed. (Illus.). 1973. 22.95 (ISBN 0-407-36401-3). Butterworth.

Hoffman, William. The Super Doctors. 256p. 1981. 12.95 (ISBN 0-02-552010-5). Macmillan.

Hoffmann-la Roche Anniversary Symposium, Basil, Switzerland, 1971. The Challenge of Life: Biomedical Progress & Human Values. Kunz, Robert M. & Fehr, Hans, eds. 456p. 1972. 16.50x (ISBN 3-7643-0589-4). Intl Pubns Serv.

Institute of Laboratory Animal Resources. Animal Models for Biomedical Research, No. 3. LC 76-607190. (Illus.). 1970. pap. 5.75 (ISBN 0-309-01854-4). Natl Acad Pr.

--Animal Models for Biomedical Research, No. 4. LC 76-607190. (Illus., Orig.). 1971. pap. text ed. 6.25 (ISBN 0-309-01918-4). Natl Acad Pr.

International Congress on Medicinal Plant Research, Section A, University of Munich, Germany, September 6-10, 1976. New Natural Products & Plant Drugs with Pharmacological, Biological or Therapeutical Activity: Proceedings. Wagner, H. K. & Wolff, P. M., eds. (Proceeding in Life Sciences Ser.). (Illus.). 1977. 39.40 (ISBN 0-387-08292-1). Springer-Verlag.

Jaques Cattell Press, ed. Research Programs in the Medical Sciences. 816p. 1980. 79.95 (ISBN 0-8352-1293-9). Bowker.

Kennedy, H. E. & Bevan, W., eds. International Communication for Biomedical Research: Journal: Health Communications & Informatics, Vol. 6, Nos. 3-4. (Illus.). 112p. 1980. pap. 11.50 (ISBN 3-8055-0974-X). S Karger.

Levine, Robert J. Clinical Research: Ethical & Regulatory Considerations. (Illus.). text ed. write for info. (ISBN 0-8067-1111-6). Urban & S.

Linscott, William D. Linscott's Directory of Immunological & Biological Reagents. 2nd ed. 120p. 1981. 25.00x (ISBN 0-9604920-1-1). W D Linscott.

Mainland, Donald. Mainland's Notes on Biometry in Medical Research. Miller, M. Clinton, 3rd, ed. LC 78-21121. (Biometry Imprint Ser.: Vol. 4). 1978. 41.75 (ISBN 0-8357-0364-9, IS-00067, Biometry Imprint Series Press). Univ Microfilms.

--Mainland's Statistical Ward Rounds. Miller, M. Clinton, III, ed. LC 79-10434. (Biometry Imprint Ser.: Vol. 5). 1979. 19.75 (ISBN 0-8357-0403-3, IS-00078). Univ Microfilms.

Martin, M. W. Miracles in Medicine. LC 73-80419. (Illus.). 1974. 9.95 (ISBN 0-8246-0159-9). Jonathan David.

Medical Research Index, 2 vols. 5th ed. LC 45-718. 1200p. 1979. Set. 175.00x (ISBN 0-8002-2386-1). Intl Pubns Serv.

Medical Research Index, 2 vols. 4th ed. LC 45-718. 1200p. 1971. Set. 85.00x (ISBN 0-8002-1715-2). Intl Pubns Serv.

Medical Research Index: A Guide to World Medical Research Including Dentistry, Nursing, Pharmacy, Psychiatry, & Surgery, 2 vols. 1322p. Set. 195.00 (ISBN 0-686-75641-X, Pub. by Longman). Gale.

Merlis, S., ed. Non-Scientific Constraints on Medical Research. LC 72-133882. 114p. 1972. pap. 2.50 (ISBN 0-911216-17-0). Raven.

Montagna, William. Nonhuman Primates in Biomedical Research. LC 76-7881. (Wesley W. Spink Lectures on Comparative Medicine: Vol. 3). (Illus.). 1976. 9.50x (ISBN 0-8166-0793-1). U of Minn Pr.

Muller-Berat, M. Progress in Differentiation Research. 1976. 75.75 (ISBN 0-444-11200-6, North-Holland). Elsevier.

Murphy, Edmond A. Probability in Medicine. LC 78-10611. 1979. text ed. 19.95x (ISBN 0-8018-2135-5). Johns Hopkins.

Mushkin, Selma J. Biomedical Research: Costs & Benefits. LC 79-19889. 448p. 1979. reference 35.00 (ISBN 0-88410-549-0). Ballinger Pub.

New York Academy of Medicine. Perspectives in Medicine. LC 75-152204. (Essay Index Reprint Ser.). 1949. 15.00 (ISBN 0-8369-2813-X). Arno.

Noone, P., ed. Sisomicin: An International Round-Table Discussion. (Royal Society of Medicine International Congress & Symposium Ser.). 80p. 1981. 10.50 (ISBN 0-12-793125-2). Acad Pr.
Nossal, G. J. Medical Science & Human Goals. 1976. text ed. 17.75x (ISBN 0-8419-5801-7). Holmes & Meier.
Oborne, D. J. Research in Psychology & Medicine: Vol. 2., Social Aspects: Attitudes, Communication, Care & Training. LC 79-42933. 1980. 29.00 (ISBN 0-12-523702-2). Acad Pr.
Oborne, D. J., et al. Research in Psychology & Medicine: Vol. 1, Physical Aspects: Pain, Stress, Diagnosis and Organic Damage. LC 79-42933. 1980. 29.00 (ISBN 0-686-73080-1). Acad Pr.
Osborn, John F. Statistical Exercises in Medical Research. LC 79-12451. 1979. 18.95x (ISBN 0-470-26744-5). Halsted Pr.
Parslow, R. D. & Green, R. Elliot, eds. Computer Graphics in Medical Research & Hospital Administration. LC 77-137741. 100p. 1971. 25.00 (ISBN 0-306-30518-6, Plenum Pr). Plenum Pub.
Pinckney, Edward, compiled by. The Encyclopedia of Medical Tests. 1978. pap. 4.95 (ISBN 0-671-79057-9, Wallaby). PB.
Ratcliff, John D. Modern Miracle Men. facsimile ed. LC 79-37770. (Essay Index Reprint Ser). Repr. of 1939 ed. 22.00 (ISBN 0-8369-2619-6). Arno.
Round Table Conference of CIOM-WHO-UNESCO, Geneva, Oct., 1969. Medical Research-Priorities & Responsibilities: Proceedings. 156p. 1970. pap. 3.60 (ISBN 92-4-156031-2, 1358). World Health.
Science Policy and Biomedical Research Symposium, Paris, 1968. Proceedings. (Science Policy Studies & Documents Ser., No. 16). (Orig.). 1969. pap. 2.50 (ISBN 92-3-100751-3, UNESCO). Unipub.
Selye, Hans. In Vivo: The Case for Supramolecular Biology. 1967. 5.95x (ISBN 0-87140-849-X). Liveright.
Sheps, Cecil G. & Taylor, Eugene E. Needed Research in Health & Medical Care. 1954. 15.00x (ISBN 0-8078-0665-X). U of NC Pr.
Shryock, Richard H. American Medical Research Past & Present. Cohen, I. Bernard, ed. LC 79-7989. (Three Centuries of Science in America Ser.). 1980. Repr. of 1947 ed. lib. bdg. 27.00x (ISBN 0-405-12571-2). Arno.
Smith, K. G. Insects & Other Arthropods of Medical Importance. LC 74-594820. 1973. 52.25 (ISBN 0-471-99684-X, Pub. by Wiley-Interscience). Wiley.
Stein, Franklin. Anatomy of Research in Allied Health. 272p. 1982. pap. text ed. 12.50x (ISBN 0-87073-007-X). Schenkman.
Strickland, Stephen P. Politics, Science, & Dread Disease: A Short History of the United States Medical Research Policy. LC 72-78427. (Commonwealth Fund Publications Ser). 472p. 1972. 16.50x (ISBN 0-674-68955-0). Harvard U Pr.
Summit, Robert & Bergsma, Daniel, eds. Recent Advances & New Syndromes. (Alan R. Liss, Inc. Ser.: Vol. 14, No. 6B). 1978. 40.00 (ISBN 0-686-23950-4). March of Dimes.
Thompson, John D. Applied Health Services Research. LC 75-12482. (Illus.). 1977. 19.95 (ISBN 0-669-00028-0). Lexington Bks.
Towse, G. & Towse, G., eds. Progress with Domperidone, a Gastrokinetic & Anti-Emetic Agent: Proceedings. (Royal Society of Medicine International Congress & Symposium Ser.). 110p. 1981. 19.00 (ISBN 0-12-794643-8). Acad Pr.
Visscher, Maurice B. Ethical Constraints & Imperatives in Medical Research. (American Lectures in Behavioral Science & Law Ser.). 128p. 1975. 12.50 (ISBN 0-398-03404-4). C C Thomas.
Volk, Bruno W. & Aronson, S. M., eds. Sphingolipids, Sphingolipidoses, & Allied Disorders. LC 71-188925. (Advances in Experimental Medicine & Biology Ser.: Vol. 19). 697p. 1972. 45.00 (ISBN 0-306-39019-1, Plenum Pr). Plenum Pub.
Wandelt. Guide for the Beginning Researcher. (Illus.). 1970. pap. 12.50 (ISBN 0-8385-3510-0). ACC.
Wechsler, Henry, et al, eds. The Horizons of Health. 1977. text ed. 20.00x (ISBN 0-674-40630-3); pap. 7.95x (ISBN 0-674-40631-1). Harvard U Pr.
--The Social Context of Medical Research. 1981. 29.50 (ISBN 0-88410-730-2). Ballinger Pub.
Weissbach, Herbert & Kunz, Robert. Dimension in Health Research: Search for the Medicines of Tomorrow. 1978. 23.50 (ISBN 0-12-744260-X). Acad Pr.
World Health Organization. Medical Research Programme of the World Health Organization, 1958-1963. (Also avail. in French, Russian & Spanish). 1964. 9.20 (ISBN 92-4-156021-5). World Health.
--Medical Research Programme of the World Health Organization, 1964-1968. (Also avail. in French, Russian & Spanish). 1969. 13.60 (ISBN 92-4-156022-3). World Health.
Zwar, Desmond. The Bio-Adventures: The Drama of Medical Research. LC 80-6168. 288p. 1981. 14.95 (ISBN 0-8128-2807-0). Stein & Day.

MEDICAL RESEARCH–JUVENILE LITERATURE

Berger, Melvin. Disease Detectives. LC 77-26589. (Scientists at Work Ser.). (Illus.). (gr. 4 up). 1978. 8.95 (ISBN 0-690-03907-7, TYC-J); PLB 8.79 (ISBN 0-690-03908-5). Har-Row.
Eberle, Irmengarde. Modern Medical Discoveries. 3rd ed. LC 68-17084. (gr. 5-9). 1968. 8.95 (ISBN 0-690-55271-8, TYC-J). Har-Row.

MEDICAL RESEARCH ETHICS

see Medical Ethics

MEDICAL SCHOOLS

see Medical Colleges

MEDICAL SCREENING

Benson, E. S. & Strandjord, P. E., eds. Multiple Laboratory Screening. 1969. 39.50 (ISBN 0-12-089050-X). Acad Pr.
Berwick, Donald M., et al. Cholesterol, Children, & Heart Disease: An Analysis of Alternatives. (Illus.). 416p. 1980. 32.95x (ISBN 0-19-502669-1). Oxford U Pr.
Cohen, Bernice H., et al. Genetic Issues in Public Health & Medicine. (Illus.). 512p. 1978. 34.50 (ISBN 0-398-03659-4). C C Thomas.
Hart, C. Screening in General Practice. (Illus.). 320p. 1975. pap. text ed. 17.50x (ISBN 0-443-01208-3). Churchill.
Mass Health Examinations. (Public Health Paper: No. 45). (Also avail. in French & Spanish). 1971. pap. 2.80 (ISBN 92-4-130045-0). World Health.
Raine. Medico-Social Management of Inherited Metabolic Diseases. (Illus.). 1977. 39.50 (ISBN 0-8391-1103-7). Univ Park.
Rosenfeld, I. Complete Medical Examination. 1979. pap. 6.95 (ISBN 0-380-46391-1, 46391). Avon.
Shipp, Audrey, ed. Tuberculin Skin Test Reaction Amon Adults 25-74 Years: United States, 1971-1972. (Ser. 11 No. 204). 1977. pap. 1.75 (ISBN 0-8406-0086-0). Natl Ctr Health Stats.

MEDICAL SECRETARIES

Alcazar, Carol C. Medical Typist's Guide for Histories & Physicals. 2nd ed. 1974. spiral bdg. 7.00 (ISBN 0-87488-976-6). Med Exam.
Berkeley, S. G. & Jackson, B. E. Your Career As a Medical Secretary-Transcriber. LC 74-34233. 194p. 1975. 14.95 (ISBN 0-471-07020-3, Pub. by Wiley Medical). Wiley.
Bredow, Miriam. Handbook for the Medical Secretary. 4th ed. (Illus.). 1959. pap. 4.50 (ISBN 0-07-007413-5, SP). McGraw.
--Medical Office Procedures. Orig. Title: Medical Secretarial Procedures. (Illus.). 416p. 1973. pap. text ed. 13.50 (ISBN 0-07-007425-9, G); instructor's manual & key 6.50 (ISBN 0-07-007426-7). McGraw.
Byers, Edward E. Ten Thousand Medical Words, Spelled & Divided for Quick Reference. 128p. 1972. text ed. 5.28 (ISBN 0-07-009503-5, G). McGraw.
Carlin, Harriette L. Medical Secretary Medi-Speller: A Transcription Aid. 260p. 1973. pap. 11.50 (ISBN 0-398-02579-7). C C Thomas.
Chernok, Norma B. Your Future in Medical Assisting. LC 67-10176. (Careers in Depth Ser). (gr. 7 up). 1979. PLB 5.97 (ISBN 0-8239-0359-1). Rosen Pr.
Doyle, Jean M. & Dennis, Robert L. The Complete Handbook for Medical Secretaries & Assistants. 2nd ed. 1978. pap. text ed. 15.95 (ISBN 0-316-18082-3, Little Med Div). Little.
Eshom, Myreta. Medical Secretary's Manual. 2nd ed. (Illus.). 560p. 1977. 15.00 (ISBN 0-8385-6259-0). ACC.
Frye, Marianne E., et al. Medical Secretary-Receptionist Simulation Project. Frazier, Lois E., ed. LC 78-78187. 1979. pap. text ed. 5.25 (ISBN 0-87350-313-9); tchr's ed. 19.75 (ISBN 0-87350-316-3); wkbk. 14.75 (ISBN 0-87350-319-8). Milady.
Kinn, Mary E. & Bradley, Hila M. Student Workbook to Accompany the Medical Office Assistant. 233p. 1976. 8.95 (ISBN 0-7216-5438-X). Saunders.
McConnico, Charles T. Medical Transcriptionist Handbook. 256p. 1972. text ed. 12.75 (ISBN 0-398-02367-0). C C Thomas.
Merriam-Webster Editorial Staff. Webster's Medical Office Handbook. 1979. 10.95 (ISBN 0-87779-035-3). Merriam.
Pitman Medical Dictation. 6.60 (ISBN 0-8224-0049-9). Pitman Learning.
Root, Kathleen B. & Byers, E. E. Medical Secretary: Terminology & Transcription. 3rd ed. 1967. 15.20 (ISBN 0-07-053586-8, G); student transcript 4.95 (ISBN 0-07-053589-2). McGraw.
--Medical Typing Practice. 2nd ed. 1967. 7.75 (ISBN 0-07-053585-X, G). McGraw.
Rowe, Leah. Medical Dictation with Foreign Accents. McFadden, S. Michele, ed. 1978. 120.00 (ISBN 0-89262-017-X). Career Pub.
Rudman, Jack. Medical Stenographer. (Career Examination Ser.: C-1368). (Cloth bdg. avail. on request). text ed. 8.00 (ISBN 0-8373-1368-6). Natl Learning.
Siegfried, W. Typing Medical Forms. 1969. 8.12 (ISBN 0-07-057342-5, G). McGraw.
Szulec, Jeannette & Szulec, Z. Syllabus for the Surgeon's Secretary. 3rd ed. (Illus.). 1980. 38.00 (ISBN 0-913092-03-7). Medical Arts.

MEDICAL SERVICE, PREPAID

see Medical Care, Prepaid

MEDICAL SERVICES

see Medical Care

MEDICAL SOCIAL WORK

see also Charities, Medical; Psychiatric Social Work; Voluntary Health Agencies

American Hospital Association. Manual on Hospital Chaplaincy. 96p. 1970. pap. 8.75 (ISBN 0-87258-060-1, 1515). Am Hospital.
Arco Editorial Board. Hospital Care Investigator Trainee: Social Case Worker 1. LC 67-23369. (Orig.). 1968. lib. bdg. 7.50 (ISBN 0-668-01832-1); pap. 5.00 (ISBN 0-668-01674-4). Arco.
Bartlett, Harriett M. Common Base of Social Work Practice. LC 72-116893. 224p. (Orig.). 1970. pap. 6.95x (ISBN 0-87101-054-2, CBO-054-C). Natl Assn Soc Wkrs.
Bracht, Neil F. Social Work in Health Care: A Guide to Professional Practice. LC 78-7881. 1978. 22.95 (ISBN 0-917724-04-6); pap. 13.95 (ISBN 0-917724-05-4). Haworth Pr.
Brown, Robert G., et al. Experience with a Patient Planning Organization: An Interim Analysis. 34p. 1961. pap. text ed. 1.50 (ISBN 0-89143-054-7). U NC Inst Res Soc Sci.
Browne, J. A. & Kirlin, Betty A. Rehabilitation Services & the Social Work Role: Challenge for Change. (Rehabilitation Medicine Library Ser.). 336p. 1981. lib. bdg. 23.50 (ISBN 0-683-01091-3). Williams & Wilkins.
Buxton, Shirley. Manual for the Department of Social Service. LC 77-73334. 1977. pap. 4.50 (ISBN 0-87125-037-3). Cath Health.
Cabot, Richard C. Social Service & the Art of Healing. LC 73-84257. (NASW Classics Ser). 192p. 1973. pap. text ed. 5.00 (ISBN 0-87101-062-3, CBC-062-I). Natl Assn Soc Wkrs.
--Social Work: Essays on the Meeting-Ground of Doctor & Social Worker. LC 76-180561. (Medicine & Society in America Ser). 224p. 1972. Repr. of 1919 ed. 12.00 (ISBN 0-405-03940-9). Arno.
Development of Professional Standards Review for Hospital Social Work. LC 77-334. 60p. (Orig.). 1976. pap. 8.75 (ISBN 0-87258-206-X, 1560). Am Hospital.
Estes, Richard J. Social Work in Health Care. (Allied Health Professions Monograph). 1981. 15.00 (ISBN 0-87527-266-5). Green.
Ettling, John. The Germ of Laziness: Rockefeller Philanthropy & Public Health in the New South. LC 81-4174. (Illus.). 272p. 1981. text ed. 18.50x (ISBN 0-674-34990-3). Harvard U Pr.
Fromstein, Roberta H. & Curtis, Jacqueline. Psychosocial Intervention for Hospital Discharge Planning. (Illus.). 352p. 1981. 21.75 (ISBN 0-398-04538-0). C C Thomas.
Goldstine, Dora, ed. Expanding Horizons in Medical Social Work. LC 54-11423. 1955. 9.50x (ISBN 0-226-30164-8). U of Chicago Pr.
--Readings in the Theory & Practice of Medical Social Work. LC 54-8906. (Midway Reprint Ser). 345p. 1974. pap. 12.50x (ISBN 0-226-30162-1). U of Chicago Pr.
Kerson, Toba S. Medical Social Work: The Pre-Professional Paradox. 320p. 1981. text ed. 19.50x (ISBN 0-8290-0237-5). Irvington.
--Social Work in Health Settings: Policy & Practice. 1981. text ed. 15.95x (ISBN 0-582-28221-7). Longman.
Orcutt, Ben A., et al, eds. Social Work & Thanatology. LC 79-22448. 300p. 1980. lib. bdg. 22.00 (ISBN 0-405-12621-2). Arno.
Rudman, Jack. Medical Social Work Coordinator. (Career Examination Ser.: C-2578). (Cloth bdg. avail. on request). pap. 12.00 (ISBN 0-8373-2578-1). Natl Learning.
--Medical Social Worker. (Career Examination Ser.: C-521). (Cloth bdg. avail. on request). pap. 10.00 (ISBN 0-8373-0521-7). Natl Learning.
--Senior Social Services Medical Assistance Specialist. (Career Examination Ser.: C-2432). (Cloth bdg. avail. on request). pap. 12.00 (ISBN 0-8373-2432-7). Natl Learning.
--Social Services Medical Assistance Specialist. (Career Examination Ser.: C-2431). (Cloth bdg. avail. on request). pap. 10.00 (ISBN 0-8373-2431-9). Natl Learning.
--Supervisor (Medical & Psychiatric Social Work) (Career Examination Ser.: C-1052). (Cloth bdg. avail. on request). pap. 12.00 (ISBN 0-8373-1052-0). Natl Learning.
Society for Hospital Social Work Directors of the American Hospital Association. Quality & Quantity Assurance for Social Workers in Health Care: A Training Manual. LC 80-26488. (Illus.). 96p. (Orig.). 1980. manual 27.50 (ISBN 0-87258-325-2, 2100). Am Hospital.
Stambaugh, Harriett, ed. Social Work on Pediatric Settings. (Social Work in Health Care Ser.: Vol. 1). 350p. 1981. text ed. 22.95 (ISBN 0-917724-29-1). Haworth Pr.
Thorman, George. Guide to Clinical Social Work. (Illus.). 180p. 1981. pap. 14.75 (ISBN 0-398-04372-8). C C Thomas.

MEDICAL SOCIOLOGY

see Social Medicine

MEDICAL SPECIALIZATION

see Medicine-Specialties and Specialists

MEDICAL STATISTICS

see also Diseases-Reporting
also subdivision Statistics, Medical under names of countries, cities, etc., e.g. United States-Statistics, Medical

Armitage, P. Sequential Medical Trials. 2nd ed. LC 75-2211. 194p. 1975. 28.95 (ISBN 0-470-03323-1). Halsted Pr.
--Statistical Methods in Medical Research. 509p. 1971. 36.95 (ISBN 0-471-03320-0). Halsted Pr.
Bahn, Anita K. Basic Medical Statistics. LC 72-6822. (Illus.). 320p. 1972. text ed. 23.00 (ISBN 0-8089-0782-4). Grune.
Bailey, Norman T. Mathematics, Statistics & Systems for Health. LC 77-1307. (Wiley Ser. in Probability & Mathematical Statistics: Applied Probability & Statistics). 222p. 1977. 33.25 (ISBN 0-471-99500-2, Pub. by Wiley-Interscience). Wiley.
Brown, Byron W., Jr. & Hollander, Myles. Statistics: A Biomedical Introduction. LC 77-396. (Probability & Mathematical Statistics Ser). 1977. 26.00 (ISBN 0-471-11240-2, Pub. by Wiley-Interscience). Wiley.
Bruch, Hans A. & Caviers, Luis M. Vital Statistics Systems in Five Developing Countries. Shipp, Audrey, ed. (Ser. 2: No. 79). 1979. pap. text ed. 1.95 (ISBN 0-8406-0169-7). Natl Ctr Health Stats.
Burdette, Walter J. & Gehan, Edmund A. Planning & Analysis of Clinical Studies. (Illus.). 116p. 1970. 15.25 (ISBN 0-398-00257-6). C C Thomas.
Castle. Statistics in Operation 1E. 1979. pap. text ed. 8.25 (ISBN 0-443-01951-7). Churchill.
Cohen, Bernice H., et al. Selected Genetic Markers of Blood & Secretions for Youth 12-17 Years of Age, United States. (Ser. 11: No. 168). 1979. pap. text ed. 1.75 (ISBN 0-8406-0171-9). Natl Ctr Health Stats.
Colton, Theodore. Statistics in Medicine. LC 73-1413. 400p. 1974. pap. 14.95 (ISBN 0-316-15250-1). Little.
Croxton, Frederick E. Elementary Statistics: With Applications in Medicine & the Biological Sciences. (Illus.). 1953. pap. 4.50 (ISBN 0-486-60506-X). Dover.
Danchik, Kathleen M. Physician Visits, Volume & Interval Since Last Visit, U.S. 1971. LC 72-20716. (Data from the Health Interview Survey Ser. 10: No. 97). 55p. 1975. pap. text ed. 1.15 (ISBN 0-8406-0032-1). Natl Ctr Health Stats.
Danchik, Kathleen M. & Schoenborn, Charlotte A. Highlights: National Survey of Personal Health Practices & Consequences, United States, 1979. Olmsted, Mary, ed. (Ser. 10: No. 137). 50p. 1981. pap. 1.75 (ISBN 0-8406-0218-9). Natl Ctr Health Stats.
Dixon, W. J., ed. BMD: Biomedical Computer Programs. new ed. Orig. Title: BMD & BMD: X-Series Supplement (2 Books) (Orig.). 1973. pap. 14.95x (ISBN 0-520-02426-5). U of Cal Pr.
Duncan, Robert C., et al. Introductory Biostatistics for the Health Sciences. LC 76-44291. 1977. 9.95 (ISBN 0-471-01604-7, Pub. by Wiley Medical). Wiley.
Dundon, Mary L. The Cooperative Health Statistics System: Its Mission & Program. Cox, Klaudia, ed. (Ser. 4: No. 19). 1977. pap. text ed. 1.75 (ISBN 0-8406-0092-5). Natl Ctr Health Stats.
Feinstein, Alvan R. Clinical Biostatistics. LC 77-3703. (Illus.). 1977. text ed. 22.50 (ISBN 0-8016-1563-1). Mosby.
Fitzpatrick Lectures for the Years 1941 & 1943, Royal College of Physicians of London in February 1943 & Greenwood, Major. Medical Statistics from Graunt to Farr. Rosenkrantz, Barbara G., ed. LC 76-25665. (Public Health in America Ser.). (Illus.). 1977. Repr. of 1948 ed. lib. bdg. 10.00x (ISBN 0-405-09820-0). Arno.
Glantz, Stanton A. Primer of Biostatistics. (Illus.). 384p. 1981. pap. text ed. 9.95 (ISBN 0-07-023370-5, HP). McGraw.

Gleeson, Geraldine A. Health Interview Survey Procedure 1957-1974. Stevenson, Taloria, ed. LC 74-32057. (Programs & Collected Procedures Ser. 2: No. 11). 55p. 1975. pap. text ed. 1.15 (ISBN 0-8406-0037-2). Natl Ctr Health Stats.

Gross, Alan J. & Clark, Virginia A. Survival Distributions: Reliability Applications in the Biomedical Sciences. LC 75-6806. (Probability & Mathematical Statistics Ser). 331p. 1975. 36.00x (ISBN 0-471-32817-0, Pub. by Wiley-Interscience). Wiley.

Hoffman, Elizabeth. The Sources of Mortality Changes in Italy Since Unification. Bruchey, Stuart, ed. LC 80-2811. (Dissertations in European Economic History II). (Illus.). 1981. lib. bdg. 25.00x (ISBN 0-405-13995-0). Arno.

Jack, Susan S. & Ries, Peter W. Current Estimates from the Health Interview Survey: United States-1979. Cox, Klaudia, ed. (Ser. 10: No. 136). 55p. 1981. pap. text ed. 1.75 (ISBN 0-8406-0219-7). Natl Ctr Health Stats.

Kilpatrick, S. Statistical Principles in Health Care Information. 2nd ed. 1977. 16.95 (ISBN 0-8391-1107-X). Univ Park.

Knapp, Rebecca G. Basic Statistics for Nurses. LC 77-26950. 308p. 1978. pap. 11.95 (ISBN 0-471-03545-9, Wiley Medical). Wiley.

Kozak, Lola J. The Status of Hospital Discharge Data in Six Countries. Olmstead, Mary, ed. (Ser. 2: No. 80). 50p. 1980. pap. 1.75 (ISBN 0-8406-0186-7). Natl Ctr Health Stats.

Lancaster, H. O. An Introduction to Medical Statistics. LC 73-11323. (Ser. in Probability & Mathematical Statistics). 305p. 1974. 36.00 (ISBN 0-471-51250-8, Pub. by Wiley-Interscience). Wiley.

Lee, Elisa T. Statistical Methods for Survival Data Analysis. LC 80-24720. 557p. 1980. text ed. 28.95 solutions manual (ISBN 0-534-97987-4). Lifetime Learn.

Lowe, Charles R. & Lwanga, S. K., eds. Health Statistics: A Manual for Teachers of Medical Students. (Illus.). 1978. pap. text ed. 11.95x (ISBN 0-19-261134-8). Oxford U Pr.

Mainland, Donald. Mainland's Elementary Medical Statistics. Miller, M. Clinton, 3rd, ed. LC 78-26409. (Biometry Imprint Ser.: Vol. 3). 1978. 27.75 (ISBN 0-8357-0349-5, IS-00066, Biometry Imprint Series Press). Univ Microfilms.

--Mainland's Statistical Ward Rounds. Miller, M. Clinton, III, ed. LC 79-10434. (Biometry Imprint Ser.: Vol. 5). 1979. 19.75 (ISBN 0-8357-0403-3, IS-00078). Univ Microfilms.

Maxwell, A. E. Basic Statistics for Medical & Social Science Students. 126p. 1978. pap. text ed. 5.95x (ISBN 0-412-15580-X, Pub. by Chapman & Hall England). Methuen Inc.

Miller, M. Clinton, III, ed. Mainland's Notes from a Laboratory of Medical Statistics, 2 vols. LC 79-22619. (Biometry Imprint Ser.: Vol. 6). 1064p. 1979. Set. 68.00 (ISBN 0-8357-0477-7, IS-00098, Pub. by Biometry Imprint); Vol. 1. (ISBN 0-8357-0483-1); Vol. 2. (ISBN 0-8357-0484-X). Univ Microfilms.

National Center for Health Statistics. Ambulatory Medical Care Records: Uniform Basic Data Set-Final Report. LC 74-6288. (Documents & Committee Reports Ser. 4: No. 16). 54p. 1974. pap. text ed. 1.50 (ISBN 0-8406-0016-X). Natl Ctr Health Stats.

--Hospitals: A County & Metropolitan Area Data Book, 1972. LC 73-20403. 268p. 1975. pap. 3.00 (ISBN 0-8406-0035-6). Natl Ctr Health Stats.

Osborn, John F. Statistical Exercises in Medical Research. LC 79-12451. 1979. 18.95x (ISBN 0-470-26744-5). Halsted Pr.

Pearch, Nancy D. Data Systems of the National Center for Health Statistics. Olmstead, Mary, ed. (Series 1: No. 16). 50p. 1981. pap. text ed. 1.75 (ISBN 0-8406-0232-4). Natl Ctr Health Stats.

Reader's Digest Special. Medical Miracles. 240p. (Orig.). 1981. pap. 2.75 (ISBN 0-686-73596-X). Berkley Pub.

Reichertz, P. L. & Goos, G., eds. Informatics & Medicine. LC 77-660. (Medizinische Informatik und Statistik: Vol. 3). 1977. pap. 40.80 (ISBN 0-387-08120-8). Springer-Verlag.

Rosenkrantz, Barbara G., ed. Selections from Public Health in Reports and Papers: American Public Health Association (1873-1883) an original anthology ed. LC 76-4065. (Public Health in America Ser.). 1977. Repr. lib. bdg. 23.00x (ISBN 0-405-09838-3). Arno.

Rutherford, Margaret. The Model State Health Statistics Act: A Model State Law for the Collection, Sharing, & Confidentiality of Health Statistics. (Ser. 4: No. 21). 1979. pap. 1.75 (ISBN 0-8406-0168-9). Natl Ctr Health Stats.

Sanchez, Marcus & Moien, Mary. Utilization of Short-Stay Hospitals by Persons Discharged with Alcohol-Related Diagnoses: United States, 1976. Cox, Klaudia, ed. (Ser. 13: No. 47). 50p. 1980. pap. text ed. 1.75 (ISBN 0-8406-0187-5). Natl Ctr Health Stats.

Stevenson, Taloria, ed. Statistics Needed to Ascertain the Effects of the Environment on Health. (Series 4: No. 20). 1977. pap. 1.95 (ISBN 0-8406-0093-3). Natl Ctr Health Stats.

Tanur, J. M., et al, eds. Statistics: A Guide to Biological & Health Sciences. 1977. pap. text ed. 5.95x (ISBN 0-8162-8564-0). Holden-Day.

Von Fraunhofer, J. A. & Murray, J. J. Statistics in Medical, Dental & Biological Studies. 120p. 1981. 25.00x (ISBN 0-905402-00-6, Pub. by Tri-Med England). State Mutual Bk.

Weise, Frieda O., ed. Health Statistics: A Guide to Information Sources. LC 80-12039. (Health Affairs Information Guide Ser.: Vol. 4). 1980. 36.00 (ISBN 0-8103-1412-6). Gale.

WHO Expert Committee on Health Statistics. Geneva, 1970, 14th. Statistical Indicators for the Planning & Evaluation of Public Health Programmes: Report. (Also avail. in Spanish). 1971. pap. 2.00 (ISBN 92-4-120472-9). World Health.

Wilder, Charles S. Acute Conditions, Incidence & Associated Disability, U. S., July 1972 - June 1973. Shipp, Audrey M., ed. LC 74-26702. (Data from the Health Interview Survey Ser. 10: No. 98). 63p. 1975. pap. 1.25 (ISBN 0-8406-0033-X). Natl Ctr Health Stats.

Wilder, Mary H. Differentials in Health Characteristics by Marital Status, U. S. 1971-72. Stevenson, Taloria, ed. LC 75-34249. (Ser. 10: No. 104). 52p. 1976. pap. text ed. 1.50 (ISBN 0-8406-0054-2). Natl Ctr Health Stats.

World Health Statistics Annual. Incl. Vol. 1. 1968. 1971. pap. 29.60 (ISBN 92-4-067681-3); Vols. 2 & 3. 1969, 2 vols. 1972-73. Vol. 2. pap. 9.60 (ISBN 92-4-067692-9); Vol. 3. pap. 12.00 (ISBN 92-4-067693-7); Vols. 2 & 3. 1970, 2 vols. 1973-74. Vol. 2. pap. 9.60 (ISBN 92-4-067702-X); Vol. 3. pap. 12.00 (ISBN 92-4-067703-8); Vols. 1-3. 1971, 3 vols. 1975. Vol. 1. pap. 40.00 (ISBN 92-4-067711-9); Vol. 2. pap. 22.40 (ISBN 92-4-067712-7); Vol. 3. pap. 12.80 (ISBN 0-686-16945-X); Vols. 1-3. 1972, 3 vols. 1975-76. Vol. 1. pap. 51.20 (ISBN 92-4-067721-6); Vol. 2. pap. 12.80 (ISBN 92-4-067722-4); Vol. 3. pap. 12.80 (ISBN 92-4-067723-2). World Health.

MEDICAL STUDENTS

Becker, Howard S., et al. Boys in White: Student Culture in Medical School. Repr. of 1961 ed. lib. bdg. 34.50x (ISBN 0-8290-0371-1). Irvington.

Becker, Howard S., et al, eds. Boys in White: Student Culture in Medical School. rev. ed. LC 76-26951. 456p. 1976. pap. text ed. 7.95 (ISBN 0-87855-622-2). Transaction Bks.

Bloom, Samuel W. Power & Dissent in the Medical School. LC 73-8356. 1973. pap. text ed. 4.95 (ISBN 0-02-904250-X). Free Pr.

Chen, Ronald. Foreign Medical Graduates in Psychiatry: Issues & Problems. LC 79-17189. 448p. 1980. 26.95 (ISBN 0-87705-485-1). Human Sci Pr.

Fredericks, Marcel A. & Mundy, Paul. Making It in Med School: Biography of a Medical Student. 144p. 1980. pap. 3.95 (ISBN 0-8294-0302-7). Loyola.

Funkenstein, Daniel H. Medical Students, Medical Schools & Society During Five Eras: Factors Affecting the Career Choices of Physicians, 1958-1976. LC 77-19063. 1978. 17.50 (ISBN 0-88410-704-3). Ballinger Pub.

Gibson, William C. Young Endeavour: Contributions to Science by Medical Students of the Past Four Centuries. (Illus.). 312p. 1958. ed. spiral bdg. 27.50photocopy (ISBN 0-398-00677-6). C C Thomas.

Hayward, Oliver S. & Thomson, Elizabeth, eds. The Journal of William Tully: Medical Student at Dartmouth, 1808-1809. (Illus.). 1977. 17.50 (ISBN 0-88202-175-3). N Watson.

Knight. Medical Student: Doctor in the Making. (Illus.). 1973. pap. 9.50 (ISBN 0-8385-6275-2). ACC.

Mamot, Patricio R. Foreign Medical Graduates in America. 196p. 1974. 12.75 (ISBN 0-398-02751-X). C C Thomas.

Thomas, Caroline Bedell, et al. An Atlas of Figure Drawings - III. Incl. Vol. 1. An Index of Rorschach Responses, Studies on the Pshchological Characteristics of Medical Students. (Illus.). 787p. 1964. o. p. 40.00x (ISBN 0-686-76931-7); Vol. 2. An Index of Responses to the Group Rorschach Test, Studies on the Psychological Characteristics of Medical Students. (Illus.). 548p. 1965. (Illus.). 922p. 1966. Vol. 3. 45.00x (ISBN 0-8018-0624-0). Johns Hopkins.

MEDICAL SUPPLIES

see also Medical Instruments and Apparatus

Keithwood Directory of Hospital & Surgical Supply Dealers. 302p. 1980. 45.00 (ISBN 0-686-27082-7). Keithwood.

Phillips, G. Briggs & Miller, William S., eds. Industrial Sterilization: International Symposium, Amsterdam, 1972. LC 72-97473. (Illus.). 420p. 1973. 19.75 (ISBN 0-8223-0299-3). Duke.

Probst, Calvin, ed. Hospital Purchasing Guide: Nieteen Eighty Two. 6th ed. (Annual Ser.). 1982. pap. text ed. 95.00 (ISBN 0-933916-06-X). IMS Comm.

Rudman, Jack. Medical Purchasing Specialist. (Career Examination Ser.: C-2448). (Cloth bdg. avail. on request). pap. 10.00 (ISBN 0-8373-2448-3). Natl Learning.

Smith, E. J., ed. Hospital Consumables: Reference for Medical Surgical Products. LC 80-14970. (Illus.). 702p. 1981. loose-leaf 192.00 (ISBN 0-87619-925-2). R J Brady.

--Hospital Consumables: Reference for Medical Surgical Products. (Illus.). 652p. 1980. text ed. 145.00 (ISBN 0-87619-715-2). R J Brady.

MEDICAL TECHNOLOGISTS

Alter, Aaron A., et al. Medical Technology Examination Review Book, Vol. 1. 4th ed. 1977. spiral bdg. 9.50 (ISBN 0-87488-451-9). Med Exam.

Atkinson, Betty J. The Medical Assistant: Clinical Practice. LC 76-5301. 1976. pap. 8.00 (ISBN 0-8273-0351-3); instructor's guide 1.60 (ISBN 0-8273-0352-1). Delmar.

Austrin, Miriam G., et al. Workbook for Medical Assistants. (Illus.). 198p. 1980. pap. text ed. 11.45 (ISBN 0-8016-0409-5). Mosby.

Bonewit, Kathy. Clinical Competencies for the Medical Assistant: A Workbook. 359p. 1981. 11.95 (ISBN 0-8036-0963-9). Davis Co.

--Clinical Procedures for Medical Assistants. 1979. text ed. 18.50 (ISBN 0-7216-1846-4). Saunders.

Boone, Patricia Z. Laboratory Procedures for the Medical Assistant. 1981. 15.00 (ISBN 0-8036-1003-3). Davis Co.

Bowers, Warner F. & Dimendberg, David C. Emergency Medical Technician Examination Review Book, Vol. 1. 1969. spiral bdg. 9.50 (ISBN 0-87488-465-9). Med Exam.

Challenor, Bernard, et al. Physician's Assistant Examination Review Book. 1975. pap. 12.50 (ISBN 0-87488-422-5). Med Exam.

Cooper, Marian & Bredow, Miriam. The Medical Assistant. 4th ed. (Illus.). 1978. text ed. 15.95 (ISBN 0-07-012751-4); instructor's manual 3.50 (ISBN 0-07-012753-0); wkbk. 7.95 (ISBN 0-07-012752-2). McGraw.

Cotton. Aid for Medical Assistants. (Medical Economics Books). 1975. 8.50 (ISBN 0-442-84031-4). Van Nos Reinhold.

Cotton, H. & Martin, N. Aid for the Medical Assistant. 1975. 9.95 (ISBN 0-87489-003-9). Med Economics.

Doyle, Jean M. & Dennis, Robert L. The Complete Handbook for Medical Secretaries & Assistants. 2nd ed. 1978. pap. text ed. 15.95 (ISBN 0-316-18082-3, Little Med Div). Little.

Dreizen, LaVerne & Audet, Thelma. Medical Assistant's Examination Review Book, Vol. 1. 2nd. ed. 1979. 9.50 (ISBN 0-87488-490-X). Med Exam.

Fordney, Marilyn T. & Follis, Joan J. The Administrative Medical Assistant. LC 81-2141. 450p. 1981. 13.95 (ISBN 0-471-06380-0, Pub. by Wiley Med). Wiley.

Frederick, Portia M. & Kinn, Mary E. The Medical Office Assistant: Administrative & Clinical. 5th ed. (Illus.). 707p. 1981. text ed. 22.50 (ISBN 0-7216-3863-5). Saunders.

--Medical Office Assistant: Administrative & Clinical. 4th ed. LC 73-89176. (Illus.). 735p. 1974. text ed. 17.95 (ISBN 0-7216-3862-7). Saunders.

Hall & Yenerich. Business Administration for the Medical Assistant. LC 74-8637. (Illus.). 1976. 8.95 (ISBN 0-940012-03-0). Colwell Co.

Hardy, C. & Martin, N. Your Roles As a Medical Assistant. 1974. 9.50 (ISBN 0-87489-044-6). Med Economics.

Hardy, Clyde & Martin, Nancy. Your Roles As a Medical Assistant. (Medical Economics Books). 1974. 8.50 (ISBN 0-442-84020-9). Van Nos Reinhold.

Lawton, M. Murray, et al. Lawton's & Foy's Textbook for Medical Assistants. 4th ed. LC 80-15524. (Illus.). 456p. 1980. text ed. 18.95 (ISBN 0-8016-2893-8). Mosby.

Lee, Leslie. The Lab Aide. LC 75-38567. (Illus.). 150p. 1976. pap. 9.45 (ISBN 0-8016-2912-8). Mosby.

Lindsey, Bonnie J. The Administrative Medical Assistant. 184p. 1979. pap. text ed. 10.95 (ISBN 0-87619-435-8). R J Brady.

--Clinical Medical Assistant. (Illus.). 169p. (Orig.). 1980. pap. text ed. 9.95 (ISBN 0-87619-714-4). R J Brady.

McMinn, A. & Russell, G. J. Training of Medical Laboratory Technicians: A Handbook for Tutors. (Offset Pub.: No. 21). (Also avail. in French). 1975. pap. 6.00 (ISBN 92-4-170021-1). World Health.

Mummah, Hazel & Smith, Marsella. The Geriatric Assistant. (Illus.). 320p. 1980. pap. text ed. 11.95 (ISBN 0-07-044015-8, HP). McGraw.

Perry, Henry B. & Breitner, Bina. Physician Assistants: Their Contribution to Health Care. 1981. 24.95 (ISBN 0-89885-066-5). Human Sci Pr.

Raphael, Stanley. Lynch's Medical Laboratory Technology: A Filmstrip Presentation. (Illus.). 1977. pap. text ed. 75.00 (ISBN 0-7216-9921-9). Saunders.

Ring, Alvin M. Laboratory Assistants Examination Review Book, Vol. 1. 3rd ed. 1979. spiral bdg. 9.50 (ISBN 0-87488-455-1). Med Exam.

Rudman, Jack. Cardio-Pulmonary Technician. (Career Examination Ser.: C-1159). (Cloth bdg. avail. on request). pap. 12.00 (ISBN 0-686-66496-5). Natl Learning.

--Clinical Laboratory Investigator. (Career Examination Ser.: C-2098). (Cloth bdg. avail. on request). 1976. pap. 8.00 (ISBN 0-8373-1196-9). Natl Learning.

--Medical Laboratory Technician. (Career Examination Ser.: C-2323). (Cloth bdg,. avail. on request). pap. 10.00 (ISBN 0-8373-2323-1). Natl Learning.

--Medical Technical Assistant. (Career Examination Ser.: C-492). (Cloth bdg. avail. on request). pap. 8.00 (ISBN 0-8373-0492-X). Natl Learning.

--Medical Technician. (Career Examination Ser.: C-512). (Cloth bdg. avail. on request). pap. 10.00 (ISBN 0-8373-0512-8). Natl Learning.

--Medical Technician Instructor. (Career Examination Ser.: C-1370). (Cloth bdg. avail. on request). pap. 12.00 (ISBN 0-8373-1370-8). Natl Learning.

--Medical Technician Trainee. (Career Examination Ser.: C-1371). (Cloth bdg. avail. on request). pap. 10.00 (ISBN 0-8373-1371-6). Natl Learning.

--Medical Technologist. (Career Examination Ser.: C-493). (Cloth bdg. avail. on request). pap. 12.00 (ISBN 0-8373-0493-8). Natl Learning.

--Physician's Assistant. (Career Examination Ser.: C-2557). (Cloth bdg. avail. on request). pap. 10.00 (ISBN 0-8373-2557-9). Natl Learning.

--Senior Medical Laboratory Technician. (Career Examination Ser.: C-2496). (Cloth bdg. avail. on request). pap. 10.00 (ISBN 0-8373-2496-3). Natl Learning.

Schapiro, Melvin & Kuritsky, Joel. The Gastroenterology Assistant: A Laboratory Manual. (Illus.). 112p. 1972. photocopy ed. spiral 11.75 (ISBN 0-398-02618-1). C C Thomas.

Schwarzrock, Shirley P. & Ward, Donovan F. Effective Medical Assisting. 2nd ed. 700p. 1976. text ed. write for info. (ISBN 0-697-05661-9); wkbk. wire coil avail. (ISBN 0-697-05662-7); instrs.' manual wire coil avail. (ISBN 0-697-05663-5). Wm C Brown.

Semrad, Alice. Comprehensive Review for Medical Technologists. 2nd ed. LC 78-31823. 1979. pap. text ed. 13.95 (ISBN 0-8016-4487-9). Mosby.

White, William D. Public Health & Private Gain: The Economics of Licensing Clinical Laboratory Personnel. LC 78-55998. (Illus.). 1979. text ed. 14.95 (ISBN 0-88425-014-8). Maaroufa Pr.

MEDICAL TECHNOLOGY

see also Medicine, Clinical

Alba. Alba's Medical Technology Board Examination Review, Vol. I. 9th ed. (Illus.). 1980. pap. text ed. 20.00 (ISBN 0-910224-05-6). Berkeley Sci.

--Alba's Medical Technology Board Examination Review, Vol. II. 4th ed. LC 72-172446. (Illus.). 1978. pap. text ed. 17.00 (ISBN 0-910224-02-1). Berkeley Sci.

American Hospital Association. Technology Evaluation & Acquisition Methods (TEAM) for Hospitals. LC 79-21859. (Illus.). 212p. 1979. 200.00 (ISBN 0-87258-293-0, 1288). Am Hospital.

Anderson, Shauna C. Introductory Laboratory Exercises for Medical Technologists. LC 77-8819. (Illus.). 1978. pap. text ed. 8.50 (ISBN 0-8016-0173-8). Mosby.

Assembly of Engineering, Institute of Medicine, National Research Council. Medical Technology & the Health Care System: A Study of the Diffusion of Equipment-Embodied Technology. 1979. pap. text ed. 10.75 (ISBN 0-309-02865-5). Natl Acad Pr.

Banta, David. Toward Rational Technology in Medicine: Considerations for Health Policy. (Health Care & Society Ser.: No. 5). 1981. text ed. 28.50 (ISBN 0-8261-3200-6); pap. text ed. cacelled (ISBN 0-8261-3201-4). Springer Pub.

Bowers, Warner F & Dimendberg, David C. Emergency Medical Technician Examination Review, Vol. 2. 1972. spiral bdg. 9.50 (ISBN 0-87488-466-7). Med Exam.

Brown, J. H. The Health Care Dilemma. LC 78-3891. 183p. 1978. 19.95 (ISBN 0-87705-360-X). Human Sci Pr.

Coltey, Roger W. Survey of Medical Technology. LC 77-2155. (Illus.). 1978. pap. text ed. 13.95 (ISBN 0-8016-1020-6). Mosby.

Critser, James R., Jr. Cardiac Technology. (Ser. 10 CT-80). 1981. 75.00 (ISBN 0-914428-81-0). Lexington Data.
--Medical Technology: Advanced Medical Apparatus-Systems. (Ser 10AMA-77). 1978. 300.00 (ISBN 0-914428-46-2). Lexington Data.
Davis, Audrey B. Medicine & Its Technology: An Introduction to the History of Medical Instrumentation. LC 80-25202. (Contributions in Medical History: No. 7). (Illus.). 224p. 1981. lib. bdg. 37.50 (ISBN 0-313-22807-8, DMT/). Greenwood.
Doucet, Lorraine. Medical Technology Review. (Illus.). 446p. 1981. pap. text ed. 11.50 (ISBN 0-397-50459-4, JBL-Med-Nursing). Har-Row.
Doucet, Lorraine D. & Packard, Albert E. Medical Technology Examination Review. LC 79-12071. 1979. pap. text ed. 11.75x (ISBN 0-397-52088-3, JBL-Med-Nursing). Har-Row.
Driggs. Problem-Directed & Medical Information Systems. 1979. 21.00 (ISBN 0-8151-2855-X). Year Bk Med.
Driver, Robienetta & Feeley, Mary A. The Revolution in Medical Technology Education. 68p. 1974. text ed. 10.25 (ISBN 0-398-02960-1). C C Thomas.
Educational Research Council of America. Medical Technologist. rev. ed. Kunze, Linda J. & Marchak, John P., eds. (Real People at Work Ser: E). (Illus.). 1976. pap. text ed. 2.25 (ISBN 0-89247-035-6). Changing Times.
Egdahl, Richard H. & Gertman, Paul M. Technology & the Quality of Health Care. LC 78-7307. (Illus.). 336p. 1978. text ed. 31.00 (ISBN 0-89443-025-4). Aspen Systems.
Ellison, David L. The Bio-Medical Fix: Human Dimensions of Bio-Medical Technologies. LC 77-91104. 1978. lib. bdg. 15.95x (ISBN 0-313-20038-6, ELB/). Greenwood.
Emlet, Harry E., ed. Challenges & Prospects for Advanced Medical Systems. (Illus.). 1978. 26.50 (ISBN 0-8151-3117-8, Pub. by Symposia Special). Year Bk Med.
Erlich, et al. Business Administration for the Medical Assistant. 2nd ed. LC 81-67045. (Illus.). 1981. 8.95 (ISBN 0-940012-01-4). Colwell Co.
French, Ruth. Guide to Diagnostic Procedures. 1980. text ed. 11.95 (ISBN 0-07-022146-4); pap. text ed. 8.95 (ISBN 0-07-022147-2). McGraw.
Goldman, J., ed. Health Care Technology Evaluation. (Lecture Notes in Medical Informatics: Vol. 6). 1980. pap. 13.10 (ISBN 0-387-09561-6). Springer-Verlag.
Gordon, Gerald & Fisher, G. Lawrence, eds. The Diffusion of Medical Technology: Policy & Research Planning Perspectives. LC 75-17638. 176p. 1975. text ed. 16.50 (ISBN 0-88410-129-0). Ballinger Pub.
Gordon, Theodore J. Life-Extending Technologies: A Technology Assessment. 1980. 33.00 (ISBN 0-08-023132-2). Pergamon.
Hahnefeld, I. W. Systematisierung von Infusionsloesungen und Grundlagen der Infusionstherapie. (Beitraege Zu Infusionstherapie und Klinische Ernaehrung: Band 5). (Illus.). 112p. 1980. pap. 15.00 (ISBN 3-8055-1395-X). S Karger.
Hayward, Mary & Clark, Connie. Medical Science for Medical Assistants. 1982. text ed. 16.95 (ISBN 0-686-75040-3). Macmillan.
Hinman. Advanced Medical Systems: An Assessment of the Contributions. 1979. 23.75 (ISBN 0-8151-4461-X). Year Bk Med.
Hossaini, Ali A., et al. Medical Technology Examination Review. LC 78-1743. (Arco Medical Review Ser.). 1978. pap. text ed. 10.00 (ISBN 0-668-04365-2). Arco.
McNeil, Barbara J. & Cravalho, Ernest G. Critical Issues in Medical Technology. 200p. 1981. 19.95 (ISBN 0-86569-070-7). Auburn Hse.
Medical Economics Company. Medical-Surgical Tips-Techniques. (Illus.). 1975. pap. 12.50 (ISBN 0-87489-089-6). Med Economics.
Nassif, Janet Z. Health Profession Careers in Medicine's New Technology. 2nd ed. LC 78-11386. Orig. Title: Medicine's New Technology: A Career Guide. 1979. lib. bdg. 9.95 (ISBN 0-668-04443-8); pap. write for info. Arco.
Nicholson, J. P., ed. Scientific Aids in Hospital Diagnosis. 288p. 1976. 35.00 (ISBN 0-306-30938-6, Plenum Pr). Plenum Pub.
Paul, Grace. Your Future in Medical Technology. (Careers in Depth Ser.). (Illus.). (gr. 7 up). 1979. PLB 5.97 (ISBN 0-8239-0481-4). Rosen Pr.
Reynolds, Moira D. Aim for a Job in the Medical Laboratory. LC 70-183733. (Aim High Vocational Guidance Ser.). (Illus.). 160p. (gr. 7 up). 1972. PLB 5.97 (ISBN 0-8239-0261-7). Rosen Pr.
Roald, Albert & Harry, Hahnewald, eds. Dictionary of Medical Technology: English, German, Spanish, French, Russian, Polish, Hungarian, Czechoslovakian, Technik-Woerterbuch. 1978. 45.00x (ISBN 0-8002-0410-7). Intl Pubns Serv.
Russell, Louise. Technology in Hospitals: Medical Advances & Their Diffusion. (Studies in Social Economics). 1979. 11.95 (ISBN 0-8157-7630-6); pap. 4.95 (ISBN 0-8157-7629-2). Brookings.
Russell, Louise B. & Burke, Carol S. Technological Diffusion in the Hospital Sector. LC 75-37308. 240p. 1976. 8.00 (ISBN 0-89068-007-8). Natl Planning.
Spiegel, Allen, et al, eds. Medical Technology, Health Care & the Consumer. LC 79-25539. 352p. 1980. 29.95x (ISBN 0-87705-498-3). Human Sci Pr.
Stocking, Barbara & Morrison, Stuart L. The Image & the Reality: A Case Study of the Impact of Medical Technology. (Nuffield Publications Ser.). (Illus.). 1978. pap. text ed. 11.50x (ISBN 0-19-721220-4). Oxford U Pr.
Tischer, Robert G., et al. Problem Solving in Medical Technology & Microbiology. LC 79-11337. (Illus.). 1979. pap. text ed. 25.00 (ISBN 0-89189-068-8, 45-7-010-00). Am Soc Clinical.
Wagner, G., et al, eds. Technology & Health: Man & World Proceedings. (Lecture Notes in Medical Informatics Ser.: Vol. 7). 243p. 1981. pap. 20.70 (ISBN 0-387-10230-2). Springer Verlag.
Wasley, G. D., ed. Clinical Laboratory Techniques. 1973. text ed. 13.95 (ISBN 0-02-859690-0). Macmillan.
Widmann, Frances K. Clinical Interpretation of Laboratory Tests. 8th ed. LC 78-21975. (Illus.). 1979. pap. text ed. 12.95 (ISBN 0-8036-9322-2). Davis Co.
Williams, B., ed. Computer Aids to Clinical Decisions, Vol. II. 224p. 1981. 59.95 (ISBN 0-8493-5576-1). CRC Pr.
Williams, Ben T., ed. Computer Aids to Clinical Decisions. 1981. Vol. I, 192pgs. 54.95 (ISBN 0-8493-5575-3); Vol. II, 224pgs. 54.95 (ISBN 0-8493-5576-1). CRC Pr.
Williams, M. Ruth & Lindberg, David S. An Introduction to the Profession of Medical Technology. 3rd ed. LC 79-672. (Illus.). 128p. 1979. pap. 7.00 (ISBN 0-8121-0667-9). Lea & Febiger.

MEDICAL TELEVISION
see Television in Medicine

MEDICAL THERMOGRAPHY

Atsumi, Kazuhiko, ed. Medical Thermography. 396p. 1973. 37.00x (ISBN 0-86008-076-5, Pub. by U of Tokyo Pr). Intl Schol Bk Serv.
Benziger, Theodore H., ed. Temperature, 2 pts. Incl. Pt. 1. Arts & Concept. 50.00 (ISBN 0-12-786141-6); Pt. 2. Thermal Homeostasis. 55.00 (ISBN 0-12-786142-4). (Benchmark Papers in Human Physiology: Vols. 9 & 10). 1977. Acad Pr.

MEDICAL TOPOGRAPHY
see Medical Geography

MEDICAL ULTRASONICS
see Ultrasonics in Medicine

MEDICAL VIROLOGY
see Virus Diseases

MEDICAL WRITING

Berger, Karen & Fields, Willa. Pocket Guide to Health Assessment. (Illus.). 1980. pap. text ed. 11.95 (ISBN 0-8359-5582-6). Reston.
Bradbury, Peggy F. Transcriber's Guide to Medical Terminology. 1973. spiral bdg. 7.00 (ISBN 0-87488-972-3). Med Exam.
Calnan, James & Barabas, Andras. Writing Medical Papers. 1973. pap. 10.00x (ISBN 0-433-05005-5). Intl Ideas.
Davis, P. Medical Dictation & Transcription. 2nd ed. LC 80-27720. 468p. 1981. pap. 12.95 (ISBN 0-471-06023-2, Pub. by Wiley Med). Wiley.
Davis, Phyllis & Hershelman, N. L. Medical Shorthand. 2nd ed. LC 80-29003. 323p. 1981. pap. 12.95 (ISBN 0-471-06024-0). Wiley.
Diehl, Marcy O. & Fordney, Marilyn T. Medical Transcribing: Techniques & Procedures. LC 78-52727. (Illus.). 1979. pap. text ed. 18.95 (ISBN 0-7216-3079-0). Saunders.
Dirckx, John H. Dx & Rx: A Physician's Guide to Medical Writing. (Medical Publications). 1977. lib. bdg. 12.95 (ISBN 0-8161-2100-1). G K Hall.
Fishbein, Morris. Medical Writing: The Technic & the Art. 4th ed. (Illus.). 216p. 1978. 13.75 (ISBN 0-398-02279-8). C C Thomas.
Huber, Jack T. Report Writing in Psychology & Psychiatry. (Orig.). 1961. pap. text ed. 10.95 scp (ISBN 0-06-042971-2, HarpC). Har-Row.
The Landmark Series of Medical & Scientific Articles, 26 bks. (Landmark Ser.). 1978. Set. 520.00x (ISBN 0-685-51731-4). Irvington.
Lock, S. Thorne's Better Medical Writing. 2nd ed. 1977. 13.95 (ISBN 0-471-03062-7, Pub. by Wiley-Medical). Wiley.
Lynch, Barbara S. & Chapman, Charles F. Writing for Communication in Science & Medicine, or Out of Your Mind with Comprehensive Assurance. 336p. 1980. text ed. 18.95 (ISBN 0-442-24959-4). Van Nos Reinhold.
Methold, Kenneth & Methold, Chuntana. Practice in Medical English. (English As a Second Language Bk.). 136p. 1975. pap. text ed. 4.75x (ISBN 0-582-55057-2). Longman.
Moser, Robert H. & Di Cyan, Erwin. Adventures in Medical Writing. (American Lecture Medical Writing & Communication Ser.). 76p. 1970. 7.75 (ISBN 0-398-01358-6). C C Thomas.
Nature Has a Remedy. (Illus., Orig.). 1979. pap. 9.95 (ISBN 0-913300-19-5). Unity Pr.
O'Connor, Andrea. Writing for Nursing Publications. LC 76-14600. 1976. pap. text ed. 6.50x (ISBN 0-913590-36-3). C B Slack.
Pearce, G. H. The Medical Report & Testimony. 104p. 1980. 35.00x (ISBN 0-686-69978-5, Pub. by Beaconsfield England). State Mutual Bk.
Pottenger Portfolio: Fifty-Five Reprints of Medical Papers of Dr. Francis M. Pottenger, Jr. 40.00 (ISBN 0-916764-03-6). Price-Pottenger.
Price Portfolio: Forty-Six Reprints of Medical Papers of Dr. Weston A. Price. 1978. 53.00 (ISBN 0-916764-04-4). Price-Pottenger.
Robinson, Alice M. & Notter, Lucille. Clinical Writing for Health Professionals. (Illus.). 160p. (Orig.). 1981. pap. 7.95 (ISBN 0-87619-893-0). R J Brady.
Smither, Effie B. Gregg Medical Shorthand Manual & Dictionary. 1953. 10.60 (ISBN 0-07-058933-X, G). McGraw.
Sternberg, Robert. Writing the Psychology Paper. LC 77-9250. 1977. pap. text ed. 3.95 (ISBN 0-8120-0772-7). Barron.
Thorne, Charles. Better Medical Writing. 180p. 1971. pap. 19.75 (ISBN 0-8089-0679-8). Grune.

MEDICARE
see Insurance, Health

MEDICATION, ANTISEPTIC
see Antiseptic Medication

MEDICATION, ORAL
see Oral Medication

MEDICI, CATHERINE DE
see Catherine De Medici, Consort of Henry 2nd, King of France, 1519-1589

MEDICI, COSIMO DE, 1389-1464

Vernon, K. Dorothea. Cosimo De' Medici. LC 72-112800. 1970. Repr. of 1899 ed. 10.75 (ISBN 0-8046-1066-5). Kennikat.

MEDICI, LORENZO DE, IL MAGNIFICO, 1449-1492

Carpenter, Edith. Lorenzo DeMedici: An Historical Portrait. 1978. Repr. of 1893 ed. lib. bdg. 22.50 (ISBN 0-8495-0760-X). Arden Lib.
Lee, Charles L. Lorenzo De' Medici & the Renaissance. LC 69-18118. (Horizon Caravel Bks.). 154p. (YA) (gr. 7 up). 1969. PLB 12.89 (ISBN 0-06-024173-X, HarpJ). Har-Row.
Lipari, Angelo. Dolce Stil Novo According to Lorenzo De'Medici. LC 72-1732. (Yale Romanic Studies: No. 12). Repr. of 1936 ed. 26.75 (ISBN 0-404-53212-8). AMS Pr.
Mee, Charles L., Jr. & Walker, John. Lorenzo De'Medici & the Renaissance. (Horizon Caravel Bks). (Illus.). 153p. (gr. 6 up). 1969. 9.95 (ISBN 0-8281-0000-4, J036-0, Dist. by Har-Row); PLB 12.89 (ISBN 0-06-024173-X, Dist. by Har-Row). Am Heritage.
Sturm, Sara. Lorenzo de' Medici. (World Authors Ser.: Italy: No. 288). 1974. lib. bdg. 12.50 (ISBN 0-8057-2609-8). Twayne.

MEDICI, MARIE DE
see Marie De Medicis, Consort of Henry 4th, King of France, 1573-1642

MEDICI, HOUSE OF

Acton, Harold. The Last Medici. rev. ed. (Illus.). 416p. 1980. Repr. of 1958 ed. 22.50 (ISBN 0-500-25074-X). Thames Hudson.
--The Pazzi Conspiracy: The Plot Against the Medici. 1979. 14.95 (ISBN 0-500-25064-2). Thames Hudson.
Baldini, Baccio. Discorso Sopra la Mascherata Della Genealogia Delg'Iddei, Repr. Of 1565 Ed. Bd. with Discorso Sopra Li Dei De'Gentili. Zucchi, Jacopo. Repr. of 1602 ed. LC 75-27852. (Renaissance & the Gods Ser.: Vol. 10). (Illus.). 1976. lib. bdg. 73.00 (ISBN 0-8240-2059-6). Garland Pub.
Brion, Marcel. The Medici. 1969. 25.00 (ISBN 0-236-17727-3, Pub. by Paul Elek). Merrimack Bk Serv.
Bullard, Melissa M. Filippo Strozzi & the Medici: Favour & Finance in Sixteenth-Century Florence & Rome. LC 79-51822. (Cambridge Studies in Early Modern History). 216p. 1980. 24.50 (ISBN 0-521-22301-6). Cambridge U Pr.
Canfield, Cass. Outrageous Fortunes: The Story of the Medici, the Rothschilds, & J. Pierpont Morgan. LC 80-24299. (Illus.). 108p. 1981. 10.95 (ISBN 0-15-170513-5). HarBraceJ.
De Roover, Raymond A. Rise & Decline of the Medici Bank: 1397-1494. LC 63-11417. (Studies in Business History: No. 21). (Illus.). 1963. 20.00x (ISBN 0-674-77145-1). Harvard U Pr.
Hale, J. R. Florence & the Medici: The Pattern of Control. (Illus.). 1978. 14.95 (ISBN 0-500-25059-6). Thames Hudson.
Hibbert, Christopher. House of Medici: Its Rise & Fall. LC 79-26508. (Illus.). 364p. 1980. pap. 6.95 (ISBN 0-688-05339-4, Quill). Morrow.
--The House of Medici: Its Rise & Fall. LC 74-15763. (Illus.). 352p. 1975. pap. 6.95 (ISBN 0-688-05339-4). Morrow.
Kent, Dale. The Rise of the Medici: Faction in Florence 1420-1434. 1978. 59.00x (ISBN 0-19-822520-2). Oxford U Pr.
Nagler, A. M. Theatre Festivals of the Medici, 1539-1637. LC 76-8447. 1976. Repr. of 1964 ed. lib. bdg. 25.00 (ISBN 0-306-70779-9). Da Capo.
Ross, Janet. Lives of the Early Medici As Told in Their Correspondence. 1977. lib. bdg. 59.95 (ISBN 0-8490-2175-8). Gordon Pr.
Schevill, Ferdinand. The Medici. 240p. 1981. Repr. of 1950 ed. lib. bdg. 35.00 (ISBN 0-8495-4952-3). Arden Lib.
--Medici. (Illus.). 5.00 (ISBN 0-8446-2874-3). Peter Smith.
Solerti, Angelo. Musica, Ballo E Drammatica Alla Corte Medicea Dal 1600 Al 1637. LC 67-12470. (It). 1968. Repr. of 1905 ed. 30.00 (ISBN 0-405-08987-2). Arno.
Young, G. F. The Medici, 2 vols. Repr. of 1913 ed. Set. 100.00 (ISBN 0-685-76645-4). Norwood Edns.

MEDICINAL PLANTS
see Botany, Medical

MEDICINE
see also Abnormalities, Human; Anatomy; Aviation Medicine; Bacteriology; Biomedical Engineering; Botany, Medical; Chemistry, Medical and Pharmaceutical; Chiropractic; Climatology, Medical; Dentistry; Diseases–Causes and Theories of Causation; Diseases–Reporting; Electricity in Medicine; Family Medicine; Folk Medicine; Health; Health Resorts, Watering-Places, etc.; Histology; Homeopathy; Hospitals; Hypnotism; Materia Medica; Mind and Body; Missions, Medical; Nosology; Nurses and Nursing; Osteopathy; Pathology; Pharmacology; Pharmacy; Physiology; Podiatry; Quacks and Quackery; Surgery; Tropical Medicine; Women in Medicine;
also headings beginning with the word Medical

Abraham, Sidney, et al. Weight by Height & Age for Adults, 18-74 Years, United States, 1971-1974. Cox, Kaludia, ed. (Ser. 11: No. 208). 1978. pap. text ed. 1.75 (ISBN 0-8406-0141-7). Natl Ctr Health Stats.
Aloisi, Ralph M. Principles of Immunodiagnostics. (Illus.). 1979. pap. text ed. 15.95 (ISBN 0-8016-0118-5). Mosby.
Alstead, Stanley & Girdwood, Ronald H., eds. Textbook of Medical Treatment. 14th ed. (Illus.). 546p. 1978. text ed. 47.50 (ISBN 0-443-01586-4). Churchill.
Alvarez, Walter C., intro. by. Inglenook Doctor Book. 1981. pap. 1.50 (ISBN 0-87178-423-8). Caroline Hse.
American Medical Association. American Medical Directory: Update to the 27th Edition. 812p. 1981. text ed. 75.00 (ISBN 0-88416-351-2). Wright-PSG.
Anderson, J., ed. Medical Informatics Europe 78: First Congress of the European Federation for Medical Informatics, Proceedings, Cambridge, England, Sept. 4-8, 1978. (Lecture Notes in Medical Informatics: Vol. 1). (Illus.). 1978. pap. 32.30 (ISBN 0-387-08916-0). Springer-Verlag.
Anderson, John. The Multiple Choice in Medicine. 1976. 11.00x (ISBN 0-272-79376-0). State Mutual Bk.
Barber, B., ed. Medical Informatics, Berlin, Nineteen Seventy-Nine. (Lecture Notes in Medical Informatics: Vol. 5). 1980. pap. 44.30 (ISBN 0-387-09549-7). Springer-Verlag.
Baum, H. & Gergely, J., eds. Molecular Aspects of Medicine, 6 pts, Vol. 1. Incl. Pt. 1. Radioimmunoassay & Reproductive Endocrinology. 1976. pap. text ed. 8.00 (ISBN 0-08-021518-1); Pt. 2. Haemoglobin Structure & Functions: Its Relevance in Biochemistry & Medicine. 1977; Pt. 3. Oedema in the Newborn. Barnes, ed. 1977. pap. text ed. 9.25 (ISBN 0-08-021538-6); Pt. 4. Enzymic Regulation & Its Clinical Significance. 1977. pap. text ed. 9.25 (ISBN 0-08-022642-6). Pergamon.
Bayt, Phyllis T. Administering Medications. (Health Occupations Ser.). 1981. pap. 10.95 (ISBN 0-672-61522-3). Bobbs.
Beeson, Paul B., et al. Cecil Textbook of Medicine, 2 vols. 15th ed. LC 77-16994. 1979. text ed. 49.00 single vol. ed. (ISBN 0-7216-1663-1); Vol. 1. text ed. 30.00 (ISBN 0-7216-1664-X); Vol. 2. text ed. 46.00 (ISBN 0-7216-1666-6); Set. text ed. 60.00 (ISBN 0-7216-1667-4). Saunders.
Berman, Edgar. The Solid Gold Stethoscope. 1978. pap. 2.25 (ISBN 0-345-28623-5). Ballantine.
Besser, G. M., ed. Advanced Medicine: Proceedings of the 13th Annual Symposium of Advanced Medicine 1977. (Illus.). 1977. 34.95x (ISBN 0-8464-0111-8). Beekman Pubs.

Birch, C. Allan, et al. The House Physician's Handbook. 5th ed. (Illus.). 336p. 1980. pap. text ed. 12.50 (ISBN 0-443-02117-1). Churchill.

Bloom. The Language of Medicine in English. (English for Careers Ser.). (gr. 10 up). 1981. pap. text ed. 3.50 (ISBN 0-88345-351-7). Regents Pub.

Bowers, John Z. & Purcell, Elizabeth F., eds. Advances in American Medicine, 2 vols. LC 75-43445. (Essays at the Bicentennial). (Illus.). 1976. 25.00 (ISBN 0-914362-17-8). J Macy Foun.

Bradoury, Parnell. The Mechanics of Healing. 17.00x (ISBN 0-8464-0624-1). Beekman Pubs.

Breckenridge, A. M. Advanced Medicine: Topics in Therapeutics No. 1. (Pitman Medical Conference Reports Ser.). (Illus.). 200p. 1975. pap. 22.00x (ISBN 0-8464-0114-2). Beekman Pubs.

Bright, Timothy. A Treatise Wherein Is Declared the Sufficiencie of English Medicines, for Cure of All Diseases, Cured with Medicine. LC 77-6860. (English Experience Ser.: No. 854). 1977. Repr. of 1580 ed. lib. bdg. 6.00 (ISBN 90-221-0854-6). Walter J Johnson.

British Postgraduate Medical Federation. The Scientific Basis of Medicine: Annual Reviews. Incl. 1966. text ed. 6.75x (ISBN 0-685-37476-9); 1967, 1968 & 1970. text ed. 9.00x ea.; 1973. text ed. 13.50x (ISBN 0-485-23816-0). Athlone Pr). Humanities.

Browne, Thomas. Religio Medici & Other Works. Martin, Leonard C., ed. 1964. 37.50x (ISBN 0-19-811429-X). Oxford U Pr.

Buck, Albert H. The Dawn of Modern Medicine. LC 75-23687. Repr. of 1920 ed. 28.50 (ISBN 0-404-13240-5). AMS Pr.

Bullough, Bonnie, et al, eds. The Management of Common Human Miseries: A Text for Primary Health Care Practitioners. LC 78-24072. 1979. text ed. 26.50 (ISBN 0-8261-2190-X). Springer Pub.

Burton, J. L. Aids to Undergraduate Medicine. 3rd ed. (Aids to... Ser.). (Illus.). 1980. pap. text ed. 8.25 (ISBN 0-443-02159-7). Churchill.

Cabot, Richard C. Social Service & the Art of Healing. LC 73-84257. (NASW Classics Ser). 192p. 1973. pap. text ed. 5.00 (ISBN 0-87101-062-3, CBC-062-I). Natl Assn Soc Wkrs.

Cahill, Kevin M. The Untapped Resource: Medicine & Diplomacy. LC 76-156971. 1971. 4.95x (ISBN 0-88344-522-0). Orbis Bks.

Cassell, Eric J. The Healer's Art. 1979. pap. 2.95 (ISBN 0-14-005276-3). Penguin.

Ceccio, Joseph F., ed. Medicine in Literature: An Anthology for Reading & Writing. LC 77-17721. (English & Humanities Ser.). 1978. pap. text ed. 9.95x (ISBN 0-582-28051-6). Longman.

Chapman, J. B. Dr. Schuessler's Biochemistry. 1973. 11.50 (ISBN 0-685-76563-6, Pub. by Thorsons). Formur Intl.

Chernin, Dennis, et al. Ancient & Modern Medicine: A Preventive & Therapeutic Synthesis. 200p. (Orig.). Date not set. pap. price not set (ISBN 0-89389-068-5). Himalayan Intl.

CIBA Foundation. Medical Care of Prisoners & Detainees. (CIBA Foundation Symposium Ser.:.No. 16). 244p. 1973. 18.00 (ISBN 0-444-15013-7, Excerpta Medica). Elsevier.

Combs, C. Murphy, ed. Illustrated Family Medical Encyclopedia: Based on Parr's Medical Encyclopedia. LC 76-16457. (Illus.). 1976. 10.95 (ISBN 0-8326-2213-3, 7499). Delair.

Conn, Howard F., ed. Current Therapy Nineteen Eighty. LC 49-8328. (Illus.). 988p. 1980. text ed. 29.50 (ISBN 0-7216-2708-0). Saunders.

Consumer Reports Editors. The Medicine Show. rev. & updated ed. 384p. 1980. 10.00 (ISBN 0-394-51106-9); pap. 5.95 (ISBN 0-394-73887-X). Pantheon.

Cooper, J. R. Dental Problems in Medical Practice. 1976. pap. text ed. 21.00x (ISBN 0-433-06425-0). Intl Ideas.

Creger, W. P., et al, eds. Annual Review of Medicine, Vol. 25. LC 51-1659. (Illus.). 1974. text ed. 17.00 (ISBN 0-8243-0525-6). Annual Reviews.

--Annual Review of Medicine: Selected Topics in the Clinical Sciences, Vol. 32. LC 51-1659. (Illus.). 1981. 20.00 (ISBN 0-8243-0532-9). Annual Reviews.

Creger, William P., et al, eds. Annual Review of Medicine: Selected Topics in the Clinical Sciences, Vol. 30. LC 51-1659. (Illus.). 1979. text ed. 17.00 (ISBN 0-8243-0530-2). Annual Reviews.

Daggett, P. R. Practical Medicine. 1976. 19.50 (ISBN 0-8151-2204-7). Year Bk Med.

Devries, Herbert & Briley, Michael. Health Science. LC 78-27588. (Illus.). 1978. text ed. 13.95 (ISBN 0-87620-380-2); inst. manual avail. (ISBN 0-87620-381-0). Goodyear.

Dewhurst, Kenneth & Reeves, Nigel. Friedrich Schiller--Medicine, Psychology, & Literature: With the First English Edition of His Complete Medical & Psychological Writings. LC 76-14308. 1978. 32.75x (ISBN 0-520-03250-0). U of Cal Pr.

Dixon, Bernard. Beyond the Magic Bullet: The Real Story of Medicine. LC 77-11811. 1978. 10.00 (ISBN 0-06-011062-7, HarpT). Harper-Row.

Doe, John. The Healers. 228p. 1969. 6.50x (ISBN 0-09-096230-3). Intl Pubns Serv.

Dubos, Rene & Escande, Jean-Paul. The Quest: Reflections on Medicine, Science & Mankind. LC 79-3347. 128p. 1980. Repr. of 1979 ed. 9.95 (ISBN 0-15-175705-4). HarBraceJ.

East, Edward M., ed. Biology in Human Affairs. LC 72-313. (Essay Index Reprint Ser.). Repr. of 1931 ed. 21.00 (ISBN 0-8369-2790-7). Arno.

Eisenbach, Rina. Calculating & Administering Medications. rev. ed. LC 78-711. (Illus.). 131p. 1978. 6.50 (ISBN 0-8036-3080-8). Davis Co.

Eisenberg, John M. & Williams, Sarkey V. The Physicians Practice. LC 80-13691. 274p. 1980. 21.50 (ISBN 0-471-05469-0, Pub. by Wiley Med). Wiley.

Elling, Ray, ed. Traditional & Modern Medical Systems. (Illus.). 100p. 1981. 14.80 (ISBN 0-08-028097-8). Pergamon.

Elliott-Binns, C. Medicine: The Forgotten Art? 1978. 17.00x (ISBN 0-8464-0625-X). Beekman Pubs.

Elstein, Arthur S., et al. Medical Problem Solving. LC 77-21505. 1978. 22.50x (ISBN 0-674-56125-2). Harvard U Pr.

Fabrini, A. & Steinberger, E., eds. Recent Progress in Andrology. (Proceedings of the Serono Symposia: Vol. 14). 1979. 51.50 (ISBN 0-12-247350-7). Acad Pr.

Firestein, Gary S. & Harrell, Robert A. The Effective Scutboy. LC 80-25057. (Illus.). 96p. 1981. pap. text ed. 7.50x (ISBN 0-668-05159-0, 5159). Arco.

Flagle, Charles D., ed. Advanced Medical Systems: Issues & Challenges. LC 75-30423. (Illus.). 271p. 1975. text ed. 19.95 (ISBN 0-8151-3250-6, Pub. by Symposia Special). Year Bk Med.

Ford, G., et al. The Use of Medical Literature: A Preliminary Survey. 1981. pap. 30.00x (ISBN 0-905984-51-X, Pub. by Brit Lib England). State Mutual Bk.

Foster, Daniel. A Layman's Guide to Modern Medicine. 1980. 14.95 (ISBN 0-671-24366-7). S&S.

Fox, M. & Schnabel, T. It's Your Body - Know What the Doctor Ordered: Your Complete Guide to Medical Testing. 1979. 10.00 (ISBN 0-13-507624-2). P-H.

Franklin, Jon & Doelp, Alan. Shocktrauma. 1980. 9.95 (ISBN 0-312-71741-5). St Martin.

Friedenwald, Harry. Jews & Medicine & Jewish Luminaries in Medical History, 3 Vols. rev. ed. 1967. 45.00x (ISBN 0-87068-053-6). Ktav.

Gerrick, David J. Footnotes to Medicine. 172p. 1980. 10.95 (ISBN 0-916750-21-3). Dayton Labs.

Gots & Kaufman. People's Hospital Book. 1981. pap. 3.95 (ISBN 0-380-53058-9, 53058). Avon.

Griffith, H. Winter. Instructions for Patients. LC 74-6684. (Illus.). 360p. 1975. pap. text ed. 39.50 (ISBN 0-7216-4281-0). Saunders.

Gross, Verlee E. The Structure of Medical Terms. 3rd, rev. ed. 208p. 1968. pap. 11.00x (ISBN 0-912256-00-1). Halls of Ivy.

Guicheney, Peirre. Qu'est-Ce Que le Medecin? Etude Psychologique De la Relation Medecin-Malade. (Interaction-L'homme et Son Environnement Sociales Ser.: No. 1). 225p. (Fr.). 1974. pap. text ed. 17.75x (ISBN 90-2797-324-5). Mouton.

Harvey, A. M., ed. The Principles & Practice of Medicine. 20th ed. (Illus.). 1569p. 1980. 39.50 (ISBN 0-8385-7930-2). ACC.

The Health Sciences Videolog. LC 78-74188. 1981. pap. 49.50 (ISBN 0-88432-069-3, Pub. by Mord Media). Video-Forum.

Hector, Winifred & Malpas, J. S. Textbook of Medicine for Nurses. 3rd ed. (Illus.). 1977. pap. text ed. 21.95x (ISBN 0-433-14214-6). Intl Ideas.

Hoffman. Fundamenta Medicinae. 142p. 1970. text ed. 15.00 (ISBN 0-685-56996-9). N Watson.

Horrobin, David. Medical Hubris: A Reply to Ivan Illich. LC 80-66836. 146p. 1980. 9.95 (ISBN 0-88831-080-3); pap. 6.95 (ISBN 0-88831-086-2). Eden Med Res.

Hulke, Malcolm, ed. The Encyclopedia of Alternative Medicine & Self-Help. LC 78-21115. 1979. 12.95x (ISBN 0-8052-3713-5); pap. 6.95 (ISBN 0-8052-0623-X). Schocken.

Hunderfund, Richard. Magic, Myths & Medicine. (Illus.). 1980. 13.95x (ISBN 0-89863-036-3). Star Pub CA.

Hunter, John. The Works of John Hunter, 5 vols. Palmer, James F., ed. LC 75-23726. Repr. of 1837 ed. Set. 230.00 (ISBN 0-404-13560-9). AMS Pr.

Jacobson, Bertil & Webster, John G. Medicine & Clinical Engineering. LC 76-13842. (Illus.). 1977. text ed. 29.95 (ISBN 0-13-572966-1). P-H.

Jaeger, Edmund C. A Source-Book of Medical Terms. (Illus.). 170p. 1953. photocopy ed. spiral 14.75 (ISBN 0-398-04295-0). C C Thomas.

Jokl, Ernst. Medical Sociology & Cultural Anthropology of Sport & Physical Education. (American Lecture in Sports Medicine). (Illus.). 176p. 1964. photocopy ed. spiral 17.50 (ISBN 0-398-00936-8). C C Thomas.

Kaufmann, H. J., ed. Medical Imaging One. (Karger Highlights, Medical Imaging). (Illus.). vi, 142p. 1980. pap. 9.00 (ISBN 3-8055-3056-0). S Karger.

Kett, Joseph F. The Formation of the American Medical Profession: The Role of Institutions, 1780-1860. LC 80-14326. xi, 217p. 1980. Repr. of 1968 ed. lib. bdg. 22.00x (ISBN 0-313-22428-5, KEFO). Greenwood.

Kleeberg, J. Eide und Bekenntnisse in der Medizin. (Illus.). 1979. pap. 17.00 (ISBN 3-8055-3041-2). S Karger.

Klein, Norman, ed. Culture, Curers, & Contagion. LC 79-10888. (Anthropology Ser.). 256p. 1979. pap. text ed. 6.95x (ISBN 0-88316-531-7). Chandler & Sharp.

Korn, Errol R. & Johnson, Karen. Visualization: The Uses of Imagery in the Health Professions. (Illus.). 250p. 1981. 29.50 (ISBN 0-88416-300-8). Wright-PSG.

Korostoff, Edward, ed. Research in Dental & Medical Materials. LC 70-94081. 154p. 1969. 29.50 (ISBN 0-306-30427-9, Plenum Pr). Plenum Pub.

The Landmark Series of Medical & Scientific Articles, 26 bks. (Landmark Ser.). 1978. Set. 520.00x (ISBN 0-685-51731-4). Irvington.

Lant, A. F., ed. Advanced Medicine - XI: Proceedings of the 11th Annual Symposium on Advanced Medicine 1975. (Illus.). 450p. (Orig.). 1975. pap. text ed. 34.95x (ISBN 0-8464-0112-6). Beekman Pubs.

LaPatra, Jack. Healing: The Coming Revolution in Holistic Medicine. 1978. 9.95 (ISBN 0-07-036359-5, GB). McGraw.

Lee, Ruth M. Orientation to Health Services. LC 77-15094. 1978. pap. 8.85 (ISBN 0-672-61434-0); tchr's manual 3.33 (ISBN 0-672-61435-9). Bobbs.

Lewis, J. G. Introduction to Medicine: 100 Topics. (Illus.). 1975. 17.95x (ISBN 0-433-19253-4). Intl Ideas.

Licht, Sidney, ed. Arthritis & Physical Medicine. LC 74-76392. 522p. 1969. 18.50 (ISBN 0-686-65364-5, Bub. by Williams & Wilkins). Krieger.

Lieberman, Leo, et al. CLEP: The Five General Examinations. LC 81-7895. 512p. 1981. lib. bdg. 12.00 (ISBN 0-668-05136-1, 5143); pap. 6.00 (ISBN 0-668-05143-4). Arco.

Lucas, Richard. Nature's Medicines. pap. 3.00 (ISBN 0-87980-105-0). Wilshire.

Luongo, Edward P. American Medicine in Crisis. LC 72-136013. 1971. 9.95 (ISBN 0-8022-2042-8). Philos Lib.

McCleery, Robert S. One Life, One Physician. 1971. 5.00 (ISBN 0-8183-0144-9). Pub Aff Pr.

McInnes, Betty. The Vital Signs with Related Clinical Measurement: A Programmed Approach. 3rd ed. (Illus.). 1979. pap. 9.50 (ISBN 0-8016-3333-8). Mosby.

Major, Ralph H. The Doctor Explains. 1931. 20.00 (ISBN 0-8274-4235-1). R West.

Martin, M. W. Miracles in Medicine. LC 73-80419. (Illus.). 1974. 9.95 (ISBN 0-8246-0159-9). Jonathan David.

Medical Hulacha for Everyone. Date not set. 8.95 (ISBN 0-87306-218-3). Feldheim.

Medicina Para Que Te Mejores. rev. ed. 128p. (Span.). 1980. pap. 1.50 (ISBN 0-87067-920-1, Melrose Sq). Holloway.

Memmler, Ruth L. & Wood, Dena L. Workbook for the Human Body in Health & Disease. 2nd ed. 1977. pap. 6.75x (ISBN 0-397-54197-X, JBL-Med-Nursing). Har-Row.

Mendelsohn, Robert. Confessions-Medical Heretic. 9.95 (ISBN 0-686-29809-8). Cancer Bk Hse.

Mergerson, David. Medicine As a Career. 12.50x (ISBN 0-392-06398-0, LTB). Sportshelf.

Millingen, J. G. Curiosities of Medical Experience. LC 72-83373. 1969. Repr. of 1839 ed. 24.00 (ISBN 0-8103-3487-9). Gale.

Mitchell, T. W. The Psychology of Medicine. 1922. 30.00 (ISBN 0-8274-4240-8). R West.

Moss, D. W. & Butterworth, P. J. Enzymology & Medicine. (Illus.). 200p. 1974. pap. text ed. 19.95x (ISBN 0-8464-0382-X). Beekman Pubs.

Mudlark, Ichabod. Gustave Dore's Primer on the Medical Profession. (Illus.). 164p. 1981. 15.00 (ISBN 0-87527-298-3). Green.

Murphy, Edmond A. The Logic of Medicine. LC 75-36952. (Illus.). 368p. 1976. 20.00x (ISBN 0-8018-1724-2). Johns Hopkins.

National Library of Medicine. Cumulated Index Medicus, Volume 11, 1970. LC 74-8462. 1974. Repr. of 1971 ed. Set. 325.00x (ISBN 0-405-06190-0, Co Pub by New York Times). Arno.

New York Academy Of Medicine. Frontiers in Medicine. facs. ed. LC 70-142675. (Essay Index Reprint Ser). 1951. 15.00 (ISBN 0-8369-2113-5). Arno.

--Medicine & Science. facs. ed. Galdston, Iago, ed. LC 75-142679. (Essay Index Reprint Ser). 1954. 13.00 (ISBN 0-8369-2122-4). Arno.

--Medicine Today: The March of Medicine, 1946 (Laity Lectures, No. 11) facsimile ed. LC 71-167393. (Essay Index Reprint Ser). Repr. of 1947 ed. 15.00 (ISBN 0-8369-2469-X). Arno.

Nolen, William A. A Surgeon's Book of Hope. 288p. 1980. 12.95 (ISBN 0-698-11044-7). Coward.

Norton, Alan. New Dimensions of Medicine. Tyerman, Donald, ed. (Twentieth Century Studies). 1971. 11.00x (ISBN 0-8426-1453-2). Verry.

Panati, Charles. Breakthroughs: Astonishing Advances in Your Lifetime in Medicine, Science, & Technology. 1980. 12.95 (ISBN 0-395-28221-7). HM.

Pappworth. A Primer of Medicine. 4th ed. LC 77-30428. (Primer Ser.). 1978. 27.50 (ISBN 0-407-62603-4). Butterworth.

Patrick, Edward A. Decision Analysis in Medicine: Methods & Applications. 352p. 1979. 79.95 (ISBN 0-8493-5255-X). CRC Pr.

Peschel, Enid R., ed. Medicine & Literature. 1980. 17.95 (ISBN 0-88202-127-3); text ed. 12.95 (ISBN 0-686-77693-3). N Watson.

Phillips. Basic Life Support: Skills Manual. LC 77-8351. 1977. pap. 13.95 (ISBN 0-87618-883-8). R J Brady.

Powell, Eric F. The Natural Home Physician. LC 79-50415. Date not set. 8.95 (ISBN 0-448-16558-9); pap. 5.95 (ISBN 0-686-76823-X). G&D.

Practical Medical Halacha. Date not set. 5.00 (ISBN 0-87306-221-3). Feldheim.

Rabey, Graham. Analytic Medicine. 75p. text ed. 14.95 (ISBN 0-8391-1418-4). Univ Park.

Rabinowitz, Peter M., ed. Talking Medicine: America's Doctors Tell Their Stories. 1981. 14.95 (ISBN 0-393-01397-9). Norton.

Read, A. E. & Barritt, D. W., eds. Modern Medicine. 600p. 1975. pap. text ed. 32.00x (ISBN 0-8464-0637-3). Beekman Pubs.

Read, Alan E., et al, eds. Modern Medicine. (Illus.). 1977. pap. 14.75 (ISBN 0-668-04124-2). Arco.

Reyment, Richard. Morphometric Methods in Biostratigraphy. LC 79-41521. 1980. 36.50 (ISBN 0-12-586980-0). Acad Pr.

Reynolds, Moira D. The Outstretched Hand-Advances in Modern Medicine. (Illus.). 140p. 1980. lib. bdg. 7.97 (ISBN 0-8239-0502-0). Rosen Pr.

Ribeiro, Leonidio. Brazilian Medical Contributions. 1976. lib. bdg. 69.95 (ISBN 0-8490-1548-0). Gordon Pr.

Riegelman, Richard K. Studying a Study & Testing a Test: How to Read the Medical Literature. 1981. pap. text ed. write for info. (ISBN 0-316-74518-9). Little.

Rigg, C. Andrew & Shearin, Robert B., eds. Adolescent Medicine. 1980. write for info. (ISBN 0-8151-7341-5). Symposia Special.

Robertson, Thomas S., et al. Televised Medicine Advertising & Children. 21.95 (ISBN 0-03-049161-4). Praeger.

Rudman, Jack. Medical Conduct Investigator. (Career Examination Ser.: C-2287). (Cloth bdg. avail. on request). 1977. 16.00 (ISBN 0-8373-2287-1). Natl Learning.

--Medical Sciences Knowledge Profile Examination (MSKP) (Admission Test Ser.: AT-86). (Cloth bdg. avail. on request). pap. 17.95 (ISBN 0-686-68260-2). Natl Learning.

Sayers, William T. Body, Soul & Blood: Recovering the Human in Medicine. LC 79-56194. 112p. 1980. pap. 4.95 (ISBN 0-935718-00-1). Asclepiad.

Scagliotta, Edward G. An L D Program That Works. LC 75-13492. 1979. pap. 9.95 (ISBN 0-87804-319-5). Mafex.

Schifferes, Justus J. The Family Medical Encyclopedia. 2nd rev. ed. 1977. pap. 2.50 (ISBN 0-671-81227-0). PB.

Scorer, Gordon & Wing, Antony, eds. Decision Making in Medicine: The Practice of Its Ethics. (Illus.). 1979. 25.00 (ISBN 0-8151-7584-1). Year Bk Med.

Scott, Ronald B. & Fraser, James. The Medical Annual, 1979-1980. (Illus.). 1979. pap. 35.00 (ISBN 0-8151-7689-9). Year Bk Med.

Senger, H., ed. The Blue Light Syndrome: Proceedings. (Life Sciences Ser.). (Illus.). 700p. 1980. 49.00 (ISBN 0-387-10075-X). Springer-Verlag.

Shenker, I. R., ed. Adolescent Medicine: Selected Topics. (Illus.). 1978. text ed. 35.00 (ISBN 0-913258-53-9). Thieme-Stratton.

Silver, George A. A Spy in the House of Medicine. LC 76-2184. 320p. 1976. 21.75 (ISBN 0-912862-18-1). Aspen Systems.

Singer, Phillip, ed. Traditional Healing: New Science or New Colonialism?, Essays in Critique of Medical Anthropology. LC 75-18490. (Trado-Medical Bks.). 250p. 1977. 17.50 (ISBN 0-914970-36-4). Conch Mag.

Steiner, Rudolf. Common Ailments & Their Natural Remedies. 1973. lib. bdg. 59.95 (ISBN 0-87968-557-3). Krishna Pr.

Thayer, William S. Osler, & Other Papers. facs. ed. LC 78-84342. (Essay Index Reprint Ser). 1931. 19.50 (ISBN 0-8369-1111-3). Arno.

University of Montpellier Faculty of Medicine. Polyphonie Du XIIIe Siecle, 4 vols. LC 80-2191. (Illus.). Repr. of 1939 ed. 365.00 (ISBN 0-404-19040-5). AMS Pr.

The Use of Medical Literature. 1981. 21.00x (ISBN 0-905984-51-X, Pub. by Brit Lib England). State Mutual Bk.

Vander Salm, Thomas J., et al. Atlas of Bedside Procedures. LC 79-65313. 1979. pap. text ed. 18.95 (ISBN 0-316-89605-5). Little.

Van Liere, Edward J. Medical & Other Essays. 1966. 5.00 (ISBN 0-685-30825-1). McClain.

Wallis, Roy & Morley, Peter, eds. Marginal Medicine. LC 76-43129. 1977. 8.95 (ISBN 0-02-933740-2). Free Pr.

Wasco, James E. Not for Doctors Only: Breakthrough Reports from the Medical Front. 12.95 (ISBN 0-201-08297-7); pap. 7.95 (ISBN 0-201-08298-5). A-W.

Werts, Margaret F. & Shilling, Charles W. Underwater Medicine & Related Sciences: A Guide to the Literature. Incl. Vol. 1. 695p. 1973. 75.00 (ISBN 0-306-65161-0); Vol. 2. 662p. 1975. 75.00 (ISBN 0-306-67412-2). LC 73-80326. IFI Plenum.

Willeford, George. Medical Word Finder. 2nd ed. 1976. 12.95 (ISBN 0-13-573519-X). P-H.

Wolf, Stewart & Berle, Beatrice B. Limits of Medicine: The Doctor's Job in the Coming Era. LC 78-1438. 167p. 1978. 22.50 (ISBN 0-306-31136-4, Plenum Pr). Plenum Pub.

Wood, Clive, ed. Cardiovascular Medicine Controversies. 83p. 1979. pap. 13.50 (ISBN 0-8089-1134-1). Grune.

MEDICINE–ABBREVIATIONS

Cole, Frank. Doctor's Shorthand. LC 71-132176. 1970. 9.95 (ISBN 0-7216-2643-2). Saunders.

Kerr, Avice H. Medical Hieroglyphs. LC 75-131216. 1970. 14.75 (ISBN 0-918558-01-8). Enterprise Calif.

--Medical Hieroglyphs. LC 75-131216. 1970. 14.75 (ISBN 0-918558-01-8). Enterprise Calif.

Roody, Peter, et al. Medical Abbreviations & Acronyms. 1976. pap. text ed. 6.95 (ISBN 0-07-053604-X, HP). McGraw.

Schertl, Albrecht. Abbreviations in Medicine. 204p. 1977. pap. 20.00 (ISBN 3-7940-7017-8, Pub. by K G Saur). Gale.

White, Wallace F. Language of the Health Sciences: A Lexical Guide to Word Parts, Word Roots, & Their Meanings. LC 77-9310. 1977. pap. 12.95 (ISBN 0-471-02159-8, Pub. by Wiley Medical). Wiley.

MEDICINE–ADDRESSES, ESSAYS, LECTURES

Advanced Medical Symposia, 11th, 1975 & Royal College of Physicians. Proceedings. Lant, A. F., ed. (Illus.). 1975. pap. text ed. 26.00x (ISBN 0-685-83067-5). State Mutual Bk.

Advanced Medicine Symposia, 10th, 1974 & Royal College of Physicians. Proceedings. Ledingham, J. G., ed. (Illus.). 1974. pap. text ed. 30.00x (ISBN 0-685-83066-7). State Mutual Bk.

Advanced Medicine Symposia, 7th, 1971. Proceedings. Boucher, I. A., ed. 1971. pap. text ed. 17.00x (ISBN 0-685-83065-9). State Mutual Bk.

Allbutt, T. C. Greek Medicine in Rome. LC 69-13230. Repr. of 1921 ed. 30.00 (ISBN 0-405-08201-0, Pub. by Blom). Arno.

Aring, Charles D. Understanding Physician: Writings of Charles D. Aring, M.D. rev. ed. LC 73-143469. 1971. Repr. text ed. 8.95x (ISBN 0-8143-1440-6). Wayne St U Pr.

Baron, D., et al, eds. Recent Advances in Medicine, No. 17. LC 77-3899. (Recent Advances in Medicine Ser.). (Illus.). 1978. 31.25x (ISBN 0-443-01316-0). Churchill.

Bruess, Clint E. & Fisher, J. Thomas. Selected Readings in Health. (Illus.). 1970. pap. text ed. 8.95 (ISBN 0-02-315700-3, 31570). Macmillan.

Cahill, Kevin M. Irish Essays. LC 80-80550. 140p. 1980. 9.00 (ISBN 0-89444-028-4). John Jay Pr.

Cohn, Alfred E. Medicine, Science & Art. facs. ed. LC 72-86742. (Essay Index Reprint Ser). 1931. 16.50 (ISBN 0-8369-1126-1). Arno.

--No Retreat from Reason. LC 68-8198. (Essay & General Literature Index Reprint Ser). 1969. Repr. of 1931 ed. 11.50 (ISBN 0-8046-0083-X). Kennikat.

Creger, William P., et al, eds. Annual Review of Medicine: Selected Topics in the Clinical Sciences, Vol. 28. LC 51-1659. (Illus.). 1977. text ed. 17.00 (ISBN 0-8243-0528-0). Annual Reviews.

--Annual Review of Medicine: Seleoted Topics in the Clinical Sciences, Vol. 29. LC 51-1659. (Illus.). 1978. text ed. 17.00 (ISBN 0-8243-0529-9). Annual Reviews.

Cushing, Harvey W. Consecratio Medici & Other Papers. facsimile ed. LC 70-99688. (Essay Index Reprint Ser). 1928. 19.00 (ISBN 0-8369-1565-8). Arno.

Edmunds, H. Tudor, et al, eds. Some Unrecognized Factors in Medicine. LC 75-28092. 211p. 1976. pap. 3.25 (ISBN 0-8356-0471-3, Quest). Theos Pub Hse.

Ehrenreich, John, ed. The Cultural Crisis of Modern Medicine. LC 78-465. (Modern Reader Paperback Ser.). 1979. pap. 5.95 (ISBN 0-85345-515-5, PB5155). Monthly Rev.

Galdston, Iago. Medicine in Transition. LC 65-24425. 1965. 8.00x (ISBN 0-226-27961-8). U of Chicago Pr.

Galdston, Iago, ed. Man's Image in Medicine & Anthropology. LC 63-19871. (Institute of Social & Historical Medicine Monographs: No. 4). 1963. text ed. 20.00 (ISBN 0-8236-3120-6). Intl Univs Pr.

--Medicine & Mankind. facs. ed. LC 70-142632. (Essay Index Reprint Ser). 1936. 15.00 (ISBN 0-8369-2108-9). Arno.

--Medicine & the Other Disciplines. LC 59-15725. 1960. text ed. 10.00 (ISBN 0-8236-3300-4). Intl Univs Pr.

Gregg, Alan. For Future Doctors. LC 57-11207. 1957. 5.50x (ISBN 0-226-30737-9). U of Chicago Pr.

--For Future Doctors. LC 57-11207. 1963. pap. 1.50 (ISBN 0-226-30738-7, P126, Phoen). U of Chicago Pr.

Haldane, John B. Possible Worlds: And Other Papers. facsimile ed. LC 75-167351. (Essay Index Reprint Ser). Repr. of 1928 ed. 18.00 (ISBN 0-8369-2452-5). Arno.

Havard, C. W. Lectures in Medicine. LC 67-27241. (Illus.). 382p. 1967. 10.50 (ISBN 0-87527-041-7). Green.

Hawley, Paul R. New Discoveries in Medicine: Their Effect on the Public Health. facsimile ed. LC 76-37922. (Essay Index Reprint Ser). Repr. of 1950 ed. 16.00 (ISBN 0-8369-2594-7). Arno.

Holmes, Oliver W. Medical Essays: 1842-1882. 1977. Repr. of 1893 ed. lib. bdg. 35.00 (ISBN 0-8495-2216-1). Arden Lib.

Jelly, Oliver. Ditchcraft, & Essays Around Medicine. 212p. 1965. 6.25x (ISBN 0-85307-054-7). Intl Pubns Serv.

Langdon-Brown, Walter. Thus We Are Men. facs. ed. LC 79-86768. (Essay Index Reprint Ser). 1938. 18.00 (ISBN 0-8369-1148-2). Arno.

Lasagna, Louis. Doctor's Dilemmas. LC 70-105025. (Essay Index Reprint Ser). 1962. 18.00 (ISBN 0-8369-1669-7). Arno.

McLachlan, Gordon. Problems & Progress in Medical Care: Essays on Current Research, Vol. 5. 5th ed. (Nuffield Publications). 1971. 5.75x (ISBN 0-19-721361-8). Oxford U Pr.

Marcus, Donald M., ed. The Harvey Lectures, Series 73. (Serial Publication). 1979. 24.00 (ISBN 0-12-312073-X). Acad Pr.

Meade, Gordon M., ed. Frontiers of Medicine. LC 77-3334. 232p. 1977. 32.50 (ISBN 0-306-31048-1, Plenum Pr). Plenum Pub.

Mendelsohn, Robert S. Confessions of a Medical Heretic. 1979. 9.95 (ISBN 0-8092-7726-3). Contemp Bks.

Middleton, William S. Values in Modern Medicine. LC 72-1379. (Illus.). 314p. 1972. 15.00x (ISBN 0-299-06220-1). U of Wis Pr.

New York Academy of Medicine. Future in Medicine: The March of Medicine, 1949, Laity Lectures, No. 14. facsimile ed. LC 74-167391. (Essay Index Reprint). Repr. of 1950 ed. 15.00 (ISBN 0-8369-2465-7). Arno.

--Landmarks in Medicine. facs. ed. LC 74-142676. (Essay Index Reprint Ser). 1939. 19.00 (ISBN 0-8369-2114-3). Arno.

--March of Medicine Laity Lectures, No. 4. facsimile ed. LC 78-142677. (Essay Index Reprint Ser). Repr. of 1940 ed. 15.00 (ISBN 0-8369-2212-3). Arno.

--March of Medicine, Laity Lectures No. 5. facs. ed. LC 78-142677. (Essay Index Reprint Ser). 1941. 15.00 (ISBN 0-8369-2115-1). Arno.

--March of Medicine, Laity Lectures No. 6. facs. ed. LC 78-142677. (Essay Index Reprint Ser). 1941. 15.00 (ISBN 0-8369-2116-X). Arno.

--March of Medicine, Laity Lectures No. 7. facs. ed. LC 78-142677. (Essay Index Reprint Ser). 1943. 16.00 (ISBN 0-8369-2117-8). Arno.

--March of Medicine: Lectures to the Laity, 1943. facsimile ed. LC 78-142677. (Essay Index Reprint Ser). Repr. of 1943 ed. 15.00 (ISBN 0-8369-2466-5). Arno.

--March of Medicine: Lectures to the Laity, 1944. facsimile ed. LC 78-142677. (Essay Index Reprint Ser). Repr. of 1945 ed. 12.00 (ISBN 0-8369-2467-3). Arno.

--Medicine & Anthropology. facs. ed. Galdston, Iago, ed. LC 71-142678. (Essay Index Reprint Ser). 1959. 15.00 (ISBN 0-8369-2118-6). Arno.

--Medicine in a Changing Society. facs. ed. Galdston, Iago, ed. LC 70-142680. (Essay Index Reprint Ser). 1956. 15.00 (ISBN 0-8369-2123-2). Arno.

--Medicine in the Postwar World: The March of Medicine, 1947, Laity Lectures, No. 12. facsimile ed. LC 78-167392. (Essay Index Reprint Ser). Repr. of 1948 ed. 12.00 (ISBN 0-8369-2468-1). Arno.

--Milestones in Medicine. facs. ed. LC 73-142681. (Essay Index Reprint Ser). 1938. 17.00 (ISBN 0-8369-2119-4). Arno.

--Perspectives in Medicine. LC 75-152204. (Essay Index Reprint Ser.). 1949. 15.00 (ISBN 0-8369-2813-X). Arno.

Newman, George. Interpreters of Nature: Essays. facs. ed. LC 68-20325. (Essay Index Reprint Ser). 1927. 15.50 (ISBN 0-8369-0741-8). Arno.

Osler, William. Aequanimitas. 3rd ed. 1932. 17.95 (ISBN 0-07-047915-1, HP). McGraw.

--A Way of Life. 1937. 4.50x (ISBN 0-06-141860-9, Harper Medical). Har-Row.

Peters, D. K., ed. Advanced Medicine-XII: Proceedings of the 12th Annual Symposium of Advanced Medicine, 1976. (Illus.). 1976. pap. 34.95x (ISBN 0-8464-0117-7). Beekman Pubs.

Pottenger Portfolio: Fifty-Five Reprints of Medical Papers of Dr. Francis M. Pottenger, Jr. 40.00 (ISBN 0-916764-03-6). Price-Pottenger.

Power, D'Arcy. Selected Writings 1877-1930. LC 78-95632. (Illus.). Repr. of 1931 ed. 19.50x (ISBN 0-678-03750-7). Kelley.

Price Portfolio: Forty-Six Reprints of Medical Papers of Dr. Weston A. Price. 1978. 53.00 (ISBN 0-916764-04-4). Price-Pottenger.

Riesman, David. Medicine in Modern Society. LC 77-92513. (Essay Index in Reprint Ser.). 1978. Repr. 18.50x (ISBN 0-8486-3010-6). Core Collection.

Selzer, Richard. Mortal Lessons: Notes on the Art of Surgery. 1978. pap. 4.95 (ISBN 0-671-24074-9, Touchstone Bks). S&S.

Smith, Stephen. Doctor in Medicine & Other Papers on Professional Subjects. LC 74-180590. (Medicine & Society in America Ser). 318p. 1972. Repr. of 1872 ed. 17.00 (ISBN 0-405-03972-7). Arno.

Stevenson, Lloyd. G. & Multhauf, Robert P., eds. Medicine, Science, & Culture: Historical Essays in Honor of Owsei Temkin. LC 68-15445. (Illus.). 312p. 1968. 20.00x (ISBN 0-8018-0615-1). Johns Hopkins.

Symposium, C. H. Boehringer Sohn, May 1974. The Creative Process in Science & Medicine: Proceedings. Krebs, H. A., ed. (International Congress Ser.: No. 355). 138p. 1975. pap. 34.25 (ISBN 0-444-15174-5, Excerpta Medica). Elsevier.

Symposium, International Norgestrel, 2nd. Proceedings. Fairweather, D. V., ed. (International Congress Ser.: No. 344). 125p. 1975. pap. 19.50 (ISBN 0-444-15159-1, Excerpta Medica). Elsevier.

Taliaferro, William H., ed. Medicine & the War. facsimile ed. LC 70-37923. (Essay Index Reprint Ser: Charles R. Walgreen Foundation Lectures). Repr. of 1944 ed. 21.00 (ISBN 0-8369-2629-3). Arno.

Thomas, Lewis. The Medusa & the Snail. 1980. pap. 7.95 (ISBN 0-8161-3102-3, Large Print Bks). G K Hall.

Virchow, Rudolf L. Disease, Life, & Man: Selected Essays. Rather, Lelland J., tr. 1958. 12.50x (ISBN 0-8047-0557-7). Stanford U Pr.

Visscher, Maurice B., ed. Chemistry & Medicine: Papers Presented at the Fiftieth Anniversary of the Founding of the Medical School of the University of Minnesota. facs. ed. LC 67-30234. (Essay Index Reprint Ser). 1940. 19.00 (ISBN 0-8369-0962-3). Arno.

Warshofsky, Fred, ed. Twenty-First Century: The New Age of Exploration, Vol. 1. (Twentyfirst Century Ser). (Illus.). 1969. 6.95 (ISBN 0-670-73582-5). Viking Pr.

MEDICINE–APHORISMS

Here are entered only the older medical works made up of short percepts and instructions, e.g. Aphorisms of Hippocrates.

Hippocrates. Amorphismes Ypocras De Martin De Saint-Gille. Lafeuille, Germaine, ed. 1954. pap. 12.00 (ISBN 0-527-01123-1). Kraus Repr.

MEDICINE–APPARATUS

see Medical Instruments and Apparatus

MEDICINE–AUTHORSHIP

see Medical Writing

MEDICINE–BIBLIOGRAPHY

see also Information Storage and Retrieval Systems–Medicine

Adams, Scott. Medical Bibliography in an Age of Discontinuity. 244p. 1981. 21.50 (ISBN 0-912176-09-1). Med Lib Assn.

Almagro, Bertha R. Early American Medical Imprints 1668-1820: Subject, Name & Format Index to the Microfilm Collection. 1981. write for info. (ISBN 0-89235-027-X). Res Pubns Conn.

American Hospital Association. Catalog of the Library of the American Hospital Association, Asa S. Bacon Memorial Chicago Library, 5 vols. 1976. Set. lib. bdg. 460.00 (ISBN 0-8161-1210-X). G K Hall.

American Medical Association, Division of Library & Archival Services. Index to Medical Socioeconomic Literature, 1962-1970, 4 vols. 1980. lib. bdg. 295.00 (ISBN 0-8161-0338-0). G K Hall.

Ash, Lee. Serial Publications Containing Medical Classics. 2nd ed. 1979. 25.00 (ISBN 0-9603990-0-3). Antiquarium.

Blake, John B. & Roos, Charles, eds. Medical Reference Works, 1679-1966: A Selected Bibliography. LC 67-30664. 1967. 10.00 (ISBN 0-912176-02-4). Med Lib Assn.

Brodman, Estelle. The Development of Medical Bibliography. 226p. 1981. Repr. of 1954 ed. 8.25 (ISBN 0-912176-00-8). Med Lib Assn.

Cumulated Index Medicus, Vol. 9, 1968, 5 vols. 8925p. 1969. Set. 185.00 (ISBN 0-405-00975-5). Arno.

Dunlap, Alice, et al, eds. Hospital Literature Index: 1980 Cumulative Annual, Vol. 36. 704p. 1981. 90.00 (ISBN 0-87258-348-1, 1389). Am Hospital.

Fulton, John F. The Great Medical Bibliographers: A Study in Humanism. LC 76-30508. (The Historical Library, Yale University School of Medicine: No. 26). (Illus.). 1977. Repr. of 1951 ed. lib. bdg. 15.00 (ISBN 0-8371-9436-9, FUGM). Greenwood.

Gross, Samuel D. History of American Medical Literature from Seventeen Seventy Six to the Present Time. 85p. 1972. Repr. of 1876 ed. 19.50 (ISBN 0-8337-1466-X). B Franklin.

Hospital Literature Subject Headings Transition Guide to Medical Subject Headings. LC 78-14972. 236p. 1978. pap. text ed. 22.50 (ISBN 0-87258-242-6, 1858). Am Hospital.

Kerker, Ann E. & Murphy, Henry T., eds. Comparative & Veterinary Medicine: A Guide to the Resource Literature. LC 72-7989. 324p. 1973. 29.50x (ISBN 0-299-06330-5). U of Wis Pr.

Kyed, James M. & Matarazzo, James H., eds. Scientific, Engineering & Medical Societies Publications in Print 1978-1979. 3rd ed. LC 79-17264. 1979. 35.00 (ISBN 0-8352-1212-2). Bowker.

Medical Books & Serials in Print, 1981. 10th ed. 1650p. 1981. 55.00 (ISBN 0-8352-1356-0). Bowker.

Medical Books for the Layperson: An Annotated Bibliography. Philbrook, Marilyn M., ed. 1976. 2.00 (ISBN 0-89073-047-4). Boston Public Lib.

Mersky, Roy, et al. A Manual on Medical Literature for Law Librarians: A Handbook & Annotated Bibliography. LC 73-7475. 216p. 1974. 17.50x (ISBN 0-87802-101-9, Dist. by Oceana). Glanville.

Meyer, Klaus. Bibliographie zur Osteuropaeischen Geschichte. 760p. 1972. 60.00x (ISBN 3-447-01437-7). Intl Pubns Serv.

Morton. Use of Medical Literature. 2nd ed. 1978. 64.95 (ISBN 0-408-70916-2). Butterworth.

National Library of Medicine. Cumulative Index Medicus, Vol. 13, 8 vols. LC 74-8462. 1975. 410.00x (ISBN 0-405-06650-3). Arno.

--National Library of Medicine Catalog, 1960-1965, 6 Vols. 1966. Set. 120.00x (ISBN 0-87471-233-5). Rowman.

Neu, John, et al, eds. Chemical, Medical, & Pharmaceutical Books Printed Before 1800: In the Collections of the University of Wisconsin Libraries. 288p. 1965. 22.00x (ISBN 0-299-03680-4). U of Wis Pr.

New York Academy of Medicine. Author Catalog of the Library of the New York Academy of Medicine, Second Supplement. 1979. lib. bdg. 500.00 (ISBN 0-8161-1181-2). G K Hall.

--Author Catalog of the Library of the New York Academy of Medicine, 43 Vols. 1969. Set. lib. bdg. 3180.00 (ISBN 0-8161-0829-3). G K Hall.

--Author Catalog of the Library of the New York Academy of Medicine, 1st Suppl, 4 vols. 1974. Set. lib. bdg. 475.00 (ISBN 0-8161-0851-X). G K Hall.

--Subject Catalog of the Library of the New York Academy of Medicine, Second Supplement. 1979. lib. bdg. 500.00 (ISBN 0-8161-1182-0). G K Hall.

--Subject Catalog of the Library of the New York Academy of Medicine, 34 Vols. 1969. Set. lib. bdg. 2590.00 (ISBN 0-8161-0826-9). G K Hall.

--Subject Catalog of the Library of the New York Academy of Medicine, 1st Supplement, 4 vols. 1974. Set. lib. bdg. 495.00 (ISBN 0-8161-0184-1). G K Hall.

New York Academy of Medicine, Illustration Catalog. 3rd. enlarged ed. 1976. lib. bdg. 30.00 (ISBN 0-8161-0038-1). G K Hall.

Pallatz, Harold. Therapy Book Locator Guide. LC 75-29787. 1975. 1.50 (ISBN 0-915068-00-1). Ideal World.

Parkinson, E. M. Catalogue of Medical Books, Fourteen Eighty to Seventeen Hundred, in Manchester University Library. 406p. 1972. 111.50x (ISBN 0-7190-1246-5, Pub. by Manchester U Pr England). State Mutual Bk.
Philbrook, Marilyn M., compiled by. Medical Books for the Layperson: An Annotated Bibliography, Supplement. 1978. pap. 2.00 (ISBN 0-89073-060-1). Boston Public Lib.
Publications of the World Health Organization, 1958-1962: A Bibliography. 125p. (Eng. & Fr.). 1964. 5.60 (ISBN 92-4-152001-9). World Health.
Publications of the World Health Organization, 1963-1967: A Bibliography. 152p. (Eng. & Fr.). 1969. 8.00 (ISBN 92-4-152002-7). World Health.
Richmond, Joy S., compiled by. Medical Reference Works, 1679-1966: Supplement 2, 1969-1972. LC 67-30664. 1973. pap. 6.95 (ISBN 0-912176-05-9). Med Lib Assn.
--Medical Reference Works, 1679-1966: Supplement 3, 1973-1974. LC 67-30664. 89p. 1975. pap. 4.95 (ISBN 0-912176-07-5). Med Lib Assn.
Singer, C. & Sigerist, H. E., eds. Essays on the History of Medicine Presented to Karl Sudhoff on the Occasion of His Seventieth Birthday, November 26th, 1923. facs. ed. LC 68-8459. (Essay Index Reprint Ser). 1924. 23.00 (ISBN 0-8369-0431-1). Arno.
Swanson, Gerald, ed. Medical Book Guide: 1974. 950p. 1974. lib. bdg. 70.00 (ISBN 0-8161-6804-0). G K Hall.
Thornton, John L. Select Bibliography of Medical Biography. 2nd ed. LC 75-500919. (Illus.). 170p. 1970. 7.50x (ISBN 0-85365-094-2). Intl Pubns Serv.
Warren, Kenneth S. Schistosomiasis: The Evolution of a Medical Literature 1852-1972. 1200p. 1974. 60.00x (ISBN 0-262-23057-7). MIT Pr.

MEDICINE–BIOGRAPHY
see also Health Officers; Nurses and Nursing; Physicians; Surgeons
Assali, Nicholas S. A Doctor's Life. LC 79-1808. 1979. 12.95 (ISBN 0-15-126161-X). HarBraceJ.
Aub, Joseph C. & Hapgood, Ruth K. Pioneer in Modern Medicine: David Linn Edsall of Harvard. LC 78-145896. (Illus.). 1970. 16.50x (ISBN 0-674-66875-8). Harvard U Pr.
Bergler, Edmund. Selected Papers of Edmund Bergler. 992p. 1969. 9.75 (ISBN 0-8089-0057-9). Grune.
Black, Herbert. Doctor, Teacher, Hospital Chief: Dr. Sam Proger & the New England Medical Center. (Illus.). 360p. 1981. 14.95 (ISBN 0-87106-960-1). Globe Pequot.
Corner, George W., Sr. The Seven Ages of a Medical Scientist: An Autobiography. LC 81-51143. (Illus.). 406p. 1981. 25.00x (ISBN 0-8122-7811-9). U of Pa Pr.
Eberson, Frederick. Profiles: Giants in Medicine. (Illus.). 120p. (Orig.). 1980. pap. 5.95 (ISBN 0-934616-11-6). Valkyrie Pr.
Greer, Virginia. Emergency: The True Story of a Woman's Faith & Service As an Emergency Room Volunteer. LC 76-50468. 1977. 5.95 (ISBN 0-915684-16-0). Christian Herald.
Hathaway, Esse V. Partners in Progress. facs. ed. LC 68-29213. (Essay Index Reprint Ser.). 1968. Repr. of 1935 ed. 16.00 (ISBN 0-8369-0518-0). Arno.
Hellstedt, Leone M. Women Physicians of the World: Autobiographies of Medical Pioneers. (Illus.). 1978. text ed. 26.50 (ISBN 0-07-027954-3, HP). McGraw.
Hoffman, William. The Super Doctors. 256p. 1981. 12.95 (ISBN 0-02-552010-5). Macmillan.
Ingle, Dwight J., ed. Dozen Doctors: Autobiographic Sketches. LC 63-20908. (Illus.). 1963. 11.50x (ISBN 0-226-38331-8). U of Chicago Pr.
International Medical Who's Who: A Biographical Guide in Medical Research, 2 vols. 1301p. Set. 235.00 (ISBN 0-686-75640-1, Pub. by Longman). Gale.
Jaques Cattell Press, ed. Biographical Directory of the American Public Health Association. LC 79-6967. 1207p. 1979. 54.50 (ISBN 0-8352-1160-6). Bowker.
Kelly, Howard A. & Burrage, Walter L. Dictionary of American Medical Biography: In One Volume. LC 78-13906. 1978. Repr. of 1928 ed. Set. lib. bdg. 75.00 (ISBN 0-89341-513-8). Longwood Pr.
Lanning, John T. Pedro de la Torre: Doctor to Conquerors. LC 73-83909. 160p. 1974. 10.00 (ISBN 0-8071-0064-1). La State U Pr.
MacFarlane, Gwyn. Howard Florey: The Making of a Great Scientist. (Illus.). 1979. 18.95x (ISBN 0-19-858161-0). Oxford U Pr.
Newman, George. Interpreters of Nature: Essays. facs. ed. LC 68-20325. (Essay Index Reprint Ser). 1927. 15.50 (ISBN 0-8369-0741-8). Arno.
Pepper, William. The Medical Side of Benjamin Franklin. (Illus.). 137p. 1970. Repr. of 1910 ed. 15.00 (ISBN 0-87266-039-7). Argosy.
Stone, R. French. Biographies of Eminent American Physicians & Surgeons. 1973. lib. bdg. 45.00 (ISBN 0-87821-145-4). Milford Hse.
Talbott, John H. A Biographical History of Medicine: Excerpts & Essays on the Men & Their Work. LC 78-109574. (Illus.). 1224p. 1970. 110.00 (ISBN 0-8089-0657-7). Grune.
Thornton, John L. Select Bibliography of Medical Biography. 2nd ed. LC 75-500919. (Illus.). 170p. 1970. 7.50x (ISBN 0-85365-094-2). Intl Pubns Serv.
Walker, M. E. Pioneers of Public Health: The Story of Some Benefactors of the Human Race. facs. ed. LC 68-26483. (Essay Index Reprint Ser). 1930. 18.00 (ISBN 0-8369-0965-8). Arno.
Walsh, James J. Makers of Modern Medicine. LC 70-107741. (Essay Index Reprint Ser). 1907. 19.50 (ISBN 0-8369-1538-0). Arno.
Who's Who in Medicine: Germany, Austria, Switzerland. 108.00 (ISBN 3-921220-30-0). Adler.
Wilson, Dorothy C. Dr. Ida: Passing on the Torch of Life. 1976. pap. 3.50 (ISBN 0-377-84221-4). Friend Pr.

MEDICINE–CASES, CLINICAL REPORTS, STATISTICS
Balint, Michael. The Doctor, His Patient & the Illness. 2nd ed. 1963. text ed. 20.00 (ISBN 0-8236-1380-1). Intl Univs Pr.
Characteristics of the Population in New York City Health Areas: Family Composition, No. 3. 1973. 4.00 (ISBN 0-86671-014-0). Comm Coun Great NY.
Eron, Carol. The Virus That Ate Cannibals: Six Great Medical Detective Stories. 1981. 12.95 (ISBN 0-02-536250-X). Macmillan.
Gerrick, David J. & McDonald, Susan. Anomalies & Curiosities of Medical Practice. 114p. 1981. pap. 7.75 (ISBN 0-916750-78-7). Dayton Labs.
Lieberman, Arnold. Case Capsules: The Droll, Directing, Devilish, Definitely Different. (Illus.). 356p. 1964. ed. spiral bdg. 29.75photocopy (ISBN 0-398-01127-3). C C Thomas.
McKusick, Victor A., ed. Medical Genetic Studies of the Amish: Selected Papers. LC 76-47386. (Illus.). 528p. 1978. 29.50x (ISBN 0-8018-1934-2). Johns Hopkins.
Ober, William B. Boswell's Clap & Other Essays: Medical Analyses of Literary Men's Afflictions. LC 78-16018. (Illus.). 320p. 1979. 19.95 (ISBN 0-8093-0889-4). S Ill U Pr.
Pearce, G. H. The Medical Report & Testimony. (Illus.). 1979. text ed. 17.95x (ISBN 0-04-610012-1). Allen Unwin.
Pickering, George. Creative Malady. 336p. 1976. pap. 3.95 (ISBN 0-440-54995-7, Delta). Dell.
Roueche, Berton. The Orange Man. LC 70-160696. 1971. 7.95 (ISBN 0-316-75951-1). Little.
Winslow, John H. Darwin's Victorian Malady: Evidence for Its Medically Induced Origin. LC 70-161989. (Memoirs Ser.: Vol. 88). 1971. pap. 2.50 (ISBN 0-87169-088-8). Am Philos.

MEDICINE–COLLECTED WORKS
Bell, Whitfield J., Jr. The Colonial Physician & Other Essays. new ed. LC 75-6652. (Illus.). 236p. 1975. text ed. 16.00 (ISBN 0-88202-024-2, Sci Hist). N Watson.
Benedek, G. B. & Villars, F. M. Physics with Illustrative Examples from Medicine & Biology, 2 vols. 1974. 15.95 ea. Vol. 1 (ISBN 0-201-00551-4). Vol. 2 (ISBN 0-201-00558-1). A-W.
Charcot, Jean M. Oeuvres completes, 9 vols. LC 70-169463. Repr. of 1894 ed. Set. 290.00 (ISBN 0-404-10000-7); 32.50 ea. AMS Pr.
Hippocrates. Medical Works, 4 vols. Incl. Vol. 1. Ancient Medicine, Airs, Waters, Places, Epidemics 1 & 2. Oath, Precepts, Nutriment (ISBN 0-674-99162-1); Vol. 2. Prognostic. Regimen in Acute Diseases. Sacred Disease. Art, Breaths, Law, Decorum; Vol. 3. On Wounds in the Head. in the Surgery. on Fractures, on Joints, Mochlikon; Vol. 4. Nature of Man. Regimen in Health. Humours. Amorphisms. Regimen 1-3. Dreams. (Includes On the Universe by Heracleitus and a General Index) (ISBN 0-674-99166-4). (Loeb Classical Library: No. 147-150). 11.00x (ISBN 0-686-76944-9). Harvard U Pr.
Parkinson, E. M. Catalogue of Medical Books, Fourteen Eighty to Seventeen Hundred, in Manchester University Library. 406p. 1972. 111.50x (ISBN 0-7190-1246-5, Pub. by Manchester U Pr England). State Mutual Bk.
Ravitch, Mark M., ed. The Papers of Alfred Blalock, 2 Vols. (Illus.). 1966. 85.00x (ISBN 0-8018-0544-9). Johns Hopkins.
Rush, Benjamin. Medical Inquiries & Observations, 4 vols. in 2. 4th ed. LC 76-180588. (Medicine & Society in America Ser). 1070p. 1972. Repr. of 1815 ed. 45.00 set (ISBN 0-405-03968-9). Arno.
Sherrington, Charles. Selected Writings of Sir Charles Sherrington. Denny-Brown, D., ed. (Illus.). 1979. 42.00x (ISBN 0-19-920104-8). Oxford U Pr.

MEDICINE–CONGRESSES
Annual Meeting of the Society for Advanced Medical Systems, 8th, Boston. Advanced Medical Systems: The 3rd Century: Proceedings. Hinman, ed. LC 77-74875. (Illus.). 1977. 21.50 (ISBN 0-8151-4459-8, Pub. by Symposia Special). Year Bk Med.
Gordon, R. A., et al, eds. International Symposium on Malignant Hyperthermia. (Illus.). 512p. 1973. 32.75 (ISBN 0-398-02549-5). C C Thomas.
National Medicological Symposium, 1975. Proceedings. 1975. 7.00 (ISBN 0-89970-073-X, OP-436). AMA.
Washington-Alaska Regional Medical Program Conference, Everett, Wash, 1973. Multitesting Database Acquisition: Current Approaches; Proceedings. LC 73-16454. 197p. 1973. 6.00 (ISBN 0-917054-06-7). Med Communications.

MEDICINE–COST OF MEDICAL CARE
see Medical Care, Cost Of

MEDICINE–DATA PROCESSING
Aikawa, Jerry K. & Pinfield, Edward R. Computerizing a Clinical Laboratory. (Illus.). 112p. 1973. 12.75 (ISBN 0-398-02847-8). C C Thomas.
Alperovitch, A., et al, eds. Evaluation of Efficacy of Medical Action. 536p. 1979. 73.25 (ISBN 0-444-85379-0). Elsevier.
American Medical Association, et al. Computer Assisted Medical Practice: AMA's Role. 1971. pap. 1.75 (ISBN 0-89970-028-4, OP377). AMA.
American Nuclear Society Topical Conference, Final Progra, Mayaguez, PR, April 30-May 4, 1978. Computers in Activation Analysis & Gamma-Ray Spectroscopy: Proceedings. Carpenter, B. Stephen, et al, eds. LC 79-19600. (DOE Symposium Ser.). 904p. 1979. pap. 15.00 (ISBN 0-686-75575-8); microfiche 3.00 (ISBN 0-686-75576-6). DOE.
Anderson, J., et al, eds. Medical Data Processing. 1977. 52.50x (ISBN 0-8448-1081-9). Crane-Russak Co.
Automated Education Center. An Annotated Bibliography of Biomedical Computer Applications. LC 79-120081. 19.00 (ISBN 0-686-02008-1). Mgmt Info Serv.
Ball, Marion J. Selecting a Computer System for the Clinical Laboratory. (Illus.). 132p. 1971. text ed. 18.75 (ISBN 0-398-02221-6). C C Thomas.
Ball, Marion J., ed. How to Select a Computerized Hospital Information System. (Data Processing in Medicine: Vol. 2). (Illus.). 1973. 35.50 (ISBN 3-8055-1465-4). S Karger.
Basmajian, et al. Computers in Electromyography. (Computers in Medicine Ser.). 1975. 15.95 (ISBN 0-407-50005-7). Butterworth.
Brandejs, J. F., ed. Computer Assisted Physicians Offices. (Health Communications & Informatics: Vol. 5, No. 2, 1979). (Illus.). 1979. softcover 11.50 (ISBN 3-8055-3063-3). S Karger.
Brandejs, Jan F. & Pace, Graham. Physician's Primer on Computers: Private Practice. LC 75-39315. (Illus.). 1979. 18.50 (ISBN 0-669-00431-6). Lexington Bks.
Caceres, C. A., ed. Clinical Electrocardiography & Computers: A Symposium Vol. 1970. 58.50 (ISBN 0-12-153840-0). Acad Pr.
Cady. Computer Techniques in Cardiology. (Biomedical Engineering & Instrumentation Ser.: Vol. 4). 1979. 45.00 (ISBN 0-8247-6743-8). Dekker.
Cardus, D. & Vallbona, C., eds. Computers & Mathematical Models in Medicine: Proceedings. (Lecture Notes in Medical Information Ser.: Vol. 9). 315p. 1981. pap. 26.50 (ISBN 0-387-10278-7). Springer-Verlag.
Cavill, I., et al. Computers in Hematology. (Computers in Medicine Ser.). 1975. 7.95 (ISBN 0-407-00037-2). Butterworth.
Chorafas, Dimitris N. Computer in der Medizin. (IS-Informations-Systeme). (Illus.). 127p. 1973. 29.50x (ISBN 3-11-004031-X). De Gruyter.
Coblentz, A. M. & Walter, J. R., eds. Systems Science in Health Care. LC 77-21046. 1978. text ed. 35.00 (ISBN 0-89433-067-5). Petrocelli.
Coles, E. C. Guide to Medical Computing. (Computers in Medicine Ser.). (Illus.). 112p. 1973. 8.95 (ISBN 0-407-54800-9). Butterworth.
Computer Information Services, Chicago Hospital Council. Shared Hospital Computer Services Evaluation. 165p. 1975. 15.00 (ISBN 0-686-68578-4, 14912). Hospital Finan.
Computers in Radiotherapy: 1968 2nd International Conference. 1980. 9.00x (ISBN 0-686-69946-7, Pub. by Brit Inst Radiology England). State Mutual Bk.
Computers in the Control of Treatment Units: Applications of Modern Technology in Radiotherapy. 1980. 10.00x (ISBN 0-686-69945-9, Pub. by Brit Inst Radiology England). State Mutual Bk.
Conference on Clinically Oriented Documentation of Laboratory Data, Buffalo, 1971. Clinically Oriented Documentation of Laboratory Data. Gabrieli, E. R., ed. 1972. 47.00 (ISBN 0-12-271850-X). Acad Pr.
Covvey, H. Dominic. Computers in the Practice of Medicine, Pt. 2: Issues in Medical Computing. LC 79-14099. 1980. text ed. 20.00 (ISBN 0-201-01249-9). A-W.
Covvey, H. Dominic & McAlister, Neil H. Computers in the Practice of Medicine, Pt. 1. LC 79-10499. 1980. text ed. 20.00 (ISBN 0-201-01251-0). A-W.
Dixon, W. J. & Brown, M. B., eds. BMDP-79: Biomedical Computer Programs, P-Series. rev. ed. 1979. 18.50x (ISBN 0-520-03569-0). U of Cal Pr.
DuBoulay, G. H., ed. Considerations About the Use of Computers in Radiodiagnostic Departments. 1980. 45.00x (ISBN 0-686-69947-5, Pub. by Brit Inst Radiology England). State Mutual Bk.
Eden, Henry S. & Eden, Murray. Microcomputers in Patient Care. LC 81-1999. (Illus.). 191p. 1981. 28.00 (ISBN 0-8155-0849-2). Noyes.
Elder, T. & Neill, W., eds. Biomedical Technology in Hospital Diagnosis. LC 74-189281. 528p. 1972. text ed. 105.00 (ISBN 0-08-015576-6). Pergamon.
Enlander, Derek. Computers in Medicine: An Introduction. LC 80-12221. (Illus.). 124p. 1980. pap. text ed. 13.95 (ISBN 0-8016-1525-9). Mosby.
Enslein, K., ed. Data Acquisition & Processing in Biology & Medicine: Proceedings. Incl. Vol. 3. Rochester Conference, 1963 (ISBN 0-08-010904-7); Vol. 4. Rochester Conference, 1964; Vol. 5. Rochester Conference, 1966 (ISBN 0-08-012671-5). Vols. 3 & 5. 25.00 ea. Pergamon.
Forsythe, Alan B., ed. Control Language Summary. (BMDP Statistical Software). 56p. (Orig.). 1980. pap. 3.00 (ISBN 0-935386-01-7). UCLA Dept Biomath.
Garrett, Raymond. Hospital Computer Systems & Procedures: Vol. 2, Medical Systems. (Computer Science Ser). 1976. 13.95 (ISBN 0-442-80338-9). Van Nos Reinhold.
--Hospitals: A Systems Approach. 224p. 1973. 16.95x (ISBN 0-442-80238-2). Van Nos Reinhold.
Gonzalez, Carlos F., et al. Computed Brain & Orbital Tomography: Technique & Interpretation. LC 76-28530. (Wiley Series in Diagnostic & Therapeutic Radiology). 1976. 55.00x (ISBN 0-471-01692-6, Pub. by Wiley-Medical). Wiley.
Grams, Ralph Raymond. Problem Solving, Systems Analysis, & Medicine. (Illus.). 244p. 1972. Set. 31.00 (ISBN 0-398-02298-4); companion volume - Systems Analysis wkbk. incl. (ISBN 0-398-02566-5). C C Thomas.
Harris, Kenneth W. & French, Dwight K. A Methodological Study of the Quality of Mortality Medical Coding. Cox, Klaudia, ed. (Series 2: No. 81). 1979. pap. text ed. 1.75 (ISBN 0-8406-0164-6). Natl Ctr Health Stats.
Herman, G. T. & Natterer, F., eds. Mathematical Aspects of Computerized Tomography: Proceedings. (Lecture Notes in Medical Information Ser.: Vol. 8). 309p. 1981. pap. 26.50 (ISBN 0-387-10277-9). Springer-Verlag.
Hill, D. W. Principles of Electronics in Medical Research. 2nd ed. (Illus.). 1973. 22.95 (ISBN 0-407-36401-3). Butterworth.
ITASA Conference, Boden, Austria, 1974. Systems Aspects of Health Planning: Proceedings. Thompson, M. & Bailey, N. J., eds. LC 74-28994. 347p. 1975. 39.00 (ISBN 0-444-10841-6, North-Holland). Elsevier.
Jacquez, John A. Computer Diagnosis & Diagnostic Methods: The Proceedings of the Second Conference on the Diagnostic Process, University of Michigan. (Illus.). 400p. 1972. 29.75 (ISBN 0-398-02521-5). C C Thomas.
Koza, Russell C., et al, eds. Health Information Systems Evaluation. LC 74-75391. (Illus.). 352p. 1974. text ed. 15.00x (ISBN 0-87081-060-X). Colo Assoc.
Krieg, Arthur F., et al. Clinical Laboratory Computerization. (Illus.). 1971. 19.50 (ISBN 0-8391-0096-5). Univ Park.
Lindberg, Donald A. The Computer & Medical Care. (Illus.). 224p. 1971. 17.50 (ISBN 0-398-01131-1). C C Thomas.
--The Growth of Medical Information Systems in the United States. LC 79-1555. 208p. 1979. 21.95 (ISBN 0-669-02911-4). Lexington Bks.
Ludwig, Herbert R. Computer Applications & Techniques in Clinical Medicine. 327p. 1974. 24.50 (ISBN 0-471-55356-5, Pub. by Wiley). Krieger.

Macfarlane, P. W. & Lawrie, D. Introduction to Automated Electrocardiogram Interpretation. (Computers in Medicine Ser.). 1974. 9.50x (ISBN 0-407-21899-8). Butterworth.
Park, W. M. & Reece, B. L. Fundamental Aspects of Medical Thermography. 1980. 18.00x (ISBN 0-686-69949-1, Pub. by Brit Inst Radiology England). State Mutual Bk.
Peth, C. F., et al. Application Design Manual for a Hospital Admitting System. 1977. 6.00 (ISBN 0-918118-13-1). MUMPS.
Pryor, T. Allan & Bailey, James J., eds. Computerized Interpretation of the IV. 395p. (Orig.). 1980. pap. text ed. 10.00 (ISBN 0-939204-05-3, 79-01). Eng Found.
Raviv, J., et al, eds. Computer Aided Tomography & Ultrasonics in Medicine. 1979. 49.00 (ISBN 0-444-85299-9, North Holland). Elsevier.
Ritchie, Robert F., ed. Automated Immunoanalysis, Pt. 1. (Clinical Chemistry & Biochemical Analysis Ser.). 1978. 42.50 (ISBN 0-8247-6678-4). Dekker.
Robida, Donald G. COMAPS: A Computer-Aided Pharmacy System. 1976. 7.50 (ISBN 0-918118-11-5). MUMPS.
Role of Computers in Radiotherapy. 1968. pap. 13.00 (ISBN 92-0-111668-3, ISP203, IAEA). Unipub.
Schade, J. & Smith, J., eds. Computers & Brains. (Progress in Brain Research: Vol. 33). 1971. 56.00 (ISBN 0-444-40855-X, North Holland). Elsevier.
Schneider, W. & Sagvall Hein, A. -L., eds. Computational Linguistics in Medicine: Proceedings of the IFIP Working Conference on Computational Linguistics in Medicine. 1978. 31.75 (ISBN 0-444-85040-6, North-Holland). Elsevier.
Shires, David B. Computer Technology in the Health Sciences. (Illus.). 160p. 1974. text ed. 14.75 (ISBN 0-398-03005-7). C C Thomas.
Spohr, Mark. Physician's Guide to Microcomputers. 1981. 18.95 (ISBN 0-8359-5548-6). Reston.
Stacy, Ralph W. & Waxman, Bruce. Computers in Biomedical Research, 4 vols. 1965-1964. Vol. 1. 58.50 (ISBN 0-12-662301-5); Vol. 2. 53.50 (ISBN 0-12-662302-3); Vol. 3. 53.50 (ISBN 0-12-662303-1); Vol. 4. 1974. 50.00 (ISBN 0-12-662304-X). Acad Pr.
Sterling, Theodor D. & Pollack, Seymour V. Computers & the Life Sciences. LC 65-27765. (Illus.). 1965. 20.00x (ISBN 0-231-02744-3). Columbia U Pr.
Stroke, George W., et al, eds. Ultrasonic Imaging & Holography: Medical, Sonar, & Optical Applications. LC 74-1371. 642p. 1974. 49.50 (ISBN 0-306-30762-6, Plenum Pr). Plenum Pub.
Szolovits, Peter, ed. Artificial Intelligence in Medicine. (AAAS Selected Symposium: No. 51). 130p. 1981. lib. bdg. 15.00x (ISBN 0-89158-900-7). Westview.
Tolan, Gil D. & Pryor, T. Allan, eds. Computerized Interpretation of the ECG V. 234p. (Orig.). 1980. pap. 15.00 (ISBN 0-939204-06-1, 80-13). Eng Found.
Toren, E. Clifford & Eggert, Arthur A., eds. Computers in the Clinical Laboratory. (Clinical & Biochemical Analysis Ser.: Vol. 8). 1978. 24.50 (ISBN 0-8247-6694-6). Dekker.
Van Egmond, J., et al, eds. Information Systems for Patient Care: Proceedings of the IFIP Working Conference on Information Systems for Patient Care Review, Analysis & Evaluation. 1976. 53.75 (ISBN 0-7204-0463-0, North-Holland). Elsevier.
Warner, Homer R. Computer-Assisted Medical Decision-Making. LC 79-52788. 1979. 27.50 (ISBN 0-12-735750-5). Acad Pr.
Weller, Charles, ed. Computer Applications in Health Care Delivery. LC 76-10867. (Illus.). 192p. 1976. text ed. 22.00 (ISBN 0-8151-9214-2, Pub. by Symposia Special). Year Bk Med.
Wiederhold, G. Databases for Health Care. (Lecture Notes in Medical Informatics Ser.: Vol. 12). 75p. 1981. pap. 11.90 (ISBN 0-387-10709-6). Springer-Verlag.
Wood, R. G. Computers in Radiotherapy: Physical Aspects. (Computers in Medicine Ser.). 1974. 9.95 (ISBN 0-407-50002-2). Butterworth.
Zielstorff, Rita. Computers in Nursing. LC 80-80813. (Nursing Dimensions Administration Ser.: Vol. I, No. 3). 236p. 1980. pap. text ed. 10.95 (ISBN 0-913654-66-3). Nursing Res.
Zimmerman, Joan & Rector, Alan. Computers for the Physician's Office. 1978. 47.00 (ISBN 0-471-27888-2). Res Stud Pr.

MEDICINE–DICTIONARIES

Albert, Ronald & Hahnewald, Harry, eds. Eight Language Dictionary of Medical Technology. LC 78-40828. 1979. 75.00 (ISBN 0-08-023763-0). Pergamon.
Andelman, S., ed. Home Medical Encyclopedia, 4 vols. 1979. 54.50 (ISBN 0-685-67807-5). Porter.
Armengol, Joseph, et al, eds. English-Spanish Guide for Medical Personnel. 1966. pap. 3.50 (ISBN 0-87488-721-6). Med Exam.
Blacque-Belair, Alain. Dictionnaire Medicine, Clinique, Pharmacologique et Therapeutique. 2nd ed. 1938p. (Fr.). 1978. 79.95 (ISBN 0-686-56920-2, M-6036). French & Eur.
Blakiston. Blakiston's Gould Medical Dictionary. 4th ed. (Illus.). 1979. Trade ed. 35.00 (ISBN 0-07-005703-6, HP); text ed. 26.95 (ISBN 0-07-005700-1). McGraw.
--Blakiston's Pocket Medical Dictionary. 4th ed. Gennaro, Alphonso R., ed. 1979. 17.95 (ISBN 0-07-005715-X, SP); text ed. 15.95 (ISBN 0-07-005714-1). McGraw.
Boericke, William. Materia Medica with Repertory. 1976. 12.50 (ISBN 0-685-76567-9, Pub. by Harjeet). Formur Intl.
Bolander, B. O. Instant Medical Dictionary. (Career Institute Instant Reference Library). 1970. 2.95 (ISBN 0-531-02009-6). Watts.
Bolander, Donald O., et al. Instant Medical Spelling Dictionary. LC 77-124400. 1970. 3.95 (ISBN 0-911744-10-X). Career Inst.
Bongiovanni, Gail. Medical Spanish. 1977. pap. text ed. 6.95 (ISBN 0-07-006470-9, HP). McGraw.
Bonvalot, Marie. Le Vocabulaire Medical De Base, 2 vols. 447p. (Fr.). 1972. Set. pap. 25.00 (ISBN 0-686-56925-3, M-6043). French & Eur.
Bordes, Gerard. Grande Encyclopedie Atlas De la Medecine, 9 vols. 320p. (Fr.). 1976. Set. 495.00 (ISBN 0-686-57312-9, M-6291). French & Eur.
Burney, Leroy E., et al, eds. Medical Aid Encyclopedia for the Home. (Illus.). 1964. 12.50 (ISBN 0-87396-003-3). Stravon.
Byers, Edward E. Gregg Medical Shorthand Dictionary. 1975. 13.75 (ISBN 0-07-009504-3, G). McGraw.
Carpovich, Eugene A. Russian-English Biological & Medical Dictionary. 2nd ed. LC 58-7915. 1960. 20.00 (ISBN 0-911484-01-9). Tech Dict.
Chapman. Medical Dictionary for the Lay Person. 1982. pap. 2.95 (ISBN 0-8120-2247-5). Barron.
Chevallier, J. Cando Medical et Pharmaceutique. 2nd ed. 996p. (Fr.). 1974. 79.95 (ISBN 0-686-56947-4, M-6069). French & Eur.
--Precis De Terminologie Medicale. 2nd ed. 208p. (Fr.). 1977. 19.95 (ISBN 0-686-56948-2, M-6070). French & Eur.
Collin, Mary A. Medical Terminology & the Body Systems. 1974. pap. text ed. 10.00x (ISBN 0-06-140663-5, Harper Medical). Har-Row.
Combs, C. Murphy, ed. Illustrated Medical Dictionary. (Medical Adviser Ser.). (Illus.). 1979. pap. 3.95 (ISBN 0-8326-2237-0, 7455). Delair.
Critchley, Macdonald, ed. Butterworths Medical Dictionary. 2nd, unabridged ed. 1980. pap. text ed. 39.95 (ISBN 0-407-00193-X). Butterworth.
--Butterworths Medical Dictionary. 2nd ed. LC 77-30154. 1978. 159.95 (ISBN 0-407-00061-5). Butterworth.
Delamare, J. & Delamare, Th. Dictionnaire Francais-Anglais et Anglais-Francais des Termes Techniques de Medecine. 714p. (Eng.-Fr.). 1970. 39.95 (ISBN 0-686-56980-6, M-6107). French & Eur.
Delamare, Jean V. Dictionary of Medical Terms: English-French & French-English. LC 73-540414. 710p. 1970. 52.50x (ISBN 0-8002-0196-5). Intl Pubns Serv.
Delamarre. Dictionnaire Francais-Anglais et Anglais-Francais des Termes Techniques De Medecine. 49.95 (ISBN 0-685-36680-4). French & Eur.
Diccionario de Medicina de Urgencia. 2nd ed. 208p. (Espn.). 1977. 6.95 (ISBN 84-352-0174-0, S-13672). French & Eur.
Diccionario Medico: De Bosillo. 2nd ed. 632p. (Espn.). 1974. leatherette 18.50 (ISBN 84-345-1017-0, S-13673). French & Eur.
Diccionario Terminologico De Ciencias Medicas. 11th ed. 1088p. (Espn.). 1978. 52.50 (ISBN 84-345-1206-8, S-13674). French & Eur.
Dictionnaire de Medecine Flammarion. 930p. (Fr.). 1975. 75.00 (ISBN 0-686-57099-5, M-6123). French & Eur.
Domart, Andre, ed. Petit Larousse De la Medecine. Bourneuf, Jacques. 852p. (Fr.). 1976. 42.50 (ISBN 0-686-57075-8, M-6448). French & Eur.
Domart, Andr e01 & Bourneuf, Jacques. Larousse de la M e01decine, 3 vols. 1728p. 1971. Set. 225.00 (ISBN 0-686-57120-7, M-6166). French & Eur.
Domart, Andr e01 & Bourneuf, Jacques, eds. Larousse De la M e01decine, 2. 515p. (Fr.). 87.50 (ISBN 0-686-56993-8, M-6333). French & Eur.
Dorland's Illustrated Medical Dictionary. 26th ed. (Illus.). 1800p. text ed. 32.50 (ISBN 0-7216-3150-9); indexed 37.50 (ISBN 0-7216-3151-7). Saunders.
Dorland's Illustrated Medical Dictionary. 25th ed. (Illus.). 1748p. 1974. deluxe ed. 40.00 (ISBN 0-7216-3149-5); text ed. 29.00 (ISBN 0-7216-3148-7). Saunders.
Dorland's Medical Dictionary: Shorter Edition. LC 79-67113. (Illus.). 768p. 1980. 14.95 (ISBN 0-7216-3142-8). Saunders.
Dorland's Pocket Medical Dictionary. 22st ed. LC 76-19604. (Illus.). 1977. thumb-indexed 11.95 (ISBN 0-7216-3162-2); plain 9.95 (ISBN 0-7216-3163-0). Saunders.
Dox, Ida, et al. Melloni's Illustrated Medical Dictionary. (Illus.). 1979. 18.95 (ISBN 0-683-02642-9). Williams & Wilkins.
Duden-Woerterbuch Medizinischer Fachausdrucke. 2nd ed. (Ger.). 25.95 (ISBN 3-411-00943-8, M-7346, Pub. by Bibliographisches Institut). French & Eur.
Duncan, A. S., et al, eds. Dictionary of Medical Ethics. 496p. 1981. 24.50 (ISBN 0-8245-0038-5). Crossroad NY.
Duncan, Helen A. Duncan's Dictionary for Nurses. LC 74-121974. (Illus.). 1971. pap. text ed. 6.25 (ISBN 0-8261-1121-1). Springer Pub.
Education & Training Systems Division of the Robert J. Brady Co. Brady's Programmed Orientation to Medical Terminology. 1970. pap. text ed. 7.50x (ISBN 0-397-54096-5, JBL-Med-Nursing). Har-Row.
Enciclopedia Medica Familiar, 2 vols. 596p. (Espn.). 1977. Set. 45.00 (ISBN 84-7017-348-0, S-50557). French & Eur.
Enciclopedia Medica Familiar, 2 vols. 5th ed. 448p. (Espn.). 1979. Set. pap. 47.95 (ISBN 84-278-0483-0, S-50532). French & Eur.
L' Encyclopedie Des Medecines Naturelles et Des Secrets De Sante. 606p. (Fr.). 1976. 29.95 (ISBN 0-686-57143-6, M-6200). French & Eur.
Encyclopedie Medicale De la Famille, 3 vols. 1200p. (Fr.). 1976. Set. 295.00 (ISBN 0-686-57162-2, M-6221). French & Eur.
Encyclopedie Medicale Quillet. (Fr.). 82.50 (ISBN 0-686-57163-0, M-6222). French & Eur.
Espinosa. Spanish for Doctors & Nurses. 1978. 10.95 (ISBN 0-8151-3147-X). Year Bk Med.
Fachredaktion. Woerterbuch Medizinischer Fachausdruecke. 2nd ed. (Ger.). 1973. 25.00 (ISBN 3-13-437802-7, M-6913). French & Eur.
Finch, Bernard, ed. Multilingual Guide for Medical Personnel. 1967. spiral bdg. 4.50 (ISBN 0-87488-961-8). Med Exam.
Finnegan, Edward G., ed. New Webster's Medical Dictionary: Vest Pocket Edition. 1980. pap. 1.95 (ISBN 0-8326-0048-2, 6453). Delair.
Fishbein, Morris. Dr. Fishbein's Popular Illustrated Medical Encyclopedia. LC 78-18133. (Illus.). 1979. Repr. of 1977 ed. 14.95 (ISBN 0-385-14190-4). Doubleday.
--Modern Home Dictionary of Medical Words: With Descriptions, Uses & Standards of Commonly Used Tests. LC 74-18845. 240p. 1976. pap. 1.95 (ISBN 0-385-01105-9, Dolp). Doubleday.
Fishbein, Morris, ed. The New Illustrated Medical and Health Encyclopedia: Spanish Language Edition, 2 vols. 1967. 29.95 (ISBN 0-87475-180-2). Stuttman.
Fishbein, Morris & Fishbein, Justin, eds. Fishbein's Illustrated Medical & Health Encyclopedia, 4 vols. LC 77-79746. (Home Library Edition). (Illus.). 1977. 39.95 (ISBN 0-87475-230-2). Stuttman.
--Fishbein's Illustrated Medical & Health Encyclopedia: Family Health Guide Edition. LC 78-53643. 1978. 24.95 (ISBN 0-87475-250-7). Stuttman.
--New Illustrated Medical & Health Encyclopedia: International Unified Edition, 22 vols. 1981. 131.56 (ISBN 0-87475-200-0). Stuttman.
Fishbein, Morris, M.D. Handy Home Medical Adviser & Concise Medical Encyclopedia. rev. ed. LC 72-92209. 394p. 1973. 7.95 (ISBN 0-385-01817-7). Doubleday.
Fort, J. A. Compendio De Anatomia Descriptiva. 546p. (Espn.). pap. 8.95 (ISBN 84-252-0222-1, S-50272). French & Eur.
Franks. Simplified Medical Dictionary. (Medical Economics Books). 1977. 12.50x (ISBN 0-442-84028-4). Van Nos Reinhold.
Franks, R. & Swartz, H. Simplified Medical Dictionary. 1977. 14.50 (ISBN 0-87489-054-3). Med Economics.
Franks, Richard. Simplified Medical Dictionary. 1977. pap. text ed. 12.52 (ISBN 0-8273-1786-7). Delmar.
Gardner, A. Ward. Good Housekeeping Dictionary of Symptoms. (Illus.). 1978. pap. 5.95 (ISBN 0-448-14731-9, Today Press). G&D.
Garnier, Marcel & Delamare, Jean. Dictionnaire des Termes Techniques De Medecine. 19th ed. 1340p. (Fr.). 1978. 35.00 (ISBN 0-686-57190-8, M-6262). French & Eur.
Gladstone. Vocabulaire De Medecine et Des Sciences Connexes Anglais-Francais-Anglais. 21.95 (ISBN 0-685-36682-0). French & Eur.
Gladstone, W. J. Dictionnaire Anglais-Francais des Sciences Medicales et Paramedicales. 1154p. (Fr.). 1978. 95.00 (ISBN 0-686-56787-0, M-6583, Pub. by Maloine). French & Eur.
--Dictionnaire Anglais-Francais des Sciences Medicales et Paramedicales. (Eng.-Fr.). 1978. 99.95 (ISBN 0-686-57303-X, M-6277). French & Eur.
Gomez, Joan. A Dictionary of Symptoms. Gersh, Marvin, ed. LC 68-16039. 1977. pap. 5.95 (ISBN 0-8128-1949-7). Stein & Day.
Good Housekeeping Concise Medical Encyclopedia. (Illus.). 384p. 1981. 14.95 (ISBN 0-87851-044-3). Hearst Bks.
Grant's Atlas. 7th ed. Bd. with Stedman's Medical Dictionary. 23rd ed. 1978. Set. 61.00 (ISBN 0-683-00213-9). Williams & Wilkins.
Gross, Verlee E. Three Hundred English Words Using Medical Word Components. 40p. (Orig.). 1972. pap. 3.00x (ISBN 0-912256-04-4). Halls of Ivy.
Habibi, B. Deutsch - Persisches Fachwoerterbuch Fuer Naturwissenschaft, Medezin und Landwirtschaft. 240p. (Ger.). 1964. pap. 17.50 (ISBN 3-447-00354-5, M-7331, Pub. by Harrassowitz). French & Eur.
Hahnemann, Samuel. Organon of Medicine. Boericke, William, tr. 1974. 9.00 (ISBN 0-685-76569-5, Pub. by Harjeet). Formur Intl.
Herbert, W. J. & Wilkinson, P. C. Diccionario De Inmunologia. 256p. (Espn.). 1974. leather 28.50 (ISBN 84-7092-106-1, S-50055). French & Eur.
Hitti, Jusuf. Medical English, Arabic Dictionary. (Illus.). 1973. 35.00x (ISBN 0-86685-067-8). Intl Bk Ctr.
Hitti, Yusuf K. Hitti's English-Arabic Medical Dictionary. 1967. 35.00x (ISBN 0-8156-6004-9, Am U Beirut). Syracuse U Pr.
Howell, G. & Perez Y Sabido, J. Spanish-English Handbook. 1977. pap. 9.95 (ISBN 0-87489-073-X). Med Economics.
Hughes, Harold K. A Dictionary of Abbreviations in Medicine & the Health Sciences. 1977. 25.95 (ISBN 0-669-00688-2). Lexington Bks.
Iribarren Reta, Mercedes. Diccionario Humano. 2nd ed. 552p. (Espn.). 1975. pap. 9.95 (ISBN 84-85000-33-1, S-50088). French & Eur.
Jedraszko, Sabina. Polish-English Medical Dictionary. 432p. 1980. vinyl 40.00x (ISBN 0-569-08616-7, Pub. by Collet's). State Mutual Bk.
Jeharned. Medical Terminology Made Easy. 2nd ed. 352p. 1968. text ed. 9.00 (ISBN 0-917036-06-9). Physicians Rec.
Kamenetz, Herman L. & Kamenetz, Georgette. Dictionnaire de Medecine Physique de Reeducation et Readaptation Fonctionelles. 208p. (Fr.). 1972. 19.95 (ISBN 0-686-56986-5, M-6324). French & Eur.
Kaps, Urban. Medizinisches Woerterbuch. (Ger.). pap. 7.50 (ISBN 0-686-56632-7, M-7555, Pub. by Bruno Wilkens). French & Eur.
Kay, Margarita. Southwestern Medical Dictionary: Spanish-English & English-Spanish. LC 76-54591. 1977. pap. text ed. 4.50x (ISBN 0-8165-0529-2). U of Ariz Pr.
Keller, Sally. English-Khmer Medical Dictionary. (Workpapers of North Dakota: Vol. XX, Suppl. 2). 1976. pap. 4.00 (ISBN 0-88312-744-X); microfiche 2.20 (ISBN 0-88312-341-X). Summer Inst Ling.
Kelly, Emerson C., ed. Encyclopedia of Medical Sources. LC 78-158127. 476p. 1948. 17.50 (ISBN 0-683-04556-3, Pub. by Williams & Wilkins). Krieger.
Larousse And Co. Larousse medical illustre. (Illus., Fr.). 72.50x (ISBN 2-03-008500-6, 3912). Larousse.
Larrauri, A. Dictionary of Oto-Rhino-Laryngology in Five Languages: English-French-Spanish-German-Italian. LC 71-501781. 1008p. 1971. 60.00x (ISBN 0-8002-0197-3). Intl Pubns Serv.
Lee-Delisle, Dora. English-Hungarian, Hungarian-English Medical Dictionary. 18.00 (ISBN 0-87557-040-2, 042-2X). Saphrograph.
Lejeune & Bunjes. Woerterbuch fuer Aerzte. 2nd ed. (Dictionary for Physicians). 1968. pap. 55.00 (ISBN 3-13-370502-4, M-6924). French & Eur.
Lejeune, F. & Bunjes, W. E. Dictionary for Physicians. 2nd ed. 459p. (Eng. -Ger.). 1968. 55.00 (ISBN 3-13-370502-4, M-7106). French & Eur.
Lepine, Pierre. Dictionnaire Francais-Anglais et Anglais-Francais des Termes Medicaux et Biologiques. 2nd ed. 896p. (Fr.-Eng.). 1974. 65.00 (ISBN 0-686-57292-0, M-4665). French & Eur.
Lucchesi, Mario. Dizionario Medico Ragionato Inglese-Italiano: Termini, Abbreviazioni, Sigle, Eponimi e Sinonimi Medici, Medico-Biologici e Delle Specializzazionni Mediche. 1490p. 1978. 98.00x (ISBN 0-913298-52-2). S F Vanni.

Manuila, A. & Nicole, M. Dictionnaire Francais de Medecine et de Biologie, Vol. 1. 866p. (Fr.). 1970. 175.00 (ISBN 0-686-57032-4, M-6392). French & Eur.
Manuila, A & Nicole, M. Dictionnaire Francais de Medecine el de Biologie, Vol. 2. (Fr.). 1971. 175.00 (ISBN 0-686-57033-2, M-6393). French & Eur.
Manuila, A., et al. Dictionnaire Francais de Medicine el de Biologie, Vol. 4. 580p. (Fr.). 1975. 130.00 (ISBN 0-686-57035-9, M-6395). French & Eur.
Manuila, L., et al. Petit Dictionnaire Medical. 566p. (Fr.). 1978. pap. 29.95 (ISBN 0-686-57036-7, M-6396). French & Eur.
Martin, M. W. A Concise Dictionary of Medicine. LC 74-23215. (Illus.). 1975. 8.95 (ISBN 0-8246-0193-9). Jonathan David.
Mauila, A., et al. Dictionnaire Francais de Medicine el de Biologie, Vol. 3. 1200p. (Fr.). 1972. 195.00 (ISBN 0-686-57034-0, M-6394). French & Eur.
The Medical and Health Sciences Word Book. 1977. 6.95 (ISBN 0-395-25409-4). HM.
Medical Dictionary. pap. 1.35 (ISBN 0-686-00474-4). Dennison.
Medical Directory 1980. 1980. text ed. 90.00 (ISBN 0-443-02067-1). Churchill.
Medizin Von A Boz Z. 464p. (Ger.). 1973. pap. 48.00 (ISBN 0-686-56631-9, M7553, Pub. by Herder). French & Eur.
Merriam-Webster Editorial Staff, ed. Webster's Medical Speller. 400p. 1975. 3.95 (ISBN 0-87779-037-X). Merriam.
Meyer-Camberg, Ernst. Das Praktische Lexikon der Naturheilkunde. (Ger.). 1977. pap. 15.95 (ISBN 3-570-06579-0, M-7594, Pub. by Mosaik/VVA). French & Eur.
Miller, Benjamin F. & Keane, Claire B. Encyclopedia & Dictionary of Medicine & Nursing. LC 73-103569. (Illus.). 1972. text ed. 18.95 (ISBN 0-7216-6357-5); student ed. 15.95 (ISBN 0-7216-6358-3). Saunders.
--Encyclopedia & Dictionary of Medicine & Nursing. LC 73-103569. (Illus.). 1972. text ed. 18.95 (ISBN 0-7216-6357-5); student ed. 15.95 (ISBN 0-7216-6358-3). Saunders.
Miller, Sigmund. Symptoms: The Complete Home Medical Encyclopedia. (Illus.). 1976. 18.95 (ISBN 0-690-01125-3). T Y Crowell.
Mills, Dorothy H. & Martinez, Jorge C. Dictionary for the Health Professional: English-Spanish-Spanish-English. LC 79-90820. (Illus.). 300p. 1981. pap. 16.00 (ISBN 0-935356-03-7). Mills Pub Co.
Mills, Dorothy H., et al. Spanish Vocabulary & Structure for the Health Professional, Bk. 1. 2nd ed. LC 80-54900. (Illus.). 146p. (Eng., Span.). 1981. pap. text ed. 18.00 (ISBN 0-935356-02-9). Mills Pub Co.
Mitchell Beazly Pub. Ltd. The Pocket Medical Encyclopedia & First Aid Guide. 1979. pap. 3.95 (ISBN 0-671-24671-2). S&S.
Mommsen. Diccionario Medico Labor Para la Familia. (Espn.). 1979. write for info. (ISBN 84-335-6007-7, S-50063). French & Eur.
Mommsen, H. Diccionario Medico Labor para la Familia. 5th ed. 816p. (Espn.). 1976. 45.00 (ISBN 84-335-6000-X, S-12337). French & Eur.
Morini, Simona. Enciclopedia De la Salud y la Belleza. 448p. (Espn.). 1977. pap. 12.25 (ISBN 0-686-57335-8, S-50037). French & Eur.
Nelson's New Compact Medical Dictionary. 1978. 1.95 (ISBN 0-8407-5635-6). Nelson.
Neuman, Maurice. Dictionnaire des Medicaments. 432p. (Fr.). 1971. pap. 27.50 (ISBN 0-686-56745-5, M-6424). French & Eur.
The New American Medical Dictionary & Health Manual. 1975. pap. 2.25 (ISBN 0-685-57129-7, Pub. by NAL). Formur Intl.
New Webster's Medical Dictionary. (Handy Reference Bks.). (Orig.). 1981. pap. 3.50 (ISBN 0-8326-0057-1, 6483). Delair.
Oeter, D. Herder - Lexikon Medizin. 2nd ed. 240p. (Ger.). pap. 15.95 (ISBN 0-686-56479-0, M-7446, Pub. by Herder). French & Eur.
Ogden, Margaret S., ed. Liber De Diversis Medicinis in the Thornton Manuscript. (Early English Text Society Ser.). (Illus.). 1938. 12.50x (ISBN 0-19-722207-2). Oxford U Pr.
Parry, S. Chalmers. Polyglot Medical Questionaire. 2nd ed. 1972. 16.95x (ISBN 0-433-05450-6). Intl Ideas.
Pauchet, V. & Dupret, S. Atlas Manual de Anatomia. 6th ed. Rodrigo Garcia, Ignacio, ed. 518p. (Esp n13.). 1978. pap. 16.75 (ISBN 84-252-0221-3, S-12343, French & Eur). French & Eur.
Pearce, Evelyn, et al. Medical & Nursing Dictionary & Encyclopaedia. new ed. 545p. 1975. text ed. 15.95 (ISBN 0-571-04843-9, Pub. by Faber & Faber). Merrimack Bk Serv.
Perlemuter, L. Dictionnaire Pratique De Therapeutique Medicale, 3. 2nd ed. Obraska, P., ed. 1032p. (Fr.). 1978. 79.95 (ISBN 0-686-57067-7, M-6439). French & Eur.
Perlemuter, Leon & Cenac, Arnaud. Dictionnaire Pratique De Medecine Clinique. 1830p. (Fr.). 1977. 99.50 (ISBN 0-686-57068-5, M-6440). French & Eur.
Piscitelli, Nicola. Diccionario Atlas De Anatomia Humana. 256p. (Espn.). 1974. pap. 13.25 (ISBN 84-307-8290-7, S-50259). French & Eur.
Pollak, Kurt. Knaurs Lexikon der Modernen Medizin. (Ger.). 1972. 17.50 (ISBN 3-426-03329-1, M-7519, Pub. by Druckenmueller). French & Eur.
Poujol, F. A. Dictionnaire de Medecine Pratique. Migne, J. P., ed. (Nouvelle Encyclopedie Theologique Ser.: Vol. 17). 552p. (Fr.). Date not set. Repr. of 1862 ed. lib. bdg. 71.00x (ISBN 0-89241-264-X). Caratzas Bros.
Prada Becares, Juan. Diccionario Terminologia Medica Explicada. 128p. (Espn.). 1977. pap. 9.95 (ISBN 84-400-3894-1, S-50111). French & Eur.
Pschyrembel, Willibald. Klinisches Woerterbuch Mit Klinischen Syndromen. 253 rev. ed. (Illus., Ger.). 1977. 26.50x (ISBN 3-11-007018-9). De Gruyter.
Rayner, Claire. Everything Your Doctor Would Tell You If He Had the Time. (Illus.). 1980. 14.95 (ISBN 0-399-12482-9). Putnam.
Rigal, Waldo A. The Inverted Medical Dictionary. LC 73-84126. 1976. 20.00x (ISBN 0-87762-203-5); pap. 14.50x (ISBN 0-87762-170-5). Technomic.
Riley, P. A. & Cunningham, P. J. The Faber Pocket Medical Dictionary. 3rd ed. Forsythe, Elizabeth, ed. (Illus.). 408p. 1979. 4.95 (ISBN 0-571-04999-0, Pub. by Faber & Faber). Merrimack Bk Serv.
Roca, Castells A., et al. Enciclopedia de la Salud. 6th ed. 1043p. (Espn.). 1974. leatherette 70.00 (ISBN 84-252-0220-5, S-13678). French & Eur.
Roper, Nancy. New American Pocket Medical Dictionary. 1978. pap. 5.95 (ISBN 0-684-15923-6, SL820, ScribT). Scribner.
--The New American Pocket Medical Dictionary. LC 78-3857. (Illus.). 1978. pap. text ed. 5.50 (ISBN 0-443-08013-5). Churchill.
Rothenberg, Robert. The New American Medical Dictionary & Health Manual. (Illus.). 552p. 1975. 10.95 (ISBN 0-517-52141-5). Crown.
--New American Medical Dictionary & Health Manual. rev. ed. pap. 3.50 (ISBN 0-451-09867-6, E9867, Sig). NAL.
Rowe, Leah. Medical Sound-Alikes. McFadden, S. Michele, ed. 1978. pap. text ed. 5.95x (ISBN 0-89262-016-1). Career Pub.
Ruiz Torres, Francisco. Diccionario Espanol-Ingles, Ingles-Espanol. 3rd ed. 714p. (Span.-Eng.). 1978. pap. 41.95 (ISBN 84-205-0455-6, S-12408). French & Eur.
--Vocabulario Ingles-Espanol, Espanol-Ingles de Medicina. 300p. (Eng.-Span.). 1979. pap. 10.75 (ISBN 84-205-0625-7, S-50091). French & Eur.
Salvat Medicina, Enciclopedia De Conocimientos Basicos, 10 vols. 3000p. (Espn.). 1974. Set. 320.00 (ISBN 84-7137-380-7, S-50559). French & Eur.
Schertel, A. Abkuerzungen in der Medizin. 198p. (Ger., Eng. & Fr., Abbreviations in Medicine). 1974. pap. 18.95 (ISBN 3-7940-3014-1, M-7292, Pub. by Vlg. Dokumentation). French & Eur.
Schmidt, J. E. English Word Power for Physicians & Other Professionals: A Vigorous & Cultured Vocabulary. 240p. 1971. 19.75 (ISBN 0-398-01666-6). C C Thomas.
--Paramedical Dictionary: A Practical Dictionary for the Semi-Medical & Ancillary Medical Professions. 1974. 14.25 (ISBN 0-398-01672-0); pap. 10.75 (ISBN 0-398-02902-4). C C Thomas.
--Police Medical Dictionary. 256p. 1968. 19.75 (ISBN 0-398-01673-9). C C Thomas.
--Practical Nurses' Medical Dictionary: A Cyclopedic Medical Dictionary for Practical Nurses, Vocational Nurses, & Nurses' Aides. 300p. 1968. 11.75 (ISBN 0-398-01675-5). C C Thomas.
--Structural Units of Medical & Biological Terms: A Convenient Guide, in English, to the Roots, Stems, Prefixes, Suffixes, & Other Combining Forms Which Are the Building Blocks of Medical & Related Scientific Words. 180p. 1969. text ed. 11.75 (ISBN 0-398-01676-3). C C Thomas.
--Visual Aids for Paramedical Vocabulary. (Illus.). 196p. 1973. 10.75 (ISBN 0-398-02609-2). C C Thomas.
Segatore, Luigi & Poli, Gianangelo. Diccionario Medico. 5th ed. 1282p. (Espn.). 1975. 44.95 (ISBN 84-307-8013-0, S-12357). French & Eur.
Settar, G. Worldwide Medical Interpreter: English, Vol. 1. 1977. pap. 12.00 (ISBN 0-87489-101-9). Med Economics.
--Worldwide Medical Interpreter: Greek, Vol. 12. 1977. pap. 12.00 (ISBN 0-87489-112-4). Med Economics.
--Worldwide Medical Interpreter: Italian, Vol. 6. 1977. pap. 12.00 (ISBN 0-87489-106-X). Med Economics.
Sliosberg, A. Elsevier's Medical Dictionary. rev. 2nd ed. LC 72-97436. 1452p. 1975. 134.25 (ISBN 0-444-41103-8). Elsevier.
Smith, Genevieve L. & Davis, Phyllis E. Quick Medical Terminology. LC 72-4193. (Wiley Self-Teaching Guides Ser). 248p. 1972. 6.95 (ISBN 0-471-80198-4); cassettes 7.95 (ISBN 0-471-80201-8). Wiley.
Standard Medical Almanac. 1st ed. LC 76-52851. 1977. 39.50 (ISBN 0-8379-4001-X). Marquis.
Stedman. Stedman's Medical Dictionary. 22nd ed. 1585p. 1972. 12.95 (ISBN 0-683-07919-0, Pub. by Williams & Wilkins). Krieger.
Stedman's Medical Dictionary. (Illus.). 1750p. 1981. lib. bdg. 30.00 (ISBN 0-683-07915-8). Williams & Wilkins.
Stedman's Medical Dictionary. 23rd ed. (Illus.). 1678p. 1976. 32.00 (ISBN 0-683-07924-7). Williams & Wilkins.
Tabery, Julia J., et al. Communicating in Spanish for Medical Personnel. LC 73-17667. 600p. 1975. pap. text ed. 15.95 (ISBN 0-316-83101-8); tapes 25.00 (ISBN 0-316-83102-6); pap. text ed. 30.00 incl. text & tapes (ISBN 0-316-83103-4). Little.
Terminologie et Lexicographie Medicales. 60p. (Fr.). 1967. pap. 17.50 (ISBN 0-686-57229-7, M-6530). French & Eur.
Thomas, Clayton L., ed. Taber's Cyclopedic Medical Dictionary. 14th ed. (Illus.). 1818p. 1981. 14.95 (ISBN 0-8036-8307-3); Thumb-indexed Edition. text ed. 17.50 (ISBN 0-8036-8306-5). Davis Co.
Thomson, Robert. The Grosset Encyclopedia of Natural Medicine. LC 79-56186. (Illus.). 1980. pap. 9.95 (ISBN 0-448-14897-8). G&D.
Thomson, William A., ed. Black's Medical Dictionary. 32nd rev. ed. LC 79-54106. (Illus.). 1979. text ed. 22.95x (ISBN 0-06-490437-7). B&N.
Thomson, William A. R., ed. Black's Medical Dictionary. 31st, rev & enl. ed. (Illus.). 1979. Repr. of 1976 ed. text ed. 18.50x (ISBN 0-06-490443-1). B&N.
Torres, Francisco R. Spanish-Espagnol-Ingles. pap. 55.95 (ISBN 84-205-0455-6). Larousse.
Touati, Maurice A. Lexique Francais Des Abreviations et Formules Medico-Chirurgicales Courantes. 142p. (Fr.). 1969. 12.50 (ISBN 0-686-57234-3, M-6535). French & Eur.
Tutsch, D. Lexikon der Medizinischen Fachsprache, 2 vols. 388p. (Ger.). 1970. Set. pap. 9.95 (ISBN 3-499-16126-5, M-7249). French & Eur.
Tutsch, Dagobert. Lexikon der Medizin. (Ger.). 1975. 19.95 (ISBN 3-541-07081-1, M-7250). French & Eur.
Ullstein Lexikon der Medizin. (Ger.). 1970. 22.50 (ISBN 3-550-06017-3, M-7674, Pub. by Ullstein Verlag/VVA). French & Eur.
Unseld, D. Medizinisches Woerterbuch der Deutschen und Englischen Sprache. 6th rev. ed. 519p. (Eng. & Ger., Medical Dictionary of the German and English Language). 1971. 33.50 (ISBN 3-8047-0415-8, M-7556, Pub. by Wissenschaftlicher Vlg.). French & Eur.
Unseld, D. W. Medical Dictionary. (Ger-Eng, Eng-Ger.). 1971. 31.50 (ISBN 3-8047-0415-8). Adler.
Urdang. Urdang Dictionary of Current Medical Terms. LC 80-22916. 455p. 1981. 12.95 (ISBN 0-471-05853-X, Pub. by Wiley Med). Wiley.
Veillon, E. & Nobel, A. Medizinisches Woerterbuch. 5th rev. ed. 1330p. (Ger., Fr. & Eng., Medical Dictionary). 1969. 105.00 (ISBN 3-456-00200-9, M-7554, Pub. by H. Huber). French & Eur.
--Spanisches Supplement Zu Medizinisches Woerterbuch. (Ger.). 1971. 48.00 (ISBN 3-456-00271-8, M-7623, Pub. by H. Huber Vlg.). French & Eur.
Vocabulaire De Medecine et Des Sciences Connexes: Francais-Anglais, Anglais-Francais. 298p. (Fr.-Eng.). 1971. 37.50 (ISBN 0-686-57281-5). French & Eur.
Von Schaldach, Herbert. DTV Woerterbuch der Medizin, Vol. 1. 5th ed. (Ger.). 1973. pap. 7.95 (ISBN 3-423-03028-3, M-7342, Pub. by DTV Deutscher Taschenbuch Vlg.). French & Eur.
--DTV Woerterbuch der Medizin, Vol. 2. 5th ed. (Ger.). 1973. pap. 7.95 (ISBN 3-423-03029-1, M-7343, Pub. by DTV Deutscher Taschenbuch Vlg.). French & Eur.
--DTV Woerterbuch der Medizin, Vol. 3. 5th ed. (Ger.). 1973. pap. 7.95 (ISBN 3-423-03030-5, M-7344, Pub. by DTV Deutscher Taschenbuch Vlg.). French & Eur.
Wakeley, Cecil, ed. The Faber Medical Dictionary. 2nd ed. LC 74-15700. 483p. 1974. 18.50 (ISBN 0-397-58142-4). Lippincott.
Wingate, Peter. Penguin Medical Encyclopedia. (Reference Ser.). (Illus.). 1972. pap. 4.95 (ISBN 0-14-051048-6). Penguin.
Zlotnicki, B. Lexikon Medicum. (Eng., Rus., Fr., Ger., Lat. & Pol., Medical Dictionary). 1973. 92.00 (ISBN 3-7945-0324-4, M-7194). French & Eur.
Zlotnickiego, Boleslaw. Lexicon Medicum. 1604p. (Eng., Rus., Fr., Ger., Lat. & Pol.). 1976. 95.00 (ISBN 0-686-57263-7, M-6576). French & Eur.
Zoltnicki, B. Medical Dictionary. (Eng., Rus., Fr., Ger., Lat. & Pol.). 1973. 92.50 (ISBN 3-7945-0324-4, M-7552, Pub. by Schattauer). French & Eur.

MEDICINE–EARLY WORKS

Albertus Magnus. The Boke of Secretes. LC 76-28227. (English Experience Ser: No. 116). 168p. 1969. Repr. of 1525 ed. 15.00 (ISBN 90-221-0116-9). Walter J Johnson.
Freind, John. History of Physick: From the Time of Galen to the Beginning of the Sixteenth Century, 2 Vols. 4th ed. Repr. of 1750 ed. Set. 55.00 (ISBN 0-404-07987-3). AMS Pr.
Guido, De Cauliaco. Guydos Questions Newly Corrected. LC 68-54627. (English Experience Ser.: No. 35). 390p. 1968. Repr. of 1579 ed. 50.00 (ISBN 90-221-0035-9). Walter J Johnson.
Leibowitz, J. O. & Marcus, Shlomo, eds. Moses Maimonides on the Causes of Symptoms. LC 71-187873. 1974. 24.00x (ISBN 0-520-02224-6). U of Cal Pr.
Paracelsus. Selected Writings. 2nd ed. Jacobi, J., ed. Gutterman, Norman, tr. (Bollingen Ser.: Vol. 28). (Illus.). 1958. 18.00x (ISBN 0-691-09810-7). Princeton U Pr.
Rudman, Jack. National Medical Boards (NMB) Pt. 2, Pt. 2. (Admission Test Ser.: ATS-23B). (Cloth bdg. avail. on request). pap. 13.95 (ISBN 0-8373-5023-9). Natl Learning.
Siegel, R. E. Galen on the Affected Parts: Translation from the Greek Text with Explanatory Footnoots. 1976. pap. 54.00 (ISBN 3-8055-2201-0). S Karger.
Thompson, Reginald C., ed. Assyrian Medical Texts from the Originals in the British Museum. LC 78-72766. (Ancient Mesopotamian Texts & Studies). Repr. of 1923 ed. 30.00 (ISBN 0-404-18220-8). AMS Pr.
Vigo, Johannes de. The Most Excellent Workes of Chirurgerye Made M. T. Vignon. Traheron, B., tr. LC 68-54639. (English Experience Ser.: No. 67). 540p. 1968. Repr. of 1543 ed. 83.00 (ISBN 90-221-0067-7). Walter J Johnson.

MEDICINE–EXAMINATIONS, QUESTIONS, ETC.

Alba. Alba's Medical Technology Board Examination Review, Vol. I. 9th ed. (Illus.). 1980. pap. text ed. 20.00 (ISBN 0-910224-05-6). Berkeley Sci.
--Alba's Medical Technology Board Examination Review, Vol. II. 4th ed. LC 72-172446. (Illus.). 1978. pap. text ed. 17.00 (ISBN 0-910224-02-1). Berkeley Sci.
Arco Editorial Board. Science Review for Medical College Admission Test. LC 78-24576. (Illus.). 1979. pap. text ed. 12.95 (ISBN 0-668-04705-4, 4705-4). Arco.
Baker, Michael A., ed. Medicine. 7th ed. (Medical Examination Review Ser.: Vol. 2). 1980. pap. 8.50 (ISBN 0-87488-102-1). Med Exam.
Bhardwaj, Ved B. Medical Examinations: A Preparation Guide. (Illus.). 1979. pap. 9.00 (ISBN 0-668-03944-2). Arco.
Bowers, Warner F., et al. ECFMG Examination Review. 4th ed. LC 76-9880. 1976. Pt. 1. pap. 11.75 (ISBN 0-87488-120-X); Pt. 2. pap. 11.75 (ISBN 0-87488-121-8). Med Exam.
Bramson, Morris & Solomon, Lawrence. New MCAT. new ed. LC 78-2312. 1978. pap. 5.95 (ISBN 0-671-18990-5). Monarch Pr.
Brown. Barron's How to Prepare for the New Medical College Admission Test (McAt) 1980. pap. 6.50 (ISBN 0-8120-2190-8). Barron.
Crow, Marjorie & Lounsbury, Patricia F. Practice Tests for the L. P. N. LC 80-39735. 112p. (Orig.). 1981. pap. text ed. 7.50x (ISBN 0-668-05189-2, 5189). Arco.
DeKornfeld, Thomas J. & Finch, Jay S. Respiratory Care Case Studies, Vol. 1. 2nd ed. 1976. spiral bdg. 12.75 (ISBN 0-87488-019-X). Med Exam.
DeMyer, William, ed. Psychiatry-Neurology: PreTest Self-Assessment & Review. (Illus.). 250p. (Orig.). 1981. pap. 25.00 (ISBN 0-07-051660-X, HP). McGraw.
Dwyer, John, ed. Medicine: PreTest Self-Assessment & Review. LC 77-86707. (Clinical Sciences: PreTest Self-Assessment & Review Ser.). (Illus.). 1978. pap. 9.95 (ISBN 0-07-051601-4). McGraw-Pretest.
Dwyer, John M., ed. Medicine: PreTest Self-Assessment & Review. 2nd ed. (Illus.). 225p. 1981. pap. 9.95 (ISBN 0-07-050971-9, HP). McGraw.
Fleming, P. R., ed. Twelve Hundred MCQs in Medicine. 168p. 1980. pap. text ed. 11.50 (ISBN 0-443-01571-6). Churchill.

Frolich, Edward D. Rypin's Medical Licensure Examinations. 13th ed. (Illus.). 1054p. 1981. text ed. 35.00 (ISBN 0-397-52091-3, JBL-Med-Nursing). Har-Row.
Gabriel, Roger & Gabriel, Cynthia. Medical Data Interpretation for MRCP. 1978. pap. 6.95 (ISBN 0-407-00134-4). Butterworth.
Hubbard, John P. Measuring Medical Education: The Tests & the Experience of the National Board of Medical Examiners. 2nd ed. LC 77-19174. (Illus.). 187p. 1978. text ed. 12.00 (ISBN 0-8121-0625-3). Lea & Febiger.
King, Thomas C., ed. Surgery: PreTest Self-Assessment & Review. 2nd ed. (Illus.). 250p. 1981. pap. 9.95 (ISBN 0-07-050972-7, HP). McGraw.
Lipman, Richard P., ed. Pediatrics: PreTest Self-Assessment & Review. 2nd ed. (Illus.). 250p. 1981. pap. 9.95 (ISBN 0-07-050973-5, HP). McGraw.
Lloyd, G. E., ed. Hippocratic Writings. (Classics Ser). 1978. pap. 4.95 (ISBN 0-14-040031-1, Pelican). Penguin.
McCaulley, Mary H. Application of the Myers-Briggs Type Indicator to Medicine & Other Health Professions, 2 vols. Incl. Monograph I. 554p. 1978. pap. 20.00 (ISBN 0-935652-03-5); Monograph II. 288p. 1977. pap. 15.00 (ISBN 0-935652-04-3). (Illus.). 842p. (Orig.). Set. pap. 30.00 (ISBN 0-935652-05-1). Ctr Applications Psych.
Nelson, J. Craig, ed. Psychiatry: PreTest Self-Assessment & Review. 2nd ed. (Illus.). 225p. 1981. 9.95 (ISBN 0-07-050974-3, HP). McGraw.
Pappworth, M. H. Passing Medical Exams. 1975. 9.95 (ISBN 0-407-00013-5). Butterworth.
PreTest for Physicians Preparing for the American Board of Internal Medicine Certifying Examination. 3rd ed. LC 77-78735. (Pretest Ser.). (Illus.). 1977. pap. 27.50 (ISBN 0-07-079142-2). McGraw-Pretest.
PreTest for Physicians Preparing for the ECFMG Examination. 2nd ed. (Pretest Series). (Illus.). 1976. pap. 27.50 (ISBN 0-07-079140-6). McGraw-Pretest.
Pretest Self-Assessment & Review Series. new ed. Incl. Anatomy (ISBN 0-07-050791-0); Biochemistry (ISBN 0-07-050796-1); Epidemiology & Public Health (ISBN 0-07-050797-X); Microbiology. 2nd ed (ISBN 0-07-050966-2); Pathology (ISBN 0-07-050794-5); Physiology (ISBN 0-07-050792-9). 1976. 9.50 ea. (HP). McGraw.
Pretest Series. PreTest for Students Preparing for the National Board Examination, Pt. 1. 4th ed. LC 77-78442. (Illus.). 1977. pap. 17.95 (ISBN 0-07-079138-4). McGraw-Pretest.
Pretest Series, ed. PreTest for Physicians Preparing for the VISA Qualifying Examination. LC 78-59990. (Illus.). 1978. pap. 27.50 (ISBN 0-07-079141-4). McGraw-Pretest.
--PreTest for Students Preparing for the National Board Examination, Pt. II. 4th ed. LC 77-78442. 1978. pap. 17.95 (ISBN 0-07-079139-2). McGraw-Pretest.
Pretest Series Editors. Pretest for Physicians Preparing for the Federation Licensing Examination Flex. 3rd ed. LC 78-71293. (Illus.). 1979. pap. 27.50 (ISBN 0-07-079143-0). McGraw-Pretest.
PreTest Service Inc. Family Practice: PreTest Self-Assessment & Review. Catlin, Robin J., ed. (Illus.). 250p. (Orig.). 1981. pap. 27.50 (ISBN 0-07-051652-9). McGraw.
Rudman, Jack. AMRA Medical Record Administrator National Registration Examination (RRA) (Admission Test Ser.: ATS-84). (Cloth bdg. avail. on request). pap. 17.95 (ISBN 0-8373-5084-0). Natl Learning.
--AMRA Medical Record Technician National Registration Examination (ART) (Admission Test Ser.: ATS-85). (Cloth bdg. avail. on request). pap. 13.95 (ISBN 0-8373-5085-9). Natl Learning.
--Educational Commission for Foreign Medical Graduates English Test (ECFMG-ET) (Admission Test Ser.: ATS-43). (Cloth bdg. avail. on request). pap. 9.95 (ISBN 0-8373-5043-3). Natl Learning.
--Medical Aide. (Career Examination Ser.: C-1364). (Cloth bdg. avail. on request). pap. 8.00 (ISBN 0-8373-1364-3). Natl Learning.
--Medical Assistant. (Career Examination Ser.: C-1365). (Cloth bdg. avail. on request). pap. 8.00 (ISBN 0-8373-1365-1). Natl Learning.
--Medical Assisting. (Occupational Competency Examination Ser.: OCE-26). (Cloth bdg. avail. on request). pap. 9.95 (ISBN 0-8373-5726-8). Natl Learning.
--Medical Services Specialist. (Career Examination Ser.: C-2746). (Cloth bdg. avail. on request). 1980. pap. 12.00 (ISBN 0-8373-2746-6). Natl Learning.
--National Medical Boards (NMB) Pt. 1, Pt. 1. (Admission Test Ser.: ATS-23A). (Cloth bdg. avail. on request). pap. 13.95 (ISBN 0-8373-5023-9). Natl Learning.
--Physician. (Career Examination Ser.: C-1392). (Cloth bdg. avail. on request). pap. 14.00 (ISBN 0-8373-1392-9). Natl Learning.
--Staff Physician. (Career Examination Ser.: C-1493). (Cloth bdg. avail. on request). pap. 14.00 (ISBN 0-8373-1493-3). Natl Learning.
Schuchmann, John A., et al. Physical Medicine & Rehabilitation Review. LC 79-21717. (Orig.). 1980. pap. text ed. 15.00 (ISBN 0-668-04723-2). Arco.
Schwartz, Seymour I., et al, eds. Principles of Surgery: PreTest Self-Assessment & Review with CME Examination. 260p. (Orig.). 1981. 70.00 (ISBN 0-07-079036-1, HP). McGraw.
Seibel, Hugo & Guyer, Kenneth E. Barron's How to Prepare for the New Medical College Admission Test (MCAT) LC 80-15470. 1981. pap. text ed. 6.50 (ISBN 0-8120-2190-8). Barron.
Swartz, William H., ed. Obstetrics & Gynecology: PreTest Self-Assessment & Review. 2nd ed. (Illus.). 225p. 1981. pap. 9.95 (ISBN 0-07-050975-1, HP). McGraw.
Tarlow, David M. Student Guide to the Medical College Admission Test. 3rd ed. LC 78-53092. (Illus.). 1981. pap. 9.00 (ISBN 0-931572-00-2). Datar Pub.
Turner, Elizabeth, ed. Chemistry for Medical Technologists: PreTest Self-Assessment & Review. (Illus.). 200p. (Orig.). 1981. pap. 9.95 (ISBN 0-07-051655-3, HP). McGraw.
Verby, John E. Family Practice Specialty Board Recertification Review. 3rd ed. 1978. spiral bdg. 16.50 (ISBN 0-87488-309-1). Med Exam.
Wisch, Nathaniel, ed. Comprehensive. 3rd ed. (Medical Examination Review Books: Vol. 1). 1972. spiral bdg. 15.00 (ISBN 0-87488-101-3). Med Exam.
Wright, Arthur W., ed. Rypins' Medical Licensure Examinations. 12th ed. LC 65-18856. 1024p. 1975. text ed. 32.50 (ISBN 0-397-52066-2). Lippincott.
Young, K., et al, eds. The MRCGP Study Book. 150p. 1981. PLB 37.00 (ISBN 0-906141-13-3, Pub. by Update Pubns England); pap. 31.50 (ISBN 0-686-28845-9). Kluwer Boston.

MEDICINE–FEES

see Medical Fees

MEDICINE–FORMULAE, RECEIPTS, PRESCRIPTIONS

see also Dispensatories; Medicines, Patent, Proprietary, etc.; Pharmacopoeias; Pharmacy

Al-Kindi. Medical Formulary or Agrabadhinx of Al-Kindi. Levey, Martin, tr. (Medieval Science Pubns., No. 7). 1966. 32.50x (ISBN 0-299-03600-6). U of Wis Pr.
Bartilucci, A. & Durgin, J. Giving Medications Correctly & Safely. 1978. pap. 9.95 (ISBN 0-87489-216-3). Med Economics.
Brendle, T. R. Folk Medicine of the Pennsylvania Germans: The Non-Occult Cures. LC 71-15633. Repr. of 1935 ed. 15.00x (ISBN 0-678-03753-1). Kelley.
British National Formulary 1981, Vol. 1. 400p. 11.00 (ISBN 0-85369-140-1). Rittenhouse.
Burack, Richard. The New Handbook of Prescription Drugs. rev. ed. 1975. pap. 2.95 (ISBN 0-345-27162-9). Ballantine.
Dirckx, John H. Dx & Rx: A Physician's Guide to Medical Writing. (Medical Publications). 1977. lib. bdg. 12.95 (ISBN 0-8161-2100-1). G K Hall.
Long, James W. The Essential Guide to Prescription Drugs. rev. ed. LC 76-5141. 863p. Date not set. pap. 8.95 (ISBN 0-06-090715-0, CN715, CN). Har-Row.
Petulengro, Gipsy. Romany Remedies & Recipes. LC 80-20035. 126p. 1980. Repr. of 1972 ed. lib. bdg. 9.95x (ISBN 0-89370-616-7). Borgo Pr.
Pharmaceutical Society of Great Britain, ed. British National Formulary, No. 1. 400p. 1981. 11.00 (ISBN 0-85369-140-1). Rittenhouse.
Pharmaceutical Society of Great Britain. British National Formulary: 1976-1978. 1981. 11.00 (ISBN 0-85369-140-1, Pub. by Pharmaceutical). Rittenhouse.
Rosenberg, J. Prescriber's Guide to Drug Interactions. 1978. pap. 12.95 (ISBN 0-87489-143-4). Med Economics.
Schonfeld, H., ed. Reports on Ceftriaxone (RocephinR) (Journal Chemptherapy: Vol. 27, Suppl. 1). (Illus.). iv, 104p. 1981. pap. 17.50 (ISBN 3-8055-3034-X). S Karger.
Strauss, Steven. Your Prescription & You. 4th ed. 1980. pap. 2.95 (ISBN 0-933916-01-9). IMS Comm.

MEDICINE–HANDBOOKS, MANUALS, ETC.

Alfred and Alfred. Medical Handbook for the Layman. 5.95 (ISBN 0-685-02562-4). Borden.
American Medical Directory, 4 vols. 26th ed. 1974. 125.00 set (ISBN 0-89970-022-5, OP-64). AMA.
Andelman, S., ed. Home Medical Encyclopedia, 4 vols. 1979. 54.50 (ISBN 0-685-67807-5). Porter.
Andelman, Samuel L. The New Home Medical Encyclopedia, 4 vols. LC 71-116070. (Illus.). 1400p. 1973. 35.00 (ISBN 0-8129-0260-2). Times Bks.
Aschenbrener, Thomas D. & Mosan, Paul. Physicians Assistant Examination Review. LC 78-26893. 144p. 1980. pap. text ed. 12.00 (ISBN 0-668-04026-2). Arco.
Austin, Glenn. Parents' Medical Manual. LC 78-2759. (Illus.). 1978. 15.95 (ISBN 0-13-650317-9, Spec); pap. 8.95 (ISBN 0-13-650309-8). P-H.
Ayres, Stephen. Medical Resident's Manual. 4th ed. 512p. 1981. 15.00 (ISBN 0-8385-6253-1). ACC.
Berkow, Robert, ed. Merck Manual of Diagnosis & Therapy. 13th ed. LC 1-31760. (Illus.). 1980p. 1977. 14.50 (ISBN 0-911910-02-6). Merck.
Berkowitz, Richard L., et al. Handbook for Prescribing Medications During Pregnancy. 1981. pap. text ed. 11.95 (ISBN 0-316-09173-1). Little.
Bernstein, Arthur. Intern's Manual. 4th ed. (Illus.). 1971. pap. 12.95 (ISBN 0-8151-0712-9). Year Bk Med.
Bernstein, Ellen, ed. Medical & Health Annual, 1982. 448p. (YA) 1981. write for info. (ISBN 0-85229-386-0). Ency Brit Inc.
Byrne, Claire J., et al. Laboratory Tests: Implications for Nurses & Allied Health Professionals. 1981. 13.95 (ISBN 0-201-00088-1, Med-Nurse). A-W.
Carding, David K., ed. Family Medical Handbook. 2nd ed. 226p. 1981. 14.95 (ISBN 0-571-18027-2, Pub. by Faber & Faber). Merrimack Bk Serv.
Chatton, Milton J., ed. Handbook of Medical Treatment. 16th ed. LC 62-13251. 1979. pap. text ed. 10.50 (ISBN 0-930010-03-5). Jones Med.
Collins, R. Douglas. Illustrated Manual of Diagnosis of Systemic Diseases. LC 71-157908. (Illus.). 320p. 1972. 41.50 (ISBN 0-397-50281-8, JBL-Med-Nursing). Har-Row.
Darvill, Fred T., Jr. Mountaineering Medicine: A Wilderness Medical Guide. 9th ed. 60p. 1980. pap. 1.95 (ISBN 0-915740-04-4). Darvill Outdoor.
Eknoyan. Medical Procedures Manual. Date not set. price not set (ISBN 0-8151-3053-8). Year Bk Med.
Evans, Wayne O. & Cole, Johnathan O. Your Medicine Chest: A Consumer's Guide to the Effects of Prescription & Non Prescription Drugs. LC 78-7497. 1978. pap. 5.95 (ISBN 0-316-25823-7). Little.
The Extended Care Facility: A Handbook for the Medical Staff. 1967. pap. 2.00 (ISBN 0-89970-041-1, OP-157). AMA.
Francke, Donald E., ed. Handbook of I.V. Additive Reviews. Incl. 1970. (Illus.). 50p (ISBN 0-914768-03-4); 1971. (Illus.). 60p (ISBN 0-914768-04-2); 1972. (Illus.) (ISBN 0-914768-05-0); 1973. (Illus.). 68p (ISBN 0-914768-06-9). pap. 3.75 ea. Drug Intl Pubns.
Galton, Lawrence. Medical Advances. 1979. pap. 2.95 (ISBN 0-14-005021-3). Penguin.
Goldring, David. The Camp Physician's Manual. (Illus.). 192p. 1967. ed. spiral bdg. 19.75photocopy (ISBN 0-398-00695-4). C C Thomas.
Golightly, Cecilia K. Creative Problem Solving for Health Care Professionals. 250p. 1981. text ed. write for info. (ISBN 0-89443-371-7). Aspen Systems.
Good Housekeeping Editors. Family Health & Medical Guide. LC 78-51129. (Illus.). 960p. 1979. 22.95 (ISBN 0-87851-023-0). Hearst Bks.
Hardy, Richard E. & Cull, John G., eds. Therapeutic Needs of the Family. (American Lectures in Social & Rehabilitation Psychology Ser.). 256p. 1974. 15.75 (ISBN 0-398-03048-0). C C Thomas.
Hoole, Axalla J., et al. Patient Care Guidelines for Family Nurse Practitioners. 1976. pap. 11.95 (ISBN 0-316-37221-8). Little.
Horrobin, D. International Handbook of Medical Science. 1972. 17.50 (ISBN 0-8391-0573-8). Univ Park.
Inglenook Doctor Book. 1975. pap. 1.50 (ISBN 0-87178-423-8). Brethren.
Jaggi, O. P. Home Medical Handbook. 128p. 1979. 10.00x (ISBN 0-86125-102-4, Pub. by Orient Longman India). State Mutual Bk.
Jensen, Bernard D. Doctor-Patient Handbook. 1.95 (ISBN 0-686-29762-8). Cancer Bk Hse.
Kean, B. H. & Tucker, Harold A. The Traveler's Health Guide. (Illus.). 236p. 1965. photocopy ed. spiral 19.75 (ISBN 0-398-00989-9). C C Thomas.
--The Traveler's Medical Guide for Physicians. (Illus.). 444p. 1966. photocopy ed. spiral 38.75 (ISBN 0-398-00988-0). C C Thomas.
Kraytman, Maurice. Guide to Clinical Reasoning. 560p. 1981. pap. text ed. 13.95 (ISBN 0-07-035451-0, HP). McGraw.
Krupp, Marcus A., et al. Physician's Handbook. 19th ed. LC 41-9970. 758p. 1979. lexotone cover 9.00 (ISBN 0-87041-021-0). Lange.
Kuhne, Paul. Home Medical Encyclopedia. 1977. pap. 1.95 (ISBN 0-449-13598-5, GM). Fawcett.
Leone, Nicholas C. & Phillips, Elisabeth C. The Farmer's & Rancher's Medical Guide. 1980. 12.95 (ISBN 0-679-51025-7). McKay.
The Luyties Reference Handbook. 1975. pap. 1.25 (ISBN 0-685-76573-3). Formur Intl.
McElhinney, Thomas K. Human Values Teaching Programs for Health Professionals. 200p. 1981. 12.95 (ISBN 0-87426-051-5). Whitmore.
Oliver, J. H. Proven Remedies. 1949. pap. 2.95 (ISBN 0-7225-0110-2, Pub. by Thorsons). Formur Intl.
Pallatz, Harold. The Health Anthology of Medical Facts & Fallacies, Vol. 1. LC 73-91100. 172p. 1974. 6.50 (ISBN 0-685-41244-X). Ideal World.
Petersen, William F. Hippocratic Wisdom: For Him Who Wishes to Pursue Properly the Science of Medicine: A Modern Appreciation of Ancient Scientific Wisdom. (Illus.). 286p. 1946. pap. write for info. (ISBN 0-398-04390-6). C C Thomas.
Physician's Handbook on Medical Certification: Death, Birth, Fetal Death. 1979. pap. 4.95 (ISBN 0-916524-14-0). US Direct Serv.
Rorvik, David. Good Housekeeping Woman's Medical Guide. 1976. pap. 1.95 (ISBN 0-380-00566-2, 28886). Avon.
Sehnert, Keith W. & Eisenberg, Howard. How to Be Your Own Doctor - Sometimes. LC 74-18875. (Illus.). 416p. 1981. pap. 7.95 (ISBN 0-448-12027-5). G&D.
Singer, Charles. From Magic to Science. 1960. 6.00 (ISBN 0-8446-2944-8). Peter Smith.
Smith, J. Instant Medical Advisor. (Career Institute Instant Reference Library). 1970. 3.95 (ISBN 0-531-02011-8). Watts.
Stoppard, Miriam. Healthcare: With an A to Z of Common Medical Complaints & How to Treat Them. (Illus.). 208p. 1980. 17.50x (ISBN 0-297-77724-6, Pub. by Weidenfeld & Nicolson England). Biblio Dist.
Thurber, Packard & Thurber, Packard, Jr. Claims Medical Manual. 3rd ed. (Illus., Orig.). 1960. pap. 5.95 (ISBN 0-87015-094-4). Pacific Bks.
Wagman, Richard J. New Complete Medical & Health Encyclopedia, 4 vols. LC 77-81669. 1977. Set. lib. bdg. 42.50 (ISBN 0-89434-007-7). Purnell Ref Bks.
Washburn, Kenneth B. Physical Medicine & Rehabilitation - a Practitioner's Guide. 1976. spiral bdg. 12.00 (ISBN 0-87488-713-5). Med Exam.
Wechsler, Henry. Handbook of Medical Specialities. LC 74-19051. 1976. pap. text ed. 12.95 (ISBN 0-87705-232-8); pap. text ed. 9.95 (ISBN 0-87705-292-1). Human Sci Pr.
Wels, Byron G. The Medicine Cabinet. Brady, Frank, ed. (Illus.). 1978. 9.95 (ISBN 0-8437-3407-8); pap. 6.95 (ISBN 0-8437-3408-6). Hammond Inc.
Williams, Roger. Physician's Handbook. 7.95 (ISBN 0-686-30002-5). Cancer Bk Hse.
Wingate, Peter. The Penguin Medical Encyclopedia. lib. bdg. 12.50x (ISBN 0-88307-483-4). Gannon.
World Book-Childcraft International, Inc. The World Book Illustrated Home Medical Encyclopedia, 4 vols. LC 79-56907. (Illus.). 1038p. 1980. write for info. (ISBN 0-7166-2060-X). World Bk-Childcraft.

MEDICINE–HISTORY

see also Medicine, Ancient; Medicine, Arabic; Medicine, Egyptian; Medicine, Medieval; also similar headings

Allbutt, Thomas C. The Historical Relations of Medicine & Surgery to the End of the 16th Century. LC 75-23672. Repr. of 1905 ed. 14.00 (ISBN 0-404-13225-1). AMS Pr.
Almagro, Bertha R. Early American Medical Imprints 1668-1820: Subject, Name & Format Index to the Microfilm Collection. 1981. write for info. (ISBN 0-89235-027-X). Res Pubns Conn.
Altschule, Mark D. What Medicine Is About: Using Its Past to Improve Its Future. (Library Associates Historical Publications). 100p. 1975. 7.95 (ISBN 0-686-15547-5). F A Countway.
Baas, John H. History of Medicine, 2 vols. LC 70-154541. 1971. Repr. of 1889 ed. Set. leather bdg. 65.00 (ISBN 0-88275-983-3); lib. bdg. 51.50 set (ISBN 0-88275-001-1). Krieger.
Bakay, Louis. The Treatment of Head Injuries in the Thirty Years War (1618 to 1648) Joannis Scultetus & His Age. (Illus.). 120p. 1971. ed. spiral bdg. 14.50photocopy (ISBN 0-398-00082-4). C C Thomas.
Baker, Jim. Frontier Medicine. 3rd ed. (Jim Baker's Historical Handbooks). (Illus.). 48p. (Orig.). (gr. 5-12). 1975. pap. 1.50 (ISBN 0-914482-02-5). Ohio Hist Soc.

Berman, Jacob K., ed. The Western Surgical Association 1891-1900: Impressions & Selected Transactions. LC 76-23164. 1976. 30.00 (ISBN 0-915144-23-9). Hackett Pub.
Bettmann, Otto L. Pictorial History of Medicine. (Illus.). 336p. 1979. pap. 16.00 (ISBN 0-398-00149-9). C C Thomas.
Blanton, Wyndham B. Medicine in Virginia in the 18th Century. LC 80-12669. Repr. of 1931 ed. 64.50 (ISBN 0-404-13238-3). AMS Pr.
Booth, Emmons R. History of Osteopathy, & Twentieth Century Medical Practice: Memorial Edition. LC 74-29281. Repr. of 1924 ed. 60.00 (ISBN 0-404-13401-7). AMS Pr.
Bowers, John Z. & Purcell, Elizabeth F., eds. Aspects of the History of Medicine in Latin America. (Illus.). 196p. pap. 4.00 (ISBN 0-914362-29-1). J Macy Foun.
Brieger, Gert H., ed. Theory & Practice in American Medicine: Historical Studies from the "Journal of the History of Medicine & Allied Sciences". (Illus.). 1976. 15.00 (ISBN 0-88202-158-3, Sci Hist); pap. 9.95 (ISBN 0-686-67911-3). N Watson.
Buck, Albert H. The Growth of Medicine from the Earliest Times to About 1800. LC 75-23688. Repr. of 1917 ed. 52.50 (ISBN 0-404-13241-3). AMS Pr.
Camac, C. N. Imhotep to Harvey: Backgrounds of Medical History. LC 77-13043. 1977. Repr. of 1931 ed. lib. bdg. 35.00 (ISBN 0-89341-135-3). Longwood Pr.
Canniff, William. The Medical Profession in Upper Canada, 1753-1850. LC 75-23690. Repr. of 1894 ed. 56.50 (ISBN 0-404-13242-1). AMS Pr.
Cartwright, Frederick F. A Social History of Medicine. LC 76-41898. (Themes in British Social History Ser.). 1977. pap. text ed. 10.95x (ISBN 0-582-48394-8). Longman.
Cash, Philip, et al, eds. Medicine in Colonial Massachusetts, 1620-1820. LC 80-68589. (Illus.). xxiv, 425p. 1981. 25.00x (ISBN 0-686-72705-3, Colonial Soc MA). U Pr of Va.
Castiglioni, Arturo. A History of Medicine. LC 73-81219. 1216p. 1973. 40.00x (ISBN 0-87668-103-8). Aronson.
Caulfield, Ernest. The Infant Welfare Movement in the Eighteenth Century. (Historia Medicinae). (Illus.). Repr. of 1931 ed. lib. bdg. 15.00x (ISBN 0-87991-704-0). Porcupine Pr.
Chuinard, Eldon G. Only One Man Died: The Medical Aspects of the Lewis & Clark Expedition. 2nd ed. LC 78-73417. (Western Frontiermen Ser.: No. 19). (Illus.). 444p. 1980. 29.00 (ISBN 0-87062-128-9). A H Clark.
Cipolla, C. M. Public Health & the Medical Profession in Renaissance Italy. LC 25-22984. (Illus.). 1976. 23.95 (ISBN 0-521-20959-5). Cambridge U Pr.
Clarke, Edwin, ed. Modern Methods in the History of Medicine. 1971. text ed. 45.50x (ISBN 0-485-11121-7, Athlone Pr). Humanities.
Clendening, Logan. Source Book of Medical History. 1942. pap. 6.50 (ISBN 0-486-20621-1). Dover.
Clendening, Logan, ed. Source Book of Medical History. 10.75 (ISBN 0-8446-1871-3). Peter Smith.
Coffin, Margaret. Death in Early America: The History & Folklore of Customs & Superstitions of Early Medicine, Funerals, Burials & Mournings. (Illus.). (YA) 1976. 8.95 (ISBN 0-525-66482-3). Elsevier-Nelson.
Cohen, Daniel. The Last Hundred Years: Medicine. Katz, Herbert M., ed. (Illus.). 160p. (gr. 5 up). 1981. 8.95 (ISBN 0-87131-356-1). M Evans.
Comrie, John D. History of Scottish Medicine, 2 vols. 2nd ed. LC 75-23698. Repr. of 1932 ed. Set. 87.50 (ISBN 0-404-13320-7). AMS Pr.
Cordasco, Francesco. American Medical Imprints, 1820-1910: A Checklist of Publications Illustrating the History & Progress of Medical Science & Education & the Healing Arts in the United States. 850p. 1981. 75.00 (ISBN 0-940198-01-0). Junius-Vaughn.
Craigie, E. Horne & Gibson, William C. The World of Ramon y Cajal: With Selections from His Nonscientific Writings. (American Lecture History of Medicine & Science). (Illus.). 308p. 1968. ed. spiral bdg. 27.50photocopy (ISBN 0-398-00354-8). C C Thomas.
Curtis, John G. Harvey's Views on the Use of the Circulation of the Blood. (Historia Medicinae). (Illus.). Repr. of 1915 ed. lib. bdg. 15.00x (ISBN 0-87991-701-6). Porcupine Pr.
Dana, Charles L. The Peaks of Medical History. 2nd ed. LC 75-23703. (Illus.). Repr. of 1928 ed. 27.50 (ISBN 0-404-13255-3). AMS Pr.
Davis, Audrey B. Circulation Physiology & Medical Chemistry in England, 1650-1680. (Illus.). 263p. 1973. 10.00x (ISBN 0-87291-059-8). Coronado Pr.
Dawson, George G. Healing: Pagan & Christian. LC 75-23704. Repr. of 1935 ed. 26.50 (ISBN 0-404-13256-1). AMS Pr.
Dawson, Warren R. The Beginnings: Egypt & Assyria. LC 75-23650. (Clio Medica: No. 1). Repr. of 1930 ed. 9.50 (ISBN 0-404-58901-4). AMS Pr.
De Baz, Petros. The Story of Medicine. LC 74-84858. (Illus.). 100p. 1975. 6.00 (ISBN 0-8022-2154-8). Philos Lib.
Debus, Allen G. English Paracelsians. LC 66-15981. (Oldbourne History of Science Ser). 1968. 8.50x (ISBN 0-226-13977-8). U of Chicago Pr.
Desaive, Jean-Paul, et al. Medecins, Climat & Epidemies a la Fin Du XVIIIe Siecle. (Civilisations & Societes: No. 29). (Illus.). 1972. pap. 30.00x (ISBN 90-2797-013-0). Mouton.
Divided Legacy: A History of the Schism in Medical Thought, 3 vols. Incl. Vol. 1. The Patterns Emerge: Hippocrates to Paracelsus. Coulter, Harris L. 1975 (ISBN 0-916386-01-5); Vol. 2. Progress & Regress: J. B. Van Helmont to Claude Bernard. 1977 (ISBN 0-916386-02-3); Vol. 3. Science & Ethics in American Medicine, 1800-1914. Coulter, Harris L (ISBN 0-916386-03-1). LC 73-75718. 1976. 22.50x ea.; Set. 67.50x (ISBN 0-916386-00-7). Wehawken Bk.
Dolan, John P. & Adams-Smith, William N. Health & Society: A Documentary History of Medicine. LC 77-13478. 1978. 12.95 (ISBN 0-8164-9324-3). Continuum.
Duffy, John. The Healers: A History of American Medicine. LC 78-27222. 1979. pap. 7.50 (ISBN 0-252-00743-3). U of Ill Pr.
Durbin, Paul T., ed. A Guide to the Culture of Science, Technology, & Medicine. LC 79-7582. 1980. 45.00 (ISBN 0-02-907820-2). Free Pr.
Eastwood, Bruce. Directory of Audio-Visual Sources: History of Science, Medicine & Technology. 160p. 1979. 17.95 (ISBN 0-88202-185-0). N Watson.
Ebbell, B., tr. The Papyrus Ebers: The Greatest Egyptian Medical Document. (Historia Medicinae). Repr. of 1937 ed. lib. bdg. 15.00x (ISBN 0-87991-712-1). Porcupine Pr.
Eberson, Frederick. Early Medical History of Pinellas Peninsula. LC 78-50560. (Illus.). 1978. 10.00 (ISBN 0-912760-67-2). Valkyrie Pr.
--Early Physicians of the West. LC 79-63659. 1979. 6.95 (ISBN 0-912760-92-3). Valkyrie Pr.
Edgar, Irving I. The Origins of the Healing Art. LC 77-82611. (Illus.). 1978. 9.50 (ISBN 0-8022-2214-5). Philos Lib.
Elgood, Cyril. Medicine in Persia. LC 75-23665. (Clio Medica: No. 14). (Illus.). Repr. of 1934 ed. 14.50 (ISBN 0-404-58914-6). AMS Pr.
Elkinton, Russell J. & Clark, Robert A. The Quaker Heritage in Medicine. (Illus.). 1978. pap. 3.95 (ISBN 0-910286-68-X). Boxwood.
Estes, J. Worth. Hall Jackson & the Purple Foxglove: Medical Practice & Research in Revolutionary America, 1760-1820. LC 79-63083. (Illus.). 309p. 1979. text ed. 20.00x (ISBN 0-87451-173-9). U Pr of New Eng.
Fellman, Anita C. & Fellman, Michael. Making Sense of Self: Medical Advice Literature in Late Nineteenth-Century America. LC 81-51141. 224p. 1981. 16.50x (ISBN 0-8122-7810-0). U of Pa Pr.
Foucault, Michael. Birth of the Clinic: An Archeology of Medical Perception. LC 74-3389. 1974. pap. 2.95 (ISBN 0-394-71097-5, V-97, Vin). Random.
Foucault, Michel. Birth of the Clinic: An Archaeology of Medical Perception. LC 73-3493. 1973. 8.95 (ISBN 0-394-48321-9). Pantheon.
Friedenwald, Harry. Jews & Medicine & Jewish Luminaries in Medical History, 3 Vols. rev. ed. 1967. 45.00x (ISBN 0-87068-053-6). Ktav.
Fujikawa, Yu. Japanese Medicine. LC 75-23663. (Clio Medica: 12). Orig. Title: Geschichte der Medizin in Japan. (Illus.). Repr. of 1934 ed. 15.00 (ISBN 0-404-58912-X). AMS Pr.
Galdston, Iago. Progress in Medicine. LC 76-39166. (Essay Index Reprint Ser.). 1940. 19.50 (ISBN 0-8369-2689-7). Arno.
--The Social & Historical Foundations of Modern Medicine. Fox, Thomas, frwd. by. LC 81-1896. 160p. 1981. 17.50 (ISBN 0-87630-259-2). Brunner-Mazel.
Gantt, William A. Russian Medicine. LC 75-23669. (Clio Medica: 20). (Illus.). 1978. Repr. of 1937 ed. 19.00 (ISBN 0-404-58920-0). AMS Pr.
Garrison, Fielding H. History of Medicine. 4th ed. LC 29-3665. (Illus.). 1960. Repr. of 1929 ed. 29.00 (ISBN 0-7216-4030-3). Saunders.
Gelfand, Toby. Professionalizing Modern Medicine: Paris Surgeons & Medical Science & Institutions in the Eighteenth Century. LC 79-8955. (Contributions in Medical History: No. 6). (Illus.). xviii, 271p. 1980. lib. bdg. 29.95 (ISBN 0-313-21488-3, GPM/). Greenwood.
Gibson, James E. Dr. Bodo Otto & the Medical Background of the American Revolution. (Illus.). 342p. 1937. ed. spiral bdg. 27.50photocopy (ISBN 0-398-04265-9). C C Thomas.
Gordon, Maurice R. Aesculapius Comes to the Colonies. LC 70-101590. (Illus.). 1969. Repr. of 1949 ed. 17.50 (ISBN 0-87266-014-1). Argosy.
Green, John R. Medical History for Students. (Illus.). 202p. 1968. 12.50 (ISBN 0-398-00722-5). C C Thomas.
Grob, Gerald N. Edward Jarvis & the Medical World of Nineteenth-Century America. LC 78-3771. 1978. 15.00x (ISBN 0-87049-239-X). U of Tenn Pr.
Grossinger, Richard. Planet Medicine: From Stone Age Shamanism to Post-Industrial Healing. LC 79-7073. 1980. pap. 5.95 (ISBN 0-385-14053-3, Anch). Doubleday.
Haberling, Wilhelm. German Medicine. LC 75-23664. (Clio Medica: 13). (Illus.). Repr. of 1934 ed. 17.25 (ISBN 0-404-58913-8). AMS Pr.
Haggard, Howard. Devils, Drugs & Doctors. (Illus.). 1980. Repr. 25.00 (ISBN 0-89182-024-8). Charles River.
Haggard, Howard W. Doctor in History. LC 79-99342. (Essay Index Reprint Ser). 1934. 25.00 (ISBN 0-8369-1654-9). Arno.
--The Doctor in History. 1935. 25.00 (ISBN 0-8274-4207-6). R West.
--Mystery, Magic & Medicine: The Rise of Medicine from Superstition to Science. 1978. Repr. of 1933 ed. lib. bdg. 20.00 (ISBN 0-8414-4788-8). Folcroft.
Haigh, Elizabeth L. Xavier Bechat & Medical Theory of the Eighteenth Century. (Studies in the History of Science: No. 6). (Illus.). 1979. lib. bdg. 18.95x (ISBN 0-89102-146-9). B Franklin.
Hake, Thomas G. Memoirs of Eighty Years. LC 73-131509. Repr. of 1892 ed. 24.50 (ISBN 0-404-03025-4). AMS Pr.
Haller, John S., Jr. American Medicine in Transition, 1840-1910. LC 80-14546. (Illus.). 334p. 1981. 27.95 (ISBN 0-252-00806-5). U of Ill Pr.
Harington, John, tr. The School of Salernum: Regimen Santitatis Salernitanum: the English Version. 1978. Repr. of 1920 ed. lib. bdg. 35.00 (ISBN 0-8495-2336-2). Arden Lib.
Harris, Bernice K., ed. Southern Home Remedies. (Illus.). 1968. 6.50 (ISBN 0-930230-22-1). Johnson NC.
Hathaway, Esse V. Partners in Progress. facs. ed. LC 68-29213. (Essay Index Reprint Ser.). 1968. Repr. of 1935 ed. 16.00 (ISBN 0-8369-0518-0). Arno.
Hawkins, Cora F. Buggies, Blizzards, & Babies. facsimile ed. 1971. pap. 9.45x (ISBN 0-8138-2245-9). Iowa St U Pr.
Hayward, Oliver S. & Thomson, Elizabeth, eds. The Journal of William Tully: Medical Student at Dartmouth, 1808-1809. (Illus.). 1977. 17.50 (ISBN 0-88202-175-3). N Watson.
Heagerty, John J. Four Centuries of Medical History in Canada & a Sketch of the Medical History of Newfoundland, 2 vols. LC 75-23719. Repr. of 1928 ed. 65.00 set (ISBN 0-404-13160-3). AMS Pr.
Heidel, William A. Hippocratic Medicine. Cohen, I. Bernard, ed. LC 80-2129. (Development of Science Ser.). (Illus.). 1981. lib. bdg. 15.00x (ISBN 0-405-13878-4). Arno.
Henslow, George. Medical Works of the Fourteenth Century, Together with a List of Plants Recorded in Contemporary Writings, with Their Identifications. LC 72-82036. 278p. 1972. Repr. of 1899 ed. lib. bdg. 21.00 (ISBN 0-8337-1666-2). B Franklin.
Hertzler, Arthur E. The Horse & Buggy Doctor. 1938. 25.00 (ISBN 0-8274-4218-1). R West.
Hirsch, August. Geschichte Der Medicischen Wissenschaften in Deutschland. 1893. 41.50 (ISBN 0-384-23360-0). Johnson Repr.
Hixson, Joseph. History of the Human Body: A Five Thousand Year Mystery Told with Pictures. LC 65-17179. (Illus., Orig.). 1966. 10.00x (ISBN 0-8154-0115-9). Cooper Sq.
Howell, William B. Medicine in Canada. LC 75-23659. (Clio Medica: 9). (Illus.). Repr. of 1933 ed. 16.00 (ISBN 0-404-58909-X). AMS Pr.
International Symposium on Society, Medicine & Law, Jerusalem, March 1972. Proceedings. Karplus, H., ed. 204p. 1973. 14.75 (ISBN 0-444-41176-3, North Holland). Elsevier.
Jarcho, Saul, ed. Essays & Notes on the History of Medicine. LC 76-11770. 1976. 20.00 (ISBN 0-88202-066-8). N Watson.
Jayne, Walter A. Healing Gods of Ancient Civilizations. 1925. 47.50x (ISBN 0-686-51398-3). Elliots Bks.
King, Lester S. Growth of Medical Thought. (Midway Reprint Ser). 1974. Repr. of 1963 ed. 14.00x (ISBN 0-226-43703-5). U of Chicago Pr.
--The Medical World of the Eighteenth Century. LC 58-7332. 366p. 1971. Repr. of 1958 ed. lib. bdg. 12.50 (ISBN 0-88275-032-1). Krieger.
--The Philosophy of Medicine: The Early Eighteenth Century. LC 77-24645. 1977. 22.50x (ISBN 0-674-66585-6). Harvard U Pr.
Klawans, Harold L. The Acromegaly of Maximinus & Other Essays. 1981. text ed. 20.00 (ISBN 0-89004-684-0). Raven.
Konkle, Burton A. Standard History of the Medical Profession of Philadelphia. 2nd corr. & enl. ed. LC 75-17803. Repr. of 1897 ed. 67.50 (ISBN 0-404-13201-4). AMS Pr.
Krumbhaar, Edward B., ed. Clio Medica: A Series of Primers on the History of Medicine, 22 vols. Repr. of 1939 ed. Set. 340.00 (ISBN 0-404-58900-6). AMS Pr.
Laignel-Lavastine, Maxime. French Medicine. LC 75-23666. (Clio Medica: 15). (Illus.). Repr. of 1934 ed. 16.50 (ISBN 0-404-58915-4). AMS Pr.
Lassek, Arthur M., Sr. The Unique Legacy of Doctor Hughlings Jackson. 152p. 1970. photocopy ed. spiral 29.75 (ISBN 0-398-01084-6). C C Thomas.
Latham, R. G. Works of Thomas Sydenham, 2 vols. 670p. 1974. Repr. 60.00 (ISBN 0-87821-250-7). Milford Hse.
Leavitt, Judith W. & Numbers, Ronald L., eds. Sickness & Health in America: Readings in the History of Medicine & Public Health. LC 78-53288. 464p. 1978. 27.50 (ISBN 0-299-07620-2); pap. 10.95 (ISBN 0-299-07624-5). U of Wis Pr.
Lesky, Erna. The Vienna Medical School of the Nineteeth Century. LC 76-24938. 1977. text ed. 24.50x (ISBN 0-8018-1908-3). Johns Hopkins.
Lobban, R. D. Edinburgh & the Medical Revolution. LC 78-51669. (Cambridge Introduction to the History of Mankind Ser.). (Illus.). (YA) 1980. pap. 3.95 (ISBN 0-521-22028-9). Cambridge U Pr.
Lyons, Albert S. & Petrucelli, R. Joseph. Medicine: An Illustrated History. (Illus.). 1978. 75.00 (ISBN 0-8109-1054-3). Abrams.
McKechnie, R. E., II. Strong Medicine: A History of Healing on the Northwest Coast. 10.50 (ISBN 0-88894-074-2, Pub. by Douglas & McIntyre); pap. 6.50 (ISBN 0-88894-011-4, Pub. by Douglas & McIntyre). Intl Schol Bk Serv.
McLachlan, Gordon & McKeown, Thomas, eds. Medical History & Medical Care: A Symposium of Perspectives. (Nuffield Publications). 1971. 9.75x (ISBN 0-19-721362-6). Oxford U Pr.
McManus, J. F. A. The Fundamental Ideas of Medicine: A Brief History of Medicine. (The Carl Vernon Weller Lecture). (Illus.). 128p. 1963. ed. spiral bdg. 12.50photocopy (ISBN 0-398-01269-5). C C Thomas.
Macmichael, William. The Gold-Headed Cane. 7th ed. (Illus.). 205p. 1953. photocopy ed. spiral 18.75 (ISBN 0-398-04351-5). C C Thomas.
Mather, Cotton. The Angel of Bethesda. Jones, Gordon W., ed. LC 72-185323. 384p. 1972. 19.95x (ISBN 0-8271-7220-6, Dist. by U Pr of Va). Am Antiquarian.
Mermier, Guy R. & DuBruck, Edelgard E., eds. Fifteenth Century Studies, Vol. 2. LC 79-640105. 1979. pap. 17.25 (ISBN 0-8357-0392-4, SS-00085). Univ Microfilms.
Morley, Peter & Wallis, Roy, eds. Culture & Curing: Anthropological Perspectives on Traditional Medical Beliefs & Practices. LC 78-62194. (Contemporary Community Health Ser.). (Illus.). 1979. 14.95 (ISBN 0-8229-1136-1); pap. 5.95 (ISBN 0-8229-5325-0). U of Pittsburgh Pr.
Neuberger, Max. History of Medicine, 2 vols. bd. in 1. (Historia Medicinae Ser.). (X, 404pp. vol. 1; 135pp. vol. 2). Repr. of 1970 ed. lib. bdg. 37.50x (ISBN 0-87991-066-6). Porcupine Pr.
Neuburger, Max. Essays in the History of Medicine. (Historia Medicinae). Repr. of 1930 ed. lib. bdg. 15.00x (ISBN 0-87991-711-3). Porcupine Pr.
New York Academy Of Medicine. Landmarks in Medicine. facs. ed. LC 74-142676. (Essay Index Reprint Ser). 1939. 19.00 (ISBN 0-8369-2114-3). Arno.
Nissenbaum, Stephen. Sex, Diet & Debility in Jacksonian America: Sylvester Graham & Health Reform. LC 79-8280. (Contributions in Medical History: No. 4). xvii, 198p. 1980. lib. bdg. 22.95 (ISBN 0-313-21415-8, NSY/). Greenwood.
Noell, Anna M. Free Show Tonight: A/History of a Medicine Show Family of the Twenties and Thirties. Date not set. price not set (ISBN 0-9602422-3-6). Noells Ark.
Numbers, Ronald L. & Leavitt, Judith W. Wisconsin Medicine: Historical Perspectives. LC 80-52297. (Illus.). 224p. 1981. 18.50x (ISBN 0-299-08430-2). U of Wis Pr.
O'Hara-May, Jane. The Elizabethan Dyetary of Health. (Illus.). 1977. 18.50x (ISBN 0-87291-074-1). Coronado Pr.

Osborn, June, ed. Influenza in America 1918-1976: History, Science, & Politics. LC 77-14344. 1977. lib. bdg. 12.00 (ISBN 0-88202-176-1). N Watson.
Osler, Sir William. The Evolution of Modern Medicine: A Series of Lectures Delivered at Yale University on the Silliman Foundation in April, 1913. LC 77-140610. (Medicine & Society in America Ser.). (Illus.). 264p. 1972. Repr. of 1922 ed. 16.00 (ISBN 0-405-02805-9). Arno.
Pennsylvania University Bicentennial Conference. Studies in the History of Science. Speiser, E. A. & Neugebauer, Otto, eds. LC 68-26202. Repr. of 1941 ed. 9.25 (ISBN 0-8046-0358-8). Kennikat.
Peterson, M. Jeanne. The Medical Profession in Mid-Victorian London. LC 76-48362. 1978. 26.75x (ISBN 0-520-03343-4). U of Cal Pr.
Price, Douglas B. & Twombly, Neil J. Phantom Limb Phenomenon - A Medical, Folkloric, & Historical Study: Texts & Translations of 10th to 20th Century Miracle Accounts. Osborne, Mary C, et al, trs. 526p. 1979. pap. text ed. 6.95 (ISBN 0-87840-168-7). Georgetown U Pr.
Pusey, William A. A Doctor of the 1870's & 80's. (Illus.). 153p. 1931. photocopy ed. spiral 14.95 (ISBN 0-398-04398-1). C C Thomas.
--The History & Epidemiology of Syphilis. (Illus.). 110p. 1933. pap. 10.75 (ISBN 0-398-04400-7). C C Thomas.
Quebbeman, Frances E. Medicine in Territorial Arizona. 1966. 7.50 (ISBN 0-685-67968-3). AZ Hist Foun.
Reiser, S. J. Medicine & the Reign of Technology. LC 77-87389. (Illus.). 1978. 21.50 (ISBN 0-521-21907-8). Cambridge U Pr.
Reiser, Stanley J. Medicine & the Reign of Technology. LC 77-87389. (Illus.). 317p. (Orig.). 1981. pap. 8.95 (ISBN 0-521-28223-3). Cambridge U Pr.
Riese, Hertha, ed. Historical Explorations in Medicine & Psychiatry. LC 78-17231. 1978. text ed. 22.95 (ISBN 0-8261-2290-6). Springer Pub.
Riesman, David. Medicine in Modern Society. LC 77-92513. (Essay Index in Reprint Ser.). 1978. Repr. 18.50x (ISBN 0-8486-3010-6). Core Collection.
--The Story of Medicine in the Middle Ages. (Historia Medicinae Ser.). (Illus.). Repr. of 1935 ed. lib. bdg. 25.00x (ISBN 0-87991-713-X). Porcupine Pr.
Rosenberg, Charles E., ed. Medicine & Society in America, 47 bks. 1972. Set. 804.00 (ISBN 0-405-03930-1). Arno.
Rumbaut, Ruben D. John of God: His Place in the History of Psychiatry & Medicine. LC 77-91668. 1978. pap. 5.95 (ISBN 0-89729-198-0). Ediciones.
Schwabe, Calvin W. Cattle, Priests, & Progress in Medicine, Vol. 4. LC 77-84547. (Wesley W. Spink Lectures on Comparative Medicine). (Illus.). 1978. 19.75x (ISBN 0-8166-0825-3). U of Minn Pr.
Shryock, R. H. The Development of Modern Medicine: An Interpretation of the Social & Scientific Factors Involved. LC 79-5401. 1980. 17.50 (ISBN 0-299-07530-3); pap. 7.50 (ISBN 0-299-07534-6). U of Wis Pr.
Shryock, Richard H. Medicine & Society in America: 1660-1860. LC 60-6417. 1962. pap. 4.95 (ISBN 0-8014-9093-6, CP93). Cornell U Pr.
Sigerist, Henry A. A History of Medicine, 2 vols. Incl. Vol. 1. Primitive & Archaic Medicine. 1951. 25.00 (ISBN 0-19-500102-8); Vol. 2. Early Greek, Hindu & Persian Medicine. 1961. 20.00x (ISBN 0-19-500103-6). Oxford U Pr.
Sigerist, Henry E. Civilization & Disease. 1962. pap. 3.95 (ISBN 0-226-75723-4, P511, Phoen). U of Chicago Pr.
Singer, C. & Sigerist, H. E., eds. Essays on the History of Medicine Presented to Karl Sudhoff on the Occasion of His Seventieth Birthday, November 26th, 1923. facs. ed. LC 68-8459. (Essay Index Reprint Ser). 1924. 23.00 (ISBN 0-8369-0431-1). Arno.
Smith, Stephen. The City That Was. Bd. with The Report of the General Committee of Health, New York City, 1806. LC 73-1827. (History of Medicine Ser.: No. 36). 1973. Repr. of 1911 ed. 11.00 (ISBN 0-8108-0598-7). Scarecrow.
Smith, Wesley D. The Hippocratic Tradition. LC 78-20977. (History of Science Ser.). 1979. 17.50x (ISBN 0-8014-1209-9). Cornell U Pr.
Stern, Bernhard J. Social Factors in Medical Progress. LC 68-57582. (Columbia University. Studies in the Social Sciences: No. 287). Repr. of 1927 ed. 12.50 (ISBN 0-404-51287-9). AMS Pr.
Stewart, Miller J. Moving the Wounded: Litters, Cacolets & Ambulance Wagons, U.S. Army, 1776-1876. LC 79-838949. (Illus.). 134p. (Orig.). 1980. pap. 17.50 (ISBN 0-88342-245-X). Old Army.
Stookey, Byron. A History of Colonial Medical Education: In the Province of New York, with Its Subsequent Development (1767-1830) (Illus.). 312p. 1962. photocopy ed. spiral 29.50 (ISBN 0-398-01866-9). C C Thomas.
Sudhoff, Karl. Essays in the History of Medicine. Garrison, Fielding H., ed. (Historia Medicinae). (Illus.). Repr. of 1926 ed. lib. bdg. 20.00x (ISBN 0-87991-714-8). Porcupine Pr.
Temkin, Owsei. The Double Face of Janus & Other Essays in the History of Medicine. LC 76-47380. (Illus.). 562p. 1977. 24.00x (ISBN 0-8018-1859-1). Johns Hopkins.
Thomas Cantimpratensis: Liber De Natura Rerum. Editio Princeps Secundum Codices Manuscriptos, 2pts, Pt. 1. 1973. 85.30x (ISBN 3-11-003789-0). De Gruyter.
Thompson, C. J. Magic & Healing. LC 73-2850. (Illus.). 176p. 1973. Repr. of 1947 ed. 22.00 (ISBN 0-8103-3275-2). Gale.
Thorndike, Lynn. Science & Thought in the Fifteenth Century. (Illus.). 1967. Repr. of 1929 ed. 14.95 (ISBN 0-02-853480-8). Hafner.
Underwood, E. Ashworth, ed. Science, Medicine, & History, 2 vols. LC 74-26300. (History, Philosophy & Sociology of Science Ser). (Illus.). 1975. Repr. Set. 78.00x (ISBN 0-405-06624-4); 39.00x ea. Vol. 1 (ISBN 0-405-06640-6). Vol. 2 (ISBN 0-405-06641-4). Arno.
Unschuld, Paul. Medical Ethics in Imperial China: A Study in Historical Anthropology. LC 78-80479. (Comparative Studies of Health Systems & Medical Care). 1979. 18.50x (ISBN 0-520-03543-7). U of Cal Pr.
Van Liere, Edward J. & Dodds, Gideon S. History of Medical Education in West Virginia. (Illus.). 1965. 6.00 (ISBN 0-685-30826-X). McClain.
Venzmer, Gerhard. Five Thousand Years of Medicine. LC 79-163511. (Illus.). 1972. 10.95 (ISBN 0-8008-2755-4). Taplinger.
Vess, David M. Medical Revolution in France, 1789-1796. LC 74-14916. 216p. 1975. 12.00 (ISBN 0-8130-0439-X). U Presses Fla.
Vogel, Morris J. & Rosenberg, Charles E., eds. The Theraputic Revolution: Essays on the Social History of American Medicine. LC 79-5044. (Illus.). 1979. 18.50 (ISBN 0-8122-7773-2). U of Pa Pr.
Waring, Joseph I. A History of Medicine in South Carolina. Incl. 1670-1825. Repr. of 1964 ed. 15.00 (ISBN 0-685-51868-X); 1825-1900. Repr. of 1967 ed. 15.00 (ISBN 0-685-51869-8); 1900-1970. Repr. of 1971 ed. 10.00 (ISBN 0-685-51870-1). Repr. Reprint.
Webster, Charles, ed. Biology, Medicine & Society Eighteen Forty to Nineteen Forty. LC 80-41752. (Past & Present Publications Ser.). 344p. Date not set. price not set (ISBN 0-521-23770-X). Cambridge U Pr.
--Health, Medicine & Mortality in the Sixteenth Century. LC 78-73234. (Cambridge Monographs on the History of Medicine). (Illus.). 1979. 42.50 (ISBN 0-521-22643-0). Cambridge U Pr.
Wheelwright, Edith G. Medicinal Plants & Their History. (Illus.). 6.50 (ISBN 0-8446-5258-X). Peter Smith.
Wilbur, C. Keith M. D. Revolutionary Medicine, Seventeen Hundred to Eighteen Hundred. LC 80-82790. (Illus.). 88p. (Orig.). 1980. pap. 8.95 (ISBN 0-87106-041-8). Globe Pequot.
Wilder, Alexander. History of Medicine: A Brief Outline of Medical History & Sects of Physicians. LC 74-29303. Repr. of 1901 ed. 65.00 (ISBN 0-404-13427-0). AMS Pr.
Wilson, R. N. A History of Medicine. 1979. Repr. of 1930 ed. lib. bdg. 12.50 (ISBN 0-8495-5744-5). Arden Lib.
Wiseman, Richard. Of Wounds, of Gun-Shot Wounds of Fractures & Luxations. 1977. text ed. 22.00 (ISBN 0-901571-81-4). State Mutual Bk.
Woglom, William H. Discoverers for Medicine. facsimile ed. LC 78-156733. (Essay Index Reprint Ser). Repr. of 1949 ed. 15.00 (ISBN 0-8369-2432-0). Arno.
Woodall, John. The Surgeon's Mate, Sixteen Hundred Seventeen. 1977. text ed. 18.00x (ISBN 0-906230-15-2). State Mutual Bk.
Youngson, A. J. The Scientific Revolution in Victorian Medicine. LC 78-31705. 1979. text ed. 25.00x (ISBN 0-8419-0479-0). Holmes & Meier.

MEDICINE–INFORMATION SERVICES

Beardsley, Richard, ed. The Videolog in the Health Sciences. 1980-81 ed. (Videolog Ser.). 1981. pap. 49.50 (ISBN 0-88432-069-3). J Norton Pubs.
Fenna, D., et al. The Stockholm County Medical Information System. (Lecture Notes in Medical Informatics Ser.: Vol. 2). 1979. pap. 11.30 (ISBN 0-387-08950-0). Springer-Verlag.
Grams, Ralph R. Medical Information Systems: The Laboratory Module. LC 78-71496. (Illus.). 1979. 39.50 (ISBN 0-89603-004-0). Humana.
Hodge, Melville H. Medical Information Systems: A New Resource for Hospitals. LC 77-12739. 216p. 1977. 25.75 (ISBN 0-912862-47-5). Aspen Systems.
Neal, Helen. Better Communications for Better Health. LC 62-15058. 224p. 1962. 20.00x (ISBN 0-231-02584-X). Columbia U Pr.
Thompson, Gene E. & Handelman, Ira. Health Data & Information Management. (Illus.). 1978. 29.95 (ISBN 0-409-95008-4). Butterworth.
World Conference on First Medical Informatics, Aug. 5-10, 1974. Medinfo 1974: Proceedings. Anderson, J. & Forsythe, J. M., eds. LC 74-83267. 1192p. 1975. 146.50 (ISBN 0-444-10771-1, North-Holland). Elsevier.
World Conference on Medical Informatics, 2nd. MEDINFO 77: Proceedings. Shires, D. B. & Wolf, H. K., eds. (IFIP Ser.). 1977. 127.00 (ISBN 0-7204-0754-0, North-Holland). Elsevier.

MEDICINE–INSTRUMENTS

see Medical Instruments and Apparatus; Surgical Instruments and Apparatus

MEDICINE–JUVENILE LITERATURE

see also Physicians–Juvenile Literature

Abels, Harriette S. Future Medicine. Schroeder, Howard, ed. LC 80-15523. (Our Future World Ser.). (Illus.). 48p. (Orig.). (gr. 6-9). 1980. PLB 6.95 (ISBN 0-89686-086-8); pap. 3.25 (ISBN 0-89686-095-7). Crestwood Hse.
Brown, Paula S. The Incredible Body Machine. (Three-Two-One Contact Bks.). (Illus.). 48p. (gr. 4-7). 1981. pap. 5.95 (ISBN 0-394-84773-3). Random.
Cohen, Daniel. The Last Hundred Years: Medicine. Katz, Herbert M., ed. (Illus.). 160p. (gr. 5 up). 1981. 8.95 (ISBN 0-87131-356-1). M Evans.
Eberle, Irmengarde. Modern Medical Discoveries. 3rd ed. LC 68-17084. (gr. 5-9). 1968. 8.95 (ISBN 0-690-55271-8, TYC-J). Har-Row.
Freeman, Dorothy R., et al. Very Important People Behind the Scenes in Medical Work. LC 73-6847. (Very Important People Ser.). (Illus.). 64p. (gr. 4-8). 1973. PLB 8.65 (ISBN 0-516-07456-3, Elk Grove Bks). Childrens.
--Very Important People Who Print & Publish. LC 73-5582. (Very Important People Ser.). (Illus.). 64p. (gr. 4-8). 1973. PLB 8.65 (ISBN 0-516-07460-1, Elk Grove Bks). Childrens.
Gottfried, Rosalie. Getting into American Medical-Veterinary Schools: A Practical "How to" Guide. LC 77-93397. (gr. 10 up). 1978. pap. text ed. 5.50x (ISBN 0-931084-01-6). Argee Pub.
Keyes, Fenton. Your Future in a Paramedic Career. (Careers in Depth Ser.). (Illus.). (gr. 7-12). 1981. PLB 5.97 (ISBN 0-8239-0486-5). Rosen Pr.
Lappin, Myra & Feinglass, Sanford. Need a Doctor? (On Your Own Ser.). (Illus.). 64p. (gr. 7-12). 1981. pap. text ed. 3.10 (ISBN 0-915510-58-8). Janus Bks.
London, Carolyn. Hospitals, Doctors, Nurses & Mystery Workers. LC 75-10915. (Illus.). 96p. (gr. 4-6). 1976. PLB 6.95 (ISBN 0-07-038657-9, GB). McGraw.
Martin, M. W. Let's Talk About the New World of Medicine. LC 72-91738. (Illus.). 76p. (gr. 3-6). 1973. PLB 4.95 (ISBN 0-8246-0149-1). Jonathan David.
Newman, Gerry, compiled by. Encyclopedia of Health & the Human Body. (Illus.). (gr. 7 up). 1977. PLB 16.90 s&l (ISBN 0-531-01331-6). Watts.
Rockwell, Harlow. My Doctor. LC 72-92442. (Illus.). 24p. (ps-2). 1973. 8.95 (ISBN 0-02-777480-5). Macmillan.

MEDICINE–LAWS AND LEGISLATION

see Medical Laws and Legislation

MEDICINE–MATHEMATICAL MODELS

Ackerman, Eugene & Gatewood, Lael C. Mathematical Models in the Health Sciences: A Computer-Aided Approach. 1979. 23.50x (ISBN 0-8166-0864-4). U of Minn Pr.
Banks, H. T. Modelling & Control in the Biomedical Sciences. LC 75-25771. (Lecture Notes in Biomathematics: Vol. 6). v, 114p. 1975. pap. 9.50 (ISBN 0-387-07395-7). Springer-Verlag.
Berger, J., et al, eds. Mathematical Models in Medicine. (Lecture Notes in Biomathematics: Vol. 11). 1976. soft cover 15.30 (ISBN 0-387-07802-9). Springer-Verlag.
Gurland, John, ed. Stochastic Models in Medicine & Biology. (Mathematics Research Center Pubns., No. 10). 410p. 1964. 22.50 (ISBN 0-299-03150-0). U of Wis Pr.
Iosifescu, M. & Tautu, P. Stochastic Processes & Application in Biology & Medicine, Pt. 1: Theory. LC 73-77733. (Biomathematics, Ser.: Vol. 3). 331p. 1973. 36.50 (ISBN 0-387-06270-X). Springer-Verlag.
--Stochastic Processes & Applications in Biology & Medicine, Pt. 2: Models. LC 73-77733. (Biomathematics, Ser.: Vol. 4). 337p. 1973. 39.70 (ISBN 0-387-06271-8). Springer-Verlag.
McIntosh, J. A. & McIntosh, R. P. Mathematical Modelling & Computers in Endocrinology. (Monographs on Endocrinology: Vol. 16). (Illus.). 370p. 1980. 48.40 (ISBN 0-387-09693-0). Springer-Verlag.
Shipley, Reginald A. & Clark, Richard E. Tracer Methods for in Vitro Kinetics: Theory & Applications. 1972. 37.50 (ISBN 0-12-640250-7). Acad Pr.

MEDICINE–MATHEMATICS

Bailey, Norman T. Mathematics, Statistics & Systems for Health. LC 77-1307. (Wiley Ser. in Probability & Mathematical Statistics: Applied Probability & Statistics). 222p. 1977. 33.25 (ISBN 0-471-99500-2, Pub. by Wiley-Interscience). Wiley.
Bila, Dennis, et al. Mathematics for Health Occupations. 1978. pap. text ed. 17.95 (ISBN 0-87626-570-0). Winthrop.
Campbell, June & Campbell, Joe B. Laboratory Mathematics: Medical & Biological Applications. 2nd ed. LC 79-24996. (Illus.). 1980. pap. text ed. 12.95 (ISBN 0-8016-0702-7). Mosby.
Curren, Anna M. Math for Meds: A Programmmed Text. 3rd ed. LC 76-43259. 1979. pap. text ed. 6.95 (ISBN 0-918082-01-3). Wallcur Inc.
Glantz, Stanton A. Mathematics for Biomedical Applications. LC 77-20320. 1979. 37.50x (ISBN 0-520-03599-2). U of Cal Pr.
Hayden, Jerome D. & Davis, Howard T. Mathematics for Health Careers. LC 78-59567. (Health Occupations Ser.). (gr. 10). 1980. pap. text ed. 14.40 (ISBN 0-686-59748-6); instructor's guide 1.75 (ISBN 0-8273-1717-4). Delmar.
Hoppensteadt, Frank C., ed. Mathematical Aspects of Physiology. LC 81-1315. (Lectures in Applied Mathematics Ser.: No. 19). Date not set. 38.00 (ISBN 0-8218-1119-3). Am Math.
Jackson, Herbert L. Mathematics of Radiology & Nuclear Medicine. LC 70-107201. (Illus.). 180p. 1971. 12.00 (ISBN 0-87527-019-0). Green.
McHenry, Ruth W. Self-Teaching Tests in Arithmetic for Nurses. 10th. ed. LC 80-10859. (Illus.). 1980. pap. text ed. 9.45 (ISBN 0-8016-2505-X). Mosby.
Martinson, Ida M. & Kepner, Gordon R. Mathematics for Health Professionals. LC 77-8276. 1977. pap. text ed. 11.95 (ISBN 0-8261-1870-4). Springer Pub.
Medications & Mathematics for the Nurse. 288p. 1981. text ed. 13.95 (ISBN 0-442-21882-6). Van Nos Reinhold.
Murrell, Sandra & Olsen, Paul. Mathematics for the Health Sciences. (Developmental & Precalculus Math Ser.). (Illus.). 432p. 1981. pap. text ed. 13.95 (ISBN 0-201-04647-4). A-W.
Ranicki, Andrew. Exact Sequences in the Algebraic Theory of Surgery. LC 80-18277. (Mathematical Notes: No. 26). 516p. 1981. pap. 12.50x (ISBN 0-691-08276-6). Princeton U Pr.
Readey, Helen & Readey, William. Mathematical Concepts for Nursing: A Workbook. LC 79-20751. 1980. 7.95 (ISBN 0-201-06166-X). A-W.
Sackheim, George I., et al. Programmed Mathematics for Nursing. 4th ed. 1979. pap. text ed. 8.95 (ISBN 0-02-405190-X). Macmillan.
Shugar, G., et al. Basic Mathematics for Allied Health. 1975. pap. 9.95x (ISBN 0-02-478500-8, 47850). Macmillan.
Simon, William. Mathematical Techniques for Biology & Medicine. rev. ed. LC 77-24347. (Illus.). 1977. pap. text ed. 9.95x (ISBN 0-262-69057-8). MIT Pr.
Taylor, Thomas J. Medical Mathematics. LC 74-79839. (Allied Health Ser). 1975. pap. 4.55 (ISBN 0-672-61393-X). Bobbs.
Waterhouse, Marian. Practical Mathematics in Allied Health: A Textbook for the Medical Disciplines. LC 79-15317. (Illus.). 256p. 1979. spiral bdg. 15.95 (ISBN 0-8067-2121-9). Urban & S.
Weaver, Mabel E. & Koehler, Vera J. Programmed Mathematics of Drugs & Solutions: Nineteen Seventy-Nine Revision with Intravenous Rate Calculations & Mathematics Pretest. LC 79-10790. 1979. pap. text ed. 4.95x (ISBN 0-397-54232-1). Lippincott.

MEDICINE–MISCELLANEA

From Bed to Verse. 1958. 2.95 (ISBN 0-917036-11-5). Physicians Rec.
Hoover, John E., ed. Dispensing of Medication. 8th ed. 1976. 22.00 (ISBN 0-912734-07-8). Mack Pub.
Larsen, Henning. An Old Icelandic Medical Miscellany. LC 75-23736. Repr. of 1931 ed. 28.50 (ISBN 0-404-13293-6). AMS Pr.
Pearl, Raymond. To Begin with: Being Prophylaxis Against Pedantry. LC 75-12708. 144p. 1976. Repr. of 1930 ed. 4.95 (ISBN 0-88275-327-4). Krieger.

Ziegler, A. Doctor's Administrative Program, 6 vols. Incl. Dap 1. Patient Contract & Public Relations (ISBN 0-87489-150-7); Dap 2. Bookkeeping & Tax Reports (ISBN 0-87489-151-5); Dap 3. Insurance & Third-Party-Payable Claims (ISBN 0-87489-152-3); Dap 4. Correspondence (ISBN 0-87489-153-1); Billing & Collections; Dap 6. Patient Records Control (ISBN 0-87489-155-8). 1978. Set. write for info. (ISBN 0-87489-158-2); Ea. Vol. write for info.

MEDICINE–MORAL AND RELIGIOUS ASPECTS

see Medical Ethics; Medicine and Religion

MEDICINE–PERIODICALS

Chen, Ching-Chih. Biomedical Scientific & Technical Book Reviewing. LC 76-20480. 1976. 10.00 (ISBN 0-8108-0939-7). Scarecrow.

Cumulative Index to Obstetrics & Gynecology: 1973-1977, Vols. 41-50. new ed. LC 78-60655. 1978. 33.50 (ISBN 0-88471-041-6). Numarc Bk Corp.

Cumulative Index to the American Journal of Pathology: Part 1, 1962-1970, Vols. 41-60. new ed. LC 77-88503. 1977. 37.50 (ISBN 0-88471-039-4). Numarc Bk Corp.

Fox, Theodore. Crisis in Communication: The Functions & Future of Medical Journals. (Heath Clark Lectures 1963). 1965. text ed. 2.50x (ISBN 0-485-26316-5, Athlone Pr). Humanities.

Lane, Nancy D. & Kammerer, Kathryn L. Writer's Guide to Medical Journals. LC 74-23210. 352p. 1975. text ed. 25.00 (ISBN 0-88410-119-3). Ballinger Pub.

Morton, Leslie T. How to Use a Medical Library. 6th ed. 1979. pap. 11.95x (ISBN 0-433-22451-7). Intl Ideas.

Waserman, Manfred & Clausen, Carol T., eds. Index to the Journal of the History of Medicine & Allied Sciences: 1948-1975, Vols I-xXX. 1977. 17.50 (ISBN 0-685-52438-8); pap. text ed. 10.00 (ISBN 0-685-52439-6). N Watson.

MEDICINE–PHILOSOPHY

Boss, Medard, ed. Existential Foundation of Medicine & Psychology. LC 77-74786. 1979. 30.00x (ISBN 0-87668-277-8). Aronson.

Brody, Howard. Placebos & the Philosophy of Medicine: Clinical, Conceptual, & Ethical Issues. LC 79-18481. 1980. lib. bdg. 13.50x (ISBN 0-226-07531-1). U of Chicago Pr.

Brown, Stephen G. & DiSaisa, Philip J. Cancer of the Cervix. (Oncologic Ser.: Vol. 14). (Illus.). 308p. 1981. pap. 50.00 (ISBN 0-08-027465-X). Pergamon.

Cassell, Eric J. The Healer's Art: A New Approach to the Doctor-Patient Relationship. 1976. 8.95 (ISBN 0-397-01098-2, JBL-Med-Nursing). Har-Row.

Clark-Kennedy, A. E. Man, Medicine, & Morality. 1969. 17.50 (ISBN 0-208-00972-8, Archon). Shoe String.

Durbin, Paul T., ed. A Guide to the Culture of Science, Technology, & Medicine. LC 79-7582. 1980. 45.00 (ISBN 0-02-907820-2). Free Pr.

Englehardt, H. Tristram, Jr., et al, eds. Clinical Judgment: A Critical Appraisal. (Philosophy & Medicine Ser.). 1979. 29.50 (ISBN 90-277-0952-1, Pub. by Reidel Holland). Kluwer Boston.

Flynn, Patricia A. The Healing Continuum: Journeys in the Philosophy of Holistic Health. (Illus.). 568p. 1980. 16.95 (ISBN 0-87619-670-9). R J Brady.

Foucault, Michael. Birth of the Clinic: An Archeology of Medical Perception. LC 74-3389. 1974. pap. 2.95 (ISBN 0-394-71097-5, V-97, Vin). Random.

Foucault, Michel. Birth of the Clinic: An Archaeology of Medical Perception. LC 73-3493. 1973. 8.95 (ISBN 0-394-48321-9). Pantheon.

Guirdham, Arthur. The Psyche in Medicine. 242p. 25.00x (ISBN 0-85978-031-7, Pub. by Spearman England). State Mutual Bk.

Illich, Ivan. Medical Nemesis: The Expropriation of Health. 1977. pap. 2.75 (ISBN 0-553-10596-5, 13371-3). Bantam.

King, Lester S. The Philosophy of Medicine: The Early Eighteenth Century. LC 77-24645. 1977. 22.50x (ISBN 0-674-66585-6). Harvard U Pr.

Luongo, Edward P. American Medicine in Crisis. LC 72-136013. 1971. 9.95 (ISBN 0-8022-2042-8). Philos Lib.

Maurois, Andre. De la Morale Medicale. pap. 8.95 (ISBN 0-685-36930-7). French & Eur.

Murphy, Edmond A. Skepsis, Dogma, & Belief: Uses & Abuses in Medicine. LC 80-8870. 176p. 1981. text ed. 14.95x (ISBN 0-8018-2510-5). Johns Hopkins.

Muturana, Humberto & Varela, Francisco. Autopoiesis & Cognition: The Realization of the Living. (Boston Studies in the Philosophy of Science Ser.: No. 42). 140p. 1980. lib. bdg. 29.00 (ISBN 90-277-1015-5, Pub. by Reidel Holland); pap. 14.50 (ISBN 90-277-1016-3). Kluwer Boston.

Pellegrino, Edmund D. & Thomasma, David C. A Philosophical Basis of Medical Practice: Toward a Philosophy & Ethic of the Healing Professions. (Illus.). 368p. 1981. 19.95 (ISBN 0-19-502790-6). Oxford U Pr.

--A Philosophical Basis of Medical Practice: Toward a Philosophy & Ethic of the Healing Professions. (Illus.). 368p. 1981. text ed. 11.95x (ISBN 0-19-502789-2). Oxford U Pr.

Rhodes, Philip. The Value of Medicine. 1977. text ed. 15.95x (ISBN 0-04-610004-0). Allen Unwin.

Rogers, William R. & Barnard, David, eds. Nourishing the Humanistic in Medicine: Interactions with the Social Sciences. LC 78-26222. (Contemporary Community Health Ser.). (Illus.). 1979. 10.95 (ISBN 0-8229-3395-0). U of Pittsburgh Pr.

Scientific American Editors. Life & Death & Medicine: A Scientific American Book. LC 73-16097. (Illus.). 1973. pap. text ed. 7.95x (ISBN 0-7167-0891-4). W H Freeman.

Sigerist, Henry E. Civilization & Disease. 1962. pap. 3.95 (ISBN 0-226-75723-4, P511, Phoen). U of Chicago Pr.

Spicker, Stuart F., ed. Organism, Medicine, & Metaphysics. (Philosophy & Medicine Ser.: No. 7). 1978. lib. bdg. 34.00 (ISBN 90-277-0823-1, Pub. by Junk Pubs Netherlands). Kluwer Boston.

Temkin, Owsei. Galenism: Rise & Decline of a Medical Philosophy. LC 72-12411. (History of Science Ser.). (Illus.). 240p. 1973. 22.50x (ISBN 0-8014-0774-5). Cornell U Pr.

Tubesing, Donald A. Wholistic Health: A Whole Person Approach to Primary Health Care. LC 78-3466. 1978. 22.95 (ISBN 0-87705-370-7). Human Sci Pr.

Yanovsky, V. S. Medicine, Science & Life. LC 77-99304. 1978. 10.00 (ISBN 0-8091-0235-8). Paulist Pr.

MEDICINE–PICTORIAL WORKS

Bettmann, Otto L. Pictorial History of Medicine. (Illus.). 336p. 1979. pap. 16.00 (ISBN 0-398-00149-9). C C Thomas.

Karolevitz, Robert F. Doctors of the Old West. encore ed. LC 67-20239. (Illus.). 1967. 9.95 (ISBN 0-87564-301-9). Superior Pub.

Netter, Frank H., illus. The C I B A Collection of Medical Illustrations, 7 vols. Incl. Vol. 1. Nervous System. 24.50x (ISBN 0-914168-01-0); Vol. 2. Reproductive System. 34.00x (ISBN 0-914168-02-9); Vol. 3, Pt. 1. Digestive System: Upper Digestive Tract. 27.00x (ISBN 0-914168-03-7); Vol. 3, Pt. 2. Digestive System: Lower Digestive Tract. 29.50x (ISBN 0-914168-04-5); Vol. 3, Pt. 3. Digestive System: Liver, Biliary Tract & Pancreas. 25.00x (ISBN 0-914168-05-3); Vol. 4. Endocrine System & Selected Metabolic Diseases. 34.00x (ISBN 0-914168-06-1); Vol. 5. Heart. 42.00x (ISBN 0-914168-07-X); Vol. 6. Kidneys, Ureters & Urinary Bladder. 44.00x (ISBN 0-914168-08-8). LC 53-2151. (Illus.). 1974. Set. 288.00x (ISBN 0-914168-00-2). C I B A Pharm.

Smith, C. C. Human Diseases in Color. (Illus.). 1978. 32.95 (ISBN 0-87489-188-4). Med Economics.

Wood, Phyllis. Scientific Illustration: A Guide to Biological, Zoological, & Medical Rendering Techniques, Design, Printing, & Display. 1979. 17.95 (ISBN 0-442-29532-4). Van Nos Reinhold.

MEDICINE–POPULAR WORKS

see Medicine, Popular

MEDICINE–PRACTICE

see also Bloodletting; Children–Diseases; Clinics; Communicable Diseases; Diagnosis; Electrotherapeutics; Group Medical Practice; Gynecology; Hydrotherapy; Infants–Diseases; Malpractice; Massage; Mechanotherapy; Nurses and Nursing; Obstetrics; Osteopathy; Therapeutics;

also names of diseases and groups of diseases, e.g. Bronchitis, Fever, Nervous System–Diseases

Aviado, Domingo M. Pharmacologic Principles of Medical Practice. 8th ed. LC 72-84836. 1366p. Date not set. Repr. of 1977 ed. 35.00 (ISBN 0-686-76753-5). Krieger.

Balliett, G. Getting Started in Private Practice. 1978. 21.50 (ISBN 0-87489-134-5). Med Economics.

--How to Close a Medical Practice. 1978. 21.50 (ISBN 0-87489-142-6). Med Economics.

Beck, Leif C. The Physician's Office. LC 77-87555. (Illus.). 1977. 14.95 (ISBN 0-444-90020-9). Excerpta-Princeton.

Beland, Irene L. & Passos, Joyce Y. Clinical Nursing. 3rd ed. (Illus.). 1086p. 1975. text ed. 24.95 (ISBN 0-02-307900-2). Macmillan.

Blech, Gustavus M. & Lynch, Charles. Medical Tactics & Logistics. (Illus.). 205p. 1934. ed. spiral bdg. 18.50photocopy (ISBN 0-398-04208-X). C C Thomas.

Bullough, Vern L. The Development of Medicine As a Profession. LC 76-56850. 132p. 1966. 20.00 (ISBN 0-686-65683-0). N Watson.

Cartwright, Ann. Patients & Their Doctors: A Study of General Practice. (Reports of the Institute of Community Studies). 1967. 23.50 (ISBN 0-7100-3919-0). Routledge & Kegan.

Castelnuovo-Tedesco, Pietro. The Twenty-Minute Hour. 184p. 1965. 14.95 (ISBN 0-316-13178-4). Little.

Cotton, H. Medical Practice Management. rev. ed. 1977. 23.95 (ISBN 0-87489-098-5). Med Economics.

Cousins, Norman. Anatomy of an Illness As Perceived by the Patient. 176p. 1981. pap. 4.95 (ISBN 0-553-01293-2). Bantam.

Directory of Self-Assessment Programs for Physicians. 3rd ed. 1974. 1.25 (ISBN 0-89970-034-9, OP-414). AMA.

Dopson, Laurence. The Changing Scene in General Practice. 248p. 1971. 10.00x (ISBN 0-85307-089-X). Intl Pubns Serv.

Fox, Donna R., ed. Private Practice. LC 78-151465. viii, 34p. 1971. pap. text ed. 1.50x (ISBN 0-8134-6256-8, 6256). Interstate.

Freidson, Eliot. Patient's Views of Medical Practice. (Midway Reprint Ser.). 268p. 1980. pap. text ed. 10.00x (ISBN 0-226-26223-5). U of Chicago Pr.

GAP Committee on Family. Case History Method in the Study of Family Process, Vol. 7. LC 62-2872. (Report No. 76). 1970. pap. 5.00 (ISBN 0-87318-105-0, Pub. by Adv Psychiatry). Mental Health.

Glasser, Morton & Pelto, Gretel H. Medical Merry-Go-Round: A Plea for Reasonable Medicine. 1980. pap. 6.90 (ISBN 0-913178-54-3). Redgrave Pub Co.

Goldberger, Emanuel. How Physicians Think: An Analysis of Medical Diagnosis & Treatment. (Illus.). 200p. 1965. ed. spiral bdg. 19.75photocopy (ISBN 0-398-00690-3). C C Thomas.

Hale, Geoffrey & Roberts, Nesta. A Doctor in Practice. 1974. 10.25x (ISBN 0-7100-7745-9). Routledge & Kegan.

Harvey, A. M., ed. The Principles & Practice of Medicine. 20th ed. (Illus.). 1569p. 1980. 39.50 (ISBN 0-8385-7930-2). ACC.

Houston, J. C., et al. Short Textbook of Medicine. 6th ed. (Illus., Orig.). 1980. pap. 14.75 (ISBN 0-397-58266-8, JBL-Med-Nursing). Har-Row.

Isselbacher, Kurt J., et al. Harrison's Principles of Internal Medicine. 400p. 1981. text ed. 30.00 (ISBN 0-07-032131-0). McGraw.

LaDou, Joseph & Likens, James D. Medicine & Money: Physicians As Businessmen. LC 77-2332. 1977. 16.50 (ISBN 0-88410-145-2). Ballinger Pub.

Margolis, Simon. The Practice of Medicine: A Self Assessment Guide. 2nd ed. (Illus.). 428p. 1980. pap. 15.95 (ISBN 0-8385-7877-2). ACC.

Mathews, Joseph M. How to Succeed in the Practice of Medicine. LC 74-180582. (Medicine & Society in America Ser). (Illus.). 244p. 1972. Repr. of 1905 ed. 12.00 (ISBN 0-405-03959-X). Arno.

Meislin, Harvey W. & Dresnick, Stephen J. Skills & Procedures of Emergency & General Medicine. 250p. 1982. text ed. 29.95 (ISBN 0-8359-7009-4). Reston.

Mettler, Fred A. The Medical Sourcebook. (Illus.). 1000p. 1960. 45.00 (ISBN 0-316-56828-7). Little.

Noble, John, ed. Primary Care & the Practice of Medicine. LC 75-41569. 1976. text ed. 19.95 (ISBN 0-316-61148-4). Little.

Oaks, Wilbur W., ed. Critical Care Medicine. LC 74-10537. (The Twenty-Eighth Hahnemann Symposium). (Illus.). 480p. 1974. 59.25 (ISBN 0-8089-0834-0). Grune.

Price, F. W. Price's Textbook of the Practice of Medicine. 12th ed. Scott, Ronald B., ed. (Illus.). 1978. text ed. 85.00x (ISBN 0-19-263209-4). Oxford U Pr.

Rachman, S., ed. Contributions to Medical Psychology. 1977. text ed. 25.00 (ISBN 0-08-020511-9). Pergamon.

Snapper, Isadore & Kahn, Alvin I. Bedside Medicine. 2nd ed. LC 66-25993. 856p. 1967. 70.75 (ISBN 0-8089-0433-7). Grune.

Snodgrass, Wilfred. Fundamentals of Family Practice. LC 74-11093. (Illus.). 640p. 1974. text ed. 37.50 (ISBN 0-8036-7960-2). Davis Co.

Sullivan, Robert J. Medical Record & Index Systems for Community Practice. LC 78-31817. (Rural Health Center Ser.). (Illus.). 1979. reference 14.50 (ISBN 0-88410-540-7); pap. 8.95 (ISBN 0-88410-546-6). Ballinger Pub.

Taylor, Robert B. Common Problems in Office Practice. 1972. 12.95x (ISBN 0-06-142541-9, Harper Medical). Har-Row.

--The Practical Art of Medicine. (Illus.). 1972. 12.95x (ISBN 0-06-142543-5, Harper Medical). Har-Row.

Tournier, Paul. Healing of Persons. LC 65-10704. 1965. 11.95 (ISBN 0-06-068350-3, HarpR). Har-Row.

Understanding Modern Medical Practice. (Illus.). 208p. 1981. pap. 9.95 (ISBN 0-87851-043-5). Hearst Bks.

Wilkins, Robert W. & Levinsky, Norman G. Medicine: Essentials of Clinical Practice. 2nd ed. 1978. text ed. 25.00 (ISBN 0-316-94091-7); pap. text ed. 16.95 (ISBN 0-316-94090-9). Little.

Zabarenko, Lucy, et al. Primary Medical Practice: A Psychiatric Evaluation. LC 67-26018. (Illus.). 272p. 1968. 11.75 (ISBN 0-87527-090-5). Green.

MEDICINE–QUOTATIONS, MAXIMS, ETC.

Strauss, Maurice B., ed. Familiar Medical Quotations. 968p. 1968. 19.95 (ISBN 0-316-81915-8). Little.

MEDICINE–READERS

see Readers–Medicine

MEDICINE–RESEARCH

see Medical Research

MEDICINE–SOCIAL ASPECTS

see Social Medicine

MEDICINE–SOCIETIES, ETC.

Source Collective. Organizing for Health Care: A Tool for Change. LC 74-254. (Source Catalog Ser., No. 3). 256p. 1974. pap. 5.95 (ISBN 0-8070-2179-2, BP503). Beacon Pr.

Stauffer, Robert B. The Development of an Interest Group: The Philippine Medical Association. 1966. 4.00x (ISBN 0-8248-0436-8). U Pr of Hawaii.

MEDICINE–SPECIALTIES AND SPECIALISTS

Directory Medical Specialist, 1981-1982, 3 vols. 20th ed. 1981. 180.00 set (ISBN 0-8379-0520-6). Marquis.

Featherstone, Donald F. & Allen, Rona. Dancing Without Danger: The Prevention & Treatment of Ballet Dancing Injuries. LC 76-88259. (Illus.). 1970. 9.95 (ISBN 0-498-06995-8). A S Barnes.

Gibson, William C. Creative Minds in Medicine: Scientific, Humanistic, & Cultural Contributions by Physicians. (Illus.). 256p. 1963. ed. spiral bdg. 22.75photocopy (ISBN 0-398-00676-8). C C Thomas.

Rosen, George. The Specialization of Medicine with Particular Reference to Opthalmology. LC 79-180586. (Medicine & Society in America Ser). 106p. 1972. Repr. of 1944 ed. 9.00 (ISBN 0-405-03966-2). Arno.

Stevens, Rosemary. American Medicine & the Public Interest. LC 77-151592. 1971. pap. 7.95 (ISBN 0-300-01744-8, Y264). Yale U Pr.

Stillman, Richard. Medical Specialities: Reveiw & Assessment. 448p. 1981. 15.00 (ISBN 0-8385-6267-1). ACC.

Stillman, Richard M. Medical Specialties: Review & Assessment. 1981. pap. 12.50 (ISBN 0-686-72395-3). ACC.

Terminology for Medical Specialties. 1975. pap. 12.00 (ISBN 0-686-10812-4). Preston.

MEDICINE–STUDY AND TEACHING

see also Psychiatry–Study and Teaching; Television in Medical Education

Abrams, Robert, et al. FLEX Review. LC 80-83395. 1980. pap. 21.50 (ISBN 0-87488-158-7). Med Exam.

Acheson, E. D., ed. Medicine: An Outline for the Intending Student. (Outlines Ser). 1970. cased 14.00 (ISBN 0-7100-6866-2); pap. 7.95x (ISBN 0-7100-6867-0). Routledge & Kegan.

American Academy of Pediatrics. Child Health Services & Pediatric Education: Report of the Committee for the Study of Child Health Services. facsimile ed. LC 74-1661. (Children & Youth Ser.). 304p. 1974. Repr. of 1949 ed. 18.00x (ISBN 0-405-05943-4). Arno.

Becker, Howard S., et al. Boys in White: Student Culture in Medical School. Repr. of 1961 ed. lib. bdg. 34.50x (ISBN 0-8290-0371-1). Irvington.

Bloom, A., ed. Whittington Postgraduate Medicine. 1974. Repr. of 1975 ed. 13.95 (ISBN 0-407-93500-2). Butterworth.

Boucher Hayes, T. A., et al. The MRCGP Study Book. 175p. 1980. text ed. 25.50 (ISBN 0-906141-13-3, Pub by MTP Pr England); pap. text ed. 21.50 (ISBN 0-906141-31-1, Pub. by MTP Pr England). Kluwer Boston.

Daum, Susan L., ed. Guide to Audiovisual Resources for the Health Care Field. 1981 ed. 200p. (Orig.). 1981. 18.00 (ISBN 0-939450-00-3). Med Info Pubns.

Effective Continuing Education: How to. 1978. pap. 10.00 (ISBN 0-912452-10-2). Am Phys Therapy Assn.

Flexner, Abraham. Medical Education in the United States & Canada. LC 78-180575. (Medicine & Society in America Ser). 368p. 1972. Repr. of 1910 ed. 16.00 (ISBN 0-405-03952-2). Arno.

Franklin, D. A. & Newman, G. B. A Guide to Medical Mathematics. LC 73-15859. (Illus.). 453p. 1973. 29.95 (ISBN 0-470-27520-0). Halsted Pr.

Gerrick, David J. Individualized Learning Materials in Medicine: A Guide to AV Materials in Health Sciences. 1975. pap. 13.95 (ISBN 0-916750-29-9). Dayton Labs.

Grob, Gerald N., ed. Psychiatry & Medical Education: Two Studies, 2 vols. in one. LC 78-22582. (Historical Issues in Mental Health Ser.). (Illus.). 1979. Repr. lib. bdg. 42.00x (ISBN 0-405-11934-8). Arno.

Holcomb, J. D. & Garner, A. E. Improving Teaching in Medical Schools: A Practical Handbook. 240p. 1973. 12.75 (ISBN 0-398-02821-4). C C Thomas.

Knight, James A. Doctor-to-Be: Coping with the Trials & Triumphs of Medical School. 2nd ed. 288p. 1981. 12.95 (ISBN 0-8385-1722-6). ACC.

Knopke, Harry J. & Diekelmann, Nancy L. Approaches to Teaching in the Health Sciences. LC 78-52503. 1978. text ed. 11.95 (ISBN 0-201-01656-7). A-W.

Knowles, John H., ed. Teaching Hospital: Evolution & Contemporary Issues. LC 66-21338. 1966. 8.95x (ISBN 0-674-86955-9). Harvard U Pr.

Mann, W. N. Conybeare's Textbook of Medicine. 16th ed. LC 73-92327. (Illus.). 832p. 1975. text ed. 45.00x (ISBN 0-443-01245-8). Churchill.

Myers, J. Arthur. Masters of Medicine: An Historical Sketch of the College of Medical Sciences of the University of Minnesota, 1888-1966. LC 68-8890. (Illus.). 942p. 1968. 15.00 (ISBN 0-87527-058-1); pap. 10.00 (ISBN 0-685-24021-5). Green.

Nassif, R. E. & Thaddeus, J. D., eds. Education for Health Manpower in the Middle East. 1967. pap. 12.95x (ISBN 0-8156-6006-5, Am U Beirut). Syracuse U Pr.

Reader, George G. & Goss, Mary E., eds. Comprehensive Medical Care & Teaching: A Report on an Experimental Program of the New York Hospital-Cornell Medical Center. LC 67-23762. 391p. 1968. 27.50x (ISBN 0-8014-0352-9). Cornell U Pr.

Shugar, Gershon J., et al. How to Get into Medical & Dental School. 3rd ed. LC 80-23397. 192p. 1981. lib. bdg. 12.00 (ISBN 0-668-05105-1); pap. 6.95 (ISBN 0-668-05112-4). Arco.

Sinclair, David C. Basic Medical Education. 212p. 1972. text ed. 13.50x (ISBN 0-19-264913-2). Oxford U Pr.

University of Natal-Conference on Medical Education Durban - July 1964. Medical Education in South Africa: Proceedings. Reid, J. V. & Wilmot, A. J., eds. 1965. 18.00x (ISBN 0-8426-1384-6). Verry.

Werkman, Sidney L. Role of Psychiatry in Medical Education: An Appraisal & a Forecast. LC 66-10810. (Commonwealth Fund Publications Ser). (Illus.). 1966. 10.00x (ISBN 0-674-77730-1). Harvard U Pr.

MEDICINE–STUDY AND TEACHING–CANADA

Flexner, Abraham. Medical Education in the United States & Canada. LC 78-180575. (Medicine & Society in America Ser). 368p. 1972. Repr. of 1910 ed. 16.00 (ISBN 0-405-03952-2). Arno.

MEDICINE–TERMINOLOGY

Alter, Aaron A., et al. Medical Technology Examination Review Book, Vol. 2. 4th ed. 1978. spiral bdg. 9.50 (ISBN 0-87488-452-7). Med Exam.

Angela. Daffy Definitions of Medical Terms. Date not set. 5.95 (ISBN 0-533-04834-6). Vantage.

Austin, D. & Crosfield, T. English for Nurses. (English As a Second Language Bk.). (Illus.). 138p. 1976. pap. text ed. 4.50x (ISBN 0-582-55019-X); tchrs' notes 2.25x (ISBN 0-582-55244-3). Longman.

Bernthal, Patricia J. & Spiller, James D. Understanding the Language of Medicine: A Programmed Learning Text. (Illus.). 300p. 1981. pap. text ed. 14.95x (ISBN 0-19-502879-1). Oxford U Pr.

Birmingham, Jacqueline J. Medical Terminology: A Self-Learning Module. (Illus.). 448p. 1981. pap. text ed. 11.95 (ISBN 0-07-005386-3, HP). McGraw.

Brady, R. J. Medical Terminology: A Programmed Orientation to. (Illus.). 1970. pap. 10.95 (ISBN 0-87618-074-8). R J Brady.

Bredow, Miriam. Handbook for the Medical Secretary. 4th ed. (Illus.). 1959. pap. 4.50 (ISBN 0-07-007413-5, SP). McGraw.

--Medical Office Procedures. Orig. Title: Medical Secretarial Procedures. (Illus.). 416p. 1973. pap. text ed. 13.50 (ISBN 0-07-007425-9, G); instructor's manual & key 6.50 (ISBN 0-07-007426-7). McGraw.

Caldwell, Esther & Hegner, Barbara R. Foundation for Medical Communication. (Illus.). 1978. text ed. 16.95 (ISBN 0-87909-299-8); pap. text ed. 12.95 (ISBN 0-87909-298-X); instrs'. manual avail. Reston.

Carlin, Harriette L. Medical Secretary Medi-Speller: A Transcription Aid. 260p. 1973. pap. 11.50 (ISBN 0-398-02579-7). C C Thomas.

Chabner, Davi-Ellen. The Language of Medicine: A Write-in Text Explaining Medical Terms. 2nd ed. (Illus.). 600p. 1981. text ed. 16.95 (ISBN 0-7216-2479-0). Saunders.

Charles Press Handbook of Current Medical Abbreviatons. 1977. 6.95 (ISBN 0-913486-80-9). Charles.

Cooper, E. S. The Language of Medicine: A Guide for Stenotypists. 1977. pap. 9.95 (ISBN 0-87489-045-4). Med Economics.

Davies, P. M. Medical Terminology in Hospital Practice. 3rd ed. 1979. pap. 16.95x (ISBN 0-433-07183-4). Intl Ideas.

Delamare, Jean V. Dictionary of Medical Terms: English-French & French-English. LC 73-540414. 710p. 1970. 52.50x (ISBN 0-8002-0196-5). Intl Pubns Serv.

Dirckx, John H. The Language of Medicine: Its Evolution, Structure & Dynamics. 1976. pap. 10.95x (ISBN 0-06-140689-9, Harper Medical). Har-Row.

Dunmore, Charles W. & Fleischer, Rita M. Medical Terminology: Exercise in Etymology. 1977. pap. text ed. 11.95 (ISBN 0-8036-2945-1). Davis Co.

Fisher, J. Patrick. Basic Medical Terminology. LC 74-77820. (Allied Health Ser). 1975. pap. text ed. 12.20 (ISBN 0-672-61385-9); tchr's manual 6.67 (ISBN 0-672-61386-7); tape cassette 96.45 (ISBN 0-672-61387-5). Bobbs.

Frenay, Agnes C. Understanding Medical Terminology. 6th ed. LC 77-73986. 1977. pap. text ed. 9.00 (ISBN 0-87125-038-1). Cath Health.

Garb, Solomon, et al. Abbreviations & Acronyms in Medicine & Nursing. LC 75-29483. 1976. text ed. 9.95 (ISBN 0-8261-2001-6); pap. text ed. 4.95 (ISBN 0-8261-2000-8). Springer Pub.

Garber, A. Brent & Sparks, Leroy. Learn-a-Term. LC 77-82026. 168p. 1977. pap. text ed. 16.50 (ISBN 0-912862-48-3). Aspen Systems.

Gross, Verlee E. Mastering Medical Terminology: Textbook of Anatomy, Diseases, Anomalies & Surgeries with English Translation & Pronunciation. 6th ed. LC 78-85804. (Illus.). 440p. (Orig., Prog. Bk.). 1969. pap. text ed. 16.00x (ISBN 0-912256-01-X). Halls of Ivy.

Hawkins, Clifford F. Speaking & Writing in Medicine: The Art of Communication. (American Lecture Living Chemistry). (Illus.). 178p. 1967. photocopy ed. spiral 18.50 (ISBN 0-398-00804-3). C C Thomas.

Jeharned. Medical Terminology Made Easy. 2nd ed. 352p. 1968. text ed. 9.00 (ISBN 0-917036-06-9). Physicians Rec.

Johnson, Carrie E. Medical Spelling Guide: A Reference Aid. 560p. 1966. 14.75 (ISBN 0-398-00931-7). C C Thomas.

Kantrowitz, Martin P., et al. Que Paso? An English-Spanish Guide for Medical Personnel. 3rd ed. LC 78-55709. (Illus.). 1978. pap. 2.95 (ISBN 0-8263-0488-5). U of NM Pr.

Kinn, Mary E. Review of Medical Terminology. 1980. 9.00 (ISBN 0-913258-73-3). Thieme Stratton.

Lee, Richard V. & Hofer, Doris J. How to Divide Medical Words. LC 71-181983. 237p. 1972. 5.95x (ISBN 0-8093-0558-5). S Ill U Pr.

Levinson, Philip J. & Sloan, Christine. Auditory Processing & Language: Clinical & Research Perspectives. 256p. 1980. 19.50 (ISBN 0-8089-1305-0). Grune.

Lewis, Carolyn D. Medical Latin. (YA) (gr. 12). 2.50x (ISBN 0-8338-0040-X). M Jones.

Lexique des Termes Medicaux. (Fr.). pap. 14.95 (ISBN 0-686-56722-6, M-6362). French & Eur.

Lorenzini, Jean. Medical Phrase Index. 1978. 28.50 (ISBN 0-87489-149-3); pap. 22.95 (ISBN 0-87489-198-1). Med Economics.

McCulloch, James A. Medical Greek & Latin Workbook. 174p. 1977. pap. 8.50 (ISBN 0-398-01249-0). C C Thomas.

Maclean, Joan. English in Basic Medical Science. (English in Focus Ser.). (Illus.). 1975. pap. text ed. 6.95x (ISBN 0-19-437515-3); tchr's ed. 11.00x (ISBN 0-19-437503-X). Oxford U Pr.

Manuila, A., ed. Progress in Medical Terminology. (Illus.). xiii, 116p. 1981. pap. 47.50 (ISBN 3-8055-2112-X). S Karger.

Marie, Joseph. Medical Vocabulary. 59.95 (ISBN 0-8490-0597-3). Gordon Pr.

Martins, Jose M. English for the Foreign Physician. (Illus.). 136p. 1974. photocopy ed. spiral 12.75 (ISBN 0-398-01227-X). C C Thomas.

Nybakken, Oscar E. Greek & Latin in Scientific Terminology. 1959. 10.50 (ISBN 0-8138-0720-4). Iowa St U Pr.

Park-Davis & Company. Medical Word Building. 1970. pap. 7.95 (ISBN 0-87489-043-8). Med Economics.

Parke, Davis & Company. Medical Word Building. (Medical Economics Books). 1970. 6.50 (ISBN 0-442-84015-2). Van Nos Reinhold.

Patterson, Sandra R. & Thompson, Lawrence S. Medical Terminology from Greek & Latin. LC 77-93780. 1978. 15.00x (ISBN 0-87875-138-6). Whitston Pub.

Prendergast, Alice. Medical Terminology: A Text-Workbook. LC 76-62907. 1977. pap. text ed. 11.95 (ISBN 0-201-05966-5, Med-Nurse); instr's man. 9.95 (ISBN 0-201-05967-3). A-W.

Prichard, Robert W. & Robinson, Robert E. Twenty Thousand Medical Words. 288p. 1972. 6.50 (ISBN 0-07-050873-9, HP); pap. 4.95 (ISBN 0-07-050874-7). McGraw.

Radcliff, Ruth K. & Ogden, Shelia J. Nursing & Medical Terminology: A Workbook. LC 76-17597. (Illus.). 1977. pap. text ed. 12.50 (ISBN 0-8016-3714-7). Mosby.

Richey, Jim. Medical Language. (Survival Vocabulary Ser.). (Illus.). 48p. (gr. 7 up). 1980. pap. text ed. 2.45 (ISBN 0-915510-48-0). Janus Bks.

Rickards, Ralph. Understanding Medical Terms: A Self-Instructional Course. (Illus.). 112p. 1980. pap. text ed. 7.95 (ISBN 0-443-02029-9). Churchill.

Rimer, Evelyn H. Harbeck's Glossary of Medical Terms. (Orig.). pap. 5.95 (ISBN 0-87465-016-X). Pacific Coast.

Roland, Charles G. The Master-Word in Medicine: A Study in Rhetoric. (Illus.). 1972. photocopy ed. spiral 6.75 (ISBN 0-398-02393-X). C C Thomas.

Root, Kathleen B. & Byers, E. E. Medical Secretary: Terminology & Transcription. 3rd ed. 1967. 15.20 (ISBN 0-07-053586-8, G); student transcript 4.95 (ISBN 0-07-053589-2). McGraw.

Schmidt, J. E. Analyzer of Medical-Biological Words: A Clarifying Dissection of Medical Terminology, Showing How It Works, for Medics, Paramedics, Students, & Visitors from Foreign Countries. 224p. 1973. 10.75 (ISBN 0-398-02682-3). C C Thomas.

--Index of Paramedical Vocabulary. (Illus.). 324p. 1974. pap. 10.75 (ISBN 0-398-02833-8). C C Thomas.

--Visual Aids for Paramedical Vocabulary. (Illus.). 196p. 1973. 10.75 (ISBN 0-398-02609-2). C C Thomas.

Sloane, Sheila B. The Medical Word Book: A Spelling & Vocabulary Guide to Medical Transcription. LC 72-86455. (Illus.). 923p. 1973. pap. 13.95 (ISBN 0-7216-8364-9). Saunders.

Smith, G. L. & Davis, P. E. Medical Terminology. 4th ed. LC 80-17970. 325p. 1981. pap. 13.95 (ISBN 0-471-05827-0, Pub. by Wiley Med). Wiley.

Spatola, Anthony L. Mastering Medical Language. (Illus.). 464p. 1981. pap. text ed. 15.95 (ISBN 0-13-560151-7). P-H.

Steen, Edwin B. Abbreviations in Medicine. 4th ed. 1978. pap. 10.95 (ISBN 0-02-859430-4). Macmillan.

Stegeman, Wilson. Medical Terms Simplified. LC 75-12977. (Illus.). 305p. 1975. pap. text ed. 12.95 (ISBN 0-8299-0062-4). West Pub.

Stein, Harold A., et al. Manual of Opthalmic Terminology. (Illus.). 218p. 1982. pap. text ed. 15.00 (ISBN 0-8016-4769-X). Mosby.

Strand, Helen R. An Illustrated Guide to Medical Terminology. 110p. 1968. 15.00 (ISBN 0-683-08006-7); pap. 7.75 (ISBN 0-685-91060-1, Pub. by W & W). Krieger.

Tebben, Joseph. Medical & Technical Terminology. 1975. pap. text ed. 4.50 (ISBN 0-88429-013-1). Collegiate Pub.

Teitelbaum & Johnson. Mangled Medicine Definitions We Doubt You Learned in School. (Medical Economics Books). 1972. 4.50 (ISBN 0-442-84017-9). Van Nos Reinhold.

Terminology for Medical Specialties. 1975. pap. 12.00 (ISBN 0-686-10812-4). Preston.

Tessier, Claudia J. The Surgical Word Book. LC 81-40485. 507p. pap. text ed. 14.95 (ISBN 0-7216-8805-5). Saunders.

Tyrrell & Blake, William. Medical Terminology for Medical Students. (Illus.). 176p. 1979. 16.00 (ISBN 0-398-03810-4); pap. 10.75 (ISBN 0-398-03820-1). C C Thomas.

Urdang. Urdang Dictionary of Current Medical Terms. LC 80-22916. 455p. 1981. 12.95 (ISBN 0-471-05853-X, Pub. by Wiley Med). Wiley.

Vaisrub, S. Medicine's Metaphors: Messages & Menaces. 1977. 9.95 (ISBN 0-87489-011-X). Med Economics.

Veillon, E. & Nobel, A. Medizinisches Woerterbuch. 5th rev. ed. 1330p. (Ger., Fr. & Eng., Medical Dictionary). 1969. 105.00 (ISBN 3-456-00200-9, M-7554, Pub. by H. Huber). French & Eur.

Volkell, Randolph Z. Quick Legal Terminology. LC 79-13647. (Self-Teaching Guides Ser.). 1979. pap. text ed. 5.95 (ISBN 0-471-03786-9). Wiley.

Wain, Harry. The Story Behind the Word: Some Interesting Origins of Medical Terms. 352p. 1958. photocopy ed. spiral 34.75 (ISBN 0-398-02001-9). C C Thomas.

Warren, Kenneth S., ed. Coping with the Biomedical Literature: A Primer for the Scientist & the Clinician. 246p. 1981. 26.95 (ISBN 0-03-057036-0); pap. 13.95 (ISBN 0-03-057034-4). Praeger.

White, Wallace F. Language of the Health Sciences: A Lexical Guide to Word Parts, Word Roots, & Their Meanings. LC 77-9310. 1977. pap. 12.95 (ISBN 0-471-02159-8, Pub. by Wiley Medical). Wiley.

Willeford, George. Medical Word Finder. 1967. 12.95 (ISBN 0-13-573501-7, Parker). P-H.

Woolley, LeGrand H. Medical-Dental Terminology: Syllabus. 2nd ed. 1974. pap. text ed. 6.10 (ISBN 0-89420-003-8, 217705); cassette recordings 177.70 (ISBN 0-89420-162-X, 196700). Natl Book.

Young, Clara G. Student's Workbook for Learning Medical Terminology Step by Step. 2nd ed. LC 79-11068. (Illus.). 1979. 11.50 (ISBN 0-8016-5658-3). Mosby.

MEDICINE–TERMINOLOGY–PROGRAMMED INSTRUCTION

Bennett, A., et al, eds. Selected Medical Terminology. Orig. Title: Medical Terminology for Hospital Employees. (Orig.). 1968. text ed. 18.00 (ISBN 0-686-00455-8). Preston.

Byers, Edward E. Ten Thousand Medical Words, Spelled & Divided for Quick Reference. 128p. 1972. text ed. 5.28 (ISBN 0-07-009503-5, G). McGraw.

Lea, J. Terminology & Communication Skills in the Health Sciences. 1975. pap. 7.95 (ISBN 0-87909-821-X). Reston.

MEDICINE–TROPICS

see Tropical Medicine

MEDICINE–VOCATIONAL GUIDANCE

Alperin, Stanley & Alperin, Melvin. One Hundred Twenty Careers in the Health Care Field. LC 79-53587. 320p. 1980. reference 22.50 (ISBN 0-88410-709-4). Ballinger Pub.

Bluestone, Naomi. So You Want to Be a Doctor? The Realities of Pursuing Medicine As a Career. LC 81-2545. 256p. (gr. 7 up). 1981. 12.95 (ISBN 0-688-00739-2). Lothrop.

Bowers, John Z. & Rosenheim, Lord, eds. Migration of Medical Manpower. LC 73-156291. (Illus.). 194p. 1972. 9.00 (ISBN 0-914362-01-1). J Macy Foun.

Bransford, Kent. The No-Nonsense Guide to Get You into Medical School. LC 78-11160. 1979. 8.95 (ISBN 0-671-18412-1); pap. write for info. Sovereign Bks.

Cavallaro, Ann. The Physician's Associate: A New Career in Health Care. LC 78-2369. (gr. 7 up). 1978. Repr. 7.95 (ISBN 0-525-66598-6). Elsevier-Nelson.

Coombs, Robert H. & Vincent, Clark E., eds. Psychosocial Aspects of Medical Training. (Illus.). 584p. 1971. 33.00 (ISBN 0-398-00343-2). C C Thomas.

Davis, Mary. Careers in a Medical Center. LC 72-7657. (Early Career Bks). (Illus.). 36p. (gr. 2-5). 1973. 4.95 (ISBN 0-8225-0310-7). Lerner Pubns.

De Craemer, Willy & Fox, Renee C. The Emerging Physician: A Sociological Approach to the Development of a Congolese Medical Profession. LC 67-26615. (Studies Ser.: No. 19). 1968. pap. 4.50 (ISBN 0-8179-3192-9). Hoover Inst Pr.

Dopson, Laurence. The Changing Scene in General Practice. 248p. 1971. 10.00x (ISBN 0-85307-089-X). Intl Pubns Serv.

Englebardt, Stanley L. Jobs in Health Care. LC 73-4939. (Exploring Careers Ser). (Illus.). 96p. (gr. 5 up). 1973. 7.25 (ISBN 0-688-75001-X). Lothrop.

Fenten, D. X. Ms.-M. D. (Illus.). (gr. 7 up). 1973. 5.25 (ISBN 0-664-32524-6). Westminster.

Freidson, E. Doctoring Together: A Study of Professional Social Control. 1976. 25.00 (ISBN 0-444-99017-8, Pub. by Elsevier). Greenwood.

Freidson, Eliot. Profession of Medicine: A Study of the Sociology of Applied Knowledge. 1970. text ed. 23.50 scp (ISBN 0-06-042205-X, HarpC). Har-Row.

Gottlieb, Marvin I., et al. Basic Sciences. 6th ed. (Medical Examination Review Book Ser.: Vol. 3). 1974. spiral bdg. 8.50 (ISBN 0-87488-103-X). Med Exam.

Gray, Jane. Medicine. LC 74-76181. (Professions Ser.). (Illus.). 168p. 1974. 5.95 (ISBN 0-7153-6623-8). David & Charles.

Health Professions Educational Association. Committee of Presidents, ed. A Guide to Education for the Health Professions. LC 79-11155. 1979. pap. 4.95 (ISBN 0-87491-242-3). Acropolis.

Heffel, Leonard E. Opportunities in Osteopathic Medicine Today. LC 74-78786. (Illus.). 144p. (gr. 9-12). 1974. PLB 6.60 (ISBN 0-8442-6463-6); pap. text ed. 4.95 (ISBN 0-8442-6462-8). Natl Textbk.

Kalb, S. William. Your Future As a Physician. LC 79-110288. (Careers in Depth Ser). (gr. 7 up). 1971. PLB 5.97 (ISBN 0-8239-0258-7). Rosen Pr.

Kantor, Herman I. Doctors Must Invest! a Primer on Where! LC 72-94163. (Illus.). 144p. 1974. 10.00 (ISBN 0-87527-110-3). Green.

Keyes, Fenton. Your Future in a Paramedic Career. (Careers in Depth Ser.). (Illus.). (gr. 7-12). 1981. PLB 5.97 (ISBN 0-8239-0486-5). Rosen Pr.

Kimbrall, Mary E. Introduction to Health Careers. (gr. 7-10). 1975. pap. text ed. 5.28 activity ed (ISBN 0-87345-179-1). McKnight.

Klein, Kenneth. Getting Better: A Medical Student's Story. 324p. 1981. 12.95 (ISBN 0-316-49838-6). Little.

Knight, James A. Doctor-to-Be: Coping with the Trials & Triumphs of Medical School. 2nd ed. 288p. 1981. 12.95 (ISBN 0-8385-1722-6). ACC.

Lebowitz, Gordon. Exploring Health Careers Ser., Bk. 3: Careers in Therapy, Medical Technology & Nutrition. new ed. (Illus.). 144p. 1974. wkbk 3.00 (ISBN 0-87005-126-1); tchrs' guide 1.50 (ISBN 0-87005-131-8). Fairchild.

Lee, Essie. Careers in the Health Field. rev. ed. LC 74-9681. (Career Bks.). (Illus.). 192p. (gr. 7 up). 1974. PLB 7.29 (ISBN 0-671-32513-2). Messner.

Lippard, Vernon W., intro. by. The Greater Medical Profession. LC 73-77542. (Illus.). 253p. 1973. pap. 7.50 (ISBN 0-914362-04-6). J Macy Foun.

Miller, George E. Educating Medical Teachers. (Commonwealth Fund Publications). (Illus.). 240p. 1980. 15.00x (ISBN 0-674-23775-7). Harvard U Pr.

Milles, George. Health Careers & Medical Sciences. LC 74-79837. (Allied Health Ser). 1975. pap. 5.50 (ISBN 0-672-61384-0). Bobbs.

Naseem, Attia & Mustafa, Kamil. Medical Careers Planning. (Illus.). 1977. pap. text ed. 27.95 (ISBN 0-917364-01-5). Bur Health Hosp.

Nassif, Janet Z. Handbook of Health Careers: A Guide to Employment Opportunities. LC 79-23027. 352p. 1980. 29.95 (ISBN 0-87705-489-4); pap. 12.95 (ISBN 0-87705-413-4). Human Sci Pr.

Parry, N. C. Rise of the Medical Profession: A Study in Collective Social Mobility. 1976. 17.50x (ISBN 0-85664-224-X). Intl Pubns Serv.

Petersen, William F. Hippocratic Wisdom: For Him Who Wishes to Pursue Properly the Science of Medicine: A Modern Appreciation of Ancient Scientific Wisdom. (Illus.). 286p. 1946. pap. write for info. (ISBN 0-398-04390-6). C C Thomas.

Quinn, Carin. Your Career As a Physician. LC 79-802. 1979. pap. 3.95 (ISBN 0-668-04742-9, 4742); pap. 3.50 (ISBN 0-668-04753-4, 4753). Arco.

Rambo, Beverly J. & Watson, Diane. Your Career in Health Care. 1976. 8.95 (ISBN 0-07-051166-7, G). McGraw.

Schneller, Eugene S. The Physician's Assistant. LC 76-11974. 1978. 18.95 (ISBN 0-669-00715-3). Lexington Bks.

Seide, Diane. Careers in Medical Science. LC 73-13538. 176p. (YA) (gr. 9 up). 1973. 7.95 (ISBN 0-525-66312-6). Elsevier-Nelson.

Silva, Yvan J. Career Development for Foreign Medical Graduates in the United States. (Illus.). 160p. 1973. photocopy ed. spiral 15.75 (ISBN 0-398-02669-6). C C Thomas.

Sulz, Harry. Grantwriting for Health Professionals. 1981. pap. write for info. (ISBN 0-316-82196-9). Little.

Winn, Charles S., et al. Exploring Health Occupations. (Careers in Focus Ser.). 1976. text ed. 5.32 (ISBN 0-07-071027-9, G); tchr's. manual & key 3.30 (ISBN 0-07-071028-7); worksheets 3.68 (ISBN 0-07-071056-2). McGraw.

Wischnitzer, Saul. Barron's Guide to Allied Health Science Careers. Date not set. pap. text ed. 4.95 (ISBN 0-8120-2427-3). Barron.

--Barron's Guide to Medical & Dental Schools. 286p. 1981. pap. text ed. 4.95 (ISBN 0-8120-2427-3). Barron.

--Barron's Guide to Medical, Dental & Allied Health Science Careers. rev. ed. LC 76-41772. (gr. 12). 1977. pap. 6.50 (ISBN 0-8120-0719-0). Barron.

Would You Like to Be a Medical Doctor? 48p. (gr. 4-6). 1980. 2.95 (ISBN 0-686-31327-5). Unica Inc.

Zimmermann, Barbara & Smith, David B. Careers in Health: The Professionals Give You the Inside Picture About Their Jobs. LC 78-53788. 1979. 11.95 (ISBN 0-8070-2578-X); pap. 4.95 (ISBN 0-8070-2579-8, BP588). Beacon Pr.

MEDICINE–YEAR BOOKS

Annual Epidemiological & Vital Statistics. Incl. 1939-1946, Part 1 - Vital Statistics & Causes of Death. 124p. (Eng. & Fr.). 1951; 1939-1946, Part 2 - Causes of & Deaths from Notifiable Diseases. 202p. (Eng. & Fr.). 1952. pap. 7.20 (ISBN 0-686-09191-4); 1947-1949, Part 1 - Vital Statistics & Causes of Death. 746p. (Eng. & Fr.). 1952; 1947-1949, Part 2 - Causes of & Deaths from Notifiable Diseases. 291p. (Eng. & Fr.). 1953; 1950, Part 1 - Vital Statistics & Causes of Death. 371p. (Eng. & Fr.). 1953; 1950, Part 2 - Causes of & Death from Notifiable Diseases. 163p. (Eng. & Fr.). 1954; 1951. 506p. (Eng. & Fr.). 1954. pap. 13.60 (ISBN 0-686-09196-5); 1952. 543p. (Eng. & Fr.). 1955. pap. 13.60 (ISBN 0-686-09197-3); 1953. 571p. (Eng. & Fr.). 1956; 1954. 617p. (Eng. & Fr.). 1957; 1955; 1956. 705p. (Eng. & Fr.). 1959. pap. 16.40 (ISBN 0-686-09201-5); 1957. 669p. (Eng. & Fr.). 1960. pap. 16.40 (ISBN 0-686-09202-3); 1958. 855p. (Eng. & Fr.). 1961. pap. 21.60 (ISBN 0-686-09203-1); 1959. 736p. (Eng. & Fr.). 1962. pap. 18.80 (ISBN 0-686-09204-X); 1960. 876p. (Eng, Fr, Rus.). 1963. pap. 26.80 (ISBN 0-686-09205-8); 1961. 741p. (Eng, Fr, Rus.). 1964. pap. 24.00 (ISBN 0-686-09206-6). World Health.

Coventry, Mark B., ed. Year Book of Orthopedics Nineteen Eighty-One. Date not set. price not set (ISBN 0-8151-1881-3). Year Bk Med.

Creger, W. P., et al, eds. Annual Review of Medicine, Vol. 24. LC 51-1659. (Illus.). 1973. text ed. 17.00 (ISBN 0-8243-0524-8). Annual Reviews.

--Annual Review of Medicine, Vol. 25. LC 51-1659. (Illus.). 1974. text ed. 17.00 (ISBN 0-8243-0525-6). Annual Reviews.

--Annual Review of Medicine: Selected Topics in the Clinical Sciences, Vol. 26. LC 51-1659. (Illus.). 1975. text ed. 17.00 (ISBN 0-8243-0526-4). Annual Reviews.

Creger, William P., et al, eds. Annual Review of Medicine: Selected Topics in the Clinical Sciences, Vol. 27. LC 51-1659. (Illus.). 1976. text ed. 17.00 (ISBN 0-8243-0527-2). Annual Reviews.

--Annual Review of Medicine: Selected Topics in the Clinical Sciences, Vol. 31. LC 51-1659. (Illus.). 1980. text ed. 17.00 (ISBN 0-8243-0531-0). Annual Reviews.

Rogers, David E. Year Book of Medicine Nineteen Eighty-One. Date not set. price not set (ISBN 0-8151-7443-8). Year Bk Med.

Rogers, David E., et al. Year Book of Medicine, 1980. (Illus.). 640p. 1980. 29.95 (ISBN 0-8151-7441-1). Year Bk Med.

Schwartz, Seymour I., ed. Year Book of Surgery Nineteen Eighty-One. Date not set. price not set (ISBN 0-8151-7620-1). Year Bk Med.

Scott, Ronald B. & Fraser, James. Medical Annual 1980-1981. 1980. 37.50 (ISBN 0-8151-7690-2). Year Bk Med.

Scott, Ronald B & Fraser, James. The Medical Annual 1981-82. 352p. 1981. pap. text ed. 37.50 (ISBN 0-7236-0602-1). Wright-PSG.

Winek, C. L. Toxicology Annual. Vol. 1, 1975. 39.50 (ISBN 0-8247-6310-6); Vol. 2, 1977. 39.50 (ISBN 0-8247-6594-X); Vol. 3, 1979. 39.50 (ISBN 0-8247-6773-X). Dekker.

MEDICINE–15TH-18TH CENTURY

Adelmann, Howard B., ed. & tr. from It. The Correspondence of Marcello Malpighi, 5 vols. Incl. Vol. 1. 1-214 Letters, 1658-1669; Vol. 2. 214-431 Letters, 1670-1683; Vol. 3. 432-724 Letters, 1684-1688; Vol. 4. 725-824 Letters, 1689-1692; Vol. 5. 825-1050 Letters, 1693-1694. LC 73-9867. (History of Science Ser). 2316p. 1975. boxed set 95.00x (ISBN 0-8014-0802-4). Cornell U Pr.

Alessio. The Secretes of Alexis of Piemount. Warde, W., tr. from Fr. LC 74-28825. (English Experience Ser.: No. 707). 1975. Repr. of 1558 ed. 21.00 (ISBN 90-221-0707-8). Walter J Johnson.

Alessio, Piemontese. A Booke Conteining...Experienced Medicines: The Fourth & Finall Booke of His Secretes. Androse, R., tr. LC 77-6846. (English Experience Ser.: No. 841). 1977. Repr. of 1569 ed. lib. bdg. 20.00 (ISBN 90-221-0841-4). Walter J Johnson.

--The Second Part of the Secretes of Maister Alexis of Piemont. Ward, W., tr. LC 77-6843. (English Experience Ser.: No. 839). 1977. Repr. of 1563 ed. lib. bdg. 17.50 (ISBN 90-221-0839-2). Walter J Johnson.

Bailey, Walter. A Short Discourse of the Three Kindes of Peppers in Common Use. LC 77-38145. (English Experience Ser.: No. 425). 48p. Repr. of 1588 ed. 7.00 (ISBN 90-221-0425-7). Walter J Johnson.

--Two Treatises Concerning the Perservation of Eye-Sight. LC 74-28827. (English Experience Ser.: No. 709). 1975. Repr. of 1616 ed. 5.00 (ISBN 90-221-0709-4). Walter J Johnson.

Baker, George. Oleum Magistrale. LC 72-171. (English Experience Ser.: No. 123). 104p. 1969. Repr. of 1574 ed. 16.00 (ISBN 9-0221-0123-1). Walter J Johnson.

Banister, John. A Needfull, New & Necessarie Treatise of Chyrugerie. LC 73-171732. (English Experience Ser.: No. 300). 276p. Repr. of 1575 ed. 22.00 (ISBN 90-221-0300-5). Walter J Johnson.

Blanton, Wyndham. Medicine in Virginia in the Seventeenth Century. LC 77-180556. (Medicine & Society in America Ser). (Illus.). 430p. 1972. Repr. of 1930 ed. 19.00 (ISBN 0-405-03936-0). Arno.

Borde, Andrew. The Breuiary of Helthe, for All Maner of Syckenesses & Diseases, the Whiche May Be in Man, or Woman Deth Folowe, 2 pts. LC 71-38106. (English Experience Ser.: No. 362). 356p. 1971. Repr. of 1547 ed. Set. 50.00 (ISBN 90-221-0362-5). Walter J Johnson.

Bullein, William. Bulleins Bulwarke of Defence Againste All Sickness, Sorness & Woundes. LC 73-37139. (English Experience Ser.: No. 350). (Illus.). 488p. 1971. Repr. of 1562 ed. 83.00 (ISBN 90-221-0350-1). Walter J Johnson.

Chaplin, Arnold. Medicine in England During the Reign of George III. LC 75-23695. Repr. of 1919 ed. 15.50 (ISBN 0-404-13244-8). AMS Pr.

Clowes, William. A Profitable & Necessarie Booke of Observations. LC 73-171740. (English Experience Ser.: No. 366). 1971. Repr. of 1596 ed. 33.50 (ISBN 90-221-0366-8). Walter J Johnson.

--A Right Fruteful Treatise for the Artificiall Cure of Struma. LC 72-25835. (English Experience Ser.: No. 238). 68p. 1970. Repr. of 1602 ed. 9.50 (ISBN 90-221-0238-6). Walter J Johnson.

--A Short & Profitable Treatise Touching the Cure of the Morbus Gallicus by Unctions. LC 75-38166. (English Experience Ser.: No. 443). 118p. 1972. Repr. of 1579 ed. 16.00 (ISBN 90-221-0443-5). Walter J Johnson.

Debus, A. G. Man & Nature in the Renaissance. LC 77-91085. (Cambridge History of Science Ser.). (Illus.). 1978. 22.95 (ISBN 0-521-21972-8); pap. 7.95x (ISBN 0-521-29328-6). Cambridge U Pr.

Dewhurst, Kenneth. Dr. Thomas Sydenham (1624-1689) His Life & Original Writings. LC 66-19348. (Wellcome Institute of the History of Medicine). 1966. 21.75x (ISBN 0-520-00320-9). U of Cal Pr.

Du Chesne, Joseph. The Practise of Chymicall, & Hermeticall Physicke, for the Preservation of Health. Timme, T., tr. from Lat. LC 74-28847. (English Experience Ser.: No. 728). 1975. Repr. of 1605 ed. 15.00 (ISBN 90-221-0728-0). Walter J Johnson.

Gale, Thomas. Certaine Workes of Chirurgerie. LC 79-38108. (English Experience Ser.: No. 420). (Illus.). 200p. 1971. Repr. of 1563 ed. 74.00 (ISBN 90-221-0420-6). Walter J Johnson.

Gesner, Conrad. The Newe Iewell of Health. LC 73-171759. (English Experience Ser.: No. 381). 540p. 1971. Repr. of 1576 ed. 51.00 (ISBN 90-221-0381-1). Walter J Johnson.

--The Treasure of Euonymus: Conteyninge the Hid Secretes of Nature. Morwyng, P., tr. LC 63-6477. (English Experience Ser.: No. 97). 408p. 1969. Repr. of 1559 ed. 45.00 (ISBN 90-221-0097-9). Walter J Johnson.

Gottfried, Robert S. Epidemic Disease in Fifteenth Century England: The Medical Response & the Demographic Consequences. (Illus.). 1978. 19.50 (ISBN 0-8135-0861-4). Rutgers U Pr.

Gutta Podagrica: A Treatise of the Gout, Perused by P. H. Dr. in Physick. LC 72-25642. (English Experience Ser.: No. 319). 1971. Repr. of 1633 ed. 9.50 (ISBN 9-0221-0319-6). Walter J Johnson.

Harward, Simon. Harwards Phlebotomy: Or, a Treatise of Letting the Blood. LC 72-6000. (English Experience Ser.: No. 526). 152p. 1973. Repr. of 1601 ed. 16.00 (ISBN 90-221-0526-1). Walter J Johnson.

Hieronymus, Von Brunschwig. A Most Excellent Homish Apothecarye. LC 68-54620. (No. 43). 1968. Repr. of 1561 ed. 21.00 (ISBN 90-221-0043-X). Walter J Johnson.

In This Tretyse That Is Cleped Gouernayle of Helthe. LC 72-200. (English Experience Ser.: No. 192). 1969. Repr. of 1489 ed. 11.50 (ISBN 90-221-0192-4). Walter J Johnson.

Jorden, Edward. A Briefe Discourse of a Disease Called the Suffocation of the Mother. LC 77-171768. (English Experience Ser.: No. 392). 58p. 1971. Repr. of 1603 ed. 7.00 (ISBN 90-221-0392-7). Walter J Johnson.

Maddison, Francis & Pelling, Margaret, eds. Linacre Studies: Essays on the Life & Work of Thomas Linacre. (Illus.). 1977. 79.00x (ISBN 0-19-858150-5). Oxford U Pr.

Piemontese, Allesio. The Thyrde & Last Parte of the Secretes of Maister Alexis of Piemont. Warde, W., tr. LC 77-6844. (English Experience Ser.: No. 840). 1977. Repr. of 1566 ed. lib. bdg. 17.50 (ISBN 90-221-0840-6). Walter J Johnson.

Simotta, George. The Theatre of the Planetary Houres for All the Days of the Yeare. Baker, G., tr. from Greek. LC 73-171791. (English Experience Ser.: No. 414). 40p. 1971. Repr. of 1631 ed. 6.00 (ISBN 90-221-0414-1). Walter J Johnson.

Skene, John. Ane Breve Descriptioun of the Pest. LC 72-38109. (English Experience Ser.: No. 415). 1971. Repr. of 1586 ed. 7.00 (ISBN 90-221-0415-X). Walter J Johnson.

Webster, Charles. The Great Instauration: Science, Medicine & Reform 1626-1660. LC 76-4550. 630p. 1976. text ed. 45.00x (ISBN 0-8419-0267-4). Holmes & Meier.

Webster, Charles, ed. Health, Medicine & Mortality in the Sixteenth Century. LC 78-73234. (Cambridge Monographs on the History of Medicine). (Illus.). 1979. 42.50 (ISBN 0-521-22643-0). Cambridge U Pr.

Wesley, John. Primitive Remedies. new ed. LC 73-77410. Orig. Title: Primitive Physick. (Illus.). 144p. (Orig.). 1973. pap. 2.25 (ISBN 0-912800-04-6). Woodbridge Pr.

MEDICINE–AFGHANISTAN

Buck, Alfred A., et al. Health & Disease in Rural Afghanistan. LC 77-186935. (The Johns Hopkins Monographs in International Health). (Illus.). 270p. 1972. 12.00x (ISBN 0-912752-00-9). York Pr.

MEDICINE–AFRICA

Ademuwagun, Z. A., et al, eds. African Therapeutic Systems. 1979. 30.00 (ISBN 0-918456-25-8). African Studies Assn.

Appiah-Kubi, Kofi. Man Cures, God Heals: Religion & Medical Practice Among the Akans of Ghana. (Illus.). 224p. 1981. text ed. 25.00 (ISBN 0-86598-011-X). Allanheld.

Bhagwandeen, S. B. Clinico-Pathological Manifestations of Schistomiasis in the African & Indian in Durban. (Illus.). 207p. 1968. 15.00x (ISBN 0-8426-0435-9). Verry.

Bossert, T. & Dunlop, D., eds. Selected Issues in Health Policies in Africa & Latin America. 82p. 1981. 17.50 (ISBN 0-08-024723-7). Pergamon.

Durodola, James I. Scientific Insights into Yoruba Traditional Medicine. (Traditional Healing Ser.). 1981. 27.50 (ISBN 0-932426-17-4). Trado-Medic.

Feierman, Steven, compiled by. Health & Society in Africa: A Working Bibliography. (Archival & Bibliographic Ser.). 1978. pap. 20.00 (ISBN 0-918456-16-9, Crossroads). African Studies Assn.

Gottlieb, Manuel. Health Care Financing in Mainland Tanzania. (Foreign & Comparative Studies, Eastern African Ser.: No. 20). 104p. (Orig.). 1975. pap. text ed. 4.50 (ISBN 0-915984-17-2). Syracuse U Foreign Comp.

Harley, George W. Native African Medicine with Special Reference to Its Practice in the Mano-Tribe of Liberia. 294p. 1970. Repr. of 1941 ed. 28.50x (ISBN 0-7146-1671-0, F Cass Co). Biblio Dist.

Imperato, Pascal J. A Wind in Africa. LC 73-24001. (Illus.). 363p. 1975. 12.50 (ISBN 0-87527-139-1). Green.

Janzen, John M. The Quest for Therapy in Lower Zaire. (Comparative Studies of Health Systems & Medical Care). 1978. 26.50x (ISBN 0-520-03295-0). U of Cal Pr.

Johnson. An Essay on West African Therapeutics. (Traditional Healing Ser.: No. 7). 1981. 17.50 (ISBN 0-686-76824-8, Trado-Medic Bks); lib. bdg. 39.50 deluxe ed. (ISBN 0-932426-19-0). Conch Mag.

Johnson, O. An Essay on West African Therapeutics. Singer, Philip & Titus, Elizabeth A., eds. 1981. 17.50 (ISBN 0-932426-09-3); lib. bdg. 39.50 (ISBN 0-932426-19-0). Trado-Medic.

Ki-Zerbo, J., ed. African Traditional Medicine & Pharmacopoeia. (Traditional Healing Ser.). 750p. 1981. 100.00 (ISBN 0-932426-22-0). Conch Mag.

Parry, E. H. Principles of Medicine in Africa. (Illus.). 1976. text ed. 29.95x (ISBN 0-19-264223-5). Oxford U Pr.

Traditional Medicine in Zaire. 39p. 1980. pap. 5.00 (ISBN 0-88936-222-X, IDRC 137, IDRC). Unipub.

Ulin, Priscilla & Segall, Marshall, eds. Traditional Health Care Delivery in Contemporary Africa. LC 80-27442. (Foreign & Comparative Studies - African Ser.: No. 35). 100p. 1980. pap. 8.00x (ISBN 0-915984-57-1). Syracuse U Foreign Comp.

Van Amelsvoort, Vincent. Medical Anthropology in African Newspapers: An Annotated Facsimile Edition from the Third World. 116p. 1976. pap. text ed. 9.25x (ISBN 90-6234-105-5). Humanities.

MEDICINE–ASIA

Dutt, Ashok K., ed. Contemporary Perspectives on the Medical Geography of South & Southeast Asia. (Illus.). 78p. 1980. pap. 20.00 (ISBN 0-08-026762-9). Pergamon.

Huckins, Anne, ed. Staying Healthy in Asia. (Illus.). 96p. (Orig.). 1979. pap. 2.50 (ISBN 0-917704-15-0). Volunteers Asia.

Kimball, Linda A. Borneo Medicine: The Healing Art of Indigenous Brunei Malay Medicine. LC 79-25123. (Illus.). 418p. (Orig.). 1979. pap. 23.25 (ISBN 0-8357-0495-5, SS-00123). Univ Microfilms.

Kleinman, Arthur, et al, eds. Culture & Healing in Asian Societies. (University Books Program). 1978. lib. bdg. 22.50 (ISBN 0-8161-8248-5). G K Hall.

Leslie, Charles, ed. Asian Medical Systems: A Comparative Study. LC 73-91674. 1976. 26.75x (ISBN 0-520-02680-2); pap. 8.95x (ISBN 0-520-03511-9). U of Cal Pr.

Lock, Margaret M. East Asian Medicine in Urban Japan: Varieties of Medical Experience. 1980. 24.00x (ISBN 0-520-03820-7). U of Cal Pr.

Madan, T. N., et al. Doctors & Society: Three Asian Case Studies. 1980. text ed. 22.50x (ISBN 0-7069-0814-7, Pub. by Vikas India). Advent NY.

Robinson, Aletha. The Lao Handbook of Maternal & Child Health. 1980. pap. 1.95 (ISBN 0-9602790-1-6). The Garden.

MEDICINE–AUSTRALIA

Ford, Sir Edward. Bibliography of Australian Medicine Seventeen Ninety to Nineteen Hundred. (Illus.). 1976. 40.00x (ISBN 0-424-00022-9, Pub. by Sydney U Pr). Intl Schol Bk Serv.

Hetzel, et al. Better Health for Aborigines? 1974. 15.00 (ISBN 0-7022-0897-3). U of Queensland Pr.

McGlashan, N. D., ed. Health Problems in Australia & New Zealand. 180p. 1980. 20.00 (ISBN 0-08-026103-5). Pergamon.

MEDICINE–BURMA

MacDonald, Keith N. The Practice of Medicine Among the Burmese. LC 77-87505. Repr. of 1879 ed. 26.00 (ISBN 0-404-16837-X). AMS Pr.

MEDICINE–CANADA

Brecher. The Rays: A History of Radiology in the United States & Canada. LC 69-19071. 522p. 1977. Repr. of 1969 ed. 21.50 (ISBN 0-88275-926-4). Krieger.

Canniff, William. The Medical Profession in Upper Canada, 1753-1850. LC 75-23690. Repr. of 1894 ed. 56.50 (ISBN 0-404-13242-1). AMS Pr.

Clute, Kenneth F. The General Practitioner: A Study of Medical Education & Practice in Ontario & Nova Scotia. LC 63-4464. 566p. 1963. 40.00x (ISBN 0-8020-7032-9). U of Toronto Pr.

Heagerty, John J. Four Centuries of Medical History in Canada & a Sketch of the Medical History of Newfoundland, 2 vols. LC 75-23719. Repr. of 1928 ed. 65.00 set (ISBN 0-404-13160-3). AMS Pr.

Howell, William B. Medicine in Canada. LC 75-23659. (Clio Medica: 9). (Illus.). Repr. of 1933 ed. 16.00 (ISBN 0-404-58909-X). AMS Pr.

Lasor, B. & Elliot, M. Issues in Canadian Nursing. 1977 (ISBN 0-13-506238-1). pap. 9.25 (ISBN 0-13-506238-1). P-H.

McKechnie, R. E., II. Strong Medicine: A History of Healing on the Northwest Coast. 10.50 (ISBN 0-88894-074-2, Pub. by Douglas & McIntyre); pap. 6.50 (ISBN 0-88894-011-4, Pub. by Douglas & McIntyre). Intl Schol Bk Serv.

Rozovsky, Lorne E. Canadian Patient's Book of Rights. LC 79-8942. 176p. 1980. 14.95 (ISBN 0-385-15377-5); pap. 8.95 (ISBN 0-385-15383-X). Doubleday.

Shortt, S. E., ed. Medicine in Canadian Society: Historical Perspectives. 400p. 1981. 23.95x (ISBN 0-7735-0356-0); pap. 11.95 (ISBN 0-7735-0369-2). McGill-Queens U Pr.

MEDICINE–CHINA

Berk, William R., ed. Chinese Healing Arts: Internal Kung-Fu. LC 79-1566. (Illus.). 240p. 1979. pap. 8.95 (ISBN 0-915238-29-2). Peace Pr.

Bowers, John Z. Western Medicine in a Chinese Palace: Peking Union Medical College, 1917-1951. LC 72-96069. (Illus.). 250p. 1973. 10.00 (ISBN 0-914362-06-2). J Macy Foun.

Bowers, John Z. & Purcell, Elizabeth F., eds. Medicine & Society in China. LC 72-96069. (Illus.). 196p. 1974. pap. 7.50 (ISBN 0-914362-09-7). J Macy Foun.

Bullock, Mary B. An American Transplant: The Rockefeller Foundation & Peking Union Medical College. LC 77-83098. 280p. 1981. 17.50x (ISBN 0-520-03559-3). U of Cal Pr.

Chang Shu-Ting. The Chinese Mushroom (Volvariella volvacea) Morphology, Cytology, Genetics, Nutrition, & Cultivation. (Illus.). 118p. 1972. 8.95 (ISBN 0-295-95743-3, Pub by Chinese Univ Hong Kong). U of Wash Pr.

Dimond, E. Grey. More Than Herbs & Acupuncture. 224p. 1975. 7.95 (ISBN 0-393-06400-X). Norton.

Dogan, Mattei & Rokkan, Stein, eds. Social Ecology. 458p. (Paperback edition of Quantitative Ecological Analysis in the Social Sciences). 1974. pap. 6.95x (ISBN 0-262-54022-3). MIT Pr.

Eong & Wu. History of Chinese Medicine. 1977. 16.00 (ISBN 0-89986-000-1). E Langstaff.

Fulder, Stephen. Tao of Medicine. (Illus.). 1981. pap. 8.95 (ISBN 0-89281-027-0). Inner Tradit.

Huard, Pierre & Wong, Ming. Chinese Medicine. (Illus., Orig.). 1968. pap. 2.45 (ISBN 0-07-030785-7, SP). McGraw.

Hyatt, Richard. Chinese Herbal Medicine: Ancient Art & Modern Science. LC 77-87891. 1978. 12.95 (ISBN 0-8052-3682-1). Schocken.

Lu, Gwei-Djen & Needham, J. Celestial Lancets: History & Rationale of Acupuncture & Moxa. LC 79-41734. (Illus.). 400p. 1980. 97.50 (ISBN 0-521-21513-7). Cambridge U Pr.

Needham, Joseph. Clerks & Craftsmen in China & the West: Lectures & Addresses on the History of Science & Technology. (Illus.). 1970. 65.00 (ISBN 0-521-07235-2). Cambridge U Pr.

Ohsawa, George. Book of Judgment. rev. ed. 1980. pap. 5.95 (ISBN 0-918860-31-8). G Ohsawa.

Read, Bernard E. Chinese Materia Medica: Dragon & Snake Drugs. lib. bdg. 75.00 (ISBN 0-8490-3063-3). Krishna Pr.

Revolutionary Health Council of Hunan Province. A Barefoot Doctor's Manual. (Illus.). 384p. 1981. pap. 11.95 (ISBN 0-914842-52-8). Madrona Pubs.

Risse, G. B. Modern China & Traditional Chinese Medicine. 176p. 1973. 12.75 (ISBN 0-398-02816-8). C C Thomas.

Sidel, Victor W. & Sidel, Ruth. Serve the People: Observations on Medicine in the People's Republic of China. LC 74-6185. (Illus.). 336p. 1974. pap. 5.95 (ISBN 0-8070-2175-X, BP501). Beacon Pr.

Silverstein, Martin E., et al, eds. Acupuncture & Moxibustion: A Handbook for the Barefoot Doctors of China. LC 74-26919. 1975. 7.00x (ISBN 0-8052-3585-X); pap. 2.95 (ISBN 0-8052-0476-8). Schocken.

Smith, F. P. Chinese Materia Medica: Vegetable Kingdom. 99.50 (ISBN 0-87968-469-0). Krishna Pr.

Wong, Chi-Min & Lien-Teh, Wu. History of Chinese Medicine, Being a Chronicle of Medical Happenings in China from Ancient Times to the Present Period. LC 73-38570. Repr. of 1936 ed. 45.00 (ISBN 0-404-07990-3). AMS Pr.

Wong, K. C. & Lien-Teh, Wu. History of Chinese Medicine, 2 vols. 1976. lib. bdg. 250.00 (ISBN 0-8490-3062-5). Gordon Pr.

MEDICINE–CHINA–1949-

Bowers, John Z. & Purcell, Elizabeth F., eds. Medicine & Society in China. LC 72-96069. (Illus.). 196p. 1974. pap. 7.50 (ISBN 0-914362-09-7). J Macy Foun.

Committee of Scholarly Communication with the People's Republic of China, National Research Council. Herbal Pharmacology in the People's Republic of China: A Trip Report of the American Herbal Pharmacology Delegation. LC 75-39772. v, 169p. 1975. pap. 8.00 (ISBN 0-309-02438-2). Natl Acad Pr.

Horn, Joshua S. Away with All Pests: An English Surgeon in People's China, 1954-1969. LC 73-142988. (Illus.). 1971. pap. 3.95 (ISBN 0-85345-199-0, PB1990). Monthly Rev.

Sidel, Victor W. & Sidel, Ruth. Serve the People: Observations on Medicine in the People's Republic of China. LC 73-89604. (Illus.). 317p. 1973. 10.00 (ISBN 0-914362-08-9). J Macy Foun.

Wegman, Myron E., et al, eds. Public Health in the People's Republic of China. LC 73-87519. (Illus.). 354p. 1973. pap. 7.50 (ISBN 0-914362-07-0). J Macy Foun.

MEDICINE–CUBA

Danielson, Roswell S. Cuban Medicine. LC 76-1768. 247p. 1978. 14.95 (ISBN 0-87855-114-X). Transaction Bks.

MEDICINE–EGYPT

Ebbell, B., tr. The Papyrus Ebers: The Greatest Egyptian Medical Document. (Historia Medicinae). Repr. of 1937 ed. lib. bdg. 15.00x (ISBN 0-87991-712-1). Porcupine Pr.

Rural Health Care in Egypt. 40p. 1980. pap. 5.00 (ISBN 0-88936-179-7, IDRC TS15, IDRC). Unipub.

MEDICINE–FRANCE

Du Mesnil & Mangenot. Etude d'Hygiene et d'Economie Sociale. Enquete sur les Logements, Professions, Salaires et Budgets. (Conditions of the 19th Century French Working Class Ser.). 166p. (Fr.). 1974. Repr. of 1899 ed. lib. bdg. 50.00x (ISBN 0-8287-0295-0, 1114). Clearwater Pub.

Forster, Robert & Ranum, Orest, eds. Medicine & Society in France. Forster, Elborg & Ranum, Patricia M., trs. LC 79-16851. (Annales Ser.: Vol. 6). 1980. 15.00x (ISBN 0-8018-2305-6); pap. text ed. 5.95 (ISBN 0-8018-2306-4). Johns Hopkins.

Laignel-Lavastine, Maxime. French Medicine. LC 75-23666. (Clio Medica: 15). (Illus.). Repr. of 1934 ed. 16.50 (ISBN 0-404-58915-4). AMS Pr.

Lebrun, Francois. Les Hommes et la Mort En Anjou Aux 17e et 18e Siecles: Essai De Demographie et De Psychologie Historiques. (Civilisations et Societes: No. 25). (Illus.). 1971. pap. 56.25x (ISBN 90-2796-904-3). Mouton.

Packard, Francis R. Guy Patin & the Medical Profession in Paris in the XVIIth Century. LC 78-95624. (Illus.). Repr. of 1924 ed. 17.50x (ISBN 0-678-03759-0). Kelley.

Richardson, Robert G. Larrey: Surgeon to Napoleon's Imperial Guard. (Illus.). 276p. 1975. 15.00 (ISBN 0-7195-3103-9). Transatlantic.

Vess, David M. Medical Revolution in France, 1789-1796. LC 74-14916. 216p. 1975. 12.00 (ISBN 0-8130-0439-X). U Presses Fla.

Wickersheimer, Charles A. La Medicine et les medecins en France a l'epoque de la Renaissance. LC 75-23770. (Fr.). Repr. of 1906 ed. 55.50 (ISBN 0-404-13396-7). AMS Pr.

MEDICINE–GERMANY

Foster, Charles R., ed. Comparative Public Policy & Citizen Participation: Energy, Education, Health & Local Governance in the U. S. A. & Germany. (Pergamon Policy Studies). 1980. 29.50 (ISBN 0-08-024624-9). Pergamon.

Haberling, Wilhelm. German Medicine. LC 75-23664. (Clio Medica: 13). (Illus.). Repr. of 1934 ed. 17.25 (ISBN 0-404-58913-8). AMS Pr.

Hirsch, August. Geschichte Der Medicischen Wissenschaften in Deutschland. 1893. 41.50 (ISBN 0-384-23360-0). Johnson Repr.

Who's Who in Medicine: Germany, Austria, Switzerland. 108.00 (ISBN 3-921220-30-0). Adler.

MEDICINE–GREAT BRITAIN

Berlant, Jeffrey L. Profession & Monopoly: A Study of Medicine in the United States & Great Britain. LC 74-76381. 1975. 23.75x (ISBN 0-520-02734-5). U of Cal Pr.

Bettany, George T. Eminent Doctors, 2 vols. facsimile ed. LC 76-39663. (Essay Index Reprint Ser.). 36.00 (ISBN 0-8369-2747-8). Arno.

Cartwright, Frederick F. A Social History of Medicine. LC 76-41898. (Themes in British Social History Ser.). 1977. pap. text ed. 10.95x (ISBN 0-582-48394-8). Longman.

Chaplin, Arnold. Medicine in England During the Reign of George III. LC 75-23695. Repr. of 1919 ed. 15.50 (ISBN 0-404-13244-8). AMS Pr.

Comrie, John D. History of Scottish Medicine, 2 vols. 2nd ed. LC 75-23698. Repr. of 1932 ed. Set. 87.50 (ISBN 0-404-13320-7). AMS Pr.

Creighton, C. History of Epidemics in Britain, 2 vols. 2nd rev ed. (Illus.). 75.00x set (ISBN 0-7146-1294-4, F Cass Co). Biblio Dist.

Debus, Allen G. English Paracelsians. LC 66-15981. (Oldbourne History of Science Ser). 1968. 8.50x (ISBN 0-226-13977-8). U of Chicago Pr.

Debus, Allen G., ed. A Symposium Held at UCLA in Honor of C. D. O'Malley. (Illus.). 1974. 25.75x (ISBN 0-520-02226-2). U of Cal Pr.

Geison, Gerald L. Michael Foster & the Cambridge School of Physiology: The Scientific Enterprise in Late Victorian Society. LC 77-85539. 1978. text ed. 30.00 (ISBN 0-691-08197-2). Princeton U Pr.

Goodman, John C. National Health Care in Great Britain: Lessons for the U. S. A. LC 79-55246. 200p. (Orig.). 1980. lib. bdg. 11.95 (ISBN 0-933028-05-9); pap. 6.95 (ISBN 0-933028-04-0). Fisher Inst.

Gottfried, Robert S. Epidemic Disease in Fifteenth Century England: The Medical Response & the Demographic Consequences. (Illus.). 1978. 19.50 (ISBN 0-8135-0861-4). Rutgers U Pr.

Hale-White, William. Great Doctors of the Nineteenth Century. LC 74-108639. (Essay Index Reprint Ser). 1935. 18.00 (ISBN 0-8369-1575-5). Arno.

--Keats As Doctor & Patient. LC 72-193726. 1938. lib. bdg. 6.45 (ISBN 0-8414-4868-X). Folcroft.

Harington, John, tr. The School of Salernum: Regimen Santitatis Salernitanum: the English Version. 1978. Repr. of 1920 ed. lib. bdg. 35.00 (ISBN 0-8495-2336-2). Arden Lib.

Harward, Simon. Harwards Phlebotomy: Or, a Treatise of Letting the Blood. LC 72-6000. (English Experience Ser.: No. 526). 152p. 1973. Repr. of 1601 ed. 16.00 (ISBN 90-221-0526-1). Walter J Johnson.

Hyman, Stanley. Supplies Management for Health Services. 250p. 1981. 30.00x (ISBN 0-85664-707-1, Pub. by Croom Helm Ltd England). Biblio Dist.

Lancaster, Arnold. Nursery & Midwifery Sourcebook. 304p. 1980. 25.00x (ISBN 0-686-69979-3, Pub. by Beaconsfield England). State Mutual Bk.

Mencher, Samuel. Private Practice in Britain. 95p. 1967. pap. text ed. 5.00x (ISBN 0-686-70856-3, Pub. by Bedford England). Renouf.

Moore, Norman. The History of the Study of Medicine in the British Isles. LC 75-23746. Repr. of 1908 ed. 17.50 (ISBN 0-404-13352-5). AMS Pr.

Pelling, Margaret. Cholera, Fever & English Medicine, 1825 - 1865. (Historical Monographs). 1978. text ed. 29.95x (ISBN 0-19-821872-9). Oxford U Pr.

Power, D'Arcy. Medicine in the British Isles. LC 75-23651. (Clio Medica: No. 2). Repr. of 1930 ed. 17.00 (ISBN 0-404-58902-2). AMS Pr.

Rhodes, Philip. The Value of Medicine. 1977. text ed. 15.95x (ISBN 0-04-610004-0). Allen Unwin.

Smith, Francis B. The People's Health Eighteen Thirty-Nineteen Ten. LC 78-13095. 1979. text ed. 39.50x (ISBN 0-8419-0448-0). Holmes & Meier.

U. K. Health Markets. 100p. 1981. 120.00x (ISBN 0-686-71959-X, Pub. by Euromonitor). State Mutual Bk.

Webster, Charles, ed. Health, Medicine & Mortality in the Sixteenth Century. LC 78-73234. (Cambridge Monographs on the History of Medicine). (Illus.). 1979. 42.50 (ISBN 0-521-22643-0). Cambridge U Pr.

Wilson, R. McNair. British Medicine. 1979. Repr. of 1941 ed. lib. bdg. 10.00 (ISBN 0-8495-5743-7). Arden Lib.

Woodward, John & Richards, David. Health Care & Popular Medicine in 19th Century England: Essays in Social History. LC 76-26910. 1977. text ed. 24.50x (ISBN 0-8419-0286-0). Holmes & Meier.

MEDICINE–GREECE, MODERN

Blum, Richard H. & Blum, Eva. Health & Healing in Rural Greece. 1965. 10.00x (ISBN 0-8047-0250-0). Stanford U Pr.

Phillips, D. E. Aspects of Greek Medicine. LC 72-89956. (Illus.). 256p. 1973. text ed. 18.95 (ISBN 0-312-05670-2). St Martin.

MEDICINE–INDIA

Bhagavat Simhaji. A Short History of Aryan Medical Science. LC 75-23683. Repr. of 1896 ed. 23.00 (ISBN 0-404-13236-7). AMS Pr.

Dash, Bhagan & Kashyap, Lalitesh. Basic Principles of Ayurveda. 655p. 1980. 37.00x (ISBN 0-391-02208-3). Humanities.

Djurfeldt, Linberg S. Pills Against Poverty: A Study of the Introduction of Western Medicine in a Tamil Village. 1981. 11.00x (ISBN 0-8364-0681-8, Pub. by Macmillan India). South Asia Bks.

Djurjeldt, Goran & Lindberg, Staffan. Pills Against Poverty: A Study of the Introduction of Western Medicine in a Tamil Village. (Scandinavian Institute of Asian Studies Monograph: No. 23). 1976. pap. text ed. 13.75x (ISBN 0-7007-0093-5). Humanities.

Hoernle, August F. Studies in the Medicine of Ancient India Pt. 1: Osteology, or the Bones of the Human Body. LC 75-23723. Repr. of 1907 ed. 24.50 (ISBN 0-404-13281-2). AMS Pr.

Jolly, J. Indian Medicine. Kashikar, C. Ct., tr. from Ger. LC 78-911076. 1977. Repr. of 1901 ed. 13.50x (ISBN 0-8002-0242-2). Intl Pubns Serv.

Jolly, Julius. Indian Medicine. rev ed. Kashikar, C. G., tr. from Ger. 1978. 16.00x (ISBN 0-8364-0216-2). South Asia Bks.

Khory, R. N. & Katrak, N. N. Materia Medica of India & Their Therapeutics. 809p. 1981. Repr. of 1903 ed. text ed. 56.25x (ISBN 0-391-02264-4, Pub. by Concept India). Humanities.

Kirkpatrick, Joanna. The Sociology of an Indian Hospital Ward. 1980. 14.00x (ISBN 0-8364-0588-9). South Asia Bks.

Mehta, R. K. Handbook of Veterinary Pharmacy, Toxicology, & Pharmacotherapeutic Index. (Illus.). 183p. 1973. 7.50x (ISBN 0-8002-0908-7). Intl Pubns Serv.

Sinha, Phulgenda. The Yogic Cure for Common Diseases. rev., enl. ed. (Orient Paperbacks Ser.). 204p. 1981. pap. 4.95 (ISBN 0-86578-076-5). Ind-US Inc.

Venkataratnam, R. Medical Sociology in an Indian Setting. 1979. 19.00x (ISBN 0-8364-0557-9, Pub. by Macmillan India). South Asia Bks.

Vohora, S. B. & Khan, S. Y. Animal Origin Drugs Used in Unani Medicine. LC 79-903036. 1980. text ed. 22.50x (ISBN 0-7069-0768-X, Pub. by Vikas India). Advent NY.

MEDICINE–IRAN

Elgood, Cyril. Medicine in Persia. LC 75-23665. (Clio Medica: No. 14). (Illus.). Repr. of 1934 ed. 14.50 (ISBN 0-404-58914-6). AMS Pr.

Richter-Bernburg, Lutz. Persian Medical Manuscripts at the University of California, Los Angeles. LC 77-94986. (Humana Civilitas Ser.: Vol. 4). (Illus.). xxi, 297p. 1978. 45.00 (ISBN 0-89003-026-X). Undena Pubns.

MEDICINE–IRELAND

Finnane, Mark. Insanity & the Insane in Post-Famine Ireland. (Illus.). 242p. 1981. 25.00x (ISBN 0-389-20212-6). B&N.

Wilde, Jane F. Ancient Cures, Charms & Usages of Ireland. LC 74-137347. 1970. Repr. of 1890 ed. 24.00 (ISBN 0-8103-3599-9). Gale.

MEDICINE–ISRAEL

Polgi. Traditional Healing & Medical Therapy in Israel. (Traditional Healing Ser.: No. 8). 1979. cancelled (ISBN 0-932426-13-1, Trado-Medic Bks). Conch Mag.

MEDICINE–ITALY

Castiglioni, Arturo. Italian Medicine. Krumbhaar, E. B., tr. LC 75-23656. (Clio Medica: No. 6). (Illus.). Repr. of 1932 ed. 12.00 (ISBN 0-404-58906-5). AMS Pr.

MEDICINE–JAPAN

Bowers, John Z. Western Medical Pioneers in Feudal Japan. LC 73-86098. (Josiah Macy Foundation Ser). 256p. 1970. 16.50x (ISBN 0-8018-1081-7). Johns Hopkins.

--When the Twain Meet: The Rise of Western Medicine in Japan. LC 80-22356. (Henry E. Sigerist Supplement to the Bulletin of the History of Medicine Ser.: No. 5). 192p. 1981. text ed. 14.00x (ISBN 0-8018-2432-X). Johns Hopkins.

Fujikawa, Yu. Japanese Medicine. LC 75-23663. (Clio Medica: 12). Orig. Title: Geschichte der Medizin in Japan. (Illus.). Repr. of 1934 ed. 15.00 (ISBN 0-404-58912-X). AMS Pr.

Ohashi, Watari. Do-It-Yourself Shiatsu. Lindner, Vicki, ed. 1976. pap. 6.95 (ISBN 0-525-47416-1). Dutton.

Ohsawa, George. Book of Judgment. rev. ed. 1980. pap. 5.95 (ISBN 0-918860-31-8). G Ohsawa.

Ontani, F. One Hundred Years of Health Progress in Japan: Progress in Japan. 130p. 1971. pap. 16.00x (ISBN 0-89955-342-7, Pub. by Japan Sci Soc Japan). Intl Schol Bk Serv.

Ueda, Y., ed. Current Research in Nephrology in Japan. (Contributions to Nephrology: Vol. 4). 1976. 29.50 (ISBN 3-8055-2383-1). S Karger.

MEDICINE–KOREA

Cheong Yeon Ha. Primary Health Care in Korea: An Approach to Evaluation. 198p. 1981. text ed. 12.00x (ISBN 0-8248-0763-4, Korea Devel Inst). U Pr of Hawaii.

Hall, Sherwood. With Stethoscope in Asia: Korea. LC 77-81765. 1981. Repr. of 1978 ed. 15.95 (ISBN 0-930696-01-8). MCL Assocs.

Soh, C. T. Korea. (Geomedical Monographs: Vol. 6). (Illus.). 270p. 1980. 57.90 (ISBN 0-387-09128-9). Springer-Verlag.

MEDICINE–LATIN AMERICA

Bossert, T. & Dunlop, D., eds. Selected Issues in Health Policies in Africa & Latin America. 82p. 1981. 17.50 (ISBN 0-08-024723-7). Pergamon.

Bowers, John Z. & Purcell, Elizabeth F., eds. Aspects of the History of Medicine in Latin America. (Illus.). 196p. pap. 4.00 (ISBN 0-914362-29-1). J Macy Foun.

Martin, Paul. Island of Immunity: Health Secrets from the Andes. (Illus.). 176p. Date not set. 15.00 (ISBN 0-8159-5828-5). Devin.

Moll, Aristides A. Aesculapius in Latin America. LC 76-101589. (Illus.). 1969. Repr. of 1944 ed. 17.50 (ISBN 0-87266-022-2). Argosy.

Wilson, Charles M. Ambassadors in White. LC 77-153258. (Essay & General Literature Index Reprint Ser). 1971. Repr. of 1942 ed. 15.00 (ISBN 0-8046-1510-1). Kennikat.

Woods, Clyde M. & Graves, Theodore D. The Process of Medical Change in a Highland Guatemalan Town. LC 72-97396. (Latin American Studies Ser.: Vol. 21). 61p. 1973. pap. text ed. 5.00 (ISBN 0-87903-021-6). UCLA Lat Am Ctr.

MEDICINE–MEXICO

Howard, David. Royal Indian Hospital of Mexico City. (Special Studies: No. 21). 99p. 1980. pap. text ed. 5.95x (ISBN 0-87918-045-5). ASU Lat Am St.

--The Royal Indian Hospital of Mexico City. (Special Studies 20 Ser.: No. 20). 99p. 1981. pap. 5.95 (ISBN 0-87918-045-5). ASU Lat Am St.

MEDICINE–NORTH VIETNAM

McMichael, Joan, ed. Health Care for the People: Studies from Vietnam. 352p. (Orig.). 1980. pap. 6.95 (ISBN 0-932870-04-X). Alyson Pubns.

MEDICINE–RUSSIA

Desmaisons. Psychiatry in Russia & Spain: An Original Anthology. LC 75-16729. (Classics in Psychiatry Ser.). (Fr. & Ger.). 1976. 18.00x (ISBN 0-405-07452-2). Arno.

Gantt, William A. Russian Medicine. LC 75-23669. (Clio Medica: 20). (Illus.). 1978. Repr. of 1937 ed. 19.00 (ISBN 0-404-58920-0). AMS Pr.

Knaus, William A. Inside Russian Medicine. 416p. 1981. 14.95 (ISBN 0-89696-115-X). Everest Hse.

--Inside Russian Medicine. LC 79-50420. 1980. 10.95 (ISBN 0-448-14958-3). G&D.

Lauterbach, Wolf. Soviet Psychotherapy. Date not set. 24.01 (ISBN 0-08-024291-X). Pergamon.

Navarro, Vincente. Social Security & Medicine in the USSR: A Marxist Critique. LC 77-227. (Illus.). 1977. 17.95 (ISBN 0-669-01452-4). Lexington Bks.

Podolsky, Edward. Red Miracle. LC 70-167402. (Essay Index Reprint Ser.). 1947. 20.00 (ISBN 0-8369-2818-0). Arno.

Podrabinek, Alexander. Punitive Medicine. Lehrman, Alexander, tr. from Rus. (Illus.). 236p. 1980. 12.95 (ISBN 0-89720-022-5). Karoma.

Saunders, Leon Z. The Evolution of Veterinary Pathology in Russia, Eighteen Hundred Sixty to Nineteen Hundred Thirty. (Illus.). 328p. 1980. 27.50x (ISBN 0-686-65255-X). Cornell U Pr.

Tabakov, George A. Medicine in the United States & the Soviet Union. 1962. 5.95 (ISBN 0-8158-0194-7). Chris Mass.

Training & Utilization of Feldshers in the USSR. (Public Health Paper: No. 56). (Also avail. in French, Russian & Spanish). 1974. pap. 2.00 (ISBN 92-4-130056-6). World Health.

MEDICINE–ST. HELENA

Shine, I. Serendipity in St. Helena. 1970. 34.00 (ISBN 0-08-012794-0). Pergamon.

MEDICINE–SPAIN

Chinchilla, Anastasio. Anales Historicos De la Medicina En General y Biografico-Bibliograficos De la Espanola En Particular, 4 vols. (Sources of Science Ser., No. 8). (Span.). 1967. Repr. of 1846 ed. Set. 215.50 (ISBN 0-384-08850-3). Johnson Repr.

Desmaisons. Psychiatry in Russia & Spain: An Original Anthology. LC 75-16729. (Classics in Psychiatry Ser.). (Fr. & Ger.). 1976. 18.00x (ISBN 0-405-07452-2). Arno.

Hernandez Morejon, Antonio. Historia Bibliografica De La Medicina Espanola, 7 Vols. LC 67-34768. (Sources of Science Ser: No. 9). (Span). 1968. Repr. 281.50 (ISBN 0-384-22570-5). Johnson Repr.

MEDICINE–TIBET

Clifford, Terry. The Diamond Healing: Tibetan Buddhist Medicine & Psychiatry. 196p. 1981. pap. 7.95 (ISBN 0-87728-528-4). Weiser.

Finckh, Elisabeth. Foundations of Tibetan Medicine, Vol. 1. 1980. 22.50x (ISBN 0-7224-0162-0, Pub. by Watkins England). State Mutual Bk.

Rechung, Ven. Rinpoche Tibetan Medicine. 346p. 1976. pap. 6.95 (ISBN 0-520-03048-6, CAL 320). U of Cal Pr.

MEDICINE–UNITED STATES

Alperin, Stanley & Alperin, Melvin, eds. U. S. Medical Directory. 4th ed. LC 72-92344. 1977-1978. 45.00x (ISBN 0-916524-04-3). US Direct Serv.

Berlant, Jeffrey L. Profession & Monopoly: A Study of Medicine in the United States & Great Britain. LC 74-76381. 1975. 23.75x (ISBN 0-520-02734-5). U of Cal Pr.

Blanton, Wyndham. Medicine in Virginia in the Seventeenth Century. LC 77-180556. (Medicine & Society in America Ser). (Illus.). 430p. 1972. Repr. of 1930 ed. 19.00 (ISBN 0-405-03936-0). Arno.

Blanton, Wyndham B. Medicine in Virginia in the Seventeenth Century. LC 73-746. (Illus.). 436p. 1973. Repr. of 1930 ed. 22.00 (ISBN 0-87152-109-1). Reprint.

--Medicine in Virginia in the 18th Century. LC 80-12669. Repr. of 1931 ed. 64.50 (ISBN 0-404-13238-3). AMS Pr.

Bordley, James, III & Harvey, A. McGehee. Two Centuries of American Medicine: 1776-1976. LC 75-19841. (Illus.). 750p. 1976. text ed. 35.00 (ISBN 0-7216-1873-1). Saunders.

Bowditch, Nathaniel I. A History of the Massachusetts General Hospital to August 5, 1851. 2nd ed. LC 74-180558. (Medicine & Society in America Ser). (Illus.). 768p. 1972. Repr. of 1872 ed. 34.00 (ISBN 0-405-03938-7). Arno.

Brecher. The Rays: A History of Radiology in the United States & Canada. LC 69-19071. 522p. 1977. Repr. of 1969 ed. 21.50 (ISBN 0-88275-926-4). Krieger.

Brieger, Gert H., ed. Medical America in the Nineteenth Century: Readings from the Literature. LC 76-165053. 348p. 1972. 20.00x (ISBN 0-8018-1237-2). Johns Hopkins.

--Theory & Practice in American Medicine: Historical Studies from the "Journal of the History of Medicine & Allied Sciences". (Illus.). 1976. 15.00 (ISBN 0-88202-158-3, Sci Hist); pap. 9.95 (ISBN 0-686-67911-3). N Watson.

Brown, E. Richard. Rockefeller Medicine Men: Medicine & Capitalism in America. LC 78-65461. 1979. 12.95 (ISBN 0-520-03817-7); pap. 4.95 (ISBN 0-520-04269-7). U of Cal Pr.

Burnham, John C. Psychoanalysis & American Medicine, 1894-1918: Medicine, Science, & Culture. LC 67-31293. (Psychological Issues Monograph: No. 20, Vol. 5, No. 4). (Orig.). 1967: text ed. 11.00 (ISBN 0-8236-5100-2). Intl Univs Pr.

Burrow, James G. Organized Medicine in the Progressive Era: The Move Toward Monopoly. LC 77-894. 1977. text ed. 14.50x (ISBN 0-8018-1918-0). Johns Hopkins.

Clarke, Edward H. Century of American Medicine, 1776-1876. LC 77-168275. (Research & Source Works Ser.: No. 843). 1971. Repr. of 1876 ed. lib. bdg. 23.50 (ISBN 0-8337-0584-9). B Franklin.

Cordasco, Francesco. American Medical Imprints, 1820-1910: A Checklist of Publications Illustrating the History & Progress of Medical Science & Education & the Healing Arts in the United States. 850p. 1981. 75.00 (ISBN 0-940198-01-0). Junius-Vaughn.

Derbyshire, Robert C. Medical Licensure & Discipline in the United States. LC 78-17712. 1978. Repr. of 1969 ed. lib. bdg. 16.75x (ISBN 0-313-20528-0, DEML). Greenwood.

Disease & Society in Provincial Massachusetts, Collected Accounts 1736-1939. LC 73-180563. (Medicine & Society in America Ser). 176p. 1972. 17.00 (ISBN 0-405-03948-4). Arno.

Drake, Daniel. Physician to the West: Selected Writings of Daniel Drake on Science & Society. Shapiro, Henry D. & Miller, Zane L., eds. LC 73-94071. (Illus.). 464p. 1970. 18.00x (ISBN 0-8131-1197-8). U Pr of Ky.

Duffy, John. The Healers: A History of American Medicine. LC 78-27222. 1979. pap. 7.50 (ISBN 0-252-00743-3). U of Ill Pr.

Eberson, Frederick. Early Physicians of the West. LC 79-63659. 1979. 6.95 (ISBN 0-912760-92-3). Valkyrie Pr.

Ellis, John H. Medicine in Kentucky. LC 76-51156. (Kentucky Bicentennial Bookshelf Ser.). (Illus.). 112p. 1977. 5.95 (ISBN 0-8131-0232-4). U Pr of Ky.

Estes, J. Worth. Hall Jackson & the Purple Foxglove: Medical Practice & Research in Revolutionary America, 1760-1820. LC 79-63083. (Illus.). 309p. 1979. text ed. 20.00x (ISBN 0-87451-173-9). U Pr of New Eng.

Foster, Charles R., ed. Comparative Public Policy & Citizen Participation: Energy, Education, Health & Local Governance in the U. S. A. & Germany. (Pergamon Policy Studies). 1980. 29.50 (ISBN 0-08-024624-9). Pergamon.

Ginzberg, Eli & Ostow, Miriam. Men, Money & Medicine. LC 79-101134. 291p. 1969. 17.50x (ISBN 0-231-03366-4). Columbia U Pr.

Gross, Samuel D. History of American Medical Literature from Seventeen Seventy Six to the Present Time. 85p. 1972. Repr. of 1876 ed. 19.50 (ISBN 0-8337-1466-X). B Franklin.

Haller, John S., Jr. American Medicine in Transition, 1840-1910. LC 80-14546. (Illus.). 334p. 1981. 27.95 (ISBN 0-252-00806-5). U of Ill Pr.

Hawes, Lloyd E. Benjamin Waterhouse, M. D., First Professor of the Theory of Physics at Harvard & Introducer of Cowpox Vaccination into America. Incl. A Concordance of Dr. Waterhouse's Horus Siccus. Estes, J. Worth. (Boston Medical Library Studies). (Illus.). 55p. 1974. 3.50 (ISBN 0-686-00002-1). F A Countway.

Jirka, Frank J. American Doctors of Destiny. LC 76-121482. (Essay Index Reprint Ser). 1940. 24.00 (ISBN 0-8369-1759-6). Arno.

Jonas, Steven. Medical Mystery: The Training of Doctors in the United States. 1979. 15.00 (ISBN 0-393-06437-9). Norton.

Karolevitz, Robert F. Doctors of the Old West. encore ed. LC 67-20239. (Illus.). 1967. 9.95 (ISBN 0-87564-301-9). Superior Pub.

Kaufman, Martin. Homeopathy in America: The Rise & Fall of a Medical Heresy. LC 79-149741. 216p. 1971. 15.00x (ISBN 0-8018-1238-0). Johns Hopkins.

Knowles, John H., ed. Doing Better & Feeling Worse. 1977. 9.95 (ISBN 0-393-06419-0); pap. text ed. 5.95 (ISBN 0-393-06423-9). Norton.

Konkle, Burton A. Standard History of the Medical Profession of Philadelphia. 2nd corr. & enl. ed. LC 75-17803. Repr. of 1897 ed. 67.50 (ISBN 0-404-13201-4). AMS Pr.

Maclachlan, John M. Planning Florida's Health Leadership: Florida's Hospitals & Nurses. LC 54-63166. (Medical Center Study Ser: Vol. 4). (Illus.). 1954. pap. 1.50 (ISBN 0-8130-0150-1). U Presses Fla.

--Planning Florida's Health Leadership: Health & the People in Florida. LC 54-62971. (Medical Center Study Ser: Vol. 3). (Illus.). 1954. pap. 1.50 (ISBN 0-8130-0151-X). U Presses Fla.

Maloof, Louis J. Planning Florida's Health Leadership: Medical Education in the University. LC 54-9612. (Medical Center Study Ser: Vol. 5). 1955. pap. 1.50 (ISBN 0-8130-0158-7). U Presses Fla.

Meyer, Clarence. American Folk Medicine. LC 73-4300. 1973. 3.95 (ISBN 0-685-72759-9, Pub. by NAL). Formur Intl.

Mullan, Fitzhugh. White Coat, Clenched Fist: The Political Education of an American Physician. 1976. 12.95 (ISBN 0-02-587910-3). Macmillan.

Nissenbaum, Stephen. Sex, Diet & Debility in Jacksonian America: Sylvester Graham & Health Reform. LC 79-8280. (Contributions in Medical History: No. 4). xvii, 198p. 1980. lib. bdg. 22.95 (ISBN 0-313-21415-8, NSY/). Greenwood.

Reedy, Barry L. The New Health Practitioners in America: A Comparative Study. 1978. text ed. 17.50 (ISBN 0-8464-0671-3). Beekman Pubs.

Risse, Guenter B., et al, eds. Medicine Without Doctors: Home Health Care in American History. 1977. pap. 8.95 (ISBN 0-88202-165-6). N Watson.

Rogers, David E. American Medicine: Challenge for the 1980's. LC 78-16183. 1978. 14.50 (ISBN 0-88410-530-X). Ballinger Pub.

Rothstein, William G. American Physicians in the Nineteenth Century: From Sects to Science. LC 77-186517. 377p. 1972. 25.00x (ISBN 0-8018-1242-9). Johns Hopkins.

Shafer, Henry B. American Medical Profession, 1783-1850. LC 68-58619. (Columbia University. Studies in the Social Sciences: No. 417). Repr. of 1936 ed. 21.00 (ISBN 0-404-51417-0). AMS Pr.

Shryock, Richard H. Medicine in America: Historical Essays. 324p. 1966. 22.00x (ISBN 0-8018-0592-9). Johns Hopkins.

Simpson, Howard N. Invisible Armies: The Impact of Disease on American History. LC 80-682. 300p. 1980. 12.95 (ISBN 0-672-52659-X). Bobbs.

Stevens, Rosemary. American Medicine & the Public Interest. LC 77-151592. 1971. pap. 7.95 (ISBN 0-300-01744-8, Y264). Yale U Pr.

Stookey, Byron. A History of Colonial Medical Education: In the Province of New York, with Its Subsequent Development (1767-1830) (Illus.). 312p. 1962. photocopy ed. spiral 29.50 (ISBN 0-398-01866-9). C C Thomas.

Tabakov, George A. Medicine in the United States & the Soviet Union. 1962. 5.95 (ISBN 0-8158-0194-7). Chris Mass.

Thacher, James. American Medical Biography, 2 Vols. 2nd ed. LC 67-25447. (American Medicine Ser). 1967. Repr. of 1828 ed. lib. bdg. 55.00 (ISBN 0-306-70944-9). Da Capo.

Thacher, James & Williams, Stephen W. American Biographies of 1828-1845, 2 Vols. (Illus.). 1967. Set. lib. bdg. 40.00 (ISBN 0-87821-005-9). Milford Hse.

Toner, Joseph M. Contributions to the Annals of Medical Progress & Medical Education in the United States Before & During the War of Independence. LC 73-143662. (Research & Source Works Ser.: No. 628). 1971. Repr. of 1874 ed. lib. bdg. 20.50 (ISBN 0-8337-3547-0). B Franklin.

Vogel, Morris J. & Rosenberg, Charles E., eds. The Theraputic Revolution: Essays on the Social History of American Medicine. LC 79-5044. (Illus.). 1979. 18.50 (ISBN 0-8122-7773-2). U of Pa Pr.

Walsh, James J. History of Medicine in New York: Three Centuries of Medical Progress, 5 vols. LC 75-23765. Repr. of 1919 ed. 125.00 set (ISBN 0-404-13440-8). AMS Pr.

MEDICINE, ANCIENT

see also Medicine, Egyptian; Medicine, Greek and Roman; Paleopathology

Avicenna. A Treatise on the Canon of Medicine of Avicenna. LC 73-12409. Repr. of 1930 ed. 45.00 (ISBN 0-404-11231-5). AMS Pr.

Budge, E. A. Wallis. Herb-Doctors & Physicians in the Ancient World: The Divine Origin of the Craft of the Herbalist. 1978. 10.00 (ISBN 0-89005-252-2); pap. 6.00 (ISBN 0-685-91071-7). Ares.

Chernin, Dennis, et al. Ancient & Modern Medicine: A Preventive & Therapeutic Synthesis. 200p. (Orig.). Date not set. pap. price not set (ISBN 0-89389-068-5). Himalayan Intl.

Edelstein, Ludwig. Ancient Medicine: Selected Papers of Ludwig Edelstein. Temkin, Owsei & Temkin, C. Lilian, eds. 496p. 1967. 27.50x (ISBN 0-8018-0183-4). Johns Hopkins.

Koecher, Franz. Die Babylonisch-assyrische Medizin in Texten und Untersuchungen: Erster Teil: Keilschrifttexte, 6 vols. Incl. Vols. 1-3. Keilschrifttexte aus Assur: Teile 1-3. 1963-64. per vol. 36.25x (ISBN 0-685-24220-X). Vol. 1 (ISBN 3-11-000111-X). Vol. 2 (ISBN 3-11-000112-8). Vol. 3 (ISBN 3-11-000113-6); Vol. 4. Keilschrifttexte aus Assur: Teil 4: Babylon, Nippur, Sippar, Uruk und Unbekannter Herkunft. (Illus.). 38p. 1971. 61.00x (ISBN 3-11-001596-X). (Ger.). De Gruyter.

Kutumbiah, P. The Evolution of Scientific Medicine. 404p. 1979. cased with jacket 15.00x (ISBN 0-86125-060-5, Pub. by Orient Longman India). State Mutual Bk.

Lang, Mabel. Cure & Cult in Ancient Corinth: A Guide to the Asklepieion. (American Excavations in Old Corinth, Corinth Notes: No. 1). (Illus.). 1977. pap. 1.50x (ISBN 0-685-88666-2). Am Sch Athens.

Lawn, Brian, ed. The Prose Salernitan Questions: An Anonymous Collection Dealing with Science & Medicine Written by an Englishman Circa 1200, with an Appendix of Ten Related Collections. (British Academy: Auctores Britannici Medii Aevi: Vol. V). 1979. 89.00x (ISBN 0-19-725978-2). Oxford U Pr.

Majno, Guido. The Healing Hand: Man & Wound in the Ancient World. LC 74-80730. (Commonwealth Fund Publications Ser). 528p. 1974. 25.00 (ISBN 0-674-38330-3). Harvard U Pr.

Morley, Peter & Wallis, Roy, eds. Culture & Curing: Anthropological Perspectives on Traditional Medical Beliefs & Practices. LC 78-62194. (Contemporary Community Health Ser.). (Illus.). 1979. 14.95 (ISBN 0-8229-1136-1); pap. 5.95 (ISBN 0-8229-5325-0). U of Pittsburgh Pr.

Schwabe, Calvin W. Cattle, Priests, & Progress in Medicine, Vol. 4. LC 77-84547. (Wesley W. Spink Lectures on Comparative Medicine). (Illus.). 1978. 19.75x (ISBN 0-8166-0825-3). U of Minn Pr.

Smith, Wesley D. The Hippocratic Tradition. LC 78-20977. (History of Science Ser.). 1979. 17.50x (ISBN 0-8014-1209-9). Cornell U Pr.

Wilde, Jane F. Ancient Cures, Charms & Usages of Ireland. LC 74-137347. 1970. Repr. of 1890 ed. 24.00 (ISBN 0-8103-3599-9). Gale.

MEDICINE, ANGLO-SAXON

Payne, Joseph F. English Medicine in the Anglo-Saxon Times. LC 75-23749. (Illus.). Repr. of 1904 ed. 14.50 (ISBN 0-404-13355-X). AMS Pr.

MEDICINE, ARABIC

Al-Kindi. Medical Formulary or Agrabadhinx of Al-Kindi. Levey, Martin, tr. (Medieval Science Pubns., No. 7). 1966. 32.50x (ISBN 0-299-03600-6). U of Wis Pr.

Browne, Edward G. Arabian Medicine. LC 79-2852. (Illus.). 138p. 1981. Repr. of 1962 ed. 16.00 (ISBN 0-8305-0028-6). Hyperion Conn.

Campbell, Donald E. Arabian Medicine & Its Influence on the Middle Ages, 2 vols. LC 74-180330. Repr. of 1926 ed. Set. 30.00 (ISBN 0-404-56235-3). AMS Pr.

Hilton-Simpson, Melville W. Arab Medicine & Surgery: A Study of the Healing Art in Algeria. LC 75-23721. Repr. of 1922 ed. 14.50 (ISBN 0-404-13279-0). AMS Pr.

Leclerc, Lucien. Histoire De la Medicine Arabe, 2 vols in 1. LC 76-164482. (Research & Source Works Ser: No. 18). (Fr). 1971. Repr. of 1876 ed. lib. bdg. 58.00 (ISBN 0-8337-2040-6). B Franklin.

Shahine, Y. A. The Arab Contribution to Medicine. (Carreras Arab Lectures Ser.: No. 5). (Illus.). 52p. 1976. pap. text ed. 2.50x (ISBN 0-582-78014-4). Longman.

MEDICINE, BIBLICAL

see Bible–Medicine, Hygiene, etc.

MEDICINE, BOTANIC

Bach, Edward. The Bach Flower Remedies. LC 79-87679. 1979. 5.95 (ISBN 0-87983-192-8); pap. 4.95 (ISBN 0-87983-193-6). Keats.

Challem, Jack J. Spirulina: Green Gold of the Future. (Good Health Guide Ser.). 48p. 1981. pap. price not set (ISBN 0-87983-262-2). Keats.

Clymer, R. Swinburne. Nature's Healing Agents. 5th new & rev. ed. 1973. 6.95 (ISBN 0-686-05880-1). Philos Pub.

Committee of Scholarly Communication with the People's Republic of China, National Research Council. Herbal Pharmacology in the People's Republic of China: A Trip Report of the American Herbal Pharmacology Delegation. LC 75-39772. v, 169p. 1975. pap. 8.00 (ISBN 0-309-02438-2). Natl Acad Pr.

Fox, William. Every Man His Own Doctor: The Botanic System Guide to Better Health. 1974. lib. bdg. 69.95 (ISBN 0-685-51387-4). Revisionist Pr.

Jackson, Mildred & Teague, Terri. The Handbook of Alternatives to Chemical Medicine. Macdonald, Alexandra, ed. LC 77-155218. 1975. pap. 5.95 (ISBN 0-932516-01-7). Lawton-Teague.

Lucas, Richard. Secrets of the Chinese Herbalists. 1978. pap. 3.95 (ISBN 0-346-12338-0). Cornerstone.

Passwater, Richard A. Evening Primrose Oil & Your Health. (Good Health Guide Ser.). 48p. 1981. pap. price not set (ISBN 0-87983-263-0). Keats.

Thomson, Robert. Natural Medicine. 1978. 10.95 (ISBN 0-07-064513-2, GB). McGraw.

Valnet, Jean. Aromatherapy: The Treatment of Illness with the Essences of Plants. 1980. 25.00x (ISBN 0-85027-141-X, Pub. by Daniel Co England). State Mutual Bk.

Weeks, Nora. The Medical Discoveries of Edward Bach, Physician. LC 79-88118. 1979. pap. 4.95 (ISBN 0-87983-197-9). Keats.

Williams, Trevor I. Drugs from Plants. 1980. lib. bdg. 49.95 (ISBN 0-8490-3162-1). Gordon Pr.

MEDICINE, CHINESE

Committee of Scholarly Communication with the People's Republic of China, National Research Council. Herbal Pharmacology in the People's Republic of China: A Trip Report of the American Herbal Pharmacology Delegation. LC 75-39772. v, 169p. 1975. pap. 8.00 (ISBN 0-309-02438-2). Natl Acad Pr.

Dimond, E. Grey. More Than Herbs & Acupuncture. 224p. 1975. 7.95 (ISBN 0-393-06400-X). Norton.

Huard, Pierre & Wong, Ming. Chinese Medicine. (Illus., Orig.). 1968. pap. 2.45 (ISBN 0-07-030785-7, SP). McGraw.

Hume, Edward H. The Chinese Way in Medicine. LC 74-10103. (China Studies: from Confucius to Mao Ser). (Illus.). 189p. 1975. Repr. of 1940 ed. 18.00 (ISBN 0-88355-168-3). Hyperion Conn.

Hu Shiu-Ying. An Enumeration of Chinese Materia Medica. 200p. 1981. 21.50 (ISBN 0-295-95744-1, Pub by Chinese Univ Hong Kong). U of Wash Pr.

John E. Fogarty International Center for Advanced Study in the Health Sciences, tr. from Chinese. The Barefoot Doctor's Manual: The American Translation of the Official Chinese Paramedical Manual. LC 77-364. (Illus.). 1977. lib. bdg. 12.90 (ISBN 0-914294-91-1); pap. 7.95 (ISBN 0-914294-92-X). Running Pr.

Kao, Frederick F. & Kao, John J., eds. Chinese Medicine: New Medicine. (Illus.). 1977. 17.00 (ISBN 0-88202-174-5). N Watson.

Keys, John. Chinese Herbs: Their Botany, Chemistry & Pharmacodynamics. LC 75-35399. 1976. 15.00 (ISBN 0-8048-1179-2). C E Tuttle.

Kleinman, Arthur, et al, eds. Culture & Healing in Asian Societies: Anthropological & Cross-Cultural Medical Studies. LC 77-2706. 480p. 1978. pap. text ed. 11.25x (ISBN 0-87073-573-X). Schenkman.

Lucas, Richard. Secrets of the Chinese Herbalists. 1978. pap. 3.95 (ISBN 0-346-12338-0). Cornerstone.

Morse, William R. Chinese Medicine. LC 75-23661. (Clio Medica: 11). (Illus.). Repr. of 1938 ed. 17.50 (ISBN 0-404-58911-1). AMS Pr.

Okanishi, Tameto. Research on Medical Works Before the Sung Dynasty. 1976. 25.00 (ISBN 0-89986-310-8). E Langstaff.

Porkert, Manfred. The Theoretical Foundations of Chinese Medicine: Systems of Correspondence. LC 73-4960. (Asian Science Ser.: No. 3). 1974. pap. 12.00 (ISBN 0-262-66040-7). MIT Pr.

Read, Bernard E. Animal Drugs. 1976. Repr. of 1931 ed. 4.50 (ISBN 0-89986-308-6). E Langstaff.

--Chinese Medicinal Plants from the Pen T'sao Kang Mu. 1977. 7.50 (ISBN 0-89986-317-5). E Langstaff.

--Famine Foods List in the Chiu Huang Pen Ts'ao. 1977. 4.50 (ISBN 0-89986-318-3). E Langstaff.

--Insect Drugs, Dragon & Snake Drugs, Fish Drugs. 1977. 7.50 (ISBN 0-89986-321-3). E Langstaff.

--Turtle & Shellfish Drugs, Avian Drugs, Minerals & Stones. 1977. 7.50 (ISBN 0-89986-330-2). E Langstaff.

Series of Classics in Acupuncture & Cauterization, 6 vols. 1976. 34.50 (ISBN 0-89986-307-8). E Langstaff.

The Stone Monkey: An Alternative, Chinese-Scientific Reality. LC 81-11063. (Illus.). 422p. 1981. 15.00 (ISBN 0-688-00665-5); pap. 7.95 (ISBN 0-688-00732-5). Morrow.

Stuart, G. A. Vegetable Kingdom. 1976. Repr. of 1911 ed. 8.00 (ISBN 0-89986-309-4). E Langstaff.

Unschuld, Paul. Medical Ethics in Imperial China: A Study in Historical Anthropology. LC 78-80479. (Comparative Studies of Health Systems & Medical Care). 1979. 18.50x (ISBN 0-520-03543-7). U of Cal Pr.

Wade, Carlson. Health Secrets from the Orient. 1973. pap. 3.95 (ISBN 0-13-384503-6, Reward). P-H.

Ware, James R., tr. from Chinese. Alchemy, Medicine, & Religion in the China of A. D. 320: The Nei P'ien of Ko Hung (Pao-p'u tzu) 416p. 1981. pap. 6.00 (ISBN 0-486-24088-6). Dover.

MEDICINE, CLERICAL

see Pastoral Medicine

MEDICINE, CLINICAL

see also Charities, Medical; Clinical Enzymology; Diagnosis; Medical Laboratories; Medical Technologists; Medical Technology; Pathology; Radioactivation Analysis; Surgery–Cases, Clinical Reports, Statistics

Acheson, Keith & Gall, Meredith. Techniques in the Clinical Supervision of Teachers. 1980. pap. text ed. 9.95x (ISBN 0-582-28121-0). Longman.

Achterberg, Jeanne & Lawlis, Frank. Bridges of the Bodymind. LC 80-16596. (Illus.). 1980. text ed. 19.50 (ISBN 0-918296-14-5). Inst Personality & Ability.

Adams, E. B. A Companion to Clinical Medicine in the Tropics & Subtropics. (Illus.). 1979. text ed. 27.50x (ISBN 0-19-261180-1). Oxford U Pr.

Arab, L., et al. Ernaehrung und Gesundheit. (Beitraege zu Infusionstherapie und Klinische Ernaehrung: Band 7). (Illus.). xii, 204p. 1981. pap. 24.00 (ISBN 3-8055-2384-X). S Karger.

Barnett, Roy N. Clinical Laboratory Statistics. 2nd ed. (Series in Laboratory Medicine). 224p. 1979. 22.50 (ISBN 0-316-08196-5). Little.

Beck. Clinical Reasoning. Date not set. price not set (ISBN 0-8151-0597-5). Year Bk Med.

Bellville, J. Weldon & Weaver, Charles S. Techniques in Clinical Physiology: A Survey of Methods in Anesthesiology. LC 1-30791. (Illus.). 1969. 22.50 (ISBN 0-02-307910-X, 30791). Macmillan.

Black, D. A., ed. Notes on Clinical Method. 148p. 1971. 12.00x (ISBN 0-7190-0484-5, Pub. by Manchester U Pr England). State Mutual Bk.

Blankenship, June & Campbell, Joe B. Laboratory Mathematics: Medical & Biological Applications. LC 75-15598. (Illus.). 288p. 1976. pap. text ed. 10.95 (ISBN 0-8016-0700-0). Mosby.

Bralow, S. Philip, ed. Basic Research & Clinical Medicine. (Illus.). 304p. 1981. text ed. 33.50 (ISBN 0-07-007150-0, Co-Pub by Hemisphere Pub). McGraw.

Buss, David H., et al. Clinical Pathology Continuing Education Review. LC 79-91972. 1980. pap. 14.75 (ISBN 0-87488-320-2). Med Exam.

Cluff, Leighton E., et al. Clinical Problems with Drugs. (Major Problems in Internal Medicine Ser., Vol. 5). (Illus.). 308p. 1975. text ed. 18.00 (ISBN 0-7216-2613-0). Saunders.

Cutler, Paul. Problem Solving in Clinical Medicine. (Illus.). 388p. 1979. 22.95 (ISBN 0-683-02251-2). Williams & Wilkins.

Delp, Mahlon H. & Manning, Robert T. Major's Physical Diagnosis: An Introduction to the Clinical Process. 9th ed. (Illus.). 650p. 1981. text ed. write for info. (ISBN 0-7216-3002-2). Saunders.

Dickerson, John W. & Lee, H. A. Nutrition in the Clinical Management of Disease. 1978. 37.50 (ISBN 0-8151-2451-1). Year Bk Med.

Dietschy, John M., ed. Disorders of the Gastrointestinal Tract; Disorders of the Liver; Nutritional Disorders. LC 75-45266. (The Science & Practice of Clinical Medicine Ser.). (Illus.). 432p. 1976. 34.50 (ISBN 0-8089-0716-6). Grune.

DiSaia, Philip J. & Creasman, William T. Clinical Gynecologic Oncology. LC 80-18687. (Illus.). 478p. 1980. text ed. 30.50 (ISBN 0-8016-1314-0). Mosby.

Draper, George, et al. Human Constitution in Clinical Medicine. (Psychology Ser). 1969. Repr. of 1914 ed. 18.50 (ISBN 0-384-12755-X). Johnson Repr.

Eastham, R. D. Biochemical Values in Clinical Medicine. 6th ed. 1979. pap. 12.95 (ISBN 0-8151-3007-4). Year Bk Med.

--Laboratory Guide to Clinical Diagnosis. 1976. 12.95 (ISBN 0-8151-3003-1). Year Bk Med.

Essex, Benjamin J. Diagnostic Pathways in Clinical Medicine. 2nd ed. (Medicine in the Tropics Ser.). (Illus.). 1981. pap. text ed. 19.00 (ISBN 0-443-02059-0). Churchill.

Fabian, Leonard W. Decade of Clinical Progress. (Illus.). 1971. text ed. 15.00 (ISBN 0-8036-3315-7). Davis Co.

Feinstein, Alvan R. Clinical Judgment. LC 67-19517. 422p. 1974. Repr. of 1967 ed. 16.95 (ISBN 0-88275-141-7). Krieger.

Fisher, Jack C. & Wachtel, Thomas. Clinical Procedures: A Concise Guide for Students of Medicine. 2nd ed. (Illus.). 240p. 1980. 13.50 (ISBN 0-683-03240-2). Williams & Wilkins.

Ford, Michael J. & Munro, John F. Practical Procedures in Clinical Medicine. (Illus.). 144p. 1981. pap. text ed. 11.00 (ISBN 0-443-02120-1). Churchill.

Gaarder, Kenneth R. & Montgomery, Penelope S. Clinical Biofeedback: A Clinical Manual in Behavioral Medicine. 2nd. ed. (Illus.). 288p. pap. 24.95 (ISBN 0-683-03401-4). Williams & Wilkins.

Galen, P. S. & Gambino, S. R. Beyond Normality: The Predictive Value & Efficiency of Medical Diagnosis. LC 75-25915. 1975. 26.00x (ISBN 0-471-29047-5, Pub. by Wiley Medical). Wiley.

Ginsburg, A. David. Clinical Reasoning in Patient Care. 224p. 1980. pap. text ed. 12.75 (ISBN 0-06-140915-4, Harper Medical). Har-Row.

Halsted, Charles H. & Halsted, James A. The Laboratory in Clinical Medicine. (Illus.). 1184p. Date not set. text ed. price not set (ISBN 0-7216-4479-1). Saunders.

Hart, Gordon M. The Process of Clinical Supervision. 224p. 1981. pap. text ed. 18.95 (ISBN 0-8391-1700-0). Univ Park.

Harvey, A. McGehee. Science at the Bedside: Clinical Research in American Medicine, 1905-1945. LC 80-28786. 496p. 1981. text ed. 17.50x (ISBN 0-8018-2562-8). Johns Hopkins.

Hillman, Robert S., et al. Introduction to Clinical Medicine. (Illus.). 512p. Date not set. pap. text ed. 12.95 (ISBN 0-07-028910-7). McGraw.

Hoffman, William S. The Biochemistry of Clinical Medicine. 4th ed. (Illus.). 1970. 27.50 (ISBN 0-8151-4537-3). Year Bk Med.

Horler, A. & Foster, J. B. Progress in Clinical Medicine. 7th ed. 1978. 35.00x (ISBN 0-443-01697-6). Churchill.

Hudak, Carolyn, et al. Clinical Protocols: A Guide for Nurses & Physicians. LC 75-43685. 1976. pap. text ed. 11.95x (ISBN 0-397-54179-1, JBL-Med-Nursing). Har-Row.

Kamath, S. H. Clinical Biochemistry for Medical Technologists. LC 77-155035. 259p. 1972. 13.95 (ISBN 0-316-48253-6). Little.

--Clinical Biochemistry for Medical Technologists. LC 77-155035. 259p. 1972. 13.95 (ISBN 0-316-48253-6). Little.

King, Maurice. A Medical Laboratory for Developing Countries. (Illus.). 1973. pap. text ed. 22.50x (ISBN 0-19-264910-8). Oxford U Pr.

Krug, Samuel E., ed. Psychological Assessment in Medicine. LC 77-71889. 1977. 17.25 (ISBN 0-918296-07-2). Inst Personality & Ability.

Lapuerta, Leopoldo. Blood Gases in Clinical Practice. (Illus.). 132p. 1976. 16.75 (ISBN 0-398-03527-X). C C Thomas.

Lawson, A. M., et al, eds. Current Developments in the Clinical Applications of HPLC, GC & MS. 1981. 51.50 (ISBN 0-12-439650-X). Acad Pr.

Lowinson, Joyce A. Clinical Problems & Perspectives: Substance Abuse. (Illus.). 885p. Date not set. price not set. Williams & Wilkins.

Ludwig, Herbert R. Computer Applications & Techniques in Clinical Medicine. 327p. 1974. 24.50 (ISBN 0-471-55356-5, Pub. by Wiley). Krieger.

Lyle, Carl & Bianchi, Raymond. Common Clinical Perplexities. LC 78-71347. 1979. spiral 9.50 (ISBN 0-87488-958-8). Med Exam.

McGuire, Christine H. Clinical Simulations: Selected Problems in Patient Management. 2nd ed. 424p. 1976. pap. 27.00 (ISBN 0-8385-1161-9). ACC.

Margolis, Carmi Z. & Shapiro, Donald L. Newborn Management: Decision Trees & Management Problems. (Illus., Orig., With work sheets). 1977. pap. 11.50 (ISBN 0-913178-60-8). Redgrave Pub Co.

Mason, Stuart & Swash, Michael. Hutchinson's Clinical Methods. 17th ed. (Illus.). 495p. 1980. 14.50 (ISBN 0-397-58270-6, JBL-Med-Nursing). Har-Row.

Mukherjee, Kanai L. Introductory Mathematics for the Clinical Laboratory. LC 78-10915. (Illus.). 1979. pap. text ed. 20.00 (ISBN 0-89189-069-6, 45-9-006-00). Am Soc Clinical.

Mukherjee, Kanai Lai. Review of Clinical Laboratory Methods: A Key Word Index System. LC 79-15463. (Illus.). 1979. pap. text ed. 14.95 (ISBN 0-8016-3589-6). Mosby.

Naish, John M., et al. The Clinical Apprentice. 5th ed. (Illus.). 1978. 15.00 (ISBN 0-8151-6322-3). Year Bk Med.

Nath, R. L. Practice of Biochemistry in Clinical Medicine. 262p. 1981. 30.00x (ISBN 0-686-72963-3, Pub. by Oxford & IBH India). State Mutual Bk.

National Board of Medical Examiners & American Institutes for Research. The Definition of Clinical Competence in Medicine: Performance Dimensions & Rationales for Clinical Skill Areas. 1976. pap. 5.00 (ISBN 0-89785-545-0). Am Inst Res.

Nay, W. Robert. Multimethod Clinical Assessment. LC 79-57. 363p. 1979. 22.95x (ISBN 0-470-26654-6). Halsted Pr.

Payton, Otto D. Research: Validation of Clinical Practice. LC 78-26362. 1979. pap. text ed. 10.95 (ISBN 0-8036-6798-1). Davis Co.

Petrie, J. C. & McIntyre, Neil, eds. The Problem-Orientated Medical Record in Clinical Practice. 1979. pap. text ed. 22.50 (ISBN 0-443-01405-1). Churchill.

Phillips, C. I. & Wolfe, J. N. Clinical Practice & Economics. pap. 14.95x (ISBN 0-8464-0251-3). Beekman Pubs.

Pinel, Philippe. The Clinical Training of Doctors: An Essay of 1793. Weiner, Dora B., ed. & tr. from Fr. LC 80-14500. (The Henry E. Sigerist Supplements to the Bulletin of the History of Medicine, New Ser.: No. 3). 108p. 1981. pap. text ed. 7.50x (ISBN 0-8018-2448-6). Johns Hopkins.

Powell, David J. Clinical Supervision. LC 79-20586. 1979. manual 19.95x (ISBN 0-87705-406-1); trainee wkbk. 7.95x (ISBN 0-87705-407-X). Human Sci Pr.

Practical Solutions to a Complex Problem: Identification of Multiple Alloantibodies in the Presence of a Strong Cold Autoantibody. 32p. 1973. 6.00 (ISBN 0-685-48761-X). Am Assn Blood.

Ravel, Richard. Clinical Laboratory Medicine. 3rd ed. (Illus.). 531p. 1978. pap. 18.95 (ISBN 0-8151-7096-3). Year Bk Med.

Reneman, Robert S. & Strackee, Jan, eds. Data in Medicine. (Instrumentation & Techniques in Clinical Medicine Ser.: No. 1). 1979. lib. bdg. 54.00 (ISBN 90-247-2150-4, Pub. by Martinus Nijhoff Netherlands). Kluwer Boston.

Robbins, Dennis & Dyer, Allen R. Ethical Dimensions of Clinical Medicine. (Illus.). 176p. 1981. 19.75 (ISBN 0-398-04503-8). C C Thomas.

Sanjivi, K. S. Profiles of Clinical Practice. 400p. 1979. 15.00x (ISBN 0-86125-210-1, Pub. by Orient Longman India). State Mutual Bk.

Schwartz, E. E. The Radiology of Complications in Medical Practice. (Illus.). 480p. 1981. lib. bdg. 48.00 (ISBN 0-683-07571-3). Williams & Wilkins.

Shankar, P. S. Manual of Clinical Methods. 1981. 40.00x (ISBN 0-686-72956-0, Pub. by Oxford & IBH India). State Mutual Bk.

Stefanini, Mario, ed. Progress in Clinical Pathology, Vols. 2-4. Incl. Vol. II. (Illus.). 392p. 1969. 69.25 (ISBN 0-8089-0476-0); Vol. III. (Illus.). 424p. 1969. 69.25 (ISBN 0-8089-0477-9); Vol. IV. 352p. 1972. 69.25 (ISBN 0-8089-0766-2). LC 66-11412. (Vol. 1 o.p.). Grune.

Strickland, William D. & Wilder, Aldridge D., Jr. Clinical Chairside Assisting. 3rd ed. (Dental Assisting Manuals: No. 8). 160p. 1980. 10.00 (ISBN 0-8078-1382-6). U of NC Pr.

--Clinical Sciences. 3rd ed. (Dental Assisting Manuals: No. 7). 140p. 1980. 10.00 (ISBN 0-8078-1381-8). U of NC Pr.

Taylor, D. & Whamond, J. Non-Invasive Clinical Measurement. 1977. 39.50 (ISBN 0-8391-1114-2). Univ Park.

Tilkian, Sarko M., et al. Clinical Implications of Laboratory Tests, Nineteen Seventy-Nine. 2nd ed. LC 78-16221. (Illus.). 1979. pap. text ed. 12.95 (ISBN 0-8016-4962-5). Mosby.

Toren, E. Clifford & Eggert, Arthur A., eds. Computers in the Clinical Laboratory. (Clinical & Biochemical Analysis Ser.: Vol. 8). 1978. 24.50 (ISBN 0-8247-6694-6). Dekker.

Tyrer, J. H. & Eadie, M. J. The Astute Physician: How to Think in Clinical Medicine. 1976. pap. text ed. 15.75 (ISBN 0-444-41425-8). Elsevier.

Walker, et al. Clinical Methods. 2nd ed. 1980. 39.95 (ISBN 0-409-95190-0). Butterworth.

Weinstein, Milton C. & Fineberg, Harvey V. Clinical Decision Analysis. (Illus.). 400p. 1980. text ed. 215.00 (ISBN 0-7216-9166-8). Saunders.

Wells, Roe, ed. The Microcirculation in Medicine. 1973. 53.50 (ISBN 0-12-743750-9). Acad Pr.

Westlake, G., ed. Automation & Management in the Clinical Laboratory. (Illus.). 1975. 19.50 (ISBN 0-8391-0627-0). Univ Park.

Wodarski, John S. The Role of Research in Clinical Practice. 208p. 1981. pap. text ed. 16.95 (ISBN 0-8391-1667-5). Univ Park.

Wood, Matthew T. & Burkes, E. Jeff, Jr. Preclinical Sciences. 3rd ed. (Dental Assisting Manuals: No. 3). 130p. 1980. 7.00 (ISBN 0-8078-1377-X). U of NC Pr.

Zakus, Sharron. Clinical Skills & Assisting Techniques for the Medical Assistant. LC 80-27135. (Illus.). 351p. 1981. pap. text ed. 15.95 (ISBN 0-8016-5672-9). Mosby.

Zimmerman, Irla L., et al. Clinical Interpretation of the Wechsler Adult Intelligence Scale. LC 72-11825. 224p. 1972. 17.00 (ISBN 0-8089-0780-8). Grune.

MEDICINE, CLINICAL–EXAMINATIONS, QUESTIONS, ETC.

Alter, Aaron A., et al. Medical Technology Examination Review Book, Vol. 1. 4th ed. 1977. spiral bdg. 9.50 (ISBN 0-87488-451-9). Med Exam.

MEDICINE, CLINICAL–LABORATORY MANUALS

see also Blood–Analysis and Chemistry; Pathology–Laboratory Manuals; Urine–Analysis and Pathology

Bauer, John D., et al. Clinical Laboratory Methods. 8th ed. LC 73-6928. 1974. pap. 36.50 (ISBN 0-8016-0507-5). Mosby.

Bodanza, Mary F. Clinical & Laboratory Procedures in the Physicians Office. 500p. 1982. 14.95 (ISBN 0-471-06497-1, Pub. by Wiley Med). Wiley.

Collins, R. Douglas. Illustrated Manual of Laboratory Diagnosis. LC 74-23530. (Illus.). 344p. 1975. 45.00 (ISBN 0-397-50340-7, JBL-Med-Nursing). Har-Row.

Edwards, Gabrielle I. & Cimmino, Marion. Laboratory Techniques for High Schools: A Worktext of Biomedical Methods. rev. ed. LC 75-23111. (gr. 10-12). 1975. pap. text ed. 5.95 (ISBN 0-8120-0649-6). Barron.

--Tecnicas De Laboratorio: Un Texto De Trabajo De Metodos Biomedicos. Casasnovas, Sonia, tr. from Eng. (Span.). (gr. 9-12). 1976. pap. text ed. 6.50 (ISBN 0-8120-0551-1); free tchr's manual with class order 1.25 (ISBN 0-8120-0702-6). Barron.

Garnett, Theodosia V. & Barbata, Jean C. A Collection of Laboratory Specimens & Diagnostic Procedures. (Quality Paperback: No. 310). (Orig.). 1964. pap. 1.95 (ISBN 0-8226-0310-1). Littlefield.

Hepler, Opal. Manual of Clinical Laboratory Methods. 4th ed. (Illus.). 416p. 1977. pap. 22.50 spiral (ISBN 0-398-03057-X). C C Thomas.

Keidel, W. D. & Neff, W. D., eds. Clinical & Special Topics, Part 3. (Handbook of Sensory Physiology: Vol. 5). (Illus.). 1976. 157.00 (ISBN 0-387-07129-6). Springer-Verlag.

Natelson, Samuel. Techniques of Clinical Chemistry. 3rd ed. (Illus.). 980p. 1971. 49.75 (ISBN 0-398-01384-5). C C Thomas.

Papaincolaou, George N. Atlas of Exfoliative Cytology. LC 52-12251. (Commonwealth Fund Publications Ser). (Illus.). 458p. 1954-60. 30.00x (ISBN 0-674-05150-5); 1956 suppl. 1 10.00x (ISBN 0-674-05151-3). Harvard U Pr.

St. Mary's Medical Center Staff. Clinical Laboratory Manual. Armstrong, Shirley, ed. LC 74-27940. 1975. pap. 14.00 (ISBN 0-87125-024-1). Cath Health.

Shih, Vivian. Laboratory Techniques for the Detection of Hereditary Metabolic Disorders. LC 73-78164. (Uniscience Ser). 125p. 1973. 34.95 (ISBN 0-8493-5013-1). CRC Pr.

Strand, Marcella M. & Elmer, Lucille A. Clinical Laboratory Tests: A Manual for Nurses. 2nd ed. LC 79-29765. 1980. pap. text ed. 7.50 (ISBN 0-8016-4827-0). Mosby.

Wasley, G. D., ed. Clinical Laboratory Techniques. 1973. text ed. 13.95 (ISBN 0-02-859690-0). Macmillan.

Widmann, Frances K. Clinical Interpretation of Laboratory Tests. 8th ed. LC 78-21975. (Illus.). 1979. pap. text ed. 12.95 (ISBN 0-8036-9322-2). Davis Co.

Winsten, Seymour & Dalal, Fram R. Manual of Clinical Laboratory Procedures for Non-Routine Problems. 151p. 1972. 18.95 (ISBN 0-87819-735-4). CRC Pr.

MEDICINE, CLINICAL–TABLES, ETC.

Lippert, Herbert & Lehmann, H. Peter, eds. SI Units in Medicine. Lehmann, H. L., tr. from Ger. LC 77-17354. Orig. Title: SI Einheiten in der Medizin. (Illus.). 220p. 1978. spiral bdg. 14.50 (ISBN 0-8067-1101-9). Urban & S.

Thomas, Harry. Handbook of Pharmaceutical & Clinical Measurement & Analysis. 1977. text ed. 29.95 (ISBN 0-87909-335-8). Reston.

MEDICINE, COMMUNICATION IN

see Communication in Medicine

MEDICINE, DENTAL

see Teeth–Diseases; Therapeutics, Dental

MEDICINE, EGYPTIAN

Bryan, Cyril. Ancient Egyptian Medicine: The Papyrus Ebers. 224p. 1974. 12.50 (ISBN 0-89005-004-X). Ares.

Dawson, Warren R. The Beginnings: Egypt & Assyria. LC 75-23650. (Clio Medica: No. 1). Repr. of 1930 ed. 9.50 (ISBN 0-404-58901-4). AMS Pr.

Ghalioungui, Paul. The House of Life: Magic & Medical Science in Ancient Egypt. rev. ed. (Illus.). 198p. 1974. 22.50 (ISBN 0-8390-0144-4). Allanheld & Schram.

Hurry, Jamieson B. Imhotep, the Vizier & Physician of King Zoser & Afterwards the Egyptian God of Medicine. 2nd rev. ed. LC 75-23727. Repr. of 1928 ed. 19.00 (ISBN 0-404-13285-5). AMS Pr.

MEDICINE, EXPERIMENTAL

see also Human Experimentation in Medicine; Medical Research

Academy Forum, National Academy of Science. Experiments & Research with Humans: Values in Conflicts. LC 75-13985. (Illus.). 224p. 1975. pap. 7.00 (ISBN 0-309-02347-5). Natl Acad Pr.

Bernard, Claude. An Introduction to the Study of Experimential Medicine. LC 57-3629. 1957. lib. bdg. 10.50 (ISBN 0-88307-618-7). Gannon.

--Introduction to the Study of Experimental Medicine. Greene, Henry C., tr. 1957. pap. 3.25 (ISBN 0-486-20400-6). Dover.

Boyland, Eric, et al. On Cancer & Hormones: Essays in Experimental Biology. LC 62-13921. (Illus.). 1962. 13.00x (ISBN 0-226-06941-9). U of Chicago Pr.

Chowdhury, Tushar K. & Weiss, A. Kurt, eds. Concanavalin A. LC 75-4528. (Advances in Experimental Medicine & Biology Ser.: Vol. 55). 360p. 1975. 29.50 (ISBN 0-306-39055-8, Plenum Pr). Plenum Pub.

Conference on Experimental Medicine & Surgery in Primates, 2nd, New York, 1969. Medical Primatology, 1970: Proceedings. Goldsmith, E. I. & Moor-Jankowski, J., eds. 1971. 167.75 (ISBN 3-8055-1227-9). S Karger.

Cranefield, Paul F. Claude Bernard's Revised Edition of His Introduction a L'etude De la Medicine Experimental. LC 76-10183. 1976. lib. bdg. 50.00 (ISBN 0-88202-153-2). N Watson.

Dalton, John C. John Call Dalton on Experimental Method: An Original Anthology. Cohen, I. Bernard, ed. LC 79-7957. (Three Centuries of Science in America Ser.). 1980. lib. bdg. 15.00x (ISBN 0-405-12538-0). Arno.

Gay, W. I., ed. Methods of Animal Experimentation, 5 vols. Vol. 1. 1965. 50.00 (ISBN 0-12-278001-9); Vol. 2. 1965. 56.50 (ISBN 0-12-278002-7); Vol. 3. 1968. 61.00 (ISBN 0-12-278003-5); Vol. 4. 1973. 56.00 (ISBN 0-12-278004-3); Vol. 5. 1974. 56.00 (ISBN 0-12-278005-1). Acad Pr.

Gill, John L. Design & Analysis of Experiments in the Animal & Medical Sciences, Vol. 3. (Illus.). 1978. pap. text ed. 8.50 (ISBN 0-8138-0110-9). Iowa St U Pr.

Glynn, L. E. & Schlumberger, H. D., eds. Experimental Models of Chronic Inflammatory Diseases. 1977. 43.80 (ISBN 0-387-08095-3). Springer-Verlag.

Gray, Bradford H. Human Subjects in Medical Experimentation: A Sociological Study of the Conduct & Regulation of Clinical Research. LC 74-20638. (Health, Medicine & Society Ser). 320p. 1975. 18.95 (ISBN 0-471-32325-X, Pub. by Wiley-Interscience). Wiley.

Hershey, Nathan & Miller, Robert D. Human Experimentation & the Law. LC 76-2179. 180p. 1976. 27.50 (ISBN 0-912862-19-X). Aspen Systems.

Hills, B. A. Gas Transfer in the Lung. (Monographs in Experimental Biology: No. 19). (Illus.). 200p. 1974. 38.50 (ISBN 0-521-20167-5). Cambridge U Pr.

Levy, Charlotte. The Human Body & the Law. LC 75-14041. (Legal Almanac Ser.). 128p. 1975. text ed. 5.95 (ISBN 0-379-11101-2). Oceana.

Mitruka, Brij M. Gas Chromatographic Applications in Microbiology & Medicine. LC 74-18002. 492p. 1975. 55.50 (ISBN 0-471-61183-2). Krieger.

Protection of Human Rights in the Light of Scientific & Technological Progress in Biology & Medicine: 8th CIOMS Round Table Conference. (Also avail. in French). 1974. 12.40 (ISBN 92-4-056007-6). World Health.

Sperlinger, David. Animals in Research: New Perspectives in Animal Experimentation. 384p. 1980. 46.50 (ISBN 0-471-27843-2, Pub. by Wiley-Interscience). Wiley.

Wooldridge, P. J. & Leonard, R. C. Methods of Clinical Experimentation to Improve Patient Care. LC 77-11072. (Illus.). 1978. pap. text ed. 10.00 (ISBN 0-8016-5622-2). Mosby.

MEDICINE, FORENSIC

see Medical Jurisprudence

MEDICINE, GREEK AND ROMAN

Allbutt, T. C. Greek Medicine in Rome. LC 69-13230. Repr. of 1921 ed. 30.00 (ISBN 0-405-08201-0, Pub. by Blom). Arno.

Brock, Arthur J., ed. Greek Medicine, Being Extracts Illustrative of Medical Writing from Hippocrates to Galen. LC 76-179302. (Library of Greek Thought: No. 8). Repr. of 1929 ed. 16.00 (ISBN 0-404-07806-0). AMS Pr.

Celsus. De Medicina, 3 Vols. (Loeb Classical Library: No. 292, 304, 336). 11.00x ea. Vol. 1 (ISBN 0-674-99322-5). Vol. 2 (ISBN 0-674-99335-7). Vol. 3 (ISBN 0-674-99370-5). Harvard U Pr.

Daremberg, Charles. La Medecine: Histoire & Doctrines. 2nd ed. LC 75-13257. (History of Ideas in Ancient Greece Ser.). (Fr.). 1976. Repr. of 1865 ed. 29.00x (ISBN 0-405-07300-3). Arno.

Dioscorides, Pedanius. Greek Herbal. Gunther, Robert T., ed. Goodyear, J., tr. (Illus.). 1968. Repr. of 1933 ed. 23.00 (ISBN 0-02-843930-9). Hafner.

Divided Legacy: A History of the Schism in Medical Thought, 3 vols. Incl. Vol. 1. The Patterns Emerge: Hippocrates to Paracelsus. Coulter, Harris L. 1975 (ISBN 0-916386-01-5); Vol. 2. Progress & Regress: J. B. Van Helmont to Claude Bernard. 1977 (ISBN 0-916386-02-3); Vol. 3. Science & Ethics in American Medicine, 1800-1914. Coulter, Harris L (ISBN 0-916386-03-1). LC 73-75718. 1976. 22.50x ea.; Set. 67.50x (ISBN 0-916386-00-7). Wehawken Bk.

Durling, R. J., ed. Galenus Latinus I. (Ars Medica: Vol. 6). 1976. text ed. 91.75x (ISBN 3-11-005759-X). De Gruyter.

Edelstein, L. The Hippocratic Oath. 90p. 1979. 10.00 (ISBN 0-89005-272-7). Ares.

Elliott, James S. Outlines of Greek & Roman Medicine. LC 77-91526. 1977. Repr. of 1914 ed. lib. bdg. 20.00 (ISBN 0-89341-502-2). Longwood Pr.

Furley, David J. & Wilkie, J. S., eds. Galen: On Respiration and the Arteries,an Edition with English Translation & Commentary of De Usu Respirationis, an in Arteriis Natura Sanguis Contineatur,De Usu Pulsum, & De Causis Respirationis. LC 81-47130. 300p. 1982. 24.00x (ISBN 0-691-08286-3). Princeton U Pr.

Grensemann, Hermann. Knidische Medizin, Part 1: Die Testimonien zur aeltesten knidischen Lehre und Analysen knidischer Schriften im Corpus Hippocraticum. (Ars Medica, Sect. 2, Griechisch-Lateinische Medizin, Vol. 4). 1974. 79.50x (ISBN 3-11-004141-3). De Gruyter.

Harris, C. R. The Heart & the Vascular System in Ancient Greek Medicine: From Alcmaeon to Galen. (Illus.). 500p. 1971. 89.00x (ISBN 0-19-858135-1). Oxford U Pr.

Hippocrates. Amorphismes Ypocras De Martin De Saint-Gille. Lafeuille, Germaine, ed. 1954. pap. 12.00 (ISBN 0-527-01123-1). Kraus Repr.

--Medical Works, 4 vols. Incl. Vol. 1. Ancient Medicine, Airs, Waters, Places, Epidemics 1 & 2. Oath, Precepts, Nutriment (ISBN 0-674-99162-1); Vol. 2. Prognostic. Regimen in Acute Diseases. Sacred Disease. Art, Breaths, Law, Decorum; Vol. 3. On Wounds in the Head. in the Surgery. on Fractures, on Joints, Mochlikon; Vol. 4. Nature of Man. Regimen in Health. Humours. Amorphisms. Regimen 1-3. Dreams. (Includes On the Universe by Heracleitus and a General Index) (ISBN 0-674-99166-4). (Loeb Classical Library: No. 147-150). 11.00x (ISBN 0-686-76944-9). Harvard U Pr.

Jones, W. H. Philosophy & Medicine in Ancient Greece. 100p. 1979. 10.00 (ISBN 0-89005-286-7). Ares.

Lang, Mabel. Cure & Cult in Ancient Corinth: A Guide to the Asklepieion. (American Excavations in Old Corinth, Corinth Notes: No. 1). (Illus.). 1977. pap. 1.50x (ISBN 0-685-88666-2). Am Sch Athens.

Lund, Fred B. Greek Medicine. LC 75-23668. (Clio Medica: 18). (Illus.). Repr. of 1936 ed. 14.50 (ISBN 0-404-58918-9). AMS Pr.

Moon, Robert O. Hippocrates & His Successors in Relation to the Philosophy of Their Time. LC 75-23745. Repr. of 1923 ed. 18.50 (ISBN 0-404-13351-7). AMS Pr.

Preiser, Gerd. Allgemeine Krankheitsbeeichnungen Im Corpus Hippocraticum: Bedeutung und Gebrauch Von Nousos und Nosema. (Ars Medica, Abt. 2 - Griechisch-Lateinische Medizin). 1976. text ed. 53.50x (ISBN 3-11-001830-6). De Gruyter.

Scarborough, John. Roman Medicine. Scullard, H. H., ed. LC 72-81596. (Aspect of Greek & Roman Life Ser). (Illus.). 1970. 25.00x (ISBN 0-8014-0525-4). Cornell U Pr.

Singer, Charles J. Greek Biology & Greek Medicine. LC 75-23760. Repr. of 1922 ed. 14.50 (ISBN 0-404-13366-5). AMS Pr.

Smith, Wesley D. The Hippocratic Tradition. LC 78-20977. (History of Science Ser.). 1979. 17.50x (ISBN 0-8014-1209-9). Cornell U Pr.

Taylor, Henry O. Greek Biology & Greek Medicine. LC 63-10282. (Our Debt to Greece & Rome Ser). Repr. of 1930 ed. 7.50x (ISBN 0-8154-0235-X). Cooper Sq.

MEDICINE, HINDU

Bhagavat Simhaji. A Short History of Aryan Medical Science. LC 75-23683. Repr. of 1896 ed. 23.00 (ISBN 0-404-13236-7). AMS Pr.

Chowry, Muthu D. The Antiquity of Hindu Medicine & Civilization. LC 77-91534. 1977. lib. bdg. 12.50 (ISBN 0-89341-507-3). Longwood Pr.

Dash, V. & Kashyap, L., eds. Materia Medica of Ayurveda. 1980. text ed. 38.00x (ISBN 0-391-01813-2). Humanities.

Girindranath Mukhopadhyaya. The Surgical Instruments of the Hindus, 2 vols. LC 75-23714. Repr. of 1914 ed. 47.50 set (ISBN 0-404-13340-1). AMS Pr.

Muthu, D. Chowry. The Antiquity of Hindu Medicine & Civilization. LC 73-165989. (Illus.). 112p. 1972. Repr. of 1931 ed. lib. bdg. 10.00 (ISBN 0-87821-041-5). Milford Hse.

Rationality, Theory, & Experimentation in Ayurvedic Medicine. 35p. 1980. pap. 5.00 (ISBN 92-808-0106-6, TUNU097, UNU). Unipub.

Thakkur, Chandrasekhar. Introduction to Ayurveda: The Science of Life. rev. ed. LC 74-75522. 1974. 7.95 (ISBN 0-88231-057-7). ASI Pubs Inc.

MEDICINE, INDUSTRIAL

see also Disability Evaluation; Industrial Health; Industrial Nursing; Industrial Ophthalmology; Labor and Laboring Classes–Medical Care; Occupational Diseases

Covalt, Donald A., ed. Rehabilitation in Industry: A Modern Monograph in Industrial Medicine. LC 58-10361. (Illus.). 166p. 1958. 27.00 (ISBN 0-8089-0104-4). Grune.

Egdahl, R. H. & Walsh, D. C., eds. Health Services & Health Hazards: The Employee's Need to Know. LC 78-18241. (Springer Ser. on Industry & Health Care: Vol. 4). (Illus.). 1978. pap. 13.90 (ISBN 0-387-90335-6). Springer-Verlag.
Gardner, A. Ward. Current Approaches to Occupational Medicine. (Illus.). 1979. 43.50 (ISBN 0-8151-9093-X). Year Bk Med.
International Labour Organization. Encyclopedia of Occupational Health, 2 vols. LC 74-39329. (Illus.). 1972. Set. 68.50 (ISBN 0-07-079555-X, P&RB). McGraw.
Shepard, William P. The Physician in Industry. Stein, Leon, ed. LC 77-70532. (Work Ser.). 1977. Repr. of 1961 ed. lib. bdg. 22.00x (ISBN 0-405-10200-3). Arno.
Shilling, Charles W. Radiation; Use & Control in Industrial Application. LC 59-14821. (Illus.). 232p. 1960. 26.00 (ISBN 0-8089-0425-6). Grune.
Slaney, Brenda, ed. Occupational Health Nursing. 177p. 1980. 22.00x (ISBN 0-85664-779-9, Pub. by Croom Helm Ltd England). Biblio Dist.
Tyrer, F. H. & Lee, K. A Synopsis of Occupational Medicine. 1979. pap. 18.50 (ISBN 0-8151-8903-6). Year Bk Med.
Waldron, H. A. Lecture Notes on Occupational Medicine. 2nd ed. (Blackwell Scientific Pubns.). (Illus.). 1979. softcover 14.75 (ISBN 0-632-00144-5). Mosby.
Zenz, Carl, ed. Developments in Occupational Medicine. (Illus.). 448p. 1980. 45.75 (ISBN 0-8151-9862-0). Year Bk Med.
--Occupational Medicine: Principles & Practical Applications. (Illus.). 944p. 1975. 68.95 (ISBN 0-8151-9864-7). Year Bk Med.

MEDICINE, INTERNAL
see Internal Medicine; Medicine–Practice

MEDICINE, LEGAL
see Medical Jurisprudence

MEDICINE, MAGIC, MYSTIC, AND SPAGIRIC
see also Aphrodisiacs; Folk Medicine
Albertus Magnus. The Boke of Secretes. LC 76-28227. (English Experience Ser: No. 116). 168p. 1969. Repr. of 1525 ed. 15.00 (ISBN 90-221-0116-9). Walter J Johnson.
Albertus Magnus, St. The Book of Secrets, of the Virtues of Herbs, Stones & Certain Beasts. Best, Michael R. & Brightman, Frank H., eds. (Studies in Tudor & Stuart Literature). 1973. 22.00x (ISBN 0-19-812502-X). Oxford U Pr.
Burnett, Mary W. Principles of Occult Healing. 135p. 1981. pap. 5.00 (ISBN 0-89540-072-3, SB-072). Sun Pub.
Calhoun, Mary. Medicine Show: Conning People & Making Them Like It. LC 75-25417. (Illus.). (gr. 5-8). 1976. PLB 9.89 (ISBN 0-06-020929-1, HarpJ); PLB 9.89 (ISBN 0-06-020930-5). Har-Row.
Coddington, Mary. In Search of the Healing Energy. (Warner Destiny Book). (Orig.). 1978. pap. 2.25 (ISBN 0-446-82575-1). Warner Bks.
Dawson, George G. Healing: Pagan & Christian. LC 75-23704. Repr. of 1935 ed. 26.50 (ISBN 0-404-13256-1). AMS Pr.
Esho, F. O. African (Yoruba) Case Studies in the Application of Metaphysical, Herbal, & Occult Therapies. (Traditional Healing Ser.: Vol. 4). (Illus.). Date not set. 22.50x (ISBN 0-932426-03-4); pap. text ed. 12.50x (ISBN 0-932426-07-7). Trado-Medic.
Evans-Pritchard, Edward E. Witchcraft, Oracles & Magic Among the Azande. 1937. 52.50x (ISBN 0-19-823103-2). Oxford U Pr.
Hohman, G. Pow-Wows. 1.95 (ISBN 0-685-22072-9). Wehman.
Jacob, Dorothy. Cures & Curses. (Illus.). 1966. 5.50 (ISBN 0-8008-2100-9). Taplinger.
Johnson, Obed S. A Study of Chinese Alchemy. LC 74-352. (Gold Ser.: Vol. 12). 156p. 1974. Repr. of 1928 ed. 10.00x (ISBN 0-405-05914-0). Arno.
Kiev, Ari, ed. Magic, Faith, & Healing: Studies in Primitive Psychiatry Today. LC 64-16960. 1974. pap. text ed. 6.95 (ISBN 0-02-917130-X). Free Pr.
Lambo, J. O. Catalogue of African Herbs. (Traditional Healing Ser.: Vol. 5). Date not set. 39.50 (ISBN 0-932426-04-2). Trado-Medic.
Lorusso, Julia & Glick, Joel. Healing Stoned: The Therapeutic Use of Gems & Minerals. 3rd ed. 1979. pap. 6.95 (ISBN 0-914732-05-6). Bro Life Bks.
McTeer, Ed. Fifty Years As a Low Country Witch Doctor. 1976. 6.95 (ISBN 0-685-71861-1). Beaufort.
Maple, Eric. The Ancient Art of Occult Healing. (Paths to Inner Power Ser.). 1974. pap. 1.25 (ISBN 0-87728-231-5). Weiser.
Middleton, John, ed. Magic, Witchcraft, & Curing. LC 75-44038. (Texas Press Sourcebooks in Anthropology: No. 7). 358p. 1976. pap. 7.95x (ISBN 0-292-75031-5). U of Tex Pr.
Powell, Eric F. The Natural Home Physician. LC 79-50415. Date not set. 8.95 (ISBN 0-448-16558-9); pap. 5.95 (ISBN 0-686-76823-X). G&D.
Propolis, the Eternal Natural Healer. 1981. 5.00 (ISBN 0-9600356-4-8). F Murat.
Rivers, William H. Medicine, Magic & Religion. LC 76-44784. Repr. of 1924 ed. 13.75 (ISBN 0-404-15967-2). AMS Pr.
Rodinson, Maxime. Magie, Medecine et Possession a Gondar. (Le Monde D'outre-Mer Passe & Present, Documents: No. 5). 1967. pap. 19.50x (ISBN 90-2796-189-1). Mouton.
Singer, Charles. From Magic to Science. 1960. 6.00 (ISBN 0-8446-2944-8). Peter Smith.
Sperber, Perry A. Drugs, Doctors, Demons & Disease. LC 70-111808. 1973. 15.50 (ISBN 0-87527-127-8). Green.
--Drugs, Doctors, Demons & Disease. LC 70-111808. 294p. 1973. 15.50 (ISBN 0-87527-127-8). Fireside Bks.
Thesen, Karen. Country Remedies. LC 78-24701. (Illus.). 1979. pap. 4.95 (ISBN 0-06-090687-1, CN687, CN). Har-Row.
Thomen, August A. Doctors Don't Believe It: Why Should You? 1941. 20.00 (ISBN 0-8274-4266-1). R West.
--Don't Believe It! Says the Doctor. 1935. 20.00 (ISBN 0-8274-4265-3). R West.
Thompson, C. J. Magic & Healing. LC 73-2850. (Illus.). 176p. 1973. Repr. of 1947 ed. 22.00 (ISBN 0-8103-3275-2). Gale.

MEDICINE, MEDIEVAL
see also Botany–Pre-Linnean Works; Herbs; Medicine, Anglo-Saxon; Medicine, Arabic
Albertus Magnus, St. The Book of Secrets, of the Virtues of Herbs, Stones & Certain Beasts. Best, Michael R. & Brightman, Frank H., eds. (Studies in Tudor & Stuart Literature). 1973. 22.00x (ISBN 0-19-812502-X). Oxford U Pr.
Campbell, Anna M. Black Death & Men of Learning. LC 31-29792. Repr. of 1931 ed. 18.50 (ISBN 0-404-01368-6). AMS Pr.
Campbell, Donald E. Arabian Medicine & Its Influence on the Middle Ages, 2 vols. LC 74-180330. Repr. of 1926 ed. Set. 30.00 (ISBN 0-404-56235-3). AMS Pr.
Cummins, Patricia W. A Critical Edition of Le Regime Tresutile et Tresproufitable Pour Conserver et Garder la Sante du Corps Humain. LC 76-25778. (North Carolina Studies in Romance Languages & Literatures: 177). 1976. 24.50 (ISBN 0-8357-0182-4, IS-00013, Pub. by U of North Carolina at Chapel Hill). Univ Microfilms.
Fort, George F. Medical Economy During the Middle Ages. LC 71-95625. Repr. of 1883 ed. 19.50x (ISBN 0-678-03758-2). Kelley.
Freeman, Margaret B. Herbs for the Mediaeval Household, for Cooking, Healing & Divers Uses. LC 43-18177. (Illus.). 1943. 4.95 (ISBN 0-87099-067-5, Pub. by Metro Mus Art). NYGS.
Henslow, George. Medical Works of the Fourteenth Century, Together with a List of Plants Recorded in Contemporary Writings, with Their Identifications. LC 72-82036. 278p. 1972. Repr. of 1899 ed. lib. bdg. 21.00 (ISBN 0-8337-1666-2). B Franklin.
Hughes, Muriel J. Women Healers in Medieval Life & Literature. facs. ed. LC 68-57322. (Essay Index Reprint Ser). 1943. 15.00 (ISBN 0-8369-0552-0). Arno.
Jacob, Dorothy. Cures & Curses. (Illus.). 1966. 5.50 (ISBN 0-8008-2100-9). Taplinger.
Kealey, Edward J. Medieval Medicus: A Social History of Anglo-Norman Medicine. LC 80-21870. (Illus.). 208p. 1981. text ed. 16.50x (ISBN 0-8018-2533-4). Johns Hopkins.
Miller, Elaine. Sources in Medieval Medicine: A Bibliography. 1981. lib. bdg. 20.00 (ISBN 0-8240-9527-8). Garland Pub.
Neaman, Judith S. Suggestion of the Devil. 1976. Repr. of 1975 ed. lib. bdg. 13.50 (ISBN 0-374-96038-0). Octagon.
Ratti, Oscar & Westbrook, Adele, trs. from Ital. The Medieval Health Handbook: Tacuinum Sanitatis. Arano, Luisa C. LC 75-21725. (Illus.). 156p. 1976. 30.00 (ISBN 0-8076-0808-4). Braziller.
Richards, Peter. The Medieval Leper: And His Northern Heirs. (Illus.). 178p. 1977. 18.50x (ISBN 0-87471-960-7). Rowman.
Rowland, Beryl. Medieval Woman's Guide to Health: The First English Gynecological Handbook. Rowland, Beryl, tr. Robbins, Rossell H. LC 80-82201. (Illus.). 194p. 1981. 17.50x (ISBN 0-87338-243-9). Kent St U Pr.
Spink, Martin S. & Lewis, Geoffrey, eds. Albucasis on Surgery & Instruments: A Definitive Edition of the Arabic Text, with English Translation & Commentary. LC 68-10498. (Welcome Institute of the History of Medicine & Near Eastern Center UCLA). (Illus.). 1973. 78.50x (ISBN 0-520-01532-0). U of Cal Pr.
Walsh, James J. Medieval Medicine. LC 75-23766. Repr. of 1920 ed. 19.00 (ISBN 0-404-13393-2). AMS Pr.

MEDICINE, MILITARY
see also Disability Evaluation; First Aid in Illness and Injury; Medicine, Naval; Surgery, Military; also subdivision Medical and sanitary affairs under the names of wars and campaigns, e.g. World War, 1939-1945–Medical and Sanitary Affairs
Ashburn, Percy M. A History of the Medical Department of the United States Army. LC 75-23675. Repr. of 1929 ed. 38.50 (ISBN 0-404-13228-6). AMS Pr.
Blanco, Richard L. Wellington's Surgeon General: Sir James McGrigor. LC 74-75477. xiv, 227p. 1974. 12.75 (ISBN 0-8223-0318-3). Duke.
Fishbein, Morris, ed. Doctors at War. LC 72-4477. (Essay Index Reprint Ser.). Repr. of 1945 ed. 36.00 (ISBN 0-8369-2943-8). Arno.
Futrell, Robert F. Development of Aeromedical Evacuation in the USAF, 1909-1960, Vol. 2. (USAF Historical Studies: No. 23). 1960. pap. 30.00x (ISBN 0-89126-051-X). MA-AH Pub.
Holland, Mary A. Our Army Nurses. LC 72-78752. 1895. Repr. 22.00 (ISBN 0-403-02043-3). Somerset Pub.
Maisel, Albert Q. Miracles of Military Medicine. facsimile ed. LC 70-167382. (Essay Index Reprint Ser). Repr. of 1943 ed. 21.00 (ISBN 0-8369-2561-0). Arno.
Medical Advisor's Handbook. (Illus.). 290p. 1977. pap. 6.00 (ISBN 0-87364-095-0). Paladin Ent.
Pottle, Frederick A. Stretchers: The Story of a Hospital Unit on the Western Front. 1929. 34.50x (ISBN 0-685-89785-0). Elliots Bks.
Richardson, Robert G. Larrey: Surgeon to Napoleon's Imperial Guard. (Illus.). 276p. 1975. 15.00 (ISBN 0-7195-3103-9). Transatlantic.
Steiner, Paul E. Physician-Generals in the Civil War: A Study in Nineteenth Mid-Century American Medicine. (Illus.). 216p. 1966. photocopy ed. spiral 21.50 (ISBN 0-398-01853-7). C C Thomas.
Sternberg, George M. Sanitary Lessons of the War & Other Papers. Rosenkrantz, Barbara G., ed. LC 76-40647. (Public Health in America Ser.). 1977. Repr. of 1912 ed. lib. bdg. 12.00x (ISBN 0-405-09832-4). Arno.
Tobey, James A. The Medical Department of the Army: Its History, Activities & Organization. LC 72-3061. (Brookings Institution. Institute for Government Research. Service Monographs of the U.S. Government: No. 45). Repr. of 1927 ed. 18.00 (ISBN 0-404-57145-X). AMS Pr.
U.S. Surgeon-General's Office. The Medical Department of the United States Army from 1775 to 1873. Brown, Harvey E., ed. LC 75-23763. Repr. of 1873 ed. 26.50 (ISBN 0-404-13369-X). AMS Pr.

MEDICINE, NAVAL
see also First Aid in Illness and Injury; Medicine, Military
Accident Prevention on Board Ship at Sea & in Port. 2nd ed. 1978. pap. 11.40 (ISBN 92-2-101837-7). Intl Labour Office.
Counter, R. T. The Yachtsman's Doctor. 148p. 1980. 27.00 (ISBN 0-245-53425-3, Pub. by Nautical England). State Mutual Bk.
Gordon, Maurice B. Naval & Maritime Medicine During the American Revolution. LC 76-52769. 1978. 17.50 (ISBN 0-685-78818-0, 911566-12). Ventnor.
International Medical Guide for Ships. (Illus.). 404p. (Eng, Fr, Rus, & Span.). 1967. 20.80 (ISBN 92-4-154018-4). World Health.
Roddis, Louis H. A Short History of Nautical Medicine. LC 75-23757. Repr. of 1941 ed. 30.50 (ISBN 0-404-13363-0). AMS Pr.
Wallett, Tim. Shark Attack & Treatment of Victims in Southern African Waters. 1980. 25.00x (ISBN 0-686-69986-6, Pub. by Bailey & Swinton South Africa). State Mutual Bk.

MEDICINE, OCCULT
see Medicine, Magic, Mystic, and Spagiric

MEDICINE, OCCUPATIONAL
see Medicine, Industrial

MEDICINE, ORTHOMOLECULAR
see Orthomolecular Medicine

MEDICINE, PASTORAL
see Pastoral Medicine

MEDICINE, POPULAR
see also Folk Medicine; Medicine–Dictionaries
About Your Medicines--Consumer Edition, 1981. 416p. 1981. pap. 4.50 (ISBN 0-686-30200-1). USPC.
Alfred, J. Tyrone & Cannon-Alfred, C. Medical Handbook for the Layman. 1969. 5.95 (ISBN 0-686-00411-6). Alfred.
Anthony, Richard. How to Perform Your Own Urinalysis Without a Doctor for Under Fifty Cents. (Illus.). pap. 10.00 (ISBN 0-916976-00-9). P I Industries.
Austin, Glenn. Parents' Medical Manual. LC 78-2759. (Illus.). 1978. 15.95 (ISBN 0-13-650317-9, Spec); pap. 8.95 (ISBN 0-13-650309-8). P-H.
Barnard, Christiaan & Illman, John, eds. The Body Machine. (Illus.). 1981. 19.95 (ISBN 0-517-54500-4). Crown.
Bennett, Hal & Samuels, Michael. The Well-Body Book. (YA) 1973. pap. 8.95 (ISBN 0-394-70969-1). Random.
Berland, Theodore & Spellberg, Mitchell A. Living with Your Ulcer. LC 77-145432. (Griffin Paperback Ser.). (Illus.). 1974. 5.95 (ISBN 0-312-49210-3, L63000); pap. 3.95 (ISBN 0-312-49245-6). St Martin.
Better Homes & Gardens Editors, ed. Better Homes & Gardens Family Medical Guide. rev. ed. (Illus.). 1084p. 1973. 24.95 (ISBN 0-696-00342-2). Meredith Corp.
Biviano, Ronald S. Medical Conditions & Terms Made Simple. LC 80-68397. 100p. (Orig.). 1981. pap. 10.00 (ISBN 0-9605476-0-6). Biviano.
Brown, Warren J., ed. Patients' Guide to Medicine: From the Drugstore Through the Hospital. 9th ed. 1981. pap. 7.95 (ISBN 0-912522-71-2). Aero-Medical.
Burney, Leroy E., et al, eds. Medical Aid Encyclopedia for the Home. (Illus.). 1964. 12.50 (ISBN 0-87396-003-3). Stravon.
Consumer Reports Editors. The Medicine Show. (YA) 1974. 8.50 (ISBN 0-394-49577-2); pap. 3.95 (ISBN 0-394-73032-1). Pantheon.
De Preaumont, Charles. La Medecine a portee de la main. (Collection que faire?). (Illus.). 1978. pap. 7.95x (ISBN 2-03-001201-7). Larousse.
Diagram Group. The Body Manual: A Complete Family Guide. LC 79-21673. (Illus.). 1980. 16.95 (ISBN 0-448-22214-0). Paddington.
Drummond, Hugh. Dr. Drummond's Spirited Guide to Health Care in a Dying Empire. LC 80-994. 352p. 1980. pap. 2.95 (ISBN 0-394-17674-X, BC44?, BC). Grove.
Eichenlaub, John E. A Minnesota Doctor's Home Remedies for Common & Uncommon Ailments. 3rd ed. LC 80-27588. 271p. 1981. 12.95 (ISBN 0-13-584532-7). P-H.
--A Minnesota Doctor's Home Remedies for Common & Uncommon Ailments. 1976. 9.95 (ISBN 0-13-584557-2, Reward); pap. 3.95 (ISBN 0-13-584490-8). P-H.
Eiseman, Ben. What Are My Chances? LC 79-67118. (Illus.). 1980. text ed. 14.95 (ISBN 0-7216-3344-7). Saunders.
Family Health: Care & Management at Home. 1976. 9.75 (ISBN 0-7207-0889-3). Transatlantic.
Fellman, Anita C. & Fellman, Michael. Making Sense of Self: Medical Advice Literature in Late Nineteenth-Century America. LC 81-51141. 224p. 1981. 16.50x (ISBN 0-8122-7810-0). U of Pa Pr.
Ferguson, L. Kracer & Kerr, John H. Explain It to Me, Doctor. LC 69-14856. 1971. 16.50 (ISBN 0-397-55951-8, JBL-Med-Nursing). Har-Row.
Ferguson, Tom. Medical Self-Care: Access to Health Tools. LC 80-14678. 320p. 1980. 19.95 (ISBN 0-671-40033-9); pap. 8.95 (ISBN 0-671-44816-1). Summit Bks.
Fishbein, Morris. Modern Home Medical Adviser: Your Health & How to Preserve It. LC 69-10978. 1969. 15.95 (ISBN 0-385-01095-8). Doubleday.
Fishbein, Morris & Fishbein, Justin, eds. New Illustrated Medical & Health Encyclopedia: International Unified Edition, 22 vols. 1981. 131.56 (ISBN 0-87475-200-0). Stuttman.
Foster, Daniel W. Modern Medicine: A Doctor Explains to the Layman. 1981. 11.95 (ISBN 0-671-24366-7). S&S.
Frank, Arthur & Frank, Stuart. The People's Handbook of Medical Care. LC 72-2718. 1972. 10.00 (ISBN 0-394-47925-4). Random.
Gardner, A. Ward. Good Housekeeping Dictionary of Symptoms. (Illus.). 1978. pap. 5.95 (ISBN 0-448-14731-9, Today Press). G&D.
Gerrick, David J. Medical Whodunits' (gr. 7 up). 1979. pap. text ed. 4.95 (ISBN 0-685-96976-2). Dayton Labs.
Gomez, Joan. A Dictionary of Symptoms. Gersh, Marvin, ed. LC 68-16039. 1977. pap. 5.95 (ISBN 0-8128-1949-7). Stein & Day.
Hackett, Earl. Blood. LC 72-88895. 1973. 9.95 (ISBN 0-8415-0215-3). Dutton.
Hawes, Richard. The Poore-Mans Plaster-Box. LC 74-80183. (No. 664). 44p. 1974. Repr. of 1634 ed. 5.00 (ISBN 90-221-0664-0). Walter J Johnson.
Ho, Betty Y. Scientific Guide to Peaceful Living. LC 77-142457. (Illus., Orig.). 1973. pap. 7.50 (ISBN 0-9600148-2-9). Juvenescent.
The Homesteaders Handbook of Rare Cures & Priceless Recipes. LC 79-15515. 8.95 (ISBN 0-912216-08-5). Angel Pr.
Jarvis, D. C. Folk Medicine: A Vermont Doctor's Guide to Good Health. LC 58-6454. 1958. 5.95 (ISBN 0-03-027410-9). HR&W.
John E. Fogarty International Center for Advanced Study in the Health Sciences, tr. from Chinese. The Barefoot Doctor's Manual: The American Translation of the Official Chinese Paramedical Manual. LC 77-364. (Illus.). 1977. lib. bdg. 12.90 (ISBN 0-914294-91-1); pap. 7.95 (ISBN 0-914294-92-X). Running Pr.

Johnson, T. C. Doctor! What You Should Know About Health Care Before You Call a Physician. 432p. 1975. 8.95 (ISBN 0-07-032664-9, GB). McGraw.

Katz, Robert S. Medical Tests You Can Do Yourself. LC 77-9522. (Illus.). 1978. pap. 5.95 (ISBN 0-8069-8502-X). Sterling.

Lipp, Martin R. The Bitter Pill: Doctors, Patients & Failed Expectations. LC 79-1673. 288p. 1980. 10.95 (ISBN 0-06-012649-3, HarpT). Har-Row.

Lust, Benedict. About Herbs: Nature's Medicine. 1980. pap. 1.95 (ISBN 0-87904-045-9). Lust.

Marchetti, Albert. Common Cures for Common Ailments. LC 77-16114. 1978. 10.95 (ISBN 0-8128-2317-6). Stein & Day.

Mellor, Constance. Natural Remedies for Common Ailments. 134p. 1980. 10.95 (ISBN 0-8464-1073-7). Beekman Pubs.

Mendelsohn, Robert S. Confessions of a Medical Heretic. 304p. 1980. pap. 3.25 (ISBN 0-446-36158-5). Warner Bks.

Miller, Benjamin & Galton, Lawrence. Complete Medical Guide. 4th rev. ed. 1978. 19.95 (ISBN 0-671-24107-9). S&S.

Miller, Jonathan. The Body in Question. (Illus.). 1979. 19.95 (ISBN 0-394-50280-9). Random.

Moody, Charles S. Backwoods Surgery & Medicine. 1974. Repr. of 1910 ed. pap. 9.50 (ISBN 0-8466-6034-2, SJU 34). Shorey.

Nichols, Thomas L. Esoteric Anthropology: The Mysteries of Man. LC 75-180585. (Medicine & Society in America Ser). (Illus.). 350p. 1972. Repr. of 1853 ed. 16.00x (ISBN 0-405-03962-X). Arno.

Noell, Anna M. Free Show Tonight: A/History of a Medicine Show Family of the Twenties and Thirties. Date not set. price not set (ISBN 0-9602422-3-6). Noells Ark.

Nourse, Alan E. The Ladies' Home Journal Family Medical Guide. LC 72-9099. (Illus.). 1088p. 1973. 25.00 (ISBN 0-06-013223-X, HarpT). Har-Row.

Oppenheim, Mike. Commonsense Health: A Doctor's Frank Prescriptions for Getting the Best Care for Less. 1981. 5.95 (ISBN 0-686-73457-2). Seaview Bks.

Plutarch. The Governaunce of Good Helthe, Erasmus Beynge Interpretoure. LC 68-54657. (English Experience Ser.: No. 16). 32p. 1968. Repr. of 1530 ed. 7.00 (ISBN 90-221-0016-2). Walter J Johnson.

Pomerantz, Virginia & Schultz, Dodi. Mothers & Fathers Medical Encyclopedia. rev. ed. (Illus.). 1978. pap. 2.50 (ISBN 0-451-07779-2, E7779, Sig). NAL.

Prevention Magazine Staff. Encyclopedia of Common Diseases. LC 75-35754. 1976. 19.95 (ISBN 0-87857-113-2); deluxe ed. 21.95 (ISBN 0-87857-150-7). Rodale Pr Inc.

Robinson, David & Henry, Stuart. Self-Help & Health: Mutual Aid for Modern Problems. 164p. 1977. 21.95x (ISBN 0-85520-167-3, Pub. by Martin Robertson England). Biblio Dist.

Rosenberg, M. M. Encyclopedia of Medical Self-Help: Medicine for the Millions. 1981. 24.95 (ISBN 0-87781-227-6); lib. bdg. 18.71 (ISBN 0-685-70332-0). Pubs Agency.

Rosenfeld, Isadore. The Complete Medical Exam. 1978. 11.95 (ISBN 0-671-22844-7). S&S.

Smith, Jeanne & Rossman, Isadore. Instant Medical Advisor. LC 77-137337. 1970. 3.95 (ISBN 0-911744-08-8). Career Inst.

Steincrohn, Peter J. Ask Dr. Steincrohn: What You Always Wanted to Ask Your Doctor & Didn't. 1979. 6.95 (ISBN 0-87491-298-9). Acropolis.

Taylor, Robert B. Dr. Taylor's Self-Help Medical Guide. 1977. 9.95 (ISBN 0-87000-370-4). Arlington Hse.

--Dr. Taylor's Self-Help Medical Guide. 1978. pap. 2.25 (ISBN 0-451-08124-2, E8124, Sig). NAL.

MEDICINE, PREVENTIVE

see also Bacteriology; Immunity; Medicine, State; Pathology; Public Health; Serumtherapy

Annual Conference for Psychosomatic Research, 20th, London, Nov. 15-16, 1976. The Psychosomatic Approach to Prevention of Disease: Proceedings. Carruthers, M. & Priest, R., eds. 1978. pap. text ed. 22.00 (ISBN 0-08-022253-6). Pergamon.

Arnold, Charles B., et al. Advances in Disease Prevention, Vol. I. 1981. text ed. price not set (ISBN 0-8261-2830-0); pap. text ed. price not set (ISBN 0-8261-2831-9). Springer Pub.

Bircher-Brenner, M. The Prevention of Incurable Disease. LC 78-61330. 1978. pap. 3.95 (ISBN 0-87983-186-3). Keats.

--The Prevention of Incurable Disease. LC 78-61330. 1978. pap. 3.95 (ISBN 0-87983-186-3). Keats.

Bommarito, James W. Preventive & Clinical Management of Troubled Children. 301p. 1977. pap. text ed. 11.25 (ISBN 0-8191-0180-X). U Pr of Amer.

Bruce, Nigel. Teamwork for Preventive Care, Vol. 1. LC 80-41095. (Social Policy Research Monographs). 241p. 1980. 55.00 (ISBN 0-471-27883-1, Pub. by Wiley-Interscience). Wiley.

Chang, Robert S. Preventive Health Care. 1981. lib. bdg. 28.00 (ISBN 0-8161-2165-6, Hall Medical). G K Hall.

Cheraskin, E. & Ringsdorf, W. M., Jr. Predictive Medicine. LC 77-73617. (Illus.). 1977. pap. 5.95 (ISBN 0-87983-150-2). Keats.

Clark, Duncan W. & Macmahon, Brian, eds. Preventive & Community Medicine. 2nd ed. 1981. pap. text ed. 24.95 (ISBN 0-316-14596-3). Little.

Clark, L. Roy & Locke, Sam. How to Survive Your Doctor's Care. Straubing, Harold E., ed. (Illus.). 80p. 1981. pap. 4.95 (ISBN 0-87786-005-X). Gold Penny.

Clark, Linda. Handbook of Natural Remedies. 9.95 (ISBN 0-686-29893-4); pap. 2.50 (ISBN 0-686-29894-2). Cancer Bk Hse.

Claveau, Paul. Medecine Preventive et Hygiene Publique. (Fr). 1966. pap. 12.00x (ISBN 2-7637-6318-9, Pub. by Laval). Intl Schol Bk Serv.

Coe, Rodney M. & Brehm, Henry P. Preventive Health Care for Adults: A Study of Medical Practice. 1972. 6.00 (ISBN 0-8084-0040-1); pap. 2.45 (ISBN 0-8084-0041-X, B59). Coll & U Pr.

Davies, J. B. Community Health, Preventive Medicine, & Social Services: Concise Medical Textbook. 4th ed. (Illus.). 1979. pap. text ed. 14.95 (ISBN 0-02-857560-1). Macmillan.

Diekelman, Nancy. Primary Health Care of the Well Adult. (Illus.). 1977. pap. text ed. 8.50 (ISBN 0-07-016879-2, HP). McGraw.

Donsbach, Kurt W. Preventive Organic Medicine. LC 76-2979. (Pivot Health Book). 1976. pap. 2.50 (ISBN 0-87983-122-7). Keats.

Editors of Prevention Magazine. The PREVENTION Guide to Surgery & Its Alternatives. 576p. 1980. 16.95 (ISBN 0-87857-304-6). Rodale Pr Inc.

Gegan, Robert A. I Rejected Bypass Surgery for a Better Life. (Illus.). 300p. (Orig.). 1981. pap. 6.95x (ISBN 0-686-30204-4). Consumer Info Pubns.

Germann, Donald R. Too Young to Die. LC 74-84337. 1974. 9.95 (ISBN 0-87863-081-3). Farnswth Pub.

Gray, J. A. Man Against Disease: Preventive Medicine. (Opus Ser.). 1979. text ed. 18.95x (ISBN 0-19-219140-3); pap. text ed. 10.95x (ISBN 0-19-289127-8). Oxford U Pr.

Harper, Harold W. & Culbert, Michael L. How You Can Beat the Killer Diseases. LC 77-10782. 1978. 9.95 (ISBN 0-87000-387-9). Arlington Hse.

The Healing Art of Clara Walter. 64p. (Orig.). 1981. pap. 2.95 (ISBN 0-932870-08-2). Alyson Pubns.

Howard, Joanice. Preventive Medicine. (Science & Technical Readers Ser.). (Orig.). 1981. pap. text ed. 2.95x (ISBN 0-435-29003-7). Heinemann Ed.

Isacson, Peter. Public Health & Preventive Medicine Continuing Education Review. 1980. pap. 15.00 (ISBN 0-87488-348-2). Med Exam.

Leavell, Hugh R., et al. Preventive Medicine for the Doctor in His Community: An Epidemiological Approach. LC 78-25872. 700p. 1979. Repr. of 1958 ed. lib. bdg. 24.50 (ISBN 0-88275-815-2). Krieger.

Lewy, Robert. Preventive Primary Medicine: Reducing the Major Causes of Mortality. 1980. pap. text ed. 9.95 (ISBN 0-316-52401-8). Little.

McCance. Preventing Aging. 1981. write for info. (ISBN 0-87527-223-1). Green.

McKeown, Thomas. The Role of Medicine: Dream, Mirage or Nemesis? LC 79-84025. 180p. 1980. 16.00x (ISBN 0-691-08235-9); pap. 5.95 (ISBN 0-691-02362-X). Princeton U Pr.

Madsen. Preventing Childhood Epilepsy. 280p. 1980. 21.50 (ISBN 0-87527-221-5). Green.

Mathur, J. S. Introduction to Social & Preventive Medicine. 500p. 1981. 30.00x (ISBN 0-686-72954-4, Pub. by Oxford & IBH India). State Mutual Bk.

Miller, Benjamin F. & Galton, Lawrence. The Family Book of Preventive Medicine. 9.95 (ISBN 0-685-54311-0, Pub by Weathervane). Formur Intl.

Moss, Abigail J. & Wilder, Mary H. Use of Selected Medical Procedures Assoc. with Preventive Care. Knox, Kathleen, ed. (Series 10: No. 110). 1976. pap. 1.75 (ISBN 0-8406-0078-X). Natl Ctr Health Stats.

Newsholme, Arthur. Evolution of Preventative Medicine. LC 75-23748. Repr. of 1927 ed. 19.50 (ISBN 0-404-13354-1). AMS Pr.

Nutrition & Food Preparation & Preventive Care & Maintenance. (Lifeworks Ser.). 1981. 4.96 (ISBN 0-07-037094-X). McGraw.

Papaioannou, A. N. The Prevention of Breast Cancer. 1981. write for info. (ISBN 0-87527-227-4). Green.

Penalver, Rafael A. Public Health & Preventative Medicine Review. LC 78-31347. 1979. pap. 10.00 (ISBN 0-668-04690-2). Arco.

Prenatal & Perinatal Immunohematology. 1981. write for info. (ISBN 0-914404-66-0). Am Assn Blood.

Racker, Efriam. Science & the Cure of Diseases: Letters to Members of Congress. LC 79-84012. 1979. 13.50x (ISBN 0-691-08243-X); pap. text ed. 6.50 (ISBN 0-691-02363-8). Princeton U Pr.

Rosen, George. Preventive Medicine in the United States, 1900-1975, Trends & Interpretations. LC 75-35978. (Illus.). 128p. 1976. lib. bdg. 15.00 (ISBN 0-88202-103-6, Sci Hist); pap. text ed. 6.95 (ISBN 0-685-63141-9). N Watson.

Schainblatt, Alfred H. Monitoring the Outcomes of State Chronic Disease Control Programs: Some Initial Suggestions. (An Institute Paper). 60p. 1977. pap. 4.00 (ISBN 0-87766-205-3, 19800). Urban Inst.

Schneiderman, Lawrence J. The Practice of Preventive Health Care. 1981. 29.95 (ISBN 0-201-07183-5, 170Y00, Med-Nurse). A-W.

Scopes, Nigel, ed. Pest & Disease Control Handbook. 250p. 1979. 35.00x (ISBN 0-901436-42-9, Pub. by Brit Crop Protection England). Intl Schol Bk Serv.

Sehnert, Keith W. & Eisenberg, Howard. How to Be Your Own Doctor - Sometimes. LC 74-18875. (Illus.). 416p. 1981. pap. 7.95 (ISBN 0-448-12027-5). G&D.

Smithurst, B. A. Fundamentals of Social & Preventative Medicine. (Illus.). 170p. 1976. 15.00x (ISBN 0-7022-0989-9); pap. 9.95x (ISBN 0-7022-0996-1). U of Queensland Pr.

Trowell, H. C. & Burkitt, D. P., eds. Western Diseases: Their Emergence & Prevention. LC 80-28917. (Illus.). 480p. 1981. text ed. 40.00 (ISBN 0-674-95020-8). Harvard U Pr.

Wain, Harry. A History of Preventive Medicine. 420p. 1970. text ed. 42.50 (ISBN 0-398-02000-0). C C Thomas.

Walczak, Michael & Ehrich, Benjamin B. Nutrition & Well-Being. LC 76-18447. 1977. 8.95 (ISBN 0-87881-054-4); pap. 6.50 (ISBN 0-87881-055-2). Mojave Bks.

West, Raymond O., ed. Public Health & Preventive Medicine. 6th ed. (Medical Examination Review Book Ser.: Vol .6). 1975. spiral bdg. 8.50 (ISBN 0-87488-106-4). Med Exam.

MEDICINE, PRIMITIVE

see also Folk Medicine; Indians of North America–Medicine; Medicine-Man; ; Medical Anthropology; Paleopathology

Ackerknecht, Erwin H. Medicine & Ethnology: Selected Essays. LC 79-154896. 1971. 16.50x (ISBN 0-8018-1307-7). Intl Pubns Serv.

Ciba Foundation. CIBA Foundation Symposium 49: Health & Disease in Tribal Societies. 1977. 34.75 (ISBN 0-444-15271-7, Excerpta Medica). Elsevier.

Devereux, George. A Study of Abortion in Primitive Societies. rev. ed. LC 75-10572. 390p. 1976. text ed. 22.50 (ISBN 0-8236-6245-4); pap. text ed. 5.95 (ISBN 0-8236-8311-7, 026245). Intl Univs Pr.

Field, Margaret J. Religion & Medicine of the Ga People. LC 76-44718. 1977. Repr. of 1937 ed. 27.50 (ISBN 0-404-15923-0). AMS Pr.

Hewat, Matthew L. Bantu Folk Lore. LC 77-129948. Repr. of 1906 ed. 10.00x (ISBN 0-8371-4992-4, Pub. by Negro U Pr). Greenwood.

Jayne, Walter A. The Healing Gods of Ancient Civilizations. LC 75-23728. Repr. of 1925 ed. 49.00 (ISBN 0-404-13286-3). AMS Pr.

MacDonald, Christina. Medicines of the Maori. LC 74-187827. (Illus.). 142p. 1973. 10.40x (ISBN 0-8002-0082-9). Intl Pubns Serv.

Maddox, John L. The Medicine Man: A Sociological Study of the Character & Evolution of Shamanism. LC 75-23737. Repr. of 1923 ed. 28.00 (ISBN 0-404-13294-4). AMS Pr.

Ngubane, Harriet. Body & Mind in Zulu Medicine: An Ethnography of Health & Disease in Nyuswa-Zulu Thought & Practice. (Studies in Anthropology Ser.). 1977. 27.50 (ISBN 0-12-518250-3). Acad Pr.

MEDICINE, PSYCHOSOMATIC

see also Enuresis; Iatrogenic Diseases; Pediatrics–Psychosomatic Aspects; Psychological Manifestations of General Disease; also subdivision Diseases–Psychosomatic Aspects under names of organs and regions of the body, e.g. Skin–Diseases–Psychosomatic Aspects

Alexander, Franz. Psychosomatic Medicine. 1965. 4.45 (ISBN 0-393-00300-0, NortonC). Norton.

Alexander, Franz, et al, eds. Psychosomatic Specificity: Experimental Study & Results, Vol. 1. LC 68-16711. 1968. 10.00x (ISBN 0-226-67356-1). U of Chicago Pr.

Ammon, Gunter. Psychoanalysis & Psychosomatics. Ray, Susan, tr. from Ger. LC 78-12589. 1979. pap. text ed. 16.95 (ISBN 0-8261-2301-5). Springer Pub.

Anderson, Robert A. Stress Power: How to Turn Tension into Energy. LC 78-8308. 225p. 1978. 14.95 (ISBN 0-87705-328-6); pap. 8.95 (ISBN 0-89885-093-2). Human Sci Pr.

Annual Conference for Psychosomatic Research, 20th, London, Nov. 15-16, 1976. The Psychosomatic Approach to Prevention of Disease: Proceedings. Carruthers, M. & Priest, R., eds. 1978. pap. text ed. 22.00 (ISBN 0-08-022253-6). Pergamon.

Association for Research in Nervous Mental Disease. Life Stress & Bodily Disease. 1968. 32.75 (ISBN 0-02-846360-9). Hafner.

Bakal, Donald A. Psychology & Medicine: Psychobiological Dimensions of Health & Illness. LC 78-23439. 1979. text ed. 19.95 (ISBN 0-8261-2580-8); pap. text ed. 11.50 (ISBN 0-8261-2581-6). Springer Pub.

Becker, Marshall H. The Health Belief Model & Personal Health Behavior. 1976. pap. 9.00x (ISBN 0-913590-34-7). C B Slack.

Bellak, Leopold. Psychology of Physical Illness. LC 52-14496. 256p. 1952. 31.25 (ISBN 0-8089-0045-5). Grune.

Birk, Lee, ed. Biofeedback: Behavioral Medicine. 210p. 1974. Repr. 29.50 (ISBN 0-8089-0832-4). Grune.

Christie, Margaret J. & Mellett, Peter. Foundations of Psychosomatics. 432p. 1981. 44.40 (ISBN 0-471-27855-6, Pub. by Wiley-Interscience). Wiley.

Ciba Foundation. Physiology, Emotion & Psychosomatic Illness. (Ciba Foundation Symposium: No. 8). 1973. 31.00 (ISBN 0-444-10402-X, Excerpta Medica). Elsevier.

Committee from the Editorial Board of Psychosomatic Medicine, ed. Psychosomatic Classics: Selected Papers from Psychosomatic Medicine, 1939-1958. 1972. pap. 21.25 (ISBN 3-8055-1232-5). S Karger.

Dunbar, Helen F. Emotions & Bodily Changes: A Survey of Literature on Psychosomatic Interrelationships, 1910-1953. 4th ed. LC 75-16699. (Classics in Psychiatry Ser.). 1976. Repr. of 1954 ed. 68.00x (ISBN 0-405-07426-3). Arno.

--Psychosomatic Diagnosis. (Psychology Ser). 1968. Repr. of 1948 ed. 38.50 (ISBN 0-384-13285-5). Johnson Repr.

Garner, H. H: Psychosomatic Management of the Patient with Malignancy. 144p. 1966. photocopy ed. spiral 14.50 (ISBN 0-398-00651-2). C C Thomas.

Grinker, Roy R. Psychosomatic Concepts. LC 73-8934. 224p. 1974. 20.00x (ISBN 0-87668-107-0). Aronson.

Hutschnecker, Arnold A. The Will to Live. 1966. pap. 4.95 (ISBN 0-346-12259-7). Cornerstone.

Ikemi, Y. & Ishikawa, H., eds. Psychosomatic Medicine: A Core Approach to Clinical Medicine. (Illus.). 1979. pap. 78.00 (ISBN 3-8055-3022-6). S Karger.

International Congress of Psychosomatic Medicine, 4th, Paris, Sept. 1970. Psychotherapeutic Action of the Physician: Proceedings, Vol. 21, Nos. 1-6. Chertok, L. & Sapir, M., eds. (Illus.). 1973. Repr. 51.50 (ISBN 3-8055-1482-4). S Karger.

Jacobson, Edmund. Modern Treatment of Tense Patients: Including the Neurotic & Depressed with Case Illustrations, Follow-Ups, & EMG Measurements. (Illus.). 484p. 1970. text ed. 45.50 photocopy ed. (ISBN 0-398-00910-4). C C Thomas.

Katz, Roger C. & Zlutnik, Steven, eds. Behavior Therapy & Health Care. LC 74-7331. 1975. 23.00 (ISBN 0-686-77052-8); pap. text ed. 14.50 (ISBN 0-08-017828-6). Pergamon.

Kimball, C. P. & Krakowski, A. J., eds. The Teaching of Psychosomatic Medicine & Consultation-Liason Psychiatry. (Bibliotheca Psychiatrica: No. 159). 1979. pap. 49.75 (ISBN 3-8055-2955-4). S Karger.

Kroger, William S. Psychosomatic Obstetrics, Gynecology & Endocrinology: Including Diseases of Metabolism. (American Lecture Gynecology & Obstetrics). (Illus.). 848p. 1962. photocopy ed. spiral 79.50 (ISBN 0-398-01052-8). C C Thomas.

Kurtsin, I. T. Theoretical Principles of Psychosomatic Medicine. Kaner, N., tr. from Rus. LC 75-5587. 257p. 1976. 59.95 (ISBN 0-470-51100-1). Halsted Pr.

Lachman, Sheldon J. Psychosomatic Disorders: A Behavioristic Interpretation. LC 78-37936. (Approaches to Behavior Pathology Ser.). 208p. 1972. pap. text ed. 11.95 (ISBN 0-471-51146-3). Wiley.

Lambert, Vickie A. & Lambert, Clinton E., Jr. The Impact of Physical Illness & Related Mental Health Concepts. (Illus.). 1979. pap. 13.95 ref. ed. (ISBN 0-13-451732-6). P-H.

Layden, Milton. Escaping the Hostility Trap: The One Sure Way to Deal with Impossible People. LC 76-54672. 1977. 7.95 (ISBN 0-13-283580-0). P-H.

Levi, Lennart. Society, Stress, & Disease: The Productive & Reproductive Age-Male-Female Roles & Relationships, Vol. 3. (Illus.). 1978. 67.50x (ISBN 0-19-261306-5). Oxford U Pr.

Linn, Louis, ed. Frontiers in General Hospital Psychiatry. LC 61-10147. 1961. text ed. 22.50 (ISBN 0-8236-2080-8); pap. text ed. 5.95 (ISBN 0-8236-8055-X, 022080). Intl Univs Pr.

Lipowski, Z, ed. Psychosocial Aspects of Physical Illness. (Advances in Psychosomatic Medicine: Vol. 8). 1972. 70.75 (ISBN 3-8055-1339-9). S Karger.

Lipowski, Z. J., et al, eds. Psychosomatic Medicine: Current Trends & Clinical Applications. (Illus.). 1977. text ed. 23.95x (ISBN 0-19-502169-X). Oxford U Pr.

Ludwig, Alfred O., et al. Psychosomatic Aspects of Gynecological Disorders: Seven Psychoanalytic Case Studies. LC 69-18039. (Commonwealth Fund Publications Ser). 1969. text ed. 7.95x (ISBN 0-674-72215-9). Harvard U Pr.

Nelson, James B. Rediscovering the Person in Medical Care: Patient, Family, Physician, Nurse, Chaplain, Pastor. LC 76-3858. (Orig.). 1976. pap. 4.95 (ISBN 0-8066-1534-6, 10-5450). Augsburg.

Peete, Don C. The Psychosomatic Genesis of Coronary Artery Disease. (Illus.). 240p. 1955. photocopy ed. spiral 24.00 (ISBN 0-398-01466-3). C C Thomas.

Pelletier, Kenneth. Mind As Healer Mind As Slayer. 1977. pap. 5.95 (ISBN 0-440-55592-2, Delta). Dell.

Pelletier, Kenneth R. Mind As Healer Mind As Slayer. 1977. 10.00 (ISBN 0-440-05591-1, Sey Lawr). Delacorte.

Pierloot, R. A., ed. Recent Research in Psychosomatics. (Psychotherapy & Psychosomatics: Vol. 18, No. 1-6). (Illus.). viii, 376p. 1970. Repr. 68.50 (ISBN 3-8055-1219-8). S Karger.

Rather, L. J. Mind & Body in Eighteenth Century Medicine: A Study Based on Jerome Gaub's De Regimine Mentis. (Wellcome Institute of the History of Medicine). 1965. 24.00x (ISBN 0-520-01049-3). U of Cal Pr.

Schindler, John. How to Live Three Hundred & Sixty Five Days a Year. 1954. pap. 3.95 (ISBN 0-13-416792-9, Parker). P-H.

Seguin, C. Alberto. Introduction to Psychosomatic Medicine. 1970. text ed. 20.00 (ISBN 0-8236-2760-8); pap. text ed. 5.95 (ISBN 0-8236-8090-8, 022760). Intl Univs Pr.

Shands, Harley C. Semiotic Approaches to Psychiatry. (Approaches to Semiotics Ser: No. 2). 1970. text ed. 52.50x (ISBN 90-2790-506-1). Mouton.

Simons, Richard C. & Pardes, Herbert. Understanding Human Behavior in Health & Illness. 2nd ed. (Illus.). 733p. 1981. 29.95 (ISBN 0-686-77743-3, 7740-6). Williams & Wilkins.

Smith, Nancy A. All I Need Is Love. LC 77-6036. (Orig.). 1977. pap. 2.75 (ISBN 0-87784-723-1). Inter-Varsity.

Snyder, Solomon H. Biological Aspects of Mental Disorder. 272p. 1980. 13.95x (ISBN 0-19-502715-9). Oxford U Pr.

Soubiran, Andre. Open Letter to a Woman of Today. Abbott, Elizabeth, tr. (Open Letter Ser). (Orig.). 1968. pap. 2.25 (ISBN 0-685-11969-6, 13). Heineman.

Steadman, Alice T. Who's the Matter with Me? (Illus.). 1977. pap. 4.95 (ISBN 0-87516-225-8). De Vorss.

Szurek, S. A. & Berlin, I. N., eds. Psychosomatic Disorders & Mental Retardation in Children. LC 67-26457. (Langley Porter Child Psychiatry Ser: Vol. 3). (Orig.). 1968. pap. 6.95x (ISBN 0-8314-0018-8). Sci & Behavior.

Trotter, Thomas. A View of the Nervous Temperment. LC 75-16735. (Classics in Psychiatry Ser.). 1976. Repr. of 1807 ed. 18.00x (ISBN 0-405-07456-5). Arno.

Usdin, Gene, ed. Psychiatric Medicine. LC 77-10139. 1977. 20.00 (ISBN 0-87630-151-0). Brunner-Mazel.

Whatmore, George B. & Kohli, Daniel R. The Physiopathology & Treatment of Functional Disorders. LC 74-17154. (Illus.). 258p. 1974. 30.25 (ISBN 0-8089-0851-0). Grune.

Wittkower, Eric D. & Warnes, Hector, eds. Psychosomatic Medicine: Its Clinical Applications. (Illus.). 1977. text ed. 21.50x (ISBN 0-06-142768-3, Harper Medical). Har-Row.

Wolf, Stewart & Goodell, Helen. Behavioral Science in Clinical Medicine. (Illus.). 256p. 1976. 19.75 (ISBN 0-398-03444-3). C C Thomas.

Wolters, W. H. & Sinnema, G., eds. Psychosomatics & Biofeedback. 1979. pap. 13.00 (ISBN 90-313-0348-8, Pub. by Martinus Nijhoff Netherlands). Kluwer Boston.

Youngs, David D. & Ehrhardt, Anke A. Psychosomatic Obstetrics & Gynecology. (Illus.). 306p. 1980. 19.50 (ISBN 0-8385-8041-6). ACC.

MEDICINE, PSYCHOSOMATIC-CASES, CLINICAL REPORTS, STATISTICS

Helen Vale Foundation. Is Your Sickness Real? Mind-Made Disease. Yogendra, Shrivi-Vijayadev, ed. 1978. 7.95 (ISBN 0-02-621400-8). Macmillan.

Reichsman, F., ed. Epidemiologic Studies in Psychosomatic Medicine. (Advances in Psychosomatic Medicine: Vol. 9). (Illus.). 1977. 34.25 (ISBN 3-8055-2654-7). S Karger.

Slote, Alfred. Termination: The Closing at Baker Plant. LC 69-13100. 360p. 1969. 11.50 (ISBN 0-87944-219-0). Inst Soc Res.

MEDICINE, ROMAN

see Medicine, Greek and Roman

MEDICINE, RURAL

see also Health, Rural

Browne, David D. The Wind & the Book: Memoirs of a Country Doctor. 1976. 16.50x (ISBN 0-522-84099-X, Pub. by Melbourne U Pr). Intl Schol Bk Serv.

Dekock, John B. Extending Family Practice Medical Services to 24 Hours in Rural Areas: Studies of a Demonstration Model. (Illus.). 1975. pap. 3.95 (ISBN 0-916552-05-5). Acoma Bks.

Nolan, Robert L. & Schwartz, Jerome L., eds. Rural & Appalachian Health. 272p. 1973. 16.75 (ISBN 0-398-02605-X). C C Thomas.

Wallack, Stanley S. & Kretz, Sandra E. Rural Medicine: Obstacles & Solutions for Self-Sufficiency. LC 79-48057. (The University Health Policy Consortium Ser.). (Illus.). 208p. 1981. 19.95x (ISBN 0-669-03691-9). Lexington Bks.

MEDICINE, SOCIAL

see Social Medicine

MEDICINE, STATE

see also Charities, Medical; Medical Jurisprudence; Medicine, Preventive; Public Health

Committee for Economic Development. Building a National Health-Care System. LC 73-75244. 105p. 1973. pap. 2.00 (ISBN 0-87186-049-X). Comm Econ Dev.

Falk, Isidore Sydney. Security Against Sickness. LC 79-38822. (FDR & the Era of the New Deal Ser). 424p. 1972. Repr. of 1936 ed. lib. bdg. 37.50 (ISBN 0-306-70447-1). Da Capo.

Heidenheimer, Arnold J. & Elvander, Nile, eds. The Shaping of the Swedish Health System. LC 80-12410. 256p. 1980. write for info. (ISBN 0-312-71627-3). St Martin.

Lynch, Matthew J. & Raphael, Stanley S. Medicine & the State. (Illus.). 480p. 1969. photocopy ed. spiral 47.75 (ISBN 0-686-71882-8). C C Thomas.

Reverby, Susan & Rosner, David, eds. Health Care in America: Essays in Social History. (Illus.). 1979. 15.00x (ISBN 0-87722-153-7); pap. 7.95x (ISBN 0-87722-171-5). Temple U Pr.

Rumsey, Henry W. Essays on State Medicine. Rosenkrantz, Barbara G., ed. LC 76-40641. (Public Health in America Ser.). 1977. Repr. of 1856 ed. lib. bdg. 24.00x (ISBN 0-405-09829-4). Arno.

Shapiro, Eileen C. & Lowenstein, Leah M. Becoming a Physician: Development of Values & Attitudes in Medicine. LC 79-10958. 1979. reference 22.50 (ISBN 0-88410-527-X). Ballinger Pub.

MEDICINE, STATE-GREAT BRITAIN

Cooper, Michael. Rationing Health Care. LC 74-32600. 150p. 1975. 21.95 (ISBN 0-470-17119-7). Halsted Pr.

Navarro, Vicente. Class Struggle, the State & Medicine: An Historical & Contemporary Analysis of the Medical Sector in Great Britain. 1978. lib. bdg. 16.95 (ISBN 0-88202-122-2). N Watson.

MEDICINE, STATE-RUSSIA

Hyde, Gordon. The Soviet Health Service: Historical & Comparative Study. 356p. 1974. 20.00x (ISBN 0-8464-0872-4); pap. 12.95x (ISBN 0-686-77084-6). Beekman Pubs.

Navarro, Vincente. Social Security & Medicine in the USSR: A Marxist Critique. LC 77-227. (Illus.). 1977. 17.95 (ISBN 0-669-01452-4). Lexington Bks.

Podolsky, Edward. Red Miracle. LC 70-167402. (Essay Index Reprint Ser.). 1947. 20.00 (ISBN 0-8369-2818-0). Arno.

MEDICINE, SUBMARINE

see Submarine Medicine

MEDICINE, TROPICAL

see Tropical Medicine

MEDICINE, VETERINARY

see Veterinary Medicine

MEDICINE AND ART

see also Anatomy, Artistic; Medical Illustration

Andrews, William. Doctor in History, Literature, Folklore. LC 74-99779. 1970. Repr. of 1896 ed. 22.00 (ISBN 0-8103-3595-6). Gale.

Coen, Rena N. Medicine in Art. LC 79-84408. (Fine Art Books). (Illus.). (gr. 5-11). 1970. PLB 4.95 (ISBN 0-8225-0166-X). Lerner Pubns.

Sigerist, Henry E. Civilization & Disease. 1962. pap. 3.95 (ISBN 0-226-75723-4, P511, Phoen). U of Chicago Pr.

Zigrosser, Carl. Medicine & the Artist. LC 69-17472. 1970. lib. bdg. 13.50 (ISBN 0-88307-291-2). Gannon.

--Medicine & the Artist. (Illus.). 1970. pap. 5.50 (ISBN 0-486-22133-4). Dover.

MEDICINE AND CHRISTIANITY

see Medicine and Religion

MEDICINE AND PSYCHOLOGY

see also Medicine, Psychosomatic; Psychiatry

Bakal, Donald A. Psychology & Medicine: Psychobiological Dimensions of Health & Illness. LC 78-23439. 1979. text ed. 19.95 (ISBN 0-8261-2580-8); pap. text ed. 11.50 (ISBN 0-8261-2581-6). Springer Pub.

Bergsma, Jurrit & Thomasma, David. Health Care: Its Psychosocial Dimensions. Orig. Title: The Other Side of Medicine. (Illus.). 225p. 1981. text ed. 15.50 (ISBN 0-391-01630-X). Duquesne.

Broskowski, Anthony, et al, eds. Linking Health & Mental Health: Coordinating Care in the Community. LC 81-8875. (Sage Annual Reviews of Community Mental Health: Vol. 5). 320p. 1981. 22.50 (ISBN 0-8039-1600-0). Sage.

Cassell, Eric J. The Healer's Art: A New Approach to the Doctor-Patient Relationship. 1976. 8.95 (ISBN 0-397-01098-2, JBL-Med-Nursing). Har-Row.

Collins, Mattie. Communication in Health Care: Understanding & Implementing Effective Human Relationships. LC 76-30551. (Illus.). 1977. pap. text ed. 10.00 (ISBN 0-8016-1021-4). Mosby.

Lambert, Vickie A. & Lambert, Clinton E., Jr. The Impact of Physical Illness & Related Mental Health Concepts. (Illus.). 1979. pap. 13.95 ref. ed. (ISBN 0-13-451732-6). P-H.

Mayerson, Evelyn W. Putting the Ill at Ease. (Illus.). 1976. pap. 16.00 (ISBN 0-06-141710-6, Harper Medical). Har-Row.

Mowbray, R. M., et al. Psychology in Relation to Medicine. 5th ed. (Illus.). 1979. pap. 14.50 (ISBN 0-443-01773-5). Churchill.

Noble, Daniel. Elements of Psychological Medicine. LC 78-72815. (Brainedness, Handedness, & Mental Abilities Ser.). Repr. of 1855 ed. 32.50 (ISBN 0-404-60885-X). AMS Pr.

Oyle, Irving. The Healing Mind. LC 74-10069. (Illus.). 128p. 1974. pap. 5.95 (ISBN 0-912310-80-4). Celestial Arts.

Sierles, Frederick. Clinical Behavioral Science. 1981. text ed. write for info. (ISBN 0-89335-131-8). Spectrum Pub.

Stone, George C., et al. Health Psychology-A Handbook: Theories, Applications, & Challenges of a Psychological Approach to the Health Care System. LC 79-83580. (Social & Behavioral Science Ser.). 1979. 29.95x (ISBN 0-87589-411-9). Jossey-Bass.

Williams, Redford B., ed. Behavioral Approaches to Medical Treatment. Gentry, W. Doyle. LC 76-30327. 1977. 18.50 (ISBN 0-88410-136-3). Ballinger Pub.

Wolf, Stewart & Goodell, Helen. Behavioral Science in Clinical Medicine. (Illus.). 256p. 1976. 19.75 (ISBN 0-398-03444-3). C C Thomas.

MEDICINE AND RELIGION

see also Christian Science; Faith-Cure; Hallucinogenic Drugs and Religious Experience; Mental Healing; Pastoral Medicine; Psychiatry and Religion

Barton, Richard T. Religious Doctrine & Medical Practice. 106p. 1958. ed. spiral bdg. 9.75photocopy (ISBN 0-398-00100-6). C C Thomas.

Belgum, David, ed. Religion & Medicine. facs. ed. 1967. pap. 11.25x (ISBN 0-8138-2290-4). Iowa St U Pr.

Bennett, George. The Heart of Healing. LC 72-5838. 128p. 1973. pap. 2.50 (ISBN 0-8170-0574-9). Judson.

Brand, Paul & Yancey, Philip. Fearfully & Wonderfully Made. (Illus.). 224p. 1980. 9.95 (ISBN 0-310-35450-1). Zondervan.

Brena, Steven. Pain & Religion: A Psychophysiological Study. (Illus.). 176p. 1972. 14.75 (ISBN 0-398-02242-9). C C Thomas.

Byron, Ralph L. & Lockerbie, Jeanette. Surgeon of Hope. 1977. 6.95 (ISBN 0-8007-0837-7). Revell.

Dawson, George G. Healing: Pagan & Christian. LC 75-23704. Repr. of 1935 ed. 26.50 (ISBN 0-404-13256-1). AMS Pr.

Dowling, Michael J. Health Care & the Church. Koenig, Robert E., ed. LC 77-1242. (Doing the Word Resource Ser.). (Orig.). 1977. pap. text ed. 3.95 (ISBN 0-8298-0333-5). Pilgrim NY.

Fichter, Joseph H. Religion & Pain: The Spiritual Dimensions of Health Care. 128p. 1981. 9.95 (ISBN 0-8245-0102-0). Crossroad NY.

Hamilton, Michael P. & Reid, Helen F. A Hospice Handbook. (Orig.). 1980. pap. 4.95 (ISBN 0-8028-1820-X). Eerdmans.

Hefley, Jim. Life in the Balance. 1980. pap. 3.95 (ISBN 0-88207-797-X). Victor Bks.

Heyer, Robert, ed. Medical-Moral Problems. LC 77-83556. 1977. pap. 2.45 (ISBN 0-8091-2058-5). Paulist Pr.

Koop, C. Everett. The Right to Live: the Right to Die. 1976. pap. 2.95 (ISBN 0-8423-5593-6). Tyndale.

MacFarlane, Gwyn. Howard Florey: The Making of a Great Scientist. (Illus.). 1979. 18.95x (ISBN 0-19-858161-0). Oxford U Pr.

McMillen, S. I. None of These Diseases. 1963. 7.95 (ISBN 0-8007-0231-X); pap. 2.50 (ISBN 0-8007-8030-2, Spire Bks). Revell.

Miller, Jonas E. Prescription for Total Health & Longevity. 1979. 2.95 (ISBN 0-88270-353-6). Logos.

O'Donnell, Thomas J. Medicine & Christian Morality. LC 75-41471. 1976. 7.95 (ISBN 0-8189-0323-6). Alba.

Parker, Paul E. & Enlow, David R. What's a Nice Person Like You Doing Sick? LC 74-82838. (Illus.). 80p. 1974. pap. 1.50 (ISBN 0-88419-082-X). Creation Hse.

Pink, Arthur W. Divine Healing. pap. 0.75 (ISBN 0-685-00742-1). Reiner.

Religious Aspects of Medical Care: A Handbook of Religious Practices of All Faiths. 2nd ed. LC 78-21467. 1978. pap. 7.00 (ISBN 0-87125-047-0). Cath Health.

Rosenbaum, Ernest H., et al. Rehabilitation Exercises for the Cancer Patient. (Illus., Orig.). 1979. pap. 4.95 (ISBN 0-915950-37-5). Bull Pub.

--Sexuality & Cancer. (Orig.). 1980. pap. 2.95 (ISBN 0-915950-39-1). Bull Pub.

Rosner, F. Medicine in the Bible & the Talmud: Selections from Classical Jewish Sources. (Library of Jewish Law & Ethics: Vol. 5). 15.00x (ISBN 0-87068-326-8). Ktav.

Sayers, William T. Body, Soul & Blood: Recovering the Human in Medicine. LC 79-56194. 112p. 1980. pap. 4.95 (ISBN 0-935718-00-1). Asclepiad.

Shriver, Donald W., Jr., ed. Medicine & Religion: Strategies of Care. LC 79-23420. (Contemporary Community Health Ser.). 1980. pap. 10.95 (ISBN 0-8229-3412-4). U of Pittsburgh Pr.

Smith, C. Raimer. Physician Examines the Bible. 4.25 (ISBN 0-8022-1593-9). Philos Lib.

Thielicke, Helmut. The Doctor as Judge of Who Shall Live & Who Shall Die. Cooperrider, Edward A., tr. from Ger. LC 75-42836. 48p. (Orig.). 1976. pap. 1.00 (ISBN 0-8006-1228-0, 1-1228). Fortress.

Wilkinson, John. Health & Healing: Studies in New Testament Principles. 220p. 1980. 15.00x (ISBN 0-905312-08-2, Pub. by Scottish Academic Pr Scotland). Columbia U Pr.

MEDICINE AND SPORTS

see Sports Medicine

MEDICINE IN ART

see Medicine and Art

MEDICINE IN LITERATURE

see also Physicians in Literature

Maurois, Andre, et al. Endocrinologie et Litterature: Textes des Exposes Inaugureaux du Cours de Perfectionnement d'Endocrinologie (17 Juin 1949, 24 Juin 1957, 28 Juin 1965) 55p. 1972. 15.95 (ISBN 0-686-55491-4). French & Eur.

Sergeant, Howard. Poems from the Medical World. 192p. 1980. 19.95 (ISBN 0-85200-289-0). Wright-PSG.

Trautman, Joanne, ed. Healing Arts in Dialogue: Medicine & Literature. (Medical Humanities Ser.). 232p. 1981. price not set (ISBN 0-8093-1028-7). S Ill U Pr.

MEDICINE-MAN

see also Shamanism

Bourke, John G. The Medicine Men of the Apache. LC 71-175003. (Illus.). 150p. 12.00 (ISBN 0-87026-049-9). Westernlore.

Corlett, William T. The Medicine-Man of the American Indian & His Cultural Background. LC 75-23699. Repr. of 1935 ed. 33.50 (ISBN 0-404-13249-9). AMS Pr.

--Medicine Man of the Early American Indian & His Cultural Background. (Illus.). 369p. 1935. photocopy spiral ed. 34.50 (ISBN 0-398-04233-0). C C Thomas.

John Lame Deer & Erdoes, Richard. Lame Deer Seeker of Visions: The Life of a Sioux Medicine Man. 1976. pap. 3.50 (ISBN 0-685-62001-8, 80391). WSP.

Mails, Thomas E. Fool's Crow. 1980. pap. 3.50 (ISBN 0-380-52175-X, 52175, Discus). Avon.

MEDICINES, PATENT, PROPRIETARY, ETC.

Adams, Samuel H. The Great American Medicine Fraud: A Series of Articles on the Patent Medicine Evil. 1976. Repr. of 1905 ed. 25.00 (ISBN 0-403-05771-X, Regency). Scholarly.

Cook, James. Remedies & Rackets: The Truth About Patent Medicines Today. LC 75-39284. (Getting & Spending: the Consumer's Dilemma). 1976. Repr. of 1958 ed. 15.00x (ISBN 0-405-08059-X). Arno.

Critser, James R., Jr. Clinical Assays. (Ser. 10CA-79). 122p. 1980. 80.00 (ISBN 0-914428-65-9). Lexington Data.

Graedon, Joe. The People's Pharmacy. 1977. pap. 5.95 (ISBN 0-380-00902-1, 76299). Avon.

Kallet, Arthur & Schlink, F. J. One Hundred Million Guinea Pigs: Dangers in Everyday Foods, Drugs, & Cosmetics. LC 75-39252. (Getting & Spending: the Consumer's Dilemma). 1976. Repr. of 1933 ed. 18.00x (ISBN 0-405-08025-5). Arno.

McNamara, Brooks. Step Right up. LC 73-20522. 256p. 1976. 6.95 (ISBN 0-385-02959-4). Doubleday.

Patent Medicine. (Americana Books Ser.). (Illus.). 1973. 1.50 (ISBN 0-911410-34-1). Applied Arts.

Proprietary Drugs. (BTA Studies). 200p. 1980. 450.00 (ISBN 0-686-31556-1). Busn Trend.

Washburn, Robert C. The Life & Times of Lydia E. Pinkham. LC 75-39280. (Getting & Spending: the Consumer's Dilemma). (Illus.). 1976. Repr. of 1931 ed. 16.00x (ISBN 0-405-08055-7). Arno.

Young, James H. The Toadstool Millionaires: A Social History of Patent Medicines in America Before Federal Regulations. (Illus.). 312p. 1972. 20.00x (ISBN 0-691-04568-2); pap. 8.50 (ISBN 0-691-00577-X, 272). Princeton U Pr.

MEDICINES, PHYSIOLOGICAL EFFECT OF
see Pharmacology

MEDICOLEGAE HEMATOLOGY
see Forensic Hematology

MEDIEVAL ARCHAEOLOGY
see Archaeology, Medieval

MEDIEVAL ARCHITECTURE
see Architecture, Medieval

MEDIEVAL ART
see Art, Medieval

MEDIEVAL CIVILIZATION
see Civilization, Medieval

MEDIEVAL EDUCATION
see Education, Medieval

MEDIEVAL HISTORY
see Middle Ages–History

MEDIEVAL LITERATURE
see Literature, Medieval

MEDIEVAL PAINTING
see Painting, Medieval

MEDIEVAL PAINTINGS
see Paintings, Medieval

MEDIEVAL PHILOSOPHY
see Philosophy, Medieval

MEDIEVAL POETRY
see Poetry, Medieval

MEDIEVAL SCULPTURE
see Sculpture, Medieval

MEDIEVAL SECTS
see Sects, Medieval

MEDINET-ABU

Edgerton, William F., ed. Medinet Habu Graffiti. LC 42-23005. (Oriental Institute Pubns. Ser: No. 36). (Illus.). 1937. 40.00x (ISBN 0-226-62133-2). U of Chicago Pr.

Hughes, George R. Medinet Habu - Epigraphic Survey: The Temple Proper, Part Three, the Third Hypostyle Hall, All Rooms Accessible from It, with Friezes of Scenes from the Roof Terraces & Exterior Walls of the Temple. LC 30-22847. (Oriental Institute Pubns. Ser). 1964. 65.00x (ISBN 0-226-62196-0, OIP93). U of Chicago Pr.

--Medinet Habu - Epigraphic Survey: The Temple Proper, Part Two, the Re Chapel, the Mortuary Complex, & Adjacent Rooms with Miscellaneous Material from Pylons, the Forecourts & the First Hypostyle Hall, Vol. 6. LC 30-22847. (Oriental Institute Pubns. Ser). 1963. 65.00x (ISBN 0-226-62185-5, OIP84). U of Chicago Pr.

Iobst, F. Murray & Muehleisen, John. Do You? (Illus.). write for info. LJB Found.

Nelson, Harold H. Medinet Habu - Epigraphic Survey: The Calendar, the Slaughterhouse, & Minor Records of Ramses III, Vol. 3. LC 30-6904. (Oriental Institute Pubns. Ser: No. 23). 1934. 70.00x (ISBN 0-226-62119-7, OIP23). U of Chicago Pr.

Nelson, Harold H. & Holscher, Uvo. Medinet Habu, Nineteen Twenty Four-Twenty Eight. LC 29-13423. (Illus.). 1929. pap. 5.00x (ISBN 0-226-62320-3, OIC5). U of Chicago Pr.

--Work in Western Thebes: Nineteen Thirty-One to Thirty-Three. LC 35-6021. (Illus.). 1934. pap. 8.00x (ISBN 0-226-62334-3, OIC18). U of Chicago Pr.

MEDITATION

Here are entered works on meditation or mental prayer as a method of promoting the spiritual life. Works that contain collections of meditations are entered under the heading Meditations.
see also Contemplation; Retreats; Transcendental Meditation

Addington, Jack & Addington, Cornelia. The Joy of Meditation. LC 78-75078. 1979. pap. 3.95 (ISBN 0-87516-292-4). De Vorss.

Ajaya, Swami. Yoga Psychology: A Practical Guide to Meditation. rev. ed. LC 76-374539. 1978. pap. 3.95 (ISBN 0-89389-052-9). Himalayan Intl Inst.

Ajaya, Swami, ed. Meditational Therapy. (Orig.). 1977. pap. 2.95 (ISBN 0-89389-032-4). Himalayan Intl Inst.

Akins, W. R. & Nurnberg, H. George. How to Meditate Without Attending a TM Class. 136p. 1976. 6.95 (ISBN 0-517-52636-0). Crown.

Alberione, James. Mystical Union with God Through the Degrees of Prayer. 1978. pap. 1.50 (ISBN 0-8198-0379-0). Dghtrs St Paul.

Alcantara, S. Peter. A Golden Treatise of Mental Prayer. Hollings, G. S., ed. 1978. 2.95 (ISBN 0-8199-0690-5). Franciscan Herald.

Aldan, Daisy. Foundation Stone Meditation by Rudolf Steiner. 1981. pap. 1.75 (ISBN 0-916786-53-6). St George Bk Serv.

Alexander, Frank J. In the Hours of Meditation. pap. 1.75 (ISBN 0-87481-162-7). Vedanta Pr.

Alibrandi, Tom. The Meditation Handbook. LC 75-36083. 176p. (Orig.). 1976. pap. 1.25 (ISBN 0-89041-072-0, 3072). Major Bks.

Allen, Marcus, et al. Reunion: Tools for Transformation. rev. ed. LC 80-19554. (Illus.). 95p. 1978. pap. 4.95 (ISBN 0-931432-01-4). Whatever Pub.

Arya, Pandit U. Superconcious Meditation. 2nd ed. LC 74-187862. 1977. pap. 3.50 (ISBN 0-89389-035-9). Himalayan Intl Inst.

Aveling, Harry, tr. Arjuna in Meditation. 1976. 14.00 (ISBN 0-89253-799-X); flexible cloth 8.00 (ISBN 0-89253-800-7). Ind-US Inc.

Bailey, Alice A. From Intellect to Intuition. 1972. 7.50 (ISBN 0-85330-008-9); pap. 4.25 (ISBN 0-85330-108-5). Lucis.

Ballentine, R. M., ed. Theory & Practice of Meditation. (Orig.). 1976. pap. 1.95 (ISBN 0-89389-017-0). Himalayan Intl Inst.

Besnard, A. M. Your Name Is Written in Heaven. 3.95 (ISBN 0-87193-093-5). Dimension Bks.

Blofeld, John. Gateway to Wisdom: Taoist & Buddhist Contemplative & Healing Yogas Adapted for Western Students of the Way. LC 79-67685. (Illus.). 1980. pap. 6.95 (ISBN 0-394-73878-0). Shambhala Pubns.

Boylan, Dom E. Difficulties in Mental Prayer. 144p. 1966. pap. 2.95 (ISBN 0-8091-1542-5). Paulist Pr.

Budhananda, Swami. The Mind & Its Control. 119p. (Orig.). 1972. pap. 1.00 (ISBN 0-87481-128-7). Vedanta Pr.

Carrington, Patricia. Freedom in Meditation. LC 76-6240. 1978. pap. 3.50 (ISBN 0-385-12407-4, Anch). Doubleday.

Cassianus, Joannes. Spiritual Life, a Guide for Those Seeking Perfection. 1977. pap. 3.95 (ISBN 0-686-19234-6). Eastern Orthodox.

Chang, Stephen T. & Miller, Richard C. The Book of Internal Exercises. LC 78-18320. (Illus., Orig.). 1978. pap. 6.95 (ISBN 0-89407-017-7). Strawberry Hill.

Chaudhuri, Haridas. Philosophy of Meditation. 2nd ed. 88p. 1974. pap. 3.50 (ISBN 0-89744-994-0, Pub. by Cultural Integration). Auromere.

Chinmoy, Sri. Meditation: Man-Perfection in God-Satisfaction. (Illus.). 1979. pap. 4.95 (ISBN 0-88497-444-8). Aum Pubns.

Clowney, Edmund P. Christian Meditation. 1979. pap. 2.50 (ISBN 0-934532-06-0). Presby & Reformed.

Cohen, Daniel. Meditation: What It Can Do for You. LC 77-6499. (Illus.). (gr. 7 up). 1977. 5.95 (ISBN 0-396-07471-5). Dodd.

Conze, Edward. Buddhist Meditation. (Unwin Bks.). 190p. 1972. pap. 5.50 (ISBN 0-04-294073-7). Allen Unwin.

Cooke, Grace. Meditation. 1955. 6.50 (ISBN 0-85487-011-3). De Vorss.

Dass, Ram. Journey of Awakening: A Meditor's Guidebook. 1978. pap. 3.50 (ISBN 0-553-14782-X). Bantam.

Daughters of St Paul. Moments of Decision. 1976. 5.00 (ISBN 0-8198-0445-2); pap. 4.00 (ISBN 0-8198-0446-0). Dghtrs St Paul.

Davis, Roy E. An Easy Guide to Meditation. 1978. 3.95x (ISBN 0-87707-208-6). CSA Pr.

DeGroat, Florence. Universal Man. LC 80-69413. 117p. 1981. pap. 5.50 (ISBN 0-87516-428-5). De Vorss.

Devas, Dominic. Treatise on Prayer & Meditation. Repr. of 1926 ed. lib. bdg. 25.00 (ISBN 0-8495-1026-0). Arden Lib.

Dhiravamsa. The Way of Non-Attachment: The Practice of Insight Meditation. LC 76-48761. 1977. 6.95 (ISBN 0-8052-3644-9). Schocken.

Downing, Jim. Meditation: The Bible Tells You How. LC 76-24064. 1976. pap. 2.50 (ISBN 0-89109-422-9, 14225). NavPress.

Eastcott, Michal J. I: The Story of the Self. LC 80-51552. (Illus.). 201p. (Orig.). 1980. pap. 5.50 (ISBN 0-8356-0541-8, Quest). Theos Pub Hse.

Easwaran, Eknath. Instrucciones En la Meditacion. 1980. pap. 1.00 (ISBN 0-915132-23-0). Nilgiri Pr.

--Instructions in Meditation. 1972. pap. 1.00 (ISBN 0-915132-09-5). Nilgiri Pr.

--Meditation: Commonsense Directions for an Uncommon Life. LC 78-10935. 1978. pap. 5.00 (ISBN 0-915132-16-8). Nilgiri Pr.

Edwards, F. Henry. Meditation & Prayer. LC 79-23708. 1980. pap. 9.75 (ISBN 0-8309-0271-6). Herald Hse.

Emmons, Michael L. The Inner Source: A Guide to Meditative Therapy. LC 78-466. 1978. 10.95 (ISBN 0-915166-47-X); pap. 6.95 (ISBN 0-915166-48-8). Impact Pubs Cal.

Enzler, Clarence. In the Presence of God. pap. 4.95 (ISBN 0-87193-055-2). Dimension Bks.

Fuller, Clifford. Thoughts While Meditating. pap. 1.00 (ISBN 0-87516-197-9). De Vorss.

Fuller, Joy. The Glorious Presence. LC 81-65753. 168p. (Orig.). 1981. pap. 7.25 (ISBN 0-87516-449-8). De Vorss.

Gangulee, N. & Eliot, T. S. Thoughts for Meditation: A Way to Recovery from Within. 59.95 (ISBN 0-8490-1208-2). Gordon Pr.

Gardner, Adelaide. Meditation: A Practical Study. LC 68-5856. 1968. pap. 2.95 (ISBN 0-8356-0105-6, Quest). Theos Pub Hse.

Gawain, Shakti. Creative Visualization. LC 79-13760. (Illus.). 158p. 1978. pap. 5.95 (ISBN 0-931432-02-2). Whatever Pub.

Gidlow, Elsa. Makings for Meditation. (Illus.). 1973. 2.00 (ISBN 0-9606568-0-4). Druid Heights.

Goldstein, Joseph. The Experience of Insight, a Natural Unfolding. LC 75-20304. (Mindful Ser.). 1976. pap. 5.95 (ISBN 0-913300-05-5). Unity Pr.

Goleman, Daniel. The Varieties of the Meditative Experience. LC 76-46306. 1977. pap. 4.50 (ISBN 0-525-47448-X). Dutton.

--Varieties of the Meditative Experience. LC 78-539. (Irvington Social Relations Ser.). 1978. 12.50 (ISBN 0-470-99191-7). Halsted Pr.

Govinda, Lama A. Creative Meditation & Multi-Dimensional Consciousness. LC 75-31616. (Illus.). 288p. (Orig.). 1976. 11.00x (ISBN 0-8356-0475-6, Quest); pap. 6.50 (ISBN 0-8356-0472-1, Guest). Theos Pub Hse.

Grammer, Grethe. Psychic Meditation. (Illus.). 1976. pap. 7.00 (ISBN 0-89351-008-4). Western Her Texas.

Green, Richard J. Meditation, The Highway to Happiness. 3rd ed. 40p. 1980. pap. 2.00 (ISBN 0-87516-407-2). De Vorss.

Griffiths, Bede. Return to the Center. 1976. 8.95 (ISBN 0-87243-064-2). Templegate.

Haddon, David & Hamilton, Vail. TM Wants You. (Direction Bks). 160p. 1976. pap. 1.95 (ISBN 0-8010-4151-1). Baker Bk.

Hanson, Virginia, ed. Approaches to Meditation. 160p. (Orig.). 1973. pap. 2.50 (ISBN 0-8356-0436-5, Quest). Theos Pub Hse.

Helleberg, Marilyn. Beyond T.M. A Practical Guide to the Lost Tradition of Christian Meditation. LC 80-82811. 144p. (Orig.). 1981. pap. 6.95 (ISBN 0-8091-2325-8). Paulist Pr.

Hills, C., ed. The Secrets of Spirulina. LC 80-22087. 224p. 1980. 6.95 (ISBN 0-916438-38-4). Univ of Trees.

Hills, Christopher. Into Meditation Now: A Course on Direct Enlightenment. LC 79-5124. (Illus.). 106p. 1979. pap. 5.95 (ISBN 0-916438-30-9). Univ of Trees.

Himalayan Institute. Meditation in Christianity. 2nd ed. LC 79-92042. 1979. pap. 1.95 (ISBN 0-89389-063-4). Himalayan Intl Inst.

Ho, Van H. Moving Meditation: Enlightenment of the Mind & Total Fitness. LC 79-88748. (Illus.). 214p. 1979. pap. 12.00 (ISBN 0-9602904-1-9). V H Ho.

How to Meditate Perfectly. 2.95 (ISBN 0-686-12818-4). Lotus Ashram.

Hua, Ellen K., adapted by. Kung Fu Meditations & Chinese Proverbial Wisdom. LC 73-7731. (Illus.). 1973. 3.95 (ISBN 0-87407-511-4); pap. 2.50 (ISBN 0-87407-200-X, FPI). Thor.

Humphries, Christmas. Concentration & Meditation. 343p. 1981. pap. 10.00 (ISBN 0-89540-068-5). Sun Pub.

Ibish, Yusuf & Wilson, Peter L., eds. Traditional Modes of Contemplation & Action. 1978. 25.00 (ISBN 0-87773-729-0). Great Eastern.

Johnston, William. Silent Music: The Science of Meditation. LC 73-18688. 1979. pap. 4.95 (ISBN 0-06-064196-7, RD 293, HarpR). Har-Row.

Jones-Ryan, Maureen. Meditation Without Frills: A Woman's Workbook. LC 76-16206. 152p. 1976. text ed. 10.00x (ISBN 0-87073-797-X); pap. 4.95x (ISBN 0-87073-798-8). Schenkman.

Jorban, E. Meet Your Guru: How to Unlock Your Soul. 1977. 4.00 (ISBN 0-682-48836-4). Exposition.

Jyotir Maya Nanda, Swami. Concentration & Meditation. (Illus.). 1971. 6.99 (ISBN 0-934664-03-X). Yoga Res Foun.

--Mantra, Kirtana, Yantra & Tantra. (Illus.). 1974. pap. 3.99 (ISBN 0-934664-06-4). Yoga Res Foun.

Kaplan, Aryeh. Meditation & Kabbalah. 244p. 1981. cloth 20.00 (ISBN 0-87728-365-6). Weiser.

--Meditation & the Bible. 1981. pap. 7.95 (ISBN 0-87728-517-9). Weiser.

--Meditation & the Bible. 1978. Repr. of 1978 ed. 15.00 (ISBN 0-87728-364-8). Weiser.

Kaushik, R. P. Energy Beyond Thought. LC 76-39623. 1977. 8.95 (ISBN 0-918038-03-0); pap. 3.95 (ISBN 0-918038-02-2). Journey Pubns.

--Light of Exploration. LC 76-39622. 1977. 7.95 (ISBN 0-918038-01-4); pap. 3.95 (ISBN 0-918038-00-6). Journey Pubns.

Kelsey, Morton T. The Other Side of Silence: A Guide to Christian Meditation. LC 76-9365. 324p. 1976. pap. 7.95 (ISBN 0-8091-1956-0). Paulist Pr.

Kim, Ashida. Secrets of the Ninja. (Illus.). 160p. 1981. 14.95 (ISBN 0-87364-234-1). Paladin Ent.

Kravette, Steve. Complete Meditation. (Illus.). 356p. (Orig.). 1981. pap. 9.95 (ISBN 0-914918-28-1). Para Res.

Krishna, Gopl. The Awakening of Kundalini. 1975. pap. 3.25 (ISBN 0-525-47398-X). Dutton.

Lamsa, George M. Pearls of Wisdom. 1978. pap. 2.50 (ISBN 0-87516-270-3). De Vorss.

Langford, Anne. Meditation for Little People. LC 75-46191. (Illus.). 40p. (gr. k-4). 1976. pap. 2.50 (ISBN 0-87516-211-8). De Vorss.

Leen, Edward. Progress Through Mental Prayer. 1978. pap. 2.45 (ISBN 0-88479-012-6). Arena Lettres.

Lesh, Terry. Meditation for Young People. LC 77-2215. (Illus.). (gr. 7 up). 1977. 7.25 (ISBN 0-688-41801-5); PLB 6.96 (ISBN 0-688-51801-X). Lothrop.

LeShan, Lawrence. How to Meditate: A Guide to Self-Discovery. LC 74-6210. 1974. 8.95 (ISBN 0-316-52155-8). Little.

--How to Meditate: A Guide to Self-Discovery. 176p. 1975. pap. 2.95 (ISBN 0-553-20463-7). Bantam.

Luk, Charles. Secrets of Chinese Meditation. (Illus.). 1970. pap. 3.95 (ISBN 0-87728-066-5). Weiser.

Lyman, Frederick C. Posture of Contemplation. LC 68-54973. 1969. 3.95 (ISBN 0-8022-2258-7). Philos Lib.

Mann, Mildred. Lecture Series. Incl. Series 1. Developing Your Awareness, 12 vols. 2.50 ea.; 30.00 set (ISBN 0-89369-009-0); Series 2. Being & Becoming, 12 vols. 2.50 ea.; 30.00 set (ISBN 0-89369-022-8); Series 3. Decreeing Your Good, 12 vols. 2.50 ea.; 30.00 set (ISBN 0-89369-035-X); Series 4. Wisdom Is Yours, 12 vols. 2.50 ea. (ISBN 0-89369-048-1); 30.00 set, by subscription 24.00 (ISBN 0-685-48572-2). 30.00 set (ISBN 0-686-57706-X). Soc Pragmatic.

Mason, Russell E. Brief Outlines for Relaxation Training (& Meditative Relaxation) (Brief Outlines Ser: No. 1). 1973. pap. 5.00 (ISBN 0-89533-022-9, 0-1). F I Comm.

Massy, Robert. You Are What You Breathe: The Negative Ion Story. 32p. 1980. 1.00 (ISBN 0-916438-41-4). Univ of Trees.

Mehta, Rohit. Science of Meditation. 1978. 7.50 (ISBN 0-89684-007-7, Pub. by Motilal Banarsidass India); pap. 4.95 (ISBN 0-89684-008-5). Orient Bk Dist.

Merritt, Jane Hamilton. A Meditator's Diary. 1977. pap. 1.75 (ISBN 0-671-81467-2). PB.

Merton, Thomas. The Asian Journal of Thomas Merton. Stone, Naomi B., et al, eds. LC 71-103370. (Illus.). 448p. 1973. 12.50 (ISBN 0-8112-0464-2); pap. 6.95 (ISBN 0-8112-0570-3, NDP394). New Directions.

--New Seeds of Contemplation. rev. ed. LC 61-17869. 1972. pap. 3.95 (ISBN 0-8112-0099-X, DP337). New Directions.

--What Is Contemplation? 1978. pap. 4.95 (ISBN 0-87243-128-2). Templegate.

Meserve, Harry C. The Practical Meditator. 144p. 1981. 16.95 (ISBN 0-87705-506-8); professional 16.95 (ISBN 0-686-73762-8). Human Sci Pr.

Michaels, Louis. The Words of Jesus: Arranged for Meditation. 1977. 6.95 (ISBN 0-87243-071-5). Templegate.

Miller, John. The Compassionate Teacher: How to Teach & Learn with Your Whole Self. 192p. 1981. 10.95 (ISBN 0-13-154468-3); pap. 5.95 (ISBN 0-13-154450-0). P-H.

Moffatt, Doris. Christian Meditation. The Better Way. LC 78-64842. 1979. pap. 3.95 (ISBN 0-915684-44-6). Christian Herald.

Moments of Meditation. 2.95 (ISBN 0-442-82343-6). Peter Pauper.

Monks of the Ramakrishna Order. Meditation. Bhavyananda, Swami, ed. 1977. pap. 10.00 (ISBN 0-7025-0019-4). Vedanta Pr.

Muktananda. Meditate. LC 80-20477. 84p. 1980. 9.95x (ISBN 0-87395-471-8, MUME); pap. 4.95x (ISBN 0-87395-472-6, MUME-P). State U NY Pr.

Muktananda, Swami. Siddha Meditation. pap. 2.95 (ISBN 0-914602-22-5). SYDA Found.

Murray, Andrew. Waiting on God. pap. 1.95 (ISBN 0-8024-0026-4). Moody.

Naranjo, Claudio & Ornstein, Robert E. On the Psychology of Meditation. 1977. pap. 2.50 (ISBN 0-14-004420-5). Penguin.

Newhouse, Flower A. Gateways into Light. LC 74-75517. 160p. 1974. pap. 6.50 (ISBN 0-910378-09-6). Christward.

Oliver, Fay C. Christian Growth Through Meditation. 128p. 1976. pap. 3.50 (ISBN 0-8170-0716-4). Judson.

Om! Meditation & Tranquility. 2.95 (ISBN 0-442-82354-1). Peter Pauper.

Oriental Meditation. 1976. 2.95 (ISBN 0-442-82568-4). Peter Pauper.

Orso, Kathryn W. As We Love & Forgive: Resources for the Lenten Season. (Orig.). 1975. pap. 4.05 (ISBN 0-89536-007-1). CSS Pub.

Pearce, Joseph C. The Bond of Power. 224p. 1981. 11.50 (ISBN 0-525-06950-X). Dutton.

Peck, Robert L. American Meditation & Beginning Yoga. 1976. 4.50 (ISBN 0-685-71846-8). Personal Dev Ctr.

Pennington, M. Basil. The Centering Prayer: Renewing an Ancient Christian Prayer Form. LC 78-22348. 1980. 8.95 (ISBN 0-385-14562-4). Doubleday.

Petersen, W. P. & Fehr, Terry. Meditation Made Easy. (Concise Guides Ser.). (Illus.). (gr. 6 up). 1979. s&l 6.90 (ISBN 0-531-02894-1). Watts.

Progoff, Ira. The Practice of Process Meditation. 348p. 1981. pap. 7.95 (ISBN 0-87941-009-4). Dialogue Hse.

--The Practice of Process Meditation: The Intensive Journal Way to Spiritual Experience. 1980. 12.95 (ISBN 0-87941-008-6); pap. 7.95, 1981 (ISBN 0-87941-009-4). Dialogue Hse.

--The Well & the Cathedral: With an Introduction on Its Use in the Practice of Meditation. 2nd ed. LC 76-20823. (Entrance Meditation Ser.). 1977. 8.95 (ISBN 0-87941-004-3); pap. 3.95 2nd ed. rev. 1981 (ISBN 0-87941-011-6). Dialogue Hse.

Prophet, Elizabeth C., intro. by. Prayer & Meditation. LC 76-28086. (Illus., Orig.). 1978. pap. 4.95 (ISBN 0-916766-19-5). Summit Univ.

Puryear, Herbert B. & Thurston, Mark. Meditation & the Mind of Man. rev. ed. 1975. pap. 4.95 (ISBN 0-87604-105-5). ARE Pr.

Rajneesh, Bhagwan S. Meditation: The Art of Ecstasy. (Orig.). 1976. pap. 5.95 (ISBN 0-06-090529-8, CN529, CN). Har-Row.

--Meditation: The Art of Ecstasy. Bharti, Ma S., ed. 1978. pap. 2.95 (ISBN 0-06-080394-0, P394, PL). Har-Row.

--Only One Sky: On the Tantric Way of Tilopa's Song of Mahamudra. LC 76-11869. 1976. pap. 6.95 (ISBN 0-525-47440-4). Dutton.

Ray, David. Art of Christian Meditation. 1979. pap. 1.95 (ISBN 0-671-82385-X). PB.

--The Art of Christian Meditation. 1977. pap. 3.95 (ISBN 0-8423-0087-2). Tyndale.

Reps, Paul. Ten Ways to Meditate. (Illus.). 64p. 1981. bonus ed. 9.95 (ISBN 0-8348-0163-9). Weatherhill.

Riccardo, Martin V. Mystical Consciousness: Exploring an Extraordinary State of Awareness. 1977. pap. 3.50 (ISBN 0-686-19170-6). MVR Bks.

Rieker, Hans-Ulrich. The Secret of Meditation. new ed. LC 74-24001. 176p. 1974. pap. 3.95 (ISBN 0-87728-245-5). Weiser.

Rittlemeyer, Friedrich. Meditation: Guidance of the Inner Life. 1981. pap. 9.50 (ISBN 0-903540-45-2, Pub. by Floris Books). St George Bk Serv.

Rogers, John. Inner Worlds of Meditation. LC 76-56625. pap. 3.00 (ISBN 0-88238-977-7). Baraka Bk.

Romney, Rodney R. Journey to Inner Space: Finding God-In-Us. LC 79-18822. (Orig.). 1980. pap. 4.95 (ISBN 0-687-20590-5). Abingdon.

Rozman, Deborah A. Meditating with Children: New Age Meditations for Children. LC 76-10480. (Illus.). 160p. (Orig.). 1975. pap. 5.95 (ISBN 0-916438-23-6). Univ of Trees.

--Meditation for Children. LC 75-28766. 160p. 1976. pap. 5.95 (ISBN 0-89087-150-7). Celestial Arts.

Sadhu. Meditation. pap. 4.00 (ISBN 0-87980-096-8). Wilshire.

Saliers, Don E. The Soul in Paraphrase: Prayer & the Religious Affections. 160p. 1980. 8.95 (ISBN 0-8164-0121-7). Seabury.

Saraydarian, Haroutiun. Science of Meditation. 1971. 10.00 (ISBN 0-911794-29-8); pap. 8.00 (ISBN 0-911794-30-1). Aqua Educ.

Satprakashananda, Swami. Meditation: Its Process, Practice, & Culmination. LC 76-15722. 264p. 1976. 8.50 (ISBN 0-916356-55-8). Vedanta Soc St Louis.

Savary, Louis M. & Scheihing, Theresa O. Our Treasured Heritage: Teaching Christian Meditation to Children. LC 81-7818. 176p. 1981. 9.95 (ISBN 0-8245-0078-4). Crossroad NY.

Schwarz, Jack. The Path of Action. LC 77-2247. 1977. pap. 4.95 (ISBN 0-525-47466-8). Dutton.

Sechrist, Elsie. Meditation - Gateway to Light. rev. ed. 53p. 1972. pap. 1.95 (ISBN 0-87604-062-8). ARE Pr.

Seifert, Harvey. Explorations in Meditation & Contemplation. LC 81-50601. 144p. (Orig.). 1981. pap. 4.50x (ISBN 0-8358-0427-5). Upper Room.

Shapiro, Deane H., Jr. & Walsh, Roger N., eds. The Art & Science of Meditation. 600p. 29.95 (ISBN 0-202-25133-0). Aldine Pub.

Shapiro, Deane, Jr. Meditation: Self-Regulation Strategy & Altered States of Consciousness. 1980. 19.95 (ISBN 0-202-25132-2). Aldine Pub.

Siddheswarananda, Swami. Meditation According to Yoga-Vedanta. pap. 2.95 (ISBN 0-87481-467-7). Vedanta Pr.

Silva, Jose & Miele, Philip. The Silva Mind Control Method. 1978. pap. 2.95 (ISBN 0-671-43343-1). PB.

Simmons, Patricia A. Between You & Me, God. LC 74-79486. 1974. pap. 3.95 (ISBN 0-8054-4412-2). Broadman.

Singh, Kirpal. The Light of Kirpal. LC 80-52537. 496p. 1980. pap. 12.00 (ISBN 0-89142-033-9). Sant Bani Ash.

--Self-Introspection - Meditation. Seader, Ruth, ed. (The Teachings of Kirpal Singh Ser., Vol. 11). iv, 170p. (Orig.). 1975. 3.50 (ISBN 0-89142-021-5). Sant Bani Ash.

Smith, Howard E. Self-Discovery Through Meditation: A Guide to Western Techniques. 1978. cancelled (ISBN 0-8092-7932-0). Contemp Bks.

Smith, Robert A. The Right Side: With Effective Meditation. 1967. 2.95 (ISBN 0-912128-06-2). Pubns Living.

Spurgeon, Charles H. Spurgeon's Morning & Evening. 736p. 1980. large print kivar 8.95 (ISBN 0-310-32927-2). Zondervan.

Sri Chinmoy. Meditation: Man's Choice & God's Voice, Pt. 2. 53p. 1974. pap. 2.00 (ISBN 0-685-53061-2). Aum Pubns.

Stahl, Carolyn. Opening to God: Guided Imagery Meditation on Scripture. LC 77-87403. 1977. 3.50x (ISBN 0-8358-0357-0). Upper Room.

Steinbrecher, Edwin C. The Inner Guide Meditation. 4th ed. LC 78-60489. (Illus.). 1978. 12.95 (ISBN 0-685-65266-1); pap. 6.75 (ISBN 0-685-65267-X). Blue Feather.

Stevens, Edward. An Introduction to Oriental Mysticism. 1974. pap. 2.95 (ISBN 0-8091-1798-3). Paulist Pr.

Stone, Justin F. The Joys of Meditation. (Illus.). 94p. 1976. pap. 3.50 (ISBN 0-89540-001-4, SB-001). Sun Pub.

--Meditation for Healing. 1977. 10.00 (ISBN 0-89540-043-X, SB-043). Sun Pub.

Stone, Justine F. Climb the Joyous Mountain: Living the Meditative Way. 94p. 1975. 3.50 (ISBN 0-89540-007-3, SB-007). Sun Pub.

Straughn, R. A. Meditation Techniques of the Kabalists, Vedantins & Taoists. 1976. pap. 6.95 (ISBN 0-917650-02-6). Maat Pub.

Subramuniya. The Fine Art of Meditation. pap. 1.00 (ISBN 0-87516-356-4). De Vorss.

--The Meditator. (On the Path Ser.). (Illus.). 72p. 1973. pap. 2.00 (ISBN 0-87516-351-3). De Vorss.

Swami Rama, et al. Faces of Meditation. Agnihotri, S. N., ed. O'Brien, Justin, ed. 1978. pap. 1.95 (ISBN 0-89389-044-8). Himalayan Intl Inst.

The, G-Jo Institute. Meditative Relaxation. 1980. pap. 4.50 (ISBN 0-916878-13-9). Falkynor Bks.

Tilmann, Klemens. The Practice of Meditation. LC 77-72469. 139p. 1977. pap. 3.95 (ISBN 0-8091-2043-7). Paulist Pr.

Time for Reflection. 1968. 2.95 (ISBN 0-442-82434-3). Peter Pauper.

Trungpa, Chogyam. Meditation in Action. (Clear Light Ser). (Orig.). 1969. pap. 3.50 (ISBN 0-394-73025-9). Shambhala Pubns.

Tulku, Tarthang. Gesture of Balance: A Guide to Awareness, Self-Healing & Meditation. LC 75-5255. (Illus.). 1976. 12.95 (ISBN 0-913546-17-8); pap. 6.95 (ISBN 0-913546-16-X). Dharma Pub.

Vamos, William J. The Life That Listens: A Workbook for Personal Meditation & Group Dialogue. 1980. 5.95 (ISBN 0-8499-2871-0). Word Bks.

Van Over, Raymond. Total Meditation: Mind Control Techniques from a Small Planet in Space. (Illus.). 1978. pap. 4.95 (ISBN 0-02-067900-9, Collier). Macmillan.

Vaughn, Ruth. Even When I Cry. 96p. 1975. pap. 2.95 (ISBN 0-8024-2389-2). Moody.

Vivekananda, Swami. Meditation & Its Methods According to Swami Vivekananda. Chetanananda, Swami, compiled by. LC 75-36392. (Orig.). 1976. pap. 3.50 (ISBN 0-87481-030-2). Vedanta Pr.

Watts, Alan. Meditation. 1976. pap. 2.95 (ISBN 0-515-05842-4). Jove Pubns.

--Om: Creative Meditations. LC 79-54101. 1980. pap. 5.95 (ISBN 0-89087-257-0). Celestial Arts.

Weber, Nellie B. Dew Drops. 3.95 (ISBN 0-686-12668-8, BE-175). Evangel Indiana.

West, Serene. Very Practical Meditation. LC 79-20249. (Orig.). 1981. pap. 4.95 (ISBN 0-89865-006-2, Unilaw). Donning Co.

White, John, ed. What Is Meditation? LC 73-81126. 280p. 1974. pap. 2.95 (ISBN 0-385-07638-X, Anch). Doubleday.

Whitehead, Carleton. Creative Meditation. 128p. 1975. 6.95 (ISBN 0-396-07139-2). Dodd.

Whitehill, James. Enter the Quiet: Everyone's Way to Meditation. LC 79-2996. (Illus.). 192p. (Orig.). 1980. pap. 5.95 (ISBN 0-06-069365-7, RD 312). Har-Row.

Wood, Ernest. Concentration: An Approach to Meditation. LC 67-2874. pap. 2.75 (ISBN 0-8356-0176-5, Quest). Theos Pub Hse.

Yatiswarananda, Swami. Meditation & Spiritual Life. 700p. 1980. 18.95 (ISBN 0-87481-403-0). Vedanta Pr.

MEDITATION (BUDDHISM)

Blofeld, John. Gateway to Wisdom: Taoist & Buddhist Contemplative & Healing Yogas Adapted for Western Students of the Way. LC 79-67685. (Illus.). 1980. pap. 6.95 (ISBN 0-394-73878-0). Shambhala Pubns.

Buksbazen, John D. To Forget the Self: An Illustrated Guide to Zen Meditation. LC 76-9475. (The Zen Writings Ser.: Vol. 3). (Illus.). 1977. pap. 7.95x (ISBN 0-916820-03-3). Center Pubns.

Fast, Howard. The Art of Zen Meditation. LC 77-6222. (Illus.). 48p. 1977. pap. 2.95 (ISBN 0-915238-15-2). Peace Pr.

Guenther, Herbert V. Philosophy & Psychology in the Abhidharma. LC 75-40259. 282p. 1981. pap. 6.95 (ISBN 0-87773-081-4). Great Eastern.

Gyatso, Geshe. Meaningful to Behold. Landaw, Jonathan, ed. Norbu, Tenzin, tr. from Tibetan. 365p. (Orig.). 1981. pap. 12.95 (ISBN 0-86171-003-7). Great Eastern.

Kongtrul, Jamgon. The Torch of Certainty. Hanson, Judith, tr. from Tibetan. LC 76-53359. (Illus.). 179p. (Orig.). 1981. pap. 7.95 (ISBN 0-87773-101-2). Great Eastern.

Lerner, Eric. Journey of Insight Meditation: A Personal Experience of the Buddha's Way. LC 76-49726. 1978. 8.95x (ISBN 0-8052-3648-1); pap. 3.95 (ISBN 0-8052-0593-4). Schocken.

Mountain, Marian. The Zen Environment: The Impact of Zen Meditation. 288p. 1981. 10.95 (ISBN 0-688-00350-8). Morrow.

Reps, Paul. Ten Ways to Meditate: Bonus Edition. (Illus.). 64p. 1981. 9.95 (ISBN 0-8348-0163-9, Pub. by John Weatherhill Inc Tokyo). C E Tuttle.

Sanadi, Lalita. Mantra Meditation. rev. ed. D'Auri, Laura, ed. (Illus.). 160p. 1981. pap. cancelled (ISBN 0-87407-204-2, FP-4). Thor.

Sekida, Katsuki. Zen Training: Methods & Philosophy. Grimstone, A. V., ed. LC 75-17573. (Illus.). 252p. 1975. 10.00 (ISBN 0-8348-0111-6); pap. 7.95 (ISBN 0-8348-0114-0). Weatherhill.

Swearer, Donald K. Secrets of the Lotus: Studies in Buddhist Meditation. Alexandre, C., ed. 1971. Macmillan.

Thich Nhat Hanh. The Miracle of Mindfulness! A Manual on Meditation. LC 76-7747. 1976. pap. 4.95 (ISBN 0-8070-1119-3, BP546). Beacon Pr.

Tulku, Tarthang. Kum Nye Relaxation, Vols. 1 & 2. (Nyingma Psychology Ser.). 1978. 14.95 ea. Vol. 1 (ISBN 0-913546-10-0). Vol. 2 (ISBN 0-913546-74-7). pap. 6.95 ea. Vol. 1 (ISBN 0-913546-25-9). Vol. 2 (ISBN 0-913546-75-5). Dharma Pub.

Watts, Alan. The Art of Contemplation. LC 72-10174. 1973. 3.95 (ISBN 0-394-70963-2). Pantheon.

MEDITATIONS

Here are entered works containing thoughts or reflections on spiritual truths. Works on the nature of meditation are entered under the heading Meditation.

see also Devotional Calendars; Devotional Literature; Jesus Christ–Devotional Literature; Spiritual Exercises;

also subdivisions Meditations under Bible, Jesus Christ, Lord's Supper, and similar headings

Alberione, James. Thoughts. 1973. 3.00 (ISBN 0-8198-0332-4). Dghtrs St Paul.

Allport, Gordon W. Waiting for the Lord: 33 Meditations on God & Man. 1978. 5.95 (ISBN 0-02-501700-4). Macmillan.

Ames, Louisa A. Meditations for Youth. 1980. pap. 3.95 (ISBN 0-89293-059-4). Beta Bk.

Anderson, Richard. Inspirational Meditations for Sunday Church School Teachers. 1980. pap. 2.25 (ISBN 0-570-03810-3, 12-2919). Concordia.

Arnold, Eberhard, et al. The Heavens Are Opened. LC 73-20715. (Illus.). 190p. 1974. 9.95 (ISBN 0-87486-113-6). Plough.

Asquith, Glenn H. Footprints in the Sand. 96p. 1975. pap. 2.95 (ISBN 0-8170-0676-1). Judson.

Baba, Meher. Meher Miniatures for Daily Living. Bodman, William C., compiled by. (Illus.). 1978. 8.95 (ISBN 0-915828-16-2). Sufism Reorien.

Bachelard, Gaston. Poetics of Reverie: Childhood, Language & the Cosmos. 1971. pap. 4.95x (ISBN 0-8070-6413-0, BP375). Beacon Pr.

Baker, Pat A. In This Moment. LC 76-28802. 1977. 4.95 (ISBN 0-687-19445-8). Abingdon.

Barclay, William. Meditations on Communicating the Gospel. 1971. pap. 1.95x (ISBN 0-8358-0253-1). Upper Room.

Barnett, Joe R. Just for Today. (Direction Bks.). pap. 1.95 (ISBN 0-8010-0785-2). Baker Bk.

Barwig, Regis N. Waiting for Rain: Meantime Reflections on the Life of Religious Consecration. 1975. pap. 5.00 (ISBN 0-686-18875-6). Benziger Sis.

Bellett, J. G. Short Meditations, 3 vols. Date not set. pap. 8.00 set (ISBN 0-686-30738-0); pap. 2.95 ea. Believers Bkshelf.

Benham, Arliss R. Long Way Back. pap. 1.50 (ISBN 0-8010-0782-8). Baker Bk.

Bennett, Dink. Living Reflections. LC 75-3948. (Illus.). 48p. 1975. 2.95 (ISBN 0-87239-042-X, 3016). Standard Pub.

--Moments with My Master. LC 75-3949. (Illus.). 48p. 1975. 2.95 (ISBN 0-87239-043-8, 3037). Standard Pub.

Best Wedding Meditations. 1972. 3.50 (ISBN 0-89536-015-2). CSS Pub.

Bittleston, Adam. Meditative Prayers for Today. 5th ed. 1975. 3.75 (ISBN 0-900285-00-1, Pub. by Floris Books). St George Bk Serv.

Bjorge, James R. And Heaven & Nature Sings. (Illus.). 1977. pap. 4.95 (ISBN 0-570-03047-1, 6-1172). Concordia.

Blofeld, John. Gateway to Wisdom: Taoist & Buddhist Contemplative & Healing Yogas Adapted for Western Students of the Way. LC 79-67685. (Illus.). 1980. pap. 6.95 (ISBN 0-394-73878-0). Shambhala Pubns.

Bloom, Anthony. Meditations. 3.95 (ISBN 0-87193-010-2). Dimension Bks.

Bodo, Murray. Song of the Sparrow: Meditations & Poems to Pray by. (Illus.). 187p. (Orig.). 1976. pap. 2.75 (ISBN 0-912228-26-1). St Anthony Mess Pr.

Boff, Leonardo. The Way of the Cross: Way of Justice. LC 79-23776. Orig. Title: Via-Sacra Da Justica. 1980. pap. 4.95 (ISBN 0-88344-701-0). Orbis Bks.

Bowness, C. The Practice of Meditation. (Paths to Inner Power Ser.). pap. 2.50 (ISBN 0-87728-151-3). Weiser.

Boyd, Malcolm. Am I Running with You, God? 1978. lib. bdg. 10.95 (ISBN 0-8161-6577-7, Large Print Bks). G K Hall.

Bradford, John. Writings of John Bradford...Martyr, 1555, 2 Vols. Repr. of 1853 ed. Set. 76.00 (ISBN 0-384-05440-4). Johnson Repr.

Brenneman, H. G. Meditaciones Para la Nueva Madre. 1978. 2.35 (ISBN 0-311-40032-9). Casa Bautista.

Brenneman, Helen G. Morning Joy. LC 80-26449. 80p. 1981. pap. 3.95 (ISBN 0-8361-1942-8). Herald Pr.

Brokering, Herbert. Lord, If. 1977. pap. 2.50 (ISBN 0-570-03046-3, 6-1171). Concordia.

Brokering, Herbert F. Pilgrimage to Renewal. 96p. (Orig.). 1979. pap. 1.95 (ISBN 0-03-053791-6). Winston Pr.

Bryant, Al. Climbing the Heights. 1974. large print kivar 6.95 (ISBN 0-310-22067-X). Zondervan.

--Daily Meditations with F. B. Meyer. 1979. 8.95 (ISBN 0-8499-0148-0). Word Bks.

Bull, Henry, ed. Christian Prayers & Holy Meditations. 1842. 17.00 (ISBN 0-384-06285-7). Johnson Repr.

Butts, Mary. Lo, the Winter Is Past. 1978. 6.95 (ISBN 0-533-03581-3). Vantage.

Caddy, Eileen. Footprints on the Path. 150p. 1981. pap. 7.00 (ISBN 0-905249-54-2, Pub. by Findhorn-Thule Scotland). Hydra Bk.

--Foundations of Findhorn. 154p. 1981. pap. 3.95 (ISBN 0-905249-29-1, Pub. by Findhorn-Thule Scotland). Hydra Bk.

--God Spoke to Me. 128p. 1981. pap. 4.95 (ISBN 0-905249-53-4, Pub. by Findhorn-Thule Scotland). Hydra Bk.

--The Spirit of Findhorn. LC 75-36747. (Illus.). 1979. pap. 4.95 (ISBN 0-06-061291-6, RD 296, HarpR). Har-Row.

Caldwell, Louis O. Good Morning Lord: Meditations for Modern Marrieds. (Good Morning Lord Ser.). 1974. 3.95 (ISBN 0-8010-2351-3). Baker Bk.

Cambell, Morgan G. Best of G. Cambell Morgan. (Best Ser.). pap. 3.95 (ISBN 0-8010-6068-0). Baker Bk.

Campbell, Anthony. Seven States of Consciousness: Vision of Possibilities Suggested by the Teaching of Maharishi Mahesh Yogi. LC 73-9078. (Orig.). 1974. pap. 2.50 (ISBN 0-06-080289-8, P289, PL). Har-Row.

Carretto, Carlo. Summoned by Love. Neame, Alan, tr. from Italian. LC 78-962. 1978. 7.95 (ISBN 0-88344-470-4); pap. 4.95 (ISBN 0-88344-472-0). Orbis Bks.

Carson, Mary. The Mom's I-Feel-Guilty-When-I-Don't-Take-Time-to-Talk-to-God Meditation Book. (Illus., Orig.). 1980. pap. 1.50 (ISBN 0-89570-189-8). Claretian Pubns.

Catoir, John T. We Dare to Believe: An Exploration of Faith in the Modern World. LC 77-169055. (Illus.). 260p. 1972. 5.95 (ISBN 0-8199-0431-7). Franciscan Herald.

Cavert, Walter D. Remember Now. (Festival Bks). 1979. pap. 2.25 (ISBN 0-687-36127-3). Abingdon.

Chaney, Robert. The Inner Way. LC 75-32224. 145p. 1975. pap. 4.95 (ISBN 0-918936-00-4). Astara.

Chapman, J. Wilbur. Secret of a Happy Day. (Direction Bks.). 1979. pap. 1.95 (ISBN 0-8010-2435-8). Baker Bk.

Chiampi, Luke. Rebuild My Church. LC 72-87090. 105p. 1972. pap. 0.95 (ISBN 0-8199-0502-X). Franciscan Herald.

Chinmoy, Sri. Aspiration & Gods Hour. 63p. (Orig.). 1977. pap. 2.00 (ISBN 0-88497-397-2). Aum Pubns.

--Aspiration-Glow & Dedication-Flow, 2 pts. (Orig.). 1977. Pt. 1, 60p. pap. text ed. 2.00 (ISBN 0-88497-386-7); Pt. 2, 70p. pap. 2.00 (ISBN 0-686-68529-6). Aum Pubns.

--Beauty-Drops. 51p. (Orig.). 1975. pap. 2.00 (ISBN 0-88497-224-0). Aum Pubns.

--Creation & Perfection. 49p. (Orig.). 1976. pap. 2.00 (ISBN 0-88497-320-4). Aum Pubns.

--Ego & Self-Complacency. 54p. (Orig.). 1977. pap. 2.00 (ISBN 0-88497-381-6). Aum Pubns.

--Father's Day: Father with His European Children. 54p. (Orig.). 1976. pap. 2.00 (ISBN 0-88497-297-6). Aum Pubns.

--Four Intimate Friends: Insincerity, Impurity, Doubt & Self-Indulgence. 59p. (Orig.). 1977. pap. 2.00 (ISBN 0-88497-382-4). Aum Pubns.

--Great Masters & the Cosmic Gods. 61p. (Orig.). 1977. pap. 2.00 (ISBN 0-88497-395-6). Aum Pubns.

--The Inner Journey. 52p. (Orig.). 1977. pap. 2.00 (ISBN 0-88497-377-8). Aum Pubns.

--Inner Progress & Satisfaction-Life. 54p. (Orig.). 1977. pap. 2.00 (ISBN 0-88497-373-5). Aum Pubns.

--Inspiration-Garden & Aspiration-Leaves. 58p. (Orig.). 1977. pap. 2.00 (ISBN 0-88497-379-4). Aum Pubns.

--Justice-Light & Satisfaction-Delight. (Soulful Questions & Fruitful Answers on Law & Justice). 41p. (Orig.). 1977. pap. 2.00 (ISBN 0-88497-338-7). Aum Pubns.

--The Master's Inner Life. 68p. (Orig.). 1977. pap. 2.00 (ISBN 0-88497-393-X). Aum Pubns.

--My Maple Tree. 121p. (Orig.). 1974. pap. 3.00 (ISBN 0-685-41607-0). Aum Pubns.

--Opportunity & Self-Transcendance. 64p. (Orig.). 1977. pap. 2.00 (ISBN 0-88497-375-1). Aum Pubns.

--Perfection & Transcendence. 60p. (Orig.). 1977. pap. 2.00 (ISBN 0-88497-372-7). Aum Pubns.

--Perseverence & Aspiration. 54p. (Orig.). 1976. pap. 2.00 (ISBN 0-88497-333-6). Aum Pubns.

--The Significance of a Smile. 52p. (Orig.). 1977. pap. 2.00 (ISBN 0-88497-367-0). Aum Pubns.

--Something, Somehow, Somewhere, Someday. 70p. (Orig.). 1973. pap. 2.00 (ISBN 0-88497-025-6). Aum Pubns.

--Soul-Education for the Family-World. 89p. (Orig.). 1977. pap. 3.00 (ISBN 0-88497-390-5). Aum Pubns.

--The Souls Evolution. 63p. (Orig.). 1977. pap. 2.00 (ISBN 0-88497-396-4). Aum Pubns.

--Supreme - His Four Children. LC 72-188849. 1973. pap. 3.00 (ISBN 0-8303-0121-6). Fleet.

--Transformation of the Ego. 52p. (Orig.). 1977. pap. 2.00 (ISBN 0-88497-371-9). Aum Pubns.

--A Twentieth-Century Seeker. 62p. (Orig.). 1977. pap. 2.00 (ISBN 0-88497-385-9). Aum Pubns.

Christopher. Our New Age: Words for the People. 1st ed. LC 77-72309. (Illus., Orig.). 1977. pap. 2.95 (ISBN 0-916940-01-2). World Light.

Clark, Miles. Glenn Clark: His Life & Writings. LC 75-6877. 160p. (Orig.). 1975. pap. 3.95 (ISBN 0-687-14810-3). Abingdon.

Clark, Vivian. If Only I Could Fly. pap. 1.95 (ISBN 0-8010-2442-0). Baker Bk.

Clark, Wayne C. God Is My Strength. 1977. pap. 1.25 (ISBN 0-8170-0763-6); pap. 12.00 per dozen (ISBN 0-686-77289-X). Judson.

Coburn, John B. Feeding Fire. LC 80-81103. 62p. 1980. 6.95 (ISBN 0-8192-1281-4). Morehouse.

Colman, Henry, ed. Divine Meditations (Sixteen Forty) 1979. 20.00 (ISBN 0-300-02305-7). Yale U Pr.

Comeau, Bill. Doubters & Dreamers. 1973. pap. 1.25x (ISBN 0-8358-0278-7). Upper Room.

Conners, Kenneth W. Lord, Have You Got a Minute? LC 78-15297. 1979. pap. 4.95 (ISBN 0-8170-0816-0). Judson.

Cook, Charles, ed. Daily Meditations for Prayer. Gift Ed. 7.95 (ISBN 0-89107-160-1). Good News.

Cooke, Grace. The Illumined Ones. (Illus.). 1966. 8.95 (ISBN 0-85487-003-2). De Vorss.

Cowman, Charles E. Cumbres De Inspiracion. Robleto, Adolfo, tr. 1979. Repr. of 1977 ed. pap. 3.00 (ISBN 0-311-40026-4). Casa Bautista.

Cowman, Mrs. Charles E. Traveling Toward Sunrise. large print ed. 272p. 1975. 6.95 (ISBN 0-310-22547-7). Zondervan.

Cox, Frank L. Bedside Meditations. 1967. pap. 1.00 (ISBN 0-686-22198-2). Firm Foun Pub.

Crawley-Boevey, Mateo. Meditaciones. (Span.). 1978. 2.00 (ISBN 0-8198-4706-2); pap. 1.00 (ISBN 0-8198-4707-0). Dghtrs St Paul.

Creme, Benjamin. Messages from Maitreyea the Christ. 209p. 1980. pap. 5.00 (ISBN 0-936604-01-8). Tara Ctr.

--The Reappearance of the Christ & the Masters of Wisdom. 253p. 1980. pap. 5.00 (ISBN 0-936604-00-X). Tara Ctr.

Criswell, W. A. Abiding Hope. 320p. 1981. 9.95 (ISBN 0-310-43840-3). Zondervan.

Crouch, Janie O. All Things New. 1976. 4.95 (ISBN 0-686-75243-0); pap. 2.95 (ISBN 0-686-75244-9). Firm Foun Pub.

Cuffee, James W. Spiritual Automobile. Knickerbocker, Charles, ed. 1980. 4.75 (ISBN 0-682-48997-2). Exposition.

Curtis, Donald. Master Meditations. LC 76-47422. 1977. pap. 3.25 (ISBN 0-87707-185-3). CSA Pr.

Cushing, Richard J. Meditations for Religious. 1959. 3.00 (ISBN 0-8198-0102-X). Dghtrs St Paul.

Dean, H. B. Bible Quotes & Comments. rev. ed. LC 74-28727. (Fountain Bks). Orig. Title: Bible Digest. 96p. 1975. pap. 1.95 (ISBN 0-87239-040-3, 2295). Standard Pub.

--More Bible Quotes & Comments. LC 74-28726. (Fountain Bks). 96p. 1975. pap. 1.95 (ISBN 0-87239-041-1, 2296). Standard Pub.

De Balaguer, Josemaria E. The Way. 9th ed. Orig. Title: Camino. 1979. pap. 4.95 (ISBN 0-933932-01-4). Scepter Pubs.

DeFoucauld, Charles. Meditations of a Hermit: The Spiritual Writings of Charles deFoucauld. Balfour, Charlotte, tr. 224p. (Orig.). 1981. pap. 7.95 (ISBN 0-88344-325-2). Orbis Bks.

DePree, Gladis & DePree, Gordon. Stars & Firelight. 112p. (Orig.). 1981. pap. 3.95 (ISBN 0-310-44121-8). Zondervan.

Dillard, Annie. Holy the Firm. 1978. lib. bdg. 10.95 (ISBN 0-8161-6571-8, Large Print Bks). G K Hall.

Dixon, A. C. Beyond the Sunset. pap. 1.25 (ISBN 0-686-74102-1). Baker Bk.

Doerffler, Alfred. The Mind at Ease. rev. ed. LC 75-43869. (Large Print Ser.). 104p. 1976. pap. 4.50 (ISBN 0-570-03040-4, 6-1163). Concordia.

Donne, John. Devotions: Upon Emergent Occasions. Bd. with Death's Duel. 1959. pap. 3.95 (ISBN 0-472-06030-9, 30, AA). U of Mich Pr.

Doty, William L. Waiting for the Lord. LC 76-45384. 1977. 4.95 (ISBN 0-8189-0338-4). Alba.

Drescher, John M. Follow Me. LC 78-153967. 1971. 3.95 (ISBN 0-8361-1637-2); pap. 2.95 (ISBN 0-8361-1706-9). Herald Pr.

--Spirit Fruit. rev. ed. LC 73-21660. 376p. 1978. pap. 5.95 (ISBN 0-8361-1867-7). Herald Pr.

Drouin, Francis M. Sounding Solitude. 1971. 3.95 (ISBN 0-8189-0204-3). Alba.

Dubay, Thomas. Dawn of a Consecration. 1964. 4.00 (ISBN 0-8198-0034-1). Dghtrs St Paul.

Duddington, John W. Ferial Christianity. 1977. 8.95 (ISBN 0-533-02803-5). Vantage.

Dukes, Ona B. & Johnston, Beverly. Lord, What Are You Doing Next Tuesday? 1978. pap. 2.95 (ISBN 0-8272-2114-2). Bethany Pr.

Dunn, James A. Mustard Meditations: Seeds for Christian Growth. 1974. pap. 2.45 (ISBN 0-89570-090-5). Claretian Pubns.

Eareckson, Joni & Estes, Steve. A Step Further. 1978. 6.95 (ISBN 0-310-23970-2). Zondervan.

Eastman, Dick. Hour That Changes the World. (Direction Bks.). pap. 1.95 (ISBN 0-8010-3337-3). Baker Bk.

Edman, V. Raymond. But God! 1980. large print 5.95 (ISBN 0-310-24047-6). Zondervan.

Edwards, Alexis. Guidelines. 1981. pap. 2.50 (ISBN 0-905249-07-0, Pub. by Findhorn-Thule Scotland). Hydra Bk.

Emmons, Helen B. The Mature Heart. new ed. (Large-Print Editions Ser.). 1977. 6.95 (ISBN 0-687-23779-3). Abingdon.

Emswiller, Tom N. The Click in the Clock: Meditations for Junior Highs. 128p. (Orig.). (gr. 7-9). 1981. pap. 5.95 (ISBN 0-8298-0470-6). Pilgrim NY.

Evely, Louis. That Man Is You. Bonin, Edmond, tr. LC 63-23494. 297p. 1964. pap. 3.95 (ISBN 0-8091-1697-9). Paulist Pr.

Everest, Quinton J. Prescription for Today. pap. 4.95 (ISBN 0-686-12669-6, BE-173). Evangel Indiana.

Fair, Harold. Class Devotions: For Use with the 1980-81 International Lessons. (Orig.). 1980. pap. 3.50 (ISBN 0-687-08620-5). Abingdon.

Farrell, Edward. Celtic Meditations. 3.95 (ISBN 0-87193-033-1). Dimension Bks.

Fields, Wilbur. Let Us Draw Near. 1965. spiral bdg. 2.95 (ISBN 0-89900-114-9). College Pr Pub.

Fifty-Two Gospel Meditations: Modern Pilgrim. 1979. 9.95 (ISBN 0-88347-117-5). Thomas More.

Finney, Charles G. Principles of Prayer. Parkhurst, L. G., ed. 112p. (Orig.). 1980. pap. 2.95 (ISBN 0-87123-468-8, 210468). Bethany Hse.

Flatt, Bill. From Worry to Happiness. pap. 2.95 (ISBN 0-8010-3495-7). Baker Bk.

Foote, Arthur. Taking Down the Defenses. LC 76-7743. 1977. pap. 3.95 (ISBN 0-8070-1117-7, BP541). Beacon Pr.

Francois De Sales. Oeuvres: Introduction a la Vie Devote & Traite de l'Amour de Dieu, etc. (Saint). 2024p. 46.95 (ISBN 0-686-56512-6). French & Eur.

Freeman, James D. Of Time & Eternity. LC 81-51069. 200p. 1981. 3.95 (ISBN 0-87159-122-7). Unity Bks.

Frost, Gerhard. Homing in the Presence: Meditations for Daily Living. 1978. pap. 4.95 (ISBN 0-03-043921-3). Winston Pr.

Gibble, Kenneth L. Yeast, Salt & Secret Agents. 1979. pap. 4.95 (ISBN 0-87178-968-X). Brethren.

Gillet, Lev. In Thy Presence. LC 77-1040. 144p. 1977. pap. 2.95 (ISBN 0-913836-34-6). St Vladimirs.

Gordon, Arthur. Touch of Wonder. 256p. 1974. 9.95 (ISBN 0-8007-0695-1). Revell.

Gordon, S. D. What It Will Take to Change the World. (Direction Books Ser.). pap. 1.95 (ISBN 0-8010-3746-8). Baker Bk.

Graham, Munir & Torre Bueno, Laura, eds. Index to the Sayings of Hazrat Inayat Khan. (The Collected Works of Hazrat Inayat Khan). 144p. (Orig.). Date not set. pap. 3.95 (ISBN 0-930872-23-1, 1009P). Sufi Order Pubns.

Grogok, N. B. Meditations on the Divine Liturgy. 1913. 8.50 (ISBN 0-8414-4691-1). Folcroft.

Grol, Lini R. Heartsongs. 1981. 4.95 (ISBN 0-8010-3764-6). Baker Bk.

Gromacki, Robert G. Stand United in Joy. pap. 5.95 (ISBN 0-8010-3760-3). Baker Bk.

Gunn, John R. Good Morning, Lord: Devotions on the Hope of Glory. (Good Morning, Lord Ser.). 1977. 2.45 (ISBN 0-8010-3706-9). Baker Bk.

Hagin, Kenneth, Jr. The Past Tense of God's Word. 1980. pap. 0.50 (ISBN 0-89276-706-5). Hagin Ministry.

Hallesby, O. God's Word for Today: A Daily Devotional for the Whole Year. Carlsen, Clarence J., tr. LC 78-67940. 1979. pap. 2.95 (ISBN 0-8066-1682-2, 10-2741). Augsburg.

Hames. Deeper Things. pap. 2.25 (ISBN 0-686-12864-8). Schmul Pub Co.

Hamilton, Elizabeth. The Voice of the Spirit: The Spirituality of St. John of the Cross. LC 76-53609. 1977. pap. 2.95 (ISBN 0-87973-686-0). Our Sunday Visitor.

Hanson, Muriel. Honey & Salt. 2nd ed. LC 78-185512. 1971. pap. text ed. 1.50 (ISBN 0-911802-26-6). Free Church Pubns.

Harless, Dan. Fireside Chats. pap. 3.95 (ISBN 0-8010-4235-6). Baker Bk.

Harrell, Irene. Prayerables. 1972. pap. 0.95 (ISBN 0-87680-910-7, 90010). Word Bks.

Harrison, Norman B. His Comfort. 1973. pap. 0.75 (ISBN 0-911802-32-0). Free Church Pubns.

--His Joy. 1973. pap. 0.75 (ISBN 0-911802-35-5). Free Church Pubns.

--His Peace. 1972. pap. 0.75 (ISBN 0-911802-29-0). Free Church Pubns.

--Suffering. 1965. pap. 0.75 (ISBN 0-911802-34-7). Free Church Pubns.

Haslam, Robert B. Peepholes on Life. 1977. pap. 3.25 (ISBN 0-89367-017-0). Light & Life.

Havner, Vance. Hope Thou in God. 1978. 7.95 (ISBN 0-8007-0902-0). Revell.

Hazrat Inayat Khan. Aphorisms. (The Collected Works of Hazrat Inayat Khan). 128p. (Orig.). Date not set. pap. 4.95 (ISBN 0-930872-22-3, 1008P). Sufi Order Pubns.

--The Bowl of Saki. LC 80-54276. (The Collected Works of Hazrat Inayat Khan). 144p. (Orig.). 1981. pap. 4.95 (ISBN 0-930872-20-7, 1007P). Sufi Order Pubns.

Hendricks, Geoffrey. Between Two Points. (Illus.). 1976. pap. 7.50 (ISBN 0-685-91421-6). Printed Edns.

--Ring Piece. (Illus.). 1973. pap. 3.50 (ISBN 0-87110-098-3). Printed Edns.

Hersey, Jean. The Touch of the Earth. 1981. 12.95 (ISBN 0-8164-2306-7). Seabury.

Hill, Jeanne. Daily Breath. LC 77-92454. 1978. 3.95 (ISBN 0-8499-0064-6, 0064-6). Word Bks.

Hodge, Charles. Way of Life. (Summit Bks.). pap. 2.95 (ISBN 0-8010-4181-3). Baker Bk.

Hodgson, Joan. Our Father. (Illus.). (ps-3). 1977. pap. 2.50 (ISBN 0-85487-040-7). De Vorss.

Holmes, Marjorie. Beauty in Your Own Backyard. (Illus.). 1980. pap. 1.95 (ISBN 0-553-11429-8). Bantam.

Hong, Edna. The Downward Ascent. LC 78-66942. 1979. pap. 3.50 (ISBN 0-8066-1679-2, 10-1955). Augsburg.

Hughes, Phillip E. Hope for a Despairing World. (Canterbury Bks.). pap. 2.95 (ISBN 0-8010-4159-7). Baker Bk.

Hulme, William E. Let the Spirit in: Practicing Christian Devotional Meditation. LC 78-26739. 1979. 5.95 (ISBN 0-687-21379-7). Abingdon.

Huntley, Frank L. Bishop Joseph Hall & Protestant Meditation in Seventeenth-Century England: A Study, with Texts of the Art of Divine Meditation (1606) & Occasional Meditations (1633) (Medieval & Renaissance Texts & Studies: 1). (Illus.). 234p. (Orig.). 1981. 11.95 (ISBN 0-86698-000-8); pap. 5.95 (ISBN 0-86698-005-9). Medieval.

Husserl. Cartesian Meditations. 1977. pap. 13.00 (ISBN 90-247-0068-X, Pub. by Martinus Nijhoff Netherlands). Kluwer Boston.

--Cartesianische Meditationen und Pariser Vortrage: Photomechanischer Nachdruck. (Husserliana Ser: No. 1). 1973. lib. bdg. 29.00 (ISBN 90-247-0214-3, Pub. by Martinus Nijhoff Netherlands). Kluwer Boston.

Ikerman, Ruth C. A Little Book of Comfort. LC 75-34421. 80p. 1976. 4.50 (ISBN 0-687-22145-5). Abingdon.

Ironside, H. A. The Continual Burnt Offering. 210p. 1981. pap. 4.50 (ISBN 0-87213-353-2). Loizeaux.

Jennings, Don. Light from Many Candles. 1977. softbound 4.95 (ISBN 0-87069-213-5). Wallace-Homestead.

Jess, Mary. Lights from the Chapel Window. (Direction Bks.). pap. 1.25 (ISBN 0-8010-5064-2). Baker Bk.

Johnson, C. Phillip. Will a Man Rob God? 1981. pap. 3.00 (ISBN 0-933184-29-8). Flame Intl.

Johnson, David. Guidelines: Thoughts on Christian Living. 1978. softbound 4.95 (ISBN 0-87069-226-7). Wallace-Homestead.

Johnson, Lois W. Gift in My Arms: Thoughts for New Mothers. LC 77-72448. 1977. pap. 2.95 (ISBN 0-8066-1586-9, 10-2549). Augsburg.

Jones, E. Stanley. Christian Maturity. (Festival Bks.). 1980. pap. 2.25 (ISBN 0-687-07453-3). Abingdon.

--How to Be a Transformed Person. (Festival Books). 1978. pap. 2.25 (ISBN 0-687-17724-3). Abingdon.

Jones, Mike. Sometimes I Wonder How to Thank Him. LC 75-26325. (Stories That Win Ser.). 1976. pap. 0.95 (ISBN 0-8163-0266-9, 19424-1). Pacific Pr Pub Assn.

Joness, Russell B. Gold from Golgotha. (Orig.). 1978. pap. 1.50 (ISBN 0-89228-024-7). Impact Bks MO.

Joyce, Robert. Thoughts to Ponder. 1980. 6.00 (ISBN 0-8198-7305-5); pap. 5.00 (ISBN 0-8198-7306-3). Dghtrs St Paul.

Julian Of Norwich. Enfolded in Love: Daily Readings with Julian of Norwich. Julian Shrine Members, tr. 96p. (Orig.). 1981. pap. 4.95 (ISBN 0-8164-2318-0). Seabury.

Kagawa, Toyohiko. Meditations. LC 78-12761. 1979. Repr. of 1950 ed. lib. bdg. 15.00x (ISBN 0-313-21180-9, KAMD). Greenwood.

Kahn, Hazrat I. Nature Meditations. LC 80-50829. (Collected Works of Hazrat Inayat Khan Ser.). (Illus.). 128p. (Orig.). 1980. pap. 5.00 (ISBN 0-930872-12-6). Sufi Order Pubns.

Keefe, Carolyn. Freedom for Me & Other Human Creatures. LC 77-83333. 1977. 5.95 (ISBN 0-8499-0037-9, 0037-9). Word Bks.

Keen, Sam. Beginnings Without End. LC 75-9321. 1977. pap. 3.95 (ISBN 0-06-064265-3, RD 245, HarpR). Har-Row.

Kemper, Frederick & Bass, George M. You Are My Beloved Sermon Book. 1980. pap. 6.95 (ISBN 0-570-03821-9, 12-2761). Concordia.

Keshavadas, Sadguru S. Gayatri, the Highest Meditation. 1979. 6.50 (ISBN 0-533-03188-5). Vantage.

Klenck, Robert H. Words Fitly Spoken: Reflections & Prayers. LC 79-13449. 1979. 7.95 (ISBN 0-396-07764-1, 07764-1, Dist. by W.W. Norton). Dembner Bks.

Knight, David M. Meditations for Priests. 1978. write for info. (ISBN 0-915488-05-1). Clarity Pub.

Koyama, Kosuke. Fifty Meditations. LC 77-7026. (Illus.). 1979. pap. 4.95 (ISBN 0-88344-134-9). Orbis Bks.

Krishanta. Thought Has Wings. 1975. pap. 4.95 (ISBN 0-87613-039-2). New Age.

Krishnamurti, J. Meditations. LC 79-1784. 1979. gift box 10.95 (ISBN 0-06-064851-1, HarpR). Har-Row.

Krummacher, F. W. The Suffering Savior. 1978. pap. 8.95 (ISBN 0-8024-8427-1). Moody.
Kung, Hans. The Church-Maintained in Truth: A Theological Meditation. 87p. 1980. 6.95 (ISBN 0-8245-0209-4). Crossroad NY.
Lang, Paul H. The Golden Days. LC 75-43871. (Large Print Ser.). 96p. 1976. pap. 4.50 (ISBN 0-570-03041-2, 6-1164). Concordia.
Lauterbach, William A. Through Cloud & Sunshine. (Illus.). 1979. 4.95 (ISBN 0-570-03056-0, 6-1181). Concordia.
Leclercq, Jacques. This Day Is Ours. Livingstone, Dinah, tr. LC 80-50314. Orig. Title: Le Jour de L'Homme. 160p. 1980. pap. 6.95 (ISBN 0-88344-504-2). Orbis Bks.
Lehn, Cornelia. Peace Be with You. LC 80-70190. (Illus.). 126p. 1981. 9.95 (ISBN 0-87303-061-3). Faith & Life.
Lenzkes, Susan L. When the Handwriting on the Wall Is Brown Crayon. 128p. (Orig.). 1981. pap. 2.95 (ISBN 0-310-43632-X). Zondervan.
Lorrance, Arleen. Musings for Meditation. LC 76-14783. (Illus.). 180p. (Orig.). 1976. pap. 2.50 (ISBN 0-916192-03-2). L P Pubns.
Lubich, Chiara. Meditations. LC 74-79452. 1974. pap. 1.95 (ISBN 0-911782-20-6). New City.
McCandless, Oleta R. Instant Help for Special Occasions. (Paperback Program Ser.). 1978. pap. 3.95 (ISBN 0-8010-6047-8). Baker Bk.
McCarroll, Tolbert. Notes from the Song of Life: Spiritual Reflections. LC 77-7135. (Illus.). 1977. pap. 4.95 (ISBN 0-89087-200-7). Celestial Arts.
McClain, Ernest G. Meditations Through the Quran: Tonal Images in an Oral Culture. LC 81-82124. (Illus.). 180p. 1981. 12.95 (ISBN 0-89254-009-5). Nicolas-Hays.
McKinney, Donald. Living with Joy. LC 76-8203. 1976. 4.95 (ISBN 0-687-22375-X). Abingdon.
McKuen, Rod. The Outstretched Hand: Poems, Prayers, & Meditations. LC 78-20589. 160p. 1980. 7.95 (ISBN 0-06-250568-8, HarpR). Har-Row.
Maclean, Dorothy. The Living Silence. 1981. pap. 4.50 (ISBN 0-905249-08-9, Pub. by Findhorn-Thule Scotland). Hydra Bk.
--To Hear the Angels Sing. 218p. 1981. pap. 6.50 (ISBN 0-905249-42-9, Pub. by Findhorn-Thule Scotland). Hydra Bk.
McMahon, Edwin H. & Campbell, Peter. Please Touch. 1969. pap. 4.95 (ISBN 0-685-30611-9). Andrews & McMeel.
Macquarrie, John. The Humility of God. 1978. pap. 4.65 (ISBN 0-664-24200-6). Westminster.
Mainprize, Don. Meditations for Teachers. (Good Morning Lord Ser.). 3.95 (ISBN 0-8010-5959-3). Baker Bk.
Mainprize, Donald. Good Morning, Lord: Meditations for Teachers. (Good Morning Lord Ser). 1974. 3.95 (ISBN 0-8010-5959-3). Baker Bk.
Makrakis, Apostolos. Orthodox Christian Meditations (Spiritual Discourses for the Orthodox Christians) Orthodox Christian Educational Society, ed. Cummings, Denver, tr. from Hellenic. 143p. (Orig.). 1965. pap. 2.00x (ISBN 0-938366-22-X). Orthodox Chr.
Manton, Joseph E. Stumbling Toward Heaven. LC 78-71262. 1979. pap. 3.95 (ISBN 0-87973-626-7). Our Sunday Visitor.
Martin, George. Your Word: Scripture Meditations. 144p. (Orig.). 1980. pap. 2.25 (ISBN 0-89283-090-5). Servant.
Martin, Paul. Good Morning, Lord: Devotions for Young People. (Good Morning, Lord Ser.). 1974. 3.95 (ISBN 0-8010-5958-5). Baker Bk.
Mattson, Lloyd. Devotions for Men. (Good Morning Lord Ser.). 2.45 (ISBN 0-686-74074-2). Baker Bk.
Maxwell, John E. Christian Meditations for Campers. 1978. pap. 2.75 (ISBN 0-89536-296-1). CSS Pub.
May, Leland C. Good Morning Lord: Meditations for College Students. (Good Morning Lord Ser.). 64p. (Orig.). 1981. 3.95 (ISBN 0-8010-6116-4). Baker Bk.
Meditation: Humanity's Race & Divinity's Grace, Pt. 2. 1974. 2.00 (ISBN 0-685-61446-8). Aum Pubns.
Meditations: Food for the Soul. 1.00 (ISBN 0-685-61447-6). Aum Pubns.
Meditations of My Heart. (Gifts of Gold Ser.). 3.50 (ISBN 0-442-82497-1). Peter Pauper.
Mendes, Reva. Words for the Quiet Moments. 35p. 1973. pap. 1.00 (ISBN 0-87516-185-5). De Vorss.
Merton, Thomas. Thoughts in Solitude. 124p. 1976. pap. 2.95 (ISBN 0-374-51325-2, N524). FS&G.
Metz, Johannes B. & Moltmann, Jurgen. Meditations on the Passion. LC 78-70823. 1979. pap. 1.75 (ISBN 0-8091-2184-0). Paulist Pr.
Meyer, F. B. Devotions & Prayers of F.B. Meyer. (Direction Bks.). pap. 1.95 (ISBN 0-8010-6084-2). Baker Bk.
Michelino. The Keys to Truth. 1977. 5.00 (ISBN 0-8022-2194-7). Philos Lib.
Middleton, R. A. The Gift of Love. LC 76-2241. 128p. 1976. 3.95 (ISBN 0-8054-5145-5). Broadman.
Moody, Dwight L., ed. Thoughts for the Quiet Hour. pap. 1.95 (ISBN 0-8024-8729-7). Moody.
Morgan, Elise N. The Angel of the Presence. (Meditation Ser.). 1922. 3.00 (ISBN 0-87516-327-0). De Vorss.
--The Illimitable One. (Meditation Ser.). 1934. 3.00 (ISBN 0-87516-329-7). De Vorss.
--Now This Day. 1948. 3.00 (ISBN 0-87516-330-0). De Vorss.
--That We May Be Willing to Receive. (Meditation Ser.). 1938. 3.00 (ISBN 0-87516-331-9). De Vorss.
--The Way. (Meditation Ser.). 1972. 3.00 (ISBN 0-87516-332-7). De Vorss.
--Your Own Path. (Meditation Ser.). 1928. 3.00 (ISBN 0-87516-333-5). De Vorss.
Morning, Evening Thoughts. 1967. 2.95 (ISBN 0-442-82345-2). Peter Pauper.
Mother Teresa. A Gift for God: Prayers & Meditations. LC 76-351371. 96p. 1980. 6.95 (ISBN 0-06-068233-7). Har-Row.
Mow, Anna B. Springs of Love. LC 79-11186. 1979. pap. 1.95 (ISBN 0-87178-810-1). Brethren.
Muehl, William. All the Damned Angels. LC 77-185414. 1972. 4.95 (ISBN 0-8298-0230-4). Pilgrim NY.
Muktananda, Swami. I Am That: The Science of Hamsa from Vijnana Bhairava, Vol. 24. (Illus., Orig.). 1978. pap. 3.50 (ISBN 0-914602-27-6). SYDA Found.
--I Welcome You All with Love. (Illus., Orig.). 1978. pap. 1.25 (ISBN 0-914602-59-4). SYDA Found.
Mullen, Tom. Birthdays, Holidays, & Other Disasters. 1978. pap. 1.95 (ISBN 0-8499-4105-9, 4105-9, Key Word Bks). Word Bks.
Murphy, Elspeth C. Chalkdust: Prayer Meditations for a Teacher. 1978. 4.95 (ISBN 0-8010-6065-6). Baker Bk.
Murphy, Joseph. Special Meditations for Health, Wealth, Love. pap. 1.50 (ISBN 0-87516-336-X). De Vorss.
Murray, Andrew. The Best of Andrew Murray. (Best Ser.). pap. 3.45 (ISBN 0-8010-6069-9). Baker Bk.
My Book of Feelings. 1977. 6.95 (ISBN 0-8065-0585-0). Citadel Pr.
My Favorite Prayers & Reflections. 1973. plastic 4.00 (ISBN 0-8198-0276-X). Dghtrs St Paul.
Myers, Victor A. The Story I Love to Tell: Meditations for the '80s. 140p. (Orig.). 1980. pap. 5.95 (ISBN 0-937172-02-2). Kindinger.
Nadzo, Stefan C. There Is a Way: Mediations for a Seeker. LC 80-66831. (Illus.). 129p. (Orig.). 1980. pap. 5.95 (ISBN 0-937226-00-9). Eden's Work.
Nee, Watchman. Table in the Wilderness. 1969. pap. 2.95 (ISBN 0-87508-422-2). Chr Lit.
Neighbour, Ralph W., ed. Golden Nuggets. 1969. 3.95 (ISBN 0-529-00800-9, A3475N). Collins Pubs.
Nelson, Ruth Y. You Can Make a Difference: American Mother of the Year Shares the Secret of Dynamic Christian Living. LC 74-77678. 112p. (Orig.). 1974. pap. 2.95 (ISBN 0-8066-1429-3, 10-7412). Augsburg.
Nethery, Susan. A Mother Shares: Meditations on Parenting. 128p. 1981. 4.95 (ISBN 0-8010-6736-7). Baker Bk.
Newman, John H. Blessed Art Thou Among Women. 2.45 (ISBN 0-87193-076-5). Dimension Bks.
Nixon, David. The Year of the Locust. 138p. (Orig.). 1980. pap. 3.95 (ISBN 0-8341-0675-2). Beacon Hill.
Noonan, Hugh. Companion to the Clams. 1980. pap. 12.50 (ISBN 0-8199-0680-8). Franciscan Herald.
Nouwen, Henri J. Out of Solitude. (Illus.). 64p. 1974. pap. 1.75 (ISBN 0-87793-072-4). Ave Maria.
Oates, Wayne E. Nurturing Silence in a Noisy Heart. LC 78-20089. (Illus.). 1979. 7.95 (ISBN 0-385-14787-2, Galilee). Doubleday.
O'Collins, Gerald. A Month with Jesus. pap. 2.95 (ISBN 0-87193-097-8). Dimension Bks.
Oda, Stephanie C., compiled by. To Everything There Is a Season: Writings That Celebrate Life's Many Joys. (Illus.). 1979. boxed 4.95 (ISBN 0-8378-1705-6). Gibson.
Ogilvie, Lloyd. Let God Love You. 1978. pap. 3.95 (ISBN 0-8499-2831-1, 2831-1). Word Bks.
Ogilvie, Lloyd J. God's Best for My Life. LC 81-82390. 390p. (Orig.). 1981. 9.95 (ISBN 0-89081-293-4, 2934). Harvest Hse.
Osgood, DeWitt S. Preparing for the Latter Rain. LC 73-75219. 144p. 1973. pap. 4.50 (ISBN 0-8127-0070-8). Review & Herald.
Owens, Virginia S. A Taste of Creation. 1980. pap. 4.50 (ISBN 0-8170-0865-9). Judson.
Palms, Roger C. God's Promises for You. 1977. pap. 3.95 (ISBN 0-8007-0888-1). Revell.
Paramananda, Swami. Concentration & Meditation. 8th ed. 1974. pap. 2.25 (ISBN 0-911564-07-1). Vedanta Ctr.
Pate, Billie. Rags, Tags, & Gentle Tears. 64p. (gr. 9-12). 1973. pap. 1.95 (ISBN 0-8054-5315-6). Broadman.
Pearson, Nancy & Spiegelberg, Stanley, trs. To Live Within: The Story of Five Years with a Himalayan Guru. 284p. 1974. 12.50 (ISBN 0-04-291008-0). Allen Unwin.
Peguy, Charles. Pensees. pap. 1.95 (ISBN 0-685-37035-6). French & Eur.
Perry, Oberlin W., Sr. & Perry, Chandler R. Inspirational Readings. 1978. 6.95 (ISBN 0-533-03528-7). Vantage.
Peterman, Ruth. My World Was Too Small. 1974. pap. 1.45 (ISBN 0-8423-4658-9). Tyndale.
Petty, Jo, compiled by. Words of Silver & Gold. 1977. gift-boxed 7.95 (ISBN 0-8007-0867-9). Revell.
Phillips, Margaret. Songs of the Good Earth. LC 79-10731. 62p. 1980. pap. 4.95 (ISBN 0-88289-221-5). Pelican.
Plantinga, Cornelius, Jr. Beyond Doubt: A Devotional Response to Questions of Faith. LC 80-10647. (Illus.). 256p. (Orig.). 1980. pap. text ed. 4.95 (ISBN 0-933140-12-6). Bd of Pubns CRC.
Poganski, Donald J. Forty Object Lessons. LC 72-86233. 160p. 1973. pap. 3.50 (ISBN 0-570-03148-6, 12-2283). Concordia.
Preston, Geoffrey. Hallowing the Time: Meditations on the Cycle of the Christian Liturgy. LC 80-82253. 176p. (Orig.). 1980. pap. 5.95 (ISBN 0-8091-2339-8). Paulist Pr.
Progoff, Ira. The Well & the Cathedral. rev. ed. LC 76-20823. 166p. 1981. pap. 3.95 (ISBN 0-87941-011-6). Dialogue Hse.
Quoist, Michael. Prayers. 1975. pap. 4.95 (ISBN 0-380-00406-2, 51375). Avon.
Quoist, Michel. Prayers. 179p. 1974. 6.95 (ISBN 0-8362-0233-3). Andrews & McMeel.
Rainford, Marcus. Our Lord Prays for His Own. 1978. pap. 8.95 (ISBN 0-8024-6195-6). Moody.
Rees, Wilbur E. Three Dollars Worth of God. LC 77-151044. 1971. 2.95 (ISBN 0-8170-0505-6). Judson.
Rev. Viola Rothacker. Precious Jewels. 1979. 6.50 (ISBN 0-533-03832-4). Vantage.
Riess, Walter. Christ's Love Will Make You Live. rev. ed. LC 72-97345. 1973. 2.50 (ISBN 0-570-03156-7, 12-2541). Concordia.
Rockness, Miriam H. Keep These Things, Ponder Them in Your Heart: Reflections of a Mother. LC 78-14656. 1979. 7.95 (ISBN 0-385-14824-0, Galilee). Doubleday.
Roeck, Alan L. Twenty-Four Hours a Day for Everyone. LC 78-52007. (Orig.). 1977. pap. 5.95 (ISBN 0-89486-040-2). Hazelden.
Rosemergy, Jim. A Recent Revelation. LC 81-50146. 137p. 1981. 3.95 (ISBN 0-87159-002-6). Unity Bks.
Russell, Marjorie H. Handbook of Christian Meditation. 1978. pap. 4.95 (ISBN 0-8159-5713-0). Devin.
St. Catherine Of Siena. The Dialogue of St. Catherine of Siena. Thorold, Algar, tr. from It. & intro. by. 1976. pap. 4.00 (ISBN 0-89555-037-7, 150). TAN Bks Pubs.
Saint Bernard. Medytacons of Saynt Bernarde. LC 77-6855. (English Experience Ser.: No. 847). 1977. Repr. of 1496 ed. lib. bdg. 8.00 (ISBN 90-221-0847-3). Walter J Johnson.
Samples, B. Mind of Our Mother: Toward Holonomy & Planetary Consciousness. 1981. 11.95 (ISBN 0-201-06667-X); pap. 6.95 (ISBN 0-201-06668-8). A-W.
Saraydarian, Torkom. I Was. 1981. pap. 7.00 (ISBN 0-911794-43-3). Aqua Educ.
--Psyche & Psychism, 2 vols. 1981. Set. 50.00 (ISBN 0-911794-06-9); Set. pap. 35.00 (ISBN 0-911794-07-7). Aqua Educ.
Sayers, Dorothy L. A Matter of Eternity. Sprague, Rosamond K., ed. 128p. 1973. 2.95 (ISBN 0-8028-1681-9). Eerdmans.
Schaeffer, Francis & Schaeffer, Edith. Everybody Can Know. 1975. 6.95 (ISBN 0-8423-0785-0). Tyndale.
Schaffer, Ulrich. For the Love of Children. LC 79-2984. 128p. (Orig.). 1980. pap. 3.95 (ISBN 0-06-067084-3, RD 310, HarpR). Har-Row.
--Love Reaches Out. LC 75-70810. 96p. (Orig.). 1976. pap. 3.95 (ISBN 0-06-067080-0, RD320, HarpR). Har-Row.
Scripture Union. Every Day: Bible Readings for Each Day of the Year. LC 72-4169. 1972. 3.95 (ISBN 0-87981-015-7). Holman.
Seaman, William R. The Many-Sided Cross: A Personal Retreat. 1977. 5.95 (ISBN 0-533-02796-9). Vantage.
Seamands, John T. Power for the Day: 108 Meditations from Matthew. LC 75-45044. 112p. 1976. pap. 3.50 (ISBN 0-687-33265-6). Abingdon.
Sechrist, Elsie. Meditation: Der Weg Zum Licht. Kronberger, Helge F., tr. from Eng. (Illus.). 53p. (Ger.). 1980. pap. 6.00 (ISBN 0-87604-131-4). ARE Pr.
Sedore, Marva J. To Walk & Not Faint. LC 80-65433. 160p. (Orig.). 1980. pap. 5.95 (ISBN 0-915684-65-9). Christian Herald.
Seymour, Peter, compiled by. Moments Bright & Shining: Three Hundred & Sixty-Five Thoughts to Enjoy Day by Day. (Illus.). 1979. boxed 4.95 (ISBN 0-8378-1706-4). Gibson.
--Reflections: Quiet Thoughts to Sample & Savor at Bedtime. (Illus.). 1979. boxed 4.95 (ISBN 0-8378-1704-8). Gibson.
Sharp, Don. Forty-Six Sharp Points. LC 75-38224. (New Life Ser.). 96p. 1976. pap. 1.95 (ISBN 0-87239-092-6, 40038). Standard Pub.
Shepherd, J. Barrie. A Diary of Prayer: Daily Meditations on the Parables of Jesus. LC 80-27037. 1981. pap. 5.95 (ISBN 0-664-24352-5). Westminster.
Shrader, Elizabeth H. & Hand, Katherine. Meditations on Ancient Wisdom. 1977. pap. 1.75 (ISBN 0-685-82000-9). Creative Pr.
Sibley, Celestine. Small Blessings. 1978. lib. bdg. 10.95 (ISBN 0-8161-6570-X, Large Print Bks). G K Hall.
--Small Blessings. LC 76-42394. 1977. 7.95 (ISBN 0-385-12318-3). Doubleday.
Skogsbergh, Helga. Time to Reflect. 1965. 2.95 (ISBN 0-910452-11-3). Covenant.
Smith, Jean L. Take More Joy. LC 73-87023. (Illus.). 95p. (Orig.). 1974. pap. 4.95 (ISBN 0-88489-054-6). St Marys.
Snowden, Rita F. On the Tip of My Tongue. 1973. pap. 1.75x (ISBN 0-8358-0283-3). Upper Room.
Sophrony, Archimandrite. His Life Is Mine. Edmonds, Rosemary, tr. from Russian. LC 76-56815. 128p. 1977. pap. 4.95 (ISBN 0-913836-33-8). St Vladimirs.
Spangler, David. The Laws of Manifestation. 112p. 1981. pap. 4.50 (ISBN 0-905249-16-X, Pub. by Findhorn-Thule Scotland). Hydra Bk.
--Links with Space. 1981. pap. 2.95 (ISBN 0-905249-33-X, Pub. by Findhorn-Thule Scotland). Hydra Bk.
Spiritual Diary. 2nd ed. 368p. (Orig.). 1981. pap. 5.95 (ISBN 0-89389-073-1). Himalayan Intl Inst.
Spurgeon, Charles H. Morning & Evening. 1980. 10.95 (ISBN 0-310-32920-5); large print 8.95 (ISBN 0-310-32927-2). Zondervan.
Sri Aurobindo. The Mother: With Letters on the Mother & Translations of Prayers & Meditations. 1972. 8.50 (ISBN 0-89071-258-1). Matagiri.
Stine, Peter. Sense of God: Meditations for Thinking Christians. 128p. 1980. 4.95 (ISBN 0-8010-8183-1). Baker Bk.
Subramuniya. Gems of Wisdom. (Illus.). 234p. 1973. 7.00 (ISBN 0-87516-346-7); pap. 5.00 (ISBN 0-87516-345-9). De Vorss.
--Raja Yoga. (Illus.). 193p. 1973. 7.00 (ISBN 0-87516-348-3); pap. 5.00 (ISBN 0-87516-347-5). De Vorss.
--Reflections. (On the Path Ser.). (Illus.). 72p. 1969. pap. 2.00 (ISBN 0-87516-354-8). De Vorss.
Taliaferro, Margaret. Do You Ever Have Questions Like These? LC 78-61448. (Illus.). 1979. 7.95 (ISBN 0-385-14789-9, Galilee). Doubleday.
Teilhard De Chardin, Pierre. Reflexions et Prieres dans L'espace-temps. 13.95 (ISBN 0-685-36601-4). French & Eur.
--Sur L'amour. pap. 6.25 (ISBN 0-685-36602-2). French & Eur.
--Sur le Bonheur. pap. 6.25 (ISBN 0-685-36603-0). French & Eur.
Ten Boom, Corrie. Each New Day. 1977. 9.95 (ISBN 0-8007-0894-6); pap. 2.50 (ISBN 0-8007-8403-0, Spire Bks). Revell.
Tengbom, Mildred & Tengbom, Luverne. Fill My Cup, Lord: Meditations on Word Pictures in the New Testament. LC 78-66944. 1979. pap. 3.95 (ISBN 0-8066-1681-4, 10-2308). Augsburg.
The Mother. Prayers & Meditations. rev. ed. Aurobindo, Sri, tr. from Fr. 380p. (Orig.). 1979. pap. 10.00 (ISBN 0-89744-998-3, Sri Aurobindo Ashram Trust India). Auromere.
Thought for the Day. 1978. plastic comb bdg. 2.25 (ISBN 0-89389-041-3). Himalayan Intl Inst.
Thurman, Howard. The Centering Moment. LC 80-67469. 1980. pap. 3.95 (ISBN 0-913408-64-6). Friends United.
Tilman, Klemens. Meditation in Depth. LC 78-78332. 1979. pap. 4.95 (ISBN 0-8091-2204-9). Paulist Pr.
Tulku, Tarthang. Crystal Mirror, Vol. I. (Illus.). 1971. pap. 4.95 (ISBN 0-913546-04-6). Dharma Pub.
--Crystal Mirror, Vol. II. (Illus.). 1972. pap. 5.95 (ISBN 0-913546-00-3). Dharma Pub.
--Crystal Mirror, Vol. III. (Illus.). 1974. pap. 6.95 (ISBN 0-913546-05-4). Dharma Pub.
Turro, James C. Reflections: Path to Prayer. 1972. 7.50 (ISBN 0-8091-8754-X). Paulist Pr.
Unruh, Fred. Questions I'd Like to Ask God. LC 80-67504. (Illus.). 64p. 1980. tchr's. guide 3.95 (ISBN 0-87303-041-9). Faith & Life.

Upper Room Disciplines 1982. (Orig.). 1981. pap. 3.25x (ISBN 0-8358-0407-0). Upper Room.
Valery, Paul. Mauvaises Pensees et Autres. pap. 6.95 (ISBN 0-685-36618-9). French & Eur.
Van Nuys, Roscoe. Whole Man. LC 77-145467. 1971. 5.95 (ISBN 0-8022-2050-9). Philos Lib.
Van Zeller, Hubert. Letters to a Soul. 1976. 7.95 (ISBN 0-87243-067-7). Templegate.
--To Be in Christ. LC 81-9793. (Illus.). 112p. 1981. 9.95 (ISBN 0-8245-0086-5). Crossroad NY.
Vass, Winifred K. Thirty-One Banana Leaves. LC 74-7617. 64p. 1975. 3.95 (ISBN 0-8042-2582-6). John Knox.
Vishnewski, Stanley. Meditations-Dorothy Day. LC 73-133570. 1970. pap. 2.95 (ISBN 0-8091-1636-7). Paulist Pr.
Vuilleumier, Marion. Meditations by the Sea. LC 79-18830. (Orig.). 1980. pap. 4.95 (ISBN 0-687-24082-4). Abingdon.
Wagner, Clarence M. Seeds of Faith. (Vol. 11). 100p. 1981. pap. 4.00x (ISBN 0-937498-02-5). Tru-Faith.
Walchars, John. Voices on Fire: A Book of Meditations. LC 81-7767. 250p. 1981. pap. 7.95 (ISBN 0-8245-0094-6). Crossroad NY.
Walker, Alan. Jesus the Liberator. LC 73-6804. 128p. 1973. 3.95 (ISBN 0-687-20199-3). Abingdon.
Wang, Leland. Arrows of the Lord. 1957. pap. 0.60 (ISBN 0-87213-918-2). Loizeaux.
Ward, Benedicta, tr. Prayers & Meditations of St. Anselm. (Classics Ser.). 1979. pap. 2.95 (ISBN 0-14-044278-2). Penguin.
Weenink, Allan J. Only the Wounded Can Serve: Select Communion Meditations. (Orig.). 1977. pap. 5.05 (ISBN 0-89536-179-5). CSS Pub.
West, Darla L. Love Every Month. (Illus.). 48p. (Orig.). 1981. pap. 4.95 (ISBN 0-9604344-4-5). Sunrise Pub OR.
Whaley, Catrina P. Share My Meditations. 1967. 2.95 (ISBN 0-8010-9560-3). Baker Bk.
White Eagle. Prayer in the New Age. 1957. 2.95 (ISBN 0-85487-041-5). De Vorss.
Wiersbe, Warren. His Name Is Wonderful. 1976. 3.95 (ISBN 0-8423-1435-0); pap. 1.95 (ISBN 0-8423-1437-7). Tyndale.
--Thoughts for Men on the Move. 1970. pap. 1.50 (ISBN 0-8024-0132-5). Moody.
Wiersbe, Warren W. Bumps Are What You Climb on. 1980. pap. 3.95 (ISBN 0-8010-9629-4). Baker Bk.
Willis, Elbert. Private Praise. 1977. 1.00 (ISBN 0-89858-009-9). Fill the Gap.
Wilson, Jim. Meditation & the Fulness of Life. 1974. pap. text ed. 4.50 (ISBN 0-227-67810-9). Attic Pr.
Wilson, Leland. Living with Wonder. LC 76-19543. 1977. pap. 3.25 (ISBN 0-87680-839-9, 98097). Word Bks.
Wolf, William J., compiled by. Thomas Traherne's Centuries of Meditation. 1980. 1.60 (ISBN 0-686-28796-7). Forward Movement.
Zunkel, Cleda S. Cornbread & Milk. 128p. (Orig.). 1980. pap. 2.25 (ISBN 0-87178-160-3). Brethren.

MEDITERRANEAN DISEASE
see Thalassemia

MEDITERRANEAN RACE
see also Greeks

Davis, John. People of the Mediterranean: An Essay in Comparative Social Anthropology. (Library of Man). 1976. 17.00x (ISBN 0-7100-8412-9). Routledge & Kegan.
Sergi, Giuseppe. Mediterranean Race: A Study of the Origin of European Peoples. LC 68-112231. (Illus.). 1967. pap. text ed. 11.00x (ISBN 90-6234-038-5). Humanities.

MEDITERRANEAN REGION

Aspects of Brackish Water Fish & Crustacean Culture in the Mediterranean. 135p. 1981. pap. 8.75 (ISBN 92-5-000964-X, F2103, FAO). Unipub.
Beny, Roloff. Odyssey: Mirror of the Mediterranean. LC 81-47220. (Illus.). 360p. 1981. 70.00 (ISBN 0-06-014879-9, HarpT). Har-Row.
Burrell, R. Michael & Cottrell, Alvin J. Politics, Oil, & the Western Mediterranean. LC 73-638. (The Washington Papers: No. 7). 80p. 1973. write for information 4.00 (ISBN 0-8039-0259-X). Sage.
Fire & Fuel Management in Mediterranean-Climate Ecosystems: Research Priorities & Programmes. (MAB Technical Note: No. 11). 1979. pap. 6.25 (ISBN 92-3-101688-1, U920, UNESCO). Unipub.
Gellner, Ernest & Waterbury, John, eds. Patrons & Clients. LC 77-4726. 1977. text ed. 16.95 (ISBN 0-910116-99-7). Am U Field.
Johl, S. S. & De Clerq, C. Irrigation & Agricultural Development. LC 80-40435. (Illus.). 386p. 1980. 58.00 (ISBN 0-08-025675-9). Pergamon.
Kent, Maxwell. The Mediterranean Revolution: Changing Patterns in the Economic & Political World's Power & Dominion. (Illus.). 1977. 41.25 (ISBN 0-89266-020-1). Am Classical Coll Pr.
Learning About People & Cultures. Incl. The Mediterranean Rim (ISBN 0-88343-636-1); Southeast Asia (ISBN 0-88343-646-9); India (ISBN 0-88343-644-2). (People & Cculture Ser.). (gr. 9 up). 1974-76. 5.28 ea.; tchrs' manual 1.50 ea. McDougal-Littell.
Lewis, Archibald R. Naval Power & Trade in the Mediterranean: A.D. 500-1100. (Princeton Studies in History: Vol. 5). 1970. Repr. of 1951 ed. 18.50 (ISBN 0-384-32470-3). Johnson Repr.
Lewis, Jesse W., Jr. The Strategic Balance in the Mediterranean. LC 75-37446. 1976. pap. 6.25 (ISBN 0-8447-3197-8). Am Enterprise.
Lord, Walter E. England & France in the Mediterranean 1660-1830. LC 73-110902. 1970. Repr. of 1901 ed. 14.00 (ISBN 0-8046-0894-6). Kennikat.
Luttwak, Edward N. & Weinland, Robert G. Sea Power in the Mediterranean: Political Utility & Military Constraints. LC 78-62800. (The Washington Papers: No. 61). 96p. 1979. pap. 4.00 (ISBN 0-8039-1126-2). Sage.
Marriner, John. Mariner in the Mediterranean. 1967. 12.50x (ISBN 0-8002-1702-0). Intl Pubns Serv.
Mediterranean. (Winston Mine Editions). 1970. text ed. 6.00 (ISBN 0-685-33389-2, HoltC). HR&W.
Mediterranean Forest & Maquis: Ecology, Conservation & Management. (MAB Technical Notes: No. 2). (Illus.). 1977. pap. 5.25 (ISBN 92-3-101388-2, U370, UNESCO). Unipub.
Peristiany, J. G. Honour & Shame: The Values of Mediterranean Society. LC 66-11886. (Midway Reprint Ser). 266p. 1974. pap. 10.00x (ISBN 0-226-65714-0). U of Chicago Pr.
Peristiany, J. G., ed. Mediterranean Family Structure. LC 75-20833. (Cambridge Studies in Social Anthropology: No. 13). (Illus.). 434p. 1976. 39.95 (ISBN 0-521-20964-1). Cambridge U Pr.
Reitzel, William. Mediterranean: Its Role in American Foreign Policy. LC 71-79310. 1969. Repr. of 1948 ed. 12.50 (ISBN 0-8046-0531-9). Kennikat.
Selected Bibliography on Studies & Research Relevant to Pollution in the Mediterranean. (FAO Fisheries Technical Paper: No. 165). 1977. pap. 7.50 (ISBN 92-5-000253-X, F897, FAO). Unipub.
Siegfried, Andre. The Mediterranean. Hemming, Doris, tr. LC 78-59042. (Illus.). 1979. Repr. of 1948 ed. 19.00 (ISBN 0-88355-714-2). Hyperion Conn.
Van Nieuwenhuijze, C. A., ed. Emigration & Agriculture in the Mediterranean Basin. LC 72-86184. (Institute of Social Studies, Paperback Ser: No. 8). (Illus.). 188p. 1972. pap. text ed. 22.75x (ISBN 90-2792-220-9). Mouton.
Williams, Ann, ed. Prophecy & Millenarianism. (Illus.). 368p. 1981. text ed. 60.00x (ISBN 0-582-36136-2). Longman.

MEDITERRANEAN REGION–ANTIQUITIES

Davis, J. Rogers & Webster, T. B. Cesnola Terracottos in the Stanford University Museum. (Studies in Mediterranean Archaeology Ser.: No. XVI). (Illus.). 1964. pap. text ed. 5.75x (ISBN 91-8505-815-7). Humanities.
Frankel, David. Middle Cypriote White Painted Pottery: An Analytical Study of the Decoration. (Studies in Mediterranean Archaeology Ser.: No. XLII). (Illus.). 1974. pap. text ed. 11.25x (ISBN 91-85058-60-2). Humanities.
Hanfmann, George M. From Croesus to Constantine: The Cities of Western Asia Minor & Their Arts in Greek & Roman Times. LC 73-80574. (Jerome Lecture Ser: No. 10). (Illus.). 1974. text ed. 15.00x (ISBN 0-472-08420-8). U of Mich Pr.
Hellbing, L. Alasia Problems. (Studies in Mediterranean Archaeology: No. 57). 1979. pap. text ed. 35.00x (ISBN 9-1850-5890-4). Humanities.
Kaplan, M. F. The Origin & Distribution of Tell el-Yahudiyeh Ware. (Studies in Mediterranean Archaeology Ser.: Vol. LXII). 336p. 1981. pap. text ed. 84.00x (ISBN 91-85058-49-1, Pub. by Paul Astroms Sweden). Humanities.
Laffineur, Robert. Les Vases En Metal Precieux a L'epoque Mycenienne. (Studies in Mediterranean Archaeology Pocket Bks.: No. 4). (Illus.). 1977. pap. text ed. 21.00x (ISBN 91-85058-73-4). Humanities.
Levi, Doro. The Recent Excavations at Phaistos. (Studies in Mediterranean Archaeology Ser.: No. XI). (Illus.). 1964. pap. text ed. 10.00x (ISBN 0-391-02033-1). Humanities.
McBurney, C. B. Haua Fteah & the Stone Age of the South-East Mediterranean. 1968. 99.00 (ISBN 0-521-06915-7). Cambridge U Pr.
McCaslin, Dan E. Stone Anchors in Antiquity: Coastal Settlements & Maritime Trade-Routes in the Eastern Mediterranean Ca. 1600-1050 B.C. 145p. 1981. pap. text ed. 42.00x (ISBN 91-85058-96-3, Pub. by Paul Astroms Sweden). Humanities.
Masson, Emilia. Cyprominoica: Reportoires Documents De Ras Sharma. (Studies in Mediterranean Archaeology: Vol. XXXI, Pt. 2). (Illus., Orig.). 1974. pap. text ed. 16.75x (ISBN 91-85058-43-2). Humanities.
Merker, Gloria S. The Hellenistic Sculpture of Rhodes. (Studies in Mediterranean Archaeology Ser.: No. XL). (Illus.). 1973. pap. text ed. 14.00x (ISBN 91-85058-58-0). Humanities.
Negbi, Ora. The Hoards of Goldwork from Tell el Ajjul. (Studies in Mediterranean Archaeology Ser.: No. XXV). (Illus.). 1970. pap. text ed. 14.00x (ISBN 0-391-01990-2). Humanities.
Papadopoulos, Athanasios. Excavations at Aigion Nineteen Seventy. (Studies in Mediterranean Archaeology Ser.: No. XLVI). (Illus.). 1976. pap. text ed. 56.00x (ISBN 91-85058-68-8). Humanities.
Roos, Paavo. The Rock Tombs of Caunus No. One: The Architecture. (Studies in Mediterranean Archaeology Ser.: No. XXXIV 1). 1972. pap. text ed. 28.00x (ISBN 91-85058-52-1). Humanities.
--The Rock Tombs of Caunus No. Two: The Finds. (Studies in Mediterranean Archaeology Ser: No. XXXIV 2). (Illus.). 1974. pap. text ed. 11.25x (ISBN 91-85058-53-X). Humanities.
Rose, J. Holland. The Mediterranean in the Ancient World. 1980. 10.00 (ISBN 0-89005-204-2). Ares.
Simpson, R. H. & Dickinson, O. P. A Gasetteer of Aegean Civilisation in the Bronze Age. (Studies in Mediterranean Archaeology: No. LII). (Orig.). 1979. pap. text ed. 56.00x (ISBN 91-85058-81-5). Humanities.
Stark, Freya. Alexander's Path. 1975. 18.50 (ISBN 0-7195-1332-4). Transatlantic.
--Dust in the Lion's Paw. 1975. 22.00 (ISBN 0-7195-1334-0). Transatlantic.
--Rome on the Euphrates. 1975. 28.50 (ISBN 0-7195-1335-9). Transatlantic.
--Zodiac Arch. 1975. 14.00 (ISBN 0-7195-1784-2). Transatlantic.
Tengvig, Olaf T. & Astrom, Paul. Hala Sultan Tekke No. Two: The Cape Kiti Survey, An Underwater Archaeological Survey. (Studies in Mediterranean Archaeology Ser.: No. XLV, Pt. 2). (Illus.). 1975. pap. text ed. 10.00x (ISBN 91-85058-66-1). Humanities.
Trump, D. H. The Prehistory of the Mediterranean. LC 79-56617. (Illus.). 320p. 1981. pap. 6.95x (ISBN 0-300-02700-1). Yale U Pr.
--The Prehistory of the Mediterranean. LC 79-56617. (Illus.). 1980. 25.00x (ISBN 0-300-02538-6). Yale U Pr.
Wells, P. S. Culture Contact & Culture Change. LC 80-40212. (New Studies in Archaeology). (Illus.). 195p. 1981. 24.95 (ISBN 0-521-22808-5). Cambridge U Pr.
Wistrand, Erik. Politik Och Literatur I Antikens Rom. (Studies in Mediterranean Archaeology Pocket Bk.: No. 7). 1978. pap. text ed. 14.00x (ISBN 91-85058-82-3). Humanities.

MEDITERRANEAN REGION–DESCRIPTION AND TRAVEL

Bristow, Philip. Down the Spanish Coast. 196p. 1980. 12.00x (ISBN 0-245-52935-7, Pub. by Nautical England). State Mutual Bk.
Davis, Richard H. Rulers of the Mediterranean. facsimile ed. LC 76-38788. (Essay Index Reprint Ser). Repr. of 1893 ed. 22.00 (ISBN 0-8369-2645-5). Arno.
Digby, Kenelm. Journal of a Voyage into the Mediterranean A.D. 1628. 1868. 15.50 (ISBN 0-384-11770-8). Johnson Repr.
Digby, Kenlem, ed. Journal of a Voyage into the Mediterranean, 1628. LC 72-164832. (Camden Society, London. Publications, First Ser.: No. 96). Repr. of 1868 ed. 14.00 (ISBN 0-404-50196-6). AMS Pr.
Facaros, Dana & Pauls, Michael. Mediterranean Island Hopping: The Italian Islands, Corsica & Malta. (Travel Ser.). (Illus.). 500p. 1981. pap. 17.95 (ISBN 0-88254-589-2). Hippocrene Bks.
--Mediterranean Island Hopping: The Spanish Islands. (Illus.). 304p. 1981. pap. 14.95 (ISBN 0-88254-588-4). Hippocrene Bks.
Garth, Sheridan H. Pageant of the Mediterranean. rev. ed. (Illus.). 1962. 9.95 (ISBN 0-8038-5690-3). Hastings.
Isreal, John & Lundt, Henry. Journal of a Cruize in the U.S. Ship Delaware 74 in the Mediterranean in the Years 1833 & 34. Davis, Moshe, ed. LC 77-70707. (America & the Holy Land Ser.). (Illus.). 1977. Repr. of 1835 ed. lib. bdg. 12.00x (ISBN 0-405-10257-7). Arno.
Pardey, Lin & Pardey, Larry. Seraffyn's Mediterranen Adventure. (Illus.). 1981. 18.95 (ISBN 0-393-03266-3). Norton.

MEDITERRANEAN REGION–HISTORY

Best, Jan & De Vries, Nanny, eds. Interaction & Acculturation in the Mediterranean. (Publications of the Henri Frankfort Foundation Ser.: Vol. 6). 221p. 1981. pap. text ed. 45.75x (ISBN 90-6032-194-4, Pub. by B R Gruner Netherlands). Humanities.
Braudel, Fernand. The Mediterranean & the Mediterranean World in the Age of Philip Second, 2 vols. rev. 2nd ed. Reynolds, Sian, tr. from Fr. (Illus.). 1418p. 1976. Vol. 1. pap. 8.95 (ISBN 0-06-090566-2, CN566, CN); Vol. 2. pap. 9.95 (ISBN 0-06-090567-0, CN567, CN). Har-Row.
Davis, John. People of the Mediterranean: An Essay in Comparative Social Anthropology. (Library of Man). 1976. 17.00x (ISBN 0-7100-8412-9). Routledge & Kegan.
De Belot, Raymond. The Struggle for the Mediterranean, 1939-1945. (Illus.). Repr. of 1951 ed. lib. bdg. 15.00x (ISBN 0-8371-1067-X, BEME). Greenwood.
Doria, Charles & Lenowitz, Harris, eds. Origins: Creation Texts from the Ancient Mediterranean. LC 74-18844. 384p. 1976. pap. 4.95 (ISBN 0-385-01922-X, Anch). Doubleday.
Field, James A., Jr. America & the Mediterranean World, 1776-1882. LC 68-11440. 1969. 28.50x (ISBN 0-691-04590-9); pap. 5.95 (ISBN 0-691-00586-9). Princeton U Pr.
Halpern, Paul G. Mediterranean Naval Situation, 1908-1914. LC 79-131469. (Historical Studies: No. 86). 1971. 20.00x (ISBN 0-674-56462-6). Harvard U Pr.
Holt, P. M., ed. The Eastern Mediterranean Lands in the Period of the Crusades. 112p. 1977. text ed. 18.00 (ISBN 0-85668-091-5, Pub. by Aris & Phillips England). Humanities.
Lazenby, J. F. Hannibal's War: A Military History of the Second Punic War. (Illus.). 1978. 29.00x (ISBN 0-85668-080-X, Pub. by Aris & Phillips). Intl Schol Bk Serv.
Markotic, Vladimir, ed. Ancient Europe & the Mediterranean. 196p. 1977. text ed. 58.00x (ISBN 0-85668-083-4, Pub. by Aris & Phillips England). Humanities.
Pine, L. G. The Middle Sea: A Short History of the Mediterranean. LC 73-5097. (Illus.). 298p. 1973. 9.95 (ISBN 0-498-01399-5). A S Barnes.
Rose, John H. Mediterranean in the Ancient World. Repr. of 1934 ed. lib. bdg. 15.00x (ISBN 0-8371-1933-2, ROME). Greenwood.
Runciman, Steven. Sicilian Vespers. 1958. 35.50 (ISBN 0-521-06167-9). Cambridge U Pr.
Sandars, N. K. The Sea Peoples: Warriors of the Ancient Mediterranean. (Aspects of Greek & Roman Life Ser.). (Illus.). 1978. 16.95 (ISBN 0-500-02085-X). Thames Hudson.
Saul, Norman E. Russia & the Mediterranean 1797-1807. LC 72-96755. 1970. 9.75x (ISBN 0-226-73540-0). U of Chicago Pr.
Stark, Freya. Alexander's Path. 1975. 18.50 (ISBN 0-7195-1332-4). Transatlantic.
--Dust in the Lion's Paw. 1975. 22.00 (ISBN 0-7195-1334-0). Transatlantic.
--Rome on the Euphrates. 1975. 28.50 (ISBN 0-7195-1335-9). Transatlantic.
--Zodiac Arch. 1975. 14.00 (ISBN 0-7195-1784-2). Transatlantic.
Swain, James E. The Struggle for the Control of the Mediterranean Prior to 1848: A Study in Anglo-French Relations. LC 72-85010. 152p. 1973. Repr. of 1933 ed. 12.00 (ISBN 0-8462-1677-9). Russell.
Trump, D. H. The Prehistory of the Mediterranean. LC 79-56617. (Illus.). 320p. 1981. pap. 6.95x (ISBN 0-300-02700-1). Yale U Pr.
Ward, William A., ed. The Role of Phoenicians in the Interaction of Mediterranean Civilizations. 1968. 22.95x (ISBN 0-8156-6011-1, Am U Beirut). Syracuse U Pr.

MEDIUMS
see Spiritualism

MEDRYANSKY, LASZIO, 1825-1919

Pataky-Brestyanszky, I. Mednyanszky. Horn, Zsuzanna, tr. (Illus.). 1968. pap. 25.00 (ISBN 0-8283-1121-8). Branden.

MEDULLA OSSIUM
see Marrow

MEDUSAE

Agassiz, Louis. On the Principles of Classification in the Animal Kingdom; on the Structure of the Halcyonoid Polypi, on the Morphology of the Medus. 1976. Repr. of 1850 ed. 30.00 (ISBN 0-403-05825-2, Regency). Scholarly.
Jacobson, Morris K. & Franz, David R. Wonders of Jellyfish. LC 77-92326. (Wonders Ser.). (Illus.). (gr. 5 up). 1978. 5.95 (ISBN 0-396-07560-6). Dodd.
Russell, Frederick S. Medusae of the British Isles II. 1970. 75.00 (ISBN 0-521-07293-X). Cambridge U Pr.
Sheperd, Elizabeth. Jellyfishes. (Illus.). (gr. 4-6). 1969. PLB 6.48 (ISBN 0-688-51055-8). Lothrop.

Shih, C. T. A Guide to the Jellyfish of Canadian Atlantic Waters. (Illus.). 1977. pap. text ed. 5.00x (ISBN 0-660-00017-2, 56366-9, Pub. by Natl Mus Canada). U of Chicago Pr.
Waters, John F. A Jellyfish Is Not a Fish. LC 77-26594. (Let's-Read-&-Find-Out Bk.). (Illus.). (gr. k-3). 1979. 8.95 (ISBN 0-690-03888-7, TYC-J); PLB 8.79 (ISBN 0-690-03889-5). Har-Row.

MEEK, JOSEPH LAFAYETTE, 1810-1875

Vestal, Stanley. Joe Meek, the Merry Mountain Man. LC 52-5211. (Illus.). 1963. pap. 6.50 (ISBN 0-8032-5206-4, BB 154, Bison). U of Nebr Pr.
Victor, Frances F. The River of the West: Life & Adventure in the Rocky Mountains & Oregon. LC 74-83523. (Illus.). 602p. 1974. Repr. of 1870 ed. 15.00 (ISBN 0-914418-02-5). Brooks-Sterling.

MEERUT, INDIA (CITY)

Hutchinson, Lester. Conspiracy at Meerut. LC 78-39303. (Conspiracy: Historical Perspectives). 1972. Repr. of 1935 ed. 10.00 (ISBN 0-405-04154-3). Arno.
Palmer, Julian A. Mutiny Outbreak at Meerut in 1857. (Cambridge South Asian Studies: No. 2). 1966. 19.95 (ISBN 0-521-05901-1). Cambridge U Pr.

MEETINGS

see also Committees; Discussion; Forums (Discussion and Debate); Leadership; Parliamentary Practice

Bibliographic Guide to Conference Publications: 1976. (Bibliographic Guides Ser.). 1976. lib. bdg. 95.00 (ISBN 0-8161-6824-5). G K Hall.
Boy Scouts of America. Group Meeting Sparklers. (Illus.). Repr. of 1962 ed. pap. text ed. 0.50x (ISBN 0-8395-3122-2, 3122). BSA.
Bradford, Leland P. Making Meetings Work: A Guide for Leaders & Group Members. LC 76-16886. 122p. 1976. pap. 12.50 (ISBN 0-88390-122-6). Univ Assocs.
Burke, W. Warner & Beckhard, Richard, eds. Conference Planning. 2nd ed. LC 76-124090. 174p. 1962. pap. 10.00 (ISBN 0-88390-118-8). Univ Assocs.
Carnes, William T. Let's Have a Meeting: Guidelines to Successful Deliberative Conferences. 13.95 (ISBN 0-07-010117-5). McGraw.
Cavalier, Richard. Achieving Objectives in Meetings. 218p. 1973. 14.95x (ISBN 0-9601096-1-7). Program Counsel.
Dunsing, Richard J. You & I Have Got to Stop Meeting This Way. (Illus.). 1978. 10.95 (ISBN 0-8144-5472-0). Am Mgmt.
Finkel, Coleman. Professional Guide to Successful Meetings. 1976. 17.50 (ISBN 0-89047-016-2). Herman Pub.
Gordon, Myron. Making Meetings More Productive. LC 80-52335. (Illus.). 192p. 1980. 10.95 (ISBN 0-8069-0206-X); lib. bdg. 9.89 (ISBN 0-8069-0207-8). Sterling.
Guth, Chester & Shaw, Stanley. How to Put on Dynamic Meetings. (Illus.). 160p. 1980. 15.95 (ISBN 0-8359-2968-X). Reston.
Hegarty, Edward J. How to Run Better Meetings. rev. ed. LC 79-29642. 328p. 1981. Repr. of 1957 ed. 14.50 (ISBN 0-89874-115-7). Krieger.
Herbert, J. Conference Terminology. 2nd ed. 1976. 24.50 (ISBN 0-444-41354-5). Elsevier.
Hoge, Carol S. Better Meetings: A Handbook for Trainers of Policy Councils & Other Decision-Making Groups. 102p. 1975. 5.00 (ISBN 0-89269-011-9, 105). Humanics Ltd.
How to Conduct a Meeting. 5.95x (ISBN 0-686-02557-1); pap. 2.65x (ISBN 0-686-02558-X). Dun.
How to Contribute to Business Meetings. pap. 12.00 (ISBN 0-686-02535-0). Preston.
Howell, William S. & Bormann, Ernest G. Presentational Speaking for Business & the Professions. (Auer Ser). 1971. text ed. 20.95 scp (ISBN 0-06-042928-3, HarpC); tchrs. manual avail. (ISBN 0-06-362977-1). Har-Row.
Jones, James. Meeting Management: A Professional Approach. Schott, Connie, ed. LC 78-74192. 1978. text ed. 17.95 (ISBN 0-933268-00-9). Bayard Pubns.
Jones, Martin. How to Organize Meetings: A Handbook for Better Workshop, Seminar and Conference Management. LC 80-28310. 138p. 1981. pap. 6.95 (ISBN 0-8253-0011-8). Beaufort Bks NY.
Jorgensen, James D., et al. Solving Problems in Meetings. LC 79-21782. 112p. 1981. 13.95 (ISBN 0-88229-521-7). Nelson-Hall.
Kirpatrick, Donald L. How to Plan & Conduct Productive Business Meetings. 1976. 65.50 (ISBN 0-85013-085-9). Dartnell Corp.
Long, Fern. All About Meetings. LC 67-14396. 1967. 6.00 (ISBN 0-379-00285-X). Oceana.
Lord, Robert W. Running Conventions, Conferences & Meetings. 400p. 1981. 21.95 (ISBN 0-8144-5643-X). Am Mgmt.
Madsen, Paul O. The Person Who Chairs the Meeting. (Illus.). 96p. (Orig.). 1973. tanalin 2.95 (ISBN 0-8170-0582-X). Judson.
O'Connor, Rochelle. Company Planning Meetings, Report No. 788. (Illus.). v, 50p. (Orig.). 1980. pap. 22.50 (ISBN 0-8237-0224-3). Conference Bd.
Redden, Martha R., et al. Barrier-Free Meetings: A Guide for Professional Associations. LC 76-54431. (Illus.). 1976. pap. 4.00 (ISBN 0-87168-229-X). AAAS.
Renton, Michael. Getting Better Results from the Meetings You Run. LC 80-51792. (Illus.). 95p. 1980. pap. text ed. 5.95 (ISBN 0-87822-214-6, 2146). Res Press.
Schindler-Rainman, Eva & Lippitt, Ronald. Taking Your Meetings Out of the Doldrums. LC 75-41890. (Illus.). 100p. 1975. 9.50 (ISBN 0-88390-136-6). Univ Assocs.
Snell, Frank. How to Hold a Better Meeting. (Orig.). 1979. pap. 2.95 (ISBN 0-346-12409-3). Cornerstone.
--How to Win the Meeting. 1979. 8.95 (ISBN 0-8015-3896-3, Hawthorn); pap. 4.95 (ISBN 0-8015-3897-1, Hawthorn). Dutton.
Swanson, Gerald, ed. Conference Publications Guide: 1974. 850p. 1974. lib. bdg. 65.00 (ISBN 0-8161-6801-6). G K Hall.
This, Leslie E. The Small Meeting Planner. 2nd ed. 254p. 1979. 12.95 (ISBN 0-87201-806-7). Gulf Pub.
Tropman, John E., et al. Essentials of Committee Management. LC 79-1484. (Illus.). 1979. 18.95x (ISBN 0-88229-515-2); pap. 9.95x (ISBN 0-88229-731-7). Nelson-Hall.
Welty, Joe. Welty's Book of Procedures for Meetings, Boards, Committees & Officers. 1981. 9.95 (ISBN 0-89803-086-2). Caroline Hse.
Welty, John D. Welty's Meeting Processes. 1981. 9.95 (ISBN 0-89803-086-2). Green Hill.
Winn, Larry J. The Chairman's Rule Book: Running a Meeting in the Twentieth Century. 128p. 1981. pap. 8.95 (ISBN 0-86616-012-4). Greene.

MEETINGS, CHURCH

see Church Meetings

MEETINGS, CORPORATE

see Corporate Meetings

MEGALITHIC MONUMENTS

Brown, Peter. Megaliths, Myths, & Men. 1978. pap. 4.95 (ISBN 0-06-090578-6, CN578, CN). Har-Row.
Brown, Peter L. Megaliths, Myths & Men: An Introduction to Astro-Archaeology. LC 76-15090. (Illus.). 324p. (YA) (gr. 10 up). 1976. 13.95 (ISBN 0-8008-5187-0). Taplinger.
Caponigro, Paul, commentary by. & photos by Megaliths: Photographs by Paul Caponigro. (Illus.). 120p. 1982. 75.00 (ISBN 0-89381-079-7). Aperture.
Michell, John. Secrets of the Stones: The Story of Astro-Archaeology. 1977. pap. 2.95 (ISBN 0-14-004491-4). Penguin.
Renfrew, Colin. Before Civilization. 1973. 12.95 (ISBN 0-394-48193-3). Knopf.
Service, Alastair & Bradbury, Jean. Megaliths & Their Mysteries. (Illus.). 1979. 14.95 (ISBN 0-02-609730-3). Macmillan.
Thom, Alexander. Megalithic Lunar Observatories. 1971. 32.50x (ISBN 0-19-858132-7). Oxford U Pr.
--Megalithic Sites in Britain. (Illus.). 1967. 39.50x (ISBN 0-19-813148-8). Oxford U Pr.
Van Der Hoop, Abraham N. Megalithic Remains in South Sumatra. Shirlaw, William, tr. LC 77-87515. Repr. of 1932 ed. 45.00 (ISBN 0-404-16783-7). AMS Pr.
Wernick, Robert. The Monument Builders. (The Emergence of Man Ser.). (Illus.). 160p. 1973. 9.95 (ISBN 0-8094-1312-4); lib. bdg. avail. (ISBN 0-685-48123-9). Time-Life.

MEGALOPTERA

see Neuroptera

MEGAVITAMIN THERAPY

see Orthomolecular Medicine

MEHER BABA, 1894-1969

Anzar, Naosherwan. The Beloved. (Illus.). 1974. 12.00 (ISBN 0-913078-16-6). Sheriar Pr.
Baba, Meher. Beams from Meher Baba on the Spiritual Panorama. LC 58-59805. 1958. 2.00 (ISBN 0-915828-05-7). Sufism Reoriented.
--The Narrow Lane. Le Page, William, ed. 148p. 1979. pap. 2.95 (ISBN 0-913078-39-5). Sheriar Pr.
Baba, Meher, et al. Treasures from the Meher Baba Journals. Haynes, Jane B., ed. LC 79-92169. (Illus.). 246p. 1980. pap. 6.95 (ISBN 0-913078-37-9). Sheriar Pr.
Craske, Margaret. The Dance of Love: My Life with Meher Baba. LC 80-53859. 180p. 1980. pap. 6.95 (ISBN 0-913078-40-9). Sheriar Pr.
Duce, Ivy O. How a Master Works. 1976. 17.95 (ISBN 0-396-07390-5). Dodd.
--How a Master Works. LC 75-17037. 1975. 17.95 (ISBN 0-915828-01-4). Sufism Reoriented.
Hopkinson, Tom & Hopkinson, Dorothy. Much Silence: Meher Baba, His Life & Works. 192p. 1975. 7.95 (ISBN 0-396-07141-4). Dodd.
Irani, Mani S. Eighty-Two Family Letters. new ed. 300p. 1976. pap. 8.95 (ISBN 0-913078-25-5). Sheriar Pr.
Kalchuri, Bhau. Let's Go to Meherabad. 120p. 1981. 10.95 (ISBN 0-940700-12-3); pap. 5.95 (ISBN 0-940700-11-5). Meher Baba Info.
Natu, Bal. Glimpses of the God-Man, Meher Baba, Vol. 1 (1943-48) LC 76-57047. 1977. pap. 6.95 (ISBN 0-915828-12-X). Sufism Reoriented.
--Glimpses of the God-Man, Meher Baba, Vol. 2: Jan. 1949-Jan. 1952. (Illus.). 406p. 1979. pap. 7.95 (ISBN 0-913078-38-7). Sheriar Pr.
Schloss, Malcolm & Purdom, Charles. Three Incredible Weeks with Meher Baba. Frederick, Filis, ed. (Illus.). 1979. pap. 5.95 (ISBN 0-913078-36-0). Sheriar Pr.

MEI, LAN-FANG, 1894-1961

Zung, Cecilia S. Secrets of the Chinese Drama. LC 63-23194. (Illus.). 1937. 23.00 (ISBN 0-405-09112-5). Arno.

MEIERKHOL'D, VSEVOLOD EMIL'EVICH, 1874-1940

Hoover, Marjorie L. Meyerhold: The Art of Conscious Theater. LC 73-93175. (Illus.). 256p. 1974. 22.50x (ISBN 0-87023-124-3). U of Mass Pr.

MEIGGS, HENRY, 1811-1877

Stewart, Watt. Henry Meiggs, Yankee Pizarro. LC 72-182723. Repr. of 1946 ed. 21.00 (ISBN 0-404-06265-2). AMS Pr.

MEIGRET, LOUIS, 16TH CENTURY

Shipman, G. R. Vowel Phonemes of Meigret. 1953. pap. 6.00 (ISBN 0-527-01450-8). Kraus Repr.

MEIJI, EMPEROR OF JAPAN, 1852-1912

Craig, Albert M. Chosho in the Meiji Restoration. 2nd ed. (Harvard Historical Monographs: No. 47). 424p. 1973. text ed. 16.50x (ISBN 0-674-12850-8). Harvard U Pr.
Sladen, Douglas. Queer Things About Japan, to Which Is Added a Life of the Emperor of Japan. 4th ed. LC 68-26607. (Illus.). 1968. Repr. of 1913 ed. 24.00 (ISBN 0-8103-3500-X). Gale.
Wilson, Robert A. Genesis of the Meiji Government in Japan, 1868-1871. LC 78-6546. (University of California Publications in History: Vol. 56). 1978. Repr. of 1957 ed. lib. bdg. 18.50x (ISBN 0-8371-9091-6, WIGM). Greenwood.

MEINECKE, FRIEDRICH, 1862-

Pois, Robert A. Friedrich Meinecke & German Politics in the Twentieth Century. LC 70-157818. 192p. 1972. 24.00x (ISBN 0-520-02045-6). U of Cal Pr.
Sterling, Richard W. Ethics in a World of Power: The Political Ideas of Friedrich Meinecke. 1958. 21.50x (ISBN 0-691-07507-7). Princeton U Pr.

MEININGER (TROOP OF ACTORS)

DeHart, Steven. The Meininger Theater, Seventeen Seventy-Six to Nineteen Twenty-Six. Beckerman, Bernard, ed. LC 81-11453. (Theater & Dramatic Studies: No. 4). 1981. price not set (ISBN 0-8357-1227-3, Pub. by UMI Res Pr). Univ Microfilms.
Grube, Max. Story of Meininger. Cole, Wendell, ed. Koller, Anne M., tr. LC 63-23352. (Bks of the Theatre: No. 4). (Illus.). 1963. 8.95x (ISBN 0-87024-027-7). U of Miami Pr.

MEINONG, ALEXIUS RITTER VON HANDSCHUCHSHEIM, 1853-1920

Bergmann, Gustav. Realism: A Critique of Brentano & Meinong. 468p. (Orig.). 1967. 25.00x (ISBN 0-299-04330-4); pap. 9.95x (ISBN 0-299-04334-7). U of Wis Pr.
Grossmann, Reinhardt. Meinong. (Arguments of the Philosophers Ser.). 1974. 20.00 (ISBN 0-7100-7831-5). Routledge & Kegan.
Lindenfield, David. The Transformation of Positivism: Alexius Meinong & European Thought, 1880-1920. LC 79-65775. 304p. 1981. 25.00x (ISBN 0-520-03994-7). U of Cal Pr.
Linsky, Leonard. Referring. 1967. text ed. 9.00x (ISBN 0-7100-3636-1). Humanities.

MEIOSIS

Anderson, Everett, et al. The Meiotic Process, I: Pairing, Recombination & Chromosome Movements. LC 72-6123. (Illus.). 189p. 1972. 29.50x (ISBN 0-8422-7019-1). Irvington.
Callebaut, M., et al. Meiosis: Current Research, 4 vols, Vol. 4. LC 72-6751. 244p. 1972. text ed. 24.50x (ISBN 0-8422-7041-8). Irvington.
Melnyk, P. L., et al. Meiosis: Current Research, 4 vols, Vol. 3. 1972. 24.50x (ISBN 0-8422-7036-1). Irvington.
Stack, Stephen M. & Lamb, B. C. The Meiotic Process, II: Pairing, Recombination, & Chromosome Movement. LC 72-6123. 208p. 1972. text ed. 29.50x (ISBN 0-8422-7031-0). Irvington.
Sybenga, J. Meiotic-Configurations. LC 75-17562. (Monographs on Theoretical & Applied Genetics: Vol. 1). (Illus.). 270p. 1975. 37.10 (ISBN 0-387-07347-7). Springer-Verlag.

MEIR, GOLDA (MABOVITZ), 1898-

Davidson, Margaret. The Golda Meir Story. rev. ed. (Illus.). 240p. (gr. 3-7). 1981. 10.95 (ISBN 0-684-16877-4). Scribner.
--The Golda Meir Story. LC 75-39297. 212p. (gr. 5 up). 1976. reinforced bdg. 6.95 (ISBN 0-684-14610-X, ScribJ). Scribner.
Gibson, William. Golda. LC 77-15889. 1978. 8.95 (ISBN 0-689-10876-1). Atheneum.
Slater, Robert. Golda: The Uncrowned Queen of Israel. 320p. 1981. 16.95 (ISBN 0-8246-0244-7). Jonathan David.

MEIR OF ROTHENBURG, RABBI

Agus, Irving A. Rabbi Meir of Rothenburg: His Life & Work, 2 Vols. in 1. rev. ed. 1970. 35.00x (ISBN 0-87068-026-9). Ktav.

MEISSEN PORCELAIN

Berling, K., ed. Meissen China, an Illustrated History. 12.50 (ISBN 0-8446-4621-0). Peter Smith.
Ducret, Siegfried. Meissen Porcelain. (World in Color Ser). (Illus.). 48p. 1975. 3.95 (ISBN 0-88254-337-7). Hippocrene Bks.
Syz, Hans, et al. Catalogue of the Hans Syz Collection, Vol. 1: Meissen Porcelain & Hausmalerei. LC 76-608122. (Illus.). 607p. 1980. 80.00 (ISBN 0-87474-168-8). Smithsonian.
Walcha, Otto. Meissen Porcelain. 1981. 60.00 (ISBN 0-399-11749-0). Putnam.

MEISTERSINGER

see also Minnesingers

Friedman, Clarence W. Prefigurations in Meistergesang. LC 75-140020. (Catholic University of America Studies in German Ser.: No. 18). Repr. of 1943 ed. 17.00 (ISBN 0-404-50238-5). AMS Pr.
Goldron, Romain. Minstrels & Masters: The Triumph of Polyphony. LC 68-1789. 1968. Volume 3 4.95 (ISBN 0-385-02342-1). Doubleday.
Linker, Robert W. Music of the Minnesinger & Early Meistersinger. LC 73-181946. (North Carolina University. Studies in the Germanic Languages & Literatures: No. 32). Repr. of 1962 ed. 18.50 (ISBN 0-404-50932-0). AMS Pr.
Schroeder, M. J. Mary-Verse in "Meistergesang". (Catholic University Studies in German: No. 16). 1970. Repr. of 1942 ed. 23.50 (ISBN 0-404-50236-9). AMS Pr.
Taylor, Archer. Literary History of Meistergesang. 1937. pap. 8.00 (ISBN 0-527-89050-2). Kraus Repr.

MEKONG RIVER AND VALLEY

Resources for the Future Staff. Agricultural Development in the Mekong Basin: Goals, Priorities, & Strategies. LC 70-158820. (Resources for the Future Ser.). 118p. 1971. pap. 2.50x (ISBN 0-8018-1294-1). Johns Hopkins.

MELANCHOLIA

see also Depression, Mental; Manic-Depressive Psychoses

MELANCHOLY

Bright, Timothy. A Treatise of Melancholie, Containing the Causes Thereof. LC 72-176. (English Experience Ser.: No. 212). 1969. Repr. of 1586 ed. 35.00 (ISBN 90-221-0212-2). Walter J Johnson.
Burton, Robert. Anatomy of Melancholy. Peters, Joan R., ed. LC 79-5052. (Milestones of Thought Ser.). (Abridged). 1980. pap. 4.95 (ISBN 0-8044-6069-8). Ungar.
--Anatomy of Melancholy, 3 Vols. Shilleto, A. R., ed. LC 75-39565. Repr. of 1893 ed. Set. 87.50 (ISBN 0-404-07822-2). AMS Pr.
--The Anatomy of Melancholy. Jackson, Holbrook, ed. (Rowman & Littlefield University Library). 547p. 1972. 23.50x (ISBN 0-87471-672-1). Rowman.
--The Anatomy of Melancholy: What It Is. LC 72-178. (English Experience Ser.: No. 301). 746p. 1971. Repr. of 1621 ed. 72.00 (ISBN 90-221-0301-3). Walter J Johnson.
--The Anatomy of Melancholy: What It Is, with All the Kinds, Causes, Symptoms, Prognostickes & Severall Cures of It. Jackson, Holbrook, ed. 1977. pap. 7.95 (ISBN 0-394-72422-4, Vin). Random.
Evans, Bergen. The Psychiatry of Robert Burton. LC 72-4487. 1972. Repr. of 1944 ed. lib. bdg. 13.50x (ISBN 0-374-92638-7). Octagon.
Ewing, S. B. Burtonian Melancholy in the Plays of John Ford. LC 77-96156. 1969. Repr. of 1940 ed. lib. bdg. 11.00x (ISBN 0-374-92660-3). Octagon.
Fox, Ruth. The Tangled Chain: The Structure of Disorder in the Anatomy of Melancholy. LC 75-17296. 1976. 18.50x (ISBN 0-520-03085-0). U of Cal Pr.
Haslam, John. Observations on Madness & Melancholy: Including Practical Remarks on Those Diseases Together with Cases, & an Account of the Morbid Appearances on Dissection. 2nd. enl. ed. LC 75-16707. (Classics in Psychiatry Ser.). 1976. Repr. of 1809 ed. 20.00x (ISBN 0-405-07432-8). Arno.
Sickels, Eleanor M. Gloomy Egoist. LC 76-76008. 1969. Repr. of 1932 ed. lib. bdg. 20.00x (ISBN 0-374-97429-2). Octagon.

Tellenbach, Hubertus. Melancholy: History of the Problem: Endogeneity; Typology; & Clinical Features. Eng, E., tr. from Ger. 1980. text ed. 25.00x (ISBN 0-391-00860-9). Duquesne.

MELANCHTHON, PHILIPP, 1497-1560

Aland, Kurt. Four Reformers: Luther, Melanchthon, Zwingli, Calvin. Schaaf, James L., tr. LC 79-50091. 176p. 1979. pap. 4.95 (ISBN 0-8066-1709-8, 10-2364). Augsburg.

Fagerberg, Holsten. A New Look at the Lutheran Confession. Lund, Gene J., tr. 336p. 1981. 14.50 (ISBN 0-570-03223-7, 15-2121). Concordia.

Hildebrandt, Franz. Melanchthon: Alien or Ally. LC 46-3804. 1968. Repr. of 1946 ed. 10.00 (ISBN 0-527-40600-7). Kraus Repr.

Manschreck, Clyde L. Melanchthon: The Quiet Reformer. LC 73-21263. (Illus.). 350p. 1975. Repr. of 1958 ed. lib. bdg. 19.50x (ISBN 0-8371-6131-2, MAMQ). Greenwood.

Richard, James W. Philip Melanchthon, the Protestant Preceptor of Germany. LC 72-82414. 1974. Repr. of 1898 ed. lib. bdg. 25.50 (ISBN 0-8337-4341-4). B Franklin.

MELANESIA

Allen, M. R., ed. Vanuatu: Politics, Economics & Ritual in Island Melanesia. LC 81-65767. (Studies in Population). 1981. write for info. (ISBN 0-12-051450-8). Acad Pr.

Barclay, Glen. A History of the Pacific. LC 78-51996. 1978. 14.95 (ISBN 0-8008-3902-1). Taplinger.

Barrau, Jacques. Subsistence Agriculture in Melanesia, 2 vols. 1958-1961. Repr. of 1958 ed. Vol. 1. pap. 10.00 (ISBN 0-527-02327-2); Vol. 2. pap. 9.00 (ISBN 0-527-02331-0). Kraus Repr.

Bayliss-Smith, Timothy & Feachem, Richard, eds. Subsistence & Survival: Rural Ecology in the Pacific. 1978. 68.00 (ISBN 0-12-083250-X). Acad Pr.

Belshaw, Cyril S. Changing Melanesia: Social Economics of Culture Contact. LC 76-44881. (Illus.). 1976. lib. bdg. 15.25x (ISBN 0-8371-9039-8, BELM). Greenwood.

Brookfield, H. C. Colonialism, Development & Independence. LC 72-75305. (Illus.). 232p. 1972. 27.50 (ISBN 0-521-08590-X). Cambridge U Pr.

Codrington, R. H. The Melanesians: Their Anthropology & Folk-Lore. (Illus.). 419p. 1972. pap. 4.50 (ISBN 0-486-20258-5). Dover.

Diole, Philippe. The Forgotten of the Pacific. Bernard, Jack, tr. from Fr. LC 77-6830. 1978. 12.95 (ISBN 0-8120-5129-7). Barron.

Huxley, Thomas H. & Huxley, Julian S. Diary of the Voyage of H. M. S. Rattlesnake. Repr. of 1936 ed. 18.00 (ISBN 0-527-43860-X). Kraus Repr.

Rivers, William H., ed. Essays on the Depopulation of Melanesia. LC 74-96470. Repr. of 1922 ed. 14.00 (ISBN 0-404-05357-2). AMS Pr.

Rodman, Margaret & Cooper, Matthew. The Pacification of Melanesia. LC 79-11040. (Association for Social Anthropology in Oceania Monograph: No. 7). 1979. 22.25 (ISBN 0-472-02703-4, IS-00075, The University of Michigan Press). Univ Microfilms.

Worsley, Peter. The Trumpet Shall Sound: A Study of Cargo Cults in Melanesia. LC 67-26995. (Illus.). 1968. pap. 5.95 (ISBN 0-8052-0156-4). Schocken.

MELANESIAN LANGUAGES

see also Austronesian Languages; Fijian Language; Mono Language; Motu Language; Nguna Language; Papuan Languages; Wagap Language

Codrington, Robert H. The Melanesian Languages. LC 75-32811. Repr. of 1885 ed. 46.50 (ISBN 0-404-14115-3). AMS Pr.

Hall, Robert A. Melanesian Pidgin English: Grammar, Texts, Vocabulary. LC 75-35114. Repr. of 1943 ed. 19.50 (ISBN 0-404-14131-5). AMS Pr.

King, Copland. A Grammar & Dictionary of the Binandere Language, Mamba River...Papua. Bd. with A Grammar & Dictionary of the Wedau Language. LC 75-35129. Repr. of 1927 ed. 15.50 (ISBN 0-404-14145-5). AMS Pr.

Peekel, Gerhard. Grammatik der Neu-Mecklenburgischen Sprache, Speziell der Pala-Sprache. LC 75-35147. Repr. of 1909 ed. 18.50 (ISBN 0-404-14163-3). AMS Pr.

Ray, Sidney H. A Comparative Study of the Melanesian Island Languages. LC 75-35151. Repr. of 1926 ed. 52.00 (ISBN 0-404-14166-8). AMS Pr.

Ray, Sidney H. & Haddon, Alfred C. A Study of the Languages of Torres Straits. LC 75-35153. Repr. of 1893 ed. 27.00 (ISBN 0-404-14168-4). AMS Pr.

Ray, Sidney H. & Riley, E. B. A Grammar of the Kiwai Language, Fly Delta, Papua, with a Kiwai Vocabulary. LC 75-35152. Repr. of 1933 ed. 15.00 (ISBN 0-404-14167-6). AMS Pr.

MELANESIANS

see also Rotumans

Brown, George. Melanesians & Polynesians. LC 71-174440. (Illus.). Repr. of 1910 ed. 17.00 (ISBN 0-405-08308-4, Blom Pubns). Arno.

Carroll, Vern, ed. Pacific Atoll Populations. LC 75-1264. (Asao Monograph Ser.: No. 3). (Illus.). 550p. 1975. text ed. 20.00x (ISBN 0-8248-0354-X, Eastwest Ctr). U Pr of Hawaii.

Errington, Frederick K. Karavar: Masks & Power in a Melanesian Ritual. Turner, Victor, ed. Repr. of 1974 ed. text ed. 20.00x (ISBN 0-8290-0339-8). Irvington.

Ivens, W. G. Melanesians of the South-East Solomon Islands. LC 74-174430. (Illus.). Repr. of 1927 ed. 25.00 (ISBN 0-405-08662-8). Arno.

Seligman, Charles G. The Melanesians of British New Guinea. LC 75-35160. Repr. of 1910 ed. 71.00 (ISBN 0-404-14174-9). AMS Pr.

Swindler, Daris R. A Racial Study of the West Nakanai. (Museum Monographs). (Illus.). 39p. 1962. soft bound 4.00 (ISBN 0-934718-16-4). Univ Mus of U PA.

MELANIN

Kettlewell, Bernard. The Evolution of Melanism: The Study of a Recurring Necessity, with Special Reference to Industrial Melanism in the Lepidoptera. (Illus.). 448p. 1973. 69.00x (ISBN 0-19-857370-7). Oxford U Pr.

Nicolaus, Rodolfo A. Melanins. LC 68-56378. (Chemistry of Natural Products Ser.). (Illus.). 312p. 1968. 42.50x (ISBN 0-8002-0849-8). Intl Pubns Serv.

MELANOMA

Ariel, Irving M. Malignant Melanoma. (Illus.). 544p. 1981. 48.50 (ISBN 0-8385-6114-4). ACC.

Clark, Wallace H., et al, eds. Human Malignant Melanoma. (Clinical Oncology Monographs). 528p. 1979. 49.50 (ISBN 0-8089-1110-4). Grune.

Conference On The Biology Of Normal And A-Typical Pigment Cell Growth - 4th - Houston - Texas - 1957. Pigment Cell Biology: Proceedings. Gordon, Myron, ed. 1959. 64.00 (ISBN 0-12-290950-X). Acad Pr.

Conference On The Biology Of Normal And A-Typical Pigment Cell Growth - 3rd - New York - 1951. Pigment Cell Growth: Proceedings. Gordon, Myron, ed. 1953. 48.50 (ISBN 0-12-290956-9). Acad Pr.

International Pigment Cell Conference, 9th, Houston, Tex., Pt. 1, Jan. 1975. Melanomas: Basic Properties & Clinical Behavior: Proceedings. Riley, V., ed. (Pigment Cell: Vol. 2). (Illus.). 476p. 1977. 91.75 (ISBN 3-8055-2369-6). S Karger.

International Pigment Cell Conference - 6th. Structure & Control of the Melanocyte: Proceedings. Della Porta, G. & Muehlbock, O., eds. (Illus.). 1966. 46.20 (ISBN 0-387-03676-8). Springer-Verlag.

Kopf, Alfred W., et al. Malignant Melanoma. LC 78-71687. (Illus.). 256p. 1979. 57.25x (ISBN 0-89352-040-3). Masson Pub.

Milton, G. W. Malignant Melanoma of the Skin & Mucous Membrane. LC 76-30318. (Illus.). 1977. text ed. 43.75 (ISBN 0-443-01422-1). Churchill.

MELANOPHORES

see Chromatophores

MELBA, DAME NELLIE, 1861-1931

Hetherington, John. Melba. (Illus.). 320p. (Orig.). 1973. pap. 5.95 (ISBN 0-571-10286-7, Pub. by Faber & Faber). Merrimack Bk Serv.

Murphy, Agnes G. Melba: A Biography. LC 74-24162. (Illus.). Repr. of 1909 ed. 22.50 (ISBN 0-404-13057-7). AMS Pr.

MELBOURNE–DESCRIPTION

White, Osmar & De'Lisle, Gordon. Melbourne. LC 68-133732. (Illus.). 1968. 21.00x (ISBN 0-8002-0896-X). Intl Pubns Serv.

White, Osmar & Newton-John, Susan. Melbourne for Everyone. 1975. pap. 1.95 (ISBN 0-85885-027-3). David & Charles.

MELBOURNE–HISTORY

Barrett, Bernard. The Civic Frontier. LC 79-670360. 1979. 25.00x (ISBN 0-522-84171-6, Pub. by Melbourne U Pr). Intl Schol Bk Serv.

Davison, Graeme. The Rise & Fall of Marvellous Melbourne. 1979. pap. 13.50x (ISBN 0-522-84191-0, Pub. by Melbourne U Pr). Intl Schol Bk Serv.

MELBOURNE–SOCIAL CONDITIONS

Henderson, F., et al. People in Poverty: A Melbourne (Australia) Survey. 1970. 9.00 (ISBN 0-8426-1299-8). Verry.

MELBOURNE, UNIVERSITY OF

Russell, K. F. The Melbourne Medical School 1862-1962. 1977. 30.00x (ISBN 0-522-84113-9, Pub. by Melbourne U Pr). Intl Schol Bk Serv.

MELBOURNE, WILLIAM LAMB, 2ND VISCOUNT, 1779-1848

Cecil, David. Melbourne. LC 76-138583. 1971. Repr. of 1954 ed. lib. bdg. 19.25x (ISBN 0-8371-5782-X, CEME). Greenwood.

--Melbourne. (Power & Personality Ser.). (Illus.). 1979. pap. 6.95 (ISBN 0-517-53782-6, Dist. by Crown). Crown.

Hoge, James O. & Olney, Clarke, eds. The Letters of Caroline Norton to Lord Melbourne. LC 74-12344. (Illus.). 1974. 10.75 (ISBN 0-8142-0208-X). Ohio St U Pr.

Melbourne, W. L. Lord Melbourne's Papers. Sanders, L., ed. Repr. of 1889 ed. 20.00 (ISBN 0-527-62850-6). Kraus Repr.

MELBOURNE CHURCH OF ENGLAND GIRL'S GRAMMAR SCHOOL, SOUTH YARRA, AUSTRALIA

Cunningham, K. S. & Ross, D. J. Australian School at Work. (Australian Council for Educational Research). 1967. pap. 7.00x (ISBN 0-8426-1223-8). Verry.

MELENDEZ VALDES, JUAN, 1754-1817

Cox, R. Merritt. Juan Melendez Valdes. (World Authors Ser.: Spain: No. 302). 1974. lib. bdg. 10.95 (ISBN 0-8057-2918-6). Twayne.

MELIES, GEORGE

Frazer, John. Artificially Arranged Scenes: The Films of George Melies. 1979. lib. bdg. 28.00 (ISBN 0-8161-8368-6). G K Hall.

MELIOLA

Stevens, Frank L. The Genus Meliola in Porto Rico. (University of Illinois Biological Monographs: Vol. 2, No. 4). Repr. of 1916 ed. pap. 6.00 (ISBN 0-384-58110-2). Johnson Repr.

MELLO, FRANCISCO MANUEL DE, 1608-1666

Prestige, Ed. D. Francisco Manuel De Mello. 1922. 2.50 (ISBN 0-87535-012-7). Hispanic Soc.

MELLON FAMILY

Hersh, Burton. The Mellon Family: A Fortune in History. LC 77-18797. (Illus.). 1978. 14.95 (ISBN 0-688-03297-4). Morrow.

Mellon, Thomas. Thomas Mellon & His Times. 1885. 32.00 (ISBN 0-527-62950-2). Kraus Repr.

MELODIC DICTATION

see Musical Dictation

MELODRAMA

Disher, M. W. Blood & Thunder. LC 73-21683. (English Literature Ser., No. 33). 1974. lib. bdg. 49.95 (ISBN 0-8383-1761-8). Haskell.

Gerould, Daniel, ed. Melodrama. LC 79-52615. (New York Literary Forum Ser.). (Illus.). 296p. (Orig.). 1980. pap. 12.50x (ISBN 0-931196-06-X). NY Lit Forum.

Grimsted, David. Melodrama Unveiled: American Theater & Culture, 1800-1850. LC 68-15575. 1968. 11.50x (ISBN 0-226-30901-0). U of Chicago Pr.

Heilman, Robert B. The Iceman, the Arsonist, & the Troubled Agent: Tragedy & Melodrama on the Modern Stage. LC 72-10391. 376p. 1973. 13.95 (ISBN 0-295-95253-9). U of Wash Pr.

--Tragedy & Melodrama: Versions of Experience. LC 68-11038. 340p. 1968. 13.50 (ISBN 0-295-97893-7). U of Wash Pr.

Metastasio, Pietro. Three Melodramas. Fucilla, Joseph G., tr. LC 80-51017. (Studies in Romance Languages: No. 24). 164p. 1981. 11.00x (ISBN 0-8131-1400-4). U Pr of Ky.

Rahill, Frank. World of Melodrama. LC 66-25466. 1967. 16.95x (ISBN 0-271-73113-3). Pa St U Pr.

Sherrill, Rowland A. The Prophetic Melville. LC 78-20436. 227p. 1979. 17.00x (ISBN 0-8203-0455-7). U of Ga Pr.

Smith, James L. Melodrama. (Critical Idiom Ser.). 90p. 1973. 7.50x (ISBN 0-416-79330-4); pap. 5.50x (ISBN 0-416-79340-1). Methuen Inc.

Smith, James L., ed. Victorian Melodramas: Seven English, French & American Melodramas. (Rowman & Littlefield University Library). (Illus.). 252p. 1976. 17.50x (ISBN 0-87471-767-1). Rowman.

Steele, William P. The Character of Melodrama. 1968. pap. 2.00 (ISBN 0-89101-017-3). U Maine Orono.

MELODY

Borisoff, Alexander. How to Write a Melody. 119p. 1980. pap. 9.95 (ISBN 0-938170-01-5). Wimbledon Music.

Chenoweth, Vida. Melodic Perception & Analysis: A Manual on Ethnic Melody. 132p. 1973. pap. 6.00 (ISBN 0-7263-0239-2); microfiche 1.60 (ISBN 0-88312-356-8). Summer Inst Ling.

DeZeeuw, Anne M. & Foltz, Roger E. Sight Singing: Melodic Structures in Functional Tonality. 1978. pap. text ed. 7.95 (ISBN 0-88408-103-6). Sterling Swift.

Gal, Hans. Franz Schubert & the Essence of Melody. 1977. 8.95 (ISBN 0-8008-2992-1, Crescendo). Taplinger.

Gibson, Jon. Melody III, Book II. pap. 10.00 (ISBN 0-89439-003-1). Printed Matter.

Holst, Imogen. Tune: The Structure of Melody. 1969. 5.75 (ISBN 0-8079-0126-1); pap. 2.95 (ISBN 0-8079-0127-X). October.

Noske, Frits R. French Song from Berlioz to DuParc: The Origins & Development of the Melodie. Benton, Rita, tr. LC 68-11171. (Illus.). 1970. pap. 6.95 (ISBN 0-486-22104-0). Dover.

Ricigliano, Daniel A. Melody & Harmony in Contemporary Songwriting. LC 78-51645. 1978. pap. text ed. 12.50 (ISBN 0-935058-01-X); wrbk. 8.50 (ISBN 0-935058-02-8). Donato Music.

Sachs, Curt. The Wellsprings of Music. Kunst, Jaap, ed. LC 77-23410. 1977. pap. 4.95 (ISBN 0-306-80073-X). Da Capo.

Siegmeister, Elie. Harmony & Melody, 2 vols. Incl. The Diatonic Style. 1965. Vol. 1 (ISBN 0-534-00245-5); Modulation, Chromatic & Modern Styles. 1966. Vol. 2 (ISBN 0-534-00247-1). 19.95x ea.; wkbks. 9.95x ea. Wadsworth Pub.

Szabolcsi, Bence. History of Melody. (Illus.). 1965. 19.95 (ISBN 0-312-38150-6). St Martin.

Warburton, Annie O. Melody Writing & Analysis. LC 78-5698. viii, 188p. 1978. Repr. of 1960 ed. lib. bdg. 17.25x (ISBN 0-313-20426-8, WAMW). Greenwood.

Whitney, Maurice. One Hundred Fifty Progressive Exercises for Melodic Dictation. (For use with Backgrounds in Music Theory). 1954. pap. 1.95 (ISBN 0-02-872880-7). Schirmer Bks.

MELON, JEAN FRANCOIS, 1675-1738

Bouzinac, J. Les Doctrines economiques au dix-huitieme siecle, Jean-Francois Melon, economiste. LC 70-121597. (Research & Source Ser.: No. 499). (Fr). 1970. Repr. of 1906 ed. lib. bdg. 18.50 (ISBN 0-8337-0344-7). B Franklin.

MELTING POINTS

see also Solidification

International Conference on Special Melting. LC 79-5175. 1979. cancelled (ISBN 0-89500-029-6). Sci Pr.

MELVILLE, HERMAN, 1819-1891

Abel, Darrel. Barron's Simplified Approach to Melville. 1964. pap. text ed. 1.50 (ISBN 0-8120-0178-8). Barron.

--Barron's Simplified Approach to Melville's Moby Dick. LC 65-25679. 1965. pap. 1.50 (ISBN 0-8120-0179-6). Barron.

Alexander, Joyce & Alexander, Dorsey, illus. The Sea: Excerpts from Herman Melville. 1970. pap. 3.00 (ISBN 0-912020-15-6). Turtles Quill.

Anderson, Charles R., ed. Journal of a Cruise to the Pacific Ocean, 1842-1844, in the Frigate United States with Notes on Herman Melville. LC 70-158282. Repr. of 1937 ed. 16.50 (ISBN 0-404-00356-7). AMS Pr.

Arvin, Newton. Herman Melville. LC 72-7818. (Illus.). 316p. 1973. Repr. of 1950 ed. lib. bdg. 17.75x (ISBN 0-8371-6524-5, ARHM); pap. 5.95 (ISBN 0-8371-8952-7, ARH:). Greenwood.

Babcock, C. Merton. Some Expressions from Herman Melville. Bd. with A Word-Finder List for Whiz Mob. Maurer, David W; Louis Pound: In Memoriam. (Publications of the American Dialect Society: No. 31). 41p. 1959. pap. 1.50x (ISBN 0-8173-0631-5). U of Ala Pr.

Bennett, John. Struck Leviathan: Poems on Moby Dick. LC 70-130668. (Breakthrough Bks). (Illus.). 1970. 5.00x (ISBN 0-8262-0099-0); pap. 3.50 (ISBN 0-8262-0183-0). U of Mo Pr.

Bernstein, John. Pacifism & Rebellion in the Writings of Herman Melville. LC 74-16813. 1974. Repr. of 1964 ed. lib. bdg. 20.00 (ISBN 0-8414-3295-3). Folcroft.

Bickley, R. Bruce. The Method of Melville's Short Fiction. LC 74-28904. 1975. 9.75 (ISBN 0-8223-0334-5). Duke.

Boswell, Jeanetta. Herman Melville & the Critics: A Checklist of Criticism, 1900-1978. LC 80-25959. (Author Bibliographies Ser.: No. 53). 259p. 1981. 13.50 (ISBN 0-8108-1385-8). Scarecrow.

Branch, Watson G., ed. Melville: The Critical Heritage. (The Critical Heritage Ser.). 1974. 38.00x (ISBN 0-7100-7774-2). Routledge & Kegan.

Braswell, William. Melville's Religious Thought. LC 73-324. ix, 154p. 1973. Repr. lib. bdg. 14.00x (ISBN 0-374-90945-8). Octagon.

Bredahl, A. Carl, Jr. Melville's Angles of Vision. LC 73-185795. (U of Fla. Humanities Monographs Ser.: No. 37). 1972. pap. 3.00 (ISBN 0-8130-0351-2). U Presses Fla.

Brodhead, Richard H. Hawthorne, Melville & the Novel. LC 75-5071. (Phoenix Ser). 1977. pap. 4.50 (ISBN 0-226-07523-0, P730, Phoen). U of Chicago Pr.

Canaday, Nicholas, Jr. Melville & Authority. LC 68-65060. (U of Fla. Humanities Monographs: No. 28). 1968. pap. 3.50 (ISBN 0-8130-0041-6). U Presses Fla.

Charters, Ann. Olson, Melville: A Study in Affinity. (Illus.). 1968. 5.00 (ISBN 0-685-19074-9, Pub. by Oyez); pap. 2.50 (ISBN 0-685-19075-7). SBD.

Chase, Richard, ed. Melville: A Collection of Critical Essays. (Orig.). 1962. 10.95 (ISBN 0-13-574293-5, Spec). P-H.

Cliff's Notes Editors. Moby Dick Notes. (Orig.). pap. 2.25 (ISBN 0-8220-0852-1). Cliffs.

Cohen, Hennig & Cahalan, James, eds. A Concordance to Melville's Moby Dick, 3 vols. LC 78-5602. 1978. Set. 143.25 (ISBN 0-8357-0306-1, IS-00055, Pub. by the Melville Society). Univ Microfilms.

Cultra, Quen. Queequeg's Odyssey. LC 77-10366. (Illus.). 1977. 10.00 (ISBN 0-914090-38-0). Chicago Review.

Curl, Vega. Pasteboard Masks: Fact As Spiritual Symbol in the Novels of Hawthorne & Melville. LC 72-193943. 1931. lib. bdg. 10.00 (ISBN 0-8414-2432-2). Folcroft.

Davis, Merrell R. Melville's Mardi: A Chartless Voyage. (Yale Studies in English Ser.: No. 119). 1967. Repr. of 1952 ed. 16.50 (ISBN 0-208-00069-0, Archon). Shoe String.

Daws, Gavan. A Dream of Islands. (Illus.). 1980. 14.95 (ISBN 0-393-01293-X). Norton.

De Onis, Jose. Melville y el Mundo Hispanico. (UPREX, E. Literarios: No. 38). pap. 1.85 (ISBN 0-8477-0038-0). U of PR Pr.

Dillingham, William B. An Artist in the Rigging: The Early Work of Herman Melville. LC 79-156038. x, 171p. 1972. 12.50x (ISBN 0-8203-0276-7). U of Ga Pr.

--Melville's Short Fiction, 1853-1856. LC 76-28922. 390p. 1977. 20.00x (ISBN 0-8203-0411-5). U of Ga Pr.

Dryden, Edgar A. Melville's Thematics of Form: The Great Art of Telling the Truth. LC 68-55612. (Illus.). 240p. 1981. pap. 5.95 (ISBN 0-8018-2619-5). Johns Hopkins.

Edinger, Edward F. Melville's Moby-Dick: A Jungian Commentary. LC 78-6146. 1978. 3.95 (ISBN 0-8112-0690-4). New Directions.

Emerson, O. B. Billy Budd Notes. Bd. with Typee Notes. (Orig.). 1968. pap. 1.75 (ISBN 0-8220-0238-8). Cliffs.

Finklestein, Dorothee M. Melville's Orienda. LC 77-120252. 1970. Repr. lib. bdg. 17.00x (ISBN 0-374-92741-3). Octagon.

Fisher, Marvin. Going Under: Melville's Short Fiction & the American 1850's. LC 77-2986. 1977. 17.50x (ISBN 0-8071-0267-9). La State U Pr.

Flibbert, Joseph. Melville & the Art of Burlesque. LC 74-80748. (Melville Studies in American Culture: No. 3). 163p. (Orig.). 1976. pap. text ed. 17.25x (ISBN 90-6203-268-0). Humanities.

Franklin, H. Bruce. The Wake of the Gods: Melville's Mythology. 1963. 12.50x (ISBN 0-8047-0137-7). Stanford U Pr.

Freeman, John. Herman Melville. LC 73-18099. (American Literature, No. 49). 1974. lib. bdg. 49.95 (ISBN 0-8383-1733-2). Haskell.

Friedman, Maurice. Problematic Rebel: Melville, Dostoievsky, Kafka, Camus. rev. ed. LC 72-101360. 1970. pap. 3.95 (ISBN 0-226-26396-7, P358, Phoen). U of Chicago Pr.

Gale, Robert L. Plots & Characters - Melville. 300p. 1972. pap. 2.95 (ISBN 0-262-57032-7). MIT Pr.

Gardner, John F. Melville's Vision of America: A New Interpretation of Moby Dick. LC 77-80051. (Illus.). 1977. pap. 1.50 (ISBN 0-913098-07-8). Myrin Institute.

Geist, Stanley. Herman Melville. 1966. lib. bdg. 8.50x (ISBN 0-374-93022-8). Octagon.

Gilman, William H. Melville's Early Life & Redburn. LC 77-173545. 1972. Repr. of 1951 ed. 23.00 (ISBN 0-8462-1632-9). Russell.

Gilmore, M., ed. Twentieth Century Interpretations of Moby Dick. 1977. 8.95 (ISBN 0-13-586057-1, Spec); pap. 2.45 (ISBN 0-13-586032-6, Spec). P-H.

Giono, Jean. Pour Saluer Melville. 184p. 1941. 5.95 (ISBN 0-686-53982-6). French & Eur.

Gleim, William S. Meaning of Moby Dick. LC 62-13834. 1962. Repr. of 1938 ed. 9.50 (ISBN 0-8462-0186-0). Russell.

Gray, Valeria B. Invisible Man's Literary Heritage: Benito Cereno & Moby Dick. (Costerus New Ser.: No. XII). 1978. pap. text ed. 16.75x (ISBN 90-6203-652-X). Humanities.

Grejda, Edward S. The Common Continent of Men: Racial Equality in the Novels of Herman Melville. LC 74-80067. 1974. 12.00 (ISBN 0-8046-9073-1, Natl U). Kennikat.

Haberstroh, Charles J. Melville & Male Identity. LC 78-75178. 152p. 1980. 14.50 (ISBN 0-8386-2321-2). Fairleigh Dickinson.

Hayford, Harrison & Parker, Hershel, eds. Moby-Dick As Doubloon. 1970. pap. text ed. 6.95x (ISBN 0-393-09883-4, NortonC). Norton.

Heffernan, Thomas F. Stove by a Whale: Owen Chase & the Essex. 256p. 1981. 19.95 (ISBN 0-8195-5052-3). Wesleyan U Pr.

Herbert, T. Walter, Jr. Moby-Dick & Calvinism: A World Dismantled. 1977. 14.00 (ISBN 0-8135-0829-0). Rutgers U Pr.

Hetherington, Hugh W. Melville's Reviewers: British & American, 1846-1891. LC 73-86720. (Illus.). xii, 304p. 1975. Repr. of 1961 ed. 20.00 (ISBN 0-8462-1744-9). Russell.

Hillway, Tyrus. Directory of Melville Dissertations. 1971. Repr. of 1962 ed. lib. bdg. 7.50 (ISBN 0-8414-5084-6). Folcroft.

--Herman Melville. rev. ed. (United States Authors Ser.: No. 37). 1979. lib. bdg. 9.95 (ISBN 0-8057-7256-1). Twayne.

--Herman Melville. rev. ed. (Twayne United States Authors Ser.). 1979. lib. bdg. 9.50 (ISBN 0-8057-7256-1). G K Hall.

--Herman Melville. LC 78-11937. (Twayne's U. S. Authors Ser.). 177p. 1979. pap. text ed. 4.95 (ISBN 0-672-61504-5). Bobbs.

--Herman Melville. (Twayne's United States Authors Ser). 1963. pap. 3.45 (ISBN 0-8084-0156-4, T37, Twayne). Coll & U Pr.

--Melville & the Whale. 1971. Repr. of 1950 ed. lib. bdg. 6.50 (ISBN 0-8414-5085-4). Folcroft.

Hillway, Tyrus & Mansfield, Luther S., eds. Moby-Dick Centennial Essays. LC 53-12917. 1953. 5.95 (ISBN 0-87074-078-4). SMU Press.

Howard, Leon. Herman Melville. (Pamphlets on American Writers Ser: No. 13). (Orig.). 1961. pap. 1.25x (ISBN 0-8166-0251-4, MPAW13). U of Minn Pr.

--Herman Melville: A Biography. 368p. 1981. pap. 7.95 (ISBN 0-520-00575-9, CAL 20). U of Cal Pr.

Inge, Thomas M. Bartleby the Inscrutable: A Collection of Commentary on Herman Melville's Tale "Bartleby the Scrivener". 334p. 1979. 19.50 (ISBN 0-208-01756-9, Archon). Shoe String.

Irey, Eugene F., compiled by. Moby Dick Index-Concordance (Adjunct) (Complete Works of Herman Melville Ser.). 172p. 1978. 9.00 (ISBN 0-87532-035-X). Hendricks House.

Jaffe, David. The Stormy Petrel & the Whale: Some Origins of Moby-Dick. LC 77-351492. 1976. pap. 2.50 (ISBN 0-9601782-1-X). D Jaffe.

James, C. L. Mariners, Renegades & Castaways. 2nd ed. xvi, 154p. 1978. pap. 3.00 (ISBN 0-935590-10-2). Bewick Edns.

Karcher, Carolyn L. Shadow Over the Promised Land: Slavery, Race, & Violence in Melville's America. LC 79-14861. 1980. text ed. 30.00x (ISBN 0-8071-0565-1); pap. 8.95x (ISBN 0-8071-0595-3). La State U Pr.

Kenny, Vincent. Herman Melville's "Clarel". A Spiritual Autobiography. 288p. 1973. 18.50 (ISBN 0-208-01226-5, Archon). Shoe String.

Keyssar, Alexander. Melville's Israel Potter: Reflections on the American Dream. LC 76-99522. (LeBaron Russell Briggs Prize Honors Essays in English Ser: 1969). 1969. text ed. 2.50x (ISBN 0-674-56475-8). Harvard U Pr.

Knapp, Joseph G. Tortured Synthesis: The Meaning of Melville's Clarel. LC 70-150099. 1971. 6.50 (ISBN 0-8022-2051-7). Philos Lib.

Levin, Harry. The Power of Blackness: Hawthorne, Poe, Melville. LC 80-83221. xxii, 263p. 1980. pap. 6.95x (ISBN 0-8214-0581-0). Ohio U Pr.

Leyda, Jay, ed. Melville Log: A Documentary Life of Herman Melville with Supplementary Chapter, 2 Vols. LC 73-8156. 1969. Repr. of 1951 ed. 35.00 (ISBN 0-87752-063-1). Gordian.

Mani, Lakshmi. The Apocalyptic Vision in Nineteenth Century Fiction: A Study of Cooper, Hawthorne, & Melville. LC 80-69060. 348p. 1981. lib. bdg. 20.75 (ISBN 0-8191-1602-5); pap. text ed. 11.75 (ISBN 0-8191-1603-3). U Pr of Amer.

Mason, Ronald. The Spirit Above the Dust: A Study of Herman Melville. 269p. Repr. of 1951 ed. 12.00 (ISBN 0-911858-19-9). Appel.

Melville, Herman. Billy Budd with Reader's Guide. (Amsco Literature Program). (gr. 10-12). 1971. pap. text ed. 3.92 (ISBN 0-87720-810-7); tchr's ed. 2.60 (ISBN 0-87720-910-3). AMSCO Sch.

--Family Correspondence of Herman Melville. Paltsits, Victor H., ed. (American Literature, No. 49). 1976. lib. bdg. 51.95 (ISBN 0-8383-2111-9). Haskell.

--Herman Melville: Authentic Anecdotes of Old Zack. Starosciak, Kenneth, ed. & intro. by. 1973. pap. 3.50x (ISBN 0-686-02647-0). K Starosciak.

Melville, Hermann. Journal of a Visit to Europe & the Levant, 1856-57. Horsford, Howard C., ed. LC 75-27655. (Princeton Studies in English Ser.: No.35). (Illus.). 1976. Repr. of 1955 ed. lib. bdg. 19.50x (ISBN 0-8371-8448-7, MEJV). Greenwood.

Metcalf, Eleanor M. Herman Melville, Cycle & Epicycle. Repr. of 1953 ed. lib. bdg. 19.75x (ISBN 0-8371-3340-8, MEHM). Greenwood.

Miller, Edwin H. Melville. LC 75-7958. 1976. pap. 7.95 (ISBN 0-89255-008-2). Persea Bks.

Miller, James E., Jr. A Reader's Guide to Herman Melville. 1973. lib. bdg. 14.50x (ISBN 0-374-95704-5). Octagon.

Miller, Perry. The Raven & the Whale: The War of Words & Wits in the Era of Poe & Melville. 370p. 1973. Repr. of 1956 ed. lib. bdg. 20.75x (ISBN 0-8371-6707-8, MIRW). Greenwood.

Minnigerode, Meade. Some Personal Letters of Herman Melville & a Bibliography. facs. ed. LC 78-75511. (Select Bibliographies Reprint Ser). 1922. 15.00 (ISBN 0-8369-5013-5). Arno.

Monarch Notes on Melville's Billy Budd. 1965. pap. 1.75 (ISBN 0-671-00686-X). Monarch Pr.

Monarch Notes on Melville's Moby Dick. (Orig.). pap. 1.95 (ISBN 0-671-00623-1). Monarch Pr.

Moore, Maxine. That Lonely Game: Melville, "Mardi", & the Almanac. LC 75-8578. 240p. 1975. 15.00x (ISBN 0-8262-0175-X). U of Mo Pr.

Mushabac, Jane. Melville's Humor: A Critical Study. 224p. 1981. 19.50 (ISBN 0-208-01910-3, Archon). Shoe String.

Nechas, James W. Synonomy, Repetition, & Restatement in the Vocabulary of Herman Melville's Moby-Dick. 1979. lib. bdg. 30.00 (ISBN 0-8482-1981-3). Norwood Edns.

--Synonomy, Repitition & Restatement in the Vocabulary of Herman Melville's Moby Dick. 286p. 1980. Repr. of 1978 ed. lib. bdg. 30.00 (ISBN 0-8414-6311-5). Folcroft.

Olson, Charles. Call Me Ishmael. LC 58-5531. 1966. pap. 3.50 (ISBN 0-87286-036-1). City Lights.

Percival, Milton O. Reading of Moby Dick. 1967. Repr. lib. bdg. 12.00x (ISBN 0-374-96403-3). Octagon.

Pommer, Henry F. Milton & Melville. LC 70-122752. (Illus.). 1970. Repr. of 1950 ed. lib. bdg. 11.00x (ISBN 0-8154-0338-0). Cooper Sq.

Rampersad, Arnold. Melville's Israel Potter: A Pilgrimage & Progress. 133p. 1969. 4.95 (ISBN 0-87972-000-X); pap. 1.95x (ISBN 0-87972-001-8). Bowling Green Univ.

Rosenberry, Edward H. Melville. (Illus.). 1979. 18.00x (ISBN 0-7100-8989-9). Routledge & Kegan.

--Melville & the Comic Spirit. LC 71-96168. 1970. Repr. of 1955 ed. lib. bdg. 14.50x (ISBN 0-374-96916-7). Octagon.

Rountree, Thomas J., ed. Critics on Melville. LC 74-143456. (Readings in Literary Criticism Ser: No. 12). 1972. 5.95x (ISBN 0-87024-193-1). U of Miami Pr.

Sachs, Viola. La Contre-Bible de Melville: Moby-Dick Dechiffre. 122p. 1975. pap. text ed. 21.25x (ISBN 90-2797-586-8). Mouton.

Sachs, Viola, ed. Le Blanc et le Noir chez Melville et Faulkner. 291p. (French.). 1975. pap. text ed. 34.50x (ISBN 90-2797-961-8). Mouton.

Scorza, Thomas J. In the Time Before Steamships: Billy Budd, the Limits of Politics & Modernity. LC 78-54746. 210p. 1979. 15.00 (ISBN 0-87580-071-8). N Ill U Pr.

Sealts, Merton M., Jr. The Early Lives of Melville: Nineteenth-Century Biographical Sketches & Their Authors. LC 74-5906. 296p. 1974. 25.00x (ISBN 0-299-06570-7). U of Wis Pr.

--Melville As Lecturer. LC 73-12808. 1957. lib. bdg. 17.50 (ISBN 0-8414-7629-2). Folcroft.

Sedgwick, William E. Herman Melville: The Tragedy of Mind. LC 62-10694. 1962. Repr. of 1944 ed. 18.00 (ISBN 0-8462-0272-7). Russell.

Seltzer, Leon F. The Vision of Melville & Conrad. LC 78-108735. xxxvi, 132p. 1970. 12.00x (ISBN 0-8214-0065-7). Ohio U Pr.

Solomon, Pearl C. Dickens & Melville in Their Time. LC 74-13307. 1975. 12.50x (ISBN 0-231-03889-5). Columbia U Pr.

Squire, J. C. Books Reviewed: Shakespeare, Melville & Byron. 293p. 1981. Repr. of 1922 ed. lib. bdg. 20.00 (ISBN 0-8495-4953-1). Arden Lib.

Stein, William B. Poetry of Melville's Late Years: Time, History, Myth, & Religion. LC 73-91203. 1970. 19.00 (ISBN 0-87395-056-9); pap. 8.95 (ISBN 0-87395-075-5); microfiche 19.00 (ISBN 0-686-66542-2). State U NY Pr.

Stern, Milton R. The Fine-Hammered Steel of Herman Melville. LC 57-6959. 1968. pap. 4.95 (ISBN 0-252-78408-1). U of Ill Pr.

Stone, Geoffrey. Melville. 336p. 1976. Repr. of 1949 ed. lib. bdg. 17.50x (ISBN 0-374-97632-5). Octagon.

Sweeney, Gerard M. Melville's Use of Classical Mythology. (Melville Studies in American Culture: Vol. 5). 169p. (Orig.). 1976. pap. text ed. 11.50x (ISBN 90-6203-258-3). Humanities.

Tanselle, G. Thomas. A Checklist of the Editions of Moby Dick, 1851-1976. 1976. pap. 3.50 (ISBN 0-686-53821-8). Newberry.

Thompson, L. Mellville's Quarrel with God. 1973. 24.00x (ISBN 0-691-06108-4). Princeton U Pr.

Vincent, Howard P. The Tailoring of Melville's White Jacket. 240p. 1970. 12.95x (ISBN 0-8101-0310-9). Northwestern U Pr.

--The Trying-Out of Moby Dick. LC 80-16962. (Illus.). 417p. 1980. pap. 8.50x (ISBN 0-87338-247-1). Kent St U Pr.

Walker, Franklin. Irreverent Pilgrims: Melville, Browne & Mark Twain in the Holy Land. LC 74-10644. (Illus.). 246p. 1974. 13.50 (ISBN 0-295-95344-6). U of Wash Pr.

Way, Brian. Herman Melville: Moby Dick. Daiches, D., ed. (Studies in English Literature). 1978. pap. 3.95x (ISBN 0-7131-5983-9). Dynamic Learn Corp.

Weaver, Herbert. Divining the Primary Sense: Micro-Communication in Art & Nature. 1978. 14.00 (ISBN 0-7100-8734-9). Routledge & Kegan.

Wegener, Larry E., ed. A Concordance to Herman Melville's Clarel: A Poem & Pilgrimage in the Holy Land, 3 vols. LC 79-10581. 1979. Set. 130.50 (ISBN 0-8357-0404-1, IS-00079). Univ Microfilms.

Willett, Ralph. Merrill Studies in Pierre. LC 75-165984. 1971. pap. text ed. 2.50x (ISBN 0-675-09642-1). Merrill.

Wright, Nathalia. Melville's Use of the Bible. 1969. lib. bdg. 13.00x (ISBN 0-374-98778-5). Octagon.

MELVILLE, HERMAN, 1819-1891–BIBLIOGRAPHY

Boswell, Jeanetta. Herman Melville & the Critics: A Checklist of Criticism, 1900-1978. LC 80-25959. (Author Bibliographies Ser.: No. 53). 259p. 1981. 13.50 (ISBN 0-8108-1385-8). Scarecrow.

Sealts, Merton M., Jr. The Early Lives of Melville: Nineteenth-Century Biographical Sketches & Their Authors. LC 74-5906. 296p. 1974. 25.00x (ISBN 0-299-06570-7). U of Wis Pr.

Smith, J. E. Bibliographic Sketch of Herman Melville. 35.00 (ISBN 0-87968-734-7). Gordon Pr.

MELVILLE, HERMAN, 1819-1891–JUVENILE LITERATURE

Keyes, Charlotte E. High on the Mainmast: The Life of Herman Melville. 1966. 3.50 (ISBN 0-8084-0157-2). Coll & U Pr.

MEMBERSHIP CORPORATIONS

see Corporations, Nonprofit

MEMBRANES (BIOLOGY)

see also Plasma Membranes

Abrahamsson, Sixten & Pascher, Irmin, eds. Structure of Biological Membranes. (Nobel Foundation Symposium Ser.). (Illus.). 580p. 1977. 49.50 (ISBN 0-306-33704-5, Plenum Pr). Plenum Pub.

Adelman, William J., Jr., ed. Biophysics & Physiology of Excitable Membranes. 1971. text ed. 31.50x (ISBN 0-442-20264-4). Van Nos Reinhold.

--Biophysics & Physiology of Excitable Membranes. 1971. text ed. 31.50x (ISBN 0-442-20264-4). Van Nos Reinhold.

Agin, Daniel, ed. Perspectives in Membrane Biophysics: A Tribute to Kenneth S. Cole. 1972. 54.00x (ISBN 0-677-15210-8). Gordon.

Altura, B. M., ed. Vascular Endothelium & Basement Membranes. (Advances in Microcirculation: Vol. 9). (Illus.). 1979. 76.75 (ISBN 3-8055-3054-4). S Karger.

Andreoli, Thomas E., et al, eds. Physiology of Membrane Disorders. LC 78-4071. (Illus.). 1148p. 1978. 75.00 (ISBN 0-306-31054-6, Plenum Pr). Plenum Pub.

--Membrane Physiology. 482p. 1980. pap. text ed. 19.95 (ISBN 0-306-40432-X, Plenum Pr). Plenum Pub.

Avery, J., ed. Membrane Structure and Mechanisms of Biological Energy Transduction. LC 72-95064. 600p. 1974. 47.50 (ISBN 0-306-30718-9, Plenum Pr). Plenum Pub.

Azzi, A., et al, eds. Membrane Proteins: A Laboratory Manual. (Illus.). 250p. 1981. pap. 19.80 (ISBN 0-387-10749-5). Springer-Verlag.

Azzone, G. F., ed. Mechanisms in Bioenergetics. 1973. 48.50 (ISBN 0-12-068960-X). Acad Pr.

Beers, Roland F., Jr. & Bassett, Edward G., eds. Cell Membrane Receptors for Viruses, Antigens & Antibodies, Polypeptide Hormones, & Small Molecules. LC 75-25108. (Miles International Symposium Ser.: No.9). 1976. 49.50 (ISBN 0-89004-091-5). Raven.

Berridge, Michael J. & Oschman, James L. Transporting Epithelia. (Monographs in the Ultrastructure of Cells & Organisms Ser.). 1972. 19.50 (ISBN 0-12-454135-6). Acad Pr.

Bittar, E. Edward. Membrane Structure & Function, 3 vols. LC 79-14969. (Membrane Structure & Function Ser.). 1980. Vol. 1. 27.50 (ISBN 0-471-03816-4, Pub. by Wiley-Interscience); Vol. 2. 43.50 (ISBN 0-471-03817-2); Vol. 3. 22.50 (ISBN 0-471-03818-0). Wiley.

--Membrane Structure & Function, Vol. 4. (Membrane Structure & Function Ser.). 246p. 1981. 37.50 (ISBN 0-471-08774-2, Pub. by Wiley-Interscience). Wiley.

Blank, M. Surface Chemistry of Biological Systems. LC 70-110799. (Advances in Experimental Medicine & Biology Ser., Vol. 7). 340p. 1970. 37.50 (ISBN 0-306-39007-8, Plenum Pr). Plenum Pub.

Bolis, L., et al. Permeability & Function of Biological Membranes. 1970. 23.75 (ISBN 0-444-10031-8, North-Holland). Elsevier.

Bolis, Liana, et al, eds. Membranes & Disease. LC 75-30235. 424p. 1976. 39.00 (ISBN 0-89004-082-6). Raven.
Borsellino, Antonio, et al, eds. Developments in Biophysical Research. 365p. 1981. 42.50 (ISBN 0-306-40627-6, Plenum Pr). Plenum Pub.
Boulpaep, Emele L., ed. Current Topics in Membranes & Transport: Vol. 13, Cellular Mechanisms of Renal Tubular Ion Transport. LC 70-117091. (Serial Publication). 1980. 45.00 (ISBN 0-12-153313-1). Acad Pr.
Bradshaw, Ralph A., et al, eds. Surface Membrane Receptors: Interface Between Cells & Their Environment. LC 76-25821. (NATO Advanced Study Institutes Ser., Series A: Life Sciences: Vol. 11). 482p. 1976. 39.50 (ISBN 0-306-35611-2, Plenum Pr). Plenum Pub.
Bronner, E. & Kleinzeller, A., eds. Current Topics in Membranes & Transport, Vol. 12. (Serial Publication). 1979. 47.50 (ISBN 0-12-153312-3). Acad Pr.
Bronner, Felix & Kleinzeller, Annost, eds. Current Topics in Membranes & Transport, Vols. 1-9, 11. Incl. Vol. 1. 1970. 38.00 (ISBN 0-12-153301-8); Vol. 2. 1971. 38.00 (ISBN 0-12-153302-6); Vol. 3. 1972. 56.00 (ISBN 0-12-153303-4); Vol. 4. 1974. 55.00 (ISBN 0-12-153304-2); Vol. 5. 1974. 55.00 (ISBN 0-12-153305-0); Vol. 6. 1975. 52.50 (ISBN 0-12-153306-9); Vol. 7. 1975. 52.50 (ISBN 0-12-153307-7); Vol. 8. 1976. 54.00 (ISBN 0-12-153308-5); Vol. 9. 1977. 59.00 (ISBN 0-12-153309-3); Vol. 11. 1978. 55.50 (ISBN 0-12-153311-5). Acad Pr.
Bronner, Felix, et al, eds. Current Topics in Membranes & Transport, Vol. 14. 1980. 49.50 (ISBN 0-12-153314-X). Acad Pr.
Cadenhead, D. A. & Danielli, James F., eds. Progress in Surface & Membrane Science, Vol. 12. 1979. 55.50 (ISBN 0-12-571812-8); lib. ed. 71.50 (ISBN 0-12-571880-2); microfiche 40.00 (ISBN 0-12-571881-0). Acad Pr.
Capaldi. Membrane Proteins in Energy Transduction. (Membrane Proteins Ser.: Vol. 2). 1979. 48.50 (ISBN 0-8247-6817-5). Dekker.
Cereijido, Marcelino & Rotunno, Catalina A. Introduction to the Study of Biological Membranes. 1970. 44.50 (ISBN 0-677-02410-X). Gordon.
Chance, Britton, et al, eds. Probes of Structure & Function of Macromolecules & Membranes, 2 Vols. 1971. Vol. 1. 49.50 (ISBN 0-12-167801-6); Vol. 2. 49.50 (ISBN 0-12-167802-4); Set. 81.00 (ISBN 0-685-02417-2). Acad Pr.
Chapman, D. Biological Membranes, Vol. 4. Date not set. price not set (ISBN 0-12-168545-4). Acad Pr.
Cone, Richard A. & Dowling, John E., eds. Membrane Transduction Mechanisms. LC 78-65280. (Society of General Physiologists Ser.). 248p. 1979. text ed. 29.00 (ISBN 0-89004-236-5). Raven.
Conference Held at Silver Spring, Maryland, Mar. 1978. Membrane Mechanisms of Drugs of Abuse: Proceedings. Abood, Leo G. & Sharp, Charles W., eds. LC 78-19682. (Progress in Clinical & Biological Research: Vol. 27). 280p. 1979. 22.00 (ISBN 0-8451-0027-0). A R Liss.
Conference on Membranes, Viruses & Immune Mechanisms in Experimental & Clinical Diseases, University of Minnesota, June, 1972. Membranes & Viruses in Immunopathology: Proceedings. Day, Stacey B. & Good, Robert A., eds. 1973. 47.00 (ISBN 0-12-207250-2). Acad Pr.
Cook, G. M. & Stoddart, R. W. Surface Carbohydrates of the Eukaryatic Cell. 1974. 55.00 (ISBN 0-12-186850-8). Acad Pr.
Coral Gables Conference On Physical Principles Of Biological Membranes - University Of Miami - 1968. Proceedings. Snell, F., et al, eds. 1970. 55.50x (ISBN 0-677-13680-3). Gordon.
Critser, James R., Jr. Membrane Separation Processes. (Ser. 5-79). 1980. 110.00 (ISBN 0-914428-72-1). Lexington Data.
--Membrane Separation Processes (1973) (Ser. 5-73). 1974. 100.00 (ISBN 0-914428-20-9). Lexington Data.
Deamer, David W., ed. Light Transducing Membranes: Structure, Function & Evolution. 1978. 26.50 (ISBN 0-12-207650-8). Acad Pr.
De Duve, C. & Hayaishi, O., eds. Tocopherol, Oxygen & Biomembranes: Proceedings of the International Symposium on Tocopheral, Oxygen & Biomembranes, Lake Yamanaka, Japan, Sept. 1977. 1978. 52.25 (ISBN 0-444-80043-3, Biomedical Pr). Elsevier.
DeFelice, Louis J. Introduction to Membrane Noise. 490p. 1981. 39.50 (ISBN 0-306-40513-X, Plenum Pr). Plenum Pub.
Edelman, Gerald M., ed. Molecular Machinery of the Membrane. 75p. 1976. pap. text ed. 4.95x (ISBN 0-262-55006-7). MIT Pr.
Eisenman, George, ed. Membranes: Lipid Bilayers & Biological Membranes: Dynamic Properties, Vol. 3. 536p. 1975. 65.00 (ISBN 0-8247-6178-2). Dekker.
--Membranes,, Vol. 2: Lipid Bilayers & Antibiotics. 576p. 1973. 65.00 (ISBN 0-8247-6049-2). Dekker.
Erwin, Joseph A., ed. Lipids & Biomembranes of Eukaryotic Microorganisms. (Cell Biology Ser.). 1973. 52.50 (ISBN 0-12-242050-0). Acad Pr.
Estrada, Sergio & Gitler, Carlos, eds. Perspectives in Membrane Biology. 1974. 48.50 (ISBN 0-12-243650-4). Acad Pr.
FEBS Meeting, Amsterdam, August, 1972, Eighth. Mitochondria & Membranes: Proceedings, Vol. 28. 1973. 31.00 (ISBN 0-444-10423-2, North-Holland). Elsevier.
Feldherr, C. M., et al. Nuclear Membrane & Nucleocytoplastic Interchange. (Protoplasmatologia: Vol. 5, Pt. 2). (Illus.). 1964. Springer-Verlag.
Finean, J. B., et al. Membranes & Their Cellular Functions. 2nd ed. LC 78-9016. 1978. pap. text ed. 14.95 (ISBN 0-470-26389-X). Halsted Pr.
Fleischer, S., et al, eds. The Molecular Biology of Membranes. LC 78-2207. (Illus.). 363p. 1978. 29.50 (ISBN 0-306-31114-3, Plenum Pr). Plenum Pub.
Fox, C. Fred & Fox, C. Fred, eds. Membrane Research: Icn-Ucla Symposium in Molecular Biology, 1972. 1972. 47.50 (ISBN 0-12-263650-3). Acad Pr.
Gel'man, N. S., et al. Biomembranes, Vol. 6: Bacterial Membranes & the Respiratory Chain. LC 75-4531. (Illus.). 275p. 1975. 30.00 (ISBN 0-306-39806-0, Plenum Pr). Plenum Pub.
Gesellschaft Fuer Biologische Chemie, 22nd Colloquium, Mossbach Baden, 1971. The Dynamic Structure of Cell Membranes: Proceedings. Wallach, D. F. & Fischer, H., eds. (Illus.). 240p. 1972. 26.00 (ISBN 0-387-05669-6). Springer-Verlag.
Giebisch, G., ed. Transport Across Multi - Membrane Systems. (Membrane Transport in Biology: Vol. 3). (Illus.). 1978. 85.50 (ISBN 0-387-08596-3). Springer-Verlag.
Glossman, Hartmut, et al. Structural & Functional Nature of Biomembranes, I. 1972. 24.00x (ISBN 0-8422-7044-2). Irvington.
Green, David E. & Baum, Harold. Energy & the Mitochondrion. 1970. 12.95 (ISBN 0-12-297950-8). Acad Pr.
Grell, E., ed. Membrane Spectroscopy. (Molecular Biology, Biochemistry, & Biophysics Ser.: Vol. 31). (Illus.). 512p. 1981. 87.40 (ISBN 0-387-10332-5). Springer-Verlag.
Harrison, R. & Lunt, G. Biological Membranes: Their Structure & Function. LC 75-43543. (Tertiary Level Biology Ser). 264p. 1976. pap. text ed. 18.95 (ISBN 0-470-15220-6). Halsted Pr.
Harrison, Roger & Lunt, George G. Biological Membranes: Their Structure & Function. 2nd ed. LC 80-14062. (Tertiary Level Biology Ser). 288p. 1980. pap. text ed. 24.95x (ISBN 0-470-26971-5). Halsted Pr.
Haslam, J. Membrane Assembly. (Outline Studies in Biology Ser.). 1981. pap. 5.95x (ISBN 0-412-13940-5, Pub. by Chapman & Hall). Methuen Inc.
Hatefi, D., ed. The Structural Basis of Membrane Function. 1976. 36.50 (ISBN 0-12-332450-5). Acad Pr.
Heinz, Erich. Electrified Potentials in Biological Membrane Transport. (Molecular Biology, Biochemistry, & Biophysics Ser.: Vol. 33). (Illus.). 100p. 1981. 32.90 (ISBN 0-387-10928-5). Springer-Verlag.
Hendry. Membrane Physiology & Cell Exciting. 1981. 10.95 (ISBN 0-8151-4267-6). Year Bk Med.
Hendy, Bruce. Membrane Physiology & Cell Excitation. 160p. 1980. 30.00x (ISBN 0-686-69935-1, Pub. by Croom Helm England). State Mutual Bk.
Hofer, M. Transport Across Biological Membranes. Hoggett, J. G., tr. (Cellular & Developmental Biology Ser.). 184p. 1981. text ed. 36.00 (ISBN 0-273-08480-1). Pitman Pub MA.
Hoffman, Joseph F., ed. Membrane Transport Processes, Vol. 1. LC 76-19934. 488p. 1978. 43.50 (ISBN 0-89004-170-9). Raven.
Hope, A. B. Ion Transport & Membranes: A Biophysical Outline. (Illus.). 1971. 15.00 (ISBN 0-8391-0608-4). Univ Park.
Hughes, R. C. Membrane Glycoproteins. 1976. 64.95 (ISBN 0-408-70705-4). Butterworth.
Hwang, S. & Kammermeyer, K. Membranes in Separations, Vol. 7. (Techniques of Chemistry). 559p. 1975. 70.00 (ISBN 0-471-93268-X). Wiley.
ICN-UCLA Symposium on Transmembrane Signaling, Keystone, Colorado, February, 1978. Transmembrane Signaling: Proceedings. Bitensky, M., et al, eds. LC 79-5061. (Progress in Clinical & Biological Research Ser.: Vol. 31). 804p. 1979. 78.00x (ISBN 0-8451-0031-9). A R Liss.
Immunochemistry of the Cell Membrane, Ravello, 1975. Proceedings. Comoglio, P. M., et al, eds. (Experimental Cell Biology: Vol. 44, Nos. 3-6). 1977. 45.00 (ISBN 3-8055-2754-3). S Karger.
International Colloquium, Paris, October 14-15, 1977. Biochemistry & Pathology of Basement Membranes. Robert, L., ed. (Frontiers of Matrix Biology: Vol. 7). (Illus.). 1979. 94.00 (ISBN 3-8055-2894-9). S Karger.
International Conference on Biology Membranes, Gargano, Italy, June 20-27, 1971-Fourth Meeting, et al. Role of Membranes in Secretory Processes: Proceedings. Bolis, L. & Keynes, R. D., eds. 1973. 49.00 (ISBN 0-444-10403-8, North-Holland). Elsevier.
International Symposium Held at the Battelle Seattle Research Center Seattle, WA, Nov. 4-6, 1974, et al. Molecular Aspects of Membrane Phenomena. Kabak, H. R. & Neurath, H., eds. LC 75-25772. (Illus.). 400p. 1975. 35.10 (ISBN 0-387-07448-1). Springer-Verlag.
International Symposium on Function & Molecular Aspects of Biomembrane Transport, Italy, April 1979. Function & Molecular Aspects of Biomembrane Transport: Proceedings. Quagliariello, E., et al, eds. (Developments in Bioenergetics & Biomembranes Ser.: Vol. 3). 526p. 1979. 68.50 (ISBN 0-444-80149-9, North Holland). Elsevier.
Jain, Mahendra K. & Wagner, Roger C. Introduction to Biological Membranes. LC 79-16690. 1980. 35.50 (ISBN 0-471-03471-1, Pub. by Wiley-Interscience). Wiley.
Jamieson, G. A. & Robinson, D. M., eds. Mammalian Cell Membranes, 5 vols. (Illus.). 1977. text ed. 159.95 set (ISBN 0-686-25573-9). Butterworth.
Kates, Morris & Kuksis, Arnis, eds. Membrane Fluidity: Biophysical Techniques & Cellular Regulation. LC 79-93347. (Experimental Biology & Medicine Ser.). (Illus.). 448p. 1980. 54.50 (ISBN 0-89603-020-2). Humana.
Korn, Edward D., ed. Methods in Membrane Biology, Vol. 10. (Illus.). 227p. 1979. 29.50 (ISBN 0-306-40126-6, Plenum Pr). Plenum Pub.
Kotyk, Arnost & Janacek, Karel. Biomembranes: An Interdisciplinary Approach, Vol. 9. 348p. 1977. 38.50 (ISBN 0-306-39809-5, Plenum Pr). Plenum Pub.
--Cell Membrane Transport: Principles & Techniques. 2nd ed. LC 71-107538. 583p. 1975. 47.50 (ISBN 0-306-30799-5, Plenum Pr). Plenum Pub.
Kruckeberg, Walter C., et al, eds. Erythrocyte Membranes II: Recent Clinical & Experimental Advances. LC 81-2768. (Progress in Clinical & Biological Research Ser.: Vol. 56). 302p. 1981. 32.00 (ISBN 0-8451-0056-4). A R Liss.
Lakshminarayanaiah, N. Transport Phenomena in Membranes. 1969. 63.50 (ISBN 0-12-434250-7). Acad Pr.
Leclerc, J. C, et al. Cell Surface Alteration As a Result of Malignant Transformation, No. 1. LC 72-10066. (Illus.). 220p. 1973. text ed. 23.00x (ISBN 0-8422-7055-8). Irvington.
Lee, E. & Smith, E., eds. Biology & Chemistry of Eucaryotic Cell Surfaces. 1974. 36.00 (ISBN 0-12-441550-4). Acad Pr.
Leive, Loretta, ed. Bacterial Membranes & Walls. (Microbiology Ser.: Vol. 1). 520p. 1973. 65.00 (ISBN 0-8247-6085-9). Dekker.
Lengerova, Alena. Membrane Antigens. (Illus.). 1977. 38.80 (ISBN 0-685-85899-5). Adler.
Lubec, G., ed. The Glomerular Basement Membrane. (Illus.). vii, 434p. 1981. 93.50 (ISBN 3-8055-2952-X). S Karger.
Mackey, M. C. Ion Transport Through Biological Membranes: An Integrated Theoretical Approach. (Lecture Notes in Biomathematics Ser.: Vol. 7). 256p. 1976. pap. 13.80 (ISBN 0-387-07532-1). Springer-Verlag.
Maddy, A. H., ed. Biochemical Analysis of Membranes. LC 75-40188. 513p. 1976. 63.00x (ISBN 0-412-12440-8, Pub. by Chapman & Hall England). Methuen Inc.
Manson, Lionel A., ed. Biomembranes. Incl. Vol. 1. 293p. 1971. 29.50 (ISBN 0-306-39801-X); Vol. 2. 302p. 1971. 29.50 (ISBN 0-306-39802-8); Vol. 5. 284p. 1974. 27.50 (ISBN 0-306-39805-2); Vol. 7. 257p. 1975. 29.50 (ISBN 0-306-39807-9); Vol. 8. 244p. 1976. 27.50 (ISBN 0-306-39808-7); Vol. 10. 253p. 1979. 29.50 (ISBN 0-306-40216-5). (Illus., Plenum Pr). Plenum Pub.
Martonosi, Anthony, ed. The Enzymes of Biological Membranes, Vols. 1-4. Incl. Vol. 1. Physical & Chemical Techniques. 257p. 1976. 27.50 (ISBN 0-306-35031-9); Vol. 2. Biosynthesis of Cell Components. 654p. 1976. 49.50 (ISBN 0-306-35032-7); Vol. 3. Membrane Transport. 459p. 1976. 42.50 (ISBN 0-306-35033-5); Vol. 4. Electron Transport Systems & Receptors. 431p. 1976. 37.50 (ISBN 0-306-35034-3). (Illus., Plenum Pr). Plenum Pub.
Methods in Membrane Biology, Vols. 1-10. Incl. Vol. 1. 241p. 1974. 27.50 (ISBN 0-686-65013-1); Vol. 2. 363p. 1974. 32.50 (ISBN 0-306-36802-1); Vol. 3. Plasma Membranes. 246p. 1975. 24.50 (ISBN 0-306-36803-X); Vol. 4. Biophysical Approaches. 298p. 1975. 27.50 (ISBN 0-306-36804-8); Vol. 5. Transport. 199p. 1975. 25.00 (ISBN 0-306-36805-6); Vol. 6. 248p. 1976. 29.50 (ISBN 0-306-36806-4); Vol. 7. 267p. 1976. 32.50 (ISBN 0-306-36807-2); Vol. 8. 368p. 1977. 32.50 (ISBN 0-306-36808-0); Vol. 9. Vol. 9. 406p. 1978. 35.00 (ISBN 0-306-36809-9); Vol. 10. 227p. 1979. 29.50 (ISBN 0-306-40126-6). LC 73-81094. (Illus., Plenum Pr). Plenum Pub.
Miller, M. W., et al, eds. Membrane Toxicity. LC 77-1562. (Advances in Experimental Medicine & Biology Ser: Vol. 84). 553p. 1977. 45.00 (ISBN 0-306-39084-1, Plenum Pr). Plenum Pub.
Mukohata, Yusuo & Packer, Lester, eds. Cation Flux Across Biomembranes. 1979. pap. text ed. 40.00 (ISBN 0-12-511050-2). Acad Pr.
Mullins, L. J., compiled by. Annual Reviews Reprints: Cell Membranes, 1975-1977. LC 78-55105. (Illus.). 1978. pap. text ed. 12.00 (ISBN 0-8243-2501-X). Annual Reviews.
Nakao, M. Organization of Energy Transducing Membranes. 1973. 49.50 (ISBN 0-8391-0718-8). Univ Park.
Nakao, M., ed. Active Transport. (Selected Papers in Biochemistry Ser.: Vol. 9). (Illus.). 1972. 19.50 (ISBN 0-8391-0619-X). Univ Park.
Nicolis, G. & Lefever, R., eds. Membranes, Dissipative Structures & Evolution. LC 74-23611. (Advances in Chemical Physics Ser: Vol. 29). 390p. 1975. 50.00 (ISBN 0-471-63792-0, Pub. by Wiley-Interscience). Wiley.
Ovchinnikov, Y. A., et al. Membrane Active Complexones. (BBA Library Ser.: Vol. 12). 1975. 127.00 (ISBN 0-444-41159-3, North Holland). Elsevier.
Oxender, Dale & Fox, C. Fred, eds. Molecular Aspects of Membrane Transport: Proceedings of the ICN-UCLA Symposium Held at Keystone, Col., Mar. 1977. LC 78-541. (Progress in Clinical & Biological Research: Vol. 22). 612p. 1978. 67.00 (ISBN 0-8451-0022-X). A R Liss.
Packer, L., et al, eds. Bioenergetics of Membranes: Proceedings, Spetsai, 10-15 July, 1977. 1978. 80.50 (ISBN 0-444-80016-6, North Holland). Elsevier.
Parsons, D. S., ed. Biological Membranes. (Illus.). 220p. 1975. text ed. 19.50x (ISBN 0-19-855469-9). Oxford U Pr.
Porcellati, Giuseppe & Di Jeso, Fernando, eds. Membrane-Bound Enzymes. LC 70-151767. (Advances in Experimental Medicine & Biology Ser.: Vol. 14). 281p. 1971. 32.50 (ISBN 0-306-39014-0, Plenum Pr). Plenum Pub.
Poste, G. & Nicolson, G. L., eds. Membrane Fusion. (Cell Surface Reviews Ser: Vol. 5). 1978. 120.00 (ISBN 0-444-00262-6, North-Holland). Elsevier.
Prince, L. M. & Sears, D. F., eds. Biological Horizons in Surface Science. 1973. 63.00 (ISBN 0-12-565850-8). Acad Pr.
Racker, Efraim, ed. Membranes of Mitochondria & Chloroplasts. LC 72-97168. (ACS Monograph: No. 165). 1970. 28.50 (ISBN 0-8412-0287-7). Am Chemical.
Rocha e Silva, M. & Suarez-Kurtz, G., eds. Concepts of Membranes in Regulation & Excitation. LC 74-21984. 239p. 1975. 22.50 (ISBN 0-89004-031-1). Raven.
Roth, Juergen. The Lectins: Molecular Probes in Cell Biology & Membrane Research. (Experimental Pathology Ser.). (Illus.). 1978. 37.50x (ISBN 0-8002-0373-9). Intl Pubns Serv.
Rothfield, Lawrence I., ed. Structure & Function of Biological Membranes. (Molecular Biology Ser.). 1971. 60.50 (ISBN 0-12-598650-5). Acad Pr.
Saier, M. H., Jr. & Stiles, C. D. Molecular Dynamics in Biological Membranes. LC 75-12923. (Heidelberg Science Library: Vol. 22). (Illus.). 95p. (Orig.). 1976. pap. 8.80 (ISBN 0-387-90142-6). Springer-Verlag.
Salanki, J., et al, eds. Physiology of Excitable Membranes: Proceedings of the 28th International Congress of Physiological Sciences, Budapest, 1980. LC 80-41853. (Advances in Physiological Sciences: Vol. 4). (Illus.). 350p. 1981. 40.00 (ISBN 0-08-026816-1). Pergamon.
Sanadi, D. Rao, ed. Chemical Mechanisms in Bioenergetics. LC 76-26707. (ACS Monograph: 172). 1976. 33.00 (ISBN 0-8412-0274-5). Am Chemical.
Schaefer, G. & Klingenberg, M., eds. Energy Conservation in Biological Membranes: April 6-8, 1978, Mosbach, Germany. (Colloquium Mosbach Ser.: Vol. 29). (Illus.). 1979. 39.30 (ISBN 0-387-09079-7). Springer-Verlag.

Schultz, Stanley G. Principles of Membrane Transport. LC 79-54015. (IUPAB Biophysics Ser.: No. 2). (Illus.). 1980. 22.50 (ISBN 0-521-22992-8); pap. 8.50x (ISBN 0-521-29762-1). Cambridge U Pr.
Selegny, Eric. Charged & Reactive Polymers. Incl. Vol. 3. Charged Gels & Membranes, Pt. 1. lib. bdg. 63.00 (ISBN 90-277-0665-4); Vol. 4. Charged Gels & Membranes, Pt. 2. lib. bdg. 45.00 (ISBN 90-277-0666-2). LC 76-6086. 1976 (Pub. by Reidel Holland). Kluwer Boston.
Semenza, G. & Carafoli, E., eds. Biochemistry of Membrane Transport: FEBS Symposium Number 42. (Proceedings in Life Sciences). 1977. 44.30 (ISBN 0-387-08082-1). Springer-Verlag.
Smyth, D. H., ed. Biomembranes, 2 vols. Incl. Vol. 4A. Intestinal Absorption. 553p (ISBN 0-306-39891-5); Vol. 4B. Intestinal Absorption. LC 72-77043. 459p (ISBN 0-306-39892-3). LC 72-77043. 1974. 47.50 ea. (Plenum Pr). Plenum Pub.
Snell, F. Physical Principles of Biological Membranes. 1970. 55.50x (ISBN 0-677-13680-3). Gordon.
Snell, F. M. & Noell, W. K., eds. Transcellular Membrane Potentials & Ionic Fluxes. (Life Sciences Ser). 1964. 32.50x (ISBN 0-677-10520-7). Gordon.
Societe de Chimie Physique, International Meeting, 29th, Orsay, Oct. 1976. Electrical Phenomena at Biological Membrane Level: Proceedings. Roux, E., ed. 1977. 88.00 (ISBN 0-444-41572-6). Elsevier.
Stevens, Charles F. & Tsien, Richard W., eds. Ion Permeation Through Membrane Channels, Vol. 3. LC 76-19934. 168p. 1979. text ed. 16.00 (ISBN 0-89004-224-1). Raven.
Symposium Held at the University of Nebraska Medical School, Omaha, Nebr., May, 1972. The Role of Membranes in Metabolic Regulation: Proceedings. Mehlman, Myron A. & Hanson, Richard W., eds. 1972. 47.00 (ISBN 0-12-487840-7). Acad Pr.
Thompson, Guy A. Regulation of Membrane Lipid Metabolism. 256p. 1980. 64.95 (ISBN 0-8493-5427-7). CRC Pr.
Tien, H. Ti. Bilayer Lipid Membranes (Blm) Theory & Practice. 672p. 1974. 64.75 (ISBN 0-8247-6048-4). Dekker.
Tosteson, D. C., ed. Concepts & Models. (Membrane Transport in Biology Ser.: Vol. 1). (Illus.). 1978. 94.10 (ISBN 0-387-08687-0). Springer-Verlag.
--Transport Across Single Biological Membranes. LC 78-17668. (Membrane Transport in Biology: Vol. 2). (Illus.). 1978. 85.50 (ISBN 0-387-08780-X). Springer-Verlag.
Tribe, M. A., et al. Cell Membranes. LC 75-7217. (Basic Biology Course Ser: Bk. 5). (Illus.). 84p. 1976. text ed. 23.95 (ISBN 0-521-20737-1); pap. text ed. 8.50x (ISBN 0-521-20738-X). Cambridge U Pr.
Trump, Benjamin F. & Arstila, Antti U., eds. Pathobiology of Cell Membranes, Vol. 2. LC 74-27793. 1980. 49.50 (ISBN 0-12-701502-7). Acad Pr.
Tzagoloff, Alexandre, ed. Membrane Biogenesis: Mitochondria, Chloroplasts & Bacteria. LC 75-4744. (Illus.). 460p. 1975. 39.50 (ISBN 0-306-30825-8, Plenum Pr). Plenum Pub.
Wallach, D. F. Membrane Molecular Biology of Neoplastic Cells. 1976. 94.25 (ISBN 0-444-41359-6, North Holland). Elsevier.
Wallach, D. F. & Winzler, R. J. Evolving Strategies & Tactics in Membrane Research. LC 73-21715. (Illus.). 450p. 1974. 44.90 (ISBN 0-387-06576-8). Springer-Verlag.
Weissmann, Gerald & Claiborne, Robert, eds. Cell Membranes: Biochemistry, Cell Biology & Pathology. (Illus.). 296p. 1975. text ed. 17.95 (ISBN 0-913800-06-6). HP Pub Co.
Yagi, Kunio. Structure & Function of Biomembranes. 1979. 46.00x (ISBN 0-89955-134-3, Pub. by Japan Sci Soc). Intl Schol Bk Serv.

MEMBRANES (TECHNOLOGY)

BCC Staff. Membrane & Membrane Technology Patents: Patent Printouts for Membrane Market Opportunities. 1980. 150.00 (ISBN 0-89336-247-6). BCC.
Bier, Milan, ed. Membrane Processes in Industry & Biomedicine. LC 72-149647. 313p. 1971. 32.50 (ISBN 0-306-30528-3, Plenum Pr). Plenum Pub.
Cadenhead, D. A., ed. Progress in Surface & Membrane Science, Vol. 13. (Serial Publication). 1979. 48.50 (ISBN 0-12-571813-6); lib. bdg. 59.00 (ISBN 0-12-571882-9); microfiche 31.50 (ISBN 0-12-571883-7). Acad Pr.
Cadenhead, D. A. & Danielli, J. F., eds. Progress in Surface & Membrane Science, Vol. 14. (Serial Publication Ser.). 1981. 41.00 (ISBN 0-12-571814-4); lib. ed. 53.50 (ISBN 0-12-571884-5); microfiche 29.00 (ISBN 0-12-571885-3). Acad Pr.
Critser, James R., Jr. Membrane Separation Processes. (Series 5-80). 221p. 1981. 110.00 (ISBN 0-914428-76-4). Lexington Data.
--Membrane Separation Processes. Incl. Index & Abstracts 1967-1971. 285:00 (ISBN 0-914428-10-1). (No.5-6771). 1972. Lexington Data Inc.
--Membrane Separation Processes. (Ser. 5-78). 1979. 110.00 (ISBN 0-914428-60-8). Lexington Data.
--Membrane Separation Processes. (Ser. 5-77). 1978. 110.00 (ISBN 0-914428-54-3). Lexington Data.
--Membrane Separation Processes (1972) (Ser. 5-72). 120p. 1973. 100.00 (ISBN 0-914428-13-6). Lexington Data.
--Membrane Separation Processes (1974) (Ser. 5-74). 1975. 110.00 (ISBN 0-914428-25-X). Lexington Data.
--Membrane Separation Processes (1975) (Ser. No. 5-75). 1976. 110.00 (ISBN 0-914428-33-0). Lexington Data.
--Membrane Separation Processes: 1976. (No. 5-76). 1977. 110.00 (ISBN 0-914428-51-9). Lexington Data.
Dutka. Membrane Filtration. (Pollution Engineering & Technology Ser.: Vol. 17). 632p. 1981. 69.50 (ISBN 0-8247-1164-5). Dekker.
Evolving Membrane Market, P-041. 1980. 800.00 (ISBN 0-89336-052-X). BCC.
Flinn, J. E. Membrane Science & Technology: Industrial, Biological, & Waste Treatment Processes. LC 77-118126. 234p. 1970. 29.50 (ISBN 0-306-30484-8, Plenum Pr). Plenum Pub.
Hatefi, D., ed. The Structural Basis of Membrane Function. 1976. 36.50 (ISBN 0-12-332450-5). Acad Pr.
Hwang, S. & Kammermeyer, K. Membranes in Separations, Vol. 7. (Techniques of Chemistry). 559p. 1975. 70.00 (ISBN 0-471-93268-X). Wiley.
Iberall, A. & Schindler, A. Physics of Membrane Transport. LC 73-87972. (Illus.). 266p. (Orig.). 1973. pap. 6.00 (ISBN 0-914780-02-6). Gen Tech Serv.
Kent, P. W., ed. Membrane Mediated Information, Vols. 1 & 2. 1974. 22.50 ea. Vol. 1 (ISBN 0-444-19540-8). Vol. 2 (ISBN 0-444-19539-4). Elsevier.
Lacey, Robert & Loeb, Sidney, eds. Industrial Processing with Membranes. LC 78-21889. 360p. 1979. Repr. of 1972 ed. lib. bdg. 25.00 (ISBN 0-88275-788-1). Krieger.
Lakshminarayanaiah, N. Transport Phenomena in Membranes. 1969. 63.50 (ISBN 0-12-434250-7). Acad Pr.
London Chemical Engineering Congress, Second Session, 1977. Advance in Enzyme & Membrane Technology: Proceedings, No. 51. 100p. 1981. 70.00x (ISBN 0-85295-103-5, Pub. by Inst Chem Eng England). State Mutual Bk.
Meares, P., ed. Membrane Separation Processes. 1976. 122.00 (ISBN 0-444-41446-0). Elsevier.
Membrane Processes for Industry, Symposium, May 19-20,1966. Proceedings. Feazel, Charles E. & Lacey, Robert E., eds. LC 66-30620. (Illus.). 268p. 1966. pap. 5.00 (ISBN 0-940824-00-0). S Res Inst.
Otto, Frei. Tensile Structures. 490p. 1973. pap. 19.95 (ISBN 0-262-65005-3). MIT Pr.
Scott, Jeanette, ed. Membrane & Ultrafiltration Technology: Recent Advances. LC 79-24503. (Chemical Tecnology Review Ser.: No. 147). (Illus.). 1980. 48.00 (ISBN 0-8155-0784-4). Noyes.
Selegny, Eric. Charged & Reactive Polymers. Incl. Vol. 3. Charged Gels & Membranes, Pt. 1. lib. bdg. 63.00 (ISBN 90-277-0665-4); Vol. 4. Charged Gels & Membranes, Pt. 2. lib. bdg. 45.00 (ISBN 90-277-0666-2). LC 76-6086. 1976 (Pub. by Reidel Holland). Kluwer Boston.
Tuwiner, Sidney B. Diffusion & Membrane Technology. LC 62-20783. (ACS Monograph: No. 156). 1962. 33.50 (ISBN 0-8412-0284-2). Am Chemical.
Zimand, Savel. Modern Social Movements. 69.95 (ISBN 0-87700-188-X). Revisionist Pr.

MEMOIRS

see Autobiography; Biography; also subdivision Correspondence, Reminiscences, etc. under classes of people, e.g. Actors–Correspondence, reminiscences, etc.; subdivision History–Sources under names of countries; subdivision Personal Narratives under names of wars, diseases, etc. e.g. World War, 1939-1945–Personal Narratives

MEMORANDA

see Memorandums

MEMORANDUMS

Uris, Auren. Memos for Managers. LC 74-14650. 288p. 1975. 10.00 (ISBN 0-690-00648-9). T Y Crowell.

MEMORIAL SERVICE

see also Funeral Service

Silverman, Morris. Memorial Service at the Cemetery. pap. 0.50 (ISBN 0-685-64878-8). Prayer Bk.

MEMORIAL TABLETS

see Sepulchral Monuments

MEMORIALS

see also Anniversaries; Holidays; Monuments

Beltz, George F. Memorials of the Most Noble Order of the Garter from Its Foundation to the Present Time. LC 72-178572. Repr. of 1841 ed. 35.00 (ISBN 0-404-56527-1). AMS Pr.
Dixon, J. M. The Spiritual Meaning of "in Memoriam". 1920. Repr. 15.00 (ISBN 0-8274-3495-2). R West.
Geological Society of America, ed. Memorials: Nineteen Seventy-Seven Decedents. LC 73-76887. (Vol. 9). (Illus.). 1979. pap. 9.00x (ISBN 0-8137-8077-2). Geol Soc.
Memorials: Nineteen Seventy-Eight Descendents, Vol. 10. LC 73-76887. (Illus.). 1980. pap. 10.00x (ISBN 0-8137-8078-0). Geol Soc.

MEMORY

see also Eidetic Imagery

Adam, G. Perception, Consciousness, Memory: Reflections of a Biologist. LC 73-20153. 215p. 1980. 22.50 (ISBN 0-306-30776-6, Plenum Pr). Plenum Pub.
Adam, G., ed. Biology of Memory. LC 73-154700. 250p. 1971. 29.50 (ISBN 0-306-30535-6, Plenum Pr). Plenum Pub.
Adams, Jack. Learning & Memory: An Introduction. rev. ed. 1980. 19.50x (ISBN 0-256-02314-X). Dorsey.
Adams, Jack A. Human Memory. (Psychology Ser). 1967. 18.50 (ISBN 0-07-000307-6, C). McGraw.
Aldrich, Bailey. Crowding Memories. 1920. 25.00 (ISBN 0-8274-2123-0). R West.
Anderson, John R. & Bower, Gordon H. Human Associative Memory: A Brief Edition. LC 79-28349. 288p. 1980. pap. text ed. 14.95x (ISBN 0-89859-020-5). L Erlbaum Assocs.
Aristotle. Aristotle de Sensu & de Memoria. Ross, George R., tr. LC 72-9301. (The Philosophy of Plato & Aristotle Ser.). (Gr. & Eng.). Repr. of 1906 ed. 17.00 (ISBN 0-405-04856-4). Arno.
Atkinson, William W. Memory Culture. 92p. 1976. Repr. of 1903 ed. 6.00 (ISBN 0-911662-61-8). Yoga.
Baddeley, Alan D. The Psychology of Memory. LC 75-36769. (Topics in Cognition Ser.). (Illus.). 1976. text ed. 10.95x (ISBN 0-465-06736-0); pap. text ed. 7.95x (ISBN 0-465-06737-9). Basic.
Barton, Helen B. Nervous Tension, Behavior & Body Function. LC 65-10567. 1965. 6.00 (ISBN 0-8022-0078-8). Philos Lib.
Bergson, Henri. Matter & Memory. (Muirhead Library of Philosophy). 1978. text ed. 16.50x (ISBN 0-391-00924-9). Humanities.
Beritashvili, I. S. Vertebrate Memory. LC 74-157930. 143p. 1971. 25.00 (ISBN 0-306-30524-0, Plenum Pr). Plenum Pub.
Bibliography of Memory. 1979. text ed. 44.00x (ISBN 0-391-01603-2). Humanities.
Birnbuam, Isabel M. & Parker, Elizabeth S., eds. Alcohol & Human Memory. LC 77-15653. 1977. 12.95 (ISBN 0-470-99339-1). Halsted Pr.
Botwinick, Jack & Storandt, Martha. Memory, Related Functions & Age. (Illus.). 208p. 1974. 18.75 (ISBN 0-398-03143-6). C C Thomas.
Bower, Gordon, ed. Human Memory: Basic Processes. 1977. 19.00 (ISBN 0-12-121050-2). Acad Pr.
Bransford, John D. Human Cognition: Learning, Understanding & Remembering. 1979. pap. text ed. 12.95x (ISBN 0-534-00699-X). Wadsworth Pub.
Brenner, Benjamin. Effect of Immediate & Delayed Praise & Blame Upon Learning & Recall. LC 70-176588. (Columbia University. Teachers College. Contributions to Education: No. 620). Repr. of 1934 ed. 17.50 (ISBN 0-404-55620-5). AMS Pr.
Bridgeman, Bruce, et al, eds. Readings on Fundamental Issues on Learning & Memory. 1977. pap. text ed. 12.50x (ISBN 0-685-81867-5). Whitehall Co.
Brown, J. Recall & Recognition. LC 75-8770. 1976. 48.00 (ISBN 0-471-11229-1, Pub. by Wiley-Interscience). Wiley.
Brown, Mark. Memory Matters. LC 77-71252. (Illus.). 1977. 14.50x (ISBN 0-8448-1091-6). Crane-Russak Co.
Burdett, Osbert. Memory & Imagination. 1935. Repr. 17.50 (ISBN 0-8274-2721-2). R West.
Buzan, Tony. Speed Memory. (Illus.). 160p. 1981. 11.00 (ISBN 0-7153-7365-X). David & Charles.
--Use Both Sides of Your Brain. 1976. pap. 6.95 (ISBN 0-525-47436-6). Dutton.
Cermak, Laird S. & Craik, Fergus I. Levels of Processing in Human Memory. LC 78-27848. 1979. 24.95x (ISBN 0-470-26651-1). Halsted Pr.
Cofer, Charles N., ed. The Structure of Human Memory. LC 76-2581. (Psychology Ser.). (Illus.). 1976. pap. text ed. 9.95x (ISBN 0-7167-0715-2). W H Freeman.
Conditioning Your Memory. 144p. 1975. pap. 1.95 (ISBN 0-346-12196-5). Cornerstone.
Conference on Learning, Remembering & Forgetting, 3rd. Proceedings: Readiness to Remember, 2 pts. Kimble, D. P., ed. Incl. Vol. 1. 354p. 63.25x (ISBN 0-677-14420-2); Vol. 2. 310p. 63.25x (ISBN 0-677-14430-X). 762p. 1969. Set. 111.75x (ISBN 0-677-13420-7). Gordon.
Congress of the Hungarian Pharmacological Society, 1st, Budapest, 1971. Symposium on Pharmacology of Learning & Retention. 103p. 1975. 10.00x (ISBN 963-05-0191-0). Intl Pubns Serv.
Corning, W. C. & Ratner, S. C., eds. Chemistry of Learning: Invertebrate Research. LC 67-25103. 468p. 1967. 42.50 (ISBN 0-306-30305-1, Plenum Pr). Plenum Pub.
Culbertson, James T. Sensations, Memories & the Flow of Time: A Theory of Subjective States - Reductive Materialism Using a Spacetime Analysis. LC 75-30170. (Illus.). 1976. 8.00x (ISBN 0-916298-01-9). Cromwel.
De Schonen, Scania. La Memoire: Connaissance Active du Passe. LC 73-86214. (Connaissance et Language Ser: No. 3). 335p. (Fr.). 1975. pap. text ed. 39.50x (ISBN 90-2797-606-6). Mouton.
Deutsch, D. & Deutsch, J. A., eds. Short-Term Memory. 1975. 35.50 (ISBN 0-12-213350-1). Acad Pr.
Deutsch, J. A., ed. The Physiological Basis of Memory. 1973. 42.50 (ISBN 0-12-213450-8). Acad Pr.
Donahoe, John W. & Wessells, Michael G. Learning, Language, & Memory. (Illus.). 1979. text ed. 19.50 scp (ISBN 0-06-041685-8, HarpC); instructor's manual avail. (ISBN 0-06-361699-8). Har-Row.
Drucker- Colin, R. R. & McGaugh, J. L. Neurobiology of Sleep & Memory. 1977. 33.50 (ISBN 0-12-222350-0). Acad Pr.
Dudley, Geoffrey. Increase Your Learning Power. pap. 2.00 (ISBN 0-87980-085-2). Wilshire.
Dutta, S. & Kanunga, R. N. Affect & Memory: A Reformulation. LC 75-8628. 148p. 1975. text ed. 25.00 (ISBN 0-08-018270-4). Pergamon.
Ellis, Henry C. Fundamentals of Human Learning, Memory & Cognition. 2nd ed. (Fundamentals of Psychology Ser.). 240p. 1978. pap. text ed. write for info. (ISBN 0-697-06623-1); tchrs.' manual avail. (ISBN 0-686-67920-2). Wm C Brown.
Ellis, Henry C., et al. Psychology of Learning & Memory. LC 78-16292. (Illus.). 1979. text ed. 18.95 (ISBN 0-8185-0267-3). Brooks-Cole.
Eysenck, Michael W. Human Memory: Theory, Research & Individual Differences. 1977. text ed. 18.25 (ISBN 0-08-020405-8). Pergamon.
Fillenbaum, Samuel. Syntactic Factors in Memory? (Janua Linguarum Ser. Minor: No. 168). 1973. pap. text ed. 17.00x (ISBN 0-686-22590-2). Mouton.
Freud, Sigmund. Psychopathology of Everyday Life. 1952. pap. 1.75 (ISBN 0-451-61656-1, ME1656, Ment). NAL.
--Zur Psychopathologie Des Alltagslebens. 1968. 2.50 (ISBN 0-685-06617-7). Assoc Bk.
Gallant, Roy A. Memory: How It Works & How to Improve It. LC 79-6342. (Illus.). 128p. (gr. 7 up). 1980. 8.95 (ISBN 0-590-07613-2, Four Winds). Schol Bk Serv.
Gattegno, Caleb. Evolution and Memory. 1976. pap. 10.00 (ISBN 0-87825-072-7). Ed Solutions.
George A. Talland Memorial Conference. New Directions in Memory & Aging: Proceedings. Poon, Leonard W., et al, eds. LC 79-27548. (Illus.). 572p. 1980. text ed. 36.00x (ISBN 0-89859-035-3). L Erlbaum Assocs.
Gibbs, M. E. & Mark, R. F. Inhibition of Memory Formation. LC 73-82140. 554p. 1973. 45.00 (ISBN 0-306-30750-2, Plenum Pr). Plenum Pub.
Ginet, C. Knowledge, Perception, & Memory. LC 75-8602. (Philosophical Studies: No. 5). 207p. 1975. 39.50 (ISBN 90-277-0574-7, Pub. by Reidel Holland). Kluwer Boston.
Gratarolus, Gulielmus. The Castel of Memorie. LC 72-38109. (English Experience Ser.: No. 382). 128p. 1971. Repr. of 1562 ed. 13.00 (ISBN 90-221-0382-X). Walter J Johnson.
Gregg, Vernon. Human Memory. (Essential Psychology Ser.). 1975. pap. 4.50x (ISBN 0-416-81980-X). Methuen Inc.
Gruneberg, M. M., et al, eds. Practical Aspects of Memory. 1979. 55.00 (ISBN 0-12-305050-2). Acad Pr.
Gruneberg, Michael & Morris, Peter, eds. Applied Problems in Memory. 1979. 36.00 (ISBN 0-12-305150-9). Acad Pr.
Gruneberg, Michael M. & Morris, Peter, eds. Aspects of Memory. 1978. 18.95x (ISBN 0-416-70550-2); pap. 11.95x (ISBN 0-416-71350-5). Methuen Inc.
Halacy, D. S., Jr. Man & Memory: Breakthrough in the Science of the Human Mind. LC 74-95962. (Illus.). 1970. 10.95 (ISBN 0-06-011728-1, HarpT). Har-Row.

Halbwachs, Maurice. Les Cadres Sociaux De la Memoire. 2nd ed. (Archontes: No. 5). 298p. 1976. pap. text ed. 36.25x (ISBN 90-2797-902-2). Mouton.

--Les Cadres Sociaux De la Memoire: The Social Framework of Memory. LC 74-25758. (European Sociology Ser.). 310p. 1975. Repr. 17.00x (ISBN 0-405-06512-4). Arno.

--The Collective Memory. Ditter, Francis J., Jr. & Ditter, Vida Y., trs. from Fr. LC 74-18576. 256p. (Orig.). 1980. pap. 5.95 (ISBN 0-06-090800-9, CN 800, CN). Har-Row.

Harcum, E. Rae. Serial Learning & Paralearning. 464p. 1975. 16.50 (ISBN 0-471-35137-7, Pub. by Wiley). Krieger.

Harmon, Glynn. Human Memory & Knowledge: A Systems Approach. LC 72-809. (Contributions in Librarianship & Information Science: No. 6). (Illus.). 159p. 1973. lib. bdg. 15.00 (ISBN 0-8371-6379-X, HAH/). Greenwood.

Hastie, Reid, et al, eds. Person Memory: The Cognitive Basis of Social Perception. LC 80-10327. (Illus.). 320p. 1980. text ed. 24.95x (ISBN 0-89859-024-8). L Erlbaum Assocs.

Herriot, Peter. Attributes of Memory. (Methuen's Manuals of Psychology Ser.). 1974. pap. 10.95x (ISBN 0-416-70330-5). Methuen Inc.

Herriot, Peter, et al. Organization & Memory. 1973. pap. 3.50x (ISBN 0-416-77590-X). Methuen Inc.

Higbee, Kenneth. Your Memory: How It Works & How to Improve It. 1977. 13.95 (ISBN 0-13-980144-8, Spec); pap. 3.95 (ISBN 0-13-980136-7). P-H.

Hintzman, Douglas L. The Psychology of Learning & Memory. LC 77-16295. (Psychology Ser.). (Illus.). 1978. text ed. 19.95x (ISBN 0-7167-0035-2). W H Freeman.

Il'yuchenok, R. Pharmacology of Behavior & Memory. LC 76-11831. 1976. 22.50 (ISBN 0-470-15116-1). Halsted Pr.

Jarman, Ronald F. & Das, J. P. Issues in Developmental Disabilities. LC 80-12931. 136p. (Orig.). 1980. pap. 11.50 (ISBN 0-8357-0524-2, SS-00136). Univ Microfilms.

John, E. Roy. Mechanisms of Memory. 1967. text ed. 21.95 (ISBN 0-12-385850-X). Acad Pr.

Kail, Robert. The Development of Memory in Children. LC 79-12262. (Psychology Ser.). (Illus.). 1979. text ed. 14.95x (ISBN 0-7167-1097-8); pap. text ed. 7.95x (ISBN 0-7167-1098-6). W H Freeman.

Kellett, Michael. How to Improve Your Memory & Concentration. new ed. (How to Ser.). (Illus.). 1975. pap. 2.95 (ISBN 0-671-18732-5). S&S.

--Memory Power. LC 80-52338. (Illus.). 128p. (Orig.). 1980. 12.95 (ISBN 0-8069-0210-8); lib. bdg. 11.69 (ISBN 0-8069-0211-6); pap. 5.95 (ISBN 0-8069-8946-7). Sterling.

Kennedy, R. A. & Wilkes, Alan, eds. Studies in Long Term Memory. LC 74-13149. 358p. 1975. 55.95 (ISBN 0-471-46905-X, Pub. by Wiley-Interscience). Wiley.

Kimble, D. P. Learning, Remembering & Forgetting, Experience & Capacity. 1972. 14.25x (ISBN 0-677-65085-X). Gordon.

Kimble, Daniel P., ed. Anatomy of Memory: Proceedings. LC 64-8098. (Orig.). 1965. pap. 4.35x (ISBN 0-8314-0004-8). Sci & Behavior.

Kintsch, W. Memory & Cognition. LC 76-49031. 490p. 1977. 24.95 (ISBN 0-471-48072-X). Wiley.

Klatzky, Roberta L. Human Memory: Structures & Processes. 2nd ed. LC 79-20895. (A Series of Books in Psychology). (Illus.). 1980. text ed. 19.95x (ISBN 0-7167-1113-3); pap. text ed. 9.95x (ISBN 0-7167-1114-1). W H Freeman.

Kohler, Wolfgang. Dynamics in Psychology. 1940. 5.95x (ISBN 0-87140-902-X); pap. 2.95 (ISBN 0-87140-077-4). Liveright.

Kosslyn, Stephen M. Image & Mind. LC 80-10329. (Illus.). 515p. 1980. text ed. 20.00x (ISBN 0-674-44365-9). Harvard U Pr.

Krymow, Virginia P. Remember Anything You Want. LC 77-75039. 1977. pap. 3.00 (ISBN 0-918838-00-2). Arlotta.

Loftus, Elizbeth. Memory: Surprising New Insights into How We Remember & Why We Forget. (Illus.). 224p. 1980. (ISBN 0-201-04473-0); pap. 5.95 (ISBN 0-201-04474-9). A-W.

Luria, A. R. Mind of a Mnemonist: A Little Book About a Vast Memory. Solotaroff, Lynn, tr. LC 68-15918. 1968. 12.50x (ISBN 0-465-04615-0). Basic.

--The Neuropsychology of Memory. Haigh, B., tr. LC 76-10186. 1976. 22.95 (ISBN 0-470-15107-2). Halsted Pr.

McGaugh, James L. Learning & Memory. (Illus.). pap. 3.95 (ISBN 0-87843-608-1). Albion.

McGaugh, James L. & Herz, Michael J. Memory Consolidation. LC 78-167987. (Psychology Ser). (Illus.). 1971. text ed. 10.50 (ISBN 0-87843-603-0). Albion.

MacLean, Paul D. A Triune Concept of the Brain & Behaviour: The Clarence M. Hincks Memorial Lectures, 1969. Campbell, D. & Boag, T. J., eds. LC 72-90742. 1973. 15.00x (ISBN 0-8020-3299-0). U of Toronto Pr.

Maggio, Elio. Psychophysiology of Learning & Memory. 196p. 1971. photocopy ed. spiral 19.75 (ISBN 0-398-01198-2). C C Thomas.

Malcolm, Norman. Memory & Mind. LC 76-28017. 1977. 17.50x (ISBN 0-8014-1018-5). Cornell U Pr.

Mark, Richard F. Memory & Nerve Cell Connections: Criticisms & Contributions from Developmental Neurophysiology. (Illus.). 160p. 1974. pap. text ed. 7.95x (ISBN 0-19-857129-1). Oxford U Pr.

Martinez, J. L., et al, eds. Endogenous Peptides & Learning & Memory Processes. (Behavioral Biology Ser.). 1981. price not set (ISBN 0-12-474980-1). Acad Pr.

Matlin, Margaret & Stang, David. The Pollyanna Principle: Selectivity in Language, Memory, & Thought. LC 78-25548. 1979. text ed. 15.50 (ISBN 0-87073-815-1); pap. text ed. 7.95 (ISBN 0-87073-817-8). Schenkman.

Melton, Arthur W. & Martin, Edwin, eds. Coding Processes in Human Memory. LC 72-5431. 448p. 1972. text ed. 12.95x (ISBN 0-470-59335-0). Halsted Pr.

Meyer, B. The Organization of Prose & Its Effects on Memory. (N-H Studies in Theoretical Poetics Ser.: Vol. 1). 249p. 1975. pap. 22.00 (ISBN 0-444-10946-3, North-Holland). Elsevier.

Murdock, Bennet B., Jr. Human Memory: Theory & Data. LC 74-888. 1974. 12.95x (ISBN 0-470-62525-2). Halsted Pr.

Nilsson, Lars-Goran. Perspectives on Memory Research: Essays in Honor of Uppsala University's 500th Anniversary. LC 78-23461. 1979. 24.95 (ISBN 0-470-26586-8). Halsted Pr.

Noordman-Vonk, W. Retrieval from Semantic Memory. (Springer Ser. in Language & Communications: Vol. 5). (Illus.). 1979. 17.30 (ISBN 0-387-09219-6). Springer-Verlag.

Norman, D. A. Models of Human Memory. 1970. text ed. 42.50 (ISBN 0-12-521350-6). Acad Pr.

Norman, Donald A. Learning & Memory. (Illus.). 1982. text ed. price not set (ISBN 0-7167-1299-7); pap. text ed. price not set (ISBN 0-7167-1300-4). W H Freeman.

--Memory & Attention: An Introduction to Human Information Processing. 2nd ed. LC 76-236. 262p. 1976. pap. text ed. 11.95x (ISBN 0-471-65137-0). Wiley.

Ornstein, Peter A., ed. Memory Development in Children. LC 78-15562. 1978. 18.00 (ISBN 0-470-26490-X). Halsted Pr.

Paivio, Allan. Imagery & Verbal Processes. LC 73-150787. 608p. 1979. text ed. 29.95x (ISBN 0-89859-069-8). L Erlbaum Assocs.

Palombo, Stanley R. Dreaming & Memory: A New Information-Processing Model. LC 78-53812. 1978. text ed. 15.00x (ISBN 0-465-01708-8). Basic.

Parente, Frederick J., et al. Ellis, Bennett, Daniel, & Rickert's Psychology of Learning & Memory: Study Guide. (Orig.). 1979. pap. text ed. 5.95 (ISBN 0-8185-0369-6). Brooks-Cole.

Paul, I. H. Studies in Remembering: The Reproduction of Connected & Extended Verbal Material. (Psychological Issues Monograph: No. 2, Vol. 1, No. 2). (Orig.). 1959. text ed. 11.00 (ISBN 0-8236-6240-3). Intl Univs Pr.

Piaget, Jean, et al. Memory & Intelligence. Pomerans, Arnold J., tr. LC 72-89197. 448p. 1974. text ed. 12.50x (ISBN 0-465-04445-X). Basic.

Piazza, Robert, ed. Readings in Perception & Memory. (Special Education Ser.). (Illus., Orig.). 1978. pap. text ed. 10.95 (ISBN 0-89568-086-6). Spec Learn Corp.

Posner, Michael I. Cognition: An Introduction. 208p. 1974. pap. text ed. 7.95x (ISBN 0-673-07860-4). Scott F.

Pribram, Karl & Broadbent, Donald, eds. Biology of Memory. 1970. 38.00 (ISBN 0-12-564350-0). Acad Pr.

Puff, C. Richard, ed. Memory Organization & Structure. LC 79-21039. 1979. 31.50 (ISBN 0-12-566750-7). Acad Pr.

Rapaport, David. Emotions & Memory. rev. ed. LC 78-165548. (Menninger Foundation Monograph Ser.: No. 2). 296p. 1972. text ed. 22.50 (ISBN 0-8236-1660-6); pap. text ed. 5.95x (ISBN 0-8236-8034-7, 021660). Intl Univs Pr.

Ribot, Theodule A. Diseases of Memory. Smith, W. H. & Snell, M. M., trs. Bd. with Diseases of Personality. Repr. of 1891 ed; Diseases of the Will. Repr. of 1894 ed. (Contributions to the History of Psychology, Vol. I, Pt. C: Medical Psychology). 1978. Repr. of 1882 ed. 30.00 (ISBN 0-89093-165-8). U Pubns Amer.

Richardson, John T. Mental Imagery & Human Memory. LC 79-26849. 180p. 1980. 19.95 (ISBN 0-312-52975-9). St Martin.

Rony, Peter R. Logic & Memory Experiments: Using TTL Integrated Circuits. Incl. Bk. 1. pap. 10.95 (ISBN 0-672-21542-X); Bk. 2. pap. 10.95 (ISBN 0-672-21543-8). LC 78-57209. 1978. Bks 1 & 2. pap. 19.95 (ISBN 0-672-21544-6). Sams.

Rosenzweig, Mark R. & Bennett, Edward L., eds. Neural Mechanisms of Learning & Memory. LC 75-35780. 1000p. 1976. text ed. 37.50x (ISBN 0-262-18076-6). MIT Pr.

Seamon, John G. Memory & Cognition: An Introduction. (Illus.). 1980. text ed. 14.95x (ISBN 0-19-502642-X); pap. text ed. 7.95x (ISBN 0-19-502643-8). Oxford U Pr.

Seamon, John G., ed. Human Memory: Contemporary Readings. (Illus.). 464p. 1980. text ed. 19.95x (ISBN 0-19-502738-8); pap. text ed. 11.95x (ISBN 0-19-502739-6). Oxford U Pr.

Seymour, P. H. Human Visual Cognition. 1979. 25.00x (ISBN 0-312-39966-9). St Martin.

Shepard, Odell. The Joys of Forgetting. 1928. Repr. 20.00 (ISBN 0-8274-2638-0). R West.

Shulman, Harvey G. Presentation Rate, Retention Interval, & Encoding in Short-Term Recognition Memory for Homonyms, Synonyms, & Identical Words. LC 70-135077. 125p. 1969. 22.00 (ISBN 0-686-01929-6). Mgmt Info Serv.

Slamecka, Norman J., ed. Human Learning & Memory: Selected Readings. (Orig.). 1967. pap. 8.95x (ISBN 0-19-501054-X). Oxford U Pr.

Smirnov, A. A. Problems of Psychology of Memory. LC 72-83045. (Monographs in Psychology Ser.). (Illus.). 338p. 1973. 39.50 (ISBN 0-306-30574-7, Plenum Pr). Plenum Pub.

Smith, Brian. Memory. (Muirhead Library of Philosophy). 1978. Repr. of 1966 ed. text ed. 12.00x (ISBN 0-391-00565-0). Humanities.

Sorabji, Richard. Aristotle on Memory. LC 72-79966. (Illus.). x, 122p. 1972. 8.00 (ISBN 0-87057-137-0, Pub. by Brown U Pr). U Pr of New Eng.

Spear, Norman E. The Processing of Memories: Forgetting & Retention. (Experimental Psychology Ser.). 1978. 29.95 (ISBN 0-470-26290-7). Halsted Pr.

Spear, Norman E. & Campbell, Byron A., eds. Ontogeny of Learning & Memory. LC 79-19045. 321p. 1979. 19.95x (ISBN 0-470-26849-2). Halsted Pr.

Stevick, Earl. Memory, Meaning & Method. LC 76-2032. 1976. 10.95 (ISBN 0-88377-053-9). Newbury Hse.

Tarpy, Roger & Mayer, Richard. Readings in Learning & Memory. 1979. pap. text ed. 7.95x (ISBN 0-673-15110-7). Scott F.

Tarpy, Roger M. & Mayer, Richard E. Foundations of Learning & Memory. 1978. text ed. 15.95x (ISBN 0-673-15074-7). Scott F.

Torda, C. Memory & Dreams: A Modern Physics Approach. LC 81-50331. (Illus.). 453p. 1980. 24.50 (ISBN 0-686-30443-8); pap. 19.50 (ISBN 0-686-30444-6). Walters.

Torda, Clara. Memory & Dreams: A Modern Physics Approach. (Illus.). 453p. 1980. 24.00 (ISBN 0-686-31514-6); pap. 19.50 (ISBN 0-940412-03-9). W Torda.

Tulving, Endel & Donaldson, Wayne, eds. Organization of Memory. 1972. 43.00 (ISBN 0-12-703650-4). Acad Pr.

Underwood, G. Attention & Memory. LC 75-17614. 231p. 1976. text ed. 34.00 (ISBN 0-08-019615-2); pap. text ed. 14.00 (ISBN 0-08-018754-4). Pergamon.

Ungar, G. Molecular Mechanisms in Memory & Learning. LC 70-107543. 296p. 1970. 29.50 (ISBN 0-306-30452-X, Plenum Pr). Plenum Pub.

Weisberg, Robert W. Memory, Thought, & Behavior. LC 79-56. (Illus.). 1979. text ed. 16.95x (ISBN 0-19-502583-0). Oxford U Pr.

Wenestam, Claes-Goran. Qualitative Differences in Retention. (Goteborg Studies in Educational Sciences: No. 35). 1980. pap. text ed. 12.75x (ISBN 91-7346-082-6). Humanities.

Werner, Victor. Short-Cut Memory: Improve Your Memory in 26 Easy Lessons. 1975. Repr. 4.95 (ISBN 0-917200-10-1). ESPress.

Wickelgren, Wayne A. Learning & Memory. (Experimental Psychology Ser.). 1977. 19.95 (ISBN 0-13-527663-2). P-H.

Willis, John. The Art of Memory... As It Dependeth Upon Places & Ideas. LC 73-6172. (English Experience Ser.: No. 634). 104p. 1973. Repr. of 1621 ed. 7.00 (ISBN 90-221-0634-9). Walter J Johnson.

Wingfield, Arthur. Human Learning & Memory: An Introduction. LC 78-18197. 1978. text ed. 17.50 scp (ISBN 0-06-047149-2, HarpC). Har-Row.

Wingfield, Arthur & Byrnes, Dennis L. The Psychology of the Human Memory. 429p. 1981. pap. 10.95 (ISBN 0-12-759650-X). Acad Pr.

Wold, Astri H. Decoding Oral Language. (European Monographs in Social Psychology Ser.). 1977. 35.50 (ISBN 0-12-336250-4). Acad Pr.

Yates, Francis A. The Art of Memory. LC 66-22770. xvi, 400p. 1974. pap. 7.50 (ISBN 0-226-95001-8, P615, Phoen). U of Chicago Pr.

Young, Chesley V. The Magic of a Powerful Memory. rev. & abr. ed. LC 80-70955. 256p. 1981. Repr. of 1971 ed. 10.95 (ISBN 0-8119-0416-4). Fell.

Young, J. Z. Evolution of Memory. Head, J. J., ed. LC 76-28270. (Carolina Biology Readers Ser.). (Illus.). (gr. 11-12). 1976. pap. 1.65 (ISBN 0-89278-233-1, 45-9633). Carolina Biological.

Young, Morris N. & Gibson, Walter B. How to Develop an Exceptional Memory. pap. 4.00 (ISBN 0-87980-058-5). Wilshire.

Zechmeister, Eugene B. & Nyberg, Stanley E. Human Memory: An Introduction to Research & Theory. 384p. (Orig.). 1981. pap. text ed. 11.95 (ISBN 0-8185-0458-7). Brooks-Cole.

Zippel, H. P., ed. Memory & Transfer of Information. LC 73-80325. 582p. 1973. 42.50 (ISBN 0-306-30743-X, Plenum Pr). Plenum Pub.

MEMORY, DISORDERS OF

see also Aphasia

Ajmone-Marsan, Cosimo & Matthies, H., eds. Neuronal Plasticity & Memory Formation. (International Brain Research Organization Monograph: Vol. 9). 1981. text ed. 55.00 (ISBN 0-89004-681-6). Raven.

Kihlstrom, John F. & Evans, Frederick J., eds. Functional Disorders of Memory. LC 79-1049. (The Experimental Psychology Ser.). 1979. 24.95 (ISBN 0-470-26698-8). Halsted Pr.

Luria, A. R. Mind of a Mnemonist: A Little Book About a Vast Memory. Solotaroff, Lynn, tr. LC 68-15918. 1968. 12.50x (ISBN 0-465-04615-0). Basic.

Zehv, William. Memory & the Older Adult: Dynamics of Memory Dysfunction Techniques to Cope with Forgetfulness. 175p. (Orig.). 1981. pap. 7.95x (ISBN 0-686-29703-2). Desert Pub CA.

MEMORY DEVICES

see Magnetic Memory (Calculating-Machines)

MEMORY TRAINING

see Mnemonics

MEMOS

see Memorandums

MEMPHIS, TENNESSEE

American Institute Of Law And Criminology. Journal of the American Institute of Law & Criminology. LC 71-154571. (Police in America Ser). 1971. Repr. of 1910 ed. 12.00 (ISBN 0-405-03361-3). Arno.

Capers, Gerald M., Jr. The Biography of a River Town: Memphis--Its Heroic Age. 2nd ed. (Illus.). 318p. 1980. Repr. of 1966 ed. 17.50 (ISBN 0-937130-09-5); signed ltd. ed. 27.50 (ISBN 0-937130-10-9). Burke's Bk Store.

Coppock, Paul R. Memphis Memoirs. LC 80-24019. (Illus.). 265p. 1980. 14.95 (ISBN 0-87870-110-9). Memphis St Univ.

Crawford, Charles W. Yesterday's Memphis. LC 76-10384. (Historic Cities Ser: No. 25). (Illus.). 160p. 1976. 9.95 (ISBN 0-912458-69-0). E A Seemann.

Davies-Rodgers, Ellen. The Great Book: Calvary Protestant Episcopal Church. Memphis, Tennessee 1832-1972. 1973. 25.00 (ISBN 0-685-84989-9). Plantation.

Hamilton, G. P. The Bright Side of Memphis. (Illus.). 294p. 1978. Repr. of 1908 ed. 20.00 (ISBN 0-937130-06-0). Burke's Bk Store.

Keating, J. M. & Vedder, O. F. History of the City of Memphis & Shelby County Tennessee, 2 vols. (Illus.). 1977. Repr. of 1888 ed. Set. ltd. boxed ed. 75.00 (ISBN 0-937130-04-4). Burke's Bk Store.

McLean, Virginia O. The Memphis Guide. LC 81-90083. (Illus.). 250p. (Orig.). 1981. pap. price not set (ISBN 0-9606046-0-X). Redbird.

Miller, William D. Memphis During the Progressive Era, Nineteen Hundred to Nineteen Seventeen. LC 58-21437. (Illus.). xiv, 242p. 1957. 12.50 (ISBN 0-87057-043-9, Pub. by Brown U Pr). U Pr of New Eng.

Roper, James E. The Founding of Memphis, 1818-1820. (Illus.). 100p. 1970. 7.00 (ISBN 0-937130-07-9). Burke's Bk Store.

Sigafoos, Robert A. Cotton Row to Beale Street: A Business History of Memphis. LC 79-89889. (Illus.). 1979. 21.95 (ISBN 0-87870-068-4). Memphis St Univ.

Sorrels, William W. Memphis' Greatest Debate: A Question of Water. LC 74-130973. 1970. 7.50x (ISBN 0-87870-005-6). Memphis St Univ.

Tucker, David M. Memphis Since Crump: Bossism, Blacks, & Civic Reformers, 1948-1968. LC 79-12211. (Illus.). 1980. 10.50 (ISBN 0-87049-282-9). U of Tenn Pr.

United States House of Representatives - 39th 1st Session - Select Committee on Memphis Riots & Massacres. Report of Memphis Riots & Massacres. (Basic Afro-American Reprint Library). Repr. of 1866 ed. 18.50 (ISBN 0-384-62870-2). Johnson Repr.
United States 39th Congress, 1st Session, 1865-1866 House. Memphis Riots & Massacres: House Report No. 101. facsimile ed. LC 79-89439. (Black Heritage Library Collection). Repr. of 1866 ed. 15.25 (ISBN 0-8369-8673-3). Arno.
U.S. House of Representatives. Memphis Riots & Massacres: Report Submitted by E.B. Washburne, 39th Congress First Session, House Report No. 101. LC 79-90202. (Mass Violence in America Ser). Repr. of 1866 ed. 14.00 (ISBN 0-405-01316-7). Arno.

MEMPHIS, EL PASO, AND PACIFIC RAILROAD COMPANY

Taylor, Virginia H. The Franco-Texan Land Company. (M. K. Brown Range Life Ser.: No. 7). (Illus.). 345p. 1969. 15.00 (ISBN 0-292-78417-1). U of Tex Pr.

MEN

see also Masculinity (Psychology)

Avedon, Burt. Ah, Men! LC 78-74675. 1980. 10.95 (ISBN 0-89479-048-X). A & W Pubs.
Carriere, Anne-Marie. Le Dictionnaire des Hommes. 252p. (Fr.). 1962. 8.95 (ISBN 0-686-56845-1, M-6623). French & Eur.
Chesler, Phyllis. About Men. 320p. 1980. pap. 3.95 (ISBN 0-553-12272-X). Bantam.
Conway, Jim. Men in Mid-Life Crisis. 1981. pap. 4.95 (ISBN 0-89191-145-6). Caroline Hse.
Cosmopolitan's Guide to Marvelous Men. 1977. pap. 3.00 (ISBN 0-87980-336-3). Wilshire.
Dubrin, Andrew J. The New Husbands & How to Become One. LC 76-15359. 1976. 14.95 (ISBN 0-88229-358-3). Nelson-Hall.
Eno, Susan. The Truth About What Women Want in Men. LC 79-23043. 1980. 10.95 (ISBN 0-688-03594-9). Morrow.
Fast, Julius. Incompatability of Men & Women & How to Overcome It. LC 70-164549. 192p. 1971. 5.95 (ISBN 0-87131-065-1). M Evans.
Goldberg, Herb. The New Male: From Self-Destruction to Self-Care. 1980. pap. 2.95 (ISBN 0-451-09339-9, E9339, Sig). NAL.
Goldberg, Steven. The Inevitability of Patriarchy. 1973. pap. 3.25 (ISBN 0-688-05175-8). Morrow.
Harter, Jim. Men: A Pictorial Archive from Nineteenth-Century Sources. 10.00 (ISBN 0-8446-5769-7). Peter Smith.
--Men: A Pictorial Archive from Nineteenth-Century Sources. (Pictorial Archive Ser.). (Illus., Orig.). 1980. pap. 4.50 (ISBN 0-486-23952-7). Dover.
Hoffman, Susanna. The Classified Man: Twenty-Two Types of Men (& What to Do About Them) 1981. pap. 4.95 (ISBN 0-399-50544-X, Perigee). Putnam.
--The Classified Man: Twenty-Two Types of Men (and What to Do About Them) LC 79-25249. (Illus.). 1980. 10.95 (ISBN 0-698-11014-5). Coward.
Hogan, Dennis. Transitions & Social Change: The Early Lives of American Men. (Studies in Population Ser.). 1981. price not set (ISBN 0-12-352080-0). Acad Pr.
Holliday, Laurel. The Violent Sex: Male Psychobiology & the Evolution of Consciousness. LC 78-7344. (Illus.). 1978. pap. 4.95 (ISBN 0-931458-01-3). Bluestocking.
Kanowitz, Leo. Equal Rights: The Male Stake. 168p. 1981. 19.95 (ISBN 0-8263-0594-6); pap. 9.95 (ISBN 0-8263-0595-4). U of NM Pr.
Karsk, Roger & Thomas, Bill. Working with Men's Groups, Vol. 1. new ed. 1979. pap. 6.50 (ISBN 0-686-25093-1). New Comm Pr.
Kriegel, Leonard. Of Men & Manhood. LC 79-63621. 1979. 10.95 (ISBN 0-8015-0248-9, Hawthorn). Dutton.
Landham, Sonny. The Total Man. LC 79-11128. 1981. 15.95 (ISBN 0-87949-157-4). Ashley Bks.
Lazarre, Jane. On Loving Men. 1980. 8.95 (ISBN 0-8037-6518-5). Dial.
Lyon, Harold C., Jr. Tenderness Is Strength: From Machismo to Manhood. LC 76-26242. 1978. 8.95 (ISBN 0-06-012713-9, HarpT). Har-Row.
McMorrow, Fred. Midolescence: The Dangerous Years. LC 74-78999. 285p. 1974. 10.95 (ISBN 0-8129-0481-8). Times Bks.
Naifeh, Steven W. & Smith, Gregory W. Moving up in Style: The Successful Man's Guide to Impeccable Taste. 1980. 10.95 (ISBN 0-312-55070-7). St Martin.
Place, Stan & Kagan, Julia. Manworks: A Guide to Style. 1980. 16.95 (ISBN 0-442-26560-3). Van Nos Reinhold.
Pleck, Joseph H. & Sawyer, Jack, eds. Men & Masculinity. 192p. 1974. 8.95 (ISBN 0-13-574319-2, Spec); pap. 3.45 (ISBN 0-13-574301-X, Spec). P-H.
Post, Henry. The Ultimate Man. 1978. pap. 6.95 (ISBN 0-425-03755-X, Windhover). Berkley Pub.
Preston, Samuel H. Older Male Mortality & Cigarette Smoking. LC 76-4875. (Population Monograph Ser.: No. 7). (Illus.). 1976. Repr. of 1970 ed. lib. bdg. 15.00x (ISBN 0-8371-8870-X, PROM). Greenwood.
Rappaport, Doreen, et al. A Man Can Be. (Illus.). 32p. (gr. 4-8). 1981. 9.95 (ISBN 0-89885-046-0). Human Sci Pr.
Robertiello, Richard C. A Man in the Making: Grandfathers, Fathers, & Sons. LC 79-15709. 1979. 9.95 (ISBN 0-399-90056-X). Marek.
Seymour, John. On My Own Terms. 2nd ed. 240p. 1980. 22.00 (ISBN 0-571-18016-7, Pub. by Faber & Faber). Merrimack Bk Serv.
Stearns, Peter N. Be a Man! Males in Modern Society. LC 79-11847. (Illus.). 1979. text ed. 23.95x (ISBN 0-8419-0435-9); pap. text ed. 10.75x (ISBN 0-8419-0587-8). Holmes & Meier.
Swerdloff, Peter. Men & Women. (Human Behavior Ser.). 176p. 1975. 9.95 (ISBN 0-8094-1924-6); lib. bdg. avail. (ISBN 0-685-53585-1). Time-Life.
Unbecoming Men: A Men's Conciousness-Raising Group Writes on Oppression & Themselves. (Illus., Orig.). 1971. pap. 2.50 (ISBN 0-87810-015-6). Times Change.
Wagenvoord, James, ed. Men: A Book for Women. 1978. pap. 7.95 (ISBN 0-380-40212-2, 76026). Avon.
Wishard, Bill & Wishard, Laurie. Men's Rights: A Handbook for the 80's. LC 80-20194. 264p. 1980. 12.95 (ISBN 0-89666-011-7); pap. 6.95 (ISBN 0-89666-012-5). Cragmont Pubns.

MEN-PHOTOGRAPHY

see Photography of Men

MEN-PRAYER-BOOKS AND DEVOTIONS

Krutza, William J. Devotionals for Modern Men. (Ultra Bks Ser.). 1968. 3.50 (ISBN 0-8010-5319-6). Baker Bk.
--Dynamic Devotionals for Men. (Ultra Bks Ser.). 1970. 3.50 (ISBN 0-8010-5306-4). Baker Bk.
La Haye, Tim. Understanding the Male Temperament: What Every Man Would Like to Tell His Wife About Himself...but Won't. 1977. 7.95 (ISBN 0-8007-0863-6); pap. 4.95 (ISBN 0-8007-5009-8, Power Bks). Revell.

MEN-SEXUAL BEHAVIOR

Bertels, Frank. The First Book on Male Liberation & Sex Equality. (Illus.). 415p. 1981. luxury hardcover 25.00 (ISBN 0-932574-05-X); pap. 15.00 (ISBN 0-932574-06-8). Brun Pr.
Botwin, Carol & Fine, Jerome. The Love Crisis: Hit & Run Lovers, Sexual Stingies, Unreliables, Kinkies, & Other Typical Men of Today. 256p. 1980. pap. 2.95 (ISBN 0-553-20431-9). Bantam.
The Fanta Sex Report: Male Impotency & Psychic-Impotency. (Orig.). 1980. pap. 4.95 (ISBN 0-89260-157-4). Hwong Pub.
Friday, Nancy. Men in Love, Male Sexual Fantasies: The Triumph of Love Over Rage. 1981. pap. 3.50 (ISBN 0-440-15404-9). Dell.
Frieze, Irene H., et al. Women & Sex Roles: Social Psychological Perspective. 1978. 13.95 (ISBN 0-393-01163-1); pap. 10.95x (ISBN 0-393-09063-9); instr's manual free (ISBN 0-393-95168-5). Norton.
Koranyi, Erwin K. Transsexuality in the Male: The Spectrum of Gender Dysphoria. (Behavioral Science & Law Ser.). (Illus.). 192p. 1980. text ed. 18.75 (ISBN 0-398-03924-0). C C Thomas.
McNary, Arthur H. The Way Men Love: A Study into the Emotional Subconscious. (Illus.). 1979. 39.45 (ISBN 0-89920-001-X). Am Inst Psych.
Malone, Michael. Heroes of Eros: Male Sexuality in the Movies. 1979. pap. 9.95 (ISBN 0-525-47552-4). Dutton.
Milsten, Richard. Male Sexual Function: Myth, Fantasy, Reality. 1979. pap. 2.50 (ISBN 0-380-44990-0, 44990). Avon.
Morin, Jack. Men Loving Themselves. (Illus.). 104p. 1980. pap. 9.00 (ISBN 0-9602324-5-1). Down There Pr.
Petras, John W. Sex: Male-Gender: Masculine. LC 74-32335. 265p. 1975. pap. text ed. 7.95x (ISBN 0-88284-019-3). Alfred Pub.
Pietropinto, Anthony & Simenauer, Jacqueline. Beyond the Male Myth. 1978. pap. 2.95 (ISBN 0-451-09040-3, E9040, Sig). NAL.
Rowan, Robert L. Men & Their Sex. (Illus.). 159p. 1979. 12.50 (ISBN 0-934200-01-7); pap. 6.95 (ISBN 0-686-77788-3). Irvington.
Weber, Eric. How to Pick up Girls! 1981. pap. 4.95 (ISBN 0-914094-00-9). Caroline Hse.
Zilbergeld, Bernie. Male Sexuality: A Guide to Sexual Fulfillment. 1978. pap. 3.95 (ISBN 0-553-20450-5). Bantam.

MEN IN LITERATURE

Friedman, Maurice. To Deny Our Nothingness: Contemporary Images of Man. LC 77-92748. 1978. pap. 6.95 (ISBN 0-226-26337-1, P754, Phoen). U of Chicago Pr.
Janaro, R. P. Human Worth. LC 72-91162. 1973. text ed. 10.95 (ISBN 0-03-086591-3, HoltC). HR&W.
Kriegel, Leonard. Of Men & Manhood. LC 79-63621. 1979. 10.95 (ISBN 0-8015-0248-9, Hawthorn). Dutton.
Mickelson, Anne Z. Thomas Hardy's Women & Men: The Defeat of Nature. LC 76-28366. 1976. 10.00 (ISBN 0-8108-0985-0). Scarecrow.
Todd, Janet, ed. Men by Women. LC 80-20702. (Women & Literature Ser.). 270p. 1981. text ed. 24.50x (ISBN 0-8419-0732-3); pap. text ed. 15.00x (ISBN 0-8419-0733-1). Holmes & Meier.

MEN NURSES

Brown, R. G. The Male Nurse. 139p. 1973. pap. text ed. 5.00x (ISBN 0-7135-1879-0, Pub. by Bedford England). Renouf.

MENANDER, OF ATHENS

Goldberg, Sander M. The Making of Menander's Comedy. LC 80-5322. 1980. 20.00x (ISBN 0-520-04250-6). U of Cal Pr.
Gomme, A. W. & Sandbach, F. H. Menander: A Commentary. 1973. 68.00x (ISBN 0-19-814197-1). Oxford U Pr.
Webster, T. Birth of Modern Comedy of Manners, No. 1. (Australian Humanities Research Council Occasional Paper Ser.: No. 1). 1959. pap. 2.00x (ISBN 0-424-05690-9, Pub. by Sydney U Pr). Intl Schol Bk Serv.
Webster, T. B. The Birth of Modern Comedy of Manners. LC 74-32030. 1959. lib. bdg. 8.50 (ISBN 0-8414-9369-3). Folcroft.
--An Introduction to Menander. 211p. 1974. text ed. 27.50x (ISBN 0-06-497504-5). B&N.

MENARD, LOUIS NICOLAS, 1822-1901

Peyre, Henri. Louis Menard. LC 72-1694. (Yale Romanic Studies: No. 5). Repr. of 1932 ed. 28.00 (ISBN 0-404-53205-5). AMS Pr.

MENCIUS, d. 289 B.C.

Richards, Ivor A. Mencius on the Mind: Experiments in Multiple Definition. LC 79-2838. (Illus.). 1981. Repr. of 1932 ed. 16.50 (ISBN 0-8305-0015-4). Hyperion Conn.
Wei, Francis C. The Political Principles of Mencius. 1977. lib. bdg. 59.95 (ISBN 0-8490-2452-8). Gordon Pr.

MENCKEN, HENRY LOUIS, 1880-1956

Bewley, Marius. Complex Fate: Hawthorne, Henry James, & Some American Writers. LC 67-28474. 1967. Repr. of 1954 ed. 9.00 (ISBN 0-87752-008-9). Gordian.
Bode, Carl. Mencken. LC 72-11997. (Arcturus Books Paperbacks). (Illus.). 474p. 1973. pap. 8.95 (ISBN 0-8093-0627-1). S Ill U Pr.
--Mencken. LC 69-11515. (Illus.). 474p. 1969. 12.50x (ISBN 0-8093-0376-0). S Ill U Pr.
--The New Mencken Letters. 1977. 19.95 (ISBN 0-8037-1379-7). Dial.
Boyd, E. H. L. Mencken. LC 74-1446. (American Literature Ser., No. 49). 1974. lib. bdg. 46.95 (ISBN 0-8383-2038-4). Haskell.
Boyd, Ernest. H. L. Mencken. LC 73-16171. 1927. 15.00 (ISBN 0-8414-9860-1). Folcroft.
Cooke, Alistar. Six Men. 1978. pap. 2.75 (ISBN 0-425-04689-3, Dist. by Putnam). Berkley Pub.
De Casseres, Benjamin. Mencken & Shaw: The Anatomy of America's Voltaire & England's Other John Bull. 1930. Repr. 25.00 (ISBN 0-8274-2727-1). R West.
Dorsey, John, ed. On Mencken. LC 80-7639. 320p. 1980. 15.00 (ISBN 0-394-51253-7). Knopf.
Douglas, George H. H. L. Mencken: Critic of American Life. 1978. 17.50 (ISBN 0-208-01693-7, Archon). Shoe String.
Fecher, Charles A. Mencken: A Study of His Thought. LC 77-21154. 1978. 15.00 (ISBN 0-394-41354-7). Knopf.
Frey, Carrol. Bibliography of the Writings of H. L. Mencken. LC 76-22789. 1924. lib. bdg. 10.00 (ISBN 0-8414-4227-4). Folcroft.
Goldberg, Isaac. Man Mencken: A Biographical & Critical Survey. LC 68-54271. Repr. of 1925 ed. 27.00 (ISBN 0-404-02857-8). AMS Pr.
Harrison, Joseph B. Short View of Menckenism. LC 77-3997. 1927. lib. bdg. 7.50 (ISBN 0-8414-4918-X). Folcroft.
Hobson, Fred C., Jr. Serpent in Eden: H. L. Mencken & the South. 258p. 1974. 17.00x (ISBN 0-8078-1224-2). U of NC Pr.
Johns, Bud. Ombibulous Mister Mencken. LC 68-8421. (Illus.). 1968. bds. 3.95 (ISBN 0-912184-01-9). Synergistic Pr.
Kemler, Edgar. Irreverent Mister Mencken. 7.75 (ISBN 0-8446-0165-9). Peter Smith.
La Monte, Robert R. & Mencken, H. L. Men Versus the Man: A Correspondence Between Robert Rives La Monte, Socialist & H. L. Mencken, Individualist. LC 79-172220. (Right Wing Individualist Tradition in America Ser). 1972. Repr. of 1910 ed. 17.00 (ISBN 0-405-00429-X). Arno.
Manchester, William. H. L. Mencken: Disturber of the Peace. 1962. pap. 0.95 (ISBN 0-02-004830-0, Collier). Macmillan.
Mencken, H. L. A Choice of Days. Galligan, Edward L., ed. LC 80-7645. 352p. 1980. 12.95 (ISBN 0-394-50795-9). Knopf.
--H. L. Mencken on Music. Cheslock, Louis, ed. LC 61-13949. 1975. pap. 3.95 (ISBN 0-02-871550-0). Schirmer Bks.
Nolte, William H. H. L. Mencken, Literary Critic. LC 66-18117. 296p. 1967. pap. 2.95 (ISBN 0-295-97877-5, WP31). U of Wash Pr.
--H. L. Mencken, Literary Critic. LC 66-18117. 1966. lib. bdg. 17.50x (ISBN 0-8195-3063-8, Pub. by Wesleyan U Pr). Columbia U Pr.
Rascoe, Burton, et al. H. L. Mencken. LC 73-9953. 1920. Repr. lib. bdg. 7.50 (ISBN 0-8414-2585-X). Folcroft.
Singleton, Marvin K. H. L. Mencken & the American Mercury Adventure. LC 62-10053. 1962. 12.75 (ISBN 0-8223-0160-1); pap. 8.50 (ISBN 0-8223-0351-5). Duke.
Wagner, Philip. H. L. Mencken. (Pamphlets on American Writers Ser: No. 62). (Orig.). 1966. pap. 1.25x (ISBN 0-8166-0408-8, MPAW62). U of Minn Pr.
Williams, W. H. H. L. Mencken. (United States Authors Ser.: No. 297). 1977. lib. bdg. 10.95 (ISBN 0-8057-7200-6). Twayne.
Wingate, Phillip J. H. L. Mencken's Un-Neglected Anniversary. LC 79-91602. 80p. 1980. 6.00 (ISBN 0-935968-07-5). Holly Pr.

MENDAEANS

see Mandaeans

MENDE

Migeod, Frederick W. View of Sierra Leone. LC 76-100269. (Illus.). Repr. of 1926 ed. 17.00x (ISBN 0-8371-2858-7). Greenwood.

MENDE LANGUAGE

Aginsky, Ethel G. A Grammar of the Mende Language. 1935. pap. 6.00 (ISBN 0-527-00766-8). Kraus Repr.

MENDEL, GREGOR JOHANN, 1822-1884

Sootin, Harry. Gregor Mendel: Father of the Science of Genetics. LC 59-7933. (Illus.). (gr. 7-10). 1958. 7.95 (ISBN 0-8149-0409-2). Vanguard.
Stern, Curt & Sherwood, Eva R., eds. The Origin of Genetics: A Mendel Source Book. LC 66-27948. (Illus.). 1966. pap. text ed. 8.95x (ISBN 0-7167-0655-5). W H Freeman.
Whittow, John B. Disasters. LC 79-5236. 405p. 1980. 18.95 (ISBN 0-8203-0499-9). U of Ga Pr.

MENDEL'S LAW

see also Genetics; Heredity; Hybridization

Fincham, J. R. A Study of Genetic Recombination. rev. ed. Head, J. J., ed. LC 77-75593. (Carolina Biology Readers Ser.). (Illus.). (gr. 11 up). 1982. pap. 1.65 (ISBN 0-89278-202-1, 45-9602). Carolina Biological.
Morgan, Thomas H. The Mechanism of Mendelian Heredity. 1972. Repr. of 1915 ed. 31.00 (ISBN 0-384-40136-8). Johnson Repr.

MENDELSOHN, ERICH, 1887-1953

Von Eckardt, Wolf. Eric Mendelsohn. LC 60-14514. (Masters of World Architecture Ser). (Illus.). 1960. pap. 3.95 (ISBN 0-8076-0230-2). Braziller.

MENDELSSOHN, MOSES, 1729-1786

Altmann, Alexander. Moses Mendelssohn: A Biographical Study. LC 72-12430. 988p. 1973. 25.00x (ISBN 0-8173-6860-4). U of Ala Pr.
Mendelssohn, Moses. Moses Mendelssohn: Selections from His Writings. Jospe, Eva, ed. LC 74-34046. (B'nai B'rith Jewish Heritage Classics). 256p. 1975. 10.00 (ISBN 0-670-48993-X). Viking Pr.
Walter, H. Moses Mendelssohn: Critic & Philosopher. LC 73-2230. (The Jewish People; History, Religion, Literature Ser.). Repr. of 1930 ed. 17.00 (ISBN 0-405-05291-X). Arno.

MENDELSSOHN FAMILY

Hensel, Sabastian. Mendelssohn Family, 1729-1847, from Letters & Journals, 2 Vols. 1882. 29.00 (ISBN 0-403-00119-6). Scholarly.
Hensel, Sebastian. Mendelssohn Family from Letters & Journals, 2 Vols. LC 68-25290. (Studies in Music, No. 42). 1969. Repr. of 1882 ed. lib. bdg. 69.95 (ISBN 0-8383-0304-8). Haskell.
--Mendelssohn Family Seventeen Twenty-Nine to Eighteen Forty-Seven from Letters & Journals, 2 Vols. 2nd ed. Klingemann, Carl, et al, trs. LC 68-31000. (Illus.). 1968. Repr. of 1882 ed. Set. lib. bdg. 31.50x (ISBN 0-8371-0104-2, HEMF). Greenwood.

MENDELSSOHN-BARTHOLDY, FELIX, 1809-1847

Colson, Percy. Victorian Portraits. facs. ed. LC 68-16921. (Essay Index Reprint Ser). 1932. 15.00 (ISBN 0-8369-0328-5). Arno.
Devrient, Eduard. My Recollections of Felix Mendelssohn-Bartholdy & His Letters to Me. Macfarren, Natalia, tr. LC 72-163799. 307p. 1972. Repr. of 1869 ed. 35.00x (ISBN 0-8443-0002-0). Vienna Hse.
Edwards, Frederick G. The History of Mendelssohn's Oratorio Elijah. LC 74-24073. Repr. of 1896 ed. 16.00 (ISBN 0-404-12901-3). AMS Pr.
Grove, George. Beethoven, Schubert, Mendelssohn. LC 76-181167. 394p. 1951. Repr. 25.00 (ISBN 0-403-08979-4). Scholarly.
Hathaway, Joseph W. An Analysis of Mendelssohn's Organ Works. LC 74-24107. Repr. of 1898 ed. 14.50 (ISBN 0-404-12956-0). AMS Pr.

Hiller, Ferdinand. Mendelssohn: Letters & Recollections. Von Glehn, M. E., tr. LC 70-163790. 470p. 1972. Repr. of 1874 ed. 35.00x (ISBN 0-8443-0003-9). Vienna Hse.

Horton, John. Mendelssohn Chamber Music. LC 72-551. (BBC Music Guides Ser.: No. 24). (Illus.). 64p. (Orig.). 1972. pap. 2.95 (ISBN 0-295-95251-2). U of Wash Pr.

Jacob, Heinrich E. Felix Mendelssohn & His Times. Winston, Richard & Winston, Clara, trs. LC 73-3024. (Illus.). 356p. 1973. Repr. of 1963 ed. lib. bdg. 19.75x (ISBN 0-8371-6823-6, JAFM). Greenwood.

Jenkins, David & Visocchi, Mark. Mendelssohn in Scotland. 1979. 17.95 (ISBN 0-903443-18-X, Pub. by Hamish Hamilton England). David & Charles.

Kaufman, Schima. Mendelssohn: A Second Elijah. LC 78-110829. (Illus.). 1971. Repr. of 1934 ed. lib. bdg. 17.75x (ISBN 0-8371-3229-0, KAME). Greenwood.

--Mendelssohn: A Second Elijah. LC 78-110829. (Illus.). 1971. Repr. of 1934 ed. lib. bdg. 17.75x (ISBN 0-8371-3229-0, KAME). Greenwood.

Kaufman, Schlems. Mendelssohn: A Second Eliph. lib. bdg. 17.00 (ISBN 0-403-08985-9). Scholarly.

Kupferberg, Herbert. Felix Mendelssohn: His Life, His Family, His Music. LC 72-1172. (Encore Edition). 1972. 2.95 (ISBN 0-684-15414-5, ScribT). Scribner.

--Felix Mendelssohn: His Life, His Family, His Music. 5.95 (ISBN 0-684-12952-3). Brown Bk.

Lampadius, W. A. Life of Felix Mendelssohn Bartholdy. Gage, William L., tr. LC 77-92443. 1978. Repr. of 1865 ed. lib. bdg. 25.00 (ISBN 0-89341-427-1). Longwood Pr.

Mason, Daniel G. Romantic Composers. LC 73-119654. Repr. of 1906 ed. 14.00 (ISBN 0-404-04223-6). AMS Pr.

--Romantic Composers. Repr. of 1906 ed. lib. bdg. 15.75x (ISBN 0-8371-4096-X, MARC). Greenwood.

Mendelssohn, Felix. Letters of Felix Mendelssohn Bartholdy from Italy & Switzerland. Wallace, Grace, tr. LC 77-2022. 1978. Repr. of 1869 ed. lib. bdg. 30.00 (ISBN 0-89341-429-8). Longwood Pr.

--Letters of Felix Mendelssohn Bartholdy from 1833 to 1847. Bartholdy-Mendelssohn, ed. Wallace, Grace, tr. LC 77-92441. 1978. Repr. of 1868 ed. lib. bdg. 30.00 (ISBN 0-685-86665-3). Longwood Pr.

Moshansky, Mozelle. Mendelssohn: His Life & Times. LC 78-53224. (Life & Times of the Composer Ser.). (Illus.). 1981. pap. cancelled (ISBN 0-8467-0488-9, Pub by Midas Bks); pap. 9.95 (ISBN 0-8467-0461-7). Hippocrene Bks.

Radcliffe, Philip. Mendelssohn. rev ed. (Master Musicians Ser). (Illus.). 224p. 1976. Repr. 11.00x (ISBN 0-460-03123-6, Pub. by J. M. Dent England). Biblio Dist.

--Mendelssohn. rev. ed. (Master Musicians Ser.: No. M180). (Illus.). 1976. pap. 7.95 (ISBN 0-8226-0715-8). Littlefield.

Selden-Goth, G., ed. Felix Mendelssohn: Letters. LC 73-86922. (Composers' Letters Ser.: No. 2). (Illus.). 400p. 1973. pap. 10.00x (ISBN 0-8443-0108-6). Vienna Hse.

Targan, Barry. Harry Belten & the Mendelssohn Violin Concerto. LC 75-17705. (Iowa School of Letters Award for Short Fiction Ser: 1975). 288p. 1975. 8.95 (ISBN 0-87745-060-9); pap. 5.95 (ISBN 0-87745-061-7). U of Iowa Pr.

Thompson, Frances A. Mendelssohn & His Friends in Kensington: Letters from Fanny & Sophy Horsley. Gotch, Rosamund B., ed. LC 74-24241. Repr. of 1934 ed. 17.50 (ISBN 0-404-13115-8). AMS Pr.

Werner, Eric. Mendelssohn: A New Image of the Composer & His Age. Newlin, Dika, tr. from Ger. LC 78-1750. (Illus.). 1978. Repr. of 1963 ed. lib. bdg. 39.00 (ISBN 0-313-20302-4, WEMN). Greenwood.

MENDES PINTO, FERNAO, b. 1509

Gowen, Herbert H. Five Foreigners in Japan. facs. ed. LC 67-28735. (Essay Index Reprint Ser). 1936. 18.00 (ISBN 0-8369-0491-5). Arno.

MENDESIA, GRACIA, 1510-1569

Roth, Cecil. House of Nasi: Dona Gracia. Repr. of 1948 ed. lib. bdg. 15.00x (ISBN 0-8371-2388-7, BOND). Greenwood.

Stadtler, Bea. Story of Dona Gracia Mendes. LC 70-83166. (Illus.). (gr. 6-9). 1969. 4.50 (ISBN 0-8381-0734-6). United Syn Bk.

MENDICANT ORDERS

see Friars

MENDING

see Repairing; Sewing

MENDIP HILLS

Atthill, Robin. Mendip: A New Study. LC 76-45509. (Illus.). 1977. 28.00 (ISBN 0-7153-7297-1). David & Charles.

--Old Mendip. (Old... Ser.). (Illus.). 6.50 (ISBN 0-7153-4050-6). David & Charles.

MENDOZA, ANTONIO DE, CONDE DE TENDILLA, 1480-1552

Aiton, Arthur S. Antonio De Mendoza, First Viceroy of New Spain. LC 66-24664. (Illus.). 1967. Repr. of 1927 ed. 8.50 (ISBN 0-8462-0783-4). Russell.

MENDOZA, BERNARDINO DE, 1540-1604

Jensen, DeLamar. Diplomacy & Dogmatism: Bernardino De Mendoza & the French Catholic League. LC 63-20769. (Illus.). 1964. 17.50x (ISBN 0-674-20800-5). Harvard U Pr.

MENDOZA, DIEGO HURTADO DE, 1503-1575

Spivakovsky, Erika. Son of the Alhambra: Diego Hurtado de Mendoza, 1504-1575. (Illus.). 466p. 1971. 19.50x (ISBN 0-292-70093-8). U of Tex Pr.

MENDOZA, ARGENTINE REPUBLIC (PROVINCE)-POLITICS AND GOVERNMENT

Strout, Richard R. Recruitment of Candidates in Mendoza Province, Argentina. (James Sprunt Studies in History & Political Science: Vol. 50). 1968. pap. text ed. 6.00x (ISBN 0-8078-5050-0). U of NC Pr.

MENELIK 2ND, NEGUS OF ETHIOPIA

Berkeley, George F. Campaign of Adowa & the Rise of Menelik. LC 76-76477. (Illus.). Repr. of 1902 ed. 20.75x (ISBN 0-8371-1132-3, Pub. by Negro U Pr). Greenwood.

Darkwah, R. H. Menelik of Ethiopia. (African Historical Biographies Ser.). 1972. pap. text ed. 2.75x (ISBN 0-435-94466-5). Heinemann Ed.

Marcus, Harold G. The Life & Times of Menelik II: Ethiopia 1844-1913. (Oxford Studies in African Affairs). (Illus.). 1975. 29.95x (ISBN 0-19-821674-2). Oxford U Pr.

MENENDEZ DE AVILES, PEDRO, 1519-1574

Lyon, Eugene. The Enterprise of Florida: Pedro Menendez de Aviles & the Spanish Conquest of 1565-1568. LC 76-29612. (Illus.). 1976. 10.00 (ISBN 0-8130-0533-7). U Presses Fla.

Solis De Meras, Gonzalo. Pedro Menendez de Aviles. McAlister, Lyle N., ed. Connor, Jeannette T., tr. LC 64-19155. (Floridiana Facsimile & Reprint Ser). 1964. Repr. of 1567 ed. 16.00 (ISBN 0-8130-0214-1). U Presses Fla.

MENIERE'S DISEASE

Harrison, M. Spencer & Naftalin, Lionel. Meniere's Disease: Mechanism & Management. (American Lecture Living Chemistry). (Illus.). 244p. 1968. photocopy ed. spiral 22.50 (ISBN 0-398-00786-1). C C Thomas.

MENINGIOMA

Cushing, Harvey & Eisenhardt, Louise. The Meningiomas: Their Classification, Regional Behaviour, Life History, & Surgical End Results. (Illus.). 802p. 1938. ed. spiral bdg. 74.50photocopy (ISBN 0-398-04239-X). C C Thomas.

Deutsche Gesellschaft Fuer Neurochirurgie, 25th, Bochum, Germany, September 1974. Proceedings. Klug, W., et al, eds. LC 75-8941. (Advances in Neurosurgery Ser.: Vol. 2). (Illus.). 500p. 1975. pap. 44.20 (ISBN 0-387-07237-3). Springer-Verlag.

Nager, George T. Meningiomas Involving the Temporal Bone: Clinical & Pathological Aspects. (Illus.). 192p. 1964. photocopy ed. spiral 19.50 (ISBN 0-398-01381-0). C C Thomas.

MENINGITIS

Berggren, Sture. Etudes Sur la Meningite Otogene Purulente Generalisse. Repr. of 1920 ed. pap. 18.50 (ISBN 0-384-03990-1). Johnson Repr.

Freeman, John M. Practical Management of Meningomyelocele. (Illus.). 1974. 29.50 (ISBN 0-8391-0639-4). Univ Park.

Lehmann-Grube, F., ed. Lymphocytic Choriomeningitis. LC 70-167276. (Virology Monographs: Vol. 10). 1971. 23.20 (ISBN 0-387-81017-X). Springer-Verlag.

Meningococcal Infections: A Report. (World Health Statistics Ser: Vol. 21, No. 7). (Eng. & Fr.). 1968. pap. 2.80 (ISBN 0-686-09181-7). World Health.

Parsons, Malcolm. Tuberculosis Meningtis: A Handbook for Clinicians. LC 78-40807. (Illus.). 1979. text ed. 12.95x (ISBN 0-19-261166-6). Oxford U Pr.

WHO Study Group. Cerebrospinal Meningitis Control: Report. (Technical Report Ser.: No. 588). (Also avail. in French & spanish). 1976. pap. 2.40 (ISBN 92-4-120588-1). World Health.

MENINGO-ENCEPHALOMYELITIS

see Encephalomyelitis

MENKEN, ADAH ISAACS, 1835-1868

Lesser, Allen. Enchanting Rebel. LC 72-85325. (Illus.). 296p. 1973. Repr. of 1947 ed. 14.50 (ISBN 0-8046-1746-5). Kennikat.

MENNO SIMONS, 1496-1561

Horst, Irvin B. A Bibliography of Menno Simons. 1962. 45.00x (ISBN 0-8361-1104-4). Herald Pr.

Vernon, Louise A. Night Preacher. LC 73-94378. (Illus.). (gr. 3-8). 1969. pap. 2.95 (ISBN 0-8361-1774-3). Herald Pr.

MENNONITE COOKERY

see Cookery, American

MENNONITES

see also Amish

Bartel, Floyd. A New Look at Church Growth. LC 79-53523. 1979. pap. 2.95 (ISBN 0-87303-027-3). Faith & Life.

Bender, Harold S. & Smith, C. Henry, eds. Mennonite Encyclopedia, 4vols. 1956-1969. Set. 90.00x (ISBN 0-8361-1018-8); 25.00x ea. Vol. 1 (ISBN 0-8361-1118-4). Vol. 2 (ISBN 0-8361-1119-2). Vol. 3 (ISBN 0-8361-1120-6). Vol. 4 (ISBN 0-8361-1121-4). Herald Pr.

Clemens, Lois G. Woman Liberated. (Conrad Grebel Ser). 1971. 4.95 (ISBN 0-8361-1634-8). Herald Pr.

Cummings, Mary L., ed. Full Circle: Stories of Mennonite Women. LC 78-66879. 1978. pap. 5.25 (ISBN 0-87303-014-1). Faith & Life.

Davies, B. String of Amber: The Heritage of the Mennonites. (Illus.). 1973. 12.50 (ISBN 0-685-47308-2). Heinman.

Derstine, Gerald & Layman, Joanne. Following the Fire. 1980. 7.95 (ISBN 0-88270-362-5). Logos.

Drescher, John M. Now Is the Time to Love. LC 73-123411. 1970. 3.95 (ISBN 0-8361-1626-7); pap. 1.50 (ISBN 0-8361-1641-0). Herald Pr.

Dyck, C. J., ed. Complete Concordances & Texts of the Fourteenth Centiry Aragonese Manuscripts of Juan Fernandez De Heredia. (Mennonite Central Committee Ser.: Vol. 4). 408p. (Orig.). 1981. pap. 7.95 (ISBN 0-686-31622-3). Herald Pr.

Dyck, Cornelius J. Twelve Becoming, Biographies of Mennonite Disciples from the Sixteenth to the Twentieth Century. LC 73-75174. 1973. pap. 4.50 (ISBN 0-87303-865-7). Faith & Life.

Erb, Paul. South Central Frontiers. LC 74-12108. (Studies in Anabaptist & Mennonite History, No. 17). (Illus.). 448p. 1974. 14.95x (ISBN 0-8361-1196-6). Herald Pr.

Eshleman, H. Frank. Historic Background & Annals of the Swiss & German Pioneer Settlers of Southeastern Pennsylvania & of Their Remote Ancestors. LC 77-86809. 1969. Repr. of 1917 ed. 17.50 (ISBN 0-8063-0105-8). Genealog Pub.

Good, Merle & Good, Phyllis. Twenty Most Asked Questions About the Amish & Mennonites. LC 79-55280. (People's Place Booklet Ser.). (Illus., Orig.). 1979. pap. 2.95 (ISBN 0-934672-00-8). Good Bks PA.

Hartzler, Jonas S. Mennonites in the World War; or, Nonresistance Under Test. LC 76-137543. (Peace Movement in America Ser). 246p. 1972. Repr. of 1922 ed. lib. bdg. 14.25x (ISBN 0-89198-071-7). Ozer.

Hershberger, Guy F., ed. Recovery of the Anabaptist Vision. LC 58-10992. 1957. 7.95 (ISBN 0-8361-1421-3). Herald Pr.

Hertzler, Daniel. Mennonite Education - Why & How: A Model Study for Mennonite Education. LC 73-172267. 1971. pap. 2.00 (ISBN 0-8361-1655-0). Herald Pr.

Hiebert, Clarence. The Holdeman People: The Church in Christ, Mennonite, 1869-1969. LC 72-94133. 1973. 17.95 (ISBN 0-87808-411-8). William Carey Lib.

Hiebert, Clarence, ed. Brothers in Deed to Brothers in Need. new ed. LC 74-76588. (Illus.). 486p. 1974. 20.00 (ISBN 0-87303-037-0). Faith & Life.

Horsch, John. Mennonites in Europe: Mennonite History, Vol. 1. (Illus.). 1950. 12.95 (ISBN 0-8361-1395-0). Herald Pr.

Hostetler, John A. Mennonite Life. rev. ed. (Illus., Orig.). 1959. pap. 1.50 (ISBN 0-8361-1394-2). Herald Pr.

Hostetler, John A. & Huntinton, Gertrude E. Children in Amish Society: Socialization & Community Education. LC 72-157454. (Case Studies in Education & Culture). 1971. pap. text ed. 4.95 (ISBN 0-03-077750-X, HoltC). HR&W.

Kauffman, J. Howard & Harder, Leland. Anabaptists Four Centuries Later. 400p. 1975. 9.95x (ISBN 0-8361-1136-2); pap. 6.95x (ISBN 0-8361-1137-0). Herald Pr.

Kennel, Leroy. Mennonites: Who & Why. 1966. pap. 0.50 (ISBN 0-8361-1396-9). Herald Pr.

Kraybill, Donald B. Ethnic Education: The Impact of Mennonite Schooling. LC 77-81022. 1977. soft bdg. 10.00 (ISBN 0-88247-480-4). R & E Res Assoc.

Lapp, John A. The Mennonite Church in India: 1897-1962. 248p. 1972. 8.95x (ISBN 0-8361-1122-2). Herald Pr.

Mecenseffy, Grete. Osterreichische Tauferakten Two. (Tauferakten Kommission Ser.). 45.00x (ISBN 0-8361-1192-3). Herald Pr.

The Mennonite Quarterly Review: Goshen, Ind., 1927-1976, Vols. 1-50. Set. lib. bdg. 2000.00 (ISBN 0-686-77268-7); lib. bdg. 40.00 ea. AMS Pr.

Miller, Clara B. To All Generations. LC 77-24926. 1977. 6.95 (ISBN 0-8361-1825-1). Herald Pr.

Redekop, Calvin. Strangers Become Neighbors. (Studies in Anabaptist & Mennonite History Ser.: No. 22). (Illus.). 312p. 1980. 19.95x (ISBN 0-8361-1228-8). Herald Pr.

Redekop, Calvin W. The Old Colony Mennonites: Dilemmas of Ethnic Minority Life. LC 69-13192. (Illus.). 302p. 1969. 20.00x (ISBN 0-8018-1020-5). Johns Hopkins.

Reed, Kenneth. Mennonite Soldier. LC 74-1355. 512p. 1974. 6.95 (ISBN 0-8361-1734-4). Herald Pr.

Rodgers, Harrell. Community Conflict, Public Opinion, & the Law. LC 70-80412. 1969. pap. text ed. 3.95x (ISBN 0-675-09440-2). Merrill.

Ruth, John L. Conrad Grebel: Son of Zurich (Biography) LC 75-8829. 160p. 1975. 6.95 (ISBN 0-8361-1767-0). Herald Pr.

Schelbert, Leo. Swiss Migration to America: The Swiss Mennonites. Cordasco, Francesco, ed. LC 80-891. (American Ethnic Groups Ser.). 1981. lib. bdg. 35.00x (ISBN 0-405-13452-5). Arno.

Seguy, J. Les Assemblees Anabaptistes-Mennonites De France. 1977. 89.00x (ISBN 90-279-7524-8). Mouton.

Shenk, Wilbert R., compiled by. Bibliography of Henry Venn's Printed Writings. (Mennonite Missionary Studies: Pt. 4). 1975. pap. 3.75x (ISBN 0-8361-1203-2). Herald Pr.

Smith, Tilman R. Boards: Purposes, Organization, Procedures. LC 78-62628. 1978. pap. 1.50 (ISBN 0-8361-1862-6). Herald Pr.

Wenger, John C. They Met God. LC 64-15344. 1964. 3.75 (ISBN 0-8361-1489-2). Herald Pr.

MENNONITES-BIBLIOGRAPHY

Smucker, Donovan E., ed. The Sociology of Canadian Mennonites, Hutterites & Amish: A Bibliography with Annotations. 232p. 1977. text ed. 11.00 (ISBN 0-88920-052-1, Pub. by Laurier U Pr Canada). Humanities.

Springer, Nelson & Klassen, A. J., eds. Mennonite Bibliography, 2 vols. LC 77-9105. 1977. Set. 118.00x (ISBN 0-8361-1208-3). Herald Pr.

MENNONITES-CATECHISM AND CREEDS

Erb, Paul. We Believe. LC 69-15831. (Orig.). 1969. pap. 2.95 (ISBN 0-8361-1587-2). Herald Pr.

Harder, Helmut. Guide to Faith. LC 79-50682. 1979. pap. 3.95 (ISBN 0-87303-022-2). Faith & Life.

Kauffman, Milo. The Way of True Riches. LC 79-83505. (Mennonite Faith Ser: No. 6). 1979. pap. 0.95 (ISBN 0-8361-1885-5). Herald Pr.

Mennonite Church. Mennonite Confession of Faith. (Orig.). 1963. pap. 0.60 (ISBN 0-8361-1314-4). Herald Pr.

MENNONITES-DOCTRINAL AND CONTROVERSIAL WORKS

Burkholder, J. R. & Redekop, Calvin, eds. Kingdom, Cross, & Community. LC 76-29663. 1976. 14.95x (ISBN 0-8361-1139-7). Herald Pr.

Coffman, John S. & Funk, J. F., eds. Confession of Faith & Minister's Manual. 1890. 3.95 (ISBN 0-8361-1354-3). Herald Pr.

Detweiler, Richard C. Mennonite Statements on Peace. (Orig.). 1968. pap. 1.50 (ISBN 0-8361-1581-3). Herald Pr.

Fairfield, James G. All That We Are We Give. LC 77-14510. 1977. pap. 3.95 (ISBN 0-8361-1839-1). Herald Pr.

Kauffman, Daniel, ed. Doctrines of the Bible. 1928. 9.95 (ISBN 0-8361-1358-6). Herald Pr.

Lederach, Paul M. Teaching in the Congregation. (Mennonite Faith Ser: No. 7). 1979. pap. 0.95 (ISBN 0-8361-1886-3). Herald Pr.

--A Third Way. LC 80-26280. 152p. 1980. pap. 6.95 (ISBN 0-8361-1934-7). Herald Pr.

Waltner, James. This We Believe. LC 68-20281. 1968. pap. 2.50 (ISBN 0-87303-845-2). Faith & Life.

Wenger, J. C. The Book We Call the Bible. LC 79-89440. (Mennonite Faith Ser.: No. 8). 1980. pap. 0.95 (ISBN 0-8361-1908-8). Herald Pr.

--El Camino de la Paz. Casas, Arnoldo J., ed. Vilela, Ernesto S., tr. LC 79-89311. (Mennonite Faith Ser.: No. 4). (Span.). 1979. pap. 0.95x (ISBN 0-8361-1226-1). Herald Pr.

--El Camino de una Nueva Vida. Casas, Arnold J., ed. Vilela, Ernesto S., tr. LC 79-89310. (Mennonite Faith Ser.: No. 3). (Span.). 1979. pap. 0.95x (ISBN 0-8361-1224-5). Herald Pr.

--Como Surgieron los Menonitas. Casas, Arnold J., ed. Vilela, Ernesto S., tr. LC 79-89306. (Mennonite Faith Ser.: No. 1). (Span.). 1979. pap. 0.95x (ISBN 0-8361-1222-9). Herald Pr.

--Los Discipulos de Jesus. Casas, Arnoldo J., ed. Vilela, Ernesto S., tr. LC 79-89308. (Mennonite Faith Ser.: No. 5). (Span.). 1979. pap. 0.95x (ISBN 0-8361-1225-3). Herald Pr.

--A Faith to Live by. LC 79-89441. (Mennonite Faith Ser.: No. 9). 1980. pap. 0.95 (ISBN 0-8361-1909-6). Herald Pr.

--Que Creen los Menonitas. Casas, Arnoldo J., ed. Vilela, Ernesto S., tr. from Eng. LC 79-89307. (Mennonite Faith Ser.: No. 2). (Span.). 1979. pap. 0.95x (ISBN 0-8361-1223-7). Herald Pr.
--What Mennonites Believe. LC 77-86338. (Mennonite Faith Ser.: No. 2). 1977. pap. 0.95 (ISBN 0-8361-1833-2). Herald Pr.
Wenger, John C., ed. Complete Writings of Menno Simons: Circa 1496-1561. Verduin, Leonard, tr. LC 55-9815. 1956. 22.50 (ISBN 0-8361-1353-5). Herald Pr.
Yoder, Edward. Estudios De Doctrina Christiana: Dios. Jesucristo, el Espiritu Santo, Pt. 1. 1973. pap. 0.60x (ISBN 0-8361-1190-7). Herald Pr.
--Estudios De Doctrina Christiana: El Hombre: Su Pecado, Salvation y Destino Eterno, Pt. 2. 1973. 0.60x (ISBN 0-8361-1191-5). Herald Pr.

MENNONITES–HISTORY

Bartel, Floyd. A New Look at Church Growth. LC 79-53523. 1979. pap. 2.95 (ISBN 0-87303-027-3). Faith & Life.
Dyck, C. J. An Introduction to Mennonite History. LC 81-1958. 400p. 1981. 12.95 (ISBN 0-8361-1955-X). Herald Pr.
Dyck, Cornelius J. From the Files of the MCC. LC 80-10975. (MCC Story Ser.). 1980. pap. 3.95x (ISBN 0-8361-1229-6). Herald Pr.
--Responding to Worldwide Needs. LC 80-10975. (MCC Story Ser.). 1980. pap. 3.95x (ISBN 0-8361-1230-X). Herald Pr.
--Witness & Service in North America. LC 80-10975. (MCC Story Ser.). 1980. pap. 3.95x (ISBN 0-8361-1231-8). Herald Pr.
Dyck, Cornelius J., ed. Mennonite Central Committee Story Series. pap. 10.65x (ISBN 0-8361-1232-6). Herald Pr.
Fast, Heinhold. Quellen Zur Geschichte der Taufer in der Schweiz, Vol. 2: Ostschweiz. (Ger.). 1974. 59.00x (ISBN 0-8361-1197-4). Herald Pr.
Goertz, Hans-Jurgen, ed. Umstrittenes Taufertum 1525-1975. 1975. 22.50x (ISBN 0-8361-1128-1). Herald Pr.
Good, Merle. These People Mine. LC 73-6196. 1973. pap. 1.25 (ISBN 0-8361-1718-2). Herald Pr.
Hershberger, Guy F. War, Peace & Nonresistance. rev. ed. LC 53-7586. 1969. 12.95 (ISBN 0-8361-1449-3). Herald Pr.
Hertzler, Daniel. From Germantown to Steinbach. 248p. 1981. pap. 7.95 (ISBN 0-8361-1949-5). Herald Pr.
Horst, Samuel L. Mennonities in the Confederacy: A Study in Civil War Pacifism. LC 67-15991. (Illus.). 1967. 6.95x (ISBN 0-8361-1180-X). Herald Pr.
Juhnke, James C. A People of Two Kingdoms. new ed. LC 74-84697. (Mennonite Historical Ser.). (Illus.). 221p. 1975. 7.95 (ISBN 0-87303-662-X). Faith & Life.
Keller, Frank R. Preparation for Covenant Life. LC 79-53522. 1979. pap. 4.95x (ISBN 0-87303-018-4). Faith & Life.
MacMaster, Richard K., et al. Conscience in Crisis. LC 78-27530. (Studies in Anabaptist & Mennonite History: No. 20). 1979. 17.95x (ISBN 0-8361-1213-X). Herald Pr.
Meet the Mennonites. (Pennsylvania Dutch Books Ser.). (Illus.). 1961. 1.50 (ISBN 0-911410-05-8). Applied Arts.
Paetkau, Paul, et al. God-Man-Land. LC 78-55244. 1978. 5.25 (ISBN 0-87303-008-7). Faith & Life.
Pannabecker, Samuel F. Open Doors. LC 75-9417. (Mennonite Historical Ser.). (Illus.). 432p. 1975. 18.50 (ISBN 0-87303-636-0). Faith & Life.
Rimland, Ingrid. The Wanderers. 1977. 8.95 (ISBN 0-570-03266-0, 15-2712). Concordia.
Ruth, John L. Twas Seeding Time. LC 76-41475. 1976. pap. 4.95 (ISBN 0-8361-1800-6). Herald Pr.
Schlabach, Theron F. Gospel Versus Gospel. LC 79-15888. 352p. 1980. 14.95x (ISBN 0-8361-1220-2). Herald Pr.
Schmid, Walter & Von Murat, Leonhard. Quellen Zur Geschichte der Taufer in der Schweiz, Vol. 1: Zurich. 1952. PLB 9.00x (ISBN 0-8361-1152-4). Herald Pr.
Smith, C. Henry. Story of the Mennonites. Krahn, Cornelius, ed. LC 81-65130. (Illus.). 589p. 1981. pap. 17.95 (ISBN 0-87303-069-9). Faith & Life.
Wenger, J. C. How Mennonites Came to Be. LC 77-86332. (Mennonite Faith Ser.: No. 1). 1977. pap. 0.95 (ISBN 0-8361-1832-4). Herald Pr.
Wenger, John C. Compendio De Historia y Doctrina Menonitas. Suarez, Ernesto, tr. Orig. Title: Glimpses of Mennonite History & Doctrine. (Span). 1960. pap. 2.50x (ISBN 0-8361-1148-6). Herald Pr.
--Mennonite Church in America. LC 66-23903. (Mennonite History Vol. 2). 1967. 12.95x (ISBN 0-8361-1179-6). Herald Pr.

MENNONITES–HYMNS

Ausbund. Das ist: Etliche schone Christliche Lieder, wie sie in dem Gefangnis zu Passau in dem Schloss von den Schweitzer-Brudern und von anderen rechtglaubigen Christen hin und her gedichtet worden. facsimile ed. (Mennonite Songbks., American Ser.: Vol. 1). x, 818p. 1971. Repr. of 1742 ed. 62.50 (ISBN 90-6027-244-7, Pub. by Frits Knuf Netherlands). Pendragon NY.
--Etliche schone christliche Gesang, wie dieselbigen zu Passau von der Schweizer Brudern in der Gefenknus im Schloss durch gottliche Gnade gedicht und gesungen worden. facsimile ed. (Mennonite Songbks., German Ser.: Vol. 1). 1973. Repr. of 1564 ed. 25.00 (ISBN 90-6027-160-2, Pub. by Frits Knuf Netherlands). Pendragon NY.
Brunk, J. D., ed. Church & Sunday School Hymnal with Supplement. (532 hymns & songs, & 50 german songs, words only, 1902; supplement 1911). 1902. 5.50x (ISBN 0-8361-1110-9). Herald Pr.
Coffman, S. F., ed. Church Hymnal. (657 hymns). 1927. 5.50x (ISBN 0-8361-1106-0). Herald Pr.
Hostetler, Lester & Yoder, Walter E., eds. Mennonite Hymnal. LC 69-18131. 1969. 6.95x (ISBN 0-87303-515-1). Faith & Life.
Joris, David. Een Geestelijck Liedt-Boexcken: Inholdende Veel Schoone Sinrijcke Christelijcke Liedekens - Dock Troostlijcke Nieuwe-Jaren - Claech Unde Lof-Sanghen-Ter Eeren Godes. (Mennonite Songbooks, Dutch Ser.: Vol. 1). 1971. 20.00 (ISBN 90-6027-242-0, Pub. by Frits Knuf Netherlands). Pendragon NY.

MENNONITES–JUVENILE LITERATURE

Smucker, Barbara C. Henry's Red Sea. LC 55-7810. (Illus.). (gr. 4-9). 1955. 2.95 (ISBN 0-8361-1372-1). Herald Pr.

MENNONITES–MISSIONS

Graber, J. D. The Church Apostolic. LC 60-14171. (Conrad Grebel Lecture Ser.). 1960. 4.00 (ISBN 0-8361-1347-0). Herald Pr.
Juhnke, James C. A People of Mission: A History of General Conference Mennonite Overseas Missions. LC 78-74809. 1979. pap. 5.95 (ISBN 0-87303-019-2). Faith & Life.

MENNONITES–SERMONS

Fast, Aganetha. The Power of Christ's Love in China. LC 71-188251. 134p. 1972. pap. 2.00 (ISBN 0-87303-667-0). Faith & Life.
Kaufman, Edmond G. Living Creatively. LC 66-20385. 1966. 2.95 (ISBN 0-87303-445-7). Faith & Life.
Mast, Russell L. Lost & Found: The Search for Significance. (YA) (gr. 9 up). 1963. 3.00 (ISBN 0-8361-1480-9). Herald Pr.

MENNONITES–SOCIAL LIFE AND CUSTOMS

Denlinger, Martha. Real People. (Illus.). 96p. 1975. pap. 2.25 (ISBN 0-8361-1756-5). Herald Pr.
Kaufman, Gordon D. Nonresistance & Responsibility, & Other Mennonite Essays. (Institute of Mennonite Studies: No. 5). 1979. pap. 7.95 (ISBN 0-87303-024-9). Faith & Life.

MENNONITES IN RUSSIA

Belk, Fred R. The Great Trek of the Russian Mennonites to Central Asia, 1880-1884. LC 75-28340. (Studies in Anabaptist & Mennonite History: Vol. 18). (Illus.). 232p. 1976. 12.95x (ISBN 0-8361-1103-6). Herald Pr.
Harder, Geraldine G. When Apples Are Ripe. LC 73-160722. (Illus.). 1972. 4.95 (ISBN 0-8361-1656-9); pap. 3.95 (ISBN 0-8361-1694-1). Herald Pr.
Klassen, Elizabeth S. Trailblazer for the Brethren. LC 78-11994. 1978. pap. 6.95x (ISBN 0-8361-1214-8). Herald Pr.
Neufeld, Dietrich. A Russian Dance of Death. Reimer, Al, tr. from Ger. (Illus.). 1978. pap. 7.95 (ISBN 0-8361-1863-4). Herald Pr.
Toews, John B. Lost Fatherland. LC 67-23294. (Study in Anabaptist & Mennonite History No. 12). (Illus.). 1967. 9.95x (ISBN 0-8361-1183-4). Herald Pr.

MENOMINEE INDIANS

see Indians of North America–Northwest, Old

MENOMINEE LANGUAGE

Bloomfield, Leonard. Menomini Texts. LC 73-3548. (American Ethnological Society. Publications: No. 12). Repr. of 1928 ed. 39.50 (ISBN 0-404-58162-5). AMS Pr.
--The Menominio Language. 1962. 47.50x (ISBN 0-686-50049-0). Elliots Bks.

MENOPAUSE

see also Climacteric

Beard, Robert J., ed. The Menopause: A Guide to Current Research & Practice. (Illus.). 1976. 32.50 (ISBN 0-8391-0943-1). Univ Park.
Beedell, Suzanne. Menopause Questions & Answers. 1977. pap. 1.95 (ISBN 0-89437-002-2). Baronet.
Campbell, S., ed. The Management of Menopause & Post-Menopausal Years. (Illus.). 1976. 39.50 (ISBN 0-8391-0931-8). Univ Park.
Clausen, Muriel C. Menopause: Vitamins & You. 105p. (Orig.). 1980. pap. 4.75 (ISBN 0-9603664-1-5). M C Clausen.
--Premenopause. 53p. 1979. pap. 6.25 (ISBN 0-9603664-0-7). M C Clausen.
Clay, Vidals. Women: Menopause & Middle Age. 1977. perfect bdg. 5.00 (ISBN 0-912786-37-X). Know Inc.
Cooke, I. D. The Role of Estrogen-Progestogen in the Management of the Menopause. 148p. text ed. 17.50 (ISBN 0-8391-1370-6). Univ Park.
Cooper, Wendy. Don't Change: A Biological Revolution for Women. LC 74-26959. 192p. 1975. 7.95 (ISBN 0-8128-1783-4). Stein & Day.
Davis, M. Edward & Meilach, Dona. Doctor Discusses Menopause & Estrogens. (Illus.). 1980. pap. 2.50 (ISBN 0-910304-26-2). Budlong.
Eskin, Bernard A., ed. The Menopause: Comprehensive Management. LC 80-80302. (Illus.). 224p. 1980. 27.50x (ISBN 0-89352-085-3). Masson Pub.
Evans, Barbara. Change of Life. LC 79-89935. (Illus.). 1980. pap. cancelled (ISBN 0-89793-012-6). Hunter Hse.
Gray, Madeline. The Changing Years: The Menopause Without Fear. rev. ed. LC 77-16917. 280p. 1981. 13.95 (ISBN 0-385-12635-2). Doubleday.
--Changing Years: The Menopause Without Fear. 1970. pap. 1.95 (ISBN 0-451-08429-2, J8429, Sig). NAL.
Greenblatt, Robert B., et al. The Menopausal Syndrome. LC 74-6093. 231p. 1974. 15.00 (ISBN 0-8463-0136-9). Krieger.
Haspels, A. A. Psychosomatics in Per-Menopause. 124p. text ed. 14.95 (ISBN 0-8391-1379-X). Univ Park.
Hutton, Isabel E. Woman's Prime of Life. 1959. 3.95 (ISBN 0-87523-031-8). Emerson.
Jern, Helen Z. Hormone Therapy of the Menopause & Aging. (Illus.). 196p. 1973. text ed. 15.75 (ISBN 0-398-02744-7). C C Thomas.
Nachtigall, Lila & Heilman, Joan. The Lila Nachtigall Report: The Intelligent Woman's Guide to Menopause, Estrogen, & Her Body. LC 77-6653. 1977. 7.95 (ISBN 0-399-11992-2). Putnam.
Norman, William H. & Scaramella, Thomas J. Mid-Life: Developmental & Clinical Issues. LC 79-24367. 1980. 17.50 (ISBN 0-87630-221-5). Brunner-Mazel.
Pasetto, N. & Paoletti, R. The Menopause & Postmenopause. 322p. text ed. 29.95 (ISBN 0-8391-4116-5). Univ Park.
Reitz, Rosetta. Menopause: A Positive Approach. 1979. pap. 3.50 (ISBN 0-14-005120-1). Penguin.
--Menopause: A Positive Approach. LC 77-6115. 1977. 9.95 (ISBN 0-8019-6442-3). Chilton.
Rose, Louisa, et al, eds. The Menopause Book. Cornell, Elizabeth & Kemeny, Nancy. 272p. 1980. pap. 5.95 (ISBN 0-8015-4995-7, Hawthorn). Dutton.
Van Keep, ed. Consensus of Menopause Research. 1977. 29.50 (ISBN 0-8391-0984-9). Univ Park.
Voda, Ann M., et al, eds. Changing Perspectives on Menopause. (Illus.). 464p. 1981. text ed. 45.00x (ISBN 0-292-71069-0). U of Tex Pr.
Weideger, Paula. Menstruation & Menopause: The Physiology & Psychology, the Myth & the Reality. 1976. 12.95 (ISBN 0-394-49647-7). Knopf.
Wilson, Robert A. Feminine Forever. LC 66-11166. (Illus.). 224p. 1966. 8.95 (ISBN 0-87131-049-X). M Evans.
Workshop Conference Geneva, Oct., 1974. Estrogens in the Post-Menopause. Van Keep, P. A. & Lauritzen, C., eds. (Frontiers of Hormone Research: Vol. 3). x, 234p. 1975. 45.50 (ISBN 3-8055-2187-1). S Karger.

MENORAH

Yarden, L. Tree of Light: A Study of the Menorah, the Seven-Branched Lampstand. LC 79-127780. (Illus.). 1971. 27.50x (ISBN 0-8014-0596-3). Cornell U Pr.

MENOTTI, GIAN CARLO, 1911-

Grieb, Lyndal C. The Operas of Gian Carlo Menotti, 1937-1972: A Selective Bibliography. LC 74-16310. 1974. 10.00 (ISBN 0-8108-0743-2). Scarecrow.
Gruen, John. Menotti: A Biography. LC 77-9304. (Illus.). 1978. 16.95 (ISBN 0-02-546320-9). Macmillan.

MEN'S CLOTHING

see also individual articles of apparel

Bennett-England, Rodney. Dress Optional, the Revolution in Menswear. LC 68-29951. (Illus.). 1968. 10.25 (ISBN 0-8023-1177-6). Dufour.
Brummell, George B. Male & Female Costume. Parker, Eleanor, ed. LC 71-177521. (Illus.). Repr. of 1932 ed. 22.00 (ISBN 0-405-08314-9, Blom Pubns). Arno.
Byrde, Penelope. The Male Image: Men's Fashion in Britain 1300-1970. 240p. 1980. text ed. 37.50x (ISBN 0-7134-0860-X). Humanities.
Carlsen, Peter & Wilson, William. Manstyle: The GQ Guide to Fashion, Fitness, & Grooming. (Illus.). 1977. 14.95 (ISBN 0-517-53076-7); pap. 8.95 (ISBN 0-517-53077-5). Potter.
Coleman, Elizabeth A. Of Men Only: Men's & Boys' Fashions, 1750-1975. (Illus.). 32p. 1975. pap. 3.95 (ISBN 0-87273-053-0). Bklyn Mus.
Designing Mens & Boys Garments. rev. ed. (Master Designs System Ser.). (Illus.). 1981. loose-leaf binding 20.00 (ISBN 0-686-21211-8). Master Design.
Doblin, F. Men's Garment Designing & Grading. rev. ed. (Illus.). Date not set. 25.00 (ISBN 0-686-30449-7). Master Design.
Fairchild Market Research Division. Men's Clothing, Tailored Sportswear, Rainwear. (Fairchild Fact File Ser.). 1979. pap. 10.00 (ISBN 0-87005-325-6). Fairchild.
--Men's Furnishings & Work Wear. (Fairchild Fact Files Ser.). (Illus.). 50p. 1981. pap. text ed. 10.00 (ISBN 0-87005-387-6). Fairchild.
--Men's Furnishings, Career - Work Wear. (Fairchilds Fact File Ser.). 1979. pap. 10.00 (ISBN 0-87005-318-3). Fairchild.
--Men's Sportswear & Casual Wear. (Fact File Ser). 1978. pap. 10.00 (ISBN 0-87005-251-9). Fairchild.
Hix, Charles. How to Dress Your Man. 192p. 1981. 9.95 (ISBN 0-517-54543-8); pap. 4.95 (ISBN 0-517-54544-6); twelve copy pre-pack 59.40 (ISBN 0-686-74647-3). Crown.
Kawashima, Masaaki. Fundamentals of Men's Fashion Design: A Guide to Tailored Clothes. rev. ed. LC 73-91066. (Illus.). 224p. 1976. 14.50x (ISBN 0-87005-105-9). Fairchild.
--Men's Outerwear Design. LC 77-79658. (Illus.). 1978. text ed. 14.50 (ISBN 0-87005-196-2). Fairchild.
Lyle, D. Clothing for Young Men. LC 78-135579. 1970. pap. 2.50 (ISBN 0-686-00148-6, 261-08302). Home Econ Educ.
Place, Stan & Kagan, Julia. Manworks: A Guide to Style. 1980. 16.95 (ISBN 0-442-26560-3). Van Nos Reinhold.
Rinehart, Jane & Shewbart, B. J. How to Make Men's Clothes. LC 74-12706. 216p. 1975. 10.00 (ISBN 0-385-01850-9). Doubleday.
Roberts, Edmund. Fundamentals of Men's Fashion Design: A Guide to Casual Clothes. new ed. LC 75-13691. (Illus.). 224p. 1975. 14.50x (ISBN 0-87005-104-0). Fairchild.
Sirkis, Susan B. Men's Fashions: 1776-1850. (Wish Booklets Ser.: Vol. 20). (Illus.). 60p. 1977. pap. 5.50x (ISBN 0-913786-20-9). Wish Bklets.
Tailoring & Repairing. rev. ed. (Modern Custom Tailoring for Men Ser.). (Illus.). 1981. loose-leaf binding 10.00 (ISBN 0-686-21215-0). Master Design.
U. K. Menswear Markets. 1981. 150.00x (ISBN 0-686-71963-8, Pub. by Euromonitor). State Mutual Bk.

MEN'S ETIQUETTE

see Etiquette for Men

MENS REA

see Criminal Intent

MENSTRUAL CYCLE

see Menstruation

MENSTRUATION

see also Menopause

Budoff, Penny W. No More Menstrual Cramps & Other Good News. 1981. pap. 4.95 (ISBN 0-14-005938-5). Penguin.
Dalton, Katharina. Once a Month. LC 79-88572. (Illus.). 1979. pap. 4.95 (ISBN 0-89793-005-3). Hunter Hse.
Dalton, Katherina. Premenstrual Syndrome & Progesterone Therapy. 1977. 17.50 (ISBN 0-8151-2265-9). Year Bk Med.
Dan, Alice, et al. The Menstrual Cycle: A Synthesis of Interdisciplinary Research, Vol. 1. LC 80-18837. (Illus.). 1980. text ed. 28.00 (ISBN 0-8261-2630-8). Springer Pub.
Dawood, M. Yusoff. Dysmenorrhea. (Illus.). 293p. 1981. lib. bdg. 42.00 (ISBN 0-683-02364-0). Williams & Wilkins.
Debrovner, Charles. Premenstrual Tension: A Multidisciplinary Approach. 1981. 19.95 (ISBN 0-89885-019-3). Human Sci Pr.
Elgin, Kathleen & Osterritter, John F. Twenty-Eight Days. LC 73-77779. (Illus.). 64p. (gr. 5 up). 1973. 6.95 (ISBN 0-679-20220-X). McKay.
Friedman, Nancy. Everything You Must Know About Tampons. (Illus.). 172p. 1981. pap. 2.50 (ISBN 0-425-05140-4). Berkley Pub.
Gardner-Loulan, JoAnn, et al. Period. LC 79-25897. (Illus.). 104p. 1981. pap. 6.00 (ISBN 0-912078-69-3). New Glide.
Gerrick, David J. Menstrual Problems in Teenagers. 1979. pap. text ed. 20.00 (ISBN 0-685-96978-9). Dayton Labs.
Givens, James R. Endocrine Causes of Menstrual Disorders. (Illus.). 1978. 37.50 (ISBN 0-8151-3526-2). Year Bk Med.
Hollingworth, Leta. Functional Periodicity: Experimental Study of the Mental & Motor Abilities of Women During Menstruation. LC 76-177604. (Columbia University. Teachers College. Contributions to Education: No. 69). Repr. of 1914 ed. 17.50 (ISBN 0-404-55069-X). AMS Pr.

Komnenich, Pauline, et al, eds. The Menstrual Cycle, Vol. 2: Research & Implications for Women's Health. 256p. 1981. text ed. 25.50 (ISBN 0-8261-2980-3). Springer Pub.
Lein, Allen. The Cycling Female: Her Menstrual Rhythm. LC 78-23675. (Illus.). 1979. pap. text ed. 7.95x (ISBN 0-7167-1038-2). W H Freeman.
Lever, Judy & Haynes, Brian. Premenstrual Tension. 192p. 1981. 12.95 (ISBN 0-07-037445-7, GB). McGraw.
Maddux, Hilary C. Menstruation. rev. ed. (Women's Library). 272p. 1981. pap. 2.50 (ISBN 0-440-05582-2). Dell.
--Menstruation. Tucker, Tarvez, ed. (Women's Library). (Illus.). 213p. 1975. 5.95 (ISBN 0-686-11658-5, 440-5840-6); pap. 2.95 (ISBN 0-686-11659-3). Tobey Pub.
Nourse, Alan. Menstruation: Just Plain Talk. (gr. 4 up). PLB 6.90 (ISBN 0-686-65171-5). Watts.
Shuttle, Penelope & Redgrove, Peter. Wise Wound: Eve's Curse & Everywoman. LC 78-6402. 1978. 9.95 (ISBN 0-399-90024-1). Marek.
Storch, Marsha L. & Nolan, Joan D. How to Relieve Cramps & Other Menstrual Problems. 128p. 1981. pap. 3.95 (ISBN 0-89480-191-0). Workman Pub.
Subak-Sharpe, Genelle, et al. Freedom from Menstrual Cramps. (Orig.). 1981. pap. price not set (ISBN 0-671-43714-3). PB.
Voelckers, Ellen. Girls' Guide to Menstruation. LC 74-20590. (MS Ser). (Illus.). 128p. (gr. 7-12). 1975. PLB 5.97 (ISBN 0-8239-0313-3). Rosen Pr.
Vollman, Rudolf F. Menstrual Cycle. LC 76-28947. (Major Problems in Obstetrics & Gynecology Ser.: Vol. 7). (Illus.). 1977. text ed. 15.00 (ISBN 0-7216-9075-0). Saunders.
Weideger, Paula. Menstruation & Menopause: The Physiology & Psychology, the Myth & the Reality. 1976. 12.95 (ISBN 0-394-49647-7). Knopf.

MENSURATION

see also Area Measurement; Colorimetry; Gaging; Geodesy; Measuring Instruments; Physical Measurements; Planimeter; Surveying; Tolerance (Engineering); Weights and Measures
also subdivision Measurement under special subjects, e.g. Altitudes–Measurement

Agrometeorology of the Maize (Corn) Crop. (Illus.). 1978. pap. 55.00 (ISBN 92-63-10481-6, WMO 481, WMO). Unipub.
ASTM Standards on Precision & Accuracy for Various Applications. 1977. pap. 10.25 (ISBN 0-686-50152-7, 03-511077-34). ASTM.
Barry, B. Austin. Construction Measurements. LC 72-13073. (Practical Construction Guides Ser.). 352p. 1973. 29.50 (ISBN 0-471-05428-3, Pub. by Wiley-Interscience). Wiley.
--Errors in Practical Measurement in Science, Engineering & Technology. LC 78-9751. 183p. 1978. 23.50- (ISBN 0-471-03156-9, Pub. by Wiley-Interscience). Wiley.
Bragg, Gordon M. Principles of Experimentation & Measurement. (Illus.). 192p. 1974. 18.95 (ISBN 0-13-701169-5). P-H.
Busch & Wilkie Bros. Foundation. Fundamentals of Dimensional Metrology. LC 64-12593. 428p. 1966. 10.80 (ISBN 0-8273-0193-6); instructor's guide 1.60 (ISBN 0-8273-0197-9). Delmar.
Clason, W. E. Elsevier's Dictionary of Measurement & Control. 1977. 144.00 (ISBN 0-444-41582-3). Elsevier.
Conaway, Judith. The Discovery Book of Size. LC 76-46471. (Discovery Ser.). (Illus.). (gr. k-3). 1977. PLB 9.85 (ISBN 0-8172-0252-8). Raintree Pubs.
Conference on Instruments & Measurements. Proceedings, 2 vols. Von Koch, H. & Ljungberg, G., eds. Incl. Vol. 1. Chemical Analysis, Electric Quantities, Nucleonics & Process Control. 50.00 (ISBN 0-12-725701-2); Vol. 2. Nuclear Instrumentation, Measurement of Electric & Magnetic Quantities, Reactor Control. 59.50 (ISBN 0-12-725702-0). 1961. Acad Pr.
Farago, Francis T. Handbook of Dimensional Measurement. LC 68-55069. (Illus.). 400p. 1968. 36.00 (ISBN 0-8311-1025-2). Indus Pr.
Gardner, R. P. & Ely, R. L. Radioisotope Measurement Applications in Engineering. 496p. 1967. 21.50 (ISBN 0-442-35576-9, Pub. by Van Nos Reinhold). Krieger.
Gray, B. F. Measurements, Instrumentation & Data Transmission. LC 76-49922. (Illus.). 1977. text ed. 13.50x (ISBN 0-582-41065-7); pap. text ed. 9.50x (ISBN 0-582-41066-5). Longman.
Hackworth, Robert D. & Howland, Joseph. Introductory College Mathematics: Indirect Measurement. LC 75-23620. 72p. 1976. pap. text ed. 2.95 (ISBN 0-7216-4413-9). HR&W.
Hinrichs, Roy S. Measuring. LC 80-67036. (Industrial Arts Ser.). 96p. 1981. pap. 4.60 (ISBN 0-8273-1916-9). Delmar.
Hunter, Richard S. The Measurement of Appearance. LC 75-20429. 348p. 1975. 36.50 (ISBN 0-471-42141-3, Pub. by Wiley-Interscience). Wiley.
Hutchinson, J. M. & Mann, W. B., eds. Metrology Needs in the Measurement of Environmental Radioactivity: Seminar Sponsered by the International Committee for Radionuclide Metrology. (Illus.). 1980. pap. 35.00 (ISBN 0-08-022943-3). Pergamon.
I.S.A. Spring Industry-Oriented Conference, May 2-5, 1977, Anaheim, CA. Metrology in Industrial Instrumentation: Proceedings. 1977. 5.00 (ISBN 0-87664-365-9). Instru Soc.
Krantz, David H., et al. Foundations of Measurement, Vol. 1: Additive & Polynomial Representations. 1971. 51.50 (ISBN 0-12-425401-2). Acad Pr.
Leblanc, John F., et al. Mathematics-Methods Program: Measurement. (Mathematics Ser.). (Illus.). 144p. 1976. pap. text ed. 3.50 (ISBN 0-201-14620-7); instr's man. 1.50 (ISBN 0-201-14621-5). A-W.
Measurements. (Machine Tool Ser.: Vol. 1). 1974. pap. text ed. 3.95x (ISBN 0-88462-242-8). Ed Methods.
Mikhail, Edward M. & Gracie, Gordon. Analysis & Adjustment of Survey Measurements. 368p. 1980. text ed. 28.50 (ISBN 0-442-25369-9). Van Nos Reinhold.
Zebrowski, Ernest, Jr. Fundamentals of Physical Measurement. 1978. pap. text ed. 12.95 (ISBN 0-87872-173-8). Duxbury Pr.
Zupko, Ronald E. British Weights & Measures: A History from Antiquity to the Seventeenth Century. 266p. 1977. 21.50 (ISBN 0-299-07340-8, 734). U of Wis Pr.

MENSURATION–JUVENILE LITERATURE

Bowden, Joan C. My Measuring Book. (Golden Play & Learn Bk). (Illus.). 14p. (ps). 1980. pap. 2.95 (ISBN 0-307-10729-9). Western Pub.
Ellison, Elise. Fun with Lines & Curves. LC 72-1095. (Craft Ser.). (Illus.). 160p. (gr. 3-12). 1972. PLB 7.44 (ISBN 0-688-51527-4); pap. 2.95 (ISBN 0-688-45527-1). Lothrop.
Kohn, Bernice. Everything Has a Shape & Everything Has a Size. (Illus.). (ps-2). 1966. PLB 4.95 (ISBN 0-13-293530-9); pap. 1.50 (ISBN 0-13-293548-1). P-H.
Luce, Marnie. Measurement: How Much? How Many? How Far? LC 68-56707. (Math Concept Bks). (gr. 3-6). 1969. PLB 3.95 (ISBN 0-8225-0578-9). Lerner Pubns.

MENTAL ABILITY AND AGE

see Age and Intelligence

MENTAL ARITHMETIC

see Arithmetic, Mental

MENTAL ASSOCIATION

see Association of Ideas

MENTAL CHRONOMETRY

see Time Perception

MENTAL CULTURE

see Mental Discipline

MENTAL DEFICIENCY

see also down'S Syndrome; Inefficiency, Intellectual; Mentally Handicapped

Accardo. Pediatrician & the Developmentally Delayed Child. 1978. 14.95 (ISBN 0-8391-1331-5). Univ Park.
Adams, Henry E. & Boardman, William K. Advances in Experimental Clinical Psychology. 230p. 1972. 21.00 (ISBN 0-08-016399-8). Pergamon.
Allen, David F. & Allen, Victoria S. Ethical Issues in Mental Retardation: Tragic Choices-Living Hope. LC 79-19747. 1979. pap. 5.95 (ISBN 0-687-12011-X). Abingdon.
Allen, Robert M. & Cortazzo, Arnold D. Psychosocial & Educational Aspects & Problems of Mental Retardation. 136p. 1970. pap. 14.75 photocopy ed. spiral (ISBN 0-398-00031-X). C C Thomas.
Allen, Robert M., et al. Theories of Cognitive Development: Implications for the Mentally Retarded. LC 72-92899. (Illus.). 1973. 9.95x (ISBN 0-87024-249-0). U of Miami Pr.
Allen, Robert M., et al, eds. The Role of Genetics in Mental Retardation. LC 73-143453. (Illus.). 1971. 7.95x (ISBN 0-87024-197-4). U of Miami Pr.
American Medical Association. Mental Retardation: A Handbook for the Primary Physician. 3rd ed. 134p. 1976. pap. 2.00 (ISBN 0-686-15736-2, OP-314). AMA.
Association for Research in Nervous Mental Disease-Dec. 1959. Mental Retardation: Proceedings, Vol. 39. (Illus.). 1969. Repr. of 1962 ed. 30.25 (ISBN 0-02-846420-6). Hafner.
Attwell, Arthur A. & Clabby, D. A. The Retarded Child: Answers to Questions Parents Ask. LC 72-182924. 139p. 1975. pap. 9.80x (ISBN 0-87424-120-0). Western Psych.
Barr, Martin W. Mental Defectives: Their History, Treatment & Training. LC 73-2383. (Mental Illness & Social Policy; the American Experience Ser.). Repr. of 1904 ed. 24.00 (ISBN 0-405-05191-3). Arno.
Bellak, Leopold, ed. Psychiatric Aspects of Minimal Brain Dysfunction in Adults. 224p. 1979. 21.50 (ISBN 0-8089-1192-9). Grune.
Berg, J. M., et al. The DeLange Syndrome. LC 72-124065. 1970. 22.00 (ISBN 0-08-016125-1). Pergamon.
Bergsma, Daniel, ed. X-Linked Mental Retardation & Verbal Disability. (Symposia Ser.: Vol. 10, No. 1). 11.50 (ISBN 0-686-10022-0). March of Dimes.
Boullin, David J. Serotonin in Mental Abnormalities. LC 77-1828. 1978. 51.95 (ISBN 0-471-99501-0, Pub. by Wiley-Interscience). Wiley.
Brinkhurst, R. O. A Guide for the Identification of British Aquatic Oligochaeta. 2nd ed. 1971. 11.00x (ISBN 0-900386-15-0, Pub. by Freshwater Bio). State Mutual Bk.
Buchwald, Nathaniel A. & Brazier, Mary A., eds. Brain Mechanisms in Mental Retardation: Based Upon a Symposium. (UCLA Forum in Medical Sciences: No. 18). 1975. 31.00 (ISBN 0-12-139050-0). Acad Pr.
Button, James E. Communications Research in Learning Disabilities & Mental Retardation. 356p. 1979. pap. text ed. 22.50 (ISBN 0-8391-1262-9). Univ Park.
Carter, Charles H. Handbook of Mental Retardation Syndromes. 3rd ed. (Illus.). 432p. 1979. text ed. 26.25 (ISBN 0-398-03090-1). C C Thomas.
Carver, John N. & Carver, Nellie E. The Family of the Retarded Child. LC 72-85384. (Segregated Settings & the Problem of Change Ser.: No. 2). 156p. 1972. 12.00x (ISBN 0-8156-8079-1). Syracuse U Pr.
A Century of Concern: A History of the American Association on Mental Deficiency 1876-1976. 1976. pap. 9.90x (ISBN 0-686-23877-X). Am Assn Mental.
Chinn, Philip C., et al. Mental Retardation: A Life Cycle Approach. 2nd ed. LC 78-31835. 1979. text ed. 18.95 (ISBN 0-8016-0968-2). Mosby.
Clarke, A. D. & Clarke, Ann M. Mental Retardation & Behavioral Research. (Illus.). 1973. 17.50x (ISBN 0-443-00952-X). Churchill.
Clarke, Ann M. & Clarke, A. D., eds. Mental Deficiency: The Changing Outlook. 3rd ed. LC 75-6314. 1975. 25.00 (ISBN 0-02-905620-9). Free Pr.
Cleland, Charles. Mental Retardation: A Developmental Approach. (Spec. Educ. Ser.). 1978. ref. ed. 19.95x (ISBN 0-13-576504-8). P-H.
Cobb, Henry V. The Forecast of Fulfillment: A Review of Research on Predictive Assessment of the Adult Retarded for Social & Vocational Adjustment. LC 72-3084. (Illus.). 176p. 1972. 5.00x (ISBN 0-8077-1168-3). Tchrs Coll.
Craft, Michael, ed. Tredgold's Mental Retardation. 12th ed. (Illus.). 1980. text ed. 50.00 (ISBN 0-02-857430-3). Macmillan.
Crome, L. C. & Stern, J. Pathology of Mental Retardation. 2nd ed. (Illus.). 1972. 39.50x (ISBN 0-443-00927-9). Churchill.
Curry, Judith B. & Peppe, Kathryn K., eds. Mental Retardation: Nursing Approaches to Care. LC 77-26307. 1978. pap. text ed. 11.50 (ISBN 0-8016-1196-2). Mosby.
Das, J. P. & Baine, David. Mental Retardation for Special Educators. (Illus.). 332p. 1978. 27.50 (ISBN 0-398-03665-9); pap. 18.50 (ISBN 0-398-03666-7). C C Thomas.
Davitz, Joel R., et al. Terminology & Concepts in Mental Retardation. LC 62-61261. (Orig.). 1964. pap. text ed. 5.00x (ISBN 0-8077-1233-7). Tchrs Coll.
Deserrano, Irma G. Manual Para la Preparacion De Informes y Tesis. LC 76-11003. 1980. 6.25 (ISBN 0-8477-2311-9); pap. 5.00 (ISBN 0-8477-2312-7). U of PR Pr.
Edgerton, Robert B. Mental Retardation. LC 78-27199. (Developing Child Ser.). (Illus.). 1979. text ed. 7.95x (ISBN 0-674-56885-0); pap. 3.95 (ISBN 0-674-56886-9). Harvard U Pr.
Ellis, Norman, ed. International Review of Research in Mental Retardation, Vol. 10. (Serial Publication Ser.). 1981. write for info. Acad Pr.
Ellis, Norman R., ed. Handbook of Mental Deficiency, Psychological Theory & Research. 2nd ed. LC 79-18891. (Illus.). 816p. 1979. text ed. 45.00x (ISBN 0-89859-002-7). L Erlbaum Assocs.
--International Review of Research in Mental Retardation. Incl. Vol. 1. 1966. 44.00 (ISBN 0-12-366201-X); Vol. 2. 1966. 44.00 (ISBN 0-12-366202-8); Vol. 3. 1968. 44.00 (ISBN 0-12-366203-6); Vol. 4. 1970. 44.00 (ISBN 0-12-366204-4); Vol. 5. 1971. 44.00 (ISBN 0-12-366205-2); Vol. 6. 1973. 44.00 (ISBN 0-12-366206-0); Vol. 9. 1978. 29.00 (ISBN 0-12-366209-5). Acad Pr.
Flanigan, Patrick J., et al. Orientation to Mental Retardation: A Programmed Text. (Illus.). 216p. 1973. 13.75 (ISBN 0-398-00584-2). C C Thomas.
Flores, Zella K. The Relation of Language Difficulty to Intelligence & School Retardation in a Group of Spanish-Speaking Children. LC 74-833371. 1975. Repr. of 1926 ed. soft bdg. 8.00 (ISBN 0-88247-355-7). R & E Res Assoc.
Frankenstein, C. Impaired Intelligence: Pathology & Rehabilitation. 1970. 37.50 (ISBN 0-677-02810-5). Gordon.
GAP Committee on Mental Retardation. Basic Considerations in Mental Retardation: A Preliminary Report, Vol. 4. LC 62-2872. (Report No. 43). 1959. pap. 2.00 (ISBN 0-87318-056-9, Pub. by Adv Psychiatry). Mental Health.
--Mild Mental Retardation: A Growing Challenge to the Physician, Vol. 6. LC 62-2872. (Report No. 66). 1967. pap. 3.00 (ISBN 0-87318-091-7, Pub. by Adv Psychiatry). Mental Health.
--Psychiatric Consultation in Mental Retardation, Vol. 10. LC 79-6358. (Publication: No. 104). 1979. pap. 4.00 (ISBN 0-87318-142-5, Pub. by Adv Psychiatry). Mental Health.
Gearheart, Bill R. & Litton, Freddie W. The Trainable Retarded: A Foundations Approach. 2nd ed. LC 78-13959. (Illus.). 1979. 16.95 (ISBN 0-8016-1761-8). Mosby.
Goddard, Henry H. Feeble-Mindedness. LC 76-39391. (Select Bibliographies Reprint Series). 1972. Repr. of 1914 ed. 40.25 (ISBN 0-8369-9907-X). Arno.
--Feeble-Mindedness: Its Causes & Consequences. LC 73-2401. (Mental Illness & Social Policy; the American Experience Ser.). Repr. of 1926 ed. 32.00 (ISBN 0-405-05207-3). Arno.
--The Kallikak Family: A Study in the Heredity of Feeble-Mindedness. LC 73-2966. (Classics in Psychology Ser.). Repr. of 1931 ed. 9.00 (ISBN 0-405-05139-5). Arno.
Groff, Catherine A., ed. Mental Retardation. LC 73-11194. 1973. pap. text ed. 12.50x (ISBN 0-8422-0335-4). Irvington.
Grossman, Herbert J., ed. Manual on Terminology & Classification in Mental Retardation. 3rd ed. LC 77-87576. 1977. 14.85x (ISBN 0-686-23878-8). Am Assn Mental.
Hardy, Richard E. & Cull, John G., eds. Mental Retardation & Physical Disability: A Book of Readings. (American Lectures in Social & Rehabilitation Psychology Ser.). (Illus.). 264p. 1974. 14.75 (ISBN 0-398-02879-6). C C Thomas.
Heber, Rick. Epidemiology of Mental Retardation. (Illus.). 136p. 1970. 11.75 (ISBN 0-398-00817-5). C C Thomas.
Hollis, John H., ed. Developmental Deficiencies: A Comparative Approach. new ed. (Illus.). 1973. text ed. 26.50x (ISBN 0-8422-5077-8); pap. text ed. 9.50x (ISBN 0-8422-0279-X). Irvington.
Holmes, Lewis B., et al. Mental Retardation: An Atlas of Diseases with Associated Physical Abnormalities. (Illus.). 1972. text ed. 42.00 (ISBN 0-02-356470-9). Macmillan.
Ingalls, Robert P. Mental Retardation: The Changing Outlook. LC 77-23359. 1978. text ed. 22.95x (ISBN 0-471-42716-0). Wiley.
Jastak, Joseph F. & MacPhee, Halsey M. Mental Retardation, Its Nature & Incidence: A Population Survey of the State of Delaware. LC 62-19658. 184p. 10.00 (ISBN 0-87413-103-0). U Delaware Pr.
Jordan, Thomas E. The Mentally Retarded. 4th ed. 1976. text ed. 19.95x (ISBN 0-675-08616-7). Merrill.
Jordan, Thomas E., ed. Perspectives in Mental Retardation. LC 66-11153. 272p. 1966. 10.00x (ISBN 0-8093-0208-X). S Ill U Pr.
Judge, Clifford. Retarded Australians. 1975. pap. 15.00x (ISBN 0-522-84082-5, Pub. by Melbourne U Pr). Intl Schol Bk Serv.
Karrer, Rathe. Developmental Psychophysiology of Mental Retardation: Concepts & Studies. (Illus.). 528p. 1976. 35.50 (ISBN 0-398-03414-1). C C Thomas.
Kauffman, James M. & Payne, James S., eds. Mental Retardation: Introduction & Personal Perspectives. new ed. (Special Education Ser). 456p. 1975. text ed. 18.50x (ISBN 0-675-08728-7). Merrill.
Kekstadt, H. & Primrose, D. A. Mental Subnormality. (Modern Practical Nursing Ser: NO. 15). (Illus.). 1975. pap. text ed. 9.95x (ISBN 0-685-83644-4). Intl Ideas.
Khanna, J. L. Brain Damage & Mental Retardation: A Psychological Evaluation. 2nd ed. (Illus.). 232p. 1973. 12.75 (ISBN 0-398-02631-9). C C Thomas.
Kirman, B. H. Mental Retardation. 1968. 3.50 (ISBN 0-08-013371-1). Pergamon.
Kurtz, Richard A. Social Aspects of Mental Retardation. LC 76-42693. 1977. 18.95 (ISBN 0-669-01054-5). Lexington Bks.
Langone, John. Goodbye to Bedlam: Understanding Mental Illness & Retardation. 160p. (gr. 7-12). 1974. 7.95 (ISBN 0-316-51421-7). Little.

McFie, J. Assessment of Organic Intellectual Impairment. 1976. 26.00 (ISBN 0-12-481950-8). Acad Pr.
Maloney, Michael P. & Ward, Michael P. Mental Retardation & Modern Society. (Illus.). 1979. text ed. 12.95x (ISBN 0-19-502473-7). Oxford U Pr.
Menolascino, Frank J. & Egger, Michael L. Medical Dimensions of Mental Retardation. LC 76-16503. (Illus.). 1978. 9.95x (ISBN 0-8032-0900-2). U of Nebr Pr.
Menolascino, Frank J., ed. Psychiatric Aspects of the Diagnosis & Treatment of Mental Retardation. LC 69-20313. 1971. pap. 9.00x (ISBN 0-87562-029-9). Spec Child.
Meyers, C. Edward, ed. Quality of Life in Severely & Profoundly Mentally Retarded People: Research Foundations for Improvement. LC 77-91506. (AAMD Monograph Ser.: No. 3). 1978. 15.95x (ISBN 0-686-23879-6). Am Assn Mental.
--Sociobehavioral Studies in Mental Retardation. LC 73-88389. (AAMD Monograph Ser.: No. 1). 1976. 7.15x (ISBN 0-686-16814-3). Am Assn Mental.
Meyers, Robert. Like Normal People. (Illus.). 1978. 9.95 (ISBN 0-07-041761-X, GB). McGraw.
Milunsky, Aubrey. Prevention of Genetic Disease & Mental Retardation. LC 74-21015. (Illus.). 450p. 1975. 29.00 (ISBN 0-7216-6395-8). Saunders.
Mittler, P., ed. Research to Practice in Mental Retardation: IASSMD Proceedings, 3 vols. 1977. Vol. 1. 29.50 (ISBN 0-8391-1122-3); Vol. 2. 29.50 (ISBN 0-8391-1123-1); Vol. 3. 29.50 (ISBN 0-8391-1124-X). Univ Park.
Mittler, Peter. Frontiers of Knowledge in Mental Retardation, Vol. 2. 368p. 1981. text ed. 34.50 (ISBN 0-8391-1637-3). Univ Park.
Mittler, Peter, ed. Frontiers of Knowledge in Mental Retardation. 494p. 1981. text ed. 34.50 (ISBN 0-8391-1636-5). Univ Park.
Moore, Byron C. & Moore, Susan. Mental Retardation: Causes & Prevention. 1977. pap. text ed. 6.95 (ISBN 0-675-08535-7); 6 cassettes & 6 filmstrips 155.00 (ISBN 0-675-08534-9); 2-5 sets 95.00, 6 or more sets 75.00 (ISBN 0-685-74287-3); instructor's manual 3.95 (ISBN 0-686-67616-5). Merrill.
Moore, Byron C., et al. Introduction to Mental Retardation Syndromes & Terminology. 184p. 1978. 14.50 (ISBN 0-398-03718-3); pap. 8.75 (ISBN 0-398-03719-1). C C Thomas.
Moran, Roberto F. Manual of Mental Subnormality. 1968. 8.75 (ISBN 0-8477-2900-1). U of PR Pr.
Murray, Robert F., Jr., et al, eds. The Genetic, Metabolic & Developmental Aspects of Mental Retardation. (Illus.). 366p. 1972. 23.50 (ISBN 0-398-02531-2). C C Thomas.
Neisworth, John & Smith, Robert. Retardation: Issues, Assessment & Intervention. (Series in Special Education). (Illus.). 1978. text ed. 18.95 (ISBN 0-07-046201-1, C); instructor's manual 3.95 (ISBN 0-07-046202-X). McGraw.
Osler, Sonia F. & Cooke, Robert E., eds. The Biosocial Basis of Mental Retardation. (Illus.). 168p. 1965. 12.00x (ISBN 0-8018-0511-2). Johns Hopkins.
Penrose, L. C. A Clinical & Genetic Study of 1280 Cases of Mental Defect: The Colchester Study. 162p. Date not set. Repr. of 1981 ed. price not set (ISBN 0-89874-191-2). Krieger.
Plog, Stanley C., ed. The Year Two Thousand & Mental Retardation. (Current Topics in Mental Health Ser.). (Illus.). 240p. 1980. 19.95 (ISBN 0-306-40252-1, Plenum Pr). Plenum Pub.
Pope, Lillie. An Introductory Course in Learning Disabilities. 1976. kit 77.00 (ISBN 0-87594-146-X, 2600). Book-Lab.
Pressey, Sidney L. & Pressey, Luella C. Mental Abnormality & Deficiency: An Introduction to the Study of Problems of Mental Health. 1979. Repr. of 1927 ed. lib. bdg. 30.00 (ISBN 0-8495-4353-3). Arden Lib.
Sackett, Gene P., ed. Observing Behavior, Vol. 1. LC 77-25276. 1977. 29.50 (ISBN 0-8391-1167-3). Univ Park.
--Observing Behavior, Vol. 2. LC 77-25276. 1977. 14.95 (ISBN 0-8391-1168-1). Univ Park.
Sellin, Donald F. Mental Retardation: Nature, Needs, & Advocacy. 1979. text ed. 20.95 (ISBN 0-205-05989-9, 2459892); tests avail. (ISBN 0-205-05990-2, 2459906). Allyn.
Slater, Eliot & Cowie, Valerie. Genetics of Mental Disorders. (Oxford Monographs on Medical Genetics). (Illus.). 1971. text ed. 37.50x (ISBN 0-19-264130-1). Oxford U Pr.
Smith, Robert. Introduction to Mental Retardation. 1971. 14.50 (ISBN 0-07-058903-8, C). McGraw.
Stephen, E. Residential Care for the Mentally Retarded. 64p. 1970. pap. 6.25 (ISBN 0-08-016106-5). Pergamon.
Stevens, Harvey A. & Heber, Rick, eds. Mental Retardation: A Review of Research. LC 64-15808. 1964. 17.50x (ISBN 0-226-77388-4). U of Chicago Pr.
Thorne, G. D. Understanding the Mentally Retarded. 1965. 10.50 (ISBN 0-07-064526-4, HP). McGraw.
Tymchuk, Alexander J. The Mental Retardation Dictionary. LC 73-80058. 149p. 1980. pap. 11.80x (ISBN 0-87424-125-1). Western Psych.
WHO Expert Committee on Mental Health, Geneva, 1967. Organization of Services for the Mentally Retarded: A Report. (Technical Report Ser: No. 392). 55p. 1968. pap. 2.00 (ISBN 92-4-120392-7, 1140). World Health.
Wortis, Joseph, ed. Mental Retardation & Developmental Disabilities: An Annual Review. Incl. Vol. 5. 1973; Vol. 6. 1974 (ISBN 0-685-57356-7); Vol. 7. 1975 (ISBN 0-685-57357-5); Vol. 8. 1976 (ISBN 0-685-57358-3); Vol. 9. 1977; Vol. 10. 1978; Vol. 11. LC 73-647002. 1979 (ISBN 0-87630-214-2). LC 75-86629. Vols. 6-11. 20.00 ea. Brunner-Mazel.

MENTAL DEFICIENCY–PROGRAMMED INSTRUCTION

Ehlers, Walter H. & Krishef, Curtis H. An Introduction to Mental Retardation - a Programmed Text. 2nd ed. (Special Education Ser.). 1977. pap. text ed. 16.95 (ISBN 0-675-08526-8). Merrill.
Flanigan, Patrick J., et al. Orientation to Mental Retardation: A Programmed Text. (Illus.). 216p. 1973. 13.75 (ISBN 0-398-00584-2). C C Thomas.
Gilmore, Alden S. & Rich, Thomas A. Mental Retardation: A Programmed Manual for Volunteer Workers. (Illus.). 152p. 1973. 9.75 (ISBN 0-398-00681-4). C C Thomas.

MENTAL DEPRESSION

see Depression, Mental

MENTAL DISCIPLINE

see also Education; Memory; Mnemonics; Self-Culture

Dorr, Darwin, et al. The Psychology of Discipline: Six Approaches to Discipline. 1981. pap. text ed. 27.50 (ISBN 0-8236-5581-4). Intl Univs Pr.
Edwin, B. Psycho-Yoga: The Practice of Mind Control. 1969. pap. 2.95 (ISBN 0-8065-0071-9). Citadel Pr.
Harrison, Allan E. Discipline at Home - Made Simple. LC 78-65644. (Orig., Prog. Bk.). 1979. pap. 4.95 (ISBN 0-89626-017-8). HEMECO.
--Discipline at School - Made Easy. LC 78-65645. (Orig., Prog. Bk.). 1979. pap. 8.95 (ISBN 0-89626-018-6). HEMECO.
Healy, William. Mental Conflicts & Misconduct. (Educational Ser.). 1920. Repr. 15.00 (ISBN 0-685-43070-7). Norwood Edns.
Howard, V. Secrets of Mental Magic. 1974. pap. 3.95 (ISBN 0-13-797985-1, Reward). P-H.
Kolesnik, Walter B. Mental Discipline in Modern Education. 1958. pap. 4.75x (ISBN 0-299-01674-9). U of Wis Pr.
Lorayne, Harry. Secrets of Mind Power. 1975. pap. 1.50 (ISBN 0-451-06712-6, W6712, Sig.). NAL.
Murphy, Joseph. Power of Your Subconscious Mind. 1963. 9.95 (ISBN 0-13-685958-5, Reward); pap. 3.95 (ISBN 0-13-685925-9). P-H.
Perry, William G. Forms of Intellectual & Ethical Development in the College Years. LC 70-107334. 1970. pap. text ed. 12.95 (ISBN 0-03-081326-3, HoltC). HR&W.
Wright, Norman. Answer to Discipline. LC 76-21113. (Answer Ser.). 1976. pap. 1.25 (ISBN 0-89081-061-3, 0613). Harvest Hse.

MENTAL DISEASES

see Mental Illness; Psychology, Pathological; Psychoses

MENTAL HEALING

see also Christian Science; Faith-Cure; Medicine, Magic, Mystic, and Spagiric; Mental Suggestion; Mind and Body; New Thought; Psychotherapy; Subconsciousness; Therapeutics, Suggestive

Addington, Jack E. Secret of Healing. 1979. pap. 6.95 (ISBN 0-911336-80-X). Sci of Mind.
Apsler, Alfred. From Witch Doctor to Biofeedback: The Story of Healing by Suggestion. LC 76-56425. 192p. (gr. 7 up). 1977. PLB 7.29 (ISBN 0-671-32832-8). Messner.
Baars, Conrad W. & Terruwe, Anna A. Psychic Wholeness & Healing: Using All the Powers of the Human Psyche. LC 81-4964. 245p. (Orig.). 1981. pap. 5.95 (ISBN 0-8189-0410-0, Pub. by Alba Bks). Alba.
Bailes, Frederick. Healing Power of Balanced Emotions. 1972. pap. 2.95 (ISBN 0-87516-124-3). De Vorss.
--Healing the Incurable. 1972. pap. 0.75 (ISBN 0-87516-126-X). De Vorss.
--The Secret of Healing. pap. 0.75 (ISBN 0-87516-163-4). De Vorss.
--What Is This Power That Heals. pap. 0.75 (ISBN 0-87516-171-5). De Vorss.
--Your Mind Can Heal You. LC 78-128864. 206p. 1975. pap. 4.95 (ISBN 0-87516-201-0). De Vorss.
Bartow, Donald W. The Adventures of Healing: How to Use New Testament Practices & Receive New Testament Results. rev. ed. 371p. 1981. pap. 5.95 (ISBN 0-938736-02-7). Life Enrich.
Beierle, Herbert L. Quiet Healing Zone. 1980. 10.00 (ISBN 0-686-23897-4). U of Healing.
Bennett, George. The Heart of Healing. LC 72-5838. 128p. 1973. pap. 2.50 (ISBN 0-8170-0574-9). Judson.
Bennett, Hal Z. The Doctor Within. 160p. 1981. 11.95 (ISBN 0-517-54178-5); pap. 5.95 (ISBN 0-517-54299-4). Potter.
Bibb, Benjamin O. & Weed, Joseph J. Amazing Secrets of Psychic Healing. 1976. 9.95 (ISBN 0-13-023846-5). P-H.
Bigger, Jama K. Then Came a Miracle. 192p. 1981. 8.95 (ISBN 0-8007-1275-7). Revell.
Bissonnier, Henri. The Pedagogy of Resurrection: The Christian Formation of the Handicapped. LC 79-52104. 232p. 1979. pap. 6.95 (ISBN 0-8091-2214-6). Paulist Pr.
Blauer, Stephen. Rejuvenation: Dr. Ann Wigmore's Complete Diet & Health Program. 197p. pap. 4.95 (ISBN 0-686-29390-8). Hippocrates.
Blomgren, David K. The Laying on of Hands & Prophecy of the Presbytery. (Illus.). 100p. 1979. pap. 5.25 (ISBN 0-914936-36-0). Bible Pr.
Bowser, Milton & Bukowinski, George. Back to Normal. (Illus.). 131p. (Orig.). 1980. pap. 5.00 (ISBN 0-940178-01-X). Sitare Inc.
Brennan, R. O. & Hosier, Helen K. Coronary? Cancer? God's Answer: Prevent It. LC 79-84719. 1979. pap. 3.95 (ISBN 0-89081-181-4, 1814). Harvest Hse.
Bulle, Florence. Lord of the Valleys: Overcoming Suffering by Faith. LC 72-85630. 240p. 1972. pap. 3.95 (ISBN 0-912106-01-8). Logos.
Cayce, H. L. Gifts of Healing. rev. ed. 1976. pap. 1.50 (ISBN 0-87604-070-9). ARE Pr.
Chaitow, Boris R. My Healing Secrets. 1980. 11.75x (ISBN 0-85032-163-8, Pub. by Daniel Co England). State Mutual Bk.
Chang, Stephen T. & Miller, Richard C. The Book of Internal Exercises. LC 78-18320. (Illus., Orig.). 1978. pap. 6.95 (ISBN 0-89407-017-7). Strawberry Hill.
Cheney, Vance. What It Is That Heals. 1980. 18.50x (ISBN 0-686-64693-2, Pub. by Daniel Co England). State Mutual Bk.
Cooke, Ivan. Healing by the Spirit. 1955. 12.00 (ISBN 0-85487-039-3). De Vorss.
Coxhead, Nona. Mindpower. 1979. pap. 2.95 (ISBN 0-14-004585-6). Penguin.
Curtiss, Harriette & Homer, F. Four-Fold Health. 1936. 4.95 (ISBN 0-87516-304-1). De Vorss.
Dawson, George G. Healing: Pagan & Christian. LC 75-23704. Repr. of 1935 ed. 26.50 (ISBN 0-404-13256-1). AMS Pr.
Denning, Melita & Phillips, Osborne. The Llewellyn Practical Guide to Psychic Self-Defense & Well Being. LC 80-84235. (Llewellyn Practical Guide Ser.). 253p. (Orig.). 1981. pap. 5.95 (ISBN 0-87542-190-3). Llewellyn Pubns.
Dethlefsen, Thorwald. Voices from Other Lives: Reincarnation As a Source of Healing. LC 76-30454. 252p. 1977. 7.95 (ISBN 0-87131-233-6). M Evans.
Drakeford, John W. The Awesome Power of the Healing Thought. 1981. 6.95 (ISBN 0-8054-5294-X). Broadman.
Evans, Warren F. The Mental-Cure. LC 74-29292. Repr. of 1869 ed. 21.50 (ISBN 0-404-13411-4). AMS Pr.
Evensen, Ken L. Healing Love: The Inner Power of All Things. 9.95 (ISBN 0-533-04807-9). Vantage.
Fillmore, Charles. Christian Healing. 1909. 2.95 (ISBN 0-87159-017-4). Unity Bks.
Folz, Joe. Psychic Healers of the Philippines. 1981. pap. 2.95 (ISBN 0-88270-508-3). Logos.
Forbes, Alec. Try Being Healthy. 1980. 15.00x (ISBN 0-85032-140-9, Pub. by Daniel Co England). State Mutual Bk.
Ford, Norman. Minding Your Body. LC 81-66774. 180p. 1981. pap. 7.95 (ISBN 0-914398-30-X). Autumn Pr.
Fricker, E. G. God Is My Witness: The Story of the World-Famous Healer. LC 76-50557. 1977. 8.95 (ISBN 0-8128-2179-3). Stein & Day.
Gardner, Arthur C., ed. How to Cope with Pain. LC 78-72914. 1978. 1.95x (ISBN 0-9602152-1-2). A C Gardner.
Gordon, Richard. Your Healing Hands: The Polarity Experience. LC 78-12527. (Illus., Orig.). 1978. pap. 6.95 (ISBN 0-913300-07-1). Unity Pr.
Hagin, Kenneth E. Laying on of Hands. 1980. pap. 0.50 mini bk. (ISBN 0-89276-250-0). Hagin Ministries.
Hall, Manly P. Mysticism & Mental Healing. pap. 1.75 (ISBN 0-89314-336-7). Philos Res.
Harris, Anastas. Journal of Holsitic Health: Vol.6. LC 78-59776. (Illus.). 144p. 1981. pap. 12.00 (ISBN 0-939410-07-9). Mandala Holistic.
Heidenreich, Alfred. Healings in the Gospels. 1980. pap. 8.95 (ISBN 0-903540-36-3, Pub. Floris Books). St George Bk Serv.
Holland, David. Miracle That Heals. 1956. 8.00 (ISBN 0-685-08739-5). Croydon.
Holzer, Hans. Psychic Healing. (Orig.). 1979. pap. 2.25 (ISBN 0-532-23123-6). Woodhill.
Hover, Robert H. How to Direct the Life Force to Dispel Mild Aches & Pains. LC 79-88460. 96p. (Orig.). 1979. pap. 7.00 (ISBN 0-934414-01-7). Hover.
Hunt, Roland. The Seven Keys to Colour Healing. 124p. 1971. 7.25x (ISBN 0-8464-1063-X). Beekman Pubs.
Jaegers, Beverly C. The Magic Power of Healing: Learn to Heal Yourself. 1979. pap. 3.00 (ISBN 0-89861-019-2). Esoteric Pubns.
Janov, Arthur. Prisoners of Pain: Unlocking the Power of the Mind to End Suffering. LC 79-8501. 288p. 1980. 11.95 (ISBN 0-385-15791-6, Anchor Pr). Doubleday.
Joy, W. Brugh. Joy's Way. LC 78-62795. 1979. 11.95 (ISBN 0-87477-084-X); pap. 6.95 (ISBN 0-87477-085-8). J P Tarcher.
Judd, Wayne. Healing: Faith or Fraud. (Uplook Ser.). 1978. pap. 0.75 (ISBN 0-8163-0199-9, 08303-0). Pacific Pr Pub Assn.
Khan, Inayat. The Development of Spiritual Healing. 3rd ed. LC 78-65080. pap. 3.50 (ISBN 0-900217-15-4, Pub. by Sufi Pub Co England). Hunter Hse.
--Healing & the Mind World. (Sufi Message of Hazrat Inayat Khan Ser.: Vol. 4). 1979. 6.95 (ISBN 90-6077-952-5, Pub. by Servire BV Netherlands). Hunter Hse.
King, Serge. Imagineering for Health. LC 80-53949. 211p. (Orig.). 1981. pap. 4.95 (ISBN 0-8356-0546-9, Quest). Theos Pub Hse.
Kingston, Beryl. Lifting the Curse. 1980. 17.50x (ISBN 0-85223-176-8, Pub. by Telford England). State Mutual Bk.
Kligman, Gail. Calus: Symbolic Transformation in Romanian Ritual. LC 80-21372. (Chicago Originals Ser.). (Illus.). 240p. 1981. lib. bdg. 14.00x (ISBN 0-226-44221-7). U of Chicago Pr.
Kraft, Dean. Portrait of a Psychic Healer. 192p. 1981. 10.95 (ISBN 0-686-69592-5). Putnam.
Kuhlman, Kathryn. From Medicine to Miracles. LC 78-67100. 1978. pap. 1.50 (ISBN 0-87123-383-5, 200383). Bethany Hse.
--How Big Is God? LC 74-12775. 96p. (Orig.). 1974. pap. 1.95 (ISBN 0-87123-222-7, 200222). Bethany Hse.
LaPatra, Jack. Healing: The Coming Revolution in Holistic Medicine. LC 77-78674. 1978. 8.95 (ISBN 0-913374-75-X). SF Bk Co.
Larsori, Muriel. You Are What You Think. pap. 1.95 (ISBN 0-89728-063-6, 658463). Omega Pubns OR.
Lawson-Wood, D. & Lawson-Wood, J. Progressive Vitality & Dynamic Posture. 1980. 17.00x (ISBN 0-85032-135-2, Pub. by Daniel Co England). State Mutual Bk.
Leuser, David V. How to Send Healing Energy: Diccionari Enciclopedic D'abast Universal, 8 vols. 3500p. (Cata.). 1974. Set. 300.00 (ISBN 84-345-3560-2, S-50517). French & Eur.
Linn, Sr. Mary J., et al. Healing the Dying. LC 79-53111. 128p. 1979. pap. 3.50 (ISBN 0-8091-2212-X). Paulist Pr.
Linn, Matthew L. & Linn, D. Healing of Memories: Prayers & Confession-Steps to Inner Healing. LC 74-17697. 112p. (Orig.). 1974. pap. 2.50 (ISBN 0-8091-1854-8). Paulist Pr.
Los, Pieter. An Entire New Healing Approach. 1981. 8.95 (ISBN 0-533-04361-1). Vantage.
MacNutt, Francis. The Power to Heal. LC 77-77845. 256p. 1977. pap. 3.95 (ISBN 0-87793-133-X). Ave Maria.
Maloney, George A. Broken but Loved: Healing Through Christ's Power. LC 81-1802. 126p. (Orig.). 1981. pap. 5.95 (ISBN 0-8189-0411-9). Alba.
Masters, Roy. The Satin Principle. LC 78-78158. 1978. pap. 6.50 (ISBN 0-933900-05-8). Foun Human Under.
Meek, George W., ed. Healers & the Healing Process. LC 77-5251. (Illus., Orig.). 1977. pap. 5.75 (ISBN 0-8356-0498-5, Quest). Theos Pub Hse.
Miller, Roberta D. Psychic Massage. (Illus.). 224p. (Orig.). 1975. pap. 7.95 (ISBN 0-06-090353-8, CN353, CN). Har-Row.
Minor, Malcolm. Healing & the Abundant Life. LC 79-7614. 108p. 1979. pap. 3.95 (ISBN 0-8192-1258-X). Morehouse.
Muramoto, Naboru. Healing Ourselves. LC 72-97039. 1973. 4.95 (ISBN 0-685-72760-2, Pub. by Avon). Formur Intl.
New Age of Healing. 96p. 1980. pap. 3.50 (ISBN 0-911336-78-8). Sci of Mind.
Otto, Herbert A. & Knight, James W., eds. Dimensions in Wholistic Healing: New Frontiers in the Treatment of the Whole Person. LC 78-27071. 1979. 25.95x (ISBN 0-88229-513-6); pap. text ed. 14.95x (ISBN 0-88229-697-3). Nelson-Hall.

Oyle, Irving. Time, Space & Mind. LC 76-11339. 128p. (Orig.). 1976. pap. 5.95 (ISBN 0-89087-122-1). Celestial Arts.

Palmer, Lacie A. God Gave Me Miracle Hands. 1981. 5.95 (ISBN 0-533-04578-9). Vantage.

Paramananda, Swami. Spiritual Healing. 4th ed. 1975. pap. 2.25 (ISBN 0-911564-10-1). Vedanta Ctr.

Ponder, Catherine. Healing Secret of the Ages. 1967. pap. 3.95 (ISBN 0-13-384396-3, Reward). P-H.

Powell, Eric F. The Natural Home Physicians. 1980. 20.50x (ISBN 0-85032-189-1, Pub. by Daniel Co England). State Mutual Bk.

Price, Richard. Your Body Heals Itself. 128p. 1981. pap. 12.00x (ISBN 0-906379-10-5, Pub. by Jupiter England). State Mutual Bk.

Puryear, Meredith. Healing Through Meditation & Prayer. rev. ed. 1978. pap. 2.95 (ISBN 0-87604-104-7). ARE Pr.

Ramacharaka, Yogi. Psychic Healing. 7.00 (ISBN 0-911662-07-3). Yoga.

Reed, William S. Doctor's Thoughts on Healing. pap. 0.75 (ISBN 0-910924-33-3). Macalester.

Saraydarian, Torkom. Healing. 1981. 15.00 (ISBN 0-911794-08-5); pap. 12.00 (ISBN 0-911794-09-3). Aqua Educ.

Satya-Miriam. Healing & Transformation: The Opening of the Rose. Berg, Sona, intro. by. LC 78-64490. (Illus.). 1978. pap. 4.95 (ISBN 0-88238-987-4). Baraka Bk.

Saxon, Edgar J. A Sense of Wonder. 1980. 17.50x (ISBN 0-85207-136-1, Pub. by Daniel Co England). State Mutual Bk.

Sheats, Morris. You Can Be Emotionally Healed. rev. ed. 1978. pap. 1.95 (ISBN 0-930718-21-6). Harvest Pr Texas.

Sherman, Harold. Your Power to Heal. 1978. pap. 1.75 (ISBN 0-449-14007-5, GM). Fawcett.

Simpson, Albert B. Lord for the Body. pap. 2.50 (ISBN 0-87509-027-3). Chr Pubns.

Sladek, Marti. Two Weeks with the Psychic Surgeons. LC 76-45732. (Illus.). 1977. 8.95 (ISBN 0-917816-01-3). Doma.

Sperry, Robert M. The Joy of Healing. LC 77-93681. 1978. 9.95 (ISBN 0-914350-29-3). Vulcan Bks.

Stapleton, Ruth C. The Experience of Inner Healing. (gr. 7-12). 1979. lib. bdg. 13.95 (ISBN 0-8161-6776-1). G K Hall.

Steiner, Lee R. Psychic Self-Healing for Psychological Problems. LC 76-56849. (Illus.). 176p. 1977. 8.95 (ISBN 0-13-732677-7). P-H.

Stevens, Henry B. The Recovery of Culture. 1980. 19.00x (ISBN 0-85207-102-7, Pub. by Daniel Co England). State Mutual Bk.

Syllabus, University of Healing. 1980. 0.25 (ISBN 0-686-27971-9). U of Healing.

Tisserand, R. B. Aromatherapy: The Art of Aromatherapy. 1980. 15.00x (ISBN 0-85207-140-X, Pub. by Daniel Co. England). State Mutual Bk.

Wagner, James K. Blessed to Be a Blessing. LC 80-52615. 144p. (Orig.). 1980. pap. 4.50x (ISBN 0-8358-0410-0). Upper Room.

Wallace, Amy & Henkin, Bill. The Psychic Healing Book. LC 77-16019. 224p. 1981. pap. 4.95 (ISBN 0-914728-34-2). Wingbow Pr.

Wallace, Amy & Henkin, William. The Psychic Healing Book. 1977. 8.95 (ISBN 0-440-07194-1). Delacorte.

Waterman, LeRoy H. Let There Be Light: A Guide to Divine Healing. 63p. 1979. 4.50 (ISBN 0-8059-2691-7). Dorrance.

White Eagle. Heal Thyself. 1962. 3.95 (ISBN 0-85487-015-6). De Vorss.

--Spiritual Unfoldment One. 1942. 5.95 (ISBN 0-85487-012-1). De Vorss.

--Spiritual Unfoldment Two. 1969. 5.95 (ISBN 0-85487-001-6). De Vorss.

--Sunrise. 1958. 3.50 (ISBN 0-85487-016-4). De Vorss.

WHO Technical Conference, Stockholm, 1969. Mental Health of Adolescents & Young Persons. A Report. (Public Health Papers Ser: No. 41). 72p. 1971. pap. 2.80 (ISBN 92-4-130041-8, 13). World Health.

Wigmore, Ann. Spiritual Diet. (Health Digest Ser.: No. 152). 64p. pap. 1.50 (ISBN 0-686-29396-7). Hippocrates.

Wolf, William. Healers, Gurus, Spiritual Guide. LC 76-2180. 1969. pap. 6.50 (ISBN 0-933900-07-4). Foun Human Under.

Worrall, Ambrose A. & Worrall, Olga N. Explore Your Psychic World. LC 79-85062. 1970. pap. 3.95 (ISBN 0-06-069686-9, HarpR); pap. 3.95 (ISBN 0-06-069686-9, RD 156). Har-Row.

Yogananda, Paramahansa. Scientific Healing Affirmations. 11th ed. 1962. pap. 1.50 (ISBN 0-87612-140-7); pap. 1.50 Span. ed. (ISBN 0-87612-141-5); pap. 6.00 German ed. (ISBN 3-87041-241-0); pap. 4.25 Italian ed. (ISBN 0-87612-143-1). Self Realization.

Zweig, Stefan. Mental Healers: Franz Anton Mesmer, Mary Baker Eddy, Sigmund Freud. LC 62-19082. 12.50 (ISBN 0-8044-2995-2); pap. 6.95 (ISBN 0-8044-6996-2). Ungar.

MENTAL HEALTH

see also Community Mental Health Services; Emotions; Happiness; Mental Health Personnel; Mental Health Services; Mental Illness; Personality; Psychiatry; Psychology; Psychology, Pathological; Relaxation; Self-Actualization (Psychology); Social Psychiatry; Stress (Psychology); Success

Ackerman, Nathan W. Psychodynamics of Family Life: Diagnosis & Treatment of Family Relationships. LC 58-13043. 1958. pap. 5.95x (ISBN 0-465-09503-8, TB5004). Basic.

Alain, pseud. Alain on Happiness. Cottrell, Robert D. & Cottrell, Jane E., trs. from Fr. LC 76-186356. Orig. Title: Propos Sur le Bonheur. 272p. 1973. 10.50 (ISBN 0-8044-5033-1); pap. 4.95 (ISBN 0-8044-6004-3). Ungar.

Allen, Richard C., ed. Mental Health in America: The Years of Crisis. LC 78-71070. (Illus.). 1979. 12.50 (ISBN 0-8379-4901-7). Marquis.

Allen, Robert & Cartier, Marsha, eds. The Mental Health Almanac: 1978-79. new ed. 403p. 1978. lib. bdg. 27.50 (ISBN 0-8240-7018-6, Garland STPM Pr). Garland Pub.

Amada, Gerald. Mental Health & Authoritarianism on the College Campus. LC 79-66480. 1979. pap. text ed. 12.00 (ISBN 0-8191-0831-6). U Pr of Amer.

--Mental Health on the Community College Campus. 157p. 1977. pap. text ed. 8.50 (ISBN 0-8191-0357-8). U Pr of Amer.

Arkoff, Abe. Adjustment & Mental Health. 1968. 15.95 (ISBN 0-07-002221-6, C); questions 3.95 (ISBN 0-07-002223-2). McGraw.

Arola, Paavo. Are You Confused. 5.95 (ISBN 0-686-29848-9). Cancer Bk Hse.

Ascheim, Barbara, et al. Development of Special Mental Health Technical Assistance Materials for Self-Help Groups in Particular Populations. 57p. 1978. pap. 2.60 (ISBN 0-89785-000-9). Am Inst Res.

Ash, Philip, ed. Volunteers for Mental Health. LC 73-10368. 1973. 28.00x (ISBN 0-8422-5121-9); pap. text ed. 7.95x (ISBN 0-8422-0322-2). Irvington.

Association For Supervision And Curriculum Development. Learning & Mental Health in the School. LC 44-6213. 1966. pap. 5.00 (ISBN 0-87120-037-6, 610-17674). Assn Supervision.

Ayd, Frank J., ed. Medical, Moral & Legal Issues in Mental Health Care. 220p. 1974. 12.50 (ISBN 0-683-00295-3, Pub. by W & W). Krieger.

Barton, John & Barton, Margaret. Emotions Can Heal, Emotions Can Harm. rev. 2nd ed. Orig. Title: Loving Affirmations. (Illus.). 157p. 1978. pap. 5.00 (ISBN 0-937216-02-X). J&M Barton.

Barton, Walter E. & Barton, Gail M. Mental Health Administration: Principles & Practice, 2 vols. 1982. in prep. Vol. 1 (ISBN 0-89885-061-4). Vol. 2 (ISBN 0-89885-062-2). Human Sci Pr.

Beiser, Morton, et al, eds. Today's Priorities in Mental Health: Knowing & Doing. (Illus.). 1978. 37.75 (ISBN 0-8151-0646-7, Pub. by Symposia Special). Year Bk Med.

Bellak, Leopold & Barten, Harvey H., eds. Progress in Community Mental Health, Vol. 1. LC 69-15739. 280p. 1969. 33.50 (ISBN 0-8089-0047-1). Grune.

Berkowitz, Morton I. A Primer on School Mental Health Consultation. 132p. 1975. 12.75 (ISBN 0-398-03342-0). C C Thomas.

Bhatia, B. D. & Craig, M. Elements of Psychology & Mental Hygiene for Nurses in India. 376p. 1979. 10.00x (ISBN 0-86125-051-6, Pub. by Orient Longman India). State Mutual Bk.

Birren, James E. & Sloane, R. Bruce, eds. Handbook of Mental Health & Aging. (Illus.). 1980. text ed. 72.00 (ISBN 0-13-380261-2). P-H.

Bloom, Bernard L. Changing Patterns of Psychiatric Care. LC 74-8850. 360p. 1975. text ed. 29.95 (ISBN 0-87705-209-3). Human Sci Pr.

Blum, Richard H. & Ezekiel, Jonathan. Clinical Records for Mental Health Services: A Guide to the Study & Development of Clinical Records Systems Including a Manual of Model Forms & Procedures. 176p. 1962. ed. spiral bdg. 14.75photocopy (ISBN 0-398-00179-0). C C Thomas.

Bowlby, J. Maternal Care & Mental Health. 2nd ed. (Monograph Ser: No. 2). 194p. (Eng, Fr, & Span.). 1952. 7.20 (ISBN 92-4-140002-1). World Health.

Bradburn, Norman M. Structure of Psychological Well-Being. LC 67-27388. (NORC Monographs in Social Research Ser.: No. 15). (Illus.). 1969. 12.95x (ISBN 0-202-25029-6). NORC.

Bragg, Paul C. & Bragg, Patricia. Building Powerful Nerve Force. 9th ed. LC 79-76538. pap. 2.95 (ISBN 0-87790-003-5). Health Sci.

Brigham, Amariah. Observations on the Influence of Religion Upon the Health & Physical Welfare of Mankind. LC 73-2389. (Mental Illness & Social Policy; the American Experience Ser.). Repr. of 1835 ed. 17.00 (ISBN 0-405-05197-2). Arno.

Brockbank, Reed & Westby-Gibson, D., eds. Mental Health in a Changing Community. LC 66-22942. 176p. 1966. 22.75 (ISBN 0-8089-0073-0). Grune.

Broskowski, Anthony, et al, eds. Linking Health & Mental Health. LC 81-8875. (Sage Annual Reviews in Community Health Ser.: Vol. 5). (Illus.). 320p. 1981. pap. 9.95 (ISBN 0-8039-1601-9). Sage.

Burnham, William H. The Normal Mind: An Introduction to Mental Hygiene & the Hygiene of School Instruction. 1978. Repr. of 1925 ed. lib. bdg. 30.00 (ISBN 0-8492-3539-1). R West.

Burrow, Trigant. A Search for Man's Sanity. Grob, Gerald N., ed. LC 78-22553. (Historical Issues in Mental Health Ser.). 1979. Repr. of 1958 ed. lib. bdg. 40.00x (ISBN 0-405-11907-0). Arno.

Cahow, Clark R. People, Patients & Politics. Grob, Gerald N., ed. LC 78-22554. (Historical Issues in Mental Health Ser.). (Illus.). 1979. lib. bdg. 18.00x (ISBN 0-405-11908-9). Arno.

Caplan, Gerald. Principles of Preventive Psychiatry. LC 64-10248. 1964. 12.95x (ISBN 0-465-06344-6). Basic.

Caprio, Frank S. Helping Yourself with Psychiatry. pap. 2.00 (ISBN 0-87980-050-X). Wilshire.

Carone, Pasquale, et al, eds. The Emotionally Troubled Employee: A Challenge to Industry. LC 76-26603. 1976. 12.00 (ISBN 0-87395-801-2). State U NY Pr.

Carroll, Herbert A. Mental Hygiene: Dynamics of Adjustment. 5th ed. 1969. text ed. 18.95x (ISBN 0-13-576314-2). P-H.

Chamberlin, Judi. On Our Own: Patient-Controlled Alternatives to the Mental Health System. 1979. pap. 4.95 (ISBN 0-07-010451-4, SP). McGraw.

Chen, Peter W. Chinese-Americans View Their Mental Health. LC 77-81019. 1977. soft bdg. 10.00 (ISBN 0-88247-476-6). R & E Res Assoc.

Chesler, Phyllis. Women & Madness. 1973. pap. 2.95 (ISBN 0-380-01627-3, 50559). Avon.

Chicorel, Marietta, ed. Chicorel Index to Mental Health Book Reviews, 1976, Vol. 26. annual ed. (Chicorel Index Ser). 1977. text ed. 85.00 ca. (ISBN 0-934598-08-8). Am Lib Pub Co.

--Chicorel Index to Mental Health Book Reviews, 1974 Annual, Vol. 26. 1981. 85.00 (ISBN 0-934598-81-9). Am Lib Pub Co.

--Chicorel Index to Mental Health Book Reviews, 1975 Annual, Vol. 26. 1981. 85.00 (ISBN 0-934598-82-7). Am Lib Pub Co.

Chu, Franklin & Trotter, Sharland. The Madness Establishment: Ralph Nader's Study Group Report on the National Institute of Mental Health. LC 73-83701. 320p. 1974. 8.95 (ISBN 0-670-44734-X, Grossman). Viking Pr.

Coan, Richard W. Hero, Artist, Sage, or Saint? A Survey of Views on What Is Variously Called Mental Health, Normality Maturity, Self-Actualization, & Human Fulfillment. LC 76-57751. 1977. 22.50x (ISBN 0-231-03806-2); pap. 9.00x (ISBN 0-231-08355-6). Columbia U Pr.

Cohen, Raquel & Ahearn, Frederick. Handbook for Mental Health Care of Disaster Victims. 120p. 1980. text ed. 12.95x (ISBN 0-8018-2427-3). Johns Hopkins.

Community Mental Health Centers. (Task Force Report: No. 4). 1972. 5.00 (ISBN 0-685-37537-4, P185-0). Am Psychiatric.

Corson, S. A. & Corson, E. O'Leary. Ethology & Nonverbal Communication in Mental Health: An Interdisciplinary Biopsychosocial Exploration. LC 79-41689. (International Ser. in Biopsychosocial Sciences). (Illus.). 290p. 1980. 48.00 (ISBN 0-08-023728-2). Pergamon.

Cosgrove, Mark P. & Mallory, James D., Jr. Mental Health: A Christian Approach. 1977. pap. 3.95 (ISBN 0-310-35721-7). Zondervan.

Coudert, Jo. Advice from a Failure. LC 65-26996. 1965. 25.00 (ISBN 0-8128-1005-8); pap. 1.95 (ISBN 0-686-66543-0). Stein & Day.

Coursey, Robert D., ed. Program Evaluation for Mental Health: Methods, Strategies and Participants. LC 77-5634. 432p. 1977. 37.00 (ISBN 0-8089-1019-1). Grune.

Craig, Paul. My Look at Life Itself. 1978. 6.95 (ISBN 0-533-03444-2). Vantage.

Crawford, Fred R., ed. Exploring Mental Health Parameters, Vol. I. LC 73-93794. 1974. pap. 6.50 (ISBN 0-89937-014-4, Pub by Paje Publishing, Inc.). Ctr Res Soc Chg.

--Exploring Mental Health Parameters, Vol. III. LC 80-67929. (Orig.). 1980. pap. 8.00 (ISBN 0-89937-030-6). Ctr Res Soc Chg.

Crawford, Jeffrey L., et al. Computer Application in Mental Health: A Source Book. 1980. write for info. (ISBN 0-88410-712-4). Ballinger Pub.

Cumming, Elaine & Cumming, John H. Closed Ranks: An Experiment in Mental Health Education. LC 57-9073. (Commonwealth Fund Publications Ser). 1957. 10.00x (ISBN 0-674-13600-4). Harvard U Pr.

Curtis, W. Robert. The Future Use of Social Networks in Mental Health. LC 79-18997. (The Client As a Social Network Ser.). 1979. pap. 3.95 (ISBN 0-89995-033-7). Social Matrix.

Cusworth, D. C. Biochemical Screening in Relation to Mental Retardation. LC 73-129632. 1971. pap. 7.00 (ISBN 0-08-016416-1). Pergamon.

D'Ambrosio, Richard. Leonora. 1978. 9.95 (ISBN 0-07-015226-8, GB). McGraw.

Davis, James A. Education for Positive Mental Health: A Review of Existing Research & Recommendations for Future Studies. LC 64-15607. (Monographs in Social Research: No. 5). 1965. 7.95x (ISBN 0-202-09009-4). NORC.

Dawley, Harold. Freedom from Fear. (Illus.). 256p. 1980. pap. 2.50 (ISBN 0-448-17186-4, Tempo). Ace Bks.

Day, Stacey B., et al. Biopsychosocial Health. 225p. 1980. pap. 15.00 (ISBN 0-934314-02-0). Intl Found Biosocial Dev.

DeCusa, Nicolas. Idiota de Mente. Miller, Clyde L., tr. LC 77-812. (Bilingual Editions of Classics in Philosophy & Science: Ser. 3). 1980. 20.00 (ISBN 0-913870-65-X). Abaris Bks.

De Langre, Jacques. Food Consciousness for Spiritual Development. LC 80-84993. (Illus., Orig.). 1980. pap. 6.00 (ISBN 0-916508-05-6). Happiness Pr.

Deutsch, Albert, ed. Encyclopedia of Mental Health. LC 63-7150. 1970. Repr. of 1963 ed. 45.00 (ISBN 0-8108-0357-7). Scarecrow.

Di Bella, Geoffrey A., et al. Partial Hospital Programs: A Comprehensive Guide. 450p. 1981. 30.00 (ISBN 0-87630-270-3). Brunner-Mazel.

Dorwart, R. A. & Meyers, W. R. Citizen Participation in Mental Health. 1981. write for info. (ISBN 0-398-04522-4). C C Thomas.

Driver, Helen I., et al. Counseling & Learning Through Small-Group Discussion. library ed. (Illus.). 1970. lib. bdg. 8.95 (ISBN 0-910982-02-3). Monona.

Dudley, Donald M. & Welke, Elton. How to Survive Being Alive. 1979. pap. 1.95 (ISBN 0-451-08958-8, J8958, Sig). NAL.

Dunn, Halbert L. High Level Wellness. 7th ed. (Positive Health Bookshelf, Vol. 1). 1972. 8.95 (ISBN 0-87948-002-5); pap. 5.95 (ISBN 0-685-06827-7). Beatty.

Egenter, Richard & Matussek, Paul. Moral Problems & Mental Health. 1967. 4.95 (ISBN 0-8189-0095-4). Alba.

Ellis, Albert & Abrams, Eliot. Comprehensive Treatment of Major Mental Disorders. (General Psychology Ser.). Date not set. 17.50t (ISBN 0-08-025538-8). Pergamon.

Engelhardt, H. Tristram & Spicker, Stuart F., eds. Mental Health: Philosophical Perspectives. LC 77-24974. (Philosophy & Medicine Ser.: No. 4). 1977. lib. bdg. 29.00 (ISBN 90-277-0828-2, Pub. by Reidel Holland). Kluwer Boston.

Fabriant, Benjamin, et al. To Enjoy Is to Live: Psychotherapy Explained. LC 76-40141. 1977. 15.95 (ISBN 0-88229-148-3). Nelson-Hall.

Felicetti, Daniel A. Mental Health & Retardation Politics: The Mind Lobbies in Congress. LC 74-14042. (Illus.). 218p. 1975. text ed. 22.95 (ISBN 0-275-09930-X). Praeger.

Ferman, Louis A. & Gordus, Jeanne P., eds. Mental Health & the Economy. LC 79-25809. 1979. text ed. 8.50 (ISBN 0-911558-69-1); pap. text ed. 6.25 (ISBN 0-911558-68-3). Upjohn Inst.

Fink, David H. Release from Nervous Tension. (Orig.). 1962. pap. 4.95 (ISBN 0-671-21248-6, Fireside). S&S.

Finney, Joseph. Culture Change, Mental Health & Poverty. 1970. pap. 2.95 (ISBN 0-671-20548-X, Touchstone Bks). S&S.

Fisher, Walter, et al. Human Services: The Third Revolution in Mental Health. LC 74-75481. (Illus.). 360p. 1974. 14.50x (ISBN 0-88284-013-4). Alfred Pub.

Freedman, Daniel X., ed. Yearbook of Psychiatry & Applied Mental Health, 1981. 1981. 39.95 (ISBN 0-8151-3328-6). Year Bk Med.

Freedman, Daniel X., et al, eds. Year Book of Psychiatry & Applied Mental Health, 1979. 1979. 36.50 (ISBN 0-8151-3325-1). Year Bk Med.

Freudenberger, Herbert J. & Richelson, Geraldine. Burn-Out. 224p. 1981. pap. 3.95 (ISBN 0-553-20048-8). Bantam.

Fromme, Allan. The Book for Normal Neurotics. 1981. 10.95 (ISBN 0-374-11544-3). FS&G.

Fryrear, Jerry L. & Fleshman, Robert. Videotherapy in Mental Health. (Illus.). 352p. 1981. pap. text ed. 36.50 (ISBN 0-398-04117-2). C C Thomas.

Furst, Bruno. Stop Forgetting. Furst, Lotte & Storm, Gerrit, eds. LC 79-7401. (Illus.). 1979. pap. 6.95 (ISBN 0-385-15401-1). Doubleday.
GAP Committee on International Relations. Self-Involvement in the Middle East Conflict, Vol. 10. LC 78-12608. (Publication: No. 103). 1978. pap. 6.00 (ISBN 0-87318-140-9, Pub. by Adv Psychiatry). Mental Health.
Gary, Lawrence E., ed. Mental Health: A Challenge to the Black Community. 1978. text ed. 12.00 (ISBN 0-8059-2493-0). Dorrance.
Gilbert, Jeanne G. & Sullivan, Catherine M. The Mental Health Aide. LC 76-14843. 1976. pap. text ed. 5.75 (ISBN 0-8261-2180-2). Springer Pub.
Gilbert, Ruth. Public Health Nurse & Her Patient. 2nd rev. ed. LC 51-12517. (Commonwealth Fund Publications Ser). 1951. 17.50x (ISBN 0-674-72300-7). Harvard U Pr.
Giordano, Joseph. Ethnicity & Mental Health: Research & Recommendations. 1980. pap. 2.00 (ISBN 0-87495-006-6). Am Jewish Comm.
Giordano, Joseph & Giordano, Grace P. The Ethno-Cultural Factor in Mental Health: A Literature Review & Bibliography. 1977. pap. 2.25 (ISBN 0-87495-007-4). Am Jewish Comm.
Gladstone, William. Test Your Own Mental Health. 1979. pap. 1.95 (ISBN 0-451-08757-7, J8757, Sig). NAL.
Glasscote, R. M. & Fishman, M. E. Mental Health on the Campus: A Field Study. 216p. 1973. 8.50 (ISBN 0-685-77454-6, P202-0). Am Psychiatric.
Glasser, William. Mental Health or Mental Illness: Psychiatry for Practical Action. 1970. pap. 2.50 (ISBN 0-06-080149-2, P149, PL). Har-Row.
Goldberg, Jacob A. Social Aspects of the Treatment of the Insane. LC 77-78005. (Columbia University. Studies in the Social Sciences: No. 221). Repr. of 1921 ed. 19.50 (ISBN 0-404-51221-6). AMS Pr.
Goldberg, Joan & Hymowitz, Ellen. Mental Health Activities in the Classroom: A Handbook. LC 77-71458. 31p. 1977. pap. text ed. 9.90x (ISBN 0-87424-149-9). Western Psych.
Greenblatt, M., et al, eds. Poverty & Mental Health: PRR 21. 275p. 1967. pap. 5.00 (ISBN 0-685-24868-2, P021-0). Am Psychiatric.
Griffin, J. D., et al. Mental Hygiene: A Manual for Teachers. 1978. Repr. of 1940 ed. lib. bdg. 25.00 (ISBN 0-8495-1920-9). Arden Lib.
Grob, Gerald N., ed. Historical Issues in Mental Health Series, 45 bks. (Illus.). 1979. Repr. lib. bdg. 988.00x set (ISBN 0-405-11900-3). Arno.
Groves, Ernest R. Understanding Yourself: The Mental Hygiene of Personality. (gr. 7 up). 1941. 7.95 (ISBN 0-87523-044-X). Emerson.
Gurin, Gerald, et al. Americans View Their Mental Health. Grob, Gerald N., ed. LC 78-22564. (Historical Issues in Mental Health Ser.). (Illus.). 1979. Repr. of 1960 ed. lib. bdg. 30.00x (ISBN 0-405-11918-6). Arno.
Gutteneag, Marcia. The Evaluation of Training in Mental Health. LC 74-8506. 1975. 16.95 (ISBN 0-87705-161-5). Human Sci Pr.
Haas, Harold I. El Cristiano Frente a los Problemas Mentales. De Molina, Sara Pais, tr. 1977. Repr. of 1975 ed. 2.25 (ISBN 0-311-42500-3). Casa Bautista.
Haefner, H., ed. Estimating Needs for Mental Health Care: A Contribution of Epidemiology. (Illus.). 1979. pap. 21.30 (ISBN 0-387-09425-3). Springer-Verlag.
Halpern, Reuben & Halpern, Joshua. Live Your Health: The Art & Practice of Holistic Healing. (Healing Arts Ser.). 220p. 1980. 10.95 (ISBN 0-89496-028-8); pap. 5.95 (ISBN 0-89496-020-2). Ross Bks.
Harris, Thomas. I'm OK-You're OK. 1973. pap. 2.75 (ISBN 0-380-00772-X, 52795). Avon.
Harris, Thomas A. I'm Ok-You're Ok: A Practical Guide to Transactional Analysis. LC 69-13495. (Illus.). 1969. 10.95 (ISBN 0-06-002385-6, HarpT). Har-Row.
Heath, Douglas H. Maturity & Competence: A Transcultural View. 1977. 19.95 (ISBN 0-470-99072-4). Halsted Pr.
Heinroth, Johann Christian. Textbook of Disturbances of Mental Life. Incl. Theory. (Vol. I); Practice. (Vol. II). 1975. 28.50x (ISBN 0-8018-1485-5). Johns Hopkins.
Hirschowitz, R. G. & Levy, B., eds. The Changing Mental Health Scene. LC 75-42398. 382p. 1976. 27.50 (ISBN 0-470-14981-7). Halsted Pr.
Hosler, Virginia N. & Fadely, Jack L. Holistic Mental Health for Tomorrow's Children: For Teachers & Mental Health Workers. (Illus.). 314p. 1981. 26.75 (ISBN 0-398-04472-4). C C Thomas.
Hutchenecker, Arnold A. Will to Happiness. rev. ed. 1970. text ed. 4.95 (ISBN 0-671-27063-X). Trident.
Hutschnecker, Arnold A. The Will to Live. 1966. pap. 4.95 (ISBN 0-346-12259-7). Cornerstone.
Hyman, Ruth B. & Woog, Pierre. Current Non-Projective Instruments for the Mental Health Field. 1978. looseleaf 25.50 (ISBN 0-915260-08-5). Atcom.
Jahoda, Marie. Current Concepts in Positive Mental Health. Grob, Gerald N., ed. LC 78-22567. (Historical Issues in Mental Health Ser.). 1979. Repr. of 1958 ed. lib. bdg. 12.00x (ISBN 0-405-11921-6). Arno.
Jansen, Elly, ed. The Therapeutic Community: Outside the Hospital. 392p. 1980. 31.50x (ISBN 0-85664-967-8, Pub. by Croom Helm Ltd England). Biblio Dist.
Johnson, Wendell. People in Quandaries: The Semantics of Personal Adjustment. 1946. text ed. 20.95 scp (ISBN 0-06-043380-9, HarpC). Har-Row.
Joint Commission on Mental Illness & Health. Action for Mental Health. Grob, Gerald N., ed. LC 78-22569. (Historical Issues in Mental Health Ser.). 1979. Repr. of 1961 ed. lib. bdg. 24.00x (ISBN 0-405-11922-4). Arno.
Jones, C. D. Hominology: Psychiatry's Newest Frontier. (Illus.). 216p. 1975. 16.00 (ISBN 0-398-03244-0). C C Thomas.
Kahn, Marvin W. Basic Methods for Mental Health Practitioners. 350p. 1981. text ed. 15.95 (ISBN 0-87626-052-0, W0520-4). Winthrop.
Kellam, Sheppard G., et al. Mental Health & Going to School. LC 74-10341. xvi, 214p. 1975. text ed. 11.00x (ISBN 0-226-42968-7). U of Chicago Pr.
Keller, Peter A. & Murray, Dennis J. Handbook of Rural Community Mental Health. 1981. 29.95 (ISBN 0-89885-065-7). Human Sci Pr.
Keyes, Fenton. Your Future in a Mental Health Career. (Careers in Depth Ser.). (Illus.). 180p. (gr. 7-12). 1981. PLB 5.97 (ISBN 0-8239-0362-1). Rosen Pr.
Kieffer. Mental Health & Industry. LC 80-18057. 1980. 22.95 (ISBN 0-87705-085-6). Human Sci Pr.
Kirkpatrick, Edwin A. Mental Hygiene for Effective Living. (Educational Ser.). 1934. Repr. 10.00 (ISBN 0-685-43623-3). Norwood Edns.
Koocher, Gerald P., ed. Children's Rights & the Mental Health Professions. LC 76-16062. (Personality Processes Ser.). 259p. 1976. 29.95 (ISBN 0-471-01736-1, Pub. by Wiley-Interscience). Wiley.
Kornhauser, Arthur. Mental Health of the Industrial Worker: A Detroit Study. LC 75-11966. 366p. 1975. Repr. of 1965 ed. 16.00 (ISBN 0-88275-295-2). Krieger.
Kotinsky, Ruth & Witmer, Helen L. Community Programs for Mental Health: Theory, Practice, Evaluation. LC 55-11030. (Commonwealth Fund Publications Ser). 1955. 18.50x (ISBN 0-674-15151-8). Harvard U Pr.
Kramer, M. Application of Mental Health Statistics: Uses in Mental Health Programmes of Statistics Derived from Psychiatric Service & Selected Vital & Morbidity Records. (Illus.). 112p. 1969. pap. 4.80 (ISBN 92-4-156013-4, 1141). World Health.
Kremer, Bruce. Mental Health in the Schools. 2nd ed. 340p. 1981. lib. bdg. 20.75 (ISBN 0-8191-1572-X); pap. text ed. 11.75 (ISBN 0-8191-1573-8). U Pr of Amer.
Kupfer, David J., et al. Mental Health Information Systems: Design and Implementation. (Library & Information Science Ser.: Vol. 19). 1976. 27.75 (ISBN 0-8247-6445-5). Dekker.
--Mental Health Information Systems: Design and Implementation. (Library & Information Science Ser.: Vol. 19). 1976. 27.75 (ISBN 0-8247-6445-5). Dekker.
Kurpius, DeWayne J., et al, eds. Supervision of Applied Training: A Comparative Review. LC 76-28640. 1977. lib. bdg. 17.50x (ISBN 0-8371-9288-9, KSA/). Greenwood.
Lancaster, Jeanette, ed. Community Mental Health Nursing: An Ecological Perspective. LC 79-26185. (Illus.). 1980. pap. text ed. 11.45 (ISBN 0-8016-2816-4). Mosby.
Lauffer, Armand. Practice of Continuing Education in the Human Services. (Illus.). 1977. text ed. 12.95 (ISBN 0-07-036625-X, C). McGraw.
Lawrence, Margaret M. The Mental Health Team in the Schools. LC 79-140048. 1971. text ed. 19.95 (ISBN 0-87705-015-5). Human Sci Pr.
Lawton, George, ed. New Goals for Old Age. LC 76-169390. (Family in America Ser). 230p. 1972. Repr. of 1943 ed. 14.00 (ISBN 0-405-03868-2). Arno.
Leedy, Jack J., ed. Compensation in Psychiatric Disability & Rehabilitation. (Illus.). 384p. 1971. 36.75 (ISBN 0-398-02186-4). C C Thomas.
Levinson, Harry. Emotional Health in the World of Work. rev ed. 298p. 1964. pap. 7.95 (ISBN 0-916516-03-2). Levinson Inst.
Levinson, Harry, et al. Men, Management, & Mental Health. LC 62-19218. 1962. 10.00x (ISBN 0-674-56700-5). Harvard U Pr.
Levitt, Morton & Rubenstein, Ben, eds. Mental Health Field: A Critical Appraisal. LC 79-135397. 1971. 14.95x (ISBN 0-8143-1438-4). Wayne St U Pr.
Lieberman, E. James, ed. Mental Health: The Public Health Challange. 1975. pap. 6.00x (ISBN 0-87553-075-3, 021). Am Pub Health.
Lindvig, Elise. Nutrition & Mental Health. LC 79-65602. 170p. (Orig.). 1979. pap. 5.95 (ISBN 0-89301-064-2). U Pr of Idaho.
Looff, David H. Appalachia's Children: The Challenge of Mental Health. LC 78-132830. 208p. 1971. 11.00 (ISBN 0-8131-1241-9); pap. 6.50 (ISBN 0-8131-0144-1). U Pr of Ky.
Low, Abraham A. Lectures to Relatives of Former Patients. 1967. 6.95 (ISBN 0-8158-0139-4). Chris Mass.
--Mental Health Through Will-Training. 20th ed. 1976. 10.95 (ISBN 0-8158-0001-0). Chris Mass.
McQuade, Walter & Aikman, Ann. Stress. 256p. 1975. pap. 2.95 (ISBN 0-553-20469-6, C13591-0). Bantam.
Magoon, T. M., et al. Mental Health Counsellors at Work. 1971. 32.00 (ISBN 0-08-006422-1). Pergamon.
Maki, Lillian. Mother, God, & Mental Health. LC 79-92840. 1980. pap. 4.95 (ISBN 0-8323-0353-4). Binford.
Malamud, Daniel I. & Machover, Solomon. Toward Self-Understanding: Group Techniques in Self-Confrontation. (American Lecture Psychology Ser.). 288p. 1975. 15.50 (ISBN 0-398-01204-0). C C Thomas.
Manderscheid, Ronald W. & Manderscheid, Frances E., eds. Systems Science & the Future of Health. LC 76-8743. (Illus.). 1976. pap. 12.00 (ISBN 0-916964-01-9). Groome Ctr.
Mannino, F. V., et al, eds. The Practice of Mental Health Consultation. 255p. 1975. 13.95 (ISBN 0-470-56774-0). Halsted Pr.
Martin, Alfred. Mental Health: Psychotherapy of Tomorrow. (Synthesis Ser.). 125p. 1980. pap. 1.50 (ISBN 0-8199-0370-1). Franciscan Herald.
Mathes, Eugene W. From Survival to the Universe: Values & Psychological Well-Being. LC 81-9583. 232p. 1981. text ed. 18.95x (ISBN 0-88229-595-0); pap. text ed. 9.95x (ISBN 0-88229-790-2). Nelson-Hall.
Mathews, Arthur G. Take It Easy: The Art of Conquering Your Nerves. (Illus.). 1945. 7.95 (ISBN 0-911378-25-1). Sheridan.
May, Gerald G. Simply Sane. 1977. lib. bdg. 7.95 (ISBN 0-8161-6516-5, Large Print Bks). G K Hall.
Mechanic, David. Mental Health & Social Policy. 2nd ed. (Ser. in Social Policy). 1980. pap. text ed. 10.95 (ISBN 0-13-576025-9). P-H.
Menninger, Karl. Human Mind. rev. ed. 1945. 17.95 (ISBN 0-394-42964-8). Knopf.
Mental Health in the Classroom. 1968. 2.50 (ISBN 0-917160-05-3). Am Sch Health.
Miller, Donald. Bodymind: The Whole Person Health Book. LC 73-20280. (Illus.). 224p. 1974. pap. 4.50 (ISBN 0-13-079616-6). P-H.
Mishara, Brian & Patterson, Robert. Consumer's Handbook of Mental Health: How to Find, Select & Use Help. 1979. pap. 2.25 (ISBN 0-451-08608-2, E8608, Sig). NAL.
Moloney, James C. Battle for Mental Health. 1952. 3.50 (ISBN 0-8022-1135-6). Philos Lib.
Morgan, Arthur J. & Johnston, Mabyl K. Mental Health & Mental Illness. 2nd ed. LC 76-14855. 1976. pap. 11.75 (ISBN 0-397-54189-9, JBL-Med-Nursing). Har-Row.
Mosak, Harold H. On Purpose: Collected Papers. LC 76-42942. 1977. pap. 8.00x (ISBN 0-918560-19-5). A Adler Inst.
Mosak, Harold H. & Laude, Edward J. Professional Issues in the Delivery of Mental Health Services: A Syllabus. 1976. pap. 2.00x (ISBN 0-918560-05-5). A Adler Inst.
Mosey, Anne Cronin. Three Frames of Reference for Mental Health. LC 77-140200. 241p. 1970. 21.95 (ISBN 0-913590-00-2). C B Slack.
Muller, C., ed. Ecology & Mental Health. (Psychiatria Clinica: Vol. 7, Nos. 4-5). 100p. 1974. 33.75 (ISBN 3-8055-2212-6). S Karger.
Myerson, Abraham. Speaking of Man. Grob, Gerald N., ed. LC 78-22577. (Historical Issues in Mental Health Ser.). 1979. Repr. of 1950 ed. lib. bdg. 18.00x (ISBN 0-405-11929-1). Arno.
Neuman, Fredric. Caring: Home Treatment for the Emotionally Disturbed. 245p. 1980. 10.95 (ISBN 0-8037-0969-2). Dial.
Norback, Judith. Mental Health Yearbook & Directory, 1979-1980. 1979. pap. text ed. 39.50 (ISBN 0-442-26065-2). Van Nos Reinhold.
Offer, Daniel & Sabshin, Melvin. Normality: Clinical & Theoretical Concepts of Mental Health. rev. ed. LC 74-79288. 1974. 11.50x (ISBN 0-465-05147-2). Basic.
Owens, Charles E. Mental Health & Black Offenders. LC 78-19588. 208p. 1980. 21.95 (ISBN 0-669-02645-X). Lexington Bks.
Park, Clara C. & Shapiro, Leon N. You Are Not Alone: Understanding & Dealing with Mental Illness. 1979. 15.00 (ISBN 0-316-69073-2); pap. 6.95 (ISBN 0-316-69075-9). Little.
Parker, Beulah. Mental Health In-Service Training: Some Practical Guidelines for the Psychiatric Consultant. LC 68-26388. 1968. text ed. 13.50 (ISBN 0-8236-3360-8). Intl Univs Pr.
Payne, Dorris B. Psychiatric-Mental Health Nursing. 2nd. ed. Clunn, Patricia A., ed. LC 77-71852. (Nursing Outline Ser.). 1977. pap. 8.50 spiral bdg. (ISBN 0-87488-379-2). Med Exam.
Pepper, Bertram, et al, eds. The Social Setting of Mental Health. LC 75-7259. (Illus.). 1976. text ed. 17.50x (ISBN 0-465-07918-0). Basic.
Posovac, Emil J. Impacts of Program Evaluation on Mental Health Care. (Westview Special Studies in Health Care). 1979. lib. bdg. 23.25x (ISBN 0-89158-271-1). Westview.
Pothier, Patricia C. Mental Health Counseling with Children: A Guide for Beginning Counselors. LC 75-30296. 1976. pap. text ed. 12.95 (ISBN 0-316-71483-6). Little.
Price, Richard H., et al, eds. Prevention in Mental Health: Research, Policy, & Practice. LC 80-14676. (Sage Annual Reviews of Community Mental Health: Vol. 1). (Illus.). 320p. 1981. 22.50 (ISBN 0-8039-1468-7); pap. 9.95 (ISBN 0-8039-1469-5). Sage.
Prien, Erich P., et al. Mental Health in Organizations: Personal Adjustment & Constructive Intervention. LC 78-16757. 1978. 16.95x (ISBN 0-88229-175-0). Nelson-Hall.
Rapopart, Robert N. & Rapopart, Rhona. Community As Doctor. Grob, Gerald N., ed. LC 78-22587. (Historical Issues in Mental Health Ser.). (Illus.). 1979. Repr. of 1960 ed. lib. bdg. 20.00x (ISBN 0-405-11938-0). Arno.
Rathbone, R. S. & Rathbone, E. Health & the Nature of Man. 1971. 9.95 (ISBN 0-07-051205-1, C); pap. 9.95 (ISBN 0-07-051206-X); instructors' manual 2.95 (ISBN 0-07-051207-8). McGraw.
Readings in Mental Health Education. 1976. 5.00x (ISBN 0-685-67032-5, 244-25830). AAHPERD.
Ribble, Margaretha A. The Rights of Infants: Early Psychological Needs & Their Satisfaction. 2nd ed. LC 65-24832. 1965. 15.00x (ISBN 0-231-02849-0). Columbia U Pr.
Richardson, Herbert W., ed. New Religions & Mental Health: Understanding the Issues. (Symposium Ser.: Vol. 5). (Orig.). 1980. soft cover 11.95x (ISBN 0-88946-910-5). E Mellen.
Riess, Bernard F., ed. New Directions in Mental Health, 2 Vols. LC 68-25832. 1968. Vol. I. 32.50 (ISBN 0-8089-0379-9); Vol. II. 36.25 (ISBN 0-8089-0380-2). Grune.
Roberts, Leigh M., et al, eds. Comprehensive Mental Health: The Challenge of Evaluation. (Illus.). 1968. 27.50x (ISBN 0-299-05000-9). U of Wis Pr.
Rudman, Jack. Health Two: Personal Health, Emotional-Social Aspects. (ACT Proficiency Examination Program: PEP-34). 14.95 (ISBN 0-8373-5584-2); pap. 9.95 (ISBN 0-8373-5534-6). Natl Learning.
--Mental Health Aide. (Career Examination Ser.: C-1372). (Cloth bdg. avail. on request). pap. 10.00 (ISBN 0-8373-1372-4). Natl Learning.
--Mental Health Geriatric Consultant. (Career Examination Ser.: C-1582). (Cloth bdg. avail. on request). pap. 12.00 (ISBN 0-8373-1582-4). Natl Learning.
--Mental Hygiene Therapy Assistant. (Career Examination Ser.: C-2188). (Cloth bdg. avail. on request). pap. 10.00 (ISBN 0-8373-2188-3). Natl Learning.
--Mental Hygiene Treatment Group Leader. (Career Examination Ser.: C-1885). (Cloth bdg. avail. on request). pap. 10.00 (ISBN 0-8373-1885-8). Natl Learning.
--Senior Mental Health Worker. (Career Examination Ser.: C-1925). (Cloth bdg. avail. on request). 10.00 (ISBN 0-8373-1925-0). Natl Learning.
Sankar, D. Siva, ed. Mental Health in Children, Vol. 3. LC 74-27252. 1976. 37.50 (ISBN 0-9600290-9-5). PJD Pubns.
Sanker, D. Siva, ed. Mental Health in Children, Vol. 2. LC 74-27252. 1976. 37.50 (ISBN 0-9600290-8-7). PJD Pubns.
Sauber, S. Richard. Preventive Educational Intervention for Mental Health. LC 73-11002. 144p. 1973. text ed. 16.50 (ISBN 0-88410-154-1). Ballinger Pub.
Schaffer, Kay F. Sex-Role Issues in Mental Health. LC 79-53872. (Clinical & Professional Psychology Ser.). 1980. pap. text ed. 7.95 (ISBN 0-201-06762-5). A-W.
Schainblatt, Alfred H. Monitoring the Outcomes of State Mental Health Treatment Programs: Some Initial Suggestions. (An Institute Paper). 86p. 1977. pap. 4.00 (ISBN 0-87766-202-9, 19400). Urban Inst.

Schindler, John. How to Live Three Hundred & Sixty Five Days a Year. 1954. pap. 3.95 (ISBN 0-13-416792-9, Parker). P-H.

Schwab, John J. Social Order & Mental Health: The Florida Health Study. LC 78-13105. 1979. 17.50 (ISBN 0-87630-185-5). Brunner-Mazel.

Sedgwick, Rae. Family Mental Health: Theory & Practice. LC 80-20160. (Illus.). 296p. 1980. pap. text ed. 10.45 (ISBN 0-8016-4447-X). Mosby.

A Selective Guide to Audiovisuals for Mental Health & Family Life Education. 4th ed. LC 78-71072. 1979. pap. 24.50 (ISBN 0-8379-5101-1). Marquis.

A Selective Guide to Publications for Mental Health & Family Life Education. 4th ed. LC 78-71071. 1979. pap. 34.50 (ISBN 0-8379-5001-5). Marquis.

Shore, Milton F. & Mannino, Fortune V., eds. Mental Health & Social Change, No. 7. LC 74-26634. (AMS Studies in Modern Society). 23.50 (ISBN 0-404-11277-3). AMS Pr.

Sicherman, Barbara. Quest for Mental Health in America, Eighteen Eighty to Nineteen Seventeen. Grob, Gerald N., ed. LC 78-22589. (Historical Issues in Mental Health Ser.). 1979. lib. bdg. 30.00x (ISBN 0-405-11940-2). Arno.

Silverman, Wade H. Community Mental Health: A Sourcebook for Professionals & Advisors. 450p. 1981. 39.95 (ISBN 0-03-057006-9). Praeger.

Simmons, Roberta G., ed. Research in Community & Mental Health: An Annual Compilation of Research, Vol. 1. 1979. lib. bdg. 37.50 (ISBN 0-89232-063-X). Jai Pr.

Smith, William D., et al. Minority Issues in Mental Health. LC 77-83032. (Topics in Clinical Psychology). (Illus.). 1978. pap. text ed. 6.95 (ISBN 0-201-07478-8). A-W.

Sobey, Francine. Nonprofessional Revolution in Mental Health. LC 71-118355. 1970. 15.00x (ISBN 0-231-03304-4). Columbia U Pr.

Sourcebook on Mental Health. 2nd ed. 660p. 1981. cancelled (ISBN 0-8379-4802-9). Marquis.

Sourcebook on Mental Health. LC 78-65722. 1979. pap. 29.50 (ISBN 0-8379-4801-0). Marquis.

Srole, Leo. Mental Health in the Metropolis: The Midtown Manhattan Study. Fisher, Anita K., ed. (Illus.). 8.50 (ISBN 0-8446-5247-4). Peter Smith.

Srole, Leo & Fisher, Anita K., eds. Mental Health in the Metropolis: The Midtown Manhattan Study. LC 77-76507. 1978. 28.50x (ISBN 0-8147-7782-1). NYU Pr.

Srole, Leo, et al. Mental Health in the Metropolis, Bk. 2. 1977. pap. 7.50x (ISBN 0-06-131915-5, TB 1915, Torch). Har-Row.

Stahler, Gerald J. & Tash, William R. Innovative Approaches to Mental Health Evaluation. 1981. price not set (ISBN 0-12-663020-8). Acad Pr.

Stainback, William & Stainback, Susan. Educating Children with Severe Maladaptive Behaviors. 320p. 1980. 24.50 (ISBN 0-8089-1269-0). Grune.

Stanton, Esther. Clients Come Last: Volunteers & Welfare Organizations. LC 71-103484. 192p. 1970. 15.00x (ISBN 0-8039-0063-5). Sage.

Stein, L. I. & Test, M. A., eds. Alternatives to Mental Hospital Treatment. LC 77-17576. 335p. 1978. 27.50 (ISBN 0-306-31120-8, Plenum Pr). Plenum Pub.

Stein, Laszlo K., et al, eds. Deafness & Mental Health. 272p. 1981. 29.50 (ISBN 0-8089-1347-6, 794328). Grune.

Stolten, Jane Henry. The Mental Health Worker. 1981. pap. text ed. 9.95 (ISBN 0-316-81744-9). Little.

Stone, Alan A. Malpractice & the Mental Health Professions. LC 78-19812. Date not set. 15.00 (ISBN 0-465-04329-1). Basic.

Sue, Stanley & Moore, Thomas. The Pluralistic Society: A Community Mental Health Perspective. Bloom, Bernard, ed. (Community Psychology Ser.: Vol. 9). 1982. in prep. (ISBN 0-89885-055-X). Human Sci Pr.

Tancredi, Lawrence P. & Slaby, Andrew E. Ethical Policy in Mental Health Care: The Goals of Psychiatric Intervention. LC 77-1996. 1977. 20.00 (ISBN 0-88202-102-8). N Watson.

Thackery, Milton G. & Skidmore, Rex A. Introduction to Mental Health: Field & Practice. (P-H Series in Social Work Practice). (Illus.). 1979. text ed. 18.95 (ISBN 0-13-487801-9). P-H.

Trower, Peter, et al. Social Skills & Mental Health. LC 77-10544. (Contemporary Community Health Ser.). 1978. 14.95x (ISBN 0-8229-1131-0). U of Pittsburgh Pr.

Turnbull, H. Rutherford, III, ed. Consent Handbook. LC 77-75282. 1977. pap. 4.40 (ISBN 0-686-24120-7). Am Assn Mental.

Valletutti, P. Preventing Physical & Mental Disabilities. 1979. 19.50 (ISBN 0-8391-1381-1). Univ Park.

Veroff, Joseph, et al. Mental Health in America. LC 80-68959. 1981. 37.50x (ISBN 0-465-04479-4). Basic.

Wall, W. D. Education & Mental Health. 1967. Repr. 4.50 (ISBN 0-685-20784-6, U190, UNESCO). Unipub.

Wallin, E. Wallace. The Mental Health of the School Child. (Educational Ser.). 1914. Repr. 20.00 (ISBN 0-685-43534-2). Norwood Edns.

Wallin, J. Wallace. Personality Maladjustments & Mental Hygiene. (Educational Ser.). 1935. Repr. 25.00 (ISBN 0-685-43535-0). Norwood Edns.

Weekes, Claire. Hope & Help for Your Nerves. 1978. pap. 2.50 (ISBN 0-553-14672-6). Bantam.

Wesley, Roland. Aspects of Mental Health: A Guide to Understanding the Meaning of Mental Illness. 1979. pap. 4.95 (ISBN 0-686-25245-4). Carlinshar.

Westemeyer, Joseph, ed. Anthropology & Mental Health. (World Anthropology Ser.). 1977. 24.00x (ISBN 0-202-90044-4). Beresford Bk Serv.

Westlake, Robert J., ed. Shaping the Future of Mental Health Care. LC 76-3437. 1976. text ed. 17.50 (ISBN 0-88410-133-9). Ballinger Pub.

White, Ellen G. Mind, Character, & Personality: Guidelines to Mental & Spiritual Health, 2 vols. (Christian Home Library). 1978. 5.95 ea. Vol. 1 (ISBN 0-8127-0148-8). Vol. 2 (ISBN 0-8127-0149-6). Review & Herald.

White, William A. The Mental Hygiene of Childhood. Grob, Gerald N., ed. LC 78-22595. (Historical Issues in Mental Health Ser.). 1979. Repr. of 1919 ed. lib. bdg. 14.00x (ISBN 0-405-11945-3). Arno.

Whittington, H. G. Psychiatry in the American Community. LC 66-24393. 1969. Repr. of 1966 ed. text ed. 25.00 (ISBN 0-8236-5460-5). Intl Univs Pr.

WHO Expert Committee on Mental Health. Geneva, 1974, 16th. Organization of Mental Health Services in Developing Countries: Report. (Technical Report Ser.: No. 564). (Also avail. in French & Spanish). 1975. pap. 2.40 (ISBN 92-4-120564-4). World Health.

WHO Seminar on the Organization of Mental Health Services, Addis Ababa, 1973. Mental Health Services in Developing Countries: Papers. Baasher, T. A., et al, eds. (Offset Pub.: No. 22). (Also avail. in French). 1975. pap. 7.20 (ISBN 92-4-170022-X). World Health.

Wiener, A. W. Mental Health for the Nonprofessional. 88p. 1980. 9.75 (ISBN 0-398-04010-9); pap. 5.95 (ISBN 0-398-04011-7). C C Thomas.

Williams, Thomas A. & Johnson, James H. Mental Health in the Twenty-First Century. LC 78-20270. 208p. 1979. 21.95x (ISBN 0-669-02718-9). Lexington Bks.

Wilson, John P. The Rights of Adolescents in the Mental Health System. LC 77-4542. 1978. 24.95 (ISBN 0-669-01485-0). Lexington Bks.

Wise, Robert. How Not to Go Crazy. 160p. (Orig.). 1980. pap. 3.95 (ISBN 0-89081-237-3). Harvest Hse.

Witty, Paul A., ed. Mental Health in Modern Education. (National Society for the Study of Education Yearbooks Ser: No. 54, Pt. 2). 1955. pap. 4.50x (ISBN 0-226-60034-3). U of Chicago Pr.

Wolberg, Lewis R. & Kildahl, John P. The Dynamics of Personality. LC 75-91600. 336p. 1970. 31.75 (ISBN 0-8089-0539-2). Grune.

Wookfolk, Robert I. & Richardson, Frank C. Stress, Sanity & Survival. 1979. pap. 2.25 (ISBN 0-451-09716-5, E9716, Sig). NAL.

Yale University Division of Student Mental Hygiene Staff. Psychosocial Problems of College Men. Wedge, Bryant M., ed. LC 72-85303. 304p. 1973. Repr. of 1958 ed. 15.00 (ISBN 0-8046-1710-4). Kennikat.

MENTAL HEALTH–BIBLIOGRAPHY

Chicorel Index to Mental Health Book Reviews: 1979 Annual, Vol. 26. 400p. 1980. 85.00 (ISBN 0-934598-79-7). Am Lib Pub Co.

Chicorel Index to Mental Health Book Reviews: 1977 Annual, Vol. 26. 400p. 1978. 85.00 (ISBN 0-934598-77-0). Am Lib Pub Co.

Chicorel Index to Mental Health Book Reviews: 1978 Annual, Vol. 26. 400p. 1980. 85.00 (ISBN 0-934598-08-8). Am Lib Pub Co.

DiCaprio, Nicholas S. Adjustment: Fulfilling Human Potentials. (Illus.). 1980. text ed. 15.95 (ISBN 0-13-004101-7). P-H.

Driver, Edwin D. The Sociology & Anthropology of Mental Illness: A Reference Guide. rev. ed. LC 71-103476. 504p. 1972. pap. 20.00x (ISBN 0-87023-062-X). U of Mass Pr.

Mental Health Materials Center, ed. Current Audiovisuals for Mental Health Education. 2nd ed. LC 78-71134. 1979. pap. 8.50 (ISBN 0-8379-5201-8). Marquis.

Schwartz, Steven J. & Ferrarone, Stephen F. Community Mental Health & the Law: An Annotated Bibliography. LC 80-18872. 256p. 1981. 24.50x (ISBN 0-8290-0239-1). Irvington.

MENTAL HEALTH–EUROPE

May, A. R. Mental Health Services in Europe. (Offset Pub.: No. 23). (Also avail. in French). 1976. pap. 4.80 (ISBN 92-4-170023-8). World Health.

MENTAL HEALTH–GREAT BRITAIN

Jones, Kathleen. A History of the Mental Health Services. (International Library of Social Policy). 422p. 1972. 30.00x (ISBN 0-7100-7452-2). Routledge & Kegan.

MENTAL HEALTH–ISRAEL

Weinberg, A. A. Migration & Belonging: A Study in Mental Health & Personal Adjustment in Israel. LC 62-1150. 1961. 22.50x (ISBN 90-247-0511-8). Intl Pubns Serv.

MENTAL HEALTH ASSOCIATES

see Allied Mental Health Personnel

MENTAL HEALTH CLINICS

see Psychiatric Clinics

MENTAL HEALTH CONSULTATION

see Psychiatric Consultation

MENTAL HEALTH LAWS

see also Insanity–Jurisprudence; Narcotic Addicts

Allen, Richard C., et al, eds. Readings in Law and Psychiatry. rev. ed. LC 74-24384. (Illus.). 848p. 1975. 30.00x (ISBN 0-8018-1692-0). Johns Hopkins.

Amary, Issam B. The Rights of the Mentally Retarded - Developmentally Disabled to Treatment & Education. (Illus.). 216p. 1980. text ed. 17.50 (ISBN 0-398-03946-1). C C Thomas.

Association Of The Bar Of The City Of New York. Mental Illness & Due Process: Report & Recommendations on Admissions to Mental Hospitals Under New York Law. (Illus.). 1962. 24.50x (ISBN 0-8014-0298-0). Cornell U Pr.

Bardach, Eugene. The Implementation Game: What Happens After a Bill Becomes Law. 1977. 20.00x (ISBN 0-262-02125-0); pap. 4.95x (ISBN 0-262-52049-4). MIT Pr.

--The Skill Factor in Politics: Repealing the Mental Commitment Laws in California. LC 79-157820. 300p. 1972. 20.00x (ISBN 0-520-02042-1). U of Cal Pr.

Barton, Walter E. & Sanborn, Charlotte J., eds. Law & the Mental Health Professions: Friction at the Interface. LC 77-90226. 1978. text ed. 17.50 (ISBN 0-8236-2950-3). Intl Univs Pr.

Bevilacqua, Joseph J. Changing Government Policies for the Mentally Diabled: Changing Government Policies for the Mentally Disabled. 1981. price not set professional reference (ISBN 0-88410-384-6). Ballinger Pub.

Blandford, G. Fielding. Insanity & Its Treatment: Lectures on the Treatment, Medical & Legal, of Insane Patients. LC 75-16684. (Classics in Psychiatry Ser.). 1976. Repr. of 1871 ed. 26.00x (ISBN 0-405-07416-6). Arno.

Briggs, L. Vernon. Occupation As a Substitute for Restraint in the Treatment of the Mentally Il: A History of the Passage of Two Bills Through the Massachusetts Legislature. LC 72-2387. (Mental Illness & Social Policy; the American Experience Ser.). Repr. of 1923 ed. 14.00 (ISBN 0-405-05195-6). Arno.

Briggs, Lloyd V. Two Years' Service on the Reorganized State Board of Insanity in Massachusetts, August, 1914 to August, 1916. Grob, Gerald N., ed. LC 78-22551. (Historical Issues in Mental Health Ser.). (Illus.). 1979. Repr. of 1930 ed. lib. bdg. 40.00x (ISBN 0-405-11905-4). Arno.

Brody, Baruch A. & Englehardt, H. Tristram. Mental Illness: Law & Public Policy. (Philosophy & Medicine Ser.: No. 5). 276p. 1980. lib. bdg. 29.00 (ISBN 0-686-27528-4, Pub. by Reidel Holland). Kluwer Boston.

Dix, George, et al. Texas Mental Health Commitments. LC 77-91216. (Texas Law Monograph Ser.: No. 1). 195p. 1978. pap. 10.00 (ISBN 0-938160-18-4). State Bar TX.

Ennis, Bruce J. & Emery, Richard D. The Rights of Mental Patients. 1972. pap. 2.50 (ISBN 0-380-01859-4, 77024, Discus). Avon.

Fersch, Ellsworth A., Jr. Law, Psychology, & the Courts: Rethinking Treatment of the Young & the Disturbed. 184p. 1979. 17.50 (ISBN 0-398-03874-0). C C Thomas.

Friedman, Paul. The Rights of Mentally Retarded Persons. 1976. pap. 2.50 (ISBN 0-380-00868-8, 54064, Discus). Avon.

GAP Committee on Psychiatry & the Law. Laws Governing Hospitalization of the Mentally Ill, Vol. 6. LC 62-2872. (Report: No. 61). 1966. pap. 1.00 (ISBN 0-87318-086-0, Pub. by Adv Psychiatry). Mental Health.

Greenland, Cyril. Mental Illness & Civil Liberty. 126p. 1970. pap. text ed. 5.00x (ISBN 0-7135-1826-X, Pub. by Bedford England). Renouf.

Haavik, Sarah F. & Menninger, Karl A., 2nd. Sexuality, Law, & the Developmentally Disabled Person: Legal & Clinical Aspects of Marriage, Parenthood, & Sterilization. LC 81-777. 210p. (Orig.). 1981. pap. text ed. 13.95 (ISBN 0-933716-21-4). P H Brookes.

Hamilton, Charles G. Any Resemblance. 1980. 7.00 (ISBN 0-934800-05-7). Gregg-Hamilton.

--Concerned Leaders: Mental Health Legislation in Mississippi. 152p. (Orig.). 1980. pap. 10.00 (ISBN 0-934800-09-X). Gregg-Hamilton.

Horowitz, Allen. The Social Control of Mental Illness. (Studies on Law & Social Control Ser.). 1981. price not set (ISBN 0-12-356180-9). Acad Pr.

Jacobs, James B. Individual Rights & Institutional Authority: Prisons, Mental Hospitals, Schools, & Military: Cases & Materials. (Contemporary Legal Education Ser.). 1979. text ed. 18.50 (ISBN 0-672-83706-4). Bobbs.

Katz, Jay, et al. Psychoanalysis, Psychiatry & Law. LC 65-27757. 1967. text ed. 35.00 (ISBN 0-02-917200-4). Free Pr.

Kittrie, Nicholas N. The Right to be Different: Deviance & Enforced Therapy. LC 73-156930. (Illus.). 480p. 1972. 27.50x (ISBN 0-8018-1052-3); pap. 5.95x (ISBN 0-8018-1319-0). Johns Hopkins.

Koren, John. Summaries of State Laws Relating to the Insane. Grob, Gerald N., ed. LC 78-22570. (Historical Issues in Mental Health Ser.). 1979. Repr. of 1917 ed. lib. bdg. 16.00x (ISBN 0-405-11923-2). Arno.

Maggio, Elio. The Psychiatry-Law Dilemma. 1980. 13.95 (ISBN 0-533-04795-1). Vantage.

Pearlstein, S. Psychiatry, the Law & Mental Health. 2nd ed. LC 67-16050. (Legal Almanac Ser: No. 30). 1967. 5.95 (ISBN 0-379-11030-X). Oceana.

Pritchard, David A. Mental Health Law in Mississippi. LC 78-62247. 1978. pap. text ed. 11.25 (ISBN 0-8191-0568-6). U Pr of Amer.

Rollin, H. The Mentally Abnormal Offender & the Law. 1969. 15.00 (ISBN 0-08-013385-1); pap. 7.00 (ISBN 0-08-013384-3). Pergamon.

Rubin, Jeffrey. Economics, Mental Health, & the Law. LC 78-19571. (Illus.). 1978. 17.95 (ISBN 0-669-02629-8). Lexington Bks.

Schwartz, Steven J. & Ferrarone, Stephen F. Community Mental Health & the Law: An Annotated Bibliography. LC 80-18872. 256p. 1981. 24.50x (ISBN 0-8290-0239-1). Irvington.

Singletary, Ernest E., et al. Law Briefs on Litigation & the Rights of Exceptional Children, Youth, & Adults. 1977. pap. text ed. 16.75 (ISBN 0-8191-0188-5). U Pr of Amer.

Special Committee, New York City Bar Association & Fordham University School Of Law. Mental Illness, Due Process & the Criminal Defendant. LC 68-19789. 1968. 25.00 (ISBN 0-8232-0780-3). Fordham.

Stone, Alan. Mental Heath & the Law: A System in Transition. LC 76-51937. 1976. 20.00x (ISBN 0-87668-288-3). Aronson.

Turnbull, H. Rutherford. Law & the Mentally Handicapped in North Carolina. 1979. 10.00 (ISBN 0-686-17565-4). U of NC Inst Gov.

Van Hoose, William H. & Kottler, Jeffrey A. Ethical & Legal Issues in Counseling & Psychotherapy. LC 76-50712. (Social & Behavioral Science Ser.). 1977. text ed. 14.95x (ISBN 0-87589-317-1). Jossey-Bass.

Woody, Robert H. Legal Aspects of Mental Retardation: A Search for Reliability. 144p. 1974. 12.75 (ISBN 0-398-03243-2). C C Thomas.

MENTAL HEALTH LAWS–GREAT BRITAIN

Jones, Kathleen. A History of the Mental Health Services. (International Library of Social Policy). 422p. 1972. 30.00x (ISBN 0-7100-7452-2). Routledge & Kegan.

Wexler, David B. Mental Health Law: Major Issues. 265p. 1981. 25.00 (ISBN 0-306-40538-5, Plenum Pr). Plenum Pub.

MENTAL HEALTH PERSONNEL

see also Clinical Psychology; Psychiatric Nursing; Psychiatric Social Work; Psychiatrists

Arco Editorial Board. Hospital Attendant. 4th ed. LC 77-25342. (Orig.). 1978. pap. 6.00 (ISBN 0-668-00012-0). Arco.

--Staff Attendant. 11th ed. LC 67-27077. 1967. lib. bdg. 6.50 (ISBN 0-668-01739-2). Arco.

Cherniss, Cary. Staff Burnout: Job Stress in the Human Services. LC 80-19408. (Sage Studies in Community Mental Health: Vol. 2). (Illus.). 200p. 1980. 20.00 (ISBN 0-8039-1338-9); pap. 9.95 (ISBN 0-8039-1339-7). Sage.

Grace, Helen K. & Camilleri, Dorothy. Mental Health Nursing: A Socio-Psychological Approach. 2nd ed. 592p. 1981. pap. text ed. write for info. (ISBN 0-697-05517-5); instrs.' manual avail. (ISBN 0-697-05518-3). Wm C Brown.

Kanno, Charles K. & Scheidemandel, Patricia L. Salary Ranges of Personnel Employed in State Mental Hospitals & Community Mental Health Centers-1970. pap. 5.00 (ISBN 0-685-24871-2, P156-0). Am Psychiatric.

Matthews, Daryl B. Disposable Patients. LC 77-25778. 128p. 1980. 14.95 (ISBN 0-669-02164-4). Lexington Bks.

Neal, Margo C. & Cohen, Patricia F. Nursing Care Planning Guides for Psychiatric & Mental Health. 1980. pap. 15.95 (ISBN 0-935236-15-5). Nurseco.

Neal-Schuman. National Director of Mental Health. LC 80-80661. 1980. 49.50 (ISBN 0-471-03886-5, Pub. by Wiley-Interscience). Wiley.

Robin, Stanley & Wagenfeld, Morton, eds. Paraprofessionals in the Human Services. (Community Psychology Ser.: Vol. 6). 320p. 1980. 29.95 (ISBN 0-87705-490-8). Human Sci Pr.

Rudman, Jack. Psychiatric Therapy Aide. (Career Examination Ser.: C-2124). (Cloth bdg. avail. on request). 1977. pap. 10.00 (ISBN 0-8373-2124-7). Natl Learning.

Youkeles, Merrill, et al. Helping People: Preparing to Enter a Mental Health Career. 192p. 1981. 13.95 (ISBN 0-13-386185-6); pap. 6.95 (ISBN 0-13-386177-5). P-H.

MENTAL HEALTH RESEARCH
see Psychiatric Research

MENTAL HEALTH SERVICES
see also Community Mental Health Services; Halfway Houses; Psychiatric Hospitals

Alley, Sam, et al, eds. Paraprofessionals in Mental Health: Theory & Practice. LC 79-11115. 336p. 1979. 29.95 (ISBN 0-87705-420-7). Human Sci Pr.

Berger, Gilda. Mental Illness. (Illus.). 144p. (gr. 9 up). 1981. lib. bdg. 8.90 (ISBN 0-531-04343-6). Watts.

Borgman, Robert D. Social Conflict & Mental Health Services. 356p. 1979. 27.00 (ISBN 0-398-03742-6); pap. 20.25 (ISBN 0-398-03743-4). C C Thomas.

Feldman, Saul. The Administration of Mental Health Services. 2nd ed. (Illus.). 544p. 1980. 49.75 (ISBN 0-398-03942-9). C C Thomas.

Gap Committee on Preventive Psychiatry. Mental Health & Primary Medical Care, Vol. 10. LC 80-19016. (Publication Ser.: No. 105). pap. 4.00 (ISBN 0-686-71039-8, 105, Mental Health Materials Center). Mental Health.

Glasscote, Raymond M., et al. Alternate Services - Their Role in Mental Health: A Field Study of Free Clinics, Runaway Houses, Counseling Centers & the Like. 1975. pap. 10.00 (ISBN 0-685-63942-8, P209-0). Am Psychiatric.

Gottlieb, Benjamin, ed. Social Networks & Social Support in Community Mental Health. (Sage Studies in Community Mental Health: Vol. 4). 300p. 1981. 20.00 (ISBN 0-8039-1669-8); pap. 9.95 (ISBN 0-8039-1670-1). Sage.

Katz, Elias, et al, eds. Mental Health Services for the Mentally Retarded. (Illus.). 292p. 1972. 17.50 (ISBN 0-398-02516-9). C C Thomas.

LaCharite, Norman & Dahlke, Arnold E. Improving Information Gathering for Hotlines: A Case Study. 1975. pap. 2.50 (ISBN 0-89785-210-9). Am Inst Res.

Laska, Eugene M., et al. Information Support for Mental Health Programs: An International Perspective. 1982. in prep. (ISBN 0-89885-083-5). Human Sci Pr.

MacMurray, Val D. Citizen Evaluation of Mental Health Services. LC 76-7616. 1976. 19.95 (ISBN 0-87705-293-X); pap. 6.95 (ISBN 0-87705-356-1). Human Sci Pr.

Massey, Craig. Ajustarse O Autodestruirse. 128p. 1981. pap. 1.95 (ISBN 0-8024-0148-1). Moody.

Mental Health Services, Information & Referral Directory, 4 vols. 1st ed. Set. 139.50 (ISBN 0-916270-25-4). Ready Ref Pr.

Miller, Kent S. The Criminal Justice & Mental Health Systems: Conflict & Collusion. LC 80-12755. 144p. 1980. 20.00 (ISBN 0-89946-032-1). Oelgeschlager.

Morrison, James K. A Consumer Approach to Community Psychology. LC 79-1172. 320p. 1979. 19.95x (ISBN 0-88229-458-X). Nelson-Hall.

Peck, Harris B., et al. A New Pattern for Mental Health Services in a Children's Court. (American Lecture Psychology). 96p. 1958. photocopy ed. spiral 9.75 (ISBN 0-398-04386-8). C C Thomas.

Ryback, Ralph S., et al. The Problem Oriented Record in Psychiatry & Mental Health Care. 2nd ed. Longabaugh, Richard & Fowler, Robert D., eds. 288p. 1981. pap. 32.50 (ISBN 0-8089-1308-5, 793701). Grune.

Vallance, Theodore. Mental Health Services in Transition: A Policy Sourcebook. Sabre, R. Michael & Sabre, Ru Michael, eds. 1980. 24.95 (ISBN 0-87705-700-1). Human Sci Pr.

Yates, B. T. Improving Effectiveness & Reducing Costs in Mental Health. (Illus.). 240p. 1980. 19.75 (ISBN 0-398-03971-2). C C Thomas.

MENTAL HEALTH VOLUNTEERS
see Volunteer Workers in Mental Health

MENTAL HOSPITALS
see Psychiatric Hospitals

MENTAL HYGIENE
see Mental Health

MENTAL ILLNESS
Here are entered popular works and works on regional or social aspects of mental disorders. Works on the legal aspects of mental illness are entered under Insanity. Systematic descriptions of mental disorders are entered under Psychology, Pathological. Works on clinical aspects of mental disorders, including therapy, are entered under Psychiatry.
see also Mental Deficiency; Mental Health; Mentally Ill; Minnesota Multiphasic Personality Inventory; Paranoia; Psychiatry; Psychology, Pathological

Abse, D. W. Hysteria & Related Mental Disorders. (Illus.). 1966. 18.95 (ISBN 0-8151-0005-1). Year Bk Med.

Alesen, Lewis A. Mental Robots. LC 57-13125. 1957. pap. 1.50 (ISBN 0-87004-000-6). Caxton.

Arnstein. When a Parent Is Mentally Ill: What to Say to Your Child. rev. ed. 1974. 1.25 (ISBN 0-87183-245-3). Child Study.

Arnstein, Helene S. When a Parent Is Mentally Ill: What to Say to Your Child. 36p. 1974. pap. 1.25 (ISBN 0-686-12282-8). Jewish Bd Family.

Barrett, James E., ed. Stress & Mental Disorder. LC 79-2202. (American Psychopathological Association Ser.). 1979. text ed. 28.00 (ISBN 0-89004-384-1). Raven.

Bates, Erica M. & Wilson, Paul R. Mental Disorder or Madness: Alternative Theories. 257p. 1980. 24.95x (ISBN 0-7022-1388-8); pap. 15.75x (ISBN 0-7022-1389-6). U of Queensland Pr.

Beers, Clifford W. A Mind That Found Itself. 5th ed. LC 80-5256. (Contemporary Communities Health Ser). 232p. 1981. 12.95 (ISBN 0-8229-3442-6); pap. 5.95 (ISBN 0-8229-5324-2). U of Pittsburgh Pr.

The Beginnings of Mental Hygiene in America: Three Selected Essays, 1833-1850. LC 73-2385. (Mental Illness & Social Policy; the American Experience Ser.). 26.00 (ISBN 0-405-05193-X). Arno.

Bennett, George. When the Mental Patient Comes Home. LC 79-23809. (Christian Care Books). 1980. pap. 5.95 (ISBN 0-664-24295-2). Westminster.

Berkley, Henry J. A Treatise on Mental Diseases. Grob, Gerald N., ed. LC 78-22549. (Historical Issues in Mental Health Ser.). (Illus.). 1979. Repr. of 1900 ed. lib. bdg. 40.00x (ISBN 0-405-11903-8). Arno.

Bloom, Bernard L. Changing Patterns of Psychiatric Care. LC 74-8850. 360p. 1975. text ed. 29.95 (ISBN 0-87705-209-3). Human Sci Pr.

--Psychiatric Patient Rights & Patient Advocacy: Issues & Evidence. (Community Psychology Ser.: Vol. 7). 1982. in prep. Human Sci Pr.

Brenner, M. Harvey. Mental Illness & the Economy. LC 72-85144. 320p. 1973. 16.50x (ISBN 0-674-56875-3). Harvard U Pr.

Brown, J. A. The Distressed Mind. Repr. of 1946 ed. 10.00 (ISBN 0-89987-044-9). Darby Bks.

Butterworth, C. A. & Skidmore, D. Caring for the Mentally Ill in the Community. 160p. 1980. 27.00x (ISBN 0-686-69924-6, Pub by Croom Helm England). State Mutual Bk.

Caine, T. M. & Smail, D. J. Treatment of Mental Illness: Science, Faith & the Therapeutic Community. LC 78-88569. 1969. text ed. 15.00 (ISBN 0-8236-6648-4). Intl Univs Pr.

Carpenter, William B. Principles of Mental Physiology: With Their Applications to the Training & Discipline of the Mind & the Study of Its Morbid Conditions. rev. ed. LC 78-72792. Repr. of 1900 ed. 55.00 (ISBN 0-404-60856-6, BF161). AMS Pr.

Cheraskin, E. Psychodietetics. 1976. pap. 2.25 (ISBN 0-553-12023-9). Bantam.

Cheraskin, Emanuel, et al. Psycho-Dietetics: Food As the Key to Emotional Health. LC 74-78529. 1974. 8.95 (ISBN 0-8128-1725-7). Stein & Day.

Clark, Robert A. Mental Illness in Perspective. 101p. (Orig.). 1973. 3.75 (ISBN 0-910286-34-5); pap. 2.95 (ISBN 0-910286-29-9). Boxwood.

Clarke, A. D. & Lewis, M. M., eds. Learning, Speech & Thought in the Mentally Retarded. (Illus.). 92p. 1972. 6.95 (ISBN 0-407-24950-8). Butterworth.

Cockerham, William C. Sociology of Mental Disorder. (Ser. in Sociology). (Illus.). 300p. 1981. text ed. 19.95 (ISBN 0-13-820886-7). P-H.

Cole, J. O., et al, eds. Depression: Biology, Psychodynamics, & Treatment. LC 77-13161. (Illus.). 262p. 1977. 22.50 (ISBN 0-306-31062-7, Plenum Pr). Plenum Pub.

Combe, Andrew. Observations on Mental Derangement: Being an Application of the Principles of Phrenology to the Elucidation of the Causes, Symptoms, Nature, Treatment of Insanity. LC 72-161928. (History of Psychology Series). Repr. of 1834 ed. 35.00x (ISBN 0-8201-1089-2). Schol Facsimiles.

Connolly, Mary G. Mental Illness & Use of Community Res. LC 74-28600. 1975. soft bdg. 9.00 (ISBN 0-88247-326-3). R & E Res Assoc.

Crocetti, Guido M., et al. Contemporary Attitudes Toward Mental Illness. LC 73-80071. (Contemporary Community Health Ser.). 1974. 10.95x (ISBN 0-8229-3273-3). U of Pittsburgh Pr.

Dayton, Neil A. New Facts on Mental Disorders. Grob, Gerald N., ed. LC 78-22558. (Historical Issues in Mental Health Ser.). (Illus.). 1979. Repr. of 1940 ed. lib. bdg. 30.00x (ISBN 0-405-11912-7). Arno.

Deutsch, Albert, ed. Encyclopedia of Mental Health. LC 63-7150. 1970. Repr. of 1963 ed. 45.00 (ISBN 0-8108-0357-7). Scarecrow.

Easson, William M. Psychiatry: Patient Management Review. LC 76-41171. 1977. pap. 8.00 (ISBN 0-668-04058-0). Arco.

Eastwood, Robin. Relation between Physical & Mental Illness: The Physical Status of Psychiatric Patients at a Multiphasic Screening Survey. LC 74-76877. 1974. 12.50x (ISBN 0-8020-3323-7). U of Toronto Pr.

Eaton, William. The Sociology of Mental Disorders. 1979. 19.95 (ISBN 0-03-046466-8). Praeger.

Erikson, Joan M., et al. Activity, Recovery, Growth: The Communal Role of Planned Activities. (Illus.). 1976 10.95 (ISBN 0-393-01126-7, Norton Lib); pap. 4.95 1978 (ISBN 0-393-00886-X). Norton.

Faris, Robert E. & Dunham, H. Warren. Mental Disorders in Urban Areas. LC 65-16168. 1965. pap. 2.45 (ISBN 0-226-23816-4, P183, Phoen). U of Chicago Pr.

Fein, Rashi. Economics of Mental Illness. Grob, Gerald N., ed. LC 78-22559. (Historical Issues in Mental Health Ser.). (Illus.). 1979. Repr. of 1958 ed. lib. bdg. 12.00x (ISBN 0-405-11913-5). Arno.

Felix, Robert H. Mental Illness: Progress & Prospects. LC 67-20278. 110p. 1967. 12.50x (ISBN 0-231-03055-X). Columbia U Pr.

Finkel, Norman J. Mental Illness & Health: Its Legacy Tensions, & Changes. 128p. 1976. pap. text ed. 7.95 (ISBN 0-02-337700-3, 33770). Macmillan.

Finnane, Mark. Insanity & the Insane in Post-Famine Ireland. (Illus.). 242p. 1981. 25.00x (ISBN 0-389-20212-6). B&N.

Freemon, Frank R. Organic Mental Disease. LC 79-23180. (Illus.). 248p. 1981. text ed. 30.00 (ISBN 0-89335-109-1). Spectrum Pub.

Gallagher, Bernard J., III. Sociology of Mental Illness. (Ser. in Sociology). (Illus.). 1980. text ed. 17.95 (ISBN 0-13-820928-6). P-H.

GAP Committee on Preventive Psychiatry. Problems of Estimating Changes in Frequency of Mental Disorders, Vol. 4. (Report No. 50). 1961. pap. 2.00 (ISBN 0-87318-067-4, Pub. by Adv Psychiatry). Mental Health.

GAP Committee on Psychiatry & the Community. The Chronic Mental Patient in the Community: Vol. 10. LC 78-55381. (Publication No. 102). 1978. pap. 4.00 (ISBN 0-87318-139-5, Pub. by Adv Psychiatry). Mental Health.

Gardner, William I. Behavior Modification in Mental Retardation: The Education & Rehabilitation of the Mentally Retarded Adolescent & Adult. LC 79-149839. 1971. 27.95x (ISBN 0-202-25000-8). Aldine Pub.

Gilman, Sander L. Seeing the Insane: A Cultural History of Psychiatric Illustration. (Illus.). 500p. 1981. 50.00 (ISBN 0-87630-233-9). Brunner-Mazel.

Glossary of Mental Disorders & Guide to Their Classification - for Use in Conjunction with the International Classification of Diseases. 8th rev. ed. (Also avail. in French & Spanish). 1974. pap. 4.80 (ISBN 92-4-154036-2). World Health.

Glover, Jonathan. Responsibility. (International Library of Philosophy and Scientific Method). 1970. text ed. 23.25x (ISBN 0-391-00097-7). Humanities.

Goldbeck, W. B. Mental Illness Programs for Employees. (Springer Ser. in Industry & Health Care: Vol. 9). 250p. 1980. pap. 12.00 (ISBN 0-387-90479-4). Springer-Verlag.

Goldberg, David & Huxley, Peter. Mental Illness in the Community. 1980. 25.00x (ISBN 0-422-76740-9, Pub. by Tavistock); pap. 11.95x (ISBN 0-422-76750-6). Methuen Inc.

Grob, Gerald N., ed. Public Policy & Mental Illness: Four Investigations, 1915-1939, an Original Anthology. LC 78-22585. (Historical Issues in Mental Health Ser.). (Illus.). 1979. lib. bdg. 44.00x (ISBN 0-405-11936-4). Arno.

Grob, Gerald N., et al, eds. Mental Illness & Social Policy: The American Experience, 41 bks. 1973. Set. 1044.50 (ISBN 0-405-11900-3). Arno.

Grusky, Oscar & Pollner, Melvin. The Sociology of Mental Illness. 1981. pap. text ed. 15.95 (ISBN 0-03-053211-6, HoltC). HR&W.

Hannah, Gerald T., et al, eds. Preservation of Client Rights: A Handbook for Practitioners Providing Therapeutic, Educational, & Rehabilitative Services. LC 80-1644. (Illus.). 1981. 25.00 (ISBN 0-02-913820-5). Free Pr.

Himwich, Harold E. Biochemistry, Schizophrenias & Affective Illnesses. LC 77-2015. (Illus.). 514p. 1977. 24.50 (ISBN 0-88275-524-2). Krieger.

Hoch, Paul. Differential Diagnosis in Clinical Psychiatry. LC 72-76812. 1972. 40.00x (ISBN 0-87668-053-8). Aronson.

Hollingshead, A. B. & Redlich, F. C. Social Class & Mental Illness: A Community Study. LC 58-6076. 1958. pap. 18.95 (ISBN 0-471-40685-6). Wiley.

Hudgens, Richard W. Psychiatric Disorders in Adolescents. LC 74-3431. 234p. 1974. 12.50 (ISBN 0-686-65363-7). Krieger.

Hunter, Marvin H., et al. The Retarded Child from Birth to Five: A Multi-Disciplinary Approach for Child & Family. LC 70-179783. (John Day Bk.). 320p. 1972. 10.95 (ISBN 0-381-98127-4, A66100). T Y Crowell.

Insel, Paul M., ed. Environmental Variables & the Prevention of Mental Illness. LC 79-3521. 240p. 1980. 25.95x (ISBN 0-669-03457-6). Lexington Bks.

Janov, Arthur. The Anatomy of Mental Illness. 1977. pap. 2.95 (ISBN 0-425-03642-1, Windhover). Berkley Pub.

Kaplan, Howard B. The Sociology of Mental Illness. 1972. 7.50x (ISBN 0-8084-0355-9); pap. 4.45 (ISBN 0-8084-0356-7, B61). Coll & U Pr.

Karlsson, John L. Inheritance of Creative Intelligence. LC 77-19297. 1978. text ed. 18.95x (ISBN 0-88229-391-5); pap. text ed. 9.95x (ISBN 0-88229-607-8). Nelson-Hall.

Keehn, J. D. The Origins of Madness: The Psychopathology of Animal Life. (Illus.). 1979. text ed. 52.00 (ISBN 0-08-023725-8). Pergamon.

Landis, Carney & Page, James D. Modern Society & Mental Disease. Grob, Gerald N., ed. LC 78-22571. (Historical Issues in Mental Health Ser.). (Illus.). 1979. Repr. of 1938 ed. lib. bdg. 14.00x (ISBN 0-405-11924-0). Arno.

Leon, Gloria R. Case Studies in Deviant Behavior: An Interactional Perspective. 2nd ed. 1977. pap. 13.95 (ISBN 0-205-05847-7, 795847-1). Allyn.

Lewis, Helen B. Freud & Modern Psychology: The/Emotional Basis of Mental Illness, Vol. 1. (Emotions Personality & Psychotherapy Ser.). 240p. 1981. 19.50 (ISBN 0-306-40525-3, Plenum Pr). Plenum Pub.

Linton, Ralph. Culture & Mental Disorders. 152p. 1956. photocopy ed. spiral 13.75 (ISBN 0-398-04342-6). C C Thomas.

Low, Abraham A. Lectures to Relatives of Former Patients. 1967. 6.95 (ISBN 0-8158-0139-4). Chris Mass.

Luber, Raymond F. & Anderson, Carol. Family Intervention with Psychiatric Patients. 1982. in prep. (ISBN 0-89885-031-2). Human Sci Pr.

McCulloch, J. Wallace & Prins, Herschel A. Signs of Stress: The Social Problems of Psychiatric Illness. (Psychiatric Topics for Community Workers Ser.). 207p. 1978. 14.00x (ISBN 0-7130-0165-8, Pub. by Woburn Pr England). Biblio Dist.

McNeil, E. Quiet Furies: Man & Disorder. 1967. pap. text ed. 8.95 (ISBN 0-13-749770-9). P-H.

Malzberg, Benjamin. Social & Biological Aspects of Mental Disease. Grob, Gerald N., ed. LC 78-22573. (Historical Issues in Mental Health Ser.). (Illus.). 1979. Repr. of 1940 ed. lib. bdg. 22.00x (ISBN 0-405-11926-7). Arno.

Malzberg, Benjamin & Lee, Everett S. Migration & Mental Disease. LC 56-8063. 1956. pap. 3.00 (ISBN 0-527-03307-3). Kraus Repr.

Martin, L. E. Mental Health-Mental Illness: Revolution in Progress. 1970. pap. 6.95 (ISBN 0-07-040644-8, C). McGraw.

Martin, W. R., ed. Drug Addiction I: Morphine, Sedative-Hypnotic & Alcohol Dependence. (Handbook of Experimental Pharmacology: Vol. 45, Pt. 1). (Illus.). 1977. 131.60 (ISBN 0-387-08170-4). Springer-Verlag.

Martindale, Don & Martindale, Edith. Social Dimensions of Mental Illness, Alcoholism, & Drug Dependence. LC 72-133499. 332p. lib. bdg. 15.95 (ISBN 0-8371-5175-9, MAM/); pap. 5.95 (ISBN 0-8371-8924-1). Greenwood.

Mason, Robert L., et al. The Clergyman & the Psychiatrist: When to Refer. LC 77-22597. 248p. 1978. 16.95x (ISBN 0-88229-260-9). Nelson-Hall.

Maudsley, Henry. Responsibility in Mental Disease. Bd. with Treatise on Insanity. (Contributions to the History of Psychology Ser., Vol. III, Pt. C: Medical Psychology). 1978. Repr. of 1876 ed. 30.00 (ISBN 0-89093-167-4). U Pubns Amer.

May, James V. Mental Diseases: A Public Health Problem. Grob, Gerald N., ed. LC 78-22574. (Historical Issues in Mental Health Ser.). 1979. Repr. of 1922 ed. lib. bdg. 32.00x (ISBN 0-405-11927-5). Arno.

Miles, Agnes. The Mentally Ill in Contemporary Society. 224p. 1981. 25.00x (ISBN 0-312-52981-3). St Martin.
Mishara, Brian & Patterson, Robert. A Consumer's Guide to Mental Health. LC 77-23461. 1977. 9.95 (ISBN 0-8129-0711-6). Times Bks.
Moreau, J. J., et al. Hashish & Mental Illness. Peters, H. & Nahas, G., eds. Barnett, G. J., tr. from Fr. LC 76-107227. Orig. Title: Du Haschish et De l'Alienation Mentale. 267p. 1973. pap. 18.00 (ISBN 0-911216-14-6). Raven.
Morgan, Arthur J. & Johnston, Mabyl K. Mental Health & Mental Illness. 2nd ed. LC 76-14855. 1976. pap. 11.75 (ISBN 0-397-54189-9, JBL-Med-Nursing). Har-Row.
Myerson, Abraham. The Inheritance of Mental Diseases. LC 75-16724. (Classics in Psychiatry Ser.). 1976. Repr. of 1925 ed. 19.00x (ISBN 0-405-07448-4). Arno.
National Research Council, the Committee on Psychiatric Investigations. The Problem of Mental Disorder. Grob, Gerald N., ed. LC 78-22580. (Historical Issues in Mental Health Ser.). 1979. Repr. of 1934 ed. lib. bdg. 24.00x (ISBN 0-405-11932-1). Arno.
Naylor, Phyllis. Crazy Love: An Autobiographical Account of Marriage & Madness. LC 76-56359. 1977. 7.95 (ISBN 0-688-03178-1). Morrow.
New York State Commission to Investigate Provision for the Mentally Deficient. Report of the State Commission to Investigate Provision for the Mentally Deficient. LC 75-17234. (Social Problems & Social Policy Ser.). (Illus.). 1976. Repr. of 1915 ed. 67.00x (ISBN 0-405-07503-0). Arno.
Nicholi, Armand M., Jr., ed. The Harvard Guide to Modern Psychiatry. 1978. 35.00x (ISBN 0-674-37566-1, Belknap Pr). Harvard U Pr.
Orley, John H. Culture & Mental Illness: A Study from Uganda. (East African Studies Ser.: No. 36). 82p. 1970. 5.00x (ISBN 0-8002-0619-3). Intl Pubns Serv.
Penrose, L. C. A Clinical & Genetic Study of 1280 Cases of Mental Defect: The Colchester Study. 162p. Date not set. Repr. of 1981 ed. price not set (ISBN 0-89874-191-2). Krieger.
Perfect, William. Annals of Insanity: Comprising a Selection of Curious & Interesting Cases in the Different Species of Lunacy, Melanchol, or Madness. LC 75-16726. (Classics in Psychiatry Ser.). 1976. Repr. of 1808 ed. 19.00x (ISBN 0-405-07449-2). Arno.
Plunkett, Richard J. & Gordon, John E. Epidemiology & Mental Ilness. Grob, Gerald N., ed. LC 78-22581. (Historical Issues in Mental Health Ser.). 1979. Repr. of 1960 ed. lib. bdg. 12.00x (ISBN 0-405-11933-X). Arno.
Pollock, Horatio M. Mental Disease & Social Welfare. LC 75-17237. (Social Problems & Social Policy Ser.). (Illus.). 1976. Repr. of 1941 ed. 13.00x (ISBN 0-405-07506-5). Arno.
Price, R. H. & Denner, Bruce, eds. Making of a Mental Patient. LC 73-235. 1973. pap. 7.95 (ISBN 0-03-085652-3, HoltC). HR&W.
Priest, Robert G. & Steinert, J. Insanity: A Study of Major Psychiatric Disorders. (Psychiatric Topics for Community Workers Ser.). 397p. 1978. 14.00x (ISBN 0-7130-0163-1, Pub. by Woburn Pr England). Biblio Dist.
Readings in Emotional & Behavioral Disorders. (Special Education Ser.). 1978. pap. text ed. 10.95 (ISBN 0-89568-007-6). Spec Learn Corp.
Robins, Lee N., et al, eds. The Social Consequences of Psychiatric Illness. LC 80-11090. 1980. 25.00 (ISBN 0-87630-226-6). Brunner-Mazel.
Rosen, George. Madness in Society. LC 68-13112. 1968. 12.50x (ISBN 0-226-72640-1). U of Chicago Pr.
--Madness in Society: Chapters in the Historical Sociology of Mental Illness. LC 68-13112. 352p. 1980. pap. 7.50 (ISBN 0-226-72642-8, P913). U of Chicago Pr.
Russell, Harold E. & Beigel, Allan. Understanding Human Behavior for Effective Police Work. LC 75-7261. (Illus.). 1976. 14.95x (ISBN 0-465-08861-9). Basic.
Sandler, Merton, ed. Mental Illness in Pregnancy & the Puerperium. (Illus.). 1979. text ed. 21.95x (ISBN 0-19-261150-X). Oxford U Pr.
Scheff, Thomas J. Being Mentally Ill: A Sociological Theory. LC 66-15207. 210p. 1966. pap. text ed. 6.95x (ISBN 0-202-30252-0). Aldine Pub.
--Being Mentally Ill: A Sociological Theory. LC 66-15207. 210p. 1966. pap. text ed. 6.95x (ISBN 0-202-30252-0). Aldine Pub.
Scheff, Thomas J., ed. Mental Illness & Social Processes. (Readers in Social Problems Ser). (Orig.). 1967. pap. 11.50 (ISBN 0-06-045762-7, HarpC). Har-Row.
Scheper-Hughes, Nancy. Saints, Scholars, & Schizophrenics: Mental Illness in Rural Ireland. LC 77-71067. 1979. 16.95 (ISBN 0-520-03444-9). U of Cal Pr.
Schwab, J. J. & Schwab, M. E. Sociocultural Roots of Mental Illness: An Epidemiological Survey. (Topics in General Psychiatry Ser.). (Illus.). 336p. 1978. 27.50 (ISBN 0-306-31089-9, Plenum Pr). Plenum Pub.
Schwartz, Arthur N., ed. Etiology of Mental Disorders. (Technical Bibliographies on Aging). 1975. 2.25 (ISBN 0-88474-081-1). USC Andrus Geron.
Scull, Andrew. Museums of Madness: The Social Organization of Insanity in Nineteenth Century England. LC 78-73732. (Illus.). 1979. 17.95x (ISBN 0-312-55355-2). St Martin.
Serban, George, ed. Cognitive Defects in the Development of Mental Illness. LC 77-94739. 1978. 25.00 (ISBN 0-87630-167-7). Brunner-Mazel.
Shagass, Charles, et al, eds. Psychopathology & Brain Dysfunction. LC 76-55487. (American Psychopathological Association Ser). 399p. 1977. 28.00 (ISBN 0-89004-120-2). Raven.
Siegler, Miriam & Osmond, Humphrey. Models of Madness, Models of Medicine. 1976. pap. 5.95x (ISBN 0-06-131953-8, TB 1953, Torch). Har-Row.
Simmons, Ozzie G. Work & Mental Illness: Eight Case Studies. 271p. 1965. 11.50 (ISBN 0-471-79198-9, Pub. by Wiley). Krieger.
Slater, Eliot & Cowie, Valerie. Genetics of Mental Disorders. (Oxford Monographs on Medical Genetics). (Illus.). 1971. text ed. 37.50x (ISBN 0-19-264130-1). Oxford U Pr.
Smith, Selwyn M. & Koranyi, Erwin K. Self-Assessment of Current Knowledge in Forensic & Organic Psychiatry. 1978. spiral bdg. 15.00 (ISBN 0-87488-235-4). Med Exam.
Snell, H. Mental Disorder: An Introductory Textbook for Nurses. (Illus.). 1977. pap. text ed. 8.95x (ISBN 0-04-610005-9). Allen Unwin.
Snyder, Solomon H. Biological Aspects of Mental Disorder. (Illus.). 272p. 1981. pap. 6.95x (ISBN 0-19-502888-0). Oxford U Pr.
Southard, Elmer E. & Jarrett, Mary C. The Kingdom of Evils: Psychiatric Social Work Presented in One Hundred Case Histories. LC 73-2417. (Mental Illness & Social Policy; the American Experience Ser.). Repr. of 1922 ed. 32.00 (ISBN 0-405-05227-8). Arno.
Spitzer, S. P. & Denzin, N. K. Mental Patient: Studies in the Sociology of Deviance. 1968. pap. text ed. 10.50 (ISBN 0-07-060332-4, C). McGraw.
Steiner, Lee R. Psychic Self-Healing for Psychological Problems. LC 76-56849. (Illus.). 176p. 1977. 8.95 (ISBN 0-13-732677-7). P-H.
Szasz, Thomas. The Manufacture of Madness. 1977. pap. 5.95 (ISBN 0-06-090560-3, CN 560, CN). Har-Row.
Szasz, Thomas S. The Myth of Mental Illness: Foundations of a Theory of Personal Conduct. rev. ed. LC 73-14296. 352p. 1974. 12.95 (ISBN 0-06-014196-4, HarpT). Har-Row.
--The Myth of Mental Illness: Foundations of a Theory of Personal Conduct. rev. ed. 320p. 1974. pap. 2.95 (ISBN 0-06-080330-4, P330, PL). Har-Row.
Szasz, Thomas S., M.D. Ideology & Insanity - Essays on the Psychiatric Dehumanization of Man. LC 72-84397. 1970. pap. 2.95 (ISBN 0-385-02033-3, A704, Anch). Doubleday.
Talbott, John. The Chronic Mentally Ill: Treatment, Programs, Systems. LC 80-24874. 384p. 1981. 32.95 (ISBN 0-87705-086-4). Human Sci Pr.
Tessler, Richard & Goldman, Howard. The Chronically Mentally Ill in the Community: The NIMH Initiative. 1981. price not set professional ref. (ISBN 0-88410-379-X). Ballinger Pub.
Thurnam, John. Observations & Essays on the Statistics of Insanity. LC 75-16734. (Classics in Psychiatry Ser.). 1976. Repr. of 1845 ed. 20.00x (ISBN 0-405-07455-7). Arno.
Townsend, John M. Cultural Conceptions & Mental Illness: A Comparison of Germany & America. LC 77-22342. (Illus.). 1978. lib. bdg. 11.00x (ISBN 0-226-81098-4). U of Chicago Pr.
Trick, I. & Obcarskas, S. Understanding Mental Illness & Its Nursing. 1976. pap. 15.00 (ISBN 0-272-79385-X). State Mutual Bk.
Tsuang, Ming T. & VanderMey, Randall. Genes & the Mind: Inheritance of Mental Illness. (Illus.). 158p. 1980. text ed. 12.95x (ISBN 0-19-261268-9). Oxford U Pr.
Upham, Thomas C. Outlines of Imperfect & Disordered Mental Action. LC 73-2426. (Mental Illness & Social Policy; the American Experience Ser.). Repr. of 1868 ed. 12.00 (ISBN 0-405-05235-9). Arno.
Usdin, Earl, et al. Enzymes & Neurotransmitters in Mental Disease: Based on a Symposium Held at the Technion Faculty of Medicine, Haifa, Israel August 28-30 1979. LC 80-40130. 650p. 1980. 98.00 (ISBN 0-471-27791-6, Pub. by Wiley-Interscience). Wiley.
Watson, George. Nutrition & Your Mind: The Psychochemical Response. (Illus.). 1972. 9.95 (ISBN 0-06-014525-0, HarpT). Har-Row.
Wertheimer, F. I. & Hesketh, Florence E. The Significance of the Physical Constitution in Mental Disease: Medicine Monographs, Vol. X. Grob, Gerald N., ed. LC 78-22594. (Historical Issues in Mental Health Ser.). (Illus.). 1979. Repr. of 1926 ed. lib. bdg. 10.00x (ISBN 0-405-11944-5). Arno.
WHO Scientific Group. Geneva, 1968. Biochemistry of Mental Disorders: Report. (Technical Report Ser.: No. 427). (Also avail. in French). 1969. pap. 2.00 (ISBN 92-4-120427-3). World Health.
Wigan, Arthur L. A New View of Insanity: The Duality of the Mind Proved by the Structure, Functions, & Diseases of the Brain, & by the Phenomena of Mental Derangement. LC 78-72829. (Brainedness, Handedness, & Mental Ability Ser.). Repr. of 1844 ed. 37.50 (ISBN 0-404-60897-3). AMS Pr.
Wolman, Benjamin B., ed. Clinical Diagnosis of Mental Disorders: A Handbook. LC 78-14969. (Illus.). 933p. 1978. 50.00 (ISBN 0-306-31141-0, Plenum Pr). Plenum Pub.
Youdim, M. B. Aromatic Amino Acid Hydroxylases & Mental Disease. LC 79-40642. 1980. 87.50 (ISBN 0-471-27606-5, Pub. by Wiley-Interscience). Wiley.

MENTAL ILLNESS–DIAGNOSIS

Barlow, David H., ed. Behavioral Assessment of Adult Disorders. LC 80-14673. (The Guilford Behavioral Assessment Ser.). 500p. 1981. 25.00 (ISBN 0-89862-140-2). Guilford Pr.
Bates, Erica. Models of Madness. 1978. 19.95x (ISBN 0-7022-1069-2); pap. 9.95x (ISBN 0-7022-1068-4). U of Queensland Pr.
Crow, Gary A. Children at Risk: A Handbook of the Signs & Symptoms of Early Childhood Difficulties. LC 77-87859. 1978. 12.95x (ISBN 0-8052-3675-9). Schocken.
DiMascio, A. & Goldberg, H. Emotional Disorders: Diagnosis & Pharmacological Treatment. 3rd ed. 1980. 15.95 (ISBN 0-87489-255-4). Med Economics.
Freedman, Alfred M. & Kaplan, Harold I., eds. Diagnosing Mental Illness: Evaluation in Psychiatry & Psychology. LC 78-178071. (Studies in Human Behavior Ser). 1972. pap. 4.95x (ISBN 0-689-70282-5, HB1). Atheneum.
Goldberg, Martin. A Guide to Psychiatric Diagnosis & Understanding for the Helping Professions. (Quality Paperback: No. 283). 181p. (Orig.). 1974. pap. 2.95 (ISBN 0-8226-0283-0). Littlefield.
Klein, Donald F. & Davis, John M. Diagnosis & Drug Treatment of Psychiatric Disorders. LC 69-14459. 480p. 1969. 18.50 (ISBN 0-686-65354-8). Krieger.
Lazare, Aaron. Outpatient Psychiatry: Diagnosis & Treatment. 1979. 39.95 (ISBN 0-683-04850-3). Williams & Wilkins.
Meehl, Paul E. Psychodiagnosis: Selected Papers. LC 72-95440. (Illus.). 334p. 1973. 20.00x (ISBN 0-8166-0685-4). U of Minn Pr.
--Psychodiagnosis: Selected Papers. 1977. pap. 5.95 (ISBN 0-393-00855-X, N855, Norton Lib). Norton.
Morison, Alexander. The Physiognomy of Mental Diseases. 2nd ed. LC 75-16723. (Classics in Psychiatry Ser.). (Illus.). 1976. Repr. of 1843 ed. 15.00x (ISBN 0-405-07447-6). Arno.
Olson, Harry A. Early Recollections: Their Use in Diagnosis & Psychotherapy. (Illus.). 416p. 1979. text ed. 29.75 (ISBN 0-398-03826-0). C C Thomas.
Pepper, Bertram, et al, eds. The Social Setting of Mental Health. LC 75-7259. (Illus.). 1976. text ed. 17.50x (ISBN 0-465-07918-0). Basic.
Perucci, Robert & Targ, Dena B. Identifying Mental Illness: The Role of Social Networks. 200p. 1981. 19.95 (ISBN 0-86569-095-2). Auburn Hse.
Pfohl, Stephen J. Predicting Dangerousness. LC 77-25742. (Illus.). 1978. 21.50 (ISBN 0-669-01509-1). Lexington Bks.
Rapaport, David, et al. Diagnostic Psychological Testing. LC 68-16993. 1968. text ed. 30.00 (ISBN 0-8236-1260-0). Intl Univs Pr.
Scheff, Thomas J. Labeling Madness. 192p. 1975. 8.95 (ISBN 0-13-517367-1, Spec); pap. 3.95 (ISBN 0-13-517359-0, Spec). P-H.

MENTAL ILLNESS–PERSONAL NARRATIVES

Anderson, Anna E. Pain: The Essence of a Mental Illness. 1979. 5.00 (ISBN 0-682-49527-1). Exposition.
Ansite, Pat. No Longer Lonely. 1977. pap. 2.95 (ISBN 0-89728-048-2, 670689). Omega Pubns OR.
Cameron, Doug. How to Survive Being Committed to a Mental Hospital. LC 79-66488. 143p. 1980. 7.95 (ISBN 0-533-04399-9). Vantage.
Drory, Irene. Another World. 1978. 5.95 (ISBN 0-533-03343-8). Vantage.
Fountain, Toby. Dying on Third Base. Date not set. 6.95 (ISBN 0-533-04182-1). Vantage.
Gardiner, Muriel, ed. The Wolf Man: With the Case of the Wolf Man by Sigmund Freud. LC 70-151227. 1971. pap. 5.95x (ISBN 0-465-09501-1, TB-5002). Basic.
Golann, Stuart, et al. The Bethlehem Diaries: Student - Mental Patient Encounters. LC 74-12420. 240p. 1980. text ed. 22.50x (ISBN 0-8290-0241-3); pap. text ed. 8.95 (ISBN 0-8290-0242-1). Irvington.
Gordon, Barbara. I'm Dancing As Fast As I Can. LC 78-20165. 1979. 9.95 (ISBN 0-06-011499-1, HarpT). Har-Row.
Gotkin, Janet & Gotkin, Paul. Too Much Anger, Too Many Tears: A Personal Triumph Over Psychiatry. LC 73-90175. 395p. 1975. 10.95 (ISBN 0-8129-0421-4); pap. 4.95 (ISBN 0-8129-6279-6). Times Bks.
Goulet, Robert. Madhouse. LC 72-13318. 1973. 4.95 (ISBN 0-87955-304-9). O'Hara.
Grainger, Roger. Watching for Wings: Theology & Mental Illness in a Pastoral Setting. 1978. pap. 7.50 (ISBN 0-232-51421-6). Attic Pr.
Kaplan, Bert, ed. The Inner World of Mental Illness: A Series of First Person Accounts of What It Was Like. (Orig.). 1964. pap. text ed. 17.50 scp (ISBN 0-06-043480-5, HarpC). Har-Row.
Lair, Jacqueline C. & Lechler, Walther H. I Exist, I Need, I'm Entitled: A Story of Love, Courage & Survival. LC 79-8011. 240p. 1980. 8.95 (ISBN 0-385-15632-4). Doubleday.
Naylor, Phyllis. Crazy Love. 1978. pap. 1.95 (ISBN 0-451-08077-7, J8077, Sig). NAL.
Perceval, John. Perceval's Narrative: A Patient's Account of His Psychosis, 1830-1832. Bateson, Gregory, ed. 1961. 16.50x (ISBN 0-8047-0052-4). Stanford U Pr.
Peterson, Dale, ed. A Mad People's History of Madness. LC 81-50430. (Contemporary Community Health Ser.). 320p. 1982. 19.95 (ISBN 0-8229-3444-2); pap. 8.95 (ISBN 0-8229-5331-5). U of Pittsburgh Pr.
Shields, Mary L. Sea Run: Surviving My Mother's Madness. 1981. 11.95 (ISBN 0-87223-665-X). Seaview Bks.
Sutherland, N. S. Breakdown. LC 75-37885. 288p. 1977. 10.00 (ISBN 0-8128-1941-1). Stein & Day.

MENTAL ILLNESS–RESEARCH

see Psychiatric Research

MENTAL ILLNESS–GHANA

Field, Margaret J. Search for Security: An Ethno - Psychiatric Study of Rural Ghana. 1970. pap. 2.95 (ISBN 0-393-00508-9, Norton Lib). Norton.

MENTAL ILLNESS–GREAT BRITAIN

Clarke, Basil. Mental Disorder in Earlier Britain. 1975. 50.00 (ISBN 0-7083-0562-8). Verry.
Diamond, Hugh W. Face of Madness. Gilman, Sander L., ed. 1977. pap. 5.95 (ISBN 0-8065-0604-0). Citadel Pr.

MENTAL ILLNESS AND ART

see Art and Mental Illness

MENTAL ILLNESS AND LAW

see Insanity–Jurisprudence

MENTAL ILLNESS IN ART

see Psychiatry in Art

MENTAL INSTITUTIONS

see Mentally Handicapped–Institutional Care; Psychiatric Hospitals

MENTAL MECHANISMS

see Defense Mechanisms (Psychology)

MENTAL-MOTOR RELATIONSHIP IN EDUCATION

see Perceptual-Motor Learning

MENTAL PRAYER

see Meditation

MENTAL RETARDATION

see Mental Deficiency

MENTAL RETARDATION FACILITIES

Blatt, Burton, et al. The Family Papers: A Return to Purgatory. (Illus.). 1980. pap. text ed. 8.95x (ISBN 0-582-28154-7). Longman.
Cunningham, Cliff & Sloper, Patricia. Helping Your Exceptional Baby: A Practical & Honest Approach to Raising a Mentally Handicapped Child. (Illus.). 1980. 12.95 (ISBN 0-394-51044-5). Pantheon.
Roos, Philip. Shaping the Future. 169p. pap. text ed. 12.95 (ISBN 0-8391-1547-4). Univ Park.
Scheerenberger, R. C. Managing Residential Facilities for the Developmentally Disabled. (Illus.). 320p. 1975. 22.75 (ISBN 0-398-03199-1). C C Thomas.
Thaw, J. Program Innovation in Facilities for the Mentally Retarded. Date not set. 12.50 (ISBN 0-685-32569-5). Univ Park.

MENTAL STEREOTYPE

see Stereotype (Psychology)

MENTAL SUGGESTION

see also Animal Magnetism; Autogenic Training; Brain-Washing; Hypnotism; Mental Healing; Therapeutics, Suggestive

Atkinson, William W. Mental Influence. pap. 1.00 (ISBN 0-911662-42-1). Yoga.
Baudouin, Charles. Suggestion & Autosuggestion. LC 76-25523. (Educational Ser.). 1920. Repr. 45.00 (ISBN 0-8482-0259-7). Norwood Edns.
--Suggestions & Autosuggestions. 1978. Repr. of 1920 ed. lib. bdg. 45.00 (ISBN 0-8495-0350-7). Arden Lib.

Brooks, C. Harry. The Practice of Autosuggestion by the Method of Emile Cove. 120p. 1981. write for info. (ISBN 0-89540-076-6, SB-076). Sun Pub.

Caprio, Frank S. & Berger, Joseph R. Helping Yourself with Self-Hypnosis. 1971. pap. 2.50 (ISBN 0-446-31073-5). Warner Bks.

--Helping Yourself with Self-Hypnosis. LC 63-10671. 1963. pap. 3.95 (ISBN 0-13-386623-8, Reward). P-H.

Coue, Emile. Self-Mastery Through Conscious Autosuggestion. 1922. 4.50 (ISBN 0-04-130005-X). Allen Unwin.

Curtis, David. Learn While You Sleep. 2nd ed. LC 60-15692. 1964. 5.00 (ISBN 0-87212-007-4); pap. 2.95 (ISBN 0-87212-008-2). Libra.

Hall, Manly P. Right Thinking. pap. 1.75 (ISBN 0-89314-350-2). Philos Res.

Hull, Clark L. Hypnosis & Suggestibility: An Experimental Approach. LC 33-30268. (Century Psychology Ser.). (Illus.). 1933. pap. text ed. 12.95x (ISBN 0-89197-223-4). Irvington.

Lewis, H. Spencer. Mental Poisoning. 1976. 6.25 (ISBN 0-686-00389-6). AMORC.

Lindner, Peter G. Mind Over Platter. pap. 3.00 (ISBN 0-87980-099-2). Wilshire.

Long, Max F. Self-Suggestion & the New Huna Theory of Mesmerism & Hypnosis. 1958. pap. 3.95 (ISBN 0-87516-048-4). De Vorss.

Lozanov, G. Suggestology & Outlines of Suggestopedy. (Psychic Studies). 1978. 19.25 (ISBN 0-677-30940-6). Gordon.

Nideffer, Robert M. & Sharpe, Roger C. A.C.T. Attention Control Training-How to Get Control of Your Mind Through Total Concentration. LC 78-15906. 1979. pap. 4.95 (ISBN 0-87223-543-2, Dist. by Har-Row). Wideview Bks.

Ousby, William J. Self-Hypnosis & Scientific Self-Suggestion. 1969. pap. 1.75 (ISBN 0-668-01815-1). Arco.

Powers, Melvin. Mental Power Thru Sleep Suggestion. pap. 3.00 (ISBN 0-87980-097-6). Wilshire.

Romen, A. S. Self-Suggestion & Its Influence on the Human Organism. Lewis, A. S. & Forsky, V., eds. (Illus.). 220p. 1980. 22.50 (ISBN 0-87332-195-2). M E Sharpe.

Sidis, Boris. The Psychology of Suggestion: A Research into the Subconscious Nature of Man & Society. LC 73-2415. (Mental Illness & Social Policy; the American Experience Ser.). Repr. of 1899 ed. 19.00 (ISBN 0-405-05225-1). Arno.

Simmons, Rachel. A Study of a Group of Children of Exceptionally High Intelligence Quotient in Situations Partaking of the Nature of Suggestion. LC 71-177781. (Columbia University. Teachers College. Contributions to Education: No. 788). Repr. of 1940 ed. 17.50 (ISBN 0-404-55788-0). AMS Pr.

Veeder, Gerry K. The Influence of Subliminal Suggestion on the Response to Two Films. LC 79-6689. (Dissertations on Film, 1980 Ser.). 1980. lib. bdg. 15.00x (ISBN 0-405-12921-1). Arno.

Wagner, Robert & Adams, Howard. Magic Dungeon Mentalism. 1972. 7.50 (ISBN 0-915926-06-7). Magic Ltd.

MENTAL TELEPATHY
see Thought-Transference

MENTAL TESTS
see Educational Tests and Measurements; Intelligence Tests; Psychological Tests

MENTAL TESTS–APPARATUS AND INSTRUMENTS
see Psychological Apparatus

MENTAL TYPES
see Typology (Psychology)

MENTALLY HANDICAPPED
see also Church Work with the Mentally Handicapped; Cookery for the Mentally Handicapped; Inefficiency, Intellectual; Mental Deficiency

Anders, Rebecca. A Look at Mental Retardation. LC 75-38466. (Lerner Awareness Bks.). (Illus.). 36p. (gr. 3-6). 1976. PLB 4.95 (ISBN 0-8225-1303-X). Lerner Pubns.

Anderson, Camilla. Society Pays. LC 71-186178. 256p. 1962. 6.95 (ISBN 0-8027-0373-9). Walker & Co.

Attwell, Arthur A. & Jamison, Colleen B. The Mentally Retarded: Answers to Questions About Sex. LC 76-48563. 153p. 1977. pap. 9.90x (ISBN 0-87424-143-X). Western Psych.

Barlow, Charles F. Mental Retardation & Related Disorders. LC 77-14933. (Contemporary Neurology Ser.: No. 17). 1978. text ed. 25.00 (ISBN 0-8036-0615-X). Davis Co.

Baroff, George S. Mental Retardation: Nature, Cause & Management. LC 74-14877. 504p. 1974. 17.95 (ISBN 0-470-05404-2); pap. text ed. 9.95x (ISBN 0-470-01370-2). Halsted Pr.

Begab, Michael J. & Haywood, H. Carl, eds. Psychosocial Influences in Retarded Performance, Vol. 1. (Issues & Theory in Development Ser.). 352p. 1981. pap. text ed. 29.95 (ISBN 0-8391-1634-9). Univ Park.

--Psychosocial Influences in Retarded Performance, Vol. 2. (Strategies for Improving Competence Ser.). 352p. 1981. pap. text ed. 29.95 (ISBN 0-8391-1635-7). Univ Park.

Begab, Michael J. & Richardson, Stephen A., eds. The Mentally Retarded & Society: A Social Science Perspective. (Illus.). 500p. 1975. 17.50 (ISBN 0-8391-0751-X). Univ Park.

Benson, Tony. Living & Laughing with the Retarded. 1980. 6.95 (ISBN 0-8062-1551-8). Carlton.

Berry, Paul, ed. Language & Communication in the Mentally Handicapped. (Illus.). 1976. 18.50 (ISBN 0-8391-0925-3). Univ Park.

Blake, Kathryn. The Mentally Retarded: An Educational Psychology. (Special Education Ser.). (Illus.). 416p. 1976. 19.95x (ISBN 0-13-576280-4). P-H.

Bogdan, Robert & Taylor, Steven. Inside Out: The Social Meaning of Mental Retardation. 256p. 1981. 14.95 (ISBN 0-8020-2432-7). U of Toronto Pr.

Brolin, Don E. Vocational Preparation of Retarded Citizens. (Illus.). 320p. 1976. text ed. 18.95 (ISBN 0-675-08667-1). Merrill.

Browning, Philip L. Mental Retardation: Rehabilitation & Counseling. (Illus.). 464p. 1974. 24.75 (ISBN 0-398-03006-5). C C Thomas.

Byars, Betsy. The Summer of the Swans. 1974. pap. 1.75 (ISBN 0-380-00098-9, 50526, Camelot). Avon.

Carpenter, Robert D. Thanks Doctor. LC 72-78231. 200p. 1972. pap. text ed. 4.95 (ISBN 0-9600576-1-7). RDC Pubs.

Carter, Charles H. Medical Aspects of Mental Retardation. 2nd ed. (Illus.). 912p. 1978. 72.00 (ISBN 0-398-03613-6). C C Thomas.

Cleland, Charles C. The Profoundly Mentally Retarded. LC 79-1258. 1979. text ed. 17.95 (ISBN 0-13-729566-9). P-H.

Cleland, Charles C. & Swartz, Jon D. Mental Retardation - Approaches to Institutional Change. LC 69-19945. 288p. 1969. 37.75 (ISBN 0-8089-0100-1). Grune.

Cobb, Henry V. The Forecast of Fulfillment: A Review of Research on Predictive Assessment of the Adult Retarded for Social & Vocational Adjustment. LC 72-3084. (Illus.). 176p. 1972. 5.00x (ISBN 0-8077-1168-3). Tchrs Coll.

Conley, Ronald. The Economics of Mental Retardation. LC 72-12345. 390p. 1973. 22.50x (ISBN 0-8018-1410-3). Johns Hopkins.

Craft, Ann & Craft, Michael. Handicapped Married Couples: A Welsh Study of Couples Handicapped from Birth by Mental, Physical of Personality Disorder. 1979. 25.00x (ISBN 0-7100-0417-7). Routledge & Kegan.

Craft, M. & Miles, L. Patterns of Care for the Mentally Subnormal. 1967. 22.00 (ISBN 0-08-012265-5); pap. 10.75 (ISBN 0-08-012264-7). Pergamon.

Craft, Michael & Craft, Ann. Sex & the Mentally Handicapped. 1978. 12.50x (ISBN 0-7100-8847-7). Routledge & Kegan.

Cunningham, Cliff & Sloper, Patricia. Helping Your Exceptional Baby: A Practical & Honest Approach to Raising a Mentally Handicapped Child. (Illus.). 1980. 12.95 (ISBN 0-394-51044-5). Pantheon.

Davies, Stanley P. Social Control of the Mentally Deficient. LC 75-17215. (Social Problems & Social Policy Ser.). (Illus.). 1975. Repr. of 1930 ed. 24.00x (ISBN 0-405-07486-7). Arno.

Davies, Stanley P. & Ecob, E. G. The Mentally Retarded in Society. 2nd ed. LC 58-59911. 248p. 1959. 17.50x (ISBN 0-231-02220-4). Columbia U Pr.

De La Cruz, F. & LaVeck, G. D., eds. Human Sexuality & the Mentally Retarded. LC 72-92057. 1973. 15.00 (ISBN 0-87630-063-8). Brunner-Mazel.

Dickerson, Martha U. Social Work Practice with the Mentally Retarded. Turner, Francis J. & Strean, Herbert S., eds. LC 80-2316. (Fields of Practice Ser.). 1981. text ed. 14.95 (ISBN 0-02-907430-4). Free Pr.

Doucette, John & Freedman, Ruth. Progress Tests for the Developmentally Disabled: An Evaluation. LC 79-55773. 1979. text ed. 27.50 (ISBN 0-89011-539-7). Abt Assoc.

Dunbar, Robert E. Mental Retardation. (First Bks). (Illus.). (gr. 4-6). 1978. PLB 6.90 (ISBN 0-531-01491-6). Watts.

Dutton, Gordon. Mental Handicap. (Postgraduate Psychiatry Ser.). 230p. 1975. 16.95 (ISBN 0-407-00035-6). Butterworth.

Eden, D. J. Mental Handicap. 128p. 1976. pap. 11.25x (ISBN 0-04-371042-5). Intl Pubns Serv.

Edgerton, Robert B. The Cloak of Competence: Stigma in the Lives of the Mentally Retarded. LC 67-14116. 1967. pap. 6.95x (ISBN 0-520-01899-0). U of Cal Pr.

Felicetti, Daniel A. Mental Health & Retardation Politics: The Mind Lobbies in Congress. LC 74-14042. (Illus.). 218p. 1975. text ed. 22.95 (ISBN 0-275-09930-X). Praeger.

Feuerstein, Reuven. The Dynamic Assessment of Retarded Performers: The Learning Potential, Assessment Device, Theory, Instruments & Techniques. 1979. 24.50 (ISBN 0-8391-1505-9). Univ Park.

Flanigan, Patrick J., et al. Orientation to Mental Retardation: A Programmed Text. (Illus.). 216p. 1973. 13.75 (ISBN 0-398-00584-2). C C Thomas.

Friedman, Paul. The Rights of Mentally Retarded Persons. 1976. pap. 2.50 (ISBN 0-380-00868-8, 54064, Discus). Avon.

Fulton, Robert T. & Lloyd, Lyle L., eds. Auditory Assessment of the Difficult-to-Test. 297p. 1975. 19.95 (ISBN 0-686-74200-1). Krieger.

Gibson, David & Brown, Roy I. Managing the Severely Retarded: A Sampler. (Illus.). 500p. 1976. 32.75 (ISBN 0-398-03513-X). C C Thomas.

Gibson, John. Mental Nursing Examination Questions & Answers. 4th ed. 224p. 1978. pap. 6.95 (ISBN 0-571-04967-2, Pub. by Faber & Faber). Merrimack Bk Serv.

Gilmore, Alden S. & Rich, Thomas A. Mental Retardation: A Programmed Manual for Volunteer Workers. (Illus.). 152p. 1973. 9.75 (ISBN 0-398-00681-4). C C Thomas.

Gottleib, J. Educating Mentally Retarded Persons: Social & Behavioral Aspects. 1980. 17.50 (ISBN 0-8391-1522-9). Univ Park.

Grossman, Frances K. Brothers & Sisters of Retarded Children: An Exploratory Study. LC 73-170664. (Special Education & Rehabilitation Monograph: No. 9). 1972. text ed. 9.50x (ISBN 0-8156-2154-X). Syracuse U Pr.

Gunzburg, H. C. Experiments in the Rehabilitation of the Mentally Handicapped. 21.95 (ISBN 0-407-17080-4). Butterworth.

--Social Competence & Mental Handicap. 2nd ed. (Illus.). 1973. text ed. 13.50 (ISBN 0-02-857880-5). Macmillan.

Gunzburg, H. C. & Gunzburg, Anna L. Mental Handicap & Physical Environment. (Illus.). 1973. text ed. 16.50 (ISBN 0-02-857890-2). Macmillan.

Hallas, Charles H. The Care & Training of the Mentally Handicapped. 6th ed. (Illus.). 1978. 19.95 (ISBN 0-8151-4105-X). Year Bk Med.

Hannah, Marta, et al. SCIL: Systematic Curriculum for Independent Living, 4 vols. 1977. Set. binders 165.00x (ISBN 0-87879-187-6). Acad Therapy.

Hardy, Richard E. & Cull, John G., eds. Severe Disabilities: Social & Rehabilitation Approaches. (American Lectures in Social & Rehabilitation Psychology Ser.). 336p. 1974. 19.75 (ISBN 0-398-02943-1). C C Thomas.

Hawley, Gloria H. How to Teach the Mentally Retarded. 1978. pap. 2.25 (ISBN 0-88207-180-7). Victor Bks.

Heaton-Ward, W. Alan. Left Behind: A Study of Mental Handicap. (Psychiatric Topics for Community Workers Ser.). 242p. 1978. 14.00x (ISBN 0-7130-0164-X, Pub. by Woburn Pr England). Biblio Dist.

Heber, Rick. Epidemiology of Mental Retardation. (Illus.). 136p. 1970. 11.75 (ISBN 0-398-00817-5). C C Thomas.

Hollingsworth, J. Selwyn. Mental Retardation, Cerebral Palsy, & Epilepsy in Alabama: A Sociological Analysis. LC 77-23418. (Illus.). 240p. 1978. 16.75x (ISBN 0-8173-2500-X). U of Ala Pr.

Iavanainen, Matti. A Study on the Origins of Mental Rehabilitation. (Clinics in Developmental Medicine Ser.: Vol. 51). 173p. 1974. 23.00 (ISBN 0-685-59045-3, JBL-Med-Nursing). Lippincott.

Ingalls, Robert P. Mental Retardation: The Changing Outlook. LC 77-23359. 1978. text ed. 22.95x (ISBN 0-471-42716-0). Wiley.

Isaacson, Robert. Meeting the Needs of the Retarded. 1977. pap. 2.95 (ISBN 0-913592-94-3). Argus Comm.

Jacobs, Jerry. Mental Retardation: A Phenomenological Approach. (Illus.). 244p. 1980. 24.50 (ISBN 0-398-04062-1); pap. 16.75 (ISBN 0-398-04063-X). C C Thomas.

Jansma, Paul, ed. The Psychomotor Domain & the Seriously Handicapped. LC 80-6299. (Illus.). 502p. (Orig.). 1981. lib. bdg. 30.00 (ISBN 0-8191-1718-8); pap. text ed. 19.25 (ISBN 0-8191-1719-6). U Pr of Amer.

Jarvis, Edward. Insanity & Idiocy in Massachusetts: Report of the Commission on Lunacy, 1855. LC 72-134950. (Commonwealth Fund Publications Ser). 1971. 16.50x (ISBN 0-674-45480-4). Harvard U Pr.

Jones, Kathleen. Opening the Door: A Study of New Policies for the Mentally Handicapped. (International Library of Social Policy Ser.). 1975. 22.50 (ISBN 0-7100-8139-1). Routledge & Kegan.

Jordan, Thomas E. The Mentally Retarded. 4th ed. 1976. text ed. 19.95x (ISBN 0-675-08616-7). Merrill.

Kanner, L. A History of the Care & Study of the Mentally Retarded. (Illus.). 160p. 1974. pap. 7.50 (ISBN 0-398-03038-3). C C Thomas.

Katz, Alfred H., ed. Mental Retardation & Social Work Education. LC 61-15754. 1961. 2.95x (ISBN 0-8143-1172-5). Wayne St U Pr.

Katz, Elias. Retarded Adult at Home. LC 74-123867. (Illus., Orig.). 1970. pap. 6.50 (ISBN 0-87562-019-1). Spec Child.

Katz, Elias, et al, eds. Mental Health Services for the Mentally Retarded. (Illus.). 292p. 1972. 17.50 (ISBN 0-398-02516-9). C C Thomas.

Kindred, Michael, et al. The Mentally Retarded Citizen & the Law: The President's Committee on Mental Retardation. LC 74-21489. 1976. 25.00 (ISBN 0-02-916860-0). Free Pr.

Kirman, B. H. Mental Handicap. (Illus.). 164p. 1975. 15.00x (ISBN 0-8464-0627-6). Beekman Pubs.

Kurtz, Richard A. Social Aspects of Mental Retardation. LC 76-42693. 1977. 18.95 (ISBN 0-669-01054-5). Lexington Bks.

Laus, Michael D. Travel Instruction for the Handicapped. 164p. 1977. 14.75 (ISBN 0-398-03637-3). C C Thomas.

McCormack. Prevention of Mental Retardation & Other Developmental Disabilities. (Pediatric Habilitation Ser.: Vol. 1). 680p. 1980. 49.75 (ISBN 0-8247-6950-3). Dekker.

Macklin, R. & Gaylin, W., eds. Mental Retardation & Sterilization: A Problem of Competency & Paternalism. (Hastings Center Ser. in Ethics). 237p. 1981. 19.50 (ISBN 0-306-40689-6, Plenum Pr). Plenum Pub.

MacMillan, Donald. Mental Retardation in School & Society. 1977. text ed. 17.95 (ISBN 0-316-54270-9); tchr's manual free (ISBN 0-316-54271-7). Little.

Malin, Nigel, et al. Services for the Mentally Handicapped in Britain. 266p. 1980. boards 30.00x (ISBN 0-85664-869-8, Pub. by Croom Helm Ltd England). Biblio Dist.

Mamula, Richard A. & Newman, Nate. Community Placement of the Mentally Retarded: A Handbook for Community Agencies and Social Work Practitioners. (Illus.). 156p. 1973. 10.75 (ISBN 0-398-02704-8); pap. 6.75 (ISBN 0-398-02761-7). C C Thomas.

Matson, J. L. Philosophy & Care of the Mentally Retarded: A Worldwide Status Report. 120p. 1981. pap. 13.80 (ISBN 0-08-028093-5). Pergamon.

Mattinson, Janet. Marriage & Mental Handicap: A Study of Subnormality in Marriage. LC 70-137335. (Contemporary Community Health Ser). 1971. 9.95 (ISBN 0-686-31671-1). U of Pittsburgh Pr.

Menolascino, Frank J. Challenges in Mental Retardation: Progressive Ideology & Services. LC 76-6947. 1977. text ed. 29.95 (ISBN 0-87705-295-6). Human Sci Pr.

Mercer, Jane R. Labeling the Mentally Retarded. 1973. pap. 7.95x (ISBN 0-520-02428-1). U of Cal Pr.

Meyers, C. Edward, ed. Quality of Life in Severely & Profoundly Mentally Retarded People: Research Foundations for Improvement. LC 77-91506. (AAMD Monograph Ser.: No. 3). 1978. 15.95x (ISBN 0-686-23879-6). Am Assn Mental.

Mittler, P., ed. Research to Practice in Mental Retardation: IASSMD Proceedings, 3 vols. 1977. Vol. 1. 29.50 (ISBN 0-8391-1122-3); Vol. 2. 29.50 (ISBN 0-8391-1123-1); Vol. 3. 29.50 (ISBN 0-8391-1124-X). Univ Park.

Mittler, Peter, ed. Psychological Assessment of Mental & Physical Handicaps. 886p. 1974. pap. 30.00x (ISBN 0-422-75600-8, Pub. by Tavistock England). Methuen Inc.

Morgenstern, Murry & Michal-Smith, Harold. Psychology in the Vocational Rehabilitation of the Mentally Retarded. 100p. 1973. text ed. 8.75 (ISBN 0-398-02696-3). C C Thomas.

Neisworth, John & Smith, Robert. Retardation: Issues, Assessment & Intervention. (Series in Special Education). (Illus.). 1978. text ed. 18.95 (ISBN 0-07-046201-1, C); instructor's manual 3.95 (ISBN 0-07-046202-X). McGraw.

Neisworth, John T. & Smith, Robert M. Modifying Retarded Behavior. (Illus.). 200p. 1973. text ed. 18.50 (ISBN 0-395-14049-8, 3-40420). HM.

O'Connor, N. Language, Cognitive Deficits, and Retardation. 376p. 1975. 33.95 (ISBN 0-407-00007-0). Butterworth.

Paul, James M., et al, eds. Deinstitutionalization: Program & Policy Development. (Special Education & Rehabilitation Monograph: No. 12). 1977. 13.95x (ISBN 0-8156-0132-8). Syracuse U Pr.

Popovich, Dorothy. A Prescriptive Behavioral Checklist for Severely & Profoundly Retarded. 416p. (Orig.). 1981. pap. text ed. 19.95 (ISBN 0-8391-4148-3). Univ Park.

--A Prescriptive Behavioral Checklist for the Severely & Profoundly Retarded, Vol. II. 352p. 1981. pap. text ed. 19.95 (ISBN 0-8391-4147-5). Univ Park.

Raynes, Norma V., et al. Organisational Structure & the Care of the Mentally Retarded. LC 79-83740. (Praeger Special Studies Ser.). 240p. 1979. 24.95 (ISBN 0-03-051516-5). Praeger.

Readings in Mental Handicaps. rev. ed. (Special Education Ser.). (Illus.). 224p. 1981. pap. text ed. 10.95 (ISBN 0-89568-195-1). Spec Learn Corp.

Readings in Mental Retardation. (Special Education Ser.). 1978. pap. text ed. 10.95 (ISBN 0-89568-002-5). Spec Learn Corp.

Redey, George & Spatz, Eugene. A Comprehensive Diagnostic Test to Evaluate Motor & Cognitive Ability for the Ambulatory Severely Mentally Retarded. LC 76-23718. 100p. 1976. vynil trade 5.00 (ISBN 0-935484-00-0). Universe Pub Co.

Rosen, Marvin & Clark, Gerald R., eds. The History of Mental Retardation: Collected Papers, 2 vols. (Illus.). 700p. 1975. 24.50 ea. (ISBN 0-8391-0827-3). Vol. 2 (ISBN 0-685-56047-3). Univ Park.

Rothstein, Jerome H., ed. Mental Retardation: Readings & Resources. 2nd ed. LC 70-143317. 1971. text ed. 13.50 (ISBN 0-03-084408-8, HoltC). Hr&W.

Sarason, Seymour B. & Doris, John. Educational Handicap, Public Policy, & Social History: A Broadened Perspective on Mental Retardation. LC 78-3203. 1979. 15.95 (ISBN 0-02-927920-8). Free Pr.

Schiefelbusch, Richard, ed. Language of the Mentally Retarded. (Illus.). 1972. 17.95 (ISBN 0-8391-0629-7). Univ Park.

Schlanger, Bernard. Mental Retardation. LC 73-9613. (Studies in Communicative Disorders Ser.). 1973. pap. 2.50 (ISBN 0-672-61289-5). Bobbs.

Schrader, Paul & Elms, Roslyn. Guidelines for Family Care Home Operators. LC 72-85087. 1972. pap. text ed. 5.95 (ISBN 0-8261-1270-6). Springer Pub.

Schulman. Focus on the Retarded Adult: Programs & Services. LC 79-17181. 1979. pap. 18.95 (ISBN 0-8016-4367-8). Mosby.

Segal, S. S., compiled by. Mental Handicap: A Select Annotated Bibliography. (Bibliographic Ser.). (Orig.). 1972. pap. text ed. 2.25x (ISBN 0-901225-90-8, NFER). Humanities.

Special Learning Corp., ed. Mentally Handicapped: Reference Book. (Special Education Ser.). (Illus., Orig.). 1981. pap. text ed. 64.00 (ISBN 0-89568-114-5). Spec Learn Corp.

Special People...Getting to Know Them: Resources in Mental Retardation. 1.00 (ISBN 0-686-70272-7). Boston Public Lib.

Szymanski, Ludwik S., ed. Emotional Disorders of Mentally Retarded Persons. 287p. pap. text ed. 18.95 (ISBN 0-8391-1514-8). Univ Park.

Viscardi, Henry, Jr. Abilities Story. LC 67-17282. (Illus.). 1971. 5.95 (ISBN 0-8397-0079-2). Eriksson.

Welsh, Marion E. Tales from a Human Warehouse. LC 77-88592. 1979. pap. 5.95 (ISBN 0-8283-1714-3). Branden.

Wills, Richard H. The Institutionalized Severely Retarded: A Study of Activity & Interaction. (Illus.). 208p. 1973. 13.75 (ISBN 0-398-02755-2). C C Thomas.

Wortis, Joseph, ed. Mental Retardation & Developmental Disabilities, Vol. XII. LC 73-647002. 200p. 1981. 20.00 (ISBN 0-87630-263-0). Brunner-Mazel.

Zaetz, Jay L. Organization of Sheltered Workshop Programs for the Mentally Retarded Adult. (Illus.). 248p. 1971. 24.75 (ISBN 0-398-02158-9). C C Thomas.

MENTALLY HANDICAPPED–EDUCATION

Amada, Gerald. Mental Health & Authoritarianism on the College Campus. LC 79-66480. 1979. pap. text ed. 12.00 (ISBN 0-8191-0831-6). U Pr of Amer.

Amary, Issam B. The Rights of the Mentally Retarded - Developmentally Disabled to Treatment & Education. (Illus.). 216p. 1980. text ed. 17.50 (ISBN 0-398-03946-1). C C Thomas.

Baker, Maryn. The Short Change Game: How to Stop the School from Depriving Your Retarded or Handicapped Child. 1981. 11.95 (ISBN 0-87949-211-2). Ashley Bks.

Balthazar, Earl E. Training the Retarded: A Manual for Parents, Teachers, & Home Trainers. (Orig.). 1976. pap. 5.00 (ISBN 0-89106-010-3, 5188). Consulting Psychol.

Evans, Sharon & Denney, M. Ray. Reading Achievement Program for the Moderately & Severely Retarded. LC 74-81202. xviii, 30p. 1974. pap. text ed. 2.50 (ISBN 0-8134-1665-5, 1665). Interstate.

Feldman, Stephen J. Vocational Training for the Mentally Retarded. (Special Education Ser.). (Illus., Orig.). 1978. pap. text ed. 10.95 (ISBN 0-89568-084-X). Spec Learn Corp.

Goldstein, Edward. Selective Audio-Visual Instruction for Mentally Retarded Pupils. (Illus.). 116p. 1964. ed. spiral bdg. 12.50photocopy (ISBN 0-398-00697-0). C C Thomas.

Kelly, George V. & Farrar, Harry. Garden of Hope: Laradon Hall. (Illus.). 240p. 1980. 12.50 (ISBN 0-87108-561-5); pap. 7.50 (ISBN 0-87108-562-3). Pruett.

Kent, Louise R. Language Acquisition Program for the Retarded or Multiply Impaired. (Illus., Orig.). 1974. pap. text ed. 10.95 spiral bd. (ISBN 0-87822-121-2). Res Press.

Kissinger, Ellen M. A Sequential Curriculum for the Severely & Profoundly Mentally Retarded-Multi-Handicapped. 276p. 1981. pap. 22.75 spiral (ISBN 0-398-04145-8). C C Thomas.

Leeming, Ken, et al. Teaching Language & Communication to the Mentally Retarded. 1979. 32.50x (ISBN 0-416-60051-4). Methuen Inc.

Leslie, Kathy, ed. Special Education. rev. ed. (Special Education Ser.). (Illus.). 1979. pap. text ed. 10.95 (ISBN 0-89568-120-X). Spec Learn Corp.

Lombardo, Victor S. Paraprofessionals in Special Education. (Illus.). 304p. 1980. text ed. 24.50 (ISBN 0-398-04105-9). C C Thomas.

McClennen, Sandra E., et al. Social Skills for Severely Retarded Adults: An Inventory & Training Program. LC 80-51546. 265p. 1980. 3-ring binder 36.95 (ISBN 0-87822-220-0, 2200). Res Press.

McDonald, Lillie B. Programmed: An Introduction of Concept of a Language Arts Unit for Advanced Educatable Mentally Retarded. LC 79-89926. 1979. pap. text ed. 4.75 (ISBN 0-8191-0853-7). U Pr of Amer.

Mittler, Peter. Frontiers of Knowledge in Mental Retardation, Vol. 2. 368p. 1981. text ed. 34.50 (ISBN 0-8391-1637-3). Univ Park.

Mittler, Peter, ed. Frontiers of Knowledge in Mental Retardation. 494p. 1981. text ed. 34.50 (ISBN 0-8391-1636-5). Univ Park.

Newman & Feldman, eds. Educable Mentally Handicapped. (Special Education Ser.). (Illus., Orig.). 1979. pap. text ed. 10.95 (ISBN 0-89568-105-6). Spec Learn Corp.

--Trainable Mentally Handicapped. (Special Education Ser.). (Illus., Orig.). 1979. pap. 10.95 (ISBN 0-89568-106-4). Spec Learn Corp.

Payne, James S. & Patton, James R. Mental Retardation. (Special Education Ser.). (Illus.). 480p. 1981. text ed. 20.95 (ISBN 0-675-08027-4); instr's manual 3.95 (ISBN 0-686-77725-5). Merrill.

Payne, James S., et al. Strategies for Teaching the Mentally Retarded. 2nd ed. (Special Education Ser.). 368p. 1981. text ed. 17.95 (ISBN 0-675-08067-3). Merrill.

Riggar, T. F. & Riggar, S. W. Career Education & Rehabilitation for the Mentally Handicapped. (Illus.). 288p. 1980. text ed. 24.75 (ISBN 0-398-04137-7). C C Thomas.

Rudman, Jack. Education of the Mentally Retarded. (National Teacher Examination Ser.: NT-24). (Cloth bdg. avail. on request). pap. 9.95 (ISBN 0-686-53780-7). Natl Learning.

Salvia, John & Ysseldyke, James E. Assessment in Special & Remedial Education. 2nd ed. (Illus.). 576p. 1981. text ed. 19.50 (ISBN 0-395-29694-3); instr's manual 1.00 (ISBN 0-686-77663-1). HM.

Stangvik, Gunnar. Self-Concept & School Segregation. (Goteborg Studies in Educational Sciences: No. 28). (Illus.). 1979. pap. text ed. 22.50x (ISBN 91-7346-064-8). Humanities.

Vanuxem, Mary. Education of Feeble-Minded Women. LC 73-177681. (Columbia University. Teachers College. Contributions to Education: No. 174). Repr. of 1925 ed. 17.50 (ISBN 0-404-55174-2). AMS Pr.

Watson, Luke S., Jr. Teaching Social-Recreational Skills to Mentally Retarded & Psychotic Children & Adults: A Manual of Game Programs. 3.60 (ISBN 0-686-75265-1). Behavior Mod Tech.

Wehman, Paul. Helping the Mentally Retarded Acquire Play Skills: A Behavioral Approach. (Illus.). 244p. 1977. 17.50 (ISBN 0-398-03604-7). C C Thomas.

MENTALLY HANDICAPPED–EMPLOYMENT

Bellamy, G. Thomas. Vocational Habilitation of Severely Retarded Adults. 241p. pap. text ed. 16.50 (ISBN 0-8391-1296-3). Univ Park.

Connis, Richard T. Training the Mentally Handicapped for Employment: A Comprehensive Manual. LC 81-1979. 1981. 18.95 (ISBN 0-89885-001-0). Human Sci Pr.

Feldman, Stephen J. Vocational Training for the Mentally Retarded. (Special Education Ser.). (Illus., Orig.). 1978. pap. text ed. 10.95 (ISBN 0-89568-084-X). Spec Learn Corp.

Gold, Marc. Marc Gold: "Did I Say That?". Articles & Commentary on the Try Another Way System. LC 80-51793. (Illus.). 347p. 1980. pap. text ed. 15.95 (ISBN 0-87822-219-7, 2197). Res Press.

Jacobs, Angeline M., et al. Handbook for Job Placement of Mentally Retarded Workers: Training, Opportunities, & Career Areas. LC 78-20654. (Garland Mental Retardation Ser.). 352p. 1979. lib. bdg. 27.50 (ISBN 0-8240-7061-5). Garland Pub.

Rusch, Frank R. & Mithaug, Dennis E. Vocational Training for Mentally Retarded Adults: A Behavior Analytic Approach. LC 79-66178. (Illus., Orig.). 1980. pap. text ed. 8.95 (ISBN 0-87822-203-0); Program Forms 3.95 (ISBN 0-87822-204-9); book & program forms 12.95 (ISBN 0-87822-212-X). Res Press.

Zaetz, Jay L. Occupational Activities Training Manual: For Severely Retarded Adults. (Illus.). 124p. 1969. photocopy ed. spiral 12.50 (ISBN 0-398-02138-4). C C Thomas.

MENTALLY HANDICAPPED–INSTITUTIONAL CARE

see also Mental Retardation Facilities; Psychiatric Hospitals

Alperin, Stanley & Alperin, Melvin, eds. Directory of Inpatient Facilities for the Mentally Retarded. 1976. 14.50 (ISBN 0-916524-02-7). US Direct Serv.

Blatt, Burton, et al. The Family Papers: A Return to Purgatory. (Illus.). 1980. pap. text ed. 8.95x (ISBN 0-582-28154-7). Longman.

Cormier, Bruno, ed. The Watchers & the Watched: A Study of the Guards & Prisoners in a Therapeutic Community. 1975. write for info. (ISBN 0-912766-13-1). Tundra Bks.

Dix, Dorothea L. On Behalf of the Insane Poor: Selected Reports 1843-1852. LC 78-137163. (Poverty U.S.A. Historical Record Ser). 1971. Repr. of 1843 ed. 21.00 (ISBN 0-405-03101-7). Arno.

Fanning, John W. A Common Sense Approach to Community Living Arrangements for the Mentally Retarded. (Illus.). 112p. 1975. 12.50 (ISBN 0-398-03300-5). C C Thomas.

Gibson, John & French, Thomas. Nursing the Mentally Retarded. 4th ed. 184p. 1978. 11.95 (ISBN 0-571-04959-1, Pub. by Faber & Faber); pap. 5.95 (ISBN 0-571-04941-9). Merrimack Bk Serv.

Glick, Ira D. & Hargreaves, William A. Psychiatric Hospital Treatment for the Nineteen Eighties. LC 77-26995. 1979. 18.95 (ISBN 0-669-01502-4). Lexington Bks.

Golann, S. & Fremouw, W. J., eds. The Right to Treatment for Mental Patients. LC 76-18917. 1976. 16.95 (ISBN 0-470-15172-2). Halsted Pr.

Hannah, Gerald T., et al, eds. Preservation of Client Rights: A Handbook for Practitioners Providing Therapeutic, Educational, & Rehabilitative Services. LC 80-1644. (Illus.). 1981. 25.00 (ISBN 0-02-913820-5). Free Pr.

Hazard, Thomas R. Report on the Poor & Insane in Rhode-Island. LC 73-2403. (Mental Illness & Social Policy; the American Experience Ser.). Repr. of 1851 ed. 9.50 (ISBN 0-405-05209-X). Arno.

McLaughlin, B. E. Long-Term Results of Psychiatric Out-Patient Treatment. 96p. 1965. photocopy ed. spiral 9.75 (ISBN 0-398-01265-2). C C Thomas.

Perrucci, Robert. Circle of Madness: On Being Insane & Institutionalized in America. 192p. 1974. pap. 3.45 (ISBN 0-13-133876-5, Spec). P-H.

Perske, R., ed. Mealtimes for Severely & Profoundly Retarded Persons. (Illus.). 1977. 11.95 (ISBN 0-8391-1152-5). Univ Park.

Seguin, Edward. Idiocy & Its Treatment by the Physiological Method. LC 79-12541. Repr. of 1866 ed. 19.50x (ISBN 0-678-00731-4). Kelley.

MENTALLY HANDICAPPED–LAWS AND LEGISLATION

see Mental Health Laws

MENTALLY HANDICAPPED–REHABILITATION

Askenasy, Alexander. Attitudes Towards Mental Patients. (New Babylon, Studies in the Social Sciences). 1974. text ed. 34.10x (ISBN 90-2797-891-3). Mouton.

Birenbaum, Arnold & Seiffer, Samuel. Resettling Retarded Adults in a Managed Community. LC 75-19765. 150p. 1976. text ed. 24.95 (ISBN 0-275-55520-8). Praeger.

Blackwell, Marian. Care of the Mentally Retarded. 1979. 15.95 (ISBN 0-316-09890-6). Little.

Blatt, Burton. In & Out of Mental Retardation. 392p. 1981. pap. text ed. 19.95 (ISBN 0-8391-1664-0). Univ Park.

Blatt, Burton & Kaplan, Fred. Christmas in Purgatory. 1974. 3.50 (ISBN 0-937540-00-5, HPP-3). Human Policy Pr.

Browning, Philip L. Rehabilitation & the Retarded Offender. (Illus.). 360p. 1976. 22.50 (ISBN 0-398-03481-8). C C Thomas.

Burton. Trainable Mentally Retarded. 1976. 15.50 (ISBN 0-675-08591-8). Merrill.

Butterworth, C. A. & Skidmore, D. Caring for the Mentally Ill in the Community. 128p. 1981. 24.50x (ISBN 0-7099-0071-6, Pub. by Croom Helm Ltd England). Biblio Dist.

Cleland, Charles C. The Profoundly Mentally Retarded. LC 79-1258. 1979. text ed. 17.95 (ISBN 0-13-729566-9). P-H.

Cornwall, Thomas & Cornwall, Judson. Please Accept Me. pap. 2.50 (ISBN 0-88270-391-9). Logos.

Crain, Cynthia D. Movement & Rhythmic Activities for the Mentally Retarded. (Illus.). 136p. 1981. 14.75 (ISBN 0-398-04174-1). C C Thomas.

Daniels, Lloyd K., ed. Vocational Rehabilitation of the Mentally Retarded: A Book of Readings. (Illus.). 648p. 1974. text ed. 37.75 (ISBN 0-398-02582-7). C C Thomas.

Daubert, James R. & Rothert, Eugene A., Jr. Horticultural Therapy for the Mentally Handicapped. (Illus.). 128p. 1981. pap. 10.00 (ISBN 0-939914-04-2). Chi Horticult.

Ginglend, David R. & Carlson, Bernice W. Ready to Work? Development of Occupational Skills, Attitudes, & Behaviors with Mentally Retarded Persons. LC 76-58841. 1977. 6.95 (ISBN 0-687-35559-1). Abingdon.

Gollay, Elinor, et al. Coming Back: The Community Experiences of Deinstitutionalized Mentally Retarded People. LC 78-68165. 1978. text ed. 19.50 (ISBN 0-89011-512-5). Abt Assoc.

Haavik, Sarah F. & Menninger, Karl A., 2nd. Sexuality, Law, & the Developmentally Disabled Person: Legal & Clinical Aspects of Marriage, Parenthood, & Sterilization. LC 81-777. 210p. (Orig.). 1981. pap. text ed. 13.95 (ISBN 0-933716-21-4). P H Brookes.

Hackett, Layne C. Movement Exploration & Games for the Mentally Retarded. 1970. pap. text ed. 4.95 (ISBN 0-917962-19-2). Peek Pubns.

Hardy, Richard E. & Cull, John G., eds. Modification of Behavior of the Mentally Retarded: Applied Principles. (American Lectures in Social & Rehabilitation Psychology Ser.). 180p. 1975. text ed. 16.75 (ISBN 0-398-03136-3). C C Thomas.

Haywood, H. Care & Newbrough, J. R., eds. Living Environments for Developmentally Retarded Persons. 360p. 1981. pap. text ed. 29.95 (ISBN 0-8391-1663-2). Univ Park.

Heshusius, Lous. Meaning in Life As Experienced by Persons Labeled Retarded in a Group Home: Their Quest to Be. (Illus.). 176p. 1980. 19.50 (ISBN 0-398-04064-8); pap. 15.75 (ISBN 0-398-04079-6). C C Thomas.

International Seminar on Vocational Rehabilitation for Mentally Retarded Persons, 2nd. Proceedings. Hollander, E. & Soloyanis, G., eds. LC 78-55690. 1978. pap. 5.50x (ISBN 0-686-23880-X). Am Assn Mental.

Katz, Elias. The Retarded Adult in the Community. (Illus.). 292p. 1977. 17.50 (ISBN 0-398-00981-3). C C Thomas.

Kelly, George V. & Farrar, Harry. Garden of Hope: Laradon Hall. (Illus.). 240p. 1980. 12.50 (ISBN 0-87108-561-5); pap. 7.50 (ISBN 0-87108-562-3). Pruett.

Kiernan, C. C. & Woodford, F. P., eds. Behaviour Modification with the Severely Retarded. (The Institute for Research into Mental & Multiple Handicap Study Group: 8). 1976. 41.50 (ISBN 0-444-15191-5, Excerpta Medica). Elsevier.

Larsen, Judith K., et al. Critical Behaviors in the Care of the Mentally Retarded: Vol. I, Behavior of Nurses. (AIR Monograph: No. 5). 1969. pap. 5.50 (ISBN 0-89785-208-7). Am Inst Res.

--Critical Behaviors in the Care of the Mentally Retarded: Vol. II, Behavior of Attendants. (AIR Monograph: No. 5). 1969. pap. 5.50 (ISBN 0-89785-209-5). Am Inst Res.

Litton, Freddie W. Education of the Trainable Mentally Retarded: Curriculum, Methods, Materials. LC 77-10772. (Illus.). 1978. text ed. 16.95 (ISBN 0-8016-3023-1). Mosby.

Matson, J. L. Philosophy & Care of the Mentally Retarded: A Worldwide Status Report. 120p. 1981. pap. 13.80 (ISBN 0-08-028093-5). Pergamon.

Matson, J. L. & McCartney, J. R., eds. Handbook of Behavior Modification with the Mentally Retarded. (Applied Clinical Psychology Ser.). 415p. 1981. 39.50 (ISBN 0-306-40617-9, Plenum Pr). Plenum Pub.

Menolascino, Frank J. Challenges in Mental Retardation: Progressive Ideology & Services. LC 76-6947. 1977. text ed. 29.95 (ISBN 0-87705-295-6). Human Sci Pr.

Popovich, D. Prescriptive Behavior Checklist, Vol. I. (Illus.). 1977. 17.95 (ISBN 0-8391-1100-2). Univ Park.

Raynes, Norma V., et al. Organisational Structure & the Care of the Mentally Retarded. 192p. 1980. 25.00x (ISBN 0-85664-532-X, Pub. by Croom Helm England). State Mutual Bk.

Readings in Vocational Training for the Mentally Retarded. (Special Education Ser.). 1978. pap. 10.95 (ISBN 0-89568-084-X). Spec Learn Corp.

Riggar, T. F. & Riggar, S. W. Career Education & Rehabilitation for the Mentally Handicapped. (Illus.). 288p. 1980. text ed. 24.75 (ISBN 0-398-04137-7). C C Thomas.
Sanders, Richard M. Behavior Modification in a Rehabilitation Facility. LC 75-5866. (Illus.). 127p. 1975. 8.95x (ISBN 0-8093-0718-9); pap. 3.95 (ISBN 0-8093-0719-7). S Ill U Pr.
Schifani, John W. Practical Stategies in Working with Trainable Mentally Retarded. 111p. 1977. pap. text ed. 7.00 (ISBN 0-8191-0028-5). U Pr of Amer.
Seligman, Milton. Group Counseling & Group Psychotherapy with the Handicapped. 415p. 1981. pap. text ed. 25.95 (ISBN 0-8391-1691-8). Univ Park.
Thompson, Travis & Grabowski, John, eds. Behavior Modification of the Mentally Retarded. 2nd ed. (Illus.). 576p. 1977. text ed. 17.95 (ISBN 0-19-502052-9); pap. text ed. 10.95x (ISBN 0-19-502053-7). Oxford U Pr.

MENTALLY HANDICAPPED, COOKERY FOR THE
see Cookery for the Mentally Handicapped

MENTALLY HANDICAPPED CHILDREN
see also Mentally Ill Children; Slow Learning Children;
also names of particular institutions

Allen, Robert M. & Cortazzo, Arnold D. Psychosocial & Educational Aspects & Problems of Mental Retardation. 136p. 1970. pap. 14.75 photocopy ed. spiral (ISBN 0-398-00031-X). C C Thomas.
Alpern, Gerald D. & Boll, Thomas J., eds. Education & Care of Moderately & Severely Retarded Children. LC 71-170090. (Orig.). 1971. pap. text ed. 9.00x (ISBN 0-87562-030-2). Spec Child.
Amary, Issam B. Creative Recreation for the Mentally Retarded. (Illus.). 128p. 1975. 14.75 (ISBN 0-398-03292-0). C C Thomas.
Avedon, Elliott M. Socio-Recreative Programming for the Retarded: A Handbook for Sponsoring Groups. LC 64-15576. (Orig.). 1964. pap. 3.50 (ISBN 0-8077-1041-5). Tchrs Coll.
Babington, Caroline H. Parenting & the Retarded Child. (Illus.). 224p. 1981. 14.95 (ISBN 0-398-04539-9). C C Thomas.
Baker, Betty S. A Study of Social Status, Personality Characteristics, & Motor Ability of Mentally Handicapped Girls. LC 74-28604. 1975. soft bdg. 8.00 (ISBN 0-88247-311-5). R & E Res Assoc.
Baldwin, Victor L., et al. Isn't It Time He Outgrew This? or A Training Program for Parents of Retarded Children. (Illus.). 230p. 1980. 13.50 (ISBN 0-398-02636-X). C C Thomas.
Baptista, Bob & Baptista, Martha. Ric. 150p. 1981. 7.95 (ISBN 0-8024-7351-2). Moody.
Baranyay, E. P. Mentally Handicapped Adolescent: The Slough Project of the National Society for Mentally Handicapped Children. 1971. text ed. 22.00 (ISBN 0-08-016271-1). Pergamon.
Beter, Thais R. & Cragin, Wesley E. The Mentally Retarded Child & His Motor Behavior: Practical Diagnosis & Movement Experiences. (Illus.). 208p. 1972. 19.75 (ISBN 0-398-02230-5). C C Thomas.
Blodgett, Harriet E. & Warfield, Grace J. Understanding Mentally Retarded Children. LC 59-12295. (Illus., Orig.). 1959. pap. text ed. 2.95x (ISBN 0-89197-457-1). Irvington.
Boersma, Frederic J. & Muir, Walter. Eye Movements & Information Processing in Mentally Retarded Children. (Modern Approaches to the Diagnosis & Instruction of Multi-Handicapped Children Ser.: Vol. 14). 100p. 1975. text ed. 21.50 (ISBN 90-237-4125-0, Pub. by Swets Pub Serv Holland). Swets North Am.
Braginsky, D. D. & Braginsky, B. M. Hansels & Gretels: Studies of Children in Institutions for the Mentally Retarded. LC 71-138669. 1971. pap. text ed. 6.95 (ISBN 0-03-080047-1, HoltC). HR&W.
Brewer, Garry D. & Kakalik, James S. Handicapped Children: Strategies for Improving Services. (Illus.). 1978. 21.95 (ISBN 0-07-007680-4, P&RB). McGraw.
Brightman, Alan. Like Me. 3.95 (ISBN 0-686-31420-4). NACAC.
Brubakken, David M., et al. Treatment of Psychotic & Neurologically Impaired Children: A Systems Approach. 288p. 1980. text ed. 17.50 (ISBN 0-442-26647-2). Van Nos Reinhold.
Bull, Inez. Retarded Child. LC 72-94851. 1973. 5.00 (ISBN 0-682-47652-8). Exposition.
Carlson, Bernice & Ginglend, David R. Play Activities for the Retarded Child. (Illus.). 1961. 6.95 (ISBN 0-687-31636-7). Abingdon.
Carson, Mary. Guide for Friends, Neighbors, & Relatives of Retarded Children. (Illus.). 1977. pap. 2.45 (ISBN 0-89570-107-3). Claretian Pubns.
Cooper, Brian, ed. Assessing the Handicaps & Needs of Mentally Retarded Children. LC 81-66374. 1981. price not set (ISBN 0-12-188020-6). Acad Pr.
Copeland, Mildred, et al. Occupational Therapy for Mentally Retarded Children: Guidelines for Occupational Therapy Aides & Certified Occupational Therapy Assistants. (Illus.). 1976. 15.95 (ISBN 0-8391-0930-X). Univ Park.
Craig, Mary. Blessings. LC 79-84041. 1979. 6.95 (ISBN 0-688-03456-X). Morrow.
Cunningham, Cliff & Sloper, Patricia. Helping Your Exceptional Baby: A Practical & Honest Approach to Raising a Mentally Handicapped Child. (Illus.). 1980. 12.95 (ISBN 0-394-51044-5). Pantheon.
Das, J. P. & Baine, David. Mental Retardation for Special Educators. (Illus.). 332p. 1978. 27.50 (ISBN 0-398-03665-9); pap. 18.50 (ISBN 0-398-03666-7). C C Thomas.
Deich, Ruth F. & Hodges, Patricia M. Language Without Speech. LC 77-27371. (Illus.). 1978. 15.00 (ISBN 0-87630-166-9). Brunner-Mazel.
Dempsey, John J. Community Services for Retarded Children: The Consumer-Provider Relationship. (Illus.). 350p. 1975. 18.50 (ISBN 0-8391-0812-5). Univ Park.
Deppe, Phillip, et al. The High Risk Child: A Guide for Concerned Parents. 224p. 1981. 12.95 (ISBN 0-02-531010-0). Macmillan.
Dickerson, Martha U. Our Four Boys: Foster Parenting Retarded Teenagers. 1978. pap. 7.95 (ISBN 0-8156-0155-7). Syracuse U Pr.
Dix, Dorothea L. On Behalf of the Insane Poor: Selected Reports 1843-1852. LC 78-137163. (Poverty U.S.A. Historical Record Ser). 1971. Repr. of 1843 ed. 21.00 (ISBN 0-405-03101-7). Arno.
Doman, Glenn. What to Do About Your Brain Injured Child. LC 72-92202. 312p. 1974. 9.95 (ISBN 0-385-02139-9). Doubleday.
Drew, Clifford J. & Hardman, Michael L. Mental Retardation: Social & Education Perspectives. LC 73-26680. (Illus.). 1977. pap. 12.00 (ISBN 0-8016-1462-7). Mosby.
Eden, David. Mental Handicap: An Introduction. LC 75-34375. 128p. 1976. 15.95 (ISBN 0-470-01373-7). Halsted Pr.
Farber, B. Effects of a Severely Mentally Retarded Child on Family Integration. 1959. pap. 6.00 (ISBN 0-527-01578-4). Kraus Repr.
--Family Organization and Crisis: Maintenance of Integration in Families with a Severely Mentally Retarded Child. 1960. pap. 5.00 (ISBN 0-527-01583-0). Kraus Repr.
Fassler, Joan. One Little Girl. 7.95 (ISBN 0-686-31421-2). NACAC.
Fernald, Grace M. Remedial Techniques in Basic School Subjects. 1943. text ed. 15.95 (ISBN 0-07-020540-X, C). McGraw.
Flory, Charles D. Physical Growth of Mentally Deficient Boys. 1936. pap. 7.00 (ISBN 0-527-01491-5). Kraus Repr.
Flowers, Ann M. Helping the Child with a Learning Disability-Suggestions for Parents. 1969. pap. text ed. 0.30x (ISBN 0-8134-1133-5, 1133). Interstate.
Fotheringham, John & Morris, Joan. Understanding the Preschool Retarded Child. 1976. pap. text ed. 4.25x (ISBN 0-8077-8006-5). Tchrs Coll.
Gallagher, J. J. Comparison of Brain-Injured and Non-Brain-Injured Mentally Retarded Children on Several Psychological Variables. 1957. pap. 5.00 (ISBN 0-527-01570-9). Kraus Repr.
Gath, Ann. Down's Syndrome & the Family: The Early Years. 1978. 20.50 (ISBN 0-12-277450-7). Acad Pr.
Glasscote, Raymond M., et al. Children & Mental Health Centers: Programs, Problems, Prospects, 1972. 257p. 1972. pap. 7.50 (ISBN 0-686-76966-X, P172-0). Am Psychiatric.
Glazzard, Margaret H. Meet Lance: Trainable Mentally Retarded. 1978. 8.95 (ISBN 0-89079-035-3). H & H Ent.
Grossman, Frances K. Brothers & Sisters of Retarded Children: An Exploratory Study. LC 73-170664. (Special Education & Rehabilitation Monograph: No. 9). 1972. text ed. 9.50x (ISBN 0-8156-2154-X). Syracuse U Pr.
Harrison, Saul I. & McDermott, John F., eds. Childhood Psychopathology: An Anthology of Basic Readings. LC 76-141808. 900p. 1972. text ed. 30.00 (ISBN 0-8236-0776-3). Intl Univs Pr.
Healy, William. Mental Conflicts & Misconduct. LC 69-16237. (Criminology, Law Enforcement, & Social Problems Ser.: No. 88). 1969. Repr. of 1917 ed. 12.50 (ISBN 0-87585-088-X). Patterson Smith.
Heisler, Verda. A Handicapped Child in the Family: A Guide for Parents. LC 71-168847. 176p. 1972. 25.00 (ISBN 0-8089-0734-4). Grune.
Holle, Britta. Motor Development in Children Normal & Retarded. 1977. pap. 23.00 (ISBN 0-397-60509-9, Pub by Blackwell Scientific). Mosby.
Hollingworth, Leta S. The Psychology of Subnormal Children. 1979. Repr. of 1926 ed. lib. bdg. 25.00 (ISBN 0-8495-2264-1). Arden Lib.
Hutt, Max L. & Gibby, Robert G. The Mentally Retarded Child: Development, Training, & Education. 4th ed. 1979. text ed. 20.95 (ISBN 0-205-06520-1, 2465205). Allyn.
Isaacson, Robert. The Retarded Child: A Guide for Parents & Friends. LC 73-94483. 1974. pap. 2.95 (ISBN 0-913592-35-8). Argus Comm.
Ishtiaq, Kishwar. Mentally Retarded Children: A Social-Psychological Study. 1977. text ed. 12.00x (ISBN 0-8426-1042-1). Verry.
Johnson, Vicki M. & Werner, Roberta A. Step-by-Step Learning Guide for Older Retarded Children. 1977. pap. 9.95x (ISBN 0-8156-2181-7). Syracuse U Pr.
Kirk, Samuel A., et al. You & Your Retarded Child: A Manual for Parents of Retarded Children. 2nd ed. LC 67-20824. (Pacific Books Paperbounds, PB-2). (Orig.). 1968. 7.95 (ISBN 0-87015-160-6); pap. 4.95 (ISBN 0-87015-161-4). Pacific Bks.
Kirman, Brian H. The Mentally Handicapped Child. LC 73-6174. 240p. 1973. 7.95 (ISBN 0-8008-5188-9). Taplinger.
Klein, Gerda. The Blue Rose. LC 74-9383. (Illus.). 64p. (gr. 3-7). 1974. 8.95 (ISBN 0-88208-047-4); pap. 3.95 (ISBN 0-88208-048-2). Lawrence Hill.
Kline, Judy. Children Move to Learn: A Guide to Planning Gross Motor Activities. 1977. pap. text ed. 4.95 (ISBN 0-88450-771-8, 2036-B). Communication Skill.
Koch, Richard & Koch, Kathryn J. Understanding Your Mentally Retarded Child: A New Approach. (Illus.). 1974. 10.95 (ISBN 0-394-48547-5). Random.
Kronick, Doreen. Social Development of Learning Disabled Persons: Examining the Effects & Treatments of Inadequate Interpersonal Skills. LC 81-81960. (Social & Behavioral Science Ser.). Date not set. text ed. price not set (ISBN 0-87589-499-2). Jossey-Bass.
Larsen, Hanne. Don't Forget Tom. LC 77-20953. (John Day Bk.). (Illus.). (gr. k-4). 1978. PLB 7.89 (ISBN 0-381-99554-2, TYC-J). T Y Crowell.
Levinson, Abraham. The Mentally Retarded Child. rev. & enl. ed. LC 77-25884. (Illus.). 1978. Repr. of 1965 ed. lib. bdg. 19.00x (ISBN 0-313-20123-4, LEMR). Greenwood.
Levinson, Elizabeth J. Retarded Children in Maine: A Survey & Analysis. 1962. pap. 2.00 (ISBN 0-89101-008-4). U Maine Orono.
Linde, T. F. & Kopp, T. Training Retarded Babies & Preschoolers. (Illus.). 200p. 1974. 17.50 (ISBN 0-398-02825-7). C C Thomas.
Loewy, Herta. More About the Backward Child. 1959. 3.75 (ISBN 0-8022-0989-0). Philos Lib.
Love, Harold D. The Mentally Retarded Child & His Family. (Illus.). 216p. 1973. text ed. 11.25 (ISBN 0-398-02728-5); pap. text ed. 7.95 (ISBN 0-398-02760-9). C C Thomas.
McIntyre, Barbara. Informal Dramatics: A Language Arts Activity for the Special Pupil. LC 63-15035. (Illus.). 1963. pap. 4.50x (ISBN 0-87076-803-4). Stanwix.
MacKay, R. J. Mental Handicap in Child Health Practice. (Postgraduate Pediatric Ser.). 1976. 19.95x (ISBN 0-407-00113-1). Butterworth.
McLean, J. E. & Yoder, D. E., eds. Language Intervention with the Retarded. (Illus.). 1972. 19.50 (ISBN 0-8391-0675-0). Univ Park.
Manocha, Sohan L. Malnutrition & Retarded Human Development. (Illus.). 400p. 1972. 39.50 (ISBN 0-398-02548-7). C C Thomas.
Meers, Hilda. Helping Our Children Talk. LC 75-43561. (Longman Early Childhood Education Ser.). 1977. text ed. 10.00x (ISBN 0-582-25014-5); pap. text ed. 8.95x (ISBN 0-582-25010-2). Longman.
Menolascino, Frank J., ed. Psychiatric Aspects of the Diagnosis & Treatment of Mental Retardation. LC 69-20313. 1971. pap. 9.00x (ISBN 0-87562-029-9). Spec Child.
Menolascino, Frank J. & Pearson, Paul H., eds. Beyond the Limits: Innovations in Services for the Severely & Profoundly Retarded. LC 74-84668. 1974. pap. 8.50x (ISBN 0-87562-053-1). Spec Child.
Monkman, Marjorie M. A Milieu Therapy Program for Behaviorally Disturbed Children. (Illus.). 312p. 1972. 19.75 (ISBN 0-398-02363-8). C C Thomas.
Montgomery, Patricia & Richter, Eileen. Sensorimotor Integration for Developmentally Disabled Children: A Handbook. LC 76-62660. 83p. 1977. pap. 11.40x (ISBN 0-87424-142-1). Western Psych.
Moran, Joan M. & Kalakian, Leonard. Movement Experiences for the Mentally Retarded or Emotionally Disturbed Child. 2nd ed. LC 77-70931. 1977. text ed. 15.95x (ISBN 0-8087-1386-8). Burgess.
Moxley, David, et al. Socialization Games for Mentally Retarded Adolescents & Adults. (Illus.). 112p. 1981. spiral 12.75 (ISBN 0-398-04545-3). C C Thomas.
Myers, Donald G., et al. The Right-to-Education Child: A Curriculum for the Severely & Profoundly Mentally Retarded. (Illus.). 248p. 1978. 14.00 (ISBN 0-398-02923-7). C C Thomas.
Nason, Donna. Child of Hope & Dreams: More About Tara. 1978. pap. 4.95 (ISBN 0-8423-6920-1). Tyndale.
New York Institute for Child Development & Walsh, Richard. Treating Your Hyperactive & Learning Disabled Child: What You Can Do. LC 76-23750. (Illus.). 1979. 8.95 (ISBN 0-385-12508-9, Anchor Pr). Doubleday.
Noland, Robert L. Counseling Parents of the Mentally Retarded: A Sourcebook. (Illus.). 420p. 1978. 16.75 (ISBN 0-398-01405-1). C C Thomas.
Ochroch, Ruth. Diagnosis & Treatment of Children with Minimal Brain Dysfunction: A Clinical Approach. 304p. 1981. professional 29.95x (ISBN 0-87705-503-3). Human Sci Pr.
Ominsky, Elaine. Jon O: A Special Boy. LC 76-41735. (Illus.). (gr. 1-4). 1977. 8.95 (ISBN 0-13-510453-X). P-H.
O'Neil, Sally M., et al. Behavioral Approaches to Children with Developmental Delays. (Illus.). 1977. pap. 9.50 (ISBN 0-8016-3709-0). Mosby.
Perske, Robert & Perske, Martha. New Directions for Parents of Persons Who Are Retarded. LC 74-28016. (Illus.). 64p. 1973. pap. 1.95 (ISBN 0-687-27734-5). Abingdon.
Pevsner, Maria S. Oligophrenia: Mental Deficiency in Children. LC 61-11207. (Illus.). 406p. 1961. 42.50 (ISBN 0-306-10562-4, Consultants). Plenum Pub.
Pollock, Morris P. & Pollock, Miriam. New Hope for the Retarded. (Special Education Ser). (Illus.). 1953. 4.50 (ISBN 0-87558-019-X); pap. 2.75 (ISBN 0-87558-020-3). Porter Sargent.
Popovich, D. Prescriptive Behavior Checklist, Vol. I. (Illus.). 1977. 17.95 (ISBN 0-8391-1100-2). Univ Park.
Popovich, Dorothy & Laham, Sandra L., eds. The Adaptive Behavior Curriculum: Prescriptive Behavior Analyses for Moderately, Severely, & Profoundly Handicapped Students, Vol. 2. LC 80-39511. 352p. (Orig.). 1981. pap. text ed. 15.95 (ISBN 0-933716-17-6). P H Brookes.
Pritchard, Miriam C. The Mechanical Ability of Subnormal Boys. LC 70-177167. (Columbia University. Teachers College. Contributions to Education: No. 699). Repr. of 1937 ed. 17.50 (ISBN 0-404-55699-X). AMS Pr.
Proceedings of the Regional Institute on the Blind Child Who Functions on a Retarded Level. 1969. 4.50 (ISBN 0-89128-030-8, PCP030). Am Foun Blind.
Riesz, Elizabeth. First Years of a Down's Syndrome Child. LC 78-52436. 1978. pap. 11.00x (ISBN 0-87562-059-0). Spec Child.
Robinson, Halbert B. & Robinson, Nancy M. The Mentally Retarded Child. 2nd ed. (Psychology Ser.). (Illus.). 672p. 1976. text ed. 21.00 (ISBN 0-07-053202-8, C); instructor's manual 4.95 (ISBN 0-07-053203-6). McGraw.
Ross, Bette M. Our Special Child: A Guide to Successful Parenting of Handicapped Children. LC 80-54815. 192p. 1981. 12.95 (ISBN 0-8027-0678-9). Walker & Co.
Rotatori, Anthony F. & Fox, Robert. Behavioral Weight Reduction Program for Mentally Handicapped Persons. 232p. (Orig.). 1981. pap. text ed. 19.95 (ISBN 0-8391-1661-6). Univ Park.
Rothstein, Jerome H., ed. Mental Retardation: Readings & Resources. 2nd ed. LC 70-143317. 1971. text ed. 13.50 (ISBN 0-03-084408-8, HoltC). Hr&W.
Sobol, Harriet L. My Brother Steven Is Retarded. 5.95 (ISBN 0-686-31422-0). NACAC.
--My Brother Steven Is Retarded. LC 76-46996. (Illus.). (gr. 3-6). 1977. 7.95 (ISBN 0-02-785990-8). Macmillan.
Szurek, S. A. & Berlin, I. N., eds. Psychosomatic Disorders & Mental Retardation in Children. LC 67-26457. (Langley Porter Child Psychiatry Ser: Vol. 3). (Orig.). 1968. pap. 6.95x (ISBN 0-8314-0018-8). Sci & Behavior.
Upton, G., ed. Physical & Creative Activities for the Mentally Handicapped. LC 77-82519. (Illus.). 1979. 13.95x (ISBN 0-521-21778-4). Cambridge U Pr.
Von Hilsheimer, George. Understanding Young People in Trouble. rev. ed. LC 76-114037. (Illus.). 200p. 1974. pap. 4.50 (ISBN 0-87491-391-8). Acropolis.
White, Robin. The Special Child: A Parents' Guide to Mental Disabilities. LC 78-5656. 1978. 8.95 (ISBN 0-316-93597-2). Little.

Wilkin, David. Caring for the Mentally Handicapped Child. 192p. 1980. 30.00x (ISBN 0-85664-648-2, Pub. by Croom Helm England). State Mutual Bk.
--Caring for the Mentally Handicapped Child. 223p. 1979. 30.00x (ISBN 0-85664-648-2, Pub. by Croom Helm Ltd England). Biblio Dist.
Wilton, Keri M. & Boersma, Frederic J. Eye Movements, Surprise Reactions & Cognitive Development. (Modern Approaches to the Diagnosis & Instruction of Multi-Handicapped Children: Vol. 13). 78p. 1973. text ed. 17.75 (ISBN 90-237-4117-X, Pub. by Swets Pub Serv Holland). Swets North Am.
Wunderlich, Christof. The Mongoloid Child: Recognition & Care. Tinsley, Royal L., Jr., et al, trs. from Ger. LC 76-15755. 1977. 12.50x (ISBN 0-8165-0610-8); pap. 5.95x (ISBN 0-8165-0519-5). U of Ariz Pr.
Young, Meredith. The Mentally Defective Child. (Educational Ser.). 1916. Repr. 15.00 (ISBN 0-685-43631-4). Norwood Edns.
Zuckerman, Lawrence & Yura, Michael T. Raising the Exceptional Child. LC 79-63620. 1979. 11.95 (ISBN 0-8015-6220-1, Hawthorn). Dutton.

MENTALLY HANDICAPPED CHILDREN–EDUCATION

see also Religious Education of Mentally Handicapped Children

Adams, Jane L. An Education Curriculum for the Moderately, Severely & Profoundly Mentally Handicapped Pupil. 2nd ed. 96p. 1980. pap. 11.75 (ISBN 0-398-03264-5). C C Thomas.
Ahrens, Michael. Activities for Intellectually Handicapped Children. LC 76-357014. 1975. 6.10x (ISBN 0-7233-0423-8). Intl Pubns Serv.
Allen, Robert M. & Cortazzo, Arnold D. Psychosocial & Educational Aspects & Problems of Mental Retardation. 136p. 1970. pap. 14.75 photocopy ed. spiral (ISBN 0-398-00031-X). C C Thomas.
American Alliance for Health, Physical Education, & Recreation. Resource Guide in Sex Education for the Mentally Retarded. 80p. 1971. pap. 4.00x (ISBN 0-685-23972-1, 244-25134). AAHPERD.
Baker, Bruce L., et al. Toward Independent Living: A Skills Training Series for Children with Special Needs. LC 80-51922. (Steps to Independence Ser.). (Illus.). 118p. 1980. pap. text ed. 7.95 spiral bdg. (ISBN 0-87822-221-9, 2219). Res Press.
Barrett, Albert M. When Thinking Begins: Lessons Learned from Helping Preaverage Intelligence Individuals. (Illus.). 84p. 1973. text ed. 8.75 (ISBN 0-398-02770-6). C C Thomas.
Baumgartner, Bernice B. Helping Every Trainable Mentally Retarded Child. LC 75-2494. 1975. pap. 5.00x (ISBN 0-8077-2472-6). Tchrs Coll.
Bennett, Annette. A Comparative Study of Subnormal Children in Elementary Grades. LC 76-176552. (Columbia University. Teachers College. Contributions to Education: No. 510). Repr. of 1932 ed. 17.50 (ISBN 0-404-55510-1). AMS Pr.
Berdine, William H. & Cegelka, Patricia T. Teaching the Trainable Retarded. (Special Education Ser.). 312p. 1980. text ed. 16.95 (ISBN 0-675-08200-5). Merrill.
Blackhurst & Berdine. An Introduction to Special Education. 1981. text ed. 18.95 (ISBN 0-316-09060-3); tchrs'. manual free (ISBN 0-316-09061-1). Little.
Blake, Kathryn. Teaching the Retarded. LC 73-13719. (Special Education Ser.). (Illus.). 384p. 1974. 18.95 (ISBN 0-13-895276-0). P-H.
Boersma, Frederic J. & Muir, Walter. Eye Movements & Information Processing in Mentally Retarded Children. (Modern Approaches to the Diagnosis & Instruction of Multi-Handicapped Children Ser.: Vol. 14). 100p. 1975. text ed. 21.50 (ISBN 90-237-4125-0, Pub. by Swets Pub Serv Holland). Swets North Am.
Bookbinder, Susan R. Mainstreaming: What Every Child Needs to Know About Disabilities, The Meeting Street School Curriculum Guide for Grades 1-4. Schleifer, Maxwell J. & Griffin, John, eds. 1978. pap. 6.95 (ISBN 0-930958-02-0). Exceptional Parent.
Broady, K. O. School Provision for Individual Differences. LC 71-176591. (Columbia University. Teachers College. Contributions to Education: No. 395). Repr. of 1930 ed. 17.50 (ISBN 0-404-55395-8). AMS Pr.
Brown, Alpha. One Hundred & One Practical Activities for Use in Classes of Pupils Who Are Retarded. 1970. pap. 2.95x (ISBN 0-88323-058-5, 156). Richards Pub.
Browning, Robert M. Teaching the Severely Handicapped Child: Basic Skills for the Developmentally Disabled. 300p. 1980. text ed. 19.95 (ISBN 0-205-06877-4). Allyn.
Brutten, Milton, et al. Something's Wrong with My Child: A Parents' Book About Children with Learning Disabilities. LC 73-5876. 1973. 8.95 (ISBN 0-15-183737-6). HarBraceJ.
Buist, Charlotte A. & Schulman, Jerome L. Toys & Games for Educationally Handicapped Children. 240p. 1976. pap. 18.75 (ISBN 0-398-00250-9). C C Thomas.
Carpenter, Robert D. Why Can't I Learn. LC 73-76060. 1972. 6.95 (ISBN 0-8307-0226-1); pap. 4.95 (ISBN 0-8307-0224-5). RDC Pubs.
Champlin, John & Champlin, Connie. Books, Puppets & the Mentally Retarded Student. (Illus.). 162p. (Orig.). 1981. pap. 9.95 (ISBN 0-938594-00-1). Spec Lit Pr.
Chaney, Clara M. & Miles, Nancy R. Remediating Learning Problems: A Developmental Curriculum. LC 73-92372. 244p. 1974. pap. text ed. 9.95x (ISBN 0-675-08816-X). Merrill.
Cleverdon, Dorthy & Rosenzweig, Louis E. A Work Play Program for the Trainable Mentally Deficient. pap. 1.00 (ISBN 0-936426-02-0). Play Schs.
Comley, John, ed. Behaviour Modification with the Retarded Child. 1975. pap. 15.95x (ISBN 0-433-06410-2). Intl Ideas.
Das, J. P. & Baine, David. Mental Retardation for Special Educators. (Illus.). 332p. 1978. 27.50 (ISBN 0-398-03665-9); pap. 18.50 (ISBN 0-398-03666-7). C C Thomas.
Davis, G. P. What Shall the Public Schools Do for the Feeble Minded? (Harvard Studies in Education: Vol. 10, Pt. 1). 1927. pap. 15.50 (ISBN 0-384-11005-3). Johnson Repr.
Davis, William F. Educator's Resource Guide to Special Education: Terms-Laws-Tests-Organizations. 270p. 1980. text ed. 19.95 (ISBN 0-205-06876-6). Allyn.
De Vore, M. Susan. Individualized Learning Program for the Profoundly Retarded. (Illus.). 256p. 1978. pap. 18.50 (ISBN 0-398-03728-0). C C Thomas.
Dickinson, Pamela I. Music with ESN Children. (General Ser.). 144p. 1976. pap. text ed. 13.75x (ISBN 0-85633-085-X, NFER). Humanities.
Drew, Clifford J. & Hardman, Michael L. Mental Retardation: Social & Education Perspectives. LC 73-26680. (Illus.). 1977. pap. 12.00 (ISBN 0-8016-1462-7). Mosby.
Dunn, L. & Capobianco, R. J. Studies of Reading & Arithmetic in Mentally Retarded Boys. 1954. pap. 8.00 (ISBN 0-527-01560-1). Kraus Repr.
Eden, D. J. Mental Handicap: An Introduction. (Unwin Education Bks.). 1976. pap. text ed. 7.95x (ISBN 0-04-371042-5). Allen Unwin.
Eden, David. Mental Handicap: An Introduction. LC 75-34375. 128p. 1976. 15.95 (ISBN 0-470-01373-7). Halsted Pr.
Educable Mentally Retarded Student in the Secondary School. LC 75-1431. (What Research Says to the Teacher Ser.). 1975. pap. 1.00 (ISBN 0-8106-1033-7). NEA.
Educational Research Council of America. Special Education Teacher. rev. ed. Kunze, Linda J. & Marchak, John P., eds. (Real People at Work Ser: E). (Illus.). 1977. pap. text ed. 2.25 (ISBN 0-89247-033-X). Changing Times.
Erickson, Marion J. Mentally Retarded Child in the Classroom. (Orig.). 1965. text ed. 3.95 (ISBN 0-02-334000-2, 33400). Macmillan.
--Teaching the Retarded Child: A Developmental Approach. LC 79-18475. 228p. 1979. lib. bdg. 22.50 (ISBN 0-8240-7169-7). Garland Pub.
Fielding, P. M., ed. A National Directory of Four Year Colleges, Two Year Colleges & Post High School Training Programs for Young People with Learning Disabilities. 4th ed. 1981. 15.95 (ISBN 0-686-19675-9). PIP.
Frankel, Max G., et al. Functional Teaching of the Mentally Retarded. 2nd ed. (Illus.). 288p. 1975. 18.50 (ISBN 0-398-03361-7). C C Thomas.
Frankenstein, C. Impaired Intelligence: Pathology & Rehabilitation. 1970. 37.50 (ISBN 0-677-02810-5). Gordon.
Freeland, Kenneth H. High School Work Study Program for the Retarded: Practical Information for Teacher Preparation & Program Organization & Operation. (Illus.). 120p. 1974. text ed. 11.50 (ISBN 0-398-00611-3). C C Thomas.
Gardner, James E. Paraprofessional Work with Troubled Children. LC 75-8731. 1975. 12.95 (ISBN 0-470-29150-8). Halsted Pr.
Garton, Malinda D. Teaching the Educable Mentally Retarded: Practical Methods. 2rd ed. (Illus.). 356p. 1974. 14.75 (ISBN 0-398-00654-7). C C Thomas.
Gearheart, Bill R. Learning Disabilities: Educational Strategies. 2nd ed. LC 76-28435. (Illus.). 1977. text ed. 15.50 (ISBN 0-8016-1767-7). Mosby.
--Teaching the Learning Disabled: A Combined Task & Process Approach. new ed. LC 75-42478. (Illus.). 304p. 1976. 15.95 (ISBN 0-8016-1762-6). Mosby.
Gillespie, Patricia H. & Johnson, Lowell. Teaching Reading to the Mildly Retarded Child. LC 73-88245. 1974. text ed. 17.50 (ISBN 0-675-08859-3). Merrill.
Gillham, Bill. The First Words Language Programme. 96p. 1980. 20.00x (ISBN 0-686-69972-6, Pub. by Beaconsfield England). State Mutual Bk.
--First Words Language Programme. (Illus.). 1979. text ed. 15.95x (ISBN 0-04-371059-X). Allen Unwin.
Ginglend, David R. & Stiles, Winifred E. Music Activities for Retarded Children. (Illus., Orig.). 1965. pap. 7.95 (ISBN 0-687-27309-9). Abingdon.
Gold, Marc. Try Another Way Training Manual. LC 80-52142. 105p. (Orig.). 1980. pap. 5.95 (ISBN 0-87822-222-7, 2227). Res Press.
Goldstein, Arnold P. Prescriptions for Child Mental Health & Education. 1978. text ed. 44.00 (ISBN 0-08-022250-1); pap. text ed. 10.95 (ISBN 0-08-022249-8). Pergamon.
Goldstein, Herbert & Seigle, Dorothy M. Curriculum Guide for Teachers of the Educable Mentally Handicapped. pap. text ed. 6.95x (ISBN 0-8134-1350-8, 1350). Interstate.
Gordon, Michael Lewis, et al. Helping the Trainable Mentally Retarded Child Develop Speech & Language: A Guidebook for Parents, Teachers & Paraprofessionals. 80p. 1979. 8.75 (ISBN 0-398-02453-7). C C Thomas.
Guess, Doug, et al. Functional Speech & Language Training for the Severely Handicapped, Part 1. 1976. 8.95 (ISBN 0-89079-023-X); scoring forms set 2.00 (ISBN 0-89079-024-8). H & H Ent.
Hannah, Marta, et al. SCIL: Systematic Curriculum for Independent Living, 4 vols. 1977. Set. binders 165.00x (ISBN 0-87879-187-6). Acad Therapy.
Hanson, M. Teaching Your Downs-Syndrome Infant. 1978. 14.95 (ISBN 0-8391-1258-0). Univ Park.
Haring, Norris G. & Brown, Louis J., eds. Teaching the Severely Handicapped, 2 vols. LC 76-25992. (Illus.). Vol. 1, 1976 320pps. 27.25 (ISBN 0-8089-0945-2); Vol. 2, 1977 224pps. 29.25 (ISBN 0-8089-0980-0); Set. 52.25 (ISBN 0-686-57860-0). Grune.
Heath, Earl J. Mentally Retarded Student & Guidance. (Guidance Monograph). 1970. pap. 2.40 (ISBN 0-395-09946-3, 9-78846). HM.
Holbrook, David. English for the Rejected. (Orig.). 1964. pap. 9.95x (ISBN 0-521-09215-9). Cambridge U Pr.
Hutt, Max L. & Gibby, Robert G. The Mentally Retarded Child: Development, Training, & Education. 4th ed. 1979. text ed. 20.95 (ISBN 0-205-06520-1, 2465205). Allyn.
Hyatt, Ralph & Rolnick, Norma, eds. Teaching the Mentally Handicapped Child. LC 74-2323. 352p. 1974. text ed. 24.95 (ISBN 0-87705-158-5). Human Sci Pr.
Ingalls, Robert P. Mental Retardation: The Changing Outlook. LC 77-23359. 1978. text ed. 22.95x (ISBN 0-471-42716-0). Wiley.
Jackson, S. E. & Taylor, G. R. School Organization for the Mentally Retarded: Basic Guides. 2nd ed. (Illus.). 160p. 1973. 13.75 (ISBN 0-398-02742-0). C C Thomas.
Jeffree, Dorothy & McConkey, Roy. Let Me Speak: Learning Games for the Retarded Child. LC 77-73825. (Illus.). 1977. 7.95 (ISBN 0-8008-4646-X). Taplinger.
Johnson, Vicki M. & Werner, Roberta A. Step-by-Step Learning Guide for Older Retarded Children. 1977. pap. 9.95x (ISBN 0-8156-2181-7). Syracuse U Pr.
--A Step-by-Step Learning Guide for Retarded Infants & Children. LC 75-22172. (Illus.). 208p. 1975. pap. 9.95x (ISBN 0-8156-2174-4). Syracuse U Pr.
Jolles, Isaac & Southwick, Selma I. Clinical Approach to Training the Educable Mentally Retarded: A Handbook. LC 70-95255. (Professional Handbook Ser.). (Illus.). 31p. 1971. pap. 8.10x (ISBN 0-87424-113-8). Western Psych.
Kirk, Samuel A., et al. Teaching Reading to Slow & Disabled Learners. LC 77-77655. (Illus.). 1978. text ed. 17.75 (ISBN 0-395-25821-9). HM.
Kneedler, Rebecca D. & Tarver, Sara G. Changing Perspectives in Special Education. 1977. pap. text ed. 12.50 (ISBN 0-675-08529-2). Merrill.
Kolstoe, Oliver P. Teaching Educable Mentally Retarded Children. 2nd ed. LC 75-23456. 1976. text ed. 18.95 (ISBN 0-03-089724-6, HoltC). HR&W.
Kolstoe, Oliver P. & Frey, Roger M. High School Work-Study Program for Mentally Subnormal Students. LC 65-12396. 188p. 1965. 5.95x (ISBN 0-8093-0183-0). S Ill U Pr.
Koppitz, Elizabeth M. Children with Learning Disabilities: A Five Year Follow-up Study. LC 70-167977. 256p. 1971. 26.00 (ISBN 0-8089-0726-3). Grune.
Lambert, Nadine M., et al. The Educationally Retarded Child: Comprehensive Assessment & Planning for Slow Learners & Educable Mentally Retarded Pupils. LC 74-5099. (Illus.). 256p. 1974. 25.50 (ISBN 0-8089-0836-7). Grune.
Lane, Harlan. The Wild Boy of Aveyron. (Illus.). 384p. 1976. 16.50x (ISBN 0-674-95282-0); pap. 6.95x (ISBN 0-674-95300-2). Harvard U Pr.
Learning Through Curriculum Modification: A Blueprint for Teaching the Mentally Retarded. LC 75-25322. pap. 9.95 (ISBN 0-87804-261-X). Mafex.
Levy, Harold B. Square Pegs, Round Holes: The Learning-Disabled Child in the Classroom & at Home. LC 73-3422. (Illus.). 288p. 1973. 8.95 (ISBN 0-316-52232-5); pap. 3.95 (ISBN 0-316-52233-3). Little.
--Square Pegs, Round Holes: The Learning-Disabled Child in the Classroom & at Home. LC 73-3422. (Illus.). 288p. 1973. 8.95 (ISBN 0-316-52232-5); pap. 3.95 (ISBN 0-316-52233-3). Little.
Lippman, Leopold & Goldberg, I. Ignacy. Right to Education: Anatomy of the Pennsylvania Case & Its Implications for Exceptional Children. LC 73-78038. 1973. text ed. 8.00 (ISBN 0-8077-2401-7); pap. text ed. 5.25 (ISBN 0-8077-2406-8). Tchrs Coll.
Mainord, James C. & Love, Harold D. Teaching Educable Mentally Retarded Children: Methods & Materials. (Illus.). 276p. 1975. 13.75 (ISBN 0-398-02646-7). C C Thomas.
Malmquist, E. Reading & Writing Disabilities in Children. Date not set. price not set (ISBN 0-07-039825-9, C). McGraw.
Mann, Lester & Sabatino, David A., eds. The First Review of Special Education, 2 vols. 605p. 1973. Set. 47.50 (ISBN 0-8089-0884-7). Grune.
--The Second Review of Special Education. 405p. 1974. 26.00 (ISBN 0-8089-0885-5). Grune.
Marsh, George E., et al. The Learning Disabled Adolescent: Program Alternatives in the Secondary School. new ed. LC 77-18050. (Illus.). 1978. text ed. 16.95 (ISBN 0-8016-3118-1). Mosby.
Mather, June. Learning Can Be Child's Play: How Parents Can Help Slower-Than-Average Preschool Children Learn & Develop Through Play Experiences. LC 76-20610. (Illus.). 64p. 1976. pap. 3.95 (ISBN 0-687-21317-7). Abingdon.
Matson, J. L. & McCartney, J. R., eds. Handbook of Behavior Modification with the Mentally Retarded. (Applied Clinical Psychology Ser.). 415p. 1981. 39.50 (ISBN 0-306-40617-9, Plenum Pr). Plenum Pub.
Mays, Maxine. Student Teaching in Special Classes for the Mentally Retarded. (Illus.). 108p. 1974. pap. 7.75 (ISBN 0-398-02861-3). C C Thomas.
Mercer, Cecil D. & Snell, Martha E. Learning Theory Research in Mental Retardation: Implications for Teaching. (Special Education Ser.). 1976. text ed. 21.95x (ISBN 0-675-08531-4). Merrill.
Mithaug, Dennis E. Prevocational Training for Retarded Students. (Illus.). 384p. 1981. text ed. 29.50 (ISBN 0-398-04111-3). C C Thomas.
Molloy, Julia S. & Matkin, A. M. Your Developmentally Retarded Child Can Communicate: A Guide for Parents & Teachers in Speech, Languages, & Nonverbal Communication. (John Day Bk.). 1975. 8.95 (ISBN 0-381-97102-3). T Y Crowell.
Mott, Mary. Teaching the Pre-Academic Child: Activities for Children Displaying Difficulties of Processing Information. 188p. 1974. text ed. 13.75 (ISBN 0-398-03083-9). C C Thomas.
Mullins, June & Wolfe, Suzanne. Special People Behind the Eight-Ball. LC 74-92371. 1975. 9.95 (ISBN 0-87804-255-5); pap. 7.95 (ISBN 0-685-90519-5). Mafex.
Myers, Donald G., et al. The Right-to-Education Child: A Curriculum for the Severely & Profoundly Mentally Retarded. (Illus.). 248p. 1978. 14.00 (ISBN 0-398-02923-7). C C Thomas.
Myers, Patricia L. & Hammill, Donald D. Methods for Learning Disorders. 2nd ed. LC 75-37504. 1976. text ed. 23.95 (ISBN 0-471-62751-8). Wiley.
Panyan, Marion C. New Ways to Teach New Skills. (Managing Behavior Ser.: Part 4). 1975. 4.00 (ISBN 0-89079-004-3). H & H Ent.
Paul, James L., et al. Mainstreaming: A Practical Guide. 1977. 9.95x (ISBN 0-8156-0136-0). Syracuse U Pr.
Perry, Natalie. Teaching the Mentally Retarded Child: Enlarged to Survey All Trainable Retardates & Their Social Needs. 2nd ed. LC 73-20246. 750p. 1974. 20.00x (ISBN 0-231-03652-3). Columbia U Pr.
Peterson, Daniel. Functional Mathematics for the Mentally Retarded. LC 70-188780. text ed. 21.50x (ISBN 0-675-09097-0). Merrill.
Popovich, D. Prescriptive Behavior Checklist, Vol. I. (Illus.). 1977. 17.95 (ISBN 0-8391-1100-2). Univ Park.
Readings in Special Education. (Special Education Ser.). 1978. pap. text ed. 10.95 (ISBN 0-89568-000-9). Spec Learn Corp.

Rolett, Karin. Organizing Community Resources in Sexuality Counseling & Family Planning for the Retarded: a Community Workers' Manual. 1976. pap. 3.00 (ISBN 0-89055-118-9). Carolina Pop Ctr.
Rothstein, Jerome H., ed. Mental Retardation: Readings & Resources. 2nd ed. LC 70-143317. 1971. text ed. 13.50 (ISBN 0-03-084408-8, HoltC). Hr&W.
Rudman, Jack. Children with Retarded Mental Development (C.R. M. D.) (Teachers License Examination Ser.: T-8). (Cloth bdg. avail. on request). pap. 10.00 (ISBN 0-8373-8008-1). Natl Learning.
Sapir, Selma & Nitzburg, Ann, eds. Children with Learning Problems. LC 73-79078. 1973. 25.00 (ISBN 0-87630-073-5). Brunner-Mazel.
Seguin, Edward. Report on Education. LC 76-39942. (History of Psychology Ser.). 1976. Repr. of 1880 ed. 23.00x (ISBN 0-8201-1282-8). Schol Facsimiles.
Shanker, Uday. Exceptional Children: India. 1977. text ed. 13.50x (ISBN 0-8426-0949-0). Verry.
Smith, Robert M. Clinical Teaching. 2nd ed. (Illus.). 448p. 1974. text ed. 15.50 (ISBN 0-07-058906-2, C). McGraw.
Sniff, William F. A Curriculum for the Mentally Retarded Young Adult. 180p. 1973. 10.75 (ISBN 0-398-01804-9). C C Thomas.
Sussman, Ellen J. Art Projects for the Mentally Retarded Child. (Illus.). 108p. 1976. 10.75 (ISBN 0-398-03535-0); pap. 7.00 (ISBN 0-398-03534-2). C C Thomas.
Systematic Instruction for Retarded Children: The Illinois Program. Incl. Part I, Teacher-Parent Guide. Chalfant, James C. & Silikovitz, Ronald G. pap. text ed. 1.00x (ISBN 0-8134-1557-8, 1557); Part II, Systematic Language Instruction. Tawney, James W. & Hipsher, Lee W. pap. text ed. 4.95x (ISBN 0-8134-1558-6, 1558); Part III, Self-Help Instruction. Linford, Maxine D., et al. pap. text ed. 3.25x (ISBN 0-8134-1559-4, 1559); Part IV, Motor Performance & Recreation Instruction. Linford, Anthony G. & Jeanrenaud, Claudine Y. pap. text ed. 2.95x (ISBN 0-8134-1560-8, 1560). 1972. Interstate.
Talbot, Mabel E. Edouard Seguin: A Study of an Educational Approach to the Treatment of Mentally Defective Children. LC 64-23753. 1964. pap. text ed. 3.50x (ISBN 0-8077-2242-1). Tchrs Coll.
Tarnopol, Lester, ed. Learning Disorders in Children: Diagnosis, Medication, Education. 1971. 14.95 (ISBN 0-316-83200-6). Little.
A Teacher's Reference Guide to PL 94-142. 50p. 1978. pap. 3.00 (ISBN 0-686-63703-8). NEA.
Van Hattum, Rolland J. Developmental Language Programming for the Retarded. new ed. 1978. text ed. 20.50 (ISBN 0-205-06452-3). Allyn.
Van Osdol, Bob M. Procedures for Teaching the Mentally Retarded. 1973. 2.95 (ISBN 0-89301-006-5). U Pr of Idaho.
Van Osdol, Bob M. & Perryman, Patricia, eds. Special Education: A New Look. 350p. 1974. text ed. 29.50x (ISBN 0-8422-5181-2); pap. text ed. 8.75x (ISBN 0-8422-0417-2). Irvington.
Wabash Center for the Mentally Retarded. Guide for Early Developmental Training. 1977. pap. text ed. 21.95 (ISBN 0-205-05810-8). Allyn.
Waite, Kathleen B. Educable Mentally Retarded Child: Guidance & Curriculum. (Illus.). 592p. 1971. text ed. 54.75 (ISBN 0-398-02002-7). C C Thomas.
--The Trainable Mentally Retarded Child. (Illus.). 336p. 1972. photocopy ed. spiral 32.75 (ISBN 0-398-02433-2). C C Thomas.
Walsh, Sara R. & Holzberg, Robert. Understanding & Educating the Deaf-Blind-Severely & Profoundly Handicapped: An International Perspective. (Illus.). 336p. 1981. 27.75 (ISBN 0-398-04514-3). C C Thomas.
Ward, David. Sing a Rainbow: Musical Activities with Mentally Handicapped Children. (Illus.). 64p. (Orig.). 1979. pap. text ed. 8.95x (ISBN 0-19-317416-2). Oxford U Pr.
Warner, Frank & Thrapp, Robert, eds. Readings in Controversial Issues in Education of the Mentally Retarded. 1972. 29.50x (ISBN 0-8422-5007-7). Irvington.
Watson, Luke S., Jr. Teaching Social-Recreational Skills to Mentally Retarded & Psychotic Children & Adults: A Manual of Game Programs. 3.60 (ISBN 0-686-75265-1). Behavior Mod Tech.
Watson, Marjorie. Mainstreaming the Educable Mentally Retarded. new ed. LC 75-12964. (Developments in Classroom Instruction Ser.). 56p. 1975. pap. text ed. 4.00 (ISBN 0-8106-1800-1). NEA.
Wheeler, Alan H. & Fox, Wayne L. Teacher's Guide to Writing Instructional Objectives. rev. ed. (Managing Behavior Ser.: Part 5). 1977. 4.00 (ISBN 0-89079-042-6). H & H Ent.
Wilton, Keri M. & Boersma, Frederic J. Eye Movements, Surprise Reactions & Cognitive Development. (Modern Approaches to the Diagnosis & Instruction of Multi-Handicapped Children: Vol. 13). 78p. 1973. text ed. 17.75 (ISBN 90-237-4117-X, Pub. by Swets Pub Serv Holland). Swets North Am.
Wirtz, Morvin A. Administrator's Handbook of Special Education. (Illus.). 184p. 1977. 18.75 (ISBN 0-398-03542-3). C C Thomas.
Withrow, Frank B. & Nygren, Carolyn J. Language Curriculum & Materials for the Handicapped Learner. 1976. text ed. 17.95 (ISBN 0-675-08615-9). Merrill.
Witty, Paul A., ed. Educationally Retarded & Disadvantaged. (National Society for the Study of Education Yearbooks Ser: No. 66, Pt. 1). 1967. 7.50x (ISBN 0-226-60086-6). U of Chicago Pr.
Wrasman, Marilyn W. & Haag, Diana B. Speak for Yourself. Ring, Constance, tr. (Illus.). 106p. 1976. pap. text ed. 4.95 (ISBN 0-914296-57-4). Activity Rec.

MENTALLY HANDICAPPED CHILDREN–PERSONAL NARRATIVES

Buck, Pearl S. Child Who Never Grew. (Special Education Bks). 1950. 3.95 (ISBN 0-381-98020-0, A12200, JD-J). Har-Row.
Hill, Archie. Closed World of Love. 1978. pap. 1.75 (ISBN 0-380-39917-2, 39917). Avon.
Hutchison, Becky & Farish, Kay. Lisa. (Orig.). 1980. pap. 4.95 (ISBN 0-88270-440-0). Logos.
Jennings, Jane. Why Joy? Learning to Love My Special Child. LC 77-90122. 1978. 6.95 (ISBN 0-915684-35-7). Christian Herald.
Lind, Miriam S. No Crying He Makes. pap. 1.50 (ISBN 0-686-31408-5). NACAC.
Lofland, Sandra J. The Sharing of My Love. new ed. LC 76-27966. (Illus.). 88p. 1977. 5.95 (ISBN 0-910812-20-9); pap. 2.95 (ISBN 0-910812-23-3). Johnny Reads.
Moise, Lotte E. As up We Grew with Barbara. LC 79-25649. 1980. 8.95 (ISBN 0-87518-194-5). Dillon.
Monty, Shirlee. May's Boy. 8.95x (ISBN 0-8407-4091-3). Warner Bks.
Murray, J. B. & Murray, Emily. And Say What He Is: The Life of a Special Child. LC 75-5810. 304p. 1975. 12.00x (ISBN 0-262-13115-3); pap. 4.95 (ISBN 0-262-63069-9). MIT Pr.
Schultz, Edna M. Kathy. Orig. Title: They Said Kathy Was Retarded. 1972. pap. 2.95 (ISBN 0-8024-4525-X). Moody.
Worswick, Marilyn & Selle, Robert. Thank You Davey; Thank You, God. LC 77-84089. 1978. pap. 3.50 (ISBN 0-8066-1614-8, 10-6244). Augsburg.

MENTALLY HANDICAPPED CHILDREN–GREAT BRITAIN

Kirman, Brian H. The Mentally Handicapped Child. LC 73-6174. 240p. 1973. 7.95 (ISBN 0-8008-5188-9). Taplinger.

MENTALLY HANDICAPPED IN LITERATURE

see also Insanity in Literature

Baskin, Barbara H. & Harris, Karen H. Notes from a Different Drummer: A Guide to Juvenile Fiction Portraying the Handicapped. LC 77-15067. 1977. 17.50 (ISBN 0-8352-0978-4). Bowker.
MacMurchy, Helen. Almosts: A Study of the Feeble Minded. LC 77-115325. 1971. Repr. of 1920 ed. 12.50 (ISBN 0-8046-1116-5). Kennikat.

MENTALLY ILL

see also Mental Illness; Mentally Handicapped

Campbell, C. M. Destiny & Disease in Mental Disorders. 1977. lib. bdg. 59.95 (ISBN 0-8490-1710-6). Gordon Pr.
Cawte, John. Cruel, Poor & Brutal Nations: The Assessment of Mental Health in an Australian Aboriginal Community by Short-Stay Psychiatric Field Team Methods. LC 72-188979. (Illus.). 200p. 1972. 12.00x (ISBN 0-8248-0207-1). U Pr of Hawaii.
Dain, Norman. Concepts of Insanity in the United States, 1789-1865. 1964. 18.50 (ISBN 0-8135-0443-0). Rutgers U Pr.
Goffman, Erving. Asylums: Essays on the Social Situation of Mental Patients & Other Inmates. LC 61-13812. pap. 4.50 (ISBN 0-385-00016-2, A277, Anch). Doubleday.
Grob, Gerald N., ed. The Mentally Ill in Urban America: An Original Anthology. LC 78-22575. (Historical Issues in Mental Health Ser.). (Illus.). 1979. lib. bdg. 38.00x (ISBN 0-405-11928-3). Arno.
--The National Association for the Protection of the Insane & the Prevention of Insanity, 2 vols. in one. LC 78-22578. (Historical Issues in Mental Health Ser.). 1979. Repr. lib. bdg. 12.00x (ISBN 0-405-11930-5). Arno.
Jarvis, Edward. Insanity & Idiocy in Massachusetts: Report of the Commission on Lunacy, 1855. LC 72-134950. (Commonwealth Fund Publications Ser). 1971. 16.50x (ISBN 0-674-45480-4). Harvard U Pr.
Keating, Paul R., ed. What You Should Know About Emotions & Mental Health. LC 74-75985. 128p. 1975. pap. 1.50 (ISBN 0-87983-082-4). Keats.
Lowenthal, Marjorie F. & Berkman, Paul L. Aging & Mental Disorder in San Francisco: A Social Psychiatric Study. LC 67-13168. (Social & Behavioral Science Ser.). 1967. 18.95x (ISBN 0-87589-001-6). Jossey-Bass.
Rappeport, Jonas R. The Clinical Evaluation of the Dangerousness of the Mentally Ill. 140p. 1967. photocopy ed. spiral 14.00 (ISBN 0-398-01550-3). C C Thomas.
Robison, Dale W. Wisconsin & the Mentally Ill. Grob, Gerald N., ed. LC 78-22588. (Historical Issues in Mental Health Ser.). 1979. lib. bdg. 22.00x (ISBN 0-405-11939-9). Arno.
Saul, Leon J. The Childhood Emotional Pattern in Marriage. LC 78-17400. 1979. text ed. 15.95x (ISBN 0-442-27359-2). Van Nos Reinhold.

MENTALLY ILL–CARE AND TREATMENT

see also Church Work with the Mentally Ill

Abroms, Gene M. & Greenfield, Norman S., eds. New Hospital Psychiatry: Proceedings of a Conference. LC 77-137633. 1971. 42.00 (ISBN 0-12-042850-4). Acad Pr.
Bailey, David S. & Dreyer, Sharon O. Therapeutic Approaches to the Care of the Mentally Ill. LC 77-3152. 290p. 1977. pap. text ed. 8.95 (ISBN 0-8036-0550-1). Davis Co.
Bryan, William A. Administrative Psychiatry. LC 58-14143. 1958. Repr. of 1936 ed. 11.00x (ISBN 0-8154-0034-9). Cooper Sq.
Conolly, J. Inquiry Concerning the Indications of Insanity with Suggestions for the Better Protection & Care of the Insane. (Illus.). 469p. 1964. Repr. of 1830 ed. 25.00x (ISBN 0-8464-0515-6). Beekman Pubs.
Conolly, John. The Treatment of the Insane Without Mechanical Restraints. LC 73-2392. (Mental Illness & Social Policy; the American Experience Ser.). Repr. of 1856 ed. 19.00 (ISBN 0-405-05200-6). Arno.
Coser, Rose L. Training in Ambiguity: Learning Through Doing in a Mental Hospital. LC 78-54109. (Illus.). 1979. 15.95 (ISBN 0-02-906580-1). Free Pr.
Dain, Norman. Clifford W. Beers: Advocate for the Insane. LC 79-24290. (Contemporary Community Health Ser.). 1980. 19.95 (ISBN 0-8229-3419-1). U of Pittsburgh Pr.
Deutsch, Albert. The Mentally Ill in America: A History of Their Care & Treatment from Colonial Times. 2nd ed. LC 49-7527. 535p. 1949. 23.50x (ISBN 0-231-01656-5). Columbia U Pr.
DiMascio, A. & Goldberg, H. Emotional Disorders: Diagnosis & Pharmacological Treatment. 3rd ed. 1980. 15.95 (ISBN 0-87489-255-4). Med Economics.
Glasscote, R. M. Partial Hospitalization for the Mentally Ill: A Study of Programs & Problems. 187p. 1969. pap. 5.00 (ISBN 0-685-24873-9, P204-1). Am Psychiatric.
Goldberg, Jacob A. Social Aspects of the Treatment of the Insane. LC 77-78005. (Columbia University. Studies in the Social Sciences: No. 221). Repr. of 1921 ed. 19.50 (ISBN 0-404-51221-6). AMS Pr.
Gordon, Richard E. & Gordon, Katherine. Systems of Treatment for the Mentally Ill: Filling the Gaps. 400p. 1981. 34.50 (ISBN 0-8089-1338-7, 791675). Grune.
Graham, Thomas F. Parallel Profiles. 4.95 (ISBN 0-8199-0082-6, L38621). Franciscan Herald.
Grimes, John M. Institutional Care of Mental Patients in the United States. Grob, Gerald N., ed. LC 78-22563. (Historical Issues in Mental Health Ser.). 1979. Repr. of 1934 ed. lib. bdg. 12.00x (ISBN 0-405-11917-8). Arno.
--When Minds Go Wrong. 1954. 4.95 (ISBN 0-8159-7206-7). Devin.
Grob, Gerald N. Mental Institutions in America: Social Policy to 1875. LC 72-92868. 1973. 15.95 (ISBN 0-02-913040-9). Free Pr.
Hankoff, L. D. Emergency Psychiatric Treatment: A Handbook of Secondary Prevention. 100p. 1969. 8.75 (ISBN 0-398-00771-3). C C Thomas.
Hoenig, J. & Hamilton, M. W. De-Segregation of the Mentally Ill. (International Library of Sociology & Social Reconstruction). 1969. text ed. 14.50x (ISBN 0-7100-6505-1). Humanities.
Hoenig, J. & Hamilton, Marian. Desegregation of the Mentally Ill. (International Library of Sociology & Social Reconstruction). 1969. text ed. 17.95x (ISBN 0-8464-0318-8). Beekman Pubs.
Horwitz, Elinor L. Madness, Magic, and Medicine: The Treatment and Mistreatment of the Mentally Ill. LC 76-54760. 1977. 7.95 (ISBN 0-397-31723-9, JBL-Med-Nursing). Har-Row.
Jacob, Norma. From One to Another. LC 59-8917. (Orig.). 1959. pap. 0.30 (ISBN 0-87574-102-9). Pendle Hill.
Kanno, Charles & Scheidemandel, Patricia L. The Mentally Ill Offender: A Survey of Treatment Programs. 76p. 1969. pap. 3.00 (ISBN 0-685-24860-7, P244-0). Am Psychiatric.
Kramer, B. M. Day Hospital. LC 62-12473. (Illus.). 120p. 1962. pap. 12.00 (ISBN 0-8089-0245-8). Grune.
Lion, John R. Evaluation & Management of the Violent Patient: Guidelines in the Hospital & Institution. 88p. 1972. 8.75 (ISBN 0-398-02542-8). C C Thomas.
Margolis, Philip M. Patient Power. 176p. 1973. 12.75 (ISBN 0-398-02839-7). C C Thomas.
Mori, Allen A. & Masters, Lowell F. Teaching the Severely Mentally Retarded: Adaptive Skills Training. LC 79-27489. 407p. 1980. text ed. 26.50 (ISBN 0-89443-173-0). Aspen Systems.
Morris, Grant H. The Mentally Ill & the Right to Treatment. 148p. 1970. photocopy ed. spiral 14.75 (ISBN 0-398-01350-0). C C Thomas.
Morrison, James R. Your Brother's Keeper: A Guide for Families of the Mentall Ill. LC 79-27810. 352p. 1981. 20.95 (ISBN 0-88229-563-2). Nelson-Hall.
Paul, Gordon L. & Lentz, Robert J. Psychosocial Treatment of Chronic Mental Patients: Milieu vs. Social-Learning Programs. 1978. 25.00x (ISBN 0-674-72112-8). Harvard U Pr.
Peszke, Michael A. Involuntary Treatment of the Mentally Ill: The Problem of Autonomy. (American Lectures in Behavioral Science & Law). (Illus.). 176p. 1975. 14.75 (ISBN 0-398-03373-0). C C Thomas.
Pollock, Horatio M. Family Care of Mental Patients: A Review of Systems of Family Care in America & Europe. LC 75-17236. (Social Problems & Social Policy Ser.). (Illus.). 1976. Repr. of 1936 ed. 14.00x (ISBN 0-405-07505-7). Arno.
Raymond, Margaret, et al. The Healing Alliance: A New View of the Family's Role in the Treatment of Emotional Problems. 1977. pap. 3.95x (ISBN 0-393-00807-X, Norton Lib). Norton.
Report of a Conference Held in January 1979. The Chronic Mental Patient: Problems, Solutions, & Recommendations for a Public Policy. Talbott, John A., ed. LC 78-73984. 1979. pap. 11.00x (ISBN 0-685-95862-0, P242-0). Am Psychiatric.
Richard H.Lamb & Associates. Community Survival for Long-Term Patients. LC 75-44883. (Social & Behavioral Science Ser.). (Illus.). 208p. 1976. 13.95x (ISBN 0-87589-274-4). Jossey-Bass.
Rock, Ronald, et al. Hospitalization & Discharge of the Mentally Ill. LC 68-54010. 1968. 12.50x (ISBN 0-226-72336-4). U of Chicago Pr.
Roosens, Eugeen. Mental Patients in Town Life: Geel - Europe's First Therapeutic Community. LC 79-15386. (Sage Library of Social Research: Vol. 90). 199p. 1979. 20.00x (ISBN 0-8039-1330-3); pap. 9.95 (ISBN 0-8039-1331-1). Sage.
Russell, William L. The New York Hospital: A History of the Psychiatric Service, 1771-1936. LC 73-2414. (Mental Illness & Social Policy; the American Experience Ser.). Repr. of 1945 ed. 27.00 (ISBN 0-405-05224-3). Arno.
Schrader, Paul & Elms, Roslyn. Guidelines for Family Care Home Operators. LC 72-85087. 1972. pap. text ed. 5.95 (ISBN 0-8261-1270-6). Springer Pub.
Schwartz, Morris S. Social Approaches to Mental Patient Care. LC 64-13736. 1964. 20.00x (ISBN 0-231-02698-6). Columbia U Pr.
Slavson, S. R. Because I Live Here: The Theory & Practice of Vita-Erg Ward Therapy with Deteriorated Psychotic Women. LC 70-125477. 1970. text ed. 25.00 (ISBN 0-8236-0490-X). Intl Univs Pr.
Swazey, Judith P. Chlorpromazine in Psychiatry: A Study of Therapeutic Innovation. 519p. 1974. 27.50x (ISBN 0-262-19130-X). MIT Pr.
Trick, I. & Obcarskas, S. Understanding Mental Illness & Its Nursing. 1976. pap. 15.00 (ISBN 0-272-79385-X). State Mutual Bk.
Tulipan, Alan B. & Heyder, Dietrich W. Outpatient Psychiatry in the 1970's. LC 70-109608. (POCA Perspectives Ser., No. 2). 1970. 10.00 (ISBN 0-87630-026-3). Brunner-Mazel.
Ulmer, Raymond A. On the Development of a Token Economy Mental Hospital Treatment Program. LC 75-37984. (Clinical Psychology Ser.). 1976. 17.95 (ISBN 0-470-01393-1). Halsted Pr.

MENTALLY ILL–CASES, CLINICAL REPORTS, STATISTICS

Estroff, Sue E. Making It Crazy: An Ethnography of Psychiatric Clients in an American Community. LC 79-64660. 338p. 1981. 16.50 (ISBN 0-520-03963-7). U of Cal Pr.
McCord, William & McCord, J. Psychopathy & Delinquency. 240p. 1956. 22.50 (ISBN 0-8089-0274-1). Grune.

MENTALLY ILL–HOSPITALS

see Psychiatric Hospitals

MENTALLY ILL–LEGAL STATUS, LAWS, ETC.

see Insanity–Jurisprudence; Mental Health Laws

MENTALLY ILL–PERSONAL NARRATIVES
see Mental Illness–Personal Narratives
MENTALLY ILL–REHABILITATION

Angrist, Shirley S., et al. Women After Treatment: A Study of Former Mental Patients & Their Normal Neighbors. LC 68-20043. 1968. 21.00x (ISBN 0-89197-471-7); pap. text ed. 5.95x (ISBN 0-89197-472-5). Irvington.

Black, Bertram J. Principles of Industrial Therapy for the Mentally Ill. LC 73-88017. 200p. 1970. 33.25 (ISBN 0-8089-0062-5). Grune.

Blum, Lawrence P. & Kujoth, Richard K. Job Placement of the Emotionally Disturbed. LC 75-185399. 1972. 14.50 (ISBN 0-8108-0468-9). Scarecrow.

Budson, Richard D. The Psychiatric Halfway House: A Handbook of Theory & Practice. LC 77-74548. (Contemporary Community Health Ser.). 1978. 10.95 (ISBN 0-8229-3350-0). U of Pittsburgh Pr.

Dencker, Sven-Jonas. Hospital Based Community Support Services Recovering Chronic Schizophrenics, No. 2. (International Exchange of Information in Rehabilitation Ser.). 83p. 1980. write for info. (ISBN 0-939986-03-5). World Rehab Fund.

Dunham, H. Warren. Social Realities & Community Psychiatry. LC 74-10967. 252p. 1976. 24.95 (ISBN 0-87705-215-8). Human Sci Pr.

Fink, Max, et al, eds. Psychobiology of Convulsive Therapy. LC 73-21990. 1974. 11.95 (ISBN 0-470-25901-9). Halsted Pr.

Glasscote, R. M., et al. Halfway Houses for the Mentally Ill: A Study of Programs & Problems. 244p. 1971. 7.50 (ISBN 0-685-24870-4, P203-0). Am Psychiatric.

--Rehabilitating the Mentally Ill in the Community: A Study of Psychosocial Rehabilitation Centers. 214p. 1971. 7.50 (ISBN 0-685-24869-0, P-157-0). Am Psychiatric.

Goldstein, Arnold P., et al. Applying Structured Learning Therapy. LC 76-16518. 1977. text ed. 27.50 (ISBN 0-08-021109-7); pap. text ed. 15.00 (ISBN 0-08-021108-9). Pergamon.

Gottesfeld, Harry. Alternative to Psychiatric Hospitalization. LC 77-7318. 1979. 12.95 (ISBN 0-470-99188-7). Halsted Pr.

Hardy, Richard E. & Cull, John G., eds. Modification of Behavior of the Mentally Ill: Rehabilitation Approaches. (American Lectures in Social & Rehabilitation Psychology Ser.). (Illus.). 248p. 1974. text ed. 18.50 (ISBN 0-398-03052-9). C C Thomas.

Kraus, Ernest A. Pathways Back to the Community. LC 71-100099. 1970. Set. pap. 18.50 (ISBN 0-8261-1093-2); 3.95 (ISBN 0-686-66539-2). Springer Pub.

Lamb, H. Richard, et al. Rehabilitation in Community Mental Health. LC 76-168989. (Social & Behavioral Science Ser.). 1971. 15.95x (ISBN 0-87589-107-1). Jossey-Bass.

Leedy, Jack J., ed. Compensation in Psychiatric Disability & Rehabilitation. (Illus.). 384p. 1971. 36.75 (ISBN 0-398-02186-4). C C Thomas.

Meislin, Jack. Rehabilitation Medicine & Psychiatry. (Illus.). 564p. 1976. 32.75 (ISBN 0-398-03432-X). C C Thomas.

Mithaug, Dennis E. Prevocational Training for Retarded Students. (Illus.). 384p. 1981. text ed. 29.50 (ISBN 0-398-04111-3). C C Thomas.

Raush, Harold L. & Raush, Charlotte L. Halfway House Movement: A Search for Sanity. LC 68-18037. (Century Psychology Ser). 1968. 18.95x (ISBN 0-89197-197-1); pap. text ed. 6.95x (ISBN 0-89197-198-X). Irvington.

A Selective Guide to Audiovisuals for Mental Health & Family Life Education. 4th ed. LC 78-71072. 1979. pap. 24.50 (ISBN 0-8379-5101-1). Marquis.

A Selective Guide to Publications for Mental Health & Family Life Education. 4th ed. LC 78-71071. 1979. pap. 34.50 (ISBN 0-8379-5001-5). Marquis.

Smith, Christopher J. Geography & Mental Health. Natoli, Salvatore J., ed. LC 76-29269. (Resource Papers for College Geography Ser.). 1977. pap. text ed. 4.00 (ISBN 0-89291-119-0). Assn Am Geographers.

Walthall, Joe E. & Love, Harold D. Habilitation of the Mentally Retarded Individual. (Illus.). 224p. 1974. 13.75 (ISBN 0-398-02908-3). C C Thomas.

Wansbrough, Nancy & Cooper, Philip. Open Employment After Mental Illness. 1980. 22.95x (ISBN 0-422-76620-8, Pub. by Tavistock). Methuen Inc.

MENTALLY ILL CHILDREN

Bachrach, Ann W. & Swindle, Fay L. Developmental Therapy for Young Children with Autistic Characteristics. LC 77-16370. 1978. pap. 16.95 (ISBN 0-8391-1186-X). Univ Park.

Benson, Hazel B. Behavior Modification & the Child: An Annotated Bibliography. LC 79-7358. (Contemporary Problems of Childhood: No. 3). 1979. lib. bdg. 27.50 (ISBN 0-313-21489-1, BBM/). Greenwood.

Clarizio, Harvey F. & McCoy, George F. Behavioral Disorders in Children. 2nd ed. 1976. scp 20.95 (ISBN 0-690-00853-8, HarpC). Har-Row.

Crow, Gary A. Children at Risk: A Handbook of the Signs & Symptoms of Early Childhood Difficulties. LC 77-87859. 1978. 12.95x (ISBN 0-8052-3675-9). Schocken.

Eissler, Ruch S., et al, eds. Psychoanalytic Assessment: The Diagnostic Profile: an Anthology of the Psychoanalytic Study of the Child. Freud, Anna & Kris, Marianne. LC 75-32280. 373p. 1977. 30.00x (ISBN 0-300-01980-7); pap. 8.95 (ISBN 0-300-01981-5). Yale U Pr.

Erickson, Marilyn T. Child Psychopathology: Assessment, Etiology & Treatment. 2nd ed. 1981. ref. ed. 19.95 (ISBN 0-13-131102-6). P-H.

Faas, Larry A. Emotionally Disturbed Child: A Book of Readings. (Illus.). 400p. 1975. 22.75 (ISBN 0-398-00539-7). C C Thomas.

Fraser. Children in Conflict: Growing up in Northern Ireland. LC 73-92721. 1977. 10.00x (ISBN 0-465-01043-1). Basic.

Frederic, Helene & Malinsky, Martine. Martin. McGreal, John & Lipshitz, Susan, trs. from Fr. Orig. Title: Martin: un Enfant Battait Sa Mere. 108p. 1981. 16.95 (ISBN 0-7100-0814-7). Routledge & Kegan.

Glasscote, Raymond M., et al. Children & Mental Health Centers: Programs, Problems, Prospects, 1972. 257p. 1972. pap. 7.50 (ISBN 0-686-76966-X, P172-0). Am Psychiatric.

Goldfarb, William, et al. Psychotic Children Grown up: A Prospective Follow-Up Study in Adolescence & Adulthood. Meyers, Donald & Pressman, Paul, eds. LC 77-93594. 1979. 9.95 (ISBN 0-87705-331-6). Human Sci Pr.

Harrison, Saul I. & McDermott, John F., eds. Childhood Psychopathology: An Anthology of Basic Readings. LC 76-141808. 900p. 1972. text ed. 30.00 (ISBN 0-8236-0776-3). Intl Univs Pr.

Jenkins, Richard L. & Harms, Ernest, eds. Understanding Disturbed Children: Professional Insights into Their Psychiatric & Developmental Problems. LC 74-84846. 1976. text ed. 18.15 (ISBN 0-87562-057-4); pap. 12.00x (ISBN 0-87562-054-X). Spec Child.

Kahan, V. L. Mental Illness in Childhood: A Study in Residential Treatment. 219p. 1971. 10.00 (ISBN 0-685-24731-7, JBL-Med-Nursing). Har-Row.

Kauffman, James M. Characteristics of Children's Behavior Disorders. 1977. text ed. 18.95 (ISBN 0-675-08557-8). Merrill.

Kaufman, Barry N. Giant Steps. LC 78-10687. 1979. 9.95 (ISBN 0-698-10956-2). Coward.

Kohn, Martin. Social Competence, Symptoms, & Underachivement in Childhood: A Longitudinal Perspective. LC 77-5011. 1977. 18.95 (ISBN 0-470-99151-8). Halsted Pr.

Kovar, Lillian C. Wasted Lives: A Study of Children in Mental Hospitals & Their Families. LC 78-23248. 1979. 16.95 (ISBN 0-470-26564-7). Halsted Pr.

Lacey, P. R. Life with the Mentally Sick Child. LC 71-97950. 1970. 11.25 (ISBN 0-08-006978-9); pap. 5.75 (ISBN 0-08-006977-0). Pergamon.

Love, Harold D. The Emotionally Disturbed Child: A Parent's Guide: for Parents Who Have Problem Children. 120p. 1970. photocopy ed. spiral 11.50 (ISBN 0-398-01149-4). C C Thomas.

McDevitt, John B. & Settlage, Calvin F., eds. Separation-Individuation: Essays in Honor of Margaret S. Mahler. LC 78-143378. 1971. text ed. 30.00 (ISBN 0-8236-6065-6). Intl Univs Pr.

Mason, Robert L., Jr., et al. The Emotionally Troubled Child. 196p. 1976. 18.50 (ISBN 0-398-03557-1). C C Thomas.

Mattick, William E. Effectiveness of Cumulative School Records in the Early Indentification of Emotionally Handicapped Children. LC 74-29573. 1975. soft bdg. 8.00 (ISBN 0-88247-312-3). R & E Res Assoc.

Monkman, Marjorie M. A Milieu Therapy Program for Behaviorally Disturbed Children. (Illus.). 312p. 1972. 19.75 (ISBN 0-398-02363-8). C C Thomas.

Morrison, Delmont, et al. Sensory-Motor Dysfunction & Therapy in Infancy & Early Childhood. (Illus.). 288p. 1978. 17.50 (ISBN 0-398-03766-3). C C Thomas.

Noland, Robert L. Counseling Parents of the Emotionally Disturbed Child. (Illus.). 452p. 1972. 16.75 (ISBN 0-686-71891-7). C C Thomas.

Park, Clara C. The Siege: The First Eight Years of an Autistic Child. 1972. pap. 3.95 (ISBN 0-316-69072-4, Pub. by Atlantic Monthly Pr). Little.

Parker, Audrey. We Still Love You, Bob. LC 79-50947. 1979. 7.95 (ISBN 0-915684-34-9). Christian Herald.

Quay, Herbert C. & Werry, John S. Psychopathological Disorders of Childhood. 2nd ed. LC 78-24238. 1979. text ed. 24.95 (ISBN 0-471-04268-4). Wiley.

Stewart, Patricia R. Children in Distress: American & English Perspectives. LC 76-189. (Sage Library of Social Research: Vol. 26). (Illus.). 285p. 1976. 20.00 (ISBN 0-8039-0573-4); pap. 9.95x (ISBN 0-8039-0574-2). Sage.

Swain, John. Spit Once for Luck: Fostering Julie, a Disturbed Child. 1978. 9.95 (ISBN 0-236-40091-6, Pub. by Paul Elek). Merrimack Bk Serv.

Thrasher, Jean H. Group Behavior & Social Development of Psychotic Children: An Exploration. 39p. 1965. pap. text ed. 1.50 (ISBN 0-89143-050-4). U NC Inst Res Soc Sci.

Wahler, Robert G., et al. Ecological Assessment of Child Problem Behavior. 1976. pap. text ed. 7.25 (ISBN 0-08-019586-5). Pergamon.

Weber, George H. & Haberlein, Bernard J., eds. Residential Treatment of Emotionally Disturbed Children. LC 78-189948. (Child Care Ser). 350p. 1973. text ed. 29.95 (ISBN 0-87705-067-8). Human Sci Pr.

Whittaker, James K. & Trieschman, Albert E., eds. Children Away from Home: A Sourcebook in Residential Treatment. LC 72-140014. 1972. 29.95x (ISBN 0-202-36010-5). Aldine Pub.

Williams, F. & Wood, N. Developmental Art Therapy. 1977. 12.95 (ISBN 0-8391-1140-1). Univ Park.

Wolman, Benjamin B., ed. Handbook of Treatment of Mental Disorders in Childhood & Adolescence. LC 77-7928. (Illus.). 1978. ref. ed. 45.00 (ISBN 0-13-382234-6). P-H.

Yates, Elizabeth. Skeezer: Dog with a Mission. 1974. pap. 1.50 (ISBN 0-380-00105-5, 48223). Avon.

MENTALLY ILL CHILDREN–EDUCATION

Apter, Steven J., ed. Focus on Prevention: The Education of Children Labeled Emotionally Disturbed. 1978. pap. 5.00x (ISBN 0-8156-8100-3). Syracuse U Pr.

Damren, Betty R., et al. Training Effective Teachers: A Competency-Based Practicum Model for Teachers of Emotionally Disturbed Children. 53p. 1975. pap. text ed. 4.00x (ISBN 0-89039-134-3). Ann Arbor Pubs.

Dupont, Henry, ed. Educating Emotionally Disturbed Children: Readings. 2nd ed. LC 74-23502. 1975. text ed. 14.95 (ISBN 0-03-089626-6, HoltC). HR&W.

Foster, Genevieve W., et al. Child Care Work with Emotionally Disturbed Children. LC 74-158185. (Contemporary Community Health Ser.). 1971. 10.95x (ISBN 0-8229-3231-8). U of Pittsburgh Pr.

Hewett & Taylor. The Emmotionally Disturbed Child in the Classroom. 2nd ed. 416p. 1980. text ed. 19.95 (ISBN 0-205-06725-5, 2467259). Allyn.

John, Ronald O. Segregated Class Placement vs. Heterogeneous Class Placement of Emotionally & Perceptually Handicapped Children. LC 74-29575. 1975. soft bdg. 8.00 (ISBN 0-88247-315-8). R & E Res Assoc.

Kohen-Raz, R. From Chaos to Reality: An Experiment of Reeducation of Emotionally Disturbed Immigrant Youth in a Kibbutz. 1972. 21.50x (ISBN 0-677-03250-1). Gordon.

MacCracken, Mary. Lovey - a Very Special Child. LC 76-15389. 1976. 10.95 (ISBN 0-397-01129-6). Har-Row.

Macracken, Mary. A Circle of Children. (RL 9). 1975. pap. 1.95 (ISBN 0-451-08807-7, J8807, Sig). NAL.

Mosier, Doris & Park, Ruth. Teacher-Therapist: A Handbook for Teachers of Emotionally Impaired Students. 1979. pap. text ed. 10.95 (ISBN 0-87620-889-8). Goodyear.

Newcomer. Understanding & Teaching Emotionally Disturbed Children. new ed. 456p. 1979. text ed. 19.95 (ISBN 0-205-06843-X, 2468433). Allyn.

Pappanikou, A. J. & Paul, James L., eds. Mainstreaming Emotionally Disturbed Children. (Special Education & Rehabilitation Monograph: No. 10). 1977. 12.95x (ISBN 0-8156-0131-X); pap. 9.95x (ISBN 0-8156-2246-5). Syracuse U Pr.

Regier, Margaret I. You Don't Like Me Anymore. (Illus.). 109p. (Orig.). 1979. pap. 3.00 (ISBN 0-940644-01-0). River Hse.

Rhodes, William C. Emotionally Disturbed Student & Guidance. (Guidance Monograph). 1970. pap. 2.40 (ISBN 0-395-09947-1). HM.

Roberts, Brian & Furneaux, Barbara, eds. Autistic Children. (Special Needs in Education Ser.). 1979. pap. 7.95 (ISBN 0-7100-0348-X). Routledge & Kegan.

Rosen, Esther K. A Comparison of the Intellectual & Educational Status of Neurotic & Normal Children in Public Schools. LC 78-177208. (Columbia University. Teachers College. Contributions to Education: No. 188). Repr. of 1925 ed. 17.50 (ISBN 0-404-55188-2). AMS Pr.

Shelby, Madge E. Teaching the Learning Disabled & Emotionally Disturbed Child. 120p. (Orig.). 1979. pap. text ed. 4.50 (ISBN 0-935648-00-3). Halldin Pub.

MENTALLY RETARDED
see Mentally Handicapped
MENTALLY RETARDED CHILDREN
see Mentally Handicapped Children
MENUHIN, YEHUDI, 1916-

Daniels, Robin. Conversations with Menuhin. 1980. 14.95 (ISBN 0-312-16943-4). St Martin.

Magidoff, Robert. Yehudi Menuhin. LC 73-10753. (Illus.). 319p. 1974. Repr. of 1955 ed. lib. bdg. 16.00x (ISBN 0-8371-7020-6, MAYM). Greenwood.

Menuhin, Yehudi. Unfinished Journey. 1977. 15.00 (ISBN 0-394-41051-3). Knopf.

Rolfe, Lionel M. The Menuhins: A Family Odyssey. LC 78-13051. 1978. 11.95 (ISBN 0-915572-22-2). Panjandrum.

MENUS
see also Buffets (Cookery); Breakfasts; Caterers and Catering; Dinners and Dining; Luncheons

Aubery, Ronald. A Royal Chef's Notebook. LC 79-313122. (Illus.). 152p. 1978. 12.50x (ISBN 0-905418-28-X). Intl Pubns Serv.

Beard, James. Menus for Entertainment. 1979. pap. 2.50 (ISBN 0-440-15569-X). Dell.

Betty Crocker's Dinner for Two. 256p. 1975. pap. 2.50 (ISBN 0-553-13867-7, C13867-7). Bantam.

Blair, Eulilia C. Fish & Seafood Dishes for Foodservice Menu Planning. LC 75-25636. (Foodservice Menu Planning Ser.). 240p. 1975. 17.95 (ISBN 0-8436-2086-2). CBI Pub.

Carson, Byrta R. & Ramee, Marue C. How You Plan & Prepare Meals. 2nd ed. (gr. 7-12). 1968. text ed. 14.24 (ISBN 0-07-010161-2, W). McGraw.

Chamberlain, Narcissa G. & Chamberlain, Narcisse. French Menus for Parties. (Illus.). 9.95 (ISBN 0-8038-2256-1). Hastings.

Chamberlain, Samuel, et al. Chamberlain Sampler of American Cooking. (Illus.). 1961. 9.95 (ISBN 0-8038-1088-1). Hastings.

Chang, Constance D. Chinese Menu Cookbook. LC 72-144257. 1971. 6.95 (ISBN 0-385-00658-6). Doubleday.

Chu, Grace Z. Pleasures of Chinese Cooking. 1962. 9.95 (ISBN 0-671-58010-8); pap. 4.95 (ISBN 0-671-22181-7). S&S.

--The Pleasures of Chinese Cooking. (Illus.). 239p. 1975. pap. 3.95 (ISBN 0-671-22181-7, Fireside). S&S.

Claiborne, Craig. New York Times Menu Cook Book. (Illus.). 1966. 17.95 (ISBN 0-06-010791-X, HarpT). Har-Row.

Clarke, H. C. Menu Terminology. 1969. pap. 5.25 (ISBN 0-08-006525-2). Pergamon.

Eckstein, Eleanor. Menu Planning. 2nd ed. (Illus.). text ed. 22.50 (ISBN 0-87055-260-0). AVI.

Elkon, Juliette & Ross, Elaine. Menus for Entertaining. 1960. 9.95 (ISBN 0-8038-4617-7). Hastings.

Ellison, Al. Ellison's French Menu Reader. 168p. 1977. pap. 2.95 (ISBN 0-930580-00-1). Liberty Pub.

--Ellison's Latin American Menu Reader. 1978. pap. 2.95 (ISBN 0-930580-06-0). Ellison Ent.

--Ellison's Mexican Menu Reader. 1977. pap. 2.95 (ISBN 0-930580-04-4). Ellison Ent.

--Ellison's Portuguese Menu Reader. Date not set. pap. 2.95 (ISBN 0-930580-07-9). Ellison Ent.

--Ellison's Swiss Menu Reader. 1978. pap. 2.95 (ISBN 0-930580-05-2). Ellison Ent.

Family Weekly. Cooking by the Calendar: A Family Weekly Cookbook. LC 78-58167. 1978. 10.95 (ISBN 0-8129-0786-8). Times Bks.

Gilchrist, Joelyn & Wood, Jacqueline. The Campus Survival Cookbook. (Illus.). 160p. 1973. o.p. 5.95 (ISBN 0-688-00030-4); pap. 4.95 (ISBN 0-688-05030-1). Morrow.

Graham, Susan. Quick Simple Meals. (Leisure Plan Bks). 1971. pap. 2.95 (ISBN 0-600-01354-5). Transatlantic.

Groceman, Wanda C. To My Daughter, with Love. LC 73-152079. (Illus.). 192p. (Orig.). 1972. pap. 4.95 (ISBN 0-911954-24-4). Nitty Gritty.

Groff, Betty. Betty Groff's Country Goodness Cookbook. LC 80-1093. (Illus.). 336p. 1981. 17.95 (ISBN 0-385-12120-2). Doubleday.

Hillman, Libby. Menu-Cookbook for Entertaining. LC 68-8524. (Illus.). 1968. 8.95 (ISBN 0-8208-0211-5). Hearthside.

Institute Publishing Company. Thoughts for Buffets. 1958. 11.95 (ISBN 0-395-07825-3). HM.

--Thoughts for Festive Foods. 1964. 15.00 (ISBN 0-395-07827-X). HM.

--Thoughts for Food. 12.95 (ISBN 0-395-07824-5). HM.

Iowa State Department of Health. Simplified Diet Manual. 4th ed. 120p. 1975. pap. text ed. 7.50x (ISBN 0-8138-1430-8). Iowa St U Pr.

Kaiser, Ralph. Menu Converter. 2.95, gift ed. (ISBN 0-685-06579-0); pap. 1.95 (ISBN 0-685-06580-4). Assoc Bk.

Kreck, Lothar A. Menus: Analysis & Planning. LC 74-28068. (Illus.). 200p. 1975. 17.95 (ISBN 0-8436-2050-1). CBI Pub.

Long, John, et al, eds. Menus of the Valley's Finest Restaurants: Nineteen Eighty-Two Edition. 176p. 1981. pap. 5.95 (ISBN 0-930380-13-4, 0148-4133). Quail Run.

McLean, Beth B. Meal Planning & Service. rev. ed. (Illus.). (gr. 9-12). 1964. text ed. 15.48 (ISBN 0-87002-218-0). Bennett IL.

Miller, Jack E. Menu Pricing. LC 76-18255. 1976. pap. 7.95 (ISBN 0-8436-2100-1). CBI Pub.

Null, Gary, et al. Food Combining Handbook. 1973. pap. 1.75 (ISBN 0-515-05779-7, V3202). Jove Pubns.

Robertson, Ellen H. Magic Menu. (Illus., Orig.). pap. 1.00 (ISBN 0-685-07371-8). Borden.

Ross, Elaine. Low Calorie Menus for Entertaining. 1970. 7.75 (ISBN 0-8038-4271-6). Hastings.

Seaberg, Albin G. Menu Design: Merchandising & Marketing. 3rd ed. 396p. 1981. text ed. 24.95 (ISBN 0-8436-2222-9). CBI Pub.

--Menu Design, Merchandising & Marketing. 2nd ed. LC 72-149403. 1973. 23.95 (ISBN 0-8436-0572-3). CBI Pub.

Shank, Dorothy E., et al. Guide to Modern Meals. 2nd ed. (American Home & Family Ser). (gr. 10-12). 1970. text ed. 14.80 (ISBN 0-07-056404-3, W). McGraw.

Tracy, Marian. Delicious Main-Course Dishes: 200 Recipes. 1978. pap. 3.00 (ISBN 0-486-23664-1). Dover.

Treat, Nola & Richards, Lenore. Quantity Cookery. 4th rev. ed. 1967. 12.95 (ISBN 0-316-85251-1). Little.

Van Zuylen, Guirne. Eating with Wine. (Illus.). 1972. 8.95 (ISBN 0-571-09958-0). Transatlantic.

Visick, H. E. & Van Kleek, Peter E. Menu Planning: A Blueprint for Better Profits. (Illus.). 176p. 1973. pap. text ed. 6.95 (ISBN 0-07-067063-3, G). McGraw.

Waldner, George K. & Mitterhauser, Klaus. Professional Chef's Book of Buffets. 1968. 23.95 (ISBN 0-8436-0505-7). CBI Pub.

Weaver, Ann A. Planning Meals & Shopping. (Young Homemakers at Work Ser). (gr. 7-12,RL 2.5). 1970. pap. 3.20 (ISBN 0-8224-5450-5); tchrs.' manual free (ISBN 0-8224-7676-2). Pitman Learning.

Wenzel, George L. Wenzel's Menu Maker. (Illus.). 1500p. 1970. text ed. 110.00 (ISBN 0-685-04751-2). Radio City.

Wenzel, William, Jr. Wenzel's Menu Maker. 2nd ed. LC 79-13732. 1979. 110.00 (ISBN 0-8436-2135-4). CBI Pub.

Wheat Flour Institute. Winning Sandwiches for Menu Makers. Thomas, Kathleen M., ed. LC 76-45621. (Illus.). 1976. 19.95 (ISBN 0-8436-2123-0). CBI Pub.

Zaccarell, Herman E. Cookbook That Tells You How. LC 75-6894. 1972. 16.95 (ISBN 0-8436-2078-1). CBI Pub.

--Cookbook That Tells You How. LC 75-6894. 1972. 16.95 (ISBN 0-8436-2078-1). CBI Pub.

MENZEL, ADOLF FRIEDRICH ERDMANN VON, 1815-1905

Von Menzel, Adolph F. Drawings of Menzel. Longstreet, Stephen, ed. (Master Draughtsman Ser). (Illus., Orig.). treasure trove bdg. 6.47x (ISBN 0-685-07275-4); pap. 2.95 (ISBN 0-685-07276-2). Borden.

MENZIES, ROBERT GORDON, 1894-

Hazelhurst, Cameron. Menzies Observed. LC 77-78556. 1979. text ed. 19.95x (ISBN 0-86861-320-7). Allen Unwin.

Holt, Edgar. Politics Is People - the Men of the Menzies Era. (Illus.). 1969. 7.50x (ISBN 0-8426-1307-2). Verry.

Perkins, Kevin. Menzies - Last of the Queen's Men. (Illus.). 1968. 10.50x (ISBN 0-8426-1467-2). Verry.

MEO

see Miao People

MEPHITIS

see Skunks

MEPROBAMATE

Wittenborn, J. R. Response to Meprobamate-A Predictive Analysis. LC 70-107228. 113p. 1970. 13.50 (ISBN 0-911216-11-1). Raven.

MERAUKESE LANGUAGE

see Marindinese Language

MERCADO COMUN CENTROAMERICANO

Maritano, Nino. Latin American Economic Community: History, Policies & Problems. LC 68-27581. 1970. 9.95x (ISBN 0-268-00357-2). U of Notre Dame Pr.

Nugent, Jeffrey B. Economic Integration in Central America: Empirical Investigations. LC 74-6832. (Illus.). 226p. 1975. 15.00x (ISBN 0-8018-1451-0). Johns Hopkins.

MERCANTILE BUILDINGS

see also Department Stores; Office Buildings; Stores, Retail

Design for Modern Merchandising Stores: Stores, Shopping Centers, Showrooms. LC 76-142927. (An Architectural Record Book). (Illus.). 247p. Repr. of 1954 ed. lib. bdg. 24.00x (ISBN 0-8371-5929-6, ARMM). Greenwood.

MERCANTILE LAW

see Commercial Law

MERCANTILE SYSTEM

see also Balance of Trade; Free Trade and Protection

Buck, Philip W. Politics of Mercantilism. 1964. lib. bdg. 15.00x (ISBN 0-374-91083-9). Octagon.

Cole, Charles W. French Mercantilism, 1683-1700. 1965. lib. bdg. 17.00x (ISBN 0-374-91824-4). Octagon.

--French Mercantilist Doctrines Before Colbert. LC 79-96178. 1970. Repr. of 1931 ed. lib. bdg. 14.50x (ISBN 0-374-91805-8). Octagon.

Cunningham, William. The Growth of English Industry & Commerce, 3 vols. in 2. Incl. Vol. 1. Early & Middle Ages. 5th ed; Vol. 2. Modern Times: the Mercantile System. 4th ed; Vol. 3. Modern Times: Laissez Faire. 4th ed. LC 66-21667. Repr. of 1907 ed. Set. 50.00x (ISBN 0-678-00288-6). Kelley.

Dionnet, Georges. Le Neomercantilisme Au Dix-Huitieme Siecle et Au Debut Du Dix-Neuvieme Siecle. LC 73-146140. (Research & Source Works Ser.: No. 625). 1971. Repr. of 1901 ed. lib. bdg. 21.00 (ISBN 0-8337-0867-8). B Franklin.

Ekelund, Robert B., Jr. & Tollison, Robert D. Mercantilism As a Rent-Seeking Society: Economic Regulation in Historical Perspectives. LC 81-40398. (Tex A&M University Economic Ser.). 176p. 1981. 17.50x (ISBN 0-89096-120-4). Tex A&M Univ Pr.

Furniss, Edgar S. Position of the Laborer in a System of Nationalism. LC 58-3121. Repr. of 1920 ed. 15.00x (ISBN 0-678-00093-X). Kelley.

Hause, E. Malcolm. Puritan Mercantilism. LC 77-73535. 1977. 2.65 (ISBN 0-89301-043-X). U Pr of Idaho.

Horne, Thomas A. The Social Thought of Bernard Mandeville: Virtue & Commerce in Early Eighteenth Century England. LC 77-13573. 1978. 15.00x (ISBN 0-231-04274-4). Columbia U Pr.

Mishkin, David J. The American Colonial Wine Industry: An Economic Interpretation, 2 vols. (Dissertations in American Economic History). (Illus.). 1975. Vol. 1. 21.00x (ISBN 0-405-07209-0); Vol. 2. 40.00x (ISBN 0-405-07210-4); set (ISBN 0-405-07208-2). Arno.

Mun, Thomas. England's Treasure by Forraign Trade. LC 74-370398. Repr. of 1664 ed. 10.00x (ISBN 0-678-06274-9). Kelley.

Reber, Vera B. British Mercantile Houses in Buenos Aires, 1810-1880. LC 78-15743. (Studies in Business History: No. 29). (Illus.). 1979. 17.50x (ISBN 0-674-08245-1). Harvard U Pr.

Schmoller, Gustav F. Mercantile System. LC 65-26377. Repr. of 1897 ed. 10.00x (ISBN 0-678-00252-5). Kelley.

Schuyler, Robert L. Fall of the Old Colonial System: A Study in British Free Trade, 1770-1870. 1966. Repr. of 1945 ed. 19.50 (ISBN 0-208-00254-5, Archon). Shoe String.

Suviranta, Bruno. Theory of the Balance of Trade in England. LC 67-28342. Repr. of 1923 ed. 13.50x (ISBN 0-678-00328-9). Kelley.

Thomas, Parakunnel J. Mercantilism & the East India Trade. LC 66-5362. Repr. of 1926 ed. 19.50x (ISBN 0-678-05197-6). Kelley.

MERCEDES AUTOMOBILE

see Automobiles, Foreign-Types-Mercedes

MERCENARIES (SOLDIERS)

see Mercenary Troops

MERCENARY TROOPS

Bidwell, Shelford. Swords for Hire: European Mercenaries in Eighteenth Century India. (Illus.). 258p. 1972. 15.00x (ISBN 0-7195-2432-6). Transatlantic.

--Swords for Hire: European Mercenaries in 18th-Century India. (Illus.). 268p. 1972. 15.00x (ISBN 0-7195-2432-6). Intl Pubns Serv.

Dempster, Chris & Tomkins, Dave. Fire Power. 500p. 1981. 13.95 (ISBN 0-312-29115-9). St Martin.

Griffith, G. T. The Mercenaries of the Hellenistic World. pap. 6.00 (ISBN 0-89005-085-6). Ares.

Griffith, Guy T. The Mercenaries of the Hellenistic World. LC 75-41123. Repr. of 1935 ed. 19.50 (ISBN 0-404-14667-8). AMS Pr.

Mallin, Jay & Brown, Robert K. Merc: American Soldiers of Fortune. 1980. pap. 2.50 (ISBN 0-451-09529-4, E9529, Sig). NAL.

--MERC: American Soldiers of Fortune. 1979. 17.95 (ISBN 0-02-579330-6). Macmillan.

Schlight, John. Monarchs & Mercenaries: A Reappraisal of the Importance of Knight Service in Norman & Early Angevin England. LC 68-15335. (Studies in British History & Culture). 103p. 1968. 6.00x (ISBN 0-8147-0376-3). NYU Pr.

Steiner, Rolf & Berges, Yves G. The Last Adventure. LC 77-19070. 1978. 9.95 (ISBN 0-316-81239-0). Little.

MERCER, HENRY CHAPMAN, 1856-1930

Gemmill, Helen. The Mercer Mile: The Story of Dr. Henry C. Mercer's Three Concrete Buildings. (Illus.). 28p. 1972. pap. 1.25 (ISBN 0-685-47445-3). Bucks Co Hist.

MERCERSBURG THEOLOGY

Maxwell, Jack M. Worship & Reformed Theology: The Liturgical Lessons of Mercersburg. LC 75-45492. (Pittsburgh Theological Monographs: No. 10). 1976. pap. 8.50 (ISBN 0-915138-12-3). Pickwick.

MERCHANDISE

see Commercial Products

MERCHANDISE, BRANDED

see Branded Merchandise

MERCHANDISE, DISPLAY OF

see Display of Merchandise

MERCHANDISING

Bohlinger, Maryanne S. Merchandise Buying: Principles & Applications. 450p. 1977. text ed. write for info. (ISBN 0-697-08014-5); instr's man. 1.00 (ISBN 0-686-67600-9). Wm C Brown.

Cardella, Carol A. Salespersons Guide to Merchandising. 44p. 1978. 8.00 (ISBN 0-86718-041-2). Natl Assn Home Builders.

Carlo & Murphy. Merchandising Mathmatics. 136p. 1981. pap. 6.60 (ISBN 0-8273-1416-7); instructor's guide 2.10 (ISBN 0-8273-1417-5). Delmar.

Carty, Richard. Visual Merchandising -- Principles & Practice. 1978. text ed. 8.95 (ISBN 0-87350-255-8); wkbk. 4.95 (ISBN 0-87350-256-6). Milady.

Copeland, Melvin T. Principles of Merchandising. Assael, Henry, ed. LC 78-277. (Century of Marketing Ser.). 1978. Repr. of 1924 ed. lib. bdg. 22.00x (ISBN 0-405-11182-7). Arno.

Corbman, Bernard P. & Krieger, Murray. Mathematics of Retail Merchandising. 2nd ed. 450p. 1972. 21.95 (ISBN 0-471-06587-0). Ronald Pr.

Cushman, Ronald A. & Daggett, Willard. Retail Merchandising. (Co-Operative Education Workbook Series). 1975. 4.50 (ISBN 0-87005-153-9). Fairchild.

Cushman, Ronald A. & Daggett, Willard R. Retail Merchandising Teacher's Manual. (Co-Operative Education Workbook Series). 1975. 2.50 (ISBN 0-87005-156-3). Fairchild.

Dorr, Eugene, et al. Merchandising. 2nd ed. (Occupational Manuals & Projects in Marketing Ser.). 1977. pap. text ed. 5.48 (ISBN 0-07-017615-9, G); tchr's manual & key 3.00 (ISBN 0-07-017616-7). McGraw.

Dyer, Lee, ed. Merchandising in Action. (Illus.). 13.95 (ISBN 0-911790-07-1). Prog Grocer.

Fulkerson, Katherine. The Merchandise Buyers' Game. 1981. pap. text ed. 3.95 (ISBN 0-933836-13-9). Simtek.

Hall. Language of Advertising & Merchandising in English. (English for Careers Ser.). (gr. 10 up). 1982. pap. text ed. 3.50 (ISBN 0-88345-352-5). Regents Pub.

Hall, Elvajean. Jobs in Marketing & Distribution. LC 73-17711. (Exploring Careers Ser.). (Illus.). 96p. (gr. 5 up). 1974. 7.25 (ISBN 0-688-75009-5). Lothrop.

Kahrl, William L. Menu Planning Merchandising. LC 78-57195. 1978. 5.95 (ISBN 0-912016-71-X). Lebhar Friedman.

Kneider, A. P. Mathematics of Merchandising. 2nd ed. (Illus.). 320p. 1981. pap. text ed. 15.95 (ISBN 0-686-63445-4). P-H.

Krieger, Murray. The Complete Dictionary of Buying & Merchandising. 125p. 1980. pap. text ed. 3.95 (ISBN 0-686-60189-0, M47780). Natl Ret Merch.

--Merchandising Math for Profit: An Executive Handbook. LC 68-17412. (Illus.). 1968. pap. 4.50 (ISBN 0-87005-044-3). Fairchild.

Luick, John F. & Ziegler, William L. Sales Promotion & Modern Merchandising. 1968. pap. text ed. 7.95 (ISBN 0-07-038998-5, C). McGraw.

Masser, Barry Z. Thirty-Six Thousand Dollars a Year in Your Own Home Merchandising Business. (Illus.). 1978. 9.95 (ISBN 0-13-918987-4, Parker). P-H.

Merchandising Arithmetic for Retail Training. 35p. 1971. soft bdg 4.00 (ISBN 0-685-44076-1, P50071). Natl Ret Merch.

Merchandising Challenges & Opportunities. (Study Units Ser.). 1977. pap. 9.00 (ISBN 0-89401-113-8). Didactic Syst.

Meyer, Jerold S. & Harling, Edwin L. Merchandise Control & Budgeting. 111p. 1969. soft bdg. 10.75 (ISBN 0-685-44046-X, M44566). Natl Ret Merch.

Mills, Kenneth H. & Paul, Judith E. Applied Visual Merchandising. (Illus.). 320p. 1982. reference 19.95 (ISBN 0-13-043331-4). P-H.

National Retail Merchants Assn. Visual Merchandising. 1976. 20.95 (ISBN 0-685-68116-5, S656-76). Natl Ret Merch.

National Retail Merchants Association. OCR: A Users Guide. (U1478 Ser.). (Illus.). 41p. 1978. pap. 4.00 (ISBN 0-685-63515-5). Natl Ret Merch.

Orange Blossom Opportunity. 93p. soft bdg. 7.00 (ISBN 0-685-45925-X, M44870); members 5.00 (ISBN 0-685-45926-8). Natl Ret Merch.

Packard, Sidney & Axelrod, Nathan. Concepts & Cases in Fashion Buying & Merchandising. LC 76-50439. 1977. text ed. 10.00 (ISBN 0-87005-182-2). Fairchild.

Parts & Service Merchandising. LC 74-83611. 10.00 (ISBN 0-87359-006-6). Northwood Inst.

Peltz, Leslie R. Merchandising Mathematics. LC 79-494. 1979. pap. 9.50 (ISBN 0-672-97273-5); tchr's manual 3.33 (ISBN 0-672-97274-3). Bobbs.

Shuch, Milton L. Retail Buying & Merchandising: A Decision Making Approach. 400p. 1982. pap. 16.95 (ISBN 0-686-76615-6). Winthrop.

Taylor, Charles G. Merchandise Assortment Planning. 100p. 16.00 (ISBN 0-685-45924-1, M45470). Natl Ret Merch.

Tolman, Ruth. Fashion Marketing & Merchandising, Vol. 2. (Illus.). 372p. 1974. 19.95 (ISBN 0-87350-251-5). Milady.

--Guide to Fashion Merchandise Knowledge, Vol. 1. (Illus.). 1973. text ed. 19.95 (ISBN 0-87350-250-7). Milady.

Troxell, Mary D. & Stone, Elaine. Fashion Merchandising. 3rd ed. LC 80-25077. (Gregg McGraw-Hill Marketing Ser.). (Illus.). 480p. 1981. 16.95 (ISBN 0-07-065280-5); instr's manual & key 4.00 (ISBN 0-07-065281-3). McGraw.

Verbatim Report: Has the Basement a Future. 55p. soft bdg. 5.50 (ISBN 0-685-45927-6, M45268). Natl Ret Merch.

Wingate, Isabel B., et al. Know Your Merchandise: For Retailers & Consumers. 4th ed. (Illus.). 544p. 1975. text ed. 15.96 (ISBN 0-07-070985-8, G); tchr's ed. 3.50 (ISBN 0-07-070986-6). McGraw.

MERCHANT ADVENTURERS OF ENGLAND

John, Wheeler. A Treatise of Commerce. Wilkins, Mira, ed. LC 76-29979. (European Business Ser.). 1977. Repr. of 1931 ed. lib. bdg. 28.00x (ISBN 0-405-09745-X). Arno.

Latimer, John. History of the Society of Merchant Venturers of the City of Bristol, with Some Account of the Anterior Merchants' Guilds. LC 79-129470. (Research & Source Works Ser: No. 534). (Illus.). 1970. Repr. of 1903 ed. lib. bdg. 23.50 (ISBN 0-8337-2016-3). B Franklin.

Lingelbach, William E. Merchant Adventurers of England, Their Laws & Ordinances with Other Documents. LC 71-172190. (Selected Essays in History, Economics & Social Science Ser: No. 315). 298p. 1972. Repr. of 1902 ed. lib. bdg. 26.50 (ISBN 0-8337-2111-9). B Franklin.

MERCHANT COMPANIES

see Colonial Companies; Gilds

MERCHANT MARINE

see also Cargo Ships; Coastwise Navigation; Coastwise Shipping; Free Ports and Zones; Harbors; Insurance, Marine; Merchant Seamen; Merchant Ships; Shipping; Ships Papers; Steamboats and Steamboat Lines

Anderson, Robert E. The Merchant Marine & World Frontiers. LC 78-5585. (Illus.). xvii, 205p. 1978. Repr. of 1945 ed. lib. bdg. 20.50x (ISBN 0-313-20437-3, ANMM). Greenwood.

Cranwell, John P. Spoilers of the Sea. facsimile ed. LC 78-93331. (Essay Index Reprint Ser). 1941. 25.00 (ISBN 0-8369-1563-1). Arno.

Crump, Irving. Our Merchant Marine Academy, Kings Point. LC 74-5553. (Illus.). 236p. 1975. Repr. of 1958 ed. lib. bdg. 16.00x (ISBN 0-8371-7511-9, CRMA). Greenwood.

Dictionnaire Francais-Anglais, Anglais-Francais des Termes et Locutions de la Marine Marchande. (Fr.-Eng.). 25.00 (ISBN 0-686-57108-8, M-6140). French & Eur.

Gorter, Wytze. United States Shipping Policy. LC 77-6767. 1977. Repr. of 1956 ed. lib. bdg. 18.00x (ISBN 0-8371-9657-4, GOUS). Greenwood.

Goss, R. O., ed. Advances in Maritime Economics. LC 76-1135. (Illus.). 1977. 49.50 (ISBN 0-521-21232-4). Cambridge U Pr.

Hall. The Language of the Merchant Marine in English. (English for Careers Ser.). (gr. 10 up). 1978. pap. text ed. 3.50 (ISBN 0-88345-347-9). Regents Pub.

Healey, James C. Foc's'le & Glory-Hole: A Study of the Merchant Seaman & His Occupation. Repr. of 1936 ed. lib. bdg. 15.00 (ISBN 0-8371-2539-1, HEFG). Greenwood.

Herndon, James. Sorrowless Times. 1981. 12.95 (ISBN 0-671-24321-7). S&S.

James, Richard & Plant, Richard M. The Multiple Choice Examinations for Chief Mate & Master: Study Guide. LC 76-48096. (Illus.). 1976. 25.00x (ISBN 0-87033-232-5). Cornell Maritime.
--The Multiple Choice Examinations for Third & Second Mates: Study Guide. 3rd ed. LC 79-1735. 1979. pap. 20.00x (ISBN 0-87033-252-X). Cornell Maritime.
MacArthur, Walter. Last Days of Sail on the West Coast. facs. ed. (Illus.). pap. 14.00 (ISBN 0-8466-0191-5, SJS191). Shorey.
MacEwen. Blue Book of Questions & Answers for Third Mates. 2nd ed. LC 65-25384. (Illus.). 1965. pap. 6.00x (ISBN 0-87033-008-X). Cornell Maritime.
MacEwen, W. A. Blue Book of Questions & Answers for Second Mate, Chief Mate & Master. LC 62-15957. (Illus.). 320p. 1969. pap. 8.50x (ISBN 0-87033-007-1). Cornell Maritime.
McLintock, Gordon E. Your Future in the Merchant Marine. LC 66-10995. (Careers in Depth Ser.). (Illus.). (gr. 7 up). 1968. PLB 5.97 (ISBN 0-8239-0050-9). Rosen Pr.
Mangone, Gerard J. Marine Policy for America: The United States at Sea. LC 77-243. 1977. 26.95 (ISBN 0-669-01432-X). Lexington Bks.
Riesenberg, Felix, Jr. Sea War: The Story of the United States Merchant Marine in World War II. LC 74-4660. (Illus.). 320p. 1974. Repr. of 1956 ed. lib. bdg. 17.00x (ISBN 0-8371-7479-1, RISW). Greenwood.
Rudman, Jack. Able Seaman. (Career Examination Ser.: C-1). (Cloth bdg. avail. on request). pap. 8.00 (ISBN 0-8373-0001-0). Natl Learning.
--Deckhand. (Career Examination Ser.: C-190). (Cloth bdg. avail. on request). pap. 8.00 (ISBN 0-8373-0190-4). Natl Learning.

MERCHANT MARINE–ACCOUNTING
see Shipping–Accounting

MERCHANT MARINE–CARGO
see Ships–Cargo

MERCHANT MARINE–HISTORY
Albion, Robert G. & Pope, Jennie B. Sea Lanes in Wartime: The American Experience, 1775-1945. 2nd ed. 1968. 22.50 (ISBN 0-208-00286-3, Archon). Shoe String.
Bunker, John G. Liberty Ships. LC 79-6103. (Navies & Men Ser.). (Illus.). 1980. Repr. of 1972 ed. lib. bdg. 25.00x (ISBN 0-405-13032-5). Arno.
Clark, William H. Ships & Sailors: The Story of Our Merchant Marine. LC 74-22736. (Illus.). Repr. of 1938 ed. 21.00 (ISBN 0-404-58488-8). AMS Pr.
Garitee, Jerome R. The Republic's Private Navy: The American Privateering Business As Practiced by Baltimore During the War of 1812. LC 76-41487. (American Maritime Library: Vol. 8). (Illus.). 356p. 1977. 17.50 (ISBN 0-8195-5004-3); limited ed. 35.00 (ISBN 0-8195-5005-1). Mystic Seaport.
Henderson, Daniel M. Yankee Ships in China Seas. LC 76-128258. (Essay Index Reprint Ser). 1946. 20.00 (ISBN 0-8369-1950-5). Arno.
Newell, Gordon. The H. W. McCurdy Marine History of the Pacific Northwest 1966 Through 1976. LC 76-51827. (Illus.). 1977. 100.00x (ISBN 0-87564-220-9). Superior Pub.
Spears, John R. The Story of the American Merchant Marine. 1977. lib. bdg. 55.95 (ISBN 0-8490-2689-X). Gordon Pr.

MERCHANT MARINE–LAW
see Maritime Law

MERCHANT MARINE–OFFICERS
see also Shipmasters
Turpin, Edward A. & MacEwen, William A. Merchant Marine Officer's Handbook. 4th ed. LC 60-14988. (Illus.). 1965. 20.00x (ISBN 0-87033-056-X). Cornell Maritime.

MERCHANT MARINE–RATES
see Shipping–Rates

MERCHANT MARINE–CUBA
Escarpenter, Claudio. Economics of International Ocean Transport: The Cuban Case Before 1958. 208p. 1965. 17.50x (ISBN 0-299-03590-5). U of Wis Pr.

MERCHANT MARINE–GREAT BRITAIN
Gee, Joshua. Trade & Navigation of Great Britain Considered. 4th ed. LC 71-97977. Repr. of 1738 ed. 14.50x (ISBN 0-678-00576-1). Kelley.

MERCHANT MARKS
see Trade-Marks

MERCHANT SEAMEN
see also Boatmen
Collins, John J. Bargaining at the Local Level. LC 73-81503. 1974. 15.00 (ISBN 0-8232-0972-5). Fordham.
Healey, James C. Foc's'le & Glory-Hole: A Study of the Merchant Seaman & His Occupation. Repr. of 1936 ed. lib. bdg. 15.00 (ISBN 0-8371-2539-1, HEFG). Greenwood.
Herndon, James. Sorrowless Times. 1981. 12.95 (ISBN 0-671-24321-7). S&S.
Hohman, Elmo P. Seamen Ashore: A Study of the United Seamen's Service & of Merchant Seamen in Port. (Merchant Seamen's Ser.: No. 2). 1952. 12.50x (ISBN 0-686-17410-0). R S Barnes.
Kitchen, Jonathan S. The Employment of Merchant Seamen. 658p. 1980. 150.00x (ISBN 0-85664-527-3, Pub. by Croom Helm Ltd England). Biblio Dist.
Moreby, D. H. Personnel Management in Merchant Ships. 1968. 27.00 (ISBN 0-08-012993-5); pap. 14.00 (ISBN 0-08-012992-7). Pergamon.
Norris, Martin J. The Law of Seamen, 3 vols. 3rd ed. LC 74-112518. 1970. Set. 144.00 (ISBN 0-686-14494-5). Lawyers Co-Op.
Rubin, Charles. The Log of Rubin the Sailor. LC 73-77809. 336p. 1973. pap. 2.25 (ISBN 0-7178-0387-2). Intl Pub Co.
Sherar, Mariam G. Shipping Out. LC 72-78239. 1973. pap. 6.00x (ISBN 0-87033-173-6). Cornell Maritime.
Taylor, Paul S. Sailors' Union of the Pacific. LC 70-156427. (American Labor Ser., No. 2). 1971. Repr. of 1923 ed. 12.00 (ISBN 0-405-02946-2). Arno.
Weintraub, Hyman G. Andrew Furuseth, Emancipator of the Seamen. (Institute of Industrial Relations, UC Berkeley). 1959. 24.00x (ISBN 0-520-01322-0). U of Cal Pr.

MERCHANT SEAMEN'S SONGS
see Sea Songs

MERCHANT SHIPS
see also Cargo Ships; Clipper-Ships; Ocean Liners; Packets; Steamboats and Steamboat Lines; Tankers; Work Boats
Arkenbout Schokker, J. C., et al. The Design of Merchant Ships. 600p. 1959. 250.00x (ISBN 0-85950-086-1, Pub. by Stam Pr England). State Mutual Bk.
Carr, Frank C. The Medley of Mast & Sail: a Camera Record, Vol. 2. LC 76-62879. 1977. 23.95 (ISBN 0-87021-939-1). Naval Inst Pr.
Clegg, W. Paul & Styring, John S. British Nationalized Shipping 1947-1968. LC 68-26163. 1968. 15.00x (ISBN 0-678-05587-4). Kelley.
Colby, C. B. Ships of Commerce: Liners, Tankers, Freighters, Floating Grain Elevators, Tugboats. (Illus.). (gr. 4-7). 1963. PLB 5.29 (ISBN 0-698-30312-1). Coward.
Ellis, Chris. Famous Ships of World War Two. LC 76-52987. (Arco Color Books). (Illus.). 1977. 7.95. (ISBN 0-668-04225-7, 4225). Arco.
Greenhill, Basil. The Life & Death of the Merchant Sailing Ships. (The Ship Series, National Maritime Museum). (Illus.). 1980. 9.95 (ISBN 0-11-290317-7). Sheridan.
Greenway, Ambrose. Comecon Merchant Ships. 2nd ed. (Illus.). 180p. 1981. text ed. 20.00x (ISBN 0-911378-34-0). Sheridan.
--Soviet Merchant Ships. 4th ed. (Illus.). 224p. 1981. text ed. 20.00x (ISBN 0-911378-33-2). Sheridan.
Hornsby, D. T., ed. Merchant Ships: Newbuildings. 1977. 14.50 (ISBN 0-85038-059-6, Pub by Kogan Pg). Nichols Pub.
Jarvis, R. C. & Craig, R. Liverpool Registry of Merchant Ships. 278p. 1967. 33.00x (ISBN 0-686-63740-2, Pub. by Manchester U Pr England). State Mutual Bk.
MacGregor, David R. Merchant Sailing Ships, Seveteen Seventy-Five to Eighteen Fifteen. (Illus.). 218p. 1981. 21.95 (ISBN 0-87021-942-1). Naval Inst Pr.
Medley of Mast & Sail Two: A Camera Record. 2nd ed. LC 80-85162. (Illus.). 473p. 1981. 29.95 (ISBN 0-87021-940-5). Naval Inst Pr.
Merchant Ship Search & Rescue Manual (MERSAR) 55p. 1980. pap. 14.00 (ISBN 92-801-1111-6, IMCO72, IMCO). Unipub.
Munro-Smith, R. Merchant Ship Types. LC 74-79180. (Illus.). 260p. 1975. 27.00 (ISBN 0-900976-26-8, Pub. by Inst Marine Eng). Intl Schol Bk Serv.
Pursey, H. J. Merchant Ship Construction. 1981. 40.00x (ISBN 0-85174-144-4, Pub. by Nautical England). State Mutual Bk.
Rinke, Hans. Woerterbuch der Seeschiffahrt, Vol. 1. 2nd ed. (Eng. -Ger., Dictionary of Merchant Shipping). 1975. 25.00 (ISBN 3-19-006294-3, M-6958). French & Eur.
--Woerterbuch der Seeschiffahrt, Vol. 2. 2nd ed. (Ger. -Eng., Dictionary of Merchant Shipping). 27.50 (ISBN 3-19-006295-1, M-6957). French & Eur.
Talbot-Booth, E. C. Talbot-Booth's Merchant Ships, Vol. 2. 1978. 25.00x (ISBN 0-89397-046-8). Nichols Pub.
--Talbot-Booth's Merchant Ships, Vol. 3. 1979. 47.50x (ISBN 0-89397-047-6). Nichols Pub.
Talbot-Booth, E. G., ed. Talbot-Booth's Merchant Ships, Vol. 1. 1978. 27.50 (ISBN 0-89397-030-1). Nichols Pub.
Taylor, D. A. Merchant Ship Construction. (Illus.). 240p. 1980. text ed. 39.95 (ISBN 0-408-00408-8). Butterworth.

MERCHANT SHIPS–CARGO
see Ships–Cargo

MERCHANT SHIP'S PAPERS
see Ships Papers

MERCHANT VENTURERS' SOCIETY, BRISTOL, ENGLAND
Latimer, John. History of the Society of Merchant Venturers of the City of Bristol, with Some Account of the Anterior Merchants' Guilds. LC 79-129470. (Research & Source Works Ser: No. 534). (Illus.). 1970. Repr. of 1903 ed. lib. bdg. 23.50 (ISBN 0-8337-2016-3). B Franklin.

MERCHANTMEN
see Merchant Ships

MERCHANTS
see also Commission Merchants
Atherton, Lewis E. Frontier Merchant in Mid-America. LC 70-155845. 1971. 12.00x (ISBN 0-8262-0530-5). U of Mo Pr.
--The Pioneer Merchant in Mid-America. LC 75-77700. (American Scene Ser). 1969. Repr. of 1939 ed. 19.50 (ISBN 0-306-71338-1). Da Capo.
Bourne, H. R. English Merchants: Memoirs in Illustration of the Progress of British Commerce, 2 Vols. in 1. LC 14-5863. 1866. 42.00 (ISBN 0-527-10400-0). Kraus Repr.
Bruchey, Stuart W. Robert Oliver, Merchant of Baltimore, 1783-1819. Carosso, Vincent P., ed. LC 78-18954. (Small Business Enterprise in America Ser.). 1979. Repr. of 1956 ed. lib. bdg. 28.00x (ISBN 0-405-11458-3). Arno.
Dart, Margaret S. Yankee Traders at Sea & Ashore. 1965. 3.00 (ISBN 0-87164-011-2). William-F.
Fogdall, Alberta B. Royal Family of the Columbia. (Illus.). 1978. 14.95 (ISBN 0-87770-168-7). Ye Galleon.
Gill, Conrad. Merchants & Mariners of the Eighteenth Century. LC 78-5810. (Illus.). 1978. Repr. of 1961 ed. lib. bdg. 15.75x (ISBN 0-313-20386-5, GIMM). Greenwood.
Goris, Jan A. Etude Sur Les Colonies Marchandes Meridionales a Anvers De 1488 a 1567, 2 vols. in 1. 1925. 46.50 (ISBN 0-8337-1390-6). B Franklin.
Harrington, Virginia D. The New York Merchant on the Eve of the Revolution. 1964. 7.50 (ISBN 0-8446-1224-3). Peter Smith.
Hedges, James B. Browns of Providence Plantations: The Colonial Years. LC 52-5032. (Illus.). 399p. 1968. Repr. of 1952 ed. text ed. 18.00x (ISBN 0-87057-109-5, Pub. by Brown U Pr). U Pr of New Eng.
--Browns of Providence Plantations: The Nineteenth Century. LC 68-23790. (Illus.). 345p. 1968. text ed. 18.00x (ISBN 0-87057-110-9, Pub. by Brown U Pr). U Pr of New Eng.
Horlick, Allan S. Country Boys & Merchant Princes: The Social Control of Young Men in New York. LC 73-2887. 278p. 1975. 18.00 (ISBN 0-8387-1361-0). Bucknell U Pr.
Hunt, Freeman, ed. Lives of American Merchants 2 Vols. LC 66-21679. Repr. of 1856 ed. 40.00x set (ISBN 0-678-00294-0). Kelley.
Jones, Lowell. Diary of a Gems Merchant. (Illus.). 1978. write for info. (ISBN 0-9602074-0-6). L Jones.
Kedar, Benjamin Z. Merchants in Crisis: Genoese & Venetian Men of Affairs & the Fourteen-Century Depression. LC 75-43320. (Economic History Ser.). 1976. 22.50x (ISBN 0-300-01941-6). Yale U Pr.
Lavine, Sigmund A. Famous Merchants. LC 65-15969. (Illus.). (gr. 7 up). 1965. 5.95 (ISBN 0-396-05140-5). Dodd.
Magnin, Cyril & Sheff, David. Call Me Cyril. (Illus.). 256p. 1980. 12.95 (ISBN 0-07-039492-X). McGraw.
Marshall, P. J. East Indian Fortunes: The British in Bengal in the Eighteenth Century. (Illus.). 1976. 45.00x (ISBN 0-19-821566-5). Oxford U Pr.
Meir's Directory of Exporters & Importers 1977-78. 1977. 25.00x (ISBN 0-8002-1312-2). Intl Pubns Serv.
The Merchants Avizo. LC 70-7710. (English Experience Ser.: No. 98). 1969. Repr. of 1607 ed. 9.50 (ISBN 90-221-0098-7). Walter J Johnson.
Mines, Mattison. Muslim Merchants: The Economic Behaviour of an Indian-Muslim Community. LC 72-907244. 136p. 1972. 7.50x (ISBN 0-8002-1739-X). Intl Pubns Serv.
Nolte, Vincent. Fifty Years in Both Hemispheres: Or, Reminiscences of the Life of a Former Merchant. facsimile ed. LC 75-37903. (Select Bibliographies Reprint Ser). Repr. of 1854 ed. 24.00 (ISBN 0-8369-6741-0). Arno.
Origo, Iris. The Merchant of Prato: Francesco di Marco Datini. 1979. Repr. lib. bdg. 24.00x (ISBN 0-374-96149-2). Octagon.
Papenfuse, Edward C. In Pursuit of Profit: The Annapolis Merchants in the Era of the American Revolution, 1763-1805. LC 74-6835. (Maryland Bicentennial Ser.). (Illus.). 320p. 1975. 20.00x (ISBN 0-8018-1573-8). Johns Hopkins.
Pelcovits, Nathan A. Old China Hands & the Foreign Office. LC 78-76003. 1969. Repr. of 1948 ed. lib. bdg. 16.00x (ISBN 0-374-96365-7). Octagon.
Pringle, Robert. The Letterbook of Robert Pringle, 1737-1745, 2 Vols. Edgar, Walter B., ed. LC 72-183905. 1972. Set. lib. bdg. 47.50x (ISBN 0-87249-121-8); Vol. 1. (ISBN 0-87249-240-0); Vol. 2. (ISBN 0-87249-241-9). U of SC Pr.
Redford, Arthur. Manchester Merchants & Foreign Trade, 2 vols. Incl. Vol. 1. 1794-1858. xii, 251p; Vol. 2. 1850-1939. 304p. Repr. of 1956 ed. LC 73-1675. 30.00x (ISBN 0-678-00750-0). Kelley.
Sapori, Armando. Italian Merchant in the Middle Ages. 1970. pap. text ed. 3.95x (ISBN 0-393-09956-3, NortonC). Norton.
Scoville, Joseph A. Old Merchants of New York City, 5 Vols. LC 68-28645. 1968. Repr. of 1870 ed. Set. lib. bdg. 105.00x (ISBN 0-8371-0214-6, SCOM). Greenwood.
Sheldon, Charles D. The Rise of the Merchant Class in Tokugawa Japan, 1600-1868: An Introductory Survey. LC 72-97536. xiv, 220p. (With a new introduction & appendix). 1973. Repr. of 1958 ed. 18.00 (ISBN 0-8462-1725-2). Russell.
Shofner, Jerrell H. Daniel Ladd: Merchant Prince of Frontier Florida. LC 77-21789. 1978. 8.50 (ISBN 0-8130-0546-9). U Presses Fla.
Singh, S. B. European Agency Houses in Bengal, 1783-1833. 1966. 6.75x (ISBN 0-8426-1538-5). Verry.
Socolow, Susan M. Merchants of Buenos Aires, Seventeen Seventy-Eight to Eighteen Hundred & Ten. LC 77-85216. (Cambridge Latin American Studies: No. 30). (Illus.). 1979. 35.50 (ISBN 0-521-21812-8). Cambridge U Pr.
Stoddard, William O. Men of Business. LC 72-3490. (Essay Index Reprint Ser.). Repr. of 1893 ed. 26.00 (ISBN 0-8369-2927-6). Arno.
Thrupp, Sylvia L. Merchant Class of Medieval London. 1962. pap. 5.95 (ISBN 0-472-06072-4, 72, AA). U of Mich Pr.
Tolles, Frederick B. James Logan & the Culture of Provincial America. Handlin, Oscar, ed. LC 77-2783. (The Library of American Biography). 1978. Repr. of 1957 ed. lib. bdg. 20.50x (ISBN 0-313-20197-8, TOJL). Greenwood.
Waterbury, John. North for the Trade: The Life & Times of a Berber Merchant. LC 70-174453. (Illus.). 200p. 1972. 24.75x (ISBN 0-520-02134-7). U of Cal Pr.
Willan, Thomas S. Muscovy Merchants of 1555. LC 72-85754. Repr. of 1953 ed. 12.50x (ISBN 0-678-00929-5). Kelley.

MERCIER, ERNEST, 1878-
Kuisel, Richard F. Ernest Mercier: French Technocrat. LC 67-22604. 1967. 26.75x (ISBN 0-520-00679-8). U of Cal Pr.

MERCIER, LOUIS-SEBASTIEN, 1740-1814
Pusey, William W. Louis-Sebastien Mercier in Germany. LC 39-31447. (Columbia University. Germanic Studies, New Ser.: No. 8). Repr. of 1939 ed. 19.00 (ISBN 0-404-50458-2). AMS Pr.

MERCURIUS
Lopez-Pedraza, Rafael. Hermes & His Children. (Seminar Ser.). (Orig.). 1978. pap. 8.00 (ISBN 0-88214-113-9). Spring Pubns.

MERCURY (PLANET)
Chapman, Clark R. Inner Planets. LC 76-58914. (Illus.). 1977. 9.95 (ISBN 0-684-14898-6, ScribT). Scribner.

MERCURY
Daniel, J. W., et al. Mercury Poisoning, No. 2. LC 72-13563. (Illus.). 220p. 1972. text ed. 29.50x (ISBN 0-8422-7073-6). Irvington.
Data Profile on Mercury. (IRPTC Data Profile Ser.: No. 3). 198p. 1981. pap. 20.00 (ISBN 0-686-69541-0, UNEP 42, UNEP). Unipub.
D'Itri, Patricia A. & D'Itri, Frank M. Mercury Contamination: A Human Tragedy. LC 76-58478. (Environmental Science and Technology: a Wiley-Interscience Series of Texts and Monographs). 311p. 1977. 24.50 (ISBN 0-471-02654-9, Pub. by Wiley-Interscience). Wiley.
Elbert, Lisa. Mercury Poisoning in Man. (Illus.). 1978. 20.00 (ISBN 0-685-89667-6, CX-10). Dayton Labs.
Environmental Studies Board. An Assessment of Mercury in the Environment. 1978. pap. 8.00 (ISBN 0-309-02736-5). Natl Acad Pr.
Frei, R. W. & Hutzinger, Otto, eds. Analytical Aspects of Mercury & Other Heavy Metals in the Environment. LC 73-88229. (Current Topics in Environmental & Toxicological Chemistry Ser.). 210p. 1975. 37.50x (ISBN 0-677-15890-4). Gordon.
Friberg, Lars T. & Vostal, Jaroslav J. Mercury in the Environment. LC 74-21911. (Uniscience Ser). 1972. 47.95 (ISBN 0-87819-004-X). CRC Pr.
Galus, Z. & Guminsky, C. Metals in Mercury: Solubilities of Solids. (Solubility Data Ser.). Date not set. 100.01 (ISBN 0-08-023921-8). Pergamon.

Kelkar, S. A. Occupational Exposure to Mercury. xi, 112p. 1980. text ed. 15.95x (ISBN 0-86590-001-9). Apt Bks.
Lange-Koval, Ernst E. & Wilhelm, Kurt. Dictionnaire Pratique Mercure: Francais-Allemand, Allemand-Francais. (Fr. & Ger.). 1964. 24.95 (ISBN 0-686-56992-X, M-6332). French & Eur.
Mayz, Eusebio, et al. Mercury Poisoning, No. 1. new ed. LC 72-13563. (Illus.). 220p. 1972. text ed. 29.50x (ISBN 0-8422-7072-8). Irvington.
Mercury Contamination in Man & His Environment. (Technical Reports Ser.: No. 137). (Illus.). 181p. (Orig.). 1973. pap. 16.75 (ISBN 92-0-115172-1, IDC 137, IAEA). Unipub.
Miller, Morton W. & Clarkson, Thomas W. Mercury, Mercurials & Mercaptans. (Illus.). 404p. 1973. 27.50 (ISBN 0-398-02600-9). C C Thomas.
Pay-Costa, M. Dictionnaire Pratique Mercure: Francais-Espagnol, Espagnol-Francais. 2nd ed. 1024p. (Fr.-Span.). 1966. 24.95 (ISBN 0-686-57200-9, M-6471). French & Eur.
Ragsdale, Kenneth B. Quicksilver: Terlingua & the Chisos Mining Company. LC 75-4081. 368p. 1976. 14.50 (ISBN 0-89096-013-5). Tex A&M Univ Pr.
Roxburgh, Nigel. Policy Responses to Resource Depletion: A Case of Mercury, Vol. 21. Walter, Ingo & Altman, Edward I., eds. (Contemporary Studies in Economic & Financial Analysis Ser.). 1980. lib. bdg. 29.50 (ISBN 0-89232-093-1). Jai Pr.
Urwin, Kenneth. Dictionnaire Pratique Mercure: Francais-Anglais, Anglais-Francais. 1216p. (Fr.-Eng.). 1968. 24.90 (ISBN 0-686-57239-4, M-6540). French & Eur.
The Use of Mercury & Alternative Compounds As Seed Dressings. (Agricultural Studies: No. 95). 29p. 1975. pap. 4.50 (ISBN 0-685-54033-2, F489, FAO). Unipub.
Whitaker, Arthur P. Huancavelica Mercury Mine: A Contribution to the History of the Bourbon Renaissance in the Spanish Empire. 1971. Repr. of 1941 ed. lib. bdg. 15.00 (ISBN 0-8371-5240-2, WHHM). Greenwood.

MERCURY COMPOUNDS

Aven, M. & Prener, J. S. Physics & Chemistry of Two - Six Compounds. 1967. 97.75 (ISBN 0-444-10134-9, North-Holland). Elsevier.
Willardon, Robert & Beer, A. C., eds. Semiconductors & Semimetals, Vol. 18: Mercury Cadmium Telluride. 1981. price not set (ISBN 0-12-752118-6). Acad Pr.

MERCURY PROJECT

see Project Mercury

MERCY, CORPORAL WORKS OF

see Corporal Works of Mercy

MERCY DEATH

see Euthanasia

MERCY SEAT

see Ark of the Covenant

MEREDITH, GEORGE, 1828-1909

Abbott, M. W. Browning & Meredith. 1979. 28.50 (ISBN 0-685-94328-3). Porter.
Abbott, Mary W. Browning & Meredith. 1904. lib. bdg. 7.50 (ISBN 0-8414-2960-X). Folcroft.
--Browning & Meredith. Some Points of Similarity. 55p. 1980. Repr. of 1904 ed. lib. bdg. 10.00 (ISBN 0-8495-0150-4). Arden Lib.
Able, Augustus. George Meredith & Thomas Love Peacock: A Study in Literary Influence. 1933. lib. bdg. 15.00 (ISBN 0-8414-2864-6). Folcroft.
--George Meredith & Thomas Love Peacock. 1977. 16.50 (ISBN 0-685-86330-1). Porter.
Able, Augustus H. George Meredith & Thomas Love Peacock: A Study in Literary Influence. LC 78-90364. (New Index). 1970. Repr. of 1933 ed. 7.50 (ISBN 0-87753-000-9). Phaeton.
--George Meredith & Thomas Love Peacock. 59.95 (ISBN 0-8490-0224-9). Gordon Pr.
--George Meredith & Thomas Love Peacock. 1978. Repr. of 1933 ed. lib. bdg. 15.00 (ISBN 0-8495-0128-8). Arden Lib.
Bailey, Elmer J. Novels of George Meredith. LC 75-163892. (Studies in George Meredith, No. 21). 1971. Repr. of 1908 ed. lib. bdg. 33.95 (ISBN 0-8383-1312-4). Haskell.
Barrie, James M. George Meredith. LC 74-8046. 1909. lib. bdg. 7.50 (ISBN 0-8414-3192-2). Folcroft.
--George Meredith. 1978. Repr. of 1909 ed. lib. bdg. 8.50 (ISBN 0-8495-0445-7). Arden Lib.
Barrie, James M. & Hardy, Thomas. George Meredith: A Tribute. 59.95 (ISBN 0-8490-0223-0). Gordon Pr.
Beach, Joseph W. Comic Spirit in George Meredith: An Interpretation. LC 62-16694. 1963. Repr. of 1911 ed. 7.00 (ISBN 0-8462-0317-0). Russell.
Bedford, H. The Heroines of George Meredith. 59.95 (ISBN 0-8490-0300-8). Gordon Pr.
Bedford, Herbert. Heroines of George Meredith. LC 78-160742. (Illus.). 1971. Repr. of 1914 ed. 12.50 (ISBN 0-8046-1555-1). Kennikat.
Beer, Gillian. Meredith: A Change of Masks, a Study of the Novels. 1970. text ed. 23.25x (ISBN 0-485-11122-5, Athlone Pr). Humanities.
Booth, Thornton Y. Mastering the Event: Commitment to Fact in George Meredith's Fiction. 66p. (Orig.). 1967. pap. 3.00 (ISBN 0-87421-033-X). Utah St U Pr.
Bruckl, Renate. Structural & Thematic Analysis of George Meredith's Novel "Diana of the Crossways". (Salzburg Studies in English Literature: Romantic Reassessment Ser.: No. 73). 1978. pap. text ed. 25.00x (ISBN 0-391-01332-7). Humanities.
Butcher, Alice M. Memories of George Meredith. 1973. Repr. of 1919 ed. 6.50 (ISBN 0-8274-1329-7). R West.
--Memories of George Meredith, O. M. LC 72-103172. 1970. Repr. of 1919 ed. 10.00 (ISBN 0-8046-0809-1). Kennikat.
Butcher, Lady. Memories of George Meredith O.M. 1978. Repr. of 1919 ed. lib. bdg. 25.00 (ISBN 0-8495-0334-5). Arden Lib.
Chislett, William. George Meredith: A Study & an Appraisal. LC 68-905. (Studies in Fiction, No. 34). 1969. Repr. of 1925 ed. lib. bdg. 48.95 (ISBN 0-8383-0526-1). Haskell.
Crees, J. H. George Meredith. 238p. 1981. Repr. of 1918 ed. lib. bdg. 25.00 (ISBN 0-89984-114-7). Century Bookbindery.
--George Meredith. 238p. 1980. lib. bdg. 20.00 (ISBN 0-8495-0786-3). Arden Lib.
--George Meredith. LC 67-30812. (Studies in Fiction, No. 34). 1969. Repr. of 1918 ed. lib. bdg. 49.95 (ISBN 0-8383-0712-4). Haskell.
--George Meredith. 1973. Repr. of 1918 ed. 20.00 (ISBN 0-8274-1330-0). R West.
--Meredith Revisited & Other Essays. LC 67-30813. (Studies in Fiction, No. 34). 1969. Repr. of 1921 ed. lib. bdg. 28.95 (ISBN 0-8383-0713-2). Haskell.
Curle, R. H. Aspects of George Meredith. LC 71-176496. (English Biography Ser., No. 31). 1972. Repr. of 1908 ed. lib. bdg. 52.95 (ISBN 0-8383-1363-9). Haskell.
Curle, Richard H. Aspects of George Meredith. LC 72-91349. 1970. Repr. of 1908 ed. 8.50 (ISBN 0-87753-012-2). Phaeton.
Ellis, S. M. George Meredith. LC 75-163502. (Studies in George Meredith, No. 21). 1971. Repr. of 1919 ed. lib. bdg. 59.95 (ISBN 0-8383-1311-6). Haskell.
--George Meredith. 1973. Repr. of 1919 ed. 17.75 (ISBN 0-8274-1328-9). R West.
--George Meredith: His Life & Friends in Relation to His Work. LC 73-11362. 1920. lib. bdg. 17.75 (ISBN 0-8414-1914-0). Folcroft.
Esdaile, Arundell. Bibliography & Various Readings, George Meredith. LC 72-4494. (Studies in George Meredith, No. 21). 1972. Repr. of 1911 ed. lib. bdg. 56.95 (ISBN 0-8383-1511-9). Haskell.
--Bibliography of the Writings in Prose & Verse of George Meredith. LC 74-23912. 1907. lib. bdg. 10.00 (ISBN 0-8414-3945-1). Folcroft.
Fletcher, Ian, ed. Meredith Now: Some Critical Essays. 1971. 22.75x (ISBN 0-7100-7061-6). Routledge & Kegan.
Forman, Maurice B. Bibliography of Writings of George Meredith & Meredithiana. LC 78-122982. (Studies in George Meredith, No. 21). (2 vol set). 1970. Repr. lib. bdg. 89.95 (ISBN 0-8383-1114-8). Haskell.
--George Meredith: Some Early Appreciations. LC 70-86014. 1969. Repr. of 1909 ed. 12.50 (ISBN 0-8046-0609-9). Kennikat.
Galland, Rene. George Meredith & British Criticism. 120p. 1980. Repr. lib. bdg. 20.00 (ISBN 0-89987-301-4). Darby Bks.
--George Meredith & British Criticism. LC 75-35557. 1975. Repr. of 1923 ed. lib. bdg. 22.50 (ISBN 0-8414-4583-4). Folcroft.
--George Meredith, les Cinquante Premiers Annees. LC 78-145025. 1971. Repr. of 1923 ed. 20.00 (ISBN 0-403-00972-3). Scholarly.
Goodell, Margaret M. Three Satirists of Snobbery: Thackeray, Meredith, Proust. 59.95 (ISBN 0-8490-1212-0). Gordon Pr.
--Three Satirists of Snobbery: Thackery, Meredith, Proust. LC 76-25175. 1939. lib. bdg. 12.75 (ISBN 0-685-10830-9). Folcroft.
Gretton, M. Writings & Life of George Meredith. LC 70-117580. (Studies in George Meredith, No. 21). 1970. Repr. of 1926 ed. lib. bdg. 32.95 (ISBN 0-8383-1013-3). Haskell.
Hammerton, J. A. George Meredith. LC 73-179268. (Studies in George Meredith, No. 21). 1971. Repr. of 1911 ed. lib. bdg. 69.95 (ISBN 0-8383-1369-8). Haskell.
--George Meredith. LC 73-16288. 1911. Repr. lib. bdg. 22.75 (ISBN 0-8414-4799-3). Folcroft.
Henderson, M. George Meredith. 59.95 (ISBN 0-8490-0222-2). Gordon Pr.
Henderson, M. Sturge. George Meredith. 324p. 1980. Repr. of 1907 ed. lib. bdg. 30.00 (ISBN 0-89987-013-9). Darby Bks.
--George Meredith: Novelist, Poet, Reformer. new ed. 1979. Repr. of 1907 ed. lib. bdg. 25.00 (ISBN 0-8492-5328-4). R West.
--George Meredith: Novelist, Poet, Reformer. LC 75-160760. 1971. Repr. of 1907 ed. 15.00 (ISBN 0-8046-1579-9). Kennikat.
Jerrold, Walter C. George Meredith: An Essay Towards Appreciation. LC 74-23633. 1974. Repr. of 1902 ed. lib. bdg. 20.00 (ISBN 0-8414-5325-X). Folcroft.
Kelvin, Norman. A Troubled Eden: Nature & Society in the Works of George Meredith. 1961. 12.50x (ISBN 0-8047-0039-7). Stanford U Pr.
Le Gallienne, Richard. George Meredith. 1894. Repr. lib. bdg. 25.00 (ISBN 0-8414-5793-X). Folcroft.
Lindsay, J. George Meredith. 1973. Repr. of 1956 ed. 25.00 (ISBN 0-8274-0095-0). R West.
Lindsay, Jack. George Meredith, His Life & Work. LC 73-9718. 424p. 1973. Repr. of 1956 ed. 40.00 (ISBN 0-527-57230-6). Kraus Repr.
Lucas, E. V. Reading, Writing & Remembering: A Literary Record. Meredith, James, Dickens, Thackeray, Conrad, & Hardy. Repr. of 1932 ed. lib. bdg. 30.00 (ISBN 0-8495-3315-5). Arden Lib.
Lynch, H. George Meredith. LC 73-128572. (Studies in George Meredith, No. 21). 1972. Repr. of 1891 ed. lib. bdg. 47.95 (ISBN 0-8383-0906-2). Haskell.
--George Meredith: A Study. 1973. Repr. of 1891 ed. 12.50 (ISBN 0-8274-0104-3). R West.
Lynch, Hannah. George Meredith. 170p. 1980. Repr. of 1891 ed. lib. bdg. 10.00 (ISBN 0-8495-3335-X). Arden Lib.
--George Meredith. LC 73-8799. 1891. Repr. lib. bdg. 9.75 (ISBN 0-8414-2280-X). Folcroft.
McCullen, Maurice & Sawin, Lewis. A Dictionary of the Characters in George Meredith's Fiction. LC 75-42886. (Reference Library of the Humanities Ser.: Vol. 48). 1976. lib. bdg. 24.50 (ISBN 0-8240-9952-4). Garland Pub.
McKechnie, James. Meredith's Allegory: The Shaving of Shagpat, Interpreted. LC 78-8927. 1973. Repr. of 1910 ed. 25.00 (ISBN 0-8492-1723-7). R West.
Meredith, George. Letters of George Meredith: Collected & Edited by His Son, 2 vols. 1912. Repr. 20.00 set (ISBN 0-8274-2839-1). R West.
Moffatt, James. George Meredith: A Primer to the Novels. LC 72-86044. 1969. Repr. of 1909 ed. 15.00 (ISBN 0-8046-0628-5). Kennikat.
--George Meredith: A Primer to the Novels. 1973. Repr. of 1909 ed. 14.50 (ISBN 0-8274-1325-4). R West.
Olmsted, John C. George Meredith: An Annotated Bibliography 1925-1975. LC 77-83354. (Library of Humanities Reference Bks.: No. 99). 1978. lib. bdg. 21.00 (ISBN 0-8240-9841-2). Garland Pub.
Peel, Robert. The Creed of a Victorian Pagan. 1972. lib. bdg. 8.00x (ISBN 0-374-96348-7). Octagon.
Photiades, Constantin. George Meredith. LC 79-113318. 1970. Repr. of 1913 ed. 12.75 (ISBN 0-8046-1029-0). Kennikat.
Priestley, John B. George Meredith. LC 70-131807. 1970. Repr. of 1926 ed. 14.00 (ISBN 0-403-00694-5). Scholarly.
Sassoon, Siegfried. Meredith. LC 68-26214. 1969. Repr. of 1948 ed. 12.75 (ISBN 0-8046-0404-5). Kennikat.
--Meredith. 1979. Repr. of 1948 ed. lib. bdg. 25.00 (ISBN 0-8492-8089-3). R West.
Sawin, Lewis. A Concordance to the Poetry of George Meredith. 1981. lib. bdg. 125.00 (ISBN 0-8240-9521-9). Garland Pub.
Shaheen, Mohammad. George Meredith: A Reappraisal of the Novels. 1981. 19.50x (ISBN 0-389-20022-0). B&N.
Sitwell, Osbert. Novels of George Meredith & Some Notes on the English Novel. LC 72-10858. (Studies in Fiction, No. 34). 1970. pap. 9.95 (ISBN 0-8383-0070-7). Haskell.
--The Novels of George Meredith & Some Notes on the English Novel. LC 77-8479. 1977. lib. bdg. 7.50 (ISBN 0-8414-7661-6). Folcroft.
Strong, Archibald T. Three Studies in Shelley & an Essay on Nature in Wordsworth & Meredith. LC 76-21867. 1921. lib. bdg. 14.00 (ISBN 0-8414-7737-X). Folcroft.
--Three Studies in Shelley & an Essay on Nature in Wordsworth & Meredith. 1968. Repr. of 1921 ed. 16.50 (ISBN 0-208-00665-6, Archon). Shoe String.
Thomas, W. B. George Meredith in Great Victorians. Massingham, H. J. & Massingham, H., eds. 1973. Repr. of 1932 ed. 40.00 (ISBN 0-8274-0510-3). R West.
Thompson, Lawrance. Comic Principle in Sterne, Meredith, Joyce. LC 76-42316. 1954. lib. bdg. 12.50 (ISBN 0-8414-8622-0). Folcroft.
Trevelyan, G. M. The Poetry & Philosophy of George Meredith. 1973. Repr. of 1907 ed. 7.50 (ISBN 0-8274-0500-6). R West.
Turquet-Miles, Gladys R. Meredith & the Cosmic Spirit. LC 77-22365. 1977. Repr. of 1925 ed. lib. bdg. 8.50 (ISBN 0-8414-8631-X). Folcroft.
Williams, David. George Meredith: His Life & Lost Love. 1978. 25.00 (ISBN 0-241-89630-4, Pub. by Hamish Hamilton England). David & Charles.
Williams, Ioan, ed. Meredith: The Critical Heritage. 1971. 28.75x (ISBN 0-7100-6961-8). Routledge & Kegan.
Wilt, Judith. The Readable People of George Meredith. 284p. 1975. 17.50x (ISBN 0-691-06275-7). Princeton U Pr.
Woods, Alice. Some of George Meredith's Poems. LC 73-513. 1973. lib. bdg. 8.50 (ISBN 0-8414-1577-3). Folcroft.
Wright, Walter F. Art & Substance in George Meredith: A Study in Narrative. LC 80-14417. vii, 211p. 1980. Repr. of 1953 ed. lib. bdg. 19.00x (ISBN 0-313-22514-1, WRAS). Greenwood.

MERGER OF CORPORATIONS

see Consolidation and Merger of Corporations

MERIMEE, PROSPER, 1803-1870

Johnston, G. Prosper Merimee: A Mask & a Face. 59.95 (ISBN 0-8490-0904-9). Gordon Pr.
Smith, Maxwell A. Prosper Merimee. (World Authors Ser.: France: No. 249). lib. bdg. 10.95 (ISBN 0-8057-2612-8). Twayne.
Trahard. La Vieillesse de Prosper Merimee (1854-1870) 26.25 (ISBN 0-685-34945-4). French & Eur.
Trahard, Pierre & Josserand, Pierre. Bibliographie Des Oeuvres De Prosper Merimee. LC 71-154650. (Bibliography & Reference Ser.: No. 420). 1971. Repr. of 1929 ed. lib. bdg. 26.50 (ISBN 0-8337-3565-9). B Franklin.
Watt, E. A. The Love Letters of a Genius: Being a Translation of Prosper Merimee's "Lettres a une Inconnue. 1978. Repr. of 1905 ed. lib. bdg. 35.00 (ISBN 0-8495-5647-3). Arden Lib.

MERINIDES

see Beni Marin Dynasty

MERISTEM

see Plant Cells and Tissues; Growth (Plants)

MERIT (CHRISTIANITY)

see also Reward (Theology)

Cooper, A. An Inquiry Concerning Virtue on Merit. Walford, E., ed. 152p. 1977. 24.95x (ISBN 0-7190-0657-0, Pub. by Manchester U Pr England). State Mutual Bk.

MERIT (JEWISH THEOLOGY)

Marmorstein, Arthur. Doctrine of Merits in Old Rabbinic Literature & the Old Rabbinic Doctrine of God, 3 vols. in one. rev. ed. 1968. Repr. 35.00x (ISBN 0-87068-087-0). Ktav.

MERIT SYSTEM

see Civil Service Reform

MERLEAU-PONTY, MAURICE, 1908-1961

Cooper, Barry. Merleau-Ponty & Marxism: From Terror to Reform. LC 78-16829. 1979. 25.00x (ISBN 0-8020-5435-8). U of Toronto Pr.
Kruks, Sonia. The Political Philosophy of Merleau-Ponty. (Harvester Philosophy Now Ser.: No. 13). 149p. 1981. text ed. 41.00x (ISBN 0-391-02226-1, Pub. by Harvester England). Humanities.
Kwant, Remy C. Phenomenology of Expression. Koren, Henry J., tr. LC 68-59089. 1978. Repr. of 1969 ed. text ed. 10.00x (ISBN 0-391-00876-5). Humanities.
Lapointe, Francois H. & Lapointe, Claire C. Maurice Merleau-Ponty & His Critics: An International Bibliography (1942-1976) Including a Bibliography of His Writings. LC 75-42885. (Reference Library in the Humanities: No. 51). 1976. lib. bdg. 21.00 (ISBN 0-8240-9949-4). Garland Pub.
Mallin, Samuel B. Merleau-Ponty's Philosophy. LC 79-64078. 1979. 25.00x (ISBN 0-300-02275-1). Yale U Pr.
O'Neill, John. Perception, Expression, & History: The Social Phenomenology of Maurice Merleau-Ponty. 1970. 9.95x (ISBN 0-8101-0299-4). Northwestern U Pr.
Sheridan, James F., Jr. Once More from the Middle: A Philosophical Anthropology. LC 72-85543. ix, 157p. 1973. 9.50x (ISBN 0-8214-0108-4). Ohio U Pr.

MERLIN

Geoffrey of Monmouth. History of the Kings of Britain. Dunn, Charles W., ed. Evans, Sebastian, tr. 1958. pap. 3.95 (ISBN 0-525-47014-X). Dutton.
--Galfredi Monumentensis Historia Britonum. Giles, John A., ed. 1966. 24.00 (ISBN 0-8337-1344-2). B Franklin.
Lovelich, Henry. Merlin, Pts. 1 & 2. Kock, E. A., ed. (EETS, ES Ser.: Nos. 93, 112). Repr. of 1904 ed. Pt. 1. 22.00 (ISBN 0-527-00184-8); Pt. 2. 13.00 (ISBN 0-527-00185-6). Kraus Repr.
--Merlin, a Middle-English Metrical Version of a French Romance, Pt. III. (EETS. OS Ser.: No. 185). Repr. of 1932 ed. 16.00 (ISBN 0-527-00183-X). Kraus Repr.
Nye, Robert. Merlin. LC 78-26799. 1979. 10.00 (ISBN 0-399-12331-8). Putnam.
Parry, John J., ed. Brut Y Brenhinedd, Cotton Cleopatra Version. 1937. 12.00 (ISBN 0-910956-10-3). Medieval Acad.

Paton, Lucy A., ed. Prophecies De Merlin, 2 Vols. 1926-1927. Set. pap. 48.00 (ISBN 0-527-70100-9). Kraus Repr.

Rowley, William. Birth of Merlin. LC 74-133731. (Tudor Facsimile Texts. Old English Plays: No. 145). Repr. of 1910 ed. 31.50 (ISBN 0-404-53445-7). AMS Pr.

Sommer, H. Oskar, ed. L' Estoire de Merlin. (Vulgate Version of the Arthurian Romances: No. 2). Repr. of 1908 ed. 57.50 (ISBN 0-404-17632-1). AMS Pr.

MERLO, THECLA, 1894-1964

Daughters Of St. Paul. Woman of Faith. (Illus.). 1965. 3.00 (ISBN 0-8198-0179-8). Dghtrs St Paul.

MERMAN, ETHEL, 1908-

Merman, Ethel & Eells, George. Merman: An Autobiography. 1979. pap. text ed. 2.50 (ISBN 0-425-04261-8). Berkley Pub.

MEROE

Crowfoot, J. W. & Griffith, F. L. Island of Meroe & Meroitic Inscriptions, Pt. 1: Soba to Dangel. (Archaeological Survey of Egypt Ser.: 19th Memoir). (Illus.). 1976. Repr. of 1911 ed. 32.00x (ISBN 0-901212-35-0, Pub. by Aris & Phillips). Intl Schol Bk Serv.

Zabkar, L. V. Apedemak Lion God of Meroe. 216p. 1975. text ed. 23.50 (ISBN 0-85668-027-3, Pub. by Aris & Phillips England); pap. text ed. 13.50 (ISBN 0-85668-045-1, Pub. by Aris & Phillips England). Humanities.

MEROMORPHIC FUNCTIONS

see Functions, Meromorphic

MEROVINGIANS

see also France–History–to 987

Thierry, Augustin. Tales of Early Franks: Episodes from Merovingian History. Jenkins, M. F., tr. from Fr. LC 76-21314. 192p. 1977. 12.95x (ISBN 0-8173-8558-4). U of Ala Pr.

MERRIAM, LUCIUS SALISBURY, 1867-1893

Hollander, Jacob H., et al. A Memorial of Lucius S. Merriam. LC 78-63828. (Johns Hopkins University. Studies in the Social Sciences. Twelfth Ser. 1894: 2). Repr. of 1894 ed. 11.50 (ISBN 0-404-61088-9). AMS Pr.

MERRICK, JOHN, 1862 or 3-1890

Howell, Michael & Ford, Peter. The True History of the Elephant Man. 1980. 20.00x (ISBN 0-85031-353-8, Pub. by Allison & Busby England). State Mutual Bk.

--The True History of the Elephant Man. (Illus.). 194p. 1980. 9.95 (ISBN 0-85031-353-8, Pub. by Allison & Busby England). Schocken.

Montagu, Ashley. The Elephant Man: A Study in Human Dignity. rev. ed. (Illus.). 1979. pap. 4.95 (ISBN 0-525-47617-2). Dutton.

Sparks, Christine. The Elephant Man. 288p. 1980. pap. 2.75 (ISBN 0-345-29136-0). Ballantine.

MERRILD, KNUD

Miller, Henry. Knud Merrild: A Holiday in Paint. 8.50 (ISBN 0-685-43107-X). Norwood Edns.

MERRIMAC (FRIGATE)

Davis, William C. Duel Between the First Ironclads. (Illus.). 216p. 1981. pap. 7.95 (ISBN 0-8071-0868-5). La State U Pr.

White, Elsberry V. The First Iron-Clad Naval Engagement in the World: The Merrimac & the Monitor. (Illus.). 1906. wrappers 12.50 (ISBN 0-686-17397-X). R S Barnes.

MERRIMACK RIVER AND VALLEY

Davis, Frances P. A Fearful Innocence. LC 81-11793. (Illus.). 1981. 14.95 (ISBN 0-87338-260-9). Kent St U Pr.

Karabatsos, James. A Word-Index to a Week on the Concord & Merrimack Rivers. LC 80-2510. Repr. of 1971 ed. 18.50 (ISBN 0-404-19058-8). AMS Pr.

Randall, Peter. Newburyport & the Merrimack. LC 81-66562. (Illus.). 1981. pap. 4.95 (ISBN 0-89272-088-3). Down East.

Thoreau, Henry D. The Concord & the Merrimack. Lunt, Dudley C., ed. (Masterworks of Literature Ser). (Illus.). 1954. pap. 3.95x (ISBN 0-8084-0089-4, M9). Coll & U Pr.

--Week on the Concord & Merrimack Rivers. (Apollo Eds.). (YA) (gr. 9-12). pap. 4.95 (ISBN 0-8152-0118-4, A118). T Y Crowell.

MERRIMAN, HENRY SETON

see Scott, Hugh Stowell, 1862-1903

MERRY-GO-ROUND

Fried, Frederick. A Pictorial History of the Carousel. LC 64-17409. (Illus.). 1978. 19.95 (ISBN 0-498-06170-1). A S Barnes.

Thomas, Art. Merry-Go-Rounds. LC 81-3825. (Carolrhoda on My Own Bks.). (Illus.). 48p. (gr. k-3). 1981. PLB 5.95 (ISBN 0-87614-168-8, AACR2). Carolrhoda Bks.

MERRYMOUNT PRESS, BOSTON

Smith, Julian P. & Bianchi, Daniel B. Bibliography of the Merrymount Press, Eighteen Ninety-Three to Nineteen Forty-Nine. LC 75-28553. (Illus.). 400p. 1975. 30.00 (ISBN 0-915346-10-9). A Wofsy Fine Arts.

Updike, Daniel B. & Smith, Julian P. Notes on the Merrymount Press & Its Work. LC 73-10387. (Illus.). 287p. 1973. Repr. of 1934 ed. lib. bdg. 25.00 (ISBN 0-87821-066-0). Milford Hse.

MERSEY VALLEY–ECONOMIC CONDITIONS

Harris, John R., ed. Liverpool & Merseyside. LC 68-21449. (Illus.). 1969. 25.00x (ISBN 0-678-05016-3). Kelley.

MERTON, THOMAS, 1915-1968

Bailey, Raymond. Thomas Merton on Mysticism. LC 74-32570. 280p. 1976. pap. 1.95 (ISBN 0-385-12071-0, Im). Doubleday.

Baker, James T. Thomas Merton: Social Critic. LC 76-132827. 184p. 1971. 10.00 (ISBN 0-8131-1238-9). U Pr of Ky.

--Under the Sign of the Waterbearer: A Life of Thomas Merton. 1976. pap. 2.95 (ISBN 0-915216-15-9). Love Street.

Cashen, Richard A. Solitude in the Thought of Thomas Merton. (Cistercian Studies: No. 40). 208p. 1981. 15.50 (ISBN 0-87907-840-5); pap. 5.50 (ISBN 0-87907-940-1). Cistercian Pubns.

Dell'Isola, Frank. Thomas Merton: A Bibliography. rev. ed. LC 74-79148. (Serif Ser.: No. 31). 250p. 1975. 9.00x (ISBN 0-87338-156-4). Kent St U Pr.

Finley, James. Merton's Palace of Nowhere. LC 78-58738. 160p. 1978. pap. 2.95 (ISBN 0-87793-159-3). Ave Maria.

Forest, James H. Thomas Merton: A Pictorial Biography. LC 80-82249. (Illus.). 112p. (Orig.). 1980. pap. 5.95 (ISBN 0-8091-2284-7). Paulist Pr.

Furlong, Monica. Merton: A Biography. 352p. 1981. pap. 3.95 (ISBN 0-553-20299-5). Bantam.

--Merton: A Biography. LC 79-3588. (Illus.). 320p. 1980. 12.95 (ISBN 0-06-063079-5, HarpR). Har-Row.

Griffin, John H. Hermitage Journals. 270p. 1981. 15.00 (ISBN 0-8362-3909-1). Andrews & McMeel.

--A Hidden Wholeness: The Visual World of Thomas Merton. 1979. pap. 7.95 (ISBN 0-395-28520-8). HM.

--A Hidden Wholeness: The Visual World of Thomas Merton. LC 72-120827. (Illus.). 1977. 25.00 (ISBN 0-910220-90-5). Larlin Corp.

Hart, Patrick. Thomas Merton, Monk: A Monastic Tribute. 240p. 1976. pap. 1.95 (ISBN 0-385-11244-0, Im). Doubleday.

Hart, Patrick, ed. The Message of Thomas Merton. (Cistercian Studies: No. 42). 1981. write for info. (ISBN 0-87907-842-1). Cistercian Pub.

Higgins, John J. Thomas Merton on Prayer. 200p. 1975. pap. 2.45 (ISBN 0-385-02813-X, Im). Doubleday.

Labrie, Ross. The Art of Thomas Merton. LC 79-1341. 1979. pap. 8.00 (ISBN 0-912646-55-1). Tex Christian.

Leclercq, Jean, intro. by. Thomas Merton on St. Bernard. (Cistercian Studies: No. 9). 1980. 13.95 (ISBN 0-87907-809-X); pap. 4.95 (ISBN 0-87907-909-6). Cistercian Pubns.

Lentfoehr, Sr. Therese. Words & Silence: On the Poetry of Thomas Merton. LC 78-21475. 1979. 12.50 (ISBN 0-8112-0712-9); pap. 4.95 (ISBN 0-8112-0713-7, NDP472). New Directions.

Malits, Elena. The Solitary Explorer: Thomas Merton's Transforming Journey. LC 80-7744. 192p. (Orig.). 1980. pap. 6.95 (ISBN 0-06-065411-2, RD 331, HarpR). Har-Row.

Merton, Thomas. The Seven Storey Mountain. LC 78-7109. 1978. pap. 6.95 (ISBN 0-15-680679-7, Harv). HarBraceJ.

--The Seven Storey Mountain. 1978. Repr. lib. bdg. 17.50x (ISBN 0-374-95568-9). Octagon.

Merton, Thomas & Griffin, John H. Thomas Merton Studies Center: Three Essays. 1969. 10.00 (ISBN 0-87775-022-X). Unicorn Pr.

Nouwen, Henri J. Thomas Merton: Contemplative Critic. LC 80-8898. 176p. 1981. pap. 3.95 (ISBN 0-06-066324-3, RD 357, HarpR). Har-Row.

Palmer, Parker J. In the Belly of a Paradox, the Thought of Thomas Merton. LC 78-71769. 1979. pap. 1.10x (ISBN 0-87574-224-6). Pendle Hill.

Patnaik, Deba, ed. Geography of Holiness: The Photography of Thomas Merton. LC 80-18604. 1980. 17.50 (ISBN 0-8298-0401-3). Pilgrim NY.

Shannon, William H. Thomas Merton's Dark Path: The Inner Experience of a Contemplative. 1981. text ed. 12.95 (ISBN 0-374-27636-6). FS&G.

Sussman, Cornelia & Sussman, Irving. Thomas Merton. LC 80-924. 176p. 1980. pap. 3.95 (ISBN 0-385-17172-2, Im). Doubleday.

Sussman, Irving & Sussman, Cornelia. Thomas Merton: The Daring Young Man on the Flying Belltower. LC 76-34236. 192p. (gr. 7 up). 1976. 7.95 (ISBN 0-02-788630-1, 78863). Macmillan.

Twomey, Gerald, ed. Thomas Merton: Prophet in the Belly of a Paradox. LC 78-61717. 1978. 9.95 (ISBN 0-8091-0268-4). Paulist Pr.

Woodcock, George. Thomas Merton: Monk & Poet. 1978. 7.95 (ISBN 0-374-27636-6); pap. 3.95 (ISBN 0-374-51487-9). FS&G.

MERU (AFRICAN TRIBE)

Moore, Sally F. & Puritt, Paul. The Chagga & Meru of Tanzania. O'Barr, W. M, ed. LC 78-309993. (Ethnographic Survey of Africa: East Central Africa: Vol. 18). (Illus.). 1977. pap. 15.00x (ISBN 0-85302-051-5). Intl Pubns Serv.

MESA VERDE NATIONAL PARK

Fewkes, Jesse W. Antiquities of the Mesa Verde National Park, Cliff Palace. Repr. of 1911 ed. 19.00 (ISBN 0-403-03510-4). Scholarly.

--Antiquities of the Mesa Verde National Park; Spruce - Tree House. Repr. of 1909 ed. 19.00 (ISBN 0-403-03511-2). Scholarly.

Nordenskiold, Gustaf E. The Cliff Dwellers of the Mesa Verde, Southwestern Colorado: Their Pottery & Implements. Morgan, D. Lloyd, tr. from Swedish. LC 72-5006. (Antiquities of the New World Ser.: Vol. 12). (Illus.). Repr. of 1893 ed. 97.50 (ISBN 0-404-57312-6). AMS Pr.

MESABA RANGE, MINNESOTA

Landis, Paul H. Three Iron Mining Towns: A Study in Cultural Change. LC 72-112555. (Rise of Urban America). 1970. Repr. of 1938 ed. 9.00 (ISBN 0-405-02462-2). Arno.

MESCALINE

Kluver, Heinrich. Mescal & Mechanisms of Hallucinations. LC 66-20593. 1967. 5.75x (ISBN 0-226-44505-4). U of Chicago Pr.

--Mescal & Mechanisms of Hallucinations. LC 66-20593. xviii, 108p. 1966. pap. 1.50 (ISBN 0-226-44506-2, P531, Phoen). U of Chicago Pr.

Michaux, Henri. Miserable Miracle. Varese, Louise, tr. (Orig.). 1963. pap. 1.95 (ISBN 0-87286-033-7). City Lights.

MESENCEPHALON

Zapletal, B. Open Messencephalotomy & Thalamotomy for Intractable Pain. LC 75-82429. (Illus.). 1969. 33.70 (ISBN 0-387-80936-8). Springer-Verlag.

MESENCHYME

see also Reticulo-Endothelial System

Fleischmajer, P. & Billingham, R. Epithelial Mesenchymal Interactions. 340p. 1968. 17.50 (ISBN 0-683-03260-7, Pub. by Williams & Wilkins). Krieger.

MESLIER, JEAN, 1664-1729

Morehouse, Andrew R. Voltaire & Jean Meslier. LC 72-1716. (Yale Romanic Studies: No. 9). Repr. of 1936 ed. 11.00 (ISBN 0-404-53209-8). AMS Pr.

MESMER, FRANZ ANTON, 1734-1815

Zweig, Stefan. Mental Healers: Franz Anton Mesmer, Mary Baker Eddy, Sigmund Freud. LC 62-19082. 12.50 (ISBN 0-8044-2995-2); pap. 6.95 (ISBN 0-8044-6996-2). Ungar.

MESMERISM

see also Animal Magnetism; Hypnotism; Mental Healing; Mental Suggestion; Mind and Body; Therapeutics, Suggestive

Darnton, Robert. Mesmerism & the End of the Enlightenment in France. LC 68-25607. (Illus.). 1968. 12.50x (ISBN 0-674-56950-4). Harvard U Pr.

--Mesmerism: The End of the Enlightenment in France. LC 68-25607. (Illus.). 1971. pap. 5.95 (ISBN 0-8052-0269-2). Schocken.

D'Assier, Adolphe. Posthumous Humanity. Olcott, H. S., ed. & tr. from French. LC 81-50204. (Secret Doctrine Reference Ser.). 384p. 1981. Repr. of 1887 ed. 15.95 (ISBN 0-913510-36-X). Wizards.

Elliotson, John. Numerous Cases of Surgical Operations Without Pain in the Mesmeric State. Bd. with Mesmerism in India; Philosophy of Sleep. (Contributions to the History of Psychology Ser., Vol. X, Pt. A: Orientations). 1978. Repr. of 1843 ed. 30.00 (ISBN 0-89093-159-3). U Pubns Amer.

--Numerous Cases of Surgical Operations Without Pain in the Mesmeric State. LC 74-29290. Repr. of 1843 ed. 10.00 (ISBN 0-404-13409-2). AMS Pr.

Esdaile, James. Mesmerism in India. Bd. with Numerous Cases of Surgical Operations; The Philosophy of Sleep. (Contributions to the History of Psychology Ser., Vol. X, Pt. A: Orientations). 1978. Repr. of 1846 ed. 30.00 (ISBN 0-89093-159-3). U Pubns Amer.

--Mesmerism in India, & Its Practical Application in Surgery & Medicine. LC 74-29291. Repr. of 1846 ed. 20.00 (ISBN 0-404-13410-6). AMS Pr.

--Mesmerism in India: And Its Practical Application in Surgery & Medicine. LC 75-16702. (Classics in Psychiatry Ser.). 1976. Repr. of 1846 ed. 18.00x (ISBN 0-405-07429-8). Arno.

--Natural & Mesmeric Clairvoyance: With the Practical Application of Mesmerism in Surgery & Medicine. LC 75-7378. (Perspectives in Psychical Research Ser.). 1975. Repr. of 1852 ed. 18.00x (ISBN 0-405-07028-4). Arno.

Gregory, William. Animal Magnetism: Or Mesmerism & Its Phenomena. 5th ed. LC 75-7384. (Perspectives in Psychical Research Ser.). 1975. Repr. of 1909 ed. 15.00x (ISBN 0-405-07032-2). Arno.

Haddock, Joseph W. Somnolism & Psycheism: Or the Science of the Soul & the Phenomena of Nervation. 2nd ed. LC 75-7386. (Perspectives in Psychical Research Ser.). (Illus.). 1975. Repr. of 1851 ed. 16.00x (ISBN 0-405-07034-9). Arno.

Kaplan, Fred. Dickens & Mesmerism: The Hidden Springs of Fiction. LC 75-2994. (Illus.). 276p. 1975. 17.50 (ISBN 0-691-06291-9). Princeton U Pr.

Long, Max F. Self-Suggestion & the New Huna Theory of Mesmerism & Hypnosis. 1958. pap. 3.95 (ISBN 0-87516-048-4). De Vorss.

Mesmer, Franz A. Mesmerism: A Translation of the Original Medical & Scientific Writings of F. A. Mesmer, M.D. Bloch, George, tr. from Lat., Fr. & Ger. LC 80-14736. 176p. 1980. 11.50 (ISBN 0-913232-88-2). W Kaufmann.

Tatar, Maria M. Spellbound: Studies on Mesmerism & Literature. LC 78-51199. 1978. 21.00 (ISBN 0-691-06377-X). Princeton U Pr.

MESOLITHIC PERIOD

Burkitt, M. C. Our Early Ancestors: An Introductory Study of Mesolithic, Neolithic, & Copper Age Cultures in Europe & Adjacent Regions. LC 72-80142. (Illus.). Repr. of 1926 ed. 15.00 (ISBN 0-405-08331-9, Blom Pubns). Arno.

Woodman, Peter C. The Mesolithic in Ireland: Hunter-Gatherers in an Insular Environment. 1978. 35.00x (ISBN 0-86054-042-1, Pub. by BAR). State Mutual Bk.

MESONS

see also Muons

AIP Conference, Philadelphia, April, 1972. Experimental Meson Spectroscopy 1972: Proceedings, No. 8. Kwan-Wu Lai & Rosenfeld, A. H., eds. LC 72-88226. (Illus.). 489p. 1972. 14.00 (ISBN 0-88318-107-X). Am Inst Physics.

Baltay, Charles & Rosenfeld, Arthur H., eds. Experimental Meson Spectroscopy. LC 78-137009. (Illus.). 664p. 1970. 32.50x (ISBN 0-231-03477-6). Columbia U Pr.

Barnes, P. D., et al, eds. Meson-Nuclear Physics-1976: Carnegie-Mellon Conference. LC 76-26811. (AIP Conference Proceedings: No. 33). 1976. 24.75 (ISBN 0-88318-132-0). Am Inst Physics.

Bransden, B. H. & Moorhouse, R. Gordon. The Pion-Nucleon System. (Illus.). 552p. 1973. 35.00 (ISBN 0-691-08115-8); pap. 12.50 (ISBN 0-691-08129-8). Princeton U Pr.

Brittin, Wesley E., et al, eds. Boulder Lecture Notes in Theoretical Physics, 1965: Vol. 8-B, Fundamental Particles & High Energy Physics. 1966. 93.00x (ISBN 0-677-13080-5). Gordon.

Cence, Robert J. Pion-Nucleon Scattering. LC 66-11964. (Investigations in Physics Ser.: No. 11). (Illus.). 1969. 15.00 (ISBN 0-691-08068-2). Princeton U Pr.

Eisenberg, Judah M. & Koltun, Daniel S. Theory of Meson Interactions with Nuclei. LC 79-24653. 1980. 42.50 (ISBN 0-471-03915-2, Pub. by Wiley-Interscience). Wiley.

Hungerford, E. V., III, ed. Meson-Nuclear Physics - Nineteen Seventy-Nine. LC 79-53978. (AIP Conference Proceedings: No. 54). (Illus.). 1979. lib. bdg. 27.75 (ISBN 0-88318-153-3). Am Inst Physics.

Kabir, P. K. C. P. Puzzle. LC 68-124833. (Illus.). 1968. 27.50 (ISBN 0-12-393150-9). Acad Pr.

Lichtenberg, D. B. Meson & Baryon Spectroscopy. rev. ed. (Illus.). 1965. pap. 8.20 (ISBN 0-387-90000-4). Springer-Verlag.

Marin, B. R., et al. Pion-Pion Interactions in Physics. 1976. 73.00 (ISBN 0-12-474740-X). Acad Pr.

Nelipa, N. F. Photoproduction & Scattering of Pi-Mesons. (Russian Tracts on the Physical Sciences Ser). (Illus.). 1961. 21.50x (ISBN 0-677-20430-2). Gordon.

Paul, E., et al. Elementary Particle Physics. (Tracts in Modern Physics Ser.: Vol. 79). (Illus.). 1976. 35.10 (ISBN 0-387-07778-2). Springer-Verlag.

Rho, M. & Wilkinson, D., eds. Mesons in Nuclei, 3 vols. 1979. Set Of 3 Vols. 186.50 (ISBN 0-444-85052-X, North Holland); Vol. 1. 88.00 (ISBN 0-444-85255-7); Vol. 2. 73.25 (ISBN 0-444-85256-5); Vol. 3. 73.25 (ISBN 0-444-85257-3). Elsevier.

Sakurai, J. J. Currents & Mesons. LC 69-15230. (Chicago Lectures in Physics Ser). 1969. pap. 7.00 (ISBN 0-226-73383-1). U of Chicago Pr.

Skobel'tsyn, D. V., ed. Photomesic & Photonuclear Processes. LC 67-27904. (P. N. Lebedev Physics Institute Ser.: Vol. 34). 227p. 1967. 35.00 (ISBN 0-306-10791-0, Consultants). Plenum Pub.

Von Goeler, Eberhard & Weinstein, Roy, eds. Experimental Meson Spectroscopy, 1977. LC 77-94049. 456p. 1977. 22.00x (ISBN 0-930350-00-6). NE U Pr.

MESOPOTAMIA

see Iraq

MESOPOTAMIAN ART

see Art, Mesopotamian

MESOPOTAMIAN POTTERY

see Pottery, Ancient

MESOTRONS
see Mesons
MESOZOIC PERIOD
see Geology, Stratigraphic–Mesozoic
MESSALLINA, VALERIE–FICTION
Graves, Robert. Claudius the God. 1977. pap. 3.95 (ISBN 0-394-72537-9, Vin). Random.
MESSENGERS
Rudman, Jack. Messenger. (Career Examination Ser.: C-495). (Cloth bdg. avail. on request). pap. 6.00 (ISBN 0-8373-0519-5). Natl Learning.
MESSERSCHMITT AIRPLANES
Aeronautical Staff. Messerschmitt ME109. LC 65-24307. (Aero Ser: Vol. 1). (Illus.). 1965. pap. 3.00 (ISBN 0-8168-0500-8). Aero.
Boyne, Walter J. Messerschmitt Me 262: Arrow to the Future. (Illus.). 192p. (Orig.). 1980. 19.95 (ISBN 0-87474-276-5); pap. 9.95 (ISBN 0-87474-275-7). Smithsonian.
Craig, James. Messerschmitt B F One Hundred Nine. LC 67-14198. (Famous Aircraft Ser). (Illus.). 1968. pap. 3.95 (ISBN 0-668-01666-3). Arco.
Feist, Uwe & Hirsch, R. S. Messerschmitt BF110. LC 67-21486. (Aero Ser: Vol. 16). (Illus.). 1967. pap. 3.00 (ISBN 0-8168-0560-1). Aero.
--Messerschmitt ME262. LC 67-16733. (Aero Ser.: Vol. 14). (Illus.). 1967. pap. 3.00 (ISBN 0-8168-0552-0). Aero.
Grinsell, Robert. Messerschmitt BF 109, Bk. 3. (Crown's World War II Fighter Planes Ser.). 1981. 15.95 (ISBN 0-517-54256-0). Crown.
Maloney, Edward T. The Messerschmitt Me-262. (Illus.). 56p. 1980. pap. 6.95 (ISBN 0-9600248-5-9, Pub. by WW Two). Aviation.
Maloney, Edward T. & Feist, Uwe. Messerschmitt ME163. LC 67-27870. (Aero Ser: Vol. 17). 1968. pap. 3.00 (ISBN 0-8168-0564-4). Aero.
Nowarra, Heinz J. Messerschmitt 109, a Famous German Fighter. LC 63-14331. (Harleyford Ser). (Illus.). 1963. 18.95 (ISBN 0-8168-6375-X). Aero.
Rice, M. S., ed. Messerschmitt Me.262: Pictorial & Design Study Including the Pilot Handbook. (Illus.). 64p. 1973. pap. 5.95 (ISBN 0-87994-020-4, Pub. by AvPubns). Aviation.
Shores, Christopher F. Battle of Britain. Cooksey, Peter G. & Ward, Richard, eds. LC 77-93935. (Aircam Aviation Ser). (Illus., Orig.). 1969. pap. 2.95 (ISBN 0-668-02119-5). Arco.
Van Ishoven, Armand. Messerschmitt BF 109 at War. (Illus.). 1977. 17.50x (ISBN 0-7110-0770-5). Intl Pubns Serv.
MESSIAH
Here are entered general works on the conception of a messiah. Works dealing with prophecies in the Old Testament concerning a messiah are entered under Messiah–Prophecies. Works identifying Jesus Christ with the Messiah are entered under Jesus Christ–Messiahship.
see also Superman
Chwolsohn, D. Die Ssabier und der Ssabismus, 2 Vols. 1856. 69.50 (ISBN 0-384-09053-2). Johnson Repr.
Cresson, Warder. The Key of David: David the True Messiah. Davis, Moshe, ed. LC 77-70671. (America & the Holy Land Ser.). (Illus.). 1977. Repr. of 1852 ed. lib. bdg. 20.00x (ISBN 0-405-10239-9). Arno.
Gratus, Jack. The False Messiahs: Prophets of the Millennium. LC 75-29890. 284p. 1976. 10.95 (ISBN 0-8008-2588-8). Taplinger.
Greenstone, Julius H. The Messiah Idea in Jewish History. LC 70-97284. 347p. 1972. Repr. of 1906 ed. lib. bdg. 19.00x (ISBN 0-8371-2606-1, GRMI). Greenwood.
Levey, Samson H. The Messiah: An Aramoic Interpretation. 1974. 20.00x (ISBN 0-87820-402-4, Pub. by Anti-Defamation League). Ktav.
Robinson, John M. Pagan Christs. 1967. 5.95 (ISBN 0-8216-0136-9). Univ Bks.
Sarachek, Joseph. The Doctrine of the Messiah in Medieval Jewish Literature. LC 68-20900. 352p. 1975. pap. 8.75 (ISBN 0-87203-061-X). Hermon.
Schatz, Elihu A. Proof of the Accuracy of the Bible. LC 73-10726. (Illus.). xxvi, 740p. 1973. 15.00x (ISBN 0-8246-0161-0). Jonathan David.
Scholem, Gershom. The Messianic Idea in Judaism: And Other Essays on Jewish Spirituality. LC 70-130212. 384p. 1972. 15.00x (ISBN 0-8052-3369-5); pap. 5.95 (ISBN 0-8052-0362-1). Schocken.
Schwartz, Howard. The Captive Soul of the Messiah. 1980. 7.50 (ISBN 0-917146-24-7, Pub. by Cauldron). SBD.
Silver, Abba H. History of Messianic Speculation in Israel from the First Through the Seventeenth Centuries. 1959. 8.50 (ISBN 0-8446-2937-5). Peter Smith.
Wallis, Wilson D. Messiahs: Their Role in Civilization. 217p. Repr. of 1943 ed. lib. bdg. 15.00x (ISBN 0-87991-114-X). Porcupine Pr.
MESSIAH–PROPHECIES
Hengstenberg, E. W. Christology of the Old Testament. Arnold, T. K., tr. from Ger. LC 77-129739. (Kregel Reprint Library). 1973. 12.95 (ISBN 0-8254-2812-2). Kregel.
Lindsay, Gordon. The Key to Israel's Future-The Forgotten Covenant. 1.00 (ISBN 0-89985-191-6). Christ Nations.
--Messiah Witness-Israel's Destiny & Coming Deliverer. 0.95 (ISBN 0-89985-187-8). Christ Nations.
Spurgeon, Charles H. Christ in the Old Testament. (Treasury of Spurgeon & Life & Work of Our Lord). 13.95 (ISBN 0-8010-8150-5). Baker Bk.
Wilson, T. Ernest. The Messianic Psalms. LC 77-27503. (Orig.). 1978. pap. 2.95 (ISBN 0-87213-963-8). Loizeaux.
MESSIANIC CULTS
see Nativistic Movements
MESSIANISM, AMERICAN
Cherry, C. God's New Israel: Religious Interpretations of American Destiny. 1971. pap. 12.95 (ISBN 0-13-357335-4). P-H.
Moorhead, James H. American Apocalypse: Yankee Protestants & the Civil War, 1860-1869. LC 77-14360. 1978. 22.50x (ISBN 0-300-02152-6). Yale U Pr.
Weinberg, Albert K. Manifest Destiny: A Study of Nationalist Expansionism in American History. LC 75-41293. Repr. of 1935 ed. 41.50 (ISBN 0-404-14706-2). AMS Pr.
MESSIANISM, POLITICAL
Talmon, J. L. Political Messianism: The Romantic Phase. LC 60-14071. 1960. 38.50x (ISBN 0-89197-892-5). Irvington.
METABOLIC ANTAGONISTS
see Antimetabolites
METABOLIC DISORDERS
see Metabolism, Disorders of
METABOLIC INHIBITORS
see Enzyme Inhibitors
METABOLISM
see also Amino Acid Metabolism; Antimetabolites; Bioenergetics; Calcium Metabolism; Carbohydrate Metabolism; Carbohydrates in the Body; Cell Metabolism; Deficiency Diseases; Dormancy (Biology); Drug Metabolism; Electrolyte Metabolism; Energy Metabolism; Fat Metabolism; Fatty Acid Metabolism; Gamma Globulin; Glucose Metabolism; Glycoside Metabolism; Iron Metabolism; Lipid Metabolism; Mevalonic Acid Metabolism; Microbial Metabolites; Mineral Metabolism; Nitrogen Metabolism; Noradrenalin Metabolism; Nucleic Acid Metabolism; Nutrition; Phosphorus Metabolism; Plants–Metabolism; Protein Metabolism; Sodium Metabolism; Strontium Metabolism; Tissue Metabolism; Urea; Vitamin Metabolism; Water Metabolism
Bakhle, Y. S. & Vane, J. R., eds. Metabolic Functions of the Lung, Vol. 4. (Lung Biology in Health & Disease). 1977. 39.50 (ISBN 0-8247-6383-1). Dekker.
Balstrino, Philip. Fat & Skinny. LC 74-12306. (A Let's-Read-&-Find-Out Science Bk). (Illus.). (gr. k-3). 1975. 8.95 (ISBN 0-690-00454-0, TYC-J); PLB 8.79 (ISBN 0-690-00665-9). Har-Row.
Banks, P., et al. The Biochemistry of the Tissues. 2nd ed. LC 75-26739. 493p. 1976. 67.50 (ISBN 0-471-05471-2, Pub. by Wiley-Interscience); pap. 25.00 (ISBN 0-471-01923-2, Pub. by Wiley-Interscience). Wiley.
Beers, Roland F. & Bassett, Edward G., eds. Nutritional Factors: Modulating Effects on Metabolic Processes. (Miles International Symposium Ser.: Vol. 13). 1981. text ed. 55.00 (ISBN 0-89004-592-5). Raven.
Beets, M. G., ed. Structure-Activity Relationships in Human Chemoreception. (Illus.). 1978. text ed. 71.30x (ISBN 0-85334-746-8, Pub. by Applied Science). Burgess-Intl Ideas.
Biochemical Society Symposium, 27th. Metabolic Roles of Citrate: Proceedings. Goodwin, T. W., ed. LC 68-17671. (Illus.). 1968. 23.50 (ISBN 0-12-289878-8). Acad Pr.
Brown, J. H. Integration & Coordination of Metabolic Processes: A Systems Approach to Endocrinology. (Illus.). 1978. text ed. 18.95x (ISBN 0-442-20940-1). Van Nos Reinhold.
Chance, Britton, ed. Energy-Linked Functions of Mitochondria. 1963. 34.00 (ISBN 0-12-167862-8). Acad Pr.
Cohen, Margo P. & Foa, Piero P., eds. Special Topics in Endocrinology & Metabolism, Vol. 1. 154p. 1979. 18.00x (ISBN 0-8451-0700-3). A R Liss.
--Special Topics in Endocrinology & Metabolism, Vol. 2. 174p. 1981. 24.00 (ISBN 0-8451-0701-1). A R Liss.
Cunningham, Earlene B. Mechanisms of Metabolism. (Illus.). 1977. text ed. 26.00 (ISBN 0-07-014927-5, C). McGraw.
Denton, R. M. & Pogson, C. I. Metabolic Regulation. LC 76-13455. (Outline Studies in Biology). 64p. 1976. pap. text ed. 5.95x (ISBN 0-412-13150-1, Pub. by Chapman & Hall England). Methuen Inc.
Dhalla, N. & Sano, Toyomi, eds. Heart Function & Metabolism. (Recent Advances in Studies of Cardiac Structure & Metabolism Ser: Vol. 11). 1977. 57.50 (ISBN 0-8391-0671-8). Univ Park.
Dorfman, Ralph & Ungar, F., eds. Metabolism of Steroid Hormones. 1965. 72.50 (ISBN 0-12-221150-2). Acad Pr.
European Nutrition Conference, 2nd, Munich, 1976. Abstracts. Zoellner, N., et al, eds. (Nutrition & Metabolism: Vol. 20, No. 3). 1976. 22.25 (ISBN 3-8055-2441-2). S Karger.
--Proceedings. Incl. Vol. 21, Nos. 1-3. Main Papers. 54.00 (ISBN 3-8055-2704-7); Vol. 21, No. 4. Round Table on Comparison of Dietary Recommendation in Different European Countries. 9.00 (ISBN 3-8055-2705-5); Vol. 21, Suppl. 1. Short Communications. 54.00 (ISBN 3-8055-2636-9). (Nutrition & Metabolism: Vol. 21, Nos. 1-4 & Suppl. 1). 1977. complete 76.75 (ISBN 3-8055-2681-4). S Karger.
Felig, P., et al. Endocrinology & Metabolism. 1981. 75.00 (ISBN 0-07-020387-3). McGraw.
Finkle, Bernard J. & Runeckles, Victor C., eds. Phenolic Compounds & Metabolic Regulation. LC 66-29065. 157p. 1967. 19.50 (ISBN 0-306-50023-X, Plenum Pr). Plenum Pub.
Fishman, William H., ed. Metabolic Conjugation & Metabolic Hydrolysis, 3 vols. LC 79-107556. 1970-73. Vol. 1. 64.00 (ISBN 0-12-257601-2); Vol. 2. 87.50 (ISBN 0-12-257602-0); Vol. 3. 62.50 (ISBN 0-12-257603-9); Set. 173.50 (ISBN 0-685-03086-5). Acad Pr.
Freinkel, Norbert, ed. The Year in Metabolism, 1977. (Illus.). 468p. (Annual). 1978. 22.50 (ISBN 0-306-32002-9, Plenum Pr). Plenum Pub.
Gati, T., et al, eds. Nutrition-Digestion-Metabolism: Proceedings of the 28th International Congress of Physiological Sciences, Budapest, 1980. LC 80-42185. (Advances in Physiological Sciences Ser.: Vol. 12). (Illus.). 400p. 1981. 50.00 (ISBN 0-08-026825-0). Pergamon.
Gilmour, D. Biochemistry of Insects. 1961. 42.00 (ISBN 0-12-284050-X). Acad Pr.
Greenberg, D. M., ed. Metabolic Pathways. 3rd ed. Incl. Vol. 1. 1967. 63.50, by subscription 63.50 (ISBN 0-12-299251-2); Vol. 2. 1968. 55.50, by subscription 55.50 (ISBN 0-12-299252-0); Vol. 3. 1969. 75.50, by subscription 75.50 (ISBN 0-12-299253-9); Vol. 4. 1970. 63.50, by subscription 63.50 (ISBN 0-12-299254-7); Vol. 5. Vogel, Henry J., ed. 1971. 68.00, by subscription 68.00 (ISBN 0-12-299255-5); Vol. 6. Hokin, L. E., ed. 1972. 79.00 (ISBN 0-12-299256-3). Acad Pr.
Greten, H., ed. Lipoprotein Metabolism. (Illus.). 180p. 1976. pap. 15.30 (ISBN 0-387-07635-2). Springer-Verlag.
Hathway, D. E., ed. Foreign Compound Metabolism in Mammals, Vols. 1-4. Incl. Vol. 1. 1960-69 Literature. 1970. 45.00 (ISBN 0-85186-008-7); Vol. 2. 1970-71 Literature. 1972. 45.00 (ISBN 0-85186-018-4); Vol. 3. 1972-73 Literature. 1975. 65.00 (ISBN 0-85186-028-1); Vol. 4. 1974-75 Literature. 1977. 67.50 (ISBN 0-85186-038-9). LC 72-623875. Am Chemical.
Herbert, R. B. Biosynthesis of Secondary Metabolites. 1981. 38.00x (ISBN 0-412-16370-5, Pub. by Chapman & Hall); pap. 17.50x (ISBN 0-412-16380-2). Methuen Inc.
Herman, Robert H., et al, eds. Principles of Metabolic Control in Mammalian Systems. (Illus.). 690p. 1980. 35.00 (ISBN 0-306-40261-0, Plenum Pr). Plenum Pub.
Hodges, Robert E., ed. Human Nutrition-A Comprehensive Treatise, Vol. 4: Nutrition-Metabolic & Clinical Applications. (Illus.). 500p. 1979. 37.50 (ISBN 0-306-40203-3, Plenum Pr). Plenum Pub.
Hollwich, F. The Influence of Ocular Light Perception on Metabolism in Man & Animal. LC 78-17076. (Topics in Environmental Physiology & Medicine). (Illus.). 1979. 39.40 (ISBN 0-387-90315-1). Springer-Verlag.
Hutter, R., et al, eds. Antibiotics & Other Secondary Metabolites: Biosynthesis & Production. 1979. 42.50 (ISBN 0-12-363250-1). Acad Pr.
International Commission on Radiological Protection. The Metabolism of Compounds of Plutonium & Other Actinides. (ICRP Publication Ser.: No. 19). 66p. 1973. pap. 9.00 (ISBN 0-08-017119-2). Pergamon.
International Symposium Biologische Anstalt Helgoland, 3rd, 1967. Quantitative Biology of Metabolism: Models of Metabolism, Metabolic Parameters, Damage to Metabolism, Metabolic Control. Locker, A., ed. LC 68-55620. (Illus.). 1969. pap. 34.90 (ISBN 0-387-04301-2). Springer-Verlag.
International Symposium, 2nd, Jerusalem, 1974. Bilirubin Metabolism in the Newborn. Bergsma, D., et al, eds. (International Congress Ser.: No. 380). 1976. 59.50 (ISBN 0-444-15216-4, Excerpta Medica). Elsevier.
Katzman, Robert & Pappius, Hanna. Brain Electrolytes & Fluid Metabolism. 419p. 1973. 36.50 (ISBN 0-683-04522-9, Pub. by W & W). Krieger.
Keleti. Mathematical Models of Metabolic Regulation. 1976. 17.00 (ISBN 0-9960001-2-7, Pub. by Kaido Hungary). Heyden.
Keleti, Tamas & Lakatos, Zsuzsanna, eds. Mathematical Models of Metabolic Regulation. 1976. 17.50x (ISBN 9-6305-0919-9). Intl Pubns Serv.
Kervran, C. L. Biological Transmutations. (Illus.). 180p. 1980. text ed. 14.95 (ISBN 0-8464-1069-9). Beekman Pubs.
Klachko, et al. Hormones & Energy Metabolism. LC 78-23943. (Advances in Experimental Medicine & Biology Ser.: Vol. 111). 212p. 1979. 25.00 (ISBN 0-306-40070-7, Plenum Pr). Plenum Pub.
Kluge, M. & Ting, I. P. Crassulacean Acid Metabolism: Analysis of an Ecological Adaptation. LC 78-12658. (Ecological Studies: Vol. 30). (Illus.). 1979. 44.80 (ISBN 0-387-08979-9). Springer-Verlag.
Kremer, William F. & Kremer, Laura. The Doctors' Metabolic Diet. 1976. pap. 1.75 (ISBN 0-380-00726-6, 29991). Avon.
Lamb, Lawrence E. Metabolics: Putting Your Food Energy to Work. LC 74-1829. (Illus.). 256p. 1974. 12.95 (ISBN 0-06-012484-9, HarpT). Har-Row.
Larner, Joseph. Intermediary Metabolism & Its Regulation. (Modern Biochemistry Ser). 1971. pap. 13.95 ref. ed (ISBN 0-13-470641-2). P-H.
Levine, R. & Luft, R., eds. Advances in Metabolic Disorders, Vols. 1-6. Incl. Vol. 1. 1964 (ISBN 0-12-027301-2); Vol. 2. 1965; Vol. 3. 1968 (ISBN 0-12-027303-9); Vol. 4. 1970 (ISBN 0-12-027304-7); Vol. 5. 1971 (ISBN 0-12-027305-5); Vol.6. 1972 (ISBN 0-12-027306-3). 55.00 ea. Acad Pr.
Levine, R. & Tuft, R., eds. Advances in Metabolic Disorders: Supplements. Incl. Suppl. 1. Early Diabetes: A Symposium. Camerini-Davalos, R. A. & Cole, H. S., eds. 1970. 56.00 (ISBN 0-12-027361-6); Suppl. 2. Vascular & Neurological Changes in Early Diabetes. Camerini-Davalos, Rafael A. & Cole, Harold S., eds. 1973. 58.00 (ISBN 0-12-027362-4). Acad Pr.
Luckner, Martin. The Secondary Metabolism of Plants & Animals. 1972. 60.50 (ISBN 0-12-459050-0). Acad Pr.
McMurray, W. C. Essentials of Human Metabolism. (Illus.). 1977. pap. text ed. 19.50x (ISBN 0-06-141641-X, Harper Medical). Har-Row.
Magill, Jane M. & Moore, John B., Jr. Experiments in Metabolism. 1979. pap. text ed. 3.95x plastic comb. bdg. (ISBN 0-89641-013-7); perfect bdg. (ISBN 0-89641-070-6). American Pr.
Mann, J. Secondary Metabolism. (Chemistry Ser.). (Illus.). 1978. text ed. 36.00 (ISBN 0-19-855506-7). Oxford U Pr.
Manner, Harold. Metabolic Therapy "A". 0.75 (ISBN 0-686-29836-5). Cancer Bk Hse.
Maxwell, Morton H. & Kleeman, Charles R., eds. Clinical Disorders of Fluid & Electrolyte Metabolism. 3rd ed. (Illus.). 1979. text ed. 60.00 (ISBN 0-07-040994-3, HP). McGraw.
Mora, Jaime & Palacios, Rafael, eds. Glutamine: Metabolism, Enzymology & Regulation. 1980. 28.00 (ISBN 0-12-506040-8). Acad Pr.
Newsholme, E. A. & Start, C. Regulation of Metabolism. LC 72-5721. 349p. 1973. text ed. 43.95 (ISBN 0-471-63530-8, Pub. by Wiley-Interscience); pap. 18.25 (ISBN 0-471-63531-6). Wiley.
O'Riordan, J. L. Recent Advances in Endocrinology & Metabolism, No. 1. LC 77-30086. (Recent Advances in Endocrinology & Metabolism Ser.). (Illus.). 1978. 29.50x (ISBN 0-443-01651-8). Churchill.
Passonneau, Janet V. & Hawkins, Richard A. Cerebral Metabolism & Neural Function. (Illus.). 370p. 1980. lib. bdg. 57.00 (ISBN 0-683-06788-5). Williams & Wilkins.
Phipps, D. A. Metals & Metabolism, No. 26. (Oxford Chemistry Ser). (Illus.). 1976. pap. 12.50x (ISBN 0-19-855413-3). Oxford U Pr.
Pories, Walter J., et al, eds. Clinical Applications of Zinc Metabolism. (Illus.). 320p. 1975. text ed. 36.25 (ISBN 0-398-02968-7). C C Thomas.
Prasad, Ananda S. Zinc Metabolism. (Illus.). 484p. 1966. photocopy ed. spiral 49.50 (ISBN 0-398-01518-X). C C Thomas.
Racker, Efraim, ed. Cellular Metabolism & Infections: Symposium. 1954. 25.50 (ISBN 0-12-574650-4). Acad Pr.
Ramsay, I. Synopsis of Endocrinology & Metabolism. 2nd ed. (Illus.). 1980. 21.95 (ISBN 0-8151-7033-5). Year Bk Med.
Ramsden, David B. Peripheral Metabolism & Action of Thyroid Hormones, Vol. 2. (Annual Research Reviews). 1978. 28.80 (ISBN 0-88831-029-3). Eden Med Res.
Roe, Francis J., ed. Metabolic Aspects of Food Safety. LC 72-142181. 1971. 55.50 (ISBN 0-12-592550-6). Acad Pr.

Salvatore, Francesco, et al, eds. The Biochemistry of Adenosylmethionine. LC 76-25565. 1977. 38.50x (ISBN 0-231-03895-X). Columbia U Pr.
Schiff, Leon, et al. Bile Salt Metabolism. (Illus.). 320p. 1969. photocopy ed. spiral 31.75 (ISBN 0-398-01661-5). C C Thomas.
Shaltiel, S., ed. Metabolic Interconversion of Enzymes 1975: Fourth International Symposium Held in Arab, April 27th-May 2nd, 1975. (Proceedings in Life Sciences). (Illus.). 1976. 39.40 (ISBN 0-387-07888-6). Springer-Verlag.
Sink, John D., ed. The Control of Metabolism. LC 73-12935. (Illus.). 328p. 1974. 17.50x (ISBN 0-271-01124-6). Pa St U Pr.
Sols, A. & Grisolia, S., eds. Metabolic Regulation & Enzyme Action. 1970. 60.50 (ISBN 0-12-654550-2). Acad Pr.
Srere, Paul A. & Estabrook, Ronald W., eds. Microenvironments & Metabolic Compartmentation. 1978. 35.50 (ISBN 0-12-660550-5). Acad Pr.
Staunton, J. Primary Metabolism: A Mechanistic Approach. (Illus.). 1978. text ed. 28.50x (ISBN 0-19-855460-5). Oxford U Pr.
Stoddart, R. W. Polysaccharide Metabolism. 224p. 1980. 35.00x (ISBN 0-85664-807-8, Pub. by Croom Helm England). State Mutual Bk.
Sword, J. P. & Waddell, A. W., eds. Standard Operating Procedures in Metabolism & Analytic Medicine. (Standard Operating Procedures Ser.: Vol. 4). 300p. 1981. 84.50 (ISBN 0-8391-1641-1). Univ Park.
Szymendera, Janusz. Bone Mineral Metabolism in Cancer. LC 75-104194. (Recent Results in Cancer Research: Vol. 27). (Illus.). 1970. 21.70 (ISBN 0-387-04992-4). Springer-Verlag.
Tager, J. M., et al, eds. Use of Isolated Liver Cells & Kidney Tabules in Metabolic Studies: Proceedings. 1976. 58.75 (ISBN 0-444-10925-0, North-Holland). Elsevier.
Tepperman, Jay. Metabolic & Endocrine Physiology. 4th ed. (Illus.). 1980. 21.95 (ISBN 0-8151-8755-6); pap. 17.95 (ISBN 0-8151-8756-4). Year Bk Med.
Thurman, Ronald, ed. Alcohol & Aldehyde Metabolizing Systems. (Advances in Experimental Medicine & Biology Ser.). 335p. 1980. 75.00 (ISBN 0-306-40476-1, Plenum Pr). Plenum Pub.
Thurman, Ronald G., et al, eds. Alcohol & Aldehyde Metabolizing Systems, 3 vols. (Johnson Foundation Colloquia Ser.). 1974-78. Vol. 1. 44.00 (ISBN 0-12-691450-8); Vol. 2. 47.00 (ISBN 0-12-691402-8); Vol. 3. 47.00 (ISBN 0-12-691403-6); Set. 112.00 (ISBN 0-686-77325-X). Acad Pr.
Wagner, R. P. Genetics & Metabolism. 2nd ed. 673p. 1964. 18.52 (ISBN 0-471-91412-6, Pub. by Wiley). Krieger.
Walker, William F. & Johnston, Ivan A. Metabolic Basis of Surgical Care. (Illus.). 1971. 17.95x (ISBN 0-433-34580-2). Intl Ideas.
Weil, William B., Jr. Fluid & Electrolyte Metabolism in Infants & Children: A Unified Approach. 336p. 1978. 37.00 (ISBN 0-8089-1028-0). Grune.
Whitney, Eleanor N. & Hamilton, Eva M. Understanding Nutrition. (Illus.). 1977. text ed. 18.50 (ISBN 0-8299-0052-7); instrs.' manual avail. (ISBN 0-8299-0583-9). West Pub.
Wildenthal, Kern, et al, eds. Regulation of Cardiac Metabolism. LC 76-1516. (AHA Monograph: No. 49). 1976. pap. 4.00 (ISBN 0-87493-050-2, 73-035A). Am Heart.
Wilkinson, A. W. Metabolism & Response to Injury. (Illus.). 1976. 28.50 (ISBN 0-8151-9322-X). Year Bk Med.
Wilmore, D. W. Metabolic Management of the Critically Ill. (Reviewing Surgical Topics Ser.). (Illus.). 278p. 1977. 22.50 (ISBN 0-306-31046-5, Plenum Pr). Plenum Pub.
Witzmann, Rupert F. Steroids: The Keys to Life. 288p. 1981. text ed. 28.50 (ISBN 0-442-29590-1). Van Nos Reinhold.
Worth, H. G. & Curnow, D. H. Metabolic Pathways in Medicine. (Illus.). 144p. 1981. 26.50x (ISBN 0-7131-4336-3). Intl Ideas.
Xenobiotic Metabolism: In Vitro Studies. LC 79-789. (Symposium Ser.: No. 97). 1979. 28.50 (ISBN 0-8412-0486-1). Am Chemical.

METABOLISM, DISORDERS OF

see also Acidosis; Amyloidosis; Calcification; Diabetes; Galactosemia; Metabolism, Inborn Errors of; Obesity; Porphyria; Uric Acid

Advances in Metabolic Disorders. Incl. Vol. 7. Levine, R. & Luft, R., eds. 1974. 55.00 (ISBN 0-12-027307-1); Vol. 8. Somatomedins & Some Other Growth Factors. Levine, R. & Luft, R., eds. 1975. 57.00 (ISBN 0-12-027308-X); lib. ed. 73.50 (ISBN 0-12-027384-5); microfiche 41.50 (ISBN 0-12-027385-3); Vol. 9. International Studies in the Epidemiology of Diabetes. Levine, R. & Bennett, P., eds. 1978. 59.00 (ISBN 0-12-027309-8); 1978. lib. ed. 75.50 (ISBN 0-12-027386-1); microfiche 42.50 (ISBN 0-12-027387-X). (Serial Publication). Acad Pr.
Association for Research in Nervous & Mental Disease. Brain Dysfunction in Metabolic Disorders, Vol. 53. Plum, Fred, ed. LC 74-79190. 1974. 34.50 (ISBN 0-911216-81-2). Raven.
Bacchus, Habeeb. Essentials of Metabolic Disease & Endocrinology. (Illus.). 1976. 26.50 (ISBN 0-8391-0866-4). Univ Park.
Berwick, Donald M., et al. Cholesterol, Children, & Heart Disease: An Analysis of Alternatives. (Illus.). 416p. 1980. 32.95x (ISBN 0-19-502669-1). Oxford U Pr.
Bodansky, Oscar. Biochemistry of Human Cancer. 1975. 60.50 (ISBN 0-12-109850-8). Acad Pr.
Bondy, Philip K. & Rosenberg, Leon E. Diseases of Metabolism. 8th ed. LC 78-52722. (Illus.). 1979. text ed. 75.00 (ISBN 0-7216-1844-8). Saunders.
Dickens, Frank, et al, eds. Carbohydrate Metabolism & Its Disorders, 2 Vols. 1968. Vol. 1. 84.50 (ISBN 0-12-214901-7); Vol. 2. 62.50 (ISBN 0-12-214902-5). Acad Pr.
Elsdon-Dew, R. W., et al, eds. The Cardiovascular, Metabolic & Psychological Interface. (Royal Society of Medicine International Congress & Symposium Ser.: No. 14). 86p. 1979. pap. 13.50 (ISBN 0-8089-1219-4). Grune.
Evers, P. & Evers, J. Sixty Recipes-M.S.-Metabolic Diseases. 1.00 (ISBN 0-686-29840-3). Cancer Bk Hse.
Farid, Nadir R., ed. HLA in Endocrine & Metabolic Disorders. 1981. price not set (ISBN 0-12-247780-4). Acad Pr.
Frost, Harold M. Bone Remodeling & Its Relationship to Metabolic Bone Diseases: Orthopaedic Lectures, Vol. 3. (Illus.). 225p. 1973. 22.50 (ISBN 0-398-02588-6). C C Thomas.
Gerrick, David J. Troubles at the Metabolic Mill-Ketosis. (Illus.). 1978. 20.00 (ISBN 0-916750-70-1). Dayton Labs.
Haddad, H. M., ed. Metabolic Eye Disease. (Illus.). 464p. 1975. 53.25 (ISBN 0-398-03169-X). C C Thomas.
Jansky, L. & Musacchia, X. J. Regulation of Depressed Metabolism & Thermogenesis. (American Lectures in Environmental Studies). (Illus.). 304p. 1976. 30.25 (ISBN 0-398-03502-4). C C Thomas.
Lee, H. A., ed. Parenteral Nutrition in Acute Metabolic Illness. 1974. 73.00 (ISBN 0-12-441750-7). Acad Pr.
Levine, R. & Luft, R., eds. Advances in Metabolic Disorders, Vols. 1-6. Incl. Vol. 1. 1964 (ISBN 0-12-027301-2); Vol. 2. 1965; Vol. 3. 1968 (ISBN 0-12-027303-9); Vol. 4. 1970 (ISBN 0-12-027304-7); Vol. 5. 1971 (ISBN 0-12-027305-5); Vol.6. 1972 (ISBN 0-12-027306-3). 55.00 ea. Acad Pr.
Levine, R. & Tuft, R., eds. Advances in Metabolic Disorders: Supplements. Incl. Suppl. 1. Early Diabetes: A Symposium. Camerini-Davalos, R. A. & Cole, H. S., eds. 1970. 56.00 (ISBN 0-12-027361-6); Suppl. 2. Vascular & Neurological Changes in Early Diabetes. Camerini-Davalos, Rafael A. & Cole, Harold S., eds. 1973. 58.00 (ISBN 0-12-027362-4). Acad Pr.
Levine, Rachmiel & Luft, Rolf, eds. Advances in Metabolic Disorders, Vol. 10. Date not set. price not set (ISBN 0-12-027310-1); price not set lib ed. (ISBN 0-12-027388-8); price not set microfiche (ISBN 0-12-027389-6). Acad Pr.
McMurray, W. C. Essentials of Human Metabolism. (Illus.). 1977. pap. text ed. 19.50x (ISBN 0-06-141641-X, Harper Medical). Har-Row.
Paige, David M. & Bayless, Theodore M., eds. Lactose Digestion: Clinical & Nutritional Implications. LC 81-1537. (Illus.). 320p. 1981. text ed. 22.50x (ISBN 0-8018-2647-0). Johns Hopkins.
Rose, Leslie I. & Lavine, Robert L., eds. New Concepts in Endocrinology & Metabolism. LC 77-9314. (The 39th Hahnemann Symposium on Endocrinology). 192p. 1977. 33.50 (ISBN 0-8089-1028-0). Grune.
Snapper, I. Rare Manifestations of Metabolic Bone Disease: Their Practical Importance. (American Lecture Metabolism). (Illus.). 103p. 1952. photocopy ed. spiral 11.75 (ISBN 0-398-04415-5). C C Thomas.
Ugolev, A. M. Physiology & Pathology of Membrane Digestion. LC 68-19186. 226p. 1968. 32.50 (ISBN 0-306-30327-2, Plenum Pr). Plenum Pub.
W., tr. Metabolic Disorders, Methods of Examination. (Developments in Ophthalmology: Vol. 4). (Illus.). vi, 228p. 1981. 99.50 (ISBN 3-8055-2014-X). S Karger.
Walker, William F. & Johnston, Ivan A. Metabolic Basis of Surgical Care. (Illus.). 1971. 17.95x (ISBN 0-433-34580-2). Intl Ideas.
Wilson, Robert F. Fluids, Electrolytes, & Metabolism. 148p. 1975. pap. 11.50 (ISBN 0-398-02643-2). C C Thomas.

METABOLISM, INBORN ERRORS OF

Belfiore, F. Enzyme Regulation & Metabolic Diseases. (Illus.). xxiv, 880p. 1981. 149.25 (ISBN 3-8055-0005-X). S Karger.
Bickel, H., et al, eds. Neonatal Screening for Inborn Errors of Metabolism. (Illus.). 300p. 1980. 50.70 (ISBN 0-387-09779-1). Springer-Verlag.
Burman, D. Inherited Disorders of Carbohydrate Metabolism. Holton, J. B. & Pennock, C. A., eds. (Society for the Study of Inborn Errors in Metabolism Ser.: No. 16). 433p. text ed. 39.50 (ISBN 0-8391-1476-1). Univ Park.
Ellis. Inborn Errors of Metabolism. 1980. 8.95 (ISBN 0-8151-3104-6). Year Bk Med.
Ellis, Roland, ed. Inborn Errors of Metabolism. 112p. 1980. 30.00x (ISBN 0-686-69931-9, Pub. by Croom Helm England). State Mutual Bk.
Goldberg, Morton F., ed. Genetic & Metabolic Eye Disease. 1974. 60.00 (ISBN 0-316-31923-6). Little.
Harkness, R. A. & Cockburn, F., eds. The Cultured Cell & Inherited Metabolic Disease. LC 77-21651. 1977. 29.50 (ISBN 0-8391-1160-6). Univ Park.
Hers, H. G. & Van Hoof, F., eds. Lysosomes & Storage Diseases. 1973. 81.00 (ISBN 0-12-342850-5). Acad Pr.
Hommes, F. A., ed. Inborn Error of Metabolism. 1973. 57.50 (ISBN 0-12-354550-1). Acad Pr.
Kelly, Sally. Biochemical Methods in Medical Genetics. (Amer. Lec in Laboratory Medicine Ser.). (Illus.). 352p. 1977. 22.25 (ISBN 0-398-03630-6). C C Thomas.
Konigsmark, Bruce W. & Gorlin, Robert J. Genetic & Metabolic Deafness. LC 75-22734. (Illus.). 1976. text ed. 34.50 (ISBN 0-7216-5489-4). Saunders.
Raine. Medico-Social Management of Inherited Metabolic Diseases. (Illus.). 1977. 39.50 (ISBN 0-8391-1103-7). Univ Park.
Raine, N. The Treatment of Inherited Metabolic Disease. LC 74-19903. 294p. 1975. 17.50 (ISBN 0-444-19516-5). Elsevier.
Shih, Vivian. Laboratory Techniques for the Detection of Hereditary Metabolic Disorders. LC 73-78164. (Uniscience Ser). 125p. 1973. 34.95 (ISBN 0-8493-5013-1). CRC Pr.
Stanbury, John B. & Wyngaarden, James B. The Metabolic Basis of Inherited Disease. (Illus.). 1977. text ed. 69.00 (ISBN 0-07-060725-7, HP). McGraw.
WHO Scientific Group, Geneva, 1967. Screening of Inborn Errors of Metabolism: A Report. (Technical Report Ser: No. 401). 57p. 1968. pap. 2.00 (ISBN 92-4-120401-X, 701). World Health.

METAL-AMMONIA COMPOUNDS

Lagowski, J. J. & Sienko, M. J., eds. Metal-Ammonia Solutions: Proceedings of the International Conference on the Nature of Metal-Ammonia Solution, Ithaca, N.Y., 1969. 522p. 1976. 79.00 (ISBN 0-08-020794-4). Pergamon.
Thompson, J. C. Electrons in Liquid Ammonia. (Monographs on the Physics & Chemistry of Materials). (Illus.). 1976. 74.00x (ISBN 0-19-851343-7). Oxford U Pr.
Wendlandt, W. W. & Smith, J. P. Thermal Properties of Transition Metal Ammine Complexes. 1967. 29.50 (ISBN 0-444-40630-1). Elsevier.

METAL BONDING

see also Ceramic to Metal Bonding

American Welding Society. Modern Joining Processes. text ed. 10.00 (ISBN 0-685-65947-X); instr's manual 2.50 (ISBN 0-685-65948-8); slides 105.00 (ISBN 0-685-65949-6). Am Welding.
Cotton, F. Albert & Walton, Richard A. Multiple Bonds Between Metal Atoms. 400p. 1982. 35.00 (ISBN 0-471-04686-8, Pub. by Wiley-Interscience). Wiley.
Lindberg, Roy A. & Braton, Norman R. Welding & Other Joining Processes. 544p. 1976. text ed. 29.95 (ISBN 0-205-05000-X, 3250008). Allyn.
Taylor, M. J. Metal to Metal Bonded States of the Main Group Elements. 1975. 34.00 (ISBN 0-12-684650-2). Acad Pr.

METAL CARBONYLS

Braterman, P. S. Metal Carbonyl Spectra. 1975. 48.00 (ISBN 0-12-125850-5). Acad Pr.
Inorganic Chemistry Metal Carbonyl Chemistry. (Topics in Current Chemistry: Vol. 71). (Illus.). 1977. 40.40 (ISBN 0-387-08290-5). Springer-Verlag.

METAL CASTINGS

Ammen, C. W. The Complete Handbook of Sand Casting. (Illus.). 1979. pap. 7.95 (ISBN 0-8306-1043-X, 1043). TAB Bks.
--The Metalcaster's Bible. (Illus.). 434p. 1980. 15.95 (ISBN 0-8306-9970-8); pap. 9.95 (ISBN 0-8306-1173-8, 1173). TAB Bks.
Flinn, Richard A. Fundamentals of Metal Casting. 1963. 20.95 (ISBN 0-201-02020-3). A-W.
Gulaev, B. B., ed. Gases in Cast Metals. LC 65-15007. 257p. 1965. 45.00 (ISBN 0-306-10726-0, Consultants). Plenum Pub.
Herrmann, E. & Hoffmann, D. Handbook on Continuous Casting. (Illus.). 758p. 1980. lib. bdg. 625.00 (ISBN 3-87017-134-0, Pub. by DGM Metallurgy Germany). IR Pubns.
Mujherjee, P. C. Fundamentals of Metal Casting Technology. 857p. 1981. 40.75x (ISBN 0-686-72949-8, Pub. by Oxford & IBH India). State Mutual Bk.
Strauss, K. Applied Science in the Casting of Metals. 1970. 50.00 (ISBN 0-08-015711-4). Pergamon.

METAL CATALYSTS

Anderson, J. R. Structure of Metallic Catalysts. 1975. 74.00 (ISBN 0-12-057150-1). Acad Pr.
Happel, et al. Base Metal Oxide Catalysts for the Petrochemical, Petroleum, & Chemical Industries. (Firm orders only). 375.00 (ISBN 0-8247-6437-4). Dekker.
Hata, Kazud. New Hydrogenating Catalysts: Urushibara Catalysts. LC 72-2652. 247p. 1972. 21.95 (ISBN 0-470-35890-4). Halsted Pr.
Sheldon, Roger & Kochi, Jay. Metal-Catalyzed Oxidations of Organic Compounds: Mechanistic Principles & Synthetic Methodology Including Bio-Chemical Process. 1981. price not set (ISBN 0-12-639380-X). Acad Pr.

METAL CLEANING

see also Metals–Pickling

Handbook of Vapor Degreasing. 1976. pap. 6.00 (ISBN 0-686-52055-6, 04-310010-15). ASTM.

METAL COLORING

see Metals–Coloring

METAL CORROSION

see Corrosion and Anti-Corrosives

METAL CRYSTALS

Cotterill, P. & Mould, P. R. Recrystallization & Grain Growth in Metals. LC 75-33874. 1976. 38.95 (ISBN 0-470-17527-3). Halsted Pr.
Kripyakevich, I. P. Systematic Classification of Types of Intermetallic Structures. LC 64-24934. 35p. 1964. 20.00 (ISBN 0-306-10683-3, Consultants). Plenum Pub.
Ovsienko, D. E., ed. Growth & Imperfections of Metallic Crystals. LC 68-13058. (Illus.). 268p. 1968. 35.00 (ISBN 0-306-10801-1, Consultants). Plenum Pub.

METAL CURTAIN WALLS

see Walls

METAL-CUTTING

see also Electric Metal-Cutting; Metal-Cutting Tools; Oxyacetylene Welding and Cutting; Ultrasonic Metal-Cutting

Bellows, Guy. Chemical Machining. (Machining Process Ser.: MDC 77-102). (Illus.). 76p. 1977. pap. 8.00 (ISBN 0-936974-04-4). Metcut Res Assocs.
--Machining: A Process Checklist. 2nd ed. (Machining Process Ser. MDC 78-100). (Illus.). 28p. 1978. pap. 3.50 (ISBN 0-936974-05-2). Metcut Res Assocs.
--Nontraditional Machining Guide. (Machining Process Ser.: MDC 76-101). (Illus.). 76p. (Orig.). 1976. pap. 8.00 (ISBN 0-936974-03-6). Metcut Res Assocs.
Fundamentals of Metal Cutting. (Machine Tool Ser.: Vol. 4). 1974. pap. text ed. 3.95x (ISBN 0-88462-245-2). Ed Methods.
Gough, P. J. Swarf & Machine Tools. 1970. 8.95 (ISBN 0-09-102240-1, Pub. by Hutchinson). Merrimack Bk Serv.
Johnson, Harold V. Technical Metals. rev. ed. (gr. 10-12). 1973. text ed. 19.96 (ISBN 0-87002-139-7); wrbk. 6.40 (ISBN 0-87002-147-8). Bennett IL.
Kronenberg, M. Machining Science & Applications. 1966. text ed. 60.00 (ISBN 0-08-011627-2). Pergamon.
Morris, Ralph C. Air Conditioning Cutter's Ready Reference. rev ed. LC 73-148571. (Illus.). 363p. 1971. 24.50 (ISBN 0-912524-02-2). Busn News.
Postnikov, S. N. Electrophysical & Electrochemical Phenomena in Friction, Cutting, & Lubrication. Teague, Ben, tr. 1978. text ed. 21.50x (ISBN 0-442-26624-3). Van Nos Reinhold.
Rogers, J. W. & Millan, W. H. Coil Slitting. LC 73-7903. 127p. 1973. pap. text ed. 9.25 (ISBN 0-08-017696-8). Pergamon.
Rosenwald, Lessing J., pref. by. Fifteenth Century Woodcuts & Metalcuts. LC 65-28226. (Illus.). write for info. (ISBN 0-685-89721-4). Natl Gallery Art.
Runck, Robert R., ed. Premachining Planning & Tool Presetting. LC 67-28208. (Manufacturing Data Ser). (Illus.). 1967. pap. 8.25x (ISBN 0-87263-008-0). SME.
Technical Staff of the Machinability Data Center, ed. Machining Data Handbook, 2 vols. 3rd ed. LC 80-81480. (Illus.). 1980. Set. 150.00x (ISBN 0-936974-00-1). Metcut Res Assocs.
Thompson, Frank E., Jr. Diving, Cutting & Welding in Underwater Salvage Operations. LC 70-92687. (Illus.). 1944. pap. 4.00x (ISBN 0-87033-139-6). Cornell Maritime.
Trent, E. M. Metal Cutting. 1977. 34.95 (ISBN 0-408-10603-4). Butterworth.

Wilson, John F. Practice & Theory of Electrochemical Machining. 266p. 1981. Repr. of 1971 ed. lib. bdg. write for info. (ISBN 0-89874-229-3). Krieger.

METAL-CUTTING TOOLS

Deshpande, D. L. Basic Tools. 64p. 1981. 5.00x (ISBN 0-86125-499-6, Pub. by Orient Longman India). State Mutual Bk.

Ebendorf, Robert, et al. Cutting Edge. Sperath, Albert F., ed. LC 81-620014. (Illus.). 66p. (Orig.). 1981. pap. 5.00 (ISBN 0-939058-01-4). Kentucky Arts.

Freeman, Henry G. Dictionary of Metal-Cutting Machine Tools, 2 Vols. (Eng-Ger. & Ger-Eng.). 1965. 61.75 ea. (ISBN 3-7736-5095-7). Adler.

--Dictionary of Metal-Cutting Machine Tools. 561p. (Eng. -Ger.). 1965. leatherette 72.00 (ISBN 3-7736-5095-7, M-7110). French & Eur.

Ham, Inyong & Bhattacharyya, Amitabha. Design of Cutting Tools: Use of Metal Cutting Theory. LC 68-29237. (Manufacturing Data Ser). (Illus.). 1969. 11.00x (ISBN 0-87263-014-5). SME.

Heiler, Toni. Dictionnaire Technique Illustre Des Outils Coupants Pour L'usinage Des Metaux. 474p. (Fr., Ger., Eng., It. & Span.). 1965. 69.95 (ISBN 0-686-57326-9, M-6313). French & Eur.

King, Alan G. & Wheildon, William M., Jr. Ceramics in Machining Processes. 1966. 55.00 (ISBN 0-12-407650-5). Acad Pr.

Pollack, Herman. Tool Design. (Illus.). 528p. 1976. 19.95 (ISBN 0-87909-840-6); students manual avail. Reston.

Swinehart, Haldon J., ed. Cutting Tool Material Selection. LC 68-27332. (Manufacturing Data Ser). (Illus., Orig.). 1968. pap. 8.25x (ISBN 0-87263-010-2). SME.

Trent, E. M. Metal Cutting. 1977. 34.95 (ISBN 0-408-10603-4). Butterworth.

METAL DETECTORS

Garrett, Charles, et al. Electronic Prospecting. Nelson, Bettye, ed. LC 76-11380. (Guidebook Ser.). 1979. pap. 3.95 (ISBN 0-915920-38-7). Ram Pub.

Hardigree, Peggy. Strike It Rich! Treasure Hunting with Metal Detectors. (Illus.). 224p. 1980. 10.95 (ISBN 0-517-54216-1, Harmony); pap. 5.95 (ISBN 0-517-54160-2, Harmony). Crown.

Lagal, Roy. Detector Owner's Field Manual. Nelson, Bettye, ed. LC 75-44706. (Illus.). 150p. (Orig.). 1976. pap. 6.95 (ISBN 0-915920-40-9). Ram Pub.

Lagal, Roy & Garrett, Charles. The Complete VLF-TR Metal Detector Handbook: All About Ground Canceling Metal Detectors. Nelson, Bettye, ed. LC 78-60309. 1979. pap. 7.95 (ISBN 0-915920-32-8). Ram Pub.

LeGaye, E. S. Electronic Metal Detector Handbook. LC 72-100686. (Illus.). 1969. pap. 8.00 (ISBN 0-685-70350-9). Western Her Texas.

Traister, John E. & Traister, Robert J. How to Build Metal-Treasurer Locators. LC 77-7510. (Illus.). 1977. pap. 5.95 (ISBN 0-8306-6909-4, 909). TAB Bks.

METAL ENGRAVERS

see Engravers

METAL FOILS

see also Aluminum Foil

Marshall, Cyril. Foilcraft. LC 77-7573. (Illus.). 160p. 1977. 12.95 (ISBN 0-8117-0647-8). Stackpole.

METAL FURNITURE

see also Wrought-Iron

METAL INDUSTRIES

see Metal Trade; Metal-Work; Mineral Industries

METAL IONS

Bensen, D. Mechanisms of Oxidation by Metal Ions. (Reaction Mechanisms in Organic Chemistry Monograph: 10). 1976. 41.50 (ISBN 0-444-41325-1). Elsevier.

Burgess, John. Metal Ions in Solutions. (Chemical Science). 481p. 1980. pap. 32.95x (ISBN 0-470-26987-1). Halsted Pr.

Dhar, Sanat K., ed. Metal Ions in Biological Systems: Studies of Some Biomedical & Environmental Problems. LC 73-15981. (Advances in Experimental Medicine & Biology Ser.: Vol. 40). 306p. 1973. 29.50 (ISBN 0-306-39040-X, Plenum Pr). Plenum Pub.

Perrin, D. D., ed. Stability Constants of Metal-Ion Complexes, Pt. B: Organic Ligands. (Chemical Data Ser.: No. 22). 1280p. 1979. 225.00 (ISBN 0-08-020958-0). Pergamon.

Sigel. Metal Ions in Biological Systems. (Metal Ions & Biological Systems Ser.: Vol. 12). 400p. 1981. 57.50 (ISBN 0-8247-1429-6). Dekker.

--Metal Ions in Biological Systems, Vol. 13. 440p. 1981. price not set (ISBN 0-8247-1504-7). Dekker.

--Metal Ions in Biological Systems, Vol. 11: Metal Complexes As Anticancer Agents. 440p. 1980. 55.00 (ISBN 0-8247-1004-5). Dekker.

--Metal Ions in Biological Systems, Vol. 9: Amino Acids & Derivatives As Ambivalent Liquids. 1979. 34.50 (ISBN 0-8247-6875-2). Dekker.

--Metal Ions in the Biological Systems, Vol. 10: Carcinogenicity & Metal Ions. 304p. 1980. 49.75 (ISBN 0-8247-6980-5). Dekker.

--Metal Ions in the Biological Systems, Vol. 8: Nucleotides & Derivatives--Their Ligating Ambivalency. 1979. 32.75 (ISBN 0-8247-6843-4). Dekker.

Sigel, Helmut, ed. Metal Ions in Biological Systems Vol. 5: Reactivity of Coordination Compounds, Vol. 5. 416p. 1976. 49.75 (ISBN 0-8247-6032-8). Dekker.

Spiro, Thomas G. Copper Proteins. (Metal Ions in Biology Ser.). 356p. 1981. 37.50 (ISBN 0-471-04400-8, Pub. by Wiley-Interscience). Wiley.

Spiro, Thomas G., ed. Metal Ion Activation of Dioxygen. LC 79-13808. (Metal Ions in Biology Ser.: Vol. 2). 1980. 35.50 (ISBN 0-471-04398-2, Pub. by Wiley-Interscience). Wiley.

METAL OXIDES

see Metallic Oxides

METAL POWDERS

Brakanova, I. T. Environmental Hazards of Metals: Toxicity of Powdered Metals & Metal Compounds. LC 73-83905. (Studies in Soviet Science - Physical Sciences Ser.). (Illus.). 277p. 1975. 35.00 (ISBN 0-306-10897-6, Consultants). Plenum Pub.

Invenson, V. A. Densification of Metal Powders During Sintering. LC 72-94822. (Studies in Soviet Science - Physical Sciences Ser.). 242p. 1973. 45.00 (ISBN 0-306-10881-X, Consultants). Plenum Pub.

METAL-ROLLING

see Rolling (Metal-Work)

METAL SCULPTURE

Benton, Suzanne. The Art of Welded Sculpture. 1975. 13.95 (ISBN 0-442-20692-5). Van Nos Reinhold.

Faulkner, Trevor. The Thames & Hudson Manual of Direct Metal Sculpture. (Illus.). 1980. pap. 16.95 (ISBN 0-500-68015-9). Thames Hudson.

--The Thames & Hudson Manual of Direct Metal Sculpture. (Illus.). 1978. 14.95 (ISBN 0-500-67015-3). Thames Hudson.

Hale, Nathan C. Welded Sculpture. (Illus.). 1968. 14.95 (ISBN 0-8230-5700-3). Watson-Guptill.

Lynch, John. How to Make Mobiles. (Illus.). (gr. 4 up). 1953. 5.00 (ISBN 0-670-38433-X, Studio). Viking Pr.

Mehta, Rustam J., intro. by. Masterpieces of Indian Bronzes & Metal Sculpture. (Illus.). 46p. 1971. 20.00x (ISBN 0-8002-1705-5). Intl Pubns Serv.

Meilach, Dona & Seiden, Donald. Direct Metal Sculpture: Creative Techniques & Appreciation. (Arts & Crafts Ser.). (Illus.). 1969. 12.95 (ISBN 0-517-02448-9). Crown.

METAL SPRAYING

see also Metals–Finishing

Recommended Practices for Metallizing Inside Diameters of Machinery Parts: C2.10-63. 1.50 (ISBN 0-685-66009-5). Am Welding.

METAL STAMPING

see also Dies (Metal-Working); Drawing (Metal Work); Forging; Power Presses

Gilchrist, Jack. Hidden Profits in Stamping: A Creative Materials Management Guide. LC 77-2145. 1977. 21.50 (ISBN 0-8436-0818-8). CBI Pub.

METAL SURFACES

see Metals–Surfaces

METAL TO CERAMIC BONDING

see Ceramic to Metal Bonding

METAL TRADE

see also Hardware;

also Iron Industry and Trade; Steel Industry and Trade, and similar headings

Andrews, Jack. The Edge of the Anvil. LC 77-15115. 1977. 11.95 (ISBN 0-87857-186-8); pap. 8.95 (ISBN 0-87857-195-7). Rodale Pr Inc.

Arnett, Harold E. & Smith, Donald L. Metal Finishing Industry: Framework for Success. (Michigan Business Reports: No. 60). (Illus.). 1977. pap. 5.50 (ISBN 0-87712-182-6). U Mich Busn Div Res.

Boothroyd, Geoffrey. Fundamentals of Metal Machining & Machine Tools. (Illus.). 350p. 1975. text ed. 18.95 (ISBN 0-07-006498-9, C); solutions manual 3.95 (ISBN 0-07-006502-0). McGraw.

Burke, John L. & Weiss, Volker, eds. Advances in Metal Processing. (Sagamore Army Materials Research Conference Ser.: Vol. 25). 375p. 1981. 45.00 (ISBN 0-306-40651-9, Plenum Pr). Plenum Pub.

Dettner, H. Fachwoerterbuch Fuer der Metalloberflaechenveredelung. 391p. (Ger. - Eng., Dictionary of Metal Refining). 1969. 20.95 (ISBN 3-87749-011-5, M-7397, Pub. by G. Siemens). French & Eur.

Granbeck, Marilyn. Looking Forward to a Career: Metals & Plastics. 2nd ed. LC 74-864. (Looking Forward to a Career Ser.). (Illus.). (gr. 6 up). 1974. PLB 6.95 (ISBN 0-87518-068-X). Dillon.

Granick, David. Soviet Metal-Fabricating & Economic Development: Practice Versus Policy. 382p. 1967. 22.50x (ISBN 0-299-04290-1). U of Wis Pr.

McLendon, Gordon. Get Really Rich in the Coming Super Metals Boom. 1981. 12.95 (ISBN 0-671-43225-7). S&S.

Muhly, James D. Copper & Tin: The Distribution of Mineral Resources & the Nature of the Metals Trade in the Bronze Age, Including Supplement. new ed. (Connecticut Academy of Arts & Sciences Transaction Ser.: Vol. 43 & 46). 380p. 1976. 19.50 (ISBN 0-208-01573-6, Archon). Shoe String.

Nuclear Techniques in the Basic Metal Industries. LC 73-164980. (Proceedings Ser.). (Illus.). 634p. (Orig.). 1973. pap. 48.75 (ISBN 92-0-060073-5, ISP314, IAEA). Unipub.

Soltow, James H. Origins of Small Business: Metal Fabricators & Machinery Makers in New England, 1890-1957. LC 65-27429. (Transactions Ser.: Vol. 55, Pt. 10). 1965. pap. 1.00 (ISBN 0-87169-560-X). Am Philos.

Trainer, Glynnis. The Metalworking Industry. 200p. 1981. cancelled (ISBN 0-86569-062-6). Auburn Hse.

METAL-WORK

see also Architectural Metal Work; Art Metal-Work; Brazing; Copperwork; Electroplating; Forging; Founding; Goldwork; Home Workshops; Metal Sculpture; Metal Stamping; Metal-Working Lubricants; Metals–Coloring; Metals–Finishing; Plate-Metal Work; Sheet-Metal Work; Silverwork; Solder and Soldering; Steelwork; Welding

Accurso, Frank. Machine Trades Projects & Procedures: Standard & Metric. LC 77-8691. 1978. pap. text ed. 9.50 (ISBN 0-672-97101-1); tchr's manual 3.33 (ISBN 0-672-97155-0). Bobbs.

Adams, Jeannette T. The Metalworking Handbook: Principles & Procedures. LC 75-23577. (Illus.). 1976. lib. bdg. 12.50 (ISBN 0-668-03857-8). Arco.

American Society Of Mechanical Engineers. ASME Handbook: Metals Engineering: Processes. 1958. 38.50 (ISBN 0-07-001514-7, P&RB). McGraw.

Ammen, C. W. The Complete Handbook of Sand Casting. (Illus.). 1979. pap. 7.95 (ISBN 0-8306-1043-X, 1043). TAB Bks.

Armstrong, L. & Guy, P. K. Metalcraft Today. 1975. pap. text ed. 5.00x (ISBN 0-435-75700-8). Heinemann Ed.

Avitzur, Betzalel. Metal Forming: Processes & Analysis. rev. ed. LC 78-2767. 522p. 1979. lib. bdg. 26.50 (ISBN 0-88275-673-7). Krieger.

Bedford, John R. Basic Course of Practical Metalwork. (gr. 9-12). pap. text ed. 8.95 (ISBN 0-7195-0079-6). Transatlantic.

--Metalcraft: Theory & Practice. (Illus.). (gr. 9 up). 1968. text ed. 8.95 (ISBN 0-7195-2251-X). Transatlantic.

Bell, J., et al, eds. General Welding & Cutting. (Engineering Craftsmen: No. F10). (Illus.). 1976. spiral bdg. 26.00x (ISBN 0-85083-330-2). Intl Ideas.

Biringuccio, Vannoccio. Pirotechnia. 1966. pap. 4.95x (ISBN 0-262-52017-6). MIT Pr.

Blandford, Percy W. The Practical Handbook of Blacksmithing & Metalworking. (Illus., Orig.). 15.95 (ISBN 0-8306-9947-3); pap. 11.95 (ISBN 0-8306-1179-7, 1179). TAB Bks.

Blaser, Werner. Filigree Architecture: Metal & Glass Construction. (Illus.). 216p. (Eng. Fr. & Ger.). 1980. pap. 19.00 (ISBN 0-89192-298-9). Interbk Inc.

Blazynski, T. Z. Metal Forming: Tool Profiles & Flow. LC 75-42156. 1976. 52.95 (ISBN 0-470-15003-3). Halsted Pr.

Boy Scouts Of America. Metalwork. LC 19-600. (Illus.). 36p. (gr. 6-12). 1969. pap. 0.70x (ISBN 0-8395-3312-8, 3312). BSA.

Boyd, T. Gardner. Metalworking. 120p. 1981. write for info. (ISBN 0-87006-258-1). Goodheart.

Bradley, Ian. The Drilling Machine. (Illus.). 157p. 1973. 10.00x (ISBN 0-85242-263-6). Intl Pubns Serv.

--Metal Working Tools, & Their Uses. (Illus.). 1978. pap. 7.50x (ISBN 0-85242-599-6). Intl Pubns Serv.

--The Shaping Machine. (Illus.). 100p. 1973. 8.00x (ISBN 0-85242-323-3). Intl Pubns Serv.

Bragdon, Charles R. Metal Decorating from Start to Finishes. LC 61-17350. (Illus.). 1969. 5.95 (ISBN 0-87027-065-6). Wheelwright.

Burton, Malcolm S. Applied Metallurgy for Engineers. 1956. text ed. 21.95 (ISBN 0-07-009292-3, C). McGraw.

Business Communications Co. Advanced Metal Working Technologies, GB-052. 1979. 750.00 (ISBN 0-89336-230-1). BCC.

Chapman, W. A. Workshop Technology, Pt. 1. 5th ed. (Illus.). 1976. pap. 14.95x (ISBN 0-7131-3269-8). Intl Ideas.

Cook, N. H. Manufacturing Analysis. 1966. 19.95 (ISBN 0-201-01211-1). A-W.

Cooley, R. H. Complete Metalworking Manual. LC 66-12058. (gr. 9-12). 1967. lib. bdg. 12.95 (ISBN 0-668-01406-7). Arco.

Cuzner, Bernard. A First Book of Metal-Work. 192p. 1980. 11.00x (ISBN 0-905418-54-9, Pub. by Gresham England). State Mutual Bk.

--A First Book of Metal-Work. 2nd ed. (Illus.). 162p. 1979. pap. 7.50x (ISBN 0-905418-54-9). Intl Pubns Serv.

Daniele, Joseph W. Early American Metal Projects. LC 75-130495. 14.00 (ISBN 0-87345-142-2). McKnight.

Darling, Sharon S. & Casterline, Gail F. Chicago Metalsmiths. LC 77-76503. (Illus.). 1977. 15.00 (ISBN 0-226-80781-9, 10412-5). U of Chicago Pr.

Dieter, George. Mechanical Metallurgy. 2nd ed. (Illus.). 1976. text ed. 26.50 (ISBN 0-07-016891-1, C); instructor's manual 4.95 (ISBN 0-07-016892-X). McGraw.

Din Standards on Stamped Parts. 235.00 (ISBN 0-686-28194-2, 10924-3/67). Heyden.

Doyle, L. E., et al. Manufacturing Processes & Materials for Engineers. 2nd ed. 1969. text ed. 26.95 (ISBN 0-13-555862-X). P-H.

Dragoo, Alva W. General Shop Metalwork. rev. ed. (gr. 8-9). 1964. pap. text ed. 5.00 (ISBN 0-87345-109-0). McKnight.

Eary, Donald F. & Johnson, G. E. Process Engineering: For Manufacturing. (Illus.). 1962. text ed. 22.95 (ISBN 0-13-723122-9). P-H.

Ezra, A. A. Principles & Practice of Explosive Metalworking. LC 73-166058. (Illus.). 270p. 1973. 35.00x (ISBN 0-901994-05-7). Intl Pubns Serv.

Fabricated Structural Metal Products. (Industrial Equipment & Supplies Ser.). 1980. 295.00 (ISBN 0-686-31545-6). Busn Trend.

Feirer & Lindbeck. Basic Metalwork. (gr. 9-12). 1978. 6.00 (ISBN 0-87002-289-X); pap. 4.32 (ISBN 0-87002-240-7). Bennett IL.

--Metalwork: S.I. Metric Edition. 1979. text ed. 13.28 (ISBN 0-87002-292-X); student guide 5.28 (ISBN 0-87002-316-0). Bennett IL.

Feirer, John L. General Metals. rev. 5th ed. (Industrial Education Ser.). (Illus.). 480p. (gr. 9-10). 1980. text ed. 17.32 (ISBN 0-07-020380-6, W); study guide 4.20 (ISBN 0-07-020382-2); tchrs. resource guide 3.96 (ISBN 0-07-020381-4). McGraw.

--Machine Tool Metalworking. 2nd ed. Gilmore, D. E., ed. LC 72-10166. (Illus.). 568p. (gr. 10-12). 1973. text ed. 14.75 (ISBN 0-07-020369-5). McGraw.

Feirer, John L. & Lindbeck, John R. Metalwork. rev. ed. (gr. 7-9). 1970. 12.60 (ISBN 0-87002-017-X); student guide 3.28 (ISBN 0-87002-048-X). Bennett IL.

Fifer, Bill. Metal Projects, Book 2. 96p. 1981. 4.80 (ISBN 0-87006-172-0). Goodheart.

Fisch, Arline M. Textile Techniques in Metal. 168p. 1975. 17.95 (ISBN 0-442-22400-1). Van Nos Reinhold.

Fischer, J. Precious Metal Plating. (Illus.). 285p. 1964. 17.50x (ISBN 0-85218-012-8). Intl Pubns Serv.

Flood, Charles R. Welding & Metal Fabrication. 1981. text ed. price not set (ISBN 0-408-00448-7). Butterworth.

Forte, Imogene, et al. Center Stuff for Nooks, Crannies & Corners. LC 77-670124. (The Learning Center Set). (gr. 2-6). 1973. pap. text ed. 10.95 (ISBN 0-913916-07-2, IP 07-2). Incentive Pubns.

Giachino, Joseph W. Basic General Metals. (gr. 9-12). 1969. text ed. 6.96 (ISBN 0-02-817070-9). Macmillan.

Gingery, David J. The Dividing Head & Deluxe Accessories. LC 80-66142. (Build Your Own Metal Working Shop from Scrap: Bk. 6). (Illus.). 112p. (Orig.). 1981. pap. 7.95 (ISBN 0-9604330-5-8). D J Gingery.

--The Metal Lathe. LC 80-66142. (Build Your Own Metal Working Shop from Scrap Ser.: Bk. 2). (Illus.). 128p. (Orig.). 1980. pap. 7.95 (ISBN 0-9604330-1-5). D J Gingery.

--The Metal Shaper. LC 80-66142. (Build Your Own Metal Working Shop from Scrap: Bk. 3). (Illus.). 84p. (Orig.). 1980. pap. 6.95 (ISBN 0-9604330-2-3). D J Gingery.

Graham, Gregory S. Metalworking: An Introduction. 1980. text ed. 17.95 (ISBN 0-534-00843-7, Breton Pubs). Wadsworth Pub.

Greek & Roman Metalware: An Exhibition Catalogue. (Illus.). 1976. pap. 4.00 (ISBN 0-685-70549-8). Walters Art.

Hoffmanner, A. L., ed. Metal Forming: Interrelation Between Theory & Practice. LC 70-171698. 503p. 1971. 49.50 (ISBN 0-306-30554-2, Plenum Pr). Plenum Pub.

Hummel, Charles F. With Hammer in Hand: The Dominy Craftsmen of East Hampton, New York. LC 67-27362. (Illus.). 255p. 1976. Repr. 25.00 (ISBN 0-8139-0124-3, Pub. by Winterthur Museum). U Pr of Va.

IBM Education Department. Precision Measurement in the Metal Working Industry. rev. ed. (Illus.). 1952. pap. 8.50x (ISBN 0-8156-2194-9). Syracuse U Pr.

An Introduction to Working with Metal. LC 77-88953. (Drake Home Craftsman Ser.). (Illus.). 1978. pap. 5.95 (ISBN 0-8069-8452-X, 019720). Sterling.

Johnson, Harold V. Technical Metals. rev. ed. (gr. 10-12). 1973. text ed. 19.96 (ISBN 0-87002-139-7); wrbk. 6.40 (ISBN 0-87002-147-8). Bennett IL.

Koenigsberger, T. & Tobias, S. A., eds. Proceedings of the Sixteenth Machine Tool Design & Research Conference. LC 76-5219. (International Machine Tool Design & Research Conference Ser.). 599p. 1976. text ed. 109.95 (ISBN 0-470-15100-5). Halsted Pr.

Kramer, Karl R. & Kramer, Nora. Coppercraft & Silver Made at Home. (Illus.). 6.50 (ISBN 0-8446-0170-5). Peter Smith.

Kraskovska, L'Udmila. Roman Bronze Vessels from Slovakia. 1978. 10.00x (ISBN 0-86054-020-0, Pub. by BAR). State Mutual Bk.

Kronquist, Emil F. Metalwork for Craftsmen: A Step-by-Step Guide with 55 Projects. Orig. Title: Art Metalwork. 7.50 (ISBN 0-8446-0171-3). Peter Smith.

Lippmann, H., ed. Engineering Plasticity: Theory of Metal Forming Processes. (CISM International Centre for Mechanical Sciences Ser.: Vol. 139). (Illus.). 1979. pap. 57.90 (ISBN 0-387-81429-9). Springer-Verlag.

Little, R. & Little, S. Basic Book of Metalworking. (Illus.). 1979. 6.00 (ISBN 0-8269-1885-9). Am Technical.

Little, Richard L. Metalworking Technology. (Illus.). 1976. text ed. 15.95 (ISBN 0-07-038097-X, G). McGraw.

Los Angeles Unified School District. Metalworking. Vorndran, Richard A., ed. LC 77-73297. 96p. (gr. 7-9). 1978. pap. text ed. 4.40 (ISBN 0-02-820420-4). Glencoe.

Ludwig, Oswald A. & McCarthy, Willard J. Metalwork Technology & Practice. rev. & 5th ed. (Illus.). (gr. 11-12). 1975. text ed. 17.28 (ISBN 0-87345-123-6); study guide 5.00 (ISBN 0-87345-118-X); ans key avail. (ISBN 0-685-04228-6). McKnight.

McCarthy, Willard J. & Repp, Victor. Machine Tool Technology. (Illus.). (gr. 11-12). 1979. text ed. 18.60 (ISBN 0-87345-143-0); Study Guide 1. 3.68 (ISBN 0-87345-144-9); Study Guide 2. 3.68 (ISBN 0-87345-145-7); ans. key avail. McKnight.

Machine Tool & Design Research International Conference, 14th. Proceedings. Tobias, S. A. & Tobias, S. A., eds. 1974. 114.95 (ISBN 0-470-49746-7). Halsted Pr.

McKnight Staff Members & Miller, Wilbur R. Metalworking. LC 78-53387. (Basic Industrial Arts Ser.). (Illus.). 1978. 6.00 (ISBN 0-87345-792-7); softbound 4.48 (ISBN 0-87345-784-6). McKnight.

Marshall, Cyril. Foilcraft. LC 77-7573. (Illus.). 160p. 1977. 12.95 (ISBN 0-8117-0647-8). Stackpole.

Maryon, Herbert. Metalwork & Enamelling. 4th ed. (Illus.). 1971. pap. 5.00 (ISBN 0-486-22702-2). Dover.

--Metalwork & Enamelling: A Practical Treatise on Gold & Silversmiths' Work & Their Allied Crafts. 5th & rev. ed. (Illus.). 7.00 (ISBN 0-8446-0198-5). Peter Smith.

Metals. (Focus Ser.). 36p. 1973. pap. 1.75 (ISBN 0-686-11067-6). Am Indus Arts.

Mitgutsch, Ali. From Ore to Spoon. LC 80-28862. (Carolrhoda Start to Finish Bks.). Orig. Title: Vom Erz Zum Loffel. (Illus.). 24p. (ps-3). 1981. PLB 5.95 (ISBN 0-87614-161-0). Carolrhoda Bks.

Noel Hume, Ivor. James Geddy & Sons: Colonial Craftsmen. LC 70-115038. (Archaeological Ser: No. 5). (Illus., Orig.). 1970. pap. 2.25 (ISBN 0-910412-10-3). Williamsburg.

North American Metalworking Research Conference, 7th, & Manufacturing Engineering Transactions, 1979. Proceedings. LC 79-63779. (Illus.). 1979. 65.00 (ISBN 0-87263-037-4). SME.

Nutting, W. Checklist of E. A. Reproductions. LC 73-96940. 1969. 3.95 (ISBN 0-87282-087-4). Century Hse.

Paul, A. Materials & Processes in Manufacturing: Lab Manual. 1969. 3.95x (ISBN 0-02-393200-7). Macmillan.

Pitts, Lynn F. Roman Bronze Figurines from the Civitates of the Catuvellavni & Trinovantes. 1979. 24.00x (ISBN 0-86054-045-6, Pub. by BAR). State Mutual Bk.

Pollack, Herman. Manufacturing & Machine Tool Operations. 2nd ed. (Illus.). 1979. ref. 21.95 (ISBN 0-13-555771-2). P-H.

Pracna, Charles F. Hobby Metalcraft. 1978. 5.00 (ISBN 0-682-49048-2). Exposition.

Punter, Ian. Projects & Designs in Metalwork. (Illus.). 96p. 1981. 14.00 (ISBN 0-7134-3510-0, Pub. by Batsford England). David & Charles.

Read, R. R., ed. Automation in the Metal Finishing Industry. LC 77-360143. (Illus.). 146p. (Orig.). 1976. pap. 15.00x (ISBN 0-901994-84-7). Intl Pubns Serv.

Recommendations for Tube & Welding: Tubular Heat Transfer Equipment: Ferrous Materials, Pt. 1. 1973. 21.00 (ISBN 0-85501-388-5). Heyden.

Ross, R. B. Handbook of Metal Treatments & Testing. LC 77-3929. 467p. 1977. text ed. 37.95x (ISBN 0-419-10960-9, Pub. by Tavistock England). Methuen Inc.

Rowe, G. W. Principles of Industrial Metalworking Processes. 1977. 67.50x (ISBN 0-8448-1219-6). Crane-Russak Co.

Rowe, Geoffrey W. Introduction to the Principles of Metalworking. (Illus.). 1955. 10.00 (ISBN 0-312-43225-9). St Martin.

Rowlands, M. J. The Production & Distribution of Metal-Work in the Middle Bronze Age in Southern Britain. 1976. 35.00x (ISBN 0-904531-44-9, Pub. by BAR). State Mutual Bk.

Ruley, M. J. Practical Metal Projects. (gr. 9 up). text ed. 13.28 (ISBN 0-87345-137-6). McKnight.

--Projects in General Metalwork. (gr. 9 up). 1969. text ed. 13.28 (ISBN 0-87345-135-X). McKnight.

Rykalin, N., et al. Laser Machinig and Welding. (Illus.). 1979. 48.00 (ISBN 0-08-022724-4). Pergamon.

Schwartz, M. M. Metals Joining Manual. (Illus.). 1979. 22.50 (ISBN 0-07-055720-9, P&RB). McGraw.

Scott, Peter. The Thames & Hudson Manual of Metalworking. (Illus.). 1980. pap. 9.95 (ISBN 0-500-68012-4). Thames Hudson.

--The Thames & Hudson Manual of Metalworking. (Illus.). 1978. 16.95 (ISBN 0-500-67012-9). Thames Hudson.

Seppa, Heikki. Form Emphasis for Metalsmiths. LC 78-1091. (Illus.). 1978. pap. 9.50 (ISBN 0-87338-212-9). Kent St U Pr.

Smith, Ernest. Working in Precious Metals. 414p. 1981. 35.00x (ISBN 0-7198-0032-3, Pub. by Northwood Bks). State Mutual Bk.

Smith, Ernest A. Working in Precious Metals. (Illus.). 1978. 24.00x (ISBN 0-7198-0032-3). Intl Ideas.

Smith, Robert E. Patternmaking & Founding. (gr. 9 up). 1959. pap. 5.00 (ISBN 0-87345-020-5). McKnight.

Society of Manufacturing Engineers. Tool & Manufacturing Engineers Handbook. 3rd ed. Dallas, D. B., ed. (Illus.). 1976. 59.50 (ISBN 0-07-059558-5, P&RB). McGraw.

Society of North American Goldsmiths. Metalsmith Papers. 96p. (Orig.). 1980. pap. text ed. 12.00 (ISBN 0-9604446-0-2). SNAG.

Squires, William T. The Metal Craftsman Handbook. 1981. cancelled (ISBN 0-89606-050-0). Green Hill.

Stewart, Richard. Modern Design in Metal. (Illus.). 1979. 18.00 (ISBN 0-7195-3537-9). Transatlantic.

Theophilus. On Divers Arts: The Foremost Medieval Treatise on Painting, Glassmaking, & Metalwork. Hawthorne, John G. & Smith, Cyril S., trs. from Latin. (Illus.). 1979. pap. text ed. 5.00 (ISBN 0-486-23784-2). Dover.

Thomas, G. H. Metalwork Technology. (gr. 9 up). 1970. 10.95x (ISBN 0-7195-2654-X). Transatlantic.

Trainer, Glynnis. The Metalworking Industry. 200p. 1981. cancelled (ISBN 0-86569-062-6). Auburn Hse.

Tubby, Pamela. Working with Metal. LC 78-65662. (Illus.). 1979. 11.95 (ISBN 0-690-01816-9); pap. 5.95 (ISBN 0-690-01826-6, TYC-T). T Y Crowell.

Tustison, F. E., et al. Metalwork Essentials. rev. ed. 1962. 6.00 (ISBN 0-02-829540-4). Glencoe.

U.S. Metal Processing & Fabrication Seminar. Proceedings. Silva, R. M., ed. 1974. pap. 40.00 (ISBN 0-912426-03-9). Univ Tech.

Von Frauenhofer, J. A. Basic Metal Finishing. (Illus.). 1976. 25.00 (ISBN 0-8206-0205-1). Chem Pub.

Walker, John R. Exploring Metalworking. 272p. 1981. 10.96 (ISBN 0-87006-199-2); wkbk. 3.20 (ISBN 0-87006-169-0). Goodheart.

--Exploring Metalworking. LC 75-31808. 1976. text ed. 10.96 (ISBN 0-87006-199-2); wkbk. 3.20 (ISBN 0-87006-169-0). Goodheart.

--Machining Fundamentals. LC 77-22648. (Illus.). 1977. text ed. 15.32 (ISBN 0-87006-236-0). Goodheart.

--Metal Projects, Bk. 1. (Illus.). 1966. pap. 4.80 (ISBN 0-87006-153-4). Goodheart.

--Metal Projects, Bk. 3. LC 77-21602. (Illus.). pap. 4.80 (ISBN 0-87006-238-7). Goodheart.

--Metal Projects, Book 1. 112p. 1981. 4.80 (ISBN 0-87006-153-4). Goodheart.

--Metal Projects, Book 3. 96p. 1981. 4.80 (ISBN 0-87006-238-7). Goodheart.

--Modern Metalworking. (Illus.). 520p. 1981. 14.64 (ISBN 0-87006-334-0). Goodheart.

--Modern Metalworking. LC 76-22559. 1976. text ed. 14.64 (ISBN 0-87006-212-3); wkbk. 3.20 (ISBN 0-87006-223-9). Goodheart.

Waller, John A. Press Tools & Presswork. (Illus.). 1980. 39.95 (ISBN 0-86108-005-X). Herman Pub.

Watkins, M. T. Metal Forming, 2 pts. Incl. Pt. 1. Forging & Related Processes. pap. 9.95x (ISBN 0-19-859134-9); Pt. 2. Pressing & Related Processes. pap. 11.50x (ISBN 0-19-859144-6). (Engineering Design Guides Ser.). (Illus.). 1977. Oxford U Pr.

Wilson, D. M. Anglo-Saxon Ornamental Metalwork, Seven Hundred to Eleven Hundred, in the British Museum. 248p. 1981. 60.00 (ISBN 0-7141-1300-X, Pub. by Brit Mus Pubns England). State Mutual Bk.

Working with Metal. (Home Repair & Improvement Ser.). (Illus.). 128p. 1981. 10.95 (ISBN 0-8094-3470-9). Time-Life.

METAL-WORK–BIBLIOGRAPHY

Johnson, W., et al. Plane Strain Slip Line Fields for Metal Deformation Processes: A Source Book & Bibliography. (Illus.). 270p. 1981. 40.00 (ISBN 0-08-025452-7). Pergamon.

METAL-WORK–DICTIONARIES

Clason, W. E. Elsevier's Dictionary of Metallurgy & Metal Working. (Eng, Fr, Sp, It, Dutch, & Ger.). 1978. 144.00 (ISBN 0-444-41695-1). Elsevier.

METAL-WORK–HISTORY

Branigan, Keith. Aegean Metalwork in the Early & Middle Bronze Age. (Oxford Monographs on Classical Archaeology). (Illus.). 192p. 1974. 54.00x (ISBN 0-19-813213-1). Oxford U Pr.

Cellini, Benvenuto. Due trattati. (Documents of Art & Architectural History Series 2: Vol. 3). 148p. (Italian). 1980. Repr. of 1569 ed. 27.50x (ISBN 0-89371-203-5). Broude Intl Edns.

Herrmann, Hans-Volkmar. Kessel der Orientalisierenden Zeit: Olympische Forshungen. (Vol. 2, Pt. 2: Vol. 11, Pt. 2). (Illus.). 1979. write for info. (ISBN 3-11-007209-2). De Gruyter.

Knauth, Percy. The Metalsmiths. (The Emergence of Man Ser.). (Illus.). 1974. 9.95 (ISBN 0-8094-1308-6); lib. bdg. avail. (ISBN 0-685-48124-7). Time-Life.

Mitchell, James R., ed. Antique Metalware. LC 77-70771. (Antiques Magazine Library). (Illus.). 1977. pap. 7.95 (ISBN 0-87663-970-8). Universe.

Nicholson, Susan M. Catalogue of the Prehistoric Metalwork in Merseyside County Museums. (Worknotes Ser.: No. 2). (Illus.). 148p. (Orig.). 1981. pap. 12.50x (ISBN 0-87474-675-2, Pub. by Dept. of Prehistoric Archaeology, U of Liverpool). Smithsonian.

Wixom, William D. Renaissance Bronzes: From Ohio Collections. LC 75-30966. (Illus.). 196p. 1975. pap. 15.00x (ISBN 0-910386-24-2, Pub. by Cleveland Mus Art). Ind U Pr.

METAL-WORKERS

see also Iron and Steel Workers

Educational Research Council of America. Metal Molder. rev. ed. Braverman, Jack R. & Marchak, John P., eds. (Real People at Work Ser: B). (Illus.). 1976. pap. text ed. 2.25 (ISBN 0-89247-017-8). Changing Times.

Goldmark, Josephine & Hopkins, Mary D. Comparison of an Eight-Hour Plant & a Ten-Hour Plant: U.S. Public Health Bulletin, No. 106. Stein, Leon, ed. LC 77-70495. (Work Ser.). 1977. Repr. of 1920 ed. lib. bdg. 15.00x (ISBN 0-405-10168-6). Arno.

Social & Labour Practices of Some European-Based Multinationals in the Metal Trades. 1976. 14.25 (ISBN 92-2-101474-6). Intl Labour Office.

METAL-WORKING LUBRICANTS

Fourth International Conference on Jet Cutting Technology. Proceedings, 2 vols. Stephens, H. S., ed. (Illus.). 1979. Set. pap. text ed. 68.00 (ISBN 0-900983-79-5, Dist. by Air Science Co.). BHRA Fluid.

Gough, P. J. Swarf & Machine Tools. 1970. 8.95 (ISBN 0-09-102240-1, Pub. by Hutchinson). Merrimack Bk Serv.

Kalpakjian, S. & Jain, S. C., eds. Metalworking Lubrication. 259p. 1980. 40.00 (ISBN 0-686-69857-6, H00159). ASME.

Olds, W. J. Lubricants, Cutting Fluids & Coolants. LC 72-83305. 1973. 19.95 (ISBN 0-8436-0812-9). CBI Pub.

Springborn, R. K., ed. Cutting & Grinding Fluids: Selection & Application. LC 67-17077. (Manufacturing Data Ser). 1967. pap. 8.75 (ISBN 0-87263-001-3). SME.

Third International Symposium on Jet Cutting Technology. Proceedings. 1977. text ed. 65.00 (ISBN 0-900983-55-8, Dist. by Air Science Co.). BHRA Fluid.

METAL-WORKING MACHINERY

see also Machine-Tools

Electrical Standard for Metalworking Machine Tools. (Seventy Ser). 52p. 1974. pap. 3.00 (ISBN 0-685-44178-4, 70). Natl Fire Prot.

Gingery, David J. The Charcoal Foundry, Bk. 1. LC 80-661412. (Build Your Own Metal Working Shop from Scrap Ser.). (Illus.). 72p. (Orig.). 1980. pap. 6.95 (ISBN 0-9604330-0-7). D J Gingery.

--Designing & Building the Sheet Metal Brake, Bk. 7. LC 80-66142. (Build Your Own Metal Working Shop from Scrap Ser.). (Illus.). 52p. (Orig.). 1980. pap. 6.95 (ISBN 0-9604330-6-6). D J Gingery.

Harris, William T. Chemical Milling: The Technology of Cutting Materials by Etching. (Oxford Series on Advanced Manufacturing). (Illus.). 1977. 74.00x (ISBN 0-19-859115-2). Oxford U Pr.

METALLIC ALLOYS

see Alloys

METALLIC CERAMICS

see Ceramic Metals

METALLIC COMPOSITES

see also Alloys

Daul, Von C., et al. Landolt-Bornstein: Part A-Atoms, Inorganic Radicals & Radicals in Metal Complexes. LC 62-53136. (Numerical Data & Functional Relationships in Science & Technology Ser.). (Illus.). 227.20 (ISBN 0-387-08019-8). Springer-Verlag.

Din Standards for Testing of Metallic Materials: Sampling, Acceptance, Testing Machines, Mechanical-Technological Test Methods. 525.00 (ISBN 0-686-28170-5, 10054-6/19). Heyden.

METALLIC FILMS

see also Vapor-Plating

Anderson, J. C., ed. Chemisorption & Reactions on Metallic Films, 2 vols. (Physical Chemistry Ser: Vol. 24). 1971. Vol. 1. 88.00 (ISBN 0-12-058001-2); Vol. 2. 51.50 (ISBN 0-12-058002-0). Acad Pr.

Diggle, John W., ed. Oxides & Oxide Films, Vol. 1. (Anodic Behavior of Metals & Semiconductors Ser.). 560p. 1972. 56.00 (ISBN 0-8247-1143-2). Dekker.

--Oxides & Oxide Films, Vol. 2. (Anodic Behavior of Metals & Semiconductors Ser.). 416p. 1973. 49.00 (ISBN 0-8247-6066-2). Dekker.

METALLIC OXIDES

Agajanian, A. H., ed. MOSFET Technology--a Comprehensive Bibliography. 305p. 1980. 95.00 (ISBN 0-306-65193-9). IFI Plenum.

Bradley, D. C., et al. Metal Alkoxides. 1979. 83.50 (ISBN 0-12-124250-1). Acad Pr.

Diggle, John W., ed. Oxides & Oxide Films, Vol. 1. (Anodic Behavior of Metals & Semiconductors Ser.). 560p. 1972. 56.00 (ISBN 0-8247-1143-2). Dekker.

--Oxides & Oxide Films, Vol. 2. (Anodic Behavior of Metals & Semiconductors Ser.). 416p. 1973. 49.00 (ISBN 0-8247-6066-2). Dekker.

Elmasry, M. I. Digital MOS Integrated Circuits. 450p. 1981. 36.00 (ISBN 0-471-86202-9, Pub. by Wiley Interscience); pap. 23.50 (ISBN 0-471-86203-7). Wiley.

Freeman, A. J., et al, eds. International Conference on Magnetic Alloys & Oxides: Haifa, Israel, August 1977. 1978. 102.50 (ISBN 0-444-85162-3, North-Holland). Elsevier.

Fromhold, A., Jr. Theory of Metal Oxidation: Defects in Crystalline Solids, Vol. 2. write for info. (ISBN 0-444-85381-2, North-Holland). Elsevier.

Fromhold, A. T. Theory of Metal Oxidation: Volume 1 - Fundamentals. LC 75-23121. (Defects in Crystalline Solids: Vol. 9). (Illus.). 80.50 (ISBN 0-444-10957-9, North-Holland). Elsevier.

Jarzebski, Z. M. Oxide Semiconductors. LC 73-6971. 304p. 1974. 42.00 (ISBN 0-08-016968-6). Pergamon.

Kofstad, Per. Nonstoichiometry, Diffusion, & Electrical Conductivity in Binary Metal Oxides. LC 74-177885. 382p. 1972. 31.50 (ISBN 0-471-49776-2, Pub. by Wiley). Krieger.

Lancaster, Don. CMOS Cookbook. LC 76-42874. (Illus.). 1977. pap. 10.50 (ISBN 0-672-21398-2). Sams.

Lenk, J. Manual for M. O. S. Users. 1975. 18.95 (ISBN 0-87909-478-8). Reston.

Nicollian, E. H. & Brews, J. R. MOS (Metal Oxide Semiconductor) Physics & Technology. 1000p. 1981. 75.00 (ISBN 0-471-08500-6, Pub. by Wiley-Interscience). Wiley.

Richman, Paul. MOS Field-Effect Transistors & Integrated Circuits. LC 73-9892. 259p. 1973. pap. text ed. 30.50 (ISBN 0-471-72030-5, Pub. by Wiley-Interscience). Wiley.

Vijh. Oxides & Oxide Films: The Anodic Behavior of Metals & Semiconductors, Vol. 6. 368p. Date not set. price not set. Dekker.

Vol'nov, I. I. Peroxides, Superoxides & Ozonides of Alkali & Alkaline Earth Metals. LC 66-22125. (Monographs in Inorganic Chemistry Ser.). 146p. 1966. 35.00 (ISBN 0-306-30259-4, Plenum Pr). Plenum Pub.

METALLIC SURFACES

see Metals–Surfaces

METALLOCHROMY

see Metals–Coloring

METALLOGRAPHY

see also Electron Metallography; Metal Crystals; Metals–Surfaces; X-Rays–Industrial Applications

Beraha, E. & Shipigler, B. Color Metallography. (TN 690.b47). 1977. 68.00 (ISBN 0-87170-045-X). ASM.

Chadwick, G. A. & Smith, D. A., eds. Grain Boundary Structure & Properties. (Material Science & Technology Ser.). 1976. 67.00 (ISBN 0-12-166250-0). Acad Pr.

Einspruch, Norman G., ed. Microstructure Science & Engineering, 2 vols. 1981. Vol. 1. 47.00 (ISBN 0-12-234101-5); Vol. 2. subscription price 40.00 (ISBN 0-12-234102-3). Acad Pr.

Emel'yanova, V. S. & Evstyukhin, A. I., eds. High Purity Metals & Alloys: Fabrication,Properties, and Testing. LC 67-19386. 175p. 1967. 35.00 (ISBN 0-306-10793-7, Consultants). Plenum Pub.

Frier, William T. Elementary Metallurgy. 2nd ed. (Illus.). 1952. text ed. 17.95 (ISBN 0-07-022419-6, G). McGraw.

Gabriel, Michael. Micrographics 1900-1977: A Bibliography. LC 79-83891. 1978. PLB 19.00 (ISBN 0-933474-01-6). Minn Scholarly.

Gifkins, R. C. Optical Microscopy of Metals. 1970. 17.50 (ISBN 0-444-19667-6). Elsevier.

Institution of Metallurgists. The Structure of Metals: A Modern Conception. 1959. 8.25x (ISBN 0-677-60580-3). Gordon.

International Metallographic Society, 7th Annual Meeting. Microstructural Science, Vol. 3, 2 Pts. Proceedings. French, P. M., et al, eds. LC 73-10895. (Microstructural Science Ser.). 1050p. 1975. Set. 100.00 (ISBN 0-444-00161-1, North Holland). Elsevier.

Kehl, George L. Principles of Metallographic Laboratory Practice. 3rd ed. (Metallurgy & Metallurgical Engineering Ser.). (Illus.). 1949. text ed. 23.95 (ISBN 0-07-033479-X, C). McGraw.

Lambert. De Ferri Metallographia: Recent Examination Methods in Metallography & the Metallography of Welds, Vol. 4. 1980. write for info. (ISBN 0-85501-165-3). Heyden.

McCall, J. L. & French, P. M., eds. Interpretive Techniques for Microstructural Analysis. LC 77-2333. 201p. 1977. 29.50 (ISBN 0-306-31036-8, Plenum Pr). Plenum Pub.

--Metallography As a Quality Control Tool. 345p. 1980. 39.50 (ISBN 0-306-40423-0, Plenum Pr). Plenum Pub.

--Metallography in Failure Analysis. 309p. 1978. 35.00 (ISBN 0-306-40012-X, Plenum Pr). Plenum Pub.

McCall, J. L. & Mueller, William, eds. Microstructural Analysis: Tools & Techniques. 343p. 1973. 35.00 (ISBN 0-306-30748-0, Plenum Pr). Plenum Pub.

McCall, J. L. & Mueller, William M., eds. Metallographic Specimen Preparation: Optical & Electron Microscopy. LC 74-8391. 358p. 1974. 35.00 (ISBN 0-306-30791-X, Plenum Pr). Plenum Pub.

Martin, J. W. & Doherty, R. D. Stability of Microstructure in Metallic Systems. LC 75-38179. (Cambridge Solid State Science Ser.). (Illus.). 298p. 1980. pap. 17.50x (ISBN 0-521-29883-0). Cambridge U Pr.

Metallography--a Practical Tool for Correlating the Structure & Properties of Materials. 1974. 24.25 (ISBN 0-686-52020-3, 04-557000-28). ASTM.

National Micrographics Assn. Practice for Operational Procedures: Inspection & Quality Control of First-Generation Silver-Gelatin Microfilm of Documents (NMA MS23-1979) rev. ed. 1979. pap. text ed. 10.00 (ISBN 0-89258-067-4). Natl Micrograph.

Petzow, Gunter. Metallographic Etching. 1978. 24.00 (ISBN 0-87170-002-6). ASM.

Phillips, Victor A. Modern Metallographic Techniques & Their Applications. 550p. (Orig.). 1971. 43.50 (ISBN 0-471-68780-4). Krieger.

Rostoker, William & Dvorak, J. R. Interpretation of Metallographic Structures. 1964. 54.00 (ISBN 0-12-598250-X). Acad Pr.

Rudman, Jack. Micrographics Technician. (Career Examination Ser.: C-2761). (Cloth bdg. avail. on request). 1980. pap. 10.00 (ISBN 0-8373-2761-X). Natl Learning.

Smallman, R. E. & Ashbee, K. H. Modern Metallography. 1966. 13.75 (ISBN 0-08-011571-3); pap. 6.25 (ISBN 0-08-011570-5). Pergamon.

Smith, Charles. Micrographics Handbook. LC 78-2561. 1978. 29.00 (ISBN 0-89006-061-4). Artech Hse.

Stereology & Quantitative Metallography. 180p. 1973. 9.75 (ISBN 0-8031-0095-7, STP504). ASTM.

Stevens, Fred. Analysis of Metal Finishing Effluents & Effluent Treatment Solutions. LC 72-425010. 112p. 1968. 10.00x (ISBN 0-85218-025-X). Intl Pubns Serv.

Technical Meeting of the International Metallographic Society, 6th, et al. Microstructural Science: Proceedings, Vol. 2. Fritzke, Gerald P. & Richardson, James H., eds. LC 73-10885. 256p. 1975. 45.00 (ISBN 0-444-00147-6, North Holland). Elsevier.

Tolansky, S. Multiple Beam Interference Microscopy of Metals. 1970. 25.50 (ISBN 0-12-692650-6). Acad Pr.

--Multiple-Beam Interferometry of Surfaces & Films. (Illus.). 1971. pap. text ed. 3.00 (ISBN 0-486-62215-0). Dover.

Warren, B. E. X-Ray Diffraction. (Metallurgy & Materials Ser). (Illus.). 1969. 20.95 (ISBN 0-201-08524-0). A-W.

Yemel'Yanov, V. S. & Yevstyukhin, A. I., eds. Metallurgy & Metallography of Pure Metals. 1962. 74.75x (ISBN 0-677-20530-9). Gordon.

METALLOIDS

see Semimetals

METALLOORGANIC COMPOUNDS

see Organometallic Compounds

METALLURGICAL ANALYSIS

see also Alloys; Assaying; Chemistry, Analytic; Mineralogy, Determinative

German Society of Metallurgy, ed. Acoustic Emission. Nicoll, A. R., tr. (Illus.). 385p. 1980. 63.00 (ISBN 3-88355-030-2, Pub. by DGM Metallurgy Germany). IR Pubns.

Meyers, Mare A. & Murr, Lawrence E., eds. Shock Waves & High-Strain-Rate Phenomena in Metals: Concepts & Applications. 1101p. 1981. 95.00 (ISBN 0-306-40633-0, Plenum Pr). Plenum Pub.

Mining & Metallurgy Group Symposium, 4th, October 1975, Milwaukee, WI. Instrumentation in the Mining & Metallurgy Industries: Proceedings, Vol. 3. LC 73-82889. 1976. pap. text ed. 10.00 (ISBN 0-87664-278-4). Instru Soc.

Smaill, J. S. Metallurgical Stereographic Projections. 37.50 (ISBN 0-9960017-3-5, Pub by. a Hilger England K). Heyden.

METALLURGICAL FURNACES

see also Refractory Materials

Krivandin, V. & Markov, B. Metallurgical Furnaces. 1980. 11.50 (ISBN 0-8285-1830-0, Pub. by Mir Pubs Russia). Imported Pubns.

METALLURGICAL PLANTS

International Tailing Symposium, 1st. Tailing Disposal Today Vol. 1: Proceedings. Argall, George O., Jr. & Aplin, C. L., eds. LC 73-78129. (A World Mining Book). (Illus.). 864p. 1973. 37.50 (ISBN 0-87930-020-5). Miller Freeman.

Lueth & Koenig, Horst. Planning of Iron & Steelworks. 3rd ed. Cockburn, Gordon, tr. LC 67-28563. (Illus.). 1967. 33.50 (ISBN 0-387-03924-4). Springer-Verlag.

METALLURGICAL PLANTS–AUTOMATION

Balshin, M. Y. & Kiparisov, S. S. General Priciples of Power Metallurgy. 1980. 7.50 (ISBN 0-8285-1834-3, Pub. by Mir Pubs Russia). Imported Pubns.

METALLURGY

see also Alloys; Chemical Engineering; Chemistry, Technical; Electrometallurgy; Hydrometallurgy; Metals; Metals–Heat Treatment; Metals–Pickling; Metals at High Temperatures; Metals at Low Temperatures; Physical Metallurgy; Powder Metallurgy; Refractory Materials; Smelting; Vacuum Metallurgy; Zone Melting also names of metals, with or without the subdivision Metallurgy

Alcock, C. B. Principles of Pyrometallurgy. 1977. 55.00 (ISBN 0-12-048950-3). Acad Pr.

Allan, J. W. Persion Metal Technology: 700-300ad. 208p. 1979. 60.00x (ISBN 0-686-75550-2, Pub. by Ashmolean Mus Oxford). State Mutual Bk.

Allen, Dell K. Metallurgy Theory & Practice. (Illus.). 1969. 18.00 (ISBN 0-8269-3500-1). Am Technical.

American Welding Society. Introductory Welding Metallurgy. text ed. 10.00 (ISBN 0-685-65950-X); instr's manual 2.50 (ISBN 0-685-65951-8); slides 105.00 (ISBN 0-685-65952-6). Am Welding.

BCC Staff. Powder, Metallurgy: Gb-041. 1977. 550.00 (ISBN 0-89336-113-5). BCC.

Belyaev, A. I., ed. Surface Phenomena in Metallurgical Processes. LC 65-11335. 288p. 1965. 37.50 (ISBN 0-306-10704-X, Consultants). Plenum Pub.

Birau, N. & Schlott, W., eds. Melatonin - Current Status & Perspectives: Proceedings of an International Symposium on Melatonin, Held in Bremen, F. R. Germany, September 18-30, 1980. (Advances in the Biosciences Ser.: Vol. 29). (Illus.). 420p. 1981. 65.00 (ISBN 0-08-026400-X). Pergamon.

Boy Scouts of America. Metals Engineering. LC 19-600. (Illus.). 64p. (gr. 6-12). 1972. pap. 0.70x (ISBN 0-8395-3269-5, 3269). BSA.

Bradbury, Samuel, ed. Source Book on Powder Metallurgy. 1979. 38.00 (ISBN 0-87170-030-1). ASM.

Brown, Donald. Metallurgy. LC 80-68584. (Mechanical Ser.). (Illus.). 272p. (Orig.). 1981. pap. text ed. 8.00 (ISBN 0-8273-1769-7); text ed. write for info. instr's. guide (ISBN 0-8273-1770-0). Delmar.

Burkin, A. R. Topics in Non-Ferrous Extractive Metallurgy. LC 80-17435. (Critical Reports on Applied Chemistry Ser.: Vol. 1). 134p. 1980. 28.95 (ISBN 0-470-27016-0). Halsted Pr.

Burkin, A. R., ed. Leaching & Reduction in Hydrometallurgy. 109p. 1980. 80.00x (ISBN 0-900488-27-1, Pub. by Inst Mining England). State Mutual Bk.

Burton, Malcolm S. Applied Metallurgy for Engineers. 1956. text ed. 21.95 (ISBN 0-07-009292-3, C). McGraw.

Butts, Allison. Metallurgical Problems. 2nd ed. (Metallurgy & Metallurgical Engineering Ser.). 1943. text ed. 20.50 (ISBN 0-07-009420-9, C); answers 1.50 (ISBN 0-07-009450-0). McGraw.

--Metallurgical Problems. LC 79-9867. 460p. 1981. Repr. of 1971 ed. lib. bdg. write for info. (ISBN 0-88275-915-9). Krieger.

Carlin, R. L., ed. Transition Metal Chemistry: A Series of Advances, Vol. 4. 1968. 43.50 (ISBN 0-8247-1079-7). Dekker.

Carter, Giles F. Principles of Physical & Chemical Metallurgy. 1979. 42.00 (ISBN 0-87170-079-4). ASM.

Case Histories in Failure Analysis. 1979. 62.00 (ISBN 0-87170-078-6). ASM.

Centre National de la Recherche Scientifique. New Physical & Chemical Properties of Metals of Very High Purity. (Illus.). 1965. 104.00x (ISBN 0-677-10060-4). Gordon.

Chaplin, Jack W. Metal Manufacturing Technology. (gr. 10 up). 1976. text ed. 15.72 (ISBN 0-87345-132-5). McKnight.

Chemical Compositions & Rupture Strengths of Superstrength Alloys. 25p. 1970. pap. 3.50 (ISBN 0-8031-0137-6, 05-009050-20). ASTM.

Christian, J. W. Theory of Transformations in Metals & Alloys., Part 1: Equilibrium & General Kinetic Theory. 2nd ed. LC 74-22470. 564p. 1975. text ed. 57.00 (ISBN 0-08-018031-0). Pergamon.

Compilation & Index of Trade Names, Specifications, & Producers of Stainless Alloys & Superalloys. 57p. 1979. pap. 5.25 (ISBN 0-8031-0138-4, 05-045010-02). ASTM.

Cottrell, Alan. An Introduction to Metallurgy. LC 75-21731. 1975. pap. 19.50x (ISBN 0-8448-0767-2). Crane-Russak Co.

Coudurier, L. & Wilkomirsky, I. Fundamentals of Metallurgical Processes. 1978. text ed. 52.00 (ISBN 0-08-019612-8); pap. text ed. 17.00 (ISBN 0-08-019654-3). Pergamon.

Educational Research Council of America. Metallurgical Technician. rev. ed. Ferris, Theodore N. & Marchak, John P., eds. (Real People at Work Ser: C). 1976. pap. text ed. 2.25 (ISBN 0-89247-029-1). Changing Times.

Electron Beam Metallurgical Processing Seminar 2nd. Proceedings. LC 72-90075. 1972. pap. 35.00 (ISBN 0-912426-02-0). Univ Tech.

Emel'yanova, V. S. & Evstyukhin, A. I., eds. High Purity Metals & Alloys: Fabrication,Properties, and Testing. LC 67-19386. 175p. 1967. 35.00 (ISBN 0-306-10793-7, Consultants). Plenum Pub.

Fitterer, G. Applications of Fundamental Thermodynamics to Metallurgical Processes. 1967. 93.00x (ISBN 0-677-10815-X). Gordon.

Foss. Basic Metallurgy. Date not set. text ed. price not set (ISBN 0-685-67274-3). Bennett IL.

Frier, William T. Elementary Metallurgy. 2nd ed. (Illus.). 1952. text ed. 17.95 (ISBN 0-07-022419-6, G). McGraw.

Gaskell, David R. Metallurgical Thermodynamics. 2nd ed. (Materials Engineering Ser.). 560p. 1981. text ed. 29.95 (ISBN 0-07-022946-5); solutions manual 11.95 (ISBN 0-07-022947-3). McGraw.

Geiger, G. H. & Poirier, D. R. Transport Phenomena in Metallurgy. LC 75-164648. 1973. text ed. 27.95 (ISBN 0-201-02352-0). A-W.

Gilchrist, J. D. Extraction Metallurgy. 2nd ed. 1978. 50.00 (ISBN 0-08-021711-7); pap. 17.00 (ISBN 0-08-021712-5). Pergamon.

Goodenough, J. B., ed. Metal Complexes. (Structure & Bonding Ser.: Vol. 44). (Illus.). 202p. 1981. 56.70 (ISBN 0-387-10494-1). Springer-Verlag.

Gordon & Breach. Metallurgical Principles for Engineers. 5th ed. 1962. pap. 9.95 (ISBN 0-592-04707-5). Butterworth.

Habashi, F. Progress in Extractive Metallurgy Series, Vol. 1. 248p. 1973. 52.25 (ISBN 0-677-12220-9). Gordon.

--Progress in Extractive Metallurgy Series, Vol. 2. 1981. write for info. (ISBN 0-677-15730-4). Gordon.

Habashi, Fathi. Chalcopyrite: Its Chemistry & Metallurgy. (Illus.). 1978. text ed. 25.95x (ISBN 0-07-025383-8, C). McGraw.

--General Principles. (Principles of Extractive Metallurgy Ser.: Vol. 1). 424p. 1970. 62.25 (ISBN 0-677-01770-7). Gordon.

Hall, Eugene J. The Language of Mining & Metallurgy in English. (English for Careers Ser.). (gr. 10 up). 1978. pap. text ed. 3.50 (ISBN 0-88345-332-0). Regents Pub.

Hanes, H. D., et al. Hot Isostatic Processing. (Metals & Ceramics Information Ctr. Ser. (Mcic)). (Illus.). 104p. 1979. 31.00 (ISBN 0-935470-03-4). Battelle.

Higgins, G. & Thomas, V. The Principles of Metallurgical Structures. write for info. Pergamon.

Hoek, E. & Bray, J. W. Rock Slope Engineering. 2nd ed. 402p. 1980. 60.00x (ISBN 0-900488-36-0, Pub. by Inst Mining England). State Mutual Bk.

Hornbogen, E. & Zum-Gahr, K. H., eds. Metallurgical Aspects of Wear. 380p. 1981. 65.00 (ISBN 0-686-30010-6, Pub. by DGM Metallurgy Germany); pre-pub price 55.00 (ISBN 0-686-30011-4). IR Pubns.

Hoyt, Samuel L. Men of Metals. 1979. 18.00 (ISBN 0-87170-059-X). ASM.

Hyslop, Marjorie R. A Brief Guide to Sources of Metals Information. LC 72-87893. (Illus.). ix, 180p. 1973. text ed. 6.00 (ISBN 0-87815-008-0). Info Resources.

Institution Of Metallurgists. Progress in Metallurgical Technology. (Illus.). 1960. 15.00x (ISBN 0-677-60150-6). Gordon.

Instrumentation in the ISA Mining & Metallurgy Industries, 3rd, Duluth, 1974. Proceedings, Vol. 2. LC 73-82889. (Illus.). 83p. pap. 10.00 (ISBN 0-87664-251-2, MM2). Instru Soc.

Interfacial Segregation. Johnson, W. C., ed. 1979. 58.00 (ISBN 0-87170-004-2). ASM.

International Tailing Symposium Second, Denver, Colorado, 1978. Tailing Disposal Today: Proceedings, Vol. 2. Argall, George O., Jr., ed. LC 73-78129. (A World Mining Book). (Illus.). 600p. 1979. 37.50 (ISBN 0-87930-106-6). Miller Freeman.

Japanese Standards Association. JIS Handbook: Ferrous Materials & Metallurgy. 1143p. 1973. pap. 37.50x (ISBN 0-8002-1617-2). Intl Pubns Serv.

--JIS Handbook: Non-Ferrous Metals & Metallurgy. 1194p. 1976. pap. 37.50x (ISBN 0-8002-1618-0). Intl Pubns Serv.

Jeffes, J. H. & Tait, R. J., eds. Physical Chemistry of Process Metallurgy: The Richardson Conference. 266p. 1980. 100.00x (ISBN 0-900488-22-0, Pub. by Inst Mining England). State Mutual Bk.

Johnson, Carl G. & Weeks, William R. Metallurgy. 5th ed. (Illus.). 1977. text ed. 15.00 (ISBN 0-8269-3482-X); student guide 4.60 (ISBN 0-8269-3484-6). Am Technical.

Jones, M. J., ed. Commonwealth Mining & Metallurgical Congress, Hong Kong, 1978, Eleventh: Proceedings. 818p. 1980. 80.00x (ISBN 0-900488-45-X, Pub. by Inst Mining England). State Mutual Bk.

--Complex Metallurgy 1978. 143p. 1980. 100.00x (ISBN 0-900488-42-5, Pub. by Inst Mining England). State Mutual Bk.

--Process Engineering of Pyrometallurgy. 105p. 1980. 50.00x (ISBN 0-900488-23-9, Pub. by Inst Mining England). State Mutual Bk.

Kovacs, T. Principles of X-Ray Metallurgy. LC 73-81852. 185p. 1969. 24.50 (ISBN 0-306-30414-7, Plenum Pr). Plenum Pub.

Kubaschewski, O. Metallurgical Thermochemistry. 5th ed. 1979. text ed. 75.00 (ISBN 0-08-020897-5); pap. text ed. 28.00 (ISBN 0-08-022107-6). Pergamon.

Kuczynski, ed. Sintering Processes. (Materials Sciences Research Ser.: Vol. 13). 585p. 1980. 55.00 (ISBN 0-306-40336-6, Plenum Pr). Plenum Pub.

Leslie, William C. The Physical Metallurgy of Steels. (M-H Materials Science & Engineering Ser.). 368p. 1981. text ed. 34.50 (ISBN 0-07-037780-4). McGraw.

Lifshits, I. M., et al, eds. Electron Theory of Metals. LC 79-188919. (Illus.). 320p. 1973. 45.00 (ISBN 0-306-10873-9, Consultants). Plenum Pub.

Linnert, G. E. Welding Metallurgy, 2 vols. Vol. 1-fundamentals. 15.00 (ISBN 0-685-65961-5); Vol. 2-technology. 20.00 (ISBN 0-685-65962-3). Am Welding.

McCall, R., ed. Microstructural Science, Vol. 1. 1974. 45.00 (ISBN 0-444-00141-7, North Holland). Elsevier.

Mander, M. R. & Pargeter, F. W. Metals & Alloys. 1974. pap. text ed. 5.00x (ISBN 0-435-65966-9); tchr's guide 5.00x (ISBN 0-435-65967-7). Heinemann Ed.

Martin, J. W. & Hull, R. A. Elementary Science of Metals. LC 73-75479. (Wykeham Science Ser.: No. 1). 1974. 9.95x (ISBN 0-8448-1103-3). Crane Russak Co.

Metals for Engineering Craftsmen. 1980. 30.00x (ISBN 0-686-75587-1, Pub. by CoSira Pubns). State Mutual Bk.

Metzbower, Edward A., ed. Applications of Lasers in Materials Processing. 1979. 32.00 (ISBN 0-87170-084-0). ASM.

Miller, J. D., ed. Microbiological Aspects of Metallurgy. 1971. 24.95 (ISBN 0-444-19645-5). Elsevier.

Mitgutsch, Ali. From Ore to Spoon. LC 80-28862. (Carolrhoda Start to Finish Bks.). Orig. Title: Vom Erz Zum Loffel. (Illus.). 24p. (ps-3). 1981. PLB 5.95 (ISBN 0-87614-161-0). Carolrhoda Bks.

Moffatt, William G. Handbook of Binary Phase Diagrams, 3 vols. (Illus.). 1030p. 1981. 175.00 (ISBN 0-931690-00-5). GE Tech Marketing.

--The Index to Binary Phase Collections. 1980. 85.00 (ISBN 0-931690-12-9). GE Tech Marketing.

Molten Salt Electrolysis in Metal Production. 1980. 59.00x (ISBN 0-900488-39-5, Pub. by Inst Mining England). State Mutual Bk.

Moore. Principles of Chemical Metallurgy. 1981. text ed. 48.95 (ISBN 0-408-00567-X); pap. text ed. 24.95 (ISBN 0-408-00430-4). Butterworth.

Mueller, William M. & Shaw, Milton C., eds. Energetics in Metallurgical Phenomena, 4 Vols. Vol. 1, 1965. 87.50x (ISBN 0-677-00570-9); Vol. 2 1965. 45.25x (ISBN 0-677-01010-9); Vol. 3 1967. 45.25x (ISBN 0-677-11120-7); Vol. 4 1968. 83.75x (ISBN 0-677-11680-2). Gordon.

Mulholland, James A. A History of Metals in Colonial America. LC 80-15130. (Illus.). xiv, 215p. 1981. text ed. 17.50x (ISBN 0-8173-0052-X); pap. text ed. 8.95x (ISBN 0-8173-0053-8). U of Ala Pr.

Mullins, W. & Shaw, M. C. Metal Transformations. 1968. 63.75x (ISBN 0-677-10900-8). Gordon.

Murr, Lawrence E. Interfacial Phenomena in Metals & Alloys. 400p. 1975. text ed. 24.50 (ISBN 0-201-04884-1); pap. text ed. 14.50 (ISBN 0-201-04885-X). A-W.

Murr, Lawrence E., et al, eds. Metallurgical Applications of Bacterial Leaching & Related Microbiological Phenomena. 1978. 42.00 (ISBN 0-12-511150-9). Acad Pr.

Nabarro, F. R. N., ed. Dislocations in Metallurgy. (Dislocations in Solids Ser.: Vol. IV). 464p. 1979. 88.00 (ISBN 0-444-85025-2, North Holland). Elsevier.

Neely, John. Practical Metallurgy & Materials of Industry. LC 78-19166. 1979. text ed. 23.95 (ISBN 0-471-02962-9); tchrs. manual o.p. avail. (ISBN 0-471-05121-7). Wiley.

Newton, J. Extractive Metallurgy. 532p. 1959. 33.95x (ISBN 0-471-63591-X). Wiley.

Nutt, Merle C. Metallurgy & Plastics for Engineers. LC 76-19249. 1977. text ed. 35.00 (ISBN 0-08-021684-6). Pergamon.

Parker, R. H. An Introduction to Chemical Metallurgy: In SI-Metric Units. 2nd ed. 1978. text ed. 52.00 (ISBN 0-08-022125-4); pap. text ed. 14.00 (ISBN 0-08-022126-2). Pergamon.

Pehlke, R. M. Unit Processes of Extractive Metallurgy. 1973. 22.95 (ISBN 0-444-00130-1). Elsevier.

Plansee Seminar De Re Metallica - 3rd - Reutte - 1958. Lectures Held at the Third Plansee Seminar. Benesovsky, F., ed. (Illus.). 465p. 1959. pap. 29.00 (ISBN 0-387-80520-6). Springer Verlag.

Pollack. Material Science & Metallurgy. 3rd ed. (Illus.). 416p. 1980. text ed. 21.95 (ISBN 0-8359-4280-5). Reston.

--Materials Science & Metallurgy. 2nd ed. 1977. text ed. 18.95 (ISBN 0-87909-480-X); students manual avail. Reston.

Pryor, E. J. Mineral Processing. 3rd ed. (Illus.). 1974. Repr. of 1965 ed. 63.50x (ISBN 0-444-20010-X). Intl Ideas.

Recent Advances in Mining & Processing of Low-Grade Submarginal Mineral Deposits. LC 76-11771. 1977. text ed. 25.00 (ISBN 0-08-021051-1). Pergamon.

Rhines, Frederick N. Phase Diagrams in Metallurgy: Their Development & Applications. 1956. text ed. 23.00 (ISBN 0-07-052070-4, C). McGraw.

Rigney, D. A. & Glaeser, W. A., eds. Source Book on Wear Control Technology. 1978. 38.00 (ISBN 0-87170-028-X). ASM.

Ritcey, G. M. & Ashbrook, A. W. Solvent Extraction: Priciples & Applications to Process Metallurgy, Pt. II. (Process Metallurgy Ser.: Vol. 1). 1979. 95.25 (ISBN 0-444-41771-0). Elsevier.

Rohde, R. W., ed. Metallurgical Effects at High Strain Rates. 700p. 1973. 55.00 (ISBN 0-306-30754-5, Plenum Pr). Plenum Pub.

Rollason, E. C. Metallurgy for Engineers. 4th ed. (Illus.). 1973. pap. 18.95x (ISBN 0-7131-3282-5). Intl Ideas.

Rosenqvist, Terkel. Principles of Extractive Metallurgy. (Illus.). 576p. 1974. text ed. 25.00 (ISBN 0-07-053847-6, C); solutions manual 2.50 (ISBN 0-07-053848-4). McGraw.

Rubin, A. J. Aqueous-Environmental Chemistry of Metals. LC 74-78805. (Illus.). 400p. 1976. 36.00 (ISBN 0-250-40060-X). Ann Arbor Science.

Rudman, Jack. Metallurgist. (Career Examination Ser.: C-496). (Cloth bdg. avail. on request). pap. 8.00 (ISBN 0-8373-0496-2). Natl Learning.

Samsonov, G. V. & Kislyi, P. S. High-Temperature Non-Metallic Thermocouples & Sheaths. LC 65-26628. 133p. 1967. 29.50 (ISBN 0-306-10765-1, Consultants). Plenum Pub.

Sastry, K. V., ed. Agglomeration Seventy-Seven. LC 76-58569. (Illus.). 1977. text ed. 35.00x (ISBN 0-89520-045-7). Soc Mining Eng.

Schuhmann, R. Metallurgical Engineering Vol. 1. Engineering Principles. (Illus.). 1952. 22.95 (ISBN 0-201-06770-6). A-W.

Shchelov, A. Fundamentals of Metallogenic Analysis. 335p. 1979. 9.60 (ISBN 0-8285-1526-3, Pub. by Mir Pubs Russia). Imported Pubns.

Shrager, Arthur M. Elementary Metallurgy & Metallography. 2nd ed. (Illus.). 1961. pap. text ed. 5.00 (ISBN 0-486-60138-2). Dover.

--Elementary Metallurgy & Metallography. (Illus.). 7.50 (ISBN 0-8446-2934-0). Peter Smith.

Sixth Mining & Metallurgy Instrumentation Symposium November 2-4, 1977, Salt Lake City. Instrumentation in the Mining & Metallurgy Industries: Proceedings, Vol. 5. Kurzinski, E. F., ed. LC 73-82889. (Illus.). 1977. 20.00 (ISBN 0-87664-368-3). Instru Soc.

Slater, R. A. Engineering Plasticity: Theory & Its Application to Metal Forming, Processes. LC 73-10606. 1977. text ed. 48.95 (ISBN 0-470-79647-2). Halsted Pr.

Smith, Norman F. Inside Story of Metal. LC 77-10768. (Illus.). 192p. (gr. 7 up). 1977. PLB 7.79 (ISBN 0-671-32860-3). Messner.

Sohn, H. Y. & Wadsworth, M. E., eds. Rate Processes of Extractive Metallurgy. (Illus.). 430p. 1978. 42.50 (ISBN 0-306-31102-X, Plenum Pr). Plenum Pub.

Spalding, D. Brian & Afgan, Naim H., eds. Heat & Mass Transfer in Metallurgical Systems. LC 80-27193. (International Center for Heat & Mass Transfer Ser.). (Illus.). 758p. 1981. text ed. 85.50 (ISBN 0-89116-169-4). Hemisphere Pub.

Stevenson, E. J. Extractive Metallurgy: Recent Advances. LC 77-77021. (Chemical Technology Review Ser.: No. 93). (Illus.). 1977. 39.00 (ISBN 0-8155-0668-6). Noyes.

Szekely, Julian & Themelis, Nickolas J. Rate Phenomena in Process Metallurgy. LC 72-140554. 784p. 1971. 57.00 (ISBN 0-471-84303-2, Pub. by Wiley-Interscience). Wiley.

Taubenblat, Pierre W. Copper Base Powder Metallurgy. LC 80-81464. (New Perspectives in Powder Metallurgy Ser.: Vol. 7). (Illus.). 232p. 1980. 42.00 (ISBN 0-918404-47-9). Metal Powder.

Tomlenov, A. D., ed. Plastic Flow of Metals, Vol. 2. LC 75-131886. 94p. 1972. 25.00 (ISBN 0-306-17162-7, Consultants). Plenum Pub.

Upadhyaya, G. S & Dube, R. K. Problems in Metallurgical Thermodynamics & Kinetics. LC 77-7376. 1977. text ed. 26.00 (ISBN 0-08-020865-7); pap. text ed. 14.50 (ISBN 0-08-020864-9). Pergamon.

Vogel, F. L., Jr., ed. Resonance & Relaxation in Metals. 2nd rev. ed. 423p. 1964. 42.50 (ISBN 0-306-30183-0, Plenum Pr). Plenum Pub.

Volsky, A. & Sergievskaya, E. Theory of Metallurgical Processes. 1978. 10.00 (ISBN 0-8285-1926-9, Pub. by Mir Pubs Russia). Imported Pubns.

Warner, J. C., et al, eds. Metallurgy of Uranium & Its Aloys. (National Nuclear Energy Ser.: Div. IV, Vol. 12). 208p. 1953. write for info.; microfilm 10.00 (ISBN 0-686-75855-2). DOE.

Waseda, Yoshio. The Structure of Non-Crystalline Materials. (Illus.). 304p. 1980. text ed. 44.50 (ISBN 0-07-068426-X, C). McGraw.

Webster, D. & London, G., eds. Beryllium Science & Technology, 2 vols. (Illus.). 1979. Vol. 1, 475p. 49.50 (ISBN 0-306-40106-1, Plenum Pr); Vol. 2. 49.50 (ISBN 0-306-40136-3). Plenum Pub.

Weinberg, F., ed. Tools & Techniques in Physical Metallurgy, Vol. 1. 1970. 59.00 (ISBN 0-8247-1764-3). Dekker.

Weiss, Alfred, ed. World Mining & Metals Technology. LC 76-19748. (Illus.). 1976. text ed. 35.00x (ISBN 0-89520-036-8). Soc Mining Eng.

Westwood, W. & Cooper, B. S. Analytical Methods in Use in Non-Ferrous Mining & Metallurgy: A Selective Review. 54p. 1980. 25.00x (ISBN 0-686-71769-4, Pub. by Inst Mining England). State Mutual Bk.

Wilkes, P. Solid State Theory in Metallurgy. LC 72-180020. (Illus.). 480p. (Orig.). 1973. 68.50 (ISBN 0-521-08454-7); pap. 19.95x (ISBN 0-521-09699-5). Cambridge U Pr.

Winkler, O. & Bakish, R. Vacuum Metallurgy. LC 74-118258. (Illus.). 906p. 1971. 134.25 (ISBN 0-444-40857-6). Elsevier.

Wohlrabe, Raymond A. Metals. LC 64-19046. (Introducing Modern Science Books Ser). (Illus.). (gr. 7-9). 1964. 8.95 (ISBN 0-397-30764-0). Lippincott.

Yemel'Yanov, V. S. & Yevstyukhin, A. I., eds. Metallurgy & Metallography of Pure Metals. 1962. 74.75x (ISBN 0-677-20530-9). Gordon.

METALLURGY-AUTOMATION

see Metallurgical Plants-Automation

METALLURGY-BIBLIOGRAPHY

Spande, Dennis, compiled by. A Historical Perspective on Metallurgy: A Bibliography. (Archival & Bibliographic Ser.). 1978. pap. 10.00 (ISBN 0-918456-13-4, Crossroads). African Studies Assn.

METALLURGY-DICTIONARIES

Bader, Oliver & Theret, Michel. Diccionario Enciclopedico de Metalurgia. 960p. (Span., Fr. & Eng.). 1975. 44.95 (ISBN 84-7146-054-8, S-50132). French & Eur.

Cagnacci & Schwicker, A. International Dictionary of Metallurgy, Mineralogy, Geology & the Mining Oil Industries. (Eng, Ger, Fr, Ital.). 1970. 54.50 (ISBN 0-07-009580-9, P&RB). McGraw.

Cagnacci-Schwicker, Angelo. Dictionnaire International de Metallurgie, Mineralogie, Geologie et Industries Extractives, 2 vols. 1530p. (Fr.). 1969. Set. 95.00 (ISBN 0-686-56933-4, M-6054). French & Eur.

Clason, W. E. Elsevier's Dictionary of Metallurgy & Metal Working. (Eng, Fr, Sp, It, Dutch, & Ger.). 1978. 144.00 (ISBN 0-444-41695-1). Elsevier.

Deruguine, Tanya. Russian-English Dictionary of Metallurgy & Allied Sciences. 18.00 (ISBN 0-8044-4185-5). Ungar.

Gagnacci-Schwicker, A. & Schwicker. International Dictionary of Metallurgy, Mineralogy, Geology and the Mining and Oil Industries. 1530p. (Eng., Fr., Ger. & It.). 1970. 88.00 (ISBN 3-7625-0751-1, M-7482, Pub. by Bauverlag). French & Eur.

Tottle, C. R. Encyclopedia of Metallurgy & Materials. 512p. 1980. 54.00x (ISBN 0-686-71794-5, Pub. by Macdonald & Evans). State Mutual Bk.

Woerterbuch Fuer Metallurgie, Mineralogie, Geologie, Bergbau und die Oelindustrie. (Eng. , Fr. , Ger. & It., Dictionary of Metallurgy, Mineralogy, Geology, Mining and Oil Industry). 1970. 88.00 (ISBN 3-7625-0751-1, M-6912). French & Eur.

METALLURGY-EARLY WORKS TO 1800

Agricola, Georgius. De Re Metallica. (Illus.). 1912. 17.95 (ISBN 0-486-60006-8). Dover.

Biringuccio, Vannoccio. Pirotechnia. 1966. pap. 4.95x (ISBN 0-262-52017-6). MIT Pr.

METALLURGY-HISTORY

Conference at Dumbarton Oaks, October 18 & 19, 1975. Pre-Columbian Metallurgy of South-America: Proceedings. Benson, Elizabeth P., ed. LC 79-49261. (Illus.). 107p. 1979. 20.00x (ISBN 0-88402-094-0, Ctr Pre-Columbian). Dumbarton Oaks.

Healy, J. F. Mining & Metallurgy in the Greek & Roman World. (Aspects of Greek & Roman Life Ser.). (Illus.). 1978. 19.95 (ISBN 0-500-40035-0). Thames Hudson.

Parr, James G. Man, Metals, & Modern Magic. LC 77-25186. 1978. Repr. of 1958 ed. lib. bdg. 22.25x (ISBN 0-313-20122-6, PAMM). Greenwood.

METALLURGY-LABORATORY MANUALS

Ormandy, P. G. An Introduction to Metallurgical Laboratory Techniques. LC 68-18530. 1968. 11.25 (ISBN 0-08-012560-3). Pergamon.

Selected ASTM Standards for Metallurgy Students. 1965. pap. 2.00 (ISBN 0-8031-0027-2, 03-000365-00). ASTM.

METALLURGY, PHYSICAL

see Physical Metallurgy

METALLURGY, POWDER

see Powder Metallurgy

METALLURGY, VACUUM

see Vacuum Metallurgy

METALORGANIC COMPOUNDS

see Organometallic Compounds

METALS

see also Alloys; Assaying; Earths, Rare; Free Electron Theory of Metals; Intermetallic Compounds; Light Metals; Liquid Metals; Metallic Composites; Metallic Films; Metallic Oxides; Metallography; Mineralogy; Nonferrous Metals; Passivity (Chemistry); Precious Metals; Semimetals; Solder and Soldering; Transition Metals

also particular metals and metal groups, e.g. Iron

Abrikosov, A. A. Introduction to the Theory of Normal Metals. (Solid State Physics: Suppl. 12). 1972. 49.50 (ISBN 0-12-607772-X). Acad Pr.

American Bureau of Metal Statistics Inc. ABMS Non-Ferrous Metal Data Publication. annual ed. 1978. 25.00 (ISBN 0-685-91837-8). Am Bur Metal.

American Bureau of Metal Statistics Editorial Staff, ed. Fifty-Second Annual Yearbook. 1973. 25.00 (ISBN 0-685-39802-1). Am Bur Metal.

American Bureau of Metal Statistics Inc. Non-Ferrous Metal Data Yearbook, 1979. (Illus.). 1980. yrbk. 25.00 (ISBN 0-686-61434-8). Am Bur Metal.

American Bureau of Metal Statistics Staff, compiled by. Year Book of the American Bureau of Metal Statistics. annual 1972. 25.00 (ISBN 0-910064-05-9). Am Bur Metal.

--Year Book of the American Bureau of Metal Statistics. LC 21-15719. 1973. 25.00 (ISBN 0-910064-06-7). Am Bur Metal.

American Society Of Mechanical Engineers. ASME Handbook: Metals Engineering-Design. 2nd ed. 1964. 53.50 (ISBN 0-07-001518-X, P&RB). McGraw.

--ASME Handbook: Metals Properties. (Illus.). 1956. 38.50 (ISBN 0-07-001513-9, P&RB). McGraw.

American Welding Society. Filler Metal Comparison Charts: A5.0. 5th ed. LC 78-54738. 1978. pap. 15.00 (ISBN 0-87171-156-7). Am Welding.

Avitzur. Metal Forming. (Manufacturing, Engineering, & Materials Processing Ser.: Vol. 4). 224p. 1980. 29.50 (ISBN 0-8247-6847-7). Dekker.

Basolo, Fred & Pearson, R. G. Mechanisms of Inorganic Reactions. 2nd ed. LC 66-28755. 701p. 1967. 45.00 (ISBN 0-471-05545-X, Pub. by Wiley-Interscience). Wiley.

BCC Staff. Major Metals & Metal Substitutes, GB-019. 1978. 550.00 (ISBN 0-89336-084-8). BCC.

Beck, H. & Gundtherodt, H. J., eds. Classy Metals, Vol. 1. (Topics in Applied Physics Ser.: Vol. 46). (Illus.). 350p. 1981. 48.00 (ISBN 0-387-10440-2). Springer-Verlag.

--Glassy Metals I. (Topics in Applied Physics: Vol. 46). (Illus.). 350p. 1981. 48.00 (ISBN 0-387-10440-2). Springer-Verlag.

Beer, S., ed. Liquid Metals: Chemistry & Physics. (Monographs & Textbks in Material Science: Vol. 4). 784p. 1972. 75.00 (ISBN 0-8247-1032-0). Dekker.

Blatt, J., et al. Thermoelectric Power of Metals. (Illus.). 264p. 1976. 32.50 (ISBN 0-306-30907-6, Plenum Pr). Plenum Pub.

Brandt, N. B. & Chudinov, S. M. Electronic Structure of Metals. 336p. 1973. 5.75 (ISBN 0-8285-0778-3, Pub. by Mir Pubs Russia). Imported Pubns.

Bunshah, R. F., ed. Techniques of Metals Research, Vol. 1. 802p. 1968. 51.00 (ISBN 0-470-12197-1, Pub. by Wiley). Krieger.

--Techniques of Metals Research, Vol. 2, Pt. 2. 502p. 1981. Repr. of 1968 ed. write for info. (ISBN 0-89874-306-0). Krieger.

--Techniques of Metals Research, Vol. 5, Pt. 2. 1981. Repr. of 1970 ed. write for info. (ISBN 0-89874-308-7). Krieger.

--Techniques of Metals Research: Techniques for the Direct Observation of Structure & Imperfections, Vol. 2, Pt. 1. LC 80-27162. 497p. 1981. Repr. of 1968 ed. write for info. (ISBN 0-89874-305-2). Krieger.

--Techniques of Metals Research: Techniques Involving Extreme Environment, Nondestructive Techniques, Computer Methods in Metals Research, & Data Analysis, Vol. 7, Pt. 2. 427p. 1976. 53.50 (ISBN 0-471-12241-6). Krieger.

--Techniques of Metals Research: Techniques of Material Preparation & Handling, Vol. 1, Pt 1. 385p. 1968. 28.00 (ISBN 0-470-12195-5). Krieger.

Bunshaw, R. F., ed. Techniques of Metals Research: Measurement of Mechanical Properties, Vol. 5, Pt. 1. LC 80-26986. 474p. 1981. Repr. of 1970 ed. write for info. (ISBN 0-89874-307-9). Krieger.

Burke, John J. & Weiss, Volker, eds. Ultrafine-Grain Metals. (Sagamore Army Materials Research Conference Proceedings Ser.: Vol. 16). 442p. 1970. 35.00 (ISBN 0-306-34516-1, Plenum Pr). Plenum Pub.

Carlin, Richard L., ed. Transition Metal Chemistry: A Series of Advances, Vol. 1. 1966. 39.75 (ISBN 0-8247-1076-2). Dekker.

Chalmers, Bruce. Principles of Solidification. LC 76-18772. 336p. 1977. Repr. of 1964 ed. 16.95 (ISBN 0-88275-446-7). Krieger.

Chisholm, Malcolm, ed. Reactivity of Metal-Metal Bonds. LC 81-361. (ACS Symposium Ser.: No. 155). 1981. 39.00 (ISBN 0-8412-0624-4). Am Chemical.

Cookson, William. Advanced Methods for Sheet Metal Work. 6th ed. (Illus.). 1975. 21.00x (ISBN 0-291-39427-2). Intl Ideas.

Coqblin, B. The Electronic Structure of Rare-Earth Metals & Alloys: The Magnetic Heavy Rare-Earths. 1978. 100.50 (ISBN 0-12-188150-4). Acad Pr.

Cotterill, P. & Mould, P. R. Recrystallization & Grain Growth in Metals. LC 75-33874. 1976. 38.95 (ISBN 0-470-17527-3). Halsted Pr.

Darken, Lawrence S. & Gurry, R. W. Physical Chemistry of Metals. (Metallurgy & Metallurgical Engineering Ser.). 1953. text ed. 25.95 (ISBN 0-07-015355-8, C). McGraw.

De, Anil K., et al. Solvent Extraction of Metals. 1970. 19.50x (ISBN 0-442-22065-0). Van Nos Reinhold.
Dickson, H., et al, eds. Thin Plate Working, Vol. 1. 2nd ed. (Illus.). 1977. 15.95x (ISBN 0-686-65561-3). Vol. 1 (ISBN 0-85083-387-6). Vol. 2 (ISBN 0-85083-047-8). Intl Ideas.
Din Standards: International Comparison of Standard-Materials--Steel & Cast Iron. 90.00 (ISBN 0-686-28196-9, 11131-X). Heyden.
Din Standards: Metallic Cast Materials: Standards on Quality Specifications, Dimensional Variations, Test Methods. 292.00 (ISBN 0-686-28188-8, 10708-3/53). Heyden.
D'Isa, Frank A. Mechanics of Metals. 1968. 20.95 (ISBN 0-201-01550-1). A-W.
Doyle, L. E., et al. Manufacturing Processes & Materials for Engineers. 2nd ed. 1969. text ed. 26.95 (ISBN 0-13-555862-X). P-H.
Drucker, Harvey & Wildung, Robert E. Biological Implications of Metals in the Environment. LC 77-1039. (ERDA Symposium Ser.). 692p. 1977. pap. 12.50 (ISBN 0-686-75775-0); microfiche 3.00 (ISBN 0-686-75776-9). DOE.
Dugdale, J. S. Electrical Properties of Metals & Alloys. (Structures & Properties of Solids: No. 5). (Illus.). 1978. 27.95x (ISBN 0-7131-2523-3, Pub. by Edward Arnold); pap. 12.95x (ISBN 0-7131-2524-1, Pub. by Edward Arnold). Intl Schol Bk Serv.
Espe, W. Materials of Vacuum Technology, 3 vols. Incl. Vol. 1. Metals & Metalloids. 1966. text ed. 77.50 (ISBN 0-08-010862-8); Vol. 2. Silicates & Oxides. 1968; Vol. 3. Auxiliary Materials. 1968. text ed. 67.50 (ISBN 0-08-013224-3). Pergamon.
European Metals Directory. 2nd ed. 770p. 1971. 27.50x (ISBN 0-900542-04-7). Intl Pubns Serv.
Fast, Johan D. Interaction of Metals & Gases, Vol. 1. Thermodynamics & Phase Relations. 1965. 49.50 (ISBN 0-12-249801-1). Acad Pr.
Ferreira, R., et al. Less Abundant Metals. LC 67-11280. (Structure & Bonding Ser.: Vol. 31). (Illus.). 1976. 23.10 (ISBN 0-387-07964-5). Springer-Verlag.
Formatibility Topics: Metallic Materials. 1978. 27.75 (ISBN 0-686-52059-9, 04-647000-23). ASTM.
Furrer, A., ed. Crystal Field Effects in Metals & Alloys. LC 76-55802. 365p. 1977. 45.00 (ISBN 0-306-31008-2, Plenum Pr). Plenum Pub.
Grant, Nicholas J. & Giessen, Bill C., eds. Rapidly Quenched Metals. 1976. text ed. 30.00x (ISBN 0-262-07066-9). MIT Pr.
Haasen, P., et al, eds. Strength of Metals & Alloys: International Conference on the Strength of Metals & Alloys, 5th, Aachen, 1979, 3 vols. LC 79-40131. (Illus.). 1980. Set. 260.00 (ISBN 0-08-023265-5). Pergamon.
Hampel, Clifford A., ed. Rare Metal Handbook. 2nd ed. LC 61-10449. 732p. 1971. Repr. of 1961 ed. 37.50 (ISBN 0-88275-024-0). Krieger.
Harrison, Walter A. Pseudopotentials in the Theory of Metals. (Frontiers in Physics Ser.: No. 25). 1966. 12.50 (ISBN 0-8053-3731-8, Adv Bk Prog). Benjamin-Cummings.
Hauffe, Karl. Oxidation of Metals. LC 63-17648. 452p. 1965. 45.00 (ISBN 0-306-30200-4, Plenum Pr). Plenum Pub.
Hawkins, Clifford. Absolute Configuration of Metal Complexes. 349p. 1971. 31.00 (ISBN 0-471-36280-8, Pub. by Wiley). Krieger.
Hehner, Nels E. & Ritchie, Everett J. Grid Metal Manual for Storage Batteries. (Avail. in eng. & span.). 1973. 15.00 (ISBN 0-685-56652-8). IBMA Pubns.
Hoffmanner, A. L., ed. Metal Forming: Interrelation Between Theory & Practice. LC 70-171698. 503p. 1971. 49.50 (ISBN 0-306-30554-2, Plenum Pr). Plenum Pub.
Hurd, C. M. Electrons in Metals. LC 80-11429. 344p. 1981. Repr. of 1975 ed. lib. bdg. write for info. (ISBN 0-89874-157-2). Krieger.
International School of Physics "Enrico Fermi" Course LXI, Varenna, July 8-20, 1974. Atomic Structure & Mechanical Properties of Metals: Proceedings. Caglioti, G., ed. 1976. 112.25 (ISBN 0-7204-0490-8, North-Holland); by subscription 86.75 (ISBN 0-685-74299-7). Elsevier.
Johnson. Technical Metals. (gr. 9-12). 1981. text ed. 20.20 (ISBN 0-87002-313-6); wkbk. 3.44 (ISBN 0-87002-322-5). Bennett IL.
Jolly, William L., ed. Metal Ammonia Solutions. LC 72-80134. (Benchmark Papers in Inorganic Chemistry Ser.). 1972. 47.00 (ISBN 0-12-786785-6). Acad Pr.
Jones, M. J. Advances in Extractive Metallurgy & Refining. 635p. 1980. 75.00x (ISBN 0-900488-06-9, Pub. by Inst Mining England). State Mutual Bk.
--Advances in Extractive Metallurgy 1977. 244p. 1980. 75.00x (ISBN 0-900488-37-9, Pub. by Inst Mining England). State Mutual Bk.
Kazanas, H. C. Properties & Uses of Ferrous & Nonferrous Metals. rev. ed. LC 78-70035. (Illus.). 1979. pap. 4.25x (ISBN 0-911168-39-7); instrs'. guide & answer bk. 1.50x (ISBN 0-911168-40-0). Prakken.
Keller, H. J., ed. The Chemistry & Physics of One-Dimensional Metals. (NATO Advanced Study Institutes Ser. Series B: Physics, Vol. 25). 426p. 1977. 45.00 (ISBN 0-306-35725-9, Plenum Pr). Plenum Pub.
Khan, M. M. & Martell, Arthur E. Homogeneous Catalysis by Metal Complexes, 2 vols. Incl. Vol. 1. Activation of Small Inorganic Molecules. 67.00 (ISBN 0-12-406101-X); Vol. 2. Activation of Alkenes & Alkynes. 43.50 (ISBN 0-12-406102-8). 1974. 90.50 set (ISBN 0-685-72440-9). Acad Pr.
Kimura, H. & Maddin, R. Quench Hardening in Metals. LC 74-140489. (Defects in Crystalline Solids Ser.: Vol. 3). (Illus.). 133p. 1971. 19.50 (ISBN 0-444-10114-4, North-Holland). Elsevier.
Lappert, M. F., et al. Metal & Metalloid Amides: Synthesis, Structure & Physical & Chemical Properties. 1979. 149.95 (ISBN 0-470-26573-6). Halsted Pr.
Lashko, N. F. & Lashko, S. V. Soldadura Indirecta De Metales. 378p. (Span.). 1979. 10.50 (ISBN 0-8285-1488-7, Pub. by Mir Pubs Russia). Imported Pubns.
Lefax Pub. Co. Editors. Metals. (Lefax Data Bks.: No. 621). (Illus.). looseleaf bdg. 3.00 (ISBN 0-685-14158-6). Lefax.
Lifshits, I. M., et al, eds. Electron Theory of Metals. LC 79-188919. (Illus.). 320p. 1973. 45.00 (ISBN 0-306-10873-9, Consultants). Plenum Pub.
McCracken, G. M., et al, eds. Plasma Surface Interactions in Controlled Fusion Devices: Proceedings of the Third Int'l. Conference, U. K., 1978. 1978. 156.00 (ISBN 0-444-85212-3, North Holland). Elsevier.
McLean, D. Mechanical Properties of Metals. LC 75-11898. 430p. 1977. Repr. of 1962 ed. 20.50 (ISBN 0-88275-298-7). Krieger.
Malatesta, Li & Cenini, S. Zerovalent Compounds of Metals. 1975. 42.00 (ISBN 0-12-466350-8). Acad Pr.
Maniloff, Jack, et al, eds. Effects of Metals on Cells, Subcellular Elements, & Macromolecules. (Illus.). 416p. 1970. text ed. 28.75 (ISBN 0-398-01210-5). C C Thomas.
Mehrotra, R. C., et al. Metal Diketonates & Allied Deviratives. 1978. 64.50 (ISBN 0-12-488150-5). Acad Pr.
Metal Bulletin Handbook 1979. 12th ed. LC 70-2106. (Illus.). 1979. 47.50x (ISBN 0-900542-32-2). Intl Pubns Serv.
Metal Statistics. (Illus.). 1980. 35.00 (ISBN 0-87005-240-3). Am Metal Mkt.
Metals for Engineering Craftsmen. 1980. 30.00x (ISBN 0-686-75587-1, Pub. by CoSira Pubns). State Mutual Bk.
Metals Handbook, Properties & Selection: Nonferrous Alloys & Pure Metals. 1979. 62.00 (ISBN 0-87170-008-5). ASM.
MiCon Seventy-Eight: Optimization of Processing, Properties & Service Performance Through Microstructural Control. (Special Technical Publications Ser.). 677p. 1979. 59.50x (ISBN 0-686-76058-1, 672, 04-672000-28). ASTM.
Miller, Rex & Morrisey, Thomas J. Metal Technology. LC 74-77817. 1976. 16.50 (ISBN 0-672-97623-4); tchr's guide 3.33 (ISBN 0-672-97625-0); lab bk. 3.95 (ISBN 0-672-97624-2). Bobbs.
Mott, Nevill F. & Jones, H. Theory of the Properties of Metals & Alloys. 1936. pap. 6.00 (ISBN 0-486-60456-X). Dover.
Mulholland, James A. A History of Metals in Colonial America. LC 80-15130. (Illus.). xiv, 215p. 1981. text ed. 17.50x (ISBN 0-8173-0052-X); pap. text ed. 8.95x (ISBN 0-8173-0053-8). U of Ala Pr.
Muns, George F. How to Find & Identify the Valuable Metals. 1977. 6.95 (ISBN 0-8059-2390-X). Dorrance.
Parish, R. V. The Metallic Elements. 1977. pap. text ed. 21.00x (ISBN 0-582-44278-8). Longman.
Peckner, Donald, ed. Strengthening of Metals. 256p. 1964. 13.95 (ISBN 0-442-15534-4, Pub. by Van Nos Reinhold). Krieger.
Petty, E. R. Physical Metallurgy of Engineering Materials. (Modern Metallurgical Texts: No. 6). 1968. text ed. 16.50 (ISBN 0-444-19835-0). Elsevier.
Phipps, D. A. Metals & Metabolism, No. 26. (Oxford Chemistry Ser). (Illus.). 1976. pap. 12.50x (ISBN 0-19-855413-3). Oxford U Pr.
Potts, Daniel L. International Metallic Materials Cross Reference. 108p. 1978. 34.50 (ISBN 0-931690-09-9). GE Tech Marketing.
Quill, Lawrence L., ed. The Chemistry & Metallurgy of Miscellaneous Materials. (National Nuclear Energy Ser.: Division IV, Vol. 19c). 172p. 1955. write for info.; microfilm 10.00 (ISBN 0-686-75740-8). DOE.
Raymond, Kenneth N., ed. Bioinorganic Chemistry II. LC 77-22225. (Advances in Chemistry Ser.: No. 162). 1977. 54.50 (ISBN 0-8412-0359-8). Am Chemical.
Sarkar, A. D. Wear of Metals. 1976. 23.00 (ISBN 0-08-019738-8); pap. 11.25 (ISBN 0-08-019737-X). Pergamon.
Savitsky, Evgeny M. The Influence of Temperature on the Mechanical Properties of Metals & Alloys. Sherby, Oleg D., ed. 1961. 15.00x (ISBN 0-8047-0054-0). Stanford U Pr.
Schroeder, Henry A. The Poisons Around Us: Toxic Metals in Food, Air, & Water. LC 73-15283. 160p. 1974. 8.50x (ISBN 0-253-16675-6). Ind U Pr.
Schwarzkopf, P. Living Metals. (Illus.). 1962. 20.00 (ISBN 0-685-12028-7). Heinman.
Semerdjiev, Stefan. Metal-to-Metal Adhesive Binding. 1970. 19.00x (ISBN 0-8464-0629-2). Beekman Pubs.
Sharp, D. W. Transition Metals, Pt. 1. Emeleus, H. J., ed. (Mtp International Review of Science-Inorganic Chemistry Ser. 1: Vol. 5). (Illus.). 1972. 29.50 (ISBN 0-8391-1008-1). Univ Park.
Sittig, Marshall. Metal & Inorganic Waste Reclaiming Encyclopedia. LC 80-21669. (Pollution Tech. Rev. 70; Chem. Tech. Rev. 175). (Illus.). 591p. (Orig.). 1981. 54.00 (ISBN 0-8155-0823-9). Noyes.
Smith, Ivan C. & Carson, Bonnie L., eds. Trace Metals in the Environment, Vol. 6: Cobalt. 1172p. 1981. text ed. 49.50 (ISBN 0-250-40362-5). Ann Arbor Science.
Smith, Norman F. Inside Story of Metal. LC 77-10768. (Illus.). 192p. (gr. 7 up). 1977. PLB 7.79 (ISBN 0-671-32860-3). Messner.
Smith, Robert E. Patternmaking & Founding. (gr. 9 up). 1959. pap. 5.00 (ISBN 0-87345-020-5). McKnight.
Smithells, C. J. Metals Reference Book, 3 vols. in 1. 4th ed. LC 67-23290. 1250p. 1967. 99.50 (ISBN 0-306-65131-9). IFI Plenum.
Smithells, C. J., ed. Metals Reference Book. 5th ed. 1976. 160.00 (ISBN 0-408-70627-9). Butterworth.
Suryanarayana, C., compiled by. Rapidly Quenched Metals--a Bibliography: 1973-1979. 310p. 1980. 75.00 (ISBN 0-306-65194-7). IFI Plenum.
Szekely, Julian. Fluid Flow Phenomena in Metals Processing. 1979. 58.00 (ISBN 0-12-680840-6). Acad Pr.
Tamamushi, R. Kinetic Parameters of Electrode Reactions of Metallic Compounds. 1976. pap. 34.00 (ISBN 0-08-020991-2). Pergamon.
Taylor, R. H. Magnetic Ions in Metals: A Review of Thier Study by Electron Spin Resonance. LC 76-53798. 1977. 21.95 (ISBN 0-470-99024-4). Halsted Pr.
Toth, Louis E. Transition Metal Carbides & Nitrides. (Refractory Materials Ser.: Vol. 7). 1971. 47.00 (ISBN 0-12-695950-1). Acad Pr.
Unified Numbering System for Metals & Alloys. 1977. pap. 49.00 (ISBN 0-686-50148-9, 05-056001-01). ASTM.
Waldron, H. A. Metals in the Environment. LC 79-42814. 1980. 60.00 (ISBN 0-12-731850-X). Acad Pr.
Webster, John. Metallograph: History of Metals, Wherein Is Declared the Signs of Ores & Minerals Both Before & After Digging. LC 77-6544. (History of Geology Ser.). Repr. of 1671 ed. lib. bdg. 25.00x (ISBN 0-405-10462-6). Arno.
Wyatt, Oliver H. & Dew-Hughes, D. Metals, Ceramics & Polymers. LC 70-178286. (Illus.). 500p. 1974. 86.50 (ISBN 0-521-08238-2); pap. 24.50x (ISBN 0-521-09834-3). Cambridge U Pr.
Zener, Clarence M. Elasticity & Anelasticity of Metals. LC 48-3902. (Illus.). 1948. 9.00x (ISBN 0-226-98054-5). U of Chicago Pr.
Ziman, John M. Physics of Metals, Vol. 1: Electrons. LC 69-10436. (Illus.). 1969. 49.50 (ISBN 0-521-07106-2). Cambridge U Pr.

METALS–ANALYSIS

see also Gases in Metals

Barrett, C. S. & Massalski, T. B. Structure of Metals: Crystallographic Methods, Principles & Data. 3rd rev. ed. LC 80-49878. (International Ser. on Materials Science & Technology: Vol. 14). (Illus.). 675p. 1980. 65.00 (ISBN 0-08-026171-X); pap. 20.00 (ISBN 0-08-026172-8). Pergamon.
Bridgman, P. W. The Thermodynamics of Electrical Phenomena in Metals & a Condensed Collection of Thermodynamic Formulas. (Illus.). 8.00 (ISBN 0-8446-1737-7). Peter Smith.
Burger, K. Organic Reagents in Metal Analysis. 270p. 1973. text ed. 42.00 (ISBN 0-08-016929-5). Pergamon.
Dederichs, P. H., et al. Metals: Phonon States of Elements. Electron States & Fermi Surfaces of Alloys. Hellwege, K. H. & Olsen, J. L., eds. (Landolt-Boernstein Ser.: Vol. 13, Group III). (Illus.). 500p. 1981. 361.80 (ISBN 0-387-09774-0). Springer-Verlag.
Frei, R. W. & Hutzinger, Otto, eds. Analytical Aspects of Mercury & Other Heavy Metals in the Environment. LC 73-88229. (Current Topics in Environmental & Toxicological Chemistry Ser.). 210p. 1975. 37.50x (ISBN 0-677-15890-4). Gordon.
Harrison, P. M. & Hoare, R. J. Metals in Biochemistry. LC 79-41813. 80p. 1980. pap. 5.95 (ISBN 0-412-13160-9, 6361, Pub. by Chapman & Hall England). Methuen Inc.
Maccioli, Frank J. & Risby, Terence H. Determination of Toxic Metals & Metalloids in Ambient Air. LC 77-88470. (Penn State Studies: No. 42). (Illus.). 1978. pap. 3.95x (ISBN 0-271-00532-7). Pa St U Pr.
Quantitative Texture Analysis. 350p. 1981. 65.00 (ISBN 3-88355-032-9, Pub. by DGM Metallurgy Germany); pre-pub price 55.00 (ISBN 0-686-30012-2). IR Pubns.
Risby, Terence H., ed. Ultratrace Metal Analysis in Biological Sciences. LC 78-31903. (Advances in Chemistry Ser: No. 172). 1979. 36.50 (ISBN 0-8412-0416-0). Am Chemical.
Sandell, E. B. & Onishi, Hiroshi. Photometric Determination of Traces of Metals: General Aspects. 4th ed. LC 77-18937. (Chemical Analysis Ser.). 1978. 68.50 (ISBN 0-471-03094-5, Pub. by Wiley-Interscience). Wiley.

METALS–BIBLIOGRAPHY

American Craft Council. Metal: A Bibliography. rev. ed. 1977. 4.70 (ISBN 0-88321-037-1). Am Craft.
Suryanarayana, C. Rapidly Quenched Metals: A Bibliography, 1973-1979. 1980. 75.00 (ISBN 0-306-65194-7). Plenum Pub.

METALS–BRITTLENESS

Hydrogen Embrittlement Testing. 1974. 29.75 (ISBN 0-686-52048-3, 04-543000-26). ASTM.

METALS–CLEANING

see Metal Cleaning

METALS–COLORING

see also Metal-Work

Angier, R. H. Firearms Blueing & Browning. 160p. 1936. 9.95 (ISBN 0-686-76905-8). Stackpole.
Hiorns, Arthur H. Metal-Colouring & Bronzing. 2nd ed. LC 79-8613. Repr. of 1911 ed. 33.50 (ISBN 0-404-18477-4). AMS Pr.
Shearman, William M. Metal Alloys & Patinas for Casting: For Metalsmiths, Jewelers & Sculptors. LC 76-28729. (Illus.). 1976. pap. 6.00 (ISBN 0-87338-193-9). Kent St U Pr.

METALS–CORROSION

see Corrosion and Anti-Corrosives

METALS–CREEP

Conway, J. B. Stress-Rupture Parameters: Origin, Calculation, & Use. 1969. 63.75x (ISBN 0-677-01860-6). Gordon.
Evaluations of the Elevated Temperature Tensile & Creep Rupture Properties of 12 to 27 Percent Chromium Steels. (Data Ser.). 330p. 1980. soft cover 24.00x (ISBN 0-686-76094-8, 59, 05-059000-40). ASTM.
Rosenfield, A. R., et al, eds. Dislocation Dynamics. LC 68-11937. (Series in Materials Science & Engineering). (Illus.). 1968. text ed. 55.00 (ISBN 0-07-053807-7, P&RB). McGraw.

METALS–DEFECTS

Damask, A. C. & Dienes, G. J. Point Defects in Metals. 1963. 59.50x (ISBN 0-677-00190-8). Gordon.
Dederichs, P. H. & Zeller, R. Point Defect in Metals II: Dynamical Properties & Diffusion Controlled Reactions. (Springer Tracts in Modern Physics: Vol. 87). 1979. 39.60 (ISBN 0-387-09623-X). Springer-Verlag.
Girifalco, L. A. & Welch, D. O. Point Defects & Diffusion in Strained Metals. (Orig.). 1967. 45.25 (ISBN 0-677-01400-7). Gordon.
Head, A. K., et al. Computed Electron Micrographs & Defect Indentification. LC 72-93092. (Defects in Crystalline Solids: Vol. 7). 410p. 1975. 58.75 (ISBN 0-444-10462-3, North-Holland). Elsevier.
Hirsch, P. B. The Physics of Metals, Vol. 2: Defects. LC 74-14439. (Illus.). 304p. 1976. 68.50 (ISBN 0-521-20077-6). Cambridge U Pr.
Liebfried, G. & Breuer, N. Atomic Structure & Dynamics of Point Effects in Metals 1: Introduction to the Theory. LC 77-24475. (Springer Tracts in Modern Physics: Vol. 81). (Illus.). 1978. 51.40 (ISBN 0-387-08375-8). Springer-Verlag.
Peterson, N. L. & Siegel, R. W., eds. Properties of Atomic Defects in Metals: Proceedings of the International Conference on the Properties of Atomic Defects in Metals, Argonne, Illinois, U.S.A. 1978. 185.50 (ISBN 0-444-85146-1, North-Holland). Elsevier.
Thompson, M. W. Defects & Radiation Damage in Metals. LC 69-10434. (Cambridge Monographs on Physics). (Illus.). 1969. 60.50 (ISBN 0-521-07068-6); pap. 18.50x (ISBN 0-521-09865-3). Cambridge U Pr.

METALS–DETECTION

see Metal Detectors

METALS-DICTIONARIES

Longan, Tang & Zenglian, Ni. English-Chinese Dictionary of Metals & Their Heat Treatment. LC 81-1279. iii, 266p. 1981. pap. 24.50 (ISBN 0-8311-1081-3). Indus Pr.

Simons, Eric N. Dictionary of Ferrous Metals. (Illus.). 1971. 14.00 (ISBN 0-584-10059-0). Transatlantic.

METALS-DIFFUSION COATINGS

see Diffusion Coatings

METALS-EROSION

Characterization & Determination of Erosion Resistance. 1970. 28.75 (ISBN 0-8031-0029-9, 04-474000-29). ASTM.

Erosion: Prevention & Useful Application. (Special Technical Publications Ser.). 637p. 1979. 55.00x (ISBN 0-686-76040-9, 664, 04-664000-29). ASTM.

Erosion, Wear & Interfaces with Corrosion. 1974. 35.00 (ISBN 0-686-52022-X, 04-567000-29). ASTM.

METALS-EXTRUSION

Heute, F. U. Isothermal Extrusion of Heavy Metals. 90p. 1981. text ed. 30.00 (ISBN 0-686-30009-2, Pub. by DGM Metallurgy Germany). IR Pubns.

Janssen, L. P. Twin Screw Extrusion. (Chemical Engineering Monographs: Vol. 7). 1977. 41.50 (ISBN 0-444-41629-3). Elsevier.

METALS-FAILURE

see Metals-Fracture

METALS-FATIGUE

see also Stress Corrosion

also Steel-Fatigue, and similar headings

Achievement of High Fatigue Resistance in Metals & Alloys. 1970. 28.75 (ISBN 0-8031-0030-2, 04-467000-30). ASTM.

Baker, T. J. The Failure Diagnosis in Ferrous Metals. (Illus.). Date not set. price not set (ISBN 0-408-70812-3). Butterworth.

Barer, R. D. & Peters, B. F. Why Metals Fail - Selected Case Histories. 1970. 60.50x (ISBN 0-677-02630-7). Gordon.

Colangelo, Vito J. & Heiser, F. A. Analysis of Metallurgical Failures. LC 73-19773. (Science & Technology of Materials Ser). 384p. 1974. 36.00 (ISBN 0-471-16450-X, Pub. by Wiley-Interscience). Wiley.

Cyclic Stress-Strain & Plastic Deformation Aspects of Fatigue Crack Growth. 1977. 25.00 (ISBN 0-686-52025-4, 04-637000-30). ASTM.

Fatigue & Fracture Toughness--Cyrogenic Behavior. 1974. 20.25 (ISBN 0-686-52046-7, 04-556000-30). ASTM.

Fatigue & Microstructure. 1979. 64.00 (ISBN 0-87170-075-1). ASM.

Finkel'shtein, B. N. Relaxation Phenomena in Metals & Alloys. LC 62-21590. 244p. 1963. 45.00 (ISBN 0-306-10664-7, Consultants). Plenum Pub.

Frost, N. E., et al. Metal Fatigue. (Oxford Engineering Science Ser). 1975. 89.00x (ISBN 0-19-856114-8). Oxford U Pr.

Fuchs, H. O. & Stephens, R. I. Metal Fatigue in Engineering. LC 80-294. 1980. 33.95 (ISBN 0-471-05264-7, Pub. by Wiley-Interscience). Wiley.

Handbook of Fatigue Testing. 1974. 17.25 (ISBN 0-686-52030-0, 04-566000-30). ASTM.

The Influence of State of Stress on Low-Cycle Fatigue of Structural Materials: A Literature Survey & Interpretive Report. 1974. pap. 5.25 (ISBN 0-686-52031-9, 04-549000-30). ASTM.

Localized Corrosion - Cause of Metal Failure. 322p. 1972. 22.50 (ISBN 0-8031-0110-4, STP516). ASTM.

Madayag, A. G. Metal Fatigue: Theory & Design. 1969. 37.50 (ISBN 0-471-56315-3, Pub. by Wiley-Interscience). Wiley.

Manual on Low Cycle Fatigue Testing. 1970. 12.50 (ISBN 0-8031-0035-3, 04-465000-30). ASTM.

Manual on Statistical Planning & Analysis for Fatigue Experiments. 1975. 15.00 (ISBN 0-686-52029-7, 04-588000-30). ASTM.

Metal Fatigue Damage - Mechanism, Detection, Avoidance & Repair. 351p. 1971. 21.00 (ISBN 0-8031-0109-0, STP495). ASTM.

Plane Strain Crack Toughness Testing of High Strength Metallic Materials. (Special Technical Publications Ser.). 134p. 1967. 5.50x (ISBN 0-686-76051-4, 410, 04-410000-30). ASTM.

References on Fatigue, 1965-1966. 1968. 11.00 (ISBN 0-8031-0132-5, 04-009160-30). ASTM.

Sors, L. Fatigue Design of Machine Components. 224p. 1971. text ed. 42.00 (ISBN 0-08-016138-3). Pergamon.

Stress Corrosion Cracking of Metals: A State of the Art. 172p. 1972. 11.75 (ISBN 0-8031-0096-5, STP518). ASTM.

Use of Computers in the Fatigue Laboratory. 1976. 20.00 (ISBN 0-686-52026-2, 04-613000-30). ASTM.

METALS-FINISHING

see also Enamel and Enameling; Metal Cleaning

Benninghoff, H. Index of Chemicals. 1974. 122.00 (ISBN 0-444-41075-9). Elsevier.

Dettner, H. W. Elsevier's Dictionary of Metal Finishing & Corrosion. 1971. 39.00 (ISBN 0-444-40938-6). Elsevier.

Dettner, Heinz W. Metal Finishing Dictionary: German-English & English-German. 1960. 15.00x (ISBN 3-87749-011-5). Intl Pubns Serv.

Duffy, J. I., ed. Electroless & Other Nonelectrolytic Plating Techniques: Recent Developments. LC 80-19494. (Chemical Tech. Rev. 171). (Illus.). 366p. 1981. 45.00 (ISBN 0-8155-0818-2). Noyes.

Dyachenko, P. E., et al. Actual Contact Area Between Touching Surfaces. LC 64-13145. 1964. 22.50 (ISBN 0-306-10678-7, Consultants). Plenum Pub.

Fraunhofer, J. A. Instrumentation in Metal Finishing. 1975. 14.95x (ISBN 0-236-31005-4, Pub. by Paul Elek). Merrimack Bk Serv.

Reid, F. H. & Goldie, W. Gold Plating Technology. 630p. 1980. 89.00x (ISBN 0-901150-02-9, Pub. by Electrochemical Scotland). State Mutual Bk.

Society Of Manufacturing Engineers. Surface Preparation & Finishes for Metals. Murphy, J. A., ed. 1971. 35.50 (ISBN 0-07-059557-7, P&RB). McGraw.

Such, Dennis T. Nickel & Chromium Plating. 1972. pap. text ed. 34.95 (ISBN 0-408-00086-4). Butterworth.

METALS-FRACTURE

see also Metals-Brittleness; Metals-Fatigue

Baker, T. J. The Failure Diagnosis in Ferrous Metals. (Illus.). Date not set. price not set (ISBN 0-408-70812-3). Butterworth.

Colangelo, Vito J. & Heiser, F. A. Analysis of Metallurgical Failures. LC 73-19773. (Science & Technology of Materials Ser). 384p. 1974. 36.00 (ISBN 0-471-16450-X, Pub. by Wiley-Interscience). Wiley.

Collins, J. A. Failure of Materials in Mechanical Design: Analysis, Prediction, Prevention. LC 80-20674. 629p. 1981. 39.95 (ISBN 0-471-05024-5, Pub. by Wiley-Interscience). Wiley.

Cracks & Fracture. 1976. 51.75 (ISBN 0-686-52039-4, 04-601000-30). ASTM.

Fatigue & Fracture Toughness--Cyrogenic Behavior. 1974. 20.25 (ISBN 0-686-52046-7, 04-556000-30). ASTM.

Flaw Growth & Fracture. 1977. 49.75 (ISBN 0-686-52036-X, 04-631000-30). ASTM.

Fractography--Microscopic Cracking Process. 1976. 27.50 (ISBN 0-686-52040-8, 04-600000-30). ASTM.

Fractography in Failure Analysis. 1978. 36.50 (ISBN 0-686-52034-3, 04-645000-30). ASTM.

Fracture Toughness Evaluation by R-Curve Methods. 118p. 1973. pap. 9.75 (ISBN 0-8031-0106-6, STP527). ASTM.

Hahn, G. T. & Kanninen, M. F., eds. Fast Fracture & Crack Arrest. 1977. 42.50 (ISBN 0-686-52037-8, 04-627000-30). ASTM.

Henry, Guy. Fractography & Microfractography, Vol. 5. (Illus., Eng, German, & French.). 1979. 175.00 (ISBN 0-85501-166-1). Heyden.

Kocanda, S. Fatigue Failure of Metals. 384p. 1978. 40.00x (ISBN 90-286-0025-6). Sijthoff & Noordhoff.

McCall, J. L. & French, P. M., eds. Metallography in Failure Analysis. 309p. 1978. 35.00 (ISBN 0-306-40012-X, Plenum Pr). Plenum Pub.

Mechanics of Crack Growth. 1976. 45.25 (ISBN 0-686-52042-4, 04-590000-30). ASTM.

National Materials Advisory Board, National Research Council. Rapid Inexpensive Tests for Determining Fracture Toughness. LC 76-39632. 1976. pap. 8.25 (ISBN 0-309-02537-0). Natl Acad Pr.

Plane Strain Crack Toughness Testing of High Strength Metallic Materials. (Special Technical Publications Ser.). 134p. 1967. 5.50x (ISBN 0-686-76051-4, 410, 04-410000-30). ASTM.

Properties Related to Fracture Toughness. 1976. pap. 15.00 (ISBN 0-686-52038-6, 04-605000-30). ASTM.

Resistance to Plane-Stress Fracture (R-Curve Behavior) of A 572 Structural Steel. 1976. soft cover 5.25 (ISBN 0-686-52041-6, 04-591000-30). ASTM.

Review of Developments in Plane Strain Fracture Toughness Testing. 1970. 18.25 (ISBN 0-8031-0037-X, 04-463000-30). ASTM.

METALS-HEAT TREATMENT

see also Tempering

Brooks, Charlie R. Heat Treatment of Ferrous Alloys. (Illus.). 1979. text ed. 24.50x (ISBN 0-07-008076-3). McGraw.

Dovey, D. M., et al. Heat Treatment of Metals. 1963. 7.50 (ISBN 0-201-01609-5, Adv Bk Prog). A-W.

Gabe, D. R. Principles of Metal Surface Treatment & Protection. 2nd ed. (International Ser. on Materials Science & Technology: Vol. 28). (Illus.). 1978. text ed. 36.00 (ISBN 0-08-022703-1); pap. text ed. 14.00 (ISBN 0-08-022707-4). Pergamon.

Harris, J. N. The Shaping & Heat Treatment of Metals. write for info.; pap. write for info. (ISBN 0-685-25019-9). Pergamon.

Lord. Advances in Electric Heat Treatment of Metals. (Electrotechnology Ser.: Vol. 7). 1981. text ed. 39.95 (ISBN 0-250-40481-8). Ann Arbor Science.

Ross, R. B. Handbook of Metal Treatments & Testing. LC 77-3929. 467p. 1977. text ed. 37.95x (ISBN 0-419-10960-9, Pub. by Tavistock England). Methuen Inc.

Wilson, R. Metallurgy & Heat Treatment of Tool Steels. 1976. 47.50 (ISBN 0-07-084453-4). McGraw.

METALS-HIGH ENERGY FORMING

see High Energy Forming

METALS-JUVENILE LITERATURE

Brooks, Anita. Picture Book of Metals. LC 78-147271. (Pictures Aids to World Geography Ser). (Illus.). (gr. 4-7). 1972. 6.89 (ISBN 0-381-99933-5, A61225, JD-J). Har-Row.

Coombs, Charles. Gold & Other Precious Metals. LC 81-38414. (Illus.). 128p. (gr. 4-6). 1981. 7.95 (ISBN 0-688-00542-X); PLB 7.63 (ISBN 0-688-00543-8). Morrow.

Radford, Don. Metals: Background Information. LC 77-83004. (Science 5-13 Ser.). (Illus.). 1977. pap. text ed. 8.25 (ISBN 0-356-04104-2). Raintree Child.

--Metals: Stages 1 & 2. LC 77-83004. (Science 5-13). (Illus.). 1977. pap. text ed. 8.25 (ISBN 0-356-04103-4). Raintree Child.

Smith, Norman. If It Shines, Clangs & Bends, Its Metal. LC 79-227. (Science Is What & Why Ser.). (Illus.). (gr. 2-4). 1980. PLB 5.99 (ISBN 0-698-30717-8). Coward.

Story of Metals. (Illus.). Arabic 2.50x (ISBN 0-86685-227-1). Intl Bk Ctr.

Wohlrabe, Raymond A. Metals. LC 64-19046. (Introducing Modern Science Books Ser). (Illus.). (gr. 7-9). 1964. 8.95 (ISBN 0-397-30764-0). Lippincott.

METALS-MICROSCOPIC STRUCTURE

see Metallography

METALS-OPTICAL PROPERTIES

Skolbel'Tsyn, D. V., ed. Optical Properties of Metals & Intermolecular Interactions. LC 72-94827. (P. N. Lebedev Physics Institute Ser.: Vol. 55). (Illus.). 228p. 1973. 35.00 (ISBN 0-306-10880-1, Consultants). Plenum Pub.

METALS-PICKLING

Mulcahy, E. W. The Pickling of Steels. LC 74-154842. (Illus.). 95p. 1973. 13.50x (ISBN 0-901994-20-0). Intl Pubns Serv.

Straschill, M. Max. Modern Practice in Pickling of Metals. 1964. 35.00x (ISBN 0-85218-010-1). Intl Pubns Serv.

METALS-RADIATION EFFECTS

see Metals, Effect of Radiation On

METALS-RADIOGRAPHY

see Radiography, Industrial

METALS-RECYCLING

Recovery of Metals from Shredding Operations & Wire & Cable Chopping. 7.50 (ISBN 0-686-23293-3). Natl Recycling.

Recycling Aluminum. (Illus.). 36p. 1981. pap. text ed. 10.00 (ISBN 0-686-30234-6). Natl Recycling.

Recycling Copper & Brass. (Illus.). 36p. 1980. pap. text ed. 10.00 (ISBN 0-686-30232-X). Natl Recycling.

Recycling Precious Metals. (Illus.). 24p. Date not set. pap. text ed. 9.50 (ISBN 0-686-30233-8). Natl Recycling.

METALS-SURFACE PROPERTIES

see Metals-Surfaces

METALS-SURFACES

see also Corrosion and Anti-Corrosives; Diffusion Coatings; Lubrication and Lubricants; Metal Bonding; Metals-Finishing

Carter. Metallic Coatings for Corrosion Control. 1977. text ed. 31.95 (ISBN 0-408-00270-0). Butterworth.

Derouane, E. G. & Lucas, A. A., eds. Electronic Structure & Reactivity of Metal Surfaces. LC 76-10692. (NATO Advanced Study Institutes Ser. B: Physics, Vol. 16). 633p. 1976. 55.00 (ISBN 0-306-35716-X, Plenum Pr). Plenum Pub.

Din Standards: Testing of Metallic Materials-Physical Test Methods-Testing of Coatings, Corrosion, Structive Test Methods: Testing of Metallic Materials-Physical Test Methods-Testing of Coatings, Corrosion, Climate, Non-Destructive Test Methods. 306.00 (ISBN 0-686-28191-8, 10791-5/56). Heyden.

Gomer, R., ed. Interactions on Metal Surfaces, Vol. 4. LC 75-1281. (Topics in Applied Physics Ser). (Illus.). 340p. 1975. 42.60 (ISBN 0-387-07094-X). Springer-Verlag.

METALS-TESTING

see also Metals-Fatigue; Metals-Fracture

Behavior of Metals at Elevated Temperatures. 6.00 (ISBN 0-685-28343-7). Philos Lib.

Glazov, V. M. & Vigdorovich, V. N. Microhardness of Metals & Semiconductors. LC 70-128504. 226p. 1971. 35.00 (ISBN 0-306-10848-8, Consultants). Plenum Pub.

Hydrogen Embrittlement Testing. 1974. 29.75 (ISBN 0-686-52048-3, 04-543000-26). ASTM.

Impact Testing of Metals. 1970. 21.25 (ISBN 0-8031-0038-8, 04-466000-23). ASTM.

Manual on Low Cycle Fatigue Testing. 1970. 12.50 (ISBN 0-8031-0035-3, 04-465000-30). ASTM.

Nondestructive Rapid Identification of Metals & Alloys by Spot Tests. 1973. pap. 4.00 (ISBN 0-686-52063-7, 04-550000-24). ASTM.

Review of Developments in Plane Strain Fracture Toughness Testing. 1970. 18.25 (ISBN 0-8031-0037-X, 04-463000-30). ASTM.

Rosenfield, A. R., et al, eds. What Does the Charpy Test Really Tell Us? 1978. 32.00 (ISBN 0-87170-027-1). ASM.

Ross, R. B. Handbook of Metal Treatments & Testing. LC 77-3929. 467p. 1977. text ed. 37.95x (ISBN 0-419-10960-9, Pub. by Tavistock England). Methuen Inc.

Selection & Use of Wear Tests for Metals. 1977. pap. 10.75 (ISBN 0-686-52057-2, 04-615000-23). ASTM.

METALS-TOXICOLOGY

Berman, E. Toxic Metals & Their Analysis. 304p. 1980. 29.00 (ISBN 0-85501-468-7). Heyden.

Friberg, L., et al, eds. Handbook of the Toxicology of Metals. Vouk, V. 700p. 1980. 117.00 (ISBN 0-444-80075-1, North Holland). Elsevier.

Goyer, Robert A. & Mehlman, Myron A., eds. Advances in Modern Toxicology: Toxicoloby of Trace Elements, Vol. 2. (Advances in Modern Toxicology Ser.). 1977. 24.50 (ISBN 0-470-99049-X). Halsted Pr.

Lee, Douglas H., ed. Metallic Contaminants & Human Health: Fogarty International Center Proceedings, (Environmental Science Ser.: No. 2). 1972. 23.00 (ISBN 0-12-440660-2). Acad Pr.

Leeper, G. W. Managing Heavy Metals on the Land. (Pollution Engineering & Technology Ser: Vol. 6). 1977. 16.75 (ISBN 0-8247-6661-X). Dekker.

Nordberg, G. F. Effects & Dose-Response Relationships of Toxic Metals. 1976. 120.50 (ISBN 0-444-41370-7, North Holland). Elsevier.

Oehme. Toxicity of Heavy Metals, Pt. 1. (Hazardous & Toxic Substances Ser.: Vol. 2). 1978. 49.50 (ISBN 0-8247-6718-7). Dekker.

--Toxicity of Heavy Metals in the Environment, Pt. 2. (Hazardous & Toxic Substances Ser.: Vol. 2). 1979. 49.50 (ISBN 0-8247-6719-5). Dekker.

Peterson, Howard B. & Monk, Ralph. Vegetation & Metal Toxicity in Relation to Mine & Mill Waste: An Annotated Bibliography Useful in Evaluating Available Literature. 75p. 1967. pap. 0.50 (ISBN 0-87421-057-7). Utah St U Pr.

Williams, D. F., ed. Systemic Aspects of Biocompatibility. 1981. Vol. 1, 272 Pgs. 74.95 (ISBN 0-8493-6621-6); Vol. 2, 224 Pgs. 62.95 (ISBN 0-8493-6622-4). CRC Pr.

METALS, EFFECT OF RADIATION ON

Arifov, U. A. Interaction of Atomic Particles with a Solid Surface. LC 79-76223. 374p. 1969. 45.00 (ISBN 0-306-10831-3, Consultants). Plenum Pub.

Corbett, James W. & Ianniello, Louis C., eds. Radiation-Induced Voids in Metals. LC 72-600048. (AEC Symposium Ser.). 884p. 1972. pap. 9.00 (ISBN 0-686-75858-7); microfiche 3.00 (ISBN 0-686-75859-5). DOE.

Effects of Radiation on Substructure & Mechanical Properties of Metals & Alloys. 1973. 49.50 (ISBN 0-686-52080-7, 04-529000-35). ASTM.

Irradiation Effects on Structural Alloys for Nuclear Reactor Applications. 1971. 49.25 (ISBN 0-8031-0014-0, 04-484000-35). ASTM.

Irradiation Effects on the Microstructure on Properties of Metals. 1976. 49.00 (ISBN 0-686-52077-7, 04-611000-35). ASTM.

Peterson, N. L. & Harkness, S. D., eds. Radiation Damage in Metals. (TA 460.r23). 1976. 38.00 (ISBN 0-87170-055-7). ASM.

Properties of Reactor Structural Alloys After Neutron or Particle Irradiation. 1976. 59.50 (ISBN 0-686-52078-5, 04-570000-35). ASTM.

Radiation Effects Information Generated on the ASTM Reference Correlation-Monitor Steels. 1974. pap. 9.75 (ISBN 0-686-52081-5, 05-054000-35). ASTM.

Thompson, M. W. Defects & Radiation Damage in Metals. LC 69-10434. (Cambridge Monographs on Physics). (Illus.). 1969. 60.50 (ISBN 0-521-07068-6); pap. 18.50x (ISBN 0-521-09865-3). Cambridge U Pr.

METALS, EFFECT OF TEMPERATURE ON

see also Metals at High Temperatures; Metals at Low Temperatures; Thermionic Emission

Elevated Temperature Testing Problem Areas. 1971. pap. 5.50 (ISBN 0-8031-0062-0, 04-488000-40). ASTM.

Smith, G. V., ed. Characterization of Materials for Service at Elevated Temperatures, MPC-7. (Bk. No. G00134). 536p. 1978. 50.00 (ISBN 0-685-37564-1). ASME.

METALS, FREE ELECTRON THEORY OF

see Free Electron Theory of Metals

METALS, GASES IN

see Gases in Metals

METALS, HEAT RESISTANT

see Heat Resistant Alloys

METALS, NONFERROUS
see Nonferrous Metals
METALS, POWDERED
see Metal Powders
METALS, TRANSMUTATION OF
see Alchemy; Transmutation (Chemistry)
METALS AT HIGH TEMPERATURES
see also Heat Resistant Alloys; Nimonic Alloys

Bradley, Elihu F., ed. Source Book on Materials for Elevated-Temperature Applications. 1979. 38.00 (ISBN 0-87170-081-6). ASM.

Elevated Temperature Properties As Influenced by Nitrogen Additions to Types 304 & 316 Austenitic Stainless Steels. 121p. 1973. pap. 10.50 (ISBN 0-8031-0112-0, STP522). ASTM.

Elevated Temperature Static Properties of Wrought Carbon Steel. 47p. 1972. pap. 3.00 (ISBN 0-8031-0107-4, STP503). ASTM.

An Evaluation of the Elevated-Temperature Tensile & Creep-Rupture Properties of Wrought Carbon Steel. 1969. pap. 6.00 (ISBN 0-8031-0063-9, 05-011001-40). ASTM.

Smith, G. V., ed. Properties of Steel Weldments for Elevated Temperature Pressure Containment Applications: MPC-9. 1978. 30.00 (ISBN 0-685-66811-8, H00133). ASME.

Toropov, N. A. & Barzakovskii, V. P. High-Temperature Chemistry of Silicates & Other Oxide Systems. LC 65-25264. 216p. 1966. 34.50 (ISBN 0-306-10749-X, Consultants). Plenum Pub.

METALS AT LOW TEMPERATURES

Fatigue & Fracture Toughness--Cyrogenic Behavior. 1974. 20.25 (ISBN 0-686-52046-7, 04-556000-30). ASTM.

METALS IN THE BODY
see also Chelation Therapy

Brewer, George J. & Prasad, Ananda S., eds. Zinc Metabolism: Current Aspects in Health & Disease. LC 77-3584. (Progress in Clinical & Biological Research: Vol. 14). 372p. 1977. 30.00x (ISBN 0-8451-0014-9). A R Liss.

Committee on Medical & Biological Effects of Environmental Pollutants. Nickel. 1975. pap. 15.00 (ISBN 0-309-02314-9). Natl Acad Pr.

Eisler, ed. Trace Metal Concentrations in Marine Organisms. 3500p. text ed. 195.00 (ISBN 0-08-025975-8). Pergamon.

Maniloff, Jack, et al, eds. Effects of Metals on Cells, Subcellular Elements, & Macromolecules. (Illus.). 416p. 1970. text ed. 28.75 (ISBN 0-398-01210-5). C C Thomas.

Powell, L. Metals & the Liver. (Liver; Normal Function & Disease Ser.: Vol. 1). 1978. 38.50 (ISBN 0-8247-6740-3). Dekker.

Sigel, Helmut, ed. Metal Ions in Biological Systems, Vol. 3: High Molecular Complexes. 304p. 1974. 39.75 (ISBN 0-8247-6030-1). Dekker.

--Metal Ions in Biological Systems, Vol. 4: Metal Ions As Probes. 272p. 1974. 39.75 (ISBN 0-8247-6031-X). Dekker.

--Metal Ions in Biological Systems, Vol. 7: Iron in Model & Natural Compounds. 1978. 44.50 (ISBN 0-8247-6708-X). Dekker.

Williams, D. F., ed. Systemic Aspects of Biocompatibility. 1981. Vol. 1, 272 Pgs. 74.95 (ISBN 0-8493-6621-6); Vol. 2, 224 Pgs. 62.95 (ISBN 0-8493-6622-4). CRC Pr.

METALWORK
see Metal-Work
METAMATHEMATICS
see also Logic, Symbolic and Mathematical

Lorenzen, Paul. Metamathematique. Grize, J. B., tr. (Mathematiques et Sciences De L'homme: No. 6). 1967. pap. 10.00x (ISBN 90-2796-316-9). Mouton.

Nagel, Ernest & Newman, James R. Godel's Proof. LC 58-5610. 1958. 13.50 (ISBN 0-8147-0324-0); pap. 5.00x (ISBN 0-8147-0325-9). NYU Pr.

Rasiowa, Helena. The Mathematics of Metamathematics. (Monographs in Mathematics Ser: No. 41). 519p. 1970. 22.50x (ISBN 0-8002-1712-8). Intl Pubns Serv.

Sanderson, J. G. A Relational Theory of Computing. (Lecture Notes in Computer Science: Vol. 82). 147p. 1980. pap. 11.80 (ISBN 0-387-09987-5). Springer-Verlag.

METAMORPHIC ROCKS
see Rocks, Metamorphic
METAMORPHISM (GEOLOGY)
see also Rocks, Metamorphic

Ernst, W. G., ed. Subduction Zone Metamorphism. LC 74-25224. (Benchmark Papers in Geology Ser: No. 19). 1975. 55.00 (ISBN 0-12-786448-2). Acad Pr.

Ernst, W. G., et al. Comparative Study of Low-Grade Metamorphism in the California Coast Ranges & the Outer Metamorphic Belt of Japan. LC 74-98022. (Memoir: No. 124). (Illus.). 1970. 20.00x (ISBN 0-8137-1124-X). Geol Soc.

French, Bevan M. Progressive Contact Metamorphism of the Biwabik Iron-Formation, Mesabi Range, Minnesota. LC 68-66592. (Bulletin: No. 45). (Illus.). 1968. 4.50x (ISBN 0-8166-0478-9). Minn Geol Survey.

Larsen, Leonard H., et al, eds. Igneous & Metamorphic Geology: A Volume in Honor of Arie Poldervaart. LC 68-55355. (Memoir: No. 115). (Illus.). 1969. 30.00x (ISBN 0-8137-1115-0). Geol Soc.

Miyashiro, A. Metamorphism & Metamorphic Belts. LC 72-13983. 1978. pap. 32.95 (ISBN 0-470-99390-1). Halsted Pr.

Turner, Francis J. Metamorphic Petrology. 2nd ed. LC 79-27496. (International Earth & Planetary Sciences Ser.). (Illus.). 512p. 1980. text ed. 29.95 (ISBN 0-07-065501-4, C). McGraw.

Weaver, Charles E. & Beck, Kevin E. Clay Water Diagenesis During Burial: How Mud Becomes Gneiss. LC 74-153907. (Special Paper: No. 134). (Illus., Orig.). 1971. pap. 6.50x (ISBN 0-8137-2134-2). Geol Soc.

METAMORPHOSIS
see also Insects–Metamorphosis

Gilbert, Lawrence I. & Frieden, Earl, eds. Metamorphosis: A Problem in Developmental Biology. rev. 2nd ed. 530p. 1981. text ed. 39.50 (ISBN 0-306-40692-6, Plenum Pr). Plenum Pub.

METAMORPHOSIS (IN RELIGION, FOLK-LORE, ETC.)
see also Leopard Men; Witchcraft; Werewolves

Massey, Irving. The Gaping Pig: Literature & Metamorphoses. LC 74-22967. 1976. 20.00x (ISBN 0-520-02887-2). U of Cal Pr.

Skulsky, Harold. Metamorphosis: The Mind in Exile. LC 80-29526. 244p. 1981. text ed. 16.50 (ISBN 0-674-57085-5). Harvard U Pr.

Summers, Anthony J. Metamorphosis. 1979. 2.75 (ISBN 0-918476-06-2). Cornerstone Pr.

METAMORPHOSIS (INSECTS)
see Insects–Development
METAPHOR
see also Simile

Abraham, Werner. A Linguistic Approach to Metaphor. 1977. pap. text ed. 3.50x (ISBN 90-316-0001-6). Humanities.

Berry, Ralph. The Shakespearean Metaphor: Studies in Language & Form. 128p. 1978. 17.50x (ISBN 0-8476-6047-8). Rowman.

Buck, Gertrude. The Metaphor. 1978. Repr. of 1899 ed. lib. bdg. 10.00 (ISBN 0-8495-0439-2). Arden Lib.

Hawkes, Terence. Metaphor. (Critical Idiom Ser.). 1972. pap. text ed. 5.50 (ISBN 0-416-09030-3). Methuen Inc.

Homan, Sidney. When the Theater Turns to Itself: The Aesthetic Metaphor in Shakespeare. LC 80-65453. 240p. 1981. 19.50 (ISBN 0-8387-5009-5). Bucknell U Pr.

Jennings, J. G. Essay on Metaphor in Poetry. LC 72-194447. 1915. lib. bdg. 8.50 (ISBN 0-8414-5379-9). Folcroft.

Johnson, Mark, ed. Philosophical Perspectives on Metaphor. LC 81-872. 352p. 1981. 29.50x (ISBN 0-8166-1056-8); pap. 10.95 (ISBN 0-8166-1057-6). U of Minn Pr.

Keach, Benjamin. Preaching from the Types & Metaphors of the Bible. LC 78-165059. (Kregel Reprint Library). 1975. 19.95 (ISBN 0-8254-3008-9). Kregel.

Lakoff, George & Johnson, Mark. Metaphors We Live by. LC 80-10783. xiv, 242p. 1981. 5.95 (ISBN 0-226-46801-1, Phoen). U of Chicago Pr.

--Metaphors We Live By. LC 80-10783. 1980. 13.95 (ISBN 0-226-46800-3). U of Chicago Pr.

Levin, Samuel R. The Semantics of Metaphor. LC 77-4550. (Illus.). 1977. text ed. 12.00x (ISBN 0-8018-1981-4). Johns Hopkins.

Machineworks: Vito Acconci, Alice Aycock, Kay Larsond, Dennis Oppenheim, Janet Kardon. (Illus.). 1980. pap. 8.00 (ISBN 0-904540-26-X). U of Pa Contemp Art.

Mendelson, Danuta. Metaphor in Babel's Short Stories. 140p. 1981. 17.50 (ISBN 0-88233-702-5). Ardis Pubs.

Monaco, Richard & Briggs, John. The Logic of Poetry. (Illus.). 448p. 1974. pap. text ed. 9.95 (ISBN 0-07-042682-1, C). McGraw.

Mooij, J. J. A. A Study of Metaphor. (North-Holland Linguistics Ser.: Vol. 27). 1976. 24.50 (ISBN 0-7204-6209-6, North-Holland). Elsevier.

O'Dell, George C. Simile & Metaphor in the English & Scottish Ballads. LC 74-28467. 1892. lib. bdg. 10.00 (ISBN 0-8414-6512-6). Folcroft.

Ortony, Andrew, ed. Metaphor & Thought. LC 78-32011. (Illus.). 1979. 45.00 (ISBN 0-521-22727-5); pap. 13.95x (ISBN 0-521-29626-9). Cambridge U Pr.

Ricoeur, Paul. The Rule of Metaphor: Multi-Disciplinary Studies of the Creation of Meaning in Language. Czerny, Robert, tr. 1977. 25.00 (ISBN 0-8020-5326-2); pap. 14.50 (ISBN 0-8020-6447-7). U of Toronto Pr.

Rogers, Robert. Metaphor: A Psychoanalytic View. LC 77-80477. 1978. 14.95x (ISBN 0-520-03548-8). U of Cal Pr.

Sacks, Sheldon, ed. On Metaphor. LC 79-5080. 1979. pap. 5.95 (ISBN 0-226-73334-3, P856, Phoen). U of Chicago Pr.

Sahlins, Marshall. Historical Metaphors & Mythical Realities: Structure in the Early History of the Sandwich Islands Kingdom. LC 80-28649. 96p. 1981. pap. text ed. 5.95x (ISBN 0-472-02721-2). U of Mich Pr.

Sapir, J. David & Crocker, J. Christopher, eds. The Social Use of Metaphor: Essays on the Anthropology of Rhetoric. LC 76-53200. 1977. 16.00x (ISBN 0-8122-7725-2). U of Pa Pr.

Shibles, Warren. Analysis of Metaphor in the Light of W. M. Urban's Theories. LC 78-159471. 1971. pap. 5.75 (ISBN 0-912386-12-6). Language Pr.

--Metaphor: An Annotated Bibliography & History. LC 72-157087. 1971. lib. bdg. 15.00 (ISBN 0-912386-00-2). Language Pr.

Stanford, William B. Greek Metaphor. xi, 156p. Repr. of 1936 ed. 18.50 (ISBN 0-384-57474-2). Johnson Repr.

Thomas, Owen. Metaphor & Related Subjects. (Orig.). 1969. pap. text ed. 2.25 (ISBN 0-685-19745-X). Phila Bk Co.

Vaisrub, S. Medicine's Metaphors: Messages & Menaces. 1977. 9.95 (ISBN 0-87489-011-X). Med Economics.

Wheelwright, Philip. Metaphor & Reality. LC 62-8971. (Midland Bks.: No. 122). 204p. 1962. pap. 4.95x (ISBN 0-253-20122-5). Ind U Pr.

Williams, Charles A. A Manual of Chinese Metaphor. LC 71-138094. Repr. of 1920 ed. 17.50 (ISBN 0-404-56969-2). AMS Pr.

METAPHYSICAL SOCIETY, LONDON

Brown, Alan W. The Metaphysical Society: Victorian Minds in Crisis, 1869-1880. LC 73-8422. xiv, 372p. 1973. Repr. of 1947 ed. lib. bdg. 20.00x (ISBN 0-374-91008-1). Octagon.

METAPHYSICS
see also Absolute, the; Causation; Cosmology; Form (Philosophy); God; Hylomorphism; Knowledge, Theory Of; Ontology; Space and Time; Substance (Philosophy); Sufficient Reason; Values

Alexander, Hartley B. Nature & Human Nature: Essays Metaphysical & Historical. LC 75-3018. (Philosophy in America Ser.). Repr. of 1923 ed. 41.50 (ISBN 0-404-59011-X). AMS Pr.

--The Problem of Metaphysics & the Meaning of Metaphysical Explanation. LC 72-38480. Repr. of 1902 ed. 14.00 (ISBN 0-404-00322-2). AMS Pr.

Anderson, James F. Introduction to the Metaphysics of St. Thomas Aquinas. LC 53-6515. 1969. pap. 2.95 (ISBN 0-89526-970-8). Regnery-Gateway.

Anscombe, G. E. Collected Philosophical Papers: Metaphysics & the Philosophy of Mind, Vol. 2. 288p. 1981. 32.50x (ISBN 0-8166-1080-0); pap. 11.95x (ISBN 0-8166-1081-9). U of Minn Pr.

Aristotle. Metaphysica. Jaeger, Werner, ed. (Oxford Classical Texts Ser). 1957. 24.00x (ISBN 0-19-814513-6). Oxford U Pr.

--Metaphysics, 2 Vols. rev. ed. Ross, W. David, ed. 1924. Set. 105.00x (ISBN 0-19-814107-6). Oxford U Pr.

--Metaphysics. Hope, Richard, tr. 1960. pap. 4.95 (ISBN 0-472-06042-2, 42, AA). U of Mich Pr.

--Metaphysics, Bks. 4-6. Kirwan, Christopher, tr. (Clarendon Aristotle Ser.). 214p. 1971. 16.95x (ISBN 0-19-872027-0). Oxford U Pr.

--Metaphysics, Bks 1-9. (Loeb Classical Library: No. 271). 11.00x (ISBN 0-674-99299-7). Harvard U Pr.

--Metaphysics, Bks 10-14. Bd. with Oeconomica, Bks 1-3; Magna Moralia, Bks 1 & 2. (Loeb Classical Library: No. 287). 11.00x (ISBN 0-674-99317-9). Harvard U Pr.

--Metaphysics: Books M & N. Annas, Julia, ed. (Clarendon Aristotle Ser.). 1976. 29.95x (ISBN 0-19-872085-8). Oxford U Pr.

Armstrong, Robert L. Metaphysics & British Empiricism. LC 78-109602. xviii, 169p. 1970. 13.50x (ISBN 0-8032-0750-6). U of Nebr Pr.

Ayer, Alfred J. Metaphysics & Common Sense. LC 79-89830. 288p. 1970. text ed. 8.00x (ISBN 0-87735-507-X). Freeman C.

Bass, Virginia. Dimensions of Man's Spirit. (Illus.). 280p. 1975. pap. 12.00 (ISBN 0-911336-60-5). Sci of Mind.

Bennett, John G. Existence. 1977. 3.95 (ISBN 0-900306-40-8, Pub. by Coombe Springs Pr). Claymont Comm.

--The First Liberation. 1976. 2.50 (ISBN 0-900306-32-7, Pub. by Coombe Springs Pr). Claymont Comm.

--Food. 1978. 2.50 (ISBN 0-900306-45-9, Pub. by Coombe Springs Pr). Claymont Comm.

--The Foundations of Moral Philosophy, Vol. 2. (The Dramatic Universe). 10.95 (ISBN 0-900306-42-4, Pub. by Coombe Springs Pr). Claymont Comm.

--Hazard. 1976. 3.95 (ISBN 0-900306-33-5, Pub. by Coombe Springs Pr). Claymont Comm.

--History, Vol. 4. (The Dramatic Universe Ser.). 10.95 (ISBN 0-900306-44-0, Pub. by Coombe Springs Pr). Claymont Comm.

--Man & His Nature, Vol. 3. (The Dramatic Universe Ser.). 10.95 (ISBN 0-900306-42-4, Pub. by Coombe Springs Pr). Claymont Comm.

--Material Objects. 1977. 2.50 (ISBN 0-900306-35-1, Pub. by Coombe Springs Pr). Claymont Comm.

--Noticing. 1976. 2.50 (ISBN 0-900306-31-9, Pub. by Coombe Springs Pr). Claymont Comm.

--Talks on Beelzebub's Tales. 1977. 4.95 (ISBN 0-900306-36-X, Pub. by Coombe Springs Pr). Claymont Comm.

Berdiaev, Nikolai A. The Beginning & the End. French, R. M., tr. from Russian. LC 76-6083. 1976. Repr. of 1952 ed. lib. bdg. 16.50x (ISBN 0-8371-8837-7, BEBE). Greenwood.

Bergson, Henri. The Creative Mind: An Introduction to Metaphysics. 256p. 1974. pap. 3.45 (ISBN 0-8065-0421-8). Citadel Pr.

--An Introduction to Metaphysics. 2nd ed. Hulme, T. E., tr. LC 49-3135. 1955. pap. 1.95 (ISBN 0-672-60171-0, LLA10). Bobbs.

--An Introduction to Metaphysics: The Creative Mind. (Quality Paperback: No. 164). 1975. pap. 3.95 (ISBN 0-8226-0164-8). Littlefield.

Bergson, Henri L. Creative Evolution. Mitchell, Arthur, tr. LC 74-28524. 453p. 1975. Repr. of 1944 ed. lib. bdg. 25.00x (ISBN 0-8371-7917-3, BECEV). Greenwood.

--Creative Mind. Andison, Mabelle L., tr. LC 68-19264. Repr. of 1946 ed. lib. bdg. 20.75x (ISBN 0-8371-0310-X, BECM). Greenwood.

Berndtson, Arthur. Power, Form, & Mind. LC 80-65658. 296p. 1981. 24.50 (ISBN 0-8387-5010-9). Bucknell U Pr.

Bharata Krsna Tirthaji Maharaj. Vedic Metaphysics. 1978. Repr. 15.00 (ISBN 0-89684-337-8). Orient Bk Dist.

Bluthardt, O. D. Kindergarten of the Universe: Introduction to the Realm of Metaphysics & Reincarnation. 1979. 6.95 (ISBN 0-533-04009-4). Vantage.

Blyth, John W. Whitehead's Theory of Knowledge. LC 73-9672. 112p. 1973. Repr. of 1941 ed. 18.00 (ISBN 0-527-09100-6). Kraus Repr.

Bowen, Francis. The Principles of Metaphysical & Ethical Science Applied to the Evidences of Religion. 1976. Repr. 60.00 (ISBN 0-685-71115-3, Regency). Scholarly.

Bowne, Borden P. Metaphysics... rev. ed. LC 75-948. (Philosophy in America Ser.). Repr. of 1898 ed. 31.50 (ISBN 0-404-59072-1). AMS Pr.

Braden, Charles S. Spirits in Rebellion: The Rise & Development of New Thought. LC 63-13245. 584p. 1980. Repr. of 1963 ed. 10.00 (ISBN 0-87074-025-3). SMU Press.

Bradley, Francis H. Appearance & Reality: A Metaphysical Essay. 1930. 32.50x (ISBN 0-19-824109-7). Oxford U Pr.

Brokmeyer, Henry C. A Mechanics Diary. LC 75-3090. Repr. of 1910 ed. 18.00 (ISBN 0-404-59088-8). AMS Pr.

Brungardt, Helen. Contemplation: The Activity of Mystical Consciousness. 2nd ed. 72p. 1980. pap. 3.00 (ISBN 0-87707-220-5). Red Earth.

Buchler, Justus. Toward a General Theory of Human Judgment. LC 79-51886. 1980. pap. 5.00 (ISBN 0-486-23874-1). Dover.

Bunge, Mario. Metascientific Queries. (American Lecture Philosophy). (Illus.). 328p. 1959. pap. 24.50 photocopy ed. spiral (ISBN 0-398-00251-7). C C Thomas.

Burton, Asa. Essays on Some of the First Principles of Metaphysicks, Ethicks, & Theology. LC 73-4839. (History of Psychology Ser). 440p. 1973. Repr. of 1824 ed. lib. bdg. 43.00x (ISBN 0-8201-1114-7). Schol Facsimiles.

Burtt, Edwin A. Metaphysical Foundations of Modern Physical Science. 2nd ed. (International Library of Psychology, Philosophy & Scientific Method). 1967. Repr. of 1932 ed. text ed. 27.50x (ISBN 0-7100-3032-0); pap. text ed. 5.95x (ISBN 0-391-01633-4). Humanities.

Butchvarov, Panayot. Being Qua Being: A Theory of Identity, Existence & Predication. LC 78-13812. 288p. 1979. 15.00x (ISBN 0-253-13700-4). Ind U Pr.

Calkins, Mary W. The Persistent Problems of Philosophy. LC 75-3096. (Philosophy in America). Repr. of 1925 ed. 44.50 (ISBN 0-404-59092-6). AMS Pr.

Calkins, Mary W., ed. The Metaphysical System of Hobbes. 2nd ed. xxv, 187p. 1974. 12.95 (ISBN 0-87548-045-4); pap. 4.95 (ISBN 0-87548-045-4). Open Court.

Campbell, Keith. Metaphysics: An Introduction. 1976. pap. text ed. 10.95x (ISBN 0-8221-0175-0). Dickenson.

Carra, Massimo, et al. Metaphysical Art. Tisdall, Caroline, tr. (World of Art Ser.). (Illus.). 1971. text ed. 9.95 (ISBN 0-19-520008-X). Oxford U Pr.

Clayton, William R. Matter & Spirit. LC 80-81694. 136p. 1981. 8.75 (ISBN 0-8022-2368-0). Philos Lib.

Collingwood, R. J. Essay on Metaphysics. LC 71-183823. 354p. 1972. pap. 4.95 (ISBN 0-89526-996-1). Regnery-Gateway.

Collingwood, Robin G. An Essay on Metaphysics. 364p. 1940. 34.95x (ISBN 0-19-824121-6). Oxford U Pr.

Connelly, R. J. Whitehead Vs. Hartshorne: Basic Metaphysical Issues. LC 80-69053. 172p. (Orig.). 1981. lib. bdg. 17.75 (ISBN 0-8191-1420-0); pap. text ed. 9.00 (ISBN 0-8191-1421-9). U Pr of Amer.

Corey, Arthur. Behind the Scenes with the Metaphysicians. 7.50 (ISBN 0-87516-014-X). De Vorss.

Dass, Ram. The Only Dance There Is. LC 74-6963. 200p. 1976. Repr. 17.50x (ISBN 0-87668-237-9). Aronson.

DeGeorge, R. T. Classical & Contemporary Metaphysics: A Source Book. 332p. 1962. 12.50 (ISBN 0-03-011310-5, Pub. by HR&W). Krieger.

Deroko, Yovan. Legend of the Truant Tree. (Illus.). 112p. 1981. 6.50 (ISBN 0-682-49804-1). Exposition.

Descartes, Rene. Meditations Metaphysiques. 7th ed. 320p. 1974. 12.95 (ISBN 0-686-55675-5). French & Eur.

--Meditations of Descartes. Veitch, John, tr. from Fr. & Lat. xxxii, 249p. 1966. 15.00 (ISBN 0-87548-042-X). Open Court.

Descartes, Rene & Robinet, Andre. Cogito 75: Meditations Metaphysiques. 156p. 1976. 19.95 (ISBN 0-686-55667-4). French & Eur.

Deutsch, Eliot. Humanity & Divinity: An Essay in Comparative Metaphysics. LC 76-128081. 1970. 10.00x (ISBN 0-87022-190-6). U Pr of Hawaii.

Diggs, Bernard J. Love & Being: An Investigation into the Metaphysics of St. Thomas Aquinas. 180p. 1947. 6.75 (ISBN 0-913298-45-X). S F Vanni.

Donato, Sri. The Unicorn. Morningland Publications, Inc., ed. (Illus.). 207p. (Orig.). 1981. pap. 10.00 (ISBN 0-935146-16-4). Morningland.

Donato, Sri & Donato, Gopi G. Oneness, Vol. III. Morningland Publications, Inc., ed. 167p. 1981. pap. 7.95 spiral bdg. (ISBN 0-935146-58-X). Morningland.

Duns Scotus, John. Philosophical Writings of John Duns Scotus. Wolter, Allan, tr. 1964. pap. 4.95 (ISBN 0-672-60432-9, LLA194). Bobbs.

Elliott, John G. Matter, Life & Evolution. LC 77-74876. (Orig.). 1977. 4.95 (ISBN 0-918892-01-5); pap. 2.95 (ISBN 0-918892-02-3). Gibson Hiller.

Emmet, Dorothy M. Whitehead's Philosophy of Organism. LC 81-4141. (Illus.). xliii, 291p. 1981. Repr. of 1966 ed. lib. bdg. 29.50x (ISBN 0-313-23070-6, EMWP). Greenwood.

Esposito, Joseph L. Evolutionary Metaphysics: The Development of Peirce's Theory of Catagories. LC 80-15736. (Illus.). x, 252p. 1980. 17.00x (ISBN 0-8214-0551-9). Ohio U Pr.

Fackenheim, Emil L. Metaphysics & Historicity. (Aquinas Lecture). 1961. 6.95 (ISBN 0-87462-126-7). Marquette.

French, Peter, et al, eds. Studies in Metaphysics. (Midwest Studies in Philosophy: Vol. 4). 1979. text ed. 29.50x (ISBN 0-8166-0887-3); pap. text ed. 12.00x (ISBN 0-8166-0888-1). U of Minn Pr.

Frossmann, Ludwig, ed. The Metaphysical Conceptions of Henry Bergson. (Illus.). 117p. 1981. 31.45 (ISBN 0-89920-030-3). Am Inst Psych.

Fuchs, W. F. Phenomenology & the Metaphysics of Presence. (Phaenomenologica Ser: No. 69). 1976. pap. 18.50 (ISBN 90-247-1822-8, Pub. by Martinus Nijhoff Netherlands). Kluwer Boston.

Fulda, Hans F., et al. Kritische Darstellung der Metaphysik. (Suhrkamp Taschenbuecher Wissenschaft: Vol. 315). 152p. (Orig.). 1980. pap. text ed. 5.85 (ISBN 3-518-07915-8, Pub. by Suhrkamp Verlag Germany). Suhrkamp.

Fullerton, George S. System of Metaphysics. LC 68-23290. Repr. of 1968 ed. lib. bdg. 32.00x (ISBN 0-8371-0079-8, FUSM). Greenwood.

--System of Metaphysics. 1968. Repr. of 1904 ed. 31.00 (ISBN 0-403-00125-0). Scholarly.

George, Conrad. Open a New Door. (Illus.). 1979. pap. 3.50 (ISBN 0-87516-374-2). De Vorss.

Gunn, Giles, ed. New World Metaphysics: Readings on the Religious Meaning of the American Experience. 500p. 1981. 19.95 (ISBN 0-19-502873-2); pap. text ed. 8.95 (ISBN 0-19-502874-0). Oxford U Pr.

Gyan, Gopi. The Book of Numbers. Morningland Publications, Inc., ed. 620p. (Orig.). 1980. pap. 10.00 (ISBN 0-935146-13-X). Morningland.

Hakim, K. A. Metaphysics of Rumi. 1959. 3.60x (ISBN 0-87902-061-X). Orientalia.

Hall, Manly P. First Principles of Philosophy. 7.50 (ISBN 0-89314-508-4). Philos Res.

--Man, the Grand Symbol of the Mysteries. 12.50 (ISBN 0-89314-513-0); pap. 8.95 (ISBN 0-89314-389-8). Philos Res.

--Soul in Egyptian Metaphysics. pap. 1.75 (ISBN 0-89314-355-3). Philos Res.

--Visions & Metaphysical Experiences. pap. 1.75 (ISBN 0-89314-378-2). Philos Res.

Hamilton, Edward J. The Human Mind, a Treatise in Mental Philosophy. LC 75-3156. 1976. Repr. of 1883 ed. 49.50 (ISBN 0-404-59162-0). AMS Pr.

Hamilton, William. Lectures on Metaphysics & Logic, 4 Vols. Repr. of 1861 ed. Set. 462.40 (ISBN 3-7728-0170-6). Adler.

Harmon, Frances A. The Social Philosophy of the St. Louis Hegelians. LC 75-3159. 1976. Repr. of 1943 ed. 16.00 (ISBN 0-404-59164-7). AMS Pr.

Harris, William T. Hegel's Doctrine of Reflection. LC 75-3160. Repr. of 1881 ed. 22.50 (ISBN 0-404-59165-5). AMS Pr.

Hartshorne, Charles. Aquinas to Whitehead: Seven Centuries of Metaphysics of Religion. LC 76-5156. (Aquinas Lectures Ser.). 1976. 6.95 (ISBN 0-87462-141-0). Marquette.

Hegel, Georg W. The Metaphysical Vision of the Roman World. (Essential Library of the Great Philosophers). (Illus.). 121p. 1980. deluxe ed. 49.85 (ISBN 0-89266-265-4). Am Classical Coll Pr.

--The Metaphysics of the Jewish, the Aegyptian & the Assyrian Spirit. (Illus.). 177p. 1981. 57.85 (ISBN 0-89266-280-8). Am Classical Coll Pr.

Heidegger, Martin. Kant & the Problem of Metaphysics. 6.50 (ISBN 0-8446-2233-8). Peter Smith.

Henle, Robert J. Method in Metaphysics. (Aquinas Lecture). 1950. 6.95 (ISBN 0-87462-115-1). Marquette.

Holmes, Jesse H. As We See It from Here, Vol. IV. LC 79-90910. (Life's Energy Fields Ser.). (Illus.). 146p. 1980. 9.75 (ISBN 0-935436-03-0). Metascience.

Jones, Gilbert. The Metaphysics of the Thinking Thought in Its Effort to Gain Control of the External Universe. (Illus.). 1978. 31.50 (ISBN 0-89266-088-0). Am Classical Coll Pr.

Kant, Immanuel. Fortschritte der Metaphysics: Progress in Metaphysics. Humphrey, Ted B., tr. LC 77-86225. (The Janus Library: Series 4). 1981. 20.00 (ISBN 0-913870-59-5). Abaris Bks.

--Grounding for the Metaphysics of Morals. Ellington, James W., tr. from Ger. (HPC Philosophical Classics Ser.). 125p. 1981. lib. bdg. 12.50 (ISBN 0-915145-01-4); pap. text ed. 2.50 (ISBN 0-915145-00-6). Hackett Pub.

--Prolegomena to Any Future Metaphysics. rev. ed. LC 51-10279. 1950. pap. 3.95 (ISBN 0-672-60187-7, LLA27). Bobbs.

--Prolegomena to Any Future Metaphysics That Will Be Able to Present Itself As a Science. Lucas, P. Gray, tr. (Philosophical Classics Ser.). 155p. 1978. pap. 8.00x (ISBN 0-686-74075-0). B&N.

--Prolegomena to Any Future Metaphysics That Will Be Able to Come Forward As Science. new ed. Ellington, J. W., ed. Carus, Paul, tr. LC 76-51051. 1977. 12.50 (ISBN 0-915144-33-6); pap. 2.50 (ISBN 0-915144-25-5). Hackett Pub.

Kraus, Elizabeth M. The Metaphysics of Experience: A Companion to Whitehead's "Process & Reality. LC 78-70564. 1979. 20.00 (ISBN 0-8232-1038-3); pap. 8.00 (ISBN 0-8232-1039-1). Fordham.

Lafferty, Theodore T. Nature & Values: Pragmatic Essays in Metaphysics. LC 78-120586. 250p. 1976. 19.50x (ISBN 0-87249-193-5). U of SC Pr.

Lamprecht, Sterling P. Metaphysics of Naturalism. LC 67-18049. (Century Philosophy Ser.). 1967. 24.00x (ISBN 0-89197-302-8). Irvington.

--Nature & History. 1966. Repr. of 1950 ed. 14.50 (ISBN 0-208-00229-4, Archon). Shoe String.

Lazerowitz, Morris. Structure of Metaphysics. 1963. text ed. 17.75x (ISBN 0-7100-3148-3). Humanities.

Lehrer, K., ed. Analysis & Metaphysics: Essays in Honor of R. M. Chisholm. LC 75-5500. (Philosophical Studies: No. 4). 316p. 1975. 58.00 (ISBN 90-277-0571-2, Pub. by Reidel Holland). Kluwer Boston.

Leibniz, Gottfried W. Discourse on Metaphysics. 2nd ed. Montgomery, George R., tr. from Fr. Bd. with Correspondence with Arnauld; Monadology. LC 51-45405. xxiii, 272p. 1973. 15.00 (ISBN 0-87548-029-2); pap. 6.95 (ISBN 0-87548-030-6). Open Court.

Letchworth, L. Tom. Sun of Superlove. LC 80-53694. (Illus.). 120p. (Orig.). (gr. 7 up). 1980. pap. 3.95 (ISBN 0-9602334-1-5). Superlove.

Levin, Michael E. Metaphysics & the Mind-Body Problem. (Clarendon Library of Logic & Philosophy). 1979. 36.00x (ISBN 0-19-824415-0). Oxford U Pr.

Loeb, Louis E. From Descartes to Hume: Continental Metaphysics & the Development of Modern Philosophy. 1981. 24.50x (ISBN 0-8014-1289-7). Cornell U Pr.

Loewenberg, Jacob. Reason & the Nature of Things. LC 58-6818. (Paul Carus Lecture Ser.). xiv, 382p. 1959. 19.95 (ISBN 0-87548-105-1). Open Court.

Lord Easu. Book of Revelations for the Aquarian Age. Rodehaver, Gladys K., compiled by. (Illus., Orig.). 1980. pap. 6.95 (ISBN 0-930208-19-6). Mangan Bks.

McCormick, John F. Scholastic Metaphysics. 1928. text ed. 2.90 (ISBN 0-8294-0092-3). Loyola.

McCosh, James. First & Fundamental Truths: Being a Treatise on Metaphysics. LC 75-3255. Repr. of 1889 ed. 25.50 (ISBN 0-404-59242-2). AMS Pr.

--Ideas in Nature Overlooked by Dr. Tyndall. LC 75-3256. Repr. of 1875 ed. 18.50 (ISBN 0-404-59243-0). AMS Pr.

MacKinnon, D. M. The Problem of Metaphysics. LC 73-79309. 180p. 1974. 23.50 (ISBN 0-521-20275-2). Cambridge U Pr.

McLean, George, ed. Man & Nature. 1979. 9.95 (ISBN 0-19-561093-8). Oxford U Pr.

Mahadevan, T. M. P., ed. Spiritual Perspectives: Essays in Mysticism & Metaphysics. 303p. 1975. lib. bdg. 15.00 (ISBN 0-89253-021-9). Ind-US Inc.

Marcel, Gabriel. Metaphysical Journal. Wall, Bernard, tr. 1967. pap. 3.95 (ISBN 0-89526-962-7). Regnery-Gateway.

--Royce's Metaphysics. Ringer, Virginia & Ringer, Gordon, trs. from Ger. LC 74-33746. 180p. 1975. Repr. of 1956 ed. lib. bdg. 15.00 (ISBN 0-8371-7978-5, MARO). Greenwood.

Maritain, Jacques. Distinguer Pour Unir: Les Degres du Savoir. 8th ed. 946p. 1959. 32.50 (ISBN 0-686-56350-6). French & Eur.

--A Preface to Metaphysics: Seven Lectures on Being. facsimile ed. LC 74-157346. (Select Bibliographies Reprint Ser). Repr. of 1939 ed. 13.00 (ISBN 0-8369-5807-1). Arno.

Martin, R. M. Logic, Language & Metaphysics. LC 74-133025. 1971. 12.50x (ISBN 0-8147-5350-7). NYU Pr.

Martin, William O. Metaphysics & Ideology. (Aquinas Lecture). 1959. 6.95 (ISBN 0-87462-124-0). Marquette.

Meyer, Hans. Natur und Kunst Bei Aristotles. pap. 9.50 (ISBN 0-384-38430-7). Johnson Repr.

Mills, Kenneth G. Near to the Fire: A Spontaneous Unfoldment. 1979. pap. 14.95 (ISBN 0-919842-04-6); cassette incl. Sun-Scape Pubns.

Noonan, John P. General Metaphysics. LC 57-6669. 1957. text ed. 2.90 (ISBN 0-8294-0089-3). Loyola.

Norman, Ruth E. Bridge to Heaven. 1969. 8.95 (ISBN 0-932642-10-1). Unarius.

--The Epic. (Tesla Speaks Ser.: No. 13). (Illus.). 1977. 7.95x (ISBN 0-932642-36-5). Unarius.

--Keys to the Universe & the Mind. (Tesla Speaks Ser.: Vol. 11). (Illus.). 1977. 12.50 (ISBN 0-932642-34-9). Unarius.

--Mars Underground Cities Discovered. (Tesla Speaks Ser.: Vol. 12). (Illus.). 1977. 7.95 (ISBN 0-932642-35-7); pap. 6.95 (ISBN 0-932642-46-2). Unarius.

--Whispers of Love on Wings of Light. (Tesla Speaks Ser.: No. 10). (Illus.). 1975. 8.95 (ISBN 0-932642-33-0); pap. 6.95 (ISBN 0-932642-44-6). Unarius.

Norman, Ruth E. & Spaegel, Vaughn. Uriel & the Masters Speak, Vol. I. (Tesla Speaks Ser.: No. 9). (Illus.). 1978. 9.95 (ISBN 0-932642-31-4). Unarius.

Norman, Ruth E., et al. The Masters Speak, 2 vols. (Tesla Speaks Ser.: No. 8). (Illus.). 1975. 8.95 ea.; Vol. 1. (ISBN 0-932642-30-6); Vol. 2. (ISBN 0-932642-29-2). Unarius.

Origen. On First Principles: Being Koetschau's Text of the De Principiis. Butterworth, G. W., tr. 7.50 (ISBN 0-8446-2685-6). Peter Smith.

Ortega Y Gasset, Jose. Some Lessons in Metaphysics. LC 76-80025. 1970 5.50x (ISBN 0-393-08591-0); pap. 4.95 (ISBN 0-393-00514-3, Norton Lib.). Norton.

Our Knowledge of the External World. 2nd ed. 251p. 1926. 17.95x (ISBN 0-04-121008-5). Allen Unwin.

Owens, Joseph C. Saint Thomas & the Future of Metaphysics. (Aquinas Lecture). 1957. 6.95 (ISBN 0-87462-122-4). Marquette.

Parker, DeWitt H. Experience & Substance: An Essay in Metaphysics. LC 68-19292. 1968. Repr. of 1941 ed. lib. bdg. 17.25x (ISBN 0-8371-0606-0, PAES). Greenwood.

Peck, Paul L. Basic Spiritual Metaphysics. LC 78-61984. 1978. 11.95 (ISBN 0-87881-079-X); pap. text ed. 9.25 (ISBN 0-87881-080-3). Mojave Bks.

--Intermediate Spiritual Metaphysics. LC 78-61985. (Spiritual Metaphysics Ser.: Vol. 2). 1979. 13.95 (ISBN 0-87881-081-1); pap. 11.95 (ISBN 0-87881-082-X). Mojave Bks.

Pepper, Stephen C. Concept & Quality. LC 66-19679. (Paul Carus Lecture Ser). xiv, 662p. 1966. 25.00 (ISBN 0-87548-095-0). Open Court.

--World Hypotheses: A Study in Evidence. 1970. pap. 6.95x (ISBN 0-520-00994-0, CAMPUS31). U of Cal Pr.

Percival, Harold W. Thinking & Destiny. LC 47-1811. 1978. 15.95 (ISBN 0-911650-01-6); deluxe ed. 18.95 in 2 vols. (ISBN 0-911650-02-4); pap. 8.95 (ISBN 0-911650-06-7). Word Foun.

Piguet. De L'esthetique a la Metaphysique. (Phaenomenologica Ser: No. 3). 1959. lib. bdg. 29.00 (ISBN 90-247-0236-4, Pub. by Martinus Nijhoff Netherlands). Kluwer Boston.

Plamondon, Ann L. Whitehead's Organic Philosophy of Science. LC 78-16682. 1979. 19.00x (ISBN 0-87395-387-8). State U NY Pr.

Poole, Cecil A. In Search of Reality. 112p. 1980. pap. 5.25 (ISBN 0-686-27980-8). AMORC.

Potter, Karl, ed. Indian Metaphysics & Epistemology: The Tradition of Nyaya-Vaisesika up to Gangesa. Encyclopedia of Indian Philosophies. LC 77-85558. 1977. 35.00 (ISBN 0-691-07183-7). Princeton U Pr.

Quotidomine, Francis. Basic Metaphysics: Concepts of Men's Spiritual & Psychic Naturalism. 1978. 4.25 (ISBN 0-87164-075-9). William-F.

Ra, Bo Yin. Bo Yin Ra: About My Books, Concerning My Name, & Other Texts. Reichenbach, B. A., tr. from Ger. LC 76-27910. 1977. pap. 1.75 (ISBN 0-915034-00-X). Kober Pr.

Rabinowics, Wlodzimierz. Universalizability. (Synthese Library: No. 141). 1979. lib. bdg. 24.00 (ISBN 90-277-1020-1, Pub. by Reidel Holland). Kluwer Boston.

Ramsey, Ian T., ed. Prospect for Metaphysics: Essays of Metaphysical Exploration. Repr. of 1961 ed. lib. bdg. 15.00x (ISBN 0-8371-2557-X, RAME). Greenwood.

Rescher, Nicholas. A Theory of Possibility: A Constructivistic & Conceptualistic Account of Possible Individuals & Possible Worlds. LC 75-10540. 1975. 19.95x (ISBN 0-8229-1122-1). U of Pittsburgh Pr.

Reuscher, John A. Essays on the Metaphysical Foundation of Personal Identity. LC 80-6067. 111p. 1981. lib. bdg. 16.50 (ISBN 0-8191-1471-5); pap. text ed. 7.25 (ISBN 0-8191-1472-3). U Pr of Amer.

Richmond, James. Theology & Metaphysics. LC 72-159483. 1971. 6.50x (ISBN 0-8052-3411-X). Schocken.

Ross, Stephen D. Philosophical Mysteries. LC 80-26837. (Ser. in Philosophy). 160p. 1981. text ed. 34.00x (ISBN 0-87395-524-2, ROPM); pap. text ed. 9.95x (ISBN 0-87395-525-0, ROPM-P). State U NY Pr.

--Transition to an Ordinal Metaphysics. 162p. 1980. 29.00 (ISBN 0-87395-434-3, ROTO); pap. 9.95 (ISBN 0-87395-435-1). State U NY Pr.

Sabzavari, Hadi Ibn Mahdi. The Metaphysics of Haji Mulla Hadi Sabzavari. Izutsu, Toshihiku & Mohaghegh, Mehdi, trs. from Persian. LC 76-18174. 300p. 1977. lib. bdg. 25.00x (ISBN 0-88206-011-2). Caravan Bks.

St. John, Gladys. Listening Across the Border. 1981. 8.95 (ISBN 0-533-04797-8). Vantage.

Samek, Robert A. Meta Phenomenon. LC 80-81699. 300p. 1981. 15.00 (ISBN 0-8022-2372-9). Philos Lib.

Sastri, M. N. Outlines of Hindu Metaphysics. 1976. 10.00x (ISBN 0-88386-854-7). South Asia Bks.

Sellars, Wilfrid. Philosophical Perspectives: Metaphysics & Epistemology. 1979. lib. bdg. 21.00 (ISBN 0-917930-25-8); pap. text ed. 6.50x (ISBN 0-917930-05-3). Ridgeview.

Shastra, M. N. Hindu Metaphysics. 247p. 1978. Repr. of 1904 ed. text ed. 15.00 (ISBN 0-89684-121-9, Pub. by Cosmo Pubns India). Orient Bk Dist.

Slote, Michael A. Metaphysics & Essence. LC 74-25322. 160p. 1975. 10.00x, USA (ISBN 0-8147-7761-9). NYU Pr.

Soll, Ivan. Introduction to Hegel's Metaphysics. LC 75-85447. 1969. 7.50x (ISBN 0-226-76794-9); pap. 5.00x (ISBN 0-226-76795-7). U of Chicago Pr.

Sontag, Frederick. Existentialist Prolegomena: To a Future Metaphysics. LC 68-11315. 1969. 9.00x (ISBN 0-226-76819-8). U of Chicago Pr.

Sprague, Elmer. Metaphysical Thinking. 1978. pap. 5.95x (ISBN 0-19-502263-7). Oxford U Pr.

Stace, Walter T. Nature of the World: An Essay in Phenomenalist Metaphysics. Repr. of 1940 ed. lib. bdg. 15.00 (ISBN 0-8371-1039-4, STNW). Greenwood.

--Theory of Knowledge & Existence. Repr. of 1932 ed. lib. bdg. 18.50x (ISBN 0-8371-4343-8, STTK). Greenwood.

Strawson, P. F. Individuals: An Essay in Descriptive Metaphysics. 1964. pap. text ed. 11.95x (ISBN 0-416-68310-X). Methuen Inc.

Strong, Edward W. Procedure & Metaphysics: A Study in the Philosophy of Mathematical-Physical Science in the 16- 17 Century. 301p. 1977. Repr. of 1936 ed. lib. bdg. 19.50 (ISBN 0-915172-28-3). Richwood Pub.

Syz, Hans C. Of Being & Meaning. LC 80-82648. 64p. 1981. 6.00 (ISBN 0-8022-2374-5). Philos Lib.

Taylor, Richard. Introductory Readings in Metaphysics. 1979. pap. text ed. 11.50 (ISBN 0-13-502302-5). P-H.

--Metaphysics. 2nd ed. LC 73-5748. (Foundations of Philosophy Ser). 133p. 1974. pap. 7.95 ref. ed. (ISBN 0-13-578468-9). P-H.

Teloh, Henry. The Development of Plato's Metaphysics. LC 80-17160. 264p. 1981. 18.75x (ISBN 0-271-00268-9). Pa St U Pr.

Thompson, Ian. Paul Tillich's Theory of Meaning, Truth, & Logic. 250p. 1981. 30.00x (ISBN 0-85224-388-X, Pub. by Edinburgh U Pr Scotland). Columbia U Pr.

Thornton, Henry D. The Metaphysics of the Womb. (Illus.). 141p. 1981. 49.85 (ISBN 0-89266-271-9). Am Classical Coll Pr.

Tuala. Tuala Speaks. Tamalelagi, Jeanne, ed. LC 80-67870. 220p. (Orig.). 1980. pap. 8.95 (ISBN 0-87516-425-0). De Vorss.

Twitchell, Paul. Anitya. (Illus.). 1969. 9.95 (ISBN 0-914766-01-5). IWP Pub.

--Coins of Gold. 1972. 9.95 (ISBN 0-914766-02-3). IWP Pub.

--Dialogues with the Master. 1970. pap. 2.95 (ISBN 0-914766-03-1). IWP Pub.

--Drums of ECK. 1970. pap. 2.50 (ISBN 0-914766-04-X). IWP Pub.

--The ECK Vidya: The Ancient Science of Prophecy. 237p. 1972. 3.50 (ISBN 0-914766-07-4). IWP Pub.

--The Far Country. 1971. pap. 4.95 (ISBN 0-914766-08-2). IWP Pub.

--The Shariyat-Ki-Sugmad. 1971. Vol. 1 1970. kivar bdg. 6.95 (ISBN 0-914766-13-9); Vol. 2 1971. 6.95 (ISBN 0-914766-14-7). IWP Pub.

--Stranger by the River. 176p. 1970. pap. 5.95 (ISBN 0-914766-16-3). IWP Pub.

--The Tiger's Fang. 1967. pap. 2.50 (ISBN 0-914766-17-1). IWP Pub.

--Way of Dharma. 1970. pap. 3.95 (ISBN 0-914766-18-X). IWP Pub.

--Der Zahn Des Tigers. 1979. pap. 5.00 (ISBN 0-914766-45-7). IWP Pub.

University Of California Philosophical Union - 1923-1924. Essays in Metaphysics: Lectures. (Publications in Philosophy Ser: Vol. 5). 1924. pap. 17.00 (ISBN 0-685-13425-3). Johnson Repr.

Urban, Wilbur M. The Intelligible World: Metaphysics & Value. LC 75-3415. Repr. of 1929 ed. 24.50 (ISBN 0-404-59412-3). AMS Pr.

--The Intelligible World: Metaphysics & Value. LC 76-51208. 1977. Repr. of 1929 ed. lib. bdg. 26.75x (ISBN 0-8371-9437-7, URIW). Greenwood.

Ushenko, Andrew P. Power & Events: An Essay on Dynamics in Philosophy. Repr. of 1946 ed. lib. bdg. 15.25x (ISBN 0-8371-1041-6, USPE). Greenwood.

Van Hook, John E. Systematic Philosophy: An Overview of Metaphysics Showing the Development from the Greeks to the Contemporaries with Specified Directions & Projections. (Illus.). 1979. 7.50 (ISBN 0-682-49398-8, University). Exposition.

Van Inwagen, Peter, ed. Time & Cause: Essays Presented to Richard Taylor. (Philosophical Studies Series in Philosophy: No. 19). vii, 300p. 1980. lib. bdg. 34.00 (ISBN 90-277-1048-1, Pub. by Reidel Holland). Kluwer Boston.

Van Nuys, Kelvin. Is Reality Meaningful. LC 65-26973. 1966. 10.00 (ISBN 0-8022-1763-X). Philos Lib.

Varma, V. P. The Political Philosophy of Sri Aurobindo. 2nd ed. 1976. Repr. of 1960 ed. text ed. 13.50x (ISBN 0-8426-0873-7). Verry.

Vaught, Carl J., ed. Essays in Metaphysics. LC 71-121785. 1970. 14.95x (ISBN 0-271-00123-2). Pa St U Pr.

Versfeld, Marthinus. An Essays on the Metaphysics of Descartes. LC 68-26210. 1968. Repr. of 1940 ed. 10.00 (ISBN 0-8046-0481-9). Kennikat.

Wallack, F. Bradford. The Epochal Nature of Process in Whitehead's Metaphysics. LC 79-22898. 1980. lib. bdg. 34.00 (ISBN 0-87395-404-1); pap. 12.95 (ISBN 0-87395-454-8). State U NY Pr.

Walsh, W. H. Kant's Criticism of Metaphysics. 1975. 12.50x (ISBN 0-85224-283-2, Pub. by Edinburgh U Pr Scotland). Columbia U Pr.

--Kant's Criticism of Metaphysics. 1976. pap. 4.50 (ISBN 0-226-87215-7, P688, Phoen). U of Chicago Pr.

Walsh, William H. Metaphysics. LC 66-26470. (Orig.). 1966. pap. 2.25 (ISBN 0-15-659305-X, H055, Hbgr). HarBraceJ.

Warrington, John, ed. Aristotle's Metaphysics. Date not set. 9.95x (ISBN 0-460-01000-X, Evman). Biblio Dist.

Weinberg, Julius R. & Yandell, Keith E., eds. Metaphysics. LC 73-148058. 1971. pap. text ed. 9.75x (ISBN 0-03-085668-X). Irvington.

Wellek, Rene, ed. James Burnett Monboddo (1714-1799) Antient Metaphysics, 6 Vol., 1779-99. LC 75-11236. (British Philosophers & Theologians of the 17th & 18th Centuries Ser.). 1977. lib. bdg. 42.00 (ISBN 0-8240-1789-7). Garland Pub.

Wells, Norman. Metaphysical Disputation, Xxxi, De Ento Finito, on Finite Being. Date not set. price not set. Marquette.

White Eagle. The Living Word of St. John. new ed. 208p. 1979. 13.95 (ISBN 0-85487-044-X). De Vorss.

Whiteley, C. H. Introduction to Metaphysics. LC 77-1892. (Repr. of 1950 ed.). 1977. text ed. 13.00x (ISBN 0-391-00711-4). Humanities.

Wilbur, James B. Spinoza's Metaphysics: Essays in Critical Appreciation. (Philosophia Spinozae Perennis: Spinoza's Philosophy & Its Relevance). 1976. pap. text ed. 20.75x (ISBN 90-232-1361-0). Humanities.

Wilson, Joseph H. The Primer of Life. 1980. 10.00 (ISBN 0-533-04565-7). Vantage.

Wippel, John F. The Metaphysical Thought of Godfrey of Fontaines: A Study in Late Thirteenth-Century Philosophy. 1981. 27.95 (ISBN 0-8132-0556-5). Cath U Pr.

Wolfe, W. Thomas. And the Sun Is up: Kundalini Rises in the West. (Illus.). 1978. pap. 4.95 perfect bdg. (ISBN 0-932312-00-4). Academy Hill.

Wood, Robert E., ed. Future of Metaphysics. LC 70-116094. 320p. (Orig.). 1972. 10.00 (ISBN 0-8129-6136-6, QP 120). Times Bks.

Woodbridge, F. J. Realm of Mind: An Essay in Metaphysics. Repr. of 1926 ed. 13.00 (ISBN 0-527-97850-7). Kraus Repr.

METAPHYSICS–DICTIONARIES

Apostle, H. G. Aristotle's Metaphysics. LC 79-88598. (Apostle Translations of Aristotle's Works Ser.: Vol. 1). 1979. text ed. 19.20x (ISBN 0-9602870-0-0); pap. text ed. 6.60x (ISBN 0-9602870-1-9). Peripatetic.

Fillmore, Charles. Revealing Word. 1959. 3.95 (ISBN 0-87159-137-5). Unity Bks.

Yott, Donald H. Man & Metaphysics. 1980. pap. 5.95 (ISBN 0-87728-488-1). Weiser.

METAPSYCHOLOGY

see Psychical Research; Spiritualism

METASTASIO, PIETRO ANTONIO DOMENICO BUONAVENTURA, 1698-1782

Burney, Charles. Memoirs of the Life & Writings of the Abate Metastasio, 3 Vols. LC 76-162295. (Music Ser). 1971. Repr. of 1796 ed. lib. bdg. 95.00 (ISBN 0-306-71110-9). Da Capo.

Stendhal. Vie de Haydn, de Mozart et de Metastase. 48.00 (ISBN 0-686-55083-8). French & Eur.

Stendhal, et al. Haydn, Mozart et Metatase. (Illus.). 9.95 (ISBN 0-686-55061-7). French & Eur.

METASTASIS

Day, Stacey B., et al, eds. Cancer Invasion & Metastasis: Biologic Mechanisms & Therapy. LC 77-83695. (Progress in Cancer Research & Therapy Ser: Vol. 5). 540p. 1977. 43.50 (ISBN 0-89004-184-9). Raven.

Garattini, S. & Franchi, G., eds. Chemotherapy of Cancer Dissemination & Metastasis. LC 72-96335. (Monographs of the Mario Negri Institute for Pharmacological Research). (Illus.). 400p. 1973. 34.50 (ISBN 0-911216-46-4). Raven.

Leighton, Joseph S. Spread of Cancer: Pathogenesis, Experimental Methods, Interpretations. (Orig.). 1967. 31.50 (ISBN 0-12-441950-X); pap. 19.50 (ISBN 0-12-441951-8). Acad Pr.

Stansly, Philip G. & Sato, Hamo, eds. Cancer Metastasis: Approaches to the Mechanism, Prevention, & Treatment. LC 77-13866. (Gann Monographs on Cancer: Vol. 20). 1977. 44.50 (ISBN 0-8391-1185-1). Univ Park.

Weiss, L. The Cell Periphery, Metastasis, & Other Contact Phenomena. Neuberger, A. & Tatum, E. L., eds. (Frontiers of Biology Ser.: Vol. 7). 1968. 34.25 (ISBN 0-444-10304-X, North-Holland). Elsevier.

--Fundamental Aspects of Metastasis. 1976. 68.50 (ISBN 0-444-11022-4, North-Holland). Elsevier.

Weiss, Leonard & Gilbert, Harvey. Bone Metastasis. 1980. lib. bdg. 55.00 (ISBN 0-8161-2129-X, Hall Medical). G K Hall.

--Pulmonary Metastasis. 1978. lib. bdg. 29.95 (ISBN 0-8161-2107-9). G K Hall.

Weiss, Leonard, et al. Brain Metastasis. (Medical Books). 1980. lib. bdg. 48.50 (ISBN 0-8161-2119-2, Hall Medical). G K Hall.

METAZOA

Clark, Robert B. Dynamics in Metazoan Evolution: The Origin of the Coelom & Segments. 1964. 45.00x (ISBN 0-19-854353-0). Oxford U Pr.

Grasse, Pierre P. & Tetry, Andree. Zoologie: Metazoaires II, Vol. 2. (Methodique Ser.). 1056p. 39.95 (ISBN 0-686-56435-9). French & Eur.

Smith, D. C. & Tiffon, Y., eds. Nutrition in the Lower Metazoa: Proceedings. (Illus.). 192p. 1980. 35.00 (ISBN 0-08-025904-9). Pergamon.

Tetry, Andree. Zoologie: Metazoaires III, Vol. 3. (Methodique Ser.). 1336p. 48.95 (ISBN 0-686-56436-7). French & Eur.

METEORIC GLASS

see Tektite

METEORITES

see also Meteors

Berger, Melvin. Comets, Meteors & Asteroids. (Illus.). 64p. (gr. 10 up). 1981. PLB 6.99 (ISBN 0-399-61148-7). Putnam.

Buchwald, Vagn F. Handbook of Iron Meteorites: Their History, Distribution, Composition & Structure, 3 vols. 1976. boxed set 250.00x (ISBN 0-520-02934-8). U of Cal Pr.

Directory of Meteorite Collections & Meteorite Research. 1968. pap. 7.00 (ISBN 92-3-000716-1, U162, UNESCO). Unipub.

Dodd, Robert T. Meteorites: A Chemical-Petrologic Synthesis. LC 80-25327. (Illus.). 368p. Date not set. price not set (ISBN 0-521-22570-1). Cambridge U Pr.

Fodor, R. V. Meteorites: Stones from the Sky. LC 76-12513. (Illus.). (gr. 2-5). 1976. 5.95 (ISBN 0-396-07369-7). Dodd.

Furneaux, Rupert. The Tungus Event. 1979. pap. 1.50 (ISBN 0-8439-0619-7, Leisure Bks). Nordon Pubns.

Huss, Glenn I. The Huss Collection of Meteorites of the American Meteorite Laboratory. (Illus.). 1976. pap. 1.00x (ISBN 0-910096-06-6). Am Meteorite.

Keil, Klaus & Gomes, Celso P. Brazilian Stone Meteorites. LC 80-5333. (Illus.). 192p. 1981. 20.00x (ISBN 0-8263-0543-1). U of NM Pr.

Kuiper, Gerard P. & Middlehurst, Barbara M., eds. Moon, Meteorites & Comets. LC 62-18117. (Solar System Ser: Vol. 4). 1963. 33.00x (ISBN 0-226-45928-4). U of Chicago Pr.

LeMaire, T. R. Stones from the Stars: The Unsolved Mysteries of Meteorites. LC 79-21158. 204p. 1980. 9.95 (ISBN 0-13-846881-8). P-H.

Lunar & Planetary Institute, compiled by. Proceedings: Eleventh Lunar & Planetary Science Conference, Houston, Texas, March 17-21, 1980, 3 vols. (Geochimica & Cosmochimica Acta: Suppl. 14). 3000p. 1981. Set. 200.00 (ISBN 0-08-026314-3). Pergamon.

McCall, G. J. Meteorites & Their Origins. 352p. 1973. 13.95 (ISBN 0-7153-5560-0, Pub. by Wiley). Krieger.

--Meteorites & Their Origins. LC 72-7640. 352p. 1973. 19.95 (ISBN 0-470-58115-8). Halsted Pr.

McCall, G. J., ed. Meteorite Craters. (Benchmark Papers in Geology: Vol. 36). 1977. 51.50 (ISBN 0-12-787026-1). Acad Pr.

Mason, Brian. Handbook of Elemental Abundances in Meteorites: Reviews in Cosmochemistry & Allied Subjects. LC 71-148927. (Illus.). 564p. 1971. 117.25 (ISBN 0-677-14950-6). Gordon.

--Handbook of Elemental Abundances in Meteorites: Reviews in Cosmochemistry & Allied Subjects. LC 71-148927. (Illus.). 564p. 1971. 117.25 (ISBN 0-677-14950-6). Gordon.

Moore, C. B. Meteorites. (Earth Science Curriculum Project Pamphlet Ser). 1971. pap. 3.20 (ISBN 0-395-02624-5, 2-14610). HM.

Nagy, B. Carbonaceous Meteorites. LC 73-89156. (Developments in Solar System & Space Science Ser: Vol. 1). 747p. 1975. 109.75 (ISBN 0-444-41189-5). Elsevier.

Nininger, H. H. Arizona's Meteorite Crater. (Illus.). 1965. 7.50 (ISBN 0-910096-01-5); pap. 4.50 (ISBN 0-910096-02-3). Am Meteorite.

--Ask a Question About Meteorites. (Illus.). 1961. pap. 2.00 (ISBN 0-910096-03-1). Am Meteorite.

--A Comet Strikes the Earth. rev. ed. (Illus.). 1969. pap. 2.00 (ISBN 0-910096-04-X). Am Meteorite.

--Find a Falling Star. LC 72-83710. (Illus.). 352p. 1976. 8.95 (ISBN 0-8397-2229-X); pap. 5.95 (ISBN 0-8397-2230-3). Eriksson.

Olsen, Edward J. Meteorites: The Poor Man's Space Probe. LC 73-163905. (Augustana College Library Occasional Papers: No. 11). 1973. pap. 1.00 (ISBN 0-910182-34-5). Augustana Coll.

Pearl, Richard M. Fallen from Heaven: Meteorites & Man. 1975. pap. 2.75 (ISBN 0-686-14945-9). Earth Science.

Peck, Ellis L. Space Rocks & Buffalo Grass. (Illus., Orig.). 1979. pap. 8.95 (ISBN 0-686-25743-X). Peach Enterprises.

Ramdohr, P. The Opaque Minerals in Stony Meteorites. 1973. 68.50 (ISBN 0-444-41067-8). Elsevier.

Sears, D. W. The Nature & Origin of Meteorites. LC 78-10127. (Monographs on Astronomical Subjects). (Illus.). 1979. 19.75 (ISBN 0-19-520121-3). Oxford U Pr.

Shand, S. James. Eruptive Rocks: Their Genesis, Composition, Classification, & Their Relation to Ore Deposits. 3rd ed. (Illus.). 1969. Repr. of 1949 ed. 17.50 (ISBN 0-02-852120-X). Hafner.

Symposium on Meteorite Research,Vienna,Austria,August 7-13,1968. Meteorite Research: Proceedings. Millman, P. N., ed. (Astrophysic & Space Science Library: No.12). 941p. 1969. lib. bdg. 89.50 (ISBN 90-277-0132-6, Pub. by Reidel Holland). Kluwer Boston.

Wasson, J. T. Meteorites: Classification & Properties. LC 74-4896. (Minerals, Rocks & Inorganic Materials Ser.: Vol. 10). (Illus.). 370p. 1974. 36.70 (ISBN 0-387-06744-2). Springer-Verlag.

Wood, J. A. Meteorites & the Origin of Planets. (International Ser. in the Earth & Planetary Sciences). 1968. text ed. 10.00 (ISBN 0-07-071581-5, C); pap. text ed. 8.00 (ISBN 0-07-071580-7). McGraw.

METEOROLOGICAL INSTRUMENTS

see also Altimeter; Barometer; Meteorological Satellites; Thermometers and Thermometry

Commission for Instruments & Methods of Observation, 6th Session. Abridged Final Report of the Sixth Session. 98p. (Orig.). 1974. pap. 20.00 (ISBN 0-685-40958-9, 363, WMO). Unipub.

Commission for Instruments & Methods of Observations: Abridged Final Report of the Seventh Session. 1977. pap. 25.00 (ISBN 92-63-10490-5, WMO 490, WMO). Unipub.

Middleton, W. E. Knowles. Invention of the Meteorological Instruments. LC 68-31640. (Illus.). 362p. 1969. 23.50x (ISBN 0-8018-1003-5). Johns Hopkins.

Performance Requirements Ofaerological Instruments. (Technical Note Ser.). pap. 6.50 (ISBN 0-685-57274-9, WMO). Unipub.

Thaller, M. Instrument Development Inquiry. 2nd ed. (No. 232). 1977. pap. 15.00 (ISBN 0-685-77319-1, WMO). Unipub.

METEOROLOGICAL LIBRARIES

see also Information Storage and Retrieval Systems–Meteorology

METEOROLOGICAL LITERATURE SEARCHING

see Information Storage and Retrieval Systems-Meteorology

METEOROLOGICAL MAPS

see Meteorology–Charts, Diagrams, etc.

METEOROLOGICAL OBSERVATIONS

see Meteorology–Observations

METEOROLOGICAL OBSERVATORIES

see Meteorological Stations

METEOROLOGICAL OPTICS

see also Auroras; Rainbow; Refraction; Twilight

Divari, Nikolai B., ed. Atmospheric Optics, Vol.1. LC 67-10534. 178p. 1970. 32.50 (ISBN 0-306-10837-2, Consultants). Plenum Pub.

Elsaesser, H. & Fechtig, H., eds. Interplanetary Dust & Zodiacal Light. LC 78-2597. 1976. pap. 21.20 (ISBN 0-387-07615-8). Springer-Verlag.

Greenler, Robert. Rainbows, Halos & Glories. LC 80-143722. (Illus.). 304p. 1980. 24.95 (ISBN 0-521-23605-3). Cambridge U Pr.

McCartney, Earl J. Optics of the Atmosphere: Scattering by Molecules & Particles. LC 76-10941. (Pure & Applied Optics Ser). 1976. 43.00 (ISBN 0-471-01526-1, Pub. by Wiley-Interscience). Wiley.

Marchuk, G. I., et al. Monte Carlo Methods in Atmospheric Optics. (Springer Ser. in Optical Sciences: Vol. 12). (Illus.). 1979. 29.80 (ISBN 0-387-09402-4). Springer-Verlag.

Minnaert, M. Nature of Light & Colour in the Open Air. 1948. pap. text ed. 5.00 (ISBN 0-486-20196-1). Dover.

Pyldmaa, V. K. Actinometry & Atmospheric Optics. 392p. 1971. 25.00x (ISBN 0-7065-1125-5, Pub. by IPST). Intl Schol Bk Serv.

Report of the Second Planning Meeting for the West African Monsoon Experiment & Report of the Preparatory Meeting of the WAMEX Scientific & Management Regional Committee. (GARP Special Report Ser.: No. 27). 1978. pap. 25.00 (ISBN 0-685-60680-5, W 394, WMO). Unipub.

Rozenberg, Georgii V. Twilight: A Study in Atmospheric Optics. LC 65-11345. 368p. 1966. 34.50 (ISBN 0-306-30220-9, Plenum Pr). Plenum Pub.

Tricker, R. A. Introduction to Meteorological Optics. 1971. 22.50 (ISBN 0-444-19700-1). Elsevier.

METEOROLOGICAL RESEARCH

American Sunbeam Staff. Weather Made to Whose Order? (Illus.). 56p. Date not set. self cover 2.00 (ISBN 0-918700-04-3). Duverus Pub.

Catalogue of Meteorological Data for Research, Pt. IV. 117p. 1980. pap. 17.00 (ISBN 0-686-65617-2, W448, WMO). Unipub.

Catalogue of Meteorological Data for Research, Pt.2. 1970. pap. 20.00 (ISBN 0-685-36784-3, WMO 174, WMO). Unipub.

Davis, Ray J. & Grant, Lewis, eds. Weather Modification: Technology & Law. LC 78-55519. (AAAS Selected Symposia Ser.). 1978. lib. bdg. 17.50x (ISBN 0-89158-153-7). Westview.

First GARP Global Experiment; Global Atmospheric Research Programme: Report. (Garp Special Report: No. 16). 46p. (List of participants). 1975. pap. 15.00 (ISBN 0-685-62850-7, WMO). Unipub.

The Global Weather Experiment Nineteen Seventy-Eight to Seventy-Nine. 44p. 1981. pap. 4.00 (ISBN 0-686-73706-7, W488, WMO). Unipub.

Information on the Application of Meteorological Satellite Data in Routine Operations & Research: Abstracts, Annual Summaries & Bibliographies, Suppl. No. 3. (Global Observing System & Satellite Sub-System Ser.). 110p. 1980. pap. 5.00 (ISBN 0-686-62999-X, W-455, WMO). Unipub.

Joint Organizing Committe,Eleventh Session. GARP Report. (Illus.). 1976. pap. 40.00 (ISBN 0-685-66360-4, WMO). Unipub.

Mihara, Yoshiaki, ed. Agricultural Meteorology of Japan. LC 74-78859. 216p. 1974. text ed. 22.50x (ISBN 0-8248-0337-X, Eastwest Ctr). U Pr of Hawaii.

The Monsoon Experiment. (GARP Publications Series: No. 18). 1977. pap. 25.00 (ISBN 0-685-77321-3, WMO). Unipub.

Pre-GATE Tests & Studies for the GARP Atlantic Tropical Experiment. (GATE Report Ser.: No. 2). (Illus.). 1974. pap. 25.00 (ISBN 0-685-50564-2, WMO). Unipub.

Preliminary Scientific Results of the GARP Atlantic Tropical Experiment, 2 vols. (GATE Report: No. 14). (Illus.). 761p. 1975. pap. 40.00 ea. (WMO). Unipub.

Report of the Seventh Session of the Tropical Experiment Board: Global Atmospheric Research Programme. (GARP Special Report: No. 15). 1975. pap. 15.00 (ISBN 0-685-57619-1, WMO). Unipub.

Report of the Sixth Session of the Tropical Experiment Board. (GARP Special Report Ser.: No. 12). 17p. (Orig.). 1974. pap. 15.00 (ISBN 0-685-50563-4, WMO). Unipub.

Report of the Third Session of WMO Executive Committee Inter-Govern-Mental Panel on the First GARP Global Experiment. 1976. pap. 15.00 (ISBN 0-685-74525-2, WMO). Unipub.

Report on the Field Phase of the GARP Atlantic Tropical Experiment: Summary of Data Collected. (GATE Report: No. 19). (Illus.). 219p. 1975. pap. 40.00 (ISBN 0-685-57618-3, WMO). Unipub.

Report on the Field Phase of the GARP Tropical Experiment Scientific Programme. (GATE Report: No. 16). (Illus.). 1975. pap. 40.00 (ISBN 0-685-57616-7, WMO). Unipub.

Scientific Results of the Air Mass Transformation Experiment (AMTEX) (GARP Publication Ser.: No. 24). 236p. 1981. pap. 40.00 (ISBN 0-686-75497-2, W494, WMO). Unipub.

Smith, C. V., ed. Meteorological Observations in Animal Experiments. (Technical Note Ser.). (Orig.). 1970. pap. 6.00 (ISBN 0-685-04918-3, WMO). Unipub.

WMO Executive Committee Inter-Governmental Panel on the First GARP Global Experimental. Report. (GARP Special Report Ser.: No. 17). (Illus.). 47p. 1976. pap. 15.00 (ISBN 0-685-66359-0, WMO). Unipub.

METEOROLOGICAL SATELLITES

see also Meteorological Instruments; Meteorological Stations; Tiros (Meteorological Satellite)

Applications of Satellite Data to Aeronautical Meteorology. (WMO Ser.: No.413). (Illus.). 93p. 1976. pap. 32.00 (ISBN 92-63-10413-1, WMO). Unipub.

Information on the Application of Meteorological Satellite Data on Routine Operations: Abstracts, Annual Summaries & Bibliographies. (World Weather Watch Ser). (Illus.). 1978. pap. 34.00 (ISBN 92-63-10475-1, WMO); 1st suppl. 34.00 (ISBN 0-686-67960-1). Unipub.

Integrated Global Ocean Station System: General Plan & Implementation Program for Phase 1. (Marine Science Affairs Ser.: No. 2). 1970. pap. 2.00 (ISBN 0-685-02470-9, WMO). Unipub.

A Pilot Study on the Application of Geosynchronous Meteorological Satellite Data to Very Short Range Terminal Forecasting. 1970. pap. 5.00 (ISBN 0-299-97031-0). U of Wis Pr.

Planning of Meteorological Station Networks. (Technical Note Ser.). 1970. pap. 10.00 (ISBN 0-685-02473-3, WMO). Unipub.

The Role of Satellites in WMO Programmes in the 1980's. (Planning Report Ser: No. 36). 1978. pap. 41.00 (ISBN 92-63-10494-8, W382, WMO). Unipub.

Satellite Data Requirements for Marine Meteorological Services. (Reports on Marine Science Affairs Ser.: No. 14). 46p. 1981. pap. 17.00 (ISBN 92-63-10548-0, W482, WMO). Unipub.

Specifications for Vertical Temperature & Moisture Sounder for the Synchronous Meteorological Satellites. 1972. pap. 5.00 (ISBN 0-299-97043-4). U of Wis Pr.

Synchronous Meteorological Satellite Sounder Specification: Final Report Under NASA Contract NHS5-216071. pap. 5.00 (ISBN 0-299-97050-7). U of Wis Pr.

The Use of Satellite Pictures in Weather Analysis & Forecasting. rev. ed. (Technical Note Ser.: No. 124). (Illus.). 275p. (Orig.). 1976. pap. 60.00 (ISBN 0-685-34562-9, 333, WMO). Unipub.

Visual Channel Data Analysis for Synchronous Meteorological Satellite: Scientific Report on NOAA-NESS. 1974. pap. 7.50 (ISBN 0-299-97053-1). U of Wis Pr.

World Meteorological Organization. Planning of the Global Telecommunication System. (World Weather Watch Planning Report Ser.: No. 16). 1966. pap. 6.00 (ISBN 0-685-22330-2, WMO). Unipub.

--Role of Meteorological Satellites in the World Weather Watch. (World Weather Watch Planning Report Ser.: No. 18). 1967. pap. 14.00 (ISBN 0-685-22336-1, WMO). Unipub.

World Weather Watch: Eighth Status Report on Implementation. (WMO Ser: No. 447). (Illus.). 140p. 1977. pap. 25.00 (ISBN 92-63-10447-6, WMO). Unipub.

METEOROLOGICAL STATIONS

see also Meteorological Satellites

Basic Synoptic Network of Observing Stations. (Illus.). 1979. pap. 45.00 (ISBN 0-685-90698-1, WMO 217, WMO). Unipub.

Gandin, L. S., et al. Design of Optimum Networks for Aerological Observing Stations. (World Weather Watch Planning Report Ser.: No. 21). 1969. pap. 12.00 (ISBN 0-685-22301-9, WMO). Unipub.

Instrument & Observing Problems in Cold Climates. (Technical Note Ser.). 30p. (Orig.). 1974. pap. 10.00 (ISBN 92-63-10384-4, WMO). Unipub.

Integrated Global Ocean Station System: General Plan & Implementation Program for Phase 1. (Marine Science Affairs Ser.: No. 2). 1970. pap. 2.00 (ISBN 0-685-02470-9, WMO). Unipub.

International List of Selected, Supplementary & Auxiliary Ships. (No. 47). 1977. pap. 21.00 (ISBN 0-685-77320-5, WMO). Unipub.

North Atlantic Ocean Stations Vessels Manual. (Technical Pubns.: No. 414). 21p. 1975. pap. 30.00 (ISBN 92-63-10414-X, WMO). Unipub.

Planning of Meteorological Station Networks. (Technical Note Ser.). 1970. pap. 10.00 (ISBN 0-685-02473-3, WMO). Unipub.

WMO Technical Conference, Washington, D.C., 14-19 February 1975. Automated Meteorological Systems: Proceedings, No. 420. (Illus.). 380p. 1975. pap. 58.00 (ISBN 92-63-10420-4, WMO). Unipub.

World Meteorological Organization. Chart Processing Functions of Regional Meteorological Centres. (World Weather Watch Planning Report Ser.: No. 12). 1966. pap. 6.00 (ISBN 0-685-22294-2, WMO). Unipub.

METEOROLOGISTS

see also Meteorology As a Profession

Compton, Grant. What Does a Meteorologist Do? (What Do They Do Ser.). (Illus.). 80p. (gr. 5 up). 1981. PLB 5.95 (ISBN 0-396-07931-8). Dodd.

Guide to Meteorological Instrument & Observing Practices. 4th ed. pap. 56.00 (ISBN 0-685-02929-8, WMO). Unipub.

Machine Processing of Hydrometeorological Data. (Technical Note Ser.). (Illus., Orig.). 1971. pap. 15.00 (ISBN 0-685-02043-6, 275, WMO). Unipub.

Meteorological Services of the World. 300p. 1972. pap. 34.00 (ISBN 0-685-23711-7, 2, WMO). Unipub.

Satellite & Computer Applications to Synoptic Meteorology. (Illus., Orig.). 1971. pap. 15.00 (ISBN 0-685-02041-X, 283, WMO). Unipub.

Selected Papers on Meteorology As Related to the Human Environment. (Special Environmental Report Ser.: No. 2). (Illus.). 151p. (Orig.). 1972. pap. 30.00 (ISBN 0-685-24967-0, WMO). Unipub.

Witty, Margot & Witty, Ken. A Day in the Life of a Meteorologist. LC 80-54098. (Illus.). 32p. (gr. 4 up). 1981. PLB 6.89 (ISBN 0-89375-450-1); pap. 2.50 (ISBN 0-89375-451-X). Troll Assocs.

WMO Basic Documents (Excluding the Technical Regulations), 1971 Ed. (Illus.). 177p. (Orig.). 1975. pap. 24.00 (ISBN 0-685-23605-6, 15, WMO). Unipub.

METEOROLOGY

see also Air; Atmosphere; Atmospheric Electricity; Atmospheric Pressure; Atmospheric Temperature; Atomic Energy and Meteorology; Climatology; Clouds; Droughts; Evaporation; Floods; Hail; Humidity; Hurricanes; Hydrometeorology; Hygrometry; Jet Stream; Lightning; Magnetism, Terrestrial; Meteorology As a Profession; Micrometeorology; Numerical Weather Forecasting; Radar Meteorology; Radio Meteorology; Rain and Rainfall; Rainbow; Seasons; Snow; Solar Radiation; Storms; Sun-Spots; Thunderstorms; Tornadoes; Typhoons; Van Allen Radiation Belts; Weather; Weather Control; Weather Forecasting; Weather Lore; Weathering; Winds

also headings beginning with the word Meteorological

Abraham, F. & Tiller, W. A., eds. An Introduction to Computer Simulation in Applied Science. LC 72-83047. 220p. 1972. 25.00 (ISBN 0-306-30579-8, Plenum Pr). Plenum Pub.

The Achievement & the Challenge. (WMO Ser.: No. 410). (Illus.). 1976. pap. 6.00 (ISBN 92-63-10410-7, W177, WMO). Unipub.

Air Pollutants, Meteorology & Plant Injury. (Technical Note Ser.). 1968. pap. 35.00 (ISBN 0-685-02471-7, WMO). Unipub.

American Meteorological Society - Boston. Cumulated Bibliography & Index to Meteorological & Geoastrophysical Abstracts: 1950-1969. 1972. Author Sequence, 5 Vols. 1340.00 (ISBN 0-685-01570-X). Dec. Class, 4 Vols (ISBN 0-8161-0183-3). G K Hall.

--Cumulated Bibliography & Index to Meteorological & Geoastrophysical Abstracts, 1950-1969: Author Sequence, 5 vols. 1972. 800.00 (ISBN 0-8161-0942-7). G K Hall.

Annual Report: Nineteen Seventy-Seven. 1977. pap. 20.00 (ISBN 92-63-10502-2, WMO 502, WMO). Unipub.

Annual Report of the World Meteorological Organization, 1974. (Illus.). 177p. 1975. pap. text ed. 20.00 (ISBN 92-63-20412-8, WMO412, WMO). Unipub.

Anthes, Richard A. Weather Around Us. (Physical Science Ser.). 1976. pap. text ed. 7.95 (ISBN 0-675-08635-3); Set Of 4. cassettes & filmstrips 135.00 (ISBN 0-675-08634-5). Merrill.

Application of Meteorology to Marine Interests. (Marine Science Affairs Ser.: No. 8). (Illus.). 54p. 1973. pap. 12.00 (ISBN 0-685-39014-4, 352, WMO). Unipub.

Applications of Meteorology to Economic & Social Development. 130p. (Orig.). 1974. pap. 28.00 (ISBN 92-63-10375-5, WMO 375, WMO). Unipub.

Atkinson, B. W., ed. Dynamical Meteorology: An Introductory Selection. 1981. 27.50x (ISBN 0-416-73830-3); pap. 12.95x (ISBN 0-416-73840-0). Methuen Inc.

The Atlantic Tropical Experiment - GATE. (Illus.). 44p. (Orig.). 1974. pap. 6.00 (ISBN 0-685-51933-3, WMO 390, WMO). Unipub.

Barry, R. G. & Chorley, R. J. Atmosphere, Weather & Climate. 3rd ed. LC 78-58311. 432p. 1976. pap. text ed. 14.95x (ISBN 0-416-70420-4, Pub. by Chapman & Hall England). Methuen Inc.

Basic Documents (Excluding Technical Regulations), Edition 1975. (Basic Documents Ser.: No. 2). 179p. 1976. pap. 24.00 (ISBN 0-685-67382-0, WMO 15, WMO). Unipub.

Battan, Louis J. Fundamentals of Meteorology. 1979. 19.95 (ISBN 0-13-341131-1). P-H.

Belousov, S. L. Computer Processing of Meteorological Data. 216p. 1971. 17.50x (ISBN 0-7065-1130-1, Pub. by IPST). Intl Schol Bk Serv.

Benefit & Cost Analysis of Hydrological Forecasts: A State-of-the-Art-Report. (Operational Hydrology Report Ser.: No. 3). (Illus.). 33p. 1973. pap. 12.00 (ISBN 0-685-39011-X, 341, WMO). Unipub.

Bernard, Etienne A. Compendium of Lecture Notes for Training Personnel in the Applications of Meteorology to Economic & Social Development. (WMO Ser: No. 382). (Illus.). 186p. 1977. pap. 25.00 (ISBN 92-63-10382-8, WMO). Unipub.

Bernard, Harold. The Greenhouse Effect. 1980. 15.95 (ISBN 0-88410-633-0). Ballinger Pub.

Berry, Frederic A., et al. Handbook of Meteorology. 1947. 55.00 (ISBN 0-07-005030-9, P&RB). McGraw.

Blair, T. & Fite, R. Weather Elements: Text in Elementary Meteorology. 5th ed. 1965. ref. ed. 19.95 (ISBN 0-13-947721-7). P-H.

The Boundary-Layer Sub-Programme for the GARP Atlantic Tropical Experiment. (GATE Report Ser.: No. 5). (Illus.). 127p. (Orig.). 1974. pap. 20.00 (ISBN 0-685-41365-9, WMO). Unipub.

A Brief Survey of Meteorology As Related to the Biosphere. (Special Environmental Report Ser.: No. 4). 54p. (Orig.). 1974. pap. 12.00 (ISBN 92-63-10372-0, WMO372, WMO). Unipub.

Brief Survey of WMO Activities Relating to the Human Environment. (Special Environmental Report Ser.: No. 1). 1971. pap. 2.00 (ISBN 0-685-02479-2, WMO). Unipub.

Catalogue of Meteorological Data for Research, Pt.1. 1965. pap. 30.00 with binder (ISBN 0-685-36783-5, WMO). Unipub.

Catalogue of Meteorological Data for Research, Pt.2. 1970. pap. 20.00 (ISBN 0-685-36784-3, WMO 174, WMO). Unipub.

The Central Programme for the GARP Atlantic Tropical Experiment. (GATE Report Ser.: No. 3). (Illus.). 35p. (Orig.). 1974. pap. 10.00 (ISBN 0-685-41363-2, WMO). Unipub.

Chassany, Jean-Philippe. Dictionnaire de Meteorologie Populaire. 416p. (Fr.). 1970. 35.00 (ISBN 0-686-56945-8, M-6067). French & Eur.

Chelius, Carl R. & Frentz, Henry J. A Basic Meteorology Exercise Manual. rev. ed. (Illus.). 1978. 8.50 (ISBN 0-8403-1623-2). Kendall-Hunt.

Circulation in the Stratosphere, Mesosphere, & Lower Thermoshpere. (Technical Note Ser.). 1965. pap. 18.00 (ISBN 0-685-36785-1, WMO 176, WMO). Unipub.

Cole, Alan. Introduction to the Atmosphere Lab Manual. 1980. loose leaf shrink wrapped 4.75 (ISBN 0-88252-110-1). Paladin Hse.

Cole, Franklyn W. Introduction to Meteorology. 3rd ed. LC 79-1212. 1980. text ed. 23.95 (ISBN 0-471-04705-8). Wiley.

Collins, Richard. Flying the Weathermap. (Illus.). 1979. 12.50 (ISBN 0-440-02610-5, E Friede). Delacorte.

Commission for Aeronautical Meteorology: Abridged Final Report of the Sixth Session, Montreal, 26 April-14 May 1976. (Illus.). 1977. pap. 25.00 (ISBN 92-63-10452-2, WMO 452, WMO). Unipub.

Commission for Basic Systems Abridged Final Report of the Extraordinary Session. 202p. 1981. pap. 25.00 (ISBN 92-63-10569-3, W496, WMO). Unipub.

Commission for Marine Meteorology, 6th Session. Abridged Final Report of the Sixth Session. 117p. 1973. pap. 20.00 (ISBN 0-685-39010-1, 344, WMO). Unipub.

Commission for Special Applications of Meteorology & Climatology: Abridged Final Report of the Seventh Session. 1978. pap. 25.00 (ISBN 0-685-93702-X, W413, WMO). Unipub.

Committee on Atmospheric Sciences. Atmospheric Sciences: Problems & Applications. 1977. pap. 7.75 (ISBN 0-309-02626-1). Natl Acad Pr.

Comparison of Sensors & Telemetry for Meteorological Rockets. (Illus.). 102p. 1975. pap. 20.00 (ISBN 92-63-10395-X, WMO 395, WMO). Unipub.

The Compatibility of Upper-Air Data. 1979. pap. 20.00 (ISBN 92-63-10512-X, WMO 512, WMO). Unipub.

Compendium of Meteorology: Aeronautical Meteorology, Vol. 2, Pt. 2. 1978. pap. 14.00 (ISBN 0-685-94614-2, W364, WMO). Unipub.

Compendium of Meteorology for Use by Class One & Class Two Meteorological Personnel. Incl. Pt. 1. Dynamic Meteorology. (Illus.). 334p. pap. write for info. (ISBN 0-685-40085-9); Pt. 2. Physical Meteorology. (Illus.). 211p. pap. 25.00 (ISBN 0-685-40086-7). (Orig.). 1974 (364, WMO). Unipub.

Compendium of Meteorology: General Hydrology, Vol. II, Pt. 1. (WMO Ser: No. 364). (Illus.). 42p. 1978. pap. 10.00 (ISBN 0-685-86542-8, W359, WMO). Unipub.

Compendium of Meteorology: Marine Meteorology, Vol. 3. 121p. 1979. pap. 11.00 (ISBN 0-686-60082-7, W441, WMO). Unipub.

Compendium of Meteorology: Synoptic Meteorology, Vol. 1, Pt. 3. 1978. pap. 32.00 (ISBN 0-685-66640-9, WMO 364, WMO). Unipub.

Compendium of Meteorology: Vol. II Part 4-Tropical Meteorology. 428p. 1979. pap. 30.00 (ISBN 0-686-74027-0, W484, WMO). Unipub.

Compendium of Training Facilities in Environmental Problems Related to Meteorological & Operational Hydrology. (Illus.). 1978. pap. 22.00 (ISBN 92-63-10489-1, WMO 489, WMO). Unipub.

Consolidated Report on the Voluntary Assistance Programme Including Project Approved for Circulation in 1978. 1979. pap. 15.00 (ISBN 92-63-10525-1, W427, WMO). Unipub.

The Convection Sub-Programme for the GARP Atlantic Tropical Experiment. (GATE Report Ser.: No. 7). (Illus.). 83p. (Orig.). 1974. pap. 25.00 (ISBN 0-685-50568-5, WMO). Unipub.

Crawford, William P. Mariner's Weather. (Illus.). 1979. 22.95 (ISBN 0-393-03221-3). Norton.

Cross, Frank L, Jr. & Forehand, David, eds. Air Pollution Meteorology. LC 75-26075. (Environmental Monograph). (Illus.). 18p. 1976. 10.00 (ISBN 0-87762-177-2). Technomic.

Decker, Fred W. The Weather Workbook. rev ed. 1979. pap. 8.00x (ISBN 0-931778-01-8). Weather Wkbk.

Dobryshman, E. M. Review of Forecast Verification Techniques. (Technical Note Ser.). 51p. 1973. pap. 10.00 (ISBN 0-685-34863-6, 303, WMO). Unipub.

Dolgin, I. M. & Gavrilova, L. A. Meteorological Conditions in the Arctic During the International Year of the Quiet Sun. 122p. 1971. 11.50 (ISBN 0-7065-1126-3, Pub. by IPST). Intl Schol Bk Serv.

Donn, William L. Meteorology. 3rd ed. 1965. text ed. 14.95 (ISBN 0-07-017598-5, G). McGraw.

--Meteorology. 4th ed. (Illus.). 608p. 1975. text ed. 19.95 (ISBN 0-07-017599-3, G). McGraw.

Doronin, Yu. P. Thermal Interaction of the Atmosphere & the Hydrosphere in the Arctic. 252p. 1971. 25.00x (ISBN 0-7065-1037-2, Pub. by IPST). Intl Schol Bk Serv.

Durst, F., et al. Principles & Practices of Laser-Doppler Anemometry. 1976. 46.00 (ISBN 0-12-225250-0). Acad Pr.

Dutton, John A. The Scientific Objectives, Philosophy & Management of the MOCAT Project. LC 77-136104. 141p. 1969. 14.00 (ISBN 0-686-01914-8). Mgmt Info Serv.

Eagleman, Joe R. Meteorology: The Atmosphere in Action. (Illus.). 384p. 1980. text ed. 20.95 (ISBN 0-442-21908-3); instr's. manual 2.95 (ISBN 0-442-25764-3); slides 199.95 (ISBN 0-442-20391-8). Van Nos Reinhold.

Eighth World Meteorological Congress Abridged Report with Resolutions. 253p. 1980. pap. 45.00 (ISBN 92-63-10533-2, WMO 451, WMO). Unipub.

Eliassen, Arnt. Meteorology: An Introductory Course, 2 vols. 1977. Vol. I. pap. 22.00x (ISBN 82-00-02392-3, Dist. by Columbia U Pr); Vol. II. pap. 15.50x (ISBN 82-00-02411-3). Universitet.

Executive Committee, 27th Session, Geneva May 26-30, 1975. Proceedings: Abridged Report with Resolutions. (WMO Ser.: No. 417). 135p. 1975. pap. 25.00 (ISBN 92-63-10417-4, WMO). Unipub.

Extraordinary Session, Budapest 1976. Regional Association Six, Europe: Abridged Final Report. (No. 456). (Illus.). 1977. pap. 25.00 (ISBN 92-63-10456-5, WMO). Unipub.

Fairbridge, R., ed. Encyclopedia of Atmospheric Sciences & Astrogeology. (Encyclopedia of Earth Sciences Ser: Vol. II). 1967. 58.00 (ISBN 0-12-786458-X). Acad Pr.

Fickett, E. D. Meteorology. Repr. of 1900 ed. pap. 2.00 (ISBN 0-8466-0029-3, SJS29). Shorey.

Filippov, V. V. Quality Control Procedures for Meteorological Use. (World Weather Watch Planning Report Ser.: No. 26). 1968. pap. 12.00 (ISBN 0-685-22334-5, WMO). Unipub.

Flohn, N. Climate & Weather. (Illus., Orig.). 1968. pap. 3.95 (ISBN 0-07-021325-9, SP). McGraw.

From, Lester D. & Staver, Allen E. Fundamentals of Weather: A Workbook Approach. 1979. pap. text ed. 15.50 (ISBN 0-8403-2023-X). Kendall-Hunt.

Gates, Ernest S. Meteorology & Climatology. 4th ed. (Illus.). 1972. pap. text ed. 17.95x (ISBN 0-245-52869-5). Intl Ideas.

Geiger, Rudolf. Climate Near the Ground. 4th ed. Scripta Technica Inc, tr. LC 64-23191. 1965. 30.00x (ISBN 0-674-13500-8). Harvard U Pr.

Gordon, Adrian H. & Taylor, Ronald C. Computations of Surface Layer Air Trajectories, & Weather, in the Oceanic Tropics. LC 72-92065. (International Indian Ocean Expedition Meterological Monographs: No. 7). (Illus.). 128p. 1975. text ed. 15.00x (ISBN 0-8248-0253-5, Eastwest Ctr). U Pr of Hawaii.

Haltiner, G. J. & Martin, F. L. Dynamical & Physical Meteorology. 1957. text ed. 25.00 (ISBN 0-07-025640-3, C). McGraw.

Harvey, J. G. Atmosphere & Ocean: Our Fluid Environments. LC 77-377903. 1978. pap. 14.50x (ISBN 0-8448-1293-5). Crane-Russak Co.

Hess, Seymour L. Introduction to Theoretical Meteorology. LC 78-27897. 380p. 1979. Repr. of 1959 ed. lib. bdg. 20.00 (ISBN 0-88275-857-8). Krieger.

Hetman, F. The Language of Forecasting. 556p. 1971. 57.75x (ISBN 0-677-62140-X). Gordon.

Hobbs, William H. Exploring About the North Pole of the Winds. LC 68-55196. (Illus.). Repr. of 1930 ed. lib. bdg. 18.75x (ISBN 0-8371-0478-5, HONP). Greenwood.

Holton, James R. Introduction to Dynamic Meteorology. 2nd ed. LC 79-6956. (International Geophysics Ser.). 1979. 22.00 (ISBN 0-12-354360-6). Acad Pr.

Hydrological Application of Atmospheric Vapour-Flux Analyses. (WMO Ser: No. 476). (Illus.). 1978. pap. 10.00 (ISBN 92-63-10476-X, WMO). Unipub.

International Global Data-Processing System Plan to Support the First GARP Global Experiment: Annexes. 22p. 1979. pap. 18.00 (ISBN 92-63-10469-7, W355, WMO). Unipub.

International Noctilucent Cloud Observation Manual. 1970. pap. 8.00 (ISBN 0-685-02467-9, WMO). Unipub.

The International Radiometersonde Intercomparison Programme (1970-71) (Technical Note Ser.). (Illus.). 127p. 1973. pap. 20.00 (ISBN 0-685-39018-7, 358, WMO). Unipub.

Jehan, L. F. Dictionnaire d'astronomie de Physique et de Meteorologie. Migne, J. P., ed. (Encyclopedie Theologique Ser.: Vol. 42). 780p. (Fr.). Date not set. Repr. of 1850 ed. lib. bdg. 99.00x (ISBN 0-89241-247-X). Caratzas Bros.

Kellogg, William W. & Schware, Robert. Climate Change & Society: Consequences of Increasing Atmospheric Carbon Dioxide. (Special Study Ser.). 170p. (Orig.). 1981. lib. bdg. 15.00x (ISBN 0-86531-179-X); pap. 8.00x (ISBN 0-86531-180-3). Westview.

Kemp, J. F. & Young, P. Notes on Meteorology. 3rd ed. (Young & Kemp Ser.). 88p. 1971. pap. 9.50x (ISBN 0-540-00369-7). Sheridan.

Kibel', I. A., ed. Collection of Articles on Dynamic Meteorology. LC 60-9255. (Soviet Research in Geophysics Ser.: Trudy No. 37). 1960. 30.00 (ISBN 0-306-10622-1, Consultants). Plenum Pub.

Lamb, Hubert H. Climate: Present, Past & Future, Vol. 1. (Illus.). 1972. 100.00x (ISBN 0-416-11530-6). Methuen Inc.

Leavy, Thomas A. Basic Meteorology Lab Manual. 2nd ed. 1969. pap. text ed. 4.00 (ISBN 0-910042-06-3). Allegheny.

Lecturers Presented at the IMO-WMO Centenary Conferences. (Technical Note Ser.: No. 130). (Illus.). 139p. (Orig.). 1974. pap. 50.00 (ISBN 0-685-41364-0, 370, WMO). Unipub.

Lounsbury, John F. A Workbook for Weather & Climate. 3rd ed. 144p. 1973. write for info. (ISBN 0-697-05253-2); tchr's manual avail. (ISBN 0-686-66894-4). Wm C Brown.

Lutgens, F. & Tarbuck, E. Atmosphere: An Introduction to Meteorology. 1979. 19.95 (ISBN 0-13-050104-2). P-H.

Lutgens, Frederick K. & Tarbuck, Edward J. The Atmosphere: An Introduction to Meteorology. (Illus.). 496p. 1982. text ed. 20.95 (ISBN 0-13-050120-4). P-H.

Lynch, David K., intro. by. Atmospheric Phenomena: Readings from Scientific American. LC 79-26987. (Illus.). 175p. 1980. text ed. 17.95x (ISBN 0-7167-1165-6); pap. 8.95x (ISBN 0-7167-1166-4). W H Freeman.

McGraw-Hill Encyclopedia of Science & Technology Staff. McGraw-Hill Encyclopedia of Ocean & Atmospheric Sciences. Parker, Sybil P., ed. (Illus.). 1979. write for info. (ISBN 0-07-045267-9). McGraw.

McIntosh, D. H. Meteorological Glossary. (Illus.). 1972. 25.00 (ISBN 0-8206-0228-0). Chem Pub.

McIntosh, D. H., et al. Essentials of Meteorology. (Wykeham Science Ser.: No. 3). 1973. pap. 11.75x (ISBN 0-8448-1354-0). Crane-Russak Co.

Makhon'Ko, K. P. & Malakhov, S. G., eds. Nuclear Meteorology. Baruch, A. & Olaru, H., trs. from Rus. Orig. Title: Yadernaya Meteorologiya. (Illus.). 380p. 1974. lib. bdg. 39.50x (ISBN 0-7065-1445-9, Pub. by IPST). Intl Schol Bk Serv.

Meade, P. J. Meteorological Aspects of Peaceful Uses of Atomic Energy, Pt. 1. (Technical Note Ser.). 1968. pap. 7.00 (ISBN 0-685-22320-5, WMO). Unipub.

Meteorological Aspects of Air Pollution. (Technical Note Ser.: No. 106). (Illus., Orig.). 1970. pap. 12.00 (ISBN 0-685-04917-5, WMO). Unipub.

Meteorological Factors in Air Pollution. (Technical Note Ser.). 1970. pap. 10.00 (ISBN 0-685-02472-5, WMO). Unipub.

Meteorology & the Human Environment. (Special Environmental Report: No. 13). 1979. pap. 6.00 (ISBN 92-63-10517-0, W425, WMO). Unipub.

Meteorology & the Human Environment. (Illus.). 52p. (Orig.). 1972. pap. 2.00 (ISBN 0-685-24050-9, 313, WMO). Unipub.

Michigan University Greenland Expeditions 1926-1933. Reports of the Greenland Expeditions of the University of Michigan, 2 Vols. LC 68-55203. (Illus.). 1968. Repr. of 1941 ed. Set. lib. bdg. 45.50x (ISBN 0-8371-3850-7, MUGE). Greenwood.

Middleton, W. E. Vision Through the Atmosphere. (Scholarly Reprint Ser.). 1980. Repr. of 1952 ed. 37.50x (ISBN 0-8020-7107-4). U of Toronto Pr.

Miller, A. Austin & Parry, M. Everyday Meteorology. 1975. 14.95 (ISBN 0-09-121910-8, Pub. by Hutchinson). Merrimack Bk Serv.

Miller, Albert & Anthes, Richard A. Meteorology. 4th ed. (Physics & Physical Science Ser.). 176p. 1980. pap. text ed. 7.95 (ISBN 0-675-08181-5). Merrill.

Miller, Albert & Thompson, Jack. Elements of Meteorology. 3rd ed. 1979. text ed. 19.95 (ISBN 0-675-08293-5); instructor's manual o. p. 3.95 (ISBN 0-686-67289-5). Merrill.

Miller, Forrest R. & Keshavamurthy, R. N. Structure of an Arabian Sea Summer Monsoon System. LC 67-29576. (International Indian Ocean Expedition Meteorological Monographs: No. 1). (Illus.). 1968. 10.00x (ISBN 0-8248-0070-2, Eastwest Ctr). U Pr of Hawaii.

Morel, P. Dynamic Meteorology: Lectures Delivered at the Centre Nationole D'Etudes Spatiales, Lannion, France, Aug. 7-Sept. 12, 1970. LC 72-78425. 621p. 1973. lib. bdg. 60.50 (ISBN 90-277-0344-2, Pub. by Reidel Holland). Kluwer Boston.

Moses, L. & Tomikel, John. Basic Meteorology, an Introduction to the Science. (Illus.). 130p. Date not set. pap. text ed. 7.50 (ISBN 0-910042-39-X). Allegheny.

Murphy, Allan H. & Katz, Richard W., eds. Probability, Statistics, & Decision Making in Meteorology. 450p. (Orig.). Nov., 1981. lib. bdg. 28.50x (ISBN 0-86531-152-8); Oct., 1981. pap. text ed. 15.00x (ISBN 0-86531-153-6). Westview.

National Research Council. Introductory Meteorology. 1918. 32.50x (ISBN 0-686-51405-X). Elliots Bks.

Neiburger, Morris, et al. Understanding Our Atmospheric Environment. LC 72-4753. (Illus.). 1973. text ed. 20.95x (ISBN 0-7167-0257-6). W H Freeman.

Nicholson, James R. Meteorological Data Catalogue. (International Indian Ocean Expedition Meteorological Monographs: No. 3). (Illus.). 1969. 12.00x (ISBN 0-8248-0082-6, Eastwest Ctr). U Pr of Hawaii.

Parameterization of Sub-Grid Scale Processes. (GARP Publications Ser: No. 8). (Illus.). 101p. 1973. pap. 12.00 (ISBN 0-685-34858-X, WMO). Unipub.

Petterssen, Sverre. Introduction to Meteorology. 3rd ed. LC 68-15476. 1968. text ed. 19.00 (ISBN 0-07-049720-6, C). McGraw.

--Weather Analysis & Forecasting, 2 vols. 2nd ed. Incl. Vol. 1. Motion & Systems. text ed. 22.00 (ISBN 0-07-049685-4); Vol. 2. Weather & Systems. text ed. 17.00 (ISBN 0-07-049686-2). 1956 (C). McGraw.

Polar Subprogram. (GARP Publications Ser: No. 19). 47p. 1978. pap. 15.00 (ISBN 0-685-60678-3, W392, WMO). Unipub.

Powers of Nature. LC 76-57002. (Special Publication Ser.: No. XII). (Illus.). 1978. 6.95 (ISBN 0-87044-234-1); lib. bdg. 8.50 (ISBN 0-87044-239-2). Natl Geog.

Problems in Dynamic Meteorology. 1970. pap. 10.00 (ISBN 0-685-02474-1, WMO). Unipub.

Proceeding of the Wmo Symposium on Meteorology As Related to Urban & Regional Land-Use Planning. (Illus.). 1977. pap. text ed. 22.50 (ISBN 92-63-10444-1, WMO). Unipub.

Proceedings of the Meeting of Education & Training in Meteorological Aspects of Atmospheric Pollution & Related Environmental Problems. 1978. pap. 40.00 (ISBN 0-685-93141-2, W379, WMO). Unipub.

Proulx, Gerard J. Standard Dictionary of Meteorological Sciences: English-French - French-English. 320p. 1971. 22.00 (ISBN 0-7735-0066-9). McGill-Queens U Pr.

Quantitative Meteorological Data from Satellites. (Technical Note Ser.: No. 166). 1980. pap. 20.00 (ISBN 92-63-10531-6, W445, WMO). Unipub.

Radiation Sub-Programme for the GARP Atlantic Tropical Experiment. (GATE Report Ser.: No. 4). (Illus.). 109p. (Orig.). 1974. pap. 25.00 (ISBN 0-685-40089-1, WMO). Unipub.

Rahn, James J. Making Weather Work for You: A Practical Guide for Gardener & Farmer. (Illus.). 1979. pap. 7.95 (ISBN 0-88266-159-0). Garden Way Pub.

Rainey, R. C. & Aspilden, C. Meteorology & the Migration of Desert Locusts. (Technical Note Ser.). 1963. pap. 25.00 (ISBN 0-685-22324-8, WMO). Unipub.

Regional Association Five, South-West Pacific: Abridged Final Report of the Sixth Session. 94p. (Orig.). 1974. pap. 25.00 (ISBN 92-63-10380-1, WMO 380, WMO). Unipub.

Regional Association Five, South-West Pacific: Abridged Final Report of the Seventh Session. (JaKarta 18-26). 1978. pap. 25.00 (ISBN 92-63-10516-2, WMO 516, WMO). Unipub.

Regional Association Four, North & Central America: Abridged Final Report of the Sixth Session. 192p. (Orig.). 1974. pap. 25.00 (ISBN 0-685-50565-0, 377, WMO). Unipub.

Regional Association Four, North & Central: Abridged Final Report of the Seventh Session. (Illus.). 1978. pap. 25.00 (ISBN 92-63-10479-4, WMO). Unipub.

Regional Association One, Africa: Abridged Final Report of the Sixth Session. 188p. (Orig.). 1974. pap. 25.00 (ISBN 92-63-10367-4, WMO). Unipub.

Regional Association One, Africa: Abridged Final Report of the Seventh Session. 1978. pap. 25.00 (ISBN 92-63-10503-0, W398, WMO). Unipub.

Regional Association Six Europe: Abridged Final Report of the Seventh Session. 1979. pap. 25.00 (ISBN 92-63-10522-7, W422, WMO). Unipub.

Reifsnyder, William E. Weathering the Wilderness: The Sierra Club Guide to Practical Meteorology. LC 79-20859. (Outdoor Guides Ser.). (Illus.). 272p. 1980. pap. 8.95 (ISBN 0-87156-266-9). Sierra.

Remote Sensing of Snow & Ice. (Technical Papers in Hydrology: No. 19). 54p. 1980. pap. 7.50 (ISBN 92-3-101730-6, U976, UNESCO). Unipub.

Report of the Eighth Session of the Joint Organizing Committee. (GATE Report Ser.). 130p. 1973. pap. 14.00 (ISBN 0-685-39020-9, WMO). Unipub.

Report of the Fifteenth Session of the Joint Organizing Committee. 1979. pap. 25.00 (ISBN 0-686-52509-4, W432, WMO). Unipub.

Report of the Fifth Session of the Tropical Experiment Board. (GARP Special Report Ser.: No. 11). 21p. (Orig.). 1974. pap. 15.00 (ISBN 0-685-41137-0, WMO). Unipub.

Report of the Fifth Session of WMO Executive Committee Inter-Governmental Panel on the First GARP Global Experiment. (GARP Special Report Ser.). (Illus.). 45p. 1978. pap. 15.00 (ISBN 0-685-27460-8, W-383, WMO). Unipub.

Report of the First Session of the Wamex Scientific & Management Committee. (GARP Special Report Ser.: No. 31). 1979. pap. 15.00 (ISBN 0-686-52645-7, W426, WMO). Unipub.

Report of the Fourteenth Session of the Joint Organizing Committee. 1978. pap. 40.00 (ISBN 0-685-66642-5, W 404, WMO). Unipub.

Report of the Fourth Planning Meeting for the Monsoon Experiment (MONEX) (GARP Special Report Ser.: No. 28). 1978. pap. 40.00 (ISBN 0-685-65240-8, W402, WMO). Unipub.

Report of the Fourth Session of the Tropical Experiment Board. (GARP Special Report Ser.: No. 9). (Illus.). 1973. pap. 14.00 (ISBN 0-685-39013-6, WMO). Unipub.

Report of the Fourth Session of WMO Executive Committee Inter-Governmental Panel on the First Garp Global Experiment. (Garp Special Report: No. 24). 1977. pap. 25.00 (ISBN 0-685-86035-3, WMO). Unipub.

Report of the Ninth Session of the Joint Organizing Committee. (Gate Report Ser.). (Orig.). 1974. pap. 10.00 (ISBN 0-685-50264-3, WMO). Unipub.

Report of the Sixth Session of WMO Executive Committee, Inter-Governmental Panel on the First Garp Global Experiment. 1978. pap. 25.00 (ISBN 0-685-90700-7, W 411, WMO). Unipub.

Report of the Third Planning Meeting for the Monsoon Experiment: New Delhi, Feb.-Mar., 1977. (GARP Special Report: No. 25). 26p. 1978. pap. 25.00 (ISBN 0-685-87432-X, WMO). Unipub.

Report on Special Observing Systems for the First GARP Global Experiment. (GARP Special Report Ser.: No. 10). (Illus.). 33p. 1973. pap. 6.00 (ISBN 0-685-39023-3, WMO). Unipub.

Requirements for Marine Meteorological Services. (Marine Science Affairs Ser.: No. 4). pap. 3.00 (ISBN 0-685-27887-5, WMO 288, WMO). Unipub.

Resolutions of Congress & the Executive Committee. 1979. pap. 35.00 (ISBN 92-63-10508-1, W415, WMO). Unipub.

Richason, Benjamin F., Jr., ed. Laboratory Manual for Introduction to Remote Sensing of the Environment. (Pacesetter Ser). (Illus.). 1978. pap. text ed. 9.95 (ISBN 0-8403-1898-7). Kendall Hunt.

Riehl, Herbert. Introduction to the Atmosphere. 3rd ed. (Illus.). 1978. text ed. 18.00 (ISBN 0-07-052656-7, C). McGraw.

Rodier, J. Bibliography of African Hydrology. 1963. 11.50 (ISBN 92-3-000541-X, U47, UNESCO). Unipub.

Role of Meteorological Services in Economic Development in Africa. 1969. pap. 15.00 (ISBN 0-685-36790-8, WMO). Unipub.

Rudman, Jack. Senior Meteorologist. (Career Examination Ser.: C-2201). (Cloth bdg. avail. on request). pap. 10.00 (ISBN 0-8373-2201-4). Natl Learning.

Saucier, Walter J. Principles of Meteorological Analysis. LC 55-7314. (Illus.). 1955. 17.50x (ISBN 0-226-73533-8). U of Chicago Pr.

Scientific Lectures Presented at the Seventh World Meteorlogical Congress. (WMO Ser: No. 435). (Illus.). 1977. pap. 16.00 (ISBN 92-63-10435-2, WMO). Unipub.

Sedunov, Yu. S. Physics of Drop Formation in the Atmosphere. Greenberg, P., ed. Lederman, D., tr. from Rus. LC 74-8198. 234p. 1974. 32.95 (ISBN 0-470-77111-9). Halsted Pr.

Seminar on Synoptic Analysis & Forecasting in the Tropics of Asia & the Southwest Pacific, Singapore, Dec. 1970. Proceedings. 1972. pap. 55.00 (ISBN 0-685-36789-4, 321, WMO). Unipub.

Shaw, William N. Manual of Meteorology, 4 vols. LC 77-10238. Repr. of 1936 ed. 130.00 set (ISBN 0-404-16230-4). AMS Pr.

Sloane, Eric. Look at the Sky & Tell the Weather. LC 79-84157. 1979. pap. 4.95 (ISBN 0-8015-4665-6, Hawthorn). Dutton.

Sorkina, A. I. Atmospheric Circulation & the Related Wind Fields Over the North Pacific. (Illus.). 224p. 1971. 14.50x (ISBN 0-7065-1132-8, Pub. by IPST). Intl Schol Bk Serv.

Suckling, Philip & Doyon, Roy. Studies in Weather & Climate. 200p. 1981. pap. text ed. 10.95 (ISBN 0-89892-043-4). Contemp Pub Co of Raleigh.

A Survey of Meteorological & Hydrological Data Available in Six Sahelian Countries of West Africa. Incl. A Survey of Studies in Meteorology & Hydrology in the Sudano-Sahelian Zone of West Africa. 119p. (Orig.). 1974. pap. 15.00 (ISBN 0-685-50567-7, 379, WMO). Unipub.

Sutton, Oliver G. Challenge of the Atmosphere. (Illus.). Repr. of 1961 ed. lib. bdg. 15.00x (ISBN 0-8371-2327-5, SUAT). Greenwood.

Symposium on Forest Meteorology. Proceedings. 233p. 1980. pap. text ed. 10.00 (ISBN 92-63-00527-3, W447, WMO). Unipub.

The Synoptic-Scale Sub-Programme for the GARP Atlantic Tropical Experiment. (GATE Report Ser.: No. 6). (Illus.). 68p. (Orig.). 1974. pap. 15.00 (ISBN 0-685-41435-3, WMO). Unipub.

Taylor, Geoffrey I. Scientific Papers, 4 vols. Batchelor, G. K., ed. Incl. Vol. 1. Mechanics of Solids. 90.00 (ISBN 0-521-06608-5); Vol. 2. Meteorology, Oceanography & Turbulent Flow. 1960. 90.00 (ISBN 0-521-06609-3); Vol. 3. Aerodynamics & the Mechanics of Projectiles & Explosions. 1963. 90.00 (ISBN 0-521-06610-7); Vol. 4. Mechanics of Fluids: Miscellaneous Topics. (Illus.). 1971. 90.00 (ISBN 0-521-07995-0). Cambridge U Pr.

Technical Conference of Hydrological & Meteorological Services. Abridged Final Report. 1970. pap. 8.00 (ISBN 0-685-02478-4, 282, W95, WMO). Unipub.

Technical Conference of Hydrological & Meteorological Services, Geneva, 1970. Scientific Papers. (Illus.). 123p. (Orig.). 1972. pap. 10.00 (ISBN 0-685-24966-2, 304, WMO). Unipub.

Technical Regional Conference, Santiago, 1970. Funcion de los Servicios Meteorologicos en el Desarpollo Economico de America Latina: Proceedings. (Illus.). 356p. (Orig., Span.). 1973. pap. 19.00 (ISBN 0-685-39520-0, 314, WMO). Unipub.

Technical Regulations, 2 vols. (Basic Documents Ser.: No. 49). (Vol. I, 95 p.; Vol. II, 45 p.). 1980. Set. sheets in binder 40.00 (ISBN 0-686-61622-7, WMO). Vol. I, General. Vol. II, Hydrology. Unipub.

Technical Regulations. Incl. Vol. 1. General Regulations, 1971 Edition. with binder 30.00 (ISBN 0-685-57266-8); Vol. 2. Meteorological Service for International Air Navigation. 3rd ed. with binder 30.00 (ISBN 0-685-57267-6); Operational Hydrology, 1971 Edition. with binder 4.00 (ISBN 0-685-57268-4); with binder 19.50 (ISBN 0-685-57269-2, VOL. 1 & VOL. 3). (Illus., 49, WMO). Unipub.

Technical Regulations. Incl. Vol. 1. General; Vol. 3. Hydrology. (Basic Documents Ser.: No. 2). 1976. 2 vols. in 1 50.00 (ISBN 0-685-67384-7, WMO). Unipub.

Tenth Status Report on Implementation. 1978. pap. 25.00 (ISBN 0-685-95369-6, W419, WMO). Unipub.

Thirtieth Session of the Executive Committee: Abridged Report with Resolutions. (Geneva May 25-15 June 1978). 1979. pap. 25.00 (ISBN 92-63-10514-6, W409, WMO). Unipub.

Thirty-First Session of the Executive Committee, WMO. 151p. 1980. pap. 25.00 (ISBN 92-63-10534-0, W443, WMO). Unipub.

Thirty-Second Session of the Executive Committee. 186p. 1981. pap. 25.00 (ISBN 92-63-10556-1, W476, WMO). Unipub.

Thomopoulos, N. Applied Forecasting Methods. 1980. 25.00 (ISBN 0-13-040139-0). P-H.

Twenty-Eighth Session of the Executive Committee, Geneva, 1976: Abridged Report with Resolutions. (WMO Ser: No. 445). 449p. 1977. pap. 25.00 (ISBN 92-63-10445-X, WMO). Unipub.

Twenty-Fifth Session of the Executive Committee: Abridged Report with Resolutions. 182p. (Orig.). 1974. pap. 25.00 (ISBN 0-685-40245-2, 365, WMO). Unipub.

Twenty Ninth Session of the Executive Committee: Geneva, 26 May-15 June, 1977. (Illus.). 1978. pap. 25.00 (ISBN 92-63-10483-2, W-361, WMO). Unipub.

Twenty-Sixth Session of the Executive Committee: Abridged Report with Resolutions. 270p. (Orig.). 1974. pap. 25.00 (ISBN 92-63-10387-9, WMO). Unipub.

U. S. Environmental Data Service. Weather Atlas of the United States. LC 74-11931. 1975. 44.00 (ISBN 0-8103-1048-1). Gale.

U. S. Weather Normals Related to Heating & Cooling Needs. LC 77-3859. Date not set. cancelled (ISBN 0-8103-1025-2). Gale.

Upper Air Sounding Studies: Studies on Radiosonde Performance & Manual Computation of Radiowinds, 2 vols. in one, No. 140. (Illus.). 159p. 1975. pap. 25.00 (ISBN 92-63-10394-1, WMO). Unipub.

Villeneuve, G. O. & Ferland, M. G. Glossaire De Meteorologie et De Climatologie. LC 75-501061. 560p. (Fr.). 1974. 29.95 (ISBN 0-686-57246-7, M-6552). French & Eur.

Villeneuve, G. Oscar, et al, eds. Glossaire De Meteorologie et De Climatologie. 560p. 1975. 25.00x (ISBN 2-7637-6680-3, Pub. by Laval). Intl Schol Bk Serv.

Vinnichenko, N. K., et al. Turbulence in the Free Atmosphere. 2nd ed. (Illus.). 325p. 1980. 49.50 (ISBN 0-306-10959-X, Consultants). Plenum Pub.

Vinnichenko, N. K., et al, eds. Turbulence in the Free Atmosphere. LC 72-157935. (Illus.). 260p. 1973. 42.50 (ISBN 0-306-10857-7, Consultants). Plenum Pub.

Wallington, C. E. Meteorology for Glider Pilots. 3rd ed. (Illus.). 331p. 1980. 24.00 (ISBN 0-7195-3303-1). Transatlantic.

Webb, Willis L. Mesometeorology at El Paso. 1972. pap. 5.00 (ISBN 0-87404-033-7). Tex Western.

WEFAX: A Weather Data Communications Experiment. (World Weather Watch Planning Report Ser.: No. 23). 1968. pap. 6.00 (ISBN 0-685-02476-8, WMO). Unipub.

Weinzierl, Edward. Laboratory Manual in Weather & Climate. 1980. coil bdg. 7.95 (ISBN 0-88252-006-7). Paladin Hse.

Weisbecker, Leo. The Impacts of Snow Enhancement: Technology Assessment of Winter Orographic Snowpack Augumentation in the Upper Colorado River Basin. LC 74-9871. 1974. pap. 14.95x (ISBN 0-8061-1223-9). U of Okla Pr.

Weisberg, Joseph S. Meteorology: The Earth & Its Weather. 2nd ed. (Illus.). 432p. 1981. text ed. 20.95 (ISBN 0-395-29516-5); instr's manual 1.00 (ISBN 0-395-29517-3). HM.

--Meteorology: The Earth & Its Weather. LC 75-26094. (Illus.). 320p. 1976. text ed. 18.95 (ISBN 0-395-20673-1); inst. manual 1.50 (ISBN 0-395-20674-X). HM.

The West African Monsoon Experiment (WAMEX) (GARP Publications Ser.: No. 21). 1978. pap. 15.00 (ISBN 0-685-65241-6, W401, WMO). Unipub.

WMO Conference 1976. Commission for Basic Systems: Abridged Final Report of the Extraordinary Session. (WMO: 457). (Illus.). 1977. pap. 25.00 (ISBN 92-63-10457-3, WMO). Unipub.

Wmo-Ecafe Regional Conference, Bangkok, 14-21 August 1973. The Role of Meteorological Services in the Economic Development of Asia & the South-West Pacific: Proceedings, No. 422. (Illus.). 172p. 1976. pap. 26.00 (ISBN 92-63-10422-0, WMO). Unipub.

WMO Technical Conference on Instruments & Methods of Observation. (Illus.). 1978. pap. 40.00 (ISBN 92-63-10480-8, WMO). Unipub.

World Meteorological Organization. Annual Report, 1972. (Annual Report Ser.). (Illus.). 141p. 1973. pap. 20.00 (ISBN 0-685-39021-7, 348, WMO). Unipub.

--Collection, Storage & Retrieval of Meteorological Data. (World Weather Watch Planning Report Ser.: No. 28). 1969. pap. 8.00 (ISBN 0-685-22296-9, WMO). Unipub.

--Economic Benefits of National Meteorological Services. (World Weather Watch Planning Report Ser.: No. 27). 1968. pap. 10.00 (ISBN 0-685-22302-7, WMO). Unipub.

--International Meteorological Vocabulary. (Eng., Fr., Rus. & Span.). 1966. pap. 40.00 (ISBN 0-685-22313-2, WMO). Unipub.

--Introduction to GARP. (GARP Publications Ser.: No. 1). 1969. pap. 5.00 (ISBN 0-685-22314-0, WMO). Unipub.

--Scope of the Nineteen Seventy-Two to Nineteen Seventy-Five Plan. (World Weather Watch Planning Report Ser.: No. 30). 1969. pap. 12.00 (ISBN 0-685-22337-X, WMO). Unipub.

--Statistical Analysis & Prognosis in Meteorology. (Technical Note Ser.). 1966. pap. 41.00 (ISBN 0-685-22343-4, WMO). Unipub.

World Meteorological Organization Congress, 6th, Geneva, 1971. Abridged Report with Resolutions. 229p. (Orig.). 1972. pap. 35.00 (ISBN 0-685-24968-9, 292, WMO). Unipub.

World Weather Watch: The Plan & Implementation Programme, 1976-1979. (WMO Ser.: No. 418). (Illus.). 52p. 1975. pap. 16.00 (ISBN 92-63-10418-2, WMO). Unipub.

METEOROLOGY–CHARTS, DIAGRAMS, ETC.

Catalogue of Meteorological Data for Research, Pt. 3. 250p. 1972. pap. 50.00 with binder (ISBN 0-685-29207-X, WMO). Unipub.

Conversion of Grid-Point Data into Meteorological Maps with a Mini-Computer System. (World Weather Watch Report: No. 37). 27p. 1980. pap. 5.00 (ISBN 9-2631-0553-7, W469, WMO). Unipub.

Decker, Fred W. Weather Map Study. rev ed. 1979. pap. 1.25x (ISBN 0-931778-00-X). Weather Wkbk.

Lahey, James F., et al. Atlas of Five Hundred Mb Wind Characteristics for the Northern Hemisphere. 96p. 1958. wired bdg. 50.00x (ISBN 0-299-01703-6). U of Wis Pr.

--Atlas of Three Hundred Mb Wind Characteristics for the Northern Hemisphere. 128p. 1960. wired bdg. 50.00x (ISBN 0-299-01963-2). U of Wis Pr.

Wahl, Eberhard W. & Lahey, James F. Seven Hundred MB Atlas for the Northern Hemisphere: Five-Day Mean Heights, Standard Deviations, & Changes. LC 69-5. 1969. plastic comb. bdg. 50.00x (ISBN 0-299-05383-0). U of Wis Pr.

METEOROLOGY–DATA PROCESSING

Belousov, S. L. Computer Processing of Meteorological Data. 216p. 1971. 17.50x (ISBN 0-7065-1130-1, Pub. by IPST). Intl Schol Bk Serv.

Catalogue of Computer Programs in Meteorology. (WMO Ser.: No. 409). 1976. pap. 60.00 (ISBN 92-63-10409-3, WMO). Unipub.

Conversion of Grid-Point Data into Meteorological Maps with a Mini-Computer System. (World Weather Watch Report: No. 37). 27p. 1980. pap. 5.00 (ISBN 9-2631-0553-7, W469, WMO). Unipub.

Guide on the Global Data-Processing System, Vol. 1. (WMO: No. 305). (Illus.). 1976. pap. 32.00 (ISBN 0-685-68974-3, WMO). Unipub.

Manual on the Global Data-Processing System, Vol. II: Regional Aspects. 74p. 1981. pap. 7.00 (ISBN 0-686-69635-2, W475, WMO). Unipub.

Neilon, J. R. & Terauchi, E. Standards & Procedures for Presentation of Processed Data in Digital Form. (World Weather Watch Planning Report Ser.: No. 29). 1969. pap. 10.00 (ISBN 0-685-22342-6, WMO). Unipub.

WMO Conference 1976. Commission for Basic Systems: Abridged Final Report of the Extraordinary Session. (WMO: 457). (Illus.). 1977. pap. 25.00 (ISBN 92-63-10457-3, WMO). Unipub.

World Meteorological Organization. Data Processing by Machine Methods. (Technical Note Ser.). 1966. pap. 8.00 (ISBN 0-685-22297-7, WMO 184, WMO). Unipub.

--Data Processing for Climatological Purposes. (Technical Note Ser.: No. 100). 1969. pap. 18.00 (ISBN 0-685-22298-5, WMO 242, WMO). Unipub.

--Data Processing in Meteorology. (Technical Note Ser.). 1966. pap. 11.00 (ISBN 0-685-22299-3, WMO 180, WMO). Unipub.

METEOROLOGY–EARLY WORKS TO 1800

Aristotle. Meteorologica. (Loeb Classical Library: No. 397). 1952. 11.00x (ISBN 0-674-99436-1). Harvard U Pr.

Nostradamus, Michael. The Prognostication for 1559. LC 78-26331. (English Experience Ser.: No. 186). 96p. 1969. Repr. of 1558 ed. 14.00 (ISBN 90-221-0186-X). Walter J Johnson.

METEOROLOGY–HISTORY

Frisinger, H. Howard. The History of Meteorology: To 1800. (Illus.). 1977. 15.00 (ISBN 0-88202-036-6, Sci Hist). N Watson.

Heninger, S. K. Hand Book of Renaissance Meteorology. LC 69-10106. 1969. Repr. of 1960 ed. lib. bdg. 14.25x (ISBN 0-8371-0472-6, HERM). Greenwood.

Middleton, W. E. History of the Theories of Rain & Other Forms of Precipitation. LC 66-15982. (Oldburne History of Science Ser). 1968. 8.00x (ISBN 0-226-52497-3). U of Chicago Pr.

One Hundred Years of International Co-Operation in Meteorology: A Historical Review, 1873-1973. (Illus.). 53p. (Orig.). 1973. pap. 10.00 (ISBN 0-685-34560-2, 345, WMO). Unipub.

METEOROLOGY–INDIAN OCEAN REGION

Bruun Memorial Lectures. (Intergovernemtal Oceanographic Commission Technical Ser.; No. 10). (Illus.). 43p. (Orig.). 1973. pap. 3.25 (ISBN 92-3-101014-X, U61, UNESCO). Unipub.

Hastenrath, Stefan & Lamb, Peter J. The Climatic Atlas of the Indian Ocean, 2 vols. LC 78-65016. (Illus.). 100.00 (ISBN 0-299-07814-0). U of Wis Pr.

Seminar on Synoptic Analysis & Forecasting in the Tropics of Asia & the Southwest Pacific, Singapore, Dec. 1970. Proceedings. 1972. pap. 55.00 (ISBN 0-685-36789-4, 321, WMO). Unipub.

METEOROLOGY–INTERNATIONAL COOPERATION

Annual Report of the World Meteorological Organization 1979. 191p. 1980. pap. 25.00 (ISBN 92-63-10552-9, W467, WMO). Unipub.

Consolidated Report on the Voluntary Co-Operation Programme Including Projects Approved for Circulation in 1979. 28p. 1980. pap. 15.00 (ISBN 92-63-10545-6, W465, WMO). Unipub.

Field Phase of the GARP Atlantic Tropical Experiment - Meteorological Atlas: Report, No. 17. (Illus.). 179p. 1975. pap. 25.00 (ISBN 0-685-62387-4, WMO). Unipub.

GATE. Report on the Field Phase of the Garp Atlantic Tropical Experiment Operations. (GATE Report: No. 15). (Illus.). 148p. 1976. pap. 25.00 (ISBN 0-685-65022-7, WMO). Unipub.

Guide on the Global Data Processing System, Vol. 2: Preparation of Synoptic Weather Charts & Diagrams. (Illus.). 60p. (Orig.). 1972. pap. 12.00 (ISBN 0-685-25259-0, 305, WMO). Unipub.

Manual on the Global Observing System. 80p. 1980. pap. 20.00 (ISBN 92-63-10544-8, W468, WMO). Unipub.

Modelling for the First GARP Global Experiment. (Garp Publications Ser.: No. 14). (Illus.). 259p. (Orig.). 1974. pap. 40.00 (ISBN 0-685-50807-2, WMO). Unipub.

National Academy Of Sciences. Feasibility of a Global Observation & Analysis Experiment. 1966. pap. 5.00 (ISBN 0-309-01290-2). Natl Acad Pr.

One Hundred Years of International Co-Operation in Meteorology: A Historical Review, 1873-1973. (Illus.). 53p. (Orig.). 1973. pap. 10.00 (ISBN 0-685-34560-2, 345, WMO). Unipub.

Papers Presented at the WMO Technical Conference on Regional & Global Observation of Atmospheric Pollution Relative to Climate. (Special Environmental Report Ser.: No. 14). 398p. 1980. pap. 31.00 (ISBN 92-63-10549-9, W466, WMO). Unipub.

Remote Sensing in the Sudan. 36p. 1978. pap. 3.50 (ISBN 0-88936-159-2, TS9, IDRC). Unipub.

Report of the First Session of the Intergovernmental Planning Commission. (GARP Special Report: No. 36). 85p. 1981. pap. 15.00 (ISBN 0-686-73318-5, W490, WMO). Unipub.

Report of the Meeting on Drifting Buoys for the First GARP Global Experiment. (Garp Special Report Ser.: No. 13). (Illus.). 80p. (Orig.). 1974. pap. 15.00 (ISBN 0-685-50808-0, WMO). Unipub.

Seventh World Meteorological Congress, Geneva, April 23-May 1975. Report: WMO No. 428. 230p. 1976. pap. 30.00 (ISBN 92-63-10428-X, WMO). Unipub.

Symposium, 2nd, Geneva, Aug 13-17, 1973. Joint IOC-WMO Planning Group for IGOSS (Integrated Global Ocean Station System) Proceedings. 60p. (Orig.). 1974. pap. 5.50 (ISBN 0-685-40088-3, WMO). Unipub.

Twenty Years of WMO Assistance. (Illus.). 187p. (Orig.). 1973. pap. 10.00 (ISBN 0-685-34561-0, 338, WMO). Unipub.

WMO Helps the Developing Countries. 85p. 1973. pap. 2.00 (ISBN 0-685-29205-3, 307, WMO). Unipub.

World Meteorological Congress, Eighth. Proceedings. 261p. 1980. pap. 30.00 (ISBN 92-63-10547-2, W472, WMO). Unipub.

World Weather Watch: Consolidated Report on the Voluntary Assistance Programme Including Projects Approved for Circulation in 1975. (WMO: No. 437). 1976. pap. 15.00 (ISBN 92-63-10437-9, WMO). Unipub.

World Weather Watch: Sixth Status Report on Implementation. (World Weather Watch Report Ser.). (Illus.). 225p. (Orig.). 1974. pap. 25.00 (ISBN 0-685-40087-5, 360, WMO). Unipub.

METEOROLOGY–JUVENILE LITERATURE

Breiter, Herta S. Weather. LC 77-27239. (Read About Science Ser.). (Illus.). (gr. k-3). 1978. PLB 11.15 (ISBN 0-8393-0079-4). Raintree Child.

Gribbin, John. Our Changing Climate. 128p. (gr. 5-8). 1978. 6.95 (ISBN 0-571-10696-X, Pub. by Faber & Faber). Merrimack Bk Serv.

London, Julius. Weather & Climate. LC 59-13618. (Illus.). (gr. 4-6). 1960. PLB 6.95 (ISBN 0-87396-012-2). Stravon.

Spar, Jerome. Way of the Weather. LC 66-30641. (Creative Science Ser). (gr. 4-9). 1967. PLB 7.95 (ISBN 0-87191-013-6). Creative Ed.

Sutcliffe, Reginald C. Weather & Climate. (Advancement of Science Series). (Illus.). 1967. 5.95x (ISBN 0-393-06329-1). Norton.

Zim, Herbert S. Lightning & Thunder. (Illus.). (gr. 3-7). 1952. PLB 6.00 (ISBN 0-688-31481-3). Morrow.

METEOROLOGY-MISCELLANEA

Fort, Charles. The Book of the Damned. Del Rey, Lester, ed. LC 75-406. (Library of Science Fiction). 1975. lib. bdg. 17.50 (ISBN 0-8240-1411-1). Garland Pub.

METEOROLOGY-OBSERVATIONS

see also Aeronautics in Meteorology; Astronautics in Meteorology; Meteorological Stations

Badgley, F. I., et al. Profiles of Wind, Temperature, & Humidity Over the Arabian Sea. LC 70-129539. (International Indian Ocean Expedition Meteorological Monographs: No. 6). (Illus.). 1972. text ed. 12.00x (ISBN 0-8248-0101-6, Eastwest Ctr). U Pr of Hawaii.

Basic Synoptic Network of Observing Stations. 1978. pap. 45.00 (ISBN 0-685-42367-0, WMO). Unipub.

Brooks, Charles E. & Carruthers, N. Handbook of Statistical Methods in Meteorology. LC 77-10222. Repr. of 1953 ed. 30.50 (ISBN 0-404-16202-9). AMS Pr.

Comparison of Climate of the United States & Europe: Especially Poland & Her Baltic Coast. 288p. 1945. 8.00 (ISBN 0-686-31659-2). Polish Inst Arts.

Guide on the Global Observing System. (WMO Ser: No. 365). (Illus.). 1978. pap. 42.00 (ISBN 0-685-87430-3, WMO 488, WMO). Unipub.

Kellogg, W. W. Meteorological Soundings in the Upper Atmosphere. (Technical Note Ser.). 1964. pap. 8.00 (ISBN 0-685-22322-1, WMO). Unipub.

Michigan University Greenland Expeditions 1926-1933. Reports of the Greenland Expeditions of the University of Michigan, 2 Vols. LC 68-55203. (Illus.). 1968. Repr. of 1941 ed. Set. lib. bdg. 45.50x (ISBN 0-8371-3850-7, MUGE). Greenwood.

The Use of Satellite Imagery in Tropical Cyclone Analysis. (WMO Ser: No. 473). (Illus.). 1978. pap. 25.00 (ISBN 92-63-10473-5, W-369, WMO). Unipub.

WMO Technical Conference on Instruments & Methods of Observation. (Illus.). 1978. pap. 40.00 (ISBN 92-63-10480-8, WMO). Unipub.

World Meteorological Organization. Meteorology in the Indian Ocean. 1965. pap. 2.00 (ISBN 0-685-22325-6, WMO). Unipub.

World Weather Watch: Consolidated Report on the Voluntary Assistance Programme Including Projects Approved for Circulation in 1973. (World Weather Watch Planning Report Ser.). 170p. (Orig.). 1974. pap. 15.00 (ISBN 92-63-10374-7, WMO). Unipub.

World Weather Watch: Consolidated Report on the Voluntary Assistance Program Including Projects Approved for Circulation in 1974. 218p. 1975. pap. 15.00 (ISBN 92-63-10404-2, WMO). Unipub.

World Weather Watch: Eighth Status Report on Implementation. (WMO Ser: No. 447). (Illus.). 140p. 1977. pap. 25.00 (ISBN 92-63-10447-6, WMO). Unipub.

World Weather Watch: Seventh Status Report on Implementation. (Illus.). 1975. pap. 25.00 (ISBN 92-63-10401-8, WMO). Unipub.

METEOROLOGY-PERIODICITY

see also Dendrochronology

METEOROLOGY-RESEARCH

see Meteorological Research

METEOROLOGY-STUDY AND TEACHING

Byers, Horace R. General Meteorology. 4th ed. (Illus.). 550p. 1974. text ed. 21.00 (ISBN 0-07-009500-0, C). McGraw.

Compendium of Meteorological Training Facilities. (WMO Ser: No. 240). (Illus.). 1978. pap. 25.00 (ISBN 0-685-86364-6, WMO). Unipub.

Conference on Meteorological Education & Training in Developing Countries in Africa. Proceedings. (Illus.). 362p. 1972. pap. 20.00 (ISBN 0-685-23600-5, 300, WMO). Unipub.

Guidelines for the Education & Training of Meteorological Personnel. (Orig.). 1969. pap. 15.00 (ISBN 0-685-04912-4, WMO 258, WMO). Unipub.

Guidelines for the Education & Training of Personnel in Meteorology & Operational Hydrology. (WMO Ser: No. 258). (Illus.). 1978. pap. 20.00 (ISBN 0-685-87431-1, W-373, WMO). Unipub.

Kazeck, M. & Bridwell, J. Weather Workbook. 1971. pap. 3.80x (ISBN 0-87563-045-6). Stipes.

Lounsbury, John F. A Workbook for Weather & Climate. 3rd ed. 144p. 1973. write for info. (ISBN 0-697-05253-2); tchr's manual avail. (ISBN 0-686-66894-4). Wm C Brown.

WMO-IAMAP Symposium on Education & Training in Meteorology & Meteorological Aspects of Environmental Problems, Caracas, February 1975. Proceedings. (WMO Ser.: No. 432). (Illus.). 321p. 1976. pap. 50.00 (ISBN 92-63-10432-8, WMO). Unipub.

WMO-IAMAP Symposium on Higher Education & Training. Proceedings. (Orig.). 1971. pap. 20.00 (ISBN 0-685-00378-7, WMO). Unipub.

World Weather Watch: Consolidated Report on the Voluntary Assistance Programme Including Projects Approved for Circulation in 1973. (World Weather Watch Planning Report Ser.). 170p. (Orig.). 1974. pap. 15.00 (ISBN 92-63-10374-7, WMO). Unipub.

World Weather Watch: Consolidated Report on the Voluntary Assistance Program Including Projects Approved for Circulation in 1974. 218p. 1975. pap. 15.00 (ISBN 92-63-10404-2, WMO). Unipub.

World Weather Watch: Seventh Status Report on Implementation. (Illus.). 1975. pap. 25.00 (ISBN 92-63-10401-8, WMO). Unipub.

METEOROLOGY-ANTARCTIC REGIONS

Kuhn, M., et al. The Radiation Budget at Plateau Station, Antarctica: Paper 5 in Meteorological Studies at Plateau Station, Antarctica. Businger, Joost A., ed. (Antarctic Research Ser.: Vol. 25). 1977. pap. 13.00 (ISBN 0-87590-139-5). Am Geophysical.

Lettau, H., et al. Air Temperature & Two-Dimensional Wind Profiles in the Lowest 32 Meters As a Function of Bulk Stability, Stability Related Wind Spiraling in the Lowest 32 Meters, & Variations of Temperature & Air Motion in the 0 to 32m Layer at Plateau Station, Antartica: Papers 6, 7, & 8 in Meteorological Studies at Plateau Station, Antarctica. Businer, Joost A., ed. (Antarctic Research Ser.: Vol. 25). 1977. pap. 10.50 (ISBN 0-87590-140-9). Am Geophysical.

Rubin, M. J., ed. Studies in Antarctic Meteorology. LC 66-6578. (Antarctic Research Ser.: Vol. 9). 1966. 14.00 (ISBN 0-87590-109-3). Am Geophysical.

METEOROLOGY, AGRICULTURAL

see also Crops and Climate

Agricultural Meteorology. 357p. (Orig.). 1972. pap. 35.00 (ISBN 0-685-26758-X, 310, W112, WMO). Unipub.

Agroclimatology Survey of Semiarid Area in Africa. (Technical Note Ser.). pap. 15.00 (ISBN 0-685-57271-4, WMO 210, WMO). Unipub.

Agrometeorological Crop Monitoring & Forecasting. (FAO Plant Production & Protection Paper Ser.: No. 17). 67p. 1980. pap. 6.00 (ISBN 92-5-100807-8, F1875, FAO). Unipub.

Board on Agriculture & Renewable Resources, National Research Council. Climate & Food: Climatic Fluctuation & U. S. Agricultural Production. LC 76-46195. 1976. pap. 7.75 (ISBN 0-309-02522-2). Natl Acad Pr.

Commission for Agricultural Meteorology: Abridged Final Report of the Seventh Session. 65p. 1980. pap. 25.00 (ISBN 92-63-10546-4, W467, WMO). Unipub.

Commission for Agricultural Meteorology: Abridged Final Report of the 6th Session. 79p. 1975. pap. 25.00 (ISBN 92-63-10402-6, WMO 402, WMO). Unipub.

The Economic Value of Agrometeorological Information & Advice. (Technical Note Ser.: No. 164). 52p. 1981. pap. 10.00 (ISBN 92-63-10526-X, W478, WMO). Unipub.

Geiger, Rudolf. Climate Near the Ground. 4th ed. Scripta Technica Inc, tr. LC 64-23191. 1965. 30.00x (ISBN 0-674-13500-8). Harvard U Pr.

Lecture Notes for Training Class II & Class III Agricultural Meteorological Personnel. 260p. 1980. pap. 18.00 (ISBN 92-63-10551-0, W485, WMO). Unipub.

Rice & Weather. (WMO Ser.: No. 423). (Illus.). 40p. 1976. pap. 12.00 (ISBN 92-63-10423-9, WMO). Unipub.

Rosenberg, Norman J. Microclimate: The Biological Environment. LC 74-8952. 336p. 1974. 23.50 (ISBN 0-471-73615-5, Pub. by Wiley-Interscience). Wiley.

Seemann, J., et al. Agrometeorology. LC 79-9757. (Illus.). 1979. 56.60 (ISBN 0-387-09331-1). Springer-Verlag.

Smith, L. P. Methods in Agricultural Meteorology. LC 74-21868. (Developments in Atmospheric Science Ser: Vol. 3). 210p. 1975. 51.25 (ISBN 0-444-41286-7). Elsevier.

Soya Bean & Weather. 1978. pap. 20.00 (ISBN 92-63-10498-0, W396, WMO). Unipub.

U. S. Department of Agriculture. Climate & Man: Nineteen Forty-One Yearbook of Agriculture, House Document No. 27, 77th Congress, 1st Session. LC 74-6297. 1248p. 1975. Repr. of 1941 ed. 68.00 (ISBN 0-8103-4016-X). Gale.

Wang Jen-Yu & Barger, Gerald L., eds. Bibliography of Agricultural Meteorology. 686p. 1962. 45.00x (ISBN 0-299-02510-1). U of Wis Pr.

World Weather Watch & Meteorological Service to Agriculture. (World Weather Watch Planning Report Ser.: No. 22). 1967. pap. 4.00 (ISBN 0-685-02477-6, WMO). Unipub.

METEOROLOGY, MARITIME

see also Hurricanes; Typhoons

Blanchard, Duncan C. From Raindrops to Volcanoes: Adventures with Sea Surface Meteorology. LC 80-19134. (Science Study Ser.: Selected Topics in Atmospheric Sciences). (Illus.). xii, 180p. 1980. Repr. of 1967 ed. lib. bdg. 19.75x (ISBN 0-313-22638-5, BLFR). Greenwood.

Bowditch, Nathaniel. Marine Weather. LC 79-799. 1979. pap. 6.00 (ISBN 0-668-04455-1). Arco.

--Waves, Wind & Weather: Selected from American Practical Navigator. (Nautical Ser.). (Illus.). 1977. 7.95 (ISBN 0-679-50753-1). McKay.

Burgess, C. R. Meteorology for Seamen. metric ed. 1981. 30.00x (ISBN 0-85174-315-3, Pub. by Nautical England). State Mutual Bk.

Commission for Marine Meteorology. (WMO Ser: No. 462). 1977. pap. 25.00 (ISBN 92-63-10462-X, WMO). Unipub.

Compendium of Lecture Notes in Marine Meteorology for Class III & Class IV Personnel. (WMO Technical Publications Ser.: No. 434). (Illus.). 1976. pap. 25.00 (ISBN 92-63-10434-4, WMO). Unipub.

Donn, William L. Meteorology. 3rd ed. 1965. text ed. 14.95 (ISBN 0-07-017598-5, G). McGraw.

--Meteorology. 4th ed. (Illus.). 608p. 1975. text ed. 19.95 (ISBN 0-07-017599-3, G). McGraw.

Guide to Marine Meteorological Services. 1978. pap. 27.00 (ISBN 92-63-10471-9, W-362, WMO). Unipub.

Handbook on Wave Analysis & Forecasting. (No. 446). (Illus.). 1977. pap. 37.00 (ISBN 92-63-10446-8, WMO). Unipub.

Hastenrath, Stefan & Lamb, Peter J. Heat Budget Atlas of the Tropical Atlantic & Eastern Pacific Oceans. LC 77-91052. (Illus.). 1978. pap. text ed. 50.00x (ISBN 0-299-07584-2). U of Wis Pr.

Maury, Matthew F. Physical Geography of the Sea, & Its Meteorology. Leighly, John, ed. LC 63-10870. (The John Harvard Library). (Illus.). 1963. pap. 8.95x (ISBN 0-674-66652-6). Harvard U Pr.

Meteorological Aspects of Ice Accretion on Ships. (Marine Science Affairs Ser.: No. 10). 34p. 1975. pap. 10.00 (ISBN 0-685-55843-6, WMO). Unipub.

Methods of Forecasting the State of Sea on the Basis of Meteorological Data. (Technical Note Ser.). 1962. pap. 12.00 (ISBN 0-685-36786-X, WMO). Unipub.

The Monsoon Experiment. (GARP Publications Series: No. 18). 1977. pap. 25.00 (ISBN 0-685-77321-3, WMO). Unipub.

Motte, R. Weather Routeing of Ships. 150p. 1972. 9.50x (ISBN 0-540-00382-4). Sheridan.

Papers Presented at the WMO Technical Conference on the Applications of Marine Meteorology to the High Seas & Coastal Zone Development. (Illus.). 1977. pap. 40.00 (ISBN 92-63-10454-9, WMO). Unipub.

Regional Association II (Asia) Abridged Final Report of the Seventh Session: Geneva, 2-12 June 1980. 145p. 1980. pap. 25.00 (ISBN 92-63-10567-7, W486, WMO). Unipub.

Roll, Hans U. Physics of the Marine Atmosphere. (International Geophysics Ser.: Vol. 7). 1965. 50.00 (ISBN 0-12-593650-8). Acad Pr.

Seiches et Denivellations Causees par le vent dans lacs, baies, mers, estuaires. (Technical Note Ser.). pap. 12.00 (ISBN 0-685-57270-6, WMO). Unipub.

Watts, Alan. Basic Windcraft. 1976. 5.95 (ISBN 0-396-07326-3). Dodd.

Whelpley, Donald A. Weather, Water & Boating. LC 61-12540. (Illus.). 1961. 5.00 (ISBN 0-87033-133-7). Cornell Maritime.

Williams, Jerome, et al. Sea & Air: The Marine Environment. 2nd ed. LC 72-93196. 1973. 13.50x (ISBN 0-87021-596-5). Naval Inst Pr.

World Meteorological Organization. Global Data-Processing System & Meteorological Service to Shipping. (World Weather Watch Planning Report Ser.: No. 15). 1966. pap. 12.00 (ISBN 0-685-22305-1, WMO). Unipub.

METEOROLOGY AND ATOMIC ENERGY

see Atomic Energy and Meteorology

METEOROLOGY AS A PROFESSION

Berry, Frederic A. & Frank, Sidney. Your Future in Meteorology. LC 62-11570. (Careers in Depth Ser). (gr. 7 up). PLB 5.97 (ISBN 0-8239-0051-7). Rosen Pr.

Educational Research Council of America. Meteorologist. rev. ed. Kunze, Linda J. & Marchak, John P., eds. (Real People at Work Ser: G). (Illus.). 1976. pap. text ed. 2.25 (ISBN 0-89247-054-2). Changing Times.

Guide to the Qualifications & Training of Meteorological Personnel Employed in the Provision of Meteorological Services for International Air Navigation. pap. 12.00 (ISBN 0-685-57277-3, 114, WMO). Unipub.

Harris, Miles F. & American Meteorological Society. Opportunities in Meteorology. rev. ed. LC 77-184504. (Illus.). 184p. 1972. lib. bdg. 6.60 (ISBN 0-685-27224-9); pap. 4.95 (ISBN 0-685-27225-7). Natl Textbk.

How to Become a Meteorologist. (Illus., Orig.). 1970. pap. 2.00 (ISBN 0-685-04913-2, WMO). Unipub.

Rudman, Jack. Meteorologist. (Career Examination Ser.: C-497). (Cloth bdg. avail. on request). pap. 10.00 (ISBN 0-8373-0497-0). Natl Learning.

METEOROLOGY IN AERONAUTICS

see also Aeronautics in Meteorology

Aviation Book Company Editors. Aviation Weather Maps. 1968. pap. 0.75 (ISBN 0-685-55077-X). Aviation.

--Flying & the Weather. 1971. pap. 1.25 (ISBN 0-685-55074-5). Aviation.

--Temperature, Pressure, & the Wind. 1966. pap. 0.75 (ISBN 0-685-55076-1). Aviation.

Aviation Hail Problem (Includes Other Notes on Forecasting for Jet Aircraft) (Technical Note Ser.: Nos. 37-40). pap. 17.00 (ISBN 0-685-57276-5, WMO109, WMO). Unipub.

Boyes, Lindy. Pilot's Weather Guide. 1962. pap. 7.95 (ISBN 0-8306-9928-7); pap. 4.95 (ISBN 0-8306-2226-8, 2226). TAB Bks.

Dabberdt, Walter F. The Whole Air Weather Guide. (Illus.). 1976. pap. 3.50 (ISBN 0-686-70932-2, Pub. by Solstice). Aviation.

Dickson, Ron R. Weather & Flight: An Introduction to Meteorology for Pilots. 176p. 1981. 14.95 (ISBN 0-13-947119-7); pap. 5.95 (ISBN 0-13-947101-4). P-H.

Federal Aviation Administration. Aviation Weather. 2nd ed. (Pilot Training Ser.). (Illus.). 219p. 1975. pap. 7.00 (ISBN 0-89100-160-3, E*A-A*C61-006A). Aviation Maintenance.

--Aviation Weather Services. 3rd ed. (Pilot Training Ser.). (Illus.). 123p. 1979. pap. 4.50 (ISBN 0-89100-161-1, E*A-A*C61-0045B). Aviation Maintenance.

Flying Magazine Editors. Flying Wisdom. 1979. 13.95 (ISBN 0-442-22452-4). Van Nos Reinhold.

Handbook of Meteorological Forecasting for Soaring Flight. (Technical Note Ser.: No. 158). 1978. pap. 18.00 (ISBN 92-63-10495-6, W399, WMO). Unipub.

Jones, R. P., et al. Meteorological Problems in the Design & Operation of Supersonic Aircraft. (Technical Note Ser.). 1967. pap. 9.00 (ISBN 0-685-22321-3, WMO). Unipub.

Nelson, John. Practical Guide to Aviation Weather. 1976. pap. 3.95 (ISBN 0-8306-2228-4, 2228). TAB Bks.

Reithmaier, Larry. Weather Briefing Guide for Pilots. LC 75-94968. (Pilot Guides). pap. 1.00 (ISBN 0-8168-7212-0). Aero.

Use of Weather Radar for Aviation. (Technical Note Ser.: No. 110). (Illus., Orig.). 1970. pap. 8.00 (ISBN 0-685-04926-4, WMO). Unipub.

Utilization of Aircraft Meteorological Reports. (Technical Notes: No. 141). (Illus.). 34p. 1975. pap. 10.00 (ISBN 92-63-10400-X, WMO). Unipub.

World Meteorological Organization. Aeronautical Meteorology. (Technical Note Ser.: No. 95). 1969. pap. 60.00 (ISBN 0-685-22293-4, WMO227, W62, WMO). Unipub.

--Global Data-Processing System & Meteorological Service to Shipping. (World Weather Watch Planning Report Ser.: No. 15). 1966. pap. 12.00 (ISBN 0-685-22305-1, WMO). Unipub.

--Manual on Meteorological Observing in Transport Aircraft. 1978. pap. 4.00 (ISBN 92-63-12197-4, W393, WMO). Unipub.

METEORS

see also Meteorites

Cristescu, Cornelia & Klepczynski, W. J., eds. Asteroids, Comets, Meteoric Matter: Proceedings. (Illus.). 333p. 1975. text ed. 50.00x (ISBN 0-87936-008-9). Scholium Intl.

Hornberger, Theodore. A Goodly Gallerye: William Fulke's Book of Meteors. LC 78-68390. (Memoirs Ser.: Vol. 130). 1979. pap. 6.00 (ISBN 0-87169-130-2). Am Philos.

IAU Symposium, 33rd, Tatranska Lomnica, Czechoslovakia, 1967. Physics & Dynamics of Meteors: Proceedings. Kresak, L. & Millman, P. M., eds. LC 68-26965. (IAU Symposia). 525p. 1968. lib. bdg. 53.00 (ISBN 90-277-0127-X, Pub. by Reidel Holland). Kluwer Boston.

McDonnell, J. A., ed. Cosmic Dust. LC 77-2895. 1978. text ed. 127.95 (ISBN 0-471-99512-6, Pub. by Wiley-Interscience). Wiley.

Nelson, Harry E. The Resistance of the Air to Stone-Dropping Meteors. LC 53-12359. (Augustana College Library Ser.: No. 24). 1953. pap. 3.00 (ISBN 0-910182-19-1). Augustana Coll.

Schiaparelli, G. V. Le Opere Publicate per Cura Della Reale Specola Di Brera, Vols. 1-11. (Sources of Science Ser). (It). Repr. of 1930 ed. Set. 339.00 (ISBN 0-384-53780-4). Johnson Repr.

METER

see Musical Meter and Rhythm; Versification

METER (STANDARD OF LENGTH)

see Metric System

METERS, ELECTRIC

see Electric Meters

METERS, FLOW
see Flow Meters
METERS, PARKING
see Parking Meters
METERS, WATER
see Water-Meters
METHADONE HYDROCHLORIDE
Bourne, Peter. Methadone: Benefits & Shortcomings. LC 75-35491. (Monograph). 1975. 1.25 (ISBN 0-686-17308-2). Drug Abuse.
Chambers, Carl D. & Brill, Leon, eds. Methadone: Experiences & Issues. LC 72-6122. 411p. 1973. text ed. 29.95 (ISBN 0-87705-072-4). Human Sci Pr.
Danaceau, Paul. Methadone Maintenance: The Experience of Four Programs. LC 73-81224. (Monograph). 109p. 1973. 1.25 (ISBN 0-686-05696-5). Drug Abuse.
Nelkin, Dorothy. Methadone Maintenance: A Technological Fix. LC 72-96071. (Science, Technology & Society Ser). 192p. 1973. pap. 1.95 (ISBN 0-8076-0680-4). Braziller.
Newman, R. G. Methadone Treatment in Narcotic Addiction: Program Management,Findings, & Prospects for the Future. 1977. 33.50 (ISBN 0-12-517050-5). Acad Pr.
Wilmarth, S. S. & Avram, A. Therapeutic Effectiveness of Methadone Maintenance Programs in the USA. (Offset Pub.: No. 3). (Also avail. in French). 1974. pap. 6.80 (ISBN 92-4-170003-3). World Health.
METHANE
Emcon Associates. Methane Generation & Recovery from Landfills. LC 80-67725. 139p. 1980. 14.95 (ISBN 0-250-40360-9). Ann Arbor Science.
Meynell, Peter-John. Methane: Planning a Digester. LC 77-87893. (Orig.). 1978. pap. 4.95 (ISBN 0-8052-0586-1). Schocken.
Rutan, Al. The Do's & Don't's of Methane: Gas Production for Self Sufficiency. rev. ed. (Illus.). 165p. 1979. pap. 15.00 (ISBN 0-936222-02-6). Rutan Pub.
Stafford, D. A., et al. Methane Production from Waste Organic Matter. LC 78-31274. 1980. 79.95 (ISBN 0-8493-5223-1). CRC Pr.
Wise, Donald L., ed. Fuel Gas Production from Biomass, 2 vols. 1981. Vol. I, 288 Pgs. 76.95 (ISBN 0-8493-5990-2); Vol. II, 272 Pgs. 74.95 (ISBN 0-8493-5991-0). CRC Pr.
METHEMOGLOBINEMIA
Kiese, M. Methemoglobinemia: A Comprehensive Treatise. LC 74-11694. (Uniscience Ser.). 260p. 1974. 49.95 (ISBN 0-87819-054-6). CRC Pr.
METHIONINE
Shapiro, Stanley K. & Schlenk, Fritz, eds. Transmethylation & Methionine Biosynthesis. LC 64-24975. 1965. 16.50x (ISBN 0-226-75039-6). U of Chicago Pr.
METHOD OF LEAST SQUARES
see Least Squares
METHOD OF STUDY
see Study, Method Of
METHOD OF WORK
see Methods Engineering; Work
METHODISM
see also Camp-Meetings; Perfection
Dearing, Trevor. Wesleyan & Tractarian Worship. 1966. text ed. 8.50x (ISBN 0-8401-0531-2). Allenson-Breckinridge.
Gill, Frederick C. The Romantic Movement & Methodism: A Study of English Romanticism & the Evangelical Revival. 1978. Repr. of 1937 ed. lib. bdg. 25.00 (ISBN 0-8492-4910-4). R West.
Gowland, D. A. Methodist Secessions: The Origins of Free Methodism in Three Lancashire Towns. 192p. 1979. 42.00x (ISBN 0-7190-1335-6, Pub. by Manchester U Pr England). State Mutual Bk.
Green, Richard. Anti-Methodist Publications Issued During the 18th Century. LC 71-83701. 175p. 1974. Repr. of 1902 ed. lib. bdg. 22.50 (ISBN 0-8337-1436-8). B Franklin.
Harmon, Nolan B. The Encyclopedia of World Methodism. rev. ed. 2816p. 1974. 89.50 (ISBN 0-687-11784-4). Abingdon.
Hassing, Arne. Religion & Power: The Case of Methodism in Norway. (Jesse Lee Prize Ser.). (Illus.). 300p. 1980. 15.00 (ISBN 0-915466-03-1). United Meth Archives.
Lee, Umphrey. Our Fathers & Us: The Heritage of the Methodists. LC 58-14109. 1958. 4.00 (ISBN 0-87074-088-1). SMU Press.
Moore, M. H. Sketches of the Pioneers of Methodism in North Carolina & Virginia. 1977. Repr. of 1884 ed. 10.95 (ISBN 0-87921-039-7). Attic Pr.
Rowe, Kenneth E., ed. Methodist Union Catalog Pre-1976 Imprints, 20 vols. Vol. I, A-bj. LC 75-33190. 1975. 25.00 (ISBN 0-8108-0880-3). Scarecrow.
Shepherd, T. B. Methodism & the Literature of the 18th Century. LC 68-4718. (Studies in Comparative Literature, No. 35). 1969. Repr. of 1940 ed. lib. bdg. 49.95 (ISBN 0-8383-0680-2). Haskell.
Simpson, Matthew. Encyclopedia of Methodism, 2 vols. 1977. lib. bdg. 250.00 (ISBN 0-8490-1766-1). Gordon Pr.
Swaney, Charles B. Episcopal Methodism & Slavery with Sidelights on Ecclesiastical Politics. LC 69-16562. 356p. 1926. Repr. 17.75x (ISBN 0-8371-1006-8, Pub. by Negro U Pr). Greenwood.
Taylor, Ernest R. Methodism & Politics, 1791-1851. LC 73-94149. xii, 227p. 1975. Repr. of 1935 ed. 16.00 (ISBN 0-8462-1781-3). Russell.
Thomas, Issac L. Methodism & the Negro. LC 75-155415. (Illus.). Repr. of 1910 ed. 16.75x (ISBN 0-8371-6111-8, Pub. by Negro U Pr). Greenwood.
Watson, Philip S., ed. Message of the Wesleys: A Reader of Instruction. (Orig.). 1964. pap. 1.95 (ISBN 0-02-089700-6). Macmillan.
Williams, John P. Social Adjustment in Methodism. LC 76-177639. (Columbia University. Teachers College. Contributions to Education: No. 765). Repr. of 1938 ed. 17.50 (ISBN 0-404-55765-1). AMS Pr.
METHODISM–HISTORY
Baker, Frank. From Wesley to Asbury: Studies in Early American Methodism. LC 75-39454. 1976. 12.75 (ISBN 0-8223-0359-0). Duke.
Baker, George C., Jr. Introduction to the History of Early New England Methodism. LC 70-95393. 1969. Repr. of 1941 ed. 16.00 (ISBN 0-404-00466-0). AMS Pr.
Barr. Early Methodist Under Persecution. pap. 4.95 (ISBN 0-686-23582-7). Schmul Pub Co.
Daniels, W. H. Illustrated History of Methodism. 1977. lib. bdg. 75.00 (ISBN 0-8490-2036-0). Gordon Pr.
Graham, J. H. Black United Methodists: Retrospect & Prospect. 1979. 7.95 (ISBN 0-533-04023-X). Vantage.
Halevy, Elie. Birth of Methodism in England. Semmel, Bernard, tr. LC 72-131959. 1971. 6.00x (ISBN 0-226-31309-3). U of Chicago Pr.
Hayes, A. J. & Gowland, D. A. Scottish Methodism in the Early Victorian Period: The Scottish Correspondence of the Reverend Jabez Bunting, 1800-1857. 160p. 1981. 18.00x (ISBN 0-85224-412-6, Pub. by Edinburgh U Pr Scotland). Columbia U Pr.
Jones, Charles E. Perfectionist Persuasion: The Holiness Movement & American Methodism, 1867-1936. LC 74-1376. (ATLA Monograph: No. 5). (Illus.). 1974. 10.00 (ISBN 0-8108-0747-5). Scarecrow.
Lee, Umphrey. Historical Backgrounds of Early Methodist Enthusiasm. LC 31-18047. (Columbia University. Studies in the Social Sciences: No. 339). Repr. of 1931 ed. 17.50 (ISBN 0-404-51339-5). AMS Pr.
McCulloh, Gerald O. Ministerial Education in the American Methodist Movement. LC 80-69028. (An Informed Ministry Ser.: 200 Years of American Methodist Thought). (Illus.). 342p. (Orig.). 1980. pap. 3.95 (ISBN 0-938162-00-4). United Meth Educ.
Nottingham, Elizabeth K. Methodism & the Frontier: Indiana Proving Ground. LC 41-19465. Repr. of 1941 ed. 7.00 (ISBN 0-404-04798-X). AMS Pr.
Sweet, William W. Methodism in American History. rev. ed. LC 54-5943. 1954. 6.50 (ISBN 0-687-25081-1). Abingdon.
Thrall, Homer S. A Brief History of Methodism in Texas. 1978. Repr. of 1889 ed. 10.95 (ISBN 0-87921-042-7). Attic Pr.
Wilder, Franklin. The Methodist Riots: The Testing of Charles Wesley. (Illus.). 160p. 1982. 8.00 (ISBN 0-89962-236-4). Todd & Honeywell.
METHODIST CHURCH
Baker, Frank. The Methodist Pilgrim in England. 3rd rev ed. LC 75-44553. (Illus.). 112p. 1976. smyth sewn 5.95 (ISBN 0-914960-07-5). Academy Bks.
Bishop, John. Methodist Worship: In Relation to Free Church Worship. rev. ed. LC 75-20379. xvii, 173p. 1976. lib. bdg. 6.95 (ISBN 0-89177-001-1). Scholars Studies.
Byrne, Donald E. No Foot of Land: Folklore of American Methodist Itinerants. LC 75-1097. (ATLA Monograph: No. 6). (Illus.). 370p. 1975. 15.00 (ISBN 0-8108-0798-X). Scarecrow.
Chreitzberg, Abel M. Early Methodism in the Carolinas. LC 70-187362. (Illus.). 378p. 1972. Repr. of 1897 ed. 18.00 (ISBN 0-87152-090-7). Reprint.
Dunkle, William F., Jr. & Quilian, Joseph D., Jr. Companion to the Book of Worship. LC 71-120595. 1970. 6.95 (ISBN 0-687-09258-2). Abingdon.
Harmon, Nolan B. Understanding the United Methodist Church, 1977 Edition. LC 73-20001. 1974. pap. 4.95 (ISBN 0-687-43005-4). Abingdon.
Keysor, Charles W. Our Methodist Heritage. LC 73-88675. 144p. 1973. pap. 2.50 (ISBN 0-912692-27-8). Cook.
Mills, Edward L. Plains, Peaks & Pioneers. (Illus.). 1947. 8.95 (ISBN 0-8323-0035-7). Binford.
Moore, John M. Long Road to Methodist Union. 1958. 3.00 (ISBN 0-687-22597-3). Abingdon.
Morrow, Ralph E. Northern Methodism & Reconstruction. ix, 269p. 1956. 5.00 (ISBN 0-87013-018-8). Mich St U Pr.
Norwood, Frederick A. The Story of American Methodism. LC 74-10621. 448p. 1974. pap. 14.95 (ISBN 0-687-39640-9); pap. 10.95 (ISBN 0-687-39641-7). Abingdon.
Norwood, Frederick A., ed. Methodist Discipline of Seventeen Ninety-Eight: Including the Annotations of Thomas Coke & Francis Asbury. LC 78-74848. 198p. 1979. pap. 8.95 (ISBN 0-914960-17-2, Pub. by Academy Bks). C E Tuttle.
Norwood, John H. The Schism in the Methodist Episcopal Church, 1844. LC 76-10284. (Perspectives in American Hist. Ser.: No. 33). 255p. Repr. of 1923 ed. lib. bdg. 15.00x (ISBN 0-87991-357-6). Porcupine Pr.
Posey, Walter B. The Development of Methodism in the Old Southwest: 1783-1824. LC 73-18408. (Perspectives in American History: No. 19). (Illus.). Repr. of 1933 ed. lib. bdg. 15.00x (ISBN 0-87991-339-8). Porcupine Pr.
Ramsden, William E. The Church in a Changing Society. LC 79-24274. (Into Our Third Century Ser.). (Orig.). 1980. pap. 3.95 (ISBN 0-687-08250-1). Abingdon.
Rowe, Kenneth E., ed. Methodist Union Catalog: Pre-1976 Imprints, Che-Dix, Vol. 3. LC 75-33190. 1978. 25.00 (ISBN 0-8108-1067-0). Scarecrow.
Schell, Edwin, ed. Methodist Conference Minutes & Traveling Preachers: Seventeen Seventy-Three to Seventeen Ninety-Four. LC 79-51893. Date not set. pap. 9.25 (ISBN 0-914960-18-0). Academy Bks.
Shipp, Albert M. The History of Methodism in South Carolina. LC 70-187373. 652p. 1972. Repr. of 1884 ed. 21.00 (ISBN 0-87152-101-6). Reprint.
Shockley, Grant S., et al. Black Pastors & Churches in United Methodism. 1976. pap. 1.00 (ISBN 0-89937-005-5). Ctr Res Soc Chg.
Short, Roy H. History of the Council of Bishops of the United Methodist Church, 1939 to 1979. LC 80-16423. 320p. 1980. 10.95 (ISBN 0-687-17190-3). Abingdon.
--United Methodism in Theory & Practice. LC 74-13016. 208p. 1974. 5.95 (ISBN 0-687-43009-7). Abingdon.
Smith, Warren T. Harry Hosier: Circuit Rider. LC 80-54008. 64p. 1980. pap. 2.95x (ISBN 0-8358-0422-4). Upper Room.
Stokes, Mack B. Major United Methodist Beliefs. rev. & enl. ed. LC 77-173955. 128p. (Orig.). 1971. pap. 1.25 (ISBN 0-687-22923-5). Abingdon.
Straughn, James H. Inside Methodist Union. 1958. 3.00 (ISBN 0-687-19030-4). Abingdon.
Towlson, Clifford W. Moravian & Methodist. 1957. 15.00x (ISBN 0-8401-2387-6, 8401-2387-6). Allenson-Breckinridge.
Tuell, Jack M. The Organization of the United Methodist Church. rev. ed. LC 76-55784. (Orig.). 1977. pap. 4.95 (ISBN 0-687-29443-6). Abingdon.
Waltz, Alan K. Images of the Future. LC 79-25028. (Into Our Third Century Ser.). (Orig.). 1980. pap. 2.95 (ISBN 0-687-18689-7). Abingdon.
Wearmouth, Robert F. Methodism & the Working-Class Movements of England 1800-1850. LC 73-139523. Repr. of 1937 ed. 15.00x (ISBN 0-678-00829-9). Kelley.
Wesley, John. Works of John Wesley, 14 vols. Set. 149.50 (ISBN 0-8010-9616-2). Baker Bk.
METHODIST CHURCH–BIOGRAPHY
Allen, Charles L. What I Have Lived by: An Autobiography. 1976. 5.95 (ISBN 0-8007-0805-9); lmtd gift ed 9.95 (ISBN 0-8007-0806-7). Revell.
Brooks, Robert R., ed. Sicilian Rebel. (Illus.). 1979. 6.95 (ISBN 0-915466-02-3); pap. 4.00 (ISBN 0-686-51182-4). United Meth Archives.
Fiester, Mark. Look for Me in Heaven: The Life of John Lewis Dyer. (Illus.). 400p. 1980. 19.95 (ISBN 0-87108-564-X). Pruett.
Gramling, Roger M. A Ministry of Hope: Portrait of Arthur J. Moore. LC 79-67099. 112p. (Orig.). 1979. pap. 3.50x (ISBN 0-8358-0395-3). Upper Room.
Holder, Ray. William Winans: Methodist Leader in Antebellum Mississippi. LC 76-26967. 1976. 7.95x (ISBN 0-87805-027-2). U Pr of Miss.
Spellman, Norman W. Growing a Soul: The Story of A. Frank Smith. LC 78-20876. 1979. 15.00 (ISBN 0-87074-171-3). SMU Press.
METHODIST CHURCH–CLERGY
Bauman, Mark K. Warren Akin Candler: The Conservative As Idealist. LC 80-22230. 290p. 1981. 16.00 (ISBN 0-8108-1368-8). Scarecrow.
Shockley, Grant S., et al. Black Pastors & Churches in United Methodism. 1976. pap. 1.00 (ISBN 0-89937-005-5). Ctr Res Soc Chg.
Ward, W. R., ed. Early Victorian Methodism: The Correspondence of the Jabez Bunting, 1830-1858. 1976. 35.00x (ISBN 0-19-713140-9). Oxford U Pr.
METHODIST CHURCH–DOCTRINAL AND CONTROVERSIAL WORKS
Baker, Eric W. Faith of a Methodist. 1959. 2.00 (ISBN 0-687-12711-4). Abingdon.
Green, Richard. Anti-Methodist Publications Issued During the 18th Century. LC 71-83701. 175p. 1974. Repr. of 1902 ed. lib. bdg. 22.50 (ISBN 0-8337-1436-8). B Franklin.
Knox, Lloyd H., compiled by. Faith & Life of a Free Methodist. 1976. pap. 2.00 (ISBN 0-89367-003-0). Light & Life.
Stokes, Mack B. Major United Methodist Beliefs. rev. & enl. ed. LC 77-173955. 128p. (Orig.). 1971. pap. 1.25 (ISBN 0-687-22923-5). Abingdon.
METHODIST CHURCH–MISSIONS
Davey, Cyril J. March of Methodism. 1952. 3.75 (ISBN 0-8022-0345-0). Philos Lib.
Shaw, Barnabas. Memorials of South Africa. LC 71-109358. Repr. of 1840 ed. 18.75x (ISBN 0-8371-3737-3, Pub. by Negro U Pr). Greenwood.
--Memorials of South Africa. facsimile ed. 1970. Repr. of 1840 ed. 21.00x (ISBN 0-8426-0181-3). Verry.
METHODIST CHURCH–SERMONS
Bishop, John. A Word in Season. LC 79-958. 1979. pap. 3.95 (ISBN 0-687-46129-4). Abingdon.
Payne, Daniel A. Sermons & Addresses, Eighteen Fifty Three to Eighteen Ninety One. LC 70-38458. (Religion in America, Ser. 2). 1972. 14.00 (ISBN 0-405-04079-2). Arno.
METHODIST EPISCOPAL CHURCH
Duvall, Sylvanus M. Methodist Episcopal Church & Education up to 1869. LC 79-176735. (Columbia University. Teachers College. Contributions to Education: No. 284). Repr. of 1928 ed. 17.50 (ISBN 0-404-55284-6). AMS Pr.
Hagood, L. M. Colored Man in the Methodist Episcopal Church. facs. ed. LC 77-149868. (Black Heritage Library Collection Ser). 1890. 17.50 (ISBN 0-8369-8631-8). Arno.
Hagood, Lewis M. Colored Man in the Methodist Episcopal Church. LC 73-111577. Repr. of 1890 ed. 17.50x (ISBN 0-8371-4602-X, Pub. by Negro U Pr). Greenwood.
Harris, William L. Constitutional Powers of the General Conference: With a Special Application to the Subject of Slave Holding. facs. ed. LC 74-146265. (Black Heritage Library Collection Ser). 1860. 10.25 (ISBN 0-8369-8740-3). Arno.
Jones, Donald G. The Sectional Crisis & Northern Methodism: A Study in Piety, Political Ethics & Civil Religion. LC 78-9978. 1979. lib. bdg. 16.50 (ISBN 0-8108-1175-8). Scarecrow.
Scott, Orange. Grounds of Secession from the M. E. Church. LC 71-82219. (Anti-Slavery Crusade in America Ser). 1969. Repr. of 1848 ed. 12.00 (ISBN 0-405-00659-4). Arno.
Williams, John P. Social Adjustment in Methodism. LC 76-177639. (Columbia University. Teachers College. Contributions to Education: No. 765). Repr. of 1938 ed. 17.50 (ISBN 0-404-55765-1). AMS Pr.
METHODIST EPISCOPAL CHURCH–MISSIONS
Lee, Daniel & Frost, Joseph H. Ten Years in Oregon. LC 72-9457. (The Far Western Frontier Ser.). (Illus.). 348p. 1973. Repr. of 1844 ed. 18.00 (ISBN 0-405-04985-4). Arno.
METHODIST EPISCOPAL CHURCH, SOUTH–HISTORY
Farish, Hunter D. Circuit Rider Dismounts, a Social History of Southern Methodism 1865-1900. LC 77-87534. (American Scene Ser). 1969. Repr. of 1938 ed. 35.00 (ISBN 0-306-71450-7). Da Capo.
Finley, James B. Sketches of Western Methodism: Biographical, Historical & Miscellaneous Illustrative of Pioneer Life. LC 79-83419. (Religion in America, Ser. 1). 1969. Repr. of 1954 ed. 22.00 (ISBN 0-405-00244-0). Arno.
Jones, John G. Methodism in Mississippi, 2 Vols. in 1. 15.00 (ISBN 0-685-08192-3). Claitors.
Walker, Clarence E. A Rock in a Weary Land: A History of the African Methodist Episcopal Church During the Civil War & Reconstruction. 188p. 1982. 18.95 (ISBN 0-8071-0883-9). La State U Pr.
METHODIST PUBLISHING HOUSE, NASHVILLE
Pilkington, James P. Methodist Publishing House: A History, Vol. 1. LC 68-21894. (Illus.). 1968. 7.50 (ISBN 0-687-26700-5). Abingdon.
METHODIUS, SAINT, ABP. OF MORAVIA, d. 885
Dvornik, Francis. Legendes de Constantin et de methode vues de Byzance. (Russian Ser: No. 12). 1969. Repr. of 1933 ed. 20.00 (ISBN 0-87569-009-2). Academic Intl.
METHODOLOGY
see also Analysis (Philosophy); Classification of Sciences; Problem Solving; Research;

also subdivision Methodology under special subjects, e.g. Science-methodology; Theology-Methodology

Ackoff, R. L. Scientific Method: Optimizing Applied Research Decisions. LC 62-10914. 464p. 1962. 29.95 (ISBN 0-471-00297-6). Wiley.

Brenner, Michael, et al, eds. The Social Contexts of Method. LC 77-17903. 1978. 19.95x (ISBN 0-312-73165-5). St Martin.

Butts, Robert E. & Hintikka, Jaakko, eds. Basic Problems in Methodology & Linguistics. (Western Ontario Ser: No. 11). 1977. lib. bdg. 53.00 (ISBN 90-277-0829-0, Pub. by Reidel Holland). Kluwer Boston.

--Historical & Philosophical Dimensions of Logic, Methodology & Philosophy of Science. (Western Ontario Ser: No. 12). 1977. lib. bdg. 56.00 (ISBN 90-277-0831-2, Pub. by Reidel Holland). Kluwer Boston.

Cohen, Morris R. Reason & Nature. 1978. pap. 6.50 (ISBN 0-486-23633-1). Dover.

Cohen, Morris R. & Nagel, Ernest. Introduction to Logic. LC 62-21468. 1962. pap. 2.95 (ISBN 0-15-645125-5, H008, Hbgr). HarBraceJ.

Collingwood, Robin G. Essay on Philosophical Method. 1933. 36.00x (ISBN 0-19-824123-2). Oxford U Pr.

Costello, Harry T. Josiah Royce's Seminar Nineteen Thirteen to Nineteen Fourteen: As Recorded in the Notebooks of Harry T. Costello. Smith, Grover, ed. LC 81-4213. (Illus.). xxiii, 209p. 1981. Repr. of 1963 ed. lib. bdg. 25.00x (ISBN 0-313-23080-3, COJR). Greenwood.

D'Alembert, Jean L. Preliminary Discourse to the Encyclopedia of Diderot. Schwab, Richard & Rex, Walter, trs. LC 63-21831. (Orig.). 1963. 6.50 (ISBN 0-672-51037-5); pap. 5.50 (ISBN 0-672-60276-8, LLA88). Bobbs.

DeGeorge, Richard T. The Philosopher's Guide to Sources, Research Tools, Professional Life, and Related Fields. LC 79-91437. 220p. 1980. 20.00x (ISBN 0-7006-0200-3). Regents Pr Ks.

DeLucca, John. Reason & Experience: Dialogues in Modern Philosophy. LC 72-91229. 450p. 1973. text ed. 10.95x (ISBN 0-87735-517-7). Freeman C.

Feyerabend, Paul. Against Method. (Illus.). 1978. pap. 6.75 (ISBN 0-86091-700-2, Pub by NLB). Schocken.

Feyerabend, Paul & Maxwell, Grover, eds. Mind, Matter & Method: Essays in Philosophy & Science in Honor of Herbert Feigl. LC 66-13467. 1966. 17.50x (ISBN 0-8166-0379-0). U of Minn Pr.

Galtung, Johan. Methodology & Ideology: Vol. 1, Theory & Methods of Social Research. (Orig.). 1977. pap. text ed. 16.00x (ISBN 87-7241-373-5). Humanities.

--Methodology & Ideology: Vol. 2, Theory & Method of Social Research. 1980. pap. 20.75x (ISBN 0-391-01133-2). Humanities.

Gandillac, Maurice, et al. Entretiens Sur les Notions De Genese et De Structure: Centre Culturel International De Cerisy-la-Salle, Juillet-Aout 1959. (Congres et Colloques: No. 9). 1965. pap. 23.50x (ISBN 90-2796-094-1). Mouton.

Hare, R. M. Essays on Philosophical Method. LC 76-182286. (New Studies in Practical Philosophy). 1972. 12.95x (ISBN 0-520-02178-9). U of Cal Pr.

International Congress of Logic, Methodology and Philosophy of Science - 1960. Logic, Methodology & Philosophy of Science: Proceedings. Nagel, Ernest, et al, eds. 1962. 25.00x (ISBN 0-8047-0096-6). Stanford U Pr.

Kaiser, C. Hillis. Essay on Method. LC 68-26208. 1969. Repr. of 1952 ed. 11.75 (ISBN 0-8046-0245-X). Kennikat.

Leonard, H. S. Principles of Reasoning: An Introduction to Logic, Methodology & the Theory of Signs. 5.75 (ISBN 0-8446-2452-7). Peter Smith.

Lomer, Gerhard R. The Concept of Method. LC 70-177005. (Columbia University. Teachers College. Contributions to Education: No. 34). Repr. of 1910 ed. 17.50 (ISBN 0-404-55034-7). AMS Pr.

Martin, William O. Order & Integration of Knowledge. LC 68-54425. (Illus.). 1968. Repr. of 1957 ed. lib. bdg. 15.75x (ISBN 0-8371-0161-1, MAKN). Greenwood.

Menger, Karl. Selected Papers in Logic & Foundations, Didactics, & Economics. (Vienna Circle Collection: No. 10). 1978. lib. bdg. 58.00 (ISBN 90-277-0320-5, Pub. by Reidel Holland); pap. 29.00 (ISBN 90-277-0321-3, Pub. by Reidel Holland). Kluwer Boston.

Pap, Arthur. A Priori in Physical Theory. LC 68-10936. 1968. Repr. of 1946 ed. 7.50 (ISBN 0-8462-1094-0). Russell.

Popper, Karl R. Conjectures & Refutations: The Growth of Scientific Knowledge. 1968. pap. 7.50x (ISBN 0-06-131376-9, TB1376, Torch). Har-Row.

Sloman, Aaron. The Computer Revolution in Philosophy: Philosophy, Science & Models of Mind. (Harvester Studies in Cognitive Science). 1978. text ed. 27.25x (ISBN 0-391-00830-7); pap. text ed. 15.50x (ISBN 0-391-00831-5). Humanities.

Suppes, P., et al. Logic, Methodology & Philosophy of Science IV. (Studies in Logic & the Foundation of Mathematics: Vol. 74). 1974. 73.25 (ISBN 0-444-10491-7, North-Holland). Elsevier.

Weiss, Paul. First Considerations: An Examination of Philosophical Evidence. LC 77-23242. 320p. 1977. 13.85 (ISBN 0-8093-0797-9). S Ill U Pr.

Wolff, Christian. Preliminary Discourse on Philosophy in General. Blackwell, Richard, tr. LC 63-20239. (Orig.). 1963. pap. 2.50 (ISBN 0-672-60395-0, LA167). Bobbs.

Zallen, Harold. Ideas Plus Dollars: Research Methodology & Funding. 2nd ed. LC 79-55737. (Illus.). 1980. 12.95 (ISBN 0-686-71018-5). Academic World.

METHODS ENGINEERING

Albano, Charles. TA on the Job. 1976. pap. 2.95 (ISBN 0-06-080385-1, P385, PL). Har-Row.

Bowditch, James & Buono, Anthony. Improving the Quality of Worklife: A Survey Methodology. 200p. 1981. 19.95 (ISBN 0-86569-067-7). Auburn Hse.

Edwards, Richard C. Contested Terrain: The Transformation of the Workplace in America. LC 78-19942. 256p. 1980. pap. 4.95 (ISBN 0-465-01413-5). Basic.

Glossop, R. H. Method Study & the Furniture Industry. LC 75-112711. 1970. 21.00 (ISBN 0-08-015653-3). Pergamon.

Guest, Robert H. Innovative Work Practices. (Studies in Productivity-Highlights of the Literature: Vol. 21). (Orig.). Date not set. pap. 25.00 (ISBN 0-89361-031-3). Work in Amer.

Hackman, J. Richard & Oldham, Greg R. Work Redesign. LC 79-8918. 1980. pap. text ed. 7.95 (ISBN 0-201-02779-8). A-W.

Krick, Edward V. Methods Engineering. LC 62-8775. (Illus.). 530p. 1962. text ed. 31.95x (ISBN 0-471-50754-7). Wiley.

McCarthy, Maureen E. & Rosenberg, Gail S. Work Sharing Case Studies. 300p. 1981. write for info. Upjohn Inst.

Maule, H. G. & Weiner, J. S., eds. Human Factors in Work Design & Production. 138p. 1977. 29.95 (ISBN 0-470-99074-0). Halsted Pr.

Methods Improvement & Work Controls. pap. 12.00 (ISBN 0-686-02538-5). Preston.

Mumford, Enid & Weir, Mary. Computer Systems in Work Design: The Ethnics Method: Effective Technical & Human Implementation of Computer Systems. LC 78-32068. 1979. 38.95 (ISBN 0-470-26656-2). Halsted Pr.

Ross, Lynne. Work Simplification in Food Service: Individualized Instruction. LC 73-171164. (Orig., Prog. Bk.). 1972. text ed. 6.95x (ISBN 0-8138-0785-9). Iowa St U Pr.

Zinck, W. Clements. Dynamic Work Simplification. LC 62-13255. 1971. Repr. of 1962 ed. 12.50 (ISBN 0-88275-056-9). Krieger.

METHUEN, JOHN, 1650-1706

Francis, A. D. Methuens & Portugal. 1966. 53.50 (ISBN 0-521-05028-6). Cambridge U Pr.

METHUEN, PAUL SANFORD, 1845-1932

Francis, A. D. Methuens & Portugal. 1966. 53.50 (ISBN 0-521-05028-6). Cambridge U Pr.

METHYL GROUPS

see also Transmethylation

Aviado, Domingo M., et al. Methyl Chloroform & Trichloroethylene in the Environment. Golberg, Leon, ed. LC 76-16138. (Solvents in the Environment Ser.). 1976. 32.95 (ISBN 0-87819-098-8). CRC Pr.

Salvatore, Francesco, et al, eds. The Biochemistry of Adenosylmethionine. LC 76-25565. 1977. 38.50x (ISBN 0-231-03895-X). Columbia U Pr.

METHYLATION

see also Transmethylation

Paik, Woon Ki & Sangduk Kim. Protein Methylation. LC 79-19557. (Biochemistry: a Series of Monographs). 1980. 38.50 (ISBN 0-471-04867-4, Pub. by Wiley-Interscience). Wiley.

Usdin, E. & Borchardt, R. T., eds. Transmethylation. LC 78-27647. (Developments in Neuroscience Ser.: Vol. 5). 1979. 55.00 (ISBN 0-444-00310-X, North Holland). Elsevier.

METIS REBELLION, 1869-1870

see Red River Rebellion, 1869-1870

METIS REBELLION, 1885

see Riel Rebellion, 1885

METOPOSCOPY

see Physiognomy

METRIC RINGS

see Banach Algebras

METRIC SPACES

see also Distance Geometry

Aubin, Jean-Pierre. Applied Abstract Analysis. LC 77-2382. (Pure & Applied Mathematics, a W-I Ser. of Texts, Monographs & Tracts). 263p. 1977. 38.50 (ISBN 0-471-02146-6, Pub. by Wiley-Interscience). Wiley.

Billingsley, P. Convergence of Probability Measures. (Probability & Mathematical Statistics Tracts: Probability & Statistics Section). 253p. 1968. 31.00 (ISBN 0-471-07242-7, Pub. by Wiley-Interscience). Wiley.

Blumenthal, Leonard M. & Menger, Karl. Studies in Geometry. LC 74-75624. (Illus.). 1970. text ed. 25.95x (ISBN 0-7167-0437-4). W H Freeman.

Borsuk, Karol. Theory of Shape. LC 76-359585. 379p. 1975. 37.50x (ISBN 0-8002-2343-8). Intl Pubns Serv.

Comfort, W. W. & Negrepontis, S. Continuous Pseudometrics. (Lecture Notes in Pure & Applied Mathematics Ser.: Vol. 14). 136p. 1975. 17.75 (ISBN 0-8247-6294-0). Dekker.

Copson, Edward T. Metric Spaces. (Cambridge Tracts in Mathematics & Mathematical Physics). 1968. 23.95 (ISBN 0-521-04722-6). Cambridge U Pr.

Kaplansky, Irving. Set Theory & Metric Spaces. 2nd ed. LC 77-7344. 1977. text ed. 8.50 (ISBN 0-8284-0298-1). Chelsea Pub.

Nadler, Sam B., Jr. & Quinn, J. Embeddability & Structure Properties of Real Curves. LC 72-4343. (Memoirs: No. 125). 74p. 1972. pap. 7.60 (ISBN 0-8218-1825-2, MEMO-125). Am Math.

Pierce, R. S. Compact Zero-Dimensional Metric Spaces of Finite Type. LC 72-11822. (Memoirs: No. 130). 68p. 1972. pap. 7.20 (ISBN 0-8218-1830-9, MEMO-130). Am Math.

Schaffer, Juan J. Geometry of Spheres in Normed Spaces. (Lecture Notes in Pure & Applied Math Ser: Vol. 20). 1976. 29.75 (ISBN 0-8247-6554-0). Dekker.

Sutherland, Wilson A. Introduction to Metric & Topological Spaces. (Illus.). 196p. 1975. 24.95x (ISBN 0-19-853155-9); pap. 13.95x (ISBN 0-19-853161-3). Oxford U Pr.

Wells, J. H. & Williams, L. R. Embeddings & Extensions in Analysis. LC 74-31234. (Ergebnisse der Mathematik und Ihrer Grenzgebiete Ser.: Vol. 84). 125p. 1975. text ed. 19.20 (ISBN 0-387-07067-2). Springer-Verlag.

METRIC SYSTEM

see also Weights and Measures

Acosta de Gonzalez, Fe. El Sistema Metrico (Modulo) (Coleccion Uprex; Serie Pedagogia: No. 57). (Span.). 1979. pap. text ed. 3.80 (ISBN 0-8477-2743-2). U. of PR Pr.

Adams, Herbert F. SI Metric Units: An Introduction. 120p. (Orig.). 1974. pap. 3.95 (ISBN 0-07-000295-9, SP). McGraw.

Adams, Priscilla, ed. Examining the Metric Issues. 85p. 1976. pap. 4.00 (ISBN 0-916148-08-4). Am Natl.

Adjuncts to ASTM Standards: Metric Practice Guide. 42p. 1979. softcover 5.00x (ISBN 0-686-76017-4, E 380-79, 06-503807-41). ASTM.

Albracht, James & Kurtz, Ray. Introduction to AG Metrics. text ed. 16.75 (ISBN 0-8134-1999-9). Interstate.

Alton, E. V. & Gersting, J. L. Module SI: Metric System. Ablon, L. J., et al, eds. LC 76-58669. (Ser. in Mathematical Modules). 1977. pap. text ed. 4.95 (ISBN 0-8465-0266-6). Benjamin-Cummings.

American Metric Journal Editors. Metric in a Nutshell. Hopkins, Robert A., ed. LC 76-19477. 1977. 6.95 (ISBN 0-917240-06-5). Am Metric.

American National Metric Council. Managing & Metrication in Business & Industry. 1976. 30.75 (ISBN 0-8247-6469-2). Dekker.

Anastasiou, C., et al. Reading About Science I: SI Metric. (Reading About Science Ser.). (gr. 7-8). Date not set. pap. text ed. price not set (ISBN 0-685-86065-5, Pub. by HR&W Canada). HR&W.

Antoine, Valerie. Guidance for Using Metric System (SI Version) 39p. 1976. pap. 6.00 (ISBN 0-914548-23-9). Soc Tech Comm.

Armbruster, Frank O. Think Metrics. rev. ed. (Illus.). 1974. pap. 1.50 (ISBN 0-912300-45-0, 45-0). Troubador Pr.

ASME Orientation & Guide for Use of Si (Metric) Units. 8th ed. 1978. pap. text ed. 2.00 (ISBN 0-685-41936-3, E00058). ASME.

Bailey, Harold J. Measurement & the Metric System. 1976. pap. text ed. 4.50 (ISBN 0-8403-1475-2). Kendall-Hunt.

Baird, Eva-Lee & Wyler, Rose. Going Metric the Fun Way. LC 77-16895. (Illus.). (gr. 8-9). 1980. 7.95a (ISBN 0-385-13641-2); PLB (ISBN 0-385-13642-0). Doubleday.

Barnard, Frederick A. The Metric System of Weights & Measures. 1976. Repr. of 1872 ed. 25.00 (ISBN 0-403-06321-3, Regency). Scholarly.

Barnett, Carne. Metric Ease. (Illus.). 79p. (Orig.). (gr. 4-9). 1975. wkbk. 4.95 (ISBN 0-88488-039-7). Creative Pubns.

Barron's Technical Staff, compiled by. Barron's Metric Conversion Tables. LC 76-8425. (Barron's Educational Ser.). 224p. 1976. pap. text ed. 4.50 (ISBN 0-8120-0659-3). Barron.

Bartlett, David F., ed. The Metric Debate. LC 79-53270. 12.50x (ISBN 0-87081-083-9). Colo Assoc.

Batchelder, J. W. Metric Madness: One Hundred Fifty Reasons for Not Converting to the Metric System. (Illus.). 250p. 1981. 12.95 (ISBN 0-8159-6220-7); pap. 5.95 (ISBN 0-8159-6219-3). Devin.

Bates & Fullerton. How to Think Metric. LC 74-75325. (gr. 5-12). 1974. pap. 3.95 (ISBN 0-8224-3763-5). Pitman Learning.

Behrens, June. True Book of Metric Measurement. LC 74-23231. (True Books). 48p. (gr. k-3). 1975. PLB 9.25 (ISBN 0-516-01146-4). Childrens.

Benedict, John T. Metrication for the Manager. Boselovic, Len, ed. LC 77-84932. (Illus.). 1977. pap. text ed. 4.50 (ISBN 0-916148-12-2). Am Natl.

Berggren, Don. The Magnificent Metric System: A Magical Guide to the Marvels of Metrics. LC 76-40527. (Illus., Orig.). 1976. pap. 2.95 (ISBN 0-912800-34-8). Woodbridge Pr.

Bitter, G., et al. Discovering Metric Measure, Bk. 1. 1974. 4.00 (ISBN 0-07-005506-8, W). McGraw.

Bitter, Gary G. & Metos, Thomas H. Exploring with Metrics. LC 75-25520. (Illus.). 64p. (gr. 3-5). 1975. PLB 6.29 (ISBN 0-671-32745-3). Messner.

Boselovic, Len, ed. Metric Editorial Guide. 3rd rev. ed. 1979. pap. text ed. 3.00 (ISBN 0-916148-13-0). Am Natl.

Bowles, D. Richard. Make Way for Metrication. LC 72-13331. (Math Concepts Bks). (Illus.). 56p. (gr. 6-10). 1975. PLB 4.95 (ISBN 0-8225-0583-5). Lerner Pubns.

Branley, Franklyn M. Measure with Metric. LC 74-4056. (Young Math Ser.). (Illus.). 40p. (gr. k-3). 1975. PLB 8.79 (ISBN 0-690-01117-2, TYC-J); (TYC-J); filmstrip with record 11.95 (ISBN 0-690-00996-8); filmstrip with cassette 14.95 (ISBN 0-690-00997-6). Har-Row.

--Think Metric! LC 72-78279. (Illus.). (gr. 3-6). 1973. 8.95 (ISBN 0-690-81861-0, TYC-J); PLB 8.79 (ISBN 0-690-81862-9). Har-Row.

Brooks, Stewart M. Going Metric. LC 75-29691. (Illus.). 128p. 1976. 6.95 (ISBN 0-498-01702-8). A S Barnes.

Brown, Sam E. Activities for Teaching Metrics in Kindergarden. LC 77-95155. 1978. pap. text ed. 7.00 (ISBN 0-8191-0462-0). U Pr of Amer.

Brownlee, Juanita. Tangram Geometry in Metric. (Illus., Orig.). (gr. 5-10). 1976. pap. 4.95 (ISBN 0-918932-43-2, 0140701407). Activity Resources.

Canada Yearbook Nineteen Seventy-Six to Nineteen Seventy-Seven. 1979. 23.00 (ISBN 0-660-00761-4, SSC 106, SSC). Unipub.

Cardwell, Richard L. The Metrics Are Coming! The Metrics Are Coming! (Illus.). 132p. 1975. 6.95 (ISBN 0-8059-2142-7). Dorrance.

Carrell, Mary J. Understanding the Metric System. 1978. pap. text ed. 2.50x (ISBN 0-88323-140-9, 229). Richards Pub.

Chisholm, L. J. Units of Weight & Measure: International (Metric) & U. S. Customary. LC 74-20726. (Illus.). 256p. 1975. Repr. of 1967 ed. 22.00 (ISBN 0-8103-4163-8). Gale.

--Units of Weight & Measure: International (Metric) & U. S. Customary. LC 74-20726. (Illus.). 256p. 1975. Repr. of 1967 ed. 22.00 (ISBN 0-8103-4163-8). Gale.

Clark, Alice & Leitch, Carol. Amusements in Developing Metric Skills. (Illus.). (gr. 6-12). pap. 4.95 (ISBN 0-910974-69-1); 47 duplicating masters 10.95 (ISBN 0-685-40577-X). Midwest Pubns.

Consumer Liaison Committee of the American National Metric Council. Metric Reference for Consumers. 1976. pap. text ed. 2.50 (ISBN 0-916148-10-6). Am Natl.

Consumer Liaison Committee of the Council. Metrication & the Consumer: The Issue of Deception in the Marketplace. Boselovic, Len, ed. (Illus.). 1977. pap. text ed. 0.40 (ISBN 0-916148-11-4). Am Natl.

Corbett, John, ed. Basic Metric Style Manual for Secretaries. new ed. 1976. pap. 2.95x (ISBN 0-912702-04-4). Global Eng.

Creston, Paul. Rational Metric Notation: The Mathematical Basis of Meters, Symbols, a Note-Values. 1979. 7.50 (ISBN 0-682-49052-0, University). Exposition.

Croft, J. H. Going Metric in Catering. 1969. pap. 4.20 (ISBN 0-08-006512-0). Pergamon.

Cuming, Pamela. Managing Metrics. LC 77-77736. 1978. pap. text ed. 8.95 (ISBN 0-201-01109-3). A-W.

Danloux-Dumesnils, M. The Metric System: A Critical Study of Its Principles & Practice. 1969. pap. text ed. 4.25x (ISBN 0-485-12013-5, Athlone Pr). Humanities.

Deming, Richard. Metric Power: Why & How We Are Going Metric. LC 74-5039. 192p. (gr. 5 up). 1974. 7.95 (ISBN 0-525-66380-0). Elsevier-Nelson.

Donovan, Frank. Let's Go Metric. (Illus.). 192p. 1974. 6.95 (ISBN 0-679-40057-5, Weybright). McKay.

Earl, Gladys, et al. Make It Metric: Food Principles Laboratory Manual. 1979. text ed. 10.95x spiral bdg. (ISBN 0-8087-0526-1). Burgess.

Editors of Hamlyn Publishing Group. Instant Metric Conversion Tables. LC 75-24712. 144p. 1979. 2.50 (ISBN 0-89196-001-5, Domus Bks). Quality Bks IL.

Educational Materials Sector Committee of the American National Metric Council. Metric Guide for Educational Materials: A Handbook for Teachers, Writers & Publishers. 1977. pap. text ed. 3.00 (ISBN 0-916148-09-2). Am Natl.

Fairweather, Leslie & Sliwa, Jan A. VNR Metric Handbook. (Illus.). 206p. 1969. pap. 7.95x (ISBN 0-442-22364-1). Van Nos Reinhold.

Faubert, Janet & Reed, Suzanne W. The Metric System. Reed, Suzanne W., ed. LC 74-80545. (Science Ser.). (Illus., Orig.). (gr. 6-9). 1975. pap. text ed. 3.25 (ISBN 0-88301-153-0). Pendulum Pr.

Feirer. SI Metric Handbook. 1977. text ed. 25.00 (ISBN 0-87002-908-8). Bennett IL.

Feirer, John. SI Metric Handbook. (Illus.). 1977. 27.50 (ISBN 0-87002-908-8, ScribT). Scribner.

Follendore, Joan S. You Can Learn Metric Easily. (Illus., Orig.). 1976. pap. 1.00 (ISBN 0-916546-01-2). Racz Pub.

Forster, M., et al. Reading About Science II: SI Metric. (Reading About Science Ser.). (YA) (gr. 8-9). Date not set. text ed. price not set (ISBN 0-03-920069-8, Pub. by HR&W Canada). HR&W.

Forte, Imogene & Pangle, Mary A. Metric Mastery. (Illus.). 1977. dup. master 3.95 (ISBN 0-913916-38-2, IP 38-2). Incentive Pubns.

Forte, Imogene & Pangle, Mary Ann. Metric Magic. LC 77-72888. (Illus.). 1977. pap. text ed. 5.95 (ISBN 0-913916-37-4, IP 37-4). Incentive Pubns.

Foster, Lowell W. Geo-Metrics: The Metric Application of Geometric Tolerancing. (Illus.). 300p. 1974. 14.95 (ISBN 0-201-01989-2); pocket guide 9.95 (ISBN 0-201-01987-6). A-W.

Free, Woodrow W. A Short History of the Metric System of Weights & Measures. 1977. 4.50 (ISBN 0-533-02208-8). Vantage.

Frey, Paul R. Metric America: Math & Measures. 1980. pap. 6.95 (ISBN 0-672-97363-4); instructors guide 3.33 (ISBN 0-672-97364-2). Bobbs.

Friesth, E. Richard. Metrication in Manufacturing. LC 77-21838. (Illus.). 373p. 1978. 22.00 (ISBN 0-8311-1120-8). Indus Pr.

Gagnadre, Marius F. Condensation of Decimal & Metrical Systems: Jumelex Method. 1980. 5.95 (ISBN 0-533-04392-1). Vantage.

Gilbert, Thomas F. & Gilbert, Marilyn B. Thinking Metric. 2nd ed. LC 77-20190. (Self-Teaching Guide Ser.). 141p. 1978. pap. text ed. 5.95 (ISBN 0-471-03427-4). Wiley.

Gilleo, Alma. About Grams. LC 77-23285. (Metric Bk.). (Illus.). (gr. 1-4). 1977. 5.95 (ISBN 0-913778-84-2); pap. 2.75 (ISBN 0-89565-061-4). Childs World.

--About Liters. LC 77-23260. (Metric Bk.). (Illus.). (gr. 1-4). 1977. 5.95 (ISBN 0-913778-85-0); pap. 2.75 (ISBN 0-89565-062-2). Childs World.

--About Meters. LC 77-23261. (Metric Bk.). (Illus.). (gr. 1-4). 1977. 5.95 (ISBN 0-913778-86-9); pap. 2.75 (ISBN 0-89565-063-0). Childs World.

--About the Metric System. LC 77-23253. (Metric Bk.). (Illus.). (gr. 1-4). 1977. 5.95 (ISBN 0-913778-88-5). Childs World.

--About the Thermometer. LC 77-23182. (A Metric Book). (Illus.). (gr. 1-4). 1977. PLB 5.95 (ISBN 0-913778-87-7); pap. 2.75 (ISBN 0-89565-064-9). Childs World.

Gise, Jean & Hovey, Carla. Metrics All Around. (gr. 1-6). 1976. pap. 4.95 (ISBN 0-918932-35-1). Activity Resources.

Glaser, Anton. Neater by the Meter: An American Guide to the Metric System. LC 73-88193. (Illus.). 112p. (Orig.). 1974. 7.50 (ISBN 0-9600324-3-6); pap. 3.50 (ISBN 0-9600324-4-4). A Glaser.

Going Metric: Guidelines for the Mathematics Teacher, Grades K-8. LC 75-31956. 1975. pap. 2.80 (ISBN 0-87353-055-1). NCTM.

Green, M. H. Metric Conversion Handbook. 1978. text ed. 18.50 (ISBN 0-8206-0229-9). Chem Pub.

Haas, Frederick C. Living in a Metric America. Pearce, C. Glenn, ed. LC 77-71582. (Illus.). 1977. pap. 2.95 (ISBN 0-9601180-1-2). Haas.

Hackworth, Robert D. & Howland, Joseph. Introductory College Mathematics: Metric Measure. LC 75-23629. 65p. 1976. pap. text ed. 2.95 (ISBN 0-7216-4422-8). HR&W.

Hallamore, Elisabeth. The Metric Book of Amusing Things to Do. 96p. (gr. 4-9). 1975. pap. text ed. 2.50 (ISBN 0-8120-0660-7). Barron.

Hartsuch, Paul J. Think Metric Now! A Step-by-Step Guide to Understanding & Applying the Metric System. 1975. pap. 1.50 (ISBN 0-14-004010-2). Penguin.

Hazlett, Ewing G., compiled by. Metric System of Weights & Measures Made Easy for Home, School & Shop. 1974. pap. 1.95 (ISBN 0-686-11479-5). Cordova.

Higgins, Jon L., ed. A Metric Handbook for Teachers. LC 74-13468. 144p. 1974. pap. 4.25 (ISBN 0-87353-077-2). NCTM.

Hilts, Michael E. Basic Consumer Metrics. (Illus.). 1979. pap. text ed. 3.95x (ISBN 0-916780-15-5). CES.

Hirsch, S. Carl. Meter Means Measure: The Story of the Metric System. 144p. (gr. 7 up). 1973. PLB 6.95 (ISBN 0-670-47365-0). Viking Pr.

Holmberg, Verda. The Metric System of Measurement. (Illus., Orig.). (gr. 4-9). 1973. pap. 5.95 (ISBN 0-918932-34-3). Activity Resources.

Hopkins, R. A. Metric Practice Guide for News Reporting & Broadcasting. 3.95 (ISBN 0-917240-05-7). Am Metric.

Hopkins, Robert A. The International SI System & How It Works. 3rd rev. ed. LC 73-94128. (AMJ Publication: B.1). 300p. 1977. 14.20 (ISBN 0-686-22829-4). Am Metric.

Iehl, Betty J. & Gruenberger, Joyce. Mastering Metric Measures. 1977. pap. 2.95 (ISBN 0-671-18756-2). Monarch Pr.

Jones, M. J. A Guide to Metrication. 1969. pap. 7.00 (ISBN 0-08-006539-2). Pergamon.

Karim, G. A. & Hamilton, A. B. Metrication for the E&P Professional. LC 81-80668. (Illus.). 109p. 1981. text ed. 22.50 (ISBN 0-934634-03-3); pap. text ed. 14.50 (ISBN 0-934634-09-2). Intl Human Res.

Keller, J. J. Metric System Guide: Definitions & Terminology, Vol. 5. rev. ed. Laux, Patricia, ed. LC 75-18705. 400p. 1978. looseleaf 59.00 (ISBN 0-934674-08-6). J J Keller.

--Metric System Guide: Legislation & Regulatory Activities, Vol. 2. rev. ed. Laux, Patricia, ed. LC 75-18702. 450p. 1978. loose leaf 59.00 (ISBN 0-934674-05-1). J J Keller.

--Metric System Guide: Metric Units Edition, Vol. 3. rev. ed. Laux, Patricia, ed. LC 75-18703. 450p. 1978. 59.00 (ISBN 0-934674-06-X). J J Keller.

--Metric System Guide: References Sources, Vol. 4. rev. ed. Laux, Patricia, ed. LC 75-18704. 400p. 1978. loose leaf 59.00 (ISBN 0-934674-07-8). J J Keller.

Keller, John J. Metric Manual: Development, Regulations, Tables, References, Definitions for Metrication in the U.S.A. Laux, Patricia, et al, eds. LC 74-31864. 362p. 1976. loose leaf 35.00 (ISBN 0-934674-29-9). J J Keller.

--Metric Manual: Development, Regulations, Tables, References, Definitions for Metrication in the U. S. A. Laux, Patricia, et al, eds. LC 75-17164. 352p. 1976. softcover 14.00 (ISBN 0-934674-30-2). J J Keller.

--Metric System Guide: Metrication in the United States, Vol. 1. rev. ed. LC 75-25158. 468p. 1978. loose leaf 59.00 (ISBN 0-934674-04-3). J J Keller.

--Metrication Handbook. Laux, Patricia, et al, eds. (Illus.). 144p. 1974. spiral bdg 15.00 (ISBN 0-934674-32-9). J J Keller.

--Metrication Handbook. Laux, Pat, ed. LC 75-17164. (Illus.). 140p. 1975. softcover 3.95 (ISBN 0-934674-33-7). J J Keller.

Kelly, Gerard W. Metric System Simplified. LC 77-93317. 96p. (gr. 4 up). 1974. 5.95 (ISBN 0-8069-3058-6); PLB 5.89 (ISBN 0-8069-3059-4). Sterling.

Kempf, Albert F. & Richards, Thomas J. The Metric System Made Simple. LC 75-36631. 144p. 1977. 3.50 (ISBN 0-385-11032-4, Made). Doubleday.

King, Franklin J. & King, Forrest. Learning & Teaching the Metric System of Measuring: A Handbook. new ed. 1978. pap. text ed. 21.95 (ISBN 0-205-06169-9). Allyn.

Kurtz, V. Ray. Metrics for Elementary & Middle Schools. 120p. 1978. pap. 4.50 (ISBN 0-686-63709-7, 1714-5-06). NEA.

--Teaching Metric Awareness. LC 75-22174. (Illus.). 125p. 1976. pap. text ed. 7.00 (ISBN 0-8016-2811-3). Mosby.

Kverneland, Knut O. World Metric Standards for Engineering. LC 77-25875. (Illus.). 760p. 1978. 47.50 (ISBN 0-8311-1113-5). Indus Pr.

Lamm, Joyce. Let's Talk About the Metric System. LC 73-80415. (Illus.). 128p. (gr. 3-6). 1974. 5.95 (ISBN 0-8246-0158-0). Jonathan David.

Laux, Patricia. The Modernized Metric System... Explained. LC 75-2632. (Illus.). 1975. pap. 0.50 (ISBN 0-934674-34-5). J J Keller.

--Official Metric System, Charts, Definitions, Terms: Clarified & Explained. LC 72-21966. (Illus.). 80p. 1976. soft cover 1.00 (ISBN 0-934674-35-3). J J Keller.

Laux, Patricia, ed. Metric Yearbook: Metrication in the United States--Progress in Industry, Education & Government During 1977. LC 76-4217. 1978. pap. 25.00 (ISBN 0-934674-31-0). J J Keller.

Lay, Richard A. Measuring the Metric Way. (Illus.). 1975. pap. text ed. 2.50x (ISBN 0-88323-123-9, 211). Richards Pub.

Leaf, Munro. Metric Can Be Fun. LC 75-29223. (gr. 1-3). 1976. 8.79 (ISBN 0-397-31679-8, JBL-J); pap. 1.95 (ISBN 0-397-31680-1). Har-Row.

LeMaraic, A. L. & Ciaramella, J. P. Basic Guide to the Metric System. LC 75-25312. 1976. 6.95 (ISBN 0-913768-06-5, 913065). Metric Media Bk.

--The Complete Metric System with the International System of Units 51. LC 72-97799. 1974. 6.95x (ISBN 0-913768-00-6, 913006). Metric Media Bk.

--The Metric System for Beginners. LC 74-3812. 1974. 5.95 (ISBN 0-913768-02-2, 913022). Metric Media Bk.

--The Metric System for Elementary Schools. LC 75-25312. 1976. 6.95 (ISBN 0-913768-09-X, 913090). Metric Media Bk.

--The Metric Systems for Secondary Schools. LC 74-10176. 1975. 6.95 (ISBN 0-913768-04-9, 913049). Metric Media Bk.

--The Teacher's Guide to the Metric System. LC 74-3811. 1974. text ed. 5.95 (ISBN 0-913768-01-4). Metric Media Bk.

LeMaraic, A. L. & Ciaramella, J. P., eds. The Metric Encyclopedia. LC 74-9235. 8.95 (ISBN 0-913768-03-0). Metric Media Bk.

Lerro, Joseph, Jr. Metric System. (Illus.). 48p. 1975. pap. 6.95 (ISBN 0-89047-042-1, MSLP). Herman Pub.

Lindbeck. Metric Practices in Drafting. 1979. pap. 2.64 (ISBN 0-87002-298-9). Bennett IL.

Lippert, Herbert & Lehmann, H. Peter, eds. SI Units in Medicine. Lehmann, H. L., tr. from Ger. LC 77-17354. Orig. Title: SI Einheiten in der Medizin. (Illus.). 220p. 1978. spiral bdg. 14.50 (ISBN 0-8067-1101-9). Urban & S.

Loose, Frances F. Matrics: Reusable Edition. (gr. 9-12). 1975. wkbk. 3.00x (ISBN 0-89039-128-9). Ann Arbor Pubs.

--Matrics: Teacher's Guide. 1975. 1.00x (ISBN 0-89039-129-7). Ann Arbor Pubs.

Lowe, Kenneth E. Metrication for the Pulp & Paper Industry. LC 74-20165. (A Pulp & Paper Book). (Illus.). 192p. 1975. 35.00 (ISBN 0-87930-034-5). Miller Freeman.

Lytle, R. J. American Metric Construction Handbook. LC 75-6257. (Illus.). 1976. pap. 14.95 (ISBN 0-912336-14-5). Structures Pub.

Mahoney, Susan & Mills, Richard G. Metric Measurement. LC 76-731369. (Illus.). 1976. pap. text ed. 103.00 (ISBN 0-89290-128-4, 507-SAR-SATC). Soc for Visual.

Managing Metrication in Business & Industry. 203p. 1976. 37.00 (ISBN 0-8247-6469-2). Am Natl.

Maritime Transportation Research Board, National Research Council. Maritime Metrication: A Recommended Metric Conversion Plan for the U.S. Maritime Industry. LC 76-1348. 121p. 1976. pap. 5.25 (ISBN 0-309-02447-1). Natl Acad Pr.

Masat, Francis E. & Page, Charles H. Teaching the Metric System--with Activities. LC 76-16273. (Professional Education Ser.). (Illus.). 1977. pap. text ed. 2.25 (ISBN 0-88224-100-1). Cliffs.

Mason & Lange. Plaid for Using the Metric System. 1976. pap. 4.95 (ISBN 0-256-01772-7, 15-1178-00). Learning Syst.

Mathews, J. P. Was Tammy Thinking Metric? 1978. 4.95 (ISBN 0-533-03122-2). Vantage.

Mechtly, E. H. The International System of Units. 1977. pap. 1.20x (ISBN 0-87563-139-8). Stipes.

Meter: A Handbook of Activities to Motivate the Teaching of the Metric System. (The Spice Ser.). 1975. 6.50 (ISBN 0-89273-118-4). Educ Serv.

Meter Duplicating Masters: Metric System, 3 vols. (Spice Ser.). 1976. 5.95 ea. Vol. 1, Grades K-3 (ISBN 0-89273-541-4). Vol. 2, Grades 3-6 (ISBN 0-89273-542-2). Vol. 3, Grades 6-8 (ISBN 0-89273-543-0). Educ Serv.

Metric Conversion in the Construction Industries: Planning, Coordination & Timing. 62p. 1980. 15.00 (ISBN 0-686-70963-2). Am Natl.

Metric Conversion Scale. 1973. lot of 10 8.00 (ISBN 0-686-65406-4). Bennett IL.

Metric-English Ruler. lot of 10 4.80 (ISBN 0-686-65407-2). Bennett IL.

Metric Practice Guide. 42p. 1979. soft cover 5.00x (ISBN 0-686-76059-X, E 380-79, 06-503807-41). ASTM.

Metric Series, 9 bks. Incl. Bks. 1 & 2. Measuring Metric. Cherrington, Don; Bk. 3. Metric Fundamentals. Fearon, Arthur D (ISBN 0-912450-08-8); Bk. 4. Metrics for Home Use. Massey, Opal (ISBN 0-912450-09-6); Bk. 5. Everyday Metrics. Fearon, Arthur D (ISBN 0-912450-10-X); Bk. 6. Metrics Workshop for Teachers. Cherrington, Don (ISBN 0-912450-11-8); Bk. 7. Practical Metrics. Prescott, Elizabeth (ISBN 0-912450-12-6); Bk. 8. Technical Si Metrics. Prescott, Elizabeth (ISBN 0-912450-13-4); Bk. 9. Metric Handbook. Garner, Bruce L (ISBN 0-912450-14-2). 1974. pap. 3.50 ea.; pap. 12.95 set (ISBN 0-685-42659-9). Willow Hse.

The Metric System Guide Series, 5 vols. 29.50 ea.; 147.50 set (ISBN 0-934674-09-4). J J Keller.

The Metric System: What It Is & How to Use It. 1975. pap. 4.00 (ISBN 0-686-10810-8). Preston.

Metrication: Managing the Industrial Transition. 1975. 30.00 (ISBN 0-686-52224-9). ASTM.

Metrication: The Australian Experience. 210p. 1975. 4.00 (ISBN 0-686-70962-4). Am Natl.

Metrics Simplified. rev. ed. LC 78-4654. 1978. lib. bdg. 5.90 (ISBN 0-89471-056-7); pap. 0.95 (ISBN 0-89471-039-7). Running Pr.

Metzner, Seymour. Fifty-Five Metric Games for the Elementary Grades. (gr. 1-6). 1976. pap. 3.95 (ISBN 0-8224-2850-4). Pitman Learning.

Michaelson, M. Metric System & Metric Conversion: A Checklist of References. LC 79-83892. 1979. lib. bdg. 10.95 (ISBN 0-933474-02-4). Minn Scholarly.

Miller, David M. Understanding the Metric System: A Programed Text. new ed. (gr. 9-12). 1979. pap. text ed. 4.80 (ISBN 0-205-06581-3, 566581-7); tchrs'. guide 2.40 (ISBN 0-205-06582-1, 566582-5). Allyn.

Miller, Mary & Richardson, Toni. The Merry Metric Cookbook. (Illus., Orig.). (gr. k-3). 1974. pap. 3.50 (ISBN 0-918932-32-7). Activity Resources.

Morgenstern, Steve. Metric Puzzles, Tricks & Games. (gr. 3 up). 1978. 6.95 (ISBN 0-8069-4588-5); PLB 6.69 (ISBN 0-8069-4589-3). Sterling.

National Micrographics Association. Metric Conversion Recommendations: NMA TR1-1979. (Technical Reports Ser.). 1979. pap. text ed. 5.00 (ISBN 0-89258-063-1). Natl Micrograph.

Nentl, Jerolyn. The Gram Is. LC 76-24203. (Metrics America Ser.). (gr. 4). 1976. 5.95 (ISBN 0-913940-47-X). Crestwood Hse.

--The Liter Is. LC 76-24202. (Metrics America Ser.). (gr. 4). 1976. 5.95 (ISBN 0-913940-46-1). Crestwood Hse.

--The Meter Is. LC 76-24200. (Metrics America Ser.). (gr. 4). 5.95 (ISBN 0-913940-45-3). Crestwood Hse.

--Metric System Is. LC 76-24199. (Metrics America Ser.). (gr. 4). 1976. 5.95 (ISBN 0-913940-44-5). Crestwood Hse.

Nentle, Jerolyn. The Celsius Thermometer. LC 76-24205. (Metrics America Ser.). (gr. 4). 1976. 5.95 (ISBN 0-913940-48-8). Crestwood Hse.

Now You Know About: Measuring - the Metric Way, 5 bks. 86.00 set (ISBN 0-87827-213-5); cassettes avail.; records avail. (ISBN 0-87827-212-7). Ency Brit Ed.

Oppert, J. Moving to Metrics in Home Economics. LC 77-81325. 1977. 2.50 (ISBN 0-686-20043-8, 26108430). Home Econ Educ.

Ostergard, Susan, et al. The Metric World: A Survival Guide. LC 75-6919. (Illus.). 176p. 1975. pap. text ed. 10.50 (ISBN 0-8299-0059-4); instrs.' manual avail. (ISBN 0-8299-0605-3). West Pub.

Paquin, Joseph R. Fractions to Millimeters. LC 75-28052. 48p. 1975. pap. 4.50 (ISBN 0-8311-1109-7). Indus Pr.

Parker, Don H., et al. The Metric System: Syllabus. 1974. pap. text ed. 16.50 units of 10 (ISBN 0-89420-052-6, 280222); cassette recordings 18.15 (ISBN 0-89420-163-8, 280000). Natl Book.

--The Metric System: Syllabus. 1974. pap. text ed. 16.50 units of 10 (ISBN 0-89420-052-6, 280222); cassette recordings 18.15 (ISBN 0-89420-163-8, 280000). Natl Book.

Pedde, Lawrence D., et al. Metric Manual. rev. ed. (Illus.). 1979. 28.00 (ISBN 0-8103-1020-1). Gale.

Perica, Lou & Boselovic, Len, eds. Guidelines for Writers of SI Metric Standards & Other Documents. 1975. pap. text ed. 8.00 (ISBN 0-916148-04-1). Am Natl.

Perrin, Helen. Warne's Metric Conversion Tables. LC 73-89830. 112p. 1974. 11.95 (ISBN 0-7232-1761-0). Warne.

Ploutz, Paul F. The Metric System: Content & Methods. 2nd ed. (Elementary Education Ser.). 1977. pap. text ed. 8.95 (ISBN 0-675-08538-1). Merrill.

Qasim, S. H. SI Units in Engineering & Technology. 1977. pap. 7.00 (ISBN 0-08-021278-6). Pergamon.

Quinn, Daniel & Cook, Emilie C. Beginning Metric Measurement Learning Module. 1974. pap. text ed. 230.00 (ISBN 0-89290-132-2, CM-53). Soc for Visual.

Rahn, Joan E. The Metric System. LC 75-29445. (Illus.). (gr. 6-9). 1976. 6.95 (ISBN 0-689-30510-9). Atheneum.

Reid, Jane. Metrics for Everyday Use. new ed. LC 74-24660. 24p. (gr. 7-12). 1975. pap. text ed. 2.60 (ISBN 0-87002-216-4). Bennett IL.

Richardson, Terry. A Guide to Metrics. LC 78-61695. (Illus.). 1978. pap. 12.00x (ISBN 0-911168-38-9). Prakken.

Richardson, Toni & Miller, Mary. Making Metric Maneuvers. (Orig.). (gr. 2-7). 1973. pap. 5.95 (ISBN 0-918932-27-0). Activity Resources.

Richmond, Doug. Metrics for Mechanics & Other Practical People. 2nd ed. LC 75-11122. 1974. 6.00 (ISBN 0-915004-02-X); pap. 4.00 (ISBN 0-685-64932-6). Dos Reals Pub.

Rinehart, John S. Go Metric. new ed. (Illus.). 32p. 1976. pap. 1.75 (ISBN 0-913270-65-2). HyperDynamics.

Rockcastle, Verne, et al. S.T.E.M. Space, Time, Energy, Matter-Metric Edition. rev., metric ed. Incl. Bk. 1. (gr. 1). text ed. 8.04 (ISBN 0-201-06081-7); Bk. 2. (gr. 2). text ed. 8.04 (ISBN 0-201-06082-5); Bk. 3. (gr. 3). text ed. 9.16 (ISBN 0-201-06083-3); tchr's ed. 18.40 (ISBN 0-201-06093-0); Bk 4. (gr. 4). text ed. 9.88 (ISBN 0-201-06084-1); tchr's. ed. 18.64 (ISBN 0-201-06094-9); Bk. 5. (gr. 5). text ed. 11.00 (ISBN 0-201-06085-X); tchr's. ed. 19.40 (ISBN 0-201-06095-7); Bk. 6. (gr. 6). text ed. 11.00 (ISBN 0-201-06086-8); tchr's. ed. 20.12 (ISBN 0-201-06096-5). (gr. 1-6). 1977 (Sch Div). A-W.

Ronningen, Helmer A. Metrics: Measurement for Tomorrow. (Illus.). 78p. 1972. pap. 1.50 (ISBN 0-02-093920-5, Collier). Macmillan.

Roper, Ann. Metric Recipes for the Classroom. 1977. 3.95 (ISBN 0-88488-084-2). Creative Pubns.

Ross, Frank, Jr. The Metric System: Measures for All Mankind. LC 74-14503. (Illus.). 128p. (gr. 7-10). 1974. 10.95 (ISBN 0-87599-198-X). S G Phillips.

Sanitation Details in SI Metric, 2 vols. (Illus.). 1977. 27.50x set, spiral binding (ISBN 0-686-65560-5). Vol. 1 (ISBN 0-7198-2610-1). Vol. 2. Intl Ideas.

Schell, F. Practical Problems in Mathematics--Metric System. LC 78-73133. 1975. pap. text ed. 5.00 (ISBN 0-8273-1418-3); instructor's guide 1.60 (ISBN 0-8273-1419-1). Delmar.

Schimizzi, Ned V. Mastering the Metric System. (Orig.). 1975. pap. 1.75 (ISBN 0-451-61735-5, ME1735, Ment). NAL.

Schleiden, Hans W. Tabellenbuch zur Umrechnung metrischer Masse in englische Masse; Tables for the Conversion Metric System of Measurement to the British System. (Technischer Verlag Herbert Cram). (Ger.-Eng.). 1961. 24.00x (ISBN 3-11-005632-1). De Gruyter.

Schlein, Miriam. Metric: The Modern Way to Measure. LC 74-22169. (gr. 3-7). 1977. pap. 1.95 (ISBN 0-15-253188-2, VoyB). HarBraceJ.

--Metric: The New Measurement. LC 74-22169. (gr. 6 up). 1975. 6.75 (ISBN 0-15-253187-4, HJ). HarBraceJ.

Schubert, Paul & Semioli, William, trs. Conversion Tables for SI Metrication. LC 74-1104. (Illus.). 360p. 1974. 25.00 (ISBN 0-8311-1104-6). Indus Pr.

Segan, Anne. One Meter Max. (Illus.). (ps-2). 1979. PLB 7.95 (ISBN 0-13-636076-9). P-H.

Sheperak, Rita & DeBruin, Jerry. Metric Math Book. (gr. k-8). 1976. 11.95 (ISBN 0-916456-08-0, GA63). Good Apple.

Shimek, William J. The Celsius Thermometer. LC 74-11898. (The Early Metric Ser.). (Illus.). 32p. (gr. 2-5). 1975. PLB 4.95 (ISBN 0-8225-0589-4). Lerner Pubns.

--The Gram. LC 74-11897. (The Early Metric Ser.). (Illus.). 32p. (gr. 2-5). 1975. PLB 4.95 (ISBN 0-8225-0588-6). Lerner Pubns.

--The Liter. LC 74-11895. (The Early Metric Ser.). (Illus.). 32p. (gr. 2-5). 1975. PLB 4.95 (ISBN 0-8225-0587-8). Lerner Pubns.

--The Meter. LC 74-11894. (The Early Metric Ser.). (Illus.). 32p. (gr. 2-5). 1975. PLB 4.95 (ISBN 0-8225-0586-X). Lerner Pubns.

--The Metric System. LC 74-11893. (The Early Metric Ser.). (Illus.). 32p. (gr. 2-5). 1975. PLB 4.95 (ISBN 0-8225-0585-1). Lerner Pubns.

Silverman, Helene. The Kid's Book of Metrics. 1977. pap. 0.95 (ISBN 0-448-14137-X, Tempo). Ace Bks.

Sleeper, Ann, compiled by. The Concise Metric Conversion Tables. (Illus.). 1980. pap. 2.25 (ISBN 0-385-14044-4, Dolp). Doubleday.

Smoley, C. K. Smoley's Metric Four Combined Tables. Smoley, E. R. & Smoley, N. G., eds. 1400p. 1976. thumb-indexed 30.00 (ISBN 0-911390-08-1). Smoley.

Sohns, Marvin L. & Buffington, Audrey V. El Libro De Medicion. (Illus.). 212p. (Span.). 1980. pap. 9.95 (ISBN 0-86582-029-5). Enrich.

Stecher, A., et al. Running Water: Si Metric. (Examining Your Environment Ser.). (gr. 4-8). 1978. pap. text ed. 5.31 (ISBN 0-03-922298-5, Pub. by HR&W Canada). HR&W.

Steinke, Don C. Thirty Days to Metric Mastery: For People Who Hate Math. (Illus., Orig.). 1981. pap. 6.95x (ISBN 0-9605344-0-7). Hse of Charles.

Stevens, B. Teaching the Metric System in the Foreign Language Classroom. (Language in Education Ser.: No. 32). 1980. pap. 5.50x (ISBN 0-87281-131-X). Ctr Appl Ling.

Stoecker, W. F. Using SI Units (Standard International Metric) in Heating, Air Conditioning, & Refrigeration. LC 74-26697. (Illus.). 1975. 7.50 (ISBN 0-912524-12-X). Busn News.

Stover, Allan C. You & the Metric System. LC 74-2593. (Illus.). 96p. (gr. 5 up). 1974. 4.50 (ISBN 0-396-06965-7). Dodd.

Teaching Classroom Metric. LC 76-22299. (AMJ Publication: B5.2). 145p. 1977. 7.45 (ISBN 0-917240-07-3). Am Metric.

Technical Book Division of Barron's. Metrics Made Easy. (Illus.). 1976. pap. text ed. 0.95 (ISBN 0-8120-0706-9). Barron.

Technical Division, Barron's Educational Ser., compiled by. Metric Converter. 1976. pap. text ed. 1.25 (ISBN 0-8120-0707-7). Barron.

Thornburg, Kathy R. & Thornburg, James L. Metric Magic. new ed. LC 77-93666. (Illus.). 1978. pap. text ed. 9.00x (ISBN 0-89334-014-6). Humanics Ltd.

Turner, Rufus P. Metrics for the Millions. LC 73-90288. (Illus.). 1974. pap. 3.95 (ISBN 0-672-21036-3). Sams.

Tutt, Patricia & Adler, David. VNR Metric Handbook of Architectural Standards. 504p. 1980. 29.95 (ISBN 0-442-25189-0); pap. 19.95 (ISBN 0-442-24902-0). Van Nos Reinhold.

U. S. Department of Commerce & Hopkins, R. A. NBS Metric Practice Guide & Style Manual. 3.95 (ISBN 0-917240-04-9). Am Metric.

Wallach, Paul. Meet the Metric System. (gr. 5-12). 1980. pap. 3.96 (ISBN 0-8224-4463-1); teacher's guide free (ISBN 0-8224-4464-X). Pitman Learning.

Wandmacher, C. Metric Units in Engineering--Going SI. LC 77-17935. (Illus.). 1978. 25.00 (ISBN 0-8311-1121-6). Indus Pr.

Washington, Allyn J. Basic Technical Mathematics with Calculus: Metric Version. 3rd ed. LC 77-71471. 1978. pap. text ed. 22.95 (ISBN 0-8053-9523-7); instr's guide 8.95 (ISBN 0-8053-9524-5). Benjamin-Cummings.

Whitman, Nancy C. & Braun, Frederick G. The Metric System: A Laboratory Approach for Teachers. LC 77-22793. 1978. pap. text ed. 12.95 (ISBN 0-471-02763-4). Wiley.

Willert, Frederic. My Metric Measurement Manual. rev. ed. (Illus.). 1975. Pgs. 120. write for info. tchrs. ed. (ISBN 0-9601144-2-4); Pgs. 88. write for info. wkbk. (ISBN 0-9601144-1-6). Pauper Pr.

Woolley, Leslie. Drainage Details in SI Metric. (Illus.). 1978. 13.50x (ISBN 0-7198-2520-2). Intl Ideas.

Young, Lorelle & Bielefeld, Carole. Hometrics. (Illus.). (gr. 7 up). 1977. pap. 4.95 (ISBN 0-933358-01-6). Enrich.

Zim, Herbert S. & Skelly, James R. Metric Measure. LC 74-702. (Illus.). 64p. (gr. 3-7). 1974. PLB 6.48 (ISBN 0-688-30118-5). Morrow.

Zupko, Ronald E. French Weights & Measures Before the Revolution: A Dictionary of Provincial & Local Units. LC 78-3249. 256p. 1979. 22.50x (ISBN 0-253-32480-7). Ind U Pr.

METRIC TOPOLOGY

see Distance Geometry

METRICS

see Versification

METRO-GOLDWYN-MAYER, INC.

Buscombe, Ed, ed. & intro. by. MGM. (BFI Dossiers Ser.: No. 1). (Orig.). 1980. pap. 6.00 (ISBN 0-918432-33-2). NY Zoetrope.

Carey, Gary. All the Stars in Heaven: The Story of Louis B. Mayer & Metro-Goldwyn-Mayer. (Illus.). 1980. 18.50 (ISBN 0-525-05245-3). Dutton.

Eames, John D. The MGM Story: The Complete History of Fifty Roaring Years, 1924-1974. (Illus.). 384p. (YA) 1976. 25.00 (ISBN 0-517-52389-2); pap. 12.95 (ISBN 0-517-53811-3). Crown.

METROLOGY

see Mensuration; Weights and Measures

METROPOLITAN AREAS

see also Metropolitan Finance; Metropolitan Government; Open Spaces; Suburbs; Urban Renewal

also names of metropolitan areas, e.g. Chicago Metropolitan Area

Abler, Ronald, ed. A Comparative Atlas of America's Great Cities: Twenty Metropolitan Regions. LC 76-14268. (Illus.). 500p. 1976. 95.00x (ISBN 0-8166-0767-2). U of Minn Pr.

Berry, Brian J. Social Burdens of Environmental Pollution: Comparative Metropolitan Data Source. LC 76-40419. 1977. 27.50 (ISBN 0-88410-427-3). Ballinger Pub.

Bollens, John C. & Schmandt, Henry J. The Metropolis: Its People, Politics & Economic Life. 4th ed. 432p. 1981. scp 14.95 (ISBN 0-06-040794-8, HarpC). Har-Row.

Boyer, Richard & Savageau, David. Places Rated Almanac. (Illus.). 384p. 1981. 19.95 (ISBN 0-528-81114-2); pap. 11.95 (ISBN 0-528-88033-0). Rand.

Chinitz, Benjamin, ed. City & Suburb. LC 76-1850. 181p. 1976. Repr. of 1965 ed. lib. bdg. 14.00x (ISBN 0-8371-8679-X, CHCS). Greenwood.

Clawson, Marion, ed. Modernizing Urban Land Policy. LC 72-12365. (Resources for the Future Ser). (Illus.). 255p. 1973. 16.50x (ISBN 0-8018-1491-X). Johns Hopkins.

Cleaveland, Frederic N., et al. Congress & Urban Problems: A Casebook on the Legislative Process. 405p. 1969. 14.95 (ISBN 0-8157-1474-2); pap. 5.95 (ISBN 0-8157-1473-4). Brookings.

Colman, William G. Cities, Suburbs & States: Governing & Financing Urban America. LC 75-2810. (Illus.). 1975. 17.95 (ISBN 0-02-906490-2). Free Pr.

Connery, R. H. & Leach, R. H. The Federal Government & Metropolitan Areas. LC 77-74936. (American Federalism-the Urban Dimension). 1978. Repr. of 1960 ed. lib. bdg. 18.00x (ISBN 0-405-10483-9). Arno.

Cook, Gillian. Spatial Dynamics of Business Growth in the Witwatersrand. LC 73-92654. (Research Papers Ser.: No. 157). (Illus.). 143p. 1975. pap. 8.00 (ISBN 0-89065-064-0). U Chicago Dept Geog.

Cooper, James R. & Guntermann, Karl L. Real Estate & Urban Land Analysis. LC 73-10397. (Special Ser. in Real Estate & Urban Land Economics). (Illus.). 544p. 1974. 32.95 (ISBN 0-669-90415-5). Lexington Bks.

Crawford, Fred R. Civil Aggression & Urban Disorders. 1967. pap. 1.00 (ISBN 0-89937-024-1). Ctr Res Soc Chg.

Crawford, Fred R., ed. Violence & Dissent in Urban America. 1970. pap. 2.00 (ISBN 0-89937-022-5, Southern Newspapers Publishers Association Foundation). Ctr Res Soc Chg.

Danielson, Michael N. Federal-Metropolitan Politics & the Commuter Crisis. LC 65-16197. (Metropolitan Politcs Ser.). (Illus.). 244p. 1965. 16.00x (ISBN 0-231-02782-6). Columbia U Pr.

--The Politics of Exclusion. LC 76-7609. 443p. 1976. 22.50x (ISBN 0-231-03697-3); pap. 10.00x (ISBN 0-231-08342-4). Columbia U Pr.

Duhl, Leonard, ed. Urban Condition. 1969. pap. 2.95 (ISBN 0-671-20243-X, Touchstone Bks). S&S.

Duke, Richard. Metropolis: The Urban Systems Game Starter Kit. 1976. 37.50x (ISBN 0-442-80344-3). Van Nos Reinhold.

Duncan, Beverly & Lieberson, Stanley. Metropolis & Region in Transition. LC 78-92350. 320p. 1970. 22.50x (ISBN 0-8039-0051-1). Sage.

Duncan, Otis D., et al. Metropolis & Region. LC 77-86393. (Resources for the Future, Inc. Publications). Repr. of 1960 ed. 37.50 (ISBN 0-404-60331-9). AMS Pr.

Eells, John M. LAFCO Spheres of Influence: Effective Planning for the Urban Fringe. (Working Paper: 77-3). 1977. pap. 5.00x (ISBN 0-685-87445-1). Inst Gov Stud Berk.

Emenhiser, Jedon A., ed. Rocky Mountain Urban Politics. 166p. (Orig.). 1971. pap. 5.00 (ISBN 0-87421-041-0). Utah St U Pr.

Fiser, Webb S. Mastery of the Metropolis. LC 80-23244. x, 168p. 1981. Repr. of 1962 ed. lib. bdg. 17.50x (ISBN 0-313-22732-2, FIMAM). Greenwood.

Greer, Scott A. Governing the Metropolis. LC 81-4211. xi, 153p. 1981. Repr. of 1966 ed. lib. bdg. 18.50x (ISBN 0-313-23038-2, GRGM). Greenwood.

Guggenheimer, Elinor C. Planning for Parks & Recreation Needs in Urban Areas. 10.95 (ISBN 0-685-60137-4, Pub by Twayne). Cyrco Pr.

Hall, Peter. World Cities. 2nd ed. (Illus.). 1979. pap. 3.95 (ISBN 0-07-025607-1, SP). McGraw.

Hawley, Amos H. & Zimmer, Basil G. The Metropolitan Community: Its People & Government. LC 77-92358. 160p. 1970. 15.00 (ISBN 0-8039-0066-X). Sage.

Heller, Walter, et al. Revenue Sharing & the City. Perloff, Harvey S. & Nathan, Richard P., eds. LC 77-86396. (Resources for the Future, Inc. Publications). Repr. of 1968 ed. 14.50 (ISBN 0-404-60333-5). AMS Pr.

Heller, Walter W., et al. Revenue Sharing & the City. LC 68-16164. (Resources for the Future Ser). 124p. (Orig.). 1968. pap. 2.50x (ISBN 0-8018-0266-0). Johns Hopkins.

Jackson, John E., ed. Public Needs & Private Behavior in Metropolitan Areas. LC 75-6732. 1975. text ed. 17.50 (ISBN 0-88410-035-9). Ballinger Pub.

Leven, Charles L., ed. The Mature Metropolis. LC 77-10363. 1978. 24.95 (ISBN 0-669-01844-9). Lexington Bks.

MacGillivray, Lois. Decision-Related Research on the Organization of Service Delivery Systems in Metropolitan Areas: Fire Protection. LC 79-83819. 1979. codebook 34.00 (ISBN 0-89138-985-7). ICPSR.

Martin, R. C. The Cities & the Federal System. LC 77-74949. (American Federalism-the Urban Dimension). 1978. Repr. of 1965 ed. lib. bdg. 15.00x (ISBN 0-405-10495-2). Arno.

Martin, Roscoe C., et al. Decisions in Syracuse. Repr. of 1961 ed. lib. bdg. 19.00 (ISBN 0-8371-0160-3, MADS). Greenwood.

National Academy of Science, National Research Council. Toward an Understanding of Metropolitan America. LC 72-2097. 124p. 1975. pap. text ed. 8.50 scp (ISBN 0-06-385492-9, HarpC). Har-Row.

O'Donoghue, Patrick. Decision-Related Research on the Organization of Service Delivery Systems in Metropolitan Areas: Public Health. LC 79-83820. 1979. codebook 14.00 (ISBN 0-89138-984-9). ICPSR.

Pollakowski, Henry O. Urban Housing Markets & Residential Location. LC 78-20609. 1981. price not set (ISBN 0-669-02773-1). Lexington Bks.

Rodwin, Lloyd, ed. The Future Metropolis. LC 61-9964. 1968. 6.00 (ISBN 0-8076-0147-0). Braziller.

Sands, Gary. Land-Office Business: Land & Housing Prices in Rapidly Growing Metropolitan Areas. 1981. price not set (ISBN 0-669-04859-3). Lexington Bks.

Schneider, Kenneth R. On the Nature of Cities: Toward Enduring & Creative Human Environments. LC 78-62556. (Social & Behavioral Science Ser.). 1979. text ed. 19.95x (ISBN 0-87589-391-0). Jossey-Bass.

Street, David, et al. Handbook of Contemporary Urban Life: An Examination of Urbanization, Social Organization & Metropolitan Politics. LC 78-1155. (Social & Behavioral Science Ser.). (Illus.). 1978. text ed. 29.95x (ISBN 0-87589-372-4). Jossey-Bass.

Ullman, Edward L., et al. The Economic Base of American Cities. rev. ed. LC 72-631496. 71p. 1971. pap. 7.50 (ISBN 0-295-95125-7). U of Wash Pr.

U.S. Advisory Commission on Intergovernmental Relations. Metropolitan America: Challenge to Freedom. LC 77-74942. (American Federalism-the Urban Dimension). 1978. Repr. of 1966 ed. lib. bdg. 12.00x (ISBN 0-405-10489-8). Arno.

Von Eckardt, Wolf. The Challenge of Megalopolis. LC 64-9998. 1964. pap. 4.00 (ISBN 0-527-02845-2). Kraus Repr.

Williams, O. P. Metropolitan Political Analysis. LC 70-136275. 1971. 7.95 (ISBN 0-02-935300-9). Free Pr.

METROPOLITAN AREAS–BIBLIOGRAPHY

President's Commission for a National Agenda: Panel on Policies & Prospects for Metropolitan & Nonmetropolitan America. Urban America in the Eighties: Perspectives & Prospects. 127p. 1981. pap. 6.95 (ISBN 0-87855-883-7). Transaction Bks.

METROPOLITAN FINANCE

Break, George F., ed. Metropolitan Financing: Principles & Practice. LC 77-77437. 346p. 1978. 25.00 (ISBN 0-299-07280-0). U of Wis Pr.

Campbell, A. K. & Sacks, S. Metropolitan America. LC 67-14373. 1967. 12.95 (ISBN 0-02-905230-0). Free Pr.

Oates, Wallace E., ed. Financing the New Federalism: Revenue Sharing, Conditional Grants, & Taxation. LC 75-19367. (The Governance of Metropolitan Regions, Resources for the Future Ser.: No. 5). (Illus.). 176p. 1975. 12.00x (ISBN 0-8018-1782-X); pap. 3.95x (ISBN 0-8018-1772-2). Johns Hopkins.

Oberman, Joseph & Bingham, Robert. Planning & Managing the Economy of the City: Policy Guidelines for the Metropolitan Mayor. LC 72-79544. (Special Studies in U.S. Economic, Social & Political Issues Ser.). 1972. 29.50x (ISBN 0-275-06160-4). Irvington.

Sackrey, Charles. The Political Economy of Urban Poverty. 172p. 1972. pap. 4.95x (ISBN 0-393-09410-3, NortonC). Norton.

METROPOLITAN GOVERNMENT

see also Municipal Corporations; Metropolitan Finance; Municipal Government; Special Districts;

also names of metropolitan areas, e.g. Chicago Metropolitan Area

Bent, Alan E. Escape from Anarchy: A Strategy for Urban Survival. LC 72-80172. 204p. 1972. 8.95x (ISBN 0-87870-010-2). Memphis St Univ.

Bollens, John C. & Schmandt, Henry J. The Metropolis: Its People, Politics & Economic Life. 4th ed. 432p. 1981. scp 14.95 (ISBN 0-06-040794-8, HarpC). Har-Row.

Bromage, Arthur W., ed. Political Representation in Metropolitan Agencies. LC 74-4656. (University of Michigan, Michigan Governmental Studies: No. 42). 102p. 1974. Repr. of 1962 ed. lib. bdg. 15.00x (ISBN 0-8371-7475-9, BRAG). Greenwood.
Courtney, Phoebe. Beware Metro & Regional Government. 5th ed. LC 73-85483. 1973. 1.50 (ISBN 0-686-08992-8). Ind American.
Emenhiser, Jedon A., ed. Rocky Mountain Urban Politics. 166p. (Orig.). 1971. pap. 5.00 (ISBN 0-87421-041-0). Utah St U Pr.
Fischer, John. Vital Signs, U. S. A. LC 74-15823. 210p. 1975. 10.00 (ISBN 0-06-011247-6, HarpT). Har-Row.
Florestando & Marando. The States & the Metropolis. 176p. 1981. 13.75 (ISBN 0-686-72703-7). Dekker.
Hallman, Howard W. Neighborhood Government in a Metropolitan Setting. LC 74-78562. (Library of Social Research: Vol. 12). 256p. 1974. 20.00 (ISBN 0-8039-0419-3); pap. 9.95x (ISBN 0-8039-0418-5). Sage.
--Small & Large Together: Governing the Metropolis. LC 77-15428. (Sage Library of Social Research: Vol. 56). 309p. 1977. 20.00 (ISBN 0-8039-0898-9); pap. 9.95 (ISBN 0-8039-0899-7). Sage.
Harrigan, John J. & Johnson, William C. Governing the Twin Cities Region: The Metropolitan Council in Comparative Perspective. LC 78-3194. (Illus.). 1978. 14.95x (ISBN 0-8166-0838-5); pap. 5.95x (ISBN 0-8166-0849-0). U of Minn Pr.
Hawkins, Brett. Politics & Urban Policies. LC 77-151612. (Policy Analysis Ser). 1971. 7.95 (ISBN 0-672-51474-5); pap. 4.95 (ISBN 0-672-61060-4). Bobbs.
Hawley, Willis D. Blacks & Metropolitan Governance: The Stakes of Reform. LC 72-5145. 34p. (Orig.). 1972. pap. 1.50x (ISBN 0-87772-153-X). Inst Gov Stud Berk.
Herman, Harold. New York State & the Metropolitan Problem. LC 63-7856. 1963. 12.00x (ISBN 0-8122-7382-6). U of Pa Pr.
Hindman, Jo. Blame Metro - When Urban Renewal Strikes, When Laws Oppress. LC 66-29557. (Illus., Orig.). 1966. pap. 2.50 (ISBN 0-87004-063-4). Caxton.
--Terrible Thirteen Hundred & Thirteen Revisited. LC 63-9066. (Orig.). 1963. pap. 2.50 (ISBN 0-87004-064-2). Caxton.
Horan, James F. & Taylor, G. Thomas, Jr. Experiments in Metropolitan Government. LC 77-7816. (Praeger Special Studies). 1978. 27.95 (ISBN 0-03-022336-9). Praeger.
League of Women Voters Education Fund. Supercity, Hometown U. S. A. Prospects for Two-Tier Government. 138p. 1974. pap. 1.95, 5-15 copies 1.50 ea. (ISBN 0-89959-086-1, 477, Pub. by Proeger). LWV US.
Long, Norton E. The Polity. (Reprints in Sociology Ser). lib. bdg. 24.50x (ISBN 0-685-70258-8); pap. 6.95x (ISBN 0-685-70259-6). Irvington.
Miller, Delbert C. Leadership & Power in the Bos-Wash Megalopolis. 442p. 1975. 24.50 (ISBN 0-471-60519-0, Pub. by Wiley). Krieger.
Rich, Richard, ed. Urban Service Distributions. (Orig.). 1981. pap. 5.00 (ISBN 0-918592-46-1). Policy Studies.
Stedman, Murray S., Jr. Urban Politics. 2nd ed. 1975. ref. ed. 11.00 (ISBN 0-87626-903-X); pap. text ed. 9.95 (ISBN 0-87626-902-1). Winthrop.
Teaford, Jon C. City & Suburb: The Political Fragmentation of Metropolitan Areas, 1850-1970. LC 78-20519. 1979. text ed. 15.00x (ISBN 0-8018-2202-5). Johns Hopkins.
Temple, David G. Merger Politics: Local Government Consolidation in Tidewater Virginia. LC 72-181718. 250p. 1972. 12.50x (ISBN 0-8139-0389-0). U Pr of Va.
U.S. Advisory Commission on Intergovernmental Relations. Metropolitan America: Challenge to Freedom. LC 77-74942. (American Federalism-the Urban Dimension). 1978. Repr. of 1966 ed. lib. bdg. 12.00x (ISBN 0-405-10489-8). Arno.
Williams, O. P. Metropolitan Political Analysis. LC 70-136275. 1971. 7.95 (ISBN 0-02-935300-9). Free Pr.

METROPOLITAN MUSEUM OF ART, NEW YORK CITY

Burke, Doreen B. American Painting in the Metropolitan Museum of Art: A Catalogue of Works by Artists Born Between 1846 & 1864, Vol. 3. LC 80-81074. 528p. 1981. 75.00x (ISBN 0-691-03961-5). Princeton U Pr.
The Chase, the Capture: Collecting at the Metropolitan. LC 75-34076. (Illus.). 240p. 1975. pap. 7.95 (ISBN 0-87099-139-6). Metro Mus Art.
Curatorial Staff, Metropolitan Museum of Art. Metropolitan Museum of Art: Notable Acquisitions, 1965-1975. LC 75-31761. (Illus.). 304p. 1975. pap. 15.95 (ISBN 0-87099-141-8). Metro Mus Art.
Davidson, Marshall B. The American Wing: A Guide. Stillinger, Penny, ed. (Illus.). 176p. 1980. pap. 9.95 (ISBN 0-87099-238-4). Metro Mus Art.
Geldzahler, Henry, intro. by. Jean Arp at the Metropolitan Museum of Art. LC 72-77067. (Illus.). 1972. pap. 2.95 (ISBN 0-87099-117-5). Metro Mus Art.
Hibbard, Howard. The Metropolitan Museum of Art. (Illus.). 600p. 1980. 50.00 (ISBN 0-06-011887-3, HarpT). Har-Row.
Howe, Winifred E. A History of the Metropolitan Museum of Art: With a Chapter on the Early Institutions of Art in New York. LC 76-168422. (Metropolitan Museum of Art Publications in Reprint). (Illus.). 380p. 1972. Repr. of 1913 ed. 27.00 (ISBN 0-405-02260-3). Arno.
Metropolitan Museum of Art Curatorial Staff. Great Paintings from the Metropolitan Museum of Art. (Library of Great Museums Ser). (Illus.). 1959. 40.00 (ISBN 0-8109-0296-6). Abrams.
Metropolitan Museum of Art, New York. Library Catalog of The Metropolitan Museum of Art (New York), Suppl. 6. 1975. lib. bdg. 115.00 (ISBN 0-8161-1126-X); lib. bdg. 175.00 suppl. 7, 1977 (ISBN 0-8161-0028-4). G K Hall.
Metropolitan Museum of Art (New York) Library Catalog of the Metropolitan Museum of Art. 2nd ed. 1980. lib. bdg. 4650.00 (ISBN 0-8161-0295-3). G K Hall.
Ragghianti, Licia C. Metropolitan Museum of Art, New York. LaFarge, Henry, ed. LC 77-17667. (Great Museums of the World Ser). (Illus.). 1978. 16.95 (ISBN 0-88225-241-0). Newsweek.
Schwartz, Marvin D. American Furniture of the Colonial Period. LC 76-18763. (Illus.). 1976. 6.95 (ISBN 0-87099-149-3). Metro Mus Art.
Young, Bonnie. A Walk Through the Cloisters. (Illus.). 144p. (Orig.). 1979. 14.95 (ISBN 0-670-74922-2, Pub by Metro Mus Art). Viking Pr.

METROPOLITAN OPERA

see New York (City)–Metropolitan Opera

METROPOLITAN REGIONAL COUNCIL

Aron, Joan B. The Quest for Regional Cooperation: A Study of the New York Metropolitan Regional Council. LC 69-16738. (California Studies in Urbanization & Environmental Design). 1969. 22.75x (ISBN 0-520-01505-3). U of Cal Pr.

METROPOLITAN TRANSPORTATION

see Urban Transportation

METROPOLITANS

Hale, Charles R. Metropolitan Innocent of Moscow, the Apostle of Alaska. pap. 1.00 (ISBN 0-686-05655-8). Eastern Orthodox.

METS (BASEBALL CLUB)

see New York Baseball Club (National League, Mets)

METTERNICH-WINNEBURG, CLEMENS LOTHAR WENZEL, FURST VON, 1773-1859

De Grunwald, C. Metternich. Todd, D., tr. 1977. lib. bdg. 59.95 (ISBN 0-8490-2231-2). Gordon Pr.
De Sauvigny, Guillaume. Metternich & His Times. 1962. text ed. 12.50x (ISBN 0-232-48202-0). Humanities.
Kissinger, Henry A. World Restored: Europe After Napoleon. 8.00 (ISBN 0-8446-2384-9). Peter Smith.
Kraeche, Ennos E. Metternich's German Policy, Vol. 2, The Contest With Alexander, 1818-1848. Date not set. price not set (ISBN 0-691-05186-0). Princeton U Pr.
Kraehe, Enno E., ed. The Metternich Controversy. LC 77-6762. (European Problem Studies). 142p. 1977. pap. text ed. 5.50 (ISBN 0-88275-562-5). Krieger.
Reinerman, Alan J. Austria & the Papacy in the Age of Metternich: Between Conflict & Cooperation, 1809-1830. (Vol. 1). 1979. 24.95 (ISBN 0-8132-0548-4). Cath U Pr.
Schroeder, Paul W. Metternich's Diplomacy at Its Zenith, 1820-1823. Repr. of 1962 ed. lib. bdg. 15.00x (ISBN 0-8371-2471-9, SCME). Greenwood.
--Metternich's Diplomacy at Its Zenith, 1820-1823. LC 62-9794. 306p. 1977. pap. text ed. 12.50x (ISBN 0-292-75034-X). U of Tex Pr.
Webster, C. K. Palmerston, Metternich & the European System: 1830-1841. LC 74-34457. (Studies in Philosophy, No. 40). 1972. Repr. of 1934 ed. lib. bdg. 19.95 (ISBN 0-8383-0135-5, 8383-135-1). Haskell.

METZGER, MAX JOSEF, 1887-1944

Swidler, Leonard. Blood Witness for Unity & Peace: The Life of Max Joseph Metzger. 3.95 (ISBN 0-87193-077-3). Dimension Bks.

METZLER, LLOYD APPLETON

Horwich, George & Samuelson, Paul A., eds. Trade, Stability, & Macroeconomics: Essays in Honor of Lloyd A. Metzler. (Economic Theory & Mathematical Economics Ser.). 1974. 43.00 (ISBN 0-12-356750-5). Acad Pr.

MEVALONIC ACID METABOLISM

Biochemical Society Symposium, 29th. Natural Substances Formed Biologically from Mevalonic Acid: Proceedings. Goodwin, T. W., ed. 1970. 26.50 (ISBN 0-12-289865-6). Acad Pr.

MEXICAN AMERICANS

Here are entered works on American citizens of Mexican descent or works concerned with Mexican American minority groups. Works on immigration from Mexico, braceros, etc. are entered under Mexicans in the United States.
see also Mexicans in the United States

Achor, Shirley. Mexican Americans in a Dallas Barrio. LC 77-22434. 1978. pap. 6.95x (ISBN 0-8165-0533-0). U of Ariz Pr.
Acuna, Rodolfo. Occupied America: A History of Chicanos. 2nd ed. 1980. pap. text ed. 11.50 (ISBN 0-06-380352-6, HarpC). Har-Row.
Aguirre, Adalberto, Jr. An Experimental Sociolinguistic Study of Chicano Bilingualism. LC 78-62239. 1978. soft cover 9.00 (ISBN 0-685-65842-2). R & E Res Assoc.
Aguirre, Rueben E. Teaching the Chicano-Mexican American Cultural Heritage in the Elementary School: A Teacher's Guide, 2 pts. 1977. tchr's guide 6.00 ea.; Pt. 1. (ISBN 0-88247-470-7); Pt. 2. (ISBN 0-88247-471-5). R & E Res Assoc.
Alexander, T. John. Spanish Surname Recent Migrant Families: Life Cycle, Family, Socioeconomics & Housing Status. LC 78-68462. 1979. perfect bdg. 8.00 (ISBN 0-88247-555-X). R & E Res Assoc.
Ambrecht, Biliana C. Politicizing the Poor: The Legacy of the War on Poverty in a Mexican American Community. LC 74-31501. 1976. 29.95 (ISBN 0-275-05900-6). Praeger.
Baird, Frank L., ed. Mexican Americans: Political Power, Influence, or Resource. (Graduate Studies: No. 14). (Illus., Orig.). 1977. pap. 7.00 (ISBN 0-89672-024-1). Tex Tech Pr.
Baral, David P. Achievement Levels Among Foreign-Born & Native-Born Mexican American Students. LC 77-81020. 1977. soft bdg. 8.00 (ISBN 0-88247-472-3). R & E Res Assoc.
Baron, Augustine, Jr. The Utilization of Mental Health Services by Mexican-Americans: A Critical Analysis. LC 78-68460. 1979. perfect bdg. 11.00 (ISBN 0-88247-557-6). R & E Res Assoc.
Baron, Augustine, Jr., ed. Explorations in Chicano Psychology. 240p. 1981. 24.95 (ISBN 0-03-058016-1). Praeger.
Barrera, Mario. Race & Class in the Southwest: A Theory of Racial Inequality. LC 78-62970. 1979. text ed. 15.95x (ISBN 0-268-01600-3). U of Notre Dame Pr.
Baty, Roger M. Re-Educating Teachers for Cultural Awareness: Preparation for Educating Mexican-American Children in Northern California. LC 75-173278. (Special Studies in U.S. Economic, Social & Political Issues). 1971. 28.50x (ISBN 0-89197-917-4). Irvington.
Beeson, Margaret, et al. Hispanic Writers in French Journals: An Annotated Bibliography. LC 77-93922. (SSSAS Bibliographies: No. 102). 1978. pap. 15.00 (ISBN 0-89295-002-1). Society Sp & Sp-Am.
Benitez, Mario A. & Villarreal, Lupita G. The Education of the Mexican American: A Selected Bibliography. 270p. 1979. 9.50 (ISBN 0-89417-353-7, Co-Pub. by Dissemination & Assessment). Natl Clearinghse Bilingual Ed.
Blair, Phillip M. Job Discrimination & Education: An Investment Analysis, a Case Study of Mexican-Americans in Santa Clara County, California. LC 70-180842. (Special Studies in U.S. Economic, Social & Political Issues). 1972. 26.50x (ISBN 0-89197-807-0). Irvington.
Blawis, Patricia B. Tijerina & the Land Grants: Mexican Americans in Struggle for Their Heritage. LC 79-175178. (Orig.). 1971. 6.95 (ISBN 0-7178-0336-8); pap. 2.65 (ISBN 0-7178-0337-6). Intl Pub Co.
Bookman, C. J. Chicano Bibliography. 1974. 59.95 (ISBN 0-87968-398-8). Gordon Pr.
Boulette, Teresa R. Determining Needs & Appropriate Counseling Approaches for Mexican-American Women: A Comparison of Therapeutic Listening & Behavioral Rehearsal. LC 75-36572. 1976. perfect bdg. softcover 9.00 (ISBN 0-88247-374-3). R & E Res Assoc.
Briggs, Vernon M., Jr. Chicanos & Rural Poverty. (PSEW Ser.: No. 16). 1973. text ed. 7.50x (ISBN 0-8018-1473-1). Johns Hopkins.
--The Mexico-United States Border: Public Policy & Chicano Economic Welfare. (Studies in Human Resource Development: No. 2). 30p. (Orig.). 1974. pap. 4.00 (ISBN 0-87755-200-2). U of Tex Busn Res.
Briggs, Vernon M., Jr., et al. The Chicano Worker. LC 76-28237. (Illus.). 145p. 1977. text ed. 10.00x (ISBN 0-292-71040-2); pap. text ed. 5.95 (ISBN 0-292-71055-0). U of Tex Pr.
Brophy, A. Blake. Foundlings on the Frontier: Racial & Religious Conflict in Arizona Territory, 1904-1905. LC 79-187824. (Southwest Chronicles). 1972. pap. 2.00 (ISBN 0-8165-0319-2). U of Ariz Pr.
Bruce-Novoa. Chicano Authors: Inquiry by Interview. (Illus.). 306p. 1980. lib. bdg. 15.95x (ISBN 0-292-71059-3); pap. text ed. 7.95x (ISBN 0-292-71062-3). U of Tex Pr.
Bullington, Bruce. Heroin Use in the Barrio. LC 76-40403. 1977. 19.95 (ISBN 0-669-01042-1). Lexington Bks.
Cabrera, Y. Arturo. Emerging Faces: The Mexican-Americans. LC 79-135153. 1978. pap. 6.95x (ISBN 0-932848-02-8). Sierra Pubns CO.
--Minorities in Higher Education. LC 78-68819. 1978. pap. 7.95x (ISBN 0-932848-01-X). Sierra Pubns CO.
Cabrera, Y. Arturo & Perea, Jose A. Community College Conflict: Chicano Under Fire. LC 78-56755. (Illus.). 1979. pap. 5.95x (ISBN 0-932848-03-6). Sierra Pubns CO.
Cabrera, Y. Arturo, ed. Strategies for the Education of Chicanos. LC 78-52129. 1978. pap. 6.95x (ISBN 0-932848-00-1). Sierra Pubns Co.
Camarillo, Albert. Chicanos in a Changing Society: From Mexican Pueblos to American Barrios in Santa Barbara & Southern California, 1848-1930. LC 79-10687. 1979. pap. 7.95x (ISBN 0-674-11396-9). Harvard U Pr.
Campa, Arthur. Hispanic Folklore Studies of Arthur Campa: An Original Anthology. Cortes, Carlos E., ed. & intro. by. LC 76-1475. (Chicano Heritage Ser.). (Illus.). 1976. 35.00x (ISBN 0-405-09536-8). Arno.
Carpenter, Roy L. Misfortunes of a Chicano: A Novel of Identity. 1977. 6.25 (ISBN 0-87164-125-9). William-F.
Carter, Thomas P. & Segura, Roberto D. Mexican Americans in School: A Decade of Change. LC 77-95391. (Illus.). 1979. pap. 9.95 (ISBN 0-87447-061-7, 252201). College Bd.
Castaneda, Alfredo, et al, eds. Mexican Americans & Educational Change. LC 73-14196. (The Mexican American Ser.). 424p. 1974. 24.00x (ISBN 0-405-05671-0). Arno.
Castillo, Pedro & Camarillo, Albert. Furia y Muerte: Los Bandidos Chicanos. (Monograph Ser: No. 4). (Illus.). 1973. pap. 2.75 (ISBN 0-89551-003-0). UCLA Chicano Stud.
Ceja, Manuel V. Methods of Orientation of Spanish-Speaking Children to an American School. LC 73-76005. pap. 8.00 (ISBN 0-88247-207-0). R & E Res Assoc.
Chang, Dorothy K. A Guide of Understanding & Teaching of Mexican-American Adolescents. LC 73-78064. pap. 8.00 (ISBN 0-685-40365-3). R & E Res Assoc.
Clark, Margaret. Health in the Mexican-American Culture: A Community Study. 2nd ed. 1970. 18.50x (ISBN 0-520-01666-1); pap. 3.85 (ISBN 0-520-01668-8, CAL192). U of Cal Pr.
Cliinchy, Everett R., Jr. Equality of Opportunity for Latin-Americans in Texas. LC 73-14199. (The Mexican American Ser.). 224p. 1974. 16.00x (ISBN 0-405-05673-7). Arno.
Coles, Robert. Eskimos, Chicanos, Indians. (Children of Crisis Ser.: Vol.4). 1978. 15.00 (ISBN 0-316-15162-9, Atlantic-Little, Brown). Little.
Communist Party Twentieth National Convention. La Lucha De los Chicanos Por la Liberacion: La Posicion Del Partido Comunista. 24p. (Span.). 1972. pap. 0.40 (ISBN 0-87898-092-X). New Outlook.
Cooke, Edwin D., Jr. Interpersonal Orientation of Elementary Teachers with Mexican-American Pupils. LC 74-76566. 1975. Repr. of 1967 ed. soft bdg. 9.00 (ISBN 0-88247-352-2). R & E Res Assoc.
Cooper, Elizabeth K. Attitude of Children & Teachers Toward Mexican, Negro & Jewish Minorities. LC 72-86399. pap. 7.00 (ISBN 0-88247-184-8). R & E Res Assoc.
Cortes, Carlos E., ed. Church Views of the Mexican American. LC 73-14198. (The Mexican American Ser.). (Illus.). 58p. 1974. Repr. 38.00x (ISBN 0-405-05672-9). Arno.
--Education & the Mexican American. LC 73-14201. (The Mexican American Ser.). 1974. Repr. 30.00x (ISBN 0-405-05675-3). Arno.
--Juan N. Cortina: Two Interpretations. LC 73-14204. (The Mexican American Ser.). (Illus.). 1974. Repr. 12.00x (ISBN 0-405-05678-8). Arno.
--The Mexican American, 21 vols. 1974. 495.00 set (ISBN 0-405-05670-2). Arno.
--The Mexican American & the Law. LC 73-14207. 1974. Repr. 20.00x (ISBN 0-405-05681-8). Arno.
--Mexican American Bibliographies. LC 73-14421. (The Mexican American Ser.). 1974. Repr. 22.00x (ISBN 0-405-05682-6). Arno.
--Mexican Labor in the United States. LC 73-14208. (The Mexican American Ser.). (Illus.). 480p. 1974. Repr. 26.00x (ISBN 0-405-05683-4). Arno.

--The New Mexican Hispano. LC 73-14210. (The Mexican American Ser.). (Illus.). 510p. 1974. Repr. 30.00x (ISBN 0-405-05684-2). Arno.
Cortes, Carlos E., et al, eds. The Chicano Heritage, 55 vols. 1976. 1359.00x (ISBN 0-405-09480-9). Arno.
Cotera, Martha P. The Chicana Feminist. 68p. 1977. pap. 5.00x (ISBN 0-931738-01-6). Info Systems.
--Diosa y Hembra: History & Heritage of Chicanas in the U.S. 202p. 1976. pap. 5.95x (ISBN 0-931738-00-8). Info Systems.
--Mexican American Directory of Austin, Texas, 1980. Cunningham, Nella, ed. (Orig.). 1979. pap. 9.00x (ISBN 0-931738-05-9). Info Systems.
Coy, Harold. Chicano Roots Go Deep. LC 75-11434. (Illus.). 224p. (gr. 7 up). 1975. 5.95 (ISBN 0-396-07186-4). Dodd.
Crow, John E. Mexican Americans in Contemporary Arizona: A Social & Demographic View. LC 75-1813. 1975. soft bdg 8.00 (ISBN 0-685-64831-1). R & E Res Assoc.
Curtis, Walt. Mala Noche. (Illus.). 1977. pap. 0.60 (ISBN 0-685-79529-2). Out of the Ashes.
Davidson. Chicano Prisoners: The Key to San Quentin. LC 74-8668. (Case Studies in Cultural Anthropology). 1974. pap. text ed. 4.95 (ISBN 0-03-091616-X, HoltC). HR&W.
Davis, James A. Do People Like Me Have Any Control Over Politics? A Study of the Locus of Political Control As Perceived by Mexican-American Adolescents of South Texas. LC 80-65614. 140p. 1981. perfect bdg. 11.50 (ISBN 0-86548-029-X). Century Twenty One.
De Leon, Arnoldo. Apuntes Tejanos: Vol. 1, an Index of Items Related to Mexican-Americans in Nineteenth Century Texas Extracted from the San Antonio Express (1869-1900) & the San Antonio Herald (1855-1878) LC 78-13013. 1978. pap. 18.00 (ISBN 0-8357-0356-8, SS-00071). Univ Microfilms.
--Apuntes Tejanos: Vol. 2, An Index of Items Related to Mexican Americans in Nineteenth Century Texas. LC 78-13013. 1978. pap. 19.75 (ISBN 0-8357-0363-0, SS-00077). Univ Microfilms.
--The Tejano Community, Eighteen Thirty-Six to Nineteen Hundred. (Illus.). 288p. 1981. 19.95x (ISBN 0-8263-0586-5). U of NM Pr.
De Tevis, Rose, et al, eds. El Oro y el Futuro del Pueblo. (Illus.). 155p. 1979. pap. 5.00 (ISBN 0-918358-11-6). Pajarito Pubns.
Dunn, Lynn P. Chicanos: A Study Guide & Source Book. LC 74-31537. 1975. soft bdg 6.00 (ISBN 0-88247-307-7). R & E Res Assoc.
Duran, Livie I. & Bernard, H. Russell. Introduction to Chicano Studies: A Reader. (Illus.). 512p. 1973. pap. text ed. 9.95 (ISBN 0-02-330830-3, 33083). Macmillan.
Elsasser, Nan, et al. Las Mujeres: Conversations from an Hispanic Community. (Women's Lives - Women's Work Ser.). (Illus.). 192p. (gr. 11 up). 1981. 14.95 (ISBN 0-912670-84-3, Co-Pub. by McGraw); pap. 5.95 (ISBN 0-912670-70-3). Feminist Pr.
Emiliano Zapata: Mini Play. (History of Mexico Ser). (gr. 5 up). 1977. 3.00 (ISBN 0-89550-357-3). RIM.
Fernandex, Luis F. A Forgotten American. 56p. 1.50 (ISBN 0-686-74905-7). ADL.
Fincher, E. B. Spanish-Americans As a Political Factor in New Mexico, 1912-1950. LC 73-14202. (The Mexican American Ser.). 332p. 1974. 19.00x (ISBN 0-405-05676-1). Arno.
Foley, Douglas E., et al. From Peones to Politicos: Ethnic Relations in a South Texas Town, 1900-1977. LC 77-93094. (Mexican American Monographs: No. 3). 287p. 1978. pap. 7.50x (ISBN 0-292-72423-3). U of Tex Pr.
Francis, Jessie D. An Economic & Social History of Mexican California (1822-1846) Chiefly Economic, Vol. 1, 2 vols. in 1. Cortes, Carlos E., ed. LC 76-1238. (Chicano Heritage Ser.). 1976. Repr. lib. bdg. 48.00x (ISBN 0-405-09502-3). Arno.
Galarza, Ernesto, et al. Mexican-Americans in the Southwest. LC 77-10039. (Illus.). (gr. 9-12). 1970. pap. text ed. 3.50 (ISBN 0-87461-020-6). McNally.
Garcia, F. Chris. The Chicano Political Experience: Three Perspectives. LC 76-177716. 1977. pap. text ed. 5.95 (ISBN 0-87872-124-X). Duxbury Pr.
Garcia, F. Chris, ed. La Causa Politica: A Chicano Politics Reader. LC 73-22582. 456p. 1974. text ed. 14.95 (ISBN 0-268-00542-7, 85-05422); pap. 6.95 (ISBN 0-268-00543-5, 85-05430). U of Notre Dame Pr.
--Chicano Politics: Readings. LC 72-11569. 225p. 1973. text ed. 24.50x (ISBN 0-8422-5076-X); pap. text ed. 9.50x (ISBN 0-8422-0274-9). Irvington.
Garcia, Richard A. The Chicanos in America, 1540-1974: Chronology & Fact Book. LC 76-42300. 1977. 8.50 (ISBN 0-379-00516-6). Oceana.
--Political Ideology: A Comparative Study of Three Chicano Youth Organizations. LC 76-27003. 1977. soft bdg. 9.00 (ISBN 0-88247-419-7). R & E Res Assoc.
Garcia-Avyens, Francisco. Quien Sabe? A Preliminary List of Chicano Reference Materials. (Bibliography & Reference Ser.: No. 11). 136p. (Orig.). 1981. pap. text ed. 6.00 (ISBN 0-89551-000-6). UCLA Chicano Stud.
Garza, Eugenio D. & Ockerman, Janet D. Adolescent Mexican American Student Attitudes of Self-Concept, Locus of Control & Family Ideology in the Lower Rio Grande Valley of Texas. LC 78-68454. 1979. perfect bdg. 8.00 (ISBN 0-685-94961-3). R & E Res Assoc.
Garza, Roberto J. Contemporary Chicano Theatre. 1975. 16.95x (ISBN 0-268-00709-8); pap. 5.95x (ISBN 0-268-00710-1). U of Notre Dame Pr.
Getty, Harry T. Interethnic Relationships in the Community of Tucson. Cortes, Carlos E., ed. LC 76-1259. (Chicano Heritage Ser.). (Illus.). 1976. 17.00x (ISBN 0-405-09503-1). Arno.
Gonzalez, Calos. An Overview of the Mestizo Heritage: Implications for Teachers of Mexican-American Children. LC 75-38306. 1976. perfect bdg. softcover 8.00 (ISBN 0-88247-379-4). R & E Res Assoc.
Gonzalez, Nancie L. Spanish-Americans of New Mexico: A Heritage of Pride. LC 75-89517. 1969. pap. 5.95 (ISBN 0-8263-0154-1). U of NM Pr.
Grebler, Leo, et al. Mexican American People: The Nation's Second Largest Minority. LC 73-81931. 1970. 30.00 (ISBN 0-02-912800-5). Free Pr.
Griffith, Beatrice. American Me. LC 72-14087. (Illus.). 341p. 1973. Repr. of 1948 ed. lib. bdg. 19.00x (ISBN 0-8371-6756-6, GRAN). Greenwood.
Guzman, Ralph C. The Political Socialization of the Mexican American People. Cortes, Carlos E., ed. LC 76-1264. (Chicano Heritage Ser.). (Illus.). 1976. 17.00x (ISBN 0-405-09504-X). Arno.
Haro, Carlos M. Mexicano-Chicano Concerns & School Desegragation in Los Angeles. (Monograph Ser.: No. 9). (Illus.). 98p. (Orig.). 1979. pap. 4.95 (ISBN 0-89551-012-X). Ucla Chicano Stud.
Heller, Celia S. New Converts to the American Dream? Mobility Aspirations of Young Mexican Americans. 1972. 7.50 (ISBN 0-8084-0038-X); pap. 2.95 (ISBN 0-8084-0039-8, B56). Coll & U Pr.
Henshel, Anne-Marie. The Forgotten Ones: A Sociological Study of Anglo & Chicano Retardates. 285p. 1972. 15.00x (ISBN 0-292-72403-9). U of Tex Pr.
Hernandez, Carrol A., et al. Chicanos: Social & Psychological Perspectives. 2nd ed. LC 75-37769. (Illus.). 376p. 1976. pap. 12.00 (ISBN 0-8016-5316-9). Mosby.
Hernandez-Chavez, Eduardo, et al. El Lenguaje de los Chicanos: Regional & Social Characteristics of Language Used by Mexican-Americans. LC 73-84649. 1975. pap. 8.75x (ISBN 0-87281-033-X). Ctr Appl Ling.
Hill, et al. Aspects of the Mexican American Experience: An Original Anthology. Cortes, Carlos E., ed. & intro. by. LC 76-1473. (Chicano Heritage Ser.). (Illus.). 1976. 37.00x (ISBN 0-405-09534-1). Arno.
Hirsch, Herbert & Gutierrez, Armando. Learning to Be Militant: Ethnic Identity & the Development of Political Militance in a Chicano Community. LC 76-55960. 1977. soft bdg. 10.00 (ISBN 0-88247-438-3). R & E Res Assoc.
Hundley, Norris, Jr., ed. The Chicano: Essays from the Pacific Historical Review. LC 75-2354. 168p. 1975. 21.75 (ISBN 0-87436-212-1); pap. 9.75 (ISBN 0-87436-213-X). ABC-Clio.
Jarratt, et al. The Mexican Experience in Texas: An Original Anthology. Cortes, Carlos, ed. LC 76-7305. (Chicano Heritage Ser.). (Illus.). 1976. lib. bdg. 20.00x (ISBN 0-405-09540-6). Arno.
Johnson, Henry S. & Hernandez-M, William J., eds. Educating the Mexican American. 1971. tanalin 6.95 (ISBN 0-8170-0497-1). Judson.
Jones, Lamar B. Mexican-American Labor Problems in Texas. LC 73-163941. 1972. pap. 7.00 (ISBN 0-88247-150-3). R & E Res Assoc.
Kibbe, Pauline R. Latin Americans in Texas. LC 73-14205. (The Mexican American Ser.). (Illus.). 338p. 1974. Repr. 18.00x (ISBN 0-405-05679-6). Arno.
Lamb, Ruth S. Mexican Americans: Sons of the Southwest. LC 75-99258. (Illus., Orig.). 1970. pap. text ed. 8.95 (ISBN 0-912434-03-1). Ocelot Pr.
Lampe, Philip E. Comparative Study of Assimilation of Mexican-Americans: Parochial Schools Versus Public Schools. LC 75-18128. 1975. soft bdg. 9.00 (ISBN 0-88247-359-X). R & E Res Assoc.
Landolt, Robert G. The Mexican-American Workers of San Antonio, Texas. Cortes, Carlos E., ed. LC 76-1291. (Chicano Heritage Ser.). (Illus.). 1976. 22.00x (ISBN 0-405-09509-0). Arno.
Lane, John H., Jr. Voluntary Associations Among Mexican Americans in San Antonio, Texas: Organizational & Leadership Characteristics. Cortes, Carlos E., ed. LC 76-1292. (Chicano Heritage Ser.). 1976. 13.00x (ISBN 0-405-09510-4). Arno.
Larralde, Carlos. Mexican American Movements & Leaders. LC 76-4705. (Illus.). 229p. 1976. pap. text ed. 5.95 (ISBN 0-89260-026-8). Hwong Pub.
LBJ School of Public Affairs. Health of Mexican - Americans in South Texas. LC 79-88345. (Policy Research Project Report Ser.: No. 32). 1979. 6.00 (ISBN 0-89940-628-9). LBJ Sch Public Affairs.
Lee, Isaiah. Medical Care in a Mexican American Community. LC 76-4706. (Illus.). 186p. 1976. pap. text ed. 5.95 (ISBN 0-89260-024-1). Hwong Pub.
Lindborg, Kristina & Ovando, Carlos J. Five Mexican-American Women in Transition: A Case Study of Migrants in the Midwest. LC 76-56558. 1977. soft bdg. 8.00 (ISBN 0-88247-444-8). R & E Res Assoc.
Lucero-White, et al. Hispano Culture of New Mexico: An Original Anthology. Cortes, Carlos E., ed. & intro. by. LC 76-5929. (Chicano Heritage Ser.). (Illus.). 1976. 15.00x (ISBN 0-405-09537-6). Arno.
Ludwig, Edward W. & Santibanez, James, eds. Chicanos: Mexican American Voices. (Orig.). 1971. pap. 2.95 (ISBN 0-14-021356-2, Pelican). Penguin.
Macias, Reynaldo F., ed. Perspectivas En Chicano Studies. 254p. (Orig.). 1978. pap. 5.00 (ISBN 0-89551-021-9). Ucla Chicano Stud.
Macklin, Barbara J. Structural Stability & Culture Change in a Mexican-American Community. Cortes, Carlos E., ed. LC 76-1249. (Chicano Heritage Ser.). 1976. 17.00x (ISBN 0-405-09513-9). Arno.
McNamara, Patrick. Mexican-Americans in Los Angeles County: A Study in Acculturation. LC 75-167579. 1975. Repr. of 1957 ed. soft bdg. 8.00 (ISBN 0-88247-362-X). R & E Res Assoc.
Madsen, W. Mexican Americans of South Texas. 2nd. ed. LC 73-2824. (Case Studies in Cultural Anthropology). 1973. pap. 4.95 (ISBN 0-03-008431-8, HoltC). HR&W.
Maldonado, Lionel A. & Byrne, David R. The Social Ecology of Chicanos in Utah. LC 78-89. (Social Organization of the Community Ser.). 1978. pap. text ed. 2.95x (ISBN 0-87414-006-4). U of Iowa Pr.
Marin, Christine. A Spokesman of the Mexican American Movement: Rodolfo "Corky" Gonzales & the Fight for Chicano Liberation, 1966-1972. LC 76-24723. 1977. soft bdg. 7.00 (ISBN 0-88247-423-5). R & E Res Assoc.
Martinez, Gilbert T. & Edwards, Jane. The Mexican American. LC 72-2751. 184p. (gr. 7-12). 1973. pap. text ed. 5.10 (ISBN 0-395-14261-X). HM.
Martinez, J. L., Jr., ed. Chicano Psychology. 1978. 12.50 (ISBN 0-12-475650-6). Acad Pr.
Martinez, Julio A., compiled by. Chicano Scholars & Writers: A Bio-Bibliographical Directory. LC 78-32076. 589p. 1979. 29.00 (ISBN 0-8108-1205-3). Scarecrow.
Martinez, Oscar J. The Chicanos of El Paso. (Southwestern Studies: No. 59). 1980. pap. text ed. 3.00 (ISBN 0-87404-118-X). Tex Western.
Meier, Matt S. & Rivera, Feliciano. The Chicanos: A History of Mexican Americans. 1972. pap. 5.95 (ISBN 0-8090-1365-7, AmCen). Hill & Wang.
--Readings on La Raza: The Twentieth Century. 1974. pap. 5.95 (ISBN 0-8090-0110-1, AmCen). Hill & Wang.
Meier, Matt S. & Rivera, Feliciano, eds. Dictionary of Mexican American History. LC 80-24750. (Illus.). 472p. 1981. lib. bdg. 35.00 (ISBN 0-313-21203-1, NMD/). Greenwood.
Melville, Margarita B. Twice a Minority: Mexican-American Woman. LC 80-11177. (Illus.). 1980. pap. text ed. 12.45 (ISBN 0-8016-3386-9). Mosby.
Mirande, Alfredo & Enriquez, Evangelina. La Chicana: The Mexican-American Woman. LC 79-13536. x, 284p. 1981. pap. 6.95 (ISBN 0-226-53160-0). U of Chicago Pr.
--La Chicana: The Mexican-American Woman. LC 79-13536. (Illus.). x, 284p. 1981. pap. 6.95 (ISBN 0-226-53160-0). U of Chicago Pr.
Montaner, Carlos A. El Ojo Del Ciclon. LC 78-67009. (Colleccion De Estudios Hispanicos). 215p. 1979. pap. 4.95 (ISBN 0-89729-212-X). Ediciones.
Montenegro, Marilyn. Chicanos & Mexican-Americans: Ethnic Self-Identification & Attitudinal Differences. LC 75-36558. 1976. perfect bdg. softcover 8.00 (ISBN 0-88247-386-7). R & E Res Assoc.
Moore, Joan, et al. Homeboys: Gangs, Drugs & Prison in the Barrios of Los Angeles. LC 78-11808. (Illus.). 1979. 19.50x (ISBN 0-87722-121-9); pap. 8.95 (ISBN 0-87722-114-6). Temple U Pr.
Moore, Joan W. Mexican Americans. 2nd ed. (Ethnic Groups in American Life Ser.). 208p. 1976. pap. text ed. 8.95x (ISBN 0-13-579508-7). P-H.
Morales, Armando. Ando Sangrando: A Study of Mexican-American Police Conflict. rev. ed. LC 72-78160. (Illus.). 152p. 1973. 7.95x (ISBN 0-913638-00-5, Pub. by Burdick). Intl Schol Bk Serv.
Murguia, Edward. Assimilation, Colonialism & the Mexican American People. (Mexican American Monographs: No. 1). 136p. 1975. pap. 3.25x (ISBN 0-292-77520-2). U of Tex Pr.
Murray, Winifred. A Socio-Cultural Study of 118 Mexican Families Living in a Low-Rent Public Housing Project in San Antonio, Texas. Cortes, Carlos E., ed. LC 76-1275. (Chicano Heritage Ser.). 1976. Repr. of 1954 ed. lib. bdg. 10.00x (ISBN 0-405-09515-5). Arno.
Museum of International Folk Art. Days of Plenty, Days of Want: Spanish Folklife & Art in New Mexico. Cuesta, Benedicto, tr. (Eng. & Span.). 1976. pap. 2.00 (ISBN 0-89013-109-0). Museum NM Pr.
National Secreteriat & Hispanic Teams. Communidades Eclesiales de Base, Experiencia en los Estados Unidos. 160p. 1981. pap. 2.95 (ISBN 0-89243-140-7). Liguori Pubns.
Nava, Julian. Mexican Americans: A Brief Look at Their History. (Illus.). 55p. pap. 0.95 (ISBN 0-686-74906-5). ADL.
--Viva la Raza: Readings on Mexican Americans. 1973. pap. text ed. 4.95x (ISBN 0-442-25918-2). D Van Nostrand.
Nicholl, Larry & Gomez, Miguel. Quality Education for Mexican Americans - Minorities. LC 80-5650. (Si, Se Puede!- Yes, It Can Be Done!). 277p. 1980. pap. text ed. 10.25 (ISBN 0-8191-1245-3). U Pr of Amer.
Nicholl, Worth L. The Rhetoric of Cultural Pluralism Vs. the Drive Toward Total Assimilation: The Mexican American Cultural Component of Federally Funded Bilingual Projects. LC 78-64358. 1978. soft cover 11.00 (ISBN 0-88247-545-2). R & E Res Assoc.
Paredes, Americo, ed. Humanidad: Essays in Honor of George I. Sanchez. (Monograph Ser: No. 6). 1977. pap. 2.50 (ISBN 0-89551-007-3). UCLA Chicano Stud.
Parigi, Sam F. A Case Study of Latin American Unionization in Austin, Texas. Cortes, Carlos E., ed. LC 76-1265. (Chicano Heritage Ser.). 1976. 23.00x (ISBN 0-405-09518-X). Arno.
Penalosa, Fernando. Class Consciousness & Social Mobility in a Mexican-American Community. LC 75-163939. 1972. pap. 7.00 (ISBN 0-88247-155-4). R & E Res Assoc.
Perales, Alonso S. Are We Good Neighbors? LC 73-14213. (The Mexican American Ser.). (Illus.). 298p. 1974. Repr. 16.00x (ISBN 0-405-05687-7). Arno.
Perspectives on Mexican-American Life. LC 73-14214. (The Mexican American Ser.). 1974. Repr. 15.00x (ISBN 0-405-05688-5). Arno.
Pettit, Arthur G. Images of the Mexican American in Fiction & Film. Showalter, Dennis E., ed. LC 79-5284. 312p. 1980. 19.50 (ISBN 0-89096-095-X); pap. 9.95 (ISBN 0-89096-115-8). Tex A&M Univ Pr.
Poggie, John J., Jr. Between Two Cultures: The Life of an American-Mexican. LC 72-84765. 1973. pap. 2.65x (ISBN 0-8165-0334-6). U of Ariz Pr.
Quintanilla, Guadalupe C. & Silman, James B. El Espiritu Siempre Eterno Del Mexico Americano. 1977. pap. text ed. 8.25 (ISBN 0-8191-0121-4). U Pr of Amer.
Ragan, Pauline K. & Simonin, Mary, eds. Black & Mexican American Aging. (Technical Bibliographies on Aging Ser: No. 2). 1977. 2.25 (ISBN 0-88474-077-3). USC Andrus Geron.
Ramirez, Manuel, 3rd & Castandea, Alfredo. Cultural Democracy, Biocognitive Development & Education. 1974. 17.50 (ISBN 0-12-577250-5). Acad Pr.
Reilly, Robert P. A Selected & Annotated Bibliography of Bicultural Classroom Materials for Mexican American Studies. LC 77-81027. 1977. soft bdg. 6.00 (ISBN 0-88247-484-7). R & E Res Assoc.
Revolutionary Communist Party, USA. The Chicano Struggle & the Struggle for Socialism. 2nd ed. (Illus.). 1979. pap. 1.50 (ISBN 0-89851-003-1). RCP Pubns.
Reyes, Ignacio. A Survey of the Problems Involved in the Americanization of the Mexican-American. LC 72-86401. pap. 7.00 (ISBN 0-88247-199-6). R & E Res Assoc.
Rivas, Gilberto L. The Chicanos: Life & Struggles of the Mexican Minority in the United States, with Readings. Martinez, Elizabeth, ed. LC 73-8056. 224p. (Bilingual). 1974. pap. 4.95 (ISBN 0-85345-329-2, PB3292). Monthly Rev.

Robinson, Barbara J. & Robinson, J. Cordell. The Mexican American: A Critical Guide to Research Aids, Vol. 1. Stueart, Robert D., ed. LC 76-5643. (Foundations in Library & Information Science Ser). 1980. lib. bdg. 39.50 (ISBN 0-89232-006-0). Jai Pr.

Rodriguez, Olga, ed. The Politics of Chicano Liberation. 1977. 12.00 (ISBN 0-87348-513-0); pap. 3.45 (ISBN 0-87348-514-9). Path Pr NY.

Rodriguez, Roy D. Mexican-American Civic Organizations: Political Participation & Political Attitudes. LC 77-91420. 1978. pap. 9.00 perfect bdg. (ISBN 0-88247-518-5). R & E Res Assoc.

Rosaldo, R., et al. Chicano: The Evolution of a People. rev. ed. LC 76-46344. 478p. 1981. pap. text ed. write for info. (ISBN 0-88275-467-X). Krieger.

Rose, Linda C. Disease Beliefs in Mexican-American Communities. LC 77-90359. 1978. pap. 8.00 perfect bdg. (ISBN 0-88247-519-3). R & E Res Assoc.

Rosenbaum, Robert J. Mexicano Resistance in the Southwest: "The Sacred Right of Self-Preservation". (Illus.). 253p. 1981. text ed. 14.95x (ISBN 0-292-77562-8). U of Tex Pr.

Rosenbaumn, Robert J. Mexicano Resistance in the Southwest: The Sacred Right of Self-Preservation. (Illus.). 253p. 1981. 14.95x (ISBN 0-292-77562-8). U of Tex Pr.

Ross, Stanley R., ed. Views Across the Border: the United States & Mexico. LC 76-57533. 1978. pap. 10.00x (ISBN 0-8263-0445-1). U of NM Pr.

Ross, Stanley R. & Chaffee, Wilber A., eds. Guide to the Hispanic American Historical Review: 1956-1975. LC 58-8501. 1980. 32.75 (ISBN 0-8223-0429-5). Duke.

Rubel, Arthur J. Across the Tracks: Mexican-Americans in a Texas City. (Hogg Foundation Research Series). (Illus.). 294p. 1966. 12.50x (ISBN 0-292-73604-5). U of Tex Pr.

Ruiz, David V. A Soul in Exile: A Chicano Lost in Occupied Land. 83p. 1981. 6.95 (ISBN 0-533-04720-X). Vantage.

Samora, Julian & Simon, Patricia V. A History of the Mexican-American People. LC 75-19877. (Illus.). 240p. 1977. text ed. 9.95x (ISBN 0-268-00545-1); pap. 5.95x (ISBN 0-268-00546-X). U of Notre Dame Pr.

Sanchez, George I. Materials Relating to the Education of Spanish-Speaking People in the United States. LC 78-149485. Repr. of 1959 ed. lib. bdg. 15.00x (ISBN 0-8371-6012-X, TLSE). Greenwood.

Sanchez, Rosaura & Cruz, Rosa M., eds. Essays on la Mujer. (Anthology Ser.: No. 1). 200p. (Orig.). 1977. pap. 6.35 (ISBN 0-89551-020-0). Ucla Chicano Stud.

Sandoval, Ruben & Strick, David. Games, Games, Games, Juegos, Juegos, Juegos: Chicano Children at Play--Games & Rhymes. (gr. 1 up). 1977. PLB 6.95 (ISBN 0-385-05438-6). Doubleday.

Saucedo, Ramedo J., compiled by. Mexican Americans in Minnesota: An Introduction to Historical Sources. LC 77-28125. 26p. 1977. pap. 2.00 (ISBN 0-87351-124-7). Minn Hist.

Servin, Manuel P. Mexican Americans. 2nd ed. LC 73-8357. Orig. Title: An Awakened Minority. 320p. 1974. pap. text ed. 7.95x (ISBN 0-02-477940-7, 47794). Macmillan.

Shelton, Edgar G., Jr. Political Conditions Among Texas Mexicans Along the Rio Grande: Thesis. LC 73-78053. 1974. soft bdg. 8.00 (ISBN 0-88247-247-X). R & E Res Assoc.

Shockley, John S. Chicano Revolt in a Texas Town. LC 73-11565. 352p. 1974. text ed. 9.95 (ISBN 0-268-00502-8); pap. text ed. 4.95x (ISBN 0-268-00500-1). U of Notre Dame Pr.

Simmen, Edward, ed. Pain & Promise: The Chicano Today. 1972. pap. 1.50 (ISBN 0-451-61507-7, MW1507, Ment). NAL.

Simmen, Edward, et al. A Comprehensive Chicano Bibliography, 1960-1972. Simmen, Edward, ed. LC 73-81559. 1973. 12.95 (ISBN 0-8363-0114-5). Jenkins.

Simmons, Ozzie G. Anglo-Americans & Mexican Americans in South Texas. LC 73-14215. (The Mexican American Ser.). (Illus.). 592p. 1974. 37.00x (ISBN 0-405-05689-3). Arno.

Steiner, Stan. La Raza: The Mexican-Americans. 1970. pap. 7.95x (ISBN 0-06-131949-X, TB1949, Torch). Har-Row.

Sunseri, Alvin. Seeds of Discord: New Mexico in the Aftermath of the American Conquest, 1846-1861. LC 78-24315. 1979. 16.95x (ISBN 0-88229-141-6). Nelson-Hall.

Takesian, Sarkis A. A Comparative Study of the Mexican-American Graduate & Dropout. LC 74-163936. 1972. pap. 7.00 (ISBN 0-88247-156-2). R & E Res Assoc.

Tatum, Charles M. A Selected & Annotated Bibliography of Chicano Studies. 2nd ed. LC 79-64044. 1979. pap. 12.00 (ISBN 0-89295-011-0). Society Sp & Sp-Am.

Teller, Charles H., et al, eds. Cuantos Somos: A Demographic Survey of the Mexican-American Population. (Mexican-American Monograph: No. 2). 254p. 1977. pap. 5.95x (ISBN 0-292-71045-3). U of Tex Pr.

Thurston, Richard G. Urbanization & Sociocultural Change in a Mexican-American Enclave. LC 73-82410. 1974. soft bdg. 9.00 (ISBN 0-88247-235-6). R & E Res Assoc.

Tijerina, Andres A. History of Mexican Americans in Lubbock County, Texas. (Graduate Studies: No. 18). 1979. 5.00 (ISBN 0-89672-067-5). Tex Tech Pr.

Tireman, L. S. Teaching Spanish-Speaking Children: Chicano Heritage Ser. Cortes, Carlos E., ed. LC 76-1591. 1976. Repr. of 1948 ed. 12.00x (ISBN 0-405-09526-0). Arno.

Trejo, Arnulfo D., ed. Bibliografia Chicana: A Guide to Information Sources. LC 74-11562. (Ethnic Studies Information Guide: Vol. 1). 240p. 1975. 36.00 (ISBN 0-8103-1311-1). Gale.

--The Chicanos: As We See Ourselves. 1979. pap. 7.50 (ISBN 0-8165-0625-6). U of Ariz Pr.

Tuck, Ruth D. Not with the Fist: Mexican-Americans in a Southwest City. LC 73-14218. (The Mexican American Ser.). 256p. 1974. Repr. 16.00x (ISBN 0-405-05691-5). Arno.

Tyler, Gus, ed. Mexican Americans Tomorrow: Educational & Economic Perspectives. LC 75-2533. 208p. (Orig.). 1975. pap. 4.95x (ISBN 0-8263-0375-7). U of NM Pr.

U. S. Commission on Civil Rights. Mexican American Education Study, 5 vols. in one. Cordasco, Francesco, ed. LC 77-90561. (Bilingual-Bicultural Education in the U. S. Ser.). 1978. Repr. of 1973 ed. lib. bdg. 28.00x (ISBN 0-405-11100-2). Arno.

Urbanski, Edmund S. Hispanic America & Its Civilizations: Spanish Americans & Anglo-Americans. Hendricks, Frances K. & Berler, Beatrice, trs. from Span. LC 77-9116. (Illus.). 1979. 15.95 (ISBN 0-8061-1431-2). U of Okla Pr.

Valencia, Atilano A. Descendants of el Siglo De Oro y Aztlan. LC 77-81029. 1977. soft bdg. 8.00 (ISBN 0-88247-486-3). R & E Res Assoc.

Vasquez, Librado K. & Vasquez, Maria E. Regional Dictionary of Chicano Slang. 111p. 1975. 13.50 (ISBN 0-8363-0083-1). Jenkins.

Vigil, Maurilio. Chicano Politics. 1977. pap. text ed. 10.75 (ISBN 0-8191-0110-9). U Pr of Amer.

Villarreal, Roberto E. Chicano Elites & Non-Elites: An Inquiry into Social & Political Change. LC 79-65247. 125p. 1979. perfect bdg. 12.00 (ISBN 0-88247-590-8). R & E Res Assoc.

Weber, David J., ed. Foreigners in Their Native Land: Historical Roots of the Mexican Americans. LC 73-77858. 1979. pap. 8.95x (ISBN 0-8263-0279-3). U of NM Pr.

Weigle, Marta. Hispanic Villages of Northern New Mexico. LC 73-89795. 1975. 18.00 (ISBN 0-89016-030-9); pap. 10.00 (ISBN 0-89016-031-7); pap. 3.00 bibliography (ISBN 0-89016-032-5). Lightning Tree.

Weiner, Sandra. Small Hands, Big Hands: Seven Stories of Mexican-American Migrant Workers & Their Families. LC 75-122925. (Illus.). (gr. 5 up). 1970. PLB 5.99 (ISBN 0-394-90442-7). Pantheon.

Wells, Gladys. Factors Influencing the Assimilation of the Mexican in Texas: Thesis. LC 73-82405. 1974. Repr. of 1941 ed. soft bdg. 7.00 (ISBN 0-88247-295-X). R & E Res Assoc.

West, Stanley A. The Mexican Aztec Society: A Mexican American Voluntary Association in Diachronic Perspective. Cortes, Carlos E., ed. LC 76-5230. (Chicano Heritage Ser.). 1976. 20.00x (ISBN 0-405-09532-5). Arno.

West, Stanley A. & Macklin, June. The Chicano Experience. (Special Studies in Contemporary Social Issues). 1979. lib. bdg. 27.75x (ISBN 0-89158-489-7). Westview.

Wolf, Bernard. In This Proud Land: The Story of a Mexican American Family. LC 78-9680. (Illus.). (gr. 3-6). 1979. 8.95 (ISBN 0-397-31815-4). Lippincott.

Woods, Frances J. Mexican Ethnic Leadership in San Antonio, Texas. Cortes, Carlos E., ed. LC 76-1623. (Chicano Heritage Ser.). 1976. Repr. of 1949 ed. 10.00x (ISBN 0-405-09533-3). Arno.

Woods, Richard D. Reference Materials on Mexican Americans: An Annotated Bibliography. LC 76-10663. 197p. 1976. 10.00 (ISBN 0-8108-0963-X). Scarecrow.

Ynigo, Alexander. Mexican-American Children in an Integrated Elementary School: Thesis. LC 74-77163. 1974. soft bdg. 7.00 (ISBN 0-88247-267-4). R & E Res Assoc.

Zeleny, Carolyn. Relations Between the Spanish-Americans & Anglo-Americans in New Mexico. LC 73-14219. (The Mexican American Ser.). (Illus.). 370p. 1974. 21.00x (ISBN 0-405-05692-3). Arno.

MEXICAN ART

see Art, Mexican

MEXICAN BALLADS AND SONGS

see also Folk-Songs, Mexican

Simmons, M. E. Mexican Corrido As a Source for Interpretive Study of Modern Mexico, 1870-1950. 1957. 31.00 (ISBN 0-527-83100-X). Kraus Repr.

MEXICAN CALENDAR

see Calendar, Mexican

MEXICAN DRAMA

Monterde Garcia Icazbalceta, Francisco. Bibliografia Del Teatro En Mexico. LC 72-132684. (Monografias Bibliograficas Mexicanas: No. 28). (Illus., Span). 1970. Repr. of 1934 ed. 43.00 (ISBN 0-8337-2440-1). B Franklin.

Niggli, Josephina. Mexican Folk Plays. Koch, Frederick H., ed. LC 76-1260. (Chicano Heritage Ser.). (Illus.). 1976. Repr. of 1938 ed. 15.00x (ISBN 0-405-09517-1). Arno.

Ravicz, Marilyn E. Early Colonial Religious Drama in Mexico. 1970. 11.95 (ISBN 0-8132-0495-X). Cath U Pr.

Trifilo, S. Samuel. Maximilian & Carlota in Mexican Drama. LC 80-12251. (Center Essay Ser.: No. 8). 1980. pap. 5.00 (ISBN 0-930450-14-0). Univ of Wis Latin Am.

Usigli, Rodolfo. Mexico in the Theater. Scott, Wilder P., tr. LC 75-38748. (Romance Monographs: No. 18). 1976. 20.00x (ISBN 84-399-4744-5). Romance.

MEXICAN DRAWINGS

see Drawings, Mexican

MEXICAN FICTION (COLLECTIONS)

see also Short Stories, Mexican

MEXICAN FICTION–BIOBIBLIOGRAPHY

Iguiniz, Juan B. Bibliografia De Novelistas Mexicanos: Ensayo Biografico, Bibliografico y Critico. (Bibliography & Reference Ser.: No. 397). 1971. Repr. of 1926 ed. lib. bdg. 30.50 (ISBN 0-8337-1799-5). B Franklin.

MEXICAN FICTION–HISTORY AND CRITICISM

Brodman, Barbara. The Mexican Cult of Death in Myth & Literature. LC 76-26105. (U of Fla. Humanities Monpgraphs: No. 44). 1976. pap. 4.00 (ISBN 0-8130-0556-6). U Presses Fla.

Langford, Walter M. The Mexican Novel Comes of Age. LC 77-160486. 239p. 1971. 8.95x (ISBN 0-268-00450-1); pap. 3.95 (ISBN 0-268-00483-8). U of Notre Dame Pr.

Larson, Ross. Fantasy & Imagination in the Mexican Narrative. LC 77-3019. 1977. pap. 8.50x (ISBN 0-87918-032-3). ASU Lat Am St.

Read, J. Lloyd. The Mexican Historical Novel,1826-1910. LC 72-85005. iii, 337p. 1973. Repr. of 1939 ed. 18.00 (ISBN 0-8462-1688-4). Russell.

Rosser, Harry L. Conflict & Transition in Rural Mexico: The Fiction of Social Realism. 174p. 1980. write for info. (ISBN 0-918456-30-4, Crossroads). African Studies Assn.

Sommers, Joseph. After the Storm: Landmarks of the Modern Mexican Novel. LC 68-23019. 1968. 5.95x (ISBN 0-8263-0098-7); pap. 3.45x (ISBN 0-8263-0232-7). U of NM Pr.

Veitch, Douglas W. Lawrence, Greene & Lowry: The Fictional Landscape of Mexico. 193p. 1978. text ed. 11.00 (ISBN 0-88920-060-2, Pub. by Laurier U Pr Canada); pap. 7.00 (ISBN 0-88920-069-6). Humanities.

MEXICAN FOLK-LORE

see Folk-Lore, Mexican

MEXICAN FOLK-SONGS

see Folk-Songs, Mexican

MEXICAN LANGUAGE

see Aztec Language

MEXICAN LEGENDS

see Legends, Mexican

MEXICAN LITERATURE

Coleman, L. F. Aspects of Indian Civilization As Revealed in Representative Mexican Novels. 59.95 (ISBN 0-87968-670-7). Gordon Pr.

De Dwyer. Chicano Voices. Adams, ed. (Multi-Ethnic Literature Ser.). (gr. 9-12). 1975. pap. text ed. 4.64 (ISBN 0-395-20579-4); instrs'. manual 3.96 (ISBN 0-395-20578-6). HM.

Flores Magon, Ricardo. Ricardo Flores Magon: Writings, 5 vols. 1979. Set. lib. bdg. 500.00 (ISBN 0-8490-2999-6). Gordon Pr.

Paredes, Americo. Mexican-American Authors. Adams, William, ed. (Multi-Ethnic Literature Ser.). (gr. 9-12). 1976. pap. text ed. 4.84 (ISBN 0-395-24041-7); inst. guide 5.28 (ISBN 0-395-24042-5). HM.

Steiner, Stan & Valdez, Luis, eds. Aztlan: An Anthology of Mexican-American Literature. 416p. Date not set. pap. 3.45 (ISBN 0-394-71770-8, Vin). Random.

MEXICAN LITERATURE–BIBLIOGRAPHY

California State Library Sutro Branch San Francisco. Catalogue of Mexican Pamphlets in the Sutro Collection 1623-1888. Radin, P. & Gans, A. I., eds. 1939-1941. 90.00 (ISBN 0-527-14400-2). Kraus Repr.

Flores, Joseph A., ed. Songs & Dreams. new ed. LC 72-80724. 137p. (Orig.). (gr. 7-12). 1972. pap. 1.75 (ISBN 0-88301-058-5). Pendulum Pr.

Iguiniz, Juan B. Bibliografia De Novelistas Mexicanos: Ensayo Biografico, Bibliografico y Critico. (Bibliography & Reference Ser.: No. 397). 1971. Repr. of 1926 ed. lib. bdg. 30.50 (ISBN 0-8337-1799-5). B Franklin.

Maciel, David R. Mexico: Selected Bibliography of Sources for Chicano Studies. (Bibliographic & Reference Ser: No. 8). 1975. pap. 1.00x (ISBN 0-89551-008-1). UCLA Chicano Stud.

Rutherford, John. An Annotated Bibliography of the Novels of the Mexican Revolution of 1910-1917. Rutherford, John, tr. LC 73-150334. 180p. (Span. & Eng.). 1972. 10.00x (ISBN 0-87875-015-0). Whitston Pub.

MEXICAN LITERATURE–HISTORY AND CRITICISM

Brushwood, John S. Mexico in Its Novel: A Nation's Search for Identity. LC 65-27534. (Texas Pan American Ser.). 306p. 1966. 12.50x (ISBN 0-292-73608-8); pap. 5.95x (ISBN 0-292-70070-9). U of Tex Pr.

Deck, Allan. Francisco Javier Alagre: A Study in Mexican Literary Criticism. 1976. pap. 9.00 (ISBN 0-8294-0337-X). Jesuit Hist.

Gonzalez Pena, Carlos. History of Mexican Literature. 3rd ed. Nance, Gusta B. & Dunstan, Florence J., trs. LC 68-24078. (Mustang Bks: No. 2). 1968. 10.00 (ISBN 0-87074-063-6); pap. 3.45 (ISBN 0-87074-064-4, MB2). SMU Press.

Grimes, Larry M. El Tabu Linguistico en Mexico: El Lenguaje erotico de los mexicanos. LC 78-52419. 1978. lib. bdg. 9.95x (ISBN 0-916950-10-7); pap. 6.95x (ISBN 0-916950-09-3). Bilingual Pr.

Harmon, Mary. Efren Hernandez: A Poet Discovered. LC 72-76854. 128p. 1972. pap. 1.00 (ISBN 0-87805-012-4). U Pr of Miss.

Langford, Walter M. The Mexican Novel Comes of Age. LC 77-160486. 1971. text ed. 18.95x (ISBN 0-268-00450-1). Irvington.

Leeder, Ellen L. Justo Sierra Y el Mar. LC 78-58669. (Coleccion Polymita Ser.). 83p. (Orig., Span.). 1979. pap. 6.95 (ISBN 0-89729-202-2). Ediciones.

Porras-Cruz, Jorge L. Vida y Obra De Luis G. Inclan. LC 76-1829. (Coleccion Mente y Palabra). 148p. (Orig., Span.). 1976. 6.00 (ISBN 0-8477-0536-6); pap. 5.00 (ISBN 0-8477-0537-4). U of PR Pr.

Renaldi, Thomas W. The Two Versions of Mariano Azuela's "Los De Abajo". A Comparative Study. 1978. lib. bdg. 69.95 (ISBN 0-8490-1396-8). Gordon Pr.

Schon, Isabel. Mexico & Its Literature for Children & Adolescents Special Studies No. 15. LC 77-4453. 1977. pap. text ed. 3.50x (ISBN 0-87918-033-1). ASU Lat Am St.

Starr, Frederick. Reading from Modern Mexican Authors. 1976. lib. bdg. 50.00 (ISBN 0-8490-0929-4). Gordon Pr.

MEXICAN LITERATURE–TRANSLATIONS FROM ENGLISH–BIBLIOGRAPHY

Cranfill, Thomas M., ed. The Muse in Mexico: A Mid-Century Miscellany. (Illus.). 182p. 1959. 10.00 (ISBN 0-292-73310-0). U of Tex Pr.

MEXICAN NATIONAL CHARACTERISTICS

see National Characteristics, Mexican

MEXICAN PAINTING

see Painting, Mexican

MEXICAN PAINTINGS

see Paintings, Mexican

MEXICAN POETRY (COLLECTIONS)

Goldberg, Isaac, ed. Mexican Poetry: An Anthology. 1977. lib. bdg. 59.95 (ISBN 0-8490-2238-X). Gordon Pr.

Green, Ernest S., ed. & tr. Mexican & South American Poems. 400p. 1974. lib. bdg. 75.00 (ISBN 0-8490-0612-0). Gordon Pr.

Nicholson, Irene. A Guide to Mexican Poetry. 96p. 1968. pap. 4.00 (ISBN 0-912434-13-9). Ocelot Pr.

Scheer, Linda & Ramirez, Miguel, eds. Anthology of Mexican Modern Poetry. 170p. 1981. 13.50 (ISBN 0-931556-06-6); pap. 4.50 (ISBN 0-931556-07-4). Translation Pr.

Underwood, Edna. Anthology of Mexican Poets. 1932. lib. bdg. 25.00 (ISBN 0-8414-8853-3). Folcroft.

Underwood, Edna W. Anthology of Mexican Poets: from the Earliest Times to the Present Day. 1979. Repr. of 1932 ed. lib. bdg. 45.00 (ISBN 0-8495-5402-0). Arden Lib.

Underwood, Edna W., ed. Anthology of Mexican Poets: From the Earliest Times to the Present Day. 1977. lib. bdg. 59.95 (ISBN 0-8490-1435-2). Gordon Pr.

MEXICAN POETRY–HISTORY AND CRITICISM

Harvey, Maria L. Cielo y Tierra En la Poesia Lirica De Manuel Alto la Guirre. LC 76-182235. 128p. (Span.). 1972. pap. text ed. 2.95x (ISBN 0-87805-007-8). U Pr of Miss.

Montross, Constance M. Virtue or Vice? Sor Juana's Use of Thomistic Thought. LC 80-6303. 136p. (Orig.). 1981. lib. bdg. 16.75 (ISBN 0-8191-1767-6); pap. text ed. 6.75 (ISBN 0-8191-1730-7). U Pr of Amer.

Perez, Maria E. Lo Americano En el Teatro De Sor Juana Ines De la Cruz. 1975. 14.00 (ISBN 0-88303-020-9); pap. 11.00 (ISBN 0-685-73221-5). E Torres & Sons.
Wogan, D. S. The Indian in Mexican Poetry. 59.95 (ISBN 0-8490-0398-9). Gordon Pr.

MEXICAN SCULPTURE
see Sculpture–Mexico

MEXICAN TALES
see Tales, Mexican

MEXICAN WAR, 1845-1848
see United States–History–War with Mexico, 1845-1848

MEXICANS IN THE UNITED STATES
see also Mexican Americans

Andersson, Theodore & Boyer, Mildred. Bilingual Schooling in the United States, 2 vols. LC 76-5907. 1976. Repr. of 1970 ed. 42.50 set (ISBN 0-87917-050-6). Blaine Ethridge.
Arnold, Charles A. Folklore, Manners & Customs of the Mexicans in San Antonio, Texas. LC 71-166049. 1970. pap. 7.00 (ISBN 0-88247-141-4). R & E Res Assoc.
Bogardus, Emory S. Mexican in the United States. LC 70-129389. (American Immigration Collection, Ser. 2). 1970. Repr. of 1934 ed. 8.00 (ISBN 0-405-00575-X). Arno.
Braddy, Haldeen. Mexico & the Old Southwest: People, Palaver, & Places. LC 71-141307. 1971. 12.50 (ISBN 0-8046-9001-4, Natl U); pap. 4.95 (ISBN 0-8046-9046-4). Kennikat.
Briggs, Vernon M., Jr. Mexican Migration & the U.S. Labor Market: A Mounting Issue for the Seventies. (Studies in Human Resource Development: No. 3). 37p. 1975. 4.00 (ISBN 0-87755-214-2). U of Tex Busn Res.
Cardoso, Lawrence. Mexican Emigration to the United States, Eighteen Ninety-Seven to Nineteen Thirty-One. 1980. pap. text ed. 8.95x (ISBN 0-8165-0659-0). U of Ariz Pr.
Committee for the Development of Subject Access to Chicano Literature. A Cumulative Index to Selected Chicano Periodicals Published Between 1967 and 1978. (Library Catalogs). 1981. lib. bdg. 60.00 (ISBN 0-8161-0363-1). G K Hall.
Copp, Nelson C. Wetbacks & Braceros. LC 78-163945. 1972. pap. 7.00 (ISBN 0-88247-144-9). R & E Res Assoc.
Corwin, Arthur F., ed. Immigrants--& Immigrants: Perspectives on Mexican Labor Migration to the United States. LC 77-84756. (Contributions in Economics & Economic History: No. 17). (Illus.). 1978. lib. bdg. 18.95x (ISBN 0-8371-9848-8, CII/). Greenwood.
Davidson, John. The Long Road North. 160p. (Orig.). 1981. pap. 5.95 (ISBN 0-932012-15-9). Texas Month Pr.
Ehrlich, Paul R., et al. The Golden Door: International Migration, Mexico, & the United States. 1981. 7.95 (ISBN 0-686-72118-7). Wideview Bks.
Flores, Raymond J. The Socio-Economic Status Trends of the Mexican People Residing in Arizona. pap. 8.00 (ISBN 0-685-40366-1). R & E Res Assoc.
Galarza, Ernesto. Barrio Boy. 1971. pap. 4.95x (ISBN 0-268-00441-2). U of Notre Dame Pr.
Gamio, Manuel. The Life Story of the Mexican Immigrant. 1972. pap. 3.50 (ISBN 0-486-22722-7). Dover.
--Mexican Immigrant: His Life Story. LC 69-18778. (American Immigration Collection Ser., No. 1). (Illus.). 1969. Repr. of 1931 ed. 8.50 (ISBN 0-405-00526-1). Arno.
--Mexican Immigration to the United States. LC 73-144233. 1971. pap. 3.00 (ISBN 0-486-22721-9). Dover.
--Mexican Immigration to the United States. LC 69-18777. (American Immigration Collection Ser., No. 1). (Illus.). 1969. Repr. of 1930 ed. 13.00 (ISBN 0-405-00525-3). Arno.
Garcia, Juan R. Operation Wetback: The Mass Deportation of Mexican Undocumented Workers in 1954. LC 79-6189. (Contributions in Ethnic Studies: No. 2). (Illus.). xvii, 268p. 1980. lib. bdg. 25.00 (ISBN 0-313-21353-4, GOW/). Greenwood.
Gerking, Shelby D. & Mutti, John H. Illegal Immigration: Economic Consequences for the United States. (A Westview Special Study Ser.). 130p. 1981. lib. bdg. 14.00 (ISBN 0-686-73325-8). Westview.
Hansen, Niles. The Border Economy: Regional Development in the Southwest. (Illus.). 237p. 1981. text ed. 17.95x (ISBN 0-292-75061-7); pap. text ed. 8.95x (ISBN 0-292-75063-3). U of Tex Pr.
Henderson, Peter V. Mexican Exiles in the Borderlands, Nineteen Ten to Thirteen. (Southwestern Studies: No. 58). 1979. pap. text ed. 3.00 (ISBN 0-87404-115-5). Tex Western.
Johnson, Kenneth F. & Ogle, Nina M. Illegal Mexican Aliens in the United States: A Teaching Manual on Impact Dimensions & Alternative Futures. LC 78-62177. 1978. pap. text ed. 9.25 (ISBN 0-8191-0575-9). U Pr of Amer.
Kirstein, Peter N. Anglo Over Bracero: A History of the Mexican Worker in the United States from Roosevelt to Nixon. LC 76-56554. 1977. soft bdg. 9.00 (ISBN 0-88247-442-1). R & E Res Assoc.
Kiser, George C. & Kiser, Martha W., eds. Mexican Workers in the United States: Historical & Political Perspectives. LC 78-55710. 1979. pap. 7.50x (ISBN 0-8263-0489-3). U of NM Pr.
Linn, George B. A Study of Several Linguistic Functions of Mexican-American Children in a Two Language Environment. LC 70-163940. pap. 7.00 (ISBN 0-88247-152-X). R & E Res Assoc.
Lopez Y Rivas, Gilberto. Conquest & Resistance: The Origins of the Chicano National Minority. LC 78-68451. 1979. perfect bdg. 9.00 (ISBN 0-88247-567-3). R & E Res Assoc.
McWilliams, Carey. Mexicans in America. LC 68-9182. 1968. pap. 2.95 (ISBN 0-8077-1794-0). Tchrs Coll.
--North from Mexico, the Spanish Speaking People of the United States. LC 68-28595. lib. bdg. 15.50x (ISBN 0-8371-0180-8, MCNM); pap. 4.95 (ISBN 0-8371-7352-3). Greenwood.
Marcoux, Fred W. Handicaps of Bi-Lingual Mexican Children. LC 73-78061. pap. 8.00 (ISBN 0-88247-229-1). R & E Res Assoc.
Martinez, John R. Mexican Immigration to the U. S. Thesis. 1957. 9.00 (ISBN 0-685-40328-9). R & E Res Assoc.
Martinez, Ruth L. The Unusual Mexican: A Study in Acculturation. LC 70-167580. pap. 7.00 (ISBN 0-88247-214-3). R & E Res Assoc.
Meguire, K. H. Educating the Mexican Child in the Elementary School. LC 73-78056. pap. 8.00 (ISBN 0-88247-231-3). R & E Res Assoc.
Mora, Magdalena & Del Castillo, Adelaida, eds. Mexican Women in the United States: Struggles Past & Present. LC 80-10682. (Occasional Papers Ser.: No. 2). (Illus.). 214p. (Orig.). 1980. pap. 12.95 (ISBN 0-89551-022-7). UCLA Chicano Stud.
Morefield, Richard H. The Mexican Adaptation in American California, 1846-1875: Thesis. 1971. Repr. of 1955 ed. 8.00 (ISBN 0-685-40330-0). R & E Res Assoc.
Morin, Raul. Among the Valiant. 7.95 (ISBN 0-685-07194-4). Borden.
Nelson, Eugene. Pablo Cruz & the American Dream: The Experiences of an Undocumented Immigrant from Mexico. LC 74-19157. (Illus.). 1977. text ed. 3.95 (ISBN 0-268-01525-2). U of Notre Dame Pr.
Park, Joseph F. Mexican Labor in Arizona During the Territorial Period. Date not set. price not set (ISBN 0-8165-0371-0). U of Ariz Pr.
Peterson, Richard H. Manifest Destiny in the Mines: A Cultural Interpretation of Anti-Mexican Nativism in California, 1848-1853. LC 75-5334. 1975. soft bdg. 9.00 (ISBN 0-88247-365-4). R & E Res Assoc.
Pinchot, Jane. Mexicans in America. rev. ed. (In America Bks.). (Illus.). 104p. (gr. 5-11). PLB 6.95g (ISBN 0-686-69989-0). Lerner Pubns.
Raat, W. Dirk. Revoltosos: Mexico's Rebels in the United States, 1903-1923. LC 80-6109. (Illus.). 368p. 1981. 22.50 (ISBN 0-89096-114-X). Tex A&M Univ Pr.
Roberts, Kenneth, et al. The Mexican Migration Numbers Game: An Analysis of the Lesko Estimate of Undocumented Migration from Mexico to the United States. (Research Report Ser.: 1978-1). 33p. 1978. pap. 4.00 (ISBN 0-87755-228-2). U of Tex Busn Res.
Rodriguez, Richard. Hunger of Memory: The Education of Richard Rodriguez. LC 81-81810. 160p. 1981. 13.95 (ISBN 0-87923-418-0). Godine.
Smith, Michael M. The Mexicans in Oklahoma. LC 79-6716. (Newcomers to a New Land Ser.: Vol. 8). (Illus.). 96p. (Orig.). 1980. pap. 3.95 (ISBN 0-8061-1631-5). U of Okla Pr.
Starr, Bill. Border Angel. 1979. 5.95 (ISBN 0-533-03670-4). Vantage.
Taylor, Paul S. Mexican Labor in the United States, 3 Vols. Repr. of 1934 ed. Set. pap. 61.00 (ISBN 0-384-59626-6). Johnson Repr.
Tireman, L. S. Teaching Spanish-Speaking Children: Chicano Heritage Ser. Cortes, Carlos E., ed. LC 76-1591. 1976. Repr. of 1948 ed. 12.00x (ISBN 0-405-09526-0). Arno.
Toney, William T. A Descriptive Study of the Control of Illegal Mexican Migration in the Southwestern U.S. LC 77-75739. 1977. 8.00 (ISBN 0-88247-465-0). R & E Res Assoc.
Urbanski, Edmund S. Hispanic America & Its Civilizations: Spanish Americans & Anglo-Americans. Hendricks, Frances K. & Berler, Beatrice, trs. from Span. LC 77-9116. (Illus.). 1979. 15.95 (ISBN 0-8061-1431-2). U of Okla Pr.
Weintraub, Sidney & Ross, Stanley R. The Illegal Alien from Mexico: Policy Choices for an Intractable Issue. 75p. 1980. pap. 3.95x (ISBN 0-292-73822-6). U of Tex Pr.
Wells, Gladys. Factors Influencing the Assimilation of the Mexican in Texas: Thesis. LC 73-82405. 1974. Repr. of 1941 ed. soft bdg. 7.00 (ISBN 0-88247-295-X). R & E Res Assoc.
Wiest, Raymond E. Mexican Farm Laborers in California: A Study of Intragroup Social Relations. LC 77-75745. 1977. 8.00 (ISBN 0-685-82441-1). R & E Res Assoc.
Withers, Charles D. Problems of Mexican Boys: Thesis. LC 74-77159. 1974. Repr. of 1942 ed. soft bdg. 8.00 (ISBN 0-88247-296-8). R & E Res Assoc.

MEXICO
see also provinces, cities and towns, etc. in Mexico

Barrett, J. Mexico. 1976. lib. bdg. 59.95 (ISBN 0-8490-2241-X). Gordon Pr.
Blake, M. Mexico. 1976. lib. bdg. 59.95 (ISBN 0-8490-2242-8). Gordon Pr.
Brocklehurst, Thomas U. Mexico Today. 1976. lib. bdg. 59.95 (ISBN 0-8490-0632-5). Gordon Pr.
Brow, Dix. Boating in Mexico. 1977. pap. 12.95 (ISBN 0-89404-003-0). Aztex.
Cantu, Caesar C. Mexico: All About the Country & Its People. (Illus.). 10.95 (ISBN 0-685-16804-2, 0-910978-3-4). Modern World.
Cleland, R. The Mexican Yearbook. 1976. lib. bdg. 59.95 (ISBN 0-8490-2240-1). Gordon Pr.
De Fornaro, Carlo. Carranza & Mexico. 1976. lib. bdg. 59.95 (ISBN 0-87968-814-9). Gordon Pr.
Downing, T. The Mexican Earth. 1976. lib. bdg. 59.95 (ISBN 0-8490-2234-7). Gordon Pr.
Enock, C. Mexico. 1976. lib. bdg. 59.95 (ISBN 0-8490-2243-6). Gordon Pr.
Fyfe, E. The Real Mexico. 1976. lib. bdg. 59.95 (ISBN 0-8490-2501-X). Gordon Pr.
Garcia Icazbalceta, Joaquin. Obras De Joaquin Garcia Icazbalceta, 10 vols. LC 68-58758. (Span). 1969. Repr. of 1898 ed. Set. 225.00 (ISBN 0-8337-1798-7). B Franklin.
Gruening, Ernest H. Mexico & Its Heritage. LC 68-9542. (Illus.). 1968. Repr. of 1940 ed. lib. bdg. 43.75x (ISBN 0-8371-0457-2, GRMH). Greenwood.
Hanke, Lewis. Mexico & the Caribbean. 2nd rev. & enl. ed. (Modern Latin America Ser: Continent in Ferment, Vol. 1). 5.00 (ISBN 0-8446-2199-4). Peter Smith.
Herring, Hubert. The Genius of Mexico. 1976. lib. bdg. 59.95 (ISBN 0-8490-0215-X). Gordon Pr.
--Renascent Mexico. 1976. lib. bdg. 59.95 (ISBN 0-8490-0944-8). Gordon Pr.
Kerr, Robert J. A Handbook of Mexican Law. 1976. lib. bdg. 59.95 (ISBN 0-8490-0280-X). Gordon Pr.
Koslow, Lawrence, ed. The Future of Mexico. LC 77-20267. 1978. 6.50 (ISBN 0-87918-040-4). ASU Lat Am St.
Kunz, Joseph L. The Mexican Expropriations. LC 43-3233. Repr. of 1940 ed. pap. 6.00 (ISBN 0-527-53600-8). Kraus Repr.
Lumholtz, Carl. Unknown Mexico, 2 vols. 500.00 (ISBN 0-8490-1249-X). Gordon Pr.
Machugh, R. Modern Mexico. 1976. lib. bdg. 59.95 (ISBN 0-8490-2268-1). Gordon Pr.
Magner, James A. Men of Mexico. facs. ed. LC 68-55849. (Essay Index Reprint Ser). 1942. 40.25 (ISBN 0-8369-0666-7). Arno.
Mexico. (Panorama Bks.). (Illus., Fr.). 3.95 (ISBN 0-685-11369-8). French & Eur.
Pan American Union, ed. Mexico. 1976. lib. bdg. 34.95 (ISBN 0-8490-0622-8). Gordon Pr.
Price, John A. Tijuana: Urbanization in a Border Culture. LC 72-12641. 208p. 1973. text ed. 6.95x (ISBN 0-268-00477-3); pap. 2.95 (ISBN 0-268-00495-1). U of Notre Dame Pr.
Quirk, Robert E. Mexico. LC 75-153437. 1971. pap. 7.95 (ISBN 0-13-579540-0, S628, Spec). P-H.
Ramos Arizpe, Miguel. Report That Dr. Miguel Ramos de Arizpe, Priest of Borbon, & Deputy in the Present General & Special Cortes of Spain for the Province of Coahuila, One of the Four Eastern Interior Provinces of the Kingdom of Mexico, Presents to the August Congress, on the Natural, Political & Civil Condition of the Provinces of Coahuila, Nuevo Leon, Nuevo Santander & Texas of the Four Eastern Interior Provinces of the Kingdom of Mexico. Benson, Nettie L., tr. & intro. by. LC 69-19011. xiii, 61p. Repr. of 1950 ed. lib. bdg. 15.00x (ISBN 0-8371-1036-X, TLRR). Greenwood.
Sanders, Thomas G. Mexico in the '70s. rev ed. Spitzer, Manon, ed. 1980. spiral bdg. 12.00 (ISBN 0-88333-003-2). Am U Field.
Sayer, Chloe. Crafts of Mexico. LC 76-51863. 1977. 9.95 (ISBN 0-385-13118-6). Doubleday.
Senior, Clarence. Land Reform & Democracy. LC 74-8261. (Illus.). 269p. 1974. Repr. of 1958 ed. lib. bdg. 14.75x (ISBN 0-8371-7563-1, SELR). Greenwood.
Simon, Kate. Mexico: Places & Pleasures. rev ed. LC 78-3317. (Illus.). 1979. 14.95 (ISBN 0-690-01653-0, Tyc-T); pap. 6.95 (ISBN 0-690-01778-2). T y Crowell.
Smith, Randolph W. Benighted Mexico. 1976. lib. bdg. 59.95 (ISBN 0-87968-721-5). Gordon Pr.
Strode, Hudson. Now in Mexico. Repr. of 1941 ed. 20.00 (ISBN 0-89987-019-8). Darby Bks.
Thompson, Wallace. The Mexican Mind: A Study of National Psychology. 1976. lib. bdg. 59.95 (ISBN 0-8490-0616-3). Gordon Pr.
Trowbridge, E. D. Mexico Today & Tomorrow. 1976. lib. bdg. 34.95 (ISBN 0-8490-0633-3). Gordon Pr.
Tweedie, Mrs. Alec. Mexico As I Saw It. 1976. lib. bdg. 59.95 (ISBN 0-8490-0624-4). Gordon Pr.
Unibook & Rubio Ortiz, Pascual, III, eds. Mexico Today. (Illus.). 320p. 1981. 21.95 (ISBN 0-02-620910-1). Macmillan.
Unibook Staff. Mexico: The Macmillan Concise Illustrated Encyclopedia. Rubio, Pascal O., 3rd, ed. (Illus.). 416p. 1981. cancelled (ISBN 0-02-620910-1). Macmillan.
Warner, L. Mexico's Progress Demands Its Price. 1976. lib. bdg. 59.95 (ISBN 0-8490-2254-1). Gordon Pr.
Wilgus, A. Curtis, ed. Caribbean: Mexico Today. LC 51-12532. (Caribbean Conference Ser: Vol. 14). 1964. 9.00 (ISBN 0-8130-0252-4). U Presses Fla.
Wright, Norman P. A Mexican Medley for the Curious. 1961. 25.00 (ISBN 0-911268-30-8). Rogers Bk.

MEXICO–ANTIQUITIES

Adams, Richard E. The Ceramics of Altar De Sacrificios. LC 72-126638. (Peabody Museum Papers: Vol. 63, No. 1). 1971. pap. text ed. 25.00 (ISBN 0-87365-180-4). Peabody Harvard.
Bernal, Ignacio. A History of Mexican Archaeology: The Vanished Civilizations of Middle America. (Illus.). 1980. 17.95 (ISBN 0-500-78008-0). Thames Hudson.
Bowditch, Charles P. Mexican & Central American Antiquities, Calendar Systems, & History. LC 74-20883. (Smithsonian Institution, Bureau of American Ethnology, Bulletin Ser.: No. 28). (Illus.). 808p. 1975. Repr. of 1904 ed. 45.00 (ISBN 0-87917-042-5). Blaine Ethridge.
Brenner, Anita. Idols Behind Altars. LC 67-19527. (Illus.). 1929. 18.00x (ISBN 0-8196-0190-X). Biblo.
Caso, Alfonso. Thirteen Masterpieces of Mexican Archaeology; Trece Obras Maestras De Arqueologia Mexicana. N. Mackie, Edith & Acosta, Jorge R., trs. from Span. LC 76-25239. (Illus., Eng. & Span.). 1976. Repr. of 1938 ed. 11.00 (ISBN 0-87917-057-3). Blaine Ethridge.
Caso, Antonio. Thirteen Masterpieces of Mexican Archaeology. 1976. lib. bdg. 59.95 (ISBN 0-8490-1194-9). Gordon Pr.
Charnay, Desire. The Ancient Cities of the New World: Being Voyages & Explorations in Mexico & Central America from 1857 to 1882. Gonina, J. & Conant, Helen S., trs. from Fr. LC 72-5004. (Antiquities of the New World: Vol. 10). (Illus.). Repr. of 1887 ed. 40.00 (ISBN 0-404-57310-X). AMS Pr.
Davies, Nigel. The Toltecs: Until the Fall of Tula. (CAI Ser.: Vol. 144). (Illus.). 1977. 22.50 (ISBN 0-8061-1394-4). U of Okla Pr.
De Zorita, Alonso. Life & Labor in Ancient Mexico: The Brief & Summary Relation of the Lords of New Spain. Keen, Benjamin, tr. 1964. 20.00 (ISBN 0-8135-0442-2). Rutgers U Pr.
DiPeso, Charles C. Casas Grandes: A Fallen Trading Center of the Gran Chichimeca, 8 vols. LC 74-82018. (Illus.). 1974. Set. 260.00 (ISBN 0-685-99080-X); Vols. 1-3. 75.00 (ISBN 0-685-99081-8); Vols. 4-8. 185.00 (ISBN 0-87358-056-7). Northland.
Drennan, Robert D. Excavations at Quachilco: A Report on the 1977 Season of the Palo Blanco Project in the Tehuacan Valley. Uribe, Carlos, tr. (Technical Reports Ser.: No. 7). (Illus., Eng. & Span., Contribution 3 in Research Reports in Archaeology). 1977. pap. 4.00x (ISBN 0-932206-16-6). U Mich Mus Anthro.
--Fabrica San Jose & Middle Formative Society in the Valley of Oaxaca. New ed. Flannery, Kent V., ed. (Memoirs, No. 8, Prehistory & Human Ecology of the Valley of Oaxaca: Vol. 4). (Illus., Orig.). 1976. pap. 8.00x (ISBN 0-932206-70-0). U Mich Mus Anthro.
Enciso, Jorge. Design Motifs of Ancient Mexico. (Illus.). 1947. pap. 3.50 (ISBN 0-486-20084-1). Dover.
Ferguson, William M. & Royce, John Q. Maya Ruins of Mexico in Color. LC 77-9110. (Illus.). 1977. 27.50 (ISBN 0-8061-1442-8). U of Okla Pr.
Gifford, James C. Prehistoric Pottery Analysis & the Ceramics of Barton Ramie in the Belize Valley. LC 75-40772. (Peabody Museum Memoirs: Vol. 18). 1976. pap. text ed. 35.00 (ISBN 0-87365-691-1). Peabody Harvard.
Graham, John A. The Hieroglyphic Inscriptions & Monumental Art of Alter De Sacrificios. LC 70-186984. (Peabody Museum Papers: Vol. 64, No. 2). 1972. pap. text ed. 15.00 (ISBN 0-87365-184-7). Peabody Harvard.

Hammond, Norman & Willey, Gordon R., eds. Maya Archaeology & Ethnohistory. (Texas Pan American Ser.). (Illus.). 310p. 1979. text ed. 23.50x (ISBN 0-292-75040-4). U of Tex Pr.

Hewett, Edgar L. Ancient Life in Mexico & Central America. LC 67-29546. (Illus.). 1968. Repr. of 1936 ed. 15.00x (ISBN 0-8196-0205-1). Biblo.

Highwater, Jamake. Journey to the Sky. LC 78-3324. (Illus.). 1978. 9.95 (ISBN 0-690-01758-8). T Y Crowell.

Holmes, W. H. Archaeological Studies Among the Ancient Cities of Mexico. (Chicago Field Museum of Natural History Fieldiana Anthropology Ser). Repr. of 1895 ed. pap. 28.00 (ISBN 0-527-01861-9). Kraus Repr.

Hunter, C. Bruce. A Guide to Ancient Maya Ruins. LC 74-5956. (Illus.). 300p. 1974. 14.95 (ISBN 0-8061-1214-X); pap. 6.95 (ISBN 0-8061-1215-8). U of Okla Pr.

--A Guide to Ancient Mexican Ruins. (Illus.). 1977. 12.95 (ISBN 0-8061-1399-5); pap. 6.95 (ISBN 0-8061-1407-X). U of Okla Pr.

Joyce, T. A. Mexican Archaeology. Repr. of 1920 ed. 24.00 (ISBN 0-527-46850-9). Kraus Repr.

Kingsborough, Edward K. Antiquities of Mexico, 9 Vols. LC 74-171542. Repr. of 1848 ed. Set. 950.00 (ISBN 0-404-03680-5). AMS Pr.

Kirkby, Ann. The Use of Land & Water Resources in the Past & Present Valley of Oaxaca. Flannery, Kent V., ed. (Memoirs No. 5, Prehistory & Human Ecology of the Valley of Caxaca Ser.: Vol. 1). (Illus.). 1973. pap. 6.00x (ISBN 0-932206-67-0). U Mich Mus Anthro.

Lange, Charles H. The Cochiti Dam Archaeological Salvage Project. (Illus.). 1968. pap. 6.95 (ISBN 0-89013-031-0). Museum NM Pr.

Lees, Susan. Sociopolitical Aspects of Canal Irrigation in the Valley of Oaxaca. Flannery, Kent V., ed. (Memoirs No. 6, Prehistory & Human Ecology of the Valley of Caxaca Ser.: Vol. 2). (Illus.). 1973. pap. 6.00x (ISBN 0-932206-68-9). U Mich Mus Anthro.

Leon & Holmes. Studies on Archaeology of Michoacan Mexico. 29p. Repr. of 1886 ed. pap. 3.75 (ISBN 0-8466-4012-0, SJ112). Shorey.

Meighan, Clement W., ed. The Archaeology of Amapa, Nayarit. LC 76-18607. (Monumenta Archaeologica: No. 2). (Illus.). 1976. 35.00 (ISBN 0-917956-01-X). UCLA Arch.

Nuttall, Zelia. Atlatl or Spear-Thrower of the Ancient Mexicans. 1891. pap. 4.00 (ISBN 0-527-01185-1). Kraus Repr.

--Official Reports on the Towns of Tequizistlan, Tepechpan, Acolman, & San Juan Teotihuacan, Sent to His Majesty Philip Second & the Council of the Indies in 1580. 1926. pap. 4.00 (ISBN 0-527-01219-X). Kraus Repr.

--Penitential Rite of the Ancient Mexicans. 1904. pap. 3.00 (ISBN 0-527-01189-4). Kraus Repr.

--Standard or Head-Dress? 1888. pap. 8.00 (ISBN 0-527-01183-5). Kraus Repr.

Nuttall, Zelia, ed. The Codex Nuttall: A Picture Manuscript from Ancient Mexico. (Illus.). 12.50 (ISBN 0-8446-5601-1). Peter Smith.

Parsons, Jeffrey R. Prehistoric Settlement Patterns in the Southern Valley of Mexico: The Chalco-Xochimilco Region. (Memoir Ser.: No. 14). (Orig.). 1981. pap. write for info. (ISBN 0-932206-88-3). U Mich Mus Anthro.

Pasztory, Esther. The Murals of Tepantitla, Teotihaucan. LC 75-23806. (Outstanding Dissertations in the Fine Arts - Native American Arts). (Illus.). 1976. lib. bdg. 45.00 (ISBN 0-8240-2000-6). Garland Pub.

Pasztory, Esther, ed. Middle Classic Mesoamerica: 400-700 A. D. (Illus.). 197p. 1978. 25.00x (ISBN 0-231-04270-1). Columbia U Pr.

Pina Chan, Roman. A Guide to Mexican Archaeology. (Illus.). 1979. pap. 5.00 (ISBN 0-912434-09-0). Ocelot Pr.

Proskouriakoff, Tatiana. Jades from the Cenote of Sacrifice, Chichen Itza, Yucatan. LC 74-77555. (Peabody Museum Memoirs: Vol. 10, No. 1). 1974. pap. text ed. 40.00 (ISBN 0-87365-682-2). Peabody Harvard.

Ruppert, Karl & Denison, John H., Jr. Archaeological Reconnaissance in Campeche, Quintana Roo, & Peten. LC 77-11517. (Carnegie Institution of Washington. Publication: No. 543). Repr. of 1943 ed. 44.00 (ISBN 0-404-16277-0). AMS Pr.

Sanders, William T. The Lowland Huasteca: Archaelogical Survey & Excavation, 1957 Field Season. (Monographs in Anthropology: No. 4). (Illus.). vii, 214p. 1978. pap. 10.50 (ISBN 0-913134-85-6). Mus Anthro Mo.

Sanders, William T. & Price, Barbara J. Mesoamerica: The Evolution of a Civilization. (Orig.). 1968. pap. text ed. 9.95x (ISBN 0-394-30789-5, RanC). Random.

Sauer, Carl O. & Brand, Donald. Aztatlan: Prehistoric Mexican Frontier on the Pacific Coast. LC 76-43816. (Ibero-Americana: No. 1). Repr. of 1932 ed. 19.50 (ISBN 0-404-15673-8). AMS Pr.

Saul, Frank P. The Human Skeletal Remains of Altar De Sacrificios: An Osteobiographic Analysis. LC 72-91442. (Peabody Museum Papers: Vol. 63, No. 2). 1972. pap. text ed. 15.00 (ISBN 0-87365-181-2). Peabody Harvard.

Sisson, Edward B. Reports of the Coxcatlan Project. Incl. First Annual Report. 1973. 4.00 (ISBN 0-939312-13-1); Second Annual Report. 1974. 3.00 (ISBN 0-939312-14-X). Peabody Found.

Smith, A. Ledyard. Excavations at Altar De Sacrificios: Architecture, Settlement, Burials & Caches. LC 72-126638. (Peabody Museum Papers: Vol. 62, No. 2). 1972. pap. 25.00 (ISBN 0-87365-178-2). Peabody Harvard.

Smith, Robert E. The Pottery of Mayapan: Including Studies of Ceramic Material from Uxmal, Kabah, & Chichen Itza. LC 73-158899. (Peabody Museum Papers: Vol. 66, Nos. 1 & 2). 1971. pap. 40.00 (ISBN 0-87365-187-1). Peabody Harvard.

Spence, Michael W., et al. Miscellaneous Studies in Mexican Pre-History. (Anthropological Papers: No. 45). (Illus.). 1972. pap. 4.00x (ISBN 0-932206-43-3). U Mich Mus Anthro.

Spinden, Herbert J. Ancient Civilizations of Mexico & Central America. 3rd rev. ed. LC 67-29554. (Illus.). 1968. Repr. of 1928 ed. 10.50x (ISBN 0-8196-0215-9). Biblo.

Thompson, J. Eric. Maya Archaeologist. (Illus.). 1975. 14.95 (ISBN 0-8061-0561-5); pap. 6.95 (ISBN 0-8061-1206-9). U of Okla Pr.

Tompkins, Peter. Mysteries of the Mexican Pyramids. LC 74-15857. (Illus.). 320p. (YA) 1976. 25.00 (ISBN 0-06-014324-X, HarpT). Har-Row.

Tozzler, Alfred M. Excavation of a Site at Santiago Auhitzotla, D.F. Mexico. Repr. of 1921 ed. cancelled (ISBN 0-685-34412-6). Scholarly.

Twenty Centuries of Mexican Art. LC 79-169322. (Museum of Modern Art in Reprint Ser.). (Illus.). 200p. 1972. Repr. of 1940 ed. 23.00 (ISBN 0-405-01580-1). Arno.

Tylor, Edward B. Anahuac or Mexico & the Mexicans Ancient & Modern. LC 66-29078. 1970. Repr. of 1861 ed. text ed. 17.00x (ISBN 0-391-01956-2). Humanities.

Whalen, Michael. Excavations at Santo Domingo Tomaltepec: Evolution of a Formative Community in the Valley of Oaxaca, Mexico. (Memoirs Ser.: No. 12, Prehistory & Human Ecology of the Valley of Oaxaca, Vol. 6). (Orig.). 1979. pap. write for info. (ISBN 0-685-94224-4). U Mich Mus Anthro.

Willey, Gordon R. The Altar De Sacrificios Excavations: General Summary & Conclusions. LC 73-77202. (Peabody Museum Papers: Vol. 64, No. 3). 1973. pap. text ed. 10.00 (ISBN 0-87365-185-5). Peabody Harvard.

--The Artifacts of Altar De Sacrificios. LC 72-93407. (Peabody Museum Papers: Vol. 64, No. 1). pap. text ed. 25.00 (ISBN 0-87365-183-9). Peabody Harvard.

Willey, Gordon R. & Smith, A. Ledyard. The Ruins of Altar De Sacrificios, Department of Peten, Guatemala: An Introduction. LC 74-82521. (Peabody Museum Papers: Vol. 62, No. 1). 1969. pap. 10.00 (ISBN 0-87365-177-4). Peabody Harvard.

Wolf, Eric R., ed. The Valley of Mexico: Studies in Pre-Hispanic Ecology & Society. LC 75-21184. (School of American Research Advanced Seminar Ser.). 337p. 1976. 20.00x (ISBN 0-8263-0398-6). U of NM Pr.

Wood, Robert D. A Travel Guide to Archaeological Mexico. (Illus.). 1979. 10.95 (ISBN 0-8038-7206-2); pap. 7.95 (ISBN 0-8038-7207-0). Hastings.

MEXICO-BIBLIOGRAPHY

California State Library Sutro Branch San Francisco. Catalogue of Mexican Pamphlets in the Sutro Collection 1623-1888. Radin, P. & Gans, A. I., eds. 1939-1941. 90.00 (ISBN 0-527-14400-2). Kraus Repr.

Cole, Garold. American Travelers' in Mexico, 1821-1975: A Descriptive Bibliography. LC 76-21469. 1978. 12.50x (ISBN 0-87875-136-X). Whitston Pub.

Cumberland, Charles C. The United States-Mexican Border: A Selective Guide to the Literature of the Region. 1960. pap. 14.00 (ISBN 0-384-10360-X). Johnson Repr.

Gunn, Drewey W. Mexico in American & British Letters: A Bibliography of Fiction & Travel Books Citing Original Editions. LC 73-20354. 1974. 10.00 (ISBN 0-8108-0692-4). Scarecrow.

Haferkorn, Henry E. The War with Mexico, 1846-1848. 1970. Repr. of 1914 ed. 21.50 (ISBN 0-8337-1529-1). B Franklin.

Lansing, Marion F. Liberators & Heroes of Mexico & Central America. facsimile ed. LC 72-152186. (Essay Index Reprint Ser). Repr. of 1941 ed. 23.00 (ISBN 0-8369-2237-9). Arno.

Puttick & Simpson. Bibliotheca Mejicana. LC 71-168027. Repr. of 1869 ed. 15.00 (ISBN 0-404-02388-6). AMS Pr.

Puttick and Simpson. Bibliotheca Mejicana. (Bibliography & Research Ser.: No. 220). 1968. Repr. of 1869 ed. 23.50 (ISBN 0-8337-0273-4). B Franklin.

Ramos, Roberto. Bibliografia De la Revolucion Mexicana, 3 vols. 1976. lib. bdg. 300.00 (ISBN 0-8490-1494-8). Gordon Pr.

Wagner, Henry R. Spanish Southwest Fifteen Forty-Two - Seventeen Ninety - Four, 2 Vols. LC 66-30073. (Quivira Society Publications, Vol. 7, 2 Pts). 1968. Repr. of 1937 ed. Set. 45.00 (ISBN 0-405-00079-0). Arno.

MEXICO-BIOGRAPHY

Abad de Santillan, Diego. Ricardo Flores Magon: Apostle of the Mexican Social Revolution. (Mexico Ser.). 1979. lib. bdg. 59.95 (ISBN 0-8490-2998-8). Gordon Pr.

Babb, Jewel & Taylor, Pat E. Border Healing Woman: The Story of Jewel Babb. 152p. 1981. text ed. 14.95x (ISBN 0-292-70729-0); pap. 5.95 (ISBN 0-292-70730-4). U of Tex Pr.

Camp, Roderic A. Mexican Political Biographies: 1935-1975. LC 74-29361. 1976. 27.50x (ISBN 0-8165-0581-0); pap. 8.95x (ISBN 0-8165-0496-2). U of Ariz Pr.

Castillo, Pedro & Camarillo, Albert. Furia y Muerte: Los Bandidos Chicanos. (Monograph Ser: No. 4). (Illus.). 1973. pap. 2.75 (ISBN 0-89551-003-0). UCLA Chicano Stud.

Decker, Robert & Marquez, Esther T. The Proud Mexicans. (Illus.). 250p. (gr. 7-12). 1976. pap. 5.25 (ISBN 0-88345-254-5). Regents Pub.

Diccionario Porrua de Historia, Biografia y Geografia de Mexico, 2 vols. (Span.). 150.00 set (ISBN 0-686-56692-0, S-12279). French & Eur.

Fernandez, Jose. Cuarenta Anos De Legislador: Biografia Del Senador Casimiro Barela. Cortes, Carlos E., ed. LC 76-1254. (Chicano Heritage Ser.). (Span.). 1976. Repr. of 1911 ed. 29.00x (ISBN 0-405-09501-5). Arno.

Harris, Charles H., 3rd. A Mexican Family Empire: The "Latifundio" of the Sanchez Navarros, 1765-186. LC 74-28274. 428p. 1975. 19.50x (ISBN 0-292-75020-X). U of Tex Pr.

Holden, William C. Teresita. LC 78-2321. (Illus.). 1978. 14.95 (ISBN 0-916144-24-0); pap. 8.95 (ISBN 0-916144-25-9). Stemmer Hse.

Lipp, Solomon. Leopoldo Zea: From Mexicanidad to a Philosophy of History. 146p. 1980. text ed. 9.75 (ISBN 0-88920-079-3, Pub. by Laurier U Pr Canada). Humanities.

MacNutt, Francis A., tr. Hernando Cortes: His Five Letters of Relations to the Emperor Charles the Fifth of Spain, 2 vols. LC 77-1155. (Beautiful Rio Grande Classics Ser.). 1977. lib. bdg. 40.00 (ISBN 0-87380-125-3). Rio Grande.

Magon, Ricardo F. Land & Liberty: Anarchist Influences in the Mexican Revolution. Poole, Dave, ed. (Orig.). 1979. pap. 5.50 (ISBN 0-932366-04-X). Black Thorn Bks.

Ortiz Y Pino, Jose. The Last Patron. Engestrom, Melissa, ed. LC 81-8817. 160p. 1981. 12.95 (ISBN 0-86534-006-4); pap. 8.95 (ISBN 0-86534-007-2). Sunstone Pr.

Parker, Morris B. Mules, Mines & Me in Mexico, Eighteen Ninety-Five to Nineteen Thirty-Two. Day, James M., ed. LC 79-15206. 1979. pap. 7.95 (ISBN 0-8165-0626-4). U of Ariz Pr.

Powell, Philip W. Mexico's Miguel Caldera: The Taming of America's First Frontier, 1548-1597. LC 76-62551. 1977. 14.95x (ISBN 0-8165-0638-8); pap. 7.95x (ISBN 0-8165-0569-1). U of Ariz Pr.

Schryer, Frans J. The Rancheros of Pisaflores: The History of a Peasant Bourgeoisie in Twentieth - Century Mexico. LC 79-20686. 1979. 20.00x (ISBN 0-8020-5466-8). U of Toronto Pr.

Spell, J. R. The Life & Works of Jose Fernandez De Lizardi. 1977. lib. bdg. 34.95 (ISBN 0-8490-2163-4). Gordon Pr.

Stagg, Albert L. The First Bishop of Sonora: Antonio de los Reyes, O.F.M. LC 75-19866. 1976. 8.50x (ISBN 0-8165-0549-7); pap. 4.50x (ISBN 0-8165-0486-5). U of Ariz Pr.

Suplemento a la Segunda Edicion Del Diccionario Pornua De Historia, Biografia y Geografia de Mexico. 496p. (Span.). 17.50 (ISBN 0-686-56693-9, S-12280). French & Eur.

Timmons, W. H. Tadeo Ortiz, Mexican Colonizer & Reformer. (Southwestern Studies Ser.: No. 43). 1974. 3.00 (ISBN 0-87404-101-5). Tex Western.

Tweedie, E. Maker of Modern Mexico: Porfirio Diaz. (Mexico Ser.). 1979. lib. bdg. 69.95 (ISBN 0-8490-2968-6). Gordon Pr.

MEXICO-BOUNDARIES

Hedrick, Basil C., et al, eds. North Mexican Frontier: Readings in Archaeology, Ethnohistory & Ethnography. LC 70-132477. 271p. 1971. 15.95x (ISBN 0-8093-0489-9). S Ill U Pr.

Marshall, T. M. History of the Western Boundary of the Louisiana Purchase, 1819-1841. LC 73-87411. (American Scene Ser). (Illus.). 1970. Repr. of 1914 ed. lib. bdg. 27.50 (ISBN 0-306-71554-6). Da Capo.

Ross, Stanley R., ed. Views Across the Border: the United States & Mexico. LC 76-57533. 1978. pap. 10.00x (ISBN 0-8263-0445-1). U of NM Pr.

MEXICO-CIVILIZATION

Collins, Michael D. Cultured Mexico. 297p. 1974. lib. bdg. 69.95 (ISBN 0-87968-973-0). Gordon Pr.

Enock, C. Reginald. Mexico: Its Ancient & Modern Civilization. 1976. lib. bdg. 59.95 (ISBN 0-8490-0629-5). Gordon Pr.

Erasmus, Charles J., et al. Contemporary Change in Traditional Communities of Mexico & Peru. Steward, Julian H., ed. LC 78-57508. 1978. pap. 6.95 (ISBN 0-252-00714-X). U of Ill Pr.

Gonzalez, Alfonso. Indice de la Cultura En Mexico: 1962-1972. LC 78-5019. 1978. 28.25 (ISBN 0-8357-0311-8, SS-00063). Univ Microfilms.

Gyles, Anna B. & Sayer, Chloe. Of God & Men: The Heritage of Ancient Mexico. LC 81-47229. (Illus.). 240p. 1981. 15.95 (ISBN 0-06-014887-X, HarpT). Har-Row.

Kennedy, John G. The Tarahumara of the Sierra Madre: Beer, Ecology & Social Organization. LC 77-86044. (Worlds of Man Ser.). (Illus.). 1978. text ed. 12.95x (ISBN 0-88295-614-0); pap. text ed. 6.95x (ISBN 0-88295-615-9). Harlan Davidson.

Lafaye, Jacques. Quetzalcoatl & Guadalupe: The Formation of Mexican National Consciousness, 1531-1813. Keen, Benjamin, tr. from Fr. LC 75-20889. 1976. lib. bdg. 22.00x (ISBN 0-226-46794-5). U of Chicago Pr.

Paz, Octavio. The Labyrinth of Solitude: Life & Thought in Mexico. Kemp, Lysander, tr. from Span. (YA) (gr. 9 up). 1962. pap. 3.95 (ISBN 0-394-17242-6, E359, Ever). Grove.

Ramos, Samuel. Profile of Man & Culture in Mexico. Earle, Peter G., tr. LC 62-9792. (Texas Pan American Ser.). 220p. 1962. 12.50x (ISBN 0-292-73340-2); pap. 4.95x (ISBN 0-292-70072-5). U of Tex Pr.

Reville, Albert. Lectures on the Origin & Growth of Religion As Illustrated by the Native Religions of Mexico & Peru. LC 77-27167. (Hibbert Lectures: 1884). Repr. of 1884 ed. 22.00 (ISBN 0-685-22190-3). AMS Pr.

Sanders, William T., et al. The Basin of Mexico: Ecological Processes in the Evolution of a Civilization. (Studies in Archeology Ser.). 1979. book & map 49.50 (ISBN 0-12-618450-X); map 17.50 (ISBN 0-12-618452-6). Acad Pr.

Simpson, Lesley B. Many Mexicos, Silver Anniversary Edition. (YA) (gr. 9 up). 1966. 20.00x (ISBN 0-520-01179-1); pap. 4.65 (ISBN 0-520-01180-5, CAL29). U of Cal Pr.

Spence, Michael W., et al. Miscellaneous Studies in Mexican Pre-History. (Anthropological Papers: No. 45). (Illus.). 1972. pap. 4.00x (ISBN 0-932206-43-3). U Mich Mus Anthro.

Wolf, Eric. Sons of the Shaking Earth. LC 59-12290. (Illus.). 1959. 15.00x (ISBN 0-226-90499-7, Phoen); pap. 4.95x (ISBN 0-226-90500-4, P90, Phoen). U of Chicago Pr.

MEXICO-DESCRIPTION AND TRAVEL

Aguiar, Walter R. Maya Land in Color. (Profiles of America Ser.). (Illus.). 1978. 7.95 (ISBN 0-8038-4703-3). Hastings.

Bandelier, A. F. Scientist on the Trail. Hammond, George P., ed. LC 67-24721. (Quivira Society Publications, Vol. 10). 1967. Repr. of 1949 ed. 12.00 (ISBN 0-405-00084-7). Arno.

Barretto, L. Bright Mexico. 1976. lib. bdg. 59.95 (ISBN 0-8490-1554-5). Gordon Pr.

Barring, G. In Mexican Waters. 1976. lib. bdg. 59.95 (ISBN 0-8490-2044-1). Gordon Pr.

Barton, M. Impressions of Mexico with Brush & Pen. 1976. lib. bdg. 59.95 (ISBN 0-8490-3064-1). Gordon Pr.

Baxter, Robert. Baxter's Mexico. 1981. 9.95 (ISBN 0-913384-42-9). Rail-Europe-Baxter.

Beals, Carleton. Mexican Maze. LC 71-156174. (Illus.). 1971. Repr. of 1931 ed. lib. bdg. 17.50x (ISBN 0-8371-6117-7, BEMM). Greenwood.

Bedford, Sybille. Sudden View: A Traveller's Tale from Mexico. LC 63-797. 1963. pap. 1.45 (ISBN 0-689-70008-3, 18). Atheneum.

Birnbaum, Stephen. Mexico, Nineteen Eighty-Two. (The Get 'em & Go Travel Guide Ser.). 704p. 1981. pap. 10.95 (ISBN 0-395-31536-0). HM.

Blichfeldt, E. A Mexican Journey. 1976. lib. bdg. 59.95 (ISBN 0-8490-2237-1). Gordon Pr.

Bose, Johanne C. Farewell to Durango: A German Lady's Diary in Mexico, 1910-1911. Blew, Robert W., ed. Bose, John C., tr. from Ger. LC 78-50471. (A Western Americana Book). (Illus., Orig.). 1978. pap. 5.00 (ISBN 0-913626-41-4). S S S Pub Co.

Boudreau, Eugene H. Move Over, Don Porfiro: Tales from the Sierra Madre. LC 75-35308. (Illus.). 96p. 1975. pap. 3.00 (ISBN 0-686-10963-5). Pleasant Hill.

--Ways of the Sierra Madre: Crafts of the Sierra Madre. LC 74-22999. (Illus.). 96p. 1974. 6.00 (ISBN 0-686-10332-7); pap. 3.00 (ISBN 0-686-10333-5). Pleasant Hill.

Bradley, Michael. Communion in Solitude: Mexico from the Corner of an Eye. LC 75-8976. (Illus.). 96p. (Eng. & Span.). 1975. 6.95 (ISBN 0-912020-41-5). Scrimshaw Calif.

Bradt, Hilary & Bradt, George. Backpacking in Mexico & Central America, Including the Darien Gap. (Backpacker Guide Ser.). (Illus.). 1981. pap. 9.95 (ISBN 0-933982-02-X). Bradt Ent.

Bruccoli, Matthew. Reconquest of Mexico: An Amiable Journey in Persuit of Cortes. LC 74-76440. 1974. 8.95 (ISBN 0-8149-0742-3). Vanguard.

Bullock, William. Six Months Residence & Travels in Mexico. LC 77-130328. (Latin-American History & Culture Ser). 1971. Repr. of 1824 ed. 17.50 (ISBN 0-8046-1392-3). Kennikat.

Butler, J. Sketches of Mexico. 1976. lib. bdg. 59.95 (ISBN 0-8490-2613-X). Gordon Pr.

Carson, W. E. Mexico, the Wonderland of the South. 1977. lib. bdg. 59.95 (ISBN 0-8490-2252-5). Gordon Pr.

Castaneda, Carlos. Journey to Ixtlan. 1973. pap. 3.95 (ISBN 0-671-21639-2, Touchstone Bks). S&S.

Champlain, Samuel De. Narrative of a Voyage to the West Indies & Mexico in the Years 1599-1602. Shaw, Norton, ed. Wilmere, Alice, tr. LC 61-30806. (Illus.). 48p. 1859. Repr. 26.00 (ISBN 0-8337-0524-5). B Franklin.

Conlen, William J. Vignettes of Mexico. 1937. 25.00 (ISBN 0-686-17227-2). Scholars Ref Lib.

Conlen, Wolliam J. Vignettes of Mexico. 1978. Repr. of 1937 ed. lib. bdg. 15.00 (ISBN 0-8495-0806-1). Arden Lib.

Corbitt, Helen, ed. Mexico Through My Kitchen Window. 1961. 10.95 (ISBN 0-395-07579-3). HM.

Cortes, Hernando, et al. Mexican Mosaic. 1978. pap. 4.95 (ISBN 0-914558-01-3). Georgetown Pr.

De Barrios, Virginia B. A Guide to Tequila, Mezcal & Pulque. 65p. 1971. pap. 3.00 (ISBN 0-912434-12-0). Ocelot Pr.

Dodge, David. Best of Mexico by Car. 1969. 5.95 (ISBN 0-02-488740-4). Macmillan.

Dunn, Mary M., ed. Humboldt's Political Essay on the Kingdom of New Spain. 1972. pap. text ed. 3.95x (ISBN 0-394-31510-3). Phila Bk Co.

Earle, Thomas. Life, Travels & Opinions of Benjamin Lundy, Including His Journeys to Texas & Mexico. LC 70-82188. (Anti-Slavery Crusade in America Ser). 1969. Repr. of 1847 ed. 13.00 (ISBN 0-405-00626-8). Arno.

Flandrau, Charles M. Viva Mexico! Gardiner, C. Harvey, ed. LC 64-18223. 1964. pap. 5.95 (ISBN 0-252-72701-0). U of Ill Pr.

Ford, Norman D. Fabulous Mexico: Where Everything Costs Less. 14th rev. ed. 192p. (Orig.). 1978. pap. 2.50 (ISBN 0-685-31471-5, 6957). Harian.

Foster, H. A Gringo in Manana Land. 1976. lib. bdg. 59.95 (ISBN 0-8490-1907-9). Gordon Pr.

Gage, Thomas. Thomas Gage's Travels in the New World. rev. ed. enl. ed. Thompson, J. Eric, ed. LC 58-6856. (American Exploration & Travel Ser.: Vol. 58). (Illus.). 1958. 17.50 (ISBN 0-8061-0881-9). U of Okla Pr.

Gillpatrick, W. The Man Who Likes Mexico. 1976. lib. bdg. 59.95 (ISBN 0-8490-2201-0). Gordon Pr.

Gorenstein, Shirley. Tepexi el Viejo: A Postclassic Fortified Site in the Mixteca-Puebla Region of Mexico. LC 73-75472. (Transactions Ser.: Vol. 63, Pt. 1). (Illus.). 1973. pap. 2.00 (ISBN 0-87169-631-2). Am Philos.

Greene, Graham. Another Mexico. 288p. 1981. 14.95 (ISBN 0-670-12892-9). Viking Pr.

Gregg, Josiah. Commerce of the Prairies. Quaife, Milo M., ed. & intro. by. 5.50 (ISBN 0-8446-2165-X). Peter Smith.

--Commerce of the Prairies. Quaife, Milo M., ed. LC 27-1450. (Illus.). 1967. pap. 4.75 (ISBN 0-8032-5076-2, BB 324, Bison). U of Nebr Pr.

--Commerce of the Prairies. Moorhead, Max, ed. (American Exploration & Travel Ser.: No. 17). (Illus.). 1974. 19.95 (ISBN 0-8061-0299-3); pap. 7.95 (ISBN 0-8061-1059-7). U of Okla Pr.

Hamilton, L. Mexican Handbook. 1976. lib. bdg. 59.95 (ISBN 0-8490-2236-3). Gordon Pr.

Hardy, R. W. Travels in Mexico, in 1825, 1826, 1827, & 1828. LC 77-388. (Beautiful Rio Grande Classics Ser.). 1977. lib. bdg. 20.00 (ISBN 0-87380-121-0). Rio Grande.

Harris, D. Here & There in Mexico. 1976. lib. bdg. 59.95 (ISBN 0-8490-1942-7). Gordon Pr.

Hawkins, John. A True Declaration of the Troublesome Voyadge of M John Hawkins to the Parties of Guynea & the West Indies. LC 73-6137. (English Experience Ser.: No. 602). 36p. 1973. Repr. of 1569 ed. 3.50 (ISBN 90-221-0602-0). Walter J Johnson.

Hortop, Job. The Travailes of an Englishman. LC 79-38203. (English Experience Ser.: No. 469). 32p. 1972. Repr. of 1591 ed. 6.00 (ISBN 90-221-0469-9). Walter J Johnson.

Jacobs, Charles & Jacobs, Babette. Mexico Travel Digest. 14th ed. (Travel Digests Ser.). (Illus.). 176p. 1981. pap. 8.95 (ISBN 0-912640-22-7). Travel Digest.

--Mexico Travel Digest. 12th ed. LC 68-22813. (Illus.). 1980. pap. 8.95 (ISBN 0-912640-22-7). Travel Digests.

Kusch, Eugen. Mexico in Pictures. 3rd ed. LC 58-59616. (Illus.). 42p. 1968. 27.50x (ISBN 3-418-00419-9). Intl Pubns Serv.

Lanier, Alison R. Update -- Mexico. LC 80-83927. (Country Orientation Ser.). 150p. (Orig.). 1980. pap. text ed. 25.00x (ISBN 0-933662-25-4). Intercult Pr.

Lumholtz, Karl. Unknown Mexico: A Record of Five Years' Exploration Among the Tribes of the Western Sierra Madre, in the Tierra Caliente of Tepic & Jalisco, & Among the Tarascos of Michoacan, 2 vols. LC 72-5010. (Antiquities of the New World Ser.: Vol. 15). (Illus.). Repr. of 1902 ed. Set. 87.50 (ISBN 0-404-57315-0). Vol. 1 (ISBN 0-404-57321-5). Vol. 2. (ISBN 0-404-57322-3); Vol. 2. (ISBN 0-404-57322-3). AMS Pr.

Lundy, Benjamin. Life, Travels & Opinions of Benjamin Lundy. LC 70-92750. Repr. of 1847 ed. 15.25x (ISBN 0-8371-2179-5, Pub. by Negro U Pr). Greenwood.

Lyon, G. F. Journal of a Residence & Tour in the Republic of Mexico, 2 Vols. LC 72-130332. (Latin-American History & Culture Ser). 1971. Repr. of 1828 ed. Set. 27.50 (ISBN 0-8046-1393-1). Kennikat.

Makens, James. Makens' Guide to Mexican Train Travel. LC 72-92706. (Illus.). 112p. 1973. pap. 3.47 (ISBN 0-686-05570-5). Le Voyageur.

Mayer, William. Early Travelers in Mexico (1534 to 1816) (Illus.). 25.00 (ISBN 0-911268-31-6). Rogers Bk.

Mexico in Pictures. (Illus.). 12.50 (ISBN 0-911268-04-9). Rogers Bk.

Miles, Beryl. Spirit of Mexico. (Illus.). 1961. 8.95 (ISBN 0-7195-0921-1). Transatlantic.

Miller, Tom. On the Border: Portraits of America's Southwestern Frontier. LC 79-2631. 224p. 1981. 12.95 (ISBN 0-06-013039-3, HarpT). Har-Row.

Moreau, Daniel, ed. Le Mexique. new ed. (Collection monde et voyages). (Illus.). 159p. (Fr.). 1973. 21.00x (ISBN 2-03-053108-1, 3900). Larousse.

Motoring in Mexico. 19th ed. 1972. pap. text ed. 1.00 (ISBN 0-8270-4830-0). OAS.

Obregon, L. The Streets of Mexico. 1976. lib. bdg. 59.95 (ISBN 0-8490-2695-4). Gordon Pr.

Pan Am's Guide to Latin America. pap. 2.50 (ISBN 0-685-37582-X). Pan Am Pubns.

Price, William & Motiekaitis, Jurgis. Pictorial Images of Mexico Today. (Illus.). 320p. 1976. 30.00 (ISBN 0-916722-00-7). Intl Pict Pubns.

Quinn, V. Beautiful Mexico. 1976. lib. bdg. 69.95 (ISBN 0-8490-1481-6). Gordon Pr.

Reid, Christian. The Land of the Sun: Vistas Mexicanas. 1976. lib. bdg. 69.95 (ISBN 0-8490-0483-7). Gordon Pr.

Ricketts, Carl E. El Lobo & Spanish Gold: A Texas Maverick in Mexico. LC 74-77508. (Illus.). 210p. 1974. 8.50 (ISBN 0-89052-006-2). Madrona Pr.

Riley, Carroll L. & Hedrick, Basil C., eds. Across the Chichimec Sea: Papers in Honor of J. Charles Kelley. LC 78-802. (Illus.). 336p. 1978. 19.95x (ISBN 0-8093-0829-0). S Ill U Pr.

Rodman, Selden. Mexican Journal: The Conquerors Conquered. LC 58-12620. (Arcturus Books Paperbacks). 315p. 1965. pap. 2.45 (ISBN 0-8093-0174-1). S Ill U Pr.

Salinas Pedraza, Jesus & Bernard, H. Russell. The Otomi: Volume I, Geography & Fauna. LC 78-55704. (Illus.). 1978. 15.00x (ISBN 0-8263-0484-2). U of NM Pr.

Saville, Marshall H., tr. Narrative of Some Things of New Spain & of the Great City of Temestitan, Mexico. Repr. of 1917 ed. 10.00 (ISBN 0-527-19721-1). Kraus Repr.

Schwatka, Frederick. In the Land of Cave & Cliff Dwellers: Travels in Northwest Mexico in 1888 & 1889. LC 77-23279. (Beautiful Rio Grande Classics Ser.). 1977. lib. bdg. 15.00 (ISBN 0-87380-123-7). Rio Grande.

Shawcross, Mike. San Cristobal de las Casas, Chiapas: City & Area Guide. 3rd ed. (Illus.). 74p. 1980. pap. 5.95 (ISBN 0-933982-16-X). Bradt Ent.

Sterling Publishing Company Editors. Mexico in Pictures. rev. ed. LC 60-14339. (Visual Geography Ser). (Illus., Orig.). (gr. 4-12). 1961. PLB 4.99 (ISBN 0-8069-1013-5). Sterling.

Thompson, J. Eric. Maya Archaeologist. (Illus.). 1975. 14.95 (ISBN 0-8061-0561-5); pap. 6.95 (ISBN 0-8061-1206-9). U of Okla Pr.

Timmons, Wilbert H., ed. John F. Finerty Reports Porfirian Mexico, 1879. LC 73-86138. 1974. 12.00 (ISBN 0-87404-041-8). Tex Western.

Tinker, Ben. Mexican Wilderness & Wildlife. LC 77-14030. (Illus.). 143p. 1978. 9.95 (ISBN 0-292-75037-4). U of Tex Pr.

Tschiffely, A. Tschiffely's Ride. 1976. lib. bdg. 34.95 (ISBN 0-8490-2777-2). Gordon Pr.

Tylor, Edward B. Anahuac or Mexico & the Mexicans Ancient & Modern. LC 66-29078. 1970. Repr. of 1861 ed. text ed. 17.00x (ISBN 0-391-01956-2). Humanities.

University of California. Publications in Geography, Vols. 1-10. Set. 354.00 (ISBN 0-685-23261-1); Set. pap. 316.00 (ISBN 0-685-23262-X). Johnson Repr.

Vigne, Godfrey T. Travels in Mexico, South America, 2 vols. LC 70-177865. (Illus.). Repr. of 1863 ed. 49.50 (ISBN 0-404-06766-2). AMS Pr.

Von Haag, Michael & Crew, Anna. A Moneywise Guide to North America Canada, USA, Mexico. rev. ed. (Travelaid Travel Bks.). (Illus., Orig.). 1978. pap. 9.95 (ISBN 0-8467-0438-2, Pub. by Two Continents). Hippocrene Bks.

Von Humboldt, Alexander. Political Essay on the Kingdom of New Spain, 4 Vols. Black, John, tr. LC 1-20796. Repr. of 1811 ed. Set. 147.50 (ISBN 0-404-03450-0). AMS Pr.

Wallenberg, Peter J. Not As a Tourist in Mexico. (Illus.). 1979. pap. 6.00 (ISBN 0-912434-24-4). Ocelot Pr.

Weekley, Richard J. Mayan Night. LC 81-65782. (Illus.). 224p. (Orig.). 1981. pap. 6.50 (ISBN 0-915392-08-9, Domina Bks). Double M Pr.

West, et al. Chart Guide for Mexico West. (Illus.). 88p. (Orig.). 1981. pap. price not set (ISBN 0-938206-05-2). ChartGuide.

Wislizenus, Frederick A. Tour to Northern Mexico with Col. Doniphan, 1846-1847. LC 74-85495. (Beautiful Rio Grande Classic Ser). (Illus.). 160p. 1969. Repr. of 1848 ed. lib. bdg. 10.00 (ISBN 0-87380-003-6). Rio Grande.

Woodcock, George. To the City of the Dead: An Account of Travels in Mexico. LC 74-31872. (Illus.). 271p. 1975. Repr. of 1957 ed. lib. bdg. 17.25x (ISBN 0-8371-7946-7, WOCI). Greenwood.

MEXICO–DESCRIPTION AND TRAVEL–GUIDEBOOKS

Barwick, Steven. The Franco Codex of the Cathedral of Mexico: Transcription & Commentary. LC 64-20256. 190p. 1965. 10.00x (ISBN 0-8093-0165-2). S Ill U Pr.

Bellamy, Frank. Mexico & Central America. LC 76-55108. 1977. 10.00 (ISBN 0-8467-0272-X, Pub. by Two Continents); pap. 6.95 (ISBN 0-8467-0336-X). Hippocrene Bks.

Birnbaum, Stephen. Mexico, 1981. (The Get 'em & Go Travel Guides). pap. 9.95 (ISBN 0-395-29747-8). HM.

Brenner, A. Your Mexican Holiday. 1976. lib. bdg. 59.95 (ISBN 0-8490-2853-1). Gordon Pr.

Campbell, R. Complete Guide & Descriptive Books of Mexico. 1976. lib. bdg. 59.95 (ISBN 0-8490-1654-1). Gordon Pr.

Conkling, Alfred R. Appleton's Guide to Mexico. 1976. lib. bdg. 59.95 (ISBN 0-8490-1443-3). Gordon Pr.

Crownover, Richard. Erotic Mexico: A Travellers Unofficial Guide. 1975. pap. 2.00 (ISBN 0-914778-11-0). Phoenix Bks.

De Mente, Boye. Insider's Guide to Rocky Point, Nogales, Guaymas, Mazatlan, & La Paz. 1975. pap. 2.00 (ISBN 0-914778-06-4). Phoenix Bks.

Fodor's Budget Mexico, 1981. 1980. pap. 5.95 (ISBN 0-679-00660-5). McKay.

Fodor's Mexico, 1981. 1980. 13.95 (ISBN 0-679-00707-5); pap. 10.95 (ISBN 0-679-00708-3). McKay.

Ford, Norman D. All of Mexico at Low Cost. new ed. 1978. pap. 3.45 (ISBN 0-685-59612-5). Harian.

Franz, Carl. The People's Guide to Camping in Mexico. (Illus.). 416p. (Orig.). 1981. pap. 10.00 (ISBN 0-912528-18-4). John Muir.

--The People's Guide to Mexico. rev. ed. LC 78-71187. (Illus.). 579p. (Orig.). 1979. pap. 9.00 (ISBN 0-912528-15-X). John Muir.

Frommer & Pasmantier. Mexico & Guatemala on Ten Dollars a Day. 1977. pap. 4.95 (ISBN 0-671-10893-X). S&S.

Gierloff-Emden, Hans G. Mexico: Eine Landeskunde. (Illus.). 634p. 1970. 96.50x (ISBN 3-11-002708-9). De Gruyter.

A Kosoy Travel Guide to Mexico, Central America & South America. (Illus.). 1981. pap. 6.95 (ISBN 0-531-02395-8). Watts.

Liebman, Seymour B. Mexico: A Country of Three Cultures. Romashko, Sandra D., ed. LC 76-46902. (Windward Full Color Travel Guide). (Illus.). 1976. pap. 2.95 (ISBN 0-89317-013-5). Windward Pub.

Mexico & Guatemala on Fifteen & Twenty Dollars a Day: 1981-82. 512p. 1981. pap. 6.95 (ISBN 0-671-41422-4). Frommer-Pasmantier.

Nagel Travel Guide to Mexico. (Nagel Travel Guide Ser.). (Illus.). 436p. 1974. 49.00 (ISBN 2-8263-0625-1). Hippocrene Bks.

Nagel's Encyclopedia Guide: Mexico. (Illus.). 576p. 1978. 49.00 (ISBN 2-8263-0625-1). Masson Pub.

Rand McNally Road Atlas: United States, Canada, Mexico. 1981. deluxe ed. 8.95 (ISBN 0-528-89205-3); pap. 5.95 (ISBN 0-528-89200-2); gift ed. 6.95 (ISBN 0-528-89203-7). Rand.

San Diego & Mexico Guide. 1979. pap. 1.95 (ISBN 0-528-84168-8). Rand.

Sunset Editors. Mexico: Travel Guide. 6th ed. LC 76-46655. (Illus.). 144p. 1977. pap. 5.95 (ISBN 0-376-06457-9, Sunset Bks). Sunset-Lane.

Wilhelm, John. John Wilhelm's Guide to Mexico. 5th ed. 1978. 12.50 (ISBN 0-07-070289-6, GB). McGraw.

MEXICO–ECONOMIC CONDITIONS

Altman, Ida & Lockhart, James, eds. Provinces of Early Mexico: Variants of Spanish American Regional Evolution. LC 76-620055. (Latin American Studies: Vol. 36). (Illus.). 1976. text ed. 12.00 (ISBN 0-87903-036-4). UCLA Lat Am Ctr.

Avila, Manuel. Tradition & Growth: A Study of Four Mexican Villages. LC 73-86134. 1969. 13.50x (ISBN 0-226-03245-0). U of Chicago Pr.

Bancroft, H. H. Resources & Development of Mexico. 1976. lib. bdg. 59.95 (ISBN 0-8490-2519-2). Gordon Pr.

Borah, Woodrow. New Spain's Century of Depression. LC 73-16181. 1951. lib. bdg. 10.00 (ISBN 0-8414-3347-X). Folcroft.

Brading, D. Miners & Merchants in Bourbon Mexico, 1763-1810. LC 74-123666. (Cambridge Latin American Studies: No. 10). (Illus.). 1971. 44.50 (ISBN 0-521-07874-1). Cambridge U Pr.

Business International Corp. Investment Strategies in Mexico: How to Deal with Mexicanization. 280p. 1980. 114.00x (ISBN 0-86010-200-9, Pub. by Graham & Trotman England). State Mutual Bk.

Callcott, Wilfrid H. Liberalism in Mexico, 1857-1929. (Illus.). 1965. Repr. of 1931 ed. 25.00 (ISBN 0-208-00278-2, Archon). Shoe String.

Camp, Roderic A. The Role of Economists in Policymaking: A Comparative Case Study of Mexico & the United States. LC 77-74318. (Institute of Government Research Ser.). 1977. pap. text ed. 1.95x (ISBN 0-8165-0526-8). U of Ariz Pr.

Cancian, Frank. Change & Uncertainty in a Peasant Community: The Maya Corn Farmers of Zinacantan. LC 72-153814. (Illus.). 1972. 12.50x (ISBN 0-8047-0787-1). Stanford U Pr.

De La Vega, John. Mexican Real Estate: Law & Practices Affecting Private U. S. Ownership. LC 75-27888. 1976. pap. 3.95 (ISBN 0-8165-0534-9). U of Ariz Pr.

De Walt, B. R. Modernization in a Mexican Ejido. LC 78-3412. (Latin American Studies: No. 33). (Illus.). 1979. 29.95 (ISBN 0-521-22064-5). Cambridge U Pr.

Dunn, Mary M., ed. Humboldt's Political Essay on the Kingdom of New Spain. 1972. pap. text ed. 3.95x (ISBN 0-394-31510-3). Phila Bk Co.

Eckstein, S. The Poverty of Revolution: The State & the Urban Poor in Mexico. 1977. 22.50 (ISBN 0-691-09367-9). Princeton U Pr.

Friedrich, Paul. Agrarian Revolt in a Mexican Village. LC 77-89627. (Illus.). 1978. pap. 5.25 (ISBN 0-226-26481-5, P832). U of Chicago Pr.

Garcia, Juan R. Operation Wetback: The Mass Deportation of Mexican Undocumented Workers in 1954. LC 79-6189. (Contributions in Ethnic Studies: No. 2). (Illus.). xvii, 268p. 1980. lib. bdg. 25.00 (ISBN 0-313-21353-4, GOW/). Greenwood.

Glade, William P., Jr. & Anderson, Charles W. Political Economy of Mexico: Two Studies. 256p. 1963. pap. 5.25x (ISBN 0-299-02894-1). U of Wis Pr.

Graham & Trotman Ltd. Business Yearbook of Brazil, Mexico & Venezuela 1980-81. 300p. 1980. 37.00x (ISBN 0-86010-242-2, Pub by Graham & Trotman England). State Mutual Bk.

Hancock, Richard H. The Role of the Bracero in the Economic & Cultural Dynamics of Mexico. 146p. 1959. pap. 2.00 (ISBN 0-912098-05-8). Cal Inst Intl St.

Hansen, Roger D. The Politics of Mexican Development. LC 77-134300. (Illus.). 298p. 1971. 20.00x (ISBN 0-8018-1193-7); pap. 4.95x (ISBN 0-8018-1651-3). Johns Hopkins.

International Bank for Reconstruction & Development. The Economic Development of Mexico. LC 77-86378. Repr. of 1953 ed. 57.50 (ISBN 0-404-60306-8). AMS Pr.

Longrigg, S., ed. Major Companies of Brazil, Mexico & Venezuela 1980-81. 450p. 1980. 114.00x (ISBN 0-86010-209-2, Pub. by Graham & Trotman England); 99.00x (ISBN 0-86010-227-0). State Mutual Bk.

Looney, Robert E. Mexico's Economy: A Policy Analysis with Forecasts to 1990. LC 78-3132. (Westview Special Studies on Latin America Ser.). 1978. lib. bdg. 29.75x (ISBN 0-89158-093-X). Westview.

Mancke, Richard B. Mexican Oil & Natural Gas: Political, Strategic & Economic Implications. LC 78-65353. 1979. 22.95 (ISBN 0-03-048451-0). Praeger.

Markiewicz, Dana. Ejido Organization in Mexico Nineteen Thirty-Four to Nineteen Seventy-Six. LC 79-620057. (Special Studies: Vol. 1). 1980. pap. text ed. 6.50 (ISBN 0-87903-501-3). UCLA Lat Am Ctr.

Mexico: National Industrial Development Plan, 2vols. 400p. 1979. Set. 66.00x (ISBN 0-686-64707-6, Pub. by Graham & Trotman England); Vol.1. 0.00; Vol. 2. 0.00 (ISBN 0-86010-187-8). State Mutual Bk.

OAS General Secretariat Executive Secretariat for Economic & Social Affairs. Short-Term Economic Reports: Mexico 1980. (Sort-Term Economic Report Ser.). 54p. (Span.). 1980. lib. bdg. 4.00 (ISBN 0-8270-1293-4). OAS.

Reyna, Jose' L. & Weinert, Richard S., eds. Authoritarianism in Mexico. LC 77-339. (Inter-American Politics Ser.: Vol. 2). 1977. text ed. 13.50x (ISBN 0-915980-64-9). Inst Study Human.

Ross, John B. The Economic System of Mexico. 130p. 1971. 5.00 (ISBN 0-912098-09-0). Cal Inst Intl St.

Schlagheck, James L., et al. The Political, Economic, & Labor Climate in Mexico. rev. ed. LC 79-92307. (Multinational Industrial Relations Ser: Latin American Studies No.4b). (Illus.). 186p. 1980. pap. 15.00 (ISBN 0-89546-019-X). Indus Res Unit-Wharton.

Shafer, Robert J. Mexican Business Organizations: History & Analysis. LC 73-629. 400p. 1973. 17.00x (ISBN 0-8156-0093-3). Syracuse U Pr.

--Mexico: Mutual Adjustment Planning. (National Planning Ser.: No. 4). (Orig.). 1966. pap. 4.25x (ISBN 0-8156-2090-X). Syracuse U Pr.

Singer, Morris. Growth, Equality, & the Mexican Experience. (Latin American Monographs: No. 16). (Illus.). 353p. 1969. 15.00x (ISBN 0-292-70011-3). U of Tex Pr.

Solis, Leopoldo. Economic Policy Reform in Mexico: A Case Study for Developing Countries. LC 80-26937. (Pergamon Press Series on International Development). 240p. 1981. 27.50 (ISBN 0-08-026330-5). Pergamon.

Stocking, George W. The Mexican Oil Problem. 1976. lib. bdg. 59.95 (ISBN 0-8490-0618-X). Gordon Pr.

Tenkte, Adriann & Wallace, Robert B. Protection & Development in Mexico. 1980. 35.00 (ISBN 0-312-65217-8). St Martin.

Thompson, John K. Financial Policy, Inflation & Economic Development: The Mexican Experience, Vol. 16. Altman, Edward I. & Walter, Ingo, eds. LC 77-7787. (Contemporary Studies in Economic & Financial Analysis). 1979. lib. bdg. 30.00 (ISBN 0-89232-084-2). Jai Pr.

Turner, John K. Barbarous Mexico. new ed. (Texas Pan American Series). (Illus.). 354p. 1969. 15.00 (ISBN 0-292-78418-X). U of Tex Pr.

Van Ginneken, Wouter. Socio-Economic Groups & Income Distribution in Mexico. 1980. 27.50x (ISBN 0-312-73941-9). St Martin.

Vellinga, Menno. Economic Development & the Dynamics of Class: Industrialization, Power & Control in Monterrey, Mexico. 1979. pap. text ed. 21.50x (ISBN 90-232-1636-9). Humanities.

Vernon, Raymond. Dilemma of Mexico's Development: The Roles of the Private & Public Sectors. LC 63-17214. (Center for International Affairs Ser). 1963. 12.50x (ISBN 0-674-20650-9). Harvard U Pr.

Wilkie, James W. The Mexican Revolution: Federal Expenditure & Social Change Since 1910. 2nd rev ed. LC 74-103072. 1970. 26.75x (ISBN 0-520-01919-9); pap. 6.50x (ISBN 0-520-01869-9, CAMPUS36). U of Cal Pr.

Williams, Edward J. The Rebirth of the Mexican Petroleum Industry: Developmental Directions & Policy Implications. LC 79-1546. 240p. 1979. 20.95 (ISBN 0-669-02908-4). Lexington Bks.

Workshop on Mexico: Management Implications of the Changing Investment Environment. 75p. 1980. pap. 5.50 (ISBN 0-686-61371-6, COA 38, COA). Unipub.

MEXICO–EMIGRATION AND IMMIGRATION

Gamio, Manuel. Mexican Immigrant: His Life Story. LC 69-18778. (American Immigration Collection Ser., No. 1). (Illus.). 1969. Repr. of 1931 ed. 8.50 (ISBN 0-405-00526-1). Arno.

--Mexican Immigration to the United States. LC 73-144233. 1971. pap. 3.00 (ISBN 0-486-22721-9). Dover.

--Mexican Immigration to the United States. LC 69-18777. (American Immigration Collection Ser., No. 1). (Illus.). 1969. Repr. of 1930 ed. 13.00 (ISBN 0-405-00525-3). Arno.

Hoffman, Abraham. Unwanted Mexican Americans in the Great Depression: Repatriation Pressures, 1929-1939. LC 73-86448. 1974. pap. 6.45x (ISBN 0-8165-0366-4). U of Ariz Pr.

Nunn, C. F. Foreign Immigrants in Early Bourbon Mexico: Seventeen Hundred to Seventeen Sixty. LC 78-1159. (Cambridge Latin American Studies: No. 31). 1979. 35.50 (ISBN 0-521-22051-3). Cambridge U Pr.

Roberts, Kenneth, et al. The Mexican Migration Numbers Game: An Analysis of the Lesko Estimate of Undocumented Migration from Mexico to the United States. (Research Report Ser.: 1978-1). 33p. 1978. pap. 4.00 (ISBN 0-87755-228-2). U of Tex Busn Res.

MEXICO–FOREIGN RELATIONS

Astiz, Carlos A., ed. Latin American International Politics: Ambitions, Capabilities & the National Interests of Mexico, Brazil & Argentina. LC 68-30668. 1969. 9.95x (ISBN 0-268-00323-8). U of Notre Dame Pr.

Bulnes, Francisco. The Whole Truth About Mexico: President Wilson's Responsibility. 1976. lib. bdg. 59.95 (ISBN 0-8490-1296-1). Gordon Pr.

Callahan, James M. American Foreign Policy in Mexican Relations. LC 66-30787. 1932. 17.50x (ISBN 0-8154-0045-4). Cooper Sq.

Carman, Michael D. U.S. Customs & the Madero Revolution. (Southwestern Studies Ser.: No. 48). 1976. 3.00 (ISBN 0-87404-105-8). Tex Western.

Condon, John C. InterAct: Mexico-United States. Renwick, George W., ed. LC 80-83092. (Country Orientation Ser.). 80p. 1980. pap. text ed. 10.00x (ISBN 0-933662-13-0). Intercult Pr.

Cronon, E. David. Josephus Daniels in Mexico. (Illus.). 1960. 11.50 (ISBN 0-299-02061-4); pap. 6.95 (ISBN 0-299-02064-9). U of Wis Pr.

David, Jules. American Political & Economic Penetration of Mexico, 1877-1920. Bruchey, Stuart & Bruchey, Eleanor, eds. LC 76-5001. (American Business Abroad Ser.). 1976. lib. bdg. 27.00x (ISBN 0-405-09269-5). Arno.

Dillon, Emile J. Mexico on the Verge. LC 78-111712. (American Imperialism: Viewpoints of United States Foreign Policy, 1898-1941). 1970. Repr. of 1921 ed. 15.00 (ISBN 0-405-02013-9). Arno.

Feller, A. H. Mexican Claims Commissions, 1923-1934. Repr. of 1935 ed. 26.00 (ISBN 0-527-28900-0). Kraus Repr.

Garber, Paul M. The Gadsden Treaty. 1959. 8.00 (ISBN 0-8446-1195-6). Peter Smith.

Gilderhus, Mark T. Diplomacy & Revolution: U. S. - Mexican Relations Under Wilson & Carranza. LC 76-26388. 1977. 10.50x (ISBN 0-8165-0630-2); pap. text ed. 4.25x (ISBN 0-8165-0561-6). U of Ariz Pr.

Gregg, Robert S. Influence of Border Troubles on Relations Between the United States & Mexico, 1876-1910. LC 72-98181. (American Scene Ser). 1970. Repr. of 1937 ed. lib. bdg. 25.00 (ISBN 0-306-71833-2). Da Capo.

Grieb, Kenneth J. United States & Huerta. LC 69-10906. (Illus.). xvi, 232p. 1969. 15.95x (ISBN 0-8032-0060-9). U of Nebr Pr.

Hanna, Alfred J. & Hanna, Kathryn A. Napoleon Third & Mexico: American Triumph Over Monarchy. LC 72-156761. (Illus.). 1971. 22.50x (ISBN 0-8078-1171-8). U of NC Pr.

Hill, Larry D. Emissaries to a Revolution: Woodrow Wilson's Executive Agents in Mexico. LC 73-81848. 424p. 1973. 25.00 (ISBN 0-8071-0055-2). La State U Pr.

Katz, Friedrich. The Secret War in Mexico: Europe, the United States, & the Mexican Revolution. LC 80-26607. 1981. lib. bdg. 30.00x (ISBN 0-226-42588-6). U of Chicago Pr.

Liss, Sheldon B. Century of Disagreement: The Chamizal Conflict 1864-1964. (Facsimile of 1965 ed.). 1967. student ed. 4.00 (ISBN 0-87419-038-X); lib. bdg. 6.00 (ISBN 0-87419-025-8). U Pr of Wash.

McBride, Robert E. Mexico & the United States. (A New American Assembly Ser.). 312p. 1981. 12.95 (ISBN 0-13-579565-6); pap. 5.95 (ISBN 0-13-579557-5). P-H.

MacCorkle, Stuart A. American Policy of Recognition Toward Mexico. LC 72-131774. 1971. Repr. of 1933 ed. 11.00 (ISBN 0-403-00661-9). Scholarly.

--American Policy of Recognition Towards Mexico. LC 70-155620. Repr. of 1933 ed. 11.50 (ISBN 0-404-04108-6). AMS Pr.

Maissin, Eugene. French in Mexico & Texas, 1838-1839. Sheppherd, J. L., tr. (Illus.). 1961. 35.00 (ISBN 0-685-05002-5). A Jones.

Manning, William R. Early Diplomatic Relations Between the United States & Mexico. LC 74-145162. 1971. Repr. of 1916 ed. 15.00 (ISBN 0-403-01090-X). Scholarly.

--Early Diplomatic Relations Between the United States & Mexico. LC 77-158857. Repr. of 1916 ed. 19.75 (ISBN 0-404-04181-7). AMS Pr.

--Early Diplomatic Relations Between the United States & Mexico. LC 68-55101. 1968. Repr. of 1916 ed. lib. bdg. 19.00x (ISBN 0-8371-0558-7, MAUM). Greenwood.

Meyer, Lorenzo. Mexico & the United States in the Oil Controversy, 1917-1942. Vasconcellos, Muriel, tr. from Span. LC 76-18690. 389p. 1977. text ed. 19.95x (ISBN 0-292-75032-3). U of Tex Pr.

Nance, Joseph M. After San Jacinto: The Texas-Mexican Frontier, 1836-1841. (Illus.). 656p. 1963. 25.00x (ISBN 0-292-73156-6). U of Tex Pr.

O'Shaughnessy, Edith. Diplomat's Wife in Mexico. LC 73-111727. (American Imperialism: Viewpoints of United States Foreign Policy, 1898-1941). 1970. Repr. of 1916 ed. 23.00 (ISBN 0-405-02042-2). Arno.

Rice, Sr. M. Elizabeth. Diplomatic Relations Between the United States & Mexico, As Affected by the Struggle for Religious Liberty in Mexico, 1925-1929. LC 73-92571. viii, 224p. Date not set. Repr. of 1959 ed. cancelled (ISBN 0-8462-1777-5). Russell.

Rippy, James F. United States & Mexico. rev. ed. LC 73-137281. Repr. of 1931 ed. 29.00 (ISBN 0-404-05337-8). AMS Pr.

Rives, George L. United States & Mexico: 1821 to 1848, 2 Vols. LC 13-20399. 1969. Repr. of 1913 ed. Set. 54.00 (ISBN 0-527-75700-4). Kraus Repr.

Schoonover, Thomas D. Dollars Over Dominion: The Triumph of Liberalism in Mexican-United States Relations, 1861-1867. LC 77-21287. 1978. 22.50x (ISBN 0-8071-0368-3). La State U Pr.

Shapira, Yoram. Mexican Foreign Policy: Under Echeverria. LC 78-58423. (The Washington Papers: No. 56). 84p. 1978. pap. 4.00 (ISBN 0-8039-1096-7). Sage.

Smith, Peter H. Mexico: The Quest for a U. S. Policy. LC 80-67612. (Illus.). 32p. (Orig.). 1980. pap. 2.00 (ISBN 0-87124-062-9). Foreign Policy.

Smith, Robert F. The United States & Revolutionary Nationalism in Mexico, 1916-1932. LC 73-182872. 1972. 15.00x (ISBN 0-226-76506-7). U of Chicago Pr.

--The United States & Revolutionary Nationalism in Mexico, 1916-1932. LC 73-182872. 1972. 15.00x (ISBN 0-226-76506-7). U of Chicago Pr.

Starr, Frederick. Mexico & the United States. 1976. lib. bdg. 50.00 (ISBN 0-8490-0623-6). Gordon Pr.

Tischendorf, Alfred P. Great Britain & Mexico in the Era of Porfiro Dias. LC 61-6224. 1961. 12.75 (ISBN 0-8223-0180-6). Duke.

Wilson, Henry L. Diplomatic Episodes in Mexico, Belgium & Chile. LC 70-123496. 1971. Repr. of 1927 ed. 15.50 (ISBN 0-8046-1383-4). Kennikat.

MEXICO–HISTORY

Alba, Victor. The Mexicans: The Making of a Nation. LC 67-20469. 1970. pap. 5.95 (ISBN 0-672-63564-X). Pegasus.

Bancroft, Hubert H. History of Mexico, 6 vols. LC 67-29422. (Works of Hubert Howe Bancroft Ser.). 1967. Repr. of 1888 ed. Set. 150.00x (ISBN 0-914888-10-2). Bancroft Pr.

--History of Mexico. 1976. lib. bdg. 59.95 (ISBN 0-8490-0336-9). Gordon Pr.

--History of the North Mexican States & Texas, 2 vols. LC 67-29422. (Works of Hubert Howe Bancroft Ser.). 1967. Repr. of 1888 ed. Set. 50.00x (ISBN 0-914888-17-X). Bancroft Pr.

Bannon, John F. Spanish Borderlands Frontier, 1513-1821. LC 74-110887. (Histories of the American Frontier Series). (Illus.). 308p. 1974. pap. 8.95x (ISBN 0-8263-0309-9). U of NM Pr.

Bartlett, John R. Personal Narratives of Explorations, 2 vols. LC 64-16598. (Beautiful Rio Grande Classics Ser). 1965. Set. lib. bdg. 40.00 (ISBN 0-87380-018-4). Rio Grande.

Bazant, J. A Concise History of Mexico from Hidalgo to Cardenas 1805-1940. (Illus.). 1977. 26.95 (ISBN 0-521-21495-5); pap. 7.95x (ISBN 0-521-29173-9). Cambridge U Pr.

Bernal, Ignacio. Mexico Before Cortez: Art, History, & Legend. (Illus.). 6.00 (ISBN 0-8446-1669-9). Peter Smith.

Bowditch, Charles P. Mexican & Central American Antiquities, Calendar Systems, & History. LC 74-20883. (Smithsonian Institution, Bureau of American Ethnology, Bulletin Ser.: No. 28). (Illus.). 808p. 1975. Repr. of 1904 ed. 45.00 (ISBN 0-87917-042-5). Blaine Ethridge.

Braddy, Haldeen. Mexico & the Old Southwest: People, Palaver, & Places. LC 71-141307. 1971. 12.50 (ISBN 0-8046-9001-4, Natl U); pap. 4.95 (ISBN 0-8046-9046-4). Kennikat.

Cameron, Charlotte. Mexico in Revolution. 1976. lib. bdg. 59.95 (ISBN 0-8490-0627-9). Gordon Pr.

Carr, H. Old Mother Mexico. 1976. lib. bdg. 59.95 (ISBN 0-8490-2369-6). Gordon Pr.

Carter, Hodding. Doomed Road of Empire: The Spanish Trail of Conquest. (American Trails Library Ser). (Illus.). 1963. 10.95 (ISBN 0-07-010182-5, P&RB). McGraw.

Carter, Robert F. & Suarez, Diamantina. Mexico: Historia Simplificada (a Simplified History) (gr. 9-12). 1977. pap. text ed. 7.95 (ISBN 0-88345-296-0). Regents Pub.

Cline, Howard F. Mexico: From Revolution to Evolution. (Royal Institute of International Affairs). 1962. pap. 5.95x (ISBN 0-19-500315-2). Oxford U Pr.

--Mexico: Revolution to Evolution, 1940 to 1960. 3rd ed. LC 81-3819. (Illus.). xiv, 375p. 1981. Repr. of 1971 ed. lib. bdg. 29.75x (ISBN 0-313-22993-7, CLME). Greenwood.

--U. S. & Mexico. LC 52-12258. 1963. pap. text ed. 4.95x (ISBN 0-689-70050-4, 40). Atheneum.

Cockcroft, James D. Intellectual Precursors of the Mexican Revolution, 1900-1913. (Latin American Monographs: No. 14). 351p. 1969. pap. 8.95x (ISBN 0-292-73808-0). U of Tex Pr.

Coerver, Don M. The Porfirian Interregnum: The Presidency of Manuel Gonzalez of Mexico, 1880-1884. LC 78-27274. (History & Culture Monograph Ser.: No. 14). (Orig.). 1978. pap. 6.95 (ISBN 0-912646-49-7). Tex Christian.

Corti, Egon C. Maximilian & Charlotte of Mexico, 2 vols. 1976. lib. bdg. 250.00 (ISBN 0-8490-0595-7). Gordon Pr.

Cosio Villegas, Daniel. American Extremes. Paredes, Americo, tr. from Span. LC 64-11188. (Texas Pan American Ser.). Orig. Title: Extremos de America. 243p. 1964. pap. 4.95x (ISBN 0-292-70069-5). U of Tex Pr.

Crawford, C. Land of the Montezumas. 1976. lib. bdg. 59.95 (ISBN 0-8490-2126-X). Gordon Pr.

Cubas, Antonio G. The Republic of Mexico in Eighteen Seventy-Six: A Political & Ethnological Division of the Population, Character, Habits, Costumes & Vocations of Its Inhabitants. (Mexico Ser.). 1979. lib. bdg. 59.95 (ISBN 0-8490-2997-X). Gordon Pr.

Cumberland, Charles C. Mexico: The Struggle for Modernity. LC 68-15891. (Latin American Histories Ser). (Orig.). 1968. pap. 5.95x (ISBN 0-19-500766-2). Oxford U Pr.

De Bekker, L. J. The Plot Against Mexico. 1976. lib. bdg. 59.95 (ISBN 0-8490-0844-1). Gordon Pr.

De Sahagun, Bernardino, as told to. The War of Conquest: How It Was Waged Here in Mexico. Anderson, Arthur J. & Dibble, Charles E., trs. from Nahuatl. (Illus.). 1981. 15.00 (ISBN 0-87480-111-7); pap. 8.00 (ISBN 0-87480-192-3). U of Utah Pr.

Detweiler, Robert & Ruiz, Ramon, eds. Liberation in the Americas: Comparative Aspects of the Independence Movements in Mexico & the United States. 1978. 10.00 (ISBN 0-916304-41-8). Campanile.

Deverdun, A. The True Mexico: Tenochtitlan. 1976. lib. bdg. 59.95 (ISBN 0-8490-2773-X). Gordon Pr.

Diccionario Porrua de Historia, Biografia y Geografia de Mexico, 2 vols. (Span.). 150.00 set (ISBN 0-686-56692-0, S-12279). French & Eur.

Dillon, E. J. Mexico on the Verge. 1976. lib. bdg. 59.95 (ISBN 0-8490-0631-7). Gordon Pr.

Duran, Livie I. & Bernard, H. Russell. Introduction to Chicano Studies: A Reader. (Illus.). 512p. 1973. pap. text ed. 9.95 (ISBN 0-02-330830-3, 33083). Macmillan.

Fastlicht, S. Tooth Mutilations & Dentistry in Pre-Columbian Mexico. LC 74-25143. 1976. text ed. cancelled (ISBN 0-88474-020-X). U of S Cal Pr.

Fehrenbach, T. R. Fire & Blood. LC 79-10158. 1979. pap. 7.95 (ISBN 0-02-032180-5, Collier). Macmillan.

Figueroa, Don Jose. Manifesto to Mexican Republic. 15.00 (ISBN 0-686-59610-2). Sullivan Bks Intl.

Friedrich, Paul. Agrarian Revolt in a Mexican Village. LC 77-89627. (Illus.). 1978. pap. 5.25 (ISBN 0-226-26481-5, P832). U of Chicago Pr.

Frost, Elsa C., et al, eds. Labor & Laborers Through Mexican History. 1979. pap. 28.50x (ISBN 9-6812-0036-5). U of Ariz Pr.

Gaither, R. Expropriation in Mexico. 1976. lib. bdg. 59.95 (ISBN 0-8490-1797-1). Gordon Pr.

Greenleaf, Richard E. Zumarraga & the Mexican Inquisition: 1536-1543. (Monograph Ser.). (Illus.). 1962. 20.00 (ISBN 0-88382-053-6). AAFH.

Greenleaf, Richard E. & Meyer, Michael C., eds. Research in Mexican History: Topics, Methodology, Sources, & a Practical Guide to Field Research. LC 72-86020. (Illus.). xiv, 226p. 1973. pap. 3.75x (ISBN 0-8032-5773-2, BB 516, Bison). U of Nebr Pr.

Guzman Y Raz Guzman, Jesus. Bibliografia de la Reforma, la Intervencion y el Imperio, 2 vols. LC 79-153568. (Monographias Bibliographicas Mexicanas: Nos. 17 & 19). (Sp.). 1973. Repr. of 1931 ed. lib. bdg. 47.00 (ISBN 0-8337-1501-1). B Franklin.

Hale, Susan. The Story of Mexico. 1976. lib. bdg. 59.95 (ISBN 0-8490-2681-4). Gordon Pr.

Hasbrouck, Louis S. Mexico from Cortez to Carranza. 1976. lib. bdg. 59.95 (ISBN 0-8490-2247-9). Gordon Pr.

Hedrick, Basil C., et al, eds. North Mexican Frontier: Readings in Archaeology, Ethnohistory & Ethnography. LC 70-132477. 271p. 1971. 15.95x (ISBN 0-8093-0489-9). S Ill U Pr.

Howard, David. Royal Indian Hospital of Mexico City. (Special Studies: No. 21). 99p. 1980. pap. text ed. 5.95x (ISBN 0-87918-045-5). ASU Lat Am St.

--The Royal Indian Hospital of Mexico City. (Special Studies 20 Ser.: No. 20). 99p. 1981. pap. 5.95 (ISBN 0-87918-045-5). ASU Lat Am St.

Jarratt, et al. The Mexican Experience in Texas: An Original Anthology. Cortes, Carlos, ed. LC 76-7305. (Chicano Heritage Ser.). (Illus.). 1976. lib. bdg. 20.00x (ISBN 0-405-09540-6). Arno.

Johnson, H. About Mexico: Past & Present. 1976. lib. bdg. 59.95 (ISBN 0-8490-1401-8). Gordon Pr.

Kelemen, P. Battlefield of the Gods: Aspects of Mexican History, Art & Exploration. 1976. lib. bdg. 59.95 (ISBN 0-87968-711-8). Gordon Pr.

Kelley, Francis C. Blood-Drenched Altars. 1976. lib. bdg. 59.95 (ISBN 0-87968-760-6). Gordon Pr.

Kibbe, Pauline R. A Guide to Mexican History. 120p. 1975. pap. 4.00 (ISBN 0-912434-11-2). Ocelot Pr.

Knowlton, Robert J. Church Property & the Mexican Reform, 1856-1910. Perry, Laurens B., ed. LC 74-28897. (The Origins of Modern Mexico Ser). (Illus.). 256p. 1976. 17.50 (ISBN 0-87580-055-6). N Ill U Pr.

Ladd, Doris M. The Mexican Nobility at Independence, 1780-1826. LC 75-720106. (Latin American Monographs: No. 40). 332p. 1976. pap. 7.95x (ISBN 0-292-75027-7). U of Tex Pr.

Langham, Thomas A. Border Trials: Ricardo Flores Magon & the Mexican Liberals. (Southwestern Studies Ser.: No. 65). 1981. pap. 3.00 (ISBN 0-87404-123-6). Tex Western.

Lieuwen, Edwin. Mexican Militarism: The Political Rise & Fall of the Revolutionary Army, 1910-1940. LC 80-28937. (Illus.). xiii, 194p. 1981. Repr. of 1968 ed. lib. bdg. 23.50x (ISBN 0-313-22911-2, LIMM). Greenwood.

McHenry, J. Patrick. Short History of Mexico. 6.00 (ISBN 0-686-66277-6). Peter Smith.

--Short History of Mexico. rev. ed. LC 75-107354. 1970. pap. 2.95 (ISBN 0-385-02391-X, C363, Dolp). Doubleday.

Magner, James A. Men of Mexico. facs. ed. LC 68-55849. (Essay Index Reprint Ser). 1942. 40.25 (ISBN 0-8369-0666-7). Arno.

Magon, Ricardo F. Land & Liberty: Anarchist Influences in the Mexican Revolution. Poole, Dave, ed. 1978. pap. 5.95 (ISBN 0-904564-17-7); pap. 5.95 (ISBN 0-904564-16-9). Carrier Pigeon.

Martin, P. Mexico of the Twentieth Century, 2 vols. 1976. lib. bdg. 200.00 (ISBN 0-8490-2249-5). Gordon Pr.

Mayer, B. Mexico: Aztec, Spanish & Republican, 2 vols. 1976. lib. bdg. 250.00 (ISBN 0-8490-2246-0). Gordon Pr.

Mayo, A. History of Mexico: From Pre-Columbia to Present. 1978. 14.95 (ISBN 0-13-390203-X). P-H.

Mexico en el Tiempo, 2 vols. (Mexico Ser.). 1979. Set. lib. bdg. 200.95 (ISBN 0-8490-2972-4). Gordon Pr.

Meyer, Michael C. & Sherman, William L. The Course of Mexican History. (Illus.). 1979. 29.95 (ISBN 0-19-502413-3); pap. text ed. 12.95x (ISBN 0-19-502414-1). Oxford U Pr.

Millan, V. Mexico Reborn. 1976. 59.95 (ISBN 0-8490-2250-9). Gordon Pr.

Morris, C. The True History of Mexico. 1976. lib. bdg. 59.95 (ISBN 0-8490-2772-1). Gordon Pr.

Nava, Julian. Viva la Raza: Readings on Mexican Americans. 1973. pap. text ed. 4.95x (ISBN 0-442-25918-2). D Van Nostrand.

Necoechea, Miguel. In Defense of Mexico. 1976. lib. bdg. 59.95 (ISBN 0-8490-2042-5). Gordon Pr.

Noll, Arthur H. From Republic to Empire: The Story of the Struggle for Constitutional Government in Mexico. 1976. lib. bdg. 59.95 (ISBN 0-8490-1867-6). Gordon Pr.

Olson, Joan & Olson, Gene. Silver Dust & Spanish Wine: A Bilingual History of Mexico. De Gutierrez, Frances A., tr. LC 78-55885. (Illus.). (gr. 9 up). 1979. pap. text ed. 8.47x (ISBN 0-913366-05-6). Windyridge.

--Silver Dust & Spanish Wine: A History of Mexico. LC 80-51869. (Illus.). 336p. (Orig.). (gr. 9 up). 1980. pap. text ed. 6.97x (ISBN 0-913366-06-4). Windyridge.

O'Shaughnessy, Edith. A Diplomat's Wife in Mexico. 1978. Repr. of 1916 ed. lib. bdg. 20.00 (ISBN 0-8492-2044-0). R West.

Palacios, E. J. The Stone of the Sun & the First Chapter of the History of Mexico. 1977. lib. bdg. 59.95 (ISBN 0-8490-2670-9). Gordon Pr.

Parker, Morris B. Mules, Mines & Me in Mexico, Eighteen Ninety-Five to Nineteen Thirty-Two. Day, James M., ed. LC 79-15206. 1979. pap. 7.95 (ISBN 0-8165-0626-4). U of Ariz Pr.

Parkes, Henry B. History of Mexico. 1969. pap. 5.95 (ISBN 0-395-08410-5, 61, SenEd). HM.

Parsons, Jeffrey R. Prehistoric Settlement Patterns in the Texcoco Region, Mexico. (Memoirs Ser.: No. 3). (Illus.). 1971. pap. 8.00x (ISBN 0-932206-65-4). U Mich Mus Anthro.

Perry, Laurens B. Juarez & Diaz: Machine Politics in Mexico. LC 76-14671. (The Origins of Modern Mexico Ser.). 467p. 1979. 25.00 (ISBN 0-87580-058-0). N Ill U Pr.

Powell, Philip W. Mexico's Miguel Caldera: The Taming of America's First Frontier, 1548-1597. LC 76-62551. 1977. 14.95x (ISBN 0-8165-0638-8); pap. 7.95x (ISBN 0-8165-0569-1). U of Ariz Pr.

Powell, T. G. Mexico & the Spanish Civil War. 240p. 1981. 17.50x (ISBN 0-8263-0546-6). U of NM Pr.

Pradeau, Alberto. Numismatic History of Mexico. LC 77-93447. (Illus.). 1978. Repr. of 1938 ed. lib. bdg. 22.50 (ISBN 0-915262-20-7). S J Durst.

Prescott, William H. Conquest of Mexico & Peru. Howell, Roger, ed. text ed. 20.00x (ISBN 0-8290-0220-0). Irvington.

Priestley, H. I. The Mexican Nation, a History. 75.00 (ISBN 0-8490-0617-1). Gordon Pr.

Priestly, H. I. Mexican Nation: A History. LC 73-79202. 1969. Repr. of 1926 ed. 17.50x (ISBN 0-8154-0292-9). Cooper Sq.

Quirk, Robert E. The Mexican Revolution, Nineteen Fourteen to Nineteen Fifteen: The Convention of Aquascalientes. LC 80-28130. 325p. 1981. Repr. of 1960 ed. lib. bdg. 27.50x (ISBN 0-313-22894-9, QUMR). Greenwood.

Reunion de Historiadores Mexicanos y Norteamericanos. Contemporary Studies in Mexican History (Investigaciones contemporaneas sobre historia de Mexico) 755p. (Eng. & Span.). 1971. 16.50x (ISBN 0-292-70125-X). U of Tex Pr.

Ricard, Robert. The Spiritual Conquest of Mexico. Simpson, Lesley B., tr. (California Library Reprint Ser: No. 57). 1974. 26.75x (ISBN 0-520-02760-4). U of Cal Pr.

Rippy, Merrill. Oil & the Mexican Revolution. 345p. 1972. 15.00 (ISBN 0-686-05004-5). E J Brill.

Rodman, Selden. A Short History of Mexico. rev. ed. LC 80-6151. 264p. 1981. 14.95 (ISBN 0-8128-2808-9). Stein & Day.

Ruiz, Ramon E. The Great Rebellion: Mexico Nineteen Hundred & Five to Nineteen Twenty-Four. 1980. 24.95 (ISBN 0-393-01323-5). Norton.

Russell, Thomas H. Mexico in Peace & War. 1976. lib. bdg. 59.95 (ISBN 0-8490-0626-0). Gordon Pr.

Sierra, Justo. The Political Evolution of the Mexican People. Ramsdell, Charles, tr. LC 69-63009. (Texas Pan American Ser.: No. 3). 426p. 1969. 17.50x (ISBN 0-292-78382-5); pap. 8.95 (ISBN 0-292-70071-7). U of Tex Pr.

Simpson, Lesley B. Many Mexicos, Silver Anniversary Edition. (YA) (gr. 9 up). 1966. 20.00x (ISBN 0-520-01179-1); pap. 4.65 (ISBN 0-520-01180-5, CAL29). U of Cal Pr.

Sinkin, Richard N. The Mexican Reform, Eighteen Fifty-Five to Eighteen Seventy-Six: A Study in Liberal Nation-Building. LC 78-620053. (No. 49). 273p. 1979. text ed. 18.95x (ISBN 0-292-75044-7); pap. text ed. 7.50x (ISBN 0-292-75045-5). U of Tex Pr.

Soleillant, Claude. Mexico: Activities & Projects in Color. LC 77-81955. (Activities & Projects Ser.). (Illus.). 96p. (English.). (gr. 3 up). 1978. 9.95 (ISBN 0-8069-4552-4); PLB 9.29 (ISBN 0-8069-4553-2). Sterling.

Soto, Shirlene A. The Mexican Woman: A Study of Her Participation in the Revolution, 1910-1940. LC 78-57992. 1979. perfect bdg. 12.00 (ISBN 0-88247-553-3). R & E Res Assoc.

Spinden, Herbert J. Ancient Civilizations of Mexico & Central America. 1977. Repr. of 1922 ed. lib. bdg. 25.00 (ISBN 0-8492-2411-X). R West.

Stephens, Kate. The Mastering of Mexico. 1977. lib. bdg. 59.95 (ISBN 0-8490-2214-2). Gordon Pr.

Taylor, John M. Maximilian & Carlotta: A Story of Imperialism. 1976. lib. bdg. 69.95 (ISBN 0-8490-0594-9). Gordon Pr.

Taylor, Paul S. American-Mexican Frontier: Nueces County, Texas. LC 73-139941. (Illus.). 1971. Repr. of 1934 ed. 15.00 (ISBN 0-8462-1569-1). Russell.

Texas University Institute of Latin American Studies. Essays in Mexican History: The Charles Wilson Hackett Memorial Volume. Cotner, Thomas E & Castaneda, Carlos E., eds. 309p. 1972. Repr. of 1958 ed. lib. bdg. 16.50x (ISBN 0-8371-6237-8, COMH). Greenwood.

Timmons, Wilbert H., ed. John F. Finerty Reports Porfirian Mexico, 1879. LC 73-86138. 1974. 12.00 (ISBN 0-87404-041-8). Tex Western.

Tompkins, Frank. Chasing Villa: The Story Behind the Pershing Expedition. 1976. lib. bdg. 69.95 (ISBN 0-87968-843-2). Gordon Pr.

Tyler, Ronnie C. The Mexican War: A Lithographic Record. LC 93-88280. (Illus.). 108p. 1974. 10.00 (ISBN 0-87611-031-6); collector's ed. o.p. 45.00 (ISBN 0-87611-032-4); portfolio of 16 prints 7.50 (ISBN 0-87611-034-0). Tex St Hist Assn.

Vaillant, George C. Aztecs of Mexico: Origin, Rise, & Fall of the Aztec Nation. lib. bdg. 12.50x (ISBN 0-88307-280-7). Gannon.

Vallens, Vivian M. Working Women in Mexico During the Porfiriato, 1880-1910. LC 77-91452. 1978. pap. 9.00 perfect bdg. (ISBN 0-88247-526-6). R & E Res Assoc.

Velarde, C. J. Under the Mexican Flag: The Mexican Struggle Outlined. 1976. lib. bdg. 59.95 (ISBN 0-8490-2783-7). Gordon Pr.

Wilkie, James W., et al, eds. Contemporary Mexico: Papers of the Fourth International Congress of Mexican History. 1976. 48.50x (ISBN 0-520-02798-1); pap. 17.75x (ISBN 0-520-02871-6, CAMPUS 144). U of Cal Pr.

Winton, G. A New Era in Old Mexico. 1976. lib. bdg. 59.95 (ISBN 0-8490-2338-6). Gordon Pr.

Wright, Marie R. Mexico: A History of Its Progress & Development in One Hundred Years. (Mexico Ser.). 1979. lib. bdg. 75.00 (ISBN 0-8490-2971-6). Gordon Pr.

MEXICO–HISTORY–FICTION

Azuela, Mariano. Two Novels of Mexico: The Flies & The Bosses. Simpson, Lesley B., tr. 1956. pap. 3.95 (ISBN 0-520-00053-6, CAL1). U of Cal Pr.

--Underdogs. Munguia, E., Jr., tr. (Orig.). pap. 1.50 (ISBN 0-451-50931-5, CW931, Sig Classics). NAL.

Leonard, Irving A. Baroque Times in Old Mexico: Seventeenth-Century Persons, Places, & Practices. LC 80-29256. (Illus.). xi, 260p. 1981. Repr. of 1978 ed. lib. bdg. 25.50x (ISBN 0-313-22826-4, LEBT). Greenwood.

Mayo, Allen. The Fortress of Miguel. 2nd ed. LC 57-12987. (Illus.). 1974. 10.95 (ISBN 0-918268-00-1). Tex-Mex.

MEXICO–HISTORY–SOURCES

Costeloe, Michael P. Mexico State Papers: 1744-1843. (Institute of Latin American Studies Monograph Ser.: No. 6). 144p. 1976. text ed. 19.50x (ISBN 0-485-17706-4, Athlone Pr). Humanities.

Hanrahan, Gene J., ed. The Madero Revolution As Reported in the Confidential Dispatches of U.S. Ambassador Henry Lane Wilson: June 1910-June 1911, & the Embassy in Mexico City. (Documents on the Mexican Revolution: Vol. 2). 1976. lib. bdg. 40.00 (ISBN 0-89712-033-7). Documentary Pubns.

Iturbide, Agustin De. The Memoirs of Agustin De Iturbide. lib. bdg. 6.00 (ISBN 0-89712-001-9). Documentary Pubns.

MEXICO–HISTORY–TO 1519

Bandelier, Adolph F. The Discovery of New Mexico by the Franciscan Monk Friar Marcos de Niza in 1539. Rodack, Madeleine T., tr. from Fr. LC 80-25083. 1981. 10.95x (ISBN 0-8165-0717-1). U of Ariz Pr.

Clavigero, Francesco S. The History of Mexico, 2 vols. Feldman, Burton & Richardson, Robert D., eds. LC 78-60908. (Myth & Romanticism Ser.: Vol. 7). (Illus.). 1979. Set. lib. bdg. 132.00 (ISBN 0-8240-3556-9). Garland Pub.

Collis, Maurice. Cortez & Montezuma. 1978. pap. 2.50 (ISBN 0-380-40402-8, 40402, Discus). Avon.

Davies, Nigel. The Toltec Heritage: From the Fall of Tula to the Rise of Tenochtitlan. LC 78-21384. (CAI Ser.: Vol. 153). (Illus.). 1980. 18.95 (ISBN 0-8061-1505-X). U of Okla Pr.

Padden, R. C. Hummingbird & the Hawk: Conquest & Sovereignty in the Valley of Mexico, 1503-1541. 1970. pap. 4.95x (ISBN 0-06-131898-1, TB1898, Torch). Har-Row.

--Hummingbird & the Hawk: Conquest & Sovereignty in the Valley of Mexico, 1503-1541. LC 67-12912. (Illus.). 1967. 6.75 (ISBN 0-8142-0100-8). Ohio St U Pr.

Sejourne, Laurette. Burning Water: Thought & Religion in Ancient Mexico. LC 76-14205. (Illus.). 1976. pap. 3.95 (ISBN 0-394-73276-6). Shambhala Pubns.

Shearer, Tony. Beneath the Moon and Under the Sun. (Illus.). 164p. 1975. 6.50 (ISBN 0-89540-042-1, SB-042). Sun Pub.

Spence, Michael W., et al. Miscellaneous Studies in Mexican Pre-History. (Anthropological Papers: No. 45). (Illus.). 1972. pap. 4.00x (ISBN 0-932206-43-3). U Mich Mus Anthro.

Vaillant, George C. Aztecs of Mexico. rev. ed. Vaillant, Suzannah B., ed. 1955. pap. 6.95 (ISBN 0-14-020200-5, Pelican). Penguin.

Wagner, H. R., tr. Discovery of New Spain in 1518 by Juan De Grijalva. Repr. of 1942 ed. 8.00 (ISBN 0-527-19731-9). Kraus Repr.

MEXICO–HISTORY–CONQUEST, 1519-1540

see also Tenochtitlan, Battle of, 1521

Aiton, Arthur S. Antonio De Mendoza, First Viceroy of New Spain. LC 66-24664. (Illus.). 1967. Repr. of 1927 ed. 8.50 (ISBN 0-8462-0783-4). Russell.

Blom, Frans. Conquest of Yucatan. LC 77-164521. 1972. Repr. of 1937 ed. 15.00x (ISBN 0-8154-0390-9). Cooper Sq.

Braden, C. S. Religious Aspects of the Conquest of Mexico. 1976. lib. bdg. 59.95 (ISBN 0-8490-2510-9). Gordon Pr.

Braden, Charles S. Religious Aspects of the Conquest of Mexico. LC 74-181914. Repr. of 1930 ed. 19.50 (ISBN 0-404-00925-5). AMS Pr.

Butterfield, M. E. Jeronimo De Aguilar Conquistador. LC 55-11361. 54p. 1969. pap. 2.50 (ISBN 0-8173-5660-6). U of Ala Pr.

Cantu, Caesar C. Cortes & the Fall of the Aztec Empire. (Illus.). 1966. 10.95 (ISBN 0-685-16803-4, 0-910978-1-3). Modern World.

Chamberlain, Robert S. Conquest & Colonization of Yucatan, 1517-1550. 1967. lib. bdg. 25.00x (ISBN 0-374-91387-0). Octagon.

Cortes, Hernando. Five Letters of Cortes. Morris, J. Bayard, tr. Orig. Title: Hernando Cortes Five Letters, 1519-1526. 1969. pap. 6.95x (ISBN 0-393-09877-X, NortonC). Norton.

Del Castillo, Bernal D. The Discovery & Conquest of Mexico. LC 71-139824. 1970. Repr. lib. bdg. 25.00x (ISBN 0-374-91307-2). Octagon.

Diaz Del Castillo, Bernal. Conquest of New Spain. Cohen, John M., tr. (Classics Ser.). (Orig.). (YA) (gr. 9 up). 1963. pap. 2.95 (ISBN 0-14-044123-9). Penguin.

--Discovery & Conquest of Mexico. 478p. 1956. pap. 8.95 (ISBN 0-374-50384-2). FS&G.

Gardiner, C. Harvey. Naval Power in the Conquest of Mexico. Repr. of 1956 ed. lib. bdg. 15.00x (ISBN 0-8371-2457-3, GANP). Greenwood.

Gardiner, Clinton H. Martin Lopez. Conquistador Citizen of Mexico. LC 73-19307. 193p. 1974. Repr. of 1958 ed. lib. bdg. 15.00x (ISBN 0-8371-7322-1, GAML). Greenwood.

Gibson, Charles. The Aztecs Under Spanish Rule: A History of the Indians of the Valley of Mexico, 1519-1810. (Illus.). 1964. 20.00x (ISBN 0-8047-0196-2); pap. 8.50x (ISBN 0-8047-0912-2). Stanford U Pr.

Gomara, Francisco Lopez de. Cortes: The Life of the Conqueror of Mexico by His Secretary Francisco Lopez de Gomara. Simpson, Lesley B., ed. & tr. LC 64-13474. 1964. pap. 5.95 (ISBN 0-520-00493-0). U of Cal Pr.

Horgan, Paul. Conquistadors in North American History. (Illus.). 303p. 1963. 7.95 (ISBN 0-374-12884-7). FS&G.

Leon-Portilla, Miguel. Broken Spears: The Aztec Account of the Conquest of Mexico. (Illus.). 1962. pap. 4.95 (ISBN 0-8070-5499-2, BP230). Beacon Pr.

Liss, Peggy K. Mexico Under Spain, Fifteen Twenty One-Fifteen Fifty Six: Society & the Origins of Nationality. LC 74-33507. xvi, 230p. 1975. 14.00x (ISBN 0-226-48495-5). U of Chicago Pr.

MacNutt, Francis A., tr. Hernando Cortes: His Five Letters of Relations to the Emperor Charles the Fifth of Spain, 2 vols. LC 77-1155. (Beautiful Rio Grande Classics Ser.). 1977. lib. bdg. 40.00 (ISBN 0-87380-125-3). Rio Grande.

Madariaga, Salvador de. Hernan Cortes: Conqueror of Mexico. LC 79-2570. (Illus.). 1979. Repr. of 1942 ed. lib. bdg. 34.75x (ISBN 0-313-22030-1, MACM). Greenwood.

Nicholson, Irene. Conquest of Mexico. (Jackdaw Ser: No. 51). (Illus.). 1968. 6.95 (ISBN 0-670-23731-0, Grossman). Viking Pr.

Padden, R. C. Hummingbird & the Hawk: Conquest & Sovereignty in the Valley of Mexico, 1503-1541. 1970. pap. 4.95x (ISBN 0-06-131898-1, TB1898, Torch). Har-Row.

--Hummingbird & the Hawk: Conquest & Sovereignty in the Valley of Mexico, 1503-1541. LC 67-12912. (Illus.). 1967. 6.75 (ISBN 0-8142-0100-8). Ohio St U Pr.

Prescott, William H. The Conquest of Mexico. Bd. with The Conquest of Peru. 1931. 5.95 (ISBN 0-394-60729-5, G29). Modern Lib.

--History of the Conquest of Mexico. abridged ed. Gardiner, C. Harvey, ed. LC 66-20592. 1966. 15.00x (ISBN 0-226-67999-3). U of Chicago Pr.
--History of the Conquest of Mexico. abr ed. Gardiner, C. Harvey, ed. 1966. pap. 7.50x (ISBN 0-226-68000-2). U of Chicago Pr.
Solis Y Rivadeneyra, Antonio De. The History of the Conquest of Mexico by the Spaniards, 2 vols. Townsend, Thomas, tr. from Span. LC 70-175990. (Eng.). Repr. of 1753 ed. Set. 49.50 (ISBN 0-404-07177-5); 25.00 ea.; Vol. 1. (ISBN 0-404-07178-3); Vol. 2. (ISBN 0-404-07179-1). AMS Pr.
Wagner, H. R. Rise of Fernando Cortes. 1944. 35.00 (ISBN 0-527-19733-5). Kraus Repr.
Wilkes, J. Herman Cortes, Conquistador in Mexico. (Introduction to the History of Mankind Ser.). (Illus.). 48p. (gr. 5-11). 1974. pap. 3.95 (ISBN 0-521-20424-0). Cambridge U Pr.

MEXICO–HISTORY–CONQUEST, 1519-1540–JUVENILE LITERATURE

O'Dell, Scott. The Feathered Serpent. (gr. 7 up). 1981. 10.95 (ISBN 0-395-30851-8). HM.

MEXICO–HISTORY–TO 1810

Aiton, Arthur S. Antonio De Mendoza, First Viceroy of New Spain. LC 66-24664. (Illus.). 1967. Repr. of 1927 ed. 8.50 (ISBN 0-8462-0783-4). Russell.
Brading, D. Miners & Merchants in Bourbon Mexico, 1763-1810. LC 74-123666. (Cambridge Latin American Studies: No. 10). (Illus.). 1971. 44.50 (ISBN 0-521-07874-1). Cambridge U Pr.
De Zorita, Alonso. Life & Labor in Ancient Mexico: The Brief & Summary Relation of the Lords of New Spain. Keen, Benjamin, tr. 1964. 20.00 (ISBN 0-8135-0442-2). Rutgers U Pr.
Harris, Charles H., 3rd. A Mexican Family Empire: The "Latifundio" of the Sanchez Navarros, 1765-186. LC 74-28274. 428p. 1975. 19.50x (ISBN 0-292-75020-X). U of Tex Pr.
Horgan, Paul. Conquistadors in North American History. (Illus.). 303p. 1963. 7.95 (ISBN 0-374-12884-7). FS&G.
Leonard, Irving A. Baroque Times in Old Mexico: Seventeenth-Century Persons, Places, & Practices. (Illus.). 1959. pap. 5.95 (ISBN 0-472-06110-0, 110, AA). U of Mich Pr.
Mathes, W. Michael, tr. Clemente Guillen, Explorer of the South: Diaries of the Overland Expeditions to Bahia Magdalena & La Paz, 1719, 1720-1721. LC 78-73364. (Bada California Travels Ser.: No. 42). 1979. 18.00 (ISBN 0-87093-242-X). Dawsons.
Mecham, John L. Francisco De Ibarra & Nueva Vizcaya. LC 68-23315. (Illus.). 1968. Repr. of 1927 ed. lib. bdg. 17.50x (ISBN 0-8371-0168-9, MEFI). Greenwood.
Moorhead, Max L. The Apache Frontier: Jacobo Ugarte & Spanish-Indian Relations in Northern New Spain, 1769-1791. LC 67-64449. (Civilization of the American Indian Ser.: No. 90). (Illus.). 1968. 15.95 (ISBN 0-8061-0787-1); pap. 7.95 (ISBN 0-8061-1312-X). U of Okla Pr.
Nunn, C. F. Foreign Immigrants in Early Bourbon Mexico: Seventeen Hundred to Seventeen Sixty. LC 78-1159. (Cambridge Latin American Studies: No. 31). 1979. 35.50 (ISBN 0-521-22051-3). Cambridge U Pr.
Tannenbaum, Frank. Peace by Revolution: An Interpretation of Mexico. LC 72-169776. (Select Bibliographies Reprint Ser.). (Illus.). Repr. of 1933 ed. 24.00 (ISBN 0-8369-5996-5). Arno.
Thomas, Alfred B., ed. Teodora De Croix & the Northern Frontier of New Spain 1776-1783. (American Exploration & Travel Ser.: No. 5). 1968. Repr. of 1941 ed. 14.95 (ISBN 0-8061-0093-1). U of Okla Pr.
Trimborn, Hermann. Quellen Zur Kulturgeschichte Des Prakolumbischen America. Repr. of 1936 ed. pap. 15.50 (ISBN 0-384-61570-8). Johnson Repr.

MEXICO–HISTORY–SPANISH COLONY–1540-1810

Altman, Ida & Lockhart, James, eds. Provinces of Early Mexico: Variants of Spanish American Regional Evolution. LC 76-620055. (Latin American Studies: Vol. 36). (Illus.). 1976. text ed. 12.00 (ISBN 0-87903-036-4). UCLA Lat Am Ctr.
Anderson, Arthur J., et al. Beyond the Codices: The Nahua View of Colonial Mexico. LC 74-29801. 225p. 1976. 24.50x (ISBN 0-520-02974-7). U of Cal Pr.
Archer, Christon I. The Army in Bourbon Mexico, 1760-1810. LC 76-57536. (Illus.). 366p. 1977. 19.95x (ISBN 0-8263-0442-7). U of NM Pr.
Brading, D. Miners & Merchants in Bourbon Mexico, 1763-1810. LC 74-123666. (Cambridge Latin American Studies: No. 10). (Illus.). 1971. 44.50 (ISBN 0-521-07874-1). Cambridge U Pr.
Fisher, Lillian E. Background of the Revolution for Mexican Independence. LC 76-151226. (Illus.). 1971. Repr. of 1934 ed. 19.00 (ISBN 0-8462-1581-0). Russell.
Gerhard, P. A Guide to the Historical Geography of New Spain. (Latin America Studies: No. 14). 1972. 84.50 (ISBN 0-521-08073-8). Cambridge U Pr.
Hu-DeHart, Evelyn. Missionaries, Miners, & Indians: Spanish Contact with the Yaqui Nation of Northwestern New Spain, 1533-1820. 1981. 19.95x (ISBN 0-8165-0740-6); pap. 9.95x (ISBN 0-8165-0755-4). U of Ariz Pr.
Konrad, Herman W. A Jesuit Hacienda in Colonial Mexico: Santa Lucia, 1576-1767. LC 79-65518. 472p. 1980. 28.50x (ISBN 0-8047-1050-3). Stanford U Pr.
Liss, Peggy K. Mexico Under Spain, Fifteen Twenty One-Fifteen Fifty Six: Society & the Origins of Nationality. LC 74-33507. xvi, 230p. 1975. 14.00x (ISBN 0-226-48495-5). U of Chicago Pr.
MacLachlan, Colin M. & Rodriguez, Jaime E. The Forging of the Cosmic Race: A Reinterpretation of Colonial Mexico. LC 78-68836. (Illus.). 408p. 1980. 25.00 (ISBN 0-520-03890-8). U of Cal Pr.
Meek, Wilbur T. The Exchange Media of Colonial Mexico. (Perspectives in Latin American History Ser.: No. 5). vi, 114p. Repr. of 1948 ed. lib. bdg. 13.50x (ISBN 0-87991-070-4). Porcupine Pr.
Powell, Philip W. Soldiers, Indians & Silver. LC 74-13634. 325p. 1975. pap. 5.95x (ISBN 0-87918-015-3). ASU Lat Am St.
Rydjord, John. Foreign Interest in the Independence of New Spain. LC 72-159223. xii, 347p. 1971. Repr. of 1935 ed. lib. bdg. 17.50x (ISBN 0-374-97001-7). Octagon.
--Foreign Interest in the Independence of New Spain: An Introduction to the War for Independence. LC 72-173541. (Illus.). 1972. Repr. of 1935 ed. 14.00 (ISBN 0-8462-1625-6). Russell.
Sauer, Carl O. Colima of New Spain in the Sixteenth Century. LC 76-9022. (Ibero-Americana Ser.: No. 29). 1976. Repr. of 1948 ed. lib. bdg. 15.00x (ISBN 0-8371-8891-1, SACO). Greenwood.
Taylor, William B. Drinking, Homicide, & Rebellion in Colonial Mexican Villages. LC 78-50475. xiv, 242p. 1981. pap. 5.95 (ISBN 0-8047-1112-7). Stanford U Pr.
--Drinking, Homicide, & Rebellion in Colonial Mexican Villages. LC 78-50475. 1979. 16.50x (ISBN 0-8047-0997-1). Stanford U Pr.
West, Robert C. The Mining Community in Northern New Spain: The Parral Mining District. LC 76-29398. Repr. of 1949 ed. 21.50 (ISBN 0-404-15331-3). AMS Pr.

MEXICO–HISTORY–1810-1861

Barker, Nancy N. French Experience in Mexico, Eighteen Twenty-One to Eighteen Sixty-One: A History of Constant Misunderstanding. LC 78-12935. 1979. 18.00x (ISBN 0-8078-1339-7). U of NC Pr.
Baylies, Francis. A Narrative of Major General Wool's Campaign in Mexico in the Years 1846, 1847, & 1848. (Illus.). Repr. of 1851 ed. 8.95 (ISBN 0-8363-0141-2). Jenkins.
Berge, Dennis E. The Mexican Republic 1847. (Southwestern Studies Ser.: No. 45). 1974. 3.00 (ISBN 0-87404-103-1). Tex Western.
Berlandier, Jean L., et al. Journey to Mexico During the Years Eighteen Twenty-Six to Eighteen Thirty-Four, 2 vols. Ohlendorf, Sheila M. & Bigelow, Josette, eds. LC 80-52705. (Illus.). 1980. boxed 75.00 (ISBN 0-87611-044-8); special limited ed. 150.00 (ISBN 0-87611-051-0). Tex St Hist Assn.
Cadenhead, Ivie E., Jr. Jesus Gonzalez Ortega & Mexican National Politics. Worcester, Donald E., ed. LC 73-161482. (History & Culture Monograph Ser.: No. 9). 161p. 1972. pap. 0.75 (ISBN 0-912646-05-5). Tex Christian.
Callcott, Wilfrid H. Santa Anna: The Story of an Enigma Who Once Was Mexico. (Illus.). 1964. Repr. of 1936 ed. 21.50 (ISBN 0-208-00533-1, Archon). Shoe String.
Cumberland, Charles C. Mexican Revolution. Incl. Genesis Under Madero. 308p. 1952. pap. 7.95x (ISBN 0-292-75017-X); The Constitutionalist Years. LC 74-38506. (Illus.). 469p. 1972. 17.50x (ISBN 0-292-75000-5); pap. 9.95x (ISBN 0-292-75016-1). (Illus.). U of Tex Pr.
De Lara, L. Gutierrez & Pinchon, Edgcumb. Mexican People: Their Struggle for Freedom. LC 75-111730. (American Imperialism: Viewpoints of United States Foreign Policy, 1898-1941). 1970. Repr. of 1914 ed. 17.00 (ISBN 0-405-02033-3). Arno.
Detweiler, Robert & Ruiz, Ramon, eds. Liberation in the Americas: Comparative Aspects of the Independence Period in Mexico & the United States. LC 77-83491. 1978. 4.00x (ISBN 0-916304-30-2). Campanile.
Flores Caballero, Romeo. Counter-Revolution: The Role of the Spaniards in the Independence of Mexico, 1804-1838. Rodriquez O., Jaime E., tr. LC 75-172037. (Illus.). xiv, 186p. 1974. 13.95x (ISBN 0-8032-0805-7). U of Nebr Pr.
Johnson, Richard A. The Mexican Revolution of Ayutla, 1854-1855. LC 74-3730. (Augustana Library Publications: No. 17). 125p. 1974. Repr. of 1939 ed. lib. bdg. 15.00x (ISBN 0-8371-7459-7, JOMR). Greenwood.
--The Mexican Revolution of Ayutla: 1854-1855. LC 40-1957. (Augustana College Library Ser.: No. 17). 1939. pap. 3.50 (ISBN 0-910182-12-4). Augustana Coll.
Maissin, Eugene. French in Mexico & Texas, 1838-1839. Sheppherd, J. L., tr. (Illus.). 1961. 35.00 (ISBN 0-685-05002-5). A Jones.
Noll, Arthur H. & McMahon, A. Philip. The Life & Times of Miguel Hidalgo y Costilla. LC 72-85003. (Illus.). 1973. Repr. of 1910 ed. 12.00 (ISBN 0-8462-1687-6). Russell.
Olliff, Conathon C. Reforma Mexico & the United States: A Search for Alternatives to Annexation, 1854-1861. 256p. 1981. 22.50 (ISBN 0-8173-0070-8). U of Ala Pr.
Rives, George L. United States & Mexico: 1821 to 1848, 2 Vols. LC 13-20399. 1969. Repr. of 1913 ed. Set. 54.00 (ISBN 0-527-75700-4). Kraus Repr.
Robertson, William S. Iturbide of Mexico. LC 68-23321. (Illus.). 1968. Repr. of 1952 ed. lib. bdg. 21.00x (ISBN 0-8371-0203-0, ROIM). Greenwood.
--Rise of the Spanish-American Republics: As Told in the Lives of Their Liberators. 1965. pap. text ed. 3.50 (ISBN 0-02-926600-9). Free Pr.
Stout, Joseph A. The Liberators: Filibustering Expeditions into Mexico, & the Last Gasp of Manifest Destiny. LC 72-83539. (Illus.). 9.50 (ISBN 0-87026-029-4). Westernlore.
Stout, Joseph A., Jr. The Liberators. (Great West & Indian Ser: Vol. 41). 9.50 (ISBN 0-87026-029-4). Westernlore.
Warren, Harris G. Sword Was Their Passport. LC 77-15077. 1971. Repr. of 1943 ed. 14.50 (ISBN 0-8046-1676-0). Kennikat.

MEXICO–HISTORY–WAR WITH UNITED STATES, 1845-1848

see United States–History–War with Mexico, 1845-1848

MEXICO–HISTORY–EUROPEAN INTERVENTION, 1861-1867

Basch, Samuel. Memories of Mexico: History of the Last Ten Months of the Empire. Oechler, Hugh M., tr. 235p. 1973. text ed. 9.00 (ISBN 0-911536-41-8). Trinity U Pr.
Case, Lynn M., ed. French Opinion on the United States & Mexico: Extracts from the Reports of the Procureurs Generaux. LC 69-19212. 1969. Repr. of 1936 ed. 22.50 (ISBN 0-208-00791-1, Archon). Shoe String.
Dabbs, Jack A. The French Army in Mexico, 1861-67: A Study in Military Government. (Studies in American History: No. 2). (Illus.). 1963. 48.75x (ISBN 90-2790-228-3). Mouton.
Dawson, Daniel. The Mexican Adventure. facsimile ed. (Select Bibliographies Reprint Ser). Repr. of 1935 ed. 24.00 (ISBN 0-8369-6682-1). Arno.
Hanna, Alfred J. & Hanna, Kathryn A. Napoleon Third & Mexico: American Triumph Over Monarchy. LC 72-156761. (Illus.). 1971. 22.50x (ISBN 0-8078-1171-8). U of NC Pr.
Miller, Robert R. Arms Across the Border: United States Aid to Juarez During the French Intervention in Mexico. LC 73-86617. (Transactions Ser.: Vol. 63, Pt. 6). (Illus.). 1973. pap. 1.00 (ISBN 0-87169-636-3). Am Philos.
Roeder, Ralph. Juarez & His Mexico: A Biographical History, 2 Vols. LC 68-23322. (Illus.). 1968. Repr. of 1947 ed. Set. lib. bdg. 40.75x (ISBN 0-8371-0204-9, ROJM). Greenwood.
Vaughan, Mary K. The State, Education, & Social Class in Mexico, 1880-1928. (Origins of Modern Mexico Ser.). 380p. 1981. 22.50 (ISBN 0-87580-079-3). N Ill U Pr.

MEXICO–HISTORY–1910-1946

see also Vera Cruz, Mexico (City)–History–American Occupation, 1914

Brading, D. A., ed. Caudillo & Peasant in the Mexican Revolution. LC 79-16593. (Cambridge Latin American Studies: No. 38). 1980. 41.50 (ISBN 0-521-22997-9). Cambridge U Pr.
Brenner, Anita & Leighton, George R. The Wind That Swept Mexico: The History of the Mexican Revolution of 1910-1942. new ed. (Texas Pan American Ser). (Illus.). 320p. 1971. 19.95 (ISBN 0-292-70106-3). U of Tex Pr.
Calvert, Peter. Mexican Revolution Nineteen Ten - Nineteen Fourteen: The Diplomacy of Anglo-American Conflict. (Cambridge Latin American Studies: No. 3). (Illus.). 1968. 39.95 (ISBN 0-521-04423-5). Cambridge U Pr.
Cumberland, Charles C. Mexican Revolution, Genesis Under Madero. LC 71-90495. Repr. of 1952 ed. lib. bdg. 19.25x (ISBN 0-8371-2126-4, CUMR). Greenwood.
Fisher, L. E. The Background of the Revolution for Mexican Independence. 1976. lib. bdg. 59.95 (ISBN 0-8490-1469-7). Gordon Pr.
Gomez-Quinones, Juan. Sembradores: Ricard Flores Magon y el Partido Liberal Mexicano, a Eulogy & Critique. (Monograph: No. 5). 1979. pap. text ed. 6.95 (ISBN 0-89551-010-3). UCLA Chicano Stud.
Greene, Graham. Another Mexico. 288p. 1981. 14.95 (ISBN 0-670-12892-9). Viking Pr.
Gregg, Robert S. Influence of Border Troubles on Relations Between the United States & Mexico, 1876-1910. LC 72-98181. (American Scene Ser). 1970. Repr. of 1937 ed. lib. bdg. 25.00 (ISBN 0-306-71833-2). Da Capo.
Guzman, Martin L. The Eagle & the Serpent. De Onis, Harriet, tr. 6.50 (ISBN 0-8446-0668-5). Peter Smith.
Hall, Linda B. Alvaro Obregon: Power & Revolution in Mexico, 1911-1920. LC 80-6110. (Illus.). 320p. 1981. 22.50 (ISBN 0-89096-113-1). Tex A&M Univ Pr.
Hanrahan, Gene Z., ed. Documents on the Mexican Revolution. Incl. Vol. I, Pts. 1 & 2. The Origins of the Revolution in Texas, Arizona, New Mexico, & California, 1910-1911. 1976 (ISBN 0-89712-034-5); Vol. II, Pts. 1 & 2. The Madero Revolution As Reported in the Confidential Dispatches of U.S. Ambassador Henry Lane Wilson, June 1910-June 1911, & the Embassy in Mexico City. 1976 (ISBN 0-89712-035-3); Vol. III, Pts. 1 & 2. The Election of Madero, the Rise of Emilano Zapata, & the Reyes Plot in Texas. 1978 (ISBN 0-89712-036-1). lib. bdg. 40.00 ea. Documentary Pubns.
--The Origins of the Revolution in Texas, Arizona, New Mexico, & California, 1910-1911. (Documents on the Mexican Revolution: Vol. 1). 1976. lib. bdg. 40.00 (ISBN 0-89712-034-5). Documentary Pubns.
Horcasitas, Fernando, ed. & tr. from Nahuatl. Life & Death in Milpa Alta: A Nahuatl Chronicle of Diaz & Zapata from the Nahuatl Recollections of Dona Luz Jiminez. LC 78-177338. (Civilization of the American Indian Ser.: Vol. 117). (Illus.). 150p. (Eng. & Nahuatl.). 1972. 9.95 (ISBN 0-8061-1001-5). U of Okla Pr.
Katz, Friedrich. The Secret War in Mexico: Europe, the United States, & the Mexican Revolution. LC 80-26607. 1981. lib. bdg. 30.00x (ISBN 0-226-42588-6). U of Chicago Pr.
Kennedy, Paul. Middle Beat: A Correspondent's View of Mexico, Guatemala, & El Salvador. LC 71-144045. (Illus.). 1971. text ed. 12.00 (ISBN 0-8077-1603-0). Tchrs Coll.
McLeish, John L. Highlights of the Mexican Revolution. 1976. lib. bdg. 5.95 (ISBN 0-8490-1950-8). Gordon Pr.
Magon, Ricardo F. Land & Liberty: Anarchist Influences in the Mexican Revolution. Poole, Dave, ed. (Orig.). 1979. pap. 5.50 (ISBN 0-932366-04-X). Black Thorn Bks.
Meyer, J. A. The Cristero Rebellion. LC 75-35455. (Cambridge Latin American Studies: No. 24). (Illus.). 1976. 32.95 (ISBN 0-521-21031-3). Cambridge U Pr.
Niemeyer, E. V., Jr. Revolution at Queretaro: The Mexican Constitutional Convention of 1916-1917. LC 73-20203. (Latin American Monographs: No. 33). (Illus.). 311p. 1974. 14.95x (ISBN 0-292-77005-7). U of Tex Pr.
O'Shaughnessy, Edith. Diplomat's Wife in Mexico. LC 73-111727. (American Imperialism: Viewpoints of United States Foreign Policy, 1898-1941). 1970. Repr. of 1916 ed. 23.00 (ISBN 0-405-02042-2). Arno.
Pinchon, Edgcumb. Viva Villa: A Recovery of the Real Pancho Villa, Peon, Bandit, Soldier, Patriot. LC 70-111729. (American Imperialism: Viewpoints of United States Foreign Policy, 1898-1941). 1970. Repr. of 1933 ed. 18.00 (ISBN 0-405-02045-7). Arno.
Reed, John. Insurgent Mexico. Repr. of 1914 ed. lib. bdg. 14.75x (ISBN 0-8371-0633-8, REIM). Greenwood.
--Insurgent Mexico. 2nd ed. LC 69-17616. 1969. pap. 1.95 (ISBN 0-7178-0099-7). Intl Pub Co.
Reyna, Jose L. & Weinert, Richard S., eds. Authoritarianism in Mexico. LC 77-339. (Inter-American Politics Ser.: Vol. 2). 1979. pap. text ed. 5.95x (ISBN 0-89727-002-9). Inst Study Human.
Ross, Stanley R., ed. Is the Mexican Revolution Dead? 2nd ed. LC 75-14017. 1975. pap. 7.95 (ISBN 0-87722-047-6). Temple U Pr.
Ruiz, Ramon-Eduardo. The Great Rebellion: Mexico Nineteen Hundred Five to Nineteen Hundred Twenty-Four. (Illus.). xii, 530p. 1981. pap. text ed. 9.95x (ISBN 0-393-95129-4). Norton.
Rutherford, John. Mexican Society During Revolution. 352p. 1971. 29.95x (ISBN 0-19-827183-2). Oxford U Pr.

Schmidt, Henry C. The Roots of Lo Mexicano: Self & Society in Mexican Thought, 1900-1934. LC 77-99280. 212p. 1978. 13.75x (ISBN 0-89096-048-8). Tex A&M Univ Pr.
Simmons, M. E. Mexican Corrido As a Source for Interpretive Study of Modern Mexico, 1870-1950. 1957. 31.00 (ISBN 0-527-83100-X). Kraus Repr.
Stagg, Albert L. The Almadas & the Alamos. LC 77-74317. 1978. 11.50x (ISBN 0-8165-0609-4); pap. 7.50 (ISBN 0-8165-0474-1). U of Ariz Pr.
Tannenbaum, Frank. Mexican Agrarian Revolution. 1968. Repr. of 1929 ed. 25.00 (ISBN 0-208-00709-1, Archon). Shoe String.
--Peace by Revolution: An Interpretation of Mexico. LC 72-169776. (Select Bibliographies Reprint Ser.). (Illus.). Repr. of 1933 ed. 24.00 (ISBN 0-8369-5996-5). Arno.
--Peace by Revolution, Mexico After 1910. LC 33-35455. (Illus.). 1933. pap. 7.50x (ISBN 0-231-08568-0). Columbia U Pr.
Vaughan, Mary K. The State, Education, & Social Class in Mexico, 1880-1928. (Origins of Modern Mexico Ser.). 380p. 1981. 22.50 (ISBN 0-87580-079-3). N Ill U Pr.
Wilkie, James W. & Michaels, Albert L., eds. Revolution in Mexico: Years of Upheaval, 1910-1940. (Borzoi Bk of Latin America). 1969. pap. text ed. 4.50x (ISBN 0-394-30477-2, KnopfC). Knopf.
Wolfskill, George & Richmond, Douglas W. Essays on the Mexican Revolution: Revisionist Views of the Leaders. (Walter Prescott Webb Memorial Lectures Ser.: No. 13). (Illus.). 158p. 1979. text ed. 9.95x (ISBN 0-292-72026-2). U of Tex Pr.
Womack, John, Jr. Zapata & the Mexican Revolution. LC 68-23947. 1970. pap. 4.95 (ISBN 0-394-70853-9, V627, Vin). Random.
--Zapata & the Mexican Revolution. (Illus.). 1968. 15.00 (ISBN 0-394-45333-6). Knopf.

MEXICO–INDUSTRY

Anderson, Rodney D. Outcasts in Their Own Land: Mexican Industrial Workers 1906-1911. Perry, Laurens B., ed. LC 74-28896. (The Origins of Modern Mexico Ser.). (Illus.). 407p. 1976. 17.50 (ISBN 0-87580-054-8). N Ill U Pr.
Fayerweather, John. Executive Overseas: Administrative Attitudes & Relationships in a Foreign Culture. LC 59-11259. 1959. 11.95x (ISBN 0-8156-2026-8). Syracuse U Pr.
Grayson, George W. The Politics of Mexican Oil. LC 80-5253. (Pitt Latin American Ser.). (Illus.). 1981. 21.95 (ISBN 0-8229-3425-6); pap. 6.95 (ISBN 0-8229-5323-4). U of Pittsburgh Pr.
Mosk, Sanford A. Industrial Revolution in Mexico. LC 73-84758. (Illus.). xii, 331p. 1975. Repr. of 1950 ed. 20.00 (ISBN 0-8462-1746-5). Russell.
Purcell, Susan K. The Mexican Profit-Sharing Decision. LC 74-84148. 224p. 1976. 30.00x (ISBN 0-520-02843-0). U of Cal Pr.
Rippy, Merrill. Oil & the Mexican Revolution. 345p. 1972. 15.00 (ISBN 0-686-05004-5). E J Brill.
Shafer, Robert J. Mexican Business Organizations: History & Analysis. LC 73-629. 400p. 1973. 17.00x (ISBN 0-8156-0093-3). Syracuse U Pr.
Texas University Institute Of Latin-American Studies. Basic Industries in Texas & Northern Mexico. (Illus.). Repr. of 1950 ed. lib. bdg. 17.25x (ISBN 0-8371-1033-5, TLIM). Greenwood.
Vellinga, Menno. Economic Development & the Dynamics of Class: Industrialization, Power & Control in Monterrey, Mexico. 1979. pap. text ed. 21.50x (ISBN 90-232-1636-9). Humanities.
West, Robert C. The Mining Community in Northern New Spain: The Parral Mining District. LC 76-29398. Repr. of 1949 ed. 21.50 (ISBN 0-404-15331-3). AMS Pr.
Workshop on Mexico: Management Implications of the Changing Investment Environment. 75p. 1980. pap. 5.50 (ISBN 0-686-61371-6, COA 38, COA). Unipub.

MEXICO–INTELLECTUAL LIFE

Motten, C. J. Mexican Silver & the Enlightenment. LC 72-120650. 1970. Repr. lib. bdg. 10.50x (ISBN 0-374-95970-6). Octagon.
Ramos, Samuel. Profile of Man & Culture in Mexico. Earle, Peter G., tr. LC 62-9792. (Texas Pan American Ser.). 220p. 1962. 12.50x (ISBN 0-292-73340-2); pap. 4.95x (ISBN 0-292-70072-5). U of Tex Pr.
Romanell, Patrick. Making of the Mexican Mind. 1967. pap. 3.25x (ISBN 0-268-00165-0). U of Notre Dame Pr.
--Making of the Mexican Mind: A Study in Recent Mexican Thought. facs. ed. LC 76-86778. (Essay Index Reprint Ser). 1952. 16.00 (ISBN 0-8369-1189-X). Arno.
Sanchez, Jose. Academias y Sociedades Literarias de Mexico. (Studies in the Romance Languages & Literatures: No. 18). 1951. pap. 13.50x (ISBN 0-8078-9018-9). U of NC Pr.
Walker, Ronald G. Infernal Paradise: Mexico & the Modern English Novel. LC 75-46046. 1978. 24.75x (ISBN 0-520-03197-0). U of Cal Pr.

MEXICO–JUVENILE LITERATURE

Deegan, Paul. Mexican Village: Life in a Zapotec Community. LC 76-140642. (World's People Ser.). (Illus.). (gr. 4-8). 1971. PLB 6.95 (ISBN 0-87191-047-0). Creative Ed.
Nevins, Albert J. Away to Mexico. LC 66-15951. (Illus.). (gr. 7-9). 1966. 4.95 (ISBN 0-396-05361-0). Dodd.
Newlon, Clarke. The Men Who Made Mexico. LC 72-12543. (Illus.). (gr. 7 up). 1973. 5.95 (ISBN 0-396-06778-6). Dodd.
Perl, Lila. Mexico, Crucible of the Americas. LC 77-20203. (Illus.). (gr. 5-9). 1978. 8.95 (ISBN 0-688-22148-3); PLB 8.59 (ISBN 0-688-32148-8). Morrow.
Rosenblum, Morris. Heroes of Mexico. LC 79-88833. (Heroes Ser). (Illus.). (gr. 7-12). 1969. 6.95 (ISBN 0-8303-0082-1). Fleet.
Toepperwein, Emilie & Toepperwein, Fritz A. Jose & the Mexican Jumping Bean. (Illus.). (gr. 4-7). 1965. PLB 2.00 (ISBN 0-910722-05-6). Highland Pr.
U. S. Committee For UNICEF. Hi Neighbor Book No. 4: Guinea, India, Iran, Mexico, Portugal. (Illus.). (gr. 4-6). 4.95 (ISBN 0-8038-2981-7); pap. 2.00 (ISBN 0-8038-2980-9). Hastings.

MEXICO–MAPS

Arbingast, Stanley A., et al. Atlas of Mexico. rev. ed. LC 75-11269. (Illus.). 1975. pap. 20.00 (ISBN 0-87755-187-1). U of Tex Busn Res.
McNally, Rand. Road Atlas: U.S., Canada & Mexico. 1977. 5.95 (ISBN 0-685-83176-0). Wehman.

MEXICO–POLITICS AND GOVERNMENT

Abad de Santillan, Diego. Ricardo Flores Magon: Apostle of the Mexican Social Revolution. (Mexico Ser.). 1979. lib. bdg. 59.95 (ISBN 0-8490-2998-8). Gordon Pr.
Ackerman, C. Mexico's Dilemma. 1976. lib. bdg. 59.95 (ISBN 0-8490-2253-3). Gordon Pr.
Anna, Timothy E. The Fall of the Royal Government in Mexico City. LC 77-17790. xxviii, 289p. 1978. 18.50x (ISBN 0-8032-0957-6). U of Nebr Pr.
Baker, Richard D. Judicial Review in Mexico: A Study of the Amparo Suit. (Latin American Monographs, No. 22). 318p. 1971. 13.50x (ISBN 0-292-70105-5). U of Tex Pr.
Benson, Nettie L., ed. Mexico & the Spanish Cortes, 1810-1822: Eight Essays. (Latin American Monograph Ser.: No. 5). 251p. 1966. 10.95x (ISBN 0-292-73606-1). U of Tex Pr.
Berry, Charles R. The Reform in Oaxaca, 1856-76: A Microhistory of the Liberal Revolution. LC 80-15378. (Illus.). xx, 282p. 1981. 20.00x (ISBN 0-8032-1158-9). U of Nebr Pr.
Bobb, Bernard E. The Viceregency of Antonio Maria Bucareli in New Spain, 1771-1779. (Texas Pan American Ser.). (Illus.). 325p. 1962. 17.50x (ISBN 0-292-73425-5). U of Tex Pr.
Callcott, Wilfrid H. Church & State in Mexico, 1822-1857. 1965. lib. bdg. 19.50x (ISBN 0-374-91235-1). Octagon.
--Liberalism in Mexico, 1857-1929. (Illus.). 1965. Repr. of 1931 ed. 25.00 (ISBN 0-208-00278-2, Archon). Shoe String.
--Liberalism in Mexico, 1857-1929. 1976. lib. bdg. 59.95 (ISBN 0-8490-2157-X). Gordon Pr.
Camp, Roderic A. Mexico's Leaders: Their Education & Recruitment. 1980. pap. text ed. 12.50x (ISBN 0-8165-0660-4). U of Ariz Pr.
Clagett, Helen L. A Guide to the Law & Legal Literature of the Mexican States. 1977. 75.00 (ISBN 0-8490-1922-2). Gordon Pr.
Coerver, Don M. The Porfirian Interregnum: The Presidency of Manuel Gonzalez of Mexico, 1880-1884. LC 78-27274. (History & Culture Monograph Ser.: No. 14). (Orig.). 1978. pap. 6.95 (ISBN 0-912646-49-7). Tex Christian.
Coleman, Kenneth M. Public Opinion in Mexico City About the Electoral System. LC 72-78930. (James Sprunt Studies Ser.). 136p. 1972. pap. text ed. 7.00x (ISBN 0-8078-5053-5). U of NC Pr.
Cronon, E. David. Josephus Daniels in Mexico. (Illus.). 1960. 11.50 (ISBN 0-299-02061-4); pap. 6.95 (ISBN 0-299-02064-9). U of Wis Pr.
Dillon, Emile J. Mexico on the Verge. LC 78-111712. (American Imperialism: Viewpoints of United States Foreign Policy, 1898-1941). 1970. Repr. of 1921 ed. 15.00 (ISBN 0-405-02013-9). Arno.
Dulles, John W. Yesterday in Mexico: A Chronicle of the Revolution, 1919-1936. (Illus.). 821p. 1961. 24.50x (ISBN 0-292-78361-2). U of Tex Pr.
Fagen, Richard R. & Tuohy, William S. Politics & Privilege in a Mexican City. xiv, 210p. 1972. 10.00x (ISBN 0-8047-0809-6); pap. 2.95 (ISBN 0-8047-0879-7, SP135). Stanford U Pr.
Fisher, Lillian E. Background of the Revolution for Mexican Independence. LC 76-151226. (Illus.). 1971. Repr. of 1934 ed. 19.00 (ISBN 0-8462-1581-0). Russell.
Friedrich, Paul. Agrarian Revolt in a Mexican Village. LC 77-89627. (Illus.). 1978. pap. 5.25 (ISBN 0-226-26481-5, P832). U of Chicago Pr.
Gilderhus, Mark T. Diplomacy & Revolution: U. S. - Mexican Relations Under Wilson & Carranza. LC 76-26388. 1977. 10.50x (ISBN 0-8165-0630-2); pap. text ed. 4.25x (ISBN 0-8165-0561-6). U of Ariz Pr.
Glade, William P. & Ross, Stanley R., eds. Criticas constructivas del sistema politico Mexicano. (Encuesta Politica Mexico: No. 2). 254p. (Eng. & Span.). 1973. pap. 5.95x (ISBN 0-292-71012-7). U of Tex Pr.
Gonzalez, Casanova P. Democracy in Mexico. 1972. pap. 4.95 (ISBN 0-19-501533-9, GB). Oxford U Pr.
Gordon, Wendell C. The Expropriation of Foreign-Owned Property in Mexico. LC 73-16647. 1975. Repr. of 1941 ed. lib. bdg. 15.00x (ISBN 0-8371-7212-8, GOPM). Greenwood.
--The Expropriation of Foreign Owned Property in Mexico. Bruchey, Stuart & Bruchey, Eleanor, eds. LC 76-5013. (American Business Abroad Ser.). 1976. Repr. of 1941 ed. 14.00x (ISBN 0-405-09281-4). Arno.
Grindle, Merilee S. Bureaucrats, Politicians, & Peasants in Mexico: A Case Study in Public Policy. LC 76-7759. 1977. 20.00x (ISBN 0-520-03238-1). U of Cal Pr.
Gutierrez De Lara, L. & Pinchon, Edgcumb. The Mexican People: Their Struggle for Freedom. 1976. lib. bdg. 59.95 (ISBN 0-8490-0619-8). Gordon Pr.
Hale, Charles A. Mexican Liberalism in the Age of Mora, 1821-1853. LC 68-13908. (Caribbean Ser.: No. 11). 1968. 30.00x (ISBN 0-300-00531-8). Yale U Pr.
Hamnett, Brian R. Politics & Trade in Southern Mexico, 1750-1821. LC 70-116839. (Latin American Studies: No. 12). (Illus.). 1971. 24.95 (ISBN 0-521-07860-1). Cambridge U Pr.
Hansen, Roger D. The Politics of Mexican Development. LC 77-134300. (Illus.). 298p. 1971. 20.00x (ISBN 0-8018-1193-7); pap. 4.95x (ISBN 0-8018-1651-3). Johns Hopkins.
Hellman, Judith A. Mexico in Crisis. LC 77-6468. 1978. text ed. 19.75x (ISBN 0-8419-0317-4); pap. text ed. 8.50x (ISBN 0-8419-0547-9). Holmes & Meier.
Johnson, Kenneth. Mexican Democracy: A Critical View. rev ed. LC 77-83473. (Praeger Special Studies). 1978. 25.95 (ISBN 0-03-027711-6); pap. 10.95 (ISBN 0-03-028151-2). Praeger.
Josephy, Alvin M., Jr. On the Hill: A History of the American, Congress. 1979. 11.95 (ISBN 0-671-25048-5). S&S.
Katz, Friedrich. The Secret War in Mexico: Europe, the United States, & the Mexican Revolution. LC 80-26607. 1981. lib. bdg. 30.00x (ISBN 0-226-42588-6). U of Chicago Pr.
Ker, Anita M. Mexican Government Publications. 1976. lib. bdg. 59.95 (ISBN 0-8490-0615-5). Gordon Pr.
Markiewicz, Dana. Ejido Organization in Mexico Nineteen Thirty-Four to Nineteen Seventy-Six. LC 79-620057. (Special Studies: Vol. 1). 1980. pap. text ed. 6.50 (ISBN 0-87903-501-3). UCLA Lat Am Ctr.
Mayagoitia, Alberto. A Layman's Guide to Mexican Law. LC 76-57534. 1977. pap. 4.95 (ISBN 0-8263-0444-3). U of NM Pr.
Moreno Sanchez, Manuel. Mexico: Nineteen Sixty-Eight to Nineteen Seventy-Two, crisis y perspectiva. (Encuesta Politica: Mexico Ser.: No. 3). 60p. (Span.). 1973. pap. 2.00x (ISBN 0-292-75009-9). U of Tex Pr.
Needler, Martin C. Politics & Society in Mexico. LC 70-153938. 1971. pap. 4.95x (ISBN 0-8263-0213-0). U of NM Pr.
OAS. Constitution of Mexico, 1917. new ed. 63p. (Orig.). 1972. pap. 2.00 (ISBN 0-8270-5580-3). OAS.
Padgett, Vincent L. The Mexican Political System. 2nd ed. LC 75-27497. (Illus.). 352p. 1976. pap. text ed. 9.75 (ISBN 0-395-20364-3). HM.
Palmer, Ann. Busted in Mexico. 1978. pap. 3.50 (ISBN 0-89540-044-8). Sun Pub.
Powell, Philip W. Soldiers, Indians & Silver. LC 74-13634. 325p. 1975. pap. 5.95x (ISBN 0-87918-015-3). ASU Lat Am St.
Reyna, Jose L. & Weinert, Richard S., eds. Authoritarianism in Mexico. LC 77-339. (Inter-American Politics Ser.: Vol. 2). 1979. pap. text ed. 5.95x (ISBN 0-89727-002-9). Inst Study Human.
Reyna, Jose' L. & Weinert, Richard S., eds. Authoritarianism in Mexico. LC 77-339. (Inter-American Politics Ser.: Vol. 2). 1977. text ed. 13.50x (ISBN 0-915980-64-9). Inst Study Human.
Robe, Stanley L. Azuela & the Mexican Underdogs. LC 76-20031. 1979. 24.00x (ISBN 0-520-03293-4). U of Cal Pr.
Ronfeldt, David F. Atencingo: The Politics of Agrarian Struggle in a Mexican Ejido. LC 74-190528. xii, 284p. 1973. 15.00x (ISBN 0-8047-0820-7). Stanford U Pr.
Ross, Stanley R. Francisco I. Madero: Apostle of Mexican Democracy. LC 79-122591. Repr. of 1955 ed. 26.50 (ISBN 0-404-05409-9). AMS Pr.
Ruiz, Ramon Eduardo. Labor & the Ambivalent Revolutionaries: Mexico 1911-1923. LC 75-29087. 154p. 1976. 12.00x (ISBN 0-8018-1728-5). Johns Hopkins.
Salamini, Heather F. Agrarian Radicalism in Veracruz, 1920-38. LC 77-26106. (Illus.). 1978. 16.50x (ISBN 0-8032-0952-5). U of Nebr Pr.
Schlagheck, James L., et al. The Political, Economic, & Labor Climate in Mexico. rev. ed. LC 79-92307. (Multinational Industrial Relations Ser: Latin American Studies No.4b). (Illus.). 186p. 1980. pap. 15.00 (ISBN 0-89546-019-X). Indus Res Unit-Wharton.
Scholes, Walter V. Mexican Politics During the Juarez Regime, 1855-1872. LC 57-63240. 1957. pap. 10.00x (ISBN 0-8262-0581-X). U of Mo Pr.
Scott, Robert E. Mexican Government in Transition. rev. ed. LC 64-18222. 1964. pap. 5.95 (ISBN 0-252-72570-0). U of Ill Pr.
Serron, Luis A. Scarcity, Exploitation, & Poverty: Malthus & Marx in Mexico. LC 79-4735. (Illus.). 1980. 19.95 (ISBN 0-8061-1460-6). U of Okla Pr.
Shafer, Robert J. Mexico: Mutual Adjustment Planning. (National Planning Ser.: No. 4). (Orig.). 1966. pap. 4.25x (ISBN 0-8156-2090-X). Syracuse U Pr.
Sierra, Justo. The Political Evolution of the Mexican People. Ramsdell, Charles, tr. LC 69-63009. (Texas Pan American Ser.: No. 3). 426p. 1969. 17.50x (ISBN 0-292-78382-5); pap. 8.95 (ISBN 0-292-70071-7). U of Tex Pr.
Sinkin, Richard N. The Mexican Reform, Eighteen Fifty-Five to Eighteen Seventy-Six: A Study in Liberal Nation-Building. LC 78-620053. (No. 49). 273p. 1979. text ed. 18.95x (ISBN 0-292-75044-7); pap. text ed. 7.50x (ISBN 0-292-75045-5). U of Tex Pr.
Smith, Peter H. Labyrinths of Power: Political Recruitment in Twentieth-Century Mexico. LC 78-51191. 1979. text ed. 28.00 (ISBN 0-691-07592-1); pap. 11.50 (ISBN 0-691-10065-9). Princeton U Pr.
Stevens, Evelyn P. Protest & Response in Mexico. 280p. 1974. 25.00x (ISBN 0-262-19128-8). MIT Pr.
Turner, John K. Barbarous Mexico. new ed. (Texas Pan American Series). (Illus.). 354p. 1969. 15.00 (ISBN 0-292-78418-X). U of Tex Pr.
Vaughan, Mary K. The State, Education, & Social Class in Mexico, 1880-1928. (Origins of Modern Mexico Ser.). 380p. 1981. 22.50 (ISBN 0-87580-079-3). N Ill U Pr.
Vellinga, Menno. Economic Development & the Dynamics of Class: Industrialization, Power & Control in Monterrey, Mexico. 1979. pap. text ed. 21.50x (ISBN 90-232-1636-9). Humanities.
Walling, W. E. The Mexican Question. 1976. lib. bdg. 59.95 (ISBN 0-8490-0620-1). Gordon Pr.

MEXICO–POPULATION

Alba, Francisco. The Population of Mexico: Trends, Issues, & Policies. 150p. 1981. text ed. 15.95 (ISBN 0-87855-359-2). Transaction Bks.
Borah, Woodrow. New Spain's Century of Depression. LC 73-16181. 1951. lib. bdg. 10.00 (ISBN 0-8414-3347-X). Folcroft.
Cook, Sherburne F. & Borah, Woodrow. Essays in Population History, 3 vols. Incl. Vols. 1 & 2. Mexico & the Caribbean. 1971. 27.50x ea. Vol. 1 (ISBN 0-520-01764-1). Vol. 2 (ISBN 0-520-02272-6); Vol. 3. Mexico & California. 1979. 25.00x (ISBN 0-520-03560-7). U of Cal Pr.
Cook, Sherburne F. & Simpson, Lesley B. The Population of Central Mexico in the Sixteenth Century. LC 76-29408. (Ibero-Americana: 31). Repr. of 1948 ed. 23.00 (ISBN 0-404-15333-X). AMS Pr.
Silvers, Arthur & Crosson, Pierre R. Rural Development & Urban Bound Migration in Mexico. LC 80-8024. (Resources for the Future Research Ser.: Paper R-17). (Illus.). 160p. (Orig.). 1980. pap. text ed. 6.95x (ISBN 0-8018-2493-1). Johns Hopkins.
Turner, Frederick C. Responsible Parenthood: Politics of Mexico's New Population Policies. LC 74-18959. 43p. (Orig.). 1974. pap. text ed. 3.25 (ISBN 0-8447-3140-4). Am Enterprise.

MEXICO–RELATIONS (GENERAL) WITH FOREIGN COUNTRIES

Cline, Howard F. U. S. & Mexico. LC 52-12258. 1963. pap. text ed. 4.95x (ISBN 0-689-70050-4, 40). Atheneum.

Fox, Annette B. The Politics of Attraction: Four Middle Powers & the United States. LC 76-27291. (Institute of War & Peace Studies). 371p. 1977. 21.00x (ISBN 0-231-04116-0). Columbia U Pr.
Garcia, Juan R. Operation Wetback: The Mass Deportation of Mexican Undocumented Workers in 1954. LC 79-6189. (Contributions in Ethnic Studies: No. 2). (Illus.). xvii, 268p. 1980. lib. bdg. 25.00 (ISBN 0-313-21353-4, GOW/). Greenwood.
Ross, Stanley R., ed. Views Across the Border: the United States & Mexico. LC 76-57533. 1978. pap. 10.00x (ISBN 0-8263-0445-1). U of NM Pr.
Shafer, Robert J. & Mabry, Donald. Neighbors - Mexico & the United States: Wetbacks & Oil. 232p. 1981. text ed. 18.95x (ISBN 0-88229-726-0); pap. 9.95 (ISBN 0-88229-781-3). Nelson-Hall.

MEXICO–SOCIAL CONDITIONS

Avila, Manuel. Tradition & Growth: A Study of Four Mexican Villages. LC 73-86134. 1969. 13.50x (ISBN 0-226-03245-0). U of Chicago Pr.
Ball, John M. Migration & the Rural Municipio in Mexico. LC 75-636482. 1971. pap. 3.00 (ISBN 0-88406-001-2). Ga St U Busn Pub.
Belshaw, Michael H. A Village Economy: Land & People of Huecorio. LC 66-28489. (Institute of Latin American Studies). (Illus.). 421p. 1967. 22.50x (ISBN 0-231-02928-4). Columbia U Pr.
Booth, George C. Mexico's School-Made Society. LC 71-94601. Repr. of 1941 ed. lib. bdg. 15.00x (ISBN 0-8371-2546-4, BOMS). Greenwood.
Callcott, Wilfrid H. Liberalism in Mexico, 1857-1929. (Illus.). 1965. Repr. of 1931 ed. 25.00 (ISBN 0-208-00278-2, Archon). Shoe String.
Cancian, Frank. Change & Uncertainty in a Peasant Community: The Maya Corn Farmers of Zinacantan. LC 72-153814. (Illus.). 1972. 12.50x (ISBN 0-8047-0787-1). Stanford U Pr.
Chase, Stuart. Mexico: A Study of Two Americans. 1931. 30.00 (ISBN 0-685-72822-6). Norwood Edns.
De Walt, B. R. Modernization in a Mexican Ejido. LC 78-3412. (Latin American Studies: No. 33). (Illus.). 1979. 29.95 (ISBN 0-521-22064-5). Cambridge U Pr.
Dillon, Emile J. Mexico on the Verge. LC 78-111712. (American Imperialism: Viewpoints of United States Foreign Policy, 1898-1941). 1970. Repr. of 1921 ed. 15.00 (ISBN 0-405-02013-9). Arno.
Elmendorf, Mary. Nine Mayan Women: A Village Faces Change. 1976. 10.00 (ISBN 0-470-23862-3); pap. 5.95 (ISBN 0-470-23864-X). Schenkman.
Erasmus, Charles J., et al. Contemporary Change in Traditional Communities of Mexico & Peru. Steward, Julian H., ed. LC 78-57508. 1978. pap. 6.95 (ISBN 0-252-00714-X). U of Ill Pr.
Frank, A. G. Mexican Agriculture: Fifteen Twenty-One to Sixteen Thirty. LC 78-6201. (Studies in Modern Capitalism Ser.). 1979. 16.95 (ISBN 0-521-22209-5). Cambridge U Pr.
Gonzalez, Casanova P. Democracy in Mexico. 1972. pap. 4.95 (ISBN 0-19-501533-9, GB). Oxford U Pr.
Gutierrez De Lara, L. & Pinchon, Edgcumb. The Mexican People: Their Struggle for Freedom. 1976. lib. bdg. 59.95 (ISBN 0-8490-0619-8). Gordon Pr.
Hopgood, James F. Settlers of Bajavista. LC 79-21191. (Papers in International Studies: Latin America Ser.: No. 7). 1979. pap. 11.00 (ISBN 0-89680-101-2). Ohio U Ctr Intl.
Kahl, Joseph A. The Measurement of Modernism: A Study of Values in Brazil & Mexico. LC 68-63239. (Latin American Monographs: No. 12). 228p. 1968. 10.00x (ISBN 0-292-78354-X); pap. 5.00x (ISBN 0-292-75019-6). U of Tex Pr.
Lewis, Oscar. Children of Sanchez. 1961. 19.95 (ISBN 0-394-41922-7). Random.
--Children of Sanchez. 1966. pap. 4.95 (ISBN 0-394-70280-8, Vin). Random.
--Five Families: Mexican Case Studies in the Culture of Poverty. LC 59-10644. 1959. 12.00x (ISBN 0-465-02466-1); pap. 4.95x (ISBN 0-465-09705-7, CN-5005). Basic.
Needler, Martin C. Politics & Society in Mexico. LC 70-153938. 1971. pap. 4.95x (ISBN 0-8263-0213-0). U of NM Pr.
Pani, A. Hygiene in Mexico. 1976. lib. bdg. 59.95 (ISBN 0-8490-2029-8). Gordon Pr.
Paz, Octavio. The Other Mexico: Critique of the Pyramid. Kemp, Lysander, tr. from Span. (Orig.). 1972. pap. 2.45 (ISBN 0-394-17773-8, B359, BC). Grove.
Reyna, Jose' L. & Weinert, Richard S., eds. Authoritarianism in Mexico. LC 77-339. (Inter-American Politics Ser.: Vol. 2). 1977. text ed. 13.50x (ISBN 0-915980-64-9). Inst Study Human.
Romanucci-Ross, Lola. Conflict, Violence, & Morality in a Mexican Village. LC 73-77391. 202p. 1973. pap. text ed. 6.95 (ISBN 0-87484-276-X). Mayfield Pub.
Ross, E. The Social Revolution in Mexico. 1976. lib. bdg. 59.95 (ISBN 0-8490-2618-0). Gordon Pr.
Saenz, M. Some Mexican Problems. 1976. lib. bdg. 59.95 (ISBN 0-8490-2628-8). Gordon Pr.
Serron, Luis A. Scarcity, Exploitation, & Poverty: Malthus & Marx in Mexico. LC 79-4735. (Illus.). 1980. 19.95 (ISBN 0-8061-1460-6). U of Okla Pr.
Tannenbaum, Frank. Peace by Revolution: An Interpretation of Mexico. LC 72-169776. (Select Bibliographies Reprint Ser.). (Illus.). Repr. of 1933 ed. 24.00 (ISBN 0-8369-5996-5). Arno.
--Peace by Revolution, Mexico After 1910. LC 33-35455. (Illus.). 1933. pap. 7.50x (ISBN 0-231-08568-0). Columbia U Pr.
Taylor, William B. Drinking, Homicide, & Rebellion in Colonial Mexican Villages. LC 78-50475. 1979. 16.50x (ISBN 0-8047-0997-1). Stanford U Pr.
Vanderwood, Paul J. Disorder & Progress: Bandits, Police, & Mexican Development. LC 80-22345. (Illus.). xx, 264p. 1981. 21.50x (ISBN 0-8032-4651-X); pap. 8.95 (ISBN 0-8032-9600-2, BB 767, Bison). U of Nebr Pr.
Van Ginneken, Wouter. Socio-Economic Groups & Income Distribution in Mexico. 1980. 27.50x (ISBN 0-312-73941-9). St Martin.
Wilkie, James W. The Mexican Revolution: Federal Expenditure & Social Change Since 1910. 2nd rev ed. LC 74-103072. 1970. 26.75x (ISBN 0-520-01919-9); pap. 6.50x (ISBN 0-520-01869-9, CAMPUS36). U of Cal Pr.
Young, James C. Medical Choice in a Mexican Village. 256p. 1981. 19.50 (ISBN 0-8135-0895-9). Rutgers U Pr.

MEXICO–SOCIAL LIFE AND CUSTOMS

Beals, Carleton. Mexican Maze. LC 71-156174. (Illus.). 1971. Repr. of 1931 ed. lib. bdg. 17.50x (ISBN 0-8371-6117-7, BEMM). Greenwood.
--Mexican Maze. LC 71-156174. (Illus.). 1971. Repr. of 1931 ed. lib. bdg. 17.50x (ISBN 0-8371-6117-7, BEMM). Greenwood.
Calderon De La Barca & Frances, Erskine. Life in Mexico During a Residence of Two Years in That Country. LC 75-41046. Repr. of 1913 ed. 27.50 (ISBN 0-404-14517-5). AMS Pr.
Calvert, Peter. The Mexicans: How They Live & Work. LC 74-17467. 168p. 1975. text ed. 8.95 (ISBN 0-03-029696-X, HoltC). HR&W.
Coit, Daniel W. Digging for Gold Without a Shovel: Letters of Daniel Wadsworth Coit from Mexico & California. Hammond, George P., ed. (Illus.). 1967. limited ed 22.50 (ISBN 0-912094-11-7). Old West.
Cook, Scott & Diskin, Martin, eds. Markets in Oaxaca. (Institute of Latin American Studies-Special Publication). 349p. 1975. 13.50x (ISBN 0-292-75014-5). U of Tex Pr.
Creel, G. Mexico: The People Next Door. 1976. lib. bdg. 59.95 (ISBN 0-8490-2251-7). Gordon Pr.
De La Fuente, Mario. I Like You Gringo-But. 1974. pap. 2.50 (ISBN 0-914778-08-0). Phoenix Bks.
Gooch, F. Face to Face with the Mexicans. 1976. lib. bdg. 59.95 (ISBN 0-8490-1798-X). Gordon Pr.
Grimes, Larry M. El Tabu Linguistico en Mexico: El Lenguaje erotico de los mexicanos. LC 78-52419. 1978. lib. bdg. 9.95x (ISBN 0-916950-10-7); pap. 6.95x (ISBN 0-916950-09-3). Bilingual Pr.
Lafaye, Jacques. Quetzalcoatl & Guadalupe: The Formation of Mexican National Consciousness, 1531-1813. Keen, Benjamin, tr. from Fr. LC 75-20889. 1976. lib. bdg. 22.00x (ISBN 0-226-46794-5). U of Chicago Pr.
Leonard, Irving A. Baroque Times in Old Mexico: Seventeenth-Century Persons, Places, & Practices. (Illus.). 1959. pap. 5.95 (ISBN 0-472-06110-0, 110, AA). U of Mich Pr.
Lewis, Oscar. Life in a Mexican Village: Tepoztlan Restudied. 8.50 (ISBN 0-8446-2469-1). Peter Smith.
--Life in a Mexican Village: Tepoztlan Restudied. LC 51-11683. (Illus.). 1963. pap. 8.95 (ISBN 0-252-72530-1). U of Ill Pr.
Madsen, William. Virgin's Children: Life in an Aztec Village Today. Repr. of 1960 ed. lib. bdg. 16.00x (ISBN 0-8371-2098-5, MAVC). Greenwood.
Miller, J. Dale & Bishop, Russell H. USA-Mexico Culture Capsules. 1977. pap. text ed. 5.95 (ISBN 0-88399-150-0). Newbury Hse.
Oehler, Mike. One Mexican Sunday. LC 80-82949. (Illus.). 112p. 1981. 8.50 (ISBN 0-9604464-1-9). Mole Pub Co.
Reck, Gregory C. In the Shadow of Tlaloc: Life in a Mexican Village. 1978. pap. 3.95 (ISBN 0-14-004872-3). Penguin.
Redfield, Robert. Tepoztlan, a Mexican Village: A Study of Folk Life. LC 30-15556. (Midway Reprint Ser). (Illus.). 1973. pap. 11.00x (ISBN 0-226-70669-9). U of Chicago Pr.
Romney, Kimball & Romney, Romaine. The Mixtecans of Juxtlahuaca, Mexico. LC 66-1706. 186p. 1973. pap. text ed. 6.50 (ISBN 0-88275-136-0). Krieger.
Ross, Corinne. Christmas in Mexico. Lopez, Jadwiga, ed. LC 76-21970. (Round the World Christmas Program Ser.). (Illus.). 1976. 7.95 (ISBN 0-7166-2002-2). World Bk-Childcraft.
Soleillant, Claude. Mexico: Activities & Projects in Color. LC 77-81955. (Activities & Projects Ser.). (Illus.). 96p. (English.). (gr. 3 up). 1978. 9.95 (ISBN 0-8069-4552-4); PLB 9.29 (ISBN 0-8069-4553-2). Sterling.
Spence, L. Mexico of the Mexicans. 35.00 (ISBN 0-8490-0630-9). Gordon Pr.
Taylor, Barbara H. Mexico: Her Daily & Festive Breads. Lamb, Ruth S., ed. LC 71-99257. (Latin American Books). (Illus., Orig.). 1969. pap. 6.95x (ISBN 0-685-08703-4, Dist. by Ocelot Pr). Creative Pr.
Winter, N. O. Mexico & Her People Today. 1977. lib. bdg. 69.95 (ISBN 0-8490-2244-4). Gordon Pr.

MEXICO (CITY)

Anna, Timothy E. The Fall of the Royal Government in Mexico City. LC 77-17790. xxviii, 289p. 1978. 18.50x (ISBN 0-8032-0957-6). U of Nebr Pr.
Janvier, Thomas. Legends of the City of Mexico. (Mexico Ser.). 1979. lib. bdg. 59.95 (ISBN 0-8490-2958-9). Gordon Pr.
Percival, Olive. Mexico City. 1976. lib. bdg. 59.95 (ISBN 0-8490-0625-2). Gordon Pr.

MEXICO (CITY)–DESCRIPTION

Arthur Frommer's Guide to Mexico City & Acapulco, 1981-82. Date not set. pap. 2.95 (ISBN 0-671-41436-4). Frommer-Pasmantier.
Carlson, Loraine. The TraveLeer Guide to Mexico City. 2nd ed. LC 80-26850. (Illus.). 224p. 1981. pap. 4.50 (ISBN 0-932554-02-4). Upland Pr.
Cervantes De Salazar, Francisco. Life in the Imperial & Loyal City of Mexico in New Spain. Shepard, Minnie L., tr. LC 79-100224. Repr. of 1953 ed. lib. bdg. 15.00x (ISBN 0-8371-3033-6, CELM). Greenwood.
Cottrell, John. Mexico City. (The Great Cities Ser.). (Illus.). 1979. 14.95 (ISBN 0-8094-3104-1). Time-Life.
--Mexico City. (The Great Cities Ser.). (Illus.). 1979. lib. bdg. 14.94 (ISBN 0-8094-3105-X); kivar bdg. 9.93 (ISBN 0-8094-3106-8). Silver.
Moldvay, Albert & Fabian, Erika. Photographing Mexico City & Acapulco. (Amphoto Travel Guide Ser.). Orig. Title: Photographer's Guide to Mexico City & Alcapulco. (Illus.). 1980. pap. 5.95 (ISBN 0-8174-2122-X). Amphoto.

MEXICO (CITY)–SOCIAL CONDITIONS

Cornelius, Wayne A. Politics & the Migrant Poor in Mexico City. LC 75-179. (Illus.). xiv, 319p. 1975. 12.50x (ISBN 0-8047-0880-0). Stanford U Pr.
Kemper, Robert V. Migration & Adaptation: Tzintzuntzan Peasants in Mexico City. LC 77-2413. (Sage Library of Social Research: Vol. 43). 1977. 20.00 (ISBN 0-8039-0687-0); pap. 9.95 (ISBN 0-8039-0688-9). Sage.
Lewis, Oscar. Children of Sanchez. 1961. 19.95 (ISBN 0-394-41922-7). Random.
--Children of Sanchez. 1966. pap. 4.95 (ISBN 0-394-70280-8, Vin). Random.
--Death in the Sanchez Family. 1969. 7.95 (ISBN 0-394-42160-4). Random.

MEXICO (CITY) MUSEO NACIONAL DE ANTROPOLOGIA

Bernel, Ignacio, et al. National Museum of Anthropology, Mexico: Art, Architecture, Archaeology, Ethnography. (Illus.). 1968. 50.00 (ISBN 0-8109-0342-3). Abrams.
Ragghianti, Carlo L. National Museum of Anthropology: Mexico City. LC 71-127833. (Great Museums of the World Ser.). 1968. 16.95 (ISBN 0-88225-233-X). Newsweek.

MEXICO (VICEROYALTY) TRIBUNAL DE MINERIA

Howe, Walter. Mining Guild of New Spain & Its Tribunal General, 1770-1821. LC 68-55634. (Illus.). 1968. Repr. of 1949 ed. lib. bdg. 21.00x (ISBN 0-8371-0486-6, HOMG). Greenwood.

MEXICO, VALLEY OF–ANTIQUITIES

De Terra, Helmut, et al. Tepexpan Man. Linton, Ralph, ed. (Illus.). 1949. pap. 15.50 (ISBN 0-384-11525-X). Johnson Repr.

MEYER, CONRAD FERDINAND, 1825-1898

Burkhard, Marianne. Conrad Ferdinand Meyer. (World Authors Ser.: No. 480 Germany). 1978. 11.95 (ISBN 0-8057-6321-X). Twayne.
Dahme, Lena F. Women in the Life & Art of Conrad Ferdinand Meyer. LC 77-163662. (Columbia University. Germanic Studies, New Ser.: No. 4). Repr. of 1936 ed. 27.00 (ISBN 0-404-50454-X). AMS Pr.
Folkers, George F., et al, trs. The Complete Narrative Prose of Conrad Ferdinand Meyer, 2 vols. 754p. 1976. Vol. 1, 1872-1879. 22.50 (ISBN 0-8387-1036-0); Vol. 2, 1881-1891. 22.50 (ISBN 0-8387-1547-8). Bucknell U Pr.
Kalischer, Erwin. Conrad Ferdinand Meyer in Seinem Verhaeltnis Zur Italienischen Renaissance. 1907. 21.00 (ISBN 0-384-28501-5); pap. 18.50 (ISBN 0-384-28500-7). Johnson Repr.
Kraeger, Heinrich. Conrad Ferdinand Meyer. Repr. of 1901 ed. 37.00 (ISBN 0-384-30366-8); pap. 34.00 (ISBN 0-384-30365-X). Johnson Repr.
Maync, Harry. Conrad Ferdinand Meyer und Sein Werk. LC 76-100522. (Ger). Repr. of 1925 ed. 27.00 (ISBN 0-404-00597-7). AMS Pr.
Weishaar, F. C. F. Meyers Angela Borgia. pap. 7.00 (ISBN 0-384-66590-X). Johnson Repr.

MEYERBEER, GIACOMO, 1791-1864

Blaze De Bury, Ange H. Meyerbeer et Son Temps. LC 80-2257. Repr. of 1865 ed. 40.50 (ISBN 0-404-18813-3). AMS Pr.
Van Dieren, Bernard. Down Among the Dead Men & Other Essays. facs. ed. LC 67-26732. (Essay Index Reprint Ser). 1935. 16.00 (ISBN 0-8369-0374-9). Arno.

MEYERSON, EMILE, 1859-1933

Boas, George. Critical Analysis of the Philosophy of Emile Meyerson. facsimile ed. LC 70-109616. (Select Bibliographies Reprint Ser). 1930. 15.00 (ISBN 0-8369-5224-3). Arno.
--Critical Analysis of the Philosophy of Emile Meyerson. LC 68-55099. (Illus.). 1968. Repr. of 1930 ed. lib. bdg. 15.00x (ISBN 0-8371-0317-7, BOEM). Greenwood.

MEYNELL, MRS. ALICE CHRISTIANA (THOMPSON) 1847-1922

Hake, Thomas G. Poems of Thomas Gordon Hake. LC 75-131504. Repr. of 1894 ed. 15.75 (ISBN 0-404-03026-2). AMS Pr.
Meynell, Viola. Alice Meynell. LC 79-145182. (Illus.). 1971. Repr. of 1929 ed. 18.00 (ISBN 0-403-00804-2). Scholarly.
--Alice Meynell: A Memoir. 1929. Repr. 19.50 (ISBN 0-8274-1841-8). R West.
Tuell, Anne K. Mrs. Meynell & Her Literary Generation. LC 75-145331. 1971. Repr. of 1925 ed. 19.00 (ISBN 0-403-01242-2). Scholarly.

MEZADA, ISRAEL

Pearlman, Moshe. Zealots of Masada: Story of a Dig. LC 67-23691. (Illus.). (gr. 7 up). 1967. pap. 2.45 (ISBN 0-684-71867-7, SL219, ScribT). Scribner.

MEZZOTINT ENGRAVING

Phillips, John M. & Parker, Barbara, eds. Discoveries of Waldron Phoenix Belknap, Jr. Concerning the Influence of the English Mezzotint on Colonial Painting. LC 55-14827. (Illus.). 1955. pap. 2.00x (ISBN 0-674-21200-2). Harvard U Pr.

MHD GENERATORS

see Magnetohydrodynamic Generators

MI-LA RAS-PA, 1038-1122

De Jong, J. W., ed. Mi la Ras Pa'i Rnam Thar: Texte Tibetian De la Vie De Milarepa. (Indo-Iranian Monographs: No. 4). 1959. 30.50x (ISBN 90-2790-052-3). Mouton.
Evans-Wentz, W. Y. Life of Milarepa. (Wisdom of the East Ser). 8.00 (ISBN 0-7195-1001-5). Paragon.
Evans-Wentz, W. Y., ed. Tibet's Great Yogi, Milarepa. 2nd ed. (Illus.). 1951. 15.95 (ISBN 0-19-501436-7). Oxford U Pr.
Lhalungpa, Lobsang. The Life of Milarepa. 1977. pap. 5.95 (ISBN 0-525-47454-4). Dutton.

MIAMI

Blackman, E. V. Miami & Dade County, Florida: Its Settlement, Progress & Achievement. LC 77-88898. (Florida County History Ser.). (Illus.). 1977. Repr. of 1921 ed. 22.50 (ISBN 0-913122-12-2). Mickler Hse.
Blum, Ethel. Miami Alive. (Span.). 1981. pap. 5.95 (ISBN 0-935572-06-6). Alive Pubns.
Buchanan, James. Miami: A Chronological & Documentary History, 1513-1977. (American Cities Chronology Ser.). 1978. 8.50 (ISBN 0-379-00616-2). Oceana.
Gabriel, Patricia. The Villagers' Book of Outstanding Homes of Miami. LC 75-31851. (Illus.). 1976. 25.00 (ISBN 0-916224-24-4). Banyan Bks.
Livingston, Elizabeth & Starbuck, Carol. Miami for Kids: A Family Guide to Greater Miami Including Everglades National Park and the Florida Keys. LC 81-65980. (Illus.). 80p. 1981. pap. 4.95 (ISBN 0-916224-63-5). Banyan Bks.
Longbrake, David B. & Nichols, Woodrow W., Jr. Sunshine & Shadows in Metropolitan Miami. LC 76-4792. (Contemporary Metropolitan Analysis Ser.). (Illus.). 1976. pap. text ed. 6.95 (ISBN 0-88410-443-5). Ballinger Pub.
Parks, Arva. Miami: The Magic City. Blakey, Ellen S., ed. LC 81-65675. (American Portrait Ser.). (Illus.). 224p. 1981. 24.95 (ISBN 0-932986-17-X). Continent Herit.
Parks, Arva M. Miami: The Magic City. Blakey, Ellen S., ed. LC 81-65675. (American Portrait Ser.). (Illus.). 224p. (YA) (gr. 11 up). 1981. 24.95 (ISBN 0-932986-17-X). Continental Herit.

Peters, Thelma. Lemon City: Pioneering on Biscayne Bay 1850-1925. LC 76-48058. (Illus.). 1976. 14.95 (ISBN 0-916224-12-0). Banyan Bks.

Richmond, Marie L. Immigrant Adaptation & Family Structure Among Cubans in Miami, Florida. Cortes, Carlos E., ed. LC 79-6220. (Hispanics in the United States Ser.). (Illus.). 1981. lib. bdg. 18.00x (ISBN 0-405-13168-2). Arno.

Smiley, Nixon. Yesterday's Miami. LC 73-80590. (Illus.). 1977. pap. 5.95 (ISBN 0-912458-78-X). E A Seemann.

MIAMI, UNIVERSITY OF

Hastings, Glen E. & Murray, Louisa. The Primary Nurse Practitioner: A Multiple Track Curriculum. LC 76-5871. 1976. 7.95 (ISBN 0-916224-04-X). Banyan Bks.

MIAMI FOOTBALL CLUB (NATIONAL LEAGUE, DOLPHINS)

May, Julian. The Miami Dolphins. (The NFL Today Ser.). (gr. 4-8). 1980. lib. bdg. 6.45 (ISBN 0-87191-725-4); pap. 2.95 (ISBN 0-89812-228-7). Creative Ed.

--Miami Dolphins. LC 74-4139. (Superbowl Champions Ser). 48p. 1974. PLB 6.45 (ISBN 0-87191-328-3); pap. 2.95 (ISBN 0-89812-088-8). Creative Ed.

--Miami Dolphins. LC 74-4139. (Superbowl Champions Ser). 48p. 1974. PLB 6.45 (ISBN 0-87191-328-3); pap. 2.95 (ISBN 0-89812-088-8). Creative Ed.

MIAMI INDIANS

see Indians of North America–Eastern States

MIAMI UNIVERSITY, OXFORD, OHIO

Visnapuu & Gaede, Inc. Fisher Hall, Miami University, Oxford, Ohio: Its Preservation Potential. (Consultant Service Grant Report). (Illus.). 25p. 1973. pap. 2.00 (ISBN 0-89133-012-7). Preservation Pr.

MIAO PEOPLE

Bernatzik, Hugo A. Akha & Miao: Problems of Applied Ethnography in Farther India. LC 73-114702. (Behavior Science Translations Ser). viii, 772p. 1970. 28.00x (ISBN 0-87536-027-0). HRAFP.

Geddes, William R. Migrants of the Mountains: The Cultural Ecology of the Blue Miao (Hmong Nyua) or Thailand. (Illus.). 1976. 37.50x (ISBN 0-19-823187-3). Oxford U Pr.

Ling, Shun-Sheng & Ruey, Yih-Fu. The Miao Tribe of Western Hurian, 3. 1976. 35.00 (ISBN 0-89986-316-7). E Langstaff.

Mickey, M. P. Cowrie Shell Miao of Kweichow. (Harvard University Peabody Museum of Archaeology & Ethnology Papers Ser). Repr. of 1947 ed. pap. 5.00 (ISBN 0-527-01282-3). Kraus Repr.

MICE

see also Jerboas

Berry, R. J., ed. Biology of the House Mouse. (Symposia of the Zoological Society of London Ser: No. 47). 756p. 1981. 88.50 (ISBN 0-12-613347-6). Acad Pr.

Brady, Irene. A Mouse Named Mus. LC 74-161651. (Illus.). 96p. (gr. 2-5). 1972. 7.95 (ISBN 0-395-13151-0); Dolphin bdg. 4.23 (ISBN 0-395-13723-3). HM.

--Wild Mouse. LC 76-14912. (Illus.). 24p. (gr. 1 up). 1976. reinforced bdg. 6.95 (ISBN 0-684-14664-9, ScribJ). Scribner.

Cooke, Tony. Exhibition & Pet Mice. 1981. 30.00x (ISBN 0-904558-25-8, Pub. by Saiga Pub). State Mutual Bk.

Elton, Charles. Voles, Mice & Lemmings. 1971. Repr. of 1942 ed. 42.00 (ISBN 3-7682-0275-5). Lubrecht & Cramer.

Foster, Henry L., et al, eds. The Mouse in Biomedical Research: History Genetics & Wild Mice, Vol. 1. (ACLAM Ser.). 1981. price not set (ISBN 0-12-262501-3). Acad Pr.

Gershwin, M. E. & Merchant, B., eds. Immunologic Defects in Laboratory Animals, 2 vols. (Vol. 1 357 pp.;vol. 2 379 pp.). 1981. Vol. 1. 37.50 (ISBN 0-306-40668-3, Plenum Pr); Vol. 2. 42.50 (ISBN 0-306-40673-X); Set. 72.50 (ISBN 0-686-73235-9). Plenum Pub.

Graham, Ada & Graham, Frank. Three Million Mice. (Illus.). 96p. (gr. 4-7). 1981. 9.95 (ISBN 0-684-17150-3, ScribJ). Scribner.

Gude, W. D., et al. Histological Atlas of the Laboratory Mouse. 146p. 1981. 25.00 (ISBN 0-306-40686-1, Plenum Pr). Plenum Pub.

Harris, Stephen. The Harvest Mouse. (Mammal Society Ser.). (Illus.). 50p. 1980. 6.95 (ISBN 0-7137-0897-2, Pub. by Blandford Pr England). Sterling.

Hirschhorn, Howard. All About Mice. (Illus.). 96p. (Orig.). 1974. pap. 2.50 (ISBN 0-87666-210-6, M-542). TFH Pubns.

Hurrell, Elaine. The Common Dormouse. (Mammel Society Ser.). (Illus.). 50p. 1980. 6.95 (ISBN 0-7137-0985-5, Pub. by Blandford Pr England). Sterling.

Jones, Tony. Encyclopedia of Pet Mice. (Illus.). 224p. 1979. 9.95 (ISBN 0-87666-910-0, H-973). TFH Pubns.

Lavine, Sigmund A. Wonders of Mice. LC 80-1018. (Wonders Ser.). (Illus.). 80p. (gr. 4 up). 1980. PLB 5.95 (ISBN 0-396-07891-5). Dodd.

LeRoi, David. Fancy Mice, Rats & Gerbils. new ed. (Pets of Today Ser.). (Illus.). (gr. 5 up). 1976. 6.00x (ISBN 0-7182-0401-8, SpS). Sportshelf.

Morse, Herbert C., ed. Origins of Inbred Mice. 1978. 48.00 (ISBN 0-12-507850-1). Acad Pr.

Oxford Scientific Films. House Mouse. LC 77-6736. (Illus.). (gr. 2 up). 1978. 7.95 (ISBN 0-399-20620-5). Putnam.

Planten, A. & Moonen, R. Meadow Mouse. (Animal Environment Ser.). (Illus.). 1979. 4.95 (ISBN 0-8120-5303-6). Barron.

Rafferty, Keen A., Jr. Methods in Experimental Embryology of the Mouse. LC 70-101642. (Illus.). 94p. 1970. 12.00x (ISBN 0-8018-1129-5). Johns Hopkins.

Saiga Editors. Mice & Rat Keeping. 1981. 10.00x (ISBN 0-86230-011-8, Pub. by Saiga Pub). State Mutual Bk.

Silverstein, Alvin & Silverstein, Virginia. Mice: All About Them. LC 79-9621. (Illus.). 160p. (gr. 4up). 1980. 9.95 (ISBN 0-397-31922-3); PLB 9.79 (ISBN 0-397-31923-1). Lippincott.

Theiler, K. The House Mouse: Development & Normal Stages from Fertilization to 4 Weeks of Age. LC 72-86714. (Illus.). 176p. 1972. 84.00 (ISBN 0-387-05940-7). Springer-Verlag.

Wirtschafter, Zoltan T. The Genesis of the Mouse Skeleton: A Laboratory Atlas. (Illus.). 192p. 1960. photocopy ed. spiral 19.50 (ISBN 0-398-02094-9). C C Thomas.

MICE–LEGENDS AND STORIES

Baker, Betty. Danby & George. LC 80-15707. (Illus.). 64p. (gr. 3-5). 1981. 7.95 (ISBN 0-688-80289-3); PLB 7.63 (ISBN 0-688-84289-5). Greenwillow.

Cunningham, Julia. A Mouse Called Junction. LC 79-9927. (Illus.). 32p. (gr. k-3). 1980. 7.95 (ISBN 0-394-84112-3); PLB 7.99 (ISBN 0-394-94112-8). Pantheon.

Oakley, Graham. The Church Mice & the Moon. LC 74-75569. (Illus.). 40p. (gr. k-3). 1974. 7.95 (ISBN 0-689-30437-4). Atheneum.

Parry, Marian, illus. City Mouse - Country Mouse & Two More Mouse Tales from Aesop. (Illus.). (gr. 2-3). 1971. pap. 1.50 (ISBN 0-590-04438-9, Schol Pap); pap. 3.50 bk. & record (ISBN 0-590-04353-6). Schol Bk Serv.

Stone, Bernard & Low, Alice. The Charge of the Mouse Brigade. LC 79-17891. (Illus.). 32p. 1980. 4.95 (ISBN 0-394-84390-8). Pantheon.

MICHAEL 8TH PALAEOLOGUS, EMPEROR OF THE EAST, 1234-1282

Geanakoplos, Deno J. Emperor Michael Palaeologus & the West, 1258-1282: A Study in Byzantine - Latin Relations. (Illus.). xii, 434p. 1973. Repr. of 1959 ed. 19.50 (ISBN 0-208-01310-5, Archon). Shoe String.

MICHAUX, HENRY, 1899-

Broome, Peter. Henri Michaux. (Athlone French Poets Ser). 1977. text ed. 19.75x (ISBN 0-485-14605-3, Athlone Pr); pap. text ed. 11.75x (ISBN 0-485-12205-7). Humanities.

La Charite, Virginia A. Henri Michaux. (World Authors Ser.: France: No. 465). 1977. lib. bdg. 11.95 (ISBN 0-8057-6302-3). Twayne.

Michaux, Henri. Au Pays De la Magie. Broome, Peter, ed. (Athlone French Poets Ser). 1977. text ed. 20.75x (ISBN 0-485-14711-4, Athlone Pr); pap. text ed. 10.75x (ISBN 0-485-12711-3). Humanities.

Shepler, Frederic J. Creatures Within: Imaginary Beings in the Work of Henri Michaux. LC 76-5630. (Physsardt Publications in Literature Ser.: No. 1). 1977. pap. 2.95x (ISBN 0-916062-00-7). Physsardt.

MICHELANGELO (BUONARROTI, MICHELANGELO), 1475-1564

Arthos, John. Dante, Michelangelo, & Milton. LC 78-32053. 1979. Repr. of 1963 ed. lib. bdg. 14.50x (ISBN 0-313-20979-0, ARDA). Greenwood.

Berti, Luciano. All the Works of Michelangelo. (Illus.). 96p. 1973. pap. 7.50x (ISBN 0-8002-0676-2). Intl Pubns Serv.

Brandes, Georg. Michelangelo: His Life, His Times, His Era. Norden, Heinz, tr. LC 67-31052. (Illus.). 1967. 18.00 (ISBN 0-8044-2071-8). Ungar.

Buonarroti, Michelangelo. Michelangelo: A Record of His Life As Told in His Own Letters & Papers. Carden, Robert W., tr. 1976. lib. bdg. 59.95 (ISBN 0-8490-2256-8). Gordon Pr.

Chastel, Andre, intro. by. The Vatican Frescoes of Michelangelo, 2 vols. Rosenthal, Raymond, tr. from Fr. LC 80-66646. (Illus.). 528p. 1980. ltd. ed. 6000.00 (ISBN 0-89659-158-1). Abbeville Pr.

Clements, Robert J. Michelangelo's Theory of Art. LC 60-14318. (Illus.). 1961. 17.50x (ISBN 0-8147-0084-5). NYU Pr.

--The Poetry of Michelangelo. LC 65-19514. (Gotham Library). 368p. (Orig.). 1965. 15.00x (ISBN 0-8147-0085-3); pap. 7.00 (ISBN 0-8147-0086-1). NYU Pr.

Condivi, Ascanio. The Life of Michelangelo. Wohl, Alice S., tr. LC 74-27197. (Illus.). 192p. 1976. 20.00 (ISBN 0-8071-0164-8). La State U Pr.

Coughlan, Robert. World of Michelangelo. (Library of Art). (Illus.). 1966. 15.95 (ISBN 0-8094-0232-7). Time-Life.

De Campos, Deoclecio Redig. Michelangelo: The Last Judgment. 1978. 100.00 (ISBN 0-385-12299-3). Doubleday.

De Tolnay, Charles Q. Michelangelo, 6 vols. Incl. Vol. 1. The Youth of Michelangelo. 1969. 60.00 (ISBN 0-691-03858-9); Vol. 2. The Sistine Ceiling. 1969. 60.00 (ISBN 0-691-03856-2); Vol. 3. The Medeci Chapel. 1970. 60.00 (ISBN 0-691-03854-6); Vol. 4. The Tomb of Julius Two. 1970. 60.00 (ISBN 0-691-03857-0); Vol. 5. The Final Period. 1970. 60.00 (ISBN 0-691-03855-4); Vol. 6. Michelangelo, Architect. 40.00 (ISBN 0-691-03853-8); Michelangelo: Sculpter-Painter-Architect. (One vol. condensation). 30.00 (ISBN 0-691-03876-7). Princeton U. Pr.

Einem, Herbert Von. Michelangelo. 2nd ed. 1973. text ed. 43.00x (ISBN 0-416-15140-X); pap. text ed. 19.95x (ISBN 0-416-18050-7). Methuen Inc.

Fairfield, Pierce A. Michelangelo's Life & His Magnetic Art. (Illus.). 1979. deluxe ed. 39.75 (ISBN 0-930582-43-8). Gloucester Art.

Furse, John. Michelangelo & His Art. (The Artist & His Art Ser.). (Illus.). 128p. 1981. 9.98 (ISBN 0-89196-094-5, Bk Value Intl). Quality Bks IL.

Gere, John A. Drawings by Michelangelo from the British Museum. LC 79-84415. (Illus.). 111p. 1979. pap. 25.00 (ISBN 0-87598-068-6). Pierpont Morgan.

Gilbert, Creighton. Michelangelo. (Color Slide Program of the Great Masters Ser). (Illus.). 1967. 17.95 (ISBN 0-07-023207-5, P&RB). McGraw.

Gilbert, Creighton, tr. from It. The Complete Poems & Selected Letters of Michelangelo. LC 79-87767. 1980. 22.00x (ISBN 0-691-03925-9); pap. 5.95 (ISBN 0-691-00324-6). Princeton U Pr.

Gladden, Washington. Witnesses of the Light. facs. ed. LC 77-84307. (Essay Index Reprint Ser). 1903. 15.75 (ISBN 0-8369-1081-8). Arno.

Grimm, H. Life of Michaelangelo, 2 vols. 200.00 (ISBN 0-8490-0533-7). Gordon Pr.

Grimm, Herman F. Life of Michael Angelo, 2 Vols. Bunnett, Fanny E., tr. Repr. of 1900 ed. Set. lib. bdg. 48.00x (ISBN 0-8371-2750-5, GRMA). Greenwood.

Hartt, Frederick. Michelangelo's Sculpture. LC 68-24045. (Illus.). 1969. 45.00 (ISBN 0-8109-0300-8). Abrams.

Hibbard, Howard. Michelangelo. LC 74-6576. (Icon Editions). (Illus.). 348p. 1975. 16.95 (ISBN 0-06-433323-X, HarpT); pap. 6.95 (ISBN 0-06-430056-0, IN-56, HarpT). Harrow.

Hickey, Dave, et al, eds. Michelangelo Pistoletto. (Illus.). 1980. pap. 5.00 (ISBN 0-686-70827-X). Inst for the Arts.

Hollanda, Francisco De. Four Dialogues on Painting. Bell, Aubrey F., tr. LC 78-20470. 1980. Repr. of 1928 ed. text ed. 14.50 (ISBN 0-88355-848-3). Hyperion Conn.

Hupka, Robert. Michelangelo: Pieta. (Illus.). 96p. 1975. pap. 4.95 (ISBN 0-517-52414-7). Crown.

Kuhn, Rudolf. Michelangelo-Die Sixtinische Decke.Beitraege ueber ihre Quellen und zu ihrer Auslegung. LC 73-91163. (Beitraege Zur Kunstgeschichte Vol. 10). (Illus.). 173p. 1975. text ed. 47.75x (ISBN 3-11-004497-8). De Gruyter.

Michelangelo. Drawings by Michelangelo. (Illus.). 6.50 (ISBN 0-8446-2581-7). Peter Smith.

--Drawings of Michelangelo. Stone, Irving, ed. (Master Draughtsman Ser). (Illus., Orig.). treasure trove bdg. 6.47x (ISBN 0-685-07277-0); pap. 2.95 (ISBN 0-685-07278-9). Borden.

--Michelangelo. Hartt, Frederick, ed. (Library of Great Painters Ser). 1965. 40.00 (ISBN 0-8109-0299-0). Abrams.

Michelangelo Pittore. (I Classici Dell'arte Ser.). (Illus.). 1977. pap. 9.95 (ISBN 0-8478-5099-4). Rizzoli Intl.

Michelangelo's "the Entombment of Christ". 1974. pap. text ed. 3.50x (ISBN 0-8277-3223-6). British Bk Ctr.

Murray, Linda. Michelangelo. (World of Art Ser.). (Illus.). 1980. 17.95x (ISBN 0-19-520163-9); pap. 9.95 (ISBN 0-19-520164-7). Oxford U Pr.

Parronchi, Allessandro. Michelangelo: The Sculptor. (Art Library Ser: Vol. 30). pap. 2.95 (ISBN 0-448-00479-8). G&D.

Phillips, Evelyn M. The Illustrated Guidebook to the Frescoes in the Sistine Chapel. (Illus.). 124p. 1981. Repr. of 1901 ed. 49.85 (ISBN 0-89901-029-6). Found Class Reprints.

Piper, David, ed. Michelangelo. Carrol, Jane, tr. LC 80-50233. (Every Painting Ser.). (Illus.). 96p. 1980. pap. 5.95 (ISBN 0-8478-0310-4). Rizzoli Intl.

Santini, Loretta. Michelangelo: Painter - Sculptor - Architect. (Illus.). 1971. 12.50x (ISBN 0-8002-0852-8). Intl Pubns Serv.

Seymour, Charles, Jr. Michelangelo's David: A Search for Identity. (Illus.). 224p. 1974. pap. 3.95 (ISBN 0-393-00735-9). Norton.

Seymour, Charles, Jr., ed. & intro. by. Michelangelo: The Sistine Chapel Ceiling. (Critical Studies in Art History). (Illus.). 243p. 1972. pap. 6.95x (ISBN 0-393-09889-3). Norton.

Steinmann, Ernst & Wittkower, Rudolf. Michelangelo - Bibliographie 1510-1926. (Illus.). 555p. 1967. Repr. of 1927 ed. 55.00x (ISBN 0-8002-1310-6). Intl Pubns Serv.

Summers, David. Michelangelo & the Language of Art. LC 80-7556. (Illus.). 532p. 1981. 47.50x (ISBN 0-691-03957-7); pap. 16.50 (ISBN 0-691-10097-7). Princeton U Pr.

Wilde, Johannes. Michelangelo: Six Lectures by Johannes Wilde. Shearman, John & Hirst, Michael, eds. (Oxford Studies in the History of Art & Architecture). (Illus.). 1979. pap. 12.95x (ISBN 0-19-817346-6). Oxford U Pr.

Wilson, Charles H. Life & Works of Michelangelo Buonarroti. Repr. of 1876 ed. 65.00 (ISBN 0-686-19837-9). Ridgeway Bks.

MICHELANGELO (BUONARROTI, MICHELANGELO), 1475-1564–FICTION

Alexander, Sidney. The Hand of Michaelangelo. LC 77-154999. 693p. 1977. pap. 10.95x (ISBN 0-8214-0235-8). Ohio U Pr.

--Michelangelo the Florentine. LC 65-25109. 464p. 1965. pap. 9.50 (ISBN 0-8214-0236-6). Ohio U Pr.

Michelangelo. Life Drawings of Michelangelo. (Dover Art Library). (Illus.). 1980. pap. 2.00 (ISBN 0-486-23876-8). Dover.

Stone, Irving. Agony & the Ecstasy. LC 61-6520. 15.95 (ISBN 0-385-01092-3). Doubleday.

--Agony & the Ecstasy. pap. 2.75 (ISBN 0-451-08276-1, E8267, Sig). NAL.

MICHELANGELO (BUONARROTI, MICHELANGELO), 1475-1564–JUVENILE LITERATURE

Coughlan, Robert. World of Michelangelo. LC 66-16540. (Library of Art Ser.). (Illus.). (gr. 6 up). 1966. 12.96 (ISBN 0-8094-0261-0, Pub. by Time-Life). Silver.

MICHELET, JULES, 1798-1874

Kaplan, Edward K. Michelet's Poetic Vision: A Romantic Philosophy of Nature, Man, & Woman. LC 76-45050. 1977. 12.50x (ISBN 0-87023-236-3). U of Mass Pr.

Kippur, Stephen A. Jules Michelet: A Study of Mind & Sensibility. 320p. (Orig.). 1980. 29.00 (ISBN 0-87395-430-0, KIJM, KIJM-P); pap. 9.95 (ISBN 0-87395-431-9). State U NY Pr.

Orr, Linda. Jules-Michelet: Nature, History, & Language. LC 76-13662. 1976. 19.50x (ISBN 0-8014-0976-4). Cornell U Pr.

Pugh, Anne R. Michelet & His Ideas on Social Reform. LC 23-13177. (Columbia University. Studies in Romance Philology & Literature: No. 34). Repr. of 1923 ed. 22.00 (ISBN 0-404-50634-8). AMS Pr.

MICHELS, ROBERT, 1876-1936

Burnham, James. Machiavellians: Defenders of Freedom. 1962. pap. 2.95 (ISBN 0-89526-946-5). Regnery-Gateway.

MICHELSON, ALBERT ABRAHAM, 1852-1931

Jaffe, Bernard. Michelson & the Speed of Light. LC 78-25969. (Illus.). 1979. Repr. of 1960 ed. lib. bdg. 16.75x (ISBN 0-313-20777-1, JAMI). Greenwood.

Livingston, Dorothy M. The Master of Light: A Biography of Albert A. Michelson. LC 72-1178. (Illus.). 1979. pap. 6.95 (ISBN 0-226-48711-3, P813, Phoen). U of Chicago Pr.

MICHENER, JAMES ALBERT, 1907-

Day, A. Grove. James Michener. (Twayne's United States Authors Ser). 1964. pap. 3.45 (ISBN 0-8084-0172-6, T60, Twayne). Coll & U Pr.

Kings, John. In Search of Centennial: Journey with James A. Michener. 1978. 14.95 (ISBN 0-394-50292-2). Random.

MICHI

see Tivi (African People)

MICHIGAN

see also names of cities, counties, etc. in Michigan

Alchin, Edmond W. Population Report, No. 1: Selected Data for Michigan, SMSA's & Counties with Reference Data for the United States. 1972. 1.75 (ISBN 0-686-16225-0). MSU-Inst Comm Devel.

--Population Report, No. 2: Selected Data for Michigan's Minor Civil Divisions by County. 1973. 1.50 (ISBN 0-686-16226-9). MSU-Inst Comm Devel.

--Population Report. No. 3: Selected Data for Michigan's Older Citizens. 1974. 2.50 (ISBN 0-686-16227-7). MSU-Inst Comm Devel.

Blois, John T. Gazetteer of the State of Michigan. facsimile ed. LC 75-87. (Mid-American Frontier Ser.). 1975. Repr. of 1838 ed. 23.00x (ISBN 0-405-06855-7). Arno.

Brennan, Martin. The Boyne Valley Vision. 1981. text ed. 26.00x (ISBN 0-85105-362-9, Dolmen Pr). Humanities.

Cosseboom, Kathy. Grosse Pointe, Michigan: Race Against Race. xiii, 167p. 1972. 7.50 (ISBN 0-87013-128-1). Mich St U Pr.
Heller, Charles F., et al. Population Patterns of Southwestern Michigan. 1974. 5.00 (ISBN 0-932826-10-5). New Issues MI.
Hendry, Fay L. Outdoor Sculpture in Kalamazoo. LC 80-7501. (Illus., Orig.). (gr. k-12). 1980. pap. 3.50 (ISBN 0-936412-01-1). Iota Pr.
--Outdoor Sculpture in Lansing. LC 80-7502. (Illus.). 153p. (Orig.). pap. 3.50x (ISBN 0-936412-02-X). Iota Pr.
House, Alvin E. & Verburg, Kenneth. Michigan County Commissioners & Human Services & Public Safety. 1976. 3.75 (ISBN 0-686-16229-3). MSU-Inst Comm Devel.
Hubbard, Bela. Memorials of a Half-Century in Michigan & the Lake Region. LC 75-23322. (Illus.). 1978. Repr. of 1888 ed. 26.00 (ISBN 0-8103-4268-5). Gale.
McCullough, Dale R. The George Reserve Deer Herd: Population Ecology of a K-Selected Species. (Illus.). 1979. lib. bdg. 16.00x (ISBN 0-472-08611-1, 08611). U of Mich Pr.
Marans, Robert W. & Wellman, John D. The Quality of Non Metropolitan Living: Evaluations, Behaviors, & Expectations of Northern Michigan Residents. LC 78-69913. (Illus.). 352p. 1978. 17.00 (ISBN 0-87944-226-3); pap. 12.00 (ISBN 0-87944-225-5). Inst Soc Res.
Meek, Forrest B. Michigan's Heartland. Date not set. 14.50 (ISBN 0-9602472-0-3). Edgewood.
Michigan. 33.00 (ISBN 0-89770-098-8). Curriculum Info Ctr.
Michigan: A Guide to the Wolverine State. LC 72-84482. 1941. 59.00 (ISBN 0-403-02172-3). Somerset Pub.
Michigan Statistical Abstract 1972. 9th. ed. LC 56-62855. 1972. pap. 4.75 (ISBN 0-87744-113-8). Mich St U Busn.
Michigan Statistical Abstract 1974. 10th ed. 705p. 1974. pap. 5.25 (ISBN 0-87744-123-5). Mich St U Busn.
Michigan Statistical Abstract: 1976. 11th ed. LC 56-62855. 1976. pap. 8.75 (ISBN 0-87744-138-3). Mich St U Busn.
Michigan Statistical Abstract: 1979. 14th ed. LC 56-62855. (MSU Business Studies Ser.). 1979. pap. 11.50 (ISBN 0-87744-161-8). Mich St U Busn.
Mother Nature's Michigan. Warbach, Oscar. (Illus., Orig.). 1976. pap. 5.50 (ISBN 0-910726-70-1). Hillsdale Educ.
Radhuber, Stanley. Beautiful Michigan. Shangle, Robert D., ed. LC 78-52648. (Illus.). 72p. 1978. 14.95 (ISBN 0-915796-10-4); pap. 7.95 (ISBN 0-915796-09-0). Beautiful Am.
Weidenaar, Reynold H. & Zeller, Ann. A Sketchbook of Michigan. (Illus.). 128p. 1980. 15.95 (ISBN 0-8010-9620-0). Baker Bk.

MICHIGAN–ANTIQUITIES

Bettarel, Robert L. & Smith, Hale G. The Moccasin Bluff Site & the Woodland Cultures of Southwestern Michigan. (Anthropological Papers: No. 49). 1973. pap. 6.00 (ISBN 0-932206-47-6). U Mich Mus Anthro.
Fitting, James E. The Archaeology of Michigan: A Guide to the Prehistory of the Great Lakes Region. LC 75-14773. (Bulletin Ser.: No. 56). (Illus.). 274p. 1975. pap. text ed. 7.50x (ISBN 0-87737-033-8). Cranbrook.
Fitting, James E., ed. The Schultz Site at Green Point: A Stratified Occupation Area in the Saginaw Valley of Michigan. (Memoirs Ser: No. 4). (Illus.). 1972. pap. 8.00x (ISBN 0-932206-66-2). U Mich Mus Anthro.
Fitting, James E., et al. Contribution to Michigan Archaeology. (Anthropological Papers: No. 32). (Illus.). 1968. pap. 3.00x (ISBN 0-932206-30-1). U Mich Mus Anthro.
Greenman, Emerson F. The Younge Site: An Archaeological Record from Michigan. (Occasional Contributions Ser.: No. 6). (Illus.). 1967. pap. 3.00x (ISBN 0-932206-01-8). U Mich Mus Anthro.
Hinsdale, W. B. Distribution of the Aboriginal Population of Michigan. (Occasional Contributions Ser.: No. 2). (Illus.). 1968. pap. 1.00x (ISBN 0-686-53050-0). U Mich Mus Anthro.
Praus, Alexis A. Bibliography of Michigan Archaeology. (Anthropological Papers Ser.: No. 22). 1964. pap. 2.00x (ISBN 0-932206-25-5). U Mich Mus Anthro.

MICHIGAN–DESCRIPTION AND TRAVEL

Andrews, Wayne. Architecture in Michigan: A Representative Photographic Survey. LC 67-26428. (Illus.). 1967. 8.95x (ISBN 0-8143-1326-4); pap. 4.95x (ISBN 0-8143-1327-2). Wayne St U Pr.
Cook, Lewis. Beautiful Michigan Waters. Shangle, Robert D., ed. (Illus.). 72p. 1981. 14.95 (ISBN 0-89802-327-0); pap. 7.95 (ISBN 0-89802-326-2). Beautiful Am.
Cook, Louis. Beautiful Michigan, Vol. II. Shangle, Robert D., ed. LC 78-105527. (Illus.). 72p. 14.95 (ISBN 0-915796-89-9); pap. 7.95 (ISBN 0-915796-88-0). Beautiful Am.
Cook, Louis & Shangle, Robert D. Beautiful: Michigan Country. (Illus.). 72p. 1980. 14.95 (ISBN 0-89802-203-7); pap. 7.95 (ISBN 0-89802-204-5). Beautiful Am.
Cross, Glenda. Friendly Fairways of Michigan. LC 78-54174. (Orig.). 1978. 4.95 (ISBN 0-686-12255-0). Friendly Fairways.
Daniel, Glenda & Sullivan, Jerry. A Sierra Club Naturlist's Guide to the North Woods of Michigan, Wisconsin, & Minnesota. (Naturalist's Guide Ser.). (Illus.). 384p. 1981. 24.95 (ISBN 0-87156-248-0); pap. 10.95 (ISBN 0-87156-277-4). Sierra.
Dodge, Roy L. Michigan Ghost Towns, Vol. 1. (Illus.). 191p. (Orig.). 5.00 (ISBN 0-934884-01-3). Glenson Pub.
--Michigan Ghost Towns, Vol. 2. (Illus.). 120p. (Orig.). 5.50 (ISBN 0-934884-03-X). Glenson Pub.
--Michigan Ghost Towns, Vol. 3. (Orig.). write for info. (ISBN 0-934884-02-1). Glenson Pub.
Duluth Superior: World's Largest Inland Seaport. 3rd ed. (Illus.). 3.95 (ISBN 0-932212-06-9). Avery Color.
Geil, Harley & Siverd. Topographical Map of the Counties of Ingham & Livingston Michigan. Thompson, Walter J., ed. LC 79-88162. (Atlas). 1979. Repr. of 1859 ed. 18.00 (ISBN 0-686-52607-4). Hist Soc Lansing & Livingston Cnty Hist Soc.
Hunziker, Barbara. Sumnerville & Pokagon, Cass County Michigan. 1977. pap. 2.00 (ISBN 0-9601340-1-8). Hunziker.
Inglis, James G. Handbook for Travelers, Northern Michigan. LC 73-89370. (Illus.). 188p. 1973. pap. 5.00 (ISBN 0-912382-12-0). Black Letter.
Jay, Charles W. My New Home in Northern Michigan. 1979. Repr. of 1874 ed. 9.50 (ISBN 0-915056-10-0). Hardscrabble Bks.
Lewis, Ferris E. Our Own State, Michigan. rev., 14th ed. LC 78-66800. (Illus.). (gr. 7-10). 1978. pap. text ed. 5.25x (ISBN 0-910726-21-3); questions & ans. for tchr's. 8.00x (ISBN 0-910726-23-X). Hillsdale Educ.
McCreary, Paul. Michigan Map Skills & Information Workbook. (Illus.). 32p. (Orig.). (gr. 6-10). 1978. wkbk. 4.50 (ISBN 0-910726-92-2). Hillsdale Educ.
Michigan. LC 77-72232. (Belding Imprint Ser.). (Illus.). 128p. (Photos & Text by Stan Osolinski). 1977. 27.50 (ISBN 0-912856-34-3). Graphic Arts Ctr.
Michigan: A Guide to the Wolverine State. LC 72-84482. 1941. 59.00 (ISBN 0-403-02172-3). Somerset Pub.
Michigan Tourist Survey, 1957. 1958. pap. 2.00 (ISBN 0-87744-048-4). Mich St U Busn.
Michigan United Conservation Clubs. Michigan County Maps & Outdoor Guide. 1977. pap. 8.00 (ISBN 0-933112-04-1). Mich United Conserv.
--Michigan Hiking & Skiing Trails. 1979. 1.75 (ISBN 0-686-65681-4). Mich United Conserv.
O'Donnell, John L. Saginaw River Port Survey, Pts. 1 & 2. pap. 2.50 ea.; Pt. 1. pap. (ISBN 0-87744-060-3); Pt. 2. pap. (ISBN 0-87744-061-1). Mich St U Busn.
Osler, Jack. Fifty Great Mini-Trips for Michigan. (Illus.). 1977. pap. 2.50 (ISBN 0-89645-002-3). Media Ventures.
Paull, Richard A. & Paull, Rachel K. Field Guide: Wisconsin & Upper Michigan Including Parts of Adjacent States - Highway Guides. (Field Guide Ser.). (Orig.). 1980. pap. text ed. 10.95 (ISBN 0-8403-2142-2). Kendall-Hunt.
Rand McNally Guide to Michigan. LC 78-58381. (Illus.). 1979. pap. 4.95 (ISBN 0-528-84212-9). Rand.
Reed, Earl H. The Dune Country. (Illus.). 1979. Repr. of 1916 ed. 10.50 (ISBN 0-915056-09-7). Hardscrabble Bks.
Santer, Richard A. Michigan: Heart of the Great Lakes. LC 76-53268. (Illus.). 1977. pap. text ed. 9.95 (ISBN 0-8403-1698-4). Kendall-Hunt.
State Industrial Directories Corp. Michigan State Industrial Directory, Nineteen Eighty-One. Date not set. pap. price not set (ISBN 0-89910-048-1). State Indus D.
Tyler, B. E. Michigan's Copper Country in Early Photos. LC 77-71925. (Illus.). 1977. pap. 4.75 (ISBN 0-912382-21-X). Black Letter.
Wermuth, Mary L. Images of Michigan. LC 80-80509. (gr. 6-8). 1981. text ed. 15.65x (ISBN 0-910726-12-4). Hillsdale Educ.

MICHIGAN–ECONOMIC CONDITIONS

Commerce Clearing House. Guidebook to Michigan Taxes: 1982. 1982. 10.00 (ISBN 0-686-76128-6). Commerce.
Cunningham, Wilbur M. Land of Four Flags. 1973. Repr. of 1961 ed. 7.50 (ISBN 0-915056-02-X). Hardscrabble Bks.
Economic & Population Base Study of the Lansing Tri-County Area. LC 60-62883. 1960. pap. 5.00 (ISBN 0-87744-021-2). Mich St U Busn.
Hazard, John L. Michigan's Commerce & Commercial Policy Study. LC 65-65321. 1965. 7.50 (ISBN 0-87744-073-5). Mich St U Busn.
House, Alvin E. & Verburg, Kenneth. Michigan County Commissioners & Economic & Physical Development. 1976. 3.75 (ISBN 0-686-16228-5). MSU-Inst Comm Devel.
Julliard, Carl L. & Stermer, Edson. Willow Run: Study of Industrialization & Cultural Inadequacy. Stein, Leon, ed. LC 77-70486. (Work Ser.). (Illus.). 1977. Repr. of 1952 ed. lib. bdg. 27.00x (ISBN 0-405-10158-9). Arno.
Kozlowski, Paul J. Business Conditions in Michigan Metropolitan Areas. LC 79-24777. 1979. pap. 4.50 (ISBN 0-911558-71-3). Upjohn Inst.
Mead, Stuart B. Michigan Local Government Accounting. 1976. 15.00 (ISBN 0-686-16232-3, GA20); 3.00 (ISBN 0-686-16233-1, GA21); tchr's manual 6.00 (ISBN 0-686-16234-X, GA22). MSU-Inst Comm Devel.
Mead, Stuart B. & Plachta, Leonard E. Michigan Local Government Bookkeeping. 2nd ed. 1975. 15.00 (ISBN 0-686-16230-7, GA10); tchr's manual 5.00 (ISBN 0-686-16231-5, GA11). MSU-Inst Comm Devel.
Michigan Business & Economic Research Bibliography: July 1970 to July 1979. 6th ed. 176p. 1981. pap. 7.00x (ISBN 0-938654-33-0). Indus Dev Inst Sci.
Michigan Governmental Accounting & Audit Guide. rev. ed. 1978. 5.00 (ISBN 0-686-16236-6). MSU-Inst Comm Devel.
Michigan Statistical Abstract 1977. 12th ed. LC 56-62855. (MSU Business Studies). 1977. pap. 10.25 (ISBN 0-87744-148-0). Mich St U Busn.
Michigan Statistical Abstract: 1980. 15th ed. LC 56-62855. (MSU Business Studies). 1980. pap. 10.95 (ISBN 0-686-70902-0). Mich St U Busn.
Sobotka, Stephen P. Profile of Michigan. LC 63-8423. 1963. 7.50 (ISBN 0-02-929830-X). Free Pr.

MICHIGAN–GENEALOGY

Jackson, Ronald V. & Teeples, Gary R. Early Michigan Census Index. LC 77-85962. (Illus.). lib. bdg. 11.00 (ISBN 0-89593-072-2). Accelerated Index.
--Michigan Census Index 1830. LC 77-85968. (Illus.). lib. bdg. 18.00 (ISBN 0-89593-073-0). Accelerated Index.
--Michigan Census Index 1840. LC 77-85969. (Illus.). lib. bdg. 28.00 (ISBN 0-89593-074-9). Accelerated Index.
--Michigan Census Index 1850. LC 77-85970. (Illus.). lib. bdg. 60.00 (ISBN 0-89593-075-7). Accelerated Index.
Smith, Lois W. Phoebe-Her Legacy of Love. Weill, Alix, ed. (Illus.). 1979. text ed. 12.95 (ISBN 0-89127-011-6). Omni Pubs.

MICHIGAN–HISTORY

Angelo, Frank. Yesterday's Michigan. LC 75-45219. (Historic States Ser.: No. 5). (Illus.). 1976. 13.95 (ISBN 0-912458-62-3). E A Seemann.
Bald, F. Clever. Michigan in Four Centuries. rev ed. (Illus.). 1961. 14.95x (ISBN 0-06-000240-9, HarpT). Har-Row.
Ballard, Ralph. Old Fort Saint Joseph. 1973. Repr. of 1949 ed. 3.50 (ISBN 0-915056-01-1). Hardscrabble Bks.
Blois, John T. Michigan Gazetteer, 1838. 418p. 1979. 18.25 (ISBN 0-686-27820-8). Bookmark.
Boyum, Burton H. Saga of Iron Mining in Michigan's Upper Peninsula. 1977. pap. 3.75 (ISBN 0-938746-03-0). Marquette Cnty Hist.
Boyum, Burton H., ed. The Mather Mine, Negaunee & Ishpeming Michigan. LC 79-89638. 1979. 18.95 (ISBN 0-938746-04-9). Marquette Cnty.
Brown, Alan S., et al. Michigan Perspectives: People, Events & Issues. LC 74-82674. (History Ser.). (Illus.). 1974. pap. text ed. 9.95 (ISBN 0-8403-0993-7). Kendall-Hunt.
Castle, Beatrice H. The Grand Island Story. Carter, James L., ed. LC 71-11186. 1974. 4.50 (ISBN 0-938746-01-4). Marquette Cnty Hist.
Catton, Bruce. Michigan. (States & the Nation Ser.). (Illus.). 224p. 1976. 12.95 (ISBN 0-393-05572-8, Co-Pub by AASLH). Norton.
--Michigan. (Illus.). 1977. pap. 1.95 (ISBN 0-393-05645-7). Norton.
Coffman, Edna M. Mackinaw City Settlers & the Savage Straits. 5.00 (ISBN 0-686-26076-7). Voyager Pr.
Cooley, Thomas M. Michigan, a History of Governments. rev. ed. LC 72-3764. (American Commonwealths: No. 5). Repr. of 1905 ed. 27.50 (ISBN 0-404-57205-7). AMS Pr.
Cunningham, Wilbur M. Land of Four Flags. 1973. Repr. of 1961 ed. 7.50 (ISBN 0-915056-02-X). Hardscrabble Bks.
Dunbar, Willis F. Michigan, a History of the Wolverine State. 1965. 12.95 (ISBN 0-8028-7003-1). Eerdmans.
--Michigan: A History of the Wolverine State. rev. ed. May, George S., rev. by. (Illus.). 24.95 (ISBN 0-8028-7043-0). Eerdmans.
Field, Leonard. How It Was: Growing up with the Century. 1980. 9.95 (ISBN 0-533-04326-3). Vantage.
Fitzpatrick, Doyle C. The King Strang Story. LC 70-140603. 1970. 7.95 (ISBN 0-685-57226-9). Natl Heritage.
Flagg, Charles A. An Index of Pioneers from Massachusetts to the West, Especially the State of Michigan. LC 74-29148. 86p. 1980. Repr. of 1915 ed. 8.50 (ISBN 0-8063-0660-2). Genealog Pub.
Gilpin, Alec R. Territory of Michigan Eighteen Hundred Five - Eighteen Hundred Thirty-Seven. 230p. 1970. 8.00 (ISBN 0-87013-155-9). Mich St U Pr.
Grand Marais. (Illus.). 4.00x (ISBN 0-686-26074-0). Voyager Pr.
Green Oak Township Historical Society. Yesteryears of Green Oak, Eighteen Thirty to Nineteen Thirty. LC 81-2270. (Illus.). xii, 338p. 1981. 22.50 (ISBN 0-936792-00-0). Green Oak Township.
Hall, Theodore P. & Farmer, Silas. Grosse Pointe on Lake Sainte Claire. LC 73-17472. 114p. 1974. Repr. of 1886 ed. 6.00 (ISBN 0-8103-3879-3). Gale.
Hayne, Coe. Baptist Trailmakers of Michigan. 1977. Repr. of 1936 ed. 6.50 (ISBN 0-915056-06-2). Hardscrabble Bks.
Heldman, Donald P. Excavations at Fort Michilimackinac: 1977 House One of the South-Southeast Rowhouse. (Archaelogical Completion Report Ser.: No. 2). (Illus.). 1978. pap. 15.00 (ISBN 0-911872-36-1). Mackinac Island.
Hubbard, Bela. Memorials of a Half-Century in Michigan & the Lake Region. LC 75-23322. (Illus.). 1978. Repr. of 1888 ed. 26.00 (ISBN 0-8103-4268-5). Gale.
Johnson, Ida A. The Michigan Fur Trade. LC 74-155928. Repr. of 1919 ed. 12.00 (ISBN 0-912382-07-4). Black Letter.
Kirk, Gordon W. The Promise of American Life: Social Mobility in a Nineteenth-Century Immigrant Community, Holland, Michigan. LC 78-50185. (Memoirs Ser.: Vol. 124). 1978. pap. 8.00 (ISBN 0-87169-124-8). Am Philos.
Kirke, et al. Michigan One Hundred Years Ago. (Sun Historical Ser.-). (Illus.). pap. 3.50 (ISBN 0-89540-053-7). Sun Pub.
Lethbridge, Alice. Well Do I Remember. (Illus.). 1976. 3.00 (ISBN 0-916536-01-7). Berwyn-London.
Lewis, Ferris E. Michigan Yesterday & Today. 9th ed. (Illus.). 591p. (gr. 10-12). 1980. text ed. 17.25x (ISBN 0-910726-52-3); tchr's ed 3.00x (ISBN 0-910726-51-5). Hillsdale Educ.
--Our Own State, Michigan. rev., 14th ed. LC 78-66800. (Illus.). (gr. 7-10). 1978. pap. text ed. 5.25x (ISBN 0-910726-21-3); questions & ans. for tchr's. 8.00x (ISBN 0-910726-23-X). Hillsdale Educ.
McConnell, David B. Discover Michigan. LC 81-6722. (Illus.). 144p. (gr. 4). 1981. text ed. 10.30x (ISBN 0-910726-07-8). Hillsdale Educ.
May, George. War Eighteen Twelve. (Illus.). 43p. (Orig.). 1962. pap. 1.50 (ISBN 0-911872-28-0). Mackinac Island.
Meek, Forrest. Michigan's Heartland, Nineteen Hundred-Nineteen Eighteen. LC 79-63276. 1979. 14.95 (ISBN 0-9602472-0-3). Edgewood.
Meek, Forrest B. Michigan's Timber Battleground. 2nd ed. 483p. lib. bdg. 9.95 softcover sewn binding (ISBN 0-9602472-1-1). Edgewood.
Michigan Ghost Towns, 3 vols. Vol. I. 5.00 (ISBN 0-932212-15-8); Vol. II. 5.50 (ISBN 0-932212-16-6); Vol. III. 5.95 (ISBN 0-932212-17-4). Avery Color.
A Michigan Reader, 2 vols. Incl. Vol. 1. Eleven Thousand B. C. to A. D. 1865. May, George & Brinks, Herbert, eds. (ISBN 0-8028-7029-5); Vol. 2. 1865 to Present. Warner, Robert & VanderHill, C. Warren, eds. (ISBN 0-8028-7030-9). 1974. pap. 4.95 ea.; pap. 9.90 2 vol. set (ISBN 0-8028-7031-7). Eerdmans.
Miller, Hazen L. Old Au Sable. 1974. 5.95 (ISBN 0-8028-7007-4). Eerdmans.
Newton, Stanley. The Story of Saulte Ste. Marie & Chippewa County. LC 74-27236. (Illus.). 199p. 1975. 12.00 (ISBN 0-912382-17-1); pap. 6.00 (ISBN 0-912382-27-9). Black Letter.
Potter, Theodore E. The Autobiography of Theodore Edgar Potter. (Michigan Heritage Library: Vol. 1). 1978. Repr. of 1913 ed. 9.95 (ISBN 0-915056-08-9). Hardscrabble Bks.
Powell, Richard R. Compromises of Conflicting Claims: A History of California Law in the Period 1760-1860. LC 77-54938. (Orig.). 1977. lib. bdg. 22.50 (ISBN 0-379-00655-3). Oceana.
Rankin, Carroll W. Dandelion Cottage. 4th ed. 1977. Repr. of 1904 ed. 4.95 (ISBN 0-938746-00-6). Marquette Cnty Hist.
Rubenstein, Bruce & Ziewacz, Lawrence. Michigan: A History of the Great Lakes State. (Orig.). 1981. pap. text ed. 11.95x (ISBN 0-88273-232-3). Forum Pr MO.
Russell, Nelson V. The British Regime in Michigan & the Old North-West 1760-1796. LC 78-10896. (Perspectives in Americn History Ser.: No. 40). xi, 302p. Repr. of 1939 ed. lib. bdg. 17.50x (ISBN 0-87991-364-9). Porcupine Pr.

Silliman, Sue I. Michigan Military Records: The D.A.R. of Mich. Historical Collection, Records of Revolutionary Soldiers, Etc. LC 79-80642. (Michigan Historical Commission Bulletin Ser: No. 12). (Illus.). 1969. Repr. of 1920 ed. 14.00 (ISBN 0-8063-0312-3). Genealog Pub.

Smeal, Lee. Michigan Historical & Biographical Index. LC 78-53704. (Illus.). Date not set. lib. bdg. price not set (ISBN 0-89593-187-7). Accelerated Index.

The Territory of Michigan, 1805-1820. (The Territorial Papers of the United States: Vol. 10). Repr. of 1942 ed. 69.50 (ISBN 0-404-01460-7). AMS Pr.

The Territory of Michigan, 1820-1829. (The Territorial Papers of the United States: Vol. 11). Repr. of 1943 ed. 69.50 (ISBN 0-404-01461-5). AMS Pr.

The Territory of Michigan, 1829-1837. (The Territorial Papers of the United States: Vol. 12). Repr. of 1945 ed. 69.50 (ISBN 0-404-01462-3). AMS Pr.

Upward, Geoffrey C. A Home for Our Heritage: The Building & Growth of Greenfield Village & Henry Ford Museum, 1929-1979. LC 79-19068. 192p. 1979. 16.95 (ISBN 0-933728-30-1, Ford Mus); pap. 9.95 (ISBN 0-933728-29-8). Edison Inst.

Vance, Mary. Historical Society Architectural Publications: Massachusetts, Michigan,Minnesota, Mississippi, Missouri. (Architecture Ser.: Bibliography A-159). 75p. 1980. pap. 8.00 (ISBN 0-686-26907-1). Vance Biblios.

Wait, S. E. Old Settlers of the Grand Traverse Region. Repr. of 1918 ed. 6.00 (ISBN 0-912382-25-2). Black Letter.

MICHIGAN-IMPRINTS

Historical Records Survey: Preliminary Check List of Michigan Imprints, 1796-1850. 1942. pap. 21.00 (ISBN 0-527-01932-1). Kraus Repr.

MICHIGAN-JUVENILE LITERATURE

Bailey, Bernadine. Picture Book of Michigan. rev. ed. (Illus.). (gr. 3-5). 1967. 5.50g (ISBN 0-8075-9524-1). A Whitman.

Carpenter, Allan. Michigan. new ed. LC 78-8001. (New Enchantment of America State Bks.). (Illus.). (gr. 4 up). 1978. PLB 10.60 (ISBN 0-516-04122-3). Childrens.

Fradin, Dennis. Michigan: In Words & Pictures. LC 79-225356. (Young People's Stories of Our States Ser.). (Illus.). 48p. (gr. 2-5). 1980. PLB 9.25 (ISBN 0-516-03922-9). Childrens.

Gringhuis, Dirk. The Eagle Pine. LC 58-7206. (Illus., Orig.). (gr. 5-8). 1969. pap. 2.75 (ISBN 0-910726-81-7). Hillsdale Educ.

Hall, E. Lorene & Kureth, Elwood J. Hi! I'm Michigan. LC 75-28621. (Illus.). 64p. (Orig.). (gr. 1-2). 1976. pap. text ed. 3.95 (ISBN 0-910726-00-0). Hillsdale Educ.

Parker, Lois & McConnell, David. A Little Peoples' Beginning on Michigan. (Illus.). 32p. (Orig.). (gr. 1-2). 1981. pap. 2.75 (ISBN 0-910726-06-X). Hillsdale Educ.

MICHIGAN-POLITICS AND GOVERNMENT

Bemis, Edward W. Local Government in Michigan & the Northwest. LC 78-63735. (Johns Hopkins University. Studies in the Social Sciences. First Ser. 1882-1883: 5). Repr. of 1883 ed. 11.50 (ISBN 0-404-61005-6). AMS Pr.

Carr, Robert W. Government of Michigan: Under the 1964 Constitution. rev. & enl. ed. LC 67-14740. 1967. pap. 3.95x (ISBN 0-472-08196-9). U of Mich Pr.

Cooley, Thomas M. Michigan, a History of Governments. rev. ed. LC 72-3764. (American Commonwealths: No. 5). Repr. of 1905 ed. 27.50 (ISBN 0-404-57205-7). AMS Pr.

Dilla, Harriette M. Politics of Michigan 1865-1878. (Columbia University Studies in the Social Sciences: No. 118). Repr. of 1912 ed. 21.50 (ISBN 0-404-51118-X). AMS Pr.

Fuller, George N., ed. Messages of the Governors of Michigan, 4 vols. LC 74-19601. Repr. of 1927 ed. Set. 167.50 (ISBN 0-404-12300-7). AMS Pr.

Gould Editorial Staff, ed. Motor Vehicle Laws of Michigan. 2nd ed. 300p. 1980. text ed. 9.00 (ISBN 0-87526-253-8). Gould.

--Penal Code of Michigan. 2nd ed. 350p. 1980. text ed. 10.50 (ISBN 0-87526-254-6). Gould.

Hagman, Harlan L. Bright Michigan Morning: The Years of Governor Tom Mason. (Illus.). 150p. (Orig.). 1981. 9.25 (ISBN 0-931600-02-2); pap. 5.50 (ISBN 0-931600-03-0). Green Oak Pr.

Hare, James M. With Malice Toward None: The Musings of a Retired Politician. 196p. 1972. 7.50 (ISBN 0-87013-168-0). Mich St U Pr.

Hotaling, Robert B. Michigan Local Planning Commissioners Handbook. 1977. 3.00 (ISBN 0-686-16224-2). MSU-Inst Comm Devel.

Lewis, Ferris E. & McConnell, David B. State & Local Government of Michigan. rev., 8th ed. LC 78-66807. (Illus.). (gr. 10-12). 1979. pap. text ed. 7.75x (ISBN 0-910726-41-8); questions & answers for tchrs. 3.00x (ISBN 0-910726-42-6). Hillsdale Educ.

Mead, Stuart B. Michigan Local Government Accounting. 1976. 15.00 (ISBN 0-686-16232-3, GA20); 3.00 (ISBN 0-686-16233-1, GA21); tchr's manual 6.00 (ISBN 0-686-16234-X, GA22). MSU-Inst Comm Devel.

Mead, Stuart B. & Plachta, Leonard E. Michigan Local Government Bookkeeping. 2nd ed. 1975. 15.00 (ISBN 0-686-16230-7, GA10); tchr's manual 5.00 (ISBN 0-686-16231-5, GA11). MSU-Inst Comm Devel.

Michigan Governmental Accounting & Audit Guide. rev. ed. 1978. 5.00 (ISBN 0-686-16236-6). MSU-Inst Comm Devel.

Michigan Laws Relating to Planning, Pts. I & II. 4th rev. ed. 1975. 6.50 (ISBN 0-686-16223-4). MSU-Inst Comm Devel.

Millspaugh, A. C. Party Organization & Machinery in Michigan Since 1890. LC 78-63962. (Johns Hopkins University. Studies in the Social Sciences. Thirty-Fifth Ser. 1917: 3). Repr. of 1917 ed. 18.50 (ISBN 0-404-61209-1). AMS Pr.

Morris, Susanne. Legislative Process in Michigan. LC 79-89030. (Illus., Orig.). 1979. pap. text ed. 3.95 (ISBN 0-910726-60-4); tchrs'. guide 3.00x (ISBN 0-910726-62-0). Hillsdale Educ.

Pollock, James K. Making Michigan's Constitution. 1963. 2.95x (ISBN 0-685-21793-0). Wahr.

Rapp, B. & Patitucci, F. Managing Local Government for Improved Performance: A Practical Approach. LC 76-25240. 1977. lib. bdg. 36.25x (ISBN 0-89158-121-9); pap. 14.50x (ISBN 0-89158-412-9). Westview.

Stieber, Carolyn. Politics of Change in Michigan. 139p. 1970. pap. text ed. 2.50x (ISBN 0-87013-148-6). Mich St U Pr.

Stollman, Gerald H. Michigan: State Legislators & Their Work. LC 77-18633. 1978. text ed. 7.50 (ISBN 0-8191-0425-6). U Pr of Amer.

MICHIGAN-SOCIAL LIFE AND CUSTOMS

Clive, Alan. State of War: Michigan in World War II. LC 79-10213. (Illus.). 1979. text ed. 15.00 (ISBN 0-472-10001-7). U of Mich Pr.

Julliard, Carl L. & Stermer, Edson. Willow Run: Study of Industrialization & Cultural Inadequacy. Stein, Leon, ed. LC 77-70486. (Work Ser.). (Illus.). 1977. Repr. of 1952 ed. lib. bdg. 27.00x (ISBN 0-405-10158-9). Arno.

Lignian, Mildred. Folks & Oaks of Olivet. new ed. (Illus.). 116p. 1975. pap. 3.50 (ISBN 0-685-55903-3). Olivet.

Marans, Robert W., et al. Waterfront Living: A Report on Permanent & Seasonal Residents in Northern Michigan. LC 76-620083. 301p. 1976. pap. text ed. 10.00 (ISBN 0-87944-218-2). Inst Soc Res.

Monroe City County Fine Arts Council. Brighten the Corner. Little, Elsie & Gibson, Catherine, eds. (Illus.). 188p. 1977. pap. 7.00x (ISBN 0-940696-00-2). Monroe County Lib.

Petersen, Eugene T. Hunters' Heritage: A History of Hunting in Michigan. Lowe, Kenneth S., ed. (Illus.). 1979. lib. bdg. 4.65 (ISBN 0-933112-01-7). Mich United Conserv.

MICHIGAN-STATE DEPARTMENT OF SOCIAL WELFARE

French, David G. Approach to Measuring Results in Social Work. LC 70-136066. xiv, 178p. Repr. of 1952 ed. lib. bdg. 15.00x (ISBN 0-8371-5216-X, FRAM). Greenwood.

MICHIGAN, UNIVERSITY OF

Babst, Earl D. & Vander Velde, Lewis G., eds. Michigan & the Cleveland Era: Sketches of University of Michigan Staff Members & Alumni Who Served the Cleveland Administrations, 1885-89,1893-97. facsimile ed. LC 70-179724. (Biography Index Reprint Ser). Repr. of 1948 ed. 25.00 (ISBN 0-8369-8092-1). Arno.

Bordin, Ruth B. University of Michigan: A Pictorial History. LC 66-17029. (Illus.). 1967. 6.50 (ISBN 0-472-16400-7). U of Mich Pr.

Davis, Phil. The University (Pictorial) LC 67-30753. 1967. 14.95 (ISBN 0-472-27900-9). U of Mich Pr.

MacInnes, Margo. A Guide to the Campus of the University of Michigan. LC 77-95134. (Illus.). 1978. pap. 3.95 (ISBN 0-472-61300-6). U of Mich Pr.

Peckham, Howard H. Making of the University of Michigan. LC 66-17028. 1967. 6.50 (ISBN 0-472-72300-6). U of Mich Pr.

Shaw, Wilfred B. Short History of the University of Michigan. 1934. 3.95x (ISBN 0-685-21804-X). Wahr.

Strode Publishers, ed. Michigan-Michigan State Joke Book. 1975. 1.98 (ISBN 0-87397-088-8). Strode.

University of Michigan, William L. Clements Library. Research Catalog of Maps of America to 1860 in the William L. Clements Library, 4 vols. 1972. Set. lib. bdg. 320.00 (ISBN 0-8161-1003-4). G K Hall.

MICHIGAN, UNIVERSITY OF-GREENLAND EXPEDITIONS, 1926-1933

Hobbs, William H. Exploring About the North Pole of the Winds. LC 68-55196. (Illus.). Repr. of 1930 ed. lib. bdg. 18.75x (ISBN 0-8371-0478-5, HONP). Greenwood.

MICHIGAN STATE UNIVERSITY

Kuhn, Madison. Michigan State: The First Hundred Years. (Illus.). 501p. 1979. 10.00x (ISBN 0-87013-222-9). Mich St U Pr.

Michigan State University,(East Lansing) Dictionary Catalog of the G. Robert Vincent Library. 1975. 50.00 (ISBN 0-8161-1149-9). G K Hall.

Stabley, Fred. W. The Spartans: A Story of Michigan State Football. LC 75-12206. (College Sports Ser.). 1975. 9.95 (ISBN 0-87397-067-5). Strode.

Strode Publishers, ed. Michigan-Michigan State Joke Book. 1975. 1.98 (ISBN 0-87397-088-8). Strode.

MICHOACAN, MEXICO

Craine, Eugene R. & Reindorp, Reginald C., eds. Chronicles of Michoacan. LC 69-16726. (Civilization of the American Indian Ser.: No. 98). (Illus.). 1970. 14.95 (ISBN 0-8061-0887-8). U of Okla Pr.

Stanislawski, Dan. Anatomy of Eleven Towns in Michoacan. (Illus.). Repr. of 1950 ed. lib. bdg. 17.25x (ISBN 0-8371-1029-7, TLSM). Greenwood.

West, Robert C. Cultural Geography of the Modern Tarascan Area. LC 77-118761. (Illus.). 77p. 1973. Repr. of 1948 ed. lib. bdg. 22.00x (ISBN 0-8371-5078-7, SMIH). Greenwood.

MICHOACANA LANGUAGE

see Tarascan Language

MICHUACANA LANGUAGE

see Tarascan Language

MICKIEWICZ, ADAM, 1798-1855

Gardner, Monica M. Adam Mickiewicz: The National Poet of Poland. LC 74-135807. (Eastern Europe Collection Ser). 1970-71. Repr. of 1911 ed. 15.00 (ISBN 0-405-02749-4). Arno.

Kridl, Manfred, ed. Adam Mickiewicz, Poet of Poland: A Symposium. Repr. of 1951 ed. lib. bdg. 15.00x (ISBN 0-8371-2783-1, KRAM). Greenwood.

Lednicki, Waclaw, ed. Adam Mickiewicz in World Literature: A Symposium. LC 76-2017. 626p. 1976. Repr. of 1956 ed. lib. bdg. 35.25x (ISBN 0-8371-8765-6, LEAM). Greenwood.

Varese, Louise. Mickiewicz: The Great Improvisation. 1956. 4.00 (ISBN 0-686-30925-1). Polish Inst Arts.

MICMAC INDIANS

see Indians of North America-Canada

MICRO COMPUTERS

see Microcomputers

MICROANALYSIS (CHEMISTRY)

see Microchemistry

MICROBALANCE

see also Vacuum Microbalance

MICROBES

see Bacteria; Bacteriology; Germ Theory of Disease; Micro-Organisms; Viruses

Andersen, C. A., ed. Microprobe Analysis. LC 72-8837. 586p. Date not set. Repr. of 1973 ed. 43.00 (ISBN 0-471-02835-5). Krieger.

MICROBIAL DISEASES IN ANIMALS

see Veterinary Microbiology

MICROBIAL DISEASES IN MAN

see Medical Microbiology

MICROBIAL DRUG RESISTANCE

see Drug Resistance in Micro-Organisms

MICROBIAL ENERGY CONVERSION

see Biomass Energy

MICROBIAL GENETICS

see also Bacterial Genetics; Drug Resistance in Micro-Organisms; Viral Genetics

Abou-Sabe, Morad A., ed. Microbial Genetics. LC 73-13002. (Benchmark Papers in Microbiology Ser.). 464p. 1973. text ed. 48.00x (ISBN 0-12-786009-6). Acad Pr.

Bainbridge, Brian W. The Genetics of Microbes. (Tertiary Level Biology Ser.). 193p. 1980. pap. 29.95x (ISBN 0-470-26995-2). Halsted Pr.

Drake, John W. Molecular Basis of Mutation. LC 73-86859. (Illus.). 1970. text ed. 20.00x (ISBN 0-8162-2450-1). Holden-Day.

Fincham, J. R. Microbial & Molecular Genetics. 2nd ed. LC 75-21729. 150p. 1976. pap. 9.95x (ISBN 0-8448-0769-9). Crane-Russak Co.

MICROBIAL METABOLITES

see also Antibiotics; Biosynthesis

Fiechter, A., ed. Microbial Metabolism. (Advances in Biochemical Engineering Ser.: Vol. 14). (Illus.). 1980. 41.20 (ISBN 0-387-09621-3). Springer-Verlag.

Gottschalk, G. Bacterial Metabolism. LC 78-7880. (Springer Ser. in Microbiology). (Illus.). 1978. 19.80 (ISBN 0-387-90308-9). Springer-Verlag.

Hutter, R., et al, eds. Antibiotics & Other Secondary Metabolites: Biosynthesis & Production. 1979. 42.50 (ISBN 0-12-363250-1). Acad Pr.

Neilands, J. B. Microbial Iron Metabolism: A Comprehensive Treatise. 1974. 68.50 (ISBN 0-12-515250-7). Acad Pr.

MICROBIAL TRANSFORMATION OF CHEMICAL COMPOUNDS

see Microbiological Synthesis

MICROBIOLOGICAL SYNTHESIS

see also Fermentation

Aaronson, Sheldon, ed. Chemcial Communication at the Microbial, Vols. I & II. 1981. Vol. I 208p. 59.95 (ISBN 0-8493-5319-X); Vol. II 208p. 59.95 (ISBN 0-8493-5320-3). CRC Pr.

Charney, William & Herzog, Hershel. Microbiological Transformation of Steroids: A Handbook. 1968. 76.50 (ISBN 0-12-169950-1). Acad Pr.

Duffy, J. I., ed. Chemicals by Enzymatic & Microbial Processes: Recent Advances. LC 80-16150. (Chemical Technology Review: No. 161). (Illus.). 386p. 1980. 48.00 (ISBN 0-8155-0805-0). Noyes.

Fonken, G. & Johnson, R. Chemical Oxidations with Microorganisms. (Oxidation in Organic Chemistry Ser.: Vol. 2). 1972. 41.50 (ISBN 0-8247-1211-0). Dekker.

Symposium on the Continuous Culture of Micro-Organisms, Fifth. Environmental Control of Cell Synthesis & Function. Dean, A. C., et al, eds. 1973. 76.00 (ISBN 0-12-208050-5). Acad Pr.

Umezawa, H. Enzyme Inhibitors of Microbial Origin. 1973. 19.50 (ISBN 0-8391-0734-X). Univ Park.

MICROBIOLOGY

see also Bacteriology; Biodegradation; Germfree Life; Industrial Microbiology; Marine Microbiology; Microbial Metabolites; Micro-Organisms; Microscope and Microscopy; Radioisotopes in Microbiology; Veterinary Microbiology; Virology; Yeast

Alexander, M., ed. Advances in Microbial Ecology, Vol. 1. (Illus.). 280p. 1977. 24.50 (ISBN 0-306-38161-3, Plenum Pr). Plenum Pub.

--Advances in Microbial Ecology, Vol. 2. (Illus.). 311p. 1978. 24.50 (ISBN 0-306-38162-1, Plenum Pr). Plenum Pub.

--Advances in Microbial Ecology, Vol. 3. (Illus.). 237p. 1979. 24.50 (ISBN 0-306-40240-8, Plenum Pr). Plenum Pub.

Alexander, Martin. Microbial Ecology. LC 71-137105. (Illus.). 511p. 1971. 29.95 (ISBN 0-471-02054-0). Wiley.

Ananthanarayan, R. & Paniker, C. K. Textbook of Microbiology. 608p. 1979. 25.00x (ISBN 0-86131-032-2, Pub. by Orient Longman India). State Mutual Bk.

Andersen, C. A., ed. Microprobe Analysis. LC 72-8837. 586p. Date not set. Repr. of 1973 ed. 43.00 (ISBN 0-471-02835-5). Krieger.

Anderson & Sobieski. Introduction to Microbiology. 2nd ed. LC 79-20560. 1980. pap. 17.95 (ISBN 0-8016-0206-8). Mosby.

Arber, W., ed. Current Topics in Microbiology & Immunology, Vol. 72. LC 15-12910. (Illus.). 200p. 1976. 44.80 (ISBN 0-387-07564-X). Springer-Verlag.

--Current Topics in Microbiology & Immunology, Vol. 78. LC 15-12910. (Illus.). 1977. 50.40 (ISBN 0-387-08499-1). Springer-Verlag.

Arber, W., et al. Current Topics in Microbiology & Immunology, Vol. 75. LC 15-12910. (Illus.). 1976. 48.10 (ISBN 3-540-08013-9). Springer-Verlag.

--Current Topics in Microbiology & Immunology, Vol. 79. LC 15-12910. 1978. 56.70 (ISBN 0-387-08587-4). Springer-Verlag.

Arber, W., et al, eds. Current Topics in Microbiology & Immunology, Vols. 40-55. Incl. Vols. 40-50 & 52-55. Chronic Infections Neuropathic Agents & Other Slow Virsus Infections. Brody, J. A., et al, eds. (Illus.). vii, 74p. 1967. 22.90 (ISBN 0-387-03754-3); Vol. 41. (Illus.). iv, 183p. 1967. 49.00 (ISBN 0-387-03755-1); Vol. 42. Insect Viruses. Maramorosch, K., ed. (Illus.). viii, 192p. 1968. 26.70 (ISBN 0-387-04071-4); Vol. 43. (Illus.). iii, 233p. (Incl. 32 pp. in German). 1968. 52.00 (ISBN 0-387-04072-2); Vol. 44. (Illus.). iii, 175p. 1968. 52.00 (ISBN 0-387-04073-0); Vol. 45. (Illus.). iii, 237p. (Incl. 61 pp. in German). 1968. 52.00 (ISBN 0-387-04074-9); Vol. 46. (Illus.). iii, 203p. (Incl. 90 pp. in German). 1968. 57.90 (ISBN 0-387-04075-7); Vol. 47. (Illus.). iii, 222p. (Incl. 29 pp. in German). 1969. 55.50 (ISBN 0-387-04445-0); Vol. 48. (Illus.). iii, 206p. 1969. 55.50 (ISBN 0-387-04446-9); Vol. 49. (Illus.). iii, 250p. 1969. 55.50 (ISBN 0-387-04447-7); Vol. 50. (Illus.). iii, 238p. 1969. 55.50 (ISBN 0-387-04448-5); Vol. 52. (Illus.). iv, 197p. 1970. 55.50 (ISBN 0-387-04787-5); Vol. 53. (Illus.). 236p. 1970. 58.50 (ISBN 0-387-05069-8); Vol. 54. (Illus.). 230p. 1971. 58.50 (ISBN 0-387-05289-5); Vol. 55. Arthropod Cell Cultures & Their Application to the Study of Viruses: Arthropod Cell Cultures & Their Application to the Study of Viruses. Weiss, E., ed. (Illus.). 340p. 1971. 49.10 (ISBN 0-387-05451-0). (Illus., Eng. & Ger.). Springer-Verlag.

--Current Topics in Microbiology & Immunology, Vol. 62. LC 73-17985. (Illus.). 170p. 1974. 35.90 (ISBN 0-387-06598-9). Springer-Verlag.

--Current Topics in Microbiology & Immunology, Vol. 63. LC 73-20915. (Illus.). 230p. 1974. 44.00 (ISBN 0-387-06599-7). Springer-Verlag.

--Current Topics in Microbiology & Immunology, Vol. 64. LC 74-3541. (Illus.). 190p. 1974. 42.20 (ISBN 0-387-06713-2). Springer-Verlag.
--Current Topics in Microbiology & Immunology, Vol. 66. LC 15-12910. (Illus.). 130p. 1974. 31.40 (ISBN 3-540-06831-7). Springer-Verlag.
--Current Topics in Microbiology & Immunology, Vol. 67. LC 15-12910. (Illus.). iv, 162p. 1975. 42.20 (ISBN 3-540-06838-4). Springer-Verlag.
--Current Topics in Microbiology & Immunology, Vol. 76. LC 15-12910. (Illus.). 1977. 48.10 (ISBN 3-540-08238-7). Springer-Verlag.
--Current Topics in Microbiology & Immunology, Vol. 77. LC 15-12910. (Illus.). 1977. 45.70 (ISBN 0-387-08401-0). Springer-Verlag.
--Current Topics in Microbiology & Immunology, Vol. 82. LC 15-12910. (Illus.). 1978. 37.50 (ISBN 0-387-08981-0). Springer-Verlag.
--Current Topics in Microbiology & Immunology, Vol. 83. LC 15-12910. (Illus.). 1978. 39.30 (ISBN 0-387-09034-7). Springer-Verlag.
--Current Topics in Microbiology & Immunology, Vol. 85. (Illus.). 1979. 50.80 (ISBN 0-387-09410-5). Springer-Verlag.
--Current Topics in Microbiology & Immunology, Vols. 86-87. (Illus.). 1980. Vol. 86. 39.30 (ISBN 0-387-09432-6); Vol. 87. 37.40 (ISBN 0-387-09433-4). Springer-Verlag.
--Current Topics in Microbiology & Immunology, Vol. 90. (Illus.). 147p. 1980. 51.90 (ISBN 0-387-10181-0). Springer-Verlag.
--Current Topics in Microbiology & Immunology, Vol. 91. (Illus.). 250p. 37.20 (ISBN 0-387-10722-3). Springer-Verlag.
Ashworth, J. M. & Smith, J. E., eds. Microbial Differentiation. (Society for General Microbiology Ser.: No. 23). (Illus.). 500p. 1973. 49.50 (ISBN 0-521-20104-7). Cambridge U Pr.
Atlas, Ronald M. & Bartha, Richard. Microbial Ecology: Fundamentals & Applications. (Life Sciences Ser.). 500p. 1981. write for info. (ISBN 0-201-00051-2). A-W.
Balows, Albert & Isenberg, Henry. Biotyping in the Clinical Microbiology Laboratory. (Amer. Lec. Clinical Microbiology). (Illus.). 128p. 1978. 12.00 (ISBN 0-398-03806-6). C C Thomas.
Baserga, Renato, et al, eds. Introduction of Macromolecules into Viable Mammalian Cells. LC 79-91743. (Wistar Symposium Ser.: Vol. 1). 354p. 1980. 26.00x (ISBN 0-8451-2000-X). A R Liss.
Bazin, M., ed. Microbial Polution Dynamics, Vol. I. 208p. 1982. price not set (ISBN 0-8493-5951-1). CRC Pr.
Beishir, Lois. Microbiology in Practice: Individualized Instruction for the Allied Health Sciences. 2nd ed. 1977. pap. text ed. 13.50 scp (ISBN 0-06-371062-5, HarpC); instrs'. manual free. Har-Row.
Benson, Harold J. Microbiological Applications: A Laboratory Manual in General Microbiology, Short Version. 3rd, ed. 1979. write for info. (ISBN 0-697-04658-3); instr. manual avail. (ISBN 0-685-91861-0). Wm C Brown.
--Microbiological Applications: A Laboratory Manual in General Microbiology, Complete Version. 3rd ed. 1979. write for info. (ISBN 0-697-04659-1); inst. manual avail. (ISBN 0-685-91874-2). Wm C Brown.
Berkeley, R. C. & Ellwood, D. C., eds. Microbial Polysaccharides & Polysaccharases. (Society for General Microbiology Ser.). 1979. 47.00 (ISBN 0-12-091450-6). Acad Pr.
Bitton, Gabriel & Marshall, Kevin C., eds. Absorption of Microorganisms to Surfaces. LC 79-19482. 439p. 1979. 37.50 (ISBN 0-471-03157-7, Pub. by Wiley-Interscience). Wiley.
Blakeman, J. P., ed. Microbial Ecology of the Phylloplane. 1981. 49.00 (ISBN 0-12-103750-9). Acad Pr.
Blough, H. A., et al. Current Topics in Microbiology & Immunology, Vol. 70. LC 75-12910. (Illus.). 140p. 1975. 35.10 (ISBN 0-387-07223-3). Springer-Verlag.
Board, R. G. & Lovelock, D. W., eds. Some Methods for Microbiological Assay. 1975. 45.50 (ISBN 0-12-108240-7). Acad Pr.
Borick, Paul M., ed. Chemical Sterilization. LC 73-4967. (Benchmark Papers in Microbiology Ser.). 368p. 1973. 40.50 (ISBN 0-12-786180-7). Acad Pr.
Brady, R. J. Microbiology: A Programmed Introduction to. (Illus.). 1969. pap. 10.95 (ISBN 0-87618-075-6). R J Brady.
Branson, Dorothy. Microbiology for the Small Laboratory. (Illus.). 80p. 1972. ed. spiral bdg. 9.50photocopy (ISBN 0-398-02576-2). C C Thomas.
Brenner, S., et al, eds. New Horizons in Industrial Microbiology: Philosophical Transactions of the Royal Society, 1980. rev. ed. (Ser. B: Vol. 290). (Illus.). 152p. text ed. 47.50x (ISBN 0-85403-146-4, Pub. by Dechema Germany). Scholium Intl.
Brock, Thomas D. & Brock, Katherine M. Basic Microbiology with Applications. 2nd ed. (Illus.). 1978. 22.95 (ISBN 0-13-065284-9). P-H.
Brock, Thomas D., ed. Milestones in Microbiology. 1975. Repr. of 1961 ed. 7.00 (ISBN 0-914826-06-9). Am Soc Microbio.
Brooks, Stewart M. A Programmed Introduction to Microbiology. 2nd ed. LC 72-88509. (Illus.). 120p. 1973. pap. text ed. 8.50 (ISBN 0-8016-0819-8). Mosby.
Brumfitt, W., ed. New Perspectives in Clinical Microbiology. 1978. lib. bdg. 31.50 (ISBN 90-247-2074-5, Pub. by Martinus Nijhoff Netherlands). Kluwer Boston.
Brumfitt, W., et al, eds. Combined Antimicrobial Therapy. (New Perspectives in Clinical Microbiology Ser.: No. 3). 1980. lib. bdg. 47.00 (ISBN 90-247-2280-2, Pub. by Martinus Nijhoff Netherlands). Kluwer Boston.
Buffaloe, Neal D. & Ferguson, Dale V. Microbiology. 2nd ed. LC 80-82842. (Illus.). 752p. 1981. text ed. 22.95 (ISBN 0-395-29649-8); lab manual 7.95 (ISBN 0-395-29652-8); instr's manual 1.00 (ISBN 0-395-29650-1); study guide 7.50 set (ISBN 0-395-29651-X). HM.
--Microbiology. LC 75-19538. (Illus.). 448p. 1976. text ed. 19.50 (ISBN 0-395-18712-5); inst. manual 1.25 (ISBN 0-395-18918-7). HM.
Bull, A. T., et al. Microbial Technology: Society for General Microbiology Symposium 29. LC 78-12206. (Illus.). 1979. 59.50 (ISBN 0-521-22500-0). Cambridge U Pr.
Bull, Alan T. & Meadow, Pauline M., eds. Companion to Microbiology: Selected Topics for Further Study. (Illus.). 1978. text ed. 35.00x (ISBN 0-582-46067-0). Longman.
Burton, Gwendolyn R. Microbiology for the Health Sciences. LC 79-1204. 1979. pap. text ed. 9.25x (ISBN 0-397-54309-3, JBL-Med-Nursing); wkbk. 4.75x (ISBN 0-685-97152-X). Har-Row.
Carlile, M. J. & Skehel, J. J., eds. Evolution in the Microbial World: Proceedings. (Illus.). 450p. 1974. 49.50 (ISBN 0-521-20416-X). Cambridge U Pr.
Carlile, M. J., et al. Molecular & Cellular Aspects of Microbial Evolution. LC 80-42172. (Society for General Microbiology Ser.: Symposium 32). (Illus.). 400p. Date not set. price not set (ISBN 0-521-24108-1). Cambridge U Pr.
Carnegie Institution of Washington Year Book, Vol. 77. (Illus.). 1978. 16.50 (ISBN 0-87279-650-7). Carnegie Inst.
Christensen, Mary L. Microbiology for Nursing & Allied Health Students. (Illus.). 624p. 1981. 39.50 (ISBN 0-398-04176-8). C C Thomas.
Clarke, R. & Bauchop, T., eds. Microbial Ecology of the Gut. 1978. 65.50 (ISBN 0-12-175550-9). Acad Pr.
Clifton, C. E., et al, eds. Annual Review of Microbiology, Vol. 26. LC 49-432. (Illus.). 1972. text ed. 17.00 (ISBN 0-8243-1126-4). Annual Reviews.
Cokelet, Giles R., et al, eds. Erythrocyte Mechanics & Blood Flow. LC 79-5473. (Kroc Foundation Ser.: Vol. 13). 285p. 1980. 30.00x (ISBN 0-8451-0303-2). A R Liss.
Collins, C. H. Microbiological Hazards. 1981. text ed. write for info. (ISBN 0-408-10650-6). Butterworth.
Cowhig, Jerry. The World Under the Microscope. (The World of Nature Ser.). (Illus.). 128p. 1973. 1.98 (ISBN 0-517-12044-5, Bounty Books). Crown.
Crabtree, Koby T. & Hinsdill, Ronald D. Fundamental Experiments in Microbiology. LC 73-89175. (Illus.). 365p. 1974. pap. 9.95 (ISBN 0-7216-2733-1). HR&W.
Current Topics in Microbiology & Immunology, Vol. 71. LC 15-12910. (Illus.). 1975. 39.00 (ISBN 0-387-07369-8). Springer-Verlag.
Current Topics in Microbiology & Immunology, Vol. 80. LC 15-12910. (Illus.). 1978. 39.30 (ISBN 0-387-08781-8). Springer-Verlag.
Current Topics in Microbiology & Immunology, Vol. 88. (Illus.). 142p. 1980. 35.20 (ISBN 0-387-09415-6). Springer-Verlag.
Daumeister, W., ed. Electron Microscopy at Molecular Dimensions. (Proceedings in Life Sciences). (Illus.). 300p. 1980. 59.80 (ISBN 0-387-10131-4). Springer-Verlag.
Davis, Bernard D. Microbiology. (Illus.). 1274p. 1980. 45.00 (ISBN 0-06-140691-0, Harper Medical). Har-Row.
Dawson, P. S., ed. Microbial Growth. LC 74-26644. (Benchmark Papers in Microbiology Ser: Vol. 8). 400p. 1975. 49.50 (ISBN 0-12-786330-3). Acad Pr.
Dean, A. C., et al, eds. Continuous Culture: Applications & New Fields. (Continuous Culture Ser.). 1976. 47.95x (ISBN 0-470-98984-X). Halsted Pr.
DECHMA, Deutsche Gesellschaft Fuer Chemisches Apparatewesen E. V., ed. Microbiology Applied to Technology: Proceedings XIIth International Congress of Microbiology. (DECHEMA Monographs: Vol. 83). 230p. (Orig.). 1979. pap. text ed. 25.80 (ISBN 3-527-10766-5). Verlag Chemie.
Deibel, Robert H. & Lindquist, John A. General Food Microbiology: Laboratory Manual. 1982. pap. price not set (ISBN 0-8087-4403-8). Burgess.
De Louvois, J., ed. Selected Topics in Clinical Bacteriology. 1976. text ed. 17.50 (ISBN 0-02-857570-9). Macmillan.
Directory. 1977. 15.00 (ISBN 0-685-88617-4). Am Soc Microbio.
Doelle, H. W., ed. Microbial Metabolism. LC 73-16370. (Benchmark Papers in Microbiology Ser). 432p. 1974. text ed. 49.50 (ISBN 0-12-786360-5). Acad Pr.
Droop, M. R. & Jannasch, H. W., eds. Advances in Aquatic Microbiology, Vol. 1. (Serial Publication). 1977. 58.00 (ISBN 0-12-003001-2). Acad Pr.
Dubos, Rene. The Professor, the Institute, & DNA. LC 76-26812. 1976. 14.50 (ISBN 0-87470-022-1). Rockefeller.
Durand, Donald P., et al. M.E.L.E. in Microbiology. 3rd ed. 1977. 5.95x (ISBN 0-8087-0458-3). Burgess.
Eddington, Arthur S. Science & the Unseen World. 56p. 1980. Repr. of 1929 ed. lib. bdg. 8.50 (ISBN 0-8495-1426-6). Arden Lib.
Editors of Scientific American, ed. Industrial Microbiology: A Scientific American Book. 1981. price not set (ISBN 0-7167-1385-3); text ed. price not set (ISBN 0-7167-1385-3); pap. price not set (ISBN 0-7167-1386-1); pap. text ed. price not set (ISBN 0-7167-1386-1). W H Freeman.
Edmonds, Paul. Microbiology: An Environmental Perspective. (Illus.). 1978. text ed. 18.95 (ISBN 0-02-333580-7). Macmillan.
Education & Training Systems Division of the Robert J. Brady Co. Brady's Programmed Introduction to Microbiology. 1969. 6.50 (ISBN 0-397-54090-6, JBL-Med-Nursing). Har-Row.
Ellwood, D. C., et al, eds. Adhesion to Microorganisms to Surfaces. (A Volume in the Special Publications of the Society for General Microbiology Ser.). 1979. 26.50 (ISBN 0-12-236650-6). Acad Pr.
Emerson, S. U., et al. Current Topics in Microbiology & Immunology, Vol. 73. LC 15-12910. 1976. 43.60 (ISBN 0-387-07593-3). Springer-Verlag.
Erlich. Geomicrobiology. 1981. 29.75 (ISBN 0-8247-1183-1). Dekker.
Farquhar, Judith & Gajdusek, D. Carleton, eds. Kuru: Early Letters & Field Notes from the Collection of D. Carleton Gajdusek. 366p. 1980. text ed. 40.00 (ISBN 0-89004-359-0). Raven.
Felkner. Microbial Testers: Probing Carcinogenesis. (Microbiology Ser.: Vol. 5). 1981. 35.00 (ISBN 0-8247-1244-7). Dekker.
Ferris, Elvira & Fong, Elizabeth. Microbiology for Health Care Carerrs. 2nd ed. LC 81-66764. (Allied Health Ser.). (Illus.). 160p. 1981. pap. text ed. 7.60 (ISBN 0-8273-1901-0); price not set (ISBN 0-8273-1902-9). Delmar.
Fiechter, A., ed. Microbial Processes. LC 72-152360. (Advances in Biochemical Engineering: Vol. 9). (Illus.). 1978. 33.60 (ISBN 0-387-08606-4). Springer-Verlag.
--New Technological Concepts. (Advances in Biochemical Engineering Ser.: Vol. 15). (Illus.). 250p. 1980. 46.50 (ISBN 0-387-09686-8). Springer-Verlag.
Fiechter, A., et al, eds. Microbiology, Theory & Application. LC 72-152360. (Advances in Biochemical Engineering Ser.: Vol. 11). 1979. 41.60 (ISBN 0-387-08990-X). Springer-Verlag.
Finegold, Sydney M., et al. Bailey & Scott's Diagnostic Microbiology: A Textbook for the Isolation & Identification of Pathogenic Microorganisms. 5th ed. LC 77-28251. (Illus.). 1978. text ed. 25.95 (ISBN 0-8016-0421-4). Mosby.
Ford, Brian J. Microbe Power. LC 76-7437. 1976. 10.00 (ISBN 0-8128-1936-5); pap. 4.95 (ISBN 0-8128-6006-3). Stein & Day.
Fourth Lepetit Colloquium Held in Cocoyoc, Mex., Nov., 1972. Possible Episomes in Eukaryotes: Proceedings. Silvestri, L., ed. LC 73-81534. 321p. 1973. pap. 49.00 (ISBN 0-444-10527-1, North-Holland). Elsevier.
Fraenkel-Conrat, H. & Wagner, R. R., eds. Comprehensive Virology, Vol. 14: Newly Characterized Vertebrate Viruses. LC 79-810. (Illus.). 562p. 1979. 45.00 (ISBN 0-306-40231-9, Plenum Pr). Plenum Pub.
Frazer, A. C., et al. Current Topics in Microbiology & Immunology, Vol. 69. (Illus.). 200p. 1975. 42.60 (ISBN 0-387-07195-4). Springer-Verlag.
Frazier, William C. Food Microbiology. 2nd ed. 1967. text ed. 18.00 (ISBN 0-07-021916-8, C). McGraw.
Frazier, William C. & Westhoff, Dennis. Food Microbiology. 3rd ed. (Illus.). 1978. text ed. 19.95 (ISBN 0-07-021917-6, C). McGraw.
Freeman, Bob A. Burrows Textbook of Microbiology. LC 77-16986. (Illus.). 1979. text ed. 39.50 (ISBN 0-7216-3869-4). Saunders.
Fudenberg, Hugh H. & Graber, Charles D. Microbiology & Immunology: A Positive Statement Manual. 1977. spiral bddg. 9.75 (ISBN 0-87488-242-7). Med Exam.
Fuerst, Robert. Frobisher & Fuerst's Microbiology in Health & Disease. 14th ed. LC 77-79391. (Illus.). 1978. text ed. 17.95 (ISBN 0-7216-3939-9). Saunders.
Gall, Lorraine S. & Riely, Phyllis E., eds. Manual for the Determination of the Clinical Role of Anaerobic Microbiology. 96p. 1981. write for info. CRC Pr.
Gaudy, Anthony & Gaudy, Elizabeth. Microbiology for Environment Science Engineers. (Water Resources & Environmental Engineering Ser.). (Illus.). 704p. 1980. 25.95 (ISBN 0-07-023035-8); solutions manual 16.50 (ISBN 0-07-023036-6). McGraw.
Gause, G. F. Microbial Models of Cancer Cells. Neuberger, A. & Tatum, E. L., eds. (Frontiers of Biology Ser.: Vol. 1). 1967. 12.25 (ISBN 0-444-10202-7, North-Holland). Elsevier.
Gauthier, Dorothy. Introductory Microbiology. 1980. spiral bdg. 8.95 (ISBN 0-88252-105-5). Paladin Hse.
Gebhardt, Louis P. & Nicholes, Paul S. Microbiology. 5th ed. LC 74-10691. 1975. text ed. 15.95 (ISBN 0-8016-1784-7); lab manual 8.50 (ISBN 0-8016-1773-1). Mosby.
Ghosh, Bijan K., ed. Organization of Prokaryotic Cell Membrane, Vols. I & II. 1981. Vol. I, 288p. 79.95 (ISBN 0-8493-5653-9); Vol. II, 256p. 74.95 (ISBN 0-8493-5654-7). CRC Pr.
Glover, S. W. & Hopwood, D. A., eds. Genetics As a Tool in Microbiology. (Society for General Microbiology Symposium: No. 31). (Illus.). 450p. 1981. text ed. 65.00 (ISBN 0-521-23748-3). Cambridge U Pr.
Gooday, G. W., et al, eds. The Eukaryotic Microbial Cell. LC 79-20741. (Society for General Microbiology Symposium: No. 30). (Illus.). 450p. 1980. 57.50 (ISBN 0-521-22974-X). Cambridge U Pr.
Gordon, John. MCQ Tutor for Students of Microbiology. 1979. pap. text ed. 15.00 (ISBN 0-8151-3805-9). Year Bk Med.
Gottfried, Sandra. Fundamentals in Laboratory Microbiology. (Illus.). 1979. pap. text ed. 8.00 (ISBN 0-910918-04-X). Lydette.
Grant, William D. & Long, P. E. Environmental Microbiology. 200p. 1981. pap. 32.95 (ISBN 0-470-27233-3). Halsted Pr.
Griffin, David H. Fungal Physiology. 392p. 1981. 32.50 (ISBN 0-471-05748-7, Pub. by Wiley-Interscience). Wiley.
Haddock, B. A. & Hamilton, W. A., eds. Microbial Energetics. LC 76-54367. (Society for General Microbiology: Symposium 27). (Illus.). 1977. 65.00 (ISBN 0-521-21494-7). Cambridge U Pr.
Heden, Carl-Goran & Illeni, Tibor, eds. Automation in Microbiology & Immunology. LC 74-12082. 610p. 1975. 50.00 (ISBN 0-471-36745-1, Pub. by Wiley). Krieger.
Hewitt, W., ed. Microbiological Assay: An Introduction to Quantitative Principles & Evaluation. 1977. 38.00 (ISBN 0-12-346450-1). Acad Pr.
Higgins, I. J. & Burns, R. G. The Chemistry & Microbiology of Pollution. 1975. 36.00 (ISBN 0-12-347950-9). Acad Pr.
Hill, I. R. & Wright, S. J., eds. Pesticide Microbiology: Microbiological Aspects of Pesticide Behavior in the Environment. 1979. 110.50 (ISBN 0-12-348650-5). Acad Pr.
Hobbs, Betty C. & Christian, J. H., eds. The Microbiological Safety of Foods. 1974. 77.00 (ISBN 0-12-350750-2). Acad Pr.
Hughes, D. E. & Rose, eds. Microbes & Biological Productivity. (Illus.). 1971. 42.50 (ISBN 0-521-08112-2). Cambridge U Pr.
Hunter, Peter. General Microbiology: The Students' Textbook. LC 76-28532. (Illus.). 500p. 1977. pap. text ed. 12.50 (ISBN 0-8016-2313-8). Mosby.
International Commission on Microbiological Specifications for Foods. Microorganisms in Foods: Vol. 2, Sampling for Microbiological Analysis: Principles & Specific Applications. LC 73-2628. 1974. 25.00x (ISBN 0-8020-2143-3). U of Toronto Pr.
International Congress of Microbiological Standardization, 12th, Annecy, 1971. Proceedings. Regamey, R. H., et al, eds. (Progress in Immunobiological Standardization: Vol. 5). 111.00 (ISBN 3-8055-1404-2). S Karger.
International Congress of Microbiological Standardization, 11th, Milan, 1968. Proceedngs. Regamey, R. H., et al, eds. (Progress in Immubobiological Standardization: Vol. 4). 1970. 129.50 (ISBN 3-8055-0400-4). S Karger.
International Symposium on Yersinia, 3rd, Montreal, September 1977. Yersinia enterocolitica. Carter, Philip B., et al, eds. (Contributions to Microbiology & Immunology: Vol. 5). (Illus.). 1979. 93.00 (ISBN 3-8055-2927-9). S Karger.

International Symposium on Yersinia, Pasteurella & Francisella, Malmoe, April 1972. Yersinia, Pasteurella & Francisella: Proceedings. Winblad, ed. (Contributions to Microbiology & Immunology: Vol. 2). 1973. 45.00 (ISBN 3-8055-1636-3). S Karger.
Johnson, Leander F. & Curl, Elroy. Methods for Research on the Ecology of Soil-Borne Plant Pathogens. LC 77-176196. 1972. text ed. 24.95x (ISBN 0-8087-1016-8). Burgess.
Joklik, et al, eds. Zinsser Microbiology. 17th ed. Willett, Hilda P. & Amost, D. Bernard. (Illus.). 1539p. 1980. 39.50 (ISBN 0-8385-9977-X). ACC.
Kaminsky, Daniel, et al. Microbiology. 3rd ed. (Nursing Examination Review Book: Vol. 7). 1974. spiral bdg. 6.00 (ISBN 0-87488-507-8). Med Exam.
Kazmier, Henry E. Basic Principles of Micro-Biology. (Orig.). 1980. pap. text ed. 13.95 (ISBN 0-8403-2170-8). Kendall-Hunt.
Kelley, Susan G. & Post, Frederick J. Basic Microbiology Techniques. (Illus.). lab. manual 6.95x (ISBN 0-89863-001-0). Star Pub CA.
Kerr, Thomas J. Applications in General Microbiology: A Laboratory Manual. 2nd ed. 224p. 1981. lab manual 9.95x (ISBN 0-89459-092-8). Hunter Hse.
Kim, Charles W., ed. Microbiology Review. 7th ed. LC 80-20088. 1980. pap. 8.50 spiral bdg. (ISBN 0-87488-203-6). Med Exam.
Kolodziej, Bruno J., et al. A Work Book for General Microbiology. 6th ed. (Orig.). 1980. pap. 8.95 (ISBN 0-8403-2146-5). Kendall Hunt.
Koneman, Elmer. Color Atlas & Textbook of Diagnostic Microbiology. 1979. text ed. 39.75 (ISBN 0-397-50405-5, JBL-Med-Nursing). Har-Row.
Kozloff & Solis. Microaggregrates: Experimental & Clinical Aspects. 1981. write for info. (ISBN 0-87527-177-4). Green.
Krueger, Robert G., et al. Introduction to Microbiology. Stewart, Charles E., Jr., ed. (Illus.). 704p. 1973. text ed. 20.95 (ISBN 0-02-366400-2). Macmillan.
Krumbein, Wolfgang E., ed. Environmental Biogeochemistry & Geomicrobiology, 3 vols. LC 77-84416. 1978. Vol. 1. 30.00 (ISBN 0-250-40218-1); Vol. 2. 30.00 (ISBN 0-250-40218-1); Vol. 3. 30.00 (ISBN 0-250-40220-3). Ann Arbor Science.
Kuchler, Robert J., ed. Animal Cell Culture & Virology. LC 74-833. (Benchmark Papers in Microbiology Ser). 464p. 1974. 50.00 (ISBN 0-12-786879-8). Acad Pr.
Lancaster, John H., et al. Microbiology: A Laboratory Science. 270p. (Orig.). pap. 8.95x lab manual (ISBN 0-89459-067-7). Hunter NC.
Lascelles, June, ed. Microbial Photosynthesis. LC 73-12684. (Benchmark Papers in Microbiology Ser.). 418p. 1973. text ed. 43.00 (ISBN 0-12-786923-9). Acad Pr.
Laskin, Allen I. & Lechevalier, Hubert. CRC Handbook of Microbiology: Fungi, Algae, Protozoa & Viruses, Vol. 2. 2d ed. 1979. 79.95 (ISBN 0-8493-7202-X). CRC Pr.
Laskin, Allen I. & Lechevalier, Hubert, eds. Handbook of Microbiology, CRC. condensed ed. LC 74-12937. 930p. 1974. pap. 19.95 (ISBN 0-87819-585-8). CRC Pr.
--Handbook of Microbiology, CRC, Vol. 1: Bacteria. 2nd ed. 770p. 1977. 69.95 (ISBN 0-8493-7201-1). CRC Pr.
--Handbook of Microbiology, CRC, Vol. 3: Microbial Composition: Amino Acids, Proteins & Nucleic Acids. 2nd ed. LC 77-12460. 1040p. 1981. 74.95 (ISBN 0-8493-7203-8). CRC Pr.
Lechene, Claude P. & Warner, Ronald, eds. Microbeam Analysis in Biology. LC 79-24948. 1980. 39.50 (ISBN 0-12-440340-9). Acad Pr.
Lee, R. E. Phycology. LC 79-25402. (Illus.). 450p. 1980. 49.50 (ISBN 0-521-22530-2); pap. 16.95 (ISBN 0-521-29541-6). Cambridge U Pr.
Lenci, Francesco & Colombetti, Giuliano, eds. Photoreception & Sensory Transduction in Aneural Organisms. (Nato Advanced Study Institutes Ser., Ser. A: Life Sciences: Vol. 33). 430p. 1980. 45.00 (ISBN 0-686-77505-8, Plenum Pr). Plenum Pub.
Livingston, Virginia. Microbiology of Cancer. 25.00 (ISBN 0-686-29788-1). Cancer Bk Hse.
Lynch, J. M. & Poole, N. J. Microbial Ecology: A Conceptual Approach. 1979. pap. 21.95 (ISBN 0-470-26533-7). Halsted Pr.
McKinney, R. E. Microbiology for Sanitary Engineers. (Sanitary & Water Resources Engineering). 1962. text ed. 24.50 (ISBN 0-07-045180-X, C). McGraw.
Margalith, Pinhas. Flavor Microbiology. (Illus.). 336p. 1981. 31.50 (ISBN 0-398-04083-4). C C Thomas.
Marshall, K. C. Interfaces in Microbial Ecology. 1976. 12.50x (ISBN 0-674-45822-2, MAIF). Harvard U Pr.
Martin, S. J. The Biochemistry of Viruses. LC 77-8231. (Texts in Chemistry & Biochemistry Ser.). (Illus.). 1978. 38.50 (ISBN 0-521-21678-8); pap. 11.50x (ISBN 0-521-29229-8). Cambridge U Pr.
Melville, T. H. & Russell, Conrad. Microbiology for Dental Students. 2nd ed. (Illus.). 1975. pap. text ed. 19.95x (ISBN 0-433-21149-0). Intl Ideas.
Methodology for Biomass Determinations & Microbial Activities in Sediments. (Special Technical Publications Ser.). 199p. 1979. 22.50x (ISBN 0-686-76103-0, 673, 04-673000-16). ASTM.
Miller, James N. Spirochetes in Body Fluids & Tissues: Manual of Investigative Methods. (Illus.). 86p. 1971. pap. 7.75 (ISBN 0-398-01312-8). C C Thomas.
Mitchell, Ralph. Introduction to Environmental Microbiology. (Illus.). 400p. 1974. ref. ed. 26.95x (ISBN 0-13-482489-X). P-H.
Mitsuhashi, S., et al, eds. Plasmids: Medical & Theoretical Aspects. (Illus.). 1977. 56.90 (ISBN 0-387-07946-7). Springer-Verlag.
Mittal, K. L., ed. Micellization, Solubilization, & Microemulsions, 2 vols. 1977. Vol. 1. 487p. 45.00 (ISBN 0-306-31023-6, Plenum Pr); Vol. 2. 945p. 45.00 (ISBN 0-306-31024-4). Plenum Pub.
Moat, Albert G. Microbial Physiology. LC 79-11323. 1979. 37.00 (ISBN 0-471-07258-3, Pub. by Wiley-Interscience). Wiley.
Moffet, Hugh L. Clinical Microbiology. 2nd ed. 1980. text ed. 19.50 (ISBN 0-397-50450-0, JBL-Med-Nursing). Har-Row.
Monod, Jacques & Borek, Ernest, eds. Of Microbes & Life. LC 71-133382. (Molecular Biology Ser). (Illus.). 312p. 1971. 20.00x (ISBN 0-231-03431-8). Columbia U Pr.
Morisita, H. & Masui, M. Saline Environment. 200p. 1980. pap. 20.00x (ISBN 0-89955-334-6, Pub. by Japan Sci Soc Japan). Intl Schol Bk Serv.
Nester, Eugene W., et al. Microbiology. 2nd ed. LC 77-10422. 1978. text ed. 26.95 (ISBN 0-03-019326-5, HoltC). HR&W.
Nicol, Hugh. Microbes & Us. 1955. 15.00 (ISBN 0-8274-4245-9). R West.
Nolte, William A. Oral Microbiology. 3rd ed. LC 77-1945. (Illus.). 1977. text ed. 31.95 (ISBN 0-8016-3688-4). Mosby.
Norris, J. R. Essays in Applied Microbiology. LC 80-42066. 380p. 1981. 36.00 (ISBN 0-471-27998-6, Pub. by Wiley-Interscience). Wiley.
Norris, J. R. & Bergan, T. Methods in Microbiology, Vol. 13. LC 68-57745. 1980. 66.00 (ISBN 0-12-521513-4). Acad Pr.
Norris, J. R. & Richmond, M. H. Essays in Microbiology. LC 78-2828. 540p. 1978. 47.25 (ISBN 0-471-99556-8, Pub. by Wiley-Interscience). Wiley.
Norris, J. R. & Bergen, T., eds. Methods in Microbiology, Vols. 10 & 11. 1978-79. Vol. 10. 60.00 (ISBN 0-12-521510-X); Vol. 11. 40.00 (ISBN 0-12-521511-8). Acad Pr.
Norris, J. R. & Ribbons, D. W., eds. Methods in Microbiology, Vol. 9. 1977. 40.00 (ISBN 0-12-521509-6). Acad Pr.
--Methods in Microbiology, Vol. 12. 1979. 32.00 (ISBN 0-12-521512-6). Acad Pr.
Norton, Cynthia F. Microbiology. LC 80-23350. (Life Sciences Ser.). (Illus.). 850p. 1981. text ed. 19.95 (ISBN 0-201-05304-7). A-W.
OAS Gerneral Secretariat Department of Scientific & Technological Affairs. Principios Generales De Microbiologia: Serie De Biologia No. 7. 2nd ed. (Biology Ser.: No. 7). 143p. 1980. text ed. 2.00 (ISBN 0-8270-1097-4). OAS.
Ooi, Wan H. Microbiology: A Laboratory Manual. 2nd ed. 1980. pap. text ed. 8.95x (ISBN 0-89641-014-5). American Pr.
Orland, Frank J. Microbiology in Clinical Dentistry. (Illus.). 250p. 1981. 23.50 (ISBN 0-88416-171-4). Wright-PSG.
Parish, J. H., ed. Developmental Biology of Prokaryotes. LC 79-10275. (Studies in Microbiology: Vol. 1). 1980. 57.50x (ISBN 0-520-04016-3). U of Cal Pr.
Payne, J. W. Microorganisms & Nitrogen Sources Transport & Utilization of Amino Acids Peptides, Proteins & Related Subjects. LC 79-42900. 870p. 1980. 135.00 (ISBN 0-471-27697-9). Wiley.
Peberdy, John F. Developmental Microbiology. LC 80-14825. (Tertiary Level Biology Ser.). 230p. 1980. pap. 32.95x (ISBN 0-470-26989-8). Halsted Pr.
Pelczar, Michael J. & Reid, Roger D. Microbiology. 3rd ed. (Illus.). 960p. 1971. text ed. 17.95 (ISBN 0-07-049226-3, C); instructor's manual 4.95 (ISBN 0-07-049228-X). McGraw.
Pelczar, Michael J., Jr., et al. Microbiology. 4th ed. 1977. te.t ed. 23.50 (ISBN 0-07-049229-8, C); instructor's manual 4.95 (ISBN 0-07-049231-X); lab. exercises 8.95 (ISBN 0-07-049230-1); illustrated chart avail. (ISBN 0-07-049233-6); study guide 5.95 (ISBN 0-07-049232-8). McGraw.
Pelczar, Michael, Jr. & Chan, E. C. S. Elements of Microbiology. 1st ed. (Illus.). 704p. (Orig.). 1981. text ed. 22.95 (ISBN 0-07-049240-9, C); 10.95 (ISBN 0-07-049241-7); instrs'. manual 9.95 (ISBN 0-07-049230-1). McGraw.
Perez-Bercoff, R., ed. The Molecular Biology of the Picronaviruses. LC 79-13845. (NATO Advanced Study Institutes Ser. A: Life Sciences: Vol. 23). 387p. 1979. 39.50 (ISBN 0-306-40192-4, Plenum Pr). Plenum Pub.
Perez-Miravete, A., ed. Behavior of Microorganisms. LC 75-78042. 301p. 1973. 35.00 (ISBN 0-306-30570-4, Plenum Pr). Plenum Pub.
Perlman, D., ed. Advances in Applied Microbiology, Vol. 17. (Serial Publication). 1974. 55.00 (ISBN 0-12-002617-1). Acad Pr.
--Advances in Applied Microbiology, Vol. 18. (Serial Publication). 1974. 55.00 (ISBN 0-12-002618-X). Acad Pr.
--Advances in Applied Microbiology, Vol. 19. (Serial Publication). 1975. 55.00 (ISBN 0-12-002619-8). Acad Pr.
--Advances in Applied Microbiology, Vol. 26. (Serial Publication). 1980. 29.50 (ISBN 0-12-002626-0). Acad Pr.
Perlman, D. & Laskin, A. I., eds. Advances in Applied Microbiology, Vol. 27. (Serial Publication). 1981. 26.00 (ISBN 0-12-002627-9). Acad Pr.
Petricciani, J. C., et al, eds. Cell Substrates: Their Use in the Production of Vaccines & Other Biologicals. LC 79-13479. (Advances in Experimental Medicine & Biology Ser.: Vol. 118). 228p. 1979. 29.50 (ISBN 0-306-40189-4, Plenum Pr). Plenum Pub.
Rahn, Joan E. Microbiology. LC 74-75843. (Rapid Reviews Ser). 128p. (Prog. Bk.). 1974. text ed. 3.95 (ISBN 0-8220-1765-2). Cliffs.
Rapid Methods & Automation in Microbiology & Immunology: A Bibliography. 250p. 24.00 (ISBN 0-904147-07-X). Info Retrieval.
Reed, G. & Rehm, H. J., eds. Biotechnology: Volume 1: Microbial Fundamentals. Date not set. text ed. 309.40 (ISBN 3-527-25763-2). Verlag Chemie.
Reed, Gerald. Prescott & Dunn's Industrial Microbiology. 4th ed. (Illus.). 1981. lib. bdg. 59.00 (ISBN 0-87055-374-7). AVI.
Reeves, John P., ed. Microbial Permeability. LC 73-4299. (Benchmark Papers in Microbiology Ser). 442p. 1973. 48.50 (ISBN 0-12-787320-1). Acad Pr.
Rimon, A., et al. Current Topics in Microbiology & Immunology, Vol. 74. LC 15-12910. 1976. 42.50 (ISBN 0-387-07657-3). Springer-Verlag.
Rose, A. H., ed. Economic Microbiology: Vol. 4, Microbial Biomass. LC 77-77361. (Economic Microbiology Ser.). 1980. 73.50 (ISBN 0-12-596554-0). Acad Pr.
--Products of Metabolism. 1978. 77.50 (ISBN 0-12-596552-4). Acad Pr.
Rose, A. H. & Morris, G., eds. Advances in Microbial Physiology, Vol. 20. LC 67-19850. 1980. 52.00 (ISBN 0-12-027720-4). Acad Pr.
Rose, Anthony H., ed. Chemical Microbiology: An Introduction to Microbial Physiology. 3rd ed. 469p. 1976. 35.00 (ISBN 0-306-30888-6, Plenum Pr). Plenum Pub.
Rudman, Jack. Anatomy, Physiology & Microbiology. (College Level Examination Ser.: CLEP-38). (Cloth bdg. avail. on request). 1977. pap. 9.95 (ISBN 0-8373-5388-2). Natl Learning.
--Assistant Microbiologist. (Career Examination Ser.: C-1811). (Cloth bdg. avail. on request). pap. 10.00 (ISBN 0-8373-1811-4). Natl Learning.
--Microbiologist. (Career Examination Ser.: C-2477). (Cloth bdg. avail. on request). pap. 10.00 (ISBN 0-8373-2477-7). Natl Learning.
--Microbiology. (College Level Examination Ser.: CLEP-35). (Cloth bdg. avail. on request). 9.95 (ISBN 0-8373-5335-1). Natl Learning.
--Senior Microbiologist. (Career Examination Ser.: C-1945). (Cloth bdg. avail. on request). pap. 10.00 (ISBN 0-8373-1945-5). Natl Learning.
Sarma, P. S., et al. Current Topics in Microbiology & Immunology, Vol. 68. LC 75-12910. (Illus.). 180p. 1975. 40.50 (ISBN 0-387-07074-5). Springer-Verlag.
Schlegel, H. G. Microbial Energy Conversion. LC 76-56894. 1977. pap. text ed. 81.00 (ISBN 0-08-021791-5). Pergamon.
Schlessinger, David, ed. Microbiology 1978. LC 74-33538. (Illus.). 1978. text ed. 22.00 (ISBN 0-914826-15-8). Am Soc Microbio.
--Microbiology 1979. (Illus.). 1979. text ed. 22.00 (ISBN 0-914826-20-4). Am Soc Microbio.
--Microbiology 1980. (Illus.). 1980. text ed. 22.00 (ISBN 0-914826-23-9). Am Soc Microbio.
--Microbiology, 1981. (Illus.). 1981. 22.00 (ISBN 0-914826-31-X). Am Soc Microbio.
Scientific American Editors. Industrial Microbiology: A Scientific American Book. 1981. price not set (ISBN 0-7167-1385-3); pap. price not set (ISBN 0-7167-1386-1). W H Freeman.
Seeley, Harry W., Jr. & VanDemark, Paul J. Selected Exercises from Microbes in Action: A Laboratory Manual of Microbiology. 3rd ed. (Illus.). 1981. 9.95x (ISBN 0-7167-1260-1); instr's manual avail. W H Freeman.
Settlemire, C. Thomas & Hughes, William. Microbiology for Health Students. (Illus.). 1978. text ed. 15.95 case (ISBN 0-8359-4360-7); instrs'. manual avail. Reston.
Shapton, D. A. & Board, R. G., eds. Safety in Microbiology. (Society for Applied Bacteriology Technical Ser.: No. 6). 1972. 38.00 (ISBN 0-12-638860-1). Acad Pr.
Skinner, F. A. & Lovelock, D. W. Identification Methods for Microbiologists, Pt. B. 2nd ed. LC 79-41203. (Society for Applied Bacteriology Technical Ser.: No.14). 1980. 39.50 (ISBN 0-12-647750-7). Acad Pr.
Skinner, F. A. & Carr, J. G., eds. The Normal Microbial Flora of Man. 1974. 42.00 (ISBN 0-12-648040-0). Acad Pr.
Skinner, Orten C. Basic Microbiology. LC 74-78590. (Allied Health Ser). 1975. pap. 7.65 (ISBN 0-672-61390-5). Bobbs.
Smith, Alice L. Principles of Microbiology. 8th ed. LC 76-30332. (Illus.). 1977. text ed. 18.95 (ISBN 0-8016-4681-2). Mosby.
Stanier, R. Y. & Rogers, H. J., eds. Relations Between Structure & Function in the Prokaryotic Cell. LC 77-21093. (Society for General Microbiology Symposium: No. 28). (Illus.). 1978. 65.00 (ISBN 0-521-21909-4). Cambridge U Pr.
Stanier, Roger, et al. Introduction to the Microbial World. (Illus.). 1979. ref. ed. 11.95 (ISBN 0-13-488049-8); lab. manual 8.95 (ISBN 0-13-488031-5). P-H.
Starr, M. P., et al, eds. Annual Review of Microbiology, Vol. 27. LC 49-432. (Illus.). 1973. text ed. 17.00 (ISBN 0-8243-1127-2). Annual Reviews.
--Annual Review of Microbiology, Vol. 32. LC 49-432. (Illus.). 1978. text ed. 17.00 (ISBN 0-8243-1132-9). Annual Reviews.
--Annual Review of Microbiology, Vol. 33. LC 49-432. (Illus.). 1979. text ed. 17.00 (ISBN 0-8243-1133-7). Annual Reviews.
Starr, Mortimer P., et al, eds. Annual Review of Microbiology, Vol. 29. LC 49-432. (Illus.). 1975. text ed. 17.00 (ISBN 0-8243-1129-9). Annual Reviews.
--Annual Review of Microbiology, Vol. 30. LC 49-432. (Illus.). 1976. text ed. 17.00 (ISBN 0-8243-1130-2). Annual Reviews.
--Annual Review of Microbiology, Vol. 31. LC 49-432. (Illus.). 1977. text ed. 17.00 (ISBN 0-8243-1131-0). Annual Reviews.
--Annual Review of Microbiology, Vol. 34. LC 49-432. (Illus.). 1980. text ed. 20.00 (ISBN 0-8243-1134-5). Annual Reviews.
--Annual Review of Microbiology, Vol. 35. LC 49-432. (Illus.). 1981. text ed. 20.00 (ISBN 0-8243-1135-3). Annual Reviews.
--Annual Review of Microbiology, Vol. 28. LC 49-432. (Illus.). 1974. text ed. 17.00 (ISBN 0-8243-1128-0). Annual Reviews.
Steinhaus, Edward A. Insect Microbiology: An Account of the Microbes Associated with Insects & Ticks. (Illus.). 1967. Repr. of 1946 ed. 23.50 (ISBN 0-02-852920-0). Hafner.
Sterbacek, Z., ed. Microbial Engineering: Proceedings of a Symposium on Advances in Microbial Engineering. 134p. 1976. 27.00 (ISBN 0-08-020795-2). Pergamon.
Stevenson, G. Biology of Fungi, Bacteria & Viruses. Barrington, E. J. & Willis, A. J., eds. (Contemporary Biology Ser). 1970. 13.95 (ISBN 0-444-19674-9). Univ Park.
Suzuki, K., ed. Radiation Biology of Microorganisms. (Selected Papers in Biochemistry, Vol. 4). 1971. 19.50 (ISBN 0-8391-0614-9). Univ Park.
Tauro, P., et al. Introductory Microbiology. 432p. Date not set. text ed. 27.50 (ISBN 0-7069-1181-4, Pub. by Vikas India). Advent NY.
Thayer, D. W., ed. Microbial Interaction with the Physical Environment. LC 75-20439. (Benchmark Papers in Microbiology Ser: Vol. 9). 431p. 1975. 42.50 (ISBN 0-12-787536-0). Acad Pr.
Tilton, Richard C., ed. Microbiology. 2nd ed. LC 79-8372. (Basic Sciences PreTest Self-Assessment & Review Ser.). (Illus.). 1979. 9.95 (ISBN 0-07-050966-2). McGraw-Pretest.
Turk, T. C. & Porter, I. A. A Short Textbook of Medical Microbiology. 4th ed. (Illus.). 1978. pap. 13.95 (ISBN 0-8151-8874-9). Year Bk Med.
Tyndall, John. Essays on the Floating-Matter of the Air in Relation to Putrefaction & Infection. Repr. of 1882 ed. 23.00 (ISBN 0-384-62270-4). Johnson Repr.
Uhlik, David J. Laboratory Manual in General Microbiology for Allied Health Personnel. 1980. pap. 8.95x (ISBN 0-8087-2109-7). Burgess.

Umbreit, Wayne W., ed. Advances in Applied Microbiology. Incl. Vol. 1. 1959. 55.00 (ISBN 0-12-002601-5); Vol. 2. 1960. 55.00 (ISBN 0-12-002602-3); Vol. 3. 1961. 55.00 (ISBN 0-12-002603-1); Vol. 4. 1962. 55.00 (ISBN 0-12-002604-X); Vol. 5. 1963. 55.00 (ISBN 0-12-002605-8); Vol. 6. 1964. 55.00 (ISBN 0-12-002606-6); Vol. 7. 1965. 55.00 (ISBN 0-12-002607-4); Vol. 8. 1966. 55.00 (ISBN 0-12-002608-2); Vol. 9. 1968. 55.00 (ISBN 0-12-002609-0); Vol. 10. Perlman, D. & Umbreit, W., eds. 1968. 55.00 (ISBN 0-12-002610-4); Vol. 11. Perlman, D., ed. 1969. 55.00 (ISBN 0-12-002611-2); Vol. 12. Perlman, D. & Umbreit, W., eds. 1970. 55.00 (ISBN 0-12-002612-0); Vol. 13. Perlman, D. & Umbreit, W., eds. 1970. 55.00 (ISBN 0-12-002613-9); Vol. 14. Perlman, D. & Umbreit, W., eds. 1971. 55.00 (ISBN 0-12-002614-7); Vol. 15. Perlman, D., ed. 1972. 55.00 (ISBN 0-12-002615-5); Vol. 16. Perlman, David, ed. 1973. 55.00 (ISBN 0-12-002616-3); Vol. 21. Perlman, David, ed. 1977. 44.50 (ISBN 0-12-002621-X); Vol. 22. Perlman, David, ed. 1977. 43.00 (ISBN 0-12-002622-8); Vol. 23. Perlman, David, ed. 1978. 34.00 (ISBN 0-12-002623-6); Vol. 24. Perlman, David, ed. 1978. 36.00 (ISBN 0-12-002624-4); Vol. 25. 1979. 31.00 (ISBN 0-12-002625-2); Vol. 26. 1980. 29.50 (ISBN 0-12-002626-0). Acad Pr.

Van Leeuwenhoek, Antony. The Select Works of Antony Van Leeuwenhork: His Microscopical Discoveries in Many Works of Nature, 2 vols in 1. Egerton, Frank N., ed. Hoole, Samuel, tr. LC 77-74236. (History of Ecology Ser.). (Illus.). 1978. Repr. of 1807 ed. lib. bdg. 42.00x (ISBN 0-405-10405-7). Arno.

Venkatsubramanian, K., ed. Immobilized Microbial Cells. LC 79-15794. (ACS Symposium Ser.: No. 106). 1979. 27.50 (ISBN 0-8412-0508-6). Am Chemical.

Volk, Wesley A. & Wheeler, Margaret F. Basic Microbiology. 4th ed. LC 79-25907. 611p. 1980. text ed. 19.50x (ISBN 0-397-54313-1). Har-Row.

Walter, William B., et al. Introduction to Microbiology. 1973. 16.95x (ISBN 0-442-29197-3). Van Nos Reinhold.

Washington, J. A. & Brewer, N. S., eds. Laboratory Procedures in Clinical Microbiology. (Illus.). 856p. 1981. flexible plastic 34.50 (ISBN 0-387-90531-6). Springer-Verlag.

Wilkinson, J. F. Introduction to Microbiology. 2nd ed. LC 75-12902. (Basic Microbiology Ser: Vol. 1). 1975. pap. text ed. 9.95 (ISBN 0-470-94649-0). Halsted Pr.

Wilson, Marion E., et al. Microbiology in Patient Care. 3rd ed. (Illus.). 1979. text ed. 19.95 (ISBN 0-02-428310-X); instrs'. manual avail. Macmillan.

Wistreich, George A. & Lechtman, Max D. Laboratory Exercises in Microbiology. 3rd ed. 1976. lab manual 8.95x (ISBN 0-02-479210-1). Glencoe.

Wyss, Orville & Eklund, C. E. Microorganisms & Man. LC 70-146674. 1971. text ed. 22.95x (ISBN 0-471-96900-1). Wiley.

Yabrov, Alexander. Interferon & Non-Specific Resistance. LC 80-13677. 376p. 1980. 39.95 (ISBN 0-87705-497-5). Human Sci Pr.

Yoshii, Zensaku, et al. Atlas of Scanning Electron Microscopy in Microbiology. (Illus.). 1976. 52.00 (ISBN 0-89640-038-7). Igaku-Shoin.

Zajic, J. E. Microbial Biogeochemistry. 1969. 37.50 (ISBN 0-12-775350-8). Acad Pr.

MICROBIOLOGY–CLASSIFICATION

Cowan, S. T. A Dictionary of Microbial Taxonomy. Hill, L. R., ed. LC 77-85705. (Illus.). 1978. 42.50 (ISBN 0-521-21890-X). Cambridge U Pr.

Goodfellow, M. & Board, R. G. Microbiological Classification & Identification. (Society for Applied Bacteriology Symposium Ser.: No. 8). 1980. 48.00 (ISBN 0-12-289660-2). Acad Pr.

MICROBIOLOGY–CULTURES AND CULTURE MEDIA

Malek, Ivan & Fencl, Zdenek, eds. Continuous Cultivation of Microorganisms: Proceedings. 1970. 63.00 (ISBN 0-12-466260-9). Acad Pr.

Olds, R. J. Color Atlas of Microbiology. (Year Book Color Atlas Ser.). (Illus.). 288p. 1975. 31.00 (ISBN 0-8151-6542-0). Year Bk Med.

Symposium on the Continuous Culture of Micro-Organisms, Fifth. Environmental Control of Cell Synthesis & Function. Dean, A. C., et al, eds. 1973. 76.00 (ISBN 0-12-208050-5). Acad Pr.

MICROBIOLOGY–DICTIONARIES

Cowan, S. T. A Dictionary of Microbial Taxonomic Usage. 1968. 7.50 (ISBN 0-934454-28-0). Lubrecht & Cramer.

Singleton, Paul & Sainsbury, Diana. Dictionary of Microbiology. LC 78-4532. 1978. 58.95 (ISBN 0-471-99658-0, Pub. by Wiley-Interscience). Wiley.

MICROBIOLOGY–HISTORY

Lechevalier, Hubert A. & Solotorovsky, Morris. Three Centuries of Microbiology. LC 73-91785. 531p. 1974. pap. text ed. 6.00 (ISBN 0-486-23035-X). Dover.

--Three Centuries of Microbiology. 11.00 (ISBN 0-8446-5057-9). Peter Smith.

Vandervliet, Glenn. Microbiology & the Spontaneous Generation Debate During the 1870's. (Illus.). 134p. 1971. 6.00x (ISBN 0-87291-020-2). Coronado Pr.

MICROBIOLOGY–LABORATORY MANUALS

Bartholomew, James W. Laboratory Textbook & Experiments in Microbiology. rev. ed. 1977. pap. text ed. 8.95 (ISBN 0-8403-1722-0). Kendall-Hunt.

Beck, J. V., et al. Laboratory Manual for General Microbiology. 3rd ed. 1979. spiral bdg. 6.95x (ISBN 0-8087-2884-9). Burgess.

Brigham Young University Microbiology Faculty. Introductory Laboratory Manual of Microbiology for Health Related Professions. 2nd ed. 1977. spiral bdg. 7.95x (ISBN 0-8087-4538-7). Burgess.

Brockman, Ellis. Laboratory Manual for Microbiology. new ed. LC 74-28777. 1980. pap. 15.00 (ISBN 0-87812-085-8). Pendell Pub.

Finstein, M. S. Pollution Microbiology: A Laboratory Manual. 184p. 1972. 14.75 (ISBN 0-8247-1190-4). Dekker.

Fuerst, Robert. Microbiology in Health & Disease: Laboratory Manual & Workbook. 6th ed. LC 77-16985. (Illus.). 1978. pap. text ed. 8.95 (ISBN 0-7216-3943-7). Saunders.

Miller, Arnold I. Microbiological Laboratory Techniques. 352p. 1976. pap. text ed. 12.95x (ISBN 0-669-98384-5). Heath.

Otero, Raymond B. Laboratory Exercises in Microbiology. 2nd ed. 1977. pap. text ed. 6.50 (ISBN 0-8403-1743-3). Kendall-Hunt.

Prier, James E. Quality Control in Microbiology. (Illus.). 300p. 1976. 17.95 (ISBN 0-8391-0766-8). Univ Park.

Seeley, Harry W., Jr. & VanDemark, Paul J. Microbes in Action: A Laboratory Manual of Microbiology. 3rd ed. (Illus.). 1981. pap. text ed. 10.95x (ISBN 0-7167-1259-8); instrs'. manual avail. W H Freeman.

Seeley, Harry W., Jr. & Van Demark, Paul J. Microbes in Action: A Laboratory Manual of Microbiology. 2nd ed. (Illus.). 1972. lab manual 9.95x (ISBN 0-7167-0689-X); tchr's manual avail. W H Freeman.

--Selected Exercises from Microbes in Action: A Laboratory Manual of Microbiology. 2nd ed. (Illus.). 1972. lab manual 8.95x (ISBN 0-7167-0690-3); teacher's manual avail. W H Freeman.

Segel, W. & Wheelis, M. Laboratory Manual to Introduction to the Microbial World. 1980. pap. 8.95 (ISBN 0-13-488031-5). P-H.

Smith, Alice L. Microbiology Laboratory Manual & Workbook. 4th ed. LC 76-30332. (Illus.). 1977. pap. 8.95 (ISBN 0-8016-4706-1). Mosby.

Wilson, Marion E., et al. Laboratory Manual & Workbook in Microbiology: Applications to Patient Care. 2nd ed. 1979. pap. text ed. 8.95 (ISBN 0-02-428370-3). Macmillan.

MICROBIOLOGY–TECHNIQUES

Aaronson, Sheldon. Experimental Microbial Ecology. 1970. 38.00 (ISBN 0-12-041050-8). Acad Pr.

Baillie, A. & Gilbert, R. J., eds. Automation, Mechanisation & Data Handling in Microbiology. (Society for Applied Bacteriology Technical Ser.: No. 4). 1970. 36.50 (ISBN 0-12-073650-0). Acad Pr.

Brenner, S., et al, eds. New Horizons in Industrial Microbiology: Philosophical Transactions of the Royal Society, 1980. rev. ed. (Ser. B: Vol. 290). (Illus.). 152p. text ed. 47.50x (ISBN 0-85403-146-4, Pub. by Dechema Germany). Scholium Intl.

Collins, C. H. & Lyne, P. Microbiological Methods. 4th ed. 1976. 24.95 (ISBN 0-408-70716-X). Butterworth.

Keleti, Georg & Lederer, William H. Handbook of Micromethods for the Biological Sciences. 1974. text ed. 15.95x (ISBN 0-442-24290-5). Van Nos Reinhold.

Mitruka, Brij M. Gas Chromatographic Applications in Microbiology & Medicine. LC 74-18002. 492p. 1975. 55.50 (ISBN 0-471-61183-2). Krieger.

Norris, J. R. & Ribbons, D. W., eds. Methods in Microbiology. Incl. Vol. 1. 1969. 87.50 (ISBN 0-12-521501-0); Vol. 2. 1970. 68.50 (ISBN 0-12-521502-9); Vol. 3A. 1970. 79.50 (ISBN 0-12-521503-7); Vol. 3B. 1970. 59.50 (ISBN 0-12-521543-6); Vol. 4. Norris, J. R., et al, eds. 1971. 100.50 (ISBN 0-12-521504-5); Vol. 5A. 1971. 69.00 (ISBN 0-12-521505-3); Vol. 5B. 1971. 62.50 (ISBN 0-685-30536-8); Vol. 6A. 1972. 93.00 (ISBN 0-12-521506-1); Vol. 6B. 1972. 60.50 (ISBN 0-12-521546-0); Vol. 7A. 1972. 77.00 (ISBN 0-12-521507-X); Vol. 7B. 1973. 60.00 (ISBN 0-12-521547-9); Vol. 8. 1973. 48.00 (ISBN 0-12-521508-8). Acad Pr.

Shapton, D. A. & Gould, G. W. Isolation Methods for Microbiologists. (Society for Applied Bacteriology Ser.: No. 3). 1969. 31.00 (ISBN 0-12-638850-4). Acad Pr.

Shapton, D. A. & Board, R. G., eds. Isolation of Anaerobes. (Society for Applied Bacteriology Technical Ser.: No. 5). 270p. 1971. 41.00 (ISBN 0-12-638840-7). Acad Pr.

Sharpe, Anthony N. & Clark, David S. Mechanizing Microbiology. (Amer. Lec. in Clinical Microbiology Ser.). (Illus.). 352p. 1978. 33.75 (ISBN 0-398-03658-6). C C Thomas.

Trotman, R. E. Technological Aids to Microbiology. (Illus.). 1978. pap. text ed. 15.95x (ISBN 0-7131-4293-6). Intl Ideas.

MICROBIOLOGY, MEDICAL

see Medical Microbiology

MICROBODIES

see also Cells

Roberts, K. & Hyams, J. S. Microtubles. LC 79-40920. 1980. 90.00 (ISBN 0-12-590750-8). Acad Pr.

MICROCALORIMETRY

see Calorimeters and Calorimetry

MICROCARDS

see also Reader-Printers (Microphotography)

MICROCHEMISTRY

see also Spot Tests (Chemistry)

Bance, S. Handbook of Practical Organic Micro-Analysis: Recommended Methods for Determining Elements & Groups. LC 80-40145. (Ellis Horwood Ser. in Analytical Chemistry). 206p. 1980. 64.95x (ISBN 0-470-26972-3). Halsted Pr.

Caldwell, William E. & King, Brooks C. Elemental Semimicro Qualitative Analysis. (Orig.). 1969. pap. text ed. 7.95 (ISBN 0-442-21005-1). Van Nos Reinhold.

Chamot, Emile M. & Mason, C. W. Handbook of Chemical Microscopy: Principles & Use of Microscopes & Accessories; Physical Methods for the Study of Chemical Problems, Vol. 1. 3rd ed. LC 58-12706. 41.50 (ISBN 0-471-14355-3, Pub. by Wiley-Interscience). Wiley.

De Bruyne, K. I., et al. Semimicro Chemistry. rev. ed. (gr. 9-12). 1966. pap. text ed. 7.96 (ISBN 0-03-052860-7); tchrs' manual 1.12 (ISBN 0-03-052865-8). HR&W.

Garrett, Alfred B., et al. Semimicro Qualitative Analysis. 3rd ed. 1966. pap. 16.95 (ISBN 0-471-00192-9). Wiley.

Gersh, Isidore, ed. Submicroscopic Cytochemistry, 2vols. Incl. Vol. 1. Protein & Nucleic Acids. 1974. 56.50 (ISBN 0-12-281401-0); Vol.2. Membranes,Mitochondria,& Connective Tissue. 1974. 42.00 (ISBN 0-12-281402-9). Set. 81.00 (ISBN 0-685-40610-5). Acad Pr.

Halpern, M. G., ed. Industrial Enzymes from Microbial Sources: Recent Advances. LC 81-1839. (Chemical Technology Review: No. 186). 1981. 45.00 (ISBN 0-8155-0843-3). Noyes.

International Union of Pure & Applied Chemistry. Microchemical Techniques: Pennsylvania, 1965. 102p. 1976. 15.00 (ISBN 0-08-020796-0). Pergamon.

Kainz, G., ed. Microtechniques-6: Proceedings of an International Symposium, Graz. 80p. 1976. 15.00 (ISBN 0-08-020797-9). Pergamon.

Klimova, V. A. Basic Methods of Organic Microanalysis. 228p. 1977. 4.50 (ISBN 0-8285-0641-8, Pub. by Mir Pubs Russia). Imported Pubns.

Korenman, I. M. Introduction to Quantitative Ultramicroanalysis. 1965. 43.00 (ISBN 0-12-420550-X). Acad Pr.

Kuck, J. A., ed. Methods in Microanalysis. Incl. Vol. 5. The Determination of Oxygen, Selenium, Chromium, & Tungsten. 1977. 96.75x (ISBN 0-677-20920-7); Vol. 6. The Determination of Sulfur. 1978. 83.75 (ISBN 0-677-20770-0). Gordon.

--Methods in Microanalysis, Vols. 1-4. Incl. Vol 1. Simultaneous Rapid Combustion. 1964. 118.75 (ISBN 0-677-10220-8); Vol 2. Wet Combustion & Catalytic Methods in Microanalysis. 1965. 93.00 (ISBN 0-677-10230-5); Vol 3. The Determination of Carbon & Hydrogen & the Use of New Combustion Catalysts. 1968. 125.00 (ISBN 0-677-20620-8); Vol. 4. The Determination of Carbon & Hydrogen in the Presence of Other Elements or Simultaneously with Them. 1969. 104.00x (ISBN 0-677-20630-5). LC 64-18800. Gordon.

Ma, T. S. & Horak, V. Microscale Manipulations in Chemistry. LC 75-20093. (Chemical Analysis Ser: Vol. 44). 480p. 1976. 48.50 (ISBN 0-471-55799-4, Pub. by Wiley-Interscience). Wiley.

Malissa, H., et al, eds. Nature, Aim & Methods of Microchemistry: Proceedings. (Illus.). 350p. pap. 57.60 (ISBN 0-387-81653-4). Springer-Verlag.

Osborne, Neville N. Microchemical Analysis of Nervous Tissue. 1974. text ed. 37.00 (ISBN 0-08-018100-7). Pergamon.

Schneider, Frank L. Qualitative Organic Microanalysis. 1964. 56.50 (ISBN 0-12-627750-8). Acad Pr.

Shinoda, Gunji, et al, eds. Proceedings of the Sixth International Conference on X-Ray Optics & Microanalysis. 928p. 1973. 63.50x (ISBN 0-86008-077-3, Pub. by U of Tokyo Pr). Intl Schol Bk Serv.

Sorum, Henry & Lagowski, Joseph J. Introduction to Semimicro Qualitative Analysis. 5th ed. LC 76-51795. (Illus.). 320p. 1977. pap. text ed. 11.95 (ISBN 0-13-496059-9). P-H.

Steyermark, Al. Quantitative Organic Microanalysis. 2nd ed. 1961. 47.50 (ISBN 0-12-670450-3). Acad Pr.

Theisen, R. Quantitative Electron Microprobe Analysis. (Illus.). 1965. 20.90 (ISBN 0-387-03415-3). Springer-Verlag.

Weisz, H. Microanalysis by the Ring Oven Technique. 2nd ed. 1970. 25.00 (ISBN 0-08-015702-5). Pergamon.

MICROCINEMATOGRAPHY

Rose, George G., ed. Cinemicrography in Cell Biology. 1963. 58.50 (ISBN 0-12-596850-7). Acad Pr.

MICROCIRCULATION

Conference of the European Society for Microcirculation, 9th, Antwerp, July 5-9, 1976. Recent Advances in Basic Microcirculatory Research: Proceedings, Pt. 1. Wolf-Heidegger, G. & Lewis, D. H., eds. (Bibliotheca Anatomica: Vol. 15). (Illus.). 1977. 118.75 (ISBN 3-8055-2757-8). S Karger.

--Recent Advances in Basic Microcirculatory Research: Proceedings, Pt. 2. Wolf-Heidegger, G. & Lewis, D. H., eds. (Bibliotheca Anatomica: Vol. 16). (Illus.). 1977. 118.75 (ISBN 3-8055-2758-6). S Karger.

Conference on Microcirculation, 6th, Aalborg, 1970. Proceedings. Ditzel, J. & Lewis, D. H., eds. (Illus.). 1971. 140.75 (ISBN 3-8055-1234-1). S Karger.

Conference on Microcirculation, 6th European, Aalborg, 1970. Microcirculatory Approaches to Current Therapeutic Problems: Lung in Shock, Organ Transplantation, Diabetic Microangiopathy. Proceedings. Ditzel, J. & Lewis, D. H., eds. (Illus.). 1971. 31.25 (ISBN 3-8055-1186-8). S Karger.

Effros, Richard, et al, eds. The Microcirculation: Current Concepts. 1981. 45.00 (ISBN 0-12-232560-5). Acad Pr.

European Conference on Microcirculation, 7th, Aberdeen, 1972, Pt. II. Clinical Aspects of Microcirculation: Proceedings. (Bibliotheca Anatomica: No. 12). (Illus.). 563p. 1973. 171.25 (ISBN 3-8055-1572-3). S Karger.

European Conference on Microcirculation, 8th, le Touquet 1974. Recent Advances in Critical Microcirculatory Research. Lewis, D. H., ed. (Bibliotheca Anatomica: Vol. 13). (Illus.). 380p. 1975. 84.50 (ISBN 3-8055-2277-0). S Karger.

Gaehtgens, P., ed. Recent Advances in Microcirculatory Research. (Bibliotheca Anatomica Ser.: No. 20). (Illus.). xvi, 740p. 1980. pap. 176.75 (ISBN 3-8055-2272-X). S Karger.

Grayson, John & Zingg, Walter, eds. Microcirculation, 2 vols. Incl. Vol. 1: Blood Vessel Interactions - Systems in Special Tissues. 420p. 1976. 42.50 (ISBN 0-306-37097-2); Vol. 2: Transport Mechanisms - Disease States. 361p. 1976. 42.50 (ISBN 0-306-37098-0). (Illus., Plenum Pr). Plenum Pub.

Gross, Joseph F., ed. Mathematics of Microcirculation Phenomena. 186p. 1980. text ed. 24.00 (ISBN 0-89004-449-X). Raven.

Harders, H., ed. Advances in Microcirculation, Vol. 3. 1970. 39.75 (ISBN 3-8055-0453-5). S Karger.

--Advances in Microcirculation, Vol. 5. (Illus.). 106p. 1973. 32.50 (ISBN 3-8055-1337-2). S Karger.

--Advances in Microcirculation, Vol. 6. (Illus.). 250p. 1975. 58.75 (ISBN 3-8055-1608-8). S Karger.

Harders, H., et al, eds. Advances in Microcirculation, Vol. 7. (Illus.). 1977. 51.00 (ISBN 3-8055-2247-9). S Karger.

International Symposium, Rottach-Egern, 1971. Hemodilution: Theoretical Basis & Clinical Application; Proceedings. Messmer, K. & Schmid-Schoenbein, H., eds. (Illus.). 313p. 1972. 42.00 (ISBN 3-8055-1306-2). S Karger.

Kaley, G. & Altura, B. M. Microcirculation, 3 vols. (Illus.). 1978. Vol. I. 52.50 (ISBN 0-8391-0966-0); Vol. II. 52.50 (ISBN 0-8391-0980-6); Vol. III. 65.00 (ISBN 0-8391-0981-4). Univ Park.
Kessler, M. Oxygen Supply. (Illus.). 1973. 49.50 (ISBN 0-8391-0742-0). Univ Park.
Messmer, K. & Fagrell, B., eds. Mikrozirkulation und arterielle Verschlusskrankheiten Muenchen, November 1980. (Illus.). 240p. 1981. pap. 24.00 (ISBN 3-8055-2417-X). S Karger.
Raynaud's Syndrom, Acrocyanosis & Cold Proteins. (Advances in Microcirculation Ser.: Vol. 10). (Illus.). xii, 240p. 1981. 90.00 (ISBN 3-8055-2790-X). S Karger.
Shepro, David & Fulton, George P. Microcirculation As Related to Shock. 1968. 44.50 (ISBN 0-12-639650-7). Acad Pr.
Symposium Held in Conjunction with the 10th European Conference on Microcirculation, Cagliari, October 24, 1978. Microcirculation in Inflammation. Irwin, J. W. & Hauck, G., eds. (Bibliotheca Anatomica: No. 17). (Illus.). 1979. pap. 29.50 (ISBN 3-8055-3016-1). S Karger.
Wiedeman, M. P., et al. An Introduction to Microcirculation. (Biophysics & Bioengineering Ser.: Vol. 3). 1981. 30.00 (ISBN 0-12-749350-6). Acad Pr.
Wiederman, Mary P., ed. Microcirculation. LC 73-22327. (Benchmark Papers in Human Physiology Ser.). 448p. 1974. 48.50 (ISBN 0-12-787760-6). Acad Pr.
Winters, William L., Jr. & Brest, Albert N. The Microcirculation: A Symposium. (Illus.). 204p. 1969. photocopy ed. spiral 19.75 (ISBN 0-398-02093-0). C C Thomas.
Wolf-Heidegger, G., ed. Current Advances in Basic & Clinical Microcirculatory Research. (Bibliotheca Anatomica: No. 18). (Illus.). 1979. 93.50 (ISBN 3-8055-3042-0). S Karger.

MICROCLIMATOLOGY

Franklin, Thomas B. Climates in Miniature: A Study in Micro-Climate & Environment. LC 79-138234. 137p. 1972. Repr. of 1955 ed. lib. bdg. 15.00x (ISBN 0-8371-5591-6, FRCM). Greenwood.
Lee, Richard. Forest Microclimatology. LC 77-21961. (Illus.). 276p. 1978. 20.00x (ISBN 0-231-04156-X). Columbia U Pr.
Rosenberg, Norman J. Microclimate: The Biological Environment. LC 74-8952. 336p. 1974. 23.50 (ISBN 0-471-73615-5, Pub. by Wiley-Interscience). Wiley.
Unwin, D. Microclimate Measurement for Ecologists. (Biological Techniques Ser.). 1981. 24.00 (ISBN 0-12-709150-5). Acad Pr.

MICROCOMPUTERS

Ahl, David H., ed. Basic Computer Games: Microcomputer Edition. LC 78-50028. (Illus.). 1978. pap. 7.95 (ISBN 0-916688-07-0). Creative Comp.
--More Basic Computer Games. LC 80-57619. (Illus.). 188p. 1980. pap. 8.95 (ISBN 0-89480-137-6). Workman Pub.
Anderson, Philip N. Computers & the Radio Amateur. (Illus.). 224p. 1982. 17.95 (ISBN 0-13-166306-2). P-H.
Artwick, B. Microcomputer Interfacing. 1980. 24.95 (ISBN 0-13-580902-9). P-H.
Barden, William, Jr. How to Buy & Use Minicomputers & Microcomputers. LC 76-19693. (Illus.). 1976. pap. 9.95 (ISBN 0-672-21351-6). Sams.
--How to Program Microcomputers. LC 77-77412. 1977. pap. 8.95 (ISBN 0-672-21459-8). Sams.
--Microcomputers for Business Applications. LC 78-64984. 1979. pap. 8.95 (ISBN 0-672-21583-7). Sams.
--Z-Eighty Microcomputer Handbook. LC 77-93166. 1978. pap. 8.95 (ISBN 0-672-21500-4). Sams.
Barna, Arpad & Porat, Dan I. Introduction to Microcomputers & Microprocessors. LC 75-31675. 108p. 1976. 17.00 (ISBN 0-471-05051-2, Pub. by Wiley-Interscience). Wiley.
Barrette, Pierre P. The Microcomputer & the School Library Media Specialist. 200p. 1981. lib. bdg. cancelled (ISBN 0-87287-226-2). Libs Unl.
Bates, William. The Computer Cookbook. 256p. 1981. pap. 8.95 (ISBN 0-13-165167-6). P-H.
Beizer, Boris. Micro-Analysis of Computer System Performance. 1978. text ed. 22.50x (ISBN 0-442-20663-1). Van Nos Reinhold.
Bennet. What Every Engineer Should Know About Microcomputers: Hardware-Software Design: a Step by Step Example. (What Every Engineer Should Know Ser.: Vol. 3). 192p. 1980. 12.75 (ISBN 0-8247-6909-0). Dekker.
Bennett, Wilma E. Checklist-Guide to Selecting a Small Computer. LC 80-13996. 1980. pap. 5.00 (ISBN 0-87576-091-0). Pilot Bks.
Bowles, K. L. Microcomputer: Problem Solving Using Pascal. LC 77-11959. 1977. pap. 9.80 (ISBN 0-387-90286-4). Springer-Verlag.
Boyce, Jefferson. Microprocessor & Microcomputer Basics. (Illus.). 1979. text ed. 18.95 (ISBN 0-13-581249-6). P-H.
Boyet, Howard. Eight Thousand Eighty Microcomputer Experiments. LC 78-606413. 416p. 1979. pap. 16.95 (ISBN 0-918398-08-8). Dilithium Pr.
--Eighty-Eighty Microcomputer Experiments. new ed. (Illus., Orig.). 1978. pap. 15.95 (ISBN 0-918398-08-8, Pub. by Dilithium). Intl Schol Bk Serv.
Bruce, Robert. Software Debugging for Microcomputers. (Illus.). 1980. text ed. 18.95 (ISBN 0-8359-7021-3); pap. text ed. 10.95 (ISBN 0-8359-7020-5). Reston.
Bursky, Dave. Components for Microcomputer System Design. 272p. 1980. pap. 12.95 (ISBN 0-8104-0975-5). Hayden.
--Microcomputer Board Data Manual. 1978. pap. 7.95 (ISBN 0-8104-0898-8). Hayden.
Burton, Philip E., ed. A Dictionary of Microcomputing. LC 76-24762. (Reference Library of Science & Technology Ser.: Vol. 5). 1980. lib. bdg. 19.50 (ISBN 0-8240-9930-3). Garland Pub.
Burton, Phillip E. A Dictionary of Mini & Micro Computing. LC 80-28272. 450p. 1981. lib. bdg. 32.50 (ISBN 0-8240-7263-4). Garland Pub.
Camp, et al. Introduction to Microcomputer Systems Principles Featuring the Six-Five-Zero-Two KIM. 1978. pap. 13.95 (ISBN 0-916460-27-4, Pub. by Matrix). Intl Schol Bk Serv.
Cannon, Don L. Fundamentals of Microcomputer Design. (Illus.). 500p. 1981. write for info. (ISBN 0-89512-050-X). Tex Instr Inc.
Cassel & Swanson. Basic Made Easy: A Guide to Programming Microcomputers & Minicomputers. (Illus.). 272p. 1980. text ed. 14.95 (ISBN 0-8359-0399-0); pap. text ed. 10.95 (ISBN 0-8359-0398-2). Reston.
Cavallari, Ford, ed. Micro-Apple. (Illus.). 224p. (Orig.). pap. 19.95 ea. Vol. 1, April 1981 (ISBN 0-938222-05-8). Vol. 2, June 1981 (ISBN 0-938222-06-6). Micro Ink.
--Micro-Apple Series, Vol. 1. 224p. 1981. spiral bdg., with computer diskette 24.95 (ISBN 0-938222-05-8). Micro Ink.
--Micro-Apple Series, Vol. 2. 224p. 1981. spiral bdg., with computer diskette 24.95 (ISBN 0-938222-06-6). Micro Ink.
Chandor, Anthony. The Facts on File Dictionary of Microcomputers. 1981. 14.95 (ISBN 0-87196-597-6). Facts on File.
Chirlian, Paul M. Microsoft FORTRAN. 325p. 1981. pap. 14.95 (ISBN 0-918398-46-0). Dilithium Pr.
Ciarcia, Steve. Ciarcia's Circuit Cellar, Vol. II. (Illus.). 190p. 1981. pap. 12.95 (ISBN 0-07-010963-X, P&RB). McGraw.
--Ciarcia's Circuit Cellar. LC 78-20920. (Illus.). 1979. pap. 8.00 (ISBN 0-931718-07-4, BYTE Bks). McGraw.
Cole, Jim. Fifty-Five Color Computer Programs for the Home, School & Office. (Illus.). 112p. (Orig.). 1982. pap. 9.95 (ISBN 0-86668-005-5). ARCsoft.
Computerist Inc. All of Micro Vol. 2: The 6502 Journal No. 7-12 Oct-Nov 78 - May 79. Tripp, Robert M., ed. (Illus.). 8.00 (ISBN 0-938222-01-5). Micro Ink.
--The Best of Micro, Vol. 1. Tripp, Robert M., et al, eds. (Illus.). 176p. (Orig.). 1978. pap. 6.00 (ISBN 0-938222-00-7). Micro Ink.
Conference of the British Educational Research Association 1980. Microcomputers in Secondary Education: Proceedings. Howe, Jim & Russ, Peter, eds. 162p. 1981. 23.50 (ISBN 0-89397-108-1). Nichols Pub.
Creason, Sam. How to Build a Microcomputer & Really Understand It. DeTray, Jeffrey D., ed. 114p. 1979. pap. 9.95 (ISBN 0-686-31436-0, BK 7325). Green Pub Inc.
Dahmke, Mark. Microcomputer Operating Systems. 240p. 1981. pap. 15.95 (ISBN 0-07-015071-0, P&RB). McGraw.
D'Angelo, Henry. Microcomputer Structures. 1981. 18.95 (ISBN 0-07-015294-2, BYTE Bks); pap. 12.95 (ISBN 0-07-015293-4). McGraw.
Danhof, Kenneth & Smith, Carol. Computing System Fundamentals: An Approach Based on Microcomputers. LC 79-14933. 1981. text ed. 21.95 (ISBN 0-201-01298-7). A-W.
Derfler, Frank, Jr. Microcomputer Data Communications Systems. 200p. 1981. 15.95 (ISBN 0-13-580720-4); lib. bdg. 8.95 (ISBN 0-13-580712-3). P-H.
Doerr, Carol. Microcomputers & the Three R's. 1979. pap. 9.75x (ISBN 0-8104-5113-1). Hayden.
Doty, Keith L. Fundamental Principles of Microcomputer Architecture. 1979. 26.95 (ISBN 0-916460-13-4, Pub by Matrix); cancelled. Intl Schol Bk Serv.
Dwyer, Thomas & Critchfield, Margot. Bit of Basic. LC 80-11428. 192p. 1980. pap. text ed. 5.95 (ISBN 0-201-03115-9). A-W.
Eden, Henry S. & Eden, Murray. Microcomputers in Patient Care. LC 81-1999. (Illus.). 191p. 1981. 28.00 (ISBN 0-8155-0849-2). Noyes.
Electronics Magazine. Microprocessors & Microcomputers: One-Chip Controllers to High-End Systems. Capece, Raymond P. & Posa, John G., eds. LC 80-11816. (Illus.). 484p. 1980. 24.50 (ISBN 0-07-019141-7, R-011); pap. text ed. 14.95 (ISBN 0-07-606670-3). McGraw.
Engineering Staff of Texas Instruments. The Bipolar Microcomputer Components Data Book. 3rd, rev. ed. LC 81-51167. 450p. 1981. pap. 6.15 (ISBN 0-89512-110-7, LCC5831). Tex Instr Inc.
Fitch, D. In Pursuit of Productivity: Making Things Happen in the Microcomputer Age. 1982. price not set (ISBN 0-201-04072-7). A-W.
Foster, Caxton C. Programming a Microcomputer: 6502. 1978. pap. text ed. 8.95 (ISBN 0-201-01995-7). A-W.
Foster, Caxton C. & Soloway, Elliot. Interfacing with the Real World. (Joy of Computing Ser.). 1981. pap. text ed. 8.95 (ISBN 0-201-01937-X). A-W.
Frederick, Franz J. Guide to Microcomputers. Assn Ed Comm Tech, ed. LC 80-68716. (Orig.). 1980. pap. 11.50 (ISBN 0-89240-038-2). Assn Ed Comm T.
Freiberger, Stephen & Chew, Paul, Jr. A Consumer's Guide to Personal Computing & Microcomputers. 2nd ed. 208p. 1980. pap. 8.95 (ISBN 0-8104-5116-6). Hayden.
Frenzel, Louis E. Getting Acquainted with Microcomputers. LC 77-93165. 1978. pap. 8.95 (ISBN 0-672-21486-5). Sams.
Frenzel, Louis E., Jr. The Howard W. Sams Crash Course in Microcomputers. LC 79-65750. 1980. pap. 17.50 (ISBN 0-672-21634-5, 21634). Sams.
Gibson, Glenn A. & Liu, Yu-Cheng. Microcomputers for Engineers & Scientists. (Illus.). 1980. text ed. 28.95 (ISBN 0-13-580886-3). P-H.
Givone, Donald D. & Roesser, Robert P. Microprocessors - Microcomputers: An Introduction. (Illus.). 1979. text ed. 22.95 (ISBN 0-07-023326-8); solns. manual 4.95 (ISBN 0-07-023327-6). McGraw.
Goldsbrough, Paul F. Microcomputer Interfacing with the 8255 PPI Chip. LC 79-63864. 1979. pap. 8.95 (ISBN 0-672-21614-0, 21614). Sams.
Goody, Roy W. Microcomputer Fundamentals. 300p. 1979. pap. text ed. 14.95 (ISBN 0-574-21540-9, 13-4540); instr's. guide avail. (ISBN 0-574-21541-7, 13-4541). SRA.
Green, Wayne, et al. The New Hobby Computers Are Here! 96p. 1976. pap. 4.95 (ISBN 0-88006-020-4, BK 7322). Green Pub Inc.
Greenfield. Architecture of Microcomputers. (Illus.). 384p. 1980. text ed. 24.95 (ISBN 0-87626-037-7). Winthrop.
Greenfield, Joseph D. Using Microprocessors & Microcomputers: The 6800 Family. LC 80-18090. (Electronic Technology Ser.). 512p. 1981. text ed. 22.95 (ISBN 0-471-02727-8). Wiley.
Grillo, John P. & Robertson, J. D. Microcomputer Systems: An Applications Approach. 275p. 1979. pap. text ed. write for info. (ISBN 0-697-08132-X); instrs.' man. avail. (ISBN 0-685-96518-X). Wm C Brown.
Gualt, J. W. & Pimmel, R. L. Introduction to Microcomputer-Based Digital Systems. (McGraw-Hill Ser. in Electronics). 1981. write for info. (ISBN 0-07-023047-1); price not set solutions manual. McGraw.
Gupton, James A. Microcomputer for External Control Devices. LC 80-67640. 1980. pap. 13.95 (ISBN 0-918398-28-2). Dilithium Pr.
Gupton, James A., Jr. Getting Down to Business with Your Microcomputer. LC 78-68552. (Illus., Orig.). 1979. pap. 9.95 (ISBN 0-933422-00-8, A100). Sourcebooks CA.
Heise, David R., ed. Microcomputers & Social Research. (Sociological Methods & Research Ser.: Vol. 9, No. 4). 11.50 (ISBN 0-686-74762-3). Sage.
Helms, Harry L., Jr. Introduction to Microcomputers for the Ham Shack. LC 79-67134. 1979. pap. 4.95 (ISBN 0-672-21681-7). Sams.
Herbert, Frank. Without Me You're Nothing: The Essential Guide to Home Computers. 1981. pap. price not set (ISBN 0-671-43964-2). PB.
Hilburn, J. L. & Julich, P. Microcomputers - Microprocessors: Hardware, Software & Applications. 1976. text ed. 25.95 (ISBN 0-13-580969-X). P-H.
Hordeski, Michael. Illustrated Dictionary of Microcomputer Terminology. (Illus.). 1978. 13.95 (ISBN 0-8306-9875-2); pap. 8.95 (ISBN 0-8306-1088-X, 1088). TAB Bks.
Huffman, Jim. Personal Computing. (Illus.). 1979. text ed. 15.95 (ISBN 0-8359-5516-8); pap. 11.95 (ISBN 0-8359-5515-X). Reston.
Introduction to Personal & Business Computing. 2 cassettes 24.95x (ISBN 0-686-74153-6). Sybex.
Jermann, William. Structure & Programming of Microcomputers. Gath, George, ed. (Illus.). 350p. 1982. text ed. 19.95 (ISBN 0-88284-175-0); avail. instructor's manual (ISBN 0-88284-178-5). Alfred Pub.
Johnson, David E., et al. Digital Circuits & Microcomputers. LC 78-13244. (Illus.). 1979. ref. ed. 25.00 (ISBN 0-13-214015-2). P-H.
Juge, Ed, et al. Some of the Best from Kilobaud Microcomputing. Gibbs, Emily A. & Perry, Jim, eds. (Illus.). 226p. 1980. pap. text ed. 10.95 (ISBN 0-686-31437-9, BK 7311). Green Pub Inc.
Kater, David & Thomas, Susan. TRS-Eighty Graphics. (Illus.). 256p. 1981. pap. 12.95 (ISBN 0-07-033303-3, P&RB). McGraw.
Khambata, Adi J. Microprocessors-Microcomputers: Architecture, Software & Systems. 672p. 1982. text ed. 19.95 (ISBN 0-471-06490-4). Wiley.
Kitsz, Dennis B. The Custom TRS-80 & Other Mysteries. Perry, Jim, ed. (TRS-80 Information Ser.: Vol. III). 300p. (Orig.). 1981. pap. 29.95 (ISBN 0-936200-02-2). IJG Inc.
Kraft, George D. & Toy, Wing N. Microprogrammed Control & Reliable Design of Small Computers. (Illus.). 248p. 1981. text ed. 23.95 (ISBN 0-13-581140-6). P-H.
--Mini-Microcomputer Hardware Design. (Illus.). 1978. ref. ed. 26.95 (ISBN 0-13-583807-X). P-H.
Lane, John E. Choosing Programs for Microcomputers. 138p. (Orig.). 1980. pap. 22.50x (ISBN 0-85012-255-4). Intl Pubns Serv.
--Operating Systems for Microcomputers. (Computing in the Eighties: No. 1). 77p. (Orig.). 1981. pap. 10.00x (ISBN 0-85012-277-5). Intl Pubns Serv.
Laurie, Peter. The Micro Revolution. (Illus.). 240p. 1981. text ed. 12.50x (ISBN 0-87663-361-0); pap. 7.95 (ISBN 0-87663-560-5). Universe.
Learning Achievement Corp. MATCH Microcomputer Software Program. 1981. 350.00 (ISBN 0-07-037117-2, G). McGraw.
Lenk. How to Troubleshoot & Repair Microcomputers. 304p. 1980. pap. 7.95 (ISBN 0-8359-2981-7). Reston.
Lenk, John D. Handbook of Microprocessors, Microcomputers & Minicomputers. (Illus.). 1979. text ed. 20.95 (ISBN 0-13-380378-3). P-H.
--Handbook of Practical Microcomputer Troubleshooting. (Illus.). 1979. text ed. 19.95 (ISBN 0-8359-2757-1). Reston.
Levanthal, Lance, et al. Understanding & Programming Microcomputers. 114p. 1980. pap. text ed. 10.95 (ISBN 0-88006-024-7). Green Pub Inc.
Levanthal, Lance A. & Walsh, Colin. Microcomputer Experimentation with Intel SDK-85. 1980. text ed. 16.95 (ISBN 0-13-580860-X). P-H.
Leventhal, Lance A. Microcomputer Experimentation with the Motorola MEK 6800D2. (Illus.). 368p. 1981. text ed. 16.95 (ISBN 0-13-580761-1). P-H.
Leventhal, Lawrence A., et al. The New Hobby Computers. Force, Rich, ed. (Illus.). 96p. pap. 4.95 (ISBN 0-88006-022-0, BK 7340). Green Pub Inc.
Lewis, T. G. Software Engineering for Micros: The Electrifying Streamlined Blueprint Speedcode Method. 168p. 1979. pap. 8.50 (ISBN 0-8104-5166-2). Hayden.
Lewis, Theodore G. PASCAL Programming for the Apple. 224p. 1981. 17.95 (ISBN 0-8359-5455-2); pap. 12.95 (ISBN 0-8359-5454-4). Reston.
Liffick, Blaise, ed. Simulation: Programming Techniques, Vol. 2. LC 78-8649. 1979. pap. 6.00 (ISBN 0-931718-13-9, BYTE Bks). McGraw.
Lipovski, Gerald J. Microcomputer Interfacing: Principles & Practice. LC 79-9683. 448p. 1980. 24.95x (ISBN 0-669-03619-6). Lexington Bks.
Logan, Jimmie J. Microcomputer Software: A Project Approach. text ed. cancelled (ISBN 0-89321-380-2). Tech Pr Inc.
Lord, Kenniston W., Jr. Using the Radio Shack TRS-80 in Your Home. 480p. 1981. 21.95 (ISBN 0-442-25707-4). Van Nos Reinhold.
McCunn, Donald H. Write, Edit, & Print: Word Processing with Personal Computers. LC 80-67880. 1981. 25.95 (ISBN 0-932538-05-3); pap. 15.95 (ISBN 0-932538-06-1). Design Ent SF.
McGlynn, Daniel R. Personal Computing: Home, Professional & Small Business Applications. LC 79-1005. 1979. pap. 10.95 (ISBN 0-471-05380-5, Pub. by Wiley-Interscience). Wiley.
Micro Ink, Inc. The Best of Micro: June 1979 to May 1980, Vol. 3. Tripp, Robert M., ed. (The Best of Micro Ser.). (Illus.). 320p. (Orig.). 1980. pap. 10.00 (ISBN 0-938222-03-1). Micro Ink.

--The Best of Micro: June 1980 to May 1981, Vol.4. Tripp, Robert M., ed. (The Best of Micro Ser.). (Illus.). Date not set. pap. price not set (ISBN 0-938222-04-X). Micro Ink.
--The Best of Micro: Vol. 2, Oct-Nov 78 to May 79. Tripp, Robert M., ed. (Illus.). 224p. (Orig.). pap. 8.00 (ISBN 0-938222-02-3). Micro Ink.
Miller, Inabeth. Microcomputers in School Media Centers. 200p. 1981. 14.95x (ISBN 0-918212-51-0). Neal-Schuman.
Monoson Microsystems, Inc. CAPDAT: Computer Assisted Preparation of Data for Microcomputer Records-Processing & Retrieval. Date not set. 9.95 (ISBN 0-8283-1774-7); software 95.00 (ISBN 0-686-73210-3). Branden.
--CAPDOC: Computer Assisted Preparation of Documents for Microcomputer Word Processing & Data Entry. Date not set. 14.95 (ISBN 0-8283-1779-8); software 295.00 (ISBN 0-686-73209-X). Branden.
Moody, Robert. The First Book of Microcomputers: The Home Computer Owner's Best Friend. 1978. pap. 6.50 (ISBN 0-8104-5121-2). Hayden.
Morse Code, Baudot & ASCIL Radio Teletype Programming for the TRS-80 Model I & Model III Microcomputers. LC 81-51636. 276p. Date not set. spiral bdg. 18.00 (ISBN 0-686-31627-4). Richcraft Eng.
Newell, Sydney B. & Rohrer, Ronald A. Introduction to Microcomputing. 512p. 1981. text ed. price not set (ISBN 0-06-044802-4, HarpC). Har-Row.
Nicoud, J. D. & Wilmink, J., eds. Microcomputer Architectures: Proceedings of the Third EUROMICRO Symposium on Microprocessing Microprogramming, October 1977, Amsterdam. 1978. 44.00 (ISBN 0-444-85097-X, North-Holland). Elsevier.
--Microcomputer Architectures: Proceedings of the Third EUROMICRO Symposium on Microprocessing Microprogramming, October 1977, Amsterdam. 1978. 44.00 (ISBN 0-444-85097-X, North-Holland). Elsevier.
Ogdin, Carol A. Microcomputer Design. (Illus.). 1978. ref. ed. 18.95 (ISBN 0-13-580977-0); pap. 14.95 (ISBN 0-13-580985-1). P-H.
--Microcomputer Management & Programming. (Illus.). 1980. text ed. 24.95 (ISBN 0-13-580936-3). P-H.
--Software Design for Microcomputers. (Illus.). 1978. ref. ed. 18.95 (ISBN 0-13-821744-0); pap. 14.95 (ISBN 0-13-821801-3). P-H.
Osborne, A., et al. Micro Systems in Business. (Micro Monograph Ser.: No. 1). 122p. 1980. pap. text ed. 29.00x (ISBN 0-903796-63-5, Pub. by Online Conferences England). Renouf.
Osborne, Adam. An Introduction to Microcomputers: Vol. 0, the Beginner's Book. 2nd ed. (Intro. to Microcomputers Ser.). 240p. 1979. pap. 4.95 (ISBN 0-931988-26-8). Osborne-McGraw.
--An Introduction to Microcomputers: Vol. 1, Basic Concepts. rev. ed. 1980. pap. 12.99 (ISBN 0-931988-34-9). Osborne-McGraw.
Osborne, Adam & Kane, Jerry. An Introduction to Microcomputers: Some Real Microprocessors. (Intro. to Microcomputers Ser.: Vol. 2). (Orig.). 1978. pap. text ed. 25.00 (ISBN 0-931988-15-2). Osborne-McGraw.
--An Introduction to Microcomputers: Some Real Support Devices. 1978. pap. text ed. 15.00 (ISBN 0-931988-18-7). Osborne-McGraw.
Peatman, J. B. Microcomputer-Based Design. 1977. 29.95 (ISBN 0-07-049138-0). McGraw.
Pennington, Harvard C. TRS-Eighty Disk! And Other Mysteries. (TRS-80 Information Ser.: Vol. 1). (Illus.). 133p. (Orig.). 1979. pap. 22.50 (ISBN 0-936200-00-6). IJG Inc.
Perry, Robert L. Owning Your Home Computer. LC 81-80777. 400p. 1981. pap. 4.95 (ISBN 0-87216-919-7). Playboy Pbks.
Poirot, James & Retzlaff, Don. Microcomputer Workbook: Pet Commodore Edition. 110p. (Orig.). 1981. pap. text ed. 5.95 (ISBN 0-88408-147-8). Sterling Swift.
--Teacher's Manual to Accompany the Microcomputer Workbook: TRS-80 Ed. 124p. tchr's. ed. 3.95 (ISBN 0-88408-146-X). Sterling Swift.
Poirot, James L. Microcomputer Systems & Apple Basic. (Illus.). 150p. (Orig.). (gr. 6-12). 1980. pap. 8.95 (ISBN 0-88408-136-2). Sterling Swift.
Poirot, James L. & Retzlaff, Danold A. Microcomputer Workbook: TRS-80ed. 128p. 1979. pap. 5.95 wkbk. (ISBN 0-88408-121-4). Sterling Swift.
Pooch, U. & Chattergy, R. Designing Microcomputer Systems. (Microcomputer Ser.). 224p. 1979. pap. 10.95 (ISBN 0-8104-5679-6). Hayden.
Randall, J. E. The Use of Microcomputers for Physiological Simulation. 1980. pap. 14.50 (ISBN 0-201-06128-7). A-W.
Rao, Guthikonda V. Microprocessors & Microcomputer Systems. rev. 2nd ed. 352p. 1981. text ed. price not set (ISBN 0-442-25626-4). Van Nos Reinhold.
--Microprocessors & Microcomputer Systems. (Illus.). 1978. text ed. 24.50x (ISBN 0-442-22000-6). Van Nos Reinhold.
Rony, Peter R. & Larsen, David G. Eighty-Eighty A Bugbook: Microcomputer Interfacing & Programming. LC 77-77399. 1977. pap. 11.95 (ISBN 0-672-21447-4). Sams.
--Introductory Experiments in Digital Electronics & 8080a Microcomputer Programming & Interfacing. Incl. Vol. 1. pap. 14.95 (ISBN 0-672-21550-0); Vol. 2. pap. 13.50 (ISBN 0-672-21551-9). 1977. 2 vol. set 25.50 (ISBN 0-672-21552-7). Sams.
Rorvig, Mark E. Microcomputers & Libraries: A Guide to Technology, Products & Applications. (Professional Librarian). (Illus.). 160p. 1981. pap. 27.50 professional (ISBN 0-914236-67-9). Knowledge Indus.
Rosa, Nicolas & Rosa, Sharon. Small Computers for the Small Businessman. LC 80-68531. 340p. 1980. pap. 12.95 (ISBN 0-918398-31-2). Dilithium Pr.
Safford, Edward L., Jr. The Complete Microcomputer Systems Handbook. (Illus.). 1980. pap. 9.95 (ISBN 0-8306-1201-7, 1201). TAB Bks.
Sargent, M. & Shoemaker, R. Interfacing Microcomputers to the Real World. 1981. pap. 14.50 (ISBN 0-201-06879-6). A-W.
Sawin, Dwight H. Microprocessors & Microcomputer Systems. 1977. 21.95 (ISBN 0-669-00564-9). Lexington Bks.
Sawusch, Mark. One Thousand One Things to Do with Your Personal Computer. (Illus.). 336p. (Orig.). 1980. 12.95 (ISBN 0-8306-9963-5); pap. 7.95 (ISBN 0-8306-1160-6, 1160). TAB Bks.
Shaw, Donald R. Your Small Business Computer: Evaluating, Selecting, Financing, Installing & Operating the Hardware & Software That Fits. 272p. 1980. text ed. 19.95 (ISBN 0-442-27540-4). Van Nos Reinhold.
Sippl, C. J. & Kidd, D. A. Microcomputer Dictionary & Guide. (Illus.). 1976. 19.95 (ISBN 0-916460-01-0, Pub. by Matrix). Intl Schol Bk Serv.
Skrokov, M. Robert, ed. Mini & Microcomputer Control in Industrial Processes: Handbook of Systems Application & Strategies. 320p. 1980. text ed. 27.50 (ISBN 0-442-27643-5). Van Nos Reinhold.
Sloan, Martha E. Introduction to Minicomputers & Microcomputers. LC 78-74693. 1980. text ed. 23.95 (ISBN 0-201-07279-3). A-W.
Soucek, Branko. Microprocessors & Microcomputers. LC 75-33123. 1976. 34.00 (ISBN 0-471-81391-5, Pub. by Wiley-Interscience). Wiley.
Spencer, Donald D. Microcomputers at a Glance. LC 77-11920. (gr. 9-12). 1977. 11.95 (ISBN 0-89218-020-X); pap. 7.95 (ISBN 0-89218-021-8). Camelot Pub.
Spenser, Donald. Fun with Microcomputers & Basic. 1981. pap. 9.95 (ISBN 0-686-76720-9). Reston.
Spohr, Mark. Physician's Guide to Microcomputers. 1981. 18.95 (ISBN 0-8359-5548-6). Reston.
Summer, Claire & Levy, Walter A. The Affordable Computer: Microcomputer Applications in Business & Industry. new ed. LC 78-24672. 1979. 13.95 (ISBN 0-8144-5493-3). Am Mgmt.
--Microcomputers for Business. Orig. Title: The Affordable Computer. 1980. pap. 7.95 (ISBN 0-8144-7539-6). Am Mgmt.
Texas Instruments, Inc. Microprocessors-Microcomputers-System Design. (Texas Instruments Bk. Ser.). (Illus.). 1980. 24.50 (ISBN 0-07-063758-X, P&RB). McGraw.
Texas Instruments Learning Center Staff & Texas Instruments Personal Computer Division Staff. User's Reference Guide. rev. ed. 208p. pap. write for info. (ISBN 0-89512-048-8). Tex Instr Inc.
Thomas, James L. Microcomputers in the Schools. 300p. 1981. lib. bdg. price not set (ISBN 0-89774-001-7). Oryx Pr.
Titus, Christopher A. TEA: 8080-8085 Co-Resident Editor-Assembler. LC 79-65751. 1979. pap. 10.95 (ISBN 0-672-21628-0, 21628). Sams.
Titus, Jonathan A. TRS Interfacing, Bk. 1. LC 79-65749. 1979. pap. 8.95 (ISBN 0-672-21633-7, 21633). Sams.
Titus, Jonathan A., et al. Microcomputer-Analog Converter Software & Hardware Interfacing. LC 78-2293. (Bugbook Ser.: No. 7). 1978. pap. text ed. 8.50 (ISBN 0-89704-009-0). E & L Instru.
--Microcomputer-Analog Converter Software & Hardware Interfacing. LC 78-57201. 1978. pap. 10.50 (ISBN 0-672-21540-3). Sams.
Tocci, Ronald & Laskowski, Lester. Microprocessors & Microcomputers: Hardware & Software. 2nd ed. (Illus.). 416p. 1982. 20.95 (ISBN 0-13-581322-0). P-H.
Tompkins, W. & Webster, J., eds. Design of Microcomputer-Based Medical Instrumentation. 1981. 27.95 (ISBN 0-13-201244-8). P-H.
Townsend, Carl. How to Get Started with CP-M: Control Programs for Microcomputers. 200p. 1981. pap. 9.95 (ISBN 0-918398-32-0). Dilithium Pr.
Townsend, Carl & Miller, Merl. How to Make Money with Your Micro-Computer. LC 79-53477. 1979. pap. 9.95 (ISBN 0-89661-001-2). Robotics Pr.
--How to Make Money with Your Microcomputer. 164p. pap. 8.95 (ISBN 0-89661-001-2, Pub. by Robotics Pr). Intl Schol Bk Serv.
Tracton, Ken. How to Build Your Own Working 16-Bit Microcomputer. (Illus.). 1979. pap. 4.95 (ISBN 0-8306-9813-2, 1099). TAB Bks.
Tripp, Robert M., ed. The Best of Micro Series, Vol. 1. 176p. 1978. pap. 6.00 (ISBN 0-938222-00-7). Micro Ink.
--The Best of Micro Series, Vol. 2. 224p. 1979. 8.00 (ISBN 0-938222-02-3). Micro Ink.
--The Best of Micro Series, Vol. 3. 320p. 1980. pap. 10.00 (ISBN 0-938222-04-X). Micro Ink.
Turner, Ronald C. Real-Time Programming with Microcomputers. new ed. LC 77-80773. 1978. 18.95x (ISBN 0-669-01666-7). Lexington Bks.
Veit, Stanley S. Using Microcomputers in Business: A Guide for the Perplexed. 142p. (Orig.). 1981. pap. 9.95 (ISBN 0-686-75499-9). Hayden.
Waite, Mitchell & Pardee, Michael. Microcomputer Primer. 2nd ed. LC 79-67127. 1980. pap. 11.95 (ISBN 0-672-21653-1). Sams.
Wakerly, John F. Microcomputer Architecture & Programming. LC 80-29060. 692p. 1981. text ed. 27.95 (ISBN 0-471-05232-9). Wiley.
Warme, Paul. BASEX. LC 79-775. 1979. pap. 8.00 (ISBN 0-931718-05-8, BYTE Bks). McGraw.
--My Micro Speaks Basex & Loves It. 164p. (Orig.). 1981. pap. 9.95 (ISBN 0-8104-5187-5). Hayden.
Weber, J. R. How to Use Your Apple II Computer. LC 80-70465. (IDM's How to Use Your Microcomputer Ser.). 300p. (gr. 10-12). 1981. 19.95 (ISBN 0-938862-02-2); pap. 13.95 (ISBN 0-938862-03-0). Five Arms Corp.
--How to Use Your PET Computer. (IDM's How to Use Your Microcomputer Ser.). 300p. (gr. 10-12). 1981. 13.95 (ISBN 0-9604892-7-4); pap. 13.95 (ISBN 0-9604892-8-2). Five Arms Corp.
--How to Use Your TRS-80 Model II Computer. LC 80-70467. (IDM's How to Use Your Microcomputer Ser.). 300p. (gr. 10-12). 1981. 19.95 (ISBN 0-938862-00-6); pap. 13.95 (ISBN 0-938862-01-4). Five Arms Corp.
Weber, Jeffrey R. Accounts Payable System for Micro-Computers: Installation Guide & Disks. (IDM's Computerized Accounting System Ser.). 100p. 1981. 299.95 (ISBN 0-938862-06-5). Five Arms Corp.
--Accounts Receivable System for Micro-Computers: Installation Guide & Disks. (IDM's Computerized Accounting System Ser.). 100p. 1981. 299.95 (ISBN 0-938862-07-3). Five Arms Corp.
--CPIM, C-Basic & Microsoft BASIC. LC 81-66910. (IDM's How to Use Your Microcomputer Ser.). 300p. (Orig.). (gr. 10-12). 1981. 19.95 (ISBN 0-938862-04-9); pap. 13.95 (ISBN 0-938862-05-7). Five Arms Corp.
--General Ledger System for Micro-Computers: Installation Guide & Disks. (IDM's Computerized Accounting System Ser.). 100p. 1981. 299.95 (ISBN 0-938862-08-1). Five Arms Corp.
--Payroll System for Micro-Computers: Installation Guide & Disks. 100p. 1981. 299.95 (ISBN 0-938862-09-X). Five Arms Corp.
Webster, Anthony. Webster's Microcomputer Buyer's Guide. (Illus.). 326p. (Orig.). 1981. pap. 25.00 (ISBN 0-8104-5129-8). Hayden.
Weitzman, Cay. Distributed Micro Minicomputer Systems: Structure, Implementation & Application. (Illus.). 1980. text ed. 26.95 (ISBN 0-13-216481-7). P-H.
Welles, Kenneth B. K-2-FDOS: A Floppy Disk Operating System for the 8080. (Orig.). 1979. pap. 20.00 (ISBN 0-07-069206-8, BYTE Bks). McGraw.
Whitbread, Martin, ed. Microprocessor Applications in Business & Industry. (Topics in Microprocessing Ser.: Book One). (Illus.). 153p. 1979. pap. text ed. 25.00 (ISBN 0-7194-0010-4, Pub. by Castle Hse England). J K Burgess.
Wiatrowski, Claude A. & House, Charles H. Logic Circuits & Microcomputer Systems. Cerra, Frank J., ed. (McGraw-Hill Series in Electrical Engineering: Computer Engineering & Switching Theory-Electronics & Electronic Circuits). (Illus.). 512p. Date not set. text ed. 25.95 (ISBN 0-07-070090-7); price not set solutions manual (ISBN 0-07-070091-5). McGraw.
Wilkes, Richard P. & Hill, Stephen C. The Bee-Zero-Zero-Kay: Accessing the TRS-80 ROM (Input-Output Routines, Vol. 2. (Illus.). 156p. (Orig.). 1981. pap. 14.95 (ISBN 0-939462-01-X). Insiders Software.
Wilkes, Richard P., et al. The Book: Accessing the TRS-80 ROM (Math Routines, Vol. 1. Hill, Stephen C. & Soltoff, Roy, eds. (Illus., Orig.). 1980. pap. 14.95 (ISBN 0-939462-00-1). Insiders Software.
Wise, Kensall D., et al. Microcomputers: A Technology Forecast & Assessment to the Year 2000. LC 79-18186. (Systems Engineering & Analysis Ser.). 1980. 18.95 (ISBN 0-471-04780-5, Pub. by Wiley-Interscience). Wiley.
Witten, Ian. Communicating with Microcomputers: An Introduction to the Technology of Man-Computer Communication. LC 80-40650. (Computers & People Ser.). 1980. 18.00 (ISBN 0-12-760750-1); pap. 10.50 (ISBN 0-12-760752-8). Acad Pr.
Wordsworth, Nat. Understanding Microcomputers & Small Computer Systems. (Da Capo Quality Paperbacks Ser.). (Illus.). 312p. 1981. pap. 8.95 (ISBN 0-306-80143-4). Da Capo.
Wyand, Roy & Graham, John, eds. The International Microcomputer Software Directory. 1981. 29.95 (ISBN 0-907352-03-0). Imprint Edns.
Zaks, Rodnay. Don't: 0r How to Care for Your Computer. (Illus.). 1981. 8.95 (ISBN 0-89588-060-1). Sybex.
--Six Thousand Five Hundred & Two Games. (Illus.). 1980. pap. 12.95 (ISBN 0-89588-022-9, 0402). Sybex.
--Your First Computer. 2nd. ed. (Illus.). 1980. 7.95 (ISBN 0-89588-045-8). Sybex.

MICROCOSM AND MACROCOSM

Conger, George P. Theories of Macrocosms & Microcosms in the History of Philosophy. LC 66-27056. 1967. Repr. of 1922 ed. 7.00 (ISBN 0-8462-0865-2). Russell.
Cornford, F. M. Microcosmographia Academia. 1980. pap. 2.95 (ISBN 0-370-00145-1, Pub. by Chatto, Bodley Head & Jonathan). Merrimack Bk Serv.
Mead, G. R. The Subtle Body. 1981. 20.00x (ISBN 0-7224-0156-6, Pub. by Watkins England). State Mutual Bk.

MICROECONOMICS

see also Managerial Economics

Abraham, C. & Thomas, A. Microeconomics: Optimal Decision Making by Private Firms & Public Authorities. Jones, D. V., tr. from Fr. LC 79-188001. Orig. Title: Microeconomic, Decisions Optimal dans L'enterprise et dans la Nation. (Illus.). 507p. 1973. lib. bdg. 60.50 (ISBN 90-277-0237-3, Pub. by Reidel Holland). Kluwer Boston.
Albrecht, William P, Jr. Microeconomic Principles. (Illus.). 1979. pap. text ed. 10.95 (ISBN 0-13-581314-X); study guide & wkbk. 11.95 (ISBN 0-13-227553-8). P-H.
Armey, Richard K. Price-Theory: A Policy-Welfare Approach. (Illus.). 1977. 19.95 (ISBN 0-13-699694-9). P-H.
Asimakopulos, A. An Introduction to Economic Theory: Microeconomics. (Illus.). 1978. text ed. 16.95x (ISBN 0-19-540281-2). Oxford U Pr.
Attiyeh, Richard E., et al. Microeconomics: A Programmed Book. 3rd ed. (Illus.). 256p. pap. 9.95 ref. ed. (ISBN 0-13-581421-9). P-H.
Awh, Robert Y. Microeconomics: Theory & Applications. LC 75-38643. 1976. text ed. 25.95 (ISBN 0-471-03849-0); wkbk. 9.95 (ISBN 0-471-03853-9). Wiley.
Ayal, Eliezer B., ed. Micro Aspects of Development. LC 72-89641. (Special Studies in International Economics & Development). 1973. 34.50x (ISBN 0-275-28685-1); pap. text ed. 14.95x (ISBN 0-89197-846-1). Irvington.
Ayatey, Siegfried B. Essentials of Economic Analysis: Vol. 1, Microeconomics. LC 79-66234. 1979. pap. text ed. 10.50 (ISBN 0-8191-0803-0). U Pr of Amer.
Baird, Charles W. Prices & Markets: Microeconomics. LC 75-7737. (Illus.). 231p. 1975. text ed. 18.50 (ISBN 0-8299-0060-8). West Pub.
Barkley, Paul W. An Introduction to Microeconomics. (Illus.). 1977. pap. text ed. 13.95 (ISBN 0-15-518817-8, HC); instructor's guide avail. (ISBN 0-15-518827-5); study guide by sam cordes 5.95 (ISBN 0-15-518826-7); test bklet incl. (ISBN 0-15-518828-3). HarBraceJ.
Baumol, W. Economic Theory & Operations Analysis. 4th ed. 1977. 21.95 (ISBN 0-13-227132-X). P-H.

Beck, Roger. Microeconomic Analysis of Issues in Business, Government & Society. (Illus.). 1978. pap. text ed. 8.95 (ISBN 0-07-004253-5, C). McGraw.

Becker, Gary S. Economic Theory. 1971. text ed. 17.95 (ISBN 0-394-31492-1, KnopfC). Knopf.

Bilas, R. A. Microeconomic Theory. 2nd ed. 1971. 16.95 (ISBN 0-07-005258-1, C); instructors' manual 3.95 (ISBN 0-07-005272-7); Problems in Microeconomics 9.95 (ISBN 0-07-005263-8). McGraw.

Blair, R. D. & Kenny, L. W. Microeconomics for Managerial Decision Making. 1981. price not set (ISBN 0-07-005800-8); price not set instr's. manual (ISBN 0-07-005801-6). McGraw.

Bradley, Michael E. Microeconomics. 1980. pap. text ed. 11.95x (ISBN 0-673-15335-5); study guide 5.95x (ISBN 0-673-15286-3). Scott F.

Brennan, M. Theory of Economic Statics. 2nd ed. 1970. 19.95 (ISBN 0-13-913624-X). P-H.

Brooks, Douglas. Market Structure & Seller Profitability. 1973. 5.85x (ISBN 0-916304-08-6). Campanile.

Call, Steven T. & Holahan, William L. Microeconomics. 544p. 1980. text ed. 21.95x (ISBN 0-534-00804-6). Wadsworth Pub.

Carson, Robert B. Microeconomic Issues Today. 182p. (Orig.). 1980. text ed. 12.95 (ISBN 0-312-53175-3); write for info instrs'. manual (ISBN 0-312-53176-1); write for info. instructor's manual (ISBN 0-312-53177-X). St Martin.

Chisholm, Roger & McCarty, Marilu. Principles of Microeconomics. 2nd ed. 1981. pap. text ed. 11.95x (ISBN 0-673-15402-5). Scott F.

Cohen, Kalman J. & Cyert, Richard M. Theory of the Firm: Resource Allocation in a Market Economy. 2nd ed. (Illus.). 640p. 1975. 21.95 (ISBN 0-13-913798-X). P-H.

David, Paul A. & Reder, Melvin W., eds. Nations & Households in Ecnomic Growth: Essays in Honor of Moses Abramovitz. 1973. 50.00 (ISBN 0-12-205050-9). Acad Pr.

Dernburg, Thomas F. & McDougall, Duncan. Macroeconomics. 5th ed. 1976. text ed. 16.95 (ISBN 0-07-016526-2, C). McGraw.

Dewey, Donald. Microeconomics: The Analysis of Prices & Markets. (Illus.). 352p. 1975. 12.95x (ISBN 0-19-501828-1). Oxford U Pr.

Dixon, P. B., et al. Notes & Problems in Microeconomic Theory. (Advanced Textbooks in Economics: Vol. 15). 318p. 1980. text ed. 36.75 (ISBN 0-444-85325-1, North Holland). Elsevier.

Dolan, Edwin G. Basic Microeconomics: Understanding Prices & Markets. 2nd ed. 400p. 1980. pap. text ed. 13.95 (ISBN 0-03-051281-6). Dryden Pr.

Douglas, Evan J. Intermediate Microeconomic Analysis: Theory & Applications. (Illus.). 576p. 1982. text ed. 21.95 (ISBN 0-13-470708-7). P-H.

Eggert, Jim. Investigating Microeconomics. LC 79-16480. (Illus.). 136p. 1979. 8.95 (ISBN 0-913232-62-9); pap. 4.95 (ISBN 0-913232-61-0). W Kaufmann.

Eichner, A. S. The Megacorp & Oligopoly. LC 75-17115. (Illus.). 450p. 1976. 35.50 (ISBN 0-521-20885-8). Cambridge U Pr.

Eichner, Alfred S. The Megacorp & Oligopoly. LC 79-92295. 365p. 1980. pap. 8.95 (ISBN 0-87332-168-5). M E Sharpe.

Farquhar, J. D. & Heidensohn, K. The Market Economy. 160p. 18.00x (ISBN 0-86003-004-0, Pub. by Allan Pubs England); pap. 9.00x (ISBN 0-86003-103-9). State Mutual Bk.

Fels, et al. Casebook of Economic, Microeconomic Problems & Policies: Practice in Thinking. 4th ed. 112p. 1978. 5.95 (ISBN 0-8299-0479-4); staff notes avail. West Pub.

Fels, Rendig, et al. Microeconomic Problems & Policies. 4th ed. 1978. pap. text ed. 5.95 (ISBN 0-8299-0192-2). West Pub.

Focus Microeconomics. (Annual Editions Ser.). (Illus.). 224p. (Orig.). 1976. pap. text ed. 4.95 (ISBN 0-87967-139-4). Dushkin Pub.

Forester, Tom, ed. The Microelectronics Revolution: The Complete Guide to the New Technology & Its Impact on Society. 1981. 25.00 (ISBN 0-262-06075-2); pap. 12.50 (ISBN 0-262-56021-6). MIT Pr.

George, K. D. & Shorey, John. The Allocation of Resources: Theory & Politics. (Illus.). 1978. text ed. 25.00x (ISBN 0-04-300073-8); pap. text ed. 11.50x (ISBN 0-04-300074-6). Allen Unwin.

Gill, Richard T. Economics & the Private Interest: An Introduction to Microeconomics. 2nd ed. LC 75-22754. 288p. 1976. pap. text ed. 10.95 (ISBN 0-87620-248-2); student guide 5.25x (ISBN 0-87620-249-0). Goodyear.

Gisser, Micha. Intermediate Price Theory: Analysis, Issues & Applications. (Illus.). 672p. 1981. text ed. 18.95 (ISBN 0-07-023312-8, C); instructor's manual 7.50 (ISBN 0-07-023313-6). McGraw.

Glahe, Fred R. & Lee, Dwight R. Microeconomics: Theory & Applications. 558p. 1981. text ed. 20.95 (ISBN 0-15-558623-8). HarBraceJ.

Golladay, Frederick L. Microeconomics: Problems, Principles & Priorities. LC 78-52927. 1978. 10.95 (ISBN 0-8053-3306-1). Benjamin-Cummings.

Goodman, John C. & Dolan, Edwin G. Economics of Public Policy: The Micro View. (Illus.). 1979. pap. text ed. 9.50 (ISBN 0-8299-0238-4); instrs.' manual avail. (ISBN 0-8299-0481-6). West Pub.

Gould, J. P. & Ferguson, C. E. Microeconomic Theory. 5th ed. 1980. 19.95x (ISBN 0-256-02157-0). Irwin.

Graham, Daniel A. Microeconomics: The Analysis of Choice. 1980. text ed. 17.95 (ISBN 0-669-02273-X). Heath.

Gravelle, H. & Rees, R. Microeconomics. 2nd ed. (Modern Economic Series). (Illus.). 1981. pap. text ed. 25.00x (ISBN 0-582-44075-0). Longman.

Greenhut, Melvin L. A Theory of the Firm in Economic Space. LC 71-112946. (Illus.). 389p. 1974. Repr. of 1970 ed. text ed. 15.00x (ISBN 0-914872-00-1). Austin Pr.

Gwartney, James D. Microeconomics: Public & Private Sector Choice. 2nd ed. 1980. 12.95 (ISBN 0-12-311070-X). Acad Pr.

Hadar, Josef. Elementary Theory of Microeconomic Behavior. 2nd ed. LC 70-171435. 1974. text ed. 18.95 (ISBN 0-201-02672-4). A-W.

Hartley, Keith & Tisdell, C. An Introduction to Microeconomic Policy. 408p. 1982. 54.95 (ISBN 0-471-28026-7, Pub. by Wiley-Interscience); pap. 17.95 (ISBN 0-471-28027-5, Pub. by Wiley-Interscience). Wiley.

Haveman, Robert H. & Hollenbeck, Kevin, eds. Microeconomic Simulation Models for Public Policy Analysis: Vol. 1 Distributional Impacts, Vol. 1. LC 79-8866. (Institute for Research on Poverty Monograph). 1980. 29.50 (ISBN 0-12-333201-X). Acad Pr.

Havemen, Robert H. The Market System: An Introduction to Microeconomics. 4th ed. LC 80-21972. (Introduction to Economics Ser.). 280p. 1981. text ed. 11.95 (ISBN 0-471-08530-8). Wiley.

Heilbroner, R. & Thorou, L. Understanding Microeconomics. 5th ed. 1981. pap. 10.95 (ISBN 0-13-936567-2); pap. 7.95 study guide (ISBN 0-13-233296-5). P-H.

Heineke, J. Microeconomics for Business Decisions: Theory & Application. 1976. text ed. 18.95 (ISBN 0-13-581389-1). P-H.

Hemenway, David. Prices & Choices: Microeconomic Vignettes. LC 77-2733. 1977. cloth 15.00 (ISBN 0-88410-663-2); pap. 9.95 (ISBN 0-88410-660-8). Ballinger Pub.

Henderson, James & Quandt, Richard E. Microeconomic Theory. 3rd ed. (Illus.). 1980. 20.50 (ISBN 0-07-028101-7); instructor's manual avail. (ISBN 0-07-044123-5). McGraw.

Hey, John D. Uncertainty in Microeconomics. LC 79-63434. 1979. cobee 19.00x (ISBN 0-8147-3398-0); pap. 9.50x cobee (ISBN 0-8147-3399-9). NYU Pr.

Heyne, Paul & Johnson, Thomas. Toward Understanding Microeconomics. LC 76-22434. 1976. pap. text ed. 11.95 (ISBN 0-574-19270-0, 13-2270); instr's guide avail. (ISBN 0-574-19256-5, 13-2256). SRA.

Hines, Lawrence G. The Persuasion of Price: Introductory Microeconomics. (Illus.). 1977. pap. text ed. 9.95 (ISBN 0-87626-661-8). Winthrop.

Hirshleifer, Jack. Price Theory & Applications. 2nd ed. (Illus.). 1980. text ed. 21.00 (ISBN 0-13-699710-4). P-H.

Howe, Charles W. Natural Resource Economics: Issues Analysis & Policy. LC 78-24174. 1979. text ed. 25.95x (ISBN 0-471-04527-6). Wiley.

Jhingan, M. L. Micro-Economic Theory. 1979. text ed. 25.00x (ISBN 0-7069-0569-5, Pub. by Vikas India). Advent NY.

Joshi, J. M. Theory of Value, Distribution & Welfare Economics. 1980. text ed. 20.00x (ISBN 0-7069-0689-6, Pub. by Vikas India). Advent NY.

Kaish, Stanley. Microeconomics: Logic, Tools, & Analysis. 448p. 1976. text ed. 21.50 scp (ISBN 0-06-043456-2, HarpC); instructor's manual free (ISBN 0-06-363460-0). Har-Row.

Kessel, Reuben A. Essays in Applied Price Theory. Coase, R. H. & Merton, Miller H., eds. LC 80-12974. 1980. write for info. U of Chicago Pr.

Kogiku, K. C. Microeconomic Models. LC 78-11695. 320p. 1981. Repr. of 1971 ed. lib. bdg. write for info. (ISBN 0-88275-781-4). Krieger.

Kohler, Heinz. Intermediate Microeconomics: Theory & Applications. text ed. 19.95 (ISBN 0-673-15277-4). Scott F.

Koutsoyiannis, A. Modern Microeconomics. 2nd ed. (Illus.). 1979. 19.95x (ISBN 0-312-54103-1). St Martin.

Krauss, Melvyn B. & Johnson, Harry G. General Equilibrium Analysis. LC 74-18213. 1975. text ed. 9.75 (ISBN 0-202-06069-1). Beresford Bk Serv.

Kuehn, Douglas. Takeovers & the Theory of the Firm: An Empirical Analysis for the United Kingdom 1957-69. 189p. 1975. 29.75x (ISBN 0-8419-5000-8). Holmes & Meier.

Laffont, Jean-Jacques. Essays in the Economics of Uncertainty. LC 79-19771. (Harvard Economic Studies: Vol. 149). 1980. text ed. 12.50x (ISBN 0-674-26555-6). Harvard U Pr.

Laidler, David. Introduction to Microeconomics. 2nd ed. 330p. 1981. pap. 18.50 (ISBN 0-470-27243-0). Halsted Pr.

--Introduction to Microeconomics. LC 75-7268. 1975. 11.95x (ISBN 0-465-03544-2). Basic.

Layard, Richard, et al. Microeconomic Theory. (Illus.). 1978. text ed. 18.95 (ISBN 0-07-036786-8, C). McGraw.

Leibenstein, Harvey. Beyond Economic Man: A New Approach to Micro-Economic Theory. (Illus.). 288p. 1976. 16.50x (ISBN 0-674-06891-2); pap. 6.95 (ISBN 0-674-06892-0). Harvard U Pr.

Lindauer, John. Microeconomics: A Modern View. LC 77-79398. 1979. pap. text ed. cancelled (ISBN 0-7216-5779-6). HR&W.

Linder, Marc. The Anti-Samuelson. Incl. Vol. I. Macroeconomics: Basic Problems of Capitalist Economy (ISBN 0-916354-14-8) (ISBN 0-916354-15-6); Vol. II. Microeconomics: Money & Banking (ISBN 0-916354-16-4) (ISBN 0-916354-17-2). 1977. 20.00 ea.; pap. text ed. 6.95 ea. Urizen Bks.

Lipsey, Richard G. & Steiner, Peter O. Economics, Vol. II: Microeconomics. 5th ed. LC 78-25645. 1979. pap. text ed. 14.95 scp (ISBN 0-06-043981-5, HarpC); scp study guide 6.50 (ISBN 0-06-043983-1). Har-Row.

Lo De Meza, David & Osborne, Michael. Problems in Price Theory. LC 80-16597. (Illus.). xiv, 302p. 1980. lib. bdg. 25.00 (ISBN 0-226-14293-0). U of Chicago Pr.

Lumsden, Keith, et al. Microeconomics: A Programmed Book. 4th ed. (Illus.). 272p. 1982. 9.95 (ISBN 0-13-581397-2). P-H.

Lyall, Katharine C. Microeconomic Issues of the 70s: Exercises in Applied Price Theory. 2nd ed. 1978. pap. text ed. 8.95 scp (ISBN 0-06-044116-X, HarpC); solutions manual avail. (ISBN 0-06-364104-6). Har-Row.

McCain, R. Markets, Decisions & Organizations: Intermediate Microeconomic Theory. 1980. 21.95 (ISBN 0-13-557884-1). P-H.

McCloskey, Donald N. The Applied Theory of Price. 1982. text ed. 20.95 (ISBN 0-686-75014-4). Macmillan.

Mahanty, Aroop K. Intermediate Microeconomics with Applications. 1980. 17.95 (ISBN 0-12-465150-X). Acad Pr.

Main, Robert S. & Baird, Charles W. Elements of Microeconomics. (Illus.). 1977. pap. text ed. 11.95 (ISBN 0-8299-0136-1). West Pub.

Malinvaud, E. Lectures on Microeconomic Theory. (Advanced Textbooks on Economics Ser: Vol. 2). 1972. text ed. 18.00 (ISBN 0-444-10389-9, North-Holland). Elsevier.

Mansfield, Edwin. Microeconomic Problems. 3rd ed. 1979. pap. text ed. 5.95x (ISBN 0-393-95004-2). Norton.

--Microeconomic Problems: Case Studies and Exercises for Review. 4th ed. 1981. pap. text ed. price not set (ISBN 0-393-95212-6). Norton.

--Microeconomics: Theory and Application. 4th ed. (Illus.). 1981. price not set (ISBN 0-393-95218-5); price not set instr's. manual (ISBN 0-393-95218-5). Norton.

--Microeconomics: Theory & Applications. 2nd ed. 500p. 1975. text ed. 12.95x (ISBN 0-393-09244-5). Norton.

--Microeconomics: Theory & Applications. shorter 2nd ed. (Illus.). 400p. 1975. text ed. 12.50x (ISBN 0-393-09190-2). Norton.

--Microeconomics: Theory & Applications. 3rd ed. (Illus.). 1979. text ed. 17.95x (ISBN 0-393-95002-6); text ed. 17.45x shorter ed. (ISBN 0-393-95010-7); instrs'. manual 3.95x (ISBN 0-393-95044-1). Norton.

--Principles of Microeconomics. 400p. 1974. pap. text ed. 6.75x (ISBN 0-393-09265-8). Norton.

--Principles of Microeconomics. 2nd ed. (Illus.). 1977. pap. text ed. 9.95x (ISBN 0-393-09113-9); readings, issues & cases 4.95x (ISBN 0-393-09102-3); study guide 4.95x (ISBN 0-393-09109-0); test item file gratis (ISBN 0-393-09105-8); transparency masters gratis (ISBN 0-393-09099-X). Norton.

--Principles of Microeconomics: Readings, Issues & Cases. 3rd ed. Mansfield, Edwin, ed. 1980. pap. 4.95 (ISBN 0-393-95144-8); study guide 3.95 (ISBN 0-393-95147-2); instructor's manual free (ISBN 0-393-95124-3); test item file free (ISBN 0-393-95125-1); transparency masters free (ISBN 0-393-95131-6). Norton.

Mansfield, Edwin, ed. Micro-Economics: Selected Readings. 2nd ed. (Illus.). 550p. 1975. pap. text ed. 8.95x (ISBN 0-393-09253-4). Norton.

--Microeconomic Problems. 1971. pap. text ed. 4.25x (ISBN 0-393-09390-5). Norton.

--Microeconomics: Selected Readings. 1971. pap. text ed. 6.95x (ISBN 0-393-09989-X). Norton.

--Microeconomics: Selected Readings. 3rd ed. 1979. pap. text ed. 10.95x (ISBN 0-393-95015-8). Norton.

--Principles of Macroeconomics. 2nd ed. Incl. Reading, Issues, & Cases. 1974. pap. text ed. 3.25x (ISBN 0-393-09271-2). 1977. pap. text ed. 4.95x (ISBN 0-393-09108-2). Norton.

Martin, Leonard W. Principles of Economics: Micro. LC 79-13493. (Grid Series in Economics). 1980. pap. text ed. 10.95 (ISBN 0-88244-190-6). Grid Pub.

Meyer, Robert A., Jr. Microeconomic Decisions. LC 75-30259. (Illus.). 384p. 1976. text ed. 18.95 (ISBN 0-395-19855-0). HM.

Microeconomic Theory. 2nd ed. LC 77-81247. 694p. 1978. text ed. 21.95 (ISBN 0-03-020831-9). Dryden Pr.

Miller, Ervin. The Microeconomic Effects of Monetary Policy. LC 77-17980. 1978. 17.50 (ISBN 0-312-53173-7). St Martin.

Miller, Roger L. Intermediate Microeconomics: Theories, Issues, & Applications. (Illus.). 1977. text ed. 16.95 (ISBN 0-07-042150-1); instructor's manual 4.95 (ISBN 0-07-042151-X); study guide 6.95 (ISBN 0-07-042152-8); transparency masters 15.00 (ISBN 0-07-042153-6). McGraw.

Mittra, Sid, ed. Dimensions of Microeconomics: A Book of Reading. 1971. pap. 6.95 (ISBN 0-685-55631-X, 31425). Phila Bk Co.

Morishima, M. The Economic Theory of Modern Society. Anthony, D. W., tr. from Japanese. LC 75-39375. (Illus.). 332p. 1976. 49.50 (ISBN 0-521-21088-7); pap. 15.95x (ISBN 0-521-29168-2). Cambridge U Pr.

Neel, Richard E. Readings in Price Theory. 1973. pap. text ed. 7.40 (ISBN 0-538-08010-8, H01). SW Pub.

Nicholson, Walter. Intermediate Microeconomics & Application. 2nd ed. LC 78-56197. 1979. text ed. 22.95 (ISBN 0-03-041481-4). Dryden Pr.

Nickson, Jack W. Economics & Social Choice: Microeconomics. 1975. 10.95 (ISBN 0-07-046519-3, C); instructors' manual 5.95 (ISBN 0-07-046520-7). McGraw.

North, Douglas C. & Miller, Roger L. The Economics of Public Issues. 5th ed. 192p. 1980. pap. text ed. 5.50 scp (ISBN 0-06-044875-X, HarpC); instructor's manual free. Har-Row.

O'Donoghue, Patrick & Roberts, Tanya. Microsets: Putting Economic Theory to Work. 1980. text ed. 6.95x (ISBN 0-393-95141-3). Norton.

Orme, Michael. Micros--A Pervasive Force: A Study of the Impact of Microelectronics on Business & Society 1946-1990. LC 79-23839. 214p. 1978. 35.95x (ISBN 0-470-26891-3). Halsted Pr.

Orr, Daniel. Property, Markets, & Government Intervention: A Textbook in Microeconomic Theory & Its Current Applications. LC 75-19565. (Illus.). 464p. 1976. pap. text ed. 14.95 (ISBN 0-87620-728-X). Goodyear.

Phelps, Edmund S., ed. The Microeconomic Foundations of Employment & Inflation Theory. 1973. 13.95x (ISBN 0-393-09326-3). Norton.

Polkinghorn, R. Stephen. Micro-Theory & Economic Choices. 1979. 18.95x (ISBN 0-256-02143-0). Irwin.

Quirk, James P. Intermediate Microeconomics. LC 75-34009. (Illus.). 448p. 1976. text ed. 19.95 (ISBN 0-574-19265-4, 13-2265); instr's guide avail. (ISBN 0-574-19266-2, 13-2266); mathematical notes 3.95 (ISBN 0-574-19267-0, 13-2267). SRA.

Quirk, James P. & McDougall, Duncan. Microeconomics. 1981. pap. text ed. 13.95 (ISBN 0-574-19410-X, 13-2410); instr's guide avail. (ISBN 0-574-19411-8, 13-2411). SRA.

Rader, Trout. Theory of Microeconomics. 1972. text ed. 22.50 (ISBN 0-12-575050-1). Acad Pr.

Redman, John C. & Redman, Barbara J. Microeconomics: Resource Allocation & Price Theory. (Illus.). 1981. text ed. 19.50 (ISBN 0-87055-367-4). AVI.

Reynolds, Lloyd G. Microeconomics: Analysis & Policy. 3rd. ed. 1979. pap. 12.95x (ISBN 0-256-02172-4); review guide & wkbk. 6.50x (ISBN 0-256-02169-4). Irwin.

Rosenberg, Alexander. Microeconomic Laws: A Philosophical Analysis. LC 75-33547. 1976. 14.95x (ISBN 0-8229-3314-4). U of Pittsburgh Pr.

Rudman, Jack. Introductory Micro- & Macroeconomics. (College Level Examination Ser.: CLEP-42). 1977. 14.95 (ISBN 0-8373-5342-4); pap. 9.95 (ISBN 0-8373-5392-0). Natl Learning.

--Introductory Microeconomics. (College Level Examination Ser.: CLEP-40). 1977. 14.95 (ISBN 0-8373-5340-8); pap. 9.95 (ISBN 0-686-67795-1). Natl Learning.

Russell, R. R. & Wilkinson, M. Microeconomics: A Synthesis of Modern & Neoclassical Theory. (Economics Ser.). 1979. text ed. 28.95 (ISBN 0-471-94652-4). Wiley.
Salvatore, Dominick. Microeconomic Theory. 256p. (Orig.). 1974. pap. text ed. 4.95 (ISBN 0-07-054495-6, SP). McGraw.
Sawyer, Malcolm C. Theories of the Firm. LC 79-14662. 1979. 18.95x (ISBN 0-312-79703-6). St Martin.
Schneider, Harold K. Economic Man: The Anthropology of Economics. LC 73-8493. (Illus.). 1974. 12.95 (ISBN 0-02-927940-2). Free Pr.
Schumacher, E. F. Small Is Beautiful: Economics As If People Mattered. LC 73-12710. 304p. (YA) 1976. 9.95 (ISBN 0-06-013801-7, HarpT). Har-Row.
Shone, Ronald. Applications in Intermediate Microeconomics. LC 81-6441. 288p. 1981. 35.95 (ISBN 0-470-27221-X). Halsted Pr.
Smith, Kerry V., ed. Advances in Applied Micro-Economics, Vol. 1. 300p. 1981. 34.50 (ISBN 0-89232-171-7). Jai Pr.
Solmon, Lewis C. Microeconomics. 3rd ed. LC 79-25515. 528p. 1980. pap. text ed. 12.95 (ISBN 0-201-07218-1); student guide avail. (ISBN 0-201-07221-1). A-W.
Spencer, Milton H. Contemporary Microeconomics. 4th ed. 1980. text ed. 13.95x (ISBN 0-87901-115-7); study guide 5.95 (ISBN 0-87901-111-4). H S Worth.
Stigum, Marcia L. Problems in Microeconomics. 1975. pap. 11.95x (ISBN 0-256-01734-4). Irwin.
Stilwell, Frank J. Normative Economics: An Introduction to Microeconomic Theory & Radical Critiques. 162p. 1975. pap. text ed. 10.75 (ISBN 0-08-018300-X). Pergamon.
Theil, Henri. The System-Wide Approach to Microeconomics. LC 78-31999. xii, 260p. 1981. pap. 6.95 (ISBN 0-226-79438-5, Phoen). U of Chicago Pr.
--The System-Wide Approach to Microeconomics. LC 78-31999. 1980. lib. bdg. 23.00x (ISBN 0-226-79437-7). U of Chicago Pr.
Thomas, Robert P. Microeconomic Applications. 272p. 1981. pap. text ed. 7.95x (ISBN 0-534-00968-9). Wadsworth Pub.
Varian, Hal E. Microeconomic Analysis. 1978. pap. text ed. 19.95x (ISBN 0-393-09036-1); pap. text ed. 7.95 exercise applications (ISBN 0-393-95078-6). Norton.
Vickerman, R. W. Spatial Economic Behavior: The Microeconomic Foundations of Urban & Transport Economics. LC 79-25872. 200p. 1980. 25.00x (ISBN 0-312-74002-6). St Martin.
Watson, Donald S. & Getz, Malcolm. Price Theory in Action. 4th ed. LC 81-80260. 448p. 1981. pap. text ed. 12.95 (ISBN 0-395-30058-4); write for info. instr's manual (ISBN 0-395-30057-6). HM.
Watson, Donald S. & Holman, Mary A. Price Theory & Its Uses. 4th ed. LC 76-14003. (Illus.). 1976. text ed. 18.50 (ISBN 0-395-24422-6); inst. manual 1.25 (ISBN 0-395-24423-4). HM.
Waud, Roger N. Microeconomics. (Illus.). 1980. text ed. 14.95 scp (ISBN 0-06-046966-8, HarpC); scp study guide 6.50 (ISBN 0-06-046988-9). Har-Row.
Weintraub, E. R. Microfoundations. LC 78-16551. (Cambridge Surveys of Economic Literature Ser.). 1979. 26.50 (ISBN 0-521-22305-9); pap. 7.95x (ISBN 0-521-29445-2). Cambridge U Pr.
Wilson, J. Holton. Microeconomics: Concepts & Applications. 443p. 1981. text ed. 20.95 scp (ISBN 0-912212-13-6, HarpC); inst. manual avail. Har-Row.

MICROELECTRONICS

see also Integrated Circuits; Miniature Electronic Equipment; Printed Circuits

Agajanian, A. H. Microelectronic Packaging: A Bibliography. 1979. 75.00 (ISBN 0-306-65183-1). IFI Plenum.
Ahmed, H. & Nixon, W. C., eds. Microcircuit Engineering. LC 79-8907. (Illus.). 1980. 47.50 (ISBN 0-521-23118-3). Cambridge U Pr.
Barron, Iann & Curnow, R. C. Future with Microelectronics. 1979. 17.50x (ISBN 0-89397-055-7). Nichols Pub.
Berman, Herbert J. & Hebert, Normand C. Ion-Selective Microelectrodes. LC 74-14914. (Advances in Experimental Medicine & Biology Ser.: Vol. 50). 202p. 1974. 25.00 (ISBN 0-306-39050-7, Plenum Pr). Plenum Pub.
Berting, Jan, et al, eds. The Socio-Economic Impact of Microelectronics: International Conference on Socio-Economic Problems & Potentialities of Microelectronics, Sept. 1979, Zandvoort, Netherlands. LC 80-49810. (Vienna Centre Ser.). (Illus.). 263p. 1980. 54.00 (ISBN 0-08-026776-9). Pergamon.
Bessant, J. R., et al. The Impact of Microelectronics: A Review of the Literature. LC 80-54414. (Illus.). 174p. 1981. text ed. 25.00x (ISBN 0-87663-729-2, Pica Special Studies). Universe.
Brewer, George R., ed. Electron Beam Technology in Microelectric Fabrication. LC 79-8856. 1980. 36.50 (ISBN 0-12-133550-X). Acad Pr.
Colclaser, R. A. Microelectronics Process & Device Design. 333p. 1980. 26.95 (ISBN 0-471-04339-7). Wiley.
CSE Microelectronics Group. Microelectronics: Capitalist Technology & the Working Class. 1981. text ed. 21.00x (ISBN 0-906336-16-3, Pub. by CSE Bks England); pap. text ed. 7.75x (ISBN 0-906336-17-1, Pub. by CSE Bks England). Humanities.
Douglas-Young, John. Technician's Guide to Microelectronics. (Illus.). 1978. 14.95 (ISBN 0-13-898650-9, Parker). P-H.
Eastman Kodak. Kodak Microelectronics Seminar - Interface '79, G-102: Proceedings. (Illus.). 180p. 1980. pap. 4.50 (ISBN 0-87985-246-1). Eastman Kodak.
Eastman Kodak Company. Interface Seventy-Two Microelectronics Seminar. LC 73-78245. (Illus.). 64p. 1973. pap. 2.00 (ISBN 0-87985-068-X, P-312). Eastman Kodak.
--Proceedings of the Kodak Microelectronics Seminar, Interface Seventy-Six. 1977. pap. 3.50 (ISBN 0-87985-186-4, G-47). Eastman Kodak.
--Proceedings of the Kodak Microelectronics Seminar, Interface '75. 100p. 1976. pap. 3.50 (ISBN 0-87985-180-5, G-45). Eastman Kodak.
Eastman Kodak Company, ed. Proceedings of the Kodak Microelectronics Seminar-Interface '77. 1978. pap. 3.50 (ISBN 0-87985-215-1, G-48). Eastman Kodak.
Electronics Magazine. Applying Microprocessors. 1977. 23.50 (ISBN 0-07-019160-3, P&RB). McGraw.
--Microelectronics Interconnection & Packaging. Lyman, Jerry, ed. LC 79-21990. (Illus.). 320p. 1979. pap. 12.95 (ISBN 0-07-606600-2, R-927). McGraw.
--Microelectronics Interconnection & Packaging. (Electronics Book Ser.). (Illus.). 1980. 19.95 (ISBN 0-07-019184-0). McGraw.
Englebardt, Stanley L. Miracle Chip: The Microelectronic Revolution. LC 79-2422. (Illus.). (gr. 5 up). 1979. 7.25 (ISBN 0-688-41908-9); PLB 6.96 (ISBN 0-688-51908-3). Lothrop.
Ghandhi, Sorab K. Theory & Practice of Microelectronics. LC 68-28501. (Illus.). 1968. 41.00x (ISBN 0-471-29718-6, Pub. by Wiley-Interscience). Wiley.
Gore, W., ed. Microcircuits & their Applications. 1970. 65.50x (ISBN 0-677-61390-3). Gordon.
Green, K. & Coombs, Rod. The Effects of Microelectronic Technologies on Employment Prospects. 209p. 1980. text ed. 36.75x (ISBN 0-566-00418-6, Pub. by Gower Pub Co England). Renouf.
Hallmark, Clayton. Microelectronics. LC 75-41723. (Illus.). 266p. 1976. 8.95 (ISBN 0-8306-6794-6); pap. 5.95 (ISBN 0-8306-5794-0, 794). TAB Bks.
Homes, P. J. & Loasby, R. C. Handbook of Thick Film Technology. 430p. 1980. 85.00x (ISBN 0-901150-05-3, Pub. by Electrochemical Scotland). State Mutual Bk.
The Impact of Micro-Electronics. 109p. 1981. pap. 11.25 (ISBN 92-2-102378-8, ILO 154, ILO). Unipub.
Index of the Proceedings of Interface Microelectronics Seminars, G-101. 52p. 1979. pap. 3.25 (ISBN 0-87985-237-2). Eastman Kodak.
Jowett, C. E. Application of Engineering in Microelectronic Industries. 184p. 1975. text ed. 22.00x (ISBN 0-220-66278-9, Pub. by Busn Bks England). Renouf.
--The Engineering of Microelectronic Thin & Thick Films. (Illus.). 1978. 29.95 (ISBN 0-333-18655-9, Pub. by Macmillan Pr). Intl Schol Bk Serv.
Kabaservice, Thomas P. Applied Microelectronics. (Electrical Engineering Ser.). (Illus.). 1977. text ed. 26.00 (ISBN 0-8299-0143-4). West Pub.
Keonjian, Edward, ed. Microelectronics: Theory, Design, & Fabrication. (Illus.). 1963. 33.50 (ISBN 0-07-034135-4, P&RB). McGraw.
Kodak Microelectronics Seminar, INTERFACE Nineteen Eighty, G-130: Proceedings. (Illus.). 132p. 1981. pap. 4.50 (ISBN 0-87985-292-5). Eastman Kodak.
Kodak Microelectronics Seminar-Interface 1974, San Diego, Ca., Oct 21-22, 1974. Proceedings. (Illus.). 92p. 1975. pap. 3.50 (ISBN 0-87985-148-1, G-41). Eastman Kodak.
Lavallee, M., et al. Glass Microelectrodes. 446p. 1969. 39.00 (ISBN 0-471-51885-9, Pub. by Wiley). Krieger.
McLean, J. Michael. The Impact of the Microelectronics Industry on the Structure of the Canadian Economy. 50p. 1979. pap. text ed. 3.00x (ISBN 0-920380-22-0, Pub. by Inst Res Pub Canada). Renouf.
Martin, A. G. & Stephenson, F. W. Linear Microelectronic Systems. 242p. 1974. 22.50x (ISBN 0-8448-0886-5). Crane-Russak Co.
Meyer, C., et al. Analysis & Design of Integrated Circuits. LC 68-8035. (Illus.). 1968. text ed. 27.50 (ISBN 0-07-041723-7, C). McGraw.
Microelectronics Dictionary. 288p. 1980. pap. 28.70x (ISBN 3-18-419069-2, Pub. by VDI Verlag Germany). Renouf.
Milek, J. T. Handbook of Electronic Materials: Pt. 1 Silicon Nitride for Microelectric Applications, Pt. 2 Applications & Devices, Vol. 6. LC 76-147312. 117p. 1972. 37.50 (ISBN 0-306-67106-9). IFI Plenum.
Miller, L. F. Thick Film Technology & Chip Joining. (Processes & Materials in Electronics Ser.). 226p. 1972. 34.25x (ISBN 0-677-03440-7). Gordon.
Millman, Jacob. Microelectronics: Digital & Analog Circuits & Systems. (Illus.). 1979. text ed. 26.95 (ISBN 0-07-042327-X, C); solution manual 6.95 (ISBN 0-07-042328-8); transparency masters 9.95 (ISBN 0-07-042329-6); transparency masters for solution manual avail. (ISBN 0-07-042339-3). McGraw.
Norman, Colin. Microelectronics at Work: Productivity & Jobs in the World Economy. LC 80-53425. (Worldwatch Papers). 1980. pap. 2.00 (ISBN 0-916468-38-0). Worldwatch Inst.
Planer, G. & Phillips, L. Thick Film Circuits: Applications & Technology. LC 72-87040. 159p. 1973. 16.50x (ISBN 0-8448-0112-7). Crane-Russak Co.
Purves, R. D. Microelectrode Methods for Intracellular Recording & Ionophoresis. (Biological Techniques Ser.). 1981. 24.00 (ISBN 0-12-567950-5). Acad Pr.
Rada, Juan. The Impact of Microelectronics: A Tentative Appraisal of Information Technology. International Labour Office, ed. viii, 109p. (Orig.). 1980. 15.70 (ISBN 9-2210-2383-4); pap. 10.00 (ISBN 9-2210-2378-8). Intl Labour Office.
REA Staff. Modern Microelectronics: Circuit Design, IC Applications, Fabrication Technology, 2 vols. 2nd ed. (Illus.). 2048p. 1981. Set. 39.75 (ISBN 0-87891-520-6). Res & Educ.
Rikoski, R. A. Hybrid Microelectronic Circuits: The Thick Film. 217p. 1973. 16.75 (ISBN 0-471-72200-6, Pub. by Jw). Krieger.
Roddy, D. Introduction to Microelectronics. 2nd ed. 1978. text ed. 30.00 (ISBN 0-08-022687-6); pap. text ed. 14.00 (ISBN 0-08-022688-4). Pergamon.
Rosenthal, Murray P. Mini-Micro Soldering & Wire Wrapping. 1978. pap. 5.20 (ISBN 0-8104-0864-3). Hayden.
Scarlett, J. A. Printed Circuit Boards for Microelectronics. 2nd ed. 330p. 1980. 70.00x (ISBN 0-901150-08-8, Pub. by Electrochemical Scotland). State Mutual Bk.
Scientific American Editors. Microelectronics: A Scientific American Book. LC 77-13955. (Illus.). 1977. pap. text ed. 8.95x (ISBN 0-7167-0066-2). W H Freeman.
Seminar on Microelectronics-Interface, Atlanta, Oct. 29-30, 1973. Proceedings. Eastman Kodak Co., ed. (Illus.). 72p. 1974. pap. 3.00 (ISBN 0-87985-091-4, G-35). Eastman Kodak.
Stout, David F. & Kaufman, Milton. Handbook of Microcircuit Design & Application. (Illus.). 1979. 32.50 (ISBN 0-07-061796-1, P&RB). McGraw.
Swords-Isherwood, N. Microelectronics of the Engineering Industry. 300p. 1980. 32.50x (ISBN 0-89397-094-8). Nichols Pub.
Sykova, Eva, et al, eds. Ion-Selective Microelectrodes & Their Use in Excitable Tissues. 360p. 1981. 39.50 (ISBN 0-306-40723-X, Plenum Pr). Plenum Pub.
Till, William C. & Luxon, James T. Integrated Circuits: Materials, Devices & Fabrication. (Illus.). 512p. 1982. 32.95 (ISBN 0-13-469031-1). P-H.
Topfer, Morton L. Thick Film Microelectronics. 1971. 17.95x (ISBN 0-442-28564-7). Van Nos Reinhold.
Towers, T. D. Hybrid Microelectronics. LC 76-53092. 1977. 19.50x (ISBN 0-8448-1080-0). Crane-Russak Co.
Twiss, Brian C., ed. The Managerial Implication of Microelectronics. 200p. 1982. 17.50x (ISBN 0-8448-1406-7). Crane-Russak Co.
Vears. Microelectronics Systems One: Checkbook. 1981. text ed. 15.95 (ISBN 0-408-00638-2). Butterworth.
Ward, Brice. Microprocessor-Microprograming Handbook. LC 75-31466. (Illus.). 294p. 1975. 12.95 (ISBN 0-8306-5785-1); pap. 8.95 (ISBN 0-8306-4785-6, 785). TAB Bks.
Whitbread, Martin, ed. Microprocessor Applications in Business & Industry. (Topics in Microprocessing Ser.: Book One). (Illus.). 153p. 1979. pap. text ed. 25.00 (ISBN 0-7194-0010-4, Pub. by Castle Hse England). J K Burgess.

MICROELEMENTS

see Trace Elements

MICROENCAPSULATION

Kondo, A. & Van Valkenburg, J. W. Microcapsule Processing & Technology. 22.50 (ISBN 0-8247-6857-4). Dekker.
Nixon, J. R., ed. Microencapsulation. (Drugs and the Pharmaceutical Science Ser.: Vol. 3). 224p. 1976. 27.50 (ISBN 0-8247-6338-6). Dekker.
Vandegaer, Jan E., ed. Microencapsulation: Processes & Applications. LC 74-6125. 180p. 1974. 25.00 (ISBN 0-306-30788-X, Plenum Pr). Plenum Pub.

MICROFICHES

see also Microfilms; Periodicals on Microfilm

Carroll, Walter J., ed. Educational Media Catalogs on Microfiche: 1979-80. 175.00x (ISBN 0-88367-301-0). Olympic Media.

MICROFILM

see also Periodicals on Microfilm

Bahr, Alice H. Microforms: The Librarians' View, 1978-79. 2nd ed. LC 78-10645. (The Professional Librarian Ser). 1978. pap. 24.50x (ISBN 0-914236-25-3). Knowledge Indus.
Luther, Frederic. MicroFilm: A History, 1839 to 1900. 1981. Repr. of 1959 ed. 25.00x (ISBN 0-913672-34-3). Microform Rev.
Mann, James H. Reducing Made Easy: The Elments of Microfilm. LC 76-25335. 12.00 (ISBN 0-87716-069-4, Pub. by Moore Pub Co). F Apple.
National Center for State Courts. Microfilm & the Courts: Guide for Court Managers. (Courts' Equipment Analysis Project Ser.). 1976. pap. 4.50 (ISBN 0-89656-007-4, R0026G). Natl Ctr St Courts.
--Microfilm & the Courts: Reference Manual. (Courts Equipment Analysis Project Ser.). 1976. 45.00 (ISBN 0-89656-008-2, R0026R). Natl Ctr St Courts.
National Micrographics Assn. Format & Coding for Computer Output Microfilm: ANSI-NMA MS2-1978. 1978. 7.00 (ISBN 0-89258-054-2). Natl Micrograph.
--Microfilm Readers: ANSI-NMA MS20-1979. 1980. 6.00 (ISBN 0-89258-061-5). Natl Micrograph.
--Specifications for Sixteen & Thirty-Five Millimeter Microfilms in Roll Form: ASNI-NMA MS14-1978. 1978. 5.00- (ISBN 0-89258-052-6). Natl Micrograph.
National Micrographics Association. Test Target for Use in Microrecording Engineering Graphics on 35-MM Microfilm. (Standards Ser.). 1980. pap. 5.00 (ISBN 0-89258-068-2, N*M*A M*S 24-1980). Natl Micrograph.
Saffady, William. Computer-Output Microfilm: Its Library Applications. LC 78-18416. 1978. pap. 11.00 (ISBN 0-8389-3217-7). ALA.
Scribner, Paul. An Introduction to Computer-Output Microfilm. rev. ed. Farmer, Jean W., ed. (Consumer Ser.). Orig. Title: Fundamentals of COM. 1980. pap. text ed. 7.00 (ISBN 0-89258-070-4, C103). Natl. Micrograph.
Spigai, Frances G. Invisible Medium: State of the Art of Microform & a Guide to the Literature. 1973. 6.50 (ISBN 0-685-33433-3). Am Soc Info Sci.
Veaner, Allen B. Evaluation of Micropublications. LC 73-138700. (LTP Publication: No. 17). 1971. pap. 4.00 (ISBN 0-8389-3128-6). ALA.

MICROFILM APERTURE CARD SYSTEMS

Bohl, Marilyn. Introduction to IBM Direct Access Storage Devices. 320p. 1981. text ed. 12.95t (ISBN 0-574-21140-3, 13-4140). SRA.

MICROFILM BOOKS

see Books on Microfilm

MICROFILMING

see Microphotography

MICROFILMS

see also Books on Microfilm; Reader-Printers (Microphotography)

Baumann, Roland & Wallace, Diane S. Guide to the Microfilm Collections in the Pennsylvania State Archives. 117p. 1980. pap. 5.00 (ISBN 0-89271-013-6). Pa Hist & Mus.
Bingham, Marie B. & Hoole, W. Stanleycompiled by. A Catalog of the Yucatan Collection on Microfilm in the University of Alabama Libraries. LC 72-4602. 1972. 8.95x (ISBN 0-8173-9512-1). U of Ala Pr.
Cruse, Larry & Warren, Sylvia B., eds. Microcartography: Applications for Archives & Libraries. (Western Association of Map Libraries, Occasional Papers: No. 6). 1981. text ed. write for info. (ISBN 0-939112-07-8). Western Assn Map.
Index to the Guide to the Microfilm of the Records of Pennsylvania's Revolutionary Governments. 77p. 1980. pap. 4.00 (ISBN 0-89271-012-8). Pa Hist & Must.

Majumdar, Gopal K. Newspaper Microfilming: A Plea for Newsprint Documentation. LC 75-912353. 1974. 11.50x (ISBN 0-8364-0439-4). South Asia Bks.

National Micrographics Assn. Practice for Operational Procedures: Inspection & Quality Control of First-Generation Silver-Gelatin Microfilm of Documents (NMA MS23-1979) rev. ed. 1979. pap. text ed. 10.00 (ISBN 0-89258-067-4). Natl Micrograph.

Wainwright, Nicholas B. Guide to the Microfilm Edition of the Thomas Penn Papers. 1968. pap. 1.00 (ISBN 0-685-38544-2). Pa Hist Soc.

MICROFORM READER-PRINTERS

see Reader-Printers (Microphotography)

MICROFORMS

see also Microfilms; Microphotography

American Library Association. Bookdealer-Library Relations Committee. Guidelines for Handling Library Orders for Microforms. LC 76-58322. 1977. 2.00 (ISBN 0-8389-3193-6). ALA.

American National Standards Institute, Standards Committee Z39 on Library Work, Documentation of Related Publishing Practices. American National Standard Advertising of Micropublications. 1975. 2.00 (ISBN 0-686-15233-6, Z39.26). ANSI.

American National Standards Institute, Standards Committee Z39 on Library Work, Documentation & Related Publishing Practices. American National Standard Compiling U. S. Microform Publishing Statistics. 1979. 3.50 (ISBN 0-686-28241-8, Z39.40). ANSI.

Ashby, P. & Campbell, R. Microform Publishing. 1979. text ed. 36.95 (ISBN 0-408-10606-9). Butterworth.

Boss, Richard. Developing Microform Reading Facilities. (Library Micrographics Management Ser.). 175p. 1981. 40.00x (ISBN 0-913672-09-2). Microform Rev.

Carleton, Ardis, ed. Guide to Microforms in Print: Author-Title 1980. LC 61-7082. 1980. 49.50x (ISBN 0-913672-35-1). Microform Rev.

--Guide to Microforms in Print: Subject. 1980. LC 62-21624. 1980. 49.50x (ISBN 0-913672-36-X). Microform Rev.

Carleton, Ardis V., ed. Guide to Microforms in Print: Author-Title, 1981. LC 61-7082. 900p. 1981. 84.50x (ISBN 0-913672-40-8). Microform Rev.

--Guide to Microforms in Print: Subject, 1981. LC 62-21624. 1400p. 1981. 89.50x (ISBN 0-913672-44-0). Microform Rev.

--Guide to Microforms in Print: Supplement, 1981. 175p. 1981. 45.00x (ISBN 0-913672-42-4). Microform Rev.

--Microform Market Place Nineteen Eighty to Nineteen Eighty-One. 4th ed. 250p. 1980. pap. text ed. 20.95x (ISBN 0-913672-37-8). Microform Rev.

Cluff, E. Dale. Microforms. Duane, James E., ed. LC 80-21457. (The Instructional Media Library: Vol. 7). (Illus.). 104p. 1981. 13.95 (ISBN 0-87778-167-2). Educ Tech Pubns.

Columbia University Oral History Collection: Index to Part 1 of the Microform Edition. 1979. text ed. 195.00 (ISBN 0-667-00612-5). Microfilming Corp.

Cook, Patsy A., ed. New York Times Oral History Guide, No. 2. 134p. 1979. pap. 17.50 (ISBN 0-667-00620-6). Microfilming Corp.

Costigan, Daniel M. Micrographic Systems. 2nd ed. Meyer, Ellen T., ed. (Reference Ser.). 1980. text ed. 29.50 (ISBN 0-89258-021-6, R016). Natl Micrograph.

Courtot, Marilyn E. & Meyer, Ellen T. An Introduction to Microform Indexing & Retrieval Systems. rev. ed. (Consumer Ser.). 1980. pap. text ed. 7.00 (ISBN 0-89258-071-2, C104). Natl Micrograph.

Cumulative Microform Reviews 1972-1976. 1979. lib. bdg. 75.00x (ISBN 0-913672-27-0). Microform Rev.

Diaz, Albert J. Microforms in Libraries: A Reader. (Library Micrographics Management Ser.: No. 1). (Illus.). 440p. 1975. 20.95x (ISBN 0-913672-03-3). Microform Rev.

Dodson, Suzanne C. Microform Research Collections: A Guide. (Microform Review Series in Library Micrographics Management: No. 8). 1978. 35.00x (ISBN 0-913672-21-1). Microform Rev.

Fair, Judy, ed. Microforms Management in Special Libraries: A Reader. LC 78-13494. (Microform Review Series in Library Micrographics Management: No. 5). 1979. 21.95x (ISBN 0-913672-15-7). Microform Rev.

Field, Ronald M. A Guide to Micropublishing. 1975. pap. 6.00 (ISBN 0-914548-18-2). Soc Tech Comm.

Fleischer, Eugene B. A Style Manual for Citing Microform & Nonprint Media. LC 78-9375. 1978. pap. 5.00 (ISBN 0-8389-0268-5). ALA.

Gabriel, Michael R. & Roselle, William C. The Microform Revolution in Libraries, Vol. 3. Stueart, Robert D., ed. LC 76-5646. (Foundations in Library & Information Science Ser.). 1980. lib. bdg. 32.50 (ISBN 0-89232-008-7). Jai Pr.

Guide to Microforms in Print 1976. LC 61-7082. 1976. pap. 15.00x (ISBN 0-910972-56-7). Microform Rev.

Hawkins, Reginald. Production of Micro-Forms. Shaw, Ralph, ed. & pref. by. LC 75-17838. (State of the Library Art Ser.: Vol. 5, Pt. 1). 208p. 1975. Repr. of 1960 ed. lib. bdg. 15.00 (ISBN 0-8371-8235-2, HAPM). Greenwood.

Hernon, Peter. Microforms & Government Information. LC 81-4393. (Library Micrographics Management Ser.: No. 6). 1981. 28.95x (ISBN 0-913672-12-2). Microform Rev.

Meckler, Alan M. Microform Market Place 1976-1977: An International Directory of Micropublishing. rev. ed. LC 75-39839. 1976. pap. 14.95x (ISBN 0-913672-05-X). Microform Rev.

Microform Review Inc. The Micropublishers' Trade List Annual 1976. rev. ed. 1976. 80.00x (ISBN 0-913672-06-8). Microform Rev.

The Micropublishers' Trade List Annual 1979. 1979. 89.50x (ISBN 0-913672-28-9). Microform Rev.

National Micrographics Assn. Document Mark (Blip) Used in Image Mark Retrieval Systems: ANSI-NMA MS8-1979. 1980. 6.00 (ISBN 0-89258-060-7). Natl Micrograph.

--Identification of Microforms: ANSI-NMA MS19-1978. 1978. 5.00 (ISBN 0-89258-051-8). Natl Micrograph.

--An Introduction to Micrographics. rev. ed. Meyer, Ellen T., ed. (Consumer Ser.). 1980. pap. 7.00 (ISBN 0-89258-069-0, C101). Natl Micrograph.

--Practice for Uniform Product Disclosure for Unitized Microform Readers (Microfiche, Jackets & Image Cards) NMA MS22-1979. 1980. 5.00 (ISBN 0-89258-057-7). Natl Micrograph.

New, Peter G. Reprography for Librarians. (Illus.). 109p. (Orig.). 1975. 12.50 (ISBN 0-208-01373-3, Linnet). Shoe String.

O'Hara, Deborah, ed. The Micropublishers' Trade List Annual, 1980. 14000p. 1980. 98.50x (ISBN 0-913672-38-6). Microform Rev.

--Micropublishers' Trade List Annual, 1981. 14000p. 1981. 115.00x (ISBN 0-913672-43-2). Microform Rev.

Reichmann, Felix & Tharpe, Josephine M. Bibliographic Control of Microforms. LC 72-2463. 256p. 1972. lib. bdg. 14.95 (ISBN 0-8371-6423-0, RCM/). Greenwood.

Rubin, Jack. A History of Micrographics. Farmar, Jean W., ed. (Reference Ser.). 1980. 22.50 (ISBN 0-89258-066-6, R012). Natl Micrograph.

Saffady, William. Micrographics. LC 78-1309. (Library Science Text Ser.). 1978. 22.50x (ISBN 0-87287-175-4). Libs Unl.

Short, Jeanne, ed. Microform Market Place 1978-79: An International Directory of Micropublishers. 3rd ed. 1978. pap. 16.95x (ISBN 0-913672-22-X). Microform Rev.

--Microform Review: Index 1972-1976, 5 vols. 1976. 35.00x (ISBN 0-913672-10-6). Microform Rev.

--Micropublishers' Trade List Annual 1977. rev. ed. 1977. 80.00x (ISBN 0-913672-19-X). Microform Rev.

Subject Guide to Microforms in Print 1976. rev ed. LC 62-21624. 1976. pap. text ed. 15.00x (ISBN 0-913672-08-4). Microform Rev.

Swanson, Edward, compiled by. A Manual of AACR 2 Examples for Microforms. 50p. 1981. pap. 6.00 (ISBN 0-936996-09-9). Soldier Creek.

Teague, S. J. Microform Librarianship. 2nd ed. (Illus.). 1979. 19.95 (ISBN 0-408-70930-8). Butterworth.

Veaner, Allen B. Studies in Micropublishing: 1853-1976. 440p. 1977. 24.50x (ISBN 0-913672-07-6). Microform Rev.

Veaner, Allen B. & Meckler, Alan M., eds. International Microforms in Print: A Guide to Microforms of Non-United States Micropublishers 1974-1975. 105p. 1974. pap. text ed. 10.00x (ISBN 0-913672-01-7). Microform Rev.

Walsh, John, ed. Guide to Microforms in Print: Supplement 1979. 1979. lib. bdg. 25.00x (ISBN 0-913672-32-7). Microform Rev.

Walsh, John J. Guide to Microforms in Print: Author-Title 1979. rev ed. LC 61-7082. 1979. 49.50x (ISBN 0-913672-30-0). Microform Rev.

Walsh, John J., ed. Guide to Microforms in Print: Author-Title 1978 (Incorporating International Microforms in Print) rev. ed. LC 71-7082. 1978. 49.50x (ISBN 0-913672-23-8). Microform Rev.

--Guide to Microforms in Print: Subject 1979. rev ed. LC 62-21624. 1979. 49.50x (ISBN 0-913672-31-9). Microform Rev.

--Guide to Microforms in Print: Subject 1978 (Incorporating International Microforms in Print) rev. ed. LC 62-21624. 1978. 49.50x (ISBN 0-913672-24-6). Microform Rev.

Walsh, John J, ed. Guide to Microforms in Print 1977. rev. ed. LC 61-7082. 1977. 35.00x (ISBN 0-913672-13-0). Microform Rev.

Walsh, John J., ed. Subject Guide to Microforms in Print 1977. rev. ed. LC 62-21624. 1977. 35.00x (ISBN 0-913672-14-9). Microform Rev.

Walsh, Patricia M., ed. Serials Management & Microforms. LC 78-13179. (Library Micrographics Management Ser.: No. 4). 1979. 21.50x (ISBN 0-913672-11-4). Microform Rev.

MICROGRAPHIC ANALYSIS

see Metallography; Microscope and Microscopy

MICROMANOMETER

see Manometer

MICROMETEOROLOGY

Goudriaan, J. Crop Micrometeorology: A Simulation Study. (Simulation Monographs). 1977. pap. 30.00 (ISBN 90-220-0614-X, Pub. by PUDOC). Unipub.

Pagen, Dennis. Flying Conditions. rev. ed. (Illus.). 124p. (Orig.). 1979. pap. 6.95 (ISBN 0-936310-03-0). Black Mntn.

Smith, L. P., ed. The Application of Micrometeorology to Agricultural Problems. (Technical Note Ser.: No. 119). 74p. (Orig.). 1972. pap. 10.00 (ISBN 0-685-25258-2, 298, WMO). Unipub.

Sutton, O. G. Micrometeorology: A Study of Physical Processes in the Lowest Layers of the Earth's Atmosphere. LC 76-56803. (Illus.). 346p. 1977. Repr. of 1953 ed. lib. bdg. 15.00 (ISBN 0-88275-488-2). Krieger.

MICROMINIATURIZATION (ELECTRONICS)

see Microelectronics; Miniature Electronic Equipment

MICRONESIA

Alkire, William H. An Introduction to the Peoples & Cultures of Micronesia. LC 76-7650. 1977. pap. 4.95 (ISBN 0-8465-0279-8). Benjamin-Cummings.

Anderson, Atholl. Birds of a Feather: Osteological & Archaeological Papers from the South Pacific in Honor of R. J. Scarlett. 1979. 55.00x (ISBN 0-86054-062-6, Pub. by BAR). State Mutual Bk.

Barclay, Glen. A History of the Pacific. LC 78-51996. 1978. 14.95 (ISBN 0-8008-3902-1). Taplinger.

Caldwell, John C. Let's Visit Micronesia: Trust Territory of the Pacific Islands. LC 76-84730. (Let's Visit Ser). (Illus.). (gr. 3-7). 1969. PLB 7.89 (ISBN 0-381-99885-1, A43050, JD-J). Har-Row.

Clyde, Paul H. Japan's Pacific Mandate. LC 67-27586. Repr. of 1935 ed. 11.50 (ISBN 0-8046-0081-3). Kennikat.

De Smith, Stanley A. Microstates & Micronesia: The Problems of America's Pacific Islands & Other Minute Territories. LC 74-92526. (Studies in Peaceful Change: Vol. 4). (Illus.). 1970. 10.00x (ISBN 0-8147-0118-3). NYU Pr.

Edmonds, I. G. Micronesia: Pebbles in the Sea. LC 73-22689. 1974. 6.95 (ISBN 0-672-51815-5). Bobbs.

Fanning, Edmund. Voyages to the South Seas & to the Northwest Coast of America. enl. ed. 1970. Repr. of 1838 ed. 14.95 (ISBN 0-87770-012-5). Ye Galleon.

Faulkner, Douglas. This Living Reef. LC 73-92293. (Illus.). 196p. 1974. 27.50 (ISBN 0-8129-0455-9). Times Bks.

Gale, Roger W. The Americanization of Micronesia: A Study of the Consolidation of the U. S. Role in the Pacific. LC 78-68800. 1979. pap. text ed. 12.00 (ISBN 0-8191-0703-4). U Pr of Amer.

Heine, Carl. Micronesia at the Crossroads: A Reappraisal of the Micronesian Political Dilemma. LC 73-78977. 256p. 1974. 12.00x (ISBN 0-8248-0273-X, Eastwest Ctr); pap. 2.95 (ISBN 0-8248-0278-0). U Pr of Hawaii.

Hughes, Daniel T. & Lingenfelter, Sherwood, eds. Political Development in Micronesia. LC 74-8161. (Illus.). 1974. 15.00 (ISBN 0-8142-0197-0). Ohio St U Pr.

Johnson, Margaret & Johnson, Roy. Life & Legends of Micronesia. (Illus.). 104p. 1980. 7.50 (ISBN 0-930230-40-X). Johnson NC.

Lewis, David. We, the Navigators: The Ancient Art of Landfinding in the Pacific. LC 72-82139. (Illus.). 368p. 1975. pap. 5.95 (ISBN 0-8248-0394-9). U Pr of Hawaii.

McHenry, Donald F. Micronesia: Trust Betrayed. LC 75-42570. 276p. 1975. 10.00 (ISBN 0-87003-000-0). Carnegie Endow.

Marshall, Mac. Weekend Warriors: Alcohol in a Micronesian Culture. Edgerton, Robert B. & Langness, L. L., eds. LC 78-64597. (Explorations in World Ethnology Ser.). 1979. pap. 6.95 (ISBN 0-87484-455-X). Mayfield Pub.

Marshall, Mac & Nason, James D. Micronesia 1944-1974: A Bibliography of Anthropological & Related Source Materials. LC 75-28587. (Behavior Science Bibliographies Ser). 348p. 1975. 18.00x (ISBN 0-87536-215-X). HRAFP.

Morrell, Benjamin, Jr. A Narrative of Four Voyages to the South Sea, Eighteen Twenty-Two to Eighteen Thirty-One. 492p. 1970. Repr. of 1832 ed. 35.00 (ISBN 0-8398-1268-X). Parnassus Imprints.

Nufer, Harold F. Micronesia Under American Rule: An Evaluation of the Strategic Trusteeship 1947-77. 1978. 15.00 (ISBN 0-682-49021-0, University). Exposition.

O'Brien, Frederick. Mystic Isles of the South Seas. 1978. Repr. of 1921 ed. lib. bdg. 25.00 (ISBN 0-8492-2042-4). R West.

--White Shadows in the South Seas. 1920. 20.00 (ISBN 0-685-72769-6). Norwood Edns.

Pinchot, Gifford. To the South Seas; the Cruise of the Schooner Mary Pinchot to the Galapogos, the Marquesas, & the Tuamotu Islands, & Tahiti. LC 70-174094. (Illus.). xiv, 500p. 1972. Repr. of 1930 ed. 28.00 (ISBN 0-8103-3933-1). Gale.

Tetens, Alfred. Among the Savages of the South Seas: Memoirs of Micronesia, 1862-1868. Spoehr, Florence M., tr. from Ger. LC 58-6708. (Illus.). 1958. 10.00x (ISBN 0-8047-0518-6). Stanford U Pr.

Waldo, Myra. Myra Waldo's Travel Guide to the South Pacific, 1981. (Illus.). 360p. 1981. pap. 8.95 (ISBN 0-02-098920-2, Collier). Macmillan.

Yanaihara, Tadao. Pacific Islands Under Japanese Mandate. LC 75-41304. (Institute of Pacific Relations). 1977. Repr. of 1940 ed. 27.50 (ISBN 0-404-14636-8). AMS Pr.

--Pacific Islands Under Japanese Mandate. LC 76-18921. (Institute of Pacific Relations: International Research Ser). (Illus.). 312p. 1976. Repr. of 1940 ed. lib. bdg. 21.00x (ISBN 0-8371-8667-6, YAPI). Greenwood.

MICRONESIAN ART

see Art, Micronesian

MICRONESIAN LANGUAGES

see also Chamorro Language; Malayan Languages; Marshall Language; Melanesian Languages

Jensen, John T., et al. Yapese-English Dictionary. LC 76-47495. (Pali Language Texts: Micronesia). (Orig.). 1977. pap. text ed. 7.50x (ISBN 0-8248-0517-8). U Pr of Hawaii.

--Yapese Reference Grammar. LC 76-40952. (PALI Language Texts: Micronesia). (Orig.). 1977. pap. text ed. 15.00x (ISBN 0-8248-0476-7). U Pr of Hawaii.

Lee, Kee-Dong. Kusaiean Reference Grammar. LC 75-6863. (PALI Language Texts: Micronesia). 554p. 1975. pap. text ed. 14.50x (ISBN 0-8248-0355-8). U Pr of Hawaii.

Sohn, Ho-Min. Woleaian Reference Grammar. (PALI Language Texts: Micronesia). 336p. (Orig.). 1975. pap. text ed. 12.50x (ISBN 0-8248-0356-6). U Pr of Hawaii.

MICRO-ORGANISMS

see also Bacteria; Fungi; Microbiology; Microscope and Microscopy; Protozoa; Soil Micro-Organisms; Viruses

Acker, Robert F. & Schaechter, Moselio, eds. Patentability of Microorganisms: Issues & Questions. 66p. (Orig.). 1981. pap. text ed. 6.00 (ISBN 0-914826-36-0). Am Soc Microbio.

Alexander, M., ed. Advances in Microbial Ecology, Vol. 4. 330p. 1980. 31.50 (ISBN 0-306-40493-1, Plenum Pr). Plenum Pub.

Bergersen, F. J., ed. Methods for Evaluating Biological Nitrogen Fixation. LC 79-41785. 702p. 1980. 114.00 (ISBN 0-471-27759-2, Pub. by Wiley-Interscience). Wiley.

Brieger, E. M. Structure & Ultrastructure of Microorganisms. 1963. 43.00 (ISBN 0-12-134350-2). Acad Pr.

Brock, Th. D. Thermophilic Microorganisms & Life at High Temperatures. LC 78-6110. (Springer Ser. in Microbiology). (Illus.). 1978. 29.80 (ISBN 0-387-90309-7). Springer-Verlag.

Brock, Thomas D. Biology of Microorganisms. 3rd ed. LC 78-13707. 1979. text ed. 26.95 (ISBN 0-13-076778-6). P-H.

Burges, H. D., ed. Microbial Control of Pests & Plant Diseases, 1970 to 1980. 960p. 1981. 99.50 (ISBN 0-12-143360-9). Acad Pr.

Cairns, John, Jr., ed. Aquatic Microbial Communities. (LC 76-052711). 1977. lib. bdg. 60.00 (ISBN 0-8240-9860-9, Garland STPM Pr). Garland Pub.

Cold Spring Harbor Symposia On Quantitative Biology. Heredity & Variation in Microorganisms: Proceedings, Vol. 11. Repr. of 1946 ed. 22.00 (ISBN 0-384-22475-X). Johnson Repr.

Dawes, I. W. & Sutherland, I. W. Microbial Physiology. (Basic Microbiology Ser.: Vol. 4). 1976. pap. text ed. 16.95 (ISBN 0-470-15159-5). Halsted Pr.

De Kruif, Paul. Microbe Hunters. LC 67-34588. 1966. pap. 3.25 (ISBN 0-15-659413-7, Harv). HarBraceJ.

Dixon, Bernard. Magnificent Microbes. LC 75-14678. 1979. pap. 4.95 (ISBN 0-689-70589-1, 250). Atheneum.

Egami, F. & Nakamura, K. Microbial Ribonucleases. LC 68-8784. (Molecular Biology, Bichemistry, & Biophysics Ser.: Vol. 6). 1969. 20.90 (ISBN 0-387-04657-7). Springer-Verlag.

Eisenstein, Edward M., ed. Aneural Organisms. LC 74-28345. (Advances in Behavioral Biology Ser.: Vol. 13). 145p. 1975. 25.00 (ISBN 0-306-37913-9, Plenum Pr). Plenum Pub.
Food & Nutrition Board, National Research Council. Prevention of Microbial & Parasitic Hazard Associated with Processed Foods: A Guide for the Food Processor. 1975. pap. 5.75 (ISBN 0-309-02345-9). Natl Acad Pr.
Fuller, R., ed. Microbial Ultrastructure. 1977. 54.50 (ISBN 0-12-269450-3). Acad Pr.
Garbutt, J. W. & Bartlett, A. J. Experimental Biology with Micro-Organisms. 1972. pap. text ed. 4.95 (ISBN 0-408-70228-1); teachers' guide 12.95 (ISBN 0-408-70240-0). Butterworth.
Giesy, John P., ed. Microcosms in Ecological Esearch: Proceedings. LC 80-23472. (DOE Symposium Ser.). 1980. 27.50 (ISBN 0-686-75572-3). DOE.
Haddock, B. A. & Hamilton, W. A., eds. Microbial Energetics. LC 76-54367. (Society for General Microbiology: Symposium 27). (Illus.). 1977. 65.00 (ISBN 0-521-21494-7). Cambridge U Pr.
Hammond. Antibiotics & Antimicrobial Action. (Studies in Biology: No. 90). 1978. 5.95 (ISBN 0-7131-2684-1). Univ Park.
Hawker, Lilian A. & Linton, Alan H., eds. Micro-Organisms. 400p. 1979. pap. text ed. 24.95 (ISBN 0-8391-1308-0). Univ Park.
Heden, Carl-Goran & Illeni, Tibor, eds. New Approaches to the Identification of Microorganisms. LC 74-11484. 466p. 1975. 36.25 (ISBN 0-471-36746-X, Pub. by Wiley). Krieger.
Heinrich, Milton R., ed. Extreme Environments: Mechanisms of Microbial Adaptation. 1976. 34.50 (ISBN 0-12-337850-8). Acad Pr.
Hollaender, Alexander, ed. Genetic Engineering for Nitrogen Fixation. LC 77-8998. (Basic Life Sciences Ser.: Vol. 9). 538p. 1977. 37.50 (ISBN 0-306-36509-X, Plenum Pr). Plenum Pub.
Hugo, W. B., ed. Inhibition & Destruction of the Microbial Cell. 1971. 119.50 (ISBN 0-12-361150-4). Acad Pr.
Iizuka, Hiroshi, ed. Culture Collection of Microoganisms. (Illus.). 1970. 35.00 (ISBN 0-8391-0018-3). Univ Park.
International Commission on Microbiological Specifications for Foods. Microorganisms in Foods: Their Significance & Methods of Enumeration, Vol. 1. 2nd ed. LC 77-17842. 1978. 30.00x (ISBN 0-8020-2293-6). U of Toronto Pr.
Ishikawa, T. Growth & Differentiation in Microorganisms. 1977. 52.50 (ISBN 0-8391-1134-7). Univ Park.
Jennings, Robert K. & Acker, Robert F. Protistan Kingdom: Protists & Viruses. 1970. pap. text ed. 4.95x (ISBN 0-442-24134-8). Van Nos Reinhold.
Johnson, Leander F. & Curl, Elroy. Methods for Research on the Ecology of Soil-Borne Plant Pathogens. LC 77-176196. 1972. text ed. 24.95x (ISBN 0-8087-1016-8). Burgess.
Kuznetsov, S. I., ed. Geologic Activity of Microorganisms. LC 62-12850. 112p. 1962. 30.00 (ISBN 0-306-10537-3, Consultants). Plenum Pub.
Leiva, Manuel R. Relacion Hospedante-Parasito Mecanismo De Patogenicidad De los Microorganismos. (Serie Biologia: No. 14). 91p. 1981. pap. 2.00 (ISBN 0-8270-1322-1). OAS.
Lloyd, David. The Mitochondria of Microorganisms. 1975. 90.00 (ISBN 0-12-453650-6). Acad Pr.
Loutit, M. W. & Miles, J. A., eds. Microbial Ecology. LC 78-14480. (Proceedings in Life Sciences). (Illus.). 1978. 41.40 (ISBN 0-387-08974-8). Springer-Verlag.
Martinsson, Anders. Evolution & Morphology of the Trilobita, Trilobitoidea, & Merostomata. 1975. pap. 70.00x (ISBN 82-00-04963-9, Dist. by Columbia U Pr). Universitet.
Microorganic Matter in Water. 1969. pap. 9.25 (ISBN 0-8031-0066-3, 04-448000-16). ASTM.
Microorganismos. (Serie De Biologia: No. 6). (Span.). 1968. pap. 1.25 (ISBN 0-8270-6065-3). OAS.
O'Day, D. H. & Horgen, P. A., eds. Sexual Interactions in Eukaryotic Microbes. LC 80-39593. (Cell Biology Ser.). 1981. 45.00 (ISBN 0-12-524160-7). Acad Pr.
Olds, R. J. Color Atlas of Microbiology. (Year Book Color Atlas Ser.). (Illus.). 288p. 1975. 31.00 (ISBN 0-8151-6542-0). Year Bk Med.
Overbeck, Juergen, et al, eds. Proceedincs of the Workshop on Measurement of Microbial Activities in the Carbon Cycle of Freshwaters: Proceedings. (Ergabnisse der Limonogie: Vol. 12). (Illus.). 170p. (Orig.). 1979. pap. 45.00x (ISBN 3-510-47010-9). Intl Pubns Serv.
Payne, J. W. Microorganisms & Nitrogen Sources Transport & Utilization of Amino Acids Peptides, Proteins & Related Subjects. LC 79-42900. 870p. 1980. 135.00 (ISBN 0-471-27697-9). Wiley.
Peppler, Henry J. & Perlman, David, eds. Microbial Technology, Vol. 1: Microbial Processes. 2nd ed. LC 78-67883. 1979. 50.50 (ISBN 0-12-551501-4). Acad Pr.
Rainbow, Cyril & Rose, A. H., eds. Biochemistry of Industrial Microorganisms. 1964. 91.50 (ISBN 0-12-576050-7). Acad Pr.
Reissig, J. L., ed. Receptors & Recognition, Ser. B, Vol. 3: Microbial Interactions. LC 77-22325. 1977. text ed. 39.95x (ISBN 0-412-14310-0, Pub. by Chapman & Hall England). Methuen Inc.
Rose, A. H., ed. Advances in Microbial Physiology. Incl. Vol. 11. 1974. 51.00 (ISBN 0-12-027711-5); Vol. 12. 1975. 58.00 (ISBN 0-12-027712-3); Vol. 13. 1976. 52.00 (ISBN 0-12-027713-1). (Serial Publication). Acad Pr.
--Economic Microbiology, Vol. 5: Microbial Enzymes & Transformations. 1981. 121.00 (ISBN 0-12-596555-9). Acad Pr.
Rose, A. H. & Morris, Gareth, eds. Advances in Microbial Physiology, Vol. 21. LC 67-19850. (Serial Publication). 1981. 64.50 (ISBN 0-12-027721-2). Acad Pr.
Rose, A. H., et al, eds. Advances in Microbial Physiology. Incl. Vol. 1. 1967; Vol. 2. 1968. 34.50 (ISBN 0-12-027702-6); Vol. 3. 1969. 40.00 (ISBN 0-12-027703-4); Vol. 4. 1970. 56.50 (ISBN 0-12-027704-2); Vol. 5. 1970. 45.00 (ISBN 0-12-027705-0); Vol. 6. 1971. 58.50 (ISBN 0-12-027706-9); Vol. 7. Rose, A. H. & Tempest, D. W., eds. 1972. 48.00 (ISBN 0-12-027707-7); Vol. 8. 1972. 43.50 (ISBN 0-12-027708-5); Vol. 9. 1973. 40.50 (ISBN 0-12-027709-3); Vol. 10. 1973. 48.00 (ISBN 0-12-027710-7); Vol. 14. 1977. 66.00 (ISBN 0-12-027714-X); Vol. 15. 1977. 71.00 (ISBN 0-12-027715-8); Vol. 16. 1978. 52.00 (ISBN 0-12-027716-6); Vol. 17. 1978. 63.50 (ISBN 0-12-027717-4). Acad Pr.
Rossmoore, Harold W. Microbes, Our Unseen Friends. LC 76-17795. 1976. 12.95 (ISBN 0-8143-1561-5); pap. 4.95 (ISBN 0-8143-1602-6). Wayne St U Pr.
Schlegel, H. G. Microbial Energy Conversion. LC 76-56894. 1977. pap. text ed. 81.00 (ISBN 0-08-021791-5). Pergamon.
Sebek, O. K. & Laskin, A. I., eds. Genetics of Industrial Microorganisms. (Illus.). 1979. 12.00 (ISBN 0-914826-19-0). Am Soc Microbio.
Shilo, Moshe, ed. Strategies of Microbial Life in Extreme Environments, LSRR 13. (Dahlem Workshop Reports Ser.: L.S.R.R. No. 13). 1979. pap. 42.40 (ISBN 0-89573-082-0). Verlag Chemie.
Stanier, R. & Doudoroff, M. The Microbial World. 4th ed. (Illus.). 1976. ref. ed. 28.95x (ISBN 0-13-581025-6). P-H.
Waste Recovery by Micro-Organisms. 1978. pap. 13.25 (ISBN 0-685-65236-X, UM 36, UNESCO). Unipub.
Weinberg, E. D. Microorganisms & Minerals. (Microbiology Ser.: Vol. 3). 1977. 54.50 (ISBN 0-8247-6581-8). Dekker.
Weiner, Jack. Microorganism Control. LC 76-57836. (Bibliographic Ser.: No. 276). 1977. pap. 23.00 (ISBN 0-87010-051-3). Inst Paper Chem.
Whitney, P. J. Microbial Plant Pathology. LC 76-20406. (Studies in the Biological Sciences Ser.). (Illus.). 1977. 12.50x (ISBN 0-87663-722-5). Universe.

MICRO-ORGANISMS–JUVENILE LITERATURE

Anderson, Lucia. The Smallest Life Around Us. LC 77-15858. (Illus.). (gr. 2-4). 1978. reinforced lib. bdg. 7.95 (ISBN 0-517-53227-1). Crown.
Binet, Alfred. Psychic Life of Micro-Organisms. 1971. Repr. 6.00x (ISBN 0-87556-025-3). Saifer.
Patent, Dorothy H. Microscopic Animals & Plants. LC 74-7575. (Illus.). 160p. (gr. 4-6). 1974. 8.95 (ISBN 0-8234-0247-9). Holiday.

MICRO-ORGANISMS, EFFECT OF DRUGS ON

Barry, Arthur L. The Antimicrobic Susceptibility Test: Principles & Practices. LC 76-18846. (Illus.). 236p. 1976. text ed. 11.00 (ISBN 0-8121-0530-3). Lea & Febiger.
Bondi, et al, eds. The Clinical Lab As an Aid in Chemotherapy of Infectious Diseases. 1977. 19.50 (ISBN 0-8391-0967-9). Univ Park.
Schnitzer, Robert J. & Grunberg, Emanuel. Drug Resistance of Microorganisms. 1957. 37.50 (ISBN 0-12-628450-4). Acad Pr.

MICRO-ORGANISMS, PATHOGENIC

see also Medical Microbiology

Burges, H. D. & Hussey, N. W. Microbial Control of Insects & Mites. 1970. 82.00 (ISBN 0-12-143350-1). Acad Pr.
Day, Stacey B., et al, eds. Miscellaneous Papers of the Bell Museum of Pathobiology. LC 73-91360. (Orig.). 1973. pap. 2.50 (ISBN 0-912922-05-2). U of Minn Bell.
Dickinson, C. H. & Lucas, J. A. Plant Pathology & Plant Pathogens. LC 77-8689. (Basic Microbiology Ser.: Vol. 6). 1977. pap. 13.95 (ISBN 0-470-99212-3). Halsted Pr.
Finegold, Sydney M., et al. Bailey & Scott's Diagnostic Microbiology: A Textbook for the Isolation & Identification of Pathogenic Microorganisms. 5th ed. LC 77-28251. (Illus.). 1978. text ed. 25.95 (ISBN 0-8016-0421-4). Mosby.
Lovell, Reginald. Aetiology of Infective Diseases: With Special Reference to the Subsidiary & Important Non-Specific Factors. viii, 136p. 1959. 3.50x (ISBN 0-87013-041-2). Mich St U Pr.
Schuhardt, Vernon T. Pathogenic Microbiology: The Biology & Prevention of Selected Bacterial, Fungal, Rickettsial, & Viral Diseases of Clinical Importance. 1978. (JBL-Med-Nursing); pap. text ed. 15.25x (ISBN 0-397-47370-2). Har-Row.
Smith, H. & Pearce, J. H., eds. Microbial Pathogenicity in Man & Animals: Proceedings. LC 75-177940. (Illus.). 1972. 50.50 (ISBN 0-521-08430-X). Cambridge U Pr.
Zadoks, Jan C. & Schein, Richard D. Epidemiology & Plant Disease Management. (Illus.). 1979. text ed. 22.95x (ISBN 0-19-502451-6); pap. text ed. 10.95x (ISBN 0-19-502452-4). Oxford U Pr.

MICROPALEONTOLOGY

Funnell, B. M. & Riedel, W. R. Micropalaeontology of Oceans. 1971. 145.00 (ISBN 0-521-07642-0). Cambridge U Pr.
Haq, B. U. & Boersma, A. Introduction to Marine Micropaleontology. 1978. 24.50 (ISBN 0-444-00267-7, North Holland). Elsevier.
Pierce, Richard L. Lower Upper Cretaceous Plant Microfossils from Minnesota. LC 61-64045. (Bulletin: No. 42). (Illus.). 1961. 3.75x (ISBN 0-8166-0257-3). Minn Geol Survey.
Ramsay, A. T. Oceanic Micropalaeontology, Vol. 1. 1977. 120.00 (ISBN 0-12-577301-3). Acad Pr.
Swain, F. M., ed. Stratigraphic Micropaleontology of Atlantic Basin & Borderlands. (Developments in Paleontology & Stratigraphy). 1977. 66.00 (ISBN 0-444-41554-8). Elsevier.
Takayanagi, Yokichi & Saito, Tsunemasa, eds. Progress in Micropaleontology. LC 76-370684. 1976. 35.00 (ISBN 0-913424-08-0); ltd. ed 58.00 (ISBN 0-685-65402-8). Am Mus Natl Hist.
Tappan, Helen. The Paleobiology of Plant Protists. LC 80-14675. (Geology Ser.). (Illus.). 1980. text ed. 95.00x (ISBN 0-7167-1109-5). W H Freeman.

MICROPHONE

Clifford, Martin. Microphones: How They Work & How to Use Them. LC 77-79349. (Illus.). 1977. 10.95 (ISBN 0-8306-7875-1); pap. 7.95 (ISBN 0-8306-6875-6, 875). TAB Bks.
Du Moncel, Theodore A. The Telephone, the Microphone, & the Phonograph. LC 74-4673. (Telecommunications Ser). (Illus.). 282p. 1974. Repr. of 1879 ed. 17.00x (ISBN 0-405-06039-4). Arno.
Eargle, John. The Microphone Handbook. 1981. 28.50 (ISBN 0-686-31835-8). Elar Pub Co.
Gayford, M. L. Electroacoustics. (STC Monograph Ser). 1971. 25.00 (ISBN 0-444-19649-8). Elsevier.
Nisbett, Alec. The Use of Microphones. (Media Manuals Ser.). 1974. pap. text ed. 9.95 (ISBN 0-240-50861-0). Focal Pr.
Wile, Frederic W. Emile Berliner: Maker of the Microphone. LC 74-4699. (Telecommunications Ser). (Illus.). 380p. 1974. Repr. of 1926 ed. 21.00x (ISBN 0-405-06062-9). Arno.

MICROPHOTOGRAPHY

Here are entered works on the photographing of objects of any size upon a microscopic or very small scale. To be distinguished from Photomicrography, the photographing of minute objects enlarged by means of the microscope.
see also Filmstrips; Reader-Printers (Microphotography)

Barrett, W. J. Thirty-Five mm Microfilming for Drawing Offices. (Reprographic Library). Date not set. 8.95 (ISBN 0-8038-7092-2). Hastings.
--Thirty-Five mm Microfilming for Drawing Offices. (Illus.). 135p. 1970. 7.95 (ISBN 0-240-50698-7). Focal Pr.
Hawkins, Reginald. Production of Micro-Forms. Shaw, Ralph, ed. & pref. by. LC 75-17838. (State of the Library Art Ser.: Vol. 5, Pt. 1). 208p. 1975. Repr. of 1960 ed. lib. bdg. 15.00 (ISBN 0-8371-8235-2, HAPM). Greenwood.
Mezher, Glen C. & Turner, Jeffrey H. Micrographic Film Technology: Roll-1979. (Illus.). 96p. 1979. 12.00 (ISBN 0-89258-059-3). Natl Micrograph.
National Micrographics Assn. All About Microfilm Cameras, No. C006, 1977. (Consumer Ser.). (Illus.). 1977. 5.00 (ISBN 0-686-63662-7). Natl Micrograph.
--Document Mark (Blip) Used in Image Mark Retrieval Systems: ANSI-NMA MS8-1979. 1980. 6.00 (ISBN 0-89258-060-7). Natl Micrograph.
--Format & Coding for Computer Output Microfilm: ANSI-NMA MS2-1978. 1978. 7.00 (ISBN 0-89258-054-2). Natl Micrograph.
--Guide to Micrographic Equipment: R015-1979. 7th ed. 1979. 25.00 (ISBN 0-89258-053-4). Natl Micrograph.
--Measuring COM Recording Speeds: MS21-1979. 1979. 5.00 (ISBN 0-89258-058-5). Natl Micrograph.
--Microfilming Newspapers: ANSI-NMA MS111-1977. 1978. 6.00 (ISBN 0-89258-050-X). Natl Micrograph.
--Practice for Uniform Product Disclosure for Unitized Microform Readers (Microfiche, Jackets & Image Cards) NMA MS22-1979. 1980. 5.00 (ISBN 0-89258-057-7). Natl Micrograph.
--Specifications for Sixteen & Thirty-Five Millimeter Microfilms in Roll Form: ASNI-NMA MS14-1978. 1978. 5.00- (ISBN 0-89258-052-6). Natl Micrograph.

MICROPROCESSORS

Adams. Master Handbook of Microprocessor Chips. 378p. 16.95 (ISBN 0-8306-1299-8); pap. 9.95 (ISBN 0-8306-1276-9, 1299). TAB Bks.
Adams, C. K. A Beginner's Guide to Computers & Microprocessors--with Projects. (Illus.). (gr. 10 up). 1978. 10.95 (ISBN 0-8306-9890-6); pap. 7.95 (ISBN 0-8306-1015-4, 1015). TAB Bks.
Agrawala, Ashok K. Foundations of Microprogramming: Architecture, Software & Applications. 1976. 27.50 (ISBN 0-12-045150-6). Acad Pr.
Andrews, Michael. Programming Microprocessor Interface for Control & Instrumentation. (Illus.). 368p. 1982. 26.95 (ISBN 0-13-597260-4). P-H.
Arnold, James T. Simplified Digital Automation with Microprocessors. LC 78-51242. 1979. 29.50 (ISBN 0-12-063750-2). Acad Pr.
Aspinall, D., ed. The Microprocessor & Its Application. LC 78-54572. (Illus.). 402p. 1980. pap. 14.95 (ISBN 0-521-29798-2). Cambridge U Pr.
--The Microprocessor & Its Application. LC 78-54572. (Illus.). 1978. 47.50 (ISBN 0-521-22241-9). Cambridge U Pr.
Aspinall, David & Dagless, Erik, eds. Introduction to Microprocessors. 1977. 19.00 (ISBN 0-12-064550-5). Acad Pr.
Aumiaux, M. The Use of Microprocessors. LC 79-42904. (Wiley Ser. in Computing). 198p. 1980. 36.00 (ISBN 0-471-27689-8, Pub. by Wiley Interscience). Wiley.
Auslander, David & Sagues, Paul. Microprocessors for Measurement & Control. 300p. (Orig.). 1981. pap. 15.99 (ISBN 0-931988-57-8). Osborne-McGraw.
Baldin, J. N. Microprocessors for Industry. 1981. text ed. price not set (ISBN 0-408-00517-3). Butterworth.
Banerji, Dilip & Raymond, Jacque. Elements of Microprogramming. (Illus.). 416p. 1982. text ed. 24.50 (ISBN 0-13-267146-8). P-H.
Barna, Arpad & Porat, Dan I. Introduction to Microcomputers & Microprocessors. LC 75-31675. 108p. 1976. 17.00 (ISBN 0-471-05051-2, Pub. by Wiley-Interscience). Wiley.
Barnaal, Dennis. Digital & Microprocessor Electronics for Scientific Application. 1981. pap. text ed. 13.95 (ISBN 0-534-01043-1, Breton Pubs). Wadsworth Pub.
Bibbero, Robert J. Microprocessors in Instruments & Control. LC 77-9929. 301p. 1977. 23.00 (ISBN 0-471-01595-4, Pub. by Wiley-Interscience). Wiley.
Bishop, Ron. Basic Microprocessors & Sixty-Eight Hundred. 1979. pap. 14.95 (ISBN 0-8104-0758-2). Hayden.
Bit-Slice. 500p. 59.95x (ISBN 0-686-74160-9). Sybex.
Bogart, Theodore F. LaPlace Transforms & Control Systems Theory for Technology, Including Microprocessor Control System. 592p. 1982. text ed. 22.95 (ISBN 0-471-09044-1); price not set solutions manual (ISBN 0-471-86325-4). Wiley.
Bowen & Behr. The Logical Design of Multiple Microprocessor Systems. (Illus.). 272p. 1980. text ed. 22.95 (ISBN 0-13-539908-4). P-H.
Boyce, Jefferson. Microprocessor & Microcomputer Basics. (Illus.). 1979. text ed. 18.95 (ISBN 0-13-581249-6). P-H.
--Microprocessor & Microcomputer Basics. (Illus.). 1979. text ed. 18.95 (ISBN 0-13-581249-6). P-H.
Boyet, Howard & Katz, Ron. MA-Two: Microprocessor Applications Experiments, Reference Book, Vol. 2. LC 79-12376. (Technibook Ser.). (Illus.). 1979. pap. text ed. 9.00 (ISBN 0-89704-027-9, 345-6003). E & L Instru.

--MA-Two: Microprocessor Applications Experiments, Vol. I. LC 79-12376. (Technibook Ser.). (Illus.). 1979. pap. text ed. 16.00 (ISBN 0-89704-026-0, 345-6002); Set. pap. text ed. 23.00 (ISBN 0-89704-028-7, 345-6003). E & L Instru.

Brunner, Herb. Introduction to Microprocessors. 1981. text ed. 17.95 (ISBN 0-8359-3247-8); instr's. manual free (ISBN 0-8359-3248-6). Reston.

Bursky, Dave. Microprocessor Systems Design & Applications. 192p. pap. 10.95 (ISBN 0-8104-0976-3). Hayden.

Burton, D. P. & Dexter, A. L. Microprocessor Systems Handbook. LC 77-88133. (Illus.). 1977. text ed. 9.50 (ISBN 0-916550-04-4). Analog Devices.

Camp, R. D., et al. Microprocessor Systems Engineering. 1979. 26.95 (ISBN 0-916460-26-6, Pub. by Matrix). Intl Schol Bk Serv.

Cannon, Don L. & Luecke, Gerald. Understanding Microprocessors. LC 78-57029. (Understanding Ser.). (Illus.). 288p. (Orig.). 1979. pap. 4.95 (ISBN 0-89512-021-6, LCB 4023). Tex Instr Inc.

Chalmers, R. A. Microprocessors in Analytical Chemistry, Vol. 27, No. 7b. 64p. 1981. pap. 23.00 (ISBN 0-08-026284-8). Pergamon.

Chandor, Anthony. The Penguin Dictionary of Microprocessors. 192p. 1981. pap. 5.95 (ISBN 0-14-051100-8). Penguin.

Chattergy, Rahul & Pooch, Udo. Sixteen-Bit Microprocessors. 256p. 1982. text ed. 19.95 (ISBN 0-8359-7003-5). Reston.

Clementson, Alan & Clewett, A. J., eds. Management, Operational Research & the Micro. 96p. 1981. pap. 14.00 (ISBN 0-08-025842-5). Pergamon.

Coffron, J. Understanding & Troubleshooting the Microprocessors. 1980. 19.95 (ISBN 0-13-936625-3). P-H.

Coffron, James W. Practical Hardware Details for 8080, 8085, Z80, & 6800 Microprocessor Systems. (Illus.). 352p. 1981. text ed. 21.95 (ISBN 0-13-691089-0). P-H.

--Practical Troubleshooting for Microprocessors. (Illus.). 256p. 1981. text ed. 19.95 (ISBN 0-13-694273-3). P-H.

Cohn, David L. & Melsa, James L. A Step by Step Introduction to 8080 Microprocessor Systems. LC 77-21762. 1977. pap. 8.95 (ISBN 0-918398-04-5). Dilithium Pr.

Colin, Andrew. Programming for Microprocessors. 1979. text ed. 21.95 (ISBN 0-408-00320-0). Butterworth.

Cooper, J. Microprocessor Background for Management Personnel. 208p. 1981. 14.95 (ISBN 0-13-580829-4). P-H.

Crane, John. Laboratory Experiments for Microprocessor Systems. (Illus.). 192p. 1980. pap. text ed. 10.95 (ISBN 0-13-519694-9). P-H.

Davis, Thomas. Experimentation with Microprocessor Applications. (Orig.). 1980. pap. text ed. 10.95 (ISBN 0-8359-1812-2). Reston.

Debenham, Michael J. Microprocessors: An Introduction to the Principles & Applications. 1979. 21.00 (ISBN 0-08-024206-5); pap. 9.50 (ISBN 0-08-024207-3). Pergamon.

Designing a Microprocessor System. 2 cassettes 29.95x (ISBN 0-686-74156-0). Sybex.

Dollhuff, Terry. Sixteen-Bit Microprocessor Architecture. (Illus.). 1979. text ed. 24.95 (ISBN 0-8359-7001-9). Reston.

Duncan, F. Microprocessor Programming & Software Development. 1979. 29.95 (ISBN 0-13-581405-7). P-H.

Electronic Design. Microprocessor Basics. Elphick, Michael, ed. (Illus.). 1977. pap. 13.95 (ISBN 0-8104-5763-6). Hayden.

Electronics Magazine. Applying Microprocessors. Scrupski, Stephen E. & Altman, Laurence, eds. LC 76-30685. (Illus.). 191p. 1977. pap. text ed. 9.95 (ISBN 0-07-099705-5, R-701). McGraw.

--Microprocessors. Altman, Laurence, ed. (Illus.). 1975. pap. text ed. 8.95 (ISBN 0-07-019171-9, R-520). McGraw.

--Microprocessors. Aitman, L., ed. 1975. 23.50x (ISBN 0-07-019171-9, P&RB). McGraw.

--Microprocessors & Microcomputers: One-Chip Controllers to High-End Systems. Capece, Raymond P. & Posa, John G., eds. LC 80-11816. (Illus.). 484p. 1980. 24.50 (ISBN 0-07-019141-7, R-011); pap. text ed. 14.95 (ISBN 0-07-606670-3). McGraw.

Felsen, Jerry. Personal Computer Systems: Analysis, Design & Applications. LC 77-83511. Date not set. pap. text ed. 15.00 (ISBN 0-916376-02-8). CDS Pub.

Fiore, Vito, et al. Sixty-Eight Hundred Family Book. 1982. text ed. 14.95 (ISBN 0-8359-7005-1). Reston.

Fohl, F. C. A Microprocessor Course. 1979. 15.00 (ISBN 0-07-091039-1, P&RB). McGraw.

Fohl, Mark E. A Microprocessor Course. (Illus.). 218p. text ed. 15.00 (ISBN 0-89433-072-1). Petrocelli.

Forester, Tom, ed. The Microelectronics Revolution: The Complete Guide to the New Technology & Its Impact on Society. (Illus.). 608p. 1981. 25.00x (ISBN 0-262-06075-2); pap. 12.50 (ISBN 0-262-56021-6). MIT Pr.

Garland, Harry. Introduction to Microprocessor System Design. (Illus.). 1979. pap. text ed. 13.00 (ISBN 0-07-022870-1, C). McGraw.

Garrett, Patrick H. Analog Systems for Microprocessors & Minicomputers. (Illus.). 1978. 19.50 (ISBN 0-87909-035-9); instructor's manual free. Reston.

Ghani, Noordin & Farrell, Edward. Microprocessor System Debugging. LC 80-40950. (Computer Engineering Ser.). 143p. 1981. 43.50 (ISBN 0-471-27860-2, Pub. by Wiley-Interscience). Wiley.

Gilmore, Charles M. Beginner's Guide to Microprocessors. (Illus.). 1977. 8.95 (ISBN 0-8306-7995-2); pap. 5.95 (ISBN 0-8306-6995-7, 995). TAB Bks.

--Introduction to Microprocessors. LC 80-26115. (Basic Skills in Electricity & Electronics). 320p. 1981. pap. 14.96 (ISBN 0-07-023301-2); lab manual 8.96 (ISBN 0-07-023302-0). McGraw.

Gise, Peter. Microprocessor Interfacing. 288p. 1982. text ed. 19.95 (ISBN 0-8359-4364-X). Reston.

Givone, Donald D. & Roesser, Robert P. Microprocessors - Microcomputers: An Introduction. (Illus.). 1979. text ed. 22.95 (ISBN 0-07-023326-8); solns. manual 4.95 (ISBN 0-07-023327-6). McGraw.

Goldsbrough, Paul. Technibook IV: Microprocessor Interfacing with the 8255 PPI Chip with Experiments. Blacksburg Group, ed. LC 79-63864. (Technibook Ser.). pap. text ed. 8.50 (ISBN 0-89704-006-6). E & L Instru.

Goodman, Robert L. Troubleshooting Microprocessors & Digital Logic. (Illus., Orig.). 1980. 13.95 (ISBN 0-8306-9950-3); pap. 8.95 (ISBN 0-8306-1183-5, 1183). TAB Bks.

Graham, Neil. Microprocessor Programming for Computer Hobbyists. (Illus.). 1977. 12.95x (ISBN 0-8306-7952-9); pap. 8.95x (ISBN 0-8306-6952-3, 952). TAB Bks.

Greenfield, Joseph D. Using Microprocessors & Microcomputers: The 6800 Family. LC 80-18090. (Electronic Technology Ser.). 512p. 1981. text ed. 22.95 (ISBN 0-471-02727-8). Wiley.

Hall, Douglas V. & Hall, Marybelle B. Experiments in Microprocessors & Digital Systems. (Illus.). 176p. 1981. 7.95x (ISBN 0-07-025576-8, G). McGraw.

Hanna, F. K. Advanced Techniques for Micro-Processor Systems. (Illus.). 1980. 36.00 (ISBN 0-906048-31-1). Inst Elect Eng.

Hartley, M. G. & Buckley, S., eds. The Challenge of Microprocessors: Selected Readings for Engineering Educators. 208p. 1979. 33.00x (ISBN 0-7190-0757-7, Pub. by Manchester U Pr England). State Mutual Bk.

Hartmann, A. C. A Concurrent Pascal Compiler for Minicomputers. Goos, G. & Hartmanis, J., eds. (Lecture Notes in Computer Science Ser.: Vol. 50). 1977. soft cover 8.40 (ISBN 0-387-08240-9). Springer-Verlag.

Healey, Martin. Minicomputers & Microprocessors. LC 76-11606. 1976. pap. 19.50x (ISBN 0-8448-0970-5). Crane-Russak Co.

Heffer, D. E. & King, G. A. Basic Principles & Practice of Microprocessors. 192p. 1981. 19.95 (ISBN 0-470-27164-7). Halsted Pr.

Heiserman, David L. Miniprocessors: From Calculators to Computers. 1978. pap. 8.95 (ISBN 0-8306-6971-X, 971). TAB Bks.

Hemenway, Jack E. RA Sixty Eight Hundred ML: An M6800 Relocatable Macro Assembler. LC 78-22084. (Illus.). 1979. pap. 25.00 (ISBN 0-07-582022-6, BYTE Bks). McGraw.

Hilburn, J. L. & Julich, P. Microcomputers - Microprocessors: Hardware, Software & Applications. 1976. text ed. 25.95 (ISBN 0-13-580969-X). P-H.

Hohenstein, C. Louis. Computer Peripherals for Minicomputers, Microprocessos & Personal Computers. (Illus.). 320p. 1980. 19.50 (ISBN 0-07-029451-8, P&RB). McGraw.

Hordeski, Michael F. Microprocessor Cookbook. (Illus.). 1979. 12.95 (ISBN 0-8306-9778-0); pap. 6.95 (ISBN 0-8306-1053-7, 1053). TAB Bks.

Industrial Microprocessor System. 500p. 59.95x (ISBN 0-686-74161-7). Sybex.

Intel Marketing Communications. The Eighty Eighty-Eighty Eighty-Five Microprocessor Book. LC 78-16936. (Intel Ser.). 1980. 22.50 (ISBN 0-471-03568-8, Pub. by Wiley-Interscience). Wiley.

Introduction to Microprocessors. 2 cassettes 29.95x (ISBN 0-686-74154-4). Sybex.

Katzan, Harry. Microprogramming Primer. Feigenbaum, Edward, ed. (Computer Science Ser). (Illus.). 1977. text ed. 22.95 (ISBN 0-07-033387-4, C); instructor's manual 4.95 (ISBN 0-07-033388-2). McGraw.

Kershaw, John D. Microprocessor Technology. 1980. text ed. 19.95x (ISBN 0-534-00748-1, Breton Pubs). Wadsworth Pub.

Khambata, Adi J. Microprocessors-Microcomputers: Architecture, Software & Systems. 672p. 1982. text ed. 19.95 (ISBN 0-471-06490-4). Wiley.

Klingman, Ed. Microprocessor Systems Design. LC 76-45190. (Illus.). 1977. 27.95 (ISBN 0-13-581413-8). P-H.

Kraft, George D. & Toy, Wing N. Microprogrammed Control & Reliable Design of Small Computers. (Illus.). 248p. 1981. text ed. 23.95 (ISBN 0-13-581140-6). P-H.

Krieger, Morris, et al. Structured Microprocessor Programming. LC 79-67229. (Illus., Orig.). 1979. pap. 20.00 (ISBN 0-917072-18-9). Yourdon.

Krutz, Ronald L. Microprocessors & Logic Design. LC 79-17874. 467p. 1980. text ed. 27.95 (ISBN 0-471-02083-4). Wiley.

Kuecken, John A. Handbook of Microprocessor Applications. (Illus.). 308p. (Orig.). 1980. 14.95 (ISBN 0-8306-9935-X); pap. 8.95 (ISBN 0-8306-1203-3). Tab Bks.

Leahy, William F. Microprocessor Architecture & Programming. LC 77-1552. 237p. 1977. 28.50 (ISBN 0-471-01889-9, Pub. by Wiley-Interscience). Wiley.

Lenk, John D. Handbook of Microprocessors, Microcomputers & Minicomputers. (Illus.). 1979. text ed. 20.95 (ISBN 0-13-380378-3). P-H.

--Handbook of Microprocessors, Microcomputers & Minicomputers. (Illus.). 1979. text ed. 20.95 (ISBN 0-13-380378-3). P-H.

Leventhal, Lance A. Introduction to Microprocessors: Software, Hardware, Programming. LC 78-7800. (Illus.). 1978. ref. ed. 28.95 (ISBN 0-13-487868-X). P-H.

--The Six-Eight Hundred Microprocessor: A Self-Study Course with Applications. (gr. 10 up). 1978. pap. text ed. 9.55 (ISBN 0-8104-5120-4). Hayden.

Lin, Wen C., ed. Microprocessors: Fundamentals & Applications. (IEEE Press Selected Reprint Ser.). 1977. text ed. 26.95 (ISBN 0-471-03115-1); pap. text ed. 17.50 (ISBN 0-471-03114-3, Pub. by Wiley-Interscience). Wiley.

--Microprocessors: Fundamentals & Applications. LC 76-53223. 1977. 26.95 (ISBN 0-87942-093-6). Inst Electrical.

McGlynn, Daniel R. Microprocessors: Technology, Architecture & Applications. LC 76-137. 1976. 19.95 (ISBN 0-471-58414-2, Pub. by Wiley-Interscience). Wiley.

McKay, Charles W. Digital Circuits: A Preparation for Microprocessors. LC 77-13058. (Illus.). 1978. ref. 19.95 (ISBN 0-13-212175-1). P-H.

Markets for Microprocessor-Based Products, G-036. 1977. 525.00 (ISBN 0-89336-079-1). BCC.

Melsa, James & Cohn, David. Step by Step Introduction to 8080 Microprocessor Systems. 1977. pap. 7.95 (ISBN 0-918398-04-5, Pub. by Dilithium). Intl Schol Bk Serv.

Mick, John & Brick, James. Bit-Slice Microprocessor Design. (Illus.). 416p. 1980. 18.50 (ISBN 0-07-041781-4, P&RB). McGraw.

Microprocessor Interfacing. 500p. 59.95x (ISBN 0-686-74162-5). Sybex.

Microprocessor Lexicon: With Ten Language Vocabulary. (Illus.). 140p. 1981. pap. 3.95x (ISBN 0-89588-067-9). Sybex.

Microprocessor Programming. 500p. 89.95x (ISBN 0-686-74158-7). Sybex.

Microprocessors. 500p. cassettes 89.95x (ISBN 0-686-74157-9). Sybex.

Morse, Stephen P. The Eighty Eighty-Six Primer: An Introduction to Its Architecture, System Design & Programming. 224p. 1980. pap. 10.95 (ISBN 0-8104-5165-4). Hayden.

Motorola Inc. Microprocessor Applications Manual. 1975. 38.00 (ISBN 0-07-043527-8, P&RB). McGraw.

Muchow, Kenneth & Deem, Bill. Microprocessor Principles, Programming & Interfacing. 1982. text ed. 18.95 (ISBN 0-8359-4383-6); instrs.' manual avail. (ISBN 0-8359-4384-4). Reston.

Nabavi, C. D. The Engineering of Microprocessor Systems: Guidelines on System Development. LC 79-40952. 1979. 21.00 (ISBN 0-08-025435-7); pap. 7.25 (ISBN 0-08-025434-9). Pergamon.

National Computing Centre. High-Level Languages for Microprocessor Projects. Taylor, David & Morgan, Lyndon, eds. (Illus.). 279p. (Orig.). 1980. pap. 37.50x (ISBN 0-85012-233-3). Intl Pubns Serv.

--Impact of Microprocessors on British Business. LC 80-478324. 72p. (Orig.). 1979. pap. 15.00x (ISBN 0-85012-232-5). Intl Pubns Serv.

--The Uses of Microprocessors. Simons, G. L., ed. (Illus.). 260p. (Orig.). 1980. pap. 32.50x (ISBN 0-85012-240-6). Intl Pubns Serv.

Nauful, Eli S., ed. Microprocessor Abstracts. 1979. 60.00 (ISBN 0-686-09563-4). Nauful.

Nauful, Eli S., compiled by. A Microprocessor Bibliography. 1976. pap. 5.00 (ISBN 0-686-18861-6). Nauful.

Nichols, Joseph C., et al. Z-Eighty Microprocessor Programming & Interfacing, 2 bks. LC 79-63822. 1979. Bk. 1. pap. 11.95 (ISBN 0-672-21609-4); Bk. 2. pap. 14.95 (ISBN 0-672-21610-8, 21610); Set. pap. 24.95 (ISBN 0-672-21611-6). Sams.

Nichols, K. G. & Zaluska, E. J. Theory & Practice of Microprocessors. (Computer Systems Engineering Ser.). 384p. 1981. 36.50x (ISBN 0-8448-1384-2); pap. 18.50x (ISBN 0-8448-1410-5). Crane-Russak Co.

Nicoud, J. D. & Wilmink, J., eds. Microcomputer Architectures: Proceedings of the Third EUROMICRO Symposium on Microprocessing Microprogramming, October 1977, Amsterdam. 1978. 44.00 (ISBN 0-444-85097-X, North-Holland). Elsevier.

Olesky, J. & Rutkowski, G. Microprocessors & Digital Computer Technology. 1981. 22.95 (ISBN 0-13-581116-3). P-H.

Osborne, Adam. The Osborne Four & Eight Bit Microprocessor Handbook. 600p. 1981. pap. text ed. 19.95 (ISBN 0-931988-42-X). Osborne-McGraw.

--The Osborne Sixteen-Bit Microprocessor Handbook. 500p. 1981. pap. 19.95 (ISBN 0-931988-43-8). Osborne-McGraw.

--The Sixty-Eight Thousand Microprocessor Handbook. 200p. (Orig.). 1981. pap. 6.99 (ISBN 0-931988-41-1). Osborne-McGraw.

Poe, Elmer. Using the 6800 Microprocessor. LC 77-93168. 1978. 6.95 (ISBN 0-672-21512-8). Sams.

Programming Microprocessors. 2 cassettes 29.95x (ISBN 0-686-74155-2). Sybex.

Ramirez, E. V. & Weiss, M. Microprocessing Fundamentals: Hardware & Software. 1980. 13.95 (ISBN 0-07-051172-1). McGraw.

Rao, Guthikonda V. Microprocessors & Microcomputer Systems. rev. 2nd ed. 352p. 1981. text ed. price not set (ISBN 0-442-25626-4). Van Nos Reinhold.

--Microprocessors & Microcomputer Systems. (Illus.). 1978. text ed. 24.50x (ISBN 0-442-22000-6). Van Nos Reinhold.

Rich, Lloyd. Understanding Microprocessors. (Illus.). 336p. 1980. text ed. 17.95 (ISBN 0-8359-8057-X). Reston.

Ross, P. J. A Simple Microprocessor System for Field Data Acquisition & Display. 1980. 10.00x (ISBN 0-643-02487-5, Pub. by CSJRO Australia). State Mutual Bk.

Rutkowski, George B. & Olesky, Jerome E. Microprocessor & Digital Computer Technology. (Illus.). 416p. 1981. text ed. 22.95 (ISBN 0-13-581116-3). P-H.

Sawin, Dwight H. Microprocessors & Microcomputer Systems. 1977. 21.95 (ISBN 0-669-00564-9). Lexington Bks.

Scanlon, L. Aim Sixty-Five Laboratory Manual. 179p. 1981. pap. text ed. 7.95 (ISBN 0-471-06488-2). Wiley.

Schindler, Max. Microprocessor Software Design. 304p. 1980. pap. 14.50 (ISBN 0-8104-5190-5). Hayden.

SEMINEX Technical Seminar & Exhibition, London, England, March 26-30, 1979. Semiconductor & Microprocessor Technology 1979: Selected Papers. Dummer, G. W. A., ed. (Illus.). 252p. 1980. pap. 50.00 (ISBN 0-08-026134-5). Pergamon.

Severe Environment-Military Microprocessor System. 500p. 59.95x (ISBN 0-686-74159-5). Sybex.

Short, K. Microprocessors & Programmed Logic. 1980. 28.95 (ISBN 0-13-581173-2). P-H.

Simons, G. L. Introducing Microprocessors. (Illus., Orig.). 1979. pap. 20.00x (ISBN 0-85012-209-0). Intl Pubns Serv.

Simpson, W. D., et al. Ninety Nine Hundred Family System Design Book. new ed. LC 78-58005. (Microprocessor Ser.). (Illus.). 1978. pap. 19.50 (ISBN 0-89512-026-7, LCC4400). Tex Instr Inc.

Singh, M. G., et al. Applied Industrial Control--an Introduction. (International Ser. on Systems & Control: Vol. 1). (Illus.). 450p. 1980. 52.00 (ISBN 0-08-024764-4); pap. 21.00 (ISBN 0-08-024765-2). Pergamon.

Sippl, Charles J. Microcomputer Handbook. (Computer Science Ser.). 350p. 1977. 19.95x (ISBN 0-442-80324-9). Van Nos Reinhold.

Sokolowsky, P. Grundlagen der Rechnertechnik Mit Einer Einfuhrung in Microprozessoren. (Interdisciplinary Systems Research Ser.: No. 52). 200p. (Ger.). 1978. pap. 18.00 (ISBN 3-7643-0993-8). Birkhauser.

Soucek, Branko. Microprocessors & Microcomputers. LC 75-33123. 1976. 34.00 (ISBN 0-471-81391-5, Pub. by Wiley-Interscience). Wiley.

Stout, David F. Microprocessor Applications. (Illus.). 448p. 1982. 32.50 (ISBN 0-07-061798-8). McGraw.

Streitmatter & Fiore. Microprocessors: Theory & Application. (Illus.). 1979. text ed. 18.95 (ISBN 0-8359-4371-2); students manual avail. (ISBN 0-8359-4372-0). Reston.

Streitmatter, Gene. Microprocessor Software: Programming Concepts & Techniques. (Illus.). 400p. 1981. text ed. 18.95 (ISBN 0-8359-4375-5). Reston.

Taub, Herbert. Digital Circuits & Microprocessors. (Electrical Engineering Ser.). (Illus.). 608p. 1981. text ed. 26.95x (ISBN 0-07-062945-5, C); solutions manual 12.95 (ISBN 0-07-062946-3). McGraw.

Texas Instruments Inc. Electronic Power Control & Digital Techniques. (Illus.). 1976. 21.50 (ISBN 0-07-063752-0, P&RB). McGraw.

Texas Instruments, Inc. Microprocessors-Microcomputers-System Design. (Texas Instruments Bk. Ser.). (Illus.). 1980. 24.50 (ISBN 0-07-063758-X, P&RB). McGraw.

Tocci, Ronald & Laskowski, Lester. Microprocessors & Microcomputers: Hardware & Software. 2nd ed. (Illus.). 416p. 1982. 20.95 (ISBN 0-13-581322-0). P-H.

Tocci, Ronald J. & Laskowski, Lester P. Microprocessors & Microcomputers: Hardware & Software. (Illus.). 1979. text ed. 18.95 (ISBN 0-13-581330-1). P-H.

Torrero, Edward A., ed. Microprocessors: New Directions for Designers. (Illus.). 144p. 1975. pap. text ed. 11.85 (ISBN 0-8104-5777-6). Hayden.

Veronis, A. Microprocessors: Design & Applications. 1978. 18.95 (ISBN 0-87909-493-1). Reston.

Weisbecker, Joe. Home Computers Can Make You Rich. 1980. pap. 7.10 (ISBN 0-8104-5177-8). Hayden.

Whitbread, Martin, ed. Microprocessor Applications in Business & Industry. (Topics in Microprocessing Ser.: Book One). (Illus.). 153p. 1979. pap. text ed. 25.00 (ISBN 0-7194-0010-4, Pub. by Castle Hse England). J K Burgess.

Whitebread, Martin. Microprocessor Software. (Topics in Microprocessing Bk No.2). (Illus.). 150p. 1980. pap. text ed. 23.50 (ISBN 0-7194-0013-9, Pub. by Castle Hse England). J. K. Burgess.

Wilmink, J. & Sami, M., eds. Microprocessing & Microprogramming: Second Symposium, Venice, 1976. 1977. 36.75 (ISBN 0-7204-0557-2, North-Holland). Elsevier.

Zaks, Rodnay. From Chips to Systems: An Introduction to Microprocessors. 4th ed. (Illus.). 420p. 1981. pap. 14.95x (ISBN 0-89588-063-6). Sybex.

Zarrella, John. Operating Systems: Concepts & Principles. LC 79-122639. (Microprocessor Software Engineering Concepts Ser.). (Illus.). 156p. (Orig.). 1979. pap. 7.95 (ISBN 0-935230-00-9). Microcomputer Appns.

--System Architecture. LC 80-82932. (Microprocessor Software Engineering Concepts Ser.). (Illus.). 240p. (Orig.). 1980. pap. 9.95 (ISBN 0-935230-02-5). Microcomputer Appns.

--Word Processing & Text Editing. LC 80-114189. (Microprocessor Software Engineering Concepts Ser.). (Illus.). 156p. 1980. pap. 7.95 (ISBN 0-935230-01-7). Microcomputer Appns.

Zarrella, John, ed. Microprocessor Operating Systems. LC 81-80864. 220p. 1981. pap. price not set (ISBN 0-935230-03-3). Microcomputer Appns.

Zissos, D. System Design with Microprocessors. 1979. 17.50 (ISBN 0-12-781750-6). Acad Pr.

MICROPUBLICATIONS

see Microforms

MICRORADIOGRAPHY

Mueller, G. Mikroradiographische Untersuchungen zur Mineralisation der Knochen Fruehgeborener und junger Saeuinge, 1980. (Journal: Acta Anatomica: Vol. 108, Suppl. 64). (Illus.). iv, 44p. 1981. pap. 27.00 (ISBN 3-8055-1719-X). S Karger.

MICROSCOPE AND MICROSCOPY

see also Biological Apparatus and Supplies; Chemical Microscopy; Electron Microscope; Field-Ion Microscope; Fluorescence Microscopy; Histology; Interference Microscope; Microbiology; Microcinematography; Micropaleontology; Microscopy, Medical; Petrographic Microscope; Phase Microscope; Photomicrography; Stains and Staining (Microscopy); X-Ray Microscope

American Microscopical Society Symposium, 1980. Artificial Substrates: Proceedings. Cairns, John, Jr., ed. 1981. text ed. write for info. Ann Arbor Science.

Annual Book of ASTM Standards, 1981: Emission, Molecular & Mass Spectroscopy; Chromatography; Resinography; Microscopy; Computerized Systems, Pt. 42. 672p. 1981. 30.00 (ISBN 0-686-76010-7, 01-042081-39). ASTM.

Becker, R. P. & Johari, O. Scanning Electron Microscopy 1980. No. II. LC 72-626068. (Illus.). xiv, 658p. 50.00 (ISBN 0-931288-12-6). Scanning Electron.

Bennett, J. E., et al. Microstructural Science, Vol. 6. 1978. 45.00 (ISBN 0-444-00257-X, North Holland). Elsevier.

Bracegirdle, Brian. A History of Microtechnique. LC 77-78658. (Illus.). 1978. 49.50x (ISBN 0-8014-1117-3). Cornell U Pr.

Bradbury, S. The Microscope Past & Present. 1969. pap. text ed. 7.75 (ISBN 0-08-013249-9). Pergamon.

Brandt, W. H. The Student's Guide to Optical Microscopes. LC 75-23251. (Illus.). 53p. 1975. pap. 3.50 (ISBN 0-913232-22-X). W Kaufmann.

Burns, Willard A. & Bretschneider, Ann. Thin Is in: Plastic Embedding of Tissue for Light Microscopy. LC 81-10876. (Illus.). 50p. 1981. text ed. 35.00 (ISBN 0-89189-083-1, 16-1-030-00). Am Soc Clinical.

Carona, Philip B. Microscope & How to Use It. (Illus.). 68p. 1970. pap. 5.95 (ISBN 0-87201-563-7). Gulf Pub.

Clay, Reginald S. & Court, T. H. The History of the Microscope. (Illus.). 60.00 (ISBN 0-87556-605-7). Saifer.

Clay, Reginald S. & Court, Thomas H. The History of the Microscope. LC 77-6994. 1977. Repr. of 1932 ed. lib. bdg. 30.00 (ISBN 0-89341-143-4). Longwood Pr.

Cosslett, V. E. & Barer, R., eds. Advances in Optical & Electron Microscopy. Vol. 1. 1966. 44.50 (ISBN 0-12-029901-1); Vol. 2. 1968. 66.00 (ISBN 0-12-029902-X); Vol. 3. 1969. 45.50 (ISBN 0-12-029903-8); Vol. 4. 1971. 67.00 (ISBN 0-12-029904-6); Vol. 5. 1973. 61.00 (ISBN 0-12-029905-4); Vol. 6, 1976. 52.50 (ISBN 0-12-029906-2); Vol. 7, 1979. 57.00 (ISBN 0-12-029907-0). Acad Pr.

Cosslett, Vernon E. Modern Microscopy, Or, Seeing the Very Small. (Illus.). 192p. (YA) (gr. 9-12). 1968. pap. 3.95 (ISBN 0-8014-9065-0, CP65). Cornell U Pr.

Craig, James R. & Vaughan, David J. Ore Microscopy & Ore Petiography. LC 80-39786. 406p. 1981. 29.95 (ISBN 0-471-08596-0, Pub. by Wiley-Interscience). Wiley.

Delly, John G., ed. Teaching Microscopy, Vol. 52. LC 76-39606. (Illus.). 1977. 15.00 (ISBN 0-904962-05-9). Microscope Pubns.

Eisner, G. Biomicroscopy of the Peripheral Fundus: An Atlas & Textbook. LC 73-83243. (Illus.). 191p. 1973. text ed. 78.50 (ISBN 0-387-06374-9). Springer-Verlag.

Filer, E. W., et al, eds. Microstructural Science. (Microstructural Science Ser.: Vol. 4). 1976. 45.00 (ISBN 0-444-00184-0, North Holland). Elsevier.

Ford, Brian J. The Optical Microscope Manual. LC 72-94378. 1973. 13.00x (ISBN 0-8448-0157-7). Crane-Russak Co.

Freund, Hugo. Applied Ore Microscopy. 1966. 39.95 (ISBN 0-02-339710-1, 33971). Macmillan.

Geisert, Paul. Understanding the Microscope. (EMI Programed Biology Ser.). 1967. pap. text ed. 2.50x (ISBN 0-88462-018-2). Ed Methods.

Glossary of Micrographics. (TR2-1980). 1980. 9.00 (ISBN 0-89258-065-8). Natl Micrograph.

Goldstein, Joseph I. & Yakowitz, Harvey, eds. Practical Scanning Electron Microscopy. LC 74-34162. (Illus.). 582p. 1975. 35.00 (ISBN 0-306-30820-7, Plenum Pr). Plenum Pub.

Gray, Peter. Use of the Microscope. (Illus.). 1967. text ed. 7.95 (ISBN 0-07-024208-9, C). McGraw.

Hall, Cecil E. Introduction to Electron Microscopy. LC 80-39788. 410p. 1981. Repr. of 1966 ed. lib. bdg. price not set (ISBN 0-89874-302-8). Krieger.

Harris, James R., ed. Electron Microscopy of Protein, 2 vols. 1981. price not set; Vol. 1. (ISBN 0-12-327601-2); Vol. 2. (ISBN 0-12-327602-0). Acad Pr.

Hartshorne, Norman H. The Microscopy of Liquid Crystals, Vol. 48. LC 73-91899. 1974. 11.00 (ISBN 0-904962-03-2). Microscope Pubns.

Hayat, M. A. Principles & Techniques of Electron Microscopy. 544p. 1980. text ed. 34.50 (ISBN 0-8391-1602-0). Univ Park.

Hayat, M. Arif. Principles & Techniques of Electron Microscopy Biological Applications, Vol. 8. 1978. text ed. 27.50x (ISBN 0-442-25693-0). Van Nos Reinhold.

--Principles & Techniques of Electron Microscopy, Vol. 3. 1973. 19.95x (ISBN 0-442-25674-4). Van Nos Reinhold.

Headstrom, Richard. Adventures with a Hand Lens. 1976. pap. 3.00 (ISBN 0-486-23330-8). Dover.

--Adventures with a Microscope. (Illus.). 6.75 (ISBN 0-8446-5584-8). Peter Smith.

James, J. Light Microscopic Techniques in Biology & Medicine. 1976. lib. bdg. 53.00 (ISBN 90-247-1900-3, Pub. by Kluwer Nijhoff Netherlands). Kluwer Boston.

Johari, Om & Becker, R. P., eds. Scanning Electron Microscopy 1980, No. III. LC 72-62608. (Illus.). xx, 670p. 50.00 (ISBN 0-931288-13-4). Scanning Electron.

Koehler, J. K. Advanced Techniques in Biological Electron Microscopy 2. 1978. 31.20 (ISBN 0-387-08503-3). Springer-Verlag.

Lankester, Edwin. Half-Hours with the Microscope. LC 71-170346. 1898. Repr. 24.00 (ISBN 0-403-01482-4). Scholarly.

Le May, I., et al, eds. Microstructural Science, Vol. 7. 1979. 45.00 (ISBN 0-444-00338-X, North Holland). Elsevier.

McCall, J. L. & Mueller, William M., eds. Metallographic Specimen Preparation: Optical & Electron Microscopy. LC 74-8391. 358p. 1974. 35.00 (ISBN 0-306-30791-X, Plenum Pr). Plenum Pub.

McCrone, Walter C., et al. Polarized Light Microscopy. LC 78-61047. (Illus.). 1979. 37.50 (ISBN 0-250-40262-9). Ann Arbor Science.

McLaughlin, Robert B. Accessories for the Light Microscope, Vol. 16. LC 74-79374. (Illus.). 1975. 15.00 (ISBN 0-904962-00-8). Microscope Pubns.

Marmasse, Claude. Microscopes & Their Uses. 344p. 1980. 19.50 (ISBN 0-677-05510-2). Gordon.

National Micrographics Assn. Guide to Micrographic Equipment: R015-1979. 7th ed. 1979. 25.00 (ISBN 0-89258-053-4). Natl Micrograph.

Padgitt, Donald L. A Short History of the Early American Microscopes, Vol. 12. LC 74-30750. (Illus.). 1975. 11.00 (ISBN 0-904962-04-0). Microscope Pubns.

Perfil'ev, B. V., et al. Applied Capillary Microscopy: The Role of Microorganisms in the Formation of Iron-Manganese Deposits. LC 65-15003. 130p. 1965. 27.50 (ISBN 0-306-10724-4, Consultants). Plenum Pub.

Riemer, Marvin F. Microscope & the World of Science. LC 62-12342. (Illus.). 334p. 1964. 5.95 (ISBN 0-89046-033-7). Herman Pub.

Rochow, T. G. & Rochow, E. G. An Introduction to Microscopy: By Means of Light, Electrons, X-Rays, or Ultrasound. LC 78-7529. (Illus.). 383p. 1979. 29.50 (ISBN 0-306-31111-9, Plenum Pr). Plenum Pub.

Roper, Freeman C. Catalogue of Works on the Microscope & of Those Referring to Microscopical Subjects in the Library of Freeman C. S. Roper. LC 79-65242. 1979. Repr. of 1865 ed. 15.00x (ISBN 0-935164-00-6). N T Smith.

Rudman, Jack. Senior Micrographics Operator. (Career Examination Ser.: C-2760). (Cloth bdg. avail. on request). 1980. pap. 12.00 (ISBN 0-8373-2760-1). Natl Learning.

--Senior Micrographics Technician. (Career Examination Ser.: C-2762). (Cloth bdg. avail. on request). 1980. pap. 12.00 (ISBN 0-8373-2762-8). Natl Learning.

Saffady, William, ed. International File of Micrographics Equipment & Accessories Nineteen Seventy-Nine to Nineteen Eighty. 2nd ed. 1979. binder 250.00 (ISBN 0-913672-33-5). Microform Rev.

--International File of Micrographics Equipment & Accessories, 1977-1978. 1977. binder 250.00x (ISBN 0-913672-25-4). Microform Rev.

Scanga, Franco, ed. Atlas of Electron Microscopy. 1964. 85.50 (ISBN 0-444-40507-0, North Holland). Elsevier.

Smith, H. G. Minerals & the Microscope. 1956. pap. text ed. 7.95x (ISBN 0-04-549002-3). Allen Unwin.

Stehli, Georg. The Microscope & How to Use It. LC 70-107464. 1970. lib. bdg. 9.50 (ISBN 0-88307-631-4). Gannon.

Stehli, George. Microscope & How to Use It. (Illus.). 1970. pap. 2.50 (ISBN 0-486-22575-5). Dover.

Stoiber, Richard E. & Morse, Stearns A. Microscopic Identification of Crystals. rev. ed. 286p. 1981. Repr. of 1972 ed. lib. bdg. 16.50 (ISBN 0-89874-276-5). Krieger.

Tarniewski, Marke. The New Regime: The Structure of Power in Eastern Europe. (Allison & Busby Title in the Motive Ser.). 224p. 1981. 18.95 (ISBN 0-8052-8115-0, Pub. by Allison & Busby England); pap. 8.95 (ISBN 0-686-73580-3). Schocken.

Thomas, Gareth & Goringe, Michael J. Transmission Electron Microscopy of Materials. LC 79-449. 388p. 1979. 28.95 (ISBN 0-471-12244-0, Pub. by Wiley-Interscience). Wiley.

Tribe, M. A., et al. Light Microscopy. (Basic Biology Course Ser: Bk. 1). (Illus.). 128p. 1975. 29.95 (ISBN 0-521-20656-1); pap. text ed. 9.75x (ISBN 0-521-20556-5). Cambridge U Pr.

Turner, Gerard L. Collecting Microscopes. (The Christies International Collectors Ser.). (Illus.). 128p. 1980. 14.95 (ISBN 0-8317-5950-X, Mayflower Bks). Smith Pubs.

Wade, Glen, ed. Acoustic Imaging: Cameras, Microscopes, Phased Arrays & Holographic Systems. LC 76-21. 325p. 1976. 32.50 (ISBN 0-306-30914-9, Plenum Pr). Plenum Pub.

Weiner, Jack. Microscopy of Pulp & Paper. 2nd ed. LC 64-7525. (Bibliographic Ser.: No. 177, Supplement 2). 1976. pap. 25.00 (ISBN 0-87010-036-X). Inst Paper Chem.

Wied, George & Bahr, Gunter F. Introduction to Quantitative Cytochemistry, 2. 1970. 67.50 (ISBN 0-12-748852-9). Acad Pr.

Wischnitzer, Saul. Introduction to Electron Microscopy. 3rd ed. LC 80-15266. 320p. 1981. 39.50 (ISBN 0-08-026298-8). Pergamon.

Zieler, H. Wolfgang. The Optical Performance of the Light Microscope, Vols. 14 & 15. LC 72-85238. (Illus.). 1972-74. 22.00 set (ISBN 0-904962-01-6); 11.00 ea. (ISBN 0-904962-02-4). Microscope Pubns.

MICROSCOPE AND MICROSCOPY–JUVENILE LITERATURE

Grillone, Lisa & Gennaro, Joseph. Small Worlds Close up. LC 77-15860. (Illus.). (gr. 3-5). 1978. 7.95 (ISBN 0-517-53289-1). Crown.

Headstrom, Richard. Adventures with a Microscope. (Illus.). 1977. pap. 3.00 (ISBN 0-486-23471-1). Dover.

Johnson, Gaylord & Bleifeld, Maurice. Hunting with the Microscope. rev. ed. LC 79-10271. (Illus.). (gr. 7 up). 1980. lib. bdg. 8.95 (ISBN 0-668-04973-1); pap. 3.95 (ISBN 0-668-04783-6). Arco.

Klein, Aaron E. The Complete Beginner's Guide to Microscopes & Telescopes. LC 78-22334. (Illus.). 224p. 1980. 9.95a (ISBN 0-385-14854-2); PLB (ISBN 0-385-14855-0). Doubleday.

Microscopes. (How & Why Wonder Books Ser.). (gr. 4-6). pap. 1.00 (ISBN 0-685-56723-0). Wonder.

Provenzo, Eugene F., Jr. & Provenzo, Asterie B. Rediscovering Astronomy. LC 80-17210. (Young Inventor's Ser.). (Illus.). 128p. 1980. 14.95 (ISBN 0-916392-61-9). Oak Tree Pubns.

Selsam, Millicent E. Greg's Microscope. LC 63-8002. (Science I Can Read Books). (Illus.). (gr. k-3). 1963. PLB 7.89 (ISBN 0-06-025296-0, HarpJ). Har-Row.

Wolberg, Barbara J. Zooming in: Photographic Discoveries Under the Microscope. LC 73-18631. 64p. (gr. 5-8). 1974. 7.75 (ISBN 0-15-299970-1, HJ). HarBraceJ.

MICROSCOPE AND MICROSCOPY–TECHNIQUE

Burrells, W. Microscope Technique: A Comprehensive Handbook for General & Applied Microscopy. LC 77-26687. (Illus.). 1977. 27.50x (ISBN 0-85242-511-2). Intl Pubns Serv.

--Microscope Techniques: A Comprehensive Handbook for General & Applied Microscopy. LC 77-26687. 1978. 34.95 (ISBN 0-470-99376-6). Halsted Pr.

Goodhew, P. J. Speciman Preparation in Materials Science. (Practical Methods in Electron Microscopy: Vol. 1, Pt. 2). 18.00 (ISBN 0-444-10412-7, North-Holland). Elsevier.

Gray, Peter. Encyclopedia of Microscopy & Micro-Technique. 1973. text ed. 36.50 (ISBN 0-442-22812-0). Van Nos Reinhold.

--Handbook of Basic Microtechnique. 3rd ed. 1964. text ed. 19.00 (ISBN 0-07-024206-2, C). McGraw.

--The Microtomists Formulary & Guide. LC 74-23818. 808p. 1975. Repr. of 1954 ed. 39.50 (ISBN 0-88275-247-2). Krieger.

Grimstone, A. V. & Skaer, R. J. A Guidebook to Microscopical Methods. LC 70-182027. (Illus.). 150p. 1972. 29.95 (ISBN 0-521-08445-8); pap. 8.95x (ISBN 0-521-09700-2). Cambridge U Pr.

Johansen, Donald A. Plant Microtechnique. (Botanical Sciences Ser.). 1940. text ed. 28.50 (ISBN 0-07-032540-5, C). McGraw.

Kiernan, K. A. Histological & Histochemical Methods: Theory & Practice. (Illus.). 400p. Date not set. 70.00 (ISBN 0-08-024936-1); pap. 25.00 (ISBN 0-08-024935-3). Pergamon.

McClung, C. E. & Jones, R. McClung, eds. Handbook of Microscopical Technique for Workers in Animal & Plant Tissues. 3rd, rev. ed. (Illus.). 1964. Repr. of 1950 ed. 26.25 (ISBN 0-02-849050-9). Hafner.

McLaughlin, Robert B. Special Methods in Light Microscopy, Vol. 17. LC 77-86749. (Illus.). 1977. 25.00 (ISBN 0-904962-06-7). Microscope Pubns.

Meek, G. A. & Elder, H. Y., eds. Analytical & Quantitative Methods in Microscopy. LC 76-22983. (Society for Experimental Biology Seminar Ser: No. 3). (Illus.). 1977. 42.50 (ISBN 0-521-21404-1); pap. 15.95x (ISBN 0-521-29141-0). Cambridge U Pr.

Needham, George H. The Practical Use of the Microscope. (Illus.). 520p. 1977. 28.75 (ISBN 0-398-03645-4). C C Thomas.

Ruthmann, August. Methods in Cell Research. LC 79-87008. (Illus.). 1969. 25.00x (ISBN 0-8014-0544-0). Cornell U Pr.

Sjostrand, Fritiof S. Electron Microscopy of Cells & Tissues. Vol. 1, 1967. 58.00, by subscription 43.50 (ISBN 0-12-647550-4). Acad Pr.

Southworth, H. N. & Hull, R. A. Introduction to Modern Microscopy. LC 74-32488. (Wykeham Science Ser.: No.34). 1975. 8.60x (ISBN 0-8448-1161-0). Crane-Russak Co.

Turney, C., et al. Sydney Micro Skills, Series 2 Handbook: Explaining, Introductory Procedures & Closure, Advanced Questioning. (Teaching Skills Development Project). 171p. 1975. pap. 5.00x (ISBN 0-424-00008-3, Pub. by Sydney U Pr). Intl Schol Bk Serv.

Wied, George. Introduction to Quantitative Cytochemistry. 1966. 71.50 (ISBN 0-12-748850-2). Acad Pr.

Willey, R. L. Microtechniques: A Laboratory Guide. 1971. pap. text ed. 6.25x (ISBN 0-02-427790-8). Macmillan.

MICROSCOPIC ANALYSIS

see Metallography; Microscope and Microscopy

MICROSCOPIC ANATOMY

see Histology

MICROSCOPIC ORGANISMS

see Micro-Organisms

MICROSCOPY, CHEMICAL

see Chemical Microscopy

MICROSCOPY, MEDICAL

see also Microsurgery

Ash, Eric, ed. Scanned Image Microscopy. LC 80-41580. 1981. 44.50 (ISBN 0-12-065180-7). Acad Pr.

Carter, H. W., et al. Clinical Applications of the Scanning Electron Microscope. Johari, Om & Becker, R. P., eds. (Illus.). 1980. pap. 10.00x (ISBN 0-931288-16-9). Scanning Electron.

Culling, C. F. Modern Microscopy: Elementary Theory & Practice. 1974. 8.95 (ISBN 0-407-75400-8). Butterworth.

Electron Microscopy in Human Medicine, Vol. 7: Digestive System. (Electron Microscopy in Human Medicine Ser.). 250p. 1980. 58.00 (ISBN 0-07-032507-3, HP). McGraw.

Freeman, James A. & Beeler, Myrton F. Laboratory Medicine-Clinical Microscopy. 2nd ed. (Illus.). 405p. Date not set. price not set (ISBN 0-8121-0822-1). Lea & Febiger.

Hall, T. A., et al. X-Ray Microscopy in Clinical & Experimental Medicine. (American Lecture Living Chemistry). (Illus.). 336p. 1972. pap. 33.50 (ISBN 0-398-02458-8). C C Thomas.

Johannessen, Jan V. Electron Microscopy in Human Medicine: Cellular Pathology, Vol. 2. (Illus.). 1978. text ed. 34.50 (ISBN 0-07-032503-0, HP). McGraw.

--Electron Microscopy in Human Medicine: Instrumentation & Techniques, Vol. 1. (Electron Microscopy in Human Medicine). (Illus.). 1978. text ed. 56.00 (ISBN 0-07-032501-4, HP). McGraw.

--Electron Microscopy in Human Medicine: Vol. 6, Nervous System, Sensory Organs, & Respiratory Tract. (Electron Microscopy in Human Medicine Ser.). (Illus.). 368p. 1980. text ed. 74.50 (ISBN 0-07-032506-5, HP). McGraw.

--Electron Microscopy in Human Medicine: Vol. 8, the Liver, Gallbladder & Biliary Ducts. (Illus.). 1979. text ed. 48.00 (ISBN 0-07-032499-9). McGraw.

Johannessen, Jans V. Electron Microscopy in Human Medicine: Vol. 3, Infectous Agents. (Electron Microscopy in Human Medicine Ser.). 450p. 1981. text ed. 88.50 (ISBN 0-07-032503-0, HP). McGraw.

--Electron Microscopy in Human Medicine: Vol. 9, Urogenital System & Breast. (Illus.). 396p. 1980. text ed. 74.00 (ISBN 0-07-032508-1, HP). McGraw.

Lang, W. H. & Muchel, F. ZEISS-Microscopes for Microsurgery. (Illus.). 144p. 1981. 29.80 (ISBN 0-387-10784-3). Springer-Verlag.

Mackay, Bruce. Introduction to Diagnostic Electron Microscopy. 384p. 1981. 24.95 (ISBN 0-8385-7860-8). ACC.

Mandal, Anil K. Electron Microscopy of the Kidney in Renal Disease & Hypertension: A Clinicopathological Approach. LC 78-24409. (Illus.). 472p. 1978. 32.50 (ISBN 0-306-40110-X, Plenum Pr). Plenum Pub.

Schmidt, W. J. & Keil, A. Polarization Microscopy of Dental Tissues. Middle, P., tr. 604p. 1971. 87.00 (ISBN 0-08-010787-7). Pergamon.

MICROSOMES

Coon, Minor J., ed. Microsomes, Drug Oxidations & Chemical Carcinogenesis, Vol. I. LC 80-11363. 1980. 39.50 (ISBN 0-12-187701-9). Acad Pr.

--Microsomes, Drug Oxidations & Chemical Carcinogenesis, Vol. 2. LC 80-11363. 1980. 41.00 (ISBN 0-12-187702-7). Acad Pr.

Estabrook, R., et al, eds. Microsomes & Drug Oxidations. 486p. 1973. 30.00 (ISBN 0-683-02918-5, Pub. by W & W). Krieger.

Gillette, James R., et al, eds. Microsomes & Drug Oxidations: Proceedings. 1969. 47.00 (ISBN 0-12-283650-2). Acad Pr.

Ullrich, Volker, et al, eds. Microsomes & Drug Oxidations. 1977. text ed. 90.00 (ISBN 0-08-021523-8). Pergamon.

MICROSPORIDIA

Kudo, Roksabro. A Biologic & Taxonomic Study of the Microsporidia. (Illinois Biological Monographs: Vol. 9). Repr. of 1924 ed. 18.50 (ISBN 0-384-30600-4). Johnson Repr.

MICROSTRIP

see Microwave Wiring

MICROSURGERY

Acland, Robert D. Microsurgery Practice Manual. LC 79-17533. (Illus.). 1979. pap. text ed. 14.95 (ISBN 0-8016-0076-6). Mosby.

Andrews, Albert H., Jr., ed. Microscopic & Endoscopic Surgery with the Carbon Dioxide Laser. 1982. write for info. (ISBN 0-88416-211-7). Wright-PSG.

Charles, Steven. Vitreous Microsurgery. (Illus.). 280p. 1981. lib. bdg. 30.00 (ISBN 0-683-01550-8). Williams & Wilkins.

Daniel, Rollin K. & Terzls, Julia. Reconstructive Microsurgery. 1977. 55.00 (ISBN 0-316-17255-3). Little.

Drotar, David L. Microsurgery: Revolution in the Operating Room. LC 81-3850. (Illus.). 224p. 1981. 9.95 (ISBN 0-8253-0056-8). Beaufort Bks NY.

Girard, Louis J. Advanced Techniques in Ophthalmic Microsurgery: Corneal Surgery, Vol. II. LC 78-31773. (Illus.). 305p. 1980. text ed. 83.50 (ISBN 0-8016-1835-5). Mosby.

International Microsurgical Society, 5th, Germany, Oct. 1978. Microsurgery: Proceedings. Lie, T. S., ed. (International Congress Ser.: No. 465). 1979. 78.00 (ISBN 0-444-90077-2, Excerpta Medica). Elsevier.

Kleensasser, O. Microlaryngoscopy & Endolaryngeal Microsurgery. 192p. 1979. pap. text ed. 64.50 (ISBN 0-8391-1350-1). Univ Park.

Kletter, G. The Extra-Intracranial Bypass Operation for Prevention & Treatment of Stroke. (Illus.). 1979. 51.50 (ISBN 0-387-81522-8). Springer-Verlag.

Lang, W. H. & Muchel, F. ZEISS-Microscopes for Microsurgery. (Illus.). 144p. 1981. 29.80 (ISBN 0-387-10784-3). Springer-Verlag.

Laws, Edward R., et al, eds. The Management of Pituitary Adenomas & Related Lesions, with Emphasis on Transphenoidal Microsurgery. 448p. 1981. 42.50 (ISBN 0-8385-6122-5). ACC.

Peerless, S. & McCormick, C. W., eds. Microsurgery for Cerebral Ischemia. (Illus.). 362p. 1981. 89.80 (ISBN 0-387-90495-6). Springer-Verlag.

Reyniak, J. Victor & Lauersen, Niels H., eds. Principles of Microsurgical Techniques in Infertility. LC 81-3045. 225p. 1981. text ed. price not set (ISBN 0-306-40781-7, Plenum Med Bk). Plenum Pub.

Roper-Hall, M. J., ed. Methods, Indications & Results of Microsurgical Procedures. (Developments in Opthamology Ser.: Vol. 5). (Illus.). viii, 170p. 1981. pap. 63.00 (ISBN 3-8055-2711-X). S Karger.

Seeger, W. Microsurgery of the Brain, 2 vols. (Illus.). 750p. 1980. Set. 215.00 (ISBN 0-387-81573-2). Springer-Verlag.

Shambough International Workshop on Middle Ear Microsurgery & Fluctuant Hearing Loss. Proceedings. Shambaugh, George E. & Shea, John J., eds. 1981. 49.95 (ISBN 0-87397-183-3). Strode.

Silber, Sherman. Microsurgery. (Illus.). 1979. 59.95 (ISBN 0-683-07753-8). Williams & Wilkins.

Troutman, Richard C. Microsurgery of the Anterior Segment of the Eye: Volume I: Introduction & Basic Techniques. LC 74-12453. 1974. 56.50 (ISBN 0-8016-5107-7). Mosby.

MICROTECHNIQUE

see Microscope and Microscopy–Technique

MICROTONES

see also Musical Intervals and Scales; Music, Oriental

MICROWAVE AMPLIFICATION BY STIMULATED EMISSION OF RADIATION

see Masers

MICROWAVE AMPLIFICATION BY VARIABLE REACTANCE

see Parametric Amplifiers

MICROWAVE CIRCUITS

Allen, J. L. & Medley, M. W., Jr. Microwave Circuit Design Using Programmable Calculators. (Illus.). 279p. 1980. 40.00 (ISBN 0-89006-089-4). Artech Hse.

Edwards, T. C. Foundations for Microstrip Circuit Design. LC 80-41687. 304p. 1981. 41.00 (ISBN 0-471-27944-7, Pub. by Wiley-Interscience). Wiley.

Grivet, P. Physics of Transmission Lines at High & Very High Frequencies, Vol. 1. (Fr). 1970. 72.00 (ISBN 0-12-303601-1). Acad Pr.

Gunston, M. A. Microwave Transmission-Line Impedance Data. 1972. 19.95x (ISBN 0-442-02898-9). Van Nos Reinhold.

Gupta, K. C. & Singh, A., eds. Microwave Integrated Circuits. LC 74-8772. 380p. 1974. 20.95 (ISBN 0-470-33640-4). Halsted Pr.

Hallmark, Clayton. Microwave Oven Service & Repair. (Illus.). 1977. pap. 12.95 (ISBN 0-8306-6962-0, 962). TAB Bks.

Helszajn, J. Passive & Active Microwave Circuits. LC 78-5787. 1978. 39.00 (ISBN 0-471-04292-7, Pub. by Wiley-Interscience). Wiley.

Howes, M. J. & Morgan, D. V., eds. Microwave Devices: Device Circuit Interaction. LC 75-15887. (Solid State Devices & Circuits Ser.). 426p. 1976. 60.50 (ISBN 0-471-41729-7, Pub. by Wiley-Interscience). Wiley.

Kurokawa, K. Introduction to the Theory of Microwave Circuits. (Electrical Science Ser.). 1969. 55.50 (ISBN 0-12-429550-9). Acad Pr.

Liao, S. Microwave Devices & Circuits. 1980. 32.95 (ISBN 0-13-581207-0). P-H.

Watson, H. A. Microwave Semiconductor Devices & Their Circuit Applications. LC 68-17197. 1968. 42.50 (ISBN 0-07-068475-8, P&RB). McGraw.

MICROWAVE COMMUNICATION SYSTEMS

see also Closed-Circuit Television; Mobile Radio Stations; Radiotelephone

Colloquium of Microwave Communication, 5th, Budapest, 1970. Proceedings, 5 vols. rev. ed. Bognar, G., ed. LC 65-40139. 1974. Set. 75.00x (ISBN 963-05-0300-X). Intl Pubns Serv.

Feher, K. Digital Communications: Microwave Applications. 1981. 28.00 (ISBN 0-13-214080-2). P-H.

Jakes, William C., et al. Microwave Mobile Communications. LC 74-13401. 640p. 1974. 49.00 (ISBN 0-471-43720-4, Pub. by Wiley-Interscience). Wiley.

Malherbe, J. A. Microwave Transmission Line Filters. LC 78-31243. (Illus.). 1979. 30.00 (ISBN 0-89006-063-0). Artech Hse.

Panter, P. F. Communication Systems Design: Line-of-Sight & Tropo-Scatter Systems. 1972. 37.50 (ISBN 0-07-048436-8, P&RB). McGraw.

MICROWAVE COOKERY

Allison, Sonia. Book of Microwave Cookery. LC 77-91467. (Illus.). 1978. 6.50 (ISBN 0-7153-7525-3). David & Charles.

Batcher, Joyce. Microwaving with a Gourmet Flair. Hamernik, Arlene, ed. (Illus.). 67p. 1979. pap. 2.00 (ISBN 0-9602930-1-9). Microwave Helps.

Benoit, Jehane. The Microwave Cook Book. (Illus.). 240p. 1975. 10.95 (ISBN 0-07-082291-3, GB). McGraw.

Better Homes & Gardens Bks., ed. Better Homes & Gardens Microwave Cook Book. LC 75-38241. (Illus.). 96p. 1976. 4.95 (ISBN 0-696-00840-8). Meredith Corp.

Better Homes & Gardens Books Editors. Better Homes & Gardens More from Your Microwave. (Illus.). 96p. 1980. 4.95 (ISBN 0-696-00615-4). Meredith Corp.

Betty Crocker's Microwave Cooking. (Betty Crocker Ser.). 1977. (Golden Pr); pap. 2.95 (ISBN 0-307-09921-0). Western Pub.

Business Communications Co. Convenience Foods & Microwave, GA-044: Directions. 1980. 725.00 (ISBN 0-89336-227-1). BCC.

Chalpin, Lila. A New Look at Microwave Cooking. 1981. 8.95 (ISBN 0-916752-04-6). Caroline Hse.

--A New Look at Microwave Cooking. LC 76-41144. (Illus.). 1976. 8.95 (ISBN 0-916752-04-6). Dorison Hse.

Clark, Diane. Diane Clark's Microwave Cookbook: Gourmet Meals with Fast, Easy, Preparation. Schrader, C., ed. 256p. 1981. 15.50 (ISBN 0-8015-2023-1, 01505-450, Hawthorn). Dutton.

Collins, Val. Microwave Baking. (Illus.). 128p. 1980. 17.95 (ISBN 0-7153-8018-4). David & Charles.

--The Microwave Fruit & Vegetable Cookbook. LC 81-65958. (Illus.). 120p. 1981. 17.95 (ISBN 0-7153-8199-7). David & Charles.

Culinary Arts Institute Staff, ed. Microwave Cooking. LC 76-53103. (Adventures in Cooking Ser.). (Illus.). 1977. pap. 3.95 (ISBN 0-8326-0568-9, 2513). Delair.

Deacon, Richard. Microwave Cookery. 1978. pap. 2.95 (ISBN 0-553-20223-5). Bantam.

--Richard Deacon's Microwave Cookery. LC 73-93782. (Illus.). 160p. 1977. pap. 5.95 (ISBN 0-912656-73-5). H P Bks.

Dixon, Geraldine B. Guidelines to Microwave Cooking. (Illus., Orig.). 1980. pap. 6.95 (ISBN 0-89305-028-8). Anna Pub.

Dlugosch, Sharon & Battcher, Joyce. Food Processor Recipes for Conventional & Microwave Cooking. LC 78-74899. 1979. pap. 3.95 (ISBN 0-918420-03-2); pap. 12.00 tchrs' manual (ISBN 0-918420-04-0). Brighton Pubns.

Farm Journal Food Editors. Farm Journal's Country-Style Microwave Cookbook. LC 80-19928. 128p. (Orig.). 1980. pap. 3.50x (ISBN 0-89795-012-7). Farm Journal.

Favorite Recipes from the Microwave Times. (Illus.). 1980. 6.95 (ISBN 0-918620-20-1). Recipes Unltd.

Foltz, John, et al, eds. Microwave Cooking: It's Not Magic. LC 77-20466. (Illus.). 1977. 9.95 (ISBN 0-930380-03-7). Quail Run.

Frigidaire. Microwave Cooking in Multiple Speeds. 256p. 1980. 12.95 (ISBN 0-385-13233-6). Doubleday.

General Electric Co. General Electric Microwave Guide & Cookbook. (Illus.). 1978. 10.95 (ISBN 0-394-50044-X). Random.

Gordon A. Friesen International, Inc. The Ready Foods Systems for Health Care Facilities. LC 72-95360. 1973. 14.95 (ISBN 0-8436-0562-6). CBI Pub.

Hamernik, Arlene. Lesson Plan for "Basic Microwave Cooking". 1979. Repr. of 1977 ed. 10.00 (ISBN 0-9602930-2-7). Microwave Helps.

--One Hundred One Microwave Favorites Plus Four. rev. ed. (Illus.). 82p. 1979. spiral bdg. 2.95x (ISBN 0-9602930-4-3). Microwave Help.

Harris, Barbara. Let's Cook Microwave! 3rd ed. LC 79-84435. 208p. 1979. 5.25x (ISBN 0-685-65148-7). B Harris.

Harshberger, Claudette. The Way of the Microwave - Como Trabajo el Microonda. Borunda, Alfredo, tr. 120p. (Orig., Span. & Eng.). 1981. pap. 6.50 (ISBN 0-9606100-0-6). Pan Prods.

The Kenmore Microwave Cookbook. 1979. write for info. (ISBN 0-87502-066-6). Benjamin Co.

Kenmore Microwave Cooking. (Illus.). 160p. 1981. 9.95 (ISBN 0-8317-5954-2, Rutledge Pr). Smith Pubs.

Kenmore Microwave Cooking. 1981. write for info. (ISBN 0-87502-084-4). Benjamin Co.

Kuse, James & Luedtke, Ralph D., eds. Guide to Microwave Cooking. 1978. pap. 2.95 (ISBN 0-89542-658-7). Ideals.

Laws, Phe. The Complete Guide to Great Microwave Cooking. (Illus.). 1980. pap. 5.95 (ISBN 0-8256-3827-5, Hidden Hse). Music Sales.

--International Gourmet Cooking with Microwave. 288p. 1981. spiral bdg. 6.95 (ISBN 0-8256-3811-9, Hidden Hse). Music Sales.

--International Gourmet Cooking with Microwave. LC 76-12163. 1976. pap. 5.95 (ISBN 0-8256-3811-9, Hidden Hse). Music Sales.

Leising, Marlene. Everyday & Gourmet Microwave Cookbook. 196p. 1980. pap. 7.95 (ISBN 0-9606096-0-1). Micro Magic.

Litton. Exciting World of Microwave Cooking. (Illus.). 1976. 8.95 (ISBN 0-442-24829-6); pap. 6.95 (ISBN 0-442-84832-3). Van Nos Reinhold.

--Microwave Cooking: Adapting Recipes. 1979. 10.95 (ISBN 0-442-24845-8). Van Nos Reinhold.

--Microwave Cooking: Everyday Dinners in Half an Hour. 1980. 10.95 (ISBN 0-442-24851-2). Van Nos Reinhold.

--Microwave Cooking on a Diet. 160p. 1981. 10.95 (ISBN 0-442-24526-2). Van Nos Reinhold.

--Microwave Cooking Step-by-Step. 1979. 10.95 (ISBN 0-442-84094-2). Van Nos Reinhold.

--Microwave Meats Step-by-Step. 1979. 10.95 (ISBN 0-442-24846-6). Van Nos Reinhold.

Litton, From. Microwave Cooking: Convenience Foods. 160p. 1981. 10.95 (ISBN 0-442-25710-4). Van Nos Reinhold.

McDonald, Marie. Australian Microwave Cookbook. rev. ed. (Illus.). 1979. 13.75 (ISBN 0-589-50025-2, Pub. by Reed Books Australia). C E Tuttle.

McNett, Dorothy. The Microwave Way. LC 78-53321. (Illus.). 1978. pap. 2.50 (ISBN 0-915942-11-9). Owlswood Prods.

Majors, Judith S. Sugar Free.. Microwavery. LC 80-67167. pap. 6.95 (ISBN 0-9602238-3-5). Apple Pr.

Microwave Cooking. LC 78-52221. 1979. pap. 7.95 (ISBN 0-88332-113-0, 8153). Larousse.

Microwave Cooking: Fruits & Vegetables. (Litton Microwave Ser.). 1981. 10.95 (ISBN 0-686-71503-9). Van Nos Reinhold.

Microwave Miracles. (Orig.). 9.95 (ISBN 0-87502-043-7); pap. 5.95 (ISBN 0-87502-042-9). Benjamin Co.

Microwave Party Cookbook. 1976. 2.95 (ISBN 0-442-82571-4). Peter Pauper.

More from Your Microwave. 1981. 4.95 (ISBN 0-696-00615-4). BH&G.

Morris, Sally. Microwave Cooking. Walsh, Jackie, ed. LC 76-3428. (Illus.). 192p. (Orig.). 1976. pap. 4.95 (ISBN 0-911954-36-8). Nitty Gritty.

Napleton, Lewis. Guide to Microwave Catering. 3rd ed. (Illus.). 1976. pap. 11.95x (ISBN 0-7198-2523-7). Intl Ideas.

--Microwave Recipe Book. (Illus.). 1977. 19.95x (ISBN 0-7198-2641-1). Intl Ideas.

The New Magic of Microwave Cookbook. 256p. 1981. 8.95 (ISBN 0-307-49266-4, Golden Pr). Western Pub.

Palmer, Carol. Easy Does It: Microwave Main Dishes. 200p. (Orig.). 1980. pap. 8.95 (ISBN 0-89716-056-8). Peanut Butter.
Ronzio, Camille & Wilkinson, Trina. Microwave Delights. 4th, rev. ed. (Illus.). 206p. Date not set. pap. price not set. Cam-Tri Prods.
Sabin, A. Ross, ed. Range Service (Gas, Electric, Microwave) (Illus.). 253p. (gr. 11). 1979. 20.00 (ISBN 0-938336-06-1). Whirlpool.
Sadlack, Janet L. Enjoying Microwave Cooking. LC 75-3715. (Illus.). 1975. 4.95 (ISBN 0-918620-02-3); pap. 3.95 (ISBN 0-918620-01-5). Recipes Unltd.
--Microwave Meals Made Easy. LC 76-45673. (Illus.). 1976. 4.95 (ISBN 0-918620-12-0); pap. 3.95 (ISBN 0-918620-11-2). Recipes Unltd.
Sanderson, Marie C. & Schroeder, Rosella J. It's Not Really Magic: Microwave Cooking for Young People. LC 79-24795. (Doing & Learning Bks.). (Illus.). 104p. (gr. 5 up). 1981. PLB 7.95 (ISBN 0-87518-196-1). Dillon.
Schur, Sylvia. The Tappan Creative Cookbook for Microwave Ovens & Ranges. 1981. pap. 2.95 (ISBN 0-451-09742-4, Sig). NAL.
--The Tappan Creative Cookbook for Microwave Ovens & Ranges. 1977. pap. 3.95 (ISBN 0-452-25146-X, Z5146, Plume). NAL.
Scott, Maria L. & Scott, Jack Denton. Mastering Microwave Cooking. (Illus.). 1976. pap. 2.75 (ISBN 0-553-20427-0). Bantam.
Scribner, Ginger. The Quick & Easy Microwave Oven Cookbook. 1977. pap. 2.95 (ISBN 0-346-12279-1). Cornerstone.
Sims, Dorothy & Malone, Barbara. The Food Processor-Microwave Oven Cookbook. (Illus.). 1980. 12.95 (ISBN 0-8256-3189-0, Quick Fox). Music Sales.
Stand-up & Cook Books: Microwave. (Illus.). 1979. pap. 2.95 (ISBN 0-517-53573-4). Crown.
Stehle, Audrey P. Microwave Cooking Made Easy: A Step-by-Step Guide 400 Microwave-Tested Recipes. LC 78-55871. (Illus.). 1978. 9.95 (ISBN 0-8487-0485-1). Oxmoor Hse.
Sunset Editors. Microwave Cook Book. 2nd ed. LC 80-53481. (Illus.). 96p. 1981. pap. 3.95 (ISBN 0-376-02504-2, Sunset Books). Sunset-Lane.
Wheeler, Grace. Microwave Cooking My Way: It's a Matter of Time. Rand, Elizabeth, ed. LC 80-53591. (Illus.). 240p. 1981. plastic comb bdg. 8.95 (ISBN 0-914488-25-2). Rand-Tofua.
Wooding, Loyta. The Microwave Oven Cookbook. 320p. 1976. pap. 1.95 (ISBN 0-671-80563-0). PB.

MICROWAVE DEVICES
see also Klystrons; Masers; Microwave Circuits; Microwave Communication Systems; Microwave Tubes; Oscillators, Microwave; Parametric Amplifiers; Traveling-Wave Tubes
Fox, J., ed. Microwave Research Institute Symposia. Incl. Vol. 1. Modern Network Synthesis. 1952. 23.00 (ISBN 0-470-27093-4); Vol. 4. Modern Advances in Microwave Techniques. LC 55-12897. 1955; Vol. 5. Modern Network Synthesis. LC 56-2590. 1956; Vol. 6. Nonlinear Circuit Analysis. LC 55-3575. 1956; Vol. 9. Millimeter Waves. LC 60-10073. 1960; Vol. 11. Electromagnetics & Fluid Dynamics of Gaseous Plasma. LC 62-13174. 1962. 36.00 (ISBN 0-470-27423-9); Vol. 13. Optical Lasers. LC 63-22084; Vol. 15. System Theory. LC 65-28522. 1965. 36.00 (ISBN 0-470-27430-1); Vol. 17. Modern Optics. LC 67-31757. 1967; Vol. 19. Computer Processing in Communications. LC 77-122632. 1970; Vol. 20. Submillimeter Waves. 1971; Vol. 21. Computers & Automata. 1972. 37.95 (ISBN 0-471-27438-0); Vol. 22. Computer Communications. 1972. 41.95 (ISBN 0-471-27439-9); Vol. 24. Computer Software Engineering. 1977. 44.95 (ISBN 0-470-98948-3). Pub. by Wiley-Interscience). Wiley.
Gandhi, Om P. Microwave Engineering & Applications. (Illus.). 543p. 1981. 60.00 (ISBN 0-08-025589-2); pap. 24.50 (ISBN 0-08-025588-4). Pergamon.
Garver, Robert. Microwave Diode Control Devices. LC 74-82596. 1976. 29.00 (ISBN 0-89006-022-3). Artech Hse.
Howes, M. J. & Morgan, D. V., eds. Microwave Devices: Device Circuit Interaction. LC 75-15887. (Solid State Devices & Circuits Ser.). 426p. 1976. 60.50 (ISBN 0-471-41729-7, Pub. by Wiley-Interscience). Wiley.
--Microwave Solid State Devices & Applications. (Illus.). 1980. 40.00 (ISBN 0-906048-39-7, Pub. by Peregrinus England). Inst Elect Eng.
Liao, S. Microwave Devices & Circuits. 1980. 32.95 (ISBN 0-13-581207-0). P-H.
Soohoo, Ronald F. Microwave Electronics. LC 75-127893. (Engineering Ser). 1971. text ed. 19.95 (ISBN 0-201-07086-3). A-W.
Tri T. Ha. Solid-State Microwave Amplifier Design. LC 81-21. 326p. 1981. 37.50 (ISBN 0-471-08971-0). Wiley.

MICROWAVE MEASUREMENTS
Kuzmin, A. D. & Salomonovich, A. E. Radioastronomical Methods of Antenna Measurements. (Electrical Science Monographs). 1967. 31.50 (ISBN 0-12-431150-4). Acad Pr.
Lance, Algie L. Introduction to Microwave Theory & Measurements. 1964. text ed. 14.50 (ISBN 0-07-036104-5, G); answer key 0.25 (ISBN 0-07-036105-3). McGraw.
Wentworth Institute. Laboratory Manual for Microwave Measurements. (Illus.). 1971. pap. text ed. 9.95 (ISBN 0-13-521211-1). P-H.

MICROWAVE METEOROLOGY
see Radio Meteorology

MICROWAVE OSCILLATORS
see Oscillators, Microwave

MICROWAVE RADIO
see Radio, Short Wave

MICROWAVE RELAY SYSTEMS
see Radio Relay Systems

MICROWAVE SPECTROSCOPY
Carrington, Alan. Microwave Spectroscopy of Free Radicals. 1974. 44.00 (ISBN 0-12-160750-X). Acad Pr.
Chantry, G. W. Modern Aspects of Microwave Spectroscopy. LC 78-73876. 1980. 103.00 (ISBN 0-12-168150-5). Acad Pr.
Ingram, D. J. Spectroscopy at Radio & Microwave Frequencies. 2nd ed. LC 67-26701. 534p. 1967. 49.50 (ISBN 0-306-30625-5, Plenum Pr). Plenum Pub.
Martin, D. H., ed. Spectroscopic Techniques for Far Infra-Red Submillimeter & Millimeter Waves. 1967. 49.00 (ISBN 0-444-10244-2, North-Holland). Elsevier.
Townes, C. H. & Schawlow, A. L. Microwave Spectroscopy. LC 74-83620. (Illus.). 720p. 1975. pap. text ed. 8.00 (ISBN 0-486-61798-X). Dover.
Varma, Ravi & Hrubesh, Lawrence W. Chemical Analysis by Microwave Rotational Spectroscopy. LC 78-17415. (Chemical Analysis Series of Monographs on Analytical Chemistry & Its Application). 1979. 31.50 (ISBN 0-471-03916-0, Pub. by Wiley-Interscience). Wiley.
Weissberger, Arnold, et al, eds. Techniques of Organic Chemistry: Microwave Molecular Spectra, Vol. 9, Pt. 2. LC 80-16243. 747p. 1970. 67.50 (ISBN 0-471-93161-6). Krieger.
Wilmhurst, T. H. Electron Spin Resonance Spectrometers. LC 68-8257. (Monographs on Electron Spin Resonance Ser.). 280p. 1968. 29.50 (ISBN 0-306-30372-8, Plenum Pr). Plenum Pub.

MICROWAVE TUBES
Dix, C. H. & Aldous, W. H. Microwave Valves. 15.00x (ISBN 0-592-02728-7). Transatlantic.
International Congress Of Microwave Tubes - 5th - Paris - 1964. Microwave Tubes: Proceedings. 1965. 115.50 (ISBN 0-12-461550-3). Acad Pr.
Kleen, Werner J. Electronics of Microwave Tubes. Lindsay, P. A., et al, trs. 1958. 46.00 (ISBN 0-12-412550-6). Acad Pr.
Okress, E., ed. Crossed-Field Microwave Devices, 2 Vols. 1961. Vol. 1. 55.25 (ISBN 0-12-525301-X); Vol. 2. 54.25 (ISBN 0-12-525302-8). Acad Pr.
Okress, Ernest, ed. Microwave Power Engineering, 2 Vols. (Electrical Science Ser). 1968. Vol. 1. 53.00 (ISBN 0-12-525350-8). Acad Pr.
Wosnik, J., ed. Microwave Tubes: Proceedings of a Congress. 1961. 98.00 (ISBN 0-12-764550-0). Acad Pr.

MICROWAVE WIRING
Bahl, I. J. & Bhartia, P. Microstrip Antennas. (Illus.), 355p. 1980. 40.00 (ISBN 0-89006-098-3). Artech Hse.

MICROWAVES
see also Microwave Devices; Microwave Measurements; Microwave Spectroscopy; Microwave Tubes; Microwave Wiring; Quantum Electronics
Angelakos, Diogenes J. & Everhart, Thomas E. Microwave Communications. (Electrical & Electronic Eng. Ser). 1967. 26.95 (ISBN 0-07-001789-1, C). McGraw.
Baden-Fuller, A. J. Microwaves: An Introduction to Microwave Theory & Techniques. 1979. 41.00 (ISBN 0-08-024228-6); pap. 16.25 (ISBN 0-08-024227-8). Pergamon.
Brodeur, Paul. Zapping of America: Microwaves. 11.95 (ISBN 0-686-29878-0). Cancer Bk Hse.
--The Zapping of America: Microwaves, Their Deadly Risk & the Cover-up. (Illus.). 1977. 14.95 (ISBN 0-393-06427-1); pap. 4.95 (ISBN 0-393-00931-9). Norton.
Business Communications Co. The Microwave Industry, G-020: Trends, Developments. 1981. 875.00 (ISBN 0-89336-275-1). BCC.
Collin, Robert E. Foundations for Microwave Engineering. 1966. 27.95 (ISBN 0-07-011801-9, C). McGraw.
Cornbleet, Sidney. Microwave Optics: The Optics of Microwave Antenna Design. (Pure & Applied Physics Ser.). 1977. 66.00 (ISBN 0-12-189650-1). Acad Pr.
Fox, J., ed. Microwave Research Institute Symposia. Incl. Vol. 1. Modern Network Synthesis. 1952. 23.00 (ISBN 0-470-27093-4); Vol. 4. Modern Advances in Microwave Techniques. LC 55-12897. 1955; Vol. 5. Modern Network Synthesis. LC 56-2590. 1956; Vol. 6. Nonlinear Circuit Analysis. LC 55-3575. 1956; Vol. 9. Millimeter Waves. LC 60-10073. 1960; Vol. 11. Electromagnetics & Fluid Dynamics of Gaseous Plasma. LC 62-13174. 1962. 36.00 (ISBN 0-470-27423-9); Vol. 13. Optical Lasers. LC 63-22084; Vol. 15. System Theory. LC 65-28522. 1965. 36.00 (ISBN 0-470-27430-1); Vol. 17. Modern Optics. LC 67-31757. 1967; Vol. 19. Computer Processing in Communications. LC 77-122632. 1970; Vol. 20. Submillimeter Waves. 1971; Vol. 21. Computers & Automata. 1972. 37.95 (ISBN 0-471-27438-0); Vol. 22. Computer Communications. 1972. 41.95 (ISBN 0-471-27439-9); Vol. 24. Computer Software Engineering. 1977. 44.95 (ISBN 0-470-98948-3). Pub. by Wiley-Interscience). Wiley.
Goldblith, Samuel A. & Decareau, Robert V. An Annotated Bibliography on Microwaves: Their Properties, Production, & Application to Food Processing. 1973. 21.50x (ISBN 0-262-07049-9). MIT Pr.
Grantham, Donald J. Antennas, Transmission Lines, & Microwaves. LC 77-25369. (The Grantham Electronics-with-Mathematics Ser.: Vol. 6). (Illus.). 1977. pap. text ed. 15.95x (ISBN 0-915668-06-8). G S E Pubns.
Gupta, K. C. Microwaves. LC 80-11904. 256p. 1980. 14.95x (ISBN 0-470-26966-9). Halsted Pr.
Heald, M. A. & Wharton, C. B. Plasma Diagnostics with Microwaves. LC 77-13781. 470p. 1978. Repr. of 1965 ed. 23.50 (ISBN 0-88275-626-5). Krieger.
Helszajn, J. Nonreciprocal Microwave Junctions & Circulators. LC 75-5588. 368p. 1975. 34.95 (ISBN 0-471-36935-7, Pub. by Wiley-Interscience). Wiley.
Hewlitt-Packard. Microwave Theory & Applications. 1969. 23.95 (ISBN 0-13-581488-X). P-H.
Kerns, D. M. & Beatty, R. W. Basic Theory of Waveguide Junctions & Introductory Microwave Network Analysis. 1967. text ed. 17.25 (ISBN 0-08-012064-4). Pergamon.
Kraszewski, Andreej. Microwave Gas Discharge Devices. Benson, F. A., ed. (Illus.). 1969. 21.25x (ISBN 0-592-02780-5). Transatlantic.
Lance, Algie L. Introduction to Microwave Theory & Measurements. 1964. text ed. 14.50 (ISBN 0-07-036104-5, G); answer key 0.25 (ISBN 0-07-036105-3). McGraw.
Laverghetta, Thomas. Microwave Measurements & Techniques. LC 75-31383. 1976. 36.00 (ISBN 0-89006-053-3). Artech Hse.
Lin, James C. Microwave Auditory Effects & Applications. (Illus.). 232p. 1978. 29.75 (ISBN 0-398-03704-3). C C Thomas.
Microwave Miracles. (Orig.). 9.95 (ISBN 0-87502-043-7); pap. 5.95 (ISBN 0-87502-042-9). Benjamin Co.
Multi-Power Microwave Miracles. 1978. write for info (ISBN 0-87502-061-5). Benjamin Co.
Okress, E., ed. Crossed-Field Microwave Devices, 2 Vols. 1961. Vol. 1. 55.25 (ISBN 0-12-525301-X); Vol. 2. 54.25 (ISBN 0-12-525302-8). Acad Pr.
Okress, Ernest, ed. Microwave Power Engineering, 2 Vols. (Electrical Science Ser). 1968. Vol. 1. 53.00 (ISBN 0-12-525350-8). Acad Pr.
Peyton, Mary F., ed. Biological Effects of Microwave Radiation. LC 61-11807. 333p. 1961. 35.00 (ISBN 0-306-30113-X, Plenum Pr). Plenum Pub.
Saad, Theodore, ed. The Microwave Engineers' Handbook, 2 vols. LC 76-168891. 1971. 43.00 set (ISBN 0-89006-004-5); Vol. 1. 26.00 (ISBN 0-89006-002-9); Vol. 2. 26.00 (ISBN 0-89006-003-7). Artech Hse.
Skobel'tsyn, D. V., ed. Microwave-Plasma Interactions. (P. N. Lebedev Physics Institute Ser.: Vol. 73). (Illus.). 140p. 1975. 42.50 (ISBN 0-306-10915-8, Consultants). Plenum Pub.
Sodha, M. S. & Srivastava, N. C. Microwave Propagation in Ferrimagnetics. 350p. 1981. text ed. 45.00 (ISBN 0-306-40716-7, Plenum Pr). Plenum Pub.
Solymar, L. A Review of the Principles of Electrical & Electronic Engineering. Incl. Vol. 1. Principles of Heavy Current Engineering. LC 73-15220. 115p. 1974. pap. text ed. 9.95x (ISBN 0-412-11660-X); Vol. 2. From Circuits to Computers. LC 73-15221. 184p. 1974. pap. text ed. 9.95x (ISBN 0-412-11670-7); Vol.3. Modern Physical Electronics. LC 73-15223. 213p. 1975. pap. text ed. 9.95x (ISBN 0-412-11680-4); Vol. 4. Microwaves, Communications & Radar. LC 73-15224. 190p. 1975. pap. text ed. 10.50x (ISBN 0-412-11690-1). Pub. by Chapman & Hall England). Methuen Inc.
Tyler, Paul E., ed. Biologic Effects of NonIonizing Radiation. (Annals of the New York Academy of Sciences: Vol. 247). 1975. 62.75x (ISBN 0-89072-761-9). NY Acad Sci.
Von Aulock, Wilhelm H., ed. Handbook of Microwave Ferrite Materials. (Illus.). 1965. 51.00 (ISBN 0-12-723350-4). Acad Pr.
Wheeler, Gershon. Introduction to Microwaves. (Illus.). 1963. ref. ed. 18.95 (ISBN 0-13-487843-4). P-H.
Young, Leo, ed. Advances in Microwaves. Incl. Vol. 1. 1966. 60.00 (ISBN 0-12-027901-0); Vol. 2. 1967. 60.00 (ISBN 0-12-027902-9); Vol. 3. 1968. 60.00 (ISBN 0-12-027903-7); Vol. 4. 1969. 60.00 (ISBN 0-12-027904-5); Vol. 5. 1970. 60.00 (ISBN 0-12-027905-3); Vol. 6. 1971. 60.00 (ISBN 0-12-027906-1); Vol. 7. 1971. 60.00 (ISBN 0-12-027907-X); Suppl. 1. Theory & Design of Microwave Filters & Circuits. Matsumoto, A. 1970. 46.50 (ISBN 0-12-027961-4). Acad Pr.

MID-CONTINENT AREA POWER PLANNERS
Nelson, W. Stewart. Mid-Continent Area Power Planners: A New Approach to Planning in the Electric Power Industry. LC 68-63563. 1968. 5.00 (ISBN 0-87744-080-8). Mich St U Busn.

MIDDLE AGE
see also Aging; Climacteric; Longevity; Old Age
Barks, Herb. Prime Time. 144p. 1981. pap. 3.95 (ISBN 0-8407-5768-9). Nelson.
Blanda, George & Herskowitz, Mickey. Over Forty Feeling Great & Looking Good. 1978. 9.95 (ISBN 0-671-22472-7). S&S.
Blanton, Smiley & Gordon, Arthur. Now or Never: The Promise of the Middle Years. 192p. 1976. pap. 1.95 (ISBN 0-346-12217-1). Cornerstone.
Block, Marilyn. Women Over Forty: Visions & Realities. LC 80-20774. (Focus on Women Ser.: No. 4). 176p. 1980. text ed. 19.95 (ISBN 0-8261-3000-3); pap. text ed. 11.95 (ISBN 0-8261-3001-1). Springer Pub.
Brody, Jean & Osborne, Gail B. The Twenty Year Phenomenon. 1980. 11.95 (ISBN 0-671-25042-6). S&S.
Burkitt, Ann. Life Begins at Forty: How to Make Sure You Enjoy Middle Age. 1977. pap. 1.95 (ISBN 0-09-129101-1, Pub. by Hutchinson). Merrimack Bk Serv.
Cagan, Maxwell S. Medianetics: Dynamic Living in Your Middle Years. LC 75-22570. 204p. 1975. 8.95 (ISBN 0-913264-20-2). Douglas-West.
Clinebell, Howard J. Growth Counseling for Mid-Years Couples. Stone, Howard W., ed. LC 76-7863. (Creative Pastoral Care & Counseling Ser.). 1977. pap. 3.25 (ISBN 0-8006-0558-6, 1-558). Fortress.
Conway, Jim. Men in Mid-Life Crisis. 1981. pap. 4.95 (ISBN 0-89191-145-6). Caroline Hse.
--Men in Mid-Life Crisis. LC 78-67098. 1978. text ed. 4.95 (ISBN 0-89191-145-6). Cook.
Conway, Sally. You & Your Husband's Mid-Life Crisis. 1981. pap. 4.95 (ISBN 0-89191-318-1). Caroline Hse.
Cooper, Cary & Torrington, Derek. After Forty: The Time for Achievement. 208p. 1981. 23.25 (ISBN 0-686-74676-7, Pub. by Wiley Interscience). Wiley.
Davitz, Joel & Davitz, Lois. Making It: Forty & Beyond, Surviving the Mid-Life Crisis. 1979. pap. 6.95 (ISBN 0-03-051561-0). Winston Pr.
Donahugh, Donald. The Middle Years. 320p. text ed. 14.95 (ISBN 0-7216-3144-4). Saunders.
Donohugh, Donald. The Middle Years. 1981. 14.95 (ISBN 0-03-057658-X). Saunders.
Eichorn, Dorothy, et al, eds. Present & Past in Middle Life. LC 80-70589. 1981. write for info. (ISBN 0-12-233680-1). Acad Pr.
Entine, Alan D. & Mueller, Jean E. Perspectives on Mid-Life. (Technical Bibliographies on Aging Ser. 2). 1977. 2.25 (ISBN 0-88474-076-5). USC Andrus Geron.
Farrell, Michael P. & Rosenberg, Stanley. Men at Midlife. LC 81-3624. 200p. 1981. 19.95 (ISBN 0-86569-073-1). Auburn Hse.
Figler, Homer R. Overcoming Executive Midlife Crisis. LC 77-29206. 1978. 14.95 (ISBN 0-471-04147-5, Pub. by Wiley-Interscience). Wiley.
Fiske, Marjorie. Middle Age: The Prime of Life. (Life Cycle Ser.). 1980. pap. text ed. 4.95 scp (ISBN 0-06-384749-3, HarpC). Har-Row.
Fogarty, Michael P. Forty to Sixty: How We Waste the Middle Aged. LC 76-357985. 1975. pap. 12.50x (ISBN 0-7199-0904-X). Intl Pubns Serv.
Genne, William. Living in the Middle Years. (Christian Living Ser). 16p. 1976. pap. 0.30 (ISBN 0-8170-0728-8). Judson.
Girdano, Daniel A. Better Late Than Never: How Men Can Avoid a Midlife Fitness Crisis. (Illus.). 256p. 1981. 12.95t (ISBN 0-13-074773-4, Spec); pap. 5.95b (ISBN 0-13-074765-3). P-H.
Hallberg, Edmond C. The Gray Itch. 1978. 8.95 (ISBN 0-8128-2439-3). Stein & Day.
Heidi, Gloria. Winning the Age Game. 1977. pap. 6.95 (ISBN 0-89104-061-7). A & W Pubs.

Hickman, Martha W. The Growing Season. LC 80-68983. 128p. (Orig.). 1980. pap. 4.50x (ISBN 0-8358-0411-9). Upper Room.
Kinderlehrer, Jane. How to Feel Younger, Longer. LC 74-13909. (Illus.). 228p. 1974. 8.95 (ISBN 0-87857-083-7); pap. 6.95 (ISBN 0-87857-278-3). Rodale Pr Inc.
LeShan, Eda. The Wonderful Crisis of Middle Age. 320p. 1974. pap. 2.95 (ISBN 0-446-93746-0). Warner Bks.
Liveseu, Herbert. Second Chance: How to Change Your Career in Mid-Life. 1979. pap. 2.25 (ISBN 0-451-08469-1, E8469, Sig). NAL.
McMorrow, Fred. Midolescence: The Dangerous Years. LC 74-78999. 285p. 1974. 10.95 (ISBN 0-8129-0481-8). Times Bks.
Maitland, David J. Against the Grain: Coming Through Mid-Life Crisis. 200p. 1981. 11.95 (ISBN 0-8298-0461-7). Pilgrim NY.
Merriam, Sharan B. Coping with Male Mid-Life: A Systematic Analysis Using Literature As a Data Source. LC 80-5124. 137p. 1980. pap. text ed. 7.50 (ISBN 0-8191-1051-5). U Pr of Amer.
Miller, Luree. Late Bloom: New Lives for Women. LC 78-25983. 1979. 8.95 (ISBN 0-448-22687-1). Paddington.
Morley, David C. Halfway up the Mountain. 1979. 7.95 (ISBN 0-8007-1060-6). Revell.
Musgrave, Beatrice & Menell, Zoe, eds. Change & Choice: Women & Middle Age. 186p. 1980. text ed. 18.50x (ISBN 0-7206-0539-3). Humanities.
Neugarten, Bernice L., ed. Middle Age & Aging: A Reader in Social Psychology. LC 68-55150. 1968. 25.00x (ISBN 0-226-57381-8); pap. 10.00x (ISBN 0-226-57382-6). U of Chicago Pr.
Newton, Kathleen & Looney, Gerald. Doctor Discussses Making the Mid-Years the Prime of Life. (Illus.). 1978. pap. 2.50 (ISBN 0-685-46333-8). Budlong.
Nudel, Adele. For the Woman Over Fifty: A Practical Guide for a Full & Vital Life. LC 77-91047. 1978. 12.50 (ISBN 0-8008-2967-0). Taplinger.
Olson, Richard P. Mid-Life: A Time to Discover, a Time to Decide. 160p. 1980. pap. 5.95 (ISBN 0-8170-0859-4). Judson.
Raber, Chester A. Middle Age: A Test of Time. LC 66-23904. (Family Life Ser.). (Orig.). 1966. pap. 0.35 (ISBN 0-8361-1530-9). Herald Pr.
Ray, David. The Forty Plus Handbook. 1979. 5.25 (ISBN 0-8499-2850-8). Word Bks.
Rogers, Dorothy. The Adult Years: An Introduction to Aging. (Illus.). 1979. text ed. 19.95 (ISBN 0-13-008987-7). P-H.
Rubin, Lillian B. Women of a Certain Age: The Midlife Search for Self. LC 79-1681. 1979. 10.95 (ISBN 0-06-013706-1, HarpT). Har-Row.
Smith, Richard K. Forty-Nine & Holding. LC 75-11179. (Illus.). 1975. 7.95 (ISBN 0-89430-023-7). Morgan-Pacific.
Sparks, James A. Friendship After Forty. LC 80-10629. 144p. 1980. 7.95 (ISBN 0-687-13520-6). Abingdon.
Stevenson, Joanne S. Issues & Crises During Middlescence. (Illus.). 230p. 1977. pap. 12.75 (ISBN 0-8385-4409-6). ACC.
Tamir, Lois M. Men in Their Forties: The Transition to Middle Age. Date not set. price not set (ISBN 0-8261-3630-3). Springer Pub.
Taylor, Robert. The Now Doctor's Guide for Adults: Welcome to the Middle Years. LC 76-39649. (Illus.). 1978. pap. 6.95 (ISBN 0-87491-271-7). Acropolis.
Tengbom, Mildred. The Bonus Years. LC 74-14180. 160p. (Orig.). 1975. pap. 3.95 (ISBN 0-8066-1463-3, 10-0782). Augsburg.
Troll, et al. Looking Ahead: A Woman's Guide to the Problems & Joys of Growing Older. 1977. 10.95 (ISBN 0-13-540310-3, Spec); pap. 4.95 (ISBN 0-13-540302-2). P-H.
Utlan. Your Middle Years: A Doctor's Guide for Today's Woman. 12.95 (ISBN 0-8385-9938-9); pap. 5.95 (ISBN 0-8385-9937-0). ACC.
Vedder, Clyde B., ed. Problems of the Middle-Aged. 216p. 1965. photocopy ed. spiral 16.75 (ISBN 0-398-01974-6). C C Thomas.
Viorst, Judith. How Did I Get to Be Forty... & Other Atrocities. 1976. 5.95 (ISBN 0-671-22366-6). S&S.
Waldo, Myra. The Prime of Life & How to Make It Last. 1980. 14.95 (ISBN 0-02-622690-1). Macmillan.
Wallis, J. H. Challenge of Middle Age. 1972. 8.50 (ISBN 0-7100-2250-6). Routledge & Kegan.
Wax, Judith. Starting in the Middle. LC 78-16809. 1979. 8.95 (ISBN 0-03-020296-5). HR&W.
Weaver. Strategies for the Second Half of Life: Not a Retirement Book. 1980. 12.95 (ISBN 0-531-09922-9, C23). Watts.
Weaver, Peter. Strategies for the Second Half of Life. 1981. pap. 3.50 (ISBN 0-451-09814-5, E9814, Sig). NAL.
Westoff, Leslie A. Breaking Out of the Middle-Age Trap. 1981. pap. 3.50 (ISBN 0-451-11210-5, AE 1210, Sig). NAL.
White, Jerry & White, Mary. Christian in Mid-Life. LC 80-83388. (Orig.). 1980. pap. 5.95 (ISBN 0-89109-448-2). NavPress.

MIDDLE AGE AND EMPLOYMENT

see Age and Employment

MIDDLE AGES

see also Architecture, Medieval; Art, Medieval; Church History–Middle Ages, 600-1500; Civilization, Medieval; Geography, Medieval; Literature, Medieval; Renaissance; Science, Medieval

Allen, Judson B. Friar As Critic: Literary Attitudes in the Later Middle Ages. LC 77-123037. 1971. 11.50 (ISBN 0-8265-1158-9). Vanderbilt U Pr.
Bachrach, B. S., ed. The Medieval Church: Success or Failure? (European Problem Ser.). 120p. 1972. pap. text ed. 5.50 (ISBN 0-03-085185-8, Pub. by HR&W). Krieger.
Baker, Derek & Millward, J. S., eds. Early Middle Ages, Eight Seventy One-Twelve Sixteen: Portraits & Documents. (Portraits & Documents Ser.). 1968. pap. text ed. 2.00x (ISBN 0-09-075642-8). Humanities.
Baldwin, John W. The Scholastic Culture of the Middle Ages: 1000-1300. LC 70-120060. (Civilization & Society Ser). 192p. 1971. pap. 5.95x (ISBN 0-669-62059-9). Heath.
Bark, William C. Origins of the Medieval World. 1958. 10.00x (ISBN 0-8047-0513-5); pap. 2.95x (ISBN 0-8047-0514-3). Stanford U Pr.
Bartlett, Bede. Social Theories of the Middle Ages, 1200-1250. 1976. lib. bdg. 59.95 (ISBN 0-8490-2619-9). Gordon Pr.
Bishop, Morris. Middle Ages. abr. ed. LC 70-95728. Orig. Title: Horizon Book of the Middle Ages. 1970. pap. 5.95 (ISBN 0-07-005466-5, SP). McGraw.
Cairns, Trevor. Middle Ages. (Cambridge Introduction to the History of Mankind Ser.: Bk. 4). (Illus.). 1971. 5.95 (ISBN 0-521-07726-5). Cambridge U Pr.
Caples, C. B., et al. A Medieval Miscellany. (Rice University Studies: Vol. 62, No. 2). (Illus.). 120p. (Orig.). 1976. pap. 4.25x (ISBN 0-89263-228-3). Rice Univ.
Centre National De la Recherche Scientifique, Paris, ed. International Directory of Medievalists, 2 vols. 5th ed. 1979. 140.00 (ISBN 0-89664-046-9, Pub. by K G Saur). Gale.
Chandler, Alice. Dream of Order: The Medieval Ideal in Nineteenth-Century English Literature. LC 69-10413. 1970. 16.50x (ISBN 0-8032-0704-2). U of Nebr Pr.
Childs, Wendy R. Anglo-Castilian Trade in the Later Middle Ages. (Illus.). 264p. 1978. 23.50x (ISBN 0-8476-6071-0). Rowman.
Church, R. W. The Beginning of the Middle Ages. 1977. lib. bdg. 59.95 (ISBN 0-8490-1484-0). Gordon Pr.
Clogan, Paul M., ed. Medievalia et Humanistica: Studies in Medieval & Renaissance Culture. (New Ser.: No. 10). 1981. 25.00x (ISBN 0-8476-6944-0). Rowman.
Coulton, George G. Life in the Middle Ages. Cambridge U Pr.
Crump, C. G. & Jacob, E. F., eds. Legacy of the Middle Ages. (Legacy Ser.). (Illus.). 1926. 29.50x (ISBN 0-19-821907-5). Oxford U Pr.
Cutts, Edward L. Scenes & Characters of the Middle Ages. 1977. lib. bdg. 59.95 (ISBN 0-8490-2569-9). Gordon Pr.
--Scenes & Characters of the Middle Ages. LC 77-23575. 1977. Repr. of 1922 ed. lib. bdg. 45.00 (ISBN 0-89341-160-4). Longwood Pr.
--Science & Characters of the Middle Ages. 552p. 1981. Repr. of 1926 ed. lib. bdg. 40.00 (ISBN 0-8495-0876-2). Arden Lib.
Dales, Richard C. The Intellectual Life of Western Europe in the Middle Ages. LC 79-5515. 1980. pap. text ed. 9.25 (ISBN 0-8191-0900-2). U Pr of Amer.
De Loy Jameson, Raymond, pseud. Trails of the Troubadors. LC 78-102837. 1970. Repr. of 1927 ed. 12.50 (ISBN 0-8046-0752-4). Kennikat.
Dobson, R. B. Durham Priory, Fourteen Hundred to Fourteen Fifty. LC 72-89809. (Studies in Medieval Life & Thought). 390p. 1973. 53.95 (ISBN 0-521-20140-3). Cambridge U Pr.
Emerton, Ephraim. An Introduction to the Study of the Middle Ages (375-814) 1978. Repr. of 1900 ed. lib. bdg. 35.00 (ISBN 0-8482-0713-0). Norwood Edns.
Frantz, Alison. The Middle Ages in the Athenian Agora. (Excavations of the Athenian Agora Picture Bks.: No. 7). (Illus.). 1961. pap. 1.50x (ISBN 0-87661-607-4). Am Sch Athens.
Funck-Bretano. The Middle Ages. O'Neill, Elizabeth, tr. 1979. Repr. of 1926 ed. lib. bdg. 35.00 (ISBN 0-8495-1644-7). Arden Lib.
Gies, Joseph & Gies, Frances. Women in the Middle Ages. 264p. 1980. pap. 3.95 (ISBN 0-06-464037-X, BN 4000, BN). Har-Row.
Hauck, Karl, ed. Fruhmittelaterliche Studien, Vol. 11. (Illus.). 1977. 123.25x (ISBN 3-11-007076-6). De Gruyter.
Hearnshaw, Fossey J., ed. Medieval Contributions to Modern Civilization. LC 66-25917. 1966. Repr. of 1921 ed. 10.00 (ISBN 0-8046-0198-4). Kennikat.
Heer, Friedrick. Medieval World: Europe Eleven Hundred to Thirteen Fifty. 1964. pap. 3.50 (ISBN 0-451-61919-6, ME1919, Ment). NAL.
Hoyt, Robert S., ed. Life & Thought in the Early Middle Ages. LC 67-15065. (Illus.). 1967. pap. 1.95x (ISBN 0-8166-0464-9, MP11). U of Minn Pr.
Huizinga, J. Waning of the Middle Ages. LC 54-4529. pap. 3.95 (ISBN 0-385-09288-1, A42, Anch). Doubleday.
Huizinga, Johan. Waning of the Middle Ages: Study of the Forms of Life, Thought & Art in France & the Netherlands in the 14th & 15th Centuries. (Illus.). 1924. 25.00 (ISBN 0-312-85540-0). St Martin.
Hunt, R. W. The History of Grammar in the Middle Ages. Bursell-Hall, G. L., ed. xxxvi, 214p. 1980. 25.00 (ISBN 90-272-0896-4, SIHOL 5). Benjamins North Am.
Jones, L. W., ed. Classical & Mediaeval Studies in Honor of Edward Kennard Rand, Presented Upon the Completion of His Fortieth Year of Teaching. facs. ed. LC 68-57312. (Essay Index Reprint Ser). 1938. 19.50 (ISBN 0-8369-0312-9). Arno.
Kantorowicz, Ernst H. Selected Studies. LC 65-25431. 12.50 (ISBN 0-685-71745-3). J J Augustin.
King, P. D. Law & Society in the Visigothic Kingdom. LC 77-179163. (Cambridge Studies in Medieval Life & Thought: Third Ser., No. 5). 320p. 1972. 44.50 (ISBN 0-521-08421-0). Cambridge U Pr.
Laistner, Max L. Intellectual Heritage of the Early Middle Ages. 1966. lib. bdg. 17.00x (ISBN 0-374-94712-0). Octagon.
LaMonte, John L. World of the Middle Ages: A Reorientation of Medieval History. (Illus.). 1949. 34.50x (ISBN 0-89197-473-3); pap. text ed. 19.50x (ISBN 0-89197-980-8). Irvington.
Lexikon des Mittelalters. (Ger.). 1977. pap. 25.00 (ISBN 3-7608-8801-1, M-7206). French & Eur.
Lievsay, John L., ed. Medieval & Renaissance Studies, No. 2. LC 66-25361. 1968. 9.75 (ISBN 0-8223-0107-5). Duke.
--Medieval & Renaissance Studies, No. 4. LC 66-25361. 1970. 11.75 (ISBN 0-8223-0227-6). Duke.
Lyon, Bryce, ed. High Middle Ages, 1000-1300. LC 64-21207. (Orig.). 1964. pap. text ed. 7.95 (ISBN 0-02-919480-6). Free Pr.
Queller, D. Office of the Ambassador in the Middle Ages. 1967. 19.00x (ISBN 0-691-04530-5). Princeton U Pr.
Rand, Edward K. Founders of the Middle Ages. 1928. pap. 5.00 (ISBN 0-486-20369-7). Dover.
Southern, Richard W. Making of the Middle Ages. (Illus.). 1953. 20.00x (ISBN 0-300-00967-4); pap. 4.95x 1961 (ISBN 0-300-00230-0, Y46). Yale U Pr.
Stubbs, W. Historical Introductions to the Rolls Series. LC 68-25267. (British History Ser., No. 30). 1969. Repr. of 1902 ed. lib. bdg. 45.95 (ISBN 0-8383-0243-2). Haskell.
Townsend, W. J. The Great Schoolmen of the Middle Ages. 1977. lib. bdg. 39.95 (ISBN 0-8490-1903-6). Gordon Pr.
Trismosin, Solomon. Splendor Solis: A.D. 1582. (Illus.). 104p. 1976. 12.50 (ISBN 0-911662-57-X). Yoga.
Zbozny, Frank T., ed. Annuale Mediaevale, Vol. 18. 1978. pap. text ed. 13.50x (ISBN 0-391-01220-7). Humanities.

MIDDLE AGES–BIBLIOGRAPHY

Chevalier, C. Ulysse. Repertoire Des Sources Historiques Du Moyen Age: Bio-Bibliographie, 2 vols. 2nd ed. 1905-07. Set. 118.00 (ISBN 0-527-16700-2). Kraus Repr.
Chevalier, Ulysse. Repertoire Des Sources Historiques Du Moyen Age: Topo-Bibliographie, 2 Vols. 2nd ed. 1894-1903. Set. 90.00 (ISBN 0-527-16710-X). Kraus Repr.
Ker, N. R., ed. Medieval Libraries of Great Britain - a List of Surviving Books. 424p. 1964. 19.95x (ISBN 0-8464-0626-8). Beekman Pubs.
Phillips, Jill. Annus Mirabilis: A Bibliography of Medieval Times. (Bibliographies for Librarians Ser.). 1980. lib. bdg. 75.00 (ISBN 0-8490-1398-4). Gordon Pr.
Pontifical Institute of Mediaeval Studies, Toronto. Dictionary Catalog of the Library of the Pontifical Institute of Mediaeval Studies: First Supplement. (Library Catalogs-Bib. Guides). 1979. lib. bdg. 125.00 (ISBN 0-8161-1061-1). G K Hall.
Rouse, Richard H., ed. Serial Bibliographies for Medieval Studies. LC 68-31637. (UCLA Center for Medieval & Renaissance Studies). 1969. 22.50x (ISBN 0-520-01456-1). U of Cal Pr.

MIDDLE AGES–HISTORIOGRAPHY

Archambault, Paul. Seven French Chroniclers: Witnesses to History. LC 73-16652. 224p. 1974. 12.00x (ISBN 0-8156-0099-2). Syracuse U Pr.

MIDDLE AGES–HISTORY

see also Chivalry; Civilization, Medieval; Crusades; Europe–History–476-1492; Feudalism; Fifteenth Century; Fourteenth Century; Holy Roman Empire; Knights and Knighthood; Migrations of Nations; Monasticism and Religious Orders; Thirteenth Century; Twelfth Century

Adams, G. B. Civilization During the Middle Ages. 75.00 (ISBN 0-87968-873-4). Gordon Pr.
Adams, George B. Medieval & Modern History. 1901. 15.00 (ISBN 0-8482-7276-5). Norwood Edns.
Allen, Michael J. B., ed. Marsilio Ficino & the Phaedran Charioteer, No. 14. (Center for Medieval & Renaissance Studies, UCLA). 1981. 30.00x (ISBN 0-520-04222-0). U of Cal Pr.
An Archepiscopal Election in the Middle Ages: Jacob II Swinka of Gniezno. 37p. 1963. 3.00 (ISBN 0-686-30941-3). Polish Inst Arts.
Ashton, Eliyahu. Studies on the Levantine Trade in the Middle Ages. 372p. 1980. 60.00x (ISBN 0-86078-020-1, Pub. by Variorum England). State Mutual Bk.
Atiya, Aziz S. Crusade in the Later Middle Ages. LC 67-28472. (Illus.). 1965. 22.00 (ISBN 0-527-03700-1). Kraus Repr.
Bagley, J. J. Medieval People. (People in Period Ser.). 1978. 16.95 (ISBN 0-7134-1046-9, Pub. by Batsford England). David & Charles.
Barber, Richard. The Reign of Chivalry. (Illus.). 208p. 1980. 27.50 (ISBN 0-312-66994-1). St Martin.
Baring-Gould, S. Old Century Life. 59.95 (ISBN 0-8490-0754-2). Gordon Pr.
Becker, Marvin B. Medieval Italy: Constraints & Creativity. LC 80-8376. 256p. 1981. 17.50x (ISBN 0-253-15294-1). Ind U Pr.
Bernheimer, Richard. Wild Men in the Middle Ages. LC 70-120229. 1970. Repr. lib. bdg. 15.50x (ISBN 0-374-90616-5). Octagon.
Bowsky, William M., ed. Studies in Medieval & Renaissance History, Vol. 1. LC 63-22098. 1964. 15.00x (ISBN 0-8032-0651-8). U of Nebr Pr.
--Studies in Medieval & Renaissance History, Vol. 4. LC 63-22098. 1967. 13.95x (ISBN 0-8032-0654-2). U of Nebr Pr.
--Studies in Medieval & Renaissance History, Vol. 5. LC 63-22098. 1968. 14.50x (ISBN 0-8032-0655-0). U of Nebr Pr.
Brown, R. Allen. The Origins of Modern Europe: The Medieval Heritage of Western Civilization. LC 72-11597. 1973. pap. 5.95x (ISBN 0-88295-705-8). Harlan Davidson.
Bullough, Vern & Brundage, James, eds. Sex in the Middle Ages. LC 80-85227. (New Concepts in Human Sexuality Ser.). 250p. 1980. 17.95 (ISBN 0-87975-141-X); pap. 9.95 (ISBN 0-87975-151-7). Prometheus Bks.
--Sexual Practices & the Medieval Church. LC 80-85227. (New Concepts in Human Sexuality Ser.). 350p. 1981. 18.95 (ISBN 0-87975-141-X); pap. 9.95 (ISBN 0-87975-151-7). Prometheus Bks.
The Cambridge Medieval History, 9 vols. Incl. Vol. 1. The Christian Roman Empire & the Foundation of the Teutonic Kingdoms. 59.95 (ISBN 0-521-04532-0); Vol. 2. The Rise of the Saracens & the Foundation of the Western Empire. 69.95 (ISBN 0-521-04533-9); Vol. 3. Germany & the Western Empire. 64.95 (ISBN 0-521-04534-7); Vol. 4, Pt. 1. The Byzantine Empire. 2nd ed. Hussey, J. M. & Nicol, D. M., eds. 1966. 87.95 (ISBN 0-521-04535-5); Vol. 4, Pt. 2. Government Church & Civilization. 59.95 (ISBN 0-521-04536-3); Vol. 5. Contest of Empire & Papacy. 77.95 (ISBN 0-521-04537-1); Vol. 6. Victory of the Papacy. 77.95 (ISBN 0-521-04538-X); Vol. 7. Decline of the Empire & Papacy. 77.95 (ISBN 0-521-04539-8); Vol. 8. The Close of the Middle Ages. 77.95 (ISBN 0-521-04540-1). Cambridge U Pr.
Carlyle, Alexander J. Political Liberty: A History of the Conception in the Middle Ages & Modern Times. LC 80-18967. viii, 220p. 1980. Repr. of 1963 ed. lib. bdg. 19.75x (ISBN 0-313-21482-4, CAPL). Greenwood.
Cate, James L. & Anderson, E. N. Medieval & Historiographical Essays in Honor of James Westfall Thompson. LC 66-25904. Repr. of 1938 ed. 17.00 (ISBN 0-8046-0072-4). Kennikat.
Cheyette, Frederic, ed. Lordship & Community in Medieval Europe. LC 75-12657. 448p. 1975. Repr. of 1968 ed. 14.50 (ISBN 0-88275-283-9). Krieger.
Church, R. W. The Beginning of the Middle Ages. 1978. Repr. of 1892 ed. lib. bdg. 20.00 (ISBN 0-8492-3977-X). R West.

Clifford, Alan. The Middle Ages. Yapp, Malcolm, et al, eds. (World History Ser.). (Illus.). (gr. 10). 1980. Repr. of 1977 ed. lib. bdg. 5.95 (ISBN 0-89908-028-6); pap. text ed. 1.95 (ISBN 0-89908-003-0). Greenhaven.

Coulton, G. G. Some Problems in Medieval Historiography. 1974. lib. bdg. 59.95 (ISBN 0-8490-1079-9). Gordon Pr.

Daniel, Walter. The Life of Ailred of Rievaulx. Powicke, Maurice, ed. 1979. 22.00x (ISBN 0-19-822256-4). Oxford U Pr.

Davidson, Audrey E. & Rastall, Richard. The Quasi-Dramatic St. John Passions from Scandinavia & Their Medieval Background. (Early Drama, Art, & Music Monograph: No. 3). (Illus.). viii, 135p. 1981. 16.95 (ISBN 0-918720-13-3); pap. 8.95 (ISBN 0-918720-14-1). Medieval Inst.

Davis, Georgene W. The Inquisition at Albi, 1229-1300. 322p. 1974. Repr. of 1948 ed. lib. bdg. 17.50x (ISBN 0-374-92075-3). Octagon.

Davison, Ellen S. Forerunners of Saint Francis & Other Studies. Richards, Gertrude R., ed. LC 77-85270. Repr. of 1927 ed. 34.50 (ISBN 0-404-16120-0). AMS Pr.

Delbruck, Hans. Das Mittelalter. LC 80-2677. Repr. of 1907 ed. 63.50 (ISBN 0-404-18559-2). AMS Pr.

Doehaerd. Early Middle Ages in the West: Economy & Society. (Europe in the Middle Ages: Vol. 13). 1978. 34.25 (ISBN 0-444-85091-0, North-Holland). Elsevier.

Drew, Katherine F. The Lombard Laws. (Middle Ages Ser). 240p. 1973. 16.00x (ISBN 0-8122-7661-2); pap. 5.95x (ISBN 0-8122-1055-7, Pa Paperbacks). U of Pa Pr.

Dupin, Henri. La Courtoisie au Moyen Age: (d'apres les textes du XII et du XIII siecle) LC 78-63496. Repr. of 1931 ed. 21.50 (ISBN 0-404-17144-3). AMS Pr.

Emerton, E. Medieval Europe, Eight Hundred Fourteen-Thirteen Hundred: An Introduction to the Study of the Middle Ages, 2 vols. Set. 250.00 (ISBN 0-8490-0599-X). Gordon Pr.

Emerton, Ephraim. An Introduction to the Study of the Middle Ages: 375-814. 1979. Repr. of 1895 ed. lib. bdg. 30.00 (ISBN 0-8495-1325-1). Arden Lib.

--An Introduction to the Study of the Middle Ages. 17.50 (ISBN 0-686-17010-5). Quality Lib.

Ennen, E. The Medieval Town. (Europe in the Middle Ages Selected Studies Ser.: Vol. 8). 1978. 39.00 (ISBN 0-444-85133-X, North-Holland). Elsevier.

Erickson, Carolly. The Medieval Vision: Essays in History & Perception. LC 75-10179. 256p. 1976. text ed. 14.95 (ISBN 0-19-501964-4); pap. text ed. 5.95x (ISBN 0-19-501963-6). Oxford U Pr.

Essays in History Presented to Reginald Lane Poole. facs. ed. LC 67-30186. (Essay Index Reprint Ser). 1927. 20.00 (ISBN 0-8369-0424-9). Arno.

Falco, Giorgio. The Holy Roman Republic: A Historic Profile of the Middle Ages. Kent, K. V., tr. from Italian. LC 80-19696. Orig. Title: La Santa Romana Republica. 336p. 1980. Repr. of 1965 ed. lib. bdg. 35.00x (ISBN 0-313-22395-5, FAHR). Greenwood.

Fisher, Herbert A. The Medieval Empire, 2 vols. Repr. Set. lib. bdg. cancelled (ISBN 0-403-00409-8). Scholarly.

Fourquin, G. The Anatomy of Popular Rebellion in the Middle Ages. (Europe in the Middle Ages - Selected Studies: Vol. 12). 1978. 31.75 (ISBN 0-444-85006-6, North-Holland). Elsevier.

Gabel, Leona, ed. The Renaissance Reconsidered: Progress. LC 64-5397. (Studies in History: No. 44). 1964. pap. 3.00 (ISBN 0-87391-004-4). Smith Coll.

Galbraith, V. H. The Anonimalle Chronicle, Thirteen Thirty-Three to Thirteen Eighty-One. 266p. 1927. 37.00x (ISBN 0-7190-0398-9, Pub. by Manchester U Pr England). State Mutual Bk.

Garcia-Antezana, Jorge. Libro De Buen Amor: Concordancia Completa De los Codices De Salamanca, Toledo y Gayoso. 1100p. (Span.). 1981. 75.00x (ISBN 0-8020-2413-0). U of Toronto Pr.

Garnier, H. L' Idee du Juste Prix Chez les Theologiens et Cannonistes du Moyen Age. LC 79-122228. 164p. (Fr.). 1973. Repr. of 1900 ed. lib. bdg. 20.50 (ISBN 0-8337-1286-1). B Franklin.

Geankoplos, Deno J. Byzantine East & Latin West: Two Worlds of Christendom in Middle Ages & Renaissance. (Illus.). 1976. Repr. of 1966 ed. 12.50 (ISBN 0-208-01615-5, Archon). Shoe String.

Genicot, Leopold. L' Economie Rurale Namuroise au Bas Moyen Age (1199-1429, 2 vols. LC 80-2028. Repr. of 1943 ed. Set. 79.50 (ISBN 0-404-18565-7). Vol. 1 (ISBN 0-404-18566-5). Vol. 2 (ISBN 0-404-18567-3). AMS Pr.

Gillon, Edmund V., Jr. Middle Ages: Dover Coloring Book. (gr. 2-6). pap. 1.75 (ISBN 0-486-22743-X). Dover.

Gottschalk, Louis, et al. History of Mankind: Cultural & Scientific Development - Vol. 4: the Foundations of the Modern World, 1300-1775, 2 pts. 1969. Pt. 1. text ed. 30.00x (ISBN 0-04-900007-1); Pt. 2. text ed. 30.00x (ISBN 0-04-900009-8). Allen Unwin.

Grant, M. Dawn of the Middle Ages: A. D. 476-816. 1981. 45.00 (ISBN 0-07-024076-0). McGraw.

Graves, Frank P. A History of Education During the Middle Ages. 1980. lib. bdg. 75.00 (ISBN 0-87968-164-0). Gordon Pr.

Guillaume De Nangis. Chronique Latine De Guillaume De Nangis 1113 a 1300, 2 Vols. Geraud, H., ed. Set. 71.00 (ISBN 0-384-20360-4); Set. pap. 61.50 (ISBN 0-384-20361-2). Johnson Repr.

Hampson, Robert Rt. Medii Aevi Kalendarium or Dates Charters Customs of the Middle Ages, 2 vols. LC 76-29824. Repr. of 1841 ed. Set. 59.50 (ISBN 0-404-16970-8). AMS Pr.

Hauck, Karl, ed. Fruehmittelalterliche Studien. Jahrbuch Des Instituts Fuer Fruehmittelalter-Forschung der Universitaet Muenster, Vol. 10. (Illus.). 1976. 104.75x (ISBN 3-11-006728-5). De Gruyter.

Helmold Priest Of Bosau. Chronicle of the Slavs. Tschan, Francis J., tr. 1967. lib. bdg. 17.00x (ISBN 0-374-98018-7). Octagon.

Hollister, C. Warren. Medieval Europe: A Short History. 5th ed. 375p. 1982. text ed. 17.00 (ISBN 0-471-08447-6). Wiley.

--Odysseus to Columbus: A Synopsis of Classical & Medieval History. LC 74-2428. 352p. 1974. pap. text ed. 12.95 (ISBN 0-471-40689-9). Wiley.

Hoyt, Robert S. & Chodorow, Stanley. Europe in the Middle Ages. 3rd ed. (Illus.). 1976. pap. text ed. 20.95 (ISBN 0-15-524712-3, HC). HarBraceJ.

Ide, Arthur F. Woman in the European Middle Ages. rev. ed. (Woman in History: Vol. 12). (Illus.). 70p. 1981. 11.00 (ISBN 0-86663-063-5); pap. 7.95 (ISBN 0-86663-064-3). Ide Hse.

Jordon, William C., et al, eds. Order & Innovation in the Middle Ages: Essays in Honor of Joseph R. Strayer. LC 75-30196. 1976. 32.50 (ISBN 0-691-05231-X). Princeton U Pr.

Kantorowicz, Ernst H. The King's Two Bodies. LC 57-5448. (Illus.). 608p. 1981. pap. 9.95 (ISBN 0-691-02018-3). Princeton U Pr.

Keen, Maurice. Pelican History of Medieval Europe. 1969. pap. 3.50 (ISBN 0-14-021085-7, Pelican). Penguin.

Kemp-Welch, Alice. Of Six Medieval Women. 189p. 1972. Repr. of 1913 ed. 10.00 (ISBN 0-87928-028-X). Corner Hse.

Koerner, Kohrad, et al, eds. Studies in Medieval Linguistic Thought, Vol. 26. (Studies in the History of Linguistics). vi, 321p. 1980. 41.00 (ISBN 90-272-4508-8). Benjamins North Am.

Kurland, Gerald. Western Civilization, One (to 1500) (Monarch College Outlines). pap. 4.95 (ISBN 0-671-08045-8). Monarch Pr.

--Western Civilization, Two (from 1500) (Monarch College Outlines). pap. 4.95 (ISBN 0-671-08050-4). Monarch Pr.

Lane, Peter. The Middle Ages. 96p. 1980. 14.95 (ISBN 0-7134-0033-1, Pub. by Batsford England). David & Charles.

Lea, Henry C. The Duel & the Oath. (Middle Ages Ser). Orig. Title: Superstition & Force. 1974. 14.00x (ISBN 0-8122-7681-7); pap. 6.95x (ISBN 0-8122-1080-8). U of Pa Pr.

Le Goff, Jacques. Time, Work, & Culture in the Middle Ages. Goldhammer, Arthur, tr. LC 79-25400. 1980. lib. bdg. 22.50x (ISBN 0-226-47080-6). U of Chicago Pr.

Lot, Ferdinand. L Art Militaire et les Armees Au Moyen Age En Europe et Dans le Proche Orient, 2 vols. LC 80-2017. Date not set. Repr. of 1946 ed. 90.00 (ISBN 0-404-18603-3). AMS Pr.

Lot, Ferdinand Vols., ed. Histoire Des Institutions Francaises Au Moyen Age, Publiee Sous la Direction De Ferdinand Lot et Robert Fawtier. LC 80-2204. Date not set. Repr. of 1957 ed. 110.00 (ISBN 0-404-18606-8). AMS Pr.

McCall, Andrew. The Medieval Underworld. (Illus.). 329p. 1979. 22.00 (ISBN 0-241-10018-6, Pub. by Hamish Hamilton England). David & Charles.

McGarry, Daniel D. Medieval History & Civilization. (Illus.). 896p. 1976. text ed. 20.95 (ISBN 0-02-379100-4). Macmillan.

McNeill, William H. & Houser, Schuyler O., eds. Medieval Europe. (Oxford Readings in World History Ser: Vol. 8). 1971. pap. 5.95x (ISBN 0-19-501312-3). Oxford U Pr.

Makdisi, George. Islam & the Medieval West: Aspects of Intercultural Relations. Semaan, Khalil I., ed. LC 79-18678. 1979. lib. bdg. 34.00 (ISBN 0-87395-409-2); pap. 12.95 (ISBN 0-87395-455-6). State U NY Pr.

Marsilius Of Padua. Defensor Pacis. Gewirth, Alan, tr. (Medieval Academy Reprints for Teaching Ser.). 1980. pap. 6.00x (ISBN 0-8020-6412-4). U of Toronto Pr.

Meyer, O. & Klauser, R. Clavis Mediaevalis: Kleines Woerterbuch der Mittelalterforschung. 312p. (Ger.). 1966. 22.50 (ISBN 3-447-00239-5, M-7323, Pub. by Harrassowitz). French & Eur.

Minorsky, Vladimir. The Turks, Iran & the Caucasus in the Middle Ages. 368p. 1980. 69.00x (ISBN 0-86078-028-7, Pub. by Variorum England). State Mutual Bk.

Miskimin, Harry A., et al, eds. The Medieval City. LC 77-76302. 1977. 25.00x (ISBN 0-300-02081-3). Yale U Pr.

Mitteis, H. The State in the Middle Ages. (N-H Medieval Translations Ser.: Vol. 1). 380p. 1975. pap. 31.75 (ISBN 0-444-10789-4, North-Holland). Elsevier.

Mollet, Michel & Wolff, Philippe. Popular Revolutions of the Late Middle Ages. Lytton-Sells, A. L., tr. (Great Revolutions Ser.). (Illus.). 323p. (Orig.). 1973. pap. text ed. 10.95x (ISBN 0-04-940041-X). Allen Unwin.

Morrison, Karl F. Europe's Middle Ages: Five Sixty-Five to Fifteen Hundred. 1970. pap. 7.95x (ISBN 0-673-05792-5). Scott F.

Moss, Henry S. The Birth of the Middle Ages, Three Ninety-Five to Eight Fourteen. LC 80-24038. (Illus.). xvi, 291p. 1980. Repr. of 1964 ed. lib. bdg. 29.75x (ISBN 0-313-22708-X, MOBM). Greenwood.

--Birth of the Middle Ages: 395-814. (Illus.). 1935. pap. 4.95x (ISBN 0-19-500260-1). Oxford U Pr.

Mundy, J. Europe in the High Middle Ages: 1150-1309. (A General History of Europe Ser.). (Illus.). 628p. pap. text ed. 14.50x (ISBN 0-582-48194-5). Longman.

Mundy, John H., et al. Essays in Medieval Life & Thought. LC 65-25472. 1955. 12.00x (ISBN 0-8196-0159-4). Biblo.

Murray, Alexander. Reason & Society. 1978. 49.50x (ISBN 0-19-822540-7). Oxford U Pr.

Newton, A. P. Travel & Travellers in the Middle Ages. 59.95 (ISBN 0-8490-1228-7). Gordon Pr.

Oxford Essays in Medieval History, Presented to Herbert Edward Salter. facs. ed. LC 68-22115. (Essay Index Reprint Ser). 1934. 15.00 (ISBN 0-8369-0760-4). Arno.

Paetow, Louis J. Guide to the Study of Medieval History. rev. ed. LC 80-81364. Repr. of 1931 ed. 55.00 (ISBN 0-527-69101-1). Kraus Repr.

Paul The Deacon. History of the Lombards. Foulke, William D., tr. LC 72-80382. (Middle Ages Ser). 1974. 20.00x (ISBN 0-8122-7671-X); pap. 6.95x (ISBN 0-8122-1079-4). U of Pa Pr.

Pearsall, Derek & Salter, Elizabeth. Landscapes & Seasons of the Medieval World. LC 73-77945. 1973. 30.00 (ISBN 0-8020-2110-7). U of Toronto Pr.

Peters, Edward M. Europe: The World of the Middle Ages. (Illus.). 1977. text ed. 24.95 (ISBN 0-13-291898-6). P-H.

Piltz, Anders. The World of Medieval Learning. Jones, David, tr. (Illus.). 310p. 1981. 30.00x (ISBN 0-389-20206-1). B&N.

Pirenne, Henri. Early Democracies in the Low Countries: Urban Society & Political Conflict in the Middle Ages & the Renaissance. Saunders, J. V., tr. Orig. Title: Belgian Democracy. 1971. pap. 1.95 (ISBN 0-393-00565-8, Norton Lib). Norton.

--Economic & Social History of Medieval Europe. Clegg, I. E., tr. LC 37-28587. 1956. pap. 2.75 (ISBN 0-15-627533-3, HB14, Harv). HarBraceJ.

Platt, Colin. The Atlas of Medieval Man. (Illus.). 1980. 22.50 (ISBN 0-312-05993-0). St Martin.

Pontifical Institute of Mediaeval Studies, Ontario. Dictionary Catalogue of the Library of the Pontifical Institute of Mediaeval Studies: First Supplement, 5 vols. 1979. Set. lib. bdg. 125.00 (ISBN 0-8161-1061-1). G K Hall.

Poole, Austin L. Obligations of Society in the Twelfth & Thirteenth Centuries: The Ford Lectures Delivered in the University of Oxford in Michaelmas Term. LC 80-2007. Repr. of 1946 ed. 18.50 (ISBN 0-404-18587-8). AMS Pr.

Power, Eileen. Medieval People. 10th rev. & enl. ed. 210p. 1963. 13.50x (ISBN 0-686-77583-X). B&N.

Power, Eileen & Poston, M. Medieval Women. LC 75-7212. (Illus.). 144p. 1976. pap. 5.50x (ISBN 0-521-09946-3). Cambridge U Pr.

Powicke, Frederick M. Ways of Medieval Life & Thought. LC 64-13394. (Illus.). 1949. 9.50x (ISBN 0-8196-0137-3). Biblo.

Previte-Orton, C. W. Outlines of Medieval History. 2nd ed. LC 64-25837. 1916. 14.00x (ISBN 0-8196-0147-0). Biblo.

--The Shorter Cambridge Medieval History, 2 vols. Incl. Vol. 1. The Later Roman Empire to the Twelfth Century. (Illus.). 644p (ISBN 0-521-20962-5). pap. (ISBN 0-521-09976-5); Vol. 2. The Twelfth Century to the Renaissance. (Illus.). 558p. pap. (ISBN 0-521-09977-3). (Medieval History Ser). 1975. 53.95 ea.; pap. 15.95 ea. Cambridge U Pr.

Previte-Orton, C. W., ed. The Shorter Cambridge Medieval History, 2 vols. Set. 89.50 (ISBN 0-521-05993-3); Set. pap. 27.95 (ISBN 0-521-08758-9). Cambridge U Pr.

Pronay, Nicholas & Taylor, John. Parliamentary Texts of the Later Middle Ages. 240p. 1980. 44.00 (ISBN 0-19-822368-4). Oxford U Pr.

Rand, E. M. Founders of the Middle Ages. 7.50 (ISBN 0-8446-2779-8). Peter Smith.

Renna, Thomas J. The West in the Early Middle Ages: Three Hundred to Ten Fifty. 150p. 1977. pap. text ed. 7.50 (ISBN 0-8191-0238-5). U Pr of Amer.

Reuter, T. The Medieval Nobility. (Europe in the Middle Ages Ser.: Vol 14). 1978. 40.00 (ISBN 0-444-85136-4, North Holland). Elsevier.

Rice, Edward. The High Middle Ages. 128p. 1963. 2.95 (ISBN 0-374-29520-4). FS&G.

Schlight, John. Monarchs & Mercenaries: A Reappraisal of the Importance of Knight Service in Norman & Early Angevin England. LC 68-15335. (Studies in British History & Culture). 103p. 1968. 6.00x (ISBN 0-8147-0376-3). NYU Pr.

See, Henri E. Les Classes Rurales et le Regime Domanial En France Au Moyen Age. LC 80-2003. 1981. Repr. of 1901 ed. 61.50 (ISBN 0-404-18594-0). AMS Pr.

Sellery, G. C. & Krey, A. C. Medieval Foundations of Western Civilization. LC 68-24116. (World History Ser., No. 48). (Illus.). 1968. Repr. 74.95 (ISBN 0-8383-0926-7). Haskell.

Simons, Gerald. Barbarian Europe. LC 68-54209. (Great Ages of Man). (Illus.). (gr. 6 up). 1968. PLB 11.97 (ISBN 0-8094-0380-3, Pub. by Time-Life). Silver.

Southeastern Institute of Medieval & Renaissance Studies, Summer 1974. Medieval & Renaissance Studies: Proceedings, No.6. Randall, Dale B., ed. LC 66-25461. 1976. 8.75 (ISBN 0-8223-0379-5). Duke.

Southern, R. W., ed. Essays in Medieval History. 1968. 17.95 (ISBN 0-312-26250-7). St Martin.

Stubbs, William. Seventeen Lectures on the Study of Medieval & Modern History. 1967. 25.00 (ISBN 0-86527-219-0). Fertig.

Swanson, R. N. Universities, Academics & the Great Schism. LC 78-56764. (Cambridge Studies in Medieval Life & Thought: 3rd Ser., No. 12). 1979. 38.50 (ISBN 0-521-22127-7). Cambridge U Pr.

Syme, Ronald. Some Arval Brethren. 140p. 1980. 29.00x (ISBN 0-19-814831-3). Oxford U Pr.

Taylor, Charles H., ed. Anniversary Essays in Mediaeval History, by Students of Charles Homer Haskins: Presented on His Completion of Forty Years of Teaching. facs. ed. LC 67-30194. (Essay Index Reprint Ser). 1929. 20.00 (ISBN 0-8369-0155-X). Arno.

Thompson, James W. The Middle Ages: Three Hundred to Fifteen Hundred, 2 vols. LC 70-145875. (Illus.). 1972. Repr. of 1932 ed. lib. bdg. 37.50x (ISBN 0-8154-0380-1). Cooper Sq.

Tierney, Brian & Painter, Sidney. Western Europe in the Middle Ages, 300-1475. 3rd ed. 1978. text ed. 19.95x (ISBN 0-394-32180-4). Random.

Tillinghast, William. Epitome of Ancient, Medieval & Modern History. 1883. Repr. 20.00 (ISBN 0-685-43262-9). Norwood Edns.

Tipton, C., ed. Nationalism in the Middle Ages. (European Problem Ser.). 128p. 1972. pap. 5.50 (ISBN 0-03-084157-7, Pub. by HR&W). Krieger.

Trehanne, R. F. The Baronial Plan of Reform, Twelve Fifty-Eight to Twelve Sixty-Three. 494p. 1932. 42.00x (ISBN 0-7190-0397-0, Pub. by Manchester U Pr England). State Mutual Bk.

Turnbull, S. R. The Mongols. (Men at Arms Ser.). (Illus.). 1981. pap. 7.95 (ISBN 0-85045-372-0, Pub. by Osprey England). Hippocrene Bks.

Ullmann, Walter. Jurisprudence in the Middle Ages. 390p. 1980. 75.00x (ISBN 0-86078-065-1, Pub. by Variorum England). State Mutual Bk.

--The Papacy & Political Ideas in the Middle Ages. 408p. 1980. 60.00x (ISBN 0-902089-87-0, Pub. by Variorum England). State Mutual Bk.

Vitalis, Orderic. Ecclesiastical History of Orderic Vitalis, Vol. 6, Books 11, 12, 13. Chibnall, Marjorie, ed. & tr. 640p. 1978. text ed. 75.00x (ISBN 0-19-822242-4). Oxford U Pr.

Wall, James T. From the Law of Moses to the Magna Carta: Essays in Ancient & Medieval History. LC 79-66236. 1979. pap. text ed. 7.50 (ISBN 0-8191-0801-4). U Pr of Amer.

Wallace-Hadrill, J. M. Barbarian West: The Early Middles Ages, A. D. 400-1000. pap. 3.95x (ISBN 0-06-131061-1, TB1061, Torch). Har-Row.
Wapnewski, Peter, intro. by. Deutsches Mittelalter. 1000p. (Ger.). text ed. 13.00 (ISBN 3-458-04945-2, Pub. by Insel Verlag Germany). Suhrkamp.
Wattenbach, W., ed. Die Chronik Fredegars und der Frankenkoenige, die Lebensbeschreibungen des Abtes Columban, der Bischoefe Arnulf, Leodegar und Eligius, der Koenigin Balthilde. 2nd ed. Abel, Otto, tr. (Die Geschichtschreiber der Deutschen Vorzeit Ser: Vol. 11). (Ger.). pap. 15.50 (ISBN 0-384-00104-1). Johnson Repr.
Zbozny, Frank, ed. Annuale Mediaevale, Nineteen. 97p. 1979. pap. text ed. 13.50x (ISBN 0-686-73994-9). Humanities.
Zimmermann, Albert, ed. Begriff der repraesentatio im Mittelalter: Stellvertretung, Symbol, Zeichen, Bild. (Illus.). 390p. 1971. 75.00x (ISBN 3-11-003751-3). De Gruyter.

MIDDLE AGES–HISTORY–OUTLINES, SYLLABI, ETC.

Beazley, Charles R. A Note-Book of Mediaeval History, A. D. 323 - A. D. 1453. facsimile ed. LC 70-160957. (Select Bibliographies Reprint Ser). Repr. of 1917 ed. 16.00 (ISBN 0-8369-5824-1). Arno.
McGarry, Daniel D. & Wahl, James A. Outline of Medieval History. (Quality Paperback: No. 7). (Orig.). 1968. pap. 2.95 (ISBN 0-8226-0007-2). Littlefield.
Magill, Frank N., ed. Great Events from History, 3 vols. (Ancient & Medieval Ser.). 1975. 95.00 set (ISBN 0-89356-104-5). Salem Pr.
Marban, Edilberto. Ancient & Medieval History. (Blue Bks.). pap. 1.25 (ISBN 0-671-18102-5). Monarch Pr.
Munro, Dana C. A Syllabus of Medieval History, Three Hundred Ninety-Five to Thirteen Hundred. 1980. lib. bdg. 49.95 (ISBN 0-8490-3193-1). Gordon Pr.

MIDDLE AGES–HISTORY–SOURCES

Brentano, Robert. Early Middle Ages. LC 64-21204. 1964. pap. text ed. 6.95 (ISBN 0-02-904670-X). Free Pr.
Cave, Roy C. & Coulson, Herbert H. Source Book for Medieval Economic History. LC 64-25840. 1936. 12.00x (ISBN 0-8196-0145-4). Biblo.
Davis, R. H. & Wallace-Hadrill, J. M., eds. The Writing of History in the Middle Ages: Essays Presented to Richard William Southern. (Illus.). 520p. 1981. 66.50 (ISBN 0-19-822556-3). Oxford U Pr.
Henderson, Ernest F. Historical Documents of the Middle Ages. 477p. 1980. Repr. of 1907 ed. lib. bdg. 45.00 (ISBN 0-8495-2269-2). Arden Lib.
--Select Historical Documents of the Middle Ages. LC 68-57867. (Bohn's Antiquarian Library Ser). 1968. Repr. of 1892 ed. 7.50 (ISBN 0-404-50016-1). AMS Pr.
Henderson, Ernest F., ed. Select Historical Documents of the Middle Ages. LC 65-15247. 1892. 10.50x (ISBN 0-8196-0149-7). Biblo.
Krochalis, Jeanne & Peters, Edward, eds. The World of Piers Plowman. LC 75-11167. (Middle Ages Ser). 1975. pap. 8.95x (ISBN 0-8122-1085-9, Pa Paperbks). U of Pa Pr.
Martene, Edmund & Durand, Ursin, eds. Thesaurus Novus Anecdotorum Seu Collectio Monumentorum, 5 Vols. folio ed. LC 68-56785. (Research & Source Works Ser: No. 274). (Lat). 1969. Repr. of 1717 ed. Set. 450.00 (ISBN 0-8337-2253-0). B Franklin.
Ogg, Frederic A. A Sourcebook of Medieval History. LC 71-187412. 504p. 1972. Repr. of 1907 ed. lib. bdg. 17.50x (ISBN 0-8154-0405-0). Cooper Sq.
Ogg, Frederic A., ed. A Source Book of Mediaeval History. 504p. 1981. Repr. of 1908 ed. lib. bdg. 50.00 (ISBN 0-89760-631-0). Telegraph Bks.
Sawyer, P. H. Charters of Burton Abbey. (Anglo-Saxon Charters Ser.). (Illus.). 1979. 39.50x (ISBN 0-19-725940-5). Oxford U Pr.
Thatcher, Oliver J. & McNeal, E. H. Source Book for Medieval History. LC 70-149676. Repr. of 1905 ed. 30.00 (ISBN 0-404-06363-2). AMS Pr.
Thorndike, Lynn, tr. University Records & Life in the Middle Ages. (Columbia University Records of Civilization Ser.). 476p. 1975. pap. text ed. 6.95x (ISBN 0-393-09216-X). Norton.
Tierney, Brian, ed. The Middle Ages: Sources of Medieval History, Vol. 1. 3rd ed. 1978. pap. text ed. 7.95 (ISBN 0-394-32151-0). Knopf.
Van Caenegem, R. C. Guide to the Sources of Medieval History. (Europe in the Middle Ages - Selected Studies: Vol. 2). 1978. 56.00 (ISBN 0-7204-0743-5, North-Holland). Elsevier.

MIDDLE AGES–JUVENILE LITERATURE

Cairns, Trevor, ed. Barbarians, Christians, & Muslims. LC 73-20213. (Cambridge Introduction to History Ser.). (Illus.). 104p. (gr. 5 up). 1975. PLB 8.95g (ISBN 0-8225-0803-6). Lerner Pubns.
Jacobs, David. Master Builders of the Middle Ages. LC 69-13692. (Horizon Caravel Bks.). 154p. (YA) (gr. 7 up). 1969. 9.95 (ISBN 0-06-022803-2, HarpJ); PLB 12.89 (ISBN 0-06-022804-0). Har-Row.
Koenig, Alma J. Gudrun. Bell, Anthea, tr. LC 79-917. (gr. 7 up). 1979. 8.25 (ISBN 0-688-41899-6); PLB 7.92 (ISBN 0-688-51899-0). Lothrop.
Lewis, Brenda R. Growing up in the Dark Ages. LC 79-56478. (Growing up Ser.). (Illus.). 72p. (gr. 7 up). 1980. text ed. 14.95 (ISBN 0-7134-3362-0, Pub. by Batsford England). David & Charles.
Unstead, R. J. Living in a Castle. LC 73-1664. (Illus.). 44p. (gr. 4 up). 1973. PLB 5.95 (ISBN 0-201-08495-3, A-W Childrens). A-W.
--Living in a Medieval City. LC 73-1666. (Illus.). 44p. (gr. 4 up). 1973. PLB 5.95 (ISBN 0-201-08499-6, A-W Childrens). A-W.
Wise, William A. Monsters of the Middle Ages. (See & Read Storybooks). (Illus.). (gr. k-3). 1971. PLB 6.29 (ISBN 0-399-60472-3). Putnam.

MIDDLE AGES IN LITERATURE

Benson, Larry D. & Leyerle, John, eds. Chivalric Literature: Essays on Relations Between Literature & Life in the Later Middle Ages. LC 80-17514. (Studies in Medieval Culture 14). (Illus.). 176p. 1980. 17.95 (ISBN 0-918720-08-7). Medieval Inst.
Dakyns, Jannie R. The Middle Ages in French Literature 1851-1900. new ed. (Oxford Modern Languages & Literature Monographs). 364p. 1973. 29.95x (ISBN 0-19-815522-0). Oxford U Pr.
Ward, Patricia A. The Medievalism of Victor Hugo. LC 74-28421. (Penn State Studies: No. 39). 148p. 1975. pap. 3.95x (ISBN 0-271-01182-3). Pa St U Pr.

MIDDLE ATLANTIC STATES

Country Inns: Mid Atlantic, 1981-1982. 1981. 4.95 (ISBN 0-89102-233-3). B Franklin.
Hitchcock, Anthony & Lindgren, Jean. Country Inns of the Middle Atlantic States. 1979. pap. 4.95 (ISBN 0-89102-157-4). B Franklin.
Meacham, Mary, ed. Readings for Young People: The Middle Atlantic. 8.00 (ISBN 0-686-74733-X). ALA.

MIDDLE CLASSES

see also Proletariat

Bensman, Joseph & Vidich, Arthur. The New American Society: The Revolution of the Middle Class. LC 70-143566. 448p. 1971. pap. 15.00 (ISBN 0-8129-0167-3); pap. 3.45 (ISBN 0-8129-6229-X). Times Bks.
Berdyaev, Nicolas. Bourgeois Mind, & Other Essays. facs. ed. LC 67-22072. (Essay Index Reprint Ser). 1934. 10.00 (ISBN 0-8369-0198-3). Arno.
Bill, Valentine T. The Forgotten Class. LC 75-25485. 1976. Repr. of 1959 ed. lib. bdg. 15.50x (ISBN 0-8371-8426-6, BIFOC). Greenwood.
Bonarius, Han, et al, eds. Personal Construct & Psychology. 300p. 1981. 30.00x (ISBN 0-312-60228-6). St Martin.
Caudwell, Christopher. Studies & Further Studies in a Dying Culture. LC 77-142989. 1972. 10.00 (ISBN 0-85345-145-1, CL-1451); pap. 6.95 (ISBN 0-85345-218-0, PB-2180). Monthly Rev.
Coston, Henry, ed. Dictionnaire des Dynasties Bourgecises et du Monde des Affaires. 599p. (Fr.). 1975. 55.00 (ISBN 0-686-56839-7, M-6617). French & Eur.
Davidson, James D. The Squeeze. LC 79-28411. 1980. 11.95 (ISBN 0-671-40084-3). Summit Bks.
Filene, Peter. Men in the Middle: Coping with the Problems of Work & Family in the Lives of Middle Aged Men. 160p. 1981. 10.95 (ISBN 0-686-71982-4); pap. 5.95 (ISBN 0-13-574491-1). P-H.
Frazier, E. Franklin. Black Bourgeoisie. 1965. pap. text ed. 6.95 (ISBN 0-02-910580-3). Free Pr.
--Black Bourgeoisie: The Rise of a New Middle Class in the United States. (Orig.). 1962. pap. 1.95 (ISBN 0-02-095600-2, Collier). Macmillan.
Garrard, J., et al, eds. The Middle Class in Politics. 380p. 1978. text ed. 29.00x (ISBN 0-566-00225-6, Pub. by Gower Pub Co England). Renouf.
Ginzberg, Eli, et al. The Middle-Class Negro in the White Man's World. LC 67-26364. 1967. 15.00x (ISBN 0-231-03096-7); pap. 5.00x (ISBN 0-231-08596-6). Columbia U Pr.
Holcombe, Arthur N. Middle Classes in American Politics. LC 64-66396. 1965. Repr. of 1940 ed. 8.50 (ISBN 0-8462-0568-8). Russell.
Kreml, William P. The Middle Class Burden. LC 79-51943. (Illus.). 1979. 11.95 (ISBN 0-89089-134-6); pap. 4.95 (ISBN 0-89089-135-4). Carolina Acad Pr.
Lowe, Donald M. Essays in the History of Bourgeois Perception. LC 81-7529. 1981. price not set (ISBN 0-226-49428-4). U of Chicago Pr.
Mills, C. Wright. White Collar: American Middle Classes. 1956. pap. 6.95 (ISBN 0-19-500677-1, GB). Oxford U Pr.
--White Collar: The American Middle Classes. 1951. 17.95 (ISBN 0-19-500024-2). Oxford U Pr.
Moraze, Charles. The Triumph of the Middle Classes: A Political & Social History of Europe in the Nineteenth Century. 6.50 (ISBN 0-8446-4448-X). Peter Smith.
Raines, John C. Illusions of Success. LC 74-22525. 96p. 1975. 5.95 (ISBN 0-8170-0650-8). Judson.
Raynor, John & King, Roger. The Middle Class. 2nd ed. (Aspects of Modern Sociology Ser.). 256p. (Orig.). 1981. pap. text ed. 9.50x (ISBN 0-582-29525-4). Longman.
Rodgers, Daniel T. The Work Ethic in Industrial America: 1850-1920. LC 77-81737. 1978. lib. bdg. 15.00x (ISBN 0-226-72351-8). U of Chicago Pr.
Sennett, Richard. Families Against the City: Middle Class Homes of Industrial Chicago, 1872-1890. LC 73-115190. (Joint Center for Urban Studies Publications Ser). (Illus.). 1970. 14.00x (ISBN 0-674-29225-1). Harvard U Pr.
Sombart, Werner. The Quintessence of Capitalism. 1967. 28.50 (ISBN 0-86527-162-3). Fertig.
Sprigg, Christopher. Studies in a Dying Culture. LC 73-10763. 228p. 1973. Repr. of 1938 ed. lib. bdg. 15.00 (ISBN 0-8371-7031-1, SPDC). Greenwood.
Varenne, Herve. Americans Together: Structured Diversity in a Midwestern Town. LC 77-10109. 1977. pap. text ed. 10.25x (ISBN 0-8077-2519-6). Tchrs Coll.
Weber, William. Music & the Middle Class: The Social Structure of Concert Life in London, Paris, & Vienna Between 1830 & 1848. LC 75-22197. 1976. 24.50x (ISBN 0-8419-0218-6). Holmes & Meier.
Wiebe, Robert H. Search for Order: 1877-1920. LC 66-27609. (Making of America Ser.). 333p. 1966. pap. 5.95 (ISBN 0-8090-0104-7, AmCen). Hill & Wang.
Wilson, John O. After Affluence: Resolving the Middle Class Crisis. LC 80-7752. 192p. 1980. 9.95 (ISBN 0-06-250970-5, HarpR). Har-Row.

MIDDLE CLASSES–AFRICA

Binder, Leonard. In a Moment of Enthusiasm: Political Power & the Second Stratum in Egypt. LC 77-15480. (Illus.). 1978. lib. bdg. 25.00x (ISBN 0-226-05144-7). U of Chicago Pr.
Kuper, Leo. African Bourgeoisie: Race, Class, & Politics in South Africa. (Illus., Orig.). 1965. pap. 5.95x (ISBN 0-300-00145-2, Y142). Yale U Pr.

MIDDLE CLASSES–ASIA

Chang, Chung-Li. Chinese Gentry: Studies on Their Role in 19th-Century Chinese Society. LC 55-6738. (Washington Paperbacks on Russia & Asia: No. 4). (Illus.). 272p. 1967. 12.50 (ISBN 0-295-73743-3); pap. 3.95 (ISBN 0-295-97891-0, PAI.3). U of Wash Pr.
Eberhard, W. Conquerors & Rulers: Social Forces in Medieval China. 2nd rev. ed. 1970. 27.50 (ISBN 0-685-12002-3). Heinman.
Vogel, Ezra F. Japan's New Middle Class: The Salary Man & His Family in a Tokyo Suburb. new enl. ed. 1971. 24.50x (ISBN 0-520-02092-8); pap. 6.95x (ISBN 0-520-02100-2, CAMPUS72). U of Cal Pr.

MIDDLE CLASSES–EUROPE

Barber, Elinor G. Bourgeoisie in Eighteenth Century France. 1955. 13.00x (ISBN 0-691-09309-1); pap. 4.95 (ISBN 0-691-02801-X, 98). Princeton U Pr.
Hovde, B. J. Scandinavian Countries, 1720-1865, 2 Vols. LC 75-159055. 1971. Repr. of 1948 ed. Set. 35.00x (ISBN 0-8046-1678-7). Kennikat.
Miller, Michael B. The Bon Marche: Bourgeois Culture & the Department Store, 1869 to 1920. LC 80-36797. (Illus.). 250p. 1980. 13.50 (ISBN 0-691-05321-9). Princeton U Pr.
Riche, Pierre. Daily Life in the World of Charlemagne. McNamara, Jo Ann, tr. from Fr. LC 78-53330. (Middle Ages Ser.). (Illus.). 1978. 22.00 (ISBN 0-8122-7751-1); pap. 9.95x (ISBN 0-8122-1096-4). U of Pa Pr.
Rorig, Fritz. The Medieval Town. Matthew, D. J., tr. 1967. 24.50x (ISBN 0-520-01088-4); pap. 6.95x (ISBN 0-520-01579-7, CAMPUS23). U of Cal Pr.
Volkov, Shulamit. The Rise of Popular Antimodernism in Germany: The Urban Master Artisans, 1873-1896. LC 77-85571. 1978. text ed. 30.00 (ISBN 0-691-05264-6). Princeton U Pr.

MIDDLE CLASSES–GREAT BRITAIN

Bonham, John. The Middle Class Vote. LC 74-11985. (Illus.). 210p. 1974. Repr. of 1954 ed. lib. bdg. 15.00x (ISBN 0-8371-7709-X, BOMI). Greenwood.
Crossick, Geoffrey, ed. The Lower-Middle Class in Britain, 1870-1914. LC 76-25410. 1977. 17.95x (ISBN 0-312-49980-9). St Martin.
Simpson, M. A. & Lloyd, T. H., eds. Middle Class Housing in Britain. (Illus.). 1977. 17.50 (ISBN 0-208-01606-6, Archon). Shoe String.
Wright, Louis B. Middle Class Culture in Elizabethan England. 733p. 1980. Repr. of 1935 ed. lib. bdg. 45.00x (ISBN 0-374-98780-7). Octagon.

MIDDLE CLASSES–LATIN AMERICA

Johnson, John J. Political Change in Latin America: The Emergence of the Middle Sectors. 1958. 15.00x (ISBN 0-8047-0528-3). Stanford U Pr.

MIDDLE CLASSES IN LITERATURE

Caudwell, Christopher & Sprigg, C. St. John. Romance & Realism: A Study in English Bourgeois Literature. LC 78-120752. 1970. 12.50 (ISBN 0-691-06195-5). Princeton U Pr.
Giraud, Raymond. Unheroic Hero in the Novels of Stendahl, Balzac & Flaubert. 1969. lib. bdg. 14.50x (ISBN 0-374-93154-2). Octagon.
Rapp, Catherine. Burgher & Peasant. LC 75-140039. (Catholic University Studies in German Ser.: No. 7). Repr. of 1936 ed. 17.00 (ISBN 0-404-50227-X). AMS Pr.

MIDDLE EAST

see Near East

MIDDLE ENGLISH

see English Language–Middle English, 1100-1500; English Literature (Collections)–Middle English (1100-1500)

MIDDLE HIGH GERMAN LANGUAGE

see German Language–Middle High German, 1050-1500

MIDDLE SCHOOLS

Alexander, William M. & George, Paul. Exemplary Middle School. 1981. pap. text ed. 9.95 (ISBN 0-03-052301-X, HoltC). HR&W.
Bondi, Joseph. Developing Middle Schools: A Guidebook. LC 72-85841. 171p. 1972. 24.00x (ISBN 0-8422-5098-0); pap. text ed. 8.95x (ISBN 0-8290-0656-7). Irvington.
--Developing Middle Schools: A Guidebook. 1977. pap. 6.50x (ISBN 0-87655-549-0). Whitehall Co.
Bough, Max E. & Hamm, Russell L., eds. The American Intermediate School: A Book of Readings. LC 73-88718. 212p. 1974. pap. 4.95x (ISBN 0-8134-1620-5, 1620). Interstate.
Burrows, L. J. The Middle School: High Road or Dead End. (New Education Ser.). 231p. 1978. 17.50x (ISBN 0-7130-0149-6, Pub. by Woburn Pr England). Biblio Dist.
Casteel, J. Doyle. Learning to Think & Choose Decision Making Episodes for the Middle Grades. LC 77-16050. 1978. text ed. 12.95 (ISBN 0-87620-525-2); pap. text ed. 10.95 (ISBN 0-87620-524-4). Goodyear.
Curtis, Thomas E. & Bidwell, Wilma W. Curriculum & Instruction for Emerging Adolescents. LC 76-9327. (Illus.). 1977. text ed. 13.95 (ISBN 0-201-00902-1). A-W.
Grooms. Perspectives on The Middle School. 1967. pap. text ed. 2.95 (ISBN 0-675-09732-0). Merrill.
Heath, Phillip A. & Weible, Thomas. Developing Social Responsibility in the Middle School: A Unit Teaching Approach. 72p. 1979. pap. 4.75 (ISBN 0-686-63711-9, 1516-9-06). NEA.
Jones, James C. The Middle School. 1978. 8.95 (ISBN 0-533-03518-X). Vantage.
Joyce, William W. & Alleman-Brooks, Janet E. Teaching Social Studies in the Elementary & Middle Schools. new ed. LC 78-10691. 1979. text ed. 18.95 (ISBN 0-03-045046-2, HoltC). HR&W.
Kindred, et al. The Middle School Curriculum: A Practitioner's Handbook. 2nd. ed. 225p. 1980. text ed. 18.95 (ISBN 0-205-06993-2). Allyn.
Klingele, William E. Teaching in Middle Schools. 1979. text ed. 17.95 (ISBN 0-205-06526-0, 236526X). Allyn.
McGlasson, Maurice. The Middle School: Whence? What? Whither? (Fastback Ser.: No. 22). (Orig.). 1973. pap. 0.75 (ISBN 0-87367-022-1). Phi Delta Kappa.
Manning, Maryann M. & Manning, Gary L. Reading Instruction in the Middle School: A Whole School Approach. 96p. 1979. pap. 4.50 (ISBN 0-686-63713-5, 1707-2-06). NEA.
NAIS Middle School Task Force: Initial Position Paper & Accompanying Papers. 1975. pap. 3.25 (ISBN 0-934338-17-5). NAIS.
Sale, Larry L. Introduction to Middle School Teaching. 1979. text ed. 15.95 (ISBN 0-675-08279-X). Merrill.
Sweat, Clifford H., ed. Why the Junior High-Middle School: Its Basic Function. 1977. pap. text ed. 3.95x (ISBN 0-8134-1947-6, 1947). Interstate.

MIDDLE STATES

Christopher, Bob & Christopher, Ellen. Christopher's America on Fifteen to Twenty-Five Dollars a Night: Mid-West States. 80p. (Orig.). Date not set. pap. 3.95 (ISBN 0-930570-04-9). Travel Discover.
Wertenbaker, Thomas J. Middle Colonies. LC 63-17541. (Founding of American Civilization Ser). (Illus.). Repr. of 1938 ed. 15.00x (ISBN 0-8154-0254-6). Cooper Sq.

MIDDLE STATES–HISTORY
Bemis, Edward W. Cooperation in the Middle States. LC 78-63781. (Johns Hopkins University. Studies in the Social Sciences. Sixth Ser. 1888: 2-3). Repr. of 1888 ed. 11.50 (ISBN 0-404-61046-3). AMS Pr.
Pownall, Thomas. A Topographical Description of the Dominions of the United States of America. Mulkearn, Lois, ed. LC 75-22835. (America in Two Centuries Ser). 1975. Repr. of 1949 ed. 15.00x (ISBN 0-405-07706-8). Arno.
Thompson, D. G. Gateway to a Nation: The Middle Atlantic States. 1956. 6.00 (ISBN 0-87233-857-6). Bauhan.
MIDDLE STONE AGE
see Mesolithic Period
MIDDLE TEMPLE, LONDON
Finkelpearl, Philip J. John Marston of the Middle Temple: An Elizabethan Dramatist in His Social Setting. LC 69-12722. (Illus.). 1969. 15.00x (ISBN 0-674-47860-6). Harvard U Pr.
MIDDLE WEST
Andrews, Clarence. Growing up in the Midwest. 168p. 1981. 11.25 (ISBN 0-8138-0250-4). Iowa St U Pr.
Atherton, Lewis. Main Street on the Middle Border. 1972. pap. 4.95 (ISBN 0-8129-6213-3). Times Bks.
Campbell, Ballard C. Representative Democracy: Public Policy & Midwestern Legislatures in the Late Nineteenth Century. 267p. 1980. text ed. 20.00x (ISBN 0-674-76275-4). Harvard U Pr.
Clark, Thomas D. The Rampaging Frontier. LC 75-17477. 350p. 1976. Repr. of 1939 ed. lib. bdg. 15.00x (ISBN 0-8371-8313-8, CLRF). Greenwood.
Clarke, James S. Life in the Middle West: History of Life in the Nineteen Hundred's-Civil War Experiences. 1981. pap. 12.95 (ISBN 0-910924-90-2). MaCalester.
Dopp, Pearl. From the Top of a Secret Tree. (Illus., Orig.). 1979. pap. 5.95 (ISBN 0-931762-11-1). J Phunn.
Flanagan, John T., ed. America Is West: An Anthology of Middle-Western Life & Literature. LC 71-106687. (Illus.). vii, 677p. Repr. of 1945 ed. lib. bdg. 25.25x (ISBN 0-8371-3358-0, FLAW). Greenwood.
Gates, Paul W. Landlords & Tenants on the Prairie Frontier: Studies in American Land Policy. (Illus.). 338p. 1973. 22.50x (ISBN 0-8014-0763-X). Cornell U Pr.
Havighurst, Walter, ed. Midwest & Great Plains. rev. ed. LC 78-54255. (United States Ser). (Illus.). (gr. 5 up). 1979. text ed. 9.93 1-4 copies (ISBN 0-88296-070-9); 5 or more 7.94 (ISBN 0-685-14490-9); tchrs'. annotated ed. 13.68 (ISBN 0-88296-347-3). Fideler.
Jensen, Richard. Winning of the Midwest: Social & Political Conflict, 1888-1896. LC 71-149802. 1971. 12.50x (ISBN 0-226-39825-0). U of Chicago Pr.
Klein, Jerry. Played in Peoria. (Illus.). 176p. 1980. 11.95 (ISBN 0-933180-14-4). Kickapoo.
McAvoy, Thomas T., ed. Midwest: Myth or Reality. 1961. 4.95x (ISBN 0-268-00177-4). U of Notre Dame Pr.
Meacham, Mary, ed. Readings for Young People: The Midwest. 10.50 (ISBN 0-686-74732-1). ALA.
Merrill, Horace S. Bourbon Democracy of the Middle West, 1865-1896. LC 53-8592. (Americana Library Ser: No. 2). (Illus.). 1969. 10.50 (ISBN 0-295-97857-0, AL2); pap. 2.95 (ISBN 0-295-95032-3, ALP2). U of Wash Pr.
Paden, Irene D. Wake of the Prairie Schooner. LC 43-15419. (Arcturus Books Paperbacks). (Illus.). 535p. 1970. pap. 2.95 (ISBN 0-8093-0462-7). S Ill U Pr.
Reid, Loren. Finally It's Friday: School & Work in Mid-America, 1921-1933. LC 80-27453. 288p. 1981. 14.00 (ISBN 0-8262-0330-2). U of Mo Pr.
Salisbury, Al & Salisbury, Jane. Here Rolled the Covered Wagons. encore ed. LC 48-3934. (Illus.). 10.95 (ISBN 0-87564-309-4). Superior Pub.
Shannon, Fred A. Appraisal of Walter Prescott Webb's "the Giant Plains. LC 78-12508. (Critiques of Research in the Social Sciences: No. III). 1979. Repr. of 1940 ed. lib. bdg. 17.75x (ISBN 0-313-21211-2, SHWP). Greenwood.
Shaw, Albert. Cooperation in the Northwest. LC 78-63782. (Johns Hopkins University. Studies in the Social Sciences. Sixth Ser. 1888: 4-6). Repr. of 1888 ed. 13.25 (ISBN 0-404-61047-1). AMS Pr.
Szymanski, Ronald, ed. America in Literature: The Midwest. LC 79-4078. 238p. (gr. 9-12). 1979. pap. text ed. 6.50 (ISBN 0-684-16137-0, SSP-43). Scribner.
The Territory South of the River Ohio, 1790-1796. (The Territorial Papers of the United States: Vol. 4). Repr. of 1936 ed. 69.50 (ISBN 0-404-01454-2). AMS Pr.
Thomson, J. S., ed. Personalities of the West & Midwest, Sixth Edition. rev. ed. LC 68-56857. (Personalities of the West & Midwest Ser.). 1979. 39.95 (ISBN 0-934544-07-7). Am Biog Inst.
--Personalities of the West & Midwest. 7th ed. 500p. 1981. 54.95x (ISBN 0-934544-07-7, Pub. by Intl Biog Ctr). Biblio Dist.
--Personalities of the West & Midwest. 7th rev. ed. LC 68-56857. 1982. 44.95 (ISBN 0-934544-08-5). Am Biog Inst.
Varenne, Herve. Americans Together: Structured Diversity in a Midwestern Town. LC 77-10109. 1977. pap. text ed. 10.25x (ISBN 0-8077-2519-6). Tchrs Coll.
Youngdale, James. Third Party Footprints. (Illus.). 10.00 (ISBN 0-87018-064-9). Ross.
MIDDLE WEST–DESCRIPTION AND TRAVEL
The Amoco Motor Club Guide to Mini-Vacations in the Midwest. (The Amoco Motor Club Guides to Mini-Vacations). (Illus.). 1980. 14.95 (ISBN 0-8092-7126-5); pap. 6.95 (ISBN 0-8092-7125-7). Contemp Bks.
Atwater, Caleb. Remarks Made on a Tour to Prairie du Chien: Thence to Washington City in 1829. fascimile ed. LC 75-82. (Mid-American Frontier Ser.). 1975. Repr. of 1831 ed. 19.00x (ISBN 0-405-06851-4). Arno.
Brown, R., et al. Agricultural Mid-West. 1975. pap. text ed. 3.95x (ISBN 0-435-34065-4). Heinemann Ed.
Caldwell, Erskine. Afternoons in Mid-America. (Illus.). 1976. 8.95 (ISBN 0-396-07376-X). Dodd.
Country Inns: Mid-West & Rocky Mountains, 1981-1982. 1981. 4.95 (ISBN 0-89102-210-4). B Franklin.
Drury, John. Historic Midwest Houses. LC 77-78084. (Illus.). 1977. pap. 6.95 (ISBN 0-226-16551-5). U of Chicago Pr.
Fodor's Midwest 1980. (Fodor's Travel Guide Ser.). (Illus.). 1980. 11.95 (ISBN 0-679-00455-6); pap. 8.95 (ISBN 0-679-00456-4). McKay.
Hitchcock, Anthony & Lindgren, Jean. Country Inns of the Midwest & Rocky Mountain States. 1979. pap. 4.95 (ISBN 0-89102-159-0). B Franklin.
Hutton, Graham. Midwest at Noon. (Midway Reprint Ser). 368p. 1975. pap. 10.50x (ISBN 0-226-36343-0). U of Chicago Pr.
Janovy, John, Jr. Back in Keith Country. (Illus.). 208p. 1981. 10.95 (ISBN 0-312-06483-7). St Martin.
Kern, Ben. One Hundred Trips, Places to Drive in the Upper Midwest. 2nd ed. LC 78-12839. (Illus.). 1979. pap. 6.95 (ISBN 0-87518-170-8). Dillon.
Nash, Linda & Nash, Steve. Chicago & Beyond: Twenty-Six Bike Tours. 224p. 1981. pap. 6.95 (ISBN 0-8329-1561-0). New Century.
Palzer, Bob & Palzer, Jody. Whitewater; Quietwater: A Guide to the Wild Rivers of Wisconsin, Upper Michigan, & Northeast Minnesota. 3rd ed. LC 77-81575. (Illus.). 160p. 1977. pap. 7.95 (ISBN 0-916166-02-3). Evergreen Paddleways.
Steele, Eliza R. A Summer Journey in the West. facsimile ed. LC 75-123. (Mid-American Frontier Ser.). 1975. Repr. of 1841 ed. 18.00x (ISBN 0-405-06888-3). Arno.
Sullivan, Jerry & Daniel, Glenda. Hiking Trails in the Midwest. rev. ed. (Illus.). 1980. pap. 7.95 (ISBN 0-8092-7007-2). Contemp Bks.
Whitman, John. The Best Free Attractions in the Midwestern States. Grooms, Kathe, ed. (The Best Free Attractions Ser.). (Illus.). 160p. (Orig.). 1981. pap. 3.95 (ISBN 0-915658-37-2). Meadowbrook Pr.
Winchester, Simon. American Heartbeat: Some Notes from a Midwestern Journey. 202p. 1976. 12.50 (ISBN 0-571-10878-4). Transatlantic.
MIDDLEBURY COLLEGE
Anderson, George K. Breadloaf School of English: The First Fifty Years. 1969. pap. 3.50x (ISBN 0-910408-15-7). Coll Store.
Freeman, Stephen A. Middlebury College Foreign Language Schools, Nineteen Fifteen to Nineteen Seventy: The Story of a Unique Idea. (Orig.). 1975. pap. 5.95x (ISBN 0-910408-17-3). Coll Store.
Morrison, Theodore. Middlebury College Breadloaf Writers' Conference: The First Thirty Years. 1976. pap. 3.95x (ISBN 0-910408-18-1). Coll Store.
MIDDLEHAM, YORK, ENGLAND–COLLEGIATE CHURCH
Atthill, William L., ed. Documents Relating to the Foundation & Antiquities of the Collegiate Church of Middleham in the County of York. LC 70-161702. (Camden Society, London. Publications, First Ser.: No. 38). Repr. of 1847 ed. 14.00 (ISBN 0-404-50138-9). AMS Pr.
--Documents Relating to the Foundation & Antiquities of the Collegiate Church of Middleham, County of York. (Camden Society Ser.: Vol. 38). 15.50 (ISBN 0-384-02270-7). Johnson Repr.
MIDDLESEX, ENGLAND
Baker, T. F., ed. The Victoria History of the Counties of England: Middlesex, Vol. 6. (Illus.). 248p. 1980. 129.00x (ISBN 0-19-722750-3). Oxford U Pr.
Lovell, Percy & Marcham, William, eds. Parish of St. Pancras, Pt. 1. LC 76-37851. (London County Council. Survey of London: No. 17). Repr. of 1936 ed. 74.50 (ISBN 0-404-51667-X). AMS Pr.
Murray, I. G. Victorian & Edwardian Middlesex. 1977. 22.50 (ISBN 0-7134-0181-8, Pub. by Batsford England). David & Charles.
Norden, John. Speculi Britanniae; the Description of Hartfordshire. LC 74-171778. (English Experience Ser.: No. 403). 38p. 1971. Repr. of 1598 ed. 7.00 (ISBN 90-221-0403-6). Walter J Johnson.
--Speculum Britanniae: The First Parte, a Description of Middlesex. LC 70-171777. (English Experience Ser.: No. 402). 58p. 1971. Repr. of 1593 ed. 8.00 (ISBN 90-221-0402-8). Walter J Johnson.
Wood, Sara, ed. Middlesex. (The Domesday Book Ser). (Illus.). 62p. 1976. 15.00x (ISBN 0-8476-1270-8). Rowman.
MIDDLESEX COUNTY, NEW JERSEY
Miers, Earl S. Where the Raritan Flows. 1964. 9.50 (ISBN 0-8135-0465-1). Rutgers U Pr.
MIDDLETON, CHARLES, 2ND EARL OF, 1650-1719
Jones, George H. Charles Middleton: The Life & Times of a Restoration Politician. LC 67-25532. 1967. 12.75x (ISBN 0-226-40947-3). U of Chicago Pr.
MIDDLETON, DREW, 1913-
Middleton, Drew. Where Has Last July Gone? LC 73-79922. 284p. 1973. 7.95 (ISBN 0-8129-0392-7). Times Bks.
MIDDLETON, RICHARD BARHAM, 1882-1911
Savage, Henry. Richard Middleton: The Man & His Work. LC 70-160780. 1971. Repr. of 1922 ed. 13.00 (ISBN 0-8046-1612-4). Kennikat.
--Richard Middleton: The Man & His Work. 1973. lib. bdg. 20.00 (ISBN 0-8414-8163-6). Folcroft.
MIDDLETON, THOMAS, d. 1627
Asp, Carolyn. A Study of Thomas Middleton's Tragicomedies. (Salzburg Studies in English Literature, Jacobean Drama Studies: No. 28). 282p. 1974. pap. text ed. 25.00x (ISBN 0-391-01303-3). Humanities.
Baines, Barbara J. The Lust Motif in the Plays of Thomas Middleton. (Salzburg Studies in English Literature, Jacobean Drama Studies: No. 29). 160p. 1973. pap. text ed. 25.00x (ISBN 0-391-01306-8). Humanities.
Barker, Richard H. Thomas Middleton. LC 74-12880. 216p. 1975. Repr. of 1958 ed. lib. bdg. 14.75x (ISBN 0-8371-7767-7, BATM). Greenwood.
Brittin, Norman A. Thomas Middleton. (English Authors Ser.: No. 139). lib. bdg. 10.95 (ISBN 0-8057-1388-3). Twayne.
Cherry, Caroline L. The Most Unvaluedst Purchase: Women in the Plays of Thomas Middleton. (Salzburg Studies in English Literature, Jacobean Drama Studies: No. 34). 114p. 1973. pap. text ed. 25.00x (ISBN 0-391-01342-4). Humanities.
Covatta, Anthony. Thomas Middleton's City Comedies. LC 72-3261. 187p. 1974. 15.00 (ISBN 0-8387-1196-0). Bucknell U Pr.
Dunkel, Wilbur D. Dramatic Technique of Thomas Middleton in His Comedies of London Life. LC 66-27062. 1967. Repr. of 1925 ed. 6.50 (ISBN 0-8462-0979-9). Russell.
Ellis, Havelock. Thomas Middleton: Best Plays of Old Dramatists, 2 vols. Repr. Set. lib. bdg. 69.00 (ISBN 0-403-00123-4). Scholarly.
Hallett, Charles A. Middleton's Cynics. (Salzburg Studies in English Literature, Jacobean Drama Studies Ser.: No. 47). 308p. 1975. pap. text ed. 25.00x (ISBN 0-391-01396-3). Humanities.
Jackson, MacD. P. Studies in Attribution: Shakespeare & Middleton. (SSEL Jacobean Drama Studies: No. 79). (Orig.). 1979. pap. text ed. 25.00x (ISBN 0-391-01699-7). Humanities.
Lake, D. J. The Canon of Thomas Middleton's Plays. LC 74-25651. (Illus.). 354p. 1975. 49.50 (ISBN 0-521-20741-X). Cambridge U Pr.
McElroy, John F. Parody & Burlesque in the Tragicomedies of Thomas Middleton. (Salzburg Studies in English Literature, Jacobean Drama Studies: No. 19). 1972. pap. text ed. 25.00x (ISBN 0-391-01479-X). Humanities.
Middleton, Thomas. Thomas Middleton: With an Introduction by A. C. Swinburne, 2 vols. Repr. of 1904 ed. 40.00 (ISBN 0-403-04311-5). Somerset Pub.
--The Widow: A Critical Edition. Levine, Robert T., ed. (Salzburg Studies in English Literature, Jacobean Studies Drama Ser.: No. 56). 260p. 1975. pap. text ed. 25.00x (ISBN 0-391-01482-X). Humanities.
--Women Beware Women. Gill, Roma, ed. (New Mermaids Ser.). 1980. pap. 5.95x (ISBN 0-393-90047-9). Norton.
Price, George R. Thomas Middleton: Michaelmas Term & a Trick to Catch the Old One. (Studies in English Literature: No. 91). 227p. 1976. pap. text ed. 42.50x (ISBN 0-686-22606-2). Mouton.
Rowe, George E., Jr. Thomas Middleton & the New Comedy Tradition. LC 79-4289. 1979. 16.95x (ISBN 0-8032-3853-3). U of Nebr Pr.
Schoenbaum, Samuel. Middleton's Tragedies. LC 71-128191. 1970. Repr. of 1955 ed. text ed. 10.00 (ISBN 0-87752-132-8). Gordian.
MIDDLETON, TROY H., 1889-
Price, Frank J. Troy H. Middleton: A Biography. LC 73-90869. (Illus.). 416p. 1974. 25.00x (ISBN 0-8071-0067-6). La State U Pr.
MIDDLEWICH, ENGLAND–HISTORY–SOURCES
Vernon, William. Middlewich Chartulary, 2 Vols. Repr. of 1944 ed. 19.50 ea. (ISBN 0-384-64375-2). Johnson Repr.
MIDGES
see Diptera
MIDGET (AUTOMOBILE)
see Automobiles, Foreign–Types–Midget
MIDGETS
see Dwarfs
MIDHAT, PASA, 1822-1884
Midhat, Ali H. The Life of Midhat Pasha. LC 73-6290. (The Middle East Ser.). Repr. of 1903 ed. 18.00 (ISBN 0-405-05348-7). Arno.
MIDLAND, TEXAS–ANTIQUITIES
Wendorf, Fred, et al. The Midland Discovery: A Report on the Pleistocene Human Remains from Midland, Texas. LC 79-161036. (Illus.). 1955. Repr. lib. bdg. 15.00 (ISBN 0-8371-5944-X, WEMD). Greenwood.
MIDLAND RAILWAY COMPANY
Barnes, E. G. Midland Main Line 1875-1922. LC 70-473273. (Illus.). 1969. 13.50x (ISBN 0-678-06029-0). Kelley.
--Rise of the Midland Railway 1844-1874. LC 76-83157. (Illus.). 1969. 13.50x (ISBN 0-678-06000-2). Kelley.
Ellis, C. Hamilton. Midland Railway. (Illus.). pap. 5.75x (ISBN 0-392-03937-0, SpS). Sportshelf.
Williams, Frederick S. Midland Railway. 5th ed. LC 68-23400. (Illus.). Repr. of 1888 ed. 19.50x (ISBN 0-678-05745-1). Kelley.
MIDLANDS
Wood, Peter A. Industrial Britain: West Midlands. 1976. 9.50 (ISBN 0-7153-7032-4). David & Charles.
MIDLER, BETTE
Baker, Rob. Bette Midler. rev. ed. 1979. pap. 2.25 (ISBN 0-445-04494-2). Popular Lib.
Midler, Bette. A View from a Broad. (Illus.). 1980. 12.95 (ISBN 0-671-24780-8). S&S.
MIDRASH
see also Tannaim
Breuer, Salomon. Chochmo U'Mussar, Vol. 3: Bamidbar-Devarim. Breuer, Jacob, tr. from Ger. Orig. Title: Belehre und Mahnung. 1977. 9.75 (ISBN 0-87306-036-9). Feldheim.
The Complete Set of Midrash Rabba: Hebrew & English, 18 vols. 185.00 (ISBN 0-87559-160-4). Shalom.
Fischel, Henry A. Essays in Greco-Roman & Related Talmudic-Midrashic Literature. 1974. 39.50x (ISBN 0-87068-260-1). Ktav.
Frankel, Israel. Peshat in Talmudic & Midrashic Literature. 1956. 12.50 (ISBN 0-87203-055-5). Hermon.
Maftechoth Hamidrash Rabba: Keys to the Midrash Rabba. 27.50 (ISBN 0-87559-159-0). Shalom.
Midrash Bamidbar Rabba: Numbers Rabba, Hebrew & English, 4 vols. 60.00 (ISBN 0-87559-153-1). Shalom.
Midrash Devorim Rabba: Deuteronomy, Hebrew & English. 15.00 (ISBN 0-87559-154-X). Shalom.
Midrash Eicha Rabba: Lamentation Rabba, Hebrew & English. 15.00 (ISBN 0-87559-157-4). Shalom.
Midrash Esther Rabba & Midrash Ruth Rabba: Hebrew & English. 15.00 (ISBN 0-87559-155-8). Shalom.
Midrash Koheleth Rabba: Ecclesiastes Rabba, Hebrew & English. 15.00 (ISBN 0-87559-158-2). Shalom.
Midrash Shemoth Rabba: Exodus Rabba, Hebrew & English, 2 vols. 30.00 (ISBN 0-87559-151-5). Shalom.
Midrash Shirashirim Rabba: Songs of Rabba, Hebrew & English. 15.00 (ISBN 0-87559-156-6). Shalom.
Midrash Vayikra Rabba: Leviticus Rabba, Hebrew & English, 2 vols. 30.00 (ISBN 0-87559-152-3). Shalom.
Strack, Hermann L. Introduction to the Talmud & Midrash. LC 59-7191. (Temple Books). 1969. pap. text ed. 5.95x (ISBN 0-689-70189-6, T10). Atheneum.
Wilken, Robert L., ed. Aspects of Wisdom in Judaism & Early Christianity. LC 74-27888. 234p. 1975. text ed. 13.95x (ISBN 0-268-00577-X, 85-05778). U of Notre Dame Pr.

MIDRASH-FOLK-LORE
see Folk-Lore, Jewish
MIDRASH-TRANSLATIONS INTO ENGLISH
The Complete Set of Midrash Rabba: Hebrew & English, 18 vols. 185.00 (ISBN 0-87559-160-4). Shalom.
Lauterbach, Jacob Z., intro. by. & tr. from Heb. Mekilta De-Rabbi Ishmael, 3 vols. LC 75-40823. (JPS Library of Jewish Classics). 808p. 1976. pap. 13.50 (ISBN 0-8276-0078-X, 382). Jewish Pubn.
Maftechoth Hamidrash Rabba: Keys to the Midrash Rabba. 27.50 (ISBN 0-87559-159-0). Shalom.
Midrash Bamidbar Rabba: Numbers Rabba, Hebrew & English, 4 vols. 60.00 (ISBN 0-87559-153-1). Shalom.
Midrash Devorim Rabba: Deuteronomy, Hebrew & English. 15.00 (ISBN 0-87559-154-X). Shalom.
Midrash Eicha Rabba: Lamentation Rabba, Hebrew & English. 15.00 (ISBN 0-87559-157-4). Shalom.
Midrash Esther Rabba & Midrash Ruth Rabba: Hebrew & English. 15.00 (ISBN 0-87559-155-8). Shalom.
Midrash Koheleth Rabba: Ecclesiastes Rabba, Hebrew & English. 15.00 (ISBN 0-87559-158-2). Shalom.
Midrash Shemoth Rabba: Exodus Rabba, Hebrew & English, 2 vols. 30.00 (ISBN 0-87559-151-5). Shalom.
Midrash Shirashirim Rabba: Songs of Rabba, Hebrew & English. 15.00 (ISBN 0-87559-156-6). Shalom.
Midrash Vayikra Rabba: Leviticus Rabba, Hebrew & English, 2 vols. 30.00 (ISBN 0-87559-152-3). Shalom.
Montefiore, C. G. & Loewe, H., eds. A Rabbinic Anthology. LC 73-91340. 1970. pap. 15.95 (ISBN 0-8052-0442-3). Schocken.
Rappaport, S. A. Treasury of the Midrash. 1969. 15.00x (ISBN 0-87068-100-1). Ktav.
MIDWAY, BATTLE OF, 1942
Fuchida, Mitsuo & Okumiya, Masatake. Midway, the Battle That Doomed Japan: The Japanese Navy's Story. Kawakami, Clarke & Pineau, Roger, eds. LC 55-9027. (Illus.). 1955. 14.95 (ISBN 0-87021-372-5). Naval Inst Pr.
Gay, George. Sole Survivor. 15.00 (ISBN 0-686-31603-7). Midway Pubs.
Mercer, Charles. Miracle at Midway. LC 77-24116. (Illus.). (gr. 6-8). 1977. 7.95 (ISBN 0-399-20612-4). Putnam.
Peck, Ira. Battle of Midway. (gr. 7 up). 1977. pap. 1.50 (ISBN 0-590-01437-4, Schol Pap). Schol Bk Serv.
Skipper, G. C. Battle of Midway. LC 80-17495. (World at War Ser.). (Illus.). 48p. (gr. 3 up). 1980. PLB 8.65 (ISBN 0-516-04782-5); pap. 2.95 (ISBN 0-516-44782-3). Childrens.
Smith, Chester L. Midway Four June Nineteen Forty-Two. LC 67-9501. 1967. soft bdg. 2.75 (ISBN 0-685-06837-4, 911970-01). Bede.
MIDWESTERN STATES
see Middle West
MIDWIFERY
see Obstetrics
MIDWIVES
see also Women Physicians
Anderson, Kathleen. Midwives. (Illus., Orig.). 1981. pap. cancelled (ISBN 0-917982-19-3). Cougar Bks.
Aveling, James H. English Midwives: Their History & Prospects. LC 75-23678. Repr. of 1872 ed. 16.00 (ISBN 0-404-13231-6). AMS Pr.
Brennan, Barbara & Heilman, Joan R. The Complete Book of Midwifery. 1977. pap. 4.95 (ISBN 0-525-03180-4). Dutton.
Buss, Fran L. La Partera: Story of a Midwife. 1980. 10.95x (ISBN 0-472-09322-3); pap. 6.95 (ISBN 0-472-06322-7). U of Mich Pr.
Davis, Elizabeth. A Guide to Midwifery: Heart & Hands. (Illus., Orig.). 1981. pap. 9.00 (ISBN 0-912528-22-2). John Muir.
Donegan, Jane B. Women & Men Midwives: Medicine, Morality, & Misogyny in Early America. LC 77-87968. (Contributions in Medical History: No. 2). (Illus.). 1978. lib. bdg. 22.50x (ISBN 0-8371-9868-2, DMA/). Greenwood.
Flatto, Edwin. Manual for Midwives: Step by Step Instructions for Natural Home & Emergency Childbirth. 1979. pap. 8.95 (ISBN 0-935540-02-4). Plymouth Pr.
Forbes, Thomas R. The Midwife & the Witch. LC 79-8099. Repr. of 1966 ed. 26.50 (ISBN 0-404-18411-1). AMS Pr.
Lancaster, Arnold. Nursing & Midwifery Sourcebook. (Illus., Orig.). 1979. pap. text ed. 12.50x (ISBN 0-04-610013-X). Allen Unwin.
Myles, Margaret. Textbook for Midwives. 9th ed. (Illus.). 870p. 1981. text ed. 40.00 (ISBN 0-443-02011-6); pap. text ed. 29.75 (ISBN 0-443-02010-8). Churchill.
Noall, Clair. Guardians of the Hearth: Utah's Pioneer Midwives & Women Doctors. LC 74-78028. 1974. 6.95 (ISBN 0-88290-030-7). Horizon Utah.
Prince, Joyce & Adams, Margaret E. Minds, Mothers & Midwives. 1978. pap. 12.50 (ISBN 0-443-01553-8). Churchill.
Roch, Sara E. Midwifery Revision. (Illus.). 352p. 1980. text ed. 10.00 (ISBN 0-443-01964-9). Churchill.
MIER EXPEDITION, 1842
Green, Thomas J. Journal of the Texian Expedition Against Mier. LC 72-9447. (The Far Western Frontier). (Illus.). 516p. 1973. Repr. of 1845 ed. 23.00 (ISBN 0-405-04975-7). Arno.
McCutchan, Joseph D. Mier Expedition Diary: A Texan Prisoner's Account. Nance, Joseph M., ed. (Elma Dill Russell Spencer Foundation Ser.: No. 8). 270p. 1978. 15.00 (ISBN 0-292-74006-9). U of Tex Pr.
Stapp, William P. The Prisoners of Perote. (Barker Texas History Center Ser: No. 1). (Illus.). 1977. 10.95 (ISBN 0-292-76442-1). U of Tex Pr.
Walker, Samuel H. Samuel H. Walker's Account of the Mier Expedition. Sibley, Marilyn M., ed. LC 78-63306. (Illus.). 1978. 10.00 (ISBN 0-87611-040-5); special collector's edition 40.00 (ISBN 0-87611-038-3). Tex St Hist Assn.
MIES VAN DER ROHE, LUDWIG, 1886-1969
Blake, Peter. The Master Builders: Le Corbusier, Mies Van der Rohe, Frank Lloyd Wright. new ed. (Illus.). 432p. 1976. pap. 5.95 (ISBN 0-393-00796-0, N796, Norton Lib). Norton.
Dunster, David, et al, eds. Mies Van der Rohe. LC 79-92594. (Architectural Monographs). (Illus.). 112p. (Orig.). 1980. pap. 16.50 (ISBN 0-8478-0295-7). Rizzoli Intl.
Glaeser, Ludwig. Mies Van der Rohe: Furniture & Drawings. LC 76-24509. (Illus.). 1977. pap. 6.95 (ISBN 0-87070-555-5). Museum Mod Art.
Gropius, et al. Four Great Makers of Modern Architecture: Gropius, le Corbusier, Mies Van der Rohe, Wright. LC 78-130312. (Architecture & Decorative Art Ser.: Vol. 37). 1970. Repr. of 1963 ed. lib. bdg. 29.50 (ISBN 0-306-70065-4). Da Capo.
Johnson, Philip C. Mies Van der Rohe. (Illus.). 1978. pap. 9.95 (ISBN 0-87070-560-1, Pub. by Museum Mod Art). NYGS.
Spaeth, David A. Ludwig Mies van der Rohe. LC 77-83355. (Library of Humanities Reference Bks.: No. 115). 1981. lib. bdg. 32.50 (ISBN 0-8240-9830-7). Garland Pub.
MIGNE, JACQUES PAUL, 1800-1875
Garnier, Freres. Catalogue General Des Ouvrages Edites Par l'Abbe Migne. LC 71-168926. 1967. Repr. of 1885 ed. 22.50 (ISBN 0-8337-2386-3). B Franklin.
MIGRAINE
Brainard, John B. Control of Migraine. 1979. pap. 3.95 (ISBN 0-393-00933-5). Norton.
--Control of Migraine. 1977. 10.95 (ISBN 0-393-06421-2). Norton.
Dell'Aquila, Lucy. Migraine Headaches: I Get Them No More (A Migraine Prevention Without Drugs) 1978. 10.00 (ISBN 0-533-03586-4). Vantage.
Diamond, Seymour, et al, eds. Vasoactive Substances Relevant to Migraine. (Illus.). 112p. 1975. 14.50 (ISBN 0-398-03348-X). C C Thomas.
Di Fiore, Frank R. You Can Conquer Your Headaches. (Illus.). 66p. (Orig.). 1980. pap. 10.00 (ISBN 0-932896-03-0). Westcliff Pubns.
Gosling, Nalda. Herbs for Headaches & Migraine. LC 80-50750. (Everybody's Home Herbal Ser.). (Illus.). 64p. (Orig.). 1980. pap. 1.95 (ISBN 0-394-73946-9). Shambhala Pubns.
Greene, Raymond, ed. Current Concepts in Migraine Research. LC 77-83690. 181p. 1978. 22.50 (ISBN 0-89004-199-7). Raven.
Hanington, Edda. How to Cope with Migraine Headaches. LC 74-22596. 1975. pap. 4.95 (ISBN 0-8069-8510-0). Sterling.
--Migraine. LC 76-11273. 1976. 11.50x (ISBN 0-87762-198-5). Technomic.
Hills, Hilda C. Good Food to Fight Migraine. LC 80-81098. 240p. 1981. 10.95 (ISBN 0-87983-255-X). Keats.
--Good Food to Fight Migraine. LC 80-84434. 240p. 1981. pap. 7.95 (ISBN 0-87983-251-7). Keats.
Mathew, R. J., ed. Treatment of Migraine: Pharmacological & Biofeedback Considerations. (Illus.). 170p. 1981. text ed. 25.00 (ISBN 0-89335-148-2). SP Med & Sci Bks.
Migraine Symposium, 1st, London, 1966. Background to Migraine: Proceedings. Smith, R., ed. LC 68-9472. (Illus.). 1967. 8.10 (ISBN 0-387-91011-5). Springer-Verlag.
Migraine Symposium, 2nd, London, 1967. Background to Migraine: Proceedings. Smith, R., ed. (Illus.). 1969. 4.80 (ISBN 0-387-91028-X). Springer-Verlag.
Migraine Symposium, 4th, London, 1971. Background to Migraine: Proceedings. Cumings, J. N., ed. (Illus.). 1971. 7.40 (ISBN 0-387-91086-7). Springer-Verlag.
Migraine Symposium, 5th, London, 1972. Background to Migraine: Proceedings. Cumings, J. N., ed. 1973. 24.20 (ISBN 0-387-91115-4). Springer Verlag.
Pearce, John. Migraine: Clinical Features, Mechanisims & Management. (American Lecture Living Chemistry). (Illus.). 116p. 1969. photocopy ed. spiral 11.75 (ISBN 0-398-01457-4). C C Thomas.
Rose, Clifford F. & Gawel, M. Migraine: The Facts. (Illus.). 150p. 1980. text ed. 11.95x (ISBN 0-19-261161-5). Oxford U Pr.
Sacks, Oliver W. Migraine: The Evolution of a Common Disorder. 1973. 17.95x (ISBN 0-520-01802-8); pap. 2.95 (ISBN 0-520-02484-2). U of Cal Pr.
Saper, Joel R. Migraine: Classification, Diagnosis & Treatment. 1982. write for info. (ISBN 0-88416-282-6, 282). Wright-PSG.
Speer, Frederic. Migraine. LC 76-25172. (Illus.). 1977. 13.95x (ISBN 0-88229-301-X); pap. 7.95 (ISBN 0-88229-467-9). Nelson-Hall.
Young, Victor A. Migraine Prevention. LC 78-61831. 156p. 1978. 7.95 (ISBN 0-9603694-0-6). V Young.
MIGRANT LABOR
see also Labor Mobility; Migration, Internal
Alexander, T. John. Spanish Surname Recent Migrant Families: Life Cycle, Family, Socioeconomics & Housing Status. LC 78-68462. 1979. perfect bdg. 8.00 (ISBN 0-88247-555-X). R & E Res Assoc.
Anderson, Henry P. The Bracero Program in California: With Particular Reference to Health Status, Attitudes, & Practices. Cortes, Carlos E., ed. LC 76-1225. (Chicano Heritage Ser.). (Illus.). 1976. 19.00x (ISBN 0-405-09482-5). Arno.
Anderson, Nels. Men on the Move. LC 74-7427. (FDR & the Era of the New Deal Ser.). xii, 357p. 1974. Repr. of 1940 ed. lib. bdg. 37.50 (ISBN 0-306-70588-5). Da Capo.
The Aspirations of Young Migrant Workers in Western Europe. (Educational Studies & Documents Ser: No. 21). 38p. 1976. pap. 2.50 (ISBN 92-3-101333-5, U42, UNESCO). Unipub.
Calles, Rudy. Champion Prune Pickers: Migrant Worker's Dilemma. (Illus., Orig.). 1979. pap. 2.95 (ISBN 0-89260-145-0). Hwong Pub.
Cheyney, Arnold B., ed. The Ripe Harvest: Educating Migrant Children. LC 73-158927. 256p. 1972. 11.95x (ISBN 0-87024-206-7). U of Miami Pr.
Coalson, George O. The Development of the Migratory Farm Labor System in Texas, 1900-1954. LC 76-24727. 1977. soft bdg. 9.00 (ISBN 0-88247-413-8). R & E Res Assoc.
Coles, Robert. Children of Crisis, Vol. 2: Migrants, Mountaineers & Sharecroppers. (Children of Crisis Ser.). (Illus.). 1972-73. 15.00 (ISBN 0-316-15171-8, Pub. by Atlantic Monthly Pr); pap. 8.95 (ISBN 0-316-15176-9). Little.
--Uprooted Children: The Early Life of Migrant Farm Workers. LC 70-98270. (Horace Mann Lecture Ser). 1970. 7.95 (ISBN 0-8229-3192-3). U of Pittsburgh Pr.
Collins, Doreen. Social Policy of the European Economic Community. LC 75-22282. 286p. 1975. 30.95 (ISBN 0-470-16583-9). Halsted Pr.
Croutch, Albert. Housing Migratory Agricultural Workers in California, 1913-1948. LC 74-31764. 1975. soft bdg. 8.00 (ISBN 0-88247-331-X). R & E Res Assoc.
Daniel, Cletus E. Bitter Harvest: A History of California Farmworkers, 1870-1941. LC 80-25664. 368p. 1981. 19.50x (ISBN 0-8014-1284-6). Cornell U Pr.
Day, James F. Migrant Education. LC 75-7967. 96p. 1975. 6.00 (ISBN 0-8022-2169-6). Philos Lib.
Dunbar, Tony & Kravitz, Linda. Hard Traveling: Migrant Farm Workers in America. LC 76-2056. 1976. text ed. 16.50 (ISBN 0-88410-293-9). Ballinger Pub.
The Education of Migrant Workers & Their Families. (Education Studies & Documents: No. 27). 1979. pap. 3.25 (ISBN 92-3-101536-2, U870, UNESCO). Unipub.
The Education of Migrant Workers' Children. 192p. 1981. pap. text ed. 18.95 (ISBN 90-265-0364-4, Pub. by Swets Pub Serv Holland). Swets North Am.
Fisher, Donald J. A Historical Study of the Migrant in California. LC 73-78057. pap. 8.00 (ISBN 0-88247-225-9). R & E Res Assoc.
Galarza, Ernesto. Merchants of Labor: The Mexican Bracero Story. (gr. 9-12). 1966. text ed. 10.00 (ISBN 0-87461-023-0); pap. text ed. 5.95 (ISBN 0-87461-024-9). McNally.
Goldfarb, Ronald L. Migrant Farm Workers: A Castle of Despair. 232p. 1981. text ed. 16.00 (ISBN 0-8138-1790-0). Iowa St U Pr.
Hathway, Marion. The Migratory Worker & Family Life. LC 77-169386. (Family in America Ser). 258p. 1972. Repr. of 1934 ed. 13.00 (ISBN 0-405-03863-1). Arno.
Heaps, Willard A. Wandering Workers: The Story of American Migrant Farm Workers & Their Problems. LC 68-9061. (gr. 7 up). 1968. 4.95 (ISBN 0-517-50184-8). Crown.
Holland, Ruth. Forgotten Minority: America's Tenant Farmers & Migrant Workers. LC 75-119144. (Illus.). (gr. 5-8). 1970. 8.95 (ISBN 0-02-744390-6, CCPr). Macmillan.
International Labour Conference, 67th Session & International Labour Office. Maintenance of Migrant Workers' Rights in Social Security. (Revision of Convention No. 48, Report VII, No. 2. 96p. (Orig.). 1981. pap. 10.00 (ISBN 92-2-102410-5). Intl Labour Office.
International Labour Office, Geneva. Migrant Workers. 196p. (Orig.). 1980. pap. 14.25 (ISBN 92-2-102093-2). Intl Labour Office.
Iowa State University of Science & Technology Center for Agricultural & Economic Adjustment. Labor Mobility & Population in Agriculture. LC 74-7535. 1977. Repr. of 1961 ed. lib. bdg. 16.75x (ISBN 0-8371-7584-4, IOLM). Greenwood.
King-Stoops, Joyce B. Migrant Education: Teaching the Wandering Ones. LC 80-82678. (Fastback Ser.: No. 145). 1980. pap. 0.75 (ISBN 0-87367-145-7). Phi Delta Kappa.
Koch, William H., Jr. Dignity of Their Own. (Orig.). 1966. pap. 1.95 (ISBN 0-377-46011-7). Friend Pr.
Laite, Julian. Industrial Development & Migrant Labour in Latin America. 1981. text ed. 25.00x (ISBN 0-292-73826-9). U of Tex Pr.
Levy, Jacques E. Cesar Chavez: Autobiography of La Causa. (Illus.). 546p. 1975. 19.95 (ISBN 0-393-07494-3). Norton.
McWilliams, Carey. Factories in the Field. LC 70-177593. (Illus.). 1971. pap. 4.95 (ISBN 0-87905-005-5). Peregrine Smith.
--Factories in the Field. LC 70-177593. (Illus.). 1971. pap. 4.95 (ISBN 0-87905-005-5). Peregrine Smith.
--Factories in the Field: The Story of the Migratory Farm Labor in California. 1969. Repr. of 1939 ed. 19.50 (ISBN 0-208-00679-6, Archon). Shoe String.
--Ill Fares the Land: Migrants & Migratory Labor in the United States. Cortes, Carlos E., ed. LC 76-1255. (Chicano Heritage Ser.). 1976. Repr. of 1942 ed. 24.00x (ISBN 0-405-09514-7). Arno.
Nelkin, Dorothy. On the Season: Aspects of the Migrant Labor System. LC 76-632774. (Paperback Ser.: No. 8). 98p. 1971. pap. 2.25 (ISBN 0-87546-041-0); pap. 5.25 special hard bdg. o.p (ISBN 0-87546-277-4). NY Sch Indus Rel.
Newby, Elizabeth. A Migrant with Hope. LC 76-53980. 1977. 5.50 (ISBN 0-8054-7218-5). Broadman.
Niejolt, G. Thomas-Lycklama. On the Road for Work: Migratory Workers on the East Coast of the United States. (Ser. on the Development of Societies: Vol. VII). 224p. 1980. lib. bdg. 16.00 (ISBN 0-89838-043-X). Kluwer Boston.
Power, Jonathan. Western Europe's Migrant Workers. (Minority Rights Group: No. 28). 1976. pap. 2.50 (ISBN 0-89192-085-4). Interbk Inc.
Power, Jonathan, et al. Migrant Workers in Western Europe & the United States. LC 78-41199. 1979. 28.00 (ISBN 0-08-023385-6); pap. 12.75 (ISBN 0-08-023384-8). Pergamon.
Rist, Ray C. Guestworkers in Germany: Prospects for Pluralism. LC 78-6282. (Praeger Special Studies). 1978. 27.95 (ISBN 0-03-040766-4). Praeger.
Rivett, Kenneth, ed. Australia & the Non-White Migrant. 327p. 1975. 27.50x (ISBN 0-522-84078-7, Pub. by Melbourne U Pr.). Intl Schol Bk Serv.
Sabot, R. H., ed. Migration & the Labor Market in Developing Countries. (Westview Special Studies in Social, Political, & Economic Development). 350p. 1981. lib. bdg. 31.25x (ISBN 0-89158-763-2). Westview.
Salt, John & Clout, Hugh, eds. Migration in Post-War Europe: Geographical Essays. (Illus.). 1976. 37.50x (ISBN 0-19-874027-1). Oxford U Pr.
Shannon, Lyle & Shannon, Magdaline. Minority Migrants in the Urban Community: Mexican-American & Negro Adjustment to Industrial Society. LC 72-84055. 352p. 1973. 24.00 (ISBN 0-8039-0158-5). Sage.
Shotwell, Louisa R. The Harvesters: The Story of the Migrant People. 1979. Repr. of 1961 ed. lib. bdg. 14.50x (ISBN 0-374-97388-1). Octagon.
U. S. Department of Labor. Farm Labor Fact Book. Repr. of 1959 ed. lib. bdg. 15.00 (ISBN 0-8371-2275-9, FALF). Greenwood.

United States Works Progress Administration. Migratory Workers of the Southwest: Consisting of "Migratory Cotton Pickers in Arizona" (1939), "The Pecan Shellers of San Antonio" (1940) & "Mexican Migratory Workers of South Texas" (1941, 3 vols. in 1. LC 78-10233. 1978. Repr. of 1941 ed. lib. bdg. 22.50x (ISBN 0-313-20685-6, USMW). Greenwood.
Webb, John N. Migratory-Casual Worker. LC 73-165690. (FDR & the Era of the New Deal Ser.). 1971. Repr. of 1937 ed. lib. bdg. 15.00 (ISBN 0-306-70339-4). Da Capo.
--Transient Unemployed. LC 71-166337. (FDR & the Era of the New Deal Ser.). 1971. Repr. of 1935 ed. lib. bdg. 15.00 (ISBN 0-306-70335-1). Da Capo.
Weiner, Sandra. Small Hands, Big Hands: Seven Stories of Mexican-American Migrant Workers & Their Families. LC 75-122925. (Illus.). (gr. 5 up). 1970. PLB 5.99 (ISBN 0-394-90442-7). Pantheon.
Whiteford, Scott. Workers from the North: Plantations, Bolivian Labor, & the City in Northwest Argentina. (Latin American Monographs: No. 54). (Illus.). 201p. 1981. text ed. 25.00 (ISBN 0-292-79015-5). U of Tex Pr.
Wiest, Raymond E. Mexican Farm Laborers in California: A Study of Intragroup Social Relations. LC 77-75745. 1977. 8.00 (ISBN 0-685-82441-1). R & E Res Assoc.

MIGRANT LABOR–AFRICA

Birks, J. S. & Sinclair, C. A. International Migration & Development in the Arab Region. International Labour Office, ed. (Illus.). 175p. (Orig.). 1980. 19.95 (ISBN 9-22-102252-8); pap. 14.25 (ISBN 9-22-102251-X). Intl Labour Office.
Murray, Colin. Families Divided: The Impact of Migrant Labour in Lesotho. (African Studies: No. 29). (Illus.). 236p. Date not set. price not set (ISBN 0-521-23501-4). Cambridge U Pr.
Wilson, Francis. Migrant Labour in South Africa: Report to the South African Council of Churches. (Illus.). pap. 10.00 (ISBN 0-86975-017-8, Pub by Ravan Press). Three Continents.

MIGRANT LABOR–GREAT BRITAIN

Phizacklea, Annie & Miles, Bob. Labour & Racism. 256p. 1980. 30.00 (ISBN 0-7100-0678-0); pap. 18.50 (ISBN 0-7100-0679-9). Routledge & Kegan.

MIGRATION, INTERNAL

see also Cities and Towns–Growth; Emigration and Immigration; Labor Mobility; Land Settlement; Rural-Urban Migration

Alexander, T. John. Spanish Surname Recent Migrant Families: Life Cycle, Family, Socioeconomics & Housing Status. LC 78-68462. 1979. perfect bdg. 8.00 (ISBN 0-88247-555-X). R & E Res Assoc.
Ball, John M. Migration & the Rural Municipio in Mexico. LC 75-636482. 1971. pap. 3.00 (ISBN 0-88406-001-2). Ga St U Busn Pub.
Beenstock, Michael. Health, Migration & Development. 192p. 1980. text ed. 27.75x (ISBN 0-566-00369-4, Pub. by Gower Pub Co England). Renouf.
Bock, P. G. & Rothenberg, Irene F. Internal Migration Policy & New Towns: The Mexican Experience. LC 78-31918. 1979. 10.00 (ISBN 0-252-00744-1). U of Ill Pr.
Brandes, Stanley H. Migration, Kinship & Community: Tradition & Transition in a Spanish Village. 1975. 32.00 (ISBN 0-12-125750-9). Acad Pr.
Brown, Alan A. & Neuberger, Egon. Internal Migration: A Comparative Perspective. 1977. 47.50 (ISBN 0-12-137350-9). Acad Pr.
Brown, David L. & Wardwell, John M., eds. New Directions in Urban-Rural Migration: The Population Turnaround in Rural America. (Studies in Population). 1980. 29.50 (ISBN 0-12-136380-5). Acad Pr.
Burford, Roger L. Net Migration for Southern Counties: 1940 to 1950 & 1950 to 1960. LC 63-63170. (Research Monograph: No. 24). 1963. spiral bdg. 5.00 (ISBN 0-88406-040-3). Ga St U Busn Pub.
Burnley, I. H., et al, eds. Mobility & Community Change in Australia. (Studies in Society & Culture). (Illus.). 286p. 1981. text ed. 30.25x (ISBN 0-7022-1446-9). U of Queensland Pr.
Cebula, Richard J. The Determinants of Human Migration. LC 79-2271. 160p. 1979. 18.95 (ISBN 0-669-03096-1). Lexington Bks.
De Jong, Gordon F. & Gardner, Robert W., eds. Migration Decision Making: Multidisciplinary Approaches to Microlevel Studies in Developed Studies in Developed & Developing Countries. (PPS on International Development). (Illus.). 370p. 1981. 37.50 (ISBN 0-08-026305-4). Pergamon.
Duchac, Rene. La Sociologie Des Migrations Aux Etats-Unis Societe, Mouvements Sociaux & Ideologies. (Premier Serie, Etudes: No. 15). 1974. pap. 35.50 (ISBN 90-2797-191-9). Mouton.
Eaton, Joseph W., ed. Migration & Social Welfare. LC 72-144344. 256p. (Orig.). 1971. pap. text ed. 5.00x (ISBN 0-87101-617-6, CBO-617-C). Natl Assn Soc Wkrs.
The Effects of Rural-Urban Migration on Women's Role & Status in Latin America. (Reports & Papers in the Social Sciences Ser.: No. 41). 1979. pap. 3.25 (ISBN 92-3-101578-8, U901, UNESCO). Unipub.
Fligstein, Neil. Going North: Migration of Blacks & Whites from the South, 1900-1950. (Quantitative Studies in Social Relations). 1981. write for info. (ISBN 0-12-260720-1). Acad Pr.
Forman, Sylvia H., et al. New Approaches to the Study of Migration. Guillet, David & Uzzell, Douglas, eds. (Rice University Studies, Vol. 62: No. 3). 181p. 1976. pap. 4.25x (ISBN 0-89263-229-1). Rice Univ.
Frisbie, W. Parker & Poston, Dudley L., Jr. Sustenance Organization & Migration in Nonmetropolitan America. LC 78-61. (Social Organization of the Community Ser.). 1978. pap. 3.25x (ISBN 0-87414-007-2). U of Iowa Pr.
Grandstaff, Peter J. Interregional Migration in the U.S.S.R. Economic Aspects, 1959 to 1970. LC 78-57233. 1980. 14.75 (ISBN 0-8223-0413-9). Duke.
Granfield, Michael L. An Econometric Model of Residential Location. LC 75-2246. 158p. 1975. text ed. 17.50 (ISBN 0-88410-410-9). Ballinger Pub.
Greenwood, Michael. Migration & Economic Growth in the United States: National, Regional & Metropolitan Perspectives. LC 80-1773. (Studies in Urban Economics). 1981. 24.00 (ISBN 0-12-300650-3). Acad Pr.
Hansen, Niles M. Location Preferences, Migration, & Regional Growth: A Study of the South & Southwest United States. LC 72-76449. (Special Studies in U.S. Economic, Social, & Political Issues). 1973. 34.00x (ISBN 0-275-06650-9). Irvington.
Holbrook, Stewart H. Yankee Exodus: An Account of Migration from New England. LC 50-7972. (Illus.). 440p. 1968. Repr. of 1950 ed. 11.50 (ISBN 0-295-73726-3). U of Wash Pr.
Houseman, Gerald L. The Right of Mobility. (National Univ. Pubns. Multi-Disciplinary in the Law Studies). 1979. 12.50 (ISBN 0-8046-9239-4). Kennikat.
Jackson, John A., ed. Migration. LC 70-85720. (Sociological Studies: No. 2). (Illus.). 1969. 22.95 (ISBN 0-521-07645-5). Cambridge U Pr.
Jansen, C. J. Readings in the Sociology of Migration. LC 72-105954. 1970. 21.00 (ISBN 0-08-006915-0); pap. 11.25 (ISBN 0-08-006914-2). Pergamon.
Johnson, Daniel M. & Campbell, Rex R. Black Migration in America: A Social Demographic History. LC 80-16919. (Social & Economic Demograpghy Studies: No. 4). (Illus.). viii, 190p. 1981. 16.75 (ISBN 0-8223-0442-2); pap. 8.95 (ISBN 0-8223-0449-X). Duke.
Jones, Douglas L. Village & Seaport: Migration & Society in Eighteenth-Century Massachusetts. LC 80-54469. (Illus.). 240p. 1981. text ed. 15.00x (ISBN 0-87451-200-X). U Pr of New Eng.
Jones, Marcus E. Black Migration in the United States with Emphasis on Selected Central Cities. LC 79-93299. 140p. 1980. 11.00 (ISBN 0-86548-014-1). Century Twenty One.
Julliard, Carl L. & Stermer, Edson. Willow Run: Study of Industrialization & Cultural Inadequacy. Stein, Leon, ed. LC 77-70486. (Work Ser.). (Illus.). 1977. Repr. of 1952 ed. lib. bdg. 27.00x (ISBN 0-405-10158-9). Arno.
Kennedy, Louise V. Negro Peasant Turns Cityward. LC 68-58597. (Columbia University Studies in the Social Sciences: No. 329). Repr. of 1930 ed. 14.00 (ISBN 0-404-51329-8). AMS Pr.
Kerr, Clark. Migration to the Seattle Labor Market Area, 1940-1942. Repr. of 1942 ed. lib. bdg. 15.00x (ISBN 0-8371-3058-1, KEMS). Greenwood.
Kiser, Clyde V. Sea Island to City: A Study of St. Helena Islanders in Harlem & Other Urban Centers. LC 32-34112. (Columbia University Studies in the Social Sciences: No. 368). Repr. of 1932 ed. 16.50 (ISBN 0-404-51368-9). AMS Pr.
--Sea Island to City: A Study of St. Helena Islanders in Harlem & Other Urban Centers. LC 69-15525. (Studies in American Negro Life Ser). 1969. pap. 3.45 (ISBN 0-689-70118-7, NL16). Atheneum.
Kono, Shigemi & Shio, Mitsuru. Inter-Prefectural Migration in Japan, 1956-1961. 1965. 5.25x (ISBN 0-210-27141-8). Asia.
Kubat, Daniel, ed. The Politics of Migration Policies: The First World in the 1970's. LC 77-93185. 1979. pap. 9.95x (ISBN 0-913256-34-X, Dist. by Ozer). Ctr Migration.
Kuper, Hilda & California University at los Angeles African Studies Center, eds. Urbanization & Migration in West Africa. LC 76-51201. (Illus.). 1977. Repr. of 1965 ed. lib. bdg. 17.00x (ISBN 0-8371-8762-1, KUUM). Greenwood.
Lang, Edith M. The Effects of Net Interregional Migration on Agricultural Income Growth: The United States, 1850-1860. LC 75-2585. (Dissertations in American Economic History). (Illus.). 1975. 15.00x (ISBN 0-405-07205-8). Arno.
Lively, C. E. & Taeuber, Conrad. Rural Migration in the United States. LC 71-165601. (FDR & the Era of the New Deal Ser.). 1971. Repr. of 1939 ed. pap. 19.50 (ISBN 0-306-70351-3). Da Capo.
McNeill, William H. & Adams, Ruth S. Human Migration: Patterns & Policies. LC 77-23685. 1978. 22.50x (ISBN 0-253-32875-6). Ind U Pr.
McWilliams, Carey. Ill Fares the Land: Migrants & Migratory Labor in the United States. Cortes, Carlos E., ed. LC 76-1255. (Chicano Heritage Ser.). 1976. Repr. of 1942 ed. 24.00x (ISBN 0-405-09514-7). Arno.
Marker, Gordon A. Internal Migration & Economic Opportunity: France, 1872-1911. Bruchey, Stuart, ed. LC 80-2815. (Dissertations in European Economic History II). (Illus.). 1981. lib. bdg. 25.00x (ISBN 0-405-13999-3). Arno.
Mayer, Kurt B. & Goldstein, Sidney. Migration & Economic Development in Rhode Island. LC 58-10480. (Illus.). viii, 64p. 1958. pap. 5.00 (ISBN 0-87057-051-X, Pub. by Brown U Pr). U Pr of New Eng.
Migration & Rural Development. (FAO Economic & Social Development Paper Ser.: No. 3). 1979. pap. 7.50 (ISBN 92-5-100611-3, F1513, FAO). Unipub.
Pernia, Ernesto D. Urbanization, Population Growth & Economic Deveopment in the Philippines. (Studies in Population & Urban Demography: No. 3). 1977. lib. bdg. 19.95 (ISBN 0-8371-9721-X, PEU/). Greenwood.
Plaut, Thomas R. Net Migration into Texas & Its Regions: Trends & Patterns. (Research Reports Ser.: 79-1). (Illus., Orig.). 1979. pap. text ed. 4.00 (ISBN 0-87755-239-8). U of Tex Busn Res.
Pryor, Robin, Jr., ed. Migration & Development in South-East Asia: A Demographic Perspective. (Illus.). 376p. 1979. text ed. 39.95x (ISBN 0-19-580420-1). Oxford U Pr.
Ramsey, Robert W. Carolina Cradle: Settlement of the Northwest Carolina Frontier, 1747-1762. 1964. 12.95 (ISBN 0-8078-0934-9). U of NC Pr.
Ravenstein, E. G. The Laws of Migration: Papers 1 & 2. LC 75-38142. (Demography Ser.). (Illus.). 1976. Repr. of 1889 ed. 10.00x (ISBN 0-405-07995-8). Arno.
Raymond, Ronald R., Jr., et al. Grow Your Roots Anywhere, Anytime. Date not set. 12.95 (ISBN 0-686-77634-8). Wyden.
Recommendations on Statistics of International Migration. (Statistical Papers Ser. M: No. 58). 73p. 1979. pap. 6.00 (ISBN 0-686-68967-4, UN79/17/18, UN). Unipub.
Reynolds, Lloyd G. Structure of Labor Markets: Wage & Labor Mobility in Theory & Practice. LC 73-109302. (Illus.). 1971. Repr. of 1951 ed. lib. bdg. 26.50x (ISBN 0-8371-3845-0, RELM). Greenwood.
Richmond, Anthony & Kubat, Daniel, eds. Internal Migration: The New World & the Third World. LC 75-42537. (Sage Studies in International Sociology: Vol. 4). 320p. 1976. 22.50x (ISBN 0-8039-9960-7); pap. 9.95x (ISBN 0-8039-9974-7). Sage.
Riddell, Barry J. Spatial Dynamics of Modernization in Sierra Leone: Structure, Diffusion & Response. 1970. 7.95x (ISBN 0-8101-0309-5). Northwestern U Pr.
Rogers, Andrei. Introduction to Multiregional Mathematical Demography. LC 74-34027. 203p. 1975. 16.50 (ISBN 0-471-73035-1, Pub. by Wiley). Krieger.
Rose, Arnold M. Migrants in Europe: Problems of Acceptance & Adjustment. LC 76-76162. 1969. 10.00x (ISBN 0-8166-0542-4). U of Minn Pr.
Roseman, Curtis C. Changing Migration Patterns Within the United States. Natoli, Salvatore J., ed. LC 76-57033. (Resource Papers for College Geography Ser.). (Illus.). 1977. pap. text ed. 4.00 (ISBN 0-89291-123-9). Assn Am Geographers.
Rowan, William. The Riddle of Migration. 1977. lib. bdg. 59.95 (ISBN 0-8490-2523-0). Gordon Pr.
Rural Poor in the Great Depression: Three Studies. LC 70-137177. (Poverty U.S.A. Historical Record Ser). 1971. Repr. of 1938 ed. 32.00 (ISBN 0-405-03133-5). Arno.
Salt, John & Clout, Hugh, eds. Migration in Post-War Europe: Geographical Essays. (Illus.). 1976. 37.50x (ISBN 0-19-874027-1). Oxford U Pr.
Salvatore, Dominick. Internal Migration & Economic Development: A Theoretical & Empirical Study. LC 81-40066. 74p. 1981. lib. bdg. 15.75 (ISBN 0-8191-1640-8); pap. text ed. 6.75 (ISBN 0-8191-1641-6). U Pr of Amer.
Schwind, Paul J. Migration & Regional Development in the United States, 1950-1960. LC 77-13850. (Research Papers Ser.: No. 133). (Illus., Orig.). 1971. pap. 8.00 (ISBN 0-89065-040-3, 133). U Chicago Dept Geog.
Scott, Emmett J. Negro Migration During the War. LC 69-18555. (American Negro: His History & Literature Ser., No 2). 1969. Repr. of 1920 ed. 9.50 (ISBN 0-405-01891-6). Arno.
Thomas, Robert N. & Hunter, John M., eds. Internal Migration Systems in the Developing World with Special Reference to Latin America. (University Bks.). 1980. lib. bdg. 19.95 (ISBN 0-8161-8414-3). G K Hall.
Thompson, Warren S. Research Memorandum on Internal Migration in the Depression. LC 70-162840. (Studies in the Social Aspects of the Depression). 98p. 1971. Repr. of 1937 ed. 12.00 (ISBN 0-405-00843-0). Arno.
Trends & Characteristics of International Migrations Since 1950. (Demographic Studies: No. 64). 172p. 1979. pap. 12.00 (ISBN 0-686-68977-1, UN78/13/5, UN). Unipub.
United States Congress, House Select Committee to Investigate Migration of Destitute Citizens. Interstate Migrations: A Report. (FDR & the Era of the New Deal Ser.). 1975. Repr. of 1941 ed. lib. bdg. 55.00 (ISBN 0-306-70711-X). Da Capo.
United States Department of Labor. Migration of Workers. (FDR & the Era of the New Deal Ser.). 1975. Repr. of 1938 ed. lib. bdg. 25.00 (ISBN 0-306-70712-8). Da Capo.
Vickery, William E. The Economics of the Negro Migration: 1900-1960. Bruchey, Stuart, ed. LC 76-45121. (Nineteen Seventy-Seven Dissertations Ser.). (Illus.). 1977. lib. bdg. 19.00x (ISBN 0-405-09932-0). Arno.
White, James W., ed. The Urban Impact of Internal Migration. LC 79-16544. (Comparative Urban Studies Project: No. 5). 1979. pap. text ed. 5.50 (ISBN 0-89143-047-4). U NC Inst Res Soc Sci.
Woodson, Carter G. Century of Negro Migration. LC 69-16770. (Illus.). 1969. Repr. of 1918 ed. 9.00 (ISBN 0-8462-1319-2). Russell.

MIGRATION, JEWISH

see Jews–Migrations

MIGRATION, RURAL-URBAN

see Rural-Urban Migration

MIGRATION OF ANIMALS

see Animal Migration

MIGRATION OF BIRDS

see Birds–Migration

MIGRATION OF FISHES

see Fishes–Migration

MIGRATION OF INSECTS

see Insects–Migration

MIGRATION OF PLANTS

see Plants–Migration

MIGRATIONS OF MAN

see Man–Migrations

MIGRATIONS OF NATIONS

see also Barbarian Invasions of Rome; Germanic Tribes; Jews–Migrations; Man–Migrations

Bury, John B. Invasion of Europe by the Barbarians. 1967. pap. 5.95 (ISBN 0-393-00388-4). Norton.
--Invasion of Europe by the Barbarians. LC 63-8359. 1963. Repr. of 1928 ed. 16.00 (ISBN 0-8462-0319-7). Russell.
Cairns, Trevor. Barbarians, Christians & Muslims. LC 69-11024. (Cambridge Introduction to the History of Mankind Ser.: Bk. 3). 1970. 5.95 (ISBN 0-521-07360-X). Cambridge U Pr.
Clastres, Helene. The Land Without Evil: Tupi-Guarani Prophetism. Grenez-Brovender, Jacqueline, tr. 160p. 1981. 18.50x (ISBN 0-8476-6271-3). Rowman.
Hammond, Nicholas G. Migrations & Invasions in Greece & Adjacent Areas. LC 76-17379. (Illus.). 1977. 28.00 (ISBN 0-8155-5047-2, NP). Noyes.
Horiuchi, Yoshitaka, et al. Afro-Asian, Japanese, & Euro-American Contributions to Mankind & Civilization Yestermorrow, Vol. 1. 1981. 9.50 (ISBN 0-533-04486-3). Vantage.
Lanning, James W. The Old Colony Mennonites of Bolivia. (Illus.). 130p. 1972. pap. 9.75x (ISBN 0-8361-1189-3). Herald Pr.
Musset, Lucien. The Germanic Invasions: The Making of Europe AD 400-600. James, Edward & James, Columba, trs. from Fr. LC 75-14261. (Illus.). 388p. 1975. 16.95x (ISBN 0-271-01198-X). Pa St U Pr.
Simkins, Paul D. & Wernstedt, Frederick L. Philippine Migration: The Settlement of the Digos-Padada Valley, Davao Province. (Monograph Ser.: No. 16). (Illus.). 147p. 1970. 5.75x (ISBN 0-686-30902-2). Yale U SE Asia.
Todd, Malcolm. The Barbarians. 1981. 24.00 (ISBN 0-7134-1669-6, Pub. by Batsford England). David & Charles.

Wallace-Hadrill, J. M. Barbarian West: The Early Middles Ages, A. D. 400-1000. pap. 3.95x (ISBN 0-06-131061-1, TB1061, Torch). Har-Row.

MIGRATORY BIRDS, PROTECTION OF
see Birds, Protection Of

MIGRATORY WORKERS
see Migrant Labor

MIHAILOVIC, DRAZA, 1893-1946

Martin, David. Patriot or Traitor: The Case of General Mihailovich. LC 77-83123. (Archival Documentary Publication Ser: No. 191). (Illus.). 520p. 1978. 19.00 (ISBN 0-8179-6911-X). Hoover Inst Pr.

Martin, David, intro. by. Patriot or Traitor: The Case of General Mihailovich. (Special Project Ser.: No. 29). 507p. 1981. pap. 12.50 (ISBN 0-8179-4292-0). Hoover Inst Pr.

Mihailovic, Drogoljub-Draza. The Trial of Dragoljub-Draza Mihailovic: Stenographic Record & Documents from the Trial of Dragoljub-Draza Milhailovic. 1978. Repr. of 1946 ed. lib. bdg. 19.95 (ISBN 0-89712-064-7). Documentary Pubns.

MIJE LANGUAGE
see Mixe Language

MIKE FINK
see Fink, Mike, 1770-1823

MILAN

Kendall, Paul M. & Ilardi, Vincent, eds. Dispatches, with Related Documents, of Milanese Ambassadors in France & Burgundy, 1450-1483. LC 68-20933. xlvii, 358p. 1970. Vol. 1, lvi 390p. 15.00x (ISBN 0-8214-0067-3); Vol. 2, 486p. 15.00x (ISBN 0-8214-0082-7). Ohio U Pr.

MILAN-DESCRIPTION

Chiarelli, Renzo. Get to Know Milan. (Italia Artistica Ser.). (Illus.). 64p. 1972. 7.50x (ISBN 0-8002-0823-4). Intl Pubns Serv.

How to Visit the Beauties of Milan. (Illus.). 128p. 1971. pap. 6.00x (ISBN 0-8002-1515-X). Intl Pubns Serv.

Magi, Giovanna. Looking at Milan. Zatta, Merry, tr. from Ital. (Italia Artistica Ser.). (Illus., Orig.). 1977. pap. 12.50x (ISBN 0-8002-0010-1). Intl Pubns Serv.

Ragghianti, Carlo L. Brera: Milan. LC 74-118562. (Great Museums of the World Ser.). (Illus.). 1968. 16.95 (ISBN 0-88225-226-7). Newsweek.

MILAN-HISTORY
see also Patarines

MILAN-LA SCALA

Lotti, Giorgio & Radice, Raul. La Scala. Gilbert, John, tr. from It. LC 79-87900. (Illus.). 1979. 35.00 (ISBN 0-688-03493-4). Morrow.

MILAREPA, 1038-1122
see Mi-La Ras-Pa, 1038-1122

MILES, NELSON APPLETON, 1839-1925

Marshall, J. T. Miles Expedition of Eighteen Seventy-Four-Eighteen Seventy-Five: An Eyewitness Account of the Red River Ear. White, Lonnie J., ed. (Narratives of the American West Ser.: Vol. 1). (Illus.). 1971. 7.50 (ISBN 0-88426-014-3). Encino Pr.

Miles, Nelson A. Serving the Republic: Memoirs of the Civil & Military Life of Nelson A. Miles. facsimile ed. LC 74-147786. (Select Bibliographies Reprint Ser). Repr. of 1911 ed. 23.00 (ISBN 0-8369-5632-X). Arno.

MILITARISM
see also Disarmament; Imperialism; Military Service, Compulsory

Afzelius, A. Two Studies on Roman Expansion: An Original Anthology. LC 75-7301. (Roman History Ser.). (Ger.). 1975. Repr. of 1975 ed. 22.00x (ISBN 0-405-07178-7). Arno.

Aichinger, Peter. The American Soldier in Fiction,1880-1963: A History of Attitudes Toward Warfare & the Military Establishment. 143p. 1975. 7.50 (ISBN 0-8138-0100-1). Iowa St U Pr.

Barnaby, Frank, et al, eds. Arms Uncontrolled. LC 75-2815. (Stockholm International Peace Research Institute Ser). 256p. 1975. text ed. 14.00x (ISBN 0-674-04655-2). Harvard U Pr.

Bienen, Henry, ed. The Military & Modernization. (Controversy Ser.). 242p. 1971. 9.95x (ISBN 0-202-24044-4); pap. 3.95x (ISBN 0-202-24045-2). Lieber-Atherton.

Cohen, Eliot A. Commandos & Politicians: Elite Military Units in Modern Democracies. LC 78-57287. (Studies in International Affairs: No. 40). (gr. 10 up). 1978. PLB 8.95x (ISBN 0-87674-042-5); pap. text ed. 3.95x (ISBN 0-87674-041-7). Harvard U Intl Aff.

Constant, Benjamin. De l'Esprit de Conquete. 72p. 1947. 4.95 (ISBN 0-686-54609-1). French & Eur.

Dixon, Norman F. On the Psychology of Military Incompetence. LC 76-9336. 1976. 12.50x (ISBN 0-465-05253-3). Basic.

Eide, Asbjorn & Thee, Marek, eds. Problems of Contemporary Militarism. LC 79-3379. 1980. 27.50x (ISBN 0-312-64744-1). St Martin.

Faramazian, R. Los Estados Unidos: Militarismo y Economia. 316p. (Span.). 1975. 4.15 (ISBN 0-8285-1425-9, Pub. by Progress Pubs Russia). Imported Pubns.

Faramazyan, F. A. U S A: Militarism & Economy. 271p. 1974. 3.25 (ISBN 0-8285-0387-7, Pub. by Progress Pubs Russia). Imported Pubns.

Faramazyan, R. A. U. S. A. Militarism & the Economy - A Soviet View. 271p. 1975. 12.95x (ISBN 0-8464-0941-0). Beekman Pubs.

Ferrero, Guglielmo. Militarism. LC 73-172547. Repr. of 1902 ed. 15.00 (ISBN 0-405-08500-1). Arno.

--Militarism. LC 76-147469. (Library of War & Peace; the Character & Causes of War). lib. bdg. 38.00 (ISBN 0-8240-0260-1). Garland Pub.

Fidel, Kenneth, ed. Militarism in Developing Countries. LC 74-20190. (Third World Ser.). 300p. 1975. 12.95 (ISBN 0-87855-092-5); pap. 5.95 (ISBN 0-87855-585-4). Transaction Bks.

Franklin, John H. Militant South, Eighteen Hundred to Eighteen Sixty-One. LC 56-10160. 1970. Repr. 16.50x (ISBN 0-674-57450-8, Belknap Pr). Harvard U Pr.

Howard, Michael E. Soldiers & Governments: Nine Studies in Civil-Military Relations. LC 78-1468. 1978. Repr. of 1959 ed. lib. bdg. 19.75x (ISBN 0-313-20303-2, HOSG). Greenwood.

Huntington, Samuel P. Soldier & the State: The Theory & Politics of Civil Military Relations. LC 57-6349. 1957. 25.00x (ISBN 0-674-81735-4, Belknap Pr). Harvard U Pr.

Johnson, John J., ed. The Role of the Military in Underdeveloped Countries: Papers of a Conference Sponsored by the Rand Corp. at Santa Monica, Calif. in August 1959. LC 80-25808. viii, 423p. 1981. Repr. of 1962 ed. lib. bdg. 39.75x (ISBN 0-313-22784-5, JORM). Greenwood.

Kelleher, Catherine M., ed. Political-Military Systems. LC 74-77094. (Sage Research Progress Ser. on War, Revolution & Peacekeeping: Vol. 4). 320p. 1974. 22.50 (ISBN 0-8039-0414-2); pap. 9.95 (ISBN 0-8039-0415-0). Sage.

Kohn, Richard H. Eagle & Sword: The Federalists & the Creation of the Military Establishment in America, 1783-1802. LC 74-33092. (Illus.). 1975. 13.95 (ISBN 0-02-917550-X). Free Pr.

Larson, Arthur D. Civil-Military Relations & Militarism: A Classified Bibliography Covering the United States & Other Nations of the World with Introductory Notes. 1971. Repr. 4.00 (ISBN 0-686-20807-2). KSU.

Liebknecht, Karl. Militarism & Anti-Militarism. Lock, Grahame, tr. from Ger. Orig. Title: Militarismus und Anti-Militaismus. 196p. (Orig.). 1980. pap. 5.95 (ISBN 0-904613-87-9). Writers & Readers.

--Militarism & Anti-Militarism. 1969. 16.50 (ISBN 0-86527-130-5). Fertig.

--Militarism & Anti-Militarism. 59.95 (ISBN 0-8490-0635-X). Gordon Pr.

--Militarism & Anti-Militarism. Sirnis, A., tr. 192p. 1972. pap. 2.00 (ISBN 0-486-22840-1). Dover.

--Militarism & Anti-Militarism. 5.00 (ISBN 0-8446-4571-0). Peter Smith.

--Militarism & Antimilitarism. LC 76-147521. (Library of War & Peace; Labor, Socialism & War). lib. bdg. 38.00 (ISBN 0-8240-0309-8). Garland Pub.

--Militarism & Antimilitarism: With Special Regard to the International Young Socialist Movement. Lock, Grahame, tr. from Ger. 162p. 1974. text ed. 10.00x (ISBN 0-9502495-7-2); pap. text ed. 4.00x (ISBN 0-9502495-8-0). Humanities.

McClellan, George B. The Armies of Europe: The Military Systems of England, France, Russia, Prussia, Austria, & Sardinia. 1976. lib. bdg. 59.95 (ISBN 0-8490-1450-6). Gordon Pr.

MacDonald, J. Ramsey. National Defence: A Study in Militarism. LC 70-147522. (Library of War & Peace; Labor, Socialism & War). lib. bdg. 38.00 (ISBN 0-8240-0310-1). Garland Pub.

Marxist-Leninist Party, USA. No to U. S. Imperialist War Preparations. National Executive Committee of the MLP, USA, ed. (Illus.). 1980. pap. 1.00 (ISBN 0-86714-003-8). Marxist-Leninist.

Militarism, Politics, & Working Class Attitudes in Late Nineteenth Century Europe. Incl. Army & the Democracy; Militarism in Politics. De Bloch, Jean; Armee, Est-Elle, Doit-Elle Etre la Nation? Bourelly, Jules; Working Men & War. Burt, Thomas; Der/Militarismus. Wiede, F. LC 75-147561. (Library of War & Peace; Control & Limitation of Arms). lib. bdg. 38.00 (ISBN 0-8240-0335-7). Garland Pub.

Schiller, Herbert I. & Phillips, Joseph D., eds. Super-State: Readings in the Military-Industrial Complex. LC 73-104026. 1970. 20.00 (ISBN 0-252-00096-X); pap. 6.95 (ISBN 0-252-00283-0). U of Ill Pr.

Smethurst, Richard J. A Social Basic for Prewar Japanese Militarism: The Army & the Rural Community. (Center for Japanese & Korean Studies). 1974. 30.00x (ISBN 0-520-02552-0). U of Cal Pr.

Vagts, Alfred. History of Militarism. rev. ed. LC 59-7194. 1967. pap. text ed. 8.95 (ISBN 0-02-933050-5). Free Pr.

--A History of Militarism: Civilian & Military. LC 81-4918. (Illus.). 542p. 1981. Repr. of 1959 ed. lib. bdg. 50.00x (ISBN 0-313-22961-9, VAHM). Greenwood.

Wingfield-Stratford, Esme. They That Take the Sword. LC 72-89273. 440p. 1973. Repr. of 1932 ed. 20.00 (ISBN 0-8046-1764-3). Kennikat.

MILITARISM-CHINA

Sutton, Donald S. Provincial Militarism & the Chinese Republic: The Yunnan Army, Nineteen Hundred & Five to Nineteen Twenty-Five. (Michigan Studies on China). (Illus.). 424p. 1980. 18.50x (ISBN 0-472-08813-0). U of Mich Pr.

Wilson, Andrew. Ever-Victorious Army: A History of the Chinese Campaign Under Lt. Col. C. G. Gordon & of the Suppression of the T'ai P'ing Rebellion. (Studies in Chinese History & Civilization). 395p. 1977. 24.75 (ISBN 0-89093-078-3). U Pubns Amer.

MILITARISM-GERMANY

Bilibin. Das Maerchen Vom Herrlichen Falken. (Insel Taschenbucher Fur Kinder: It 487). 64p. (Ger.). 1980. pap. text ed. 4.55 (ISBN 3-458-32187-X, Pub. by Insel Verlag Germany). Suhrkamp.

MacKsey, Kenneth. Kesselring: The Making of the Luftwaffe. 1978. 27.00 (ISBN 0-7134-0862-6, Pub. by Batsford England). David & Charles.

Ritter, Gerhard. The Sword & the Scepter: The Problem of Militarism in Germany. Norden, Heinz, tr. Incl. Vol. 1. The Prussian Tradition 1740-1890. 1969. 19.95x (ISBN 0-87024-127-3); Vol. 2. The European Powers & the Wilhelminian Empire, 1890-1914. 1970. 19.95x (ISBN 0-87024-128-1); Vol. 3. The Tragedy of Statesmanship: Bethmann Hollweg As War Chancellor (1914-1917) 1972. 19.95x (ISBN 0-87024-182-6); Vol. 4. The Reign of German Militarism & the Disaster of 1918. 1973. 19.95x (ISBN 0-87024-235-0). LC 68-31041. Set. 69.95x (ISBN 0-87024-297-0). U of Miami Pr.

MILITARISM-JAPAN

Causton, Eric E. Militarism & Foreign Policy in Japan. LC 78-63658. (Studies in Fascism: Ideology & Practice). Repr. of 1936 ed. 18.00 (ISBN 0-404-16918-X). AMS Pr.

MILITARISM-NEAR EAST

Pipes, Daniel. Slave Soldiers & Islam: The Genesis of a Military System. LC 80-23969. 272p. 1981. text ed. 25.00x (ISBN 0-300-02447-9). Yale U Pr.

Wolpin, Miles D. Militarism & Social Revolution in the Third World. LC 81-65014. 256p. 1981. text ed. 19.95 (ISBN 0-86598-021-7). Allanheld.

MILITARY ADMINISTRATION
see also Military Law

Baxter, Douglas C. Servants of the Sword: French Intendants of the Army, 1630-70. LC 75-40115. 288p. 1976. 17.50 (ISBN 0-252-00291-1). U of Ill Pr.

Cruickshank, C. G. Elizabeth's Army. 2nd ed. (Orig.). 1966. pap. 3.00x (ISBN 0-19-881148-9, OPB). Oxford U Pr.

Goldhamer, Herbert. The Soviet Soldier: Soviet Military Management at the Troop Level. LC 74-26727. 1975. 22.50x (ISBN 0-8448-0615-3); pap. 8.75x (ISBN 0-8448-0652-8). Crane-Russak Co.

Janowitz, Morris. Sociology & the Military Establishment. 3rd ed. LC 65-23742. (Sage Ser. on Armed Forces & Society: Vol. 6). 160p. 1974. 18.95 (ISBN 0-8039-0214-X); pap. 8.95 (ISBN 0-8039-0215-8). Sage.

Thompson, I. A. War & Government in Habsburg Spain 1560-1620. 1976. text ed. 36.50x (ISBN 0-485-11166-7, Athlone Pr). Humanities.

Williams, T. Harry. Americans at War: The Development of the American Military System. LC 60-8287. (Illus.). 1960. 10.00x (ISBN 0-8071-0830-8). La State U Pr.

MILITARY AERONAUTICS
see Aeronautics, Military

MILITARY AID
see Military Assistance, American

MILITARY AIRPLANES
see Airplanes, Military

MILITARY AND CIVILIAN POWER
see Civil Supremacy over the Military

MILITARY ARCHITECTURE
see also Arsenals; Fortification

Duffy, Christopher. Fire & Stone: The Science of Fortress Warfare 1660-1860. LC 74-84087. (Illus.). 200p. 1975. 17.50 (ISBN 0-88254-305-9). Hippocrene Bks.

Jones, Peter B. Hans Scharoun-A Monograph. LC 79-307585. 1979. 30.50 (ISBN 0-900406-57-7, Pub by G Fraser). Intl Schol Bk Serv.

Norwood, Richard. Fortification, or Architecture Military. LC 72-6019. (English Experience Ser.: No. 545). 1973. Repr. of 1628 ed. 15.00 (ISBN 90-221-0545-8). Walter J Johnson.

Sweeney, James B. Pictorial Guide to the Military Museums, Forts, & Historic Sites of the U. S. 320p. 1981. 19.95 (ISBN 0-517-54481-4). Crown.

Viollet-Le-Duc, Eugene. An Essay on the Military Architecture of the Middle Ages. LC 74-12651. (Illus.). 1977. Repr. of 1860 ed. lib. bdg. 19.75 (ISBN 0-8371-7747-2, VIMA). Greenwood.

MILITARY ART AND SCIENCE
see also Aeronautics, Military; Air Warfare; Armaments; Armed Forces; Armies; Arms and Armor; Atomic Warfare; Attack and Defense (Military Science); Battles; Biological Warfare; Camouflage (Military Science); Chemical Warfare; Civil Defense; Classification-Books-Military Art and Science; Disarmament; Drill and Minor Tactics; Fortification; Guerrilla Warfare; Gunnery; Imaginary Wars and Battles; Industrial Mobilization; Intrenchments; Lightning War; Logistics; Mechanization, Military; Mines, Military; Morale; Naval Art and Science; Ordnance; Psychological Warfare; Scouts and Scouting; Shooting, Military; Sieges; Signals and Signaling; Soldiers; Spies; Strategy; Street Fighting (Military Science); Tactics; Tank Warfare; Transportation, Military; Veterans; War; War Games
also headings beginning with the word Military

Abrahamsson, Bengt. Military Professionalization & Political Power. LC 79-172472. (Sage Series on Armed Forces & Society: Vol. 2). 192p. 1972. 20.00x (ISBN 0-8039-0138-0). Sage.

Angell, Norman. The Great Illusion: A Study of the Relation of Military Power to National Advantage. 1913. 25.00 (ISBN 0-686-19910-3). Quaker City.

Arkin, William. IPS Research Guide to Current Military & Strategic Affairs. 160p. 1981. pap. 5.95 (ISBN 0-89758-025-7). Inst Policy Stud.

Aston, George, ed. The Study of War for Statesmen & Citizens. LC 72-89260. 216p. 1973. Repr. of 1927 ed. 12.50 (ISBN 0-8046-1762-7). Kennikat.

Ayers, Bradley E. The War That Never Was. 1979. pap. 2.50 (ISBN 0-89041-255-3). Major Bks.

Bailey, Norman & Feder, Stuart. Operational Conflict Analysis. 1973. 7.00 (ISBN 0-8183-0145-7). Pub Aff Pr.

Balck, William. Tactics, 2 vols. 4th rev. ed. Krueger, Walter, tr. LC 70-84261. (West Point Military Library). 1977. Set. lib. bdg. 63.50x (ISBN 0-8371-9512-8, BATC); Vol. 1. lib. bdg. 37.25 (ISBN 0-8371-9513-6); Vol. 2. lib. bdg. 37.25 (ISBN 0-8371-9514-4). Greenwood.

Barrows, William, ed. The General: Twelve Nights in the Hunters' Camp. facsimile ed. LC 70-179504. (Select Bibliographies Reprint Ser). Repr. of 1869 ed. 18.00 (ISBN 0-8369-6633-3). Arno.

Blakey, Scott. Prisoner at War: The Survival of Commander Richard A. Stratton. (Illus.). 1979. pap. 2.95 (ISBN 0-14-005225-9). Penguin.

Bond, Brian. Liddell Hart: A Study of His Military Thought. (Illus.). 1977. 20.00 (ISBN 0-8135-0846-0). Rutgers U Pr.

Buck, James H., ed. Military Leadership. LC 81-9105. (Sage Research Progress Series on War, Revolution, & Peacekeeping: Vol. 10). 320p. 1981. 22.50 (ISBN 0-8039-1679-5); pap. 9.95 (ISBN 0-8039-1680-9). Sage.

Candler. Atlas of African Military Strategy. 102p. Date not set. 29.95 (ISBN 0-02-905750-7). Macmillan.

Command, Control & Communication. (Brassey's Battlefield Weapons Systems & Technology: Vol. 6). 160p. 1982. 40.00 (ISBN 0-08-028332-2); pap. 16.00 (ISBN 0-08-028333-0). Pergamon.

Cooling, Benjamin F., ed. War, Business, & World Military-Industrial Complexes. (National University Publications, Political Science Ser.). 1981. 19.50 (ISBN 0-8046-9276-9). Kennikat.

Cooper, Duff. Sergeant Shakespeare. LC 76-30696. (Studies in Shakespeare, No. 24). 1977. lib. bdg. 46.95 (ISBN 0-8383-2152-6). Haskell.

Cordier, Sherwood S. The Air & Sea Lanes of the North Atlantic: Their Security in the Nineteen Eighties. LC 81-40180. 90p. (Orig.). 1981. pap. text ed. 6.25 (ISBN 0-8191-1587-8). U Pr of Amer.

--Calculus of Power: The Current Soviet-American Conventional Military Balance in Central Europe. 3rd ed. LC 79-5435. 1980. pap. text ed. 7.50 (ISBN 0-8191-0883-9). U Pr of Amer.

Cowper, H. S. The Art of Attack. (Illus.). 1977. Repr. of 1906 ed. 24.00x (ISBN 0-7158-1212-2). Charles River Bks.

Curtis, Tony, ed. Militaria. (Illus.). 1978. 3.95 (ISBN 0-902921-49-5). Apollo.

Cuthbert, S. J. We Shall Fight in the Streets. (Illus.). 68p. 1972. pap. 5.00 (ISBN 0-87364-049-7). Paladin Ent.

Dan, Uri. The Face of Terror. 1978. pap. 1.75 (ISBN 0-8439-0526-3, Leisure Bks). Nordon Pubns.

Daniel, Donald C. & Herbig, Katherine L., eds. Strategic Military Deception. (Pergamon Policy Studies on Security Affairs). 300p. 1981. 32.51 (ISBN 0-08-027219-3). Pergamon.

De Gaulle, Charles. The Army of the Future. LC 74-5925. 1976. Repr. of 1941 ed. lib. bdg. 15.00x (ISBN 0-8371-7525-9, GAAF). Greenwood.

Delbruck, Hans. History of the Art of War Within the Framework of Political History, Vol. II: The Germans. Renfroe, Walter J., Jr., tr. from Ger. LC 72-792. (Contributions in Military History: No. 20). (Illus.). 552p. 1980. lib. bdg. 39.95 (ISBN 0-8371-8163-1, DEC/). Greenwood.

Des Pas Feuquieres, Antoine. Memoirs Historical & Military: Containing a Distinct View of All the Considerable States of Europe. LC 68-54790. 1735-1736. Repr. lib. bdg. 36.50x (ISBN 0-8371-2662-2, FEMH). Greenwood.

Dilley, Roy S. Beginner's Guide to Military Modelling. 176p. 1974. 8.95 (ISBN 0-7207-0551-7, Pub. by Michael Joseph). Merrimack Bk Serv.

Doenitz, Karl. Memoirs: Ten Years & Twenty Days. 1977. pap. 1.95 (ISBN 0-8439-0493-3, Leisure Bks). Nordon Pubns.

Downey, Robert J. & Roth, Jordon T. Weapon Retention Techniques for Officer Survival. (Illus.). 128p. 1980. text ed. 14.75 (ISBN 0-398-04108-3). C C Thomas.

Draeger, D. F. Weapons & Fighting Arts of the Indonesian Archyselage. 12.50 (ISBN 0-685-63790-5). Wehman.

Earle, Edward M., ed. Makers of Modern Strategy: Military Thought from Machiavelli to Hitler. 1943. 40.00 (ISBN 0-691-06907-7); pap. 8.95 (ISBN 0-691-01853-7). Princeton U Pr.

Eccles, Henry E. Logistics in the National Defense. LC 81-4920. (Illus.). xviii, 347p. 1981. Repr. lib. bdg. 35.00 (ISBN 0-313-22716-0, ECLO). Greenwood.

Engels, Friedrich. Engels As Military Critic: Articles Reprinted from the "Volunteer Journal" & the "Manchester Guardian of the 1860's. LC 75-26213. 1976. Repr. of 1959 ed. lib. bdg. 15.00x (ISBN 0-8371-8407-X, ENMC). Greenwood.

Enloe, Cynthia. Police, Military, & Ethnicity. LC 79-64569. 179p. 1980. text ed. 14.95 (ISBN 0-87855-302-9); pap. cancelled (ISBN 0-87855-721-0). Transaction Bks.

Farrer, J. A. Military Manners & Customs: The Laws & Observations of Warfare in Ancient & Modern Times. lib. bdg. 59.95 (ISBN 0-8490-0636-8). Gordon Pr.

Farrer, James A. Military Manners & Customs. LC 68-21771. 1968. Repr. of 1885 ed. 19.00 (ISBN 0-8103-3510-7). Gale.

Foch, Ferdinand. Principles of War. De Morinni, J., tr. LC 70-128436. Repr. of 1918 ed. 27.00 (ISBN 0-404-02439-4). AMS Pr.

Friedman, William F. Elementary Military Cryptography. rev. ed. (Cryptographic Ser.). 1976. Repr. of 1941 ed. 11.80 (ISBN 0-89412-010-7). Aegean Park Pr.

Gilbey, J. F. Secret Fighting Arts of World. 8.50 (ISBN 0-685-63779-4). Wehman.

Gonen, Rivka. Weapons & Warfare in Ancient Times. LC 72-10802. (Lerner Archaeology Ser: Digging up the Past). (Illus.). (gr. 5 up). 1976. PLB 7.95g (ISBN 0-8225-0832-X). Lerner Pubns.

Halleck, Henry W. Elements of Military Art & Science. Repr. of 1846 ed. lib. bdg. 15.00x (ISBN 0-8371-5008-6, HAMA). Greenwood.

Harkavy, Robert & Kolodziej, Edward. Security Policy: Dilemmas of Using & Controlling Military Power. 1979. pap. 5.00 (ISBN 0-918592-34-8). Policy Studies.

Harries-Jenkins, G. & Van Doorn, J., eds. The Military & the Problem of Legitimacy. LC 75-24788. (Sage Studies in International Sociology: Vol. 2). 220p. 1976. 22.50x (ISBN 0-8039-9957-7); pap. 9.95x (ISBN 0-8039-9964-X). Sage.

Hart, Basil L. Paris; or, the Future of War. LC 75-148368. (Library of War & Peace; the Character & Causes of War). lib. bdg. 38.00 (ISBN 0-8240-0460-4). Garland Pub.

Hartmann, Gregory K. Weapons That Wait: Mine Warfare in the U. S. Navy. LC 78-71766. (Illus.). 1979. 22.95 (ISBN 0-87021-753-4). Naval Inst Pr.

Hoeber, Frank. Slow to Take Offense: Bombers, Cruise Missiles, & Prudent Deterrence. LC 80-80662. (CSIS Monograph). 137p. 1980. pap. text ed. 6.95 (ISBN 0-686-70746-X). CSI Studies.

Horner, D. M. Crisis of Command. new ed. text ed. 21.95 (ISBN 0-7081-1345-1, Pub. by ANUP Australia). Bks Australia.

Hoyt, Epaphras. Practical Instructions for Military Officers. Repr. of 1811 ed. lib. bdg. 23.00x (ISBN 0-8371-5012-4, HOPI). Greenwood.

Kaldor, Mary & Eide, Ashborn. The World Military Order. LC 78-87885. 1979. 28.95 (ISBN 0-03-053371-6). Praeger.

Kim, R. Weaponless Warriors. 4.50 (ISBN 0-685-63789-1). Wehman.

Kini, K. N. Compulsory Military Training. 1980. lib. bdg. 59.95 (ISBN 0-8490-3081-1). Gordon Pr.

Kitson, Frank. Low Intensity Operations: Subversion, Insurgency, Peace-Keeping. (Illus.). xi, 208p. 1974. Repr. of 1971 ed. 16.50 (ISBN 0-208-01473-X, Archon). Shoe String.

Koistinen, Paul A. C. The Military-Industrial Complex: A Historical Perspective. LC 79-20569. 186p. 1980. 19.95 (ISBN 0-03-055766-6). Praeger.

Kourvetaris, George A. & Dobratz, Betty A. Social Origins & Political Orientations of Officer Corps in a World Perspective. (Monograph Ser. in World Affairs, Vol. 10: 1972-73 Ser., Pt. D). 4.00 (ISBN 0-87940-036-6). U of Denver Intl.

Laird, Melvin R. & Korb, Lawrence J. Problem of Military Readiness. 1980. pap. 3.75 (ISBN 0-8447-1087-3). Am Enterprise.

Langford, David. War in Two Thousand Eighty: The Future of Military Technology. LC 79-61433. (Illus.). 1979. 12.95 (ISBN 0-688-03426-8). Morrow.

Liddell Hart, Basil H. Defence of the West. LC 79-113062. x, 335p. Repr. of 1950 ed. lib. bdg. 14.75x (ISBN 0-8371-4701-8, LIDW). Greenwood.

--The Remaking of Modern Armies. LC 79-24497. 1980. Repr. of 1928 ed. lib. bdg. 25.00x (ISBN 0-313-22174-X, LHRM). Greenwood.

Little, Roger W., ed. Handbook of Military Institutions. LC 78-127989. (Sage Ser. on Armed Forces & Society: Vol. 1). 640p. 1971. 30.00x (ISBN 0-8039-0078-3). Sage.

Lopez-Reyes, Ramon R. Power & Immortality. LC 70-146911. 1971. 10.00 (ISBN 0-682-47247-6, University). Exposition.

Ludendorff, Erich Von. The General Staff & Its Problems, 2 vols. facsimile ed. Holt, F. A., tr. LC 79-165646. (Select Bibliographies Reprint Ser). Repr. of 1920 ed. Set. 42.00 (ISBN 0-8369-5955-8). Arno.

Luttwak, Edward N. Strategic Power: Military Capabilities & Political Utility. LC 76-40529. (The Washington Papers: No. 38). 70p. 1976. 4.00x (ISBN 0-8039-0659-5). Sage.

McDaniel, Norman. Yet Another Voice. 1978. pap. 1.50 (ISBN 0-8439-0516-6, Leisure Books). Nordon Pubns.

Macvey, John W. Space Weapons - Space War. LC 78-24147. (Illus.). 1979. 9.95 (ISBN 0-8128-2579-9). Stein & Day.

Mahan, Dennis H. Complete Treatise on Field Fortification. Repr. of 1836 ed. lib. bdg. 21.75 (ISBN 0-8371-0557-9, MAFF). Greenwood.

Marmont, Auguste F. Spirit of Military Institutions. Schaller, Frank, tr. Repr. of 1864 ed. lib. bdg. 15.00x (ISBN 0-8371-5018-3, MAMI). Greenwood.

Marshall, George C. Selected Speeches & Statements of General of the Army George C. Marshall. DeWeerd, H. A., ed. LC 72-10365. (FDR & the Era of the New Deal Ser.). 1973. Repr. of 1945 ed. lib. bdg. 29.50 (ISBN 0-306-70556-7). Da Capo.

Marshall, S. L. Men Against Fire: The Problem of Battle Command in Future War. 7.50 (ISBN 0-8446-2535-3). Peter Smith.

Marwah, Onkar & Pollack, Jonathan D., eds. Military Power & Policy in Asian States: Toward the 1980's. (Special Studies in Military Affairs Ser.). 1979. lib. bdg. 22.75x (ISBN 0-89158-407-2). Westview.

May, Gerald. Wolfe's Army. LC 74-76626. (Men-at-Arms Ser.). (Illus.). 40p. (Orig.). 1974. pap. 7.95 (ISBN 0-88254-232-X). Hippocrene Bks.

The Military Balance, Nineteen Seventy-Nine to Nineteen Eighty. (Annuals Ser.). (Illus.). 1980. lib. bdg. 17.95 (ISBN 0-87196-446-5). Facts on File.

Minnery, John. How to Kill. Brown, Robert K. & Lund, Peder C., eds. (Illus.). 88p. 1973. pap. 6.00 (ISBN 0-87364-003-9). Paladin Ent.

--How to Kill, Vol. II. (Illus.). 71p. 1978. pap. 6.00 (ISBN 0-87364-128-0). Paladin Ent.

Moyer, Frank A. & Scroggie, Robert J. Special Forces Combat Firing Techniques. new ed. Brown, Robert K., ed. LC 72-180974. (Illus.). 120p. 1971. 15.95 (ISBN 0-87364-010-1). Paladin Ent.

Naroll, Raoul, et al. Military Deterrence in History: A Pilot Cross-Historical Survey. LC 69-14647. 1974. 33.00 (ISBN 0-87395-047-X); microfiche 33.00 (ISBN 0-87395-147-6). State U NY Pr.

Naval Department. Underwater Demolition Team Handbook. (Illus.). 222p. 1971. pap. 9.95 (ISBN 0-87364-019-5). Paladin Ent.

Nickerson, Hoffman. Can We Limit War? LC 72-89268. 336p. 1973. Repr. of 1934 ed. 16.00 (ISBN 0-8046-1763-5). Kennikat.

Noble, Dave. The War & Peace Book. (Illus.). 96p. 1980. 14.00 (ISBN 0-904613-57-7); pap. 3.95 (ISBN 0-904613-32-1). Writers & Readers.

Oppenheimer, Martin, ed. The American Military. LC 73-78698. (Society Book Ser). 1973. 9.95 (ISBN 0-87855-056-9); pap. text ed. 3.95x (ISBN 0-87855-549-8). Transaction Bks.

Perlmutter, Amos. Political Roles & Military Rulers. 314p. 1981. 24.00x (ISBN 0-7146-3122-1, F Cass Co). Biblio Dist.

Perlmutter, Amos & Bennett, Valerie P., eds. The Political Influence of the Military: A Comparative Reader. LC 78-26154. 320p. text ed. 39.50x (ISBN 0-300-02230-1); pap. 12.95x (ISBN 0-300-02433-9). Yale U Pr.

Pierce, G. McGuire. USMC Destruction by Demolition, Incendiaries & Sabotage. (Illus.). 262p. 1974. pap. 14.95 (ISBN 0-87364-004-7). Paladin Ent.

Preston, Adrian & Denis, Peter, eds. Swords & Covenants. 254p. 1976. 15.00x (ISBN 0-87471-862-7). Rowman.

Preston, Anthony, ed. Warship, Vol. 1. LC 78-55455. (Illus.). 1978. 17.95 (ISBN 0-87021-975-8). Naval Inst Pr.

Ratti, O. & Westbrook, A. Secrets of the Samurai: A Survey of the Martial Arts of Feudal Japan. LC 72-91551. 1973. 35.00 (ISBN 0-8048-0917-8). C E Tuttle.

Royal United Services Institute for Defence Studies, London & Marriott, John, eds. International Weapon Developments: A Survey of Current Developments in Weapons Systems. LC 78-31785. (Illus.). 1979. pap. 7.95 (ISBN 0-89141-089-9). Presidio Pr.

Royal United Services Institute for Defence Studies, ed. RUSI Brassey's Defence Yearbook: 1981. 91st ed. 376p. 1980. 45.00 (ISBN 0-08-027006-9). Pergamon.

Sarkesian, Sam C., ed. Combat Effectiveness: Cohesion, Stress, & the Volunteer Military. LC 80-17486. (Sage Research Progress Ser. on War, Revolution, & Peacekeeping: Vol. 9). (Illus.). 305p. 1980. 22.50 (ISBN 0-8039-1440-7); pap. 9.95 (ISBN 0-8039-1441-5). Sage.

--The Military-Industrial Complex: A Reassessment. LC 78-183960. (Sage Research Progress Series on War, Revolution, & Peacekeeping: Vol. 2). 352p. 1972. 22.50 (ISBN 0-8039-0134-8); pap. 9.95 (ISBN 0-8039-0135-6). Sage.

Scharnhorst, Gerhard J. Military Field Pocket Book. Repr. of 1811 ed. lib. bdg. 15.00x (ISBN 0-8371-5022-1, SCFB). Greenwood.

Schelling, Thomas C. Arms & Influence. (Henry L. Stimson Lectures Ser.). 1967. pap. 5.45x (ISBN 0-300-00221-1, Y190). Yale U Pr.

--Arms & Influence. LC 76-41307. 1976. Repr. of 1966 ed. lib. bdg. 19.00x (ISBN 0-8371-8980-2, SCAI). Greenwood.

Schmidt, Steffen W. & Dorfman, Gerald A., eds. Soldiers in Politics. LC 73-92304. 320p. 1974. 12.50x (ISBN 0-87672-107-2). Geron-X.

Six Essays on Military Affairs. 1972. 2.95 (ISBN 0-8351-0356-0). China Bks.

Slow to Take Offense: Bombers, Cruise Missles & Prudent Deterrence. 136p. 1980. pap. 15.00 (ISBN 0-89206-015-8, CSIS017, CSIS). Unipub.

Smythe, John. Certain Discourses Military. Hale, J. R., ed. (Documents Ser). 1978. 13.50x (ISBN 0-918016-39-8). Folger Bks.

Sokolovskiy, V. D. Soviet Military Strategy. 3rd ed. Scott, Harriet F., tr. from Rus. LC 73-94042. (Illus.). 560p. 1975. 39.50x (ISBN 0-8448-0311-1); pap. 29.50x (ISBN 0-8448-1382-6). Crane-Russak Co.

Steer, George L. The Tree of Gernika: A Field Study of Modern War. 1974. lib. bdg. 69.95 (ISBN 0-685-51640-7). Revisionist Pr.

Stern, Ellen P., ed. The Limits of Military Intervention. LC 77-5588. (Sage Series on Armed Forces & Society: Vol. 12). 1977 (ISBN 0-8039-0810-5). pap. 12.50 (ISBN 0-8039-0811-3). Sage.

Stockholm International Peace Research Institute. Problem of Chemical & Biological Warfare: A Study of the Historical, Technical, Military, Legal & Political Aspects of CBW, & Possible Disarmament Measures, Vol. 6, Technical Aspects of Early Warning & Verification 1975. 1975. text ed. 23.50x (ISBN 0-391-00205-8). Humanities.

--Problem of Chemical & Biological Warfare: A Study of the Historical, Technical, Military, Legal & Political Aspects of CBW, & Possible Disarmament Measures, Vol. 2, CB Weapons Today. 1973. text ed. 11.75x (ISBN 0-391-00201-5). Humanities.

--Problem of Chemical & Biological Warfare: A Study of the Historical, Technical, Military, Legal & Political Aspects of CBW, & Possible Disarmament Measures, Vol. 3, C B W & International Law. 1973. text ed. 11.25 (ISBN 0-391-00202-3). Humanities.

--Problem of Chemical & Biological Warfare: A Study of the Historical, Technical, Military, Legal & Political Aspects of CBW, & Possible Disarmament Measures, Vol. 4, C. B. Disarmament Negotiations, 1920-1970. 1971. text ed. 21.50x (ISBN 0-391-00203-1). Humanities.

--World Armaments & Disarmament: SIPRI Yearbook 1977. 1977. 37.50x (ISBN 0-262-19160-1). MIT Pr.

Styers, John. Cold Steel. Schuon, Karl, ed. LC 74-81801. (Illus.). 179p. 1974. Repr. of 1952 ed. 12.95 (ISBN 0-87364-025-X). Paladin Ent.

Tiede, Roland. On the Analysis of Ground Combat. (Orig.). 1979. pap. 25.00x (ISBN 0-89126-067-6). MA-AH Pub.

Trotsky, Leon. Military Writings. Wright, John G., et al, trs. LC 72-92843. 1969. 12.00 (ISBN 0-87348-030-9); pap. 3.45 (ISBN 0-87348-029-5). Path Pr NY.

Turner. Language of the Army in English. (English for Careers Ser). (Illus.). 1978. pap. text ed. 3.50 (ISBN 0-88345-349-5). Regents Pub.

U. S. Army. Counter Sniper Guide. (Illus.). 28p. 1977. pap. 4.00 (ISBN 0-87364-069-1). Paladin Ent.

United States Bureau of Labor Statistics, U. S. Congress, Senate Committee on Military Affairs, Subcommittee on War Moblization. Wartime Technological Developments, 2 vols. in one. LC 78-22407. (American Military Experience Ser.). 1979. Repr. of 1945 ed. lib. bdg. 36.00x (ISBN 0-405-11882-1). Arno.

U.S. Army. Deal the First Deadly Blow. (Illus.). 156p. 1977. pap. 12.95 (ISBN 0-87364-126-4). Paladin Ent.

--Physical Security. (Illus.). 150p. 1977. pap. 10.00 (ISBN 0-87364-093-4). Paladin Ent.

Van Creveld, Martin L. Supplying War. LC 77-5550. 1979. pap. 9.95 (ISBN 0-521-29793-1). Cambridge U Pr.

Von Bernhardi, Friedrich. On War of Today, 2 vols. LC 78-147464. (Library of War & Peace; the Character & Causes of War). Set. lib. bdg. 38.00 (ISBN 0-8240-0255-5). Garland Pub.

Von Clausewitz, Karl. On War. Rapoport, Anatol, ed. (Classics Ser.). 1968. pap. 3.95 (ISBN 0-14-040004-4, Pelican). Penguin.

--War, Politics & Power. 1962. pap. 4.95 (ISBN 0-89526-999-6). Regnery-Gateway.

Von Dach, H. Total Resistance. LC 66-978. (Illus.). 173p. 1966. 12.95 (ISBN 0-87364-021-7). Paladin Ent.

Von Schmidt, Karl. Instructions for the Training, Employment, & Leading of Cavalry. Bell, C. Bowkler, tr. from Ger. LC 68-54805. (Illus.). viii, 232p. Repr. of 1881 ed. 15.00 (ISBN 0-8371-0647-8, SCIC). Greenwood.

Von Shelina, Viktor E. Treatise on Coast-Defence. Repr. of 1868 ed. lib. bdg. 26.50x (ISBN 0-8371-5023-X, SCCD). Greenwood.

Washbuck, John B. & Sherlock, Barbara J. To Get the Job Done. 2nd ed. LC 76-25411. 256p. Date not set. pap. 12.95x (ISBN 0-87021-709-7). Naval Inst Pr.

Weigley, Russell F., ed. New Dimensions in Military History. LC 76-4159. 419p. 1976. 14.95 (ISBN 0-89141-002-3). Presidio Pr.

Wheeler, Barry. Airforces of the World. (Illus.). 1980. (ScribT); encore ed. 4.95 (ISBN 0-686-76818-3). Scribner.

Wightman, A. S. & Velo, G., eds. Renormalization Theory. LC 75-45277. (NATO Advanced Study Institute: No. 23). 1976. lib. bdg. 39.50 (ISBN 9-0277-0668-9). Kluwer Boston.

Wright, Quincy. Study of War. 2nd ed. LC 65-5396. 1965. pap. 50.00x (ISBN 0-226-90998-0). U of Chicago Pr.

--Study of War. abr. ed. Wright, Louise L., ed. LC 64-19850. 1964. 12.00x (ISBN 0-226-90999-9). U of Chicago Pr.

--Study of War. abr. ed. Wright, Louise L., ed. LC 64-19850. 1965. pap. 3.45 (ISBN 0-226-91000-8, P185, Phoen). U of Chicago Pr.

Wylie, Joseph C. Military Strategy: A General Theory of Power Control. LC 80-36885. vii, 111p. 1980. Repr. of 1967 ed. lib. bdg. 17.50x (ISBN 0-313-22679-2, WYMS). Greenwood.

Zurcher, Louis A. & Harries-Jenkins, Gwyn, eds. Supplementary Military Forces: Reserves, Militias, Auxiliaries. LC 78-13068. (Sage Research Progress Series on War, Revolution, & Peacekeeping: Vol. 8). 278p. 1978. 20.00x (ISBN 0-8039-1109-2); pap. 9.95x (ISBN 0-8039-1110-6). Sage.

MILITARY ART AND SCIENCE–BIBLIOGRAPHY

Cockle, Maurice J. A Bibliography of Military Books up to Sixteen Forty-Two. (Illus.). xlii, 268p. 1978. Repr. of 1957 ed. 65.00 (ISBN 0-900470-70-4). Oak Knoll.

Jaehns, Max. Geschichte Der Kriegswissenschaften, Vornehmlich in Deutschland, 3 Vols. 1889-1891. 161.50 (ISBN 0-384-26634-7). Johnson Repr.

Millett, Allan R. & Cooling, B. F. Doctoral Dissertations in Military Affairs. 1972. Repr. 7.50 (ISBN 0-686-20812-9). KSU.

Pohler, Johann. Bibliotheca Historico-Militaris, 4 Vols. 1899. 271.00 (ISBN 0-8337-2793-1). B Franklin.

Weiner, Richard. Military Publications. LC 78-64584. 1979. 15.00 (ISBN 0-913046-09-4). Public Relations.

MILITARY ART AND SCIENCE-DATA PROCESSING

Huber, Reiner K., et al, eds. Military Strategy & Tactics: Computer Modeling of Land War Problems. LC 75-33040. 386p. 1975. 39.50 (ISBN 0-306-30889-4, Plenum Pr). Plenum Pub.

Severe Environment-Military Microprocessor System. 500p. 59.95x (ISBN 0-686-74159-5). Sybex.

MILITARY ART AND SCIENCE-DICTIONARIES

Centre De Documentation De L'Armement. Lexique Thematique des Descripteurs et Identificateurs. 151p. (Fr.). 1976. pap. 35.00 (ISBN 0-686-56742-0, M-6371). French & Eur.

Dictionary of U. S. Military Terms. 1963. 4.50 (ISBN 0-685-57340-0). Pub Aff Pr.

Eitzen, K. Military Eitzen. (Ger. & Eng.). 1957. pap. 15.95 (ISBN 3-87599-035-8, M-7563, Pub. by Vlg. Offene Worte). French & Eur.

Gaynor, Frank, ed. New Military & Naval Dictionary. Repr. of 1951 ed. lib. bdg. 14.25x (ISBN 0-8371-2129-9, GAMN). Greenwood.

Hanrieder, Wolfram F. & Buel, Larry V., eds. Words & Arms: A Dictionary of Security & Defense Terms with Supplementary Data. 1979. lib. bdg. 28.75 (ISBN 0-89158-383-1). Westview.

Heinl, Robert D., Jr., ed. Dictionary of Military & Naval Quotations. LC 66-22342. 1966. 16.95 (ISBN 0-87021-149-8). Naval Inst Pr.

Pooch, H. Fachwoerterbuch des Nachrichtenwesens. 280p. (Ger.). 1976. pap. 22.50 (ISBN 3-7949-0234-3, M-7390, Pub. by Fachvlg. Schiele & Schoen). French & Eur.

Quick, John. Dictionary of Weapons & Military Terms. (Illus.). 515p. 1973. 27.50 (ISBN 0-07-051057-1, P&RB). McGraw.

Ruiz Jodar, Carlos. Diccionario Espanol-Aleman, Aleman-Espanol Militar. 375p. (Espn. -Ale.). 1975. pap. 13.95 (ISBN 84-400-8515-X, S-50101). French & Eur.

Scott, H. L. Civil War Military Dictionary. Rywell, Martin, ed. (Illus.). pap. 2.00 (ISBN 0-913150-08-8). Pioneer Pr.

Scott, Henry L. Military Dictionary. Repr. of 1861 ed. lib. bdg. 25.00 (ISBN 0-8371-0648-6, SCMD). Greenwood.

The Unifying Military Dictionary, 2 parts. Incl. Part 1. Arabic-English; Part 2. English-Arabic. 1976. 44.00 ea. Intl Learn Syst.

Wells, Rowland A. Modern Dictionary of Military Technology: English-Spanish, Spanish-English. LC 76-51622. 1977. 20.00 (ISBN 0-686-19085-8). Lexicon Pr.

MILITARY ART AND SCIENCE-EARLY WORKS TO 1800

Aelianus, Tacitus. The Art of Embattailing an Army, or the Second Part of Aelian's Tacticks. Bingham, J., tr. LC 68-54605. (English Experience Ser.: No. 70). Repr. of 1629 ed. 21.00 (ISBN 90-221-0070-7). Walter J Johnson.

Aelinanus, Tacitus. The Tacticks of Aelign, or Art of Embattailing an Army. Bingham, J., tr. LC 68-54606. (English Experience Ser.: No. 14). (Illus.). Repr. of 1616 ed. 42.00 (ISBN 90-221-0014-6). Walter J Johnson.

Aeneas Tacticus. Military Essays. Bd. with Military Essays. Asclepiodotus; Military Essays. Onasander. (Loeb Classical Library: No. 156). 11.50x (ISBN 0-674-99172-9). Harvard U Pr.

Articles of Military Dicipline. LC 71-76430. (English Experience Ser.: No. 77). 16p. Repr. of 1639 ed. 7.00 (ISBN 9-0221-0077-4). Walter J Johnson.

Barker, Thomas M. The Military Intellectual & Battle: Raimondo Montecuccoli & the Thirty Years War. LC 74-837. (Illus.). 1975. 31.00 (ISBN 0-87395-250-2); microfiche 31.00 (ISBN 0-87395-251-0). State U NY Pr.

Barret, Robert. The Theorike & Practike of Moderne Warres. LC 74-26523. (English Experience Ser.: No. 155). (Illus.). 247p. 1969. Repr. of 1598 ed. 42.00 (ISBN 90-221-0155-X). Walter J Johnson.

Barwick, Humphrey. Concerning the Force & Effect of Manual Weapons of Fire. LC 74-80163. (English Experience Ser.: No. 643). 86p. 1974. Repr. of 1594 ed. 8.00 (ISBN 90-221-0643-8). Walter J Johnson.

Clayton, Giles. Approved Order of Martiall Dicipline, with Every Particular Offycer His Offyce & Dutie. LC 73-6114. (English Experience Ser.: No. 581). 84p. 1973. Repr. of 1591 ed. 9.50 (ISBN 90-221-0581-4). Walter J Johnson.

Cockle, Maurice J. A Bibliography of Military Books up to Sixteen Forty-Two. (Illus.). xlii, 268p. 1978. Repr. of 1957 ed. 65.00 (ISBN 0-900470-70-4). Oak Knoll.

Davies, Edward. The Art of War & Englands Traynings. LC 68-54633. (English Experience Ser.: No. 37). 1968. Repr. of 1619 ed. 30.00 (ISBN 90-221-0037-5). Walter J Johnson.

Digges, Leonard & Digges, Thomas. An Arithmeticall Militarie Treatise, Named Stratioticos. LC 68-27478. (English Experience Ser.: No. 71). 192p. 1968. Repr. of 1579 ed. 21.00 (ISBN 90-221-0071-5). Walter J Johnson.

Du Castel, Christine. Here Begynneth the Boke of the Fayt of Armes & of Chyualrye. Caxton, William, tr. LC 78-6332. (English Experience Ser.: No. 13). 1968. Repr. of 1489 ed. 49.00 (ISBN 90-221-0013-8). Walter J Johnson.

Frontinus, Sextus J. Stratagems & Aqueducts. (Loeb Classical Library: No. 174). 11.00x (ISBN 0-674-99192-3). Harvard U Pr.

Gates, Geffrey. The Defence of Militarie Profession. LC 72-5996. (English Experience Ser.: No. 521). 64p. 1973. Repr. of 1579 ed. 7.00 (ISBN 90-221-0521-0). Walter J Johnson.

Kellie, Thomas. Pallas Armata, or, Militarie Instructions. LC 72-209. (English Experience Ser.: No. 331). 130p. 1971. Repr. of 1627 ed. 20.00 (ISBN 90-221-0331-5). Walter J Johnson.

Macchiavelli, Niccolo. The Arte of Warre, (Certain Waies of the Orderyng of Souldiours) Whitehorne, P., tr. LC 79-26097. (English Experience Ser.: No. 135). 1969. Repr. of 1562 ed. 42.00 (ISBN 90-221-0135-5). Walter J Johnson.

Machiavelli, Niccolo. Art of War. rev. ed. Farneworth, Ellis, tr. LC 64-66078. (Orig.). 1965. pap. 6.95 (ISBN 0-672-60434-5, LLA196). Bobbs.

Procter, Thomas. Of the Knowledge & Conducte of Warres. LC 79-25921. (English Experience Ser.: No. 268). 96p. 1970. Repr. of 1578 ed. 13.00 (ISBN 90-221-0268-8). Walter J Johnson.

Prussia Kriegsministerium. Regulations for the Prussian Infantry: To Which Is Added the Prussian Tactick. LC 68-54803. Repr. of 1759 ed. lib. bdg. 25.75x (ISBN 0-8371-0625-7, PRPI). Greenwood.

Rich, Barnaby. A Path-Way to Military Practice. LC 75-25920. (English Experience Ser.: No. 177). 88p. 1969. Repr. of 1587 ed. 11.50 (ISBN 90-221-0177-0). Walter J Johnson.

Rudiments of Militarie Dicipline. LC 70-25967. (English Experience Ser.: No. 105). 14p. 1969. Repr. of 1638 ed. 7.00 (ISBN 90-221-0105-3). Walter J Johnson.

Saxe, Maurice. Reveries, or Memoirs Upon the Art of War. Repr. of 1757 ed. lib. bdg. 46.75x (ISBN 0-8371-5021-3, SARM). Greenwood.

Sun Tzu. The Art of War. Griffith, Samuel B., tr. & intro. by. 1971. pap. 4.95 (ISBN 0-19-501476-6, 361, GB). Oxford U Pr.

Turner, James. Pallas Armata. Repr. of 1683 ed. lib. bdg. 25.50x (ISBN 0-8371-0690-7, TUPA). Greenwood.

Vegetius Renatus, Flavius. The Foure Bookes of Martiall Policye. Sadler, J., tr. from Lat. LC 68-54662. (English Experience Ser.: No. 41). 132p. 1968. Repr. of 1572 ed. 16.00 (ISBN 90-221-0041-3). Walter J Johnson.

MILITARY ART AND SCIENCE-HISTORY

Adcock, Frank E. The Greek & Macedonian Art of War. LC 57-10495. (Sather Classical Lectures: No. 30). 1957. 14.75x (ISBN 0-520-02807-4); pap. 2.25 (ISBN 0-520-00005-6, CAL54). U of Cal Pr.

--Roman Art of War Under the Republic. rev ed. (Martin Classical Lectures: Vol. 8). 1970. Repr. of 1960 ed. 8.95x (ISBN 0-06-490017-7). B&N.

Albion, Robert G. Introduction to Military History. LC 75-158240. (Illus.). 1971. Repr. of 1929 ed. 29.00 (ISBN 0-404-00303-6). AMS Pr.

Barker, Thomas M. The Military Intellectual & Battle: Raimondo Montecuccoli & the Thirty Years War. LC 74-837. (Illus.). 1975. 31.00 (ISBN 0-87395-250-2); microfiche 31.00 (ISBN 0-87395-251-0). State U NY Pr.

Benson, Ragnar. Survival Poaching. (Illus.). 250p. 1980. 12.95 (ISBN 0-87364-183-3). Paladin Ent.

Boatner, Mark M. Military Customs & Traditions. LC 75-17189. 176p. 1976. Repr. of 1956 ed. lib. bdg. 19.75x (ISBN 0-8371-8299-9, BOMCT). Greenwood.

Bohme, Klaus-Richard. The Defense Policies of the Nordic Countries, Nineteen Eighteen to Nineteen Thirty-Nine. Krosby, H. Peter, tr. from Swedish. (Orig.). 1979. pap. 7.00x (ISBN 0-89126-073-0). MA-AH Pub.

Brayton, Abbott A. & Landwehr, Stephana J. The Politics of War & Peace: A Survey of Thought. LC 80-67206. 320p. (Orig.). 1981. lib. bdg. 20.50 (ISBN 0-8191-1726-9); pap. text ed. 11.50 (ISBN 0-8191-1727-7). U Pr of Amer.

Brodie, Bernard & Brodie, Fawn M. From Crossbow to H-Bomb. rev. enl. ed. LC 72-90408. (Midland Bks.: No. 161). (Illus.). 320p. 1973. pap. 2.95x (ISBN 0-253-20161-6). Ind U Pr.

Chandler, David. The Art of Warfare in the Age of Marlborough. LC 75-26934. (Illus.). 320p. 1976. 17.50 (ISBN 0-88254-366-0). Hippocrene Bks.

Chandler, David G. Atlas of Military Strategy. (Illus.). 1980. Repr. 29.95 (ISBN 0-02-905750-7). Free Pr.

Clark, Ronald W. War Winners. (Illus.). 154p. 1980. 14.95 (ISBN 0-283-98503-8, Pub. by Sidgwick & Jackson England). Presidio Pr.

Colin, Jean L. The Transformations of War. LC 77-1125. (West Point Military Library). 1977. Repr. of 1912 ed. lib. bdg. 21.00x (ISBN 0-8371-9510-1, COTW). Greenwood.

Connelly, Peter. Greece & Rome at War. (Illus.). 320p. 1981. 30.00 (ISBN 0-13-364976-8). P-H.

Contamine, Philippe. Guerre, Etat & Societe a la Fin Du Moyen Age: Etudes Sur les Armees Des Rois De France, 1337-1494. (Civilisation & Societes: No. 24). (Illus.). 1972. 58.50x (ISBN 90-2796-991-4). Mouton.

Dodge, Theodore A. Hannibal, a History of the Art of War Among the Cartaginians & Romans Down to the Battle of Pydna, 168 B.C. with a Detailed Account of the Second Punic War. 1977. Repr. 75.00 (ISBN 0-403-08284-6). Scholarly.

Dupuy, R. Ernest & Dupuy, Trevor N. The Encyclopedia of Military History. rev. ed. LC 75-6333. (Illus.). 1488p. 1977. 29.95 (ISBN 0-06-011139-9, HarpT). Har-Row.

Dupuy, T. N. Numbers, Prediction & War. LC 77-5243. (Illus.). 1979. 13.95 (ISBN 0-672-52131-8). Bobbs.

Haigh, R. H. & Turner, P. W. Defense Policy Between the Wars, Nineteen Nineteen to Nineteen Thirty-Eight, Culminating in the Munich Agreement of September 1938. (Orig.). 1979. pap. 14.00 (ISBN 0-89126-072-2). MA-AH Pub.

--Episodes in Punjab Military History in the Mid-Nineteenth Century, Culminating in the Indian Mutiny of 1857. (Orig.). 1979. pap. 18.00x (ISBN 0-89126-071-4). MA-AH Pub.

Hale, John R. The Art of War & Renaissance England. LC 79-65983. (Folger Guides to the Age of Shakespeare). 1979. pap. 3.95 (ISBN 0-918016-10-X). Folger Bks.

Herman, Vernon A. The Twentieth Century: A Military & Political Chronology. 1982. 14.95 (ISBN 0-533-04616-5). Vantage.

Humble, Richard. Famous Land Battles: From Agincourt to the Six Day War. LC 79-1527. (Illus.). 1979. 19.95 (ISBN 0-316-38145-4). Little.

Jaehns, Max. Geschichte Der Kriegswissenschaften, Vornehmlich in Deutschland, 3 Vols. 1889-1891. 161.50 (ISBN 0-384-26634-7). Johnson Repr.

Karsten, Peter, ed. The Military in America: From the Colonial Era to the Present. LC 79-7846. (Illus.). 1980. pap. text ed. 9.95 (ISBN 0-02-916740-X). Free Pr.

Kendall, Paul M. The Story of Land Warfare. LC 74-3764. (Illus.). x, 194p. 1981. Repr. of 1957 ed. lib. bdg. 21.75x (ISBN 0-8371-7463-5, KELW). Greenwood.

Koch, H. W. The Rise of Modern Warfare. (Illus.). 256p. 1981. 29.95 (ISBN 0-13-781260-4). P-H.

Lloyd, Ernest M. A Review of the History of Infantry. LC 70-84277. 1976. Repr. of 1908 ed. lib. bdg. 18.75x (ISBN 0-8371-5015-9, LLHI). Greenwood.

Lot, Ferdinand. L Art Militaire et les Armees Au Moyen Age En Europe et Dans le Proche Orient, 2 vols. LC 80-2017. Date not set. Repr. of 1946 ed. 90.00 (ISBN 0-404-18603-3). AMS Pr.

McCartney, Eugene S. Warfare by Land & Sea. LC 63-10284. (Our Debt to Greece & Rome Ser). (Illus.). Repr. of 1930 ed. 7.50x (ISBN 0-8154-0149-3). Cooper Sq.

McElwee, William. The Art of War: Waterloo to Mons. LC 74-17459. (Midland Bks.: No. 214). 352p. 1975. pap. 4.95x (ISBN 0-253-20214-0). Ind U Pr.

Morris, John. Welsh Wars of Edward First: Medieval Military History. LC 68-25253. (British History Ser., No. 30). 1969. Repr. of 1901 ed. lib. bdg. 49.95 (ISBN 0-8383-0221-1). Haskell.

Mullin, Timothy J. Training The Gunfighter. (Illus.). 1981. 24.95 (ISBN 0-87364-185-X). Paladin Ent.

National Army Museum, London, et al. War and Weapons. LC 77-838. 1977. Watts.

Newark, Timothy. Medieval Warfare: An Illustrated Introduction. (Illus.). 176p. 1981. 24.00x (ISBN 0-686-72294-9, Pub. by Jupiter England). State Mutual Bk.

Oman, Charles W. Art of War in the Middle Ages: A.D. 378-1515. rev. ed. Beeler, John H., ed. (Illus.). (YA) (gr. 9-12). 1960. pap. 4.95 (ISBN 0-8014-9062-6, CP62). Cornell U Pr.

Owen, David. Battle of Wits: A History of Psychology & Deception in Modern Warfare. 1979. 14.95x (ISBN 0-8448-1369-9). Crane-Russak Co.

Quimby, Robert S. Background of Napoleonic Warfare: The Theory of Military Tactics in Eighteenth-Century France. LC 68-59257. (Columbia University. Studies in the Social Sciences: No. 596). Repr. of 1957 ed. 19.50 (ISBN 0-404-51596-7). AMS Pr.

Ropp, Theodore. War in the Modern World. rev. ed. 1962. pap. 3.95 (ISBN 0-02-036400-8, Collier). Macmillan.

Ross, Steven. From Flintlock to Rifle: Infantry Tactics, 1740-1866. LC 77-74397. (Illus.). 218p. 1979. 15.00 (ISBN 0-8386-2051-5). Fairleigh Dickinson.

Rothenberg, Gunther E. The Art of Warfare in the Age of Napoleon. LC 77-86495. (Midland Bks.: No. 260). (Illus.). 280p. 1981. pap. 7.95x (ISBN 0-253-20260-4). Ind U Pr.

--The Art of Warfare in the Age of Napoleon. LC 77-86495. (Illus.). 280p. 1978. 15.00 (ISBN 0-253-31076-8). Ind U Pr.

Sanchez-Saavedra, E. M., compiled by. A Guide to Virginia Military Organizations in the American Revolution, 1774-1787. 1978. 15.00 (ISBN 0-88490-003-7). VA State Lib.

Senich, Peter R. Pictorial History of U.S. Sniping. (Illus.). 175p. 1980. 19.95 (ISBN 0-87364-181-7). Paladin Ent.

Smail, R. C. Crusading Warfare, 1097-1193: A Contribution to Medieval Military History. LC 67-26956. (Cambridge Studies in Medieval Life & Thought Ser). (Cambridge U Pr Library Editions). 1967. 35.50 (ISBN 0-521-21315-0); pap. 11.50 (ISBN 0-521-09730-4). Cambridge U Pr.

Smith, Myron J., Jr. Air War Chronology: Air War Chronology 1939-1945, Vol. 3, Pt. 2. new ed. (Orig.). 1979. pap. text ed. 24.00x (ISBN 0-89126-044-7). MA-AH Pub.

Spaulding, Oliver L., et al. Warfare: A Study of Military Methods from the Earliest Times. LC 72-4301. (World Affairs Ser.: National & International Viewpoints). 616p. 1972. Repr. of 1925 ed. 28.00 (ISBN 0-405-04592-1). Arno.

Swettenham, John. The Evening of Chivalry. (Illus.). 1972. pap. 3.95 (ISBN 0-660-00043-1, 56332-4, Pub. by Natl Mus Canada). U of Chicago Pr.

--The Evening of Chivalry: (Canadian War Museum Historical Publications Ser.). (Illus.). 61p. 1975. pap. 3.50 (ISBN 0-685-53615-7). Samuel Stevens.

Taylor, Frederick L. The Art of War in Italy, 1494-1529. LC 76-84284. (Illus.). 228p. 1973. Repr. of 1921 ed. lib. bdg. 21.50x (ISBN 0-8371-5025-6, TAWI). Greenwood.

Turney-High, Harry H. The Military. 1981. pap. 12.00 (ISBN 0-8158-0403-2). Chris Mass.

Van Creveld, Martin L. Supplying War: Logistics from Wallenstein to Patton. LC 77-5550. (Illus.). 1977. 27.50 (ISBN 0-521-21730-X). Cambridge U Pr.

Verbruggen, J. F. The Art of Warfare in Western Europe During the Middle Ages. new ed. (Europe in the Middle Ages: Select Studies: Vol. 1). 1977. 41.50 (ISBN 0-444-10968-4, North-Holland). Elsevier.

Warry, John. Warfare in the Classical World. (Illus.). 224p. 1981. 19.95 (ISBN 0-312-85614-8). St Martin.

--Warfare in the Classical World: An Illustrated Encyclopedia of Weapons, Warriors & Warfare in the Ancient Civilizations of Greece & Rome. LC 80-54639. (Illus.). 224p. 1981. 19.95 (ISBN 0-312-85614-8). St Martin.

Webb, Henry J. Elizabethan Military Science: The Books & the Practice. (Illus.). 256p. 1965. 25.00x (ISBN 0-299-03810-6). U of Wis Pr.

White, Gerald T. Billions for Defense: Government Financing by the Defense Plant Corporation During World War II. LC 79-10931. 1980. 16.50x (ISBN 0-8173-0018-X). U of Ala Pr.

Wintringham, Thomas H. Story of Weapons & Tactics. facs. ed. LC 79-128335. (Essay Index Reprint Ser). 1943. 16.00 (ISBN 0-8369-2093-7). Arno.

MILITARY ART AND SCIENCE-SOLDIERS HANDBOOKS

see also United States-Army-Handbooks, Manuals, etc.

Achesone, James. The Military Garden: Instructions for All Young Souldiers. LC 74-80157. (English Experience Ser.: No. 637). 36p. 1974. Repr. of 1629 ed. 5.00 (ISBN 90-221-0637-3). Walter J Johnson.

Alam, M. A. Elementary Calculations. 188p. 1981. 10.00x (ISBN 0-86125-715-4, Pub. by Orient Longman India). State Mutual Bk.

Markham, Gervase. The Solders Exercise, 3 bks. LC 74-80197. (English Experience Ser.: No. 677). 1974. Repr. of 1639 ed. 21.00 (ISBN 90-221-0677-2). Walter J Johnson.

Rhodesian Government. Rhodesian Leader's Guide. (Illus.). 55p. 1980. pap. 6.00 (ISBN 0-87364-194-9). Paladin Ent.

U.S.Government. Special Forces Handbook. (Illus.). 200p. 1977. pap. 8.00 (ISBN 0-87364-109-4). Paladin Ent.

MILITARY ART AND SCIENCE–TERMINOLOGY
Dictionary of U. S. Military Terms. 1963. 4.50 (ISBN 0-685-57340-0). Pub Aff Pr.
Garber, Max B. & Bond, P. S. A Modern Military Dictionary: Ten Thousand Technical & Slang Terms of Military Usage. 2nd ed. LC 74-31354. 1975. Repr. of 1942 ed. 22.00 (ISBN 0-8103-4208-1). Gale.
Hayward, P. H. Jane's Dictionary of Military Terms. 1976. 11.95 (ISBN 0-356-08261-X). Hippocrene Bks.
MILITARY ASSISTANCE, AMERICAN
Feuerwerger, Marvin C. Congress & Israel: Foreign Aid Decision-Making in the House of Representatives, Nineteen Sixty-Nine to Ninety Seventy-Six. LC 78-74654. (Contributions in Political Science: No. 28). (Illus.). 1979. lib. bdg. 23.95 (ISBN 0-313-21240-6, FCO/). Greenwood.
Liska, George. New Statecraft: Foreign Aid in American Foreign Policy. LC 60-6823. 1960. 8.50x (ISBN 0-226-48485-8). U of Chicago Pr.
Lyons, Gene M. Military Policy & Economic Aid: The Korean Case, 1950-1953. LC 61-7301. 1961. 4.50 (ISBN 0-8142-0088-5). Ohio St U Pr.
Pranger, Robert J. & Tahtinen, Dale R. Toward a Realistic Military Assistance Program. 48p. 1974. 4.25 (ISBN 0-8447-3147-1). Am Enterprise.
Ra'Anan, Uri, et al. Arms Transfer to the Third World: Problems & Policies. LC 77-17949. (Westview Special Studies in International Relations & U.S. Foreign Policy). 1978. lib. bdg. 38.75x (ISBN 0-89158-092-1). Westview.
Schilling, W. R. American Arms Changing Europe. 1973. 17.50x (ISBN 0-231-03704-X); pap. 7.50x (ISBN 0-231-03705-8). Columbia U Pr.
Taylor, Richard K. Blockade! Guide to Nonviolent Intervention. LC 76-30600. 1977. 6.95x (ISBN 0-88344-036-9); pap. 2.95x (ISBN 0-88344-037-7). Orbis Bks.
U. S. Commission on Organization of the Executive Branch of the Government - Task Force on Overseas Economic Operations. Overseas Economic Operations 1953-1955: A Report to the Congress. LC 68-55107. (Illus.). 1968. Repr. of 1955 ed. lib. bdg. 41.25x (ISBN 0-8371-0695-8, REOE). Greenwood.
U. S. Library Of Congress - Legislative Reference Service. U. S. Foreign Aid: Its Purposes, Scope, Administration, & Related Information. LC 68-55134. (Illus.). 1968. Repr. of 1959 ed. lib. bdg. 15.00 (ISBN 0-8371-0721-0, USFA). Greenwood.
Walterhouse, Harry F. Time to Build: Military Civic Action, Medium for Economic Development & Social Reform. LC 64-8172. (Studies in International Affairs: No. 4). (Orig.). 1964. 5.95x (ISBN 0-87249-096-3); pap. 2.25x (ISBN 0-87249-006-8). U of SC Pr.
Wolf, C., Jr. Foreign Aid: Theory & Practice in Southern Asia. (Rand Corporation Research Studies). 1960. 23.50 (ISBN 0-691-05618-8). Princeton U Pr.
MILITARY ASSISTANCE, BRITISH
Sherwig, John M. Guineas & Gunpowder: British Foreign Aid in the Wars with France, 1793-1815. LC 69-12736. (Illus.). 1969. 20.00x (ISBN 0-674-36775-8). Harvard U Pr.
MILITARY ASSISTANCE, RUSSIAN
Joshua, Wynfred & Gibert, Stephen P. Arms for the Third World: Soviet Military Aid Diplomacy. LC 78-91337. 179p. (Bibl, footnotes, index, tabs). 1969. 12.00x (ISBN 0-8018-1104-X). Johns Hopkins.
MILITARY ATTACHES
Mott, Thomas B. Twenty Years As Military Attache. Kohn, Richard H., ed. LC 78-22390. (American Military Experience Ser.). 1979. Repr. of 1937 ed. lib. bdg. 20.00x (ISBN 0-405-11867-8). Arno.
Vagts, A. Military Attache. 1967. 28.00x (ISBN 0-691-06908-5). Princeton U Pr.
MILITARY AVIATION
see Aeronautics, Military
MILITARY BALLOONS
see Balloons
MILITARY BASES
see also Military Posts; Navy-Yards and Naval Stations
Cottrell, Alvin J. & Moorer, Thomas H. Overseas Bases: Problems of Projecting American Military Power Abroad. LC 77-88453. (The Washington Papers: No. 47). 67p. 1977. 4.00 (ISBN 0-8039-0952-7). Sage.
Ellis, Christopher. Military Transport of the First World War. (Mechanical Warfare in Color Ser). (Illus.). 1970. 5.95 (ISBN 0-02-535240-7). Macmillan.
Harkavy, Robert E. Great Power Competition for Overseas Bases. 300p. Date not set. price not set (ISBN 0-08-025089-0). Pergamon.
Mattern, Carolyn J. Soldiers When They Go: The Story of Camp Randall, 1861-1865. LC 80-26238. (Illus.). 135p. 1981. 7.95 (ISBN 0-87020-206-5). State Hist Soc Wis.
Military Community: Fort Bragg, North Carolina. (gr. 2). 1974. pap. text ed. 3.80 (ISBN 0-205-03886-7, 8038864); tchrs'. guide 12.00 (ISBN 0-205-03884-0, 8038848). Allyn.
MILITARY BASES, RUSSIAN–CUBA
Kennedy, Robert. Thirteen Days. (RL 8). pap. 1.95 (ISBN 0-451-09150-7, J9150, Sig). NAL.
Kennedy, Robert F. Thirteen Days: A Memoir of the Cuban Missile Crisis. Neustadt, Richard & Allison, Graham, eds. 1971. pap. text ed. 4.95x (ISBN 0-393-09896-6, NortonC). Norton.
Russell, Bertrand. Unarmed Victory. 1963. text ed. 12.50x (ISBN 0-04-327024-7). Allen Unwin.
MILITARY BIOGRAPHY
see also Generals
Albert, Don E. General Wesley Merritt. LC 80-13126. (Illus.). 1979. 15.00 (ISBN 0-686-26105-4); deluxe ed. 40.00 (ISBN 0-686-26106-2). Presidial.
Baird, John A., Jr. Profile of a Hero: Absalom Baird, His Family, & the American Military Tradition. 1977. 7.95 (ISBN 0-8059-2460-4). Dorrance.
Biggs, Bradley. Gavin. (Illus.). 182p. 1980. 17.50 (ISBN 0-208-01748-8, Archon). Shoe String.
Carver, Michael, ed. The War Lords: Military Commanders of the 20th Century. 1976. 19.95 (ISBN 0-316-13060-5). Little.
Deweerd, Harvey A. Great Soldiers of the Two World Wars. facs. ed. LC 69-18926. (Essay Index Reprint Ser). 1941. 21.25 (ISBN 0-8369-1032-X). Arno.
Dickman, William J. Battery Rodgers. 1980. pap. 4.50 (ISBN 0-89126-094-3). MA-AH Pub.
Dodge, Thomas A. Great Captains: Showing the Influence on the Art of War of the Campaigns of Alexander, Hannibal, Caesar, Gustavus Adolphus, Frederick & Napoleon. LC 67-27591. 1889. Repr. 12.00 (ISBN 0-8046-0111-9). Kennikat.
Fuller, J. F. Memoirs of an Unconventional Soldier. 1976. lib. bdg. 59.95 (ISBN 0-8490-2223-1). Gordon Pr.
Hommer, John F. An Infantryman's Journal. (Illus.). 216p. 1981. 12.95 (ISBN 0-934588-04-X). Ranger Assocs.
Hudleston, Francis J. Warriors in Undress. facsimile ed. LC 73-93346. (Essay Index Reprint Ser). 1926. 17.00 (ISBN 0-8369-1298-5). Arno.
Liddell Hart, Basil H. Reputations Ten Years After. facs. ed. LC 68-8478. (Essay Index Reprint Ser). (Illus.). 1968. Repr. of 1928 ed. 18.00 (ISBN 0-8369-0619-5). Arno.
Lockerbie, D. Bruce. A Man Under Orders: Lieutenant General William K. Harrison. LC 78-15838. (Illus.). 1979. 8.95 (ISBN 0-06-065257-8, HarpR). Har-Row.
Loeblein, John M. Memoirs of Kelly Field, 1917-1918. 1974. pap. text ed. 6.50 (ISBN 0-89126-010-2). MA-AH Pub.
Mackay, Ruddock F. Fisher of Kilverstone. (Illus.). 559p. 1974. 19.95x (ISBN 0-19-822409-5). Oxford U Pr.
Martell, Paul & Hayes, Grace P. World Military Leaders. LC 74-78392. 268p. 1974. 32.50 (ISBN 0-8352-0785-4, Co-Pub. by T N Dupuy). Bowker.
Motto, Sytha. More Than Conquerers: Makers of History. (Illus.). 228p. 1980. 15.00 (ISBN 0-913270-88-1); ltd. signed 22.50 (ISBN 0-913270-94-6). Sunstone Pr.
Smyth, John. Leadership in Battle 1914-1918. LC 75-20132. (Illus.). 191p. 1976. 12.50 (ISBN 0-88254-365-2). Hippocrene Bks.
Stone, W. L. Campaign of Lieut. Gen. John Burgoyne & the Expedition of Lieut. Col. Barry St. Leger. LC 75-114716. (Era of the American Revolution Ser). 1970. Repr. of 1877 ed. lib. bdg. 42.50 (ISBN 0-306-71925-8). Da Capo.
Von Muenchhausen, Friedrich. At General Howe's Side, 1776-1778. LC 73-94002. (Revolutionary War Bicentennial Ser.). (Illus.). 84p. 1974. lib. bdg. 14.95 (ISBN 0-912480-09-2). Freneau.
Williams, Mike. Major Mike. 352p. 1981. pap. 2.95 (ISBN 0-441-51601-7, Pub. by Charter Bks). Ace Bks.
Zivkovic, Georg. Heer-und Flottenfuehrer der Welt - Army & Navy Leaders of the World: The Holders of the Higher Military Dignities & Offices of the European States, of the U. S. A. & Japan. LC 72-301460. 891p. 1971. 87.50x (ISBN 3-7648-0666-4). Intl Pubns Serv.
MILITARY BOUNTIES–UNITED STATES
see Bounties, Military–United States
MILITARY CAPITULATIONS
see Capitulations, Military
MILITARY CAREER
see Military Service As a Profession
MILITARY-CIVIL RELATIONS
see Militarism; Military Policy
MILITARY COMPENSATION
see Pensions, Military
MILITARY CONTRACTS
see Defense Contracts
MILITARY COSTUME
see Uniforms, Military
MILITARY CRIMES
see Military Offenses
MILITARY DEPENDENTS
see Air Force Wives; Army Wives; Navy Wives
MILITARY DESERTION
see Desertion, Military
MILITARY DISCIPLINE
see also Military Offenses; Morale
Keijzer, N. Military Obedience. 349p. 1978. 45.00x (ISBN 90-286-0508-8). Sijthoff & Noordhoff.
MILITARY DRAFT
see Military Service, Compulsory
MILITARY DRILL
see Drill and Minor Tactics
MILITARY EDUCATION
Barnard, Henry, compiled by. Military Schools & Courses of Instruction in the Science & Art of War. LC 68-54786. Repr. of 1872 ed. lib. bdg. 33.75x (ISBN 0-8371-1325-3, BAMS). Greenwood.
Collins, Arthur S., Jr. Common Sense Training. LC 77-19077. 1978. pap. 6.95 (ISBN 0-89141-067-8). Presidio Pr.
Heise, Arthur. Brass Factories. 1969. pap. 4.50 (ISBN 0-8183-0153-8). Pub Aff Pr.
Lebra, Joyce C. Japanese-Trained Armies in Southeast Asia: Independence & Volunteer Forces in World War II. LC 75-16116. 226p. 1977. 17.50x (ISBN 0-231-03995-6). Columbia U Pr.
Lovell, John P. Neither Athens nor Sparta: The American Service Academies in Transition. LC 78-9509. (Illus.). 384p. 1979. 17.50x (ISBN 0-253-12955-9). Ind U Pr.
Margiotta, Franklin D., ed. The Changing World of the American Military. (Westview Special Studies in Military Affairs). 1978. lib. bdg. 29.75x (ISBN 0-89158-331-9); pap. 12.00x (ISBN 0-89158-309-2). Westview.
Nash, Willard L. A Study of the Stated Aims & Purposes of the Departments of Military Science & Tactics & Physical Education in the Land-Grant Colleges of the United States. LC 79-177105. (Columbia University. Teachers College. Contributions to Education: No. 614). Repr. of 1934 ed. 17.50 (ISBN 0-404-55614-0). AMS Pr.
U. S. Military Academy. Centennial of the United States Military Academy at West Point, New York, 1802-1902, 2 Vols. Repr. of 1904 ed. Set. lib. bdg. 59.00x (ISBN 0-8371-2665-7, MACE). Greenwood.
Wilson, E. Raymond, ed. & intro. by. Military Training. Incl. Military Training in Schools & Colleges of the United States. Lane, Winthrop D; Universal Military Training. Villard, Oswald G; Universal Military Training & Democracy. Nasmyth, George; Militarizing Our Youth. Barnes, Roswell P; So This Is War. Smith, Tucker P. (Library of War & Peace; Conscrip. & Cons. Object.). lib. bdg. 38.00 (ISBN 0-8240-0417-5). Garland Pub.
Wise, Henry A. Drawing Out the Man: The VMI Story. LC 77-29062. 1978. 14.95x (ISBN 0-8139-0740-3). U Pr of Va.
MILITARY ENGINEERING
see also Earthwork; Electronics in Military Engineering; Fortification; Intrenchments; Military Architecture; Topographical Surveying
Ellis, Chris. German Infantry & Assault Engineer Equipment 1939-1945. 1976. pap. 6.00x (ISBN 0-85242-456-6). Intl Pubns Serv.
Liblich, Garnet Mills, ed. Qualified Products List & Sources. 60th ed. 300p. 1981. lib. bdg. 65.00 perfect bdg (ISBN 0-912702-03-6). Global Eng.
Mazmanian, Daniel A. & Nienaber, Jeanne. Can Organizations Change? Environmental Protection, Citizen Participation, & the Army Corps of Engineers. 1979. 14.95 (ISBN 0-8157-5524-4); pap. 5.95 (ISBN 0-8157-5523-6). Brookings.
MILITARY EQUIPMENT, SUPPLIES, ETC.
see Uniforms, Military;
also subdivisions Commissariat, Equipment, Supplies and stores, Uniforms under armies
MILITARY EXPLOSIVES
see Explosives
MILITARY FAMILIES
see Air Force Wives; Army Wives; Navy Wives
MILITARY FIREWORKS
Bebie, Jules. Manual of Explosives, Military Pyrotechnics & Chemical Warfare Agents. (Illus.). 1977. pap. 7.00 (ISBN 0-87364-088-8). Paladin Ent.
Kentish, Thomas. The Pyrotechnists Treasury: The Complete Art of Firework-Making. LC 76-13259. (Illus.). 242p. 1976. pap. 9.95 (ISBN 0-87364-056-X). Paladin Ent.
Macchiavelli, Niccolo. The Arte of Warre, (Certain Waies of the Orderyng of Souldiours) Whitehorne, P., tr. LC 79-26097. (English Experience Ser.: No. 135). 1969. Repr. of 1562 ed. 42.00 (ISBN 90-221-0135-5). Walter J Johnson.
MILITARY FRONTIER (TER.)
Rothenberg, Gunther. Military Border in Croatia, Seventeen Forty-Eighteen Eighty One: A Study of an Imperial Institution. LC 66-13887. 1966. 7.00x (ISBN 0-226-72944-3). U of Chicago Pr.
MILITARY GEOGRAPHY
see also Maps, Military
MILITARY GOVERNMENT
see also Military Occupation
Elgueta, Bernardo, et al. Five Years of Military Government in Chile (1973-1978) 300p. 1981. text ed. cancelled (ISBN 0-930576-40-3). E M Coleman Ent.
Fitch, John S., 3rd. The Military Coup D'etat As a Political Process: Ecuador, 1948-1966. LC 76-47381. (SHPS Ser.: No. 1, 95th Ser.). (Illus.). 1977. text ed. 17.50x (ISBN 0-8018-1915-6). Johns Hopkins.
Janowitz, Morris. Military Institutions & Coercion in the Developing Nations. LC 76-50462. 1977. pap. 3.95 (ISBN 0-226-39310-0, P174, Phoen). U of Chicago Pr.
Maginnis, John J. Military Government Journal: Normandy to Berlin. Hart, Robert A., ed. LC 75-123539. 1971. 15.00x (ISBN 0-87023-066-2). U of Mass Pr.
MILITARY HALF-TRACKS
see Half-Track Vehicles, Military
MILITARY HEALTH AND HYGIENE
see also Medicine, Military; Tropical Medicine
MILITARY HISTORY
see also Battles; Military Art and Science–History; Military Biography; Military Policy; Naval History; Sieges;
also subdivisions History, or History, military under names of countries, e.g. United States–History, Military; particuliar wars, battles, sieges, etc.; also France–Army; United States–Army, and similar headings
Adams, Charles F. Lee at Appomattox, & Other Papers. 2nd facs. ed. LC 77-134047. (Essay Index Reprint Ser). 1902. 23.00 (ISBN 0-8369-1901-7). Arno.
Banks, Arthur. A World Atlas of Military History: 1861-1945. LC 73-90857. (Illus.). 200p. 1978. 22.50 (ISBN 0-88254-454-3). Hippocrene Bks.
Beck, Phillip. Oradour: Village of the Dead. vii, 88p. 1979. 15.00 (ISBN 0-686-70591-2). Shoe String.
Beeson, Colin R. The Glider Pilot War at Home & Overseas. (Orig.). 1978. pap. 25.00x (ISBN 0-89126-063-3). MA-AH Pub.
Bohme, Klaus-Richard. The Defense Policies of the Nordic Countries, Nineteen Eighteen to Nineteen Thirty-Nine. Krosby, H. Peter, tr. from Swedish. (Orig.). 1979. pap. 7.00x (ISBN 0-89126-073-0). MA-AH Pub.
Brown, Dee A. Grierson's Raid. 261p. 1981. Repr. 17.50 (ISBN 0-686-73906-X). Pr of Morningside.
Carver, Michael, ed. The War Lords: Military Commanders of the 20th Century. 1976. 19.95 (ISBN 0-316-13060-5). Little.
Des Pas Feuquieres, Antoine. Memoirs Historical & Military: Containing a Distinct View of All the Considerable States of Europe. LC 68-54790. 1735-1736. Repr. lib. bdg. 36.50x (ISBN 0-8371-2662-2, FEMH). Greenwood.
Dixon, Norman F. On the Psychology of Military Incompetence. LC 76-9336. 1976. 12.50x (ISBN 0-465-05253-3). Basic.
Dupuy, R. Ernest & Dupuy, Trevor N. The Encyclopedia of Military History. rev. ed. LC 75-6333. (Illus.). 1488p. 1977. 29.95 (ISBN 0-06-011139-9, HarpT). Har-Row.
Earle, Edward M., ed. Makers of Modern Strategy: Military Thought from Machiavelli to Hitler. 1943. 40.00 (ISBN 0-691-06907-7); pap. 8.95 (ISBN 0-691-01853-7). Princeton U Pr.
Engels, Friedrich. Engels As Military Critic: Articles Reprinted from the "Volunteer Journal" & the "Manchester Guardian of the 1860's. LC 75-26213. 1976. Repr. of 1959 ed. lib. bdg. 15.00x (ISBN 0-8371-8407-X, ENMC). Greenwood.
Esposito, Vincent J. & Elting, John R. Military History & Atlas of the Napoleonic Wars. LC 77-14708. Repr. of 1968 ed. 49.50 (ISBN 0-404-16950-3). AMS Pr.
Featherstone, Donald F. Wargaming: Pike & Shot. LC 76-6759. (Illus.). 1976. 10.00 (ISBN 0-88254-403-9). Hippocrene Bks.
Ford, Worthington C. British Officers Serving in America, 1754-1774. 59.95 (ISBN 0-87968-792-4). Gordon Pr.
Forty, George. Fifth Army at War. (Illus.). 144p. 1980. 17.50 (ISBN 0-684-16615-1, ScribT). Scribner.
Fuller, John F. War & Western Civilization, 1832-1932. LC 72-102238. (Select Bibliographies Reprint Ser). 1932. 22.00 (ISBN 0-8369-5123-9). Arno.
Futrell, Robert F. Development of Aeromedical Evacuation in the USAF, 1909-1960, Vol. 2. (USAF Historical Studies: No. 23). 1960. pap. 30.00x (ISBN 0-89126-051-X). MA-AH Pub.

Garrett, Richard. The Raiders. 224p. 1980. 18.95 (ISBN 0-442-25873-9). Van Nos Reinhold.
Gooch, John. Armies in Europe: Military Organisation & Society, 1789-1945. 1980. 30.00 (ISBN 0-7100-0462-1). Routledge & Kegan.
Haigh, R. H. & Turner, P. W. Defense Policy Between the Wars, Nineteen Nineteen to Nineteen Thirty-Eight, Culminating in the Munich Agreement of September 1938. (Orig.). 1979. pap. 14.00 (ISBN 0-89126-072-2). MA-AH Pub.
--Episodes in Punjab Military History in the Mid-Nineteenth Century, Culminating in the Indian Mutiny of 1857. (Orig.). 1979. pap. 18.00x (ISBN 0-89126-071-4). MA-AH Pub.
Hart, B. Liddell. Strategy. 448p. 1974. pap. 3.50 (ISBN 0-451-11041-2, AE1041, Sig). NAL.
Hibbert, Christopher. Agincourt. 1978. 22.50 (ISBN 0-7134-1150-3, Pub. by Batsford England). David & Charles.
Higham, Robin, ed. Civil Wars in the Twentieth Century. LC 78-160044. 272p. 1972. 12.00x (ISBN 0-8131-1261-3). U Pr of Ky.
Higham, Robin & Kipp, Jacob W., eds. ACTA of the Washington ICMH Meeting: August 1975, No. 2. 1977. pap. text ed. 15.00 (ISBN 0-89126-026-9). MA-AH Pub.
Hogg, Ian. Fortress: A History of Military Defense. LC 76-62774. 1977. 15.00 (ISBN 0-312-29977-X). St Martin.
Howard, Michael, ed. Restraints on War: Studies in the Limitation of Armed Conflict. 1979. 24.00x (ISBN 0-19-822545-8). Oxford U Pr.
Jiricek, C. Die Heerstrasse von Begrad Nach Constantinopel und die Balkanapasse. (Ger.). 1877. text ed. 10.50x (ISBN 90-6041-100-5). Humanities.
Karsten, Peter. Law, Soldiers, & Combat. LC 77-87976. (Contributions in Legal Studies: No. 3). (Illus.). 1978. lib. bdg. 15.95x (ISBN 0-313-20042-4, KSL/). Greenwood.
Keegan, John. The Face of Battle. LC 76-10611. (Illus.). 1976. 10.95 (ISBN 0-670-30432-8). Viking Pr.
Kendall, Paul M. The Story of Land Warfare. LC 74-3764. (Illus.). x, 194p. 1981. Repr. of 1957 ed. lib. bdg. 21.75x (ISBN 0-8371-7463-5, KELW). Greenwood.
Kuethe, Allan J. Military Reform & Society in New Granada, 1773-1808. LC 77-21908. (Latin American Monographs: Ser. 2, No. 22). 1978. 11.00 (ISBN 0-8130-0570-1). U Presses Fla.
Luttwak, Edward N. The Grand Strategy of the Roman Empire: From the First Century A. D. to the Third. LC 76-17232. (Illus.). 272p. 1977. 16.00x (ISBN 0-8018-1863-X); pap. 3.95 (ISBN 0-8018-2158-4). Johns Hopkins.
McElwee, William. The Art of War: Waterloo to Mons. LC 74-17459. (Midland Bks.: No. 214). 352p. 1975. pap. 4.95x (ISBN 0-253-20214-0). Ind U Pr.
Naroll, Raoul, et al. Military Deterrence in History: A Pilot Cross-Historical Survey. LC 69-14647. 1974. 33.00 (ISBN 0-87395-047-X); microfiche 33.00 (ISBN 0-87395-147-6). State U NY Pr.
Nickerson, Hoffman. Can We Limit War? LC 72-89268. 336p. 1973. Repr. of 1934 ed. 16.00 (ISBN 0-8046-1763-5). Kennikat.
Oman, Charles W. Art of War in the Middle Ages: A.D. 378-1515. rev. ed. Beeler, John H., ed. (Illus.). (YA) (gr. 9-12). 1960. pap. 4.95 (ISBN 0-8014-9062-6, CP62). Cornell U Pr.
--A History of the Art of War in the Sixteenth Century. LC 75-41204. Repr. of 1937 ed. 42.50 (ISBN 0-404-14579-5). AMS Pr.
Polemon, John. The Second Part of the Booke of Battailes, Fought in Our Age. LC 78-38219. (English Experience Ser.: No. 483). 196p. 1972. Repr. of 1587 ed. 13.00 (ISBN 90-221-0483-4). Walter J Johnson.
Preston, Richard A. & Wise, Sidney. Men in Arms: A History of Warfare & Its Interrelationships with Western Society. rev. ed. 2nd ed. LC 76-101676. (Illus.). 440p. (Orig.). 1970. pap. text ed. 11.95 (ISBN 0-03-045681-9). Praeger.
Preston, Richard A. & Wise, Sydney F. Men in Arms: A History of Warfare & Its Interrelationships with Western Society. 4th ed. LC 78-21298. 1979. pap. text ed. 12.95 (ISBN 0-03-045681-9, HoltC). HR&W.
Richardson, Lewis F. Statistics of Deadly Quarrels. Wright, Quincy & Lienau, C. C., eds. (Illus.). 1960. 24.00 (ISBN 0-910286-10-8). Boxwood.
Ropp, Theodore. War in the Modern World. rev. ed. 1962. pap. 3.95 (ISBN 0-02-036400-8, Collier). Macmillan.
Rosenberg, Arnold. The Social Studies Student Investigates Modern Wars. (YA) 1977. PLB 7.97 (ISBN 0-8239-0379-6). Rosen Pr.
Rosengarten, Joseph G. The German Soldier in the Wars of the U. S. LC 70-167572. 10.00 (ISBN 0-88247-200-3). R & E Res Assoc.
Rowland, Dunbar. Military History of Mississippi, 1803-1898. LC 78-2454. 1978. Repr. of 1908 ed. 32.50 (ISBN 0-87152-266-7). Reprint.
Sargent, Porter. Between Two Wars, 2 vols. 1975. Set. lib. bdg. 100.00 (ISBN 0-87700-220-7). Revisionist Pr.
Saxtorph, Niels. Warriors & Weapons of Early Times in Color. (Illus.). 260p. 1980. 9.95 (ISBN 0-7137-0735-6, Pub. by Blandford Pr England). Sterling.
Sheets, Gary D. A History of Wing-Base Organization & Considerations for Change. (Orig.). 1978. pap. 15.00x (ISBN 0-89126-068-4). MA-AH Pub.
Spaulding, Oliver L., et al. Warfare: A Study of Military Methods from the Earliest Times. LC 72-4301. (World Affairs Ser.: National & International Viewpoints). 616p. 1972. Repr. of 1925 ed. 28.00 (ISBN 0-405-04592-1). Arno.
Stone, Richard G., Jr. A Brittle Sword: The Kentucky Militia, 1776-1912. LC 77-76330. (Kentucky Bicentennial Bookshelf Ser.). (Illus.). 136p. 1977. 6.95 (ISBN 0-8131-0242-1). U Pr of Ky.
Streetly, Martin. Confound & Destroy. (Illus.). 297p. 1979. 17.95 (ISBN 0-88254-560-4, Pub by Macdonald & Jane's England). Hippocrene Bks.
Thomas, Henry W. History of Doles-Cook Brigade. 1981. Repr. of 1903 ed. 35.00 (ISBN 0-686-73905-1). Pr of Morningside.
Vagts, Alfred. History of Militarism. rev. ed. LC 59-7194. 1967. pap. text ed. 8.95 (ISBN 0-02-933050-5). Free Pr.
Vickers, Robert E., Jr. The Liberators from Wendling. 1977. pap. text ed. 25.00 (ISBN 0-89126-033-1). MA-AH Pub.
Von Pivka, Otto. Armies of the Napoleonic Era. LC 78-70397. (Illus.). 1979. 17.95 (ISBN 0-8008-5471-3). Taplinger.
--Kings German Legion. LC 74-76630. (Men-at-Arms Ser). (Illus.). 40p. 1974. pap. 7.95 (ISBN 0-88254-228-1). Hippocrene Bks.
Wright, John. Military Collections at the Essex Institute. (E. I. Museum Booklet Ser.). (Illus.). 64p. 1981. pap. text ed. 4.95 (ISBN 0-88389-104-2). Essex Inst.
Young, Brigadier P. Dictionary of Battles, Vol. 1. (Illus.). 1978. 15.00 (ISBN 0-8317-2260-6, Mayflower Bks). Smith Pubs.
Young, Brigadier P. & Calvert, Brigadier M. Dictionary of Battles, Vol. 2. LC 78-23518. (Illus.). 1979. 15.00 (ISBN 0-8317-2261-4, Mayflower Bks). Smith Pubs.
Young, Peter. The Righting Man. 256p. 1981. 29.95 (ISBN 0-8317-4503-7, Rutledge Pr). Smith Pubs.
Zivkovic, Georg. Heer-und Flottenfuehrer der Welt - Army & Navy Leaders of the World: The Holders of the Higher Military Dignities & Offices of the European States, of the U. S. A. & Japan. LC 72-301460. 891p. 1971. 87.50x (ISBN 3-7648-0666-4). Intl Pubns Serv.

MILITARY HISTORY–BIBLIOGRAPHY

Library for Contemporary History - World War Library,Stuttgart. Catalog from the Library for Contemporary History - World War Library, 2 pts. Incl. Pt. 1. Alphabetical Catalog, 11 vols. 8159p. 1968. Set. 860.00 (ISBN 0-8161-0798-X); Pt. 2. Classified Catalog, 20 vols. ii, 332p. 1968. Set. 1590.00 (ISBN 0-8161-0175-2). G K Hall.
Pohler, Johann. Bibliotheca Historico-Militaris, 4 Vols. 1899. 271.00 (ISBN 0-8337-2793-1). B Franklin.
Silverthorne & Gaskin, W. D. The British Foot Guards: A Bibliography. 1960. pap. 3.00 (ISBN 0-685-63727-1). Hope Farm.

MILITARY HYGIENE

see also Medicine, Military; Tropical Medicine

MILITARY INSTALLATIONS

see Military Bases

MILITARY INTELLIGENCE

see also U-Two Incident, 1960

Armstrong, N. A. Fieldcraft, Sniping & Intelligence. (Illus.). 238p. pap. 8.00 (ISBN 0-87364-080-2). Paladin Ent.
Challener, Richard D., ed. Nineteen Twenty (Feb. Seventh - April Ninth, 1920) (United States Military Intelligence 1917-1927 Ser.). 1979. lib. bdg. 60.50 (ISBN 0-8240-3011-7). Garland Pub.
--World War One, Oct. 20, 1917-Jan. 19, 1918. (United States Military Intelligence 1917-1927 Ser.). 1979. lib. bdg. 60.50 (ISBN 0-8240-3001-X). Garland Pub.
Farago, Ladislas. War of Wits: The Anatomy of Espionage & Intelligence. LC 75-31362. (Illus.). 379p. 1976. Repr. of 1954 ed. lib. bdg. 24.00x (ISBN 0-8371-8518-1, FAWW). Greenwood.
Grant, Robert M. U-Boat Intelligence, 1914-1918. (Illus.). 1969. 16.50 (ISBN 0-208-00898-5, Archon). Shoe String.
Kahn, David. Hitler's Spies: German Military Intelligence in World War II. (Illus.). 1978. 19.95 (ISBN 0-02-560610-7). Macmillan.
Lee, William T. The Estimation of Soviet Defense Expenditures, 1955-75: An Unconventional Approach. LC 76-24357. (Special Studies). 1977. text ed. 36.50 (ISBN 0-275-56900-4). Praeger.
McGovern, William M. Strategic Intelligence & the Shape of Tomorrow. LC 74-9039. (Foundation of Foreign Affairs Ser.: No. 5). 191p. 1974. Repr. of 1961 ed. lib. bdg. 15.00 (ISBN 0-8371-7604-2, MCSI). Greenwood.
Ransom, Harry H. Intelligence Establishment. LC 70-115480. 1970. 15.00x (ISBN 0-674-45816-8). Harvard U Pr.
Wilcox, Laird M., compiled by. Bibliography on Espionage & Intelligence Operations. (Orig.). 1981. pap. text ed. 9.95 (ISBN 0-933592-23-X). Edit Res Serv.

MILITARY INTERVENTION

see Intervention (International Law)

MILITARY JUSTICE

see Courts-Martial and Courts of Inquiry

MILITARY LAW

see also Capitulations, Military; Courts-Martial and Courts of Inquiry; Martial Law; Military Administration; Military Discipline; Military Offenses; Military Privileges and Immunities; Military Service, Compulsory

Brand, C. F. Roman Military Law. 262p. 1968. 10.00x (ISBN 0-292-73393-3). U of Tex Pr.
Byrne, Edward. Military Law. 3rd ed. LC 76-1057. 224p. 1981. text ed. 21.95x (ISBN 0-87021-389-X). Naval Inst Pr.
Callan, John F. The Military Laws of the United States 1776-1858. LC 70-165125. 488p. 1858. lib. bdg. 45.00 (ISBN 0-87821-085-7). Milford Hse.
Dahl, Richard C. & Whelan, John F., eds. The Military Law Dictionary. LC 60-10208. 1960. 15.00 (ISBN 0-379-00042-3). Oceana.
Daly, James & Bergman, Lee. A Hero's Welcome: The Conscience of Sergeant James Daly VS. the United States Army. LC 74-17652. (Illus.). 288p. 1975. 8.50 (ISBN 0-672-52030-3). Bobbs.
Dowell, Cassius. Military Aid to the Civil Power. Kavass, Igor I. & Sprudz, Adolf, eds. LC 72-75030. (International Military Law & History Ser.: Vol. 1). 1972. Repr. of 1925 ed. lib. bdg. 21.50 (ISBN 0-930342-38-0). W S Hein.
Glenn, Garrard. Army & the Law. LC 72-168168. Repr. of 1943 ed. 18.00 (ISBN 0-404-02819-5). AMS Pr.
Holborn, Hajo. American Military Government: Its Organization & Policies. Kavass, Igor I. & Sprudz, Adolf, eds. LC 75-766. (International Military Law & History Ser.: Vol. 10). Repr. of 1947 ed. lib. bdg. 22.50 (ISBN 0-930342-47-X). W S Hein.
Jacobs, James B. Individual Rights & Institutional Authority: Prisons, Mental Hospitals, Schools, & Military: Cases & Materials. (Contemporary Legal Education Ser.). 1979. text ed. 18.50 (ISBN 0-672-83706-4). Bobbs.
Kohn, Richard H., ed. Military Laws of the U. S., from the Civil War Through the War Powers Act of 1973: An Original Anthology. LC 78-74063. (American Military Experience Ser.). 1979. lib. bdg. 35.00x (ISBN 0-405-11894-5). Arno.
Marks, F. Raymond. Military Lawyers, Civilian Courts, & the Organized Bar: A Case Study of the Unauthorized Practice Dilemma. 1972. pap. 2.50 (ISBN 0-685-32710-8). Am Bar Foun.
Shanor, Charles A. & Terrell, Timothy P. Military Law in a Nutshell. LC 80-165. (Nutshell Ser.). 418p. 1980. pap. text ed. 6.95 (ISBN 0-8299-2083-8). West Pub.
Wiener, Frederick B. Civilians Under Military Justice. LC 67-25530. 1967. 12.50x (ISBN 0-226-89588-2). U of Chicago Pr.
Winthrop, William. Military Law & Precedents. Kohn, Richard H., ed. LC 78-74061. (American Military Experience Ser.). 1979. Repr. of 1920 ed. lib. bdg. 64.00x (ISBN 0-405-11895-3). Arno.
--Military Law & Precedents, 2 vols, Vol. 6. 2nd ed. Kavass, Igor I. & Sprudzs, Adolf, eds. LC 79-91717. (International Military Law & History Ser.). 1111p. 1979. Repr. of 1920 ed. lib. bdg. 45.00 (ISBN 0-930342-72-0). W S Hein.

MILITARY LIFE

see Soldiers

MILITARY MANEUVERS

see also War Games

Polyaenus. The Stratagems of War. Shepherd, R., tr. 408p. 1974. 15.00 (ISBN 0-89005-020-1). Ares.

MILITARY MAPS

see also Maps, Military

MILITARY MEDICINE

see Medicine, Military

MILITARY MINIATURES

Blake, Michael. Making Model Soldiers. 1975. 8.95 (ISBN 0-09-124000-X, Pub. by Hutchinson). Merrimack Bk Serv.
Cassin-Scott, Jack. Making Model Soldiers of the World. 1977. pap. 5.95 (ISBN 0-8120-0822-7). Barron.
Consumer Guide Magazine Editors. Model Military Toys. (Orig.). 1978. pap. 2.95 (ISBN 0-06-090641-3, CN 641, CN). Har-Row.
Cummings, Richard. Make Your Own Model Forts & Castles. (Illus.). (gr. 6 up). 1977. 7.95 (ISBN 0-679-20400-8). McKay.
Dilley, Roy. Model Soldiers in Color. (Illus.). 1979. 12.95 (ISBN 0-7137-0907-3, Pub by Blandford Pr England). Sterling.
Edwards, Alan & Spinks, John. Fighting Men in Miniature. 192p. 1980. 32.95x (ISBN 0-85177-187-4, Pub. by Conway Maritime England). State Mutual Bk.
Featherstone, Donald. Better Military Modelling. LC 77-367696. (Better Sports Ser.). (Illus.). 1977. 8.50x (ISBN 0-7182-1447-1). Intl Pubns Serv.
Garratt, John G. The World Encyclopedia of Model Soldiers. LC 80-84376. (Illus.). 224p. 1981. 75.00 (ISBN 0-87951-129-X); pre-Jan. 60.00 (ISBN 0-686-73693-1). Overlook Pr.
Garrett, John. Collecting Model Soldiers. LC 74-24665. 1975. 8.95 (ISBN 0-668-03749-0). Arco.
Goodenough, Simon. Military Miniatures: The Art of Making Model Soldiers. (Illus.). 1978. 15.00 (ISBN 0-8019-6721-X); pap. 8.50 (ISBN 0-8019-6722-8). Chilton.
Mackenzie, Ian. Collecting Old Toy Soldiers. 1975. 30.00 (ISBN 0-7134-3036-2). David & Charles.
Stearns, Philip. How to Make Model Soldiers. LC 73-92267. (gr. 7 up). 5.95 (ISBN 0-668-03446-7). Arco.

MILITARY MUSEUMS

see also Arsenals

Sweeney, James B. Pictorial Guide to the Military Museums, Forts, & Historic Sites of the U. S. 320p. 1981. 19.95 (ISBN 0-517-54481-4). Crown.

MILITARY MUSIC

see also Band Music; Bands (Music)
also subdivision Songs and Music under names of wars, e.g. United States–History–Civil War, 1861-1865–Songs and Music

Adkins, H. E. Treatise on the Military Band. 1977. lib. bdg. 59.95 (ISBN 0-8490-2763-2). Gordon Pr.
Farmer, Henry G. Rise & Development of Military Music. LC 79-107801. (Select Bibliographies Reprint Ser). 1912. 16.00 (ISBN 0-8369-5204-9). Arno.
Hall, Harry H. A Johnny Reb Band from Salem. (Music Reprint 1980 Ser.). (Illus.). xi, 118p. 1980. Repr. of 1963 ed. lib. bdg. 15.00 (ISBN 0-306-76014-2). Da Capo.
Olson, Kenneth E. Music & Musket: Bands & Bandsmen of the American Civil War. LC 79-6195. (Contributions to the Study of Music & Dance: No. 1). (Illus.). xx, 299p. 1981. lib. bdg. 27.50 (ISBN 0-313-22112-X, OMM/). Greenwood.
White, William C. A History of Military Music in America. LC 73-10739. (Illus.). 272p. 1975. Repr. of 1944 ed. lib. bdg. 19.75 (ISBN 0-8371-7029-X, WHMM). Greenwood.

MILITARY OCCUPATION

see also Enemy Property; Military Government; Occupation Currency; Territory, National; World War, 1939-1945–Occupied Territories;
also subdivisions History and Politics and Government under names of territory occupied, e.g. France–History–German Occupation, 1940-1945

Fraenkel, Ernst. Military Occupation & the Rule of Law: Occupation Government in the Rhineland 1918-1923. (Institute of World Affairs Ser.). 279p. 1944. 20.00x (ISBN 0-8014-0140-2). Cornell U Pr.
Graber, Doris A. Development of the Law of Belligerent Occupation, 1863-1914. LC 68-58584. (Columbia University. Studies in the Social Sciences: No. 543). Repr. of 1949 ed. 24.50 (ISBN 0-404-51543-6). AMS Pr.

MILITARY OFFENSES

see also Desertion, Military; Mutiny; Trials (Military Offenses)

Aycock, William B. & Wurfel, Seymour W. Military Law Under the Uniform Code of Military Justice. LC 72-6929. (Illus.). 430p. 1973. Repr. of 1955 ed. lib. bdg. 29.50 (ISBN 0-8371-6507-5, AYML). Greenwood.
Bryant, Clifton D. Khaki-Collar Crime: Deviant Behavior in the Military Context. LC 79-7105. 1979. 14.95 (ISBN 0-02-904930-X). Free Pr.
Byrne, Edward M. Military Law. 2nd ed. LC 76-1057. 1976. 21.00x (ISBN 0-87021-378-4). Naval Inst Pr.
Curry, David. Sunshine Patriots: Punishment & the Vietnam Offender. Date not set. price not set. U of Notre Dame Pr.
Everett, Robinson O. Military Justice in the Armed Forces of the United States. LC 75-42097. 338p. 1976. Repr. of 1956 ed. lib. bdg. 19.50x (ISBN 0-8371-8642-0, EVMJ). Greenwood.
Gulley, Bill & Reese, Mary E. Breaking Cover. 352p. 1981. pap. 2.95 (ISBN 0-446-93938-2). Warner Bks.

MILITARY PENSIONS

see Pensions, Military

MILITARY PERSONNEL

see Soldiers

MILITARY PERSONNEL AND DRUGS
see Drugs and Military Personnel
MILITARY POLICY
see also Defense Information, Classified; Deterrence (Strategy); Militarism; Strategic Materials;
also subdivision Military Policy under names of countries, e.g. United States–Military Policy
Abbiatico, Mario. Grandi Incisioni Su Armi D'oggi. (Illus.). Repr. of 1976 ed. 30.00 (ISBN 0-686-70832-6). Arma Pr.
Askari, Hossein & Glover, Michael C. Military Expenditures & the Level of Economic Development. (Studies in International Business: No. 3). 1977. pap. 4.00 (ISBN 0-87755-272-X). U of Tex Busn Res.
Blackett, Patrick M. Studies of War: Nuclear & Conventional. LC 78-16364. (Illus.). 1978. Repr. of 1962 ed. lib. bdg. 24.75x (ISBN 0-313-20575-2, BLSW). Greenwood.
Boserup, Anders & Mack, Andrew. War Without Weapons: Non-Violence in National Defense. LC 74-26920. 192p. 1975. 6.50x (ISBN 0-8052-3581-7); pap. 2.95 (ISBN 0-8052-0484-9). Schocken.
Brodie, Bernard. Strategy in the Missile Age. (Rand Corporation Research Studies). 1959. pap. 8.95 (ISBN 0-691-01852-9). Princeton U Pr.
Cordier, Sherwood S. Calculus of Power: The Current Soviet-American Conventional Military Balance in Central Europe. 3rd ed. LC 79-5435. 1980. pap. text ed. 7.50 (ISBN 0-8191-0883-9). U Pr of Amer.
Garnett, John C., ed. Theories of Peace & Security: A Reader in Contemporary Strategic Thought. 1970. 15.95 (ISBN 0-312-79695-1); pap. 6.95 (ISBN 0-312-79660-9). St Martin.
Halle, Louis J. Choice of Survival. LC 74-7539. 147p. 1974. Repr. of 1958 ed. lib. bdg. 15.00x (ISBN 0-8371-7578-X, HACH). Greenwood.
Handel, Michael I. The Diplomacy of Surprise: Hitler, Nixon, Sadat. (Harvard Studies in International Affairs Ser.). 369p. 1981. 22.50x (ISBN 0-87674-048-4, 44); pap. 11.95x (ISBN 0-87674-049-2). Harvard U Intl Aff.
Hoeber, Frank. Slow to Take Offense: Bombers, Cruise Missiles, & Prudent Deterrence. LC 80-80662. (CSIS Monograph). 137p. 1980. pap. text ed. 6.95 (ISBN 0-686-70746-X). CSI Studies.
Holst, Johan & Nerlich, Uwe, eds. Beyond Nuclear Deterrence: New Aims, New Arms. LC 76-20283. 1977. 19.50x (ISBN 0-8448-0974-8). Crane-Russak Co.
Horton, Frank B., 3rd, et al, eds. Comparative Defense Policy. LC 73-19341. (Illus.). 616p. 1974. 30.00x (ISBN 0-8018-1581-9); pap. 7.95x (ISBN 0-8018-1597-5). Johns Hopkins.
Huntington, Samuel P. The Soldier & the State: The Theory & Politics of Civil-Military Relations. 552p. 1981. pap. 8.95 (ISBN 0-674-81736-2). Harvard U Pr.
Knorr, Klaus. On the Uses of Military Power in the Nuclear Age. (Center of International Studies Ser.). 1966. 14.00 (ISBN 0-691-05626-9). Princeton U Pr.
Knorr, Klaus, ed. Historical Dimensions of National Security Problems. LC 75-41842. (National Security Studies). 365p. (Orig.). 1976. pap. 6.95x (ISBN 0-7006-0143-0). Regents Pr KS.
Lang, Kurt. Military Sociology 1963-1969: A Trend Report & Bibliography. (Current Sociology Ser.). 1971. pap. 6.70x (ISBN 90-2796-578-1). Mouton.
Lider, Julian. On the Nature of Military Force. 1980. text ed. 44.50x (ISBN 0-566-00296-5, Pub. by Gower Pub Co England). Renouf.
Owen, David. The Politics of Defence. LC 72-76256. 260p. 1972. 7.95 (ISBN 0-8008-6406-9). Taplinger.
Schwarz, Urs. Confrontation & Intervention in the Modern World. LC 78-102940. 1970. 12.00 (ISBN 0-379-00380-5). Oceana.
Simon, Sheldon W., ed. The Military & Security in the Third World: Domestic & International Impacts. LC 77-29133. (A Westview Special Study Ser.). 1978. lib. bdg. 29.75x (ISBN 0-89158-424-2). Westview.
Singer, David J., ed. The Correlates of War I: Research Origins & Rationale. LC 77-18431. 1979. 19.95 (ISBN 0-02-928960-2). Free Pr.
Snyder, Glenn H. Deterrence & Defense: Toward a Theory of National Security. LC 75-18405. (Illus.). 294p. 1975. Repr. of 1961 ed. lib. bdg. 22.25x (ISBN 0-8371-8333-2, SNDD). Greenwood.
Sveics, V. V. Small Nation Survival. 1970. 8.50 (ISBN 0-682-47163-1, University). Exposition.
Toynbee, Philip. The Fearful Choice: A Debate on Nuclear Policy Conducted by Philip Toynbee with the Archbishop of Centerbury & Others. LC 74-11406. 112p. 1974. Repr. of 1958 ed. lib. bdg. 15.00x (ISBN 0-8371-7677-8, TOFC). Greenwood.
Walt, Lewis W. The Eleventh Hour. LC 79-83563. 1979. 9.95 (ISBN 0-89803-005-6). Caroline Hse.
Woddis, Jack. Armies & Politics. LC 77-11724. 1978. pap. 4.50 (ISBN 0-7178-0495-X). Intl Pub Co.
MILITARY POSTS
Foreman, Grant. Advancing the Frontier, 1830-1860. (Civilization of the American Indian Ser.: No. 4). (Illus.). 1968. Repr. of 1933 ed. 16.95 (ISBN 0-8061-0792-8). U of Okla Pr.
Frazer, Robert W. Forts of the West: Military Forts & Presidios & Posts Commonly Called Forts West of the Mississippi to 1898. (Illus.). 1977. pap. 5.95 (ISBN 0-8061-1250-6). U of Okla Pr.
Hart, Herbert M. Old Forts of the Northwest. Encore ed. LC 63-15215. (Illus.). 1963. 9.95 (ISBN 0-87564-314-0). Superior Pub.
--Old Forts of the Southwest. encore ed. LC 64-21316. 1964. 9.95 (ISBN 0-87564-315-9). Superior Pub.
Laird, Melvin R., et al. Who's First in Defense, the U.S. or the USSR? LC 76-26810. 1976. pap. 3.75 (ISBN 0-8447-2089-5). Am Enterprise.
Mansfield, Joseph K. Mansfield on the Condition of the Western Forts, 1853-54. Frazer, Robert W., ed. (American Exploration & Travel Ser.: Vol. 41). (Illus.). 1963. pap. 7.95 (ISBN 0-8061-1083-X). U of Okla Pr.
Paber, Stanley W., ed. Fort Churchill: Nevada Military Outpost of the 1860's. (Illus.). 1981. pap. 2.95 (ISBN 0-913814-38-5). Nevada Pubns.
Prucha, Francis Paul. A Guide to the Military Posts of the United States 1789-1895. LC 64-63571. (Illus.). 1966. Repr. of 1964 ed. 7.50 (ISBN 0-87020-088-7). State Hist Soc Wis.
MILITARY POWER
see Air Power; Armies; Disarmament; Military Art and Science; Navies; Sea-Power
MILITARY PRIVILEGES AND IMMUNITIES
McAlister, Lyle. The Fuero Militar in New Spain 1764-1800. LC 74-6753. 117p. 1974. Repr. of 1957 ed. lib. bdg. 15.00 (ISBN 0-8371-7554-2, MCFM). Greenwood.
Rivkin, Robert S. The Rights of Servicemen. (ACLU Handbook Ser). (Orig.). 1972. pap. 1.50 (ISBN 0-380-01526-9, 33365, Discus). Avon.
MILITARY PSYCHIATRY
see Psychiatry, Military
MILITARY PSYCHOLOGY
see Psychology, Military
MILITARY RECONNAISSANCE
see also Photographic Reconnaissance Systems; Scouts and Scouting; U-Two Incident, 1960
Moore, Michael L. A Review of Search & Reconnaisance Theory Literature. LC 75-131015. 104p. 1970. 22.00 (ISBN 0-686-01956-3). Mgmt Info Serv.
MILITARY RELIGIOUS ORDERS
see also Hospitalers; Templars; Teutonic Knights
MILITARY RESEARCH
see also Research; Research and Development Contracts
Hart, Guy. Challenge of War: Britain's Scientific & Engineering Contributions to World War Two. LC 70-106910. 1970. 10.95 (ISBN 0-8008-1431-2). Taplinger.
Marschak, Thomas, et al. Strategy for R & D: Studies in the Microeconomics of Development. LC 67-28248. (Econometrics & Operations Research Ser.: Vol. 8). (Illus.). 1967. 39.00 (ISBN 0-387-03945-7). Springer-Verlag.
Powder Metallurgy in Defense Technology, Vol. 3. (Defense Technology Seminar). 1977. 37.50x (ISBN 0-918404-42-8). Metal Powder.
Royal United Services Institute for Defence Studies, London, ed. Defence Yearbook 1981. 91st ed. LC 75-614843. (Illus.). 355p. 1980. 45.00x (ISBN 0-08-027006-9). Intl Pubns Serv.
Speech & Facsimile Scrambling & Decoding: Basic Text on Speech Scrambling. 1981. pap. 22.80 (ISBN 0-89412-046-8). Aegean Park Pr.
Stewart, Irvin. Organizing Scientific Research for War: The Administrative History of the Office of Scientific Research & Development. Cohen, I. Bernard, ed. LC 79-7999. (Three Centuries of Science in America Ser.). 1980. Repr. of 1948 ed. lib. bdg. 26.00x (ISBN 0-405-12587-9). Arno.
MILITARY SCHOOLS
see Military Education
MILITARY SCIENCE
see Military Art and Science
MILITARY SECRETS
see Defense Information, Classified
MILITARY SERVICE, COMPULSORY
see also Conscientious Objectors;
also subdivisions Recruiting, etc. under armies, e.g. United States–Army–Recruiting, etc.
Alotta, Robert I. Stop the Evil. LC 78-10425. (Illus.). 1978. 10.00 (ISBN 0-89141-018-X). Presidio Pr.
Anderson, Martin, ed. Conscription: A Select & Annotated Bibliography. LC 75-41906. (Bibliographical Ser.: No. 57). 472p. 1976. 19.95 (ISBN 0-8179-2571-6). Hoover Inst Pr.
Baskir, Lawrence M. & Straus, William A. Chance & Circumstance: The Draft, the War & the Vietnam Generation. (Giant Ser.). pap. 3.95 (ISBN 0-394-72749-5, V-749, Vin). Random.
Baskir, Lawrence M. & Strauss, William A. Chance & Circumstance: The Draft, the War, & the Vietnam Generation. LC 77-75000. 1978. 10.00 (ISBN 0-394-41275-3). Knopf.
Coffey, Kenneth J. Manpower for Military Mobilization. 1978. pap. 4.25 (ISBN 0-8447-3291-5). Am Enterprise.
Committee for Economic Development. Military Manpower & National Security. LC 78-189538. 48p. 1972. lib. bdg. 2.00 (ISBN 0-87186-745-1); pap. 1.00 (ISBN 0-87186-045-7). Comm Econ Dev.
Davis, James W., Jr. & Dolbeare, Kenneth M. Little Groups of Neighbors: The Selective Service System. LC 80-25861. xv, 276p. 1981. Repr. of 1968 ed. lib. bdg. 35.00x (ISBN 0-313-22777-2, DALN). Greenwood.
Dell, Roberta E. The United States Against Bergdoll: How the Government Spent Twenty Years & Millions of Dollars to Capture & Punish America's Most Notorious Draft Dodger. LC 76-55819. (Illus.). 1977. 9.95 (ISBN 0-498-02070-3). A S Barnes.
Dennis, Peter. Decision by Default: Peacetime Conscription & British Defence, 1919 - 1939. LC 72-190372. 320p. 1972. 14.75 (ISBN 0-8223-0272-1). Duke.
Gerhardt, James M. Draft & Public Policy: Issues in Military Manpower Procurement, 1945-1970. LC 70-105723. 1971. 15.00 (ISBN 0-8142-0143-1). Ohio St U Pr.
Graham, John R. Constitutional History of the Military Draft. 5.95 (ISBN 0-87018-065-7); pap. 2.95 (ISBN 0-87018-070-3). Ross.
Graham, John W. Conscription & Conscience: A History 1916-1919. LC 78-81509. Repr. of 1922 ed. 17.50x (ISBN 0-678-00507-9). Kelley.
Hayes, Denis. Conscription Conflict. LC 70-147647. (Library of War & Peace; Conscrip. & Cons. Object.). lib. bdg. 38.00 (ISBN 0-8240-0416-7). Garland Pub.
Johnson, R. Charles. Don't Sit in the Draft. 240p. (Orig.). 1980. pap. 6.95 (ISBN 0-917316-32-0). Nolo Pr.
Kasinsky, Renee G. Refugees from Militarism: Draft-Age Americans in Canada. (Littlefield, Adams Quality Paperbacks: No. 344). 1978. pap. 4.95 (ISBN 0-8226-0344-6). Littlefield.
--Refugees from Militarism: Draft-Age Americans in Canada. LC 75-46232. 350p. 1976. 14.95 (ISBN 0-87855-113-1). Transaction Bks.
Little, Roger W., ed. Selective Service & American Society. LC 68-54411. 1969. text ed. 9.95 (ISBN 0-87154-548-9). Russell Sage.
Mitchell, Memory F. Legal Aspects of Conscription & Exemption in North Carolina, 1861-1865. (James Sprunt Study in History & Political Science: Vol. 47). (Orig.). 1965. pap. text ed. 5.00x (ISBN 0-8078-5047-0). U of NC Pr.
Moore, Albert B. Conscription & Conflict in the Confederacy. 1963. text ed. 15.00x (ISBN 0-391-00459-X). Humanities.
Murdock, Eugene C. One Million Men: The Civil War Draft in the North. LC 80-14431. (Illus.). xi, 366p. 1980. Repr. of 1971 ed. lib. bdg. 29.75x (ISBN 0-313-22502-8, MUOM). Greenwood.
Norman, E. Herbert. Soldier & Peasant in Japan: The Origins of Conscription. LC 75-33572. (Institute of Pacific Relations). Repr. of 1943 ed. 12.50 (ISBN 0-404-59549-9). AMS Pr.
O'Sullivan, John & Meckler, Alan M., eds. The Draft & Its Enemies: A Documentary History. LC 74-10979. 309p. 1974. 17.50 (ISBN 0-252-00395-0). U of Ill Pr.
Tax, Sol, ed. Draft, a Handbook of Facts & Alternatives. LC 67-25517. 1967. 12.95x (ISBN 0-226-79090-8); pap. 3.95 (ISBN 0-226-79091-6). U of Chicago Pr.
Wilson, E. Raymond, ed. & intro. by. Military Training. Incl. Military Training in Schools & Colleges of the United States. Lane, Winthrop D; Universal Military Training. Villard, Oswald G; Universal Military Training & Democracy. Nasmyth, George; Militarizing Our Youth. Barnes, Roswell P; So This Is War. Smith, Tucker P. (Library of War & Peace; Conscrip. & Cons. Object.). lib. bdg. 38.00 (ISBN 0-8240-0417-5). Garland Pub.
MILITARY SERVICE, COMPULSORY–CANADA
Granatstein, J. L. Broken Promises: A History of Conscription in Canada. 1977. pap. 8.50x (ISBN 0-19-540258-8). Oxford U Pr.
MILITARY SERVICE, COMPULSORY–FRANCE
Challener, Richard D. French Theory of the Nation in Arms, 1866-1939. LC 64-66394. 1965. Repr. of 1952 ed. 8.50 (ISBN 0-8462-0565-3). Russell.
MILITARY SERVICE, VOLUNTARY
see also subdivision Recruting, enlistment, etc. under armies, navies, etc., e.g. United States–Army–Recruiting, enlistment, etc.
Bachman, Jerald G., et al. The All-Volunteer Force: A Study of Ideology in the Military. LC 77-5631. 1977. text ed. 10.95x (ISBN 0-472-08095-4); pap. 6.95x (ISBN 0-472-08096-2). U of Mich Pr.
Gottlieb, David. Babes in Arms: Youth in the Army. LC 80-15830. (Illus.). 173p. 1980. 16.95 (ISBN 0-8039-1499-7). Sage.
Hess, Karl & Reeves, Thomas. The End of the Draft: The Feasibility of Freedom. pap. 1.95 (ISBN 0-394-70870-9, V-644, Vin). Random.
Marmion, Harry A. Case Against a Volunteer Army. LC 73-143567. 128p. (Orig.). 1971. 5.95 (ISBN 0-8129-0184-3). Times Bks.
Sarkesian, Sam C. American Military Professionalism. LC 80-27027. (Pergamon Policy Studies on International Politics). 1981. 27.50 (ISBN 0-08-027178-2). Pergamon.
Underhill, Lonnie E. Genealogy Records of the First Arizona Volunteer Infantry Regiment. LC 80-24778. (Illus.). iv, 124p. 1980. pap. 18.50 (ISBN 0-933234-02-3). Roan Horse.
MILITARY SERVICE AS A PROFESSION
Fuller, J. F. Memoirs of an Unconventional Soldier. 1976. lib. bdg. 59.95 (ISBN 0-8490-2223-1). Gordon Pr.
Gates, Geffrey. The Defence of Militarie Profession. LC 72-5996. (English Experience Ser.: No. 521). 64p. 1973. Repr. of 1579 ed. 7.00 (ISBN 90-221-0521-0). Walter J Johnson.
Hummel, Dean L. The Counselor & Military Service Opportunities. (Guidance Monograph). 1973. pap. 2.40 (ISBN 0-395-14202-4). HM.
Janowitz, Morris. Professional Soldier: A Social & Political Portrait. LC 60-7090. 1960. 12.95 (ISBN 0-02-916170-3); pap. 8.95 (ISBN 0-02-916180-0). Free Pr.
MacCloskey, Monro. Your Future in the Military Services. LC 73-89978. (Careers in Depth Ser). 1979. PLB 5.97 (ISBN 0-8239-0479-2). Rosen Pr.
Millett, Allan R. The General: Robert L. Bullard & Officership in the U.S. Army, 1881-1925. LC 75-68. (Contributions in Military History: No. 10). (Illus.). 499p. 1975. lib. bdg. 19.95x (ISBN 0-8371-7957-2, MIG/). Greenwood.
Rafferty, Robert. Careers in the Military: Good Training for Civilian Life. 1980. 8.95 (ISBN 0-525-66668-0). Elsevier-Nelson.
Sarkesian, Sam C. The Professional Army Officer in a Changing Society. LC 74-10917. 230p. 1974. 18.95x (ISBN 0-911012-62-1). Nelson-Hall.
Wool, Harold. The Military Specialist: Skilled Manpower for the Armed Forces. LC 68-22676. (Illus.). 216p. 1969. 15.00x (ISBN 0-8018-0695-X). Johns Hopkins.
MILITARY SIGNALING
see Signals and Signaling
MILITARY SOCIOLOGY
see Sociology, Military
MILITARY STAFFS
see Armies–Staffs
MILITARY STATIONS
see Military Posts
MILITARY STRATEGY
see Military Art and Science; Strategy
MILITARY SURGERY
see Surgery, Military
MILITARY TACTICS
see Tactics
MILITARY TERMS
see Military Art and Science–Terminology
MILITARY TOPOGRAPHY
see also Maps, Military
MILITARY TRAINING
see Military Education
MILITARY TRAINING, UNIVERSAL
see Military Service, Compulsory
MILITARY TRIBUNALS
see Courts-Martial and Courts of Inquiry
MILITARY UNIFORMS
see Uniforms, Military
MILITARY VEHICLES
see Vehicles, Military
MILIUKOV, PAUL
Riha, Thomas. Russian European: Paul Miliukov in Russian Politics. (International Studies Ser). 1968. 10.95x (ISBN 0-268-00236-3). U of Notre Dame Pr.
MILIUTIN, DMITRII ALEKSEEVICH, GRAF, 1816-1912
Miller, Forrestt A. Dmitrii Miliutin & the Reform Era in Russia. LC 68-20545. 1968. 10.00 (ISBN 0-8265-1112-0). Vanderbilt U Pr.
MILK
see also Butter; Cheese; Cookery (Dairy Products); Milk Plants
Aihara, Herman. Milk: A Myth of Civilization. 1971. 1.50 (ISBN 0-918860-08-3). G Ohsawa.
Bahna, Sami L. & Heiner, Douglas C. Allergies to Milk. 224p. 1980. 23.50 (ISBN 0-8089-1256-9). Grune.

Campbell, J. R. & Marshall, R. T. The Science of Providing Milk for Man. (Agricultural Sciences Ser). 1975. 21.95 (ISBN 0-07-009690-2, C). McGraw.
Eckles, Clarence H., et al. Milk & Milk Products. 4th ed. (Agricultural Sciences Ser). (Illus.). 1951. text ed. 19.95 (ISBN 0-07-018959-5, C). McGraw.
Education & Training Comm. Oregon Association of Milk, Food & Environment Sanitarians, Inc. HTST Pasteurizer Operation Manual. (Illus.). 4.75x (ISBN 0-88246-057-9). Oreg St U Bkstrs.
FAO-WHO Joint Expert Committee on Milk Hygeine, 3rd, Geneva, 1969. Report. (Technical Report Ser: No. 453). 82p. 1970. pap. 2.00 (ISBN 92-4-120453-2, 1144). World Health.
Galli, C., et al, eds. Dietary Lipids & Postnatal Development. LC 73-79580. (Illus.). 286p. 1973. 27.00 (ISBN 0-911216-50-2). Raven.
Gerrick, David J. When Milk Is Dangerous. 1978. 20.00 (ISBN 0-916750-76-0, CX-4). Dayton Labs.
Hartley, Robert M. An Historical Scientific & Practical Essay on Milk, As an Article of Human Sustenance: Consideration of the Effects Consequent Upon the Unnatural Methods of Producing It for the Supply of Large Cities. Rosenkrantz, Barbara G., ed. LC 76-40629. (Public Health in America Ser.). (Illus.). 1977. Repr. of 1842 ed. lib. bdg. 20.00x (ISBN 0-405-09822-7). Arno.
Henderson, J. Lloyd. Fluid Milk Industry. 3rd ed. LC 75-137709. Orig. Title: The Market Milk Industry. (Illus.). 1971. 45.00 (ISBN 0-87055-090-X). AVI.
Judkins, Henry F. & Keener, H. A. Milk Production & Processing. LC 60-10317. 452p. 1960. 23.95 (ISBN 0-471-45276-9). Wiley.
Kon, S. K. Milk & Milk Products in Human Nutrition. 2nd ed. (Fao Nutritional Studies: No. 27). 80p. (Orig.). 1973. pap. 6.25 (ISBN 0-685-39007-1, F 277, FAO). Unipub.
Kon, S. K. & Cowie, Alfred T., eds. Milk: The Mammary Gland & Its Secretion, 2 Vols. (Illus.). 1961. Vol. 1. 56.00 (ISBN 0-12-418701-3); Vol. 2. 56.00 (ISBN 0-12-418702-1); Set. 92.00 (ISBN 0-685-05135-8). Acad Pr.
Larson, Bruce L. & Smith, Vearl R., eds. Lactation: A Comprehensive Treatise. Incl. Vol. 1, 1974. Development, Lactogenesis. 63.50 (ISBN 0-12-436701-1); subscription 63.50 (ISBN 0-686-77185-0); Vol. 2. 1974. 48.75, by subscription 41.75 (ISBN 0-12-436702-X); Vol. 3. Milk, Nutrution & Maintenance. 1974. 56.00, by subscription 56.00 (ISBN 0-12-436703-8); Vol. 4. 1978. 66.50, by subscription 66.50 (ISBN 0-12-436704-6). Acad Pr.
Lolli, Giorgio, et al. Alcohol in Italian Culture: Food & Wine in Relation to Sobriety Among Italians & Italian Americans. LC 58-9167. (Rutgers Center of Alcohol Studies: Monograph No. 3). 1958. 7.50x (ISBN 0-911290-27-3). Rutgers Ctr Alcohol.
--Alcohol in Italian Culture. 1958. 6.00x (ISBN 0-8084-0411-3). Coll & U Pr.
Lyon, Ninette & Benton, Peggie. Eggs, Milk & Cheese. 288p. 1971. 12.50x (ISBN 0-571-08302-1). Intl Pubns Serv.
McKenzie, Hugh A., ed. Milk Proteins, Vols. 1-2. 1971. Vol. 1. 71.00 (ISBN 0-12-485201-7); Vol. 2. 72.00 (ISBN 0-12-485202-5); Set. 116.00 (ISBN 0-686-76835-3). Acad Pr.
Milk & Milk Products. (Terminology Bulletin: No. 31). 95p. 1980. pap. 7.50 (ISBN 92-5-000758-2, F 1879, FAO). Unipub.
OECD. Milk, Milk Products & Egg Balances in OECD Member Countries, 1973-1978. May 1980. (Illus.). 140p. (Orig., Eng. & Fr.). 1980. pap. 11.50x (ISBN 92-64-02093-4). OECD.
Report of the Eighteenth Session of the Joint FAO-WHO Committee of Government Experts on the Code of Priniples Concerning Milk & Milk Products. (Joint FAO-WMO Food Standards Programme). 1977. pap. 8.75 (ISBN 0-685-80150-0, FAO). Unipub.

MILK-ANALYSIS AND EXAMINATION

see also Milk-Composition

Code of Principles Concerning Milk & Milk Products, International Standards & Standard Methods of Sampling & Analysis for Milk Products. 7th ed. (Codex Alimentarius Commission Reports). 127p. (Orig.). 1974. pap. 4.50 (ISBN 0-685-50042-X, F657, FAO). Unipub.
Westerhuis, J. H. Parturient Hypocalcaemia Prevention in Parurient Cows Prone to Milk Fever by Dietary Measures. new ed. (Agricultural Research Reports). 78p. 1974. pap. 14.00 (ISBN 90-220-0506-2, Pub. by PUDOC). Unipub.

MILK-BACTERIOLOGY

FAO-WHO Joint Expert Committee on Milk Hygiene 1st, Geneva, 1956. Report. (Technical Report Ser: No. 124). 54p. (Eng. & Span.). 1957. pap. 1.20 (ISBN 92-4-120124-X). World Health.
Long Ashton Symposium - Fourth, University of Bristol, September, 1974. Lactic Acid Bacteria in Beverages & Food: Proceedings. Carr, J. G., et al, eds. 1975. 68.50 (ISBN 0-12-160650-3). Acad Pr.

MILK-COMPOSITION

see also Milk-Analysis and Examination

Joint FAO-WHO Committee of Governmental Experts on the Code of Principles Concerning Milk & Milk Products. 1979. pap. 8.75 (ISBN 92-5-100131-6, F653, FAO). Unipub.
Mulder, H. & Walstra, P. The Milk Fat Globule. 296p. 1974. 36.00 (ISBN 90-220-0470-8, Pub. by PUDOC). Unipub.
Recommended International Standard for Lactose. 1970. pap. 4.50 (ISBN 0-685-36305-8, F676, FAO). Unipub.

MILK-LAW AND LEGISLATION

see Dairy Laws

MILK-MARKETING

see Milk Trade

MILK-PASTEURIZATION

Education & Training Comm. Oregon Association of Milk, Food & Environment Sanitarians, Inc. HTST Pasteurizer Operation Manual. (Illus.). 4.75x (ISBN 0-88246-057-9). Oreg St U Bkstrs.
Straus, Lina G. Disease in Milk: the Remedy Pasteurization: The Life Work of Nathan Straus. Rosenkrantz, Barbara G., ed. LC 76-40650. (Public Health in America Ser.). (Illus.). 1977. Repr. of 1917 ed. lib. bdg. 23.00x (ISBN 0-405-09833-2). Arno.

MILK-TESTING

see Milk-Analysis and Examination

MILK, DRIED

Hall, Carl W. & Hedrick, T. I. Drying of Milk & Milk Products. 2nd ed. (Illus.). 1971. text ed. 29.50 (ISBN 0-87055-107-8). AVI.
Jones, Robert E. Industry Builder: The Biography of Chester Earl Gray. (Illus.). 1948. 12.95 (ISBN 0-87015-007-3). Pacific Bks.

MILK, HUMAN

see also Breast Feeding; Infants-Nutrition

Ogra, P. L. & Dayton, Delbert H., eds. The Immunology of Breast Milk. LC 79-64434. 300p. 1979. 30.00 (ISBN 0-89004-387-6). Raven.
Symposium, Campione, Sept 1973. Milk & Lactation: Proceedings. Kretchmer, N., et al, eds. (Modern Problems in Paediatrics: Vol. 15). (Illus.). 250p. 1975. 58.75 (ISBN 3-8055-2056-5). S Karger.

MILK, PASTEURIZED

see Milk-Pasteurization

MILK FEVER IN ANIMALS

Anderson, J. J., ed. Parturient Hypocalcemia. 1970. 44.50 (ISBN 0-12-058350-X). Acad Pr.

MILK GLASS

see Glassware

MILK HYGIENE-LAW AND LEGISLATION

see Dairy Laws

MILK PLANTS

FAO-WHO Joint Expert Committee on Milk Hygiene 1st, Geneva, 1956. Report. (Technical Report Ser: No. 124). 54p. (Eng. & Span.). 1957. pap. 1.20 (ISBN 92-4-120124-X). World Health.
Hall, Carl W. & Hedrick, T. I. Drying of Milk & Milk Products. 2nd ed. (Illus.). 1971. text ed. 29.50 (ISBN 0-87055-107-8). AVI.
Standardized Pilot Milk Plants. (FAO Animal Production & Health Ser: No. 3). (Illus.). 1977. pap. 11.50 (ISBN 92-5-100089-1, F440, FAO). Unipub.

MILK PRODUCTS

see Dairy Products

MILK SUBSTITUTES

see Food Substitutes

MILK TRADE

Casalis, Jacques. Dictionnaire Laitier: Francais, Allemand, Anglais. (Fr., Ger. & Eng.). 1963. 49.95 (ISBN 0-686-56941-5, M-6063). French & Eur.
Cassels, John M. A Study of Fluid Milk Prices. LC 75-39237. (Getting & Spending: the Consumer's Dilemma). (Illus.). 1976. Repr. of 1937 ed. 19.00x (ISBN 0-405-08014-X). Arno.
Castle, Malcolm & Watkins, Paul. Modern Milk Production. (Illus.). 320p. 1979. 22.95 (ISBN 0-571-11312-5, Pub. by Faber & Faber); pap. 13.50 (ISBN 0-571-11347-8). Merrimack Bk Serv.
MacAvoy, Paul W., ed. Federal Milk Marketing Orders & Price Supports. (Ford Administration Papers). 1977. pap. 6.25 (ISBN 0-8447-3276-1). Am Enterprise.
Milk, Milk Products & Egg Balances in OECD Member Countries, 1964-1977. (Document Ser.). 250p. 1979. 16.50x (ISBN 92-64-01952-9). OECD.
Packaging, Storage & Distribution of Processed Milk. 1978. pap. 7.50 (ISBN 92-5-100566-4, F1461, FAO). Unipub.
Payment for Milk on Quality. (FAO Agricultural Studies: No. 89). 82p. (Orig.). 1973. pap. 6.00 (ISBN 0-685-39006-3, F308, FAO). Unipub.
Seehafer, M. E. Development & Manufacture of Sterilized Milk Concentrate. 1967. pap. 4.75 (ISBN 0-685-36289-2, F115, FAO). Unipub.
Spencer, Leland & Blanford, Charles. An Economic History of Milk Marketing & Pricing: Source & Reference Materials, Vol. 3. 1125p. (Orig.). 1977. pap. 38.00 (ISBN 0-686-74029-7). Grid Pub.
Spencer, Leland & Blanford, Charles J. An Economic History of Milk Marketing, Vol. I. LC 77-90779. 1977. text ed. 38.00 (ISBN 0-88244-157-4). Grid Pub.
--An Economic History of Milk Marketing, Vol. IV. LC 77-90779. 1981. text ed. 30.00 (ISBN 0-88244-116-7). Grid Pub.
--An Economic History of Milk Marketing: A Bibliography. LC 77-90779. 1973. pap. text ed. 38.00 (ISBN 0-88244-028-4). Grid Pub.
Whetstone, Linda. Marketing of Milk. (Institute of Economic Affairs, Research Monographs: No. 21). pap. 3.50 with supplement (ISBN 0-255-27606-0); supplement avail. (ISBN 0-255-36071-1). Transatlantic.

MILK TRADE-LAW AND LEGISLATION

see Dairy Laws

MILKWEED

Graham, Ada & Graham, Frank, Jr. The Milkweed & Its World of Animals. LC 74-18801. 96p. (gr. 3-5). 1976. 5.95 (ISBN 0-385-09933-9). Doubleday.

MILKY WAY

Alter, G. & Ruprecht, J. System of Open Star Clusters & Galaxy Atlas of Open Star Clusters. 1963. 42.00 (ISBN 0-12-054250-1). Acad Pr.
Blaauw, Adriaan & Schmidt, Maarten, eds. Galactic Structure. LC 64-23428. (Stars & Stellar Systems Ser: Vol. 5). (Illus.). 1965. 35.00x (ISBN 0-226-45957-8). U of Chicago Pr.
Bok, Bart J. & Bok, Priscilla F. The Milky Way. 5th ed. LC 80-22544. (Harvard Books on Astronomy Ser.). (Illus.). 384p. 1981. text ed. 20.00 (ISBN 0-674-57503-2). Harvard U Pr.
Branley, Franklyn M. Book of the Milky Way Galaxy for You. LC 65-16183. (Illus.). (gr. 3-6). 1965. PLB 9.89 (ISBN 0-690-15367-8, TYC-J). Har-Row.
Burton, W. B. The Large Scale Characteristics of the Galaxy. (International Astronomical Union: No. 84). 1979. lib. bdg. 73.50 (ISBN 90-277-1029-5, Pub. by Reidel Holland); pap. 37.00 (ISBN 90-277-1030-9, Pub. by Reidel Holland). Kluwer Boston.
IAU Symposium, 38th, Basel, Switzerland, 1969. The Spiral Tructure of Our Galaxy: Proceedings. Becker, W. & Contopoulos, G., eds. LC 75-115886. (IAU Symposia). 478p. 1970. lib. bdg. 45.00 (ISBN 90-277-0109-1, Pub. by Reidel Holland). Kluwer Boston.
NATO Advanced Study Institution, Athens, Greece, September 8-19, 1969. Structure & Evolution of the Galaxy: Proceedings. Mavaridis, L. N., ed. LC 77-135107. (Astrophysics & Space Science Library: No.22). 312p. 1971. lib. bdg. 42.00 (ISBN 90-277-0177-6, Pub. by Reidel Holland). Kluwer Boston.

MILL, HARRIET (HARDY) TAYLOR

Pappe, H. O. John Stuart Mill & the Harriet Taylor Myth. 1960. 14.00x (ISBN 0-522-83693-3, Pub. by Melbourne U Pr). Intl Schol Bk Serv.

MILL, JAMES, 1773-1836

Bain, Alexander. James Mill: A Biography. LC 66-19689. Repr. of 1882 ed. 19.50x (ISBN 0-678-00214-2). Kelley.
Burston, W. H. James Mill on Philosophy & Education. 256p. 1973. text ed. 27.50x (ISBN 0-485-11138-1, Athlone Pr). Humanities.
Cumming, Ian. James Mill on Education. 1959. 17.50 (ISBN 0-932062-37-7). Sharon Hill.
--James Mills on Education. 1978. Repr. of 1959 ed. lib. bdg. 10.00 (ISBN 0-8492-3962-1). R West.
Mazlish, Bruce. James & John Stuart Mill. LC 74-79278. 1975. text ed. 18.00x (ISBN 0-465-03630-9). Basic.
Mill, James. Utilitarian Logic & Politics: James Mill's 'Essay on Government', Macaulay's 'Critique' & the Ensueing Debate. Lively, Jack & Rees, John, eds. 1978. text ed. 29.50x (ISBN 0-19-827198-0). Oxford U Pr.
Mill, James & Mill, John S. James & John Stuart Mill on Education. Cavenagh, F. A., ed. LC 78-27822. 1979. Repr. of 1931 ed. lib. bdg. 16.00x (ISBN 0-8371-4282-2, MIOE). Greenwood.
Stephen, Leslie. English Utilitarians, 3 Vols. LC 67-29517. Repr. of 1900 ed. 50.00x (ISBN 0-678-00353-X). Kelley.
--The English Utilitarians: Jeremy Bentham, James Mill, John Stuart Mill, 3 vols. in 1. 20.00 (ISBN 0-8446-1422-X). Peter Smith.
Thompson, William. Appeal of One Half the Human Race, Women, Against the Pretensions of the Other Half, Men, to Retain Them in Political, & Thence in Civil & Domestic, Slavery. LC 71-164450. (Research & Source Works Ser: No. 567). 1970. Repr. of 1825 ed. lib. bdg. 14.50 (ISBN 0-8337-3515-2). B Franklin.
--Appeal of One Half the Human Race, Women, Against the Pretensions of the Other Half, Men. (Source Library of Women's Movement). 1970. Repr. of 1825 ed. lib. bdg. 12.00 (ISBN 0-442-81060-1). Hacker.

MILL, JOHN STUART, 1806-1873

Alexander, Edward. Matthew Arnold & John Stuart Mill. LC 65-14321. 313p. 1965. 16.00x (ISBN 0-231-02786-9). Columbia U Pr.
Alexander, Patrick P. Mill & Carlyle. 1866. lib. bdg. 10.00 (ISBN 0-8414-2968-5). Folcroft.
Bain, Alexander. John Stuart Mill: A Criticism with Personal Recollections. LC 69-16521. Repr. of 1882 ed. 9.50x (ISBN 0-678-00468-4). Kelley.
--John Stuart Mill: A Criticism with Personal Recollections. 1973. Repr. of 1882 ed. 9.95 (ISBN 0-8274-1796-9). R West.
Capaldi, Nicholas. Monarch Notes on Mill, Bentham & the Utilitarian School. (Orig.). pap. 1.95 (ISBN 0-671-00532-4). Monarch Pr.
Douglas, Charles. John Stuart Mill: A Study of His Philosophy. LC 73-11056. Repr. of 1895 ed. lib. bdg. 20.00 (ISBN 0-8414-1885-3). Folcroft.
Duncan, G. Marx & Mill: Two Views of Social Conflict & Social Harmony. 416p. 1973. 32.50 (ISBN 0-521-20257-4); pap. 9.95x (ISBN 0-521-29130-5). Cambridge U Pr.
Eisenach, Eldon J. Two Worlds of Liberalism: Religion & Politics in Hobbes, Locke, & Mill. LC 80-27255. (Chicago Original Paperback Ser.). 272p. 1981. lib. bdg. 20.00x (ISBN 0-226-19533-3). U of Chicago Pr.
Ellery, John B. John Stuart Mill. (English Authors Ser.: No. 5). 1964. lib. bdg. 10.95 (ISBN 0-8057-1392-1). Twayne.
Garforth, Francis W. Educative Democracy: John Stuart Mill on Education in Society. 268p. text ed. 27.50x (ISBN 0-19-713438-6). Oxford U Pr.
Garforth, Francis W., ed. John Stuart Mill on Education. LC 75-115230. 1971. text ed. 10.50 (ISBN 0-8077-1403-8); pap. 4.50x (ISBN 0-8077-1402-X). Tchrs Coll.
Halliday, R. J. John Stuart Mill. (Political Thinkers Ser.). 1976. text ed. 25.00x (ISBN 0-04-320113-X). Allen Unwin.
Harrison, Frederic. On Society. 1979. Repr. of 1918 ed. lib. bdg. 20.00 (ISBN 0-8482-4481-8). Norwood Edns.
--On Society. facs. ed. LC 70-142640. (Essay Index Reprint Ser). 1918. 19.50 (ISBN 0-8369-2052-X). Arno.
Hawley, Frederick B. Capital & Population. LC 68-30525. Repr. of 1882 ed. 13.50x (ISBN 0-678-00904-X). Kelley.
Hayek, F. A. John Stuart Mill & Harriet Taylor: Their Correspondence & Subsequent Marriage. 1979. Repr. of 1951 ed. lib. bdg. 40.00 (ISBN 0-8492-5349-7). R West.
Himmelfarb, Gertrude. On Liberty & Liberalism: The Case of John Stuart Mill. 1974. 8.95 (ISBN 0-394-49028-2). Knopf.
--On Liberty & Liberalism: The Case of John Stuart Mill. 1974. 8.95 (ISBN 0-394-49028-2). Knopf.
Laine, Michael. Bibliography of Works on John Stuart Mill. 176p. 1982. 25.00x (ISBN 0-8020-2414-9). U of Toronto Pr.
MacCunn, John. Six Radical Thinkers: Bentham, J. S. Mill, Cobden, Carlyle, Mazzini, T. H. Green. LC 64-20669. 1964. Repr. of 1910 ed. 7.50 (ISBN 0-8462-0502-5). Russell.
Mazlish, Bruce. James & John Stuart Mill. LC 74-79278. 1975. text ed. 18.00x (ISBN 0-465-03630-9). Basic.
Mill, James & Mill, John S. James & John Stuart Mill on Education. Cavenagh, F. A., ed. LC 78-27822. 1979. Repr. of 1931 ed. lib. bdg. 16.00x (ISBN 0-8371-4282-2, MIOE). Greenwood.
Mill, John S. Autobiography of John Stuart Mill. LC 24-27691. 240p. 1924. pap. 6.00x (ISBN 0-231-08506-0, 6). Columbia U Pr.
--Autobiography of John Stuart Mill. Stillinger, Jack, ed. 1964. pap. 3.50 (ISBN 0-395-05120-7, B22, RivEd, 3-47656). HM.
--Bibliography of the Writings of John Stuart Mill. LC 79-128997. (Northwestern University. Humanities Ser.: No. 12). Repr. of 1945 ed. 15.00 (ISBN 0-404-50712-3). AMS Pr.
Morlan, George K. America's Heritage from John Stuart Mill. LC 72-987. Repr. of 1936 ed. 17.45 (ISBN 0-404-04436-0). AMS Pr.
Morley, John. Nineteenth Century Essays. Stansky, Peter, ed. LC 73-116380. (Classics of British Historical Literature Ser). 1970. 12.00x (ISBN 0-226-53847-8). U of Chicago Pr.
Mueller, Iris W. John Stuart Mill & French Thought. facs. ed. LC 68-58805. (Essay Index Reprint Ser). 1956. 16.00 (ISBN 0-8369-0089-8). Arno.
Neff, Emery. Carlyle & Mill. 1964. lib. bdg. 20.00x (ISBN 0-374-96042-9). Octagon.
Pappe, H. O. John Stuart Mill & the Harriet Taylor Myth. 1960. 14.00x (ISBN 0-522-83693-3, Pub. by Melbourne U Pr). Intl Schol Bk Serv.

Plamenatz, John. Mill's Utilitarianism, Reprinted with a Study of "The English Utilitarians". 228p. 1981. Repr. of 1949 ed. lib. bdg. 35.00 (ISBN 0-8495-4398-3). Arden Lib.

Rickaby, Joseph J. Free Will & Four English Philosophers. facs. ed. LC 74-84333. (Essay Index Reprint Ser). 1906. 15.50 (ISBN 0-8369-1103-2). Arno.

Ritchie, David G. Principles of State Interference. facsimile ed. LC 70-94282. (Select Bibliogrpahies Reprint Ser). 1902. 17.00 (ISBN 0-8369-5060-7). Arno.

Robson, John M. Improvement of Mankind: The Social & Political Thought of John Stuart Mill. LC 68-140051. 1968. 17.50x (ISBN 0-8020-1529-8). U of Toronto Pr.

Robson, John M. & Laine, Michael, eds. James & John Stuart Mill: Papers of the Centenary Conference. LC 76-16117. 1976. 20.00x (ISBN 0-8020-5338-6). U of Toronto Pr.

Ryan, Alan. John Stuart Mill. (Orig.). 1969. pap. text ed. 3.95 (ISBN 0-685-19693-3). Phila Bk Co.

Schwartz, Pedro. The New Political Economy of J. S. Mill. LC 72-88518. 331p. 1973. 14.75 (ISBN 0-686-66809-X). Duke.

Smith, Henry. John Stuart Mill's Other Island. (Institute of Economic Affairs, Research Monographs: No. 6). pap. 2.50 (ISBN 0-685-27184-6). Transatlantic.

Spencer, Herbert, et al. John Stuart Mill: His Life & Works. LC 76-8395. 1976. Repr. of 1873 ed. lib. bdg. 15.00 (ISBN 0-8414-7845-7). Folcroft.

Stephen, Leslie. English Utilitarians, 3 Vols. LC 67-29517. Repr. of 1900 ed. 50.00x (ISBN 0-678-00353-X). Kelley.

--The English Utilitarians: Jeremy Bentham, James Mill, John Stuart Mill, 3 vols. in 1. 20.00 (ISBN 0-8446-1422-X). Peter Smith.

MILLAIS, GOLIN EVERETT, SIR, 1829-1896

Millais, Goeffroy. Sir John Everett Millais. LC 79-64343. (Illus.). 1979. pap. 9.95 (ISBN 0-8478-0231-0). Rizzoli Intl.

Spielmann, Marion H. Millais & His Works. LC 74-148306. Repr. of 1898 ed. 17.50 (ISBN 0-404-06175-3). AMS Pr.

MILLAR, JOHN, 1735-1801

Lehmann, William C. John Millar of Glascow: 1735-1801. Mayer, J. P., ed. LC 78-67364. (European Political Thought Ser.). 1979. Repr. of 1960 ed. lib. bdg. 28.00x (ISBN 0-405-11712-4). Arno.

MILLAR, KENNETH, 1915--BIBLIOGRAPHY

Bruccoli, Matthew J., ed. Kenneth Millar-Ross Macdonald: A Checklist. LC 77-39690. (Modern Authors Checklist Ser.). (Illus.). 86p. 1971. 16.00 (ISBN 0-8103-0901-7, Bruccoli Clark Book). Gale.

Bruccoli, Matthew J. & Millar, Kenneth. Kenneth Millar - Ross Macdonald: A Checklist. (Illus.). 16.00 (ISBN 0-685-77422-8). Bruccoli.

MILLAY, EDNA ST. VINCENT, 1892-1950

Brittin, Norman A. Edna St. Vincent Millay. (Twayne's United States Authors Ser). 1967. pap. 3.45 (ISBN 0-8084-0114-9, T116, Twayne). Coll & U Pr.

--Edna St. Vincent Millay. (U. S. Authors Ser.: No. 116). 1967. lib. bdg. 9.95 (ISBN 0-8057-0496-5). Twayne.

Cheney, Anne. Millay in Greenwich Village. LC 74-23424. (Illus.). 171p. 1975. 11.95x (ISBN 0-8173-7161-3). U of Ala Pr.

Gould, Jean. Poet & Her Book: The Life & Work of Edna St. Vincent Millay. LC 69-17603. (Illus.). 1969. 6.50 (ISBN 0-396-05907-4). Dodd.

Gray, James. Edna St. Vincent Millay. (Pamphlets on American Writers Ser: No. 64). (Orig.). 1967. pap. 1.25x (ISBN 0-8166-0437-1, MPAW64). U of Minn Pr.

Nierman, Judith, ed. Edna St. Vincent Millay: A Reference Guide. (Reference Publications Ser.). 1977. lib. bdg. 16.00 (ISBN 0-8161-7950-6). G K Hall.

MILLCAYAC LANGUAGE

Schuller, R. R. Discovery of a Fragment of the Printed Copy of the Work on the Millcayac Language of Chile. (Harvard University Peabody Museum of Archaeology & Ethnology Papers). Repr. of 1913 ed. pap. 3.00 (ISBN 0-527-01196-7). Kraus Repr.

MILLEDGEVILLE, GEORGIA

Bonner, James C. Milledgeville: Georgia's Antebellum Capital. LC 76-28923. 336p. 1978. 15.95 (ISBN 0-8203-0424-7). U of Ga Pr.

MILLENNIUM

see also Dispensationalism; Second Advent

Barkun, Michael. Disaster & the Millennium. LC 73-86884. 272p. 1974. 20.00x (ISBN 0-300-01725-1). Yale U Pr.

Boettner, Loraine. Millennium. 5.95 (ISBN 0-8010-0682-1). Baker Bk.

--Millennium. 5.95 (ISBN 0-87552-128-2). Presby & Reformed.

Burridge, Kenelm. New Heaven, New Earth: A Study of Millenarian Activities. (Pavilion Ser.). 191p. 1980. pap. 9.95x (ISBN 0-631-11950-7, Pub. by Basil Blackwell). Biblio Dist.

Clouse, Robert G. The Meaning of the Millennium. 212p. 1978. pap. 4.25 (ISBN 0-88469-099-7). BMH Bks.

Clouse, Robert G., ed. The Meaning of the Millennium: Four Views. 1977. pap. 4.95 (ISBN 0-87784-794-0). Inter-Varsity.

Davidson, James W. The Logic of Millennial Thought: Eighteenth-Century New England. LC 75-43315. (Yale Historical Publications Miscellany Ser.: No. 112). 1977. 25.00x (ISBN 0-300-01947-5). Yale U Pr.

Erickson, Millard J. Contemporary Options in Eschatology: A Study of the Millennium. LC 77-89406. 1977. 7.95 (ISBN 0-8010-3262-8). Baker Bk.

Feinberg, Charles L. Millenialism: The Two Major Views. 1980. 12.95 (ISBN 0-8024-6815-2). Moody.

Garrett, Clarke. Respectable Folly: Millenarians and the French Revolution in France and England. LC 74-24378. 252p. 1975. 16.00x (ISBN 0-8018-1618-1). Johns Hopkins.

Gilpin, W. Clark. The Millenarian Piety of Roger Williams. LC 78-20786. 1979. lib. bdg. 17.00x (ISBN 0-226-29397-1). U of Chicago Pr.

Harrison, John F. The Second Coming: Popular Millenarianism 1780-1850. 1979. 21.00 (ISBN 0-8135-0879-7). Rutgers U Pr.

Hopkins, Samuel. A Treatise on the Millennium. LC 70-38450. (Religion in America, Ser. 2). 162p. 1972. Repr. of 1793 ed. 10.00 (ISBN 0-405-04070-9). Arno.

Ladd, George E. Crucial Questions About the Kingdom of God. 1952. pap. 2.95 (ISBN 0-685-09270-4). Eerdmans.

Lindsay, Gordon. The Millennium. (Revelation Ser.). 1.25 (ISBN 0-89985-048-0). Christ Nations.

Murray, George L. Millennial Studies. 1975. pap. 2.95 (ISBN 0-8010-5899-6). Baker Bk.

Oliver, W. H. Prophets & Millennialists: The Uses of Biblical Prophecy in England from the 1790s to the 1840s. 1979. 17.95x (ISBN 0-19-647962-2). Oxford U Pr.

Ryrie, Charles C. Basis of the Premillennial Faith. 1954. pap. 3.95 (ISBN 0-87213-741-4). Loizeaux.

Schwartz, Hillel. Knaves, Fools, Madmen & That Subtile Effluvium: A Study of the Opposition to the French Prophets in England, 1706-1710. LC 78-1692. (U of Fla. Social Science Monographs: No. 62). 1978. pap. 5.50 (ISBN 0-8130-0505-1). U Presses Fla.

Seyer, Herman D. Millenialism. 68p. 1979. pap. 1.50 (ISBN 0-686-70690-0). H D Seyer.

Thomas, L. R. Does the Bible Teach Millennialism. pap. 2.25 (ISBN 0-685-36796-7). Reiner.

Walvoord, John F. Millennial Kingdom. 1959. 10.95 (ISBN 0-310-34090-X). Zondervan.

Weber, Timothy P. Living in the Shadow of the Second Coming: American Premillennialism 1875-1925. 1979. 15.95 (ISBN 0-19-502494-X). Oxford U Pr.

Weinstein, Donald. Savonarola & Florence: Prophecy & Patriotism in the Renaissance. LC 76-113013. 1971. 21.00x (ISBN 0-691-05184-4). Princeton U Pr.

MILLEPEDS

Williams, Stephen R. & Hefner, Robert A. Millipedes & Centipedes of Ohio. 1928. 1.00 (ISBN 0-686-30292-3). Ohio Bio Survey.

MILLER, ARTHUR, 1915-

Calandra, Denis M. Crucible Notes. (Orig.). 1968. pap. 1.95 (ISBN 0-8220-0337-6). Cliffs.

Corrigan, R., ed. Arthur Miller: A Collection of Critical Essays. 1969. 10.95 (ISBN 0-13-582973-9, Spec). P-H.

Ferres, John, ed. Twentieth Century Interpretations of The Crucible. 128p. 1972. 8.95 (ISBN 0-13-194860-1, Spec). P-H.

Hayman, Ronald. Arthur Miller. LC 75-153122. (World Dramatists Ser.). (Illus.). 10.95 (ISBN 0-8044-2374-1). Ungar.

Martin, Robert A., ed. Arthur Miller: A Collection of Critical Essays, Vol. II. 224p. 1981. 12.95 (ISBN 0-13-048801-1); pap. 4.95 (ISBN 0-13-048793-7). P-H.

Martine, James J. Critical Essays on Arthur Miller. (Critical Essays on American Literature Ser.). 1979. lib. bdg. 25.00 (ISBN 0-8161-8258-2). G K Hall.

Moss, Leonard. Arthur Miller. rev. ed. (United States Author Ser.: No. 115). (gr. 10-12). 1980. lib. bdg. 8.95 (ISBN 0-8057-7311-8). Twayne.

--Arthur Miller. (Twayne's United States Authors Ser). 1967. pap. 3.45 (ISBN 0-8084-0056-8, T115, Twayne). Coll & U Pr.

Nourse, Joan T. Monarch Notes on Miller's Crucible & View from the Bridge. (Orig.). pap. 2.25 (ISBN 0-671-00687-8). Monarch Pr.

--Monarch Notes on Miller's Death of a Salesman. (Orig.). pap. 1.95 (ISBN 0-671-00688-6). Monarch Pr.

Roberts, James L. Death of a Salesman Notes. (Orig.). pap. 1.95 (ISBN 0-8220-0382-1). Cliffs.

MILLER, ARTHUR, 1915--BIBLIOGRAPHY

Ferres, John H. Arthur Miller: A Reference Guide. (Reference Bks.). 1979. lib. bdg. 26.50 (ISBN 0-8161-7822-4). G K Hall.

Hayashi, Tetsumaro. An Index to Arthur Miller Criticism. 2nd ed. LC 76-10893. (Author Bibliographies Ser.: No. 3). 165p. 1976. 10.00 (ISBN 0-8108-0947-8). Scarecrow.

MILLER, BERTHA MAHONY

Ross, Eulalie S. A Spirited Life: Bertha Mahoney Miller & Children's Books. LC 73-84132. (Illus.). 274p. 1973. 12.00 (ISBN 0-87675-057-9). Horn Bk.

MILLER, GLENN, 1909-1944?

Simon, George T. Glenn Miller & His Orchestra. (Illus.). xiii, 473p. 1980. pap. 8.95 (ISBN 0-306-80129-9). Da Capo.

MILLER, HENRY, 1827-1916

Martin, Jay. Always Merry & Bright: The Life of Henry Miller. 1980. pap. 10.95 (ISBN 0-14-005548-7). Penguin.

Perkins, Dorothy. The Passionate Wisdom of Henry Miller: The Religious Dimension of His Life & Art. (Orig.). 1980. pap. 3.00 (ISBN 0-9604742-1-8). D J Perkins.

MILLER, HENRY, 1891-1980

Gertz, Elmer & Lewis, Felice F., eds. Henry Miller: Years of Trial & Triumph, 1962-1964: The Correspondence of Henry Miller & Elmer Gertz. LC 78-3547. (Illus.). 361p. 1978. 17.50 (ISBN 0-8093-0860-6). S Ill U Pr.

Gordon, William A. Mind & Art of Henry Miller. LC 67-12215. 1967. 17.50 (ISBN 0-8071-0512-0); pap. 6.95 (ISBN 0-8071-0142-7). La State U Pr.

Hassan, Ihab. Literature of Silence: Henry Miller & Samuel Beckett. 1967. pap. text ed. 3.95x (ISBN 0-685-39884-6). Phila Bk Co.

Martin, Jay. Always Merry & Bright: The Life of Henry Miller. (Illus.). 1978. 15.00 (ISBN 0-88496-082-X). Capra Pr.

Mathieu, Bertrand. Orpheus in Brooklyn: Orphism, Rimbaud, & Henry Miller. (Studies in American Literature: No. 31). 1976. 28.75x (ISBN 90-2793-036-8). Mouton.

Meserve, Walter. Studies in Death of a Salesman. LC 79-171570. 1972. pap. text ed. 2.95x (ISBN 0-675-09259-0). Merrill.

Miller, Henry. Book of Friends: A Tribute to Friends of Long Ago. (Illus.). 144p. 1976. 7.95 (ISBN 0-88496-050-1); pap. 3.95 (ISBN 0-88496-051-X). Capra Pr.

--Henry Miller, 3 vols. boxed set. Incl. Tropic of Cancer; Tropic of Capricorn; Black Spring. 1979. pap. 7.40 (ISBN 0-394-17094-6, B430, BC). Grove.

--Letters to Anais Nin. 14.95x (ISBN 0-8464-0563-6). Beekman Pubs.

Mitchell, Edward, ed. Henry Miller: Three Decades of Criticism. LC 78-181513. 216p. 1971. 10.00x (ISBN 0-8147-5356-6); pap. 3.95x (ISBN 0-8147-5357-4). NYU Pr.

Moore, Nicholas. Henry Miller. LC 77-8486. 1943. lib. bdg. 6.50 (ISBN 0-8414-6203-8). Folcroft.

Nelson, Jane A. Form & Image in the Fiction of Henry Miller. LC 69-10515. 1970. 11.95x (ISBN 0-8143-1400-7). Wayne St U Pr.

Renken, Maxine. Bibliography of Henry Miller. LC 72-4735. (American Literature Ser., No. 49). 1972. Repr. of 1962 ed. lib. bdg. 49.95 (ISBN 0-8383-1592-5). Haskell.

Shifreen, Lawrence J. Henry Miller: A Bibliography of Secondary Sources. LC 78-12518. (Scarecrow Author Bibliographies: No. 38). 1979. lib. bdg. 22.50 (ISBN 0-8108-1171-5). Scarecrow.

Thiebaud, Twinka, ed. Reflections. (Illus.). 128p. (Orig.). 1981. pap. 6.95 (ISBN 0-88496-166-4). Capra Pr.

Treadwell, Edward F. The Cattle King. LC 81-50165. (Illus.). xii, 375p. 1981. pap. 7.95 (ISBN 0-934136-10-6). Western Tanager.

Wickes, George. Henry Miller. (Pamphlets on American Writers Ser: No. 56). (Orig.). 1966. pap. 1.25x (ISBN 0-8166-0386-3, MPAW56). U of Minn Pr.

Wickes, George, ed. Henry Miller & the Critics. LC 63-14289. (Crosscurrents-Modern Critiques Ser.). 212p. 1963. 12.95 (ISBN 0-8093-0102-4). S Ill U Pr.

Widmer, Kingsley. Henry Miller. (Twayne's United States Authors Ser). 1963. pap. 3.45 (ISBN 0-8084-0153-X, T44, Twayne). Coll & U Pr.

--Henry Miller. (U. S. Authors Ser.: No. 44). 1963. lib. bdg. 10.95 (ISBN 0-8057-0504-X). Twayne.

MILLER, HUGH, 1802-1856

Brown, Thomas N. Life & Times of Hugh Miller. (Folklore Ser.). Repr. 25.00 (ISBN 0-8482-7394-X). Norwood Edns.

Leask, W. Keith. Hugh Miller. 153p. 1980. Repr. lib. bdg. 25.00 (ISBN 0-89987-501-7). Darby Bks.

Rosie, George. Hugh Miller: Outrage & Order. 240p. 1981. 50.00x (ISBN 0-906391-17-2, Pub. by Mainstream). State Mutual Bk.

MILLER, JOAQUIN, 1839-1913

Frost, Oscott W. Joaquin Miller. (Twayne's United States Authors Ser). 1967. pap. 3.45 (ISBN 0-8084-0177-7, T119, Twayne). Coll & U Pr.

Lawson, Benjamin S. Joaquin Miller, No. 43. LC 80-69014. (Western Writers Ser.). (Illus.). 52p. (Orig.). 1980. pap. 2.00 (ISBN 0-88430-067-6). Boise St Univ.

Longtin, Ray C. Three Far Western Writers: A Reference Guide. (Reference Bks.). 1980. lib. bdg. 32.50 (ISBN 0-8161-7832-1). G K Hall.

MILLER, ORIE O.

Erb, Paul. Orie O. Miller: The Story of a Man & an Era. LC 75-76624. 1969. 7.95 (ISBN 0-8361-1613-5). Herald Pr.

MILLER, SAMUEL FREEMAN, 1816-1890

Fairman, Charles. Mr. Justice Miller & the Supreme Court, 1862-1890. LC 66-24688. (Illus.). 1966. Repr. of 1939 ed. 12.50 (ISBN 0-8462-0801-6). Russell.

MILLER, WILLIAM, 1795-1861

Bliss, Sylvester. Memoirs of William Miller. LC 72-134374. Repr. of 1853 ed. 30.00 (ISBN 0-404-08422-2). AMS Pr.

Nichol, Francis D. The Midnight Cry: A Defense of William Miller & the Millerites. LC 72-8249. Repr. of 1944 ed. 36.00 (ISBN 0-404-11003-7). AMS Pr.

White, James. Sketches of the Christian Life & Public Labors of William Miller. LC 70-134376. Repr. of 1875 ed. 27.50 (ISBN 0-404-08424-9). AMS Pr.

MILLER ANALOGIES TEST

Bader, William & Burt, Daniel S. Miller Analogies Test. 4th ed. LC 81-152. 160p. 1981. lib. bdg. 10.00 (ISBN 0-668-04989-8); pap. 5.00 (ISBN 0-668-04990-1). Arco.

Cash, Phyllis. How to Prepare for the Miller Analogies Test (MAT) (McGraw-Hill Paperbacks). (Orig.). 1979. pap. 5.95 (ISBN 0-07-010222-8). McGraw.

Gruber, Edward C. Miller Analogies Test. 1976. pap. 4.95 (ISBN 0-671-18981-6). Monarch Pr.

Rudman, Jack. Miller Analogies Test (MAT) (Admission Test Ser.: ATS-18). 300p. 14.95 (ISBN 0-8373-5118-9); pap. 9.95 (ISBN 0-8373-5018-2). Natl Learning.

Sternberg, Robert J. Barron's How to Prepare for the Miller Analogies Test (MAT) 3rd ed. 1981. pap. text ed. 4.50 (ISBN 0-8120-2325-0). Barron.

--Barron's How to Prepare for the Miller Analogies Test (MAT) LC 77-24683. 1974. pap. 4.50 (ISBN 0-8120-0887-1). Barron.

Turner, David R., ed. Miller Analogies Test: Fourteen Hundred Analogy Questions. 3rd ed. LC 72-50. 1973. lib. bdg. 8.00 (ISBN 0-668-01115-7); pap. 5.00 (ISBN 0-668-01114-9). Arco.

MILLET, JEAN FRANCOIS, 1814-1875

Ady, Julia M. Jean Francois Millet, His Life & Letters. LC 73-155629. Repr. of 1896 ed. 28.50 (ISBN 0-404-00297-8). AMS Pr.

Fermigier, Andre. Millet. LC 7-77034. (Illus.). 1977. 50.00 (ISBN 0-8478-0120-9). Rizzoli Intl.

Langlois, Marc H. The Art & Life of Jean-Francois Millet. (Illus.). 121p. 1980. 39.75 (ISBN 0-930582-76-4). Gloucester Art.

Leveque, Jean-Jacques. Jean Francois Milet. 1977. pap. text ed. 5.95 (ISBN 0-8120-0712-3). Barron.

Pollock, Griselda. Millet. 1981. 27.00x (ISBN 0-905368-12-6, Pub. by Jupiter England). State Mutual Bk.

--Millet. 1977. 15.95 (ISBN 0-8467-0252-5, Pub. by Two Continents); pap. 9.95 (ISBN 0-8467-0251-7). Hippocrene Bks.

Smith, Charles S. Barbizon Days. facs. ed. LC 79-86784. (Essay Index Reprint Ser). 1902. 21.00 (ISBN 0-8369-1194-6). Arno.

MILLET

Hulse, Joseph, et al. Sorghum & the Millets: Their Composition & Nutritive Value. LC 79-40871. 1980. 184.00 (ISBN 0-12-361350-7). Acad Pr.

Improvement & Production of Maize, Sorghum & Millet. (FAO Plant Production & Protection Paper Ser.: Vol. 24, Nos. 1 & 2). 1980. Set. pap. 46.50 (ISBN 0-686-74540-X, F2129, FAO). Vol. 1, General Principles, 216p. Vol. 2, Breeding, Agronomy & Seed Production, 487p. Unipub.

Rachie, Kenneth O. The Millets & Minor Cereals. LC 73-22142. 1974. 10.00 (ISBN 0-8108-0700-9). Scarecrow.

Sorghum & Millet: Food Production & Use. 1979. pap. 5.00 (ISBN 0-88936-199-1, IDRC123, IDRC). Unipub.

MILLIGAN, NEBRASKA

Kutak, Robert I. Story of a Bohemian-American Village: A Study of Social Persistence & Change. LC 70-129406. (American Immigration Collection, Ser. 2). 1970. Repr. of 1933 ed. 9.00 (ISBN 0-405-00559-8). Arno.

MILLIKAN RAYS

see Cosmic Rays

MILLINERY

see also Artificial Flowers; Dress Accessories; Hats

Montagna, Pier. Key to Millinery Design. pap. 2.00 (ISBN 0-686-00704-2). Key Bks.

Tomlinson, Jill. Lady Bee's Bonnets. 32p. 1971. pap. 2.95 (ISBN 0-571-11133-5, Pub. by Faber &Faber). Merrimack Bk Serv.

MILLING (METALLURGY)

see Ore-Dressing

MILLING MACHINERY

Here are entered works on machinery used in the process of grinding, etc.

see also Flour Mills; Mills and Mill-Work

Daniels, Harold R. Press Brake & Shear Handbook. rev. ed. LC 74-13643. 184p. 1974. 19.95 (ISBN 0-8436-0815-3). CBI Pub.

Engineering Industry Training Board, ed. Training for Milling Machine Operators & Setters, 22 vols. (Illus.). 1977. Set. 38.95x (ISBN 0-89563-027-3). Intl Ideas.

Evans, Oliver. The Young Mill-Wright & Miller's Guide. LC 72-5047. (Technology & Society Ser.). (Illus.). 438p. 1972. Repr. of 1850 ed. 24.00 (ISBN 0-405-04699-5). Arno.

Lewis, Gaspar J. Cabinetmaking, Pattermaking, & Millwork. 448p. 1981. 18.95 (ISBN 0-442-24785-0). Van Nos Reinhold.

Lynch, A. J. Mineral Crushing & Grinding Circuits: Their Simulation, Design & Control. (Developments in Mineral Processing). 1977. 63.50 (ISBN 0-444-41528-9). Elsevier.

Plaster, C., et al, eds. Milling, Vol. 1. 2nd ed. (Engineering Craftsmen: No. H4). (Illus.). 1977. spiral bdg. 16.50x (ISBN 0-85083-404-X). Intl Ideas.

Spencer, A. G., ed. Milling, Vol. 2. (Engineering Craftsmen: No. H29). (Illus.). 1969. spiral bdg. 14.95x (ISBN 0-85083-060-5). Intl Ideas.

MILLING TRADE

see Flour and Feed Trade

MILLIONAIRES

see also Capitalists and Financiers; Wealth

Clark, Noel. The Millionaire Sourcebook. 1971. 9.98 (ISBN 0-685-27198-6). Claitors.

Lemann, Nicholas. The Fast Track: Texans & Other Strivers. 1981. 12.95 (ISBN 0-393-01436-3). Norton.

Rich-McCoy, Lois. Millionairess: Self-Made Women in America. LC 78-2142. 1978. 9.95 (ISBN 0-06-012852-6, HarpT). Har-Row.

Steward, Hal D. Money Making Secrets of the Millionaires. 1976. 9.95 (ISBN 0-13-600320-6, Reward); pap. 3.95 (ISBN 0-13-600296-X). P-H.

Thompson, Jacqueline. The Very Rich Book: America's Super-Millionaires & Their Money-Where They Got It, How They Spend It. LC 80-21618. (Illus.). 454p. 1981. 13.95 (ISBN 0-688-00072-X). Morrow.

MILLIPEDES

see Millepeds

MILLS, CHARLES WRIGHT

Aptheker, Herbert. The World of C. Wright Mills. LC 60-50975. 1976. Repr. of 1960 ed. 8.00 (ISBN 0-527-03003-1). Kraus Repr.

Ballard, Hoyt B. & Domhoff, G. William, eds. C. Wright Mills & "The Power Elite". 1968. pap. 4.95x (ISBN 0-8070-4185-8, BP334). Beacon Pr.

Horowitz, Irving L., ed. New Sociology: Essays in Social Science & Social Theory in Honor of C. Wright Mills. 1964. 19.95 (ISBN 0-19-500587-2). Oxford U Pr.

--New Sociology: Essays in Social Science & Social Theory in Honor of C. Wright Mills. (YA) (gr. 9 up). 1965. pap. 6.95 (ISBN 0-19-500722-0, GB). Oxford U Pr.

Howard Press. C. Wright Mills. (World Leaders Ser.). 1978. lib. bdg. 12.50 (ISBN 0-8057-7708-3). Twayne.

Scimecca, Joseph A. The Sociological Theory of C. Wright Mills. (National University Pubns. Series in American Studies). 1976. 11.50 (ISBN 0-8046-9155-X). Kennikat.

MILLS, ROBERT, 1781-1855

Gallagher, Helen M. Robert Mills: Architect of the Washington Monument, 1781-1855. LC 74-168092. Repr. of 1935 ed. 21.00 (ISBN 0-404-02668-0). AMS Pr.

MILLS (BUILDINGS)

see Factories; Flour Mills

MILLS AND MILL-WORK

see also Windmills

Apps, Jerry. Mills of Wisconsin. LC 80-24684. (Illus., Orig.). 1980. pap. 12.50 (ISBN 0-915024-22-5). Tamarack Pr.

Dunwell, Steve. The Run of the Mill. LC 78-57683. (Illus.). 1978. 14.95x (ISBN 0-87923-249-8). Godine.

Ewing, Kristine L. Mill Maintenance I: General Mill Maintenance, Fires & Explosions. LC 78-387. (Bibliographic Ser.: No. 280). 1978. pap. 30.00 (ISBN 0-87010-030-0). Inst Paper Chem.

--Mill Maintenance II: Large Machinery. LC 78-387. (Bibliographic Ser.: No. 281). 1978. pap. 13.00 (ISBN 0-87010-031-9). Inst Paper Chem.

--Mill Maintenance III: Instruments & Small Equipment. LC 78-387. (Bibliographic Ser.: No. 282). 1978. pap. 13.00 (ISBN 0-87010-032-7). Inst Paper Chem.

Hareven, Tamara K. & Langenbach, Randolph. Amoskeag: Life & Work in an American Factory-City. LC 78-52862. (Illus.). 1978. 15.00 (ISBN 0-394-49941-7). Pantheon.

Howell, Charles & Keller, Allan. The Mill at Philipsburg Manor, Upper Mills, & a Brief History of Milling. LC 75-7156. (Illus.). 1977. 15.00 (ISBN 0-912882-22-0). Sleepy Hollow.

McLaurin, Melton. Paternalism & Protest: Southern Mill Workers & Organized Labor, 1875-1905. LC 70-111261. (Contributions in Economics & Economic History, No. 3). 1971. 15.75x (ISBN 0-8371-4662-3). Greenwood.

Miller Freeman Publications, Inc. Pulping Processes: Mill Operations, Techology, & Practices. Smith, Kenneth E., ed. LC 81-81386. (Pulp & Paper Focus Bk). (Illus.). 220p. 1981. pap. 35.00 (ISBN 0-87930-126-0). Miller Freeman.

Rawson, Marion N. Little Old Mills. LC 35-22355. (Rediscovering America Ser). 1970. Repr. of 1935 ed. 19.50 (ISBN 0-384-49710-1). Johnson Repr.

Rudman, Jack. Cabinetmaking & Millwork. (Occupational Competency Examination Ser.: OCE-9). (Cloth bdg. avail. on request). pap. 9.95 (ISBN 0-8373-5709-8). Natl Learning.

Swanson, Leslie C. Old Mills in the Midwest. (Illus.). 1963. 5.95 (ISBN 0-911466-15-0). Swanson.

Uhlig, Stephen & Bhat, B. A. Choice of Technique in Maize Milling. 135p. 1980. pap. 11.50x (ISBN 0-7073-0240-4, Pub by Scottish Academic Pr Scotland). Columbia U Pr.

Zimiles, Martha & Zimiles, Murray. Early American Mills. (Illus.). 352p. 1973. 15.00 (ISBN 0-517-50060-4). Crown.

MILLSTONE VALLEY

Menzies, Elizabeth G. Millstone Valley. LC 68-57688. (Illus.). 1969. 19.50 (ISBN 0-8135-0593-3). Rutgers U Pr.

MILNE, ALAN ALEXANDER, 1882-1956

Crews, Frederick C. Pooh Perplex: A Freshman Casebook. (Illus.). 1963. bds. 2.95 (ISBN 0-525-47160-X). Dutton.

Milne, Christopher. The Enchanted Places. 1978. pap. 1.95 (ISBN 0-14-003449-8). Penguin.

Swann, Thomas B. A. A. Milne. (English Authors Ser.: No. 113). lib. bdg. 10.95 (ISBN 0-8057-1396-4). Twayne.

MILNER, ALFRED MILNER, VISCOUNT, 1854-1925

Crankshaw, Edward. The Forsaken Idea: A Study of Viscount Milner. LC 73-17918. 178p. 1974. Repr. of 1952 ed. lib. bdg. 15.00x (ISBN 0-8371-7278-0, CRFI). Greenwood.

Nimocks, Walter. Milner's Young Men: The Kindergarten in Edwardian Imperial Affairs. LC 68-8588. 1968. 12.50 (ISBN 0-8223-0122-9). Duke.

Waddams, S. M. Milner's Cases & Materials on Contracts. 3rd ed. LC 75-151396. 1977. lib. bdg. 50.00x (ISBN 0-8020-2272-3); college ed. 29.95x (ISBN 0-8020-2273-1). U of Toronto Pr.

MILTON, JOHN, 1563-1647?

Brennecke, Ernest. John Milton the Elder & His Music. LC 73-1770. 224p. 1973. Repr. lib. bdg. 14.00x (ISBN 0-374-90980-6). Octagon.

Candy, Hugh C. Milton: The Individualist in Metre. 1978. Repr. of 1924 ed. lib. bdg. 8.50 (ISBN 0-8495-0771-5). Arden Lib.

Channing, William E. The Character & Writings of John Milton. 1978. Repr. lib. bdg. 10.00 (ISBN 0-8495-0837-1). Arden Lib.

Hill, Christopher. Milton & the English Revolution. 1979. pap. 5.95 (ISBN 0-14-005066-3). Penguin.

LeComte, Edward. Milton & Sex. LC 77-1081. 154p. 1978. 15.00x (ISBN 0-231-04340-6). Columbia U Pr.

Ring, Max. John Milton & His Times. LC 76-23306. 1976. Repr. of 1889 ed. lib. bdg. 45.00 (ISBN 0-8414-7231-9). Folcroft.

MILTON, JOHN, 1608-1674

Adams, Robert M. Ikon: John Milton & the Modern Critics. LC 72-152588. 231p. 1972. Repr. of 1955 ed. lib. bdg. 15.00 (ISBN 0-8371-6021-9, ADIK). Greenwood.

--Milton & the Modern Critics. 1966. pap. 3.95 (ISBN 0-8014-9025-1, CP25). Cornell U Pr.

Allen, Don Cameron. The Harmonious Vision: Studies in Miltons Poetry. enl. ed. LC 79-117254. 166p. 1970. 12.50x (ISBN 0-8018-1191-0). Johns Hopkins.

Ames, Percy W. Milton Memorial Lectures. 1974. Repr. 22.50 (ISBN 0-8274-2738-7). R West.

--Milton Memorial Lectures 1909. LC 65-15895. (Studies in Milton, No. 22). 1969. Repr. of 1909 ed. lib. bdg. 32.95 (ISBN 0-8383-0501-6). Haskell.

Arthos, John. Dante, Michelangelo, & Milton. LC 78-32053. 1979. Repr. of 1963 ed. lib. bdg. 14.50x (ISBN 0-313-20979-0, ARDA). Greenwood.

Bailey, John. Milton. 1979. 32.50 (ISBN 0-685-94334-8). Porter.

Bailey, John C. Milton. 256p. 1980. Repr. of 1945 ed. lib. bdg. 20.00 (ISBN 0-8495-0463-5). Arden Lib.

--Milton. LC 73-12210. 1973. lib. bdg. 17.50 (ISBN 0-8414-3218-X). Folcroft.

Barker, Arthur E., ed. Milton: Modern Essays in Criticism. (Orig.). (YA) (gr. 9 up). 1965. pap. 6.95 (ISBN 0-19-500720-4, GB). Oxford U Pr.

Barnes, C. L. Parallels in Dante & Milton. LC 74-3180. 1917. lib. bdg. 5.00 (ISBN 0-8414-9926-8). Folcroft.

Beers, Henry A. Milton's Tercentenary. LC 73-39421. Repr. of 1910 ed. 7.50 (ISBN 0-404-00725-2). AMS Pr.

--Milton's Tercentenary. LC 73-9747. 1910. lib. bdg. 8.50 (ISBN 0-8414-3168-X). Folcroft.

Belloc, Hilaire. Milton. LC 78-100142. Repr. of 1935 ed. lib. bdg. 15.00 (ISBN 0-8371-3248-7, BEMI). Greenwood.

Berry, W. Grinton. John Milton. LC 73-10007. 1909. lib. bdg. 17.50 (ISBN 0-8414-3150-7). Folcroft.

Berry, William G. John Milton. 1978. Repr. of 1909 ed. lib. bdg. 20.00 (ISBN 0-8495-0407-4). Arden Lib.

Blake, William. Milton. Russell, A. & Maclagan, E., eds. LC 73-16264. 1907. lib. bdg. 10.00 (ISBN 0-8414-3345-3). Folcroft.

Bouchard, Donald F. Milton: A Structural Reading. 224p. 1974. 11.75x (ISBN 0-7735-0229-7). McGill-Queens U Pr.

Boynton, Henry W. World's Leading Poets. facs. ed. LC 68-8439. (Essay Index Reprint Ser). 1912. 18.00 (ISBN 0-8369-0238-6). Arno.

Brennecke, Ernest. John Milton the Elder & His Music. LC 73-1770. 224p. 1973. Repr. lib. bdg. 14.00x (ISBN 0-374-90980-6). Octagon.

Brooke, Stopford A. Milton. LC 70-39534. Repr. of 1879 ed. 9.00 (ISBN 0-404-01108-X). AMS Pr.

--Milton. LC 72-189881. 1973. lib. bdg. 10.00 (ISBN 0-8414-1118-2). Folcroft.

Brown, Eleanor. Milton's Blindness. 1968. lib. bdg. 14.00x (ISBN 0-374-91007-3). Octagon.

Brown, Eleanor G. Milton's Blindness. LC 73-11333. 1971. Repr. of 1934 ed. lib. bdg. 20.00 (ISBN 0-8414-3197-3). Folcroft.

Brown, George D. Syllabification & Accent in the Paradise Lost. LC 73-39543. Repr. of 1901 ed. 12.00 (ISBN 0-404-01129-2). AMS Pr.

Bush, Douglas. Paradise Lost in Our Times. 6.50 (ISBN 0-8446-1096-8). Peter Smith.

--Renaissance & English Humanism. LC 40-11006. 1939. pap. 4.00 (ISBN 0-8020-6008-0). U of Toronto Pr.

Byse, Frank. Milton on the Continent. LC 74-4225. 1903. lib. bdg. 15.00 (ISBN 0-8414-3134-5). Folcroft.

Campbell, Oscar J., et al. Studies in Shakespeare, Milton & Donne. McCartney, Eugene S., ed. LC 78-93244. (University of Michigan Publications: Vol. 1). 1970. Repr. of 1925 ed. 9.50 (ISBN 0-87753-020-3). Phaeton.

Candy, Hugh C. Milton the Individualist in Metre. 1930. lib. bdg. 7.50 (ISBN 0-685-10330-7). Folcroft.

Carpenter, William. The Life & Times of John Milton. 171p. 1980. Repr. of 1836 ed. lib. bdg. 20.00 (ISBN 0-8495-0795-2). Arden Lib.

Catalogue of an Exhibition Commemorative of the Tercentary of the Birth of John Milton: 1608-1908. 1978. Repr. of 1909 ed. lib. bdg. 17.50 (ISBN 0-8495-0114-8). Arden Lib.

Chambers, R. W. Poets & Their Critics: Langland & Milton. 1942. lib. bdg. 6.50 (ISBN 0-685-10478-8). Folcroft.

Channing, William. Character & Writings of John Milton. 1826. lib. bdg. 7.50 (ISBN 0-8414-3465-4). Folcroft.

Channing, William E. The Character & Writings of John Milton. 1978. Repr. lib. bdg. 10.00 (ISBN 0-8495-0837-1). Arden Lib.

--Remarks on the Character and Writings of John Milton. 3rd ed. LC 72-966. Repr. of 1828 ed. 12.50 (ISBN 0-404-01448-8). AMS Pr.

Charlesworth, Arthur R. Paradise Found. LC 72-91109. 1973. 7.50 (ISBN 0-8022-2104-1). Philos Lib.

Clark, Donald L. John Milton at St. Paul's School: A Study of Ancient Rhetoric in English Renaissance Education. 1964. Repr. of 1948 ed. 17.50 (ISBN 0-208-00148-4, Archon). Shoe String.

Coleridge, Samuel T. Lectures & Notes on Shakespeare & Other English Poets: Now First Collected by T. Ashe. LC 70-38347. (Select Bibliographies Reprint Ser). Repr. of 1884 ed. 25.00 (ISBN 0-8369-6764-X). Arno.

--Seven Lectures on Shakespeare & Milton. LC 68-56787. (Research & Source Works Ser.: No. 276). 1969. Repr. of 1856 ed. 13.50 (ISBN 0-8337-0618-7). B Franklin.

--Seven Lectures on Shakespeare & Milton. Collier, John P., ed. LC 72-962. Repr. of 1856 ed. 12.50 (ISBN 0-404-01617-0). AMS Pr.

Collins, J. C. Miltonic Myths & Their Authors in Studies of Poetry & Criticism. 1905. Repr. 30.00 (ISBN 0-8274-2739-5). R West.

Condee, Ralph W. Structure in Milton's Poetry: From the Foundation to the Pinnacles. LC 73-12934. 240p. 1974. 15.95x (ISBN 0-271-01133-5). Pa St U Pr.

Conklin, George N. Biblical Criticism & Heresy in Milton. LC 78-159175. x, 137p. 1971. Repr. of 1949 ed. lib. bdg. 13.50x (ISBN 0-374-91905-4). Octagon.

Cooke, John. John Milton: 1608-1674. 56p. 1980. Repr. of 1908 ed. lib. bdg. 12.50 (ISBN 0-8482-3553-3). Norwood Edns.

--John Milton: 1608-1674. LC 74-5138. 1973. Repr. of 1908 ed. lib. bdg. 10.00 (ISBN 0-8414-3549-9). Folcroft.

Corson, Hiram. Introduction to the Prose & Poetical Works of John Milton. (Illus.). 335p. Repr. of 1899 ed. 13.50 (ISBN 0-686-76942-2). Gordian.

Courthope, W. J. Essays on Milton. 1908. lib. bdg. 10.00 (ISBN 0-8414-3599-5). Folcroft.

Crump, Galbraith M. The Mystical Design of "Paradise Lost". 194p. 1975. 12.00 (ISBN 0-8387-1519-2). Bucknell U Pr.

Curry, Walter C. Milton's Ontology, Cosmogony & Physics. LC 57-5833. (Illus.). 226p. 1966. pap. 4.00x (ISBN 0-8131-0102-6). U Pr of Ky.

Daiches, David. Milton. (Orig.). 1966. pap. 4.95x (ISBN 0-393-00347-7, Norton Lib). Norton.

Darbishire, Helen. Milton's Paradise Lost. LC 74-3031. 1951. lib. bdg. 6.00 (ISBN 0-8414-3750-5). Folcroft.

Darbishire, Helen, ed. Early Lives of Milton. LC 77-144967. (Illus.). 1971. Repr. of 1932 ed. 29.00 (ISBN 0-403-00935-9). Scholarly.

De Selincourt, Ernest. English Poets & the National Ideal. LC 73-7775. 1915. lib. bdg. 15.00 (ISBN 0-8414-1879-9). Folcroft.

Dobbins, Austin C. Milton & the Book of Revelation: The Heavenly Cycle. LC 73-22715. (Studies in the Humanities Ser.: No. 7). 176p. 1975. 11.95 (ISBN 0-8173-7320-9); pap. 4.95 (ISBN 0-8173-7321-7). U of Ala Pr.

Dorian, Donald C. English Diodatis. LC 74-92175. (BCL Ser. I). Repr. of 1950 ed. 21.50 (ISBN 0-404-02146-8). AMS Pr.

Dowden, Edward. Milton in the Eighteenth Century 1701-1750. 1908. lib. bdg. 6.00 (ISBN 0-8414-3853-6). Folcroft.

Duncan, Joseph E. Milton's Earthly Paradise: A Historical Study of Eden. LC 71-187167. (Monographs in the Humanities Ser: No. 5). (Illus.). 320p. 1972. 12.50x (ISBN 0-8166-0633-1). U of Minn Pr.

Edmonds, Cyrus R. John Milton: A Biography. LC 72-194753. 1851. lib. bdg. 10.00 (ISBN 0-8414-3886-2). Folcroft.

Edmundson, George. Milton & Vondel: A Curiosity of Literature. LC 74-23571. 1974. Repr. of 1885 ed. lib. bdg. 15.00 (ISBN 0-8414-3913-3). Folcroft.

ELH, et al. Critical Essays on Milton from ELH. LC 71-93296. 290p. 1969. pap. 3.95x (ISBN 0-8018-1094-9). Johns Hopkins.

Elton, Oliver. Milton Il Penseroso. LC 73-13546. Repr. of 1891 ed. lib. bdg. 7.50 (ISBN 0-8414-3906-0). Folcroft.

Evans, Robert O. Milton's Elisions. LC 66-63842. (U of Fla. Humanities Monographs: No. 21). 1966. pap. 3.00 (ISBN 0-8130-0076-9). U Presses Fla.

Fenton, Elijah. The Life of John Milton. 8p. 1980. Repr. of 1785 ed. lib. bdg. 10.00 (ISBN 0-8492-4704-7). R West.

--The Life of John Milton. 1978. Repr. of 1977 ed. lib. bdg. 8.50 (ISBN 0-8414-1994-9). Folcroft.

Ferry, Anne D. Milton & the Miltonic Dryden. LC 68-25608. 1968. 10.00x (ISBN 0-674-57576-8). Harvard U Pr.

Firth, Charles H. Milton As an Historian. LC 74-13082. 1908. lib. bdg. 5.00 (ISBN 0-8414-4242-8). Folcroft.

Fletcher, Angus. Transcendental Masque: An Essay on Milton's Comus. LC 78-148019. (Illus.). 278p. 1972. 22.50x (ISBN 0-8014-0620-X). Cornell U Pr.

Fletcher, H. Use of the Bible in Milton's Prose. LC 75-95425. (Studies in Milton, No. 22). 1970. Repr. of 1929 ed. lib. bdg. 28.95 (ISBN 0-8383-0974-7). Haskell.

Fletcher, Harris. Grierson's Suggested Date for Milton's Ad Patrem in Scott Anniversary Papers. 1929. Repr. 25.00 (ISBN 0-8274-2450-7). R West.

Fletcher, Harris F. Milton Studies in Honor of Harris Francis Fletcher. LC 74-16488. 1974. Repr. of 1961 ed. lib. bdg. 20.00 (ISBN 0-8414-4247-9). Folcroft.

--Milton's Semitic Studies. LC 74-18236. 1973. lib. bdg. 10.00 (ISBN 0-8414-4249-5). Folcroft.

--Use of the Bible in Milton's Prose. 1973. lib. bdg. 59.95 (ISBN 0-87968-014-8). Gordon Pr.

Flower, Desmond. Voltaire's Essay on Milton. LC 77-918. 1954. lib. bdg. 6.50 (ISBN 0-8414-4186-3). Folcroft.

French, J. Milton, ed. Life Records of John Milton 1608-1674, 5 Vols. LC 66-20024. 1966. Repr. of 1958 ed. Set. 85.00 (ISBN 0-87752-039-9); 17.50 ea. Gordian.

French, Joseph M. Milton in Chancery: New Chapters in the Lives of the Poet & His Father. Repr. of 1939 ed. 29.00 (ISBN 0-403-04175-9). Somerset Pub.

Garnett, Richard. Life of John Milton. LC 77-112638. Repr. of 1890 ed. 10.00 (ISBN 0-404-02686-9). AMS Pr.
--Life of John Milton. 1890. lib. bdg. 9.75 (ISBN 0-8414-4638-5). Folcroft.
--Prose of Milton. 1894. Repr. 20.00 (ISBN 0-8274-3214-3). R West.
Gertsch, Alfred. Der Steigende Ruhm Miltons. Repr. of 1927 ed. pap. 45.50 (ISBN 0-384-18230-5). Johnson Repr.
Gilman, Wilbur E., ed. Milton's Rhetoric: Studies in His Defence of Liberty. LC 74-93243. 1970. Repr. of 1939 ed. 7.50 (ISBN 0-87753-018-1). Phaeton.
Good, John W. Studies in the Milton Tradition. LC 73-144619. Repr. of 1915 ed. 16.00 (ISBN 0-404-02862-4). AMS Pr.
--Studies in the Milton Tradition. Repr. of 1915 ed. 18.50 (ISBN 0-384-19150-9). Johnson Repr.
Grace, William J. Ideas in Milton. LC 68-12290. 1969. Repr. of 1968 ed. 2.95x (ISBN 0-268-00126-X). U of Notre Dame Pr.
Grebanier, Bernard. Barron's Simplified Approach to Milton: Paradise Lost & Other Works. 1964. pap. text ed. 1.50 (ISBN 0-8120-0180-X). Barron.
Grierson, Herbert. Criticism & Creation. LC 73-733. 1949. lib. bdg. 10.00 (ISBN 0-8414-1603-6). Folcroft.
Gurteen, Stephen H. The Epic of the Fall of Man: A Comparative Study of Caedmon, Dante & Milton. Repr. of 1896 ed. 36.00 (ISBN 0-403-04055-8). Somerset Pub.
Hall, William C. Milton & His Sonnets. LC 73-4268. 1973. lib. bdg. 5.00 (ISBN 0-8414-2071-8). Folcroft.
Hamilton, G. Rostrevor. Hero or Fool. LC 70-98995. (Studies in Milton, No. 22). 1970. pap. 12.95 (ISBN 0-8383-0038-3). Haskell.
--Hero or Fool: A Study of Milton's Satan. LC 74-16136. 1944. lib. bdg. 6.50 (ISBN 0-8414-4860-4). Folcroft.
Hamilton, John A. The Life of John Milton, Englishman. LC 74-16133. 1974. Repr. lib. bdg. 6.50 (ISBN 0-8414-4874-4). Folcroft.
--The Life of John Milton, Englishmen. 72p. 1980. Repr. lib. bdg. 15.00 (ISBN 0-8482-1230-4). Norwood Edns.
Hamilton, W. Douglas. Original Papers Illustrative of the Life & Writings of John Milton. LC 76-29043. 1859. lib. bdg. 14.95 (ISBN 0-8414-4935-X). Folcroft.
Hamilton, William D., ed. Original Papers Illustrative of the Life & Writings of John Milton. (Camden Society, London. Publications, First Ser.: No. 75). Repr. of 1859 ed. 21.00 (ISBN 0-404-50175-3). AMS Pr.
--Original Papers Illustrative of the Life & Writings of John Milton. 1859. 23.00 (ISBN 0-384-21220-4). Johnson Repr.
Harris, W. Melville. John Milton: Puritan, Patriot, Poet. LC 77-3593. lib. bdg. 5.00 (ISBN 0-8414-4919-8). Folcroft.
Hartwell, Kathleen. Lactantius & Milton. LC 74-17014. (Studies in Milton, No. 22). 1974. lib. bdg. 36.95 (ISBN 0-8383-1743-X). Haskell.
Hayley, William. Life of Milton. LC 78-122485. 1970. Repr. of 1796 ed. 37.00x (ISBN 0-8201-1081-7). Schol Facsimiles.
--The Life of Milton. LC 76-26849. Repr. of 1796 ed. lib. bdg. 16.50 (ISBN 0-8414-4739-X). Folcroft.
Herford, C. H. Dante & Milton. 1924. lib. bdg. 6.00 (ISBN 0-8414-5044-7). Folcroft.
Hieatt, A. Kent. Chaucer, Spenser, Milton: Mythopoeic Continuities & Transformations. (Illus.). 336p. 1975. 20.00x (ISBN 0-7735-0228-9). McGill-Queens U Pr.
Hillis, Newell D. Great Men As Prophets of a New Era. facs. ed. LC 68-16939. (Essay Index Reprint Ser). 1968. Repr. of 1922 ed. 13.00 (ISBN 0-8369-0541-5). Arno.
Hood, Edwin P. John Milton: The Patriot & the Poet. LC 72-190920. 1972. lib. bdg. 12.50 (ISBN 0-8414-4905-8). Folcroft.
Hudson, William H. Milton & His Poetry. LC 79-120964. (Poetry & Life Ser.). Repr. of 1914 ed. 7.25 (ISBN 0-404-52518-0). AMS Pr.
--Milton & His Poetry. LC 76-43042. 1919. lib. bdg. 7.50 (ISBN 0-8414-4909-0). Folcroft.
Hughes, Merritt Y., ed. A Variorum Commentary on the Poems of John Milton, Vol. 1. LC 70-129962. 30.00x (ISBN 0-231-08879-5). Columbia U Pr.
--A Variorum Commentary on the Poems of John Milton, Vol. 2, 3 Pts. LC 70-129962. 1972. 30.00x ea. Pt. 1 (ISBN 0-231-08880-9). Pt. 2 (ISBN 0-231-08881-7). Pt. 3 (ISBN 0-231-08882-5). Columbia U Pr.
Hunter, John. Milton's Samson Agonistes & Lycidas. 92p. 1980. Repr. of 1872 ed. text ed. 17.50 (ISBN 0-8492-5271-7). R West.
Hunter, Joseph. Milton, a Sheaf of Gleanings. LC 76-26898. 1850. lib. bdg. 8.50 (ISBN 0-8414-4737-3). Folcroft.
Hunter, William. Milton on the Nature of Man. LC 76-48905. 1946. lib. bdg. 5.00 (ISBN 0-8414-4908-2). Folcroft.
Hunter, William B., Jr., et al. Bright Essence: Studies in Milton's Theology. LC 74-161485. 1971. 15.00x (ISBN 0-87480-061-7). U of Utah Pr.
Hunter, Wm. Bridges. Milton on the Nature of Man. 1978. Repr. of 1946 ed. lib. bdg. 10.00 (ISBN 0-8492-1186-7). R West.
Hutchinson, F. E. Milton & the English Mind. LC 74-7187. (Studies in Milton, No. 22). 1974. lib. bdg. 36.95 (ISBN 0-8383-1906-8). Haskell.
--Milton & the English Mind. LC 74-28171. 1946. Repr. lib. bdg. 17.50 (ISBN 0-8414-4897-3). Folcroft.
Hyman, Lawrence. The Quarrel Within: Art & Morality in Milton's Poetry. LC 76-189559. 1972. 11.00 (ISBN 0-8046-9018-9, Natl U). Kennikat.
Ivimey, Joseph. John Milton, His Life & Times, Religious & Political Opinions. 397p. 1980. Repr. of 1833 ed. lib. bdg. 40.00 (ISBN 0-8495-2619-1). Arden Lib.
--John Milton: His Life & Times, Religious & Political Opinions. LC 72-190658. 1833. lib. bdg. 30.00 (ISBN 0-8414-5069-2). Folcroft.
Jenks, Tudor. In the Days of Milton. LC 76-170812. Repr. of 1905 ed. 19.45 (ISBN 0-404-03559-0). AMS Pr.
Keightley, Thomas. An Account of the Life, Opinions, & Writings of John Milton. 484p. 1980. Repr. of 1855 ed. lib. bdg. 50.00 (ISBN 0-8492-1495-5). R West.
--An Account of the Life, Opinions, & Writings of John Milton. LC 73-11332. 1855. Repr. lib. bdg. 45.00 (ISBN 0-8414-2222-2). Folcroft.
Kelley, Maurice. This Great Argument: A Study of Milton's De Doctrina Christiana As a Gloss Upon Paradise Lost. Repr. of 1941 ed. 22.00 (ISBN 0-403-04309-3). Somerset Pub.
Kermode, Frank, ed. The Living Milton: Essays by Various Hands. 1960. cased 12.95 (ISBN 0-7100-1666-2); pap. 6.50 (ISBN 0-7100-4640-5). Routledge & Kegan.
Kerrigan, William. The Prophetic Milton. LC 74-6118. 1974. 13.95x (ISBN 0-8139-0512-5). U Pr of Va.
Kranidas, Thomas, ed. New Essays on Paradise Lost. LC 72-82463. 1969. pap. 3.65x (ISBN 0-520-01902-4, CAMPUS51). U of Cal Pr.
Kreuder, Hans-Dieter. Milton in Deutschland: Seine Rezeption im latein-und deutschsprachigen Schrifttum zwischen 1651-1732. (Quellen und Forschungen zur Sprach-und Kulturgeschichte der germanischen Voelker). 257p. 1971. 52.50x (ISBN 3-11-003685-1). De Gruyter.
Langdon, Ida. Milton's Theory of Poetry & Fine Art. LC 65-17905. 1965. Repr. of 1924 ed. 8.50 (ISBN 0-8462-0645-5). Russell.
Larson, Martin A. Modernity of Milton. LC 76-23120. 1927. lib. bdg. 7.95 (ISBN 0-8414-5800-6). Folcroft.
--Modernity of Milton: A Theological & Philosophical Interpretation. LC 76-124764. Repr. of 1927 ed. 18.75 (ISBN 0-404-03880-8). AMS Pr.
Lauder, William. Essay on Milton's Use & Imitation of the Moderns in Paradise Lost. LC 74-172306. Repr. of 1750 ed. 16.45 (ISBN 0-404-03888-3). AMS Pr.
Lawry, Jon S. Shadow of Heaven: Matter & Stance in Milton's Poetry. LC 68-16385. 1968. text ed. 22.50x (ISBN 0-8014-0252-2). Cornell U Pr.
Lawson, McEwan. Master John Milton of the Citie of London. LC 72-10632. 1973. Repr. lib. bdg. 6.50 (ISBN 0-8414-0725-8). Folcroft.
Leach, A. F. Milton As Schoolboy & Schoolmaster. LC 76-48904. 1908. lib. bdg. 5.00 (ISBN 0-8414-5817-0). Folcroft.
Le Comte, Edward S. Yet Once More: Verbal & Psychological Pattern in Milton. Repr. of 1953 ed. 12.50 (ISBN 0-404-03918-9). AMS Pr.
Lieb, Michael & Shawcross, John T., eds. Achievements of the Left Hand: Essays on the Prose of John Milton. LC 73-79506. 404p. 1974. 17.50x (ISBN 0-87023-125-1). U of Mass Pr.
Lijegren, Sten B. Studies in Milton. LC 67-30816. (Studies in Milton, No. 22). 1969. Repr. of 1918 ed. lib. bdg. 23.95 (ISBN 0-8383-0718-3). Haskell.
Liljegren, Sten B. Studies in Milton. 1918. lib. bdg. 6.75 (ISBN 0-8414-5707-7). Folcroft.
Macaulay, Rose. Milton. LC 74-7050. (Studies in Milton, No. 22). 1974. lib. bdg. 39.95 (ISBN 0-8383-1911-4). Haskell.
Macaulay, Thomas B. Milton. Repr. of 1900 ed. lib. bdg. 15.00 (ISBN 0-8371-4094-3, MAM). Greenwood.
MacCaffrey, Isabel G. Paradise Lost As Myth. LC 59-9282. 1959. 12.50x (ISBN 0-674-65450-1). Harvard U Pr.
Mackail, John W. Bentley's Milton. LC 73-7628. 1973. lib. bdg. 5.00 (ISBN 0-8414-2343-1). Folcroft.
Manuel, M. Seventeenth Century Critics & Biographers of Milton. LC 77-23430. 1962. lib. bdg. 15.00 (ISBN 0-8414-6184-8). Folcroft.
Marsh, John F. Papers Connected with the Affairs of Milton & His Family. LC 74-22180. 1974. Repr. of 1851 ed. lib. bdg. 8.50 (ISBN 0-8414-5959-2). Folcroft.
Martin, John R. Portrait of John Milton at Princeton. LC 61-14263. (Illus.). 1961. 7.50 (ISBN 0-87811-006-2). Princeton Lib.
Martin, L. C. Thomas Warton & Early Poems of Milton. 1979. 24.50 (ISBN 0-685-62770-5, 0-911156). Porter.
--Thomas Warton & the Early Poems of Milton. LC 77-9907. 1934. lib. bdg. 5.00 (ISBN 0-8414-6096-5). Folcroft.
Martyn, Carlos. Life & Times of John Milton. LC 76-39970. 1976. Repr. of 1866 ed. lib. bdg. 30.00 (ISBN 0-8414-6009-4). Folcroft.
Martz, Louis L. Poet of Exile: A Study of Milton's Poetry. LC 79-64079. 1980. 24.50x (ISBN 0-300-02393-6). Yale U Pr.
Masson, David. Chapters from the Sixth Volume of the Life of John Milton. 1973. Repr. of 1898 ed. lib. bdg. 30.00 (ISBN 0-8414-6489-8). Folcroft.
--Life of John Milton: Narrated in Connection with the Political, Literary & Ecclesiastical History of His Time, 7 vols. 91.00 (ISBN 0-8446-1303-7). Peter Smith.
--Three Devils: Luther's, Milton's & Goethe's. LC 72-193946. 1874. lib. bdg. 17.50 (ISBN 0-8414-6495-2). Folcroft.
Masterman, J. Howard. The Age of Milton. 1906. Repr. lib. bdg. 15.00 (ISBN 0-8414-6453-7). Folcroft.
Maurice, F. D. The Friendship of Books: Spenser, Milton, Burke. 1889. Repr. 30.00 (ISBN 0-8274-2376-4). R West.
Mead, Lucia A. Milton's England. LC 76-7984. 1973. lib. bdg. 20.00 (ISBN 0-8414-6021-3). Folcroft.
Milton, John. Catalogue of an Exhibition Commemorative of the Tercentenary of the Birth of John Milton. Repr. of 1909 ed. lib. bdg. 15.00 (ISBN 0-8414-6620-3). Folcroft.
--The Latin Poems of John Milton. Repr. of 1930 ed. 19.00 (ISBN 0-403-04132-5). Somerset Pub.
--A Maske: The Earlier Versions. Sprott, S. E., ed. LC 72-97784. 1973. 30.00x (ISBN 0-8020-5287-8). U of Toronto Pr.
--Milton's Lament for Damon & His Other Latin Poems. 109p. 1980. Repr. of 1935 ed. lib. bdg. 20.00 (ISBN 0-8495-5518-3). Arden Lib.
--On the Morning of Christ's Nativity: Milton's Hymn with Illustrations by William Blake. Keynes, Geoffrey, ed. LC 77-22296. (Illus.). Repr. of 1923 ed. lib. bdg. 12.50 (ISBN 0-8414-9917-9). Folcroft.
--The Portable Milton. Bush, Douglas, ed. (Viking Portable Library: No. 44). 1955. 10.00 (ISBN 0-670-47608-0). Viking Pr.
--Portraits, Prints & Writings of John Milton. LC 73-15855. 1908. lib. bdg. 10.00 (ISBN 0-8414-6060-4). Folcroft.
Mody, Jehangir. R. P. Vondel & Milton. LC 76-29704. 1942. lib. bdg. 15.00 (ISBN 0-8414-6127-9). Folcroft.
Mordell, Albert. Dante & Other Waning Classics. LC 68-8219. 1969. Repr. of 1915 ed. 8.75 (ISBN 0-8046-0322-7). Kennikat.
Morison, William. Milton & Liberty. LC 76-27343. Repr. of 1909 ed. lib. bdg. 6.00 (ISBN 0-8414-6135-X). Folcroft.
Morris, Edward E. Milton: Tractate of Education. LC 73-13795. 1895. Repr. lib. bdg. 10.00 (ISBN 0-8414-6000-0). Folcroft.
Morris, J. W. John Milton: A Vindication from the Change of Arianism. LC 77-22943. 1862. lib. bdg. 15.00 (ISBN 0-8414-6210-0). Folcroft.
Mutschmann, H. Milton's Projected Epic on the Rise & Future Greatness of the Britannic Nation. LC 72-196843. 1936. lib. bdg. 10.00 (ISBN 0-8414-6693-9). Folcroft.
--Secret of John Milton. LC 72-194771. 1925. lib. bdg. 10.00 (ISBN 0-8414-6694-7). Folcroft.
Mutschmann, Heinrich. Milton's Eyesight & the Chronology of His Works. LC 75-163458. (Studies in Milton, No. 22). 1971. Repr. of 1924 ed. lib. bdg. 22.95 (ISBN 0-8383-1325-6). Haskell.
Myers, Ernest, ed. Selected Prose Writings of John Milton. 1973. Repr. of 1904 ed. lib. bdg. 20.00 (ISBN 0-8414-6695-5). Folcroft.
Myers, Robert H. Handel, Dryden, & Milton. 1978. Repr. of 1956 ed. lib. bdg. 20.00 (ISBN 0-8492-6708-0). R West.
Myers, Robert M. Handel, Dryden & Milton. 1956. lib. bdg. 20.00 (ISBN 0-8414-6129-5). Folcroft.
Myhr, Ivar L. Evolution & Practice of Milton's Epic Theory. LC 76-28764. 1942. lib. bdg. 8.50 (ISBN 0-8414-6106-6). Folcroft.
Nelson, James G. The Sublime Puritan: Milton & the Victorians. LC 74-8794. (Illus.). 209p. 1974. Repr. of 1963 ed. lib. bdg. 15.00 (ISBN 0-8371-7586-0, NESP). Greenwood.
Neve, Philip. Cursory Remarks on Some of the Ancient English Poets, Particularly Milton. LC 78-27474. 1889. lib. bdg. 25.00 (ISBN 0-8414-6310-7). Folcroft.
Nicolson, Marjorie H. John Milton: A Reader's Guide to His Poetry. 1971. lib. bdg. 17.50x (ISBN 0-374-96106-9). Octagon.
Oras, Ants. Blank Verse & Chronology in Milton. LC 66-63667. (U of Fla. Humanities Monographs: No. 20). 1966. pap. 3.50 (ISBN 0-8130-0169-2). U Presses Fla.
--Milton's Editors & Commentators. LC 67-31494. (Studies in Milton, No. 22). 1969. Repr. of 1931 ed. lib. bdg. 52.95 (ISBN 0-8383-0604-7). Haskell.
--Notes on Some Miltonic Usages: Their Background & Later Development. LC 72-195207. 1938. lib. bdg. 10.00 (ISBN 0-8414-6673-4). Folcroft.
Osgood, Charles G. Classical Mythology of Milton's English Poems. LC 64-8180. 1964. Repr. of 1900 ed. 8.50 (ISBN 0-87752-080-1). Gordian.
--Classical Mythology of Milton's English Poems. LC 65-15902. (Studies in Comparative Literature, No. 35). 1969. Repr. of 1900 ed. lib. bdg. 49.95 (ISBN 0-8383-0603-9). Haskell.
Parker, William R. Milton's Contemporary Reputation. LC 70-122996. (Studies in Milton, No. 22). 1970. Repr. of 1940 ed. lib. bdg. 36.95 (ISBN 0-8383-1129-6). Haskell.
--Milton's Contemporary Reputation. LC 76-24454. 1940. lib. bdg. 12.75 (ISBN 0-8414-6729-3). Folcroft.
Patrick, J. Max & Sundell, Roger H. Milton & the Art of Sacred Song. LC 78-65014. 248p. 1979. 15.00 (ISBN 0-299-07830-2). U of Wis Pr.
Patrick, J. Max, ed. SAMLA Studies in Milton: Essays on John Milton & His Works. LC 53-12340. 1953. pap. 5.95 (ISBN 0-8130-0183-8). U Presses Fla.
Patterson, Frank A., ed. The Student's Milton. rev. ed. 1930. 44.50x (ISBN 0-89197-430-X). Irvington.
Pattison, Mark. Milton. Morley, John, ed. LC 68-58393. (English Men of Letters). Repr. of 1887 ed. lib. bdg. 12.50 (ISBN 0-404-51725-0). AMS Pr.
--Milton. 1896. Repr. 12.00 (ISBN 0-8274-2735-2). R West.
Philo-Milton. Milton's Sublimity Asserted in a Poem. LC 71-174195. Repr. of 1709 ed. 5.00 (ISBN 0-404-05042-5). AMS Pr.
Plotkin, Frederick. Milton's Inward Jerusalem: "Paradise Lost" & the Ways of Knowing. LC 76-159468. (Studies in English Literature: No. 72). 155p. 1971. text ed. 21.50x (ISBN 0-686-22493-0). Mouton.
Pommer, Henry F. Milton & Melville. LC 70-122752. (Illus.). 1970. Repr. of 1950 ed. lib. bdg. 11.00x (ISBN 0-8154-0338-0). Cooper Sq.
Potter, Lois. A Preface to Milton. (Preface Bks). (Illus.). 1977. pap. text ed. 5.95x (ISBN 0-582-31508-5). Longman.
Racine, Louis. Life of Milton. LC 74-16189. 1930. lib. bdg. 15.00 (ISBN 0-8414-7258-0). Folcroft.
Radzinowicz, Mary Ann. Toward Samson Agonistes: The Growth of Milton's Mind. LC 77-85559. 1978. 32.50x (ISBN 0-691-06357-5). Princeton U Pr.
Rajan, B., ed. Milton's Paradise Lost: Bks 1 & 2. 4.50x (ISBN 0-210-31187-8). Asia.
Rajan, Balachandra. Paradise Lost & the Seventeenth Century Reader. 1967. pap. 1.95 (ISBN 0-472-06132-1, 132, AA). U of Mich Pr.
Rajan, Balachandra, ed. Paradise Lost: A Tercentenary Tribute. LC 77-429833. 1969. 12.50x (ISBN 0-8020-1605-7). U of Toronto Pr.
--The Prison & the Pinnacle. LC 72-90737. 1973. 12.50x (ISBN 0-8020-1929-3). U of Toronto Pr.
Raleigh, Walter A. Milton. LC 67-13336. 1967. Repr. of 1900 ed. 12.50 (ISBN 0-405-08873-6). Arno.
--Milton. 1973. 8.50 (ISBN 0-8274-1323-8). R West.
Raymond, Dora N. Oliver's Secretary. LC 71-174302. Repr. of 1932 ed. 26.50 (ISBN 0-404-05229-0). AMS Pr.
Reaske, Christopher. Monarch Notes on Milton's Poetry. (Orig.). pap. 1.95 (ISBN 0-671-00787-4). Monarch Pr.
Reesing, John. Milton's Poetic Art: A Mask, Lycidas, & Paradise Lost. LC 68-17632. 1968. 10.00x (ISBN 0-674-57626-8). Harvard U Pr.
Richmond, Hugh M. The Christian Revolutionary: John Milton. 1975. 19.50x (ISBN 0-520-02443-5). U of Cal Pr.
Ricks, Christopher. Milton's Grand Style. 1963. pap. 9.95x (ISBN 0-19-812090-7). Oxford U Pr.
Riggs, William G. The Christian Poet in Paradise Lost. 1972. 19.50x (ISBN 0-520-02081-2). U of Cal Pr.
Robertson, John G. Milton's Fame on the Continent. Repr. of 1908 ed. lib. bdg. 8.50 (ISBN 0-8414-7462-1). Folcroft.

Rudrum, Alan, ed. John Milton. LC 71-127553. (Modern Judgement Ser). 1970. pap. text ed. 2.50 (ISBN 0-87695-100-0). Aurora Pubs.
Saillens, E. Les Sonnets Anglais et Italians De Milton. LC 74-12230. 1930. lib. bdg. 15.00 (ISBN 0-8414-7784-1). Folcroft.
Sampson, Alden. Studies in Milton & an Essay on Poetry. LC 71-126686. 1970. Repr. of 1913 ed. 24.00 (ISBN 0-404-05555-9). AMS Pr.
Samuel, Irene. Plato & Milton. 1965. pap. 3.95 (ISBN 0-8014-9092-8, CP92). Cornell U Pr.
Sarma, M. V. The Heroic Argument: A Study of Milton's Heroic Poetry. 171p. 1971. 8.75x (ISBN 0-8426-0283-6). Verry.
Saurat, Denis. Blake & Milton. LC 65-18830. 1965. Repr. of 1935 ed. 9.50 (ISBN 0-8462-0693-5). Russell.
--Milton, Man & Thinker. LC 76-121151. (Studies in Milton, No. 22). 1970. Repr. of 1925 ed. lib. bdg. 39.95 (ISBN 0-8383-1093-1). Haskell.
--Milton: Man & Thinker. LC 73-153352. Repr. of 1925 ed. 24.50 (ISBN 0-404-05565-6). AMS Pr.
Scherpbier, H. Milton in Holland. LC 76-41928. 1933. lib. bdg. 17.50 (ISBN 0-8414-7580-6). Folcroft.
Schultz, H. Milton & Forbidden Knowledge. 1955. pap. 15.00 (ISBN 0-527-80600-5). Kraus Repr.
Seldin, Mariam. Monarch Notes on Milton's Paradise Lost. (Orig.). pap. 2.50 (ISBN 0-671-00513-8). Monarch Pr.
Senior, H. L. John Milton, the Supreme Englishman. lib. bdg. 6.00 (ISBN 0-8414-8126-1). Folcroft.
Sensabaugh, George. Milton in Early America. LC 79-14332. 1979. 13.50 (ISBN 0-87752-180-8). Gordian.
Sewell, Arthur. Study in Milton's Christian Doctrine. 1967. Repr. of 1939 ed. 17.50 (ISBN 0-208-00416-5, Archon). Shoe String.
Shawcross, John T., ed. Complete Poetry of John Milton. LC 72-150934. 1971. pap. 5.95 (ISBN 0-385-02351-0, Anch). Doubleday.
--Milton 1732-1801: The Critical Heritage. (Critical Heritage Ser.). 1972. 33.75x (ISBN 0-7100-7261-9). Routledge & Kegan.
Sherburn, George. The Early Popularity of Milton's Minor Poems. LC 73-14758. 1974. Repr. of 1919 ed. lib. bdg. 8.50 (ISBN 0-8414-7647-0). Folcroft.
Shumaker, W. Unpremeditated Verse: Feeling & Perception in Milton's Paradise Lost. 1967. 17.00x (ISBN 0-691-06134-3). Princeton U Pr.
Simmonds, James D., ed. Milton Studies, Vol. III. LC 69-12335. (Milton Studies). 1971. 15.95x (ISBN 0-8229-3218-0). U of Pittsburgh Pr.
--Milton Studies, Vol. II. LC 69-12335. (Milton Studies). 1970. 15.95x (ISBN 0-8229-3194-X). U of Pittsburgh Pr.
--Milton Studies, Vol. V. LC 69-12335. (Milton Studies). 1973. 19.95x (ISBN 0-8229-3272-5). U of Pittsburgh Pr.
--Milton Studies, Vol. VI. LC 69-12335. (Milton Studies). 1974. 19.95x (ISBN 0-8229-3288-1). U of Pittsburgh Pr.
--Milton Studies, Vol. VIII. LC 69-12335. (Milton Studies). 1975. 19.95x (ISBN 0-8229-3310-1). U of Pittsburgh Pr.
--Milton Studies, Vol. XII. LC 69-12335. (Milton Studies). (Illus.). 1979. 19.95x (ISBN 0-8229-3376-4). U of Pittsburgh Pr.
Simmonds, James D, ed. Milton Studies, Vol. IX. LC 69-12335. (Milton Studies). 1976. 19.95x (ISBN 0-8229-3329-2). U of Pittsburgh Pr.
Skeat, Walter W. John Milton's Epitaphium Damonis. LC 75-44069. 1933. lib. bdg. 10.00 (ISBN 0-8414-7644-6). Folcroft.
Slights, Camille W. The Casuistical Tradition in Shakespeare, Donne, Herbert, & Milton. LC 80-8576. 352p. 1981. 21.00 (ISBN 0-691-06463-6). Princeton U Pr.
--The Casuistical Tradition in Shakespeare, Donne, Herbert, & Milton. LC 80-8576. 352p. 1981. 21.00 (ISBN 0-691-06463-6). Princeton U Pr.
Smith, Logan P. Milton & His Modern Critics. 1967. Repr. of 1941 ed. 13.50 (ISBN 0-208-00325-8, Archon). Shoe String.
Sotheby, S. L. Ramblings in the Elucidation of the Autograph of Milton. 1974. Repr. of 1861 ed. lib. bdg. 100.00 limited ed. (ISBN 0-8414-8008-7). Folcroft.
Stevens, David H. Milton Papers. LC 75-176438. Repr. of 1927 ed. 5.00 (ISBN 0-404-06262-8). AMS Pr.
--Milton Papers. LC 76-27340. 1927. lib. bdg. 4.95 (ISBN 0-8414-7615-2). Folcroft.
Summers, Joseph H., ed. Lyric & Dramatic Milton: Selected Papers from the English Institute. LC 65-22231. 1965. 12.50x (ISBN 0-231-02863-6). Columbia U Pr.
Symmons, Charles. Life of John Milton. 3rd ed. LC 71-128979. 1970. Repr. of 1822 ed. 25.50 (ISBN 0-404-06325-X). AMS Pr.
Taylor, George C. Milton's Use of Du Bartas. 1968. Repr. lib. bdg. 12.00x (ISBN 0-374-97829-8). Octagon.
Telleen, John M. Milton Dans la Litterature Francaise. LC 75-189895. ii, 151p. (Fr.). 1972. Repr. of 1904 ed. lib. bdg. 18.50 (ISBN 0-8337-4446-1). B Franklin.
Thompson, Elbert. Essays on Milton. LC 72-195123. 1910. lib. bdg. 6.95 (ISBN 0-8414-8044-3). Folcroft.
Thompson, Elbert N. Essays on Milton. LC 68-15179. 1968. Repr. of 1914 ed. 7.00 (ISBN 0-8462-1055-X). Russell.
Thorpe, James. Milton Criticism: Selections from Four Centuries. 1966. lib. bdg. 22.50x (ISBN 0-374-97923-5). Octagon.
Tillyard, Eustace M. Milton's L'Allegro & Il Penseroso. 1932. lib. bdg. 8.50 (ISBN 0-8414-8403-1). Folcroft.
Todd, H. J. Some Account of the Life & Writings of John Milton. LC 77-22935. 1826. lib. bdg. 30.00 (ISBN 0-8414-8637-9). Folcroft.
Toland, John. Life of John Milton. LC 76-40068. 1761. lib. bdg. 25.00 (ISBN 0-8414-8619-0). Folcroft.
Trent, William P. John Milton: A Short Study of His Life & Works. LC 71-177572. Repr. of 1899 ed. 12.00 (ISBN 0-404-06523-6). AMS Pr.
--John Milton: A Short Study of His Life & Work. LC 72-187004. 1899. lib. bdg. 11.95 (ISBN 0-8414-8430-9). Folcroft.
Tuckwell, W. Lycidas: A Monograph. LC 77-22476. 1911. lib. bdg. 8.50 (ISBN 0-8414-8588-7). Folcroft.
Verity, A. W. Milton's Ode on the Morning of Christ's Nativity, L'allegro, Il Penseroso, & Lycidas. LC 73-12943. 1974. Repr. of 1931 ed. lib. bdg. 22.50 (ISBN 0-8414-9150-X). Folcroft.
Visiak, E. H. Animus Against Milton. 1945. lib. bdg. 8.50 (ISBN 0-8414-9173-9). Folcroft.
Wagenknecht, Edward. Personality of Milton. LC 71-108807. 1970. 9.95x (ISBN 0-8061-0916-5). U of Okla Pr.
Warner, Rex. John Milton. LC 72-12371. Repr. of 1949 ed. lib. bdg. 10.00 (ISBN 0-8414-9389-8). Folcroft.
Watkins, Walter B. Anatomy of Milton's Verse. 1965. Repr. of 1955 ed. 15.00 (ISBN 0-208-00170-0, Archon). Shoe String.
Werblowsky, Raphael J. Lucifer & Prometheus: A Study of Milton's Satan. LC 79-153359. Repr. of 1952 ed. 7.50 (ISBN 0-404-06906-1). AMS Pr.
Whaler, James. Counterpoint & Symbol. LC 76-117997. (Studies in Blake, No. 3). 1970. Repr. of 1956 ed. lib. bdg. 32.95 (ISBN 0-8383-1052-4). Haskell.
--Counterpoint & Symbol: An Inquiry into the Rhythm of Milton's Epic Style. LC 72-192013. 1956. lib. bdg. 25.00 (ISBN 0-8414-9668-4). Folcroft.
Williamson, George. Milton & Others. 2nd ed. LC 74-134913. 1970. 9.00x (ISBN 0-226-89937-3). U of Chicago Pr.
Williamson, George C. Milton. LC 75-19089. 1975. Repr. of 1905 ed. lib. bdg. 15.00 (ISBN 0-88305-757-3). Norwood Edns.
--Milton Tercentenary: The Portraits, Prints & Writings of John Milton. LC 72-194902. 1973. lib. bdg. 18.50 (ISBN 0-8414-9743-5). Folcroft.
Wolfe, Don M. Milton & His England. LC 76-146646. (Illus.). 1971. 20.00 (ISBN 0-691-06200-5). Princeton U Pr.
Woodberry, George E. Great Writers. facs. ed. LC 67-30236. (Essay Index Reprint Ser). 1907. 12.50 (ISBN 0-8369-1008-7). Arno.
Woodhouse, A. S. The Heavenly Muse: A Preface to Milton. Maccallum, Hugh R., ed. LC 79-185724. 1972. 27.50x (ISBN 0-8020-5247-9). U of Toronto Pr.
--Milton the Poet. LC 73-785. 1955. lib. bdg. 10.00 (ISBN 0-8414-1606-0). Folcroft.
Woodhull, Marianna. Epic of Paradise Lost. LC 72-194899. 1907. lib. bdg. 8.00 (ISBN 0-8414-9501-7). Folcroft.
Woods, M. A. Characters of Paradise Lost. LC 72-6863. 1908. lib. bdg. 20.00 (ISBN 0-8414-0133-0). Folcroft.
Young, Richard B., et al. Three Studies in the Renaissance: Sidney, Jonson, Milton. LC 69-15695. (Yale Studies in English Ser.: No. 138). 1969. Repr. of 1958 ed. 19.50 (ISBN 0-208-00780-6, Archon). Shoe String.

MILTON, JOHN, 1608-1674–ARCADES

Demaray, John G. Milton & the Masque Tradition: The Early Poems, Arcades & Comus. LC 68-14254. (Illus.). 1968. 12.50x (ISBN 0-674-57550-4). Harvard U Pr.

MILTON, JOHN, 1608-1674–AREOPAGITICA

Gilman, Wilbur E. Milton's Rhetoric, Studies in His Defense of Liberty. LC 76-25152. 1939. lib. bdg. 7.25 (ISBN 0-8414-4435-8). Folcroft.
Jebb, Richard C. Milton's Areopagitica. LC 74-28431. 1918. lib. bdg. 6.45 (ISBN 0-8414-5331-4). Folcroft.
Milton, John. Areopagitica. Jebb, Richard C., ed. LC 72-170811. Repr. of 1918 ed. 11.50 (ISBN 0-404-03556-6). AMS Pr.
Ould, Hermon, ed. Freedom of Expression. LC 73-111309. 1970. Repr. of 1944 ed. 12.50 (ISBN 0-8046-0968-3). Kennikat.

MILTON, JOHN, 1608-1674–BIBLIOGRAPHY

Boswell, Jackson C. Milton's Library. LC 74-22095. (Reference Library of the Humanities: No. 1). 300p. 1974. lib. bdg. 32.00 (ISBN 0-8240-1057-4). Garland Pub.
Fletcher, Harris F. Contributions to a Milton Bibliography Eighteen Hundred to Nineteen Hundred & Thirty. LC 73-11330. Repr. of 1931 ed. lib. bdg. 15.00 (ISBN 0-8414-1975-2). Folcroft.
--Contributions to a Milton Bibliography 1800-1930. (Illinois Studies in Language & Literature). 1969. Repr. of 1931 ed. 9.50 (ISBN 0-384-16005-0). Johnson Repr.
--Contributions to a Milton Bibliography, 1800-1930. LC 67-18300. 1967. Repr. of 1931 ed. 8.50 (ISBN 0-8462-0895-4). Russell.
Hanford, James H. & McQueen, William A. Milton. 2nd ed. LC 76-4625. (Goldentree Bibliographies in Language & Literature). 1979. text ed. 17.95x (ISBN 0-88295-571-3); pap. text ed. 12.95x (ISBN 0-88295-561-6). Harlan Davidson.
Huckabay, Calvin. John Milton: A Bibliographical Supplement. LC 60-11948. Repr. of 1960 ed. 32.50 (ISBN 0-404-04346-1). AMS Pr.
Huckabay, Calvin & Hudson, J. John Milton: An Annotated Bibliography 1929-1968. rev. ed. LC 73-98551. (Duquesne Philological Ser.: No. 1). 1970. text ed. 17.50x (ISBN 0-8207-0126-2). Humanities.
Milton, John. Catalogue of an Exhibition Commemorative of the Tercentenary of the Birth of John Milton. Repr. of 1909 ed. lib. bdg. 15.00 (ISBN 0-8414-6620-3). Folcroft.
Mutschmann, H. Milton's Eyesight & the Chronology of His Works. LC 72-194770. 1924. lib. bdg. 7.75 (ISBN 0-8414-6692-0). Folcroft.
Smith, Robert M. The Variant Issues of Shakespeare's Second Folio & Milton's First Published English Poem. LC 75-30813. 1975. Repr. of 1928 ed. lib. bdg. 10.00 (ISBN 0-8414-7544-X). Folcroft.
Thompson, Elbert N. John Milton: A Topical Bibliography. LC 70-176151. Repr. of 1916 ed. 5.00 (ISBN 0-404-06398-5). AMS Pr.
--John Milton: Topical Bibliography. LC 73-11376. 1916. lib. bdg. 6.50 (ISBN 0-8414-2693-7). Folcroft.
Williamson, George C. Milton Tercentenary: The Portraits, Prints & Writings of John Milton. LC 72-194902. 1973. lib. bdg. 18.50 (ISBN 0-8414-9743-5). Folcroft.

MILTON, JOHN, 1608-1674–COMUS

Demaray, John G. Milton & the Masque Tradition: The Early Poems, Arcades & Comus. LC 68-14254. (Illus.). 1968. 12.50x (ISBN 0-674-57550-4). Harvard U Pr.
Egerton, Alix. Milton's Comus: Being the Bridgewater Manuscript. LC 73-14760. 1910. lib. bdg. 20.00 (ISBN 0-8414-3914-1). Folcroft.
Johnson, Samuel. Johnson's Prologue to Comus Seventeen Hundred & Fifty. Repr. of 1925 ed. lib. bdg. 6.50 (ISBN 0-8414-5388-8). Folcroft.
Stevens, David H. Milton Papers. LC 75-176438. Repr. of 1927 ed. 5.00 (ISBN 0-404-06262-8). AMS Pr.
Todd, Henry J. Some Account of the Life & Writings of John Milton. 437p. 1980. Repr. of 1826 ed. lib. bdg. 50.00 (ISBN 0-8492-8406-6). R West.

MILTON, JOHN, 1608-1674–CONCORDANCES

Bradshaw, John. A Concordance to the Poetical Works of John Milton. LC 70-144894. 412p. 1972. Repr. of 1894 ed. 27.00 (ISBN 0-403-00833-6). Scholarly.
--A Concordance to the Poetical Works of John Milton. LC 77-13457. 1977. Repr. of 1894 ed. lib. bdg. 20.00 (ISBN 0-89341-452-2). Longwood Pr.
Cleveland, Charles D. Complete Concordance to the Poetical Works of John Milton. LC 76-57784. 1867. lib. bdg. 25.00 (ISBN 0-8414-3459-X). Folcroft.
Cooper, L., ed. Concordance of the Latin, Greek, & Italian Poems of John Milton. Repr. of 1923 ed. 11.00 (ISBN 0-527-19440-9). Kraus Repr.
Hudson, Gladys W. Paradise Lost: A Concordance. LC 74-127413. 1971. 28.00 (ISBN 0-8103-1002-3). Gale.
Ingram, William & Swain, Kathleen M., eds. Concordance to Milton's English Poetry. 1972. 98.00x (ISBN 0-19-811138-X). Oxford U Pr.
Lockwood, Laura E. Lexicon to the English Poetical Works of John Milton. LC 68-56596. (Bibliography & Reference Ser: No. 323). 1968. Repr. of 1907 ed. 32.00 (ISBN 0-8337-2132-1). B Franklin.

MILTON, JOHN, 1608-1674–CRITICISM AND INTERPRETATION

Allen, Don C. The Harmonious Vision: Studies in Milton's Poetry. 1979. Repr. of 1970 ed. lib. bdg. 14.00x (ISBN 0-374-90139-2). Octagon.
Barker, Arthur. Milton's Schoolmasters. 1979. 24.50 (ISBN 0-685-94335-6). Porter.
Brisman, Leslie. Milton's Poetry of Choice & Its Romantic Heirs. (Illus.). 335p. 1973. 22.50x (ISBN 0-8014-0666-8). Cornell U Pr.
Brown, Eleanor G. Milton's Blindness. LC 73-11333. 1971. Repr. of 1934 ed. lib. bdg. 20.00 (ISBN 0-8414-3197-3). Folcroft.
Burnett, Archie. Milton's Style: The Shorter Poems, Paradise Regained, & Samson Argonistes. 240p. (Orig.). 1981. text ed. 22.00x (ISBN 0-582-49128-2); pap. text ed. 10.95x (ISBN 0-582-49129-0). Longman.
Byron, May C. A Day with John Milton. LC 77-21475. 1977. Repr. of 1912 ed. lib. bdg. 15.00 (ISBN 0-685-85840-5). Folcroft.
Byse, Fanny. Milton on the Continent: A Key to L'Allegro & Il Pensaroso. 1978. Repr. of 1903 ed. lib. bdg. 12.50 (ISBN 0-8495-0432-5). Arden Lib.
Candy, Hugh C. Milton, the Individualist in Metre. 49p. 1980. Repr. lib. bdg. 8.50 (ISBN 0-89987-112-7). Darby Bks.
Carey, John & Fowler, Alastair. Poems of Milton. (Longman Annotated English Poets Ser.). 1181p. 1980. text ed. 60.00x (ISBN 0-582-48443-X). Longman.
Channing, William E. The Character & Writings of John Milton. 1978. Repr. lib. bdg. 10.00 (ISBN 0-8495-0837-1). Arden Lib.
Cohen, Kitty. The Throne & the Chariot: Studies in Milton's Hebraism. (Studies in English Literature: No. 97). 1975. text ed. 36.25x (ISBN 0-686-22628-3). Mouton.
Condee, Ralph W. Structure in Milton's Poetry: From the Foundation to the Pinnacles. LC 73-12934. 240p. 1974. 15.95x (ISBN 0-271-01133-5). Pa St U Pr.
Critical Essays on Milton from E. L. H. 7.50 (ISBN 0-8446-0565-4). Peter Smith.
Dello Buono, Carmen J. Rare Early Essays on John Milton. 204p. 1981. lib. bdg. 22.50 (ISBN 0-8482-3682-3). Norwood Edns.
Demaray, John G. Milton's Theatrical Epic: The Invention & Design of Paradise Lost. LC 79-23139. (Illus.). 1980. text ed. 16.50x (ISBN 0-674-57615-2). Harvard U Pr.
Dunbar, Pamela. William Blake's Illustrations to the Poetry of Milton. (Illus.). 282p. 59.00x (ISBN 0-19-817345-8). Oxford U Pr.
Eastland, Elizabeth W. Milton's Ethics: A Summary of a Thesis. 55p. 1980. Repr. of 1942 ed. lib. bdg. 10.00 (ISBN 0-8495-1339-1). Arden Lib.
Fiore, Peter A. Milton & Augustine: Patterns of Augustinian Thought in Milton's Paradise Lost. LC 80-17854. 144p. 1981. 14.50x (ISBN 0-271-00269-7). Pa St U Pr.
Franson, John K., ed. Milton Reconsidered: Essays in Honour of Arthur E. Baker. (Salzburg Studies in English Literature: Elizabethan & Renaissance Studies: No. 49). (Illus.). 215p. 1976. pap. text ed. 25.00x (ISBN 0-391-01378-5). Humanities.
Hill, Christopher. Milton & the English Revolution. 1978. 20.00 (ISBN 0-670-47612-9). Viking Pr.
Hill, John S. John Milton--Poet, Priest & Prophet: A Study of Divine Vocation in Milton's Poetry & Prose. 233p. 1979. 20.00x (ISBN 0-8476-6124-5). Rowman.
Hunt, Clay. Lycidas & the Italian Critics. LC 78-15344. 1979. text ed. 16.50 (ISBN 0-300-02269-7). Yale U Pr.
Kastor, Frank S. Milton & the Literary Satan. LC 74-81305. 119p. (Orig.). 1976. pap. text ed. 11.50x (ISBN 90-6203-198-6). Humanities.
Labriola, Albert C. & Lieb, Michael, eds. Eyes Fast Fixt: Current Perspectives in Milton Methodology. LC 69-12335. (Milton Studies Ser.: Vol. 7). 1975. 19.95x (ISBN 0-8229-3305-5). U of Pittsburgh Pr.
Lake, D. J. John Milton! Paradise Lost. 128p. 1981. Repr. of 1967 ed. lib. bdg. 20.00 (ISBN 0-89984-313-1). Century Bookbindery.
LeComte, Edward. Milton's Unchanging Mind: Three Essays. LC 73-83266. 132p. 1974. 11.00 (ISBN 0-8046-9060-X). Kennikat.
Lewalski, Barbara K. Milton's Brief Epic: The Genre, Meaning, & Art of Paradise Regained. LC 66-10282. xii, 436p. 1966. 16.00 (ISBN 0-87057-095-1, Pub. by Brown U Pr). U Pr of New Eng.
MacKellar, Walter, ed. Variorum Commentary on the Poems of John Milton, Vol. 4. 400p. 1975. 30.00 (ISBN 0-231-08883-3). Columbia U Pr.
Maresca, Thomas E. Three English Epics: Studies of "Troilus & Criseyde", "The Faerie Queene", & "Paradise Lost". LC 79-1080. xi, 222p. 1979. 15.95x (ISBN 0-8032-3059-1). U of Nebr Pr.
Marilla, E. L. Milton & Modern Man: Selected Essays. LC 67-17942. 149p. 1968. 7.50x (ISBN 0-8173-7307-1). U of Ala Pr.

Milner, Andrew. John Milton & the English Revolution: A Study in the Sociology of Literature. 248p. 1981. 29.50x (ISBN 0-389-20123-5). B&N.

Nelson, James G. The Sublime Puritan: Milton & the Victorians. LC 74-8794. (Illus.). 209p. 1974. Repr. of 1963 ed. lib. bdg. 15.00 (ISBN 0-8371-7586-0, NESP). Greenwood.

Osgood, C. G. The Classical Mythology of Milton's English Poems. (Reprints in History). Repr. of 1900 ed. lib. bdg. 22.50x (ISBN 0-697-00014-1). Irvington.

Patrides, C. A. & Waddington, Raymond B., eds. The Age of Milton: Backgrounds to Seventeenth-Century Literature. 400p. 1981. 60.00x (ISBN 0-686-73056-9, Pub. by Manchester U Pr England). State Mutual Bk.

Pointon, M. R. Milton & English Art, Sixteen Thirty-Eight to Eighteen Sixty. 320p. 1980. 35.00x (ISBN 0-7190-0371-7, Pub. by Manchester U Pr England); pap. 18.00x (ISBN 0-7190-0593-0). State Mutual Bk.

Rajan, B., ed. The Presence of Milton. LC 69-12335. (Milton Studies Ser: Vol. 11). (Illus.). 1978. 9.95x (ISBN 0-8229-3373-X). U of Pittsburgh Pr.

Rama Sarma, M. V. Heroic Argument: A Study of Milton's Heroic Poetry. 108p. 1979. pap. text ed. 6.25x (ISBN 0-391-01741-1). Humanities.

Roston, Murray. Milton & the Baroque. LC 79-21611. (Illus.). 1980. 24.95 (ISBN 0-8229-1138-8). U of Pittsburgh Pr.

Rudrum, Alan, ed. Milton, 1970. (Modern Judgement Ser.): 1978. 2.50 (ISBN 0-87695-100-0). Aurora Pubs.

Saurat, Denis. Milton: Man & Thinker. LC 73-153352. Repr. of 1925 ed. 24.50 (ISBN 0-404-05565-6). AMS Pr.

Shawcross, John T., ed. Milton 1732-1801: The Critical Heritage. (Critical Heritage Ser.). 1972. 33.75x (ISBN 0-7100-7261-9). Routledge & Kegan.

Simmonds, James D., ed. Milton Studies, Vol. XV. LC 69-12335. 288p. 1981. 23.95x (ISBN 0-8229-3449-3). U of Pittsburgh Pr.

--Milton Studies, Vol. XIV. LC 69-12335. (Milton Studies). (Illus.). 286p. 1980. 21.95x (ISBN 0-8229-3429-9). U of Pittsburgh Pr.

--Milton Studies, Vol. XIII. LC 69-12335. (Milton Studies). 1979. 20.95x (ISBN 0-8229-3404-3). U of Pittsburgh Pr.

--Milton Studies, Vol. X. LC 69-12335. (Milton Studies). 1977. 14.95x (ISBN 0-8229-3356-X). U of Pittsburgh Pr.

Singh, Brijraj. Milton: An Introduction. 1977. 5.50x (ISBN 0-333-90213-0). South Asia Bks.

Stein, Arnold. The Art of Presence: The Poet & Paradise Lost. 1976. 19.50x (ISBN 0-520-03167-9). U of Cal Pr.

Tayler, Edward W. Milton's Poetry: Studies in Language & Literature Ser. LC 78-12047. (Studies in Language & Literature: No. 2). 1979. text ed. 18.00x (ISBN 0-391-00863-3). Duquesne.

Visak, Edward H. Milton Agonistes: A Metaphysical Criticism. 104p. 1980. Repr. of 1923 ed. lib. bdg. 17.50 (ISBN 0-8492-2834-4). R West.

Warner, R. John Milton. LC 75-30812. (Studies in Milton, No. 22). 1975. lib. bdg. 29.95 (ISBN 0-8383-2097-X). Haskell.

Webber, Joan. Milton & His Epic Tradition. LC 78-4368. 260p. 1979. 16.50 (ISBN 0-295-95618-6). U of Wash Pr.

Whaler, James. Counterpoint & Symbol. 1978. Repr. of 1956 ed. lib. bdg. 25.00 (ISBN 0-8495-5804-2). Arden Lib.

Wittreich, Joseph A., Jr. Angel of Apocalypse: Blake's Idea of Milton. LC 74-27316. 358p. 1975. 30.00x (ISBN 0-299-06800-5). U of Wis Pr.

Wittreich, Joseph A., Jr., ed. Milton & the Line of Vision. LC 75-12215. (Illus.). 280p. 1975. 27.50x (ISBN 0-299-06910-9). U of Wis Pr.

Wood, Louis A. The Form & Origin of Milton's Antitrinitarian Conception. 1979. Repr. of 1911 ed. lib. bdg. 16.50 (ISBN 0-8495-5650-3). Arden Lib.

Woodhouse, A. S. The Heavenly Muse: A Preface to Milton. Maccallum, Hugh R., ed. LC 79-185724. 1972. 27.50x (ISBN 0-8020-5247-9). U of Toronto Pr.

MILTON, JOHN, 1608-1674–DICTIONARIES, INDEXES, ETC.

Coleridge, K. A. A Descriptive Catalogue of the Milton Collection in the Alexander Turnbull Library, Wellington, New Zealand. (Illus.). 544p. 1980. 98.00x (ISBN 0-19-920110-2). Oxford U Pr.

Gilbert, A. H. A Geographical Dictionary of Milton. 59.95 (ISBN 0-8490-0216-8). Gordon Pr.

Gilbert, Allan H. Geographical Dictionary of Milton. LC 76-25214. 1971. Repr. of 1919 ed. lib. bdg. 9.45 (ISBN 0-8414-4528-1). Folcroft.

--Geographical Dictionary of Milton. LC 68-10922. 1968. Repr. of 1919 ed. 9.50 (ISBN 0-8462-1105-X). Russell.

--A Geographical Dictionary of Milton. 1979. Repr. of 1919 ed. lib. bdg. 35.00 (ISBN 0-8495-2014-2). Arden Lib.

Hunter, William B., Jr., ed. A Milton Encyclopedia, 8 vols. Incl. Vol. 1. A-B (ISBN 0-8387-1834-5); Vol. 2. C-Ec (ISBN 0-8387-1835-3); Vol. 3. Ed-Hi (ISBN 0-8387-1836-1); Vol. 4. Ho-La (ISBN 0-8387-1837-X); Vol. 5. Le-N (ISBN 0-8387-1838-8); Vol. 6. O-Po (ISBN 0-8387-1839-6); Vol. 7. Pr-Sl (ISBN 0-8387-1840-X); Vol. 8. Sm-Z (ISBN 0-8387-1841-8). 25.00 ea.; 180.00 set (ISBN 0-685-66788-X). Bucknell U Pr.

Le Comte, Edward. Dictionary of Puns in Milton's English Poetry. 240p. 1981. 25.00x (ISBN 0-231-05102-6). Columbia U Pr.

Le Comte, Edward S. Milton Dictionary. LC 76-86175. Repr. of 1961 ed. 19.50 (ISBN 0-404-03917-0). AMS Pr.

Lockwood, Laura E. Lexicon to the English Poetical Works of John Milton. LC 72-193205. 1972. lib. bdg. 27.45 (ISBN 0-8414-5878-2). Folcroft.

Luey, Beth E. Milton Studies Index: Vols. I-XII. LC 69-12335. 1980. 16.95x (ISBN 0-8229-3389-6). U of Pittsburgh Pr.

MILTON, JOHN, 1608-1674–HISTORY OF BRITAIN

McDill, Joseph M. Milton & the Pattern of Calvinism. LC 74-19202. 1974. Repr. of 1942 ed. lib. bdg. 30.00 (ISBN 0-8414-5908-8). Folcroft.

Mutschmann, Heinrich. Milton's Projected Epic on the Rise & Future Greatness of the Britannic Nation. 1980. Repr. of 1936 ed. lib. bdg. 10.00 (ISBN 0-8492-6830-3). R West.

MILTON, JOHN, 1608-1674–JUVENILE LITERATURE

Strousse, Flora. John Milton. LC 62-13343. (gr. 7-11). 1960. 6.95 (ISBN 0-8149-0411-4). Vanguard.

MILTON, JOHN, 1608-1674–KNOWLEDGE AND LEARNING

Babb, Lawrence. Moral Cosmos of Paradise Lost. 1970. 7.50 (ISBN 0-87013-154-0). Mich St U Pr.

Bailey, Margaret L. Milton & Jakob Boehme. LC 65-15885. (Studies in Comparative Literature, No. 35). 1969. Repr. of 1914 ed. lib. bdg. 31.95 (ISBN 0-8383-0505-9). Haskell.

Banks, Theodore H. Milton's Imagery. LC 69-19874. (BCL Ser. II). Repr. of 1950 ed. 17.00 (ISBN 0-404-00498-9). AMS Pr.

Cawley, Robert R. Milton & the Literature of Travel. LC 72-114095. (Princeton Studies in English: No. 32). 1970. Repr. of 1951 ed. text ed. 7.50 (ISBN 0-87752-015-1). Gordian.

Curry, Walter C. Milton's Ontology, Cosmogony & Physics. LC 57-5833. (Illus.). 226p. 1966. pap. 4.00x (ISBN 0-8131-0102-6). U Pr of Ky.

Fletcher, Harris F. Milton's Rabbinical Readings. LC 67-30701. 1967. Repr. of 1930 ed. 8.50 (ISBN 0-87752-034-8). Gordian.

--Milton's Rabbinical Readings. 1967. Repr. of 1930 ed. 19.50 (ISBN 0-208-00335-5, Archon). Shoe String.

--Milton's Semitic Studies & Some Manifestations of Them in His Poetry. LC 66-29575. 1966. Repr. of 1926 ed. 6.00 (ISBN 0-87752-035-6). Gordian.

--Use of the Bible in Milton's Prose. 1973. lib. bdg. 59.95 (ISBN 0-87968-014-8). Gordon Pr.

Frye, Roland M. Milton's Imagery & the Visual Arts: Iconographic Tradition in the Epic Poems. LC 77-24541. 1978. text ed. 40.00 (ISBN 0-691-06349-4). Princeton U Pr.

Myhr, Ivar L. The Evolution & Practice of Milton's Epic Theory. 53p. 1980. Repr. of 1942 ed. lib. bdg. 20.00 (ISBN 0-8495-3825-4). Arden Lib.

Orchard, Thomas N. Milton's Astronomy. 1978. Repr. of 1913 ed. lib. bdg. 30.00 (ISBN 0-8495-4205-7). Arden Lib.

Spaeth, Sigmund G. Milton's Knowledge of Music. LC 72-8052. (Music Ser). 186p. 1972. Repr. of 1913 ed. lib. bdg. 22.50 (ISBN 0-306-70535-4). Da Capo.

Svendsen, Kester. Milton & Science. Repr. of 1956 ed. lib. bdg. 15.00x (ISBN 0-8371-2410-7, SVMS). Greenwood.

Warren, William F. Universe As Pictured in Milton's Paradise Lost. LC 73-12894. 1915. lib. bdg. 4.95 (ISBN 0-8414-9418-5). Folcroft.

MILTON, JOHN, 1608-1674–PARADISE LOST

Addison, Joseph. Addison: Criticisms on Paradise Lost. Cook, Albert S., ed. 1976. Repr. of 1892 ed. 15.00 (ISBN 0-403-05785-X, Regency). Scholarly.

--Criticism on Paradise Lost. Cook, Albert S., ed. LC 68-59040. 1968. Repr. of 1924 ed. 8.50 (ISBN 0-87753-001-7). Phaeton.

Anand, Shahla. Of Costliest Emblem: Paradise Lost & the Emblem Tradition. LC 78-59853. (Illus.). 1978. pap. text ed. 11.25 (ISBN 0-8191-0556-2). U Pr of Amer.

Babb, Lawrence. Moral Cosmos of Paradise Lost. 1970. 7.50 (ISBN 0-87013-154-0). Mich St U Pr.

Barnett, Pamela R. Theodore Haak, F. R. S. 1605-1690, the First German Translator of Paradise Lost. 1962. text ed. 19.00x (ISBN 0-686-22468-X). Mouton.

Berry, Boyd M. Process of Speech: Puritan Religious Writing & Paradise Lost. LC 75-36933. 304p. 1976. 19.00x (ISBN 0-8018-1779-X). Johns Hopkins.

Blessington, Francis C. Paradise Lost & the Classical Epic. 1979. 18.00 (ISBN 0-7100-0160-6). Routledge & Kegan.

Blondel, Jacques. Milton Poete De la Bible Dans le Paradis Perdu. LC 73-13668. 1959. lib. bdg. 12.50 (ISBN 0-8414-3252-X). Folcroft.

Bogholm, N. Milton & Paradise Lost. LC 74-7116. (Studies in Milton, No. 22). 1974. lib. bdg. 39.95 (ISBN 0-8383-1968-8). Haskell.

--Milton & Paradise Lost. 1932. lib. bdg. 10.75 (ISBN 0-8414-2532-9). Folcroft.

Broadbent, John. Introduction to Paradise Lost. (Milton for Schools & Colleges Ser). (Illus.). 1971. 28.50 (ISBN 0-521-08068-1); pap. 7.95x (ISBN 0-521-09639-1). Cambridge U Pr.

Broadbent, John, ed. John Milton: Paradise Lost Bks. 1-2. (Milton for Schools & Colleges Ser). (gr. 11-12). 1972. text ed. 6.95 (ISBN 0-521-08298-6). Cambridge U Pr.

Cann, Christian. Scriptural & Allegorical Glossary to Milton's Paradise Lost. Repr. of 1828 ed. 30.00 (ISBN 0-8414-0566-2). Folcroft.

--A Scriptural & Allegorical Glossary to Milton's Paradise Lost. 1978. Repr. of 1828 ed. lib. bdg. 35.00 (ISBN 0-8495-0807-X). Arden Lib.

Carter, George. The Story of Milton's Paradise. 1909. lib. bdg. 15.00 (ISBN 0-8414-1590-0). Folcroft.

Cohen, Kitty. The Throne & the Chariot: Studies in Milton's Hebraism. (Studies in English Literature: No. 97). 1975. text ed. 36.25x (ISBN 0-686-22628-3). Mouton.

Condee, Ralph W. Milton's Theories Concerning Epic Poetry. LC 77-861. 1977. lib. bdg. 6.00 (ISBN 0-8414-3421-2). Folcroft.

Considerations on Milton's Early Reading & the Prima Stamina of His Paradise Lost. 59.95 (ISBN 0-87968-933-1). Gordon Pr.

Cope, Jackson. The Metaphoric Structure of Paradise Lost. 1979. Repr. of 1962 ed. lib. bdg. 14.00x (ISBN 0-374-91920-8). Octagon.

Cowling, George H. Shelley, & Other Essays. facs. ed. LC 67-23198. (Essay Index Reprint Ser). 1936. 15.00 (ISBN 0-8369-0344-7). Arno.

Diekhoff, John S. Milton's Paradise Lost: A Commentary on the Argument. 1963. Repr. of 1946 ed. text ed. 10.00x (ISBN 0-391-00447-6). Humanities.

Douglas, John. Milton No Plagiary; or a Detection of the Forgeries. LC 72-187954. Repr. of 1756 ed. lib. bdg. 10.00 (ISBN 0-8414-0508-5). Folcroft.

Evans, J. M. John Milton's Paradise Lost, Bks. 9-10. LC 72-87438. (Milton for Schools & Colleges). 208p. 1973. 7.50 set (ISBN 0-521-20067-9). Cambridge U Pr.

--Paradise Lost & the Genesis Tradition. 1968. 22.00x (ISBN 0-19-811665-9). Oxford U Pr.

Fish, Stanley E. Surprised by Sin: The Reader in Paradise Lost. 1971. pap. 3.45 (ISBN 0-520-01897-4, CAL228). U of Cal Pr.

Frye, Northrop. The Return of Eden: Five Essays on Milton's Epics. 1975. 12.50x (ISBN 0-8020-1353-8); pap. 5.00 (ISBN 0-8020-6281-4). U of Toronto Pr.

Gardner, Helen. Reading of Paradise Lost. 1965. pap. 11.50x (ISBN 0-19-811662-4). Oxford U Pr.

Gilbert, Allan H. On the Composition of Paradise Lost. 1966. lib. bdg. 13.00x (ISBN 0-374-93059-7). Octagon.

Gurteen, S. Humphreys. Epic of the Fall of Man. LC 65-15879. (Studies in Comparative Literature, No. 35). 1969. Repr. of 1896 ed. lib. bdg. 49.95 (ISBN 0-8383-0561-X). Haskell.

Hagin, Peter. Epic Hero & the Decline of Heroic Poetry, Study of the Neoclassical English Epic with Special Reference to Milton's Paradise Lost. LC 72-191806. 1964. lib. bdg. 20.00 (ISBN 0-8414-4978-3). Folcroft.

Hamilton, K. G. Paradise Lost: A Humanist Approach. (Scholars' Library). 122p. 1981. text ed. 32.50x (ISBN 0-7022-1626-7). U of Queensland Pr.

Hamlet, Desmond M. One Greater Man: Justice & Damnation in Paradise Lost. LC 74-27670. 224p. 1976. 14.50 (ISBN 0-8387-1674-1). Bucknell U Pr.

Hayley, William. Life of Milton. LC 78-122485. 1970. Repr. of 1796 ed. 37.00x (ISBN 0-8201-1081-7). Schol Facsimiles.

Himes, John A. A Study of Milton's Paradise Lost. LC 76-17888. 1976. lib. bdg. 35.00 (ISBN 0-8414-4841-8). Folcroft.

Hollington, M. & Wilkinson, L., eds. Paradise Lost, Bks. 11, 12. LC 75-36682. (Milton for School and Colleges Ser.). (Illus.). 128p. 1976. pap. 6.95x (ISBN 0-521-21091-7). Cambridge U Pr.

Hume, Patrick. Annotations on Milton's Paradise Lost. 1595. lib. bdg. 35.00 (ISBN 0-8414-5230-X). Folcroft.

Hunter, G. K. Paradise Lost. (Unwin Critical Library). 232p. 1980. text ed. 17.95x (ISBN 0-04-800004-3). Allen Unwin.

Jacobus, Lee A. Sudden Apprehension: Aspects of Knowledge in Paradise Lost. (Studies in English Literature: No. 94). 225p. 1976. text ed. 42.50x (ISBN 90-2793-253-0). Mouton.

Kirkconnell, Watson. Celestial Cycles: The Theme of Paradise Lost in World Literature with Translations of the Major Analogues. LC 67-30308. 1967. Repr. of 1952 ed. 17.50 (ISBN 0-87752-058-5). Gordian.

Knott, John R., Jr. Milton's Pastoral Vision: An Approach to "Paradise Lost". LC 79-145576. 1971. text ed. 8.50x (ISBN 0-226-44846-0). U of Chicago Pr.

Kranidas, Thomas, ed. New Essays on Paradise Lost. LC 72-82463. 1969. pap. 3.65x (ISBN 0-520-01902-4, CAMPUS51). U of Cal Pr.

Lake, D. J. John Milton! Paradise Lost. 128p. 1981. Repr. of 1967 ed. lib. bdg. 20.00 (ISBN 0-89984-313-1). Century Bookbindery.

Lewis, Clive S. Preface to Paradise Lost. 1942. pap. 3.95x (ISBN 0-686-76896-5). Oxford U Pr.

Lieb, Michael. The Dialectics of Creation: Patterns of Birth & Regeneration in Paradise Lost. LC 71-76047. 1970. 12.00x (ISBN 0-87023-049-2). U of Mass Pr.

--Poetics of the Holy: A Reading of Paradise Lost. LC 80-29159. 450p. 1981. 28.00x (ISBN 0-8078-1479-2). U of NC Pr.

Livingston, Howard. A Dramatization Milton's Paradise Lost. 51p. (Orig.). 1980. pap. text ed. 3.50 (ISBN 0-89669-056-3). Collegium Bk Pubs.

Marilla, Esmond L. Central Problem of Paradise Lost. 1953. lib. bdg. 8.50 (ISBN 0-8414-6200-3). Folcroft.

Massey, William. Remarks Upon Milton's Paradise Lost. 276p. 1980. Repr. of 1761 ed. lib. bdg. 35.00 (ISBN 0-8492-6755-2). R West.

--Remarks Upon Milton's Paradise Lost. LC 77-4961. 1751. lib. bdg. 30.00 (ISBN 0-8414-6194-5). Folcroft.

Milton, J. Paradise Lost, Bks. 7 & 8. Aers, D. & Radzinowicz, Mary Ann, eds. LC 77-181884. (Milton for Schools & Colleges Ser). 200p. 1974. pap. text ed. 6.95x (ISBN 0-521-20457-7). Cambridge U Pr.

Milton, John. Milton's Paradise Lost. Verity, A. W., ed. LC 72-4906. 1921. lib. bdg. 65.00 (ISBN 0-8414-0012-1). Folcroft.

--Milton's "Paradise Lost.". new ed. Bentley, Richard, ed. LC 74-5237. Repr. of 1732 ed. 67.50 (ISBN 0-404-11537-3). AMS Pr.

--Paradise Lost. Elledge, Scott, ed. (Critical Editions Ser). 546p. 1975. 19.95 (ISBN 0-393-04406-8); pap. 6.95x (ISBN 0-393-09230-5). Norton.

--Paradise Lost, Bks. 5 & 6. Hodge, R. I. & MacCaffrey, I., eds. LC 75-8314. (Milton for Schools & Colleges Ser). (Illus.). 176p. 1975. pap. text ed. 6.95x (ISBN 0-521-20796-7). Cambridge U Pr.

Mutschmann, H. Further Studies Concerning the Origin of Paradise Lost. LC 77-24899. lib. bdg. 7.50 (ISBN 0-8414-6211-9). Folcroft.

Mutschmann, Heinrich. Studies Concerning the Origins of Milton's Paradise Lost. LC 79-163459. (Studies in Milton, No. 22). 1971. Repr. of 1924 ed. lib. bdg. 24.95 (ISBN 0-8383-1324-8). Haskell.

--Studies Concerning the Origins of Milton's Paradise Lost. 1924. Repr. 10.00 (ISBN 0-8274-3532-0). R West.

Orchard, Thomas N. Astronomy of Milton's Paradise Lost. LC 68-4178. (Studies in Milton, No. 22). (Illus.). 1969. Repr. of 1896 ed. lib. bdg. 49.95 (ISBN 0-8383-0672-1). Haskell.

Paskus, John M. Not Less but More Heroic: Milton's Classical & Christian Worlds. 1978. 12.00 (ISBN 0-533-03372-1). Vantage.

Patrick, John M. Milton's Conception of Sin As Developed in Paradise Lost. 1930. Repr. 10.00 (ISBN 0-8274-2740-9). R West.

Peter, John D. Critique of Paradise Lost. LC 70-121758. 1970. Repr. of 1960 ed. 15.00 (ISBN 0-208-00991-4, Archon). Shoe String.

Potter, L & Broadbent, J., eds. Paradise Lost, Bks.3,4. LC 75-36681. (Milton for Schools & Colleges Ser.). 200p. 1976. pap. 6.95x (ISBN 0-521-21150-6). Cambridge U Pr.

Revard, Stella P. The War in Heaven. LC 79-23297. (Illus.). 1980. 20.00x (ISBN 0-8014-1138-6). Cornell U Pr.

Richardson, Jonathan & Richardson, Jonathan, Jr. Explanatory Notes & Remarks on Milton's Paradise Lost. LC 77-174317. Repr. of 1734 ed. 37.50 (ISBN 0-404-05298-3). AMS Pr.

Seaman, John E. Moral Paradox of Paradise Lost. LC 74-135665. (Studies in English Literature: Vol. 61). 1971. text ed. 21.25x (ISBN 90-2791-715-9). Mouton.

Shawcross, John T. With Mortal Voice: The Creation of Paradise Lost. LC 80-51944. 224p. 1981. 15.50x (ISBN 0-8131-1450-0). U Pr of Ky.
Smith, Eric. Some Versions of the Fall: The Myth of the Fall of Man in English Literature. LC 75-185025. (Illus.). 1973. 10.95x (ISBN 0-8229-1107-8). U of Pittsburgh Pr.
Steadman, John M. Epic & Tragic Structure in Paradise Lost. LC 75-43234. 1976. lib. bdg. 15.00x (ISBN 0-226-77134-2). U of Chicago Pr.
Stein, Arnold. The Art of Presence: The Poet & Paradise Lost. 1976. 19.50x (ISBN 0-520-03167-9). U of Cal Pr.
Summers, Joseph H. The Muse's Method: An Introduction to Paradise Lost. 230p. Date not set. 11.95 (ISBN 0-86698-004-0); pap. 4.50 (ISBN 0-86698-009-1). Medieval.
Waldock, A. J. Paradise Lost & Its Critics. 1959. 7.75 (ISBN 0-8446-1463-7). Peter Smith.
Warren, William F. Universe As Pictured in Milton's Paradise Lost. LC 73-12894. 1915. lib. bdg. 4.95 (ISBN 0-8414-9418-5). Folcroft.
--Universe As Pictured in Milton's Paradise Lost: An Illustrated Study for Personal & Class Use. LC 68-59037. (Illus.). 1968. Repr. of 1915 ed. 6.00 (ISBN 0-87752-117-4). Gordian.
Weber, Burton J. Construction of Paradise Lost. LC 72-132483. (Literary Structures Ser.). 218p. 1971. 12.50x (ISBN 0-8093-0488-0). S Ill U Pr.
--Construction of Paradise Lost. LC 72-132483. (Literary Structures Ser.). 218p. 1971. 12.50x (ISBN 0-8093-0488-0). S Ill U Pr.
Wilding, M. Milton's Paradise Lost. (Sydney Studies in Literature Ser). 1969. 6.50x (ISBN 0-424-05850-2, Pub. by Sydney U Pr). Intl Schol Bk Serv.
Wilkes, Gerald A. The Thesis of Paradise Lost. LC 76-28374. 1976. Repr. of 1961 ed. lib. bdg. 17.50 (ISBN 0-8414-9514-9). Folcroft.
Woodhull, Marianna. Epic of Paradise Lost: Twelve Essays. LC 68-57833. 1968. Repr. of 1907 ed. 8.50 (ISBN 0-87752-124-7). Gordian.

MILTON, JOHN, 1608-1674–PARADISE REGAINED

Corcoran, M. I. Milton's Paradise with Reference to the Hexameral Background. 1967. pap. 4.95 (ISBN 0-8132-0335-X). Cath U Pr.
Frye, Northrop. The Return of Eden: Five Essays on Milton's Epics. 1975. 12.50x (ISBN 0-8020-1353-8); pap. 5.00 (ISBN 0-8020-6281-4). U of Toronto Pr.
Frye, Roland M. Milton's Imagery & the Visual Arts: Iconographic Tradition in the Epic Poems. LC 77-24541. 1978. text ed. 40.00 (ISBN 0-691-06349-4). Princeton U Pr.
Lewalski, Barbara K. Milton's Brief Epic: The Genre, Meaning, & Art of Paradise Regained. LC 66-10282. 448p. 1967. Repr. of 1966 ed. text ed. 16.00x (ISBN 0-87057-095-1, Pub. by Brown U Pr). U Pr of New Eng.
Meadowcourt, Richard. Milton's Paradise Regained: Two Eighteenth-Century Critiques, 2 vols. in one. Wittreich, Joseph A., Jr., ed. LC 76-161937. 1971. Repr. of 1732 ed. 35.00x (ISBN 0-8201-1087-6). Schol Facsimiles.
Milton, John. Paradise Regained, a Poem, in Four Books. LC 73-9863. Repr. of 1795 ed. lib. bdg. 40.00 (ISBN 0-8414-5950-9). Folcroft.
Pope, Elizabeth M. Paradise Regained: The Tradition & the Poem. LC 61-13783. (Illus.). 1962. Repr. of 1947 ed. 10.00 (ISBN 0-8462-0256-5). Russell.
Stein, Arnold. Heroic Knowledge: An Interpretation of "Paradise Regained" & "Samson Agonistes". 1965. Repr. of 1957 ed. 17.50 (ISBN 0-208-00317-7, Archon). Shoe String.
Weber, Burton J. Wedges & Wings: The Patterning of Paradise Regained. LC 74-20703. (Literary Structure Ser). 144p. 1975. 10.00x (ISBN 0-8093-0673-5). S Ill U Pr.

MILTON, JOHN, 1608-1674–POLITICAL AND SOCIAL VIEWS

Barker, Arthur E. Milton & the Puritan Dilemma, 1641-1660. LC 58-3195. 1942. 22.50x (ISBN 0-8020-5025-5); pap. 7.50 (ISBN 0-8020-6306-3). U of Toronto Pr.
Knight, G. Wilson. Chariot of Wrath: The Message of John Milton to Democracy at War. LC 72-196540. 1942. lib. bdg. 15.00 (ISBN 0-8414-5589-9). Folcroft.
Knight, George W. Chariot of Wrath. 1978. Repr. of 1942 ed. lib. bdg. 25.00 (ISBN 0-8495-3012-1). Arden Lib.
Morand, Paul P. Effects of His Political Life Upon John Milton. 1939. lib. bdg. 15.00 (ISBN 0-685-09929-6). Folcroft.
Ross, Malcolm M. Milton's Royalism: A Study of the Conflict of Symbol & Idea in the Poems. LC 76-102535. 1970. Repr. of 1943 ed. 8.50 (ISBN 0-8462-1185-8). Russell.
Sensabaugh, George. That Grand Whig Milton. LC 67-29815. Repr. of 1952 ed. 14.00 (ISBN 0-405-08948-1, Blom Pubns). Arno.
Sensabaugh, George F. That Grand Whig, Milton. (Stanford University. Stanford Studies in Language & Literature: No. 11). Repr. of 1952 ed. 14.50 (ISBN 0-404-51821-4). AMS Pr.
Stavely, Keith W. The Politics of Milton's Prose Style. LC 74-20086. (Studies in English Ser.: No. 185). 180p. 1975. 12.50x (ISBN 0-300-01804-5). Yale U Pr.
Wolfe, Don M. Milton in the Puritan Revolution. 1963. text ed. 15.00x (ISBN 0-391-00477-8). Humanities.

MILTON, JOHN, 1608-1674–RELIGION AND ETHICS

Acton, Henry. Religious Opinions & Example of Milton, Locke, & Newton. LC 71-158223. Repr. of 1833 ed. 11.50 (ISBN 0-404-00283-8). AMS Pr.
Barker, Arthur. Milton's Schoolmasters. LC 73-16488. 1937. lib. bdg. 6.00 (ISBN 0-8414-9887-3). Folcroft.
Barker, Arthur E. Milton & the Puritan Dilemma, 1641-1660. LC 58-3195. 1942. 22.50x (ISBN 0-8020-5025-5); pap. 7.50 (ISBN 0-8020-6306-3). U of Toronto Pr.
Charlesworth, Arthur R. Paradise Found. LC 72-91109. 1973. 7.50 (ISBN 0-8022-2104-1). Philos Lib.
Conklin, George N. Biblical Criticism & Heresy in Milton. LC 78-159175. x, 137p. 1971. Repr. of 1949 ed. lib. bdg. 13.50x (ISBN 0-374-91905-4). Octagon.
Cullen, Patrick. The Infernal Triad: The Flesh, the World & the Devil in Spenser & Milton. LC 73-16753. 300p. 1974. 21.00 (ISBN 0-691-06267-6). Princeton U Pr.
Eastland, Elizabeth W. Milton's Ethics. LC 76-26903. 1942. lib. bdg. 5.00 (ISBN 0-8414-3939-7). Folcroft.
--Milton's Ethics: A Summary of a Thesis. 1978. Repr. of 1942 ed. 10.00 (ISBN 0-8492-4400-5). R West.
Empson, W. Milton's God. LC 80-40109. 320p. 1981. pap. 15.95 (ISBN 0-521-29910-1). Cambridge U Pr.
Empson, William. Milton's God. LC 78-14409. 1978. Repr. of 1961 ed. lib. bdg. 19.50x (ISBN 0-313-21021-7, EMMG). Greenwood.
Hamlet, Desmond M. One Greater Man: Justice & Damnation in Paradise Lost. LC 74-27670. 224p. 1976. 14.50 (ISBN 0-8387-1674-1). Bucknell U Pr.
Knight, G. Wilson. Chariot of Wrath: The Message of John Milton to Democracy at War. LC 72-196540. 1942. lib. bdg. 15.00 (ISBN 0-8414-5589-9). Folcroft.
Knight, George W. Chariot of Wrath. 1978. Repr. of 1942 ed. lib. bdg. 25.00 (ISBN 0-8495-3012-1). Arden Lib.
McLachlan, Herbert. The Religious Opinions of Milton, Locke & Newton. LC 74-20740. 1974. Repr. of 1941 ed. lib. bdg. 11.95 (ISBN 0-8414-5930-4). Folcroft.
Muldrow, George M. Milton & the Drama of the Soul: A Study of the Theme of the Restoration of Man in Milton's Later Poetry. LC 76-89796. (Studies in English Literature: Vol. 51). 1970. text ed. 36.25x (ISBN 90-2790-530-4). Mouton.
Palacios, Miguel A. Islam & the Divine Comedy. 295p. 1968. Repr. of 1926 ed. 28.50x (ISBN 0-7146-1995-7, F Cass Co). Biblio Dist.
Patrides, C. A. Milton & the Christian Tradition. 1979. Repr. 19.50 (ISBN 0-208-01821-2, Archon). Shoe String.
Sewell, Arthur. Study in Milton's Christian Doctrine. LC 72-193159. 1939. lib. bdg. 6.45 (ISBN 0-8414-8118-0). Folcroft.
--Study in Milton's Christian Doctrine. 1967. Repr. of 1939 ed. 17.50 (ISBN 0-208-00416-5, Archon). Shoe String.
Whiting, George W. Milton & This Pendant World. LC 77-97259. 1969. Repr. of 1958 ed. lib. bdg. 15.00x (ISBN 0-374-98494-8). Octagon.
Wittreich, Joseph A., Jr. Visionary Poetics: Milton's Tradition & His Legacy. LC 78-52569. (Illus.). 1979. 18.50 (ISBN 0-87328-101-2). Huntington Lib.
Wood, Louis A. Form & Origin of Milton's Antitrinitarian Conception. LC 72-191655. 1911. lib. bdg. 15.00 (ISBN 0-8414-0833-5). Folcroft.

MILTON, JOHN, 1608-1674–SAMSON AGONISTES

Kreipe, Christian E. Milton's Samson Agonistes. LC 76-10958. (Ger.). 1926. lib. bdg. 20.00 (ISBN 0-8414-5458-2). Folcroft.
--Milton's Samson Agonistes. 59.95 (ISBN 0-8490-0638-4). Gordon Pr.
Krouse, Michael F. Milton's Samson & the Christian Tradition. LC 74-762. viii, 159p. 1974. Repr. of 1949 ed. lib. bdg. 15.00x (ISBN 0-374-94651-5). Octagon.
Low, Anthony. The Blaze of Noon: A Reading of "Samson Agonistes". 236p. 1974. 15.00x (ISBN 0-231-03842-9). Columbia U Pr.
--The Blaze of Noon: A Reading of "Samson Agonistes". 236p. 1974. 15.00x (ISBN 0-231-03842-9). Columbia U Pr.
Radzinowicz, Mary Ann. Toward Samson Agonistes: The Growth of Milton's Mind. LC 77-85559. 1978. 32.50x (ISBN 0-691-06357-5). Princeton U Pr.
Stein, Arnold. Heroic Knowledge: An Interpretation of "Paradise Regained" & "Samson Agonistes". 1965. Repr. of 1957 ed. 17.50 (ISBN 0-208-00317-7, Archon). Shoe String.
Visiak, E. H. Milton's Agonistes. (Studies in Milton, No. 22). 1970. pap. 12.95 (ISBN 0-8383-0102-9). Haskell.
--Milton's Agonistes: A Metaphysical Criticism. LC 77-9361. 1922. lib. bdg. 10.00 (ISBN 0-8414-9187-9). Folcroft.

MILTON, JOHN, 1608-1674–SONNETS

Berkeley, David S. Inwrought with Figures Dim: A Reading of Milton's Lycidas. (De Proprietatibus Litterarum Ser. Didactica: No. 2). 1974. pap. text ed. 22.35x (ISBN 90-2792-605-0). Mouton.
Fletcher, Harris F. John Milton's Complete Poetical Works. (Seventy-Fifth Anniversary Ser.). 1949. Vol. 3. 32.50 (ISBN 0-252-72714-2); Vol. 4. 24.50 (ISBN 0-252-72715-0). U of Ill Pr.
Nardo, Anna K. Milton's Sonnets & the Ideal Community. LC 79-17221. xiv, 213p. 1979. 15.95x (ISBN 0-8032-3302-7). U of Nebr Pr.
Sampson, Aden. Milton's Sonnets. LC 77-5662. 1886. lib. bdg. 10.00 (ISBN 0-8414-7690-X). Folcroft.
Verity, A. W. Milton's Sonnets. LC 72-11699. 1973. lib. bdg. 12.50 (ISBN 0-8414-0906-4). Folcroft.

MILTON, JOHN, 1608-1674–SOURCES

Fletcher, Harris F. The Use of the Bible in Milton's Prose. Repr. of 1929 ed. 12.50 (ISBN 0-384-16005-0). Johnson Repr.
Harding, David Philoon. Milton & the Renaissance Ovid. LC 76-47466. 1977. Repr. of 1946 ed. lib. bdg. 17.50 (ISBN 0-8414-4941-4). Folcroft.
Kirkconnell, Watson. Awake the Courteous Echo: The Themes of Comus, Lycidas, & Paradise Regained in World Literature with Translations of the Major Analogues. LC 78-185721. 340p. 1973. 20.00x (ISBN 0-8020-5266-5). U of Toronto Pr.
Mutschmann, H. Further Studies Concerning the Origin of Paradise Lost. LC 77-24899. lib. bdg. 7.50 (ISBN 0-8414-6211-9). Folcroft.

MILWAUKEE

Anderson, Harry H. & Olson, Fredrick I. Milwaukee: At the Gathering Waters. Blakey, Ellen S., ed. LC 81-65676. (American Potrait Ser.). (Illus.). 224p. 1981. 24.95 (ISBN 0-932986-18-8). Continent Herit.
Hamming, Edward. The Port of Milwaukee. LC 55-3708. (Augustana College Library Ser.: No. 25). 1953. pap. 4.00 (ISBN 0-910182-20-5). Augustana Coll.
Hoan, Daniel W. City Government: The Record of the Milwaukee Experiment. LC 74-14353. 365p. 1975. Repr. of 1936 ed. lib. bdg. 21.00x (ISBN 0-8371-7793-6, HOCI). Greenwood.
McArthur, Shirley D. North Point Historic Districts - Milwaukee. LC 80-83990. (Illus.). 260p. (Orig.). 1981. pap. write for info. (ISBN 0-9606072-0-X). N Point Hist Soc.
Schenker, Eric, et al. Port of Milwaukee: An Economic Review. (Illus.). 228p. 1967. 11.50x (ISBN 0-299-04310-X). U of Wis Pr.
Schultz, Russell E. A Milwaukee Transport Era: The Trackless Trolley Years. Sebree, Mac, ed. (Interurbans Special Ser.: 74). (Illus.). 160p. (Orig.). 1980. pap. 13.95 (ISBN 0-916374-43-2). Interurban.
Simon, Roger D. The City-Building Process: Housing & Services in New Milwaukee Neighborhoods. LC 78-56724. (Transactions Ser.: Vol. 68, Pt. 5). (Illus.). 1978. 8.00 (ISBN 0-87169-685-1). Am Philos.
Wells, Robert. This Is Milwaukee. LC 78-71508. 1978. Repr. of 1970 ed. 10.00 (ISBN 0-932476-00-7). Renaissance Bks.

MILWAUKEE–HISTORY

Anderson, Byron. A Bibliography of Master's Theses & Doctoral Dissertations on Milwaukee Topics, 1911-1977. LC 80-27261. 136p. (Orig.). 1981. pap. 5.00 (ISBN 0-87020-202-2). State Hist Soc Wis.
Anderson, Harry & Olson, Frederick I. Milwaukee Story: At the Gathering of the Waters. Blakey, Ellen S., ed. LC 81-65676. (American Portrait Ser.). (Illus.). 224p. 1981. 24.95 (ISBN 0-932986-18-8). Continental Herit.
Conzen, Kathleen N. Immigrant Milwaukee, 1836-1860. (Studies in Urban History). 1976. text ed. 16.50x (ISBN 0-674-44436-1). Harvard U Pr.
Interurban to Milwaukee: Bulletin-106. (Illus.). 1974. 15.00 (ISBN 0-915348-06-3). Central Electric.
Wells, Robert W. Yesterday's Milwaukee. LC 76-10377. (Historic Cities Ser: No. 23). (Illus.). 144p. 1976. 9.95 (ISBN 0-912458-67-4). E A Seemann.

MILWAUKEE LAKESIDE CHILDREN'S CENTER

Burmeister, Eva E. Forty Five in the Family: The Story of a Home for Children. LC 76-100147. Repr. of 1949 ed. lib. bdg. 15.00x (ISBN 0-8371-3259-2, BUFA). Greenwood.

MIMBRES VALLEY, NEW MEXICO–ANTIQUITIES

Cosgrove, Harriet S. & Cosgrove, C. B. Swarts Ruin: A Typical Mimbres Site in Southwestern New Mexico. 1932. pap. 37.00 (ISBN 0-527-01234-3). Kraus Repr.

MIME

see also Pantomime

Avital, Samuel. Mime Workbook. 2nd, rev. ed. Reed, Ken, ed. LC 77-84487. (Illus.). 176p. 1977. pap. 8.95 (ISBN 0-914794-30-2). Wisdom Garden.
Cholerton, John. The World of Mime. Date not set. pap. 2.50x (ISBN 0-392-09737-0, SpS). Sportshelf.
Davis, R. G. The San Francisco Mime Troupe: The First Ten Years. LC 74-19943. 1975. 14.00 (ISBN 0-87867-058-0); pap. 4.95 (ISBN 0-87867-059-9). Ramparts.
Decroux, Etienne. Words on Mime. 208p. 1981. 12.00x (ISBN 0-89676-045-6). Drama Bk.
Dorcy, Jean. Mime. 1961. pap. 3.95 (ISBN 0-8315-0045-X). Speller.
Dorian, Margery & Gulland, Frances. Telling Stories Through Movement. LC 73-87493. 1974. pap. 4.95 (ISBN 0-8224-6940-5). Pitman Learning.
Enters, Angna. On Mime. LC 65-21130. 1978. pap. 5.95 (ISBN 0-8195-6056-1, Pub. by Wesleyan U Pr). Columbia U Pr.
Hamblin, Kay. Mime: A Playbook of Silent Fantasy. LC 77-27705. 1978. 6.95 (ISBN 0-385-14246-3, Dolp). Doubleday.
Hausbrandt, Andrzej. Tomaszewski's Mime Theatre. (Theatre, Film & Literature Ser.). (Illus.). 176p. 1977. 12.50 (ISBN 0-306-77436-4). Da Capo.
Keysell, Pat. Mime Themes & Motifs. (Illus.). 80p. 80. Repr. of 1975 ed. 9.95 (ISBN 0-8238-0245-0). Plays.
Kipnis, Claude. The Mime Book. (Illus.). 1976. pap. 8.95 (ISBN 0-06-090283-3, CN283, CN). Har-Row.
Kitching, Jessie & Braun, Susan, eds. Dance & Mime Film & Videotape Catalog. rev. ed. (Orig.). 1980. pap. 10.95 (ISBN 0-914438-00-X). Dance Films.
Lawson, Joan. Mime: The Theory & Practice of expressive Gesture. LC 72-88968. (Illus.). 167p. pap. 7.50 (ISBN 0-87127-042-0). Dance Horiz.
Loeschke, Maravene. Mime: A Movement Technique for the Visually Handicapped. 75p. 3.50 (ISBN 0-89128-954-2, PEP954). Am Foun Blind.
Rolfe, Bari, ed. Mimes on Miming: An Anthology of Writings on the Art of Mime. (Illus.). 1980. 12.95 (ISBN 0-915572-32-X); pap. 6.95 (ISBN 0-915572-31-1). Panjandrum.
Shepard, Richmond. Mime: The Technique of Silence. LC 72-134993. (Illus.). 1979. pap. text ed. 7.50x (ISBN 0-89676-008-1). Drama Bk.
Stolzenberg, Mark. Exploring Mime. LC 79-65068. (Illus.). 1979. 10.95 (ISBN 0-8069-7028-6); lib. bdg. 9.89 (ISBN 0-8069-7029-4). Sterling.

MIMIC THEATER

see Toy Theaters

MIMICRY (BIOLOGY)

see also Color of Animals

Patent, Dorothy H. Animal & Plant Mimicry. LC 78-7457. (Illus.). (gr. 6 up). 1978. 6.95 (ISBN 0-8234-0331-9). Holiday.
Selsam, Millicent E. Hidden Animals. rev. ed. LC 72-85020. (Science I Can Read Books). (Illus.). (gr. k-3). 1969. 5.95 (ISBN 0-06-025281-2, HarpJ); PLB 7.89 (ISBN 0-06-025282-0). Har-Row.
Wickler, Wolfgang. Mimicry in Plants & Animals. (Illus., Orig.). 1968. pap. text ed. 2.95 (ISBN 0-07-070100-8, SP). McGraw.

MINACK THEATRE

Dermuth, Averill, ed. The Minack Open-Air Theatre. (Illus.). 128p. 1968. 2.50 (ISBN 0-7153-4254-1). David & Charles.

MINAS VELHAS, BRAZIL

Harris, Marvin. Town & Country in Brazil. LC 78-82364. (Columbia Univ. Contribution to Anthropology Ser.: Vol. 37). 1969. Repr. of 1956 ed. 24.00 (ISBN 0-404-50587-2). AMS Pr.

MINAUX, ANDRE

Sorlier, Charles. Minaux: Lithographer. Brabyn, Howard, tr. (Illus.). 210p. 1974. 50.00 (ISBN 0-8148-0599-X). L Amiel Pub.

MIND

see Intellect; Psychology

MIND, PEACE OF

see Peace of Mind

MIND AND BODY
see also Body, Human; Consciousness; Conversion (Psychoanalysis); Dreams; Faith-Cure; Hypnotism; Medicine, Psychosomatic; Mental Healing; Mental Suggestion; Nervous System; Personality, Disorders of; Psychoanalysis; Psychology, Pathological; Psychology, Physiological; Rolfing; Self; Sleep; Somnambulism; Subconsciousness; Temperament

Armstrong, D. M. The Nature of Mind & Other Essays. LC 80-68117. 188p. 1981. 19.50x (ISBN 0-8014-1353-2). Cornell U Pr.
Atkinson, William W. Mind Power: The Secret of Mental Magic. limited ed. limited ed. 8.00 (ISBN 0-911662-27-8). Yoga.
Bacik, James J. Apologetics & the Eclipse of Mystery: Mystagogy According to Karl Rahner. LC 80-123. 1980. 15.00 (ISBN 0-268-00592-3). U of Notre Dame Pr.
Bateson, Gregory. Mind & Nature: A Necessary Unity. 1979. 11.95 (ISBN 0-525-15590-2). Dutton.
Beebe-Center, John G. Psychology of Pleasantness & Unpleasantness. LC 65-26686. (Illus.). 1965. Repr. of 1932 ed. 10.00 (ISBN 0-8462-0669-2). Russell.
Beloff, John. Existence of Mind. 1964. pap. 1.95 (ISBN 0-8065-0159-6, 177). Citadel Pr.
Benson, Herbert. The Mind-Body Effect. 1980. pap. 2.50 (ISBN 0-425-04699-0). Berkley Pub.
Bergson, Henri. Matter & Memory. (Muirhead Library of Philosophy). 1978. text ed. 16.50x (ISBN 0-391-00924-9). Humanities.
Bindra, Dalbir, ed. The Brain's Mind: A Neuroscience Perspective on the Mind-Body Problem. (Illus.). 128p. 1980. text ed. 14.95x (ISBN 0-89876-003-8). Gardner Pr.
Biro, J. I. & Shahan, Robert W. Mind, Brain & Function: Essays in the Philosophy of Mind. LC 81-40296. 208p. 1981. 12.95 (ISBN 0-8061-1783-4). U of Okla Pr.
Borst, C. V., ed. Mind-Brain Identity Theory. LC 70-106388. (Controversies in Philosophy Ser). 1970. pap. text ed. 7.50 (ISBN 0-312-53305-5). St Martin.
Brandreth, Gyles. Amazing Facts About Your Body. LC 80-1088. (Amazing Facts Bks.). (Illus.). 32p. (gr. 5-8). 1981. pap. 2.95 (ISBN 0-686-69710-3). Doubleday.
Brown, Barbara B. Supermind: The Ultimate Energy. LC 79-2614. (Illus.). 1980. 11.95 (ISBN 0-06-010518-6, HarpT). Har-Row.
Bunge, Mario. The Mind-Body Problem: A Psychobiological Approach. (Foundations & Philosophy of Science & Technology: Vol. 1). (Illus.). 245p. 1980. 33.00 (ISBN 0-08-024720-2); pap. 14.00 (ISBN 0-08-024719-9). Pergamon.
Campbell, Keith. Body & Mind. LC 80-10126. 160p. 1980. text ed. 10.95 (ISBN 0-268-00660-1); pap. text ed. 3.50 (ISBN 0-268-00659-8). U of Notre Dame Pr.
Carington, Whately. Matter, Mind & Meaning. facsimile ed. LC 78-111818. (Essay Index Reprint Ser). 1949. 19.50 (ISBN 0-8369-1596-8). Arno.
Cheng, Chung-ying, ed. Philosophical Aspects of the Mind-Body Problem. 240p. 1975. text ed. 12.00x (ISBN 0-8248-0342-6). U Pr of Hawaii.
Clark-Kennedy, A. E. Man, Medicine, & Morality. 1969. 17.50 (ISBN 0-208-00972-8, Archon). Shoe String.
Cole, Francis V. Open up Your Mind. 1978. 10.00 (ISBN 0-533-03648-8). Vantage.
Collin, Rodney. The Theory of Conscious Harmony. 1981. 25.00x (ISBN 0-7224-0152-3, Pub. by Watkins England). State Mutual Bk.
Cousins, Norman. Anatomy of an Illness As Perceived by the Patient. 176p. 1981. pap. 4.95 (ISBN 0-553-01293-2). Bantam.
Dacey, John. Adulthood & Aging. 1981. text ed. write for info. (ISBN 0-8302-0050-9). Goodyear.
Defoggi, Ernest. Unlocking the Mystery of How the Mind Creates Time: An Engineer's Analysis. (Illus.). 1979. 8.95 (ISBN 0-9602372-1-6). E Defoggi.
Delaney, Cornelius F. Mind & Nature: A Study in the Naturalistic Philosophies of Cohen, Woodbridge & Sellars. LC 70-75150. 1969. 9.95x (ISBN 0-268-00313-0). U of Notre Dame Pr.
Descartes, Rene. Les Passions de l'Ame. 1970. 3.95 (ISBN 0-686-55677-1). French & Eur.
Descartes, Rene & Lewis, G. Meditationes, de Prima Philosophia: Meditations Metaphysiques. 178p. (Fr. & Lat.). 1967. 13.00 (ISBN 0-686-55674-7). French & Eur.
Ducasse, C. J. Critical Examination of the Belief in a Life After Death. (American Lecture Philosophy Ser). 336p. 1974. pap. 12.75 (ISBN 0-398-03037-5). C C Thomas.
--Nature, Mind & Death. (Paul Carus Lecture Ser.). xix, 514p. 1951. 22.50 (ISBN 0-87548-102-7). Open Court.
Dumont, Theron Q. The Master Mind: The Key to Mental Power, Development & Efficiency. 276p. 1980. Repr. of 1918 ed. 7.00 (ISBN 0-911662-66-9). Yoga.
Dychtwald, Ken. Bodymind. 1978. pap. 2.25 (ISBN 0-515-05561-1). Jove Pubns.
Eckstein, Gustav. The Body Has a Head. abridged ed. 464p. 1980. pap. 3.95 (ISBN 0-553-12481-1). Bantam.
Evans, C. O. Subject of Consciousness. (Muirhead Library of Philosophy). 1970. text ed. 10.00x (ISBN 0-391-00037-3). Humanities.
Faust, Verne. I Know More About You Than You Ever Dreamed Possible. LC 79-88004. 1980. 13.95 (ISBN 0-934162-00-X). Thomas Paine Pr.
Feigl, Herbert, et al, eds. Concepts, Theories & the Mind-Body Problem. LC 57-12861. (Studies in the Philosophy of Science Ser: Vol. 2). 1958. 22.50x (ISBN 0-8166-0158-5). U of Minn Pr.
Fellman, Anita C. & Fellman, Michael. Making Sense of Self: Instructing the Public About the Body & Mind in Late Nineteenth Century America. LC 81-5114. 1981. 16.50x (ISBN 0-686-73794-6). U of Pa Pr.
Feyerabend, Paul & Maxwell, Grover, eds. Mind, Matter & Method: Essays in Philosophy & Science in Honor of Herbert Feigl. LC 66-13467. 1966. 17.50x (ISBN 0-8166-0379-0). U of Minn Pr.
Findlay, John N. Psyche & Cerebrum. (Aquinas Lecture, 1972). 52p. 1972. 6.95 (ISBN 0-87462-137-2). Marquette.
Flew, Antony, ed. Body, Mind & Death. 1964. pap. 2.50 (ISBN 0-02-084840-4). Macmillan.
Fortune, Dion. The Machinery of the Mind. 1980. pap. 4.95 (ISBN 0-87728-505-5). Weiser.
Gassette, Grace & Ashton, Horace. The Key. 1977. pap. 4.95 (ISBN 0-87516-229-0). De Vorss.
Gelb, Michael. Body Learning: An Introduction to the Alexander Technique. (Illus.). 160p. 1981. 12.95 (ISBN 0-933328-03-6). Delilah Comm.
Girdano, Daniel A. & Everly, George S., Jr. Controlling Stress & Tension: A Holistic Approach. (Illus.). 1979. 12.95 (ISBN 0-13-172114-3); pap. 6.95 (ISBN 0-13-172106-2). P-H.
Greer, E. Eugene. Toward Physical Excellence. (Orig.). 1976. pap. 1.95 (ISBN 0-930718-07-0). Harvest Pr Texas.
Grings, William W. & Dawson, Michael E. Emotions & Bodily Responses: A Psychophysiological Approach. (Behavioral Biology & International Ser.). 1978. 19.50 (ISBN 0-12-303750-6). Acad Pr.
Halle, Louis J. Out of Chaos. 1977. 20.00 (ISBN 0-395-25357-8). HM.
Hampden-Turner, Charles. Maps of the Mind. LC 80-21886. (Illus.). 224p. 1981. 14.95 (ISBN 0-686-76138-3). Macmillan.
Hampshire, Stuart. Freedom of Mind & Other Essays. 1971. 17.00x (ISBN 0-691-07176-4). Princeton U Pr.
Hartman, Edwin. Substance, Body, & Soul: Aristotelian Investigations. LC 77-71984. 1977. text ed. 21.00 (ISBN 0-691-07223-X). Princeton U Pr.
Hebb, D. O. Essay on Mind. LC 79-24993. (Illus.). 176p. 1980. text ed. 19.95x (ISBN 0-89859-017-5). L Erlbaum Assocs.
Highet, Gilbert. Man's Unconquerable Mind. LC 54-6133. 138p. 1954. 11.00x (ISBN 0-231-02016-3); pap. 3.95 (ISBN 0-231-08501-X). Columbia U Pr.
Hofstadter, Douglas R. & Dennett, Daniel C. The Mind's I: Fantasies & Reflections on Self & Soul. LC 81-66099. 280p. 1981. 14.95 (ISBN 0-465-04624-X). Basic.
Hook, Sidney, ed. Dimensions of Mind: A Symposium. 1961. pap. 1.50 (ISBN 0-02-065670-X, Collier). Macmillan.
Hopkins, Emma C. Self Treatment. 1975. pap. 1.00 (ISBN 0-87516-200-2). De Vorss.
Jastrow, Robert. The Enchanted Loom: The Mind in the Universe. (Illus.). 1981. 13.95 (ISBN 0-671-43308-3). S&S.
Jones, Frank P. Body Awareness in Action: A Study of the Alexander Technique. rev. ed. LC 78-20659. (Illus.). 1979. pap. 4.95 (ISBN 0-8052-0628-0). Schocken.
--Body Awareness in Action: A Study of the Alexander Technique. LC 76-9132. (Illus.). 1976. 9.95x (ISBN 0-8052-3632-5). Schocken.
Keleman, Stanley. Your Body Speaks Its Mind. 1980. pap. 5.95 (ISBN 0-934320-01-2). Center Pr.
Kurtz, Ron & Prestera, Hector. The Body Reveals. LC 75-66800. 160p. (Orig.). 1976. pap. 6.95 (ISBN 0-06-066680-3, RD139, HarpR). Har-Row.
La Mettrie, Julien O. Man a Machine. 216p. (Fr. & Eng.). 12.95 (ISBN 0-87548-041-1); pap. 4.95 (ISBN 0-87548-041-1). Open Court.
Laszlo, Ervin. System, Structure & Experience: Toward a Scientific Theory of Mind. (Current Topics of Contemporary Thought Ser.: Vol. 1). 124p. 1969. 27.00x (ISBN 0-677-02360-X). Gordon.
Lawson, Chester A. Language, Thought, & the Human Mind. vii, 117p. 1958. 4.50 (ISBN 0-87013-035-8). Mich St U Pr.
Laycock, Thomas. Mind & Brain: Or, the Correlations of Consciousness & Organization with Their Applications to Philosophy, Zoology, Physiology, Mental Pathology & the Practice of Medicine, 2 vols. in 1. LC 75-16715. (Classics in Psychiatry Ser.). (Illus.). 1976. Repr. of 1860 ed. 52.00x (ISBN 0-405-07443-3). Arno.
Leland, Charles G. The Mystic Will. 1976. Repr. of 1907 ed. 6.00 (ISBN 0-911662-58-8). Yoga.
Lewis, C. S. A Mind Awake. LC 80-14133. 1980. pap. 3.95 (ISBN 0-15-659772-1, Harv). HarBraceJ.
Lewis, H. D. Elusive Mind. (Muirhead Library of Philosophy). 1969. text ed. 26.00x (ISBN 0-00-430013-0). Humanities.
Lloyd, G. E. & Owen, G. E., eds. Aristotle on Mind & the Senses. LC 77-9389. (Classical Studies). 1978. 38.50 (ISBN 0-521-21669-9). Cambridge U Pr.
Lovejoy, Arthur O. Revolt Against Dualism. 2nd ed. (Paul Carus Lecture Ser.). 405p. 1960. 19.95 (ISBN 0-87548-106-X); pap. 7.95 (ISBN 0-87548-107-8). Open Court.
McDougall, William. Body & Mind. LC 73-13025. (Illus.). 384p. 1974. Repr. of 1911 ed. lib. bdg. 18.75x (ISBN 0-8371-7107-5, MCBM). Greenwood.
McGlashan, Alan. Savage & Beautiful Country: The Secret Life of the Mind. LC 67-11828. 192p. 1976. pap. 3.95 (ISBN 0-88373-035-9). Stonehill Pub Co.
Macleod, William M. & Macleod, Gael S. M. I. N. D Over Weight: "How to Stay Slim the Rest of Your Life". LC 80-21001. 120p. 1981. 7.95 (ISBN 0-13-583385-X). P-H.
Mandler, George. Mind & Emotion. 296p. Date not set. Repr. of 1975 ed. lib. bdg. price not set (ISBN 0-89874-350-8). Krieger.
--Mind & Motion. 280p. 1975. pap. 12.95 (ISBN 0-471-56691-8). Krieger.
Masters, Robert & Houston, Jean. Listening to the Body. 1979. pap. 4.95 (ISBN 0-440-54960-4, Delta). Dell.
Mayer, Fred S. Why Two Worlds: Relation of Physical to Spiritual Realities. LC 78-134425. Repr. of 1934 ed. 21.00 (ISBN 0-404-08465-6). AMS Pr.
Mead, G. R. The Subtle Body. 1981. 20.00x (ISBN 0-7224-0156-6, Pub. by Watkins England). State Mutual Bk.
Miller, Don E. The Body Electric: Energy Games & Exercises for a New Age. LC 78-22463. 1979. cancelled (ISBN 0-690-01813-4). T y Crowell.
Molteni, George J. Without End... or Beginning. 1980. 3.95 (ISBN 0-8062-1467-8). Carlton.
Moore, George. The Use of the Body in Relation to the Mind. LC 78-72812. Repr. of 1849 ed. 32.50 (ISBN 0-404-60882-5). AMS Pr.
Oyle, Irving. The Healing Mind. LC 74-10069. (Illus.). 128p. 1974. pap. 5.95 (ISBN 0-912310-80-4). Celestial Arts.
--Time, Space & Mind. LC 76-11339. 128p. (Orig.). 1976. pap. 5.95 (ISBN 0-89087-122-1). Celestial Arts.
Parnell, Richard W. Behavior & Physique: An Introduction to Practical & Applied Somatometry. LC 73-20503. (Illus.). 1978. Repr. of 1958 ed. lib. bdg. 17.25x (ISBN 0-8371-7327-2, PABE). Greenwood.
Paterson, Donald G. Physique & Intellect. Repr. of 1930 ed. lib. bdg. 14.25x (ISBN 0-8371-2886-2, PAPI). Greenwood.
Pelletier, Kenneth. Mind As Healer Mind As Slayer. 1977. pap. 5.95 (ISBN 0-440-55592-2, Delta). Dell.
Pelletier, Kenneth R. Mind As Healer Mind As Slayer. 1977. 10.00 (ISBN 0-440-05591-1, Sey Lawr). Delacorte.
Pick. Mind & Body. (Warwick Press Ser.). (gr. 5 up). 1980. PLB 8.40 (ISBN 0-531-09174-0, F54). Watts.
Pratt, James B. Matter & Spirit: A Study of Mind & Body in Their Relation to the Spiritual Life. Repr. of 1922 ed. lib. bdg. 15.00x (ISBN 0-8371-3548-6, PRMS). Greenwood.
Putnam, James J. Human Motives. LC 73-2413. (Mental Illness & Social Policy; the American Experience Ser.). Repr. of 1915 ed. 12.00 (ISBN 0-405-05223-5). Arno.
Rather, L. J. Mind & Body in Eighteenth Century Medicine: A Study Based on Jerome Gaub's De Regimine Mentis. (Wellcome Institute of the History of Medicine). 1965. 24.00x (ISBN 0-520-01049-3). U of Cal Pr.
Reed, Sampson. Observations on the Growth of the Mind Including GENIUS. 5th ed. LC 72-4971. (The Romantic Tradition in American Literature Ser.). 110p. 1972. Repr. of 1859 ed. 13.00 (ISBN 0-405-04641-3). Arno.
--Observations on the Growth of the Mind with Remarks on Other Subjects. LC 78-100126. 1970. Repr. of 1838 ed. 22.00x (ISBN 0-8201-1070-1). Schol Facsimiles.
Reid, Thomas. Essays on the Active Powers of the Human Mind. 1969. pap. 3.95 (ISBN 0-262-68013-0). MIT Pr.
Rieber, Robert W. & Jay, John, eds. Body & Mind: Past, Present & Future. LC 79-6777. 1980. 19.50 (ISBN 0-12-588260-2). Acad Pr.
Rosenthal, David. Materialism & the Mind-Body Problem. LC 77-157186. (Central Issues in Philosophy Ser). (Illus.). 1971. pap. 9.50 ref. ed. (ISBN 0-13-560177-0). P-H.
Rubinoff, Lionel. Collingwood & the Reform of Metaphysics: A Study in the Philosophy of Mind. LC 73-19150. 1970. 25.00x (ISBN 0-8020-5213-4). U of Toronto Pr.
Ryle, Gilbert. Concept of Mind. 1975. 22.00x (ISBN 0-06-496042-0). B&N.
Saltzman, Barry, et al. Wholly Alive: The Handbook of Holistic Health. LC 78-67852. 1979. pap. 4.95 (ISBN 0-89087-237-6). Celestial Arts.
Samples, Bob. Metaphoric Mind. (Illus.). 218p. 1976. 9.95 (ISBN 0-201-06705-6); pap. 5.95 (ISBN 0-201-06706-4). A-W.
Sayre, Kenneth M. Cybernetics & the Philosophy of Mind. (International Library of Philosophy & Scientific Method). 350p. 1976. text ed. 18.25x (ISBN 0-391-00594-4). Humanities.
Scarf, Maggie. Body Mind Behavior. 1977. pap. 2.25 (ISBN 0-440-30765-1, 440-30765-225, LE). Dell.
Scheler, Max. Man's Place in Nature. Meyerhoff, Hans, tr. 605p. 1962. pap. 4.25 (ISBN 0-374-50252-8, N231). FS&G.
Schiller, Francis. A Mobius Strip: Fin-de-Sicle Neuropsychiatry & Paul Mobius. LC 81-40317. (Illus.). 110p. 1981. 12.50x (ISBN 0-520-04467-3). U of Cal Pr.
Selden, Bernice. The Body-Mind Book: Nine Ways to Awareness. LC 79-17571. (Illus.). 160p. (gr. 8-12). 1979. PLB 7.29 (ISBN 0-671-32918-9). Messner.
Shaffer, Jerome A. Philosophy of Mind. LC 68-24352. (Foundations of Philosophy Series). (Orig.). 1968. pap. 7.95x ref. ed. (ISBN 0-13-663724-8). P-H.
Sherrington, Charles S. Man on His Nature. 1951. 39.95 (ISBN 0-521-06436-8); pap. 11.95x (ISBN 0-521-09203-5). Cambridge U Pr.
Simeons, Albert T. Man's Presumptuous Brain. 1962. pap. 4.50 (ISBN 0-525-47109-X). Dutton.
Singer, Edgar A. Mind As Behavior & Studies in Empirical Idealism. LC 75-3386. (Philosophy in America Ser.). Repr. of 1924 ed. 22.50 (ISBN 0-404-59382-8). AMS Pr.
Smith, E. Lester, ed. Intelligence Came First. LC 74-19053. (Illus.). 200p. (Orig.). 1975. 8.50 (ISBN 0-8356-0458-6, Quest); pap. 2.95 (ISBN 0-8356-0456-X). Theos Pub Hse.
Smythies, John R., ed. Brain & Mind. (International Library of Philosophy & Scientific Method Ser.). 1965. text ed. 27.50x (ISBN 0-7100-3624-8). Humanities.
Southfield, Lawrence G. An Analysis of the Processes of the Human Mind. (Illus.). 137p. 1981. 49.75 (ISBN 0-89266-317-0). Am Classical Coll Pr.
Spicker, Stuart, ed. Philosophy of the Body: Rejections of Cartesian Dualism. 1972. 15.00 (ISBN 0-8129-0132-0, QP 118); pap. 2.95 (ISBN 0-8129-6110-2). Times Bks.
Swift, Edgar J. Mind in the Making. 329p. 1981. Repr. of 1909 ed. lib. bdg. 35.00 (ISBN 0-89984-416-2). Century Bookbindery.
Tansley, David V. Subtle Body: Essence & Shadow. (Illus.). 1977. pap. 7.95 (ISBN 0-500-81014-1). Thames Hudson.
Tart, Charles T., et al, eds. Mind at Large: Institute of Electrical & Electronic Engineers Symposia on the Nature of Extrasensory Perception. LC 79-9982. 288p. 1979. 25.95 (ISBN 0-03-050476-7). Praeger.
Taylor, Gordon R. The Natural History of the Mind. 1981. pap. 4.95 (ISBN 0-14-005703-X). Penguin.
Turner, Charles H. Maps of the Mind. 1981. 14.95 (ISBN 0-02-547740-4). Macmillan.
Tyrrell, G. N. Homo Faber: A Study of Man's Mental Evolution. LC 73-13026. 205p. 1973. Repr. of 1951 ed. lib. bdg. 15.00x (ISBN 0-8371-7110-5, TYHF). Greenwood.
Verny, Thomas & Kelly, John. The Secret Life of the Unborn Child. 256p. 1981. 12.95 (ISBN 0-671-25312-3). Summit Bks.
Villard, Sebastian C. The Forces Which Contribute to Make Man a Genius & a Hero of Mankind. (Illus.). 157p. 1981. 59.65 (ISBN 0-89266-320-0). Am Classical Coll Pr.
Von Franz, Marie-Louise. Number & Time. Dykes, Andrea, tr. from Ger. LC 73-86467. (Studies in Jungian Thought). 256p. 1974. 18.95x (ISBN 0-8101-0429-6); pap. 8.95x (ISBN 0-8101-0532-2). Northwestern U Pr.
Weissman, David. Dispositional Properties. LC 65-11655. (Philosophical Explorations Ser). 231p. 1965. 8.95x (ISBN 0-8093-0163-6). S Ill U Pr.

Williams, B. A. Problems of the Self: Philosophical Papers, 1956-1972. 240p. 1973. 35.50 (ISBN 0-521-20225-6); pap. 9.95x (ISBN 0-521-29060-0). Cambridge U Pr.
Wisdom, John. Problems of Mind & Matter. (Orig.). pap. 6.95x (ISBN 0-521-09197-7). Cambridge U Pr.
The Works of Aristotle: The Famous Philosopher. LC 73-20613. (Sex, Marriage & Society Ser.). (Illus.). 268p. 1974. Repr. 14.00x (ISBN 0-405-05792-X). Arno.

MIND-CURE
see Animal Magnetism; Christian Science; Faith-Cure; Mental Healing; Mind and Body

MIND-DISTORTING DRUGS
see Hallucinogenic Drugs

MIND-READING
see also Clairvoyance; Hypnotism; Thought-Transference
Atkinson, William W. Practical Mind Reading. pap. 1.00 (ISBN 0-911662-43-X). Yoga.
Cumberland, Stuart. A Thought-Reader's Thoughts: Being the Impressions & Confessions of Stuart Cumberland. LC 75-7373. (Perspectives in Psychical Research Ser.). 1975. Repr. of 1888 ed. 19.00x (ISBN 0-405-07024-1). Arno.
Fulves, Karl. Self-Working Mental Magic: Sixty-Seven Foolproof Mind-Reading Tricks. LC 79-50010. (Illus.). 1979. pap. 2.00 (ISBN 0-486-23806-7). Dover.

MINDANAO
Enriquez, Antonio R. Surveyors of the Liguasan Marsh. (Asian & Pacific Writing Ser.). 131p. 1981. text ed. 18.00 (ISBN 0-7022-1532-5); pap. 9.75 (ISBN 0-7022-1533-3). U of Queensland Pr.

MINDSZENTY, JOZSEF, CARDINAL, 1892-
Vecsey, Joseph & Schlafly, Phyllis. Mindszenty the Man. LC 72-93906. 1972. 2.00 (ISBN 0-686-09586-3). Pere Marquette.

MINE ACCIDENTS
see also Coal Mines and Mining–Accidents; Mine Gases
Adams, James T. Death in the Dark. LC 76-30618. 1977. Repr. of 1941 ed. lib. bdg. 12.50 (ISBN 0-8414-2884-0). Folcroft.

MINE DRAINAGE
International Mine Drainage Symposium, 1st, Denver Colorado May 1979. Mine Drainage: Proceedings. Argall, George O., Jr. & Brawner, C. O., eds. LC 79-89681. (A World Mining Bk.). (Illus.). 1979. 55.00 (ISBN 0-87930-122-8). Miller Freeman.

MINE DUSTS
see also Mine Ventilation
Measurement & Control of Respirable Dust in Mining. 1980. 11.00 (ISBN 0-309-03047-1). Natl Acad Pr.
Nettleton, M. A., et al. Coal: Current Advances in Coal Chemistry & Mining Techniques, Vol. 2. 1976. text ed. 28.00x (ISBN 0-8422-7283-6). Irvington.

MINE EXAMINATION
see also Mine Surveying; Mine Valuation; Prospecting
Parks, Roland D. Examination & Valuation of Mineral Property. 4th ed. (Illus.). 1957. 27.50 (ISBN 0-201-05730-1, Adv Bk Prog). A-W.

MINE EXPLOSIONS
see also Mine Gases

MINE GASES
Antsyferov, M. S., ed. Seismo-Acoustic Methods in Mining. LC 65-26634. 134p. 1966. 34.50 (ISBN 0-306-10752-X, Consultants). Plenum Pub.
Nettleton, M. A., et al. Coal: Current Advances in Coal Chemistry & Mining Techniques, Vol. 2. 1976. text ed. 28.00x (ISBN 0-8422-7283-6). Irvington.

MINE INSPECTION
Rudman, Jack. Federal Mine Inspector. (Career Examination Ser.: C-1283). (Cloth bdg. avail. on request). pap. 8.00 (ISBN 0-8373-1283-3). Natl Learning.

MINE MANAGEMENT
see also Mining Engineering
Crawford, John T., III & Hustrulid, William A., eds. Open Pit Planning & Design. LC 79-52269. (Illus.). 367p. 1979. text ed. 27.00x (ISBN 0-89520-253-0). Soc Mining Eng.
Institute in Mine Health & Safety, Sixth. Proceedings. Reeder, R. T., ed. (Illus.). 292p. 1981. pap. text ed. 16.00 (ISBN 0-918062-42-X). Colo Sch Mines.

MINE RAILROADS
California Central Coal Railways. Date not set. 39.95 (ISBN 0-686-75183-3). Chatham Pub CA.
Curr, John. Coal Viewer & Engine Builder's Practical Companion. LC 74-96376. (Illus.). Repr. of 1797 ed. lib. bdg. 19.50x (ISBN 0-678-05104-6). Kelley.
--Coal Viewer & Engine Builder's Practical Companion. 2nd ed. 96p. 1970. Repr. of 1797 ed. 25.00x (ISBN 0-7146-2429-2, F Cass Co). Biblio Dist.
Gilpin Gold Tram. 12.95 (ISBN 0-685-83337-2). Chatham Pub CA.
Szklarski, L. Underground Electric Haulage. 1969. 52.00 (ISBN 0-08-011663-9). Pergamon.

MINE SURVEYING
see also Mine Examination
Staley, William W. Introduction to Mine Surveying. rev. ed. (Illus.). 1964. 9.50x (ISBN 0-8047-0361-2). Stanford U Pr.
Surveying Offshore Canada Lands: For Mineral Resource Development. 1978. pap. 8.50 (ISBN 0-660-00673-1, 94, SSC). Unipub.

MINE SWEEPERS
Elliott, Peter. Allied Minesweeping in World War Two. LC 78-61581. 1979. 11.95 (ISBN 0-87021-904-9). Naval Inst Pr.

MINE VALUATION
see also Mine Examination; Prospecting
David, M. Geostatistical Ore Reserve Estimation. (Developments in Geomathematics). 1977. 39.75 (ISBN 0-444-41532-7). Elsevier.
Parks, Roland D. Examination & Valuation of Mineral Property. 4th ed. (Illus.). 1957. 27.50 (ISBN 0-201-05730-1, Adv Bk Prog). A-W.

MINE VENTILATION
Hartman, Howard L. Mine Ventilation & Air Conditioning. (Illus.). 1961. 31.50 (ISBN 0-8260-3860-3, Pub. by Wiley-Interscience). Wiley.

MINEBALAIS, HAITI
Herskovits, Melville J. Life in a Haitian Valley. 1964. lib. bdg. 18.00x (ISBN 0-374-93857-1). Octagon.

MINERAL COLLECTING
see Mineralogy–Collectors and Collecting

MINERAL INDUSTRIES
see also Ceramic Industries; Ceramics; Metallurgy; Mines and Mineral Resources; Mining Engineering; Mining Industry and Finance; also specific types of mines and mining, e.g. Coal Mines and Mining
A. J. Wilson Mining Journal Books Ltd. The Pick & the Pen. 318p. 1980. 26.00x (ISBN 0-900117-16-8, Pub. by Mining Journal England). State Mutual Bk.
Atkins, M. H. & Lowe, J. F. Economics of Pollution Control in the Non-Ferrous Metals Industry. (Illus.). 1979. 45.00 (ISBN 0-08-022458-X). Pergamon.
Barger, Harold & Schurr, Sam H. The Mining Industries, 1899-1939: A Study of Output, Employment, & Productivity. LC 75-19694. (National Bureau of Economic Research Ser.). (Illus.). 1975. Repr. 24.00x (ISBN 0-405-07575-8). Arno.
Barnes, Marvin P. Computer-Assisted Mineral Appraisal & Feasibility. LC 79-52270. (Illus.). 167p. 1980. text ed. 30.00x (ISBN 0-89520-262-X). Soc Mining Eng.
Barry, Mary J. A History of Mining on the Kenai Peninsula. LC 73-80129. (Illus.). 214p. 1973. pap. 6.95 (ISBN 0-88240-018-5). Alaska Northwest.
Bernstein, Marvin. Mexican Mining Industry, 1890-1950. LC 64-18628. 1965. 27.50 (ISBN 0-87395-016-X); microfiche 27.50 (ISBN 0-87395-117-4). State U NY Pr.
Blakey, Fred. The Florida Phosphate Industry: A History of the Development & Use of a Vital Mineral. LC 73-82345. (Wertheim Publications in Industrial Relations Ser.). 1973. text ed. 14.00x (ISBN 0-674-30670-8). Harvard U Pr.
Board on Mineral & Energy Resources. Redistribution of Accessory Elements in Mining & Mineral Processing: Coal & Oil Shale, Pt. I. 1979. pap. 9.25 (ISBN 0-309-02897-3). Natl Acad Pr.
--Redistribution of Accessory Elements in Mining & Mineral Processing: Uranium, Phosphate, & Alumina, Pt. II. 1979. pap. 12.25 (ISBN 0-309-02899-X). Natl Acad Pr.
--Technological Innovation & Forces for Change in the Mineral Industry. 1978. pap. 5.50 (ISBN 0-309-02768-3). Natl Acad Pr.
Bosson, Rex & Varon, Bension. The Mining Industry & the Developing Countries. (A World Bank Research Publication Ser.). 1977. 22.00x (ISBN 0-19-920096-3); pap. 10.95x (ISBN 0-19-920099-8). Oxford U Pr.
Boyum, Burton H., ed. The Mather Mine, Negaunee & Ishpeming Michigan. 87p. 1980. 18.95 (ISBN 0-686-29176-X). Longyear Res.
Brooks, David B., ed. Resource Economics: Selected Works of Orris C. Herfindahl. LC 74-6814. (Resources for the Future Research Report Ser). (Illus.). 346p. 1974. 24.00x (ISBN 0-8018-1645-9). Johns Hopkins.
Burt, Roger, ed. Cornish Mining. LC 70-77258. 1969. 12.50x (ISBN 0-678-05536-X). Kelley.
Cameron, Eugene N., ed. The Mineral Position of the United States, 1975-2000. LC 72-7983. (Illus.). 182p. 1973. 15.00 (ISBN 0-299-06300-3); pap. 5.95 (ISBN 0-299-06304-6). U of Wis Pr.
Canada's Mineral Trade: The Balance of Payments & Economic Development. 113p. (Orig.). 1978. pap. text ed. 5.00x (ISBN 0-88757-011-9, Pub. by Ctr Resource Stud Canada). Renouf.
Chopra, V. P. India's Industrialisation & Mineral Exports 1951-52 to 1960-61 & Projections to 1970-71. 6.50x (ISBN 0-210-22727-3). Asia.
Current Concerns in Mineral Policy. 75p. (Orig.). 1978. pap. text ed. 3.00x (ISBN 0-88757-010-0, Pub. by Ctr Resource Stud Canada). Renouf.
Currie, John M. & British Columbia Institute of Technology. Unit Operations in Mineral Processing. 1978. Repr. of 1973 ed. 15.00 (ISBN 0-918062-13-6). Colo Sch Mines.
Decade of Digital Computing in the Mineral Industry. LC 72-91452. 1969. 23.00x (ISBN 0-89520-010-4). Soc Mining Eng.
Down, C. G. & Stocks, J. Environmental Impact of Mining. LC 77-23129. 1977. 65.95 (ISBN 0-470-99086-4). Halsted Pr.
Economics of the Minerals Industries. 3rd ed. LC 72-86920. 1976. 27.00x (ISBN 0-89520-033-3). Soc Mining Eng.
Employee Relations Initiatives in Canadian Mining. 85p. (Orig.). 1979. pap. text ed. 5.00x (ISBN 0-88757-014-3, Pub. by Ctr Resource Stud Canada). Renouf.
Engineering & Mineral Journal Editors, compiled by. E-MJ Operating Handbook of Mineral Processing, Vol. II. 500p. 1980. 19.50 (ISBN 0-07-019527-7). McGraw.
Eucharius Roesslin. On Minerals & Mineral Products. (Ars Medica: Section IV, Vol. 1). 1978. 134.00x (ISBN 3-11-006907-5). De Gruyter.
Gillis, Malcolm, et al. Taxation & Mining: Nonfuel Minerals in Bolivia & Other Countries. LC 77-23806. 1978. 35.00 (ISBN 0-88410-458-3). Ballinger Pub.
Graham, Katherine A., et al. The Administration of Mineral Exploration in the Yukon & Northwest Territories. 60p. (Orig.). 1979. pap. text ed. 3.00x (ISBN 0-686-63144-7, Pub. by Ctr Resource Stud Canada). Renouf.
Herfindahl, Orris C. Three Studies in Mineral Economics. LC 77-86399. Repr. of 1961 ed. 12.00 (ISBN 0-404-60335-1). AMS Pr.
Hodges, L. K. Mining in Central & Eastern Washington. Repr. of 1897 ed. pap. 20.00 (ISBN 0-8466-1998-9, SJS134B). Shorey.
--Mining in Southern British Columbia. (Illus.). Repr. of 1897 ed. pap. 20.00 (ISBN 0-8466-1997-0, SJS134C). Shorey.
--Mining in Western Washington. (Illus.). Repr. of 1897 ed. pap. 20.00 (ISBN 0-8466-1999-7, SJS134A). Shorey.
Industrial Minerals & Rocks. 4th ed. LC 73-85689. 1975. 40.00x (ISBN 0-89520-028-7). Soc Mining Eng.
Instrumentation in the ISA Mining & Metallurgy Industries, 3rd, Duluth, 1974. Proceedings, Vol. 2. LC 73-82889. (Illus.). 83p. pap. 10.00 (ISBN 0-87664-251-2, MM2). Instru Soc.
ISA Mining & Metallurgy Instrumentation Symposium, 2nd, Toronto, June 1973. Instrumentation in the Mining & Metallurgy Industries: Proceedings, Vol. 1. Whiteside, J. A., ed. LC 73-82889. 98p. 1973. pap. text ed. 10.00 (ISBN 0-87664-213-X). Instru Soc.
Kuzvart, M. & Bohmer, M. Prospecting & Exploration for Mineral Deposits. 1978. 68.50 (ISBN 0-444-99876-4). Elsevier.
Leith, Charles K. World Minerals & World Politics. LC 74-113286. 1970. Repr. of 1931 ed. 11.50 (ISBN 0-8046-1322-2). Kennikat.
Livermore, Robert. Bostonians & Bullion: The Journal of Robert Livermore, 1892-1915. Gressley, Gene M., ed. LC 68-12703. (Illus.). xxx, 193p. 1968. 13.95x (ISBN 0-8032-0105-2). U of Nebr Pr.
McDivitt, James & Manners, Gerald. Minerals & Men: An Exploration of the World of Minerals & Metals, Including Some of the Major Problems that Are Posed. rev. & enl. ed. LC 73-8138. (Resources for the Future Ser.). (Illus.). 192p. 1974. 14.00x (ISBN 0-8018-1536-3); pap. 3.95x (ISBN 0-8018-1827-3). Johns Hopkins.
Mackenzie, Brian W. & Bolodeau, Michel L. Effects of Taxation on Base Metal Mining in Canada. 190p. (Orig.). 1979. pap. text ed. 9.50x (ISBN 0-88757-012-7, Pub. by Ctr Resource Stud Canada). Renouf.
Miller, C. George, et al. Cerre Colorade: A Case Study of the Role of Canadian Crown Corporations in Foreign Mineral Development. 60p. (Orig.). 1978. pap. text ed. 3.00x (ISBN 0-686-63142-0, Pub. by Ctr Resource Stud Canada). Renouf.
Miller, Richard K., et al. Noise Control Solutions for the Metal Products Industry. 45.00 (ISBN 0-89671-000-9). Fairmont Pr.
Mineral Industry Report, 1973: Northwest Territories 1976-1979. 1977. pap. 6.95 (ISBN 0-660-00490-9, SSC). Unipub.
Mineral Industry Trends & Economic Opportunities. (Mineral Policy Ser). 1978. pap. 2.75 (ISBN 0-685-87291-2, SSC). Unipub.
Mineral Processing in Developing Countries. 143p. 1980. pap. 7.00 (ISBN 0-686-72714-2, UN80/2B5, UN). Unipub.
Morse, G. Nuclear Methods in Mineral Exploration & Production. 1977. 53.75 (ISBN 0-444-41567-X). Elsevier.
Mular, A. L. & Bhappu, R. B., eds. Mineral Processing Plant Design. 2nd ed. LC 79-57345. (Illus.). 958p. 1980. text ed. 27.00x (ISBN 0-89520-269-7). Soc Mining Eng.
Netschert, Bruce C. The Mineral Foreign Trade of the United States in the Twentieth Century: A Study in Mineral Economics. Bruchey, Stuart, ed. LC 76-39836. (Nineteen Seventy-Seven Dissertations Ser.). (Illus.). 1977. lib. bdg. 33.00x (ISBN 0-405-09916-9). Arno.
Nickel, P. E., et al. Economic Impacts & Linkages of the Canadian Mining Industry. 141p. (Orig.). 1978. pap. text ed. 6.00x (ISBN 0-88757-007-0, Pub. by Ctr Resource Stud Canada). Renouf.
Novitzky, Alejandro. Diccionario Minero-Metalurgico-Geologico-Mineralogico-Petrografico y de Petroleo: English-Spanish-French-German-Russian. 2nd ed. 376p. 1960. indice alfabetico 30.00 (ISBN 0-8002-0155-8). Intl Pubns Serv.
O'Neil, Thomas J., ed. Application of Computers & Operations Research in the Mineral Industry: 16th International Symposium. LC 79-52273. (Illus.). 651p. 1979. text ed. 30.00x (ISBN 0-89520-261-1). Soc Mining Eng.
Paher, Stanley W. Nevada Ghost Towns & Mining Camps. LC 70-116733. (Illus.). 1970. 25.00 (ISBN 0-8310-7075-7). Howell-North.
Peterson, Richard H. The Bonanza Kings: The Social Origins & Business Behavior of Western Mining Entrepreneurs, 1870-1900. LC 76-58410. 1977. 9.95 (ISBN 0-8032-0916-9). U of Nebr Pr.
Pounds, Norman J. Ruhr: A Study in Historical & Economic Geography. LC 68-55636. (Illus.). 1968. Repr. of 1952 ed. lib. bdg. 14.25x (ISBN 0-8371-0621-4, POTR). Greenwood.
Shephers, R. Prehistoric Mining & Allied Industries. (Studies in Archaeology Science Ser.). 1981. 38.50 (ISBN 0-12-639480-6). Acad Pr.
Sittig, M. Pollution Control in the Asbestos, Cement, Glass & Allied Mineral Industries. LC 75-10353. (Pollution Technology Review Ser.: No. 19). (Illus.). 333p. 1975. 36.00 (ISBN 0-8155-0578-7). Noyes.
Sklar, Richard L. Corporate Power in an African State: The Political Impact of Multinational Mining Companies in Zambia. LC 74-81440. 1975. 30.00x (ISBN 0-520-02814-7). U of Cal Pr.
Smith, Duane A. Colorado Mining: A Photographic History. LC 76-46583. (Illus.). 176p. 1979. Repr. of 1977 ed. 17.50 (ISBN 0-8263-0437-0). U of Nm Pr.
Somasundaran, P., ed. Fine Particles Processing, 2 vols. LC 79-57344. (Illus.). 1865p. 1980. text ed. 45.00x (ISBN 0-89520-275-1). Soc Mining Eng.
Sullivan, John W. Story of Metals. (Illus.). 1951. 6.50x (ISBN 0-8138-1600-9). Iowa St U Pr.
Symposium on Computer Applications in the Mineral Industry, 10th, South Africa, 1972. Proceedings. 36.00 (ISBN 0-620-00774-5). Soc Mining Eng.
Tilton, John E. The Future of Nonfuel Minerals. 1977. 9.95 (ISBN 0-8157-8460-0). Brookings.
Voskuil, Walter H. Minerals in Modern Industry. LC 74-118424. 1970. Repr. of 1930 ed. 15.50 (ISBN 0-8046-1374-5). Kennikat.
Weiss, Alfred, ed. Computer Methods for the Eighties, in the Mineral Industry. LC 79-52274. (Illus.). 975p. 1979. text ed. 50.00x (ISBN 0-89520-257-3). Soc Mining Eng.
William Fox Mining Journal Books Ltd. Tin: The Working of a Commodity Agreement. 418p. 1980. 21.00x (ISBN 0-900117-05-2, Pub. by Mining Journal England). State Mutual Bk.
Williams, Roy E. Waste Production & Disposal in Mining, Milling & Metallurgical Industries. LC 74-20167. (A World Mining Book). (Illus.). 489p. 1975. 45.00 (ISBN 0-87930-035-3). Miller Freeman.
Wills, B. A. Mineral Processing Technology. (International Series on Materials Science & Technology: Vol. 29). (Illus.). 1979. 60.00 (ISBN 0-08-021280-8); pap. 18.50 (ISBN 0-08-021279-4). Pergamon.

MINERAL INDUSTRIES–EARLY WORKS TO 1800
Agricola, Georgius. De Re Metallica. (Illus.). 1912. 17.95 (ISBN 0-486-60006-8). Dover.
Biringuccio, Vannoccio. Pirotechnia. 1966. pap. 4.95x (ISBN 0-262-52017-6). MIT Pr.

MINERAL KING RECREATIONAL AREA, CALIFORNIA
Adler, Pat. Mineral King Guide. rev. ed. (Illus.). 48p. 1975. wrappers 1.50 (ISBN 0-910856-05-2). La Siesta.

MINERAL LAND SURVEYING
see Mine Surveying

MINERAL LANDS
see Mines and Mineral Resources; Mining Law

MINERAL METABOLISM
Adams, Ruth & Murray, Frank. Minerals: Kill or Cure. rev. ed. 366p. (Orig.). 1974. pap. 1.95 (ISBN 0-915962-16-0). Larchmont Bks.

Ashmead, DeWayne. Chelated Mineral Nutrition. 186p. (Orig.). 1981. pap. 4.95 (ISBN 0-86664-002-9). Intl Inst Nat Health.

Bronner, Felix & Coburn, Jack, eds. Disorders of Mineral Metabolism, Vol.I. 1981. price not set (ISBN 0-12-135301-X). Acad Pr.

--Disorders of Mineral Metabolism: Pathophysiology of Calcium, Phosphorus, & Magnesium, Vol. 3. 1981. price not set. Acad Pr.

Comar, C. L. & Bronner, Felix, eds. Mineral Metabolism: An Advanced Treatise, 3 vols. Incl. Vol. 1, Pt. A. Principles, Processes & Systems. 1960. 56.00 (ISBN 0-12-183201-5); Vol. 1, Pt. B. Principles, Processes & Systems. 1961. 70.00 (ISBN 0-12-183241-4); Vol. 2, Pt. A. The Elements. 1964. 78.00 (ISBN 0-12-183202-3); Set. 52.00 (ISBN 0-686-66613-5); Vol. 2, Pt. B. The Elements. 1962. 73.00 (ISBN 0-12-183242-2); 41.00 (ISBN 0-686-66614-3); Vol. 3. Supplementary Volume. 1969. 63.00 (ISBN 0-12-183250-3). 275.50 set (ISBN 0-685-23116-X). Acad Pr.

Mineral Studies with Isotopes in Domestic Animals. (Illus., Orig.). 1971. pap. 14.75 (ISBN 92-0-111371-4, ISP293, IAEA). Unipub.

Nordin, B. E. Calcium, Phosphate & Magnesium Metabolism: Clinical Physiology & Diagnostic Procedures. LC 75-13875. (Illus.). 544p. 1976. text ed. 77.00 (ISBN 0-443-01188-5). Churchill.

Trace Mineral Studies with Isotopes in Domestic Animals. 1969. pap. 9.75 (ISBN 92-0-011069-X, ISP218, IAEA). Unipub.

Wade, Carlson. Magic Minerals: Your Key to Better Health. LC 67-27851. 1970. pap. 2.50 (ISBN 0-668-02135-7). Arco.

Weinberg, E. D. Microorganisms & Minerals. (Microbiology Ser.: Vol. 3). 1977. 54.50 (ISBN 0-8247-6581-8). Dekker.

MINERAL OILS

see also Petroleum

Campbell, Lindsey. Moonie & the Oil Search. (Illus.). 12.50x (ISBN 0-392-03985-0, ABC). Sportshelf.

Din Standards for Mineral Oils & Fuels: Basic Standards. 424.00 (ISBN 0-686-28192-6, 10792-5/57). Heyden.

Din Standards for Mineral Oils & Fuels: Test Methods for Lubricants, Insulating Oils, Cooling Lubricants, Paraffins & White Oil. 186.00 (ISBN 0-686-28171-3, 10055-5/20). Heyden.

Kagler, S. H. Spectroscopic & Chromatographic Analysis of Mineral Oil, 3 vols. LC 72-4105. 559p. 1973. Set. 87.95 (ISBN 0-470-45425-3). Halsted Pr.

Wade, Harlan. El Aceite. Contreras, Mamie M., tr. from Eng. LC 78-26613. (A Book About Ser.). (Illus., Sp.). (gr. k-3). 1979. PLB 7.95 (ISBN 0-8172-1485-2). Raintree Pubs.

--L' Huile. Potvin, Claude & Potvin, Rose-Ella, trs. from Eng. (A Book About Ser.). Orig. Title: Oil. (Illus., Fr.). (gr. k-3). 1979. PLB 7.95 (ISBN 0-8172-1460-7). Raintree Pubs.

MINERAL OILS-LAW AND LEGISLATION

see Petroleum Law and Legislation

MINERAL RESOURCES

see Mines and Mineral Resources

MINERAL RESOURCES IN SUBMERGED LANDS

Leipziger, Danny M. & Mudge, James L. Seabed Mineral Resources: The Economic Interests of Developing Countries. LC 76-19076. 1976. 20.00 (ISBN 0-88410-049-9). Ballinger Pub.

Surveying Offshore Canada Lands: For Mineral Resource Development. 1978. pap. 8.50 (ISBN 0-660-00673-1, 94, SSC). Unipub.

MINERALOGICAL CHEMISTRY

Andres, U. Magnetohydrodynamic & Magnetohydrostatic Methods of Mineral Separation. 1976. 43.95 (ISBN 0-470-15014-9). Halsted Pr.

Brown, R. C., et al. The Invitro Effects of Mineral Dusts. 1980. 48.00 (ISBN 0-12-137240-5). Acad Pr.

Clark, ed. Chemistry & Physics of Minerals. pap. 7.50 (ISBN 0-686-60385-0). Polycrystal Bk Serv.

Ehlers, Ernest G. The Interpretation of Geological Phase Diagrams. LC 75-182129. (Illus.). 1972. text ed. 32.95x (ISBN 0-7167-0254-1). W H Freeman.

Helgeson, Harold C., et al. Handbook of Theoretical Activity Diagrams Depicting Chemical Equilibria in Geologic Systems Involving an Aqueous Phase at One ATM & Zero Degrees to 300 Degrees Centigrade. LC 73-97467. (Illus.). 256p. 1969. text ed. 7.50x (ISBN 0-87735-331-X). Freeman C.

International Mineral Processing Congress 1960. 1118p. 1980. 100.00x (ISBN 0-686-71770-8, Pub. by Inst Mining England). State Mutual Bk.

Jones, M. J., ed. International Mineral Processing Congress 1973. 1209p. 1980. 150.00x (ISBN 0-900488-24-7, Pub. by Inst Mining England). State Mutual Bk.

Lemery, Nicolas. Traite de l'antomoine contenant l'analyse chymique de ce mineral, et un recueil d'un grand nombre d'operations rapportees a l'academie royale des Sciences, avec les raisonnemens qu'on a cruz necessaires... 620p. 1981. Repr. of 1707 ed. lib. bdg. 235.00 (ISBN 0-8287-1465-7). Clearwater Pub.

Marfunin, A. S. Physics of Minerals & Inorganic Materials: An Introduction. Egorova, G. & Mishchenko, A. G., trs. from Russ. (Illus.). 1979. 52.30 (ISBN 0-387-08982-9). Springer-Verlag.

Marshall, C. Edmund. The Physical Chemistry & Mineralogy of Soils: Soils in Place, Vol. II. LC 64-20074. 1977. 34.50 (ISBN 0-471-02957-2, Pub. by Wiley-Interscience). Wiley.

Mining Chemicals. 1981. 950.00 (ISBN 0-89336-262-X, C-021). BCC.

Newton, R. C., et al, eds. Thermodynamics of Minerals & Melts, Vol. 1. (Advances in Physical Geochemistry Ser.). (Illus.). 272p. 1981. 39.00 (ISBN 0-387-90530-8). Springer-Verlag.

Rose, Arthur, et al. Geochemistry in Mineral Exploration. 2nd ed. 1980. pap. 30.00 (ISBN 0-12-596252-5). Acad Pr.

MINERALOGY

see also Crystallography; Gems; Meteorites; Mineralogical Chemistry; Petrology; Precious Stones; Rocks;

also names of minerals, e.g. Feldspar, Quartz

Anthony, John W., et al. The Mineralogy of Arizona. LC 75-44670. 1977. pap. text ed. 9.75x (ISBN 0-8165-0471-7). U of Ariz Pr.

Arem, Joel. Rocks & Minerals. (Knowledge Through Color Ser., No. 40). (Illus.). 160p. 1973. pap. 2.25 (ISBN 0-553-12345-9). Bantam.

Atkinson, Richard & Atkinson, Frances. The Observer's Book of Rocks & Minerals. (Illus.). 1979. 4.95 (ISBN 0-684-16221-0, ScribT). Scribner.

Bates, Robert L. Geology of the Industrial Rocks & Minerals. (Illus.). 10.00 (ISBN 0-8446-0481-X). Peter Smith.

Battey, M. H. Mineralogy for Students. 2nd ed. (Illus.). 356p. 1981. pap. text ed. 21.50x (ISBN 0-582-44005-X). Longman.

--Mineralogy for Students. (Illus.). 1975. pap. text ed. 17.95x (ISBN 0-582-44159-5). Longman.

Berry, Leonard G. & Mason, Brian. Mineralogy: Concepts, Descriptions, Determinations. LC 59-7841. (Geology Ser.). (Illus.). 1959. 26.95x (ISBN 0-7167-0203-7). W H Freeman.

Black, Joseph. Experiments Upon Magnesia Alba, Quicklime & Some Other Alcaline Substances. LC 79-8596. Repr. of 1898 ed. 13.50 (ISBN 0-404-18449-9). AMS Pr.

Bowen, Oliver E., Jr. Rocks & Minerals of the San Francisco Bay Region. (California Natural History Guides: No. 5). (Illus.). 1962. 14.95 (ISBN 0-520-03244-6); pap. 2.85 (ISBN 0-520-00158-3). U of Cal Pr.

Boyd, F. R., ed. Kimberlites, Diatremes, & Diamonds: Their Geology, Petrology & Geochemistry. LC 78-72025. 1979. 19.00 (ISBN 0-87590-212-X, SP0024). Am Geophysical.

--The Mantle Sample: Inclusions in Kimberlites & Other Volcanics. 1979. 19.00 (ISBN 0-87590-213-8, SP0025). Am Geophysical.

Brown, Vinson, et al. Rocks & Minerals of California. 3rd. rev. ed. LC 72-13423. (Illus.). 200p. (gr. 4 up). 1972. 9.95 (ISBN 0-911010-59-9); pap. 5.95 (ISBN 0-911010-58-0). Naturegraph.

Burns, R. G. Mineralogical Applications of Crystal Field Theory. LC 77-85714. (Earth Sciences Ser). (Illus.). 1969. 29.50 (ISBN 0-521-07610-2). Cambridge U Pr.

Canadian Minerals & International Economic Interdependence. (Mineral Policy Ser.). 38p. 1978. pap. 2.75 (ISBN 0-685-87290-4, SSC85, SSC). Unipub.

Canadian Minerals Yearbook, 1977. (Mineral Report Ser.: No. 27). (Illus.). 634p. 1980. 31.00 (ISBN 0-660-10295-1, SSC-1355, SSC). Unipub.

Chesterman, Charles W. The Audubon Society Field Guide to North American Rocks & Minerals. LC 78-54893. (Illus.). 1979. 9.95 (ISBN 0-394-50269-8). Knopf.

Clark, Andrew. Minerals. (Illus.). 128p. 1979. 8.95 (ISBN 0-600-36313-9). Transatlantic.

Cleaveland, Parker. An Elementary Treatise on Mineralogy & Geology. Albritton, Claude C., Jr., ed. LC 77-6513. (History of Geology Ser.). (Illus.). 1978. Repr. of 1816 ed. lib. bdg. 40.00 (ISBN 0-405-10436-7). Arno.

Correns, C. W., et al. Introduction to Mineralogy: Crystallography & Petrology. Johns, W. D., tr. LC 72-460063. (Illus.). 1969. 22.50 (ISBN 0-387-04443-4). Springer-Verlag.

Cox, K. G., et al. Introduction to the Practical Study of Crystals, Minerals & Rocks. 1969. 8.75 (ISBN 0-07-094053-3, P&RB). McGraw.

--An Introduction to the Practical Study of Crystals, Minerals, & Rocks. rev. ed. LC 74-13833. 235p. 1975. text ed. 14.95 (ISBN 0-470-18139-7). Halsted Pr.

Cronstedt, Axel F. An Essay Towards a System of Minerology, 2 vols. Von Engestrom, Gustav, tr. from Swedish. LC 79-8604. Repr. of 1788 ed. 92.50 set (ISBN 0-404-18462-6). AMS Pr.

Dana, E. S. & Ford, W. E. Textbook of Mineralogy. 4th ed. 1932. 39.95 (ISBN 0-471-19305-4). Wiley.

Dana, E. S. & Hurlbut, C. S. Minerals & How to Study Them. 3rd ed. pap. 15.95 (ISBN 0-471-19195-7). Wiley.

Dana, J. D., et al. Systems of Mineralogy, 3 vols. 7th ed. Incl. Vol. 1. Elements, Sulfides, Sulfosalts, Oxides. 1944. 53.00 (ISBN 0-471-19239-2); Vol. 2. Halides, Nitrates, Borates, Carbonates, Sulfates, Phosphates, Arsenates, Tungstates, Molybdates. 1951. 53.00 (ISBN 0-471-19272-4); Vol. 3. Silica Minerals. 1962. 28.50 (ISBN 0-471-19287-2). Pub. by Wiley-Interscience). Wiley.

Deer, W. A., et al. Rock-Forming Minerals, Vol. 2A. 2nd ed. LC 78-40451. 1979. 65.95x (ISBN 0-470-26455-1). Halsted Pr.

Deer, William A., et al. Introduction to Rock Forming Minerals. 1966. pap. 27.95 (ISBN 0-470-20516-4). Halsted Pr.

Desautels, Paul E. Rocks & Minerals. LC 73-91134. (Collector's Series: No. 1). (Illus.). 160p. 1974. 4.95 (ISBN 0-448-11540-9, MSP). G&D.

Dietrich, R. V. Mineral Tables: Hand Specimen Properties of Fifteen Hundred Minerals. 1968. 8.95 (ISBN 0-07-016895-4, C). McGraw.

El-Hinnawi, Essam E. Methods in Chemical & Mineral Microscopy. 1966. 39.00 (ISBN 0-444-40189-X). Elsevier.

Ernst, W. G. Earth Materials. (gr. 10 up). 1969. pap. text ed. 8.95 (ISBN 0-13-222604-9). P-H.

Firsoff, Val A. Gemstones of the British Isles. (Illus.). 152p. 1971. 12.50x (ISBN 0-05-002472-8). Intl Pubns Serv.

Franco, R. R. & Leprevost, A. Minerals of Brazil, 3 vols. (Illus.). 1972. Set. 150.00 (ISBN 0-685-47310-4). Heinman.

French, Bevan M. Progressive Contact Metamorphism of the Biwabik Iron-Formation, Mesabi Range, Minnesota. LC 68-66592. (Bulletin: No. 45). (Illus.). 1968. 4.50x (ISBN 0-8166-0478-9). Minn Geol Survey.

Frissel, M. J., ed. Cycling of Mineral Nutrients in Agricultural Ecosystems, Vol. 4, No. 1-2. (Developments in Agricultural & Managed-Forest Ecology: Vol. 3). 1978. Repr. 51.25 (ISBN 0-444-41660-9). Elsevier.

Frondel, Judith W. Lunar Mineralogy. LC 75-9786. 323p. 1975. 37.50 (ISBN 0-471-28289-8, Pub. by Wiley-Interscience). Wiley.

Frye, Keith. Modern Minerology. (Illus.). 336p. 1973. ref. ed. 23.95 (ISBN 0-13-595686-2). P-H.

Girard, R. M. Texas Rocks & Minerals: An Amateur's Guide. (Illus.). 109p. 1964. Repr. 2.00 (ISBN 0-686-29314-2, GB 6). Bur Econ Geology.

Greene, John C. & Burke, John G. The Science of Minerals in the Age of Jefferson. LC 78-50195. (Transactions Ser.: Vol. 68, Pt. 4). (Illus.). 1978. pap. 10.00 (ISBN 0-87169-684-3). Am Philos.

Gupta, A. & Yagi, K. Petrology & Genesis of Leucite-Bearing Rocks. (Minerals & Rocks Ser.: Vol. 14). (Illus.). 250p. 1980. 39.00 (ISBN 0-387-09864-X). Springer-Verlag.

Hammons, Lee. How to Identify Minerals. new ed. (Illus.). 1979. pap. 5.95 (ISBN 0-686-20477-8). Ariz Maps & Bks.

Harder, Herrmann. Lexikon Fuer Mineralien - und Gesteins Freunde. (Ger.). 1977. 25.00 (ISBN 3-7658-0253-0, M-7198). French & Eur.

Hardy, George W., III, ed. Royalties & Division Orders. 1977. 27.00 (ISBN 0-89419-012-1). Inst Energy.

Holland, Heinrich D. The Chemistry of the Atmosphere & Oceans. LC 77-28176. 1978. 34.00 (ISBN 0-471-03509-2, Pub. by Wiley-Interscience). Wiley.

Howell, Fred G., et al, eds. Mineral Cycling in Southeastern Ecosystems. LC 75-33463. 920p. 1975. pap. 13.60 (ISBN 0-686-75801-3); microfiche 3.00 (ISBN 0-686-75802-1). DOE.

Hurlbut, Cornelius S., Jr. & Klein, Cornelis. Manual of Mineralogy After J. D. Dana. 19th ed. LC 77-1131. 1977. 31.50 (ISBN 0-471-42226-6). Wiley.

In Situ Investigation in Soils & Rocks. 328p. 1980. 80.00x (ISBN 0-901948-30-6, Pub. by Telford England). State Mutual Bk.

Industrial Minerals & Rocks. 4th ed. LC 73-85689. 1975. 40.00x (ISBN 0-89520-028-7). Soc Mining Eng.

International Workshop on Phosphate & Other Minerals, 5th. Fifth International Workshop on Phosphate & Other Minerals: Abstracts. Massry, S. G., ed. (Mineral & Electrolyte Metabolism Journal: Vol. 6, No. 4-5, 1981). (Illus.). 52p. 1981. pap. 42.00 (ISBN 3-8055-3441-8). S Karger.

Jensen, M. L. & Bateman, A. M. Economic Mineral Deposits. 3rd rev. ed. LC 78-9852. 593p. 1981. text ed. 25.95 (ISBN 0-471-09043-3). Wiley.

Johnson, Wesley M. & Maxwell, John A. Rock & Mineral Analysis. LC 81-1659. (Chemical Analysis Ser.). 584p. 1981. 40.00 (ISBN 0-471-02743-X, Pub. by Wiley-Interscience). Wiley.

Keller, W. D. Common Rocks & Minerals of Missouri. rev. ed. LC 67-66173. (Illus.). 1961. pap. 4.00x (ISBN 0-8262-0585-2). U of Mo Pr.

Kimbler, Frank S. & Narsavage, Robert J., Jr. New Mexico Rocks & Minerals Guide. (Illus.). 128p. (Orig.). 1981. pap. 8.95 (ISBN 0-913270-97-0). Sunstone Pr.

Kobell, Franz & Ritter, V. Geschichte der Mineralogie. Repr. of 1864 ed. 41.50 (ISBN 0-384-30015-4). Johnson Repr.

Kohland, William. Mineral Identification. LC 77-73455. 1977. 9.00 (ISBN 0-910042-31-4); pap. 3.50 (ISBN 0-910042-30-6). Allegheny.

Kondo, Riki H. Rocks & Minerals. (Instant Nature Guides). (Illus.). 1979. pap. 2.95 (ISBN 0-448-12676-1). G&D.

Kostov, Ivan. Mineralogy. 1969. 29.40 (ISBN 0-934454-63-9). Lubrecht & Cramer.

Kuzin, M. & Egorov, N. Field Manual of Minerals. 194p. 1979. 8.40 (ISBN 0-8285-1516-6, Pub. by Mir Pubs Russia). Imported Pubns.

Ladurner, J. More About Minerals. (Illus.). 187p. 1972. 22.50x (ISBN 3-524-00386-9). Intl Pubns Serv.

Leake, Bernard E. Catalogue of Analyzed Calciferous & Subcalciferous Amphiboles Together with Their Nomenclature & Associated Minerals. LC 68-26496. (Special Paper: No. 98). (Illus., Orig.). 1968. pap. 9.75x (ISBN 0-8137-2098-2). Geol Soc.

Lye, Keith. Minerals & Rocks. LC 79-17802. (Arco Fact Guides in Color Ser.). (Illus.). 1980. 6.95 (ISBN 0-668-04847-6). Arco.

McConnell, D. Apatite: Its Crystal Chemistry, Mineralogy, Utilization, & Biologic Occurrences. LC 72-88060. (Applied Mineralogy Ser.: Vol. 5). (Illus.). 111p. 1973. 30.50 (ISBN 0-387-81095-1). Springer-Verlag.

MacFall, Russell P. Minerals & Gems. LC 74-28082. (Illus.). 256p. 1975. 17.50 (ISBN 0-690-00687-X). T Y Crowell.

Macintosh, E. K. Guide to the Rocks, Minerals & Gemstones of Southern Africa. (Illus.). 1976. limp bdg. 11.00x (ISBN 0-86977-062-4). Verry.

Mackenzie, W. S. & Guilford, C. Atlas of Rock-Forming Minerals in Thin Section. 98p. 1980. pap. 24.95x (ISBN 0-470-26921-9). Halsted Pr.

McQuiston, Frank W., Jr. & Shoemaker, Robert S. Primary Crushing Plant Design. (Illus.). 1978. 30.00x (ISBN 0-89520-252-2). Soc Mining Eng.

Marfunin, A. S. Spectroscopy, Luminescence & Radiation Centers in Minerals. Schiffer, W. W., tr. from Russ. (Illus.). 1979. 52.30 (ISBN 0-387-09070-3). Springer-Verlag.

Mason, Brian & Berry, L. G. Elements of Mineralogy. LC 68-13311. (Geology Ser.). (Illus.). 1968. 25.95x (ISBN 0-7167-0235-5). W H Freeman.

Matthews, William H., 3rd. Mineral, Fossil & Rock Exhibits & Where to See Them. 1977. 3.00 (ISBN 0-913312-20-7). Am Geol.

Mitchell, Richard S. Mineral Names: What Do They Mean? 1979. text ed. 13.95 (ISBN 0-442-24593-9). Van Nos Reinhold.

Moore, Nathaniel F. Ancient Mineralogy: An Inquiry Respecting Mineral Substances Mentioned by the Ancients. Albritton, Claude C., Jr., ed. LC 77-6532. (History of Geology Ser.). 1978. Repr. of 1834 ed. lib. bdg. 15.00 (ISBN 0-405-10452-9). Arno.

Nicol, A. W., ed. Physicochemical Methods of Mineral Analysis. LC 72-95070. 508p. 1975. 39.50 (ISBN 0-306-30739-1, Plenum Pr). Plenum Pub.

Pearl, Richard M. Cleaning & Preserving Minerals. 5th ed. 1980. pap. 2.75 (ISBN 0-686-14941-6). Earth Science.

--Rocks & Minerals. (Orig.). 1969. pap. 2.75 (ISBN 0-06-463260-1, EH 260, EH). Har-Row.

Phillips, W. J. & Phillips, N. Introduction to Mineralogy for Geologists. LC 79-42898. 344p. 1980. 49.50 (ISBN 0-471-27642-1); pap. 19.95 (ISBN 0-471-27795-9). Wiley.

Phillips, William. An Outline of Mineralogy & Geology: Intended for the Use of Those Who May Desire to Become Acquainted with the Elements of Those Sciences. Albritton, Claude C., Jr., ed. LC 77-6536. (History of Geology Ser.). (Illus.). 1978. Repr. of 1816 ed. lib. bdg. 12.00x (ISBN 0-405-10456-1). Arno.
Pierrot, Roland. Chemical & Determinative Tables of Mineralogy Without the Silicates. LC 79-90000. 608p. 1980. 85.00x (ISBN 0-89352-077-2). Masson Pub.
Pough, Frederick H. A Field Guide to Rocks & Minerals. 4th ed. (Peterson Field Guide Ser.). 1976. 12.95 (ISBN 0-395-24047-6); pap. 8.95 (ISBN 0-395-24049-2). HM.
Prinz, Martin, et al, eds. Simon & Schuster's Guide to Rocks & Minerals. (Illus.). 1978. 9.95 (ISBN 0-671-24396-9); pap. 7.95 (ISBN 0-671-24417-5). S&S.
Ramdohr, Paul. The Ore Minerals & Their Intergrowths, 2 vols. 2nd ed. LC 79-40745. (International Series in Earth Sciences: Vol. 35). (Illus.). 1269p. 1981. Set. 200.00 (ISBN 0-08-023801-7). Pergamon.
Rapp, G. Color of Minerals. (Earth Science Curriculum Project Pamphlet Ser). 1971. pap. 3.20 (ISBN 0-395-02620-2). HM.
Rittmann, A. Stable Mineral Assemblages of Igneous Rocks. LC 72-90269. (Minerals, Rocks, & Inorganic Materials Ser.: Vol. 7). (Illus.). 250p. 1973. 41.30 (ISBN 0-387-06030-8). Springer-Verlag.
Rogers, Austin F. & Staples, Lloyd. Introduction to the Study of Minerals. 3rd ed. LC 75-41235. Repr. of 1937 ed. 34.50 (ISBN 0-404-14699-6). AMS Pr.
Royal Society of London Publications, et al. Mineralogy: Towards the Twenty-First Century. (Illus.). 1978. text ed. 90.00x (ISBN 0-85403-092-1). Scholium Intl.
Saggerson, E. Identification Tables for Minerals in Thin Sections. 280p. 1975. pap. text ed. 12.95x (ISBN 0-582-44343-1). Longman.
Scholfield, Charles G. Homogenisation-Blending Systems Design & Control for Minerals Processing. (Bulk Materials Handling Ser.). (Illus.). 1980. 60.00x (ISBN 0-87849-030-2); pap. 40.00 (ISBN 0-87849-037-X). Trans Tech.
Shawe, Daniel R., ed. Guidebook on Fossil Fuels & Metals, Eastern Utah & Western-Southwestern Central Colorado. (Professional Contributions Ser.: No. 9). (Illus.). 150p. 1978. pap. 8.50x (ISBN 0-918062-04-7). Colo Sch Mines.
Simpson, B. Rocks & Minerals. 1966. 23.00 (ISBN 0-08-011744-9); pap. 9.00 (ISBN 0-08-011743-0). Pergamon.
Sinkankas, John. Mineralogy. 598p. 1964. pap. 12.95 (ISBN 0-442-27624-9). Van Nos Reinhold.
--Prospecting for Gemstones & Minerals. rev. ed. 398p. 1970. pap. 9.95 (ISBN 0-442-27620-6). Van Nos Reinhold.
Slaughter, M. & Earley, J. W. Mineralogy & Geological Significance of the Mowry Bentonites, Wyoming. LC 65-22397. (Special Paper: No. 83). (Illus., Orig.). 1965. pap. 6.00x (ISBN 0-8137-2083-4). Geol Soc.
Smith, H. G. Minerals & the Microscope. 1956. pap. text ed. 7.95x (ISBN 0-04-549002-3). Allen Unwin.
Smith, W. L., ed. Remote-Sensing Applications for Mineral Exploration. 1977. 71.00 (ISBN 0-12-787477-1). Acad Pr.
Somasundaran, P. & Arbiter, N., eds. Beneficiation of Mineral Fines. LC 79-91945. (Illus.). 406p. (Orig.). 1979. pap. text ed. 21.00x (ISBN 0-89520-259-X). Soc Mining Eng.
Sorrell, Charles. Rocks & Minerals. (Golden Field Guide Ser). (Illus.). 280p. 1974. (Golden Pr); pap. 4.95 (ISBN 0-307-13661-2). Western Pub.
Stone, Gregory. Prospecting for Lode Gold. (Illus.). 48p. 1975. pap. 3.95 (ISBN 0-8059-2192-3). Dorrance.
Strens, R. G., ed. The Physics & Chemistry of Minerals & Rocks. LC 75-6930. 697p. 1975. 121.75 (ISBN 0-471-83368-1, Pub by Wiley-Interscience). Wiley.
Teodorovich, G. I. Authigenic Minerals in Sedimentary Rocks. LC 60-13951. 120p. 1961. 30.00 (ISBN 0-306-10507-1, Consultants). Plenum Pub.
Todor, Dumitru N. Thermal Analysis of Minerals. Marcus, S., tr. from Romanian. (Illus.). 1976. 36.00x (ISBN 0-85626-101-7, Pub. by Abacus Pr). Intl Schol Bk Serv.
Touloukian, U. S. & Ho, C. Y. Physical Properties of Rocks & Minerals, Vol. II. (M-H-CINDAS Data Series on Material Properties). (Illus.). 576p. 1981. text ed. 44.50 (ISBN 0-07-065032-2). McGraw.
Trudinger, P. A. & Swaine, D. J., eds. Biogeochemical Cycling of Mineral-Forming Elements. LC 79-21297. (Studies in Environmental Science: Vol. 3). 616p. 1979. 97.75 (ISBN 0-444-41745-1). Elsevier.
Vanders, Iris & Kerr, Paul F. Mineral Recognition. LC 66-25223. 1967. 29.50 (ISBN 0-471-90295-0, Pub. by Wiley-Interscience). Wiley.
Van Olphen, H. & Fripiat, J. J., eds. Data Handbook for Clay Materials & Other Non-Metallic Minerals. (Illus.). 1979. text ed. 76.00 (ISBN 0-08-022850-X). Pergamon.
Voskuil, Walter H. Minerals in Modern Industry. LC 74-118424. 1970. Repr. of 1930 ed. 15.50 (ISBN 0-8046-1374-5). Kennikat.
Watson, Janet. Rocks & Minerals. 2nd rev. ed. (Introducing Geology Ser.). (Illus.). pap. text ed. 4.95x (ISBN 0-04-551031-8). Allen Unwin.
Wenk, H. R., et al, eds. Electron Microscopy in Mineralogy. (Illus.). 590p. 1976. 52.40 (ISBN 0-387-07371-X). Springer-Verlag.
Wright, Ruth V. & Chadbourne, Robert L. Gems & Minerals of the Bible. LC 76-58767. 160p. 1977. pap. 3.95 (ISBN 0-87983-139-1). Keats.
Wyllie, Peter J., ed. Ultramafic & Related Rocks. LC 78-12080. 484p. (Orig.). 1979. Repr. of 1967 ed. 35.00 (ISBN 0-88275-755-5). Krieger.
Zim, Herbert S. & Shaffer, Paul R. Rocks & Minerals. (Golden Guide Ser). (Illus.). (gr. 6 up). 1957. PLB 9.15 (ISBN 0-307-63502-3, Golden Pr); pap. 1.95 (ISBN 0-307-24499-7). Western Pub.
Zussman, J., ed. Physical Methods in Determinative Mineralogy. 2nd ed. 1978. 84.00 (ISBN 0-12-782960-1). Acad Pr.

MINERALOGY–BIBLIOGRAPHY

DeLucia, Alan A., et al. Mineral Atlas: Pacific Northwest. LC 80-52312. (Orig.). 1980. pap. 8.95 (ISBN 0-89301-072-3). U Pr of Idaho.

MINERALOGY–COLLECTING OF SPECIMENS

see Mineralogy–Collectors and Collecting

MINERALOGY–COLLECTORS AND COLLECTING

Baldwin, Charles. Colorado Gem & Mineral Collecting Localities. 1980. pap. 4.95 (ISBN 0-933472-08-0). Johnson Bks.
MacFall, Russell P. Rock Hunter's Guide. LC 78-22457. (Illus.). 1980. 12.95 (ISBN 0-690-01812-6). T Y Crowell.
Sadanaga, Ryoichi & Bunno, Michiaki, eds. The Wakabayashi Mineral Collection: At the University Museum of the University of Tokyo. new ed. 202p. 1974. 37.00x (ISBN 0-86008-115-X, Pub. by U of Tokyo Pr). Intl Schol Bk Serv.
Sanborn, William B. Handbook of Crystal & Mineral Collecting. 1966. pap. 2.00 (ISBN 0-910652-05-8). Gembooks.
Schumann, Walter. Minerals & Rocks. LC 79-301701. (Nature Guides Ser.). (Illus.). 144p. 1979. pap. 5.95 (ISBN 0-7011-2362-1, Pub. by Chatto Bodley Jonathan). Merrimack Bk Serv.
Touloukian, U. S. & Ho, C. Y. Physical Properties of Rocks & Minerals, Vol. II. (M-H-CINDAS Data Series on Material Properties). (Illus.). 576p. 1981. text ed. 44.50 (ISBN 0-07-065032-2). McGraw.

MINERALOGY–DICTIONARIES

Armanet, J. & Becquer, A. Annales des Mines: Lexique Technique Allemand-Francais. 344p. (Ger.-Fr.). 1951. 8.95 (ISBN 0-686-56901-6, M-6011). French & Eur.
Cagnacci-Schwicker, Angelo. Dictionnaire International de Metallurgie, Mineralogie, Geologie et Industries Extractives, 2 vols. 1530p. (Fr.). 1969. Set. 95.00 (ISBN 0-686-56933-4, M-6054). French & Eur.
Congres International de la Preparation des Minerais, ed. Lexique Quadrilinque de la Preparation des Minerais. 260p. (Ger., Eng., Fr. & Rus., Four-Language Lexicon of Ore Preparation). 1963. pap. 25.00 (ISBN 0-686-56795-1). French & Eur.
Deeson, A. F. The Collector's Encyclopedia of Rocks & Minerals. (Illus.). 288p. 1973. 15.00 (ISBN 0-517-50550-9). Potter.
De Michele, Vincenzo. Diccionario: Atlas De Mineralogia. 2nd ed. 216p. (Espn.). 1978. 11.50 (ISBN 84-307-8288-5, S-50260). French & Eur.
Diccionario Rioduero: Geologia y Mineralogia. 2nd ed. (Espn.). 1978. leatherette 9.95 (ISBN 0-686-57363-3). French & Eur.
Frank, Claudia. Enzyklopaedie der Minerale und Edelsteine. 304p. (Ger.). 1977. 80.00 (ISBN 3-451-17622-X, M-7058). French & Eur.
Gagnacci-Schwicker, A. & Schwicker. International Dictionary of Metallurgy, Mineralogy, Geology and the Mining and Oil Industries. 1530p. (Eng., Fr., Ger. & It.). 1970. 88.00 (ISBN 3-7625-0751-1, M-7482, Pub. by Bauverlag). French & Eur.
Hamilton, et al. Larousse Guide to Minerals, Rocks & Fossils. LC 77-71167. 1977. 15.95 (ISBN 0-88332-079-7, 8095); pap. 9.95 (ISBN 0-88332-078-9, 8094). Larousse.
Jehan, L. F. Dictionnaire de Chimie et de Mineralogie. Migne, J. P., ed. (Encyclopedie Theologique Ser.: Vol. 46). 830p. (Fr.). Date not set. Repr. of 1851 ed. lib. bdg. 105.00x (ISBN 0-89241-250-X). Caratzas Bros.
Roberts, Willard L., et al. Encyclopedia of Minerals. 858p. 1974. text ed. 74.50 (ISBN 0-442-26820-3). Van Nos Reinhold.
Woerterbuch Fuer Metallurgie, Mineralogie, Geologie, Bergbau und die Oelindustrie. (Eng., Fr., Ger. & It., Dictionary of Metallurgy, Mineralogy, Geology, Mining and Oil Industry). 1970. 88.00 (ISBN 3-7625-0751-1, M-6912). French & Eur.
Woolley, Alan, ed. The Illustrated Encyclopedia of the Mineral Kingdom. LC 77-90038. (Illus.). 1978. 19.95 (ISBN 0-88332-089-4, 8047). Larousse.

MINERALOGY–EARLY WORKS TO 1800

Caley, Earle R. & Richards, John C. Theophrastus on Stones. 1956. 6.00 (ISBN 0-8142-0033-8). Ohio St U Pr.
Gobet, Nicolas. Les Anciens Mineralogietes Du Royaume De France. Repr. of 1779 ed. 259.00 (ISBN 0-8287-0379-5). Clearwater Pub.
Schafer, Edward H. Tu Wan's Stone Catalogue of Cloudy Forest: A Commentary & Synopsis. LC 60-10361. (Illus.). 1961. 17.00x (ISBN 0-520-01143-0). U of Cal Pr.
Woodward, John. An Essay Toward a Natural History of the Earth, & Terrestrial Bodies Especially Minerals of the Sea, Rivers, & Springs: An Account of the Universal Deluge & of the Effects That It Had Upon the Earth. Albritton, Claude C., Jr., ed. LC 77-7406. (History of Geology Ser.). 1978. Repr. of 1695 ed. lib. bdg. 20.00 (ISBN 0-405-10468-5). Arno.

MINERALOGY–JUVENILE LITERATURE

Fenton, Carroll Lane & Fenton, Mildred Adams. Rocks & Their Stories. LC 51-12152. (gr. 6-9). 1951. 5.95 (ISBN 0-385-07113-2). Doubleday.
Gilbert, Miriam. Science-Hobby Book of Rocks & Minerals. rev. ed. LC 61-17403. (Science Hobby Bks). (gr. 5-10). 1968. PLB 4.95 (ISBN 0-8225-0556-8). Lerner Pubns.
Harris, Susan. Gems & Minerals. (gr. 2-4). 1980. PLB 6.90 (ISBN 0-531-03241-8). Watts.
Hyler, Nelson W. Rocks & Minerals. (How & Why Wonder Books Ser.). (Illus.). (gr. 4-6). pap. 1.00 (ISBN 0-448-05004-8). Wonder.
McGowen, Tom. Album of Rocks & Minerals. (Rand McNally "Album" Ser.). (Illus.). 64p. (gr. 4 up). 1981. 7.95 (ISBN 0-528-82400-7); PLB 7.97 (ISBN 0-528-80075-2). Rand.
Pearl, Richard M. Wonders of Rocks & Minerals. (Illus.). (gr. 4-6). 1961. PLB 5.95 (ISBN 0-396-06930-4). Dodd.
Ridpath, Ian, ed. Man & Materials: Minerals. LC 74-10558. (Illus.). 32p. (gr. 4 up). 1975. PLB 4.95 (ISBN 0-201-09032-5, 9032, A-W Childrens). A-W.
Rinkoff, Barbara. Guess What Rocks Do. LC 74-16111. (Illus.). 32p. (gr. k-3). 1975. 7.25 (ISBN 0-688-41678-0); PLB 6.96 (ISBN 0-688-51678-5). Lothrop.
White, Anne T. All About Rocks & Minerals. (Allabout Ser: No. 12). (Illus.). (gr. 4-6). 1963. PLB 5.39 (ISBN 0-394-90212-2, BYR). Random.

MINERALOGY–PICTORIAL WORKS

Tennissen, Anthony C. Colorful Mineral Identifier. LC 72-151706. (Illus.). (gr. 10 up). 1971. 9.95 (ISBN 0-8069-3040-3); PLB 9.29 (ISBN 0-8069-3041-1). Sterling.

MINERALOGY, DETERMINATIVE

see also Assaying; Chemistry, Analytic; Optical Mineralogy

Freund, Hugo. Applied Ore Microscopy. 1966. 39.95 (ISBN 0-02-339710-1, 33971). Macmillan.
Gadsen, J. A. Infrared Spectra of Minerals & Related Inorganic Compounds. 288p. 1975. 37.95 (ISBN 0-408-70665-1). Butterworth.
Heinrich, Eberhardt W. Microscopic Identification of Minerals. 1965. text ed. 24.00 (ISBN 0-07-028055-X, C). McGraw.
Karr, Clarence, ed. Infrared & Raman Spectroscopy of Lunar & Terrestrial Minerals. 1975. 63.00 (ISBN 0-12-399950-2). Acad Pr.
Liddicoat, Richard T., Jr. Handbook of Gemstone Identification. 11th ed. (Illus.). 1981. 22.75 (ISBN 0-87311-006-4). Gemological.
Maxwell, John A. Rock & Mineral Analysis. LC 68-29396. (Chemical Analysis Ser: Vol. 27). 1968. 46.50 (ISBN 0-471-57900-9, Pub. by Wiley-Interscience). Wiley.
Pearl, Richard M. How to Know the Minerals & Rocks. (RL 7). pap. 1.50 (ISBN 0-451-07240-5, W7240, Sig). NAL.
Pierrot, Roland. Chemical & Determinative Tables of Mineralogy Without the Silicates. LC 79-90000. 608p. 1980. 85.00x (ISBN 0-89352-077-2). Masson Pub.
Shelby, C. A. Heavy Minerals in the Wellborn Formation, Lee & Burleson Counties, Texas. (Illus.). 54p. 1965. 1.25 (ISBN 0-686-29337-1, RI 55). Bur Econ Geology.
Smykatz-Kloss, W. Differential Thermal Analysis: Application & Results in Mineralogy. LC 74-17490. (Minerals & Rocks Ser.: Vol. 11). (Illus.). xiv, 185p. 1975. 29.50 (ISBN 0-387-06906-2). Springer-Verlag.
Tickell, F. G. Techniques of Sedimentary Mineralogy. (Developments in Sedimentology: Vol. 4). 1965. 46.50 (ISBN 0-444-40570-4). Elsevier.
Troeger, W. E. Optical Determination of Rock-Forming Minerals. Part I: Determinative Tables. Hoffman, C., tr. from Ger. (Illus.). 1979. lib. bdg. 28.20 (ISBN 3-5106-5311-4). Lubrecht & Cramer.
Van Der Plas, Leendert. Identification of Detrital Feldspars. (Developments in Sedimentology: Vol. 6). 1966. 63.50 (ISBN 0-444-40597-6). Elsevier.
Winchell, H. Optical Properties of Minerals: A Determinative Table. 1964. 21.00 (ISBN 0-12-759150-8). Acad Pr.

MINERALOGY, OPTICAL

see Optical Mineralogy

MINERALS

see Mineralogy; Mines and Mineral Resources

MINERALS, RADIOACTIVE

see Radioactive Substances

MINERALS IN PLANTS

see Plants–Assimilation

MINERALS IN THE BODY

see also Mineral Metabolism

Adams, Ruth & Murray, Frank. Minerals: Kill or Cure. rev. ed. 366p. (Orig.). 1974. pap. 1.95 (ISBN 0-915962-16-0). Larchmont Bks.
Bosco, Dominick. The People's Guide to Vitamins & Minerals: From A to Zinc. 1980. 12.95 (ISBN 0-8092-7140-0); pap. 6.95 (ISBN 0-8092-7139-7). Contemp Bks.
Flodin, N. W. Vitamin - Trace Mineral - Protein Interactions, Vol. 2. Horrobin, D. F., ed. (Annual Research Reviews). 1980. 30.00 (ISBN 0-88831-062-5, Dist. by Pergamon). Eden Med Res.
Flodin, Nestor W. Vitamin-Trace Mineral-Protein Interactions, Vol. 3. Horribin, David F., ed. (Annual Research Reviews). 362p. 1980. 38.00 (ISBN 0-88831-085-4). Eden Med Res.
Karcioglu, Z. A. & Sarper, R. M. Zinc & Copper in Medicine. (Illus.). 696p. 1980. 59.75 (ISBN 0-398-03977-1). C C Thomas.
Kolisko, E. Lead & the Human Organism. 1980. pap. 3.95x (ISBN 0-906492-31-9, Pub. by Kolisko Archives). St George Bk Serv.
Kutsky, Roman J. Handbook of Vitamins, Minerals & Hormones. 1981. text ed. 24.50 (ISBN 0-442-24557-2). Van Nos Reinhold.
Lewis, Clara M. Nutrition: Vitamins & Minerals, Sodium & Potassium. LC 75-43830. (Illus.). 1978. pap. text ed. 7.00 (ISBN 0-8036-5622-X). Davis Co.
Massry, Shaul G., et al, eds. Phosphate & Minerals in Health & Disease. (Advances in Experimental Medicine & Biology: Vol. 128). 666p. 1980. 59.50 (ISBN 0-306-40451-6, Plenum Pr). Plenum Pub.
Mervyn, Len. Minerals & Your Health. LC 80-84442. 144p. 1981. 9.95 (ISBN 0-87983-242-8). Keats.
Pfeiffer, Carl C. Zinc & Other Micro-Nutrients. LC 77-91321. (Illus.). 1978. pap. 2.95 (ISBN 0-87983-169-3). Keats.
Prevention Magazine Editors. The Complete Book of Minerals for Health. Prevention Magazine & Padus, Emrika, eds. (Illus.). 562p. 1981. 16.95 (ISBN 0-87857-360-7). Rodale Pr Inc.
Zipkin, Isadore. Biological Mineralization. (Fundamental Mathematics Ser.). 916p. 1973. 64.50 (ISBN 0-471-98381-0). Krieger.

MINERS

see also Coal Miners

Arnot, R. Page. The Miners: One Union, One Industry: A History of the National Union of Mineworkers 1939-46. (Illus.). 1979. text ed. 30.00x (ISBN 0-04-331074-5). Allen Unwin.
Bates, Robert H. Unions, Parties, & Political Development: A Study of Mineworkers in Zambia. LC 78-158135. (Illus.). 1971. 25.00x (ISBN 0-300-01403-1). Yale U Pr.
Brown, Ronald C. Hard-Rock Miners: The Intermountain West, 1860-1920. LC 78-21778. (Illus.). 336p. 1979. 15.95 (ISBN 0-89096-066-6). Tex A&M Univ Pr.
Clark, Paul F. The Miner's Fight for Democracy: Arnold Miller & the Reform of the Mited Mine Workers. 194p. Date not set. cancelled (ISBN 0-686-30349-0); pap. cancelled (ISBN 0-686-30350-4). Cornell U Pr.
De Chungara, Domitila B. & Viezzer, Moema. Let Me Speak! Testimony of Domitila, a Woman of the Bolivian Mines. Ortiz, Victoria, tr. LC 77-91757. 235p. 1979. 12.50 (ISBN 0-85345-445-0, CL-4450); pap. 5.95 (ISBN 0-85345-485-X, PB485X). Monthly Rev.
Educational Research Council of America. Hardrock Miner. Ferris, Theodore N. & Marchak, John P., eds. (Real People at Work Ser: F). (Illus.). 1974. pap. text ed. 2.25 (ISBN 0-89247-044-5). Changing Times.
Employee Relations Initiatives in Canadian Mining. 85p. (Orig.). 1979. pap. text ed. 5.00x (ISBN 0-88757-014-3, Pub. by Ctr Resource Stud Canada). Renouf.

Fish, Lydia M. The Folklore of the Coal Miners of the Northeast of England. LC 76-25433. 1976. Set. lib. bdg. 25.00 (ISBN 0-8414-4209-6). Folcroft.

Gardner, James A. Lead King: Moses Austin. 256p. 1980. 9.95 (ISBN 0-86629-004-4). Sunrise MO.

Hochschild, Harold K. The MacIntyre Mine: From Failure to Fortune. rev. ed. (Old Township Thirty-Four Ser.). (Illus.). 27p. 1962. 2.50 (ISBN 0-686-74827-1). Adirondack Mus.

Holleman, J. F. & Biesheuvel, S. White Mine Workers in Northern Rhodesia 1959-60. LC 75-306853. (African Social Research Ser.: Vol. 6). 1973. pap. 13.50x (ISBN 0-8002-2153-2). Intl Pubns Serv.

Keiser, John. The Union Miners Cemetary. 40p. 1980. pap. 2.50 (ISBN 0-916884-09-0). C H Kerr.

Masten, Arthur H. The Story of Adirondac. (Illus.). 240p. 1968. Repr. of 1923 ed. 9.50 (ISBN 0-686-74842-5). Adirondack Mus.

Nash, June. We Eat the Mines & the Mines Eat Us: Dependency & Exploitation in Bolivian Tin Mines. LC 79-11623. 1979. 25.00x (ISBN 0-231-04710-X). Columbia U Pr.

Perrings, Charles. Black Mineworkers in Central Africa. LC 78-11413. 1979. text ed. 42.50x (ISBN 0-8419-0462-6, Africana). Holmes & Meier.

Samuel, Raphael, ed. Miners, Quarrymen & Saltworkers. (History Workshop Ser.). (Illus.). 1977. 22.00 (ISBN 0-7100-8353-X); pap. 12.50 (ISBN 0-7100-8354-8). Routledge & Kegan.

Todd, Arthur C. Cornish Miner in America. (Illus.). 1968. 15.00 (ISBN 0-87062-063-0). A H Clark.

Voynick, Stephen M. The Making of a Hardrock Miner. LC 78-56574. pap. 5.95 (ISBN 0-8310-7116-8). Howell-North.

Wallace, Robert. The Miners. LC 73-94242. (The Old West). (Illus.). (gr. 5 up). 1976. kivar 12.96 (ISBN 0-8094-1539-9, Pub. by Time-Life). Silver.

Wallace, Robert, ed. The Miners. (Old West Ser.). (Illus.). 1976. 14.95 (ISBN 0-8094-1537-2). Time-Life.

Wyman, Mark. Hard-Rock Miners: Western Miners & the Industrial Revolution, 1860-1910. LC 78-54805. 1979. 17.95 (ISBN 0-520-03678-6). U of Cal Pr.

Young, Otis E., Jr. & Lenon, Robert. Black Powder & Hand Steel: Miners & Machines on the Old Western Frontier. LC 75-4634. (Illus.). 200p. 1976. pap. 10.95 (ISBN 0-8061-1269-7). U of Okla Pr.

MINERS–SONGS AND MUSIC

Green, Archie. Only a Miner: Studies in Recorded Coal-Mining Songs. LC 78-155499. (Music in American Life Ser). (Illus.). 520p. 1972. 20.00 (ISBN 0-252-00181-8); text ed. 8.95 (ISBN 0-252-00835-9). U of Ill Pr.

Lloyd, A. A. Come All Ye Bold Miners: Ballads & Songs of the Coalfields. rev ed. 1978. Repr. of 1952 ed. text ed. 25.00x (ISBN 0-85315-412-0). Humanities.

MINERS' FEDERATION OF GREAT BRITAIN

Arnot, Robert P. Miners: A History of the Miners' Federation of Great Britain, 3 vols. Incl. Vol. 1. 1889-1910; Vol. 2. Years of Struggle from 1910 Onwards; Vol. 3. In Crisis and War, from 1930 Onwards. (Illus.). 1949-61. 50.00x set (ISBN 0-678-01368-3); 19.50x ea. Kelley.

MINERS' NYSTAGMUS

see Nystagmus

MINES, FOLK-LORE OF

see Folk-Lore of Mines

MINES, MILITARY

see also Blasting; Mines, Submarine

Goad, K. J. & Halsey, D. H. Ammunition, Grenades & Mines. (Brassey's Battlefield Weapons Systems & Technology: Vol. 3). 160p. 1982. 40.00 (ISBN 0-08-028324-1); pap. 16.00 (ISBN 0-08-028327-6). Pergamon.

Hartmann, Gregory K. Weapons That Wait: Mine Warfare in the U. S. Navy. LC 78-71766. (Illus.). 1979. 22.95 (ISBN 0-87021-753-4). Naval Inst Pr.

MINES, SUBMARINE

see also Mine Sweepers; Submarine Warfare

Elliott, Peter. Allied Minesweeping in World War Two. LC 78-61581. 1979. 11.95 (ISBN 0-87021-904-9). Naval Inst Pr.

MINES AND MINERAL RESOURCES

see also Ceramic Materials; Mineralogy; Mining Engineering; Mining Geology; Mining Industry and Finance; Mining Law; Precious Metals; Prospecting; Raw Materials;

also specific types of mines and mining, e.g. Coal Mines and Mining, Gold Mines and Mining

Anders, Gerhard, et al, eds. The Economics of Mineral Extraction. Gramm, W. Phillip. LC 79-22949. 334p. 1980. 29.95 (ISBN 0-03-053171-3). Praeger.

Beus, A. A. & Grigorian, S. V. Geochemical Exploration Methods for Mineral Deposits. Levinson, A. A., ed. Teteruk-Schneider, Rita, tr. LC 77-75045. (Illus.). 1977. 32.00x (ISBN 0-915834-03-0). Applied Pub.

Board on Mineral & Energy Resources. Redistribution of Accessory Elements in Mining & Mineral Processing: Coal & Oil Shale, Pt. I. 1979. pap. 9.25 (ISBN 0-309-02897-3). Natl Acad Pr.

--Redistribution of Accessory Elements in Mining & Mineral Processing: Uranium, Phosphate, & Alumina, Pt. II. 1979. pap. 12.25 (ISBN 0-309-02899-X). Natl Acad Pr.

Brown, J. Coggin & Key, A. K. The Mineral & Nuclear Fuels of the Indian Subcontinent & Burma. 1976. 38.00x (ISBN 0-19-560172-6). Oxford U Pr.

Bulmer, Martin, ed. Mining & Social Change. 318p. 1978. 30.00x (ISBN 0-85664-509-5, Pub. by Croom Helm Ltd England). Biblio Dist.

Burns, R. M. Conflict & Its Resolution in the Administration of Mineral Resources in Canada. 63p. (Orig.). 1976. pap. text ed. 3.50x (ISBN 0-88757-000-3, Pub. by Ctr Resource Stud Canada). Renouf.

Cargo, David N. & Mallory, Bob F. Man & His Geologic Environment. 2nd ed. LC 76-7655. 1977. text ed. 18.95 (ISBN 0-201-00894-7). A-W.

Carlson, Ellsworth C. Kaiping Mines, 1877-1912. rev. 2nd ed. LC 71-148943. (East Asian Monographs Ser: No. 3). 1971. pap. 9.00x (ISBN 0-674-49700-7). Harvard U Pr.

Carson, J. H. Early Recollections of the Mines. 59.95 (ISBN 0-8490-0074-2). Gordon Pr.

Cobbe, James. Governments & Mining Companies in Developing Countries. LC 79-4851. (Special Studies in Social, Political & Economic Development). (Illus.). 1979. lib. bdg. 26.25x (ISBN 0-89158-562-1). Westview.

COMECON's Mineral Development Potential & It's Implications for Canada. (Mineral Bulletin: No. 183). 112p. 1980. pap. 5.75 (ISBN 0-660-10204-8, SSC 137, SSC). Unipub.

Cowan, Jack C. & Weintritt, Donald J. Water - Formed Scale Deposits. 606p. 1976. 69.95x (ISBN 0-87201-896-2). Gulf Pub.

David, M. Geostatistical Ore Reserve Estimation. (Developments in Geomathematics). 1977. 39.75 (ISBN 0-444-41532-7). Elsevier.

Dawson, J. B. Kimberlites & Their Xenoliths. (Minerals & Rocks: Vol. 15). (Illus.). 252p. 1980. 47.25 (ISBN 0-387-10208-6). Springer-Verlag.

Deer, W. A., et al. Rock Forming Minerals: Vol. 1A, Orthosilicates. 2nd ed. 900p. 1981. 165.00 (ISBN 0-470-26633-3). Halsted Pr.

--Rock Forming Minerals, Vol. 5. 372p. 1962. 35.95 (ISBN 0-471-20524-9). Halsted Pr.

--Rock Forming Minerals, Vol. 1. 333p. 1962. 29.50 (ISBN 0-471-20518-4). Halsted Pr.

--Rock Forming Minerals, Vol. 4. 435p. 1963. 37.95 (ISBN 0-471-20523-0). Halsted Pr.

De Michele, Vincenzo. World of Minerals. (World of Nature Ser.). 1973. 4.98 (ISBN 0-517-12043-7, Bounty Books). Crown.

Derry, Duncan. Concise World Atlas of Geology & Mineral Deposits: Non-Metallic Minerals, Metallic Minerals & Energy Minerals. LC 80-675233. 110p. 1980. 68.95 (ISBN 0-470-26996-0). Halsted Pr.

De Vore, R. William & Carpenter, Stanley B., eds. Symposium on Surface Mining Hydrology, Sedimentology, & Reclamation. LC 79-91553. (Illus.). 353p. (Orig.). 1979. pap. 33.50 (ISBN 0-89779-024-3, UKY BU119); microfiche 4.50 (ISBN 0-89779-025-1). OES Pubns.

Dictionnaire Minier Russe-Francais. (Fr. & Rus.). 1973. pap. 25.00 (ISBN 0-686-56770-6, M-6150). French & Eur.

Engineering Mining Journal Magazine. Operating Handbook of Mineral Underground Mining, Vol. III. (Library of Operating Handbooks). 1979. 19.50 (ISBN 0-07-019521-8, P&RB). McGraw.

Fischman, Leonard L. World Mineral Trends & U. S. Supply Problems. LC 80-8025. (Resources for the Future, Inc. Research Paper R-20). (Illus.). 576p. (Orig.). 1981. pap. text ed. 15.00x (ISBN 0-8018-2491-5). Johns Hopkins.

Franco, R. R. & Leprevost, A. Minerals of Brazil, 3 vols. (Illus.). 1972. Set. 150.00 (ISBN 0-685-47310-4). Heinman.

Gary, James H., ed. Fourteenth Oil Shale Symposium Proceedings. (Illus.). 440p. 1981. pap. text ed. 18.00 (ISBN 0-918062-46-2). Colo Sch Mines.

Gaventa, John. Power & Powerlessness: Quiescence & Rebellion in an Appalachian Valley. LC 80-12988. (Illus.). 284p. 1980. 16.50 (ISBN 0-252-00772-7). U of Ill Pr.

Ghost Mines. (YA) pap. 1.50 (ISBN 0-915266-02-4). Awani Pr.

Govett, G. J. & Govett, M. H. World Mineral Supplies. (Developments in Economic Geology: Vol. 3). 1976. 58.75 (ISBN 0-444-41366-9). Elsevier.

Griffin, A. R. Mining in the East Midlands: 1550-1947. 338p. 1971. 30.00x (ISBN 0-7146-2585-X, F Cass Co). Biblio Dist.

Healy, J. F. Mining & Metallurgy in the Greek & Roman World. (Aspects of Greek & Roman Life Ser.). (Illus.). 1978. 19.95 (ISBN 0-500-40035-0). Thames Hudson.

Hodges, L. K. The Reaction of Gold & Silver. Repr. of 1897 ed. pap. 4.00 (ISBN 0-8466-1993-8, SJS134D). Shorey.

Hughes, E., ed. Jobson's Mining Year Book, 1979. LC 66-2200. 305p. 1979. 50.00x (ISBN 0-8002-2224-5). Intl Pubns Serv.

Instrumentation in the Mining & Metallurgy Industries, Vol. 4. LC 73-82889. 109p. 1976. pap. text ed. 10.00 (ISBN 0-87664-320-9). Instru Soc.

International Mine Ventilation Congress, 2nd. Proceedings. Mousset-Jones, Pierre, ed. LC 80-52943. (Illus.). 864p. 1980. 34.00x (ISBN 0-89520-271-9). Soc Mining Eng.

International Symposium on the Transportation & Handling of Minerals, 3rd Vancouver, British Columbia, Canada, Oct. 1979. Minerals Transportion: Proceedings, Vol. 3. Argall, George O., Jr., ed. LC 76-189985. (A World Mining Bk.). 1980. pap. 50.00 (ISBN 0-87930-080-9). Miller Freeman.

Jaenicke, G., et al, eds. Mining Ventures in Developing Countries. (Studies of the Transnational Law of Natural Resources: No. 1). 1979. lib. bdg. 58.00 (ISBN 90-268-1037-7, Pub. by Kluwer Law Netherlands). Kluwer Boston.

Jones, M. J. Minerals & the Environment. 803p. 1980. 150.00x (ISBN 0-900488-28-X, Pub. by Inst Mining England). State Mutual Bk.

Jordan, Amos A. & Kilmarx, Robert A. Strategic Mineral Dependence: The Stockile Dilemma. LC 79-66890. (The Washington Papers: No. 70). 83p. 1979. pap. 4.00 (ISBN 0-8039-1397-4). Sage.

Karelin, N. T. Mine Transport. 193p. 1981. 10.00x (ISBN 0-86125-796-0, Pub. by Orient Longman India). State Mutual Bk.

Kesler, S. E. Our Finite Resources. 1975. 5.95 (ISBN 0-07-034245-8, C). McGraw.

Knauth, Percy. The Metalsmiths. (The Emergence of Man Ser.). (Illus.). 1974. 9.95 (ISBN 0-8094-1308-6); lib. bdg. avail. (ISBN 0-685-48124-7). Time-Life.

Krige, D. G. Lognormal: De Wijsian Geostatistics for Ore Evaluation. 50p. 1980. 18.50x (ISBN 0-620-03006-2, Pub. by Mining Journal England). State Mutual Bk.

Kurzinski, E. F., ed. Instrumentation in the Mining & Metallurgy Industries, Vol. 6. LC 73-82889. 1978. pap. text ed. 25.00 (ISBN 0-87664-425-6). Instru Soc.

Kuzin, M. & Egorov, N. Field Manual of Minerals. 194p. 1979. 8.40 (ISBN 0-8285-1516-6, Pub. by Mir Pubs Russia). Imported Pubns.

Kuzvart, M. & Bohmer, M. Prospecting & Exploration for Mineral Deposits. 1978. 68.50 (ISBN 0-444-99876-4). Elsevier.

Lamey, C. A. Metallic & Industrial Mineral Deposits. 1966. text ed. 28.00 (ISBN 0-07-036091-X, C). McGraw.

Leith, Charles K. World Minerals & World Politics. LC 74-113286. 1970. Repr. of 1931 ed. 11.50 (ISBN 0-8046-1322-2). Kennikat.

Littlefield, Charles W. Man, Minerals, & Masters. (Illus.). 140p. 1980. pap. 5.50 (ISBN 0-89540-059-6). Sun Pub.

Mackenzie, Brian W. Canada's Competitive Positon in Copper & Zinc Markets. 60p. (Orig.). 1979. pap. text ed. 4.00x (ISBN 0-686-63143-9, Pub. by Ctr Resource Stud Canada). Renouf.

McQuiston, Frank W., Jr. & Shoemaker, Robert S. Primary Crushing Plant Design. (Illus.). 1978. 30.00x (ISBN 0-89520-252-2). Soc Mining Eng.

Martin, Jeani H. Carbide Mine Lamps. LC 77-84577. (Illus.). 1979. 17.50 (ISBN 0-498-02116-5). A S Barnes.

Measurement & Control of Respirable Dust in Mining. 1980. 11.00 (ISBN 0-309-03047-1). Natl Acad Pr.

Miers, John. Travels in Chili & La Plata, 2 Vols. LC 76-128416. Repr. of 1826 ed. Set. 67.50 (ISBN 0-404-04317-8). AMS Pr.

Mikesell, Raymond F. New Patterns of World Mineral Development. LC 79-90054. 116p. 1980. 5.00 (ISBN 0-89068-049-3). Natl Planning.

Mineral Development in the Eighties: Prospects & Problems. LC 76-53628. 64p. 1977. 3.00 (ISBN 0-902594-29-X). Natl Planning.

Mining Journal Books Ltd. Negotiation & Drafting of Mining Development Agreements. 236p. 1980. 19.00x (ISBN 0-900117-11-7, Pub. by Mining Journal England). State Mutual Bk.

Mining Journal Editors. Mining Annual Review 1980. 200p. 1980. 60.00x (ISBN 0-686-69873-8, Pub. by Mining Journal England). State Mutual Bk.

Muhly, James D. Copper & Tin: The Distribution of Mineral Resources & the Nature of the Metals Trade in the Bronze Age, Including Supplement. new ed. (Connecticut Academy of Arts & Sciences Transaction Ser.: Vol. 43 & 46). 380p. 1976. 19.50 (ISBN 0-208-01573-6, Archon). Shoe String.

Muir, W. L. Reclamation of Surface Mined Land. (Illus.). 244p. 1979. pap. 225.00 (ISBN 0-9506461-0-5, Pub. by Muir Coal Industry Info Serv England). Miller Freeman.

National Research Council. Mineral Resources & the Environment. 1975. pap. 8.25 (ISBN 0-309-02343-2). Natl Acad Pr.

Nightingale, William G., ed. Mining International Year Book 1979. 92nd ed. LC 50-18583. 715p. 1979. 55.00x (ISBN 0-900671-87-4). Intl Pubns Serv.

Nuclear Techniques & Mineral Resources. 1969. pap. 35.75 (ISBN 92-0-040069-8, ISP198, IAEA). Unipub.

Nuclear Technology & Mineral Resources 1977. (Proceedings Ser). (Illus.). 1978. pap. 68.25 (ISBN 92-0-060077-8, ISP464, IAEA). Unipub.

Park, Charles F., Jr. & Freeman, Margaret C. Earthbound: Minerals, Energy & Man's Future. 1981. 8.00x (ISBN 0-686-76140-5). Freeman C.

--Earthbound: Minerals, Energy & Man's Future. LC 73-87688. (Illus.). 1975. pap. text ed. 6.95x (ISBN 0-87735-318-2). Freeman C.

Pearson, John S. Ocean Floor Mining. LC 75-801. (Ocean Technology Review Ser: No. 2). (Illus.). 205p. 1975. 24.00 (ISBN 0-8155-0569-8). Noyes.

Persaud, Thakoor. Conflicts Between Multinational Corporations & Less Developed Countries: The Case of Bauxite Mining in the Caribbean with Special Reference to Guyana. Bruchey, Stuart, ed. LC 80-587. (Multinational Corporations Ser.). 1980. lib. bdg. 25.00x (ISBN 0-405-13378-2). Arno.

Polis, M. & O'Shea, J., eds. Automation in Mining, Mineral & Metal Processing: Proceedings of the Third IFAC Symposium, Montreal, 1980. LC 80-40809. (Illus.). 712p. 1981. 145.00 (ISBN 0-08-026164-7); pap. cancelled (ISBN 0-08-026143-4). Pergamon.

Pryor, E. J. Mineral Processing. 3rd ed. (Illus.). 1974. Repr. of 1965 ed. 63.50x (ISBN 0-444-20010-X). Intl Ideas.

Radiation Protection in Mining & Milling of Uranium & Thorium. 1976. 19.95 (ISBN 92-2-101504-1). Intl Labour Office.

Ramsey, Robert H. Men & Mines of Newmont: A Fifty Year History. 1973. lib. bdg. 12.00x (ISBN 0-374-96710-5). Octagon.

Rapid Excavation & Tunneling Conference, 1979. R E T C Proceedings, 2 vols. Hustrulid, William A. & Maevis, Alfred C., eds. LC 79-52280. (Illus.). 1819p. 1979. 55.00x (ISBN 0-89520-266-2). Soc Mining Eng.

Reed, C. B. Fuels, Minerals & Human Survival. LC 74-21575. 1978. softcover 12.50 (ISBN 0-250-40256-4). Ann Arbor Science.

Reedman, J. H. Techniques in Mineral Exploration: Popular Edition. (Illus.). 1979. 50.00x (ISBN 0-85334-851-0, Pub. by Applied Science). Burgess-Intl Ideas.

Rendu, Jo M. Introduction to Geostatistical Methods of Mineral Evaluation. 84p. 1980. 18.50x (ISBN 0-620-03313-4, Pub. by Mining Journal England). State Mutual Bk.

Ridge, J. D. Annotated Bibliographies of Mineral Deposits in Africa Asia (Exclusive of the USSR) & Australasia. 545p. 1976. text ed. 75.00 (ISBN 0-08-020459-7). Pergamon.

Riley, Charles M. Our Mineral Resources: An Elementary Textbook in Economic Geology. 4th ed. LC 76-57669. (Illus.). 348p. 1977. Repr. of 1967 ed. lib. bdg. 15.00 (ISBN 0-88275-530-7). Krieger.

Rummery, R. A. & Howes, K. M. Management of Land Affected by Mining. 172p. 1981. 50.00x (ISBN 0-643-02275-9, Pub. by CSIRO Australia). State Mutual Bk.

Schwind-Belkin, Johanna & Caley, Earle R., eds. Eucharius Rosslin in the Younger: On Minerals & Mineral Products. (Arts Medica, Abeilung IV: Landessprachliche und Mittelalterliche Medizin I). 415p. 1978. text ed. 150.00x (ISBN 3-11006-907-5). De Gruyter.

Sideri, S. & Johns, S., eds. Mining for Development in the Third World: Multinationals, State Enterprises & the International Economy. LC 80-20930. (Pergamon Policy Studies on International Development). 376p. 1981. 35.00 (ISBN 0-08-026308-9). Pergamon.

Sinclair, John. Quarrying, Opencast, & Alluvial Mining. (Illus.). 1969. 42.00x (ISBN 0-444-20040-1). Intl Ideas.

Sinkankas, John. Gemstone & Mineral Data Book. 360p. 1981. pap. 6.95 (ISBN 0-442-24709-5). Van Nos Reinhold.
Sixth Mining & Metallurgy Instrumentation Symposium November 2-4, 1977, Salt Lake City. Instrumentation in the Mining & Metallurgy Industries: Proceedings, Vol. 5. Kurzinski, E. F., ed. LC 73-82889. (Illus.). 1977. 20.00 (ISBN 0-87664-368-3). Instru Soc.
Skinner, Brian J., ed. Earth's Energy & Mineral Resources. LC 80-23495. (The Earth & Its Inhabitants: Selected Readings from American Scientist Ser.). (Illus.). 200p. 1980. pap. 8.95 (ISBN 0-913232-90-4). W Kaufmann.
Smith, David N. & Wells, Louis T., Jr. Negotiating Third World Mineral Agreements, Promises As Prologue. LC 75-29274. 1976. 22.50 (ISBN 0-88410-041-3). Ballinger Pub.
Somasundaran, P. & Arbiter, N., eds. Beneficiation of Mineral Fines. LC 79-91945. (Illus.). 406p. (Orig.). 1979. pap. text ed. 21.00x (ISBN 0-89520-259-X). Soc Mining Eng.
Sullivan, George. The Gold Hunter's Handbook. LC 80-5718. 208p. 1981. 14.95 (ISBN 0-8128-2788-0). Stein & Day.
Tanzer, Michael. The Race for Resources: Continuing Struggles Over Minerals & Fuels. LC 79-5201. 416p. 1981. 16.00 (ISBN 0-85345-540-6); pap. 6.50 (ISBN 0-85345-541-4, PB5414). Monthly Rev.
Tatsch, J. H. Mineral Deposits: Origin, Evolution, & Present Characteristics. LC 73-78206. (Illus.). 264p. 1973. text ed. 64.00 (ISBN 0-912890-01-0). Tatsch.
Todd, Arthur C. Cornish Miner in America. (Illus.). 1968. 15.00 (ISBN 0-87062-063-0). A H Clark.
Weiss, Alfred, ed. World Mining & Metals Technology. LC 76-19748. (Illus.). 1976. text ed. 35.00x (ISBN 0-89520-036-8). Soc Mining Eng.
Woerterbuch Fuer Metallurgie, Mineralogie, Geologie, Bergbau und die Oelindustrie. (Eng., Fr., Ger. & It., Dictionary of Metallurgy, Mineralogy, Geology, Mining and Oil Industry). 1970. 88.00 (ISBN 3-7625-0751-1, M-6912). French & Eur.

MINES AND MINERAL RESOURCES–DICTIONARIES

Auger, Pierre & Rousseau, Louis-Jean. Lexique Anglais-Francais De L'industrie Miniere, 1. 91p. (Eng.-Fr.). 1973. pap. 2.95 (ISBN 0-686-56905-9, M-6016). French & Eur.
Cagnacci-Schwicker, Angelo. Dictionnaire International de Metallurgie, Mineralogie, Geologie et Industries Extractives, 2 vols. 1530p. (Fr.). 1969. Set. 95.00 (ISBN 0-686-56933-4, M-6054). French & Eur.
Ersov, N. N. & Komarov, A. N., eds. Projet de Lexique Minier Russe-Francais. 183p. (Fr. & Rus.). 1972. pap. 22.50 (ISBN 0-686-56769-2, M-6468). French & Eur.
Fueyo Cuesta, Laureano. Diccionario Terminologico De Minas, Canteras y Mineralurgia. 272p. (Espn.). 1973. leather 17.95 (ISBN 84-400-6971-5, S-50112). French & Eur.
Gagnacci-Schwicker, A. & Schwicker. International Dictionary of Metallurgy, Mineralogy, Geology and the Mining and Oil Industries. 1530p. (Eng., Fr., Ger. & It.). 1970. 88.00 (ISBN 3-7625-0751-1, M-7482, Pub. by Bauverlag). French & Eur.
Wyllie, R. J. & Argall, George O., Jr., eds. World Mining Glossary of Mining, Processing & Geological Terms. LC 74-20169. (A World Mining Book). 432p. 1975. 47.50 (ISBN 0-87930-031-0). Miller Freeman.

MINES AND MINERAL RESOURCES–FOLK-LORE

see Folk-Lore of Mines

MINES AND MINERAL RESOURCES–JUVENILE LITERATURE

Mason, Brian. Treasures Underground. (Illus.). (gr. 4-6). 1960. PLB 6.95 (ISBN 0-87396-015-7). Stravon.
Ridpath, Ian, ed. Man & Materials: Minerals. LC 74-10558. (Illus.). 32p. (gr. 4 up). 1975. PLB 4.95 (ISBN 0-201-09032-5, 9032, A-W Childrens). A-W.

MINES AND MINERAL RESOURCES–LAW

see Mining Law

MINES AND MINERAL RESOURCES–TAXATION

Gillis, S. Malcolm & Beals, Ralph E. Tax & Investment Policies for Hard Minerals: Public & Multinational Enterprise in Indonesia. 1980. reference 35.00 (ISBN 0-88410-488-5). Ballinger Pub.
Resource Materials: Domsetic Taxation of Hard Minerals. 254p. 1980. pap. 30.00 (ISBN 0-686-29227-8, T159). ALI-ABA.
Young, Lewis E. Mine Taxation in the United States. Repr. of 1917 ed. 18.50 (ISBN 0-384-70400-X). Johnson Repr.

MINES AND MINERAL RESOURCES–AFRICA

De Kun, N. The Mineral Resources of Afric. 1965. 122.00 (ISBN 0-444-40163-6). Elsevier.
Holleman, J. F. & Biesheuvel, S. White Mine Workers in Northern Rhodesia 1959-60. LC 75-306853. (African Social Research Ser.: Vol. 6). 1973. pap. 13.50x (ISBN 0-8002-2153-2). Intl Pubns Serv.
Perrings, Charles. Black Mineworkers in Central Africa. LC 78-11413. 1979. text ed. 42.50x (ISBN 0-8419-0462-6, Africana). Holmes & Meier.
Postel, A. Williams. Mineral Resources of Africa. (African Handbooks Ser.: Vol. 2). (Illus.). 3.00 (ISBN 0-686-24091-X). Univ Mus of U.
South African Mining & Engineering Year Book: 1978. 27.50x (ISBN 0-8002-1994-5). Intl Pubns Serv.

MINES AND MINERAL RESOURCES–ALASKA

Anderson, Eskil. Asbestos & Jade in the Kobuk River Region of Alaska. facs. ed. 26p. Repr. of 1945 ed. pap. 3.50 (ISBN 0-8466-0037-4, SJS37). Shorey.
Tussing, Arlon R. & Erickson, Gregg K. Mining & Public Policy in Alaska: Mineral Policy, the Public Lands, & Economic Development. LC 72-629327. (Joint Institute of Social & Economic Research Ser.: No. 21). 142p. 1969. pap. 5.00 (ISBN 0-295-95118-4). U of Wash Pr.

MINES AND MINERAL RESOURCES–ASIA

Braake, Alex L. Ter. Mining in the Netherlands East Indies. Wilkins, Mira, ed. LC 76-29762. (European Business Ser.). (Illus.). 1977. Repr. of 1944 ed. lib. bdg. 10.00x (ISBN 0-405-09777-8). Arno.
Carlson, Ellsworth C. Kaiping Mines, 1877-1912. rev. 2nd ed. LC 71-148943. (East Asian Monographs Ser: No. 3). 1971. pap. 9.00x (ISBN 0-674-49700-7). Harvard U Pr.
How Japan's Metal Mining Industries Modernized. 65p. 1980. pap. 5.00 (ISBN 92-808-0083-3, TUNU089, UNU). Unipub.
Imai, Hideki, et al, eds. Geological Studies of the Mineral Deposits in Japan & East Asia. 1978. 49.50x (ISBN 0-86008-208-3, Pub. by U of Tokyo Pr). Intl Schol Bk Serv.
Technology & Labour in Japanese Coal Mining. 65p. 1980. pap. 5.00 (ISBN 92-808-0082-5, TUNU090, UNU). Unipub.
Wadia, M. D. Minerals of India. (India - Land & People Ser). (Illus.). 1966. 4.00x (ISBN 0-8426-1583-0). Verry.

MINES AND MINERAL RESOURCES–AUSTRALIA

Bambrick, Susan. Australian Minerals & Energy Policy. LC 78-74969. (Illus.). 1979. pap. text ed. 13.95 (ISBN 0-7081-1070-3, 0535, Pub. by ANUP Australia). Bks Australia.
Blainey, Geoffrey. The Rush That Never Ended: A History of Australian Mining. 3rd ed. 1978. pap. 12.95x (ISBN 0-522-84145-7, Pub. by Melbourne U Pr). Intl Schol Bk Serv.
Harris, Stuart, ed. Social & Environmental Choice: The Impact of Uranium Mining in the Northern Territory. (Centre for Resources & Environmental Studies Mongraph: No. 3). 178p. 1981. pap. text ed. 10.95 (ISBN 0-86740-169-9, 0039, Pub. by ANUP Australia). Bks Australia.
Management of Lands Affected by Mining. 172p. 1979. pap. 15.50 (ISBN 0-686-71835-6, CO 30, CSIRO). Unipub.
Prider, Rex T. Mining in Western Australia. 328p. 1980. 22.50x (ISBN 0-85564-153-3, Pub. by U of West Australia Pr Australia). Intl Schol Bk Serv.
Williams, Claire. Open Cut: The Working Class in an Australian Mining Town. (Studies in Society Ser.). write for info. Allen Unwin.

MINES AND MINERAL RESOURCES–CANADA

Boadway, R. W. & Treddenick, J. M. The Impact of the Mining Industries on the Canadian Economy. 117p. (Orig.). 1977. pap. text ed. 4.50x (ISBN 0-686-63141-2, Pub. by Ctr Resource Stud Canada). Renouf.
Canadian Minerals Yearbook 1974. 1978. 18.50 (ISBN 0-660-00963-3, SSC 109, SSC). Unipub.
Cousoneau, Eric & Richardson, Peter R. Gold: The World Industry & Canadian Corporate Strategy. 192p. (Orig.). 1979. pap. text ed. 10.00x (ISBN 0-88757-013-5, Pub. by Ctr Resource Stud Canada). Renouf.
Downing, Donald O. & Mackenzie, Brian W. Public Policy Aspects of Information Exchange in Canadian Mineral Exploration. 60p. (Orig.). 1979. pap. text ed. 3.00x (ISBN 0-686-63138-2, Pub. by Ctr Resource Stud Canada). Renouf.
The Future for Junior Mining in Canada. 175p. (Orig.). 1979. pap. text ed. 10.00x (ISBN 0-88757-018-6, Pub. by Ctr Resource Stud Canada). Renouf.
Geology & Economic Minerals of Canada, 2 pts. (Illus.). 1978. pap. 28.00 set (ISBN 0-660-00553-0, SSC 96, SSC). Unipub.
Gibbs, G. W. & Pintus, P. Health & Safety in the Canadian Mining Industry. 249p. (Orig.). 1978. pap. text ed. 12.00x (ISBN 0-88757-003-8, Pub. by Ctr Resource Stud Canada). Renouf.
International Competition & the Canadian Mineral Industries. 109p. (Orig.). 1978. pap. text ed. 5.00x (ISBN 0-88757-009-7, Pub. by Ctr Resource Stud Canada). Renouf.
Lafkas, C. & Paterson, J. G. A Survey of Resources & a Production Cycle for the Non-Ferrous Metals. 60p. (Orig.). 1978. pap. text ed. 3.00x (ISBN 0-686-63136-6, Pub. by Ctr Resource Stud Canada). Renouf.
MacDonald, Wendy. Constitutional Change & the Mining Industry in Canada. 73p. 1890. write for info. (Pub. by Ctr. Resource Stud Canada). Renouf.
Macmillan, J. A., et al. Human Resources in Canadian Mining: A Preliminary Analysis. 176p. (Orig.). 1977. pap. 8.50x (ISBN 0-88757-004-6, Pub. by Ctr Resource Stud Canada). Renouf.
Meldrum, G. H., ed. Canadian Minerals Yearbook 1976. LC 36-32389. (Illus.). 1979. 30.00x (ISBN 0-660-10074-6). Intl Pubns Serv.
Mining to Manufacturing: Links in a Chain. (Mineral Bulletin Ser.: No. MR 175). (Illus.). 1979. pap. 9.25 (ISBN 0-660-01714-8, SSC116, SSC). Unipub.
Moore, Elwood S. American Influence in Canadian Mining. Bruchey, Stuart, ed. LC 80-561. (Multinational Corporations Ser.). (Illus.). 1980. Repr. of 1941 ed. lib. bdg. 15.00x (ISBN 0-405-13358-8). Arno.
Murray, Ronald C. Provincial Mineral Policies: Saskatchewan 1944-75. 65p. (Orig.). 1978. pap. text ed. 3.50x (ISBN 0-686-63139-0, Pub. by Ctr Resource Stud Canada). Renouf.
Owen, Brian E. & Kops, W. J. The Impact of Policy Change on Decisions in the Mineral Industry. 116p. (Orig.). 1979. pap. text ed. 7.00x (ISBN 0-88757-015-1, Pub. by Ctr Resource Stud Canada). Renouf.
Prince, Michael J. Provincial Mineral Policies: Newfoundland 1945-75. 60p. (Orig.). 1977. pap. text ed. 3.50x (ISBN 0-686-63140-4, Pub. by Ctr Resource Stud Canada). Renouf.
Rate of Return Taxation of Minerals. 109p. (Orig.). 1977. pap. text ed. 5.00x (ISBN 0-88757-006-2, Pub. by Ctr Resource Stud Canada). Renouf.
Ripley, Earle A., et al. Environmental Impact of Mining in Canada. 274p. (Orig.). 1978. pap. text ed. 12.00x (ISBN 0-88757-008-9, Pub. by Ctr Resource Stud Canada). Renouf.
Shewchun, John S. & Curtis, David B. Solar Energy & the Canadian Mining Sector: A Demand Forecast. 60p. (Orig.). 1978. pap. text ed. 3.00x (ISBN 0-686-63137-4, Pub. by Ctr Resource Stud Canada). Renouf.
A Survey of Known Mineral Deposits in Canada That Are Not Being Mined. (Mineral Bulletin: No. 181). 159p. 1980. pap. 7.50 (ISBN 0-686-61081-4, SSC 138, SSC). Unipub.
Trimble, William J. The Mining Advance into the Inland Empire: A Comparative Study of the Beginnings of the Mining Industry in Idaho & Montana, Eastern Washington & Oregon & the Southern Interior of British Columbia, & of Institutions & Laws Based Upon That Industry. LC 14-31275. Repr. of 1914 ed. 19.50 (ISBN 0-384-61560-0). Johnson Repr.
Wilkinson, Bruce W. Trends in Canada's Mineral Trade. 64p. (Orig.). 1978. pap. text ed. 3.50x (ISBN 0-686-63145-5, Pub. by Ctr Resource Stud Canada). Renouf.
Wojciechowski, Margot J. Federal Mineral Policies, Nineteen Forty-Five to Seventy-Five: A Survey of Federal Activities That Affected the Canadian Mineral Industry. 87p. (Orig.). 1979. pap. 3.50x (ISBN 0-686-63135-8, Pub. by Ctr Resource Stud Canada). Renouf.

MINES AND MINERAL RESOURCES–GREAT BRITAIN

Arnot, R. Page. The Miners: One Union, One Industry: A History of the National Union of Mineworkers 1939-46. (Illus.). 1979. text ed. 30.00x (ISBN 0-04-331074-5). Allen Unwin.
Bird, R. H. Yesterday's Golcondas. 1977. 15.00 (ISBN 0-903485-37-0). State Mutual Bk.
Brown, I. J. Mines of Shropshire. 1977. 15.00 (ISBN 0-903485-32-X). State Mutual Bk.
Gough, John W. Mines of Mendip. LC 67-105992. (Illus.). Repr. of 1930 ed. 15.00x (ISBN 0-678-05688-9). Kelley.
Handy, L. J. Wages Policy in the British Coalmining Industry: A Study of National Wage Bargaining. LC 80-40229. (Department of Applied Economics Monograph: No. 27). 312p. 1981. 47.50 (ISBN 0-521-23535-9). Cambridge U Pr.
Jenkin, A. K. Mines of Devon, Vol. 1. LC 74-82834. (Illus.). 144p. 1975. 6.50 (ISBN 0-7153-6784-6). David & Charles.
Leifchild, J. R. Cornwall: Its Mines & Miners. 304p. 1968. Repr. of 1857 ed. 28.50x (ISBN 0-7146-1402-5, F Cass Co). Biblio Dist.
Lindsay, Jean. A History of the North Wales Slate Industry. 1974. 25.00 (ISBN 0-7153-6265-8). David & Charles.
Metcalfe, J. E. British Mining Fields. 91p. 1980. 35.00x (ISBN 0-900488-00-X, Pub. by Inst Mining England). State Mutual Bk.
Moore, R. Pit-Men, Preachers & Politics. LC 73-88307. 39.50x (ISBN 0-521-20356-2, 1974); pap. 12.95x (ISBN 0-521-29752-4, 1979). Cambridge U Pr.
Morrison, T. A. Cornwall's Central Mines: The Northern District, 1810-1895. 400p. 1980. 40.00x (ISBN 0-906720-10-9, Pub. by Hodge England). State Mutual Bk.
Rodgers, Peter R. Rock & Mineral Collecting in Britain. 1979. (Pub. by Faber & Faber); pap. 7.95 (ISBN 0-571-11266-8). Merrimack Bk Serv.
Trounson, J. Mining in Cornwall, Eighteen Fifty to Nineteen Sixty, Vol. 1. 80p. 1981. 12.00x (ISBN 0-903485-79-6, Pub. by Moorland). State Mutual Bk.
--Mining in Cornwall, Eighteen Fifty to Nineteen Sixty, Vol. 2. 80p. 1981. 12.00x (ISBN 0-903485-95-8, Pub. by Moorland). State Mutual Bk.

MINES AND MINERAL RESOURCES–MEXICO

Lyon, G. F. Journal of a Residence & Tour in the Republic of Mexico, 2 Vols. LC 72-130332. (Latin-American History & Culture Ser). 1971. Repr. of 1828 ed. Set. 27.50 (ISBN 0-8046-1393-1). Kennikat.
Von Humboldt, Alexander. Political Essay on the Kingdom of New Spain, 4 Vols. Black, John, tr. LC 1-20796. Repr. of 1811 ed. Set. 147.50 (ISBN 0-404-03450-0). AMS Pr.

MINES AND MINERAL RESOURCES–RUSSIA

Alexandrov, Eugene A., compiled by. Mineral & Energy Resources of the USSR: A Selected Bibliography of Sources in English. 160p. 1980. 10.00 (ISBN 0-913312-21-5). Am Geol.

MINES AND MINERAL RESOURCES–SOUTH AMERICA

Bain, Foster H. & Read, Thomas T. Ores & Industry in South America. Bruchey, Stuart & Bruchey, Eleanor, eds. LC 76-4767. (American Business Abroad Ser.). (Illus.). 1976. Repr. of 1934 ed. 24.00x (ISBN 0-405-09265-2). Arno.
Baird, Wesley. Guyana Gold: The Story of Wesley Baird, Guyana's Greatest Miner. LC 81-51666. 210p. (Orig.). 1981. 16.00x (ISBN 0-89410-192-7); pap. 7.00x (ISBN 0-89410-193-5). Three Continents.
Franco, R. R., et al, eds. Minerals of Brazil, 3 vols. Leprevost, J. & Bigarella, J. 426p. 1975. 117.00 (ISBN 0-444-99864-0). Elsevier.
Gardner, George. Travels in the Interior of Brazil. LC 75-128421. Repr. of 1846 ed. 37.50 (ISBN 0-404-02678-8). AMS Pr.
Lindgren, Waldemar. Gold & Silver Deposits in North, South America. 34p. Repr. of 1917 ed. pap. 4.95 (ISBN 0-8466-8006-8, SJG6). Shorey.
Miller, Benjamin & Singewald, Joseph T. The Deposits of South America. Wilkins, Mira, ed. LC 76-29758. (European Business Ser.). (Illus.). 1977. Repr. of 1919 ed. lib. bdg. 35.00x (ISBN 0-405-09773-5). Arno.

MINES AND MINERAL RESOURCES–UNITED STATES

see also Mines and Mineral Resources–Alaska

Albert, Herman W. Odyssey of a Desert Prospector. (Western Frontier Library: No. 35). 1974. pap. 5.95 (ISBN 0-8061-1180-1). U of Okla Pr.
Anderson, George B. One Hundred Booming Years. Row, H. J. & Stupek, D., eds. (Illus.). 305p. 1980. 32.50 (ISBN 0-9604136-0-X). Bucyrus-Erie Co.
Annual ISA Mining & Metallurgy Division Symposium & Exhibit, 8th, Phoenix, 1980. Instrumentation in the Mining & Metallurgy Industries, Vol. 7. Kurzinski, E. F., ed. LC 73-82889. 180p. 1980. pap. text ed. 25.00x (ISBN 0-87664-470-1). Instru Soc.
Arizona Industrial Minerals. 1975. 15.80 (ISBN 0-686-29528-5). Minobras.
Armes, Ethel. The Story of Coal & Iron in Alabama. LC 73-1988. (Big Business; Economic Power in a Free Society Ser.). (Illus.). Repr. of 1910 ed. 30.00 (ISBN 0-405-05072-0). Arno.
Association of American Geologists & Naturalists at Philadelphia, 1840 & 1841. Proceedings. Albritton, Claude C., ed. LC 77-6507. (History of Geology Ser.). Repr. of 1843 ed. lib. bdg. 35.00x (ISBN 0-405-10430-8). Arno.
Barnes, V. E. & Schofield, D. A. Potential Low-Grade Iron Ore & Hydraulic-Fracturing Sand in Cambrian Sandstones, Northwestern Llano Region, Texas. (Illus.). 58p. 1964. 2.00 (ISBN 0-686-29335-5, RI 53). Bur Econ Geology.
Barry, Mary J. A History of Mining on the Kenai Peninsula. LC 73-80129. (Illus.). 214p. 1973. pap. 6.95 (ISBN 0-88240-018-5). Alaska Northwest.
Bartlett, Robert V. The Reserve Mining Controversy: Science, Technology, & Environmental Quality. LC 79-48019. 312p. 1980. 17.50x (ISBN 0-253-14556-2). Ind U Pr.
Belden, L. Burr. Mines of Death Valley. (Illus.). 1966. wrappers 2.95 (ISBN 0-910856-16-8). La Siesta.

Bidwell, Percy W. Raw Materials: A Study of American Policy. LC 74-9649. (Council on Foreign Relations Ser). (Illus.). 403p. 1974. Repr. of 1958 ed. lib. bdg. 19.75x (ISBN 0-8371-7616-6, BIRM). Greenwood.
Boyum, Burton H., ed. The Mather Mine, Negaunee & Ishpeming Michigan. LC 79-89638. 1979. 18.95 (ISBN 0-938746-04-9). Marquette Cnty.
Byrd, William. Writings of Colonel William Byrd. Bassett, J. S., ed. LC 76-125631. (Research & Source Ser.: No. 518). (Illus.). 1970. Repr. of 1901 ed. lib. bdg. 32.00 (ISBN 0-8337-0442-7). B Franklin.
Colorado & Utah Industrial Minerals. 1974. 15.50 (ISBN 0-686-29527-7). Minobras.
Davis, Richard H. At a New Mining Camp: Creede of Colorado, 1892. Jones, William R., ed. (Illus.). 32p. 1977. Repr. of 1892 ed. pap. 2.00 (ISBN 0-89646-018-5). Outbooks.
DeDecker, Mary. Mines of the Eastern Sierra. (Illus.). 1966. wrappers 2.95 (ISBN 0-910856-15-X). La Siesta.
Dietrich, J. W. & Lonsdale, J. T. Mineral Resources of the Colorado River Industrial Development Association Area. (Illus.). 84p. 1958. 1.50 (ISBN 0-686-29332-0, RI 37). Bur Econ Geology.
Dobie, J. Frank. Apache Gold & Yaqui Silver. (Illus.). 1939. 9.95 (ISBN 0-316-18791-7). Little.
Dornburgh, Henry. Why the Wilderness Is Called Adirondack: The Earliest Account of Founding of the MacIntyre Mine. LC 79-25055. 1980. pap. 3.95 (ISBN 0-916346-39-0). Harbor Hill Bks.
Eargle, D. H., et al. Uranium Geology & Mines, South Texas. (Illus.). 59p. 1971. 1.75 (ISBN 0-686-29320-7, GB 12). Bur Econ Geology.
Eberhart, Philip. Guide to the Colorado Ghost Towns & Mining Camps. 4th ed. LC 59-11061. (Illus.). 496p. 1969. pap. 13.95 (ISBN 0-8040-0140-5, SB). Swallow.
Eckes, Alfred E. The United States & the Global Struggle for Minerals. LC 78-11082. 365p. 1979. text ed. 18.95x (ISBN 0-292-78506-2); pap. 8.95x (ISBN 0-292-78511-9). U of Tex Pr.
El Hult, Ruby. Treasure Hunting Northwest. LC 70-165220. 1971. 8.95 (ISBN 0-8323-0087-X). Binford.
Fielder, Mildred. A Guide to Black Hills Ghost Mines. new ed. LC 72-84340. (Illus.). 240p. 1972. 7.95 (ISBN 0-87970-125-0). North Plains.
Fisher, W. L. Rock & Mineral Resources of East Texas. (Illus.). 439p. 1965. 5.00 (ISBN 0-686-29336-3, RI 54). Bur Econ Geology.
Fossett, Frank. Colorado: Its Gold & Silver Mines, Farms & Stock Ranges, & Health & Pleasure Resorts. LC 72-9444. (The Far Western Frontier Ser.). (Illus.). 544p. 1973. Repr. of 1879 ed. 26.00 (ISBN 0-405-04973-0). Arno.
Galenson, Walter, ed. Incomes Policy: What Can We Learn from Europe? LC 72-619695. (Pierce Ser.: No. 3). 1973. 7.50 (ISBN 0-87546-048-8). NY Sch Indus Rel.
Galloway, W. E., et al. South Texas Uranium Province, Geologic Perspective. (Illus.). 81p. 1979. 3.00 (ISBN 0-686-29323-1, GB 18). Bur Econ Geology.
Gibson, Arrell M. Wilderness Bonanza: The Tri-State Mining District of Missouri, Kansas & Oklahoma. LC 77-177335. (Illus.). 350p. 1972. 16.95 (ISBN 0-8061-0990-4); pap. 8.95 (ISBN 0-8061-1033-3). U of Okla Pr.
Grimmett, Robert G. Cabal of Death. LC 77-15675. 1977. 7.50 (ISBN 0-89301-047-2). U Pr of Idaho.
Harpending, Asbury. Great Diamond Hoax & Other Stirring Incidents in the Life of Asbury Harpending. (Western Frontier Library: No. 10). (Illus.). 1958. 5.95 (ISBN 0-8061-0400-7). U of Okla Pr.
Hibbard, W., ed. United States Minerals Issues--the Seventies, a Review; the Eighties, a Preview: 6th Annual Mineral Economics Symposium, November 12, 1980, Washington DC. 1981. pap. 27.50 (ISBN 0-08-027593-1). Pergamon.
Hollister, Ovando J. The Mines of Colorado. LC 72-9452. (The Far Western Frontier Ser.). (Illus.). 454p. 1973. Repr. of 1867 ed. 21.00 (ISBN 0-405-04980-3). Arno.
Hult, Ruby E. Lost Mines & Treasures of the Pacific Northwest. 3rd. ed. LC 68-58980. (Illus.). 1968. pap. 6.50 (ISBN 0-8323-0241-4). Binford.
Jensen, David E. Minerals of New York State. LC 78-66426. (Illus.). 1978. 12.95 (ISBN 0-932142-00-1); pap. 7.95 (ISBN 0-932142-01-X). Ward Pr.
Laustsen, Jean B. & Bennett, Mary E., eds. Help One Another Cookbook, Vol. 2. LC 73-77360. 1973. spiral bdg. 4.95 (ISBN 0-87970-129-3). North Plains.
Lee, Hammons. Mineral & Gem Localities in Arizona. new ed. (Illus.). 1977. pap. 5.95 (ISBN 0-686-15520-3). Ariz Maps & Bks.
Libecap, Gary D. The Evolution of Private Mineral Rights: Nevada's Comstock Lode. LC 77-14777. (Dissertations in American Economic History Ser.). 1978. 27.00 (ISBN 0-405-11047-2). Arno.
Lord, Eliot. Comstock Miners & Mining. (Illus.). 578p. 1981. Repr. of 1959 ed. 20.00 (ISBN 0-8310-7008-0). Howell-North.
Love, Frank. Mining Camps & Ghost Towns: Along the Lower Colorado in Arizona & California. LC 73-86960. (Illus.). 240p. 8.50 (ISBN 0-87026-031-6). Westernlore.
Maxwell, R. A. Mineral Resources of South Texas: Region Served Through the Port of Corpus Christi. (Illus.). 140p. 1962. 3.50 (ISBN 0-686-29333-9, RI 43). Bur Econ Geology.
Miller, Ronald D. Mines of the High Desert. rev. ed. (Illus.). 1964. wrappers 2.95 (ISBN 0-910856-13-3). La Siesta.
Mitchell, John D. Lost Mines of the Great Southwest. (Illus.). lib. bdg. 10.00 (ISBN 0-87380-013-3). Rio Grande.
Montana Industrial Minerals. 1975. 15.20 (ISBN 0-686-29522-6). Minobras.
Mullan, John. Miner's & Travelers' Guide to Oregon, Washington, Idaho, Montana, Wyoming, & Colorado. LC 72-9461. (The Far Western Frontier Ser.). (Illus.). 158p. 1973. Repr. of 1865 ed. 13.00 (ISBN 0-405-04989-7). Arno.
Murbarger, Nell. Ghosts of the Adobe Walls: Human Interest & Historical Highlights from 400 Ghost Haunts of Old Arizona. 1977. pap. 7.95 (ISBN 0-918080-23-1). Treasure Chest.
Nevada Industrial Minerals. 1973. 13.40 (ISBN 0-686-29525-0). Minobras.
Northrop, Stuart A. Minerals of New Mexico. rev ed. LC 59-10091. (Illus.). 665p. 1959. 15.00 (ISBN 0-8263-0079-0). U of NM Pr.
Pearl, Richard M. Exploring Rocks, Minerals, Fossils in Colorado. rev. ed. LC 64-25339. (Illus.). 215p. 1969. 12.95 (ISBN 0-8040-0105-7, SB). Swallow.
Poindexter, O. F., et al. Rocks & Minerals of Michigan. (Illus.). 49p. (Orig.). 1971. pap. 3.50 (ISBN 0-910726-73-6). Hillsdale Educ.
Prieto, Carlos. Mining in the New World. (Illus.). 1973. 14.95 (ISBN 0-07-050862-3, P&RB). McGraw.
Probert, Alan. Mining in the West. 1981. pap. 8.00 (ISBN 0-89745-019-1). Sunflower U Pr.
Rickard, Thomas A. A History of American Mining. (Illus.). Repr. of 1932 ed. 23.00 (ISBN 0-384-50800-6). Johnson Repr.
Robinson, John W. Mines of the San Bernardinos. (California Mines Ser). (Illus., Orig.). 1977. pap. text ed. 2.95 (ISBN 0-910856-64-8). La Siesta.
Rodda, P. U., et al. Limestone & Dolomite Resources: Lower Cretaceous Rocks, Texas. (Illus.). 286p. 1966. 4.50 (ISBN 0-686-29338-X, RI 56). Bur Econ Geology.
Ryerson, Kathleen H. Rock Hound's Guide to Connecticut. 3rd ed. LC 68-24037. (Illus.). 1972. pap. 2.95 (ISBN 0-87106-010-8). Globe Pequot.
Shawe, Daniel R., ed. Guidebook on Fossil Fuels & Metals, Eastern Utah & Western-Southwestern Central Colorado. (Professional Contributions Ser.: No. 9). (Illus.). 150p. 1978. pap. 8.50x (ISBN 0-918062-04-7). Colo Sch Mines.
Silverberg, Robert. Ghost Towns of the American West. LC 68-17081. (Illus.). (gr. 7 up). 1968. 10.95 (ISBN 0-690-32621-1, TYC-J). Har-Row.
Smith, Duane A. & Wieler, Hank. Secure the Shadow: Lachlan McLean, Colorado Mining Photographer. LC 80-10693. (Illus.). 100p. 1980. 13.50 (ISBN 0-918062-09-8). Colo Sch Mines.
Snyder, F. G., ed. Symposium on Mineral Resources of the Southeastern United States. 1950. 14.50x (ISBN 0-87049-007-9). U of Tenn Pr.
Southern Calif. Industrial Minerals. 1973. 14.70 (ISBN 0-686-29526-9). Minobras.
Stanton, Robert B. The Hoskaninni Papers, Mining in Glen Canyon, 1897-1902. (Glen Canyon Ser.: No. 15). Repr. of 1961 ed. 20.00 (ISBN 0-404-60654-7). AMS Pr.
Trimble, William J. The Mining Advance into the Inland Empire: A Comparative Study of the Beginnings of the Mining Industry in Idaho & Montana, Eastern Washington & Oregon & the Southern Interior of British Columbia, & of Institutions & Laws Based Upon That Industry. LC 14-31275. Repr. of 1914 ed. 19.50 (ISBN 0-384-61560-0). Johnson Repr.
--The Mining Advance into the Inland Empire. 254p. Date not set. Repr. of 1914 ed. price not set (ISBN 0-87770-088-5). Ye Galleon.
Uranium Deposits of Arizona, California & Nevada. 1978. 40.30 (ISBN 0-686-29530-7). Minobras.
Uranium Deposits of the Northern U. S. Region. 1977. 37.10 (ISBN 0-686-29521-8). Minobras.
Uranium Guidebook for Wyoming. 1976. xerox copy 40.00 (ISBN 0-686-29529-3). Minobras.
Uranium Resources of the Central & Southern Rockies. 1979. 33.80 (ISBN 0-686-29531-5). Minobras.
Von Mueller, Karl. Placer Miner's Manual, 3 vols. (Illus.). 1981. Vol. 1. 8.00 (ISBN 0-89316-612-X); Vol. 1. pap. 5.00 (ISBN 0-89316-611-1); Vol. 2. 8.00 (ISBN 0-89316-614-6); Vol. 2. pap. 5.00 (ISBN 0-89316-613-8); Vol. 3. 8.00 (ISBN 0-89316-616-2); Vol. 3. pap. 5.00 (ISBN 0-89316-615-4). Exanimo Pr.
Weight, Harold O. Lost Mines of Death Valley. 3rd ed. LC 70-125556. 1970. pap. 2.50 (ISBN 0-912714-03-4). Calico Pr.
Whitney, Josiah D. Metallic Wealth of the United States. LC 74-125766. (American Environmental Studies). 1970. Repr. of 1854 ed. 23.00 (ISBN 0-405-02692-7). Arno.
Woodhouse, Philip. Monte Cristo. LC 78-71665. (Illus.). 312p. 1979. 15.00 (ISBN 0-916890-66-X). Mountaineers.
Young, Otis E., Jr. Western Mining: An Informal Account of Precious-Metals Prospecting, Placering, Lode Mining, & Milling on the American Frontier from Spanish Times to 1893. LC 76-108800. (Illus.). 1970. 16.95 (ISBN 0-8061-0909-2); pap. 7.95 (ISBN 0-8061-1352-9). U of Okla Pr.
Young, Otis E., Jr. & Lenon, Robert. Black Powder & Hand Steel: Miners & Machines on the Old Western Frontier. LC 75-4634. (Illus.). 200p. 1976. pap. 10.95 (ISBN 0-8061-1269-7). U of Okla Pr.

MINES AND MINING
see Mineral Industries; Mines and Mineral Resources; Mining Engineering; Mining Industry and Finance

MINHAGIM
see Jews–Rites and Ceremonies

MINI CAR (MORRIS MINOR)
see Automobiles, Foreign–Types–Morris Mini Minor

MINI COMPUTERS
see Minicomputers

MINIATURE CAMERAS
see also individual makes of miniature cameras, e.g. Cameras–Types–Retina, etc.

MINIATURE CAR RACING
see Model Car Racing

MINIATURE CASES
Maxym, Lucy. Russian Laquer, Legends & Fairy Tales. (Illus.). 80p. 1981. 27.50 (ISBN 0-940202-01-8). Siamese Imports.

MINIATURE COMPUTERS
see Minicomputers

MINIATURE ELECTRONIC EQUIPMENT
see also Microelectronics; Minicomputers; Printed Circuits; Transistor Radios
Comer, David J. Electronic Design with Integrated Circuits. LC 80-23365. (Electrical Engineering Ser.). (Illus.). 416p. 1981. text ed. 24.95 (ISBN 0-201-03931-1). A-W.
Freiberger, Stephen & Chew, Paul. Consumer's Guide to Personal Computing & Microcomputers. 1978. pap. 8.95 (ISBN 0-8104-5680-X). Hayden.
Harrigan, Norwell, ed. Microstate Studies, Vol. I. 1977. pap. 4.00 (ISBN 0-8130-0592-2). U Presses Fla.

MINIATURE GARDENS
see Gardens, Miniature

MINIATURE HOUSES
see Doll-Houses

MINIATURE LAMPS–CATALOGS
Smith, Frank & Smith, Ruth. Miniature Lamp. (Illus.). 288p. 1981. Repr. of 1968 ed. 18.95 (ISBN 0-916838-44-7). Schiffer.
Smith, Frank R. & Smith, Ruth E. Miniature Lamps. LC 68-57930. (Collector's Books Ser.). (Illus.). 1968. 18.95 (ISBN 0-8407-4315-7). Nelson.

MINIATURE OBJECTS
see also Architectural Models; Doll-Houses; Gardens, Miniature; Machinery–Models; Military Miniatures; Models and Modelmaking; Ship Models; Toys
also subdivision Models under names of objects, e.g. Airplanes–Models
Abels, Harriette S. Dollhouse Miniatures. LC 80-15010. (Hobbies for Everyone Ser.). (Illus.). 48p. (gr. 3 up). 1980. PLB 10.60 (ISBN 0-516-03557-6). Childrens.
Bower, John. Waterline Ship Models. 130p. 1980. 20.00x (ISBN 0-85177-050-9, Pub. by Conway Maritime England). State Mutual Bk.
Brown, Dort F. Souvenir Buildings: A Collection of Identified Miniatures, 2 vols. (Illus.). 203p. (Orig., Vol. 1, 1977, Vol. 2, 1979). pap. 5.00 set (ISBN 0-9603420-0-1). Indisota Pubs.
Consumer Guide Magazine Editors. Miniatures. LC 78-22443. (Illus.). 1980. cancelled (ISBN 0-06-090707-X, CN 707, CN). Har-Row.
Daniele, Joseph. Building Masterpiece Miniatures. (Illus.). 352p. 1981. text ed. 24.95 (ISBN 0-8117-0306-1). Stackpole.
Daniele, Joseph W. Building Colonial Furnishings, Miniatures, & Folk Art. LC 76-17006. (Illus.). 256p. 1976. 17.95 (ISBN 0-8117-0451-3). Stackpole.
--Building Miniature Furniture. (Illus.). 256p. 1981. 24.95 (ISBN 0-8117-1000-9). Stackpole.
Falk, Toby & Archer, Mildred. Indian Miniatures in the India Office Library. (Illus.). 800p. 1981. 200.00x (ISBN 0-85667-100-2, Pub. by Sotheby Parke Bernet England). Biblio Dist.
Foskett, Daphne. Collecting Miniatures. (Illus.). 500p. 1980. 62.50 (ISBN 0-902028-79-0). Antique Collect.
Foster, Bryan. Scenic Models. 192p. 1980. 32.95x (ISBN 0-85177-168-8, Pub. by Conway Maritime England). State Mutual Bk.
Greenhowe, Jean. Jean Greenhowe's Miniature Toys. 120p. 1980. 13.95 (ISBN 0-442-24338-3). Van Nos Reinhold.
--Making Musical Miniatures. (Illus.). 120p. 1980. 19.95 (ISBN 0-7134-1631-9, Pub. by Batsford England). David & Charles.
Jensen, Gerald. Early American Dollhouse Miniatures. LC 80-70383. (Illus.). 240p. 1981. 14.95 (ISBN 0-8019-7023-7); pap. 9.95 (ISBN 0-8019-7024-5). Chilton.
Lathrop, Mary L. & Lathrop, Norman M., eds. Index to How to Do It Information: 1980 Index. 1980. pap. 15.00x (ISBN 0-910868-80-8). Lathrop.
Meras, Phyllis. Miniatures: How to Make Them, Use Them, Sell Them. LC 76-16493. 1976. 12.95 (ISBN 0-395-24344-0); pap. 7.95 (ISBN 0-395-24586-9). HM.
Merrill, Virginia & Richardson, Susan M. Reproducing Period Furniture & Accessories in Miniature. Aymar, Brant, ed. 320p. 1981. 25.00 (ISBN 0-517-53816-4). Crown.
Miniature Needlepoint & Sewing Projects for Dollhouses. (Illus.). 1979. (Hawthorn); pap. 7.95 (ISBN 0-8015-5073-4). Dutton.
Pipe, Ann K. Reproducing Furniture in Miniature. LC 79-50986. (Illus.). 1979. pap. 5.95 (ISBN 0-8092-7149-4). Contemp Bks.
Poska, Valentine J. Miniature Horses. (Illus.). 48p. 1981. 24.00 (ISBN 0-686-76456-0). Mosaic Pr.
Puiboube, Daniel. The Art of Making Miniature Models. LC 77-27999. (Illus.). 1979. 15.00 (ISBN 0-668-04564-7). Arco.
Rosner, Bernard & Beckerman, Jay. Inside the World of Miniatures & Dollhouses: A Comprehensive Guide to Collecting & Creating. LC 76-16458. (Illus.). 256p. 1976. pap. 9.95 (ISBN 0-679-50620-9). McKay.
Roth, Charlene D. Making Dollhouse Accessories: Patterns & Directions for Rooms, Furniture, Animal Companions, Utensils, & Vehicles for Full-Size Dolls. (Illus.). 1977. 8.95 (ISBN 0-517-52878-9); pap. 4.95 (ISBN 0-517-52879-7). Crown.
Ruthberg, Helen. Miniature Room Settings. LC 77-14742. (Creative Crafts Ser.). (Illus.). 1978. 12.50 (ISBN 0-8019-6678-7); pap. 8.95 (ISBN 0-8019-6679-5). Chilton.
Schiffer, Herbert F. & Schiffer, Peter B. Miniature Antique Furniture. (Illus.). 25.00 (ISBN 0-685-78509-2). Schiffer.
Sirkis, Susan B. Fashioning Miniatures - One More Time. (Wish Booklets: Vol. 23). (Illus.). 52p. 1980. pap. 5.50x (ISBN 0-913786-23-3). Wish Bklets.

MINIATURE PAINTING
see also Portrait Painting
Archer, W. G. Visions of Courtly India. (Illus.). 128p. 1977. 34.00x (ISBN 0-85667-032-4, Pub. by Sotheby Parke Bernet England). Biblio Dist.
Bardo, Pamela P. English & Continental Portrait Miniatures: The Latter-Schlesinger Collection. LC 78-59762. (Illus.). 120p. 1978. pap. 7.95 (ISBN 0-89494-006-6). New Orleans Mus Art.
Boehn, Max Von. Miniatures & Silhouettes: Modes & Manners Supplement. LC 70-145772. (Illus.). 1969. Repr. of 1928 ed. 22.00 (ISBN 0-405-08279-7, Blom Pubns). Arno.
Bussagli, Mario. Indian Minatures. 1976. 8.50x (ISBN 0-333-90152-5). South Asia Bks.
Foster, Joshua J. A Dictionary of Painters of Miniatures, 1525-1850 with Some Account of Exhibitions, Collections, Sales, Etc. Foster, Ethel M., ed. 1967. Repr. of 1926 ed. 29.50 (ISBN 0-8337-1218-7). B Franklin.
London, Hannah R. Miniatures & Silhouettes of Early American Jews. LC 78-87797. (Illus.). 1969. Repr. 15.00 (ISBN 0-8048-0657-8). C E Tuttle.
Long, Basil. British Miniaturists. 1520-1860. (Illus.). 35.00x (ISBN 0-87556-209-4). Saifer.
Mayne, Arthur. British Profile Miniaturists. 132p. 1970. 19.95 (ISBN 0-571-09208-X, Pub. by Faber & Faber). Merrimack Bk Serv.
Norton(R.W.) Art Gallery. Portrait' Miniatures in Early American History: 1750-1840. LC 76-11634. 1976. pap. 3.50x (ISBN 0-913060-09-7). Norton Art.
Schidlof, Leo R. The Miniature in Europe, 4 vols. (Illus.). 1965. Set. 290.00x (ISBN 0-8002-1721-7). Intl Pubns Serv.
Selection of Portrait Miniatures in the Walters Art Gallery: A Picture Book. (Illus.). 1966. pap. 3.50 (ISBN 0-685-21836-8). Walters Art.

Wehle, Harry B. American Minatures Seventeen Thirty to Eighteen Fifty: One Hundred & Seventy-Three Portraits. LC 71-87684. (Library of American Art Ser.). 1970. Repr. of 1927 ed. lib. bdg. 27.50 (ISBN 0-306-71708-5). Da Capo.

Welch, Stuart C. Imperial Mughal Painting. LC 77-4049. (Magnificent Paperback Art Ser.). (Illus.). 1978. 19.95 (ISBN 0-8076-0870-X); pap. 9.95 (ISBN 0-8076-0871-8). Braziller.

MINIATURE PAINTING–REPRODUCTIONS, FACSIMILES, ETC.

Gamulin, Grgo & Cionini-Visani, Maria. Giorgio Giulio Clovio. (Illus.). 162p. 1980. 85.00 (ISBN 0-933516-17-7). Alpine Fine Arts.

Goodspeed, Edgar J., et al, eds. Rockefeller McCormick New Testament, 3 Vols. LC 32-30657. (Illus.). 1932. Set. 100.00x (ISBN 0-226-30379-9). U of Chicago Pr.

MINIATURE PAINTINGS

see also Miniature Cases

Azarpay, Guitty. Sogdian Painting: The Pictorial Epic in Oriental Art. 1981. 65.00x (ISBN 0-520-03765-0). U of Cal Pr.

Buchthal, Hugo. Miniature Painting in the Latin Kingdom of Jerusalem. LC 78-63329. (The Crusades & Military Orders: Second Ser.). (Illus.). Repr. of 1957 ed. 87.50 (ISBN 0-404-16249-5). AMS Pr.

Long, Basil S. British Miniaturists. (Illus.). xxxiv, 484p. 1966. Repr. of 1929 ed. 50.00 (ISBN 0-900470-51-8). Oak Knoll.

Maxym, Lucy. Russian Laquer, Legends & Fairy Tales. (Illus.). 80p. 1981. 27.50 (ISBN 0-940202-01-8). Siamese Imports.

Weitzmann, Kurt. The Miniatures of the Sacra Parallela: Parsinius Graecus 923. LC 78-70320. (Studies in Manuscript Illumination: -8). (Illus.). 1979. 60.00 (ISBN 0-691-03940-2). Princeton U Pr.

MINIATURE PINSCHERS

see Dogs–Breeds–Miniature Pinschers

MINIATURE PLANTS

see also Bonsai; Gardens, Miniature

Brian, Matthew. Dwarf Bulbs. LC 73-75749. (Illus.). 224p. 1973. 12.95 (ISBN 0-668-02964-1). Arco.

Kramer, Jack. Picture Encyclopedia of Small Plants. 1978. 11.95 (ISBN 0-8128-2497-0). Stein & Day.

McDonald, Elvin. Little Plants for Small Spaces. 1974. pap. 1.50 (ISBN 0-445-03035-6). Popular Lib.

--Little Plants for Small Spaces. LC 75-15794. (Illus.). 192p. 1975. 8.95 (ISBN 0-87131-195-X). M Evans.

Perl, Philip. Miniatures & Bonsai. Time-Life Books, ed. LC 78-20889. (Encyclopedia of Gardening Ser.). (Illus.). 1979. 12.95 (ISBN 0-8094-2641-2). Time-Life.

MINIATURE TREES

see Bonsai; Miniature Plants

MINIATURES (ILLUMINATION OF BOOKS AND MANUSCRIPTS)

see Illumination of Books and Manuscripts

MINIATURES (PORTRAITS)

see Miniature Painting

MINIATURES, MILITARY

see Military Miniatures

MINIATURIZATION (ELECTRONICS)

see Miniature Electronic Equipment

MINICOMPUTERS

see also Microcomputers; Microprocessors

Barden, William, Jr. How to Buy & Use Minicomputers & Microcomputers. LC 76-19693. (Illus.). 1976. pap. 9.95 (ISBN 0-672-21351-6). Sams.

--Z-Eighty Microcomputer Handbook. LC 77-93166. 1978. pap. 8.95 (ISBN 0-672-21500-4). Sams.

Bonelli, Robert A. The Executive Handbook to Minicomputers. (Illus.). text ed. 14.00 (ISBN 0-89433-090-X). Petrocelli.

--Increasing Profitability with Minicomputers. (Illus.). 256p. 1981. text ed. 17.50 (ISBN 0-89433-123-X). Petrocelli.

Bourne, John R. Laboratory Minicomputing. 1981. price not set (ISBN 0-12-119080-3). Acad Pr.

British Computer Society. Minicomputers: Proceedings of the Nottingham Branch Winter School. 1975. 17.50 (ISBN 0-85501-425-3). Heyden.

Brown, Carol W. The Minicomputer Simplified: An Executive's Guide to the Basics. LC 80-1031. (Illus.). 1980. 14.95 (ISBN 0-02-905130-4). Free Pr.

Brown, Helen, ed. Minicomputer Research & Applications: Proceedings of the First Conference of the HP-1000 International Users Group. (Illus.). 392p. 1981. 40.00 (ISBN 0-08-027567-2). Pergamon.

Burton, Phillip E. A Dictionary of Mini & Micro Computing. LC 80-28272. 450p. 1981. lib. bdg. 32.50 (ISBN 0-8240-7263-4). Garland Pub.

Buyers' Guide to Business Minicomputer Systems. 24.95 (ISBN 0-686-51433-5). Auerbach.

Buyers' Guide to Minicomputers. 24.95 (ISBN 0-686-51432-7). Auerbach.

Canning, Richard G. & Leeper, Nancy C. So You Are Thinking About a Small Business Computer. (Computing in Your Business Ser.). (Illus.). 100p. (Orig.). 1980. pap. 12.50 (ISBN 0-938516-01-9). Canning Pubns.

Cassel & Swanson. Basic Made Easy: A Guide to Programming Microcomputers & Minicomputers. (Illus.). 272p. 1980. text ed. 14.95 (ISBN 0-8359-0399-0); pap. text ed. 10.95 (ISBN 0-8359-0398-2). Reston.

Cluley, J. C. Programming for Minicomputers. LC 77-83270. (Computer Systems Engineering Ser.). 1978. 19.50x (ISBN 0-8448-1259-5). Crane-Russak Co.

Cooper, James W. The Minicomputer in the Laboratory: With Examples Using the PDP-11. LC 76-44255. 1977. 25.00 (ISBN 0-471-01883-X, Pub. by Wiley-Interscience). Wiley.

Donahue, Carroll & Enger, Janice. The PET-CBM Personal Computer Guide. (Orig.). 1980. pap. 15.00 (ISBN 0-931988-30-6). Osborne-McGraw.

Eadie, Donald. Minicomputers: Theory & Operation. (Illus.). 1979. 21.95 (ISBN 0-8359-4387-9). Reston.

Eckhouse, Richard H., Jr. & Morrison, L. Robert. Minicomputer Systems: Organization, Programming & Applications (PDP-11) 2nd ed. (Illus.). 1979. text ed. 26.95 (ISBN 0-13-583914-9). P-H.

Finkel, Jules. Computer-Aided Experimentation: Interfacing to Minicomputers. LC 74-22060. 422p. 1975. 42.50 (ISBN 0-471-25884-9, Pub. by Wiley-Interscience). Wiley.

Garrett, Patrick H. Analog Systems for Microprocessors & Minicomputers. (Illus.). 1978. 19.50 (ISBN 0-87909-035-9); instructor's manual free. Reston.

Gotlieb, C. C. Computers in the Home. 65p. 1978. pap. text ed. 3.00x (ISBN 0-920380-10-7, Pub. by Inst Res Pub Canada). Renouf.

Green, Roy. Using Minicomputers in Distributed Systems. (Illus.). 1978. 28.50x (ISBN 0-85012-202-3). Intl Pubns Serv.

Grillo, John P. & Robertson, J. D. Minicomputer Systems. 1981. 22.95 (ISBN 0-8436-1602-4). CBI Pub.

Grosch, Audrey N. Minicomputers in Libraries. LC 79-11134. (Professional Librarian Ser.). (Illus.). 1979. pap. 24.50x (ISBN 0-914236-19-9). Knowledge Indus.

Harrison, H. B. Structural Analysis & Design: Some Minicomputer Applications, 2 pts. (Illus.). 1980. Set. text ed. 79.00 (ISBN 0-08-023239-6); pap. text ed. 30.00 (ISBN 0-08-023240-X). Pergamon.

Harrison, Thomas J., ed. Minicomputers in Industrial Control. LC 77-93080. (Illus.). 356p. 1978. text ed. 30.00 (ISBN 0-87664-372-1). Instru Soc.

Haviland, R. P. The COMPULATOR Book: Building Super Calculators & Mini Computer Hardware with Calculator Chips. (Illus.). 1977. pap. 7.95x (ISBN 0-8306-6975-2, 975). TAB Bks.

Healey, Martin & Hebditch, David. Minicomputers in on-Line Systems. (Computer Systems Ser.). (Illus.). 352p. 1981. text ed. 22.95 (ISBN 0-87626-579-4). Winthrop.

Herbert, Frank & Barnard, Max. Without Me You're Nothing: The Essential Guide to Home Computers. 1981. 14.95 (ISBN 0-671-41287-6). S&S.

Hohenstein, C. Louis. Computer Peripherals for Minicomputers, Microprocessos & Personal Computers. (Illus.). 320p. 1980. 19.50 (ISBN 0-07-029451-8, P&RB). McGraw.

Huffman, Jim. Personal Computing. (Illus.). 1979. text ed. 15.95 (ISBN 0-8359-5516-8); pap. 11.95 (ISBN 0-8359-5515-X). Reston.

IFIP Conference on Software for Minicomputers, 1st, Hungary, 1975. Minicomputer Software: Proceedings. Bell, J. R. & Bell, C. G., eds. 1976. 36.75 (ISBN 0-444-11094-1, North-Holland). Elsevier.

Kennedy, Donald P. Minicomputers: Low-Cost Computer Power for Management. rev. ed. (Illus.). 1979. 15.95 (ISBN 0-8144-5484-4). Am Mgmt.

Lenk, John D. Handbook of Microprocessors, Microcomputers & Minicomputers. (Illus.). 1979. text ed. 20.95 (ISBN 0-13-380378-3). P-H.

Leventhal, Lance A. & Stafford, Irving. Why Do You Need a Personal Computer. LC 80-2391. (Self-Teaching Guide Ser.). 320p. 1981. pap. text ed. 8.95 (ISBN 0-471-04784-8). Wiley.

Lien, David A. Controlling the World with Your TRS-80. Gunzel, David, ed. (CompuSoft Learning Ser.). (Illus.). 600p. (Orig.). 1981. pap. price not set (ISBN 0-932760-03-1). CompuSoft.

Lin, Wen C., ed. Microprocessors: Fundamentals & Applications. LC 76-53223. 1977. 26.95 (ISBN 0-87942-093-6). Inst Electrical.

Lines, Vardell. Minicomputer Systems. (Illus.). 1980. text ed. 19.95 (ISBN 0-87626-582-4). Winthrop.

Lykos, Peter, ed. Minicomputers & Large Scale Computations. LC 77-15932. (ACS Symposium Ser.: No. 57). 1977. 24.50 (ISBN 0-8412-0387-3). Am Chemical.

McCabe, Dwight, ed. PCC's Reference Book of Personal & Home Computing, 1977. LC 77-73021. (Illus.). 1977. pap. 5.95 (ISBN 0-918790-02-6). Peoples Computer.

McGlynn, Daniel R. Microprocessors: Technology, Architecture & Applications. LC 76-137. 1976. 19.95 (ISBN 0-471-58414-2, Pub. by Wiley-Interscience). Wiley.

Mayzner, Mark S. & Dolan, Terrence R. Minicomputers in Sensory & Information Processing Research. 280p. 1978. 18.00x (ISBN 0-470-26488-8). Halsted Pr.

Meldman, Monte, et al. RISS: A Relational Data Base Management System for Minicomputers. 124p. 1981. Repr. of 1978 ed. lib. bdg. price not set (ISBN 0-89874-373-7). Krieger.

Meldman, Monte J., et al. RISS: A Relational Data Base Management System for Minicomputers. 1978. text ed. 14.95x (ISBN 0-442-25297-8). Van Nos Reinhold.

Moschytz, G. S. Active Filter Design Handbook: For Use with Programmable Pocket Calculators & Minicomputers. LC 80-40845. 324p. 1981. 45.00 (ISBN 0-471-27850-5, Pub. by Wiley-Interscience). Wiley.

Nicoud, J. D. & Wilmink, J., eds. Microcomputer Architectures: Proceedings of the Third EUROMICRO Symposium on Microprocessing Microprogramming, October 1977, Amsterdam. 1978. 44.00 (ISBN 0-444-85097-X, North-Holland). Elsevier.

Nilles, Jack M. Exploring the World of the Personal Computer. (Illus.). 256p. 1982. text ed. 15.95 (ISBN 0-13-297580-7); pap. text ed. 12.95 (ISBN 0-13-297572-6). P-H.

Osborne, Adam. A Business System Buyer's Guide. 600p. (Orig.). 1981. pap. 7.95 (ISBN 0-931988-47-0). Osborne-McGraw.

Paker, Y., ed. Minicomputers: A Reference Book for Engineers, Scientists & Managers. 1980. write for info. (ISBN 0-85626-188-2, Pub. by Abacus Pr). Intl Schol Bk Serv.

Paker, Yakup. Mini Computers: Guidelines for First Time Users. 1980. 25.00x (ISBN 0-85626-184-X, Pub. by Abacus Pr). Intl Schol Bk Serv.

Perry, Robert. Owning Your Home Computer. (The Complete Illustrated Guide Ser.). (Illus.). 256p. (Orig.). 1980. pap. 12.95 (ISBN 0-89696-093-5). Everest Hse.

Pooch, Udo W. & Chattergy, Rahul. Minicomputers: Hardware, Software, & Selection. (Illus.). 1980. text ed. 21.95 (ISBN 0-8299-0055-1). West Pub.

Poole, Lon. The Apple II User's Guide. 500p. 1981. pap. 15.00 (ISBN 0-931988-46-2). Osborne-McGraw.

Rinder, Robert M. A Practical Guide to Small Computers for Business & Professional Use. 288p. 1981. pap. 9.95 (ISBN 0-671-09259-6). Monarch Pr.

Sanderson, P. C. Minicomputers. text ed. 12.95 (ISBN 0-408-00213-1). Butterworth.

Schoeffler, James D. IBM Series 1: Small Computer Concept. 1980. pap. text ed. 10.95 (ISBN 0-574-21330-9, 13-4330). SRA.

Sippl, Charles J. & Dahl, Fred. Video Computers: How to Select, Mix, & Operate Personal Computers & Home Video Equipment. (Illus.). 256p. 1980. 15.95 (ISBN 0-13-941856-3, Spec); pap. 7.95 (ISBN 0-13-941849-0). P-H.

Skrokov, M. Robert, ed. Mini & Microcomputer Control in Industrial Processes: Handbook of Systems Application & Strategies. 320p. 1980. text ed. 27.50 (ISBN 0-442-27643-5). Van Nos Reinhold.

Sloan, Martha E. Introduction to Minicomputers & Microcomputers. LC 78-74693. 1980. text ed. 23.95 (ISBN 0-201-07279-3). A-W.

Solomon, Leslie & Veit, Stanley. Getting Involved with Your Own Computer: A Guide for Beginners. LC 77-8498. (Illus.). 1977. pap. 5.95 (ISBN 0-89490-004-8). Enslow Pubs.

Spikell, Mark A. & Snover, Stephen. Brain Ticklers: Puzzles & Pastimes for Programmable Calculators & Personal Computers. (Illus.). 160p. 1980. 13.95 (ISBN 0-13-081018-5); pap. 5.95 (ISBN 0-13-081000-2). P-H.

Thiagarajan, Sivasailam & Stolovitch, Harold D. Games with the Pocket Calculator. (gr. 3 up). 1976. pap. 3.95 (ISBN 0-918398-20-7). Dilithium Pr.

Titus, Jonathan A., et al. Microcomputer-Analog Converter Software & Hardware Interfacing. LC 78-57201. 1978. pap. 10.50 (ISBN 0-672-21540-3). Sams.

Tocci, Ronald J. & Laskowski, Lester P. Microprocessors & Microcomputers: Hardware & Software. (Illus.). 1979. text ed. 18.95 (ISBN 0-13-581330-1). P-H.

Warren, Carl & Miller, Merl. From the Counter to the Bottom Line. 1979. pap. 12.95 (ISBN 0-918398-11-8, Pub. by Dilithium). Intl Schol Bk Serv.

Warren, Jim, ed. Dr. Dobb's Journal of Computer Calisthenics & Orthodontia, Vol. 1. 1977. pap. 18.95 (ISBN 0-8104-5475-0). Peoples Computer.

Warren, Jim C., Jr., ed. National Computer Conference '78 Personal Computing Digest. (Illus.). iv, 425p. 1978. pap. 12.00 (ISBN 0-88283-011-2). AFIPS Pr.

Weitzman, Cay. Distributed Micro Minicomputer Systems: Structure, Implementation & Application. (Illus.). 1980. text ed. 26.95 (ISBN 0-13-216481-7). P-H.

--Minicomputer Systems: Structure, Implementation, & Application. (Illus.). 384p. 1974. 26.95 (ISBN 0-13-584227-1). P-H.

MINIMA

see Maxima and Minima

MINIMAX APPROXIMATION

see Chebyshev Approximation

MINIMAL ART

Battcock, Gregory, ed. Minimal Art: A Critical Anthology. 1968. pap. 7.50 (ISBN 0-525-47211-8). Dutton.

MINIMAL SURFACES

see Surfaces, Minimal

MINIMUM WAGE

see Wages–Minimum Wage

MINING

see Mineral Industries; Mines and Mineral Resources; Mining Engineering; Mining Industry and Finance

MINING, ELECTRIC

see Electricity in Mining

MINING ENGINEERING

see also Blasting; Boring; Electricity in Mining; Hydraulic Mining; Mine Surveying; Mine Ventilation; Petroleum Engineering; Strip Mining; Tunnels and Tunneling

American Society of Civil Engineers, compiled By. Current Geotechnical Practice in Mine Waste Disposal. 272p. 1979. pap. text ed. 19.25 (ISBN 0-87262-141-3). Am Soc Civil Eng.

Amstutz, G. Glossary of Mining Geology. 196p. (Eng., Span., Fr. & Ger.). 1971. 36.50 (ISBN 3-432-01667-0, M-7428, Pub. by F. Enke). French & Eur.

Baguelin, F., et al. The Pressuremeter & Foundation Engineering. (Rock & Soil Mechanics Ser.). (Illus.). 1978. 58.00x (ISBN 0-87849-019-1). Trans Tech.

Barger, Harold & Schurr, Sam H. The Mining Industries, 1899-1939: A Study of Output, Employment & Productivity. LC 72-2833. (Use & Abuse of America's Natural Resources Ser). 474p. 1972. Repr. of 1944 ed. 22.00 (ISBN 0-405-04502-6). Arno.

--The Mining Industries, 1899-1939: A Study of Output, Employment, & Productivity. LC 75-19694. (National Bureau of Economic Research Ser.). (Illus.). 1975. Repr. 24.00x (ISBN 0-405-07575-8). Arno.

Bramble, Charles A. The ABC's of Mining: The Prospector's Handbook. LC 81-80695. (Illus.). 183p. 1981. pap. 8.98 (ISBN 0-939694-00-X). Goldhound Intl.

Cancrinus, Franz L. First Principles of the Science of Mining & Salt Mining. Bordeau, Kenneth V. & Bordeau, Elvi L., trs. LC 80-65488. (Microform Publication: No. 10). 1980. 4.00x (ISBN 0-8137-6010-0). Geol Soc.

Cline, Robert L. Directory of Computer Models Applicable to the Coal Mining Industry. Raese, Jon W., ed. (Illus.). 490p. 1981. pap. text ed. 20.00 (ISBN 0-918062-44-6). Colo Sch Mines.

De Vore, R. William & Carpenter, Stanley B., eds. Symposium on Surface Mining Hydrology, Sedimentology, & Reclamation. LC 79-91553. (Illus.). 353p. (Orig.). 1979. pap. 33.50 (ISBN 0-89779-024-3, UKY BU119); microfiche 4.50 (ISBN 0-89779-025-1). OES Pubns.

Engineering Mining Journal Magazine. Operating Handbook of Mineral Underground Mining, Vol. III. (Library of Operating Handbooks). 1979. 19.50 (ISBN 0-07-019521-8, P&RB). McGraw.

Gelb, Bernard & Pliskin, Jeffrey. Energy Use in Mining: Patterns & Prospects. LC 79-851. 1979. 22.50 (ISBN 0-88410-088-X). Ballinger Pub.

Gold & Silver Cyanidation Plant Practice Monograph. 1975. 25.00x (ISBN 0-89520-027-9). Soc Mining Eng.

Green, Lewis. The Gold Hustlers. LC 77-7341. (Illus.). 1977. pap. 7.95 (ISBN 0-88240-088-6). Alaska Northwest.

Gregory, Cedric E. A Concise History of Mining. LC 80-13925. 1981. 30.00 (ISBN 0-08-023882-3). Pergamon.

Haley, K. Brian & Stone, Lawrence D., eds. Search Theory & Applications. (NATO Conference Ser. (Series II--Systems Science): Vol. 8). 260p. 1980. 35.00 (ISBN 0-306-40562-8, Plenum Pr). Plenum Pub.

Hall, Eugene J. The Language of Mining & Metallurgy in English. (English for Careers Ser.). (gr. 10 up). 1978. pap. text ed. 3.50 (ISBN 0-88345-332-0). Regents Pub.

Hardy, H. Reginald & Leighton, Frederick W. Proceedings of the Second Conference on Acoustic Emission: Microseismic Activity in Geologic Structures & Materials. (Rock & Soil Mechanics Ser.). (Illus.). 500p. 1980. 45.00x (ISBN 0-87849-032-9). Trans Tech.
Hoisting Conference: 1975. 10.50x (ISBN 0-89520-026-0). Soc Mining Eng.
Jones, A. H., ed. Mining Technology for Energy Resources Advances for the Eighties. 1978. 8.00 (ISBN 0-685-66805-3, G00140). ASME.
Lama, R. D. & Vutukuri, V. S. Handbook on Mechanical Properties of Rocks, Vol. III. (Rock & Soil Mechanics Ser.). (Illus.). 1978. 65.00x (ISBN 0-87849-022-1). Trans Tech.
--Handbook on Mechanical Properties of Rocks, Vol. IV. (Rock & Soil Mechanics Ser.). (Illus.). 1978. 65.00x (ISBN 0-87849-023-X). Trans Tech.
Lewis, Robert S. & Clark, G. B. Elements of Mining. 3rd ed. LC 64-14990. 1964. 53.95 (ISBN 0-471-53331-9). Wiley.
Li Itunda Yenge. Analysis of Bulk Flow of Materials Under Gravity Caving Process, Pt. 1: Sublevel Caving in Relation to Flow in Bins & Bunkers, Vol. 75, No. 4. Raese, Jon W., ed. LC 81-129. (Colorado School of Mines Quarterly Ser.). (Illus.). 56p. 1981. pap. 12.00 (ISBN 0-686-74853-0). Colo Sch Mines.
Mining & Metallurgy Group Symposium, 4th, October 1975, Milwaukee, WI. Instrumentation in the Mining & Metallurgy Industries: Proceedings, Vol. 3. LC 73-82889. 1976. pap. text ed. 10.00 (ISBN 0-87664-278-4). Instru Soc.
Mining Information Services. Mining Methods & Equipment. 224p. 1980. 16.50 (ISBN 0-07-039794-5). McGraw.
Mining Journal Books Ltd. Economics of Mineral Engineering. 223p. 1980. 16.00x (ISBN 0-900117-10-9, Pub. by Mining Journal England). State Mutual Bk.
Peele, R. Mining Engineers' Handbook, 2 vols. 3rd ed. (Engineering Handbook Ser.). 1941. Set. 82.50 (ISBN 0-471-67716-7, Pub. by Wiley-Interscience). Wiley.
Ramani, R. V., ed. Proceedings: Fourteenth APCOM. LC 76-58570. 1977. 25.00x (ISBN 0-89520-047-3). Soc Mining Eng.
Recent Advances in Mining & Processing of Low-Grade Submarginal Mineral Deposits. LC 76-11771. 1977. text ed. 25.00 (ISBN 0-08-021051-1). Pergamon.
Rickard, Thomas A. A History of American Mining. (Illus.). Repr. of 1932 ed. 23.00 (ISBN 0-384-50800-6). Johnson Repr.
--Man & Metals: A History of Mining in Relation to the Development of Civilization, 2 vols. in 1. LC 74-358. (Gold Ser.: Vol. 16). (Illus.). 1974. Repr. of 1932 ed. 56.00x (ISBN 0-405-05919-1). Arno.
SME Mining Engineering Handbook. LC 72-86922. 1973. 45.00x (ISBN 0-89520-021-X). Soc Mining Eng.
Stephansson, O., ed. Application of Rock Mechanics to Cut & Fill Mining. 1981. pap. text ed. 132.25 (ISBN 0-686-31378-X). IMM North Am.
Symposium on Solution Mining, 1974. Proceedings. LC 73-94005. 15.00x (ISBN 0-89520-025-2). Soc Mining Eng.
Thomas, L. J. An Introduction to Mining: Exploration, Feasibility, Extraction, Rock Mechanics. LC 73-14857. 1977. pap. 24.95 (ISBN 0-470-99220-4). Halsted Pr.
Tillson, Benjamin F. Mine Plant. (Illus.). 1976. text ed. 30.00x (ISBN 0-89520-042-2). Soc Mining Eng.
Wilson, David, ed. Design & Construction of Tailing Dams: First Seminar on Design & Construction of Tailing Dams, Nov. 6-7, 1980. (Illus.). 286p. 1981. Repr. of 1980 ed. text ed. 20.00 (ISBN 0-918062-45-4). Colo Sch Mines.

MINING ENGINEERING–BIBLIOGRAPHY

SME-AIME Cumulative Index, 1936-1968. 1972. 25.00x (ISBN 0-89520-012-0). Soc Mining Eng.

MINING GEOLOGY

Amstutz, G. C. Glossary of Mining Geology. 1971. 44.00 (ISBN 0-444-99922-1). Elsevier.
Brown, Wayne S., et al, eds. Monograph on Rock Mechanics Applications in Mining. LC 76-45924. 1977. pap. text ed. 16.50x (ISBN 0-89520-046-5). Soc Mining Eng.
Eurotunnel 1980. 1980. 79.00x (ISBN 0-900488-50-6, Pub. by Inst Mining England). State Mutual Bk.
Jones, M. J. Geology Mining & Extractive Processing of Uranium. 171p. 1980. 100.00x (ISBN 0-900488-35-2, Pub. by Inst Mining England). State Mutual Bk.
Journel, A. G. & Huijbregts, C. J. Mining Geostatistics. 1979. 93.50 (ISBN 0-12-391050-1). Acad Pr.
Metcalfe, J. E. British Mining Fields. 91p. 1980. 35.00x (ISBN 0-900488-00-X, Pub. by Inst Mining England). State Mutual Bk.

MINING INDUSTRY AND FINANCE

see also Mines and Mineral Resources; Mines and Mineral Resources–Taxation

Bain, Foster H. & Read, Thomas T. Ores & Industry in South America. Bruchey, Stuart & Bruchey, Eleanor, eds. LC 76-4767. (American Business Abroad Ser.). (Illus.). 1976. Repr. of 1934 ed. 24.00x (ISBN 0-405-09265-2). Arno.
Barger, Harold & Schurr, Sam H. The Mining Industries, 1899-1939: A Study of Output, Employment & Productivity. LC 72-2833. (Use & Abuse of America's Natural Resources Ser). 474p. 1972. Repr. of 1944 ed. 22.00 (ISBN 0-405-04502-6). Arno.
Carman, John S. Obstacles to Mineral Development: A Pragmatic View. Varon, Benison, ed. LC 78-26807. (Illus.). 1979. 28.00 (ISBN 0-08-023904-8). Pergamon.
Carpenter, Kenneth E. Speculation in Gold & Silver. LC 74-367. (Vol. 14). 1974. gold 9.00x (ISBN 0-405-05928-0). Arno.
Conrad, Robert & Hool, Bryce, eds. Taxation of Mineral Resources. LC 80-8392. (Lincoln Institute of Land Policy Book). 1980. 14.95x (ISBN 0-669-04104-1). Lexington Bks.
Davis, Shelton H. & Mathews, Robert O. The Geological Imperative: Anthropology & Development in the Amazon Basin of South America. (Illus., Orig.). 1976. pap. 3.50 (ISBN 0-932978-01-0). Anthropology Res.
Fisher, Chris. Custom, Work & Market Capitalism. 224p. 1981. 29.50x (ISBN 0-7099-1001-0, Pub. by Croom Helm Ltd England). Biblio Dist.
Guarascio, Massimo, et al, eds. Advanced Geostatistics in the Mining Industry. LC 76-13915. (Nato Mathematical& Physical Sciences Ser: No. C24). 1976. lib. bdg. 55.00 (ISBN 90-277-0669-7, Pub. by Reidel Holland). Kluwer Boston.
Howe, Walter. Mining Guild of New Spain & Its Tribunal General, 1770-1821. LC 68-55634. (Illus.). 1968. Repr. of 1949 ed. lib. bdg. 21.00x (ISBN 0-8371-0486-6, HOMG). Greenwood.
King, Joseph E. A Mine to Make a Mine: Financing the Colorado Mining Industry, 1859-1902. LC 76-51655. 240p. 1977. 13.75 (ISBN 0-89096-034-8). Tex A&M Univ Pr.
Lake, James A. Law & Mineral Wealth: The Legal Profile of the Wisconsin Mining Industry. (Illus.). 228p. 1962. 17.50x (ISBN 0-299-02580-2). U of Wis Pr.
M. Radetzki & S. Zorn Mining Journals Books Ltd. Financing Mining Projects in Developing Countries. 200p. 1980. 23.00x (ISBN 0-900117-17-6, Pub. by Mining Journal England); soft cover 17.00x (ISBN 0-686-64743-2). State Mutual Bk.
Malone, Michael P. The Battle for Butte: Mining & Politics on the Northern Frontier, 1864-1906. LC 81-51283. (Illus.). 320p. 1981. 17.95 (ISBN 0-295-95837-5). U of Wash Pr.
Marcosson, Isaac F. Anaconda. LC 75-41771. (Companies & Men: Business Enterprises in America). (Illus.). 1976. Repr. of 1957 ed. 27.00x (ISBN 0-405-08085-9). Arno.
O'Connor, Harvey. The Guggenheims: The Making of an American Dynasty. Bruchey, Stuart & Bruchey, Eleanor, eds. LC 76-5026. (American Business Abroad Ser.). (Illus.). 1976. Repr. of 1937 ed. 30.00x (ISBN 0-405-09292-X). Arno.
Reedman, J. H. Techniques in Mineral Exploration: Popular Edition. (Illus.). 1979. 50.00x (ISBN 0-85334-851-0, Pub. by Applied Science). Burgess-Intl Ideas.
The Role of Innovation in the Mining & Mining Supply Industries. (Illus.). 1977. pap. 3.85 (ISBN 0-685-81707-5, MR146, SSC). Unipub.
Shinn, Charles. Mining Camps: A Study in American Frontier Government. Paul, R. W., ed. 7.50 (ISBN 0-8446-0909-9). Peter Smith.
Wallace, Iain. The Transportation Impact of the Canadian Mining Industry. 155p. (Orig.). 1977. pap. text ed. 8.00x (ISBN 0-88757-002-X, Pub. by Ctr Resource Stud Canada). Renouf.

MINING LAW

see also Coal Mines and Mining–Laws and Legislation; Mining Leases; Petroleum Law and Legislation

Copp, Henry N. United States Mineral Lands. Bruchey, Stuart, ed. LC 78-53539. (Development of Public Land Law in the U. S. Ser.). 1979. Repr. of 1882 ed. lib. bdg. 39.00x (ISBN 0-405-11373-0). Arno.
Federal Mine Safety & Health Act of 1977. 1977. pap. 4.00 (ISBN 0-685-46986-7). Commerce.
Jaenicke, G., et al, eds. Mining Ventures in Developing Countries. (Studies of the Transnational Law of Natural Resources: No. 1). 1979. lib. bdg. 58.00 (ISBN 90-268-1037-7, Pub. by Kluwer Law Netherlands). Kluwer Boston.
Kronmiller, Theodore G., ed. The Lawfullness of Deep Seabed Mining, Vols. 1 & 2. LC 79-23232. 1980. Set. lib. bdg. 80.00 (ISBN 0-379-20461-4). Vol. 1, 521p (ISBN 0-379-20461-4). Vol. 2, 460p (ISBN 0-379-20462-2). Oceana.
Lake, James A. Law & Mineral Wealth: The Legal Profile of the Wisconsin Mining Industry. (Illus.). 228p. 1962. 17.50x (ISBN 0-299-02580-2). U of Wis Pr.
Lindley, Curtis H. A Treatise on the American Law Relating to Mines & Mineral Lands Within the Public Land States & Territories & Governing the Acquisition & Enjoyment of Mining Rights in Lands of the Public Domain, 2 vols. 2nd ed. LC 72-2853. (Use & Abuse of America's Natural Resources Ser). 1972. Repr. of 1903 ed. 98.00 (ISBN 0-405-04517-4); 49.90 ea. Vol. 1 (ISBN 0-405-04546-8). Vol. 2 (ISBN 0-405-04547-6). Arno.
Organization of American States. Mining & Petroleum Legislation. LC 78-16150. (Binder 1 & supplement). 1978. perfect binder 100.00 (ISBN 0-379-20381-2). Oceana.
--Mining & Petroleum Legislation, Release 1 & 2. 1980. 35.00 ea. (ISBN 0-379-20381-2). Oceana.
Shinn, Charles H. Land Laws of Mining Districts. LC 78-63751. (Johns Hopkins University. Studies in the Social Sciences. Second Ser. 1884: 12). Repr. of 1884 ed. 11.50 (ISBN 0-404-61020-X). AMS Pr.

MINING LEASES

see also Oil and Gas Leases

Shinn, C. H. Land Laws of Mining Districts. Repr. of 1884 ed. pap. 7.00 (ISBN 0-384-55159-9). Johnson Repr.

MINING MACHINERY

see also Electricity in Mining; Hoisting Machinery

Mining Machinery. (Machinery Studies). 1980. 335.00 (ISBN 0-686-31532-4). Busn Trend.
Stack, Barbara. Handbook of Mining & Tunnelling Machinery. 640p. 1982. 103.00 (ISBN 0-471-27937-4, Pub. by Wiley-Interscience). Wiley.

MINING PICTURES–EVALUATION

see also Moving-Picture Criticism

MINING RESEARCH

The Role of Innovation in the Mining & Mining Supply Industries. (Illus.). 1977. pap. 3.85 (ISBN 0-685-81707-5, MR146, SSC). Unipub.

MINISINK, NEW YORK, BATTLE OF, 1779

Leslie, Vernon. Battle of Minisink. LC 73-89690. 1976. 12.50x (ISBN 0-686-14953-X). T E Henderson.

MINISINK REGION–HISTORY

Hine, Charles G. The Old Mine Road. (Illus.). 1963. pap. 2.75 (ISBN 0-8135-0427-9). Rutgers U Pr.

MINISTERIAL RESPONSIBILITY

Blackwood, Andrew W. Planning a Year's Pulpit Work. (Andrew W. Blackwood Library). 240p. 1975. pap. 4.50 (ISBN 0-8010-0640-6). Baker Bk.
Kelly, George A., ed. Catholic Ministries in Our Times. 1981. 4.00 (ISBN 0-8198-1400-8); pap. 3.00 (ISBN 0-8198-1401-6). Dghtrs St Paul.
Wang Chi-Kao. Dissolution of the British Parliament 1832-1931. LC 79-127433. (Columbia University Studies in the Social Sciences: No. 396). Repr. of 1934 ed. 12.50 (ISBN 0-404-51396-4). AMS Pr.

MINISTERS (DIPLOMATIC AGENTS)

see Ambassadors; Diplomatic and Consular Service

MINISTERS OF RELIGIOUS EDUCATION

see Directors of Religious Education

MINISTERS OF STATE

see Cabinet Officers

MINISTERS OF THE GOSPEL

see Clergy

MINISTRY

see Church Work; Clergy–Office; Pastoral Theology

MINISTRY, URBAN

see City Clergy

MINKOWSKI SPACE

see Spaces, Generalized

MINKS

Adams, L. Mink Raising. (Illus.). 188p. 1979. pap. 3.00 (ISBN 0-936622-15-6). A R Harding Pub.
Committee On Animal Nutrition. Nutrient Requirements of Mink & Foxes. (Nutrient Requirements of Domestic Animals Ser.). 1968. pap. 3.50 (ISBN 0-309-01676-2). Natl Acad Pr.
Errington, Paul L. Muskrats & Marsh Management. LC 77-14177. (Illus.). x, 183p. 1978. 13.50x (ISBN 0-8032-0975-4); pap. 3.25 (ISBN 0-8032-5892-5, BB 664, Bison). U of Nebr Pr.
Liers, Emil E. A Mink's Story. LC 78-10374. (Orion Ser.). (gr. 6-9). 1979. pap. 1.95 (ISBN 0-8127-0205-0). Review & Herald.

MINNEAPOLIS

Abler, Ronald, et al. The Twin Cities of St. Paul & Minneapolis. LC 76-4801. (Contemporary Metropolitan Analysis Ser.). (Illus.). 1976. pap. text ed. 6.95 (ISBN 0-88410-434-6). Ballinger Pub.
Brambilla, Roberto & Longo, Gianni. Learning from Minneapolis, St. Paul. (Learning from the USA Ser.). (Illus.). 150p. (Orig.). Date not set. pap. 6.95 (ISBN 0-936020-03-2). Inst for Environ Action.
Dobbs, Farrell. Teamster Rebellion. LC 78-186690. (Illus.). 192p. 1972. 14.00 (ISBN 0-913460-02-8, Dist. by Path Pr NY); pap. 4.45 (ISBN 0-913460-03-6). Monad Pr.
Doche, Viviane. Cedars by the Mississippi: The Lebanese-Americans in the Twin-Cities. LC 77-81012. 1978. soft cover 12.00 (ISBN 0-88247-488-X). R & E Res Assoc.
Ervin, Jean. The Twin Cities Perceived: A Study in Words & Drawings. LC 76-7338. (Illus.). 136p. 1976. 9.95 (ISBN 0-8166-0786-9). U of Minn Pr.
Flanagan, Barbara. Minneapolis. (Illus.). 176p. 1975. pap. 4.95 (ISBN 0-685-64395-6). Nodin Pr.
French, Elizabeth S. Exploring the Twin Cities with Children. (Illus.). 1975. pap. 3.95 (ISBN 0-685-64394-8). Nodin Pr.
Harrigan, John J. & Johnson, William C. Governing the Twin Cities Region: The Metropolitan Council in Comparative Perspective. LC 78-3194. (Illus.). 1978. 14.95x (ISBN 0-8166-0838-5); pap. 5.95x (ISBN 0-8166-0849-0). U of Minn Pr.
Holbert, Sue E. & Holmquist, June D. History Tour of 50 Twin City Landmarks. LC 66-64829. (Minnesota Historic Sites Pamphlet Ser.: No. 2). (Illus.). 64p. 1966. 4.50 (ISBN 0-87351-031-3). Minn Hist.
Kane, Lucile M. Waterfall That Built a City: The Falls of St. Anthony in Minneapolis. LC 66-63543. (Illus.). 224p. 1966. 5.00 (ISBN 0-87351-026-7). Minn Hist.
Rosheim, David L. The Other Minneapolis. (Illus., Orig.). pap. 6.50 (ISBN 0-9602996-0-2). Andromeda.
Shapiro, Rachel, ed. Minneapolis-St. Paul Epicure. (Epicure Ser.). (Orig.). 1978. pap. 3.95 (ISBN 0-89716-032-0). Peanut Butter.
Walker, Charles R. American City: A Rank & File History. LC 70-156440. (American Labor Ser., No. 2). (Illus.). 1971. Repr. of 1937 ed. 20.00 (ISBN 0-405-02948-9). Arno.
Writers Program. Minnesota. Minneapolis. LC 73-3629. Repr. of 1940 ed. 8.50 (ISBN 0-404-57930-2). AMS Pr.

MINNESINGERS

see also Courtly Love; Meistersinger; Troubadours; Trouveres

Arens, Hans. Ulrichs Von Lichtenstein Frauendienst: Untersuchungen Uber Den Hofischen Sprachstil. (Ger). Repr. of 1939 ed. 14.00 (ISBN 0-384-01898-X); pap. 11.00 (ISBN 0-685-02208-0). Johnson Repr.
Kroeger, A. The Minnesingers of Germany. 59.95 (ISBN 0-8490-0640-6). Gordon Pr.
Linker, Robert W. Music of the Minnesinger & Early Meistersinger. LC 73-181946. (North Carolina University. Studies in the Germanic Languages & Literatures: No. 32). Repr. of 1962 ed. 18.50 (ISBN 0-404-50932-0). AMS Pr.

MINNESOTA

see also names of cities, counties, towns, etc. in Minnesota

Anderson, Chester G., ed. Growing Up in Minnesota: Ten Writers Remember Their Childhoods. LC 75-40546. 1976. 9.95 (ISBN 0-8166-0765-6); pap. 6.95 (ISBN 0-8166-0921-7). U of Minn Pr.
Jenks, Albert E. Minnesota's Browns Valley Man and Associated Burial Artifacts. LC 38-22478. 1937. pap. 5.00 (ISBN 0-527-00548-7). Kraus Repr.
Nelson, Lowry. Minnesota Community: Country & Town in Transition. LC 60-10191. (Illus.). 1960. 5.25x (ISBN 0-8166-0211-5). U of Minn Pr.
Parker, Nathan H. The Minnesota Handbook for 1856-7. facsimile ed. LC 75-114. (Mid-American Frontier Ser.). 1975. Repr. of 1857 ed. 9.00x (ISBN 0-405-06880-8). Arno.
Poatgieter, A. Hermina & Dunn, James T., eds. Gopher Reader 2. LC 74-12072. (Illus.). 316p. 1975. 10.95 (ISBN 0-87351-083-6). Minn Hist.
Russell, Morris C. Uncle Dudley's Odd Hours; Western Sketches, Indian Trail Echoes. LC 73-104558. Repr. of 1904 ed. lib. bdg. 14.00x (ISBN 0-8398-1768-1). Irvington.
Stuhler, Barbara. Ten Men of Minnesota & American Foreign Policy, 1898-1968. LC 73-15967. (Public Affairs Center Publications Ser). (Illus.). 263p. 1973. 8.50 (ISBN 0-87351-080-1). Minn Hist.
Treuer, Robert. The Tree Farm. 1977. 8.95 (ISBN 0-316-85273-2). Little.
Waters, Thomas F. The Streams & Rivers of Minnesota. LC 77-84166. (Illus.). 1977. 11.95 (ISBN 0-8166-0821-0). U of Minn Pr.
Wheeler, Robert C., et al. Voices from the Rapids: An Underwater Search for Fur Trade Artifacts, 1960-73. LC 75-1194. (Minnesota Historical Archaeology Ser., No. 3). (Illus.). 115p. 1975. pap. 6.50 (ISBN 0-87351-086-0). Minn Hist.
Writers Program, Minnesota. The Minnesota Arrowhead Country. LC 73-3630. (American Guide Ser.). 1941. Repr. 16.50 (ISBN 0-404-57931-0). AMS Pr.

MINNESOTA–DESCRIPTION AND TRAVEL

Andrews, Christopher C. Minnesota & Dacotah: In Letters Descriptive of a Tour Through the Northwest... facsimile ed. LC 75-81. (Mid-American Frontier Ser.). 1975. Repr. of 1857 ed. 12.00x (ISBN 0-405-06850-6). Arno.

Bolz, J. Arnold. Portage into the Past: By Canoe Along the Minnesota-Ontario Boundary Waters. (Illus.). 1960. 8.95 (ISBN 0-8166-0218-2); pap. 4.95 (ISBN 0-8166-0919-5). U of Minn Pr.

Bray, Martha C., ed. Journals of Joseph N. Nicollet: 1836-37. Fertey, Andre, tr. 288p. 1970. 16.50 (ISBN 0-87351-062-3). Minn Hist.

Buchanan, James W. Minnesota Walk Book, Vol. 3. (Illus.). 1978. pap. 4.50 (ISBN 0-931714-00-1). Nodin Pr.

Daniel, Glenda & Sullivan, Jerry. A Sierra Club Naturalist's Guide to the North Woods of Michigan, Wisconsin, & Minnesota. (Naturalist's Guide Ser.). (Illus.). 384p. 1981. 24.95 (ISBN 0-87156-248-0); pap. 10.95 (ISBN 0-87156-277-4). Sierra.

Featherstonhaugh, George W. A Canoe Voyage up the Minnay Sotor, 2 Vols. LC 71-111618. 372p. 1970. Repr. of 1847 ed. 20.00 (ISBN 0-87351-057-7). Minn Hist.

Federal Writers' Project. Minnesota: A State Guide. 545p. 1938. Repr. 49.00 (ISBN 0-403-02173-1). Somerset Pub.

Gibbon, Guy E. The Sheffield Site: An Oneota Site on the St. Croix River. LC 73-6715. (Minnesota Prehistoric Archaeology Ser., No. 10). (Illus.). 62p. 1973. pap. 4.00 (ISBN 0-87351-079-8). Minn Hist.

Holmquist, June D. & Brookins, Jean A. Minnesota's Major Historic Sites: A Guide. rev ed. LC 73-188490. (Illus.). 191p. 1972. 8.95 (ISBN 0-87351-072-0). Minn Hist.

Jaques, Florence P. Canoe Country. LC 38-27731. (Illus.). 1938. 7.95 (ISBN 0-8166-0024-4); pap. 5.95 (ISBN 0-8166-0922-5). U of Minn Pr.

Poatgieter, A. Hermina & Dunn, James T., eds. Gopher Reader 2. LC 74-12072. (Illus.). 316p. 1975. 10.95 (ISBN 0-87351-083-6). Minn Hist.

Scott, William W. & Hess, Jeffrey A. History & Architecture of Edina, Minnesota. (Illus.). 92p. 1981. pap. 6.95 (ISBN 0-9605054-0-7). City Edina.

Singley, Grover. Tracing Minnesota's Old Government Roads. LC 74-4149. (Minnesota Historic Sites Pamphlet Ser.: No. 10). (Illus.). 52p. 1974. pap. 3.95 (ISBN 0-87351-088-7). Minn Hist.

Stewart, Anne. What's a Wilderness Worth? LC 79-13781. (Story of Environmental Action Ser.). (Illus.). (gr. 7 up). 1979. PLB 8.95 (ISBN 0-87518-182-1). Dillon.

Thompson, Neil B. Minnesota's State Capitol: The Art & Politics of a Public Building. LC 74-4326. (Minnesota Historic Sites Pamphlet Ser.: No. 9). (Illus.). 100p. 1974. pap. 5.50 (ISBN 0-87351-085-2). Minn Hist.

Thoreau, Henry D. Thoreaus Minnesota Journey: Two Documents. Harding, Walter, ed. LC 80-2524. 1981. Repr. of 1962 ed. 18.50 (ISBN 0-404-19072-3). AMS Pr.

Van Zee, Ron, photos by. Minnesota. LC 75-41888. (Belding Imprint Ser.). (Illus.). 192p. (Text by Ivan Kubista). 1976. 27.50 (ISBN 0-912856-23-8). Graphic Arts Ctr.

Wechsler, Charles. Minnesota: State of Beauty. (Illus.). 96p. 1981. pap. 10.95 (ISBN 0-931714-12-5). Nodin Pr.

Will, Robin. Beautiful Minnesota. 72p. 1978. write for info. (ISBN 0-915796-61-9); pap. write for info. (ISBN 0-915796-60-0). Beautiful Am.

MINNESOTA–DESCRIPTION AND TRAVEL–GUIDEBOOK

Beymer, Robert. The Boundary Waters Canoe Area: The Western Region, Vol. 1. 2nd ed. Winnett, Thomas, ed. LC 80-52552. (Illus.). 192p. 1981. pap. 8.95 (ISBN 0-89997-005-2). Wilderness.

Buchanan, James W. Minnesota Walk Book, Vol. 2. (Illus.). 1977. pap. 3.95 (ISBN 0-685-88677-8). Nodin Pr.

--Minnesota Walk Book: A Guide to Hiking & Cross-Country Skiing in the Pioneer Region. (Minnesota Walk Book Ser.: Vol. 5). (Illus.). 59p. (Orig.). 1979. pap. 4.50 (ISBN 0-931714-07-9). Nodin Pr.

Hungry Gourmet: The Guide to Twin Cities Dining for Under Five Dollars. LC 78-18630. (Illus.). 1978. 4.95 (ISBN 0-87832-042-3). Piper.

Whitman, John. Whitman's Travel Guide to Minnesota. (Illus.). 1977. pap. 1.00 (ISBN 0-685-88678-6). Nodin Pr.

MINNESOTA–HISTORY

Blegen, Theodore C. The Land Lies Open. LC 74-27727. 246p. 1975. Repr. of 1949 ed. lib. bdg. 15.25x (ISBN 0-8371-7912-2, BLLO). Greenwood.

--Minnesota: A History of the State. 2nd ed. LC 75-6116. (Illus.). 713p. 1975. 14.95x (ISBN 0-8166-0754-0). U of Minn Pr.

Bowen, Ralph H., ed. A Frontier Family in Minnesota: Letters of Theodore & Sophie Bost, 1851-1920. (Illus.). 400p. 1981. 25.00 (ISBN 0-8166-1032-0); pap. 12.95 (ISBN 0-8166-1035-5). U of Minn Pr.

Carley, Kenneth. Minnesota in the Civil War. 3.95 (ISBN 0-87018-006-1). Ross.

Carrigan, Minnie B. Captured by the Indians: Reminiscences of Pioneer Life in Minnesota, Repr. Of 1907 Ed. Bd. with Eastern Kentucky Papers: The Founding of Harman's Station with an Account of the Indian Captivity of Mrs. Jennie Wiley. Connelley, William E. Repr. of 1910 ed. LC 75-7134. (Indian Captivities Ser.: Vol. 106). (Incl. rev. ed. of 1912). 1977. lib. bdg. 44.00 (ISBN 0-8240-1730-7). Garland Pub.

Christgau, John. Spoon. LC 77-22081. (Richard Seaver Bk). 1978. 10.95 (ISBN 0-670-66455-3). Viking Pr.

Cichy, Helen J. The Defrosting of Minnesota. LC 77-86170. 1977. 8.00 (ISBN 0-9601852-1-6). H J Cichy.

Coen, Rena N. Painting & Sculpture in Minnesota, 1820-1914. LC 75-27788. (Illus.). xiv, 178p. 1976. 19.50 (ISBN 0-8166-0771-0). U of Minn Pr.

Eubank, Nancy. A Living Past: Fifteen Historic Places in Minnesota. rev. ed. (Minnesota Historic Sites Pamphlet Ser.: No. 7). (Illus.). 32p. 1978. pap. 2.75 (ISBN 0-87351-077-1). Minn Hist.

Fearing, Jerry. The Story of Minnesota. 75p. 1977. pap. 3.50 (ISBN 0-87351-053-4). Minn Hist.

Federal Writers' Project, Minnesota. The Bohemian Flats. LC 73-3628. (American Guide Ser). Repr. of 1941 ed. 10.00 (ISBN 0-404-57929-9). AMS Pr.

Fogerty, James E., compiled by. Preliminary Guide to the Holdings of the Minnesota Regional Research Centers. LC 76-1287. (Guide Ser.: No. 1). 20p. 1975. 1.00x (ISBN 0-87351-093-3). Minn Hist.

Folwell, William W. A History of Minnesota, 4 vols. rev. ed. Incl. Vol. 1, 1956. LC 28-20894. 533p. 7.75 (ISBN 0-87351-000-3); Vol. 2, 1961. LC 28-20894. 477p. 7.75 (ISBN 0-87351-001-1); Vol. 3, 1969. LC 56-57334. 605p. 7.75 (ISBN 0-87351-002-X); Vol. 4, 1969. LC 56-57334. 575p. 6.50 (ISBN 0-87351-003-8). LC 21-20894. 1956-69. 28.00 set (ISBN 0-87351-151-4). Minn Hist.

--Minnesota, the North Star State. LC 72-3767. (American Commonwealths: No. 19). Repr. of 1908 ed. 26.00 (ISBN 0-404-57219-7). AMS Pr.

Fridley, Russell W. Minnesota. LC 66-23778. (Orig.). 1966. pap. 2.95 (ISBN 0-8077-1395-3). Tchrs Coll.

Gluek, Alvin C., Jr. Minnesota & the Manifest Destiny of the Canadian Northwest: A Study in Canadian-American Relations. LC 77-536946. 1965. 25.00x (ISBN 0-8020-5162-6). U of Toronto Pr.

Hall, Stephen P. Split Rock: Epoch of a Lighthouse. LC 77-26287. (Minn. Historic Sites Pamphlet Ser.: No. 15). (Illus.). 24p. 1978. pap. 1.50 (ISBN 0-87351-122-0). Minn Hist.

Harpole, Patricia C. & Nagle, Mary D., eds. Minnesota Territorial Census, 1850. LC 70-188492. 115p. 1972. pap. 5.00 (ISBN 0-87351-065-8). Minn Hist.

Heilbron, Bertha L. The Thirty-Second State: A Pictorial History of Minnesota. LC 54-14431. (Illus.). 306p. 1978. pap. 8.50 (ISBN 0-87351-130-1). Minn Hist.

Hess, Jeffrey A. Alexander Harkin: Dealer in Dry Goods & Groceries. LC 77-23425. (Minnesota Historic Sites Pamphlet Ser.: No. 14). (Illus.). 24p. 1977. pap. 2.00 (ISBN 0-87351-115-8). Minn Hist.

Jaques, Florence P. Snowshoe Country. (Illus.). 1979. pap. 5.95 (ISBN 0-8166-0918-7). U of Minn Pr.

Johnson, Elden. Prehistoric Peoples of Minnesota. 2nd ed. LC 73-96478. (Minnesota Prehistoric Archaeology Ser.: No. 3). 30p. 1978. pap. 2.00 (ISBN 0-87351-054-2). Minn Hist.

Kreidberg, Marjorie. Food on the Frontier: Minnesota Cooking from 1850 to 1900, with Selected Recipes. LC 75-34214. (Illus.). 313p. 1975. 10.50 (ISBN 0-87351-096-8); pap. 7.50 (ISBN 0-87351-097-6). Minn Hist.

Lass, William E. Minnesota: A History. (States & the Nation Ser.). (Illus.). 1977. 12.95 (ISBN 0-393-05651-1, Co-Pub. by AASLH); pap. 3.95 (ISBN 0-393-00937-8). Norton.

--Minnesota's Boundary with Canada: Its Evolution since 1783. LC 80-21644. (Minnesota Public Affairs Center Publication Ser.). (Illus.). 141p. 1980. 16.50 (ISBN 0-87351-147-6); pap. 8.75 (ISBN 0-87351-153-0). Minn Hist.

League of Women Voters of Minnesota. Minnesota Judiciary: Structures & Procedures. 2nd ed. (Illus.). 64p. 1981. pap. text ed. 2.00 (ISBN 0-939816-00-8). LWV MN.

Lucas, Lydia A., compiled by. Manuscripts Collections of the Minnesota Historical Society Guide, No. 3. LC 35-27911. 189p. 1977. pap. 7.00 (ISBN 0-87351-120-4). Minn Hist.

Meissner, Dennis E. Guide to the Use of the 1860 Minnesota Population Census Schedules & Index. 21p. 1978. pap. 1.00 (ISBN 0-87351-132-8). Minn Hist.

Morris, Lucy W., ed. Old Rail Fence Corners: Frontier Tales Told by Minnesota Pioneers. 344p. 1976. 8.50 (ISBN 0-87351-108-5); pap. 5.50 (ISBN 0-87351-109-3). Minn Hist.

Morse, Ann R. The Story of Minnesota: Study Guide. 16p. 1978. pap. 1.50 (ISBN 0-87351-125-5). Minn Hist.

Neill, Edward D. The History of Minnesota: From the Earliest French Explorations to the Present Time. facsimile ed. LC 75-112. (Mid-American Frontier Ser.). 1975. Repr. of 1858 ed. 35.00x (ISBN 0-405-06879-4). Arno.

Nute, Grace L. Voyageur's Highway: Minnesota's Border Lake Land. LC 65-63529. (Illus.). 113p. 1976. pap. 3.75 (ISBN 0-87351-006-2). Minn Hist.

Our Founders' Legacy. (Defrosting of Minnesota Ser.: Vol. 2). 1980. 7.75 (ISBN 0-9601852-2-4). H J Cichy.

Peterson, Clark C. The Great Hinckley Fire. (Illus.). 1980. 7.50 (ISBN 0-682-49569-7). Exposition.

Powell & Van Dyke. Minnesota & Manitoba One Hundred Years Ago. (Illus.). pap. 3.50 (ISBN 0-89540-056-1). Sun Pub.

Saucedo, Ramedo J., compiled by. Mexican Americans in Minnesota: An Introduction to Historical Sources. LC 77-28125. 26p. 1977. pap. 2.00 (ISBN 0-87351-124-7). Minn Hist.

Schaefer, Vernon J. We Ate Gooseberries: Growing up on a Minnesota Farm During the Depression. 1974. 7.00 (ISBN 0-682-47836-9). Exposition.

Stephenson, George M. John Lind of Minnesota. LC 73-130335. (Latin-American History & Culture Ser). 1971. Repr. of 1935 ed. 16.50 (ISBN 0-8046-1389-3). Kennikat.

Stewart, Anne & Roquitte, Ruth. The Land of Sky-Blue Waters. LC 78-9039. (Minnesota Adventures Ser.). (Illus.). (gr. 4-6). 1978. pap. text ed. 3.95 (ISBN 0-87518-161-9). Dillon.

--Minnesota Adventures Teacher's Guide. (Minnesota Adventures Ser.). 1979. pap. 6.95 (ISBN 0-87518-164-3). Dillon.

--A Part of These United States. LC 78-16325. (Minnesota Adventures Ser.). (Illus.). (gr. 4-6). 1979. pap. text ed. 3.95 (ISBN 0-87518-162-7). Dillon.

Stoltman, James B. The Laurel Culture in Minnesota. LC 73-4190. (Minnesota Prehistoric Archaeology Ser.: No. 8). (Illus.). x, 146p. 1973. pap. 5.50 (ISBN 0-87351-076-3). Minn Hist.

Streiff, Jan E., compiled by. Roster of Excavated Prehistoric Sites in Minnesota to 1972. LC 72-78032. (Minnesota Prehistoric Archaeology Ser.: No. 7). 38p. 1972. pap. 2.50 (ISBN 0-87351-071-2). Minn Hist.

Swanholm, Marx. Lumbering in the Last of the White-Pine States. LC 78-14221. (Minnesota Historic Sites Pamphlet Ser.: No. 17). (Illus.). 34p. 1978. 2.00 (ISBN 0-87351-131-X). Minn Hist.

Treuer, Robert. Voyageur Country: A Park in the Wilderness. LC 78-23339. (Illus.). 1979. 10.95 (ISBN 0-8166-0878-4). U of Minn Pr.

Utley, Robert G. Tales of the Old Hometown. (Illus.). 1976. 5.00 (ISBN 0-87839-030-8). North Star.

Walker, David A. Iron Frontier: The Discovery & Early Development of Minnesota's Three Ranges. (Illus.). 336p. 1979. 16.00 (ISBN 0-87351-145-X). Minn Hist.

White, Bruce M., compiled by. The Fur Trade in Minnesota: An Introductory Guide to Manuscript Sources. 61p. 1977. pap. 4.50 (ISBN 0-87351-121-2). Minn Hist.

White, Bruce M., et alcompiled by. Minnesota Votes: Election Returns by County for Presidents, Senators, Congressmen, & Governors 1857-1976. 234p. 1977. pap. 8.50 (ISBN 0-87351-107-7). Minn Hist.

Wirth, Fremont P. The Discovery & Exploitation of the Minnesota Iron Lands. Bruchey, Stuart, ed. LC 78-53544. (Development of Public Lands in the U. S. Ser.). 1979. Repr. of 1937 ed. lib. bdg. 16.00x (ISBN 0-405-11393-5). Arno.

MINNESOTA–HISTORY–BIBLIOGRAPHY

Brook, Michael, compiled by. Reference Guide to Minnesota History: A Subject Bibliography of Books, Pamphlets & Articles in English. LC 74-4222. 132p. 1974. pap. 7.50 (ISBN 0-87351-082-8). Minn Hist.

Fogerty, James E., compiled by. Manuscripts Collections of the Minnesota Regional Research Centers: Guide No. 2. 92p. 1979. pap. 4.50 (ISBN 0-87351-150-6). Minn Hist.

Matters, Marion, compiled by. Minnesota State Archives Preliminary Check List. 92p. 1979. pap. 3.00x (ISBN 0-87351-136-0). Minn Hist.

Mitau, G. Theodore. A Selected Bibliography of Minnesota Government, Politics, & Public Finance Since 1900. (Studies in Minn. Govt. & Politics). 94p. 1960. pap. 2.50 (ISBN 0-685-47099-7). Minn Hist.

Vance, Mary. Historical Society Architectural Publications: Massachusetts, Michigan,Minnesota, Mississippi, Missouri. (Architecture Ser.: Bibliography A-159). 75p. 1980. pap. 8.00 (ISBN 0-686-26907-1). Vance Biblios.

MINNESOTA–JUVENILE LITERATURE

Bailey, Bernadine. Picture Book of Minnesota. rev. ed. (Illus.). (gr. 3-5). 1967. 5.50g (ISBN 0-8075-9526-8). A Whitman.

Carpenter, Allan. Minnesota. new ed. LC 78-8000. (New Enchantment of America State Bks.). (Illus.). (gr. 4 up). 1978. PLB 10.60 (ISBN 0-516-04123-1). Childrens.

Densmore, Frances. Dakota & Ojibwe People in Minnesota. LC 77-72282. (Illus.). 55p. (gr. 7-9). 1977. pap. 3.00 (ISBN 0-87351-111-5). Minn Hist.

Fradin, Dennis. Minnesota: In Words & Pictures. LC 79-21543. (Young People's Stories of Our States Ser.). (Illus.). 48p. (gr. 2-5). 1980. PLB 9.25 (ISBN 0-516-03923-7). Childrens.

Stewart, Anne & Roquitte, Ruth. Riches from the Land. LC 78-16326. (Minnesota Adventures Ser.). (Illus.). (gr. 4-6). 1979. pap. text ed. 3.95 (ISBN 0-87518-163-5). Dillon.

MINNESOTA–POLITICS AND GOVERNMENT

Anderson, William. Intergovernmental Relations in Review. LC 73-16639. (Intergovernmental Realtions in the U.S. Research Monograph: No. 10). 178p. 1974. Repr. of 1960 ed. lib. bdg. 20.00x (ISBN 0-8371-7208-X, ANIG). Greenwood.

Bates, James D. Minnesota Legal Forms: Probate. Mason Publishing Staff, ed. 184p. 1981. ring binder 19.95 (ISBN 0-917126-98-X). Mason Pub.

Beyle, Herman C. Identification & Analysis of Attribute-Cluster-Blocs: A Technique for Use in the Investigation of Behavior in Governance. LC 77-108602. 1970. 19.50 (ISBN 0-384-04085-3). Johnson Repr.

Chrislock, Carl H. The Progressive Era in Minnesota, 1899-1918. LC 79-178677. (Public Affairs Center Publication Ser.). (Illus.). 242p. 1971. 7.50 (ISBN 0-87351-067-4). Minn Hist.

Committee for the Inauguration of Wendell R. Anderson. Governors of Minnesota: 1849-1971. (Illus.). 22p. 1971. pap. 2.00 (ISBN 0-685-47097-0). Minn Hist.

Deike, Robert J., et al. Minnesota Real Estate Law Digest. 500p. 1981. price not set (ISBN 0-917126-94-7). Mason Pub.

Gieske, Millard. Minnesota Farmer-Laborism: The Third Party Alternative. LC 79-1115. (Illus.). 1979. 15.00 (ISBN 0-8166-0890-3). U of Minn Pr.

Jerabek, Esther A., compiled by. Check List of Minnesota State Documents, 1858-1923. LC 73-186382. 216p. 1972. pap. 7.00 (ISBN 0-87351-070-4). Minn Hist.

League of Women Voters of Minnesota. Minnesota Judiciary: Structures & Procedures. 2nd ed. (Illus.). 64p. 1981. pap. text ed. 2.00 (ISBN 0-939816-00-8). LWV MN.

McFarland, Douglas D. & Keppel, William J. Minnesota Civil Practice, 4 vols. Incl. Vol. 1 (ISBN 0-917126-09-2); Vol. 2 (ISBN 0-917126-10-6); Vols. 3 & 4 (ISBN 0-917126-11-4) (ISBN 0-917126-12-2). LC 79-88507. 1979. text ed. 50.00 ea.; Set. text ed. 200.00 (ISBN 0-917126-08-4). Mason Pub.

McLean, Daniels W. Minnesota Legal Forms-Family Law. Mason Publishing Staff, ed. 150p. 1981. ring binder 24.00 (ISBN 0-917126-85-8). Mason Pub.

Mason Editorial Staff. Dunnell Minnesota Digest. rev. ed. (Dunnell Minnesota Digest Second Ser.: Vol. 13A). 400p. 1981. 50.00 (ISBN 0-917126-80-7). Mason Pub.

Mayer, George. Political Career of Floyd B. Olson. (Illus.). 1951. 10.00x (ISBN 0-8166-0071-6). U of Minn Pr.

Mitau, G. Theodore. Politics in Minnesota. rev. ed. LC 78-110660. (Illus.). 1970. 7.50x (ISBN 0-8166-0558-0); pap. 3.95x (ISBN 0-8166-0559-9). U of Minn Pr.

Newell, Robert L. Minnesota Legal Forms: Law Office Systems. Mason Publishing Staff, ed. 221p. 1981. 24.00 (ISBN 0-917126-99-8). Mason Pub.

Nichols, Donald H., et al. Driving While Intoxicated in Minnesota. 350p. 1981. 30.00 (ISBN 0-86678-000-9). Mason Pub.

Peck, Michael T. Minnesota Legal Forms: Workers' Compensation. Mason Publishing Staff, ed. 261p. 1981. ring binder 19.95 (ISBN 0-917126-97-1). Mason Pub.

Roer, Kathleen. Minnesota Legal Forms-Residential Real Estate. Mason Publishing Staff, ed. 137p. 1981. ring binder 19.95 (ISBN 0-917126-86-6). Mason Pub.

Smolka, Richard G. Election Day Registration: The Minnesota & Wisconsin Experience in 1976. LC 77-83209. 1977. pap. 4.25 (ISBN 0-8447-3263-X). Am Enterprise.

Spring Hill Center. Solar Energy & Potentials for Minnesota. Hoel, Donna & Ziegenhagen, John, eds. 1978. pap. text ed. 2.50 (ISBN 0-932676-02-2). Spring Hill.

Stewart, Anne & Roquitte, Ruth. A Part of These United States. LC 78-16325. (Minnesota Adventures Ser.). (Illus.). (gr. 4-6). 1979. pap. text ed. 3.95 (ISBN 0-87518-162-7). Dillon.

Swanholm, Marx. Alexander Ramsey & the Politics of Survival. LC 77-23371. (Minnesota Historic Sites Pamphlet Ser.: No. 13). (Illus.). 31p. 1977. pap. 2.00 (ISBN 0-87351-114-X). Minn Hist.

Toensing, Waldemar F., compiled by. Minnesota Congressmen, Legislators, & Other Elected Officials: An Alphabetical Check List, 1849-1971. LC 70-188492. 143p. 1971. pap. 3.75 (ISBN 0-87351-064-X). Minn Hist.

Weidner, Edward W. Intergovernmental Relations As Seen by Public Officials. LC 73-16645. (Intergovernmental Relations in the U.S., Research Monograph: No. 9). 162p. 1974. Repr. of 1960 ed. lib. bdg. 16.75x (ISBN 0-8371-7209-8, WEIR). Greenwood.

White, Bruce M., et alcompiled by. Minnesota Votes: Election Returns by County for Presidents, Senators, Congressmen, & Governors 1857-1976. 234p. 1977. pap. 8.50 (ISBN 0-87351-107-7). Minn Hist.

MINNESOTA, FOOTBALL CLUB (NATIONAL LEAGUE)

Batson, Larry. Alan Page. LC 74-18256. (Sports Superstars Ser). (Illus.). 32p. (gr. 3-9). 1974. PLB 5.95 (ISBN 0-87191-381-X). Creative Ed.

MINNESOTA, UNIVERSITY OF

Davis, Edith & McGinnis, Esther. Parent Education: A Survey of the Minnesota Program. LC 76-141544. (Univ. of Minnesota, the Institute of Child Welfare Monograph: No. 17). (Illus.). 153p. 1975. Repr. of 1939 ed. lib. bdg. 15.00x (ISBN 0-8371-5891-5, CWDP). Greenwood.

Gray, James. University of Minnesota, 1851-1951. (Illus.). 1951. 9.50x (ISBN 0-8166-0069-4). U of Minn Pr.

McDonald, William A. & Rapp, George R., Jr., eds. The Minnesota Messenia Expedition: Reconstructing a Bronze Age Regional Environment. LC 75-187168. (Illus.). 304p. 1972. 22.50x (ISBN 0-8166-0636-6). U of Minn Pr.

Stein, Robert A. In Pursuit of Excellence. (Illus.). 545p. 1980. 24.50 (ISBN 0-917126-13-0). Mason Pub.

Utecht, Bob. This Is Gold Country. LC 77-91022. (Illus.). 1977. pap. 3.95 (ISBN 0-87832-041-5). Piper.

MINNESOTA INFANTRY, 1ST REGIMENT, 1861-1864

Imholte, John Q. First Volunteers. 8.75 (ISBN 0-87018-029-0). Ross.

MINNESOTA MULTIPHASIC PERSONALITY INVENTORY

Ball, John C. Social Deviancy & Adolescent Personality. LC 72-12308. (Illus.). 119p. 1973. Repr. of 1962 ed. lib. bdg. 15.00 (ISBN 0-8371-6687-X, BASD). Greenwood.

Block, Jack. Challenge of Response Sets: Unconfounding Meaning, Acquiescence, & Social Desirability in the M. M. P. I. LC 65-24810. (Century Psychology Ser.). 1965. 22.50x (ISBN 0-89197-069-X); pap. text ed. 6.95x (ISBN 0-89197-070-3). Irvington.

Butcher, James N., ed. New Developments in the Use of the MMPI. LC 79-22093. (Illus.). 1979. 27.50x (ISBN 0-8166-0894-6). U of Minn Pr.

Dahlstrom, W. Grant & Dahlstrom, Leona, eds. Basic Readings on the MMPI: A New Selection on Personality Measurement. 1980. 27.50x (ISBN 0-8166-0903-9). U of Minn Pr.

Dahlstrom, W. Grant, et al. MMPI Handbook, Vol. 1: Clinical Interpretation. revised ed. LC 74-172933. (Illus.). 1972. 35.00x (ISBN 0-8166-0589-0). U of Minn Pr.

--An MMPI Handbook, Vol. 2: Research Applications. rev. ed. LC 74-26244. 624p. 1975. 35.00x (ISBN 0-8166-0725-7). U of Minn Pr.

Drake, Lewis E. & Oetting, Eugene R. MMPI Codebook for Counselors. LC 59-10187. 1959. 10.95x (ISBN 0-8166-0187-9). U of Minn Pr.

Duckworth, Jane. MMPI Interpretation Manual for Counselors & Clinicians. 2nd, rev. ed. LC 79-64500. (Illus.). 1979. pap. text ed. 11.95x (ISBN 0-915202-22-0). Accel Devel.

Faschingbauer, Thomas R. & Newmark, Charles S. Short Forms of the MMPI. LC 77-6934. 1978. 18.95 (ISBN 0-669-01641-1). Lexington Bks.

Good, Patricia K. & Brantner, John. A Practical Guide to the MMPI: An Introduction for Psychologists, Physicians, Social Workers, & Other Professionals. 1974. 9.50x (ISBN 0-8166-0706-0). U of Minn Pr.

Hathaway, Starke R. & Meehl, Paul E. Atlas for the Clinical Use of the MMPI. (Illus.). 1951. 32.50x (ISBN 0-8166-0070-8). U of Minn Pr.

Hathaway, Starke R. & Monachesi, Elio D. Adolescent Personality & Behavior: MMPI Patterns of Normal, Delinquent, Dropout & Other Outcomes. LC 63-23057. 1963. 13.95x (ISBN 0-8166-0310-3). U of Minn Pr.

--Atlas of Juvenile MMPI Profiles. LC 61-8795. 1961. 25.00x (ISBN 0-8166-0232-8). U of Minn Pr.

Lanyon, Richard I. Handbook of MMPI Group Profiles. LC 68-55387. 1968. 13.95x (ISBN 0-8166-0501-7). U of Minn Pr.

Marks, Philip A., et al. The Actuarial Use of the MMPI with Adolescents & Adults. 450p. 1974. 19.95x (ISBN 0-19-502297-1). Oxford U Pr.

Newmark, Charles S., ed. MMPI: Clinical & Research Trends. LC 79-17777. (Praeger Special Studies). 464p. 1979. 35.95 (ISBN 0-03-048926-1). Praeger.

Swenson, Wendell M., et al. An MMPI Source Book: Basic Item, Scale, & Pattern Data on 50,000 Medical Patients. LC 72-95442. 160p. 1973. 10.95x (ISBN 0-8166-0662-5). U of Minn Pr.

MINOAN VASES

see Vases-Crete

MINOAN WRITING

see Greek Language, Mycenaean; Inscriptions-Crete; Inscriptions, Linear A; Inscriptions, Linear B

MINOBE, TATSUKICHI, 1873-1948

Miller, Frank O. Minobe Tatsukichi: Interpreter of Constitutionalism in Japan. (Center for Japanese & Korean Studies, UC Berkeley). 1965. 27.00x (ISBN 0-520-00865-0). U of Cal Pr.

MINOLTA CAMERA

see Cameras-Types-Minolta

MINOR AUTOMOBILE

see Automobiles, Foreign-Types-Morris Minor

MINOR PLANETS

see Planets, Minor

MINOR PROPHETS

see Prophets

MINOR SURGERY

see Surgery, Minor

MINOR TACTICS

see Drill and Minor Tactics

MINORCA-DESCRIPTION AND TRAVEL-GUIDEBOOKS

Foss, Arthur. Ibiza & Minorca. (Illus.). 210p. 1978. 15.95 (ISBN 0-571-10487-8, Pub. by Faber & Faber); pap. 7.95 (ISBN 0-571-11220-X). Merrimack Bk Serv.

Thurson, Hazel. The Balearic Islands: Majorca, Minorca, Ibiza & Formentera. 1977. 19.95 (ISBN 0-7134-0882-0). David & Charles.

MINORESSES

see Poor Clares

MINORITES

see Franciscans

MINORITIES

see also Assimilation (Sociology); Discrimination; Ethnic Attitudes; Jews-Diaspora; Majorities; Nationalism; Population Transfers; Proportional Representation; Race Discrimination; Race Relations; Segregation; Self-Determination, National;

also names of individual races of peoples, e.g. Chinese in Foreign Countries; Germans in the United States; also subdivisions Foreign Population and Race relations under names of countries, cities, etc.

Abraham, Roger D. & Troike, Rudolph D., eds. Language & Cultural Diversity in American Education. 384p. 1972. pap. text ed. 9.95 (ISBN 0-13-522888-3). P-H.

Alcock, Antony E., et al, eds. The Future of Cultural Minorities. LC 78-13725. 1979. 19.95x (ISBN 0-312-31470-1). St Martin.

Allswang, John M. A House for All Peoples: Ethnic Politics in Chicago, 1890-1936. LC 76-119810. (Illus.). 264p. 1971. 16.00x (ISBN 0-8131-1226-5). U Pr of Ky.

--The Political Behavior of Chicago's Ethnic Groups, 1918-1932. LC 80-837. (American Ethnic Groups Ser.). 1981. lib. bdg. 29.00x (ISBN 0-405-13401-0). Arno.

Appel, John J. Immigrant Historical Societies in the United States, 1880-1950. Cordasco, Francesco, ed. LC 80-838. (American Ethnic Groups Ser.). 1981. lib. bdg. 39.00x (ISBN 0-405-13402-9). Arno.

Ashnorth, Georgina, ed. World Minorities, Vol. 2. pap. 8.95 (ISBN 0-905898-01-X). Transatlantic.

Atkinson, Donald R. & Morten, George. Counseling American Minorities: A Cross-Cultural Perspective. 1979. pap. text ed. write for info. (ISBN 0-697-06629-0). Wm C Brown.

Banks, James A. Teaching Strategies for Ethnic Studies. 2nd ed. 1979. text ed. 19.95 (ISBN 0-205-06587-2, 2365855); pap. text ed. 10.95 (ISBN 0-205-06587-2). Allyn.

Bean, Frank D. & Frisbie, W. Parker, eds. Demography of Racial & Ethnic Groups. (Studies in Population Ser.). 1978. 29.50 (ISBN 0-12-083650-5). Acad Pr.

Bengelsdorf, Winnie. Ethnic Studies in Higher Education. Cordasco, Francesco, ed. LC 77-90407. (Bilingual-Bicultural Education in the U. S. Ser.). 1978. Repr. of 1972 ed. lib. bdg. 19.00x (ISBN 0-405-11076-6). Arno.

Berger, David G. They All Look Alike. LC 75-5370. 1975. soft bdg. 9.00 (ISBN 0-685-64833-8). R & E Res Assoc.

Bernardo, Stephanie. The Ethnic Almanac. LC 78-14694. (Illus.). 576p. 1981. 19.95 (ISBN 0-385-14143-2). Doubleday.

Bertelsen, Judy S., ed. Non-State Nations in International Politics: Comparative System Analyses. LC 75-36404. 1978. text ed. 29.95 (ISBN 0-275-56320-0). Praeger.

Bettelheim, Bruno & Janowitz, M. B. Social Change & Prejudice. LC 64-11214. 1964. 15.95 (ISBN 0-02-903480-9). Free Pr.

Bodnar, John E., ed. & intro. by. The Ethnic Experience in Pennsylvania. LC 72-3257. (Illus.). 330p. 1973. 18.00 (ISBN 0-8387-1155-3). Bucknell U Pr.

Brody, Eugene B. Minority Group Adolescents in the United States. LC 78-20769. 256p. 1979. Repr. of 1968 ed. lib. bdg. 11.50 (ISBN 0-88275-849-7). Krieger.

Brooks, Charlotte, ed. The Outnumbered: Stories, Essays & Poems About Minority Groups by America's Leading Writers. (Orig.). (gr. 6-9). 1967. pap. 0.95 (ISBN 0-440-96772-4, LFL). Dell.

Brown, Francis J. One America: The History, Contributions, & Present Problems of Our Racial & National Minorities. LC 72-111566. Repr. of 1952 ed. 34.00x (ISBN 0-8371-4587-2). Greenwood.

Brown, R. Craig, ed. Minorities, Schools & Politics. LC 23-16213. (Canadian Historical Readings Ser.: No. 7). 1969. pap. 2.50x (ISBN 0-8020-1617-0). U of Toronto Pr.

Buenker, John D. & Burckel, Nicholas C. Immigration & Ethnicity: A Guide to Information Sources. LC 74-11515. (American Government & History Information Guide Ser.: Vol. 1). 1977. 36.00 (ISBN 0-8103-1202-6). Gale.

Butcher, Philip. The Minority Presence in American Literature 1600-1900, 2 vols. LC 77-5687. 1977. Vol. 1. 12.95 (ISBN 0-88258-101-5); Vol. 2. 11.95 (ISBN 0-88258-102-3); Vol. 1. pap. 7.95 (ISBN 0-88258-061-2); Vol. 2. pap. 6.95 (ISBN 0-88258-100-7). Howard U Pr.

Cazden, Courtney B., et al, eds. Functions of Language in the Classroom. LC 78-173091. 1972. pap. 10.95x (ISBN 0-8077-1142-X). Tchrs Coll.

Chandras, Kananur V. Arab, Armenian, Syrian, Lebanese, East Indian, Pakistani & Bangla Deshi Americans: A Study Guide & Source Book. LC 77-81032. 1977. soft bdg. 6.00 (ISBN 0-88247-475-8). R & E Res Assoc.

Chandras, Kananur V., ed. Racial Discrimination Against Neither-White-nor-Black American Minorities. LC 77-91409. 1978. soft cover 11.00 (ISBN 0-88247-497-9). R & E Res Assoc.

Chauhan, Shivdan Singh. Nationalities Question in USA & USSR: A Comparative Study. 1977. text ed. 9.00x (ISBN 0-8426-0948-2). Verry.

Claerbaut, David, ed. New Directions in Ethnic Studies: Minorities in America. LC 80-69329. 115p. 1981. perfect bdg. 8.50 (ISBN 0-86548-026-5). Century Twenty One.

Clarke, Susan E. & Obler, Jeffrey L., eds. Urban Ethnic Conflict: A Comparative Perspective. LC 77-686. (Comparative Urban Studies Monograph: No.3). 1976. pap. text ed. 5.50 (ISBN 0-89143-046-6). U NC Inst Res Soc Sci.

Claude, Inis L. National Minorities: An International Problem. LC 78-90486. Repr. of 1955 ed. lib. bdg. 15.00x (ISBN 0-8371-2283-X, CLMN). Greenwood.

Cole, Katherine W., ed. Minority Organizations: A National Directory. (Illus.). 1978. pap. 16.00 (ISBN 0-912048-78-6). Garrett Pk.

Collier, Joseph, ed. American Ethnics & Minorities. LC 78-70396. (Illus.). 1978. pap. text ed. 6.95x (ISBN 0-89260-076-4). Hwong Pub.

Coppa, Frank J. & Curran, Thomas J. The Immigrant Experience in America. (Immigrant Heritage of America Ser). 1977. lib. bdg. 9.95 (ISBN 0-8057-8406-3). Twayne.

Cordasco, Francesco, ed. Materials & Human Resources for Teaching Ethnic Studies. LC 77-17706. (Bilingual-Bicultural Education in the U. S. Ser.). 1978. Repr. of 1975 ed. lib. bdg. 20.00x (ISBN 0-405-11088-X). Arno.

Crockett, Harry J., Jr. & Schulman, Jerome L., eds. Achievement Among Minority Americans: A Conference Report. 148p. 1972. text ed. 11.25x (ISBN 0-87073-658-2); pap. 4.50x (ISBN 0-87073-659-0). Schenkman.

Cunningham, Barbara, ed. The New Jersey Ethnic Experience. LC 77-77851. (Illus.). 1977. 14.95 (ISBN 0-8349-7534-3). W H Wise.

Curry, Ann. Teaching About the Other Americans: Minorities in United States History. LC 80-69120. 110p. 1981. perfect bdg. 8.95 (ISBN 0-86548-028-1). Century Twenty One.

Davis, F. James. Minority-Dominant Relations: A Sociological Analysis. LC 77-90659. 1978. pap. text ed. 11.95x (ISBN 0-88295-209-9). Harlan Davidson.

--Understanding Minority Dominant Relations: Sociological Contributions. LC 77-90671. 1979. 12.95x (ISBN 0-88295-210-2). Harlan Davidson.

Dean, John P. & Rosen, Alex. Manual of Intergroup Relations. LC 56-5141. 1963. pap. 4.50x (ISBN 0-226-13933-6, Phoen). U of Chicago Pr.

Deloria, Vine, Jr. We Talk, You Listen. 1972. pap. 2.45 (ISBN 0-440-59587-8, Delta). Dell.

Dench, Geoff. Maltese in London. 1975. 25.00x (ISBN 0-7100-8067-0). Routledge & Kegan.

De Voto, Bernard A. Minority Report. facs. ed. LC 71-142619. (Essay Index Reprint Ser). 1940. 19.00 (ISBN 0-8369-2105-4). Arno.

Dinnerstein, Leonard & Jaher, Frederic C., eds. Uncertain Americans: Readings in Ethnic History. 2nd ed. 1977. pap. text ed. 5.95x (ISBN 0-19-502133-9). Oxford U Pr.

Dinnerstein, Leonard, et al. Natives & Strangers: Ethnic Groups & the Building of America. LC 78-2415. (Illus.). 1979. 15.95 (ISBN 0-19-502426-5); pap. text ed. 6.95 (ISBN 0-19-502427-3). Oxford U Pr.

Dixon, William H. White Conquest, 2 Vols. facs. ed. LC 70-138335. (Black Heritage Library Collection Ser). 1876. Set. 34.75 (ISBN 0-8369-8727-6). Arno.

Doi, Mary L., et al. Pacific-Asian American Research: An Annotated Bibliography. LC 81-4086. (Orig.). 1981. pap. write for info. (ISBN 0-934584-11-7). Pacific-Asian.

Drake, Rollen H. A Comparative Study of the Mentality & Achievement of Mexican & White Children. LC 74-147297. pap. 7.00 (ISBN 0-88247-185-6). R & E Res Assoc.

Dreyer, June. China's Forty Millions. (East Asian Ser.: No. 87). 1977. 16.50x (ISBN 0-674-11964-9). Harvard U Pr.

Dunlap, J. Diseases of Racial & Ethnic Groups. (Illus.). 1979. pap. 2.75 (ISBN 0-686-23755-2). World Intl.

Dunn, Lynn P. Asian Americans: A Study Guide & Source Book. LC 74-31620. 1975. soft bdg. 6.00 (ISBN 0-88247-304-2). R & E Res Assoc.

Dyer, Esther R. Cultural Pluralism & Children's Media. (School Media Centers: Focus on Issues & Trends: No. 1). 1979. pap. 4.50 (ISBN 0-8389-3218-5). ALA.

Ehrlich, Richard L., ed. & intro. by. Immigrants in Industrial America: 1850-1920. LC 76-56376. 1977. 12.50x (ISBN 0-8139-0678-4, Eleutherian Mills -Balch Institute). U Pr of Va.

Enloe, Cynthia. Ethnic Conflict & Political Development: An Analytic Study. (Ser. in Comparative Politics). 282p. 1973. pap. text ed. 8.95 (ISBN 0-316-24020-6). Little.

Faderman, Lillian & Bradshaw, Barbara. Speaking for Ourselves: American Ethnic Writing. 2nd ed. 625p. 1975. pap. 7.95x (ISBN 0-673-07925-2). Scott F.

Farley, John E. Majority-Minority Relations. (Illus.). 384p. 1982. 19.95 (ISBN 0-13-545574-X). P-H.

Feagin, Joe R. & Hahn, Harlan. Ghetto Revolt. 1974. pap. 9.95 (ISBN 0-02-336550-1, 33655). Macmillan.

Fischer, Eric. Minorities & Minority Problems. 1978. 15.00 (ISBN 0-533-03610-0). Vantage.

Ford, David L., Jr., ed. Readings in Minority-Group Relations. LC 74-21570. 356p. 1976. pap. 8.00 (ISBN 0-88390-094-7). Univ Assocs.

Foster, Arnold. Trouble Makers: An Anti Defamation League Report. LC 72-106872. Repr. of 1952 ed. 15.00x (ISBN 0-8371-3289-4). Greenwood.

Foster, Charles R., ed. Nations Without a State: Ethnic Minorities of Western Europe. 304p. 1980. 24.50 (ISBN 0-03-056807-2). Praeger.

Freedman, Morris & Banks, Carolyn. American Mix: The Minority Experience in America. LC 73-170857. 450p. 1972. pap. text ed. 8.50 scp (ISBN 0-397-47201-3, HarpC). Har-Row.

Fromkin, Howard L. & Sherwood, John J., eds. Intergroup & Minority Relations: An Experiential Handbook. LC 74-21569. 182p. 1976. pap. 14.50 (ISBN 0-88390-092-0). Univ Assocs.

Glazer, Nathan & Moynihan, Daniel P. Beyond the Melting Pot: The Negroes, Puerto Ricans, Jews, Italians, & Irish of New York City. 2nd rev ed. 1970. 20.00x (ISBN 0-262-07039-1); pap. 5.95 (ISBN 0-262-57022-X). MIT Pr.

Gloster, Jesse E. Minority Economic, Political & Social Development. LC 78-62738. 1978. pap. text ed. 17.25 (ISBN 0-8191-0593-7). U Pr of Amer.

Gossett, Thomas F. Race: The History of an Idea in America. LC 63-21187. 1963. 12.50 (ISBN 0-87074-065-2). SMU Press.
--Race: The History of an Idea in America. rev. ed. LC 63-21187. (Sourcebooks in Negro History Ser.). (YA) (gr. 7 up). 1965. pap. 8.50 (ISBN 0-8052-0106-8). Schocken.
Greenspan, Charlotte L. & Hirsch, Lester M. All Those Voices: The Minority Experience. 1971. pap. text ed. 8.50 (ISBN 0-02-346910-2, 34691). Macmillan.
Greer, Colin. The Divided Society: The Ethnic Experience in America. LC 73-88029. 1974. 12.50x (ISBN 0-465-01679-0); pap. text ed. 6.95x (ISBN 0-465-01680-4). Basic.
Griessman, B. E. Minorities. LC 74-28207. 399p. 1975. text ed. 15.95 (ISBN 0-03-077675-9, HoltC). HR&W.
Gross, Feliks. World Politics & Tension Areas. LC 65-19520. (Illus.). 1966. 12.50x (ISBN 0-8147-0173-6). NYU Pr.
Haksar, Urmila. Minority Protection & International Bill of Human Rights. 1974. text ed. 9.00x (ISBN 0-8426-0716-1). Verry.
Hall, Raymond L., ed. Ethnic Autonomy: Comparative Dynamics - the Americas, Europe & the Developing World. (Pergamon Policy Studies). 1979. 47.00 (ISBN 0-08-023683-9); pap. 10.95 (ISBN 0-08-023682-0). Pergamon.
Harper, Richard C. The Course of the Melting Pot Idea to 1910. Cordasco, Francesco, ed. LC 80-862. (American Ethnic Groups Ser.). 1981. lib. bdg. 39.00x (ISBN 0-405-13425-8). Arno.
Hartley, Eugene. Problems in Prejudice. LC 70-96197. 1970. Repr. of 1946 ed. lib. bdg. 11.00x (ISBN 0-374-93705-2). Octagon.
Helmer, John. Drugs & Minority Opression. LC 75-2114. 250p. 1975. 9.95 (ISBN 0-8164-9216-6). Continuum.
Henderson, George. Understanding & Counseling Ethnic Minorities. (Illus.). 552p. 1979. text ed. 24.50 (ISBN 0-398-03916-X). C C Thomas.
Hepburn, A. C. Minorities in History. 1979. 27.50x (ISBN 0-312-53423-X). St Martin.
Higham, John. Strangers in the Land: Patterns of American Nativism, 1860 to 1925. LC 80-22204. (Illus.). xiv, 431p. 1981. Repr. of 1963 ed. lib. bdg. 35.50x (ISBN 0-313-22459-5, HISL). Greenwood.
Holli, Melvin & Jones, Peter, eds. The Ethnic Frontier. 1977. pap. 7.95 (ISBN 0-8028-1705-X). Eerdmans.
Hus Sung-Shih. Minorities in Kuangsi & Kuangtung. (National Peking University & Chinese Assn. for Folklore, Folklore & Folkliterature Ser.: No. 89 & 90). (Chinese.). 13.00 (ISBN 0-89986-171-7). E Langstaff.
Institute on Minority Aging. Comprehensive Service Delivery Systems for the Minority Aged: Proceedings, Vol. 4. Stanford, E. Percil, ed. 1978. pap. 6.00 (ISBN 0-916304-40-X). Campanile.
--Retirement Concepts & Realities of Ethnic Minority Elders. Stanford, Percil E., ed. (Vol. 5). (Illus., Orig.). 1979. pap. 6.00 (ISBN 0-916304-44-2). Campanile.
Jackson, Jacquelyne J. Minorities & Aging. 272p. 1979. pap. text ed. 9.95x (ISBN 0-534-00779-1). Wadsworth Pub.
Janowsky, Oscar I. Jews & Minority Rights, 1898-1919. LC 33-31678. (Columbia University. Studies in the Social Sciences: No. 384). Repr. of 1933 ed. 24.50 (ISBN 0-404-51384-0). AMS Pr.
Josey, E. J. & Peeples, Kenneth E., Jr. Opportunities for Minorities in Librarianship. LC 77-375. 1977. 10.00 (ISBN 0-8108-1022-0). Scarecrow.
Kantrowitz, Nathan. Ethnic & Racial Segregation Patterns in the New York City Metropolis: Residential Patterns Among White Ethnic Groups, Blacks & Puerto Ricans. LC 72-86840. (Special Studies in U.S. Economic, Social & Political Issues). 1973. 29.50x (ISBN 0-275-06550-2). Irvington.
Kaplan, Roy, ed. American Minorities & Economic Opportunity. 1977. text ed. 15.95 (ISBN 0-87581-219-8, 219). Peacock Pubs.
Kennedy, Stetson. Jim Crow Guide to the U.S.A. LC 72-12558. 230p. 1973. Repr. of 1959 ed. lib. bdg. 15.00x (ISBN 0-8371-6721-3, KEJC). Greenwood.
Kinloch, Graham C. The Sociology of Minority Group Relations. LC 78-12274. (P-H Series in Sociology). (Illus.). 1979. pap. 10.95 ref.ed. (ISBN 0-13-821017-9). P-H.
Kinton, J. American Ethnic Groups Sourcebook or Supplementary Text. 5th ed. 1980. lib. bdg. 10.95 (ISBN 0-915574-16-0). Soc Sci & Soc Res.
Kolm, Richard. The Change of Cultural Identity: An Analysis of Factors Conditioning the Cultural Integration of Immigrants. Cordasco, Francesco, ed. LC 80-870. (American Ethnic Groups Ser.). 1981. lib. bdg. 25.00x (ISBN 0-405-13432-0). Arno.
Kranz, Harry. The Participatory Bureaucracy: Women & Minorities in a More Representative Public Service. LC 75-44600. (Illus.). 1976. 21.95 (ISBN 0-669-00556-8). Lexington Bks.
Leavis, Frank R. Mass Civilization & Minority Culture. LC 74-20677. 1974. Repr. of 1930 ed. lib. bdg. 7.50 (ISBN 0-8414-5730-1). Folcroft.
Levitan, Sar A., et al. Minorities in the United States. 1976. 4.50 (ISBN 0-8183-0242-9). Pub Aff Pr.
Lieberson, Stanley. Ethnic Patterns in American Cities. LC 63-7551. 1962. 15.95 (ISBN 0-02-918980-2). Free Pr.
Liu, William T., ed. Methodological Problems in Minority Research. LC 80-21325. (Orig.). 1981. pap. write for info. (ISBN 0-934584-09-5). Pacific-Asian.
Luhman, Reid & Gilman, Stuart. Race & Ethnic Relations: The Social & Political Experience of Minority Groups. 352p. 1980. pap. text ed. 13.95x (ISBN 0-534-00795-3). Wadsworth Pub.
Macartney, Carlile A. National States & National Minorities. 2nd ed. LC 68-15136. (With a new intro. & epilogue). 1968. Repr. of 1934 ed. 18.50 (ISBN 0-8462-1266-8). Russell.
McDonagh, Edward C. & Richards, Eugene S. Ethnic Relations in the United States. LC 70-154107. 408p. 1972. Repr. of 1953 ed. 30.00x (ISBN 0-8371-6070-7, MER). Greenwood.
MacIver, R. M. The More Perfect Union: A Program for the Control of Inter-Group Discrimination in the United States. 1971. Repr. of 1948 ed. 17.00 (ISBN 0-02-848760-5). Hafner.
MacIver, R. M., ed. Civilization & Group Relations. LC 68-26193. (Essay & General Literature Index Reprint Ser). 1969. Repr. of 1945 ed. 10.00 (ISBN 0-8046-0224-7). Kennikat.
--Discrimination & National Welfare. LC 68-26187. (Essay & General Literature Index Reprint Ser). 1969. Repr. of 1949 ed. 10.00 (ISBN 0-8046-0226-3). Kennikat.
MacIver, Robert M. Group Relations & Group Antagonisms. 7.50 (ISBN 0-8446-1294-4). Peter Smith.
Mack, Raymond W., ed. Race, Class & Power. 2nd ed. (Orig.). 1968. pap. text ed. 8.95x (ISBN 0-442-23361-2). Van Nos Reinhold.
McNeeley, R. L. & Pope, Carl E., eds. Race, Crime & Criminal Justice. LC 80-28347. (Perspectives in Criminal Justice Ser.: Vol. 2). (Illus.). 176p. 1981. 16.00 (ISBN 0-8039-1584-5). Sage.
--Race, Crime & Criminal Justice. LC 80-28347. (Perspectives in Criminal Justice Ser.: Vol. 2). (Illus.). 176p. 1981. pap. 7.95 (ISBN 0-8039-1585-3). Sage.
McWilliams, Carey. Brothers Under the Skin. rev. ed. 1951. pap. 3.95 (ISBN 0-316-56423-0). Little.
Makielski, S. J., Jr. Beleaguered Minorities: Cultural Politics in America. LC 73-12290. (Illus.). 1973. text ed. 18.95x (ISBN 0-7167-0789-6); pap. text ed. 9.95x (ISBN 0-7167-0788-8). W H Freeman.
Mann, Arthur. The One & the Many: Reflections on the American Identity. LC 78-27849. 1979. 12.95 (ISBN 0-226-50337-2). U of Chicago Pr.
Marden, Charles F. & Meyer, Gladys. Minorities in American Society. 5th ed. 1978. text ed. 13.95 (ISBN 0-442-23460-0). D Van Nostrand.
Medhurst, Kenneth. The Basques. (Minority Rights Group: No. 9). 1972. pap. 2.50 (ISBN 0-89192-098-6). Interbk Inc.
Meeting of the American Orthopsychiatric Assoc., 47th. On the Urban Scene: Proceedings. Levitt, Morton & Rubenstein, Ben, eds. LC 72-1440. 1972. 13.50x (ISBN 0-8143-1478-3). Wayne St U Pr.
Miller, Herbert A. School & the Immigrant. LC 71-129507. (American Immigration Collection, Ser. 2). 1970. Repr. of 1916 ed. 7.00 (ISBN 0-405-00561-X). Arno.
Miller, Wayne Charles, compiled by. A Comprehensive Bibliography for the Study of American Minorities, 2 vols. LC 74-21636. 1400p. 1976. 125.00x (ISBN 0-8147-5373-6). NYU Pr.
--A Handbook of American Minorities. LC 74-21636. 225p. 1976. 30.00x (ISBN 0-8147-5374-4). NYU Pr.
Mims, George L., ed. The Minority Administrator in Higher Education: Progress, Experiences, & Perspectives. 220p. 1981. 22.50x (ISBN 0-87073-161-0); pap. text ed. 8.95x (ISBN 0-87073-162-9). Schenkman.
Minority-Ethnic Media Guide. 1981. 75.00 (ISBN 0-685-79886-0). Directories Intl.
Mosby, Robert. The Degeneration in the Leadership in the United States As the Primary Cause for the Moral, Economic & Political Collapse of the World. (Illus.). 243p. 1976. 25.00 (ISBN 0-913314-67-6); lib. bdg. 39.50 (ISBN 0-685-66467-8). Am Classical Coll Pr.
Nevinson, Henry W. A Modern Slavery. LC 68-9583. 1968. pap. 1.95 (ISBN 0-8052-0201-3). Schocken.
Newman, William M. American Pluralism: A Study of Minority Groups & Social Theory. (Illus.). 307p. 1973. pap. text ed. 10.95 scp (ISBN 0-06-044801-6, HarpC). Har-Row.
Novak, Michael. Rise of the Unmeltable Ethnics. 1972. pap. 3.50 (ISBN 0-02-087800-1, Collier). Macmillan.
Oakland, Thomas, ed. Psychological & Educational Assessment of Minority Children. LC 77-22961. 1977. 17.50 (ISBN 0-87630-145-6). Brunner Mazel.
Orleans, Leo A. Every Fifth Child: The Population of China. LC 70-190527. 192p. 1972. 8.50x (ISBN 0-8047-0819-3). Stanford U Pr.
Ortiz, Flora I. Women, Men Minorities in Public School Administration. 256p. 1981. 24.95x (ISBN 0-686-76473-0). J F Bergin.
Packard, H. Jeremy. Minority-Majority Confrontation in America. (gr. 11-12). 1977. pap. 4.95x (ISBN 0-88334-088-7). Ind Sch Pr.
Palley, Marian & Preston, Michael, eds. Minorities & Policy Studies. 1978. pap. 5.00 (ISBN 0-918592-29-1). Policy Studies.
Palley, Marian L. & Preston, Michael B., eds. Race, Sex, & Policy Problems. (Policy Studies Organization Ser.). (Illus.). 1979. 22.95 (ISBN 0-669-01985-2). Lexington Bks.
Pennsylvania University Bicentennial Conference. Studies in Political Science & Sociology. Shih, Hu & Edwards, Newton, eds. LC 68-26201. Repr. of 1941 ed. 11.50 (ISBN 0-8046-0357-X). Kennikat.
Poatgieter, A. Hermina & Dunn, James T., eds. Gopher Reader 2. LC 74-12072. (Illus.). 316p. 1975. 10.95 (ISBN 0-87351-083-6). Minn Hist.
Radecki, Henry. Ethnic Organizational Dynamics: The Polish Group in Canada. 275p. 1979. text ed. 11.50 (ISBN 0-88920-080-7, Pub. by Laurier U Pr Canada); pap. text ed. 7.75 (ISBN 0-88920-075-0). Humanities.
Ross, Edward A. Standing Room Only? Grob, Gerald, ed. LC 76-46101. (Anti-Movements in America). 1977. Repr. of 1927 ed. lib. bdg. 21.00x (ISBN 0-405-09972-X). Arno.
Rubin, Bernard, ed. Small Voices & Great Trumpets: Minorities & the Media. 295p. 1980. 24.95 (ISBN 0-03-056973-7); pap. 9.95 (ISBN 0-03-056972-9). Praeger.
Ryan, Joseph, ed. White Ethnics: Life in Working Class America. (Human Futures Ser.). 224p. 1974. pap. 2.95 (ISBN 0-13-957704-1, Spec). P-H.
Said, Abdul A. & Simmons, Luiz R., eds. Ethnicity in an International Context. LC 74-20193. 200p. 1976. 12.95x (ISBN 0-87855-110-7). Transaction Bks.
Samuda, Ronald J. Psychological Testing of American Minorities: Issues & Consequences. LC 74-26165. 232p. (Orig.). 1975. pap. text ed. 13.50 scp (ISBN 0-06-045696-5, HarpC). Har-Row.
Saville-Troike, Muriel. A Guide to Culture in the Classroom. LC 78-61039. 67p. 1978. pap. 4.50 (ISBN 0-89763-000-9). Natl Clearinghse Bilingual Ed.
Scarpaci, Jean, ed. The Interaction of Italians & Jews in America. 1974. 4.00 (ISBN 0-686-21891-4). Am Italian.
Schaefer, Richard. Racial & Ethnic Groups. 1979. text ed. 17.95 (ISBN 0-316-77274-7); tchrs' manual free (ISBN 0-316-77275-5). Little.
Schermerhorn, Richard A. Comparative Ethnic Relations: A Framework for Theory & Research. LC 78-55043. 1979. pap. 4.95 (ISBN 0-226-73757-8, P784). U of Chicago Pr.
Seamans, Eldon L. Studies in American Minority Life. 1976. pap. text ed. 7.50 (ISBN 0-8191-0092-7). U Pr of Amer.
Seller, Maxine S. To Seek America: A History of Ethnic Life in the United States. LC 77-8248. 1977. lib. bdg. 14.95x (ISBN 0-89198-117-9); pap. text ed. 7.50x (ISBN 0-89198-118-7). Ozer.
Shannon, Lyle & Shannon, Magdaline. Minority Migrants in the Urban Community: Mexican-American & Negro Adjustment to Industrial Society. LC 72-84055. 352p. 1973. 24.00 (ISBN 0-8039-0158-5). Sage.
Shenton, James P. & Brown, Gene, eds. Ethnic Groups in American Life. LC 77-11053. (Great Contemporary Issues Ser.). 1978. lib. bdg. 35.00x (ISBN 0-405-10310-7). Arno.
Shiloh, Ailon & Selavan, Ida C., eds. Ethnic Groups of America; Their Morbidity, Mortality & Behavior Disorders, Vol. 2: The Blacks. (Illus.). 312p. 1974. 24.50 (ISBN 0-398-03022-7); pap. 17.50 (ISBN 0-398-03023-5). C C Thomas.
Shiloh, Ailon & Selevan, Ida C., eds. Ethnic Groups of America: Their Morbidity, Mortality & Behavior Disorders, Vol. 1. The Jews. (Illus.). 446p. 1973. text ed. 24.50 (ISBN 0-398-02610-6); pap. text ed. 17.50 (ISBN 0-398-02619-X). C C Thomas.
Simpson, George E. & Yinger, Milton, Jr. Racial & Cultural Minorities: An Analysis of Prejudice & Discrimination. 4th ed. 1972. text ed. 24.95 scp (ISBN 0-06-046212-4, HarpC). Har-Row.
Spicer, Edward H. & Thompson, Raymond H., eds. Plural Society in the Southwest. 380p. 1972. 5.95 (ISBN 0-913456-53-5). Interbk Inc.
Spindler, G. D. & Spindler, L. S. Urban Anthropology in the U.S. Four Cases. LC 77-16671. 1978. pap. 7.95 (ISBN 0-03-039721-9, HoltC). HR&W.
Stein, Howard F. & Hill, Robert F. The Ethnic Imperative: Examining the New White Ethnic Movement. LC 77-1694. (Illus.). 1977. 15.95 (ISBN 0-271-00508-4). Pa St U Pr.
Stone, James C. & DeNevi, Donald. Teaching Multi-Cultural Populations: Five Heritages. 1971. pap. text ed. 11.95x (ISBN 0-442-27912-4). Van Nos Reinhold.
Study on the Rights of Persons Belonging to Ethnic, Religious & Linguistic Minorities. 114p. 1979. pap. 11.00 (ISBN 0-686-61481-X, UN78-14-1, UN). Unipub.
U. S. House of Representatives, General Subcommittee on Education & Labor. United States Ethnic Heritage Studies Center. Cordasco, Francesco, ed. LC 77-90564. (Bilingual-Bicultural Education in the U. S. Ser.). 1978. Repr. of 1970 ed. lib. bdg. 25.00x (ISBN 0-405-11102-9). Arno.
Vander Zanden, James W. American Minority Relations. 3rd ed. 1972. 19.50x (ISBN 0-8260-8870-8). Wiley.
Von Vorys, Karl. Democracy Without Consensus: Communalism & Political Stability in Malaysia. 512p. 1975. 31.00x (ISBN 0-691-07571-9). Princeton U Pr.
Wagley, Charles & Harris, Marvin. Minorities in the New World: Six Case Studies. LC 58-12214. 1958. 20.00x (ISBN 0-231-02280-8); pap. 6.00x (ISBN 0-231-08557-5). Columbia U Pr.
Warner, William L. Social Systems of American Ethnic Groups. LC 75-31425. (Yankee City Series: Vol. 3). (Illus.). 318p. 1976. Repr. of 1945 ed. lib. bdg. 18.00x (ISBN 0-8371-8502-5, WAAE). Greenwood.
Washburn, David. Directory of Ethnic Studies in Pennsylvania. LC 77-28612. 1978. pap. text ed. 6.95 (ISBN 0-916002-33-0, Pub. by U Ctr Intl St). U of Pittsburgh Pr.
Washburn, David E. Ethnic Studies in Pennsylvania. LC 78-23822. (Orig.). 1978. pap. text ed. 3.95 (ISBN 0-916002-35-7, Pub. by U Ctr Intl St). U of Pittsburgh Pr.
Wasserman, Paul & Morgan, Jean, eds. Ethnic Information Sources of the United States: A Guide to Organizations, Agencies, Foundations, Institutions, Media, Commercial & Trade Bodies, Government Programs, Research Institutes, Libraries & Museums, Etc. LC 76-4642. 350p. 1976. 78.00 (ISBN 0-8103-0373-6). Gale.
Weaver, Jerry L. National Health Policy & the Underserved: Ethic Minorities, Women, & the Elderly. LC 76-6955. (Issues & Problems in Health Care). 176p. 1976. pap. 8.25 (ISBN 0-8016-5360-6). Mosby.
Weiser, Marjorie P., ed. Ethnic America. (Reference Shelf Ser.: Vol. 50, No. 2). 1978. 6.25 (ISBN 0-8242-0623-1). Wilson.
Wesley, Roland, ed. The Journal of Contemporary Minority Issues. 1979. write for info. (ISBN 0-934872-00-7). Carlinshar.
Whitaker, Ben. Biharis in Bangladesh. (Minority Rights Group: No. 11). 1972. pap. 2.50 (ISBN 0-89192-100-1). Interbk Inc.
Whitaker, Ben, ed. The Fourth World: Victims of Group Oppression. LC 72-93008. 1973. 10.00x (ISBN 0-8052-3482-9). Schocken.
Whitten, Norman E., Jr. Cultural Transformations & Ethnicity in Modern Ecuador. LC 81-4402. 850p. 1981. 33.95 (ISBN 0-252-00832-4). U of Ill Pr.
Williams, Robin M., Jr. Reduction of Intergroup Tensions. LC 47-6441. 1947. pap. 3.25 (ISBN 0-527-03285-9). Kraus Repr.
Wilson, James. Canada's Indians. (Minority Rights Group: No. 21). 1974. pap. 2.50 (ISBN 0-89192-107-9). Interbk Inc.
Wirsing, Robert G., ed. Protection of Ethnic Minorities: Comparative Perspectives. LC 80-25618. (Pergamon Policy Studies on International Politics). 350p. 1981. 39.50 (ISBN 0-08-025556-6). Pergamon.
Woolfolk, George R. The Free Negro in Texas, 1800-1860: A Study in Cultural Compromise. LC 76-48791. 1976. 20.00 (ISBN 0-8357-0192-1, SS-00020). Univ Microfilms.
Wynar, Lubomyr R. Encyclopedic Directory of Ethnic Organizations in the United States. LC 75-28150. 440p. 1975. lib. bdg. 25.00x (ISBN 0-87287-120-7). Libs Unl.
Yinger, John M. Minority Group in American Society. 1965. text ed. 10.95 (ISBN 0-07-072271-4, C); pap. text ed. 6.95 (ISBN 0-07-072270-6). McGraw.

Young, Donald. American Minority Peoples. 1932. 15.00 (ISBN 0-686-17716-9). Quality Lib.

MINORITIES–BIBLIOGRAPHY

Allworth, Edward. Soviet Asia: Bibliographies. LC 73-9061. (Illus.). 756p. 1976. text ed. 54.95 (ISBN 0-275-07540-0). Praeger.

Barton, Josef J., compiled by. Brief Ethnic Bibliography: An Annotated Guide to the Ethnic Experience in the U. S. LC 76-1282. 56p. pap. 2.75 (ISBN 0-916704-00-9). Langdon Assocs.

Buttlar, Lois & Wynar, Lubomyr R. Building Ethnic Collections: An Annotated Guide for School Media Centers and Public Libraries. LC 76-55398. 1977. lib. bdg. 22.50x (ISBN 0-87287-130-4). Libs Unl.

Calvert, Robert, Jr. Affirmative Action: A Comprehensive Recruitment Manual. LC 79-50634. 380p. 1979. pap. 15.00 (ISBN 0-912048-79-4). Garrett Pk.

Herrera, Diane, ed. Puerto Ricans & Other Minority Groups in the Continetal United States: An Annotated Bibliography. 1979. Repr. of 1973 ed. 30.00 (ISBN 0-87917-067-0). Blaine-Ethridge.

Jackson, Clara O. Bibliography of Afro-American & Other American Minorities Represented in Library & Library Related Listings. (Bibliographical Ser.: No. 9). 1972. 1.50 (ISBN 0-89977-013-4). Am Inst Marxist.

Johnson, Harry A., ed. Ethnic American Minorities: A Guide to Media & Materials. LC 76-25038. 1976. 21.50 (ISBN 0-8352-0766-8). Bowker.

Monarch Notes on Introduction to American Minority Literature. pap. 1.50 (ISBN 0-671-00962-1). Monarch Pr.

Oaks, Priscilla S. Minority Studies: An Annotated Bibliography. (Series Seventy). 200p. 1976. lib. bdg. 22.00 (ISBN 0-8161-1092-1). G K Hall.

Schlachter, Gail A. & Belli, Donna. Minorities & Women: A Guide to Reference Literature in the Social Sciences. LC 76-53061. 19.50 (ISBN 0-918276-01-2). Ref Serv Pr.

MINORITIES–ECONOMIC CONDITIONS

Blalock, Hubert M. Race & Ethnic Relations. (Foundations of Modern Sociology Ser.). (Illus.). 160p. 1982. 11.95 (ISBN 0-13-750182-X); pap. 5.95 (ISBN 0-13-750174-9). P-H.

Nelson, Esther B. A Model Community Counseling Program for Ethnic Minority Low Income Women. LC 79-65258. 140p. 1979. perfect bdg. 9.00 (ISBN 0-88247-586-X). R & E Res Assoc.

Sowell, Thomas. Markets & Minorities. LC 81-66107. 160p. 1981. 12.95 (ISBN 0-465-04398-4); pap. 5.95x (ISBN 0-465-04399-2). Basic.

Wilson, Franklin D. Residential Consumption, Economic Opportunity & Race. LC 79-51705. (Studies in Population). 1979. 19.50 (ISBN 0-12-757980-X). Acad Pr.

MINORITIES–EDUCATION

Bailey, Robert L. & Hafner, Anne L. Minority Admissions. LC 77-18360. (Illus.). 1978. 21.00 (ISBN 0-669-02095-8). Lexington Bks.

Beyond Desegregation: Urgent Issues in the Education of Minorities. LC 77-95022. 1978. pap. 6.00 (ISBN 0-87447-006-4, 211150). College Bd.

Bresnick, David, et al. Black-White-Green-Red: The Politics of Education in Ethnic America. LC 77-18306. (Educational Policy, Planning, & Theory Ser.). 1978. pap. text ed. 6.95x (ISBN 0-582-28042-7). Longman.

Cabrera, Y. Arturo. Minorities in Higher Education. LC 78-68819. 1978. pap. 7.95x (ISBN 0-932848-01-X). Sierra Pubns CO.

Cabrera, Y. Arturo & Perea, Jose A. Community College Conflict: Chicano Under Fire. LC 78-56755. (Illus.). 1979. pap. 5.95x (ISBN 0-932848-03-6). Sierra Pubns CO.

Calvert, Robert, Jr. Affirmative Action: A Comprehensive Recruitment Manual. LC 79-50634. 380p. 1979. pap. 15.00 (ISBN 0-912048-79-4). Garrett Pk.

Castaneda, Alfredo, et al. The Educational Needs of Minority Groups. LC 74-83020. (The Professional Education Ser.). 112p. (Orig.). 1974. pap. text ed. 2.75 (ISBN 0-88224-043-9). Cliffs.

Conference on Civil & Human Rights in Education, 11th. Student Displacement-Exclusion: Violations of Civil & Human Rights. LC 73-9751. 64p. 1973. pap. 1.50 (ISBN 0-8106-0543-0). NEA.

Cooke, Edwin D., Jr. Interpersonal Orientation of Elementary Teachers with Mexican-American Pupils. LC 74-76566. 1975. Repr. of 1967 ed. soft bdg. 9.00 (ISBN 0-88247-352-2). R & E Res Assoc.

Crossland, Fred E. Minority Access to College: A Ford Foundation Report. LC 73-152572. 1971. 4.95x (ISBN 0-8052-3408-X). Schocken.

Dunfee, Maxine. Ethnic Modification of the Curriculum. new ed. LC 74-129363. 51p. 1970. pap. text ed. 1.00 (ISBN 0-87120-022-8, 611-17832). Assn Supervision.

Farmer, George L. Education: The Dilemma of the Spanish-Surname American. 1968. 15.00x (ISBN 0-913330-13-2). Sun Dance Bks.

Farrell, John J. The Immigrant & the School in New York City: A Program for Citizenship. Cordasco, Francesco, ed. LC 80-845. (American Ethnic Groups Ser.). 1981. lib. bdg. 19.00x (ISBN 0-405-13417-7). Arno.

Franklin, Vincent P. The Education of Black Philadelphia: The Social & Educational History of a Minority Community, Nineteen Hundred to Nineteen Fifty. LC 79-5045. (Illus.). 1979. 19.95 (ISBN 0-8122-7769-4). U of Pa Pr.

Gilbert, Fontelle, ed. Minorities & Community Colleges. 1979. pap. 7.50 (ISBN 0-87117-091-4). Am Assn Comm Jr Coll.

Grant, Carl A., et al. The Public School & the Challenge of Ethnic Pluralism. LC 80-21315. 1981. pap. 2.95 (ISBN 0-8298-0421-8). Pilgrim NY.

Herman, Judith, ed. The Schools & Group Identity: Educating for a New Pluralism. (Illus.). 1974. pap. 1.75 (ISBN 0-87495-010-4). Am Jewish Comm.

Jones, Reginald L., ed. Mainstreaming & the Minority Child. 1976. pap. text ed. 5.00x (ISBN 0-86586-051-3). Coun Exc Child.

Krug, Mark. The Melting of the Ethnics: Education of the Immigrants, 1880-1914. LC 75-26385. (Foundation Monograph Ser.). 1976. 10.00 (ISBN 0-87367-409-X); pap. 5.00 (ISBN 0-87367-415-4). Phi Delta Kappa.

Linskie, Rosella & Rosenberg, Howard. A Handbook for Multicultural Studies in Elementary Schools, Bk. 1: Chicano, Black, Asian & Native Americans. LC 77-91289. 1978. soft cover 6.00 (ISBN 0-88247-494-4). R & E Res Assoc.

Megarry, Jacquetta, et al, eds. World Yearbook of Education 1981: Education of Minorities. 422p. 1981. 35.00x (ISBN 0-89397-105-7). Nichols Pub.

Melnick, V. L. & Hamilton, F. D. Minorities in Science: The Challenge for Change in Biomedicine. LC 77-9462. (Illus.). 296p. 1977. 19.50 (ISBN 0-306-31033-3). Plenum Pub.

Morris, Lorenzo. Elusive Equality: The Status of Black Americans in Higher Education. LC 79-2576. 1979. pap. 10.95 (ISBN 0-88258-080-9). Howard U Pr.

Morris, Lorenzo & Henry, Charles. The Chit'lin Controversy: Race & Public Policy in America. 1978. pap. text ed. 7.75 (ISBN 0-8191-0471-X). U Pr of Amer.

NAIS Admission & Minority Affairs Committees. Recruiting Minority Students. 1979. pap. 3.25 (ISBN 0-934338-41-8). NAIS.

National Association for Women Deans, Administrators & Counselors. What, Then, Is a Human Being...? 1973. pap. 3.00 (ISBN 0-686-09580-4). Natl Assn Women.

National Association of Women Deans & Counselors. Alternative Roles. 1973. pap. 3.00 (ISBN 0-686-09579-0). Natl Assn Women.

National Board on Graduate Education. Minority Group Participation in Graduate Education. LC 76-16850. 1976. pap. 7.00 (ISBN 0-309-02502-8). Natl Acad Pr.

Oakland, Thomas, ed. Psychological & Educational Assessment of Minority Children. LC 77-22961. 1977. 17.50 (ISBN 0-87630-145-6). Brunner Mazel.

Oakland, Thomas & Phillips, Beeman N., eds. Assessing Minority Group Children. LC 68-52341. 128p. 1973. text ed. 12.95 (ISBN 0-87705-154-2). Human Sci Pr.

Ockerman, Janet D. Self-Esteem & Social Anchorage of Adolescent White, Black & Mexican American Students. LC 79-65267. 135p. 1979. perfect bdg. 10.00 (ISBN 0-88247-587-8). R & E Res Assoc.

Ogbu, John. The Next Generation: An Ethnography of Education in an Urban Neighborhood. (Studies in Anthropology Ser). 1974. 25.50 (ISBN 0-12-785589-0). Acad Pr.

Olivas, Michael. The Dilemma of Access: Minorities in Two Year Colleges. LC 79-2575. 1979. 8.95 (ISBN 0-88258-079-5). Howard U Pr.

Pasternak, Michael G. Helping Kids Learn Multi-Cultural Concepts: A Handbook of Strategies. LC 79-63052. (Illus.). 1979. pap. text ed. 9.95 (ISBN 0-87822-194-8). Res Press.

Peterson, Marvin W., et al. Black Students on White Campuses: The Impacts of Increased Black Enrollments. LC 78-60965. 384p. 1978. text ed. 16.00 (ISBN 0-87944-221-2). Inst Soc Res.

Sourcebook of Equal Educational Opportunity. 2nd ed. LC 77-75482. Orig. Title: Yearbook of Equal Educational Opportunity. 1977. 39.50 (ISBN 0-8379-2902-4). Marquis.

Spolsky, Bernard, ed. The Language Education of Minority Children. 1972. pap. 10.95 (ISBN 0-912066-65-2). Newbury Hse.

Stent, Madelon D. Cultural Pluralism in Education: A Mandate for Change. new ed. Hazard, William R. & Rivlin, Harry N., eds. LC 72-92109. 1973. 13.95 (ISBN 0-13-195461-X). P-H.

Telfer, Judie. Training Minority Journalists: A Case Study of the San Francisco Examiner Intern Program. LC 73-4313. 124p. (Orig.). 1973. pap. 4.00x (ISBN 0-87772-169-6). Inst Gov Stud Berk.

Thomas, Judith A. Interethnic Sensitivity Materials for Educators Who Want to Know. 1978. pap. text ed. 10.00 (ISBN 0-8191-0387-X). U Pr of Amer.

Ulin, Richard O. The Italo-American Student in the American Public School. LC 74-17957. (Italian American Experience Ser). (Illus.). 226p. 1975. 18.00x (ISBN 0-405-06426-8). Arno.

Wargo, Michael J. & Green, Donald R., eds. Achievement Testing of Disadvantaged & Minority Students for Educational Program Evaluation. new ed. LC 78-4519. (Orig.). 1978. pap. 8.95 (ISBN 0-07-068282-8, 99814). CTB McGraw-Hill.

Watson, Bernard C. In Spite of the System: The Individual & Educational Reform. LC 74-16370. 1974. text ed. 16.00 (ISBN 0-88410-159-2). Ballinger Pub.

Weinberg, M. A Chance to Learn. LC 76-4235. (Illus.). 1977. 37.50 (ISBN 0-521-21303-7); pap. 9.95x (ISBN 0-521-29128-3). Cambridge U Pr.

White, Isaiah E. A Black Principal Looks Back with Hope. 1978. 5.95 (ISBN 0-533-03355-1). Vantage.

MINORITIES–EMPLOYMENT

see also Affirmative Action Programs

Almquist, Elizabeth M. Minorities, Gender & Work. LC 77-4537. 1979. 19.95 (ISBN 0-669-01488-5). Lexington Bks.

Bullock, Paul, ed. Minorities in the Labor Market: American Indians, Asian Americans, Blacks, & Chicanos. 1978. 5.50 (ISBN 0-89215-095-5). U Cal LA Indus Rel.

Calvert, Robert, Jr. Affirmative Action: A Comprehensive Recruitment Manual. LC 79-50634. 380p. 1979. pap. 15.00 (ISBN 0-912048-79-4). Garrett Pk.

Council on Economic Priorities & Simcich, Tina L. Women & Minorities in Banking: Shortchanged-Update. LC 76-50522. 1977. 20.95 (ISBN 0-03-040336-7). Praeger.

Directory of Career Resources for Minorities. 1st ed. 37.50 (ISBN 0-916270-16-5). Ready Ref Pr.

Glover, Robert W. Minority Enterprise in Construction. LC 77-10650. (Praeger Special Studies). 22.95 (ISBN 0-275-24070-3). Praeger.

Lecht, Leonard A. Occupational Choices & Training Needs. LC 76-24356. (Special Studies). 1977. text ed. 23.95 (ISBN 0-275-23960-8). Praeger.

Lusterman, Seymour. Minorities in Engineering: The Corporate Role. LC 79-51320. (Report Ser.: No. 756). (Illus.). 1979. pap. 15.00 (ISBN 0-8237-0192-1). Conference Bd.

Melnick, Vijaya L. & Hamilton, Franklin D., eds. Minorities in Science: The Challenge for Change in Biomedicine. LC 77-9465. 296p. 1977. softcover 6.95 (ISBN 0-306-20027-9, Rosetta). Plenum Pub.

Mizio, Emelicia & Delaney, Anita J., eds. Training for Service Delivery to Minority Clients. 1980. pap. 10.95 (ISBN 0-87304-180-1). Family Serv.

Morrison, James H. Human Factors in Supervising Minority Group Employees: Conference Leader's Guide. 207p. 1970. pap. 18.00 (ISBN 0-87373-352-5). Intl Personnel Mgmt.

MSC Associates, Inc. Affirmative Action Book. 123p. 1976. text ed. 75.00 (ISBN 0-201-00209-4). A-W.

Odegaard, Charles E. Minorities in Medicine - from Receptive Passivity to Positive Action 1966-76: Report of a Study. LC 77-75502. (Illus.). 1977. pap. 4.00 (ISBN 0-914362-20-8). J Macy Foun.

Pepper. Affirmative Action Plan Workbook for Federal Contractors. 2nd ed. 1979. pap. 45.00 (ISBN 0-917386-31-0). Exec Ent.

Reid, Peter. Affirmative Action Compliance Kit: Eed Dictionary. 1980. pap. 10.00 (ISBN 0-917386-35-3). Exec Ent.

--Affirmative Action Compliance Kit: Reference Guide. 1980. pap. 15.00 (ISBN 0-917386-34-5). Exec Ent.

--Affirmative Action Compliance Kit: Working Manual. 1980. pap. 75.00 (ISBN 0-917386-33-7). Exec Ent.

Roche, G. The Balancing Act: Quota Hiring in Higher Education. LC 74-11130. 1974. pap. 2.95 (ISBN 0-87548-305-4). Open Court.

Rosen, Doris B. Employment Testing & Minority Groups. (Key Issues Ser.: No. 6). 1970. pap. 2.00 (ISBN 0-87546-239-1). NY Sch Indus Rel.

Simmons. California Prsonnel Managers Guide to EEO Laws. 1980. pap. 25.00 (ISBN 0-917386-40-X). Exec Ent.

Solving EEO Problems. 1980. pap. 9.95 (ISBN 0-917386-36-1). Exec Ent.

Taylor, Vernon R. Employment of the Disadvantaged in the Public Service. 1971. 3.00 (ISBN 0-87373-283-9). Intl Personnel Mgmt.

Young, Donald. Research Memorandum on Minority Peoples in the Depression. LC 74-162841. (Studies in the Social Aspects of the Depression). 1971. Repr. of 1937 ed. 12.00 (ISBN 0-405-00844-9). Arno.

MINORITIES–SOCIAL CONDITIONS

Dana, Richard H. Human Services for Cultural Minorities. 300p. (Orig.). 1981. pap. text ed. 17.95 (ISBN 0-8391-1687-X). Univ Park.

Dubois, Betty Lou & Crouch, Isabel. American Minority Women in Sociolinguistic Perspective. (International Journal of the Sociology of Language Ser.: No. 17). 1978. pap. 19.00x (ISBN 90-279-7587-6). Mouton.

Institute on Minority Aging. Minority Aging Policy Issues for the 1980's: Proceedings, Vol. 7. Stanford, E. Percil, ed. (Illus.). 214p. (Orig.). 1981. pap. 7.00x (ISBN 0-916304-49-3). Campanile.

--Minority Aging Research, Old Issues-New Approaches: Proceedings, Vol. 6. Stanford, E. Percil, ed. (Illus.). 282p. (Orig.). 1980. pap. 7.00x (ISBN 0-916304-46-9). Campanile.

Instructional Aides, Inc. Minorities--a Changing Role in American Society. (Instructional Aides Ser.). 1980. 8p. pap. 9.95 (ISBN 0-936474-08-4). Instruct Aides TX.

Larson, E. Richard & McDonald, Laughlin. The Rights of Racial Minorities. 1979. pap. 1.95 (ISBN 0-380-75077-5, 75077, Discus). Avon.

Mack, Raymond W. & Duster, Troy S. Patterns of Minority Relations. 60p. 0.75 (ISBN 0-686-74878-6). ADL.

Nam, Charles B. Nationality Groups & Social Stratification: A Study of the Socioeconomic Status & Mobility of Selected European Nationality Groups in America. Cordasco, Francesco, ed. LC 80-882. (American Ethnic Groups Ser.). 1981. lib. bdg. 25.00x (ISBN 0-405-13443-6). Arno.

Spring Hill Center. Police-Minority Community Relations: The Control & Structuring of Police Discretion. Hoel, Donna & Ziegenhagen, John, eds. 1978. pap. text ed. 2.50 (ISBN 0-932676-04-9). Spring Hill.

MINORITIES–AFRICA

Gay, Kathlyn & Barnes, Ben E. The River Flows Backward. new ed. Ashton, Sylvia, ed. LC 74-76645. 1975. 12.95 (ISBN 0-87949-027-6). Ashley Bks.

Hourani, Albert H. Minorities in the Arab World. LC 77-87665. Repr. of 1947 ed. 18.50 (ISBN 0-404-16402-1). AMS Pr.

MINORITIES–ASIA

Allworth, Edward, ed. The Nationality Question in Soviet Central Asia. LC 72-85986. (Special Studies in International Politics & Government Ser.). 1973. 39.50x (ISBN 0-275-28659-2). Irvington.

Hourani, Albert H. Minorities in the Arab World. LC 77-87665. Repr. of 1947 ed. 18.50 (ISBN 0-404-16402-1). AMS Pr.

Kang, Tai S., ed. Nationalism & the Crises of Ethnic Minorities in Asia. LC 78-19295. (Contributions in Sociology: No. 34). (Illus.). 1979. lib. bdg. 19.95x (ISBN 0-313-20623-6, KNA/). Greenwood.

Thompson, Virginia M. & Adloff, Richard. Minority Problems in Southeast Asia. LC 70-102547. 1970. Repr. of 1955 ed. 13.00 (ISBN 0-8462-1483-0). Russell.

MINORITIES–AUSTRIA

Kann, Robert A. Multinational Empire: Nationalism & National Reform in the Habsburg Monarchy, 1848-1918, 2 Vols. 1964. lib. bdg. 42.50x (ISBN 0-374-94503-9). Octagon.

MINORITIES–CZECHOSLOVAK REPUBLIC

Kennan, George F. From Prague After Munich: Diplomatic Papers, 1938-1939. LC 66-26587. 1968. 20.00 (ISBN 0-691-05620-X); pap. 7.95 (ISBN 0-691-01063-3). Princeton U Pr.

Wagner, Francis. Toward a New Central Europe: A Symposium. (Illus.). 394p. 1970. 8.50 (ISBN 0-87934-002-9). Danubian.

MINORITIES–GREAT BRITAIN

Khan, Verity S., ed. Minority Families in Britain: Support & Stress. 1979. text ed. 26.00x (ISBN 0-333-26189-5). Humanities.

MINORITIES–HUNGARY

Seton-Watson, R. W. Racial Problems in Hungary. 540p. 1973. Repr. of 1908 ed. 29.50 (ISBN 0-86527-163-1). Fertig.

MINORITIES–INDIA

Schermerhorn, R. A. Ethnic Plurality in India. LC 77-75662. 1978. text ed. 12.95x (ISBN 0-8165-0612-4); pap. text ed. 6.45x (ISBN 0-8165-0578-0). U of Ariz Pr.

MINORITIES–RUSSIA
Allworth, Edward, ed. Nationality Group Survival in Multi-Ethnic States: Shifting Support Patterns in the Soviet Baltic Region. LC 77-4952. 1977. text ed. 30.95 (ISBN 0-275-24040-1). Praeger.
Chauhan, Shivdan Singh. Nationalities Question in USA & USSR: A Comparative Study. 1977. text ed. 9.00x (ISBN 0-8426-0948-2). Verry.
Dobriansky, Lev E. U. S. A. & the Soviet Myth. 6.50 (ISBN 0-8159-7005-6). Devin.
Kamenetsky, Ihor. Nationalism and Human Rights: Processes of Modernization in the USSR. LC 77-1257. (Series in Issues Studies (Ussr & East Europe): No. 1). 1977. lib. bdg. 18.50x (ISBN 0-87287-143-6). Libs Unl.
Kolarz, Walter. Russia & Her Colonies. 1967. Repr. of 1953 ed. 22.50 (ISBN 0-208-00519-6, Archon). Shoe String.
McCagg, William O. & Silver, Brian D., eds. Soviet Asian Ethnic Frontiers. LC 77-11796. (Pergamon Policy Studies). (Illus.). 1979. 36.00 (ISBN 0-08-024637-0). Pergamon.
Smal-Stocki, Roman. The Captive Nations: Nationalism of the Non-Russian Nations in the Soviet Union. 1960. pap. 1.45 (ISBN 0-8084-0068-1, B9). Coll & U Pr.
Zenkovsky, Serge A. Pan-Turkism & Islam in Russia. LC 60-5399. (Russian Research Center Studies: No. 36). 1960. 17.50x (ISBN 0-674-65350-5). Harvard U Pr.

MINORITIES–YUGOSLAVIA
Shoup, Paul. Communism & the Yugoslav National Question. LC 68-19759. (East Central European Studies). 1968. 20.00x (ISBN 0-231-03125-4). Columbia U Pr.

MINORS (LAW)
see Children–Law

MINOX CAMERA
see Cameras–Types–Minox

MINSTREL SHOWS
see Musical Revues, Comedies, etc.

MINSTRELS
see also Meistersinger; Minnesingers; Troubadours; Trouveres; Waits
Anderson, Hugh. The Colonial Minstrel. 1981. Repr. lib. bdg. 19.00 (ISBN 0-403-01502-2). Scholarly.
Bullock-Davies, C. Menestrellorum Multitudo: Minstrels at a Royal Feast. 1978. text ed. 32.50x (ISBN 0-7083-0656-X). Verry.
Duncan, Edmondstoune. Story of Minstrelsy. LC 69-16802. (Music Story Ser). 1968. Repr. of 1907 ed. 22.00 (ISBN 0-8103-4240-5). Gale.
Eckstorm, Fanny. Minstrelsy of Maine. LC 79-152248. 1971. Repr. of 1927 ed. 24.00 (ISBN 0-8103-3707-X). Gale.
Faral, Edmond. Jongleurs En France Au Moyen Age. LC 79-140971. (Reseach & Source Works Ser: No. 606). 1971. Repr. of 1910 ed. 23.50 (ISBN 0-8337-1099-0). B Franklin.
Goldron, Romain. Minstrels & Masters: The Triumph of Polyphony. LC 68-1789. 1968. Volume 3 4.95 (ISBN 0-385-02342-1). Doubleday.
Jeanroy, Alfred. Bibliographie Sommaire Des Chansonniers Francais Du Moyen Age. LC 76-162043. (Bibliography & Reference Ser.: No. 423). 1971. Repr. of 1918 ed. lib. bdg. 18.50 (ISBN 0-8337-1828-2). B Franklin.
The Minstrelsy of the Scottish Border. (Illus.). 1976. Repr. 19.00x (ISBN 0-7158-1064-2). Charles River Bks.
Moffat, Alfred. The Minstrelsy of Ireland. (Folklore Ser.). Repr. of 1897 ed. 25.00 (ISBN 0-685-43814-7). Norwood Edns.
--The Minstrelsy of Scotland. (Folklore Ser). Repr. of 1896 ed. 22.50 (ISBN 0-685-43813-9). Norwood Edns.
Moffat, Alfred & Kidson, Frank. The Minstrelsy of England. (Folklore Ser.). 1901. 25.00 (ISBN 0-685-43812-0). Norwood Edns.
Motherwool, W. Minstrelsy. 35.00 (ISBN 0-8490-0641-4). Gordon Pr.
Nathan, Hans. Dan Emmett & the Rise of Early Negro Minstrelsy. (Illus.). 1962. 24.95 (ISBN 0-8061-0540-2); pap. 12.50 (ISBN 0-8061-1423-1). U of Okla Pr.
O'Neill, Francis. Irish Minstrels & Musicians. LC 75-40336. 1975. Repr. of 1913 ed. lib. bdg. 25.00 (ISBN 0-8414-6532-0). Folcroft.
Percy, Thomas. Reliques of Ancient English Poetry, 3 Vols. Wheatley, Henry B., ed. 8.50 ea. (ISBN 0-8446-2728-3). Peter Smith.
Ritson, Joseph. A Dissertation on Romance & Minstrelsy. LC 77-94617. 1979. Repr. of 1891 ed. lib. bdg. 25.00 (ISBN 0-89341-180-9). Longwood Pr.
Sargent, B. Minstrels. LC 73-80470. (Resources of Music Ser.). (Illus.). 64p. 1974. pap. text ed. 3.95 (ISBN 0-521-20166-7). Cambridge U Pr.
Sparling, H. Halliday. Irish Minstrelsy. 1977. Repr. of 1887 ed. 20.00 (ISBN 0-89984-120-1). Century Bookbindery.
Zguta, Russell. Russian Minstrels: A History of the Skomorokhi. LC 78-53331. (Illus.). 1978. 16.00x (ISBN 0-8122-7753-8). U of Pa Pr.

MINTS
see also Coinage
Grinsell, L. V. The Bath Mint. 1973. 3.00 (ISBN 0-685-51513-3, Pub by Spink & Son England). S J Durst.
Hudgeons. The Official Price Guide to Mint Errors & Varieties. 3rd ed. (Collector Ser). (Illus.). 182p. 1981. pap. 4.95 (ISBN 0-686-69749-9, 167-05). Hse of Collectibles.
Illustrated History of the U. S. Mint. 1978. Repr. of 1881 ed. lib. bdg. 35.00 (ISBN 0-8482-0112-4). Norwood Edns.
Lapp, Warren A. & Silberman, Herbert A., eds. United States Large Cents 1793-1857. LC 74-27611. (Gleanings from the Numismatist Ser.). (Illus.). 640p. 1975. 40.00x (ISBN 0-88000-058-9). Quarterman.
Nesmith, Robert. The Coinage of the First Mint of the Americas at Mexico City 1536-1572. LC 75-1789. 1978. Repr. of 1955 ed. 35.00x (ISBN 0-88000-064-3). Quarterman.
Newell, E. T. Western Seleucid Mints. (Illus.). 1977. 40.00 (ISBN 0-89005-247-6). Ares.
Stewart, Frank H. History of the First United States Mint. LC 76-189173. (Illus.). 247p. 1974. Repr. of 1928 ed. 20.00x (ISBN 0-88000-030-9). Quarterman.

MINUTEMEN
Fisher, Dorothy C. Paul Revere & the Minute Men. (Landmark Ser.: No. 4). (Illus.). (gr. 4-6). 1950. 2.95 (ISBN 0-394-80304-3). Random.
Gross, Robert A. The Minutemen & Their World. 1976. 8.95 (ISBN 0-8090-6933-4, AmCen); pap. 4.95 (ISBN 0-8090-0120-9). Hill & Wang.

MIQUELON
Anglin, Douglas G. Saint Pierre & Miquelon Affaire of 1941: A Study in Diplomacy in the North Atlantic Quadrangle. LC 66-5251. (Illus.). 1966. 17.50x (ISBN 0-8020-5172-3). U of Toronto Pr.

MIR
Hourwich, Isaac A. Economics of the Russian Village. LC 76-127451. (Columbia University Studies in the Social Sciences: No. 5). Repr. of 1892 ed. 16.50 (ISBN 0-404-51005-1). AMS Pr.
Male, D. J. Russian Peasant Organisation Before Collectivisation. LC 70-123662. (Soviet & East European Studies). 1971. 33.50 (ISBN 0-521-07884-9). Cambridge U Pr.

MIRABEAU, HONORE GABRIEL RIQUETTI, COMTE DE, 1749-1791
Barthou, Louis. Mirabeau. LC 72-7091. (Select Bibliographies Reprint Ser.). 1972. Repr. of 1913 ed. 22.00 (ISBN 0-8369-6923-5). Arno.
Vallentin, Antonina. Mirabeau. Dickes, E. W., tr. LC 70-122070. (Illus.). Repr. of 1948 ed. 19.50x (ISBN 0-678-03173-8). Kelley.
Welch, Oliver J. Mirabeau, a Study of a Democratic Monarchist. LC 67-27662. Repr. of 1951 ed. 12.50 (ISBN 0-8046-0492-4). Kennikat.
Willert, Paul F. Mirabeau. LC 74-112822. 1970. Repr. of 1898 ed. 10.25 (ISBN 0-8046-1089-4). Kennikat.

MIRABEAU, OCTAVE
Carr, Reg. Anarchism in France: The Case of Octave Mirbeau. 1977. lib. bdg. 14.95x (ISBN 0-7735-0301-3). McGill-Queens U Pr.

MIRABEAU, VICTOR DE RIQUETTI, MARQUIS DE, 1715-1789
Brocard, Lucien. Doctrines economiques et sociales du Marquis de Mirabeau dans "L'Ami des hommes". LC 79-121220. (Research & Source Ser.: No. 500). (Fr). 1970. Repr. of 1902 ed. 23.50 (ISBN 0-8337-0379-X). B Franklin.

MIRACLE-PLAYS
see Mysteries and Miracle-Plays

MIRACLES
see also Holy Wells; Jesus Christ–Miracles; Modernist-Fundamentalist Controversy; Saints–Legends; Shrines; Supernatural
Bailey, Keith M. The Children's Bread. LC 77-83941. 1977. 5.95 (ISBN 0-87509-063-X). Chr Pubns.
Bales, James D. Miracles or Mirages. 1956. 3.00 (ISBN 0-686-21487-0). Firm Foun Pub.
Bredesen, Harald & Scheer, James F. Need a Miracle? 1979. 4.95 (ISBN 0-8007-0995-0). Revell.
Brewer, E. Cobham. A Dictionary of Miracles, Imitative, Realistic, & Dogmatic. LC 66-29783. 1966. Repr. of 1885 ed. 28.00 (ISBN 0-8103-3000-8). Gale.
Brewer, Ebenezer. A Dictionary of Miracles. 75.00 (ISBN 0-8490-0040-8). Gordon Pr.
Britten, Emma. Nineteenth Century Miracles. 1977. lib. bdg. 59.95 (ISBN 0-8490-2348-3). Gordon Pr.
Brown, William N. The Indian & Christian Miracles of Walking on the Water. LC 78-72381. Repr. of 1928 ed. 16.50 (ISBN 0-404-17243-1). AMS Pr.
Burns, R. M. The Great Debate on Miracles: From Joseph Glanvill to David Hume. LC 78-75197. 300p. 1981. 20.00 (ISBN 0-8387-2378-0). Bucknell U Pr.
Collins, J. H. Ten Miracles. 1975. pap. 0.50 (ISBN 0-8198-0479-7). Dghtrs St Paul.
A Course in Miracles. LC 76-20363. 1975. Set Of 3 Vols. incl. text, tchrs' manual wkbk. 30.00 (ISBN 0-686-23922-9). Found Inner Peace.
Fox, George. George Fox's Book of Miracles. Cadbury, Henry J., ed. LC 73-735. 161p. 1973. Repr. of 1948 ed. lib. bdg. 12.50x (ISBN 0-374-92825-8). Octagon.
Freret. Recherches sur les Miracles. (Holbach & His Friends Ser). 173p. (Fr.). 1974. Repr. of 1773 ed. lib. bdg. 51.00x (ISBN 0-8287-1407-X, 1555). Clearwater Pub.
Fridrichsen, Anton. Problem of Miracle in Primitive Christianity. Harrisville, Roy A. & Hanson, John S., trs. from Fr. LC 72-176480. 1972. 7.95 (ISBN 0-8066-1211-8, 10-5170). Augsburg.
Gregorius, Saint Les Livres Des Miracles et Autres Opuscules, 4 Vols. 1863. Set. 126.00 (ISBN 0-384-19888-0); 31.50 ea.; pap. 27.00 ea.; Set. pap. 108.00 (ISBN 0-384-19889-9). Johnson Repr.
Hunter, Charles & Hunter, Frances. Impossible Miracles. 1976. pap. 2.25 (ISBN 0-917726-05-7). Hunter Bks.
Johnston, Francis. Fatima: The Great Sign. 1980. Repr. of 1979 ed. write for info. Tan Bks Pubs.
Kelsey, Morton. The Age of Miracles. LC 78-74095. 80p. 1979. pap. 2.45 (ISBN 0-87793-169-0). Ave Maria.
Koch, Dietrich-Alex. Die Bedeutung der Wundererzaehlungen fuer die Christologie des Markusevangeliums. (Beiheft 42 zur Zeitschrift fuer die neutestamentliche Wissenschaft Ser.). 217p. 1975. 56.00x (ISBN 3-11-004783-7). De Gruyter.
Kuhlman, Kathryn. I Believe in Miracles. 1975. pap. 2.25 (ISBN 0-515-05858-0). Jove Pubns.
Lecanu, A. F. Dictionnaire des Propheties et des Miracles, 2 vols. Migne, J. P., ed. (Nouvelle Encyclopedie Theologique Ser.: Vols. 24-25). 1246p. (Fr.). Date not set. Repr. of 1852 ed. lib. bdg. 159.00x (ISBN 0-89241-268-2). Caratzas Bros.
Lewis, C. S. Miracles: A Preliminary Study. 1963. pap. 1.95 (ISBN 0-02-086820-0). Macmillan.
Lindsay, Gordon. The Miracles of Divine Discipline, Vol. 7. (Miracles in the Bible Ser.). 0.95 (ISBN 0-89985-184-3). Christ Nations.
MacDonald, George. The Miracles of Our Lord. Hein, Rolland, ed. LC 79-22261. (Wheaton Literary Ser.). 1980. pap. 4.95 (ISBN 0-87788-547-8). Shaw Pubs.
McGill, Ormond. How to Produce Miracles. LC 74-9288. 208p. 1976. 9.95 (ISBN 0-498-01553-X). A S Barnes.
Menendez, Josefa. The Way of Divine Love. LC 79-112493. 1977. pap. 7.50 (ISBN 0-89555-030-X, 104). TAN Bks Pubs.
Milagre No Corredor Da Morte. 160p. (Portuguese.). 1980. pap. 1.50 (ISBN 0-8297-0453-1). Life Pubs Intl.
Milagros De la Oracion. (Spanish Bks.). 1977. 1.75 (ISBN 0-8297-0443-4). Life Pubs Intl.
Miracles De Nostre Dame Par Personnages, 8 Vols. 1876-1893. Set. 215.50 (ISBN 0-384-39105-2); pap. 23.00 ea.; Set. pap. 185.00 (ISBN 0-685-13516-0). Johnson Repr.
Oliveira, Joseph De. Jacinta, Flower of Fatima. 192p. 1972. 4.75 (ISBN 0-911988-16-5). AMI Pr.
Rahm, Harold J. Am I Not Here. 2nd ed. 176p. 1962. 3.75 (ISBN 0-911988-23-8). AMI Pr.
Roberts, Oral. The Daily Guide to Miracles. 1977. pap. 2.50 (ISBN 0-8007-8300-X, Spire Bks). Revell.
--The Miracle of Seed Faith. 1977. pap. 1.50 (ISBN 0-8007-8299-2, Spire). Revell.
Robertson, Pat. Milagro Del Amor Agape. (Spanish Bks.). (Span.). 1978. 1.90 (ISBN 0-8297-0914-2). Life Pubs Intl.
Sanchez-Silva, J. The Miracle of Marcelino. 122p. 1963. pap. 1.95 (ISBN 0-933932-28-6). Scepter Pubs.
Schuller, Robert H. Discover the Miracles in Your Life. (Orig.). 1978. pap. 1.25 (ISBN 0-89081-136-9). Harvest Hse.
Shelly, Bruce. The Miracle of Anne. 96p. 1974. pap. 3.50 (ISBN 0-911336-55-9). Sci of Mind.
Spurgeon, Charles H. Sermons on the Miracles. 1977. Repr. of 1958 ed. limp bk. 5.95 (ISBN 0-551-05576-6). Attic Pr.
Tari, Mel & Dudley, Cliff. Like a Mighty Wind. LC 76-182854. 1978. pap. 2.50 (ISBN 0-89221-049-4). New Leaf.
Wallace, Alfred R. Miracles & Modern Spiritualism. rev. ed. LC 75-7409. (Perspectives in Psychical Research Ser.). 1975. Repr. of 1896 ed. 14.00x (ISBN 0-405-06996-0). Arno.
Warfield, B. B. Counterfeit Miracles. 1976. pap. 5.45 (ISBN 0-85151-166-X). Banner of Truth.
Wise, Robert L. When There Is No Miracle. LC 77-89394. 1978. pap. 3.95 (ISBN 0-8307-0582-1, 54-080-08); study guide 1.39 (ISBN 0-8307-0651-8, 6101518). Regal.

MIRANDA, FRANCISCO DE, 1750-1816
Miranda, Francisco De. The Diary of Francisco E Miranda: Tour of the United States, 1783-1784. Robertson, William S., ed. (Span.-eng.). 1928. limited to 1500 copies 15.00x (ISBN 0-686-17414-3). R S Barnes.
Robertson, W. Francisco De Miranda & the Revolutionizing of South America. 1976. lib. bdg. 59.95 (ISBN 0-8490-1862-5). Gordon Pr.
Robertson, William S. Life of Miranda, 2 Vols. LC 77-79203. (Illus.). 1969. Repr. of 1929 ed. 27.50x (ISBN 0-8154-0291-0). Cooper Sq.
Thorning, Joseph F. Miranda: World Citizen. 1967. 9.00 (ISBN 0-8130-0226-5). U Presses Fla.

MIRO, JOAN, 1893-
Chilo, Michel. Miro: The Artist, the Work. Schultze, Margreth C., tr. (Maeght Gallery Art Ser.). (Illus.). 1977. 7.95 (ISBN 0-8120-5175-0). Barron.
Diehl, Gaston. Joan Miro. (Q L P Ser.). (Illus.). 87p. 1974. 6.95 (ISBN 0-517-51671-3). Crown.
Greenberg, Clement. Joan Miro. LC 77-91377. (Contemporary Art Ser). Repr. of 1948 ed. 15.00 (ISBN 0-405-00728-0). Arno.
Joan Miro Lithographs: Vol. 2 (1953-1964) (Illus.). 1975. 150.00x (ISBN 0-8148-0583-3). L Amiel Pub.
Leiris, Michael & Mourlot, Fernand. Joan Miro, Lithographs, Vol. 1. (Illus.). 231p. 1972. 150.00x (ISBN 0-8148-0494-2, Pub. by Tudor). Hennessey.
Millard, Charles W. Miro: Selected Paintings. LC 79-9662. (Illus.). 94p. 1980. 20.00 (ISBN 0-87474-638-8). Smithsonian.
Miro, No. 203. (Derriere le Miroir Ser.). (Fr.). 1977. pap. 19.95 (ISBN 0-8120-0894-4). Barron.
Miro, No. 151. (The Maeght Gallery: Derriere le Miroir Ser.). (Fr.). 1977. pap. 19.95 o. p. (ISBN 0-8120-0918-5). Barron.
Miro, No. 186. (Derriere le Miroir Ser.). (Fr.). 1977. pap. 19.95 (ISBN 0-8120-0901-0). Barron.
Miro Artigas, No. 139-140. (Derriere le Miroir Ser.). (Fr.). 1977. pap. 19.95 (ISBN 0-8120-0917-7). Barron.
Penrose, Roland. Creation in Space of Joan Miro. (Illus.). 1967. 17.50x (ISBN 0-8150-0092-8). Wittenborn.
Rubin, William S. Miro in the Collection of the Museum of Modern Art. LC 72-95708. (Illus.). 1973. 17.50 (ISBN 0-87070-463-X); pap. 8.95 (ISBN 0-87070-462-1). Museum Mod Art.
Soby, James Thrall. Joan Miro. Gullon, Ricardo, tr. 8.75 (ISBN 0-8477-2106-X). U of PR Pr.
Sweeney, James J. Joan Miro. LC 78-86434. (Museum of Modern Art Publications in Reprint Ser). (Illus.). 1970. Repr. of 1941 ed. 17.00 (ISBN 0-405-01551-8). Arno.

MIRRORS
Elementary Science Study. Mirror Cards. 1975. tchr's. guide 8.36 (ISBN 0-07-018524-7, W). McGraw.
Heyne, Pamela. Today's Architectural Mirror: Interiors, Buildings, & Solar Designs. 225p. 1981. text ed. price not set (ISBN 0-442-23424-4). Van Nos Reinhold.
Morrien, Adrian. Use of a Wall Mirror. Leigh-Loohuizen, Ria, tr. 1970. pap. 2.85 (ISBN 0-912136-17-0, Pub. by Twowindows Pr). SBD.
Ruchlis, Hy. Science Projects: Mirrors. (gr. 4-9). pap. 2.50 (ISBN 0-87594-014-5, 3020). Book-Lab.
Swallow, Robert W. & Beicher, Fred. Ancient Chinese Bronze Mirrors. rev. ed. LC 76-28881. (Illus.). 1976. 17.50 (ISBN 0-89344-014-0). Ars Ceramica.

MIRRORS, MAGIC
see also Crystal-Gazing; Divination; Magic

MISCARRIAGE
see Abortion

MISCARRIAGE OF JUSTICE
see Judicial Error

MISCEGENATION
Here are entered works on marriage between persons of different races, especially between whites and Afro-Americans, and on the resulting mixture or hybridity of races.
see also Colored People (South Africa); Indians of North America–Mixed Bloods; Interracial Marriage; Marriage, Mixed; Mulattoes
Adams, Romanzo. Interracial Marriage in Hawaii: A Study of Mutually Conditioned Processes of Acculturation & Amalgamation. LC 69-14907. (Criminology, Law Enforcement, & Social Problems Ser.: No. 65). (Illus.). 1969. Repr. of 1937 ed. 12.50 (ISBN 0-87585-065-0). Patterson Smith.
--Interracial Marriage in Hawaii: A Study of the Mutually Conditioned Processes of Acculturation & Amalgamation. LC 75-96473. (BCL Ser.: No. I). Repr. of 1937 ed. 12.00 (ISBN 0-404-00293-5). AMS Pr.
Allen, William G. American Prejudice Against Color. LC 75-82165. (Anti-Slavery Crusade in America Ser). 1969. Repr. of 1853 ed. 9.00 (ISBN 0-405-00603-9). Arno.

Champly, H. White Women, Coloured Men. 59.95 (ISBN 0-8490-1293-7). Gordon Pr.

Croly, David G. Miscegenation. LC 70-104435. Repr. of 1864 ed. lib. bdg. 14.00x (ISBN 0-8398-0281-1). Irvington.

Davenport, Charles B. Race Crossing in Jamaica. LC 77-106833. Repr. of 1929 ed. 31.00x (ISBN 0-8371-3455-2). Greenwood.

Day, Caroline. Study of Some Negro-White Families in the U. S. LC 76-106857. (Illus.). Repr. of 1932 ed. 27.00x (ISBN 0-8371-3479-X, Pub. by Negro U Pr). Greenwood.

Hernton, Calvin C. Sex & Racism in America. 1966. pap. 2.95 (ISBN 0-394-17409-7, B306, BC). Grove.

Johnston, James H. Miscegenation in the Ante-Bellum South. LC 70-144642. Repr. of 1939 ed. 15.00 (ISBN 0-404-00178-5). AMS Pr.

--Race Relations in Virginia & Miscegenation in the South: 1776-1860. LC 78-87833. 1970. 15.00x (ISBN 0-87023-050-6). U. of Mass Pr.

Jones, Philip. Racial Hybridity. (Illus.). 241p. (Orig.). 1979. pap. 5.50x (ISBN 0-911038-77-9, Uriel Pubns). Noontide.

Mencke, John G. Mulattoes & Race Mixture: American Attitudes & Images, 1865-1918. Berkhofer, Robert, ed. LC 78-27611. (Studies in American History & Culture: No. 4). 1979. 29.95 (ISBN 0-8357-0984-1, Pub. by UMI Res Pr). Univ Microfilms.

Morner, Magnus. Race Mixture in the History of Latin America. 178p. 1967. pap. 4.95 (ISBN 0-316-58369-3). Little.

Reuter, Edward B. Mulatto in the United States. LC 70-100495. (Studies in Black History & Culture, No. 54). 1970. 54.95 (ISBN 0-8383-1216-0). Haskell.

--Mulatto in the United States. LC 69-16569. Repr. of 1918 ed. 17.50x (ISBN 0-8371-0938-8, Pub. by Negro U Pr). Greenwood.

--The Mulatto in the United States: Including a Study of the Role of Mixed Blood Races Throughout the World. (Basic Afro-American Reprint Ser.). 1970. Repr. of 1918 ed. 19.50 (ISBN 0-384-50330-6). Johnson Repr.

--Race Mixture: Studies in Intermarriage & Miscegenation. (Basic Afro-American Reprint Library Ser). 1970. Repr. of 1931 ed. 11.00 (ISBN 0-384-50340-3). Johnson Repr.

--Race Mixtures: Studies in Intermarriage & Miscegenation. LC 71-94486. Repr. of 1931 ed. 100.75x (ISBN 0-8371-2375-5). Greenwood.

Schultz, Alfred P. Race or Mongrel: History of the Rise & Fall of the Ancient Races of Earth. Grob, Gerald, ed. LC 76-46103. (Anti-Movements in America). 1977. Repr. of 1908 ed. lib. bdg. 21.00x (ISBN 0-405-09974-6). Arno.

Shapiro, Harry L. Race Mixture. (Orig.). 1958. pap. 2.50 (ISBN 92-3-100416-6, U509, UNESCO). Unipub.

Stember, C. H. Sexual Racism: The Emotional Barrier to an Integrated Society. 1976. 25.00 (ISBN 0-444-99034-8, Pub. by Elsevier). Greenwood.

Stonequist, Everett V. Marginal Man: A Study in Personality & Culture Conflict. LC 61-13767. 1961. Repr. of 1937 ed. 13.00 (ISBN 0-8462-0281-6). Russell.

Williams, George D. Maya-Spanish Crosses in Yucatan. 1931. pap. 12.00 (ISBN 0-527-01228-9). Kraus Repr.

MISCONDUCT IN OFFICE

see Administrative Responsibility; Corruption (In Politics); Government Liability

MISDEMEANORS (LAW)

see Criminal Law

MISES, LUDWIG VON

see Von Mises, Ludwig, 1881-

MISHIMA, YUKIO, 1925-1970

DH - TE Research Studies. Yukio Mishima: Japan's Prodigal Son. LC 75-14402. 1975. pap. 3.50 (ISBN 0-686-11972-X). Bks Intl DH-TE.

Nathan, John. Mishima: A Biography. LC 74-12184. (Illus.). 1974. pap. 3.95 (ISBN 0-316-59846-1). Little.

Stokes, Henry S. The Life & Death of Yukio Mishima. 368p. 1975. pap. 3.45 (ISBN 0-440-55033-5, Delta). Dell.

MISHNAH

Albeck, Chanoch. Einfuehrung in die Mischna. (Studia Judaica, 6). 493p. 1971. 41.75x (ISBN 3-11-006429-4). De Gruyter.

Bokser, Baruch M. Post Mishnaic Judaism in Transition: Samuel on Berakhot & the Beginnings of Gemara. Neusner, Jacob, ed. LC 80-19702. 1981. 19.50 (ISBN 0-89130-432-0, 14 00 17); pap. 15.00 (ISBN 0-89130-433-9). Scholars Pr CA.

Commentary on the Mishna. Date not set. 8.95 (ISBN 0-87306-083-0). Feldheim.

Goldworm, Hersh. Mishnah-Moed, Vol.2. (Artscroll Mishnah Ser.). 416p. 1981. 15.95 (ISBN 0-89906-254-7); pap. 12.95 (ISBN 0-89906-255-5). Mesorah Pubns.

Hoffmann, David. The First Mishna & the Controversies of the Tannaim. Forchheimer, Paul, tr. from German. Incl. The Highest Court in the City of Sanctuary. LC 77-98683. 1977. 12.50 (ISBN 0-87203-072-5). Hermon.

Neusner, Jacob. Form-Analysis & Exegesis: A Fresh Approach to the Interpretation of Mishnah. 224p. 1981. 22.50x (ISBN 0-8166-0984-5); pap. 9.95x (ISBN 0-8166-0985-3). U of Minn Pr.

--Judaism: The Evidence of the Mishnah. LC 80-26080. 432p. 1981. 25.00 (ISBN 0-226-57617-5). U of Chicago Pr.

--Learn Mishnah. LC 78-5482. (Illus.). 1978. pap. 4.95x (ISBN 0-87441-310-9). Behrman.

Rosner. Maimonides' Commentary on the Mishnah. 8.95 (ISBN 0-87306-083-0). Feldheim.

Rosner, Fred. Maimonides' Commentary on Mishnah Sanhedrin. LC 81-51800. 224p. 1981. 14.95 (ISBN 0-87203-099-7). Hermon.

Weingreen, Jacob. From Bible to Mishna: The Continuity of Tradition. LC 75-37728. 250p. 1976. text ed. 27.00x (ISBN 0-8419-0249-6). Holmes & Meier.

MISREPRESENTATION (LAW)

see Fraud

MISSALS

see also Catholic Church-Liturgy and Ritual-Missal; Illumination of Books and Manuscripts

Daughters of St Paul. My Massbook. (gr. 3 up). 1978. plastic bdg. 2.00 (ISBN 0-8198-0361-8); pap. 1.25 (ISBN 0-8198-0362-6). Dghtrs St Paul.

Grant, Raymond J. S. Cambridge, Corpus Christi College Forty One: The Loricas & the Missal. (Costerus New Ser.: No. XVII). 1979. pap. 17.25x (ISBN 90-6203-762-3). Humanities.

The New Saint Joseph Sunday Missal & Hymnal. complete ed. (Illus., References, Calendar,Bold Sense-Lines, Two Color Ordinary, Perpetual). red flexible vinyl 7.25 (ISBN 0-686-14305-1, 820/09); green cloth, colored edges 9.25 (ISBN 0-686-14306-X, 820/22-GN); black cloth hard bdg. 9.25 (ISBN 0-686-14307-8, 820/22-B); brown flexible bdg., colored edges 9.95 (ISBN 0-686-14308-6, 820/10-BN). Catholic Bk Pub.

New...Saint Joseph Children's Missal. (Illus.). black leatherette, hard bd. 1.65 (ISBN 0-686-14300-0, 806/67-B); white leatherette, hard bd. 1.65 (ISBN 0-686-14301-9, 806/67-W); black soft simulated lea., colored edges 2.25 (ISBN 0-686-14302-7, 806/42-B); white soft simulated lea., colored edges 2.25 (ISBN 0-686-14303-5, 806/42-W). Catholic Bk Pub.

Vatican Two Sunday Missal. 1974. 6.95 (ISBN 0-8198-0513-0); pap. 5.95 (ISBN 0-8198-0514-9); leatherette 7.95 (ISBN 0-8198-0515-7); genuine leather 10.95 (ISBN 0-8198-0516-5). Dghtrs St Paul.

Vatican 2 Weekday Missal. 1975. red edge 13.95 (ISBN 0-8198-0497-5); leatherette, gold edge 16.95 (ISBN 0-8198-0498-3); genuine leather 17.95 (ISBN 0-8198-0499-1). Dghtrs St Paul.

MISSELDEN, EDWARD, fl. 1608-1654

De Malynes, Gerald. Center of the Circle of Commerce. LC 66-21687. Repr. of 1623 ed. 15.00x (ISBN 0-678-00296-7). Kelley.

De Malynes, Gerard. Maintenance of Free Trade. LC 73-115927. Repr. of 1622 ed. lib. bdg. 15.00x (ISBN 0-678-00644-X). Kelley.

MISSILE GUIDANCE SYSTEMS

see Guided Missiles-Guidance Systems

MISSILES, GUIDED

see Guided Missiles

MISSING PERSONS

Cohen, Daniel. Missing: Stories of Strange Disappearances. 1980. pap. 1.95 (ISBN 0-671-56052-2). Archway.

--Missing! Stories of Strange Disappearances. LC 78-25729. (High Interest-Low Vocabulary Ser.). (Illus.). (gr. 4-9). 1979. 5.95 (ISBN 0-396-07651-3). Dodd.

--Mysterious Disappearances. LC 75-38352. (Illus.). (gr. 7 up). 1976. 5.95 (ISBN 0-396-07298-4). Dodd.

Cohn, Daniel. Missing! Stories of Strange Disappearances. (gr. 4 up). 1979. pap. 1.95 (ISBN 0-671-56052-2). Archway.

Cox, Robert & Peiffer, Kenneth. Missing Person. LC 78-12024. (Illus.). 224p. 1979. 10.95 (ISBN 0-8117-1002-5). Stackpole.

Eriksen, Ronald G. How to Find Missing Persons: A Handbook for Investigators. 1981. pap. 3.95 (ISBN 0-686-30631-7). Loompanics.

Hayman, Leroy. Thirteen Who Vanished: True Stories of Mysterious Disappearances. LC 78-26750. 160p. (gr. 7 up). 1979. PLB 8.29 (ISBN 0-671-32933-2). Messner.

Olsen, Jack. Missing Persons. LC 80-69375. 1981. 12.95 (ISBN 0-689-11133-9). Atheneum.

Payne, Jack. How to Make a Fortune in Finders' Fees. rev. ed. LC 73-80450. 176p. 1980. 10.95 (ISBN 0-8119-0346-X). Fell.

MISSIOLOGY

see Missions-Theory

MISSION OF THE CHURCH

Here are entered works on the chief objective and responsibility of the church as viewed in its entirety. Works on missionary work are entered under Missions.

see also Church and the World; Missions

Anderson, Gerald & Stransky, Thomas, eds. Mission Trends: Liberation Theologies in North America & Europe, No. 4. LC 78-70827. 1978. pap. 3.45 (ISBN 0-8028-1709-2). Eerdmans.

Armstrong, James. The Nation Yet to Be: Christian Mission & the New Patriotism. (Orig.). 1975. pap. 2.25 (ISBN 0-377-00023-X). Friend Pr.

Collins, Sheila D. & Collins, John A. In Your Midst: Perspectives on Christian Mission. (Orig.). 1980. pap. 3.25 (ISBN 0-377-00101-5). Friend Pr.

Comblin, Jose. The Meaning of Mission. Drury, John, tr. from Spanish. LC 76-41723. Orig. Title: Teologia De la Mision. 1977. 6.95x (ISBN 0-88344-304-X); pap. 4.95 (ISBN 0-88344-305-8). Orbis Bks.

Costas, Orlando E. The Integrity of Mission: The Inner Life & Outreach of the Church. LC 79-1759. 1979. pap. 3.95 (ISBN 0-06-061586-9, RD 235, HarpR). Har-Row.

Ellis, David & Gasque, W. Ward, eds. In God's Community: Essays on the Church & Its Ministry. LC 79-12847. 1979. pap. 3.95 (ISBN 0-87788-392-0). Shaw Pubs.

Escobar, Samuel & Driver, John. Christian Mission & Social Justice. LC 78-6035. (Mennonite Missionary Study Ser.: No. 5). 1978. pap. 3.95 (ISBN 0-8361-1855-3). Herald Pr.

Gatti, Enzo. Rich Church-Poor Church? O'Connell, Matthew, tr. from It. LC 74-77432. Orig. Title: Couli che Conosce il Dolore Dell'uomo. 96p. 1974. 4.95x (ISBN 0-88344-437-2). Orbis Bks.

Hesselgrave, David J. Communicating Christ Cross-Culturally. 1978. 9.95 (ISBN 0-310-36691-7). Zondervan.

Hodges, Melvin L. The Indigenous Church. rev. ed. 1976. pap. 2.00 (ISBN 0-88243-527-2, 02-0527). Gospel Pub.

Hopkins, Paul A. What Next in Mission? LC 77-21776. 1977. pap. 3.95 (ISBN 0-664-24143-3). Westminster.

Killinger, John. Steeple People & the World: Planning for Mission Through the Church. (Orig.). 1977. pap. 2.50 (ISBN 0-377-00059-0). Friend Pr.

McConkey, Dale. Goal Setting: A Guide to Achieving the Church's Mission. (Administration for Churches Ser.). 1978. pap. 1.95 (ISBN 0-8066-1651-2, 10-2558). Augsburg.

McMullen, Eleanor & Sonnenfeld, Jean. Go-Groups: Gearing up for Reaching Out. (Orig.). 1977. pap. 2.50 (ISBN 0-377-00060-4). Friend Pr.

Middleton, Robert G. Charting a Course for the Church. 1979. pap. 5.95 (ISBN 0-8170-0844-6). Judson.

Morikawa, Jitsuo. Biblical Dimensions of Church Growth. 1979. pap. 3.95 (ISBN 0-8170-0839-X). Judson.

Newbigin, Leslie. The Open Secret. 1978. pap. 4.95 (ISBN 0-8028-1752-1). Eerdmans.

Ramseyer, Robert L. Mission & the Peace Witness. LC 79-16738. (Missionary Studies Ser.: No. 7). 144p. 1979. pap. 4.95 (ISBN 0-8361-1896-0). Herald Pr.

Richardson, William J. Social Action Vs Evangelism: An Essay on the Contemporary Crisis. LC 77-22669. 1977. pap. 2.95x (ISBN 0-87808-160-7). William Carey Lib.

Schultz, Richard J. Christian's Mission. May, Edward C., ed. LC 70-119917. (Discipleship Ser). (Orig., Prog. Bk.). 1970. pap. text ed. 3.50 (ISBN 0-570-06306-X, 20-1049); tchr's ed. 2.60 (ISBN 0-570-06307-8, 20-1050). Concordia.

Simmons, Robert A. O Church Awake. 1969. 3.95 (ISBN 0-8158-0133-5). Chris Mass.

Stott, John R. Christian Mission in the Modern World. LC 75-21455. 128p. (Orig.). 1976. pap. 2.95 (ISBN 0-87784-485-2). Inter-Varsity.

Thung, Mady A. The Precarious Organisation: Sociological Explorations of the Church's Mission & Structure. (Religion & Society Ser.: No. 5). 1976. text ed. 23.50x (ISBN 0-686-22627-5). Mouton.

MISSION SERMONS

see Missions-Sermons

MISSIONARIES

Addison, James T. The Medieval Missionary. LC 76-7628. (Perspectives in European Hist. Ser.: No. 1). xiv, 176p. Repr. of 1936 ed. lib. bdg. 15.00x (ISBN 0-87991-610-9). Porcupine Pr.

Allen, Catherine. The New Lottie Moon Story. LC 79-52336. 1980. 7.95 (ISBN 0-8054-6319-4). Broadman.

Beeching, Jack. Open Path: Christian Missionaries, 1515-1914. LC 80-21270. 350p. 1981. 14.95 (ISBN 0-915520-37-0). Ross-Erikson.

Blair, William & Hunt, Bruce. The Korean Pentecost & the Sufferings Which Followed. 1977. pap. 2.95 (ISBN 0-85151-244-5). Banner of Truth.

Brister, Elaine H. The Joy of Discovery. LC 76-21567. (Illus.). 1976. bds. 3.95 (ISBN 0-8054-7217-7). Broadman.

Cannon, Joseph L. For Missionaries Only. 96p. 1975. pap. 2.95 (ISBN 0-8010-2347-5). Baker Bk.

Cauthen, Eloise G. Higher Ground. LC 77-82402. 1978. pap. 3.95 (ISBN 0-8054-7221-5). Broadman.

Christopher, Kenneth. The Merry Missionary: A Story About Philip Neri. (Stories About Christian Heroes Ser.). (Illus.). 32p. (gr. 6-9). pap. 1.95 (ISBN 0-686-63634-1). Winston Pr.

Coleman, Bernard & LaBud, Verona. Masinaigans: The Little Book. (Illus.). 368p. 1972. 10.00 (ISBN 0-686-05025-8). North Central Pub.

Collins, Marjorie A. Manual for Accepted Missionary Candidates. 2nd ed. LC 78-15314. 1979. pap. 4.45 (ISBN 0-87808-165-8). William Carey Lib.

--Manual for Missionaries on Furlough. LC 72-92747. 1978. pap. 4.45 (ISBN 0-87808-119-4). William Carey Lib.

--Who Cares About the Missionary? 160p. (Orig.). 1974. pap. 2.50 (ISBN 0-8024-9496-X). Moody.

Coole, Arthur B. A Trouble Shooter for God in China. (Illus.). 1976. 14.00x (ISBN 0-912706-05-8). Akers.

Crawford, David & Crawford, Leona. Missionary Adventures in the South Pacific. LC 67-15137. 1967. 5.50 (ISBN 0-8048-0403-6). C E Tuttle.

Creegan, Charles C. & Goodnow, Josephine A. Great Missionaries of the Church. facsimile ed. LC 73-37522. (Essay Index Reprint Ser). Repr. of 1895 ed. 22.00 (ISBN 0-8369-2541-6). Arno.

Darst, Mrs. H. W. Missions in the Mountains. (Illus.). 116p. 1979. pap. 2.50 (ISBN 0-89114-085-9). Baptist Pub Hse.

Donnelly, Joseph P. Pierre-Gibault, Missionary, 1737-1802. LC 77-156371. 1971. 8.00 (ISBN 0-8294-0203-9). Loyola.

Drury, Clifford. Sarah White Smith Diary. 1966. 11.00 (ISBN 0-87062-011-8). A H Clark.

Dugger, John W. Girl with a Missionary Heart. (Illus.). 104p. 1978. pap. 1.95 (ISBN 0-89114-074-3). Baptist Pub Hse.

Eddy, George S. Pathfinders of the World Missionary Crusade. facs. ed. LC 76-84304. (Essay Index Reprint Ser). 1945. 18.25 (ISBN 0-8369-1127-X). Arno.

Edwards, Jonathan. Life & Diary of David Brainerd. 384p. 1980. pap. 7.95 (ISBN 0-8024-4772-4). Moody.

Engelhardt, Zephyrin. Missions & Missionaries of California, 4vols. (Illus.). lib. bdg. 185.00 (ISBN 0-87821-019-9). Milford Hse.

Fell, Doris E. Lady of the Tboli. LC 79-50950. 1979. 7.95 (ISBN 0-915684-28-4). Christian Herald.

Fitts, Leroy. Lott Carey: First Black Missionary to Africa. 1978. pap. 5.95 (ISBN 0-8170-0820-9). Judson.

Fletcher, Jesse C. Living Sacrifices: A Missionary Odyssey. LC 73-93903. 1974. 4.95 (ISBN 0-8054-7210-X). Broadman.

Fox, Donald S. The White Fox of Andhra. 216p. 1978. 6.95 (ISBN 0-8059-2432-9). Dorrance.

Frizen, Edwin L., ed. Christ & Caesar in Christian Missions. Coggins, Wade T. LC 79-17124. (Orig.). 1979. pap. 5.95 (ISBN 0-87808-169-0). William Carey Lib.

Fuller, Millard. Bokotola. 1977. pap. 3.95 (ISBN 0-8096-1924-5). New Century.

Furlow, Elaine. Love with No Strings: The Human Touch in Christian Social Ministries. Hullum, Everett, ed. (The Human Touch Photo-Text Ser.: Volume Iv). (Illus.). 1977. 6.95 (ISBN 0-937170-15-1). Home Mission.

Garrand, Victor. Augustine Laure, S.J., Missionary to the Yakimas. 1977. 7.50 (ISBN 0-87770-176-8); pap. 4.95 (ISBN 0-87770-187-3). Ye Galleon.

Griffiths, Michael C. You & God's Work Overseas. pap. 0.50 (ISBN 0-87784-130-6). Inter-Varsity.

Hayden, Eric W. Traveller's Guide to Spurgeon Country. 1975. pap. 1.95 (ISBN 0-686-10527-3). Pilgrim Pubns.

Hefley, James & Hefley, Marti. Prisoners of Hope. LC 76-28840. 1976. 6.95 (ISBN 0-87509-122-9); pap. 3.95 (ISBN 0-87509-123-7). Chr Pubns.

Hembree, Ron. Mark. (Orig.). 1979. pap. 2.50 (ISBN 0-88270-403-6). Logos.

Hemenway, Ruth V. Ruth V. Hemenway, M.D. A Memoir of Revolutionary China, 1924-1941. Drake, Fred W,, ed. LC 76-45245. (Illus.). 1977. 12.50 (ISBN 0-87023-230-4). U of Mass Pr.

Hitt, Russell T. Jungle Pilot. 320p. 1973. pap. 3.95 (ISBN 0-310-26082-5). Zondervan,

Hodges, Melvin L. The Indigenous Church & the Missionary: A Sequel to the Indigenous Church. LC 77-14519. 1978. pap. 2.95 (ISBN 0-87808-151-8). William Carey Lib.
Hunter, J. H. Beside All Waters. 245p. 1964. 3.95 (ISBN 0-87509-050-8). Chr Pubns.
Jacobs, Sylvia M. A Biographical Dictionary of Black American Missionaries in Africa, Seventeen Seventy to Nineteen Seventy. 1981. lib. bdg. 35.00 (ISBN 0-8240-9367-4). Garland Pub.
Kane, J. Herbert. The Making of a Missionary. 160p. 1975. pap. 4.45 (ISBN 0-8010-5358-7). Baker Bk.
--Winds of Change in the Christian Mission. 160p. 1973. pap. 2.95 (ISBN 0-8024-9561-3). Moody.
Kapenzi, Geoffrey Z. The Clash of Cultures: Christian Missionaries & the Shona of Rhodesia. LC 78-68799. 1979. pap. text ed. 7.50 (ISBN 0-8191-0704-2). U Pr of Amer.
Kerr, James L. Wilfred Grenfell, His Life & Work. LC 73-21177. 1977. lib. bdg. 19.50x (ISBN 0-8371-6068-5, KEWG). Greenwood.
Kung, Andres. Bruce Olson: Missionary of American Colonizer? LC 80-69309. 1981. pap. 6.95 (ISBN 0-915684-83-7). Christian Herald.
Larson, Mel. One Hundred Fourteen Ways to the Mission Field. 1967. 3.95 (ISBN 0-911802-02-9); pap. 2.50 (ISBN 0-911802-03-7). Free Church Pubns.
Laveille, E. Life of Father De Smet, S. J. (1801-1873) Lindsay, Marian, tr. (Loyola Request Reprint Ser.). 398p. 1981. Repr. of 1915 ed. 8.95 (ISBN 0-8294-0372-8). Loyola.
Lee, Amy. Throbbing Drums: The Story of James H. Robinson. (Orig.). 1968. pap. 0.95 (ISBN 0-377-84141-2). Friend Pr.
Life of John Kline. 7.95 (ISBN 0-87178-118-2). Brethren.
Livingstone, David. Missionary Travels & Researches in South Africa. LC 72-5439. (Select Bibliographies Reprint Ser.). 1972. Repr. of 1857 ed. 52.00 (ISBN 0-8369-6918-9). Arno.
Lockerbie, Jeanette. When Blood Flows the Heart Grows Softer. pap. 3.95 (ISBN 0-8423-7980-0). Tyndale.
McCants, Sr. Dorothea O., ed. They Came to Louisiana: Letters of a Catholic Mission, 1854-1882. LC 72-96258. (Illus.). 1970. 17.50x (ISBN 0-8071-0903-7). La State U Pr.
Maclear, George F. Apostles of Mediaeval Europe. LC 72-624. (Essay Index Reprint Ser.). Repr. of 1869 ed. 19.50 (ISBN 0-8369-2803-2). Arno.
Mickelson, Einar H. God Can. (Illus.). 301p. 1966. 2.50 (ISBN 0-87509-086-9). Chr Pubns.
Missionary Heroes, 2 vols. pap. 3.95 ea. Schmul Pub Co.
Morrison, James H. Missionary Heroes of Africa. LC 79-89010. Repr. of 1922 ed. 13.25x (ISBN 0-8371-1738-0, Pub. by Negro U Pr). Greenwood.
Morton, Daniel O. Memoir of Rev. Levi Parsons: Late Missionary to Palestine. Davis, Moshe, ed. (America & the Holy Land Ser.). 1977. Repr. of 1824 ed. lib. bdg. 25.00x (ISBN 0-405-10271-2). Arno.
Moyer, Samuel T. They Heard the Call. LC 76-141248. (Illus.). 1970. pap. 2.00 (ISBN 0-87303-834-7). Faith & Life.
Mueller, John T. Great Missionaries to China. LC 73-38329. (Biography Index Reprint Ser). Repr. of 1947 ed. 12.75 (ISBN 0-8369-8124-3). Arno.
--Great Missionaries to the Orient. LC 78-38330. (Biography Index Reprint Ser). Repr. of 1948 ed. 12.75 (ISBN 0-8369-8125-1). Arno.
Muggeridge, Malcolm. Something Beautiful for God: Mother Teresa of Calcutta. 1977. pap. 2.45 (ISBN 0-385-12639-5, Im). Doubleday.
Murray, Andrew & Choy, Leona. Key to the Missionary Problem. (Orig.). 1980. pap. 2.95 (ISBN 0-87508-401-X). Chr Lit.
Nau, John F. Nau! Mission Inspired, the Story of Henry Nau. LC 78-72558. 1979. 8.95 (ISBN 0-915644-16-9). Clayton Pub Hse.
Nida, Eugene A. Customs & Cultures: Anthropology for Christian Missions. 2nd ed. LC 54-8976. (Applied Cultural Anthropology Ser.). 306p. 1975. Repr. of 1954 ed. 6.95x (ISBN 0-87808-723-0). William Carey Lib.
Padwick, Constance. Henry Martyn. 256p. 1980. pap. 3.50 (ISBN 0-8024-3513-0). Moody.
Page, Jesse. The Black Bishop: Samuel Adjai Crowther. LC 79-100. (Illus.). 1979. Repr. of 1908 ed. lib. bdg. 29.00x (ISBN 0-8371-4610-0, PBB&). Greenwood.
Pederson, Les. Missionary Go Home? 1980. pap. 3.50 (ISBN 0-8024-4881-X). Moody.
Poynter, Margaret. Miracle at Metlakatla. (Greatness with Faith Ser.). (Illus.). 1978. 4.95 (ISBN 0-570-07876-8, 39-1201); pap. 2.95 (ISBN 0-570-07881-4, 39-1211). Concordia.
Preheim, Marion K. Overseas Service Manual. (Illus., Orig.). 1969. pap. 1.00 (ISBN 0-8361-1591-0). Herald Pr.
Russell, H. Africa's Twelve Apostles. 1980. 6.95 (ISBN 0-8198-0702-8); pap. 5.50 (ISBN 0-8198-0703-6). Dghtrs St Paul.
Ryckman, Lucile D. Paid in Full: The Story of Harold Rykman, Missionary Pioneer to Paraguay & Brazil. (Illus.). 1979. pap. 3.75 (ISBN 0-89367-033-2). Light & Life.
Sigal, Gerald. The Jew & the Christian Missionary: A Jewish Response to Missionary Christianity. Date not set. 17.50x (ISBN 0-686-73602-8). Ktav.
Smith, Edwin W. Great Lion of Bechuanaland: The Life and Times of Roger Price, Missionary. 1957. text ed. 15.00x (ISBN 0-8401-2210-1). Allenson-Breckinridge.
Steere, Douglas V. God's Irregular - Arthur Shearly Cripps: A Rhodesian Epic. (Illus.). 1973. 5.95 (ISBN 0-281-02675-0). Pendle Hill.
Steven, Hugh. To the Ends of the Earth. LC 77-90116. 1978. pap. 2.95 (ISBN 0-915684-36-5). Christian Herald.
Taylor, Hudson & Thompson, Phyllis. God's Adventurer. (Illus.). 1978. pap. 2.25 (ISBN 0-85363-094-1). OMF Bks.
Thompson, Phyllis. Count It All Joy! LC 78-64550. 1978. pap. 2.50 (ISBN 0-87788-103-0). Shaw Pubs.
Tiltman, Marjorie. God's Adventurers. facs. ed. LC 68-16979. (Essay Index Reprint Ser). 1933. 18.00 (ISBN 0-8369-0945-3). Arno.
Trautwein, Noreen. The Everywhere Missionary. 2.98 (ISBN 0-686-12667-X, BE-150). Evangel Indiana.
Troutman, Charles. Everything You Want to Know About the Mission Field, but Are Afraid You Won't Learn Until You Get There: Letters to a Perspective Missionary. LC 76-4738. 120p. 1976. pap. 2.95 (ISBN 0-87784-717-7). Inter-Varsity.
Underwood, Joel, ed. In Search of Mission: An Interconfessional & Intercultural Quest. LC 74-12989. (The Future of the Missionary Enterprise Ser.: Dossier 9). 144p. (Orig.). 1974. pap. 3.95 (ISBN 0-89021-026-8). IDOC.
Vester, Bertha H. Our Jerusalem: An American Family in the Holy City, 1881-1949. Davis, Moshe, ed. LC 77-70752. (America & the Holy Land Ser.). 1977. Repr. of 1950 ed. lib. bdg. 22.00x (ISBN 0-405-10296-8). Arno.
Welch, Herbert. Men of the Outposts: The Romance of the Modern Christian Movement. facs. ed. LC 69-17594. (Essay Index Reprint Ser). 1937. 14.50 (ISBN 0-8369-1162-8). Arno.
Wendland, E. H. Dear Mr. Missionary. 1978. pap. 4.95 (ISBN 0-8100-0035-0, 12N1714). Northwest Pub.
Willis, John R. God's Frontiersmen: The Yale Band in Illinois. LC 79-65011. 1979. pap. text ed. 10.00 (ISBN 0-8191-0781-6). U Pr of Amer.
Wilson, Dorothy C. Apostle of Sight: The Story of Victor Rambo. 255p. 1980. 7.95 (ISBN 0-915684-54-3). Christian Herald.
Wilson, Samuel, ed. Mission Handbook: North American Protestant Ministries Overseas. 1980. 15.00 (ISBN 0-912552-34-4). MARC.
Wyker, Bertha P. Spanning the Decades: A Spiritual Pilgrimage. (Illus.). 224p. 1981. 8.50 (ISBN 0-682-49746-0). Exposition.

MISSIONARIES-APPOINTMENT, CALL, AND ELECTION

Griffiths, Michael C. Give up Your Small Ambitions. LC 70-175488. 1972. pap. 2.50 (ISBN 0-8024-2970-X). Moody.
Hunter, J. H. Beside All Waters. 245p. 1964. 3.95 (ISBN 0-87509-050-8). Chr Pubns.
McCloskey, Michael. The Formative Years of the Missionary College of Santa Cruz of Queretaro: 1683-1733. (Monograph Ser.). 1955. 10.00 (ISBN 0-88382-051-X). AAFH.
Morgan, Helen. Who'd Be a Missionary. 1972. pap. 0.50 (ISBN 0-87508-365-X). Chr Lit.
--Who'd Stay a Missionary. 1972. pap. 0.95 (ISBN 0-87508-366-8). Chr Lit.

MISSIONARIES-CORRESPONDENCE, REMINISCENCES, ETC.

Bliss, Eugene F., ed. Diary of David Zeisberger: A Missionary Among the Indians of Ohio, 2 vols. LC 73-108557. 1972. Repr. of 1885 ed. 45.00 (ISBN 0-403-00253-2). Scholarly.
Burchard, Florence & Boucher, Sharon. Someone Had to Hold the Lantern. LC 79-17836. (Crown Ser.). 1979. pap. 4.50 (ISBN 0-8127-0238-7). Review & Herald.
Crider, Virginia. Allegheny Gospel Trails. (Illus.). 1971. 5.65 (ISBN 0-87813-502-2). Christian Light.
Culpepper, Robert H. God's Calling: A Missionary Autobiography. LC 80-68643. 1981. 4.95 (ISBN 0-8054-6323-2). Broadman.
De Smet, Pierre J. Life, Letters & Travels of Father Pierre Jean de Smet, 4 vols. LC 75-83418. (Religion in America Ser. I). 1969. Repr. of 1905 ed. 75.00 set (ISBN 0-405-00237-8); Vols. 1-2. 16.50 ea. Vol. 1 (ISBN 0-405-00238-6). Vol. 2 (ISBN 0-405-00239-4). Vols. 3-4. 16.00 ea. Vol. 3 (ISBN 0-405-00240-8). Vol. 4 (ISBN 0-405-00241-6). Arno.
Elliot, Elisabeth. The Journals of Jim Elliot. 1978. 12.95 (ISBN 0-8007-0922-5). Revell.
Fife, Eric S. Against the Clock: The Story of Ray Buker, Sr., Olympic Runner & Missionary Statesman. (Illus.). 224p. (Orig.). 1981. pap. 5.95 (ISBN 0-310-24351-3). Zondervan.
Gunson, Niel, ed. Australian Reminiscences & Papers of L. E. Threlkeld, Missionary to the Aborigines 1824-1859, 2 vols. (AIAS Ethnohistory Ser.: No. 2). (Illus.). 1974. pap. text ed. 22.50x (ISBN 0-85575-031-6). Humanities.
McDowell, Catherine, ed. Letters from the Ursuline 1852-1853. LC 77-85460. 1978. 25.00 (ISBN 0-911536-69-8). Trinity U Pr.
Moffat, Robert. The Matabele Journals of Robert Moffat, 1829-1860, 2 vols. LC 74-15069. Repr. of 1945 ed. Set. 75.00 (ISBN 0-404-12111-X). AMS Pr.
Mooneyham, Stanley W. Come Walk the World. LC 77-92471. 1978. 6.95 (ISBN 0-8499-0076-X, 0076-X). Word Bks.
Quimby, Paul & Youngsberg, Norma. Yankee on the Yangtze. LC 76-49387. (Nova Ser.). 1977. pap. 4.95 (ISBN 0-8127-0131-3). Review & Herald.
Roseveare, Helen. Living Sacrifices. 1979. pap. 3.95 (ISBN 0-8024-4943-3). Moody.
Simkin, Robert L. & Simkin, Margaret. Letters from Szechwan. 1978. text ed. 8.95 (ISBN 0-914064-08-8); pap. text ed. 6.95 (ISBN 0-914064-09-6). Celo Pr.
Smith, E. Ellsworth. He Came with "Seeing" Eyes & Understanding Heart. LC 78-64757. 1980. 7.95 (ISBN 0-533-04034-5). Vantage.
Van Ess, Dorothy. Pioneers in the Arab World. 1974. pap. 3.95 (ISBN 0-8028-1585-5). Eerdmans.
Winter, Ralph D. Say Yes to Mission. pap. 0.50 (ISBN 0-87784-149-7). Inter-Varsity.

MISSIONARIES-JUVENILE LITERATURE

Carter, Virginia B. I'm Going to Be a Missionary. (Orig.). 1978. pap. 2.95 (ISBN 0-89036-103-7). Hawkes Pub Inc.
Zook, Mury R. Little Missionaries. 184p. 1979. 5.35 (ISBN 0-686-30764-X). Rod & Staff.

MISSIONARIES-VOCATION

see Missionaries-Appointment, Call, and Election

MISSIONARIES, ANGLO-SAXON

Glunz, Hans. Britannien und Bibeltext. Repr. of 1930 ed. pap. 13.50 (ISBN 0-384-18950-4). Johnson Repr.
Levison, Wilhelm. England & the Continent in the Eighth Century. (Ford Lectures Ser). 1946. 32.50 (ISBN 0-19-821232-1). Oxford U Pr.

MISSIONARIES, BRITISH

Buchan, James. The Expendable Mary Slessor. (Illus.). 272p. (Orig.). 1981. pap. 7.95 (ISBN 0-8164-2320-2). Seabury.
Mackay, A. M. A. M. Mackay: Pioneer Missionary of the Church of the Missionary Society of Uganda. (Illus.). 485p. 1970. Repr. of 1890 ed. 29.50x (ISBN 0-7146-1874-8, F Cass Co). Biblio Dist.
Oddie, G. A. Social Protest in India: British Protestant Missionaries & Social Reforms, Eighteen Fifty to Nineteen Hundred. 1979. 17.50x (ISBN 0-8364-0195-6). South Asia Bks.
Turtas, Raimondo. L' Attivita E la Politica Missionaria Della Direzione Della London Missionary Society 1795-1820. (Analecta Gregoriana, Vol. 182). (Ital.). 1971. pap. 9.75 (ISBN 0-8294-0329-9, Pub. by Gregorian U Pr). Loyola.
Wright, Louis B. Religion & Empire. 1965. lib. bdg. 14.50x (ISBN 0-374-98816-1). Octagon.

MISSIONARIES, IRISH

Dunleavy, Gareth W. Colum's Other Island: The Irish at Lindisfarne. (Illus.). 160p. 1960. 11.50x (ISBN 0-299-02120-3). U of Wis Pr.
Glunz, Hans. Britannien und Bibeltext. Repr. of 1930 ed. pap. 13.50 (ISBN 0-384-18950-4). Johnson Repr.
McDowell, Catherine, ed. Letters from the Ursuline 1852-1853. LC 77-85460. 1978. 25.00 (ISBN 0-911536-69-8). Trinity U Pr.

MISSIONARY APOLOGETICS

see Apologetics, Missionary

MISSIONARY EDUCATION

see Missions-Study and Teaching

MISSIONARY RIDGE, BATTLE OF, 1863

see also Chattanooga, Battle Of, 1863

MISSIONARY STORIES

Abrahams, Olga. Seiko. Orig. Title: The Spiders Thread. 1973. pap. 1.25 (ISBN 0-85363-112-3). OMF Bks.
Ascent to the Tribes. 1956. pap. 2.95 (ISBN 0-85363-062-3). OMF Bks.
Bagley, Val C. Mission Mania: A Cartoonist's View of the Best Two Years of Life. (Illus.). 98p. (Orig.). 1980. pap. 4.95 (ISBN 0-88290-140-0). Horizon Utah.
Bentley-Taylor, David. Java Saga. Orig. Title: Weathercocks Reward. 1975. pap. 2.25 (ISBN 0-85363-100-X). OMF Bks.
Cleator, Margaret. God Who Answers by Fire. 1968. pap. 1.00 (ISBN 0-87508-140-1). Chr Lit.
Day, Phyllis. Sold Twice. 1968. pap. 0.90 (ISBN 0-85363-078-X). OMF Bks.
Demon Gods of Thorny River. 1974. pap. 1.95 (ISBN 0-85363-098-4). OMF Bks.
Dortzbach, Karl & Dortzbach, Debbie. Kidnapped. LC 74-25708. (Illus.). 1977. pap. 1.95 (ISBN 0-06-061976-7, HJ 35, HarpR). Har-Row.
Fraser, J. D. & Allbutt, Mary E., eds. Prayer of Faith. pap. 0.90 (ISBN 0-85363-106-9). OMF Bks.
Griffiths, Michael. Don't Soft Pedal God's Call. 1968. pap. 0.60 (ISBN 0-85363-063-1). OMF Bks.
Gurtler, Mary. Nid's Exciting Day. 1961. pap. 0.90 (ISBN 0-85363-033-X). OMF Bks.
Hartshorn, Leon R. Inspirational Missionary Stories. 1976. 6.95 (ISBN 0-87747-588-1). Deseret Bk.
Holder, Philip. Captain Mahjong. 1976. pap. 2.40 (ISBN 0-85363-113-1). OMF Bks.
Hoste, D. E. If I Am to Lead. 1968. pap. 0.60 (ISBN 0-85363-068-2). OMF Bks.
Kendrick, Bv. Ben. Battle for Yanga. LC 80-20643. 127p. 1980. pap. 3.95 (ISBN 0-87227-074-2). Reg Baptist.
Kirkpatrick, Charles. Cow in the Clinic & Other Missionary Stories from Around the World. 1977. pap. 2.95 (ISBN 0-89367-016-2). Light & Life.
Kuhn, Isobel. In the Arena. 1960. pap. 3.50 (ISBN 0-85363-023-2). OMF Bks.
--Nests Above the Abyss. pap. 3.95 (ISBN 0-85363-031-3). OMF Bks.
--Stones of Fire. 1951. pap. 2.95 (ISBN 0-85363-049-6). OMF Bks.
Lane, Denis. God's Powerful Weapon. 1977. pap. 1.00 (ISBN 0-85363-117-4). OMF Bks.
Lister, Ellen. The Key. 1970. pap. 0.90 (ISBN 0-85363-080-1). OMF Bks.
Lyall, Leslie. Flame for God: John Sung. 1954. pap. 3.00 (ISBN 0-85363-026-7). OMF Bks.
--Three of China's Mighty Men. pap. 3.95 (ISBN 0-85363-090-9). OMF Bks.
Lyall, Leslie T. A Passion for the Impossible. 1965. pap. 2.40 (ISBN 0-85363-115-8). OMF Bks.
Mathews, R. Arthur. Born for Battle. 3rd ed. 1980. pap. 2.95 (ISBN 0-85363-126-3). OMF Bks.
Miller, Sheila. I Went to School in the Jungle. 1975. pap. 1.95 (ISBN 0-85363-109-3). OMF Bks.
Muira, Ayako. Shiokari Pass. 1968. 4.95 (ISBN 0-85363-099-2). OMF Bks.
Nielson, Larry. How Would You Like to See the Slides of My Mission. LC 80-82708. (Illus.). 80p. (Orig.). 1980. pap. 4.95 (ISBN 0-88290-153-2, 2040). Horizon Utah.
Nightingale, Ken. One Way Through the Jungle. pap. 2.50 (ISBN 0-85363-107-7). OMF Bks.
Precious Things of the Lasting Hills. 1938. pap. 1.20 (ISBN 0-85363-044-5). OMF Bks.
Reynolds, A. Voice of China's Christian. 1968. pap. 0.35 (ISBN 0-85363-087-9). OMF Bks.
Sanders, J. Oswald. Best That I Can Be. 1976. pap. 2.25 (ISBN 0-85363-111-5). OMF Bks.
Scherzger, Otto. The New Trail. 1963. pap. 1.35 (ISBN 0-85363-114-X). OMF Bks.
Segraves, Kelly L. Lolly. 1978. pap. 2.95 (ISBN 0-89293-024-1). Beta Bk.
Stickly, Caroline. Broken Snare. 1975. pap. 3.75 (ISBN 0-85363-102-6). OMF Bks.
Tallach, John. God Made Them Great. 1978. pap. 4.95 (ISBN 0-85151-190-2). Banner of Truth.
Taylor, Howard. James Hudson Taylor: Biography. 11.95 (ISBN 0-85363-004-6). OMF Bks.
Taylor, Mrs. Howard. Pastor Hsi. 1900. pap. 3.75 (ISBN 0-85363-040-2). OMF Bks.
--Triumph of John & Betty Stam. 1935. pap. 2.40 (ISBN 0-85363-055-0). OMF Bks.
Thompson, Phyllis. Minka & Margaret. 1976. pap. 3.00 (ISBN 0-85363-121-2). OMF Bks.
Three Men Filled with the Spirit. 1969. pap. 1.35 (ISBN 0-85363-073-9). OMF Bks.
Van Der Linden, Elly. Village on Stilts. Orig. Title: Boy from Mindoro. 1963. pap. 0.75 (ISBN 0-85363-110-7). OMF Bks.
Wallis, Kathleen. Young Ki's Adventures. 1978. pap. 1.35 (ISBN 0-85363-124-7). OMF Bks.
Wendland, E. H. Dear Mr. Missionary. 1978. pap. 4.95 (ISBN 0-8100-0035-0, 12N1714). Northwest Pub.
White, Paul. Alias Jungle Doctor: An Autobiography. 1977. pap. 6.95 (ISBN 0-85364-205-2). Attic Pr.

MISSIONS

see also Communication (Theology); Evangelistic Work; Missionaries; Radio in Missionary Work; Salvation Army; Spanish Missions of California; Spanish Missions of Mexico; Spanish Missions of New Mexico; Spanish Missions of the Southwest also subdivision Missions under names of churches, denominations, religious orders, etc. e.g. Church of England-Missions; Jesuits-Missions; Lutheran Church-Missions; Spanish Missions of California

Allen, Roland. Missionary Methods: St. Paul's or Our's? 1962. pap. 2.95 (ISBN 0-8028-1001-2). Eerdmans.

Anderson, Gerald & Stransky, Thomas, eds. Mission Trends No.5: Faith Meets Faith. LC 81-80983. 320p. (Orig.). 1981. pap. 3.95 (ISBN 0-8091-2356-8). Paulist Pr.

Anderson, Gerald H. & Stansky, Thomas. Missions Trends, No. 2. LC 75-29836. 1975. pap. 3.45 (ISBN 0-8028-1624-X). Eerdmans.

Anderson, Gerald H. & Stranskey, Thomas F. Mission Trends No. 2: "Evangelization". (Mission Trend Ser.). 1976. pap. 3.45 (ISBN 0-8091-1900-5). Paulist Pr.

Anderson, Gerald H. & Stransky, Thomas F., eds. Mission Trends No. Five: Faith Meets Faith. (Mission Trends Ser.). 320p. (Orig.). 1981. pap. 3.95 (ISBN 0-8028-1821-8). Eerdmans.

--Mission Trends, No. 1: Crucial Issues in Mission Today. LC 74-81222. (Mission Trend Ser.). (Orig.). 1974. pap. 3.45 (ISBN 0-8091-1843-2). Paulist Pr.

--Mission Trends No. 1: Current Issues in Mission Today. LC 74-81222. 1974. pap. 3.45 (ISBN 0-8028-1483-2). Eerdmans.

Barrett, Kate W. Some Practical Suggestions on the Conduct of a Rescue Home: Including Life of Dr. Kate Waller Barrett. facsimile ed. LC 74-3928. (Women in America Ser.). Orig. Title: Fifty Years Work with Girls. 186p. 1974. Repr. of 1903 ed. 15.00x (ISBN 0-405-06075-0). Arno.

Bartlett, Samuel C. Historical Sketches of the Missions of the American Board. LC 78-38436. (Religion in America, Ser. 2). 210p. 1972. Repr. of 1972 ed. 16.00 (ISBN 0-405-04057-1). Arno.

Bassham, Rodger C. Mission Theology, Nineteen Forty Eight to Nineteen Seventy-Five: Years of Worldwide Creative Tension--Ecumenical, Evangelical & Roman Catholic. 1980. 10.95 (ISBN 0-87808-330-8). William Carey Lib.

Bauer, Arthur O. Making Mission Happen. 1974. pap. 3.50 (ISBN 0-377-00019-1). Friend Pr.

Bavinck, J. H. Introduction to the Science of Missions. 1977. pap. 4.95 (ISBN 0-8010-0600-7). Baker Bk.

Bavinck, John H. Introduction to Science of Missions. 1960. pap. 4.95 (ISBN 0-87552-124-X). Presby & Reformed.

Bolton, Herbert E. Wider Horizons of American History. 1967. pap. 2.25x (ISBN 0-268-00301-7). U of Notre Dame Pr.

Booth, Philip A. Slim Fingers. 1976. pap. 1.50 (ISBN 0-87508-030-8). Chr Lit.

Braun, J. R. Is This My Neighbor? The Union Gospel Mission. (Illus.). 60p. (Orig.). 1980. pap. text ed. 8.95 (ISBN 0-933656-08-4). Trinity Pub Hse.

Burgess, E. T. Missions in a Missile Age. 1979. pap. 0.50 (ISBN 0-89114-012-3). Baptist Pub Hse.

Camp Farthest Out. Roots & Fruits of the Camp Farthest Out. 1980. 3.95 (ISBN 0-910924-89-9). Macalester.

Cervin, Russell A. Mission in Ferment. 1977. pap. 3.50 (ISBN 0-910452-33-4). Covenant.

Chambers, Oswald. So Send I You. 1973. pap. 2.25 (ISBN 0-87508-138-X). Chr Lit.

Coggins, Wade T. So That's What Missions Is All About. 128p. 1975. pap. 2.95 (ISBN 0-8024-8107-8). Moody.

Costas, Orlando E. The Church and Its Mission: A Shattering Critique from the Third World. 1975. pap. 4.95 (ISBN 0-8423-0276-X). Tyndale.

Davids, Richard C. Man Who Moved a Mountain. LC 75-99609. (Illus.). 270p. 1972. pap. 4.25 (ISBN 0-8006-1237-X, 1-1237). Fortress.

Dayton, Edward R., ed. Mission Handbook: North American Protestant Ministries Overseas. 1977. 6.00 (ISBN 0-912552-06-9). MARC.

DiGangi, Mariano. I Believe in Mission. 1979. pap. 2.95 (ISBN 0-87552-255-6). Presby & Reformed.

Dubose, Francis M., ed. Classics of Christian Missions. LC 78-53147. 1979. pap. 10.50 (ISBN 0-8054-6313-5). Broadman.

Dwight, Henry Otis, et al, eds. Encyclopedia of Missions: Descriptive, Historical, Biographical, Statistical. 2nd ed. LC 74-31438. 851p. 1975. Repr. of 1904 ed. 29.50 (ISBN 0-8103-3325-2). Gale.

Elkins, Phillip W. Church Sponsored Missions. 1974. 3.00 (ISBN 0-686-21462-5). Firm Foun Pub.

Elsbree, Oliver W. The Rise of the Missionary Spirit in America 1790-1815. LC 79-13028. (Perspectives in American History Ser.: No. 55). Repr. of 1928 ed. 15.00x (ISBN 0-87991-376-2). Porcupine Pr.

Engstrom, Ted W. What in the World Is God Doing? The New Face of Missions. 1978. 8.95 (ISBN 0-8499-0085-9). Word Bks.

Fairbank, John K., ed. The Missionary Enterprise in China & America. LC 74-82191. (Studies in American-East Asian Relations: No. 6). 442p. 1974. text ed. 20.00x (ISBN 0-674-57655-1). Harvard U Pr.

Forbes, William R. Engaging in Mission: A Study-Action Guide. (Orig.). 1980. pap. 2.25 (ISBN 0-377-00102-3). Friend Pr.

Gatti, Enzo. Rich Church-Poor Church? O'Connell, Matthew, tr. from It. LC 74-77432. Orig. Title: Couli che Conosce il Dolore Dell'uomo. 96p. 1974. 4.95x (ISBN 0-88344-437-2). Orbis Bks.

Glasser, Arthur F., et al, eds. Crucial Dimensions in World Evangelization. LC 76-42165. 1976. pap. 9.95x (ISBN 0-87808-732-X). William Carey Lib.

Goldsmith, Martin. Don't Just Stand There: The Why & How of Mission Today. LC 76-49237. 1976. pap. 2.25 (ISBN 0-87784-649-9). Inter-Varsity.

Goodykoontz, Colin B. Home Missions on the American Frontier. LC 76-120619. 1970. Repr. lib. bdg. 25.00x (ISBN 0-374-93198-4). Octagon.

Gordon, Adoniram J. Holy Spirit in Missions. pap. 2.25 (ISBN 0-87509-094-X). Chr Pubns.

Graber, J. D. The Church Apostolic. LC 60-14171. (Conrad Grebel Lecture Ser.). 1960. 4.00 (ISBN 0-8361-1347-0). Herald Pr.

Griffiths, Michael. Get Your Church Involved in Missions. 1980. pap. 0.90 (ISBN 0-686-27991-3). OMF Bks.

Gurganus, George P., ed. Guidelines for World Evangelism. 1977. 9.95 (ISBN 0-89112-040-8). Bibl Res Pr.

Hardin, Daniel C. Mission: A Practical Approach to Church-Sponsored Mission Work. LC 77-27424. 1978. pap. text ed. 4.95x (ISBN 0-87808-427-4). William Carey Lib.

Harrison, William P. Gospel Among the Slaves. LC 70-168249. Repr. of 1893 ed. 27.50 (ISBN 0-404-00263-3). AMS Pr.

Henderson, W. Guy. Passport to Missions. LC 78-57816. 1979. pap. 4.95 (ISBN 0-8054-6315-1). Broadman.

Hesselgrave, David J. Planting Churches Cross-Culturally. 1980. pap. 12.95 (ISBN 0-8010-4219-4). Baker Bk.

Hollaway, Ida Nelle. Punching Holes in the Darkness. LC 77-81521. 1978. pap. 3.25 (ISBN 0-8054-5587-6). Broadman.

Holmes, Brian, ed. Educational Policy & the Mission Schools: Case Studies from the British Empire. 1967. text ed. 16.75x (ISBN 0-7100-6002-5). Humanities.

Howard, David M. Student Power in World Missions. 2nd ed. LC 79-122918. (Orig.). 1979. pap. 2.25 (ISBN 0-87784-493-3). Inter-Varsity.

Hulbert, Terry C. World Missions Today. LC 78-68233. 1979. pap. text ed. 3.95 (ISBN 0-910566-16-X); instr's. guide by Robert E. Clark 3.95 (ISBN 0-910566-28-3). Evang Tchr.

Johnson, E. H. For a Time Like This. (Orig.). 1973. pap. 2.50 (ISBN 0-377-03001-5). Friend Pr.

Kane, J. Herbert. The Christian World Mission: Today & Tomorrow. 240p. 1981. 9.95 (ISBN 0-8010-5426-5). Baker Bk.

--Life & Work on the Mission Field. LC 80-65010. 1980. 12.95 (ISBN 0-8010-5406-0). Baker Bk.

Lacroix & De Djunkovskoy, E. Dictionnaire des Missions Catholiques, 2 vols. Migne, J. P., ed. (Troisieme et Derniere Encyclopedie Theologique Ser.: Vols. 59-60). 1545p. (Fr.). Date not set. Repr. of 1864 ed. lib. bdg. 197.50x (ISBN 0-89241-325-5). Caratzas Bros.

Lees, W. C. Second Thoughts on Missions. 1965. pap. 0.50 (ISBN 0-87508-908-9). Chr Lit.

Loewen, Jacob A. Culture & Human Values: Christian Intervention in Anthropological Perspective. Smalley, William A., ed. LC 75-12653. (Applied Cultural Anthropology Ser.). 443p. (Orig.). 1975. pap. 6.95x (ISBN 0-87808-722-2). William Carey Lib.

McBeth, Leon. Hombres Claves En las Misiones. Orig. Title: Men Who Made Missions. 128p. 1980. pap. 3.25 (ISBN 0-311-01070-9). Casa Bautista.

MacDonald, Allan J. Trade, Politics & Christianity in Africa & the East. LC 77-89007. Repr. of 1916 ed. 14.50x (ISBN 0-8371-1755-0). Greenwood.

McFadyen, J. F. The Missionary Idea in Life & Religion. 194p. Repr. of 1926 ed. text ed. 4.50 (ISBN 0-567-02180-7). Attic Pr.

McGavran, Donald A. How Churches Grow. (Orig.). 1965. pap. 6.95 (ISBN 0-377-40011-4). Friend Pr.

McGavran, Donald A., ed. Church Growth Bulletin: Second Consolidated Volume (Sept. 1969 -July 1975) LC 77-5192. 1977. pap. 7.95x (ISBN 0-87808-702-8). William Carey Lib.

--The Conciliar-Evangelical Debate: The Crucial Documents, 1964-1976. 2nd enl. ed. LC 77-1705. 1977. pap. 8.95 (ISBN 0-87808-733-8). William Carey Lib.

Matthews, Reginald L. Missionary Administration in the Local Church. 1972. 3.95 (ISBN 0-87227-002-5); pap. 2.95 (ISBN 0-87227-011-4). Reg Baptist.

Mellis, Charles J. Committed Communities: Fresh Streams for World Missions. LC 76-53548. 1976. pap. 4.95 (ISBN 0-87808-426-6). William Carey Lib.

Missions Strategy of the Local Church. 1976. pap. 2.00 (ISBN 0-912552-14-X). MARC.

Mott, John R., et al. Student Mission Power: Report of the First International Convention of the Student Volunteer Movement for Foreign Missions, 1891. LC 79-92013. 1979. pap. 6.95 (ISBN 0-87808-736-2). William Carey Lib.

Murray, Andrew & Choy, Leona. Key to the Missionary Problem. (Orig.). 1980. pap. 2.95 (ISBN 0-87508-401-X). Chr Lit.

Nelson, Marlin L., ed. Readings in Third World Missions: A Collection of Essential Documents. LC 76-45803. 1976. pap. 6.95x (ISBN 0-87808-319-7). William Carey Lib.

Nevius, John. Planting & Development of Missionary Churches. 1974. pap. 1.95 (ISBN 0-87552-346-3). Presby & Reformed.

Newbigin, Lesslie. The Household of God. (Orig.). 1954. pap. 2.25 (ISBN 0-377-33011-6). Friend Pr.

Powles, Cyril & Nelson, Rob. Mission Impossible--Unless... (Orig.). 1973. pap. 2.95 (ISBN 0-377-03009-0). Friend Pr.

Reapsome, James W., et al, eds. Evangelical Missions Quarterly, Vols. 7-9. LC 71-186301. 1973. Set. 13.95x (ISBN 0-87808-707-9). William Carey Lib.

Sao Paulo, Brazil Mission Team. Steps into the Mission Field. 1978. 5.95 (ISBN 0-686-25522-4). Firm Foun Pub.

Seamands, J. T. Tell It Well. 236p. (Orig.). 1981. pap. 6.95 (ISBN 0-8341-0684-1). Beacon Hill.

Shenk, Wilbert R., ed. The Challenge of Church Growth. (Mennonite Missionary Studies: Pt. 1). 1973. pap. 2.95x (ISBN 0-8361-1200-8). Herald Pr.

--Mission Focus: Current Issues. 488p. 1980. pap. 11.95 (ISBN 0-8361-1937-1). Herald Pr.

Simonet, Andre. Apostles for Our Time: Thoughts on Apostolic Spirituality. Bouchard, M. Angeline, tr. from Fr. LC 77-8537. 1977. pap. 4.95 (ISBN 0-8189-0354-6). Alba.

Smith, Bertha. Our Lost World. LC 80-68537. 1981. pap. 3.95 (ISBN 0-8054-6324-0). Broadman.

Starkes, M. Thomas. The Foundation for Missions. LC 80-67460. 1981. pap. 4.95 (ISBN 0-8054-6325-9). Broadman.

--Mission Two Thousand. 1979. pap. 3.00 (ISBN 0-914520-14-8). Insight Pr.

Stoesz, Samuel J. Church & Missions Alive. 1975. pap. 2.25 (ISBN 0-87509-068-0); leaders guide 0.95 (ISBN 0-87509-069-9). Chr Pubns.

Stransky, Thomas & Anderson, Gerald H., eds. Mission Trends, No. 4: Liberation Theologies. LC 78-70827. (Mission Trend Ser.). 1979. pap. 3.45 (ISBN 0-8091-2185-9). Paulist Pr.

This Land: Ours for a Season. pap. 1.95 (ISBN 0-87178-843-8). Brethren.

Tidsworth, Floyd, Jr. Planting & Growing Missions. LC 79-89866. 1979. pap. 5.95 (ISBN 0-87716-108-9, Pub. by Moore Pub Co). F Apple.

Truman, George, et al. Narrative of a Visit to the West Indies: In 1840 & 1841. facsimile ed. LC 71-38027. (Black Heritage Library Collection). Repr. of 1844 ed. 13.25 (ISBN 0-8369-8993-7). Arno.

Vierow, Duain W. On the Move with the Master: A Daily Devotional Guide on World Mission. LC 76-57679. 1977. 4.95 (ISBN 0-87808-155-0). William Carey Lib.

Wagner, C. Peter. Frontiers in Missionary Strategy. LC 72-181592. 320p. 1972. 8.95 (ISBN 0-8024-2881-9). Moody.

Wakatama, Pius. Independence for the Third World Church: An African's Perspective on Missionary Work. LC 76-21462. 116p. (Orig.). 1976. pap. 4.95 (ISBN 0-87784-719-3). Inter-Varsity.

Warren, Max. I Believe in the Great Commission. (I Believe Ser.). 1976. pap. 3.95 (ISBN 0-8028-1659-2). Eerdmans.

Weber, James K. Let's Quit Kidding Ourselves About Missions. 1979. pap. 3.50 (ISBN 0-8024-4678-7). Moody.

Weiss, G. Christian. The Heart of Missionary Theology. 1977. pap. 1.95 (ISBN 0-8024-3483-5). Moody.

Westing, Harold J., compiled by. I'd Love to Tell the World: The Challenge of Missions. LC 77-75131. 1977. pap. 2.95 (ISBN 0-916406-67-9). Accent Bks.

White, Mrs. Bob. Unto the Uttermost. (Illus.). 80p. 1978. pap. 1.00 (ISBN 0-89114-079-4). Baptist Pub Hse.

Wilson, Otto & Barratt, Robert S. Fifty Years' Work with Girls, 1883-1933: A Story of the Florence Crittenton Homes. LC 74-1717. (Children & Youth Ser.: Vol. 12). (Illus.). 513p. 1974. Repr. of 1933 ed. 33.00x (ISBN 0-405-05992-2). Arno.

Wilson, Samuel, ed. Mission Handbook: North American Protestant Ministries Overseas. 1980. 15.00 (ISBN 0-912552-34-4). MARC.

MISSIONS–BIBLICAL TEACHING

see also Kerygma

Devadutt, Vinjamuri E. Bible & the Faiths of Men. (Orig.). 1967. pap. 1.25 (ISBN 0-377-37011-8). Friend Pr.

Goerner, H. Cornell. All Nations in God's Purpose. LC 78-50360. 1979. pap. 3.95 (ISBN 0-8054-6312-7). Broadman.

Peters, George. A Biblical Theology of Missions. LC 72-77952. 384p. 1972. 12.95 (ISBN 0-8024-0709-9). Moody.

Tippett, Alan R. Church Growth & the Word of God. 1970. pap. 1.95 (ISBN 0-8028-1328-3). Eerdmans.

Weiss, G. Christian. The Heart of Missionary Theology. 1977. pap. 1.95 (ISBN 0-8024-3483-5). Moody.

MISSIONS–BIBLIOGRAPHY

Ericson, Jack T., ed. Missionary Society of Connecticut Papers, 1759-1948: A Guide to the Microform Edition. 49p. 1976. pap. 15.00 (ISBN 0-667-00289-8). Microfilming Corp.

Horvath, David G., ed. Papers of the American Home Missionary Society, 1816 (1826-1894) 1936: A Guide to the Microfilm Edition. 94p. 1975. pap. 50.00 (ISBN 0-88455-994-7). Microfilming Corp.

Missionary Research Library - New York. Dictionary Catalog of the Missionary Research Library, 17 Vols. 1967. Set. 1350.00 (ISBN 0-8161-0778-5). G K Hall.

MISSIONS–EDUCATIONAL WORK

Elliott, Arthur E. Paraguay: Its Cultural Heritage, Social Conditions & Educational Problems. LC 70-176746. (Columbia University. Teachers College. Contributions to Education: No. 473). Repr. of 1931 ed. 17.50 (ISBN 0-404-55473-3). AMS Pr.

Holmes, Brian, ed. Educational Policy & the Mission Schools: Case Studies from the British Empire. 1967. text ed. 16.75x (ISBN 0-7100-6002-5). Humanities.

Lockerbie, D. Bruce. The Education of Missionaries' Children: The Neglected Dimension of World Mission. LC 75-12726. 96p. 1975. 2.95 (ISBN 0-87808-422-3). William Carey Lib.

MISSIONS–HISTORY

Cuming, G. J., ed. Mission of the Church & the Propagation of the Faith. LC 77-108105. (Cambridge Studies in Church History: Vol. 6). 1970. 36.00 (ISBN 0-521-07752-4). Cambridge U Pr.

Cuming, G. J. & Baker, D., eds. Councils & Assemblies. LC 70-132384. (Cambridge Studies in Church History: No. 7). 1971. 47.50 (ISBN 0-521-08038-X). Cambridge U Pr.

Eddy, George S. Pathfinders of the World Missionary Crusade. facs. ed. LC 76-84304. (Essay Index Reprint Ser). 1945. 18.25 (ISBN 0-8369-1127-X). Arno.

Fear, Leona K. New Ventures-Free Methodist Missions Nineteen Sixty to Nineteen Seventy-Nine. (Orig.). 1979. pap. 3.95 (ISBN 0-89367-036-7). Light & Life.

Filbeck, David. The First Fifty Years. LC 80-65966. 400p. 1980. pap. 5.95 (ISBN 0-89900-060-6). College Pr Pub.

Hefley, James & Hefley, Marti. Unstilled Voices. LC 80-70116. 224p. 1981. 8.95 (ISBN 0-915684-85-3). Christian Herald.

Kane, J. Herbert. Global View of Christian Missions. 1971. 11.95 (ISBN 0-8010-5308-0). Baker Bk.

McBeth, Leon. Hombres Claves En las Misiones. Orig. Title: Men Who Made Missions. 128p. 1980. pap. 3.25 (ISBN 0-311-01070-9). Casa Bautista.

Mangham, Evelyn. Great Missionaries in a Great Work Leader's Guide. Schroeder, E. H., ed. (Illus.). 85p. 1970. pap. 1.75 (ISBN 0-87509-091-5). Chr Pubns.

Murray, Andrew & Choy, Leona. Key to the Missionary Problem. (Orig.). 1980. pap. 2.95 (ISBN 0-87508-401-X). Chr Lit.

Neill, Stephen. History of Christian Missions. (History of the Church). (Orig.). 1964. pap. 4.95 (ISBN 0-14-020628-0, Pelican). Penguin.

Smalley, William A., ed. Readings in Missionary Anthropology II. 2nd rev. enl. ed. LC 78-6009. (Applied Cultural Anthropology Ser.). 1978. pap. text ed. 12.95x (ISBN 0-87808-731-1). William Carey.

Tracy, Joseph, et al, eds. History of American Missions to the Heathens from Their Commencement to the Present Time. LC 35-32346. (American Studies). 1970. Repr. of 1840 ed. 38.50 (ISBN 0-384-23460-7). Johnson Repr.

Winter, Ralph D. The Twenty-Five Unbelievable Years, 1945-1969. 8th ed. LC 73-125459. (Illus.). 128p. 1974. pap. 3.95x (ISBN 0-87808-102-X). William Carey Lib.

MISSIONS–SERMONS

Simpson, Albert B. Missionary Messages. pap. 1.50 (ISBN 0-87509-029-X). Chr Pubns.

Spurgeon, Charles H. Twelve Missionary Sermons. (Charles H. Sprugeon Library). 1978. pap. 2.95 (ISBN 0-8010-8135-1). Baker Bk.

MISSIONS–STUDY AND TEACHING

Grunlan, Stephen A. & Mayers, Marvin K. Cultural Anthropology: A Christian Perspective. 1979. 8.95 (ISBN 0-310-36321-7). Zondervan.

Hughes, William. Dark Africa & the Way Out: Or, a Scheme for Civilizing & Evangelizing the Dark Continent. LC 76-90133. (Illus.). Repr. of 1892 ed. 11.75x (ISBN 0-8371-1990-1, Pub. by Negro U Pr). Greenwood.

Ward, Ted & Buker, Raymond B., Sr., eds. The World Directory of Mission-Related Educational Institutions. LC 72-94135. 906p. 1973. 19.95x (ISBN 0-87808-121-6). William Carey Lib.

MISSIONS–THEORY

Anderson, Gerald H. & Stransky, Thomas R., eds. Missions Trends No. 3. (Mission Trends Ser). (Orig.). 1976. pap. 3.45 (ISBN 0-8028-1654-1). Eerdmans.

Boer, Harry R. Pentecost & Missions. LC 61-13664. pap. 4.95 (ISBN 0-8028-1021-7). Eerdmans.

Bosch, David J. Witness to the World: The Christian Mission in Theological Perspective. LC 79-91241. (New Foundations Theological Library). 285p. (Series editors Peter Toon & Ralph Martin). 1980. 18.50 (ISBN 0-8042-3706-9, 3706-9). John Knox.

Brock, Charles. The Principles & Practice of Indigenous Church Planting. 1981. pap. 2.95 (ISBN 0-8054-6328-3). Broadman.

Comblin, Jose. The Meaning of Mission. Drury, John, tr. from Spanish. LC 76-41723. Orig. Title: Teologia De la Mision. 1977. 6.95x (ISBN 0-88344-304-X); pap. 4.95 (ISBN 0-88344-305-8). Orbis Bks.

Danielou, Jean. Salvation of the Nations. 1962. pap. 1.25x (ISBN 0-268-00244-4). U of Notre Dame Pr.

Dunn, Edmond J. Missionary Theology: Foundations in Development. LC 80-67259. 409p. 1980. lib. bdg. 21.75 (ISBN 0-8191-1209-7); pap. text ed. 13.50 (ISBN 0-8191-1210-0). U Pr of Amer.

Franciscan View of Missiology. (Franciscan Educational Conferences Ser). 1946. pap. 2.00 (ISBN 0-685-77547-X). Franciscan Herald.

Hesselgrave, David J., ed. Theology & Mission: Papers Given at Trinity Consultation No. 1. 1978. pap. 7.95 (ISBN 0-8010-4131-7). Baker Bk.

Liao, David. The Unresponsive: Resistant or Neglected? The Hakka Chinese in Taiwan Illustrate the Homogeneous Unit Principle. LC 73-175494. 1979. pap. 5.95 (ISBN 0-87808-735-4). William Carey Lib.

McGavran, Donald A., ed. Church Growth & Christian Mission. LC 65-10702. 256p. 1976. pap. 4.95x (ISBN 0-87808-728-1). William Carey Lib.

Newbigin, Lesslie. Sign of the Kingdom. 48p. (Orig.). 1981. pap. 1.95 (ISBN 0-8028-1878-1). Eerdmans.

Peters, George. A Biblical Theology of Missions. LC 72-77952. 384p. 1972. 12.95 (ISBN 0-8024-0709-9). Moody.

Rahner, Karl, ed. Re-Thinking the Church's Mission. LC 66-20894. (Concilium Ser.: Vol. 13). 160p. 6.95 (ISBN 0-8091-0127-0). Paulist Pr.

Reilly, Michael C. Spirituality for Mission. LC 78-878. 1978. pap. 8.95 (ISBN 0-88344-464-X). Orbis Bks.

Scott, Waldron. Karl Barth's Theology of Mission. Bockmuehl, Klaus, ed. (World Evangelical Fellowship: Outreach & Identity Theological Monograph). 40p. 1978. pap. 1.95 (ISBN 0-87784-541-7). Inter-Varsity.

Verkuyl, Johannes. Contemporary Missiology: An Introduction. Cooper, Dale, tr. from Dutch. 1978. 14.95 (ISBN 0-8028-3518-X). Eerdmans.

Webster, Douglas. Yes to Mission. LC 66-72166. 1966. text ed. 3.50x (ISBN 0-8401-2703-0). Allenson-Breckinridge.

MISSIONS–AFRICA

Berman, Edward H. African Reaction to Missionary Education. LC 74-22497. (Orig.). 1975. pap. text ed. 9.95x (ISBN 0-8077-2445-9). Tchrs Coll.

Bowdich, T. E. Mission from Cape Coast to Ashantee. new ed. 595p. 1966. 48.50x (ISBN 0-7146-1794-6, F Cass Co). Biblio Dist.

Bowen, Thomas J. Central Africa: Adventures & Missionary Labors in Several Countries in the Interior of Africa, from 1849-1856. LC 75-79819. (Illus.). Repr. of 1857 ed. 18.25x (ISBN 0-8371-1540-X, Pub. by Negro U Pr). Greenwood.

Brookes, Edgar H. & Vandenbosch, Amry. The City of God & the City of Man in Africa. LC 64-13998. (Illus.). 144p. 1964. 7.00x (ISBN 0-8131-1091-2). U Pr of Ky.

Buhlmann, Walbert. The Missions on Trial. Dolan, A. P., tr. LC 78-23922. 1979. pap. 5.95 (ISBN 0-88344-316-3). Orbis Bks.

Ekechi, F. K. Missionary Enterprise & Rivalry in Igboland, 1857-1914. (Illus.). 296p. 1972. 28.50x (ISBN 0-7146-2778-X, F Cass Co). Biblio Dist.

Fitts, Leroy. Lott Carey: First Black Missionary to Africa. 1978. pap. 5.95 (ISBN 0-8170-0820-9). Judson.

Fraser, Donald. New Africa. LC 78-89034. (Illus.). Repr. of 1927 ed. 12.25x (ISBN 0-8371-1914-6, Pub. by Negro U Pr). Greenwood.

Gollock, Georgina A. Daughters of Africa. LC 71-89000. (Illus.). Repr. of 1932 ed. 12.75x (ISBN 0-8371-1765-8, Pub. by Negro U Pr). Greenwood.

Hastings, Adrian. Church & Mission in Modern Africa. LC 67-30321. (Orig.). 1967. 22.50 (ISBN 0-8232-0770-6). Fordham.

Hughes, William. Dark Africa & the Way Out: Or, a Scheme for Civilizing & Evangelizing the Dark Continent. LC 76-90133. (Illus.). Repr. of 1892 ed. 11.75x (ISBN 0-8371-1990-1, Pub. by Negro U Pr). Greenwood.

Johnston, James. Missionary Landscapes in the Dark Continent. LC 72-3911. (Black Heritage Library Collection Ser.). Repr. of 1892 ed. 16.00 (ISBN 0-8369-9100-1). Arno.

Kendrick, V. Ben. Buried Alive for Christ & Other Missionary Stories. LC 78-14984. 1978. pap. 3.95 (ISBN 0-87227-061-0). Reg Baptist.

Markowitz, Marvin D. Cross & Sword: The Political Role of Christian Missions in the Belgian Congo, 1908-1960. LC 75-170209. (Publications Ser.: No. 114). 1973. 13.50 (ISBN 0-8179-6141-0). Hoover Inst Pr.

Moffat, Robert. The Matabele Journals of Robert Moffat, 1829-1860, 2 vols. LC 74-15069. Repr. of 1945 ed. Set. 75.00 (ISBN 0-404-12111-X). AMS Pr.

Mondini, A. G. Africa or Death. (Illus.). 1964. 5.00 (ISBN 0-8198-0007-4). Dghtrs St Paul.

Monsma, Timothy. An Urban Strategy for Africa. LC 79-11273. 1979. pap. 6.95 (ISBN 0-87808-430-4). William Carey Lib.

Morrison, James H. Missionary Heroes of Africa. LC 79-89010. Repr. of 1922 ed. 13.25x (ISBN 0-8371-1738-0, Pub. by Negro U Pr). Greenwood.

Okwuosa, Vincent A. In the Name of Christianity: The Missionaries in Africa. 1977. 4.50 (ISBN 0-8059-2420-5). Dorrance.

Richardson, James. Narrative of a Mission to Central Africa: 1850-1851, 2 vols. (Illus.). 360p. 1970. 85.00x set (ISBN 0-7146-1848-9, F Cass Co). Biblio Dist.

Schmelzenbach, Elmer & Parrott, Leslie. Sons of Africa. 217p. 1979. 9.95 (ISBN 0-8341-0601-9, Beacon). Nazarene.

Schon, James F. & Crowther, Samuel. Journals of the Rev. James Frederick Schon & Mr. Samuel Crowther Who with the Sanction of Her Majesty's Government; Accompanied the Expedition: Up the Niger in 1841 on Behalf of the Church Missionary Society. 2nd ed. 394p. 1970. 32.50x (ISBN 0-7146-1877-2, F Cass Co). Biblio Dist.

Westermann, Diedrich. Africa & Christianity. LC 74-15102. (Duff Lectures, 1935). Repr. of 1937 ed. 17.50 (ISBN 0-404-12151-9). AMS Pr.

MISSIONS–AFRICA, CENTRAL

Arnot, Frederick S. Garenganze or Seven Years' Pioneer Mission Work in Central Africa. rev. & 2nd ed. (Illus.). 276p. 1969. 27.50x (ISBN 0-7146-1860-8, F Cass Co). Biblio Dist.

Bowen, T. J. Adventures & Missionary Labours in Several Countries in the Interior of Africa from 1849-1856. 2nd rev. ed. 359p. 1968. Repr. of 1857 ed. 27.50x (ISBN 0-7146-1863-2, F Cass Co). Biblio Dist.

Clarke, Richard F., ed. Cardinal Lavigerie & the African Slave Trade. LC 74-77199. Repr. of 1889 ed. 17.75x (ISBN 0-8371-1283-4, Pub. by Negro U Pr). Greenwood.

Crawford, Daniel. Thinking Black: Twenty-Two Years Without a Break in the Long Grass of Central Africa. Repr. of 1913 ed. 24.75x (ISBN 0-8371-1752-6). Greenwood.

Fuller, Millard. Bokotola. 1977. pap. 3.95 (ISBN 0-8096-1924-5). New Century.

Hodges, Tony. Jehovah's Witnesses in Central Africa. (Minority Rights Group Ser.: No. 29). 16p. (Orig.). 1976. pap. 2.50 (ISBN 0-89192-120-6). Interbk Inc.

Jack, James W. Daybreak in Livingstonia: The Story of the Livingstonia Mission, British Central Africa. rev. ed. LC 79-77204. (Illus.). Repr. of 1900 ed. 20.75x (ISBN 0-8371-1308-3, Pub. by Negro U Pr). Greenwood.

Linden, Ian & Linden, Jane. Church & Revolution in Rwanda. LC 76-58329. 1977. text ed. 33.00x (ISBN 0-8419-0305-0, Africana). Holmes & Meier.

Morrison, James H. Streams in the Desert: A Picture of Life in Livingstonia. LC 79-12172. Repr. of 1919 ed. 10.50x (ISBN 0-8371-2780-7, Pub. by Negro U Pr). Greenwood.

Rowley, Henry. Story of the Universities' Mission to Central Africa. 2nd ed. LC 75-77211. (Illus.). Repr. of 1867 ed. 20.50x (ISBN 0-8371-1299-0, Pub. by Negro U Pr). Greenwood.

Wendland, E. H. Of Other Gods & Other Spirits. 1977. pap. 4.95 (ISBN 0-8100-0034-2, 12-1711). Northwest Pub.

MISSIONS–AFRICA, EAST

African Education Commission. Education in East Africa. LC 78-100256. (Illus.). Repr. of 1925 ed. 24.75x (ISBN 0-8371-2914-1, Pub. by Negro U Pr). Greenwood.

Gregory, John W. Foundation of British East Africa. LC 78-88412. Repr. of 1901 ed. 17.00x (ISBN 0-8371-1727-5, Pub. by Negro U Pr). Greenwood.

Healey, Joseph G. A Fifth Gospel: The Experience of Black Christian Values. LC 80-25033. (Illus.). 320p. (Orig.). 1981. pap. 7.95 (ISBN 0-88344-013-X). Orbis Bks.

Macdonald, Duff. Africana, Or, the Heart of Heathen Africa, 2 Vols. LC 70-82058. (Illus.). Repr. of 1882 ed. 29.00x (ISBN 0-8371-1523-X, Pub. by Negro U Pr). Greenwood.

Newman, Henry S. Banani: The Transition from Slavery to Freedom in Zanzibar & Pemba. LC 74-82320. (Illus.). Repr. of 1898 ed. 16.00x (ISBN 0-8371-1655-4, Pub. by Negro U Pr). Greenwood.

Oliver, Roland. Missionary Factor in East Africa. (Illus.). 1967. pap. text ed. 4.00x (ISBN 0-582-60847-3). Humanities.

Pringle, M. A. Journey in East Africa: Towards the Mountains of the Moon. new ed. LC 72-3957. (Black Heritage Library Collection Ser.). Repr. of 1886 ed. 25.00 (ISBN 0-8369-9105-2). Arno.

Tucker, Alfred R. Eighteen Years in Uganda & East Africa. LC 77-106884. Repr. of 1911 ed. 23.50x (ISBN 0-8371-3280-0, Pub. by Negro U Pr). Greenwood.

MISSIONS–AFRICA, SOUTH

African Education Commission. Education in East Africa. LC 78-100256. (Illus.). Repr. of 1925 ed. 24.75x (ISBN 0-8371-2914-1, Pub. by Negro U Pr). Greenwood.

Bryan, G. McLeod. Naude: Prophet to South Africa. LC 77-15746. (Orig.). 1978. pap. 5.95 (ISBN 0-8042-0942-1). John Knox.

Champion, George. Journal of Reverend G. Champion, American Missionary in Zululand, 1835-9. Booth, Alan R., ed. 1967. 10.00x (ISBN 0-8426-1189-4). Verry.

Hance, Gertrude R. Zulu Yesterday & Today: Twenty-Nine Years in South Africa. LC 79-89002. (Illus.). Repr. of 1916 ed. 16.25x (ISBN 0-8371-1743-7). Greenwood.

Latrobe, C. I. Journal of a Visit to South Africa in 1815-1816. (Illus.). 1969. Repr. of 1818 ed. 60.00x (ISBN 0-8426-1348-X). Verry.

Latrobe, Christian I. Journal of a Visit to South Africa, in Eighteen Fifteen & Eighteen Sixteen. LC 70-89040. Repr. of 1818 ed. 18.75x (ISBN 0-8371-1940-5, Pub. by Negro U Pr). Greenwood.

Livingston, David. Missionary Travels & Researches in South Africa. LC 5-15250. 1971. Repr. of 1857 ed. 54.00 (ISBN 0-384-32983-7). Johnson Repr.

Moffat, Robert. Missionary Labours & Scenes in Southern Africa. (Landmarks in Anthropology Ser). (Illus.). 1969. Repr. of 1842 ed. 27.00 (ISBN 0-384-39470-1). Johnson Repr.

Philip, John. Researches in South Africa, 2 Vols. LC 77-82065. (Illus.). Repr. of 1828 ed. 33.00x (ISBN 0-8371-3855-8). Greenwood.

Shaw, Barnabas. Memorials of South Africa. LC 71-109358. Repr. of 1840 ed. 18.75x (ISBN 0-8371-3737-3, Pub. by Negro U Pr). Greenwood.

--Memorials of South Africa. facsimile ed. 1970. Repr. of 1840 ed. 21.00x (ISBN 0-8426-0181-3). Verry.

MISSIONS–AFRICA, WEST

Bane, Martin J. Popes & Western Africa. 1968. 3.95 (ISBN 0-8189-0114-4). Alba.

Barrow, Alfred. Fifty Years in Western Africa. LC 79-92739. Repr. of 1900 ed. 10.00x (ISBN 0-8371-2193-0, Pub. by Negro U Pr). Greenwood.

Hening, Mrs. E. F. History of the African Mission of the Protestant Episcopal Church in the United States. facsimile ed. LC 77-173608. (Black Heritage Library Collection). Repr. of 1849 ed. 18.75 (ISBN 0-8369-8900-7). Arno.

McGavran, Donald A. & Riddle, Norman. Zaire: Midday in Missions. 1979. pap. 12.95 (ISBN 0-8170-0835-7). Judson.

Scott, Anna M. Day Dawn in Africa: Or Progress of the Protestant Episcopal Mission at Cape Palmas, West Africa. LC 69-18659. (Illus.). Repr. of 1858 ed. 17.00x (ISBN 0-8371-5091-4, Pub. by Negro U Pr). Greenwood.

MISSIONS–ALASKA

Aaron Ladner Lindsley: Founder of Alaska Missions. 9p. Repr. pap. 2.25 (ISBN 0-8466-0050-1, SJS50). Shorey.

Pierce, Richard A., ed. The Russian Orthodox Religious Mission in America, 1794-1837. Bearne, Colin, tr. (Alaska History Ser.: No. 11). 1977. 15.50 (ISBN 0-919642-80-2). Limestone Pr.

Savage, Alma H. Dogsled Apostles. facs. ed. LC 68-55857. (Essay Index Reprint Ser). 1942. 18.00 (ISBN 0-8369-0851-1). Arno.

Wallace, Fern. Tides of Change: A History of the Russian Orthodox Mission in Alaska. 1977. pap. 5.00 (ISBN 0-913026-78-6, Synaxis Pr). St Nectarios.

MISSIONS–ASIA

Burke, Todd & Burke, DeAnn. Anointed for Burial. 1977. pap. 2.95 (ISBN 0-88270-485-0). Logos.

Hyatt, Irwin T., Jr. Our Ordered Lives Confess. (American-East Asian Relations Ser.: No. 8). 1976. 18.50x (ISBN 0-674-64735-1). Harvard U Pr.

Mathews, Basil J., ed. East & West: Conflict or Cooperation. facs. ed. LC 67-26764. (Essay Index Reprint Ser). 1936. 12.25 (ISBN 0-8369-0694-2). Arno.

Mueller, John T. Great Missionaries to the Orient. LC 78-38330. (Biography Index Reprint Ser). Repr. of 1948 ed. 12.75 (ISBN 0-8369-8125-1). Arno.

Nelson, Marlin L. The How & Why of Third World Missions: An Asian Case Study. LC 76-47658. 1976. pap. 6.95 (ISBN 0-87808-318-9). William Carey Lib.

Wagner, C. Peter & Dayton, Edward R. Unreached Peoples, Eighty-One. (Orig.). 1981. pap. 8.95 (ISBN 0-89191-331-9). Cook.

MISSIONS–AUSTRALIA

Cato, Nancy. Mister Maloga: Daniel Matthews & His Mission, Murray River, 1864-1902. 1977. 24.95x (ISBN 0-7022-1110-9). U of Queensland Pr.

Perez, Eugene. Kalumburu: The Benedictine Mission & the Aborigines 1908-1975. (Illus.). 1978. pap. 11.50x (ISBN 0-9596887-0-6, Pub. by U of W Austral Pr). Intl Schol Bk Serv.

Tonkinson, Robert. The Jigalong Mob: Aboriginal Victors of the Desert Crusade. LC 73-85115. (Illus.). 166p. 1974. pap. 6.95 (ISBN 0-8465-7549-3). Benjamin-Cummings.

MISSIONS–BOLIVIA

Smith, W. Douglas. Toward Continuous Misson: Strategizing for the Evangelization of Bolivia. LC 77-21490. 1978. pap. 4.95 (ISBN 0-87808-321-9). William Carey Lib.

MISSIONS–BOTSWANA

Mackenzie, John. Day-Dawn in Dark Places: A Story of Wanderings & Work in Bechwanaland. LC 76-77206. (Illus.). Repr. of 1883 ed. 13.50x (ISBN 0-8371-1280-X, Pub. by Negro U Pr). Greenwood.

MISSIONS–BRAZIL

Barnes, Vera F. Miles Beyond in Brazil. 3.50 (ISBN 0-87509-104-0); pap. 2.00 (ISBN 0-87509-105-9). Chr Pubns.

Edwards, Fred E. The Role of the Faith Mission: A Brazilian Case Study. LC 79-152406. (Illus.). 76p. 1971. pap. 3.45 (ISBN 0-87808-406-1). William Carey Lib.

MISSIONS–BRITISH COLOMBIA

Lillard, Charles. Mission to Nootka. (Illus.). 119p. 1977. pap. 6.95 (ISBN 0-686-74137-4). Superior Pub.

Poynter, Margaret. Miracle at Metlakatla. (Greatness with Faith Ser.). (Illus.). 1978. 4.95 (ISBN 0-570-07876-8, 39-1201); pap. 2.95 (ISBN 0-570-07881-4, 39-1211). Concordia.

MISSIONS–BURMA

Cramer, Robert F. Hunger Fighter in Burma: The Story of Brayton Case. (Orig.). 1968. pap. 0.95 (ISBN 0-377-84111-0). Friend Pr.

Fischer, Edward. Mission in Burma: The Columban Fathers' Forty-Three Years in Kachin Country. 192p. 1980. 9.95 (ISBN 0-8164-0464-X). Seabury.

Tegenfeldt, Herman. A Century of Growth: The Kachin Baptist Church of Burma. LC 74-4415. 540p. 1974. 10.95 (ISBN 0-87808-416-9). William Carey Lib.

MISSIONS–CAMEROONS

Mackenzie, Jean K. Black Sheep: Adventures in West Africa. LC 70-89008. Repr. of 1916 ed. 14.50x (ISBN 0-8371-1761-5, Pub. by Negro U Pr). Greenwood.

MISSIONS–CANADA

Brasseur De Bourbourg, E. Ch. Histoire De Canada, De Son Eglise et De Ses Missions. (Canadiana Avant 1867: No. 4). 1968. 65.25x (ISBN 90-2796-333-9). Mouton.

Faraud, Henri J. Dix-Huit Ans Chez Les Sauvages: Voyages Et Missions De Monseigneur Henry Faraud. Repr. of 1866 ed. 23.00 (ISBN 0-384-15135-3). Johnson Repr.

Marsden, Joshua. The Narrative of a Mission to Nova Scotia, New Brunswick & the Somers Islands. Repr. of 1816 ed. 19.50 (ISBN 0-384-35430-0). Johnson Repr.

Pritchett, John P. Black Robe & Buckskin. 1960. 3.00 (ISBN 0-8084-0063-0). Coll & U Pr.

Tache, Alexandre A. Vingt Annees De Missions Dans le Nord-Ouest De L'amerique. (Canadiana Before 1867 Ser). (Fr). Repr. of 1866 ed. 14.50 (ISBN 0-384-59425-5). Johnson Repr.
--Vingt Annees De Missions Dans le Nord-Ouest De L'amerique Par Mgr. Alex. Tache Eveque De Saint-Boniface (Montreal, 1866) (Canadiana Avant 1867: NO. 21). 1970. 23.50x (ISBN 90-2796-343-6). Mouton.

MISSIONS–CHINA

Aikman, David. Love China Today. 1979. pap. text ed. 2.45 (ISBN 0-8423-3845-4). Tyndale.
Bailie, Victoria W. Bailie's Activities in China. LC 64-17671. (Illus.). 1964. 15.00x (ISBN 0-87015-128-2). Pacific Bks.
Band, Edward. Working His Purpose Out: The History of the English Presbyterian Mission, 1847-1947, CW-223. 1972. 16.85x (ISBN 0-89644-310-8, Pub. by Ch'eng Wen Taiwan). Chinese Materials.
Bohr, Paul R. Famine in China & the Missionary: Timothy Richard As Relief Administrator & Advocate of National Reform, 1876-1884. LC 72-75828. (East Asian Monographs Ser: No. 48). (Illus.). 1972. pap. 9.00x (ISBN 0-674-29425-4). Harvard U Pr.
Carlson, Ellsworth C. The Foochow Missionaries, 1847-1880. LC 72-97832. (East Asian Monographs Ser: No. 51). 1973. pap. 15.00x (ISBN 0-674-30735-6). Harvard U Pr.
Cohen, Paul A. China & Christianity: The Missionary Movement & the Growth of Chinese Antiforeignism, 1860-1870. LC 63-19135. (East Asian Ser: No. 11). (Illus.). 1963. 20.00x (ISBN 0-674-11701-8). Harvard U Pr.
Dunne, George H. Generation of Giants. 1962. 9.95x (ISBN 0-268-00109-X). U of Notre Dame Pr.
Edwards, E. H. Fire & Sword in Shansi: The Story of the Martyrdom of Foreigners & Chinese Christians. LC 74-111738. (American Imperialism: Viewpoints of United States Foreign Policy, 1898-1941). 1970. Repr. of 1903 ed. 17.00 (ISBN 0-405-02014-7). Arno.
Fairbank, John K., ed. The Missionary Enterprise in China & America. LC 74-82191. (Studies in American-East Asian Relations: No. 6). 442p. 1974. text ed. 20.00x (ISBN 0-674-57655-1). Harvard U Pr.
Fast, Aganetha. The Power of Christ's Love in China. LC 71-188251. 134p. 1972. pap. 2.00 (ISBN 0-87303-667-0). Faith & Life.
Forsythe, Sidney A. An American Missionary Community in China, 1895-1905. LC 70-178077. (East Asian Monographs Ser: No. 43). 1971. pap. 9.00x (ISBN 0-674-02626-8). Harvard U Pr.
Goforth, Jonathan. By My Spirit. 1967. pap. 3.50 (ISBN 0-87123-034-8, 210034). Bethany Hse.
Goforth, Rosalind. Goforth of China. 1969. pap. 3.95 (ISBN 0-87123-181-6, 200181). Bethany Hse.
Gulick, Edward V. Peter Parker & the Opening of China. LC 73-82628. (Harvard Studies in American-East Asian Relations: No. 3). 228p. 1974. text ed. 15.00x (ISBN 0-674-66326-8). Harvard U Pr.
Kuhn, Isobel S. Green Leaf in Drought Time. 1957. pap. 1.95 (ISBN 0-8024-0046-9). Moody.
Latourette, Kenneth S. History of Christian Missions in China. LC 66-24721. 1967. Repr. of 1929 ed. 22.50 (ISBN 0-8462-0992-6). Russell.
Legge, James. Nestorian Monument of Hsi-an Fu in Shen-Hsi, China. 1966. Repr. of 1888 ed. 5.50 (ISBN 0-8188-0062-3). Paragon.
Liu Kwang-Ching, ed. American Missionaries in China: Papers from Harvard Seminars. LC 66-31226. (East Asian Monographs Ser: No. 21). 1966. pap. 9.00x (ISBN 0-674-02600-4). Harvard U Pr.
Medhurst, W. H. China: Its State & Prospects with Especial Reference to the Spread of the Gospel. LC 72-79833. (The China Library Ser.). 1972. Repr. of 1842 ed. 29.00 (ISBN 0-8420-1379-2). Scholarly Res Inc.
Mueller, John T. Great Missionaries to China. LC 73-38329. (Biography Index Reprint Ser). Repr. of 1947 ed. 12.75 (ISBN 0-8369-8124-3). Arno.
Pfeilschifter, B. & Schmalz, N. Shen-Fu's Story. 3.50 (ISBN 0-8199-0130-X, L38787). Franciscan Herald.
Rabe, Valentin H. The Home Base of American China Missions, 1880-1920. (Harvard East Asian Monographs: Vol. 75). 1978. 15.00x (ISBN 0-674-40581-1). Harvard U Pr.
Reynolds, A. Voice of China's Christian. 1968. pap. 0.35 (ISBN 0-85363-087-9). OMF Bks.
Simkin, Robert L. & Simkin, Margaret. Letters from Szechwan. 1978. text ed. 8.95 (ISBN 0-914064-08-8); pap. text ed. 6.95 (ISBN 0-914064-09-6). Celo Pr.
Smith, Bertha. Go Home & Tell. LC 65-10342. (Orig.). 1965. pap. 4.95 (ISBN 0-8054-7202-9). Broadman.
Taylor, Howard. James Hudson Taylor: Biography. 11.95 (ISBN 0-85363-004-6). OMF Bks.
Trettel, Father Efrem. Rivers - Rice Fields - Souls. 4.50 (ISBN 0-8199-0670-0, L38690). Franciscan Herald.
Varg, Paul A. Missionaries, Chinese & Diplomats. LC 76-30301. 1977. Repr. lib. bdg. 17.50x (ISBN 0-374-98071-3). Octagon.
West, Philip. Yenching University & Sino-Western Relations, 1916-1952. (East Asian Ser.: No. 85). 1976. 17.50x (ISBN 0-674-96569-8). Harvard U Pr.
Widmer, Eric. The Russian Ecclestastical Mission in Peking During the Eighteenth Century. (East Asian Monographs: No. 69). 1976. 15.00x (ISBN 0-674-78129-5). Harvard U Pr.
Wu, Chao-Kwang. The International Aspect of the Missionary Movement in China. LC 75-41300. (Johns Hopkins University. Studies in Historical & Political Science: Extra Volumes; New Ser.: No. 11). Repr. of 1930 ed. 18.50 (ISBN 0-404-14708-9). AMS Pr.
Wyker, Bertha P. Spanning the Decades: A Spiritual Pilgrimage. (Illus.). 224p. 1981. 8.50 (ISBN 0-682-49746-0). Exposition.

MISSIONS–CONGO

Bently, W. Holman. Pioneering on the Congo, 2 Vols. (Landmarks in Anthropology Ser). 1970. Repr. of 1900 ed. Set. lib. bdg. 69.50 (ISBN 0-384-03943-X). Johnson Repr.
Burgess, Alan. Daylight Must Come. 1978. pap. 2.50 (ISBN 0-87123-107-7, 200107). Bethany Hse.
Rodeheaver, Homer A. Singing Black. LC 72-1681. Repr. of 1936 ed. 12.50 (ISBN 0-404-08330-7). AMS Pr.

MISSIONS–EAST (FAR EAST)

Richter, Julius. History of Protestant Missions in the Near East. LC 79-133822. Repr. of 1910 ed. 29.50 (ISBN 0-404-05331-9). AMS Pr.
Van Akkeren, Philip. Sri & Christ: A Study of the Indigenous Church in East Java. Mackie, Annebeth, tr. from Dutch. (World Studies of Churches in Mission). 1969. pap. 4.95 (ISBN 0-377-82981-1, Pub. by Lutterworth England). Friend Pr.

MISSIONS–ECUADOR

Elliot, Elisabeth. Through Gates of Splendor. 1981. 2.95 (ISBN 0-8423-7151-6). Tyndale.

MISSIONS–ESKIMOS

Menager, Francis M. The Kingdom of the Seal. (Illus.). 1962. 1.80 (ISBN 0-8294-0056-7). Loyola.

MISSIONS–ETHIOPIA

Gobat, Samuel. Journal of Three Years' Residence in Abyssinia. LC 72-78576. Repr. of 1851 ed. 19.00x (ISBN 0-8371-1416-0, Pub. by Negro U Pr). Greenwood.

MISSIONS–EUROPE

Andrew, Bro., et al. God's Smuggler. 1968. pap. 2.25 (ISBN 0-8007-8016-7, Spire Bks). Revell.
Andrew, Brother, et al. God's Smuggler. 1968. pap. 1.50 (ISBN 0-451-08325-3, W8325, Sig). NAL.
Maclear, George F. Apostles of Mediaeval Europe. LC 72-624. (Essay Index Reprint Ser.). Repr. of 1869 ed. 19.50 (ISBN 0-8369-2803-2). Arno.

MISSIONS–FIJI ISLANDS

Fischer, Edward. Fiji Revisited: A Columban Father's Memories of Twenty-Eight Years in the Islands. LC 81-5365. (Illus.). 1981. pap. 5.95 (ISBN 0-8245-0097-0). Crossroad NY.
Murray, Thomas. Pitcairn's Island. LC 72-281. (World History Ser., No. 48). 1972. Repr. of 1860 ed. lib. bdg. 43.95 (ISBN 0-8383-1410-4). Haskell.

MISSIONS–FINLAND

Oppermann, Charles J. English Missionaries in Sweden & Finland. (Church Historical Society Ser.: No. 26). 1937. 12.50x (ISBN 0-281-00240-1). Allenson-Breckinridge.

MISSIONS–FORMOSA

Bolton, Robert J. Treasure Island: Church Growth Among Taiwan's Urban Minnan Chinese. LC 76-20828. (Illus.). 1976. pap. 8.95 (ISBN 0-87808-315-4). William Carey Lib.

MISSIONS–GABON

Klein, Carol M. We Went to Gabon. 1974. pap. 2.95 (ISBN 0-87509-151-2). Chr Pubns.

MISSIONS–HAWAII

Krauss, Bob. The Island Way. LC 75-21944. (Illus.). 1977. 14.95 (ISBN 0-89610-026-X). Island Her.

MISSIONS–INDIA

Carmichael, Amy. Gold Cord. 1957. pap. 3.95 (ISBN 0-87508-068-5). Chr Lit.
--Mimosa. 1958. pap. 1.50 (ISBN 0-87508-074-X). Chr Lit.
Doig, Desmond. Mother Teresa: Her Work & Her People. LC 75-39857. (Illus.). 176p. 1980. pap. 9.95 (ISBN 0-06-061941-4, RD336, HarpR). Har-Row.
Ingham, Kenneth. Reformers in India, 1793-1833: An Account of the Work of Christian Missionaries on Behalf of Social Reform. LC 73-16425. xi, 150p. 1973. Repr. of 1956 ed. lib. bdg. 13.50x (ISBN 0-374-94112-2). Octagon.
Luke, P. Y. & Carman, John B. Village Christians & Hindu Culture. (World Studies of Churches in Mission). 1968. pap. 3.95 (ISBN 0-377-82851-3, Pub. by Lutterworth England). Friend Pr.
Schutte, Josef F. Valignano's Mission Principles for Japan: Vol. I (1573-1582), Pt. I - The Problem (1573-1580) Coyne, John J., tr. from Ger. LC 78-69683. (Modern Scholarly Studies About the Jesuits, in English Translations, Ser. II: No. 3). (Illus.). xxiv, 428p. 1980. 14.00 (ISBN 0-912422-36-X); pap. 12.00 smyth sewn (ISBN 0-912422-35-1). Inst Jesuit.
Walsh, Jay & Oviatt, Patricia C. Ripe Mangoes: Miracle Missionary Stories from Bangladesh. LC 78-8671. (Illus.). 1978. pap. 2.95 (ISBN 0-87227-060-2). Reg Baptist.

MISSIONS–INDONESIA

Bentley-Taylor, David. Java Saga. Orig. Title: Weathercocks Reward. 1975. pap. 2.25 (ISBN 0-85363-100-X). OMF Bks.
Tari, Mel & Tari, Noni. Gentle Breeze of Jesus. LC 78-64960. 1978. pap. 2.50 (ISBN 0-89221-056-7, 056-7). New Leaf.

MISSIONS–IRAN

Wilson, Samuel G. Persian Life & Customs. 3rd ed. LC 76-178305. Repr. of 1900 ed. 24.50 (ISBN 0-404-06996-7). AMS Pr.

MISSIONS–IRELAND

Fischer, Edward. Fiji Revisited: A Columban Father's Memories of Twenty-Eight Years in the Islands. LC 81-5365. (Illus.). 1981. pap. 5.95 (ISBN 0-8245-0097-0). Crossroad NY.

MISSIONS–ISRAEL

Carter, John T. Witness in Israel: The Story of Paul Rowden. LC 69-14369. (gr. 4-9). 1969. pap. 0.75 (ISBN 0-8054-4314-2). Broadman.
Davis, Moshe, ed. Holy Land Missions & Missionaries: An Original Anthology. LC 77-70703. (America & the Holy Land Ser.). (Illus.). 1977. lib. bdg. 15.00x (ISBN 0-405-10259-3). Arno.
Morton, Daniel O. Memoir of Rev. Levi Parsons: Late Missionary to Palestine. Davis, Moshe, ed. (America & the Holy Land Ser.). 1977. Repr. of 1824 ed. lib. bdg. 25.00x (ISBN 0-405-10271-2). Arno.

MISSIONS–JAMAICA

Phillippo, James M. Jamaica: Its Past & Present State. LC 70-109998. (Illus.). Repr. of 1843 ed. 23.75x (ISBN 0-8371-4132-X, Pub. by Negro U Pr). Greenwood.

MISSIONS–JAPAN

Francis, Mable & Smith, Gerald. One Shall Chase a Thousand. 3.95 (ISBN 0-87509-113-X); pap. 2.50 (ISBN 0-87509-114-8). Chr Pubns.
Laures, John. Catholic Church in Japan: A Short History. Repr. of 1954 ed. lib. bdg. 15.00x (ISBN 0-8371-2974-5, LACC). Greenwood.
Neve, Lloyd R. Japan: God's Door to the Far East. LC 73-78255. 1973. write for info (ISBN 0-8066-1321-1, 10-3465). Augsburg.
Schutte, Josef F. Valignano's Mission Principles for Japan: Vol. I (1573-1582), Pt. I - The Problem (1573-1580) Coyne, John J., tr. from Ger. LC 78-69683. (Modern Scholarly Studies About the Jesuits, in English Translations, Ser. II: No. 3). (Illus.). xxiv, 428p. 1980. 14.00 (ISBN 0-912422-36-X); pap. 12.00 smyth sewn (ISBN 0-912422-35-1). Inst Jesuit.

MISSIONS–KAFFRARIA

Callaway, Godfrey. Sketches of Kafir Life. LC 79-77192. (Illus.). Repr. 12.75x (ISBN 0-8371-1277-X). Greenwood.
Gibson, Alan G. Eight Years in Kaffraria, 1882-1890. LC 79-82052. (Illus.). Repr. of 1891 ed. 12.25x (ISBN 0-8371-1573-6, Pub. by Negro U Pr). Greenwood.

MISSIONS–KOREA

Fisher, James E. Democracy & Mission Education in Korea. LC 70-176773. (Columbia University. Teachers College. Contributions to Education: No. 306). Repr. of 1928 ed. 17.50 (ISBN 0-404-55306-0). AMS Pr.
Pattisson, Peter. Crisis Unawares: A Doctor Examines the Korean Church. 1981. pap. 3.95 (ISBN 0-85363-135-2). OMF Bks.

MISSIONS–LAOS

Menger, Matt. Valley of Mekong. 1970. 4.95 (ISBN 0-685-79412-1); pap. 3.95 (ISBN 0-685-79413-X). Guild Bks.
Menger, Matt J. In the Valley of the Mekong. LC 79-115966. 1970. pap. 3.95 (ISBN 0-686-18632-X). Oblate.

MISSIONS–LATIN AMERICA

Blumenschein, Marian. Home in Honduras. LC 74-82186. 1975. 7.50 (ISBN 0-8309-0125-6). Herald Hse.
Costello, Gerald M. Mission to Latin America: The Successes & Failures of a Twentieth-Century Crusade. LC 78-12974. 1979. pap. 9.95 (ISBN 0-88344-312-0). Orbis Bks.
Gage, Thomas. Thomas Gage's Travels in the New World. rev. ed. enl. ed. Thompson, J. Eric, ed. LC 58-6856. (American Exploration & Travel Ser.: Vol. 58). (Illus.). 1958. 17.50 (ISBN 0-8061-0881-9). U of Okla Pr.
Materne, Yves, ed. Indian Awakening in Latin America. 1980. pap. 5.95 (ISBN 0-377-00097-3). Friend Pr.

MISSIONS–LIBERIA

Brittan, Harriett G. Scenes & Incidents of Everyday Life in Africa. LC 70-75541. Repr. of 1860 ed. 16.00x (ISBN 0-8371-0981-7). Greenwood.
Camphor, Alexander P. Missionary Story Sketches: Folk-Lore from Africa. facsimile ed. LC 79-173603. (Black Heritage Library Collection). Repr. of 1909 ed. 20.00 (ISBN 0-8369-8915-5). Arno.
Christy, David. Ethiopia: Her Gloom & Glory. LC 73-75550. Repr. of 1857 ed. 13.00x (ISBN 0-8371-1016-5, Pub. by Negro U Pr). Greenwood.

MISSIONS–MADAGASCAR

Gow, Bonar A. Madagascar & the Protestant Impact. LC 78-11216. (Dalhousie African Studies). 1979. text ed. 42.00x (ISBN 0-8419-0463-4, Africana). Holmes & Meier.

MISSIONS–MALAWI

Fraser, Donald. African Idylls: Portraits & Impressions of Life on a Central African Mission Station. LC 78-94477. (Illus.). Repr. of 1923 ed. 12.25x (ISBN 0-8371-2354-2, Pub. by Negro U Pr). Greenwood.
--Winning a Primitive People. LC 78-107474. (Illus.). Repr. of 1914 ed. 15.25x (ISBN 0-8371-3752-7). Greenwood.
Linden, Ian & Linden, Jane. Catholics, Peasants & Chewa Resistance in Nyasaland, 1889-1939. 1974. 26.75x (ISBN 0-520-02500-8). U of Cal Pr.
McCracken, J. Politics & Christianity in Malawi 1875-1940. LC 76-27905. (Cambridge Commonwealth Ser.). (Illus.). 1977. 39.00 (ISBN 0-521-21444-0). Cambridge U Pr.

MISSIONS–MEXICO

Barnes, Vera F. Daybreak Below the Border. 1975. Repr. 2.50 (ISBN 0-87509-078-8). Chr Pubns.
Robertson, Tomas. Baja California & Its Missions. (Illus.). 1978. pap. 3.50 (ISBN 0-910856-66-4). La Siesta.
Weddle, Robert S. San Juan Bautista: Gateway to Spanish Texas. (Illus.). 485p. 1968. 17.95 (ISBN 0-292-73306-2). U of Tex Pr.

MISSIONS–NEAR EAST

Burnet, David S. & Davis, Moshe, eds. The Jerusalem Mission: Under the Direction of the American Christian Missionary Society. (America & the Holy Land Ser.). 1977. Repr. of 1853 ed. lib. bdg. 20.00x (ISBN 0-405-10233-X). Arno.
Grabill, Joseph L. Protestant Diplomacy & the Near East: Missionary Influence in American Policy, 1810-1927. LC 70-5750. (Illus.). 1971. 15.00x (ISBN 0-8166-0575-0). U of Minn Pr.
Richter, Julius. History of Protestant Missions in the Near East. LC 79-133822. Repr. of 1910 ed. 29.50 (ISBN 0-404-05331-9). AMS Pr.

MISSIONS–NEW GUINEA

Bromilow, William E. Twenty Years Among Primitive Papuans. LC 75-32800. Repr. of 1929 ed. 26.00 (ISBN 0-404-14103-X). AMS Pr.
Hall, Clarence. Miracle on the Sepik. 2nd ed. (Illus.). 100p. Date not set. pap. price not set. Full Gospel.

MISSIONS–NIGERIA

Ajayi, J. F. Christian Missions in Nigeria, 1841-1891: The Making of a New Elite. 1965. 14.95 (ISBN 0-8101-0038-X). Northwestern U Pr.
Ayandele, Emmanuel A. Missionary Impact on Modern Nigeria, 1842-1914. (Ibadan History Ser.). 1967. pap. text ed. 15.75x (ISBN 0-582-64512-3). Humanities.
Buchan, James. The Expendable Mary Slessor. (Illus.). 272p. (Orig.). 1981. pap. 7.95 (ISBN 0-8164-2320-2). Seabury.
Helser, Albert D. Education of Primitive People. LC 75-97403. Repr. of 1934 ed. 14.50x (ISBN 0-8371-2651-7, Pub. by Negro U Pr). Greenwood.
Linden, Ian. Emirs & Evangelicals. 1981. 27.50x (ISBN 0-7146-3146-9, F Cass Co). Biblio Dist.
McCaba, Joseph. The Teacher Who Laughs. LC 73-80903. 1973. pap. 2.50 (ISBN 0-87227-050-5). Reg Baptist.

MISSIONS–NORTH AMERICA

Goodykoontz, Colin B. Home Missions on the American Frontier. LC 76-120619. 1970. Repr. lib. bdg. 25.00x (ISBN 0-374-93198-4). Octagon.
Humphreys, David. Historical Account of the Incorporated Society for the Propagation of the Gospel in Foreign Parts - to the Year 1728. LC 75-83426. (Religion in America, Ser. 1). 1969. Repr. of 1730 ed. 16.00 (ISBN 0-405-00251-3). Arno.
Toepperwein, Emilie & Toepperwein, Fritz. The Missions of San Antonio. pap. text ed. 1.50 (ISBN 0-910722-12-9). Highland Pr.

MISSIONS–OCEANICA

Barrett, Ward J., tr. from Span. Mission in the Marianas: An Account of Father Diego Luis De Sanvitores & His Companions, 1669-1670. LC 74-27258. (Illus.). 72p. 1975. 8.50x (ISBN 0-8166-0747-8). U of Minn Pr.

Gunson, Niel. Messengers of Grace: Evangelical Missionaries in the South Seas 1797-1860. (Illus.). 1978. 41.00x (ISBN 0-19-550517-4). Oxford U Pr.

Hilliard, David. God's Gentlemen: A History of the Melanesian Mission, 1849-1942. (Illus.). 1978. 19.95x (ISBN 0-7022-1066-8). U of Queensland Pr.

Wiltgen, R. M. The Founding of the Roman Catholic Church in Oceania 1825-1850. LC 78-74665. (Illus.). 610p. 1980. text ed. 36.95 (ISBN 0-7081-0835-0, 0572). Bks Australia.

Yate, William. An Account of New Zealand & of the Church Missionary Society's Mission in the Northern Island. (Illus.). 330p. 1970. Repr. of 1835 ed. 22.50x (ISBN 0-87471-392-7). Rowman.

MISSIONS–PERU

Wight, Maxine C. A Story About Light. LC 79-14691. 1979. 4.00 (ISBN 0-8309-0236-8). Herald Hse.

MISSIONS–PHILIPPINE ISLANDS

Baily, Michael. Small Net in a Big Sea: The Redemptorists in the Philippines, 1905-1929. (Illus.). 7.25x (ISBN 0-686-24529-6, San Carlos Pubns); pap. 5.00x (ISBN 0-686-24530-X). Cellar.

Gambill, Sandra & Ashley, Clara. Mission Studies: Philippines. (Vacation Bible School Ser.). (Illus.). 32p. (Orig.). 1981. pap. 1.00 (ISBN 0-89114-105-7). Baptist Pub Hse.

MISSIONS–RHODESIA

Embree, Esther. Now Rings the Bell. (Illus.). 1978. pap. 3.50 (ISBN 0-89367-023-5). Light & Life.

Rotberg, Robert I. Christian Missionaries & the Creation of Northern Rhodesia, 1880-1924. 1965. 17.50x (ISBN 0-691-03009-X). Princeton U Pr.

MISSIONS–RUSSIA

Smirnoff, Eugene. Russian Orthodox Missions. pap. 3.50 (ISBN 0-686-01299-2). Eastern Orthodox.

MISSIONS–SOLOMON ISLANDS

Laracy, Hugh. Marists & Melanesians: A History of Catholic Missions in the Solomon Islands. 256p. 1976. text ed. 14.00x (ISBN 0-8248-0361-2). U Pr of Hawaii.

Tippett, Alan R. Solomon Islands Christianity: A Study in Growth & Obstruction. LC 75-15143. (Applied Cultural Anthropology Ser.). 432p. 1975. pap. 5.95x (ISBN 0-87808-724-9). William Carey Lib.

MISSIONS–SOUTH AMERICA

Rippy, J. Fred & Nelson, Jean T. Crusaders of the Jungle. LC 76-123495. 1971. Repr. of 1936 ed. 15.50 (ISBN 0-8046-1382-6). Kennikat.

Rippy, James F. Crusaders of the Jungle. LC 76-136081. (Illus.). 1971. Repr. of 1936 ed. lib. bdg. 18.25x (ISBN 0-8371-5231-3, RIJU). Greenwood.

MISSIONS–SUDAN

Boer, Jan H. Missionary Messengers of Liberation in a Colonial Context: A Case Study of the Sudan United Mission. 542p. 1979. pap. text ed. 51.50x (ISBN 90-6203-561-2). Humanities.

MISSIONS–SWEDEN

Oppermann, Charles J. English Missionaries in Sweden & Finland. (Church Historical Society Ser.: No. 26). 1937. 12.50x (ISBN 0-281-00240-1). Allenson-Breckinridge.

MISSIONS–TAHITI

Song, Choan-Seng. Christian Mission in Reconstruction: An Asian Analysis. LC 77-23237. 1977. 10.00x (ISBN 0-88344-073-3); pap. 4.95x (ISBN 0-88344-074-1). Orbis Bks.

MISSIONS–TANGANYIKA

Hore, Edward C. Missionary to Tanganyika: 1877-1888. Wolf, James B., ed. 200p. 1971. 25.00x (ISBN 0-7146-2605-8, F Cass Co). Biblio Dist.

MISSIONS–TONGA ISLANDS

Tremblay, Edward. When You Go to Tonga. (Illus.). 1954. 3.25 (ISBN 0-8198-0173-9). Dghtrs St Paul.

MISSIONS–UNITED STATES

Abell, Aaron I. Urban Impact on American Protestantism, 1865-1900. 1962. Repr. of 1943 ed. 17.50 (ISBN 0-208-00587-0, Archon). Shoe String.

Adams, Eleanor B., ed. The Missions of New Mexico, 1776: A Description by Fray Francisco Atanasio Dominguez with Other Contemporary Documents. LC 55-12223. 1975. Repr. of 1956 ed. 35.00 (ISBN 0-8263-0373-0); deluxe ed. 100.00 (ISBN 0-8263-0418-4). U of NM Pr.

Archibald, Robert R. An Economic History of the California Missions. (Monograph). 1977. 25.00 (ISBN 0-88382-063-3). AAFH.

Barton, Bruce W. The Tree at the Center of the World: The Story of the California Missions. LC 79-26434. (Illus., Orig.). 1980. lib. bdg. 19.95 (ISBN 0-915520-30-3); pap. 9.95 (ISBN 0-915520-29-X). Ross-Erikson.

Beaver, R. Pierce, ed. American Missions in Bicentennial Perspective. LC 77-7569. 1977. pap. 10.95 (ISBN 0-87808-153-4). William Carey Lib.

Berkhofer, Robert F. Salvation & the Savage: An Analysis of Protestant Missions & American Indian Response, 1787-1862. LC 77-22857. 1977. Repr. of 1965 ed. lib. bdg. 19.00x (ISBN 0-8371-9745-7, BESSA). Greenwood.

Bolton, Herbert E. Fray Juan Crespi, Missionary Explorer on the Pacific Coast, 1769-1774. LC 78-158616. Repr. of 1927 ed. 29.50 (ISBN 0-404-01838-6). AMS Pr.

Chaney, Charles L. Birth of Missions in America. LC 75-26500. 352p. 1976. pap. 7.95 (ISBN 0-87808-146-1). William Carey Lib.

Cochran, Alice C. Miners, Merchants & Missionaries: The Roles of Missionaries & Pioneer Churches in the Colorado Gold Rush & Its Aftermath, 1858-1870. LC 80-16895. (ATLA Monographs: No. 15). x, 287p. 1980. 15.00 (ISBN 0-8108-1325-4). Scarecrow.

Company for Promoting & Propagation of the Gospel of Jesus Christ in New England: The Ledger for the Years 1650-1660 & the Record Book of Meetings Between 1656 & 1686. Repr. of 1920 ed. 23.50 (ISBN 0-8337-4481-X). B Franklin.

Dryden, Cecil P. Give All to Oregon. (Illus.). 1968. 9.95 (ISBN 0-8038-2606-0). Hastings.

Dunne, Peter M. Black Robes in Lower California. (California Library Reprint Series: No. 3). (Illus.). 1968. Repr. 26.75x (ISBN 0-520-00362-4). U of Cal Pr.

Engelhardt, Zephyrin. Missions & Missionaries of California, 4vols. (Illus.). lib. bdg. 185.00 (ISBN 0-87821-019-9). Milford Hse.

Ericson, Jack T., ed. Missionary Society of Connecticut Papers, 1759-1948: A Guide to the Microform Edition. 49p. 1976. pap. 15.00 (ISBN 0-667-00289-8). Microfilming Corp.

Evans, Mac, illus. Cowboy Boots & City Slickers. (Home Mission Board Mission Studies). (Illus.). 1980. pap. 0.35 (ISBN 0-937170-01-1). Home Mission.

Gallagher, Neil. Don't Go Overseas Until You've Read This Book. LC 77-2643. 1977. pap. 3.50 (ISBN 0-87123-105-0, 210105). Bethany Hse.

Gannon, Michael V. Cross in the Sand: The Early Catholic Church in Florida, 1513-1870. LC 65-27283. 1965. Repr. 9.00 (ISBN 0-8130-0084-X). U Presses Fla.

Geary, Gerald J. The Secularization of the California Missions (1810-1846) LC 73-3572. (Catholic University of America. Studies in American Church History: No. 17). Repr. of 1934 ed. 19.25 (ISBN 0-404-57767-9). AMS Pr.

Grabill, Joseph L. Protestant Diplomacy & the Near East: Missionary Influence in American Policy, 1810-1927. LC 70-5750. (Illus.). 1971. 15.00x (ISBN 0-8166-0575-0). U of Minn Pr.

Holloway, Lee. A Treehouse in Frostburg. (Home Missions Board Mission Studies). (Illus.). 1980. pap. 1.00 (ISBN 0-937170-06-2). Home Mission.

Horvath, David G., ed. Papers of the American Home Missionary Society, 1816 (1826-1894) 1936: A Guide to the Microfilm Edition. 94p. 1975. pap. 50.00 (ISBN 0-88455-994-7). Microfilming Corp.

Hunter, Jim & Western, Robert. Guide to the Baja Missions. (Illus.). Date not set. price not set. Darwin Pubns.

Kessell, John L. Friars, Soldiers & Reformers: Hispanic Arizona & the Sonora Mission Frontier, 1767-1856. LC 75-19867. 1976. pap. 10.50 (ISBN 0-8165-0487-3). U of Ariz Pr.

--The Missions of New Mexico Since 1776. LC 79-4934. (Illus.). 320p. 1980. 45.00x (ISBN 0-8263-0514-8). U of NM Pr.

Kocher, Paul. Alabado, a Story of Old California. 1978. 6.95 (ISBN 0-8199-0689-1). Franciscan Herald.

Kocher, Paul H. California's Old Missions: The Story of the Founding of the 21 Franciscan Missions in Spanish Alta California, 1769-1823. (Illus.). 220p. 1976. 6.95 (ISBN 0-8199-0601-8). Franciscan Herald.

Lanning, John T. Spanish Missions of Georgia. (Illus.). 1971. Repr. of 1935 ed. 29.00 (ISBN 0-403-00803-4). Scholarly.

McCoy, Isaac. History of Baptist Indian Missions. LC 19-11605. 1970. Repr. of 1840 ed. 31.00 (ISBN 0-384-36590-6). Johnson Repr.

Mathieson, Moira. Shepherds of the Delectable Mountains: The Story of the Washington County Mission. 1979. 2.00 (ISBN 0-686-28792-4). Forward Movement.

Montgomery, R. G., et al. Franciscan Awatovi: The Excavation & Conjectural Reconstruction of a Seventeenth Century Spanish Mission. (Harvard University Peabody Museum of Archaeology & Ethnology Memoirs). 1949. pap. 16.00 (ISBN 0-527-01292-0). Kraus Repr.

Morfi, Fray J. History of Texas 1673-1779, 2 pts. Castaneda, Carlos E., ed. LC 67-24718. (Quivira Society Publications, Vol. 6). 1967. Repr. of 1935 ed. 25.00 (ISBN 0-405-00076-6). Arno.

Nolan, James L. Discovery of the Lost Art Treasures of California's First Mission. Pourade, Richard F., ed. LC 78-73173. (Illus.). 128p. 1978. 20.00 (ISBN 0-913938-20-3). Copley Bks.

O'Rourke, Thomas P. The Franciscan Missions in Texas (1690-1793) LC 73-3559. (Catholic University of America. Studies in American Church History: No. 5). Repr. of 1927 ed. 14.50 (ISBN 0-404-57755-5). AMS Pr.

Parsons, Francis. Early Seventeenth Century Missions of the Southwest. LC 74-32368. (Illus., Orig.). 1975. 7.50 (ISBN 0-912762-21-7); pap. 3.50 (ISBN 0-912762-20-9). King.

Robinson, Alfred. Life in California Before the Conquest. LC 68-30553. (American Scene Ser). (Illus.). 1968. Repr. of 1846 ed. lib. bdg. 35.00 (ISBN 0-306-71142-7). Da Capo.

Salpointe, J. B. Soldiers of the Cross. 1977. Repr. of 1898 ed. lib. bdg. 17.95 (ISBN 0-89712-063-9). Documentary Pubns.

Segale, Blandina. At the End of the Santa Fe Trail. 1981. Repr. of 1948 ed. lib. bdg. 25.00 (ISBN 0-89987-778-8). Darby Bks.

Six Missions of Texas. (Illus.). 1965. 15.95 (ISBN 0-87244-002-8). Texian.

Tanner, William G. Hurry Before Sundown. 1981. pap. 3.95 (ISBN 0-8054-6327-5). Broadman.

Taraval, Sigismundo. Indian Uprising in Lower California, 1734-1737. LC 79-137296. Repr. of 1931 ed. 24.00 (ISBN 0-404-06337-3). AMS Pr.

Temple, Sydney. The Carmel Mission, from Founding to Rebuilding. LC 79-57168. (Illus.). 176p. 1980. pap. 5.95 (ISBN 0-913548-71-5, Valley Calif). Western Tanager.

Weber, Francis, ed. Observations of Benjamin C. Truman on the Missions of California. LC 75-10166. (Los Angeles Miscellany Ser.: No. 9). (Illus.). 1978. 20.00 (ISBN 0-87093-309-4). Dawsons.

MISSIONS–VIETNAM

Borri, Christoforo. Cochin-China: Containing Many Admirable Rarities of That Countrey. LC 71-25710. (English Experience Ser.: No. 223). 1970. Repr. of 1633 ed. 9.50 (ISBN 90-221-0223-8). Walter J Johnson.

Hefley, James. No Time for Tombstones. 1975. pap. 2.95 (ISBN 0-8423-4720-8). Tyndale.

MISSIONS–WEST INDIES

Underhill, Edward B. West Indies: Their Social & Religious Condition. LC 73-107525. Repr. of 1862 ed. 24.75x (ISBN 0-8371-3772-1). Greenwood.

MISSIONS–ZAMBIA

International Missionary Council - Department of Social & Economic Research & Council. Modern Industry & the African. 2nd ed. Davis, J. Mearle, ed. LC 67-24749. Repr. of 1932 ed. 24.00x (ISBN 0-678-05042-2). Kelley.

International Missionary Council - Department Of Social And Economic Research. Modern Industry & the African. Davis, J. M., ed. LC 72-97369. Repr. of 1933 ed. 17.00x (ISBN 0-8371-2426-3, Pub. by Negro U Pr). Greenwood.

MISSIONS, CITY

see City Missions

MISSIONS, FOREIGN

Allen, Roland. The Spontaneous Expansion of the Church. 1962. pap. 2.95 (ISBN 0-8028-1002-0). Eerdmans.

Davey, Cyril J. March of Methodism. 1952. 3.75 (ISBN 0-8022-0345-0). Philos Lib.

Greenway, Roger S. A World to Win: Preaching World Missions Today. 128p. 1975. pap. 3.95 (ISBN 0-8010-3685-2). Baker Bk.

Kraemer, Hendrik. Christian Message in a Non-Christian World. LC 56-10732. 1969. 12.95 (ISBN 0-8254-3002-X). Kregel.

Luzbetak, Louis J. The Church & Cultures: An Applied Anthropology for the Religious Worker. LC 75-108055. (Applied Cultural Anthropology Ser). 448p. 1976. pap. 6.95x (ISBN 0-87808-725-7). William Carey Lib.

Mott, John R. The Evangelization of the World in This Generation. LC 76-38457. (Religion in America, Ser. 2). 258p. 1972. Repr. of 1900 ed. 14.00 (ISBN 0-405-04078-4). Arno.

Price, Maurice T. Christian Missions & Oriental Civilizations: A Study in Cultural Contact. 1924. 10.00x (ISBN 0-685-19286-5). Paragon.

Strong, William E. Story of the American Board: An Account of the First Hundred Years of the American Board for Foreign Missions. LC 79-83443. (Religion in America Ser). 1969. Repr. of 1910 ed. 19.50 (ISBN 0-405-00277-7). Arno.

MISSIONS, HOME

see also City Missions

Goodykoontz, Colin B. Home Missions on the American Frontier. LC 76-120619. 1970. Repr. lib. bdg. 25.00x (ISBN 0-374-93198-4). Octagon.

Horvath, David G., ed. Papers of the American Home Missionary Society, 1816 (1826-1894) 1936: A Guide to the Microfilm Edition. 94p. 1975. pap. 50.00 (ISBN 0-88455-994-7). Microfilming Corp.

MISSIONS, INDIAN

see Indians of North America–Missions; Indians of South America–Missions

MISSIONS, MEDICAL

see also Missions to Lepers

Dooley, Thomas A. Night They Burned the Mountain. (RL 10). pap. 1.50 (ISBN 0-451-08681-3, W8681, Sig). NAL.

Hasselblad, Marva & Brandon, Dorothy. Lucky-Lucky: A Nurse's Story of Life at a Hospital in Vietnam. LC 66-27488. (Illus.). 224p. 1966. 4.95 (ISBN 0-87131-014-7). M Evans.

Krimsky, Joseph. Pilgrimage & Service. Davis, Moshe, ed. LC 77-70712. (America & the Holy Land Ser.). 1977. Repr. of 1919 ed. lib. bdg. 12.00x (ISBN 0-405-10261-5). Arno.

Reynolds, Charles. Mandate for Mercy. (Orig.). 1972. pap. 2.50 (ISBN 0-377-02031-1). Friend Pr.

Roseveare, Helen. He Gave Us a Valley. LC 76-12305. 192p. (Orig.). 1976. pap. 3.95 (ISBN 0-87784-780-0). Inter-Varsity.

Salsbury, Clarence G. & Hughes, Paul. The Salsbury Story: A Medical Missionary's Lifetime of Public Service. LC 72-101100. 320p. 1969. 7.50 (ISBN 0-8165-0204-8). U of Ariz Pr.

Schweitzer, Albert. On the Edge of the Primeval Forest & More from the Primeval Forest: Experiences & Observations of a Doctor in Equatorial Africa. LC 75-41244. (Illus.). 1976. Repr. of 1948 ed. 18.50 (ISBN 0-404-14598-1). AMS Pr.

Seaton, Ronald S. & Seaton, Edith B. Here's How: Health Education by Extension. LC 76-40599. 1976. pap. 3.95 (ISBN 0-87808-150-X). William Carey Lib.

Seel, David J. Challenge & Crisis in Missionary Medicine. LC 79-16015. 1979. pap. 3.95 (ISBN 0-87808-172-0). William Carey Lib.

White, Ellen G. Counsels on Health & Instruction to Medical Missionary Workers. 1951. deluxe ed. 7.50 (ISBN 0-8163-0114-X, 03561-8). Pacific Pr Pub Assn.

--Medical Ministry. 1963. deluxe ed. 6.50 (ISBN 0-8163-0158-1, 13370-2). Pacific Pr Pub Assn.

MISSIONS, PARISH

see Parish Missions

MISSIONS TO ITALIANS

Cordasco, Francesco, ed. Protestant Evangelism Among Italians in America. LC 74-17943. (Italian American Experience Ser). (Illus.). 276p. 1975. Repr. 19.00x (ISBN 0-405-06414-4). Arno.

MISSIONS TO JEWS

see also Converts from Judaism

Burnet, David S. & Davis, Moshe, eds. The Jerusalem Mission: Under the Direction of the American Christian Missionary Society. (America & the Holy Land Ser.). 1977. Repr. of 1853 ed. lib. bdg. 20.00x (ISBN 0-405-10233-X). Arno.

Fleischner, Eva. Judaism in German Christian Theology Since 1945: Christianity & Israel Considered in Terms of Mission. LC 75-22374. (ATLA Monograph: No. 8). 1975. 10.00 (ISBN 0-8108-0835-8). Scarecrow.

Goldberg, Louis. Our Jewish Friends. 1977. pap. 3.95 (ISBN 0-8024-6217-0). Moody.

Grob, Gerald, ed. A Course of Lectures on the Jews: By Ministers of the Established Church in Glasgow. LC 76-46095. (Anti-Movements in America). 1977. lib. bdg. 28.00x (ISBN 0-405-09968-1). Arno.

Henry, Matthew. Job to Song of Solomon. (A Commentary on the Whole Bible Ser: Vol. 3). 14.95 (ISBN 0-8007-0199-2). Revell.

Manson, T. W. Only to the House of Israel? Jesus & the Non-Jews. Reumann, John, ed. LC 64-11860. (Facet Bks). 1964. pap. 1.00 (ISBN 0-8006-3005-X, 1-3005). Fortress.

Wishniesky, Dan H. Over the Stumbling Block: Inviting Jews to Jesus. LC 77-80938. 1978. pap. 1.95 (ISBN 0-8054-6216-3). Broadman.

MISSIONS TO LEPERS

Dutton, Charles J. The Samaritans of Molokai. facsimile ed. (Select Bibliographies Reprint Ser). Repr. of 1932 ed. 21.00 (ISBN 0-8369-5733-4). Arno.

Farrow, John. Damien the Leper. 1954. pap. 2.95 (ISBN 0-385-02918-7, D3, Im). Doubleday.

MISSIONS TO MORMONS

Bailey, Jack S. Inside a Mormon Mission. 190p. pap. 4.50 (ISBN 0-89036-076-6). Hawkes Pub Inc.

MISSIONS TO MUSLIMS

see also Converts from Islam

Addison, James T. The Christian Approach to the Moslem. LC 76-158227. (BCL Ser.: No. II). Repr. of 1942 ed. 24.50 (ISBN 0-404-00294-3). AMS Pr.

Marsh, Charles R. Share Your Faith with a Muslim. 1975. pap. 2.25 (ISBN 0-8024-7900-6). Moody.

VanderWerff, Lyle L. Christian Mission to Muslims-the Record: Anglican & Reformed Approaches in India & the Near East, 1800-1938. LC 77-24027. 1977. pap. 8.95 (ISBN 0-87808-320-0). William Carey Lib.

MISSISSIPPI

see also names of cities, counties, towns, etc. in Mississippi

Campbell, Clarice T. & Rogers, Oscar A. Mississippi: The View from Tougaloo. LC 78-10229. 1979. 25.00x (ISBN 0-87805-091-4); pap. 10.00x (ISBN 0-87805-092-2). U Pr of Miss.

Carpenter, Allan. Mississippi. new ed. LC 78-3400. (New Enchantment of America State Bks.). (Illus.). (gr. 4 up). 1978. PLB 10.60 (ISBN 0-516-04124-X). Childrens.

Crocker, Mary W. Historic Architecture in Mississippi. 3rd ed. LC 72-92483. (Illus.). 256p. 1977. 12.50 (ISBN 0-87805-022-1). U Pr of Miss.

Cross, Ralph D. & Wales, Robert W., eds. Atlas of Mississippi. LC 74-78569. (Illus.). 1974. 5.00x (ISBN 0-87805-061-2). U Pr of Miss.

Davidge, William F. & Hollman, Kenneth W. An Analysis of Mississippi Industrial Location Factors. 1978. 4.00 (ISBN 0-938004-02-6). U MS Bus Econ.

Federal Writers' Project. Mississippi: A Guide to the Magnolia State. 545p. 1938. Repr. 49.00 (ISBN 0-403-02174-X). Somerset Pub.

Hamilton, Charles G. Progressive Mississippi. LC 78-55059. 1978. 7.95 (ISBN 0-934800-06-5). Gregg-Hamilton.

Ingraham, Joseph H. South-West, 2 Vols. LC 68-55895. 1835. 29.00x (ISBN 0-8371-0493-9, Pub. by Negro U Pr). Greenwood.

Kempe, Helen. Pelican Guide to Old Homes of Mississippi, 2 vols. Incl. Vol. 1. Natchez & the South (ISBN 0-88289-134-0); Vol. 2. Columbus & the North (ISBN 0-88289-135-9). LC 76-20434. (Pelican Guide Ser.). (Illus.). 1977. pap. 3.95 ea. Pelican.

McDermott, John F. Seth Eastman's Mississippi: A Lost Portfolio Recovered. LC 73-2457. (Illus.). 144p. 1973. 12.50 (ISBN 0-252-00192-3). U of Ill Pr.

Mississippi. 28.00 (ISBN 0-89770-100-3). Curriculum Info Ctr.

Morgan, Albert T. Yazoo, or, On the Picket Line of Freedom in the South: A Personal Narrative. LC 68-25036. (Illus., With a new introduction by Otto H. Olsen). 1968. Repr. of 1884 ed. 13.50 (ISBN 0-8462-1153-X). Russell.

Myrick, Burny, illus. The Timeless River: A Portrait of Life on the Mississippi, 1850 to 1900. 1981. 45.00 (ISBN 0-8487-0523-8). Oxmoor Hse.

Newton, Carolyn S. & Coggin, Patricia A. Meet Mississippi. LC 75-32109. 1976. 10.00 (ISBN 0-87397-090-X). Strode.

Raban, Jonathan. Old Glory: An American Voyage. 1981. 16.95 (ISBN 0-671-25061-2). S&S.

Smith, Frank E. & Warren, Audrey. Mississippians All. LC 68-54601. 1968. 4.95 (ISBN 0-911116-22-2). Pelican.

Tunica. pap. 5.00 (ISBN 0-685-71704-6). J J Augustin.

Webb & DeJarnette. An Archeological Survey of Pickwick Basin in the Adjacent Portions of the States of Alabama, Mississippi & Tennessee. Repr. of 1942 ed. 55.00 (ISBN 0-403-03525-2). Scholarly.

Welty, Eudora. One Time, One Place. 1971. 10.95 (ISBN 0-394-47308-6). Random.

MISSISSIPPI–GENEALOGY

Biographical & Historical Memoirs of Mississippi, 2 vols. LC 78-2299. (Illus.). 1978. Repr. of 1891 ed. Set. 90.00 (ISBN 0-87152-267-5); Vol. 1. 45.00 (ISBN 0-87152-268-3); Vol. 2. 45.00 (ISBN 0-87152-269-1). Reprint.

Hammons, Ann R. Wild Bill Sullivan: King of the Hollow. LC 80-19625. 1980. 9.95 (ISBN 0-87805-127-9). U Pr of Miss.

Jackson, Ronald V. & Teeples, Gary R. Mississippi Census Index 1820. LC 77-85971. lib. bdg. 15.00 (ISBN 0-89593-076-5). Accelerated Index.

--Mississippi Census Index 1830. LC 77-85972. (Illus.). lib. bdg. 20.00 (ISBN 0-89593-077-3). Accelerated Index.

--Mississippi Census Index 1850. LC 77-85975. (Illus.). lib. bdg. 50.00 (ISBN 0-89593-079-X). Accelerated Index.

McBee, May W. The Natchez Court Records, 1767-1805. LC 79-88259. 1979. Repr. of 1953 ed. 25.00 (ISBN 0-8063-0851-6). Genealog Pub.

Wells, Dean F. & Cole, Hunter, eds. Mississippi Heroes, Vol. 1. LC 80-19704. (Illus.). 250p. 1980. 15.00 (ISBN 0-87805-128-7). U Pr of Miss.

MISSISSIPPI–HISTORY

Barlow, Estelle. Growing Up in the Depression: And Other Glimpses of My Life. 1978. 5.95 (ISBN 0-533-03047-1). Vantage.

Bettersworth, John K. Confederate Mississippi: The People & Policies of a Cotton State in Wartime. LC 78-10897. (Perspectives in American History Ser.: No. 48). (Illus.). Repr. of 1943 ed. lib. bdg. 22.50x (ISBN 0-87991-372-X). Porcupine Pr.

Biographical & Historical Memoirs of Mississippi, 2 vols. LC 78-2299. (Illus.). 1978. Repr. of 1891 ed. Set. 90.00 (ISBN 0-87152-267-5); Vol. 1. 45.00 (ISBN 0-87152-268-3); Vol. 2. 45.00 (ISBN 0-87152-269-1). Reprint.

Brown, Calvin S. Archaeology of Mississippi. LC 72-5011. (Antiquities of the New World Ser.: Vol. 16). (Illus.). Repr. of 1926 ed. 49.50 (ISBN 0-404-57316-9). AMS Pr.

Claiborne, John F. Mississippi As a Province, Territory & State. LC 78-2291. 1978. Repr. of 1880 ed. 30.00 (ISBN 0-87152-264-0). Reprint.

Claiborne, William C. Official Letter Books, 1801 to 1816, 6 Vols. Rowland, Dunbar, ed. LC 72-980. Repr. of 1917 ed. Set. 165.00 (ISBN 0-404-01600-6); 27.50 ea. AMS Pr.

Fradin, Dennis. Mississippi: In Words & Pictures. LC 80-36855. (Young People's Stories of Our States Ser.). (Illus.). 48p. (gr. 2-5). 1980. PLB 9.25 (ISBN 0-516-03924-5). Childrens.

Fulkerson, H. S. Random Recollections of Early Days in Mississippi. 1972. 7.50 (ISBN 0-685-37715-6). Claitors.

Garner, J. W. Reconstruction in Mississippi. 1964. 8.50 (ISBN 0-8446-1196-4). Peter Smith.

Garner, James W. Reconstruction in Mississippi. LC 12-1798. 1968. pap. text ed. 9.95x (ISBN 0-8071-0137-9). La State U Pr.

Gibbon, Guy E. The Mississippian Occupation of the Red Wing Area: Microfiche Edition. (Minnesota Prehistoric Archaeology Ser.: No. 13). 394p. 1979. 12.50 (ISBN 0-87351-137-9). Minn Hist.

Hall, James. A Brief History of the Mississippi Territory: To Which Is Prefixed a Summary View of the Country Between the Settlements on Cumberland River & the Territory. LC 75-46573. 90p. 1976. Repr. of 1801 ed. 13.50 (ISBN 0-87152-215-2). Reprint.

Hamilton, Charles G. There's No Place Like It. (Illus.). 240p. (Orig.). 1981. pap. 12.00 (ISBN 0-934800-11-1). Gregg-Hamilton.

Kinser, Jerry. The Cost of Mississippi: Its Past & Progress. Woolfolk, Doug, ed. 1981. 10.00 (ISBN 0-86518-018-0). Moran Pub Corp.

Lamar, Curt, ed. History of Rosedale, Mississippi, 1876-1976. LC 76-25443. 1976. 12.50 (ISBN 0-87152-246-2). Reprint.

Lang, Meredith. Defender of the Faith: The High Court of Mississippi, 1817-1875. LC 77-7971. 1977. 3.00 (ISBN 0-87805-033-7). U Pr of Miss.

Lewis, Harvey S. & Waller, E. Nolan. Commercial Banking in Mississippi, 1940-1975. 1977. pap. 3.00 (ISBN 0-938004-07-7). U MS Bus Econ.

Loewen, James L. & Sallis, Charles, eds. Mississippi: Conflict & Change. LC 74-4768. 1974. 10.00 (ISBN 0-394-48964-0); pap. 6.95 (ISBN 0-394-70929-2). Pantheon.

Logan, Marie. Mississippi-Louisiana Border Country: History of Rodney Mississippi & Environs. 1974. 9.95 (ISBN 0-685-42684-X). Claitors.

Lowry, Robert & McCardle, William H. A History of Mississippi from the Discovery of the Great River by Hernando Desoto Including the Earliest Settlement Made by the French Under Iberville Tothe Death of Jefferson Davis. LC 78-2335. 1978. Repr. of 1891 ed. 32.50 (ISBN 0-87152-265-9). Reprint.

Mathews, Walter M., ed. Mississippi Nineteen Ninety. 200p. 1981. pap. 12.50 (ISBN 0-87805-147-3). U Pr of Miss.

Mississippi in the Confederacy, 2 vols. in one. 1961. 36.00 (ISBN 0-527-64100-6). Kraus Repr.

Moore, John H. & Moore, Margaret D. Mississippi. LC 68-9254. 1970. pap. 2.95 (ISBN 0-8077-1830-0). Tchrs Coll.

Newton, Carolyn. Outdoor Mississippi. LC 73-86316. (Illus.). 240p. 1974. pap. 1.00 (ISBN 0-87805-023-X). U Pr of Miss.

Phillips, Philip. Archaeological Survey in the Lower Yazoo Basin, Mississippi: 1949-1955. LC 77-80028. (Peabody Museum Papers: Vol. 60). 1970. pap. text ed. 50.00 (ISBN 0-87365-173-1). Peabody Harvard.

Rainwater. Mississippi, Storm Center of Secession. 1973. 12.50x (ISBN 0-685-37723-7). Claitors.

Ray, William, ed. Conversations: Reynolds Price & William Ray. (Mississippi Collection Bulletin, No. 9). (Illus.). 82p. 1976. pap. 5.95x (ISBN 0-87870-086-2). Memphis St Univ.

Rietti, J. C., compiled by. Military Annals of Mississippi: Military Organizations Which Entered the Service of the Confederate States of America,from the State of Mississippi. LC 75-45377. 196p. 1976. 16.50 (ISBN 0-87152-218-7). Reprint.

Riley, Franklin L. School History of Mississippi. LC 76-68. (Illus.). 448p. 1976. Repr. of 1900 ed. 20.00 (ISBN 0-87152-219-5). Reprint.

Rowland, Dunbar. Encyclopedia of Mississippi History, 2 vols. LC 74-19619. Repr. of 1907 ed. Set. 137.50 (ISBN 0-404-12453-4). AMS Pr.

--History of Mississippi: The Heart of the South. LC 78-2541. (Illus.). 1978. Repr. of 1925 ed. Set. 150.00 (ISBN 0-87152-270-5); 37.50 ea. Vol. 1 (ISBN 0-87152-271-3). Vol. 2 (ISBN 0-87152-272-1). Vol. 3 (ISBN 0-87152-273-X). Vol. 4 (ISBN 0-87152-274-8). Reprint.

--Military History of Mississippi, 1803-1898. LC 78-2454. 1978. Repr. of 1908 ed. 32.50 (ISBN 0-87152-266-7). Reprint.

Rowland, Dunbar, ed. Mississippi: Sketches of Counties,Towns,Events,Institutions & Persons Arranged in Cyclopedic Form, 3 vols. LC 76-73. 1976. Repr. of 1907 ed. Vol. 1. 36.00 (ISBN 0-87152-220-9); Vol. 2. 36.00 (ISBN 0-87152-221-7); Vol.3. 48.00 (ISBN 0-87152-222-5); Vol. 4, Supplement. 30.00 (ISBN 0-87152-223-3). Reprint.

Sansing, David G. & Waller, Carroll. A History of the Mississippi Governor's Mansion. LC 77-12243. (Illus.). 220p. 1977. 15.00 (ISBN 0-87805-041-8). U Pr of Miss.

Sillers, Florence W., compiled by. History of Bolivar County,Mississippi. LC 76-157. (Illus.). 673p. 1976. Repr. of 1948 ed. 20.00 (ISBN 0-87152-230-6). Reprint.

Smeal, Lee. Mississippi Historical & Biographical Index. LC 78-53705. (Illus.). Date not set. lib. bdg. price not set (ISBN 0-89593-188-5). Accelerated Index.

Smith, Reid & Owens, John. The Majesty of Natchez. (Illus.). 1969. 6.95 (ISBN 0-911116-67-2). Pelican.

The Territory of Mississippi, 1798-1817. (The Territorial Papers of the United States: Vol. 5). Repr. of 1937 ed. 69.50 (ISBN 0-404-01455-0). AMS Pr.

The Territory of Mississippi, 1809-1817. (The Territorial Papers of the United States: Vol. 6). Repr. of 1938 ed. 69.50 (ISBN 0-404-01456-9). AMS Pr.

Vance, Mary. Historical Society Architectural Publications: Massachusetts, Michigan,Minnesota, Mississippi, Missouri. (Architecture Ser.: Bibliography A-159). 75p. 1980. pap. 8.00 (ISBN 0-686-26907-1). Vance Biblios.

Wier, Sadye H. & Marszalek, John F. A Black Businessman in White Mississippi, 1886-1974. LC 77-13358. (Illus.). 1977. 4.95x (ISBN 0-87805-042-6). U Pr of Miss.

Williams, E. Russ & Conerly, Luke W. Source Records from Pike County, Mississippi, Seventeen Ninety-Eight to Nineteen Ten. (Illus.). 500p. 1978. Repr. of 1909 ed. 30.00 (ISBN 0-89308-104-3). Southern Hist Pr.

Winsor, Justin. From Cartier to Frontenac: Geographical Discovery in the Interior of North America in Its Historical Relations 1534-1700. LC 79-114670. (Illus.). 1970. Repr. of 1894 ed. lib. bdg. 15.00x (ISBN 0-8154-0323-2). Cooper Sq.

MISSISSIPPI–POLITICS AND GOVERNMENT

Harris, William C. The Day of the Carpetbagger: Republican Reconstruction in Mississippi. LC 78-18779. (Illus.). 1979. 45.00 (ISBN 0-8071-0366-7). La State U Pr.

Hearon, Cleo C. Mississippi & the Compromise of 1850. LC 70-168958. Repr. of 1913 ed. 19.00 (ISBN 0-404-00061-4). AMS Pr.

Highsaw, Robert B. & Fortenberry, Charles N. The Government & Administration of Mississippi. Graves, W. Brooke, ed. LC 80-11136. (American Commonwealths Ser.: Vol. 22). (Illus.). xiv, 414p. 1980. Repr. of 1954 ed. lib. bdg. 29.75x (ISBN 0-313-22369-6, HIGA). Greenwood.

Kirwan, Albert D. The Revolt of the Rednecks: Mississippi Politics (1876-1925) 1964. 8.00 (ISBN 0-8446-1265-0). Peter Smith.

Kynerd, Thomas E. Administrative Reorganization of Mississippi Government: A Study in Politics. LC 77-8799. 1978. 3.00 (ISBN 0-87805-038-8). U Pr of Miss.

Landry, David M. & Parker, Joseph B. Mississippi Government & Politics in Transition. LC 76-13763. (Government Ser.). 1976. pap. text ed. 5.50 (ISBN 0-8403-1482-5). Kendall-Hunt.

Lynch, John R. Reminiscences of an Active Life: The Autobiography of John Roy Lynch. Franklin, John H., ed. LC 70-110669. (Negro American Biographies & Autobiographies Ser). 1970. 15.00x (ISBN 0-226-49818-2). U of Chicago Pr.

McDowell, Jennifer, ed. Black Politics: A Study & Annotated Bibliography of the Mississippi Freedom Democratic Party. LC 68-58320. 1971. pap. 6.95 (ISBN 0-930142-02-0). Merlin Pr.

Miles, Edwin A. Jacksonian Democracy in Mississippi. LC 78-107415. (American Scene Ser). 1970. Repr. of 1960 ed. lib. bdg. 25.00 (ISBN 0-306-71884-7). Da Capo.

Rainwater, Percy L. Mississippi: Storm Center of Secession, 1856-1861. LC 72-84188. (American Scene, Comments & Commentators Ser). 1969. Repr. of 1938 ed. lib. bdg. 27.50 (ISBN 0-306-71614-3). Da Capo.

Ranck, James B. Albert Gallatin Brown: Radical Southern Nationalist. LC 73-16349. (Illus.). 320p. Repr. of 1937 ed. lib. bdg. 19.50x (ISBN 0-87991-347-9). Porcupine Pr.

Satcher, Buford. Blacks in Mississippi Politics 1865-1900. LC 78-53792. 1978. pap. text ed. 9.50 (ISBN 0-8191-0513-9). U Pr of Amer.

Sumners, Cecil L. Governors of Mississippi. (Governors of the State Ser.). (Illus.). 180p. 1980. 13.95 (ISBN 0-88289-237-1). Pelican.

Swain, Martha H. Pat Harrison: The New Deal Years. LC 78-7919. (Illus.). 1978. 15.00x (ISBN 0-87805-076-0). U Pr of Miss.

Wagner, Kenneth C. Economic Development Manual. LC 77-24592. (Illus.). 1978. pap. 5.00x (ISBN 0-87805-039-6). U Pr of Miss.

MISSISSIPPI–SOCIAL CONDITIONS

Greenberg, Polly. Devil Has Slippery Shoes. LC 68-26430. 1969. 14.95 (ISBN 0-02-545480-3). Macmillan.

Hamilton, Charles G. Any Resemblance. 1980. 7.00 (ISBN 0-934800-05-7). Gregg-Hamilton.

Powdermaker, Hortense. After Freedom: A Cultural Study in the Deep South. LC 68-16415. (Studies in American Negro Life). 1968. pap. 3.45 (ISBN 0-689-70160-8, NL3). Atheneum.

Pritchard, David A. Mental Health Law in Mississippi. LC 78-62247. 1978. pap. text ed. 11.25 (ISBN 0-8191-0568-6). U Pr of Amer.

MISSISSIPPI–SOCIAL LIFE AND CUSTOMS

Fradin, Dennis. Mississippi: In Words & Pictures. LC 80-36855. (Young People's Stories of Our States Ser.). (Illus.). 48p. (gr. 2-5). 1980. PLB 9.25 (ISBN 0-516-03924-5). Childrens.

Hammons, Ann R. Wild Bill Sullivan: King of the Hollow. LC 80-19625. 1980. 9.95 (ISBN 0-87805-127-9). U Pr of Miss.

Hudson, Arthur P., ed. Humor of the Old Deep South, 2 Vols. LC 75-86026. 1970. Repr. of 1936 ed. Set. 29.50x (ISBN 0-8046-0616-1). Kennikat.

Moore, Glover. A Calhoun County, Alabama, Boy in the 1860s. Moore, Glover, Jr., ed. LC 78-15256. (Illus.). 1978. 5.00x (ISBN 0-87805-081-7). U Pr of Miss.

Pitts, J. R. The Life & Confession of the Noted Outlaw James Copeland. facsimile ed. LC 80-20865. (Illus.). 256p. 1980. Repr. of 1909 ed. 12.50 (ISBN 0-87805-125-2). U Pr of Miss.

Thigpen, S. G. Boy in Rural Mississippi. (Illus.). 1966. 5.00 (ISBN 0-685-20525-8). Thigpen.

MISSISSIPPI RIVER

Burman, Ben L. Look Down That Winding River: An Informal Profile of the Mississippi. LC 72-6610. (Illus.). 1973. 7.95 (ISBN 0-8008-4960-4). Taplinger.

Coleman, James M. Recent Coastal Sedimentation: Central Louisiana Coast. LC 67-63069. (Coastal Studies, Vol. 17). (Illus.). 1967. pap. 4.00x (ISBN 0-8071-0403-5). La State U Pr.

Daniel, Pete. Deep'n As It Come: The 1927 Mississippi River Flood. LC 76-42642. (Illus.). 1977. 12.95 (ISBN 0-19-502122-3). Oxford U Pr.

Ellet, Charles. Mississippi & Ohio Rivers, Containing Plans for the Protection of the Delta from Inundation & Investigations. LC 70-125738. (American Environmental Studies). 1970. Repr. of 1853 ed. 17.00 (ISBN 0-405-02663-3). Arno.

Mason, Philipp, ed. Schoolcraft's Expedition to Lake Itasca: The Discovery of the Source of the Mississippi. xxvi, 390p. 1958. 10.00 (ISBN 0-87013-040-4). Mich St U Pr.

Pope, John. Tour Through the Southern & Western Territories of the United States of North America, the Spanish Dominions on the River Mississippi & the Floridas, the Countries of the Creek Nations, & Many Uninhabited Parts. LC 70-146411. (First American Frontier Ser). 1971. Repr. of 1792 ed. 9.00 (ISBN 0-405-02875-X). Arno.

Wright, L. D. Circulation, Effluent Diffusion & Sediment Transport, Mouth of South Pass, Mississippi River Delta. LC 72-185845. (University Studies: Coastal Studies Ser 26). (Illus.). x, 56p. 1970. pap. 4.00x (ISBN 0-8071-0515-5). La State U Pr.

MISSISSIPPI RIVER–DESCRIPTION AND TRAVEL

Baily, Francis. Journal of a Tour in Unsettled Parts of North America in 1796 & 1797. Holmes, Jack D., ed. LC 68-21414. (Travels on the Western Waters Ser.). (Illus.). 307p. 1969. Repr. of 1856 ed. 15.00x (ISBN 0-8093-0389-2). S Ill U Pr.

Bishop, Nathaniel Holmes. Four Months in a Sneak Box: A Boat Voyage of Twenty Six Hundred Miles Down the Ohio & Mississippi Rivers. LC 71-142572. (Illus.). xii, 322p. 1976. Repr. of 1879 ed. 30.00 (ISBN 0-8103-4170-0). Gale.

Bray, Martha C., ed. Journals of Joseph N. Nicollet: 1836-37. Fertey, Andre, tr. 288p. 1970. 16.50 (ISBN 0-87351-062-3). Minn Hist.

Forman, Samuel S. Narrative of a Journey Down the Ohio & Mississippi in 1789-90 with a Memoir & Illustrative Notes by Lyman C. Draper. LC 78-146396. (First American Frontier Ser). 1971. Repr. of 1888 ed. 9.00 (ISBN 0-405-02850-4). Arno.
Lewis, Henry. Valley of the Mississippi Illustrated. Heilbron, Bertha L., ed. Poatgieter, A. H., tr. LC 67-65590. (Illus.). 423p. 1967. 39.75 (ISBN 0-87351-035-6); uncut 50.00 (ISBN 0-87351-036-4). Minn Hist.
McDermott, John F., ed. Before Mark Twain: A Sampler of Old, Old Times on the Mississippi. LC 68-25555. (Travels on the Western Waters Ser.). (Illus.). 332p. 1968. 15.00x (ISBN 0-8093-0331-0). S Ill U Pr.
Pike, Zebulon M. Account of Expeditions to the Source of the Mississippi, the Southwest, Etc, 2 vols. facsimile ed. 1965. Set. boxed 22.50 (ISBN 0-87018-049-5). Ross.
--The Journals of Zebulon Montgomery Pike, with Letters & Related Documents, 2 Vols. Jackson, Donald, ed. (American Exploration & Travel Ser.: No. 48). (Illus.). 1966. boxed 42.50 (ISBN 0-8061-0699-9). U of Okla Pr.
Pittman, Philip. The Present State of the European Settlements on the Mississippi. facsimile, new ed. McDermott, John Francis, ed. LC 76-44247. (Illus.). 221p. 1977. 24.95x (ISBN 0-87870-011-0). Memphis St Univ.
Raban, Jonathan. Old Glory: An American Voyage. 1981. 16.95 (ISBN 0-671-25061-2). S&S.
Schwaig, Robert. Odessy of the Blithe Spirit II. 200p. (Orig.). pap. 6.95 (ISBN 0-86629-024-9). Sunrise MO.
Twain, Mark. Life on the Mississippi. (Classics Ser). (gr. 9 up). pap. 0.95 (ISBN 0-8049-0055-8, CL-55). Airmont.
--Life on the Mississippi. 6.95 (ISBN 0-19-250589-0, W*C589). Oxford U Pr.

MISSISSIPPI RIVER–DISCOVERY AND EXPLORATION

Miceli, A. P. Man with the Red Umbrella. 1974. 7.95 (ISBN 0-685-42678-5). Claitors.
Ogg, Frederic. Opening of the Mississippi: A Struggle for Supremacy in the American Interior. LC 68-24990. (American History & Americana Ser., No. 47). (Illus.). 1969. Repr. of 1904 ed. lib. bdg. 49.95 (ISBN 0-8383-0223-8). Haskell.
Ogg, Frederic A. Opening of the Mississippi: A Struggle for Supremacy in the American Interior. LC 68-57500. Repr. of 1904 ed. 17.50x (ISBN 0-8154-0283-X). Cooper Sq.
--Opening of the Mississippi: A Struggle for Supremacy in the American Interior. LC 69-14017. 1969. Repr. of 1904 ed. lib. bdg. 19.25x (ISBN 0-8371-1103-X, OGOM). Greenwood.

MISSISSIPPI RIVER–HISTORY

Baldwin, Leland D. The Keelboat Age on Western Waters. LC 41-10342. 1941. 7.95 (ISBN 0-8229-1027-6). U of Pittsburgh Pr.
Capers, Gerald M. The Mississippi River: Before & After Mark Twain. 1977. 8.50 (ISBN 0-682-48845-3, Lochinvar). Exposition.
Daniel, Pete. Deep'n As It Come: The 1927 Mississippi River Flood. 1977. pap. 6.95 (ISBN 0-19-502123-1, 480, GB). Oxford U Pr.
Federal Writers Project, Mississippi. Mississippi Gulf Coast, Yesterday & Today, 1699-1939. LC 73-3631. (American Guide Ser.). Repr. of 1939 ed. 14.00 (ISBN 0-404-57932-9). AMS Pr.
Merrill, James M. Battle Flags South: Story of the Civil War Navies on Western Waters. LC 71-86652. 334p. 1970. 18.00 (ISBN 0-8386-7448-8). Fairleigh Dickinson.
Milligan, John D. Gunboats Down the Mississippi. LC 79-6119. (Navies & Men Ser.). (Illus.). 1980. Repr. of 1965 ed. lib. bdg. 20.00x (ISBN 0-405-13047-3). Arno.
Ogg, Frederic. Opening of the Mississippi: A Struggle for Supremacy in the American Interior. LC 68-24990. (American History & Americana Ser., No. 47). (Illus.). 1969. Repr. of 1904 ed. lib. bdg. 49.95 (ISBN 0-8383-0223-8). Haskell.
Samuel, Ray, et al. Tales of the Mississippi. rev ed. LC 81-5937. (Illus.). 240p. 1981. Repr. of 1955 ed. 19.95 (ISBN 0-88289-291-6). Pelican.

MISSISSIPPI RIVER–JUVENILE LITERATURE

Bulla, Clyde R. Down the Mississippi. (gr. 4-6). 1970. pap. 1.25 (ISBN 0-590-08722-3, Schol Pap). Schol Bk Serv.
Cooper, Kay. Journeys on the Mississippi. LC 80-28109. (Illus.). 96p. (gr. 4-6). 1981. PLB 8.29 (ISBN 0-671-34024-7). Messner.
Darell-Brown, Susan. The Mississippi. LC 78-62982. (Rivers of the World Ser.). (Illus.). 1978. lib. bdg. 7.95 (ISBN 0-686-51135-2). Silver.
Kjelgaard, Jim A. Explorations of Pere Marquette. (Landmark Ser.: No. 17). (Illus.). (gr. 4-6). 1951. PLB 5.99 (ISBN 0-394-90317-X). Random.

MISSISSIPPI VALLEY

Flint, Timothy. Condensed Geography & History of the Western States or the Mississippi Valley 1828, 2 Vols. LC 70-119865. 1970. Repr. of 1828 ed. 90.00x set (ISBN 0-8201-1076-0). Schol Facsimiles.
Holley, Donald. Uncle Sam's Farmers: The New Deal Communities in the Lower Mississippi Valley. LC 75-20091. 1975. 19.95 (ISBN 0-252-00510-4). U of Ill Pr.
Kirkpatrick, John E. Timothy Flint: Pioneer, Missionary, Author, Editor, 1780-1840. LC 68-56780. (Research & Source Works Ser: No. 267). 1968. Repr. of 1911 ed. 21.50 (ISBN 0-8337-1930-0). B Franklin.
McDermott, John F., ed. Western Journals of Doctor George Hunter, 1796-1805. LC 63-17662. (Transactions Ser.: Vol. 53, Pt. 4). (Illus.). 1963. pap. 2.00 (ISBN 0-87169-534-0). Am Philos.
Peck, John M. Forty Years of Pioneer Life: Memoir of John Mason Peck. Babcock, Rufus, ed. LC 65-12394. (Perspectives in Sociology Ser.). 454p. 1965. 15.00x (ISBN 0-8093-0181-4). S Ill U Pr.

MISSISSIPPI VALLEY–ANTIQUITIES

George, Gale. Upper Mississippi: Or, Historical Sketches of the Mound-Builder, the Indian Tribes, & the Progress of Civilization in the North-West. 1975. Repr. of 1867 ed. 20.00 (ISBN 0-527-03220-4). Kraus Repr.
Phillips, P., et al. Archaeological Survey in the Lower Mississippi Alluvial Valley 1940-1947. (Illus.). 1951. pap. 58.00 (ISBN 0-527-01262-9). Kraus Repr.
Schnell, Frank T. & Knight, Vernon J. Cemochechobee: Archaeology of a Mississippian Ceremonial Center on the Chattahoochee River. (Ripley P. Bullen Monographs in Anthropology & History: No. 3). 1981. write for info. (ISBN 0-8130-0710-0). U Presses Fla.
Smith, Bruce D. Middle Mississippi Exploitation of Animal Populations. (Anthropological Papers: No. 57). (Illus.). 1975. pap. 4.00x (ISBN 0-932206-55-7). U Mich Mus Anthro.
Smith, Bruce D., ed. Mississippian Settlement Patterns. (Studies in Archaeology Ser.). 1978. 42.00 (ISBN 0-12-650640-X). Acad Pr.
Squier, Ephraim G. & Davis, E. H. Ancient Monuments of the Mississippi Valley. (Illus.). Repr. of 1848 ed. 54.00 (ISBN 0-384-57250-2). Johnson Repr.
--Ancient Monuments of the Mississippi Valley. LC 72-4998. (Harvard University. Peabody Museum of Archaeology & Ethnology. Antiquities of the New World: No. 2). (Illus.). Repr. of 1848 ed. 46.50 (ISBN 0-404-57302-9). AMS Pr.

MISSISSIPPI VALLEY–DESCRIPTION AND TRAVEL

Atwater, Caleb. Remarks Made on a Tour to Prairie du Chien: Thence to Washington City in 1829. fascimile ed. LC 75-82. (Mid-American Frontier Ser.). 1975. Repr. of 1831 ed. 19.00x (ISBN 0-405-06851-4). Arno.
Brown, Samuel R. Western Gazetteer: Or Emigrant's Directory. LC 79-146380. (First American Frontier Ser). (Illus.). 1971. Repr. of 1817 ed. 17.00 (ISBN 0-405-02831-8). Arno.
Collot, Georges H. Journey in North America, 3 Vols. LC 72-1001. Repr. of 1924 ed. Set. 295.00 (ISBN 0-404-01790-8). AMS Pr.
Cutler, Jervis. Topographical Description of the State of Ohio, Indiana Territory, & Louisiana. LC 78-146388. (First American Frontier Ser). (Illus.). 1971. Repr. of 1812 ed. 12.00 (ISBN 0-405-02839-3). Arno.
--A Topographical Description of the State of Ohio, Indiana Territory, & Louisiana. Washburn, Wilcomb E., ed. LC 75-7056. (Narratives of North American Indian Captivities: Vol. 34). 1975. lib. bdg. 44.00 (ISBN 0-8240-1658-0). Garland Pub.
Flint, Timothy. Recollections of the Last Ten Years in the Valley of the Mississippi. 2nd ed. LC 68-24891. (American Scene Ser). 1968. Repr. of 1826 ed. lib. bdg. 39.50 (ISBN 0-306-71136-2). Da Capo.
--Recollections of the Last Ten Years in the Valley of the Mississippi. Brooks, George R., ed. LC 68-21413. (Travels on the Western Waters Ser). (Illus.). 367p. 1968. 15.00x (ISBN 0-8093-0332-9). S Ill U Pr.
--Recollections of the Last Ten Years: Passed in Occasional Residences & Journeyings in the Valley of the Mississippi. (American Studies). 1968. Repr. of 1826 ed. 19.50 (ISBN 0-384-16030-1). Johnson Repr.
Hall, James. Letters from the West. LC 67-10123. 1967. Repr. of 1828 ed. 41.00x (ISBN 0-8201-1024-8). Schol Facsimiles.
Imlay, Gilbert. Topographical Description of the Western Territory of North America. 3rd ed. 1797. 15.50 (ISBN 0-384-25685-6). Johnson Repr.
--Topographical Description of the Western Territory of North America. 3rd ed. LC 68-55739. (Illus.). Repr. of 1797 ed. 15.00x (ISBN 0-678-00541-9). Kelley.
Keating, Bern. Mighty Mississippi. LC 70-151944. (Special Publications Ser.). (Illus.). 1971. 6.95, avail. only from natl. geog. (ISBN 0-87044-096-9). Natl Geog.
Peck, John M. A Guide for Emigrants: Containing Sketches of Illinois, Missouri, & the Adjacent Parts. facsimile ed. LC 75-115. (Mid-American Frontier Ser.). 1975. Repr. of 1831 ed. 19.00x (ISBN 0-405-06881-6). Arno.
Prenshaw, Peggy W. & McKee, Jesse O., eds. The Sense of Place: Mississippi. LC 79-26098. (Southern Quarterly Ser.). 1980. 12.50x (ISBN 0-87805-110-4); pap. 6.00 (ISBN 0-87805-111-2). U Pr of Miss.
Schoolcraft, Henry R. Travels in the Central Portions of the Mississippi Valley. LC 1-6591. 1975. Repr. of 1825 ed. 20.00 (ISBN 0-527-03224-7). Kraus Repr.
Sealsfield, Charles. The United States of North America As They Are & the Americans As They Are. LC 70-105361. Repr. of 1828 ed. 14.50 (ISBN 0-384-54585-8). Johnson Repr.
State Industrial Directories Corp. Mississippi State Industrial Directory, Nineteen Eighty-One. Date not set. pap. price not set (ISBN 0-89910-050-3). State Indus D.
Thwaites, Reuben G., ed. Early Western Travels, 1748-1846, Vols. 19-32. Incl. Vol. 19. Ogden's Letters from Thi West, 1821-23. Bullock's Journey from New Orleans to New York, 1827. Gregg's Commerce of the Prairies, 1831-39: Pt. 1 (ISBN 0-404-06549-X); Vol. 20. Gregg's Commerce of the Prairies: Pt. 2 (ISBN 0-404-06550-3); Vol. 21. Wyeth's Oregon, or a Short History of a Long Journey, 1832. Townsend's Narrative of a Journey Across the Rocky Mountains, 1834 (ISBN 0-404-06551-1); Vols. 22-24. Maximilian, Prince of Wieds, Travel in the Interior of North America, 1832-34: Pts 1-3. Vol. 22 (ISBN 0-404-06552-X). Vol. 23 (ISBN 0-404-06553-8). Vol. 24 (ISBN 0-404-06554-6); Vol. 25. Comprising the Series of Original Paintings of Charles Bodmer to Illustrate Maximilian, Prince of Wieds Travels in the Interior of North America, 1832-34 (ISBN 0-404-06555-4); Vol. 26. Flagg's The Far West, 1836-37: Pt. 1 (ISBN 0-404-06556-2); Vol. 27. Flagg's the Far West, Pt. 2: De Smet's Letters & Sketches 1841-42 (ISBN 0-404-06557-0); Vol. 28. Farnham's Travels in the Great Western Prairies, Etc., May 21-Oct. 16, 1839: Pt. 1 (ISBN 0-404-06558-9); Vol. 29. Farnham's Travels in the Great Western Prairies, Etc., Oct. 21-Dec. 4, 1839: Pt. 2. De Smet's Oregon Missions & Travels Over the Rocky Mountains, 1845-46 (ISBN 0-404-06559-7); Vol. 30. Palmer's Journal of Travels Over the Rocky Mountains, 1845-46 (ISBN 0-404-06560-0); Vols. 31-32. Analytical Index to the Series. Vol. 31 (ISBN 0-404-06561-9). Vol. 32 (ISBN 0-404-06562-7). Repr. of 1907 ed. Set. Vols. 1-32. 805.00 (ISBN 0-404-06530-9). AMS Pr.

MISSISSIPPI VALLEY–DESCRIPTION AND TRAVEL–POETRY

Bell, Charles. Delta Return. rev. ed. LC 70-3119. 1969. 5.00 (ISBN 0-910220-04-2). Larlin Corp.

MISSISSIPPI VALLEY–HISTORY

Alvord, Clarence W. Mississippi Valley in British Politics, 2 Vols. LC 59-6233. (Illus.). 1959. Repr. of 1916 ed. Set. 22.50 (ISBN 0-8462-0108-9). Russell.
Caldwell, Norman W. The French in the Mississippi Valley: 1740-1750. LC 73-18443. (Perspectives in American History Ser.: No. 2). (Illus.). 113p. Repr. of 1941 ed. lib. bdg. 12.50x (ISBN 0-87991-330-4). Porcupine Pr.
Carter, Clarence E. Great Britain & the Illinois Country, 1763-1774. LC 73-120870. (American Bicentennial Ser). 1970. Repr. of 1910 ed. 12.00 (ISBN 0-8046-1263-3). Kennikat.
--Great Britain & the Illinois Country 1763-74. facsimile ed. LC 79-164594. (Select Bibliographies Reprint Ser). Repr. of 1910 ed. 17.00 (ISBN 0-8369-5878-0). Arno.
Eaton, John. Grant, Lincoln & the Freedman. LC 70-78763. (Illus.). Repr. of 1907 ed. 17.50x (ISBN 0-8371-1388-1, Pub. by Negro U Pr). Greenwood.
Flint, Timothy. Indian Wars of the West, Containing Biographical Sketches of Those Pioneers Who Headed the Western Setllers in Repelling the Attacks of the Savages. LC 74-146395. (First American Frontier Ser). 1971. Repr. of 1833 ed. 15.00 (ISBN 0-405-02848-2). Arno.
Havighurst, Walter H. Upper Mississippi Valley. LC 66-19220. 1966. pap. 2.95 (ISBN 0-8077-1506-9). Tchrs Coll.
Holmes, Jack D. Gayoso: The Life of a Spanish Govenor in the Mississippi Valley Seventeen Eighty-Nine to Seventeen Ninety-Nine. 8.50 (ISBN 0-8446-5835-9). Peter Smith.
Houck, Louis. Spanish Regime in Missouri: A Collection of Papers & Documents Relating to Upper Louisiana Principally Within the Present Limits of Missouri During the Dominion of Spain, from the Archives of the Indies at Seville, 2 Vols. in 1. LC 70-146403. (First American Frontier Ser). (Illus.). 1971. Repr. of 1909 ed. 40.00 (ISBN 0-405-02860-1). Arno.
Imlay, Gilbert. Topographical Description of the Western Territory of North America. 3rd ed. 1797. 15.50 (ISBN 0-384-25685-6). Johnson Repr.
--Topographical Description of the Western Territory of North America. 3rd ed. LC 68-55739. (Illus.). Repr. of 1797 ed. 15.00x (ISBN 0-678-00541-9). Kelley.
Knox, Thomas W. Camp-Fire & Cotton-Field. LC 75-84186. (American Scene Ser.). 1969. Repr. of 1865 ed. lib. bdg. 49.50 (ISBN 0-306-71782-4). Da Capo.
Konnyu, Leslie. Acacias: Hungarians of the Mississippi Valley. LC 76-6789. 1976. pap. text ed. 4.50 (ISBN 0-685-68332-X). Hungarian Rev.
Lowry, Robert & McCardle, William H. History of Mississippi from the Discovery of the Great River by Hernando De Soto. LC 70-172755. Repr. of 1891 ed. 37.50 (ISBN 0-404-04610-X). AmS Pr.
McDermott, John F., ed. The Spanish in the Mississippi Valley: 1762-1804. LC 72-75490. (Illus.). 432p. 1974. 21.00 (ISBN 0-252-00269-5). U of Ill Pr.
Monette, John W. History of the Discovery & Settlement of the Valley of the Mississippi by the Three Great European Powers Spain, France, & Great Britain, & the Subsequent Occupation Settlement & Extension of Civil Government by the United States Until the Year 1846, 2 Vols. in 1. LC 78-146408. (First American Frontier Ser). (Illus.). 1971. Repr. of 1846 ed. 50.00 (ISBN 0-405-02868-7). Arno.
Ogg, Frederic A. Opening of the Mississippi: A Struggle for Supremacy in the American Interior. LC 68-57500. Repr. of 1904 ed. 17.50x (ISBN 0-8154-0283-X). Cooper Sq.
--Opening of the Mississippi: A Struggle for Supremacy in the American Interior. LC 69-14017. 1969. Repr. of 1904 ed. lib. bdg. 19.25x (ISBN 0-8371-1103-X, OGOM). Greenwood.
Phillips, Paul C. West in the Diplomacy of the American Revolution. LC 66-24750. 1967. Repr. of 1913 ed. 8.50 (ISBN 0-8462-0947-0). Russell.
Pittman, Philip. The Present State of the European Settlements on the Mississippi. facsimile, new ed. McDermott, John Francis, ed. LC 76-44247. (Illus.). 221p. 1977. 24.95x (ISBN 0-87870-011-0). Memphis St Univ.
Riegel, R. E. & Athearn, R. G. America Moves West. 5th ed. LC 72-113832. 1971. text ed. 16.95 (ISBN 0-03-084316-2, HoltC). HR&W.
Roosevelt, Theodore. Winning of the West. Wish, Harvey, ed. & intro. by. 8.00 (ISBN 0-8446-2827-1). Peter Smith.
Samuel, Ray, et al. Tales of the Mississippi. rev ed. LC 81-5937. (Illus.). 240p. 1981. Repr. of 1955 ed. 19.95 (ISBN 0-88289-291-6). Pelican.
Shannon, Fred A. Appraisal of Walter Prescott Webb's "the Giant Plains. LC 78-12508. (Critiques of Research in the Social Sciences: No. III). 1979. Repr. of 1940 ed. lib. bdg. 17.75x (ISBN 0-313-21211-2, SHWP). Greenwood.
Sprague, Marshall. So Vast So Beautiful a Land: Louisiana & the Purchase. LC 73-21943. 1974. 12.50 (ISBN 0-316-80766-4). Little.
Surrey, Nancy M. Commerce of Louisiana During the French Regime, 1699-1763. LC 71-76702. (Columbia University. Studies in Social Sciences: No. 167). Repr. of 1916 ed. 20.00 (ISBN 0-404-51167-8). AMS Pr.
Tobin, Gregory M. The Making of a History: Walter Prescott Webb & "The Great Plains". 204p. 1976. 12.50x (ISBN 0-292-75029-3). U of Tex Pr.
Van Every, Dale. Ark of Empire: The American Frontier, 1784-1803. LC 76-1392. (Frontier People of America Ser.). 1976. Repr. of 1963 ed. 15.00x (ISBN 0-405-05543-9). Arno.
Weddle, Robert S. Wilderness Manhunt: The Spanish Search for La Salle. LC 72-1579. (Illus.). 307p. 1973. 14.95 (ISBN 0-292-79000-7). U of Tex Pr.
Whitaker, Arthur P. The Mississippi Question, 1795-1803. 8.50 (ISBN 0-8446-1476-9). Peter Smith.
--Spanish-American Frontier, 1783-1795: The Westward Movement & the Spanish Retreat in the Mississippi Valley. LC 27-23368. (Illus.). 1969. pap. 2.95x (ISBN 0-8032-5216-1, BB 398, Bison). U of Nebr Pr.
Winsor, Justin. The Mississippi Basin. LC 70-39703. (Select Bibliographies Reprint Ser.). 1972. Repr. of 1895 ed. 21.50 (ISBN 0-8369-9949-5). Arno.

--Westward Movement: The Colonies & the Republics West of the Alleghanies, 1763-1798. LC 68-56585. (Research & Source Works Ser.: No. 307). (Illus.). 1968. Repr. of 1897 ed. 29.00 (ISBN 0-8337-3821-6). B Franklin.

MISSISSIPPI VALLEY-HISTORY-SOURCES

French, Benjamin F. Historical Collections of Louisiana, Embracing Rare & Valuable Documents Relating to the Natural, Civil, & Political History of That State, 5 vols. LC 72-14380. Repr. of 1853 ed. Set. 150.00 (ISBN 0-404-11050-9); 30.00 ea. Vol. 1 (ISBN 0-404-11051-7). Vol. 2 (ISBN 0-404-11052-5). Vol. 3 (ISBN 0-404-11053-3). Vol. 4 (ISBN 0-404-11054-1). Vol. 5 (ISBN 0-404-11055-X). AMS Pr.

Mississippi Department Of Archives And History. Mississippi Provincial Archives: French Dominion, 3 Vols. Rowland, Dunbar & Sanders, A. G., eds. LC 72-172737. Repr. of 1932 ed. Set. 127.50 (ISBN 0-404-07370-0); 42.50 ea. AMS Pr.

University of Illinois at Urbana-Champaign - Library. Mereness Calendar: Federal Documents on the Upper Mississippi Valley, 1780-1890, 13 vols. 1971. Set. 1470.00 (ISBN 0-8161-0915-X). G K Hall.

MISSISSIPPI VALLEY-SOCIAL LIFE AND CUSTOMS

Baldwin, Joseph. Flush Times of Alabama & Mississippi. 1959. 8.00 (ISBN 0-8446-1589-7). Peter Smith.

McConnel, John L. Western Characters: Or, Types of Border Life in the Western States. facsimile ed. LC 75-110. (Mid-American Frontier Ser.). (Illus.). 1975. Repr. of 1853 ed. 22.00x (ISBN 0-405-06877-8). Arno.

Twain, Mark. Life on the Mississippi. (Classics Ser). (gr. 9 up). pap. 0.95 (ISBN 0-8049-0055-8, CL-55). Airmont.

--Life on the Mississippi. 6.95 (ISBN 0-19-250589-0, W*C589). Oxford U Pr.

MISSIPPIAN EPOCH

see Geology, Stratigraphic-Mississippian

MISSOURI

see also names of cities, regions, etc. in Missouri, e.g. St. Louis, Platte County

Beck, Lewis C. A Gazetteer of the States of Illinois & Missouri. fascimile ed. LC 75-84. (Mid-American Frontier Ser.). 1975. Repr. of 1823 ed. 28.00x (ISBN 0-405-06853-0). Arno.

Chapman, Carl H. The Archaelogy of Missouri, I. LC 73-92242. 320p. 1975. 20.00x (ISBN 0-8262-0160-1). U of Mo Pr.

Chapman, Carl H. & Chapman, Eleanor F. Indians & Archaeology of Missouri. LC 64-64127. (Missouri Handbook Ser.). (Illus.). 1964. pap. 4.00x (ISBN 0-8262-0589-5). U of Mo Pr.

Christensen, Parrish, et al. Missouri Heart of the Nation. LC 80-66209. 1980. text ed. 16.95x (ISBN 0-88273-237-4). Forum Pr MO.

Graham, Keith, et al, eds. Glasgow Story of a Missouri Rivertown. (Illus.). 8.00 (ISBN 0-930552-03-2). Tech Ed Serv.

Missouri. 28.00 (ISBN 0-89770-101-1). Curriculum Info Ctr.

Missouri: A Guide to the 'Show Me' State. LC 72-84486. 1941. 59.00 (ISBN 0-403-02175-8). Somerset Pub.

Mott, Frank L., ed. Missouri Reader. LC 64-14412. 1964. 15.00 (ISBN 0-8262-0024-9). U of Mo Pr.

Price, James E. & Griffin, James B. The Snodgrass Site of the Powers Phase of Southeast Missouri. (Anthropological Papers Ser.: No. 66). (Illus., Orig.). 1979. pap. 6.00x (ISBN 0-932206-77-8). U Mich Mus Anthro.

Reid, Loren. Hurry Home Wednesday: Growing up in a Small Missouri Town, 1905-1921. LC 77-25401. (Illus.). 1978. text ed. 12.95x (ISBN 0-8262-0247-0). U of Mo Pr.

Schiavo, Giovanni. The Italians in Missouri. LC 74-17951. (Italian American Experience Ser). (Illus.). 220p. 1975. Repr. 18.00x (ISBN 0-405-06421-7). Arno.

Switzler, William F. Switzler's Illustrated History of Missouri, from 1541-1877. facsimile ed. LC 75-125. (Mid-American Frontier Ser.). (Illus.). 1975. Repr. of 1879 ed. 36.00x (ISBN 0-405-06890-5). Arno.

Wetmore, Alphonso, compiled by. Gazetteer of the State of Missouri. facsimile ed. LC 75-129. (Mid-American Frontier Ser.). 1975. Repr. of 1837 ed. 24.00x (ISBN 0-405-06894-8). Arno.

MISSOURI-DESCRIPTION AND TRAVEL

Basler, Lucille. A Tour of Old Ste. Genevieve. (Illus.). 32p. 1975. pap. 1.95 (ISBN 0-935284-16-8). Patrice Pr.

Franzwa, Gregory M. The Story of Old Ste. Genevieve. 3rd ed. (Illus.). 1977. 8.95 (ISBN 0-935284-02-8); pap. 3.95 (ISBN 0-935284-03-6). Patrice Pr.

Holman, Donna, ed. Rhineland: Winter in a Missouri Rivertown. (Illus.). 191p. (Orig.). 1979. pap. text ed. 8.00 (ISBN 0-930552-02-4). Tech Ed Serv.

Lewis, Paul M. Beautiful Missouri. LC 80-14717. (Illus.). 72p. 1980. 14.95 (ISBN 0-89802-123-5); pap. 7.95 (ISBN 0-89802-122-7). Beautiful Am.

Lyle, Wes & Hall, John. Missouri: Faces & Places. (Illus.). 1977. 9.50 (ISBN 0-7006-0165-1). Regents Pr KS.

Missouri: A Guide to the 'Show Me' State. LC 72-84486. 1941. 59.00 (ISBN 0-403-02175-8). Somerset Pub.

Rafferty, Milton D. Historical Atlas of Missouri. LC 81-675048. (Illus.). 272p. 1981. 19.95 (ISBN 0-8061-1663-3); pap. 9.95 (ISBN 0-8061-1732-X). U of Okla Pr.

Schoolcraft, Henry R. A View of the Lead Mines of Missouri: Including Some Observations on the Mineralogy, Geology, Geography, Antiquities, Soil, Climate, Population & Productions of Missouri & Arkansas, & Other Sections of the Western Country. LC 72-2867. (Use & Abuse of America's Natural Resources Ser). (Illus.). 302p. 1972. Repr. of 1819 ed. 16.00 (ISBN 0-405-04534-4). Arno.

Thias, Edward J., ed. Pencil Sketches of Missouri. LC 81-50901. (Illus.). 159p. 1981. 14.95 (ISBN 0-86629-033-8). Sunrise MO.

Tixier, Victor. Tixier's Travels on the Osage Prairies. McDermott, John, ed. Salvan, Albert, tr. (American Exploration & Travel Ser: No. 4). (Illus.). 1968. Repr. of 1940 ed. 16.95 (ISBN 0-8061-0087-7). U of Okla Pr.

MISSOURI-GENEALOGY

Bryan, William S. & Rose, Robert. History of the Pioneer Families of Missouri. LC 76-55479. 1977. Repr. of 1876 ed. 20.00 (ISBN 0-8063-0753-6). Genealog Pub.

Hull, William H. Aunt Zettie's Wonderful Salve & Other Stories of the Descendants of Ebanizer B. Hull. LC 81-80641. (Illus.). 180p. (Orig.). 1981. pap. 12.95x (ISBN 0-939330-00-8). Garden Pub.

Jackson, Ronald V. & Teeples, Gary R. Missouri Census Index 1830. LC 77-85976. (Illus.). lib. bdg. 20.00 (ISBN 0-89593-080-3). Accelerated Index.

--Missouri Census Index 1840. LC 77-85977. (Illus.). lib. bdg. 39.00 (ISBN 0-89593-081-1). Accelerated Index.

--Missouri Census Index 1850. LC 77-85978. (Illus.). lib. bdg. 80.00 (ISBN 0-89593-082-X). Accelerated Index.

King, Everett M. History of Maries County, Missouri. rev. ed. (Illus.). 1967. 12.50 (ISBN 0-911208-05-4). Ramfre.

MISSOURI-HISTORY

Biographical & Historical Memoirs of Missouri. 972p. 1978. Repr. 40.00 (ISBN 0-89308-105-1, Goodspeed Pub Co). Southern Hist Pr.

Breuer. Crawford Co. & Cuba, Mo. 10.00 (ISBN 0-911208-23-2). Ramfre.

Brownlee, Richard S. Gray Ghosts of the Confederacy: Guerrilla Warfare in the West, 1861-65. LC 58-14213. (Illus.). 1958. 17.50 (ISBN 0-8071-0333-0). La State U Pr.

Bryan, William S. & Rose, Robert. History of the Pioneer Families of Missouri. LC 76-55479. 1977. Repr. of 1876 ed. 20.00 (ISBN 0-8063-0753-6). Genealog Pub.

Burright, Orrin U. The Sun Rides High: Pioneering Days in Oklahoma, Kansas & Missouri. 1974. 8.95 (ISBN 0-89015-022-2). Eakin Pubns.

Cantor, Louis. Prologue to the Protest Movement: The Missouri Sharecropper Roadside Demonstrations of 1939. LC 70-86480. 1969. 12.75 (ISBN 0-8223-0215-2). Duke.

Carr, Lucien. Missouri, a Bone of Contention. LC 72-3761. (American Commonwealth: No. 11). Repr. of 1888 ed. 26.00 (ISBN 0-404-57211-1). AMS Pr.

Chapman, Carl H. The Archaeology of Missouri, Vol. 2. LC 73-92242. 1980. text ed. 26.95x (ISBN 0-8262-0284-5). U of Mo Pr.

Chen, Stephen. Missouri in the Federal System. LC 80-54752. (Illus.). 234p. (Orig.). 1981. lib. bdg. 21.00 (ISBN 0-8191-1720-X); pap. text ed. 11.00 (ISBN 0-8191-1721-8). U Pr of Amer.

Cordry, Christopher L. Every Name Index of W. F. Johnson's 1919 History of Cooper County Missouri. LC 77-94831. 1978. 12.00x (ISBN 0-916440-05-2). VKM.

Cordry, Eugene A. History of New Lebanon, Cooper County, Missouri. LC 75-16896. (Illus.). 400p. 1976. 29.00x (ISBN 0-916440-03-6). VKM.

Cramer, Rose F. Wayne County, Missouri. (Illus.). 734p. 1972. 11.00 (ISBN 0-911208-22-4). Ramfre.

Ellison, Robert S. Independence Rock. 41p. 1975. pap. 3.00 (ISBN 0-87770-136-9). Ye Galleon.

Foerester, Bernd & Heritage Commission. Independence, Missouri. LC 78-2287. (Illus.). 1978. 12.00 (ISBN 0-8309-0203-1). Independence Pr.

Foley, William E. History of Missouri: Volume 1: 1673 T0 1820. LC 70-15584. (Missouri Sesquicentennial History Ser: Vol. 1). (Illus.). (gr. 9-12). 1971. text ed. 15.00x (ISBN 0-8262-0108-3). U of Mo Pr.

Franzwa, Gregory M. History of the Hazelwood School District. (Illus.). 1977. 9.95 (ISBN 0-935284-08-7). Patrice Pr.

--The Story of Old Ste. Genevieve. 3rd ed. (Illus.). 1977. 8.95 (ISBN 0-935284-02-8); pap. 3.95 (ISBN 0-935284-03-6). Patrice Pr.

The History of Buchanan County, Missouri. (Illus.). 1123p. 1974. Repr. of 1889 ed. 15.00 (ISBN 0-911208-25-9). Ramfre.

Houck, Louis. History of Missouri from the Earliest Explorations & Settlements Until the Admission of the State into the Union. LC 76-146402. (First American Frontier Ser). (Illus.). 1971. Repr. of 1908 ed. 56.00 (ISBN 0-405-02856-3). Arno.

--Spanish Regime in Missouri: A Collection of Papers & Documents Relating to Upper Louisiana Principally Within the Present Limits of Missouri During the Dominion of Spain, from the Archives of the Indies at Seville, 2 Vols. in 1. LC 70-146403. (First American Frontier Ser). (Illus.). 1971. Repr. of 1909 ed. 40.00 (ISBN 0-405-02860-1). Arno.

Illustrated Atlas Map of Cooper County Missouri. (Illus.). 1975. Repr. of 1877 ed. 17.00 (ISBN 0-916440-02-8). VKM.

Johnson, W. F. & Cordry, Christopher L. History of Cooper County Missouri Plus Every Name Index, 2 vols. (Illus.). 1978. Set. 55.00x (ISBN 0-916440-04-4). VKM.

Karsch, Robert F. I'm from Missouri. (gr. 7-9). 1978. pap. text ed. 3.50x saddle stitched (ISBN 0-87543-107-0). Lucas.

Kirkman, Kay & Stinnett, Roger. Joplin: A Pictorial History. Friedman, Donna R., ed. LC 80-20530. (Illus.). 192p. 1980. pap. 13.95 (ISBN 0-89865-070-4). Donning Co.

Knox, Thomas W. Camp-Fire & Cotton-Field. LC 75-84186. (American Scene Ser.). 1969. Repr. of 1865 ed. lib. bdg. 49.50 (ISBN 0-306-71782-4). Da Capo.

Kodner, Barbara. Olivette: Chronicle of a Country Village. LC 78-71855. (Illus.). 1979. 19.95 (ISBN 0-935284-11-7). Patrice Pr.

Kremer, et al. Missouri's Black Heritage. LC 79-54887. (Orig.). 1980. pap. text ed. 8.95x (ISBN 0-88273-115-7). Forum Pr MO.

McCandless, Perry. A History of Missouri, Volume II: 1820 to 1860, Vol. II. LC 76-155844. (Missouri Sequicentennial History Ser). (Illus.). 1972. 15.00x (ISBN 0-8262-0124-5). U of Mo Pr.

McCorkle, John. Three Years with Quantrell. Barton, D. S., ed. LC 67-6851. (American Biography Ser., No. 32). 1970. lib. bdg. 45.95 (ISBN 0-8383-1107-5). Haskell.

McReynolds, Edwin C. Missouri: A History of the Crossroads State. (Illus.). 1975. pap. 9.95 (ISBN 0-8061-1265-4). U of Okla Pr.

Missouri Land Claims: Chadwell/Patricia. 1976. 17.50 (ISBN 0-686-20882-X). Polyanthos.

Nagel, Paul C. Missouri: A History. (States & the Nation Ser.). (Illus.). 1977. 12.95 (ISBN 0-393-05633-3, Co-Pub. by AASLH). Norton.

Parrish, William E. A History of Missouri, Volume III: 1860 to 1875. LC 76-155844. (Missouri Sesquicentennial History Ser). (Illus.). 1973. 15.00x (ISBN 0-8262-0148-2). U of Mo Pr.

--Missouri Under Radical Rule, 1865-1870. LC 65-21794. 1965. 10.00x (ISBN 0-8262-0043-5). U of Mo Pr.

Primm, James N. Lion of the Valley: Saint Louis, Missouri. (Western Urban History Ser.: Vol. III). (Illus.). 1981. 16.95 (ISBN 0-87108-546-1). Pruett.

Report of Major General John Pope. LC 76-43557. (Civil War Monographs). 1977. Pt. 1. lib. bdg. 26.00 (ISBN 0-527-17570-6); pap. 20.00 (ISBN 0-527-17577-3); Pt. 2. lib. bdg. 23.00 (ISBN 0-527-17571-4); pap. 17.00 (ISBN 0-527-17572-2). Kraus Repr.

Shoemaker, Floyd C. Missouri's Struggle for Statehood, 1804-1821. LC 76-81467. (Illus.). 1969. Repr. of 1916 ed. 12.50 (ISBN 0-8462-1374-5). Russell.

Smeal, Lee. Missouri Historical & Biographical Index. LC 78-53706. (Illus.). Date not set. lib. bdg. price not set (ISBN 0-89593-189-3). Accelerated Index.

The Territory of Louisiana-Missouri, 1803-1806. (The Territorial Papers of the United States: Vol. 13). Repr. of 1948 ed. 69.50 (ISBN 0-404-01463-1). AMS Pr.

The Territory of Louisiana-Missouri, 1806-1814. (The Territorial Papers of the United States: Vol. 14). Repr. of 1949 ed. 69.50 (ISBN 0-404-01464-X). AMS Pr.

The Territory of Louisiana-Missouri, 1815-1821. (The Territorial Papers of the United States: Vol. 15). Repr. of 1951 ed. 69.50 (ISBN 0-404-01465-8). AMS Pr.

Terry, Dickson. There's a Town in Missouri. 136p. (Orig.). 1980. pap. 4.95 (ISBN 0-86629-016-8). Sunrise MO.

Vance, Mary. Historical Society Architectural Publications: Massachusetts, Michigan,Minnesota, Mississippi, Missouri. (Architecture Ser.: Bibliography A-159). 75p. 1980. pap. 8.00 (ISBN 0-686-26907-1). Vance Biblios.

MISSOURI-IMPRINTS

Fitzgerald, Alice I. Missouri's Literary Heritage for Children & Youth: An Annotated Bibliography of Books About Missouri. LC 81-3030. 304p. 1981. text ed. 21.00 (ISBN 0-8262-0346-9). U of Mo Pr.

Historical Records Survey: Preliminary Check List of Missouri Imprints, 1808-1850. 1937. pap. 12.00 (ISBN 0-527-01898-8). Kraus Repr.

MISSOURI-JUVENILE LITERATURE

Bailey, Bernadine. Picture Book of Missouri. rev. ed. LC 66-31256. (Illus.). (gr. 3-5). 1974. 5.50g (ISBN 0-8075-9528-4). A Whitman.

Carpenter, Allan. Missouri. LC 78-3551. (New Enchantment of America State Bks.). (Illus.). (gr. 4 up). 1978. PLB 10.60 (ISBN 0-516-04125-8). Childrens.

Fradin, Dennis. Missouri: In Words & Pictures. LC 80-12249. (Young People's Stories of Our States Ser.). (Illus.). 48p. (gr. 2-5). 1980. PLB 9.25 (ISBN 0-516-03925-3). Childrens.

MISSOURI-POLITICS AND GOVERNMENT

Brekke, Jerald. An Assessment of the Bloc Grant Provisions of the Omnibus Crime Control & Safe Streets Act of 1968: The Missouri Experience. 1977. pap. text ed. 6.75 (ISBN 0-8191-0254-7). U Pr of Amer.

Chen, Stephen. Missouri in the Federal System. LC 80-54752. (Illus.). 234p. (Orig.). 1981. lib. bdg. 21.00 (ISBN 0-8191-1720-X); pap. text ed. 11.00 (ISBN 0-8191-1721-8). U Pr of Amer.

Hathaway, Beverly W. Inventory of County Records of Missouri. LC 77-87437. (Illus.). Date not set. lib. bdg. price not set (ISBN 0-89593-163-X). Accelerated Index.

Karsch, Robert. The Government of Missouri. 14th ed. 1978. text ed. 11.95x (ISBN 0-87543-143-7). Lucas.

Karsch, Robert F. I'm from Missouri. (gr. 7-9). 1978. pap. text ed. 3.50x saddle stitched (ISBN 0-87543-107-0). Lucas.

--Missouri Under the Constitution. 5th ed. 1979. text ed. 6.95x perfect bdg. (ISBN 0-87543-149-6). Lucas.

McCurdy, Frances L. Stump, Bar & Pulpit: Speechmaking on the Missouri Frontier. LC 74-93050. 1969. 9.00x (ISBN 0-8262-0081-8). U of Mo Pr.

Matthews, Stephen F. & Levi, Donald R. Missouri Agricultural Law. 4th ed. (Lucas Text Ser). 1979. spiral bdg. 10.00x (ISBN 0-87543-132-1). Lucas.

St. Louis Board Of Education. Missouri: The Simplified Constitution. 2nd ed. 1965. 3.52 (ISBN 0-07-054452-2, W); tests 0.32 (ISBN 0-07-026220-9). McGraw.

Shoemaker, Floyd C. Missouri's Struggle for Statehood, 1804-1821. LC 76-81467. (Illus.). 1969. Repr. of 1916 ed. 12.50 (ISBN 0-8462-1374-5). Russell.

MISSOURI-SOCIAL LIFE AND CUSTOMS

Fradin, Dennis. Missouri: In Words & Pictures. LC 80-12249. (Young People's Stories of Our States Ser.). (Illus.). 48p. (gr. 2-5). 1980. PLB 9.25 (ISBN 0-516-03925-3). Childrens.

Slaughter, Steven S. History of a Missouri Farm Family: The O. V. Slaughters, 1700-1944. LC 78-9549. (Illus.). 1978. 15.00 (ISBN 0-916346-27-7). Harbor Hill Bks.

MISSOURI (BATTLESHIP)

Newell, Gordon & Smith, Allan E. Mighty Mo: A Biography of a Battleship. LC 72-87802. deluxe ed. 25.00 (ISBN 0-87564-204-7). Superior Pub.

MISSOURI, KANSAS AND TEXAS RAILROAD COMPANY

Katy Noerthwest. 26.95 (ISBN 0-685-83343-7). Chatham Pub CA.

MISSOURI, UNIVERSITY OF

Devine, Dan & Onofrio, Al. Missouri Power Football. 2nd ed. 1967. text ed. 6.95x (ISBN 0-87543-006-6). Lucas.

Stephens, Frank F. History of the University of Missouri. LC 62-7571. (Illus.). 1962. 12.00x (ISBN 0-8262-0013-3). U of Mo Pr.

MISSOURI AND NORTH ARKANSAS RAILROAD STRIKE, 1921-1923

Gooden, Orville T. Missouri & North Arkansas Railroad Strike. LC 68-57567. (Columbia University. Studies in the Social Sciences: No. 275). Repr. of 1926 ed. 21.00 (ISBN 0-404-51275-5). AMS Pr.

MISSOURI COMPROMISE

see also Kansas-Nebraska Bill

Benton, Thomas H. Historical & Legal Examination of That Part of the Decision of the Supreme Court of the U.S. in the Dred Scott Case Which Declares the Unconstitutionality of the Missouri Compromise Act & the Self-Extension of the Constitution to Territories. Repr. of 1857 ed. 11.50 (ISBN 0-384-03946-4). Johnson Repr.

Brown, Everett S., ed. Missouri Compromises & Presidential Politics, 1820-1825: From the Letters of William Plumer. Jr. LC 76-103942. (American Constitutional & Legal History Ser). 1970. Repr. of 1926 ed. lib. bdg. 17.50 (ISBN 0-306-71869-3). Da Capo.

Dixon, Susan B. History of the Missouri Compromise & Slavery in American Politics. Repr. of 1903 ed. 38.50 (ISBN 0-384-11885-2). Johnson Repr.

Moore, Glover. The Missouri Controversy, 1819-1821. LC 53-5518. (Illus.). 392p. 1966. pap. 7.00x (ISBN 0-8131-0106-9). U Pr of Ky.

--The Missouri Controversy 1819-1821. 1953. 7.75 (ISBN 0-8446-1315-0). Peter Smith.

Ray, P. Orman. Repeal of the Missouri Compromise. 1965. Repr. of 1909 ed. 12.50x (ISBN 0-910324-07-7). Canner.

MISSOURI RIVER AND VALLEY

Anderson, John. Mackinaws Down the Missouri. Barrett, Glenn, ed. (Western Text Society Ser.). 105p. 1973. 6.00 (ISBN 0-87421-059-3); pap. 4.00 (ISBN 0-87421-090-9). Utah St U Pr.

Athearn, Robert G. High Country Empire: The High Plains & Rockies. LC 60-8822. (Illus.). x, 358p. 1965. pap. 4.95 (ISBN 0-8032-5008-8, 314, Bison). U of Nebr Pr.

Brackenridge, H. M. Journal of a Voyage up the River Missouri. 1976. Repr. of 1815 ed. 15.00 (ISBN 0-527-10510-4). Kraus Repr.

Chittenden, Hiram M. Early Steamboat Navigation on the Missouri River. Repr. 12.50 (ISBN 0-87018-009-6). Ross.

De Voto, Bernard. Journals of Lewis & Clark. 1953. 22.50 (ISBN 0-395-07607-2). HM.

Gale, John. Missouri Expedition Eighteen Eighteen to Eighteen Twenty: The Journal of Surgeon John Gale with Related Documents. Nichols, Roger L., ed. LC 68-10623. (American Exploration & Travel Ser.: Vol. 56). (Illus.). 1969. 9.95 (ISBN 0-8061-0840-1). U of Okla Pr.

Lewis, Meriwether & Clark, William. History of the Expedition Under the Command of Lewis & Clark, 3 Vols. Coues, E., ed. (Illus.). Set. 35.00 (ISBN 0-8446-2468-3); 11.75 ea. Peter Smith.

--Journals of Lewis & Clark. De Voto, Bernard, ed. (Illus.). 1963. pap. 8.95 (ISBN 0-395-08380-X, 31, SenEd). HM.

--Journals of Lewis & Clark: A New Selection. Bakeless, John, ed. (Orig.). 1964. pap. 1.95 (ISBN 0-451-61665-0, MJ1665, Ment). NAL.

Mattes, Merrill J. Missouri Valley. 1971. pap. 2.95 (ISBN 0-8077-1718-5). Tchrs Coll.

Neihardt, John G. River & I. LC 68-13650. (Illus.). 1968. pap. 4.95 (ISBN 0-8032-5144-0, BB 378, Bison). U of Nebr Pr.

Nelson, Bruce. Land of the Dacotahs. LC 65-108129. (Illus.). 1964. pap. 3.95 (ISBN 0-8032-5145-9, BB 176, Bison). U of Nebr Pr.

Tabeau, Pierre-Antoine. Tabeau's Narrative of Loisel's Expedition to the Upper Missouri. (American Exploration & Travel Ser: No. 3). (Illus.). 1968. Repr. of 1939 ed. 14.95 (ISBN 0-8061-0080-X). U of Okla Pr.

Terral, Rufus. Missouri Valley. LC 73-122867. 1970. Repr. of 1947 ed. 13.00 (ISBN 0-8046-1315-X). Kennikat.

Thwaites, Rueben G., ed. Original Journals of the Lewis & Clark Expedition, 8 Vols. LC 72-88223. Repr. of 1904 ed. Set. 160.00 (ISBN 0-405-00030-8). Arno.

Vestal, Stanley. Missouri. LC 44-5196. (Illus.). 1964. pap. 4.50 (ISBN 0-8032-5207-2, BB 186, Bison). U of Nebr Pr.

Wilder, Laura I. On the Way Home. Lane, Rose W., ed. LC 62-17966. (Illus.). (gr. 7 up). 1962. 8.95 (ISBN 0-06-026489-6, HarpJ); PLB 9.89 (ISBN 0-06-026490-X). Har-Row.

MISTAKE (LAW)

see also Fraud

McKeag, Edwin C. Mistake in Contract: A Study in Comparative Jurisprudence. LC 75-76675. (Columbia University, Studies in the Social Sciences Ser.: No. 59). Repr. of 1905 ed. 16.50 (ISBN 0-404-51059-0). AMS Pr.

Verplanck, Gulian C. An Essay on the Doctrine of Contracts. LC 77-37992. (American Law Ser.: The Formative Years). 244p. 1972. Repr. of 1825 ed. 10.00 (ISBN 0-405-04039-3). Arno.

MISTAKES

see Errors; Errors, Popular

MISTRAL, FREDERIC, 1830-1914

Downer, Charles A. Frederic Mistral: Poet & Leader in Provence. LC 74-164783. (Columbia University. Studies in Romance Philology & Literature: No. 2). Repr. of 1901 ed. 19.75 (ISBN 0-404-50602-X). AMS Pr.

Ford, Harry E. Modern Provencal Phonology & Morphology Studied in the Language of Frederic Mistral. LC 72-168117. (Columbia University. Studies in Romance Philology & Literature: No. 30). Repr. of 1921 ed. 15.00 (ISBN 0-685-05898-0). AMS Pr.

Lyle, Rob. Mistral. 1953. 24.50x (ISBN 0-686-50050-4). Elliots Bks.

Olson, Selma. Ana Mistral. LC 75-263. 242p. 1975. 6.00 (ISBN 0-915392-00-3, Domina Bks); pap. 2.25 (ISBN 0-915392-01-1, Domina Bks). Double M Pr.

MISTRAL, GABRIELA

see Godoy Alcayaga, Lucila, 1889-1957

MIT

see Massachusetts Institute of Technology

MITANNI

McEwan, Calvin W., et al. Soundings at Tell Fakhariyah. LC 57-11216. (Oriental Institute Pubns. Ser: No. 79). (Illus.). 1958. 40.00x (ISBN 0-226-62180-4, OIP79). U of Chicago Pr.

MITANNIANS

see also Hurrians

MITCHELL, JOHN, 1870-1919

Berkeley, Edmund & Berkeley, Dorothy S. Dr. John Mitchell: The Man Who Made the Map of North America. LC 73-16162. (Illus.). 302p. 1974. 19.50x (ISBN 0-8078-1221-8). U of NC Pr.

Gluck, Elsie. John Mitchell, Miner: Labor's Bargain with the Gilded Age. LC 72-158853. Repr. of 1929 ed. 14.50 (ISBN 0-404-02829-2). AMS Pr.

--John Mitchell, Miner: Labor's Bargain with the Gilded Age. LC 69-13909. Repr. of 1929 ed. lib. bdg. 15.50x (ISBN 0-8371-2170-1, GLJM). Greenwood.

Mitchell, Johnny. Secret War of Captain Johnny Mitchell. LC 76-2963. 103p. 1976. 5.95 (ISBN 0-685-66076-1). Pacesetter Pr.

Turcheneske, John A., Jr., ed. The John Mitchell Papers, 1885-1919: A Guide to the Microfilm Edition. LC 75-9921. 114p. 1975. pap. 25.00 (ISBN 0-88455-197-0). Microfilming Corp.

MITCHELL, MARGARET, 1900-1949

Gemme, Leila. Monarch Notes on Mitchell's Gone with the Wind. 1975. pap. 1.95 (ISBN 0-671-00946-X). Monarch Pr.

MITCHELL, MARIA, 1818-1889

Morgan, Helen L. Maria Mitchell, First Lady of American Astronomy. LC 77-5871. (gr. 7-10). 1977. 7.95 (ISBN 0-664-32614-5). Westminster.

Wayne, Bennett, ed. & commentaries by. Women Who Dared to Be Different. LC 72-6802. (Target Ser.). (Illus.). 168p. (gr. 5-12). 1973. PLB 7.29 (ISBN 0-8116-4902-4). Garrard.

MITCHELL, MARTHA, 1918-1976

McLendon, Winzola. Martha: The Biography of Martha Mitchell. LC 77-90289. (Illus.). 1979. 12.95 (ISBN 0-394-41124-2). Random.

MITCHELL, SUSAN

Kain, Richard M. Susan L. Mitchell. LC 78-126275. (Irish Writers Ser.). 1972. 4.50 (ISBN 0-8387-7768-6); pap. 1.95 (ISBN 0-8387-7627-2). Bucknell U Pr.

MITCHELL, WESLEY CLAIR, 1874-1948

Homan, Paul T. Contemporary Economic Thought. facs. ed. LC 68-20310. (Essay Index Reprint Ser). 1928. 19.50 (ISBN 0-8369-0546-6). Arno.

Mitchell, Wesley C. Economic Essays in Honor of Wesley Clair Mitchell. LC 68-15144. (Illus.). 1968. Repr. of 1935 ed. 14.00 (ISBN 0-8462-1129-7). Russell.

MITCHELL, WILLIAM, 1879-1936

Burlingame, Roger. General Billy Mitchell: Champion of Air Defense. LC 77-26823. (They Made America Ser.). (Illus.). 1978. Repr. of 1952 ed. lib. bdg. 20.00x (ISBN 0-313-20170-6, BUGM). Greenwood.

Hurley, Alfred F. Billy Mitchell: Crusader for Air Power. new ed. LC 74-22831. (Midland Bks.: No. 180). (Illus.). 204p. 1975. 10.00x (ISBN 0-253-31203-5); pap. 2.95x (ISBN 0-253-20180-2). Ind U Pr.

Levine, Isaac D. Mitchell, Pioneer of Air Power. LC 71-169426. (Literature & History of Aviation Ser). 1971. Repr. of 1943 ed. 20.00 (ISBN 0-405-03777-5). Arno.

MITCHILL, SAMUEL LATHAM, 1764-1831

Hall, Courtney R. Scientist in the Early Republic: Samuel Latham Mitchill, 1764-1831 with Selected Mitchill Correspondence. 2nd ed. LC 66-27092. 1967. Repr. of 1934 ed. 8.00 (ISBN 0-8462-0869-5). Russell.

MITCHUM, ROBERT, 1917-

Marill, Alvin H. Robert Mitchum on the Screen. LC 76-50203. (Illus.). 1978. 19.95 (ISBN 0-498-01847-4). A S Barnes.

MITES

see also Ticks

Balogh, J. The Oribatid Genera of the World. (Illus.). 188p. (Orig.). 1972. 21.00 (ISBN 0-685-36757-6). Entomological Repr.

Cook, David. Studies on Neotropical Water Mites. (Memoir Ser.: No. 31). (Illus.). 644p. 1980. 44.00 (ISBN 0-686-27979-4). Am Entom Inst.

--Water Mite Genera & Subgenera. (Memoris Ser: No. 21). (Illus.). 860p. 1974. 55.00 (ISBN 0-686-08749-6). Am Entom Inst.

Cook, David R. Water Mites from India. (Memoirs Ser: No. 9). (Illus.). 411p. 1967. 25.00 (ISBN 0-686-17145-4). Am Entom Inst.

--The Water Mites of Liberia. (Memoirs Ser: No. 6). (Illus.). 418p. 1966. 25.00 (ISBN 0-686-17144-6). Am Entom Inst.

Evans, G. Owen, et al. The Terrestrial Acari of the British Isles: an Introduction to Their Morphology, Biology & Classification, Vol. 1: Introduction & Biology. (Illus.). 219p. 1961. Repr. of 1968 ed. 11.00x (ISBN 0-565-00696-7, Pub. by Brit Mus Nat Hist England). Sabbot-Natural Hist Bks.

Fransz, H. G. The Functional Response to Prey Density in an Acarine System. new ed. (Simulation Monographs). 143p. 1974. pap. 16.00 (ISBN 90-220-0509-7, Pub. by PUDOC). Unipub.

International Congress of Acarology-2nd. Proceedings. Evans, Owen, ed. 652p. 1969. 32.50x (ISBN 0-8002-1861-2). Intl Pubns Serv.

Jeppson, Lee R., et al. Mites Injurious to Economic Plants. LC 72-93523. (Illus.). 1975. 52.50x (ISBN 0-520-02381-1). U of Cal Pr.

McDaniel, Burruss. How to Know the Mites & Ticks. (Pictured Key Nature Ser.). 1979. write for info. wire coil (ISBN 0-697-04757-1); text ed. write for info. (ISBN 0-697-04756-3). Wm C Brown.

Michael, Albert D. British Tyroglyphidae, 2 Vols. Repr. of 1903 ed. Set. 69.50 (ISBN 0-384-38875-2). Johnson Repr.

Piffl, Eduard, ed. Proceedings of the Fourth International Congress of Arcarology. (Illus.). 752p. (Available in english, german, french). 1979. 65.00x (ISBN 963-05-1695-0). Intl Pubns Serv.

Prasad, Vikram & Cook, David. Taxonomy of Water Mite Larvae. (Memoirs Ser: No. 18). (Illus.). 326p. 1972. 22.00 (ISBN 0-686-08727-5). Am Entom Inst.

Rodriguez, J. G., ed. Recent Advances in Acarology. LC 79-17386. 1979. Vol. 1. 38.00 (ISBN 0-12-592201-9); Vol. 2. 34.50 (ISBN 0-12-592202-7). Acad Pr.

Tuttle, Donald M. & Baker, Edward W. The Spider Mites of the Southwestern United States & a Revision of the Family Tetranychidae. LC 67-30668. (Illus.). 1968. 2.00 (ISBN 0-8165-0085-1). U of Ariz Pr.

Van Der Hammen, L. A Berlese, Acari Myriopoda et Scorpiones Eighteen Hundred Eighty-Two - Nineteen Hundred Three, 12 vols. 4616p. 1980. Set. 315.00 (ISBN 90-6193-603-9, Pub. by Junk Pubs Netherlands). Kluwer Boston.

Whittington, H. B. British Trilobites of the Family Harpidae. pap. 9.50 (ISBN 0-384-68220-0). Johnson Repr.

Zakhvatkin, A. A. Arachnoidea: Tyroglyphoidea (Acari) Ratcliffe, A. & Hughes, A. M., eds. Ratcliffe, A. & Hughes, A. M., trs. 1959. 10.00 (ISBN 0-934454-09-4). Lubrecht & Cramer.

MITFORD, MARY RUSSELL, 1787-1855

Astin, Majorie. Mary Russell Mitford: Her Circle & Her Books. 1930. Repr. 15.00 (ISBN 0-8274-2685-2). R West.

Hill, Constance. Mary Russell Mitford & Her Surroundings. 1920. Repr. 30.00 (ISBN 0-8274-2686-0). R West.

Lee, Elizabeth. Mary Russell Mitford: Correspondence with Charles Boner & John Ruskin. 1973. Repr. of 1914 ed. 35.00 (ISBN 0-8274-1398-X). R West.

L'Estrange, A. G., ed. The Friendships of Mary Russell Mitford As Recorded in Letters from Her Literary Correspondence. 460p. 1981. Repr. of 1882 ed. lib. bdg. 40.00 (ISBN 0-89987-511-4). Darby Bks.

Mitford, Mary R. The Letters of Mary Russell Mitford. Johnson, Reginald B., ed. LC 77-16515. 1977. Repr. of 1925 ed. lib. bdg. 25.00 (ISBN 0-8414-5403-5). Folcroft.

Roberts, W. J. Mary Russell Mitford. 1913. Repr. 40.00 (ISBN 0-8274-2684-4). R West.

Watson, Vera. Mary Russell Mitford. 1949. Repr. 20.00 (ISBN 0-8274-2683-6). R West.

MITHAN

see Gayal

MITHRAISM

see also Zoroastrianism

Cumont, Franz. Mysteries of Mithra. (Illus.). 8.00 (ISBN 0-8446-1926-4). Peter Smith.

--The Mysteries of Mithra. 2nd ed. McCormack, Thomas J., tr. (Illus., Fr). 1911. pap. 4.00 (ISBN 0-486-20323-9). Dover.

Laeuchli, Samuel, ed. Mithraism in Ostia: Mystery Religion & Christianity in the Ancient Port of Rome. (Illus.). 1967. 11.95x (ISBN 0-8101-0138-6). Northwestern U Pr.

Speidel, Michael P. Mithras-Orion: Greek Hero & Roman Army God. (Illus.). 56p. 1980. pap. text ed. 16.00x (ISBN 90-04-06055-3). Humanities.

MITLA, MEXICO (OAXACA)

Parsons, Elsie C. Mitla: Town of the Souls, & Other Zapoteco-Speaking Pueblos of Oaxaca, Mexico. LC 36-18029. (Illus.). 1936. 17.50x (ISBN 0-226-64760-9). U of Chicago Pr.

MITOCHONDRIA

Bandlow, W., et al, eds. Genetics, Biogenetics & Bioenergetics of Mitochondria: Symposium, Sept. 1975, University of Munich, Germany. 1976. 87.50x (ISBN 3-11-006865-6). De Gruyter.

Birky, C. William, Jr., et al, eds. Genetics & Biogenesis of Mitochondria & Chloroplasts. LC 75-20271. (Ohio State University Biosciences Colloquia: No.1). (Illus.). 1976. 15.00x (ISBN 0-8142-0236-5). Ohio St U Pr.

Bucher, T., et al, eds. Genetics & Biogenesis of Chloroplasts & Mitochondria: Interdisciplinary Conference on the Genetics & Biogenesis of Chloroplasts & Mitrochondria, Munich, Germany August 2-7, 1976. 1977. 85.50 (ISBN 0-7204-0604-8, North-Holland). Elsevier.

Carafoli, E. & Roman, I. Mitochondria & Disease. (Illus.). 133p. 1980. 12.00 (ISBN 0-08-027378-5). Pergamon.

Chance, Britton, ed. Energy-Linked Functions of Mitochondria. 1963. 34.00 (ISBN 0-12-167862-8). Acad Pr.

Chappell, J. B. The Energetics of Mitochondria. rev. ed. Head, J. J., ed. LC 77-70873. (Carolina Biology Readers Ser.). (Illus.). (gr. 11 up). 1979. pap. 2.00 (ISBN 0-89278-219-6, 45-9619). Carolina Biological.

Conference, Rosa Marni, Italy, June 1973. The Biogenesis of Mitochondria: Transcriptional,Translational & Genetic Aspects, Proceedings. Kroon, A. M. & Saccone, C., eds. 1974. 44.50 (ISBN 0-12-426750-5). Acad Pr.

Ducet, G. & Lance, C. Plant Mitochondria. (Developments in Plant Biology Ser.: Vol. 1). 1978. 66.00 (ISBN 0-444-80082-4, Biomedical Pr). Elsevier.

Easton, A. J., et al. Analysis of Chondritic Material Using Selective Attack by Chlorine. (Illus.). 1981. spiral bdg. 25.00x (ISBN 0-565-00837-4, Pub. by Brit Mus Nat Hist England). Sabbot-Natural Hist Bks.

Erecinska, Maria & Wilson, David F., eds. Inhibitors of Mitochondrial Function. (International Encyclopedia of Pharmacology & Therapeutics: Section 107). (Illus.). 324p. Date not set. 80.01 (ISBN 0-08-027380-7). Pergamon.

Ernster, L. & Ernster, L., eds. Mitochondria, Structure & Function. 1970. 62.00 (ISBN 0-12-241250-8). Acad Pr.

FEBS Meeting, Amsterdam, August, 1972, Eighth. Mitochondria & Membranes: Proceedings, Vol. 28. 1973. 31.00 (ISBN 0-444-10423-2, North-Holland). Elsevier.

Green, David E. & Baum, Harold. Energy & the Mitochondrion. 1970. 12.95 (ISBN 0-12-297950-8). Acad Pr.

Lloyd, David. The Mitochondria of Microorganisms. 1975. 90.00 (ISBN 0-12-453650-6). Acad Pr.

Mehlman, Myron A. & Hanson, Richard W., eds. Energy Metabolism & the Regulation of Metabolic Processes in Mitochondria. 1972. 36.00 (ISBN 0-12-487850-4). Acad Pr.

Mitochondria 1977 - Genetics & Biogenesis of Mitochondria: Proceedings. 1977. 118.75x (ISBN 3-11-007321-8). De Gruyter.

Mitochondrial Ribosomes & Mitochondrial RNA from Yeast. (Agricultural Research Reports Ser.: 797). 1973. pap. 4.00 (ISBN 90-220-0451-1, PUDOC). Unipub.

Munn, E. A. The Structure of Mitochondria. 1974. 72.00 (ISBN 0-12-510150-3). Acad Pr.

--The Structure of Mitochondria. 1974. 72.00 (ISBN 0-12-510150-3). Acad Pr.

Prebble, J. N. Mitochondria, Chloroplasts & Bacterial Membranes. (Illus.). 1981. text ed. 30.00x (ISBN 0-582-44133-1). Longman.

Racker, Efraim, ed. Membranes of Mitochondria & Chloroplasts. LC 72-97168. (ACS Monograph: No. 165). 1970. 28.50 (ISBN 0-8412-0287-7). Am Chemical.

Saccone, C. & Kroon, A. M. The Genetic Function of Mitochondrial DNA. 1976. 51.25 (ISBN 0-7204-0586-6, North-Holland). Elsevier.

Sager, Ruth. Cytoplasmic Genes & Organelles. 1972. 29.50 (ISBN 0-12-614650-0). Acad Pr.

Saito, S., ed. Mitochondria. (Selected Papers in Biochemistry Ser.: Vol. 10). (Illus.). 1976. 16.50 (ISBN 0-8391-0620-3). Univ Park.

Slonimski, P., et al, eds. Mitochondrial Genes. (Cold Spring Harbor Monographs: Vol. 12). 550p. 1981. price not set (ISBN 0-87969-145-X). Cold Spring Harbor.

Symposium on Biochemistry & Biophysics of Mitochondrial Membranes. Biochemistry & Biophysics of Mitochondrial Membranes: Proceedings. Azzone, G. F., ed. 1972. 55.50 (ISBN 0-12-068950-2). Acad Pr.

Tandler, Bernard & Hoppel, Charles L. Mitochondria. (Monographs on the Ultrastructure of Cells & Organisms Ser.). 1972. 19.50 (ISBN 0-12-454143-7). Acad Pr.

Tedeschi, H. Mitochondria: Structure, Biogenesis & Transducing Functions. (Cell Biology Monographs: Vol. 4). (Illus.). 180p. 1976. 48.30 (ISBN 0-387-81317-9). Springer-Verlag.
Tzagoloff, Alexander. Mitochondria. (Cellular Organelles Ser.). 300p. 1982. text ed. price not set (ISBN 0-306-40799-X, Plenum Pr). Plenum Pub.
Van Dam, K. & Van Gelder, B. F., eds. Structure & Function of Energy-Transducing Membranes: Proceedings of a Workshop, Amsterdam, August, 1977. (BBA Library: Vol. 14). 1978. 55.75 (ISBN 0-444-80019-0, North Holland). Elsevier.
Wainio, Walter W. Mammalian Mitochondrial Respiratory Chain. (Molecular Biology Ser). 1971. 62.00 (ISBN 0-12-730650-1). Acad Pr.
Whittaker, P. A. & Danks, Susan M. Mitochondria: Structure, Function & Assembly. new ed. (Integrated Themes in Biology Ser.). (Illus.). 1979. pap. text ed. 11.95x (ISBN 0-582-44382-2). Longman.

MITOSIS

Little, M., et al, eds. Mitosis: Facts & Questions. LC 77-17156. (Proceedings in Life Sciences). 1977. 25.20 (ISBN 0-387-08517-3). Springer-Verlag.
Parker, Gary E., et al. Mitosis & Meiosis. 2nd ed. (EMI Programed Biology Ser.). (Illus.). (gr. 9 up). 1979. pap. 3.95x (ISBN 0-88462-010-7). Ed Methods.
Zimmerman, Arthur, et al, eds. Mitosis & Cytokinesis. (Cell Biology Ser.). Date not set. price not set (ISBN 0-12-781240-7). Acad Pr.

MITRAILLEUSES

see also Gatling Guns

MITRAL VALVE–DISEASES

see Heart–Diseases

MITSUI FAMILY

Russell, Oland D. House of Mitsui. Repr. of 1939 ed. lib. bdg. 17.25x (ISBN 0-8371-4327-6, RUHM). Greenwood.

MITSVOT

see Commandments (Judaism)

MITTENS

see Gloves

MITTON, DAMIEN, 1618-1690

Grubbs, H. A. Damien Mitton. (Elliott Monographs: Vol. 29). 1932. pap. 5.00 (ISBN 0-527-02632-8). Kraus Repr.

MIVART, ST. GEORGE JACKSON, 1827-1900

Gruber, Jacob W. A Conscience in Conflict: The Life of St. George Jackson Mivart. LC 79-17545. (Illus.). 1980. Repr. of 1960 ed. lib. bdg. 23.75x (ISBN 0-313-22041-7, GRCC). Greenwood.

MIX, TOM, 1880-1940

Nicholas, John H. Tom Mix: Riding up to Glory. LC 80-81554. (Illus.). 108p. 1980. 12.95 (ISBN 0-932154-05-0). Lowell Pr.

MIXE LANGUAGE

Van Hiatsma, Willard & Van Hiatsma, Julia. A Hierarchical Sketch of Mixe As Spoken in San Jose el Paraiso. (Publications in Linguistics & Related Fields Ser: No. 44). 1975. pap. 8.50 (ISBN 0-88312-054-2); microfiche 2.00 (ISBN 0-88312-454-8). Summer Inst Ling.

MIXED BLOODS (AMERICAN INDIANS)

see Indians of North America–Mixed Bloods

MIXED CYCLOIDS (CHEMISTRY)

see Heterocyclic Compounds

MIXED LANGUAGES

see Languages, Mixed

MIXED MARRIAGE

see Marriage, Mixed

MIXED RACE ADOPTION

see Interracial Adoption

MIXERS (MACHINERY)

see Mixing Machinery

MIXING

Chance, Britton, ed. Rapid Mixing & Sampling Techniques in Biochemistry. 1964. 42.00 (ISBN 0-12-167868-7). Acad Pr.
European Conference on Mixing, 3rd. Proceedings, 2 vols. Stephens, H. S. & Stapleton, C. A., eds. (European Conferences on Mixing Ser.). 500p. 1979. Set. PLB 73.00 (ISBN 0-906085-31-4, Dist. by Air Science Co.). BHRA Fluid.
Holland, F. A. & Chapman, F. S. Liquid Mixing & Processing in Stirred Tanks. (Illus.). 1966. 19.50 (ISBN 0-442-35139-9). Van Nos Reinhold.
Jimenez, J., ed. Role of Coherent Structures in Modelling Turbulence & Mixing: Proceedings. (Lecture Notes in Physics Ser.: Vol. 136). 393p. 1981. pap. 27.70 (ISBN 0-387-10289-2). Springer-Verlag.
Mecklenburgh, J. C. & Hartland, S. The Theory of Backmixing: The Design of Continuous Flow Chemical Plant with Backmixing. LC 74-32190. 517p. 1975. 92.25 (ISBN 0-471-59023-1, Pub. by Wiley-Interscience). Wiley.
Nagata, Shinji. Mixing: Principals & Applications. LC 75-2056. 1975. 71.95 (ISBN 0-470-62863-4). Halsted Pr.
Okubo, Akira. Oceanic Mixing. LC 73-133442. 151p. 1970. 22.00 (ISBN 0-686-01932-6). Mgmt Info Serv.
Second European Conference on Mixing. Proceedings. Stephens, H. S. & Clarke, J. A., eds. 1978. pap. 68.00 (ISBN 0-900983-69-8, Dist. by Air Science Co.). BHRA Fluid.
Sweeney, Eugene T. An Introduction & Literature Guide to Mixing. (BHRA Fluid Engineering Ser., Vol. 5). 1978. pap. 21.00 (ISBN 0-900983-77-9, Dist. by Air Science Co.). BHRA Fluid.
Symposium at Pittsburgh, Penn., June, 1974. Turbulence in Mixing Operations: Theory & Application to Mixing & Reaction. Brodkey, Robert S., ed. 1975. 42.00 (ISBN 0-12-134450-9). Acad Pr.
Uhl, Vincent & Gray, Joseph B., eds. Mixing: Theory & Practice, 2 Vols. 1966-67. 55.00 ea. Vol. 1 (ISBN 0-12-706601-2). Vol. 2 (ISBN 0-12-706602-0). Acad Pr.

MIXING MACHINERY

see also Blenders (Cookery)

Advani, L. T. Horsepower Tables for Agitator Impellers. (Illus.). 175p. 1976. 18.95x (ISBN 0-87201-368-5). Gulf Pub.

MIXTEC LITERATURE–HISTORY AND CRITICISM

Leon-Portilla, Miguel. Pre-Columbian Literatures of Mexico. Lobanov, Grace, tr. (Civilization of the American Indian Ser: Vol. 22). (Illus.). 1969. 9.95 (ISBN 0-8061-0818-5). U of Okla Pr.

MIXTURES

see also Azeotropes; Emulsions; Solution (Chemistry)

Budnikov, P. P. & Ginstling, A. M. Principles of Solid State Chemistry. 1970. 83.50x (ISBN 0-677-61250-8). Gordon.
Cornell, John A. Experiments with Mixtures: Designs, Models & the Analysis of Mixtures Data. LC 80-22153. (Probability & Mathematical Statistics Ser.). 305p. 1981. 30.95 (ISBN 0-471-07916-2, Pub. by Wiley-Interscience). Wiley.
Everitt, B. S. & Hand, D. J. Finite Mixture Distributions. (Monographs in Applied Probability & Statistics). 1981. 14.95x (ISBN 0-412-22420-8, Pub. by Chapman & Hall). Methuen Inc.
Hiza, M. J., et al. Equilibrium Properties of Fluid Mixtures: A Bibliography of Data or Fluids of Cryogenic Interest. LC 75-19000. (N S R D S Bibliographic Ser.). 160p. 1975. 45.00 (ISBN 0-306-66001-6). IFI Plenum.
Neilsen, Lawrence E. Predicting the Properties of Mixtures. 1978. 16.75 (ISBN 0-8247-6690-3). Dekker.

MNEMONICS

see also Memory

Bornstein, Arthur. Memory: Arthur Bornstein's Memory Training Course. Orig. Title: Bornstein's Miracle Memory Course. (Illus.). 1979. Repr. of 1969 ed. 20.00 (ISBN 0-686-26172-0). Bornstein Memory Schls.
Buzan, Tony. Use Both Sides of Your Brain. 1976. pap. 6.95 (ISBN 0-525-47436-6). Dutton.
Cermak, Laird S. Improving Your Memory. LC 76-26011. (McGraw-Hill Paperbacks). 1976. pap. 2.95 (ISBN 0-07-010325-9, SP). McGraw.
--Improving Your Memory. 123p. 1976. 3.95 (ISBN 0-393-01124-0). Norton.
Day, Dabney, et al. Learning to Remember: Procedures for Teaching Recall. 1978. pap. text ed. 18.50 (ISBN 0-87879-194-9). Acad Therapy.
Dudley, Geoffrey. Increase Your Learning Power. pap. 2.00 (ISBN 0-87980-085-2). Wilshire.
Hersey, William D. How to Cash in on Your Hidden Memory Power. (Illus.). 1963. 10.95 (ISBN 0-13-403204-7, Reward); pap. 3.95 (ISBN 0-13-403220-9). P-H.
Higbee, Kenneth. Your Memory: How It Works & How to Improve It. 1977. 13.95 (ISBN 0-13-980144-8, Spec); pap. 3.95 (ISBN 0-13-980136-7). P-H.
How to Double Your Memorizing Ability in 20 Minutes. (Orig.). 1977. pap. 0.45 (ISBN 0-932032-00-1). Found Pub.
Howell, John C. Dynamics of Memory Development. 224p. (Orig.). (gr. 11 up). 1981. pap. 8.95 (ISBN 0-89648-094-1). Hamilton Pr.
Kellett, Michael. How to Improve Your Memory & Concentration. new ed. (How to Ser.). (Illus.). 1975. pap. 2.95 (ISBN 0-671-18732-5). S&S.
--How to Improve Your Memory & Concentration. (How to Ser.). 1976. pap. 2.95 (ISBN 0-671-18732-5). Monarch Pr.
--Memory Power. LC 80-52338. (Illus.). 128p. (Orig.). 1980. 12.95 (ISBN 0-8069-0210-8); lib. bdg. 11.69 (ISBN 0-8069-0211-6); pap. 5.95 (ISBN 0-8069-8946-7). Sterling.
Klein, Pnina & Schwartz, Allen. A Manual for the Training of Sequential Memory & Attention. 1977. pap. 4.00 (ISBN 0-87879-168-X). Acad Therapy.
Laird, Donald A. & Laird, Eleanor C. Techniques for Efficient Remembering. 1960. 5.75 (ISBN 0-07-036075-8, GB); pap. 3.95 (ISBN 0-07-036076-6). McGraw.
Logan, Arthur L. Remembering Made Easy. LC 65-27668. 1965. pap. 1.95 (ISBN 0-668-01402-4). Arco.
Lorayne, Harry. Good Memory-Successful Student: A Guide to Remembering What You Learn. LC 73-14940. 192p. (gr. 9-12). 1974. 7.95 (ISBN 0-8407-6322-0). Elsevier-Nelson.
--How to Develop a Super-Power Memory. LC 57-7884. 217p. (gr. 9 up). 1956. 8.95 (ISBN 0-8119-0078-9). Fell.
--How to Develop a Super-Power Memory. 1974. pap. 2.50 (ISBN 0-451-09947-8, E9947, Sig). NAL.
--Remembering People: The Key to Success. LC 75-8897. 1975. 25.00 (ISBN 0-8128-1778-8). Stein & Day.
--Secrets of Mind Power. LC 61-9267. 242p. 1961. 9.95 (ISBN 0-8119-0156-4). Fell.
Lorayne, Harry & Lucas, Jerry. Memory Book. LC 73-90705. 256p. 1974. 25.00x (ISBN 0-8128-1664-1). Stein & Day.
Lucas, Jerry & Lorayne, Harry. The Memory Book. 224p. 1975. pap. 1.95 (ISBN 0-345-27808-9). Ballantine.
Luria, A. R. The Mind of a Mnemonist: A Little Book About a Vast Memory. Solotaroff, Lynn, tr. from Rus. LC 76-11237. 1976. pap. 3.95 o. p. (ISBN 0-8092-8007-8). Contemp Bks.
Mackinnon, Lillias. Music by Heart. LC 80-26551. xi, 141p. 1981. Repr. of 1954 ed. lib. bdg. 17.50x (ISBN 0-313-22810-8, MAMB). Greenwood.
Markoff, David & Dubin, Andrew. How to Remember Anything. LC 75-957. 1976. pap. 5.00 (ISBN 0-668-03929-9). Arco.
Montgomery, Robert L. Memory Made Easy: The Complete Book of Memory Training. (Illus.). 1979. 10.95 (ISBN 0-8144-5523-9). Am Mgmt.
Rudman, Jack. Supervisor's Handbook of Mnemonic Devices. (Teachers License Examination Ser.: S-10). (Cloth bdg. avail. on request). pap. 14.00 (ISBN 0-8373-8110-X). Natl Learning.
Smith, Alastair G. Irving's Anatomy Mnemonics. 4th ed. 1972. Repr. 1.50x (ISBN 0-443-00253-3). Churchill.
Suid, Murray. Demonic Mnemonics. LC 80-82982. 1981. pap. 5.95 (ISBN 0-8224-6464-0). Pitman Learning.
Vaz, Kevin S. Memory Training for Students & Executives. 1979. text ed. 7.95 (ISBN 0-7069-0813-9, Pub. by Vikas India). Advent NY.
Webster, Owen. Read Well & Remember. 1969. pap. 2.45 (ISBN 0-671-20347-9, Fireside). S&S.
Weinland, James D. How to Improve Your Memory. (Orig.). 1957. pap. 3.50 (ISBN 0-06-463273-3, EH 273, EH). Har-Row.
Yates, Frances A. Art of Memory. LC 66-22770. 1966. 20.00x (ISBN 0-226-94999-0). U of Chicago Pr.

MO TI, fl. 400 B.C.

Yi-Pac, Mei. Motse, the Neglected Rival of Confucius. LC 73-892. (China Studies). (Illus.). xi, 222p. 1973. Repr. of 1934 ed. 19.00 (ISBN 0-88355-084-9). Hyperion Conn.

MO-PEDS

see Mopeds

MOBILE, ALABAMA

Craighead, Erwin. Craighead's Mobile. Delaney, Caldwell, ed. (Illus.). 221p. 1968. 10.00 (ISBN 0-940882-10-8). Haunted Bk Shop.
Delaney, Caldwell. Confederate Mobile: A Pictorial History. LC 70-172006. (Illus.). 1971. 25.00 (ISBN 0-940882-12-4). Haunted Bk Shop.
--The Phoenix Volunteer Fire Company of Mobile, 1838-1888. (Illus., Orig.). 1967. pap. 2.00 (ISBN 0-914334-00-X). Museum Mobile.
--Remember Mobile. (Illus.). 242p. 1980. Repr. of 1948 ed. 15.00 (ISBN 0-940882-13-2). Haunted Bk Shop.
--The Story of Mobile. rev. ed. (Illus.). 352p. 1981. Repr. of 1953 ed. 15.00 (ISBN 0-940882-14-0). Haunted Bk Shop.
Hamilton, Peter J. Colonial Mobile. Summersell, Charles G., ed. LC 75-19291. (Southern Historical Series: No. 20). 896p. 1976. Repr. of 1910 ed. 25.00 (ISBN 0-8173-5228-7). U of Ala Pr.
Higginbotham, Jay. Old Mobile: Fort Louis De la Louisiana, 1702-1711. LC 77-89698. (Illus., Orig.). 1977. 25.00 (ISBN 0-914334-03-4); deluxe ed. write for info. (ISBN 0-914334-04-2). Museum Mobile.
--Old Mobile: Fort Louis de la Louisiane, 1702-1711. LC 77-89698. (Illus.). 1977. 25.00x (ISBN 0-914334-03-4); deluxe ed. write for info. (ISBN 0-913208-04-3). Rockwell.
Hill, Jackson. On Mobile Streets: A Rumor of the City. (Illus.). 1978. pap. 5.95 (ISBN 0-930642-04-X). Easter Pub.
Howard, Annie S. Enchantment in Iron: Mobile. (Illus.). 63p. 1950. 7.50 (ISBN 0-940882-06-X). Haunted Bk Shop.
John H. Friend, Inc. Fort Conde Plaza, Mobile, Alabama: Its Development As a Tourist Oriented Historical Attraction. (Consultant Service Grant Report). (Illus.). 16p. 1974. pap. 2.00 (ISBN 0-89133-016-X). Preservation Pr.
Thomason, Michael & McLaurin, Melton. Mobile American River City. 1975. 15.95 (ISBN 0-930642-00-7); pap. 8.95 (ISBN 0-930642-01-5). Easter Pub.
Walter, Eugene. Mobile Mardi Gras Annual Nineteen Forty-Eight, Vol. 1, No. 2. Plummer, Cameron, ed. (Illus.). 32p. (YA) (gr. 7 up). 1948. pap. 2.00 (ISBN 0-940882-05-1). Haunted Bk Shop.

MOBILE BAY, BATTLE OF, 1864

Smith, C. Carter, ed. Two Naval Journals: 1864-Battle of Mobile Bay. 1964. pap. 3.95 (ISBN 0-87651-210-4). Southern U Pr.

MOBILE COMMUNICATION SYSTEMS

see also Automobiles–Radio Equipment; Mobile Radio Stations; Police Communication Systems; Walkie-Talkies

Bowers, Raymond, et al, eds. Communications for a Mobile Society: An Assessment of New Technology. LC 77-28119. 432p. 1978. 30.00 (ISBN 0-8039-0960-8). Sage.
Jakes, William C., et al. Microwave Mobile Communications. LC 74-13401. 640p. 1974. 49.00 (ISBN 0-471-43720-4, Pub. by Wiley-Interscience). Wiley.
Lee, William C. Mobile Communications Engineering. (Illus.). 356p. 1981. 38.00 (ISBN 0-07-037039-7, P&RB). McGraw.

MOBILE HOME LIVING

see also Trailer Camps

Allen, Gayle & Allen, Robert F. The Complete Recreational Vehicle Cookbook: For Campers, Motor Homes, RV's, & Vans. LC 76-54176. (Orig.). 1977. pap. 4.95 (ISBN 0-89087-174-4). Celestial Arts.
Davidson, Harold A. Housing Demand: Mobile, Modular or Conventional? 1973. text ed. 17.50x (ISBN 0-442-21990-3). Van Nos Reinhold.
Fenwick, Daman C. Mobile Home Living: The Money-Saving Guide. (Illus.). 224p. 1981. 14.95 (ISBN 0-8306-9670-9, 1322); pap. 8.95 (ISBN 0-8306-1322-6). TAB Bks.
Hodes, Barnet & Roberson, G. Gale. The Law of Mobile Homes. 3rd ed. LC 73-92292. 952p. 1974. 22.00 (ISBN 0-87179-195-1). BNA.
Johnson, Sheila K. Idle Haven: Community Building Among the Working-Class Retired. LC 72-145786. (California Studies in Urbanization & Environmental Studies). 1971. 20.00x (ISBN 0-520-01909-1). U of Cal Pr.
Kneass, Jack & Myers, Marv. Ask Aunt Gabby. LC 70-154316. (Illus., Orig.). 1971. pap. 2.95 (ISBN 0-87593-082-4). Trail-R.
Newcomb, Duane. Mobile Home Gardening Manual. (Illus.). 3.95 (ISBN 0-87593-030-1). Trail-R.
Rabb, Bernard & Rabb, Judith. Good Shelter: A Guide to Mobiles, Modular, & Prefabricated Homes. LC 75-8296. (Illus.). 192p. 1976. 12.50 (ISBN 0-8129-0570-9); pap. 7.95 (ISBN 0-8129-6265-6). Times Bks.
Wilmath, Cliff. Mobile Home Living in Florida. Scott, Carroll L., ed. (Illus.). Date not set. pap. price not set (ISBN 0-915764-03-2). SunRise Hse.

MOBILE HOME PARKS

Mobile Home Communities: A Digest of Rules & Regulations. 22p. 1978. pap. 7.00 (ISBN 0-86718-068-4). Natl Assn Home Builders.
Nulsen, David & Nulsen, Robert H. Mobile Home & Recreation Vehicle Park Operation Manual: (Two Looseleaf Volumes) 1978. 129.50 (ISBN 0-87593-126-X). Trail-R.

MOBILE HOMES

see also Mobile Home Living; Mobile Home Parks

Belt, Forest & McPherson, M. Easi-Guide to Mobile Home Maintenance. LC 74-15453. (Illus.). 144p. 1975. pap. 3.50 (ISBN 0-672-21136-X). Sams.
Bernhardt, Arthur D. Building Tomorrow: The Mobile-Manufactured Housing Industry. (Illus.). 1980. text ed. 45.00x (ISBN 0-262-02134-X). MIT Pr.
Evan, John. Mobile Home Buyer's Bible. LC 79-51492. 1979. pap. 14.95 (ISBN 0-9602644-0-X). Concours Pub.
Hudson Home Magazine, ed. Practical Guide to Mobile Homes: An Affordable Home...Still a Reality. 144p. 1981. 12.95 (ISBN 0-442-25638-8). Van Nos Reinhold.
Loos, Alex & Loos, John. Chilton's Mobile Home Maintenance Guide. 1977. 9.95 (ISBN 0-8019-6455-5); pap. 7.95 (ISBN 0-8019-6516-0). Chilton.
Mobile Homes. (Five Hundred Ser). 1974. pap. 3.75 (ISBN 0-685-58221-3, 501B). Natl Fire Prot.
Nulsen, Robert & Nulsen, David. Mobile Home & Recreation Vehicle Encyclopedia. (Illus.). 1978. 17.95 (ISBN 0-685-82639-2). Trail-R.

Nutt-Powell, Thomas. Manufactured Housing: Public Sector Perceptions of Responsibilities for a Housing Opportunity. 200p. 1981. 19.95 (ISBN 0-86569-086-3). Auburn Hse.
Raskhodoff, Nicholas M. The Complete Mobile Home Book: The Guide to Manufactured Homes. LC 80-5798. 240p. 1981. 19.95 (ISBN 0-8128-2781-3). Stein & Day.
--The Complete Mobile Home Book: The Guide to Manufactured Homes. LC 80-5798. (Illus.). 240p. 1981. 19.95 (ISBN 0-8128-2781-3); pap. 10.95 (ISBN 0-8128-6137-X). Stein & Day.
Rockland, Michael A. Homes on Wheels. 192p. 1980. 12.95 (ISBN 0-8135-0892-4). Rutgers U Pr.

MOBILE RADIO STATIONS
see also Citizens Band Radio
CB Carsound, Communication Equipment. rev. ed. (Illus.). pap. 1.95 (ISBN 0-89552-002-8). DMR Pubns.

MOBILES (SCULPTURE)
Creative Educational Society Editors. How to Have Fun Making Mobiles. LC 73-18210. (Creative Craft Bks.). (Illus.). 32p. (gr. 2-5). 1973. PLB 5.95 (ISBN 0-87191-293-7). Creative Ed.
Elementary Science Study. Mobiles. 2nd ed. 1975. tchr's. guide 5.20 (ISBN 0-07-018584-0, W). McGraw.
Holz, Loretta. Mobiles You Can Make. LC 75-8994. (Illus.). 128p. (gr. 3 up). 1975. 7.75 (ISBN 0-688-41695-0); PLB 7.44 (ISBN 0-688-51695-5). Lothrop.
Mobiles. 1975. pap. 1.50 (ISBN 0-8277-4460-9). British Bk Ctr.
Morris, Victoria S. Let's Make a Mobile, Vol. 1. rev. ed. (Mobiles Ser.). 1979. pap. 3.00 (ISBN 0-914318-10-1). V S Morris.
--M & M (More & More) Mobiles, Vol. 3. rev. ed. (Mobiles Ser.). 1979. pap. 3.00 (ISBN 0-914318-11-X). V S Morris.
--More Mobiles: Math Shapes & Forms. (Mobiles Ser.: Vol. 2). (gr. 1-8). 1977. pap. 3.00 (ISBN 0-914318-03-9). V S Morris.
Parish, Peggy. Beginning Mobiles. LC-79-9950. (Ready-to-Read Handbook). (Illus.). (gr. 1-4). 1979. 6.95 (ISBN 0-02-770030-5). Macmillan.
Romberg, Jenean. Let's Discover Mobiles. (Arts & Crafts Discovery Units Ser.). (Illus.). 1974. pap. 5.95x (ISBN 0-87628-524-8). Ctr Appl Res.
Williams, Guy R. Making Mobiles. (Illus.). (gr. 7 up). 1969. 7.95 (ISBN 0-87523-167-5). Emerson.

MOBILITY
see Labor Mobility; Migration, Internal; Occupational Mobility; Social Mobility

MOBILIZATION, INDUSTRIAL
see Industrial Mobilization

MOBS
see also Crowds; Panic; Riot Control; Riots
Raper, Arthur F. The Tragedy of Lynching. LC 77-110755. 1970. pap. 4.00 (ISBN 0-486-22622-0). Dover.
--Tragedy of Lynching. LC 72-90191. (Mass Violence in America Ser). Repr. of 1933 ed. 17.00 (ISBN 0-405-01334-5). Arno.
--Tragedy of Lynching. LC 69-16568. (Illus.). Repr. of 1933 ed. 20.75x (ISBN 0-8371-1145-5). Greenwood.
--Tragedy of Lynching. LC 69-14943. (Criminology, Law Enforcement, & Social Problems Ser.: No. 25). (With a new intro. by the author). 1969. Repr. of 1933 ed. 16.00 (ISBN 0-87585-025-1). Patterson Smith.
Richards, Leonard L. Gentlemen of Property and Standing: Anti-Abolition Mobs in Jacksonian America. 1970. pap. 4.95 (ISBN 0-19-501351-4, 347, GB). Oxford U Pr.
Weinbaum, Paul O. Mobs & Demagogues: The New York Response to Collective Violence in the Early Nineteenth Century. Berkhofer, Robert, ed. LC 78-27662. (Studies in American History & Culture Ser.: No. 3). 1979. 25.95 (ISBN 0-8357-0978-7, Pub. by UMI Res Pr). Univ Microfilms.

MOCCASINS
Grainger, Sylvia. How to Make Your Own Moccasins. LC 77-4262. (gr. 5 up). 1977. 7.95 (ISBN 0-397-31754-9, JBL-J); pap. 3.95 (ISBN 0-397-31755-7). Har-Row.
Hatt, Gudmund. Moccasins & Their Relation to Arctic Footwear. LC 18-6197. 1916. pap. 7.00 (ISBN 0-527-00514-2). Kraus Repr.

MOCHA LANGUAGE
Harrison, Sheldon P. & Albert, Salich. Mokilese-English Dictionary. LC 76-41796. (PALI Language Tests Ser.: Micronesia). (Orig.). 1976. pap. text ed. 6.50x (ISBN 0-8248-0512-7). U Pr of Hawaii.

MODALITY (LOGIC)
Bellugi, U. & Studdert-Kennedy, M., eds. Signed & Spoken Language: Biological Constraints on Linguistic Form. (Dahlem Workshop Reports, Life Science Research Report Ser.: No. 19). (Illus.). 379p. (Orig.). 1980. pap. 35.70 (ISBN 0-89573-034-0). Verlag Chemie.
Boolos, G. The Unprovability of Consistency. LC 77-85710. (Illus.). 1979. 26.95 (ISBN 0-521-21879-9). Cambridge U Pr.
Chellas, Brian F. Modal Logic. LC 76-47197. 1980. 50.50 (ISBN 0-521-22476-4); pap. 15.95x (ISBN 0-521-29515-7). Cambridge U Pr.
Gabbay, Dov M. Investigations in Modal & Tense Logics with Applications to Problems in Philosophy & Linguistics. LC 76-17835. (Synthese Library: No. 92). 1976. lib. bdg. 50.00 (ISBN 90-277-0656-5, Pub. by Reidel Holland). Kluwer Boston.
Gupta, Anil. The Logic of Common Nouns: An Investigation in Quantified Modal Logic. LC 79-19684. 196p. 1980. text ed. 17.50x (ISBN 0-300-02346-4). Yale U Pr.
Hintikka, J. The Intention of Intentionality & Other New Models for Modalities. LC 75-31698. (Synthese Library: No. 90). 275p. 1975. lib. bdg. 44.75 (ISBN 90-277-0633-6); pap. 23.70 (ISBN 90-277-0634-4). Kluwer Boston.
Hintikka, K. J. Models for Modalities: Selected Essays. (Synthese Library: No. 23). 220p. 1969. lib. bdg. 26.00 (ISBN 90-277-0078-8, Pub. by Reidel Holland); pap. 16.00 (ISBN 90-277-0598-4). Kluwer Boston.
Hughes, George E. & Cresswell, Maxwell J. An Introduction to Modal Logic. 388p. 1972. pap. 12.95x (ISBN 0-416-29460-X). Methuen Inc.
Kroy, Moshe. Moral Competence: An Application of Model Logic to Nationalistic Psychology. (Studies in Philosophy Ser: No. 28). 356p. (Orig.). 1975. pap. text ed. 62.50x (ISBN 90-2793-301-4). Mouton.
Lewy, C. Meaning & Modality. LC 76-11084. 1977. 23.50 (ISBN 0-521-21314-2). Cambridge U Pr.
Linsky, L., ed. Reference & Modality. (Oxford Readings in Philosophy Ser). (Orig.). 1971. pap. text ed. 5.95x (ISBN 0-19-875017-X). Oxford U Pr.
Linsky, Leonard. Names & Descriptions. LC 76-8093. 1977. lib. bdg. 13.50x (ISBN 0-226-48441-6). U of Chicago Pr.
Loux, Michael J., intro. by. The Possible & the Actual: Readings in the Metaphysics of Modality. LC 79-7618. 1979. 22.50x (ISBN 0-8014-1238-2); pap. 7.95x (ISBN 0-8014-9178-9). Cornell U Pr.
Pieraut-Le Bonniec, Gilbert. The Development of Modal Reasoning: Genesis of Necessity & Probability Notions. LC 79-24969. (Developmental Psychology Ser.). 1980. 16.50 (ISBN 0-12-554650-5). Acad Pr.
Prior, Arthur. Past, Present & Future. 1967. 36.00x (ISBN 0-19-824311-1). Oxford U Pr.
Prior, Arthur N. Papers on Time & Tense. 1968. 29.95x (ISBN 0-19-824322-7). Oxford U Pr.
--Time & Modality. LC 78-26696. (Illus.). 1979. Repr. of 1957 ed. lib. bdg. 16.75x (ISBN 0-313-20911-1, PRTI). Greenwood.
Prior, Arthur N. & Fine, Kit. Worlds, Times & Selves. LC 76-45042. 1977. 10.00x (ISBN 0-87023-227-4). U of Mass Pr.
Reichenbach, Hans. Laws, Modalities, & Counterfactuals. LC 74-29798. Orig. Title: Nomological Statements & Admissible Operations. 1977. 21.50x (ISBN 0-520-02966-6). U of Cal Pr.
Rescher, N. Temporal Modalities in Arabic Logic. (Foundations of Language Supplementary Ser: No. 2). 50p. 1967. lib. bdg. 13.00 (ISBN 90-277-0083-4, Pub. by Reidel Holland). Kluwer Boston.
Rescher, N. & Urquhart, A. J. Temporal Logic. LC 74-141565. (Library of Exact Philosophy: Vol. 3). (Illus.). 1971. 33.90 (ISBN 0-387-80995-3). Springer-Verlag.
White, Alan R. Modal Thinking. LC 75-16811. 228p. 1975. 22.50x (ISBN 0-8014-0991-8). Cornell U Pr.

MODEL AIRPLANES
see Airplanes–Models

MODEL CAR RACING
Olney, Ross R. Auto Racing--R-C Micro Style. LC 79-23447. (Illus.). (gr. 4 up). 1980. 6.95 (ISBN 0-688-41929-1); PLB 6.67 (ISBN 0-688-51929-6). Lothrop.
Schleicher, Robert. Model Car Racing. LC 78-22138. 1979. 13.95 (ISBN 0-8019-6857-7, 6858); pap. 5.95 (ISBN 0-8019-6858-5). Chilton.
Siposs, George G. Model Car Racing by Radio Control. LC 76-185261. (Illus.). 224p. 1972. pap. 4.95 (ISBN 0-8306-1592-X, 592). TAB Bks.

MODEL CARS
see Automobiles–Models

MODEL CITIES
see City Planning

MODEL-MAKING
see Models and Modelmaking

MODEL NETWORKS
see Electric Network Analyzers

MODEL RAILROADS
see Railroads–Models

MODEL SAMPLING
see Monte Carlo Method

MODEL SCHOOLS
see Laboratory Schools

MODEL SOLDIERS
see Military Miniatures

MODEL SPACE VEHICLES
see Space Vehicles–Models

MODEL THEORY
Auerbach, Stevanne. Model Programs & Their Components. LC 76-10121. 1976. 24.95 (ISBN 0-87705-256-5). Human Sci Pr.
Bridge, Jane. Beginning Model Theory: The Completeness Theorem & Some Consequences. (Oxford Logic Guides Ser.). 1977. 27.50x (ISBN 0-19-853157-5). Oxford U Pr.
Cherlin, G. Model Theoretic Algebra Selected Topics. LC 76-15388. (Lecture Notes in Mathematics: Vol. 521). 1976. pap. 12.10 (ISBN 0-387-07696-4). Springer-Verlag.
Crossley, J. N. & Nerode, A. Combinatorial Factors. LC 73-10783. (Ergebnisse der Mathematik und Ihrer Grenzgebiete: Vol. 81). (Illus.). 160p. 1974. 21.10 (ISBN 0-387-06428-1). Springer-Verlag.
Devlin, K. J. Aspects of Constructibility. (Lecture Notes in Mathematics: Vol. 354). 240p. 1974. pap. 12.50 (ISBN 0-387-06522-9). Springer-Verlag.
Hirschfeld, J. & Wheeler, W. H. Forcing, Arithmetic, Division Rings. (Lecture Notes in Mathematics Ser.: Vol. 454). vii, 266p. 1975. pap. 13.80 (ISBN 0-387-07157-1). Springer-Verlag.
Latin American Symposium on Mathematical Logic, 3rd. Non-Classical Logics, Model Theory & Computability: Proceedings. Arruda, A., et al, eds. (Studies in Logic: Vol. 89). 1977. 34.25 (ISBN 0-7204-0752-4, North-Holland). Elsevier.
Makkai, M. & Reyes, G. First Order Categorical Logic: Model-Theoretical Methods in the Theory of Topoi & Related Categories. LC 77-13221. (Lecture Notes in Mathematics: Vol. 611). 1977. pap. text ed. 18.30 (ISBN 0-387-08439-8). Springer-Verlag.
Mal'cev, A. I. Algebraic Systems. Seckler, B. D. & Doohovskoy, A. P., trs. from Russian. (Die Grundlehren der Mathematischen Wissenschaften: Vol. 192). 320p. 1973. 50.60 (ISBN 0-387-05792-7). Springer-Verlag.
Maurer, C. & Wraith, G. C., eds. Model Theory & Topoi. (Lecture Notes in Mathematics Ser). 354p. 1975. pap. 16.50 (ISBN 0-387-07164-4). Springer-Verlag.
Morley, Michael D., ed. Studies in Model Theory. LC 73-86564. (MAA Studies: No. 8). 1973. 12.50 (ISBN 0-88385-108-3). Math Assn.
Reiss, David. The Family's Construction of Reality. LC 81-2703. (Illus.). 448p. 1981. text ed. 26.00 (ISBN 0-674-29415-7). Harvard U Pr.
Robinson, et al. Selected Papers of Abraham Robinson: Model Theory & Algebra, Vol. 1. Keisler, H. J. & Korner, S., eds. LC 77-92395. 1979. text ed. 50.00 (ISBN 0-300-02071-6). Yale U Pr.
Sacks, G. E. Saturated Model Theory. (Mathematics Lecture Series: No. 52). 1972. pap. text ed. 12.50 (ISBN 0-8053-8381-6, Adv Bk Prog). Benjamin Cummings.
Saracino, D. H. & Weispfenning, V. B., eds. Model Theory & Algebra: A Memorial Tribute to Abraham Robinson. LC 75-40483. (Lecture Notes in Mathematics: Vol. 498). 1975. pap. 20.30 (ISBN 0-387-07538-0). Springer-Verlag.
Schiffman, Susan, et al. Introduction to Multidimensional Scaling: Theory, Methods & Applications. 1981. write for info. (ISBN 0-12-624350-6). Acad Pr.
Striefel, Sebastian. How to Teach Through Modeling & Imitation. 1981. 3.25 (ISBN 0-89079-059-0). H & H Ent.

MODELING
see also Sculpture–Technique
Berensohn, Paulus. Finding One's Way with Clay. 1972. 12.95 (ISBN 0-671-21324-5). S&S.
Bruckmann, G., ed. Input-Output Approaches in Global Modeling: Proceedings of the Fifth IIASA Symposium on Global Modeling, Sept. 26-29,1977. (IIASA Proceedings: Vol. 9). (Illus.). 518p. 1980. 115.00 (ISBN 0-08-025663-5). Pergamon.
Chernoff, Goldie T. Clay Dough, Play Dough. (Illus.). (gr. 5-8). 1974. pap. 1.50 (ISBN 0-590-04548-2, Schol Pap). Schol Bk Serv.
Guide to Clay Modeling. 1976. pap. 1.50 (ISBN 0-8277-5707-7). British Bk Ctr.
Hawkinson, John. A Ball of Clay. LC 72-13350. (Illus.). 48p. (gr. 3-7). 1974. 6.95g (ISBN 0-8075-0557-9). A Whitman.
Helfman, Harry. Making Your Own Sculpture. LC 73-155992. (Illus.). (gr. 3-7). 1971. 6.25 (ISBN 0-688-21878-4); PLB 6.00 (ISBN 0-688-31878-9). Morrow.
Kenny, John B. Ceramic Sculpture. LC 56-5530. (Creative Crafts Ser). (Illus.). 1953. 13.25 (ISBN 0-8019-0162-6); pap. 8.95 (ISBN 0-8019-6052-5). Chilton.
Kowal, Dennis, Jr. & Meilach, Dona Z. Sculpture Casting. LC 72-84319. (Arts & Crafts Ser). (Illus.). 224p. 1972. 9.95 (ISBN 0-517-50059-0). Crown.
Langstaff, Nancy & Sproul, Adelaide. Exploring with Clay. Cohen, Monroe D., ed. LC 79-17398. 1979. pap. 5.50 (ISBN 0-87173-093-6). ACEI.
Lucchesi, Bruno. Modeling the Head in Clay. (Illus.). 1979. 17.95 (ISBN 0-8230-3098-9). Watson-Guptill.
Marlow, Francine. Your Career Opportunities in Modeling. (Illus.). 9.95 (ISBN 0-517-53196-8); pap. 5.95 (ISBN 0-517-53197-6). Crown.
Olson, Lynn. Sculpting with Cement: Direct Modeling in a Permanent Medium. LC 81-708. (Illus.). 109p. (Orig.). 1981. pap. 14.95 (ISBN 0-9605678-0-1). Steelstone.
Scott, John & Fisher, Eric. Approaches to Clay Modelling. LC 75-8414. (The Craft Approaches Ser). (Illus.). 80p. 1975. 7.50 (ISBN 0-8008-0281-0). Taplinger.
Seidelman, James E. & Mintonye, Grace. Creating with Clay. (gr. 1-6). 1967. 5.95g (ISBN 0-02-767160-7, CCPr). Macmillan.
Slade, Richard. Your Book of Modelling. (gr. 4 up). 1968. 5.95 (ISBN 0-571-08387-0). Transatlantic.
Zaidenberg, Arthur. The Lively Way to Modeling Sculpture: A Book for Beginners. LC 74-134676. (Illus.). (gr. 9 up). Date not set. 4.95 (ISBN 0-8149-0446-7). Vanguard.

MODELING, GEOLOGICAL
see Geological Modeling

MODELING IN WAX
see Wax Modeling

MODELS (PATENTS)
see also Machinery–Models

MODELS, ARCHITECTURAL
see Architectural Models

MODELS, ARTISTS
see also Models, Fashion
Bulliet, C. J. The Courtezan Olympia: An Intimate Survey of Artists & Their Mistress Models. 59.95 (ISBN 0-87968-955-2). Gordon Pr.

MODELS, BIOLOGICAL
see Biological Models

MODELS, CHEMICAL
see Chemical Models

MODELS, FASHION
Blanchard, Nina. How to Break into Motion Pictures, Television, Commercials & Modeling. LC 77-14890. 1978. 9.95 (ISBN 0-385-14109-2). Doubleday.
Cameron, Besty & Jewell, Diana. Lisanne: A Young Model. (Illus.). 1979. 10.95 (ISBN 0-517-53866-0). Potter.
Carter, Fred F. Free & Easy: Male & Female Poses. 1978. pap. 11.95 (ISBN 0-87314-075-3). Peter Glenn.
Cragin, Valerie. Photographic Modeling. LC 75-10066. (Photography How-to Ser.). 1977. pap. 4.50 (ISBN 0-8227-0102-2). Petersen Pub.
Glenn, Peter & Seiffert, Dorothy. Everything You Wanted to Know About Modeling: But Didn't Know Whom or Where to Ask. 1976. pap. 2.50 (ISBN 0-87314-060-5); lib. bdg. 4.00 (ISBN 0-87314-061-3). Peter Glenn.
Greene, Hal. Professional Modeling. LC 75-10231. (Illus.). 167p. 1975. perfect bdg. 7.00 (ISBN 0-9601820-1-2). Killy-Moon Pr.
Hix, Charles & Taylor, Michael. Male Model. (Illus.). 192p. 1980. pap. 7.95 (ISBN 0-312-50938-3). St Martin.
--Male Model. LC 79-16546. (Illus.). 1979. 12.95 (ISBN 0-312-50938-3). St Martin.
Krem, Viju. How to Become a Successful Model. 2nd ed. LC 77-13370. (Illus.). 1978. lib. bdg. 6.95 (ISBN 0-668-04517-5, 3625); pap. 2.95 (ISBN 0-668-04508-6). Arco.
Leigh, Dorian & Hobe, Laura. The Girl Who Had Everything. 240p. 1981. pap. 2.50 (ISBN 0-553-14264-X). Bantam.
Lenz, Bernie. The Complete Book of Fashion Modeling. (Illus.). 320p. 1969. 8.95 (ISBN 0-517-50193-7). Crown.
MacGil, Gillis. Your Future As a Model. (Careers in Depth Ser). (gr. 7 up). 1971. PLB 5.97 (ISBN 0-8239-0159-9). Rosen Pr.
Marlowe, Francine. Male Modeling: An Inside Look. (Illus.). 192p. 1980. 12.95 (ISBN 0-517-53194-1); pap. 5.95 (ISBN 0-517-53195-X). Crown.
Models Mart Directory of Model Agencies & Schools. 125p. 1980. 15.00 (ISBN 0-686-62467-X). B Klein Pubns.
Patrick, Jane G. How to Get Your Child into Commercials & Modeling. LC 79-8031. (Illus.). 264p. 1981. 11.95 (ISBN 0-385-15317-1). Doubleday.
Rose, Linda. Hands. 1980. 14.95 (ISBN 0-671-24944-4). S&S.
Seide, Diane. Looking Good: The Everything Guide to Health, Beauty & Modeling. LC 77-13619. (gr. 7 up). 1978. 7.95 (ISBN 0-525-66561-7). Elsevier-Nelson.
Sims, Naomi. How to Be a Top Model. LC 77-27680. (Illus.). 1979. 12.95 (ISBN 0-385-13361-8). Doubleday.
Tiegs, Cheryl. The Way to Natural Beauty. (Illus.). 1980. 14.95 (ISBN 0-671-24894-4). S&S.

Turner, Gerry A. The Teen Model: Fact Book. LC 80-18228. (Illus.). 224p. (gr. 7 up). 1980. PLB 9.79 (ISBN 0-671-33022-5). Messner.
Walker, Greta. Modeling Careers. (YA) 1978. pap. 1.25 (ISBN 0-440-95783-4, LFL). Dell.

MODELS, MECHANICAL
see Machinery–Models

MODELS, MILITARY
see Military Miniatures

MODELS, NUCLEAR
see Nuclear Models

MODELS AND MODELMAKING
see also Architectural Models; Engineering Models; Geological Modeling; Pattern-Making; Simulation Methods
also subdivision Models under names of objects, e.g. Automobiles–Models; and Machinery–Models; Surfaces, Models of

Alt, E. Winifred. Index to Handicrafts, Modelmaking & Workshop Projects, Suppl. 4. LC 36-27324. (The Useful Reference Ser. of Library Bks: Vol. 96). 1969. lib. bdg. 16.00x (ISBN 0-87305-096-7). Faxon.
Ashley, Roy. Matchstick Modelling. (Illus.). 80p. 1980. 10.95 (ISBN 0-7207-1150-9, Pub. by Michael Joseph). Merrimack Bk Ser V.
Birch, T. Carrington. Models & Modelmaking. Date not set. 3.00 (ISBN 0-392-09561-0, SpS). Sportshelf.
Bowen, John, ed. Scale Model Sailing Ships. (Illus.). 1978. 12.95 (ISBN 0-8317-7700-1, Mayflower Bks). Smith Pubs.
--Scale Model Warships. LC 78-25641. (Illus.). 1979. 12.95 (ISBN 0-8317-7702-8, Mayflower Bks). Smith Pubs.
Buragas, Robert. Decade of Designs, Bk. 2. (Carstens Hobby Bks.: C-19). 1970. pap. 4.00 (ISBN 0-911868-09-7). Carstens Pubns.
Chaney, Charles & Skee, Stanley. Plaster Model & Mold Making. 1978. pap. 7.95 (ISBN 0-442-21515-0). Van Nos Reinhold.
--Plaster Mold & Model Making. 144p. 1981. Repr. of 1973 ed. text ed. 13.00 (ISBN 0-89874-282-X). Krieger.
Chesneau, Roger, ed. Scale Models in Plastic. (Illus.). 1979. 14.95 (ISBN 0-684-16250-4, ScribT). Scribner.
Close, Charles M. & Frederick, Dean K. Modeling & Analysis of Dynamic Systems. LC 77-74421. (Illus.). 1978. text ed. 27.95 (ISBN 0-395-25040-4); sol. manual 2.05 (ISBN 0-395-25031-5). HM.
Colbridge, A. M. Scale Models in Balsa. (Illus.). 118p. 1972. pap. 2.95 (ISBN 0-8008-7000-X). Taplinger.
Coleman, H. S. Teach Yourself Modelcraft. Date not set. 7.50x (ISBN 0-392-08233-0, SpS). Sportshelf.
Crilley, Raymond E. & Burkholder, Charles E. Collecting Model Farm Toys of the World. (Illus.). 1979. pap. 17.95 (ISBN 0-89404-011-1). Aztex.
Dean, Bill. Bill Dean's Book of Balsa Models. rev. ed. LC 72-105134. 1970. pap. 3.95 (ISBN 0-668-02210-8). Arco.
Frank, Adolph F. Animated Scale Models Handbook. LC 80-22858. (Illus.). 160p. 1981. lib. bdg. 15.95 (ISBN 0-668-05118-3, 5118). Arco.
Himmelblau, David M. Process Analysis & Simulation: Deterministic Systems. (Illus.). 333p. 1980. pap. text ed. 24.95 (ISBN 0-88408-132-X). Sterling Swift.
Hughes, W. J. Building the Allchin. LC 79-670337. (Illus., Orig.). 1979. pap. 17.50x (ISBN 0-85242-635-6). Intl Pubns Serv.
Jackson, Albert & Day, David. The Modelmaker's Handbook. LC 80-2702. (Illus.). 352p. 1981. 19.95 (ISBN 0-394-50788-6). Knopf.
Kine, Jack. Miniature Scenic Modelling. (Illus., Orig.). 1979. pap. 7.50x (ISBN 0-85242-650-X). Intl Pubns Serv.
Kroack, Lou. Collecting & Building Model Trucks. (Modern Automotive Ser.). 1980. 14.95 (ISBN 0-8306-9720-9); pap. 9.95 (ISBN 0-8306-2057-5, 2057). TAB Bks.
Laming, Roy. Fun with Building Models. (Learning with Fun Ser.). (Illus.). 64p. 1980. text ed. 12.50x (ISBN 0-7182-1322-X, SpS). Sportshelf.
Lamit, Gary. Industrial Model Building. (Illus.). 528p. 1981. text ed. 29.95 (ISBN 0-13-461566-2). P-H.
Lathrop, Mary L. & Lathrop, Norman M., eds. Index to How to Do It Information: 1980 Index. 1980. pap. 15.00x (ISBN 0-910868-80-8). Lathrop.
Lippitt, Gordon L. Visualizing Change: Model Building & the Change Process. LC 73-81361. (Illus.). 370p. 1973. pap. 14.50 (ISBN 0-88390-125-0). Univ Assocs.
Lovell, Eleanor C. & Hall, Ruth M. Index to Handicrafts, Modelmaking & Workshop Projects. (The Useful Reference Ser of Library Bks: Vol. 57). 1936. lib. bdg. 14.00x (ISBN 0-87305-057-6). Faxon.
--Index to Handicrafts, Modelmaking & Workshop Projects, Suppl. 1. (The Useful Reference Ser of Library Bks: Vol. 70). 1943. lib. bdg. 14.00x (ISBN 0-87305-070-3). Faxon.
--Index to Handicrafts, Modelmaking & Workshop Projects, Suppl. 2. (The Useful Reference Ser of Library Bks: Vol. 79). 1950. lib. bdg. 14.00x (ISBN 0-87305-079-7). Faxon.
Maginley, C. J. Historic Models of Early America, & How to Make Them. LC 47-11432. (Illus.). (gr. 4-6). 1947. 5.95 (ISBN 0-15-234689-9, HJ). HarBraceJ.
Marshall, Percival. Model Steamer Building. (Illus.). 1976. pap. 5.00x (ISBN 0-85242-478-7). Intl Pubns Serv.
Marshall, Percival, ed. The Model Engineer & Amateur Electrician: A Journal of Mechanics & Electricity for Amateurs & Students, Vol. 1. (Illus.). 1976. Repr. of 1898 ed. 22.50x (ISBN 0-85242-476-0). Intl Pubns Serv.
Mickle, Marlin & Vogt, William, eds. Modeling & Simulation, 2 pts, Vol. 6. 1975. Pt. 1. text ed. 40.00 (ISBN 0-87664-268-7); Pt. 2. text ed. 40.00 (ISBN 0-87664-269-5); Set. text ed. 75.00 (ISBN 0-686-77252-0). Instru Soc.
Models Mart Directory. 4th ed. 1980. pap. 15.00 (ISBN 0-87314-053-2). Peter Glenn.
Philpott, Bryan. Making & Improving Plastic Models. LC 74-21510. (Illus.). 112p. 1975. 2.95 (ISBN 0-7153-6698-X). David & Charles.
Price, Brick. The Model-Building Handbook: Techniques Professionals Use. LC 80-70387. (Illus.). 224p. 1981. 13.95 (ISBN 0-8019-6862-3); pap. 8.95 (ISBN 0-8019-6863-1). Chilton.
Renner, Al G. How to Build a Better Mousetrap Car -- & Other Experimental Science Fun. LC 76-48912. 1977. 5.95 (ISBN 0-396-07419-7). Dodd.
Rivett, Patrick. Model Building for Decision Analysis. LC 79-40739. 1980. 24.75 (ISBN 0-471-27654-5, Pub. by Wiley-Interscience). Wiley.
Ruddle, John. Collectors' Guide to Britains Model Soldiers. (Illus.). 158p. 1980. 17.50x (ISBN 0-85242-568-6). Intl Pubns Serv.
Sansweet, Stephen. Science Fiction Toys & Models, Vol. I. 1980. pap. 3.95 (ISBN 0-931064-27-9). Starlog.
Schleicher, Robert. Model Car, Truck & Motorcycle Handbook. (Illus.). 1978. 13.95 (ISBN 0-8019-6626-4); pap. 7.95 (ISBN 0-8019-6627-2). Chilton.
--The Modeler's Manual. (Illus.). 192p. 1981. 14.95 (ISBN 0-8019-6996-4); pap. 9.95 (ISBN 0-8019-6997-2). Chilton.
Slade, Richard. Patterns in Space. 62p. 1969. 8.50 (ISBN 0-571-08327-7, Pub. by Faber & Faber). Merrimack Bk Serv.
Smeed, Vic E. Model Making. (Pegasus Books: No. 24). 1970. 10.50x (ISBN 0-234-77187-9). Intl Pubns Serv.
Solarbo Book of Balsa Models. 1977. pap. 10.00x (ISBN 0-85242-462-0). Intl Pubns Serv.
Stensbol, Ottar. Model Flying Handbook. LC 75-14507. (Illus.). 128p. (gr. 6 up). 1976. 9.95 (ISBN 0-8069-0088-1); PLB 9.29 (ISBN 0-8069-0089-X). Sterling.
Veenstra, Andre. Handbook of Ship Modelling. (Illus.). 240p. (Orig.). 1981. pap. 15.00x (ISBN 0-85242-714-X). Intl Pubns Serv.
Vogt, William G. & Mickle, Marlin H., eds. Modeling & Simulation, 4 pts. Incl. Pt. 1. Energy & Power System Modeling - Ecological & Biomedical Modeling; Pt. 2. Socioeconomic Modeling; Pt. 3. Control & Identification; Pt. 4. Methodology & Applications. 1978. Set. pap. text ed. 75.00 (ISBN 0-686-53136-1). Instru Soc.
Ward, Roland. The Price Guide to the Models of W. H. Goss. (Price Guide Ser.). (Illus.). 182p. 1980. 29.50 (ISBN 0-902028-20-0). Antique Collect.
Wellstead, P. E. Introduction to Physical Modelling. LC 79-50528. 1980. 43.50 (ISBN 0-12-744380-0). Acad Pr.
Wilson, Forrest. Build Your Own Moon Settlement. (Illus.). 1973. pap. 2.95 (ISBN 0-394-82606-X). Pantheon.

MODELS AND MODELMAKING–JUVENILE LITERATURE

Boy Scouts Of America. Model Design & Building. LC 19-600. (Illus.). 44p. (gr. 6-12). 1964. pap. 0.70x (ISBN 0-8395-3280-6, 3280). BSA.
Comins, Jeremy. Vans to Build from Cardboard. (Lothrop Craft Ser). (Illus.). (gr. 4 up). 1978. 7.75 (ISBN 0-688-41872-4); PLB 7.44 (ISBN 0-688-51872-9). Lothrop.
Ellis, Chris. How to Make Model Aircraft. LC 73-92268. (gr. 8 up). 5.95 (ISBN 0-668-03448-3). Arco.
Hilton, Suzanne. It's a Model World. (Illus.). 128p. (gr. 5 up). 1972. 5.95 (ISBN 0-664-32515-7). Westminster.
--It's Smart to Use a Dummy. LC 78-155902. (Illus.). (gr. 5 up). 1971. 5.50 (ISBN 0-664-32500-9). Westminster.
Lozier, Herbert. Model Making. LC 67-28893. (Creative Crafts Ser.). (Illus.). 165p. (gr. 7 up). 1967. 6.95 (ISBN 0-8019-6562-4). Chilton.
Maginley, C. J. Historic Models of Early America: & How to Make Them. LC 47-11432. (Illus.). (gr. 4-6). 1966. pap. 0.60 (ISBN 0-15-234691-0, AVB28, VoyB). HarBraceJ.
--Models of America's Past & How to Make Them. LC 69-17116. (Illus.). (gr. 4-7). 1969. 6.25 (ISBN 0-15-255051-8, HJ). HarBraceJ.
Murray, Jerry. Getting into Radio-Controlled Sports. LC 78-31751. (Illus.). (gr. 7-12). 1979. 7.95 (ISBN 0-399-20686-8). Putnam.
Stensbol, Ottar. Model Flying Handbook. LC 75-14507. (Illus.). 1979. pap. 4.95 (ISBN 0-8069-8848-7). Sterling.

MODELS AND MODELMAKING–RADIO CONTROL SYSTEMS

Drake, John A. Radio Control Helicopter Models. LC 78-670035. 1977. pap. 10.00x (ISBN 0-85242-519-8). Intl Pubns Serv.
Laidlaw-Dickson. Radio Controlled Model Car Racing. (Illus.). 136p. (Orig.). 1979. pap. 11.25x (ISBN 0-85242-675-5). Intl Pubns Serv.
Laidlaw-Dickson, D. J. Radio Control Model Cars Manual. (Illus.). 128p. (Orig.). 1979. pap. 10.00x (ISBN 0-906958-00-8). Intl Pubns Serv.
McEntee, Howard C. Radio Control Handbook. 4th, rev. ed. (Illus.). 1979. pap. 11.95 (ISBN 0-8306-9772-1, 1093). TAB Bks.
Marks, Fred & Winter, William. Basics of Radio Control Modeling. rev. ed. Angle, Burr, ed. (Illus.). 84p. (Orig.). 1979. pap. 6.50 (ISBN 0-89024-517-7). Kalmbach.
Marks, Fred M. Getting the Most from Radio Control Systems. Angle, Burr, ed. LC 80-81430. (Illus.). 88p. (Orig.). 1980. pap. 8.95 (ISBN 0-89024-550-9). Kalmbach.
Murray, Jerry. Getting into Radio-Controlled Sports. LC 78-31751. (Illus.). (gr. 7-12). 1979. 7.95 (ISBN 0-399-20686-8). Putnam.
Radio Controlled Model Boats. (Illus.). 124p. (Orig.). 1981. pap. 12.50x (ISBN 0-85242-569-4). Intl Pubns Serv.
Safford, Edward I., Jr. Model Radio Control. 3rd ed. (Illus.). 1979. 12.95 (ISBN 0-8306-9762-4); pap. 6.95 (ISBN 0-8306-1174-6, 1174). TAB Bks.
Safford, Edward L., Jr. Advanced Radio Control, Including Rockets & Robots. 2nd ed. 1980. 12.95 (ISBN 0-8306-9948-1); pap. 7.95 (ISBN 0-8306-1222-X, 1222). TAB Bks.
Schluter, Dieter. Schluter's Radio Controlled Helicopter Manual. (Illus.). 255p. (Orig.). 1981. pap. 15.00x (ISBN 0-85242-742-5). Intl Pubns Serv.
Siposs, George. RC Modeler's Handbook of Gliders & Sailplanes. LC 75-41726. (Illus.). 196p. 1976. 7.95 (ISBN 0-8306-6747-4); pap. 4.95 (ISBN 0-8306-5747-9, 747). TAB Bks.
Siposs, George G. Building & Racing Radio Control Cars & Motorcycles. Angle, Burr, ed. LC 80-84853. (Illus.). 80p. (Orig.). 1981. pap. 7.50 (ISBN 0-89024-556-8). Kalmbach.
--Model Sail & Power Boating: By Remote Control. LC 74-75213. (Illus.). 192p. 1974. 7.95 (ISBN 0-8306-4693-0); pap. 4.95 (ISBN 0-8306-3693-5, 693). TAB Bks.
Thomas, David B. Basics of Radio Control Power Boat Modeling. Burr, Angle, ed. (Illus.). 100p. (Orig.). 1981. pap. price not set (ISBN 0-89024-035-3). Kalmbach.
Vale, A. M. Radio Control Model Aircraft. 192p. 1980. 20.00x (ISBN 0-905418-04-2, Pub. by Gresham England). State Mutual Bk.
Warrin, R. H. Radio Control for Models. 2nd ed. (Illus.). 1977. text ed. 22.50x (ISBN 0-8464-0779-5). Beekman Pubs.
Whitehead, Gordon. Radio Control Scale Aircraft: Models for Everyday Flying. (Illus.). 308p. (Orig.). 1980. pap. 17.50x (ISBN 0-8002-2768-9). Intl Pubns Serv.

MODERATION

Miyamoto, Shoson. The Buddhist Philosophy of the Middle Way. 1982. 9.95 (ISBN 0-914910-07-8); pap. 6.95 (ISBN 0-914910-08-6). Buddhist Bks.

MODERN ARCHITECTURE
see Architecture, Modern

MODERN ART
see Art, Modern–20th Century; Modernism (Art)

MODERN CIVILIZATION
see Civilization, Modern

MODERN DANCE

Banes, Sally. Terpsichore in Sneakers: Post-Modern Dance. 1980. 17.95 (ISBN 0-395-28212-8); pap. 7.95 (ISBN 0-395-28689-1). HM.
Beaumont, Cyril W. & Idzikowski, Stanislas. A Manual of the Theory & Practice of Classical Theatrical Dancing (Methode Cecchetti) LC 70-17363. (Illus.). 232p. 1975. pap. 3.50 (ISBN 0-486-23223-9). Dover.
--A Manual of the Theory & Practice of Classical Theatrical Dancing (Methode Cecchetti) (Illus.). 6.75 (ISBN 0-8446-5157-5). Peter Smith.
Castle, Vernon & Castle, Irene. Modern Dancing. (Dance Ser.). 1980. Repr. of 1914 ed. 19.50 (ISBN 0-306-76050-9). Da Capo.
Cheney, Gay & Strader, Janet. Modern Dance. 2nd ed. 100p. 1975. pap. text ed. 7.50 (ISBN 0-205-04839-0, 624839X). Allyn.
Cohen, Selma J., ed. The Modern Dance: Seven Statements of Belief. LC 66-14663. (Illus.). 1969. pap. 8.95x (ISBN 0-8195-6003-0, Pub. by Wesleyan U Pr). Columbia U Pr.
Cook, Susan. The Alvin Ailey American Dance Theater. LC 78-1987. 1978. 15.95 (ISBN 0-688-03304-0); pap. 8.95 (ISBN 0-688-08304-8). Morrow.
De Sola, Carla. Learning Through Dance. LC 73-90083. 1974. pap. 7.95 (ISBN 0-8091-1807-6). Paulist Pr.
Exiner, Johanna & Lloyd, Phyllis. Teaching Creative Movement. 1974. 7.95 (ISBN 0-8238-0177-2). Plays.
Graham, Martha. The Notebooks of Martha Graham. LC 72-75416. (Illus.). 1973. 27.50 (ISBN 0-15-167265-2). HarBraceJ.
Haselbach, Barbara. Improvisation, Dance, & Movement. Murray, Margaret, tr. from Ger. Orig. Title: Improvisation, Tanz, Bewegung. 1980. Repr. of 1976 ed. pap. 19.95 (ISBN 0-918812-15-1). Magnamusic.
Hodgson, Moira. Quintet: Five American Dance Companies. (Illus.). 1979. pap. 8.95 (ISBN 0-688-08095-2). Morrow.
Horst, Louis & Russell, Carroll. Modern Dance Forms in Relation to the Other Modern Arts. LC 61-11421. (Illus.). pap. 5.50 (ISBN 0-87127-011-0). Dance Horiz.
King, Eleanor. Transformations: A Memoir - the Humphrey-Weidman Era. LC 76-44682. (Illus.). 1979. 22.50 (ISBN 0-87127-100-1). Dance Horiz.
Kriegsman, Sali Ann. Modern Dance in Ascent: The Bennington Years. (Scholarly Reference Publications Ser.). Date not set. lib. bdg. 95.00 (ISBN 0-686-73222-7). G K Hall.
Lloyd, Margaret. Borzoi Book of Modern Dance. LC 78-77181. (Illus.). 1970. pap. 10.50 (ISBN 0-87127-023-4). Dance Horiz.
McDonagh, Don. The Complete Guide to Modern Dance. LC 75-21235. 576p. 1976. 12.95 (ISBN 0-385-05055-0). Doubleday.
Martin, John. Modern Dance. LC 65-24217. pap. 4.95 (ISBN 0-87127-001-3). Dance Horiz.
Morris, Margaret. Creation in Dance & Life. (Illus.). 125p. 1972. 10.00x (ISBN 0-7206-0042-1). Intl Pubns Serv.
Mueller, John. Dance Film Directory: An Annotated & Evaluative Guide to Films on Ballet & Modern Dance. LC 78-70263. (Illus.). 103p. 1979. pap. 9.95 (ISBN 0-916622-08-8). Princeton Bk Co.
Page, Ruth. Page by Page. LC 78-65648. (Illus.). 1979. 14.95 (ISBN 0-87127-102-8). Dance Horiz.
Pease, Esther E. Modern Dance. 2nd ed. (Physical Education Activities Ser.). 96p. 1976. pap. text ed. write for info. (ISBN 0-697-07068-9). Wm C Brown.
Penrod, James & Plastino, Janice. The Dancer Prepares: Modern Dance for Beginners. 2nd, rev. ed. LC 79-91836. (Illus.). 77p. 1980. pap. text ed. 4.95 (ISBN 0-87484-340-5). Mayfield Pub.
Preston, Valerie. Handbook for Modern Educational Dance. rev. ed. (Movement & Creative Drama Ser.). 1980. pap. 10.95 (ISBN 0-8238-0247-7). Plays.
Schurman, Nona & Clark, Sharon L. Modern Dance Fundamentals. (Illus.). 352p. 1972. pap. text ed. 9.95x (ISBN 0-02-408120-5). Macmillan.
Shurr, Gertrude & Yocom, Rachael D. Modern Dance: Techniques & Teaching. LC 79-51363. (Illus.). 191p. 1980. pap. 7.50 (ISBN 0-87127-109-5). Dance Horiz.
UNESCO. Ten Years of Films on Ballet & Classical Dance, 1955-1965,Catalogue. 1968. pap. 4.25 (ISBN 92-3-100656-8, U674, UNESCO). Unipub.
Warren, Larry. Lester Horton: Modern Dance Pioneer. 1977. 13.75 (ISBN 0-8247-6503-6). Dekker.
Winearls, Jane. Modern Dance Study: Training for Modern Dance, 3 bks. 1976. pap. 3.75 ea. Bk. 4 (ISBN 0-19-321813-5). Bk. 5 (ISBN 0-19-321814-3). Bk. 6 (ISBN 0-19-321815-1). Oxford U Pr.

MODERN GEOMETRY
see Geometry, Modern

MODERN HISTORY
see History, Modern

MODERN LANGUAGES
see Languages, Modern

MODERN LITERATURE
see Literature, Modern (Collections)

MODERN MUSIC
see Music–History and Criticism–20th Century

MODERN PHILOSOPHY
see Philosophy, Modern

MODERN POETRY
see Poetry, Modern (Collections)

MODERN SCULPTURE
see also Sculpture, Modern

MODERNISM
see also Fundamentalism

Anderson, Robert R. Spanish American Modernism: A Selected Bibliography. LC 73-82616. 1970. 2.00 (ISBN 0-8165-0193-9). U of Ariz Pr.

Attir, Mustafa O., et al, eds. Directions of Change: Modernization Theory, Research, & Realities. (Special Study Ser.). 300p. (Orig.). 1981. 22.00 (ISBN 0-86531-223-0); pap. text ed. 15.00 (ISBN 0-86531-274-5). Westview.

Chiari, Joseph. Aesthetics of Modernism. 1970. text ed. 9.00x (ISBN 0-85478-172-2). Humanities.

Foundations: A Statement of Christian Belief in Terms of Modern Thought by 70 Oxford Men. facs. ed. (Essay Index Reprint Ser). 1912. 20.50 (ISBN 0-8369-2189-5). Arno.

Mathews, Shailer. Faith of Modernism. LC 71-108117. Repr. of 1924 ed. 17.50 (ISBN 0-404-04266-X). AMS Pr.

MODERNISM–CATHOLIC CHURCH

see also Americanism (Catholic Controversy)

Barmann, Lawrence F. Baron Friedrich Von Hugel & the Modernist Crisis in England. LC 77-153014. 1972. 39.00 (ISBN 0-521-08178-5). Cambridge U Pr.

Daly, Gabriel. Transcendence & Immanence: A Study in Catholic Modernism & Integralism. 266p. 1980. 37.50x (ISBN 0-19-826652-9). Oxford U Pr.

Hutchison, William R. The Modernist Impulse in American Protestantism. (Illus.). 384p. 1976. 16.50x (ISBN 0-674-58058-3). Harvard U Pr.

Lilley, Alfred L. Modernism: A Record & Review. LC 75-102575. 1970. Repr. of 1908 ed. 14.00 (ISBN 0-8046-0735-4). Kennikat.

Loisy, Alfred F. My Duel with the Vatican: The Autobiography of a Catholic Modernist. Boynton, Richard W., tr. 1968. Repr. of 1924 ed. lib. bdg. 14.75x (ISBN 0-8371-0148-4, LODV). Greenwood.

Noel, Gerard. The Anatomy of the Catholic Church: Roman Catholicism in an Age of Revolution. LC 78-22344. 1980. 10.95 (ISBN 0-385-14311-7). Doubleday.

Reardon, Bernard M., ed. Roman Catholic Modernism. 1970. 10.00x (ISBN 0-8047-0750-2). Stanford U Pr.

MODERNISM (ART)

see also Art, Abstract; Art, Modern–20th Century; Cubism; Dadaism; Expressionism (Art); Fauvism; Futurism (Art); Impressionism (Art); Post-Impressionism (Art); Surrealism

Barr, Alfred H., Jr. What Is Modern Painting. 5th rev. ed. (Illus., Orig.). 1966. pap. 2.50 (ISBN 0-87070-631-4, Pub. by Museum Mod Art). NYGS.

Bradbury, Malcolm & McFarlane, James. Modernism. (Pelican Ser.). 1978. pap. 3.95 (ISBN 0-14-021933-1). Penguin.

Duthuit, Georges. Fauvist Painters. (Documents of Modern Art Ser). (Illus.). 1950. pap. 12.50 (ISBN 0-8150-0036-7). Wittenborn.

Josipovici, Gabriel. The Lessons of Modernism: And Other Essays. 208p. 1977. 22.50x (ISBN 0-87471-957-7). Rowman.

Klee, P. On Modern Art. (Illus.). 1974. pap. 7.50 (ISBN 0-571-06682-8). Heinman.

Klee, Paul. Paul Klee on Modern Art. 64p. 1966. pap. 5.95 (ISBN 0-571-06682-8, Pub. by Faber & Faber). Merrimack Bk Serv.

Rowland, Kurt. History of the Modern Movement, Vol. 3. 80p. 1974. pap. 3.95 (ISBN 0-442-27175-1). Van Nos Reinhold.

MODERNISM (LITERATURE)

Coester, Alfred L., ed. Anthology of the Modernista Movement in Spanish America. LC 75-91347. 1970. Repr. of 1924 ed. 9.50 (ISBN 0-87752-023-2). Gordian.

Craig, George D. Modernist Trend in Spanish American Poetry. LC 78-131249. 1971. Repr. of 1934 ed. text ed. 10.00 (ISBN 0-87752-129-8). Gordian.

Faulkner, Peter. Modernism. (The Critical Idiom Ser.). 1977. pap. 5.50x (ISBN 0-416-83710-7). Methuen Inc.

Fein, John M. Modernismo in Chilean Literature: The Second Period. LC 64-25821. 1965. 9.75 (ISBN 0-8223-0055-9). Duke.

Foster, John B., Jr. Heirs to Dionysus: A Nietzschean Current in Literary Modernism. LC 81-47127. 450p. 1981. 27.50x (ISBN 0-691-06480-6). Princeton U Pr.

Goldberg, Isaac. Studies in Spanish-American Literature. 59.95 (ISBN 0-8490-1149-3). Gordon Pr.

Goldberg, Issac. Studies in Spanish American Literature. LC 67-27600. 1968. Repr. of 1920 ed. 13.50 (ISBN 0-8046-0171-2). Kennikat.

Josipovici, Gabriel. World & the Book: A Study of Modern Fiction. LC 79-170983. 1971. 10.00x (ISBN 0-8047-0797-9). Stanford U Pr.

Martins, Wilson. The Modernist Idea: A Critical Survey of Brazilian Writing in the Twentieth Century. Tomlins, Jack E., tr. from Portuguese. LC 78-24232. 1979. Repr. of 1970 ed. lib. bdg. 23.50x (ISBN 0-313-20811-5, MAID). Greenwood.

--The Modernist Idea: A Critical Survey of Brazilian Writing in the Twentieth Century. Tomlins, Jack, tr. LC 79-124529. 1971. pap. 5.95x (ISBN 0-8147-0293-7). NYU Pr.

MODERNISM IN ART

see Modernism (Art)

MODERNIST-FUNDAMENTALIST CONTROVERSY

see also Fundamentalism

Furniss, Norman F. Fundamentalist Controversy, 1919-1931. 1963. Repr. of 1954 ed. 15.00 (ISBN 0-208-00444-0, Archon). Shoe String.

Glick, Thomas, compiled by. Darwinism in Texas. LC 72-185614. (Illus.). 38p. 1972. 7.00 (ISBN 0-87959-032-7). U of Tex Hum Res.

Pius X. On the Doctrine of the Modernists. 1973. pap. 0.50 (ISBN 0-8198-0248-4). Dghtrs St Paul.

MODES, MUSICAL

see Musical Intervals and Scales

MODESTUS, d. 634 or 635

Baumstark, Anton. Die Modestianischen und Die Konstantinischen Bauten Am Heiligen Grabe Zu Jerusalem. Repr. of 1915 ed. pap. 12.50 (ISBN 0-384-03585-X). Johnson Repr.

MODIGLIANI, AMEDEO, 1884-1920

Fified, William. Modigliani. LC 75-41362. (Illus.). 1976. 11.95 (ISBN 0-688-03039-4). Morrow.

Fifield, William. Modigliani: The Biography. LC 75-41362. (Illus.). 1978. pap. 3.95 (ISBN 0-688-08039-1). Morrow.

Mann, Carol. Modigliani. LC 79-28336. (World of Art Ser.). (Illus.). 300p. 1980. 17.95 (ISBN 0-19-520198-1); pap. 9.95 (ISBN 0-19-520199-X). Oxford U Pr.

Manning, Hugo. Modigliani. 1976. 5.00 (ISBN 0-685-79210-2, Pub. by Enitharmon Pr); signed ed. 12.50 (ISBN 0-685-79211-0); pap. 3.00 (ISBN 0-685-79212-9). SBD.

Modigliani. Drawings of Modigliani. Longstreet, Stephen, ed. (Master Draughtsman Ser). treasure trove bdg. 6.47x (ISBN 0-685-07279-7); pap. 2.95 (ISBN 0-685-07280-0). Borden.

Soby, James T. Modigliani: Paintings, Drawings, Sculpture. LC 73-169318. (Museum of Modern Art Publications in Reprint). Repr. of 1951 ed. 14.00 (ISBN 0-405-01576-3). Arno.

MODJESKA, HELENA, 1840-1909

Coleman, Arthur P. & Coleman, Marion M. Wanderers Twain: Exploratory Memoir on Helen Modjeska & Henryk Sienkiewicz. LC 63-20948. (Illus.). 1964. 5.00 (ISBN 0-910366-23-3). Alliance Coll.

Coleman, Marion M. Fair Rosalind: The American Career of Helena Modjeska, 1877-1907. LC 69-10370. (Illus.). 1969. 20.00 (ISBN 0-910366-07-1). Alliance Coll.

MODJOKERTO, INDONESIA

Geertz, Clifford. Peddlers & Princes: Social Development & Economic Change in Two Indonesian Towns. LC 62-18844. (Comparative Studies of New Nations Ser.). (Illus.). 1963. 9.00x (ISBN 0-226-28513-8). U of Chicago Pr.

--Peddlers & Princes: Social Development & Economic Change in Two Indonesian Towns. LC 62-18844. (Comparative Studies of New Nations Ser). (Illus.). 1968. pap. 3.95 (ISBN 0-226-28514-6, P318, Phoen). U of Chicago Pr.

MODOC INDIANS

see Indians of North America–Northwest, Pacific

MODOC WAR, 1873

see Indians of North America–Wars–1815-1895

MODULAR ARITHMETIC

Adams, William J. Finite Mathematics: For Business & Social Science. LC 73-84448. 354p. Date not set. Repr. of 1974 ed. 14.50 (ISBN 0-536-00986-4). Krieger.

Costello, John J., et al. Finite Mathematics with Applications. 524p. 1981. text ed. 17.95 (ISBN 0-15-527400-7). HarBraceJ.

Curtis, Charles W. & Reiner, Irving. Representation Theory of Finite Groups & Associative Algebras. LC 62-16994. (Pure & Applied Mathematics Ser). 1962. 53.00 (ISBN 0-470-18975-4, Pub. by Wiley-Interscience). Wiley.

Gray. Calculus with Finite Mathematics for Social Science. 1972. 17.95 (ISBN 0-201-02573-6); instr's man. 2.00 (ISBN 0-201-02574-4). A-W.

Gregory, Robert T. Error-Free Computation: Why It Is Needed & Methods for Doing It. LC 80-23923. 152p. (Orig.). 1980. 7.50 (ISBN 0-89874-240-4). Krieger.

Hunkins, Dalton & Mugridge, Larry. Applied Finite Mathematics. LC 80-29563. 538p. 1981. write for info. (ISBN 0-87150-306-9). Prindle.

Lial, Margaret L. & Miller, Charles D. Finite Mathematics. 2nd ed. 1981. pap. text ed. 17.95x (ISBN 0-673-15536-6). Scott F.

Negus, Robert W. Fundamentals of Finite Mathematics. 416p. 1981. Repr. of 1974 ed. text ed. write for info. (ISBN 0-89874-270-6). Krieger.

Rector, Robert E. & Zwick, Earl J. Finite Mathematics & Its Applications. LC 78-69547. (Illus.). 1979. text ed. 17.50 (ISBN 0-395-27206-8); inst. manual 0.75 (ISBN 0-395-27207-6). HM.

Residue Reviews, Vol. 78. (Illus.). 143p. 1981. 23.80 (ISBN 0-387-90566-9). Springer-Verlag.

Thomas, James W. & Thomas, Ann M. Finite Mathematics. 2nd ed. 1978. text ed. 18.95 (ISBN 0-205-05996-1); instr's man. avail. (ISBN 0-205-05997-X). Allyn.

Weiss, Malcolm E. Solomon Grundy, Born on Oneday: A Finite Arithmetic Puzzle. LC 76-26560. (Young Math Ser.). (Illus.). (gr. k-3). 1977. PLB 8.79 (ISBN 0-690-01275-6, TYC-J). Har-Row.

Williams, Gareth. Practical Finite Mathematics. 1979. text ed. 18.95 (ISBN 0-205-06525-2, 566525-6). Allyn.

MODULAR ARITHMETIC–PROGRAMMED INSTRUCTION

Newmark, Joseph. Using Finite Mathematics. 608p. 1981. text ed. price not set (ISBN 0-06-385752-9, HarpC). Har-Row.

MODULAR COORDINATION (ARCHITECTURE)

Le Corbusier. The Modulor & Modulor 2. (Illus.). 336p. 1980. 25.00x (ISBN 0-674-58103-2); pap. 12.95 (ISBN 0-674-58102-4). Harvard U Pr.

Severino, Renato. Equipotential Space: Freedom in Architecture. LC 70-124863. (Illus.). 1970. 34.50x (ISBN 0-275-49170-6). Irvington.

MODULAR FIELDS

see also Modular Arithmetic; Quaternions

Chari, M. V. & Silvester, P., eds. Finite Elements in Electrical & Magnetic Field Problems. LC 79-10377. (Wiley Series in Numerical Methods in Engineering). 1980. 42.25 (ISBN 0-471-27578-6, Pub. by Wiley-Interscience). Wiley.

Hirschfield, J. W. Projective Geometries Over Finite Fields. (Oxford Mathematical Monographs). (Illus.). 1980. 59.00x (ISBN 0-19-853526-0). Oxford U Pr.

Matlis, Eben. Cotorsion Modules. LC 52-42839. (Memoirs: No. 49). 1979. pap. 10.80 (ISBN 0-8218-1249-1, MEMO-49). Am Math.

Schmidt, W. M. Equations Over Finite Fields: An Elementary Approach. (Lecture Notes in Mathematics: Vol. 536). 1976. soft cover 13.80 (ISBN 0-387-07855-X). Springer-Verlag.

Seligman, G. B. Modular Lie Algebras. LC 67-28452. (Ergebnisse der Mathematik & Ihrer Grenzgebiete: Vol. 40). 1967. 29.40 (ISBN 0-387-03782-9). Springer-Verlag.

MODULAR FUNCTIONS

see Functions, Modular

MODULATION (ELECTRONICS)

see also Radio Frequency Modulation

Betts, J. Signal Processing, Modulation & Noise. 1971. 21.95 (ISBN 0-444-19671-4). Elsevier.

Cardona, M. Modulation Spectroscopy. (Solid State Physics: Suppl. 11). 1969. 55.00 (ISBN 0-12-607771-1). Acad Pr.

Connor, F. R. Modulation. (Introductory Topics in Electronics & Telecommunication Ser.). (Illus.). 1973. pap. text ed. 11.00x (ISBN 0-7131-3303-1). Intl Ideas.

Gibson, Jerry D. & Melsa, James L. Introduction to Nonparametric Detection with Applications. (Mathematics in Science & Engineering Ser.). 1975. 46.50 (ISBN 0-12-282150-5). Acad Pr.

Schwartz, Melvin. Information, Transmission, Modulation & Noise. 2nd ed. 1970. text ed. 26.95 (ISBN 0-07-055761-6, C); solutions manual 3.50 (ISBN 0-07-020115-3). McGraw.

Steele, R. Delta Modulation Systems. LC 74-11299. 379p. 1975. 47.95 (ISBN 0-470-82104-3). Halsted Pr.

Van Trees, Harry L. Detection, Estimation & Modulation Theory, 2 pts. Incl. Pt. 1. Detection, Estimation & Linear Modulation Theory. 697p. 1968. 42.95 (ISBN 0-471-89955-0); Pt. 3. Radar - Sonar Signal Processing & Gaussian Signals in Noise. 626p. 1971. 55.95 (ISBN 0-471-89958-5). LC 67-23331. (Illus.). Wiley.

MODULATION (MUSIC)

Foote, Arthur W. Modulation & Related Harmonic Questions. LC 78-98. (Illus.). 1978. Repr. of 1919 ed. lib. bdg. 15.00x (ISBN 0-313-20301-6, FOMR). Greenwood.

Otterstrom, Thorvald. A Theory of Modulation. LC 74-34379. (Music Reprint Ser). (Illus.). viii, 162p. (Ger. & Eng.). 1975. Repr. of 1935 ed. lib. bdg. 19.50 (ISBN 0-306-70721-7). Da Capo.

MODULATION THEORY

see also Modulation (Electronics); Speech Processing Systems

Cowley, J. M., et al, eds. Modulated Structures - Nineteen Seventy-Nine. LC 79-53846. (AIP Conference Preceedings: No. 53). (Illus.). 1979. lib. bdg. 22.00 (ISBN 0-88318-152-5). Am Inst Physics.

Johns, P. B. & Rowbotham, T. R. Communication Systems Analysis. 1972. 13.95x (ISBN 0-442-24141-0). Van Nos Reinhold.

Norden, Hugo. Modulation Re-Defined. 2.50 (ISBN 0-8283-1406-3). Branden.

MODULES (ALGEBRA)

see also Modular Arithmetic; Modular Fields; Finite Groups

Anderson, W. & Fuller, K. R. Ring & Categories of Modules. LC 73-80045. (Graduate Texts in Mathematics Ser.: Vol. 13). 368p. 1973. 26.00 (ISBN 0-387-90069-1); pap. 18.70 (ISBN 0-387-90070-5). Springer-Verlag.

Auslander, M. & Bridger, M. Stable Module Theory. LC 52-42839. (Memoirs: No. 94). 1969. pap. 7.60 (ISBN 0-8218-1294-7, MEMO-94). Am Math.

Barshay, Jacob. Topics in Ring Theory. (Math Lecture Notes Ser.: No. 20). 1969. text ed. 17.50 (ISBN 0-8053-0550-5, Adv Bk Prog). Benjamin-Cummings.

Blyth, T. S. Module Theory: An Approach to Linear Algebra. (Illus.). 1977. 49.00x (ISBN 0-19-853162-1). Oxford U Pr.

Dicks, W. Groups, Trees & Projective Modules. (Lecture Notes in Mathematics: Vol. 790). 127p. 1980. pap. 9.80 (ISBN 0-387-09974-3). Springer-Verlag.

Eichler, Martin. Projective Varieties & Modular Forms. LC 78-166998. (Lecture Notes in Mathematics: Vol. 210). 1971. pap. 8.20 (ISBN 0-387-05519-3). Springer-Verlag.

Faith, C. Algebra: Rings, Modules, & Categories One. LC 72-96724. (Die Grundlehren der Mathematischen Wissenschaften: Vol. 190). (Illus.). xxiii, 565p. 1973. 26.40 (ISBN 0-387-05551-7). Springer-Verlag.

Faith, C. & Wiegand, S., eds. Module Theory: Proceedings, Seattle, August 15-18, 1977. LC 79-4636. (Lecture Notes in Mathematics: Vol. 700). 1979. pap. 13.10 (ISBN 0-387-09107-6). Springer-Verlag.

Golan, Jonathan S. Decomposition & Dimension in Module Catagories, Vol. 33. (Lecture Notes in Pure & Applied Math). 1977. 23.75 (ISBN 0-8247-6643-1). Dekker.

Gordon, M. & Green, E. L. Modules with Cores & Amalgamations of Indecomposable Modules. LC 77-3560. (Memoirs Ser: No. 187). 1977. pap. 11.60 (ISBN 0-8218-2187-3, MEMO-187). Am Math.

Hartley, B. & Hawkes, T. Rings, Modules & Linear Algebra. (Mathematics Ser.). 210p. 1970. pap. text ed. 13.95x (ISBN 0-412-09810-5, Pub. by Chapman & Hall England). Methuen Inc.

Hofmann, K. H. Lectures on Rings & Modules: Tulane University Ring & Operator Theory Year, 1970-71, Vol. 1. (Lecture Notes in Mathematics: Vol. 246). 661p. 1972. pap. 15.40 (ISBN 0-387-05760-9). Springer-Verlag.

Kertesz, A., ed. Rings, Modules & Radicals. 520p. 1973. 63.50 (ISBN 0-444-10485-2, North-Holland). Elsevier.

Lambek, Joachim. Lectures in Rings & Modules. 2nd ed. LC 75-41494. viii, 184p. 1976. 9.95 (ISBN 0-8284-1283-9). Chelsea Pub.

Maass, H. Siegel's Modular Forms & Dirichlet Series. LC 73-171870. (Lecture Notes in Mathematics: Vol. 216). 1971. pap. 14.10 (ISBN 0-387-05563-0). Springer-Verlag.

McDonald, Bernard R. Finite Rings with Identity. (Pure & Applied Mathematics Ser.: Vol. 28). 448p. 1974. 39.75 (ISBN 0-8247-6161-8). Dekker.

Matlis, E. One-Dimensional Cohen-Macaulay Rings. (Lecture Notes in Mathematics Ser.: Vol. 327). xii, 157p. 1973. pap. 10.90 (ISBN 0-387-06327-7). Springer-Verlag.

Nastasescu, C. Graded & Filtered Rings & Modules. (Lecture Notes in Mathematics: Vol. 758). 148p. 1980. pap. 12.40 (ISBN 0-387-09708-2). Springer-Verlag.

Northcott, D. G. Finite Free Resolutions. LC 75-31397. (Tracts in Mathematics Ser.: No. 71). 250p. 1976. 49.50 (ISBN 0-521-21155-7). Cambridge U Pr.

Northcott, Douglas G. Lessons on Rings, Modules & Multiplicities. LC 68-21397. 1968. 48.00 (ISBN 0-521-07151-8). Cambridge U Pr.

Osofsky, Barbara L. Homological Dimensions of Modules. LC 72-6826. (CBMS Regional Conference Series in Mathematics: No. 12). 1973. 8.20 (ISBN 0-8218-1662-4, CBMS-12). Am Math.

Robinson, D. J. Finiteness Conditions & Generalized Soluble Groups, Pt. 2. LC 74-189458. (Ergebnisse der Mathematik und Ihrer Grenzgebiete: Vol. 63). (Illus.). 275p. 1972. 29.30 (ISBN 0-387-05572-X). Springer-Verlag.

Sharpe, D. W. & Vamos, P. Injective Modules. (Cambridge Tracts in Mathematics & Mathematical Physics: No. 63). (Illus.). 250p. 1972. 32.95 (ISBN 0-521-08391-5). Cambridge U Pr.

Stenstroem, B. Rings & Modules of Quotients. (Lecture Notes in Mathematics: Vol. 237). 136p. 1971. pap. 6.30 (ISBN 0-387-05690-4). Springer-Verlag.

Williams, Gareth. Practical Finite Mathematics. 1979. text ed. 18.95 (ISBN 0-205-06525-2, 566525-6). Allyn.

MOEHLER, JOHANN ADAM, 1796-1838

Fitzer, Joseph. Moehler & Baur in Controversy Eighteen Thirty-Two to Thirty-Eight: Reformation & Counter-Reformation in the Age of Romantic Idealism. LC 74-77619. (American Academy of Religion. Studies in Religion). 1974. 7.50 (ISBN 0-88420-111-2, 010007). Scholars Pr Ca.

Savon, Herve. Johann Adam Mohler: The Father of Modern Theology. pap. 1.50 (ISBN 0-8091-1961-7). Paulist Pr.

MOENKOPI PUEBLO

Nagata, Shuichi. Modern Transformations of Moenkopi Pueblo. LC 70-76829. (Studies in Anthropology Ser: No. 6). (Illus.). 1970. pap. 10.95 (ISBN 0-252-00031-5). U of Ill Pr.

MOERIKE, EDUARD, 1804-1875

Mare, Margaret. Eduard Morike: The Man & the Poet. LC 72-7860. (Illus.). 275p. 1973. Repr. of 1957 ed. lib. bdg. 14.00x (ISBN 0-8371-6538-5, MEMO). Greenwood.

--Eduard Morike: The Man & the Poet. LC 72-7860. (Illus.). 275p. 1973. Repr. of 1957 ed. lib. bdg. 14.00x (ISBN 0-8371-6538-5, MEMO). Greenwood.

Slessarev, Helga. Eduard Morike. (World Authors Ser.: No. 72). 12.50 (ISBN 0-8057-2634-9). Twayne.

--Eduard Morike. LC 68-57244. (World Authors Ser.). 1970. lib. bdg. 12.95x (ISBN 0-8057-2634-9). Irvington.

MOESSBAUER EFFECT

Abragam, A. L Effet Mossbauer. (Documents on Medern Physics Ser). 1964. 23.25x (ISBN 0-677-00015-4). Gordon.

Applications of the Mossbauer Effect in Chemistry & Solid-State Physics. (Technical Reports Ser.: No. 50). (Illus., Orig.). 1966. pap. 16.75 (ISBN 92-0-035066-6, IDC50, IAEA). Unipub.

Bancroft, G. M. Mossbauer Spectroscopy: An Introduction for Chemists & Geochemists. LC 73-3326. 252p. 1974. text ed. 32.95 (ISBN 0-470-04665-1). Halsted Pr.

Cohen, Richard L. Applications of Mossbauer Spectroscopy, Vol. 2. 1980. 53.00 (ISBN 0-12-178402-9). Acad Pr.

Cohen, S. G. & Pasternak, M., eds. Perspectives in Mossbauer Spectroscopy. LC 72-97398. 254p. 1973. 27.50 (ISBN 0-306-30727-8, Plenum Pr). Plenum Pub.

Conference on the Application of the Mossbauer Effect, Tihany, Hungary, 1969. Proceedings. 1971. 27.50x (ISBN 0-8002-1842-6). Intl Pubns Serv.

Coulter, C. A. & Shatas, R. A., eds. Topics in Fields & Solids. 1968. 45.75 (ISBN 0-677-12740-5). Gordon.

Danon, J. Lectures on the Mossbauer Effect. LC 68-19092. (Documents on Modern Physics Ser). (Orig.). 1968. 34.75x (ISBN 0-677-01530-5). Gordon.

Dubna Conference on the Mossbauer Effect. Proceedings. 271p. 1963. 42.50 (ISBN 0-306-10662-0, Consultants). Plenum Pub.

Gol'danskii, V. I. Mossbauer Effect & Its Applications in Chemistry. LC 64-21682. 119p. 1964. 32.50 (ISBN 0-306-10677-9, Consultants). Plenum Pub.

Goldanskii, V. I. & Herber, R. H., eds. Chemical Applications of Mossbauer Spectroscopy. LC 68-18671. (Illus.). 1968. 78.50 (ISBN 0-12-287350-5). Acad Pr.

Gonser, U., ed. Moessbauer Spectroscopy II: The/Exotic Side of the Methods. (Topics in Currents Physics Ser.: Vol. 25). (Illus.). 210p. 1981. 29.60 (ISBN 0-387-10519-0). Springer-Verlag.

--Mossbauer Spectroscopy. (Topics in Applied Physics Ser.: Vol. 5). (Illus.). 240p. 1975. 38.20 (ISBN 0-387-07120-2). Springer-Verlag.

Greenwood, N. N. & Gibb, T. C. Mossbauer Spectroscopy. 659p. 1971. text ed. 59.95x (ISBN 0-412-10710-4, Pub. by Chapman & Hall England). Methuen Inc.

Gruverman, Irwin J., et al, eds. Mossbauer Effect Methodology, Vol. 9. 344p. 1974. 35.00 (ISBN 0-306-38809-X, Plenum Pr). Plenum Pub.

Herber, Rolf H., ed. Moessbauer Effect & Its Application in Chemistry. LC 67-31407. (Advances in Chemistry Ser: No. 68). 1967. 17.50 (ISBN 0-8412-0069-6). Am Chemical.

May, Leopold, ed. An Introduction to Mossbauer Spectroscopy. LC 76-137011. 203p. 1971. 25.00 (ISBN 0-306-30477-5, Plenum Pr). Plenum Pub.

Mossbauer Spectroscopy & Its Applications. (Illus.). 421p. (Orig.). 1972. pap. 32.50 (ISBN 92-0-131072-2, ISP304, IAEA). Unipub.

Perlow, Gilbert J., ed. Workshop on New Directions in Mossbauer Spectroscopy, Argonne National Lab, June 1977. LC 77-90635. (AIP Conference Proceedings: No. 38). (Illus.). 1977. lib. bdg. 15.00 (ISBN 0-88318-137-1). Am Inst Physics.

Poole, Charles P., et al. Relaxation in Magnetic Resonance: Dielectric & Mossbauer Applications. 1971. 54.00 (ISBN 0-12-561450-0). Acad Pr.

Shenoy, G. K. & Wagner, F. E., eds. Mossbauer Isomer Shifts. 1978. 117.00 (ISBN 0-7204-0314-6, North-Holland). Elsevier.

Stevens, et al, eds. Cumulative Index to the Mossbauer Effect Data Indexes. 1979. 75.00 (ISBN 0-306-65150-5). IFI Plenum.

Stevens, John & Shenoy, Gopal G., eds. Mossbauer Spectroscopy & Its Chemical Applications. (Advances in Chemistry Ser.: No. 194). 1981. price not set (ISBN 0-8412-0593-0). Am Chemical.

Stevens, John G. & Stevens, Virginia E, eds. Mossbauer Effect Data Index, 9 vols. Incl. Vol. 1. Covering the Nineteen Hundred Sixty-Six to Nineteen Hundred Sixty-Eight Literature. 522p. 1975. 95.00 (ISBN 0-306-65162-9); Vol. 2. Covering the Nineteen Sixty-Nine Literature. LC 76-146429. 292p. 1971. 95.00 (ISBN 0-306-65140-8); Vol. 3. Covering the Nineteen Seventy Literature. LC 76-146429. 382p. 1972. 95.00 (ISBN 0-306-65141-6); Vol. 4. Covering the Nineteen Seventy-One Literature. LC 76-146429. 430p. 1972. 95.00 (ISBN 0-306-65142-4); Vol. 5. Covering the Nineteen Seventy-Two Literature. LC 76-146429. 489p. 1973. 95.00 (ISBN 0-306-65143-2); Vol. 6. Covering the Nineteen Seventy-Three Literature. 496p. 1975. 95.00 (ISBN 0-306-65144-0); Vol. 7. Covering the Nineteen Seventy-Four Literature. LC 76-146429. 398p. 1975. 95.00 (ISBN 0-306-65145-9); Vol. 8. Covering the Nineteen Seventy-Five Literature. 445p. 1976. 95.00 (ISBN 0-306-65146-7); Vol. 9. Covering the Nineteen Seventy-Six Literature. 367p. 1978. 95.00 (ISBN 0-306-65149-1). IFI Plenum.

Vertes, A., et al. Mossbauer Spectroscopy. LC 79-199. (Studies in Physical & Theoretical Chemistry: Vol. 5). 416p. 1980. 73.25 (ISBN 0-444-99782-2). Elsevier.

Wertheim, G. K., et al. The Electronic Structure of Point Defects As Determined by Mossbauer Spectroscopy & by Spin Resonance. (Defects in Crystalline Solids: Vol. 4). 1972. 34.25 (ISBN 0-444-10125-X, North-Holland). Elsevier.

MOGHAL EMPIRE

see Mogul Empire

MOGOLLON INDIANS

see Indians of North America–Southwest, New

MOGUL EMPIRE

Babar, Emperor of Hindustan. Babur-Nama in English: Memoirs of Babur, 2 Vols. Beveridge, Annette S., tr. LC 72-161719. (BCL Ser.: No. I). Repr. of 1922 ed. Set. 67.50 (ISBN 0-404-00510-1). Vol. 1 (ISBN 0-404-00511-X). Vol. 2 (ISBN 0-404-00512-8). AMS Pr.

Chopra, P. N. Life & Letters Under the Mughals. LC 76-900552. 1975. 16.00x (ISBN 0-88386-742-7). South Asia Bks.

Das, H. Norris Embassy to Aurangzib, 1699-1702. Sarkar, S. C., ed. 1959. 6.50x (ISBN 0-8426-1228-9). Verry.

Edwardes, Michael. King of the World: The Collapse of the Moghul Empire in the 18th Century. LC 72-131025. 1970. 7.95 (ISBN 0-8008-4465-3). Taplinger.

Edwardes, Stephen M. & Garrett, Herbert L. Mughal Rule in India. LC 75-41084. Repr. of 1930 ed. 27.50 (ISBN 0-404-14537-X). AMS Pr.

Gokhale, B. G. Surat in the Seventeenth Century: A Study in Urban Hstory of Pre-Modern India. (Scandinavian Inst. of Asian Studies: No. 28). 1977. pap. text ed. 12.50x (ISBN 0-7007-0099-4). Humanities.

Habib, Irfan. An Atlas of the Mughal Empire: Political & Economic Maps with Detailed Notes, Bibliography, & Index. (Illus.). 120p. 1981. 69.00x (ISBN 0-19-560379-6). Oxford U Pr.

Haidar, et al. The Tarikh-I-Rashidi: A History of the Moghuls of Central Asia. Elias, N., ed. Ross, E. D., tr. (Illus.). 535p. 1974. Repr. of 1895 ed. 36.00x (ISBN 0-8002-2067-6). Intl Pubns Serv.

Haidar, Mirza M. A History of the Moghuls of Central Asia, Being the Tarikh-I-Rashidi. Elias, N., ed. Ross, E. D., tr. (Records of Asian History). (Illus.). 1972. text ed. 17.00x (ISBN 0-7007-0021-8). Humanities.

Hallissey, Robert C. The Rajput Rebellion Against Aurangzeb: A Study of the Mughal Empire in Seventeenth-Century India. LC 77-268. (Illus.). 1977. 11.50x (ISBN 0-8262-0222-5). U of Mo Pr.

Harrison, John, et al. Akbar & the Mughal Empire. Yapp, Malcolm & Killingray, Margaret, eds. (Greenhaven World History Ser.). (Illus.). 32p. (gr. 10). lib. bdg. 5.95 (ISBN 0-89908-031-6); pap. text ed. 1.95 (ISBN 0-89908-006-5). Greenhaven.

Husain, Yusuf. Two Studies in Early Mughal History. 1976. 7.50x (ISBN 0-8002-0217-1). Intl Pubns Serv.

Husain, Yusuf H. First Nizam. 1964. 9.25x (ISBN 0-210-34081-9). Asia.

Jahangir. Memoirs. Price, D., tr. (Oriental Translation Fund Ser.: No. 2). 1969. Repr. of 1829 ed. 15.50 (ISBN 0-384-26680-0). Johnson Repr.

Lai, Muni. Akbar. 380p. 1980. text ed. 17.95x (ISBN 0-7069-1076-1, Pub. by Vikas India). Advent NY.

Lal, Muni. Humayun. 1978. 14.00x (ISBN 0-7069-0645-4, Pub. by Croom Helm Ltd. England). Biblio Dist.

Lane-Poole, S. Medieval India, Under Mohammedan Rule. LC 70-132442. (World History Ser., No. 48). 1970. Repr. of 1903 ed. lib. bdg. 59.95 (ISBN 0-8383-1196-2). Haskell.

Le Strange, Guy. Mesopotamia & Persia Under the Mongols in the Fourteenth Century A.D. (Studies in Islamic History: No. 18). 104p. Repr. of 1903 ed. lib. bdg. 13.50x (ISBN 0-87991-108-5). Porcupine Pr.

Malik, Zahiruddin. A Mughal Statesman of the Eighteenth Century: Khan-I-Dauran Mir Bashshi of Mumammad Shah 1719-1739. 120p. 1973. 2.75x (ISBN 0-210-40544-9). Asia.

Markham, Clements R., ed. Hawkins' Voyages During the Reigns of Henry Eighth, Queen Elizabeth, & James First. LC 73-126271. (Hakluyt Society First Ser.: No. 57). (Illus.). 1970. 32.00 (ISBN 0-8337-2229-8). B Franklin.

Nijjar, B. S. Panjab Under the Great Mughals. 1968. 8.25x (ISBN 0-8426-0127-9). Verry.

Ojha, P. N. North India Social Life During the Mughal Period. 1975. 16.00x (ISBN 0-88386-708-7). South Asia Bks.

Orme, Robert. Historical Fragments of the Mogul Empire of the Moralttoes, & of the English Concerns in Indostan from the Year 1659. 317p. 1974. text ed. 15.00x (ISBN 0-8426-0736-6). Verry.

--Historical Fragments of the Mogul Empire. 1974. 15.00 (ISBN 0-686-20241-4). Intl Bk Dist.

Pant, Devidatt. The Commercial Policy of the Moguls. (Studies in Islamic History: No. 20). 281p. Repr. of 1930 ed. lib. bdg. 19.50x (ISBN 0-87991-078-X). Porcupine Pr.

Richards, J. F. Mughal Administration in Golconda. (Illus.). 360p. 1975. 49.00x (ISBN 0-19-821561-4). Oxford U Pr.

Sarkar, Jadunath. Fall of the Mughal Empire, 4 Vols. Repr. of 1952 ed. Set. 36.75 (ISBN 0-404-05580-X); 9.25 ea. Vol. 1 (ISBN 0-404-05581-8). Vol. 2 (ISBN 0-404-05582-6). Vol. 3 (ISBN 0-404-05583-4). Vol. 4 (ISBN 0-404-05584-2). AMS Pr.

Sharma, Sri A. A Bibliography of Mughal India: Fifteen Twenty-Six to Seventeen Hundred Seven. LC 77-10597. (Studies in Islamic History Ser.). lib. bdg. 15.00x (ISBN 0-87991-467-X). Porcupine Pr.

Sinha, Surendra N. Subah of Allahabad Under the Great Mughals: 1580-1707. LC 74-903761. 1974. 9.00x (ISBN 0-88386-603-X). South Asia Bks.

Sri Ram Sharma. The Religious Policy of the Mughal Emperors. 3rd ed. 258p. 1973. lib. bdg. 8.95x (ISBN 0-210-33935-7). Asia.

MOHAMMED, THE PROPHET, 570-632

Abbott, Nabia. Aishah: The Beloved of Mohammed. LC 73-6264. (The Middle East Ser.). Repr. of 1942 ed. 15.00 (ISBN 0-405-05318-5). Arno.

Ahmad, G. Sayings of Muhammad. 3.00x (ISBN 0-87902-036-9). Orientalia.

Ahmad, Ghazi. Sayings of Muhammad. pap. 1.25 (ISBN 0-686-18342-8). Kazi Pubns.

Ali, Syed A. The Spirit of Islam: A History of the Evolution & Ideals of Islam with a Life of the Prophet. rev ed. 515p. 1974. Repr. of 1922 ed. text ed. 17.00x (ISBN 0-391-00341-0). Humanities.

Alladin, Bilzik. Story of Mohammad the Prophet. (Illus.). (gr. 3-10). 1979. 6.25 (ISBN 0-89744-139-7). Auromere.

Andrae, Tor. Mohammed: The Man & His Faith. facsimile ed. Menzel, Theophil, tr. LC 79-160954. (Select Bibliographies Reprint Ser). Repr. of 1936 ed. 19.00 (ISBN 0-8369-5821-7). Arno.

--Mohammed: The Man & His Faith. LC 60-5489. 1977. pap. text ed. 4.95x (ISBN 0-06-130062-4, TB 62, Torch). Har-Row.

Balyuzi, H. M. Muhammad & the Course of Islam. (Illus.). 1976. 18.50 (ISBN 0-85398-060-8, 339-001-10, Pub. by G Ronald England). Baha'i.

Bermann, Richard A. The Mahdi of Alah: The Story of the Dervish, Mohammed Ahmed. John, Robin, tr. LC 80-1935. Repr. of 1932 ed. 36.00 (ISBN 0-404-18955-5). AMS Pr.

Bodley, Ronald V. Messenger: The Life of Mohammed. LC 70-92296. Repr. of 1946 ed. lib. bdg. 18.25x (ISBN 0-8371-2423-9, BOTM). Greenwood.

Dermenghem, Emile. Muhammad & the Islamic Tradition. Watt, Jean M., tr. from Fr. LC 81-47412. (Spiritual Masters Ser.). (Illus.). 192p. 1981. 12.95 (ISBN 0-87951-130-3). Overlook Pr.

Durrani, M. H. An Advisory Study of the Infallibility of the Prophets. 1.65 (ISBN 0-686-18628-1). Kazi Pubns.

The Excellent Sayings of the Prophet Muhammad & Hazrat Ali. LC 74-406. 1978. pap. 5.00 (ISBN 0-917220-02-1). Irfan.

Friedlander, Ira, ed. Submission Sayings of the Prophet Muhammad. 1977. pap. 5.95 (ISBN 0-06-090592-1, CN592, CN). Har-Row.

Glubb, John. Life & Times of Muhammad. LC 74-87954. 1970. pap. 6.95 (ISBN 0-8128-1393-6). Stein & Day.

Hamidullah, M. The First Written Constitution in the World. pap. 1.50 (ISBN 0-686-18543-9). Kazi Pubns.

Hashim, A. S. Life of Prophet Muhammad-I. (Islamic Books for Children: Bk. 4). pap. 3.00 (ISBN 0-686-18410-6); pap. 30.00 entire ser. (ISBN 0-686-18411-4). Kazi Pubns.

--Life of Prophet Muhammad-II. (Islamic Books for Children: Bk 5). pap. 3.00 (ISBN 0-686-18408-4); pap. 30.00 entire ser. (ISBN 0-686-18409-2). Kazi Pubns.

Haykal, M. H. The Life of Muhammad. Faruqi, R. I., tr. LC 76-3060. 1976. 14.75 (ISBN 0-89259-002-5). Am Trust Pubns.

Hosain, S. Who Was Muhammad? pap. 3.00 (ISBN 0-686-18418-1). Kazi Pubns.

Hussain, F. Wives of the Prophet. 4.95 (ISBN 0-686-18463-7). Kazi Pubns.

Hussain, S. A. Sayings of Muhammad, the Last Prophet. pap. 1.00 (ISBN 0-686-18340-1). Kazi Pubns.

Ishaq, I. The Life of Muhammad: A Translation of Ishaq's Sirat Rasul Allah. Guillaume, A., intro. by. 864p. 1979. pap. text ed. 12.50x (ISBN 0-19-636034-X). Oxford U Pr.

Ismail, J. W. Muhammad the Last Prophet. 3.95 (ISBN 0-686-18390-8). Kazi Pubns.

Jeffrey, Arthur, ed. Islam: Muhammad & His Religion. LC 58-9958. 1958. pap. 5.75 (ISBN 0-672-60348-9, LLA137). Bobbs.

Kelen, Betty. Muhammad: The Messenger of God. LC 75-5792. 224p. 1975. 7.95 (ISBN 0-525-66440-8). Elsevier-Nelson.

Khan, Muhammad Z. Muhammad: Seal of the Prophets. 400p. 1980. pap. 12.50 (ISBN 0-7100-0610-1). Routledge & Kegan.

Khan, S. A. Essays on the Life of Muhammad. 1968. 12.00x (ISBN 0-87902-172-1). Orientalia.

Malik, Fida H. Wives of the Prophet. 185p. (Orig.). 1981. pap. 6.50 (ISBN 0-686-31657-6) (ISBN 0-88004-005-X). Sunwise Turn.

Margoliouth, David S. Mohammed & the Rise of Islam. LC 73-38361. (Select Bibliographies Reprint Ser.). Repr. of 1905 ed. 34.00 (ISBN 0-8369-6778-X). Arno.

--Mohammed & the Rise of Islam. LC 73-14455. Repr. of 1905 ed. 30.00 (ISBN 0-404-58273-7). AMS Pr.

Margoliuth, David S. Mohammed. LC 79-2875. 151p. 1981. Repr. of 1939 ed. 14.50 (ISBN 0-8305-0044-8). Hyperion Conn.

Maududi, A. A. The Prophet of Islam. pap. 1.00 (ISBN 0-686-18420-3). Kazi Pubns.

Muir, William. The Life of Mohammad from Original Sources. new rev. ed. Weir, Thomas H., ed. LC 78-180366. Repr. of 1923 ed. 57.50 (ISBN 0-404-56306-6). AMS Pr.

Narayan, B. K. Mohammed: The Prophet of Islam, a Flame in the Desert. 250p. 1980. text ed. 27.50x (ISBN 0-8426-1662-4). Verry.

Nursi, Bediuzzaman S. The Miracles of Muhammad. LC 79-112496. 1978. pap. 2.75 (ISBN 0-933552-06-8). Risale i Nur Inst.

Pirenne, Henri. Mohammed & Charlemagne. Miall, Bernard, tr. 293p. 1974. pap. text ed. 9.50x (ISBN 0-04-940025-8). Allen Unwin.

Pool, S. L. Orations of Mohammad. pap. 1.50 (ISBN 0-686-18347-9). Kazi Pubns.

Prayers of Mohammad. (With arabic text). pap. 6.50 (ISBN 0-686-18346-0). Kazi Pubns.

Qazi, M. A. Miracles of Prophet Muhammad. pap. 2.95 (ISBN 0-686-18629-X). Kazi Pubns.

Rehman, A. Muhammad the Educator. pap. 13.00 (ISBN 0-686-18433-5). Kazi Pubns.

Rodinson, Maxime. Muhammad. Carter, Anne, tr. LC 69-20189. 1980. 15.95 (ISBN 0-394-50908-0); pap. 5.95 (ISBN 0-394-73822-5). Pantheon.

Sawar, G. Muhammed the Holy Prophet. pap. 7.95 (ISBN 0-686-18432-7). Kazi Pubns.

Siddiqui, A. H. Life of Muhammad. 5.50 (ISBN 0-686-18307-X). Kazi Pubns.

Siddiqui, N. Muhammad the Benefactor of Humanity. pap. 4.95 (ISBN 0-686-18434-3). Kazi Pubns.

Townsend, Meredith. Mahommed "the Great Arabian". 86p. 1981. Repr. of 1912 ed. lib. bdg. 20.00 (ISBN 0-89984-454-5). Century Bookbindery.

Watt, W. Montgomery. Muhammad at Medina. 1956. 24.95x (ISBN 0-19-826513-1). Oxford U Pr.

--Muhammad: Prophet & Statesman. 255p. 1974. pap. 5.95 (ISBN 0-19-881078-4, GB409, GB). Oxford U Pr.

Yamauchi, E. Jesus Zoroaster, Buddha, Socrates, Muhammad. pap. 0.50 (ISBN 0-87784-145-4). Inter-Varsity.

MOHAMMED REZA PAHLAVI, SHAH OF IRAN, 1919-1980

Bayne, E. A. Persian Kingship in Transition. LC 68-30502. 1968. 7.50 (ISBN 0-910116-65-2). Am U Field.

Forbis, William H. Fall of the Peacock Throne: The Story of Iran. (McGraw-Hill Paperbacks Ser.). (Illus.). 320p. 1981. pap. 6.95 (ISBN 0-07-021486-7). McGraw.

Hoveyda, Fereydoun. The Fall of the Shah. Liddell, Roger, tr. 1980. 9.95 (ISBN 0-671-61003-1). S&S.

Pahlavi, Mohammad R. Answer to History. LC 80-52039. 256p. 1980. 12.95 (ISBN 0-8128-2755-4). Stein & Day.

Saikal, Amin. The Rise & Fall of the Shah. LC 80-7462. 294p. 1980. 14.50 (ISBN 0-691-03118-5). Princeton U Pr.

Sale, Richard. The Sword & the Power of Gold: The Shah - a Critical Biography. 1980. 10.95 (ISBN 0-448-22982-X). Paddington.

MOHAMMEDAN

see headings beginning with the word Islamic or Muslim

MOHAMMEDAN POTTERY

see Pottery, Islamic

MOHAMMEDANISM

see Islam

MOHAMMEDANS

see Muslims

MOHAVE DESERT, CALIFORNIA

Abbey, Edward. Desert Solitaire. rev. ed. (Literature of the American Wilderness). (Illus.). 296p. 1981. Repr. of 1968 ed. 12.50 (ISBN 0-87905-070-5). Peregrine Smith.

Miller, Ron & Miller, Peggy. Mines of the Mojave. 1975. wrappers 2.50 (ISBN 0-910856-57-5). La Siesta.

MOHAVE INDIANS

see Indians of North America–Southwest, New

MOHAWK LANGUAGE

see also Iroquoian Languages

Bruyas, Jacques. Radical Words of the Mohawk Language, with Their Derivatives. LC 10-30198. (Library of American Linguistics Ser.: Vol. 10). Repr. of 1862 ed. 20.00 (ISBN 0-404-50990-8). AMS Pr.

Hale, Horatio E., ed. Iroquois Book of Rites. LC 74-83458. (Library of Aboriginal American Literature: No. 2). Repr. of 1883 ed. 20.00 (ISBN 0-404-52182-7). AMS Pr.

Postal, Paul M. Some Syntactic Rules in Mohawk. Hankamer, Jorge, ed. LC 78-66582. (Outstanding Dissertations in Linguistics Ser.). 1979. lib. bdg. 44.00 (ISBN 0-8240-9677-0). Garland Pub.

MOHAWK RIVER AND VALLEY

Grassmann, Thomas. Mohawk Indians & Their Valley. LC 74-79962. (Illus.). 1969. 25.00x (ISBN 0-87343-034-4). Magi Bks.

MacWethy, Lou D. Book of Names Especially Relating to the Early Palatines & the First Settlers in the Mohawk Valley. LC 69-17132. (Illus.). 1969. Repr. of 1933 ed. 12.50 (ISBN 0-8063-0231-3). Genealog Pub.

Penrose, Maryly B. Mohawk Valley in the Revolution: Committee of Safety Papers & Genealogical Compendium. LC 78-16942. 1978. 20.00 (ISBN 0-918940-06-0). Libty Bell Assoc.

Reid, W. Max. The Mohawk Valley: Its Legends & Its History. (Illus.). 1979. Repr. of 1901 ed. 22.50 (ISBN 0-916346-32-3). Harbor Hill Bks.

MOHEGAN INDIANS

see Indians of North America–Eastern States

MOHLA, PAKISTAN

Eglar, Zekiye S. A Punjabi Village in Pakistan. LC 60-6751. (Illus.). 240p. 1960. 17.50x (ISBN 0-231-02332-4). Columbia U Pr.

MOHLER, JOHANN ADAM, 1796-1838

see Moehler, Johann Adam, 1796-1838

MOHOLE PROJECT

Heintze, Carl. The Bottom of the Sea & Beyond. LC 74-34393. (Illus.). 128p. 1975. 7.95 (ISBN 0-525-66432-7). Elsevier-Nelson.

MOHOLY-NAGY LASZLO, 1895-1945

Kostelanetz, Richard, ed. Moholy-Nagy. LC 70-12175. (Illus.). 1978. 12.50 (ISBN 0-932360-12-2); pap. 4.95 (ISBN 0-932360-11-4). RK Edns.

Moholy-Nagy, Sibyl. Experiment in Totality. 1969. pap. 4.95 (ISBN 0-262-63042-7). MIT Pr.

MOINIDAE

Goulden, Clyde E. Systematics & Evolution of the Moinidae. LC 68-54558. (Transactions Ser.: Vol. 58, Pt. 6). (Illus.). 1968. pap. 1.50 (ISBN 0-87169-586-3). Am Philos.

MOIRE METHOD

Theocaris, P. S. Moire Fringes in Strain Analysis. 1969. text ed. 32.00 (ISBN 0-08-012974-9); pap. text ed. 15.00 (ISBN 0-08-012973-0). Pergamon.

MOISTURE

see also Condensation (Meteorology); Evaporation; Humidity

Pande. Handbook of Moisture Determination & Control: Principles, Techniques, Applications, Vol. 1. 1974. 49.50 (ISBN 0-8247-6184-7). Dekker.

Pande, A. Handbook of Moisture Determination & Control: Principles, Techniques, Applications, Vol. 3. 320p. 1975. 49.50 (ISBN 0-8247-6186-3). Dekker.

Wexler, Arnold, ed. Humidity & Moisture: Measurement & Control in Science & Industry, Vols. 1, 3 & 4. 1964-65. Vol. 1, 704 Pgs. 34.50 (ISBN 0-685-36922-6, Pub. by UNR); Vol. 3, 1977 576 Pgs. 32.50 (ISBN 0-88275-941-8, Pub. by UNR); Vol. 4, 347 Pgs. 26.00 (ISBN 0-685-36924-2). Krieger.

MOISTURE CONTROL IN BUILDINGS

see Dampness in Buildings

MOISTURE OF SOILS

see Soil Moisture

MOJICA, JOSE, 1895-

De Jesus, Gonzalo. Fray Jose De Guadalupe Mojica: Mid Guia y Mi Estrella. (Illus.). 100p. 1976. 2.00 (ISBN 0-8199-0570-4). Franciscan Herald.

Mojica, Fray Jose G. I, a Sinner. 1962. 5.95 (ISBN 0-685-10968-2, L38305). Franciscan Herald.

MOLD (BOTANY)

see Molds (Botany)

MOLD, VEGETABLE

see Humus; Soils

MOLDING (CLAY, PLASTER, ETC.)

see Modeling; Prosthesis; Sculpture–Technique

MOLDING (FOUNDING)

Dym, Joseph B. Injection Molds & Molding: A Practical Manual. 1979. text ed. 26.50 (ISBN 0-442-22223-8). Van Nos Reinhold.

Jones, David A. Blow Molding. rev. ed. LC 61-18585. 220p. 1971. Repr. of 1961 ed. 8.95 (ISBN 0-88275-027-5). Krieger.

Sarkar, A. D. Mould & Core Material for the Steel Industry. 1967. 22.00 (ISBN 0-08-012486-0); pap. 10.75 (ISBN 0-08-012487-9). Pergamon.

Whelan, A. & Craft, J. L., eds. Developments in Injection Molding, Vol. 1. (Illus.). 1978. text ed. 51.40x (ISBN 0-85334-798-0, Pub. by Applied Science). Burgess-Intl Ideas.

MOLDING (PLASTIC)

see Plastics–Molding

MOLDS (BOTANY)

see also Fungi; Myxomycetes

Christensen, Clyde M. Molds, Mushrooms, & Mycotoxins. LC 74-21808. (Illus.). 292p. 1975. 15.00x (ISBN 0-8166-0743-5). U of Minn Pr.

Froman, Robert. Mushrooms & Molds. LC 71-187936. (A Let's-Read-&-Find-Out Science Book). (Illus.). (gr. k-3). 1972. PLB 8.79 (ISBN 0-690-56603-4, TYC-J). Har-Row.

Ingold. The Biology of Mucor & Its Allies. (Studies in Biology: No. 88). 1978. 5.95 (ISBN 0-7131-2680-9). Univ Park.

Kavaler, Lucy. Mushrooms, Moulds & Miracles: The Strange World of Fungi. 5.95 (ISBN 0-686-05401-6). British Am Bks.

Malloch, David. Moulds: Their Isolation, Cultivation, & Identification. 88p. 1981. 13.95x (ISBN 0-8020-2418-1). U of Toronto Pr.

Moreau, Claude. Moulds, Toxins & Food. LC 78-8715. 1979. 73.50 (ISBN 0-471-99681-5, Pub. by Wiley-Interscience). Wiley.

Mori, Kisaku. Mushrooms As Health Foods. Orig. Title: Mushrooms & Molds-Nutritional & Medicinal Benefits. (Illus.). 112p. (Orig.). 1974. pap. 3.25 (ISBN 0-87040-332-X). Japan Pubns.

Spencer, D. N., ed. The Downy Mildews. 1981. price not set (ISBN 0-12-656860-X). Acad Pr.

Villanveva, J. R., et al, eds. Yeast, Mould & Plant Protoplasts. 1974. 60.00 (ISBN 0-12-722160-3). Acad Pr.

MOLECULAR ACOUSTICS

Nozdrev, V. F. Application of Ultrasonics in Molecular Physics. (Russian Monographs Ser). (Illus.). 1963. 104.00 (ISBN 0-677-20360-8). Gordon.

Pullman, B. Intermolecular Interactions: From Diatomics to Biopolymers. LC 77-24278. (Perspectives in Quantum Chemistry). 1977. 85.25 (ISBN 0-471-99507-X). Wiley.

MOLECULAR ASSOCIATION

Goddard, E. D., ed. Molecular Association in Biological & Related Systems. LC 68-59079. (Advances in Chemistry Ser: No. 84). 1968. 24.50 (ISBN 0-8412-0085-8). Am Chemical.

Molecular Interactions & Activity in Proteins. (CIBA Foundation Symposium Ser.: No. 60). (Illus.). 1978. 31.25 (ISBN 0-444-90040-3, Excerpta Medica). Elsevier.

MOLECULAR ASYMMETRY

see Stereochemistry

MOLECULAR BEAMS

Estermann, Immanuel, ed. Recent Research in Molecular Beams: A Collection of Papers Dedicated to Otto Stern on the Occasion of His 70th Birthday. 1959. 31.00 (ISBN 0-12-243250-9). Acad Pr.

Pamplin, Brian R. Molecular Beam Epitaxy. (Illus.). 178p. 1980. 40.00 (ISBN 0-08-025050-5). Pergamon.

Schlier, C., ed. Molecular Beams & Reaction Kinetics. (Italian Physical Society: Course No. 44). 1970. 56.50 (ISBN 0-12-368844-2). Acad Pr.

Wegener, P., ed. Molecular Beams & Low Density Gasdynamics. (Gasdynamics Ser.: Vol. 4). 1974. 47.75 (ISBN 0-8247-6199-5). Dekker.

MOLECULAR BIOLOGY

see also Genetic Code; Molecular Genetics

Agranoff, B. W., et al. Progress in Molecular & Subcellular Biology, Vol. 1. Hahn, F. E., et al, eds. (Illus.). 1970. 37.20 (ISBN 0-387-04674-7). Springer-Verlag.

Agris, Paul F., ed. Biomolecular Structure & Function. 1978. 42.00 (ISBN 0-12-043950-6). Acad Pr.

Ando, T., et al. Protamines: Isolation, Characterization, Structure & Function. LC 73-77821. (Molecular Biology, Biochemistry & Biophysics Ser: Vol. 12). (Illus.). 114p. 1973. 31.50 (ISBN 0-387-06221-1). Springer-Verlag.

Balaban, M., ed. Molecular Mechanisms of Biological Recognition. 516p. 1979. 68.50 (ISBN 0-444-80130-8). Elsevier.

Baum, H. & Gergely, J., eds. Molecular Aspects of Medicine: Vol. 1, Complete. 600p. 1978. 70.00 (ISBN 0-08-020277-2). Pergamon.

Bearman, David & Edsall, John T. Archival Sources for the History of Biochemistry & Molecular Biology: A Reference Guide & Report. 1980. 40.00 (ISBN 0-8357-0511-0, IS-00111, Pub. by Am Philos); microfiche 40.00 (ISBN 0-8357-0550-1, IS-00112). Univ Microfilms.

Benjamin, Bernard, et al, eds. Population & the New Biology. 1974. 29.50 (ISBN 0-12-088340-6). Acad Pr.

Bentley, R. Molecular Asymmetry in Biology, Vols. 1 & 2. (Molecular Biology Ser). 1969-70. Vol. 1. 47.50 (ISBN 0-12-089201-4); Vol. 2. 65.00 (ISBN 0-12-089202-2). Acad Pr.

Berliner, L. J., ed. Spin Labeling Two: Theory & Applications. LC 75-3587. (Molecular Biology Ser.). 1979. 40.00 (ISBN 0-12-092352-1). Acad Pr.

Berliner, Lawrence J., ed. Spin Labeling: Theory & Applications. (Molecular Biology Ser.: Vol. 1). 1976. 71.00 (ISBN 0-12-092350-5). Acad Pr.

Birnie, G. D. & Rickwood, D. Centrifugal Seperations in Molecular & Cell Biology. (Illus.). 1978. 29.95 (ISBN 0-408-70803-4). Butterworth.

Blecher, Melvin, ed. Methods in Receptor Research, Pt. 1. (Methods in Molecular Biology Ser.: Vol. 9). 1976. 46.50 (ISBN 0-8247-6414-5). Dekker.

Bradshaw, L. Jack. Introduction to Molecular Biological Techniques. 1966. pap. 11.95x ref. ed. (ISBN 0-13-489187-2). P-H.

Bresler, S. E. Introduction to Molecular Biology. 1970. 54.00 (ISBN 0-12-132550-4). Acad Pr.

Butler, J. A. & Noble, D., eds. Progress in Biophysics & Molecular Biology, Vols. 5-11, & 13-30. Incl. Vol. 5. 1955. Vol. 10. 62.50 (ISBN 0-08-009293-4); Vol. 6. 1956; Vol. 7. 1957; Vol. 8. 1958; Vol. 9. 1959; Vol. 10. 1960; Vol. 11. 1961; Vol. 13. 1963. 60.00 (ISBN 0-08-010028-7); Vol. 14. 1964. 60.00 (ISBN 0-08-010612-9); Vol. 15. 1965; Vol. 16. 1966. 10.50 (ISBN 0-08-011581-0); Vol. 17. 1967. 60.00 (ISBN 0-08-012046-6); Vol. 18. 1968. 60.00 (ISBN 0-08-012753-3); Vol. 19, Pt. 1. 1969. 31.00 (ISBN 0-08-013034-8); Vol. 19, Pt. 2. 1969. 31.00 (ISBN 0-08-006522-8); Vol. 19, Complete. 62.50 (ISBN 0-08-006523-6); Vol. 20. 1970. 62.50 (ISBN 0-08-006627-5); Vol. 21. 1970. 60.00 (ISBN 0-08-015696-7); Vol. 22. 1971. 60.00 (ISBN 0-08-016348-3); Vol. 23. 1971. 60.00 (ISBN 0-08-016740-3); Vol. 24. 1972. 60.00 (ISBN 0-08-016868-X); Vol. 25. 1972. 60.00 (ISBN 0-08-016935-X); Vol. 26. 1973. 62.50 (ISBN 0-08-017048-X); Vol. 27. 1973. 60.00 (ISBN 0-08-017142-7); Vol. 28. 1974. 60.00 (ISBN 0-08-018005-1); Vol. 29. 1975-76. Pt. 1. 60.00 (ISBN 0-08-019719-1); Vol. 29, Pt. 2, 1975. pap. 18.50 (ISBN 0-08-019784-1); Vol. 29, Pt. 3, 1975. pap. 18.50 (ISBN 0-08-019890-2); Vol. 29, Complete, 1976. 55.00 (ISBN 0-08-020201-2); Vol. 30. 1976. Pt. 1. 60.00 (ISBN 0-08-019972-0); Pts. 2-3. 55.00 (ISBN 0-08-020207-1); Vol. 30, Complete. pap. 22.00 (ISBN 0-686-66314-4). Pergamon.

Cairns, J., et al, eds. Phage & the Origins of Molecular Biology. LC 66-26455. (Illus.). 352p. 1966. 25.00x (ISBN 0-87969-104-2). Cold Spring Harbor.

Celis, J. E. & Smith, J. D., eds. Nonsense Mutations & Irna Suppressors. 1979. 47.50 (ISBN 0-12-164550-9). Acad Pr.

Chedd, Graham. The New Biology. LC 74-174816. (Science & Discovery Books). (Illus.). (gr. 12). 11.50 (ISBN 0-465-04998-2). Basic.

Cheung, Wai Yiu, ed. Calcium & Cell Function: Vol. 1, Calmodulin. LC 80-985. (Molecular Biology Ser.). 1980. 46.50 (ISBN 0-12-171401-2); subscription price 39.50 (ISBN 0-686-77570-8). Acad Pr.

Ciba Foundation. Submolecular Biology & Cancer. LC 79-10949. (Ciba Foundation Ser.: No. 67). 360p. 1979. 42.50 (ISBN 0-444-90078-0, Excerpta Medica). Elsevier.

Cohn, Waldo E., ed. Progress in Nucleic Acid Research & Molecular Biology, Vol. 23. LC 63-15847. 1980. 40.00 (ISBN 0-12-540023-3); lib ed. 40.00 (ISBN 0-12-540090-X); microfiche ed. 22.00 (ISBN 0-12-540091-8). Acad Pr.

--Progress in Nucleic Acid Research & Molecular Biology, Vol. 24. 1980. 32.50 (ISBN 0-12-540024-1); lib. ed. 42.50 (ISBN 0-12-540092-6); microfiche ed. 22.50 (ISBN 0-12-540093-4). Acad Pr.

--Progress in Nucleic Acid Research & Molecular Biology, Vol. 25. (Serial Publication). 1981. 29.50 (ISBN 0-12-540025-X); lib. ed. 38.50 (ISBN 0-12-540094-2); microfiche ed. 20.00 (ISBN 0-12-540095-0). Acad Pr.

Cold Spring Harbor Symposia on Quantitative Biology. Cold Spring Harbor Symposia on Quantitative Biology, Vol. 44. LC 34-8174. (Illus.). 1322p. 1980. 2 book set 130.00x (ISBN 0-87969-043-7). Cold Spring Harbor.

Crick, Francis. Of Molecules & Men. LC 66-26994. (Jesse & John Danz Lecture Ser.). 118p. 1967. pap. 3.95 (ISBN 0-295-97869-4, WP-26). U of Wash Pr.

Davidson, J. N., et al, eds. Progress in Nucleic Acid Research & Molecular Biology: An International Series. Incl. Vol. 3. 1964. 55.00 (ISBN 0-12-540003-9); Vol. 4. 1965. 55.00 (ISBN 0-12-540004-7); Vol. 5. 1966. 55.00 (ISBN 0-12-540005-5); Vol. 6. 1967. 55.00 (ISBN 0-12-540006-3); Vol. 7. 1967. 55.00 (ISBN 0-12-540007-1); Vol. 8. 1968. 55.00 (ISBN 0-12-540008-X); Vol. 9. 1969. 55.00 (ISBN 0-12-540009-8); Vol. 10. 1970. 47.00 (ISBN 0-12-540010-1); Vol. 11. 1970. 58.50 (ISBN 0-12-540011-X); Vol. 12. 1972. 46.00 (ISBN 0-12-540012-8); Vol. 13. 1973. 51.00 (ISBN 0-12-540013-6); Vol. 20. 1977. 44.50 (ISBN 0-12-540020-9); lib. ed. 63.50 (ISBN 0-12-540084-5); microfiche 31.50 (ISBN 0-12-540085-3); Vol. 21. 1978. 32.00 (ISBN 0-12-540021-7); lib. ed. 40.00 (ISBN 0-12-540086-1); microfiche 24.00 (ISBN 0-12-540087-X); Vol. 22. 1979. 40.00 (ISBN 0-12-540022-5); lib ed. o. s. i. 54.50 (ISBN 0-12-540088-8); microfiche 29.00 (ISBN 0-12-540089-6). Acad Pr.

DeRobertis, Eduardo & DeRobertis, E. M., Jr. Essentials of Cell & Molecular Biology. 1981. text ed. 20.95 (ISBN 0-03-057713-6, HoltC); study guide 7.95 (ISBN 0-03-059736-6); instr's manual 10.95 (ISBN 0-03-059734-X). HR&W.

Devons, Samuel, ed. Biology & the Physical Sciences. LC 78-80272. 379p. 1969. 23.50x (ISBN 0-231-03134-3). Columbia U Pr.

Dodson, Guy, et al, eds. Structural Studies on Molecules of Biological Interest: A Volume in Honour of Professor Dorothy Hodgkin. (Illus.). 400p. 1981. 98.00x (ISBN 0-19-855362-5). Oxford U Pr.

Dubnau, David A. The Molecular Biology of the Bacilli, Vol 1. (Molecular Biology Ser.). 1982. price not set (ISBN 0-12-222701-8). Acad Pr.

Du Praw, Ernest J., ed. Advances in Cell & Molecular Biology. Incl. Vol. 1. 1971. 46.50 (ISBN 0-12-008001-X); Vol. 2. 1972. 61.00 (ISBN 0-12-008002-8); Vol. 3. 1973. 46.50 (ISBN 0-12-008003-6). Acad Pr.

Erlich, Henry, et al. Molecular Biology of Rifomycin. 182p. 1973. text ed. 28.50x (ISBN 0-8422-7089-2). Irvington.

European Molecular Biology International Workshop, Fifth, Marine Biological Laboratory of the University of Malta, Malta, August 2-4, 1976. Structure & Function of Haemocyanin: Proceedings in Life Sciences. Bannister, J. V., ed. (Illus.). 1977. 44.60 (ISBN 0-387-08284-0). Springer-Verlag.

Evans, Anthony. Glossary of Molecular Biology. LC 74-26571. 1975. 15.95 (ISBN 0-470-24740-1). Halsted Pr.

Fasman, Gerald D., ed. Handbook of Biochemistry & Molecular Biology, CRC: Lipids, Carbohydrates, & Steroids Section, Vol. 1. 3rd ed. LC 75-29514. (Handbook Ser.). 570p. 1976. 69.95 (ISBN 0-87819-508-4). CRC Pr.

Fermi, G. & Perutz, M. F. Haemoglobin & Myoglobin. (Atlas of Molecular Structures in Biology Ser.: No. 2). (Illus.). 100p. 1981. text ed. 55.00x (ISBN 0-19-854706-4). Oxford U Pr.

Finean, J. B. & Engstrom, Arne. Biological Ultrastructure. 2nd ed. 1967. 54.00 (ISBN 0-12-256550-9). Acad Pr.

Florkin, Marcel & Schoffeniels, Ernest. A Molecular Approach to Ecology. 1969. 42.50 (ISBN 0-12-261046-6). Acad Pr.

Folco, G. & Paoletti, R., eds. Molecular Biology & Pharmacology of Cyclic Nucleotides: Proceedings of the NATO Advanced Study Institute on Cyclic Nucleotides Held in Tremezzo, Italy, September, 1977, Vol. 1. (Symposia of the Giovanni Lorenzini Foundation). 1978. 49.75 (ISBN 0-444-80041-7, Biomedical Pr). Elsevier.
Freifelder, David. Molecular Biology & Biochemistry: Problems & Applications. LC 78-18712. (Biology Ser.). (Illus.). 1978. pap. text ed. 10.95x (ISBN 0-7167-0068-9). W H Freeman.
Gaede, K. & Gaede, K., eds. Molecular Basis of Biological Activity, Vol. 1. 1972. 38.00 (ISBN 0-12-272850-5). Acad Pr.
Gaito, John. Molecular Psychobiology: A Chemical Approach to Learning & Other Behavior. (American Lecture Ser.). (Illus.). 280p. 1966. ed. spiral bdg. 24.50photocopy (ISBN 0-398-00635-0). C C Thomas.
Goldberger, R. F. Biological Regulation & Development: Molecular Organization & Cell Function, Vol. 2. 1980. 49.50 (ISBN 0-306-40486-9). Plenum Pub.
Govil, G. & Hosur, R. Confirmation of Biological Molecules. (NMR - Basic Principles & Progress Ser.: Vol. 20). (Illus.). 220p. 1981. 70.50 (ISBN 0-387-10769-X). Springer-Verlag.
Gratzer, W. B., ed. Readings in Molecular Biology Selected from Nature. 1971. pap. 4.95x (ISBN 0-262-57025-4). MIT Pr.
Guroff. Molecular Neurobiology. 1980. 53.50 (ISBN 0-8247-6862-0). Dekker.
Gutmann, Viktor. The Donor-Acceptor Approach to Molecular Interactions. LC 77-25012. 295p. 1978. 27.50 (ISBN 0-306-31064-3, Plenum Pr). Plenum Pub.
Hahn, F. E., ed. Progress in Molecular & Subcellular Biology, Vol. 3. LC 75-79748. (Illus.). 400p. 1973. 39.60 (ISBN 0-387-06227-0). Springer-Verlag.
--Progress in Molecular & Subcellular Biology, Vol. 6. (Illus.). 1978. 49.70 (ISBN 0-387-08588-2). Springer-Verlag.
Hahn, F. E., et al. Progress in Molecular & Subcellular Biology, Vol. 5. 1977. 37.80 (ISBN 0-387-08192-5). Springer-Verlag.
Hahn, F. E., et al, eds. Progress in Molecular & Subcellular Biology, Vol. 7. (Illus.). 260p. 1980. 50.80 (ISBN 0-387-10150-0). Springer-Verlag.
Haidemenkakis, A., ed. Molecular Biology. 1970. 54.50x (ISBN 0-677-14070-3). Gordon.
Hall, Marjory. The Other Girl. LC 73-18334. 184p. (gr. 5-8). 1974. 5.25 (ISBN 0-664-32542-4). Westminster.
Hanawalt, Philip C., intro. by. Molecules to Living Cells: Readings from Scientific Americans. LC 80-10814. (Illus.). 1980. text ed. 19.95x (ISBN 0-7167-1208-3); pap. text ed. 9.95x (ISBN 0-7167-1209-1). W H Freeman.
Handbook of Biochemistry & Molecular Biology, CRC: Cumulative Index. 295p. 1977. 50.00 (ISBN 0-8493-0511-X). CRC Pr.
Heinz, Erich. Electrified Potentials in Biological Membrane Transport. (Molecular Biology, Biochemistry, & Biophysics Ser.: Vol. 33). (Illus.). 100p. 1981. 32.90 (ISBN 0-387-10928-5). Springer-Verlag.
Holum, J. R. Elements of General & Biological Chemistry: An Introduction to the Molecular Basis of Life. 5th ed. 593p. 1979. 23.95 (ISBN 0-471-02224-1). Wiley.
Hood, Leroy E., et al. Molecular Biology of Eucaryotic Cells. 1975. 14.95 (ISBN 0-8053-9851-1, 39851). Benjamin-Cummings.
Hopfinger, A. J. Intermolecular Interactions & Biomolecular Organization. LC 76-26540. 1977. 37.50 (ISBN 0-471-40910-3, Pub by Wiley-Interscience). Wiley.
Hsieh, Kuo-Tsing. Modern Cell Biology. (Programed Biology Studies). (Illus.). 120p. (Orig., Prog. Bk.). 1975. pap. 4.95x (ISBN 0-88462-035-2). Ed Methods.
Huang, C. C., et al. Molecular Studies on Halogenated Deoxynucleosides. 256p. 1972. text ed. 34.50x (ISBN 0-8422-7013-2). Irvington.
Jope, Charlene A. Cellular & Molecular Laboratory Manual. 64p. 1981. pap. text ed. 4.95 (ISBN 0-8403-2353-0). Kendall-Hunt.
Judson, Horace. The Eighth Day of Creation. 8.95 (ISBN 0-671-25410-3, 25410, Touchstone). S&S.
Kaplan, J. G. The Molecular Basis of Immune Cell Function. 780p. 1979. 70.75 (ISBN 0-444-80168-5, North Holland). Elsevier.
Keith. The Aqueous Cytoplasm. (Contemporary Biophysics Ser.: Vol. 1). 1979. 29.75 (ISBN 0-8247-6760-8). Dekker.
Knight, C. A. Molecular Virology. (Illus.). 256p. 1974. text ed. 14.95 (ISBN 0-07-035112-0, C); pap. text ed. 9.95 (ISBN 0-07-035113-9). McGraw.
Knowles, Peter F., et al. Magnetic Resonance of Biomolecules: An Introduction to the Theory & Practice of NMR & ESR in Biological Systems. LC 75-4872. 343p. 1976. 41.25 (ISBN 0-471-49575-1, Pub. by Wiley-Interscience); pap. 18.95 (ISBN 0-471-01672-1). Wiley.
Kwapinski, J. B., ed. Molecular Microbiology. LC 80-11813. 494p. 1981. Repr. of 1974 ed. lib. bdg. write for info. (ISBN 0-89874-148-3). Krieger.
Laborit, Henri. Decoding the Human Message. LC 76-53312. 1977. text ed. 17.95x (ISBN 0-312-19022-0). St Martin.
Ledoux, L. Informative Molecules in Biological Systems. 1972. 39.00 (ISBN 0-444-10086-5, North-Holland). Elsevier.
Leshem, Y. The Molecular & Hormonal Basis of Plant Growth Regulation. LC 73-6802. 168p. 1974. 14.50 (ISBN 0-08-017649-6). Pergamon.
Luria, S. E. Life: The Unfinished Experiment. encore ed. LC 72-1179. (Encore Edition). 192p. 1973. pap. 0.95 (ISBN 0-684-16374-8, ScribT). Scribner.
Lwoff, Andre & Ullman, Agnes, eds. Origins of Molecular Biology: A Tribute to Jacques Monod. 1979. 23.50 (ISBN 0-12-460480-3). Acad Pr.
Meister, Alton. Advances in Enzymology & Related Areas of Molecular Biology, Vol. 52. LC 42-9213. 456p. 1981. 32.50 (ISBN 0-471-08120-5, Pub. by Wiley-Interscience). Wiley.
--Advances in Enzymology & Related Areas of Molecular Biology, Vol. 53. 350p. 1981. 35.00 (ISBN 0-471-08405-0, Pub. by Wiley-Interscience). Wiley.
Meister, Alton, ed. Advances in Enztymology & Related Areas of Molecular Biology, Vol. 44. LC 41-9213. 318p. 1976. 35.50 (ISBN 0-471-59179-3). Krieger.
--Advances in Enzymology & Related Areas of Molecular Biology. Vol. 45, 1977. 48.00 (ISBN 0-471-02726-X, Pub. by Wiley-Interscience); Vol. 46, 1978. 51.00 (ISBN 0-471-02993-9); Vol. 47, 1978. 42.50 (ISBN 0-471-04116-5); Vol. 51, 1980, 225p. 29.50 (ISBN 0-471-05653-7). Wiley.
Miami Winter Symposium. The Molecular Basis of Electron Transport. Schultz, Julius & Cameron, Bruce F., eds. 1972. 33.50 (ISBN 0-12-632650-9). Acad Pr.
Monod, Jacques. Selected Papers in Molecular Biology. Lwoff, Andre & Ullmann, Agnes, eds. 1978. 40.00 (ISBN 0-12-460482-X). Acad Pr.
Nayak, Debi, ed. The Molecular Biology of Animal Virus, Vol. 1. 1977. 49.75 (ISBN 0-8247-6533-8). Dekker.
Neuhoff, V. Micromethods in Molecular Biology. (Molecular Biology, Biochemistry & Biophysics Ser.: Vol. 14). (Illus.). xv, 428p. 1973. 59.50 (ISBN 0-387-06319-6). Springer-Verlag.
New York Academy of Sciences, Feb. 4-6, 1980. Second International Conference on Carriers & Channels in Biological Systems: Transport Proteins, Vol. 358. (Annals of the New York Academy of Sciences). 387p. 1980. 75.00x (ISBN 0-89766-105-2); pap. 75.00x (ISBN 0-89766-106-0). Ny Acad Sci.
Niederman, Robert A., ed. Molecular Biology & Protein Synthesis. LC 76-13388. (Benchmark Papers in Microbiology Ser.: Vol. 10). 1976. 46.00 (ISBN 0-12-787130-6). Acad Pr.
Noble, D. Progress in Biophysics & Molecular Biology, Vol. 34. 1979. 62.50 (ISBN 0-08-024858-6). Pergamon.
Noble, D. & Blundell, T. L. Progress in Biophysics & Molecular Biology, Vol. 36, Nos. 1-3 Complete. (Illus.). 130p. 1981. 68.00 (ISBN 0-08-028394-2). Pergamon.
Noble, D. & Blundell, T. L., eds. Progress in Biophysics & Molecular Biology, Vol. 35. (Illus.). 206p. 1981. 62.50 (ISBN 0-08-027122-7). Pergamon.
Norwick, Kenneth H. Molecular Dynamics in Biosystems. 1977. 66.00 (ISBN 0-08-020420-1). Pergamon.
Ovchinnikov, Y. A. & Kolosov, M. N., eds. Frontiers in Bioorganic Chemistry & Molecular Biology. LC 79-1188. 1979. 58.75 (ISBN 0-444-80072-7, North Holland). Elsevier.
Papaconstantinou, John & Rutter, William J., eds. Molecular Control of Proliferation & Differentiation: Thirtyfifth Symposium on the Society for Developmental Biology. 1978. 34.00 (ISBN 0-12-612981-9). Acad Pr.
Pecht, I. & Rigler, R., eds. Chemical Relaxation in Molecular Biology. (Molecular Biology, Biochemistry & Biophysics Ser: Vol. 24). 1977. 46.90 (ISBN 0-387-08173-9). Springer-Verlag.
Price, F. W. Basic Molecular Biology. 497p. 1979. 29.50 (ISBN 0-471-69729-X). Wiley.
Progress in Molecular & Subcellular Biology, Vol. 4. (Illus.). 300p. 1976. 39.40 (ISBN 0-387-07487-2). Springer-Verlag.
Pryor, William A., ed. Free Radicals in Biology, Vol. Four. 1980. 46.00 (ISBN 0-12-566504-0). Acad Pr.
Pullman, Bernard, ed. Catalysis in Chemistry & Biochemistry: Theory & Experiment. (Jerusalem Symposia: No. 12). 1979. lib. bdg. 45.00 (ISBN 90-277-1039-2, Pub. by Reidel Holland). Kluwer Boston.
--Molecular Associations in Biology. LC 68-18679. 1968. 70.00 (ISBN 0-12-566954-2). Acad Pr.
Pullman, Bernard & Weissbluth, Mitchel, eds. Molecular Biophysics. 1965. 56.00 (ISBN 0-12-566956-9). Acad Pr.
Quinn, A. J., ed. The Molecular Biology of Cell Membranes. 1976. 14.95 (ISBN 0-8391-0929-6). Univ Park.
Ramsey-Klee, Diane M., ed. Information & Control Processes in Living Systems: Molecular Coding Problems. 1967. 43.00x (ISBN 0-677-65060-4). Gordon.
Research Symposium on Complexes of Biologically Active Substances with Nucleic Acids & Their Modes of Action. Proceedings. Hahn, F. E., et al, eds. (Progress in Molecular & Subcellular Biology: Vol. 2). (Illus.). 1971. 39.80 (ISBN 0-387-05321-2). Springer-Verlag.
Rich, Alexander & Davidson, Norman, eds. Structural Chemistry & Molecular Biology: A Volume Dedicated to Linus Pauling by His Students, Colleagues, & Friends. LC 67-21127. (Illus.). 1968. 36.95x (ISBN 0-7167-0135-9). W H Freeman.
Richter, Dietmar, ed. Lipmann Symposium: Energy, Regulation & Biosynthesis in Molecular Biology. 698p. 1974. 93.50x (ISBN 3-11-004976-7). De Gruyter.
Righetti, P. J., et al, eds. Isoelectric Focusing: Lab Techniques in Biochemistry & Molecular Biology, Vol. 4, Pt. 2. 1976. pap. 20.00 (ISBN 0-444-11215-4, North-Holland). Elsevier.
Roller-Massar, Ann. Discovering the Basis of Life: An Introduction to Molecular Biology. (Illus.). 320p. 1973. pap. text ed. 8.95 (ISBN 0-07-053564-7, C). McGraw.
Salvatore, F., et al, eds. Macromolecules in the Functioning Cell. LC 78-27547. 351p. 1979. 35.00 (ISBN 0-306-40146-0, Plenum Pr). Plenum Pub.
Schmitt, F. O., et al, eds. Functional Linkage in Biomolecular Systems. LC 74-14479. 366p. 1975. 31.50 (ISBN 0-89004-006-0). Raven.
Schrodinger, Erwin. What Is Life? Bd. with Mind & Matter. pap. 8.95x (ISBN 0-521-09397-X). Cambridge U Pr.
Slavkin, Harold C., ed. The Comparative Molecular Biology of Extracellular Matrices. 1972. 43.00 (ISBN 0-12-648340-X). Acad Pr.
Societe de Chimie Physique, 23rd. Dynamic Aspects of Conformation Changes in Biological Macromolecules: Proceedings. Sadron, C., ed. LC 72-97962. 400p. 1973. lib. bdg. 79.00 (ISBN 90-277-0334-5, Pub. by Reidel Holland). Kluwer Boston.
Steele, E. J. Somatic Selection & Adaptive Evolution: On the Inheritance of Acquired Characters. rev. ed. LC 81-11419. (Illus.). 1981. lib. bdg. price not set (ISBN 0-226-77162-8); pap. price not set (ISBN 0-226-77163-6). U of Chicago Pr.
Steiner, Robert F. The Chemical Foundations of Molecular Biology. 468p. 1965. 16.00 (ISBN 0-442-07940-0, Pub. by Van Nos Reinhold). Krieger.
Strathern, Jeffrey N., et al, eds. The Molecular Biology of the Yeast Saccharomyces, 2 bk. set. LC 81-68203. (Cold Spring Harbor Laboratory Monograph: Vol. 11 a & B). 1200p. 1981. 75.00 (ISBN 0-87969-139-5); price not set. Cold Spring Harbor.
Symposium Held at the Roche Institute of Molecular Biology, Nutley, New Jersey, May, 1975. Teratomas & Differentiation: Proceedings. Sherman, Michael I. & Solter, Davor, eds. 1975. 30.00 (ISBN 0-12-638550-5). Acad Pr.
Symposium, University of Florida, Gainsville, March, 1975. Chromosomal Proteins & Their Role in the Regulation of Gene Expression: Proceedings. Stein, Gary S. & Kleinsmith, Lewis J., eds. 1975. 30.00 (ISBN 0-12-664750-X). Acad Pr.
Tedeschi, Henry. Cell Physiology: Molecular Dynamics. 1974. 23.50 (ISBN 0-12-685150-6). Acad Pr.
Timasheff, S. & Fasman, G., eds. Subunits in Biological Systems, Pt. A. (Biological Macromolecules Ser: Vol. 5). 1971. 59.50 (ISBN 0-8247-1187-4). Dekker.
Tooze, John, ed. The Molecular Biology of Tumour Viruses. LC 74-154474. (Monograph: Vol. 3). (Illus.). 743p. 1973. 35.00 (ISBN 0-87969-108-5). Cold Spring Harbor.
Vogel, Henry J., et al, eds. Organizational Biosynthesis. 1967. 48.00 (ISBN 0-12-722556-0). Acad Pr.
Vol'kenshtein, Mikhail. Molecules & Life: An Introduction to Molecular Biology. 513p. 1974. pap. 7.95 (ISBN 0-306-20007-4, Rosetta). Plenum Pub.
Vol'kenshtein, Mikhail V. Molecules & Life: An Introduction to Molecular Biology. LC 66-22787. 513p. 1970. 37.50 (ISBN 0-306-30264-0, Plenum Pr). Plenum Pub.
Wanka, F., et al. Green Algae, I: Molecular Biology. LC 73-10108. 1973. 26.00x (ISBN 0-8422-7134-1). Irvington.
Wassermann, G. D. Molecular Control of Cell Differentiation & Morphogenesis: A Systematic Theory. (Quantitative Approach to Life Science Ser.: Vol. 2). 1972. 74.75 (ISBN 0-8247-1766-X). Dekker.
Weissbach, Herbert & Pestka, Sidney, eds. Protein Biosynthesis. (Molecular Biology Ser.). 1977. 72.00 (ISBN 0-12-744250-2). Acad Pr.
Work, T. S. & Work, E. Laboratory Techniques in Biochemistry & Molecular Biology, 3 vols. LC 68-54514. (Illus.). 1969. Vol. 2. 51.25 (ISBN 0-444-10055-5, North-Holland); Vol. 3. 75.75 (ISBN 0-444-10386-4). Elsevier.
Work, T. S. & Work, E., eds. Laboratory Techniques in Biochemistry & Molecular Biology, Vol. 5. 1976. 92.75 (ISBN 0-444-11216-2, North-Holland). Elsevier.
--Laboratory Techniques in Biochemistry & Molecular Biology, Vol. 6. Incl. Pt. 1. Density Gradient Centrifugation. Hinton, R. & Dobrota, M.; An Introduction to Radioimmunoassay & Related Techniques. Chard, T. 1978. 78.00 (ISBN 0-7204-4221-4, North-Holland). Elsevier.
Zundell, George. Hydration & Intermolecular Interaction: Infrared Investigations with Polyelectrolyte Membranes. 1970. 55.00 (ISBN 0-12-782850-8). Acad Pr.

MOLECULAR DISTILLATION

see Distillation, Molecular

MOLECULAR DYNAMICS

see also Gases, Kinetic Theory Of; Irreversible Processes; Masers; Molecular Beams; Molecular Rotation; Quantum Theory; Wave Mechanics

Boutin, Henri & Yip, Sidney. Molecular Spectroscopy with Neutrons. LC 68-22823. 1968. 20.00x (ISBN 0-262-02042-4). MIT Pr.
DeTar, Delos F., ed. Molecular Mechanics: A Symposium. LC 77-14614. 1978. pap. text ed. 33.00 (ISBN 0-08-022070-3). Pergamon.
Di Bartolo, Baldassare. Radiationless Processes. (NATO Advanced Study Institutes Series B-Physical Sciences). 545p. 1981. 65.00 (ISBN 0-306-40577-6, Plenum Pr). Plenum Pub.
Evans, M. W., et al. Molecular Dynamics. 928p. 1982. 69.00 (ISBN 0-471-05977-3, Pub. by Wiley-Interscience). Wiley.
Flygare, W. H. Molecular Structure & Dynamics. LC 77-16786. (Illus.). 1978. ref. 29.95 (ISBN 0-13-599753-4). P-H.
Hopfinger, A. J. Intermolecular Interactions & Biomolecular Organization. LC 76-26540. 1977. 37.50 (ISBN 0-471-40910-3, Pub by Wiley-Interscience). Wiley.
Johnson, R. E. Introduction to Atomic & Molecular Collisions. 300p. 1981. text ed. price not set (ISBN 0-306-40787-6, Plenum Pr). Plenum Pub.
Judd, Brian R. Angular Momentum Theory for Diatomic Molecules. 1975. 43.00 (ISBN 0-12-391950-9). Acad Pr.
Lambert, J. D. Vibrational & Rotational Relaxation in Gases. (International Series of Monographs on Chemistry). (Illus.). 1978. 47.50x (ISBN 0-19-855605-5). Oxford U Pr.
Lima-De-Faria, A. Handbook of Molecular Cytology. (Frontiers of Biology Ser. Vol. 15). 1972. pap. text ed. 122.00 (ISBN 0-444-10413-5, North-Holland). Elsevier.
Lister, David G. Internal Rotation & Inversion: An Introduction to Large Amplitude Motions in Molecules. 1978. 40.50 (ISBN 0-12-452250-5). Acad Pr.
Lyubitov, Yu. N. Molecular Flow in Vessels. LC 65-20215. 164p. 1967. 29.50 (ISBN 0-306-10757-0, Consultants). Plenum Pub.
Margenau, H. & Kestner, N. Theory of Intermolecular Forces. 2nd ed. 1971. 52.00 (ISBN 0-08-016502-8). Pergamon.
Meier, D. J. Molecular Basis of Transitions & Relaxations. (Midland Macromolecular Monographs). 1978. 68.75 (ISBN 0-677-11240-8). Gordon.
Nikitin, E. E. Theory of Elementary Atomic & Molecular Processes in Gases. Kearsley, M. J., tr. (Illus.). 486p. 1974. 74.00x (ISBN 0-19-851928-1). Oxford U Pr.
Pies, W. & Weiss, A. Landolt-Boernstein Numerical Data & Functional Relationships in Science & Technology, New Series, Group 3: Crystal & Solid State Physics, Vol. 7g, References. 465p. 1974. 177.00 (ISBN 0-387-06541-5). Springer-Verlag.
Prausnitz, J. M. Molecular Thermodynamics of Fluid-Phase Equilibria. LC 69-16866. 1969. ref. ed. 32.95 (ISBN 0-13-599639-2). P-H.
Reed, Rowland I. Ion Production by Electron Impact. 1962. 37.00 (ISBN 0-12-585250-9). Acad Pr.
Reid, Eric, ed. Membranous Elements & Movement of Molecules. LC 77-77378. (Methodological Surveys Ser: Vol. 6). 1977. 59.95 (ISBN 0-470-99186-0). Halsted Pr.

Sarma, Ramaswamy H. Stereodynamics of Molecular Systems. 1979. 66.00 (ISBN 0-08-024629-X). Pergamon.

Schlier, C., ed. Molecular Beams & Reaction Kinetics. (Italian Physical Society: Course No. 44). 1970. 56.50 (ISBN 0-12-368844-2). Acad Pr.

Thyagarajan, B. S. Mechanisms of Molecular Migrations, 3 vols. Incl. Vol. 1. 1968; Vol. 2. 1968. 36.50 (ISBN 0-470-86682-9); Vol. 3. 1971. 36.50 (ISBN 0-471-86684-9). 32.50 ea. Krieger.

Watts, R. O. & McGee, I. J. Liquid State Chemical Physics. LC 76-21793. 350p. 1976. 35.50 (ISBN 0-471-91240-9). Krieger.

Yardley, James T. Introduction to Molecular Energy Transfer. LC 80-10898. 1980. 34.00 (ISBN 0-12-768550-2). Acad Pr.

MOLECULAR GENETICS

Bonner, James. Molecular Biology of Development. 1965. 7.95x (ISBN 0-19-500310-1). Oxford U Pr.

Fincham, J. R. Microbial & Molecular Genetics. 2nd ed. LC 75-21729. 150p. 1976. pap. 9.95x (ISBN 0-8448-0769-9). Crane-Russak Co.

First John Innes Symposium, Norwich, England, July, 1972. The Generation of Subcellular Structures: Proceedings. Markham, R., et al, eds. LC 73-75798. (Illus.). 372p. 1973. 41.50 (ISBN 0-444-10472-0, North-Holland). Elsevier.

Gesellschaft Fuer Biologische Chemie, 24th, Mossbach-Baden, 1973. Regulation of Transcription & Translation in Eukaryotes: Proceedings. Bautz, E., ed. (Illus.). 300p. 1973. 46.20 (ISBN 0-387-06472-9). Springer-Verlag.

Goodman, Morris & Tashian, Richard E., eds. Molecular Anthropology: Genes & Proteins in the Evolutionary Ascent of the Primates. LC 76-45445. (Advances in Primatology Ser.). (Illus.). 466p. 1977. 39.50 (ISBN 0-306-30948-3, Plenum Pr). Plenum Pub.

Hamkalo, Barbara A. & Papaconstantinou, John. Molecular Cytogenetics. LC 73-18008. 359p. 1973. 37.50 (ISBN 0-306-30765-0, Plenum Pr). Plenum Pub.

Lappe, Marc & Morison, Robert S., eds. Ethical & Scientific Issues Posed by Human Uses of Molecular Genetics, Vol. 265. (Annals of the New York Academy of Sciences). 208p. 1976. 24.00x (ISBN 0-89072-019-3). NY Acad Sci.

Leighton, Terrance & Loomis, William F., eds. The Molecular Genetics of Development. LC 80-532. (Molecular Biology Ser.). 1980. 49.50 (ISBN 0-12-441960-7). Acad Pr.

Medvedev, Zhores A. Molecular-Genetic Mechanisms of Development. LC 71-80754. 418p. 1970. 34.50 (ISBN 0-306-30403-1, Plenum Pr). Plenum Pub.

Miller, Jeffrey H. Experiments in Molecular Genetics. LC 72-78914. (Illus.). 466p. 1972. 32.00 (ISBN 0-87969-106-9). Cold Spring Harbor.

Nei, Masatoshi, ed. Molecular Population Genetics & Evolution. LC 74-84734. (Frontiers of Biology: Vol. 40). 287p. 1975. 53.75 (ISBN 0-444-10751-7, North-Holland). Elsevier.

Nierlich, Donald P., et al, eds. Molecular Mechanisms in the Control of Gene Expression, Vol. 5. 1976. 41.50 (ISBN 0-12-518550-2). Acad Pr.

Rockstein, Morris & Baker, George T., eds. Molecular Genetic Mechanisms in Aging & Development. 1972. 25.50 (ISBN 0-12-591550-0). Acad Pr.

Shugar, D., ed. Genetic Elements, Properties & Functions. 1967. 60.00 (ISBN 0-12-640950-1). Acad Pr.

Stent, Gunther S. & Calendar, Richard. Molecular Genetics: An Introductory Narrative. 2nd ed. LC 78-688. (Illus.). 1978. text ed. 27.95x (ISBN 0-7167-0048-4). W H Freeman.

Symposium On Informational Macromolecules - Rutgers University - 1962. Informational Macromolecules: Proceedings. Vogel, Henry J., et al, eds. 1963. 50.50 (ISBN 0-12-722550-1). Acad Pr.

Taylor, J. H., ed. Molecular Genetics: An Advanced Treatise, 2 pts. (Molecular Biology Ser). Pt. 1, 1962. 48.00 ea. (ISBN 0-12-684401-1). Pt. 1. Pt. 2. 55.00 (ISBN 0-12-684402-X). Acad Pr.

Taylor, J. Herbert, ed. Selected Papers on Molecular Genetics. (Perspectives in Modern Biology). (Illus., Orig.). 1965. pap. 25.00 (ISBN 0-12-684456-9). Acad Pr.

Tso, Paul O. The Molecular Biology of the Mammalian Genetic Apparatus, 2 vols. Incl. Vol. 1. 68.00 (ISBN 0-7204-0625-0); Vol. 2. 55.75 (ISBN 0-7204-0626-9). 1977. 92.50 set (ISBN 0-685-83474-3, North-Holland). Elsevier.

Wassermann, G. D. Molecular Control of Cell Differentiation & Morphogenesis: A Systematic Theory. (Quantitative Approach to Life Science Ser.: Vol. 2). 1972. 74.75 (ISBN 0-8247-1766-X). Dekker.

Watson, J. D. Molecular Biology of the Gene. 3rd ed. LC 75-14791. 1976. 23.95 (ISBN 0-8053-9609-8). Benjamin-Cummings.

Winkler, U., et al. Bacterial, Phage & Molecular Genetics. 250p. 1976. pap. 12.70 (ISBN 0-387-07602-6). Springer-Verlag.

Woodward, Dow O. & Woodward, Val. Concepts of Molecular Genetics. (Illus.). 1976. text ed. 17.95 (ISBN 0-07-071780-X, C). McGraw.

Yunis, Jorge, ed. Molecular Structure of Human Chromosomes. 1977. 39.50 (ISBN 0-12-775168-8). Acad Pr.

MOLECULAR ORBITALS

see also Molecular Structure

Ballard, R. E. Photoelectron Spectroscopy & Molecular Orbital Theory. LC 78-40817. 1979. 63.95 (ISBN 0-470-26542-6). Halsted Pr.

Bellamy, A. J. Introduction to Conservation of Orbital Symmetry: A Programmed Text. 160p. (Orig.). 1974. pap. text ed. 9.85x (ISBN 0-582-44089-0). Longman.

Borden, Weston T. Modern Molecular Orbital Theory for Organic Chemists. (Illus.). 336p. 1975. 24.95 (ISBN 0-13-595983-7). P-H.

Boschke, F., ed. Molecular Orbitals. LC 51-5497. (Topics in Current Chemistry: Vol. 23). 1971. pap. 28.40 (ISBN 0-387-05504-5). Springer-Verlag.

Csizmadia, I. G., ed. Applications of Mo Theory in Organic Chemistry. (Progress in Theoretical Organic Chemistry Ser.: Vol. 2). 1977. 83.00 (ISBN 0-444-41565-3). Elsevier.

Dewar, Michael J. Molecular Orbital Theory of Organic Chemistry. LC 68-21840. (Advanced Chemistry Ser). (Illus.). 1968. text ed. 24.00 (ISBN 0-07-016637-4, C). McGraw.

Dewar, Michael J. & Dougherty, Ralph C. The PMO Theory of Organic Chemistry. LC 74-12196. (Illus.). 576p. 1975. 42.50 (ISBN 0-306-30779-0, Plenum Pr). Plenum Pub.

--The PMO Theory of Organic Chemistry. LC 74-26609. (Illus.). 576p. 1975. pap. 12.50 (ISBN 0-306-20010-4, Rosetta). Plenum Pub.

Doggett, G. The Electronic Structure of Molecules: Theory & Application to Inorganic Molecules. 1972. 49.00 (ISBN 0-08-016588-5). Pergamon.

Fleming, I. Frontier Orbitals & Organic Chemical Reactions. LC 76-3800. 1976. 39.50 (ISBN 0-471-01820-1); pap. 15.95 (ISBN 0-471-01819-8, Pub. by Wiley-Interscience). Wiley.

Gilchrist, T. L. & Storr, R. C. Organic Reactions & Orbital Symmetry. 2nd ed. LC 78-54578. (Cambridge Texts in Chemistry & Biochemistry Ser.). (Illus.). 1979. 59.50 (ISBN 0-521-22014-9); pap. 18.95x (ISBN 0-521-29336-7). Cambridge U Pr.

Gimarc, Benjamin M. Molecular Structure & Bonding: The Qualitative Molecular Orbital Theory. 1979. 21.00 (ISBN 0-12-284150-6). Acad Pr.

Heilbronner, E. & Bock, H. The HMO Model & Its Application, 3 vols. Incl. Vol. 1. Basis & Manipulation. 46.50 (ISBN 3-527-25654-7); Vol. 2. Problems with Solutions. 41.20 (ISBN 3-527-25655-5); Vol. 3. Tables of Huckel Molecular Orbitals. 25.90 (ISBN 3-527-25656-3). 1976. Verlag Chemie.

Heilbronner, E. & Straub, P. A. HMO-Hueckel Molecular Orbitals. 1966. looseleaf bdg 53.30 (ISBN 0-387-03566-4). Springer-Verlag.

Higasi, Ken'Ichi, et al. Quantum Organic Chemistry. 358p. 1965. text ed. 18.50 (ISBN 0-470-38690-8, Pub. by Wiley). Krieger.

Jorgensen, William L. & Salem, Lionel. The Organic Chemist's Book of Orbitals. 1973. 25.50 (ISBN 0-12-390250-9); pap. 17.00 (ISBN 0-12-390256-8). Acad Pr.

Kier, Lemont B. Molecular Orbital Theory in Drug Research. LC 73-137616. (Medicinal Chemistry Ser). 1971. 46.50 (ISBN 0-12-406550-3). Acad Pr.

Kutzelnigg, W., et al. Sigma & PI Electrons in Organic Compounds. LC 51-5497. (Topics in Current Chemistry: Vol. 22). (Illus.). 1971. pap. 36.60 (ISBN 0-387-05473-1). Springer-Verlag.

Lehr, R. E. & Manchard, Alan. Orbital Symmetry Relationships. 1972. text ed. 12.50 (ISBN 0-12-441150-9); pap. text ed. 7.95 (ISBN 0-12-441156-8). Acad Pr.

Lowdin, Per-Olov & Pullman, Bernard, eds. Molecular Orbitals in Chemistry, Physics, & Biology. 1964. 77.00 (ISBN 0-12-456850-5). Acad Pr.

March, N. H., ed. Orbital Theories of Molecules & Solids. (Illus.). 402p. 1974. text ed. 39.00x (ISBN 0-19-855350-1). Oxford U Pr.

Orchin, Milton & Jaffe, H. H. Symmetry, Orbitals, & Spectra. LC 76-136720. 1971. 37.50 (ISBN 0-471-65550-3, Pub. by Wiley-Interscience). Wiley.

Pearson, Ralph G. Symmetry Rules for Chemical Reactions: Orbital Topology & Elementary Processes. LC 76-10314. 600p. 1976. 41.00 (ISBN 0-471-01495-8, Pub. by Wiley-Interscience). Wiley.

Pople, J. A. & Beveridge, D. L. Approximate Molecular Orbital Theory. 1970. text ed. 25.00 (ISBN 0-07-050512-8, C). McGraw.

Roberts, John D. Molecular Orbital Calculations. (Illus.). 1962. pap. 9.50 (ISBN 0-8053-8301-8, Adv Bk Prog). Benjamin-Cummings.

Sackheim, George I. Atomic & Molecular Orbitals. 1965. pap. 1.80x (ISBN 0-87563-002-2). Stipes.

Salem, Lionel. The Molecular Orbital Theory of Conjugated Systems. LC 66-10239. 592p. 1966. text ed. 28.50 (ISBN 0-8053-8402-2, Adv Bk Prog); pap. text ed. 18.50 (ISBN 0-8053-8401-4, Adv Bk Prog). Benjamin-Cummings.

Simmons, Howard E. & Bunnett, Joseph F., eds. Orbital Symmetry Papers. LC 74-75425. (ACS Reprint Collection). 1974. 23.50 (ISBN 0-8412-0196-X); pap. 13.25 (ISBN 0-8412-0239-7). Am Chemical.

Slater, John C. The Calculation of Molecular Orbitals. LC 78-323. 1979. 29.00 (ISBN 0-471-03181-X, Pub. by Wiley-Interscience). Wiley.

Smith, William B. Molecular Orbital Methods in Organic Chemistry - HMO & PMO: An Introduction. (Studies in Organic Chemistry: Vol. 2). 192p. 1974. 16.75 (ISBN 0-8247-6127-8). Dekker.

Steiner, E. Determination & Interpretaion of Molecular Wave Functions. LC 75-78120. (Monographs in Physical Chemistry: No. 3). 250p. 1976. 44.50 (ISBN 0-521-21037-2). Cambridge U Pr.

Streitweiser, Andrew & Owens, Peter H. Orbital & Electron Density Diagrams: An Application of Computer Graphics. (Illus.). 150p. 1973. pap. text ed. 14.95 (ISBN 0-02-418020-3). Macmillan.

Suzuki, H. Electronic Absorption Spectra & Geometry of Organic Molecules. 1967. 71.50 (ISBN 0-12-678150-8). Acad Pr.

Van Wazer, John R. & Absar, Ilyas. Electron Densities in Molecules & Molecular Orbitals. (Physical Chemistry Ser.). 1975. 28.50 (ISBN 0-12-714550-8). Acad Pr.

Wagniere, G. H. Introduction to Elementary Molecular Orbital Theory & to Semiempirical Methods. (Lecture Notes in Chemistry: Vol. 1). 1976. soft cover 8.20 (ISBN 0-387-07865-7). Springer-Verlag.

Williams, A. F. A Theoretical Approach to Inorganic Chemistry. (Illus.). 1979. 53.90 (ISBN 0-387-09073-8). Springer-Verlag.

Yates, Keith. Huckel Molecular Orbital Theory. 1978. 34.00 (ISBN 0-12-768850-1). Acad Pr.

Zahradnik, Rudolph & Pancir, Jiri. HMO Energy Characteristics. LC 75-130314. 120p. 1970. 37.50 (ISBN 0-306-65152-1). IFI Plenum.

MOLECULAR PHYSIOLOGY

see Biological Physics

MOLECULAR RAYS

see Molecular Beams

MOLECULAR REARRANGEMENTS

see Rearrangements (Chemistry)

MOLECULAR ROTATION

see also Conformational Analysis; Isomerism; Optical Rotation; Polymers and Polymerization

Kovacs, I. Rotational Structure of the Spectra of Diatomic Molecules. 1970. 25.00 (ISBN 0-444-19672-2). Elsevier.

Mizushima, Masataka. The Theory of Rotating Diatomic Molecules. 543p. 1975. 37.50 (ISBN 0-471-61187-5, Pub. by Wiley). Krieger.

Mizushima, San-Ichiro. Structure of Molecules & Internal Rotation. (Physical Chemistry Ser.: Vol. 2). 1954. 38.00 (ISBN 0-12-501750-2). Acad Pr.

Schutte, C. J. The Theory of Molecular Spectroscopy: The Quantum Mechanics & Group Theory of Vibrating & Rotating Molecules, Vol. 1. 1976. Vol. 1. 83.00 (ISBN 0-444-10627-8, North-Holland); Vol. 2. write for info. Elsevier.

Wollrab, James E. Rotational Spectra & Molecular Structure. (Physical Chemistry Ser.: Vol. 13). 1967. 57.00 (ISBN 0-12-762150-4). Acad Pr.

MOLECULAR SIEVES

see also Clathrate Compounds; Zeolites

Breck, Donald W. Zeolite Molecular Sieves: Structure, Chemistry & Use. LC 73-11028. 1974. 65.00 (ISBN 0-471-09985-6, Pub. by Wiley-Interscience). Wiley.

Katzer, James R., ed. Molecular Sieves II. LC 77-720. (ACS Symposium Ser.: No. 40). 1977. 34.50 (ISBN 0-8412-0362-8). Am Chemical.

Meier, W. M. & Uytterhoeven, J. B., eds. Molecular Sieves. LC 73-83768. (Advances in Chemistry Ser.: No. 121). 1973. 46.00 (ISBN 0-8412-0180-3). Am Chemical.

MOLECULAR SPECTRA

see also Vibrational Spectra

Allen, G. & Pritchard, H. Statistical Mechanics & Spectroscopy. LC 74-7034. 140p. 1974. pap. 16.95 (ISBN 0-470-02331-7). Halsted Pr.

Allen, H. C., Jr. & Cross, P. C. Molecular Vib-Rotors: Theory & Interpretation of High Resolution Infrared Spectra. 324p. 1963. text ed. 17.50 (ISBN 0-471-02325-6, Pub. by Wiley). Krieger.

Arndt, U. W. & Wonacott, A. J. The Rotation Method in Crystallography. 1977. 50.75 (ISBN 0-7204-0594-7, North-Holland). Elsevier.

ASTM Manual on Practices in Molecular Spectroscopy (E-13) 4th ed. 168p. 1980. soft cover 12.50x (ISBN 0-686-76089-1, 03-513079-39). ASTM.

Barrow, Gordon M. Introduction to Molecular Spectroscopy. 1962. 21.00 (ISBN 0-07-003870-8, C). McGraw.

--Structure of Molecules: An Introduction to Molecular Spectroscopy. (Orig.). 1963. pap. 7.95 (ISBN 0-8053-0521-1). Benjamin-Cummings.

Barswell, C. N. Fundamentals of Molecular Spectroscopy. 2nd ed. 1973. text ed. 15.95 (ISBN 0-07-084007-5, P&RB). McGraw.

Bellamy, L. J. The Infrared Spectra of Complex Molecules. 3rd ed. LC 75-2435. (The Infrared Spectra of Complex Molecules Ser.: Vol. 1). 433p. 1975. Vol. 1. text ed. 29.95x (ISBN 0-412-13850-6, Pub. by Chapman & Hall England). Methuen Inc.

Bingel, Werner. Theory of Molecular Spectra. LC 75-80980. (Chemische Taschenbuecher: Vol. 2). (Illus.). 1970. pap. 12.90 (ISBN 3-527-25018-2). Verlag Chemie.

Birks, J. B., ed. Organic Molecular Photophysics, 2 vols. LC 74-8594. (Monographs in Chemical Physics Ser). 600p. 1973. Vol. 1. 104.75 (ISBN 0-471-07415-2, Pub. by Wiley-Interscience); Vol. 2. 115.25 (ISBN 0-471-07421-7). Wiley.

Boutin, Henri & Yip, Sidney. Molecular Spectroscopy with Neutrons. LC 68-22823. 1968. 20.00x (ISBN 0-262-02042-4). MIT Pr.

Brittain, E. F., et al. Introduction to Molecular Spectroscopy: Theory & Experiment. 1978. pap. 20.00 (ISBN 0-12-135051-7). Acad Pr.

Bunker, Philip R. The Molecular Symmetry & Spectroscopy. LC 78-51240. 1979. 43.50 (ISBN 0-12-141350-0). Acad Pr.

Davies, Mansel, ed. Infra-Red Spectroscopy & Molecular Structure. 1963. 53.75 (ISBN 0-444-40152-0). Elsevier.

Downs, A. J., et al, eds. Essays in Structural Chemistry. LC 76-144136. 479p. 1971. 45.00 (ISBN 0-306-30525-9, Plenum Pr). Plenum Pub.

Dunford, Brian. Elements of Diatomic Molecular Spectra. LC 68-13548. (Chemistry Ser). (Illus., Orig.). 1968. pap. 10.95 (ISBN 0-201-01615-X). A-W.

European Congress on Molecular Spectroscopy, 12th, Strasbourg, 1975, et al. Molecular Spectroscopy of Dense Phases: Proceedings. Grosmann, M., et al, eds. 1976. 90.25 (ISBN 0-444-41409-6). Elsevier.

Gaydon, A. G. & Pearse, R. W. Identification of Molecular Spectra. 2nd ed. 1976. 64.00x (ISBN 0-412-14350-X, Pub. by Chapman & Hall). Methuen Inc.

Herzberg, Gerhard. Spectra & Structures of Simple Free Radicals: An Introduction to Molecular Spectroscopy. LC 70-124722. (Baker Non-Resident Lectureships in Chemistry Ser.). 240p. 1971. 25.00x (ISBN 0-8014-0584-X). Cornell U Pr.

Horak, M. & Vitek, Antonin V. Interpretation & Processing of Vibrational Spectra. LC 78-16741. 1978. 79.25 (ISBN 0-471-99504-5, Pub. by Wiley-Interscience). Wiley.

Kovacs, I. Rotational Structure of the Spectra of Diatomic Molecules. 1970. 25.00 (ISBN 0-444-19672-2). Elsevier.

Lamola, Angelo, ed. Creation & Detection of the Excited State, Vol. 1, Pt. B. 1971. 53.50 (ISBN 0-8247-1403-2). Dekker.

--Creation & Detection of the Excited State, Vol. 1, Pt. A. 1971. 59.50 (ISBN 0-8247-1402-4). Dekker.

Levine, Ira N. Molecular Spectroscopy. LC 74-30477. 480p. 1975. 35.00 (ISBN 0-471-53128-6, Pub. by Wiley-Interscience). Wiley.

Long, D. A., et al. Molecular Spectroscopy, Vols. 1-6. Incl. Vol. 1. Literature up to 1972. 1973. 49.50 (ISBN 0-85186-506-2); Vol. 2. 1972-73 Literature. 1974. 57.75 (ISBN 0-85186-516-X); Vol. 3. 1973 Literature. 1975. 66.00 (ISBN 0-85186-526-7); Vol. 4. 1974-75 Literature. 1976. 49.50 (ISBN 0-85186-536-4); Vol. 5. 1975-76 Literature. 1978. 71.50 (ISBN 0-85186-546-1). LC 72-92545. Am Chemical.

McClure, Donald S. Electronic Spectra of Molecules & Ions in Crystals. (Solid State Reprint). 1964. 10.50 (ISBN 0-12-608474-2). Acad Pr.

Mataga, N. & Kubota, T. Molecular Interactions & Electronic Spectra. 520p. 1970. 62.50 (ISBN 0-8247-1444-X). Dekker.

NATO Advanced Study Institute, Cambridge, England, September, 1979. Semiclassical Methods in Molecular Scattering & Spectroscopy: Proceedings. Child, M. S., ed. (NATO Advanced Study Institute Series C. Mathematical & Physical Sciences: No. 53). 344p. 1980. lib. bdg. 39.50 (ISBN 90-277-1082-1, Pub. by Reidel Holland). Kluwer Boston.

Penner, S. S. Quantitative Molecular Spectroscopy & Gas Emissivities. 1959. 21.50 (ISBN 0-201-05760-3). A-W.
Rao, K. N. & Mathews, C. Weldon, eds. Molecular Spectroscopy: Modern Research. 1972. 58.50 (ISBN 0-12-580640-X). Acad Pr.
Schutte, C. J. The Theory of Molecular Spectroscopy: The Quantum Mechanics & Group Theory of Vibrating & Rotating Molecules, Vol. 1. 1976. Vol. 1. 83.00 (ISBN 0-444-10627-8, North-Holland); Vol. 2. write for info. Elsevier.
Skobel'tsyn, D. V., ed. Electronic & Vibrational Spectra of Molecules. LC 68-26494. (P. N. Lebedev Physics Institute Ser.: Vol. 35). (Illus.). 217p. 1968. 32.50 (ISBN 0-306-10813-5, Consultants). Plenum Pub.
Skolbel'Tsyn, D. V., ed. Optical Properties of Metals & Intermolecular Interactions. LC 72-94827. (P. N. Lebedev Physics Institute Ser.: Vol. 55). (Illus.). 228p. 1973. 35.00 (ISBN 0-306-10880-1, Consultants). Plenum Pub.
--Research in Molecular Spectroscopy. LC 65-14628. (P. N. Lebedev Physics Institute Ser.: Vol. 27). 205p. 1965. 32.50 (ISBN 0-306-10715-5, Consultants). Plenum Pub.
Societe De Chimie Physique. Non-Radiative Transition in Molecules. 254p. 1970. 46.50x (ISBN 0-677-30610-5). Gordon.
Steinfeld, Jeffrey. Molecules & Radiation: An Introduction to Modern Molecular Spectroscopy. 1978. pap. text ed. 13.50x (ISBN 0-262-69059-4). MIT Pr.
Suzuki, H. Electronic Absorption Spectra & Geometry of Organic Molecules. 1967. 71.50 (ISBN 0-12-678150-8). Acad Pr.
Truter, M. R. & Sutton, L. E. Molecular Structure by Diffraction Methods, Vols. 1-6. LC 72-95097. Vol. 1 1973. 1971-72 literature 52.25 (ISBN 0-85186-507-0); Vol. 2 1974. 1972-73 literature 55.00 (ISBN 0-85186-517-8); Vol. 3 1975. 1973-74 literature 71.50 (ISBN 0-85186-527-5); Vol. 4 1976. 1974-75 literature 78.50 (ISBN 0-85186-537-2); Vol. 5 1977. 1975-76 literature 96.25 (ISBN 0-85186-547-X); Vol. 6 1978. 1976-77 literature 90.75 (ISBN 0-85186-557-7). Am Chemical.
Verma, R. N. Spectroscopic References to Polyatomic Molecules. 1980. 75.00 (ISBN 0-306-65190-4). Plenum Pub.
Weissberger, Arnold, et al, eds. Techniques of Organic Chemistry: Microwave Molecular Spectra, Vol. 9, Pt. 2. LC 80-16243. 747p. 1970. 67.50 (ISBN 0-471-93161-6). Krieger.

MOLECULAR STRUCTURE

Allen, G. Molecular Structures & Properties. 1973. 24.50 (ISBN 0-8391-1016-2). Univ Park.
Ballhausen, C. J. & Gray, H. B. Molecular Orbital Theory. 1964. pap. text ed. 9.50 (ISBN 0-8053-0451-7, Adv Bk Prog). Benjamin-Cummings.
Bradley & Hanson, eds. Machine Interpretations of Patterson Functions & Alternative Direct Approaches & the Austin Symposium on Gas Phase Molecular Structure. pap. 5.00 (ISBN 0-686-60373-7). Polycrystal Bk Serv.
Buckingham, A. D. Molecular Structure & Properties. (IRS Physical Chemistry Ser. Two: Vol. 2). 1975. 29.95 (ISBN 0-408-70601-5). Butterworth.
Cartmell, Edward & Fowles, G. W. Valency & Molecular Structure. (Illus.). 1966. text ed. 8.95x (ISBN 0-442-01462-7). Van Nos Reinhold.
Coulson, C. A. The Shape & Structure of Molecules. (Oxford Chemistry Ser). (Illus.). 96p. 1973. pap. text ed. 8.95x (ISBN 0-19-855421-4). Oxford U Pr.
Dunitz, Jack D. X-Ray Analysis & the Structure of Organic Molecules. LC 78-15588. (George Fisher Baker Non-Resident Lectureship Ser.). 1979. 65.00x (ISBN 0-8014-1115-7). Cornell U Pr.
Flygare, W. H. Molecular Structure & Dynamics. LC 77-16786. (Illus.). 1978. ref. 29.95 (ISBN 0-13-599753-4). P-H.
Griffiths, J. Color & Constitution of Organic Molecules. 1976. 45.00 (ISBN 0-12-303550-3). Acad Pr.
Hargittai, I. Sulphone Molecular Structures: Conformation & Geometry from Electron Diffraction & Microwave Spectroscopy; Structural Variations. LC 78-557. (Lecture Notes in Chemistry: Vol. 6). (Illus.). 1978. pap. 14.40 (ISBN 0-387-08654-4). Springer-Verlag.
Hoppe, W. & Mason, R., eds. Advances in Structure Research by Diffraction Methods, Vol. VII. 1979. 48.00 (ISBN 0-9940012-3-1, Pub. by Vieweg & Sohn Germany). Heyden.
Pauling, Linus. Nature of the Chemical Bond & the Structure of Molecules & Crystals: An Introduction to Modern Structural Chemistry. 3rd ed. (Baker Non-Resident Lectureship in Chemistry Ser.). (Illus.). 644p. 1960. 29.50x (ISBN 0-8014-0333-2). Cornell U Pr.
Wheatley, P. J. Determination of Molecular Structure. 2nd, rev. ed. 264p. 1981. pap. 5.00 (ISBN 0-486-64068-X). Dover.
Wilson, E. B., Jr., et al. Molecular Vibrations: The Theory of Infrared & Raman Vibrational Spectra. (Illus.). 1980. pap. text ed. 6.00 (ISBN 0-486-63941-X). Dover.

MOLECULAR THEORY

see also Gases, Kinetic Theory Of

Bird, G. A. Molecular Gas Dynamics. (Oxford Engineering & Science Ser.). 1976. text ed. 74.00x (ISBN 0-19-856120-2). Oxford U Pr.
Cole, G. H. An Introduction to the Statistical Theory of Classical Simple Dense Fluids. 1967. 45.00 (ISBN 0-08-010397-9). Pergamon.
Cotton, F. Albert. Chemical Applications of Group Theory. 2nd ed. LC 76-129657. 1971. 32.50 (ISBN 0-471-17570-6, Pub. by Wiley-Interscience). Wiley.
Fisher, I. Z. Statistical Theory of Liquids. Switz, Theodore, tr. LC 64-22249. 1964. pap. 17.50x (ISBN 0-226-25184-5). U of Chicago Pr.
Graovac, A., et al. Topological Approach to the Chemistry of Conjugated Molecules. (Lecture Notes in Chemistry: Vol. 4). 1977. pap. 10.70 (ISBN 0-387-08431-2). Springer-Verlag.
Green, Herbert S. The Molecular Theory of Fluids. 8.75 (ISBN 0-8446-0658-8). Peter Smith.
Guillory, William A. Introduction to Molecular Structure & Spectroscopy. 1977. text ed. 28.95 (ISBN 0-205-05718-7). Allyn.
Hirschfelder, Joseph O., et al. Molecular Theory of Gases & Liquids. LC 54-7621. 1964. 75.00 (ISBN 0-471-40065-3, Pub. by Wiley-Interscience). Wiley.
Hurley, A. C. Electron Correlation in Small Molecules. (Theoretical Chemistry Ser.). 1977. 44.00 (ISBN 0-12-362450-9). Acad Pr.
--Introduction to the Electron Theory of Small Molecules. 1977. 50.50 (ISBN 0-12-362460-6). Acad Pr.
Kieffer, William F. Mole Concept in Chemistry. 2nd ed. (Orig.). 1973. pap. text ed. 3.95x (ISBN 0-442-24402-9). Van Nos Reinhold.
Kier, L. B. & Hall, L. H. Molecular Connectivity in Chemistry & Drug Research. (Medicinal Chemistry Ser.). 1976. 45.00 (ISBN 0-12-406560-0). Acad Pr.
Kihara, T. Intermolecular Forces. LC 77-12353. 182p. 1978. 33.25 (ISBN 0-471-99583-5, Pub. by Wiley-Interscience). Wiley.
Mauskopf, Seymour. Crystals & Compounds: Molecular Structure & Composition in Nineteenth-Century French Science. LC 76-3197. (Transactions Ser.: Vol. 66, Pt. 3). (Illus.). 1976. pap. 4.50 (ISBN 0-87169-663-0). Am Philos.
Medoff, Sol & Powers, John. The Student Chemist Explores Atoms & Molecules. (YA) 1977. PLB 7.97 (ISBN 0-8239-0381-8). Rosen Pr.
Orville-Thomas, W. J., ed. Internal Rotation in Molecules. LC 73-2791. (Wiley Monographs in Chemical Physics). 608p. 1974. 105.95 (ISBN 0-471-65707-7, Pub. by Wiley-Interscience). Wiley.
Rescigno, et al, eds. Electron-Molecule & Photon-Molecule Collisions. 1979. 39.50 (ISBN 0-306-40193-2, Plenum Pr). Plenum Pub.
Schaefer, Henry F., ed. Applications of Electronic Structure Theory. (Modern Theoretical Chemistry Ser.: Vol. 4). (Illus.). 461p. 1977. 39.50 (ISBN 0-306-33504-2, Plenum Pr). Plenum Pub.
Schonland, David. Molecular Symmetry. (Illus.). 1965. 14.95 (ISBN 0-442-07423-9). Van Nos Reinhold.
Slater, John C. Quantum Theory of Molecules & Solids, Vol. 1, 3 & 4. Incl. Vol. 1. Electronic Structure of Molecules. 1963; Vol. 3. Insulators, Semiconductors & Solids. 1969; Vol. 4. The Self-Consistent Field for Molecules & Solids. 29.95 (ISBN 0-07-058038-3, C). C). McGraw.
Williams, Dudley, ed. Molecular Physics, 2pts. 2nd ed. (Methods in Experimental Physics). Pt.a, 1974. 55.50 (ISBN 0-12-476003-1); Pt.b,1974. 58.50 (ISBN 0-12-476043-0). Acad Pr.

MOLECULAR WEIGHTS

see also Atomic Weights

Billingham, N. C. Molar Mass Measurements in Polymer Science. LC 77-2823. 1977. 46.95 (ISBN 0-470-99125-9). Halsted Pr.
Dewar, M. J. & Jones, R. Computer Compilation of Molecular Weights & Percentage Compositions for Organic Compounds. 1969. 79.00 (ISBN 0-08-012707-X). Pergamon.
Division of Chemistry and Chemical Technology. Characterization of Macromolecular Structure. (Illus.). 1968. 16.00 (ISBN 0-309-01573-1). Natl Acad Pr.
Kieffer, William F. Mole Concept in Chemistry. 2nd ed. (Orig.). 1973. pap. text ed. 3.95x (ISBN 0-442-24402-9). Van Nos Reinhold.
Windholz, Martha, et al, eds. Table of Molecular Weights: A Companion Volume to the Merck Index. 9th ed. LC 77-95432. 1978. 12.00 (ISBN 0-911910-73-5). Merck.

MOLECULES

see also Dipole Moments; Energy-Band Theory of Solids; Macromolecules; Molecular Acoustics; Molecular Orbitals; Molecular Structure

Altmann, Simon L. Induced Representations in Crystals & Molecules: Point, Space & Nonrigid Molecule Groups. 1978. 55.00 (ISBN 0-12-054650-7). Acad Pr.
Ausloos, Pierre J., ed. Ion-Molecule Reactions in the Gas Phase. LC 66-28609. (Advances in Chemistry Ser: No. 58). 1966. 26.00 (ISBN 0-8412-0059-9). Am Chemical.
Bassow, H. Construction & Use of Atomic & Molecular Models. 1968. 19.50 (ISBN 0-08-012925-0); pap. 9.75 (ISBN 0-08-012924-2). Pergamon.
Bates, D. R., et al, eds. Advances in Atomic & Molecular Physics, Vols. 1-14. Incl. Vol. 1. 1965. 50.00 (ISBN 0-12-003801-3); Vol. 2. 1966. 50.00 (ISBN 0-12-003802-1); Vol. 3. 1968. 57.00 (ISBN 0-12-003803-X); Vol. 4. 1968. 57.00 (ISBN 0-12-003804-8); Vol. 5. 1969. 57.00 (ISBN 0-12-003805-6); Vol. 6. 1970. 57.00 (ISBN 0-12-003806-4); Vol. 7. 1971. 57.00 (ISBN 0-12-003807-2); Vol. 8. 1972. 57.00 (ISBN 0-12-003808-0); Vol. 9. 1974. 57.00 (ISBN 0-12-003809-9); Vol. 10. 1974. 57.00 (ISBN 0-12-003810-2); Vol. 11. 1976. 76.50 (ISBN 0-12-003311-9); lib ed. 98.50 (ISBN 0-12-003874-9); microfiche 54.50 (ISBN 0-12-003875-7); Vol. 12. 1976. 67.50 (ISBN 0-12-003812-9); lib ed. 87.00 (ISBN 0-12-003876-5); microfiche 48.50 (ISBN 0-12-003877-3); Vol. 13. 1978. 66.50 (ISBN 0-12-003813-7); lib ed. 85.00 (ISBN 0-12-003878-1); microfiche 41.50 (ISBN 0-12-003879-X); Vol. 14. 1979. 55.50 (ISBN 0-12-003814-5); lib ed. 71.50 (ISBN 0-12-003880-3); microfiche 40.00 (ISBN 0-12-003881-1). Acad Pr.
Bates, David R., ed. Atomic & Molecular Processes. (Pure & Applied Physics Ser.: Vol. 13). 1962. 60.00 (ISBN 0-12-081450-1). Acad Pr.
Benjamin-Maruzen HGS Molecular Structure Models: Generalchemistry Set. 1969. 10.95 (ISBN 0-8053-6971-6). Benjamin-Cummings.
Berne, Bruce J. & Pecora, Robert. Dynamic Light Scattering: With Applications to Chemistry, Biology & Physics. LC 75-19140. 376p. 1976. 42.50 (ISBN 0-471-07100-5, Pub. by Wiley-Interscience). Wiley.
Boschke, F. L., ed. Large Amplitude Motion in Molecules One. (Topics in Current Chemistry: Vol. 81). (Illus.). 1979. 52.30 (ISBN 0-387-09310-9). Springer-Verlag.
--Large Amplitude Motion in Molecules Two. (Topics in Current Chemistry: Vol. 82). (Illus.). 1979. 47.00 (ISBN 0-387-09311-7). Springer-Verlag.
Brand, J. C. & Speakman, J. C. Molecular Structure: The Physical Approach. 2nd ed. Tifer, J. K., ed. LC 75-8507. 1975. 35.95 (ISBN 0-470-09795-7). Halsted Pr.
Cartmell, Edward & Fowles, G. W. Valency & Molecular Structure. (Illus.). 1966. text ed. 8.95x (ISBN 0-442-01462-7). Van Nos Reinhold.
Chu, Benjamin. Molecular Forces: Based on the Baker Lectures of Peter Debye. 176p. 1967. text ed. 11.75 (ISBN 0-470-15630-9, Pub. by Wiley). Krieger.
CIAMDA Eighty: An Index to the Literature on Atomic & Molecular Collision Data Relevant to Fusion Research. 498p. 1980. pap. 31.25 (ISBN 92-0-039080-3, ISP550, IAEA). Unipub.
Clementi, E. Selected Topics in Molecular Physics. (Illus.). 1972. 40.00 (ISBN 3-527-25388-2). Verlag Chemie.
Davydov, A. S. Theory of Molecular Excitons. LC 72-75767. 313p. 1971. 35.00 (ISBN 0-306-30440-6, Plenum Pr). Plenum Pub.
Del Re, G., et al. Electronic States of Molecules & Atom Clusters. (Lecture Notes in Chemistry: Vol. 13). (Illus.). 180p. 1980. pap. 17.50 (ISBN 0-387-09738-4). Springer-Verlag.
Dmitriev, I. S. Symmetry in World of Molecules. 148p. 1979. pap. 3.00 (ISBN 0-8285-1519-0, Pub. by Mir Pubs Russia). Imported Pubns.
Engleman, R., ed. Nonradiative Decay of Ions & Molecules in Solids. 1979. 58.75 (ISBN 0-444-85244-1, North Holland). Elsevier.
Englman, R. The Jahn-Teller Effect in Molecules & Crystals. LC 77-37113. (Monographs in Chemical Physics Ser.). 370p. 1972. 64.95 (ISBN 0-471-24168-7, Pub. by Wiley-Interscience). Wiley.
Fano, U. & Fano, L. Physics of Atoms & Molecules: An Introduction to the Structure of Matter. LC 76-184808. 456p. 1973. text ed. 20.00x (ISBN 0-226-23782-6). U of Chicago Pr.
Flory, P. J. Statistical Mechanics of Chain Molecules. LC 68-21490. 1969. 37.50 (ISBN 0-470-26495-0, Pub. by Wiley-Interscience). Wiley.
Fong, Francis K. Theory of Molecular Relaxation Applications in Chemistry & Biology. LC 75-17814. 314p. 1975. 28.50 (ISBN 0-471-26555-1, Pub. by Wiley-Interscience). Wiley.
Foster, Roy, ed. Molecular Association: Including Molecular Complexes, Vol. 1. 1975. 59.50 (ISBN 0-12-262701-6). Acad Pr.
--Molecular Association: Including Molecular Complexes, Vol. 2. 1979. 112.50 (ISBN 0-12-262702-4). Acad Pr.
Fuhrhop, J. H., et al. Large Molecules. LC 67-11280. (Structure & Bonding Ser.: Vol. 18). (Illus.). 216p. 1974. 39.50 (ISBN 0-387-06658-6). Springer-Verlag.
Gribov, Lev A. Intensity Theory for Infrared Spectra of Polyatomic Molecules. LC 64-17204. 120p. 1964. 30.00 (ISBN 0-306-10689-2, Consultants). Plenum Pub.
Hudson Symposium, 9th, Plattsburgh, N.Y., Apr. 1976. Homoatomic Rings, Chains & Macromolecules of Main Group Elements: Proceedings. Rheingold, A. L., ed. 1977. 95.25 (ISBN 0-444-41634-X). Elsevier.
Inoue, S. & Stephens, R. E., eds. Molecules & Cell Movement. LC 75-16666. (Society of General Physiologists Ser.: Vol. 30). 460p. 1975. 36.00 (ISBN 0-89004-041-9). Raven.
Jukes, Thomas H. Molecules & Evolution. LC 66-19974. (Molecular Biology Ser.). (Illus.). 285p. 1968. Repr. of 1966 ed. 18.00x (ISBN 0-231-08614-8). Columbia U Pr.
Julg, A. Crystals As Giant Molecules. (Lecture Notes in Chemistry Ser.: Vol. 9). 1979. pap. 10.50 (ISBN 0-387-08946-2). Springer-Verlag.
Kimura, Katsumi. Handbook of Hei Photoelectron Spectra of Fundamental Organic Molecules. LC 81-6449. 268p. 1981. 39.95 (ISBN 0-470-27200-7). Halsted Pr.
Kirkwood, John G. Dielectrics-Intermolecular Forces-Optical Rotation. Cole, Robert H., ed. (Documents on Modern Physics Ser.). (Illus., Orig.). 1965. 34.75x (ISBN 0-677-00405-2). Gordon.
Klinkmann, Horst, et al, eds. Middle Molecules in Uremia & Other Diseases: Analytical Techniques, Metabolic Toxicity, & Clinical Aspects. (Artificial Organs: Vol. 4). 1981. 50.00 (ISBN 0-686-73132-8); pap. 30.00 (ISBN 0-686-73133-6). Intl Soc Artifical Organs.
Knewstubb, P. F. Mass Spectrometry & Ion-Molecule Reactions. LC 69-16282. (Cambridge Chemistry Textbooks Ser). (Illus.). 1969. 27.50 (ISBN 0-521-07489-4); pap. 11.50x (ISBN 0-521-09563-8). Cambridge U Pr.
Landau, L. & Kitaigorodsky, A. I. Physics for Everyone: Molecules. 224p. 1980. 6.60 (ISBN 0-8285-1725-8, Pub. by Mir Pubs Russia). Imported Pubns.
Lax, Melvin. Symmetry Principles in Solid State & Molecular Physics. LC 74-1215. 499p. 1974. (Pub. by Wiley-Interscience); pap. 23.95x (ISBN 0-471-51904-9). Wiley.
Ledoux, L. Uptake of Informative Molecules by Living Cells: Proceedings. 1972. 53.75 (ISBN 0-444-10407-0, North-Holland). Elsevier.
Maitland, Geoffrey C., et al. Intermolecular Forces: Their Origin & Determination. (International Ser. of Monographs in Chemistry). (Illus.). 450p. 1981. 129.00x (ISBN 0-19-855611-X). Oxford U Pr.
Mead, C. A. Symmetry & Chirality. LC 51-5497. (Topics in Current Chemistry: Vol. 49). (Illus.). 90p. 1974. 18.50 (ISBN 0-387-06705-1). Springer-Verlag.
Milne, Jim. Big Molecules. (Foreground Chemistry Ser.). 1972. pap. text ed. 5.00x (ISBN 0-435-64302-9). Heinemann Ed.
Mulay, L. N. & Boudreaux, E. A., eds. Theory & Applications of Molecular Diamagnetism. LC 76-4874. 321p. 1976. 28.00 (ISBN 0-471-62358-X, Pub. by Wiley). Krieger.
Mulliken, Robert & Ermler, W. C., eds. Polyatomic Molecules. LC 80-2764. 1981. write for info. (ISBN 0-12-509860-X). Acad Pr.
Mulliken, Robert S., ed. Ab Initio Calculations on Diatomic Molecules. Ermler, W. C. 1977. 29.50 (ISBN 0-12-510750-1). Acad Pr.
Neel, L., ed. Nonlinear Behaviour of Molecules, Atoms & Ions in Electric, Magnetic or Electromagnetic Fields. 1979. 88.00 (ISBN 0-444-41790-7). Elsevier.
Nye, Mary Jo. Molecular Reality: A Perspective on the Scientific Work of Jean Perrin. LC 70-171234. 1972. lib. bdg. 17.00 (ISBN 0-685-52440-X). N Watson.
Okabe, Hideo. Photochemistry of Small Molecules. LC 78-6704. 1978. 45.50 (ISBN 0-471-65304-7, Pub. by Wiley-Interscience). Wiley.
Pauling, Linus C. The Chemical Bond: A Brief Introduction to Modern Structural Chemistry. (Illus.). 278p. 1967. 25.00x (ISBN 0-8014-0332-4). Cornell U Pr.
Price, C. C. Geometry of Molecules. 1971. 6.95 (ISBN 0-07-050866-6, C); pap. 5.95 (ISBN 0-07-050867-4). McGraw.

Pullman, Bernard, ed. Quantum Mechanics of Molecular Conformations. LC 75-43927. (Perspectives in Quantum Chemistry). 1976. 70.95 (ISBN 0-471-01489-3, Pub. by Wiley-Interscience). Wiley.
Ratajczak, H. & Orville-Thomas, W. J. Molecular Interactions. Vol. 1, 448 Pp. 78.00 (ISBN 0-471-27664-2, 1-500); Vol. 2. 110.00 (ISBN 0-471-27681-2). Wiley.
Rich, Alexander & Davidson, Norman, eds. Structural Chemistry & Molecular Biology: A Volume Dedicated to Linus Pauling by His Students, Colleagues, & Friends. LC 67-21127. (Illus.). 1968. 36.95x (ISBN 0-7167-0135-9). W H Freeman.
Rossman, M. G. The Molecular Replacement Method. (International Science Review). 276p. 1972. 59.50x (ISBN 0-677-13940-3). Gordon.
Sensory Physiology & Structure of Molecules. (Structure & Bonding Ser.: Vol. 114). (Illus.). 146p. 1980. 36.80 (ISBN 0-387-09958-1). Springer-Verlag.
Societe De Chimie Physique, 24th, Paris-Orsay, July 2-6, 1973. Molecular Motions of Liquids: Proceedings. Lascombe, J., ed. LC 73-91947. 1974. lib. bdg. 105.00 (ISBN 90-277-0431-7, Pub. by Reidel Holland). Kluwer Boston.
Symposium on Quantum, Chemistry, & Biochemistry, 8th, Jerusalem, April 1975. Environmental Effects on Molecular Structure & Properties: Proceedings. Pullman, Bernard, ed. LC 75-35543. (Jerusalem Symposium on Quantum Chemistry & Biochemistry Ser.: Vol. 8). 530p. 1976. lib. bdg. 103.00 (ISBN 90-277-0604-2, Pub. by Reidel Holland). Kluwer Boston.
Symposium On Relaxation Methods In Relation To Molecular Structure - Aberystwyth - 1965. Molecular Relaxation Processes: Proceedings. Cross, R. C., ed. 1966. 33.50 (ISBN 0-12-150450-6). Acad Pr.
Van Lancker, J. L. Molecules, Cells & Disease. LC 77-893. (Springer Study Edition). 1977. pap. 18.90 (ISBN 0-387-90242-2). Springer-Verlag.
Van Wazer, John R. & Absar, Ilyas. Electron Densities in Molecules & Molecular Orbitals. (Physical Chemistry Ser.). 1975. 28.50 (ISBN 0-12-714550-8). Acad Pr.
Von Hippel, Arthur R., ed. Molecular Designing of Materials & Devices. 1965. 31.50x (ISBN 0-262-22006-7). MIT Pr.
Voronkov, M. G., et al. The Siloxane Bond. (Studies in Soviet Science--Physical Sciences Ser.). (Illus.). 500p. 1978. 65.00 (ISBN 0-306-10940-9, Consultants). Plenum Pub.
Williams, Dudley, ed. Molecular Physics, 2pts. 2nd ed. (Methods in Experimental Physics). Pt.a, 1974. 55.50 (ISBN 0-12-476003-1); Pt.b,1974. 58.50 (ISBN 0-12-476043-0). Acad Pr.
Woodward, L. A. Molecular Statistics for Students of Chemistry. (Illus.). 232p. 1975. 28.00x (ISBN 0-19-855357-9). Oxford U Pr.

MOLECULES–INTERNAL ROTATION
see Molecular Rotation

MOLES (ANIMALS)
Mellanby, Kenneth. The Mole. LC 72-2186. (The New Naturalist Ser). (Illus.). 159p. 1973. 9.95 (ISBN 0-8008-5316-4). Taplinger.
Smith, Guy N. Moles & Their Control. 1981. 25.00x (ISBN 0-904558-82-7, Pub. by Saiga Pub). State Mutual Bk.

MOLESWORTH, MARY LOUISA (STEWART), 1842-1921
Laski, Marghanita. Mrs. Ewing, Mrs. Molesworth, & Mrs. Hodgson Burnett. LC 76-11955. 1976. Repr. of 1950 ed. lib. bdg. 12.50 (ISBN 0-8414-5717-4). Folcroft.

MOLIERE, JEAN BAPTISTE POQUELIN, 1622-1673
Albanese, Ralph, Jr. Le Dynamisme De la Peur Chez Moliere: Une Analyse Socio - Culturelle De Dom Juan, Tartuffe, et L'ecole Des Femmes. LC 76-9061. (Romance Monographs: No. 19). 1976. 20.00x (ISBN 84-399-5071-3). Romance.
Arnott, Peter. Ballet of Comedians. 1971. 7.95 (ISBN 0-02-503330-1). Macmillan.
Ashton, H. A Preface to Moliere. LC 73-15535. Repr. of 1927 ed. lib. bdg. 20.00 (ISBN 0-8414-2916-2). Folcroft.
Audiberti, Jacques. Moliere. 144p. 1973. 7.95 (ISBN 0-686-54495-1). French & Eur.
Barrett, Ethel. Debout Tartuffe! Date not set. 2.00 (ISBN 0-686-76395-5). Life Pubs Intl.
Chardon, Henri. Noveaux Documents sur la vie de Moliere. Incl. Vol. 2. Noveaux documents sur les comediens de campagne, la vie de Moliere et le theatre de college dans le Maine. (Research & Source Works Ser). 728p. (Fr.). 1972. Repr. of 1905 ed. lib. bdg. 20.00 (ISBN 0-8337-0536-9). B Franklin.
Chatfield-Taylor, H. C. Moliere: A Biography. 1973. Repr. of 1907 ed. 50.00 (ISBN 0-8274-1498-6). R West.
Cismaru, Alfred. Marivaux & Moliere: A Comparison. 1977. 12.95 (ISBN 0-89672-055-1). Tex Tech Pr.
Clarke, Charles C. Moliere-Characters. LC 75-35806. 1975. Repr. of 1865 ed. lib. bdg. 30.00 (ISBN 0-8414-3399-2). Folcroft.
Davis, Harold T. & Holcomb, George L. Moliere Resumes. 250p. 1971. text ed. 6.00 (ISBN 0-911536-39-6). Trinity U Pr.
De Bury, Blaz. Moliere & the French Classical Drama. 1973. Repr. of 1846 ed. 25.00 (ISBN 0-8274-1508-7). R West.
Defaux, Gerard. Moliere, ou les Metamorphoses du Comique: De la Comedie Morale Au Triomphe De la Folie. LC 79-53401. (French Forum Monographs: No. 18). 372p. (Fr.). 1980. pap. 17.50 (ISBN 0-917058-17-8). French Forum.
Desfeuilles, Arthur. Lexique de la Langue de Moliere avec une, Vol. 1-2. (Fr). 1900. Set. 64.00 (ISBN 0-8337-4744-4). B Franklin.
--Notice Bibliographique De Moliere. Despois, Eugene & Mesnard, Paul, eds. LC 70-126412. (Bibliography & Reference Ser.: No. 343). (Fr). 1970. Repr. of 1893 ed. lib. bdg. 23.50 (ISBN 0-8337-0839-2). B Franklin.
Eustis, Alvin. Moliere As Ironic Contemplator. LC 72-94465. (De Proprietatibus Litterarum, Ser. Practica: No. 40). 231p. 1974. pap. text ed. 40.75x (ISBN 90-2792-507-0). Mouton.
Fernandez, Ramon. Moliere: The Man Seen Through the Plays. LC 79-28249. 212p. 1980. Repr. of 1958 ed. lib. bdg. 14.00x (ISBN 0-374-92739-1). Octagon.
Giucharhaud, J., ed. Moliere: A Collection of Critical Essays. 1964. 10.95 (ISBN 0-13-599712-7, Spec). P-H.
Gossman, Lionel. Men & Masks: A Study of Moliere. 325p. 1963. pap. 4.95 (ISBN 0-8018-1043-4). Johns Hopkins.
Grebanier, Bernard. Barron's Simplified Approach to Moliere. LC 64-8320. 1965. pap. text ed. 1.50 (ISBN 0-8120-0181-8). Barron.
Grene, Nicholas. Shakespeare, Jonson, Moliere: The Comic Contract. 246p. 1980. 26.50x (ISBN 0-389-20093-X). B&N.
Guicharnaud. Moliere. (Bibliotheque des Idees). 21.50 (ISBN 0-685-34244-1). French & Eur.
Herzel, Roger W. The Original Casting of Moliere's Plays. Beckerman, Bernard, ed. LC 81-7538. (Theater & Dramatic Studies: No. 1). 1981. price not set (ISBN 0-8357-1209-5, Pub. by UMI Res Pr). Univ Microfilms.
Horville, R. Don Juan De Moliere: Une Dramaturgie De Rupture. (La Collection Themes & Textes Ser.). 288p. (Orig., Fr.). 1972. pap. 6.75 (ISBN 2-03-035011-7, 2690). Larousse.
Howarth, W. D. & Thomas, J. Merlin, eds. Moliere: Stage & Study. 1973. 29.95x (ISBN 0-19-815712-6). Oxford U Pr.
Hubert, J. D. Moliere & the Comedy of Intellect. LC 62-18021. (California Library Reprint). 1974. 20.00x (ISBN 0-520-02520-2). U of Cal Pr.
Hubert, Judd D. Moliere & the Comedy of Intellect. LC 70-143558. 1971. Repr. of 1962 ed. 13.50 (ISBN 0-8462-1583-7). Russell.
Johnson, Roger, et al, eds. Moliere & the Commonwealth of Letters: Patrimony & Posterity. LC 74-77454. 1975. 5.00x (ISBN 0-87805-059-0). U Pr of Miss.
Kasparek, Jerry L. Moliere's Tartuffe: An Interpretation Based on Significant Parallels with the Traditions of Roman Satiric Literature. (Studies in the Romance Languages & Literatures Ser: No. 175). 1977. 14.50x (ISBN 0-8078-9175-4). U of NC Pr.
Klibbe, Lawrence. Monarch Notes on Moliere's Plays. (Orig.). pap. 1.95 (ISBN 0-671-00568-5). Monarch Pr.
Knutson, Harold C. An Archetypal Approach to Moliere. LC 76-15976. 1976. 20.00x (ISBN 0-8020-5348-3). U of Toronto Pr.
Lawrence, F. L. Moliere: The Comedy of Unreason, Vol. 2. 119p. 1968. pap. 7.00 (ISBN 0-912788-01-1). Tulane Romance Lang.
Mander, Gertrud. Moliere. Peters, Diana, tr. from Ger. LC 70-163147. (World Dramatists Ser.). (Illus.). 1973. 10.95 (ISBN 0-8044-2662-7). Ungar.
Marzials, Frank T. Moliere. 1973. Repr. of 1910 ed. 20.00 (ISBN 0-8492-6727-7). R West.
Masters, Brian. A Student's Guide to Moliere. 1970. pap. text ed. 5.00x (ISBN 0-435-37570-9). Heinemann Ed.
Matthews, Brander. Moliere: His Life & His Works. LC 72-84999. xii, 385p. 1973. Repr. of 1910 ed. 20.00 (ISBN 0-8462-1695-7). Russell.
Moliere, Jean B. La Critique de l'Ecole des Femmes. 1970. 2.95 (ISBN 0-686-54768-3). French & Eur.
Oliphant & Tarver, F. Moliere. 1973. Repr. of 1879 ed. 22.50 (ISBN 0-8274-0301-1). R West.
Relyea, Suzanne. Signs, Systems, & Meanings: A Contemporary Semiotic Reading of Four Moliere Plays. LC 76-8520. 1976. lib. bdg. 12.00x (ISBN 0-8195-4097-8, Pub. by Wesleyan U Pr). Columbia U Pr.
Roberts, James L. Tartuffe Notes, Misanthrope Notes & Bourgeois Gentleman Notes. (Orig.). 1968. pap. 1.95 (ISBN 0-8220-1265-0). Cliffs.
Romero, Laurence. Moliere: Traditions in Criticism. (Studies in the Romance Languages & Literatures: No. 151). 1974. pap. 10.00x (ISBN 0-8078-9151-7). U of NC Pr.
Stendhal. Moliere, Shakespeare. facsimile ed. 1930. 50.00 (ISBN 0-686-55072-2). French & Eur.
Tilley, Arthur A. Moliere. LC 68-10950. (Illus.). 1968. Repr. of 1921 ed. 11.00 (ISBN 0-8462-1086-X). Russell.
Treloar, Bronnie. Moliere: Les Precieuses Ridicules. (Studies in French Literature). 1970. pap. text ed. 3.95x (ISBN 0-7131-5500-0). Dynamic Learn Corp.
Trollope, Henry M. The Life of Moliere. LC 74-9801. 1974. Repr. of 1905 ed. lib. bdg. 50.00 (ISBN 0-8414-8581-X). Folcroft.
--The Life of Moliere. 1978. Repr. of 1905 ed. lib. bdg. 50.00 (ISBN 0-8495-5115-3). Arden Lib.
Turnell, Martin. Classical Moment: Studies of Corneille, Moliere, & Racine. LC 79-138601. (Illus.). 1971. Repr. of 1948 ed. lib. bdg. 16.00x (ISBN 0-8371-5803-6, TUCM). Greenwood.
Walker, Hallam. Moliere. (World Authors Ser.: France: No. 176). lib. bdg. 12.50 (ISBN 0-8057-2620-9). Twayne.
Waterson, Karolyn. Moliere et L'Autorite: Structures Sociales, Structures Comiques. LC 76-17257. (Monographs: No.1). 140p. (Orig.). 1976. pap. 9.50x (ISBN 0-917058-00-3). French Forum.
Wilcox, John. Relation of Moliere to the Restoration Comedy. LC 64-14719. 1938. 15.00 (ISBN 0-405-09078-1). Arno.

MOLINA, LUIS DE, 1535-1600
Costello, Frank B. The Political Philosophy of Luis De Molina, S. J. 1974. pap. 12.00 (ISBN 0-8294-0360-4). Jesuit Hist.
--Political Philosophy of Luis de Molina, S. J. 1975. 15.00 (ISBN 0-686-11872-3). Gonzaga U Pr.
Monarch Notes on Molina's the Trickster of Seville. 1976. pap. 1.50 (ISBN 0-671-00975-3). Monarch Pr.
Smith, Gerard. Freedom in Molina. 1966. 2.25 (ISBN 0-8294-0070-2). Loyola.

MOLLUSCOIDEA
see also Brachiopoda; Polyzoa

MOLLUSKS
see also Cephalopoda; Gasteropoda; Lamellibranchiata; Opisthobranchiata; Shells; Snails; Squids
Abbott, R. Tucker. The Best of the Nautilus: A Bicentennial Anthology of American Conchology. LC 75-41628. (Illus.). 280p. 1976. 13.95 (ISBN 0-915826-02-X). Am Malacologists.
Abbott, R. Tucker, ed. American Malacologists: 1975 Supplement. LC 75-15478. 110p. 1975. pap. text ed. 2.00x (ISBN 0-915826-01-1). Am Malacologists.
--Indexes to the Nautilus: Geographical, Vols. 1-90, & Scientific Names, Vols. 61-90. 1979. Set. 24.00x (ISBN 0-915826-06-2). Am Malacologists.
Abbott, R. Tucker & Young, M. E., eds. American Malacologists, 1973-1974. LC 73-87999. 1975. pap. text ed. 4.95 (ISBN 0-915826-00-3). Am Malacologists.
Arnold, Winifred H. Glossary of a Thousand & One Terms Used in Conchology. 1965. 4.50 (ISBN 0-913792-05-5). Shell Cab.
Bayer, Frederick M. & Voss, Gilbert L., eds. Studies in Tropical American Mollusks. LC 70-170142. 1971. 12.50x (ISBN 0-87024-230-X). U of Miami Pr.
Bayne, B. L., ed. Marine Mussels. LC 75-25426. (International Biological Programme Ser.: No. 10). (Illus.). 400p. 1976. 99.00 (ISBN 0-521-21058-5). Cambridge U Pr.
Blust, Robert A. The Proto-Oceanic Palatals. 1979. pap. text ed. 15.00x (ISBN 0-8248-0684-0, Pub. by Polynesian Soc). U Pr of Hawaii.
Byrne, John H. & Koester, John, eds. Molluscan Nerve Cells: From Biophysics to Behavior. LC 80-39967. (Cold Spring Harbor Reports in the Neurosciences Ser.: Vol. 1). 230p. 1980. 26.00x (ISBN 0-87969-135-2). Cold Spring Harbor.
Caum, E. L. Check-List of Hawaiian Land & Freshwater Mollusca. (BMB Ser.: No. 56). Repr. of 1928 ed. pap. 7.00 (ISBN 0-527-02162-8). Kraus Repr.
Dethier. Newberry: The Life & Times of a Maine Clam. LC 81-66267. (Illus.). (gr. 3-4). 1981. pap. 5.95 (ISBN 0-89272-085-9). Down East.
Draparnaud, Jacques P. Histoire Naturelle Des Mollusques Terrestres et Fluviatiles De la France... 172p. 1981. Repr. of 1804 ed. lib. bdg. 75.00 (ISBN 0-8287-1464-9). Clearwater Pub.
Maury, C. J. Recent Mollusks Gulf Coast. 1971. Repr. 5.00 (ISBN 0-87710-361-5). Paleo Res.
Morris, Dean. Animals That Live in Shells. LC 77-7911. (Read About Animals Ser.). (Illus.). (gr. k-3). 1977. PLB 11.15 (ISBN 0-8393-0013-1). Raintree Child.
Morton, J. E. Molluscs. (Hutchinson Biological Sciences Ser.). (Illus.). 244p. 1979. pap. text ed. 11.25 (ISBN 0-09-134161-2, Hutchinson U Lib). Humanities.
Purchon, R. D. The Biology of the Mollusca. 2nd ed. 1968. 55.50 (ISBN 0-08-021028-7). Pergamon.
Solem, Alan. The Shell Makers: Introducing Mollusks. LC 73-20315. 304p. 1974. 17.95 (ISBN 0-471-81210-2, Pub. by Wiley-Interscience). Wiley.
Thompson, T. E. Nudibranchs. (Illus., Orig.). 1976. pap. 5.95 (ISBN 0-87666-459-1, PS-696). TFH Pubns.
Van Der Spoel, S., et al, eds. Pathways in Malacology. 1979. lib. bdg. 53.00 (ISBN 90-313-0319-4, Pub. by Junk Pubs Netherlands). Kluwer Boston.
Walne, Peter R. Culture of Bivalve Molluscs: Fifty Years' Experience at Conwy. (Illus.). 190p. 24.00 (ISBN 0-85238-063-1, FN 8, FNB). Unipub.
Webb, Walter F. Foreign Land Shells. (Illus.). 1948. 7.95 (ISBN 0-910872-13-9). Lee Pubns.
--Handbook for Shell Collectors. 16th rev. ed. (Illus.). 12.00 (ISBN 0-910872-11-2). Lee Pubns.
Wilbur, Karl M. & Yonge, C. M., eds. Physiology of Mollusca, Vol. 2. 1966. Vol. 1. 63.00 (ISBN 0-12-751302-7). Acad Pr.
Zoological Society Of London - 22nd Symposium. Studies in the Structure, Physiology & Ecology of Molluscs. Fretter, ed. 1968. 52.00 (ISBN 0-12-613322-0). Acad Pr.

MOLLUSKS–PARASITES
see Parasites–Mollusks

MOLLUSKS–AUSTRALIA
MacPherson, J. Hope & Gabriel, C. J. Marine Molluscs of Victoria. 1962. 7.50x (ISBN 0-522-83665-8, Pub. by Melbourne U Pr). Intl Schol Bk Serv.

MOLLUSKS–CARIBBEAN SEA
Warmke, Germaine L. & Abbott, R. Tucker. Caribbean Seashells. (Illus.). 1961. 10.00 (ISBN 0-87098-004-1). Livingston.

MOLLUSKS–GREAT BRITAIN
Ellis, A. E. British Freshwater Bivalve Mollusca: Keys & Notes for the Identification of the Species. (A Volume in the Synopses of the British Fauna Ser.). 1978. pap. 8.50 (ISBN 0-12-236950-5). Acad Pr.

MOLLUSKS–NORTH AMERICA
Abbott, R. Tucker. American Seashells. 2nd ed. 1974. text ed. 54.50 (ISBN 0-442-20228-8). Van Nos Reinhold.
Clarke, Arthur H. The Freshwater Molluscs of Canada. (Illus.). 416p. 1981. lib. bdg. 39.95x (ISBN 0-660-00022-9, 56350-2, Pub. by Natl Mus Canada). U of Chicago Pr.
Dall, W. H. Land & Fresh Water Mollusks. Bd. with Hydroids. Nutting, C. C. (Harriman Alaska Expedition, 1899). 16.00 (ISBN 0-527-38173-X). Kraus Repr.
Keen, A. Myra & Coan, Eugene. Marine Molluscan Genera of Western North America: An Illustrated Key. 2nd ed. LC 73-80625. (Illus.). 224p. 1974. 10.00x (ISBN 0-8047-0839-8). Stanford U Pr.
Marcus, Eveline & Marcus, Ernst. American Opisthobranch Mollusks. LC 67-31694. (Studies in Tropical Oceanography Ser: No. 6). 1967. 10.00x (ISBN 0-87024-087-0). U Miami Marine.

MOLLUSKS–PACIFIC OCEAN
Carpenter, Philip P. West Coast Mollusks. Orig. Title: Catalogue of the Collection of Mazatlan Shells. 1967. Repr. of 1857 ed. 6.00 (ISBN 0-87710-371-2). Paleo Res.
MacFarland, Frank. Memoir IV: Studies of Opisthobranchiate Mollusks of the Pacific Coast of North America. Kessell, Howard L., ed. (Memoirs of the California Academy of Sciences Ser.). (Illus.). 546p. 1966. 25.00 (ISBN 0-940228-10-6). Calif Acad Sci.
Olsson, Axel A. Mollusks of the Tropical Eastern Pacific. 574p. Date not set. Repr. of 1981 ed. price not set (ISBN 0-89874-324-9). Krieger.
--Neogene Mollusks from Northwestern Ecuador. (Illus.). 1964. 12.00 (ISBN 0-87710-367-4). Paleo Res.
Tinker, Spencer W. Pacific Sea-Shells. LC 57-18069. (Illus.). 1957. bds. 7.95 (ISBN 0-8048-0464-8). C E Tuttle.

MOLLUSKS–UNITED STATES
Baker, F. C. The Fresh Water Mollusca of Wisconsin. 1973. pap. 100.00 (ISBN 3-7682-0764-1). Lubrecht & Cramer.
Baker, Frank C. The Molluscan Fauna of the Big Vermillion River, Illinois. 9.50 (ISBN 0-384-03095-5). Johnson Repr.
Bequaert, Joseph C. & Miller, Walter B. The Mollusks of the Arid Southwest. LC 72-187825. 1973. pap. 2.00 (ISBN 0-8165-0318-4). U of Ariz Pr.
Metcalf, Artie L. Late Quaternary Mollusks of the Rio Grande Valley. 1970. pap. 3.00 (ISBN 0-685-64634-3). Tex Western.

Olsson, Axel A. & Harbison, Anne. Pliocene Mollusca of Southern Florida. LC 79-14175. (Academy of Naturl Sciences Monograph: No. 8). 602p. 1979. Repr. of 1953 ed. lib. bdg. 29.50 (ISBN 0-88275-980-9). Krieger.
Perry, Louise M. & Schwengel, Jeanne S. Marine Shells of the Western Coast of Florida. rev. ed. 1955. 10.00 (ISBN 0-87710-370-4); pap. 8.00 (ISBN 0-87710-369-0). Paleo Res.
Webb, Walter F. United States Mollusca. (Illus.). 7.95 (ISBN 0-910872-12-0). Lee Pubns.

MOLLUSKS, FOSSIL
see also Ammonoidea
Agassiz, Louis. Etudes Critiques les Mollusques Fossiles: Memoire les Trigonies et Monographic Des Myes (Critical Studies on Fossil Mollusks. Gould, Stephen J., ed. LC 79-8323. (History of Paleontology Ser.). (Illus., Fr.). 1980. Repr. of 1840 ed. lib. bdg. 60.00x (ISBN 0-405-12702-2). Arno.
Carpenter, Philip P. West Coast Mollusks. Orig. Title: Catalogue of the Collection of Mazatlan Shells. 1967. Repr. of 1857 ed. 6.00 (ISBN 0-87710-371-2). Paleo Res.
Dall, W. H., et al. A Manual of the Recent & Fossil, Marine Pelecypod Mollusks of the Hawaiian Islands. Repr. of 1938 ed. 23.00 (ISBN 0-527-02261-6). Kraus Repr.
Edwards, F. E. The Eocene Mollusca, 4 Vols. 1848-55. Set. pap. 42.50 (ISBN 0-384-13860-8). Johnson Repr.
Harmer, F. W. Pliocene Mollusca, 8 Nos. 1914-24. Set. pap. 104.00 (ISBN 0-384-21390-1). Johnson Repr.
Hoare, Richard D. Desmoinesian Brachiopoda & Mollusca from Southwest Missouri. LC 61-13508. (Illus.). 1961. 10.00x (ISBN 0-8262-0545-3). U of Mo Pr.
La Rocque, Aurele. Molluscan Faunas of the Flagstaff Formation of Central Utah. LC 60-2798. (Memoir: No. 78). (Illus., Orig.). 1960. 6.00x (ISBN 0-8137-1078-2). Geol Soc.
Maury, C. J. Recent Mollusks Gulf Coast. 1971. Repr. 5.00 (ISBN 0-87710-361-5). Paleo Res.
Moore, Ellen J. Fossil Mollusks of Coastal Oregon. LC 71-634653. (Studies in Geology Ser: No. 10). (Illus.). 1971. pap. 3.95 (ISBN 0-87071-068-0). Oreg St U Pr.
Moore, Raymond C., ed. Treatise on Invertebrate Paleontology, Pt. I: Mollusca 1. LC 53-12913. (Illus.). 1960. 19.75x (ISBN 0-8137-3009-0). Geol Soc.
--Treatise on Invertebrate Paleontology, Pt. K: Mollusca 3. LC 53-12913. (Illus.). 1964. 23.75x (ISBN 0-8137-3011-2). Geol Soc.
--Treatise on Invertebrate Paleontology, Pt. N: Mollusca 6 (Bivalvia, Vols. 1-2. LC 53-12913. (Illus.). 1969. 38.25x (ISBN 0-8137-3014-7). Geol Soc.
Morris, J. & Lycett, J. Mollusca of the Great Oolite, 3 Pts. 1850-54. Set. pap. 37.50 (ISBN 0-384-40170-8). Johnson Repr.
Ostergaard, J. M. Fossil Marine Mollusks of Oahu. Repr. of 1928 ed. pap. 5.00 (ISBN 0-527-02157-1). Kraus Repr.
--Recent & Fossil Marine Molluska of Tongatabu. Repr. of 1935 ed. pap. 6.00 (ISBN 0-527-02237-3). Kraus Repr.
Sharpe, D. Mollusca of the Chalk, 4 Pts. Repr. of 1909 ed. Set. pap. 18.50 (ISBN 0-384-55070-3). Johnson Repr.
Wood, S. V. Crag Mollusca, 2 Pts in 4 Nos. Repr. of 1855 ed. Set. pap. 86.50 (ISBN 0-384-69151-X). Johnson Repr.

MOLLY MAGUIRES
Bimba, Anthony. Molly Maguires. LC 75-15046. 1970. 4.95 (ISBN 0-7178-0272-8); pap. 1.95 (ISBN 0-7178-0273-6). Intl Pub Co.
Coleman, J. Walter. The Molly Maguire Riots: Industrial Conflict in the Pennsylvania Coal Region. LC 78-89724. (American Labor, from Conspiracy to Collective Bargaining, Ser. 1). 189p. Repr. of 1936 ed. 14.50 (ISBN 0-405-02112-7). Arno.
Dewees, Francis P. Molly Maguires, the Origin, Growth, & Character of the Organization. 1877. 22.50 (ISBN 0-8337-0848-1). B Franklin.
McCabe, James D. History of the Great Riots. LC 68-56253. (Illus.). Repr. of 1877 ed. 19.50x (ISBN 0-678-00711-X). Kelley.
Pinkerton, Allan. Molly Maguires & the Detectives. LC 72-2092. (American History & Americana Ser., No. 47). 1972. 49.95 (ISBN 0-8383-1289-6). Haskell.

MOLOKAI
Farrow, John. Damien the Leper. 1954. pap. 2.95 (ISBN 0-385-02918-7, D3, Im). Doubleday.
Keesing, Felix M. Hawaiian Homesteading on Molokai. LC 75-35196. Repr. of 1936 ed. 15.50 (ISBN 0-404-14224-9). AMS Pr.
Land Study Bureau, Univ. of Hawaii. Molokai: Present & Potential Land Use. (Land Study Bureau Bulletin: No. 1). (Illus.). 90p. 1960. pap. 5.00x (ISBN 0-8248-0313-2). U Pr of Hawaii.

MOLOKANS
White, Mel. Margaret of Molokai: Biography. 1981. 8.95 (ISBN 0-8499-0294-0). Word Bks.
Young, Pauline V. Pilgrims of Russian-Town: The Community of Spiritual Christian Jumpers in America. LC 66-27375. (Illus.). 1967. Repr. of 1932 ed. 9.00 (ISBN 0-8462-1001-0). Russell.

MOLTEN METALS
see Liquid Metals

MOLTEN SALTS
see Fused Salts

MOLTKE, HELMUTH JOHANNES LUDWIG VON, COUNT, 1848-1916
Morris, William O. Moltke: A Biographical & Critical Study. LC 68-25254. (World History Ser., No. 48). 1969. Repr. of 1894 ed. lib. bdg. 37.95 (ISBN 0-8383-0222-X). Haskell.
Whitton, F. E. Moltke. LC 72-7115. (Select Bibliographies Reprint Ser.). 1972. Repr. of 1921 ed. 20.00 (ISBN 0-8369-6958-8). Arno.

MOLUCCAS
Barraud, Cecile. Tanebar-Evav. LC 78-56176. (Atelier D'anthropologie Sociale). (Illus.). 1980. 37.50 (ISBN 0-521-22386-5). Cambridge U Pr.

MOLYBDENUM
Boschke, F. L., ed. Aspects of Molybdenum & Related Chemistry. LC 78-13469. (Topics in Current Chemistry: Vol. 76). (Illus.). 1979. 43.20 (ISBN 0-387-08986-1). Springer-Verlag.
Chappell, Willard & Peterson, Kathy. Molybdenum in the Environment, Vol. 2: The Geochemistry, Cycling, & Industrial Uses of Molybdenum. 1977. 57.50 (ISBN 0-8247-6495-1). Dekker.
Chappell, Williard R. & Paterson, Kathy K. Molybdenum in the Environment, Vol. 1: The Biology of Molybdenum. 1976. 42.50 (ISBN 0-8247-6405-6). Dekker.
Elwell, W. T. & Wood, D. F. Analytical Chemistry of Molybdenum & Tungsten. 292p. 1971. text ed. 55.00 (ISBN 0-08-016673-3). Pergamon.
Molybdenum Resources Guidebook. 1980. 89.00 (ISBN 0-686-31233-3). Minobras.
Newton, William E. & Otsuka, Sei, eds. Molybdenum Chemistry of Biological Significance. 435p. 1980. 39.50 (ISBN 0-306-40352-8, Plenum Pr). Plenum Pub.
Sutulor, Alexander, ed. International Molybdenum Encyclopedia, 3 vols. Incl. Vol. 1. Resources & Production. 402p. 1978 (ISBN 0-87930-116-3); Vol. 2. Metallurgy & Processing. 375p. 1979 (ISBN 0-87930-117-1); Vol. 3. Products, Uses & Trade. 341p. 1980. (Illus.). Set. text ed. 330.00 (ISBN 0-87930-118-X). Miller Freeman.

MOLYBDENUM ALLOYS
see also Chromium-Molybdenum Steel
Coughlan, Michael P. Molybdenum & Molybdenum-Containing Enzymes. (Illus.). 1980. 94.00 (ISBN 0-08-024398-3). Pergamon.

MOMBASA
Freeman-Grenville, G. S. The Mombasa Rising Against the Portuguese, Sixteen Thirty-One: From Sworn Evidence. (British Academy-Fontes Historiae Africanae). (Illus.). 224p. 98.00x (ISBN 0-19-725992-8). Oxford U Pr.
Mombasa: The Official Handbook. LC 79-981864. (Illus.). 168p. 1971. pap. 5.00x (ISBN 0-902952-03-X). Intl Pubns Serv.

MOMENT OF FORCE
see Torque

MOMENT SPACES
Ahiezer, N. I. & Krein, M. G. Some Questions in the Theory of Moments. LC 63-22077. (Translations of Mathematical Monographs: Vol. 2). 1974. Repr. of 1962 ed. 25.60 (ISBN 0-8218-1552-0, MMONO-2). Am Math.
Karlin, Samuel & Shapley, L. S. Geometry of Moment Spaces. LC 52-42839. (Memoirs: No. 12). 1972. pap. 9.60 (ISBN 0-8218-1212-2, MEMO-12). Am Math.

MOMENTS OF INERTIA
see also Mass (Physics)

MON-KHMER LANGUAGES
see also Indochinese Languages; Khmer Language
Gregerson, Kenneth & Thomas, David, eds. Mon-Khmer Studies V. 1976. pap. 7.00 (ISBN 0-88312-788-1); microfiche 2.20 (ISBN 0-88312-358-4). Summer Inst Ling.
Jenner, Philip N., ed. Mon-Khmer Studies IX. 650p. 1980. write for info. (ISBN 0-8248-0727-8). U Pr of Hawaii.
Thomas, David D. Chrau Grammar. LC 77-127332. (Oceanic Linguistics Special Publications: No. 7). (Orig.). 1971. pap. 6.00x (ISBN 0-87022-788-2). U Pr of Hawaii.

MON LANGUAGE
see also Mon-Khmer Languages

MONACHISM
see Monasticism and Religious Orders

MONACO
De Vos, Raymond. History of the Monies Medals & Tokens of Monaco. 1978. write for info. (ISBN 0-685-51123-5); lib. bdg. 80.00x (ISBN 0-685-51124-3). S J Durst.
Jackson, Stanley. Inside Monte Carlo. LC 75-11814. (Illus.). 286p. 1975. 35.00x (ISBN 0-8128-1827-X). Stein & Day.

MONADOLOGY
see also Microcosm and Macrocosm; Pluralism
Leibniz, Gottfried. Monadology & Other Philosophical Essays. Schrecker, Paul & Schrecker, Anne, trs. LC 65-26531. (Orig.). 1965. pap. 4.95 (ISBN 0-672-60426-4, LLA188). Bobbs.
Leibniz, Gottfried W. La Monadologie. 245p. 1981. Repr. of 1881 ed. lib. bdg. 100.00 (ISBN 0-8287-1478-9). Clearwater Pub.

MONARCH BUTTERFLY
Thompson, Susan. Diary of a Monarch Butterfly. LC 75-1793. (Illus.). (gr. k-3). 1976. 6.50 (ISBN 0-8027-6267-0, Dist. by Walker & Co). Magic Circle Pr.

MONARCHS
see Kings and Rulers

MONARCHY
see also Democracy; Despotism; Divine Right of Kings; Emperors; Ministerial Responsibility; Prerogative, Royal; Sovereignty
Allen, John C. Inquiry into the Rise & Growth of the Royal Prerogative in England. new ed. 1962. Repr. of 1849 ed. 22.50 (ISBN 0-8337-0042-1). B Franklin.
Aquinas, St. Thomas. On Kingship. Phelan, Gerald B., tr. LC 78-14098. 1979. Repr. of 1949 ed. 15.00 (ISBN 0-88355-772-X). Hyperion Conn.
Dante, Alighieri. Monarchy, & Three Political Letters. Nicholl, D. & Hardie, C., trs. LC 78-20461. 1980. Repr. of 1947 ed. text ed. 15.00 (ISBN 0-88355-840-8). Hyperion Conn.
Dunbar, Louise B. A Study of "Monarchical" Tendencies in the United States from 1776 to 1801. LC 23-4276. (Illinois Studies in the Social Sciences: Vol. 10). 1970. Repr. of 1923 ed. 9.50 (ISBN 0-384-13295-2). Johnson Repr.
--Study of Monarchical Tendencies in the United States from 1776 to 1801. LC 75-131693. 1970. Repr. of 1922 ed. 12.00 (ISBN 0-403-00580-9). Scholarly.
Ferrero, Guglielmo. Peace & War. facs. ed. Pritchard, B., tr. LC 69-18927. (Essay Index Reprint Ser). 1933. 16.00 (ISBN 0-8369-0041-3). Arno.
Franklin, J. H. John Locke & the Theory of Sovereignty. LC 77-80833. (Studies in the History & Theory of Politics). 1978. 19.95 (ISBN 0-521-21758-X). Cambridge U Pr.
Lacey, Robert. Majesty: Elizabeth II & the House of Windsor. LC 76-27424. 1977. 12.95 (ISBN 0-15-155684-9). HarBraceJ.
Merbury, Charles. A Briefe Discourse of Royall Monarchie, Wherunto Is Added a Collection of Italian Proverbes, Etc. LC 70-38209. (English Experience Ser.: No. 474). 94p. 1972. Repr. of 1581 ed. 14.00 (ISBN 90-221-0474-5). Walter J Johnson.
Muret, Charlotte T. French Royalist Doctrines Since the Revolution. LC 72-8904. x, 326p. 1971. Repr. of 1933 ed. lib. bdg. 15.50x (ISBN 0-374-96025-9). Octagon.
Myers, Henry A. & Wolfram, Herwig. Medieval Kingship. 520p. 1981. text ed. 25.95x (ISBN 0-88229-633-7); pap. text ed. 13.95x (ISBN 0-88229-782-1). Nelson-Hall.
Paine, Thomas. Common Sense. (Classic Ser.). 1976. pap. 1.95 (ISBN 0-14-040032-X, Pelican). Penguin.
Rowen, Herbert H. The King's State: Proprietary Dynasticism in Early Modern France. 256p. 1980. 19.50 (ISBN 0-8135-0893-2). Rutgers U Pr.
Smith, Edward O., Jr. Crown & Commonwealth: A Study in the Official Elizabethan Doctrine of the Prince. LC 76-24258. (Transactions Ser.: Vol. 66, Pt. 8). 1976. pap. 6.00 (ISBN 0-87169-668-1). Am Philos.
Thompson, J. A. & Mejia, Arthur. Modern British Monarchy. LC 71-157104. 1971. pap. text ed. 6.95 (ISBN 0-312-53690-9). St Martin.
Yates, Frances A. Astraea: The Imperial Theme in the Sixteenth Century. (Illus.). 1975. 18.95 (ISBN 0-7100-7971-0). Routledge & Kegan.
Ziegler, Philip. Crown & People. LC 78-5397. (Illus.). 1978. 10.00 (ISBN 0-394-42124-8). Knopf.

MONASTERIES
see also Abbeys; Convents and Nunneries; Monasticism and Religious Orders; Priories; Secularization
Beckford, William. Recollections of an Excursion to the Monasteries of Alcobaca & Batalha. 24.00 (ISBN 0-87556-541-7). Saifer.
Braunfels, Wolfgang. Monasteries of Western Europe: The Architecture of the Orders. LC 73-2472. (Illus.). 263p. 1980. 35.00x (ISBN 0-691-03896-1); pap. 15.00x (ISBN 0-691-00313-0). Princeton U Pr.
Brooke, Christopher. The Monastic World. (Illus.). 1978. 49.00 (ISBN 0-236-31059-3, Pub. by Paul Elek). Merrimack Bk Serv.
Butler, Lionel & Given-Wilson, Chris. Medieval Monasteries of Great Britain. (Illus.). 416p. 1980. 19.95 (ISBN 0-7181-1614-3, Pub. by Michael Joseph). Merrimack Bk Serv.
Chavrukov, Georgy. Bulgarian Monasteries: Monuments of History, Culture & Art. 1981. 80.00x (ISBN 0-569-08507-1, Pub. by Collet's). State Mutual Bk.
Cheney, Christopher R. Episcopal Visitation of Monasteries in the Twelfth Century. rev. ed. 224p. 1981. lib. bdg. 15.00x (ISBN 0-87991-638-9). Porcupine Pr.
De Montrond, M. Dictionnaire des Abbayes et Monasteres ou Histoire Des Establissements Religieux. Migne, J. P., ed. (Troisieme et Derniere Encyclopedie Theologique Ser.: Vol. 16). 614p. (Fr.). Date not set. Repr. of 1856 ed. lib. bdg. 81.00x (ISBN 0-89241-299-2). Caratzas Bros.
Dickinson, John C. Monastic Life in Medieval England. LC 78-25804. (Illus.). 1979. Repr. of 1961 ed. lib. bdg. 18.75x (ISBN 0-313-20774-7, DIML). Greenwood.
Forsyth, George H. & Weitzmann, Kurt. The Monastery of Saint Catherine at Mount Sinai: The Church & Fortress of Justinian: Plates. LC 68-29257. (Illus.). 236p. 1973. 45.00 (ISBN 0-472-33000-4). U of Mich Pr.
Haigh, C. The Last Days of the Lancashire Monasteries & the Pilgrimage of Grace. 182p. 1969. 33.00x (ISBN 0-7190-1150-7, Pub. by Manchester U Pr England). State Mutual Bk.
Kelly, J. Thomas. Thorns on the Tudor Rose: Monks, Rogues, Vagabonds, & Sturdy Beggars. LC 76-58547. 1977. 3.00x (ISBN 0-87805-029-9). U Pr of Miss.
Leroy, Jules. Monks & Monasteries of the Near East. (Illus.). 1963. 6.75x (ISBN 0-8426-1353-6). Verry.
Libackyj, Anfir. The Ancient Monasteries of Kiev Rus. 1978. 5.95 (ISBN 0-533-02897-3). Vantage.
Little, Bryan. Abbeys & Priories of England & Wales. LC 79-213. (Illus.). 1979. text ed. 24.50x (ISBN 0-8419-0485-5). Holmes & Meier.
Matthew, Donald. The Norman Monasteries & Their English Possessions. LC 78-26293. (Oxford Historical Ser.). 1979. Repr. of 1962 ed. lib. bdg. 18.75x (ISBN 0-313-20847-6, MANM). Greenwood.
Midmer, Roy. English Mediaeval Monsteries, Ten Hundred and Sixty-Six to Fifteen Forty. LC 79-53097. 352p. 1980. 17.50 (ISBN 0-8203-0488-3). U of Ga Pr.
Morrison, Barrie M. Lalmai, a Cultural Center of Early Bengal: An Archaeological Report & Historical Analysis. LC 74-9892. (Publications on Asia of the School of International Studies: No. 24). (Illus.). 160p. 1974. 11.50 (ISBN 0-295-95342-X). U of Wash Pr.
Puhalo, Lev. Kiev Caves Paterikon: A Hagiography of the Kiev Caves Monastery. 1980. pap. 7.50 (ISBN 0-913026-80-8). St Nectarios.
Rosanow, Gora Z. Cultural Heritage of Jasna Gora. (Illus.). 1977. 13.00 (ISBN 0-912728-44-2). Newbury Bks.
Scott, Sir Walter. Monastery. 1969. 10.95x (ISBN 0-460-00136-1, Evman). Biblio Dist.
Sedgwick, Henry D. Pro Vita Monastia. 1923. 20.00 (ISBN 0-8414-8137-7). Folcroft.
Thompson, A. Hamilton. English Monasteries. LC 78-3738. 1974. Repr. of 1913 ed. lib. bdg. 12.50 (ISBN 0-8414-8646-8). Folcroft.
Unstead, R. J., ed. Monasteries. (Junior Reference Ser). (Illus.). (gr. 6-9). 1961. 7.95 (ISBN 0-7136-1043-3). Dufour.
White, L. T., Jr. Latin Monasticism in Norman Sicily. 1967. Repr. of 1938 ed. 9.00 (ISBN 0-910956-12-X). Medieval Acad.
Zouche, Robert C. Visits to Monasteries in the Levant. LC 80-2200. Repr. of 1916 ed. 45.00 (ISBN 0-404-18989-X). AMS Pr.

MONASTIC AND RELIGIOUS LIFE
see also Asceticism; Celibacy; Hermits; Perfection (Catholic); Spiritual Direction; Superiors, Religious; Vows
Alberione, James. Christ, Model & Reward of Religious. 1964. 3.25 (ISBN 0-8198-0023-6). Dghtrs St Paul.
Bale, John. The First Two Partes of the Acts or Unchaste Examples of the Englyshe Votaryes. LC 79-84086. (English Experience Ser.: No. 906). 540p. 1979. Repr. of 1560 ed. lib. bdg. 40.00 (ISBN 90-221-0906-2). Walter J Johnson.
Balla, Mother Ignatius. Our Continuing Yes. 1973. pap. 2.00 (ISBN 0-8198-0243-3). Dghtrs St Paul.
Beyer, Jean. Religious Life or Secular Institute. 1970. pap. 2.75 (ISBN 0-8294-0319-1, Pub. by Gregorian U Pr). Loyola.
Boyd, Anne. Life in a Fifteenth Century Monastery. LC 76-22452. (Cambridge Topic Bks). (Illus.). (gr. 5-10). 1978. PLB 5.95 (ISBN 0-8225-1208-4). Lerner Pubns.
Brooke, Christopher. The Monastic World. (Illus.). 1978. 49.00 (ISBN 0-236-31059-3, Pub. by Paul Elek). Merrimack Bk Serv.
Clarke, Tom. New Pentecost or New Passion? The Direction of Religious Life Today. LC 73-84049. 1974. pap. 3.95 (ISBN 0-8091-1792-4). Paulist Pr.
Cushing, Richard J. Meditations for Religious. 1959. 3.00 (ISBN 0-8198-0102-X). Dghtrs St Paul.

Cussianovich, Alejandro. Religious Life & the Poor: Liberation Theology Perspectives. Drury, John, tr. from Sp. LC 78-16740. 1979. pap. 6.95 (ISBN 0-88344-429-1). Orbis Bks.
Daughters Of St. Paul. Religious Life in the Light of Vatican 2. (Orig.). 4.00 (ISBN 0-8198-0132-1). Dghtrs St Paul.
Dondero, John P. & Frary, Thomas D. New Pressures, New Responses in Religious Life. LC 76-26585. 1979. pap. 5.95 (ISBN 0-8189-0332-5). Alba.
Doyle, Stephen C. Covenant Renewal in Religious Life: Biblical Reflections. 140p. 1976. 6.95 (ISBN 0-8199-0585-2). Franciscan Herald.
Edwards, Bruce & Fudge, Edward. A Journey Toward Jesus. 1.50 (ISBN 0-686-12687-4). E Fudge.
Fudge, Edward. Christianity Without Ulcers. pap. 3.50 (ISBN 0-686-12686-6). E Fudge.
--The Church That Pleases God. 1.50 (ISBN 0-686-12690-4). E Fudge.
Gambari, Elio. Updating of Religious Formation. LC 75-98171. 1969. pap. 2.00 (ISBN 0-8198-0168-2). Dghtrs St Paul.
Gasquet, Cardinal. Monastic Life in the Middle Ages. 59.95 (ISBN 0-8490-0657-0). Gordon Pr.
Grandaur, Georg, ed. & tr. Leben Des Abtes Eigil Von Fulda und der Aebtissin Hathumoda Von Gandersheim Nebst der Uebertragung Des Hl. Liborius und Des Hl. Vitus. (Ger). pap. 8.00 (ISBN 0-384-19640-3). Johnson Repr.
Jane, L. C., ed. The Chronicle of Jocelin of Brakeland, Monk of St. Edmundsbury: A Picture of Monastic & Social Life in the 12th Century. 1977. Repr. of 1907 ed. lib. bdg. 20.00 (ISBN 0-8414-5269-5). Folcroft.
Jenkins, Claude. The Monastic Chronicler & the Early School of St. Albans: A Lecture. LC 74-19113. 1974. Repr. of 1922 ed. lib. bdg. 20.00 (ISBN 0-8414-5320-9). Folcroft.
Kiesling, Christopher. Celibacy, Prayer & Friendship: A Making-Sense-Out-of-Life Approach. LC 77-25084. 1978. pap. 5.95 (ISBN 0-8189-0365-1). Alba.
Knowles, D. Christian Monasticism. (World University Library). (Illus., Orig.). 1969. 4.95 (ISBN 0-07-035192-9, SP); pap. 3.95 (ISBN 0-07-035191-0). McGraw.
Lackener, Bede K. The Eleventh-Century Background of Citeaux. LC 70-152484. (Cistercian Studies: No. 8). xxii, 305p. 1972. 7.50 (ISBN 0-87907-808-1). Cistercian Pubns.
Lange, Joseph & Cushing, Anthony. Called to Service. LC 75-41813. (Living Christian Community Ser). 180p. 1976. pap. 4.95 (ISBN 0-8091-1921-8). Paulist Pr.
Leclercq, Jean. Love of Learning & Desire for God: A Study of Monastic Culture. rev. ed. LC 60-53004. 1977. pap. 8.00 (ISBN 0-8232-0406-5). Fordham.
McBrien, Richard P. Who Is a Catholic? 4.95 (ISBN 0-87193-090-0). Dimension Bks.
McDonnell, Thomas P., ed. A Thomas Merton Reader. LC 74-29. 600p. 1974. pap. 4.95 (ISBN 0-385-03292-7, Im). Doubleday.
McNamee, Fintan, ed. Helping Disturbed Religious. (Symthesis Ser). pap. 0.65 (ISBN 0-8199-0393-0, L38268). Franciscan Herald.
Maloney, George. Inscape: God at the Heart of the Matter. pap. 4.95 (ISBN 0-87193-095-1). Dimension Bks.
Manning, Brennan. The Wisdom of Accepted Tenderness. casebound 5.95 (ISBN 0-87193-091-9). Dimension Bks.
Martin, Francis P. Hung by the Tongue. 1976. 1.50 (ISBN 0-89858-014-5). Fill the Gap.
Matura, Thadee. Celibacy & Community. Flood, David, tr. 1968. 3.95 (ISBN 0-8199-0118-0, L38095). Franciscan Herald.
Meissner, William W. Group Dynamics in the Religious Life. 1965. 6.95x (ISBN 0-268-00115-4). U of Notre Dame Pr.
Merton, Thomas. The Silent Life. 178p. 1975. pap. 4.50 (ISBN 0-374-51281-7). FS&G.
Mohler, James A. Heresy of Monasticism. LC 76-148683. 1971. 5.95 (ISBN 0-8189-0183-7). Alba.
Nouwen, Henri J. M. The Genesee Diary: Report from a Trappist Monastery. LC 75-38169. 192p. 1976. 9.95 (ISBN 0-385-11368-4). Doubleday.
O'Reilly, James. Lay & Religious States of Life. LC 76-43048. 1977. pap. text ed. 0.65 (ISBN 0-685-81233-2). Franciscan Herald.
Orsy, Ladislas M. Open to the Spirit. pap. 5.95 (ISBN 0-87193-086-2). Dimension Bks.
Rousseau, Phillip. Ascetics, Authority, & the Church in the Age of Jerome & Cassian. (Historical Monographs). 1978. 36.00x (ISBN 0-19-821870-2). Oxford U Pr.
Salmon, Pierre. The Abbot in Monastic Tradition. Lavoie, Claire, tr. from Fr. LC 78-158955. (Cistercian Studies: No. 14). 148p. 1972. 9.95 (ISBN 0-87907-814-6). Cistercian Pubns.
Schellenberger, Bernadin. Nomad of the Spirit: Reflections of a Young Monastic. 112p. 1981. 8.95 (ISBN 0-8245-0075-X). Crossroad NY.
Schlink, Basilea. Let Me Stand at Your Side. 2.75 (ISBN 3-872-09614-1). Evang Sisterhood Mary.
Schlitzer, Albert L. Apostolic Dimensions of the Religious Life. (Religious Life in the Modern World Ser.: Vol. 7). (Orig.). 1966. pap. 1.95x (ISBN 0-268-00008-5). U of Notre Dame Pr.
Theophane The Monk. Tales of a Magic Monastery. LC 81-9765. (Illus.). 96p. 1981. pap. 6.95 (ISBN 0-8245-0085-7). Crossroad NY.
Unstead, R. J., ed. Monasteries. (Junior Reference Ser). (Illus.). (gr. 6-9). 1961. 7.95 (ISBN 0-7136-1043-3). Dufour.
Van Der Looy, H. Rule for a New Brother. 1976. pap. 2.25 (ISBN 0-87243-065-0). Templegate.
Van De Wetering, Janwillem. The Empty Mirror: Experiences in a Japanese Zen Monastery. 1974. 7.95 (ISBN 0-395-18282-4). HM.
--A Glimpse of Nothingness: Experiences in an American Zen Commune. LC 74-31078. 192p. 1975. 8.95 (ISBN 0-395-20442-9). HM.
Van Kaam, Adrian. On Being Involved. 2.95 (ISBN 0-87193-039-0). Dimension Bks.
--Personality Fulfillment in the Religious Life. 5.95 (ISBN 0-87193-042-0). Dimension Bks.
--The Vowed Life. 9.95 (ISBN 0-87193-040-4). Dimension Bks.
Vatican Council Two. Decree on the Renewal of Religious Life. Baum, Gregory, ed. LC 66-19150. 96p. 1966. pap. 1.95 (ISBN 0-8091-1540-9). Paulist Pr.
Vineeth, V. F. Call to Integration: A New Theology of Religious Life. LC 81-5588. 144p. 1981. write for info. Crossroad NY.
Weber, Nellie B. Dew Drops. 3.95 (ISBN 0-686-12668-8, BE-175). Evangel Indiana.
Wildmon, Donald E. Nuggets of Gold. 4.95 (ISBN 0-686-12696-3). Five Star Pubs.
--Pebbles in the Sand. 4.95 (ISBN 0-686-12698-X). Five Star Pubs.
William Of St. Tierry. The Nature & Dignity of Love. Elder, E. R., ed. Davis, Thomas X., tr. from Lat. (Cistercian Fathers Ser.: No. 30). Orig. Title: De natura et dignitate amoris. 1981. 13.95 (ISBN 0-87907-330-6). Cistercian Pubns.
Willis, Elbert. Who Is Responsible for Sickness. 1978. 1.00 (ISBN 0-89858-010-2). Fill the Gap.
Wolter, Allan B. Life in God's Love. 1958. pap. 1.75 (ISBN 0-8199-0059-1, L38375). Franciscan Herald.

MONASTIC AND RELIGIOUS LIFE OF WOMEN

see also Asceticism; Celibacy; Monasticism and Religious Orders for Women; Nuns; Perfection (Catholic); Vows

Alcock, John. Spousage of a Virgin to Christ. LC 74-80158. (English Experience Ser.: No. 638). (Illus.). 19p. 1974. Repr. of 1496 ed. 3.50 (ISBN 90-221-0638-1). Walter J Johnson.
Daughters of St Paul. Blessed Kateri Takakwitha: Mohawk Maiden. 1980. 3.75 (ISBN 0-8198-1100-9); pap. 2.25 (ISBN 0-8198-1101-7). Dghtrs St Paul.
Dubay, Thomas. Dawn of a Consecration. 1964. 4.00 (ISBN 0-8198-0034-1). Dghtrs St Paul.
Griffin, Mary. The Courage to Choose: An American Nun's Story. 1975. 7.95 (ISBN 0-316-32864-2). Little.
Horstmann, C., ed. Prose Lives of Women Saints of Our Contrie of England. (EETS, OS Ser.: No.86). Repr. of 1886 ed. 14.00 (ISBN 0-527-00082-5). Kraus Repr.
MacConnell, Margaret. Open Then the Door. 1968. 5.95 (ISBN 0-685-20609-2). Transatlantic.
Mary Francis, Sr. Right to Be Merry. LC 73-6850. 1973. pap. 1.95 (ISBN 0-8199-0506-2). Franciscan Herald.
Maureen, Mary. Your Calling As a Nun: A Sense of Mission. LC 66-10997. (Careers in Depth Ser). (gr. 7 up). 1967. PLB 5.97 (ISBN 0-8239-0059-2). Rosen Pr.
Schlitzer, Albert L. Apostolic Dimensions of the Religious Life. (Religious Life in the Modern World Ser.: Vol. 7). (Orig.). 1966. pap. 1.95x (ISBN 0-268-00008-5). U of Notre Dame Pr.
Schlitzer, Albert L., ed. Psychological Dimensions of the Religious Life. (Religious Life in the Modern World Ser.: Vol. 6). (Orig.). 1966. pap. 1.95x (ISBN 0-268-00224-X). U of Notre Dame Pr.

MONASTIC POVERTY

see Monasticism and Religious Orders–Common Life

MONASTIC VOCATION

see Vocation (In Religious Orders, Congregations, etc.)

MONASTICISM AND RELIGIOUS ORDERS

see also Beghards and Beguines; Benedictines; Cistercians; Cluniacs; Dominicans; Franciscans; Friars; Hospitalers; Jesuits; Monasteries; Monastic and Religious Life; Novitiate; Recollets (Franciscan); Retreats; Superiors, Religious; Trappists; Vocation (In Religious Orders, Congregations, etc.); Vows

Assenmacher, Hugh. A Place Called Subiaco: A History of the Benedictine Monks in Arkansas. LC 77-78877. 486p. 1977. 12.95 (ISBN 0-914546-16-3). Rose Pub.
Bharati, Agahananda. The Ochre Robe: An Autobiography. 2nd ed. 300p. 1980. 14.95 (ISBN 0-915520-40-0); pap. 7.95 (ISBN 0-915520-28-1). Ross-Erikson.
Bland, C. C., tr. The Autobiography of Guibert: Abbot of Nogent-Sous-Coucy. 1979. Repr. of 1925 ed. lib. bdg. 30.00 (ISBN 0-8482-0140-X). Norwood Edns.
Brooke, Odo. Studies in Monastic Theology. (Cistercian Studies Ser.: No. 37). 1980. 8.95 (ISBN 0-87907-837-5). Cistercian Pubns.
Cabaniss, Allen, tr. from Lat. The Emperor's Monk: Contemporary Life of Benedict of Aniane by Ardo. 120p. 1981. 7.95 (ISBN 0-686-31782-3, Pub. by Stockwell England). Cistercian Pubns.
Cary-Elwes, Columbia. Law, Liberty & Love. 1950. 5.00 (ISBN 0-8159-6104-9). Devin.
Chapman, John. Saint Benedict & the Sixth Century. LC 79-109719. 239p. 1972. Repr. of 1929 ed. lib. bdg. 15.00x (ISBN 0-8371-4209-1, CHSB). Greenwood.
Corbett, Julian. Monk. facsimile ed. LC 72-154148. (Select Bibliographies Reprint Ser). Repr. of 1889 ed. 16.00 (ISBN 0-8369-5764-4). Arno.
English Benedictine Congregation Members & Rees, Daniel. Consider Your Call. (Cistercian Studies Ser.: No. 20). 447p. 1980. 17.95 (ISBN 0-87907-820-0). Cistercian Pubns.
Erasmus, Desiderius. De Contemptu Mundi. Paynell, Thomas, tr. LC 67-18715. 1967. 18.00x (ISBN 0-8201-1016-7). Schol Facsimiles.
Guigo II. Guigo II: The Ladder of Monks & Twelve Meditations. Colledge, Edmund & Walsh, James, trs. (Cistercian Studies: No. 48). 1981. pap. write for info. (ISBN 0-87907-748-4). Cistercian Pubns.
Herold, Sr. Duchesne. New Life: Preparation of Religious for Retirement. LC 73-76987. 168p. 1973. pap. 5.50 (ISBN 0-87125-007-1). Cath Health.
Hinnebusch, William A. History of the Dominican Order: Intellectual & Cultural Life to 1500, Vol. 2. new ed. LC 65-17977. 461p. 1973. 9.75 (ISBN 0-8189-0266-3). Alba.
Johnson, Penelope. Prayer, Patronage, & Power: The Abbey of la Trinite, Vendome, 1032-1187. (Illus.). 224p. 1981. text ed. 17.50x (ISBN 0-8147-4162-2). NYU Pr.
Kingsley, Rose G. The Order of St. John of Jerusalem: Past & Present. LC 76-29842. Repr. of 1918 ed. 20.00 (ISBN 0-404-15422-0). AMS Pr.
Knowles, D. Christian Monasticism. (World University Library). (Illus., Orig.). 1969. 4.95 (ISBN 0-07-035192-9, SP); pap. 3.95 (ISBN 0-07-035191-0). McGraw.
Kraus, Dorothy & Kraus, Henry. The Hidden World of the Misericords. LC 75-10869. (Illus.). 192p. 1975. 20.00 (ISBN 0-8076-0804-1). Braziller.
Leclercq, Jean. Aspects of Monasticism. (Cistercian Studies: No. 7). 1978. pap. 8.95 (ISBN 0-87907-807-3). Cistercian Pubns.
Levy, Howard S. & Yang, R. F. Monks & Nuns in a Sea of Sins. 117p. 1971. pap. 6.00x (ISBN 0-685-27150-1). Paragon.
Miller, David M. & Wertz, Dorothy C. Hindu Monastic Life: The Monks & Monasteries of Bhubaneswar. (Illus.). 320p. 1976. 22.00x (ISBN 0-7735-0190-8); pap. 9.95 (ISBN 0-7735-0247-5). McGill-Queens U Pr.
Moffitt, John, ed. New Charter for Monasticism. 1970. 12.00x (ISBN 0-268-00433-1). U of Notre Dame Pr.
Mohler, James A. Heresy of Monasticism. LC 76-148683. 1971. 5.95 (ISBN 0-8189-0183-7). Alba.
Le Moine et l'Antimoine. (Holbach & His Friends Ser). 64p. (Fr.). 1974. Repr. of 1767 ed. lib. bdg. 20.00x (ISBN 0-8287-1388-X, 1589). Clearwater Pub.
Muller, Max, ed. Sacred Books of China: Text of Taoism, 2 vols. lib. bdg. 250.00 (ISBN 0-87968-298-1). Krishna Pr.
Murphy, Sr. M. Gertrude. Saint Basil & Monasticism. LC 70-144661. Repr. of 1930 ed. 14.75 (ISBN 0-404-04543-X). AMS Pr.
Pennington, M. B., ed. One Yet Two: Monastic Tradition East & West. LC 75-26146. (Cistercian Studies Ser.: No. 29). 1976. 14.95 (ISBN 0-87907-800-6). Cistercian Pubns.
Prebish, Charles S. Buddhist Monastic Discipline: The Sanskrit Pratimoksa Sutras of the Mahasamghikas & Mulasarvastivadins. LC 74-10743. (Institute for Advanced Study of World Religions Ser.). 1975. 13.95x (ISBN 0-271-01171-8). Pa St U Pr.
Sophrony, Archimandrite. The Monk of Mount Athos: Staretz Silouan 1866-1938. LC 61-4333. 124p. 1975. pap. 3.95 (ISBN 0-913836-15-X). St Vladimirs.
Tettemer, John. I Was a Monk. LC 73-89888. pap. 1.25 (ISBN 0-8356-0300-8, Quest). Theos Pub Hse.
Turner, Samuel. Account of an Embassy to the Court of the Teshoo Lama in Tibet. (Bibliotheca Himalayica Ser). 1970. Repr. of 1806 ed. 36.00x (ISBN 0-8426-0481-2). Verry.
Veilleux, Armand, tr. Pachomian Koinonia I: The Life of St. Pachomius. (Cistercian Studies: No. 45). 524p. (Coptic Greek.). 1981. write for info.; pap. write for info. (ISBN 0-87907-945-2). Cistercian Pubns.
Weisgerber, Charles A. Psychological Assessment of Candidates for a Religious Order. LC 77-91649. 1969. pap. 2.95 (ISBN 0-8294-0019-2). Loyola.
White, L. T., Jr. Latin Monasticism in Norman Sicily. 1967. Repr. of 1938 ed. 9.00 (ISBN 0-910956-12-X). Medieval Acad.
Wishart, Alfred W. A History of Monks & Monasteries. 1977. lib. bdg. 59.95 (ISBN 0-8490-1980-X). Gordon Pr.
Zarnecki, George. The Monastic Achievement. (Illus.). 144p. 1972. pap. 3.95 (ISBN 0-07-072735-X, SP). McGraw.

MONASTICISM AND RELIGIOUS ORDERS–BIBLIOGRAPHY

Constable, Giles. Medieval Monasticism: A Select Bibliography. LC 75-42284. 1976. 15.00x (ISBN 0-8020-2200-6); pap. 7.50x (ISBN 0-8020-6280-6). U of Toronto Pr.

MONASTICISM AND RELIGIOUS ORDERS–COMMON LIFE

English Benedictine Congregation Members & Rees, Daniel. Consider Your Call. (Cistercian Studies Ser.: No. 20). 447p. 1980. 17.95 (ISBN 0-87907-820-0). Cistercian Pubns.
Van Corstanje, Auspicius. Covenant with God's Poor. 3.95 (ISBN 0-8199-0014-1). Franciscan Herald.

MONASTICISM AND RELIGIOUS ORDERS–DICTIONARIES

De Montrond, M. Dictionnaire des Abbayes et Monasteres ou Histoire Des Establissements Religieux. Migne, J. P., ed. (Troisieme et Derniere Encyclopedie Theologique Ser.: Vol. 16). 614p. (Fr.). Date not set. Repr. of 1856 ed. lib. bdg. 81.00x (ISBN 0-89241-299-2). Caratzas Bros.
Helyot, P. Dictionnaires des Ordres Religieux ou Historie des Ordres Monastiques, Religieux et Militaires, 4 vols. Migne, J. P., ed. (Encyclopedie Theologique Ser.: Vols. 20-23). 2724p. (Fr.). Date not set. Repr. of 1859 ed. lib. bdg. 347.50x (ISBN 0-89241-239-9). Caratzas Bros.

MONASTICISM AND RELIGIOUS ORDERS–EARLY CHURCH, ca. 30-600

Chadwick, Owen. John Cassian. 2nd ed. 1968. 26.50 (ISBN 0-521-04607-6). Cambridge U Pr.
Palladius. Lauasic History. Budge, E. A., tr. 1977. pap. 3.95 (ISBN 0-686-19350-4). Eastern Orthodox.

MONASTICISM AND RELIGIOUS ORDERS–EAST

Jnanatmananda, Swami. Invitation to Holy Company. Dey, J. N., tr. from Bengali. (Illus.). 1979. pap. 2.25 (ISBN 0-87481-491-X). Vedanta Pr.
Mendelson, E. Michael. Sangha & State in Burma: A Study of Monastic Sectarianism & Leadership. Ferguson, John P., ed. LC 75-13398. (Illus.). 400p. 1975. 32.50x (ISBN 0-8014-0875-X). Cornell U Pr.

MONASTICISM AND RELIGIOUS ORDERS–JUVENILE LITERATURE

Ansley, Delight. Good Ways. rev. ed. LC 59-14674. (Illus.). (gr. 7-11). 1959. 7.95 (ISBN 0-690-33757-4, TYC-J). Har-Row.

MONASTICISM AND RELIGIOUS ORDERS–MIDDLE AGES, 600-1500

Coulton, George G. Ten Medieval Studies. 7.75 (ISBN 0-8446-1132-8). Peter Smith.
Davison, Ellen S. Forerunners of Saint Francis & Other Studies. Richards, Gertrude R., ed. LC 77-85270. Repr. of 1927 ed. 34.50 (ISBN 0-404-16120-0). AMS Pr.
Dickinson, John C. Monastic Life in Medieval England. LC 78-25804. (Illus.). 1979. Repr. of 1961 ed. lib. bdg. 18.75x (ISBN 0-313-20774-7, DIML). Greenwood.
Gasquet, Francis A. Monastic Life in the Middle Ages, 1792-1806. facs. ed. LC 76-137377. (Select Bibliographies Reprint Ser). 1922. 16.00 (ISBN 0-8369-5578-1). Arno.
Hogg, James. Rewyll of Seynt Sauioure: The Syon Additions for the Brethren & the Boke of Sygnes, Vol. 3. (Salzburger Studien Zur Anglistik und Amerikanistik). 1981. pap. text ed. 38.50x (ISBN 0-391-02257-1, Pub. by Salzburg Austria). Humanities.
--The Rewyll of Seynt Sauioure: The Syon Addition for the Sisters, Vol. 4. (Salzburg Zur Anglistik und Amerikanistik). 207p. 1981. pap. text ed. 38.50x (ISBN 0-391-02258-X, Pub. by Salzburg Austria). Humanities.

Jerome, Saint. Vitas Patrum: The Lyff of the Olde Auncyent Fathers Hermytes. Caxton, W., tr. LC 77-7409. (English Experience Ser.: No. 874). 1977. Repr. of 1495 ed. lib. bdg. 99.00 (ISBN 90-221-0874-0). Walter J Johnson.
Montalembert, Charles, pseud. The Monks of the West from St. Benedict to St. Bernard, 6 vols. LC 3-11386. Repr. of 1896 ed. Set. 145.00 (ISBN 0-404-04410-7); 25.00 ea.; Vol. 1. (ISBN 0-404-04411-5); Vol. 2. (ISBN 0-404-04412-3); Vol. 3. (ISBN 0-404-04413-1); Vol. 4. (ISBN 0-404-04414-X); Vol. 5. (ISBN 0-404-04415-8); Vol. 6. (ISBN 0-404-04416-6). AMS Pr.
Zeibig, Hartmann, ed. Urkundenbuch Des Stiftes Klosterneuburg Bis Zum Ende Des Vierzehnten Jahrhunderts. (Ger). Repr. of 1857 ed. pap. 52.00 (ISBN 0-384-29875-3). Johnson Repr.

MONASTICISM AND RELIGIOUS ORDERS–RULES

Ancren Riwle: A Treatise on the Rules & Duties of Monastic Life. 1853. 46.00 (ISBN 0-685-13344-3). Johnson Repr.
Benedict, Saint Rule of Saint Benedict. Gasquet, Cardinal, tr. LC 66-30730. (Medieval Library). (Illus.). 130p. 1966. Repr. of 1926 ed. 15.00x (ISBN 0-8154-0022-5). Cooper Sq.
Eberle, Luke, tr. from Latin. & The Rule of the Master: Regula Magistri. LC 77-3986. (Cistercian Studies Ser: No. 6). 1977. 12.95 (ISBN 0-87907-806-5). Cistercian Pubns.
Flood, David & Matura, Thadee. The Birth of a Movement. LaChance, Paul & Schwartz, Paul, trs. 168p. 1975. 6.95 (ISBN 0-8199-0567-4). Franciscan Herald.
Morton, James, ed. Ancren Riwle, a Treatise on the Rules & Duties of Monastic Life from a Semi-Saxon MS. of the Thirteenth Century. LC 72-158250. (Camden Society, London. Publications, First Series: No. 1). Repr. of 1853 ed. 42.00 (ISBN 0-404-50157-5). AMS Pr.
Morton, James, tr. Nuns' Rule or the Ancren Riwle. LC 66-23314. (Medieval Library). Repr. of 1926 ed. 8.50x (ISBN 0-8154-0155-8). Cooper Sq.
Shepherd, Geoffrey, ed. Ancrene Wisse, Pts. 6 & 7. (Old & Middle English Texts). 116p. 1972. pap. 10.95x (ISBN 0-06-496228-8). B&N.
Tolkien, J. R., ed. Ancrene Wisse: English Text of the Ancrene Riwle. (Early English Text Society Ser.). 1962. 16.95x (ISBN 0-19-722249-8). Oxford U Pr.

MONASTICISM AND RELIGIOUS ORDERS–VOWS

see Vows

MONASTICISM AND RELIGIOUS ORDERS–EGYPT

Pachomius, St. History of the Monks at Tabenna. pap. 1.50 (ISBN 0-686-05644-2). Eastern Orthodox.
Veilleux, Armand. Pachomian Koinonia Third: Instructions, Letters & Other Writings, No. 47. (Cistercian Studies). 1982. price not set; pap. write for info. (ISBN 0-87907-947-9). Cistercian Pubns.
Ward, Benedicta & Russell, Norman, trs. from Gr. The Lives of the Desert Fathers: The Historia Monachorum in Aegypto. (Cistercian Studies: No. 34). 1981. 17.95 (ISBN 0-87907-834-0); pap. 8.95 (ISBN 0-87907-934-7). Cistercian Pubns.

MONASTICISM AND RELIGIOUS ORDERS–FRANCE

Chateaubriand, Rene de & Guyard, Marius Francois. Vie de Rance. 3.95 (ISBN 0-686-54375-0). French & Eur.
Matthew, Donald. The Norman Monasteries & Their English Possessions. LC 78-26293. (Oxford Historical Ser.). 1979. Repr. of 1962 ed. lib. bdg. 18.75x (ISBN 0-313-20847-6, MANM). Greenwood.
Ultee, Maarten. The Abbey of St. Germain des Pres in the Seventeenth Century. LC 81-2265. (Illus.). 224p. 1981. text ed. 20.00x (ISBN 0-300-02562-9). Yale U Pr.

MONASTICISM AND RELIGIOUS ORDERS–GERMANY

Zeibig, Hartmann, ed. Urkundenbuch Des Stiftes Klosterneuburg Bis Zum Ende Des Vierzehnten Jahrhunderts. (Ger). Repr. of 1857 ed. pap. 52.00 (ISBN 0-384-29875-3). Johnson Repr.

MONASTICISM AND RELIGIOUS ORDERS–GREAT BRITAIN

Bedford, William K. The Order or the Hospital of St. John of Jerusalem. LC 76-29831. Repr. of 1902 ed. 25.00 (ISBN 0-404-15412-3). AMS Pr.
Boyd, Anne. The Monks of Durham. LC 74-14438. (Introduction to the History of Mankind Ser). (Illus.). 48p. (gr. 6-11). 1975. text ed. 3.95 (ISBN 0-521-20647-2). Cambridge U Pr.
Dickinson, John C. Monastic Life in Medieval England. LC 78-25804. (Illus.). 1979. Repr. of 1961 ed. lib. bdg. 18.75x (ISBN 0-313-20774-7, DIML). Greenwood.
Fish, Simon. A Supplicacyon for the Beggers. LC 72-5989. (English Experience Ser.: No. 515). 16p. 1973. Repr. of 1529 ed. 6.00 (ISBN 90-221-0515-6). Walter J Johnson.
Gasquet, Francis A. English Monastic Life. LC 76-118470. 1971. Repr. of 1904 ed. 17.50 (ISBN 0-8046-1219-6). Kennikat.
--English Monastic Life. fascimile ed. LC 77-157336. (Select Bibliographies Reprint Ser). Repr. of 1904 ed. 30.00 (ISBN 0-8369-5796-2). Arno.
--Henry the Eighth & the English Monasteries, 2 vols. LC 74-39467. (Select Bibliography Reprint Series). 1972. Repr. of 1888 ed. 51.25 (ISBN 0-8369-9905-3). Arno.
King, Edwin J. The Grand Priory of the Order of the Hospital of St. John of Jerusalem in England: A Short History. LC 76-29826. Repr. of 1924 ed. 20.00 (ISBN 0-404-15420-4). AMS Pr.
Knowles, D., et al, eds. Heads of Religious Houses, England & Wales, 940-1216. LC 79-171676. 336p. 1972. 47.95 (ISBN 0-521-08367-2). Cambridge U Pr.
Knowles, David. Monastic Order in England. 2nd ed. 1963. 67.50 (ISBN 0-521-05479-6). Cambridge U Pr.
--Religious Orders in England. Incl. Vol. 1. The Old Orders. 1948. 47.50 (ISBN 0-521-05480-X); pap. 14.50 (ISBN 0-521-29566-1); Vol. 2. End of the Middle Ages. 1955. 53.50 (ISBN 0-521-05481-8); pap. 15.50 (ISBN 0-521-29567-X). Cambridge U Pr.
Knowles, David & Hadcock, R. Neville. Medieval Religious Houses in England & Wales. 2nd ed. 1972. 29.95x (ISBN 0-312-52780-2). St. Martin.
Legge, Mary D. Anglo-Norman in the Cloisters. LC 79-158505. 1971. Repr. of 1950 ed. 22.00 (ISBN 0-403-01476-X). Scholarly.
Little, Bryan. Abbeys & Priories of England & Wales. LC 79-213. (Illus.). 1979. text ed. 24.50x (ISBN 0-8419-0485-5). Holmes & Meier.
Matthew, Donald. The Norman Monasteries & Their English Possessions. LC 78-26293. (Oxford Historical Ser.). 1979. Repr. of 1962 ed. lib. bdg. 18.75x (ISBN 0-313-20847-6, MANM). Greenwood.
Milliken, E. K. English Monasticism, Yesterday & Today. 1967. 4.50x (ISBN 0-8426-1386-2). Verry.
Rees, William. A History of the Order of St. John of Jerusalem in Wales & on the Welsh Border: Including an Account of the Templars. LC 76-29839. (Illus.). Repr. of 1947 ed. 18.50 (ISBN 0-404-15427-1). AMS Pr.
Wright, Thomas. Three Chapters of Letters Relating to the Suppression of Monasteries. 31.00 (ISBN 0-384-69545-0). Johnson Repr.
Wright, Thomas, ed. Three Chapters of Letters Relating to the Suppression of Monasteries. (Camden Society, London. Publications First Ser.: No. 26). Repr. of 1843 ed. 28.00 (ISBN 0-404-50126-5). AMS Pr.
Youings, Joyce. The Dissolution of the Monasteries. (Historical Problems: Studies & Documents). 1971. pap. text ed. 9.95x (ISBN 0-04-942090-9). Allen Unwin.

MONASTICISM AND RELIGIOUS ORDERS–IRELAND

Bradshaw, B. The Dissolution of the Religious Orders in Ireland Under Henry Eighth. LC 73-83104. (Illus.). 248p. 1974. 41.50 (ISBN 0-521-20342-2). Cambridge U Pr.
Hanson, William G. The Early Monastic Schools of Ireland, Their Missionaries, Saints & Scholars. 1927. 18.00 (ISBN 0-8337-4580-8). B Franklin.
Monastic Rules of Ireland. pap. 1.50 (ISBN 0-686-05654-X). Eastern Orthodox.

MONASTICISM AND RELIGIOUS ORDERS–JAPAN

Berlin, Charles. Studies in Jewish Bibliography, History & Literature: In Honor of I. Edward Kiev. 1971. 50.00x (ISBN 0-87068-143-5). Ktav.
Van de Wetering, Janwillem. The Empty Mirror: Experiences in a Japanese Monastery. 1981. pap. 2.50 (ISBN 0-671-41610-3). WSP.

MONASTICISM AND RELIGIOUS ORDERS–NEAR EAST

Leroy, Jules. Monks & Monasteries of the Near East. (Illus.). 1963. 6.75x (ISBN 0-8426-1353-6). Verry.

MONASTICISM AND RELIGIOUS ORDERS, BUDDHIST

see also Koan

Bunnag, Jane. Buddhist Monk, Buddhist Layman: A Study of Urban Monastic Organisation in Central Thailand. LC 72-86420. (Cambridge Studies in Social Anthropology: No. 6). (Illus.). 230p. 1973. 24.95 (ISBN 0-521-08591-8). Cambridge U Pr.
De Visser, Marinus W., pseud. The Arhats in China & Japan. LC 78-70136. Repr. of 1923 ed. 27.50 (ISBN 0-404-17406-X). AMS Pr.
Dutt, Nalinaksha. Early Monastic Buddhism. 1981. Repr. of 1971 ed. 12.00x (ISBN 0-8364-0729-6, Pub. by Mukhopadhyay). South Asia Bks.
Kakhun. Lives of Eminent Korean Monks: The Haedong Kosung Chon. Lee, Peter H., tr. LC 69-18037. (Harvard-Yenching Institute Studies: No. 25). 1969. pap. text ed. 7.00x (ISBN 0-674-53662-2). Harvard U Pr.
Prebish, Charles S. Buddhist Monastic Discipline: The Sanskrit Pratimoksa Sutras of the Mahasamghikas & Mulasarvastivadins. LC 74-10743. (Institute for Advanced Study of World Religions Ser.). 1975. 13.95x (ISBN 0-271-01171-8). Pa St U Pr.
Suzuki, Daisetz T. Introduction to Zen Buddhism. 1964. pap. 2.95 (ISBN 0-394-17474-7, B341, BC). Grove.
--Manual of Zen Buddhism. (Orig.). 1960. pap. 3.95 (ISBN 0-394-17224-8, E231, Ever). Grove.
Tanahashi, Kazuaki. Monk Enku: Life & Work. LC 81-50969. (Illus.). 176p. (Orig.). 1981. pap. 7.95 (ISBN 0-394-74882-4). Shambhala Pubns.
Van de Wetering, Janwillem. The Empty Mirror: Experiences in a Japanese Monastery. 1981. pap. 2.50 (ISBN 0-671-41610-3). WSP.

MONASTICISM AND RELIGIOUS ORDERS, ISLAMIC

see also Senussites

MONASTICISM AND RELIGIOUS ORDERS, ORTHODOX EASTERN

Carthach, St. The Monastic Rule of St. Carthach: St. Mochuda the Younger. pap. 1.50 (ISBN 0-686-05656-6). Eastern Orthodox.
Murphy, Sr. M. Gertrude. Saint Basil & Monasticism. LC 70-144661. Repr. of 1930 ed. 14.75 (ISBN 0-404-04543-X). AMS Pr.
Pachomius, Saint Rule of St. Pachomius. Budge, E. A., tr. from Coptic. 1975. pap. 1.50 (ISBN 0-686-10939-2). Eastern Orthodox.
Patrinelis, Christos, et al. Stavronikita Monastery: History-Icons-Embroideries. (Illus.). 241p. 1974. 75.00 (ISBN 0-89241-076-0). Caratzas Bros.
Robinson, N. F. Monasticism in the Orthodox Church. LC 72-131506. Repr. of 1916 ed. 10.00 (ISBN 0-404-05375-0). AMS Pr.
St. John Climacus. The Ladder of Divine Ascent. rev. ed. Holy Transfiguration Monastery, tr. from Greek. LC 79-83920. (Illus.). 1979. 12.00x (ISBN 0-913026-07-7). St Nectarios.
Wallis-Budge, A. E., tr. from Syriac. The Paradise of the Fathers, 2 vols. 1979. Repr. of 1907 ed. 20.00x set (ISBN 0-913026-21-2). St Nectarios.

MONASTICISM AND RELIGIOUS ORDERS FOR WOMEN

see also Beghards and Beguines; Convents and Nunneries; Monastic and Religious Life of Women; Nuns; Sisterhoods;
also names of orders, e.g. Sisters of Mercy

Ebaugh, Helen R. Out of the Cloister: A Study of Organizational Dilemmas. 177p. 1977. text ed. 9.95x (ISBN 0-292-76007-8). U of Tex Pr.
Eckenstein, Lina. Woman Under Monasticism. 59.95 (ISBN 0-8490-1318-6). Gordon Pr.
--Woman Under Monasticism: Chapters on Saint-Lore & Convent Life Between A. D. 500 & A. D. 1500. LC 63-11028. 1963. Repr. of 1896 ed. 10.00 (ISBN 0-8462-0363-4). Russell.
Fichter, Joseph H., ed. Dimensions of Authority in the Religious Life. (Religious Life in the Modern World Ser.: Vol. 5). (Orig.). 1966. pap. 1.95x (ISBN 0-268-00079-4). U of Notre Dame Pr.
Griffiths, Michael. God's Forgetful Pilgrims: Recalling the Church to Its Reason for Being. 176p. 1975. pap. 2.95 (ISBN 0-8028-1619-3). Eerdmans.
Ludlow, John M. Woman's Work in the Church. LC 75-33300. 1976. Repr. of 1866 ed. 14.95 (ISBN 0-89201-007-X). Zenger Pub.
Morton, James, ed. Ancren Riwle, a Treatise on the Rules & Duties of Monastic Life from a Semi-Saxon MS. of the Thirteenth Century. LC 72-158250. (Camden Society, London. Publications, First Series: No. 1). Repr. of 1853 ed. 42.00 (ISBN 0-404-50157-5). AMS Pr.
Morton, James, tr. Nuns' Rule or the Ancren Riwle. LC 66-23314. (Medieval Library). Repr. of 1926 ed. 8.50x (ISBN 0-8154-0155-8). Cooper Sq.
Shepherd, Geoffrey, ed. Ancrene Wisse, Pts. 6 & 7. (Old & Middle English Texts). 116p. 1972. pap. 10.95x (ISBN 0-06-496228-8). B&N.
Tolkien, J. R., ed. Ancrene Wisse: English Text of the Ancrene Riwle. (Early English Text Society Ser.). 1962. 16.95x (ISBN 0-19-722249-8). Oxford U Pr.

MONASTICISM AND RELIGIOUS ORDERS FOR WOMEN–BIOGRAPHY

Armstrong, Karen. Through the Narrow Gate. 288p. 1981. 12.95 (ISBN 0-686-72590-5). St Martin.
Code, Joseph B. Great American Foundresses. facs. ed. LC 68-20291. (Essay Index Reprint Ser). 1929. 19.50 (ISBN 0-8369-0319-6). Arno.
Curry, Lois. Women After His Own Heart. Blanc, Claude, ed. (Illus.). 250p. 1981. 10.95 (ISBN 0-911782-37-0). New City.
Lowrey, Kathleen. Up Among the Stars. LC 73-83922. 1974. 9.95 (ISBN 0-87949-022-5). Ashley Bks.
Walsh, James J., compiled by. These Splendid Sisters. LC 75-128326. (Essay Index Reprint Ser). 1927. 16.00 (ISBN 0-8369-1856-8). Arno.

MONDALE, WALTER

Lewis, Finlay. Mondale: Portrait of an American Politician. LC 79-1672. 1980. 12.95 (ISBN 0-06-012599-3, HarpT). Har-Row.

MONDRIAN, PIETER CORNELIUS, 1872-1944

Gay, Peter. Art & Act: On Causes in History - Manet, Gropius, Mondrian. LC 75-12291. (Icon Editions). (Illus.). 320p. 1976. 20.00 (ISBN 0-06-433248-9, HarpT). Har-Row.
Jaffe, Hans L. Mondrian. (Library of Great Painters Ser). (Illus.). 1970. 40.00 (ISBN 0-8109-0325-3). Abrams.
Welsh, Robert P. Piet Mondrian's Early Career: The Naturalistic Periods. LC 76-23659. (Outstanding Disserations in the Fine Arts Ser.). 1977. lib. bdg. 56.00x (ISBN 0-8240-2738-8). Garland Pub.

MONET, CLAUDE, 1840-1926

Barskaya, Anna, compiled By. Claude Monet. (Illus.). 50p. 1980. pap. 4.95 (ISBN 0-686-62716-4, 2219-3). Abrams.
Hoog, Michael. Monet. (Masters of Art Ser.). (Illus.). 1979. pap. 3.95 (ISBN 0-8120-2152-5). Barron.
Levine, Steven Z. Monet & His Critics. LC 75-23800. (Outstanding Dissertations in the Fine Arts - 19th Century). (Illus.). 1976. lib. bdg. 45.00 (ISBN 0-8240-1995-4). Garland Pub.
Moffet, Charles S., intro. by. Monet's Years at Giverny: Beyond Impressionism. LC 78-328. (Illus.). 1978. 12.50 (ISBN 0-87099-175-2); pap. 6.95 (ISBN 0-87099-174-4). Metro Mus Art.
Monet. (The Painter & the Man Ser.). 1977. pap. 19.95 (ISBN 0-8120-5115-7). Barron.
Seitz, William C. Claude Monet: Seasons & Moments. LC 60-9682. (Museum of Modern Art Publications in Reprint Ser). (Illus.). 1970. Repr. of 1960 ed. 15.00 (ISBN 0-405-01548-8). Arno.
--Monet. LC 60-7800. (Library of Great Painters Ser). (Illus.). 1960. 40.00 (ISBN 0-8109-0326-1). Abrams.
Tucker, Paul H. Claude Monet at Argenteuil: 1871-1878. 260p. 1981. price not set. Yale U Pr.
Wildenstein, Daniel. Monet's Years at Giverny: Beyond Impressionism. LC 78-328. (Illus.). 1978. 22.50 (ISBN 0-8109-1336-4); pap. 9.95 (ISBN 0-8109-2183-9). Abrams.

MONETARY POLICY

see also Credit; Fiscal Policy

Ahearn, Daniel S. Federal Reserve Policy Reappraised, 1951-1959. LC 63-10522. 376p. 1963. 18.00x (ISBN 0-231-02575-0). Columbia U Pr.
American Assembly. U. S. Monetary Policy. facsimile & rev. ed. Jacoby, Neil H., ed. LC 79-164586. (Select Bibliographies Reprint Ser). Repr. of 1964 ed. 16.00 (ISBN 0-8369-5702-4). Arno.
Block, Fred L. The Origins of International Economic Disorder: A Study of United States International Monetary Policy from World War Two to the Present. LC 75-7190. 1977. pap. 6.95x (ISBN 0-520-03729-4). U of Cal Pr.
Bloomfield, Arthur I. Monetary Policy Under the International Gold Standard. Wilkins, Mira, ed. LC 78-3899. (International Finance Ser.). 1978. Repr. of 1959 ed. lib. bdg. 10.00x (ISBN 0-405-11204-1). Arno.
Boughton, James M. Monetary Policy & the Federal Funds Market. LC 74-172018. 1972. 14.75 (ISBN 0-8223-0287-X). Duke.
Brock, Leslie V. The Currency of the American Colonies, Seventeen Hundred to Seventeen Sixty-Four: A Study in Colonial Finance & Imperial Relations. LC 75-2576. (Dissertations in American Economic History). (Illus.). 1975. 43.00x (ISBN 0-405-07257-0). Arno.
Brothers, Dwight S. & Solis, M. Leopoldo. Mexican Financial Development. 252p. 1965. 12.95x (ISBN 0-292-73304-6). U of Tex Pr.
Brown, Brendan. The Dollar-Mark Axis: On Currency Power. LC 79-5354. 1979. 19.95x (ISBN 0-312-21623-8). St Martin.
Cagan, Phillip. The Channels of Monetary Effects on Interest Rates. (General Ser.: No. 97). 144p. 1972. 10.00x (ISBN 0-87014-235-6, Dist. by Columbia U Pr). Natl Bur Econ Res.
Carbaugh, Robert J. & Fan, Liang-Shing. The International Monetary System: History, Institutions, Analyses. LC 75-38829. (Illus.). 176p. 1976. 12.00x (ISBN 0-7006-0141-4). Regents Pr KS.

Cargil, Thomas & Garcia, Gillian. Financial Deregulation & Monetary Control: Historical Perspective & Impact of the 1980 Act. (Publication Ser.: No. 259). (Illus.). 128p. Date not set. pap. text ed. write for info. (ISBN 0-8179-7592-6). Hoover Inst Pr.
Carron, Andrew S. Regulatory Reform of Financial Institutions. 120p. 1981. pap. 5.95 (ISBN 0-8157-1297-9). Brookings.
Chick, Victoria. The Theory of Monetary Policy. rev. ed. 1977. pap. 14.50x (ISBN 0-631-18210-1, Pub. by Basil Blackwell England). Biblio Dist.
Cohen, J. Special Bibliography in Monetary Economics & Finance. 1976. 54.00x (ISBN 0-677-00690-X). Gordon.
Committee for Economic Development. Fiscal & Monetary Policies for Steady Economic Growth. LC 76-76619. 85p. 1969. lib. bdg. 2.00 (ISBN 0-87186-732-X); pap. 1.00 (ISBN 0-87186-032-5). Comm Econ Dev.
Conference of the Universities. The State of Monetary Economics: Proceedings. LC 75-19702. (National Bureau of Economic Research Ser.). (Illus.). 1975. Repr. of 1963 ed. 12.00x (ISBN 0-405-07582-0). Arno.
Crawford, Arthur W. Monetary Management Under the New Deal. LC 70-173988. (FDR & the Era of the New Deal Ser.). 380p. 1972. Repr. of 1940 ed. lib. bdg. 39.50 (ISBN 0-306-70374-2). Da Capo.
Dalgaard, Bruce R. South Africa's Impact on Britain's Return to Gold, 1925. Bruchey, Stuart, ed. LC 80-2801. (Dissertations in European Economic History II). (Illus.). 1981. lib. bdg. 18.00x (ISBN 0-405-13985-3). Arno.
Dam, Kenneth W. The Role of Rules in the International Monetary System. LC 76-47303. 1976. pap. 1.50 (ISBN 0-916770-03-6). Law & Econ U Miami.
Dauphine Conference on Money & International Money Problems, 3rd, Paris. Stabilization Policies in Interdependent Economies: Proceedings. Salin & Claassen, eds. 1972. 39.00 (ISBN 0-444-10368-6, North-Holland). Elsevier.
DeRosa, Paul & Stern, Gary H. In the Name of Money: A Professional's Guide to the Federal Reserve, Interest Rates & Money. (Illus.). 192p. 1980. 16.95 (ISBN 0-07-016521-1, P&RB). McGraw.
Edie, Lionel D. Easy Money: A Study of Low Interest Rates, Their Bearing on the Outlook for the Gold Standard & on the Problem of Curbing a Boom. 1937. 24.50x (ISBN 0-686-51374-6). Elliots Bks.
Einzig, Paul. Bankers, Statesmen & Economists. facs. ed. LC 67-30185. (Essay Index Reprint Ser). 1935. 16.00 (ISBN 0-8369-0410-9). Arno.
--A Textbook on Monetary Policy. 18.95 (ISBN 0-685-58434-8, Pub by St Martins Pr). Cyrco Pr.
Fischer, Gordon & Sheppard, David. Effects of Monetary Policy on the United States Economy: A Survey of Econometric Evidence. (Occasional Economic Studies Ser.). 1972. 2.25x (ISBN 92-64-11226-X). OECD.
Fisher, Douglas. Monetary Policy. LC 75-20330. 91p. 1976. pap. text ed. 8.95x (ISBN 0-470-25996-5). Halsted Pr.
--Money, Banking & Monetary Policy. 1980. 19.50x (ISBN 0-256-02365-4). Irwin.
Flumiani, C. M. The Gyrations of the Dollar & the Deceit of Gold. LC 73-85330. 30p. 1971. 51.25 (ISBN 0-913314-03-X). Am Classical Coll Pr.
--Silver, Gold & the Approaching Revolution in the International Monetary System. LC 74-28459. (Illus.). 90p. 1974. 57.50 (ISBN 0-913314-42-0). Am Classical Coll Pr.
--Silver, Gold & the Approaching Revolution in the International Monetary System. (Illus.). 1978. deluxe ed. 49.75 (ISBN 0-930008-10-3). Inst Econ Pol.
Fousek, Peter G. Foreign Central Banking: The Instruments of Monetary Policy. LC 72-91042. 1969. Repr. of 1957 ed. 12.50 (ISBN 0-8046-0610-2). Kennikat.
Friedman, M. Dollars & Deficits: Inflation, Monetary Policy & the Balance of Payments. 1968. pap. 11.95 (ISBN 0-13-218289-0). P-H.
Friedman, Milton. The Counter-Revolution in Monetary Theory. (Institute of Economic Affairs, Occasional Papers Ser.: No. 33). 1972. pap. 2.50 (ISBN 0-255-36007-X). Transatlantic.
--Optimum Quantity of Money & Other Essays. LC 68-8148. 1969. 24.95x (ISBN 0-202-06030-6). Aldine Pub.
Friedman, Milton & Heller, Walter H. Monetary Versus Fiscal Policy. 1969. 3.95x (ISBN 0-393-05372-5); pap. 2.95x (ISBN 0-393-09847-8). Norton.
Friedman, Milton & Schwartz, Anna J. Great Contraction, 1929-1933: Chapter Seven of "Monetary History of the United States, 1867-1960". 1965. pap. 3.95 (ISBN 0-691-00350-5, 9). Natl Bur Econ Res.
--Monetary History of the United States, 1867-1960. (Business Cycles Ser.: No. 12). 1963. 25.00 (ISBN 0-691-04147-4, Dist. by Princeton U Pr); pap. 8.95 (ISBN 0-685-17332-1). Natl Bur Econ Res.
Friedman, Milton, ed. Studies in the Quantity Theory of Money. LC 56-10999. 1973. pap. 4.75 (ISBN 0-226-26406-8, P561, Phoen). U of Chicago Pr.
Gilbert, Milton. Currency Depreciation & Monetary Policy. Wilkins, Mira, ed. LC 78-3914. (International Finance Ser.). (Illus.). 1978. Repr. of 1939 ed. lib. bdg. 12.00x (ISBN 0-405-11218-1). Arno.
Goddard, Donald. Easy Money. 1979. pap. 2.50 (ISBN 0-445-04465-9). Popular Lib.
Gold, Joseph. Legal & Institutional Aspects of the International Monetary System. Evensen, Jane B. & Oh, Jai K., eds. 1979. 17.50 (ISBN 0-686-23762-5). Intl Monetary Fund.
Goodbar, Joseph E. Managing the People's Money. 1935. 47.50x (ISBN 0-685-89765-6). Elliots Bks.
Griffiths, Brian, ed. Monetary Targets. Wood, Geoffrey E. 27.50 (ISBN 0-312-54421-9). St Martin.
Griffiths, Brian & Woods, Geoffrey E., eds. Monetary Targets. 1981. 27.50 (ISBN 0-686-71697-3). St Martin.
Hamberg, Daniel. The U. S. Monetary System: Money, Banking, & Financial Markets. 1981. text ed. 18.95 (ISBN 0-316-34096-0). Little.
Hamel, Esther V. & Kelly, Thomas L. House of Termites: Hidden People & Their Power Over Liberty & the Dollar. 2nd ed. 1972. pap. 2.00 (ISBN 0-913162-02-7). Ponderosa.
Hanson, J. L. Monetary Theory & Practice. 6th ed. (Illus.). 352p. 1978. pap. text ed. 13.95x (ISBN 0-7121-1293-6, Pub. by Macdonald & Evans England). Intl Ideas.
--An Outline of Monetary Theory. 4th ed. 160p. 1980. pap. text ed. 9.95x (ISBN 0-7121-1533-1). Intl Ideas.
Havrilesky, Thomas M. & Boorman, John T., eds. Current Issues in Monetary Theory & Policy. 2nd ed. LC 79-55733. (Illus.). 1980. pap. text ed. 15.95x (ISBN 0-88295-406-7). Harlan Davidson.
Hellman, Rainer. Gold Dollars, & the European Currency System: The Seven Year Monetary War. (Praeger Special Studies). 1979. 24.95 (ISBN 0-03-041611-6). Praeger.
Holtrop, M. W. Money in an Open Economy. lib. bdg. 44.00 (ISBN 90-207-0368-4, Pub. by Martinus Nijhoff Netherlands). Kluwer Boston.
Hosek, William R. & Zahn, Frank. Monetary Theory, Policy & Financial Markets. (Illus.). 1977. text ed. 18.95 (ISBN 0-07-030436-X, C); instructor's manual 4.95 (ISBN 0-07-030437-8). McGraw.
Hover, Craig R. The Coming Depression. LC 79-52019. (Illus.). 1979. pap. 4.95 (ISBN 0-89913-000-3). Entity Pub Co.
Hurst, James W. A Legal History of Money in the United States, 1774-1970. LC 72-86019. (Roscoe Pound Lecture Ser). xviii, 367p. 1973. 21.50x (ISBN 0-8032-0824-3). U of Nebr Pr.
Hyatt, Thomas. The Internationalization of Money. (Illus.). 1978. deluxe bdg. 41.25 (ISBN 0-930008-08-1). Inst Econ Pol.
Isaacs, Charles P. The Menace of the Money Power. 59.95 (ISBN 0-87968-291-4). Gordon Pr.
Jackendoff, Nathaniel. Money, Flow of Funds, & Economic Policy. LC 68-30892. (Illus.). 523p. 1968. 23.50 (ISBN 0-471-06632-X). Wiley.
Jackson, Terence G. Postwar Monetary Reform in Severely Damaged Economies: Its Role in Recovery from Nuclear Attack. LC 79-133439. 175p. 1969. 29.50 (ISBN 0-686-01962-8). Mgmt Info Serv.
Jelset, Christ. Money & Money Reforms. 60p. 1947. pap. 1.00 (ISBN 0-88286-041-0). C H Kerr.
Johnson, Gove G. Treasury & Monetary Policy, 1933-1938. LC 66-24711. 1967. Repr. of 1939 ed. 8.50 (ISBN 0-8462-0843-1). Russell.
Johnson, Harry G. Further Essays in Monetary Economics. LC 72-95183. (Illus.). 1973. 18.50x (ISBN 0-674-33525-2). Harvard U Pr.
Kenen, Peter, ed. Monetary System Under Flexible Exchange Rates: Global, Regional, & National. 350p. Date not set. price not set professional reference bk. (ISBN 0-88410-853-8). Ballinger Pub.
Kitson, Arthur. A Fraudulent Standard: An Exposure of the Fraudulent Character of Our Monetary Standard. 1980. lib. bdg. 59.95 (ISBN 0-8490-3099-4). Gordon Pr.
Klein, John J. Money & the Economy. 4th ed. 1978. text ed. 18.95 (ISBN 0-15-564005-4, HC). HarBraceJ.
Korteweg, P. & Van Loo, P. D., eds. The Market for Money & the Market for Credit. 1977. pap. 12.00 (ISBN 90-207-0685-3, Pub. by Martinus Nijhoff Netherlands). Kluwer Boston.
Krause, Lawrence B. Sequel to Bretton Woods: A Proposal to Reform the World Monetary System. 50p. 1971. pap. 2.95 (ISBN 0-8157-5035-8). Brookings.
Larkins, Dan. Three Hundred Billion in Loans: An Introduction to Federal Credit Programs. 1972. pap. 4.25 (ISBN 0-8447-3086-6). Am Enterprise.
Lazar, Leonard. Transnational Economic & Monetary Law Transactions & Contracts, 3 vols. LC 77-8398. 1978. looseleaf 75.00 ea. (ISBN 0-379-10215-3); 375.00 set (ISBN 0-686-77298-9). Oceana.
Lindow, Wesley. Inside the Money Market. 1972. 15.00 (ISBN 0-394-47885-1). Random.
McCulloch, J. Houston. Money & Inflation: Monetarist Approach. 121p. 1975. 7.95 (ISBN 0-12-483050-1). Acad Pr.
Machlup, Fritz, et al. International Monetary Problems. 1972. 12.25 (ISBN 0-8447-2029-1); pap. 5.25 (ISBN 0-8447-2028-3). Am Enterprise.
Maisel, Sherman J. Managing the Dollar. (Illus.). 1973. 10.95 (ISBN 0-393-05494-2). Norton.
Mayer, Thomas. Elements of Monetary Policy. 5.00 (ISBN 0-8446-2554-X). Peter Smith.
--Elements of Monetary Policy. 1968. pap. text ed. 3.95x (ISBN 0-685-77203-9). Phila Bk Co.
--The Structure of Monetarism. 1978. 11.95x (ISBN 0-393-09045-0). Norton.
Meier, Gerald M. Problems of a World Monetary Order. (Illus.). 300p. 1974. pap. text ed. 7.95x (ISBN 0-19-501801-X). Oxford U Pr.
Meigs, A. James. Free Reserves & the Money Supply. LC 62-17136. (Economic Research Studies Ser). 1962. 10.00x (ISBN 0-226-51901-5). U of Chicago Pr.
Meiselman, David M., ed. Varieties of Monetary Experience. LC 70-116027. (Economic Research Center Ser). 1971. 20.00x (ISBN 0-226-51930-9). U of Chicago Pr.
Metzler, Lloyd A. & Haberler, Gottfried. International Monetary Policies. Wilkins, Mira, ed. LC 78-3938. (International Finance Ser.). 1978. Repr. of 1947 ed. lib. bdg. 10.00x (ISBN 0-405-11239-4). Arno.
Mezneries, I. International Payments: With Special Regard to Monetary Systems. 265p. 1979. 25.00x (ISBN 90-286-0119-8). Sijthoff & Noordhoff.
Miller, Ervin. The Microeconomic Effects of Monetary Policy. LC 77-17980. 1978. 17.50 (ISBN 0-312-53173-7). St Martin.
Miller, James. A Key to Financial Survival: The Secret Investment Diary of a Portfolio Manager. LC 77-1071. 1977. pap. 2.95 (ISBN 0-87576-060-0). Pilot Bks.
Miller, Randall J. Regional Impact of Monetary Policy in the United States. LC 78-59750. (Illus.). 1978. 19.95 (ISBN 0-669-02373-6). Lexington Bks.
Mitchell, Glenn. The Collapse of the Dollar & the Approaching Catastrophe in the International World Monetary Order. (Illus.). 1978. 54.85 (ISBN 0-930008-05-7). Inst Econ Pol.
Mittra, Sid. Money & Banking: Theory, Analysis & Policy. 1970. pap. text ed. 6.95x (ISBN 0-685-84267-3). Phila Bk Co.
Monetary Targets & Inflation Control. (OECD Monetary Studies). 101p. 1979. 9.50x (ISBN 92-64-11963-9). OECD.
Mortensen, Michael H. Gold, Swiss Banks & the World Monetary Catastrophe. (Illus.). 1981. 49.65 (ISBN 0-930008-43-X). Inst Econ Pol.
Mundell, Robert. Monetary Theory: Inflation, Interest & Growth in the World Economy. LC 74-123615. (Illus.). 1971. text ed. 18.95 (ISBN 0-87620-586-4). Goodyear.
Nagatani, K. Monetary Theory. (Advanced Textbooks in Economics: Vol. 10). 1978. 29.50 (ISBN 0-444-85032-5, North-Holland). Elsevier.
Norburn, C. S. & Norburn, Russell. A New Monetary System. 1979. lib. bdg. 59.95 (ISBN 0-8490-2977-5). Gordon Pr.
Organization for Economic Cooperation & Development. Monetary Policy in Italy. (Monetary Studies Ser.: No. 2). 92p. 1973. 3.75x (ISBN 92-64-11071-2). OECD.
--Monetary Policy in the U. S. (Monetary Studies Ser.: No. 4). 216p. 1974. 9.50 (ISBN 0-686-14846-0). OECD.
Perkins, Y. O. The Macroeconomic Mix to Stop Stagflation. 1979. 27.95x (ISBN 0-470-26525-6). Halsted Pr.
Phillips, J. G. Development in Monetary Theories & Policies. 32p. 1971. pap. 2.00x (ISBN 0-424-06260-7, Pub. by Sydney U. Pr). Intl Schol Bk Serv.
Pierce, David G. & Shaw, David M. Monetary Economics: Theories, Evidence & Policy. LC 73-91530. 1974. o. p. 27.00x (ISBN 0-8448-0267-0); pap. 14.50x (ISBN 0-8448-0268-9). Crane-Russak Co.
Prager, Jonas, ed. Monetary Economics: Controversies in Theory & Policy. (Orig.). 1971. pap. text ed. 8.95 (ISBN 0-394-30827-1, RanC). Random.
Robertson, Sir Dennis H. Essays in Monetary Theory. LC 78-20487. 1980. 19.50 (ISBN 0-88355-864-5). Hyperion Conn.
Rock, James M., ed. Money, Banking & Macroeconomics: A Guide to Information Sources. LC 73-17585. (Economics Information Guide Ser.: Vol. 11). 1977. 36.00 (ISBN 0-8103-1300-6). Gale.
Rossland, Edmond C. The Utterly Irrational United States Monetary Policies & the Absolute Inevitability of a Major World Economic & Financial Crisis, 2 vols. in 1. (Illus.). 1979. deluxe ed. 61.85 (ISBN 0-930008-37-5). Inst Econ Pol.
Rowland, Benjamin M., ed. Balance of Power or Hegemony: The Interwar Monetary System. LC 75-27423. 266p. 1976. 18.50x (ISBN 0-8147-7368-0). NYU Pr.
Royal Institute Of International Affairs. Monetary Policy & the Depression. (Social & Economic History Ser). Repr. of 1933 ed. 11.50 (ISBN 0-384-52290-4). Johnson Repr.
Schmitz, W., ed. Convertibility, Multilateralism & Freedom: World Economic Policy in the Seventies. Essays in Honour of Reinhard Kamitz. LC 76-186940. 400p. 1972. 37.80 (ISBN 0-387-81056-0). Springer-Verlag.
Schulze, David L. A General Equilibrium Study of the Monetary Mechanism. LC 74-13495. (U of Fla. Social Sciences Monographs Ser.: No. 51). 1974. pap. 3.50 (ISBN 0-8130-0407-1). U Presses Fla.
Scindler, D. & Toman, J. The Laws of Armed Conflicts. rev. ed. 904p. 1980. 105.00x (ISBN 90-286-0199-6). Sijthoff & Noordhoff.
Sijben, J. J. Money & Economic Growth. 1977. lib. bdg. 29.00 (ISBN 90-207-0655-1, Martinus Nijhoff Pubs). Kluwer Boston.
Slovin, M. B. & Sushka, M. E. Interest Rates on Savings Deposits: Theory, Estimation, & Policy. LC 74-16931. (Illus.). 192p. 1975. 18.95 (ISBN 0-669-96453-0). Lexington Bks.
Stein, Herbert. Fiscal Revolution in America. LC 69-14828. (Studies in Business & Society Ser). 1969. pap. 7.95 (ISBN 0-226-77170-9). U of Chicago Pr.
Symposium on Demand Management, Globalsteuerung, 1971. Proceedings. Giersch, Herbert, ed. (Illus.). 257p. 1972. 17.50x (ISBN 3-16-334532-8). Intl Pubns Serv.
Thorn, Richard S., ed. Monetary Theory & Policy. LC 81-43023. 702p. 1981. lib. bdg. 26.75 (ISBN 0-8191-1623-8); pap. text ed. 16.00 (ISBN 0-8191-1624-6). U Pr of Amer.
Timberlake, Richard H., Jr. The Origins of Central Banking in the United States. LC 78-4622. 1978. 18.50x (ISBN 0-674-64480-8). Harvard U Pr.
U. S. Board of Governors of the Federal Reserve System. Banking & Monetary Statistics: Supplement. LC 75-41278. 1976. Repr. of 1943 ed. 82.50 (ISBN 0-404-14621-X). AMS Pr.
U. S. Senate, Executive Document. International Monetary Conference. Wilkins, Mira, ed. LC 78-3952. (International Finance Ser.: No. 58). (Illus.). 1978. Repr. of 1879 ed. lib. bdg. 54.00x (ISBN 0-405-11253-X). Arno.
Uselton, G. Lags in the Effects of Monetary Policy: A Nonparametric Analysis. (Business Economics & Finance Ser.: Vol. 2). 192p. 1974. 23.75 (ISBN 0-8247-6112-X). Dekker.
Vaish, M. C. Monetary Theory. 8th, rev., & enl. ed. (Illus.). 697p. 1978. text ed. 17.50x (ISBN 0-7069-0282-3). Intl Pubns Serv.
--Money, Banking & International Trade. 2nd, rev. ed. (Illus.). 643p. 1978. text ed. 17.50x (ISBN 0-7069-0559-8). Intl Pubns Serv.
Vane, Howard R. & Thompson, John L. Monetarism: Theory, Evidence & Policy. 1979. pap. text ed. 14.95 (ISBN 0-470-26569-8). Halsted Pr.
Wadsworth, J. E. & De Juvigny, F. Leonard. New Approaches in Monetary Policy, No. 4. (Financial & Monetary Policy Issues Ser.). 406p. 1979. 40.00x (ISBN 90-286-0848-6). Sijthoff & Noordhoff.
Walker, Pinkney C., ed. Essays in Monetary Policy in Honor of Elmer Wood. LC 65-21793. 1965. 3.75x (ISBN 0-8262-0039-7). U of Mo Pr.
Weihofen, Richard Herold. The European Monetary System...Gold..the Future Value of the Dollar...and Their Perturbing Impact Upon the Economy of the World. (Illus.). 1979. 79.45 (ISBN 0-930008-45-6). Inst Econ Pol.
Weston, Rae. Domestic & Multinational Banking: The Effect of Monetary Policy. 400p. 1980. 32.50x (ISBN 0-231-05058-5). Columbia U Pr.
Wilford, D. Sykes. Monetary Policy & the Open Economy: Mexico's Experience. LC 77-14386. (Praeger Special Studies). 1977. 22.95 (ISBN 0-03-028156-3). Praeger.
Williams, Gordon L. Financial Survival in the Age of New Money. 1981. 12.95 (ISBN 0-671-25474-X). S&S.
Wilson, R. MacNair. The Mind of Napoleon: A Study of Napoleon, Mr. Roosevelt, & the Money Power. 75.00 (ISBN 0-8490-0639-2). Gordon Pr.

Wood, Elmer. Monetary Control. 1963. 10.00 (ISBN 0-8262-0021-4). U of Mo Pr.
Wood, J. H. Commercial Bank Loan & Investment Behavior. Walters, A. A., ed. LC 75-1192. (Monographs in Applied Econometrics Ser). 153p. 1975. 30.95 (ISBN 0-471-95998-7, Pub. by Wiley-Interscience). Wiley.
Woodworth, G. Walter. Money Market & Monetary Management. 2nd ed. 1972. text ed. 31.50 scp (ISBN 0-06-047216-2, HarpC). Har-Row.
Wrightsman, Dwayne. An Introduction to Monetary Theory & Policy. 2nd ed. LC 75-22767. (Illus.). 1976. pap. text ed. 9.95 (ISBN 0-02-935560-5). Free Pr.
Yeager, Leland B., ed. In Search of a Monetary Constitution. LC 62-19227. 1962. 17.50x (ISBN 0-674-44550-3). Harvard U Pr.
Zolotas, Xenophon. International Monetary Issues & Development Policies. LC 77-90142. 1977. 28.50x (ISBN 0-8147-9654-0). NYU Pr.
Zwass, Adam. Monetary Cooperation Between East & West. LC 73-92368. 248p. 1975. 20.00 (ISBN 0-87332-057-3). M E Sharpe.

MONETARY POLICY–MATHEMATICAL MODELS

Fischer, Gordon & Sheppard, David. Effects of Monetary Policy on the United States Economy: A Survey of Econometric Evidence. (Occasional Economic Studies Ser.). 1972. 2.25x (ISBN 92-64-11226-X). OECD.
Herring, R. J. & Marston, R. C. National Monetary Policies & International Financial Markets. (Contributions to Economic Analysis: Vol. 104). 1977. 39.00 (ISBN 0-7204-0519-X, North-Holland). Elsevier.
Laidler, D. E. Essays on Money & Inflation. LC 75-22170. xiv, 246p. 1979. lib. bdg. 16.00x (ISBN 0-226-46793-7); pap. 6.95 (ISBN 0-226-46792-9, P817, Phoen). U of Chicago Pr.
Stein, Jerome L. Money & Capacity Growth. LC 73-160844. 1971. 17.50x (ISBN 0-231-03372-9). Columbia U Pr.

MONETARY POLICY–AFRICA, EAST

Newlyn, Walter T. Money in an African Context. (Studies in African Economics Ser). 1967. pap. 4.25x (ISBN 0-19-644049-1). Oxford U Pr.

MONETARY POLICY–CANADA

Wonnacott, Paul. The Floating Canadian Dollar: Exchange Flexibility & Monetary Independence. 1972. pap. 4.25 (ISBN 0-8447-3079-3). Am Enterprise.

MONETARY POLICY–CHINA

Hsiao, Katherine H. Money & Monetary Policy in Communist China. LC 77-158341. (Studies of the East Asian Institute). (Illus.). 1971. 20.00 (ISBN 0-231-03510-1). Columbia U Pr.
Kann, Edward. The Currencies of China. (Illus.). 1978. Repr. of 1926 ed. lib. bdg. 39.50 (ISBN 0-915262-22-3). S J Durst.
King, Frank H. Money & Monetary Policy in China, 1845-1895. LC 65-13847. (East Asian Ser: No. 19). (Illus.). 1965. 16.50x (ISBN 0-674-58350-7). Harvard U Pr.

MONETARY POLICY–EUROPE

Einzig, Paul & Quinn, Brian S. The Euro-Dollar System: Practice & Theory of International Interest Rates. 6th ed. LC 77-78988. 1977. 17.95x (ISBN 0-312-26741-X). St Martin.
Krause, Lawrence B. & Salant, Walter S., eds. European Monetary Unification & Its Meaning for the United States. LC 73-1084. 1973. 12.95 (ISBN 0-8157-5032-3). Brookings.
Ludlow. The Making of the European Monetary System. 1982. text ed. price not set (ISBN 0-408-10728-6). Butterworth.
Magnifico, G. European Monetary Unification. LC 73-303. 227p. 1973. 24.95 (ISBN 0-470-56525-X). Halsted Pr.
Meyer, Richard H. Bankers' Diplomacy: Monetary Stabilization in the Twenties. LC 79-111120. (Columbia Studies in Economics Ser.: No. 4). 170p. 1970. 20.00x (ISBN 0-231-03325-7). Columbia U Pr.
Organization for Economic Cooperation & Development. Monetary Policy in France. (Monetary Studies Ser.: No. 5). 106p. 1975. 5.25 (ISBN 0-686-14847-9). OECD.
Spooner, Frank C. International Economy & Monetary Movements in France, 1493-1725. rev. abr. ed. LC 70-145894. (Economic Studies: No. 138). (Illus.). 1972. 17.50x (ISBN 0-674-45840-0). Harvard U Pr.
Trezise, Philip H., ed. The European Monetary System: Its Promise & Prospects. LC 79-55581. 96p. 1979. pap. 4.50 (ISBN 0-8157-8531-3). Brookings.
Vaubel, Roland. Choice in European Monetary Union. (Occasional Paper Ser.: No. 55, Ninth Wincott Memorial Lecture). (Orig.). 1979. 3.50 (ISBN 0-255-36118-1). Transatlantic.
Zwass, Adam. Money, Banking, & Credit in the Soviet Union & Eastern Europe. LC 78-64910. 1979. 18.50 (ISBN 0-87332-124-3). M E Sharpe.

MONETARY POLICY–GERMANY

Frowen, S. F., et al. Monetary Policy & Economic Activity in West Germany. LC 77-2403. 268p. 1977. 37.50 (ISBN 0-470-99131-3). Krieger.
Frowen, S. F., et al, eds. Monetary Policy & Economic Activity in West Germany. LC 77-2403. 1977. 58.95 (ISBN 0-470-99131-3). Halsted Pr.
Hogenmiller, Peter U. The West German Mark & the New Monetary World Leadership. (Illus.). 1980. deluxe ed. 59.75 (ISBN 0-930008-56-1). Inst Econ Pol.
Organization for Economic Cooperation & Development. Monetary Policy in Germany. (Monetary Studies Ser.: No. 3). 132p. 1974. 5.25x (ISBN 92-64-11127-1). OECD.

MONETARY POLICY–GREAT BRITAIN

Asgill, John. Several Assertions Proved in Order to Create Another Species of Money. Repr. of 1696 ed. 12.50 (ISBN 0-384-02180-8). Johnson Repr.
Broadbridge, Seymour. Studies in Railway Expansion & the Capital Market in England: 1825-73. 216p. 1970. 30.00x (ISBN 0-7146-1287-1, F Cass Co). Biblio Dist.
Dalgaard, Bruce R. South Africa's Impact on Britain's Return to Gold, 1925. Bruchey, Stuart, ed. LC 80-2801. (Dissertations in European Economic History II). (Illus.). 1981. lib. bdg. 18.00x (ISBN 0-405-13985-3). Arno.
Grant, Alexander T. Study of the Capital Market in Britain from 1919-1936. 2nd ed. 320p. 1967. 32.50x (ISBN 0-7146-1224-3, F Cass Co). Biblio Dist.
Howson, Susan. Domestic Monetary Management in Britain, 1919-38. LC 75-21032. (Department of Applied Economics, Occasional Papers Ser.: No. 48). 1975. 31.00 (ISBN 0-521-21059-3); pap. 14.95x (ISBN 0-521-29026-0). Cambridge U Pr.
Jocelyn, J. Essay on Money & Bullion. LC 77-13311. 1971. Repr. of 1718 ed. 12.50 (ISBN 0-384-27540-0). Johnson Repr.
Johnson, H. G. & Nobay, A. R., eds. Issues in Monetary Economics Proceedings of the 1972 Money Study Group Conference. (Illus.). 608p. 1974. 45.00x (ISBN 0-19-877021-9). Oxford U Pr.
Liverpool, Charles J. Treatise on the Coins of the Realm. LC 67-29513. Repr. of 1880 ed. 17.50x (ISBN 0-678-00412-9). Kelley.
Moggridge, D. E. British Monetary Policy, Nineteen Twenty-Four to Nineteen Thirty-One. LC 76-169576. (Department of Applied Economics Monographs: No. 21). 1972. 42.50 (ISBN 0-521-08225-0). Cambridge U Pr.

MONETARY POLICY–GREECE, MODERN

Zolotas, Xenophon. Monetary Equilibrium & Economic Development. 1965. 16.50x (ISBN 0-691-04148-2). Princeton U Pr.

MONETARY POLICY–INDIA

Gould, B., et al. Monetarism or Prosperity? 1981. text ed. 37.50x (ISBN 0-333-30782-8, Pub. by Macmillan England); pap. text ed. 15.00x (ISBN 0-333-31973-7). Humanities.
Gupta, Suraj B. Monetary Planning for India. 252p. 1979. text ed. 14.95x (ISBN 0-19-561145-4). Oxford U Pr.

MONETARY POLICY–JAPAN

Organization for Economic Cooperation & Development. Monetary Policy in Japan. (Monetary Studies Ser.: No. 1). 108p. 1973. 3.50x (ISBN 92-64-11019-4). OECD.

MONETARY POLICY–LATIN AMERICA

Behrman, J. R. Macroeconomic Policy in a Developing Country: Chilean Experience. (Contributions to Economic Analysis: Vol. 109). 1977. 36.75 (ISBN 0-7204-0548-3, North-Holland). Elsevier.
Official External Financing in Latin American Development Strategy: Implications for the Seventies. 1973. pap. 2.00 (ISBN 0-8270-3700-7). OAS.

MONETARY POLICY–RUSSIA

Zwass, Adam. Money, Banking, & Credit in the Soviet Union & Eastern Europe. LC 78-64910. 1979. 18.50 (ISBN 0-87332-124-3). M E Sharpe.

MONETARY POLICY–SWEDEN

Eagly, Robert V. The Swedish Bullionist Controversy: P. N. Christiernin's Lectures on the High Price of Foreign Exchange in Sweden (1761) LC 74-161990. (Memoirs Ser.: Vol. 87). 1971. pap. 2.50 (ISBN 0-87169-087-X). Am Philos.

MONETARY POLICY–YUGOSLAVIA

Dimitrijevic, Dimitrije & Macesich, George. Money & Finance in Contemporary Yugoslavia. LC 72-92889. (Special Studies in International Economics & Development). 1973. 29.50x (ISBN 0-275-28725-4); pap. text ed. 18.50x (ISBN 0-89197-857-7). Irvington.

MONETARY QUESTION

see Currency Question; Money

MONETARY UNIONS

see also Sterling Area

Fratianni, Michele & Peeters, Theo, eds. One Money for Europe. LC 78-67228. (Praeger Special Studies). 1979. 24.95 (ISBN 0-03-047526-0). Praeger.
Hayek, F. A. Choice in Currency: A Way to Stop Inflation. (Occasional Paper: No. 48). 1977. pap. 4.25 (ISBN 0-255-36078-9). Transatlantic.
Johnson, Harry G. & Swoboda, Alexander K. The Economics of Common Currencies. LC 73-76382. 302p. 1973. text ed. 16.50x (ISBN 0-674-23226-7). Harvard U Pr.
Krauss, Melvyn B., ed. The Economics of Integration: A Book of Readings. 1973. pap. text ed. 14.95x (ISBN 0-04-330222-X). Allen Unwin.
McKinnon, Ronald I. Money in International Exchange: The Convertible Currency System. 1979. text ed. 13.95x (ISBN 0-19-502408-7); pap. text ed. 9.95x (ISBN 0-19-502409-5). Oxford U Pr.
Swoboda, A. K., ed. Europe & the Evolution of the International Monetary System. 1973. 25.00 (ISBN 9-0286-0173-2). Heinman.

MONEY

see also Bank Deposits; Banks and Banking; Banks and Banking, Central; Barter; Bills of Exchange; Bimetallism; Capital; Circular Velocity of Money; Coinage; Coins; Counterfeits and Counterfeiting; Credit; Currency Question; Finance; Finance, Public; Foreign Exchange; Gold; Gold Standard; Inflation (Finance); Mints; Occupation Currency; Paper Money; Precious Metals; Prices; Purchasing Power; Quantity Theory of Money; Silver; Silver Question; Social Credit; Tokens; Wealth
also names of coins, e.g. Dollar

Achterberg, E. & Lanz, K. Enzyklopadisches Lexikon Fur des Geld, Bank und Borsen Wesen, 2 vols. (Ger.). 1967. 240.00 set (ISBN 3-7819-0030-4, M-7364, Pub. by Fritz Knapp Verlag). French & Eur.
Aliber, Robert Z. Monetary Reform & World Inflation. LC 73-86713. (The Washington Papers: No. 12). 1973. 4.00x (ISBN 0-8039-0285-9). Sage.
Angell, James W. Behavior of Money: Exploratory Studies. LC 75-85140. Repr. of 1936 ed. 12.50x (ISBN 0-678-00525-7). Kelley.
--Theory of International Prices. LC 65-19644. Repr. of 1926 ed. 22.50x (ISBN 0-678-00094-8). Kelley.
Argoff, Allen. The Social Studies Student Investigates Money. (gr. 7-12). 1977. PLB 7.97 (ISBN 0-8239-0375-3). Rosen Pr.
Aronson, Jonathan D. Money & Power: Banks & the World Monetary System. LC 78-6630. (Sage Library of Social Research: No. 66). 216p. 1978. 20.00x (ISBN 0-8039-0998-5); pap. 9.95x (ISBN 0-8039-1046-0). Sage.
Auernheimer, Leonardo & Ekelund, Robert B. The Essentials of Money & Banking. 450p. 1982. 21.95 (ISBN 0-471-02103-2). Wiley.
Bailey, Samuel. Money & Its Vicissitudes in Value: As They Affect National Industry & Pecuniary Contracts. Repr. of 1837 ed. 15.00x (ISBN 0-678-00981-3). Kelley.
Barry, James A., Jr. Money Power. 1981. 12.95 (ISBN 0-8359-4637-1). Reston.
Beck, William. Money & Banking. 1980. lib. bdg. 69.95 (ISBN 0-8490-3095-1). Gordon Pr.
Berman, Peter I. Inflation & the Money Supply in the United States, 1956-1977. LC 78-4344. 1978. 14.95 (ISBN 0-669-02346-9). Lexington Bks.
Beyen, J. W. Money in a Maelstrom. Wilkins, Mira, ed. LC 73-3898. (International Finance Ser.). 1978. Repr. of 1949 ed. lib. bdg. 15.00x (ISBN 0-405-11203-3). Arno.
Blodgett, Richard E. The New York Times Book of Money. rev. ed. LC 72-88117. (Illus.). 224p. 1978. pap. 6.95 (ISBN 0-8129-6272-9). Times Bks.
Boissevain, Gideon M. Monetary Question. Warner, G. T., tr. LC 75-75564. Repr. of 1891 ed. lib. bdg. 15.00x (ISBN 0-8371-1080-7, BOMQ). Greenwood.
Borneman, Ernest, ed. The Psychoanalysis of Money. 1976. 15.00 (ISBN 0-916354-02-4); pap. 5.95 (ISBN 0-916354-03-2). Urizen Bks.
Bowen, Ian. Inflation & Social Justice. 35p. 1977. pap. 3.00x (ISBN 0-85564-056-1, Pub. by U of W Austral Pr). Intl Schol Bk Serv.
Bretton, Henry L. The Power of Money. LC 79-23484. 1980. 34.00 (ISBN 0-87395-425-4); pap. 12.95 (ISBN 0-87395-426-2). State U NY Pr.
Brough, William. Natural Law of Money. LC 76-75567. Repr. of 1896 ed. lib. bdg. 15.00x (ISBN 0-8371-1081-5, BRNL). Greenwood.
Buchanan, David. Inquiry into the Taxation & Commercial Policy of Great Britain. Repr. of 1844 ed. 19.50x (ISBN 0-678-01018-8). Kelley.
Burkett, Larry. What Husbands Wish Their Wives Knew About Money. 1977. pap. 3.50 (ISBN 0-88207-758-9). Victor Bks.
Cana Conference of Chicago. Perspectives on Money. 1973. pap. 0.35 (ISBN 0-915388-11-1, Pub. by Delaney). Buckley Pubns.
Cantelon, Willard. Money Master of the World. LC 75-38197. 1976. pap. 2.95 (ISBN 0-88270-152-5). Logos.
Cargill, Thomas F. Money, the Financial System, & Monetary Policy. (Illus.). 1979. ref. 19.95 (ISBN 0-13-600346-X). P-H.
Carson, C. Deane. Money & Finance: Readings in Theory, Policy & Institutions. 2nd ed. LC 70-37643. 1972. text ed. 21.50 (ISBN 0-471-13712-X). Wiley.
Catchings, Waddill & Roos, Charles F. Money, Men & Machines. 1953. 12.50 (ISBN 0-686-17719-3). Quest Edns.
Chaim, Bezalel. Hugo Bilgram & Louis Levy: The Battle Against the Money Monopoly. 1980. lib. bdg. 49.95 (ISBN 0-686-26596-3). Mutualist Pr.
Chandler, Lester V. The Monetary-Financial System. 1979. text ed. 20.95 scp (ISBN 0-06-041219-4, HarpC). Har-Row.
Chevalier, Michel. On the Probable Fall in the Value of Gold. Cobden, Richard, ed. LC 68-28619. Repr. of 1859 ed. lib. bdg. 15.00x (ISBN 0-8371-0045-3, CHPF). Greenwood.
Chipman, John S. The Theory of Inter-Sectoral Money Flows & Income Formation. LC 78-64212. (Johns Hopkins University. Studies in the Social Sciences. Sixty-Eighth Ser. 1950: 2). Repr. of 1851 ed. 18.00 (ISBN 0-404-61317-9). AMS Pr.
Cohen, Benjamin J. Organizing the World's Money. LC 77-72540. 1977. text ed. 11.95x (ISBN 0-465-05327-0). Basic.
Colwell, Stephen. Ways & Means of Payment. LC 65-23212. Repr. of 1859 ed. 22.50x (ISBN 0-678-00110-3). Kelley.
Coogan, Gertrude M. Money Creators. 69.95 (ISBN 0-87968-317-1). Gordon Pr.
Coughlin, Charles E. Money, Questions & Answers. 1978. pap. 4.00x (ISBN 0-911038-28-0). Noontide.
Coulter, M. B. Vermont Obsolete Notes & Scrip. (Illus.). 151p. 10.00 (ISBN 0-87637-226-4). Hse of Collectibles.
Cowperthwait, John H. Money, Silver & Finance. LC 69-19666. Repr. of 1892 ed. lib. bdg. 14.00x (ISBN 0-8371-0363-0, COMS). Greenwood.
Crawford, Arthur W. Monetary Management Under the New Deal. LC 70-173988. (FDR & the Era of the New Deal Ser.). 380p. 1972. Repr. of 1940 ed. lib. bdg. 39.50 (ISBN 0-306-70374-2). Da Capo.
Crockett, Andrew D. International Money: Issues & Analysis. 1977. 28.50 (ISBN 0-12-195750-0). Acad Pr.
--Money: Theory, Policy & Institutions. 1973. pap. text ed. 14.95x (ISBN 0-17-712206-4). Intl Ideas.
Crump, Thomas. The Phenomenon of Money. (The Library of Man). 304p. 1981. price not set (ISBN 0-7100-0856-2). Routledge & Kegan.
Culbertson, John M. Money & Banking. 2nd ed. 1976. text ed. 16.95 (ISBN 0-07-014886-4, C); instructor's manual 4.95 (ISBN 0-07-014887-2). McGraw.
Currie, Lauchlin. Supply & Control of Money in the U. S: Containing the 1934 Proposed Revision of the Monetary System of the U. S. 3rd ed. LC 67-18291. (Illus.). 199p. (With a prefatory paper by Karl Brunner). 1968. Repr. of 1934 ed. 17.50 (ISBN 0-8462-1060-6). Russell.
Darst, David M. The Handbook of the Bond & Money Markets. LC 80-36816. (Illus.). 461p. 1981. 29.95 (ISBN 0-07-015401-5, P&RB). McGraw.
Davidson, P. Earn Money at Home. (McGraw-Hill Paperback Ser.). 1981. pap. price not set (ISBN 0-07-049606-4, SP). McGraw.
Davidson, Paul. Money & the Real World. 2nd ed. 1978. pap. text ed. 16.95 (ISBN 0-470-99217-4). Halsted Pr.
Davies, Brinley. United Kingdom & the World Monetary System: Studies in the British Economy Ser. 1976. pap. text ed. 7.00x (ISBN 0-435-84350-8). Heinemann Ed.
Dayton. Your Money: Frustration or Freedom? 1979. pap. 2.95 (ISBN 0-8423-8725-0). Tyndale.
De Bodin De Saint-Laurent, Jean. Idees Monetaires et Commerciales De Jean Bodin. 1969. Repr. of 1907 ed. 20.50 (ISBN 0-8337-0314-5). B Franklin.
De Brunhoff, Suzanne. Marx on Money. 1976. 10.00 (ISBN 0-916354-43-1); pap. 4.95 (ISBN 0-916354-44-X). Urizen Bks.
De Bruyn Steinbach, Marie. How Much in Real Money: Survey of International Currency Exchange Rates. 1969. pap. 0.65x (ISBN 0-9600298-1-8). Steinbach.
Del Mar, Alexander. Science of Money. 2nd ed. LC 68-5846. (Research & Source Ser.: No. 322). 1969. Repr. of 1896 ed. 20.50 (ISBN 0-8337-0830-9). B Franklin.
--The Science of Money. 59.95 (ISBN 0-8490-1002-0). Gordon Pr.

Dennis, G. E. Monetary Economics. LC 80-40095. (Modern Economic Ser.). (Illus.). 312p. (Orig.). 1981. pap. text ed. 16.95x (ISBN 0-582-45573-1). Longman.

Donoghue, William E. & Tilling, Thomas. William E. Donoghue's Complete Money Market Guide. LC 80-8200. (Illus.). 256p. 1981. 12.95 (ISBN 0-690-02008-2, HarpT). Har-Row.

Drake, Peter J. Money, Finance & Development. 244p. 1980. 30.95x (ISBN 0-470-26992-8). Halsted Pr.

Drollinger, William C. & Drollinger, William C., Sr. You Are a Money Brain. LC 81-67503. 1981. write for info. (ISBN 0-914244-07-8). Epic Pubns.

Duesenberry, James. Money & Credit: Impact & Control. 3rd ed. LC 70-173310. (Foundations of Modern Economics Ser). (Illus.). 160p. 1972. pap. 9.95 ref. ed. (ISBN 0-13-600304-4). P-H.

Dunbar, Charles F., ed. Laws of the United States Relating to Currency, Finance & Banking from 1789 to 1891. LC 68-28627. Repr. of 1893 ed. lib. bdg. 20.25x (ISBN 0-8371-4585-6, DULU). Greenwood.

Dunkman, William E. Money, Credit & Banking. 1970. pap. text ed. 10.95x (ISBN 0-394-30170-6). Phila Bk Co.

Dwinell, Olive C. Story of Our Money. 1979. lib. bdg. 59.95 (ISBN 0-8490-3009-9). Gordon Pr.

Edwards, William E. Action Guide to Big Money Selling. 1972. 49.50 (ISBN 0-13-918698-0). Exec Reports.

Enzyklopaedisches Lexicon Fuer das Geld, Bank und Boersenwesen, 2 vols. 3rd ed. 1968. Set. 250.00 (ISBN 3-7819-0030-4, M-7086). French & Eur.

Eshag, Eprime. From Marshall to Keynes. LC 64-1849. 1963. 12.50x (ISBN 0-678-06254-4). Kelley.

Faulkner, Edward H. Uneasy Money. 114p. 1946. 7.95x (ISBN 0-8061-0149-0). U of Okla Pr.

Fisher, Douglas. Monetary Theory & the Demand for Money. LC 77-15504. 278p. 1980. pap. 21.95 (ISBN 0-470-27023-3, Pub. by Halsted Pr). Wiley.

--Monetary Theory & the Demand for Money. LC 77-15504. 1978. text ed. 21.95 (ISBN 0-470-99297-2). Halsted Pr.

--Money, Banking & Monetary Policy. 1980. 19.50x (ISBN 0-256-02365-4). Irwin.

Fitzgerald, T. H. Money Market Directory 1981: Institutional Investors & Their Portfolio Managers. 1980. 265.00 (ISBN 0-939712-00-8). Money Mkt.

Frankel, S. Herbert. Two Philosophies of Money: The Conflict of Trust & Authority. LC 77-9211. 1977. 14.95x (ISBN 0-312-82698-2). St Martin.

Frazer, William J., Jr. Crisis in Economic Theory: A Study of Monetary Policy, Analysis, & Economic Goals. LC 73-16273. 1973. 20.00 (ISBN 0-8130-0392-X); pap. 14.50x (ISBN 0-8130-0445-4). U Presses Fla.

--Liquidity Structure of Firms & Monetary Economics. LC 65-63999. (U of Fla. Social Sciences Monographs: No. 27). (Illus.). 1965. pap. 3.00 (ISBN 0-8130-0080-7). U Presses Fla.

Fry, Richard. Scheme for a Paper Currency Together with Two Petitions Written in a Boston Gaol in 1739-1740. LC 68-57129. (Research & Source Works Ser.: No. 312). 1969. Repr. of 1908 ed. 18.50 (ISBN 0-8337-1248-9). B Franklin.

Gayer, A. D., ed. Lessons of Monetary Experience: Essays in Honor of Irving Fisher. LC 70-86089. Repr. of 1937 ed. 19.50x (ISBN 0-678-00643-1). Kelley.

Goldberg, Herb & Lewis, Robert T. Money Madness. LC 77-25444. 1978. 8.95 (ISBN 0-688-03296-6). Morrow.

--Money Madness: The Psychology of Saving, Spending, Loving & Hating Money. 1979. pap. 2.75 (ISBN 0-451-09856-0, E9856, Sig). NAL.

Gordon-Cumming, M. Money in Industry. 59.95 (ISBN 0-8490-0660-0). Gordon Pr.

Gray, John. Lectures on the Nature & Use of Money. LC 68-55724. Repr. of 1848 ed. lib. bdg. 19.50x (ISBN 0-678-00828-0). Kelley.

Grieve, Robin. Money: Denarius to Decimal. (Jackdaw Ser: No. 70). (Illus.). 1971. 6.95 (ISBN 0-670-48522-5, Grossman). Viking Pr.

Grimaudet, Francois & Von Humboldt, Alexander. Fluctuations of Gold Together with the Law of Payment. LC 75-157156. (Research & Source Works Ser.: No. 722). 1971. Repr. of 1900 ed. 18.50 (ISBN 0-8337-4622-7). B Franklin.

Gurley, John G. & Shaw, Edward S. Money in a Theory of Finance. 1960. 18.95 (ISBN 0-8157-3322-4). Brookings.

Haberler, Gottfried. Money in the International Economy: A Study in Balance-Of-Payments Adjustment, International Liquidity, & Exchange Rates. 2nd ed. 1969. pap. text ed. 1.95x (ISBN 0-674-58401-5). Harvard U Pr.

Hacche, John. Economics of Money & Income. LC 77-555712. (Illus.). 1970. 11.25x (ISBN 0-435-84396-6). Intl Pubns Serv.

Haines, Walter W. Money, Prices & Policy. 2nd ed. 1966. text ed. 16.00 (ISBN 0-07-025525-3, C). McGraw.

Hamilton, Rowland. Money & Value: An Inquiry into the Means & Ends of Economic Production. LC 78-120326. Repr. of 1878 ed. lib. bdg. 19.50x (ISBN 0-678-00704-7). Kelley.

Hamilton, William. Money Should Be Fun. 1980. 9.95 (ISBN 0-395-28218-7); pap. 5.95 (ISBN 0-686-65605-9). HM.

Harris, Joseph. Essay Upon Money & Coins, Pt. 1. (History of English Economic Thought Ser). 1970. Repr. of 1757 ed. 23.00 (ISBN 0-384-21480-0). Johnson Repr.

Harvey, William H. Coin on Money, Trusts & Imperialism. LC 75-323. (The Radical Tradition in America Ser.). 184p. 1975. Repr. of 1899 ed. 16.50 (ISBN 0-88355-226-4). Hyperion Conn.

Hawtrey, Ralph G. Currency & Credit. Wilkins, Mira, ed. LC 78-3923. (International Finance Ser.). 1978. Repr. of 1919 ed. lib. bdg. 25.00x (ISBN 0-405-11226-2). Arno.

--Good & Bad Trade: An Inquiry into the Causes of Trade Fluctuations. LC 68-54735. Repr. of 1913 ed. lib. bdg. 15.00x (ISBN 0-678-00359-9). Kelley.

Hayek, F. A. Denationalisation of Money. (Hobart Paperbk: No. 70). 1977. pap. 7.50 (ISBN 0-255-36105-X). Transatlantic.

Hayek, Friedrich A. Monetary Nationalism & International Stability. LC 64-7666. Repr. of 1937 ed. 9.50x (ISBN 0-678-00047-6). Kelley.

--Monetary Theory & the Trade Cycle. LC 66-22629. Repr. of 1933 ed. 13.50x (ISBN 0-678-00176-6). Kelley.

--Prices & Production. 2nd enl. ed. LC 67-19586. Repr. of 1935 ed. 12.50x (ISBN 0-678-06515-2). Kelley.

Hayes, Michael. Money: How to Get It, Keep It, & Make It Grow. (Illus.). 1979. 15.95 (ISBN 0-8144-5503-4). Am Mgmt.

Heidensohn, Klaus, ed. The Book of Money. (Illus.). 1979. 24.95 (ISBN 0-07-027862-8, GB). McGraw.

Helfferich, Karl T. Money, 2 Vols in One. Gregory, T. E., ed. Infield, Louis, tr. LC 67-19708. Repr. of 1927 ed. Set. 25.00x (ISBN 0-678-00474-9). Kelley.

Henning, Charles, et al. Financial Markets & the Economy. 2nd ed. (Illus.). 1978. ref. 19.95 (ISBN 0-13-316083-1). P-H.

Herrick, Tracy G. Timing: Managing Your Money Through Your Life-Cycle. 255p. 1981. 13.95 (ISBN 0-89505-062-5, 21057). Argus Comm.

Hicks, John R. Critical Essays in Monetary Theory. 1967. 11.00x (ISBN 0-19-828155-2). Oxford U Pr.

Hinshaw, Randall, ed. Monetary Reform & the Price of Gold: Alternative Approaches. LC 67-24630. 176p. 1967. 12.50x (ISBN 0-8018-0274-1). Johns Hopkins.

Hosek, William R. & Zahn, Frank. Monetary Theory, Policy & Financial Markets. (Illus.). 1977. text ed. 18.95 (ISBN 0-07-030436-X, C); instructor's manual 4.95 (ISBN 0-07-030437-8). McGraw.

Hotson, John H. International Comparisons of Money Velocity & Wage Markups. LC 68-56840. (Illus.). 1968. 13.50x (ISBN 0-678-00437-4). Kelley.

Howe, John B. Monetary & Industrial Fallacies: A Dialogue. Repr. of 1878 ed. lib. bdg. 14.00x (ISBN 0-8371-1102-1, HOIF). Greenwood.

Hudgeons. Hewitt-Donln Catalog of U. S. Small Size Paper Money. 14th ed. (Collector Ser.). (Illus.). 192p. 1981. pap. 3.95 (ISBN 0-87637-112-8, 112-08). Hse of Collectibles.

--The Official Guide to Detecting Altered Counterfeit Coins & Currency. (Collector Ser.). (Illus.). 160p. (Orig.). 1981. pap. 4.95 (ISBN 0-87637-169-1, 169-01). Hse of Collectibles.

--The Official Investors Guide to Buying & Selling Gold, Silver & Diamonds. (Collector Ser.). (Illus.). 160p. (Orig.). 1981. pap. 6.95 (ISBN 0-87637-171-3, 171-03). Hse of Collectibles.

Jackendoff, Nathaniel. Money, Flow of Funds, & Economic Policy. LC 68-30892. (Illus.). 523p. 1968. 23.50 (ISBN 0-471-06632-X). Wiley.

Jevons, William S. Investigations in Currency & Finance. Foxwell, H. S., ed. LC 64-22238. (Illus.). Repr. of 1884 ed. 19.50x (ISBN 0-678-00060-3). Kelley.

John-Roger. A Consciousness of Wealth: Creating a Money Magnet. 1976. pap. 2.50 (ISBN 0-88238-951-3). Baraka Bk.

Johnson, Gove G. Treasury & Monetary Policy, 1933-1938. LC 66-24711. 1967. Repr. of 1939 ed. 8.50 (ISBN 0-8462-0843-1). Russell.

Johnson, Harry G. Macroeconomics & Monetary Theory. 214p. 1972. 16.95x (ISBN 0-202-06053-5). Aldine Pub.

Jones, David. Your Book of Money. (gr. 7 up). 1971. 6.50 (ISBN 0-571-09341-8). Transatlantic.

Kahn, Charles H. & Hanna, J. Bradley. Money Makes Sense. 2nd ed. (Illus., Orig.). 1972. pap. 4.40 (ISBN 0-8224-4515-8); tchrs' manual free (ISBN 0-8224-5210-3). Pitman Learning.

Katz, Howard S. The Paper Aristocracy. LC 76-467. (Illus.). 1976. 9.95 (ISBN 0-916728-01-3); pap. 5.95 (ISBN 0-916728-00-5). Bks in Focus.

Kemmerer, Edwin W. Seasonal Variations in the Relative Demand for Money & Capital in the United States. Bruchey, Stuart, ed. LC 80-1154. (The Rise of Commercial Banking Ser.). (Illus.). 1981. Repr. of 1910 ed. lib. bdg. 45.00x (ISBN 0-405-13660-9). Arno.

Keynes, John M. General Theory of Employment, Interest & Money. LC 36-27176. 1965. pap. 4.95 (ISBN 0-15-634711-3, H044, Hbgr). HarBraceJ.

--A Treatise on Money, 2 vols. LC 75-41162. Repr. of 1930 ed. 48.00 set (ISBN 0-404-15000-4); Vol. 1. 24.00 (ISBN 0-404-15001-2); Vol. 2. 24.00 (ISBN 0-404-15002-0). AMS Pr.

Keystrokes Series, 4 bks. 1981. Set. 22.00 (ISBN 0-88488-215-2, 10560). Creative Pubns.

Kinley, David. Money: Study of the Theory of the Medium of Exchange. LC 68-28638. 1968. Repr. of 1904 ed. lib. bdg. 25.50x (ISBN 0-8371-0515-3, KIMS). Greenwood.

--Use of Credit Instruments in Payments in the United States. LC 68-27848. Repr. of 1910 ed. 13.50x (ISBN 0-678-00546-X). Kelley.

Klise, Eugene S. Money & Banking. 5th ed. 1972. text ed. 13.25 (ISBN 0-538-06230-4). SW Pub.

Knapp, Georg F. State Theory of Money. Lucas, H. M. & Bonar, James, trs. LC 75-140544. Repr. of 1924 ed. lib. bdg. 15.00x (ISBN 0-678-00831-0). Kelley.

Krishnan-Kutty, G. Money & Banking. 1979. text ed. 9.25x (ISBN 0-391-01815-9). Humanities.

Labadie, Laurance. The Money Racket. (Men & Movements in the History & Philosophy of Anarchism Ser.). 1979. lib. bdg. 59.95 (ISBN 0-685-96406-X). Revisionist Pr.

Laidler, David E. Demand for Money: Theories & Evidence. 2nd ed. (Monetary Economic Ser). 128p. 1978. pap. text ed. 8.50 scp (ISBN 0-912212-07-1, HarpC). Har-Row.

Lancaster, Don. The Incredible Secret Money Machine. LC 78-62350. 1978. pap. 5.95 (ISBN 0-672-21562-4). Sams.

League of Nations, Secretariat. Memorandum on Currency & Central Banks: 1913-1924, 2 vols. in 1. Wilkins, Mira, ed. LC 78-3931. (International Finance Ser.). (Illus.). 1978. Repr. of 1925 ed. lib. bdg. 36.00x (ISBN 0-405-11234-3). Arno.

--Memorandum on Currency & Central Banks: 1913-1925, 2 vols. in 1. Wilkins, Mira, ed. LC 78-3930. (International Finance Ser.). (Illus.). 1978. Repr. of 1926 ed. lib. bdg. 23.00x (ISBN 0-405-11233-5). Arno.

Leijonhufvud, Axel. Information & Coordination: Essays in Macroeconomic Theory. (Illus.). 400p. 1981. text ed. 19.95x (ISBN 0-19-502814-7); pap. text ed. 11.95x (ISBN 0-19-502815-5). Oxford U Pr.

Leitch, Gordon, Jr. From Dollar to Counterfeit: The Path of American Government Dishonesty. LC 80-71064. (Illus.). 168p. (Orig.). (gr. 9-12). 1981. pap. 8.00 (ISBN 0-9605734-1-0). Bicent Era.

Lesko, Matthew. Goverment Money Book. (Handbook Ser.). 1982. pap. 3.95 (ISBN 0-14-046510-3). Penguin.

Lewinski, Jan S. Money, Credit & Prices. LC 79-51865. 1980. Repr. of 1929 ed. 15.50 (ISBN 0-88355-957-9). Hyperion Conn.

Lindahl, Erik R. Studies in the Theory of Money & Capital. LC 70-117915. (Illus.). Repr. of 1939 ed. 17.50x (ISBN 0-678-00655-5). Kelley.

Lindgren, Henry C. Great Expectations: The Psychology of Money. LC 80-14177. 262p. 1980. 12.50 (ISBN 0-913232-82-3). W Kaufmann.

Lindholm, Richard W. Money & Banking. (Quality Paperback: No. 19). (Orig.). 1969. pap. 1.95 (ISBN 0-8226-0019-6). Littlefield.

--Money Management & Institutions. 1978. pap. 7.95 (ISBN 0-8226-0334-9). Littlefield.

Locke, John. Several Papers Relating to Money, Interest & Trade, Etc. LC 67-29701. Repr. of 1696 ed. 19.50x (ISBN 0-678-00334-3). Kelley.

Lombra, Raymond E., et al. Money & the Financial System: Theory, Institutions & Policy. (Illus.). 1980. text ed. 16.95x (ISBN 0-07-038607-2); instructor's manual 5.50 (ISBN 0-07-038608-0). McGraw.

Lundberg, Erik. Study in the Theory of Economic Expansion. Repr. of 1937 ed. 15.00x (ISBN 0-678-00046-8). Kelley.

McCulloch, John R., ed. Select Collection of Scarce & Valuable Tracts on Money & Metallic Currency. LC 65-16987. Repr. of 1856 ed. 32.50x (ISBN 0-678-00147-2). Kelley.

McKinnon, Ronald I., ed. Money & Finance in Economic Growth & Development. (Business Economics & Finance Ser.: Vol. 8). 1976. 43.75 (ISBN 0-8247-6366-1). Dekker.

Makinen, Gil. Money: The Price Level & Interest Rates - an Introduction to Monetary Theory. (Illus.). 1977. ref. ed. 21.95 (ISBN 0-13-600486-5). P-H.

Mandel, Ernest. Decline of the Dollar: A Marxist View of the Monetary Crisis. LC 72-85799. 128p. 1973. 10.00 (ISBN 0-913460-04-4, Dist. by Path Pr Inc Ny). Monad Pr.

Marshall, Alfred. Money, Credit & Commerce. LC 65-16984. Repr. of 1923 ed. 19.50x (ISBN 0-678-00072-7). Kelley.

Mason, Will E. Clarification of the Monetary Standard. LC 62-20541. 1963. 16.50x (ISBN 0-271-73052-8). Pa St U Pr.

Meiselman, David M., ed. Varieties of Monetary Experience. LC 70-116027. (Economic Research Center Ser). 1971. 20.00x (ISBN 0-226-51930-9). U of Chicago Pr.

Miller, Roger L. & Manne, Henry G. Gold, Money & the Law. LC 75-20705. 160p. 1975. 12.95 (ISBN 0-202-06072-1). Beresford Bk Serv.

Mittra, Sid. Money & Banking: Theory, Analysis & Policy. 1970. pap. text ed. 6.95x (ISBN 0-685-84267-3). Phila Bk Co.

Money in Growing. 1981. 12.00x (ISBN 0-686-75418-2, Pub. by Grower Bks). State Mutual Bk.

Money Made Mysterious. 1976. pap. 3.95 (ISBN 0-911038-21-3). Noontide.

Moore, William G., Sr. Basic Business Facts: Evaluating Money Resources. 1980. pap. text ed. 1.99 (ISBN 0-934488-02-9). Williams Ent.

Morgan, E. Victor & Morgan, Ann D. Gold or Paper? (Hobart Paperbk: No. 69). 1977. pap. 4.25 (ISBN 0-255-36088-6). Transatlantic.

Moulton, Harold G. The Financial Organization of Society. facsimile ed. LC 75-2653. (Wall Street & the Security Markets Ser.). 1975. Repr. of 1930 ed. 46.00x (ISBN 0-405-06978-2). Arno.

Mundell, Robert. Monetary Theory: Inflation, Interest & Growth in the World Economy. LC 74-123615. (Illus.). 1971. text ed. 18.95 (ISBN 0-87620-586-4). Goodyear.

Myers, Margaret. Monetary Proposals for Social Reform. LC 71-110574. 1970. Repr. of 1940 ed. 18.00 (ISBN 0-404-04548-0). AMS Pr.

Myrdal, Gunnar. Monetary Equlibrium. LC 65-23216. Repr. of 1939 ed. 15.00x (ISBN 0-678-00092-1). Kelley.

Neale, Walter C. Monies in Societies. LC 76-519. (Cross-Cultural Themes Ser.). 128p. 1976. pap. text ed. 3.50x (ISBN 0-88316-525-2). Chandler & Sharp.

Newlyn, Walter T. Theory of Money. 3rd. ed. (Illus.). 1978. pap. 24.00x (ISBN 0-19-877099-5); pap. 9.95 (ISBN 0-19-877100-2). Oxford U Pr.

Niebyl, Karl H. Studies in the Classical Theories of Money. LC 70-173795. Repr. of 1946 ed. 18.75 (ISBN 0-404-04709-2). AMS Pr.

Niehans, Jurg. The Theory of Money. 1980. pap. 6.95 (ISBN 0-8018-2372-2). Johns Hopkins.

--The Theory of Money. LC 77-17247. (Illus.). 1978. text ed. 22.50x (ISBN 0-8018-2055-3). Johns Hopkins.

The Nine Deceits & the Collapse of Gold. 1976. 45.80 (ISBN 0-89266-076-7). Inst Econ Finan.

North, Dudley. Discourses Upon Trade: Principally Directed to the Cases of the Interest, Coinage, Clipping, Increase of Money. (History of English Economic Thought Ser). 1970. Repr. of 1691 ed. 12.50 (ISBN 0-384-41960-7). Johnson Repr.

Otis, George. God, Money & You. pap. 1.95 (ISBN 0-89728-034-2, 546638). Omega Pubns OR.

Owens, Od O. Living with Money. (Christian Living Ser). 16p. 1976. pap. 0.30 (ISBN 0-8170-0727-X). Judson.

Patinkin, Don. Money, Interest, & Prices: An Integration of Monetary & Value Theory. 2nd ed. 1965. text ed. 35.50 scp (ISBN 0-06-045030-4, HarpC). Har-Row.

Pepper, Gordon & Wood, Geoffrey. Too Much Money...? (Hobart Paperbk: No. 68). 1977. pap. 4.25 (ISBN 0-255-36083-5). Transatlantic.

Petievich, Gerald. Money Men & One Shot Deal. LC 79-8756. 1981. 12.95 (ISBN 0-15-169892-9). Harbracej.

Phillips, Michael, et al. The Seven Laws of Money. 1974. 7.95 (ISBN 0-394-49224-2); pap. 4.00 (ISBN 0-394-70686-2). Random.

Pick, Franz. Pick's Currency Yearbook 1974. 19th ed. LC 55-11013. 728p. 1975. 150.00x (ISBN 0-87551-274-7). Pick Pub.

--Pick's Currency Yearbook 1975-1976. 20th ed. LC 55-11013. 1976. 150.00x (ISBN 0-87551-275-5). Pick Pub.

--Pick's Currency Yearbook 1976-1977. 21st ed. LC 55-11013. 1978. 150.00 (ISBN 0-87551-276-3). Pick Pub.

--Pick's Currency Yearbook 1977-1979. 22nd ed. LC 55-11013. 1981. 180.00 (ISBN 0-87551-277-1). Pick Pub.

Pick, Franz & Sedillot, Rene. All the Monies of the World - A Chronicle of Currency Values. LC 72-154984. 1971. 80.00x (ISBN 0-87551-610-6). Pick Pub.
Pigou, Arthur C. The Veil of Money. LC 78-10214. 1979. Repr. of 1949 ed. lib. bdg. 17.50x (ISBN 0-313-20742-9, PIVM). Greenwood.
Poole, William. Money & the Economy: A Monetarist View. LC 78-52499. (Perspectives on Economics). (Illus.). 1978. 6.95 (ISBN 0-201-08364-7). A-W.
Popp, Edward E. The Great Cookie Jar: Taking the Mysteries Out of the Money System. LC 78-62961. 1978. pap. 1.95 (ISBN 0-9600358-2-6). Wis Ed Fund.
--Money, Bona Fide or Non-Bona Fide. 1970. pap. 0.50 (ISBN 0-9600358-1-8). Wis Ed Fund.
Potter, David. Understanding Money. 1972. 17.95 (ISBN 0-7134-2163-0, Pub. by Batsford England). David & Charles.
Prager, Jonas, ed. Monetary Economics: Controversies in Theory & Policy. (Orig.). 1971. pap. text ed. 8.95 (ISBN 0-394-30827-1, RanC). Random.
Radford, Charles D. What No One, but Absolutely No One Knows About Money. (Illus.). 127p. 1981. 31.25 (ISBN 0-89266-284-0). Am Classical Coll Pr.
Raguet, Condy. Treatise on Currency & Banking. 2nd ed. LC 65-26375. Repr. of 1840 ed. 17.50x (ISBN 0-678-00215-0). Kelley.
Rainwater. What Money Buys. LC 73-90139. 1974. 10.95x (ISBN 0-465-09139-3). Basic.
Ranlett, John G. Money & Banking: An Introduction to Analysis & Policy. 3rd ed. LC 77-23251. 1977. text ed. 26.50 (ISBN 0-471-70815-1). Wiley.
Riboud, Jacques. The Mechanics of Money. 1980. 25.00x (ISBN 0-312-52455-2). St Martin.
Rice, George G. My Adventures with Your Money. 1975. 8.50 (ISBN 0-685-54481-8). Bookfinger.
Richardson, Dennis W. Electric Money: Evolution of an Electronic Funds-Transfer System. 1970. pap. 4.95x (ISBN 0-262-68025-4). MIT Pr.
Ricour, Pierre. Lexique Anglais-Francais De la Banque et De la Monnaie. 87p. (Eng.-Fr.). 1973. pap. 2.95 (ISBN 0-686-57208-4, M-6486). French & Eur.
Ridgeway, William. The Origin of Metallic Currency & Weight Standards. LC 76-16440. (Illus.). 1976. Repr. of 1892 ed. text ed. 18.50 (ISBN 0-915018-14-4). Attic Bks.
Riegel, E. C. The New Approach to Freedom. new, rev. ed. MacCallum, Spencer H., ed. LC 76-24987. (Illus.). 1977. 11.95 (ISBN 0-9600300-7-7). Heather Foun.
Rietti, Mario. Money & Banking in Latin America. LC 79-4157. 1979. 24.95 (ISBN 0-03-049156-8). Praeger.
Ripley, William Z. Financial History of Virginia 1609-1776. LC 78-127449. (Columbia Social Science Studies Ser: No. 10). Repr. of 1893 ed. 10.00 (ISBN 0-404-51010-8). AMS Pr.
Rist, Charles. History of Monetary & Credit Theory from John Law to the Present Day. LC 66-21371. Repr. of 1940 ed. 19.50x (ISBN 0-678-00161-8). Kelley.
Ritter, Lawrence & Silber, William L. Money. rev., 3rd ed. LC 76-43483. 1977. 11.95 (ISBN 0-465-04714-9); pap. 4.95x (ISBN 0-465-04716-5). Basic.
Ritter, Lawrence S. & Silber, William L. Principles of Money Banking & Financial Markets. 2nd rev. ed. LC 76-43477. 1977. text ed. 13.95x (ISBN 0-465-06337-3); instrs' manual avail. (ISBN 0-465-06338-1). Basic.
Rolfe, Sidney E. & Burtle, James. The Great Wheel: The World Monetary System - a Reinterpretation. LC 73-79929. 1974. 9.95 (ISBN 0-8129-0378-1). Times Bks.
Rolfe, Sidney E. & Burtle, James L. The Great Wheel: The World, Monetary System; a Reinterpretation. LC 73-79929. (McGraw-Hill Paperbacks). 304p. 1975. pap. 4.95 (ISBN 0-07-053562-0, SP). McGraw.
Rose, Floyd E. Money Without Guilt. 1976. 2.75 (ISBN 0-686-18204-9). Rose Pubns.
Russel, Henry B. International Monetary Conferences: Their Purposes, Character & Results with a Study of the Conditions of Currency & Finance in Europe & America. LC 74-359. (Vol. 10). 477p. 1974. Repr. of 1898 ed. 25.00x (ISBN 0-405-05920-5). Arno.
Russell, Etta M. Basic Principles of Constitutional Money: A Textbook for High Schools and the General Public on the Federal Reserve Conspiracy. 1980. lib. bdg. 59.95 (ISBN 0-8490-3096-X). Gordon Pr.
Sarnoff, Paul. The Smart Investor's Guide to the Money Market. (Orig.). 1981. pap. 2.95 (ISBN 0-686-75501-4, AE1188, Sig). NAL.
Saulnier, Raymond J. Contemporary Monetary Theory. LC 70-12744. (Columbia University Studies in the Social Sciences: No. 443). Repr. of 1938 ed. 27.50 (ISBN 0-404-51443-X). AMS Pr.
Savage, Donald T. Money & Banking. LC 76-56134. 1977. text ed. 26.50x (ISBN 0-471-75519-2); tchrs. manual avail. (ISBN 0-471-02578-X). Wiley.
Senior, Nassau W. Three Lectures on the Value of Money: Delivered Before the University of Oxford in 1829. LC 75-41245. Repr. of 1840 ed. 11.50 (ISBN 0-404-14779-8). AMS Pr.
Seyd, Ernest. Bullion & Foreign Exchanges Theoretically & Practically Considered: A Defence of the Double Evaluation with Special Reference to the Proposed System of Universal Coinage. LC 74-36. (Gold Ser.: Vol. 9). 716p. 1974. Repr. of 1868 ed. 37.00x (ISBN 0-405-05921-3). Arno.
Shaw, E. R. London Money Market. 1st ed. 1975. 17.95x (ISBN 0-434-91830-X). Intl Ideas.
Sheppard, T. & Musham, J. F. Money Scales & Weights. 1977. 15.00 (ISBN 0-685-51562-1, Pub by Spink & Son England). S J Durst.
Shibley, George. The Money Question, 2 vols. 1981. Set. lib. bdg. 150.00 (ISBN 0-686-71631-0). Revisionist Pr.
Silver, Gold & the Approaching Revolution in the International Monetary Order. 1976. 45.25 (ISBN 0-913314-42-0). Inst Econ Finan.
Simmel, Georg. Philosophy of Money. Bottomore, Tom & Frisby, David, trs. from Fr. 1978. 40.00x (ISBN 0-7100-8874-4). Routledge & Kegan.
Simpson, Thomas. Money, Banking & Economic Analysis. (Illus.). 496p. 1976. 19.95 (ISBN 0-13-600247-1). P-H.
Slater, Philip. Wealth Addiction. 1980. 9.95 (ISBN 0-525-23073-4). Dutton.
Smith, Harlan M. Elementary Monetary Theory. (Orig.). 1968. pap. text ed. 3.95x (ISBN 0-685-19722-0). Phila Bk Co.
Soddy, Frederick. The Role of Money: What It Should Be, Contrasted to What It Has Become. 1976. lib. bdg. 59.95 (ISBN 0-8490-2530-3). Gordon Pr.
Spadone, Frank G. Major Variety & Oddity Guide of U. S. Coins. 8th ed. LC 80-84159. (Collector Ser.). (Illus.). 128p. 1981. pap. 4.95 (ISBN 0-87637-162-4, 162-04). Hse of Collectibles.
Spero, Herbert & Davids, Lewis E. Money & Banking. 3rd ed. (Orig.). 1970. pap. 4.95 (ISBN 0-06-460069-6, CO 69, COS). Har-Row.
Stein, Jerome L. Money & Capacity Growth. LC 73-160844. 1971. 17.50x (ISBN 0-231-03372-9). Columbia U Pr.
Steward, Hal D. Money Making Secrets of the Millionaires. 1976. 9.95 (ISBN 0-13-600320-6, Reward); pap. 3.95 (ISBN 0-13-600296-X). P-H.
Taylor, Edith C. Money: The Root of All Evil. 1978. 5.50 (ISBN 0-682-49156-X). Exposition.
Taylor, Fred M. Some Chapters on Money. LC 79-1594. 1981. Repr. of 1906 ed. 23.50 (ISBN 0-88355-899-8). Hyperion Conn.
Thomson, F. P. Money in the Computer Age. 1968. 23.00 (ISBN 0-08-012856-4); pap. 11.25 (ISBN 0-08-012855-6). Pergamon.
Thoren, Ted & Warner, Dick. The Truth in Money Book. 5.95 (ISBN 0-686-31382-8). Truth in Money.
Thorn, Richard S. Introduction to Money & Banking. LC 75-34099. 544p. 1976. text ed. 16.95x (ISBN 0-06-046614-6). Kelley.
Thorn, Richard S., ed. Monetary Theory & Policy. LC 81-43023. 702p. 1981. lib. bdg. 26.75 (ISBN 0-8191-1623-8); pap. text ed. 16.00 (ISBN 0-8191-1624-6). U Pr of Amer.
Timerlake, Richard H., Jr. & Selby, Edward B., Jr. Money & Banking. 1972. 16.95x (ISBN 0-534-00108-4). Wadsworth Pub.
Tolfree, W. Money: The Facts of Life. 1977. Repr. 7.00 (ISBN 0-85941-032-3). State Mutual Bk.
Toscano, Peter R. On Money: A Translation of "Della Moneta" by Ferdinando Galiani. LC 77-18334. 1977. 31.75 (ISBN 0-8357-0286-3, SS-00052). Univ Microfilms.
Tucker, George. Theory of Money & Banks Investigated. LC 68-23334. 1968. Repr. of 1839 ed. lib. bdg. 20.50x (ISBN 0-8371-0251-0, TUTM). Greenwood.
--Theory of Money & Banks Investigated. LC 63-23038. Repr. of 1839 ed. 18.50x (ISBN 0-678-00032-8). Kelley.
Turner, W. E. Stable Money. 1979. lib. bdg. 59.95 (ISBN 0-8490-3008-0). Gordon Pr.
U. S. Congress - House Committee On Banking And Currency. Money Trust Investigation of Financial & Monetary Conditions in the United States. Repr. of 1913 ed. lib. bdg. 86.50x (ISBN 0-8371-3181-2, MTIN). Greenwood.
Vero, Andrew J. Price Guide for Bicentennial Two Dollar Bill Cancellations. (Illus.). 1980. pap. 14.95 (ISBN 0-939368-04-8). B-Two FDC.
Vickers, Douglas. Studies in the Theory of Money, 1690-1776. LC 59-9191. 1959. 15.00x (ISBN 0-678-08048-8). Kelley.
Visser, H. The Quanity of Money. LC 75-4762. 294p. 1974. 13.95 (ISBN 0-470-90845-9, Pub. by Wiley). Krieger.
Von Mises, Ludwig. On the Manipulation of Money & Credit. new ed. Greaves, Percy L., Jr., ed. Greaves, Bettina B., tr. from Ger. LC 77-90572. 1978. 15.00 (ISBN 0-930902-01-7). Free Market.
--The Theory of Money & Credit. Batson, H. E., tr. from Ger. LC 79-25752. (Liberty Classics Ser.). 544p. 1981. 11.00 (ISBN 0-913966-70-3); pap. 5.00 (ISBN 0-913966-71-1). Liberty Fund.
Walker, Amasa. Nature & Uses of Money & Mixed Currency. Repr. of 1857 ed. lib. bdg. 15.00 (ISBN 0-8371-1120-X, WAMC). Greenwood.
Walker, Francis A. Money. LC 68-25641. Repr. of 1878 ed. 19.50x (ISBN 0-678-00395-5). Kelley.
Walsh, Correa M. The Fundamental Problem in Monetary Science. 1976. lib. bdg. 59.95 (ISBN 0-8490-1872-2). Gordon Pr.
Walters, A. A. Money in Boom & Slump. (Institute of Economic Affairs, Hobart Papers Ser.: No. 44). pap. 2.75 (ISBN 0-255-36025-8). Transatlantic.
Wasserman, M. J., et al. International Money Management. rev. ed. LC 71-173321. 1973. 16.50 (ISBN 0-8144-5285-X, 49684). Am Mgmt.
Weeden, W. B. Indian Money As a Factor in New England Civilization. Repr. of 1884 ed. pap. 7.00 (ISBN 0-384-66385-0). Johnson Repr.
Wells, David A. Robinson Crusoe's Money. Repr. of 1876 ed. lib. bdg. 15.00 (ISBN 0-8371-1086-6, WECM). Greenwood.
What Is Money: An Original Arno Press Compilation. LC 74-172227. (Right Wing Individualist Tradition in America Ser). 1972. Repr. of 1971 ed. 9.00 (ISBN 0-405-00447-8). Arno.
White, Horace. Money & Banking Illustrated by American History. Repr. of 1896 ed. lib. bdg. 19.75x (ISBN 0-8371-0749-0, WHMB). Greenwood.
Wicksell, Knut. Interest & Prices. LC 65-16993. Repr. of 1936 ed. 13.50x (ISBN 0-678-00086-7). Kelley.
--Lectures on Political Economy, 2 vols. Robbins, Lionel, ed. Classen, E., tr. Incl. Vol. 1. General Theory; Vol. 2. Money. LC 67-28341. Repr. of 1934 ed. 25.00x (ISBN 0-678-06520-9). Kelley.
Wilczynski, J. Comparative Monetary Economics: Capatalist & Socialist Monetary Systems & Their Interrelations in the Changing International Scene. (Illus.). 1978. 23.00 (ISBN 0-19-520032-2). Oxford U Pr.
Wilford, D. Sykes. Monetary Policy & the Open Economy: Mexico's Experience. LC 77-14386. (Praeger Special Studies). 1977. 22.95 (ISBN 0-03-028156-3). Praeger.
Williams, Gordon L. Financial Survival in the Age of New Money. 1981. 12.95 (ISBN 0-671-25474-X). S&S.
Wilson, Charles M. Let's Try Barter. 1976. pap. 5.95 (ISBN 0-8159-6105-7). Devin.
Wolenik, Robert. Buying & Selling Currency for Profit. rev. ed. (Illus.). 1980. pap. 5.95 (ISBN 0-8092-7452-3). Contemp Bks.
Wool, John D. Using Money Series, 4 bks. Incl. Bk. 1. Counting My Money (ISBN 0-88323-074-7, 171); Bk. 2. Making My Money Count (ISBN 0-88323-075-5, 172); Bk. 3. Buying Power (ISBN 0-88323-076-3, 173); Bk. 4. Earning, Spending & Saving (ISBN 0-88323-077-1, 174). 1973. pap. 2.50x ea.; tchr's answer key 1.00x (ISBN 0-88323-137-9, 224). Richards Pub.
Wrightsman, Dwayne. An Introduction to Monetary Theory & Policy. 2nd ed. LC 75-22767. (Illus.). 1976. pap. text ed. 9.95 (ISBN 0-02-935560-5). Free Pr.

MONEY–BIBLIOGRAPHY

Ladley, Barbara. Money & Finance: Sources of Print & Nonprint Materials. (Neal-Schuman Sourcebook Ser.). 208p. 1980. 19.95x (ISBN 0-918212-23-5). Neal-Schuman.
Masui, Mitsuzo, ed. Bibliography of Finance, 3 Vols. LC 68-56724. (Bibliography & Reference Ser.: No. 221). 1969. Repr. of 1935 ed. 99.50 (ISBN 0-8337-2296-4). B Franklin.
Rock, James M., ed. Money, Banking & Macroeconomics: A Guide to Information Sources. LC 73-17585. (Economics Information Guide Ser.: Vol. 11). 1977. 36.00 (ISBN 0-8103-1300-6). Gale.
Soetbeer, Adolf. Liraturnachweis Ueber Geld-und Muenzwesen Insbesondere Weber der Waehrungsstreit, 1871-1891. LC 72-85106. iv, 322p. 1972. Repr. of 1892 ed. lib. bdg. 32.50 (ISBN 0-8337-3304-4). B Franklin.

MONEY–HISTORY

Angell, Norman. The Story of Money. Repr. of 1930 ed. lib. bdg. 25.00 (ISBN 0-8414-3073-X). Folcroft.
Babelon, Ernest C. Origines de la monnaie considerees au point de vue economique et historique. LC 77-129030. (Research & Source Works Ser: No. 530). (Fr). 1970. Repr. of 1897 ed. lib. bdg. 16.75x (ISBN 0-8337-0142-8). B Franklin.
Breckinridge, Sophonisba P. Legal Tender: A Study in English & American Monetary History. LC 72-75566. Repr. of 1903 ed. lib. bdg. 15.00x (ISBN 0-8371-1079-3, BRLT). Greenwood.
Bullock, Charles J. Essays on the Monetary History of the United States. LC 69-18301. Repr. of 1900 ed. lib. bdg. 16.75x (ISBN 0-8371-0332-0, BUMH). Greenwood.
Burns, A. R. Money & Monetary Policy in Early Times. 1976. lib. bdg. 59.95 (ISBN 0-8490-2275-4). Gordon Pr.
Burns, Arthur R. Money & Monetary Policy in Early Times. LC 65-19645. Repr. of 1927 ed. 19.50x (ISBN 0-678-00100-6). Kelley.
Butchart, M. Money in the English Tradition, 1640-1936. 59.95 (ISBN 0-8490-0661-9). Gordon Pr.
Cannan, Edwin. Money. 155p. 1980. Repr. lib. bdg. 22.50 (ISBN 0-8495-0785-5). Arden Lib.
Carlile, William. Evolution of Modern Money. LC 69-17029. Repr. of 1901 ed. 17.50x (ISBN 0-678-00467-6). Kelley.
Carlile, William W. Evolution of Modern Money. LC 68-56766. (Research & Source Works Ser.: No. 251). 1968. Repr. of 1901 ed. lib. bdg. 20.50 (ISBN 0-8337-0475-3). B Franklin.
Davis, Andrew M. Currency & Banking in the Province of the Massachusetts-Bay, 2 Vols. LC 68-55700. (Illus.). Repr. of 1900 ed. Set. 35.00x (ISBN 0-678-00637-7). Kelley.
Del Mar, Alexander. A History of Monetary Crimes. 59.95 (ISBN 0-8490-0337-7). Gordon Pr.
--History of Money in America. 59.95 (ISBN 0-8490-0338-5). Gordon Pr.
--The History of Money in America from the Earliest Times to the Establishment of the Constitution. LC 68-58459. (Research & Source Ser.: No. 323). 1969. Repr. of 1899 ed. 20.50 (ISBN 0-8337-0827-9). B Franklin.
--History of Money in Ancient Countries from Earliest Times to the Present. 1969. Repr. of 1885 ed. 24.00 (ISBN 0-8337-0826-0). B Franklin.
--Money & Civilization. 1969. 29.00 (ISBN 0-8337-0829-5). B Franklin.
--Money & Civilization. pap. 5.00 (ISBN 0-913022-20-9). Angriff Pr.
Dickey, George E. Money, Prices & Growth: The American Experience, 1869-1896. Bruchey, Stuart, ed. LC 76-39828. (Nineteen Seventy-Seven Dissertations Ser.). (Illus.). 1977. lib. bdg. 15.00x (ISBN 0-405-09907-X). Arno.
Felt, Joseph B. Historical Account of Massachusetts Currency. LC 68-57905. (Research & Source Works Ser.: No. 223). (Illus.). 1967. Repr. of 1839 ed. 21.00 (ISBN 0-8337-1106-7). B Franklin.
Fitzgerald, Adolphus L. Thirty Years' War on Silver. LC 71-75571. Repr. of 1903 ed. lib. bdg. 19.50x (ISBN 0-8371-1083-1, FIWS). Greenwood.
Friedberg, Robert. Paper Money of the U. S. A Complete Illustrated Guide with Valuations. 10th ed. LC 76-66813. (Illus.). 328p. 1981. 19.50 (ISBN 0-8069-6074-4). Sterling.
Friedman, Milton & Schwartz, Anna J. Great Contraction, 1929-1933: Chapter Seven of "Monetary History of the United States, 1867-1960". 1965. pap. 3.95 (ISBN 0-691-00350-5, 9). Natl Bur Econ Res.
--Monetary History of the United States, 1867-1960. (Business Cycles Ser.: No. 12). 1963. 25.00 (ISBN 0-691-04147-4, Dist. by Princeton U Pr); pap. 8.95 (ISBN 0-685-17332-1). Natl Bur Econ Res.
Galbraith, John K. Money: Whence It Came, Where It Went. 408p. 1976. pap. 3.50 (ISBN 0-553-14314-X). Bantam.
Garnier, Germaine. Histoire de la Monnaie, depuis les Temps de la Plus Haute Antiquite Jusqu'au Regne de Charlemagne, 2 Vols. 1967. Repr. of 1819 ed. 44.50 (ISBN 0-8337-1285-3). B Franklin.
Gouge, William M. Fiscal History of Texas. LC 68-18226. Repr. of 1852 ed. 17.50x (ISBN 0-678-00364-5). Kelley.
--Fiscal History of Texas: An Account of Its Revenues, Debts, & Currency from the Commencement of the Revolution in 1834 to 1851-52 with Remarks on American Debts. 1969. Repr. of 1852 ed. 20.00 (ISBN 0-8337-1397-3). B Franklin.
Grierson, Philip. The Origins of Money. 1977. pap. text ed. 4.75x (ISBN 0-485-14115-9, Athlone Pr). Humanities.
Hepburn, A. Barton. History of Currency in the United States. rev. ed. LC 67-27411. Repr. of 1924 ed. 19.50x (ISBN 0-678-00311-4). Kelley.

Hepburn, Alonzo B. History of Coinage & Currency in the United States & the Perennial Contest for Sound Money. LC 68-28634. 1968. Repr. of 1903 ed. lib. bdg. 34.50 (ISBN 0-8371-0105-0). Greenwood.

Hessler, Gene. The Comprehensive Catalog of U.S. Paper Money. 3rd ed. LC 80-66208. (Illus.). 500p. 1980. lib. bdg. 30.00 (ISBN 0-931960-06-1); pap. 15.95 (ISBN 0-686-61344-9). BNR Pr.

Hurst, James W. A Legal History of Money in the United States, 1774-1970. LC 72-86019. (Roscoe Pound Lecture Ser). xviii, 367p. 1973. 21.50x (ISBN 0-8032-0824-3). U of Nebr Pr.

King, C. E. Imperial Revenue, Expenditure & Monetary Policy in the Fourth Century A.D. The Fifth Oxford Symposium on Coinage & Monetary History. 1980. 60.00x (ISBN 0-86054-084-7, Pub. by BAR). State Mutual Bk.

Laughlin, James L. History of Bimetallism in the United States. LC 68-28639. 1968. Repr. of 1897 ed. lib. bdg. 24.25x (ISBN 0-8371-0138-7, LAHB). Greenwood.

Lester, Richard. Monetary Experiments. LC 70-75796. (Illus.). Repr. of 1939 ed. 17.50x (ISBN 0-678-05547-5). Kelley.

McCusker, John J. Money & Exchange in Europe and America, 1600-1775: A Handbook. LC 76-54774. (The Institute of Early American History & Culture). (Illus.). 1978. 27.50x (ISBN 0-8078-1284-6). U of NC Pr.

Monroe, Arthur E. Monetary Theory Before Adam Smith. LC 64-66154. Repr. of 1923 ed. 15.00x (ISBN 0-678-00134-0). Kelley.

--Monetary Theory Before Adam Smith. 1923. 8.50 (ISBN 0-8446-1314-2). Peter Smith.

Murray, Andrew. Money: Christ's Perspective on the Use & Abuse of Money. 1978. pap. 1.50 (ISBN 0-87123-382-7, 200382). Bethany Hse.

Newman, Eric P. & Doty, Richard G., eds. Studies on Money in Early America. (Illus.). 216p. 1976. 10.50 (ISBN 0-89722-065-X). Am Numismatic.

Phillips, Henry. American Paper Currency, 2 Vols. in 1. LC 68-18223. (Library of Money, Banking & Finance). Repr. of 1865 ed. lib. bdg. 19.50x (ISBN 0-678-00787-X). Kelley.

--Historical Sketches of the Paper Currency of the American Colonies Prior to the Adoption of the Federal Constitution, 2 Vols. in 1. LC 68-57123. (Research & Source Works Ser: No. 314). 1969. Repr. of 1866 ed. 20.50 (ISBN 0-8337-2744-3). B Franklin.

Pick, Franz. The U. S. Dollar: 1940-1980, an Advance Obituary. LC 81-81389. (Illus.). 76p. 1981. pap. 50.00x (ISBN 0-87551-514-2). Pick Pub.

Poor, Henry V. Money & Its Laws. Repr. of 1877 ed. lib. bdg. 28.75x (ISBN 0-8371-0618-4, POML). Greenwood.

Powell, Ellis T. Evolution of the Money Market. 732p. 1966. Repr. 35.00x (ISBN 0-7146-1243-X, F Cass Co). Biblio Dist.

Quiggin, Aliston H. A Survey of Primitive Money: The Beginnings of Currency. LC 76-44779. Repr. of 1949 ed. 28.00 (ISBN 0-404-15964-8). AMS Pr.

Quiggins, A. H. Survey of Primitive Money. 1979. 30.00 (ISBN 0-686-51599-4, Pub. by Spink & Son England). S J Durst.

Ripley, William Z. Financial History of Virginia 1609-1776. 1893. 20.50 (ISBN 0-8337-2997-7. B Franklin.

Rodewald, Cosmo. Money in the Age of Tiberius. (Illus.). 154p. 1976. 17.50x (ISBN 0-87471-823-6). Rowman.

Schoenhof, J. A History of Money & Prices from the Thirteenth Century to the Beginning of the Twentieth Century. 1977. lib. bdg. 69.95 (ISBN 0-8490-1979-6). Gordon Pr.

Schuckers, J. W. Finances & Paper Money of the Revolutionary War. LC 77-74029. 1978. Repr. of 1874 ed. lib. bdg. 15.00 (ISBN 0-915262-12-6). S J Durst.

Shaw, William A. History of Currency: Twelve Fifty-Two to Eighteen Ninety-Four. 3rd ed. 1967. Repr. of 1896 ed. 29.00 (ISBN 0-8337-3243-9). B Franklin.

--History of Currency, 1251-1894. 2nd ed. LC 67-20086. Repr. of 1896 ed. 19.50x (ISBN 0-678-00256-8). Kelley.

Sumner, William G. History of American Currency. LC 68-55331. Repr. of 1874 ed. 17.50x (ISBN 0-678-00436-6). Kelley.

--History of American Currency, with Chapters on the English Bank Restriction & Austrian Paper Money. LC 68-28648. Repr. of 1874 ed. lib. bdg. 20.50x (ISBN 0-8371-0241-3, SUHA). Greenwood.

Thian, Raphael P. Register of the Confederate Debt (1880) LC 70-189169. (Illus.). 212p. 1972. Repr. of 1880 ed. 35.00x (ISBN 0-88000-002-3). Quarterman.

Vilar, Pierre. A History of Gold & Money 1450-1920. (Illus.). 1976. 21.00 (ISBN 0-902308-18-1, Pub. by NLB). Schocken.

Wade, William W. From Barter to Banking. (gr. 7 up). 1967. 3.50g (ISBN 0-02-792350-9, CCPr). Macmillan.

Webster, Pelatiah. Political Essays on the Nature & Operation of Money, Public Finances & Other Subjects, 2 vols. in 1. LC 78-77603. (Research & Source Works Ser.: No. 354). (American Classics in History & Social Science Ser, No. 82). 1969. Repr. of 1791 ed. 29.00 (ISBN 0-8337-3712-0). B Franklin.

Weiser, F. Contributions to the Monetary History of Serbia, Montenegro & Yugoslavia. 1975. 3.00 (ISBN 0-685-51550-8, Pub by Spink & Son England). S J Durst.

White, Horace. Money & Banking Illustrated by American History. Repr. of 1896 ed. lib. bdg. 19.75x (ISBN 0-8371-0749-0, WHMB). Greenwood.

Wiseley, William. A Tool of Power: The Political History of Money. LC 76-57701. 300p. 1977. 29.95 (ISBN 0-471-02235-7, Pub. by Wiley-Interscience). Wiley.

Yang, Lien-Sheng. Money & Credit in China: A Short History. LC 52-5413. (Harvard-Yenching Institute Monograph Ser: No. 12). 1952. pap. 3.50x (ISBN 0-674-58300-0). Harvard U Pr.

MONEY-JUVENILE LITERATURE

Arnold, Oren. Marvels of the U. S. Mint. LC 70-141860. (Illus.). (gr. 1 up). 1972. PLB 8.79 (ISBN 0-200-71798-7, 254701, AbS-J). Har-Row.

Cooke, David C. How Money Is Made. rev. ed. LC 72-7641. (How Things Are Made Bks.). (Illus.). (gr. 4-6). 1973. PLB 5.95 (ISBN 0-396-06652-6). Dodd.

Davis, Ken & Taylor, Tom. Kids & Cash: Solving a Parent's Dilemma. LC 79-13092. (Illus.). 1979. 8.95 (ISBN 0-916392-26-0). Oak Tree Pubns.

Eldred, Pat & Taylor, Paula. Easy Money Making Projects. (Creative Games, Projects & Activities Ser.). (Illus.). (gr. 4 up). 1979. PLB 5.95 (ISBN 0-89812-048-9); pap. 2.95 (ISBN 0-685-99627-1). Creative Ed.

Fodor, R. V. Nickels, Dimes & Dollars, How Currency Works. LC 79-22539. (Illus.). 96p. (gr. 4-6). 1980. 6.95 (ISBN 0-688-22220-X); PLB 6.67 (ISBN 0-688-32220-4). Morrow.

German, Joan W. The Money Book. (Illus.). 32p. (ps-2). 1981. 6.25 (ISBN 0-525-66726-1, 0607-180). Elsevier-Nelson.

James, Elizabeth & Barkin, Carol. Managing Your Money. LC 76-48287. (Money Ser.). (Illus.). (gr. 4-6). 1977. PLB 9.85 (ISBN 0-8172-0279-X). Raintree Pubs.

--Understanding Money. LC 76-47030. (Money Ser.). (Illus.). (gr. 2-3). 1977. PLB 9.85 (ISBN 0-8172-0277-3). Raintree Pubs.

--What Is Money? LC 76-46589. (Money Ser.). (Illus.). (gr. k-1). 1977. PLB 9.85 (ISBN 0-8172-0275-7). Raintree Pubs.

Lewis, Shari. How Kids Can Really Make Money. (Kids-Only Club Books). (Illus.). (gr. 3-6). 1979. 4.95 (ISBN 0-03-049691-8); pap. 1.95 (ISBN 0-03-049696-9). HR&W.

Mahoney, Susan & Molloy, Julia S. Money Skills Learning Module. 1977. pap. 154.00 (ISBN 0-89290-148-9, CM-92). Soc for Visual.

Morgan, Tom. Money, Money, Money: How to Get & Keep It. LC 78-1769. (Illus.). (gr. 6-8). 1978. 7.95 (ISBN 0-399-20641-8). Putnam.

Scott, Elaine. The Banking Book. LC 81-2412. (Illus.). 96p. (gr. 6-10). 1981. 8.95 (ISBN 0-7232-6202-0). Warne.

Seuling, Barbara. You Can't Count a Billion Dollars & Other Little Known Facts About Money. LC 78-22354. (Illus.). 1979. 6.95a (ISBN 0-385-12221-7); PLB (ISBN 0-385-12222-5). Doubleday.

Smith, Kenneth H. Money & Banking. LC 72-84417. (Real World of Economics Ser). Orig. Title: Banking. (Illus.). (gr. 5-11). 1970. PLB 4.95 (ISBN 0-8225-0614-9). Lerner Pubns.

MONEY-LAW

see also Banking Law; Foreign Exchange-Law

Coogan, Gertrude. Lawful Money Explained. 1979. lib. bdg. 59.95 (ISBN 0-8490-2956-2). Gordon Pr.

MONEY-PROBLEMS, EXERCISES, ETC.

Silvey, Linda. Money Matters. 1973. pap. 4.95 wkbk. (ISBN 0-88488-037-0). Creative Pubns.

MONEY-PROGRAMMED INSTRUCTION

Soracco, Lionel J., Jr. Math House Proficiency Review Tapes: Applications Involving Money, Unit D. (YA) (gr. 7 up). 1980. manual & cassettes 179.50 (ISBN 0-917792-06-8). Math Hse.

MONEY-TABLES, ETC.

McCusker, John J. Money & Exchange in Europe and America, 1600-1775: A Handbook. LC 76-54774. (The Institute of Early American History & Culture). (Illus.). 1978. 27.50x (ISBN 0-8078-1284-6). U of NC Pr.

Technical Division of Barrons Educational Series Inc. Currency Converter. Date not set. 2.95 (ISBN 0-8120-0819-7). Barron.

MONEY-ASIA

Daniel, Howard W., III. The Catalog & Guidebook of Southeast Asian Coins & Currency, Vol. 1. 2nd ed. LC 78-60307. (Illus.). 1978. pap. 17.50 (ISBN 0-931960-01-0). BNR Pr.

MONEY-AUSTRALIA

Butlin, S. Foundations of the Australian Monetary System, 1788-1851. 1969. 18.50x (ISBN 0-424-05830-8, Pub by Sydney U Pr). Intl Schol Bk Serv.

MONEY-CANADA

Canada-Public Archives. Documents Relating to Canadian Currency, Exchange & Finance During the French Period, 2 Vols. Shortt, Adam, ed. (Fr. & Eng.). 1925. Set. 63.00 (ISBN 0-8337-3256-0). B Franklin.

Cornwell, William C. Currency-the Banking Law of the Dominion of Canada with Considered Reference to Currency Reform in the United States. LC 70-75568. Repr. lib. bdg. 15.00x (ISBN 0-8371-2156-6, COCB). Greenwood.

Lester, Richard. Monetary Experiments. LC 70-75796. (Illus.). Repr. of 1939 ed. 17.50x (ISBN 0-678-05547-5). Kelley.

MONEY-CHINA

Burger, Werner. Ch'ing Cash Until Seventeen Thirty-Five. 126p. 1980. 22.50x (ISBN 0-89955-141-6, Pub. by Mei Ya China). Intl Schol Bk Serv.

Cresswell, O. D. Chinese Cash. (Illus.). 1980. Repr. of 1915 ed. 8.00 (ISBN 0-686-64438-7). S J Durst.

Hsiao, Katherine H. Money & Monetary Policy in Communist China. LC 77-158341. (Studies of the East Asian Institute). (Illus.). 1971. 20.00 (ISBN 0-231-03510-1). Columbia U Pr.

Morse, Hosea B. Trade & Administration of China. 3rd ed. LC 64-24734. (Illus.). 1967. Repr. of 1921 ed. 12.50 (ISBN 0-8462-0881-4). Russell.

MONEY-EUROPE

Cipolla, Carlo M. Money, Prices & Civilization in the Mediterranean World. LC 67-18440. (Illus.). 1967. Repr. of 1956 ed. 5.50 (ISBN 0-87752-021-6). Gordian.

Corden, W. M. Inflation, Exchange Rates, & the World Economy: Lectures on International Monetary Economics. LC 76-58331. (Studies in Business & Society). 1977. lib. bdg. 11.00x (ISBN 0-226-11583-6). U of Chicago Pr.

Encyclopedie Des Monnaies et Billets D'europe: 19e et 20e Siecles. 304p. (Fr.). 1978. 27.50 (ISBN 0-686-57144-4, M-6201). French & Eur.

Little, Jane S. Euro-Dollars: The Money Market Gypsies. LC 74-1834. (Illus.). 314p. 1975. 14.95 (ISBN 0-06-012621-3, HarpT). Har-Row.

Salin, Pascal. European Monetary Unity: For Whose Benefit? Getchell, Charles, tr. from Fr. Orig. Title: L'Unite Monetaire Europeenne: Au Profit De Qui? (Illus.). 82p. (Orig.). 1980. pap. 5.00 (ISBN 0-938864-00-9). Ipswich Pr.

Triffin, Robert. Europe & the Money Muddle: From Bilateralism to Near-Convertibility 1947-1956. LC 76-26932. (Yale Studies in Economics Ser: No. 7). 1976. Repr. of 1957 ed. lib. bdg. 24.00x (ISBN 0-8371-9026-6, TREM). Greenwood.

Tsoukalis, Loukas. The Politics & Economics of European Monetary Integration. 1977. text ed. 27.50x (ISBN 0-04-382017-4). Allen Unwin.

Van Brabant, Jozef M. East European Cooperation: The Role of Money & Finance. LC 76-2911. (Illus.). 1976. text ed. 34.50 (ISBN 0-275-56650-1). Praeger.

Wilczynski, J. Comparative Monetary Economics: Capatalist & Socialist Monetary Systems & Their Interrelations in the Changing International Scene. (Illus.). 1978. 23.00 (ISBN 0-19-520032-2). Oxford U Pr.

MONEY-FRANCE

Miskimin, Harry A. Money, Prices, & Foreign Exchange in Fourteenth Century France. LC 63-7942. 1970. Repr. of 1963 ed. 15.00 (ISBN 0-08-022307-9). Pergamon.

MONEY-GREAT BRITAIN

Baring, Frances. Observations on the Establishment of the Bank of England. Bd. with Further Observations. 16p. LC 66-21659. 81p. Repr. of 1797 ed. 11.50x (ISBN 0-678-00281-9). Kelley.

Bisschop, W. R. Rise of the London Money Market: 1640-1826. 256p. 1968. Repr. of 1826 ed. 30.00x (ISBN 0-7146-1206-5, F Cass Co). Biblio Dist.

Breckinridge, Sophonisba P. Legal Tender: A Study in English & American Monetary History. LC 72-75566. Repr. of 1903 ed. lib. bdg. 15.00x (ISBN 0-8371-1079-3, BRLT). Greenwood.

Cannan, Edwin, ed. Paper Pound of 1797-1812. 2nd ed. 72p. 1970. Repr. of 1925 ed. 24.00x (ISBN 0-7146-1210-3, F Cass Co). Biblio Dist.

Chadwick, Hector M. Studies on Anglo-Saxon Institutions. LC 63-15152. 1963. Repr. of 1905 ed. 16.00 (ISBN 0-8462-0361-8). Russell.

Dennis, G. E. Monetary Economics. LC 80-40095. (Modern Economic Ser.). (Illus.). 312p. (Orig.). 1981. pap. text ed. 16.95x (ISBN 0-582-45573-1). Longman.

Doubleday, Thomas. Financial, Monetary & Statistical History of England, from the Revolution of 1688 to the Present Time. LC 68-28626. 1968. Repr. of 1847 ed. lib. bdg. 21.00x (ISBN 0-8371-0388-6, DOFM). Greenwood.

Farrer, Thomas H. Studies in Currency Eighteen Ninety-Eight. LC 67-19961. Repr. of 1898 ed. 19.50x (ISBN 0-678-00397-1). Kelley.

Fleetwood, William. Chronicon Precosium. LC 68-55711. (Illus.). Repr. of 1745 ed. 15.00x (ISBN 0-678-00492-7). Kelley.

Hoare, Peter R. Tracts on Our Present Money System & National Bankruptcy. LC 67-27467. Repr. of 1814 ed. 17.50x (ISBN 0-678-00574-5). Kelley.

Hollis, Christopher. The Two Nations. 69.95 (ISBN 0-87968-230-2). Gordon Pr.

Josset, C. R. Money in Great Britain: A History of the Coins & Notes of the British Isles. LC 70-170671. (Illus.). 1972. 12.50 (ISBN 0-8048-1011-7). C E Tuttle.

Lavington, Frederick. English Capital Market. LC 67-30469. Repr. of 1921 ed. 15.00x (ISBN 0-678-00345-9). Kelley.

McCulloch, John R., ed. Select Collection of Scarce & Valuable Tracts & Other Publications on Paper Currency & Banking. LC 65-16986. Repr. of 1857 ed. 32.50x (ISBN 0-678-00149-9). Kelley.

--Select Collection of Scarce & Valuable Tracts on Money & Metallic Currency. LC 65-16987. Repr. of 1856 ed. 32.50x (ISBN 0-678-00147-2). Kelley.

Malthus, Thomas R. Measure of Value. Repr. of 1823 ed. 10.00x (ISBN 0-678-00603-2). Kelley.

Overstone, Samuel J. Tracts & Other Publications on Metallic & Paper Currency. LC 67-20089. Repr. of 1857 ed. 25.00x (ISBN 0-678-00902-3). Kelley.

Pennington, James. Currency of the British Colonies. LC 67-18578. Repr. of 1848 ed. 15.00x (ISBN 0-678-00260-6). Kelley.

Shaw, William A. Select Tracts & Documents Illustrative of English Monetary History 1626-1730. LC 67-19743. Repr. of 1896 ed. 15.00x (ISBN 0-678-00251-7). Kelley.

Vanderlint, Jacob. Money Answers All Things. (History of English Economic Thought Ser). Repr. of 1734 ed. 38.50 (ISBN 0-384-63883-X). Johnson Repr.

--Money Answers All Things. 1970. Repr. of 1734 ed. 28.00x (ISBN 0-8464-0640-3). Beekman Pubs.

Welham, Philip J. Monetary Circulation in the United Kingdom. LC 78-92500. 1969. 11.50x (ISBN 0-678-06251-X). Kelley.

MONEY-GREECE

Babelon, Ernest. Introduction Generale a l'etude des Monnaies de l'antiquite. Finley, Moses, ed. LC 79-4960. (Ancient Economic History). (Fr.). 1980. Repr. of 1901 ed. lib. bdg. 30.00x (ISBN 0-405-12348-5). Arno.

Letronne, Jean A. Considerations Generales sur L'evaluation Des Monnaies Grecques et Romaines. LC 77-179916. (Research & Source Works Ser.: No. 885). 154p. (Fr.). 1972. Repr. of 1817 ed. lib. bdg. 21.50 (ISBN 0-8337-2090-2). B Franklin.

MONEY-HAWAII

Medcalf, Donald & Russell, Ronald. Hawaiian Money Standard Catalog. LC 77-75830. (Illus.). 1978. 10.00 (ISBN 0-931388-00-7). AA Sales Inc.

MONEY-INDIA

Chattopadhyaya, Brajadulal. Coins & Currency Systems in South India: C. Ad 225-1300. LC 77-903086. (Illus.). 1977. 27.50x (ISBN 0-8002-0234-1). Intl Pubns Serv.

Maity, S. K. Early Indian Coins & Currency System. (Illus.). 1971. 6.75x (ISBN 0-8426-0212-7). Verry.

MONEY-ISRAEL

Haffner, Sylvia, ed. Israel's Money & Medals. 2nd ed. LC 75-46129. 1976. with supplement 25.00 (ISBN 0-685-92169-7). Am Israel Numismatic.

MONEY-JAPAN

Takizawa, Matsuyo. Penetration of Money Economy in Japan & Its Effects Upon Social & Political Institutions. LC 68-54302. (Columbia University. Studies in the Social Sciences: No. 285). Repr. of 1927 ed. 16.50 (ISBN 0-404-51285-2). AMS Pr.

MONEY-NEW ZEALAND

Blakeborough, Peter. The Coinage of New Zealand Eighteen Fourty to Nineteen Sixty-Three. Date not set. pap. 4.25x (ISBN 0-392-09186-0, ABC). Sportshelf.

MONEY-PHILIPPINE ISLANDS

Basso, Aldo P. Coins, Medals & Tokens of the Philippines. (Illus.). 144p. 1968. 5.95 (ISBN 0-912496-10-X). Shirjieh Pubs.

MONEY-ROME

Babelon, Ernest. Introduction Generale a l'etude des Monnaies de l'antiquite. Finley, Moses, ed. LC 79-4960. (Ancient Economic History). (Fr.). 1980. Repr. of 1901 ed. lib. bdg. 30.00x (ISBN 0-405-12348-5). Arno.

Del Mar, Alexander. Roman & Moslem Moneys. 59.95 (ISBN 0-8490-0968-5). Gordon Pr.
Kennett, B. Roman Money. (Illus.). 16p. 1975. pap. 2.00 (ISBN 0-916710-18-1). Obol Intl.
Letronne, Jean A. Considerations Generales sur L'evaluation Des Monnaies Grecques et Romaines. LC 77-179916. (Research & Source Works Ser.: No. 885). 154p. (Fr.). 1972. Repr. of 1817 ed. lib. bdg. 21.50 (ISBN 0-8337-2090-2). B Franklin.
Mattingly, H. AES & PECVNIA: Records of Roman Currency Down to 269 B.C. 19p. 1979. pap. 3.00 (ISBN 0-916710-51-3). Obol Intl.

MONEY–SCANDINAVIA

Lester, Richard. Monetary Experiments. LC 70-75796. (Illus.). Repr. of 1939 ed. 17.50x (ISBN 0-678-05547-5). Kelley.

MONEY–SPAIN

Hamilton, Earl J. American Treasure & the Price Revolution in Spain, 1501-1650. 1965. lib. bdg. 27.50x (ISBN 0-374-93420-7). Octagon.
La Moneda Hispanica: A Vives y Escudero, 4 vols. in 2. 1980. Repr. of 1926 ed. write for info. Attic Bks.

MONEY–SYRIA

Himadeh, Sa'id B. Monetary & Banking System of Syria. LC 77-180347. Repr. of 1935 ed. 30.00 (ISBN 0-404-56277-9). AMS Pr.

MONEY–VIRGIN ISLANDS OF THE UNITED STATES

Gilbert, James H. Trade & Currency in Early Oregon. LC 77-168145. (Columbia University. Studies in the Social Sciences: No. 68). Repr. of 1907 ed. 16.50 (ISBN 0-404-51068-X). AMS Pr.

MONEY–YUGOSLAVIA

Dimitrijevic, Dimitrije & Macesich, George. Money & Finance in Contemporary Yugoslavia. LC 72-92889. (Special Studies in International Economics & Development). 1973. 29.50x (ISBN 0-275-28725-4); pap. text ed. 18.50x (ISBN 0-89197-857-7). Irvington.

MONEY, CIRCULAR VELOCITY OF

see Circular Velocity of Money

MONEY, PRIMITIVE

see also Shell Money; Wampum

MONEY, QUANTITY THEORY OF

see Quantity Theory of Money

MONEY IN LITERATURE

Mull, Donald L. Henry James' "Sublime Economy". Money As Symbolic Center in the Fiction. LC 73-6007. 1973. 12.50x (ISBN 0-8195-4064-1, Pub. by Wesleyan U Pr). Columbia U Pr.

MONEY RAISING

see Fund Raising

MONEY SUPPLY

see Money

MONGALALLA (PROVINCE)

Nalder, Leonard F., ed. Tribal Survey of Mongalla Province. (Illus.). Repr. 12.75 (ISBN 0-8371-2862-5). Greenwood.

MONGKUT, KING OF SIAM, 1804-1868

Jumsai, M. L. King Mongkut & Sir Bowring. 240p. 1970. 12.50x (ISBN 0-685-25237-X). Paragon.
Landon, Margaret. Anna & the King of Siam. (Illus.). 1944. 12.95 (ISBN 0-381-98136-3, A05201, JD-J). Har-Row.
Moffat, Abbot L. Mongkut, the King of Siam. (Illus.). 254p. (YA) (gr. 9-12). 1968. pap. 3.95 (ISBN 0-8014-9069-3, CP69). Cornell U Pr.

MONGO (BANTU TRIBE)

Reid, Alexander J. Roots of Lomomba: Mongo Land. rev ed. 1979. 9.00 (ISBN 0-682-49008-3). Exposition.

MONGOLIA

Aberle, David F. Chahar & Dagor Mongol Bureaucratic Administration: 1912-45. LC 62-20019. (Behavior Science Monographs). xii, 117p. 1962. pap. 7.50x (ISBN 0-87536-316-4). HRAFP.
Boyle, John A., tr. from Pers. The Successors of Glengis. LC 70-135987. (Illus.). 372p. 1971. 20.00x (ISBN 0-231-03351-6). Columbia U Pr.
Friters, Gerard M. Outer Mongolia & Its International Position. LC 74-4496. 1974. Repr. of 1949 ed. lib. bdg. 17.50x (ISBN 0-374-92937-8). Octagon.
Jagchid, Sechin & Hyer, Paul. Mongolia's Culture & Society. LC 79-1438. (Illus.). 461p. 1980. 36.25x (ISBN 0-89158-390-4). Westview.
Ligeti, Louis, ed. Mongolian Studies: Dedicated to the Second International Congress of Mongolists, to Its Organizers, the Mongolian Scholars, Budapest, 1970. (Bibliotheca Orientalis Hungrica). 1970. text ed. 48.50x (ISBN 90-6032-352-1). Humanities.
Mongolia Society. Bulletin, Vols. 4-6 In 1 Vol. 1964-66. pap. 5.00 (ISBN 0-910980-02-0). Mongolia.
--Bulletin, Vols. 7-12. 4.00 ea. Mongolia.
--Newsletter, Vols. 1-3. 1962-64. pap. 5.00 (ISBN 0-910980-01-2). Mongolia.
Murphy, George G. Soviet Mongolia: A Study of the Oldest Political Satellite. 1966. 24.00x (ISBN 0-520-00906-1). U of Cal Pr.
Onon, Urgunge, ed. Mongolian Heroes of the Twentieth Century. LC 76-23980. (Asian Studies Ser.: No. 1). (Illus.). 1976. lib. bdg. 18.95 (ISBN 0-404-15402-6). AMS Pr.
Price, Ernest B. Russo-Japanese Treaties of 1907-1916. LC 76-101274. Repr. of 1933 ed. 17.50 (ISBN 0-404-05135-9). AMS Pr.
Rupen, Robert. How Mongolia Is Really Ruled: A Political History of the Mongolian People's Republic 1900-1978. Staar, Richard F., ed. LC 78-59865. (Publications Ser.: No. 212). (Illus.). 1979. pap. 7.95 (ISBN 0-8179-7122-X). Hoover Inst Pr.
Schwarz, Henry G. Bibliotheca Mongolica: Pt. 1 Works in English, French, & German. LC 78-18355. (Occasional Papers: Vol. 12). (Illus.). 1978. 18.00 (ISBN 0-914584-12-X). West Wash Univ.
Schwarz, Henry G., ed. Studies on Mongolia: Proceedings of the First North American Conference on Mongolian Studies. LC 79-4517. (Studies on East Asia: Vol. 13). (Illus.). 1979. pap. 5.50 (ISBN 0-914584-13-8). West Wash Univ.
Tang, Peter S. Russian & Soviet Policy in Manchuria & Outer Mongolia, 1911-1931. LC 59-7084. 1959. 19.75 (ISBN 0-8223-0170-9). Duke.

MONGOLIA–DESCRIPTION AND TRAVEL

Barzini, Luigi S. Peking to Paris. Barzini, Luigi, Jr., ed. Castelvecchio, tr. LC 72-6279. (Illus.). 1973. 17.50 (ISBN 0-912050-26-8, Library Pr). Open Court.
Hedin, Sven A. Across the Gobi Desert. Cant, H. J., tr. LC 68-23296. (Illus.). 1968. Repr. of 1931 ed. lib. bdg. 25.25x (ISBN 0-8371-0103-4, HEGD). Greenwood.
Lattimore, Owen. Desert Road to Turkestan. LC 70-112348. (Illus.). Repr. of 1929 ed. 27.50 (ISBN 0-404-03887-5). AMS Pr.
--Mongol Journeys. LC 72-4436. Repr. of 1941 ed. 27.50 (ISBN 0-404-10633-1). AMS Pr.
Li Chit-Chlang. The Travels of an Alchemist. Waley, Arthur, tr. from Chinese. LC 75-36098. (Illus.). 166p. 1976. Repr. of 1931 ed. lib. bdg. 15.00x (ISBN 0-8371-8614-5, LITA). Greenwood.

MONGOLIA–HISTORY

Boyle, J. A. The Mongol World Empire, 1206-1370. 316p. 1980. 60.00x (ISBN 0-86078-002-3, Pub. by Variorum England). State Mutual Bk.
Dindub, L. Brief History of Mongolia in the Autonomous Period: Mongolian Text with an Introduction & Index in English by John G. Hangin. (Special Papers Ser.: No. 6). spiral bdg. 10.00 (ISBN 0-910980-26-8). Mongolia.
Ewing, Thomas E. Between the Hammer & the Anvil? Chinese & Russian Policies in Outer Mongolia, 1911-1921. LC 80-52924. (Indiana University Uralic & Altaic Ser.: Vol. 138). 300p. 1980. 20.00 (ISBN 0-933070-06-3). Ind U Res Inst.
Friters, Gerard M. Outer Mongolia & Its International Position. LC 74-4496. 1974. Repr. of 1949 ed. lib. bdg. 17.50x (ISBN 0-374-92937-8). Octagon.
Lattimore, Owen. The Mongols of Manchuria. LC 68-9626. 1969. Repr. of 1934 ed. 25.00 (ISBN 0-86527-132-1). Fertig.
Manual of Mongolian Astrology & Divination. pap. 7.00x (ISBN 0-674-54825-6). Harvard U Pr.
Mongolian Studies Journal of the Mongolia Society, Vol. 3. 1976. pap. 10.00 (ISBN 0-910980-73-X). Mongolia.
Mongolian Studies Journal of the Mongolia Society, Vol. 4. 1977. pap. 10.00 (ISBN 0-910980-74-8). Mongolia.
Pozdneyev, Aleksei M. Religion & Ritual in Society: Lamaist Buddhism in Late 19th-Century Mongolia. Krueger, John R., ed. Raun, Alo & Raun, Linda, trs. from Rus. (Occasional Papers Ser.: No. 10). Orig. Title: Ocherki Byta Buddiiskikh Monastyrei. pap. 15.00 (ISBN 0-910980-50-0). Mongolia.
Rupen, Robert A. Mongols of the Twentieth Century. LC 63-64522. (Uralic & Altaic Ser: Vol. 37-Pt. 2). (Orig.). 1964. Pt. 2. pap. text ed. 6.00x (ISBN 0-87750-062-2). Res Ctr Lang Semiotic.
Sanjdorj, M. Manchu Chinese Colonial Rule in Northern Mongolia. LC 80-17449. 1980. 19.95 (ISBN 0-312-51249-X). St Martin.
Zhamtsarano, Ts. Ethnography & Geography of the Darkhat & Other Mongolian Minorities. (Special Papers Ser.: No. 8). 1979. spiral bdg. 15.00 (ISBN 0-910980-28-4). Mongolia.

MONGOLIAN INSCRIPTIONS

see Inscriptions, Mongolian

MONGOLIAN LANGUAGE

Binnick, Robert I. Modern Mongolian: A Transformational Syntax. 1979. 17.50x (ISBN 0-8020-5422-6). U of Toronto Pr.
Buck, Frederick H. Glossary of Mongolian Technical Terms. LC 58-59834. (American Council of Learned Societies Publications). 79p. (Orig.). 1958. pap. 3.00x (ISBN 0-87950-257-6). Spoken Lang Serv.
Chinggaltai. Grammar of the Mongol Language. LC 62-22262. 15.00 (ISBN 0-8044-0096-2). Ungar.
Erickson, Jon T. Kachinas: An Evolving Art Form? (The Heard Museum Ser.). (Illus.). 112p. (Orig.). 1981. pap. 12.95 (ISBN 0-295-95857-X, Pub. by Heard Mus). U of Wash Pr.
Poppe, Nicholas. Grammar of Written Mongolian. 1964. 40.00x (ISBN 3-447-00684-6). Intl Pubns Serv.
--Mongolian Language Handbook. LC 72-125673. (Language Handbook Ser.). 1970. pap. text ed. 5.00 (ISBN 0-87281-003-8). Ctr Appl Ling.

MONGOLIAN LANGUAGE–TEXTS

Hangin, John G. Intermediate Mongolian. (Uralic & Altaic Ser.: No. 125). 392p. (Orig.). 1975. pap. text ed. 15.00x (ISBN 0-87750-195-5). Res Ctr Lang Semiotic.
Montgomery, David C. Mongolian Newspaper Reader. LC 78-627747. (Uralic & Altaic Ser: Vol. 102). (Orig., Mongolian). 1969. pap. text ed. 9.00x (ISBN 0-87750-083-5). Res Ctr Lang Semiotic.
Supplementary Texts in Mongolian Script for First Year Reading. 1965. spiral bdg. 5.00 (ISBN 0-910980-24-1). Mongolia.

MONGOLIAN LANGUAGES

see also Mongolian Language; Ordos Language

MONGOLIAN LITERATURE

Krueger, John R., compiled by. Thirteen Kalmyk-Oirat Tales from the Bewitched Corpse Cycle. (Special Papers Ser.: No. 7). 1978. spiral bdg. 10.00 (ISBN 0-910980-27-6). Mongolia.
Poppe, Nicholas, et al. Catalogue of the Manchu-Mongol Section of Toyo Bunko. LC 65-63112. (Publications on Asia of the School of International Studies: No. 12). 391p. 1964. 20.00 (ISBN 0-295-73732-8). U of Wash Pr.
Secen, Sayang. Erdeni-Yin Tobci - Mongolian Chronicle, Pts. I-IV, Mongolian Texts, Mss. A-C. Cleaves, Francis W., ed. (Harvard-Yenching Institute Scripta Mongolia: No. 2). (Illus.). 994p. 1956. Set. pap. text ed. 25.00x (ISBN 0-674-26050-3). Harvard U Pr.

MONGOLIANS

see Mongols

MONGOLISM (DISEASE)

see down'S Syndrome

MONGOLISM–PERSONAL NARRATIVES

Cobb, Mary Ann. Lorie: A Story of Hope. LC 78-20951. 1979. pap. 3.95 (ISBN 0-8407-5677-1). Nelson.
Mussett, Hannah. The Untrodden Ways. 1976. text ed. 11.50x (ISBN 0-575-02003-2). Verry.
Roberts, Nancy. David. LC 74-3710. (Illus.). 72p. 1974. pap. 3.95 (ISBN 0-8042-2031-X). John Knox.
Wilks, John & Wilks, Eileen. Bernard: Bringing up Our Mongol Son. Stevenson, Olive, intro. by. 1974. 12.50 (ISBN 0-7100-7791-2); pap. 6.50 (ISBN 0-7100-7792-0). Routledge & Kegan.

MONGOLS

see also Mogul Empire; Monguors; Tatars

Bergmann, Benjamin. Nomadische Streifereien Unter Den Kalmuken in Den Jahren 1802 & 1803. 1969. text ed. 30.75x (ISBN 90-6234-002-4). Humanities.
Grabar, Oleg & Blair, Sheila. Epic Images & Contemporary History: The Illustrations of the Great Mongol Shahnama. LC 80-305. 1980. lib. bdg. 27.50x (ISBN 0-226-30585-6). U of Chicago Pr.
Hudson, Alfred E. Kazak Social Structure. LC 64-24363. (Yale University Publications in Anthropology Reprints Ser.: No. 20). 109p. 1964. pap. 6.00x (ISBN 0-87536-508-6). HRAFP.
Polo, Marco. The Description of the World, 2 vols. LC 74-5372. Repr. of 1938 ed. 65.00 set (ISBN 0-404-11525-X). AMS Pr.
Schwarz, Henry G. Bibliotheca Mongolica: Pt. 1 Works in English, French, & German. LC 78-18355. (Occasional Papers: Vol. 12). (Illus.). 1978. 18.00 (ISBN 0-914584-12-X). West Wash Univ.
Vreeland, Herbert H., 3rd. Mongol Community & Kinship Structure. LC 72-12334. (Illus.). 327p. 1973. Repr. of 1962 ed. lib. bdg. 17.50x (ISBN 0-8371-6734-5, VRMC). Greenwood.

MONGOLS–HISTORY

Baddeley, John F. Russia, Mongolia, China, 2 Vols. 1964. Repr. of 1919 ed. Set. 133.00 (ISBN 0-8337-0147-9). B Franklin.
Bartol'D, Vasilii V. Turkestan Down to the Mongol Invasion. 3rd ed. Minorsky, V. M., tr. LC 77-8278. xix, 513p. Repr. of 1968 ed. lib. bdg. 25.00x (ISBN 0-87991-453-X). Porcupine Pr.
Boyle, J. A. The Mongol World Empire, 1206-1370. 316p. 1980. 60.00x (ISBN 0-86078-002-3, Pub. by Variorum England). State Mutual Bk.
Curtin, Jeremiah. The Mongols: A History. LC 72-6183. 426p. 1973. Repr. of 1908 ed. lib. bdg. 26.75x (ISBN 0-8371-5445-6, CUMO). Greenwood.
De Rachewiltz, I. Papal Envoys to the Great Khans. LC 77-150327. (Illus.). 1971. 10.00x (ISBN 0-8047-0770-7). Stanford U Pr.
De Rachewiltz, Igor. Index to the Secret History of the Mongols. LC 70-183993. (Uralic & Altaic Ser: Vol. 121). 347p. (Orig.). 1972. pap. text ed. 17.50x (ISBN 0-87750-166-1). Res Ctr Lang Semiotic.
Lattimore, Owen. The Mongols of Manchuria. LC 68-9626. 1969. Repr. of 1934 ed. 25.00 (ISBN 0-86527-132-1). Fertig.
Moses, Larry W. The Political Role of Mongol Buddhism. (Indiana University Uralic & Altaic Ser.: Vol. 133). x, 299p. 1977. 14.95 (ISBN 0-933070-01-2). Ind U Res Inst.
Pelliot, Paul. Les Mongols et la Papaute, 3 pts. in 1 vol. LC 80-2365. Repr. of 1923 ed. 34.50 (ISBN 0-404-18913-X). AMS Pr.
Pokotilov, Dmitrii. History of the Eastern Mongols During the Ming Dynasty from 1368-1631. Lowenthal, Rudolf, tr. from Rus. LC 76-50087. (Perspectives in Asian History: No.1). Repr. of 1947 ed. lib. bdg. 15.00x (ISBN 0-87991-602-8). Porcupine Pr.
Polo, Marco. Travels. Wright, T., ed. Marsden, tr. LC 68-57871. (Bohn's Antiquarian Library Ser). Repr. of 1854 ed. 27.50 (ISBN 0-404-50023-4). AMS Pr.
--Travels of Marco Polo. (Classic Ser). (gr. 9 up). 1968. pap. 1.50 (ISBN 0-8049-0186-4, CL-186). Airmont.
--Travels of Marco Polo. Komroff, Manuel, ed. 1953. 6.95 (ISBN 0-87140-898-8). Liveright.
Roy, M. P. Origin Growth & Suppression of the Pindaris. (Illus.). 355p. 1973. text ed. 17.50x (ISBN 0-8426-0543-6). Verry.
Saunders, J. J. The History of the Mongol Conquests. 1971. 25.00 (ISBN 0-7100-7073-X). Routledge & Kegan.
Skelton, R. A., et al. Vinland Map & the Tartar Relation. (Illus.). 1965. 35.00x (ISBN 0-300-00959-3). Yale U Pr.
Spuler, Bertold. History of the Mongols: Based on Eastern & Western Accounts of the Thirteenth & Fourteenth Centuries. Drummond, Helga, tr. 1971. 26.75x (ISBN 0-520-01960-1). U of Cal Pr.
Washburn, Wilcomb E., ed. Vinland Map Conference: Proceedings. LC 77-152380. 1971. 12.50x (ISBN 0-226-87394-3). U of Chicago Pr.
Zhamtsarano, Ts. Ethnography & Geography of the Darkhat & Other Mongolian Minorities. (Special Papers Ser.: No. 8). 1979. spiral bdg. 15.00 (ISBN 0-910980-28-4). Mongolia.

MONGOOSES

Neal, Ernest. Uganda Quest: African Wildlife After Dark. LC 75-158843. (Illus.). 1971. 7.95 (ISBN 0-8008-7923-6). Taplinger.

MONGUORS

Schram, Louis M. Monguors of the Kansu-Tibetan Frontier Part 3: Records of the Monguor Clans, History of the Monguors in Huangchung & the Chronicles of the Lu Family. LC 54-6120. (Transactions Ser.: Vol. 51, Pt. 3). (Illus.). 1961. pap. 1.00 (ISBN 0-87169-513-8). Am Philos.

MONICA, SAINT, d. 387–FICTION

Cristiani, Leon. The Story of Monica & Her Son Augustine. 1977. 3.95 (ISBN 0-8198-0461-4); pap. 2.95 (ISBN 0-8198-0462-2). Dghtrs St Paul.

MONILIALES

Barron, George L. Genera of Hyphomycetes from Soil. LC 68-14275. 378p. 1977. Repr. of 1968 ed. 21.00 (ISBN 0-88275-004-6). Krieger.
Tubaki, K. Hyphomycetes; Their Perfect-Imperfect Connexions. 300p. 1981. lib. bdg. 15.00 (ISBN 3-7682-1267-X). Lubrecht & Cramer.

MONILIASIS

see Candidiasis

MONISM

see also Dualism; Idealism; Materialism; Pluralism

Haeckel, Ernst. Riddle of the Universe at the Close of the 19th Century. LC 6403. 1900. 16.00 (ISBN 0-403-00117-X). Scholarly.
Plekhanov, G. Development of the Monist View of History. 335p. 1974. 3.60 (ISBN 0-8285-0191-2, Pub. by Progress Pubs Russia). Imported Pubns.
Plekhanov, G. V. The Development of the Monist View of History. 317p. 1973. 5.00 (ISBN 0-7178-0371-6). Intl Pub Co.
Plekhanov, George V. Development of the Monist View of History. 350p. 1982. 19.95 (ISBN 0-87855-322-3); pap. 4.95 (ISBN 0-87855-704-0). Transaction Bks.
Plikhanou, Georgi. Development of the Monist View of History. 334p. 1972. Repr. of 1956 ed. 17.00x (ISBN 0-8464-1086-9). Beekman Pubs.
Ward, J. Naturalism & Agnosticism: The Gifford Lectures Delivered Before the University of Aberdeen in 1896-1898, 2 Vols. in 1. 4th ed. Repr. of 1899 ed. 30.00 (ISBN 0-527-94500-5). Kraus Repr.

MONITOR (IRONCLAD)

Davis, William C. Duel Between the First Ironclads. (Illus.). 216p. 1981. pap. 7.95 (ISBN 0-8071-0868-5). La State U Pr.

The Monitor: Its Meaning & Future. LC 78-70798. (Illus.). 1978. pap. 6.50 (ISBN 0-89133-071-2). Preservation Pr.
White, Elsberry V. The First Iron-Clad Naval Engagement in the World: The Merrimac & the Monitor. (Illus.). 1906. wrappers 12.50 (ISBN 0-686-17397-X). R S Barnes.

MONITORIAL SYSTEM OF EDUCATION

Kaestle, Carl F. Joseph Lancaster & the Monitorial School Movement: A Documentary History. LC 72-97206. 200p. 1973. text ed. 12.00 (ISBN 0-8077-2375-4); pap. text ed. 5.50x (ISBN 0-8077-2380-0). Tchrs Coll.
Lancaster, Joseph. Improvements in Education. 3rd ed. LC 68-56241. (Social History of Education). Repr. of 1805 ed. 13.50x (ISBN 0-678-00697-0). Kelley.
Reigart, John F. Lancasterian System of Instruction in the Schools of New York City. LC 72-89220. (American Education: Its Men, Institutions & Ideas, Ser. 1). 1969. Repr. of 1916 ed. 9.00 (ISBN 0-405-01459-7). Arno.
--The Lancasterian System of Instruction in the Schools of New York City. LC 74-177187. (Columbia University. Teachers College. Contributions to Education: No. 81). Repr. of 1916 ed. 9.00 (ISBN 0-404-55081-9). AMS Pr.

MONITORING (HOSPITAL CARE)

see also Hospital Care

Chartridge Symposium on Real-Time Computing in Patient Management, 1975. Proceedings. Date not set. 28.50 (ISBN 0-901223-88-3, Pub. by Peregrinus England). Inst Elect Eng.
Chartridge Symposium on the Management of the Acutely Ill, 1976. Proceedings. Date not set. 29.50 (ISBN 0-901223-92-1, Pub. by Peregrinus England). Inst Elect Eng.
Chertow, Bruce S., et al. Patient Management Problems: Exercises in Decision Making & Problem Solving. 318p. 1979. pap. 32.00x (ISBN 0-8385-7769-5). ACC.
Chung, E. K. Ambulatory Electrocardiography: Holter Monitor Electrocardiography. (Illus.). 1979. 26.20 (ISBN 0-387-90360-7). Springer-Verlag.
Dornette, William H., ed. Monitoring in Anesthesia. (Illus.). 424p. 1973. text ed. 25.00 (ISBN 0-8036-2725-4). Davis Co.
Gravenstein, J. S., et al, eds. Essential Noninvasive Monitoring in Anesthesia. (Illus.). 323p. 1980. 19.50 (ISBN 0-8089-1241-0). Grune.
Huch, Albert, et al, eds. Continous Transcutaneous Blood Gas Monitorin. LC 79-2586. (Alan R. Liss Ser.: Vol. 15, No. 4). 1979. 68.00 (ISBN 0-8451-1027-6). March of Dimes.
IFPtC4 Working Conference, Amsterdam, 1976. Trends in Computer-Processed Electrocardiograms: Proceedings. Van Bemmel, J. H. & Willems, J. L., eds. LC 77-1801. 1977. 56.00 (ISBN 0-7204-0723-0, North-Holland). Elsevier.
International Symposium on Biotelemetry Garmisch-Partenkirch, 4th, May 1978. Abstracts. Kimmich, H. P., ed. (Biotelemetry & Patient Monitoring: Vol. 5, No. 1). 1978. soft cover 21.00 (ISBN 3-8055-2911-2). S Karger.
Kimmich, H. P. Monitoring of Vital Parameters During Extracorporeal Circulation. (Illus.). 1981. soft cover 72.00 (ISBN 3-8055-2059-X). S Karger.
Kimmich, H. P., ed. Continuous Monitoring of Arterial Oxygen Partial Pressure. (Biotelemetry & Patient Monitoring: Vol. 6, Nos. 1-2, 1979). (Illus.). 1979. pap. 16.25 (ISBN 3-8055-0053-X). S Karger.
Lauersen, Neils H. & Hochberg, Howard. Clinical Perinatal Biochemical Monitoring. 320p. 1981. 30.00 (ISBN 0-686-77745-X, 1901-1). Williams & Wilkins.
Society of Patient Representatives of the American Hospital Association. The Patient Representative's Participation in Risk Management. (Orig.). 1980. pap. 8.75 (ISBN 0-87258-315-5, 1532). Am Hospital.
Symposium Held at St. Lucas Hospital, Amsterdam, 1973. Anxiety Factors in Comprehensive Patient Care: Proceedings. Rees, W. Linford, ed. (International Congress Ser.: No. 305). 1974. 12.75 (ISBN 0-444-15063-3, Excerpta Medica). Elsevier.
Transcutaneous Monitoring of Oxygen. (Illus.). 1978. pap. 20.00 (ISBN 3-8055-2883-3). S Karger.

MONITORING (PSYCHOLOGY)

see Vigilance (Psychology)

MONKEYS

see also Baboons; Lemurs; Macaques

Andrew, G. & Harlow, H. F. Performance of Macaque Monkeys on a Test of the Concept of Generalized Triangularity. LC 48-10876. Repr. of 1948 ed. pap. 5.00 (ISBN 0-527-24935-1). Kraus Repr.
Beattie, J. Anatomy of the Common Marmoset. LC 78-72711. Repr. of 1927 ed. 27.50 (ISBN 0-404-18281-X). AMS Pr.
Carpenter, Clarence R. A Field Study of the Behavior & Social Relations of Howling Monkeys. LC 76-44703. Repr. of 1934 ed. 22.50 (ISBN 0-404-15854-4). AMS Pr.
Emmers, Raimond & Akert, Konrad. Stereotaxic Atlas of the Brain of the Squirrel Monkey. (Illus.). 120p. 1963. 100.00x (ISBN 0-299-02690-6). U of Wis Pr.
Folk, Dean. External Neuroanatomy of Old World Monkeys (Cercopithecoidea) Szalay, F. S., ed. (Contributions to Primatology: Vol. 15). (Illus.). 1978. 35.50 (ISBN 3-8055-2834-5). S Karger.
Hershkovitz, Philip. Living New World Monkeys (Platyrrhini) With an Introduction to Primates, Vol. 1. LC 75-9059. (Illus.). 1978. 90.00x (ISBN 0-226-32788-4). U of Chicago Pr.
Hughes, Lynn, ed. Monkeys. LC 80-57619. (Illus.). 56p. 1980. 4.95 (ISBN 0-89480-098-1). Workman Pub.
Kleiman, Devra G., ed. The Biology & Conservation of the Callitrichidae. LC 78-2428. (Symposia of the National Zoological Park Ser.: No. 2). (Illus.). 1978. text ed. 35.00x (ISBN 0-87474-586-1); pap. text ed. 15.00x (ISBN 0-87474-587-X). Smithsonian.
Kluver, Heinrich. Behavior Mechanisms in Monkeys. (Illus.). 1961. pap. 1.95 (ISBN 0-226-44508-9, P503, Phoen). U of Chicago Pr.
Krieg, Wendell J. Connections of the Frontal Cortex of the Monkey. (Illus.). 320p. 1954. photocopy ed. spiral 29.75 (ISBN 0-398-01050-1). C C Thomas.
Kusama, T. & Mabuchi, M. Stereotaxic Atlas of the Brain of Macaca Fuscata. (Illus.). 1970. 125.00 (ISBN 0-8391-0011-6). Univ Park.
Langeveld, M. J. Columbus Picture Analysis of Growth Towards Maturity: A Series of 24 Pictures & a Manual. 2nd ed. 76p. 1976. 42.75 (ISBN 3-8055-2329-7). S Karger.
Milton, Katherine. The Foraging Strategy of Howler Monkeys: A Study in Economics. LC 79-27380. (Illus.). 1980. 20.00x (ISBN 0-231-04850-5). Columbia U Pr.
Monkeys & Apes. (Wild, Wild World of Animals Ser). 1976. 10.95 (ISBN 0-913948-03-9). Time-Life.
Muller, Dorothy. The Monkey Wanderu. 1978. 5.95 (ISBN 0-533-03009-9). Vantage.
Rowell, Thelma. Social Behaviour of Monkeys. lib. bdg. 9.50x (ISBN 0-88307-442-7). Gannon.
Struhsaker, Thomas T. The Red Colobus Monkey. LC 74-21339. (Wildlife Behavior & Ecology Ser.). (Illus.). xiv, 312p. 1976. 25.00x (ISBN 0-226-77769-3). U of Chicago Pr.
Williams, Leonard. Samba. LC 80-40597. (Illus.). 128p. 1980. 12.95 (ISBN 0-8052-8055-3, Pub. by Allison & Busby England); pap. 6.95 (ISBN 0-8052-8054-5). Schocken.
Ziemer, L. K. Functional Morphology of Forelimb Joints in the Wooly Monkey Lagothrix Lagothricha. Szalay, F. S., ed. (Contributions to Primatology: Vol. 14). (Illus.). 1978. 46.75 (ISBN 3-8055-2821-3). S Karger.
Zuckerman, S. The Social Life of Monkey & Apes. 356p. 1981. Repr. of 1932 ed. lib. bdg. 40.00 (ISBN 0-89984-547-9). Century Bookbindery.
--The Social Life of Monkeys & Apes. 2nd ed. (Illus.). 496p. 1981. 55.00 (ISBN 0-7100-0691-8). Routledge & Kegan.

MONKEYS–JUVENILE LITERATURE

Allen, Martha. Meet the Monkeys. LC 78-26211. (Illus.). (gr. 2-5). 1979. 6.95g (ISBN 0-13-574202-1). P-H.
Boorer, Michael. The Life of Monkeys & Apes. LC 78-56603. (Easy Reading Edition of Introduction to Nature Ser.). (Illus.). 1978. lib. bdg. 7.95 (ISBN 0-686-51143-3). Silver.
Monkeys & Apes. LC 75-40056. (Wild, Wild World of Animals). (Illus.). (gr. 5 up). 1976. lib. bdg. 11.97 (ISBN 0-685-73290-8). Silver.
Morris, Dean. Monkeys & Apes. LC 77-8148. (Read About Animals Ser.). (Illus.). (gr. k-3). 1977. PLB 11.15 (ISBN 0-8393-0005-0). Raintree Child.
Radlauer, Edward. Monkey Mania. (Ready, Get Set, Go Books). (gr. 1-4). 1977. PLB 9.25 (ISBN 0-516-07466-0, Elk Grove Bks); pap. 2.95 (ISBN 0-516-47466-9, Elk Grove Bks). Childrens.
Rau, Margaret. The Snow Monkey at Home. LC 78-31550. (Illus.). (gr. 4-7). 1979. 6.95 (ISBN 0-394-83976-5); PLB 6.99 (ISBN 0-394-93976-X). Knopf.
Rey, H. A. Cecily G. & the Nine Monkeys. (Illus.). (gr. 1-3). 1942. reinforced bdg. 7.95 (ISBN 0-395-18430-4). HM.
Thompson, Brenda & Overbeck, Cynthia. Monkeys & Apes. LC 76-22474. (First Fact Books Ser). (Illus.). (gr. k-3). 1977. PLB 7.95g (ISBN 0-8225-1358-7). Lerner Pubns.
Whitehead, Patricia. Monkeys. LC 81-11439. (Now I Know Ser.). (Illus.). 32p. (gr. k-2). 1982. PLB 7.95 (ISBN 0-89375-670-9); pap. 1.25 (ISBN 0-89375-671-7). Troll Assocs.
Zim, Herbert S. Monkeys. (Illus.). (gr. 3-7). 1955. PLB 6.48 (ISBN 0-688-31517-8). Morrow.

MONKEYS AS LABORATORY ANIMALS

Stern, J. T., Jr. Functional Myology of the Hip & Thigh of Cebid Monkeys & Its Implications for the Evolution of Erect Posture. (Bibliotheca Primatologica: No. 14). 1971. pap. 46.75 (ISBN 3-8055-1212-0). S Karger.
Tobias, Thomas J. Towards Analysis of Marmoset Motor Cortex. (Illus.). 50p. 1980. pap. text ed. 16.00 (ISBN 0-9604634-0-2). Learn Mich.

MONKS

see Monasticism and Religious Orders

MONMOUTH, BATTLE OF, 1778

Smith, Samuel S. The Battle of Monmouth. LC 64-56379. (Revolutionary War Bicentennial Ser.). (Illus.). 1964. lib. bdg. 6.95 (ISBN 0-912480-00-9). Freneau.
Stryker, William S. Battle of Monmouth. LC 79-120893. (American Bicentennial Ser). 1970. Repr. of 1927 ed. 13.75 (ISBN 0-8046-1286-2). Kennikat.
Thayer, Theodore. Washington & Lee at Monmouth: The Making of a Scapegoat. 1976. 9.95 (ISBN 0-8046-9139-8, Natl U). Kennikat.

MONMOUTH COUNTY, NEW JERSEY–HISTORY

Beekman, George C. Early Dutch Settlers of Monmouth County. 2nd ed. 1974. 12.00 (ISBN 0-686-11781-6). Morris Genealog Lib.
Hornor, William S. This Old Monmouth of Ours. LC 73-89903. 1974. 20.00 (ISBN 0-686-11780-8). Morris Genealog Lib.
Moss, George H., Jr. Double Exposure: Early Stereographic Views of Historic Monmouth County, New Jersey & Their Relationship to Pioneer Photography. LC 70-154560. (Illus.). 176p. 1971. 20.00 (ISBN 0-912396-00-8). Ploughshare Pr.
--Steamboat to the Shore: A Pictorial History of the Steamboat Era in Monmouth County, New Jersey. (Illus.). 102p. 1972. 15.00 (ISBN 0-912396-02-4). Ploughshare Pr.
Van Benthuysen, Robert F., ed. Monmouth County, New Jersey: A Bibliography of Published Works 1676-1973. 200p. 1974. 11.95 (ISBN 0-912396-04-0). Ploughshare Pr.

MONMOUTH'S REBELLION, 1685

Johnson, David. The Monmouth Rebellion. (Jackdaw Ser: No. 34). 1968. 6.95 (ISBN 0-670-48665-5, Grossman). Viking Pr.
Wigfield, W. MacDonald. The Monmouth Rebellion: A Social History Including the Complete Text of "Wade's Narrative," 1685 & "a Guide to the Battlefield of Sedgemoor". (Illus.). 176p. 1980. 24.50x (ISBN 0-389-20149-9). B&N.

MONNET, JEAN, 1888-

McKown, Dave R. The Dean: The Life of Julien Charles Monnet. LC 73-7418. (Illus.). 300p. 1973. 14.95 (ISBN 0-8061-1132-1). U of Okla Pr.
Monnet, Jean. Memoirs. LC 76-56322. 1978. 12.95 (ISBN 0-385-12505-4). Doubleday.

MONO COUNTY, CALIFORNIA

Gaines, David. Mono Lake Guidebook. (Illus.). 120p. (Orig.). 1981. pap. 3.95 (ISBN 0-939716-00-3). Mono Lake Comm.
Mitchell, Roger. Inyo-Mono Jeep Trails. (Illus.). 1969. wrappers 1.25 (ISBN 0-910856-33-8). La Siesta.

MONO LANGUAGE

see also Melanesian Languages

Wheeler, G. C. Mono-Alu Folklore: Bougainville Strait, Western Solomon Islands. LC 70-174374. Repr. of 1926 ed. 20.00 (ISBN 0-405-10049-3). Arno.

MONOCOTYLEDONS

Arber, A. Monocotyledons: A Morphological Study. (Illus.). 1961. Repr. of 1925 ed. 40.00 (ISBN 3-7682-0074-4). Lubrecht & Cramer.
Braun, E. Lucy. Monocotyledoneae: Cat-Tails to Orchids. LC 66-25170. (Vascular Flora of Ohio: No. 1). (Illus.). 1967. 10.00 (ISBN 0-8142-0028-1). Ohio St U Pr.
Brickell, C., et al. Petaloid Monocotyledons: Horticultural & Botanical Research. (Linnean Society Symposium Ser.: No.8). 1980. 71.50 (ISBN 0-12-133950-5). Acad Pr.
Dahlgren, R. M. & Clifford, H. T. The Monocotyledon: A Comparative Study. (Botanical Systematics Ser.: No. 2). 1981. price not set (ISBN 0-12-200680-1). Acad Pr.
Godfrey, Robert K. & Wooten, Jean W. Aquatic & Wetland Plants of Southeastern States: Monocotyledons. LC 76-28924. 723p. 1979. 30.00 (ISBN 0-8203-0420-4). U of Ga Pr.
Hara, H., et al. Enumeration of the Flowering Plants of Nepal: Vol. 1, Monocotyledons. (Illus.). 1978. pap. 61.50x (ISBN 0-565-00777-7, Pub. by Brit Mus Nat Hist). Sabbot-Natural Hist Bks.
Metcalfe, C. R., ed. Anatomy of the Monocotyledons, 4 vols. Incl. Vol. 1. Gramineae. 1960; Vol. 2. Palmae. Tomlinson, P. B. 1961. 49.00x (ISBN 0-19-854344-1); Vol. 3. Commelinales-Zingiberales. Tomlinson, P. B. 1969. 48.00x (ISBN 0-19-854365-4); Vol. 4. Juncales. Cutler, D. F. 1969. 42.00x (ISBN 0-19-854369-7); Vol. 5. Cyperaceae. Metcalfe, C. R. (Illus.). 610p. 1971. 62.00x (ISBN 0-19-854372-7); Vol. 6. Dioscoreales. Ayensu, E. S. (Illus.). 226p. 1972. 49.00x (ISBN 0-19-854376-X). Oxford U Pr.
Purseglove, J. W. Tropical Crops: Monocotyledons, Vol. 3. 1972-73. Pt. 2. 20.95 (ISBN 0-471-70242-0). Halsted Pr.
Rendle, Alfred B. Classification of Flowering Plants, 2 bks. Incl. Bk. 1. Gymnosperms & Monocotyledons. 72.50 (ISBN 0-521-06056-7); Bk. 2. Dicotyledons. 85.00 (ISBN 0-521-06057-5). Cambridge U Pr.
Tutin, T. G., et al. Flora Europaea: Alismataceae to Orchidaceae, Vol. 5. LC 64-24315. (Illus.). 1980. 105.00 (ISBN 0-521-20108-X). Cambridge U Pr.

MONOD, JACQUES

Chiari, Joseph. The Necessity of Being. LC 73-3338. 168p. 1973. 9.00 (ISBN 0-87752-167-0). Gordian.

MONOGENIC FUNCTIONS

see Analytic Functions

MONOGENISM AND POLYGENISM

Nott, Josiah C. Two Lectures on the Connection Between the Biblical & Physical History of Man. LC 72-78584. (Illus.). Repr. of 1849 ed. 10.50x (ISBN 0-8371-1409-8). Greenwood.
Smith, Samuel S. Essay on the Causes of the Variety of Complexion & Figure in the Human Species. Jordan, Winthrop D., ed. LC 65-19831. (The John Harvard Library). 1965. 16.50x (ISBN 0-674-26350-2). Harvard U Pr.

MONOGRAMS

see also Alphabets; Anagrams; Artists' Marks; Initials

Bergling, J. M. Art Monograms & Lettering. 18th ed. Bergling, V. C., ed. 1950. pap. 6.50 (ISBN 0-910222-03-7). Gem City Coll.
--Art Monograms & Lettering. 20th ed. Bergling, V. C., ed. LC 63-22577. 1964. 17.95 (ISBN 0-910222-02-9). Gem City Coll.
Cirker, Hayward & Cirker, Blanche. Monograms & Alphabetic Devices. (Illus.). 10.00 (ISBN 0-8446-0546-8). Peter Smith.
--Monograms & Alphabetic Devices. (Illus., Orig.). 1970. pap. 6.00 (ISBN 0-486-22330-2). Dover.
Haslam, Malcolm. Marks & Monograms of the Modern Movement, 1875-1930. LC 76-26189. 1977. 12.50 (ISBN 0-684-14828-5, ScribT). Scribner.
Hitchcock, Thomas H. & Merrick, Kenneth A. Official Monogram Painting Guide to German Aircraft, 1935-1945. (Illus.). 132p. 1980. ring bdg. 39.95 (ISBN 0-914144-29-4, Pub by Monogram Aviation Pubns). Aviation.
Ris-Pacquot, Oscar E. Dictionnaire Encyclopedique Des Marques Et Monogrammes. 1964. Repr. of 1893 ed. 51.50 (ISBN 0-8337-3003-7). B Franklin.
Turbayne, A. A. Monograms & Ciphers. LC 68-55285. (Illus.). 1968. pap. 3.00 (ISBN 0-486-22182-2). Dover.
Turbayne, A. A., et al. Monograms & Ciphers. (Illus.). 7.50 (ISBN 0-8446-3093-4). Peter Smith.

MONOLOGUE

Arnold, Morris L. Soliloquies of Shakespeare: A Study in Technic. LC 78-58273. Repr. of 1911 ed. 16.00 (ISBN 0-404-00389-3). AMS Pr.
Curry, S. S. Browning & the Dramatic Monologue. LC 65-26455. (Studies in Browning, No. 4). 1969. Repr. of 1908 ed. lib. bdg. 49.95 (ISBN 0-8383-0535-0). Haskell.
Honan, Park. Browning's Characters: A Study in Poetic Technique. 1969. Repr. of 1961 ed. 18.50 (ISBN 0-208-00793-8, Archon). Shoe String.
Langbaum, Robert. Poetry of Experience: The Dramatic Monologue in Modern Literary Tradition. 1963. pap. 4.95 (ISBN 0-393-00215-2, Norton Lib). Norton.
Roessler, Erwin W. Soliloquy in German Drama. LC 15-5583. (Columbia University. Germanic Studies, Old Ser.: No. 19). Repr. of 1915 ed. 19.00 (ISBN 0-404-50419-1). AMS Pr.
Westrom, Robert. Monologues for the Actor. 60p. (Orig.). 1978. pap. 2.50 (ISBN 0-938230-02-6, TX341-851). Westrom.

MONOLOGUES

Here are entered collections of monologues.
see also Dialogues

Beckett, Samuel. Company. LC 80-995. 64p. 1980. 8.95 (ISBN 0-394-51394-0, GP 833). Grove.
Emerson, Robert & Grumbach, Jane. Monologues for Men. LC 76-1027. 1976. 3.95x (ISBN 0-910482-78-0). Drama Bk.
--Monologues for Women. LC 76-1965. 1976. 3.95x (ISBN 0-910482-79-9). Drama Bk.
Franklin, Clay. Mixed Company. 100p. 1959. 4.50 (ISBN 0-573-60070-8). French.

Griffith, B. C., et al, eds. Monologues & Novelties. LC 70-38599. (Granger Index Reprint Ser.). Repr. of 1896 ed. 17.00 (ISBN 0-8369-6331-8). Arno.

Grumbach, Jane & Emerson, Robert. Actor's Guide to Monologues, Vol. 2. rev ed. LC 73-21893. 1981. pap. 2.95x (ISBN 0-89676-043-X). Drama Bk.

--Monologues: Men, Vol. 2. 56p. (Orig.). 1981. pap. price not set (ISBN 0-89676-065-0). Drama Bk.

--Monologues: Women, Vol. 2. 56p. (Orig.). 1981. pap. price not set. Drama Bk.

Hereford, Beatrice. Beatrice Hereford's Monologues. 80p. 1937. 4.50 (ISBN 0-573-60064-3). French.

Ireland, Norma O. Index to Monologs & Dialogs. rev. enl. ed. (The Useful Reference Ser. of Library Bks: Vol. 77). 1949. 9.00x (ISBN 0-87305-077-0). Faxon.

Karshner, Roger. Thirty Modern Monologues. 4.00 (ISBN 0-573-60078-3). French.

Marshall, Michael. Stanley Holloway: More Monologues & Songs, Vol. 2. (Illus.). 128p. 1980. pap. 6.50 (ISBN 0-241-10478-5, Pub. by Hamish Hamilton England). David & Charles.

Murray, John. Modern Monologues for Young People. rev. ed. LC 72-6277. (gr. 7 up). 1982. 12.00 (ISBN 0-8238-0255-8). Plays.

Rudnicki, Stefan, ed. Classical Monologues 1: Shakespeare. LC 79-16079. 1979. pap. 3.95x (ISBN 0-89676-021-9). Drama Bk.

--Classical Monologues 2: Shakespeare & Friends. LC 79-16079. 1980. pap. 3.95x (ISBN 0-89676-022-7). Drama Bk.

--Classical Monologues 3: The Age of Style. 128p. (Orig.). 1981. pap. 3.95x (ISBN 0-89676-036-7). Drama Bk.

--Classical Monologues 4: Shakespeare & Friends Encore. 144p. (Orig.). 1981. pap. text ed. 4.95x (ISBN 0-89676-037-5). Drama Bk.

--Classical Monologues 5: Warhorses. 96p. (Orig.). 1981. pap. text ed. 4.95x (ISBN 0-89676-038-3). Drama Bk.

Ryerson, Florence & Clements, Colin. First Person Singular. 110p. 1937. 4.50 (ISBN 0-573-60066-X). French.

Wolfe, Humbert. Dialogues & Monologues. 1928. Repr. 25.00 (ISBN 0-8274-2172-9). R West.

MONOMERS

Albright, Lyle F. Processes for Major Addition-Type Plastics & Their Monomers. 396p. 1981. Repr. of 1974 ed. lib. bdg. write for info. (ISBN 0-89874-074-6). Krieger.

Commercial Monomers & Polymers. (Plastics Studies). 1977. 525.00 (ISBN 0-89336-036-8, P-039). BCC.

Frisch, Kurt C. Cyclic Monomers. (High Polymer Ser.: Vol. 26). 1972. 43.50 (ISBN 0-471-39360-6, Pub. by Wiley). Krieger.

Leonard, Edward C. Vinyl & Diene Monomers. (High Polymer Ser.: Vol. 23, Pt. 3). 1971. 36.00 (ISBN 0-471-39330-4). Krieger.

--Vinyl & Diene Monomers. (High Polymer Ser.: Vol. 24, Pt. 2). 1971. 56.50 (ISBN 0-471-39329-0, Pub. by Wiley). Krieger.

Stille, John K. & Campbell, T. W. Condensation Monomers. (High Polymer Ser.: Vol. 27). 1972. 59.50 (ISBN 0-471-39370-3, Pub. by Wiley). Krieger.

Yocum, R. H. & Nyquist, E., eds. Functional Monomers: Their Preparation, Polymerization, & Application, Vol. 1. 736p. 1973. 79.00 (ISBN 0-8254-1810-0). Dekker.

--Functional Monomers: Their Preparation, Polymerization, & Application, Vol. 2. 832p. 1974. 79.00 (ISBN 0-8247-6080-8). Dekker.

MONOMOTAPA

Hall, Richard N. & Neal, W. G. Ancient Ruins of Rhodesia. 2nd ed. LC 71-77202. (Illus.). Repr. of 1904 ed. 31.00x (ISBN 0-8371-1275-3, Pub. by Negro U Pr). Greenwood.

Randles, W. G. L' Empire Du Monomotapa Du XV Au XIX Siecle. (Civilisations et Societes: No. 46). (Illus.). 167p. (Orig.). 1976. pap. text ed. 19.50x (ISBN 0-686-22615-1). Mouton.

Wieschoff, Heinrich A. The Zimbabwe - Monomotapa Culture in Southeast Africa. LC 76-44801. Repr. of 1941 ed. 21.50 (ISBN 0-404-15981-8). AMS Pr.

Wilmot, Alexander. Manomotapa, Rhodesia: Its Monuments & Its History from the Most Ancient Times to the Present Century. LC 76-76485. (Illus.). Repr. of 1896 ed. 14.50x (ISBN 0-8371-1136-6, Pub. by Negro U Pr). Greenwood.

MONONCHIDAE

Jensen, Harold J. & Mulvey, Ronald H. Predaceous Nematodes of Oregon. LC 68-63023. (Studies in Zoology Ser: No. 12). (Illus., Orig.). 1968. pap. 3.50 (ISBN 0-87071-112-1). Oreg St U Pr.

MONONGAHELA RIVER

Van Voorhis, John S. The Old & New Monongahela. LC 74-7529. 486p. 1974. Repr. of 1893 ed. 20.00 (ISBN 0-8063-0625-4). Genealog Pub.

MONONUCLEOSIS

Hoagland, Robert J. Infectious Mononucleosis. LC 67-16801. (Illus.). 144p. 1967. 32.25 (ISBN 0-8089-0190-7). Grune.

Infectious Mononucleosis. (Illus.). 1978. 20.00 (ISBN 0-916750-30-2). Dayton Labs.

MONOPHYSITES

see also Ethiopic Church

Chesnut, Roberta C. Three Monophysite Christologies: Severus of Antioch, Philoxenus of Mabbug, & Jacob of Sarug. (Oxford Theological Monographs). 1976. 24.95x (ISBN 0-19-826712-6). Oxford U Pr.

Lebon, Joseph. Le Monophysisme severien: Etude historique, litteraire et theologique sur la resistance monophysite au Concile de Chalcedoine jusqu'a la constitution de l'eglise jacobite. LC 77-84704. Repr. of 1909 ed. 39.00 (ISBN 0-404-16111-1). AMS Pr.

Wigram, William A. The Separation of the Monophysites. LC 77-84708. Repr. of 1923 ed. 19.50 (ISBN 0-404-16115-4). AMS Pr.

MONOPOLIES

see also Competition; Corporation Law; Oligopolies; Railroads–Consolidation; Restraint of Trade; Trusts, Industrial

Baran, Paul A. & Sweezy, Paul M. Monopoly Capital: An Essay on the American Economic & Social Order. LC 65-15269. 1968. pap. 6.50 (ISBN 0-85345-073-0, PB-0730). Monthly Rev.

Brozen, Yale. Is Government the Source of Monopoly? And Other Essays. LC 80-14176. (Cato Paper Ser.: No. 9). 80p. 1980. pap. 2.00x (ISBN 0-932790-09-7). Cato Inst.

Chamberlin, Edward H. Theory of Monopolistic Competition: A Re-Orientation of the Theory of Value. 8th ed. LC 63-649. (Economic Studies: No. 38). 1962. 18.50x (ISBN 0-674-88125-7). Harvard U Pr.

Clarkson, Kenneth W. Intangible Capital & Rates of Return. 1977. pap. 4.25 (ISBN 0-8447-3235-4). Am Enterprise.

Committee of Experts on Restrictive Business Practices. Export Cartels, 1974: Proceedings. 1974. 5.00 (ISBN 92-64-11271-5). OECD.

CPUSA. The People vs. Monopoly: Nineteen Eighty Draft Program of the Communist Part, USA. 62p. (Orig.). 1980. pap. 0.50 (ISBN 0-87898-142-X). New Outlook.

Douglas, C. H. The Monopoly of Credit. 59.95 (ISBN 0-8490-0664-3). Gordon Pr.

Ely, Richard T. Monopolies & Trust. LC 73-2505. (Big Business; Economic Power in a Free Society Ser.). Repr. of 1912 ed. 15.00 (ISBN 0-405-05087-9). Arno.

Fellner, William J. Competition Among the Few. rev. ed. LC 64-17622. Repr. of 1949 ed. 15.00x (ISBN 0-678-00042-5). Kelley.

Fouraker, Lawrence E. & Seigel, Sidney. Bargaining Behavior. LC 77-23058. 1977. Repr. of 1963 ed. lib. bdg. 24.00x (ISBN 0-8371-9738-4, FOBB). Greenwood.

Groner, Alfred M. The Monopoly Players. 1982. 13.95 (ISBN 0-87949-207-4). Ashley Bks.

Hilhorst, J. G. Monopolistic Competition, Technical Progress & Income Distribution. 1970. pap. 22.50 (ISBN 0-677-61545-0). Gordon.

International Conference on Monopolies, Mergers & Restrictive Practices - Papers & Reports - Cambridge, England - 1969. Proceedings. Heath, J. B., ed. 285p. 1973. 17.50x (ISBN 0-8002-1856-6). Intl Pubns Serv.

Lewis, W. Arthur. Overhead Costs. LC 70-113506. Repr. of 1949 ed. lib. bdg. 12.50x (ISBN 0-678-06014-2). Kelley.

Machlup, Fritz. The Economics of Sellers Competition, Vol. 2. 602p. 1952. 35.00x (ISBN 0-8018-0414-0). Johns Hopkins.

--The Political Economy of Monopoly, Vol. 1. 560p. 1952. 35.00x (ISBN 0-8018-0415-9). Johns Hopkins.

Mansfield, Edwin, ed. Monopoly Power & Economic Performance. 4th ed. (Problems of the Modern Economy Ser.). 1978. 14.95 (ISBN 0-393-05702-X); pap. 5.95x (ISBN 0-393-09013-2). Norton.

--Monopoly Power & Economic Performance. 3rd ed. LC 73-18027. (Problems of the Modern Economy Ser). (Illus.). 228p. 1974. 7.95x (ISBN 0-393-05448-9); pap. 3.25x (ISBN 0-393-09990-3). Norton.

Mason, Edward S. Economic Concentration & the Monopoly Problem. LC 57-6351. 1964. 1.95 (ISBN 0-689-70137-3). Atheneum.

Nukhovich, E. International Monopolies and the Developing Countries. 1980. 6.50 (ISBN 0-8285-1801-7, Pub. by Progress Pubs Russia). Imported Pubns.

Polanyi, George. Which Way Monopoly Policy? (Institute of Economic Affairs, Research Monographs: No. 30). pap. 2.50 (ISBN 0-255-36047-9). Transatlantic.

Robinson, Joan. Economics of Imperfect Competition. 1969. 17.95 (ISBN 0-312-23380-9); pap. 6.95 (ISBN 0-312-23345-0). St Martin.

Schmalensee, Richard. The Control of Natural Monopolies. LC 78-6061. 1979. 18.95 (ISBN 0-669-02322-1). Lexington Bks.

Siegel, Sidney & Fouraker, Lawrence E. Bargaining & Group Decision Making: Experiments in Bilateral Monopoly. LC 77-14561. 1977. Repr. of 1960 ed. lib. bdg. 14.00x (ISBN 0-8371-9837-2, SIBG). Greenwood.

Spelling, Thomas C. A Treatise on Trusts & Monopolies, Containing an Exposition of the Rule of Public Policy Against Contracts & Combinations in Restraint of Trade, & a Review of Cases, Ancient & Modern. xxvii, 274p. 1981. Repr. of 1893 ed. lib. bdg. 27.50x (ISBN 0-8377-1116-9). Rothman.

Triffin, Robert. Monopolistic Competition & General Equilibrium Theory. LC 40-12673. (Economic Studies: No. 67). 1940. 10.00x (ISBN 0-674-58650-6). Harvard U Pr.

U. S. Senate, Subcommittee on Monopoly of the Select Committee on Small Business. Foreign Legislation Concerning Monopoly & Cartel Practices. Bruchey, Stuart & Carosso, Vincent P., eds. LC 78-18983. (Small Business Enterprise in America Ser.). 1979. Repr. of 1952 ed. lib. bdg. 15.00x (ISBN 0-405-11485-0). Arno.

Wilcox, Clair. Competition & Monopoly in American Industry. Repr. of 1940 ed. lib. bdg. 20.50x (ISBN 0-8371-3173-1, WIAI). Greenwood.

Zeuthen, Frederik. Problems of Monopoly & Economic Warfare. LC 67-25998. (Illus.). Repr. of 1930 ed. 13.50x (ISBN 0-678-06522-5). Kelley.

MONOPOLIES–GERMANY

Michels, Rudolf K. Cartels, Combines & Trusts in Post-War Germany. LC 68-58607. (Columbia University. Studies in the Social Sciences: No. 306). Repr. of 1928 ed. 17.50 (ISBN 0-404-51306-9). AMS Pr.

MONOPOLIES–GREAT BRITAIN

Fitzgerald, Patrick. Industrial Combination in England. Wilkins, Mira, ed. LC 76-29996. (European Business Ser.). 1977. Repr. of 1927 ed. lib. bdg. 15.00x (ISBN 0-405-09754-9). Arno.

Levy, Hermann. Monopoly & Competition: A Study in English Industrial Organisation. Wilkins, Mira, ed. LC 76-29993. (European Business Ser.). 1977. Repr. of 1911 ed. lib. bdg. 21.00x (ISBN 0-405-09751-4). Arno.

Walshe, G. Recent Trends in Monopoly in Great Britain. (Illus.). 132p. 1974. 16.95x (ISBN 0-521-09863-7). Cambridge U Pr.

MONOPOLIES–INDIA

Indian Economic Association, Calcutta, 1966. Monopolies & Their Regulations in India. Hazari, R. K., ed. 1967. 5.00x (ISBN 0-8002-0931-1). Intl Pubns Serv.

MONOPOLIES–UNITED STATES

Alsberg, Carl L. Combination in the American Bread-Baking Industry: With Some Observations on the Mergers of 1924-25. LC 73-1987. (Big Business; Economic Power in a Free Society Ser.). Repr. of 1926 ed. 8.00 (ISBN 0-405-05071-2). Arno.

Arnold, Thurman W. The Bottlenecks of Business. LC 72-2363. (FDR & the Era of the New Deal Ser.). 352p. 1973. Repr. of 1940 ed. lib. bdg. 35.00 (ISBN 0-306-70470-6). Da Capo.

Asch, Peter. Economic Theory & the Antitrust Dilemma. LC 78-127658. (Illus.). 414p. 1970. 27.95 (ISBN 0-471-03443-6, Pub. by Wiley-Interscience). Wiley.

Brown, George T. The Gas Light Company of Baltimore: A Study of Natural Monopoly. LC 78-64162. (Johns Hopkins University. Studies in the Social Sciences. Fifty-Fourth Ser. 1936: 2). Repr. of 1936 ed. 15.00 (ISBN 0-404-61272-5). AMS Pr.

Cox, Reavis. Competition in the American Tobacco Industry, 1911-1932. LC 68-58562. (Columbia University Studies in the Social Sciences: No. 381). Repr. of 1933 ed. 26.50 (ISBN 0-404-51381-6). AMS Pr.

Fetter, Frank A. Masquerade of Monopoly. LC 66-22623. (Illus.). Repr. of 1931 ed. 19.50x (ISBN 0-678-00291-6). Kelley.

Harris, Brian F. Shared Monopoly & the Cereal Industry. LC 79-84189. 1979. pap. 6.50 (ISBN 0-87744-156-1). Mich St U Busn.

Harrison, William C. How to Move from a Competitive to a Monopolistic Market & Start Making Money. (Illus.). 110p. 1981. 43.50 (ISBN 0-918968-79-8). Inst Econ Fina.

Hawley, Ellis W. New Deal & the Problem of Monopoly. LC 65-24273. (Orig.). 1966. pap. 8.95 (ISBN 0-691-00564-8). Princeton U Pr.

Kalecki, Michal. Essays in the Theory of Economic Fluctuations. LC 70-173538. (Illus.). 1972. Repr. of 1939 ed. 18.00 (ISBN 0-8462-1629-9). Russell.

Kefauver, Estes. In a Few Hands: Monopoly Power in America. Till, Irene, ed. LC 64-18344. (Illus.). 1965. 7.95 (ISBN 0-394-43021-2). Pantheon.

Kennedy, Edward D. Dividends to Pay. LC 68-56239. Repr. of 1939 ed. 15.00x (ISBN 0-678-00522-2). Kelley.

Lindblom, Charles E. Unions & Capitalism. LC 77-121757. 1970. Repr. of 1949 ed. 19.50 (ISBN 0-208-00959-0, Archon). Shoe String.

Mueller, Willard F. Primer on Monopoly & Competition. 1970. pap. text ed. 5.95 (ISBN 0-394-30738-0). Random.

Nutter, G. Warren & Einhorn, Henry. Enterprise Monopoly in the United States, 1899-1958. LC 69-15570. 256p. 1969. 20.00x (ISBN 0-231-02974-8). Columbia U Pr.

Wilcox, Clair. Competition & Monopoly in American Industry. LC 73-158856. Repr. of 1940 ed. 18.50 (ISBN 0-404-06944-4). AMS Pr.

--Competition & Monopoly in American Industry. Repr. of 1940 ed. lib. bdg. 20.50x (ISBN 0-8371-3173-1, WIAI). Greenwood.

Winston, Ambrose P. Judicial Economics: The Doctrine of Monopoly As Set Forth by Judges of the U.S. Federal Courts in Suits Under the Anti-Trust Laws. LC 73-172240. (Right Wing Individualist Tradition in America Ser). 1972. Repr. of 1957 ed. 10.00 (ISBN 0-405-00449-4). Arno.

MONOPOLIES, PARTIAL

see Oligopolies

MONOPRINT

see Monotype (Engraving)

MONOSACCHARIDES

Stanek, Jaroslav, et al. Monosaccharides. Mayer, Karel, tr. 1964. 79.00 (ISBN 0-12-663750-4). Acad Pr.

MONOTHEISM

Albright, William Foxwell. From the Stone Age to Christianity. 2nd ed. 1957. pap. 2.50 (ISBN 0-385-09306-3, A100, Anch). Doubleday.

Fowler, William W. Roman Ideas of Deity in the Last Century Before the Christian Era. LC 75-102236. (Select Bibliographies Reprint Ser). 1914. 17.00 (ISBN 0-8369-5121-2). Arno.

Freud, Sigmund. Moses & Monotheism. Jones, Katherine, ed. 1955. pap. 2.45 (ISBN 0-394-70014-7, V14, Vin). Random.

Hack, Roy K. God in Greek Philosophy to the Time of Socrates. 1970. Repr. of 1931 ed. lib. bdg. 12.50 (ISBN 0-8337-1514-3). B Franklin.

Nelson, Julius C. Five Thousand Years Among the Gods. 1977. 6.50 (ISBN 0-533-02563-X). Vantage.

Niebuhr, H. Richard. Radical Monotheism in Western Culture. pap. 3.50x (ISBN 0-06-131491-9, TB1491, Torch). Har-Row.

MONOTHEISM (ISLAM)

see God (Islam)

MONOTREMATA

Griffiths, Mervyn. The Biology of the Monotremes. LC 78-4818. 1979. 44.50 (ISBN 0-12-303850-2). Acad Pr.

MONOTYPE (ENGRAVING)

Aspinwall, Margaret, ed. The Painterly Print: Monotypes from the Seventeenth to the Twentieth Century. (Illus.). 262p. 1980. 29.95 (ISBN 0-87099-223-6); pap. 14.95 (ISBN 0-87099-224-4). Metro Mus Art.

De Montebello, Philippe & Fontein, Jan, eds. The Painterly Print: Monotypes from the Seventeenth to the Twentieth Century. LC 80-10441. (Illus.). 261p. 1980. 37.50 (ISBN 0-8478-5323-3). Rizzoli Intl.

Marsh, Roger. Monoprints for the Artist. (gr. 10 up). 1969. pap. 7.50 (ISBN 0-85458-549-4). Transatlantic.

Morison, Stanley. Tally of Types. Crutchley, B., ed. LC 72-90486. 144p. 1973. 49.50 (ISBN 0-521-20043-1); pap. 14.95 (ISBN 0-521-09786-X). Cambridge U Pr.

Solman, Joseph. The Monotypes of Joseph Solman. (Illus.). 1977. lib. bdg. 18.95 (ISBN 0-306-77425-9). Da Capo.

MONRO, HAROLD, 1879-1932

Grant, Joy. Harold Monro & the Poetry Bookshop. LC 66-11437. 1967. 20.00x (ISBN 0-520-00512-0). U of Cal Pr.

MONROE, BILL

Rosenberg, Neil V. Bill Monroe & His Blue Grass Boys: An Illustrated Discography. (Illus.). 122p. 1974. pap. 4.50 (ISBN 0-915608-02-2). Country Music Found.

MONROE, HARRIET, 1860-1936

Williams, Ellen. Harriet Monroe & the Poetry Renaissance: The First Ten Years of Poetry, 1912-22. LC 76-45403. 1977. 16.95 (ISBN 0-252-00478-7). U of Ill Pr.

MONROE, JAMES, PRES. U. S., 1758-1831

Bond, Beverley W. The Monroe Mission to France, 1794-1796. LC 78-63920. (Johns Hopkins University. Studies in the Social Sciences. Twenty-Fifth Ser. 1907: 2-3). Repr. of 1907 ed. 14.50 (ISBN 0-404-61171-0). AMS Pr.

Cresson, William P. James Monroe. LC 75-124098. 1971. Repr. of 1946 ed. 27.50 (ISBN 0-208-01089-0, Archon). Shoe String.

Elliot, I. James Monroe, 1758-1831: Chronology, Documents, Bibliographical Aids. LC 69-15393. (Presidential Chronologies Ser.). 1969. 8.00 (ISBN 0-379-12060-7). Oceana.

Gilman, Daniel C. James Monroe. LC 80-24500. (American Statesmen Ser.). 315p. 1981. pap. 5.95 (ISBN 0-87754-187-6). Chelsea Hse.

--James Monroe. Morse, John T., Jr., ed. LC 73-128966. (American Statesmen: No. 14). Repr. of 1898 ed. 18.00 (ISBN 0-404-50864-2). AMS Pr.

Morgan, George. Life of James Monroe. LC 76-106979. Repr. of 1921 ed. 31.45 (ISBN 0-404-00594-2). AMS Pr.

Wilmerding, L., Jr. James Monroe: Public Claimant. LC 60-11525. 1960. 4.00 (ISBN 0-910294-26-7). Brown Bk.

MONROE, MARILYN, 1926-1962

Conover, David. Finding Marilyn. LC 81-47699. (Illus.). 256p. 1981. 14.95 (ISBN 0-448-12020-8). G&D.

Conway, Michael & Ricci, Mark. Films of Marilyn Monroe. (Illus.). 1968. 12.00 (ISBN 0-8065-0395-5, C265); pap. 6.95 (ISBN 0-8065-0145-6, C265). Citadel Pr.

Lembourn, Hans J. Diary of a Lover of Marilyn Monroe. LC 78-73861. 1979. 8.95 (ISBN 0-87795-216-7). Arbor Hse.

Mailer, Norman. Marilyn. LC 73-6899. (Illus.). 272p. 1981. pap. 11.95 (ISBN 0-448-11813-0). G&D.

Oppenheimer, Joel. Marilyn Lives. (Illus.). 128p. (Orig.). 1981. pap. 8.85 (ISBN 0-933328-02-8). Delilah Comm.

Pepitone, Lena & Stadiem, William. Marilyn Monroe Confidential. 1980. pap. 2.50 (ISBN 0-671-83038-4). PB.

--Marilyn Monroe Confidential. 1979. 9.95 (ISBN 0-671-24289-X). S&S.

Samuels, M. Screen Greats: Monroe. 1980. pap. 2.95 (ISBN 0-931064-32-5). Starlog.

Scaduto, Anthony. Who Killed Marilyn? 224p. 1976. pap. 1.75 (ISBN 0-532-17124-1). Woodhill.

Slatzer, Robert F. The Life & Curious Death of Marilyn Monroe. (Illus.). 1977. pap. 2.25 (ISBN 0-523-40090-X). Pinnacle Bks.

MONROE DOCTRINE

Bingham, Hiram. The Monroe Doctrine. (Latin America in the 20th Century Ser.). 1976. Repr. of 1913 ed. lib. bdg. 15.00 (ISBN 0-306-70833-7). Da Capo.

Bornholdt, Laura. Baltimore & Early Pan-Americanism: A Study in the Background of the Monroe Doctrine. LC 49-10098. (Studies in History: No. 34). 1949. pap. 3.00 (ISBN 0-87391-002-8). Smith Coll.

Chew, Benjamin. Sketch of the Politics, Relations & Statistics of the Western World. LC 77-128427. Repr. of 1827 ed. 19.50 (ISBN 0-404-01489-5). AMS Pr.

Cleland, R. One Hundred Years of the Monroe Doctrine. 1976. lib. bdg. 59.95 (ISBN 0-8490-2376-9). Gordon Pr.

Dangerfield, George. Era of Good Feelings. LC 51-14815. 1963. pap. 5.50 (ISBN 0-15-629000-6, H034, Hbgr). HarBraceJ.

Dozer, Donald. The Monroe Doctrine: Its Modern Significance. LC 75-38904. 1976. Repr. 6.50x (ISBN 0-87918-026-9). ASU Lat Am St.

Hart, Albert B. Foundations of American Foreign Policy. LC 74-109549. (Law, Politics & History Ser). 1970. Repr. of 1901 ed. lib. bdg. 32.50 (ISBN 0-306-71903-7). Da Capo.

Kennedy, S. M. The Monroe Doctrine Clause of the League of Nations Covenant. (Graduate Studies: No. 20). (Orig.). 1979. 5.00 (ISBN 0-89672-073-X). Tex Tech Pr.

Lawson, Leonard A. The Relation of British Policy to the Declaration of the Monroe Doctrine. 1972. lib. bdg. 13.50x (ISBN 0-374-94830-5). Octagon.

Logan, John A. No Transfer: An American Security Principle. 1961. 42.50x (ISBN 0-685-69838-6). Elliots Bks.

May, Ernest R. The Making of the Monroe Doctrine. 224p. 1975. text ed. 15.00x (ISBN 0-674-54340-8, Belknap Pr). Harvard U Pr.

Miller, Hugh G. Isthmian Highway: A Review of the Problems of the Caribbean. LC 76-111725. (American Imperialism: Viewpoints of United States Foreign Policy, 1898-1941). 1970. Repr. of 1929 ed. 18.00 (ISBN 0-405-02039-2). Arno.

Newton, Arthur P., ed. Sea Commonwealth, & Other Papers. Imperial Studies Ser. facs. ed. LC 68-22114. (Essay Index Reprint Ser). 1919. 11.75 (ISBN 0-8369-0742-6). Arno.

Perkins, Dexter. History of the Monroe Doctrine. rev. ed. (Illus.). 1963. 10.00 (ISBN 0-316-69933-0). Little.

--The Monroe Doctrine, 3 vols. Incl. 1823-1826. 8.00 (ISBN 0-685-22731-6); 1826-1867. 9.50 (ISBN 0-685-22732-4); 1867-1907. 9.50 (ISBN 0-685-22733-2). Set (ISBN 0-8446-1346-0). Peter Smith.

Rappaport, Armin, ed. The Monroe Doctrine. LC 76-15182. (American Problem Studies). 128p. (Orig.). 1976. pap. text ed. 5.50 (ISBN 0-88275-432-7). Krieger.

Scudder, Evarts S. Monroe Doctrine & World Peace. LC 79-159711. 1971. Repr. of 1939 ed. 10.50 (ISBN 0-8046-1672-8). Kennikat.

Tatum, Edward H., Jr. United States & Europe, 1815-1823: A Study in the Background of the Monroe Doctrine. LC 66-27160. 1967. Repr. of 1936 ed. 9.50 (ISBN 0-8462-1032-0). Russell.

MONROVIA, LIBERIA

Fraenkel, Merran. Tribe & Class in Monrovia. (International African Institute Ser.). 1964. 27.50x (ISBN 0-19-724157-3). Oxford U Pr.

MONSOONS

Duing, Walter. Monsoon Regime of the Currents in the Indian Ocean. LC 76-104320. (International Indian Ocean Expedition Oceanographic Monographs: No. 1). (Illus.). 1970. 12.00x (ISBN 0-8248-0092-3, Eastwest Ctr). U Pr of Hawaii.

Krishnamurti, T., ed. Monsoon Dynamics. (Contributions to Current Research in Geophysics Ser.: Vol. 4). 1978. text ed. 80.00x (ISBN 3-7643-0999-7). Renouf.

Lighthill, James & Pearce, R. P., eds. Monsoon Dynamics. LC 78-72091. (Illus.). 700p. 1981. 130.00 (ISBN 0-521-22497-7). Cambridge U Pr.

Ramage, C. S. Monsoon Meteorology. (International Geophysics Ser: Vol. 15). 1971. 40.00 (ISBN 0-12-576650-5). Acad Pr.

Report of the Fifth Planning Meeting for the Monsoon Experiment: Part I - Winter Monex. (GARP Special Reports Ser.: No. 30). pap. 15.00 (ISBN 0-685-95501-X, W424, WMO). Unipub.

Report of the Planning Meeting for the Monsoon: 77th Experiment. (GARP Special Report: No. 21). 1976. pap. 15.00 (ISBN 0-685-74524-4, WMO). Unipub.

Report of the Third Planning Meeting for the Monsoon Experiment: New Delhi, Feb.-Mar., 1977. (GARP Special Report: No. 25). 26p. 1978. pap. 25.00 (ISBN 0-685-87432-X, WMO). Unipub.

Summer MONEX, 5th Planning Meeting. Planning Meeting for the Monsoon Experiment MONEX. (GARP Special Report Ser.: No. 32). 74p. 1980. pap. 15.00 (ISBN 0-686-60085-1, W437, WMO). Unipub.

MONSTERS

see also Abnormalities, Human; Dragons; Dwarfs; Sea Monsters

Cohen, Daniel. Modern Look at Monsters. LC 78-121977. (Illus.). 1970. 5.95 (ISBN 0-396-06200-8). Dodd.

--Supermonsters. LC 76-48970. (Illus.). (gr. 4-9). 1977. 5.95 (ISBN 0-396-07399-9). Dodd.

Dean, Audrey V. Make a Prehistoric Monster. LC 77-76580. (Illus.). (gr. 2-7). 1977. 7.50 (ISBN 0-8008-5049-1). Taplinger.

De Menil, Dominique, intro. by. Constant Companions: An Exhibition of Mythological Animals, Demons, & Monsters. (Illus.). 1964. pap. 6.00 (ISBN 0-914412-19-1). Inst for the Arts.

Evans, Larry. How to Draw Monsters. LC 77-3731. (Illus., Orig.). (YA) 1977. pap. 3.95 (ISBN 0-912300-75-2, 75-2). Troubador Pr.

Gould, Charles. Mythical Monsters. LC 74-75474. 1969. Repr. of 1886 ed. 24.00 (ISBN 0-8103-3834-3). Gale.

--Mythical Monsters. 1976. lib. bdg. 134.95 (ISBN 0-8490-2324-6). Gordon Pr.

Laycock, George. Strange Monsters & Great Searches. LC 72-76185. 120p. (gr. 4-7). 1973. 6.95 (ISBN 0-385-03463-6). Doubleday.

McCloy, James F. & Miller, Ray, Jr. The Jersey Devil. LC 75-32056. (Illus.). 1979. cancelled (ISBN 0-912608-05-6); pap. 4.95 (ISBN 0-912608-11-0). Mid Atlantic.

Mank, Gregory W. It's Alive! the Classic Cinema Saga of Frankenstein. LC 80-26625. (Illus.). 176p. 1981. 14.95 (ISBN 0-498-02473-3). A S Barnes.

Price, Vincent & Price, V. B. Monsters. LC 77-94851. (Illus.). 192p. 1981. 25.00 (ISBN 0-448-14304-6); pap. 12.95 (ISBN 0-448-14305-4). G&D.

Soule, Gardner. The Maybe Monsters. (Illus.). (gr. 5 up). 1963. PLB 5.69 (ISBN 0-399-60457-X). Putnam.

Stoker, John. The Illustrated Frankenstein. LC 80-52336. (Illus., Orig.). 1980. pap. 6.95 (ISBN 0-8069-8916-5). Sterling.

Thompson, C. J. Mystery & Lore of Monsters. 1970. pap. 2.45 (ISBN 0-8065-0210-X). Citadel Pr.

Thorn, Ian. The Monsters. Schroeder, Howard, ed. (Illus.). 48p. (gr. 3-5). 1981. PLB 6.95 (ISBN 0-89686-188-0); pap. text ed. 2.95 (ISBN 0-89686-191-0). Crestwood Hse.

Thorne, Ian. Creature from the Black Lagoon. Schroeder, Howard, ed. (The Monsters). (Illus.). 48p. (Orig.). (gr. 3-5). 1981. PLB 6.95 (ISBN 0-89686-187-2); pap. 2.95 (ISBN 0-89686-190-2). Crestwood Hse.

--The Mummy. Schroeder, Howard, ed. (The Monsters). (Illus.). 48p. (Orig.). (gr. 3-5). 1981. PLB 6.95 (ISBN 0-89686-186-4); pap. text ed. 2.95 (ISBN 0-89686-189-9). Crestwood Hse.

Topsell, Edward. The Historie of Foure-Footed Beastes, Collected Out of All Volumes of C. Gesner, & All Other Writers to This Present Day. LC 72-6034. (English Experience Ser.: No. 561). 816p. 1973. Repr. of 1607 ed. 104.00 (ISBN 90-221-0561-X). Walter J Johnson.

Wise, William A. Monsters from Outer Space? LC 77-16504. (See & Read Science). (Illus.). 1978. PLB 6.29 (ISBN 0-399-61089-8). Putnam.

MONSTERS–JUVENILE LITERATURE

Allen, M. Real Life Monsters. 1978. 5.95 (ISBN 0-13-766568-7). P-H.

Aylesworth, Thomas G. The Story of Dragons & Other Monsters. LC 79-21550. (Illus.). 96p. (gr. 5-8). 1980. 7.95 (ISBN 0-07-002646-7, GB). McGraw.

--Werewolves & Other Monsters. LC 70-155226. (Illus.). (gr. 6 up). 1971. PLB 7.95 (ISBN 0-685-00094-X, A-W Childrens). A-W.

Baumann, Elwood D. Monsters of North America. (Illus.). (gr. 5 up). 1978. PLB 7.90 s&l (ISBN 0-531-02246-3). Watts.

Cameron, Ann. Harry (The Monster) (Illus.). 48p. 1980. 6.95 (ISBN 0-394-84162-X); PLB 6.99 (ISBN 0-394-94162-4). Pantheon.

Christensen, Nancy. Monsters: Creatures of Mystery. LC 79-55011. (Illus.). 48p. (gr. 2-8). 1980. 5.95 (ISBN 0-448-47485-9); PLB 11.85 (ISBN 0-448-13622-8). Platt.

Cohen, Daniel. Everything You Need to Know About Monsters & Still Be Able to Get to Sleep. LC 79-6589. (Illus.). 128p. (gr. 4 up). 1981. 7.95a (ISBN 0-385-15803-3); PLB (ISBN 0-385-15804-1). Doubleday.

--Greatest Monsters in the World. (Illus.). (gr. 4 up). 1977. pap. 1.50 (ISBN 0-671-29990-5). PB.

--Monsters, Giants & Little Men from Mars. LC 74-4534. 256p. (gr. 4-7). 1975. 6.95a (ISBN 0-385-03267-6); PLB (ISBN 0-385-06943-X). Doubleday.

--Monsters You Never Heard of. LC 79-23641. (High Interest, Low Vocabulary Ser.). (Illus.). (gr. 4-9). 1980. 5.95 (ISBN 0-396-07789-7). Dodd.

--Supermonsters. LC 76-48970. (Illus.). (gr. 4-9). 1977. 5.95 (ISBN 0-396-07399-9). Dodd.

Drozd, Ann M. Living Monsters. McCarthy, Patricia, ed. (Pal Paperbacks Kit A Ser.). (Illus., Orig.). (gr. 7-12). 1974. pap. text ed. 1.25 (ISBN 0-8374-3471-8). Xerox Ed Pubns.

Dynamite Monster Hall of Fame. (gr. 3-5). pap. 1.50 (ISBN 0-590-11806-4, Schol Pap). Schol Bk Serv.

Gates, Frieda. Monsters & Ghouls: Costumes & Lore. LC 79-5385. (Illus.). 48p. (gr. 4-9). 1980. PLB 8.85 (ISBN 0-8027-6379-0). Walker & Co.

Glendinning, Sally. Jimmy & Joe See a Monster. LC 74-190544. (Jimmy & Joe Ser.). (Illus.). 40p. (gr. k-3). 1972. PLB 6.48 (ISBN 0-8116-4707-2). Garrard.

Glovach, Linda & Keller, Charles. The Little Witch Presents a Monster: Joke Book. LC 76-9077. (Illus.). (gr. 2-5). 1976. PLB 4.95 (ISBN 0-13-537969-5). P-H.

Jameson, Jon. Monsters of the Mountains. (Easy-Read Facts Bks.). (Illus.). (gr. 2-4). 1979. PLB 6.90 s&l (ISBN 0-531-02269-2). Watts.

Laycock, George. Mysteries, Monsters & Untold Secrets. (Illus.). (gr. 3-7). 1980. pap. 1.50 (ISBN 0-590-31270-7, Schol Pap). Schol Bk Serv.

Lord, Suzanne. Count Morbida's Monster Quiz Book. 80p. (Orig.). (gr. 3 up). 1980. pap. 1.50 (ISBN 0-590-30621-9, Schol Pap). Schol Bk Serv.

Newton, Michael. Monsters, Mysteries & Man. (Illus.). (gr. 7 up). 1979. 8.95 (ISBN 0-201-05274-1, 5274, A-W Childrens); pap. 5.95 (ISBN 0-201-05222-9, 5222). A-W.

Nolan, Dennis. Monster Bubbles: A Counting Book. LC 76-10167. 1976. PLB 5.95 (ISBN 0-13-600635-3); pap. 1.95 (ISBN 0-13-600643-4). P-H.

Ormsby, Alan. Movie Monsters: Monster Make-up & Monster Shows to Put on. (gr. 4-7). 1975. pap. 1.25 (ISBN 0-590-02175-3, Schol Pap). Schol Bk Serv.

Rabinowich, Ellen. The Loch Ness Monster. (Easy-Read Fact Bks.). (Illus.). (gr. 2-4). 1979. PLB 6.90 s&l (ISBN 0-531-02274-9). Watts.

Radlauer, Ed. Monster Mania. LC 79-18666. (Ready, Get Set, Go Ser.). (Illus.). 32p. (gr. 1-6). 1980. PLB 9.25 (ISBN 0-516-07472-5, Elk Grove Bks.); pap. 2.95 (ISBN 0-516-47472-3). Childrens.

Shulan, Michael. The Truth About Monsters. LC 80-13490. (Monsters & Mysteries Ser.). (gr. 4-10). 1980. pap. 1.95 (ISBN 0-88436-761-4). EMC.

Simon, Seymour. Creatures from Lost Worlds. LC 78-25875. (Eerie Ser.). (Illus.). (gr. 2-4). 1979. 7.95 (ISBN 0-397-31834-0); PLB 7.89 (ISBN 0-397-31852-9). Lippincott.

--Space Monsters: From Movies, TV & Books. LC 77-3566. (gr. 4 up). 1977. 7.95 (ISBN 0-397-31765-4). Lippincott.

Thorne, Ian. The Loch Ness Monster. Schroeder, Howard, ed. LC 78-6193. (Search for the Unknown Ser.). (Illus.). (gr. 4). 1978. PLB 6.95 (ISBN 0-913940-83-6); pap. 3.25 (ISBN 0-89686-004-3). Crestwood Hse.

--Monster Tales of Native Americans. Schroeder, Howard, ed. LC 78-5234. (Search for the Unknown Ser.). (Illus.). (gr. 4). 1978. PLB 6.95 (ISBN 0-913940-85-2); pap. 2.95 (ISBN 0-89686-006-X). Crestwood Hse.

Wallace, Daisy, ed. Monster Poems. LC 75-17680. (Illus.). 32p. (gr. k-3). 1976. PLB 7.95 (ISBN 0-8234-0268-1). Holiday.

Wise, William A. Monsters of North America. LC 75-23109. (See & Read Science). (Illus.). (gr. k-4). 1978. PLB 6.29 (ISBN 0-399-60992-X). Putnam.

Woods, Geraldine & Woods, Harold. Magical Beasts & Unbelievable Monsters. LC 80-20627. (Monsters & Mysteries Ser.). (gr. 4-10). 1980. pap. 1.95 (ISBN 0-88436-765-7). EMC.

MONT BLANC

Rebuffat, Gaston. Between Heaven & Earth. Brockett, E., tr. (Illus.). 1965. 17.50 (ISBN 0-19-519058-0). Oxford U Pr.

--The Mont Blanc Massif: The 100 Finest Routes. 1975. 19.95 (ISBN 0-19-519789-5). Oxford U Pr.

Smith, Albert. Mont Blanc. 1872. 15.00 (ISBN 0-685-72781-5). Norwood Edns.

MONT SAINT MICHEL, FRANCE

Adams, Henry. Mont-Saint Michel & Chartres. LC 81-47279. (Illus.). 448p. (Orig.). 1981. 30.00x (ISBN 0-691-03971-2); pap. 6.95x (ISBN 0-691-00335-1). Princeton U Pr.

--Mont-Saint-Michel & Chartres. (Illus.). 300p. 1980. 20.00 (ISBN 0-399-12498-5). Putnam.

--Mont Saint Michel & Chartres. LC 36-27246. 1978. pap. 25.00 (ISBN 0-910220-94-8). Larlin Corp.

Bazin, Germain. Mont-Saint-Michel. LC 75-24825. (Fr.). 1978. Repr. of 1933 ed. lib. bdg. 100.00 (ISBN 0-87817-190-8). Hacker.

Luce, Simeon, ed. Chronique Du Mont-Saint-Michel 1343-1468, 2 Vols. 1879-83. Set. 55.50 (ISBN 0-384-09010-9); Set. pap. 46.00 (ISBN 0-384-09011-7). Johnson Repr.

Rene-Jacques. Mont Saint-Michel. (Panorama Bks.). 62p. (Fr.). 3.95 (ISBN 0-685-23348-0). French & Eur.

MONT SAINT MICHEL, FRANCE–FICTION

Vercel, Roger. Tides of Mont St. Michel. Wells, Warre B., tr. Repr. of 1938 ed. lib. bdg. 14.00x (ISBN 0-8371-4052-8, VEMM). Greenwood.

MONTAGNARDS (VIETNAMESE TRIBES)

Mole, Robert L. Montagnards of South Vietnam: A Study of Nine Tribes. LC 70-104198. (Illus.). 1970. pap. 3.25 (ISBN 0-8048-0724-8). C E Tuttle.

Montagnards of South Vietnam. (Minority Rights Group: No. 18). 1974. pap. 2.50 (ISBN 0-89192-104-4). Interbk Inc.

MONTAGU, MARY (PIERREPONT) WORTLEY, LADY, 1689-1762

Barry, Iris. Portrait of Lady Mary Montagu. 1928. Repr. 17.50 (ISBN 0-8274-3187-2). R West.

Gibbs, Lewis. The Admirable Lady Mary. 1949. Repr. 25.00 (ISBN 0-8274-1816-7). R West.

Halsband, Robert. Life of Lady Mary Wortley Montagu. 1956. 29.95x (ISBN 0-19-811548-2). Oxford U Pr.

Halsband, Robert, ed. Court Eclogs, Written in the Year Seventeen Sixteen: Alexander Pope's Autograph Manuscript of Poems by Lady Mary Wortley Montagu. LC 76-17311. (Illus.). 1977. ltd. ed. 25.00 (ISBN 0-87104-265-7, Co-Pub. by Readex Books). NY Pub Lib.

Melville, Lewis. Lady Mary Wortley Montagu: Her Life & Letters. Repr. 25.00 (ISBN 0-8274-3870-2). R West.

Moy, Thomas W. The Letters & Works of Lady Mary Wortley Montagu, 2 vols. Wharncliffe, Lord, ed. 1979. Repr. of 1893 ed. lib. bdg. 125.00 (ISBN 0-89984-500-2). Century Bookbindery.

Paston, George. Lady Mary Wortley Montagu & Her Times. 1907. Repr. 50.00 (ISBN 0-8274-2790-5). R West.

Ropes, Arthur R. Lady Mary Wortley Montagu. Repr. 25.00 (ISBN 0-8274-2789-1). R West.

Thanet, Octave, ed. The Best Letters of Lady Mary Wortley Montagu. 1978. Repr. of 1890 ed. lib. bdg. 30.00 (ISBN 0-8492-1879-9). R West.

MONTAGUE, ELIZABETH (ROBINSON), 1720-1800

Busse, John. Mrs. Montagu: Queen of the Blues. 1928. Repr. 15.00 (ISBN 0-8274-2774-3). R West.

Carter, Elizabeth. Letters from Mrs. Elizabeth Carter to Mrs. Montagu Between the Years 1755-1800, 3 vols. LC 73-178402. Repr. of 1817 ed. Set. 82.50 (ISBN 0-404-56720-7); 27.50 ea. AMS Pr.

Climenson, Emily J. Elizabeth Montagu: The Queen of the Bluestockings, 2 vols. 1906. Repr. Set. 85.00 (ISBN 0-8274-2239-3). R West.

Doran, John. Lady of the Last Century: Mrs. Elizabeth Montague. 2nd ed. LC 75-37690. (Illus.). Repr. of 1873 ed. 28.00 (ISBN 0-404-56744-4). AMS Pr.
--Lady of the Last Century: Mrs. Elizabeth Montagu. 1873. Repr. 19.50 (ISBN 0-8274-2791-3). R West.
Huchon, R. Mrs. Montagu & Her Friends. 1907. Repr. 35.00 (ISBN 0-8274-2775-1). R West.

MONTAGUE, JOHN, 1929-

Kersnowski, Frank. John Montague. (Irish Writers Ser.). 72p. 1975. 4.50 (ISBN 0-8387-7807-0); pap. 1.95 (ISBN 0-8387-7983-2). Bucknell U Pr.

MONTAIGNE, MICHEL EYQUEM DE, 1533-1592

Boase, Alan M. Fortunes of Montaigne: A History of the Essays in France, 1580-1669. 1970. Repr. lib. bdg. 25.00 (ISBN 0-374-90725-0). Octagon.
Bond, R. W. Montaigne: A Study. 93p. 1980. Repr. of 1906 ed. lib. bdg. 20.00 (ISBN 0-8492-3753-X). R West.
Bond, R. Warwick. Montaigne. 1973. Repr. of 1906 ed. 15.00 (ISBN 0-8274-1437-4). R West.
Boon. Montaigne, Gentilhomme et Essayiste. 18.50 (ISBN 0-685-34192-5). French & Eur.
Bowen, Barbara C. Age of Bluff: Paradox & Ambiguity in Rabelais & Montaigne. LC 71-165041. (Studies in Language & Literature Ser: No. 62). 184p. 1972. 12.50 (ISBN 0-252-00212-1). U of Ill Pr.
Cameron, Keith, ed. Montaigne & His Age. 175p. 20.00x (ISBN 0-85989-167-4, Pub. by Exeter Univ England). State Mutual Bk.
Carlyle, Thomas. Montaigne: And Other Essays, Chiefly Biographical. LC 72-13208. (Essay Index Reprint Ser.). Repr. of 1897 ed. 18.25 (ISBN 0-8369-8149-9). Arno.
Collins, W. Lucas. Montaigne. 1973. Repr. of 1879 ed. 25.00 (ISBN 0-8274-1781-0). R West.
--Montaigne. 1979. Repr. of 1879 ed. lib. bdg. 20.00 (ISBN 0-8495-0930-0). Arden Lib.
Compayre, Gabriel. Michel de Montaigne. (Educational Ser.). 1908. Repr. 20.00 (ISBN 0-685-43513-X). Norwood Edns.
--Montaigne & Education of the Judgment. 1973. Repr. of 1908 ed. 10.95 (ISBN 0-8274-1780-2). R West.
--Montaigne & the Education of the Judgement. Mansion, J. E., tr. LC 77-166439. (Research & Source Works Ser: No. 782). 1971. Repr. of 1908 ed. lib. bdg. 17.00 (ISBN 0-8337-4054-7). B Franklin.
--Montaigne & the Education of the Judgement. Mansion, J. E., tr. LC 77-166439. (Research & Source Works Ser: No. 782). 1971. Repr. of 1908 ed. lib. bdg. 17.00 (ISBN 0-8337-4054-7). B Franklin.
Conpayre, G. Montaigne & Education of the Judgement. Mansion, J. E., tr. 139p. 1980. Repr. lib. bdg. 30.00 (ISBN 0-8492-4046-8). R West.
Dowden, Edward. Michel De Montaigne. LC 77-153266. 1971. Repr. of 1905 ed. 15.00 (ISBN 0-8046-1562-4). Kennikat.
--Michel de Montaigne. 1905. lib. bdg. 30.00 (ISBN 0-8414-3852-8). Folcroft.
--Michel De Montaigne. 1977. Repr. of 1905 ed. lib. bdg. 25.00 (ISBN 0-8495-1002-3). Arden Lib.
Feis, Jacob. Shakspere & Montaigne. LC 73-130615. Repr. of 1884 ed. 17.00 (ISBN 0-404-02375-4). AMS Pr.
Frame, Donald M. & McKinley, Mary B., eds. Columbia Montaigne Conference: Papers. LC 80-70811. (French Forum Monographs: No. 27). 120p. (Orig.). 1981. pap. 9.50 (ISBN 0-917058-26-7). French Forum.
Gide, Andre. The Living Thoughts of Montaigne. 1978. Repr. of 1942 ed. 12.50 (ISBN 0-8492-4914-7). R West.
--The Living Thoughts of Montaigne. 1979. Repr. of 1939 ed. lib. bdg. 17.50 (ISBN 0-8495-2017-7). Arden Lib.
Hall, Marie-Louise. Montaigne & His Translators. 59.95 (ISBN 0-8490-0666-X). Gordon Pr.
Hallie, Philip P. The Scar of Montaigne: An Essay in Personal Philosophy. LC 66-23925. 1966. 15.00x (ISBN 0-8195-3068-9, Pub. by Wesleyan U Pr). Columbia U Pr.
Insdorf, Cecile. Montaigne & Feminism. (Studies in the Romance Languages & Literatures). (Orig.). 1978. pap. 7.00x (ISBN 0-8078-9194-0). U of NC Pr.
La Charite, Raymond C., ed. O un Amy! Essays on Montaigne in Honor of Donald M. Frame. LC 76-47501. (Monographs: No. 5). 341p. (Orig., Eng. & Fr.). 1977. pap. 15.00x (ISBN 0-917058-04-6). French Forum.
Lowndes, M. E. Michel De Montaigne. 1973. Repr. of 1898 ed. 25.00 (ISBN 0-8274-0106-X). R West.
Lowndes, Mary E. Michel De Montaigne: A Biographical Study. LC 76-18077. 1976. Repr. of 1898 ed. lib. bdg. 27.50 (ISBN 0-8414-5738-7). Folcroft.
McKinley, Mary B. Words in a Corner: Studies in Montaigne's Latin Quotations. LC 80-70810. (French Forum Monographs: No. 26). 120p. (Orig.). 1981. pap. 9.50 (ISBN 0-917058-25-9). French Forum.
Monarch Notes on Michel de Montaigne's Essays. pap. 1.95 (ISBN 0-671-00855-2). Monarch Pr.
Norton, Glyn P. Montaigne & the Introspective Mind. (Studies in French Literature: No. 22). 219p. 1974. pap. text ed. 40.00x (ISBN 90-2793-412-6). Mouton.
Norton, Grace. The Early Writings of Montaigne. 1973. Repr. of 1904 ed. 25.00 (ISBN 0-8274-0302-X). R West.
--Studies in Montaigne. 1973. Repr. of 1904 ed. 25.00 (ISBN 0-8274-0303-8). R West.
Pond, C. F. A Day Book of Montaigne. 1905. Repr. 20.00 (ISBN 0-8274-2146-X). R West.
Regosin, Richard. The Matter of My Book: Montaigne's "Essais" As the Book of the Self. LC 77-75398. 1977. 15.95x (ISBN 0-520-03476-7). U of Cal Pr.
Rider, Frederick. The Dialectic of Selfhood in Montaigne. 128p. 1973. 7.50x (ISBN 0-8047-0830-4). Stanford U Pr.
Robertson, John. Montaigne & Shakespeare & Other Essays on Cognate Questions. LC 68-24914. (Studies in Comparative Literature, No. 35). 1969. Repr. of 1909 ed. lib. bdg. 37.95 (ISBN 0-8383-0234-3). Haskell.
Robertson, John M. Montaigne & Shakespeare & Other Essays on Cognate Questions. LC 70-108429. (Research & Source Works Ser.: No. 411). 1970. Repr. of 1909 ed. lib. bdg. 22.50 (ISBN 0-8337-3022-3). B Franklin.
Sayce, R. A. Essays of Montaigne: A Critical Exploration. 1972. 16.95x (ISBN 0-8101-0392-3). Northwestern U Pr.
Sedgwick, Henry D. Essays on Great Writers. facs. ed. LC 68-29245. (Essay Index Reprint Ser). 1968. Repr. of 1903 ed. 18.00 (ISBN 0-8369-0861-9). Arno.
Sichel, Edith. Michel De Montaigne. LC 74-113322. 1970. Repr. of 1911 ed. 12.50 (ISBN 0-8046-0999-3). Kennikat.
--Michel De Montaigne. 1973. Repr. of 1911 ed. 12.00 (ISBN 0-8274-1315-7). R West.
Strowski, Fortunat. Montaigne. LC 75-168935. (Philosophy Monographs: No. 83). 364p. 1972. Repr. of 1931 ed. lib. bdg. 23.50 (ISBN 0-8337-4411-9). B Franklin.
Svitak, Ivan. The Dialectic of Common Sense: The Master Thinkers. LC 78-65849. 1979. pap. text ed. 9.75 (ISBN 0-8191-0675-5). U Pr of Amer.
Taylor, George C. Shakespeare's Debt to Montaigne. LC 68-58441. 1968. Repr. of 1925 ed. 5.00 (ISBN 0-87753-039-4). Phaeton.
Tetel, Marcel. Montaigne. LC 74-2250. (World Authors Ser.: France: No. 317). 1974. lib. bdg. 12.50 (ISBN 0-8057-2623-3). Twayne.
Villey-Desmeserets, Pierre. Influence De Montaigne Sur les Idees Pedagogiques De Locke & De Rousseau. LC 70-157527. (Research & Source Works Ser: No. 72). 1971. Repr. of 1911 ed. lib. bdg. 23.50 (ISBN 0-8337-4465-8). B Franklin.
The Web of Metaphor: Studies in the Imagery of Montaigne's Essais. LC 77-93404. (Monographs: No. 7). 191p. (Orig.). 1978. pap. 9.50x (ISBN 0-917058-06-2). French Forum.
Willis, Irene C. Montaigne. 1973. Repr. of 1927 ed. 25.00 (ISBN 0-8274-0563-4). R West.
Winter, Ian J. Montaigne's Self-Portrait & Its Influence in France, 1580-1630. LC 76-17259. (Monographs: No. 3). 140p. (Orig.). 1976. pap. 9.50x (ISBN 0-917058-02-X). French Forum.
Woodberry, George E. Great Writers. facs. ed. LC 67-30236. (Essay Index Reprint Ser). 1907. 12.50 (ISBN 0-8369-1008-7). Arno.
--Literary Essays. LC 67-27667. Repr. of 1920 ed. 11.50 (ISBN 0-8046-0510-6). Kennikat.
Young, Charles L. Emerson's Montaigne. 236p. 1980. Repr. of 1941 ed. lib. bdg. 30.00 (ISBN 0-8495-6117-5). Arden Lib.

MONTAIGNE, MICHEL EYQUEM DE, 1533-1592–BIBLIOGRAPHY

Richou, Gabriel C., ed. Inventaire de la Collection des Ounrages & Documents Reunis Par J. F. Payen & J. B. Bastide sur Michel de Montaigne. LC 70-131410. 1970. Repr. of 1878 ed. 29.00 (ISBN 0-8337-2992-6). B Franklin.

MONTALE, EUGENIO, 1896-

Almansi, Guido & Merry, Bruce. Montale: The Private Language of Poetry. 1977. 10.00x (ISBN 0-85224-298-0, Pub. by Edinburgh U Pr Scotland). Columbia U Pr.
Cary, Joseph. Three Modern Italian Poets: Saba, Ungaretti, & Montale. LC 69-18279. 1969. 15.00x (ISBN 0-8147-0077-2). NYU Pr.
Pipa, Arshi. Montale & Dante. LC 68-31650. (Monographs in the Humanities Ser: No. 4). 1968. 6.00x (ISBN 0-8166-0500-9). U of Minn Pr.
West, Rebecca J. Eugenio Montale: Poet on the Edge. LC 81-4119. 200p. 1981. text ed. 16.50x (ISBN 0-674-26910-1). Harvard U Pr.

MONTANA

see also cities, counties, towns, etc. in montana

Bailey, Bernadine. Picture Book of Montana. rev. ed. LC 65-8994. (Illus.). (gr. 3-5). 1969. 5.50g (ISBN 0-8075-9529-2). A Whitman.
Bigart, Robert. Montana: An Assessment for the Future. 1978. 5.95 (ISBN 0-686-23487-1). U of MT Pubns Hist.
Carpenter, Allan. Montana. new ed. LC 79-683. (New Enchantment of America State Bks.). (Illus.). (gr. 4 up). 1979. PLB 10.60 (ISBN 0-516-04126-6). Childrens.
Cohen, Stan B. & Houde, Frank. Missoula-Bitterroot Memory Book: A Picture Post Card History. LC 79-90794. (Illus.). 96p. 1979. pap. 5.95 (ISBN 0-933126-09-3). Pictorial Hist.
Cook, Lewis. Beautiful Montana Country. Shangle, Robert D., ed. (Illus.). 72p. 1980. 12.95 (ISBN 0-89802-205-3); pap. 6.95 (ISBN 0-89802-206-1). Beautiful Am.
Doig, Ivan. This House of Sky: Landscapes of a Western Mind. LC 78-53897. 1978. 9.95 (ISBN 0-15-190054-X). HarBraceJ.
Federal Writers' Project. Montana: A State Guide Book. 430p. 1939. Repr. 45.00 (ISBN 0-403-02176-6). Somerset Pub.
Fisher, Hank. The Floater's Guide to Montana. LC 79-52411. (Illus.). 160p. (Orig.). 1979. pap. 6.95 (ISBN 0-934318-00-X). Falcon Pr MT.
Fradin, Dennis. Montana: In Words & Pictures. LC 80-25023. (Young People's Stories of Our States Ser.). (Illus.). 48p. (gr. 2-5). 1981. PLB 9.25 (ISBN 0-516-03926-1). Childrens.
Graetz, Richard P., photos by. Montana. LC 75-34321. (Illus.). 160p. 1976. 19.95 (ISBN 0-87294-079-9). Country Beautiful.
Graetz, Rick. Beautiful Montana, Vol. II. LC 78-102354. 72p. 1979. text ed. 14.95 (ISBN 0-89802-006-9); pap. 7.95 (ISBN 0-89802-005-0). Beautiful Am.
--Beautiful Montana. Shangle, Robert D., ed. LC 78-102354. (Illus.). 1977. 14.95 (ISBN 0-915796-25-2); pap. 7.95 (ISBN 0-915796-24-4). Beautiful Am.
Hanna, Warren. Montana's Many Splendored Glacier Land. LC 76-3614. (Illus.). 1976. pap. 5.95 (ISBN 0-87564-622-0). Superior Pub.
Hart, Herbert M. Tourguide to Old Forts of Montana, Wyoming North & South Dakota, Vol. 4. (Illus.). 150p. 1980. pap. 3.95 (ISBN 0-87108-570-4). Pruett.
Howard, Joseph K., ed. Montana Margins: A State Anthology. facsimile ed. LC 73-38747. (Essay Index Reprint Ser). Repr. of 1946 ed. 28.00 (ISBN 0-8369-2652-8). Arno.
Lamb, Russell, photos by. Montana. LC 80-65132. (Belding Imprint Ser.). (Illus.). 128p. (Text by Dale Burk). 1980. 27.50 (ISBN 0-912856-58-0). Graphic Arts Ctr.
Lang, William L. & Myers, Rex. Montana: Our Land & People. (Illus.). (gr. 7-8). 1979. text ed. 13.95x (ISBN 0-87108-229-2). Pruett.
Melcher, Joan. Watering Hole: A User's Guide to Montana Bars. 128p. 1980. pap. text ed. 6.95 (ISBN 0-938314-00-9). MT Mag.
Miller, D. Ghost Towns of Montana. LC 72-95496. (Western Ghost Town Ser.). (Illus.). 1974. 17.50 (ISBN 0-87108-070-2). Pruett.
Montana. 23.00 (ISBN 0-89770-102-X). Curriculum Info Ctr.
Montana Institute of the Arts. The Arts in Montana. Merriam, Harold G., ed. LC 76-58521. (Illus.). 238p. 1977. 10.00 (ISBN 0-87842-068-1). Mountain Pr.
Peterson, Martin L. The Complete Montana Travel Guide. LC 79-88126. (Illus.). 224p. 1980. pap. 5.95 (ISBN 0-686-28763-0). Lake County.
Reese, Rick, ed. Montana Mountain Ranges. (Montana Geographic Series: No. 1). 100p. 1981. pap. write for info. (ISBN 0-938314-01-7). MT Mag.
Schneider, Bill. The Hiker's Guide to Montana. LC 79-55480. 208p. (Orig.). 1979. pap. text ed. 6.95 (ISBN 0-934318-01-8). Falcon Pr MT.
Spritzer, Donald. Waters of Wealth. (Illus.). 1979. 11.95 (ISBN 0-87108-528-3); pap. 5.95 (ISBN 0-87108-542-9). Pruett.
State Industrial Directories Corp. Montana State Industrial Directory, 1980. 1980. pap. 25.00 (ISBN 0-89910-026-0). State Indus Dir.
Stein, Bennett H., ed. Tough Trip Through Paradise 1878-1879 by Andrew Garcia. (Illus.). 1967. 6.95 (ISBN 0-395-07719-2). HM.
Stone, Albert. Selected Aspects of Montana Water Law. LC 78-5890. 88p. 1978. 17.50x (ISBN 0-87842-102-5). Mountain Pr.
Stuart, Granville. Montana As It Is. LC 72-9469. (The Far Western Frontier Ser.). 180p. 1973. Repr. of 1865 ed. 13.00 (ISBN 0-405-04996-X). Arno.
Toole, K. Ross. The Rape of the Great Plains: Northwest America, Cattle & Coal. 1976. 8.95 (ISBN 0-316-84990-1, Pub. by Atlantic Monthly Pr). Little.
--Twentieth-Century Montana: A State of Extremes. LC 75-177348. 300p. 1979. Repr. of 1972 ed. 11.95 (ISBN 0-8061-0992-0). U of Okla Pr.
Wolf, James R. Guide to the Continental Divide Trail: Southern Montana & Idaho, Vol. 2. LC 76-17632. (Guide to the Continental Divide Trail Ser.). (Illus.). 1979. pap. 8.95 (ISBN 0-934326-02-9). Continent Divide.

MONTANA–HISTORY

Brier, Warren J. & Blumberg, Nathan B., eds. A Century of Montana Journalism. LC 78-169031. 352p. 1971. 10.00 (ISBN 0-87842-023-1). Mountain Pr.
Brown, Margery H. & Griffing, Virginia. Montana. LC 77-11832. (Localized History Ser). 1971. pap. text ed. 2.95 (ISBN 0-8077-1130-6). Tchrs Coll.
Cohen, Stan B. & Miller, Donald C. Big Burn: Big Burn: the Northwest's Forest Fire of Nineteen Ten. LC 78-51507. (Illus.). 96p. 1978. pap. 4.95 (ISBN 0-933126-04-2). Pictorial Hist.
Connor, Dixie. Shining Mountain Shadows. (Illus.). 1977. pap. 5.00x (ISBN 0-918292-02-6). Griggs Print.
Cushman, Dan. Montana-the Gold Frontier. LC 73-83492. 12.95 (ISBN 0-911436-03-0). Stay Away.
Dimsdale, Thomas J. Vigilantes of Montana. (Western Frontier Library: No. 1). 1978. Repr. of 1953 ed. pap. 4.95 (ISBN 0-8061-1379-0). U of Okla Pr.
Dupuyer Centennial: By Gone Days & Modern Ways. Griggs, James K., ed. 1977. pap. write for info. (ISBN 0-918292-01-8). Griggs Print.
Farr, William & Toole, K. Ross. Montana: Images of the Past. (Illus.). 1978. 35.00 (ISBN 0-87108-514-3). Pruett.
Federal Writers' Project, Montana. Land of Nakoda. LC 73-3634. (American Guide Ser). Repr. of 1942 ed. 20.00 (ISBN 0-404-57934-5). AMS Pr.
Gutfeld, Arnon. Montana's Agony: Years of War & Hysteria, 1917-1921. LC 78-31495. (University of Florida Social Science Monographs: No. 64). 174p. 1979. pap. 6.50 (ISBN 0-8130-0629-5). U Presses Fla.
Hamilton, James M. History of Montana: From Wilderness to Statehood, 1805-1970. 2nd. rev. & enl. ed. LC 74-92542. (Illus.). 1970. 18.95 (ISBN 0-8323-0018-7). Binford.
Howard, Joseph K. Montana: High, Wide and Handsome. new ed. LC 59-9606. (Illus.). 1959. 25.00x (ISBN 0-300-00576-8). Yale U Pr.
Johnson, Dorothy M. Bloody Bozeman: The Perilous Trail to Montana's Gold. Stewart, Robert, ed. (Illus.). 1977. 9.95 (ISBN 0-07-032576-6, GB). McGraw.
Lang, William L. & Myers, Rex C. Montana: Our Land & People. 1981. pap. 11.95 (ISBN 0-87108-586-0). Pruett.
Malone, Michael P. & Roeder, Richard B. Montana: A History of Two Centuries. LC 76-7791. (Illus.). 364p. 1976. 20.00 (ISBN 0-295-95520-1); pap. 8.95 (ISBN 0-295-95756-5). U of Wash Pr.
Merriam, Harold G. The Golden Valley: Missoula to 1883. LC 77-25893. (Illus.). 48p. 1977. pap. 4.95 (ISBN 0-87842-100-9). Mountain Pr.
Miller, Don C. & Cohen, Stan B. Military & Trading Posts of Montana. LC 78-70407. (Illus.). 116p. 1978. 12.95 (ISBN 0-933126-01-8); pap. 7.95 (ISBN 0-933126-00-X). Pictorial Hist.
Montana Historical Socety, ed. Not in Precious Metals Alone: A Manuscript History of Montana. 1976. 15.95 (ISBN 0-917298-01-2); pap. 7.95 (ISBN 0-917298-02-0). MT Hist Soc.
Montana Historical Society Contributions, 10 vols. 1966. Repr. of 1876 ed. 25.00x ea.; bound set 245.00x (ISBN 0-910324-12-3). Canner.
Murphy, Jerre C. The Comical History of Montana: A Serious Story for Free People... facsimile ed. McCurry, Dan C. & Rubenstein, Richard E., eds. LC 74-30644. (American Farmers & the Rise of Agribusiness Ser.). 1975. Repr. of 1912 ed. 22.00x (ISBN 0-405-06814-X). Arno.
Old Fort Benton, Montana. 32p. 1975. pap. 3.00 (ISBN 0-87770-144-X). Ye Galleon.
Potter, Edgar. Whoa... Yuh Sonsabitches. (Illus.). 300p. 1977. pap. 6.95 (ISBN 0-918292-00-X). Superior Pub.
Randolph, Edmund. Beef, Leather & Grass. LC 80-18818. (Illus.). 286p. 1981. 14.95 (ISBN 0-8061-1517-3). U of Okla Pr.
Schneider, George A., ed. The Freeman Journal: The Infantry in the Sioux Campaign of 1876. LC 76-29573. (Illus.). 1978. 15.00 (ISBN 0-89141-060-0). Presidio Pr.
Spence, Clark C. Montana: A History. (States & the Nation Ser.). (Illus.). 1978. 12.95 (ISBN 0-393-05679-1, Co-Pub by AASLH). Norton.
--Territorial Politics & Government in Montana, 1864-89. LC 75-28343. (Illus.). 345p. 1976. 20.00 (ISBN 0-252-00460-4). U of Ill Pr.

Stuart, Granville. Pioneering in Montana: The Making of a State 1864-1887. Phillips, Paul C., ed. LC 77-7651. Orig. Title: Forty Years on the Frontier. (Illus.). 1977. 15.95x (ISBN 0-8032-0933-9); pap. 5.25 (ISBN 0-8032-5870-4, BB 648, Bison). U of Nebr Pr.
--Prospecting for Gold: From Dogtown to Virginia City, 1852-1864. Phillips, Paul C., ed. LC 77-7244. Orig. Title: Forty Years on the Frontier. (Illus.). 1977. 15.95x (ISBN 0-8032-0932-0); pap. 5.25 (ISBN 0-8032-5869-0, BB 647, Bison). U of Nebr Pr.
Toole, K. Ross. Montana: An Uncommon Land. (Illus.). 1977. Repr. of 1959 ed. 10.95 (ISBN 0-8061-0427-9). U of Okla Pr.
Waldron, Ellis & Wilson, Paul. Atlas of Montana Elections: Eighteen Eighty-Nine to Nineteen Seventy-Six. 1979. 33.00 (ISBN 0-686-23488-X); pap. 19.95 (ISBN 0-686-31714-9). U of MT Pubns Hist.
Whitehead, Bruce & Whitehead, Charlotte. Montana Bound: An Activity Approach to Teaching Montana History. (Illus.). 180p. (gr. 5-6). 1980. pap. text ed. 7.95x (ISBN 0-87108-235-7). Pruett.

MONTANA-SOCIAL LIFE AND CUSTOMS

Poston, Richard W. Small Town Renaissance: A Story of the Montana Study. LC 76-109300. 1971. Repr. of 1950 ed. lib. bdg. 15.00x (ISBN 0-8371-3843-4, POST). Greenwood.

MONTANA FORMATION

see Geology, Stratigraphic-Cretaceous

MONTANISM

De Labriolle, Pierre C. Les Sources de l'Histoire du Montanisme. LC 80-13175. (Heresies of the Early Christian & Medieval Era: Second Ser.). Repr. of 1913 ed. 31.50 (ISBN 0-404-16184-7). AMS Pr.

MONTCALM-GOZON, LOUIS JOSEPH DE, MARQUIS DE SAINT-VERAN, 1712-1759

Parkman, Francis. Montcalm & Wolfe. 6.50 (ISBN 0-8446-2702-X). Peter Smith.

MONTCHRETIEN, ANTOINE DE, 1575-1621

Dessaix, Paul. Montchretien et L'economie Politique Nationale. LC 79-146139. (Research & Source Works Ser.: No. 624). 1971. Repr. of 1901 ed. lib. bdg. 12.00 (ISBN 0-8337-0843-0). B Franklin.

MONTE CARLO METHOD

Binder, K., ed. Monte Carlo Methods in Statistical Physics. (Topics in Current Physics Ser.: Vol. 7). 1979. 37.00 (ISBN 0-387-09018-5). Springer-Verlag.
Habib, Muhammad K. Sampling Representations & Approximations for Certain Functions & Stochastic Processes. 100p. 1980. pap. 3.15 (ISBN 0-686-70755-9, 1260). U of NC Pr.
Hammersley, J. M. & Handscomb, D. C. Monte Carlo Methods. (Monographs on Applied Probability & Statistics). 178p. 1964. text ed. 15.95x (ISBN 0-412-15870-1, Pub. by Chapman & Hall England). Methuen Inc.
Judge, G. G. & Bock, M. E. The Statistical Implications of Pre-Test & Stein-Rule Estimators in Econometrics. (Studies in Mathematical & Managerial Economics: Vol. 25). 1978. 58.75 (ISBN 0-7204-0729-X, North-Holland). Elsevier.
Kleijnen, J. P. Statistical Techniques in Simulation, Pt.2. (Statistics: Textbooks & Monographs Ser.: Vol. 9). 512p. 1975. 37.50 (ISBN 0-8247-6243-6). Dekker.
Lattes, Robert. Methods of Resolution for Selected Boundary Problems in Mathematical Physics. (Documents on Modern Physics Ser). 1969. 45.25x (ISBN 0-677-30060-3). Gordon.
--Quelques Methodes De Resolutions De Problemes Aux Limites De la Physique Mathematiques. (Cours & Documents De Mathematiques & De Physique Ser). (Orig.). 1967. 44.25x (ISBN 0-677-50060-2). Gordon.
Rubenstein, Reuven Y. Simulation & the Monte Carlo Method. LC 81-1873. (Probability & Mathematical Statistics Ser.). 300p. 1981. 32.95 (ISBN 0-471-08917-6, Pub. by Wiley-Interscience). Wiley.
Sobol, I. M. Metodo De Montecarlo. 78p. (Span.). 1976. pap. 1.25 (ISBN 0-8285-1689-8, Pub. by Mir Pubs Russia). Imported Pubns.
--The Monte Carlo Method. 2nd ed. Fortini, Peter, et al, trs. from Rus. LC 73-98791. (Popular Lectures in Mathematics Ser). (Illus.). 76p. 1975. pap. text ed. 4.50x (ISBN 0-226-76749-3). U of Chicago Pr.
Spanier, Jerome & Gelbard, Ely M. Monte Carlo Principles & Neutron Transport Problems. 1969. text ed. 17.50 (ISBN 0-201-07089-8, Adv Bk Prog). A-W.

MONTE CASSINO (BENEDICTINE MONASTERY)-SIEGE, 1944

Bloch, Herbert. Monte Cassino in the Middle Ages. 1980. text ed. 100.00x (ISBN 0-674-58655-7). Harvard U Pr.
Piekalkiewicz, Janusz. The Battle for Cassino. LC 80-51757. 224p. 1980. 16.95 (ISBN 0-672-52667-0). Bobbs.

MONTEIRO, ARISTEDES

Dannett, Sylvia G. & Burkart, Rosamond H. Confederate Surgeon: Aristides Monteiro. LC 69-16207. (Illus.). (gr. 8 up). 1969. 5.95 (ISBN 0-396-05896-5). Dodd.

MONTEMEZZI, ITALO

Gilman, Lawrence. Nature in Music, & Other Studies in the Tone Poetry of Today. facs. ed. LC 67-22096. (Essay Index Reprint Ser). 1914. 13.00 (ISBN 0-8369-0475-3). Arno.

MONTENEGRO-CIVILIZATION

Boehm, Christopher. Montenegrin Social Organization & Values. LC 77-87156. 17.50 (ISBN 0-404-16895-7). AMS Pr.
Denton, William. Montenegro: Its People & Their History. LC 77-87162. 1977. Repr. of 1877 ed. 32.50 (ISBN 0-404-16896-5). AMS Pr.
Djilas, Milovan. Njegos: Poet, Prince, Bishop. Petrovich, Michael B., tr. LC 66-12915. (Illus.). 1966. 10.00 (ISBN 0-15-166480-3). HarBraceJ.

MONTEREY, CALIFORNIA

Dutton, Davis & Dutton, Judy, eds. Tales of Monterey. 1976. pap. 1.95 (ISBN 0-89174-016-3). Comstock Edns.
Fink, Augusta. Monterey County: The Dramatic Story of Its Past. LC 72-76931. 1978. 10.95 (ISBN 0-913548-60-X, Valley Calif); pap. 4.95 (ISBN 0-913548-62-6, Valley Calif). Western Tanager.
Gordon, Burton L. Monterey Bay Area: Natural History & Cultural Imprints. 2nd ed. LC 74-13912. (Illus.). 192p. 1977. pap. text ed. 5.95 (ISBN 0-910286-37-X). Boxwood.
Hicks, John & Hicks, Regina. Monterey. (A Pictorial History: No. 2). (Illus.). 64p. 1973. pap. 3.95 (ISBN 0-914606-02-6). Creative Bks.
Reinstedt, Randall A. Ghosts, Bandits & Legends of Old Monterey. LC 74-189524. (Illus.). 48p. 1974. pap. 3.50 (ISBN 0-933818-00-9). Ghost Town.
--Tales, Treasures, & Pirates of Old Monterey. LC 79-110354. (Illus.). 72p. 1976. pap. 4.95 (ISBN 0-933818-03-3). Ghost Town.
Shangle, Robert D., ed. Beautiful Monterey Peninsula & Big Sur. LC 80-20374. (Illus.). 72p. 1980. 14.95 (ISBN 0-89802-164-2); pap. 7.95 (ISBN 0-89802-163-4). Beautiful Am.
Van Nostrand, Jeanne. Monterey: Adobe Capitol of California. 1968. 14.95 (ISBN 0-910312-14-1). Calif Hist.
Wildflowers of the Monterey Area of California. (Nature & Scenic Bks.). pap. 3.50 (ISBN 0-937512-03-6). Wheelwright UT.
Writers Program, California. Monterey Peninsula. LC 73-3599. (American Guide Ser.). Repr. of 1941 ed. 19.50 (ISBN 0-404-57903-5). AMS Pr.

MONTEREY, CALIFORNIA-DESCRIPTION-VIEWS

Elliott & Moore. History of Monterey County, Eighteen Eighty One: With Illustrations, Descriptions of Its Scenery, Farms, Residences, Public Buildings, Etc. (Illus.). 1979. Repr. of 1881 ed. 24.95 (ISBN 0-913548-69-3, Valley Calif). Western Tanager.
Monterey, a Pictorial History. Date not set. price not set. Creative Bks.

MONTEREY COUNTY, CALIFORNIA

Crouch, Steve. Steinbeck Country. LC 72-95690. (Images of America Ser.). (Illus.). 192p. 1975. 18.50 (ISBN 0-517-52715-4, 527154); pap. 9.95 (ISBN 0-517-52716-2, 527162). Crown.
Knox, Maxine & Rodriguez, Mary. Making the Most of the Monterey Peninsula & Big Sur. LC 78-11589. (Illus.). 1979. pap. 5.95 (ISBN 0-89141-079-1). Presidio Pr.
--Steinbeck's Street: Cannery Row. LC 79-19443. (Illus.). 1980. pap. 6.95 (ISBN 0-89141-095-3). Presidio Pr.
Masten, Warren. How to Take a Walking Field Trip on the Monterey Peninsula & Live to Tell the Story. (Illus.). 90p. (gr. 4-12). 1981. pap. 5.00 (ISBN 0-931104-05-X). Sunflower Ink.

MONTESQUIEU, CHARLES LOUIS DE SECONDAT, BARON DE LA BREDE ET DE, 1689-1755

Althusser, Louis. Politics & History: Montesquieu, Rousseau, Hegel, Marx. 1978. pap. 5.50 (ISBN 0-902308-96-3, Pub by NLB). Schocken.
Barckhausen. Montesquieu Ses Idees et Ses Oeuvres d'apres les Papiers de La Brede. 49.90 (ISBN 0-685-34049-X). French & Eur.
Carayon, Jean. Essai sur les rapports du pouvoir politique et du pouvoir religieux chez Montesquieu. LC 75-168919. (Fr.). 1973. Repr. of 1903 ed. lib. bdg. 15.00 (ISBN 0-8337-4024-5). B Franklin.
Collins, J. Churton. Voltaire, Montesquieu & Rousseau in England. 293p. 1980. Repr. of 1908 ed. lib. bdg. 35.00 (ISBN 0-8414-3032-2). Folcroft.
Cotta, Sergio. Montesquieu E la Scienza Della Societa. Mayer, J. P., ed. LC 78-67343. (European Political Thought Ser.). (It.). 1979. Repr. of 1953 ed. lib. bdg. 42.00x (ISBN 0-405-11688-8). Arno.
Courtney, C. P. Montesquieu & Burke. LC 74-2586. 204p. 1975. Repr. of 1963 ed. lib. bdg. 15.00x (ISBN 0-8371-7406-6, COMB). Greenwood.
Dargan, Edwin P. The Aesthetic Doctrine of Montesquieu, Its Application in His Writings. (Research & Source Works Ser: No. 181). 1968. Repr. of 1907 ed. 22.50 (ISBN 0-8337-0769-8). B Franklin.
Dedieu, Joseph. Montesquieu et la Tradition Politique Anglaise En France: Les Sources Anglaises de "l'Espirit des Lois". 1969. Repr. of 1909 ed. 26.50 (ISBN 0-8337-0804-X). B Franklin.
Destutt De Tracy, Antoine L. Commentary & Review of Montesquieu's Spirit of Laws. 1967. Repr. of 1811 ed. 22.50 (ISBN 0-8337-0845-7). B Franklin.
Durkheim, Emile. Montesquieu & Rousseau: Forerunners of Sociology. 1960. pap. 3.95x (ISBN 0-472-08291-4, AA). U of Mich Pr.
Fletcher, Frank T. Montesquieu & English Politics (1750-1800) LC 79-12773. (Perspectives in European History Ser.: No. 18). 286p. Repr. of 1939 ed. lib. bdg. 17.50x (ISBN 0-87991-625-7). Porcupine Pr.
Hulliung, Mark. Montesquieu & the Old Regime. 1977. 21.50x (ISBN 0-520-03108-3). U of Cal Pr.
Jameson, Russell P. Montesquieu et l'Esclavage: Etude Sur les Origines De l'Opinion Antiesclavage En France Au Dix-Huitieme Siecle. LC 72-171409. (Research & Source Works Ser.: No. 859). 371p. (Fr., Philosophy & Religious History Monographs, No. 81). 1972. Repr. of 1911 ed. lib. bdg. 23.50 (ISBN 0-8337-4185-3). B Franklin.
Jaubert, Charles. Montesquieu Economiste. LC 76-131452. (Research & Source Works: No. 548). (Fr). 1970. Repr. of 1901 ed. lib. bdg. 20.50 (ISBN 0-8337-1825-8). B Franklin.
Levin, Lawrence M. The Political Doctrine of Montesquieu's Esprit Des Lois: Its Classical Background. 359p. 1973. Repr. of 1936 ed. lib. bdg. 19.75x (ISBN 0-8371-6569-5, LEME). Greenwood.
Montesquieu. Considerations. new ed. (Documentation thematique). (Illus.). 159p. (Orig., Fr.). 1975. pap. 2.95 (ISBN 0-685-60915-4, 228). Larousse.
Pangle, Thomas L. Montesquieu's Philosophy of Liberalism. 1974. 15.00x (ISBN 0-226-64543-6). U of Chicago Pr.
Richter, M., ed. Political Theory of Montesquieu. LC 76-4753. 400p. 1977. 29.95 (ISBN 0-521-21156-5); pap. 9.95x (ISBN 0-521-29061-9). Cambridge U Pr.
Shackleton, Robert. Montesquieu: A Critical Biography. 1961. 29.95x (ISBN 0-19-815339-2). Oxford U Pr.
Sorel, Albert. Montesquieu. LC 68-26254. 1969. Repr. of 1888 ed. 11.50 (ISBN 0-8046-0434-7). Kennikat.
Spurlin, P. M. Montesquieu in America: 1760-1801. LC 79-86287. 1969. Repr. of 1940 ed. lib. bdg. 16.50x (ISBN 0-374-97581-7). Octagon.
Tournyal Du Clos, J. Idees Financieres De Montesquieu. 1912. 10.00 (ISBN 0-8337-3562-4). B Franklin.

MONTESSORI, MARIA, 1870-1952

Boyd, William. From Locke to Montessori. 1976. Repr. 27.00 (ISBN 0-685-71143-9, Regency). Scholarly.
Fynne, Robert J. Montessori & Her Inspirers. 1977. lib. bdg. 59.95 (ISBN 0-8490-2277-0). Gordon Pr.
Harms, Valerie. Stars in My Sky: Maria Montessori, Anais Nin, Frances Steloff. LC 74-82389. (Illus.). 160p. (Orig.). (YA) 1976. 8.00 (ISBN 0-8027-0536-7, Dist. by Walker & Co). Magic Circle Pr.
--Stars in My Sky: Maria Montessori, Anais Nin, Frances Steloff. (Illus.). 1976. 8.00 (ISBN 0-8027-0536-7). Walker & Co.
Leone, Bruno. Maria Montessori: Knight of the Child. Bender, David L. & McCuen, Gary E., eds. (Focus on Famous Women Ser.). (Illus.). (gr. 3 up). 1978. 6.95 (ISBN 0-912616-47-4); read along cassette 9.95 (ISBN 0-89908-246-7). Greenhaven.
Packard, Rosa C. The Hidden Hinge. LC 74-188958. 1977. soft cover 5.95 (ISBN 0-8190-0074-4). R C Packard.
Standing, E. M. Maria Montessori. pap. 1.95 (ISBN 0-451-61694-4, MJ1694, Ment). NAL.

MONTESSORI METHOD OF EDUCATION

Bettelheim, Bruno. Children of the Dream. 1970. pap. 2.50 (ISBN 0-380-01097-6, 49130, Discus). Avon.
Blessington, John P. Let My Children Work. LC 72-79377. 200p. 1975. pap. 2.95 (ISBN 0-385-00875-9, Anch). Doubleday.
Farrow, Elvira & Hill, Carol. Montessori on a Limited Budget: A Manual for the Amateur Craftsman. LC 74-29539. (Illus.). 291p. 1975. pap. 10.00 (ISBN 0-915676-01-X). Montessori Wkshps.
Fisher, Dorothy C. Montessori for Parents. LC 65-2506. (Illus.). 258p. 1965. text ed. 8.50x (ISBN 0-8376-0170-3). Bentley.
Gitter, Lena L. Montessori Approach to Art Education. LC 73-82978. (Illus.). 1973. pap. 3.50x (ISBN 0-87562-047-7). Spec Child.
--Montessori Approach to Special Education: An Equipment, Teaching & Feedback Manual. LC 75-171955. 1971. pap. 7.95 (ISBN 0-685-90520-9). Mafex.
--Montessori Way. LC 69-20317. (Illus., Orig.). 1970. pap. 9.00x (ISBN 0-87562-018-3). Spec Child.
Hainstock, Elizabeth. The Essential Montessori. (Orig.). 1978. pap. 1.95 (ISBN 0-451-61695-2, MJ1695, Ment). NAL.
--Teaching Montessori in the Home: The School Years. 1978. pap. 3.95 (ISBN 0-452-25175-3, Z5175, Plume). NAL.
Hainstock, Elizabeth G. Teaching Montessori in the Home: The Pre-School Years. 1976. pap. 3.95 (ISBN 0-452-25128-1, Z5128, Plume). NAL.
--Teaching Montessori in the Home: The Preschool Years. 1968. 7.95 (ISBN 0-394-41018-1). Random.
Harrison, Elizabeth. Montessori & the Kindergarten. 59.95 (ISBN 0-8490-0667-8). Gordon Pr.
Hill, Carol H. Montessori for a Home Based Curriculum: A Study, with Particular Emphasis on the Day Care Education Project, Ithaca, N. Y. LC 77-93842. 1978. pap. 4.50 (ISBN 0-915676-00-1). Montessori Wkshps.
Kilpatrick, William H. Montessori System Examined. LC 70-165739. (American Education Ser, No. 2). 1971. Repr. of 1914 ed. 8.00 (ISBN 0-405-03609-4). Arno.
Lillard, Paula P. Montessori: A Modern Approach. LC 78-163334. (Illus.). 1973. 8.95x (ISBN 0-8052-3423-3); pap. 2.75 (ISBN 0-8052-0394-X). Schocken.
Malloy, Terry. Montessori & Your Child: A Primer for Parents. LC 73-90684. (Illus.). 96p. 1976. 6.00x (ISBN 0-8052-3538-8); pap. 4.95 (ISBN 0-8052-0520-9). Schocken.
Meyer, Judith W. Diffusion of an American Montessori Education. LC 74-80719. (Research Papers Ser.: No. 160). 109p. 1975. pap. 8.00 (ISBN 0-89065-067-5). U Chicago Dept Geog.
Montessori Approach to Discipline: A Manual for Teacher & Parent. LC 71-184670. 1972. pap. 4.95 (ISBN 0-87804-189-3). Mafex.
Montessori, Maria. Advanced Montessori Method, 2 vols. Incl. Vol. 1. Spontaneous Activity in Education: The Education of Children from 7 to 11. 384p. 10.00x (ISBN 0-8376-0173-8); Vol. 2. Montessori Elementary Material: The Education of Children from 7 to 11 Continued. (Illus.). 512p. 12.50x (ISBN 0-8376-0174-6). LC 64-7247. 1964. Bentley.
--Child in the Family. 1970. pap. 1.95 (ISBN 0-380-01096-8, 42648, Discus). Avon.
--Collected Works. 500.00 (ISBN 0-87968-894-7). Gordon Pr.
--Doctor Montessori's Own Handbook. LC 65-1318. (Illus.). 170p. 1964. 5.95x (ISBN 0-8376-0175-4). Bentley.
--Dr. Montessori's Own Handbook. LC 65-14827. (Illus.). 1965. pap. 3.95 (ISBN 0-8052-0098-3). Schocken.
--From Childhood to Adolescence: Including Erdkinder & the Function of the University. 2nd ed. Joosten, A. M., tr. LC 75-34878. 162p. 1976. 8.00x (ISBN 0-8052-3618-X); pap. 2.75 (ISBN 0-8052-0500-4). Schocken.
--The Montessori Elementary Material. Livingston, Arthur, tr. from It. LC 72-95664. (Illus.). 444p. 1973. pap. 6.75 (ISBN 0-8052-0380-X). Schocken.
--The Montessori Method. rev. ed. LC 64-24014. 1964. pap. 5.50 (ISBN 0-8052-0088-6). Schocken.
--The Montessori Method. (Educational Ser.). 1912. Repr. 25.00 (ISBN 0-685-43237-8). Norwood Edns.
--Montessori Method: The Education of Children from 3 to 6. LC 64-5573. (Illus.). 448p. 1964. 7.50x (ISBN 0-8376-0172-X). Bentley.
--Spontaneous Activity in Education. LC 65-18641. 1965. 9.00x (ISBN 0-8052-3248-6); pap. 4.95 (ISBN 0-8052-0097-5). Schocken.
Montessori, Mario M., Jr. Education for Human Development: Understanding Montessori. Lillard, Paula P., ed. LC 75-37042. 192p. 1977. pap. 8.95x (ISBN 0-8052-3617-1). Schocken.
Orem, R. C. & Coburn, Marjorie F. Montessori: Prescriptions for Children with Learning Disabilities. LC 77-17687. 1978. 8.95 (ISBN 0-399-11802-0). Putnam.
Standing, E. M. The Montessori Revolution in Education. LC 66-14877. (Illus.). 1966. pap. 3.95 (ISBN 0-8052-0114-9). Schocken.
Ward, Florence E. Montessori Method & the American School. LC 70-165744. (American Education Ser, No. 2). (Illus.). 1971. Repr. of 1913 ed. 16.00 (ISBN 0-405-03722-8). Arno.

Wolf, Aline D. Una Guia Para Padres Al Aula Montessori. (Illus., Sp.). 1979. 5.00 (ISBN 0-9601016-3-2). Parent-Child Pr.
--Look at the Child. LC 78-58153. (Illus.). 1978. 9.95x (ISBN 0-686-77355-1); pap. 4.95 (ISBN 0-9601016-2-4). Parent-Child Pr.
--A Parents' Guide to the Montessori Classroom. (Illus.). 1980. 3.50x (ISBN 0-9601016-0-8). Parent-Child Pr.

MONTEVERDI, CLAUDIO, 1567-1643

Arnold, Denis. Monteverdi. rev. ed. (Master Musicians Ser). (Illus.). 224p. 1975. 11.00x (ISBN 0-460-03155-4, Pub. by J. M. Dent England). Biblio Dist.
--Monteverdi. (Master Musicians: No. M153). (Illus.). 1975. pap. 7.95 (ISBN 0-8226-0716-6). Littlefield.
Arnold, Denis & Fortune, Nigel, eds. Monteverdi Companion. (Illus.). 1972. pap. 5.95 (ISBN 0-393-00636-0, Norton Lib). Norton.
Kurtzman, Jeffrey. Essays on the Monteverdi Mass & Vespers of 1610. LC 78-66039. (Rice University Studies: Vol. 64, No.4). 182p. 1979. pap. 5.50x (ISBN 0-89263-238-0). Rice Univ.
Prunieres, Henry. Monteverdi: His Life & Work. MacKie, Marie D., tr. LC 70-100830. (Illus.). 293p. 1973. Repr. of 1926 ed. lib. bdg. 14.00x (ISBN 0-8371-3996-1, PRMO). Greenwood.
Redlich, Hans F. Claudio Monteverdi: Life & Works. Dale, Kathleen, tr. Repr. of 1952 ed. lib. bdg. 15.00x (ISBN 0-8371-4003-X, REMO). Greenwood.
Schrade, Leo. Monteverdi, Creator of Modern Music. (Music Reprint Ser.). 1979. Repr. of 1950 ed. lib. bdg. 32.50 (ISBN 0-306-79565-5). Da Capo.
Stevens, Denis. Letters of Claudio Monteverdi. LC 80-66219. 432p. 1980. 45.00 (ISBN 0-521-23591-X). Cambridge U Pr.
--Monteverdi: Sacred, Secular & Occasional Music. 147p. 1978. 13.50 (ISBN 0-8386-1937-1). Fairleigh Dickinson.

MONTEZ, LOLA, 1818-1861

Cannon, M., compiled by. Lola Montes: The Tragic Story of a Liberated Woman. (Illus.). 90p. 1974. 9.50 (ISBN 0-914418-03-3). Brooks-Sterling.
Goldberg, Isaac. Queen of Hearts: The Passionate Pilgrimage of Lola Montez. LC 75-91505. 308p. 1936. 18.00 (ISBN 0-405-08563-X). Arno.
Wyndham, Horace. Magnificent Montez. LC 70-91592. (Illus.). 1935. 18.00 (ISBN 0-405-09109-5). Arno.

MONTEZUMA 1ST, EMPEROR OF MEXICO, 1390-1469

Gillmor, Frances. The King Danced in the Marketplace. LC 63-11970. (Illus.). 1978. pap. 20.00 (ISBN 0-87480-148-6). U of Utah Pr.

MONTEZUMA 2ND, EMPEROR OF MEXICO, 1480-1520

Collis, Maurice. Cortez & Montezuma. 1978. pap. 2.50 (ISBN 0-380-40402-8, 40402, Discus). Avon.

MONTEZUMA, CARLOS, 1866-1923

Arnold, Adele. Red Son Rising. LC 74-17283. (Illus.). (gr. 5 up). 1974. 6.95 (ISBN 0-87518-077-9). Dillon.
Hohler, Joanne S. Papers of Carlos Montezuma 1892-1937: Guide to a Microfilm Edition. (Guides to Historical Resources Ser.). 1975. pap. 1.50 (ISBN 0-87020-156-5). State Hist Soc Wis.

MONTFORT, SIMON OF, EARL OF LEICESTER, 1208?-1265

Bemont, Charles. Simon De Montfort, Earl of Leicester, 1208-1265. Jacob, E. F., tr. LC 74-9223. (Illus.). 303p. 1974. Repr. of 1930 ed. lib. bdg. 20.50x (ISBN 0-8371-7625-5, BESM). Greenwood.
De Rishanger, William. Chronicle of William De Rishanger, of the Barons' Wars. Halliwell, James O., ed. (Camden Society, London. Publications, First Ser.: No. 15). Repr. of 1840 ed. 17.50 (ISBN 0-404-50115-X). AMS Pr.
Labarge, Margaret W. Simon De Montfort. LC 75-22643. (Illus.). 312p. 1976. Repr. of 1963 ed. lib. bdg. 17.50x (ISBN 0-8371-8359-6, LASM). Greenwood.
Luckock. Simon de Montfort: Reformer & Rebel. 3.38 (ISBN 0-08-008757-4). Pergamon.
Rishanger, William. The Chronicle of William of Rishanger. Repr. of 1840 ed. 19.50 (ISBN 0-384-50960-6). Johnson Repr.

MONTGOMERIE, ALEXANDER, 1545-1611

Brotanek, R. Untersuchungen Ueber Das Leben Und Die Dichtungen Alexander Montgomeries. 1896. pap. 21.00 (ISBN 0-384-05955-4). Johnson Repr.

MONTGOMERY, BERNARD LAW MONTGOMERY, 1ST VISCOUNT, 1887-

Chalfont, Alun. Montgomery of Alamein. LC 76-12519. 1976. 12.95 (ISBN 0-689-10744-7). Atheneum.
Montgomery, Brian. A Field-Marshal in the Family: A Personal Biography of Montgomery of Alamein. LC 74-3873. (Illus.). 416p. 1974. 14.95 (ISBN 0-8008-2635-3). Taplinger.
Thompson, R. W. Montgomery. 160p. (Orig.). 1974. pap. 2.00 (ISBN 0-345-24294-7). Ballantine.

MONTGOMERY, EDMUND, 1835-1911

Keeton, Morris T. Philosophy of Edmund Montgomery. LC 50-8270. 1950. 6.95 (ISBN 0-87074-083-0). SMU Press.

MONTGOMERY, RICHARD, 1738-1775

Babbitt, Katharine M. Janet Montgomery: Hudson River Squire. LC 75-9600. 60p. 1975. pap. text ed. 2.45 (ISBN 0-912526-18-1). Lib Res.

MONTGOMERY, ALABAMA-RACE QUESTION

King, Martin L. Stride Toward Freedom. LC 58-7099. 1958. 10.95 (ISBN 0-06-064690-X, HarpR). Har-Row.
Meltzer, Ida S. Montgomery Bus Story. Thomas, Nestina, ed. (Ethnic Reading Ser). (Illus.). 32p. (gr. 4-9). 1972. pap. text ed. 6.75 set of ten (ISBN 0-87594-169-9, 4602). Book-Lab.

MONTGOMERY COUNTY, MARYLAND

Boyd, Thomas H. History of Montgomery County, Maryland, from Its Earliest Settlement in 1650-1879. LC 68-31727. 1972. Repr. of 1879 ed. 12.50 (ISBN 0-8063-7954-5). Regional.
Kiplinger, Austin H., ed. Portrait in Time: A Photographic Profile of Montgomery County, Maryland. LC 76-44652. (Illus.). 1976. pap. 6.95 (ISBN 0-9601094-2-0). Montgomery Co Govt.
MacMaster, Richard K. & Hiebert, Ray E. A Grateful Remembrance: The Story of Montgomery County, Maryland. 1976. 6.95 (ISBN 0-686-63842-5). Montgomery Co Govt.
Scharf, John T. History of Western Maryland: Including Biographical Sketches of Their Representative Men, 2 Vols. LC 68-26127. (Illus.). 1968. Repr. of 1882 ed. Set. 85.00 (ISBN 0-8063-7965-0). Regional.

MONTGOMERY COUNTY, VIRGINIA-HISTORY

Nell, Varney R., ed. Entitled! Free Papers in Appalachia Concerning Antebellum Freeborn Negroes & Emancipated Blacks of Montgomery County, Virginia. LC 81-80481. 102p. lib. bdg. 18.50 (ISBN 0-915156-47-4). Natl Genealogical.
Worrell, Anne L. A Brief of Wills & Marriages in Montgomery & Fincastle Counties, Virginia, 1733-1831. LC 75-34994. 1979. Repr. of 1932 ed. wrappers 5.00 (ISBN 0-8063-0707-2). Genealog Pub.

MONTHERLANT, HENRY DE, 1896-

Becker, Lucille. Henry De Montherlant: A Critical Biography. LC 70-83666. (Crosscurrents-Modern Critiques Ser.). 150p. 1970. 6.95 (ISBN 0-8093-0411-2). S Ill U Pr.
Johnson, Robert B. Henry de Montherlant. (World Authors Ser.: No. 37). 12.50 (ISBN 0-8057-2626-8). Twayne.
--Henry de Montherlant. LC 67-25202. (World Authors Ser.). 1968. lib. bdg. 12.95x (ISBN 0-8057-2626-8). Irvington.

MONTHS

Krutch, Joseph. Twelve Seasons. LC 72-134106. (Essay Index Reprint Ser). 1949. 16.00 (ISBN 0-8369-1970-X). Arno.
Scarry, Richard. All Year Long. (Golden Look-Look Bks.). (Illus.). (ps-1). 1976. PLB 5.38 (ISBN 0-307-61826-9, Golden Pr); pap. 0.95 (ISBN 0-307-11826-6). Western Pub.
Updike, John. Child's Calendar. (Illus.). (gr. k-3). 1965. PLB 4.99 (ISBN 0-394-91059-1). Knopf.

MONTICELLI, ADOLPHE JOSEPH THOMAS, 1824-1886

Alauzen, Andre & Ripert, Pierre. Monticelli. (Illus., Fr.). 1970. 60.00 (ISBN 0-912728-10-8). Newbury Bks.

MONTICELLO, VIRGINIA

Bear, James A., Jr., ed. Jefferson at Monticello. Incl. Memoirs of a Monticello Slave. Campbell, Isaac; The Private Life of Thomas Jefferson. Pierson, Hamilton W. LC 67-17629. (Illus.). 144p. 1967. pap. 2.95 (ISBN 0-8139-0022-0). U Pr of Va.
Betts, Edwin M., ed. Thomas Jefferson's Garden Book. (Memoirs Ser.: Vol. 22). (Illus.). 1944. 12.00 (ISBN 0-87169-022-5). Am Philos.
Nichols, Frederick D. & Bear, James A., Jr. Monticello: A Guide Book. (Orig.). 1967. pap. 2.95x (ISBN 0-8139-0329-7). U Pr of Va.
Richards, Norman. Story of Monticello. LC 70-100699. (Cornerstones of Freedom Ser.). (gr. 4-8). 1970. PLB 7.95 (ISBN 0-516-04627-6). Childrens.

MONTREAL-DESCRIPTION-GUIDEBOOKS

Drummond, Michael, photos by. Montreal & Its Countryside. (Illus.). 1979. 14.95 (ISBN 0-19-540308-8). Oxford U Pr.
Johnson, Bruce. Montreal Souvenirs. (Illus.). 140p. 1980. 19.95 (ISBN 0-88776-117-8). Tundra Bks.
McLean, Eric & Wilson, R. D. The Living Past of Montreal: Le Passe Vivant De Montreal. rev. ed. (Illus.). 128p. 1976. 9.95 (ISBN 0-7735-0268-8); pap. 5.95 (ISBN 0-7735-0259-9). McGill-Queens U Pr.
Toker, Franklin. The Church of Notre-Dame in Montreal: An Architectural History. LC 70-98392. (Illus.). 1970. 22.75 (ISBN 0-7735-0058-8). McGill-Queens U Pr.

MONTREAL-HISTORY

Ames, H. B. City Below the Hill. LC 78-163831. (Social History of Canada Ser.). 112p. 1972. pap. 5.00 (ISBN 0-8020-6142-7). U of Toronto Pr.
Boissevain, Jeremy. The Italians of Montreal. LC 74-17921. (Italian American Experience Ser). (Illus.). 104p. 1975. Repr. 9.50x (ISBN 0-405-06394-6). Arno.
Marsan, Jean C. Montreal in Evolution: Historical Analysis of the Development of Montreal Architecture & Urban Environment. (Illus.). 488p. 1981. 27.50x (ISBN 0-7735-0339-0). McGill-Queens U Pr.
Mouton, Claude. The Montreal Canadians. 256p. 1981. 19.95 (ISBN 0-442-29634-7). Van Nos Reinhold.
Senior, Elinor K. British Regulars in Montreal: An Imperial Garrison, 1832-1854. (Illus.). 302p. 1981. 29.95 (ISBN 0-7735-0372-2). McGill-Queens U Pr.

MONTROSE, JAMES GRAHAM, 1ST MARQUIS OF, 1612-1650

Buchan, John. Montrose: A History. LC 74-14349. (Illus.). 385p. 1975. Repr. of 1928 ed. lib. bdg. 22.75x (ISBN 0-8371-7795-2, BUMO). Greenwood.

MONTS-DE-PIETE

see Pawnbroking

MONTSHIWA, BAROLONG CHIEF, 1815-1896

Molema, S. M. Montshiwa: Barolong Chief & Patriot. 1966. 11.50x (ISBN 0-8426-1391-9). Verry.

MONUMENTAL BRASSES

see Brasses

MONUMENTAL THEOLOGY

see Bible-Antiquities; Christian Antiquities

MONUMENTS

see also Arches, Triumphal; Historical Markers; Megalithic Monuments; Pyramids; Sepulchral Monuments; Tombs

Alicu, Dorin, et al. Figured Monuments from Ulpia Traiana Sarmizegetusa. (Sarmizegetusa Monograph: No. 2). 1979. 75.00x (ISBN 0-86054-050-2, Pub. by BAR). State Mutual Bk.
Apted, M. R., et al, eds. Ancient Monuments & Their Interpretation: Essays Presented to A. J. Taylor. (Illus.). 371p. 1977. 45.00x (ISBN 0-8476-1493-X). Rowman.
Brown, Ivor & Fearon, George. Amazing Monument. 1939. Repr. 12.50 (ISBN 0-8274-1846-9). R West.
Brown, Sheldon S. Remade in America: A Grand Tour of Europe, Asia, Within the U. S. A. Blumenstein, Barbara J. & Blumenstein, Lynn, eds. LC 72-79470. (Illus.). 400p. 1972. 20.00 (ISBN 0-911068-08-2). Old Time.
Critchlow, Keith. Time Stands Still. 176p. 1980. 49.95 (ISBN 0-86092-039-9, Pub. by G Fraser England); pap. 29.95 (ISBN 0-86092-040-2). Intl Schol Bk Serv.
Dames, Michael. The Silbury Treasure: The Great Goddess Rediscovered. (Illus.). 1977. 12.95 (ISBN 0-500-05027-9). Thames Hudson.
Delbrueck, Richard. Die Consulardiptychen und verwandte Denkmaeler. (Studien Zur Spaetantiken Kunstgeschichte: Vol. 2). (Illus.). 296p. Repr. of 1929 ed. write for info. (ISBN 3-11-005704-2). De Gruyter.
Doezema, Marianne & Hargrove, June. The Public Monument & Its Audience. LC 77-25428. (Themes in Art Ser.). (Illus.). 76p. 1977. pap. 4.95x (ISBN 0-910386-38-2, Pub. by Cleveland Mus Art). Ind U Pr.
Forster, Charles. The Monuments of Assyria, Babylonia & Persia. LC 77-94577. 1979. Repr. of 1859 ed. lib. bdg. 40.00 (ISBN 0-89341-261-9). Longwood Pr.
Friedlander, Lee. The American Monument. LC 76-6715. 1976. 85.00x (ISBN 0-87130-043-5). Eakins.
The Guarding of Cultural Property: Protection of the Cultural Heritage - Technical Handbooks for Museums & Monuments. (Illus.). 40p. 1978. pap. 4.75 (ISBN 92-3-101429-3, U813, UNESCO). Unipub.
Hammond Incorporated Editors. Landmarks of Liberty. LC 77-114691. (Profile Ser). (Illus.). (gr. 7 up). 1970. 6.95 (ISBN 0-8437-3078-1). Hammond Inc.
Harris, D. V. The Geologic Story of the National Parks & Monuments. 3rd ed. 344p. 1980. pap. 19.95 (ISBN 0-471-09764-0, Pub. by Wiley Med). Wiley.
Homage to Shravana Belgola. 1981. 28.00x (ISBN 0-8364-0761-X, Pub. by Marg India). South Asia Bks.
Jackson, Earl. Tumacacori's Yesterdays. 2nd rev ed. LC 73-81365. (Popular Ser.: No. 6). (Illus.). 1973. pap. 1.50 (ISBN 0-911408-31-2). Sw Pks Mnmts.
Kraskovka, L'Udmila. Te Roman Cemetery at Gerulata Rusovce, Czechoslovakia. 10.00x (ISBN 0-904531-42-2, Pub. by BAR). State Mutual Bk.
Krythe, Maymie R. What So Proudly We Hail: All About Our American Flag, Monuments & Symbols. LC 68-15993. (YA) 1968. (HarpT); lib. bdg. 8.97 (ISBN 0-06-012464-4). Har-Row.
Preservation & Conservation: Principles & Practices. LC 75-13331. (Illus.). 547p. 1976. text ed. 17.95 (ISBN 0-89133-029-1). Preservation Pr.

MONUMENTS-PRESERVATION

Moe, Christine. Preservation & the Human Scale in New Orleans & Louisiana. rev. & enl. ed. (Architecture Ser.: A-94). 1979. pap. 8.00 (ISBN 0-686-26439-8). Vance Biblios.
Morton, Terry B., ed. Monumentum. (Illus.). 128p. (Orig.). 1976. pap. 10.00 (ISBN 0-89133-087-9). Preservation Pr.
Preserving & Restoring Monuments & Historic Buildings. LC 73-189463. (Museums & Monuments Ser., No. 14). (Illus.). 267p. 1972. 24.75 (ISBN 92-3-100985-0, U479, UNESCO); pap. (U480). Unipub.

MONUMENTS-GREAT BRITAIN

Crossley, F. H. English Church Monuments A.D. Eleven Fifty to Fifteen Fifty. LC 77-94565. 1979. Repr. of 1921 ed. lib. bdg. 35.00 (ISBN 0-89341-233-3). Longwood Pr.
Harbison, Peter. A Guide to the National Monuments of Ireland. (Illus.). 1979. limp bdg. 13.50 (ISBN 0-7171-0758-2). Irish Bk Ctr.
Hayward, R. Cleopatra's Needles. 128p. 1980. 30.00x (ISBN 0-903485-82-6, Pub. by Moorland England). State Mutual Bk.
Thom, A. & Thom, A. S. Megalithic Rings: Plans & Data for 229 Monuments in Britain. 405p. 1980. 72.00x (ISBN 0-86054-094-4, Pub. by BAR). State Mutual Bk.

MONUMENTS, NATURAL

see Natural Monuments

MONUMENTS, SEPULCHRAL

see Sepulchral Monuments

MOODY, DWIGHT LYMAN, 1837-1899

Bailey, Faith C. D. L. Moody. 1959. pap. 2.95 (ISBN 0-8024-0039-6). Moody.
Findlay, James F., Jr. Dwight L. Moody, American Evangelist: 1837-1899. LC 69-13200. 1969. 15.00x (ISBN 0-226-24925-5). U of Chicago Pr.
Fitt, A. P. Life of D. L. Moody. pap. 2.25 (ISBN 0-8024-4727-9). Moody.
Gericke, Paul. Crucial Experiences in the Life D. L. Moody. LC 78-7570. 72p. (Orig.). 1978. pap. 1.50 (ISBN 0-914520-12-1). Insight Pr.
Goodspeed, Edgar J. Full History of the Wonderful Career of Moody & Sankey, in Great Britain & America. LC 70-168154. (Illus.). Repr. of 1876 ed. 39.00 (ISBN 0-404-07227-5). AMS Pr.
Gundry, Stanley. Love Them in: The Proclamation Theology of D. L. Moody. 1976. 6.95 (ISBN 0-8024-5026-1). Moody.

MOODY, WILLIAM VAUGHN, 1869-1910

Halpern, Martin. William Vaughn Moody. (Twayne's United States Authors Ser). 1964. pap. 3.45 (ISBN 0-8084-0330-3, T64, Twayne). Coll & U Pr.
Henry, David D. William Vaughn Moody. LC 73-14578. 1934. Repr. lib. bdg. 25.00 (ISBN 0-8414-4768-3). Folcroft.
--William Vaughn Moody: A Study. 1978. Repr. of 1934 ed. lib. bdg. 25.00 (ISBN 0-8495-2378-8). Arden Lib.

MOODY BIBLE INSTITUTE OF CHICAGO

Martin, Dorothy. Moody Bible Insitute: God's Power in Action. 1977. pap. 3.95 (ISBN 0-8024-5518-2). Moody.

MOON, CHARLOTTE, 1840-1912

Hyatt, Irwin T., Jr. Our Ordered Lives Confess. (American-East Asian Relations Ser.: No. 8). 1976. 18.50x (ISBN 0-674-64735-1). Harvard U Pr.
Monsell, Helen A. Her Own Way, the Story of Lottie Moon. LC 58-9919. (gr. 4-8). 1958. 5.95 (ISBN 0-8054-4303-7). Broadman.

MOON, MILTON

Pryor, Dennis. Focus on Milton Moon. (Illus.). 1967. 12.95x (ISBN 0-7022-0054-9). U of Queensland Pr.

MOON, SUN MYUNG

Bjornstad, James. The Moon Is Not the Son: A Close Look at the Religion of Rev. Son Myung Moon. LC 76-46208. 1977. pap. 3.50 (ISBN 0-87123-380-0, 200380). Bethany Hse.
Chong Sun Kim. Rev. Sun Myung Moon. LC 78-52115. 1978. pap. text ed. 7.75 (ISBN 0-8191-0494-9). U Pr of Amer.
Horowitz, Irving L., ed. Science, Sin & Scholarship: The Politics of Reverend Moon & the Unification Church. 312p. 1980. 15.00x (ISBN 0-262-08100-8); pap. 6.95 (ISBN 0-262-58042-X). MIT Pr.
Lofland, John. Doomsday Cult: A Study of Conversion, Proselytization, & Maintenance of Faith. enl. ed. LC 77-23028. 1981. pap. text ed. 9.50x (ISBN 0-8290-0095-X). Irvington.
Tingle, Donald A. & Fordyce, Richard A. Phases & Faces of the Moon: A Critical Evaluation of the Unification Church & Its Principles. 1979. 5.00 (ISBN 0-682-49264-7). Exposition.

Yamamoto, J. Isamu. The Puppet Master: An Inquiry into Sun Myung Moon & the Unification Church. LC 76-55622. 1977. pap. 3.95 (ISBN 0-87784-740-1). Inter-Varsity.

MOON

see also Lunar Geology; Space Flight to the Moon; Tides

Asimov, Isaac. The Tragedy of the Moon. LC 73-79641. 240p. 1973. 6.95 (ISBN 0-385-07221-X). Doubleday.

Baldwin, Ralph B. Measure of the Moon. LC 62-20025. (Illus.). 1963. 20.00x (ISBN 0-226-03606-5). U of Chicago Pr.

Ball, Robert S. Time & Tide: A Romance of the Moon. 1899. 10.00 (ISBN 0-686-17418-6). Ridgeway Bks.

Brown, Ernest & Hedrick, Henry B. Tables of the Motion of the Moon, 3 vols. 1920. pap. 200.00x set (ISBN 0-685-89789-3). Elliots Bks.

Chamberlain, Joseph, ed. Reviews of Lunar Sciences. 1977. pap. 15.00 (ISBN 0-87590-220-0). Am Geophysical.

Conference on Origins of Life, 3rd, California, 1970. Planetary Astronomy: Proceedings. Margulis, L., ed. LC 72-91514. (Illus.). 268p. 1973. 24.90 (ISBN 0-387-06065-0). Springer-Verlag.

C.O.S.P.A.R International Space Science Symposium - London - Jul 26-27 1967. Moon & Planets: A Session of the Joint Open Meeting of Working Groups One, Two & Five of the Tenth Plenary Meeting of COSPAR, Vol. 2. Dollfus, A., ed. (Illus., Part Fr). 1968. 14.25x (ISBN 0-7204-0129-1). Humanities.

C.O.S.P.A.R International Space Science Symposium - 7th - Vienna. Moon & Planets: Proceedings, Vol. 1. Dollfus, A., ed. 1967. text ed. 15.00x (ISBN 0-7204-0116-X, Pub. by North Holland). Humanities.

Dow, T. W. The Moon Has No Rotation. 1958. pap. 1.00 (ISBN 0-910340-01-3). Celestial Pr.

Forbes, George. The Earth, the Sun & the Moon. 1979. Repr. of 1928 ed. lib. bdg. 12.50 (ISBN 0-8495-1627-7). Arden Lib.

--The Earth, the Sun, & the Moon. 1928. 10.00 (ISBN 0-686-17422-4). Ridgeway Bks.

French, Bevan M. The Moon Book. 1977. pap. 4.95 (ISBN 0-14-004340-3). Penguin.

Gamow, George & Stubbs, Harry G. Moon. rev ed. LC 73-137588. (Illus.). (gr. 5 up). 1971. 6.95 (ISBN 0-200-71761-8, B56491, AbS-J). Har-Row.

Goldstine, Herman H. New & Full Moons One Thousand & One B. C. to A. D. Sixteen Fifty One. LC 72-89401. (Memoirs Ser.: Vol. 94). 1973. 6.50 (ISBN 0-87169-094-2). Am Philos.

Hevelius, Johann. Selenographia, Sive Lunae Descriptio. 1968. Repr. 100.00 (ISBN 0-384-22820-8). Johnson Repr.

International Astronomical Union, 47th Symposium, Newcastle-Upon-Tyne, 1971. The Moon: Proceedings. Urey, H. C. & Runcorn, S. K., eds. LC 73-188005. (IAU Symposium Ser.: No. 47). 480p. 1972. lib. bdg. 58.00 (ISBN 90-277-0149-0, Pub. by Reidel Holland). Kluwer Boston.

International Conference on Selenodesy & Lunar Topograph,2nd,University of Manchester,England May 30-June 4,1966. Measure of the Moon: Proceedings. Kopal, Z. & Goudas, C. L., eds. (Astrophysics & Space Science Library: No.8). 479p. 1967. lib. bdg. 58.00 (ISBN 90-277-0125-3, Pub. by Reidel Holland). Kluwer Boston.

Kolisko, L. Moon & Growth of Plants. (Illus.). 1979. pap. 7.95x (ISBN 0-906492-13-0, Pub. by Kolisko Archives). St George Bk Serv.

Kopal, Z. An Introduction to the Study of the Moon. 476p. 1966. 84.25 (ISBN 0-677-01230-6). Gordon.

--The Moon in the Post-Apollo Era. LC 74-26877. (Geophysics & Astrophysics Monographs: No.7). 224p. 1974. lib. bdg. 37.00 (ISBN 90-277-0277-2, Pub. by Reidel Holland); pap. 24.00 (ISBN 90-277-0278-0). Kluwer Boston.

Kopal, Z. & Goudas, C. L. Measure of the Moon. 1967. 96.75 (ISBN 0-677-11850-3). Gordon.

Kopal, Z. & Carder, R. W., eds. The Mapping of the Moon. LC 73-88592. (Astrophysics & Space Science Library: No. 50). 1974. lib. bdg. 39.50 (ISBN 90-277-0398-1, Pub. by Reidel Holland). Kluwer Boston.

Kopal, Zdenek, ed. Physics & Astronomy of the Moon. 2nd ed. 1971. 46.50 (ISBN 0-12-419340-4). Acad Pr.

Kopel, Zdenek & Mikhailov, Z. K., eds. The Moon. 1963. 56.00 (ISBN 0-12-419362-5). Acad Pr.

Kuiper, Gerard P. & Middlehurst, Barbara M., eds. Moon, Meteorites & Comets. LC 62-18117. (Solar System Ser: Vol. 4). 1963. 33.00x (ISBN 0-226-45928-4). U of Chicago Pr.

Lieber, A. L., M.D. The Lunar Effect. LC 77-12870. 1978. 7.95 (ISBN 0-385-12897-5, Anchor Pr). Doubleday.

Lunar & Planetary Science Conference, 10th, Houston, Texas, March 19-23, 1979. Proceedings. LC 79-22554. (Illus.). 3200p. 1980. 220.00 (ISBN 0-08-025128-5). Pergamon.

Manson, Lewis A. Birth of the Moon. (Illus.). 205p. 1978. 14.95 (ISBN 0-87201-567-X). Gulf Pub.

--The Birth of the Moon. LC 76-19964. (Illus.). 1978. 14.95 (ISBN 0-930422-12-0). Dennis-Landman.

Masterson, Amanda R., ed. Index to the Proceedings of the Lunar & Planetary Science Conferences, Houston, Texas, 1970-1978. LC 79-20109. (Illus.). 325p. 1979. 33.00 (ISBN 0-08-024620-6). Pergamon.

Moore, Patrick. The Moon. Hunt, Garry, ed. (Rand McNally Library of Astronomical Atlases for Amateur & Professional Photographers). (Illus.). 96p. 1981. 14.95 (ISBN 0-528-81541-5). Rand.

--New Guide to the Moon. 1977. 12.95 (ISBN 0-393-06414-X). Norton.

--Survey of the Moon. (Illus.). 1963. 6.95 (ISBN 0-393-06330-5). Norton.

Moore, Patrick & Cattermole, Peter J. Craters of the Moon: An Observational Approach. LC 68-10883. (Illus.). 1967. 5.95 (ISBN 0-393-06355-0). Norton.

Nagel Travel Guide to the Moon. (Nagel Travel Guide Ser.). (Illus.). 176p. 1970. 23.00 (ISBN 2-8263-0059-8). Hippocrene Bks.

Newton, Robert. Moon's Acceleration & Its Physical Origins: Vol. 1, As Deduced from Solar Eclipses. LC 78-2059. 1979. 32.50x (ISBN 0-8018-2216-5). Johns Hopkins.

Pavese, C. La Lune. Thompson, A. D., ed. 208p. 1980. 15.00x (ISBN 0-7190-0771-2, Pub. by Manchester U Pr England). State Mutual Bk.

Rousseau, Pierre. Nuestra Amiga La Luna. (Span.). 1963. 4.95 (ISBN 0-914326-05-8). Orbiting Bk.

Rukl, Antonin. Moon, Mars & Venus. (Concise Guides Ser.). (Illus.). 1979. 7.95 (ISBN 0-600-36219-1). Transatlantic.

Salisbury, John W. & Glaser, Peter E., eds. Lunar Surface Layer: Materials & Characteristics: Proceedings. 1964. 44.50 (ISBN 0-12-615450-3). Acad Pr.

Schultz, Peter H. Moon Morphology: Interpretations Based on Lunar Orbiter Photography. LC 74-22176. (Illus.). 644p. 1976. 60.00x (ISBN 0-292-75036-6). U of Tex Pr.

Singer, S. Fred, ed. Physics of the Moon. (Science & Technology Ser.: Vol. 13). 1967. 25.00 (ISBN 0-87703-041-3). Am Astronaut.

Taylor, Stuart R. Lunar Science: A Post-Apollo View. LC 74-17227. 372p. 1975. text ed. 31.00 (ISBN 0-08-018274-7); pap. text ed. 16.00 (ISBN 0-08-018273-9). Pergamon.

Very, Frank W. Lunar & Terrestrial Albedoes. (Orig.). pap. 1.00 (ISBN 0-8283-1188-9). Branden.

Whipple, Fred L. Earth, Moon, & Planets. 3rd ed. LC 68-21987. (Books on Astronomy Series). (Illus.). 15.00x (ISBN 0-674-22400-0); pap. 5.95 (ISBN 0-674-22401-9). Harvard U Pr.

Wilkins, John. The Discovery of a World in the Moone. LC 70-38230. (English Experience Ser.: No. 494). 224p. 1972. Repr. of 1638 ed. 14.00 (ISBN 90-221-0494-X). Walter J Johnson.

Zim, Herbert S. The New Moon. LC 79-21896. (Illus.). 64p. (gr. 4-6). 1980. 6.50 (ISBN 0-688-22219-6); PLB 6.24 (ISBN 0-688-32219-0). Morrow.

MOON–EXPLORATION

Adler, I. & Trombka, J. I. Geochemical Exploration of the Moon & the Planets. LC 78-127039. (Physics & Chemistry in Space Ser.: Vol. 3). (Illus.). 1970. 31.20 (ISBN 0-387-05228-3). Springer-Verlag.

Cadogan, Peter. The Moon-Our Sister Planet. LC 80-41564. (Illus.). 400p. Date not set. price not set (ISBN 0-521-23684-3); pap. price not set (ISBN 0-521-28152-0). Cambridge U Pr.

Colby, C. B. Moon Exploration: Space Stations, Moon Maps, Lunar Vehicles. LC 76-125328. (Illus.). (gr. 4-7). 1970. 5.29 (ISBN 0-698-30239-7). Coward.

Hallion, Richard P. & Crouch, Tom D., eds. Apollo: Ten Years Since Tranquillity Base. LC 79-10271. (Illus.). 174p. 1979. 19.95 (ISBN 0-87474-506-3); pap. 8.95 (ISBN 0-87474-505-5). Smithsonian.

Holland, Claude V. Rover & Men on the Moon. 1973. 4.95 (ISBN 0-932092-01-2); pap. 2.98 (ISBN 0-932092-00-4). Hol-Land Bks.

Johnson, Nicholas L. Handbook of Soviet Lunar & Planetary Exploration. (Science & Technology Ser.: Vol. 47). 276p. 1979. lib. bdg. 35.00 (ISBN 0-87703-130-4); pap. text ed. 25.00 (ISBN 0-87703-131-2). Univelt Inc.

Kopal, Z. An Introduction to the Study of the Moon. 476p. 1966. 84.25 (ISBN 0-677-01230-6). Gordon.

--The Moon: An Outline of Astronomy & Physics of Our Satellite on the Eve of the Apollo Era. (Illus.). 525p. 1969. lib. bdg. 58.00 (ISBN 9-0277-0124-5, Pub. by Reidel Holland). Kluwer Boston.

Lunar & Planetary Institute, Houston, Texas, ed. Mare Crisium: The View from Luna Twenty-Four. 733p. 1979. 49.00 (ISBN 0-08-022965-4). Pergamon.

Malina, F. J. Applied Sciences Research & Utilization of Lunar Resources. 1970. 50.00 (ISBN 0-08-015565-0). Pergamon.

Newton, Robert. Moon's Acceleration & Its Physical Origins: Vol. 1, As Deduced from Solar Eclipses. LC 78-2059. 1979. 32.50x (ISBN 0-8018-2216-5). Johns Hopkins.

MOON–JUVENILE LITERATURE

Branley, Franklyn M. Moon Seems to Change. LC 60-8796. (A Let's-Read-&-Find-Out Science Bk). (Illus.). (gr. k-3). 1960. PLB 8.79 (ISBN 0-690-55485-0, TYC-J). Har-Row.

--What the Moon Is Like. LC 63-8479. (A Let's-Read-&-Find-Out Science Bk). (Illus.). (gr. k-3). 1963. pap. 2.95 (ISBN 0-690-00203-3, TYC-J); lib. bdg. 8.79 (ISBN 0-690-87860-5). Har-Row.

Collins, Jim. First to the Moon. LC 78-13611. (Famous Firsts Ser.). (Illus.). 1978. lib. bdg. 7.35 (ISBN 0-686-51106-9). Silver.

The Earth's Moon. 1981. 23.50 (ISBN 0-686-73887-X, 04920). Natl Geog.

Going to the Moon. (Learning Shelf Kits Ser.). (gr. 2-4). 1978. incl. cassete & tchrs. guide 14.95 (ISBN 0-686-74374-1, 04981). Natl Geog.

Kerrod, Robin. Race for the Moon. LC 79-2347. (The Question & Answer Bks.). (Illus.). (gr. 3-6). 1980. PLB 6.95g (ISBN 0-8225-1183-5). Lerner Pubns.

Levitin, Sonia. Who Owns the Moon? LC 73-77124. (Illus.). (ps-3). 1973. 6.95 (ISBN 0-87466-066-1); PLB 5.38 (ISBN 0-87466-005-X). Parnassus.

The Moon. (Learning Shelf Kits Ser.). (gr. 2-4). 1978. incl. cassette & tchrs. guide 14.95 (ISBN 0-686-74375-X, 04980). Natl Geog.

The Moon. (MacDonald Educational Ser.). (Illus., Arabic.). 3.50 (ISBN 0-86685-208-5). Intl Bk Ctr.

Shuttlesworth, Dorothy E. & Williams, Lee Ann. The Moon: Stepping Stone to Outer Space. LC 76-50787. (gr. 3-7). 1977. 5.95a (ISBN 0-385-12118-0); PLB (ISBN 0-385-12119-9). Doubleday.

Taylor, G. Jeffrey. A Close Look at the Moon. LC 79-24721. (Illus.). (gr. 5 up). 1980. 5.95 (ISBN 0-396-07797-8). Dodd.

Whitcomb, John C. & DeYoung, Donald B. The Moon: Its Creation, Form & Significance. 7.95 (ISBN 0-88469-102-0). BMH Bks.

MOON–PHOTOGRAPHS, MAPS, ETC.

Alter, Dinsmore. Pictorial Guide to the Moon. 3rd ed. Jackson, Joseph H., rev. by. LC 78-22452. (Illus.). 1979. pap. 6.95 (ISBN 0-690-01824-X). T Y Crowell.

Elsby, F. H. Marketing & the Sales Manager. 1969. 25.00 (ISBN 0-08-006537-6); pap. 13.25 (ISBN 0-08-006536-8). Pergamon.

Kopal, Zdenek. New Photographic Atlas of the Moon. LC 72-125480. 1970. 20.00 (ISBN 0-8008-5515-9). Taplinger.

Leonardi, Piero. Volcanoes & Impact Craters on the Moon & Mars. (Illus.). 1976. 85.50 (ISBN 0-444-99821-7). Elsevier.

Lowman, P. D., Jr. Lunar Panorama: A Photographic Guide to the Geology of the Moon. (Illus.). 1969. 25.00 (ISBN 0-685-00394-9). Heinman.

Whitaker, E. A., et al. The Rectified Lunar Atlas. LC 63-17721. (Photographic Lunar Atlas, Suppl: No. 2). (Illus.). 1964. 35.00x (ISBN 0-8165-0077-0). U of Ariz Pr.

MOON (IN RELIGION, FOLK-LORE, ETC.)

see also Moon in Literature

Harding, M. Esther. Woman's Mysteries. 1976. pap. 4.95 (ISBN 0-06-090525-5, CN525, CN). Har-Row.

Harley, Timothy. Moon Lore. Repr. of 1885 ed. 15.00x (ISBN 0-8464-0641-1). Beekman Pubs.

--Moon Lore. 1976. Repr. 13.00x (ISBN 0-85409-828-3). Charles River Bks.

Heline, Corinne. Moon in Occult Lore. pap. 0.50 (ISBN 0-87613-013-9). New Age.

O'Neill, Eugene. Moon for the Misbegotten. LC 74-5218. 1974. pap. 1.95 (ISBN 0-394-71236-6, Vin). Random.

Rush, Anne K. Moon, Moon. 1976. pap. 7.95 (ISBN 0-394-73230-8). Random.

--Moon, Moon. LC 76-16003. 1976. 15.00 (ISBN 0-685-78827-X); pap. 7.95 (ISBN 0-685-78828-8). Moon Bks.

Whitcomb, John C. & DeYoung, Donald B. The Moon: Its Creation, Form & Significance. 7.95 (ISBN 0-8010-9619-7). Baker Bk.

MOON, FLIGHT TO THE

see Space Flight to the Moon

MOON, THEORY OF

Airy, George B. Gravitation. rev. ed. 1969. pap. 2.50 (ISBN 0-911014-02-0). Neo Pr.

Godfray, Hugh. An Elementary Treatise on the Lunar Theory. Cohen, I. Bernard, ed. LC 80-2125. (Development of Science Ser.). (Illus.). 1981. lib. bdg. 12.00x (ISBN 0-405-13847-4). Arno.

MOON BASES

see Lunar Bases

MOON CARS

Zipkin, M. A. & Edwards, R. N., eds. Power Systems for Space Flight. (Progress in Astronautics & Aeronautics Ser.: Vol. 11). 1963. 29.00 (ISBN 0-12-535111-9). Acad Pr.

MOON IN LITERATURE

see also Moon (In Religion, Folk-Lore, etc.)

Eiseley, Loren. Invisible Pyramid. LC 71-123826. (Illus.). 1972. pap. 2.95 (ISBN 0-684-12732-6, SL328, ScribT). Scribner.

Mc Colley, Grant, ed. The Man in the Moone & Nuncius Inanimatus. LC 73-6816. 1937. 25.00 (ISBN 0-8414-5931-2). Folcroft.

MOON PROBES

see Lunar Probes

MOON SYSTEM

see Blind–Printing and Writing Systems

MOON WORSHIP

see Moon (In Religion, Folk-Lore, etc.)

MOONEY, THOMAS J., 1882-1942

Frost, Richard H. The Mooney Case. LC 68-13222. (Illus.). 1968. 18.50x (ISBN 0-8047-0651-4). Stanford U Pr.

Hopkins, Ernest J. What Happened in the Mooney Case. LC 73-107411. (Civil Liberties in American History Ser). 1970. Repr. of 1932 ed. lib. bdg. 27.50 (ISBN 0-306-71891-X). Da Capo.

Hunt, Henry T. Case of Thomas J. Mooney & Warren K. Billings. LC 72-122166. (Civil Liberties in American History Ser). (Illus.). 1970. Repr. of 1929 ed. lib. bdg. 42.50 (ISBN 0-306-71976-2). Da Capo.

MOONLIGHTING

see Supplementary Employment

MOON'S TYPE FOR THE BLIND

see Blind–Printing and Writing Systems

MOONSHINING

see Distilling, Illicit

MOORE, ANNE CARROLL

Sayers, Frances C. Anne Carroll Moore: A Biography. LC 72-78291. (Illus.). 320p. 1972. 8.95 (ISBN 0-689-10523-1). Atheneum.

MOORE, ARTHUR JAMES, BP. 1888-

Moore, Arthur J. Bishop to All Peoples. LC 73-6701. 144p. 1973. 5.95 (ISBN 0-687-03571-6). Abingdon.

MOORE, BRIAN, 1921-

Dahlie, Hallvard. Brian Moore. (Canada Authors Ser.: No. 632). 1981. lib. bdg. 14.95 (ISBN 0-8057-6475-5). Twayne.

Flood, Jeanne. Brian Moore. (Irish Writers Ser.). 98p. 1975. 4.50 (ISBN 0-8387-7823-2); pap. 1.95 (ISBN 0-8387-7972-7). Bucknell U Pr.

MOORE, CHARLES HERBERT, 1840-1930

Allen, Gerald. Charles Moore. (Illus.). 128p. 1980. 18.95 (ISBN 0-8230-7375-0). Watson-Guptill.

Mather, Frank A. Charles Herbert Moore, Landscape Painter. 1957. 15.00 (ISBN 0-691-03810-4). Princeton U Pr.

MOORE, EDWARD, 1712-1757

Caskey, John H. The Life & Works of Edward Moore. (Yale Studies in English Ser.: No. 75). 197p. 1973. Repr. of 1927 ed. 16.50 (ISBN 0-208-01125-0, Archon). Shoe String.

MOORE, GEORGE, 1852-1933

Cave, Richard A. A Study of the Novels of George Moore. LC 78-3471. (Irish Literary Studies Ser: No. 3). 1978. text ed. 22.50x (ISBN 0-06-491014-8). B&N.

Dunleavy, Janet E. George Moore: The Artist's Vision, the Storyteller's Art. LC 75-125793. 156p. 1973. 10.00 (ISBN 0-8387-7757-0). Bucknell U Pr.

Farrow, Anthony. George Moore. (English Authors Ser.: No. 244). 1978. 12.50 (ISBN 0-8057-6685-5). Twayne.

Ferguson, Walter D. Influence of Flaubert on George Moore. LC 74-10999. 1934. lib. bdg. 10.00 (ISBN 0-8414-4220-7). Folcroft.

Freeman, John. Portrait of George Moore in a Study of His Work. LC 78-131711. 1971. Repr. of 1922 ed. 22.00 (ISBN 0-403-00598-1). Scholarly.

--Portrait of George Moore in a Study of His Work. LC 74-4125. 1973. lib. bdg. 25.00 (ISBN 0-8414-4177-4). Folcroft.

Gilcher, Edwin, compiled by. Bibliography of George Moore. LC 72-125334. 1970. 20.00 (ISBN 0-87580-017-3). N Ill U Pr.

Godwin, G. Conversations with George Moore. LC 73-21564. (English Literature Ser., No. 33). 1974. lib. bdg. 33.95 (ISBN 0-8383-1811-8). Haskell.

Hone, Joseph M. The Life of George Moore. LC 73-141483. (Illus.). 515p. 1973. Repr. of 1936 ed. lib. bdg. 22.25x (ISBN 0-8371-5868-0, HOGM). Greenwood.

Hughes, Douglas A., ed. The Man of Wax: Critical Essays on George Moore. LC 71-124527. 1971. 12.00x (ISBN 0-8147-3380-8); pap. 3.95x (ISBN 0-8147-3381-6). NYU Pr.

Mitchell, Susan L. George Moore. LC 70-102618. (Irish Culture & History Ser). 1970. Repr. of 1916 ed. 10.50 (ISBN 0-8046-0795-8). Kennikat.

Moore, George. Letters of George Moore. LC 77-1316. 1977. lib. bdg. 17.50 (ISBN 0-8414-3980-X). Folcroft.

--Letters of George Moore (Eighteen Fifty-Two to Nineteen Thirty-Three) to His Brother Col. M. Moore National Library of Ireland Mss 2646-7. 1980. text ed. write for info. (ISBN 0-391-01200-2). Humanities.

Quiller-Couch, A. T. Adventures in Criticism: Robinson Crusoe, Charles Reade, Henery Kingsley, George Moore. 428p. 1981. Repr. of 1896 ed. lib. bdg. 30.00 (ISBN 0-89760-724-4). Telegraph Bks.

Sechler, Robert P. George Moore: A Disciple of Walter Pater. LC 76-26908. 1931. lib. bdg. 12.50 (ISBN 0-8414-7817-1). Folcroft.

Seinfelt, Frederick W. George Moore: Ireland's Unconventional Realist. 320p. 1975. 7.95 (ISBN 0-8059-2150-8). Dorrance.

Williams, I. A. George Moore. (Bibliographies of Modern Authors Ser: No. 3). lib. bdg. 8.50 (ISBN 0-8414-9734-6). Folcroft.

--George Moore: A Bibliography. 16p. 25.00 (ISBN 0-686-74427-6). Porter.

Wolfe, Humbert. George Moore. facsimile ed. LC 74-99673. (Select Bibliographies Reprint Ser). 1931. 17.00 (ISBN 0-8369-5102-6). Arno.

MOORE, GEORGE EDWARD, 1873-1958

Ambrose, Alice. Essays in Analysis. (Muirhead Library of Philosophy). 1966. text ed. 13.50x (ISBN 0-04-110001-8). Humanities.

Ambrose, Alice & Lazerowitz, Morris, eds. G. E. Moore: Essays in Retrospect. (Muirhead Library of Philosophy). 1970. text ed. 12.75x (ISBN 0-04-192023-6). Humanities.

Ayer, Alfred J. Russell & Moore: The Analytical Heritage. LC 77-133216. (William James Lectures Ser: 1970). 1971. 15.00x (ISBN 0-674-78103-1). Harvard U Pr.

Goodwin, Gerain. Conversations with George Moore. LC 73-13738. 1940. lib. bdg. 17.50 (ISBN 0-8414-4440-4). Folcroft.

Hochberg, Herbert. Thought, Fact, & Reference: The Origins & Ontology of Logical Atomism. 1978. 24.50x (ISBN 0-8166-0867-9). U of Minn Pr.

Klemke, E. D. Epistemology of G. E. Moore. (Publications in Analytic Philosophy Ser). 1969. 11.95x (ISBN 0-8101-0001-0). Northwestern U Pr.

Levy, Paul. Moore: G. E. Moore & the Cambridge Apostles. (Illus.). 366p. 1981. pap. 6.95 (ISBN 0-19-281313-7, GB 631). Oxford U Pr.

--Moore: G. E. Moore & the Cambridge Apostles. LC 79-23106. (Illus.). 368p. 1980. 18.95 (ISBN 0-03-053616-2). HR&W.

Schilpp, Paul A., ed. & intro. by. The Philosophy of G. E. Moore. LC 68-57206. (Library of Living Philosophers: Vol. Iv). 727p. 1942. 25.00 (ISBN 0-87548-136-1); Vol. 1. pap. 7.95 (ISBN 0-87548-285-6); Vol. 2. pap. 6.95 (ISBN 0-87548-281-3). Open Court.

White, Alan R. G. E. Moore: A Critical Exposition. LC 78-26069. 1979. Repr. of 1969 ed. lib. bdg. 18.75x (ISBN 0-313-20805-0, WHGM). Greenwood.

Williams, I. A. George Moore. (Bibliographies of Modern Authors Ser: No. 3). lib. bdg. 8.50 (ISBN 0-8414-9734-6). Folcroft.

MOORE, GEORGE EDWARD, 1873-1958–ETHICS

Cavarnos, Constantine. A Dialogue on G. E. Moore's Ethical Philosophy: Together with an Account of Three Talks with Moore on Diverse Philosophical Questions. 1979. 5.95 (ISBN 0-914744-43-7); pap. 2.95 (ISBN 0-914744-44-5). Inst Byzantine.

Olthius, James H. Facts, Values & Ethics. 1968. pap. text ed. 18.00x (ISBN 9-0232-0487-5). Humanities.

Sarkar, Shukla. Epistemology & Ethics of G. E. Moore: A Critical Evaluation. 202p. 1981. text ed. 15.00x (ISBN 0-391-02266-0, Pub. by Concept Pub. Co. India). Humanities.

Soghoian, Richard J. The Ethics of G. E Moore & David Hume: The Treatise As a Response to Moore's Refutation of Ethical Naturalism. LC 79-88306. 1979. pap. text ed. 7.50 (ISBN 0-8191-0774-3). U Pr of Amer.

MOORE, HENRY SPENCER, 1898-

Finn, David & Moore, Henry. Henry Moore: Sculpture & Environment. LC 76-12588. (Illus.). 1977. 65.00 (ISBN 0-8109-1313-5). Abrams.

Gilmour, Pat. Henry Moore: Graphics in the Making. (Tate Gallery Art Ser.). (Illus.). 1977. pap. 8.95 (ISBN 0-8120-0851-0). Barron.

Jianou, Ionel. Henry Moore. (Illus.). 25.00 (ISBN 0-8283-1365-2). Branden.

Levine, Gemma, illus. With Henry Moore: The Artist at Work. LC 78-20689. (Illus.). 1979. 19.95 (ISBN 0-8129-0822-8). Times Bks.

Mitchinson, David, intro. by. Henry Moore: Prints 1969-1974. LC 75-25136. (Illus.). 1975. 3.50 (ISBN 0-88397-052-X). Intl Exhibit Foun.

Moore, Henry. Drawings of Henry Moore. (Master Draughtsman Ser). (Illus.). treasure trove bdg. 6.47x (ISBN 0-685-07261-4); pap. 2.95 (ISBN 0-685-07262-2). Borden.

--Henry Moore's Sheep Sketchbook. 1980. 19.95 (ISBN 0-500-23315-2). Thames Hudson.

--Sculpture & Drawings: 1964-73, Vol. 4. 1977. 32.50x (ISBN 0-8150-0695-0). Wittenborn.

Neumann, Erich. Archetypal World of Henry Moore. Hull, R. F., tr. (Bollingen Ser.: Vol. 68). (Illus.). 1959. 16.00x (ISBN 0-691-09702-X). Princeton U Pr.

Spender, Stephen. Henry Moore: Sculptures in Landscape. (Illus.). 1979. 25.00 (ISBN 0-517-53676-5, Dist. by Crown). Potter.

Tate Gallery. The Drawings of Henry Moore. 1981. pap. 15.95 (ISBN 0-8120-2063-4). Barron.

Teague, Edward H. Henry Moore: Bibliography & Reproductions Index. LC 80-28048. (Illus.). 183p. 1981. lib. bdg. 21.00x (ISBN 0-89950-016-1). McFarland & Co.

Wingfield, Digby C. Meaning & Symbol in Three Modern Artists: Edward Munch, Henry Moore, Paul Nash. LC 55-2585. 204p. 1955. Repr. 20.00 (ISBN 0-403-04167-8). Somerset Pub.

MOORE, MARIANNE CRAIG, 1887-

Abbott, Craig S. Marianne Moore: A Descriptive Bibliography. LC 76-5922. (Pittsburgh Ser. in Bibliography). 1977. 20.00x (ISBN 0-8229-3319-5). U of Pittsburgh Pr.

Costello, Bonnie. Marianne Moore: Imaginary Possessions. LC 81-1133. 320p. 1981. text ed. 18.50x (ISBN 0-674-54848-5). Harvard U Pr.

Engel, Bernard F. Marianne Moore. (Twayne's United States Authors Ser). 1964. pap. 3.45 (ISBN 0-8084-0210-2, T54, Twayne). Coll & U Pr.

Hadas, Pamela W. Marianne Moore: Poet of Affection. 1977. 16.95x (ISBN 0-8156-2162-0). Syracuse U Pr.

Hall, Donald. Marianne Moore: The Cage & the Animal. LC 71-114171. (American Authors Ser). 1970. 8.95 (ISBN 0-672-53560-2). Pegasus.

Lane, Gary. A Concordance to the Poems of Marianne Moore. LC 72-6438. (Reference Ser., No. 44). 1972. lib. bdg. 49.95 (ISBN 0-8383-1588-7). Haskell.

Nitchie, George W. Marianne Moore: An Introduction to the Poetry. LC 79-96998. (Introductions to 20th Century American Poetry Ser.). 205p. 1969. 15.00x (ISBN 0-231-03119-X); pap. 5.00x (ISBN 0-231-08312-2). Columbia U Pr.

Sheehy, Eugene P. & Lohf, Kenneth A. Achievement of Marianne Moore. 1958. lib. bdg. 8.50 (ISBN 0-8414-8096-6). Folcroft.

Stapleton, Laurence. Marianne Moore: The Poet's Advance. LC 78-51193. (Illus.). 1978. text ed. 21.00 (ISBN 0-691-06373-7). Princeton U Pr.

Weatherhead, A. Kingsley. The Edge of the Image: Marianne Moore, William Carlos Williams, & Some Other Poets. LC 67-21198. 265p. 1967. 12.50 (ISBN 0-295-97872-4). U of Wash Pr.

MOORE, THOMAS, 1779-1852

Burke, James. The Life of Thomas Moore. Repr. 25.00 (ISBN 0-8274-2901-0). R West.

Dowden, Wilfred S., ed. The Journal of Thomas Moore, Vol. 1. LC 79-13541. (Illus.). 700p. 1982. 50.00 (ISBN 0-87413-145-6). U Delaware Pr.

Gywnn, Stephen L. Thomas More. 204p. 1980. Repr. of 1905 ed. lib. bdg. 22.50 (ISBN 0-8495-2045-2). Arden Lib.

Harpsfield, Nicholas. Life & Death of St. Thomas More. Repr. of 1932 ed. 25.00 (ISBN 0-403-04140-6). Somerset Pub.

Jones, Howard M. Harp That Once: A Chronicle of the Life of Thomas Moore. LC 75-102508. (Illus.). 1970. Repr. of 1937 ed. 15.00 (ISBN 0-8462-1498-9). Russell.

Jordan, Hoover H. Bolt Upright: The Life of Thomas Moore, 2 vols. (Salzburg Studies in English Literature, Romantic Reassessment Ser.: No. 38). (Illus.). 666p. 1975. Set. pap. text ed. 50.25x (ISBN 0-391-01440-4). Humanities.

Maccall, Seamus. Thomas Moore. 1973. Repr. of 1935 ed. 20.00 (ISBN 0-8274-0109-4). R West.

Mackey, Herbert O. The Life of Thomas Moore. LC 73-11363. 1973. lib. bdg. 6.50 (ISBN 0-8414-5968-1). Folcroft.

Moore, Thomas. Thomas Moore Anecdotes, Being Anectodes, Bon-Mots, & Epigrams. LC 74-13039. (The Raconteur Ser: Vol. 1). 1974. Repr. of 1899 ed. lib. bdg. 25.00 (ISBN 0-8414-4848-5). Folcroft.

Pollard, Alfred W. Shakespeare's Hand in the Play of Sir Thomas Moore. LC 76-131803. 229p. 1923. Repr. 25.00 (ISBN 0-403-00690-2). Scholarly.

Strong, I. A. The Minstrel Boy: A Portrait of Tom Moore. 1973. Repr. of 1937 ed. 30.00 (ISBN 0-8274-0520-0). R West.

Symington, Andrew J. Thomas Moore the Poet: His Life & Works. 1880. lib. bdg. 12.50 (ISBN 0-8414-8011-7). Folcroft.

Trench, W. F. Tom Moore: A Lecture. 1973. Repr. of 1934 ed. 10.00 (ISBN 0-8274-0501-4). R West.

MOORE, THOMAS STURGE, 1870-1944

Gwynn, Frederick L. Sturge Moore & the Life of Art. 159p. 1980. Repr. of 1952 ed. lib. bdg. 30.00 (ISBN 0-89984-249-6). Century Bookbindery.

MacCall, Seamus. Thomas More. 1978. Repr. of 1935 ed. lib. bdg. 20.00 (ISBN 0-8495-3748-7). Arden Lib.

MOORE, WILL GRAYBURN

Howarth, W. D. & Thomas, J. Merlin, eds. Moliere: Stage & Study. 1973. 29.95x (ISBN 0-19-815712-6). Oxford U Pr.

MOORISH ARCHITECTURE

see Architecture, Islamic

MOORISH ART

see Art, Islamic

MOORISH LANGUAGE (INDIA)

see Urdu Language

MOORISH POTTERY

see Pottery, Islamic

MOORS AND HEATHS

see also Fens; Marshes; Peat Bogs

Gimingham, C. H. Ecology of Heathlands. 1976. 21.95x (ISBN 0-412-14980-X, Pub. by Chapman & Hall). Methuen Inc.

Heal, O. W. & Perkins, D. F., eds. Production Ecology of Some British Moors & Montane Grasslands. (Ecological Studies: Vol. 27). (Illus.). 1978. 49.80 (ISBN 0-387-08457-6). Springer-Verlag.

Odum, Howard T. & Ewel, Katherine C., eds. Cyprus Swamps. (Center for Wetlands Research Bks.). 1981. write for info. (ISBN 0-8130-0714-3). U Presses Fla.

MOOR'S INDIAN CHARITY SCHOOL, LEBANON, CONNECTICUT

McCallum, James D., ed. Letters of Eleazar Wheelock's Indians. LC 32-6653. (Dartmouth College Manuscript Ser.: No. 1). (Illus.). 327p. 1932. text ed. 4.00x (ISBN 0-87451-003-1). U Pr of New Eng.

Richardson, Leon B., ed. An Indian Preacher in England: Being Letters & Diaries Relating to the Mission of Reverend Samson Occom & the Reverend Nathaniel Whitaker to Collect Funds in England for the Benefit of Eleazar Wheelock's Indian Charity School from Which Grew Dartmouth College. LC 34-912. (Dartmouth College Manuscript Ser.: No. 2). (Illus.). 376p. 1933. text ed. 15.00x (ISBN 0-87451-004-X). U Pr of New Eng.

MOOSE

Jenkins, Marie M. Deer, Moose, Elk, & Their Family. LC 79-2111. (Illus.). 128p. (gr. 5 up). 1979. 8.95 (ISBN 0-8234-0362-9). Holiday.

Mason, George F. Moose Group. LC 68-25625. (Famous Museum Ser). (Illus.). (gr. 6-9). 1968. PLB 5.95 (ISBN 0-8038-4634-7). Hastings.

Peterson, Randolph L. North American Moose. LC 56-1401. 280p. 1955. pap. 17.50 (ISBN 0-8020-6349-7). U of Toronto Pr.

MOPEDS

Alth, Max. All About Mopeds. LC 78-2348. (Concise Guides Ser.). (Illus.). (gr. 7 up). 1978. PLB 6.90 (ISBN 0-531-01496-7). Watts.

Bleach, Mervyn. Moped Owners Workshop Manual: Garelli Mopeds. new ed. (Owners Workshop Manuals Ser.: No. 189). 1979. 8.50 (ISBN 0-85696-189-2, Pub. by J H Haynes England). Haynes Pubns.

Clew, Jeff. Puch Maxi Mopeds Owners Workshop Manual. new ed. (Owners Workshop Manuals Ser.: No. 107). 1979. 8.50 (ISBN 0-85696-107-8, Pub. by J H Haynes England). Haynes Pubns.

Coggins, Frank W. Moped Maintenance Manual. LC 78-24727. (Illus.). 1979. 12.50 (ISBN 0-89196-054-6, Domus Bks); pap. 6.95 (ISBN 0-89196-053-8). Quality Bks IL.

Darlington, Mansur. Mobylette Mopeds Owners Workshop Manuals. (Haynes Owners Workshop Manuals: No. 258). 1976. 8.50 (ISBN 0-85696-258-9, Pub by J H Haynes England). Haynes Pubns.

Schultz, Neil. The Complete Book of Safe Moped Operation & Repair. LC 78-18144. (Illus.). 1980. pap. 4.95 (ISBN 0-385-13531-9, Dolp). Doubleday.

Scott, Ed. Batavus Moped Owner Service-Repair: 1976-1978. (Illus., Orig.). pap. 6.00 (ISBN 0-89287-199-7, M438). Clymer Pubns.

Seever, R. Mopeds. LC 78-59252. (Free Time Fun Ser.). (Illus.). (gr. 5 up). 1979. PLB 6.99 (ISBN 0-8178-5871-7). Harvey.

MORA, JOSE MARIA LUIS, 1794-1850

Hale, Charles A. Mexican Liberalism in the Age of Mora, 1821-1853. LC 68-13908. (Caribbean Ser.: No. 11). 1968. 30.00x (ISBN 0-300-00531-8). Yale U Pr.

MORAINES

see also Glaciers

MORAL CONDITIONS

see also Crimes without Victims; Sex Customs; also subdivision Moral Conditions under names of countries, cities, etc., e.g. United States–Moral Conditions

Arthur, J. Morality & Moral Controversies. 1981. pap. 11.95 (ISBN 0-13-601278-7). P-H.

Beale, Lionel S. Our Morality & the Moral Question: From the Medical Side. LC 73-20615. (Sex, Marriage & Society Ser.). 208p. 1974. Repr. of 1887 ed. 14.00x (ISBN 0-405-05793-8). Arno.

Beehler, Rodger. Moral Life. 226p. 1978. 17.50x (ISBN 0-8476-6107-5). Rowman.

Calverton, V. F. Bankruptcy of Marriage. LC 76-169403. (Family in America Ser). 344p. 1972. Repr. of 1928 ed. 20.00 (ISBN 0-405-03852-6). Arno.

Dell, Floyd. Love in the Machine Age: A Psychological Study of the Transition from Patriarchal Society. LC 73-4608. 428p. 1973. Repr. of 1930 ed. lib. bdg. 20.00x (ISBN 0-374-92104-0). Octagon.

Durkheim, Emile. On Morality & Society. Bellah, Robert N., ed. (Heritage of Sociology Ser). 1973. 15.00x (ISBN 0-226-17335-6). U of Chicago Pr.

Ehlers, Martin. Betrachtungen Uber Die Sittlichkeit der Vergnugens, 2 vols. 1973. Repr. of 1779 ed. Set. 67.50 (ISBN 0-384-13970-1). Johnson Repr.

Garcia, John D. The Moral Society. LC 75-137086. (Illus.). 325p. 1974. 8.95 (ISBN 0-87426-033-7). Whitmore.

Graham, Douglas. Moral Learning & Development. 1974. pap. 17.95 (ISBN 0-7134-2842-2, Pub. by Batsford England). David & Charles.

Great Mortalities: Methodological Studies of Demographic Crises in the Past. 373p. 1980. pap. 45.00 (ISBN 2-87040-015-2, ORD 10, Ordina). Unipub.

Grisez, Germain & Shaw, Russell. Beyond the New Morality: The Responsibilities of Freedom. LC 73-17772. 240p. 1974. 7.95x (ISBN 0-268-00533-8). U of Notre Dame Pr.

Habermehl, Laurence. Morality in the Modern World. 1976. pap. text ed. 14.95x (ISBN 0-8221-0176-9). Dickenson.

Harkness, Georgia E. The Sources of Western Morality: From Primitive Society Through the Beginning of Christianity. LC 72-10723. Repr. of 1954 ed. 21.50 (ISBN 0-404-10643-9). AMS Pr.

Kant, Immanuel. The Doctrine of Virtue: Metaphysic of Morals, Pt. II. (Works in Contin. Philos. Ser.). 1971. 5.95x (ISBN 0-686-74243-5). U of Pa Pr.

Kirchwey, Freda, ed. Our Changing Morality, a Symposium. LC 78-169389. (Family in America Ser). 254p. 1972. Repr. of 1930 ed. 14.00 (ISBN 0-405-03866-6). Arno.

Kohlberg, Lawrence. The Philosophy of Moral Development: Essays in Moral Development, Vol. 1. LC 80-8902. 256p. 1981. 20.95 (ISBN 0-06-064760-4, HarpR). Har-Row.

Lickona, Thomas, et al, eds. Moral Development & Behavior: Theory, Research & Social Issues. LC 75-29471. 1976. text ed. 22.95 (ISBN 0-03-002811-6, HoltC). HR&W.

Long, John D. Ethics, Morality, & Insurance: A Long-Range Outlook. LC 71-633786. (Sesquicentennial Insurance Ser). 1971. 8.50 (ISBN 0-685-00047-8). Ind U Busn Res.

Macbeath, Alexander. Experiments in Living: A Study of the Nature & Foundation of Ethics or Morals in the Light of Recent Work in Social Anthropology. LC 77-27180. (Gifford Lectures: 1948-49). Repr. of 1952 ed. 28.00 (ISBN 0-404-60503-6). AMS Pr.

Neblett, William. The Role of Feelings in Morals. LC 81-40105. 114p. (Orig.). 1981. lib. bdg. 18.25 (ISBN 0-8191-1752-8); pap. text ed. 8.25 (ISBN 0-8191-1753-6). U Pr of Amer.

Peters, Charles C. Motion Pictures & Standards of Morality. LC 72-124030. (Literature of Cinema Ser.: Payne Fund Studies). Repr. of 1933 ed. 9.00 (ISBN 0-405-01648-4). Arno.

Rabinowics, Wlodzimierz. Universalizability. (Synthese Library: No. 141). 1979. lib. bdg. 24.00 (ISBN 90-277-1020-1, Pub. by Reidel Holland). Kluwer Boston.

Ruf, Henry L. Moral Investigations: An Introduction to Current Moral Problems. 1977. pap. text ed. 8.75 (ISBN 0-8191-0300-4). U Pr of Amer.

Tolstoy, Leo. Why Do Men Stupefy Themselves. (East Ridge Press). (Illus.). 168p. 1978. pap. 3.50 (ISBN 0-914896-08-3). Multimedia.

Wasserstrom, Richard. Today's Moral Problems. 2nd ed. 1979. pap. text ed. 11.95 (ISBN 0-02-424820-7). Macmillan.

MORAL EDUCATION

see also Christian Education; Religious Education

Arbuthnot, Jack & Faust, David. Teaching Moral Reasoning: Theory & Practice. (Illus.). 289p. 1980. text ed. 18.95 scp (ISBN 0-06-040321-7, HarpC). Har-Row.

Barrow, Robin. Moral Philosophy for Education. 214p. (Orig.). 1975. 17.50 (ISBN 0-208-01502-7, Linnet). Shoe String.

Bayliss, William B. An Evaluation of a Plan for Character Education Involving the Use of a Pledge, an Award & a Sponsor. LC 70-176545. (Columbia University. Teachers College. Contributions to Education: No. 695). Repr. of 1936 ed. 17.50 (ISBN 0-404-55695-7). AMS Pr.

Beechel, Edith E. A Citizenship Program for Elementary Schools. LC 70-176548. (Columbia University. Teachers College. Contributions to Education: No. 335). Repr. of 1929 ed. 17.50 (ISBN 0-404-55335-4). AMS Pr.

Berkowitz, Leonard. Development of Motives & Values in the Child. LC 64-20402. (Basic Topics in Psychology: Social Psychology). 1964. 6.95x (ISBN 0-465-01613-8). Basic.

Bull, Norman J. Moral Education. LC 77-101419. 190p. 1970. 15.00x (ISBN 0-8039-0039-2). Sage.

Burgess, Patricia. Erica's School on the Hill: A Child's Journey in Moral Growth. 1978. pap. 2.95 (ISBN 0-03-043911-6). Winston Pr.

Butts, R. Freeman & Peckenpaugh, Donald H. The School's Role As Moral Authority. LC 77-89087. 1977. pap. text ed. 4.50 (ISBN 0-87120-085-6, 611-77110). Assn Supervision.

Chapman, William E. Roots of Character Education: An Exploration of the American Heritage from the Decade of the 1920s. LC 77-84299. 1977. pap. 2.95 (ISBN 0-915744-08-2). Character Res.

Chase, Larry. The Other Side of the Report Card: A How-to-Do-It Program in Affective Education. LC 74-10233. 264p. 1976. pap. text ed. 10.95 (ISBN 0-87620-653-4). Goodyear.

Cochrane, Don & Manley-Casimir, Michael, eds. Development of Moral Reasoning: Practical Approaches. LC 80-17141. 352p. 1980. 29.95 (ISBN 0-03-056209-0). Praeger.

Cochrane, Don B., et al. The Domain of Moral Education. LC 79-54303. 312p. 1979. pap. 9.95 (ISBN 0-8091-2175-1). Paulist Pr.

Colquhoun, P. A New & Appropriate System of Education for the Labouring People. 98p. 1971. Repr. of 1806 ed. 15.00x (ISBN 0-7165-1773-6, Pub. by Irish Academic Pr Ireland). Biblio Dist.

Dewey, John. Moral Principles in Education. LC 74-18472. (Arcturus Books Paperbacks). 80p. 1975. pap. 2.95 (ISBN 0-8093-0715-4). S Ill U Pr.

Dreikurs, Rudolf. Character Education & Spiritual Values in an Anxious Age. (AAI Monograph Ser.: No. 1). 1971. Repr. of 1952 ed. pap. 2.00x (ISBN 0-918560-16-0). A Adler Inst.

Durkheim, Emile. Moral Education. LC 59-6815. 1961. 12.95 (ISBN 0-02-908330-3); pap. text ed. 4.95 (ISBN 0-02-908320-6). Free Pr.

Duska, Ronald & Whelan, Mariellen. Moral Development: a Guide to Piaget & Kohlberg. LC 75-20863. 1975. pap. 4.95 (ISBN 0-8091-1892-0). Paulist Pr.

Eisenberg, et al. Sex Education & the New Morality. 1967. pap. 1.95 (ISBN 0-686-12286-0). Jewish Bd Family.

Elder, Carl A. Values & Moral Development in Children. LC 76-28842. 1977. bds. 5.95 (ISBN 0-8054-6115-9). Broadman.

Faust, Clarence H. & Feingold, Jessica, eds. Approaches to Education for Character: Strategies for Change in Higher Education. LC 70-83386. 451p. 1969. 22.50x (ISBN 0-231-03262-5). Columbia U Pr.

Ford, Edward E. & Englund, Steven. For the Love of Children. LC 77-70561. 1977. 6.95 (ISBN 0-385-12958-0); pap. 2.95 (ISBN 0-385-12959-9, Anch). Doubleday.

Forisha, Bill E. & Forisha, Barbara. Moral Development & Education. LC 76-16272. 1976. pap. text ed. 2.25 (ISBN 0-88224-089-7). Cliffs.

Fraenkel, Jack R. How to Teach About Values: An Analytic Approach. (Illus.). 176p. 1977. text ed. 12.95x (ISBN 0-13-435446-X); pap. text ed. 9.95x (ISBN 0-13-435453-2). P-H.

Gustafson, James M. Moral Education. 7.95x (ISBN 0-674-58660-3); pap. 3.25x (ISBN 0-674-58661-1). Harvard U Pr.

Hake, Edward. A Touchstone for This Time Present. LC 74-80182. (English Experience Ser.: No. 663). 96p. 1974. Repr. of 1574 ed. 7.00 (ISBN 90-221-0663-2). Walter J Johnson.

Hall, Brian. Value Clarification As Learning Process: A Sourcebook for Educators. (Educator Formation Bks). (Orig.). 1974. pap. 8.95 (ISBN 0-8091-1773-8). Paulist Pr.

Hall, Brian P. Value Clarifications As Learning Process: A Guidebook for Educators. (Educator Formation Bks). (Illus., Orig.). 1974. pap. 8.95 (ISBN 0-8091-1796-7). Paulist Pr.

Hall, Robert & Davis, John. Moral Education in Theory & Practice. LC 75-21078. 189p. 1975. 10.95 (ISBN 0-87975-052-9). Prometheus Bks.

Hall, Robert T. Moral Education: A Handbook for Teachers. 1979. pap. 6.95 (ISBN 0-03-045686-X). Winston Pr.

Harmin, Merrill. What I've Learned About Values Education. LC 76-52075. (Fastback Ser.: No. 91). 1977. pap. 0.75 (ISBN 0-87367-091-4). Phi Delta Kappa.

Harmin, Merrill, et al. Clarifying Values Through Subject Matter: Applications for the Classroom. 1973. pap. 3.95 (ISBN 0-03-008241-2, 860). Winston Pr.

Harris, Alan. Teaching Morality & Religion. (Classroom Close-Ups Ser.). 1975. pap. text ed. 6.50x (ISBN 0-04-371030-1). Allen Unwin.

Helena, Ann. The Lie. LC 77-23395. (Moods & Emotions Ser.). (Illus.). (gr. k-3). 1977. PLB 10.25 (ISBN 0-8172-0958-1). Raintree Pubs.

Horne, Herman H. Essentials of Leadership & Other Papers in Moral & Religious Education. LC 76-117808. (Essay Index Reprint Ser). 1931. 12.00 (ISBN 0-8369-1660-3). Arno.

Howe, Leland W. & Howe, Mary M. Personalizing Education: Values Clarification & Beyond. 448p. (Orig.). 1975. pap. 8.95 (ISBN 0-89104-189-3). A & W Pubs.

Hyman, Herbert H. & Wright, Charles R. Education's Lasting Influence on Values. LC 78-23376. (Illus.). 1979. lib. bdg. 12.50x (ISBN 0-226-36542-5). U of Chicago Pr.

Jensen, Larry C. That's Not Fair! Helping Children Make Moral Decisions. LC 77-7248. (Illus.). (gr. k-2). 1977. pap. 8.95 (ISBN 0-8425-0752-3). Brigham.

Johnson, Henry C., Jr. The Public School & Moral Education. LC 80-20768. (The Education of the Public & the Public School Ser.). 96p. (Orig.). 1981. pap. 3.95 (ISBN 0-8298-0420-X). Pilgrim NY.

Jones, Henry. Essays on Literature & Education. 288p. 1980. Repr. of 1924 ed. lib. bdg. 30.00 (ISBN 0-8495-2757-0). Arden Lib.

Kay, William. Moral Education: A Sociological Study of the Influence of Society, Home & School. (Illus.). 383p. 1975. 17.50 (ISBN 0-208-01465-9, Linnet). Shoe String.

Kelly, A. V. & Downey, Meriel. Moral Education: Theory & Practice. 1978. text ed. 15.70 (ISBN 0-06-318079-0, IntlDept); pap. text ed. 9.25 (ISBN 0-06-318080-4, IntlDept). Har-Row.

Kirschenbaum, Howard. Advanced Value Clarification. LC 76-50695. 188p. (Orig.). 1977. pap. 12.95 (ISBN 0-88390-132-3). Univ Assocs.

Kniker, Charles. You & Values Education. (Educational Foundations Ser.). 1977. pap. text ed. 8.50 (ISBN 0-675-08516-0). Merrill.

Kreusler, Abraham A. Contemporary Education & Moral Upbringing in the Soviet Union. LC 76-19168. 1976. 25.50 (ISBN 0-8357-0184-0, SS-00017). Univ Microfilms.

Lande, Nathaniel & Slade, Afton. Stages: Understanding How You Make Your Moral Decisions. LC 78-195000. 1979. 8.95 (ISBN 0-06-250510-6, HarpR). Har-Row.

Lodge, Oliver. Parent & Child. a Treatise on the Moral & Religious Education of Children. (Educational Ser.). 1910. Repr. 15.00 (ISBN 0-685-43094-4). Norwood Edns.

Lovasik, Lawrence G. Clean Love in Courtship. 1974. pap. 1.00 (ISBN 0-89555-095-4, 158). TAN Bks Pubs.

McCluskey, Neil Gerard. Public Schools & Moral Education. LC 74-12848. 315p. 1975. Repr. of 1958 ed. lib. bdg. 17.50x (ISBN 0-8371-7762-6, MCPS). Greenwood.

McLenighan, Valjean. I Know You Cheated. LC 77-8623. (Moods & Emotions Ser.). (Illus.). (gr. k-3). 1977. PLB 10.25 (ISBN 0-8172-0962-X). Raintree Pubs.

Munsey, Brenda, ed. Moral Development, Moral Education, & Kohlberg. LC 80-50. 478p. (Orig.). 1980. pap. 12.95 (ISBN 0-89135-020-9). Religious Educ.

Musgrave, P. W. The Moral Curriculum: A Sociological Analysis. 1978. 13.95x (ISBN 0-416-85600-4); pap. 6.95x (ISBN 0-416-85620-9). Methuen Inc.

Orso, Kathryn W. Parenthood: A Commitment in Faith. LC 75-5219. 64p. (Orig.). 1975. pap. text ed. 2.95 (ISBN 0-8192-1198-2); tchr's ed. 3.75 (ISBN 0-8192-1204-0); wkbk. 3.95 (ISBN 0-8192-1199-0). Morehouse.

Pagliuso, Susan. Understanding Stages of Moral Development: A Programmed Learning Workbook. (Orig.). 1976. pap. 6.95 (ISBN 0-8091-1960-9). Paulist Pr.

Peabody, Elizabeth P. Record of a School. LC 74-89218. (American Education: Its Men, Institutions & Ideas, Ser. 1). 1969. Repr. of 1836 ed. 18.00 (ISBN 0-405-01457-0). Arno.

Peters, R. S. Moral Development & Moral Education. 192p. 1981. pap. text ed. 8.95x (ISBN 0-04-370107-8). Allen Unwin.

Phenix, Philip H. Education & the Common Good: A Moral Philosophy of the Curriculum. LC 77-22594. 1977. Repr. of 1961 ed. lib. bdg. 22.25x (ISBN 0-8371-9728-7, PHEC). Greenwood.

Piaget, Jean. Moral Judgment of the Child. 1932. 12.95 (ISBN 0-02-925230-X); pap. text ed. 6.95 (ISBN 0-02-925240-7). Free Pr.

Piediscalzi, N., et al. Distinguishing Moral Education, Values Clarification & Religion-Studies: Proceedings. Swyhart, B., ed. LC 76-26670. (American Academy of Religion. Section Papers). 1976. pap. 4.50 (ISBN 0-89130-082-1, 010918). Scholars Pr Ca.

Purpel, David & Ryan, Kevin, eds. Moral Education...It Comes with the Territory. LC 76-18041. xix, 424p. 1976. 13.50x (ISBN 0-8211-1516-2, Co-Pub. & Co-Distrib. by McCutchan). Phi Delta Kappa.

Purpel, David E. & Ryan, Kevin, eds. Moral Education: It Comes with the Territory. LC 76-18041. 1976. 21.00 (ISBN 0-8211-1516-2); text ed. 18.90x (ISBN 0-685-71410-1). McCutchan.

Read, D., et al. Health Education: The Search for Values. 1977. 13.50 (ISBN 0-13-384511-7). P-H.

Rugh, Charles E., et al. Moral Training in the Public Schools. (Educational Ser.). Repr. of 1907 ed. 5.50 (ISBN 0-685-43184-3). Norwood Edns.

Russell, Bertrand. Education & the Good Life. new ed. LC 73-114378. 1970. pap. 4.95 (ISBN 0-87140-012-X). Liveright.

Ryan, Kevin. Questions & Answers on Moral Education. LC 81-80011. (Fastback Ser.: No. 153). 1981. pap. 0.75 (ISBN 0-87367-153-8). Phi Delta Kappa.

Savary, Louis. Integrating Values. LC 74-14306. (Orig.). 1974. pap. 2.95 (ISBN 0-8278-9061-3). Pflaum Pr.

Sayre, Joan M. & Mack, James E. Teaching Moral Values Through Behaviour Modification: Primary Level. 1974. text ed. 7.95x (ISBN 0-8134-1615-9, 1615). Interstate.

Scharf, Peter. Moral Education. LC 78-51097. (Dialogue Bks). (Illus.). 1978. pap. 7.75 (ISBN 0-931364-02-7); wkbk. 4.75 (ISBN 0-685-67201-8). Intl Dialogue Pr.

Scharf, Peter, ed. Readings in Moral Education. 1978. pap. 9.95 (ISBN 0-03-021346-0). Winston Pr.

Silver, Michael. Values Education. 128p. 1976. pap. 4.75 (ISBN 0-686-63705-4, 1810-9-06). NEA.

Simon, Sidney, et al. Values, Concepts & Techniques. 312p. 1976. pap. 5.75 (ISBN 0-686-63704-6, 0705-0-06). NEA.

Spencer, Herbert. Education-Intellectual, Moral & Physical. (Educational Ser.). 1896. Repr. 20.00 (ISBN 0-685-43181-9). Norwood Edns.

Stiles, Lindley J. & Johnson, Bruce D., eds. Morality Examined: Guidelines for Teachers. LC 77-70106. 240p. 1977. pap. text ed. 7.95x (ISBN 0-916622-02-9). Princeton Bk Co.

Sullivan, Edmund V. Moral Learning. LC 74-31726. 1975. pap. 3.95 (ISBN 0-8091-1872-6). Paulist Pr.

Superka, Douglas P., et al. Values Education Sourcebook: Conceptual Approaches, Materials Analyses, & an Annotated Bibliography. 1976. pap. 11.95 (ISBN 0-89994-176-1). Soc Sci Ed.

Symons, Jelinger C. School Economy. LC 71-78973. (Social History of Education). Repr. of 1852 ed. 15.00x (ISBN 0-678-08460-2). Kelley.

Taylor, Monica. Progress & Problems in Moral Education. (General Ser.). 239p. 1975. pap. text ed. 17.50x (ISBN 0-85633-069-8, NFER). Humanities.

Thompson, Andrew D. When Your Child Learns to Choose. LC 78-73018. (When Bks). (Illus.). 1979. pap. 2.45 (ISBN 0-87029-145-9, 20228). Abbey.

Vivekananda, Swami. Education. pap. 1.50 (ISBN 0-87481-451-0). Vedanta Pr.

Wade, Francis C. Teaching & Morality. LC 63-17962. 1963. 2.95 (ISBN 0-8294-0080-X). Loyola.

Watt, J. Rational Moral Education. Selleck, R. J., ed. (Second Century in Australian Education Ser.). 1976. pap. 6.50x (ISBN 0-522-84102-3, Pub. by Melbourne U Pr). Intl Schol Bk Serv.

Whitney, William T. Moral Education. (Educational Ser.). 1915. Repr. 5.50 (ISBN 0-685-43652-7). Norwood Edns.

Yulish, Stephen M. The Search for a Civic Religion: A History of the Character Education Movement in America, Eighteen Ninety to Nineteen Thirty-Five. LC 80-5619. 318p. 1980. lib. bdg. 19.50 (ISBN 0-8191-1173-2); pap. text ed. 11.25 (ISBN 0-8191-1174-0). U Pr of Amer.

MORAL JUDGMENT

see Judgment (Ethics)

MORAL OFFENSES

see Crimes without Victims

MORAL PHILOSOPHY

see Ethics

MORAL THEOLOGY

see Christian Ethics

MORAL VIRTUES

see Virtue and Virtues

MORALE

see also Employee Morale; Military Discipline; Psychological Warfare; Psychology, Military; War-Psychological Aspects

Darwin, Charles R. The Descent of Man. 1902. 30.00 (ISBN 0-8274-2165-6). R West.

Gardner, John. Morale. 160p. 1980. pap. 3.45 (ISBN 0-393-00977-7). Norton.

MORALES, LUIS DE, CALLED EL DIVINO, 16TH CENTURY

Banks, Louis A. Poetry & Morals. 1900. Repr. 12.50 (ISBN 0-8274-3174-0). R West.

Trapier, Elizabeth D. Luis De Morales & Leonardesque Influences in Spain. (Illus.). 1953. 2.00 (ISBN 0-87535-079-8). Hispanic Soc.

MORALITIES

see also Drama, Medieval; Mysteries and Miracle-Plays

Bevington, David M., ed. The Macro Plays. LC 72-3905. 1972. 46.00 (ISBN 0-384-34920-X). Johnson Repr.

Eccles, Mark, ed. Macro Plays: The Castle of Perseverance, Wisdom, Mankind. (Early English Text Society Ser.). 1969. 12.95x (ISBN 0-19-722265-X). Oxford U Pr.

Happe, Peter, intro. by. Four Morality Plays. 1980. pap. 6.95 (ISBN 0-14-043119-5). Penguin.

Thompson, Elbert N. English Moral Plays. LC 70-131500. Repr. of 1910 ed. 7.00 (ISBN 0-404-06397-7). AMS Pr.

MORALITIES–HISTORY AND CRITICISM

Houle, Peter J. The English Morality & Related Drama: A Bibliographical Survey. LC 70-38714. 195p. 1972. 18.50 (ISBN 0-208-01264-8, Archon). Shoe String.

--The English Morality & Related Drama: A Bibliographical Survey. LC 70-38714. 195p. 1972. 18.50 (ISBN 0-208-01264-8, Archon). Shoe String.

MacKenzie, W. Roy. English Moralities from the Point of View of Allegory. LC 68-54172. (Studies in Drama, No. 39). 1969. Repr. of 1914 ed. lib. bdg. 33.95 (ISBN 0-8383-0592-X). Haskell.

MacKenzie, William R. The English Moralities from the Point of View of Allegory. (Harvard Studies in English). Repr. of 1914 ed. 19.50 (ISBN 0-384-34880-7). Johnson Repr.

--English Moralities from the Point of View of Allegory. LC 66-29466. 1966. Repr. of 1914 ed. 8.50 (ISBN 0-87752-066-6). Gordian.

Moore, E. Hamilton. English Miracle Plays & Moralities. LC 77-100517. Repr. of 1907 ed. 17.25 (ISBN 0-404-00598-5). AMS Pr.

Potter, Robert A. English Morality Play. 1975. 22.50x (ISBN 0-7100-8033-6). Routledge & Kegan.

MORALITIES, FRENCH

Fournier, Edouard, ed. Theatre Francais Avant La Renaissance, 1430-1550. 1965. Repr. of 1872 ed. 32.00 (ISBN 0-8337-1225-X). B Franklin.

MORALITY AND RELIGION

see Religion and Ethics

MORALS

see Conduct of Life; Ethics; Moral Conditions

MORALS AND ART

see Art and Morals

MORALS AND LAW

see Law and Ethics

MORALS AND LITERATURE

see Literature and Morals

MORALS AND MUSIC

see Music and Morals

MORALS AND WAR

see War and Morals

MORAN, THOMAS, 1837-1926

Clark, Carol. Thomas Moran: Watercolors of the American West. LC 80-13459. (Illus.). 192p. 1980. 25.00 (ISBN 0-292-75059-5). U of Tex Pr.

Priehs, Timothy J. Thomas Moran: The Grand Canyon Sketches. 1978. 4.95 (ISBN 0-938216-07-4). GCNHA.

MORAND, PAUL, 1888

Lemaitre, George. Four French Novelists: Marcel Proust, Andre Gide, Jean Giraudoux, Paul Morand. LC 68-8201. (Essay & General Literature Reprint Ser). 1969. Repr. of 1938 ed. 15.00 (ISBN 0-8046-0267-0). Kennikat.

MORANDI, GIORGIO

Klepac, Lou. Morandi Etchings. 1978. 40.00x (ISBN 0-85564-140-1, Pub. by U of W Austral Pr). Intl Schol Bk Serv.

MORAVIA, ALBERTO

see Pincherle, Alberto, 1914-

MORAVIAN INDIANS

see Indians of North America–Eastern States

MORAVIANS

see also Bohemian Brethren

Ankrum, Freeman. Sidelights on Brethren History. (Illus.). 174p. 1962. 2.75 (ISBN 0-87178-788-1). Brethren.

Buchner, J. H. The Moravians in Jamaica. facsimile ed. LC 77-178470. (Black Heritage Library Collection). Repr. of 1854 ed. 15.00 (ISBN 0-8369-8918-X). Arno.

Burkey, F. T., ed. The Brethren: Growth in Life & Thought. 1975. pap. 2.95x (ISBN 0-934970-00-9). Brethren Ohio.

Coad, F. Roy. A History of the Brethren Movement: Its Origins, Its Worldwide, and Its Significance for the Present Day. rev. ed. 1976. pap. 9.50 (ISBN 0-85364-164-1). Attic Pr.

Cumnock, Frances, ed. Catalog of the Salem Congregation Music. LC 79-15173. (Illus.). 682p. 1980. 30.00x (ISBN 0-8078-1398-2). U of NC Pr.

Dekan, Jan. Moravia Magna. Trebaticka, Heather, tr. (Illus.). 192p. 1981. 42.50 (ISBN 0-89893-084-7). CDP.

Durnbaugh, Donald F. The Brethren in Colonial America. (Illus.). 659p. (YA) 1967. 13.95 (ISBN 0-87178-110-7). Brethren.

--European Origins of the Brethren. 463p. 1958. 8.95 (ISBN 0-87178-256-1). Brethren.

Fliegel, Carl J., compiled by. Index to the Records of the Moravian Mission Among the Indians of North America, 2 vols. 1970. 375.00 (ISBN 0-89235-018-0). Res Pubns Conn.

Fries, Adelaide L., ed. Records of the Moravians in North Carolina, 7 vols. Incl. Vol. 1. 1752-1771. 511p. 1968. Repr. of 1922 ed (ISBN 0-86526-056-7); Vol. 2. 1752-1775. viii, 460p. 1968. Repr. of 1925 ed (ISBN 0-86526-057-5); Vol. 3. 1776-1779. viii, 513p. 1968. Repr. of 1926 ed (ISBN 0-86526-058-3); Vol. 4. 1780-1783. v, 471p. 1968. Repr. of 1930 ed (ISBN 0-86526-059-1); Vol. 5. 1784-1792. ix, 487p. 1970. Repr. of 1941 ed (ISBN 0-86526-060-5); Vol. 6. 1793-1808. x, 566p. 1970. Repr. of 1943 ed (ISBN 0-86526-061-3); Vol. 7. 1808-1822. x, 593p. 1970. Repr. of 1947 ed (ISBN 0-86526-062-1). (Illus.). 10.00 ea. Set (ISBN 0-86526-055-9). NC Archives.

Gollin, Gillian L. Moravians in Two Worlds: A Study of Changing Communities. LC 67-19653. 302p. 1967. 20.00x (ISBN 0-231-03033-9). Columbia U Pr.

Gombosi, Marilyn. A Day of Solemn Thanksgiving: Moravian Music for the Fourth of July, 1783, in Salem, North Carolina. LC 75-6533. 1977. 22.00x (ISBN 0-8078-1275-7). U of NC Pr.

Gray, Elma E. & Gray, Leslie R. Wilderness Christians: The Moravian Mission to the Delaware Indians. LC 72-84988. (Illus.). xiv, 354p. 1973. Repr. of 1956 ed. 22.00 (ISBN 0-8462-1701-5). Russell.

Hamilton, John T. A History of the Church Known As the Moravian Church. LC 70-134379. Repr. of 1900 ed. 37.50 (ISBN 0-404-08427-3). AMS Pr.

James, Hunter. The Quiet People of the Land: A Story of the North Carolina Moravians in Revolutionary Times. LC 75-44042. (Old Salem Ser). (Illus.). 1976. 8.50 (ISBN 0-8078-1282-X). U of NC Pr.

Latrobe, C. I. Journal of a Visit to South Africa in 1815-1816. (Illus.). 1969. Repr. of 1818 ed. 60.00x (ISBN 0-8426-1348-X). Verry.

Latrobe, Christian I. Journal of a Visit to South Africa, in Eighteen Fifteen & Eighteen Sixteen. LC 70-89040. Repr. of 1818 ed. 18.75x (ISBN 0-8371-1940-5, Pub. by Negro U Pr). Greenwood.

Lehman, James H. The Old Brethren. LC 76-20274. (Illus.). 1976. pap. 2.45 (ISBN 0-87178-650-8). Brethren.

McKinnell, James. Now About Peace. (Orig.). (gr. 5-6). 1971. pap. 1.50 (ISBN 0-87178-935-3). Brethren.

Miller, Vernon. Brethren Patriots Again. pap. 3.95 (ISBN 0-87178-315-0). Brethren.

Rau, Albert G. & David, Hans T. Catalogue of Music by American Moravians, 1742-1842. LC 76-134283. Repr. of 1938 ed. 14.00 (ISBN 0-404-07206-2). AMS Pr.

Records of the Moravians in North Carolina, 4 vols. Incl. Vol. 8. 1823-1837. Fries, Adelaide L. & Rights, Douglas L., eds. xi, 756p. 1954 (ISBN 0-86526-063-X); Vol. 9. 1838-1847. Smith, Minnie J., ed. xiii, 685p. 1964 (ISBN 0-86526-064-8); Vol. 10. 1841-1856. Hamilton, Kenneth G., ed. xviii, 626p. 1966 (ISBN 0-86526-065-6); Vol. 11. 1852-1879. Hamilton, Kenneth, ed. xvi, 524p. 1969 (ISBN 0-86526-066-4). (Illus.). 10.00 ea. NC Archives.

Reichel, Levin T. Moravians in North Carolina: An Authentic History. LC 68-19907. 1968. Repr. of 1857 ed. 12.50 (ISBN 0-8063-0292-5). Genealog Pub.

Roberts, Bruce. Old Salem in Pictures. (Illus., Orig.). 1968. pap. 3.95 (ISBN 0-87461-951-3). McNally.

Ronk, A. T. History of Brethren Missionary Movements. LC 70-184490. 1971. pap. 2.25x (ISBN 0-934970-02-5). Brethren Ohio.

--History of the Brethren Church. LC 68-23554. 1968. 6.95x (ISBN 0-934970-03-3). Brethren Ohio.

Sappington, Roger. The Brethren in the New Nation. (Illus.). 1976. 13.95 (ISBN 0-87178-113-1). Brethren.

Sessler, John J. Communal Pietism Among Early American Moravians. LC 70-134387. Repr. of 1933 ed. 19.50 (ISBN 0-404-08430-3). AMS Pr.

Smith, Defost. Martyrs of the Oblong & Little Nine. 1948. 6.00 (ISBN 0-910294-11-9). Brown Bk.

Steelman, Robert, ed. Catalog of the Lititz Congregation Collection. LC 80-27511. 670p. 1981. 40.00x (ISBN 0-8078-1477-6). U of NC Pr.

Towlson, Clifford W. Moravian & Methodist. 1957. 15.00x (ISBN 0-8401-2387-6, 8401-2387-6). Allenson-Breckinridge.

Yoder, Glee. Passing on the Gift. 1978. pap. 3.95 (ISBN 0-87178-689-3). Brethren.

MORAY JAMES STEWART, 1ST EARL OF, 1531-1570–FICTION

Lee, Maurice. James Stewart, Earl of Moray: A Political Study of the Reformation in Scotland. LC 73-104251. 1971. Repr. of 1953 ed. lib. bdg. 15.25x (ISBN 0-8371-3975-9, LEJS). Greenwood.

MORBID ANATOMY

see Anatomy, Pathological

MORE, BROOKES

Brewer, Wilmon. Life & Poems of Brookes More. (Illus.). 1980. 3.00 (ISBN 0-686-77552-X). M Jones.

MORE, HANNAH, 1745-1833

Harland, Marion. Hannah More. 1900. Repr. 20.00 (ISBN 0-8274-2461-2). R West.

Hopkins, Mary A. Hannah More & Her Circle. 1947. Repr. 25.00 (ISBN 0-8274-2464-7). R West.

Johnson, R. Brimley. The Letters of Hannah More. 1925. lib. bdg. 25.00 (ISBN 0-8482-9963-9). Norwood Edns.

Jones, Mary G. Hannah More. LC 69-10110. (Illus.). 1968. Repr. of 1952 ed. lib. bdg. 15.00x (ISBN 0-8371-0506-4, JOHM). Greenwood.

Knight, Helen C. A New Memoir of Hannah More. 1853. Repr. 40.00 (ISBN 0-8274-3025-6). R West.

Meakin, Annette M. Hannah More: A Biographical Study. 1911. Repr. 40.00 (ISBN 0-8274-2463-9). R West.

Roberts, William. Memoirs of the Life of Mrs. Hannah More. 472p. 1981. Repr. of 1839 ed. lib. bdg. 75.00 (ISBN 0-8495-4640-0). Arden Lib.

Thompson, Henry. The Life of Hannah More. 1838. Repr. 50.00 (ISBN 0-8274-2886-3). R West.

Yonge, Charlotte M. Hannah More. LC 76-17900. 1976. lib. bdg. 25.00 (ISBN 0-8414-9751-6). Folcroft.

MORE, PAUL ELMER, 1864-1937

Dakin, Arthur H. Paul Elmer Moore. (Illus.). 1960. 28.00 (ISBN 0-691-06089-4). Princeton U Pr.

Duggan, Francis X. Paul Elmer Moore. LC 66-24144. (United States Authors Ser.). 1966. lib. bdg. 12.95x (ISBN 0-8057-0524-4). Irvington.

--Paul Elmer More. (Twayne's United States Authors Ser). 1966. pap. 3.45 (ISBN 0-8084-0240-4, T106, Twayne). Coll & U Pr.

Hoeveler, J. David, Jr. The New Humanism: A Critique of Modern America, 1900-1940. LC 76-25168. 1977. 13.95x (ISBN 0-8139-0658-X). U Pr of Va.

McKean, Keith F. The Moral Measure of Literature. LC 73-2339. 137p. 1973. Repr. of 1961 ed. lib. bdg. 15.00 (ISBN 0-8371-6842-2, MCMM). Greenwood.

Shafer, Robert. Paul Elmer More & American Criticism. LC 75-41246. Repr. of 1935 ed. 21.50 (ISBN 0-404-14813-1). AMS Pr.

MORE, THOMAS, SIR, SAINT, 1478-1535

Adams, Robert P. Better Part of Valor: More, Erasmus, Colet & Vives on Humanism, War, & Peace, 1496-1535. LC 61-15064. (Illus.). 368p. 1962. 12.50 (ISBN 0-295-73722-0). U of Wash Pr.

Ames, Russell. Citizen Thomas More & His Utopia. LC 68-27046. 1969. Repr. of 1949 ed. 23.00 (ISBN 0-8462-1190-4). Russell.

Bridgett, Thomas E. Life & Writings of Sir Thomas More. 1976. 61.00 (ISBN 0-685-71991-X, Regency). Scholarly.

Campbell, William E. More's Utopia & His Social Teaching. LC 72-97533. 164p. 1973. Repr. of 1930 ed. 13.00 (ISBN 0-8462-1720-1). Russell.

Chambers, R. W. Place of Saint Thomas More in English Literature & History. LC 65-15870. (English Biography Ser., No. 31). 1969. Repr. of 1937 ed. lib. bdg. 28.95 (ISBN 0-8383-0523-7). Haskell.

--The Saga & the Myth of Sir Thomas More. 1978. Repr. of 1927 ed. lib. bdg. 10.00 (ISBN 0-8495-0744-8). Arden Lib.

Chambers, Raymond W. Saga & Myth of Sir Thomas More. 1926. lib. bdg. 8.50 (ISBN 0-8414-3642-8). Folcroft.

--Thomas More. 1958. pap. 6.95x (ISBN 0-472-06018-X, 18, AA). U of Mich Pr.

Donner, Henry W. Introduction to Utopia. LC 78-94268. (Select Bibliographies Reprint Ser). 1946. 16.00 (ISBN 0-8369-5042-9). Arno.

Elliott, John W. Monarch Notes on More's Utopia. (Orig.). pap. 1.95 (ISBN 0-671-00856-0). Monarch Pr.

The Family of Sir Thomas More: Facsimiles of the Drawings by Hans Holbein the Younger in the Royal Library, Windsor Castle. (Illus.). 1977. 65.00 (ISBN 0-685-88559-3). Johnson Repr.

Flower, B. O. The Century of Sir Thomas More. 1896. Repr. 50.00 (ISBN 0-8274-2018-8). R West.

Glunz, Hans. Shakespeare und Morus. Repr. of 1938 ed. pap. 17.00 (ISBN 0-384-18960-1). Johnson Repr.

Guy, J. A. The Public Career of Sir Thomas More. LC 80-5391. 224p. 1980. 25.00x (ISBN 0-300-02546-7). Yale U Pr.

Gwynn, Stephen. Thomas Moore. LC 73-13838. 1905. Repr. lib. bdg. 15.00 (ISBN 0-8414-4448-X). Folcroft.

Hexter, Jack H. More's Utopia: The Biography of an Idea. LC 76-15177. (History of Ideas Ser.: No. 5). 1976. Repr. of 1952 ed. lib. bdg. 15.50x (ISBN 0-8371-8947-0, HEMU). Greenwood.

Heywood, Ellis. Il Moro: Ellis Heywood's Dialogue in Memory of Thomas More. Deakins, Roger L., tr. LC 75-184107. 176p. 1972. 10.00x (ISBN 0-674-58735-9). Harvard U Pr.

Hogrefe, Pearl. The Sir Thomas More Circle: A Program of Ideas & Their Impact on Secular Drama. LC 59-10553. 1959. 22.50 (ISBN 0-252-72653-7). U of Ill Pr.

Hollis, Christopher. Thomas More. 1934. Repr. 20.00 (ISBN 0-8274-3614-9). R West.

Jenkins, Claude. Sir Thomas More. 1935. Repr. 20.00 (ISBN 0-8274-3431-6). R West.

Johnson, Robbin S. More's Utopia, Ideal & Illusion. LC 75-81421. (College Ser: No. 9). 1969. 12.50x (ISBN 0-300-01129-6). Yale U Pr.

Jones, Judith P. Thomas More. (English Authors Ser.: No. 247). 1979. lib. bdg. 9.95 (ISBN 0-8057-6711-8). Twayne.

--Thomas More. (Twayne English Authors Ser.). 1979. lib. bdg. 8.95 (ISBN 0-8057-6711-8). G K Hall.

Jordan, Hoover H. Bolt Upright: The Life of Thomas Moore, 2 vols. (Salzburg Studies in English Literature, Romantic Reassessment Ser.: No. 38). (Illus.). 666p. 1975. Set. pap. text ed. 50.25x (ISBN 0-391-01440-4). Humanities.

Kautsky, Karl. Thomas More & His Utopia. Stenning, H. J., tr. LC 59-10095. 1959. Repr. of 1890 ed. 15.00 (ISBN 0-8462-0214-X). Russell.

Lawler, Thomas, et al, eds. A Dialogue Concerning Heresies: The Yale Edition of the Complete Works of St. Thomas More, Vol. 6, Pts. 1 & 2. LC 63-7949. (Illus.). 910p. 1981. Set. text ed. 80.00x (ISBN 0-300-02211-5). Yale U Pr.

Maynard, Theodore. The Humanist As Hero: The Life of Sir Thomas More. 1971. Repr. of 1947 ed. 14.75 (ISBN 0-02-849040-1). Hafner.

Morgan, Arthur E. Nowhere Was Somewhere: How History Makes Utopias & Utopias Make History. LC 76-7481. (Illus.). 1976. Repr. of 1946 ed. lib. bdg. 15.25x (ISBN 0-8371-8881-4, MONO). Greenwood.

Morison, Stanley. Likeness of Thomas More: An Iconographical Survey of Three Centuries. Barker, Nicolas, ed. (Illus.). 1964. 32.50 (ISBN 0-8232-0575-4). Fordham.

Munday, Anthony & Shakespeare, William. Sir Thomas More. LC 74-133715. (Tudor Facsimile Texts. Old English Plays: No. 65). Repr. of 1910 ed. 31.50 (ISBN 0-404-53365-5). AMS Pr.

Paul, Leslie. Sir Thomas More. facsimile ed. LC 75-128882. (Select Bibliographies Ser). Repr. of 1953 ed. 16.00 (ISBN 0-8369-5502-1). Arno.

Priest, Harold M. More's Utopia & Utopian Literature Notes. 64p. (Orig.). 1975. pap. text ed. 1.95 (ISBN 0-8220-1318-5). Cliffs.

Quincentennial Essays on St. Thomas More: Selected Papers from the Thomas More College Conference. LC 78-67288. 11.95 (ISBN 0-932530-00-1). Albion NC.

Reynolds, E. Field Is Won. (Illus.). 1969. 6.50 (ISBN 0-685-07631-8, 80622). Glencoe.

Reynolds, E. E. The Life & Death of St. Thomas More: The Field Is Won. (Illus.). 1978. text ed. 16.50x (ISBN 0-06-495854-X). B&N.

Reynolds, Ernest E. Thomas More & Erasmus. LC 65-26739. 1966. 20.00 (ISBN 0-8232-0670-X). Fordham.

Roper, William & Harpsfield, Nicholas. Lives of St. Thomas More. Reynolds, E. E., ed. 1963. 8.95x (ISBN 0-460-00019-5, Evman). Biblio Dist.

Rupp, Gordon. Thomas More: The King's Good Servant. (Illus.). 1978. 14.95 (ISBN 0-529-05494-9, RB5494). Collins Pubs.

Saint German, Christopher. Salem & Bizance. LC 73-6156. (English Experience Ser.: No. 618). 216p. 1973. Repr. of 1533 ed. 14.00 (ISBN 90-221-0618-7). Walter J Johnson.

Sargent, Daniel. Thomas More. 299p. 1980. Repr. of 1933 ed. lib. bdg. 30.00 (ISBN 0-89984-412-X). Century Bookbindery.

--Thomas More. facs. ed. LC 71-119963. (Select Bibliographies Reprint Ser). 1933. 17.00 (ISBN 0-8369-5406-8). Arno.

Stewart, Agnes M. The Life & Letters of Sir Thomas More. 365p. 1981. Repr. of 1876 ed. lib. bdg. 50.00 (ISBN 0-89984-415-4). Century Bookbindery.

Sylvester, Richard. St. Thomas More - Action & Contemplation: Proceedings. Sylvester, Richard S., ed. 1972. 15.00x (ISBN 0-300-01507-0). Yale U Pr.

Sylvester, Richard & Marc'Hadour, Germaine. Essential Articles for the Study of Thomas More. (Essential Articles Ser.). 1977. 20.00 (ISBN 0-208-01554-X, Archon). Shoe String.

Sylvester, Richard S. & Harding, Davis P., eds. Two Early Tudor Lives. Incl. The Life & Death of Cardinal Wolsey. Cavendish, George; The Life of Sir Thomas More. Roper, William. xxi, 260p. 1962. 20.00x (ISBN 0-300-00985-2); pap. 5.95x (ISBN 0-300-00239-4, Y81). Yale U Pr.

Teetgen, A. B. The Footsteps of Sir Thomas More. 126p. 1981. Repr. of 1930 ed. lib. bdg. 40.00 (ISBN 0-89984-473-1). Century Bookbindery.

Trapp, J. B. & Herbruggen, Hubertus. The King's Good Servant, Sir Thomas More 1477-1535. (Illus.). 147p. 1977. 25.00x (ISBN 0-8476-6032-X). Rowman.

Tyndale, William. An Answer to Sir Thomas More's Dialogue, the Supper of the Lord After the True Meaning of John 6 & or. 11. Repr. of 1850 ed. 25.50 (ISBN 0-384-62240-2). Johnson Repr.

Willow, Sr. Mary E. An Analysis of the English Poetry of St. Thomas More. (Bibliotheca Humanistica & Reformatorica: No. 8). 1974. text ed. 44.00x (ISBN 90-6004-316-2). Humanities.

Wilson, Derek. England in the Age of Thomas More. (Illus.). 1980. text ed. 15.50x (ISBN 0-246-10943-2). Humanities.

MORE, THOMAS, SIR, SAINT, 1478-1535–DRAMA

Bolt, Robert. Man for All Seasons. 1962. 8.95 (ISBN 0-394-40623-0). Random.

--Man for All Seasons. 1966. pap. 1.95 (ISBN 0-394-70321-9, V321, Vin). Random.

MOREAU, GUSTAV, 1826-1898

Mathieu, Pierre-Louis. Gustave Moreau: With a Catalogue of the Finished Paintings, Watercolors, & Drawings. LC 76-21928. (Illus.). 1977. 75.00 (ISBN 0-8212-0701-6, 332542). NYGS.

Moreau. (Selected Artist Art Ser). (Illus.). 1977. pap. 5.95 o. p. (ISBN 0-8120-0812-X). Barron.

Selz, Jean. Gustave Moreau. (Q. L. P. Ser.). (Illus.). 1979. 6.95 (ISBN 0-517-53449-5). Crown.

MOREAU DE SAINT-MERY, 1750-1819

Roberts, Kenneth & Roberts, Anna M., eds. Moreau De St. Mery's American Journey, 1793-1798. 5.00 (ISBN 0-385-04307-4). Doubleday.

MORELLI, DOMENICO, d. 1901

Villari, Pasquale. Studies, Historical & Critical. facs. ed. Villari, L., tr. LC 68-16983. (Essay Index Reprint Ser). 1968. Repr. of 1907 ed. 18.00 (ISBN 0-8369-0960-7). Arno.

MORELOS Y PAVON, JOSE MARIA TECLO, 1765-1815

Caruso, J. A. The Liberators of Mexico. (Illus.). 8.75 (ISBN 0-8446-1105-0). Peter Smith.

Timmons, Wilbert H. Morelos of Mexico: Priest, Soldier, Statesman. 1970. 6.00 (ISBN 0-87404-004-3). Tex Western.

MORES, ANTOINE AMEDEE MARIE VINCENT MANCA DE VALLAMBROSA, MARQUIS DE, 1858-1896

Dresden, Donald. Marquis De Mores: Emperor of the Badlands. LC 69-16720. (Illus.). 1970. 13.95x (ISBN 0-8061-0869-X). U of Okla Pr.

Tweton, D. Jerome. The Marquis De Mores: Dakota Capitalist, French Natinalist. LC 72-619655. (Illus.). 249p. 1972. 8.95 (ISBN 0-911042-17-2). N Dak Inst.

MORETO Y CAVANA, AUGUSTIN, 1618-1669

Casa, Frank P. Dramatic Craftsmanship of Moreto. LC 66-18244. (Studies in Romance Languages: No. 29). 1966. 10.00x (ISBN 0-674-21550-8). Harvard U Pr.

Castaneda, James A. Agustin Moreto. (World Authors Ser.: Spain: No. 308). 1974. lib. bdg. 12.50 (ISBN 0-8057-2633-0). Twayne.

MORGAN, CHARLES, 1795-1878

Baughman, James P. Charles Morgan & the Development of Southern Transportation. LC 68-17281. (Illus.). 1968. 10.95 (ISBN 0-8265-1114-7). Vanderbilt U Pr.

Duffin, Henry C. Novels & Plays of Charles Morgan. 1973. lib. bdg. 30.00 (ISBN 0-8414-3865-X). Folcroft.

MORGAN, DANIEL, 1736-1802

Callahan, North. Daniel Morgan: Ranger of the Revolution. LC 71-161759. Repr. of 1961 ed. 14.50 (ISBN 0-404-09017-6). AMS Pr.

Campbell, Thomas F. Daniel E. Morgan, 1877-1949: The Good Citizen in Politics. (Illus.). 1966. 10.00 (ISBN 0-8295-0054-5). UPB.

Higginbotham, Don. Daniel Morgan: Revolutionary Rifleman. 1961. 16.95 (ISBN 0-8078-0824-5); pap. 6.00 (ISBN 0-8078-1386-9). U of NC Pr.

MORGAN, EDWIN DENISON, 1811-1883

Rawley, James A. Edwin D. Morgan, 1811-1833: Merchant in Politics. LC 68-59261. (Columbia University. Studies in the Social Sciences: No. 582). Repr. of 1955 ed. 22.50 (ISBN 0-404-51582-7). AMS Pr.

MORGAN, GEORGE, 1743-1810

Savelle, Max. George Morgan: Colony Builder. LC 32-30652. Repr. of 1932 ed. 14.00 (ISBN 0-404-05567-2). AMS Pr.

MORGAN, GILBERT, 1842-1909

Boatright, Mody C. Gib Morgan: Minstrel of the Oil Fields. LC 46-815. (Texas Folklore Society Publications: No. 20). (Illus.). 1965. Repr. of 1945 ed. 5.00 (ISBN 0-87074-008-3). SMU Press.

MORGAN, HENRY, SIR, 1635-1688

Howard, Edward G. Sir Henry Morgan, the Buccaneer, 3 vols. in 2. LC 79-8136. Repr. of 1842 ed. Set. 84.50 (ISBN 0-404-61923-1). Vol. 1 (ISBN 0-404-61924-X). Vol. 2 (ISBN 0-404-61925-8). AMS Pr.

Pope, Dudley. The Buccaneer King: The Biography of the Notorious Sir Henry Morgan, 1635-1688. LC 76-12156. (Illus.). 1978. 11.95 (ISBN 0-396-07566-5). Dodd.

MORGAN, JOHN HUNT, 1825-1864

Duke, Basil W. History of Morgan's Cavalry. LC 60-8607. (Indiana University Civil War Centennial Ser.). (Illus.). 1968. Repr. of 1960 ed. write for info. (ISBN 0-527-25500-9). Kraus Repr.

Thomas, Edison H. John Hunt Morgan & His Raiders. LC 75-3553. (Kentucky Bicentennial Bookshelf Ser.). (Illus.). 136p. 1975. 6.95 (ISBN 0-8131-0214-6). U Pr of Ky.

MORGAN, JOHN PIERPONT, 1837-1913

Canfield, Cass. The Incredible Pierpont Morgan: Financier & Art Collector. LC 73-15000. (Illus.). 176p. 1974. 17.50 (ISBN 0-06-010599-2, HarpT). Har-Row.

--Outrageous Fortunes: The Story of the Medici, the Rothschilds, & J. Pierpont Morgan. LC 80-24299. (Illus.). 108p. 1981. 10.95 (ISBN 0-15-170513-5). HarBraceJ.

Corey, Lewis. House of Morgan. LC 78-94469. Repr. of 1930 ed. 32.50 (ISBN 0-404-01728-2). AMS Pr.

Hovey, Carl. The Life of J. Pierpont Morgan. facsimile ed. (Select Bibliographies Reprint Ser). Repr. of 1912 ed. 21.00 (ISBN 0-8369-6692-9). Arno.

Satterlee, Herbert L. J. Pierpont Morgan: An Intimate Portrait. facsimile ed. LC 75-2667. (Wall Street & the Security Market Ser.). (Illus.). 1975. Repr. of 1939 ed. 40.00x (ISBN 0-405-07230-9). Arno.

Sinclair, Andrew. Corsair: The Life of J. Pierpont Morgan. 1981. 15.00 (ISBN 0-316-79240-3). Little.

MORGAN, JOHN PIERPONT, 1867-1943

Forbes, John D. J. P. Morgan, Jr., Eighteen Sixty-Seven to Nineteen Forty-Three. LC 81-1787. 1981. price not set (ISBN 0-8139-0889-2). U Pr of Va.

MORGAN, LEWIS HENRY, 1818-1881

Resek, Carl. Lewis Henry Morgan, American Scholar. (Midway Reprint Ser). (Illus.). 1974. pap. 8.00x (ISBN 0-226-71012-2). U of Chicago Pr.

Stern, Bernhard J. Lewis Henry Morgan, Social Evolutionist. LC 66-24763. 1967. Repr. of 1931 ed. 7.50 (ISBN 0-8462-0855-5). Russell.

MORGAN, SYDNEY (OWENSON) LADY, 1783-1859

Morgan, Sydney O. Lady Morgan's Memoirs, 2 vols. LC 76-37705. (Women of Letters Ser.). Repr. of 1862 ed. Set. 87.50 (ISBN 0-404-56793-2). AMS Pr.

Stevenson, Lionel. Wild Irish Girl: The Life of Sydney Owenson, Lady Morgan, 1776-1859. LC 68-27864. (Illus.). 1969. Repr. of 1936 ed. 11.00 (ISBN 0-8462-1217-X). Russell.

MORGAN, THOMAS, 1543-1606

Hicks, Leo. Elizabethan Problem: Some Aspects of the Careers of Two Exile-Adventurers. LC 64-24786. 1965. 22.50 (ISBN 0-8232-0625-4). Fordham.

MORGAN FAMILY

Corey, Lewis. House of Morgan. LC 78-94469. Repr. of 1930 ed. 32.50 (ISBN 0-404-01728-2). AMS Pr.

MORGAN HORSE

Henry, Marguerite. Justin Morgan Had a Horse. LC 54-8903. (Illus.). (gr. 2-9). 1954. 6.95 (ISBN 0-528-82255-1); pap. 2.95 (ISBN 0-528-87682-1). Rand.

Mellin, Jeanne. Morgan Horse. LC 61-13021. (Illus.). 1961. pap. 7.95 (ISBN 0-8289-0153-8). Greene.

Pittenger, Peggy J. Morgan Horses. LC 67-15768. (Illus.). 1967. 7.50 (ISBN 0-668-02797-5). Arco.

Self, Margaret C. Morgan Horse in Pictures. pap. 2.00 (ISBN 0-87980-236-7). Wilshire.

MORGAN LE FAY

Paton, Lucy A. Studies in the Fairy Mythology of Arthurian Romance. 2nd enl. ed. Loomis, Roger S., ed. 1963. 22.50 (ISBN 0-8337-2683-8). B Franklin.

MORGAN'S CALVARY DIVISION (C.S.A.)

Duke, Basil W. History of Morgan's Cavalry. LC 60-8607. (Indiana University Civil War Centennial Ser.). (Illus.). 1968. Repr. of 1960 ed. write for info. (ISBN 0-527-25500-9). Kraus Repr.

MORGAN'S RAID, 1863

Thomas, Edison H. John Hunt Morgan & His Raiders. LC 75-3553. (Kentucky Bicentennial Bookshelf Ser.). (Illus.). 136p. 1975. 6.95 (ISBN 0-8131-0214-6). U Pr of Ky.

MORGANTOWN, WEST VIRGINIA-FIRST CHRISTIAN CHURCH

Core, Earl L. Morgantown Disciples. (Illus.). 1960. 8.00 (ISBN 0-87012-024-7). McClain.

MORGENTHAU, HENRY, 1891-1967

Everest, Allan S. Morgenthau, the New Deal & Silver. LC 72-2368. (FDR & the Era of the New Deal Ser.). 209p. 1973. Repr. of 1950 ed. lib. bdg. 25.00 (ISBN 0-306-70469-2). Da Capo.

MORGUES

Arco Editorial Board. Mortuary Caretaker. LC 74-31666. 1975. pap. 6.00 (ISBN 0-668-01354-0). Arco.

MORGUES (NEWSPAPER LIBRARIES)

see Newspaper Office Libraries

MORIKE, EDUARD

see Moerike, Eduard, 1804-1875

MORISCOS

Here are entered works on Muslims in Spain after about 1492 who were converted to Christianity by decree. Works on Muslims living in Spain under Christian protection before 1492 who did not convert to Christianity are entered under the heading Mudejares. Works including both Mudejares and Moriscos are entered under Moriscos.

Lea, Henry C. Moriscos of Spain. LC 68-56783. 1968. Repr. of 1901 ed. 20.50 (ISBN 0-8337-4218-3). B Franklin.

--Moriscos of Spain: Their Conversion & Expulsion. 1968. Repr. of 1901 ed. lib. bdg. 23.50x (ISBN 0-8371-0141-7, LEMS). Greenwood.

--Moriscos of Spain, Their Conversion & Expulsion. LC 68-26358. (Studies in Spanish Literature, No. 36). 1969. Repr. of 1901 ed. lib. bdg. 51.95 (ISBN 0-8383-0266-1). Haskell.

MORISON, STANLEY

Barker, Nicolas J. Stanley Morison. LC 76-189157. (Illus.). 1972. 30.00x (ISBN 0-674-83425-9). Harvard U Pr.

MORISOT, BERTHE, 1841-1895

Valery, Paul. Collected Works of Paul Valery, Vol. 12, Degas, Manet, Morisot. Matthews, Jackson, ed. Paul, David, tr. (Bollingen Ser.: Vol. 45). 1960. 15.00 (ISBN 0-691-09839-5). Princeton U Pr.

MORIZ VON CRAUN (ROMANCE)

Anderson, Robert R., ed. Wortindex und Reimregister Zum Moriz Von Craun. (Indices Verborumzum Altdeutschen Schrifttum: No. 2). (Orig., Ger.). 1976. pap. text ed. 12.00x (ISBN 90-6203-457-8). Humanities.

MORLEY, CHRISTOPHER DARLINGTON, 1890-1957

Keats-Wilde-Morley-Rosenbach. 1977. pap. 4.50 (ISBN 0-939084-03-1). Rosenbach Mus and Lib.

Oakley, Helen McK. Three Hours for Lunch: The Life & Times of Christopher Morley. LC 75-39492. 1976. 12.00 (ISBN 0-88370-005-0). Watermill Pubs.

Wallach, Mark I. & Bracker, Jon. Christopher Morley. LC 76-17922. (U.S. Authors Ser.: No. 278). 1976. lib. bdg. 10.95 (ISBN 0-8057-7178-6). Twayne.

MORLEY, JOHN, VISCOUNT, 1838-1923

Alexander, Edward. John Morley. (English Authors Ser.: No. 147). lib. bdg. 10.95 (ISBN 0-8057-1404-9). Twayne.

Braybrooke, Patrick. Lord Morley: Writer & Thinker. Repr. 17.50 (ISBN 0-8274-3862-1). R West.

--Lord Morley: Writer & Thinker. 1978. Repr. lib. bdg. 25.00 (ISBN 0-89760-035-5, Telegraph). Dynamic Learn Corp.

Hirst, Francis W. Early Life & Letters of John Morley, 2 vols. LC 75-23069. Repr. of 1927 ed. 67.50 set (ISBN 0-404-14060-2). AMS Pr.

Knickerbocker, Frances W. Free Minds: John Morley & His Friends. Repr. of 1943 ed. lib. bdg. 15.00x (ISBN 0-8371-2803-X, KNFM). Greenwood.

Morley, John. Recollections, 2 vols. 1978. Repr. of 1917 ed. lib. bdg. 50.00 (ISBN 0-8495-3727-4). Arden Lib.

--Recollections, 2 vols. LC 75-30034. Repr. of 1917 ed. 49.50 set (ISBN 0-404-14080-7). AMS Pr.

Wolpert, Stanley A. Morley & India 1906-1910. 1967. 24.50x (ISBN 0-520-01360-3). U of Cal Pr.

MORLEY, THOMAS, 1552-1603

Murphy, Catharine A. Thomas Morley: Editions of Italian Canzonets & Madrigals, 1597-98. LC 64-64160. (Florida State U. Studies: No. 42). 1964. 12.00 (ISBN 0-8130-0480-2). U Presses Fla.

MORMON TABERNACLE CHOIR

Calman, Charles J. & Kaufman, William. The Morman Tabernacle Choir. LC 79-1656. (Illus.). 1979. 14.95 (ISBN 0-06-010624-7, HarpT). Har-Row.

Petersen, Gerald A. More than Music: The Mormon Tabernacle Choir. LC 79-21122. (Illus., Orig.). 1979. pap. 7.95 (ISBN 0-8425-1736-7). Brigham.

MORMON TRAIL

Jones, Helen H. Over the Mormon Trail. LC 63-9706. (Frontiers of America Ser.). (Illus.). 128p. (gr. 3-10). 1980. PLB 8.60 (ISBN 0-516-03354-9). Childrens.

Kimball, Stanley B. Discovering Mormon Trails. LC 79-53092. 1979. 4.95 (ISBN 0-87747-756-6). Deseret Bk.

Richards, Aurelia. The Mormon Trail: In Story Form. pap. 5.95 (ISBN 0-89036-137-1). Hawkes Pub Inc.

Stegner, Wallace. Gathering of Zion: The Story of the Mormon Trail. (American Trails Ser). 1964. (GB); pap. 4.50 (ISBN 0-07-060981-0). McGraw.

MORMONS AND MORMONISM

see also Book of Mormon; Church of Jesus Christ of Latter-Day Saints; Mountain Meadows Massacre, 1857; Utah Expedition, 1857-1858

Alexander, Thomas G., ed. The Mormon People: Their Character & Traditions. (Charles Redd Monographs in Western History Ser.: No. 10). 120p. 1980. pap. 6.95 (ISBN 0-8425-1834-7). Brigham.

Allen, Edward J. The Second United Order Among the Mormons. LC 73-38483. (Columbia University Studies in the Social Sciences: No. 419). Repr. of 1936 ed. 15.00 (ISBN 0-404-51419-7). AMS Pr.

Andrew, Laurel B. The Early Temples of the Mormons: The Architecture of the Millennial Kingdom in the American West. LC 77-23971. (Illus.). 1978. 16.50 (ISBN 0-87395-358-4). State U NY Pr.

Answers for Young Latter-Day Saints. 5.95 (ISBN 0-87747-645-4). Deseret Bk.

Austin, Mildred C. Woman's Divine Destiny. LC 78-21274. 1979. 5.95 (ISBN 0-87747-733-7). Deseret Bk.

Bailey, F. My Summer in a Mormon Village. 59.95 (ISBN 0-8490-0692-9). Gordon Pr.

Barbour, Hugh. Margaret Fell Speaking. LC 76-4224. (Orig.). 1976. pap. 0.95x (ISBN 0-87574-206-8). Pendle Hill.

Barnes, Kathleen H. & Pearce, Virginia H. Forever & Ever. LC 75-28899. (Illus.). (gr. 4). 1975. 4.95 (ISBN 0-87747-603-9). Deseret Bk.

Barrett, Ivan J. Joseph Smith & the Restoration: A History of the LDS Church to 1846. rev. ed. LC 70-167990. (Illus.). 1973. pap. 9.95 (ISBN 0-8425-0672-1). Brigham.

Barron, Howard H. Judah, Past & Future: LDS Teachings Concerning God's Covenant People. LC 79-89350. 1979. 8.95 (ISBN 0-88290-121-4). Horizon Utah.

Beardall, Douglas & Beardall, Jewel, eds. Qualities of Love. (Orig.). 1978. pap. 3.95 (ISBN 0-89036-110-X). Hawkes Pub Inc.

Bennett, John C. The History of the Saints: Or an Expose of Joe Smith & Mormonism. 1976. Repr. of 1842 ed. 42.00 (ISBN 0-403-06649-2, Regency). Scholarly.

Berrett, William E. Restored Church. 8.95 (ISBN 0-87747-228-9). Deseret Bk.

Bitton, Davis. Guide to Mormon Diaries & Autobiographies. LC 77-1138. 1977. 12.95 (ISBN 0-8425-1478-3). Brigham.

Bjornstad, James. Counterfeits at Your Door. LC 78-72864. 1979. pap. text ed. 1.95 (ISBN 0-8307-0610-0, S124254). Regal.

Black, William T. Mormon Athletes. (Illus.). 6.95 (ISBN 0-87747-842-2). Deseret Bk.

The Book of Mormon: An Account Written by the Hand of Mormon, Upon Plates Taken from the Plates of Nephi. 1976. Repr. of 1830 ed. 74.00 (ISBN 0-685-70648-6, Regency). Scholarly.

Bradford, Mary L., ed. Mormon Women Speak. 1981. price not set (ISBN 0-913420-94-8). Olympus Pub Co.

Breeze, Janet. Articles of Faith for Children. 2.50 (ISBN 0-87747-017-0). Deseret Bk.

Bringhurst, Newell G. Saints, Slaves, & Blacks: The Changing Place of Black People Within Mormonism. LC 81-1093. (Contributions to the Study of Religion Ser.: No. 4). (Illus.). 256p. 1981. lib. bdg. 27.50 (ISBN 0-313-22752-7, BSB/). Greenwood.

Brough, R. Clayton. His Servants Speak: Statements by Latter-day Saint Leaders on Contemporary Topics. LC 75-17101. 298p. 1975. 9.50 (ISBN 0-88290-054-4). Horizon Utah.

Cannon, George Q. Writings from the "Western Standard". Repr. of 1864 ed. 25.00 (ISBN 0-404-01379-1). AMS Pr.

Charriere, Doris T. Hidden Treasures of the Word of Wisdom. (Orig.). 1978. pap. 5.50 (ISBN 0-89036-106-1). Hawkes Pub Inc.

Christensen, Leon N. The Little Book: Why I Am a Mormon. 1976. 12.50 (ISBN 0-8283-1606-6). Branden.

Clark, J. Reuben, Jr. Why the King James Version. LC 79-15008. (Classics in Mormon Literature Ser.). 535p. 1979. 7.95 (ISBN 0-87747-773-6). Deseret Bk.

Clayton, William. The Latter-Day Saints' Emigrant's Guide. LC 68-25859. 24p. pap. 2.25 (ISBN 0-685-37632-X). Vic.

--William Clayton's Journal: A Daily Record of the Journey of the Original Company of Mormon Pioneers from Nauveo, Illinois, to the Valley of the Great Salt Lake. LC 72-9435. (The Far Western Frontier Ser.). 380p. 1973. Repr. of 1921 ed. 20.00 (ISBN 0-405-04965-X). Arno.

Codman, John T. Mormon Country. LC 70-134392. Repr. of 1874 ed. 18.25 (ISBN 0-404-08481-8). AMS Pr.

Coleman, Gary J. A Look at Mormonism. pap. 3.95 (ISBN 0-89036-142-8). Hawkes Pub Inc.

Conkling, J. Christopher. Joseph Smith Chronology. LC 79-896. 1979. 6.95 (ISBN 0-87747-734-5). Deseret Bk.

Covey, Stephen R. Spiritual Roots of Human Relations. 1979. pap. 2.50 (ISBN 0-87747-742-6). Deseret Bk.

Cowan, Marvin W. Los Mormones: Sus Doctrinas Refutadas a la Luz De la Biblia. De La Fuente, Tomas, tr. from Eng. 1978. pap. 2.95 (ISBN 0-311-05763-2). Casa Bautista.

Creer, Leland H. Mormon Towns in the Region of the Colorado. Incl. The Activities of Jacob Hamblin in the Region of the Colorado. (Glen Canyon Ser.: Nos. 3-4). Repr. of 1958 ed. 20.00 (ISBN 0-404-60633-4). AMS Pr.

Crossfield, R. C. Book of Onias. LC 70-86503. 1969. 3.50 (ISBN 0-8022-2290-0). Philos Lib.

Crouch, Brodie. The Myth of Mormon Inspiration. 6.50 (ISBN 0-89315-158-0). Lambert Bk.

Crowther, Duane S. Prophetic Warnings to Modern America. LC 77-87431. 415p. 1977. 10.95 (ISBN 0-88290-016-1). Horizon Utah.

--Scripture Chains No. 1: Scripture Memorization Cards & Cross Reference Guides on the Apostary, Restoration, & Characterization of the True Church of Jesus Christ. Date not set. 4.95 (ISBN 0-88290-133-8). Horizon Utah.

Crowther, Jean D. Book of Mormon Puzzles & Pictures for Young Latter-Day Saints. LC 77-74495. (Books for LDS Children). (Illus.). (gr. 3 up). 1977. pap. 4.95 (ISBN 0-88290-080-3). Horizon Utah.

Dean, Bessie. Let's Learn of God's Love. LC 79-89367. (Books for LDS Children). (Illus.). (ps-3). 1979. pap. 4.95 (ISBN 0-88290-124-9). Horizon Utah.

--Let's Learn the First Principles. LC 78-70366. (Books for LDS Children). (Illus.). (ps-3). 1978. pap. 4.95 (ISBN 0-88290-104-4). Horizon Utah.

--Let's Love One Another. LC 77-74492. (Books for Lds Children Ser.). (Illus.). (ps-3). 1978. pap. 4.95 (ISBN 0-88290-077-3). Horizon Utah.

Doxey, Roy W. Latter-Day Prophets & the Doctrine & Covenants, 4 vols. LC 78-17475. 1978. Repr. of 1960 ed. pap. 15.95 set (ISBN 0-87747-717-5). Vol. 1 (ISBN 0-87747-704-3). Vol. 2 (ISBN 0-87747-705-1). Vol. 3 (ISBN 0-87747-707-8). Vol. 4 (ISBN 0-87747-708-6). Deseret Bk.

Ericksen, Ephraim E. The Psychological & Ethical Aspects of Mormon Group Life. 101p. 1974. Repr. of 1922 ed. 10.00 (ISBN 0-87480-090-0). U of Utah Pr.

Etzenhouser, R. From Palmyra, New York, Eighteen-Thirty to Independence, Missouri, Eighteen-Ninety-Four. LC 73-134393. Repr. of 1894 ed. 29.50 (ISBN 0-404-08435-4). AMS Pr.

Evans, R. C. Forty Years in the Mormon Church: Why I Left It. 1976. Repr. of 1920 ed. 6.50 (ISBN 0-89315-054-1). Lambert Bk.

Fernandez, Domingo. El Mormonismo Revelacion Divina O Invencion Humana. 1978. 0.95 (ISBN 0-311-05762-4). Casa Bautista.

Ferris, B. G. Mormons at Home. LC 70-134395. Repr. of 1856 ed. 24.00 (ISBN 0-404-08437-0). AMS Pr.

Fife, Austin & Fife, Alta. Saints of Sage & Saddle: Folklore Among the Mormons. 375p. 1981. pap. 20.00 (ISBN 0-87480-180-X). U of Utah Pr.

Flanders, Robert B. Nauvoo: Kingdom on the Mississippi. LC 65-19110. (Illus.). 374p. 1975. pap. 6.95 (ISBN 0-252-00561-9). U of Ill Pr.

Fluckiger, W. Lynn. Unique Advantages of Being a Mormon. pap. 3.95 (ISBN 0-89036-138-X). Hawkes Pub Inc.
Fox, Frank W. J. Reuben Clark: The Public Years. LC 80-17903. (J. Reuben Clark Three Vol. Ser.). (Illus.). 706p. 1980. 10.95 (ISBN 0-8425-1832-0). Brigham.
Francaviglia, Richard V. The Mormon Landscape: Existence, Creation & Perception of a Unique Image in the American West. LC 77-83791. (Studies in Social History: No. 2). (Illus.). 14.95 (ISBN 0-404-16020-4). AMS Pr.
Fraser, Gordon H. Is Mormonism Christian? 1977. pap. 2.50 (ISBN 0-8024-4169-6). Moody.
Gates, Susa Y. & Widtsoe, Leah D. The Life Story of Brigham Young. facsimile ed. LC 74-164602. (Select Bibliographies Reprint Ser). Repr. of 1930 ed. 24.00 (ISBN 0-8369-5886-1). Arno.
Gerstner, John H. Teachings of Mormonism. pap. 1.25 (ISBN 0-8010-3719-0). Baker Bk.
Gibbons, Francis M. Heber J. Grant: Man of Steel, Prophet of God. LC 79-11649. 252p. 1979. 7.95 (ISBN 0-87747-755-8). Deseret Bk.
Gospel Principles. pap. 1.95 (ISBN 0-87747-763-9). Deseret Bk.
Green, N. W. Mormonism: Its Rise, Progress & Present Condition. LC 79-134401. Repr. of 1870 ed. 32.50 (ISBN 0-404-08445-1). AMS Pr.
Gunn, Richard. The Search for Sensitivity & the Spirit. LC 80-26646. (Illus.). 216p. 1981. 7.95 (ISBN 0-87747-851-1). Deseret Bk.
Gunn, Rodger S. Mormonism: Challenge & Defense. 1979. pap. 8.95 (ISBN 0-89036-126-6). Hawkes Pub Inc.
Gunnison, John W. The Mormons: Or, Latter-Day Saints, in the Valley of the Great Salt Lake; a History of Their Rise & Progress, Peculiar Doctrines, Present Condition & Prospects, Derived from Personal Observation During a Residence Among Them. LC 70-38355. (Select Bibliographies Reprint Ser.). Repr. of 1852 ed. 14.00 (ISBN 0-8369-6772-0). Arno.
Hafen, LeRoy R. & Hafen, Ann W. Handcarts to Zion. LC 59-14279. (Illus.). 1969. 10.00 (ISBN 0-87062-027-4). A H Clark.
Halverson, Sandy. Book of Mormon Activity Book. (Illus.). 80p. (gr. 3-8). 1981. pap. 4.95 (ISBN 0-88290-188-5, 4521). Horizon Utah.
Hansen, Klaus J. Mormonism & the American Experience. LC 80-19312. (History of American Religion Ser.). 224p. 1981. 17.50 (ISBN 0-226-31552-5). U of Chicago Pr.
--Quest for Empire: The Political Kingdom of God & the Council of Fifty in Mormon History. LC 74-8002. xxii, 237p. 1974. pap. 3.95 (ISBN 0-8032-5769-4, BB 591, Bison). U of Nebr Pr.
Hartshorn, Leon, ed. Outstanding Stories by General Authorities. 6.95 (ISBN 0-87747-369-2). Deseret Bk.
Hartshorn, Leon R. Remarkable Stories from the Lives of Latter-Day Saint Women, Vol. 2. LC 75-23943. (Illus.). 286p. 1975. 6.95 (ISBN 0-87747-569-5). Deseret Bk.
Hawkes, John D. Book of Mormon Digest. 240p. 1966. pap. 4.95 (ISBN 0-89036-010-3). Hawkes Pub Inc.
Hector, Lee H. The Three Nephites: Substance & Significance of the Legend in Folklore. Dorson, Richard, ed. LC 77-70608. (International Folklore Ser.). 1977. Repr. of 1949 ed. lib. bdg. 10.00x (ISBN 0-405-10105-8). Arno.
Hemingway, Donald W. Utah & the Mormons. (Illus.). 1979. pap. 2.50 (ISBN 0-686-30193-5). D W Hemingway.
Hettrick, Ric & Hettrick, Marcia. From Among Men. LC 76-27242. 1976. 9.00 (ISBN 0-8309-0170-1). Herald Hse.
Hickman, Bill. Brigham's Destroying Angel. facsimile ed. LC 74-165642. (Select Bibliographies Reprint Ser). Repr. of 1904 ed. 18.00 (ISBN 0-8369-5951-5). Arno.
Hill, Donna. Joseph Smith: The First Mormon. LC 73-15345. 1977. 14.95 (ISBN 0-385-00804-X). Doubleday.
Hillam, Ray C., ed. By the Hands of Wise Men: Essays on the U.S. Constitution. LC 79-13702. 1979. pap. text ed. 5.95 (ISBN 0-8425-1647-6). Brigham.
Hoekema, Anthony A. The Four Major Cults. 1963. 9.95 (ISBN 0-8028-3117-6). Eerdmans.
--Mormonism. 1974. pap. 1.75 (ISBN 0-8028-1491-3). Eerdmans.
Howard, Richard P., ed. The Memoirs of President Joseph Smith III. LC 79-12281. 1979. pap. 14.00 (ISBN 0-8309-0237-6). Herald Hse.
Hullinger, Robert N., ed. Mormon Answer to Skepticism: Why Joseph Smith Wrote the Book of Mormon. LC 79-54055. 201p. (Orig.). 1980. pap. 14.95x (ISBN 0-915644-18-5). Clayton Pub Hse.
Jacobson, Jay. El Mormonismo Refutado. (Modern Doctrines Collection). 1978. Repr. of 1972 ed. 0.60 (ISBN 0-311-05030-1). Casa Bautista.
Jaussi, Laureen & Chaston, Gloria. Genealogical Records of Utah. LC 73-87713. 336p. 1974. 6.95 (ISBN 0-87747-507-5). Deseret Bk.
Johnson, Sonia. From Housewife to Heretic. LC 80-2964. 312p. 1981. 12.95 (ISBN 0-385-17493-4). Doubleday.
Kaiser, Edgar P. How to Respond to the Latter Day Saints. (The Response Ser.). 1977. 1.25 (ISBN 0-570-07680-3, 12-2669). Concordia.
Kapp, Ardeth G. Miracles in Pinafores & Bluejeans. LC 77-4268. (gr. 7-12). 1977. 5.95 (ISBN 0-87747-644-6). Deseret Bk.
Kelner, Alexis. The Mormon Chronicles: A Journal of a Gentile's Life in Zion. (Illus.). 256p. (Orig.). 1981. pap. 6.95x (ISBN 0-9604402-2-4). Dream Garden.
Kern, Louis J. An Ordered Love: Sex Roles & Sexuality in Victorian Utopias--the Shakers, the Mormons, & the Oneida Community. LC 80-10763. xv, 430p. 1981. 24.00x (ISBN 0-8078-1443-1); pap. 12.50x (ISBN 0-8078-4074-2). U of NC Pr.
Kidder, Danuiel P. Mormonism & the Mormons. 59.95 (ISBN 0-8490-0674-0). Gordon Pr.
Kimball, Spencer W. Faith Precedes the Miracle. 364p. 1972. pap. 2.50 (ISBN 0-87747-743-4). Deseret Bk.
--My Beloved Sisters. LC 79-3620. 1979. 4.95 (ISBN 0-87747-798-1). Deseret Bk.
Kirban, Salem. Mormonism. (Illus.). 1971. pap. 2.50 (ISBN 0-912582-13-8). Kirban.
Krueger, John R. An Analysis of the Names of Mormonism. 1979. pap. 3.00 (ISBN 0-911706-21-6). Selbstverlag.
Lautensach, Hermann. Das Mormoneniand Als Beispiel Eines Sozialgeographischen Raumes. Repr. of 1953 ed. pap. 15.50 (ISBN 0-384-31640-9). Johnson Repr.
Le Grand Richards. A Marvelous Work & a Wonder. 424p. 14.00 (ISBN 0-87747-686-1); pap. 1.50 (ISBN 0-87747-614-4). Deseret Bk.
Leone, Mark P. Roots of Modern Mormonism. LC 78-25965. 1979. 15.00x (ISBN 0-674-77970-3). Harvard U Pr.
Le Poidevin, Cecil G. Book of Mormon Geography: Zion Land of Promise. 1977. pap. 3.95 (ISBN 0-89036-068-5). Hawkes Pub Inc.
Lewis, Gordon. Bible, Christian & Latter Day Saints. pap. 0.75 (ISBN 0-8010-5567-9). Baker Bk.
Linn, W. A., et al. The Mormons & Mormonism, 15 vols. 1973. lib. bdg. 50.00 (ISBN 0-8490-0675-9). Gordon Pr.
Ludlow, Daniel H. Marking the Scriptures. 105p. (Orig.). 1980. pap. 3.95 (ISBN 0-87747-815-5). Deseret Bk.
Ludlow, Fitz H. Heart of the Continent. LC 74-134396. (Illus.). Repr. 35.45 (ISBN 0-404-08438-9). AMS Pr.
--Heart of the Continent. LC 74-134396. (Illus.). Repr. 35.45 (ISBN 0-404-08438-9). AMS Pr.
Lum, Dyer D. The Mormon Question in Its Economic Aspects. 1973. lib. bdg. 59.95 (ISBN 0-8490-0672-4). Gordon Pr.
McClintock, James. Mormon Settlement in Arizona. LC 78-134397. Repr. of 1921 ed. 27.00 (ISBN 0-404-08439-7). AMS Pr.
McConkie, Bruce R. Let Every Man Learn His Duty. (Illus.). 1976. pap. 1.95 (ISBN 0-87747-612-8). Deseret Bk.
McConkie, Oscar W. Aaronic Priesthood. LC 77-3609. 1977. 5.95 (ISBN 0-87747-631-4). Deseret Bk.
--Angels. LC 75-29505. 136p. 1975. 5.95 (ISBN 0-87747-572-5). Deseret Bk.
McElveen, Floyd. The Mormon Illusion. rev. ed. LC 76-57036. Orig. Title: Will the "Saints" Go Marching in? 1980. pap. text ed. 2.50 (ISBN 0-8307-0735-2, 5017807). Regal.
--The Mormon Revelations of Convenience. LC 78-72945. 1978. pap. 1.75 (ISBN 0-87123-385-1, 210385). Bethany Hse.
McElveen, Floyd C. A Ilusao Mormon. Date not set. 1.80 (ISBN 0-686-76424-2). Life Pubs Intl.
McKinlay, Lynn A. Life Eternal. 6.95 (ISBN 0-87747-147-9). Deseret Bk.
McMurrin, Sterling M. The Philosophical Foundations of Mormon Theology. 1979. pap. 5.00 (ISBN 0-87480-169-9). U of Utah Pr.
--The Theological Foundations of the Mormon Religion. LC 65-26131. 1965. pap. 10.00 (ISBN 0-87480-051-X). U of Utah Pr.
McNiff, William J. Heaven on Earth: A Planned Mormon Society. LC 72-187474. (The American Utopian Adventure Ser.). 262p. Repr. of 1940 ed. lib. bdg. 13.50x (ISBN 0-87991-001-1). Porcupine Pr.
--Heaven on Earth: A Planned Mormon Society. LC 72-8632. Repr. of 1940 ed. 14.00 (ISBN 0-404-11007-X). AMS Pr.
Marshal, Walter G. Through America: Nine Months in the United States. LC 73-13143. (Foreign Travelers in America, 1810-1935 Ser.). (Illus.). 490p. 1974. Repr. 24.00x (ISBN 0-405-05466-1). Arno.
Martin, Walter. The Maze of Mormonism. LC 78-66067. (Orig.). 1979. pap. 5.95 (ISBN 0-88449-017-3). Vision Hse.
--Mormonism. 1968. pap. 1.25 (ISBN 0-87123-367-3, 210367). Bethany Hse.
Martin, Wynetta W. Black Mormon Tells Her Story. 96p. 1972. pap. 2.00 (ISBN 0-89036-023-5). Hawkes Pub Inc.
Maxwell, Neal A. All These Things Shall Give Thee Experience. LC 79-26282. 144p. 1979. 5.95 (ISBN 0-87747-796-5). Deseret Bk.
--Of One Heart: The Glory of the City of Enoch. 64p. (Orig.). 1975. pap. 3.95 (ISBN 0-87747-604-7). Deseret Bk.
--Things As They Really Are. LC 78-26077. 1978. 6.95 (ISBN 0-87747-730-2). Deseret Bk.
Mayhew, Henry. Mormons: Or, Latter Day Saints. LC 71-134398. Repr. of 1852 ed. 24.75 (ISBN 0-404-08440-0). AMS Pr.
Meirill Library Staff. Name Index to the Library of Congress Collection of Mormon Diaries. (Western Text Society Ser.: Vol. 1, No. 2). 391p. (Orig.). 1971. pap. 11.00 (ISBN 0-87421-045-3). Utah St U Pr.
Melville, J. Keith. Conflict & Compromise: The Mormons in Mid-Nineteeth-Century American Politics. (Illus.). 1974. pap. 1.95 (ISBN 0-8425-0373-0). Brigham.
Merrell, Karen D. Tithing. 22p. (ps-2). pap. 3.95 (ISBN 0-87747-560-1). Deseret Bk.
Miller, David E. Hole in the Rock: An Epic in the Colonization of the Great American West. LC 66-22142. (Illus.). 1966. 20.00 (ISBN 0-87480-022-6). U of Utah Pr.
Miller, Ken. What the Mormons Believe. LC 81-80958. 248p. 1981. 9.95 (ISBN 0-88290-177-X, 1040). Horizon Utah.
Miner, Caroline E. & Kimball, Edward L. Camilla. LC 80-69723. (Illus.). 1980. 7.95 (ISBN 0-87747-845-7). Deseret Bk.
Missionary Set. 1978. pap. 12.95 (ISBN 0-87747-774-4). Deseret Bk.
Monson, Thomas S. Pathways to Perfection. 302p. 1973. pap. 2.95 (ISBN 0-87747-797-3). Deseret Bk.
The Mormons. LC 78-9112. (Illus.). 1978. pap. 2.95 (ISBN 0-87747-711-6). Deseret Bk.
Mouritsen, Maren, ed. Blueprints for Living: Perspectives for Latter-day Saint Women, 2 vols. 128p. 1980. pap. 5.95 ea. Vol. 1 (ISBN 0-8425-1812-6). Vol. 2 (ISBN 0-8425-1814-2). Brigham.
Mulder, William & Mortensen, A. Russell, eds. Among the Mormons: Historic Accounts by Contemporary Observers. LC 58-5825. xiv, 496p. 1973. 8.50 (ISBN 0-8032-5778-3, BB 568, Bison). U of Nebr Pr.
Nelson, John Y. Fifty Years on the Trail, a True Story of Western Life: The Adventures of John Young Nelson, As Described to Harrington O'Reilly. (Western Frontier Library: No. 22). (Illus.). 1969. Repr. of 1963 ed. 7.95 (ISBN 0-8061-0572-0). U of Okla Pr.
Nelson, Lowry. The Mormon Village: A Study in Social Origins. 59.95 (ISBN 0-8490-0673-2). Gordon Pr.
O'Dea, Thomas F. Mormons. LC 57-6984. 1957. 14.00x (ISBN 0-226-61743-2). U of Chicago Pr.
--Mormons. LC 57-6984. 1964. pap. 4.95 (ISBN 0-226-61744-0, P162, Phoen). U of Chicago Pr.
Packer, Boyd K. Eternal Love. LC 73-88635. 22p. 1973. 1.50 (ISBN 0-87747-514-8). Deseret Bk.
Parr, Lucy. True Stories of Mormon Pioneer Courage. LC 76-29310. (Orig.). (gr. 1-12). 1976. 6.95 (ISBN 0-88290-073-0). Horizon Utah.
Pelham, R. W. A Shaker's Answer. 1981. pap. 2.00 (ISBN 0-937942-09-X). Shaker Mus.
Petersen, Mark E. The Great Prologue. LC 75-14997. 136p. 1976. pap. 1.50 (ISBN 0-87747-606-3). Deseret Bk.
Peterson, Charles S. Take up Your Mission: Mormon Colonizing Along the Little Colorado River, 1870-1900. LC 72-89621. 1973. 9.50 (ISBN 0-8165-0397-4). U of Ariz Pr.
Piercy, Frederick. Route from Liverpool to the Great Salt Lake Valley. facsimile ed. Brodie, Fawn M., ed. LC 62-19223. (The John Harvard Library). 1962. 16.50x (ISBN 0-674-77956-8). Harvard U Pr.
Prayer: Compilation of Essays from General Authorities of the Church of Jesus Christ of Latter-Day Saints. 1977. pap. 1.95 (ISBN 0-87747-739-6). Deseret Bk.
Pritt, Ann F. How to Make an L.D.S. Quiet Book. 1.95 (ISBN 0-87747-116-9). Deseret Bk.
Remy, Jules & Brenchley, Julius. A Journey to Great Salt-Lake City, 2 vols. LC 75-134399. (Illus.). Repr. of 1861 ed. Set. write for info. (ISBN 0-404-08441-9). Vol. 1 (ISBN 0-404-08442-7). Vol. 2 (ISBN 0-404-08443-5). AMS Pr.
Richards, Aurelia. The Mormon Trail: In Story Form. pap. 5.95 (ISBN 0-89036-137-1). Hawkes Pub Inc.
Richards, LeGrand. Marvelous Work & a Wonder. 1.95 (ISBN 0-87747-161-4); flexible bdg. o.p. 1.25 (ISBN 0-87747-162-2); pocket black leather 8.50 (ISBN 0-87747-163-0); pocket brown leather 8.50 (ISBN 0-87747-383-8); pocket blue fab. leather 4.95 (ISBN 0-87747-458-3). Deseret Bk.
Riegel, O. U. Crown of Glory: Life of J. J. Strang, Moses, of the Mormons. 1935. 45.00x (ISBN 0-685-69857-2). Elliots Bks.
Roberts, B. H. Joseph Smith, the Prophet Teacher. Repr. leatherette 3.95 (ISBN 0-685-59814-4). Western Epics.
--Outlines of Ecclesiastical History. LC 79-9744. 1979. 7.95 (ISBN 0-87747-748-5). Deseret Bk.
Robertson, LaRae C. You Can Be a Book of Mormon Expert in Five Minutes a Day. LC 77-74494. (Illus.). 1977. pap. 5.50 (ISBN 0-88290-079-X). Horizon Utah.
Robinson, Philip S. Sinners & Saints. LC 75-134400. Repr. of 1883 ed. 25.00 (ISBN 0-404-08444-3). AMS Pr.
--Sinners & Saints. LC 75-134400. Repr. of 1883 ed. 25.00 (ISBN 0-404-08444-3). AMS Pr.
Ropp, Harry L. The Mormon Papers. LC 77-2681. (Illus., Orig.). 1977. pap. 3.95 (ISBN 0-87784-789-4). Inter-Varsity.
Ruoff, Norman D., ed. The Writings of President Frederick M. Smith, Vol. 2. LC 78-6428. 1979. pap. 7.50 (ISBN 0-8309-0239-2). Herald Hse.
Scott, Latayne C. The Mormon Mirage. 1980. 10.95 (ISBN 0-310-38910-0). Zondervan.
Shapiro, R. Gary. Exhaustive Concordance of the Book of Mormon, Doctrine & Covenants & Pearl of Great Peace. Orig. Title: Triple Concordance. 1977. 20.95 (ISBN 0-89036-085-5). Hawkes Pub Inc.
Sidney Rigdon Seventeen Ninety-Three to Eighteen Seventy-Six. 1979. 6.00 (ISBN 0-8309-0241-4). Herald Hse.
Smith, Eliza R. Biography & Family Record of Lorenzo Snow. 1975. Repr. 12.50 (ISBN 0-685-59815-2). Western Epics.
Smith, Joseph. Doctrine & Covenants of the Church of Jesus Christ of Latter-Day Saints: Containing the Revelations Given to Joseph Smith, Jun, the Prophet, for the Building up of the Kingdom of God in the Last Days. Pratt, Orson, ed. LC 69-14082. 1971. Repr. of 1880 ed. lib. bdg. 15.00 (ISBN 0-8371-4101-X, SMCC). Greenwood.
Smith, Joseph F. Teachings of the Prophet Joseph Smith. LC 76-111624. 437p. Date not set. pap. 2.50 (ISBN 0-87747-778-7). Deseret Bk.
--The Way to Perfection. 365p. 1972. 6.95 (ISBN 0-87747-300-5). Deseret Bk.
Smith, Joseph, Jr., tr. The Book of Mormon. LC 66-15423. 414p. 1973. pap. 2.50 (ISBN 0-8309-0273-2). Herald Hse.
Sondrup, Steven P., ed. Arts & Inspiration: Mormon Perspectives. LC 80-21927. (Illus.). 240p. 1980. pap. 7.95 (ISBN 0-8425-1845-2). Brigham.
Stewart, John J. Joseph Smith the Mormon Prophet. pap. 3.50 (ISBN 0-89036-082-0). Hawkes Pub Inc.
--Mormonism & the Negro. LC 78-52123. 1978. 5.50 (ISBN 0-88290-098-6). Horizon Utah.
Sturlaugson, Mary F. A Soul So Rebellious. 88p. 1980. 6.95 (ISBN 0-87747-841-4). Deseret Bk.
Talmage, James E. Articles of Faith. LC 80-22041. (Classics in Mormon Literature Edition Ser.). 537p. 1981. 8.95 (ISBN 0-87747-838-4). Deseret Bk.
--Articles of Faith. 537p. pap. 2.50 (ISBN 0-87747-662-4). Deseret Bk.
--Articles of Faith. 1970. pocket brown leather ed. 11.00 (ISBN 0-87747-374-9); pocket black leather ed. 11.00 (ISBN 0-87747-320-X); pocket blue fab. leather ed. o.s.i. 5.50 (ISBN 0-87747-457-5); black leather ed. 14.50 (ISBN 0-87747-319-6); brown leather ed. 14.50 (ISBN 0-87747-373-0); missionary ed. 6.95 (ISBN 0-87747-317-X); lib. bdg. 5.50 (ISBN 0-87747-318-8). Deseret Bk.
--Great Apostasy. 5.95 (ISBN 0-87747-384-6). Deseret Bk.
--House of the Lord. pap. 5.50 (ISBN 0-87747-112-6). Deseret Bk.
--Jesus the Christ. 804p. pap. 2.95 (ISBN 0-87747-456-7). Deseret Bk.
--Jesus the Christ. Bd. with The Articles of Faith. deluxe ed. 15.00 pocket ed. black leather (ISBN 0-87747-392-7); deluxe ed. 15.00 pocket ed. brown leather (ISBN 0-87747-394-3). Deseret Bk.
Taylor, Bill. A Tale of Two Cities: The Mormons-Catholics. 1981. pap. 4.00 (ISBN 0-933046-02-2). Little Red Hen.
Tullis, F. LaMond & King, Arthur H., eds. Mormonism: A Faith for All Cultures. LC 78-7665. (Illus.). pap. 8.95 (ISBN 0-8425-1282-9). Brigham.
Vanderhoof, Elisha W. Historical Sketches of Western New York. LC 71-134434. Repr. of 1907 ed. 14.00 (ISBN 0-404-08476-1). AMS Pr.

Wallace, Arthur. Can Mormonism Be Proved Experimentally? 2nd rev. ed. 170p. 1973. 4.00 (ISBN 0-937892-00-9); pap. 3.00 (ISBN 0-937892-01-7). LL Co.
Wallace, Arthur, compiled by. L. D. S. Children's Comments, Vol. 1. 60p. 1978. pap. 1.95 (ISBN 0-937892-03-3). LL Co.
Walton, H. Dyke. They Built with Faith: True Tales of God's Guidance in L.D.S. Chapel Building World-Wide. LC 79-89353. 1979. 5.95 (ISBN 0-88290-122-2). Horizon Utah.
Ward, Margery W., ed. A Fragment: The Autobiography of Mary Jane Mount Tanner. (Utah, the Mormons, & the West: No. 9). 1980. 15.00 (ISBN 0-87480-183-4, Tanner). U of Utah Pr.
Warenski, Marilyn. Patriarchs & Politics. (Illus.). 1978. 10.95 (ISBN 0-07-068270-4, GB). McGraw.
Warner, Ross. Fulfillment of Book of Mormon Prophecies. 1975. pap. 5.50 (ISBN 0-89036-081-2). Hawkes Pub Inc.
Warren, Rod, illus. How Do Other See You? In an LDS Ward. (Illus., Orig.). 1977. pap. 2.95 (ISBN 0-89036-101-0). Hawkes Pub Inc.
Webb, Robert C. The Real Mormonism. LC 72-2971. Repr. of 1916 ed. 29.00 (ISBN 0-404-10736-2). AMS Pr.
Werner, Morris R. Brigham Young. LC 75-351. (The Radical Tradition in America Ser). xvi, 478p. 1975. Repr. of 1925 ed. 29.50 (ISBN 0-88355-254-X). Hyperion Conn.
West, Emerson R. Profiles of the Presidents. LC 80-10455. 328p. 1980. 7.95 (ISBN 0-87747-800-7). Deseret Bk.
Whalen, William J. Latter-Day Saints in the Modern Day World. (Illus.). 1967. pap. 3.25x (ISBN 0-268-00153-7). U of Notre Dame Pr.
Whipple, Maurine. Giant Joshua. Repr. 9.95 (ISBN 0-685-59816-0). Western Epics.
Widtsoe, John A. Discourses of Brigham Young. 497p. pap. 2.50 (ISBN 0-87747-788-4). Deseret Bk.
Widtsoe, John A., ed. Discourses of Brigham Young. 7.95 (ISBN 0-87747-066-9). Deseret Bk.
Yarn, David H., Jr. The Gospel: God, Man, & Truth. LC 65-18575. (Classics in Mormon Literature). 211p. 1978. Repr. of 1965 ed. 5.95 (ISBN 0-87747-718-3). Deseret Bk.
Young, Ann E. Wife No. Nineteen: The Story of a Life in Bondage, Being a Complete Expose of Mormonism, & Revealing the Sorrows, Sacrifices & Sufferings of Women in Polygamy. LC 72-2634. (American Women Ser: Images & Realities). (Illus.). 632p. 1972. Repr. of 1875 ed. 27.00 (ISBN 0-405-04488-7). Arno.
Young, Kimball. Isn't One Wife Enough. Repr. of 1954 ed. lib. bdg. 19.75x (ISBN 0-8371-3238-X, YOOW). Greenwood.
Zimmerman, Dean. Sentence Sermons. LC 78-2568. 1978. pap. 5.95 (ISBN 0-87747-672-1). Deseret Bk.

MORMONS AND MORMONISM–FICTION

Ferris, B. G. Utah & the Mormons. LC 77-134394. Repr. of 1856 ed. 27.00 (ISBN 0-404-08436-2). AMS Pr.
Fisher, Vardis. Children of God. 1977. 12.95 (ISBN 0-918522-50-1). O L Holmes.
Gibson, Margaret W. Emma Smith: Elect Lady. LC 54-7910. 1954. pap. 5.00 (ISBN 0-8309-0256-2). Herald Hse.
Switzer, Jennie B. Elder Northfield's Home; or, Sacrificed on the Mormon Altar. facsimile ed. LC 71-164576. (American Fiction Reprint Ser). Repr. of 1882 ed. 23.00 (ISBN 0-8369-7053-5). Arno.
Weyland, Jack. First Day Forever & the Other Stories for LDS Youth. LC 80-82455. 120p. 1980. 6.95 (ISBN 0-88290-136-2, 2037). Horizon Utah.
Writers Program, Utah. Provo, Pioneer Mormon City. LC 73-3654. (American Guide Ser.). 1942. Repr. 11.50 (ISBN 0-404-57954-X). AMS Pr.

MORMONS AND MORMONISM–HISTORY

Anderson, C. LeRoy. For Christ Will Come Tomorrow Morning: The Saga of the Morrisites. 200p. 1981. price not set (ISBN 0-87421-109-3). Utah St U Pr.
Anderson, Einar. History & Beliefs of Mormonism. Orig. Title: Inside Story of Mormonism. 162p. 1981. pap. 4.95 (ISBN 0-8254-2122-5). Kregel.
Anderson, Nels. Desert Saints: The Mormon Frontier in Utah. LC 66-19134. 1942. 14.00x (ISBN 0-226-01782-6). U of Chicago Pr.
Arrington, Leonard J. & Bitton, Davis. The Mormon Experience: A History of the Latter-Day Saints. LC 80-11843. (Illus.). 404p. 1980. pap. 5.95 (ISBN 0-394-74102-1, Vin). Random.
--The Mormon Experience: A History of the Latter-Day Saints. LC 78-20561. (Illus.). 1979. 17.50 (ISBN 0-394-46566-0). Knopf.
Barron, Howard H. Orson Hyde: Missionary, Apostle, Colonizer. LC 77-74490. (Illus.). 1977. 9.95 (ISBN 0-88290-076-5). Horizon Utah.
Barron, Howard H., ed. Of Everlasting Value, Vol. 1. (Orig.). 1978. pap. 5.95 (ISBN 0-89036-129-0). Hawkes Pub Inc.
Book of Mormon. 568p. 3.95 ea. Pocket Ed., Black (ISBN 0-87747-621-7). Pocket Ed., Brown (ISBN 0-87747-622-5). Deseret Bk.
Brown, Joseph E. The Mormon Trek West. LC 77-16900. (Illus.). 1980. 35.00 (ISBN 0-385-13030-9). Doubleday.
Bushman, Claudia L., et al. Mormon Sisters: Women in Early Utah. Bushman, Claudia, ed. LC 76-53854. (Illus.). 320p. 1980. pap. 5.95 (ISBN 0-913420-95-6). Olympus Pub Co.
Canning, Ray R. & Beeton, Beverly, eds. The Genteel Gentile: Letters of Elizabeth Cumming, 1857 - 1858. (Utah, The Mormons, & The West: No. 8). 1978. 12.50 (ISBN 0-87480-163-X, Tanner). U of Utah Pr.
Carriker, Robert C. & Carriker, Eleanor R., eds. An Army Wife on the Frontier. (Utah, the Mormons, & the West Ser.: No. 6). 1975. 8.00 (ISBN 0-87480-160-5, Tanner). U of Utah Pr.
Dyer, Alvin R. The Refiner's Fire. 7.95 (ISBN 0-87747-222-X). Deseret Bk.
Ellsworth, S. George. Dear Ellen: Two Mormon Women & Their Letters. (Utah, the Mormons, & the West: No. 3). 1974. 12.00 (ISBN 0-87480-159-1, Tanner). U of Utah Pr.
Flake, Chad J., ed. A Mormon Bibliography, 1830-1930: Books, Pamphlets, Periodicals, & Broadsides Relating to the First Century of Mormonism. LC 74-22639. (Illus.). 1978. 80.00x (ISBN 0-87480-016-1). U of Utah Pr.
Foster, Lawrence. Religion & Sexuality: Three American Communal Experiments of the Nineteenth Century. 400p. 1981. 19.95 (ISBN 0-19-502794-9). Oxford U Pr.
Geddes, Joseph A. The United Order Among the Mormons (Missouri Phase) An Unfinished Experiment in Economic Organization. LC 72-8247. Repr. of 1924 ed. 17.00 (ISBN 0-404-11001-0). AMS Pr.
Gibbons, Francis M. Joseph Smith: Martyr-Prophet of God. LC 77-2019. 1977. 6.95 (ISBN 0-87747-637-3). Deseret Bk.
Grondahl, Calvin. Freeway to Perfection: A Collection of Mormon Cartoons. (Illus.). 96p. (Orig.). 1980. pap. 3.75 (ISBN 0-686-27079-7). Sunstone Found.
Hartshorn, Leon R. Classic Stories from the Lives of Our Prophets. LC 73-155235. 384p. 1975. 7.95 (ISBN 0-87747-438-9). Deseret Bk.
Hill, Marvin S. & Rooker, C. Keith. The Kirtland Economy Revisited: A Market Critique of Sectarian Economics. LC 78-3848. (Studies in Mormon History: No. 3). (Illus.). 1977. pap. 4.95 (ISBN 0-8425-1230-6). Brigham.
Howe, Eber D. Mormonism Unvailed; or, a Faithful Account of That Singular Imposition & Delusion, from Its Rise to the Present Time. LC 72-2967. Repr. of 1834 ed. 22.50 (ISBN 0-404-10730-3). AMS Pr.
Jackson, Richard H., ed. The Mormon Role in the Settlement of the West. LC 78-24728. (Charles Redd Monographs in Western History Ser.: No. 9). (Illus.). 1978. pap. 6.95 (ISBN 0-8425-1321-3). Brigham.
Kane, Elizabeth W. Twelve Mormon Homes. (Utah, the Mormons, & the West: No. 4). 1974. 12.00 (ISBN 0-87480-162-1, Tanner). U of Utah Pr.
Kimball, Stanley B. Heber C. Kimball: Mormon Patriarch & Pioneer. LC 80-21923. (Illus.). 1981. 17.95 (ISBN 0-252-00854-5). U of Ill Pr.
Larson, Gustave O. Prelude to the Kingdom: Mormon Desert Conquest, a Chapter in American Cooperative Experience. LC 78-5694. 1978. Repr. of 1947 ed. lib. bdg. 25.75x (ISBN 0-313-20452-7, LAPK). Greenwood.
Long, E. B. The Saints & the Union: Utah Territory During the Civil War. LC 80-16775. (Illus.). 292p. 1981. 17.95 (ISBN 0-252-00821-9). U of Ill Pr.
McKiernan, F. Mark & Launius, Roger D. An Early Latter Day Saint History by John Whitmer. 1980. pap. 8.00 (ISBN 0-8309-0269-4). Herald Hse.
Madsen, Carol C. & Oman, Susan S. Sisters & Little Saints. (Illus.). 1980. 6.95 (ISBN 0-87747-760-4). Deseret Bk.
Mulder, William. The Mormons in American History. (The University of Utah Frederick William Reynolds Lecture Ser.). 1981. pap. 5.00 (ISBN 0-87480-184-2). U of Utah Pr.
Reay, Lee. Incredible Passage: Through the Hole-in-the-Rock. Hechtle, Ranier, ed. (Illus.). 128p. (Orig.). 1981. 6.95 (ISBN 0-934826-05-6); pap. 4.50 (ISBN 0-934826-06-4). Meadow Lane.
Roberts, B. H. Comprehensive History of the Church of Jesus Christ of Latter-Day-Saints, 6 vols. 1978. pap. 9.95 set (ISBN 0-8425-1275-6). Brigham.
--Comprehensive History of The Church of Jesus Christ of Latter-day Saints, 6 vols plus index. (Illus.). 1965. Vols. 1-6. 9.95 ea.; Vol. 1. (ISBN 0-8425-0299-8); Vol. 2. (ISBN 0-8425-0300-5); Vol. 3. (ISBN 0-8425-0301-3); Vol. 4. (ISBN 0-8425-0482-6); Vol. 5. (ISBN 0-8425-0304-8); Vol. 6. (ISBN 0-8425-0305-6); Index. 6.95 (ISBN 0-8425-0627-6). Brigham.
Roberts, B. H., intro. by. History of the Church, 7 vols. Incl. Vol. 1 (1820-1834) 511p. 1974 (ISBN 0-87747-074-X); Vol. 2 (1834-1837) 543p. 1974 (ISBN 0-87747-075-8); Vol. 3 (1834-1839) 478p (ISBN 0-87747-076-6); Vol. 4 (1839-1842) 620p (ISBN 0-87747-077-4); Vol. 5 (1842-1843) 563p (ISBN 0-87747-078-2); Vol. 6 (1843-1844) 641p (ISBN 0-87747-079-0); Vol. 7 (period 2, The Apostolic Interregnum) 640p (ISBN 0-87747-080-4). 12.95 ea.; index 12.95 (ISBN 0-87747-291-2). Deseret Bk.
Simmonds, A. J. The Gentile Comes to Cache Valley. 143p. 1976. 6.00 (ISBN 0-87421-088-7). Utah St U Pr.
Smith, Gary. Day of Great Healing in Nauvoo. 25p. 1980. pap. 1.95 (ISBN 0-87747-811-2). Deseret Bk.
Smith, Joseph. History of the Church, 8 vols. (Vol. 7 from the Manuscript History of Brigham Young). Set. pap. 12.95 (ISBN 0-87747-725-6). Deseret Bk.
Smith, Joseph F. Essentials in Church History. LC 67-21351. (Classics in Mormon Literature Ser.). (Illus.). 604p. 1979. 9.95 (ISBN 0-87747-786-8). Deseret Bk.
Sperry, Sidney B. Book of Mormon Chronology. pap. 1.50 (ISBN 0-87747-408-7). Deseret Bk.
Spurrier, Joseph H. Great Are the Promises Unto the Isle of the Sea: The Church of Jesus Christ of Latter-day Saints in the Hawaiian Islands. (Orig.). 1978. pap. 3.95 (ISBN 0-89036-114-2). Hawkes Pub Inc.
Stegner, Wallace. Gathering of Zion: The Story of the Mormon Trail. (American Trails Ser). 1964. (GB); pap. 4.50 (ISBN 0-07-060981-0). McGraw.
--Mormon Country. LC 81-3410. x, 362p. 1981. Repr. of 1942 ed. 21.50x (ISBN 0-8032-4129-1); pap. price not set (ISBN 0-8032-9125-6, BB 778, Bison). U of Nebr Pr.
Tanner, Annie C. A Biography of Ezra Thompson Clark. (Utah, the Mormons, & the West: No. 5). 1975. 8.50 (ISBN 0-87480-156-7, Tanner). U of Utah Pr.
--A Mormon Mother: An Autobiography. (Utah, the Mormons, & the West: No. 1). 1976. pap. 5.00 (ISBN 0-87480-157-5, Tanner). U of Utah Pr.
Tanner, Jerald & Tanner, Sandra. Changing World of Mormonism. 1979. 11.95 (ISBN 0-8024-1234-3). Moody.
Taylor, Samuel W. Nightfall at Nauvoo. 1973. pap. 2.75 (ISBN 0-380-00247-7, 52696). Avon.
--The Rocky Mountain Empire: The Latter Day Saints Today. 1978. 12.95 (ISBN 0-02-616610-0). Macmillan.
Thane, James L., Jr. A Governor's Wife on the Mining Frontier. (Utah, the Mormons, & the West: No. 7). 1976. 8.50 (ISBN 0-87480-161-3, Tanner). U of Utah Pr.
Warenski, Marilyn. Patriarchs & Politics. (McGraw-Hill Paperbacks Ser.). 352p. 1980. pap. 6.95 (ISBN 0-07-068271-2). McGraw.
Wells, Merle W. Anti-Mormonism in Idaho, Eighteen Seventy-Two to Ninety-Two. LC 77-89975. (Studies in Mormon History Ser.: No. 4). 1978. pap. 7.95 (ISBN 0-8425-0904-6). Brigham.
White, Sheryl & Shangle, Robert D., eds. Mormon: One Hundred & Fifty Years. (Illus.). 72p. 1980. 14.95 (ISBN 0-89802-177-4); pap. 7.95 (ISBN 0-89802-201-0). Beautiful Am.

MORMONS AND MORMONISM–HISTORY–SOURCES

Crane, Charles. Bible & Mormon Scriptures Compared. (Illus.). 1976. pap. 2.95 (ISBN 0-89900-100-9). College Pr Pub.
Zimmerman, Dean R. I Knew the Prophets: An Analysis of the Letter of Benjamin F. Johnson to George F. Gibbs Reporting Doctrinal Views of Joseph Smith & Brigham Young. LC 76-3992. 1976. pap. 3.95 (ISBN 0-88290-065-X). Horizon Utah.

MORMONS AND MORMONISM–MISSIONS

Allred, Hugh & Allred, Steven. How to Make a Good Mission Great. 66p. 1978. pap. 1.25 (ISBN 0-87747-761-2). Deseret Bk.
Dennison, Mark A. Preparing for the Greatest Two Years of Your Life. pap. 3.95 (ISBN 0-89036-128-2). Hawkes Pub Inc.
Dyer, Alvin R. Challenge. 7.95 (ISBN 0-87747-031-6). Deseret Bk.
Passantino, Robert, et al. Answers to the Cultist at Your Door. LC 80-83850. 1981. pap. 4.95 (ISBN 0-89081-275-6). Harvest Hse.
Whetten, John D. Making the Most of Your Mission. LC 81-66421. 83p. 1981. 5.95 (ISBN 0-87747-868-6). Deseret Bk.

MORMONS AND MORMONISM–SERMONS

Burton, Alma P. Discourses of the Prophet Joseph Smith. LC 77-23977. 399p. 8.95 (ISBN 0-87747-067-7). Deseret Bk.
Hawkes, John D. Art of Achieving Success. 128p. 1971. pap. 2.95 (ISBN 0-89036-008-1). Hawkes Pub Inc.
Himes, Ellvert H. Growing in the Priesthood: Messages of Inspiration & Motivation with Personal Records of Fulfillment. LC 75-17103. (Illus.). 128p. 1975. 6.95 (ISBN 0-88290-052-8). Horizon Utah.
Richards, LeGrand. LeGrand Richards Speaks. (Illus.). 292p. 1972. 6.95 (ISBN 0-87747-469-9). Deseret Bk.
Russon, Robb. Letters to a New Elder: The Melchizedek Priesthood, Its Duty Fulfillment. pap. 2.95 (ISBN 0-89036-144-4). Hawkes Pub Inc.
Sill, Sterling W. Christmas Sermons. LC 73-86165. 184p. 1973. 5.95 (ISBN 0-87747-503-2). Deseret Bk.
Smith, Joseph F. Answers to Gospel Questions, 5 vols. 225p. 1979. Set. pap. 8.95 (ISBN 0-87747-747-7). Deseret Bk.
--Gospel Doctrine. 553p. 1975. 8.95 (ISBN 0-87747-101-0); pap. 2.50 (ISBN 0-87747-663-2). Deseret Bk.

MORMONS AND MORMONISM–SONGS AND MUSIC

Cheney, Thomas E., ed. Mormon Songs from the Rocky Mountains: A Compilation of Mormon Folksong. 224p. 1981. pap. 15.00 (ISBN 0-87480-196-6). U of Utah Pr.
Cornwall, J. Spencer. Stories of Our Mormon Hymns. 7.95 (ISBN 0-87747-247-5). Deseret Bk.
Sing with Me. (gr. 1-6). 5.00 (ISBN 0-87747-362-5). Deseret Bk.

MORMONS AND MORMONISM IN MEXICO

Palmer, David S. In Search of Cumorah. LC 80-83866. (Illus.). 300p. 1981. 9.95 (ISBN 0-88290-169-9, 1063). Horizon Utah.
Tyler, Daniel. A Concise History of the Mormon Battalion in the Mexican War, 1846-1848. LC 64-15125. (Beautiful Rio Grande Classics Ser). Repr. of 1881 ed. lib. bdg. 15.00 (ISBN 0-87380-011-7). Rio Grande.

MORNAY, PHILLIPE DE, SEIGNEUR DU PLESSIS-MARLY, CALLED DU PLESSIS-MORNAY, 1549-1623

De Mornay, Charlotte A. Memoires 2 Vols. 1869. Set. 55.50 (ISBN 0-384-40148-1); Set. pap. 46.00 (ISBN 0-384-40149-X). Johnson Repr.

MORO LANGUAGES

see Maranao Language

MOROCCAN LEGENDS

see Legends, Moroccan

MOROCCO

Abu-Lughod, Janet L. Rabat: Urban Apartheid in Morocco. LC 80-7508. (Princeton Studies on the Near East). (Illus.). 400p. 1981. 30.00 (ISBN 0-691-05315-4); pap. 12.50 (ISBN 0-691-10098-5). Princeton U Pr.
Amin, Samir. The Maghreb in the Modern World: Algeria, Tunisia, Morocco. Perl, Michael, tr. lib. bdg. 11.50x (ISBN 0-88307-293-9). Gannon.
Bensusan, S. L. Morocco. 1977. lib. bdg. 59.95 (ISBN 0-8490-2281-9). Gordon Pr.
Chiapuris, John P. The Ait Ayash of the High Moulouya Plain: Rural Social Organization in Morocco. (Anthropological Papers Ser.: No. 69). 1980. pap. 6.00x (ISBN 0-932206-83-2). U Mich Mus Anthro.
Harrell, Richard S. A Short Reference Grammar of Moroccan Arabic. (Richard Slade Harrell Arabic Ser.). 263p. 1962. pap. 8.50 (ISBN 0-87840-006-0); one cassette 5.00 (ISBN 0-87840-016-8); write for info. five-inch reel (ISBN 0-87840-017-6). Georgetown U Pr.
Hureau, Jean. Le Maroc Aujourd 'hui. (Illus.). 1976. 21.95x (ISBN 2-85258-028-4). Intl Learn Syst.
Landau, Rom. Morocco. 1967. 21.95 (ISBN 0-236-30866-1, Pub. by Paul Elek). Merrimack Bk Serv.
Loti, Pierre. Morocco. 30.00 (ISBN 0-685-64789-7). Norwood Edns.
Secretariat d'Etat au Plan et au Development Regional, Direction de la Statistique. Annuaire Statistique Du Maroc 1975. 1976. pap. 12.50x (ISBN 0-8002-2356-X). Intl Pubns Serv.
Westermarck, Eduard A. Ritual & Belief in Morocco, 2 vols. LC 66-27623. (Illus.). 1968. 25.00 (ISBN 0-8216-0144-X). Univ Bks.
Westermarck, Edvard A. Wit & Wisdom in Morocco: A Study of Native Proverbs. LC 76-44800. Repr. of 1930 ed. 26.75 (ISBN 0-404-15980-X). AMS Pr.

MOROCCO–DESCRIPTION AND TRAVEL

Aubin, E. Morocco of Today. 1977. lib. bdg. 59.95 (ISBN 0-8490-2283-5). Gordon Pr.
Barrows, David P. Berbers & Blacks: Impressions of Morocco, Timbuktu & the Western Sudan. LC 70-129938. (Illus.). Repr. of 1927 ed. 16.50x (ISBN 0-8371-1003-3, Pub. by Negro U Pr). Greenwood.

Caille, R. Travels Through Central Africa to Timuctoo & Across the Great Desert to Morocco, 1824-28, 2 vols. (Illus.). 1968. Repr. of 1830 ed. 85.00x (ISBN 0-7146-1796-2, F Cass Co). Biblio Dist.
Canetti, Elias. The Voices of Marrakesh: A Record of a Visit. Underwood, J. A., tr. from Ger. LC 78-9776. 1978. 7.95 (ISBN 0-8164-9346-4). Continuum.
De Amicis, Edmondo. Morocco: Its People & Places, 2 vols. 1976. lib. bdg. 250.00 (ISBN 0-8490-2282-7). Gordon Pr.
Fernea, Elizabeth Warnock. A Street in Marrakech. LC 74-12686. 1976. pap. 5.95 (ISBN 0-385-12045-1, Anch). Doubleday.
Hureau, Jean. Morocco Today. (J. A. Editions: Today). (Illus.). 240p. 1980. 14.95 (ISBN 0-88254-539-6, Pub. by J. A. Editions France). Hippocrene Bks.
Kay, Shirley. Morocco. (Illus.). 160p. 1981. 30.00 (ISBN 0-7043-2224-2, Pub. by Quartet England). Charles River Bks.
Kininmonth, Christopher. The Travellers' Guide to Morocco. rev. ed. (Illus.). 356p. 1981. pap. 16.95 (ISBN 0-224-01897-3, Pub. by Chatto-Bodley-Jonathan). Merrimack Bk Serv.
Launey, Andre. Morrocco. 1976. 19.95 (ISBN 0-7134-3182-2). David & Charles.
Lewis, Wyndham. Filibusters in Barbary. LC 72-2114. (English Literature Ser., No. 33). 1972. Repr. of 1932 ed. lib. bdg. 42.95 (ISBN 0-8383-1477-5). Haskell.
Loti, Pierre. Morocco. 25.00 (ISBN 0-686-17246-9). Scholars Ref Lib.
Michelin Guides & Maps. Michelin Green Guide to Maroc. 3rd ed. (Green Guide Ser.). (Fr.). 1979. pap. 7.95 (ISBN 2-06-005450-8). Michelin.
Moreau, Daniel, ed. Le Maroc. new ed. (Collection monde et voyages). (Illus.). 159p. (Fr.). 1973. 21.00x (ISBN 2-03-053111-1). Larousse.
Nagel Travel Guide to Morocco. (Nagel Travel Guide Ser.). (Illus.). 328p. 1977. 23.00 (ISBN 2-8263-0164-0). Hippocrene Bks.
Nagel's Encyclopedia Guide: Morocco. (Illus.). 328p. 1977. 23.00 (ISBN 2-8263-0164-0). Masson Pub.
Seligo, Hans. Morocco. (Panorama Bks.). (Illus., Fr). 1966. 3.50 (ISBN 0-685-11405-8). French & Eur.
Terhorst, Bernd. With the Riff Kabyles. LC 69-18998. (Illus.). Repr. of 1926 ed. 13.75x (ISBN 0-8371-4948-7). Greenwood.

MOROCCO–ECONOMIC CONDITIONS

Ashford, Douglas E. Morocco-Tunisia: Politics & Planning. LC 65-25988. (National Planning Ser.: No. 2). (Orig.). 1965. pap. 3.95x (ISBN 0-8156-2088-8). Syracuse U Pr.
Secretariat d'Etat au Plan et au Development Regional, Direction de la Statistique. Annuaire Statistique Du Maroc 1975. 1976. pap. 12.50x (ISBN 0-8002-2356-X). Intl Pubns Serv.
Stewart, Charles F. Economy of Morocco, 1912-1962. LC 64-8716. (Middle Eastern Monographs Ser: No. 12). (Illus.). 1964. pap. 6.95 (ISBN 0-674-23600-9). Harvard U Pr.
Waterbury, John. North for the Trade: The Life & Times of a Berber Merchant. LC 70-174453. (Illus.). 200p. 1972. 24.75x (ISBN 0-520-02134-7). U of Cal Pr.
Waterston, Albert. Planning in Morocco: Organization & Implementation. (World Bank Ser). 73p. 1962. pap. 3.50x (ISBN 0-8018-0664-X). Johns Hopkins.

MOROCCO–FOREIGN RELATIONS

Anderson, Eugene N. First Moroccan Crisis, 1904-1906. 1966. Repr. of 1930 ed. 23.00 (ISBN 0-208-00294-4, Archon). Shoe String.
Ashmead-Bartlett, Ellis. Passing of the Shereefian Empire. LC 78-109314. (Illus.). Repr. of 1910 ed. 31.00x (ISBN 0-8371-3565-6). Greenwood.
Barlow, Ima C. Agadir Crisis. 1971. Repr. of 1940 ed. 25.00 (ISBN 0-208-01023-8, Archon). Shoe String.
Flournoy, Francis R. British Policy Towards Morocco in the Age of Palmerston, 1830-1865. LC 74-106835. Repr. of 1935 ed. 14.75x (ISBN 0-8371-3457-9, Pub. by Negro U Pr). Greenwood.
Hall, Luella J. United States & Morocco, 1776-1956. LC 71-142233. 1971. 35.00- (ISBN 0-8108-0338-0). Scarecrow.

MOROCCO–HISTORY

see also Beni Marin Dynasty; Rif Revolt, 1921-1926

Anderson, Eugene N. First Moroccan Crisis, 1904-1906. 1966. Repr. of 1930 ed. 23.00 (ISBN 0-208-00294-4, Archon). Shoe String.
Ashmead-Bartlett, Ellis. Passing of the Shereefian Empire. LC 78-109314. (Illus.). Repr. of 1910 ed. 31.00x (ISBN 0-8371-3565-6). Greenwood.
Bidwell, Robin. Morocco Under Colonial Rule: French Administration of Tribal Areas, 1912-1956. 349p. 1973. 32.50x (ISBN 0-7146-2877-8, F Cass Co). Biblio Dist.
Bowie, Leland. The Impact of the Protege System in Morocco: 1880-1912. LC 79-633875. (Papers in International Studies: No. 11). 1970. pap. 2.75x (ISBN 0-89680-044-X). Ohio U Ctr Intl.
Braithwaite, John. History of the Revolutions in the Empire of Morocco, Upon the Death of the Late Emperor, Muley Ishmael. facs. ed. LC 74-88541. (Black Heritage Library Collection Ser). 1729. 15.25 (ISBN 0-8369-8522-2). Arno.
Burke, Edmund. Prelude to Protectorate in Morocco: Precolonial Protest & Resistance, 1860-1912. LC 75-43228. (Illus.). 1977. lib. bdg. 18.50x (ISBN 0-226-08075-7). U of Chicago Pr.
Chenier, L. S. de. Recherches Historiques sur les Maures et Histoire de l'Empire de Maroc, 3 vols. (Bibliotheque Africaine Ser.). (Fr.). 1974. Repr. of 1787 ed. lib. bdg. 371.00x (ISBN 0-8287-0184-9). Clearwater Pub.
Cigar, Norman, ed. Muhammad Al-Qadiris Nashr Al Mathani: The Chronicles. (Fontes Historiae Africanae Ser.). (Illus.). 400p. 1981. 65.00x (ISBN 0-19-725994-4). Oxford U Pr.
Cruickshank, Earl F. Morocco at the Parting of the Ways: The Story of Native Protection to 1885. LC 73-106832. Repr. of 1935 ed. 13.50x (ISBN 0-8371-3454-4, Pub. by Negro U Pr). Greenwood.
De Chenier, Louis. Present State of the Empire of Morocco, 2 Vols. in 1. 1788. 46.00 (ISBN 0-384-08620-9). Johnson Repr.
Dunton, John. A True Journall of the Sally Fleet, with the Proceedings of the Voyage. LC 71-25745. (English Experience Ser.: No. 242). 26p. 1970. Repr. of 1637 ed. 9.50 (ISBN 90-221-0242-4). Walter J Johnson.
Gilman, Antonio. A Later Prehistory of Tangier, Morocco. LC 75-20595. (American School of Prehistoric Research Bulletins Ser.: No. 29). (Illus.). 1976. pap. 17.00 (ISBN 0-87365-531-1). Peabody Harvard.
Halstead, John P. Rebirth of a Nation: Origins & Rise of Moroccan Nationalism, 1912-1944. LC 67-31566. (Middle Eastern Monographs Ser: No. 18). (Orig.). 1967. pap. 7.95x (ISBN 0-674-75000-4). Harvard U Pr.
Harris, Walter B. Morocco That Was. LC 75-106838. Repr. of 1921 ed. 18.50x (ISBN 0-8371-3460-9, Pub. by Negro U Pr). Greenwood.
Jackson, James G. Account of the Empire of Morocco & the Districts of Suse & Tafilelt. (Illus.). 328p. 1968. Repr. of 1814 ed. 35.00x (ISBN 0-7146-1820-9, F Cass Co). Biblio Dist.
Ling, Dwight L. Morocco & Tunisia: A Comparative History. LC 79-5364. 1979. pap. text ed. 9.50 (ISBN 0-8191-0873-1). U Pr of Amer.
Morsy, Magali. Les Ahansala: Examen Du Role Historique D'une Famille Maraboutique De L'atlas Marocain Au XVIIIe Siecle. (Recherches Mediterraneennes, Documents: No. 5). 1972. pap. 8.90x (ISBN 90-2797-046-7). Mouton.
Rabinow, Paul. Symbolic Domination: Cultural Symbols & Historical Change in Morocco. LC 74-7565. (Midway Reprint). 1978. pap. text ed. 8.00x (ISBN 0-226-70149-2). U of Chicago Pr.
Spencer, William. Historical Dictionary of Morocco. LC 80-21328. (African Historical Dictionaries: No. 24). 195p. 1980. 11.00 (ISBN 0-8108-1361-0). Scarecrow.
Terrasse, Henri. Histoire Du Maroc Des Origines a L'etablissment Du Protectorat Francais, 2 vols. LC 74-180381. (Fr.). Repr. of 1950 ed. 24.00 ea.; 47.50 set (ISBN 0-404-56329-5). AMS Pr.
Wilkins, George. Three Miseries of Barbary: Plague, Famine, Civill Warre. LC 77-26339. (English Experience Ser.: No. 178). 32p. 1969. Repr. of 1606 ed. 7.00 (ISBN 90-221-0178-9). Walter J Johnson.
Yahya, Dahiru. Morocco in the Sixteenth Century: Problems & Patterns in African Foreign Policy. (Ibadan History Ser.). 1981. text ed. write for info. (ISBN 0-391-01787-X). Humanities.

MOROCCO–JUVENILE LITERATURE

Martin, Rupert. Land & People of Morocco. (gr. 5-9). 1968. 6.95g (ISBN 0-02-762430-7). Macmillan.
Spencer, William. The Land & People of Morocco. rev. ed. LC 73-4906. (Portraits of the Nations Series). (Illus.). 1973. 8.95 (ISBN 0-397-31481-7). Lippincott.

MOROCCO–POLITICS AND GOVERNMENT

Al-Fasi, Alal. Independence Movements in Arab North Africa. LC 70-96201. 1969. Repr. of 1954 ed. lib. bdg. 22.50x (ISBN 0-374-90095-7). Octagon.
Scham, Alan. Lyautey in Morocco: Protectorate Administration, 1912-1925. LC 74-92680. 1970. 26.75x (ISBN 0-520-01602-5). U of Cal Pr.
Zartman, I. William. Destiny of a Dynasty: The Search for Institutions in Morocco's Developing Society. LC 64-8171. (Studies in International Affairs: No. 3). 1964. 5.95x (ISBN 0-87249-094-7). U of SC Pr.

MOROCCO–SOCIAL LIFE AND CUSTOMS

Brown, Kenneth L. People of Sale. 1976. text ed. 18.00x (ISBN 0-674-66155-9). Harvard U Pr.
Coon, Carleton S. Tribes of the Rif. (Harvard African Studies: Vol. 9). 1931. 49.00 (ISBN 0-527-01032-4). Kraus Repr.
Crapanzano, Vincent. The Hamadsha: A Study in Moroccan Ethnopsychiatry. LC 72-75529. 1973. 24.50x (ISBN 0-520-02241-6). U of Cal Pr.
--Tuhami: Portrait of a Moroccan. LC 79-24550. 1980. lib. bdg. 17.50x (ISBN 0-226-11870-3). U of Chicago Pr.
De Amicis, Edmondo. Morocco: Its People & Places, 2 vols. 1976. lib. bdg. 250.00 (ISBN 0-8490-2282-7). Gordon Pr.
Geertz, C., et al. Meaning & Order in Moroccan Society. LC 78-54327. (Illus.). 1979. 49.50 (ISBN 0-521-22175-7). Cambridge U Pr.
Hoffman, Bernard G. Structure of Traditional Moroccan Rural Society. (Studies in Social Anthropology: No. 2). 1967. text ed. 36.25x (ISBN 0-686-22465-5). Mouton.
Maher, Vanessa. Women & Property in Morocco. LC 74-80351. (Studies in Social Anthropology: No. 10). (Illus.). 164p. 1975. 27.50 (ISBN 0-521-20548-4). Cambridge U Pr.

MORONS

see Mentally Handicapped

MORPHINE

see also Heroin; Opium

Levinstein, Edward. Morbid Craving for Morphia: Die Morphiumsucht. Harrer, Charles, tr. Grob, Gerald N., ed. LC 80-1259. (Addiction in America Ser.). 1981. Repr. of 1878 ed. lib. bdg. 12.00x (ISBN 0-405-13602-1). Arno.
Waldorf, Dan, et al. Morphine Maintenance: The Shreveport Clinic, 1919-1923. LC 74-79289. (Special Studies Ser). 1974. 1.25 (ISBN 0-686-05810-0). Drug Abuse.
Way, E. L. & Adler, T. K., eds. Biological Disposition of Morphine & Its Surrogates. (WHO Bulletin Reprint). (Summary in French). 1962. pap. 2.00 (ISBN 92-4-056004-1). World Health.

MORPHOGENESIS

see also Botany–Morphology; Cell Differentiation; Morphology; Morphology (Animals)

Abercrombie, M. & Brachet, J., eds. Advances in Morphogenesis, 10 vols. Incl. Vol. 1. 1961 (ISBN 0-12-028601-7); Vol. 2. 1963 (ISBN 0-12-028602-5); Vol. 3. 1964. (ISBN 0-12-028603-3); Vol. 4. 1965 (ISBN 0-12-028604-1); Vol. 5. 1966 (ISBN 0-12-028605-X); Vol. 6. 1967 (ISBN 0-12-028606-8); Vol. 7. King, T. J., ed. 1968 (ISBN 0-12-028607-6); Vol. 8. King, T. J., ed. 1970 (ISBN 0-12-028608-4); Vol. 9. King, T. J., ed. 1971 (ISBN 0-12-028609-2); Vol. 10. 1973 (ISBN 0-12-028610-6). 55.00 ea. Acad Pr.
Bergsma, Daniel & Lenz, Widukind, eds. Morphogenesis & Malformation of the Limb: Proceedings. LC 76-55004. (Birth Defects Original Article Ser.: Vol. 13, No. 1). 1977. 41.00x (ISBN 0-8451-1008-X). A R Liss.
Bernhard, C. G. & Schade, J. Developmental Neurology. (Progress in Brain Research: Vol. 26). 1967. 53.75 (ISBN 0-444-40040-0, North Holland). Elsevier.
Bonner, John T. Morphogenesis: An Essay on Development. LC 52-5847. (Illus.). 1963. pap. 1.65 (ISBN 0-689-70021-0, 28). Atheneum.
Cau, P., et al. Morphogenesis of Thyroid Follicles in Vitro. (Advances in Anatomy Embryology & Cell Biology: Vol. 52, Pt. 2). 1976. pap. 34.30 (ISBN 0-387-07654-9). Springer-Verlag.
Connelly, Thomas G., et al, eds. Morphogenesis & Pattern Formation. 312p. 1981. 34.50 (ISBN 0-89004-635-2). Raven.
Curtis, A. S. Cell Surface: Its Molecular Role in Morphogenesis. 1967. 55.50 (ISBN 0-12-199650-6). Acad Pr.
Gorlin, Robert J., ed. Morphogenesis & Malformation of the Ear. LC 80-18892. (Alan R. Liss: Vol. 16,No. 4). 1980. 44.00 (ISBN 0-8451-1038-1). March of Dimes.
Henrici, Arthur T. Morphologic Variation & Rate of Growth of Bacteria. (Illus.). 194p. 1928. photocopy ed. spiral 18.50 (ISBN 0-398-04277-2). C C Thomas.
International Conference on Morphogenesis & Malformation, Lake Wilderness, Washington, 3rd, July 1976. Morphogenesis & Malformation of the Genital System: Proceedings. Blandau, Richard J. & Bergsma, Daniel, eds. LC 77-535. (Birth Defects Original Article Ser.: Vol. 13, No. 2). 174p. 1977. 21.00x (ISBN 0-8451-1009-8). A R Liss.
International Workshop on Morphogenesis & Malformation, 4th, Grand Canyon, Ariz., 1977. Morphogenesis & Malformation of the Cardiovascular System: Proceedings. Rosenquist, Glenn C. & Bergsma, Daniel, eds. LC 78-14527. (Birth Defects Original Article Ser.: Vol. 14, No. 7). 452p. 1978. 53.00x (ISBN 0-8451-1023-3). A R Liss.
Needham, Joseph. Biochemistry & Morphogenesis. 1942. 99.50 (ISBN 0-521-05797-3). Cambridge U Pr.
--Order & Life. 1968. pap. 4.95 (ISBN 0-262-64001-5). MIT Pr.
Pexieder, T. Cell Death in the Morphogenesis & Teratogenesis of the Heart. (Advances in Anatomy, Embryology & Cell Biology Ser.: Vol. 51, Pt. 3). (Illus.). 100p. (Orig.). 1975. pap. 42.50 (ISBN 0-387-07270-5). Springer-Verlag.
Phillips, Joy B. Development of Vertebrate Anatomy. LC 74-14876. 1975. text ed. 17.95 (ISBN 0-8016-3927-1). Mosby.
Rosenquist, Glenn C. & Bergsma, Daniel, eds. Morphogenesis & Malinformation of the Cardiovascular System. LC 78-14527. (Alan R. Liss Ser.: Vol. 14, No. 7). 1978. 46.00 (ISBN 0-8451-1023-3). March of Dimes.
Sengel, P. Morphogenesis of Skin. LC 74-25659. (Developmental & Cell Biology Ser.: No. 2). (Illus.). 300p. 1975. 69.00 (ISBN 0-521-20644-8). Cambridge U Pr.
Sinnott, Edmund G. Problem of Organic Form. 1963. 27.50x (ISBN 0-685-69864-5). Elliots Bks.
Smith, David W. Recognizable Patterns of Human Deformation: Identification & Management of Mechanical Effects on Morphogenesis. (Illus.). 240p. 1981. text ed. write for info. (ISBN 0-7216-8401-7). Saunders.
Structural Stability & Morphogenesis: An Outline of a General Theory of Models. (Illus.). 1975. 29.50 (ISBN 0-8053-9278-5, Adv Bk Prog); pap. 17.50 (ISBN 0-8053-9279-3). Benjamin-Cummings.
Thom, R. Structual Stability & Morphogenesis: An Outline of a General Theory of Models. Fowler, D. H., tr. from Fr. pap. 22.50 (ISBN 0-8053-9279-3). A-W.
Trinkaus, J. P. Cells into Organs: The Forces That Shape the Embryo. 1969. pap. 12.95x ref. ed. (ISBN 0-13-121640-6). P-H.
Wassermann, G. D. Molecular Control of Cell Differentiation & Morphogenesis: A Systematic Theory. (Quantitative Approach to Life Science Ser.: Vol. 2). 1972. 74.75 (ISBN 0-8247-1766-X). Dekker.
Wolff, E. & Lender, T., eds. Tissue Interactions During Organogenesis. (Documents in Biology Ser.: Vol. 1). 1970. 43.00x (ISBN 0-677-13010-4). Gordon.

MORPHOLOGY

see also Abnormalities, Human; Morphogenesis

Akhmanova, Olga. Phonology, Morphonology, Morphology. LC 72-159459. (Janua Linguarum, Ser. Minor: No. 101). 135p. 1971. pap. text ed. 23.50x (ISBN 90-2791-748-5). Mouton.
Blackith, R. E. & Reyment, R. A. Multivariate Morphometrics. 1972. 65.00 (ISBN 0-12-103150-0). Acad Pr.
Bookstein, F. L. The Measurement of Biological Shape & Shape Change. LC 78-15923. (Lecture Notes in Biomathematics: Vol. 24). 1978. pap. 10.30 (ISBN 0-387-08912-8). Springer-Verlag.
Brown, Tasman. Morphology of the Australian Skull: Studies by Multivariate Analysis. (AIAS Human Biology Ser.: No. 4). (Illus.). 1973. pap. text ed. 12.75x (ISBN 0-85575-027-8). Humanities.
Gierer, A. Generation of Biological Patterns & Form: Some Physical, Mathmatical & Logical Aspects. LC 50-11295. (Illus.). 48p. 1981. pap. 23.00 (ISBN 0-08-027133-2). Pergamon.
Glick, David & Rosenbaum, R., eds. Techniques of Biochemical & Biophysical Morphology, Vol. 1. 280p. 1972. 22.50 (ISBN 0-471-30800-5). Krieger.
--Techniques of Biochemical & Biophysical Morphology, Vol. 14. 536p. 1975. 30.50 (ISBN 0-471-30801-3). Krieger.
Glick, David & Rosenbaum, Robert, eds. Techniques of Biochemical & Biophysical Morphology, Vol. 3. LC 72-153. 214p. 1977. 27.50 (ISBN 0-471-02219-5, Pub. by Wiley). Krieger.
Gosline, William A. Functional Morphology & Classification of Teleostean Fishes. LC 77-151454. (Illus.). 1971. pap. text ed. 7.00x (ISBN 0-87022-300-3). U Pr of Hawaii.
Johnson, John E, Jr., ed. Current Trends in Morphological Techniques, Vols. II & III. 1981. Vol. II, 288p. 79.95 (ISBN 0-8493-5826-4); Vol. III, 272p. 75.95 (ISBN 0-686-73486-6). CRC Pr.
Khlebnikova, Irina. Oppositions in Morphology: As Exemplified in the English Tense System. LC 72-94476. (Janua Linguarum, Ser. Minor: No. 151). 185p. (Orig.). 1973. pap. text ed. 28.25x (ISBN 0-686-22547-3). Mouton.

Kurosumi, Kazumasa & Fujita, Hisao. Functional Morphology of Endocrine Glands: An Atlas of Electron Micrographs. (Illus.). 1974. 50.00 (ISBN 0-89640-020-4). Igaku-Shoin.
McArdle, J. Functional Morphology of the Hip & Thigh of the Lorisiformes. (Contributions to Primatology Ser.: Vol. 17). (Illus.). 148p. 1981. pap. 19.25 (ISBN 3-8055-1767-X). S Karger.
Matthews, P. H. Morphology: An Introduction to the Theory of Word-Structure. LC 73-91817. (Cambridge Textbooks in Linguistics Ser.). 256p. 1974. 37.50 (ISBN 0-521-20448-8); pap. 9.95x (ISBN 0-521-09856-4). Cambridge U Pr.
Mayer, Edmund. Introduction to Dynamic Morphology. 1963. 58.50 (ISBN 0-12-480650-3). Acad Pr.
Miles, R. E. & Serra, J., eds. Geometrical Probability & Biological Structures: Buffon's 200 Anniversary. (Lecture Notes in Biomathematics: Vol. 23). 1978. pap. 15.60 (ISBN 0-387-08856-3). Springer-Verlag.
Nachtigall, W. Biological Mechanisms of Attachment: The Comparative Morphology & Bioengineering of Organs for Linkage, Suction, & Adhesion. Biederman-Thorson, M. A., tr. LC 73-17936. (Illus.). 194p. 1974. 44.30 (ISBN 0-387-06550-4). Springer-Verlag.
Ohlander, Solve. Phonology, Meaning, Morphology: On the Role of Semantic & Morphological Criteria in Phonological Analysis. (Gothenburg Studies in English: No. 33). 221p. 1976. pap. text ed. 13.50x (ISBN 0-685-72010-1). Humanities.
Portmann, Adolf. Animal Forms & Patterns: A Study of the Appearance of Animals. Czech, Hella, tr. from Ger. LC 67-14962. (Illus.). 1971. 6.00x (ISBN 0-8052-3003-3); pap. 2.75 (ISBN 0-8052-0309-5). Schocken.
Rousseau, G. S. Organic Form: The Life of an Idea. 1972. 8.00x (ISBN 0-7100-7246-5). Routledge & Kegan.
Sapir, E. Notes on Chasta Costa Phonology & Morphology. (Anthropological Publications Ser.: Vol. 2-2). (Illus.). 1914. 2.00 (ISBN 0-686-24092-8). Univ Mus of U.
Sarma, Ramaswamy H. Nucleic Acid Geometry & Dynamics. LC 80-10620. (Illus.). 424p. 1980. 55.00 (ISBN 0-08-024631-1); pap. 24.50 (ISBN 0-08-024630-3). Pergamon.
Shipley, Kenneth G. & Banis, Carolyn S. Teaching Morphology Developmentally: Methods & Materials for Teaching Bound Morphology. 1981. manual 50.00 (ISBN 0-88450-728-9). Communication Skill.
Stevens, Peter S. Patterns in Nature. LC 73-19720. (Illus.). 256p. 1974. 12.50 (ISBN 0-316-81328-1, Pub. by Atlantic Monthly Pr); pap. 6.95 (ISBN 0-316-81331-1). Little.
Straub, W., ed. Current Genetic, Clinical & Morphological Problems. (Developments in Ophthalmology: Vol. 3). (Illus.). vi, 218p. 1981. pap. 94.00 (ISBN 3-8055-2000-X). S Karger.
Symposium Based on Papers Presented at the Cajal Club Meeting in Conjunction with the American Association of Anatomists, Dallas, Tex., April 1972. Neuromorphological Plasticity: Proceedings. Bernstein, J. & Goodman, D. C., eds. (Brain, Behavior & Evolution: Vol. 8, Nos. 1-2). (Illus.). 164p. 1973. Repr. 29.25 (ISBN 3-8055-1703-3). S Karger.
Ungvary. Functional Morphology of Hepatic Vascular System. 1977. 17.00 (ISBN 0-9960006-7-4, Pub. by Kaido Hungary). Heyden.
Webster, Douglas B. & Webster, Molly. Comparative Vertebrate Morphology. 1974. text ed. 23.95 (ISBN 0-12-740850-9). Acad Pr.

MORPHOLOGY (ANIMALS)
see also Abnormalities (Animals); Anatomy, Comparative; Animal Weapons; Body Size; Embryology; Growth
Albrecht, Gene H. The Craniofacial Morphology of the Sulawesi Macaques: Multivariate Analysis As a Tool in Systematics. (Contributions to Primatology: Vol. 13). (Illus.). 1977. 44.50 (ISBN 3-8055-2694-6). S Karger.
Baur, R. Morphometry of the Placental Exchange Area. LC 77-3148. (Advances in Anatomy, Embryology & Cell Biology: Vol. 53, No. 1). 1977. pap. 18.00 (ISBN 0-387-08159-3). Springer-Verlag.
Carr, Ian & Daems, W. T., eds. The Reticuloendothalial System--a Comprehensive Treatise: Morphology, Vol. 1. (Illus.). 771p. 1980. 49.50 (ISBN 0-686-62966-3, Plenum Pr). Plenum Pub.
Coleman, William, tr. & intro. by. The Interpretation of Animal Form. (The Sources of Science: No. 15). (Illus.). 191p. 1968. Repr. of 1888 ed. 15.50 (ISBN 0-384-28525-2). Johnson Repr.
Dullemeier, P. Concepts & Approaches in Animal Morphology. (Illus.). 272p. 33.70x (ISBN 90-232-1133-2, Pub. by Van Gorcum). Intl Schol Bk Serv.
Hildebrand, Milton. Analysis of Vertebrate Structure. LC 73-11486. (Illus.). 704p. 1974. text ed. 26.50x (ISBN 0-471-39580-3). Wiley.
Jollie, Malcolm. Chordate Morphology. LC 62-17800. 492p. 1973. Repr. of 1962 ed. 19.50 (ISBN 0-88275-090-9). Krieger.
Joseph, N. R. Physicochemical Anthropology, Part II: Comparative Morphology & Behavior. 1979. 58.75 (ISBN 3-8055-2951-1). S Karger.
McLaughlin, Patsy A. Comparative Morphology of Recent Crustacea. LC 79-26066. (Illus.). 1980. text ed. 23.95x (ISBN 0-7167-1121-4). W H Freeman.
Mitro, A. & Palkovits, M. Morphology of the Rat Brain Ventricles, Ependyma & Periventricular Structures. (Biblio Anatomica Ser.: No. 21). (Illus.). x, 110p. 1981. pap. 58.75 (ISBN 0-686-71647-7). S Karger.
Phillips, Joy B. Development of Vertebrate Anatomy. LC 74-14876. 1975. text ed. 17.95 (ISBN 0-8016-3927-1). Mosby.
Saunders, John T. & Manton, Sidnie M. Manual of Practical Vertebrate Morphology. 4th ed. (Illus.). 1969. pap. 15.95x (ISBN 0-19-857114-3). Oxford U Pr.
Tillmann, Bernhard. A Contribution to the Functional Morphology of Articular Surfaces. Bargmann, Wolfgang & Doerr, Wilhelm, eds. Konorza, G., tr. from Ger. LC 78-54588. (Normal & Pathologic Anatomy Ser.). (Illus.). 55p. 1978. pap. 18.00 (ISBN 0-88416-248-6). Wright-PSG.
Ziemer, L. K. Functional Morphology of Forelimb Joints in the Wooly Monkey Lagothrix Lagothricha. Szalay, F. S., ed. (Contributions to Primatology: Vol. 14). (Illus.). 1978. 46.75 (ISBN 3-8055-2821-3). S Karger.

MORPHOLOGY (PLANTS)
see Botany–Morphology

MORPHY, PAUL CHARLES, 1837-1884
Edge, Frederick M. The Exploits & Triumphs in Europe of Paul Morphy, the Chess Champion. (Illus.). 224p. 1973. pap. 2.00 (ISBN 0-486-22882-7). Dover.

MORPHY, PAUL CHARLES, 1837-1884–FICTION
Lange, Max. The Chess Genius of Paul Morphy. Falkbeer, Ernest, tr. LC 73-83322. (Chess Classics Ser.). (Illus.). 356p. 1974. pap. 3.95 (ISBN 0-88254-182-X). Hippocrene Bks.

MORRILL, JUSTIN SMITH, 1810-1898
Parker, William B. Life & Public Services of Justin Smith Morrill. LC 79-87371. (American Scene Ser). (Illus.). 1971. Repr. of 1924 ed. lib. bdg. 42.50 (ISBN 0-306-71595-3). Da Capo.

MORRIS, EARL HALSTEAD, 1889-1956
Lister, Florence C. & Lister, Robert H. Earl Morris & Southwestern Archaeology. LC 68-19737. (Illus.). 1977. pap. 6.95 (ISBN 0-8263-0455-9). U of NM Pr.

MORRIS, GEORGE SYLVESTER
Jones, Marc E. George Sylvester Morris: His Philosophical Career & Theistic Idealism. LC 68-23303. 1968. Repr. of 1948 ed. lib. bdg. 19.75x (ISBN 0-8371-0121-2, JOMC). Greenwood.

MORRIS, GOUVERNEUR, 1752-1816
Kline, Mary-Jo. Gouverneur Morris & the New Nation, 1775-1788. LC 77-14776. (Dissertations in American Economic Histoy Ser.). 1978. 28.00 (ISBN 0-405-11042-1). Arno.
Lecky, William. Historical & Political Essays. LC 76-99707. (Essay Index Reprint Ser). 1908. 18.00 (ISBN 0-8369-1973-4). Arno.
Lodge, Henry C. Historical & Political Essays. LC 72-282. (Essay Index Reprint Ser.). Repr. of 1892 ed. 15.00 (ISBN 0-8369-2801-6). Arno.
Mintz, Max M. Gouverneur Morris & the American Revolution. LC 70-108792. (Illus.). 1970. 16.95x (ISBN 0-8061-0900-9). U of Okla Pr.
Roosevelt, T. Gouverneur Morris. LC 68-24996. (American Biography Ser., No. 32). 1969. Repr. of 1889 ed. lib. bdg. 52.95 (ISBN 0-8383-0274-2). Haskell.
Roosevelt, Theodore. Gouverneur Morris. LC 80-24746. (American Statesmen Ser.). 340p. 1981. pap. 5.95 (ISBN 0-87754-188-4). Chelsea Hse.
--Gouverneur Morris. LC 70-108532. 1971. Repr. of 1898 ed. 14.00 (ISBN 0-403-00313-X). Scholarly.
--Gouverneur Morris. Morse, John T., Jr., ed. LC 76-128972. (American Statesmen: No. 8). Repr. of 1898 ed. 15.00 (ISBN 0-404-50858-8). AMS Pr.

MORRIS, JAN, 1926-
Morris, Jan. Conundrum. LC 74-525. (Helen & Kurt Wolff Bk). 1974. 6.95 (ISBN 0-15-122563-X). HarBraceJ.
--Conundrum. 1975. pap. 1.50 (ISBN 0-451-06413-5, W6413, Sig). NAL.

MORRIS, RICHARD BRANDON, 1904-
Sohner, Charles P. The People's Power: American Government & Politics Today. 575p. 1973. pap. 10.95x (ISBN 0-673-07646-6). Scott F.

MORRIS, ROBERT, 1734-1806
Chernow, Barbara A. Robert Morris: Land Speculator 1790-1801. LC 77-14762. (Dissertations in American Economic History Ser.). 1978. 25.00 (ISBN 0-405-11029-4). Arno.
Ferguson, E. James & Catanzariti, John, eds. Papers of Robert Morris, Seventeen Eighty One to Seventeen Eighty-Four, Vol. 4: January 11-April 15, 1782. LC 72-91107. (Robert Morris Papers Ser). 1978. 25.00x (ISBN 0-8229-3352-7). U of Pittsburgh Pr.
--The Papers of Robert Morris, 1781-1784, Vol. 1: February 7 - July 31, 1781. LC 72-91107. (Illus.). 1973. 22.50x (ISBN 0-8229-3267-9). U of Pittsburgh Pr.
--The Papers of Robert Morris, 1781-1784, Vol. 3: October 1, 1781-January 10, 1782. LC 72-91107. (Illus.). 1977. 23.50x (ISBN 0-8229-3324-1). U of Pittsburgh Pr.
--The Papers of Robert Morris, 1781-1784: Vol. 5; April 16-July 20, 1782. LC 72-91107. 1980. 27.50x (ISBN 0-8229-3420-5). U of Pittsburgh Pr.
Oberholtzer, Ellis P. Robert Morris: Patriot & Financier. LC 68-57120. (Research & Source Works Ser: No. 317). (Illus.). 1969. Repr. of 1903 ed. 29.00 (ISBN 0-8337-2598-X). B Franklin.
Sumner, William G. Financier & the Finances of the American Revolution, 2 Vols. 1891. Set. 38.00 (ISBN 0-8337-3460-1). B Franklin.
--Financier & the Finances of the American Revolution, 2 Vols. LC 68-18224. Repr. of 1891 ed. Set. 35.00x (ISBN 0-678-00435-8). Kelley.
Ver Steeg, Clarence L. Robert Morris: Revolutionary Financier. LC 71-120674. 276p. 1970. Repr. of 1954 ed. lib. bdg. 16.50x (ISBN 0-374-98078-0). Octagon.
Wagner, Frederick. Robert Morris, Audacious Patriot. (Illus.). (gr. 7up). 1976. 5.95 (ISBN 0-396-07281-X). Dodd.

MORRIS, ROBERT, 1931-
Compton, Michael & Sylvester, David. Robert Morris. (Tate Gallery Art Ser.). (Illus.). 1977. 4.50 (ISBN 0-8120-5143-2). Barron.
Krens, Thomas. The Drawings of Robert Morris. LC 80-8703. (Illus.). 256p. 1981. pap. 12.95 (ISBN 0-06-430111-7, IN111, BN). Har-Row.

MORRIS, SAMUEL, 1873-1893
Baldwin, Lindley. March of Faith: Samuel Morris. 1969. pap. 1.95 (ISBN 0-87123-360-6, 200360). Bethany Hse.

MORRIS, WILLIAM, 1834-1896
Arnot, R. Page. Bernard Shaw & William Morris. LC 73-4396. 1973. lib. bdg. 7.50 (ISBN 0-8414-1725-3). Folcroft.
--Bernard Shaw & William Morris. 1978. Repr. of 1957 ed. lib. bdg. 8.50 (ISBN 0-8495-0027-3). Arden Lib.
Arnot, Robert P. William Morris, the Man & the Myth. LC 76-107. 131p. 1976. Repr. of 1964 ed. lib. bdg. 15.00 (ISBN 0-8371-8652-8, ARWM). Greenwood.
Ashbee, C. B. An Endeavor Towards the Teaching of John Ruskin & William Morris. LC 73-7761. Repr. of 1901 ed. lib. bdg. 10.00 (ISBN 0-8414-2854-9). Folcroft.
Bloomfield, Paul. William Morris. LC 73-15902. 1934. lib. bdg. 25.00 (ISBN 0-8414-3322-4). Folcroft.
--William Morris. LC 70-144886. 314p. 1934. Repr. 16.00 (ISBN 0-403-00872-7). Scholarly.
Bradley, Ian. William Morris & His World. LC 78-35937. (Illus.). 1978. 10.95 (ISBN 0-684-15867-1, ScribT). Scribner.
Calhoun, Blue. The Pastoral Vision of William Morris: The Earthly Paradise. LC 74-14054. 270p. 1975. 16.00x (ISBN 0-8203-0354-2). U of Ga Pr.
Cary, Elisabeth L. William Morris, Poet, Craftsman, Socialist. 1977. Repr. 29.00 (ISBN 0-403-07268-9). Scholarly.
Cary, Elizabeth L. William Morris: Poet, Craftsmen, Socialist. LC 74-18124. 74. Repr. of 1902 ed. lib. bdg. 35.00 (ISBN 0-8414-3545-6). Folcroft.
Clutton-Brock, A. William Morris: His Work & Influence. 1978. Repr. of 1919 ed. lib. bdg. 20.00 (ISBN 0-8492-3900-1). R West.
--William Morris: His Work & Influence. 1978. Repr. of 1914 ed. lib. bdg. 20.00 (ISBN 0-8495-0849-5). Arden Lib.
Cole, G. D. William Morris As a Socialist. LC 73-17131. 1960. lib. bdg. 10.00 (ISBN 0-8414-3508-1). Folcroft.
Compton-Rickett, Arthur. William Morris: A Study in Personality. LC 73-160749. 1971. Repr. of 1913 ed. 15.00 (ISBN 0-8046-1563-2). Kennikat.
--William Morris: A Study in Personality. 1978. Repr. of 1913 ed. lib. bdg. 30.00 (ISBN 0-8495-0801-0). Arden Lib.
Compton-Rickett, R. William Morris: A Study in Personality. LC 72-195148. 1973. lib. bdg. 20.00 (ISBN 0-8414-2374-1). Folcroft.
Countess Of Warwick. William Morris: His Homes & Haunts. LC 73-13851. 1912. lib. bdg. 15.00 (ISBN 0-8414-3462-X). Folcroft.
Crane, Walter. William Morris & His Work. 1911. lib. bdg. 6.50 (ISBN 0-8414-3544-8). Folcroft.
--William Morris to Whistler. LC 73-19972. 1911. lib. bdg. 25.00 (ISBN 0-8414-3534-0). Folcroft.
Crow, Gerald H. William Morris: Designer. 120p. 1980. Repr. of 1934 ed. lib. bdg. 22.50 (ISBN 0-8492-3970-2). R West.
--William Morris, Designer. LC 75-28168. 1975. Repr. of 1934 ed. lib. bdg. 25.00 (ISBN 0-8414-3469-7). Folcroft.
Dunlap, Joseph R. The Book That Never Was: William Morris Edward Burne-Jones & "The Earthly Paradise". LC 78-156977. (Illus.). 1971. 15.00 (ISBN 0-88211-018-7). S A Russell.
Eshleman, Lloyd W. A Victorian Rebel: The Life of William Morris. LC 74-168557. xiv, 386p. 1971. Repr. of 1940 ed. lib. bdg. 20.00x (ISBN 0-374-92627-1). Octagon.
Evans, B. Ifor. William Morris & His Poetry. LC 74-23889. 1925. lib. bdg. 7.50 (ISBN 0-8414-3947-8). Folcroft.
Evans, Benjamin I. William Morris & His Poetry. LC 74-120987. (Poetry & Life Ser.). Repr. of 1925 ed. 7.25 (ISBN 0-404-52512-1). AMS Pr.
Faulkner, Peter. Against the Age: An Introduction to William Morris. (Illus.). 192p. 1980. text ed. 28.50 (ISBN 0-04-809012-3). Allen Unwin.
Faulkner, Peter, ed. William Morris: The Critical Heritage. (The Critical Heritage Ser.). 480p. 1973. 38.50 (ISBN 0-7100-7520-0). Routledge & Kegan.
Fritzsche, Gustav. William Morris' Sozialismus Und Anarchistischer Kommunismus. 1967. pap. 10.00 (ISBN 0-384-17010-2). Johnson Repr.
Gardner, Delbert R. An "Idle Singer" & His Audience: A Study of William Morris's Poetric Reputation in England, 1858-1900. (Studies in English Literature: No. 92). 135p. 1975. text ed. 25.00x (ISBN 0-686-22603-8). Mouton.
Gillington, M. C. A Day with William Morris. Repr. 10.00 (ISBN 0-8274-2155-9). R West.
Godwin, Edward & Godwin, Stephani. Warrior Bard: The Life of William Morris. LC 70-103190. 1970. Repr. of 1947 ed. 10.00 (ISBN 0-8046-0827-X). Kennikat.
--Warrior Bird: The Life of William Morris. 1978. Repr. of 1947 ed. lib. bdg. 25.00 (ISBN 0-8495-1938-1). Arden Lib.
Godwin, Edward & Godwin, Stepheni. Warrior Bard: The Life of William Morris. 176p. 1980. Repr. lib. bdg. 25.00 (ISBN 0-8492-4955-4). R West.
Hoare, Dorothy M. The Works of Morris & of Yeats in Relation to Early Saga Literature. LC 72-139476. 1971. Repr. of 1937 ed. 11.00 (ISBN 0-8462-1382-6). Russell.
--The Works of Morris & of Yeats: In Relation to Early Saga Literature. 1978. Repr. of 1937 ed. lib. bdg. 20.00 (ISBN 0-8495-2317-6). Arden Lib.
--Works of Morris & Yeats in Relation to Early Saga Literature. LC 72-193501. 1973. lib. bdg. 10.95 (ISBN 0-8414-5087-0). Folcroft.
Jackson, Holbrook. William Morris. LC 79-110848. 1971. Repr. of 1926 ed. lib. bdg. 15.00x (ISBN 0-8371-4515-5, JAwM). Greenwood.
--William Morris. LC 74-18287. 1974. Repr. of 1934 ed. lib. bdg. 8.50 (ISBN 0-8414-5318-7). Folcroft.
--William Morris & the Arts & Crafts. 59.95 (ISBN 0-8490-1306-2). Gordon Pr.
--William Morris: Craftsman-Socialist. 59p. 1980. Repr. of 1908 ed. lib. bdg. 12.50 (ISBN 0-8495-2756-2). Arden Lib.
Kirchhoff, Frederick. William Morris. (English Authors Ser.: No. 262). 1979. lib. bdg. 14.50 (ISBN 0-8057-6723-1). Twayne.
Kocmanova, Jessie. Poetic Maturing of William Morris: From the Earthly Paradise to the Pilgrim's Hope. LC 72-190712. 1964. lib. bdg. 17.50 (ISBN 0-8414-5600-3). Folcroft.
Lindsay, Jack. William Morris: His Life & Work. LC 79-13075. (Illus.). 1979. 14.95 (ISBN 0-8008-8339-X). Taplinger.
Mackail, J. W. Life of William Morris, 2 vols. in 1. LC 68-57988. 1968. Repr. of 1899 ed. 30.00 (ISBN 0-405-08767-5, Pub. by Blom). Arno.
--William Morris. 1902. lib. bdg. 5.00 (ISBN 0-8414-5938-X). Folcroft.
--William Morris & His Circle. 1907. lib. bdg. 6.75 (ISBN 0-8414-5999-1). Folcroft.
Mackail, John W. Life of William Morris. LC 79-118180. (English Biography Ser., No. 31). 1970. Repr. of 1900 ed. lib. bdg. 79.95 (ISBN 0-8383-1070-2). Haskell.
--William Morris. LC 74-20657. 1942. Repr. of 1901 ed. lib. bdg. 6.00 (ISBN 0-8414-5936-3). Folcroft.
--William Morris: An Address Delivered at Kelmscott House. LC 74-20765. 1974. Repr. of 1902 ed. lib. bdg. 6.00 (ISBN 0-8414-5938-X). Folcroft.

--William Morris: An Address Delivered at the Annual Meeting of the National Home Reading Union, 28th Oct., 1910. LC 74-20768. 1974. Repr. of 1910 ed. lib. bdg. 6.50 (ISBN 0-8414-5942-8). Folcroft.
--William Morris & His Circle. LC 79-117585. (English Literature Ser., No. 33). 1970. Repr. of 1907 ed. lib. bdg. 40.95 (ISBN 0-8383-1018-4). Haskell.
MacLeod, Robert D. William Morris: As Seen by His Contemporaries. LC 74-20769. 1974. Repr. of 1956 ed. lib. bdg. 6.00 (ISBN 0-8414-5935-5). Folcroft.
Marshall, Roderick. William Morris & His Earthly Paradises. (Illus.). 317p. 1979. 29.50x (ISBN 0-389-20085-9). B&N.
Mathews, Richard. Worlds Beyond the World: The Fantastic Vision of William Morris. LC 78-247. (The Milford Ser: Popular Writers of Today Vol. 13). 1978. lib. bdg. 8.95x (ISBN 0-89370-118-1); pap. 2.95 (ISBN 0-89370-218-8). Borgo Pr.
Meier, Paul. William Morris: The Marxist Dreamer, 2 vols. Gubb, Frank G., tr. from Fr. 1977. Set. text ed. 57.50 (ISBN 0-391-00684-3). Humanities.
Meynell, E. Portrait of William Morris. 59.95 (ISBN 0-8490-0881-6). Gordon Pr.
Morris, May. The Introductions to the Collected Works of William Morris, 2 vols. LC 73-80306. (Illus.). 800p. 1973. Set. 35.00 (ISBN 0-88211-046-2). S A Russell.
Morris, William. The Collected Letters of William Morris, Vol. I. Kelvin, Norman, ed. 648p. Date not set. 55.00 (ISBN 0-686-76571-0). Princeton U Pr.
--The Letters of William Morris to His Family & Friends. Henderson, Philip, ed. LC 75-41199. Repr. of 1950 ed. 28.25 (ISBN 0-404-14711-9). AMS Pr.
--Three Works by William Morris. Morton, A. L., ed. 1968. pap. 2.25 (ISBN 0-7178-0202-7). Intl Pub Co.
Murry, J. Middleton. William Morris in the Great Victorians. Massingham, H. J., ed. 1973. Repr. of 1932 ed. 45.00 (ISBN 0-8274-0131-0). R West.
Needham, P., ed. William Morris & the Art of the Book. (Illus.). 1976. 55.00 (ISBN 0-685-77490-2, Pub. with Oxford U Pr); pap. 27.50 (ISBN 0-87598-059-7). Pierpont Morgan.
Noyes, Alfred. William Morris. LC 72-39201. (Select Bibliographies Reprint Ser.). Repr. of 1908 ed. 14.00 (ISBN 0-8369-6803-4). Arno.
--William Morris. 1973. lib. bdg. 12.50 (ISBN 0-8414-6662-9). Folcroft.
--William Morris. LC 70-173176. Repr. of 1908 ed. 14.00 (ISBN 0-405-08822-1, Pub. by Blom). Arno.
Oberg, Charlotte H. A Pagan Prophet: William Morris. LC 77-4730. 1978. 13.95x (ISBN 0-8139-0714-4). U Pr of Va.
Phelan, Anna A. The Social Philosophy of William Morris. 207p. Repr. of 1927 ed. lib. bdg. 30.00 (ISBN 0-8495-4369-X). Arden Lib.
--The Social Philosophy of William Morris. LC 76-40079. 1976. lib. bdg. 27.50 (ISBN 0-8414-4703-9). Folcroft.
Purkis, John A. The Icelandic Jaunt: A Study of the Expeditions Made by Morris to Iceland in 1871 & 1873. LC 77-8166. 1977. Repr. of 1962 ed. lib. bdg. 10.00 (ISBN 0-8414-6792-7). Folcroft.
Sewter, A. Charles. The Stained Glass of William Morris & His Circle: A Catalogue, Vol. 2. LC 72-91307. (Studies in British Art Ser.). 344p. 1975. 125.00 (ISBN 0-300-01836-3). Yale U Pr.
--The Stained Glass of William Morris & His Circle, Vol. 1. LC 72-91307. (Studies in British Art Ser.). (Illus.). 384p. 1974. 100.00x (ISBN 0-300-01471-6). Yale U Pr.
Sparling, J. The Kelmscott Press & William Morris. 1976. lib. bdg. 39.95 (ISBN 0-8490-2114-6). Gordon Pr.
Tames, R. William Morris. (Clarendon Biography Ser.). (Illus.). pap. 3.50 (ISBN 0-912728-55-8). Newbury Bks.
Thompson, E. P. William Morris: Romantic to Revolutionary. LC 76-62712. 1978. pap. 7.95 (ISBN 0-394-73320-7). Pantheon.
Thompson, Edward P. William Morris. LC 76-62712. 1977. 17.95 (ISBN 0-394-41136-6). Pantheon.
Thompson, Paul. The Work of William Morris. 7.95 (ISBN 0-7043-3118-7, Pub. by Quartet England). Charles River Bks.
Thomson, Susan Otis. American Book Design & William Morris. LC 77-8733. (Illus.). 1977. 32.50 (ISBN 0-8352-0984-9). Bowker.
Townshend, Emily C. William Morris & the Communist Ideal. LC 74-18411. 1974. Repr. of 1934 ed. lib. bdg. 8.50 (ISBN 0-8414-8602-6). Folcroft.
Vallance, Aymer. William Morris: His Art His Writings & His Public Life. LC 77-6968. 1977. Repr. of 1898 ed. lib. bdg. 55.00 (ISBN 0-89341-208-2). Longwood Pr.
Von Helmholtz, Anna A. The Social Philosophy of William Morris. LC 74-13029. 1974. Repr. of 1927 ed. lib. bdg. 25.00 (ISBN 0-8414-9170-4). Folcroft.
Witkinson, Ray. William Morris As Designer. (Illus.). 148p. 1980. 22.50 (ISBN 0-289-70673-4). Eastview.

MORRIS, WILLIAM, 1834-1896–BIBLIOGRAPHY

Forman, H. Buxton. The Books of William Morris Described with Some Account of His Doings in Literature & in the Allied Crafts. (Illus.). xvi, 224p. 1976. Repr. of 1897 ed. 40.00 (ISBN 0-900470-74-7). Oak Knoll.
Forman, Harry B. Books of William Morris Described with Some Account of His Doings in Literature & in the Allied Arts. LC 68-58235. (Research & Source Ser.: No. 104). (Illus.). 1969. Repr. of 1897 ed. 23.50 (ISBN 0-8337-1205-5). B Franklin.
Grennan, Margaret R. William Morris, Medievalist & Revolutionary. LC 76-102500. 1970. Repr. of 1945 ed. 10.00 (ISBN 0-8462-1459-8). Russell.
Scott, Temple. A Bibliography of the Works of William Morris. 75.00 (ISBN 0-87968-742-8). Gordon Pr.
Weekley, Montague. William Morris. LC 73-908. 1934. lib. bdg. 12.50 (ISBN 0-8414-2800-X). Folcroft.

MORRIS, WRIGHT, 1910-

Crump, G. B. The Novels of Wright Morris: A Critical Interpretation. LC 77-15796. 1978. 12.95x (ISBN 0-8032-0962-2). U of Nebr Pr.
Howard, Leon. Wright Morris. LC 68-64752. (Pamphlets on American Writers Ser: No. 69). (Orig.). 1968. pap. 1.25x (ISBN 0-8166-0483-5, MPAW69). U of Minn Pr.
Knoll, Robert E., ed. Conversations with Wright Morris: Critical Views & Responses. LC 76-25497. (Illus.). 1977. 10.95x (ISBN 0-8032-0904-5); pap. 3.95 (ISBN 0-8032-5854-2, BB 630, Bison). U of Nebr Pr.
Madden, David. Wright Morris. (Twayne's United States Authors Ser). 1964. pap. 3.45 (ISBN 0-8084-0336-2, T71, Twayne). Coll & U Pr.

MORRIS-DANCE

Sharp, Cecil J. & MacIlwaine, Herbert C. The Morris Book: With a Description of Dances As Performed by the Morris-Men of England, Pts. 1-3. 1978. Repr. of 1911 ed. 17.50 (ISBN 0-85409-965-4). Charles River Bks.

MORRIS MINI MINOR AUTOMOBILE

see Automobiles, Foreign–Types–Morris Mini Minor

MORRISON, GEORGE ERNEST, 1862-1920

Lo, Hui-Min, ed. Correspondence of G. E. Morrison, 2 vols. Set. 249.00 (ISBN 0-521-08779-1); Vol. 1 1895-1912. 119.00 (ISBN 0-521-20486-0); Vol. 2 1912-1920. 150.00 (ISBN 0-521-21561-7). Cambridge U Pr.
Parker, Joseph B. Morrison Era: Reform Politics in New Orleans. LC 74-7142. 10.00 (ISBN 0-88289-009-3). Pelican.

MORRISTOWN, NEW JERSEY–HISTORY

Cataldo, Mary A., ed. Morristown: The War Years Seventeen Seventy-Five to Seventeen Eighty-Three. LC 79-64938. (Illus.). 124p. 1979. 15.95 (ISBN 0-89062-100-4, Pub. by Eastern Natl Park). Pub Ctr Cult Res.
Cataldo, Mary A. & Benvenuti, Judi, eds. Morristown: The War Years, 1775-1783. (Illus., Orig.). Date not set. pap. 15.95 (ISBN 0-915992-03-5). Eastern Acorn.

MORRO CASTLE (STEAMSHIP)

Burton, Hal. The Morro Castle: Tragedy at Sea. (Illus.). 224p. 1973. 7.95 (ISBN 0-670-48960-3). Viking Pr.

MORROW, DWIGHT WHITNEY, 1873-1931

McBride, M. M. The Story of Dwight W. Morrow. 59.95 (ISBN 0-8490-1131-0). Gordon Pr.
Nicolson, Harold. Dwight Morrow. facsimile ed. LC 75-2657. (Wall Street & the Security Markets Ser.). (Illus.). 1975. Repr. of 1935 ed. 26.00x (ISBN 0-405-06982-0). Arno.

MORSE, JEDIDIAH, 1761-1826

Morse, James K. Jedidiah Morse: A Champion of New England Orthodoxy. LC 39-11247. Repr. of 1939 ed. 10.00 (ISBN 0-404-04504-9). AMS Pr.

MORSE, SAMUEL FINLEY BREESE, 1791-1872

Mabee, Carleton. American Leonardo: A Life of Samuel F. B. Morse. LC 72-76512. (Illus.). 1969. Repr. of 1943 ed. lib. bdg. 27.50x (ISBN 0-374-95225-6). Octagon.
Morse, Edward L., ed. Samuel F.B. Morse: His Letters & Journals, 2 vols. 440p. 1980. Repr. of 1914 ed. lib. bdg. 65.00 (ISBN 0-89984-331-X). Century Bookbindery.
Morse, Samuel F. Samuel F. B. Morse: His Letters & Journals, 2 vols. Morse, Edward L., ed. LC 76-75279. (Library of American Art Ser.). (Illus.). 1080p. 1973. Repr. of 1914 ed. Set. lib. bdg. 65.00 (ISBN 0-306-71304-7). Da Capo.
Prime, Samuel I. The Life of Samuel F. B. Morse, L. L. D: Inventor of the Electro-Magnetic Recording Telegraph. LC 74-4691. (Telecommunications Ser). (Illus.). 816p. 1974. Repr. of 1875 ed. 42.00x (ISBN 0-405-06054-8). Arno.
Reid, James D. The Telegraph in America: Its Founders, Promoters & Noted Men. LC 74-7493. (Telecommunications Ser). (Illus.). 926p. 1974. Repr. of 1879 ed. 47.00 (ISBN 0-405-06056-4). Arno.

MORSE

see Walruses

MORSE CODE

Adlam, D. Code in Context. (Primary Socialization, Language & Education Ser.). 1977. 26.00 (ISBN 0-7100-8481-1). Routledge & Kegan.
International Teaching Systems Inc. International Code Training System. LC 62-21976. (Illus., Orig.). (YA) (gr. 8 up). 1971. pap. 12.95 with tape cassette (ISBN 0-672-20812-1, 20812). Sams.
Schwartz, Martin. Mastering the Morse Code. LC 57-9115. 1979. pap. 1.00 (ISBN 0-912146-02-8). AMECO.

MORT, THOMAS SUTCLIFFE, 1816-1878

Barnard, Alan. Visions & Profits: Studies in the Business Career of Thomas Sutcliffe Mort. 1961. 12.50x (ISBN 0-522-83523-6, Pub. by Melbourne U Pr). Intl Schol Bk Serv.

MORTAL SIN

see Sin, Mortal

MORTALITY

see also Children–Mortality; Death (Biology); Infants–Mortality; Insurance, Life–Mathematics; Mothers–Mortality; Violent Deaths

Alderson, Michael. International Mortality Statistics. 380p. 1981. 55.00 (ISBN 0-87196-514-3). Facts on File.
Amplification of Medical Certification of Cause of Death: Inquiries to Certifiers Concerning Incomplete or Vague Statements. 44p. (Eng. & Fr.). 1953. pap. 1.20 (ISBN 92-4-156008-8). World Health.
Arriaga, Eduardo E. Mortality Decline & Its Demographic Effects in Latin America. LC 76-4852. (Population Monograph Ser.: No. 6). (Illus.). 1976. Repr. of 1970 ed. lib. bdg. 34.75x (ISBN 0-8371-8827-X, ARLT). Greenwood.
Batten, Robert W. Mortality Table Construction. LC 77-12349. (Risk, Insurance & Security Ser.). (Illus.). 1978. 18.95 (ISBN 0-13-601302-3). P-H.
Benjamin, Bernard. Social & Economic Factors Affecting Mortality Confluence. 1965. text ed. 7.25x (ISBN 0-686-22460-4). Mouton.
Boston Medical Commission. The Sanitary Condition of Boston: The Report of a Medical Commission. Rosenkrantz, Barbara G., ed. LC 76-25655. (Public Health in America Ser.). 1977. Repr. of 1875 ed. lib. bdg. 12.00x (ISBN 0-405-09808-1). Arno.
Conde, Julien, et al. Mortality in Developing Countries. OECD Deveopment Centre, ed. (Development Centre Studies). (Orig.). 1980. Tome 1 & 2, 1266p. pap. 85.00 (ISBN 9-2640-2097-7, 41-80-05-3); Tome 3, 550p. pap. 30.00 (ISBN 9-2640-2120-5, 41-80-06-1). OECD.
Curiel, D., et al. Trends in the Study of Morbidity & Mortality. (Public Health Paper Ser: No. 27). 196p. (Eng, Fr, Rus, & Span.). 1965. pap. 3.60 (ISBN 92-4-130027-2). World Health.
Estimation of Recent Trends in Fertility & Mortality in the Republic of Korea. 1980. 3.75 (ISBN 0-309-02890-6). Natl Acad Pr.
Fertility & Mortality Changes in Thailand, 1950-1975. 1980. 3.50 (ISBN 0-309-02943-0). Natl Acad Pr.
Fisher, Irving. National Vitality, Its Wastes & Conservation. LC 75-17221. (Social Problems & Social Policy Ser.). 1976. Repr. of 1909 ed. 8.00x (ISBN 0-405-07492-1). Arno.
Foudray, Elbertie & U. S. Dept. of Commerce, Bureau of the Census. United States Abridged Life Tables: 1919-1920. LC 75-37268. (Demography Ser.). (Illus.). 1976. Repr. of 1923 ed. 10.00x (ISBN 0-405-08000-X). Arno.
Glover, James W. & U. S. Dept. of Commerce, Bureau of the Census. United States Life Tables: 1890, 1901, 1910, & 1901-1910. LC 75-37267. (Demography Ser.). (Illus.). 1976. Repr. of 1921 ed. 35.00x (ISBN 0-405-07997-4). Arno.
Harris, Kenneth W. & French, Dwight K. A Methodological Study of the Quality of Mortality Medical Coding. Cox, Klaudia, ed. (Series 2: No. 81). 1979. pap. text ed. 1.75 (ISBN 0-8406-0164-6). Natl Ctr Health Stats.
Hoffman, Elizabeth. The Sources of Mortality Changes in Italy Since Unification. Bruchey, Stuart, ed. LC 80-2811. (Dissertations in European Economic History II). (Illus.). 1981. lib. bdg. 25.00x (ISBN 0-405-13995-0). Arno.
Kitagawa, Evelyn M. & Hauser, Philip M. Differential Mortality in the United States: A Study in Socio-Economic Epidemiology. LC 72-93951. (Vital & Health Statistics Monographs, American Public Health Association). 1973. 15.00x (ISBN 0-674-20561-8). Harvard U Pr.
Morbidity from Malignant Neoplasms in Certain Countries. (World Health Statistics Ser: Vol. 15, No. 11, Vol. 17, No. 12, Vol. 18, No. 12; & Vol. 19, No. 12). pap. 3.60 ea. World Health.
Mortality from Infective & Parasitic Diseases (B1-B17) 1963-1967: A Report. (World Health Statistics Ser: Vol. 23, No. 7). (Eng. & Fr.). 1970. pap. 7.20 (ISBN 0-686-09182-5). World Health.
Mortality from Infective & Parasitic Diseases 1955-1967: A Report. (World Health Statistics Ser: Vol. 123, Nos. 4-5). (Eng. & Fr.). 1970. pap. 9.20 (ISBN 0-686-09183-3). World Health.
Preston, S. H. Mortality Patterns in National Populations: With Special Reference to Recorded Causes of Death. (Studies in Population Ser.). 1976. 26.50 (ISBN 0-12-564450-7). Acad Pr.
Preston, Samuel, et al. Causes of Death: Life Tables for National Populations. (Studies in Population). 800p. 1972. 52.00 (ISBN 0-12-785664-1). Acad Pr.
Retherford, Robert D. The Changing Sex Differential in Mortality. LC 74-19808. (Studies in Demography & Urban Population). (Illus.). 1975. lib. bdg. 15.00x (ISBN 0-8371-7848-7, RSX/). Greenwood.
Rickham, P. P., et al, eds. Causes of Postoperative Death in Children: Analysis & Therapeutic Implications. LC 79-19638. (Progress in Pediatric Surgery Ser.: Vol. 13). 1979. text ed. 34.50 (ISBN 0-8067-1513-8). Urban & S.
Sakamoto-Momiyama, Masako. Seasonality in Human Mortality: A Medico-Geographical Study. (Illus.). 1977. 19.50x (ISBN 0-86008-182-6, Pub. by U of Tokyo Pr). Intl Schol Bk Serv.
Sauer, Herbert I. Geographic Patterns in the Risk of Dying & Associated Factors United States, 1968-1972. Cox, Klaudia, ed. (Series 3: No. 18). 1980. pap. text ed. 1.70 (ISBN 0-8406-0184-0). Natl Ctr Health Stats.
Sibley, Elbridge. Differential Mortality in Tennessee, 1917-1928. LC 70-88450. Repr. of 1930 ed. 17.00x (ISBN 0-8371-1794-1, Pub. by Negro U Pr). Greenwood.
Ten Leading Causes of Death in Selected Countries. 1959-67. Vol. 12, Nos. 5-6. pap. 2.00 (ISBN 0-686-09170-1); Vol. 15, No. 1. pap. 3.60 (ISBN 0-686-09171-X); Vol. 17, Nos. 1-2. pap. 3.60 (ISBN 0-686-09172-8); Vol. 20, No. 1. pap. 3.60 (ISBN 0-686-09173-6); Vol. 20, No. 2. pap. 2.80 (ISBN 0-686-09174-4). World Health.
UN-WHO Meeting. Geneva, 1968. Programmes of Analysis of Mortality Trends & Levels: Report. (Technical Report Ser.: No. 440). (Also avail. in French, Russian & Spanish). 1970. pap. 2.00 (ISBN 92-4-120440-0). World Health.
Weaver, David C., et al. The Map Abstract of Mortality Factors Affecting the Elderly: Alabama, 1979. LC 79-14064. (Map Abstract Ser.: No. 6). 112p. 1979. pap. text ed. 7.75 (ISBN 0-8173-0016-3). U of Ala Pr.
Webster, Charles, ed. Health, Medicine & Mortality in the Sixteenth Century. LC 78-73234. (Cambridge Monographs on the History of Medicine). (Illus.). 1979. 42.50 (ISBN 0-521-22643-0). Cambridge U Pr.
Woolsey, Theodore D. Toward an Index of Preventable Mortality, Ser. 2, No. 85. Cox, Klaudia, ed. 50p. 1980. pap. text ed. 1.75 (ISBN 0-8406-0189-1). Natl Ctr Healt.

MORTAR

see also Grouting

Gutcho, M. H., ed. Cement & Mortar Technology & Additives: Developments Since 1977. LC 80-19343. (Chemical Tech. Rev. 173). 540p. (Orig.). 1981. 54.00 (ISBN 0-8155-0822-0). Noyes.
Seymour, Raymond B., ed. Plastic Mortars, Sealants, & Caulking Compounds. LC 79-19752. (ACS Symposium Ser.: No. 113). 1979. 24.25 (ISBN 0-8412-0523-X). Am Chemical.

MORTGAGE FORECLOSURE

see Foreclosure

MORTGAGE LENDING

see Mortgage Loans

MORTGAGE LOANS

see also Mortgages

Benston, George J. The Anti-Redlining Rules: An Analysis of the Federal Home Loan Bank Board's Proposed Non Discrimination Requirements. (LEC Occasional Paper). 1978. pap. text ed. 2.50 (ISBN 0-916770-06-0). Law & Econ U Miami.
Bruce, Jon W. Real Estate Finance in a Nutshell. LC 79-289. (Nutshell Ser.). 292p. 1979. pap. text ed. 6.95 (ISBN 0-314-60008-6). West Pub.

Bryant, Willis R. Mortgage Lending: Fundamentals & Practices. 2nd ed. 1962. text ed. 17.00 (ISBN 0-07-008609-5, C); instructors' handbook 4.95 (ISBN 0-07-008608-7). McGraw.
Buckley, Robert H., et al, eds. Capital Markets & the Housing Sector: Perspectives on Financial Reform. LC 77-5117. 1977. 20.00 (ISBN 0-88410-658-6). Ballinger Pub.
DeHuszar, William I. Mortgage Loan Administration. (Illus.). 480p. 1972. text ed. 17.95 (ISBN 0-07-016257-3, C). McGraw.
Dennis, Marshall. Mortgage Lending Fundamentals & Practices. (Illus.). 1981. text ed. 16.95 (ISBN 0-8359-4651-7). Reston.
Hamecs, Richard. FHA Financing for Rental Housing - Section 221 (D) (4) A Processing Guide. 281p. 1979. pap. 15.00 (ISBN 0-86718-052-8). Natl Assn Home Builders.
Johnsich, John R., intro. by. Alternate Mortgage Instruments & Financing Techniques. (Orig.). 1981. pap. 5.95 (ISBN 0-914256-14-9). Real Estate Pub.
Listokin, David & Casey, Stephen. Mortgage Lending & Race: Conceptual & Analytical Perspectives of the Urban Financing Problem. LC 79-12209. 1980. text ed. 17.95 (ISBN 0-88285-060-1). Ctr Urban Pol Res.
McLean, Andrew J. Complete Guide to Real Estate Loans. Kinsey, Thomas D., ed. 128p. (Orig.). 1980. pap. 5.95 (ISBN 0-930306-20-1). Delphi Info.
Pease, Robert H. & Kerwood, L. O., eds. Mortgage Banking. 2nd ed. 1965. text ed. 18.95 (ISBN 0-07-049126-7, C). McGraw.
Pugh, J. W. & Hippaka, William H. California Real Estate Finance. 3rd ed. (Illus.). 1978. text ed. 19.95 (ISBN 0-13-112680-6). P-H.
Schafer, Robert & Ladd, Helen F. Discrimination in Mortgage Lending. (MIT-Harvard Joint Center for Urban Studies). (Illus.). 448p. 1981. 40.00x (ISBN 0-262-19192-X). MIT Pr.
Strum, Brian J., ed. Financing Real Estate During the Inflationary 80s. LC 54-30037. 450p. (Orig.). 1981. pap. text ed. 35.00x (ISBN 0-89707-040-2). Amer Bar Assn.
Vano, Anthony F. Mortgages: Borrower, Broker & Lender. 1968. 25.00 (ISBN 0-87164-000-7). William-F.

MORTGAGES

see also Agricultural Credit; Conveyancing; Foreclosure; Housing–Finance; Liens; Mortgage Loans

Akerson, Charles B. An Introduction to Mortgage-Equity Capitalization. 1970. 3.00 (ISBN 0-911780-35-1). Am Inst Real Estate Appraisers.
Arnold, Alvin L., et al. Modern Real Estate & Mortgage Forms Checklists. LC 79-50553. 1979. 56.00 (ISBN 0-88262-280-3). Warren.
Bogue, Allan G. Money at Interest: The Farm Mortgage on the Middle Border. LC 68-10903. (Illus.). 1968. Repr. of 1955 ed. 10.00 (ISBN 0-8462-1071-1). Russell.
--Money at Interest: The Farm Mortgage on the Middle Border. LC 55-1350. 1969. pap. 4.50x (ISBN 0-8032-5018-5, BB 396, Bison). U of Nebr Pr.
Burgh, Edward M. Mortgage Investing by Life Insurance Companies. LC 80-80943. (FLMI Insurance Education Program Ser.). (Illus.). 202p. (Orig.). 1980. pap. text ed. 12.00 (ISBN 0-915322-36-6). Loma.
Burleigh, D. Robert. Double Your Money in Six Years: How to Reap Profits in Discounted Mortgages. (Illus.). 1971. 9.95 (ISBN 0-13-218818-X, Reward); pap. 3.95 (ISBN 0-13-218842-2). P-H.
Cabbell, Paul. God Bless Our Second Mortgage. (Illus.). 105p. (Orig.). 1973. pap. 3.95 (ISBN 0-87945-024-X). Fed Legal Pubns.
Complete Mortgage Payment Tables. 1979. 3.50 (ISBN 0-89471-068-0). Running Pr.
Consumer Guide to Mortgage Payments. 254p. 1981. pap. 5.95 (ISBN 0-686-30649-X). Caroline Hse.
Delphi. Advanced Mortgage Yield Tables. Kinsey, Thomas D., ed. 200p. (Orig.). 1979. pap. 15.00 (ISBN 0-930306-11-2). Delphi Info.
--Expanded Mortgage Yield Tables. Kinsey, Thomas D., ed. 200p. (Orig.). 1979. pap. 15.00 (ISBN 0-930306-10-4). Delphi Info.
--Payment Tables for Monthly Mortgages. Kinsey, Thomas D., ed. 96p. (Orig.). 1979. pap. 2.95 (ISBN 0-930306-22-8). Delphi Info.
Dennis, Marshall W. Fundamentals of Mortgage Lending. (Illus.). 1978. ref. ed. 18.95 (ISBN 0-8359-2153-0); instrs'. manual avail. (ISBN 0-8359-2154-9). Reston.
Driscoll, Clancy. Getting a Mortgage. (Illus.). 160p. 1980. 8.95 (ISBN 0-07-017852-6). McGraw.
Financial Prepayment Mortgage Yield Table, No. 159. pocket ed 5.00 (ISBN 0-685-32725-6). Finan Pub.
Financial Pub Editors, ed. Financial Pass-Through Yield & Value Tables for GNMA Mortgage-Backed Securities No. 715. 7th ed. 25.00 (ISBN 0-685-47818-1). Finan Pub.
Financial Publications. Financial Monthly Mortgage Handbook: 10 per Cent to 15 per Cent No. 158. 4th ed. 17.50 (ISBN 0-685-47820-3). Finan Pub.
Financial Publishing Co. Prepayment Mortgage Yield Table No. 435. 6th ed. 19.50 (ISBN 0-685-02555-1). Finan Pub.
Follain, James & Struyk, Raymond. Homeownership Effects of Alternate Mortgage Instruments. (An Institute Paper). 95p. 1977. pap. 6.00 (ISBN 0-87766-193-6, 18900). Urban Inst.
Glubetich, Dave. How to Grow a Moneytree. 2nd ed. Wigginton, Dave, ed. 137p. 1981. pap. 8.95 (ISBN 0-686-75065-9). Impact Pub.
Goebel, Paul R. & Miller, Norman G. Handbook of Mortgage Mathematics & Financial Tables. (Illus.). 416p. 1981. 24.95 (ISBN 0-13-380410-0); pap. 9.95 (ISBN 0-686-71764-3). P-H.
Halperin, Don A. Construction Funding: Where the Money Comes from. LC 74-11188. (Practical Construction Guides Ser). 256p. 1974. 22.95 (ISBN 0-471-34570-9, Pub. by Wiley-Interscience). Wiley.
Harvey, David C. Harvey's Law of Real Property & Title Closings, 3 vols. rev. ed. Biskind, Elliot L., ed. LC 66-23512. 1966. looseleaf with 1980 suppl. 145.00 (ISBN 0-87632-058-2). Boardman.
High Interset Mortgage Yield Tables. 1980. pap. 15.00 (ISBN 0-930306-38-4). Delphi Info.
How to Manage a Mortgage. 1976. 8.00 (ISBN 0-89982-028-X, 048400). Am Bankers.
How to Market a Mortgage. 1976. 8.00 (ISBN 0-89982-027-1, 048500). Am Bankers.
James, R. W. Land Tenure & Policy in Tanzania. LC 76-185718. 375p. 1971. pap. 6.50x (ISBN 0-8020-1808-4). U of Toronto Pr.
Johnson, Irvin E. Instant Mortgage-Equity: Extended Tables of Overall Rates. LC 80-7729. (Lexington Books Real Estate & Urban Land Economics Special Ser.). 464p. 1980. 22.95 (ISBN 0-669-03808-3). Lexington Bks.
Kass, Louis A. Mortgages (N.Y.) 1964. pap. 1.75x (ISBN 0-87526-046-2). Gould.
Mortgages & Mortgage Foreclosure in New York. rev. ed. 1975. 35.00 (ISBN 0-685-58291-4). Acme Law.
Phillips, Kenneth F. & Teitz, Michael B. Housing Conservation in Older Urban Areas: A Mortgage Insurance Approach. LC 78-181. (Research Report Ser.: No. 78-2). 39p. 1978. pap. 3.50x (ISBN 0-87772-254-4). Inst Gov Stud Berk.
Pugh, J. W. & Hippaka, William H. California Real Estate Finance. 3rd ed. (Illus.). 1978. text ed. 19.95 (ISBN 0-13-112680-6). P-H.
Rogg, Eleanor M. The Assimilation of Cuban Exiles: The Role of Community & Class. LC 74-1392. (Illus.). 250p. 1974. pap. 5.95x (ISBN 0-87945-027-4). Fed Legal Pubns.
Rudman, Jack. Mortgage Administrator. (Career Examination Ser.: C-2311). (Cloth bdg. avail. on request). 1977. pap. 10.00 (ISBN 0-8373-2311-8). Natl Learning.
--Supervising Mortgage Administrator. (Career Examination Ser.: C-2312). (Cloth bdg. avail. on request). 1977. pap. 10.00 (ISBN 0-8373-2312-6). Natl Learning.
Selzer, Richard P. & Van Dusen, Wilson. How to Make Money with Mortgage Notes. LC 77-92303. (Illus.). 1978. pap. 10.00 (ISBN 0-9601434-1-6). Philemon Found.
Sherman, Michael. The Complete Payment Book. 1978. pap. 3.25 (ISBN 0-930306-08-2). Delphi Info.
--Mortgage Yield Tables. 1978. pap. 15.00 (ISBN 0-930306-09-0). Delphi Info.
Shiels, Larry, Jr. Mortgage Credit & Closing. 1972. pap. 45.00 (ISBN 0-686-04915-2). Home Equity.
Sokol, Andrew, Jr. Contractor or Manipulator? A Guide to Contruction Financing from Beginning of Construction to Completion. rev. ed. LC 68-9511. (Illus.). 1968. 14.95x (ISBN 0-87024-091-9). U of Miami Pr.
Wiedemer, John P. Real Estate Finance. 3rd ed. (Illus.). 384p. 1980. text ed. 17.95 (ISBN 0-8359-6522-8). Reston.

MORTGAGES–TAXATION

see also Taxation of Bonds, Securities, etc.

Financial Publishing Co. Mortgage Payment Tables Nos. 167, 177, 553, 492, 592, 491. 5.00 ea. Finan Pub.
--Mortgage Values Tables No. 207. 12.50 (ISBN 0-685-02552-7). Finan Pub.

MORTIFICATION (PATHOLOGY)

see Gangrene

MORTMAIN

see also Church Lands

Wilson, Alan. Clergy Reserves of Upper Canada: A Canadian Mortmain. LC 72-353178. (Illus.). 1968. 15.00x (ISBN 0-8020-3216-8). U of Toronto Pr.

MORTON, FERDINAND JOSEPH (JELLY ROLL), 1885-1941

Dapogny, James. The Collected Piano Music of Ferdinand "Jelly Roll" Morton. 600p. (Orig.). 1981. pap. 25.00 (ISBN 0-87474-351-6). Smithsonian.
--The Collected Piano Music of Ferdinand "Jelly Roll" Morton. 750p. 1981. pap. 19.95x (ISBN 0-87474-351-6). Smithsonian.
Lomax, Alan. Mr. Jellyroll: The Fortunes of Jellyroll Morton, New Orleans Creole & 'Inventor' 1973. pap. 4.95 (ISBN 0-520-02237-8). U of Cal Pr.

MORTON, FERDINAND JOSEPH, 1885-1941–DISCOGRAPHY

Lomax, Alan. Mr. Jellyroll: The Fortunes of Jellyroll Morton, New Orleans Creole & 'Inventor' 1973. pap. 4.95 (ISBN 0-520-02237-8). U of Cal Pr.

MORTON, JULIUS STERLING, 1832-1902

Moore, Clyde B. J. Sterling Morton: Arbor Day Boy. (Childhood of Famous Americans Ser.). (Illus.). (gr. 3-7). 1962. 3.95 (ISBN 0-672-50112-0). Bobbs.
Olson, James C. J. Sterling Morton. 1972. Repr. 7.95 (ISBN 0-686-18152-2). Nebraska Hist.

MORTON, OLIVER PERRY, 1823-1877

Foulke, William D. Life of Oliver P. Morton, 2 Vols. LC 77-168129. Repr. of 1899 ed. Set. 72.50 (ISBN 0-404-04592-8); 23.00 ea. Vol. 1 (ISBN 0-404-04593-6). Vol. 2 (ISBN 0-404-04594-4). AMS Pr.

MORTON, THOMAS, 1575-1646

Morton, Thomas. New English Canaan of Thomas Morton. Adams, Charles F., ed. 1966. 26.00 (ISBN 0-8337-0013-8). B Franklin.

MORTON, WILLIAM THOMAS GREEN, 1819-1868

MacQuitty, Betty. Victory Over Pain: Morton's Discovery of Anesthesia. LC 75-107007. (Illus.). 1971. 5.95 (ISBN 0-8008-8014-5). Taplinger.

MORTUARY CUSTOMS

see Burial; Cremation; Dead; Funeral Rites and Ceremonies; Mourning Customs; Undertakers and Undertaking; Urn Burial

MORTUARY LAW

see Burial Laws

MORTUARY STATISTICS

see Infants–Mortality; Mortality; Vital Statistics

MOSAIC LAW

see Jewish Law

MOSAICS

see also Mural Painting and Decoration

Anthony, Edgar W. History of Mosaics. LC 68-9000. (Illus.). 1968. Repr. of 1935 ed. 40.00 (ISBN 0-87817-001-4). Hacker.
Avi-Yonah, Michael. The Art of Mosaics. LC 72-10793. (The Lerner Archaeology Ser.: Digging up the Past). (Illus.). 96p. 1975. PLB 7.95 (ISBN 0-8225-0828-1). Lerner Pubns.
Clarke, John R. Roman Black & White Figural Mosaics. LC 78-68553. (College Art Association Monographs: Vol. 35). (Illus.). 1979. 22.50x (ISBN 0-8147-1376-9). NYU Pr.
Demus, Otto. Byzantine Mosaic Decoration: Aspects of Monumental Art in Byzantium. (Illus.). 162p. 1976. 20.00 (ISBN 0-89241-018-3). Caratzas Bros.
DiFederico, Frank. The Mosaics of the National Shrine of the Immaculate Conception. (Illus.). 96p. 1981. 16.95 (ISBN 0-916276-09-0). Decatur Hse.
Harmon, Beatrice E. Mosaics. LC 74-144725. (Yale Ser. of Younger Poets: No. 18). Repr. of 1923 ed. 11.00 (ISBN 0-404-53818-5). AMS Pr.
Haswell, J. Mellentin. VNR Manual of Mosaic. (Illus.). 224p. 1973. 12.95 (ISBN 0-442-23197-0). Van Nos Reinhold.
Kiss. Roman Mosaics in Hungary. 1973. 10.00 (ISBN 0-9960003-0-5, Pub. by Kaido Hungary). Heyden.
Parker, Xenia L. Mosaics in Needlepoint. LC 77-5045. (Encore Edition). (Illus.). 1977. encore ed. 5.95 (ISBN 0-684-16201-6, ScribT); pap. 3.95 encore ed. (ISBN 0-684-15036-0, SL713, ScribT). Scribner.
Parlasca, Klans. Die Roemischen Mosaiken in Deutschland. (Illus.). 156p. 1970. Repr. of 1959 ed. 99.75x (ISBN 3-11-001212-X). De Gruyter.
Stephany, Konrad. Ludwig Schaffrath, Stained Glass & Mosaic. LC 77-79948. 1977. write for info. (ISBN 0-686-05497-0). C & R Loo.
Stern, Henri. Les Mosaiques De la Grande Mosquee De Cordoue. (Madrider Forschungen, Ser., Vol. 11). (Illus.). 55p. 1976. 99.75x (ISBN 3-11-002126-9). De Gruyter.
Thompson, Maurice. Hoosier Mosaics. 1972. Repr. of 1875 ed. 9.95x (ISBN 0-8422-8118-5). Irvington.
Underwood, Paul A. Kariye Djami, 4 vols. LC 65-10404. (Bollingen Ser.: Vol. 70). (Illus.). 1966. Vols. 1-3. boxed set 85.00 (ISBN 0-691-09777-1); Vol. 4, 1975. 60.00 (ISBN 0-691-09778-X); Vols. 1-4. boxed set 125.00 (ISBN 0-686-57571-7). Princeton U Pr.
Whitehouse, Helen. The Dal Pozzo Copies of the Palestrina Mosaic. 1976. 10.00x (ISBN 0-904531-48-1, Pub. by BAR). State Mutual Bk.

MOSAICS–TECHNIQUE

Luchner, Adolf. Crystal-Glass Mosaic. (Illus.). 80p. 1975. 4.75 (ISBN 0-263-70141-7). Transatlantic.
Mosaics. 1975. pap. 1.50 (ISBN 0-8277-4457-9). British Bk Ctr.
Seidelman, James E. & Mintonye, Grace. Creating Mosaics. (Illus.). (gr. 4-6). 1967. 4.95g (ISBN 0-02-767180-1, CCPr). Macmillan.
Shults, Eric. Glass, Mosaics, & Plastic. (Encore Edition). (Illus.). 1979. 3.95 (ISBN 0-684-16924-X, ScribT). Scribner.
Stribling, Mary-Lou. Mosaic Techniques: New Aspects of Fragmented Design. (Illus.). 1966. 7.95 (ISBN 0-517-02562-0, 025620). Crown.
Timmons. Designing & Making Mosaics. 1977. pap. 7.95 (ISBN 0-13-201954-X, Spec). P-H.

MOSAICISM

Gehring, W. J. Genetic Mosaics & Cell Differentiation. (Results & Problems in Cell Differentiation: Vol. 9). (Illus.). 1979. 45.10 (ISBN 0-387-08882-2). Springer-Verlag.
Russell, L. B. Genetic Mosaics & Chimeras in Mammals. LC 78-23172. (Basic Life Sciences Ser.: Vol. 12). 499p. 1978. 39.50 (ISBN 0-306-40065-0, Plenum Pr). Plenum Pub.
Stern, Curt. Genetic Mosaics & Other Essays. LC 68-21985. (John M. Prather Lectures Ser: 1965). (Illus.). 1968. text ed. 10.00x (ISBN 0-674-34650-5). Harvard U Pr.

MOSBY, JOHN SINGLETON, 1833-1916

Jones, Virgil C. Ranger Mosby. LC 44-8072. 1944. 12.95 (ISBN 0-8078-0432-0). U of NC Pr.

MOSCA, GAETANO, 1858-1941

Burnham, James. Machiavellians: Defenders of Freedom. 1962. pap. 2.95 (ISBN 0-89526-946-5). Regnery-Gateway.
Meisel, James H. The Myth of the Ruling Class: Gaetano Mosca & the "Elite". LC 80-13080. xiv, 432p. 1980. Repr. of 1962 ed. lib. bdg. 31.75x (ISBN 0-313-22346-7, MEMR). Greenwood.

MOSCHELES, CHARLOTTE (EMBDEN), d. 1889

Mendelssohn, Felix. Letters of Felix Mendelssohn to Ignaz & Charlotte Moscheles. Moscheles, Felix, ed. & tr. LC 77-107822. (Select Bibliographies Reprint Ser). 1888. 24.00 (ISBN 0-8369-5217-0). Arno.
--Letters of Felix Mendelssohn to Ignaz & Charlotte Moscheles. Moscheles, Felix, ed. LC 76-173116. (Illus.). Repr. of 1888 ed. 22.00 (ISBN 0-405-08786-1, Pub. by Blom). Arno.

MOSCHELES, IGNAZ, 1794-1870

Mendelssohn, Felix. Letters of Felix Mendelssohn to Ignaz & Charlotte Moscheles. Moscheles, Felix, ed. & tr. LC 77-107822. (Select Bibliographies Reprint Ser). 1888. 24.00 (ISBN 0-8369-5217-0). Arno.
--Letters of Felix Mendelssohn to Ignaz & Charlotte Moscheles. Moscheles, Felix, ed. LC 76-173116. (Illus.). Repr. of 1888 ed. 22.00 (ISBN 0-405-08786-1, Pub. by Blom). Arno.
Moscheles, Ignatz. Recent Music & Musicians As Described in the Diaries & Correspondence of Ignatz Moscheles. LC 73-125057. (Music Ser). 1970. Repr. of 1873 ed. lib. bdg. 32.50 (ISBN 0-306-70022-0). Da Capo.
Moscheles, Ignaz. Life of Ignaz Moscheles: With Selections from His Diaries & Correspondence, 2 vols. Moscheles, Charlotte, ed. Coleridge, A. D., tr. LC 77-94605. 1979. Repr. of 1873 ed. Set. lib. bdg. 60.00 (ISBN 0-89341-413-1). Longwood Pr.

MOSCOW

Benjamin, Walter. Moskauer Tagebuch. (Edtion Suhrkamp: Neue Folge). 200p. (Orig.). 1980. pap. text ed. 6.50 (ISBN 3-518-11020-9, Pub. by Suhrkamp Verlag Germany). Suhrkamp.
Friedland, Ann, ed. U. S. Information Moscow: Spring 1981 to Winter 1982. rev. ed. (Illus.). 507p. 1981. pap. 9.95 (ISBN 0-934192-03-0). Dimes Group.
Gruliou, Leo. Moscow. (The Great Cities Ser.). (Illus.). (gr. 6 up). 1977. PLB 11.97 (ISBN 0-8094-2275-1, Pub. by Time-Life). Silver.
Hamilton, Ian. The Moscow City Region. (Problem Regions of Europe). (Illus.). 1976. pap. text ed. 4.95x (ISBN 0-19-913191-0). Oxford U Pr.
Levin, Deana. Nikolai Lives in Moscow. (Children Everywhere Ser.: No. 5). (gr. 2-4). 1968. PLB 4.95 (ISBN 0-8038-5007-7). Hastings.
Moscow. (Panorama Bks.). (Illus., Fr.). 3.95 (ISBN 0-685-11406-6). French & Eur.

MOSCOW–DESCRIPTION

Blue Guide - Moscow & Leningrad. 1980. 39.95 (ISBN 0-528-84611-6); pap. 24.95 (ISBN 0-528-84607-8). Rand.
Bocca, Geoffrey. Moscow Scene. LC 75-34244. 192p. 1976. 25.00x (ISBN 0-8128-1912-8). Stein & Day.
Bortoli, Georges. Moscow & Leningrad Observed. Thomson, Amanda & Thomson, Edward, trs. from Fr. (Realites Ser). (Illus.). 166p. 1975. 24.95 (ISBN 0-19-519809-3). Oxford U Pr.
Chernov, V. A. Moscow: A Short Guide. 220p. 1977. 4.80 (ISBN 0-8285-0537-3, Pub. by Progress Pubs Russia). Imported Pubns.

Gruliow, Leo, ed. Moscow. (The Great Cities Ser.). 1977. 14.95 (ISBN 0-8094-2274-3). Time-Life.
Il'In, M. Architectural Monuments of Moscow 14th-17th Centuries. 1973. 35.00 (ISBN 0-685-86585-1). State Mutual Bk.
--Architectural Monuments of Moscow, 18th-19th Centuries. (Illus.). 1973. 35.00 (ISBN 0-685-86586-X). State Mutual Bk.
Kozlova, Y. The Cathedral Square in the Moscow Kremlin. 134p. 1977. 3.00 (ISBN 0-8285-0530-6, Pub. by Progress Pubs Russia). Imported Pubns.
Kuballa. Seeing the Real Moscow. 1982. pap. 7.95 (ISBN 0-8120-2180-0). Barron.
Moscow Kremlin & Red Square. 183p. 1976. 2.60 (ISBN 0-8285-0538-1, Pub. by Progress Pubs Russia). Imported Pubns.
Schecter, Jerrold, et al. An American Family in Moscow. (Illus.). 1975. 10.95 (ISBN 0-316-77301-8). Little.
Sevruk, V., ed. Moscow-Stalingrad. 279p. 1974. 4.80 (ISBN 0-8285-0485-7, Pub. by Progress Pubs Russia). Imported Pubns.
Smith, Desmond. Smith's Moscow. LC 73-20770. 1974. pap. 5.95 (ISBN 0-394-70692-7). Knopf.
Ward, Charles A. Cultural Historic Places. (Moscow & Leningrad: Cultural History & Architecture Ser.). Date not set. price not set. K G Saur.
--An Index to Buildings, Vol. 1. (Moscow & Leningrad: Cultural History & Architecture Ser.). 1980. text ed. write for info. (ISBN 0-89664-260-7). K G Saur.
--Their Development As Cultural Centers, Vol. 3. (Moscow & Leningrad: Cultural & History Architecture Ser.). 1980. write for info. K G Saur.

MOSCOW-HISTORY

De Mertens, Charles. An Account of the Plague Which Raged at Moscow, 1771. 1977. Repr. of 1799 ed. 13.50 (ISBN 0-89250-007-7). Orient Res Partners.
Fleischhacker, Hedwig. Die Staats und Voelkerrechtlichen Grundlagen der Moskauischen Aussenpolitik. Repr. of 1938 ed. 11.50 (ISBN 0-384-15970-2). Johnson Repr.
Fletcher, Harris. A Note on Two Words in Milton's History of Moscovia in Renaissance Studies in Honor of Hardin Craig. Maxwell, Baldwin, et al, eds. 1941. Repr. 25.00 (ISBN 0-8274-3045-0). R West.
Gruliow, Leo, ed. Moscow. (The Great Cities Ser.). 1977. 14.95 (ISBN 0-8094-2274-3). Time-Life.
Presniakov. Tsardom of Muscovy. (Russian Ser.: 30). 12.50 (ISBN 0-87569-025-4). Academic Intl.

MOSCOW-KREMLIN

Ascher, Abraham. The Kremlin. LC 79-163361. (Wonders of Man Ser). (Illus.). 176p. 1972. 16.95 (ISBN 0-88225-012-4). Newsweek.
Burian, Jiri & Shvidkovsky, Oleg A. The Kremlin of Moscow. LC 74-21650. (Illus.). Date not set. 25.00 (ISBN 0-312-46095-3). St Martin.
Klein, Mina C. & Klein, H. Arthur. The Kremlin: Citadel of History. (Illus.). 176p. (gr. 7 up). 1973. 8.95g (ISBN 0-02-750830-7). Macmillan.
Voyce, Arthur. The Moscow Kremlin: Its History, Architecture, & Art Treasures. LC 74-138135. xiii, 147p. Repr. of 1954 ed. lib. bdg. 41.75 (ISBN 0-8371-5708-0, VOMK). Greenwood.

MOSCOW-THEATERS

Sayler, Oliver M. Inside the Moscow Art Theatre. Repr. of 1925 ed. lib. bdg. 17.50x (ISBN 0-8371-4014-5, SAMA). Greenwood.
Stanislavski, Constantin. My Life in Art. 1952. pap. 9.95 (ISBN 0-87830-550-5). Theatre Arts.

MOSCOW, BATTLE OF, 1941-1942

Seaton, Albert. The Battle for Moscow. LC 79-93213. (World War II Ser.). (Illus.). 320p. 1980. pap. 2.50 (ISBN 0-87216-675-9). Playboy Pbks.
Shaw, John. Red Army Resurgent. Time-Life Books, ed. (World War II Ser.). (Illus.). 1980. 14.95 (ISBN 0-8094-2518-1). Time-Life.

MOSCOW MATHEMATICAL SOCIETY

Transactions of the Moscow Mathematical Society, Vol. 23 (1970, Vol. 23. LC 65-7413. 316p. 1972. text ed. 59.60 (ISBN 0-8218-1623-3, MOSCOW-23). Am Math.

MOSELEY, H. G. J., 1887-1915

Heilbron, John L. H. G. J. Moseley: The Life & Letters of an English Physicist, 1887-1915. LC 72-93519. 1974. 30.00x (ISBN 0-520-02375-7). U of Cal Pr.

MOSELLE RIVER AND VALLEY-DESCRIPTION AND TRAVEL

Cermakian, Jean. The Moselle: River & Canal from the Roman Empire to the European Economic Community. LC 75-22132. (Illus.). 1975. pap. 10.00x (ISBN 0-8020-3310-5). U of Toronto Pr.

MOSES

Allis, Oswald T. The Five Books of Moses. 1977. Repr. of 1947 ed. pap. 4.95 (ISBN 0-8010-0108-0). Baker Bk.
Andre, G. Moses, the Man of God. (Let's Discuss It Ser.). pap. 0.95 (ISBN 0-686-13259-9); pap. 9.50 per doz. (ISBN 0-686-13260-2). Believers Bkshelf.
Auerbach, Elias. Moses. Lehman, Israel O. & Barclay, R. A., trs. from Ger. LC 72-6589. 285p. 1975. text ed. 13.95x (ISBN 0-8143-1491-0). Wayne St U Pr.
Auld, A. Graeme. Joshua, Moses & the Land: Tretrateuch-Pentateuch-Hexateuch in a Generation Since 1938. 156p. 1980. Repr. text ed. 20.00x (ISBN 0-567-09306-9). Attic Pr.
Beegle, Dewey M. Moses, the Servant of Yahweh. LC 79-84558. 368p. 1972. pap. text ed. 5.95 (ISBN 0-933462-03-4). Pryor Pettengill.
Bork, Paul F. The World of Moses. LC 78-5022. (Horizon Ser.). 1978. pap. 4.95 (ISBN 0-8127-0166-6). Review & Herald.
Borne, Mortimer. Meet Moses: Fifty-Four Drawings in Color. LC 77-74180. (Illus.). 18.50 (ISBN 0-913870-39-0). Abaris Bks.
Campbell, R. K. Moses, the Man of God. tchr's lesson outline 0.50 (ISBN 0-686-13893-7); primary companion wkbk 0.40 (ISBN 0-686-13894-5); jr. companion wkbk 0.40 (ISBN 0-686-13895-3); intermediate companion wkbk 0.40 (ISBN 0-686-13896-1). Believers Bkshelf.
Conner, Kevin. Tabernacle of Moses. 1974. 6.95 (ISBN 0-914936-08-5). Bible Pr.
Freud, Sigmund. Moses & Monotheism. Jones, Katherine, ed. 1955. pap. 2.45 (ISBN 0-394-70014-7, V14, Vin). Random.
Glasson, T. Francis. Moses in the Fourth Gospel. (Studies in Biblical Theology: No. 40). 1963. prebound o.p. 8.45x (ISBN 0-8401-4040-1); pap. 5.95x (ISBN 0-8401-3040-6). Allenson-Breckinridge.
Golding, Louis. In the Steps of Moses the Lawgiver. 1937. 25.00 (ISBN 0-8414-4653-9). Folcroft.
Habel, Norman. This Old Man Called Moses. (Purple Puzzle Tree Ser). (Illus., Orig.). (ps-4). 1971. pap. 0.85 (ISBN 0-570-06512-7, 56-1212). Concordia.
Lindsay, Gordon. Moses & His Contemporaries. (Old Testament Ser.). 1.25 (ISBN 0-89985-133-9). Christ Nations.
--Moses & the Church in the Wilderness. (Old Testament Ser.). 1.25 (ISBN 0-89985-132-0). Christ Nations.
--Moses, The Deliverer. (Old Testament Ser.). 1.25 (ISBN 0-89985-131-2). Christ Nations.
--Moses the Lawgiver. (Old Testament Ser.: Vol. 10). pap. 1.25 (ISBN 0-89985-959-3). Christ Nations.
Maimonides, Moses. The Reason of the Laws of Moses. Townley, James, ed. LC 78-97294. 451p. 1975. Repr. of 1827 ed. lib. bdg. 16.75x (ISBN 0-8371-2618-5, MARL). Greenwood.
Mellinkoff, Ruth. The Horned Moses in Medieval Art & Thought. LC 77-85450. (California Studies in the History of Art: No. XIV). (Illus.). 1970. 35.00x (ISBN 0-520-01705-6). U of Cal Pr.
Meyer, F. B. Moses. 1972. pap. 2.95 (ISBN 0-87508-354-4). Chr Lit.
Moses. 1979. 0.75 (ISBN 0-8198-0586-6). Dghtrs St Paul.
Noerdlinger, Henry S. Moses & Egypt: The Documentation to the Motion Picture "the Ten Commandments". LC 56-12886. 202p. 1956. pap. 1.95 (ISBN 0-88474-007-2). U of S Cal Pr.
Offner, Hazel. Moses: A Man Changed by God. 72p. (Orig.). 1981. pap. 2.50 (ISBN 0-87784-617-0). Inter-Varsity.
Petersen, Mark E. Moses. LC 77-21553. 1977. 6.95 (ISBN 0-87747-651-9). Deseret Bk.
Polzin, Robert. Moses & the Deuteronomist: A Literary Syudy of the Deuteronomic History. 224p. 1980. 17.95 (ISBN 0-8164-0456-9); pap. 8.95 (ISBN 0-8164-2284-2). Seabury.
Ponder, Catherine. The Millionaire Moses. LC 77-71459. (The Millionaires of the Bible Ser.). 1977. pap. 3.95 (ISBN 0-87516-232-0). De Vorss.
Reid, R. J. Law of Moses & Its Lesson. pap. 0.30 (ISBN 0-87213-693-0). Loizeaux.
Torah: The Five Books of Moses. LC 62-12948. 1962. blue cloth 7.50 (ISBN 0-8276-0015-1, 51); black leather, gold edges, boxed 31.50 (ISBN 0-8276-0101-8, 52). Jewish Pubn.
Wellek, Rene, ed. The Divine Legation of Moses, 4 vols. 2nd ed. LC 75-11264. (British Philosophers & Theologians of the 17th & 18th Centuries Ser.: Vol. 62). 1978. Set. lib. bdg. 168.00 (ISBN 0-8240-1813-3); lib. bdg. 42.00 ea. Garland Pub.
Wood, P. Moses: Founder of Preventive Medicine. 1976. lib. bdg. 59.95 (ISBN 0-8490-2285-1). Gordon Pr.
Young, Bill. Moses: God's Helper. 5.50 (ISBN 0-8054-4225-1). Broadman.

MOSES-FICTION

Kayser, Rudolf. The Saints of Qumran: Stories & Essays on Jewish Themes. Zohn, Harry, ed. LC 76-20273. 188p. 1977. 14.50 (ISBN 0-8386-2024-8). Fairleigh Dickinson.

MOSES-JUVENILE LITERATURE

Baby Moses in a Basket. (Tell-a-Bible Story Ser.). (Illus.). 28p. bds. 0.69 (ISBN 0-686-68638-1, 3682). Standard Pub.
Bennett, Marian. The Story of Moses. (Mini Pop-up Bks). (Illus.). 12p. (gr. k-2). 1979. 2.50 (ISBN 0-87239-367-4, 3615). Standard Pub.
Diamond, Lucy. Moses, Prince & Shepherd. (Ladybird Ser). (Illus.). 1954. bds. 1.49 (ISBN 0-87508-850-3). Chr Lit.
Habel, Norman. When God Told Us His Name: Moses & the Burning Bush. (Purple Puzzle Tree Ser). (Illus., Orig.). (ps-4). 1971. pap. 0.85 (ISBN 0-570-06509-7, 56-1209). Concordia.
Kramer, Janice. Princess & the Baby. (Arch Bks: Set 6). 1969. laminated bdg 0.79 (ISBN 0-570-06043-5, 59-1158). Concordia.
Maniscalco, Joe. Moses. (Bible Hero Stories). (Illus.). (gr. 3-6). 1977. pap. 2.00 (ISBN 0-87239-138-8, 2725). Standard Pub.
Odor, Ruth S. Baby in a Basket. LC 79-12092. (Bible Story Books). (Illus.). (ps-3). 1979. PLB 5.50 (ISBN 0-89565-086-X). Childs World.
Saporta, Raphael. Basket in the Reeds. LC 64-25640. (Foreign Land Bks). (gr. k-7). 1965. PLB 5.95 (ISBN 0-8225-0352-2). Lerner Pubns.
Shimoni, S. Legends of Moses the Law-Giver. (Biblical Ser.). (Illus.). (gr. 1-5). 1975. 5.00 (ISBN 0-914080-08-3). Shulsinger Sales.
Warren-Roberts, Mary P. Great Escape. (Arch Bks: Set 3). 1966. laminated bdg. 0.79 (ISBN 0-570-06016-8, 59-1125). Concordia.

MOSES BEN MAIMON, 1135-1204

Baron, Salo W., ed. Essays on Maimonides. LC 79-160004. Repr. of 1941 ed. 24.50 (ISBN 0-404-00658-2). AMS Pr.
Chavel, Charles B. Ramban: His Life & Teachings. LC 63-1543. pap. 3.95 (ISBN 0-87306-037-7). Feldheim.
Cohen, Abraham. The Teachings of Maimonides. Date not set. 15.00x (ISBN 0-87068-033-1). Ktav.
Dienstag, J. I., ed. Studies in Maimonidean Medicine. (Texts, Studies & Translations in Maimonidean Thought & Scholarship: Vol.2). 35.00x (ISBN 0-87068-449-3). Ktav.
--Studies in Maimonides & Spinoza. (Texts, Studies & Translations in Maimonidean Thought & Scholarship: Vol. 3). 35.00x (ISBN 0-87068-330-6). Ktav.
Dienstag, Jacob I. Eschatology in Maimonidean Thought. Date not set. 35.00x (ISBN 0-87068-706-9). Ktav.
--Maimonides & St. Thomas Aquinas. 1974. 29.50x (ISBN 0-87068-249-0). Ktav.
--Studies in Maimonidean Science. Date not set. 35.00x (ISBN 0-87068-707-7). Ktav.
Efros, Israel I. Philosophical Terms in the Moreh Nebukim. LC 73-164764. (Columbia University. Oriental Studies: No. 22). Repr. of 1924 ed. 17.00 (ISBN 0-404-50512-0). AMS Pr.
Goldman, Solomon. The Jew & the Universe. LC 73-2200. (The Jewish People; History, Religion, Literature Ser.). Repr. of 1936 ed. 17.00 (ISBN 0-405-05265-0). Arno.
Goodman, Lenn E. RAMBAM: Readings in the Philosophy of Moses Maimonides. Patterson, David & Edelman, Lily, eds. LC 75-14476. 1978. text ed. 10.00x (ISBN 0-917232-07-0). Gee Tee Bee.
--Rambam: Readings in the Philosophy of Moses Maimonides. LC 75-14476. (B'nai B'rith Jewish Heritage Classics Ser). 576p. 1976. 10.00 (ISBN 0-670-58964-0). Viking Pr.
Haberman, Jacob. Maimonides & Aquinas. Date not set. 22.50x (ISBN 0-87068-685-2). Ktav.
--Maimonides & Aquinas: A Contemporary Appraisal. 17.50x (ISBN 0-87068-685-2). Ktav.
Heschel, Abraham J. Maimonides. Neugroschel, Joachim, tr. from Ger. 1982. 10.95 (ISBN 0-374-19874-8). FS&G.
Hyamson. Maimonides Mishneh Torah, 2 vols. Set. 21.00 (ISBN 0-87306-084-9); Vol. 2. 11.50 (ISBN 0-87306-085-7); Vol. 2 Bk. Of Adoration. 9.50 (ISBN 0-87306-086-5). Feldheim.
Katz, Steven, ed. Maimonides: Selected Essays, Original Anthology. LC 79-7176. (Jewish Philosophy, Mysticism & the History of Ideas Ser.). 1980. lib. bdg. 45.00x (ISBN 0-405-12234-9). Arno.
Letters of Maimonidies. Date not set. 10.00 (ISBN 0-686-76539-7). Feldheim.
Lieberman, Saul. Hilkhot Ha-Yerushalmi of Rabbi Moses Ben Maimon. 1947. 10.00x (ISBN 0-685-31432-4, Pub. by Jewish Theol Seminary). Ktav.
Maimonides' Commentary on Avoth. 7.95 (ISBN 0-686-52186-2). Feldheim.
Maimonides, Moses. The Book of Women: The Code of Maimonides, Bk. 4. Klein, Isaac, ed. LC 49-9495. (Judaica Ser.: No. 19). 592p. 1972. 35.00x (ISBN 0-300-01438-4). Yale U Pr.
Maimonides, Moses & Twersky, Isadore. Introduction to the Code of Maimonides (Mishneh Torah) LC 79-10347. (Yale Judaica Ser.: No. XXII). 1980. 40.00x (ISBN 0-300-02319-7). Yale U Pr.
Maimonides Octocentennial Series, Nos. 1-4. LC 73-2214. (The Jewish People; History, Religion, Literature Ser.). Repr. of 1935 ed. 12.00 (ISBN 0-405-05278-2). Arno.
Reines, Alvin J. Maimonides & Abrabanel on Prophecy. 1971. 15.00x (ISBN 0-87820-200-5, Pub. by Hebrew Union). KTAV.
Rosner, Fred. Sex Ethics in the Writings of Moses Maimonides. LC 74-75479. 225p. 1974. 7.95 (ISBN 0-8197-0365-6). Bloch.
Rosner, Fred, ed. & tr. The Medical Aphorisms of Moses Maimonides, 2 vols. in 1. 1973. 12.50x (ISBN 0-8197-0358-3). Bloch.
Strauss, Leo. Persecution & the Art of Writing. LC 73-1407. 204p. 1973. Repr. of 1952 ed. lib. bdg. 16.75x (ISBN 0-8371-6801-5, STPA). Greenwood.
Twersky, Isadore. Maimonides Reader. LC 76-160818. pap. 6.95x (ISBN 0-87441-206-4). Behrman.
Unterman, Isaac. Moses Maimonides. 245p. (Orig.). 1978. pap. 7.75 (ISBN 0-8197-0479-2). Bloch.
Weiss, Raymond L. & Butterworth, Charles E. Ethical Writings of Maimonides. LC 74-18951. 182p. 1975. 15.00x (ISBN 0-8147-0984-2). NYU Pr.

MOSES, ANNA MARY (ROBERTSON), 1860-1962

Grandma Moses: Memorial Exhibition. (Illus.). 1962. pap. 5.00 (ISBN 0-910810-17-6). Johannes.
Laing, Martha. Grandma Moses: The Grand Old Lady of American Art. Rahmas, D. Steve, ed. LC 71-190231. (Outstanding Personalities Ser: No. 13). 32p. (Orig.). (gr. 7-9). 1972. lib. bdg. 2.95 incl. catalog cards (ISBN 0-87157-513-2); pap. 1.50 vinyl laminated covers (ISBN 0-87157-013-0). SamHar Pr.

MOSES, ROBERT

Caro, Robert A. The Power Broker: Robert Moses & the Fall of New York. 1975. 9.95 (ISBN 0-394-72024-5, Vin). Random.
--The Power Broker: Robert Moses & the Fall of the New York. LC 73-20751. (Illus.). 1296p. 1974. 20.00 (ISBN 0-394-48076-7). Knopf.
Lewis, Eugene. Public Entrepreneurship: Toward a Theory of Bureaucratic Political Power. LC 79-2451. 288p. 1980. 22.50x (ISBN 0-253-17384-1). Ind U Pr.

MOSES, SINKIUSE-COLUMBIA CHIEF, 1829-1899

Ruby, Robert H. & Brown, John A. Half-Sun on the Columbia: A Biography of Chief Moses. (Civilization of the American Indian Ser.: No. 80). (Illus.). 1966. Repr. of 1965 ed. 17.95 (ISBN 0-8061-0675-1). U of Okla Pr.

MOSKOWITZ, IRA

Singer, Isaac B. Hasidim. LC 72-84288. (Illus.). 160p. 1973. 10.00 (ISBN 0-517-50047-7). Crown.

MOSLEM

see headings beginning with the word Islamic or Muslim

MOSLEMS

see Muslims

MOSO (TRIBE)

Jackson, Anthony. Na-Khi Religion: An Analytical Appraisal of the Na-Khi Ritual Texts. (Religion & Society Ser.). 1979. text ed. write for info (ISBN 90-279-7642-2). Mouton.
Li Lin-Tsan. Studies in Mo-So Tribal Stories, No. 3. (Asian Folklore & Social Life Monograph). (Chinese.). 1970. 6.60 (ISBN 0-89986-006-0). E Langstaff.
Rock, Joseph F. Ancient Na-Khi Kingdom of Southwest China, 2 Vols. LC 48-6883. (Harvard-Yenching Institute Monograph Ser: No. 8-9). (Illus.). 1947. Set. 30.00x (ISBN 0-674-03400-7). Harvard U Pr.

MOSQUES

Ingrams, Doreen. Mosques & Minarets. LC 74-12221. (The Arab World Ser). 1974. lib. bdg. 4.95 (ISBN 0-88436-115-2); pap. 2.95 (ISBN 0-88436-116-0). EMC.
Kuran, Aptullah. Mosque in Early Ottoman Architecture. LC 68-16701. (Publications of the Center for Middle Eastern Studies Ser). (Illus.). 1968. 25.00x (ISBN 0-226-46293-5). U of Chicago Pr.
Turánszky, Ilona. Azerbaijan: Mosques, Turrets, Palaces. Boros, Laszlo, tr. (Illus.). 184p. 1979. 22.50x (ISBN 963-13-0321-7). Intl Pubns Serv.

MOSQUITIA

Roberts, Orlando W. Narrative of Voyages & Excursions on the East Coast & in the Interior of Central America. Craggs, Hugh, ed. LC 65-28696. (Latin American Gateway Ser). 1965. Repr. of 1827 ed. 9.00 (ISBN 0-8130-0199-4). U Presses Fla.
Young, T. Narrative of a Residence on the Mosquito Shore. 2nd ed. Repr. of 1847 ed. 14.00 (ISBN 0-527-99700-5). Kraus Repr.

MOSQUITOES

Bard, Samuel A., pseud. Waikna, or, Adventures on the Mosquito Shore. Alleger, Daniel E., ed. LC 65-28697. (Latin American Gateway Ser.). (Illus.). 1965. Repr. of 1855 ed. 9.00 (ISBN 0-8130-0217-6). U Presses Fla.

Bates, Marston. The Natural History of Mosquitos. (Illus.). 8.25 (ISBN 0-8446-0480-1). Peter Smith.

Belkin, John N. & Heinemann, Sandra J. The Mosquitoes of the West Indies, 2 vols. 1979. Set. lib. bdg. write for info. (ISBN 0-916846-10-5). World Natural Hist.

Bohart, R. M. & Washino, R. K. Mosquitoes of California. 3rd ed. LC 77-84551. 1978. pap. 6.00x (ISBN 0-931876-15-X, 4084). Ag Sci Pubns.

Carpenter, Stanley J. & Lacasse, Walter J. Mosquitoes of North America. (California Library Reprint Ser.). (Illus.). 1974. Repr. 45.00x (ISBN 0-520-02638-1). U of Cal Pr.

Darsie, Richard F. & Ward, Ronald A. Identification & Geographical Distribution of the Mosquitoes of North America North of Mexico. LC 81-50441. (Supplements to Mosquito Systematics Ser.). (Illus.). 315p. (Orig.). 1981. 35.00 (ISBN 0-9606210-0-8); pap. 30.00 (ISBN 0-9606210-1-6). Am Mosquito.

Delfinado, Mercedes. Culicine Mosquitoes of the Philippines. (Memoris Ser: No. 7). (Illus.). 252p. 1966. 15.00 (ISBN 0-686-00417-5). Am Entom Inst.

Dobrotworsky, N. V. Mosquitoes of Victoria. 1965. 22.50x (ISBN 0-522-83584-8, Pub. by Melbourne U Pr). Intl Schol Bk Serv.

Gutsevich, A. V., et al. Fauna of the U.S.S.R. Diptera Mosquitoes-Family Culicidae. Bykhovskii, B. E., ed. Lavoott, Rose, tr. from Rus. (Fauna of the U.S.S.R. Ser.: Vol. 3, No. 4). (Illus.). iii, 403p. 1974. 35.00x (ISBN 0-7065-1475-0, Pub. by IPST). Intl Schol Bk Serv.

Harbach, R. E. & Knight, Kenneth L. Taxonomists' Glossary of Mosquito Anatomy. LC 80-83112. (Illus.). 430p. 1980. 24.95 (ISBN 0-517-54149-1). Plexus Pub.

Holstein, M. H. Biology of Anopheles Gambiae: Research in French West Africa. (Monograph Ser: No. 9). 172p. 1954. pap. 3.60 (ISBN 92-4-140009-9). World Health.

Horsfall, William R. Mosquitoes: Their Bionomics & Relation to Disease. LC 55-6089. 1972. Repr. of 1955 ed. 30.25 (ISBN 0-02-846210-6). Hafner.

Knight, Kenneth L. & Stone, Alan. A Catalog of the Mosquitos of the World, Vol. 6. 2nd ed. LC 77-82735. 1977. 20.50 (ISBN 0-686-04889-X); supplement 1978 3.35 (ISBN 0-686-28524-7). Entomol Soc.

Manual on Larval Control Operations in Malaria Programmes. (Offset Pub.: No. 1). (Also avail. in French). 1973. pap. 12.50 (ISBN 92-4-170001-7). World Health.

Marshall, J. F. The British Mosquitoes. Repr. of 1938 ed. 31.00 (ISBN 0-384-35450-5). Johnson Repr.

Matheson, Robert. Handbook of the Mosquitoes of North America. rev. 2nd ed. (Illus.). 1966. Repr. of 1944 ed. 11.95 (ISBN 0-02-848850-4). Hafner.

The Mosquitoes of Canada: Diptera; Culicidae. (The Insects & Arachnids of Canada: Pt. 6). 390p. 1980. pap. 15.00 (ISBN 0-660-10402-4, SSC 143, SSC). Unipub.

Pal, R. & Wharton, R. H., eds. Control of Arthropods: Medical & Veterinary Importance. LC 74-4172. 138p. 1974. 32.50 (ISBN 0-306-30790-1, Plenum Pr). Plenum Pub.

Service, M. W. Mosquito Ecology: Field Sampling Methods. 1976. 96.95 (ISBN 0-470-15191-9). Halsted Pr.

White, William, Jr. A Mosquito Is Born. LC 77-93319. (Sterling Nature Series). (Illus.). (gr. 5 up). 1978. 7.95 (ISBN 0-8069-3534-0); PLB 7.49 (ISBN 0-8069-3535-9). Sterling.

MOSQUITOES-EXTERMINATION

Malaria & Insecticides. Incl. Vol. 27, No. 2. 122p. 1962; Vol. 28, No. 1. 138p. 1963; Vol. 29, No. 2. 158p. 1963; Vol. 30, No. 1. 151p. 1964; Vol. 31, No. 5. 131p. 1964. (Bulletin of WHO). (Eng. & Fr.). pap. 3.60 ea. World Health.

Pampana, Emilio. Textbook of Malaria Eradication. 2nd ed. 1969. 24.00x (ISBN 0-19-264212-X). Oxford U Pr.

MOSSBAUER EFFECT

see Moessbauer Effect

MOSSES

Bartram, E. B. Manual of Hawaiian Mosses. Repr. of 1933 ed. pap. 25.00 (ISBN 0-527-02207-1). Kraus Repr.

--Mosses of the Phillipines. (Illus.). 437p. 1972. Repr. of 1939 ed. lib. bdg. 67.50x (ISBN 3-87429-033-6). Lubrecht & Cramer.

Bland, John. Forests of Lilliput: The Realm of Mosses & Lichens. LC 70-143811. (Natural History Ser). (Illus.). 1971. 9.95 (ISBN 0-13-326868-3). P-H.

Boros. An Atlas of Recent European Moss Spores. 1975. 34.50 (ISBN 0-9960002-1-6, Pub. by Kaido Hungary). Heyden.

Boros, Adam. Atlas of Recent European Moss Spores. 466p. 1975. 35.00x (ISBN 963-05-0212-7). Intl Pubns Serv.

Breen, Ruth S. Mosses of Florida: An Illustrated Manual. LC 62-19677. 1963. 15.00x (ISBN 0-8130-0613-9). U Presses Fla.

Brotherus, V. F. Hawaiian Mosses. (BMB: No. 40). Repr. of 1927 ed. pap. 6.00 (ISBN 0-527-02143-1). Kraus Repr.

--Die Laubmoose Fennoskandias. (Flora Fennica Ser.: Vol. 1). (Illus.). 635p. (Ger.). 1974. Repr. of 1923 ed. lib. bdg. 102.95x (ISBN 3-87429-078-6). Lubrecht & Cramer.

Bruch, P., et al. Brvologie Europaea, Seu Genera Muscorum Europaeorum Monographice Illustrated: Collarium, Index & Supplement. Incl. Music Europaei Novi Vel Bryologiae Supplementum. Florschuetz, P. A., pref. by.. (Illus.). Repr. of 1866 ed. 810.00 (ISBN 90-6123-220-1). Lubrecht & Cramer.

Conard, Henry S. & Redfearn, Paul L., Jr. How to Know the Mosses & Liverworts. 2nd ed. (Pict. Key Nature Ser.). 1979. wire coil avail. (ISBN 0-697-04768-7); text ed. write for info. (ISBN 0-697-04769-5). Wm C Brown.

Correns, Carl. Untersuchungen Uber Die Vermehrung der Laubmoose: Durch Brutorgane und Stecklinge. (Bryophytorum Bibliotheca: Band 7). (Illus.). 1976. pap. 48.00x (ISBN 3-7682-1060-X, Pub. by J. Cramer). Intl Schol Bk Serv.

Crum, Howard A. & Anderson, Lewis E. Mosses of Eastern North America, 2 Vols. LC 79-24789. (Illus.). 576p. 1981. 60.00x (ISBN 0-231-04516-6). Columbia U Pr.

Darlington, Henry T. Mosses of Michigan. LC 64-25250. (Bulletin Ser.: No. 47). (Illus.). 212p. 1964. text ed. 9.00x (ISBN 0-87737-024-9). Cranbrook.

Davis, Bette. The World of Mosses. LC 74-10606. (Illus.). 64p. (gr. 5 up). 1975. 6.75 (ISBN 0-688-41667-5); PLB 6.48 (ISBN 0-688-51667-X). Lothrop.

During, H. J. Taxonomical Revision of the Garovaglioideae (Pterobryaceae, Musci) (Bryophytorum Bibliotheca Ser.: No. 12). (Illus.). 1977. lib. bdg. 30.00x (ISBN 3-7682-1161-4). Lubrecht & Cramer.

Flowers, Seville. Mosses: Utah & the West. Holmgren, Arthur, ed. LC 72-96422. (Illus.). 567p. 1973. text ed. 7.95 (ISBN 0-8425-1524-0). Brigham.

Grout, A. J. Mosses with Hand Lens & Microscope. 1972. 15.00 (ISBN 0-910914-03-6). J Johnson.

Guerke, W. R. A Monograph of the Genus Jubula Dumortier. (Bryophytorum Bibliotheca: No. 17). (Illus.). 1979. pap. 20.00 (ISBN 3-7682-1213-0). Lubrecht & Cramer.

Harthill, Marion P. Common Mosses of the Pacific Coast. LC 74-31294. (Illus.). 1975. 7.25 (ISBN 0-87961-025-5); pap. 3.25 (ISBN 0-87961-024-7). Naturegraph.

Haseloff, H. P. Veraenderungen Im 002.-Gaswechsel bel Laubmoosen nach experimentellen Be-Lastungen mit Schwermetallverbingungen. (Bryohpytorum Bibliotheca 19). (Illus.). 1979. pap. text ed. 15.00x (ISBN 3-7682-1234-3). Lubrecht & Cramer.

Hedwig, J. Species Muscorum Frondosorum. (Illus.). 1960. Repr. of 1801 ed. 42.00 (ISBN 3-7682-7055-6). Lubrecht & Cramer.

Husnot, P. T. Muscologia Gallica: 1884-94, 2 parts in 1. (Illus.). 1968. 90.00 (ISBN 90-6123-082-9). Lubrecht & Cramer.

Jaeger, A. & Sauerbeck, F. Genera et Species Muscorum Systematice Disposita Seu Adumbratio Florae Muscorum Totius Orbis Terrarum, 2 vols. Repr. of 1870 ed. Set. lib. bdg. 100.00x (ISBN 3-7682-1157-6). Lubrecht & Cramer.

Johnson, Anne. Mosses of Singapore & Malaysia. 126p. 1980. pap. 7.50 (ISBN 0-8214-0547-0). Swallow.

Kramer, Wolfgang. Tortula Hedw. Sect. Rurales De Not. Pottiaceae, Musci in der Oestlichen Holarktis. (Bryophytorum Bibliotheca: 21). 250p. (Ger.). 1980. lib. bdg. 30.00x (ISBN 3-7682-1266-1). Lubrecht & Cramer.

Leitgeb, H. Utersuchungen Ueber Die Lebermoose. 1970. 100.00 (ISBN 3-7682-7187-0). Lubrecht & Cramer.

Miller, H. A., et al. Prodromus Florae Muscorum Polynesiae. with a Key to Genera. 1978. lib. bdg. 50.00x (ISBN 3-7682-1115-0). Lubrecht & Cramer.

Norris, Daniel H. Bryophytes of California. (Illus.). Date not set. pap. cancelled (ISBN 0-685-57432-6). Mad River.

Nowak, H. Revision der Laubmoosgattung Mitthyridium (Mitten) Robinson Fuer Oreanien (Calymperaceae) (Bryophytorum Bibliotheca: No. 20). (Illus., Ger.). 1981. lib. bdg. 30.00x (ISBN 3-7682-1236-X). Lubrecht & Cramer.

Smith, A. J. The Moss Flora of Britain & Ireland. LC 77-71428. (Illus.). 1978. 82.50 (ISBN 0-521-21648-6). Cambridge U Pr.

Steere, William C. The Mosses of Arctic Alaska. (Bryophytorum Bibliotheca: No. 14). (Illus.). 1978. lib. bdg. 75.00 (ISBN 3-7682-1181-9). Lubrecht & Cramer.

Steere, William C. & Crum, Howard A. New Combinations and New Taxa of Mosses Proposed by Nils Conrad Kindberg. LC 66-6394. (Memoirs of the New York Botanical Garden Ser.: Vol. 28, No. 2). 1977. pap. 20.00 (ISBN 0-89327-005-9). NY Botanical.

Suire, C., ed. Congres International De Bryologie, Bordeaux 1977: Proceedings. (Bryophytorum Bibliotheca Ser.: No. 13). (Illus.). 1978. lib. bdg. 100.00 (ISBN 3-7682-1163-0). Lubrecht & Cramer.

Sullivant, William S. Icones Muscorum, or Figures & Descriptions of Most of Those Mosses Peculiar to Eastern North America: 1864-74, 2 vols. with supplement. text ed. 60.00 (ISBN 90-6123-145-0). Lubrecht & Cramer.

Taylor, Ronald J. & Leviton, Alan E., eds. Mosses of North America. 170p. (Orig.). 1980. 11.95 (ISBN 0-934394-02-4). AAASPD.

Tixier, P. Contribution a L'etude du Genre Colo-Lejeuna. Les Colclejeuniceas de Nouvelles Caledonie. (Illus.). 1979. pap. text ed. 15.00x (ISBN 3-7682-1230-0). Lubrecht & Cramer.

Watson, E. Vernon. British Mosses & Liverworts. 2nd ed. LC 68-22665. (Illus.). 1968. 50.00 (ISBN 0-521-06741-3); pap. 29.50 (ISBN 0-521-29472-X). Cambridge U Pr.

Whittier, Henry O. Mosses of the Society Islands. LC 75-23309. (Illus.). 1976. 17.50 (ISBN 0-8130-0521-3). U Presses Fla.

MOSSI (AFRICAN PEOPLE)

Schildkrout, Enid. People of the Zongo: The Transformation of Ethnic Identities in Ghana. LC 76-47188. (Cambridge Studies in Social Anthropology: No. 20). 1978. 27.50 (ISBN 0-521-21483-1). Cambridge U Pr.

Skinner, Elliott P. The Mossi of the Upper Volta: The Political Development of a Sudanese People. LC 64-12074. (Illus.). 1964. 12.50x (ISBN 0-8047-0166-0). Stanford U Pr.

MOSSOS

see Moso (Tribe)

MOTAZILITES

see also Shiites

Ali ibn Isma'il, A. H., et al. Al ibanah 'an usul addiyanah. Klein, W. C., tr. (American Oriental Ser.: Vol. 19). 1940. pap. 12.00 (ISBN 0-527-02693-X). Kraus Repr.

MOTELS

Belasco, Warren J. Americans on the Road: From Autocamp to Motel. (Illus.). 1979. 17.50 (ISBN 0-262-02123-4); pap. 6.95 (ISBN 0-262-02123-4). MIT Pr.

Brymer, Robert A. Introduction to Hotel & Restaurant Management: A Book of Readings. 2nd ed. 1979. pap. text ed. 12.95 (ISBN 0-8403-2478-2, 40247801). Kendall-Hunt.

Buzby, Walter J. & Paine, David. Hotel & Motel Security Management. LC 76-12555. 256p. 1976. 17.95 (ISBN 0-913708-24-0). Butterworth.

Carlson, Raymond, ed. National Directory of Budget Motels. LC 75-11992. 1981. pap. 3.50 (ISBN 0-87576-051-1). Pilot Bks.

Dittmer, Paul. Accounting Practices for Hotels, Motels, & Restaurants. LC 79-142507. 1971. text ed. 17.95 (ISBN 0-672-96062-1); tchr's manual 5.00 (ISBN 0-672-26064-6); wkbk., 1972 9.95 (ISBN 0-672-96063-X). Bobbs.

Dukas, Peter. Planning Profits in the Food and Lodging Industry. 180p. 1976. 14.95 (ISBN 0-8436-2080-3). CBI Pub.

Fales, John T. Functional Housekeeping in Hotels & Motels. LC 72-142508. 1971. text ed. 14.50 (ISBN 0-672-96080-X); tchr's manual 6.67 (ISBN 0-672-96082-6); wkbk. 6.50 (ISBN 0-672-96081-8). Bobbs.

Hertzson, David. Hotel-Motel Marketing. LC 76-142509. 1971. text ed. 14.50 (ISBN 0-672-96083-4); tchr's manual 6.67 (ISBN 0-672-96085-0); wkbk. 6.95 (ISBN 0-672-96084-2). Bobbs.

Lawson, Fred. Hotels, Motels & Condominiums: Design, Planning & Maintenance. (Illus.). 1976. 54.95 (ISBN 0-8436-2109-5). CBI Pub.

Lyda, Harold. Motel-Hotel Management Directory. 1977. looseleaf 29.95 (ISBN 0-915260-06-9). Atcom.

Podd, George O. & Lesure, John D. Planning & Operating Motels and Motor Hotels. (Illus.). 1964. 16.15x (ISBN 0-8104-9437-X). Hayden.

Rushmore, Stephen. The Valuation of Hotels & Motels. 1978. 18.00 (ISBN 0-911780-44-0). Am Inst Real Estate Appraisers.

Witzky, Herbert K. Modern Hotel-Motel Management Methods. rev.,2nd ed. 1976. text ed. 15.25x (ISBN 0-8104-9467-1). Hayden.

MOTELS-EMPLOYEES

see Hotels, Taverns, etc.-Employees

MOTET

Here are entered works on the motet as a musical form.

Arnold, Denis, ed. Ten Venetian Motets. 108p. 1981. text ed. 10.75x (ISBN 0-19-353035-X). Oxford U Pr.

Aubry, Pierre. Cent Motets du XIIIe siecle, 3 vols. (Illus.). 540p. (Fr.). 1964. pap. 125.00x (ISBN 0-8450-0001-2). Broude.

De Mondonville, Jean-Joseph C. A Motet: Jubilate. Borroff, Edith, ed. (Music Reprint Ser., 1977). (Illus.). 1977. Repr. of 1961 ed. text ed. 5.75 (ISBN 0-306-77411-9). Da Capo.

Dreves, Guido M., ed. Cantiones et Muteti, 3 vols. (Illus.). 1895-1904. 50.00 ea. (ISBN 0-384-12865-3). Johnson Repr.

Lowinsky, Edward E. Secret Chromatic Art in the Netherlands Motet. Buchman, Carl, tr. LC 66-27120. (Illus.). 1967. Repr. of 1946 ed. 10.00 (ISBN 0-8462-0847-4). Russell.

Slim, H. Colin, ed. A Gift of Madrigals & Motets. LC 73-172799. (Illus.). 1973. Set Of 2 Vols. 37.50x (ISBN 0-226-76271-8); Vol. 2. pap. 8.75x (ISBN 0-226-76272-6). U of Chicago Pr.

Soriano, Francesco. The Works of Francesco Soriano: Vol. I, "Motets for Eight Voices," 1597. Kniseley, S. Phillip, ed. LC 79-25222. (Vol. 1). (Illus.). 132p. 1980. pap. 12.00 (ISBN 0-8130-0668-6). U Presses Fla.

MOTHER AND CHILD

Arcana, Judith. Our Mothers' Daughters. 1979. pap. 3.95 (ISBN 0-915288-40-0). Shameless Hussy.

Badinter, Elisabeth. Mother Love: Myth & Reality. DeGaris, Roger, tr. (Illus.). 352p. 1981. 12.95 (ISBN 0-02-504610-1). Macmillan.

Baker, Pat A. Mom, Take Time. 128p. 1976. 3.95 (ISBN 0-8010-0655-4). Baker Bk.

Bell, Robert W. & Smotherman, William F., eds. Maternal Influences & Early Behavior. new ed. LC 78-17074. (Illus.). 465p. 1980. text ed. 45.00 (ISBN 0-89335-059-1). Spectrum Pub.

Bernard, Jessie. The Future of Motherhood. 448p. 1975. pap. 2.95 (ISBN 0-14-004040-4). Penguin.

Bernard, Susan. Joyous Motherhood: A 30-Day Program for Total Communication Between the New Mother & Her Child Under Three. LC 78-21680. (Illus.). 160p. 1979. pap. 6.95 (ISBN 0-87131-272-7). M Evans.

Blumenfeld, Samuel L. The Retreat from Motherhood. 1975. 7.95 (ISBN 0-87000-304-6). Arlington Hse.

Bowlby, John. Attachment. LC 70-78464. (Attachment & Loss Ser., Vol. 1). 1969. text ed. 20.00x (ISBN 0-465-00539-X); pap. 4.95x (ISBN 0-465-09715-4, CN-5015). Basic.

--Separation: Anxiety & Anger. LC 70-78464. (Attachment & Loss Ser.: Vol. 2). 429p. 1973. text ed. 20.00x (ISBN 0-465-07691-2); pap. 4.95x (ISBN 0-465-09716-2, CN-5016). Basic.

Brazelton, T. Berry. Infants & Mothers: Individual Differences in Development. (Illus.). 1969. 12.95 (ISBN 0-440-04045-0, Sey Lawr). Delacorte.

Bricklin, Alice G. Motherlove: Natural Mothering, Birth to Three Years. Williams, Betsy, ed. LC 79-9724. 1979. lib. bdg. 12.90 (ISBN 0-89471-070-2); pap. 4.95 (ISBN 0-89471-069-9). Running Pr.

Brody, Sylvia & Axelrad, Sidney. Anxiety & Ego Formation in Infancy. LC 74-141660. 1971. text ed. 22.50 (ISBN 0-8236-0390-3). Intl Univs Pr.

Browne, J. C. Advice to the Expectant Mother. 14th ed. 64p. 1973. pap. text ed. 1.50 (ISBN 0-686-31227-9). Churchill.

Burlingham, Dorothy. Psychoanalytic Studies of the Sighted & the Blind. LC 76-184213. 1972. text ed. 25.00 (ISBN 0-8236-4510-X). Intl Univs Pr.

Clezy. Modification of the Mother-Child Interchange. 1979. 11.95 (ISBN 0-8391-1319-6). Univ Park.

Cohler, Bertram J. & Grunebaum, Henry U. Mothers, Grandmothers & Daughters: Personality & Child-Care in Three Generation Families. LC 80-17979. (Personality Processes Ser.). 456p. 1981. 24.95 (ISBN 0-471-05900-5, Pub. by Wiley-Interscience). Wiley.

Ehrenreich, Barbara & English, Deirdre. For Her Own Good: 150 Years of Expert's Advice to Women. 1979. pap. 3.95 (ISBN 0-385-12651-4, Anch). Doubleday.

Fabe, Marilyn & Wikler, Norma. Up Against the Clock: Career Women Speak on the Choice to Have Children. 1980. pap. 2.75 (ISBN 0-446-95536-1). Warner Bks.

--Up Against the Clock: Career Women Speak on the New Choice of Motherhood. 1979. 10.00 (ISBN 0-394-50221-3). Random.

Fallon, Edward B. Hey Mom. 100p. (Orig.). 1980. 7.95 (ISBN 0-935976-00-0). Midland Pub Co.

Friday, Nancy. My Mother, Myself. 1981. pap. 3.25 (ISBN 0-440-15663-7). Dell.

Friedland, Ronnie & Kort, Carol, eds. The Mother's Book. 384p. 1981. 14.95 (ISBN 0-395-30527-6); pap. 8.95 (ISBN 0-395-31134-9). HM.

Garnica, Olga K. Mother-Child Interaction Strategies. (Humanist Psychobiology & Psychiatry Ser.). Date not set. price not set (ISBN 0-08-024302-9). Pergamon.
Glickman, Beatrice M. & Springer, Nesha B. Who Cares for the Baby? Choices in Child Care. LC 77-75293. 1978. 9.95 (ISBN 0-8052-3667-8). Schocken.
Grunebaum, Henry, et al. Mentally Ill Mothers & Their Children. LC 74-5740. xxii, 346p. 1975. 15.50x (ISBN 0-226-31021-3). U of Chicago Pr.
Hall, Nor. Mothers & Daughters: Reflections on the Archetypal Feminine. 1976. pap. 2.50 (ISBN 0-685-74192-3). Rusoff Bks.
Hammer, Signe. Daughters & Mothers-Mothers & Daughters. 1976. pap. 1.75 (ISBN 0-451-08721-6, E8721, Sig). NAL.
Hawley, Gloria H. Laura's Psalm. 192p. 1981. pap. 5.95 (ISBN 0-86608-000-7, 14014P). Impact Tenn.
Howard, Linda. Mothers Are People Too. 1976. pap. 3.95 (ISBN 0-88270-190-8). Logos.
Klaus & Kennell. Maternal-Infant Bonding: The Impact of Early Separation or Loss on Family Development. LC 76-5397. Orig. Title: Care of the Family of the Normal or Sick Newborn. (Illus.). 224p. 1976. text ed. 14.95 (ISBN 0-8016-2631-5); pap. 11.95 (ISBN 0-8016-2630-7). Mosby.
Lazarre, Jane. The Mother Knot. 1977. pap. 1.95 (ISBN 0-440-35798-5, LE). Dell.
Leiderman, P. Herbert, et al, eds. Culture & Infancy: Variations in the Human Experience. (Child Psychology Ser.). 1977. 30.00 (ISBN 0-12-442050-8). Acad Pr.
Light, P. The Development of Social Sensitivity. LC 78-12415. (Illus.). 1979. 17.95 (ISBN 0-521-22372-5). Cambridge U Pr.
Loeks, Mary F. Mom's Quiet Corner. (Comtempo Ser.). 1977. pap. 0.95 (ISBN 0-8010-5576-8). Baker Bk.
Maassen, Pierce. Motherhood. pap. 0.45 (ISBN 0-686-23476-6). Rose Pub MI.
McDevitt, John B. & Settlage, Calvin F., eds. Separation-Individuation: Essays in Honor of Margaret S. Mahler. LC 78-143378. 1971. text ed. 30.00 (ISBN 0-8236-6065-6). Intl Univs Pr.
Macfarlane, Aidan. The Psychology of Childbirth. (Developing Child Ser.). 1977. 6.95x (ISBN 0-674-72105-5); pap. 3.95 (ISBN 0-674-72106-3). Harvard U Pr.
Mandell, Dale. Early Feminine Development: Current Psychoanalytic Views. 303p. 1981. text ed. 25.00 (ISBN 0-89335-135-0). Spectrum Pub.
Mitchell, Joyce S. Be a Mother & More. 224p. (Orig.). 1980. pap. 2.95 (ISBN 0-553-13926-6). Bantam.
Olsen, Paul. Sons & Mothers: Why Men Behave As They Do. LC 81-1844. 192p. 1981. 9.95 (ISBN 0-87131-338-3). M Evans.
Polansky, Norman A., et al. Roots of Futility. LC 72-5894. (Social & Behavioral Science Ser.). 1972. 16.95x (ISBN 0-87589-150-0). Jossey-Bass.
Rich, Adrienne. Of Woman Born: Motherhood As Experience & Institution. 1976. 12.95 (ISBN 0-393-08750-6). Norton.
Rockness, Miriam H. Keep These Things, Ponder Them in Your Heart: Reflections of a Mother. (Festival Ser.). 224p. 1980. pap. 1.95 (ISBN 0-687-20740-1). Abingdon.
Rue, James & Shanahan, Louise. Daddy's Girl, Mama's Boy. 1979. pap. 2.25 (ISBN 0-451-08822-0, E8822, Sig). NAL.
Rutter, Michael. The Qualities of Mothering: Material Deprivation Reassessed. LC 74-9266. 175p. 1974. Repr. 17.50x (ISBN 0-87668-183-6). Aronson.
Safran, Rose. Don't Go Dancing Mother. LC 79-64288. (Illus.). 1979. pap. 4.95 (ISBN 0-9602786-1-3). Tide Bk Pub Co.
Schaffer, Rudolph. Mothering. (Developing Child Ser.). 1977. 6.95x (ISBN 0-674-58745-6); pap. 3.95 (ISBN 0-674-58746-4). Harvard U Pr.
Seabrook, Jeremy. Mother & Son. 1980. 8.95 (ISBN 0-394-50538-7). Pantheon.
Shaffer, David & Dunn, Judy. The First Year of Life: Psychological & Medical Implications of Early Experience. LC 78-11237. (Studies in Psychiatry). 1980. 41.75 (ISBN 0-471-99734-X, Pub. by Wiley-Interscience). Wiley.
Sharmat, Marjorie W. I Want Mama. LC 74-3584. (Illus.). 32p. (gr. k-3). 1974. PLB 9.89 (ISBN 0-06-025554-4, HarpJ). Har-Row.
Snow, Catherine & Ferguson, C. Talking to Children. LC 76-11094. 1977. 35.00 (ISBN 0-521-21318-5); pap. 12.95x (ISBN 0-521-29513-0). Cambridge U Pr.
Spellman, Cathy C. Notes to My Daughters. 320p. 1981. 11.95 (ISBN 0-517-54331-1). Crown.
Stern, Daniel. The First Relationship: Infant & Mother. Bruner, Jerome, et al, eds. (Developing Child Ser.). 1977. 7.95x (ISBN 0-674-30431-4); pap. 3.95 (ISBN 0-674-30432-2). Harvard U Pr.
Ton, Mary E. For the Love of My Daughter. LC 77-87253. 1978. pap. 2.95 (ISBN 0-89191-104-9). Cook.
Van Den Berg, J. H. Dubious Maternal Affection. 110p. 1972. pap. text ed. 2.50x (ISBN 0-8207-0140-8). Duquesne.

MOTHER-GODDESSES

Bhattacharyya, N. N. Indian Mother Goddess. 2nd ed. 1977. 16.50x (ISBN 0-88386-736-2). South Asia Bks.
Presoon, James J., ed. Mother Worship: Theme & Variations. LC 81-3336. (Studies in Religion Ser.). 360p. 1982. 24.00x (ISBN 0-8078-1471-7). U of NC Pr.
Sengupta, Sudhir R. Mother Cult. 1977. 5.50x (ISBN 0-8364-0048-8). South Asia Bks.

MOTHER GOOSE

Abbey, Stella K. Mother Goose Sweeps History. LC 13-275. (Illus.). 1967. 2.99 (ISBN 0-686-00888-X). S K Abbey.
The Christian Mother Goose Treasury, Pt. II. (The Christian Mother Goose Ser.: Vol. 2). 1980. 10.95 (ISBN 0-686-31783-1). Chr Mother Goose.
Decker, Marjorie A. The Christian Mother Goose Book. (Illus.). 1981. 10.95 (ISBN 0-8007-1195-5). Revell.
--The Christian Mother Goose Treasury. (Illus.). 1981. 10.95 (ISBN 0-8007-1196-3). Revell.
--The Christian Mother Goose Treasury: Part II of the Original Christian Mother Goose Book. LC 80-69167. (Three Part Series: Vol. II). (Illus.). 112p. (gr. k-4). 1980. PLB 10.95 (ISBN 0-933724-01-2). CMG Prods.
Favorite Mother Goose Rhymes. LC 62-15042. (Illus.). (ps-2). 1978. 5.95 (ISBN 0-528-82215-2). Rand.
Miller, William A. Big Kids' Mother Goose: Christian Counselor Finds New Insights in Old Stories. LC 75-22722. (Illus.). 112p. 1976. pap. 3.25 (ISBN 0-8066-1500-1, 10-0715). Augsburg.
Mother Goose. 2.95 (ISBN 0-442-82347-9). Peter Pauper.
Mother Goose: The Original Mother Goose's Melody As First Issued by John Newbery of London, About A.D. 1760. LC 68-31093. 1969. Repr. of 1889 ed. 19.00 (ISBN 0-686-66814-6). Gale.
Mother Goose. Mother Goose in Hieroglyphics. Bleiler, E. F., ed. pap. 1.75 (ISBN 0-486-20745-5). Dover.
The Original Mother Goose Melody. lib. bdg. 69.95 (ISBN 0-8490-0778-X). Gordon Pr.
Provensen, Alice & Provensen, Martin. The Mother Goose Book. LC 76-8548. (Illus.). (gr. 1 up). 1976. (BYR); PLB 7.99 (ISBN 0-394-92122-4). Random.
Sandburg, Don. Legal Guide to Mother Goose. (Illus.). 1978. pap. 2.50 (ISBN 0-8431-0480-5). Price Stern.
Sesame Street. The Sesame Street Mother Goose. LC 75-39341. (Sesame Street Pop-up Ser.: No. 9). (Illus.). (ps-3). 1976. 4.95 (ISBN 0-394-83256-6, BYR). Random.
Wiseman, Bernard. Morris Tell Boris Mother Moose Stories & Rhymes. (Illus.). 48p. 1980. Repr. pap. 1.50 (ISBN 0-590-30999-4, Schol Pap). Schol Bk Serv.

MOTHER GOOSE-BIBLIOGRAPHY

Newbery, John, et al, eds. Original Mother Goose's Melody. LC 68-31093. 1969. Repr. of 1892 ed. 19.00 (ISBN 0-8103-3485-2). Gale.

MOTHER LODE

Minke, Pauline. Chinese in the Mother Lode, Eighteen Fifty to Eighteen Seventy. LC 73-82390. 1974. Repr. of 1960 ed. soft bdg. 7.00 (ISBN 0-88247-273-9). R & E Res Assoc.

MOTHER THERESA

Gonzalez-Balado, Jose. Always the Poor: Mother Teresa, Her Life & Message. Diaz, Olimpia, Sr., tr. from Span. 112p. (Orig.). 1980. pap. 2.50 (ISBN 0-89243-134-2). Liguori Pubns.
Lee, Betsy. Mother Teresa: Caring for All God's Children. LC 80-20286. (Taking Part Ser.). (Illus.). 48p. (gr. 3 up). 1981. PLB 6.95 (ISBN 0-87518-205-4). Dillon.
Rae, Daphne. Love Until It Hurts: The Work of Mother Teresa & Her Missionaries of Charity. LC 81-47424. (Illus., Orig.). 1981. pap. 9.95 (ISBN 0-06-066729-X, RD 368, HarpR). Har-Row.
Spink, Kathryn. The Miracle of Love: Mother Teresa of Calcutta, Her Missionaries of Charity, & Her Co-Workers. LC 81-47717. (Illus.). 256p. 1982. 14.95 (ISBN 0-06-067497-0, HarpR). Har-Row.

MOTHER-IN-LAW

see Mothers-In-Law

MOTHERS

see also Grandparents; Housewives; Love, Maternal; Maternal and Infant Welfare; Maternal Deprivation; Mother's Day; Prenatal Care; Stepmothers

American Mothers Committee, Bicentennial Project 1974-1976, compiled by. Mothers of Achievement in American History: 1776-1976. LC 76-461. (Illus.). 1976. 14.50 (ISBN 0-8048-1201-2). C E Tuttle.
Bettelheim, Bruno. Dialogues with Mothers. 1971. pap. 2.50 (ISBN 0-380-01138-7, 49874, Discus). Avon.
Bloomingdale, Teresa. I Should Have Seen It Coming When the Rabbit Died. 208p. 1980. pap. 2.50 (ISBN 0-553-20428-9). Bantam.
Blumenfeld, Samuel L. The Retreat from Motherhood. 1975. 7.95 (ISBN 0-87000-304-6). Arlington Hse.
Bowman, Jayne, compiled by. Dear Mother: Words of Thanks & Thoughts of Love. (Illus.). 1979. boxed 4.95 (ISBN 0-8378-1703-X). Gibson.
Brazelton, T. Berry. Infants & Mothers. 1972. pap. 7.95 (ISBN 0-440-54076-3, Delta). Dell.
Breen, Dana. Talking with Mothers. 232p. 1981. 30.00x (ISBN 0-906908-35-3, Pub. by Norman England). State Mutual Bk.
Bremner, Robert H., ed. Security & Services for Children: An Original Anthology, Vol. 24. LC 74-1703. (Children & Youth Ser.). 1974. 12.00x (ISBN 0-405-05980-9). Arno.
Briffault, Robert. The Mothers: A Study of the Origins of Sentiments & Institutions, 3 vols. (Anthropology Ser). Repr. of 1927 ed. Set. 115.50 (ISBN 0-384-05800-0). Johnson Repr.
Bush, Barbara. A Woman's Workshop on Motherhood. (Women's Workshop Ser.). 144p. 1981. pap. 3.95 (ISBN 0-310-43031-3, 12013P). Zondervan.
Cardozo, Arlene Rossen. Woman at Home. LC 75-40717. 192p. 1976. 6.95 (ISBN 0-385-11674-8). Doubleday.
Chesler, Phyllis. With Child: A Diary of Motherhood. LC 79-7081. 1979. 9.95 (ISBN 0-690-01835-5). T Y Crowell.
Child, Lydia. The Mother's Book. LC 73-169377. (Family in America Ser). 184p. 1972. Repr. of 1831 ed. 10.00 (ISBN 0-405-03854-2). Arno.
Chodorow, Nancy. The Reproduction of Mothering: Psychoanalysis & the Sociology of Gender. 1978. 12.95 (ISBN 0-520-03133-4); pap. 4.95 (ISBN 0-520-03892-4). U of Cal Pr.
Dufoyer, Pierre. Maternity. LC 64-21802. 1964. 3.95 (ISBN 0-8189-0087-3). Alba.
Ellis, Mrs. The Mothers of England. 1974. lib. bdg. 59.95 (ISBN 0-685-51355-6). Revisionist Pr.
Faber, Doris. The Presidents' Mothers. LC 77-9175. (Illus.). 1978. 10.00 (ISBN 0-312-64132-X). St Martin.
Hammer, Signe. Daughters & Mothers. LC 75-9211. 256p. 1975. 7.95 (ISBN 0-8129-0591-1). Times Bks.
Hartshorn, Leon R. A Mother's Love. LC 80-81506. 76p. 1980. 5.95 (ISBN 0-88290-143-5). Horizon Utah.
Heffner, Elaine. Mothering: The Emotional Experience of Motherhood After Freud & Feminism. LC 79-7799. 1980. pap. 4.95 (ISBN 0-385-15551-4, Anch). Doubleday.
--Mothering: The Emotional Experience of Motherhood After Freud & Feminism. LC 77-82946. 1978. 7.95 (ISBN 0-385-12837-1). Doubleday.
Hertz, Geraldine. The Mosaic of Motherhood. LC 77-99088. 1978. pap. 2.95 (ISBN 0-87973-732-8). Our Sunday Visitor.
Hilander, Fannee. Hold Back the Spring. 192p. 1981. 9.95 (ISBN 0-89962-037-X). Todd & Honeywell.
Holmes, Deborah A. Survival Prayers for Young Mothers. LC 76-12390. 1976. 5.25 (ISBN 0-8042-2195-2). John Knox.
Holmes, Marjorie. A Mother's World. 1979. pap. 2.50 (ISBN 0-8378-5023-1). Gibson.
Key, Ellen. The Renaissance of Motherhood. Fries, Anna E., tr. 1970. Repr. 8.50 (ISBN 0-685-55674-3). Hacker.
Kitzinger, Sheila. Giving Birth: The Parents' Emotions in Childbirth. LC 77-2518. (Orig.). 1978. pap. 4.95 (ISBN 0-8052-0573-X). Schocken.
--Women As Mothers. LC 79-4853. 1979. 8.95 (ISBN 0-394-50651-0). Random.
--Women As Mothers: How They See Themselves in Different Cultures. LC 80-11276. 256p. 1980. pap. 2.95 (ISBN 0-394-74079-3, Vin). Random.
Lakin, M. Personality Factors in Mothers of Excessively Crying Infants. 1957. pap. 4.00 (ISBN 0-527-01569-5). Kraus Repr.
Langston, Shelley & Bermont, Hubert. Mother. pap. 2.00 (ISBN 0-671-10552-3, Fireside). S&S.
Lasker, Joe. Mothers Can Do Anything. LC 72-83684. (Concept Bks.). (Illus.). 40p. (gr. k-3). 1972. 7.50g (ISBN 0-8075-5287-9). A Whitman.
Lazarre, Jane. The Mother Knot. 1977. pap. 1.95 (ISBN 0-440-35798-5, LE). Dell.
Lee, Joanna. I Want to Keep My Baby. (Orig.). (RL 10). 1977. pap. 1.75 (ISBN 0-451-09864-1, E9864, Sig). NAL.
Lessin, Roy. Moms Are God's Idea. (God's Idea Books Ser.). (Illus.). 32p. (ps-4). 1981. pap. 1.50 (ISBN 0-87123-175-1, 210175). Bethany Hse.
McBride, Angela B. The Growth & Development of Mothers. 1975. pap. 3.95 (ISBN 0-06-080328-2, CN858 CN, PL). Har-Row.
Mall, E. Jane. A Mother's Gifts: Words of Praise & Inspiration. LC 75-33082. 64p. 1976. 4.95 (ISBN 0-687-27249-1). Abingdon.
Moghissi, Kamran S. & Evans, Tommy N. Nutritional Impacts on Women. (Illus.). 1977. text ed. 18.25x (ISBN 0-06-141793-9, Harper Medical). Har-Row.
Moore, Kristin A., et al. Teenage Motherhood: Social & Economic Consequences. (An Institute Paper). 50p. 1979. pap. 4.00 (ISBN 0-87766-243-6, 24300). Urban Inst.
Neimark, Paul, et al. A Doctor Discusses Your New Baby & Your New Life. (Illus.). 1980. pap. 2.50 (ISBN 0-685-46338-9). Budlong.
Neumann, Erich. The Great Mother: An Analysis of the Archetype. Manheim, Ralph, tr. (Bollingen Ser.: Vol. 47). 628p. 1972. 28.50 (ISBN 0-691-09742-9); pap. 6.95 (ISBN 0-691-01780-8). Princeton U Pr.
Norris, Gloria & Miller, Jo Ann. The Working Mother's Complete Handbook: Everything You Need to Know to Succeed on the Job & at Home. 1979. 12.95 (ISBN 0-87690-357-X); pap. 7.95 (ISBN 0-87690-313-8). Dutton.
Oakley, Ann. Woman's Work: A History of the Housewife. LC 74-4765. 320p. 1975. 8.95 (ISBN 0-394-46097-9). Pantheon.
--Woman's Work: The Housewife, Past & Present. 1976. pap. 2.95 (ISBN 0-394-71960-3, Vin). Random.
Price, Jane. You're Not Too Old to Have a Baby. 1978. pap. 2.95 (ISBN 0-14-004910-X). Penguin.
Quadri, Lynn D. & Breckenridge, Kate. Mothercare. 1980. pap. 2.25 (ISBN 0-671-82614-X). PB.
Rich, Adrienne. Of Woman Born: Motherhood As Experience & Institution. 1976. 12.95 (ISBN 0-393-08750-6). Norton.
--Of Woman Born: Motherhood As Experience & Institution. 1977. pap. 3.95 (ISBN 0-553-20078-X). Bantam.
Rosenkrantz, Barbara G., ed. The Health of Women & Children: An Original Anthology. LC 76-43205. (Public Health in America Ser.). (Illus.). 1977. Repr. of 1977 ed. lib. bdg. 18.00x (ISBN 0-405-09876-6). Arno.
Rudy, Ann. Mom Spelled Backwards Is Tired. LC 79-55442. 190p. 1980. 9.95 (ISBN 0-672-52627-1). Bobbs.
Russo, Nancy F. Motherhood Mandate: Special Issue of Psychology of Women Quarterly. LC 79-88275. 148p. 1979. pap. text ed. 8.95x (ISBN 0-87705-463-0). Human Sci Pr.
Sapone, Edith. To You Mom. (Illus.). 1961. 3.00 (ISBN 0-8198-0162-3); pap. 2.00 (ISBN 0-8198-0163-1). Dghtrs St Paul.
Sebald, Hans. Momism: The Silent Disease of America. LC 75-45223. 386p. 1976. 15.95x (ISBN 0-88229-275-7). Nelson-Hall.
Seligman, Susan M. Now That I'm a Mother...What Do I Do for Me. 1980. 9.95 (ISBN 0-8092-7156-7); pap. 5.95 (ISBN 0-8092-7155-9). Contemp Bks.
Sibley, Celestine. Mothers Are Always Special. LC 77-101715. 1970. 6.95 (ISBN 0-385-01180-6). Doubleday.
Smith, Helen W. Survival Handbook for Preschool Mothers. 1977. pap. 2.95 (ISBN 0-695-80721-8). New Century.
Talbot, Toby. A Book About My Mother. 192p. 1980. 10.95 (ISBN 0-374-11542-7). FS&G.
Ungar, Frederick, ed. To Mother with Love: A Tribute in Great Stories. (Illus.). (gr. 11-12). 1951. (Pub. by Stephen Daye Pr); pap. 5.75 (ISBN 0-8044-6943-1). Ungar.
West, Marion B. Out of My Bondage. LC 76-5297. 128p. 1976. 3.95 (ISBN 0-8054-5144-7). Broadman.
Zanzucchi, Anne M. The Difficult Role of a Mother. Bartram, Gerry, ed. Szczesniak, Lenny, tr. from It. LC 79-84941. (Education in the Family Ser.). 1979. pap. 2.25 (ISBN 0-911782-33-8). New City.

MOTHERS-EMPLOYMENT

Boggs, Sue H. Is a Job Really Worth It? 1979. pap. 2.25 (ISBN 0-89137-522-8). Quality Pubns.
Curtis, Jean. Working Mothers. 1977. pap. 3.95 (ISBN 0-671-22753-X, Touchstone Bks). S&S.
Fogarty, Michael P., et al. Sex, Career & Family. LC 70-158823. 581p. 1970. pap. 12.50 (ISBN 0-8039-0348-0). Sage.
Greenleaf, Barbar K. & Schaffer, Lewis A. Help: A Handbook for Working Mothers. 1980. pap. 2.75 (ISBN 0-425-04462-9). Berkley Pub.
Greenleaf, Barbara K. & Schaffer, Lewis A. Help: A Handbook for Working Mothers. LC 78-3301. 1979. 11.95 (ISBN 0-690-01461-9). T Y Crowell.
Hewitt, Margaret. Wives & Mothers in Victorian Industry. LC 73-11623. (Illus.). 245p. 1975. Repr. of 1958 ed. lib. bdg. 17.75x (ISBN 0-8371-7078-8, HEWM). Greenwood.

Hoffman, Lois W. & Nye, F. Ivan. Working Mothers: An Evaluative Review of the Consequences for Wife, Husband, & Child. LC 74-6744. (Social & Behavioral Science Ser.). 240p. 1974. 16.95x (ISBN 0-87589-243-4). Jossey-Bass.

Hughes, Gwendolyn S. Mothers in Industry: Wage-Earning by Mothers in Philadelphia. Stein, Leon, ed. LC 77-70507. (Work Ser.). (Illus.). 1977. Repr. of 1925 ed. lib. bdg. 20.00x (ISBN 0-405-10177-5). Arno.

Kamerman, Sheila B. Parenting in an Unresponsive Society: Managing Work & Family Life. LC 80-641. 1980. 15.95 (ISBN 0-02-916730-2). Free Pr.

Kuzmack, Linda G. & Saloman, George. Working & Mothering. 28p. 1980. pap. 1.50 (ISBN 0-87495-030-9). Am Jewish Comm.

Lasker, Joe. Mothers Can Do Anything. LC 72-83684. (Concept Bks.). (Illus.). 40p. (gr. k-3). 1972. 7.50g (ISBN 0-8075-5287-9). A Whitman.

Norris, Gloria & Miller, Jo Ann. The Working Mother's Complete Handbook: Everything You Need to Know to Succeed on the Job & at Home. 1979. 12.95 (ISBN 0-87690-357-X); pap. 7.95 (ISBN 0-87690-313-8). Dutton.

Nye, Francis & Hoffman, Lois W. The Employed Mother in America. LC 76-4503. (Illus.). 406p. 1976. Repr. of 1963 ed. lib. bdg. 28.75x (ISBN 0-8371-8784-2, NYEM). Greenwood.

Olds, Sally W. The Mother Who Works Outside the Home. new ed. LC 75-2076. 79p. 1975. pap. 2.00 (ISBN 0-87183-188-0). Child Study.

--The Mother Who Works Outside the Home. 1975. pap. 2.00 (ISBN 0-87183-188-0). Jewish Bd Family.

Peterson, Samiha S., et al. The Two-Career Family: Issues & Alternatives. LC 78-66418. 1978. pap. text ed. 10.25 (ISBN 0-8191-0020-X). U Pr of Amer.

Pincus, Cynthia S. Double Duties: An Action Plan for the Working Wife. LC 78-5823. 1978. 8.95 (ISBN 0-89456-009-3). Chatham Sq.

Roland, Alan & Harris, Barbara. Career & Motherhood: Struggles for a New Identity. LC 78-8026. 1978. 19.95 (ISBN 0-87705-372-3). Human Sci Pr.

Ryglewicz, Hilary & Thaler, Pat Koch. Working Couples: How to Cope with Two Jobs & One Home. 1980. 9.95 (ISBN 0-671-18401-6). Sovereign Bks.

Scott, Niki. The Balancing Act: A Handbook for Working Mothers. 1978. pap. 4.95 (ISBN 0-8362-6404-5). Andrews & McMeel.

Stein, Leon, ed. Suffer the Little Children: Two Children's Bureau Bulletins, Original Anthology. LC 77-70552. (Work Ser.). (Illus.). 1977. lib. bdg. 18.00x (ISBN 0-405-10206-2). Arno.

Tittle, Carol K. Careers & Family: Sex Roles & Adolescent Life Plans. LC 81-2015. (Sage Library of Social Research: Vol. 121). 320p. 1981. 20.00 (ISBN 0-8039-1352-4). Sage.

MOTHERS–MORTALITY

Eckholm, Erik & Newland, Kathleen. Health: The Family Planning Factor. LC 76-52228. (Worldwatch Papers). 1977. pap. 2.00 (ISBN 0-916468-09-7). Worldwatch Inst.

Shapiro, Sam, et al. Infant, Perinatal, Maternal, & Childhood Mortality in the United States. LC 68-29183. (Vital & Health Statistics Monographs, American Public Health Association). (Illus.). 1968. 20.00x (ISBN 0-674-45301-8). Harvard U Pr.

MOTHERS–POETRY

Morris, J. & Adams, St. Clair. The Book of Mother Verse. 1977. Repr. of 1924 ed. 15.00 (ISBN 0-89984-069-8). Century Bookbindery.

Schauffler, Robert. Mother: In Verse & Prose. Repr. of 1916 ed. 30.00 (ISBN 0-686-18775-X). Scholars Ref Lib.

Schouffler, Robert. Mother in Verse & Prose. 1916. lib. bdg. 20.00 (ISBN 0-8414-8159-8). Folcroft.

Wiggin, Karl. An Anthology of Mother Verse. Repr. of 1919 ed. 20.00 (ISBN 0-686-18751-2). Scholars Ref Lib.

MOTHERS–RELIGIOUS LIFE

Aldrich, Doris C. Musings of a Mother. 1949. pap. 1.25 (ISBN 0-8024-5674-X). Moody.

Brenneman, H. G. Meditaciones Para la Nueva Madre. 1978. 2.35 (ISBN 0-311-40032-9). Casa Bautista.

Brenneman, Helen G. Meditations for the Expectant Mother. LC 68-12025. (Orig.). 1968. deluxe ed. 4.95 (ISBN 0-8361-1639-9); pap. 3.50 (ISBN 0-8361-1567-8). Herald Pr.

--Meditations for the New Mother. LC 53-7585. (Illus., Orig.). 1953. deluxe ed. 4.95 (ISBN 0-8361-1640-2); pap. 3.50 (ISBN 0-8361-1391-8). Herald Pr.

Edman, V. Raymond. Crisis Experiences in the Lives of Noted Christians. 1970. pap. 1.95 (ISBN 0-87123-065-8, 200065). Bethany Hse.

Hertz, Geraldine. What's in It for Mothers? LC 75-20741. 176p. (Orig.). 1975. pap. 1.75 (ISBN 0-87973-793-X). Our Sunday Visitor.

Huxhold, Harry. Magnificat. 1961. pap. 1.50 (ISBN 0-570-03679-8, 74-1007). Concordia.

Loeks, Mary F. Good Morning, Lord: Devotions for Young Mothers. (Good Morning, Lord Ser.). 1977. 3.95 (ISBN 0-8010-5566-0). Baker Bk.

Mattison, Judith. Prayers from a Mother's Heart. LC 74-14177. (Illus.). 96p. (Orig.). 1975. pap. 2.95 (ISBN 0-8066-1460-9, 10-5095). Augsburg.

Moody, Dwight L., ed. Thoughts for the Quiet Hour. pap. 1.95 (ISBN 0-8024-8729-7). Moody.

Murphy, Mary M. Creating: Reflections During Pregnancy. LC 73-90086. 64p. (Orig.). 1974. pap. 1.95 (ISBN 0-8091-1815-7). Paulist Pr.

Renfroe, Cornelia M. Kitchen Communion. LC 59-11220. (Illus.). 1959. 2.50 (ISBN 0-8042-2400-5). John Knox.

Sallee, Lynn. To God from Mom. 96p. 1975. 3.95 (ISBN 0-8010-8047-9). Baker Bk.

Wust, L. & Wust, M. Zelie Martin: Mother of the Little Flower. 5.00 (ISBN 0-8198-0649-8). Dghtrs St Paul.

MOTHERS (IN RELIGION, FOLKLORE, ETC.)

see Mother-Goddesses; Women (In Religion, Folklore, etc.)

MOTHERS, UNMARRIED

see Unmarried Mothers

MOTHERS' ADVISORY SERVICE, BALTIMORE

Cooper, Marcia M. Evaluation of the Mother's Advisory Service. 1947. pap. 5.00 (ISBN 0-527-01540-7). Kraus Repr.

MOTHER'S DAY

Dia De las Madres. 1980. pap. 0.90 (ISBN 0-311-07301-8). Casa Bautista.

Kuse, James A., ed. Mother's Day Ideals. (Illus.). 1979. pap. 2.95 (ISBN 0-89542-323-5). Ideals.

Phelan, Mary K. Mother's Day. LC 65-11646. (Holiday Ser.). (Illus.). (gr. 1-3). 1965. PLB 7.89 (ISBN 0-690-56195-4, TYC-J). Har-Row.

Wolfe, Howard H. Mothers Day & the Mothers Day Church. (Illus.). 274p. Date not set. Repr. of 1962 ed. 8.00 (ISBN 0-9600850-0-9). H H Wolfe.

MOTHERS-IN-LAW

Serb, Ann T. The Mother-in-Law. LC 77-95170. 1978. 7.95 (ISBN 0-89310-031-5); pap. 3.95 (ISBN 0-89310-032-3). Carillon Bks.

MOTHERS IN LITERATURE

Hawkes, Laura M. Quotes from Prophets on Mothers & Families. 96p. 1974. pap. 2.95 (ISBN 0-89036-016-2). Hawkes Pub Inc.

Kobler, Franz, ed. Her Children Call Her Blessed: A Portrait of the Jewish Mother. LC 55-6191. (Illus.). 16.95 (ISBN 0-8044-5562-7, Pub. by Stephen Daye Pr). Ungar.

Schouffler, Robert. Mother in Verse & Prose. 1916. lib. bdg. 20.00 (ISBN 0-8414-8159-8). Folcroft.

MOTHERS IN POETRY

see Mothers–Poetry

MOTHER'S PENSIONS

see also Child Welfare; Family Allowances

Abbott, Edith & Breckinridge, S. P. The Family & Social Service in the 1920's. LC 74-169361. (Family in America Ser). 386p. 1972. 23.00 (ISBN 0-405-03885-2). Arno.

U. S. Children'S Bureau. Child Dependency in the District of Columbia. LC 79-89061. Repr. of 1924 ed. 13.00x (ISBN 0-8371-1926-X, Pub. by Negro U Pr). Greenwood.

MOTHS

see also Caterpillars

Boorman, John. West African Butterflies & Moths. (West African Nature Handbooks Ser). (Illus., Orig.). 1970. pap. 5.00x (ISBN 0-582-60425-7). Intl Pubns Serv.

Bradley, J. D. & Fletcher, D. S. British Butterflies & Moths. 1980. 6.00x (ISBN 0-902068-08-3, Pub. by Curwen England). State Mutual Bk.

Bradley, J. D., et al. British Tortricoid Moths. Incl. Vol.1. Cochylidae & Tortricidae: Tortricidae. viii, 251p. 1973. 50.00x (ISBN 0-903874-01-6); Vol. 2. Tortrkidae: Olethreutinae. viii, 336p. 1979. 100.00x (ISBN 0-903874-06-7). (Illus., Pub. by Brit Mus Nat Hist England). Sabbot-Natural Hist Bks.

Crotch, W. J. A Silkmoth Rearer's Handbook. 165p. 1969. 30.00x (ISBN 0-686-75578-2, Pub. by Amateur Entomol Soc). State Mutual Bk.

DeTreville, Susan & DeTreville, Stan. Butterflies & Moths. (Illus.). 32p. (Orig.). 1981. pap. 3.95 (ISBN 0-89844-026-2). Troubador Pr.

Fletcher, D. S. The Generic Names of Moths of the World: Geometroidea-Apoprogonidae, Axiidae, Callidulidae, Cyclidiidae, Drepanidae, Epicopeidae, Epiplemidae, Geometridae, Pterothysanidae, Sematuridae, Thyatridae & Uranidae, Vol. Iii. Nye, I. W., ed. (Illus.). 243p. 1979. 56.50x (ISBN 0-565-00812-9, Pub. by Brit Mus Nat Hist England). Sabbot-Natural Hist Bks.

Gerardi, Michael H. & Grimm, James K. The History, Biology, Damage & Control of the Gypsy Moth. LC 72-20321. 233p. 1978. 17.50 (ISBN 0-8386-2023-X). Fairleigh Dickinson.

Heath, John, ed. The Moths & Butterflies of Great Britain & Ireland, Vol. 1. 343p. 1976. text ed. 39.95x (ISBN 0-632-00331-6). Entomological Repr.

Holland, W. J. The Moth Book: A Guide to Moths of North America. (Illus.). 13.50 (ISBN 0-8446-0145-4). Peter Smith.

--Moth Book: A Popular Guide to a Knowledge of the Moths of North America. rev. ed. Brower, A. E., ed. LC 68-22887. (Illus.). 1968. pap. 7.95 (ISBN 0-486-21948-8). Dover.

Howard, Leland O. & Fiske, William F. The Importation into the United States of the Parasites of the Gypsy Moth & the Brown-Tail Moth: Report of Progress of Previous & Concurrent Efforts of This Kind. Egerton, Frank N., 3rd, ed. LC 77-74230. (History of Ecology Ser.). (Illus.). 1978. Repr. of 1911 ed. lib. bdg. 24.00x (ISBN 0-405-10400-6). Arno.

Hsiao, H. S. Attraction of Moths to Light & to Infrared Radiation. LC 72-90348. (Illus.). 1972. 9.50 (ISBN 0-911302-21-2). San Francisco Pr.

Kettlewell, H. B. Your Book of Butterflies & Moths. (Your Book Ser.). (Illus.). 60p. 1963. 6.95 (ISBN 0-571-05576-1, Pub. by Faber & Faber). Merrimack Bk Serv.

Metzler, Eric H. Annotated Checklist & Distribution Maps of the Royal Moths & Giant Silkworm Moths (Lepidoptera: Saturniidae) in Ohio. 1980. 2.50 (ISBN 0-686-30346-6). Ohio Bio Survey.

Mitchell, Robert & Zim, Herbert S. Butterflies & Moths. (Golden Guide Ser.). (Illus.). (gr. 5 up). 1964. PLB 10.38 (ISBN 0-307-63524-4, Golden Pr); pap. 1.95 (ISBN 0-307-24413-X). Western Pub.

Nye, I. W. The Generic Names of Moths of the World, Vol. 1, Noctuoidea: Noctuidae, Agaristidae & Nolidae, Vol. 1. (Illus.). 568p. 1975. 69.00x (ISBN 0-565-00770-X, Pub. by Brit Mus Nat Hist England). Sabbot-Natural Hist Bks.

Parenti, Umberto. The World of Butterflies & Moths. LC 77-14627. (Illus.). 1978. 14.95 (ISBN 0-399-12071-8). Putnam.

Pinhey, Elliot C. G. Moths of Southern Africa. (Illus.). 273p. (Orig.). 1975. 41.25x (ISBN 0-624-00784-7). Entomological Repr.

Selman, Charles L. A Pictorial Key to the Hawkmoths (Lepidotera: Sphingidae) of Eastern United States (Except Florida) 1975. 1.50 (ISBN 0-686-30340-7). Ohio Bio Survey.

Treat, Asher E. Mites of Moths & Butterflies. LC 75-7147. (Illus.). 368p. 1975. 50.00x (ISBN 0-8014-0878-4). Comstock.

Turner, Bryan, ed. Illustrated Encyclopedia of Butterflies & Moths. (Illus.). 352p. 1979. 8.50 (ISBN 0-7064-0547-1, Mayflower Bks). Smith Pubs.

Villiard, Paul. Moths & How to Rear Them. 2nd, rev. ed. (Illus.). 9.50 (ISBN 0-8446-5254-7). Peter Smith.

--Moths & How to Rear Them. 1975. pap. 5.00 (ISBN 0-486-23119-4). Dover.

Watson, A., et al. The Generic Names of Moths of the World. Vol. II. Noctuoidea: Arctiidae, Cocytiidae, Ctenuchidae, Dilobidae, Dioptidae, Lymantriidae, Notodontidae, Strepsimanidae, Thaumetopoedae, & Thyretidae. Nye, I. W., ed. (Illus.). xiv, 228p. 1980. 58.00x (ISBN 0-565-00811-0). Sabbot-Natural Hist Bks.

Whalley, P. E. Tropical Leaf Moths. (Illus.). 1976. text ed. 67.50x (ISBN 0-565-00782-3, Pub. by Brit Mus Nat Hist). Sabbot-Natural Hist Bks.

MOTHS–JUVENILE LITERATURE

Angeles, Peter. Pouf: A Moth-une Mite. (Mini Books for Mini Hands Ser.). (Illus., Fr & Eng.). (gr. k-3). 1977. reinforced bdg. 1.95 (ISBN 0-912766-25-5). Tundra Bks.

Butterflies & Moths. (How & Why Wonder Books Ser.). (gr. 4-6). pap. 1.00 (ISBN 0-448-05037-4, 5037-4). Wonder.

Jourdan, Eveline. Butterflies & Moths Around the World. LC 80-20086. (Nature & Man Bks.). (Illus.). (gr. 5 up). 1981. PLB 8.95g (ISBN 0-8225-0567-3). Lerner Pubns.

McClung, Robert M. Gypsy Moth: Its History in America. LC 74-6245. (Illus.). (gr. 5-9). 1974. PLB 6.96 (ISBN 0-688-30124-X). Morrow.

Morris, Dean. Butterflies & Moths. LC 77-7912. (Read About Animals Ser.). (Illus.). (gr. k-3). 1977. PLB 11.15 (ISBN 0-8393-0010-7). Raintree Child.

Perry, Phyllis J. Let's Look at Moths & Butterflies. (Nature & Science Bk.). (Illus.). (gr. k-6). PLB 5.95 (ISBN 0-513-00380-0). Denison.

Sabin, Louis. Amazing World of Butterflies & Moths. (Illus.). 32p. (gr. 2-4). 1981. PLB 7.29 (ISBN 0-89375-560-5); pap. text ed. 1.95 (ISBN 0-89375-561-3). Troll Assocs.

Selsam, Millicent E. Harlequin Moth: Its Life Story. LC 75-17862. (Illus.). 48p. (gr. 2-5). 1975. 8.25 (ISBN 0-688-22049-5); PLB 7.92 (ISBN 0-688-32049-X). Morrow.

MOTILITY OF CELLS

see Cells–Motility

MOTION

see also Acceleration (Mechanics); Force and Energy; Kinematics; Liapunov Functions; Mechanical Movements; Mechanics; Movement, Psychology Of; Rotational Motion; Speed; Stability

Bickford, John H. Mechanisms for Internittent Motion. LC 75-184639. 272p. Date not set. Repr. of 1972 ed. price not set (ISBN 0-8311-1091-0). Krieger.

Buckley, Michael J. Motion & Motion's God: Thematic Variations in Aristotle, Cicero, Newton, & Hegel. LC 73-132234. 1971. 19.00 (ISBN 0-691-07124-1). Princeton U Pr.

Casper, Barry M. & Noer, Richard J. Revolutions in Physics. 1972. text ed. 14.95x (ISBN 0-393-09992-X); instructor's guide free (ISBN 0-393-09405-7). Norton.

Dow, T. W. Repeal Kepler's Laws. LC 60-13372. 1960. 5.00 (ISBN 0-910340-02-1). Celestial Pr.

--Reshape Newton's Laws. LC 64-19218. 1965. 5.00 (ISBN 0-910340-03-X). Celestial Pr.

Gardner, Robert & Webster, David. Moving Right Along: A Book of Science Experiments & Puzzlers About Motion. LC 77-15149. (gr. 3-5). 1978. 7.95a (ISBN 0-385-11642-X); PLB (ISBN 0-385-11643-8). Doubleday.

Hackett, L. C. & Jenson, R. G. A Guide to Movement Exploration. 1973. pap. text ed. 3.50 (ISBN 0-917962-04-4). Peek Pubns.

Kratz, Laura E. Movement Without Sight. 4.95 (ISBN 0-917962-27-3). Peek Pubns.

Landau, L. & Kitaigorodsky, A. I. Physics for Everyone: Physical Bodies. 248p. 1980. 6.60 (ISBN 0-8285-1716-9, Pub. by Mir Pubs Russia). Imported Pubns.

Legunn, Joel. Motion. Liberty, Gene, ed. LC 73-128852. (Understanding Bks.). Orig. Title: Investigating Motion. (gr. 6-9). 1971. PLB 7.95 (ISBN 0-87191-041-1). Creative Ed.

LeVeau, Barney. William & Lissner Biomechanics of Human Motion. 2nd ed. LC 75-44605. (Illus.). 1977. text ed. 14.50 (ISBN 0-7216-5773-7). Saunders.

Markvenas, Anthony J. Elements of Motion. Reed, Suzanne W., ed. LC 74-80552. (Science Ser.). (Illus., Orig.). (gr. 6-9). 1975. pap. text ed. 3.25 (ISBN 0-88301-152-2). Pendulum Pr.

Metheny, Elenor. Moving & Knowing: Sport, Dance, Physical Education. 1975. pap. text ed. 6.95 (ISBN 0-917962-26-5). Peek Pubns.

Morecki, A., ed. Biomechanics of Motion. (CISM-Courses & Lectures: Vol. 263). (Illus.). 217p. 1981. pap. 28.00 (ISBN 0-387-81611-9). Springer-Verlag.

Oresme, Nicole, ed. De Proportionibus Proportionum. Grant, Edward, tr. Bd. with Ad Pauca Respicientes. (Medieval Science Publications Ser). (Illus.). 488p. 1966. 50.00x (ISBN 0-299-04000-3). U of Wis Pr.

Park, David. The Image of Eternity: Roots of Time in the Physical World. LC 79-22984. 1980. lib. bdg. 14.50x (ISBN 0-87023-286-X). U of Mass Pr.

Prigogine, I. & Herman, R. Kinetic Theory of Vehicular Traffic. 1971. 22.50 (ISBN 0-444-00082-8, North Holland). Elsevier.

Ruchlis, Hyman. Orbit: Picture Story of Force & Motion. LC 58-5290. (Illus.). (gr. 5 up). 1958. PLB 8.79 (ISBN 0-06-025111-5, HarpJ). Har-Row.

Symposium on Incremental Motion & Control Systems & Devices, 8th, Annual. Proceedings. LC 73-647018. (Illus.). 1979. 39.50 (ISBN 0-931538-01-7). Incremental Motion.

Unwin, Derick. Leyes De Movimiento De Newton. (Sp.). 1970. pap. 2.00 (ISBN 0-06-317011-6, IntlDept). Har-Row.

MOTION PERCEPTION (VISION)

Epstein, W. Stability & Constancy in Visual Perception: Mechanisms & Processes. 1977. 34.95 (ISBN 0-471-24355-8). Wiley.

Kolers, Paul A. Aspects of Motion Perception. LC 73-188746. 232p. 1972. text ed. 32.00 (ISBN 0-08-016843-4). Pergamon.

MOTION-PICTURE CAMERAS

see Moving-Picture Cameras

MOTION PICTURES

see Moving-Pictures

MOTION STUDY

see Time and Motion Study

MOTIONS (LAW)

Landau, L. & Kitaigorodsky, A. I. Physics for Everyone: Physical Bodies. 248p. 1980. 6.60 (ISBN 0-8285-1716-9, Pub. by Mir Pubs Russia). Imported Pubns.

MOTIVATION (PSYCHOLOGY)

see also Achievement Motivation; Conflict (Psychology); Dissonance (Psychology); Motivation Research (Marketing); Rewards and Punishments in Education; Self-Actualization (Psychology); Threat (Psychology); Wishes

Adler, Peter. Momentum: A Theory of Social Action. LC 81-2718. (Sociological Observations Ser.: Vol. 11). (Illus.). 191p. 1981. 20.00 (ISBN 0-8039-1307-9); pap. 9.95 (ISBN 0-8039-1581-0). Sage.

Advertising Research Foundation. A Bibliography of Theory & Research Techniques in the Field of Human Motivation. LC 72-5274. 117p. 1972. Repr. of 1956 ed. lib. bdg. 15.00 (ISBN 0-8371-5723-4, BTRT). Greenwood.
Aldag, Ramon J. & Brief, Arthur P. Task Design & Employee Motivation. 1979. pap. text ed. 8.95x (ISBN 0-673-15146-8). Scott F.
Alderfer, Clayton P. Existence, Relatedness & Growth: Human Needs in Organizational Settings. LC 78-156839. 1972. 15.95 (ISBN 0-02-900390-3). Free Pr.
Anderson, Richard C. Motivation: The Master Key. LC 72-7668. (Illus.). 92p. Date not set. 7.95 (ISBN 0-913842-01-X). Correlan Pubns.
Arkes, Hal R. & Garske, John P. Psychological Theories of Motivation. 2nd ed. (Psychology Ser.). 400p. 1981. text ed. 18.95 (ISBN 0-8185-0465-X). Brooks-Cole.
--Psychological Theories of Motivation. LC 76-30413. (Illus.). 1977. text ed. 15.95 (ISBN 0-8185-0216-9); test items free (ISBN 0-685-78212-3). Brooks-Cole.
Arnold, William J., ed. Nebraska Symposium on Motivation, 1968. LC 53-11655. (Nebraska Symposia on Motivation Ser: Vol. 16). 1968. 12.50x (ISBN 0-8032-0610-0); pap. 5.95x (ISBN 0-8032-5616-7). U of Nebr Pr.
Arnold, William J. & Page, Monte M., eds. Nebraska Symposium on Motivation, 1970. LC 53-11655. (Nebraska Symposia on Motivation Ser: Vol. 18). 1971. 17.50x (ISBN 0-8032-0612-7); pap. 5.50x (ISBN 0-8032-5618-3). U of Nebr Pr.
Atkinson, John W. Introduction to Motivation. 2d ed. (Illus.). 1978. text ed. 16.95x (ISBN 0-442-00368-4). D Van Nostrand.
Barry, Ruth & Wolf, Beverly. Motives, Values, & Realities: A Framework for Counseling. LC 76-40268. 1976. Repr. of 1965 ed. lib. bdg. 18.50x (ISBN 0-8371-9066-5, WOMV). Greenwood.
Beard, Ruth & Senior, Isabel J. Motivating Students. (Routledge Education Bks.). 100p. 1980. 17.50x (ISBN 0-7100-0594-6). Routledge & Kegan.
Beck, Robert C. Motivation: Theories & Principles. 1978. ref. ed. 19.95 (ISBN 0-13-603902-2). P-H.
Bennis, Warren G., et al, eds. Leadership & Motivation: Essays of Douglas McGregor. 1966. pap. 5.95x (ISBN 0-262-63015-X). MIT Pr.
Berkowitz, Leonard. Development of Motives & Values in the Child. LC 64-20402. (Basic Topics in Psychology: Social Psychology). 1964. 6.95x (ISBN 0-465-01613-8). Basic.
Berman, Mark L., ed. Motivation & Learning: Applying Contingency Management Techniques. LC 70-160894. 222p. 1972. pap. 10.95 (ISBN 0-87778-023-4). Educ Tech Pubns.
Bolles, Robert C. Theory of Motivation. 2nd ed. 568p. 1975. text ed. 24.95 scp (ISBN 0-06-040793-X, HarpC). Har-Row.
Bower, Gordon, ed. The Psychology of Learning & Motivation: Advances in Research & Motivation, Vol. 13. LC 66-30104. (Serial Publication). 1979. 43.50 (ISBN 0-12-543313-1). Acad Pr.
Bower, Gordon & Lang, Albert R., eds. The Psychology of Learning & Motivation, Vol. 15. (Serial Publication). 1981. price not set (ISBN 0-12-543315-8). Acad Pr.
Buck, Ross W. Human Motivation & Emotion. LC 75-37893. 1976. text ed. 22.95 (ISBN 0-471-11570-3). Wiley.
Buhler, Charlotte & Massarik, Fred, eds. Course of Human Life: A Study of Goals in the Humanistic Perspective. LC 68-23550. 1968. text ed. 19.00 (ISBN 0-8261-0991-8). Springer Pub.
Burke, Kenneth. Permanence & Change: An Anatomy of Purpose. 2nd ed. LC 64-66067. 1965. pap. 7.50 (ISBN 0-672-60452-3, LLA207). Bobbs.
Coe, George A. The Motives of Men. LC 75-3112. Repr. of 1928 ed. 18.50 (ISBN 0-404-59108-6). AMS Pr.
Cofer, Charles N. & Appley, M. H. Motivation: Theory & Research. LC 64-13214. (Illus.). 1964. 34.50 (ISBN 0-471-16317-1). Wiley.
Cofer, Charles N., ed. Human Motivation: A Guide to Information Sources. rev. ed. (The Psychology Information Guide Ser.: Vol. 4). 175p. 1980. 36.00 (ISBN 0-8103-1418-5). Gale.
Cole, James K., ed. Nebraska Symposium on Motivation, 1971. LC 53-11655. (Nebraska Symposia on Motivation Ser: Vol. 19). xii, 304p. 1972. 18.50x (ISBN 0-8032-0613-5); pap. 5.50x (ISBN 0-8032-5619-1). U of Nebr Pr.
Cole, James K & Jensen, Donald D., eds. Nebraska Symposium on Motivation, 1972. LC 53-11655. (Nebraska Symposia on Motivation Ser: Vol. 20). xiv, 343p. 1973. 19.50x (ISBN 0-8032-0614-3); pap. 5.75x (ISBN 0-8032-5620-5). U of Nebr Pr.
Cole, James K. & Sonderegger, Theo B., eds. Nebraska Symposium on Motivation, 1974: Brain Research. LC 53-11655. (Nebraska Symposia on Motivation Ser: Vol. 22). xviii, 310p. 1975. 19.50x (ISBN 0-8032-0617-8); pap. 6.95x (ISBN 0-8032-5622-1). U of Nebr Pr.
Cooper, Robert. Job Motivation & Job Design. LC 74-192791. (Management in Perspective Ser.). 140p. 1977. pap. 11.50x (ISBN 0-85292-094-6). Intl Pubns Serv.
Coopersmith, Stanley. Developing Motivation in Young Children. LC 75-16006. 1975. 13.95 (ISBN 0-87843-620-0). Albion.
Day, et al. Intrinsic Motivation. (Winston Mine Editions). 1971. text ed. 6.26 (ISBN 0-685-33355-8, HoltC). HR&W.
Day, Hy I., ed. Advances in Intrinsic Motivation & Aesthetics. 503p. 1981. 42.50 (ISBN 0-306-40606-3, Plenum Pr). Plenum Pub.
--Advances in Intrinsic Motivation & Aesthetics. 500p. 1981. 42.50 (ISBN 0-306-40606-3). Plenum Pub.
Deci, Edward L. Intrinsic Motivation. LC 75-17613. (Perspectives in Social Psychology Ser.). (Illus.). 324p. 1975. 17.50 (ISBN 0-306-34401-7, Plenum Pr). Plenum Pub.
Dichter, Ernest. Getting Motivated: The Secret Behind Individual Motivations by the Man Who Was Not Afraid to Ask "Why?". LC 78-21168. (Illus.). 1979. 14.50 (ISBN 0-08-023687-1). Pergamon.
--Motivating Human Behavior. 1971. 23.95 (ISBN 0-07-016781-8, P&RB). McGraw.
Dienstbier, Richard A., ed. Nebraska Symposium on Motivation, 1978: Human Emotion. LC 53-11655. (Nebraska Symposia on Motivation Ser.: Vol. 26). 1979. 19.95x (ISBN 0-8032-2306-4); pap. 8.95x (ISBN 0-8032-7203-0). U of Nebr Pr.
Dunham, Philip J. Experimental Psychology: Theory & Practice. LC 77-5688. (Harper's Experimental Psychology Ser.). (Illus.). 1977. text ed. 20.50 scp (ISBN 0-06-041805-2, HarpC); tchrs' manual avail. (ISBN 0-06-361783-8). Har-Row.
Eckblad, Gudrun. Scheme Theory: A Conceptual Framework for Cognitive Motivational Processes. 1981. 31.50 (ISBN 0-12-229550-1). Acad Pr.
Eims, Leroy. Be a Motivational Leader. 144p. 1981. pap. 3.95 (ISBN 0-89693-008-4). Victor Bks.
Evans, Phil. Motivation. (Essential Psychology Ser.). 1975. pap. 4.50x (ISBN 0-416-83160-5). Methuen Inc.
Feldman, Shel, ed. Cognitive Consistency: Motivational Antecedents & Behavioral Consequents. 1966. 37.50 (ISBN 0-12-252650-3). Acad Pr.
Flowers, John H., ed. Nebraska Symposium on Motivation, 1980: Cognitive Processes. LC 53-11655. (Nebraska Symposium on Motivation: Vol. 28). xvi, 249p. 1981. 16.50x (ISBN 0-8032-0620-8); pap. 8.95x (ISBN 0-8032-0621-6). U of Nebr Pr.
Franken, Robert E. Human Motivation. 512p. 1981. text ed. 18.95 (ISBN 0-8185-0461-7). Brooks-Cole.
Fuller, John L. Motivation: A Biological Perspective. (Orig.). 1962. pap. text ed. 2.95 (ISBN 0-685-19747-6). Phila Bk Co.
Gale, Raymond F. Explorations into Humanness. 1977. 4.95 (ISBN 0-8158-0346-X). Chris Mass.
Gellerman, Saul W. Management by Motivation. LC 68-12699. (Illus.). 1968. 17.95 (ISBN 0-8144-5157-8). Am Mgmt.
--Motivation & Productivity. LC 63-16332. 1963. 15.95 (ISBN 0-8144-5084-9). Am Mgmt.
Hokanson, Jack E. The Physiological Bases of Motivation. 192p. 1981. pap. write for info. (ISBN 0-89874-187-4). Krieger.
Holt, Robert R., ed. Motives & Thoughts: Psychoanalytic Essays in Honor of David Rapaport. LC 67-20615. (Psychological Issues Monograph: No. 18-19, Vol. 5, Nos. 2-3). (Orig.). 1967. text ed. 19.50 (ISBN 0-8236-3480-9); pap. text ed. 16.50 (ISBN 0-8236-3460-4). Intl Univs Pr.
Irwin, Francis W. Intentional Behavior & Motivation: A Cognitive Theory. 201p. 1971. text ed. 8.95 (ISBN 0-397-47232-3, JBL-Med-Nursing). Har-Row.
Jones, Marshall R., ed. Nebraska Symposium Motivation, 1960. LC 53-11655. (Nebraska Symposia on Motivation Ser.: Vol. 8). 1960. 16.50x (ISBN 0-8032-0601-1); pap. 4.95x (ISBN 0-8032-5608-6). U of Nebr Pr.
--Nebraska Symposium on Motivation: Index to Vols. 1-6. LC 53-11655. (Nebraska Symposia on Motivation Ser.). 1960. pap. 2.95x (ISBN 0-8032-7649-4). U of Nebr Pr.
--Nebraska Symposium on Motivation, 1955. LC 53-11655. (Nebraska Symposia on Motivation Ser: Vol. 3). 1955. pap. 4.95x (ISBN 0-8032-5602-7). U of Nebr Pr.
--Nebraska Symposium on Motivation, 1956. LC 53-11655. (Nebraska Symposia on Motivation Ser: Vol. 4). 1956. pap. 5.50x (ISBN 0-8032-5603-5). U of Nebr Pr.
--Nebraska Symposium on Motivation, 1957. LC 53-11655. (Nebraska Symposia on Motivation Ser: Vol. 5). 1957. pap. 6.95x (ISBN 0-8032-5604-3). U of Nebr Pr.
--Nebraska Symposium on Motivation, 1958. LC 53-11655. (Nebraska Symposia on Motivation Ser: Vol. 6). 1958. pap. 4.95x (ISBN 0-8032-5605-1). U of Nebr Pr.
--Nebraska Symposium on Motivation, 1959. LC 53-11655. (Nebraska Symposia on Motivation Ser: Vol. 7). 1959. 11.95x (ISBN 0-8032-0600-3). U of Nebr Pr.
--Nebraska Symposium on Motivation, 1961. LC 53-11655. (Nebraska Symposia on Motivation Ser.: Vol. 9). 1962. 14.50x (ISBN 0-8032-0603-8); pap. 3.95x (ISBN 0-8032-5609-4). U of Nebr Pr.
--Nebraska Symposium on Motivation, 1962. LC 53-11655. (Nebraska Symposia on Motivation Ser: Vol. 10). 1962. 19.50x (ISBN 0-8032-0604-6). U of Nebr Pr.
--Nebraska Symposium on Motivation, 1963. LC 53-11655. (Nebraska Symposia on Motivation Ser: Vol. 11). 1963. 13.95x (ISBN 0-8032-0605-4); pap. 3.95x (ISBN 0-8032-5611-6). U of Nebr Pr.
Jung, John. Understanding Human Motivation: A Cognitive Approach. (Illus.). 1978. text ed. 19.95 (ISBN 0-02-361550-8). Macmillan.
Kaiser, Artur. Motivation Techniques. Peppe, G. & Birker, D., trs. from Ger. LC 79-89938. Orig. Title: Druck erzeugt Gegendruck. (Orig.). Date not set. pap. cancelled (ISBN 0-89793-013-4). Hunter Hse.
Klapp, Orrin E. Currents of Unrest: An Introduction to Collective Behavior. LC 76-189252. 1972. 28.00x (ISBN 0-03-085305-2); pap. text ed. 14.95x (ISBN 0-89197-717-1). Irvington.
Klein, George S. Perception, Motives & Personality. pap. text ed. write for info. (ISBN 0-685-69599-9). Phila Bk Co.
Klein, S. B. Motivation: Biosocial Approaches. 576p. 1982. text ed. 22.95 (ISBN 0-07-035051-5, C). McGraw.
Klinger, Eric. Meaning & Void: Inner Experience & the Incentives in People's Lives. LC 77-73546. (Illus.). 1977. 17.50x (ISBN 0-8166-0811-3, 0811-3); pap. 7.95x (ISBN 0-8166-0856-3, 0856-3). U of Minn Pr.
Kolesnik, Walter B. Motivation: Understanding & Influencing Human Behavior. 1978. pap. text ed. 11.95 (ISBN 0-205-05973-2, 2459736). Allyn.
Korman, Abraham K. The Psychology of Motivation. (Experimental Psychology Ser). (Illus.). 288p. 1974. ref. ed. 19.95 (ISBN 0-13-733279-3). P-H.
Laird, Donald A. What Makes People Buy. LC 75-39254. (Getting & Spending: the Consumer's Dilemma). 1976. Repr. of 1935 ed. 15.00x (ISBN 0-405-08027-1). Arno.
Landfield, Alvin W., ed. Nebraska Symposium on Motivation, 1976: Personal Construct Psychology. LC 53-11655. (Nebraska Symposia on Motivation Ser.: Vol. 24). 1977. 19.95x (ISBN 0-8032-0619-4); pap. 7.95x (ISBN 0-8032-5625-6). U of Nebr Pr.
Lawler, Edward E. Motivation in Work Organizations. LC 73-78810. (Behavioral Science in Industry Ser.). (Orig.). 1973. pap. text ed. 6.95 (ISBN 0-8185-0088-3). Brooks-Cole.
Levine, David, ed. Nebraska Symposium on Motivation, 1964. LC 53-11655. (Nebraska Symposia on Motivation Ser: Vol. 12). 1964. 17.50x (ISBN 0-8032-0606-2); pap. 4.95x (ISBN 0-8032-5612-4). U of Nebr Pr.
--Nebraska Symposium on Motivation, 1965. LC 53-11655. (Nebraska Symposia on Motivation Ser: Vol. 13). 1965. 19.50x (ISBN 0-8032-0607-0). U of Nebr Pr.
--Nebraska Symposium on Motivation, 1966. LC 53-11655. (Nebraska Symposia on Motivation Ser: Vol. 14). 1966. 14.50x (ISBN 0-8032-0608-9); pap. 4.95x (ISBN 0-8032-5614-0). U of Nebr Pr.
--Nebraska Symposium on Motivation, 1967. LC 53-11655. (Nebraska Symposium on Motivation: Vol. 15). 1967. pap. 5.95x (ISBN 0-8032-5615-9). U of Nebr Pr.
Levine, Jacob, ed. Motivation in Humor. (Controversy Ser). 182p. (Orig.). 1969. 9.95x (ISBN 0-202-25059-8); pap. 3.95 (ISBN 0-202-25060-1). Lieber-Atherton.
Lichtenberg, Philip, et al. Motivation for Child Psychiatry Treatment. LC 60-6368. (Illus.). 1960. 5.00 (ISBN 0-8462-0231-X). Russell.
Logan, Frank A. & Ferraro, Douglas P. Systematic Analyses of Learning & Motivation. LC 78-6870. 1978. text ed. 22.50x (ISBN 0-471-04130-0). Wiley.
McCay, James T. Beyond Motivation. 1973. pap. 3.95x (ISBN 0-88432-026-X). J Norton Pubs.
McDonough, Reginald. Keys to Effective Motivation. LC 77-26532. 1979. pap. 3.25 (ISBN 0-8054-3226-4). Broadman.
McReynolds, Paul, ed. Four Early Works on Motivation, 4 vols. in 1. Incl. An Inquiry Concerning Beauty, Order, etc. Hutcheson, Francis. Repr. of 1726 ed; Concerning the Constitution of Human Nature & the Supreme Good. Hutcheson, Francis. Repr. of 1755 ed; An Inquiry into the Origins of Human Affections. Long, James. Repr. of 1747 ed; A Tale of the Springs of Action. Bentham, Jeremy. Repr. of 1815 ed. LC 72-81360. (History of Psychology Ser). (Illus.). 1969. 47.00x (ISBN 0-8201-1057-4). Schol Facsimiles.
Maslow, Abraham H. Toward a Psychology of Being. 2nd ed. 1968. pap. 7.95 (ISBN 0-442-03805-4, IS-5, IB). Van Nos Reinhold.
Maslow, Abraham H., ed. Motivation & Personality. 2nd ed. 1970. pap. text ed. 17.50 scp (ISBN 0-06-044241-7, HarpC). Har-Row.
Metzger, Bert L. How to Motivate with Profit Sharing. 1977. pap. 2.00 (ISBN 0-911192-29-8). Profit Sharing.
Mischel, Theodore, ed. Human Action: Conceptual & Empirical Issues. 1969. 28.50 (ISBN 0-12-498650-1). Acad Pr.
Murrell, Hywel. Motivation at Work. (Essential Psychology Ser.). 1976. pap. text ed. 4.50x (ISBN 0-416-84090-6). Methuen Inc.
Nevin, John A. The Study of Behavior: Learning, Motivation, Emotion & Instinct. 1973. text ed. 14.95x (ISBN 0-673-05430-6). Scott F.
Nuttin, Joseph & Meili, Richard. Experimental Psychology: Vol. 5, Motivation, Emotion & Personality. 1968. 13.50x (ISBN 0-465-04719-X). Basic.
Peters, R. S. Concept of Motivation. 2nd ed. (Studies in Philosophical Psychology). 1969. pap. text ed. 9.25x (ISBN 0-391-00060-8). Humanities.
Petri, Herbert. Motivation: Theory & Research. 400p. 1981. text ed. 19.95x (ISBN 0-534-00936-0). Wadsworth Pub.
Putnam, James J. Human Motives. LC 73-2413. (Mental Illness & Social Policy; the American Experience Ser.). Repr. of 1915 ed. 12.00 (ISBN 0-405-05223-5). Arno.
Rang. Kausalitat und Motivation. (Phaenomenologica Ser: No. 53). 1973. lib. bdg. 34.00 (ISBN 90-247-1353-6, Pub. by Martinus Nijhoff Netherlands). Kluwer Boston.
Raynor, Joel O. & Entin, Elliot E. Motivation, Career Striving, & Aging. LC 80-27082. (Illus.). 496p. 1981. text ed. 24.95 (ISBN 0-89116-189-9). Hemisphere Pub.
Robinson, W. P. & Rackstraw, Susan J. A Question of Answers, 2 vols. (Primary Socialization, Language & Education Ser.). 1972. 15.00x ea.; Vol. 1. (ISBN 0-7100-6986-3); Vol. 2. (ISBN 0-7100-7068-3); Set. 28.00x (ISBN 0-685-25616-2). Routledge & Kegan.
Roy, S. K. & Menon, A. S., eds. Motivation & Organizational Effectiveness with Special Reference to India. 267p. 1975. text ed. 10.50x (ISBN 0-8426-0800-1). Verry.
Russell, Wallace A., ed. Milestones in Motivation: Contributions to the Psychology of Drive & Purpose. 1970. 23.95 (ISBN 0-13-581686-6). P-H.
Sanzotta, Donald. Motivational Theories & Applications for Managers. new ed. LC 76-41732. 1977. 11.95 (ISBN 0-8144-5430-5). Am Mgmt.
Schaefer. Motivation Process. 1977. 5.95 (ISBN 0-87626-583-2). Winthrop.
Sewell, William H. & Hauser, Robert M. Education, Occupation, and Earnings: Achievement in the Early Career. 1975. 28.50 (ISBN 0-12-637850-9). Acad Pr.
Shinn, George. Miracle of Motivation. 1981. 8.95 (ISBN 0-8423-4353-9). Tyndale.
Steers, Richard M. & Porter, Lyman W. Motivation & Work Behavior. (Illus.). 608p. 1975. text ed. 12.95 (ISBN 0-07-060940-3, C). McGraw.
Stogdill, Ralph M. Team Achievement Under High Motivation. 1963. pap. 2.00x (ISBN 0-87776-113-2, R113). Ohio St U Admin Sci.
Taylor, Charles. Explanation of Behaviour. 1964. text ed. 17.00x (ISBN 0-391-00099-3); pap. text ed. 9.75x (ISBN 0-7100-0491-5). Humanities.
Thalheimer, Ross. Reflections. LC 79-164910. 1972. 7.50 (ISBN 0-8022-2058-4). Philos Lib.
Thomson, Thomas. Cainot's Theory of Motive Power. LC 79-170348. 1890. Repr. 24.00 (ISBN 0-403-01484-0). Scholarly.
Toates, F. & Halliday, T., eds. Analysis of Motivational Processes. 1981. 40.00 (ISBN 0-12-692260-8). Acad Pr.
Toman, W. An Introduction to Psychoanalytic Theory of Motivation. 1960. text ed. 18.75 (ISBN 0-08-009485-6). Pergamon.
Ullrich, Robert. Motivation Methods That Work. 176p. 1981. 12.95 (ISBN 0-13-603860-3); pap. 5.95 (ISBN 0-13-603852-2). P-H.

Valenstein, Elliot S. Brain Stimulation & Motivation: Research & Commentary. 192p. 1973. pap. 6.95x (ISBN 0-673-05443-8). Scott F.
Valle, Fred P. Motivation: Theories & Issues. LC 75-3928. (Core Books in Psychology Ser). 1975. text ed. 15.95 (ISBN 0-685-53815-X). Brooks-Cole.
Van Houten, Ron. How to Motivate Others Through Feedback. 1980. 3.25 (ISBN 0-89079-048-5). H & H Ent.
Vernon, Magdalen D. Human Motivation. LC 69-14396. 1969. 27.50 (ISBN 0-521-07419-3); pap. 8.95x (ISBN 0-521-09580-8, 580). Cambridge U Pr.
Weiner, Bernard. Human Motivation. LC 78-20731. 480p. 1980. text ed. 20.95 (ISBN 0-03-055226-5, HoltC). HR&W.
Weiner, Bernard, ed. Cognitive Views of Human Motivation. 1974. 18.00 (ISBN 0-12-741950-0). Acad Pr.
Wenzel, William J. Motivation Training Manual. 272p. 1970. 24.95 (ISBN 0-8436-0599-5). CBI Pub.
Whitmore, D. A. & Ibbetson, J. The Management of Motivation & Renumeration. 230p. 1977. text ed. 29.50x (ISBN 0-220-66319-X, Pub. by Busn Bks England). Renouf.
Williams, Leonard. Challenge to Survival. LC 76-51920. 170p. 1977. 14.50x (ISBN 0-8147-9172-7). NYU Pr.
Wong, Roderick. Motivation: a Biobehavioral Analysis of Consummatory Activities. (Illus.). 320p. 1976. text ed. 16.50 (ISBN 0-02-429400-4). Macmillan.
Yarrow, L. J., et al. Infant & Environment: Early Cognitive & Motivational Development. LC 74-26522. 255p. 1975. 15.95 (ISBN 0-470-97178-9). Halsted Pr.
Zimbardo, Philip. The Cognitive Control of Motivation: The Consequences of Choice & Dissonance. 1969. text ed. 12.95x (ISBN 0-673-05447-0). Scott F.

MOTIVATION (PSYCHOLOGY)–TESTING

Hackman, Ray C. Motivated Working Adult. LC 68-17540. 1969. 13.00 (ISBN 0-8144-5166-7). Am Mgmt.

MOTIVATION IN EDUCATION

Alley, Stephen L. One Hundred Helps for Teachers. LC 77-26679. (Illus.). 1978. pap. 5.95x (ISBN 0-8425-0996-8). Brigham.
DeCharms, R., et al. Enhancing Motivation: A Change Project in the Classrooms. LC 75-38701. (Social Relations Ser.). 288p. 1976. 15.95 (ISBN 0-470-01392-3). Halsted Pr.
Drew, Walter F., et al. Motivating Today's Students. LC 74-16805. (Learning Handbooks Ser.). (Illus.). 1974. pap. 4.95 (ISBN 0-8224-1908-4). Pitman Learning.
Frymier, Jack. Motivation & Learning in School. LC 74-83881. (Fastback Ser.: No. 43). (Orig.). 1974. pap. 0.75 (ISBN 0-87367-043-4). Phi Delta Kappa.
Gaa, John P. Motivation in the Classroom. 1982. pap. text ed. 8.95x (ISBN 0-582-28240-3). Longman.
Hawley, Robert C. & Hawley, Isabel I. Building Motivation in the Classroom: A Structured Approach to Improving Student Achievement. LC 78-69902. 1979. pap. 10.95 (ISBN 0-913636-10-X). Educ Res MA.
Jay, M. Ellen. Involvement Bulletin Boards & Other Motivational Reading Activities. LC 76-20451. (Illus.). 1976. pap. 7.50 (ISBN 0-915794-07-1). Gaylord Prof Pubns.
Logan, Frank A. & Gordon, William C. Fundamentals of Learning & Motivation. 3rd ed. 239p. 1981. pap. text ed. write for info. (ISBN 0-697-06634-7); instrs. manual avail. (ISBN 0-697-06639-8). Wm C Brown.
McAshan, H. H. The Goals Approach to Performance Objectives. LC 74-4577. 305p. 1974. pap. text ed. 7.95 (ISBN 0-7216-5860-1). HR&W.
Maller, Julius B. Cooperation & Competition: An Experimental Study in Motivation. LC 74-177049. (Columbia University. Teachers College. Contributions to Education: No. 384). Repr. of 1929 ed. 17.50 (ISBN 0-404-55384-2). AMS Pr.
Martin, Reed & Lauridsen, David. Developing Student Discipline & Motivation: A Series for Teacher in-Service Training. (Illus., Orig.). 1974. pap. text ed. 6.95 (ISBN 0-87822-119-0). Res Press.
Meihofer, Susan S., ed. Student & the Learning Environment. 1974. pap. 4.00 (ISBN 0-8106-0627-5). NEA.
Robinson, W. P. & Rackstraw, Susan J. A Question of Answers, 2 vols. (Primary Socialization, Language & Education Ser.). 1972. 15.00x ea.; Vol. 1. (ISBN 0-7100-6986-3); Vol. 2. (ISBN 0-7100-7068-3); Set. 28.00x (ISBN 0-685-25616-2). Routledge & Kegan.
Roueche, John E. & Mink, Oscar G. Improving Student Motivation. LC 76-15016. 1976. pap. 2.95 (ISBN 0-88408-079-X). Sterling Swift.
Sandven, Johs. Projectometry. 1975. text ed. 26.00x (ISBN 8-200-04844-6, Dist. by Columbia U Pr). Universitet.
Society for Research into Higher Education, 9th, 1973. Research into Higher Education: Proceedings. Page, C. F., ed. 1974. pap. 8.00 (ISBN 0-900868-38-4). Verry.
Stainback, William C., et al. Establishing a Token Economy in the Classroom. LC 72-93476. 1973. pap. text ed. 5.95x (ISBN 0-675-09032-6). Merrill.
Thompson, John F. Using Role Playing in the Classroom. LC 78-61318. (Fastback Ser.: No. 114). 1978. pap. 0.75 (ISBN 0-87367-114-7). Phi Delta Kappa.
Venables, Ethel C. Intelligence & Motivation Among Day Release Students. (General Ser.). 168p. 1974. pap. text ed. 16.50x (ISBN 0-85633-047-7, NFER). Humanities.
Wlodkowski, Raymond J. Motivation & Teaching: A Practical Guide. 224p. 1978. pap. 8.50 (ISBN 0-686-63693-7, 0751-4-06). NEA.
Zubin, Joseph. Some Effects of Incentives: A Study of Individual Differences in Rivalry. LC 70-177605. (Columbia University. Teachers College. Contributions to Education: No. 532). Repr. of 1932 ed. 17.50 (ISBN 0-404-55532-2). AMS Pr.

MOTIVATION IN SPORTS

see Sports–Psychological Aspects

MOTIVATION RESEARCH (MARKETING)

see also Advertising–Psychological Aspects

Britt, Stewart H. Psychological Principles of Marketing & Consumer Behavior. LC 77-75658. 1978. 29.95 (ISBN 0-669-01513-X). Lexington Bks.
Cheskin, Louis. Basis for Marketing Decisions Through Controlled Motivation Research. 1961. 6.95x (ISBN 0-87140-965-8). Liveright.
--Why People Buy: Motivation Research & Its Successful Application. 1959. 6.95x (ISBN 0-87140-962-3). Liveright.
Cunningham, William H. Segmentation in the United States Compact-Car Market. (Studies in Marketing: No. 16). 1972. pap. 4.00 (ISBN 0-87755-162-6). U of Tex Busn Res.
Dichter, Ernest. Handbook of Consumer Motivations: The Psychology of the World of Objects. 1964. 24.95 (ISBN 0-07-016780-X, P&RB). McGraw.
--Packaging: The Sixth Sense. LC 73-76439. 192p. 1975. 22.50 (ISBN 0-8436-1103-0). CBI Pub.
Ferber, Robert, ed. Motivation & Market Behavior. LC 75-39244. (Getting & Spending: the Consumer's Dilemma). (Illus.). 1976. Repr. of 1958 ed. 25.00x (ISBN 0-405-08018-2). Arno.
Gellerman, Saul W. Motivation & Productivity. (AMACOM Executive Books). 1978. pap. 6.95 (ISBN 0-8144-7502-7). Am Mgmt.
Guder, Robert F. Managing for Productivity: Motivating Employees. Reilly, Harry, ed. 100p. 1980. binder 125.00 (ISBN 0-89290-090-3, SWB 111); participant 45.00 (ISBN 0-89290-089-X). Soc for Visual.
Scitovsky, Tibor. The Joyless Economy: An Inquiry into Human Satisfaction & Consumer Dissatisfaction. LC 75-16904. 1977. pap. 5.95 (ISBN 0-19-502183-5, 499, GB). Oxford U Pr.
Smith, George H. Motivation Research in Advertising & Marketing. LC 70-100175. (Illus.). 1971. Repr. of 1954 ed. lib. bdg. 19.00 (ISBN 0-8371-4023-4, SMMO). Greenwood.
--Motivation Research in Advertising & Marketing. LC 70-100175. (Illus.). 1971. Repr. of 1954 ed. lib. bdg. 19.00 (ISBN 0-8371-4023-4, SMMO). Greenwood.
Wasson, Chester R., et al. Competition & Human Behavior. LC 68-16463. (Illus., Orig.). 1968. pap. text ed. 4.95x (ISBN 0-89197-100-9). Irvington.

MOTIVE (LAW)

see also Mistake (Law)

MOTONEURON TRANSMISSION

see Neuromuscular Transmission

MOTOR ABILITY

see also Kinesiology

Ammon, Jeanne E. & Etzel, Mary E. Sensorimotor Organization in Reach & Prehension: A Developmental Model. 1977. pap. 1.00 (ISBN 0-912452-19-6). Am Phys Therapy Assn.
Barnes, Marylou R., et al. The Neurophysiological Basis of Patient Treatment: Reflexes in Motor Development, Vol. II. LC 72-87895. (Illus.). 1973. pap. 12.75x (ISBN 0-936030-01-1). Stokesville Pub.
Bizzi, Emilio. Central & Peripheral Mechanisms in Motor Control. Date not set. write for info. (ISBN 0-89004-466-X, 521). Raven.
Blane, Linda. Development of Psycho-Motor Competence: Selected Readings. LC 74-31488. 201p. 1975. 20.00x (ISBN 0-8422-5219-3); pap. text ed. 6.95x (ISBN 0-8422-0443-1). Irvington.
Capon, Jack. Successful Movement Challenges: Movement Activities for the Developing Child. Alexander, Frank & Alexander, Diane, eds. (Illus.). 129p. (Orig.). 1981. pap. 7.95 (ISBN 0-915256-07-X). Front Row.
Casebeer, Beverly B. Casebeer Program: Developing Motor Skills for Early Childhood Education. 1978. pap. 6.00x (ISBN 0-87879-203-1). Acad Therapy.
Charcot, Jean M. & Pitres, Jean A. Les Centres moteurs corticaux chez l'homme. LC 77-169465. (Illus.). Repr. of 1895 ed. 12.50 (ISBN 0-404-10013-9). AMS Pr.
Connolly. Mechanisms of Motor Skill Development. 1971. 62.50 (ISBN 0-12-185950-9). Acad Pr.
Corbin, Charles B. A Textbook of Motor Development. 2nd ed. 224p. 1980. pap. text ed. write for info. (ISBN 0-697-07266-5). Wm C Brown.
Cratty, Bryant J. Psycho-Motor Behavior in Education & Sport: Selected Papers. (Illus.). 190p. 1974. text ed. 18.50 (ISBN 0-398-03099-5). C C Thomas.
Cratty, Bryant J., et al. Movement Activities, Motor Ability & the Education of Children. (Illus.). 192p. 1970. pap. 18.75 photocopy ed. spiral (ISBN 0-398-00360-2). C C Thomas.
Desmedt, J. E., ed. Cerebral Motor Control in Man: Cerebral Event-Related Potentials. (Progress in Clinical Neurophysiology: Vol. 4). (Illus.). 1977. 70.75 (ISBN 3-8055-2712-8). S Karger.
--Spiral & Supraspinal Mechanisms of Voluntary Motor Control & Locomotion. (Progress in Clinical Neurophysiology: Vol. 8). (Illus.). x, 374p. 1980. 82.75 (ISBN 3-8055-0022-X). S Karger.
Dickinson, John. Proprioceptive Control of Human Movement. 209p. 1980. 12.00x (ISBN 0-86019-002-1, Pub. by Kimpton). State Mutual Bk.
Dubner, Ronald & Kawamura, Yojiro, eds. Oral-Facial Sensory & Motor Mechanisms. LC 75-135617. 384p. 1971. 32.50 (ISBN 0-306-50018-3, Plenum Pr). Plenum Pub.
Espenschade, Anna. Motor Performance in Adolescence. (SRCD: Vol. 5, No. 1). 1940. pap. 7.00 (ISBN 0-527-01513-X). Kraus Repr.
Feldenkrais, Moshe. Awareness Through Movement: Health Exercises for Personal Growth. LC 74-184419. 192p. 1972. 10.95 (ISBN 0-06-062345-4, HarpR). Har-Row.
Feldman. Spasticity: Disorders of Motor Control. 1980. 61.50 (ISBN 0-8151-3240-9). Year Bk Med.
Feller, Babara A. & Shipp, Audrey. Health Characteristics of Person with Chronic Activity Limitation: United States 1979. (Series 10: No. 137). 50p. 1981. pap. text ed. 1.75 (ISBN 0-8406-0229-4). Natl Ctr Health Stats.
Fiorentino, Mary R. Normal & Abnormal Development: The Influence of Primitive Reflexes on Motor Development. (Illus.). 80p. 1980. 10.75 (ISBN 0-398-02278-X). C C Thomas.
Forman, George E., ed. Action & Thought: From Sensorimotor Schemes to Symbolic Operations. (Developmental Psychology Ser.). 1981. price not set. Acad Pr.
Gardner, Joyce & La Fleur, Ida. Psychomotor Continuum. (gr. k-2). 1977. 7.00x (ISBN 0-933892-09-8). Child Focus Co.
Garland, P. B. & Hales, C. N., eds. Substrate Mobilization & Energy Provision in Man. (Symposia Ser.: No. 43). 228p. 1981. 32.00x (ISBN 0-904498-07-7, Pub. by Biochemical England). State Mutual Bk.
Glaser, G. Temporal Lobe Psychomotor Seizures. 1981. pap. text ed. write for info. (ISBN 0-443-08000-3). Churchill.
Grieve, D. W. Techniques for the Analysis of Human Movement. 177p. 1980. 18.00x (ISBN 0-86019-006-4, Pub. by Kimpton). State Mutual Bk.
Hall, Michael C. The Locomotor System: Functional Anatomy. (Illus.). 376p. 1966. photocopy ed. spiral 54.50 (ISBN 0-398-00759-4). C C Thomas.
--The Locomotor System: Functional Histology. (Illus.). 456p. 1965. photocopy ed. spiral 44.75 (ISBN 0-398-00758-6). C C Thomas.
Hall, Tom. Academic Ropes: A Perceptual-Motor Academic Program. Alexander, Frank & Alexander, Diane, eds. (Illus.). 89p. (Orig.). 1981. pap. 5.95 (ISBN 0-915256-08-8). Front Row.
--Classroom-Made Movement Materials: A Perceptual-Motor Program with Classroom-Made Materials. Alexander, Frank & Alexander, Diane, eds. (Illus.). 70p. (Orig.). 1981. pap. 5.95 (ISBN 0-915256-09-6). Front Row.
Haywood, Kathleen, et al. Motor Development. Kneer, Marian, ed. (Basic Stuff Ser.). (Illus.). 55p. (gr. k up). 1981. pap. text ed. 5.95 (ISBN 0-686-30221-4). AAHPERD.
Healy, Harriet & Stainback, Susan. The Severely Motorically Impaired Student: A Handbook for the Classroom Teacher. (Illus.). 90p. 1980. 11.75 (ISBN 0-398-04050-8); pap. 7.50 (ISBN 0-398-04061-3). C C Thomas.
Holle, Britta. Motor Development in Children Normal & Retarded. 1977. pap. 23.00 (ISBN 0-397-60509-9, Pub by Blackwell Scientific). Mosby.
Jansma, Paul, ed. The Psychomotor Domain & the Seriously Handicapped. LC 80-6299. (Illus.). 502p. (Orig.). 1981. lib. bdg. 30.00 (ISBN 0-8191-1718-8); pap. text ed. 19.25 (ISBN 0-8191-1719-6). U Pr of Amer.
Jenkins, Lulu M. A Comparative Study of Motor Achievements of Children of Five, Six & Seven Years of Age. LC 76-176903. (Columbia University. Teachers College. Contributions to Education: No. 414). Repr. of 1930 ed. 17.50 (ISBN 0-404-55414-8). AMS Pr.
Jones, Barbara S. Movement Themes: Topics for Early Childhood Learning Through Creative Movement. LC 80-65608. 115p. 1981. perfect bdg. 8.50 (ISBN 0-86548-042-7). Century Twenty One.
Kline, Judy. Children Move to Learn: A Guide to Planning Gross Motor Activities. 1977. pap. text ed. 4.95 (ISBN 0-88450-771-8, 2036-B). Communication Skill.
Lissak, K., ed. Results in Neuroanatomy, Motor Organization, Cerebral Circulation & Modelling: Recent Developments in Neurobiology in Hungary, Vol. VIII. 1981. 60.00x (ISBN 0-569-08549-7, Pub. by Collet's). State Mutual Bk.
--Results in Neuroanatomy, Motor Organization, Cerebral Circulation and Modelling. (Recent Developments of Neurobiology in Hungary: Vol. 8). 1979. 24.00 (ISBN 0-9960011-1-5, Pub. by Kaido Hungary). Heyden.
Long, John A. Motor Abilities of Deaf Children. LC 75-177009. (Columbia University. Teachers College. Contributions to Education: No. 514). Repr. of 1932 ed. 17.50 (ISBN 0-404-55514-4). AMS Pr.
McNell, Harry. Motor Adaptation & Accuracy. Repr. of 1934 ed. 30.00 (ISBN 0-89987-067-8). Darby Bks.
Magill, Richard A. Motor Learning: Concepts & Applications. 1980. text ed. write for info. (ISBN 0-697-07090-5). Wm C Brown.
Marteniuk, R. G. Information Processing in Motor Skills. LC 75-43982. 1976. text ed. 20.95 (ISBN 0-03-006091-5, HoltC). HR&W.
Morgan, ed. Ergogenic Aids & Muscular Performance. 1972. 55.00 (ISBN 0-12-506850-6). Acad Pr.
Nadeau, Claude, et al, eds. Psychology of Motor Behavior & Sport: 1979. LC 78-641529. (Illus.). 1980. text ed. 24.95x (ISBN 0-686-64327-5). Human Kinetics.
Nichols, David, et al. Motor Activities for the Underachiever. (Illus.). 150p. 1980. 13.75 (ISBN 0-398-04090-7). C C Thomas.
Oester, Y. T. & Mayer, John H., Jr. Motor Examination of Peripheral Nerve Injuries. (Illus.). 96p. 1960. photocopy ed. spiral 10.50 (ISBN 0-398-01413-2). C C Thomas.
Olson, Marjorie E. Itty the Inchworm: Motor Coordination Experiences for Children. (Illus.). 31p. (gr. k-1). 1974. pap. text ed. 2.00x (ISBN 0-89039-127-0). Ann Arbor Pubs.
Parish, Peggy. I Can--Can You, 4 bks. LC 79-26041. (Illus.). (ps). 1980. Set. 4.95 (ISBN 0-688-80279-6); write for info. pre-pack set. Greenwillow.
Peterson, Adrienne & Sedjo, Karen. CAMS Motor Program. Casto, Glendon, ed. LC 79-64724. (Curriculum & Monitoring System Ser.). 192p. (For use with early-childhood handicapped). 1979. pap. text ed. 17.20 (ISBN 0-8027-9064-X). Walker Educ.
Rarick, L., et al. The Motor Domain & Its Correlates in Educationally Handicapped Children. (Illus.). 208p. 1976. 18.95 (ISBN 0-13-604116-7). P-H.
Ridenour, Marcella V., et al. Motor Development: Issues & Applications. Ridenour, Marcella V., ed. LC 77-92489. (Illus.). 240p. 1978. text ed. 13.95 (ISBN 0-916622-06-1). Princeton Bk Co.
Roberts, Glyn & Landers, Daniel, eds. Psychology of Motor Behavior & Sport 1980. (Illus.). 1981. text ed. 12.00x (ISBN 0-931250-19-6). Human Kinetics.
Rothstein, Anne, et al. Motor Learning. Kneer, Marian, ed. (Basic Stuff Ser.: No. I, 3 of 6). (Illus.). 109p. (Orig.). 1981. pap. text ed. 5.95 (ISBN 0-686-30222-2). AAHPERD.
Ruebel, Ines. Needle & Thread. (Practical Knowledge Ser.). 96p. 1971. 5.00x (ISBN 0-7188-1784-2). Intl Pubns Serv.
Sage, George H. Introduction to Motor Behavior: A Neuro-Psychological Approach. 2nd ed. LC 76-14660. (A-W Physical Ed Ser.). 1977. text ed. 21.95 (ISBN 0-201-06766-8). A-W.
Schade, Charlene. Move with Me from A to Z. (Illus.). 72p. (gr. k-1). 1981. pap. 9.95 (ISBN 0-940156-01-6). Wright Group.
Schmidt, Richard A. Motor Skills. (Scientific Perspectives of Physical Education). 192p. 1975. pap. text ed. 10.95 scp (ISBN 0-06-045784-8, HarpC). Har-Row.

Schotland, Donald L. Diseases of the Motor Unit. (Illus.). 1981. write for info. (ISBN 0-89289-410-5). HM.

--Disorders of the Motor Unit. 992p. 1982. 70.00 (ISBN 0-471-09507-9, Pub. by Wiley Med). Wiley.

Singer, Robert N. The Learning of Motor Skills. 1982. text ed. 15.95 (ISBN 0-686-75039-X). Macmillan.

--Motor Learning & Human Performance: An Application to Motor & Movement Behaviors. 3rd ed. (Illus.). 1980. text ed. 19.95 (ISBN 0-02-410780-8). Macmillan.

Skinner, Louise. Motor Development in the Preschool Years. (Illus.). 128p. 1979. pap. 11.75 (ISBN 0-398-03835-X). C C Thomas.

Stallings, Loretta M. Motor Learning: From Theory to Practice. (Illus.). 300p. 1982. pap. text ed. 14.50 (ISBN 0-8016-4768-1). Mosby.

Steindler, Arthur. Mechanics of Normal & Pathological Locomotion in Man. (Illus.). 424p. 1935. photocopy ed. spiral 42.50 (ISBN 0-398-04416-3). C C Thomas.

Stelmach, George E., ed. Motor Control: Issues & Trends. 1976. 28.00 (ISBN 0-12-665950-8). Acad Pr.

Sturm, Timothy M., et al. Carolina Developmental Curriculum, 2 bks. Incl. Bk. 1. Activities in Gross Motor, Fine Motor & Visual Perception. pap. text ed. 32.50 (ISBN 0-8027-9076-3); Bk. 2. Activities in Reasoning, Receptive Language & Expressive Language. pap. text ed. 29.50 (ISBN 0-8027-9077-1). LC 80-52392. (For use with pre-K to Gr. 1). 1980. Walker Educ.

Talbott, Richard E. & Humphrey, Donald R., eds. Posture & Movement. LC 77-85515. 325p. 1979. text ed. 32.50 (ISBN 0-89004-259-4). Raven.

Whiting, H. T. & Whiting, Marilyn G., eds. Journal of Human Movement Studies. 1980. 35.00x (ISBN 0-686-71771-6, Pub. by Kimpton). State Mutual Bk.

Wickstrom, Ralph L. Fundamental Motor Patterns. 2nd ed. LC 76-53536. (Illus.). 209p. 1977. text ed. 9.50 (ISBN 0-8121-0583-4). Lea & Febiger.

Zacks, Sumner I. The Motor Endplate. rev. ed. LC 73-84420. 508p. 1973. Repr. of 1964 ed. 27.50 (ISBN 0-88275-113-1). Krieger.

MOTOR ABILITY-TESTING

Fredericks, H. D., et al. Teaching Research Motor-Development Scale: For Moderately & Severely Retarded Children. (Illus.). 80p. 1972. 9.75 (ISBN 0-398-02284-4). C C Thomas.

Haworth, Mary R. Primary Visual Motor Test - Manual & Test Materials. LC 78-82557. 192p. 1970. Set. 28.75 (ISBN 0-8089-0181-8); test cards 16 card set 9.25 (ISBN 0-8089-0184-2); scoring forms, 50 in pkg. 15.50 (ISBN 0-8089-0183-4); test sheets pkg. of 100 10.25 (ISBN 0-8089-0182-6). Grune.

Howard, Glenn W. A Measure of Achievement in Motor Skills of College Men in the Game Situation of Basketball. LC 72-176882. (Columbia University. Teachers College. Contributions to Education: No. 733). Repr. of 1937 ed. 17.50 (ISBN 0-404-55733-3). AMS Pr.

Jones, Lloyd M. Factorial Analysis of Ability in Fundamental Motor Skills. LC 71-176918. (Columbia University. Teachers College. Contributions to Education: No. 665). Repr. of 1935 ed. 17.50 (ISBN 0-404-55665-5). AMS Pr.

Motor Function in the Lower Extremity: Analysis by Electronic Instrumentation. (American Lecture Orthopaedic Surgery). (Illus.). 176p. 1964. photocopy ed. spiral 18.75 (ISBN 0-398-00317-3). C C Thomas.

Welford, Alan T. Ageing & Human Skill: A Report Centered on Work by the Nuffield Unit. LC 73-1409. (Illus.). 300p. 1973. Repr. of 1958 ed. lib. bdg. 20.25 (ISBN 0-8371-6799-X, WEAH). Greenwood.

MOTOR BOAT ENGINES

see also Marine Diesel Motors; Outboard Motors

Coles, Clarence & Young, Howard. Mercruiser: Stern Drive Tune-up & Repair Manual. 1980. pap. 21.95 (ISBN 0-89330-005-5). Caroline Hse.

--OMC Stern Drive: Tune-up & Repair Manual. 1980. pap. 21.95 (ISBN 0-89330-004-7). Caroline Hse.

Zadig, Ernest A. The Complete Book of Pleasure Boat Engines. LC 79-24306. (Illus.). 320p. 1980. 17.95 (ISBN 0-13-157636-4). P-H.

MOTOR-BOAT RACING

Jackson, Al & Tardy, Gene. Drag Boat Racing: The National Championships. (Sports Action Ser). (Illus.). 48p. (gr. 3-12). 1973. PLB 5.51 (ISBN 0-914844-05-9); pap. 3.95 (ISBN 0-914844-06-7). J Alden.

Stone, Jane. Challenge! The Big Thunderboats. new ed. LC 75-23408. (Illus.). 32p. (gr. 5-10). 1976. PLB 6.89 (ISBN 0-89375-003-4); pap. 2.50 (ISBN 0-89375-019-0). Troll Assocs.

MOTOR-BOATS

see also Outboard Motor-Boats; Outboard Motors

Block, Richard A., ed. Motorboat Operator License Preparation Course. rev. ed. (Illus.). 269p. 1980. pap. text ed. 18.00 (ISBN 0-934114-29-3). Marine Educ.

Boy Scouts Of America. Motorboating. LC 19-600. (Illus.). 64p. (gr. 6-12). 1962. pap. 0.70x (ISBN 0-8395-3294-6, 3294). BSA.

Cox, T. Motor Boat & Yachting Manual. 18th ed. (Illus.). 1973. 15.00 (ISBN 0-540-00966-0). Heinman.

Cox, Tom. Motor Boat & Yachting Manual. 18th ed. (Illus.). 356p. 1973. 17.95x (ISBN 0-8464-0644-6). Beekman Pubs.

Desmond, Kevin. Motorboating Facts & Feats. (Illus.). 256p. 1980. 17.95 (ISBN 0-8069-9204-2, Pub by Guinness Superlatives England). Sterling.

Ducane, Peter. High Speed Small Craft. rev. ed. 1973. 25.00 (ISBN 0-8286-0065-1). De Graff.

Fletcher, N. E. & Ladd, J. D. Family Sports Boating. (Illus.). 242p. 1972. 12.00 (ISBN 0-7207-0601-7). Transatlantic.

Gibbs, Tony & Sports Illustrated Editors. Sports Illustrated Power Boating. LC 72-13277. 1973. 5.95 (ISBN 0-397-00971-2); pap. 2.95 (ISBN 0-397-00972-0, LP81). Har-Row.

Liebers, Arthur. Motorboat Owners Handbook. pap. 1.00 (ISBN 0-686-00709-3). Key Bks.

Motor Boating & Water Skiing. 1976. pap. 2.50 (ISBN 0-8277-4888-4). British Bk Ctr.

Mudie, Colin. Power Boats. 1976. 6.95 (ISBN 0-600-37045-3). Transatlantic.

Penzer, Mark. The Powerboater's Bible. LC 76-42427. 1978. pap. 2.95 (ISBN 0-385-12669-7). Doubleday.

Robinson, Jeff, ed. Powerboat Maintenance. (Illus.). 288p. pap. text ed. 9.00 (ISBN 0-89287-069-9, B620). Clymer Pubns.

Scharff, Robert. Motor Boating. (Quick & Easy Ser). (Orig.). 1963. pap. 1.95 (ISBN 0-02-081660-X, Collier). Macmillan.

Schult, Joachim. Curious Boating Inventions. LC 74-1525. (Illus.). 150p. 1974. 14.95 (ISBN 0-8008-2103-3). Taplinger.

Warren, Nigel. Small Motor Cruisers. (Illus.). 253p. 1976. 18.50 (ISBN 0-229-11537-3). Transatlantic.

--Small Motor Cruises. 1979. 19.95x (ISBN 0-8464-0064-2). Beekman Pubs.

Wickham, Hilary & Wickham, K. J. Motor Boating: A Practical Handbook. (Illus.). 224p. 1976. 14.00 (ISBN 0-370-10347-5); pap. 10.50 (ISBN 0-370-10348-3). Transatlantic.

Zadig, Ernest. The Complete Book of Boating. 2nd ed. LC 76-16006. (Illus.). 1976. 14.95 (ISBN 0-13-157503-1). P-H.

MOTOR BUS DRIVERS

Arco Editorial Board. Bus Operator: Conductor. 5th ed. LC 76-128136. (Orig.). 1970. pap. 5.00 (ISBN 0-668-01553-5). Arco.

Rudman, Jack. Bus Driver. (Career Examination Ser.: C-2197). (Cloth bdg. avail. on request). pap. 8.00 (ISBN 0-8373-2197-2). Natl Learning.

--Bus Operator. (Career Examination Ser.: C-102). (Cloth bdg. avail. on request). pap. 8.00 (ISBN 0-8373-0102-5). Natl Learning.

--Head Bus Driver. (Career Examination Ser.: C-2198). (Cloth bdg. avail. on request). pap. 8.00 (ISBN 0-8373-2198-0). Natl Learning.

--Surface Line Operator. (Career Examination Ser.: C-789). (Cloth bdg. avail. on request). pap. 8.00 (ISBN 0-8373-0789-9). Natl Learning.

Tompkins, L. Michael. Plimpton Never Drove a School Bus. 1980. pap. 5.95 (ISBN 0-931324-02-5). La Grange.

MOTOR BUS LINES

see also Motor Bus Drivers

Anderson, Roy C. & Frankis, G. History of the Royal Blue Express Services. LC 72-91235. 1970. 12.50x (ISBN 0-678-05649-8). Kelley.

Arco Editorial Board. Surface Line Dispatcher. 4th ed. LC 78-86828. 1974. pap. 6.00 (ISBN 0-668-00140-2). Arco.

British Bus Fleets No. 12 London Transport. Date not set. pap. 3.00x (ISBN 0-392-15862-0, SpS). Sportshelf.

Cockshott, J. S. British Bus Fleets No. 9 Yorkshire Company Operators. Date not set. pap. 3.00x (ISBN 0-392-08801-0, SpS). Sportshelf.

Collins, et al. British Bus Fleets No. 4 East Anglia. Date not set. pap. 3.00x (ISBN 0-392-08703-0, SpS). Sportshelf.

Davis. British Bus Fleets No. 10 Northern. Date not set. pap. 3.00x (ISBN 0-392-08670-0, SpS). Sportshelf.

Gardiner, Hilliard. British Bus Fleets No. 2 Yorkshire Municipal Operators. Date not set. pap. 3.00x (ISBN 0-392-08751-0, SpS). Sportshelf.

Gibson & Roberson. British Bus Fleets No. 7 Midlands. Date not set. pap. 3.00x (ISBN 0-392-08748-0, SpS). Sportshelf.

Hibbs, John. Transport for Passengers. (Institute of Economic Affairs, Hobart Papers Ser.: No. 23). pap. 2.50 (ISBN 0-255-36015-0). Transatlantic.

Kennedy & Marshall. British Bus Fleets No. 11 Greater London Operators. Date not set. pap. 3.00x (ISBN 0-392-08720-0, SpS). Sportshelf.

Manual on User Benefit Analysis & Bus Transit Improvements. 1978. pap. 7.00 (ISBN 0-686-24170-3, UBA). AASHTO.

Marshall & Kennedy. British Bus Fleets No. 5 East Midlands Area. Date not set. pap. 3.00x (ISBN 0-392-08927-0, SpS). Sportshelf.

Marshall, Prince J. British Bus Fleets No. 14 Birmingham City. Date not set. pap. 3.00x (ISBN 0-392-08698-0, SpS). Sportshelf.

OECD. Bus Lanes & Busway Systems. (Road Research). 124p. (Orig.). 1977. pap. 7.00x (ISBN 92-64-11628-1). OECD.

Passingham, W. J. Romance of London's Underground. LC 72-80705. (Illus.). Repr. of 1932 ed. 25.00 (ISBN 0-405-08839-6). Arno.

Scanlon, H. D. A Lifetime of London Bus Work. 120p. 1981. 35.00x (ISBN 0-903839-33-4, Pub. by Transport). State Mutual Bk.

Sinclair, Wm. British Bus Fleets No. 15 Midland Red. Date not set. pap. 3.00x (ISBN 0-392-08734-0, SpS). Sportshelf.

Standwick. British Bus Fleets No. 16 Ribble. Date not set. pap. 3.00x (ISBN 0-392-08684-0, SpS). Sportshelf.

Townsin, A. Alan. British Double Deckers Since Nineteen Forty-Two. Date not set. pap. 3.00x (ISBN 0-392-08765-0, SpS). Sportshelf.

Turns, Keith. The Independent Bus: An Historical Survey of Some Independent Bus Operators. (Illus.). 200p. 1974. 5.95 (ISBN 0-7153-6438-3). David & Charles.

MOTOR BUSES

Anderson, R. C. History of Crosville Motor Services. LC 81-65955. (Illus.). 160p. 1981. 19.95 (ISBN 0-7153-8088-5). David & Charles.

Arco Editorial Board. Bus Maintainer - Bus Mechanic. 4th ed. LC 70-104878. 136p. (Orig.). 1972. pap. 8.00 (ISBN 0-668-00111-9). Arco.

Blacker, Ken, ed. Vintage Bus Annual, No. 1. (Illus.). 96p. 1979. 16.50x (ISBN 0-906116-09-0). Intl Pubns Serv.

Booth, Gavin. Alexander Coachbuilders. 192p. 1981. 45.00x (ISBN 0-903839-38-5, Pub. by Transport). State Mutual Bk.

Bruce, J. Graeme. London Motor Bus. (Illus.). 138p. 1973. 9.50x (ISBN 0-85329-036-9). Intl Pubns Serv.

Holding, David. A History of British Bus Services: The North East. LC 79-52370. 1979. 17.95 (ISBN 0-7153-7813-9). David & Charles.

Klapper, Charles F. Golden Age of Buses. (Illus.). 1978. 22.00 (ISBN 0-7100-8961-9). Routledge & Kegan.

McClure, Louis C. How to Build Low Cost Motor Homes. LC 72-91090. (Build-It-Yourself Plans Ser). (Illus.). 300p. (Orig.). 1975. pap. 9.95 (ISBN 0-87593-099-9). Trail-R.

Rudman, Jack. Bus Maintainer, Group A. (Career Examination Ser.: C-100). (Cloth bdg. avail. on request). pap. 8.00 (ISBN 0-8373-0100-9). Natl Learning.

--Bus Maintainer, Group B. (Career Examination Ser.: C-101). (Cloth bdg. avail. on request). pap. 8.00 (ISBN 0-8373-0101-7). Natl Learning.

--Foreman (Buses & Shops) (Career Examination Ser.: C-264). (Cloth bdg. avail. on request). pap. 8.00 (ISBN 0-8373-0264-1). Natl Learning.

Seal, Mark. Cambridge Buses. (Cambridge Town, Gown & County Ser: Vol. 26). 1978. pap. 4.50 (ISBN 0-900891-24-6). Oleander Pr.

Townsin, A. A. The Best of British Buses: Leyland Titans, 1927-1941, No. 1. 96p. 1981. 30.00x (ISBN 0-903839-56-3, Pub. by Transport). State Mutual Bk.

Turner, Tom. Birkenhead Buses. 48p. 1981. 10.00x (ISBN 0-903839-30-X, Pub. by Transport). State Mutual Bk.

MOTOR CARRIERS

see Transportation, Automotive-Laws and Regulations

MOTOR-CARS

see Automobiles

MOTOR COURTS

see Motels

MOTOR CYCLES

see Motorcycles

MOTOR DEXTERITY

see Motor Ability

MOTOR END PLATE

see Myoneural Junction

MOTOR FUELS

see also Airplanes-Fuel; Alcohol As Fuel; Jet Planes-Fuel; Liquid Fuels; Petroleum As Fuel; Petroleum Products

Colucci, Joseph M. & Gallopoulos, Nicholas E., eds. Future Automotive Fuels: Prospects, Performance, Perspective. LC 76-30757. (General Motors Research Symposia Ser.). 380p. 1977. 45.00 (ISBN 0-306-31017-1, Plenum Pr). Plenum Pub.

Frazier, Jack. Automobile Fuels of the 1980's: A Survey. (Illus.). 1978. pap. 3.95 (ISBN 0-685-87593-8). Solar Age Pr.

Gruse, William A. Motor Fuels: Performance & Testing. 288p. 1967. 18.00 (ISBN 0-442-15575-1, Pub. by Van Nos Reinhold). Krieger.

LP-Gas Engine Fuels. 140p. 1973. 4.75 (ISBN 0-8031-0104-X, STP525). ASTM.

Paul, J. K., ed. Methanol Technology & Application in Motor Fuels. LC 78-56011. (Chemical Tech. Rev. 114, Energy Tech. Rev. 31). (Illus.). 1979. 54.00 (ISBN 0-8155-0719-4). Noyes.

Proposed Methods of Test for Knock Characteristics of Motor Fuels. 1970. 8.25 (ISBN 0-686-50151-9, 12-419480-20). ASTM.

Ranney, M. W. Fuel Additives for Internal Combustion Engines--Recent Developments. LC 78-57662. (Chemical Technology Review Ser. No. 112, Energy Technology Review Ser. No. 30). 1978. 39.00 (ISBN 0-8155-0709-7). Noyes.

Whitcomb, R. M. Non-Lead Antiknock Agents for Motor Fuels. LC 75-4474. (Chemical Technology Review Ser: No. 49). 288p. (Index of patents, inventors, companies). 1975. 36.00 (ISBN 0-8155-0573-6). Noyes.

MOTOR HOMES

see Campers and Coaches, Truck

MOTOR HOTELS

see Motels

MOTOR LEARNING

see also Perceptual-Motor Learning

Ashlock, Robert B. & Humphrey, James H. Teaching Elementary School Mathematics Through Motor Learning. 168p. 1976. 16.25 (ISBN 0-398-03578-4). C C Thomas.

Barrow, Harold M. Man & Movement: Principles of Physical Education. 2nd ed. LC 77-22989. 396p. 1977. text ed. 14.00 (ISBN 0-8121-0599-0). Lea & Febiger.

Colwell, Lida C. Jump to Learn: Teaching Motor Skills for Self-Esteem to Kindergartners. (Orig.). 1975. pap. 6.95 (ISBN 0-913458-25-2). Pennant Pr.

Cratty, Bryant J. Developmental Sequences of Perceptional Motor Tasks. 1967. 3.75 (ISBN 0-914296-01-9). Activity Rec.

--Movement Behavior & Motor Learning. 3rd ed. LC 73-1938. (Health & Physical Education & Recreation Ser.). (Illus.). 512p. 1973. text ed. 11.50 (ISBN 0-8121-0425-0). Lea & Febiger.

Crews, Katherine. Music & Perceptual Motor Development. (Classroom Music Enrichment Units Ser.). (Illus.). 1974. pap. 5.95x (ISBN 0-87628-213-3). Ctr Appl Res.

Drowatzky, John N. Motor Learning: Principles & Practices. 2nd ed. LC 80-69551. Date not set. text ed. 14.95x (ISBN 0-8087-0495-8). Burgess.

Dunn, Marsha L. Pre-Scissor Skills: Skill Starters for Motor Development. (Illus.). 1979. pap. text ed. 10.00 (ISBN 0-88450-701-7, 3101-B). Communication Skill.

Engstrom, Georgianna, ed. The Significance of the Young Child's Motor Development. LC 70-177238. 55p. (Orig.). 1971. pap. text ed. 2.25 (ISBN 0-686-65517-6, 128). Natl Assn Child Ed.

Exploring Movement. Glass, Henry. (Illus.). 1966. 2.50 (ISBN 0-914296-00-0). Activity Rec.

Fiorentino, Mary R. A Basis for Sensorimotor Development-Normal & Abnormal: The Influence of Primitive, Postural Reflexes on the Development & Distribution of Tone. (Illus.). 184p. 1981. text ed. 19.75 (ISBN 0-398-04179-2). C C Thomas.

--Normal & Abnormal Development: The Influence of Primitive Reflexes on Motor Development. (Illus.). 80p. 1980. 10.75 (ISBN 0-398-02278-X). C C Thomas.

Gallahue, David L. Motor Development & Movement Experiences for Young Children. LC 75-37676. 1976. text ed. 20.95 (ISBN 0-471-29042-4). Wiley.

Humphrey, James H. Education of Children Through Motor Activity. 220p. 1975. 16.75 (ISBN 0-398-03471-0). C C Thomas.

--Teaching Elementary School Science Through Motor Learning. 144p. 1975. 11.75 (ISBN 0-398-03252-1). C C Thomas.

King, Nancy. Giving Form to Feeling. LC 74-23359. (Illus.). 320p. 1975. 8.95x (ISBN 0-910482-57-8). Drama Bk.

Lawther, John D. The Learning & Performance of Physical Skills. 2nd ed. (Illus.). 1977. text ed. 12.95 (ISBN 0-13-527325-0). P-H.

Lockhart, Ailene S. & Johnson, Joann M. Laboratory Experiments in Motor Learning. 2nd ed. 1977. pap. text ed. 8.95 (ISBN 0-8403-1662-3). Kendall-Hunt.

Motor Growth & Development. Date not set. price not set (ISBN 0-939418-20-7). Ferguson-Florissant.

Nichols, David, et al. Motor Activities for the Underachiever. (Illus.). 150p. 1980. 13.75 (ISBN 0-398-04090-7). C C Thomas.

Oxendine, J. Psychology of Motor Learning. 1968. text ed. 18.95 (ISBN 0-13-736595-0). P-H.

Schade, Charlene. Move with Me from A to Z. (Illus.). 72p. (gr. k-1). 1981. pap. 9.95 (ISBN 0-940156-01-6). Wright Group.
Schmidt, Richard A. Motor Learning & Control: A Behavioral Emphasis. (Illus.). 1981. text ed. 24.95x (ISBN 0-931250-21-8). Human Kinetics.
Singer, R. N. & Milne, C. Laboratory & Field Experiments in Motor Learning. (Illus.). 292p. 1975. 26.75 (ISBN 0-398-03262-9). C C Thomas.
Smith, Leon E., ed. Psychology of Motor Learning. LC 79-123217. 1970. soft bdg 7.50 (ISBN 0-87670-851-3). Athletic Inst.
Smith, Paul. Rope Skipping-Rhythms, Rhymes, & Routines. (Illus.). 1969. 5.95 (ISBN 0-914296-04-3); kit with lP record 12.95 (ISBN 0-685-64474-X); record only 7.95 (ISBN 0-685-64475-8). Activity Rec.

MOTOR PSYCHOLOGY
see Movement, Psychology Of

MOTOR SCOOTERS
see also names of motor scooters e.g. Vespa Motor Scooter

Butterworth, William E. Mighty Minicycles. LC 75-15040. (Free Time Fun Ser.). (Illus.). 48p. (gr. 4-8). 1976. PLB 6.99 (ISBN 0-8178-5392-8). Harvey.
Edmonds, I. G. Minibikes & Minicycles for Beginners. LC 72-11099. (Illus.). 168p. (gr. 4 up). 1973. PLB 7.61 (ISBN 0-8255-3003-2). Macrae.
Pyle, Steve. Mopeds: The Complete Guide. 1978. pap. 4.95 (ISBN 0-8128-2446-6). Stein & Day.
Webb, Bob. You & Your Motor Scooter. Date not set. 4.50x (ISBN 0-392-13576-0, SpS). Sportshelf.

MOTOR SKILL
see Motor Ability

MOTOR TRANSPORTATION
see Transportation, Automotive

MOTOR-TRUCK DRIVERS
see Highway Transport Workers

MOTOR-TRUCKS
see also Campers and Coaches, Truck; Materials Handling; Vans

Anson, Mike. Customizing Your Pickup. (Illus.). 1977. pap. 5.95 (ISBN 0-8306-6972-8, 972). TAB Bks.
Arrow & Dodge D-Fifty Pick-Ups 1979-81. LC 80-70343. (Illus.). 192p. pap. 8.95 (ISBN 0-686-70875-X). Chilton.
Asa, Donald S. Introduction to Trucking. (Illus.). 1978. pap. text ed. 7.95x (ISBN 0-685-08729-8). D & A Pub.
Baldwin, Nick. Kaleidoscope of Lorries & Vans. (Illus.). 96p. 1979. 15.00x (ISBN 0-906116-05-8). Intl Pubns Serv.
--Trucks of the Sixties & Seventies. (Transport Library). (Illus.). 64p. 1980. 13.95 (ISBN 0-7232-2364-5, Pub. by Warne Pubs England). Motorbooks Intl.
--Trucks of the Sixties & Seventies. (Warne's Transport Library). (Illus.). 1980. 10.95 (ISBN 0-7232-2364-5). Warne.
Baldwin, Nick, ed. Vintage Lorry Annual. (Illus.). 96p. 1979. 16.50x (ISBN 0-906116-07-4). Intl Pubns Serv.
Bowman, Daniel. Lift Trucks: A Practical Guide for Buyers & Users. LC 72-83304. (Illus.). 1973. 19.95 (ISBN 0-8436-1007-7). CBI Pub.
Brady, James. On-Highway Trucks: Power Trains & Suspension Systems. 624p. Date not set. text ed. 19.95 (ISBN 0-8359-5232-0). Reston.
Broehl, Wayne G., Jr. Trucks, Trouble & Triumph: The Norwalk Truck Line Company. LC 75-41749. (Companies & Men: Business Enterprises in America). (Illus.). 1976. Repr. of 1954 ed. 21.00x (ISBN 0-405-08066-2). Arno.
Burness, Tad. American Truck Spotter's Guide 1920-1970. LC 77-18535. (Illus.). 1978. pap. 13.95 (ISBN 0-87938-040-3). Motorbooks Intl.
Chevrolet-GMC Pick-Ups: Nineteen Seventy to Eighty Repair & Tune-up Guide. LC 79-8304. (New Automotive Bks.). 272p. 1980. 8.95 (ISBN 0-8019-6936-0). Chilton.
Chilton Book Company. Automotive Editorial Dept. Chilton's Repair & Tune-up Guide: For Blazer-Jimmy, 1969-1977. LC 76-53144. (Chilton's Repair & Tune up Guides). 1977. pap. 8.95 (ISBN 0-8019-6558-6). Chilton.
Chilton's Automotive Editorial Department. Chilton's Repair & Tune-up Guide for Ford Courier, 1972-1975. (Illus.). 224p. 1975. 8.95 (ISBN 0-8019-6202-1); pap. 8.95 (ISBN 0-8019-6203-X). Chilton.
--Chilton's Repair & Tune-up Guide for Toyota Hi Lux, 1970-1974. (Illus.). 224p. 1974. 8.95 (ISBN 0-8019-6204-8); pap. 8.95 (ISBN 0-8019-6205-6). Chilton.
Chilton's Automotive Editorial Dept. Chilton's Chevrolet Luv: 1972-1979, Repair & Tune-up Guide. LC 78-20241. (Repair & Tune-up Guides Ser.). 1979. pap. 8.95 (ISBN 0-8019-6815-1). Chilton.
--Chilton's Datsun Pick-Ups: 1970-1979 Repair & Tune-up Guide. LC 78-20245. (Repair & Tune-up Guides Ser.). 1979. pap. 8.95 (ISBN 0-8019-6816-X). Chilton.
--Chilton's Motor Age Professional Truck & Van Repair Manual: Gasoline & Diesel Engines. (Illus.). 1980. 27.00x (ISBN 0-8019-6925-5). Chilton.
--Chilton's Truck & Van Manual 1973-1980: Gasoline & Diesel Engines. (Illus.). 1980. 18.00 (ISBN 0-8019-6910-7). Chilton.
Chilton's Automotive Editorial Staff. Datsun Pick-Ups, 1970 to 1981. (Illus.). 1981. pap. 9.95 (ISBN 0-8019-7050-4). Chilton.
--Dodge D-50-Plymouth Arrow Pickups, 1979 to 1981. (Illus.). 1981. pap. 9.95 (ISBN 0-8019-7032-6). Chilton.
Chilton's Repair & Tune-up Guide for Chevrolet-Gmc Pick-Ups, 1970-78. (Illus.). 1978. pap. 8.95 (ISBN 0-8019-6700-7). Chilton.
Chilton's Repair & Tune-up Guide for Toyota Pick-Ups, 1970-1978. LC 77-18305. (Illus.). 1978. pap. 8.95 (ISBN 0-8019-6692-2). Chilton.
Chilton's Truck & Van Repair Manual, 1971-78. LC 77-16756. (Illus.). 1978. 18.00 (ISBN 0-8019-6698-1). Chilton.
Consumer Guide Editors. The Complete Book of Vans. 1976. pap. 1.95 (ISBN 0-671-80991-1). PB.
Davis, Grant M. & Dillard, John E., Jr. Increasing Motor Carrier Productivity: An Empirical Analysis. LC 77-7821. (Praeger Special Studies). 1977. text ed. 20.95 (ISBN 0-03-022641-4). Praeger.
Dempsey, Paul. How to Repair Lift Trucks. (Illus.). 1977. 19.95 (ISBN 0-8306-7967-7, 967). TAB Bks.
Dodge-Plymouth Vans: Nineteen Sixty Seven to Eighty Repair & Tune-up Guide. (New Automotive Bks.). 1980. 8.95 (ISBN 0-8019-6934-4). Chilton.
Drolet, Robert P. & Dowling, John R. Operator's Training Program for Powered Industrial Trucks. 2nd ed. 96p. 1981. pap. 12.95 (ISBN 0-8436-0797-1); of 10 79.50 set (ISBN 0-686-77615-1). CBI Pub.
Educational Research Council of America. Truck Mechanic. rev. ed. Ferris, Theodore N., et al, eds. (Real People at Work Ser: K). (Illus.). 1980. pap. text ed. 2.25 (ISBN 0-89247-087-9). Changing Times.
Fancher, Paul S. Research in Support of Motor Truck Brake System Design & Development. (Illus.). 141p. 1980. 12.00 (ISBN 0-686-72868-8, BRAKE). Indus Dev Inst Sci.
Fleet Owner Magazine Staff. Truck Maintenance. 256p. 1981. 24.50 (ISBN 0-07-021260-0, P&RB). McGraw.
Ford Pick-Ups: Nineteen Sixty Five to Eighty Repair Tune-up Guide. (New Automotive Bks.). 256p. 1980. 8.95 (ISBN 0-8019-6913-1). Chilton.
Georgano, G. N. & Demand, Carlo. Trucks: An Illustrated History 1892-1921. (Illus.). 1978. 24.95 (ISBN 0-8467-0500-1, Pub. by Two Continents). Hippocrene Bks.
Green, Michael, ed. Truck Facts Buyer's Guide, 1981. rev. ed. 96p. (Orig.). write for info. DMR Pubns.
Green, Michael L. Nineteen-Eighty Truck Facts. (Truck Facts, 1980). 1979. pap. 2.25 (ISBN 0-89552-062-1). DMR Pubns.
Green, Michael L., ed. New Truck & Van Prices, 1981. rev. ed. (Buyer's Guide Ser.). 96p. (Orig.). Date not set. pap. 2.50 (ISBN 0-89552-070-2). DMR Pubns.
--Nineteen Eighty New Truck & Van Prices. (Buyer's Guide Ser.). 1979. pap. 2.25 (ISBN 0-89552-061-3). DMR Pubns.
--Nineteen Seventy Nine Truck & Van Prices Buyer's Guide. (Buyer's Guide Reports Ser.). 1978. pap. 1.95 (ISBN 0-89552-052-4). DMR Pubns.
--Nineteen Seventy Nine Truck Facts. (Buyer's Guide Reports Ser.). 1978. pap. 1.95 (ISBN 0-89552-053-2). DMR Pubns.
--Used Truck & Van Prices. rev. ed. (Buyer's Guide Ser.). 96p. (Orig.). Date not set. pap. 2.25 (ISBN 0-89552-066-4). DMR Pubns.
--Used Truck & Van Prices. rev. ed. (Buyer's Guide Ser.). 1979. pap. 2.25 (ISBN 0-89552-056-7). DMR Pubns.
Holl, Adelaide. ABC of Cars, Trucks & Machines. (ps-1). 1970. 6.95 (ISBN 0-07-029561-1, GB). McGraw.
Hoy, Ray. Ford Pickups: 1969-1981 Shop Manual. (Illus.). pap. text ed. 10.95 (ISBN 0-89287-303-5, A248). Clymer Pubns.
Hull, C. Plans & Instructions for Volkswagen Van Conversions. LC 76-25173. 1976. 9.95 (ISBN 0-87593-751-9). Trail-R.
Hull, Clinton R. Plans & Instructions for Ford, Chevy, & Dodge Van Conversions. LC 76-4510. (Illus.). 1976. pap. 9.95 (ISBN 0-87593-076-X). Trail-R.
Ingram, Arthur. Off Highway & Construction Trucks. (Illus.). 160p. 1980. 17.50 (ISBN 0-7137-0960-X, Pub. by Blandford Pr England). Sterling.
Ingram, Arthur, ed. Trucks of the World Highways. (Illus.). 1979. 17.50 (ISBN 0-7137-0994-4, Pub by Blandford Pr England). Sterling.
International Tune-up-Maintenance, Scouts, Wagons, Pickups, Through 1980. (Illus.). pap. 7.95 (ISBN 0-89287-137-7, A233). Clymer Pubns.
J. J. Keller & Associates, Inc. Emergency & Trip Permit Handbook. 8th ed. LC 75-25157. 1978. cerlox bound 25.00 (ISBN 0-934674-17-5). J J Keller.
J. J. Keller & Associates, Inc. Driver's Guide to Low Underpasses. 2nd ed. LC 75-26145. 1978. pap. 6.00 perfect bdg (ISBN 0-934674-16-7). J J Keller.
--Federal Motor Carrier Safety Regulations Handbook. LC 75-1681. 1978. cerlox bdg 25.00 (ISBN 0-934674-20-5). J J Keller.
Jacobs, David. American Trucks: A Photographic Essay of American Trucks & Trucking. (Illus.). 128p. (YA) 1980. 14.95 (ISBN 0-85045-379-8, Pub. by Osprey England). Motorbooks Intl.
Jorgensen, Eric, ed. Chevy & GMC Vans Nineteen Sixty-Seven to Nineteen Eighty Shop Manual. (Illus.). pap. text ed. 10.95 (ISBN 0-89287-300-0, A239). Clymer Pubns.
--Chevy GMC Pickups Nineteen Sixty-Seven to Nineteen Eighty: Includes Suburbans Shop Manual. (Illus.). pap. text ed. 9.95 (ISBN 0-89287-207-1, A238). Clymer Pubns.
--Dodge Pickups: 1971-1980 Shop Manual. (Illus.). pap. text ed. 10.95 (ISBN 0-89287-313-2, A243). Clymer Pubns.
Jorgensen, Eric & Jorgensen, Eric, eds. Dodge & Plymouth 4-Wheel Drive Maintenance: 4-Wheel Drive Maintenance, 1965-1978. pap. 7.95 (ISBN 0-89287-289-6, A231). Clymer Pubns.
Kahn, Elliott. American Trucks of the Seventies. (Illus.). 64p. 1981. 11.95 (ISBN 0-7232-2765-9, Pub. by Warne Pubs England). Motorbooks Intl.
Karolevitz, Robert. This Was Trucking. encore ed. LC 66-25421. 1966. 9.95 (ISBN 0-87564-524-0). Superior Pub.
Keller, John J. Truck Broker Directory. 9th ed. Nelson, Harold C., ed. LC 75-25256. (Illus., Prog. Bk.). 1978. spiral bdg 25.00 (ISBN 0-934674-18-3). J J Keller.
--Trucking Safety Guide: Driver, Vehicles, Cargo, Highway. rev. ed. Quirk, Terence J., et al, eds. LC 74-3865. 1979. loose-leaf 95.00 (ISBN 0-934674-03-5). J J Keller.
Kuipers, J. F. World's Truck Catalogue: International Listings. (Illus.). Date not set. pap. 16.95 (ISBN 0-89404-013-8). Aztex.
Lahue, Kalton C. Mini-Truck Repair Manual. LC 78-51841. (Illus.). 384p. 1978. pap. 5.95 (ISBN 0-8227-5016-3). Petersen Pub.
Lustig, Loretta, illus. The Pop-up Book of Trucks. LC 73-19318. (Pop-up Ser). (Illus.). (ps-2). 1974. 4.95 (ISBN 0-394-82826-7, BYR). Random.
MacAvoy, Paul W. & Snow, John W., eds. Regulation of Entry & Pricing in Truck Transportation. LC 77-89167. 1977. pap. 8.25 (ISBN 0-8447-3261-3). Am Enterprise.
Mathieu, Joseph. Big Joe's Trailer Truck. LC 74-2538. (Picturebacks Ser). (Illus.). 32p. (Orig.). (ps-1). 1974. pap. 1.25 (ISBN 0-394-82925-5, BYR). Random.
Montville, John B. Mack, Greatest Name in Trucks. (Illus.). 1979. 24.95 (ISBN 0-89404-030-8); pap. 14.95 (ISBN 0-89404-010-3). Aztex.
--The Packard Truck: Ask the Man Who Owns One. (Illus.). 128p. 1981. pap. 14.95 (ISBN 0-89404-052-9). Aztex.
Motor Truck Repair Manual. 34th ed. (Illus.). 1400p. 1981. 24.95 (ISBN 0-87851-537-2). Hearst Bks.
Murray, Spence, ed. Chevy-GMC Pickup Repair. LC 78-61768. (Pickups & Vans Ser.). (Illus.). 1978. pap. 4.95 (ISBN 0-8227-5038-4). Petersen Pub.
--Dodge Pickup Repair. LC 79-53094. (Pickups & Vans Ser.). (Illus.). 1979. pap. 4.95 (ISBN 0-8227-5043-0). Petersen Pub.
National Directory of Full-Service, Twenty-Four-Hour Auto-Truck Stops. 1979. pap. 2.50 (ISBN 0-918734-21-5). Reymont.
Nunes, Joseph. Diesel Heavy Truck Applications & Performance Factors. (Illus.). 1980. pap. text ed. 12.95 (ISBN 0-13-211102-0). P-H.
Poteet, G. Howard. How to Live in Your Van & Love It! LC 76-14809. (Illus.). 1976. pap. 8.95 (ISBN 0-87593-022-0). Trail-R.
Proctor, Charles W. Authorities & Rights of Interstate Truckers, 2 vols. 1958. with 1961 Cum. Suppl. 35.00 (ISBN 0-87215-044-5); 1961 cum. suppl. 10.00 (ISBN 0-87215-292-8). Michie-Bobbs.
Quackenbush, Robert. City Trucks. Tucker, Kathleen, ed. (Illus.). 40p. (gr. 3-9). 1981. 7.50 (ISBN 0-8075-1163-3). A Whitman.
Radlauer, Ed. Trucks. LC 79-21853. (Ready, Get Set, Go Ser.). (Illus.). 32p. (gr. 1-6). 1980. PLB 9.25 (ISBN 0-516-07473-3, Elk Grove Bks.); pap. 2.95 (ISBN 0-516-47473-1). Childrens.
Rice, Gini. Relics of the Road. Incl. GMC Truck Gems, 1900-1950 (ISBN 0-8038-6326-8). 8.95 ea. Hastings.
--Relics of the Road: Impressive International Trucks, 1907-1947, Vol. 3. (Illus.). 174p. 1976. 8.95 (ISBN 0-8038-6335-7). Hastings.
Richards, Norman & Richards, Pat. Trucks & Supertrucks. LC 78-22350. (Illus.). (gr. 3-6). 1980. 8.95a (ISBN 0-385-14069-X); PLB (ISBN 0-385-14070-3). Doubleday.
Robinson, Jeff, ed. Chevrolet & GMC--4-Wheel Drive Maintenance: Blazer, Jimmy, Pickups & Suburbans, 1967-1979. (Illus.). pap. 7.95 (ISBN 0-89287-159-8, A230). Clymer Pubns.
--Datsun Service-Repair Handbook L521, P1521, P1620 Pickups, 1968-1980. new ed. (Illus.). pap. 10.95 (ISBN 0-89287-151-2, A-148). Clymer Pubns.
Rudman, Jack. Tractor-Trailer Operator. (Career Examination Ser.: C-1519). (Cloth bdg. avail. on request). pap. 8.00 (ISBN 0-8373-1519-0). Natl Learning.
Scott, Ed. Chevy Luv: 1972-1980--Service, Repair Handbook. (Illus.). pap. 10.95 (ISBN 0-89287-274-8, A145). Clymer Pubns.
Society of Automotive Engineers. Current Trends in Truck Suspensions. 1980. 15.00 (ISBN 0-89883-246-2). SAE.
Thomas, James H. The Long Haul: Truckers, Truck Stops, & Trucking. (Illus.). 12.95 (ISBN 0-87870-055-2); pap. 6.95 (ISBN 0-87870-057-9). Memphis St Univ.
Timms, Arthur W. Finding Out About Trucks. LC 80-14559. (Finding-Out Books). (Illus.). 96p. (gr. 4 up). 1980. PLB 7.95 (ISBN 0-89490-037-4). Enslow Pubs.
Toyota Pick-Ups Nineteen Seventy to Eighty-One. LC 80-70344. (Illus.). 224p. 1980. pap. 8.95 (ISBN 0-686-70876-8). Chilton.
Traister, John E. One Hundred & One Vantastic Ideas to Improve Your Van. (Illus.). 1979. 8.95 (ISBN 0-8306-9741-1); pap. 4.95 (ISBN 0-8306-1018-9, 1018). TAB Bks.
Truck Fire Protection Recommended Good Practices. (Five Hundred Ser). 1970. pap. 2.00 (ISBN 0-685-58224-8, 512). Natl Fire Prot.
Truck Transport (Wayside Amenities) 88p. 1980. pap. 12.00 (ISBN 92-833-1457-3, APO 84, APO). Unipub.
Type Designations, Areas of Use, Maintenance & Operation of Powered Industrial Trucks. (Five Hundred Ser). 1973. pap. 2.00 (ISBN 0-685-58223-X, 505). Natl Fire Prot.
Used Truck & Van Prices. rev. ed. (Vehicle Price Group Ser.). (Illus.). pap. 1.95 (ISBN 0-89552-005-2). DMR Pubns.
Vanderveen, Bart H. American Trucks of the Early Thirties. (Olyslager Auto Library). (Illus.). 63p. 1974. 10.95 (ISBN 0-686-76457-9, Pub. by Warne Pubs England). Motorbooks Intl.
--American Trucks of the Late Nineteen Thirties. 10.95 (ISBN 0-686-76458-7, Pub. by Warne Pubs England). Motorbooks Intl.
Vehicle Inspection Procedure Booklet & Forms. 3.50 (ISBN 0-686-31444-1); vehicle inspection forms 2.50 (ISBN 0-686-31445-X). Private Carrier.
Wagner, James K. Ford Trucks Since 1905. Dammann, George H., ed. LC 72-5765. (Automotive Ser.). (Illus.). 1978. 24.95 (ISBN 0-912612-10-X). Crestline.
Weiss, Harvey. Model Cars & Trucks & How to Build Them. LC 44-7403. (Illus.). 80p. (gr. 5 up). 1974. 10.95 (ISBN 0-690-00414-1, TYC-J). Har-Row.
Wren, James A. & Wren, Genevieve J. Motor Trucks of America. (Illus.). 1979. pap. 8.50 (ISBN 0-472-06313-8). U of Mich Pr.

MOTOR-TRUCKS–JUVENILE LITERATURE

Abrams, Kathleen S. & Abrams, Lawrence F. The Big Rigs: Trucks, Truckers, & Trucking. (Illus.). 64p. (gr. 4-6). PLB write for info. (ISBN 0-671-41897-1). Messner.
Cameron, Elizabeth. Big Book of Real Trucks. (Grosset Picture Bks.). (gr. 1-5). 1970. 2.95 (ISBN 0-448-02240-0). G&D.
Dorin, Patrick C. Yesterday's Trucks. (Superwheels & Thrill Sports Bks.). (Illus.). (gr. 4 up). 1981. PLB 6.95 (ISBN 0-8225-0502-9). Lerner Pubns.
Gibbons, Gail. Trucks. LC 81-43039. (Illus.). 32p. (ps-2). 1981. 8.95 (ISBN 0-690-04118-7, TYC-J); PLB 8.89 (ISBN 0-690-04119-5). Har-Row.
Graham, Kennon. My Little Book of Cars & Trucks. (Tell-a-Tale Readers). (Illus.). (gr. k-3). 1973. PLB 4.77 (ISBN 0-307-68473-3, Whitman). Western Pub.
Greene, Carla. Camioneros: Que Hacen? Belpre, Pura, tr. LC 69-14454. (Spanish I Can Read Books). Orig. Title: Truck Drivers: What Do They Do. (Illus., Span.). (gr. k-3). 1969. PLB 7.89 (ISBN 0-06-022100-3, HarpJ). Har-Row.
--Truck Drivers: What Do They Do. LC 67-4192. (I Can Read Books). (Illus.). (gr. k-3). 1967. PLB 7.89 (ISBN 0-06-022099-6, HarpJ). Har-Row.
Harrison, David. Let's Go, Trucks! (Illus.). 24p. (gr. k-2). 1976. PLB 5.00 (ISBN 0-307-60185-4, Golden Pr). Western Pub.
Kelley, Ken. Pickup Parade. rev. ed. LC 67-17967. (Illus.). (YA) 1969. pap. 6.95 (ISBN 0-910390-07-X). Auto Bk.

McNaught, Harry. The Truck Book. LC 77-79851. (Picturebacks Ser.). (ps-2). 1978. pap. 1.25 (ISBN 0-394-83703-7, BYR); PLB 4.99 (ISBN 0-394-93703-1). Random.
--Trucks. LC 79-63901. (Shape Bks.). (Illus.). (ps-1). 1979. 2.50 (ISBN 0-394-84268-5). Random.
--Trucks. LC 75-36463. (Illus.). 14p. (ps-1). 1976. 2.95 (ISBN 0-394-83240-X). Random.
Malone, Tyrone. The Million Dollar Truck Display. (Adventures of Tyrone Malone Ser.). (Illus.). (gr. 4 up). 1981. PLB 10.60 (ISBN 0-516-01863-9). Childrens.
--Super Boss: King of Diesel Truck Drag Racing. (Adventures of Tyrone Malone Ser.). (Illus.). (gr. 4 up). 1981. PLB 10.60 (ISBN 0-516-01861-2). Childrens.
Mann, Philip, ed. Camiones. Kreps, Georgian, tr. from Eng. (Shape Board Play Book). Orig. Title: Trucks. (Illus.). 14p. (Span.). (ps-3). 1981. bds. 3.50 plastic comb bdg (ISBN 0-89828-200-4, 5004SP). Tuffy Bks.
Marston, Hope I. Big Rigs. LC 79-21356. (Illus.). (gr. 1-4). 1980. PLB 5.95 (ISBN 0-396-07785-4). Dodd.
--Trucks, Trucking, & You. LC 78-7725. (Illus.). (gr. 5 up). 1978. 6.95 (ISBN 0-396-07602-5). Dodd.
Murray, Spence. Trucking Trends. LC 77-84296. (Pickups & Vans Ser.). (Illus., Orig.). (gr. 9-12). 1977. pap. 3.95 (ISBN 0-8227-5017-1). Petersen Pub.
Nineteen Seventy Eight New Truck & Van Prices. rev. ed. (Vehicle Price Group Ser.). 1977. pap. 1.95 (ISBN 0-89552-008-7). DMR Pubns.
Olson, Norman. I Can Read About Trucks & Cars. LC 72-96957. (Illus.). (gr. 2-4). 1973. pap. 1.25 (ISBN 0-89375-055-7). Troll Assocs.
Piper, Watty. Watty Piper's Trucks. LC 77-87558. (A Cricket Book). (Illus.). (gr. k-2). 1978. 1.95 (ISBN 0-448-46526-4). Platt.
Rich, Mark J. Diesel Trucks. LC 78-7345. (On the Move Ser.). (Illus.). (gr. 3-6). 1978. PLB 10.00 (ISBN 0-516-03881-8); pap. 2.95 (ISBN 0-516-43881-6). Childrens.
Robbins, Ken. Trucks of Every Sort. (Illus.). 48p. (gr. 2-4). 1981. lib. bdg. 8.95 (ISBN 0-517-54164-5). Crown.
Scarry, Richard, illus. Great Big Car & Truck Book. (ps-2). 1951. (Golden Pr); PLB 7.62 (ISBN 0-307-60473-X). Western Pub.
Schulz, Charles M. Snoopy's Facts & Fun Book About Trucks. LC 79-23616. (Snoopy's Facts & Fun Bks.). (Illus.). 40p. (ps-1). 1980. 2.95 (ISBN 0-394-84273-1); PLB 3.99 (ISBN 0-394-94273-6). Random.
Spizzirri, Peter M. History of the American Truck. (Illus.). 32p. (gr. 3-8). 1979. pap. 1.00 (ISBN 0-86545-018-8). Spizzirri.
Stambler, Irwin. Dream Machines: Vans & Pickups. (Illus.). 128p. (YA) (gr. 7-12). 1980. 8.95 (ISBN 0-399-20692-2). Putnam.
Stevens, Leonard A. The Trucks That Haul by Night. LC 66-10066. (Illus.). (gr. k-3). 1966. 8.79 (ISBN 0-690-83743-7, TYC-J). Har-Row.
Trucks. (Illus.). 8p. 1981. 1.50 (ISBN 0-8431-0710-3). Price Stern.
Witty, Susan. Golden Truck Book. (Golden Play & Learn Bks). (Illus.). (ps). 1969. 2.95 (ISBN 0-307-10738-8, Golden Pr). Western Pub.

MOTOR VEHICLE DRIVERS

see Highway Transport Workers; Motor Bus Drivers

MOTOR VEHICLE DRIVING

see also Automobile Driving

Liebers, Arthur. You Can Be a Professional Driver. LC 75-44019. (Vocations in Trades Ser.). (Illus.). 128p. (gr. 6 up). 1976. 6.75 (ISBN 0-688-41734-5); PLB 6.48 (ISBN 0-688-51734-X). Lothrop.

MOTOR VEHICLE OPERATORS

see Automobile Drivers

MOTOR VEHICLES

see also Automobiles; Ground-Effect Machines; Moon Cars; Motorcycles; Tracklaying Vehicles; Trafficability

Advances in Road Vehicle Aerodynamics. 1973. pap. 42.00 (ISBN 0-900983-26-4, Dist. by Air Science Co.). BHRA Fluid.
An Analysis of the Literature on Tire-Road Skid Resistance. 1973. 5.50 (ISBN 0-8031-0085-X, 04-541000-37). ASTM.
Ayres, Robert U. & McKenna, Richard P. Alternatives to the Internal Combustion Engine: Impacts on Environmental Quality. LC 74-181555. (Resources for the Future Ser). 340p. 1972. 22.50x (ISBN 0-8018-1369-7). Johns Hopkins.
Bekker, M. G. Introduction to Terrain-Vehicle Systems. LC 68-29272. (Illus.). 1969. 27.50 (ISBN 0-472-04144-4). U of Mich Pr.
Cole, Lee S. Handling Vehicle Theft Losses. 56p. (Orig.). 1979. pap. 4.00 (ISBN 0-939818-02-7). Lee Bks.
--The Investigation of Motor Vehicle Fires. 65p. 1980. pap. 5.00 (ISBN 0-939818-04-3). Lee Bks.
--Vehicle Identification: 1938-1968. 75p. 1980. pap. 5.00 (ISBN 0-939818-03-5). Lee Bks.
--Vehicle Identification: 1969-1982. 75p. (Orig.). Date not set. pap. 6.00 (ISBN 0-939818-05-1). Lee Bks.
The Corporation & the Motor Vehicle. LC 75-265. 10.00 (ISBN 0-87359-005-8). Northwood Inst.
Crouse, William H. Automotive Service Business: Operation & Management. 1972. pap. text ed. 10.95 (ISBN 0-07-014605-5, G). McGraw.
Crouse, William H. & Anglin, Donald L. Motor Vehicle Inspection. (Illus.). 1978. 17.95 (ISBN 0-07-014813-9, G); instructor's planning guide 2.00 (ISBN 0-07-014814-7); wkbk 5.95 (ISBN 0-07-014815-5). McGraw.
Dexler, Paul. Vans. LC 77-6181. (Superwheels & Thrill Sports Bks.). (Illus.). (gr. 3-9). 1977. PLB 6.95g (ISBN 0-8225-0415-4). Lerner Pubns.
Gibbs, H. G. & Richards, T. H., eds. Stress, Vibration & Noise Analysis in Vehicles. LC 75-14389. 1975. 68.95 (ISBN 0-470-29742-5). Halsted Pr.
Gould Editorial Staff. Vehicle Laws of Pennsylvania. Date not set. looseleaf 12.00 (ISBN 0-87526-233-3). Gould.
Gould Editorial Staff, ed. Motor Vehicle Laws of Michigan. 2nd ed. 300p. 1980. text ed. 9.00 (ISBN 0-87526-253-8). Gould.
Hallmark, Clayton. How to Install Everything Electronic in Cars, Boats, Planes, Trucks & RVs. (Illus.). 1978. 10.95 (ISBN 0-8306-9902-3); pap. 7.95 (ISBN 0-8306-1056-1, 1056). TAB Bks.
Hancock, Ralph. Super Machines. LC 78-2202. (Illus.). (gr. 4-9). 1978. 5.95 (ISBN 0-670-68446-5). Viking Pr.
Harrison, David, Jr. Who Pays for Clean Air: The Cost & Benefit Distribution of Federal Automobile Emission Standards. LC 75-22060. 192p. 1975. text ed. 20.00 (ISBN 0-88410-451-6). Ballinger Pub.
Hill, Harry G. Interpreting Automotive Systems. LC 75-19527. 1977. pap. 10.36 (ISBN 0-8273-1057-9); instructor's guide 1.60 (ISBN 0-8273-1058-7). Delmar.
Hurn, Richard W., ed. Approaches to Automotive Emissions Control. LC 74-22443. (ACS Symposium Ser.: No. 1). 1974. 15.50 (ISBN 0-8412-0212-5). Am Chemical.
Jane's Motor Veh. & Grnd. Supp. Equip. Date not set. 125.00x (ISBN 0-531-03954-4). Key Bk Serv.
Jensen, L. E., et al. Automotive Science. LC 76-3940. 1977. pap. 6.60 (ISBN 0-8273-1302-0); instructor's guide 1.60 (ISBN 0-8273-1303-9). Delmar.
Maintenance & Repair of Motor Vehicles. 7th ed. (Illus.). 1973. 9.00 (ISBN 92-2-100026-5). Intl Labour Office.
Miller, Denis N. & Vanderveen, Bart H. Wreckers & Recovery Vehicles. (Olyslager Auto Library). (Illus.). 74p. 1972. 11.95 (ISBN 0-7232-1466-2, Pub. by Warne Pubs England). Motorbooks Intl.
Newcomb, T. P. & Spurr, R. T. Braking of Road Vehicles. LC 68-73207. (Illus.). 1969. 12.95 (ISBN 0-8376-0031-6). Bentley.
Newton. Motor Vehicle. 10th ed. 1981. text ed. write for info. (ISBN 0-408-01118-1). Butterworth.
Patterson, D. J. & Henein, N. A. Emissions from Combustion Engines & Their Control. LC 72-77313. 360p. 1974. 30.00 (ISBN 0-250-97514-9). Ann Arbor Science.
Reizes, Haim. The Mechanics of Vehicle Collisions. (Illus.). 152p. 1973. 16.75 (ISBN 0-398-02639-4). C C Thomas.
Royal Academy of Engineering Sciences. The Motor Vehicle Nineteen Hundred & Eighty-Two Thousand. 1978. pap. 7.50x (ISBN 91-7082-153-4). Intl Pubns Serv.
Rudman, Jack. Motor Vehicle Dispatcher. (Career Examination Ser.: C-503). (Cloth bdg. avail. on request). pap. 8.00 (ISBN 0-8373-0503-9). Natl Learning.
--Motor Vehicle Inspector. (Career Examination Ser.: C-2384). (Cloth bdg. avail. on request). pap. 8.00 (ISBN 0-8373-2384-3). Natl Learning.
--Motor Vehicle Investigator. (Career Examination Ser.: C-504). (Cloth avail. on request). pap. 8.00 (ISBN 0-8373-0504-7). Natl Learning.
--Motor Vehicle License Examiner. (Career Examination Ser.: C-506). (Cloth bdg. avail. on request). pap. 8.00 (ISBN 0-8373-0506-3). Natl Learning.
--Motor Vehicle Officer. (Career Examination Ser.: C-2031). (Cloth bdg. avail. on request). pap. 8.00 (ISBN 0-8373-2031-3). Natl Learning.
Scibor-Rylski, A. J. Road Vehicle Aerodynamics. LC 74-26859. 213p. 1975. 38.95 (ISBN 0-470-75920-8); pap. 18.95x (ISBN 0-470-26655-4). Halsted Pr.
Society of Automotive Engineers. Vehicle Structured Mechanics, 3rd International Proceedings. 1979. 30.00 (ISBN 0-89883-053-2). SAE.
Stykolt, Stefan. Economic Analysis & Combines Policy: A Study of Intervention into the Canadian Market for Tires. LC 65-4198. 1965. 6.50x (ISBN 0-8020-3132-3). U of Toronto Pr.
Sully, F. K. Motor Vehicle Craft Studies: Principles, Vol. 1. 1974. text ed. 5.95 (ISBN 0-408-00133-X). Butterworth.
--Motor Vehicle Craft Studies: Workbook, Vol. 2. 1975. text ed. 4.50 (ISBN 0-408-00139-9). Butterworth.
--Motor Vehicle Mechanics Textbook. 4th ed. (Illus.). 1979. text ed. 13.95 (ISBN 0-408-00428-2). Butterworth.
U. S. Army Standard Military Motor Vehicles Nineteen Forty-Three. (Illus.). 556p. 1979. 25.00x (ISBN 0-905418-46-8). Intl Pubns Serv.
U.S. Army Standard Military Motor Vehicles, 1943. 560p. 1980. 55.00x (ISBN 0-905418-46-8, Pub. by Gresham England). State Mutual Bk.
Vanderveen, Bart H. The Observer's Army Vehicles Directory to 1940. (Illus.). 378p. 1974. 15.00 (ISBN 0-7232-1540-5, Pub. by Warne Pubs England). Motorbooks Intl.
--The Observer's Military Directory from 1945. (Illus.). 425p. 1972. 15.00 (ISBN 0-7232-1435-2, Pub. by Warne Pubs England). Motorbooks Intl.

MOTOR VEHICLES–EMISSION CONTROL DEVICES

see Motor Vehicles–Pollution Control Devices

MOTOR VEHICLES–EXHAUST CONTROL DEVICES

see Motor Vehicles–Pollution Control Devices

MOTOR VEHICLES–POLLUTION CONTROL DEVICES

Crouse, William H. & Anglin, Donald L. Automotive Emission Control. 2nd ed. (Automotive Technology Ser.). (Illus.). 1977. pap. text ed. 14.50 (ISBN 0-07-014640-3, G); wkbk. 6.25 (ISBN 0-07-014641-1); instrs planning guide 2.95 (ISBN 0-07-014642-X). McGraw.
Environmental Aspects of the Motor Vehicle & Its Use. (Industry Overview Ser.: No. 4). 1979. pap. 6.75 (ISBN 0-686-59760-5, UNEP 021, UNEP). Unipub.

MOTOR VEHICLES–RECREATIONAL USE

Anson, Mike. Customizing Your Pickup. (Illus.). 1977. pap. 5.95 (ISBN 0-8306-6972-8, 972). TAB Bks.
Barnes, F. A. Canyon Country Off-Road Vehicle Trails: Arches & la Sals Areas. new ed. LC 77-95043. (Canyon Country Ser.). (Illus.). 1978. pap. 2.50 (ISBN 0-915272-13-X). Wasatch Pubs.
Brickell, David & Cole, Lee S. Recreational Vehicle Identification. 150p. 1979. pap. 7.50 (ISBN 0-939818-01-9). Lee Bks.
Caravanning. 1976. pap. text ed. 2.50 (ISBN 0-8277-4852-3). British Bk Ctr.
Consumer Guide Editors. Van Ideas & Plans. 1979. 9.95 (ISBN 0-671-24864-2, Fireside); pap. 4.95 (ISBN 0-671-24821-9). S&S.
Coombs, Charles. Mopeding. (Illus.). (gr. 4-6). 1978. 6.95 (ISBN 0-688-22155-6); PLB 6.67 (ISBN 0-688-32155-0). Morrow.
Ebershoff-Coles, Susan & Leibenguth, Charla, eds. Motorsports: A Guide to Information Sources. LC 79-13736. (Sports, Games, & Pastimes Information Guide Ser.: Vol. 5). 1979. 36.00 (ISBN 0-8103-1446-0). Gale.
Engel, Lyle K. The Complete Book of Motor Camping. rev. ed. Vainder, Martin, ed. LC 78-7542. 1979. pap. 2.95 (ISBN 0-668-02916-1, 2916). Arco.
Four by Four & of Road Vehicles Editors. The Giant Book of Four by Four's & off-Road Vehicles. (Modern Automotive Ser.). (Illus.). 1979. 12.95 (ISBN 0-8306-9831-0); pap. 10.95 (ISBN 0-8306-2049-4, 2049). TAB Bks.
Gill, Herb. Electrical Handbook for RVs, Campers, Vans, Boats & Trailers. (Illus.). 1978. 7.95 (ISBN 0-8306-8867-6); pap. 3.95 (ISBN 0-8306-7867-0, 867). TAB Bks.
Hull, Clinton. How to Build Recreation Vehicles. LC 77-4441. (Illus.). 1977. 9.95 (ISBN 0-87593-077-8). Trail-R.
--How to Choose, Buy & Enjoy Recreation Vehicles. (Illus.). 1980. 8.95 (ISBN 0-87593-003-4). Trail-R.
Lidz, Jane. Rolling Homes: Handmade Houses on Wheels. LC 78-72506. (Illus.). 1979. 14.95 (ISBN 0-89104-128-1); pap. 7.95 (ISBN 0-89104-129-X). A & W Pubs.
Motor Sport. 1976. pap. 2.50 (ISBN 0-8277-4890-6). British Bk Ctr.
Murray, Spence, ed. Vanning Trends. LC 77-84297. (Pickups & Vans Ser.). (Illus., Orig.). 1977. pap. 3.95 (ISBN 0-8227-5015-5). Petersen Pub.
Myhill, Henry. Motor Caravanning: A Complete Guide. (Illus.). 160p. 1976. 9.75 (ISBN 0-7063-5086-3). Transatlantic.
Nulsen, David R. & Nulsen, Robert H. More Miles...Less Gas with Your Recreation Vehicle. LC 74-2042. 143p. 1975. pap. 3.95 (ISBN 0-87593-029-8). Trail-R.
Nulsen, Robert & Nulsen, David. How to Drive, Pull & Travel in RV's. LC 77-839. (Illus.). 1977. 6.95 (ISBN 0-87593-019-0). Trail-R.
--Mobile Home & Recreation Vehicle Encyclopedia. (Illus.). 1978. 17.95 (ISBN 0-685-82639-2). Trail-R.
Peterson, Franklynn & Kesselman, Judi R. The Do-It-Yourself Custom Van Book. LC 76-55657. (Illus.). 1977. o. p. 14.95 (ISBN 0-8092-7851-0); pap. 6.95 (ISBN 0-8092-7904-5). Contemp Bks.
Recreational Vehicles. (Five Hundred Ser.). 96p. 1974. pap. 3.75 (ISBN 0-685-46038-X, 501C). Natl Fire Prot.
Robinson, Jeff, ed. Recreational Vehicle Maintenance. (Illus.). 232p. pap. text ed. 8.95 (ISBN 0-89287-081-8, X930). Clymer Pubns.
RV Buyer's Catalog. 1980. pap. 5.95 (ISBN 0-671-25315-8). Woodall.
Thompson, John & Trailer Life Editors. Trailer Life's RV Repair & Maintenance Manual: The Most Comprehensive & Authoritative Technical Guide Ever Published for RVers. LC 79-66970. (Illus.). 1980. 12.98 (ISBN 0-934798-00-1); pap. 10.98 (ISBN 0-686-25972-6). TL Enterprises.
Van World Editors. Do-It-Yourselfer's Guide to Van Conversion. (Illus.). 1977. 8.95 (ISBN 0-8306-7992-8); pap. 6.95 (ISBN 0-8306-6992-2, 992). TAB Bks.
--Super Vans. (Illus.). 1977. 8.95 (ISBN 0-8306-8993-1); pap. 4.95 (ISBN 0-8306-7993-6, 993). TAB Bks.
Woodall's RV How to Guide. 1980. pap. 4.95 (ISBN 0-671-25520-7). Woodall.

MOTOR VEHICLES–SMOG CONTROL DEVICES

see Motor Vehicles–Pollution Control Devices

MOTOR VEHICLES IN WAR

see Tanks (Military Science)

MOTORCYCLE RACING

see also Racing

Bailey, Gary & Shipman, Carl. How to Win Motocross. LC 73-92958. (Illus.). 192p. 1974. pap. 5.95 (ISBN 0-912656-16-6). H P Bks.
Batson, Larry. Evel Knievel. LC 74-18302. (Sports Superstars Ser). (Illus.). 32p. (gr. 3-6). 1974. PLB 5.95 (ISBN 0-87191-385-2); pap. 2.75 o. p. (ISBN 0-89812-191-4). Creative Ed.
Briggs, Barry. Trackin' with Briggo. (Briggo Motorcycle Racing Library: No. 4). (Illus.). 128p. 1975. 12.95 (ISBN 0-285-62206-4, Pub. by Souvenir). Scholium Intl.
Carrick, Peter. Encyclopaedia of Motor-Cycle Sport. LC 76-62754. (Illus.). 224p. 1977. 10.00 (ISBN 0-312-24867-9). St Martin.
--Great Moments in Sport: Motor Cycle Racing. (Illus.). 1977. 16.95 (ISBN 0-7207-0972-5). Transatlantic.
--Hell Raisers. (Illus.). 173p. 1974. 8.75 (ISBN 0-7207-0668-8). Transatlantic.
Edmonds, I. G. BMX! Bicycle Motocross for Beginners. LC 79-4311. (Illus.). (gr. 7 up). 1979. 7.95 (ISBN 0-03-044321-0). HR&W.
--Motorcycle Racing for Beginners. (Illus.). (gr. 7-9). 1980. pap. 1.75 (ISBN 0-671-29898-4). PB.
--Motorcycle Racing for Beginners. LC 77-6273. (gr. 6 up). 1977. 6.95 (ISBN 0-03-017686-7). HR&W.
Gianatsis, Jim. Design & Tuning for Motocross. LC 80-28239. (Illus.). 128p. (Orig.). 1981. pap. write for info. (ISBN 0-87938-129-9). Motorbooks Intl.
Hudson-Evans, Richard. The Handbook of Motorcycle Sport. LC 78-2771. (Illus.). 1978. 11.95 (ISBN 0-668-04629-5, 4629). Arco.
Jonzier, Bernard. Motorcross. Bernard, Jack, tr. (Illus.). Date not set. 8.95 (ISBN 0-8120-5218-8). Barron.
Mauger, Ivan & Oakes, Peter, eds. Ivan Mauger's Speedway Spectacular. (Illus.). 136p. 1976. 11.50 (ISBN 0-7207-0780-3). Transatlantic.
Partridge, Michael. Motorcycle Pioneers: The Man, the Machines, the Events, 1860-1930. LC 76-12553. 1977. 8.95 (ISBN 0-668-04035-1). Arco.
Perry, Robin. The Trials Motorcyclist: The How to Buy, Equip, & Ride It in Observed Trials. (Illus.). 192p. 1975. 5.95 (ISBN 0-517-51880-5). Crown.
Pritchard, Anthony. The Motor Racing Year, No. 4. (Illus.). 1973. 8.95 (ISBN 0-393-08677-1). Norton.
Puleo, Nicole. Motorcycle Racing. LC 72-5421. (Superwheels & Thrill Sports Bks.). (Illus.). 48p. (gr. 3-6). 1973. PLB 6.95g (ISBN 0-8225-0401-4). Lerner Pubns.
Racing Motorcycles. LC 77-88442. (Illus.). 1978. pap. 6.95 (ISBN 0-528-88173-6). Rand.
Radlauer, Ed. Some Basics About Motorcycles. LC 78-5277. (Gemini Books Ser.). (Illus.). (gr. 3-12). 1978. PLB 9.25 (ISBN 0-516-07683-3, Elk Grove Bks); pap. 2.95 (ISBN 0-516-47683-1). Childrens.
Rae, Rusty. The World's Biggest Motorcycle Race: The Daytona 200. LC 77-92297. (Superwheels & Thrill Sports Bks.). (Illus.). (gr. 4-9). 1978. PLB 6.95g (ISBN 0-8225-0422-7). Lerner Pubns.

Seaver, David-Linn. Moto-Cross Racing. LC 78-38590. (Speed Sports Ser.). (Illus.). (gr. 9 up). 1972. 6.50 (ISBN 0-397-31294-6). Lippincott.

Spence, Jim & Brown, Gar. Motorcycle Racing in America: A Definitive Look at the Sport. LC 74-6144. (Illus.). 144p. 1977. pap. 4.95 (ISBN 0-87955-418-5). O'Hara.

Whyte, Norrie. Motor Cycle Racing Champions. LC 75-295936. 1976. 7.95 (ISBN 0-668-03910-8). Arco.

Yaw, John. Grand National Championship Races. LC 77-92293. (Superwheels & Thrill Sports Bks.). (Illus.). (gr. 4-9). 1978. PLB 6.95 (ISBN 0-8225-0424-3). Lerner Pubns.

--Motocross Motorcycle Racing. LC 77-92298. (Superwheels & Thrill Sports Bks.). (Illus.). (gr. 4-9). 1978. PLB 6.95g (ISBN 0-8225-0423-5). Lerner Pubns.

MOTORCYCLES

see also Mopeds; Motor Scooters; Motorcycling; also names of motorcycles, e.g. B.S.A. motorcycle, Honda motorcycle

Alth, Max. Motorcycles & Motorcycling. (First Bks.). (Illus.). (gr. 4 up). 1979. PLB 6.90 s&l (ISBN 0-531-02945-X). Watts.

Arctander, Erik. New Book of Motorcycles. LC 68-54470. (Illus.). 1968. Repr. of 1968 ed. lib. bdg. 3.50 (ISBN 0-668-01813-5). Arco.

Arman, Michael P. How to Buy a Used Motorcycle & Not Get Burned--Maybe. (Illus.). 1979. pap. 4.95 (ISBN 0-87799-064-6). Aztex.

Caddell, Laurie. Modern Motor Bikes. (Illus.). 1979. 12.50 (ISBN 0-7137-0989-8, Pub by Blandford Pr England). Sterling.

--Powerbikes. (Illus.). 160p. 1981. 19.95 (ISBN 0-7137-1021-7, Pub. by Blandford Pr England). Sterling.

Caddell, Laurie & Winfield, Mike. Superbikes. (Orig.). 1981. pap. 9.95 (ISBN 0-89586-067-8). H P Bks.

Clifford, Peter, ed. Motocourse 1980-1981, No. 5. (Illus.). 208p. 1981. 36.95 (ISBN 0-905138-14-7, Pub. by Hazelton England). Motorbooks Intl.

Croucher, Robert M. The Observer's Book of Motorcycles. (Illus.). 192p. 1976. 3.95 (ISBN 0-7232-1572-3, Pub. by Warne Pubs England). Motorbooks Intl.

--The Observer's Book of Motorcycles. (Illus.). 1977. 3.95 (ISBN 0-684-14951-6, ScribT). Scribner.

Dempsey, Paul. Moped Repair Handbook. (Illus.). 1977. 9.95 (ISBN 0-8306-7976-6); pap. 7.95 (ISBN 0-8306-6976-0, 976). TAB Bks.

Dunster, Mark. Motorcyles. LC 77-155954. (Rin: Pt. 7). 1978. pap. 4.00 (ISBN 0-89642-006-X). Linden Pubs.

Edmonds, I. G. Motorcycling for Beginners. LC 74-183864. (Illus.). 192p. (gr. 7 up). 1972. PLB 7.61 (ISBN 0-8255-3007-5). Macrae.

Felsen, Henry G. Living with Your First Motorcycle. 1977. pap. 2.25 (ISBN 0-425-03300-7, Windhover). Berkley Pub.

Felson, Henry G. Living with Your First Motorcycle. LC 75-29401. (Illus.). 96p. (gr. 6-8). 1976. 7.95 (ISBN 0-399-20488-1). Putnam.

Forsdyke, G. Questions & Answers on Motorcycles. pap. 3.95 (ISBN 0-408-00232-8, NB 23, Pub. by Newnes-Technical). Hayden.

Griffin, John Q. Motorcycles on the Move. LC 75-17435. (Superwheels & Thrill Sports Bks.). (Illus.). 52p. (gr. 5-10). 1976. PLB 6.95g (ISBN 0-8225-0414-6). Lerner Pubns.

Griffin, Michael M. Motorcycles: From the Inside Out (& How to Keep Them Right Side up) (Illus.). 1978. ref. ed. 12.95 (ISBN 0-13-604041-1); pap. text ed. 9.95 (ISBN 0-13-604033-0). P-H.

Hartley, Peter. The Ariel Story. (Illus.). 316p. (Orig.). 1980. pap. 17.50x (ISBN 0-85242-681-X). Intl Pubns Serv.

--Brooklands Bikes in the Twenties. (Illus.). 244p. (Orig.). 1980. pap. 17.50x (ISBN 0-85242-620-8). Intl Pubns Serv.

Hatmon, Paul W. Yesterday's Motorcycles. (Superwheels & Thrill Sports Bks.). (Illus.). (YA) (gr. 4 up). 1981. PLB cancelled (ISBN 0-8225-0429-4). Lerner Pubns.

Hough, Richard & Setright, L. J. History of the World's Motorcycles. rev. ed. LC 72-9123. (Illus.). 208p. (YA) 1973. 12.95 (ISBN 0-06-011967-5, HarpT). Har-Row.

Houlgate, Deke. All About Motorcycles. (gr. 7 up). 1976. pap. 1.25 (ISBN 0-590-00485-9, Schol Pap). Schol Bk Serv.

Jennings, Gordon. Motorcycles. LC 79-15294. (Illus.). (gr. 7 up). 1979. PLB 8.95 (ISBN 0-13-604009-8). P-H.

Kaysing, Bill. Fell's Beginner's Guide to Motorcycling. LC 76-17052. 180p. 1976. 8.95 (ISBN 0-8119-0272-2); pap. 4.95 (ISBN 0-8119-0365-6). Fell.

Kosbab, William H. Dictionary of Motorcycle Terminology. McFadden, S. Michele, ed. 300p. (Orig.). 1981. pap. text ed. 14.95 (ISBN 0-89262-044-7). Career Pub.

Macauley, Ted. The Yamaha Legend. 248p. 1980. 15.95 (ISBN 0-312-89609-3). St Martin.

Mosher, Lynn S. & Lear, George. Motorcycle Mechanics. (Illus.). 272p. 1977. 17.95 (ISBN 0-13-604090-X). P-H.

Murray, Jerry. Mo-Ped: The Wonder Vehicle. LC 76-18937. (Illus.). (gr. 5 up). 1976. 6.95 (ISBN 0-399-20540-3). Putnam.

--Moped: The Wonder Vehicle. (gr. 7-9). 1978. pap. 1.25 (ISBN 0-671-29882-8). Archway.

Naden, C. J. Cycle Chase, the Championship Season. LC 79-64638. (Illus.). 32p. (gr. 4-9). 1980. PLB 6.89 (ISBN 0-89375-249-5); pap. 2.50 (ISBN 0-89375-263-0). Troll Assocs.

--High Gear. LC 79-64637. (Illus.). 32p. (gr. 4-9). 1980. PLB 6.89 (ISBN 0-89375-248-7); pap. 2.50 (ISBN 0-89375-262-2). Troll Assocs.

--I Can Read About Motorcycles. new ed. LC 78-74657. (Illus.). (gr. 3-6). 1979. pap. 1.25 (ISBN 0-89375-212-6). Troll Assocs.

Olney, Ross R. Modern Motorcycle Superstars. LC 79-72021. (High Interest-Low Vocabulary Ser.). (Illus.). (gr. 4-9). 1980. 5.95 (ISBN 0-396-07786-2). Dodd.

Page, Victor W. Early Motorcycles: Construction, Operation, Service. LC 71-158128. (Illus.). 1971. pap. 16.00 (ISBN 0-911160-62-0). Post-Era.

Partridge, Michael. Motorcycle Pioneers: The Man, the Machines, the Events, 1860-1930. LC 76-12553. 1977. 8.95 (ISBN 0-668-04035-1). Arco.

Paulsen, Gary. Track, Enduro, & Motocross--Unless You Fall Over. LC 78-21022. (Sports on the Light Side Ser.). (Illus.). (gr. 4-6). 1979. PLB 10.65 (ISBN 0-8172-0181-5). Raintree Pubs.

Radlauer, Ed. Minibike Racing. LC 80-12627. (Ready, Get Set, Go Ser.). (Illus.). 32p. (gr. 1-6). 1980. PLB 9.25 (ISBN 0-516-07776-7, Elk Grove Bks.); pap. 2.95 (ISBN 0-516-47776-5). Childrens.

--Motorcyclopedia. LC 72-92678. (Illus.). (gr. 3-12). 1973. 4.50 (ISBN 0-8372-0298-1); pap. 3.31 (ISBN 0-8372-0885-8). Bowmar-Noble.

--Motorcyclopedia Teaching Program. (Illus.). (gr. 4 up). 1973. tchr's guide 2.25 (ISBN 0-8372-0887-4, 887). Bowmar-Noble.

--Motorcyclopedia Tech Log. (Illus.). (gr. 4 up). 1973. 12.00, set of ten (ISBN 0-8372-1891-8). Bowmar-Noble.

Radlauer, Ed & Radlauer, Ruth. Chopper Cycle Mania. LC 80-12261. (Mania Bks.). (Illus.). 32p. (gr. k-5). 1980. PLB 9.25 (ISBN 0-516-07779-1, Elk Grove Bks.); pap. 2.95 (ISBN 0-516-47779-X). Childrens.

Redman, Martin. Superbike: Modern High Performance Motorcycles. LC 74-15847. (Illus.). 120p. (YA) 1975. 9.95 (ISBN 0-06-013558-1, HarpT). Har-Row.

Renstrom, Richard. Motorcycle Milestones, Vol. 1. LC 80-66669. (Illus.). 112p. 1980. 20.00 (ISBN 0-936660-00-7); pap. 15.00 (ISBN 0-936660-01-5). Classics Unltd.

Renstrom, Richard C. Great Motorcycle Legends. (Illus.). 1977. pap. 9.95 (ISBN 0-87799-057-3). Aztex.

Rich, Mark. Custom Cycles. LC 80-26659. (On the Move Ser.). (Illus.). 48p. (gr. 3-6). 1981. PLB 10.00 (ISBN 0-516-03887-7); pap. 2.95 (ISBN 0-516-43887-5). Childrens.

Robb, Loren. Bikes. 1974. 8.70x (ISBN 0-7233-0399-1). Intl Pubns Serv.

Sagnier, Thierry. Bike! Motorcycles & the People Who Ride Them. LC 72-9151. (Illus.). 208p. 1974. (HarpT); (HarpT). Har-Row.

Sequeira, M. S. Motorcycles. LC 78-5963. (Easy-Read Fact Bks). (Illus.). (gr. 2-4). 1978. PLB 6.90 s&l (ISBN 0-531-01373-1). Watts.

Setright, L. J. Bahnstormer: The Story of BMW Motorcycles. (Illus.). 1978. 18.50 (ISBN 0-85184-021-3, Pub. by Transport Bookman Pubns. Ltd. England). Motorbooks Intl.

--Motorcycling Facts & Feats. 258p. 1980. 17.95 (ISBN 0-8069-9232-8, Pub. by Guinness Superlatives England). Sterling.

Shipman, Carl. The Boonie Book. 2nd ed. LC 73-93781. (Illus.). 192p. 1974. pap. 5.95 (ISBN 0-912656-17-4). H P Bks.

Smith, Philip H. & Morrison, John C. Scientific Design of Exhaust & Intake Systems. 3rd rev. ed. LC 72-86569. (Illus.). 294p. 1972. 12.95 (ISBN 0-8376-0309-9). Bentley.

Sparks, James C. Mini & Trail Bikes: How to Build Them Yourself. (Illus.). 1976. 9.95 (ISBN 0-87690-184-4). Dutton.

Stambler, Irwin. Minibikes & Small Cycles. (Illus.). (gr. 6-8). 1977. PLB 6.59 (ISBN 0-399-61055-3). Putnam.

Stone, Mike. Mopedaller's Handy Manual. (Modern Automotive Ser.). (Illus.). 1978. pap. 2.25 (ISBN 0-8306-2044-3, 2044). TAB Bks.

Tardy, Gene & Jackson, Al. Motorcycle: Cross-Country Racing. (Sports Action Ser.). (Illus.). (gr. 3-7). 1974. PLB 5.51 (ISBN 0-914844-00-8). J Alden.

--Motorcycle: Grand Prix Racing. (Sports Action Ser.). (Illus.). (gr. 3-7). 1974. PLB 5.51 (ISBN 0-914844-01-6). J Alden.

--Motorcycle: Moto-Cross Racing. (Sports Action Ser.). (Illus.). (gr. 3-7). 1974. PLB 5.51 (ISBN 0-914844-02-4). J Alden.

Thompson, Eric E. Motor Cycles in Color. (Color Ser.). (Illus.). 1974. 9.95 (ISBN 0-7137-0711-9, Pub. by Blandford Pr England). Sterling.

Vanderveen, Bart H. Motorcycles & Scooters from Nineteen Forty-Five. (Illus.). 64p. 1972. 10.95 (ISBN 0-686-76461-7, Pub. by Warne Pubs England). Motorbooks Intl.

Wilkinson-Latham, Robert. Cycles in Color. (Illus.). 1978. 11.95 (ISBN 0-7137-0853-0, Pub. by Blandford Pr England). Sterling.

Woollett, Mick. Lightweight Bikes. (Illus.). 64p. 1981. pap. 5.95 (ISBN 0-686-69617-4, Pub. by Batsford England). David & Charles.

Wright, Chris & Bisson, Roy. Motorcycling Fundamentals. (Fundamentals: A Series on Getting It Right First Time). (Illus.). 80p. (Orig.). 1979. pap. 10.25 (ISBN 0-589-50081-3, Pub. by Reed Books Australia). C E Tuttle.

Zonker, Patricia. Murdercycles. LC 78-12855. (Illus.). 1978. 14.95 (ISBN 0-88229-553-5); pap. 8.95 (ISBN 0-88229-610-8). Nelson-Hall.

MOTORCYCLES–MAINTENANCE AND REPAIR

Arman, Mike. Motorcycle Electrics Without Pain. (Illus.). 1980. pap. 8.00 (ISBN 0-933078-03-X). M Arman.

B M W Bavaria Owners Workshop Manual: 3.0 Thru '77. new ed. (Owners Workshop Manuals Ser.: No. 348). 1979. 10.95 (ISBN 0-85696-348-8, Pub. by J H Haynes England). Haynes Pubns.

Bacon, Roy. The Motorcycle Manual. 1977. pap. 12.50 (ISBN 0-408-00260-3). Transatlantic.

Brotherwood, Clive. Honda Owner's Workshop Manual: One Hundred & One Twenty-Five Singles '70-75. new ed. (Owners Workshop Manuals Ser.: No. 188). 1979. 8.50 (ISBN 0-85696-188-4, Pub. by J H Haynes England). Haynes Pubns.

--Triumph Owners Workshop Manual: Three-Fifty, Five Hundred Twins '53 on. new ed. (Owners Workshop Manuals Ser.: No. 137). 1979. 8.50 (ISBN 0-85696-137-X, Pub. by J H Haynes England). Haynes Pubns.

Chilton Book Company Auto. Ed. Dept. Chilton's Motorcycle Troubleshooting Guide. 2nd ed. LC 77-121. 1977. pap. 7.95 (ISBN 0-8019-6587-X, 6587). Chilton.

Chilton's Automotive Ed. Dept. Chilton's Repair & Tune-Up Guide for Honda 350-550, 1972-1977. LC 77-89115. (Chilton's Repair & Tune-up Guides). (Illus., Orig.). 1977. pap. 8.95 (ISBN 0-8019-6603-5, 6603). Chilton.

--Chilton's Repair & Tune-up Guide for Honda 750 1969-1977. LC 76-57321. (Chilton's Repair & Tune-up Guides). (Illus., Orig.). 1977. pap. 8.95 (ISBN 0-8019-6589-6, 6598). Chilton.

--Chilton's Repair & Tune-up Guide for Yamaha 360-400 1976-78. (Repair & Tune-up Guides Ser.). (Illus.). 1978. pap. 8.95 (ISBN 0-8019-6738-4). Chilton.

Chilton's Automotive Editorial Department. Chilton's Repair & Tune-up Guide, Bronco 1966-1973. LC 74-2472. (Illus.). 1974. 8.95 (ISBN 0-8019-5920-9); pap. 8.95 (ISBN 0-8019-5921-7). Chilton.

--Chilton's Repair & Tune-up Guide for Audi, 1970-1973. (Illus.). 190p. 1973. 8.95 (ISBN 0-8019-5864-4); pap. 8.95 (ISBN 0-8019-5902-0). Chilton.

--Chilton's Repair & Tune-up Guide for BMW Motorcycle Through 1972. LC 72-8340. (Illus.). 150p. 1973. 8.95 (ISBN 0-8019-5738-9); pap. 8.95 (ISBN 0-8019-6049-5). Chilton.

--Chilton's Repair & Tune-up Guide for International Scout, 1967-1973: International Scout. LC 74-5077. (Illus.). 200p. 1974. 8.95 (ISBN 0-8019-5878-4); pap. 8.95 (ISBN 0-8019-5912-8). Chilton.

--Chilton's Repair & Tune-up Guide for Moto Guzzi, 1966-1972. LC 73-17292. (Illus.). 224p. 1973. 8.95 (ISBN 0-8019-5866-0); pap. 8.95 (ISBN 0-8019-5908-X). Chilton.

--Chilton's Repair & Tune-up Guide for Norton 750 & 850, 1966-1973. LC 73-16164. (Illus.). 224p. 1973. 8.95 (ISBN 0-8019-5816-4); pap. 8.95 (ISBN 0-8019-5913-6). Chilton.

--Chilton's Repair & Tune-up Guide for Yamaha Enduros, 1968-1974. (Illus.). 1975. 8.95 (ISBN 0-8019-6085-1); pap. 8.95 (ISBN 0-8019-6086-X). Chilton.

Chilton's Automotive Editorial Dept. Chilton's Motorcycle Owner's Handbook. (Illus.). 1979. 10.95 (ISBN 0-8019-6894-1); pap. 8.95 (ISBN 0-8019-6867-4, 795). Chilton.

Chilton's Automotive Editorial Dept., ed. Chilton's Motorcycle Repair Manual. 2nd ed. LC 74-9342. (Illus.). 1976. 22.95 (ISBN 0-8019-6509-8). Chilton.

Chilton's Automotive Editorial Dept. Yamaha Six Fifty, Nineteen Seventy to Seventy-Nine. (Chilton's Repair & Tune-Up Guides). (Illus.). 1979. pap. 8.95 (ISBN 0-8019-6895-X, 6895). Chilton.

Chilton's Motorcycle Repair Manual 1981. (Illus.). 1248p. 24.95 (ISBN 0-8019-7077-6). Chilton.

Chilton's Repair & Tune-up Guide for Honda 350-360, 1968-77: Motorcycle. (Repair & Tune-up Guides Ser.). (Illus.). 1978. pap. 8.95 (ISBN 0-8019-6705-8). Chilton.

Chilton's Repair & Tune-up Guide for Kawasaki 900-1000, 1973-1977. (Repair & Tune-up Guides Ser.). (Illus.). 1978. pap. 8.95 (ISBN 0-8019-6605-1). Chilton.

Clew, Jeff. B.S.A Owner's Workshop Manual: A7-A10 Thru '63. (Owners Workshop Manuals Ser.: No. 121). 1979. 8.50 (ISBN 0-85696-121-3, Pub. by J H Haynes England). Haynes Pubns.

--Bultaco Owner's Workshop Manual: Competition Bikes '72-75. new ed. (Owners Workshop Manuals Ser.: No. 219). 1979. 8.50 (ISBN 0-85696-219-8, Pub. by J H Haynes England). Haynes Pubns.

--Harley Davidson Owners Workshop Manual: Sportster '75 on. new ed. (Owners Workshop Manuals Ser.: No. 250). 1979. 8.50 (ISBN 0-85696-250-3, Pub. by J H Haynes England). Haynes Pubns.

--Honda Owner's Workshop Manual: Fifty Ohv & Ohc '63-71. new ed. (Owners Workshop Manuals Ser.: No. 114). 1979. 8.50 (ISBN 0-85696-114-0, Pub. by J H Haynes England). Haynes Pubns.

--Honda Owner's Workshop Manual: One Twenty-Five to Two Hundred Twins '64-78. new ed. (Owners Workshop Manuals Ser.: No. 067). 1979. 8.50 (ISBN 0-900550-67-8, Pub. by J H Haynes England). Haynes Pubns.

--Honda Owner's Workshop Manual: Seven-Fifty 4 Cyl '70-79. new ed. (Owners Workshop Manuals Ser.: No. 131). 1979. 8.50 (ISBN 0-85696-131-0, Pub. by J H Haynes England). Haynes Pubns.

--Honda Owner's Workshop Manual: Sixty-Five, Seventy, Ninety Ohv & Ohc '64-73. new ed. (Owners Workshop Manuals Ser.: No. 116). 1979. 8.50 (ISBN 0-85696-116-7, Pub. by J H Haynes England). Haynes Pubns.

--Honda Owner's Workshop Manual: Two Fifty Elsinor '73-75. new ed. (Owners Workshop Manuals Ser.: No. 217). 1979. 8.50 (ISBN 0-85696-217-1, Pub. by J H Haynes England). Haynes Pubns.

--Honda Owner's Workshop Manual: Xl 250, 350 '72-75. new ed. (Owners Workshop Manuals Ser.: No. 209). 1979. 8.50 (ISBN 0-85696-209-0, Pub. by J H Haynes England). Haynes Pubns.

--Norton Owners Workshop Manual: Commando 750, 850 '68 on. new ed. (Owners Workshop Manuals Ser.: No. 125). 1979. 8.50 (ISBN 0-85696-125-6, Pub. by J H Haynes England). Haynes Pubns.

--Suzuki Owners Workshop Manual: Two-Fifty, Three-Fifty Twins '65 on. new ed. (Owners Workshop Manuals Ser.: No. 120). 1979. 8.50 (ISBN 0-85696-120-5, Pub. by J H Haynes England). Haynes Pubns.

--Triumph Owners Workshop Manual: PRE Unit Twins Thru '62. new ed. (Owners Workshop Manuals Ser.: No. 251). 1979. 8.50 (ISBN 0-85696-251-1, Pub. by J H Haynes England). Haynes Pubns.

--Triumph Owners Workshop Manual: Six-Fifty, Seven-Fifty Twins '62 on. new ed. (Owners Workshop Manuals Ser.: No. 122). 1979. 8.50 (ISBN 0-85696-122-1, Pub. by J H Haynes England). Haynes Pubns.

--Velocette Owners Workshop Manual: 350, 500 Singles Thru '70. new ed. (Owners Workshop Manuals Ser.: No. 186). 1979. 8.50 (ISBN 0-85696-186-8, Pub. by J H Haynes England). Haynes Pubns.

--Yamaha Owners Workshop Manual: TX & XS 500 Twins '73 on. new ed. (Owners Workshop Manuals Ser.: No. 308). 1978. 8.50 (ISBN 0-85696-308-9, Pub. by J H Haynes England). Haynes Pubns.

Clymer Publications. Bultaco Service Repair Handbook: 125-370cc, Through 1977. (Illus.). pap. 9.95 (ISBN 0-89287-174-1, M303). Clymer Pubns.

--Honda Service-Repair Handbook: 750cc Fours, 1969-1978. Jorgensen, Eric, ed. (Illus.). pap. 9.95 (ISBN 0-89287-167-9, M341). Clymer Pubns.

--Yamaha Service Repair Handbook: 80-175cc Enduro & Motocross, 1968-1978. (Illus.). 1979. pap. text ed. 9.95 (ISBN 0-89287-235-7, M410). Clymer Pubns.

--Yamaha: 250-500cc Enduro & Motocross, 1968-78, Service, Repair, Performance. 3rd ed. Jorgensen, Eric, ed. (Illus.). pap. 9.95 (ISBN 0-89287-276-4, M415). Clymer Pubns.

Clymer Publications, ed. Bridgestone Singles & Tweins, 50-175cc. (Illus.). 1967. pap. 3.50 (ISBN 0-89287-245-4, M301). Clymer Pubns.

Clymer Pubns. Suzuki: 380-750cc Triples, 1972-1977 Service, Repair, Maintenance. (Illus.). 1977. pap. write for info. (ISBN 0-89287-285-3, M368). Clymer Pubns.

Collett, George. Honda Owner's Workshop Manual: Four-Fifty Twins '66-78. new ed. (Owners Workshop Manuals Ser.: No. 211). 1979. 8.50 (ISBN 0-85696-211-2, Pub. by J H Haynes England). Haynes Pubns.

--Kawasaki Owners Workshop Manual: 900zi & Zib '73-79. (Owners Workshop Manuals Ser.: No. 222). 1979. 8.50 (ISBN 0-686-14951-3, Pub. by J H Haynes England). Haynes Pubns.

--Suzuki Owners Workshop Manual: GT 380, 550 3 Cyl. '72 on. new ed. (Owners Workshop Manuals Ser.: No. 216). 1979. 8.50 (ISBN 0-85696-216-3, Pub. by J H Haynes England). Haynes Pubns.

Crouse, W. H. & Anglin, D. L. Motorcycle Mechanics Workbook. 128p. 1981. 5.95 (ISBN 0-07-014782-5, W). McGraw.

Crouse, William H. & Anglin, Donald L. Workbook for Motorcycle Mechanics. (Illus.). 128p. 1982. 5.95 (ISBN 0-07-014782-5, G). McGraw.

Cunningham, Chet. Your Bike: How to Keep Your Motorcycle Running. LC 74-16626. (Illus.). (gr. 6 up). 1975. 6.95 (ISBN 0-399-20435-0). Putnam.

Daniels, Marcus. B.S.A Owner's Workshop Manual: 250 to 500 Unit Singles Thru '72. new ed. (Owners Workshop Manuals Ser.: No. 127). 1979. 8.50 (ISBN 0-85696-127-2, Pub. by J H Haynes England). Haynes Pubns.

Darlington, Mansur. B.S.A Owner's Workshop Manual: Gold Star Singles. new ed. (Owners Workshop Manuals Ser.: No. 326). 1979. 8.50 (ISBN 0-85696-326-7, Pub. by J H Haynes England). Haynes Pubns.

--Honda Owner's Workshop Manual: Gold Wing 1000 '75-77. new ed. (Owners Workshop Manuals Ser.: No. 309). 1979. 8.50 (ISBN 0-85696-309-7, Pub. by J H Haynes England). Haynes Pubns.

--Honda Owner's Workshop Manual: One Twenty Five Elsinore, Mr 175 '73-76. new ed. (Owners Workshop Manuals Ser.: No. 312). 1979. 8.50 (ISBN 0-85696-312-7, Pub. by J H Haynes England). Haynes Pubns.

--Honda Owner's Workshop Manual: Three-Sixty Twins '74-78. new ed. (Owners Workshop Manuals Ser.: No. 291). 1979. 8.50 (ISBN 0-85696-291-0, Pub. by J H Haynes England). Haynes Pubns.

--Husquarna Owner's Workshop Manual: Competition Bikes '72-75. new ed. (Owners Workshop Manuals Ser.: No. 221). 1979. 8.50 (ISBN 0-85696-221-X, Pub. by J H Haynes England). Haynes Pubns.

--Kawasaki Owner's Workshop Manual: Kz 400 Twins '74-76. (Owners Workshop Manuals Ser.: No. 281). 1979. 8.50 (ISBN 0-85696-281-3, Pub. by J H Haynes England). Haynes Pubns.

--Suzuki Owners Workshop Manual: GT 750 3 Cyl '71 on. new ed. (Owners Workshop Manuals Ser.: No. 302). 1979. 8.50 (ISBN 0-85696-302-X, Pub. by J H Haynes England). Haynes Pubns.

--Suzuki Owners Workshop Manual: Trail Bikes '71 on. new ed. (Owners Workshop Manuals Ser.: No. 218). 1979. 8.50 (ISBN 0-85696-218-X, Pub. by J H Haynes England). Haynes Pubns.

--Yamaha Owners Workshop Manual: Two-Fifty to Four Hundred Trails '68 on. new ed. (Owners Workshop Manuals Ser.: No. 263). 1978. 8.50 (ISBN 0-85696-263-5, Pub. by J H Haynes England). Haynes Pubns.

Dempsey, Paul. Motorcycle Repair Handbook. LC 76-24787. (Illus.). 1976. pap. 9.95 (ISBN 0-8306-5789-4, 789). TAB Bks.

Ducati Service-Repair Handbook: 160, 250,350, 450cc, Through 1974. (Illus.). 1974. pap. text ed. 9.95 (ISBN 0-89287-004-4, M306). Clymer Pubns.

Harley Davidson Owners Workshop Manual: Super & Electraglide Thru '77. new ed. (Owners Workshop Manuals Ser.: No. 330). 1979. 8.50 (ISBN 0-85696-330-5, Pub. by J H Haynes England). Haynes Pubns.

Honda Hawk (Motorcycle) Nineteen Seventy-Seven to Eighty Repair Tune-up Guide: Nineteen Seventy Seven to Eighty Repaair Tune-up Guide. LC 79-3245. (New Automotive Bks.). 192p. 1980. 8.95 (ISBN 0-8019-6868-2). Chilton.

Honda Owner's Workshop Manual: Xr75 '72-76. new ed. (Owners Workshop Manuals Ser.: No. 287). 1979. 8.50 (ISBN 0-85696-287-2, Pub. by J H Haynes England). Haynes Pubns.

Jorgensen, Eric. Honda: Four Fifty & Five Hundred cc Twins 1965-1977--Service, Repair, Performance. Robinson, Jeff, ed. (Illus.). pap. 9.95 (ISBN 0-89287-242-X, M333). Clymer Pubns.

--Honda Service Repair Handbook: 350-550cc Fours,1972-1978. Robinson, Jeff, ed. (Illus.). pap. 9.95 (ISBN 0-89287-287-X, M332). Clymer Pubns.

--Honda Two-Fifty & Three-Fifty cc Twins, 1964-1974: Service-Repair-Performance. pap. 9.95 (ISBN 0-89287-209-8, M322). Clymer Pubns.

Jorgensen, Eric, ed. BMW Five Hundred & Six Hundred cc Twins, Nineteen Fifty-Five to Nineteen Sixty-Nine: Service-Repair-Performance. (Illus.). pap. 9.95 (ISBN 0-89287-224-1, M308). Clymer Pubns.

--Honda: One Hundred-Three Fifty cc Four-Stroke Singles 1970-1978--Service, Repair Performance. (Illus.). pap. 9.95 (ISBN 0-89287-184-9, M315). Clymer Pubns.

--Honda One-Twenty-Five to Two Hundred cc Twins, 1964-1977: Service, Repair, Performance. (Illus.). pap. 9.95 (ISBN 0-89287-208-X, M321). Clymer Pubns.

--Honda Two-Fifty & Three-Sixty cc Twins, 1974-1977: Service-Repair-Performance. (Illus.). pap. 9.95 (ISBN 0-89287-210-1, M323). Clymer Pubns.

--Kawasaki: 250-750cc Triples 1969-1979--Service, Repair, Maintenance Handbook. 4th ed. (Illus.). 1978. pap. 9.95 (ISBN 0-89287-192-X, M353). Clymer Pubns.

--Puch Moped Owner Service-Repair: 1976-1977. (Illus.). pap. 6.00 (ISBN 0-89287-213-6, M437). Clymer Pubns.

--Suzuki GS1000 Fours: 1978-1979 Service-Repair-Performance. (Illus.). 216p. (Orig.). pap. text ed. 9.95 (ISBN 0-89287-315-9, M375). Clymer Pubns.

--Suzuki: GS400 Twins 1977-1978--Service, Repair, Performance. (Illus.). pap. 9.95 (ISBN 0-89287-237-3, M372). Clymer Pubns.

--Suzuki: GS550 Fours, 1977-1978--Service, Repair, Performance. (Illus.). pap. 9.95 (ISBN 0-89287-273-X, M373). Clymer Pubns.

--Suzuki GS750 Fours, 1977-1979: Service, Repair, Performance. (Illus.). pap. 9.95 (ISBN 0-89287-189-X, M370). Clymer Pubns.

--Suzuki: 125-400cc Singles, 1964-1979 Service, Repair, Performance. 3rd ed. (Illus.). pap. 9.95 (ISBN 0-89287-280-2, M369). Clymer Pubns.

--Suzuki: 50-120cc Singles 1964-1979--Service, Repair, Maintenance Handbook. 3rd ed. (Illus.). pap. 9.95 (ISBN 0-89287-292-6, M367). Clymer Pubns.

--Yamaha Service-Repair Handbook: 90-200cc Twins, 1966-1977. (Illus.). pap. 9.25 (ISBN 0-89287-179-2, M400). Clymer Pubns.

--Yamaha SR500 Singles: 1977-1979 Service-Repair-Performance. (Illus.). 191p. (Orig.). pap. 9.95 (ISBN 0-89287-212-8, M407). Clymer Pubns.

--Yamaha: TX500 & XS500 Twins, 1973-1978--Service, Repair, Performance. (Illus.). pap. 8.50 (ISBN 0-89287-241-1, M406). Clymer Pubns.

--Yamaha: XS360 & XS-400 Twins, 1976-78, Service, Repair, Maintenance. (Illus.). pap. 9.95 (ISBN 0-89287-170-9, M402). Clymer Pubns.

--Yamaha: XT500 & TT500 Singles, 1976-1980. (Illus.). pap. 8.50 (ISBN 0-89287-240-3, M405). Clymer Pubns.

--Yamaha: 50-100cc Rotary Valve Singles, 1963-1976--Service, Repair, Maintenance. 3rd ed. (Illus.). pap. 9.95 (ISBN 0-89287-220-9, M389). Clymer Pubns.

--Yamaha: 650cc Twins, 1979-79, Service, Repair, Performance. (Illus.). pap. 9.95 (ISBN 0-89287-233-0, M403). Clymer Pubns.

Jorgensen, Jeff, ed. BSA Service-Repair Handbook: All 500 & 650cc Unit Construction Twins. (Illus.). pap. 9.95 (ISBN 0-89287-182-2, M302). Clymer Pubns.

Jorgenson, Eric, ed. Honda Hawk: Four Hundred cc Twins 1978-1980--Service, Repair, Performance. (Illus.). pap. 9.95 (ISBN 0-89287-234-9, M334). Clymer Pubns.

Meek, Frank. Kawasaki Owners Workshop Manual: 250 & 400 3 Cyl '72-79. (Owners Workshop Manuals Ser.: No. 134). 1979. 8.50 (ISBN 0-85696-134-5, Pub. by J H Haynes England). Haynes Pubns.

--Triumph Owners Workshop Manual: Trident Bsa Rocket '60 on. new ed. (Owners Workshop Manuals Ser.: No. 136). 1979. 8.50 (ISBN 0-85696-136-1, Pub. by J H Haynes England). Haynes Pubns.

Mosher, Lynn S. & Lear, George. Motorcycle Mechanics. (Illus.). 272p. 1977. 17.95 (ISBN 0-13-604090-X). P-H.

Moto-Guzzi Owners Workshop Manual: V Twins Thru '79. new ed. (Owners Workshop Manuals Ser.: No. 339). 1979. 8.50 (ISBN 0-85696-339-9, Pub. by J H Haynes England). Haynes Pubns.

Rabone, David. Norton Owners Workshop Manual: Twins Thru '70. new ed. (Owners Workshop Manuals Ser.: No. 187). 1979. 8.50 (ISBN 0-85696-187-6, Pub. by J H Haynes England). Haynes Pubns.

--Suzuki Owners Workshop Manual: Five Hundred Twins '68 on. new ed. (Owners Workshop Manuals Ser.: No. 135). 1979. 8.50 (ISBN 0-85696-135-3, Pub. by J H Haynes England). Haynes Pubns.

Reynolds, Mark. B.S.A Owner's Workshop Manual: A50-A65 Thru '73. new ed. (Owners Workshop Manuals Ser.: No. 155). 1979. 8.50 (ISBN 0-85696-155-8, Pub. by J H Haynes England). Haynes Pubns.

--Honda Owner's Workshop Manual: Three-Fifty, Five Hundred 4 Cyl Thru '75. new ed. (Owners Workshop Manuals Ser.: No. 132). 1979. 8.50 (ISBN 0-85696-132-9, Pub. by J H Haynes England). Haynes Pubns.

Robinson, Jeff, ed. CZ Service-Repair Handbook: Single Exhaust Models-Through 1978. (Illus.). pap. text ed. 9.95 (ISBN 0-89287-102-4, M425). Clymer Pubns.

--Hodaka Service - Repair Handbook: 90-125cc Singles, 1964-1975. (Illus.). pap. text ed. 9.95 (ISBN 0-89287-005-2, M307). Clymer Pubns.

--Honda: G L-One Thousand Fours, 1975-1980--Service, Repair, Performance. (Illus.). pap. 9.95 (ISBN 0-89287-238-1, M340). Clymer Pubns.

--Husqvarna Service - Repair Handbook: 125-450cc Singles, 1966-1975. (Illus.). pap. text ed. 9.95 (ISBN 0-89287-014-1, M423). Clymer Pubns.

--Kawasaki Service - Repair Handbook: 250 & 350cc Twins, All Years. (Illus.). pap. text ed. 9.95 (ISBN 0-89287-016-8, M352). Clymer Pubns.

--Maico Service-Repair Handbook: 250-501cc Singles, 1968-1975. (Illus.). pap. text ed. 9.95 (ISBN 0-89287-019-2, M357). Clymer Pubns.

--Norton Service Repair Handbook: 750 & 850 Commandos, All Years. (Illus.). pap. 9.95 (ISBN 0-89287-158-X, M361). Clymer Pubns.

--Ossa Service - Repair Handbook: 125-250cc Singles, 1971-1978. 2nd ed. (Illus.). 160p. 1976. pap. text ed. 9.95 (ISBN 0-89287-092-3, M362). Clymer Pubns.

Schultz, Neil. Complete Guide to Motorcycle Repair & Maintenance. rev. ed. LC 79-21201. (Illus.). 224p. 1980. pap. 6.95 (ISBN 0-668-04856-5, 4856-5). Arco.

Scott, Ed. Garelli Moped Owner Service-Repair: 1976-1978. (Illus.). pap. 6.00 (ISBN 0-89287-200-4, M435). Clymer Pubns.

--Peugeot Moped Owners Service-Repair, 1976-1978. (Illus.). pap. 6.00 (ISBN 0-89287-202-0, M436). Clymer Pubns.

--Yamaha XS1100 Fours: 1978-1979 Service-Repair-Performance. (Illus.). 224p. (Orig.). 1980. pap. text ed. 9.95 (ISBN 0-89287-309-4, M411). Clymer Pubns.

Shipman, Carl. The Boonie Book. 2nd ed. LC 73-93781. (Illus.). 192p. 1974. pap. 5.95 (ISBN 0-912656-17-4). H P Bks.

--Motorcycle Tuning for Performance. LC 73-82437. (Illus.). 1973. pap. 5.95 (ISBN 0-912656-33-6). H P Bks.

Wilkins, Stewart. Honda Owner's Workshop Manual: Two Fifty & Three Fifty Twins Thru '74. new ed. (Owners Workshop Manuals Ser.: No. 133). 1979. 8.50 (ISBN 0-85696-133-7, Pub. by J H Haynes England). Haynes Pubns.

--Kawasaki Owners Workshop Manual: 500 & 750 3 Cyl Thru '76. (Owners Workshop Manuals Ser.: No. 325). 1979. 8.50 (ISBN 0-85696-325-9, Pub. by J H Haynes England). Haynes Pubns.

--Maico Owners Workshop Manual: Competition Bikes '73 on. new ed. (Owners Workshop Manuals Ser.: No. 220). 1979. 8.50 (ISBN 0-85696-220-1, Pub. by J H Haynes England). Haynes Pubns.

--MZ Owners Workshop Manual: One-Fifty, Two-Fifty Singles '70 on. new ed. (Owners Workshop Manuals Ser.: No. 253). 1979. 8.50 (ISBN 0-85696-253-8, Pub. by J H Haynes England). Haynes Pubns.

--Suzuki Owners Workshop Manual: B120 & B100p Singles '66 on. new ed. (Owners Workshop Manuals Ser.: No. 298). 1979. 8.50 (ISBN 0-85696-298-8, Pub. by J H Haynes England). Haynes Pubns.

--Suzuki Owners Workshop Manual: Gt 125, 185 Twins '74 on. new ed. (Owners Workshop Manuals Ser.: No. 301). 1979. 8.50 (ISBN 0-85696-301-1, Pub. by J H Haynes England). Haynes Pubns.

Witcomb, John. B M W Owners Workshop Manual: Series 5 & 6 Twins '70 on. new ed. (Owners Workshop Manuals Ser.: No. 249). 1979. 10.95 (ISBN 0-85696-249-X, Pub. by J H Haynes England). Haynes Pubns.

--Honda Owner's Workshop Manual: Four Hundred, Five-Fifty F 4 Cyl '73-78. new ed. (Owners Workshop Manuals Ser.: No. 262). 1979. 8.50 (ISBN 0-85696-262-7, Pub. by J H Haynes England). Haynes Pubns.

MOTORCYCLING

Alth, Max. Motorcycles & Motorcycling. (First Bks.). (Illus.). (gr. 4 up). 1979. PLB 6.90 s&l (ISBN 0-531-02945-X). Watts.

Bishop, George. The Encyclopedia of Motorcycling. 192p. 1980. 16.95 (ISBN 0-399-12557-4, Perigee); pap. 8.95 (ISBN 0-399-50491-5). Putnam.

Blom, Dick. Rider's Complete Guide to Motorcycle Touring. (Illus.). 213p. 1981. 12.95 (ISBN 0-934798-02-8). TL Enterprises.

Carrick, Peter. Encyclopaedia of Motor-Cycle Sport. LC 76-62754. (Illus.). 224p. 1977. 10.00 (ISBN 0-312-24867-9). St Martin.

--Motorcycling. (Illus.). 223p. 1980. 24.95 (ISBN 0-8069-9242-5); lib. bdg. 21.59 (ISBN 0-8069-9243-3). Sterling.

--Motorcycling. (Guinness Superlatives Ser.). (Illus.). 224p. 1980. 24.95 (ISBN 0-8069-9242-5, Pub. by Guinness Superlatives England). Sterling.

Coombs, Charles. Motorcycling. LC 68-23911. (gr. 5-9). 1968. PLB 7.25 (ISBN 0-688-21564-5); pap. 6.96 (ISBN 0-688-31564-X). Morrow.

Cutter, Robert A. The New Guide to Motorcycling. (Illus.). 1977. 7.95 (ISBN 0-668-02732-0); pap. 3.95 (ISBN 0-668-04059-9). Arco.

Davis, Anthony. Tackle Motorcycle Sport This Way. (Tackle Ser.). (Illus.). 1976. pap. 6.95x (ISBN 0-09-103521-X, SpS). Sportshelf.

Edmonds, I. G. Motorcycling for Beginners. pap. 3.00 (ISBN 0-87980-234-0). Wilshire.

Feilen, John. Motocross. LC 78-17436. (Winners Circle Ser.). (Illus.). (gr. 4). 1978. PLB 6.95 (ISBN 0-913940-79-8). Crestwood Hse.

Griffin, Michael M. Motorcycles: From the Inside Out (& How to Keep Them Right Side up) (Illus.). 1978. ref. ed. 12.95 (ISBN 0-13-604041-1); pap. text ed. 9.95 (ISBN 0-13-604033-0). P-H.

Hampton, William. Expert Motorcycling. LC 79-50978. (Illus.). 1979. o. p. 9.95 (ISBN 0-8092-7195-8); pap. 4.95 (ISBN 0-8092-7193-1). Contemp Bks.

Hudson-Evans, Richard. The Handbook of Motorcycle Sport. LC 78-2771. (Illus.). 1978. 11.95 (ISBN 0-668-04629-5, 4629). Arco.

Jackson, Bob. Street Biking: How to Ride to Save Your Hide. 1980. pap. 5.95 (ISBN 0-89586-081-3). H P Bks.

Lovin, Roger. The Complete Motorcycle Nomad: A Guide to Machines, Equipment, People & Places. (A Sports Illustrated Bk.). 1974. pap. 3.95 (ISBN 0-316-53356-4). Little.

McCoy, Duke. How to Start & Run Your Own Motorcycle Gang. 1981. pap. 7.95 (ISBN 0-686-30639-2). Loompanics.

Mosher, Lynn S. & Lear, George. Motorcycle Mechanics. (Illus.). 272p. 1977. 17.95 (ISBN 0-13-604090-X). P-H.

Motor Cycling. rev. ed. (Know the Game Ser.). (Illus.). 1974. pap. 2.50 (ISBN 0-7158-0140-6). Charles River Bks.

Motor Cycling. 1976. pap. 2.50 (ISBN 0-8277-4889-2). British Bk Ctr.

Naden, C. J. Motorcycle Challenge, Trials & Races. LC 79-52178. (Illus.). 32p. (gr. 4-9). 1980. PLB 6.89 (ISBN 0-89375-252-5); pap. 2.50 (ISBN 0-89375-253-3). Troll Assocs.

--Rough Rider. LC 79-52177. (Illus.). 32p. (gr. 4-9). 1980. PLB 6.89 (ISBN 0-89375-250-9); pap. 2.50 (ISBN 0-89375-251-7). Troll Assocs.

Patrignani, R., intro. by. Color Treasury of Motorcycle Competition. (Bounty Bk. Ser.). (Illus.). 64p. 1974. pap. 1.98 (ISBN 0-517-51433-8). Crown.

Perry, Robin. The Road Rider: A Guide to on-the-Road Motorcycling. LC 73-91519. (Illus.). 128p. 1974. 5.95 (ISBN 0-517-51501-6); pap. 2.95 (ISBN 0-517-51502-4). Crown.

Robinson, Jeff, ed. Ride, & Stay Alive. (Illus.). 128p. pap. text ed. 4.95 (ISBN 0-89287-024-9, X910). Clymer Pubns.

Roth, Bernhard A. The Complete Beginner's Guide to Motorcycling. LC 73-11719. 192p. (gr. 5-9). 1974. 6.95 (ISBN 0-385-03537-3). Doubleday.

Sagnier, Thierry. Bike! Motorcycles & the People Who Ride Them. LC 72-9151. (Illus.). 208p. 1974. (HarpT); (HarpT). Har-Row.

Shipman, Carl. How to Ride Observed Trials. LC 73-82436. (Illus.). 1973. pap. 5.95 (ISBN 0-912656-14-X). H P Bks.

Smith, Don. The Baja Run: Racing Fury. new ed. LC 75-23412. (Illus.). 32p. (gr. 5-10). 1976. PLB 6.89 (ISBN 0-89375-000-X); pap. 2.50 (ISBN 0-89375-016-6). Troll Assocs.

--Trials Bike Riding. (EP Sports Ser.). (Illus.). 112p. 1981. 12.95 (ISBN 0-8069-9050-3, Pub. by EP Publishing England). Sterling.

Taylor, Paula. World's Daredevil: Evel Knievel. (Allstars Ser.). (Illus.). (gr. 2-6). 1976. PLB 5.95 (ISBN 0-87191-478-6); pap. 2.95 (ISBN 0-89812-201-5). Creative Ed.

Tobey, Peter. Two-Wheel Travel: Motorcycle Camping & Touring. 288p. 1973. pap. 3.00 (ISBN 0-440-59156-2). Dell.

Wallach, Theresa. Easy Motorcycle Riding. rev. enlarged ed. LC 78-57787. (Illus.). 1978. 7.95 (ISBN 0-8069-4134-0); lib. bdg. 7.49 (ISBN 0-8069-4135-9). Sterling.

Williamson, Mitch. Safe Riding: Staying Alive on Your Motorcycle. LC 80-11435. 256p. 1980. pap. 7.95 (ISBN 0-89696-101-X); 11.95 (ISBN 0-89696-098-6). Everest Hse.

Yeager, Tricia. How to Be Sexy with Bugs in Your Teeth. LC 77-92986. 1978. pap. 5.95 (ISBN 0-8092-7669-0). Contemp Bks.

Yerkow, Charles. Here Is Your Hobby: Motorcycling. (Here Is Your Hobby Ser.). (Illus.). 128p. (gr. 7-12). 1973. PLB 5.29 (ISBN 0-399-60820-6). Putnam.

MOTORS
see also Automobiles–Motors; Diesel Motor; Dynamos; Electric Motors; Gas and Oil Engines; Machinery; Outboard Motors
also subdivision Motors under subjects, e.g. Automobiles–Motors
Alerich, Walter N. Electric Motor Control. 3rd ed. (Electric Trades Ser.). (Illus.). 300p. 1981. pap. text ed. 6.40 (ISBN 0-8273-1365-9); price not set instructor's guide (ISBN 0-8273-1366-7). Delmar.
Braymer, Daniel H. & Roe, A. C. Rewinding Small Motors. 3rd ed. LC 80-29580. 432p. 1981. Repr. of 1949 ed. lib. bdg. write for info. (ISBN 0-89874-291-9). Krieger.
Brewster, Albert H., Jr. How to Convert Salvage Auto Starter to Powerful DC Motor. 2nd ed. (Illus.). 1981. pap. 6.00x (ISBN 0-918166-04-7). Amonics.
The Directory of Motor Component Manufacturers in Western Europe. 1981. 165.00x (ISBN 0-686-75442-5, Pub. by European Directories England). State Mutual Bk.
Holmes, Leonard, ed. Odhams New Motor Manual. (Illus.). 320p. 1972. 7.25x (ISBN 0-600-71800-X). Transatlantic.
Motors & Generators. (Industrial Equipment & Supplies Ser.). 1980. 350.00 (ISBN 0-686-31538-3). Busn Trend.
Peterson, Franklynn. Handbook of Lawn Mower Repair. LC 75-189619. (Illus.). 1978. 9.95 (ISBN 0-87523-179-9). Emerson.
Rudman, Jack. Motor Equipment Maintenance Foreman. (Career Examination Ser.: C-2084). (Cloth bdg. avail. on request). 1977. 16.00 (ISBN 0-8373-2084-4). Natl Learning.
Stock Drive Products Staff Engineers. Handbook of Small Belt & Chain Drives, 2 vols. 1978. pap. 1.95 (ISBN 0-686-10242-8). Stock Drive.
MOTOWN
Benjaminson, Peter. The Story of Motown. LC 79-2332. (Illus.). 1979. pap. 8.95 (ISBN 0-394-17554-9, E745, Ever). Grove.
MOTT, JOHN RALEIGH, b. 1865
Hopkins, C. Howard. John R. Mott, Eighteen Sixty-Five to Nineteen Fifty-Five: A Biography. LC 79-15069. 22.50 (ISBN 0-8028-3525-2). Eerdmans.
MOTT, LUCRETIA (COFFIN), 1793-1880
Bacon, Margaret H. Valiant Friend: The Life of Lucretia Mott. (Illus.). 320p. 1980. 14.95 (ISBN 0-8027-0645-2). Walker & Co.
Cromwell, Otelia. Lucretia Mott. LC 79-139913. (Illus.). 1971. Repr. of 1958 ed. 14.00 (ISBN 0-8462-1579-9). Russell.
Greene, Dana, ed. Lucretia Mott: The Complete Speeches & Sermons. (Studies in Women & Religion: Vol. 4). 1980. soft cover 24.95 (ISBN 0-88946-968-7). E Mellen.
Hare, L. C. The Greatest American Woman: Lucretia Mott. LC 71-145069. 307p. 1972. Repr. of 1937 ed. 12.00 (ISBN 0-403-01011-X). Scholarly.
Hare, Lloyd C. The Greatest American Woman, Lucretia Mott. LC 76-109327. (Illus.). 307p. Repr. of 1937 ed. lib. bdg. 15.00x (ISBN 0-8371-3593-1, HLM&). Greenwood.
Kurland, Gerald. Lucretia Mott: Early Leader of the Women's Liberation Movement. Rahmas, D. Steve, ed. LC 72-81902. (Outstanding Personalities Ser.: No. 39). 32p. (Orig.). (gr. 7-12). 1972. lib. bdg. 2.95 incl. catalog cards (ISBN 0-87157-549-3); pap. 1.50 vinyl laminated covers (ISBN 0-87157-049-1). SamHar Pr.
MOTTOES
see also Devices; Slogans
Anson, W. S. Mottoes & Badges of Families, Regiments, Schools, Colleges, States, Towns, Livery Companies, Societies, Etc. LC 74-14502. 192p. 1975. Repr. of 1904 ed. 24.00 (ISBN 0-8103-4055-0). Gale.
Caulfield, Sophia F. House Mottoes & Inscriptions. LC 68-21758. 1968. Repr. of 1908 ed. 19.00 (ISBN 0-8103-3322-8). Gale.
Elvin, Charles N. Hand-Book of Mottoes: Borne by the Nobility, Gentry, Cities, Public Companies. LC 79-122638. (Illus.). 1971. Repr. of 1860 ed. 19.00 (ISBN 0-8103-3387-2). Gale.
--Handbook of Mottoes: Borne by the Nobility, Gentry, Cities, Public Cos., Etc. LC 70-151294. 1971. Repr. of 1860 ed. suppl. with index 15.00 (ISBN 0-8063-0481-2). Genealog Pub.
Shankle, George E. State Names, Flags, Seals, Songs, Birds, Flowers, & Other Symbols. rev. ed. LC 73-109842. (Illus.). 522p. Repr. of 1938 ed. lib. bdg. 23.50x (ISBN 0-8371-4333-0, SHSN). Greenwood.
MOTU LANGUAGE
see also Melanesian Languages
Lawes, William G. Grammar & Vocabulary of Language Spoken by Motu Tribe (New Guinea) 3rd enl. ed. LC 75-35132. 1976. Repr. of 1896 ed. 17.50 (ISBN 0-404-14148-X). AMS Pr.
MOTURIKI
Hayden, Howard. Moturiki: A Pilot Project in Community Development. LC 79-138147. (Illus.). 180p. 1972. Repr. of 1954 ed. lib. bdg. 15.00 (ISBN 0-8371-5604-1, HAMO). Greenwood.
MOULAGE
see Prosthesis
MOULD (BOTANY)
see Molds (Botany)
MOULD, VEGETABLE
see Humus
MOULDING (METAL)
see Molding (Founding)
MOULTON FAMILY
Sneller, Anne G. Vanished World. LC 64-16923. (Illus.). 1964. 6.00 (ISBN 0-8156-0037-2). Syracuse U Pr.
Whiting, Lilian. Louise Chandler Moulton: Poet & Friend. 1979. Repr. of 1910 ed. lib. bdg. 30.00 (ISBN 0-8495-5708-9). Arden Lib.
MOUND-BUILDERS
see also Hopewell Culture
Ford, James A. & Willey, Gordon. Crooks Site, a Marksville Period Burial Mound in the LaSalle Parish, Louisiana. LC 40-28710. 1975. Repr. of 1940 ed. 12.00 (ISBN 0-527-03232-8). Kraus Repr.
George, Gale. Upper Mississippi: Or, Historical Sketches of the Mound-Builder, the Indian Tribes, & the Progress of Civilization in the North-West. 1975. Repr. of 1867 ed. 20.00 (ISBN 0-527-03220-4). Kraus Repr.
King, Blanche B. Under Your Feet: The Story of the American Mound Builders. facsimile ed. LC 73-152990. (Select Bibliographies Reprint Ser). Repr. of 1939 ed. 20.00 (ISBN 0-8369-5742-3). Arno.
Steele, William O. Talking Bones: Secrets of Indian Mound Builders. LC 76-58687. (Illus.). (gr. 2-5). 1978. 8.95 (ISBN 0-06-025768-7, HarpJ); PLB 8.79 (ISBN 0-06-025769-5). Har-Row.
MOUND KEY
Schell, Rolfe F. One Thousand Years on Mound Key. rev. ed. LC 68-24198. (Illus.). 1968. 3.95 (ISBN 0-87208-001-3); pap. 1.50 (ISBN 0-87208-000-5). Island Pr.
MOUNDS
see also Earthworks (Archaeology)
Atwater, Caleb. Description of the Antiquities Discovered in the State of Ohio & Other Western States. LC 72-4997. (Harvard University. Peabody Museum of Archaeology & Ethnology. Antiquities of the New World: No. 1). (Illus.). Repr. of 1820 ed. 21.50 (ISBN 0-404-57301-0). AMS Pr.
Beauchamp, William M. Perch Lake Mounds, with Notes on Other New York Mounds & Some Accounts of Indian Trails. LC 74-7929. Repr. of 1905 ed. 14.50 (ISBN 0-404-11815-1). AMS Pr.
Claflin, W. H. Stalling's Island Mound, Columbia County, Georgia. 1931. pap. 9.00 (ISBN 0-527-01232-7). Kraus Repr.
Fox, Cyril. Life & Death in the Bronze Age: An Archaeologist's Field Work. 1959. text ed. 13.25x (ISBN 0-7100-1392-2). Humanities.
Grinsell, L. V. The Ancient Burial-Mounds of England. LC 73-13037. (Illus.). 278p. 1975. Repr. of 1953 ed. lib. bdg. 18.00x (ISBN 0-8371-7101-6, GRAB). Greenwood.
Hooton, E. A. Indian Village Site & Cemetery Near Madisonville, Ohio. 1920. pap. 12.00 (ISBN 0-527-01212-2). Kraus Repr.
Johnson, Elden. The Arvilla Complex. LC 73-5899. (Minnesota Prehistoric Archaeology Ser.: No. 9). (Illus.). 88p. 1973. pap. 6.00 (ISBN 0-87351-078-X). Minn Hist.
Lapham, Increase A. The Antiquities of Wisconsin As Surveyed & Described. LC 72-5000. (Antiquities of the New World Ser.: Vol. 4). (Illus.). Repr. of 1855 ed. 18.50 (ISBN 0-404-57304-5). AMS Pr.
Marsden, Barry M. The Early Barrow Diggers. LC 74-76137. (Illus.). 126p. 1974. 9.95 (ISBN 0-8155-5027-8, NP). Noyes.
Peabody, Charles. Exploration of Mounds, Coahoma County, Mississippi. 1904. pap. 4.00 (ISBN 0-527-01193-2). Kraus Repr.
Rowe, Chandler W. Effigy Mound Culture of Wisconsin. Repr. of 1956 ed. lib. bdg. 15.00x (ISBN 0-8371-4630-5, ROMC). Greenwood.
Schmidt, Erich F. Alishar Huyuk, Seasons of 1928-1929, Pt. 1. LC 30-14675. (Researches in Anatolia Ser: Vol. 4). 1932. 30.00x (ISBN 0-226-62115-4, OIP19). U of Chicago Pr.
--Alishar Huyuk, Seasons of 1928-1929, Pt. 2. LC 30-14678. (Researches in Anatolia Ser: Vol. 5). 1933. 20.00x (ISBN 0-226-62116-2, OIP20). U of Chicago Pr.
Sears, William H. Excavations at Kolomoki: Final Report. LC 53-7144. 144p. 1956. pap. 4.50x (ISBN 0-8203-0059-4). U of Ga Pr.
Squier, Ephraim G. & Davis, E. H. Ancient Monuments of the Mississippi Valley. LC 72-4998. (Harvard University. Peabody Museum of Archaeology & Ethnology. Antiquities of the New World: No. 2). (Illus.). Repr. of 1848 ed. 46.50 (ISBN 0-404-57302-9). AMS Pr.
Steele, William O. Talking Bones: Secrets of Indian Mound Builders. LC 76-58687. (Illus.). (gr. 2-5). 1978. 8.95 (ISBN 0-06-025768-7, HarpJ); PLB 8.79 (ISBN 0-06-025769-5). Har-Row.
Thomas, Cyrus. Work in Mound Exploration of the Bureau of Ethnology. Repr. of 1887 ed. 17.00 (ISBN 0-403-03727-1). Scholarly.
Von Der Osten, Hans H. Discoveries in Anatolia, 1930-31. LC 33-13172. (Oriental Institute Pubns. Ser). (Illus.). 1933. pap. 11.50x (ISBN 0-226-62330-0, OIC14). U of Chicago Pr.
Von Der Osten, Hans H. & Schmidt, Erich F. Alishar Huyuk, Season of 1927: Researches in Anatolia, Vol. 3, Pt. 2. LC 30-14678. (Oriental Institute Pubns. Ser: No. 7). 1932. 20.00x (ISBN 0-226-62101-4, P7). U of Chicago Pr.
Wilford, Lloyd A. Burial Mounds of the Red River Headwaters. LC 70-113818. (Minnesota Prehistoric Archaeology Ser.: No. 5). (Illus.). 36p. 1970. pap. 2.00 (ISBN 0-87351-059-3). Minn Hist.
Wilford, Lloyd A., et al. Burial Mounds of Central Minnesota: Excavation Reports. LC 70-626259. (Minnesota Prehistoric Archaeology Ser.: No. 1). (Illus.). 72p. 1969. pap. 4.25 (ISBN 0-87351-047-X). Minn Hist.
Willoughby, C. C. Turner Group of Earthworks, Hamilton County, Ohio. 1922. pap. 8.00 (ISBN 0-527-01214-9). Kraus Repr.
MOUNIER, EMMANUEL, 1905-1950
Cantin, Eileen. Mounier: A Personalist View of History. LC 73-87031. (Orig.). 1974. pap. 4.95 (ISBN 0-8091-1801-7). Paulist Pr.
MOUNT BAKER
see Baker, Mount
MOUNT DESERT ISLAND, MAINE
AMC Maine Mountain Guidebook Committee, ed. AMC Trail Guide to Mount Desert Island & Acadia National Park. 2nd ed. (Illus.). 1975. pap. 2.50 (ISBN -0910146-04-7). Appalach Mtn.
Morison, Samuel E. The Story of Mt. Desert Island, Maine. (Illus.). 1960. 5.95 (ISBN 0-316-58362-6, Pub. by Atlantic Monthly Pr). Little.
Nichols, George W. Mount Desert, 1872. Jones, William R., ed. (Illus.). 24p. 1977. Repr. of 1872 ed. pap. 2.00 (ISBN 0-89646-029-0). Outbooks.
MOUNT EVEREST
see Everest, Mount
MOUNT EVEREST EXPEDITION, 1953
Kohli, M. S. Nine Atop Everest: Story of the Indian Ascent. 1969. 17.50 (ISBN 0-8046-8813-3). Kennikat.
MOUNT FUJI
see Fuji, Mount
MOUNT HOLYOKE COLLEGE
Green, Elizabeth A. Mary Lyon & Mount Holyoke: Opening the Gates. LC 78-68857. (Illus.). 424p. 1979. text ed. 17.50x (ISBN 0-87451-172-0). U Pr of New Eng.
MOUNT HUNTINGTON
see Huntington, Mount
MOUNT HOOD
see Hood, Mount, Oregon
MOUNT KATMAI
see Katmai, Mount
MOUNT MCKINLEY
see McKinley, Mount
MOUNT MCKINLEY NATIONAL PARK
Alaska Travel Publications Editors. Exploring Alaska's Mount McKinley National Park. 2nd ed. LC 76-4404. (Illus.). 1976. 8.95 (ISBN 0-914164-04-X). Alaska Travel.
Buskirk, Steve. Mount McKinley: The Story Behind the Scenery. DenDooven, Gweneth R., ed. LC 78-57540. (Illus.). 1978. lib. bdg. 7.95 (ISBN 0-916122-52-2); pap. 3.50 (ISBN 0-916122-23-9). KC Pubns.
MOUNT RAINIER
see Rainier, Mount
MOUNT RAINIER NATIONAL PARK
Spring, Bob & Spring, Ira. The Mount Rainier National Park. LC 74-765656. (Illus.). 1974. pap. 2.95 (ISBN 0-87564-614-X). Superior Pub.
Spring, Ira & Manning, Harvey. Fifty Hikes in Mt. Rainier National Park. 2nd ed. LC 78-84752. (Illus.). 136p. (Orig.). 1978. pap. 5.95 (ISBN 0-916890-19-8). Mountaineers.
MOUNT RUSHMORE NATIONAL MEMORIAL
Borglum, Lincoln & DenDooven, Gweneth R. Mount Rushmore: The Story Behind the Scenery. LC 76-57455. (Illus.). 1977. 7.95 (ISBN 0-916122-45-X); pap. 3.00 (ISBN 0-916122-20-4). KC Pubns.
Fite, Gilbert C. Mount Rushmore. (Illus.). pap. 5.95 (ISBN 0-8061-0959-9). U of Okla Pr.
Zeitner, June C. & Borglum, Lincoln. Borglum's Unfinished Dream--Mount Rushmore. LC 76-5651. (Illus.). 1976. 10.95 (ISBN 0-87970-135-8). North Plains.
MOUNT TACOMA
see Rainier, Mount
MOUNT TAMALPAIS AND MUIR WOODS RAILROAD
Crookedest Railroad in the World. 5.75 (ISBN 0-685-83332-1). Chatham Pub CA.
Wurm, Theodore G. & Graves, Alvin C. The Crookedest Railroad in the World. 2nd ed. LC 60-53393. (Illus.). 1960. 5.75 (ISBN 0-8310-7021-8). Howell-North.
MOUNT VERNON
Bourne, Miriam A. The Children of Mount Vernon: A Guide to George Washington's Home. LC 80-974. (Illus.). 64p. (gr. 4-6). 1981. PLB 8.95 (ISBN 0-385-15535-2); pap. 4.95 (ISBN 0-385-15534-4). Doubleday.
Miller, Natalie. The Story of Mount Vernon. (Cornerstone of Freedom Ser.). (Illus.). (gr. 3-7). 1965. PLB 7.95 (ISBN 0-516-04624-1). Childrens.
MOUNT WASHINGTON, NEW HAMPSHIRE
see Washington, Mount, New Hampshire
MOUNT WHITNEY
see Whitney, Mount, California
MOUNT WILSON
Robinson, John W. Mount Wilson Story. (Illus.). 1973. wrappers 1.00 (ISBN 0-910856-53-2). La Siesta.
MOUNTAIN CLIMBING
see Mountaineering
MOUNTAIN ECOLOGY
see also Alpine Flora
Berger, Gilda. Mountain Worlds: What Lives There. (What Lives There Ser.). (Illus.). (gr. 2-5). 1978. 5.59 (ISBN 0-698-30702-X). Coward.
Brooks, Maurice. Life of the Mountains. (Our Living World of Nature Ser). (Illus.). (gr. 7 up). 1968. 9.95 (ISBN 0-07-008075-5, P&RB); by subscription. 3.95 (ISBN 0-07-046010-8). McGraw.
Flader, Susan L. Thinking Like a Mountain: Aldo Leopold & the Evolution of an Ecological Attitude Toward Deer, Wolves & Forests. LC 78-17667. (Illus.). 1978. pap. 4.50 (ISBN 0-8032-6850-5, BB 668, Bison). U of Nebr Pr.
Ricciuti, Edward R. Wildlife of the Mountains. (Wildlife Habitat Ser.). (Illus.). 1979. 18.95 (ISBN 0-8109-1757-2). Abrams.
Spring, Ira & Manning, Harvey. Mountain Flowers. LC 79-9284. (Illus.). 1979. pap. 3.95 (ISBN 0-916890-92-9). Mountaineers.
Zwinger, Ann H. & Willard, Beatrice E. Land Above the Trees: A Guide to American Alpine Tundra. LC 72-79702. (Illus.). 448p. 1972. 17.50 (ISBN 0-06-014823-3, HarpT). Har-Row.
MOUNTAIN FLORA
see Alpine Flora
MOUNTAIN LIONS
see Pumas
MOUNTAIN MEADOWS MASSACRE, 1857
Brooks, Juanita. Mountain Meadows Massacre. (Illus.). 1979. Repr. of 1962 ed. 14.95 (ISBN 0-8061-0549-6). U of Okla Pr.
MOUNTAIN RAILROADS
see also Railroads, Cable
MOUNTAIN SHEEP
see also Bighorn Sheep
Geist, Valerius. Mountain Sheep & Man in the Northern Wilds. LC 75-5481. 272p. 1975. 15.00x (ISBN 0-8014-0943-8). Cornell U Pr.
O'Connor, Jack. Sheep & Sheep Hunting. 1974. 12.95 (ISBN 0-87691-145-9). Winchester Pr.
Russell, Andy. Horns in the High Country. 1973. 10.95 (ISBN 0-394-47221-7). Knopf.
MOUNTAIN SICKNESS
Mitchell, Dick. Mountaineering First Aid: A Guide to Accident Response & First Aid Care. 2nd ed. LC 75-25341. (Illus.). 104p. 1975. pap. 3.95 (ISBN 0-916890-33-3). Mountaineers.
MOUNTAIN WHITES (SOUTHERN STATES)
Campbell, John C. The Southern Highlander & His Homeland. LC 73-2563. (Illus.). 427p. 1973. Repr. of 1921 ed. 18.00 (ISBN 0-87152-128-8). Reprint.
Caudill, Harry M. A Darkness at Dawn: Appalachian Kentucky & the Future. LC 74-7871. (Kentucky Bicentennial Bookshelf Ser.). 88p. 1976. 6.95 (ISBN 0-8131-0218-9). U Pr of Ky.
Clark, Joe. Tennessee Hill Folk. LC 72-2880. (Illus.). 96p. 1972. 8.95 (ISBN 0-8265-1183-X). Vanderbilt U Pr.
Coles, Robert. Children of Crisis, Vol. 2: Migrants, Mountaineers & Sharecroppers. (Children of Crisis Ser.). (Illus.). 1972-73. 15.00 (ISBN 0-316-15171-8, Pub. by Atlantic Monthly Pr); pap. 8.95 (ISBN 0-316-15176-9). Little.
Eaton, Allen H. Handicrafts of the Southern Highlands. (Illus.). 370p. 1973. pap. 6.95 (ISBN 0-486-22211-X). Dover.
Fetterman, John. Stinking Creek: The Portrait of a Small Mountain Community in Appalachia. 1970. pap. 3.95 (ISBN 0-525-47266-5). Dutton.

Hannum, Alberta P. Look Back with Love: A Recollection of the Blue Ridge. LC 70-89659. (Illus.). 1969. 10.00 (ISBN 0-8149-0007-0). Vanguard.
McClain, J. Dudley. Political Profiles of College Students in Southern Appalachia: Socio-Political Attitudes, Preferences, Personality & Characteristics. LC 77-84178. 1978. 11.95 (ISBN 0-89583-006-X); pap. 7.95 (ISBN 0-89583-007-8). Resurgens Pubns.
Matthews, Martin T. Experience-Worlds of Mountain People. LC 76-177060. (Columbia University. Teachers College. Contributions to Education: No. 700). Repr. of 1937 ed. 17.50 (ISBN 0-404-55700-7). AMS Pr.
Miles, Emma Bell. Spirit of the Mountains. LC 75-19222. (Tennesseana Editions Ser.). (Illus.). 256p. 1975. Repr. of 1905 ed. 8.95 (ISBN 0-87049-181-4). U of Tenn Pr.
Raine, James W. Land of Saddle-Bags: A Study of the Mountain People of Appalachia. LC 70-78223. (Illus.). 1969. Repr. of 1924 ed. 19.00 (ISBN 0-8103-0160-1). Gale.
Randolph, Vance. Ozark Magic & Folklore. Orig. Title: Ozark Superstition. 1947. pap. 4.50 (ISBN 0-486-21181-9). Dover.
Scarborough, Dorothy. Song Catcher in Southern Mountains. LC 37-4992. Repr. of 1937 ed. 18.50 (ISBN 0-404-05569-9). AMS Pr.
Shapiro, Henry D. Appalachia on Our Mind: The Southern Mountains & Mountaineers in the American Consciousness, 1870-1920. LC 77-2301. 1978. 22.50x (ISBN 0-8078-1293-5). U of NC Pr.
Sheppard, Muriel E. Cabins in the Laurel. 1935. 12.95 (ISBN 0-8078-0184-4). U of NC Pr.
Walston, Marie. These Were My Hills. LC 74-75978. (Pivot Family Reader). 144p. 1974. pap. 1.50 (ISBN 0-87983-072-7). Keats.
Weller, Jack E. Yesterday's People: Life in Contemporary Appalachia. LC 65-27012. 184p. 1965. pap. 4.00 (ISBN 0-8131-0109-3). U Pr of Ky.
West, John F. Appalachian Dawn. LC 73-77500. 1973. 9.95 (ISBN 0-87716-041-4, Pub. by Moore Pub Co). F Apple.

MOUNTAINEERING

see also Mountain Sickness; Rock Climbing; Trails

Ahluwalia, H. P. Faces of Everest. (Illus.). 1979. text ed. 50.00 (ISBN 0-7069-0563-6, Pub. by Vikas India). Advent NY.
--Higher Than Everest: Memoirs of a Mountaineer. 1975. 9.00x (ISBN 0-7069-0268-8). Intl Bk Dist.
Anderson, J. R. High Mountains & Cold Seas: A Biography of H. W. Tilman. LC 80-81520. (Illus.). 364p. 1980. 20.00 (ISBN 0-89886-008-3). Mountaineers.
Bagg, Alan. Fifty Short Climbs in the Midwest. LC 77-91194. 1978. pap. 6.95 (ISBN 0-8092-7667-4). Contemp Bks.
Banks, Mike. Mountain Climbing for Beginners. 1978. 8.95 (ISBN 0-8128-2448-2); pap. 3.95 (ISBN 0-8128-2447-4). Stein & Day.
Barker, Ralph. The Last Blue Mountain. LC 79-83801. (Illus.). 1979. pap. 7.95 (ISBN 0-916890-85-6). Mountaineers.
Beckett, T. N. The Mountains of Erewhon. (Illus.). 1978. 19.50 (ISBN 0-589-01119-7, Pub. by Reed Books Australia). C E Tuttle.
Beckey, Fred. Cascade Alpine Guide: Stevens Pass to Rainy Pass, Vol. 2. LC 77-82368. (Illus.). 1978. flexible plastic 13.95 (ISBN 0-916890-51-1). Mountaineers.
--Challenge of the North Cascades. LC 77-76453. (Illus.). 280p. 1977. pap. 6.95 (ISBN 0-916890-21-X). Mountaineers.
Beery, Donald. Call of the Mountains. (Illus.). 1973. 8.00 (ISBN 0-87012-138-3). McClain.
Bennet, Donald. Scottish Mountain Climbs. (Illus.). 192p. 1980. 30.00 (ISBN 0-7134-1048-5, Pub. by Batsford England). David & Charles.
Bernstein, Jeremy. Ascent: Of the Invention of Mountain Climbing & Its Practice. LC 78-26722. (Illus.). 1979. 9.50x (ISBN 0-8032-1154-6); pap. 3.25 (ISBN 0-8032-6052-0, BB#689, Bison). U of Nebr Pr.
--Mountain Passages. LC 78-15996. (Illus.). 1978. 12.50 (ISBN 0-8032-0983-5). U of Nebr Pr.
Blum, Arlene. Annapurna: A Woman's Place. LC 80-13288. (Illus.). 272p. 1980. 16.95 (ISBN 0-87156-236-7). Sierra.
Bonington, Chris. The Ultimate Challenge: The Hardest Way up the Highest Mountain in the World. LC 73-82322. (Illus.). 356p. 1973. 35.00 (ISBN 0-8128-1638-2). Stein & Day.
Bonington, Chris, et al. Everest -- the Hard Way. 1977. 14.95 (ISBN 0-394-40786-5). Random.
Bonney, Orrin H. & Bonney, Lorraine G. Field Book Wind River Range. rev. ed. (Illus.). 1968. pap. 5.95 with 1975 supp. (ISBN 0-685-07191-X). Bonney.
Braham, Trevor. Himalayan Odyssey. 1974. 17.95 (ISBN 0-04-910054-8). Allen Unwin.
Bridge, Raymond. Climbing: A Guide to Mountaineering. LC 75-38571. 1977. encore ed. 3.95 (ISBN 0-684-16347-0, ScribT). Scribner.
Brooks, Don. Washington Rock: A Climbing Guide. (Illus., Orig.). 1981. pap. 6.95 (ISBN 0-89886-046-6). Mountaineers.
Burdsall, Richard L. & Emmons, Arthur B., 3rd. Men Against the Clouds. LC 79-25369. (Illus.). 1980. pap. 9.95 (ISBN 0-916890-93-7). Mountaineers.
Chase, Evelyn H. Mountain Climber: Baley, 1840-1894. LC 80-23877. (Illus.). 173p. 1981. 12.95 (ISBN 0-87015-235-1). Pacific Bks.
Chouinard, Yvon. Climbing Ice. LC 77-19137. (Illus.). 1978. 15.00 (ISBN 0-87156-207-3); pap. 10.95 (ISBN 0-87156-208-1). Sierra.
Cleare, John. Mountaineering. (Illus.). 176p. 1980. 12.95 (ISBN 0-7137-0946-4, Pub. by Blandford Pr England); pap. 6.95 (ISBN 0-7137-1082-9). Sterling.
Climb to the Lost World. MacInnes, Hamish. (Illus.). 256p. 1976. pap. 2.95 (ISBN 0-14-003444-7). Penguin.
Cline, Platt. They Came to the Mountain. LC 76-10424. (Illus.). 206p. 1976. 12.50 (ISBN 0-87358-153-9). Northland.
Clyde, Norman. El Picacho Del Diablo: The Conquest of Lower California's Highest Peak, 1932 & 1937. Robinson, John W., ed. (Baja California Travels Ser.: No. 36). (Illus.). 1975. 15.00 (ISBN 0-87093-236-5). Dawsons.
Coleman, Edmund T. Mountaineering on the Pacific in 1868. Jones, William R., ed. (Illus.). 24p. 1977. Repr. of 1869 ed. pap. 2.00 (ISBN 0-89646-014-2). Outbooks.
Craig, Robert. Storm & Sorrow in the High Pamirs. 1980. 12.95 (ISBN 0-671-25154-6). S&S.
Darvill, Fred T., Jr. Mountaineering Medicine: A Wilderness Medical Guide. 9th ed. 60p. 1980. pap. 1.95 (ISBN 0-915740-04-4). Darvill Outdoor.
Davidson, Art. Minus One Hundred & Forty-Eight Degrees: The Winter Ascent of Mt. McKinley. (Illus.). 1979. pap. 4.95 (ISBN 0-89174-037-6). Comstock Edns.
De Beer, Gavin. Early Travellers in the Alps. (Illus.). 1967. 5.95 (ISBN 0-8079-0041-9); pap. 2.95 (ISBN 0-8079-0042-7). October.
Dingle, Graeme. Wall of Shadows: Jannu the New Zealand Adventure. LC 77-364274. (Illus.). 1976. 13.50x (ISBN 0-340-21450-3). Intl Pubns Serv.
Dodge, Nicholas A. A Climbing Guide to Oregon. LC 75-16654. (Illus.). 1975. pap. 8.95 (ISBN 0-911518-33-9). Touchstone Pr Ore.
Edwards, Anne, et al. Exploring the Purcell Wilderness. LC 78-71661. (Illus.). 112p. 1979. pap. 6.95 (ISBN 0-916890-75-9). Mountaineers.
Engel, Claire E. The History of Mountaineering in the Alps. LC 77-8869. (Illus.). 1977. Repr. of 1950 ed. lib. bdg. 23.50x (ISBN 0-8371-9700-7, ENHM). Greenwood.
Favour, Alpheus H. Old Bill Williams, Mountain Man. 234p. 1962. 11.95 (ISBN 0-8061-0515-1). U of Okla Pr.
Ferber, Peggy, ed. Mountaineering: The Freedom of the Hills. 3rd ed. LC 73-92374. (Illus.). 478p. 1974. 13.95 (ISBN 0-916890-01-5). Mountaineers.
Frances, Godfrey. Teach Yourself Mountain Climbing. Date not set. 7.50x (ISBN 0-392-08295-0, SpS). Sportshelf.
Fryxell, Fritiof. Mountaineering in the Tetons: The Pioneer Period, Eighteen Ninety-Eight to Nineteen Forty. 2nd ed. Smith, Phil D., ed. LC 79-83648. (Illus.). 1978. 10.95 (ISBN 0-933160-00-3); pap. 5.95 (ISBN 0-933160-01-1). Teton Bkshop.
Gervasutti, Giusto. Gervasutti's Climbs. LC 78-70839. 202p. 1979. pap. 7.95 (ISBN 0-916890-67-8). Mountaineers.
Gilbert, Richard. Mountaineering for All. (Illus.). 136p. 1981. 19.95 (ISBN 0-7134-3350-7, Pub. by Batsford England). David & Charles.
Goetzmann, William H. The Mountain Man. LC 78-51924. (Illus.). 64p. 1979. pap. 12.95 (ISBN 0-8032-7004-6, Buffalo Bill Hist. Ctr.). U of Nebr Pr.
Grodin, Joseph R., et al. High Sierra Hiking Guide to Silver Lake. 2nd ed. Winnett, Thomas, ed. LC 78-50994. (High Sierra Hiking Guide Ser.: Vol. 17). (Illus., Orig.). 1970. pap. 4.95 (ISBN 0-911824-73-1). Wilderness.
Hammond, Alan. To Climb a Sacred Mountain. (Illus.). 1979. pap. 3.95 softcover (ISBN 0-914766-47-3). IWP Pub.
Harris, Stephen. Fire & Ice: The Cascade Volcanoes. 2nd ed. LC 80-16095. (Illus.). 1980. pap. 7.95 (ISBN 0-89886-009-1). Mountaineers.
Harvard, Andrew & Thompson, Todd. Mountain of Storms: The American Expeditions to Dhaulagiri. LC 74-13924. (Illus.). 220p. 1981. pap. 9.95 (ISBN 0-87754-146-9). Chelsea Hse.
Haston, Dougal. In High Places. (Illus.). 176p. 1973. 9.95 (ISBN 0-02-548980-1). Macmillan.
Higman, Harry W. & Larrison, Earl J. Pilchuck, the Life of a Mountain. 288p. 30.00 (ISBN 0-8466-2307-2, SJS307); pap. 20.00 (ISBN 0-8466-0307-1). Shorey.
Hill, Howard. Freedom to Roam: The Struggle for Access to Britain's Moors & Mountains. 139p. 1980. 29.75x (ISBN 0-903485-77-X, Pub. by Moorland England). State Mutual Bk.
Hill, Mike. Hikers' & Climbers' Guide to the Sandia Mountains. (Illus.). 1977. pap. 5.95 (ISBN 0-933004-02-8). Adobe Pr.
Hillary, Edmund. From the Ocean to the Sky. (Illus.). 1979. 12.95 (ISBN 0-670-33172-4). Viking Pr.
Hornbein, Thomas F. Everest: The West Ridge. LC 80-16088. (Illus.). 248p. 1980. Repr. of 1965 ed. 17.50 (ISBN 0-916890-90-2). Mountaineers.
Houston, Charles S. & Bates, Robert H. K Two: The Savage Mountain. LC 78-71666. (Illus.). 1979. pap. 8.95 (ISBN 0-916890-73-2). Mountaineers.
Hunter, Jim & Shelley, Marshall. A Man Against the Mountain. 1978. pap. 1.95 (ISBN 0-89191-143-X). Cook.
Jones, Chris. Climbing in North America. LC 75-3771. 1976. 19.95 (ISBN 0-520-02976-3); pap. 9.95 (ISBN 0-520-03637-9). U of Cal Pr.
Kelsey, Joe. Climbing & Hiking in the Wind River Mountains: Wyoming. LC 79-23882. (Illus.). 400p. (Totebook). 1980. pap. 8.95 (ISBN 0-87156-267-7). Sierra.
Kelsey, Michael R. Climbers & Hikers Guide to the Worlds Mountains. (Illus.). 680p. 1981. pap. 17.95 (ISBN 0-9605824-0-1). Kelsey Pub.
King, Clarence. Mountaineering in the Sierra Nevada. LC 79-116056. 1970. pap. 6.95 (ISBN 0-8032-5716-3, BB 518, Bison). U of Nebr Pr.
King, Clarence. Mountaineering in the Kings River Country. Jones, William R., ed. (Illus.). 48p. 1978. Repr. of 1871 ed. pap. 2.95 (ISBN 0-89646-042-8). Outbooks.
King, Tom. In the Shadow of Giants: Great Mountain Ascents Past & Present. LC 77-84572. (Illus.). 1981. 11.95 (ISBN 0-498-02186-6). A S Barnes.
Kingsley, Norman. Icecraft. (Illus.). 120p. 1975. wrappers 4.95 (ISBN 0-910856-59-1). La Siesta.
Langford, N. P. The Ascent of Mt. Hayden. Jones, William R., ed. (Illus.). 1980. pap. 2.00 (ISBN 0-89646-066-5). Outbooks.
Law, Donald. Starting Mountaineering & Rockclimbing. 1977. 10.50 (ISBN 0-7153-7322-6). David & Charles.
Lee, Chip, et al. On Edge: The Life & Climb of Henry Barber. (Illus.). 250p. (Orig.). 1981. pap. 9.95 (ISBN 0-910146-35-7). Appalach Mtn.
Lewis, H. Warren. You're Standing on My Fingers. LC 78-98409. (Illus.). 1969. 5.95 (ISBN 0-8310-7076-5). Howell-North.
Lizar, Thomas. New Mexico Mountain Access. (Illus.). 95p. (Orig.). 1980. pap. 7.95 (ISBN 0-939866-02-1). Woodstone Bks.
Lowe, Jeff. The Ice Experience. 1979. pap. 7.95 (ISBN 0-8092-7511-2). Contemp Bks.
Lyman, Tom & Riviere, Bill. The Field Book of Mountaineering & Rock Climbing. (Illus.). 256p. 1975. 9.95 (ISBN 0-87691-162-9). Winchester Pr.
MacInnes, Hamish. High Drama: Mountain Rescue Stories from Four Continents. LC 81-80500. (Illus.). 224p. 1981. 12.95 (ISBN 0-89886-031-8). Mountaineers.
--International Mountain Rescue Handbook. 1981. 18.00x (ISBN 0-686-75470-0, Pub. by Constable Pubs). State Mutual Bk.
McMartin, Barbara. Old Roads & Open Peaks. (Illus.). 1977. pap. 6.95 (ISBN 0-935272-02-X). ADK Mtn Club.
McMullen, D. E. Oregon Underfoot. LC 75-9247. (Illus.). 1975. pap. cancelled (ISBN 0-911518-31-2). Touchstone Pr Ore.
Marty, Sid. Men for the Mountains. LC 81-80365. (Illus.). 272p. 1981. Repr. of 1978 ed. pap. 7.95 (ISBN 0-89886-027-X). Mountaineers.
Messner, Reinhold. The Big Walls. (Illus.). 1978. 19.95 (ISBN 0-19-520062-4). Oxford U Pr.
--K Two: Mountain of Mountains. (Illus.). 176p. 1981. 35.00 (ISBN 0-19-520253-8). Oxford U Pr.
--Seventh Grade. 1974. 9.95 (ISBN 0-19-519768-2). Oxford U Pr.
--Solo: Nanga Parbat. (Illus.). 1981. 19.95 (ISBN 0-19-520196-5). Oxford U Pr.
Molenaar, Dee. The Challenge of Rainier. rev. ed. LC 79-14923. (Illus.). 1979. pap. 9.95 (ISBN 0-916890-70-8). Mountaineers.
Moore, Terris. Mt. McKinley: The Pioneer Climbs. LC 81-1002. (Illus.). 224p. 1981. pap. 8.95 (ISBN 0-89886-021-0). Mountaineers.
Moravetz, Bruno. The Big Book of Mountaineering. (Illus.). 1981. 49.95 (ISBN 0-8120-5332-X). Barron.
Munday, Don. The Unknown Mountain. LC 75-36436. 268p. 1976. pap. 6.95 (ISBN 0-916890-38-4). Mountaineers.
Neate, W. R. Mountaineering & Its Literature. LC 80-7785. 168p. 1980. pap. 9.95 (ISBN 0-89886-004-0). Mountaineers.
Nentl, Jerolyn. Mountain Climbing. Schroeder, Howard, ed. LC 80-415. (Funseekers Ser.). (Illus.). (gr. 3-5). 1979. lib. bdg. 6.95 (ISBN 0-89686-075-2); pap. 3.25 (ISBN 0-89686-079-5). Crestwood Hse.
Paulcke, Wilhelm & Dumler, Helmut. Hazards in Mountaineering: How to Recognize & Avoid Them. Bowman, E. Noel, tr. (Illus.). 175p. 1973. 9.95 (ISBN 0-19-519718-6). Oxford U Pr.
Piggott, Margaret. Discover Southeast Alaska: With Pack and Paddle. LC 74-81954. (Illus.). 268p. (Orig.). 1975. pap. 7.95 (ISBN 0-916890-35-X). Mountaineers.
Planting the Five Star Flag on Mt. Tomur. 1979. 8.95 (ISBN 0-8351-0673-X). China Bks.
Pokorny, George, et al. International Directory of Mountaineering Clubs & Organizations. LC 79-1890. (Illus.). 162p. 1979. pap. 5.95 (ISBN 0-87842-112-2). Mountain Pr.
Pyatt, Edward. Mountains & Mountaineering Facts & Feats. (Guinness Superlatives Ser.). (Illus.). 256p. 1980. 19.95 (ISBN 0-8069-9246-8, Pub. by Guinness Superlatives England). Sterling.
Radcliffe, Peter. Land of Mountains: Hiking & Climbing in New Zealand. (Illus.). 1979. 27.50 (ISBN 0-916890-69-4). Mountaineers.
Rebuffat, Gaston. Between Heaven & Earth. Brockett, E., tr. (Illus.). 1965. 17.50 (ISBN 0-19-519058-0). Oxford U Pr.
--On Ice & Snow & Rock. Evans, Patrick, tr. from Fr. (Illus.). 1971. 19.50 (ISBN 0-19-519149-8). Oxford U Pr.
--Starlight & Storm: The Ascent of Six Great North Faces of the Alps. 1968. 8.00 (ISBN 0-19-519061-0). Oxford U Pr.
Renouf, Jane & Hulse, Stewart. First Aid for Hill Walkers & Climbers. (Illus.). 169p. 1978. pap. 5.95 (ISBN 0-14-046293-7). Bradt Ent.
Ridgeway, Rick. The Last Step: The American Ascent of K2. LC 80-19395. (Illus.). 352p. 1980. 25.00 (ISBN 0-89886-007-5). Mountaineers.
Riley, Michael J. Mountain Camping. 1979. o. p. 12.95 (ISBN 0-8092-7683-6); pap. 5.95 (ISBN 0-8092-7682-8). Contemp Bks.
Robbins, Royal. Basic Rockcraft. (Illus.). 1970. wrappers 2.95 (ISBN 0-910856-34-6). La Siesta.
Roberts, Eric. Welzenbach's Climbs. LC 81-80502. (Illus.). 270p. 1981. 14.95 (ISBN 0-89886-018-0). Mountaineers.
Robinson, John W. High Sierra Hiking Guide to Mt. Goddard. 2nd ed. Winnett, Thomas, ed. (High Sierra Hiking Guide Ser.: Vol. 10). (Illus., Orig.). 1980. pap. 4.95 (ISBN 0-89997-002-8). Wilderness.
Roper, Steve. Climbers Guide to Yosemite Valley. LC 71-157530. (Totebook Ser.). (Illus.). 320p. 1971. pap. 7.95 (ISBN 0-87156-048-8). Sierra.
Roper, Steve & Steck, Allen. Fifty Classic Climbs of North America. (Paperback Library). (Illus.). 336p. 1981. pap. 10.95 (ISBN 0-87156-292-8). Sierra.
Roscoe, D. T. Mountaineering: A Manual for Teachers & Instructors. (Illus.). 1976. 18.00 (ISBN 0-571-09456-2). Transatlantic.
Rowell, Galen. High & Wild: A Mountaineer's World. LC 79-13000. (Illus.). 1979. 29.95 (ISBN 0-87156-263-4). Sierra.
--In the Throne Room of the Mountain Gods. LC 76-21248. (Illus.). 1977. 18.50 (ISBN 0-87156-184-0). Sierra.
--Many People Come, Looking, Looking. LC 80-19394. (Illus.). 176p. 1980. 30.00 (ISBN 0-916890-86-4). Mountaineers.
Rudner, Ruth. Huts & Hikes in the Dolomites. LC 74-76314. (Totebook Ser.). (Illus.). 208p. 1974. pap. 4.95 (ISBN 0-87156-100-X). Sierra.
Rusk, C. E. Tales of a Western Mountaineer. LC 78-54427. (Illus.). 324p. 1978. pap. 7.95 (ISBN 0-916890-62-7). Mountaineers.
Schneider, Anne & Schneider, Steven. The Climber's Sourcebook. LC 75-21251. 321p. 1976. pap. 4.95 (ISBN 0-385-11081-2, Anch). Doubleday.
Schneider, Steven. High Technology: A Guide to Modern Mountaineering Equipment. 1980. 12.95 (ISBN 0-8092-7315-2); pap. 5.95 (ISBN 0-8092-7314-4). Contemp Bks.
Scott, Doug. Big Wall Climbing: Development, Techniques & Aids. (Illus.). 336p. 1974. 15.95 (ISBN 0-19-519767-4). Oxford U Pr.
Setnicka, Timothy J. Wilderness Search & Rescue: A Complete Handbook. Andrasko, Kenneth, ed. (Illus.). 640p. (Orig.). 1981. pap. 12.95 (ISBN 0-910146-21-7). Appalach Mtn.
Sherman, Paddy. Cloud Walkers. LC 78-71663. (Illus.). 1979. pap. 7.95 (ISBN 0-916890-79-1). Mountaineers.
Shipton, Eric. Mountain Conquest. LC 66-15087. (Horizon Caravel Bks.). 154p. (YA) (gr. 7 up). 1966. 9.95 (ISBN 0-06-025642-7, HarpJ). Har-Row.
Smith, Dave. Wasatch Granite. (Illus.). 1977. pap. 3.95 (ISBN 0-915272-04-0). Wasatch Pubs.

Steck, Allen & Roper, Steve, eds. Ascent: The Mountaineering Experience in Word & Image. LC 80-13855. (Illus.). 272p. (Orig.). 1980. pap. 14.95 (ISBN 0-87156-240-5). Sierra.
--Ascent 1975-76: The Mountaineering Experience in Word & Image. (Illus.). 128p. 1976. pap. 8.95 (ISBN 0-87156-189-1). Sierra.
Steele, Peter. Medical Care for Mountain Climbers. 1976. pap. 13.95x (ISBN 0-433-31560-1). Intl Ideas.
Stuck, Hudson. The Ascent of Denali. LC 77-90371. (Illus.). 1977. pap. 6.95 (ISBN 0-916890-58-9). Mountaineers.
Swinburne, Lawrence. Modern Mountain Man. 1981. lib. bdg. 7.99 (ISBN 0-8172-1570-0). Raintree Pubs.
Temple, Philip. Castles in the Air: Men & Mountains in New Zealand. LC 74-177859. (Illus.). 1973. pap. 8.50x (ISBN 0-8002-0342-9). Intl Pubns Serv.
Tenzing & Barnes, Malcom. After Everest. (Illus.). 1977. 13.50 (ISBN 0-04-920050-X). Allen Unwin.
Thompson, Phyllis T. The Use of Mountain Recreation Resources: A Comparison of Recreation & Tourism in the Colorado Rockies & the Swiss Alps. 233p. 12.00 (ISBN 0-686-64176-0). U CO Busn Res Div.
Tobias, Michael C. & Drasdo, Harold, eds. The Mountain Spirit. LC 77-20740. (Illus.). 264p. 1979. 25.00 (ISBN 0-87951-073-0). Overlook Pr.
Unsworth, Walt, ed. Peaks, Passes & Glaciers. (Illus.). 288p. 1981. 20.00 (ISBN 0-89886-044-X). Mountaineers.
Vervoorn, Aat. Beyond the Snowline. 1981. price not set (Pub. by Reed Books Australia). C E Tuttle.
Wallace, Gordon. Random Journey: Selections from the Notebook of a Longtime Wanderer. 1978. 8.95 (ISBN 0-533-03737-9). Vantage.
Wheelock, Walt. Ropes, Knots & Slings for Climbers. rev. ed. (Illus.). 1967. wrappers 1.50 (ISBN 0-910856-00-1). La Siesta.
Wheelock, Walt & Condon, T. Climbing Mount Whitney. rev. ed. (Illus.). 36p. 1978. wrappers 1.50 (ISBN 0-910856-02-8). La Siesta.
Whymper, Edward. Scrambles Amongst the Alps in the Years Eighteen Sixty to Eighteen Sixty-Nine. (Illus.). 176p. 1981. pap. 12.95 (ISBN 0-89815-055-8). Ten Speed Pr.
Widule, William & Swartling, Sven O. Climber's Guide to Devil's Lake. LC 78-65017. 208p. 1979. pap. 7.95 (ISBN 0-299-07804-3). U of Wis Pr.
Wilcox, Joe. White Winds. (Illus.). 1981. 12.95 (ISBN 0-89260-162-0); pap. 4.95 (ISBN 0-89260-163-9). Hwong Pub.
Wilson, Ken, ed. Games Climbers Play: A Collection of Mountaineering Writing. LC 80-15374. (Sierra Club Paperback Library). (Illus.). 688p. 1980. pap. 9.95 (ISBN 0-87156-301-0). Sierra.
Wolford, Feaster. Mountain Memories in Prose & Poetry. 1975. 12.00 (ISBN 0-87012-225-8). McClain.
Wood, Robert L. Men, Mules & Mountains: Lt. O'Neil's Olympic Expeditions. LC 76-15458. (Illus.). 460p. 1976. 17.50 (ISBN 0-916890-43-0). Mountaineers.

MOUNTAINEERING–JUVENILE LITERATURE

Casewit, Curtis W. The Saga of the Mountain Soldiers: The Story of the Tenth Mountain Division. LC 81-9662. (Illus.). 160p. (gr. 7 up). 1981. PLB 9.79 (ISBN 0-671-41630-8). Messner.
Gleasner. Rock Climbing. 1981. 7.95 (ISBN 0-679-20925-5). McKay.
Hargrove, Jim. Mountain Climbing. (Superwheels & Thrill Sports Bks.). (Illus.). (gr. 4 up). 1981. PLB 6.95 (ISBN 0-8225-0505-3). Lerner Pubns.
Roberts, David. Deborah: A Wilderness Narrative. LC 76-134663. (Illus.). (gr. 7-12). 8.95 (ISBN 0-8149-0677-X). Vanguard.
Shipton, Eric & Washburn, Bradford. Mountain Conquest. LC 66-15087. (Horizon Caravel Bks). (Illus.). 153p. (gr. 6 up). 1966. 9.95 (ISBN 0-06-025642-7, Dist. by Har-Row); (Dist. by Har-Row). Am Heritage.
Styles, Showell, ed. Men & Mountaineering. LC 68-25733. (gr. 6 up). 1968. 3.75 (ISBN 0-87250-221-X); PLB 3.56 (ISBN 0-87250-421-2). D White.
White, Anne T. All About Mountains & Mountaineering. (Allabout Ser: No. 41). (Illus.). (gr. 5-8). 1962. PLB 5.39 (ISBN 0-394-90241-6, BYR). Random.

MOUNTAINS

see also Geology, Structural; Mountain Ecology; Mountaineering; Photography of Mountains; Volcanoes; Watersheds
America's Magnificent Mountains, No. XV. LC 78-21447. (Illus.). 1980. 6.95 (ISBN 0-87044-281-3); lib. bdg. 8.50 (ISBN 0-87044-286-4). Natl Geog.
Barry, Roger. Mountain, Weather & Climate. 1981. 29.95x (ISBN 0-416-73730-7). Methuen Inc.
Bjorge, James R. Lord of the Mountain: Messages for Lent & Easter. LC 78-66941. 1979. pap. 3.50 (ISBN 0-8066-1687-3, 10-4110). Augsburg.
Bueler, William. Mountains of the World. LC 74-87796. (Illus.). 1977. pap. 5.95 (ISBN 0-916890-49-X). Mountaineers.
Cleare, John. World Guide to Mountains & Mountaineering. LC 78-25727. (Illus.). 1979. 19.95 (ISBN 0-8317-9546-8, Mayflower Bks). Smith Pubs.
Condry, William. The World of a Mountain. (Illus.). 96p. 1977. 8.95 (ISBN 0-571-10779-6, Pub. by Faber & Faber). Merrimack Bk Serv.
Country Beautiful Editors, ed. Great Mountains of North America. LC 75-28226. (Illus.). 208p. 1976. 25.00 (ISBN 0-87294-078-0). Country Beautiful.
Eberhart, Perry & Schmuck, Philip. Fourteeners: Colorado's Great Mountains. LC 72-75740. (Illus.). 128p. 1970. 14.00 (ISBN 0-8040-0122-7, SB); pap. 8.95 (ISBN 0-8040-0123-5, SB). Swallow.
Ecological Guidelines for Balanced Land Use: Conservation & Development in High Mountains. 40p. 1980. pap. 10.75 (ISBN 2-88032-100-X, IUCN77, IUCN). Unipub.
Fenton, Carroll L. & Fenton, Mildred. Mountains. facs. ed. LC 70-84305. (Essay Index Reprint Ser). 1942. 20.00 (ISBN 0-8369-1129-6). Arno.
Fountain, Paul. The Great Mountains & Forests of South America. 1976. lib. bdg. 59.95 (ISBN 0-8490-1902-8). Gordon Pr.
Frison-Roche, Roger & Tairraz, Pierre. Montagne (Mountain) new ed. (Larousse vie, art, cite). (Illus.). 144p. (Fr.). 1975. 29.95x (ISBN 2-03-018400-4). Larousse.
Gautrat, Jacques. Dictionnaire de la Montagne. 256p. (Fr.). 1970. pap. 8.95 (ISBN 0-686-56820-6, M-6598). French & Eur.
Ives, Jack D. & Barry, Roger G. Arctic & Alpine Environments. LC 74-2673. (Illus.). 980p. 1974. 134.00x (ISBN 0-416-65980-2). Methuen Inc.
Jerome, John. On Mountains: Thinking About Terrain. LC 78-24273. 1979. pap. 4.95 (ISBN 0-07-032535-9, SP). McGraw.
Kindersley, Anna. The Mountains of Serbia: Travels Through Inland Yugoslavia. (Illus.). 1977. 26.00 (ISBN 0-7195-3300-7). Transatlantic.
Lewis, H. Warren. You're Standing on My Fingers. LC 78-98409. (Illus.). 1969. 5.95 (ISBN 0-8310-7076-5). Howell-North.
MacInnes, Hamish. International Mountain Rescue Handbook. 1976. pap. 6.95 (ISBN 0-684-13904-9, SL552, ScribT). Scribner.
Maeder, Herbert. Mountains of Switzerland. 1968. 27.50 (ISBN 0-04-914039-6). Allen Unwin.
Mainwaring, William L. Exploring Oregon's Central & Southern Cascades. LC 79-64841. (Illus.). 1979. pap. 7.95 (ISBN 0-918832-02-0). Westridge.
Morse, Randy. The Mountains of Canada. LC 78-71667. (Illus.). 1979. 27.50 (ISBN 0-916890-74-0). Mountaineers.
National Geographic Society, ed. American Mountain People. LC 73-829. (Special Publications Ser.). (Illus.). 1973. avail. only from natl. geog. 6.95 (ISBN 0-87044-126-4). Natl Geog.
Peattie, Roderick. Mountain Geography: A Critique & Field Study. Repr. of 1936 ed. lib. bdg. 14.25x (ISBN 0-8371-2243-0, PEMG). Greenwood.
Perkis, Philip, photos by. Warwick Mountain Series. LC 78-61647. (Illus.). 1978. 24.00 (ISBN 0-932526-01-2). Nexus Pr.
Prater, Yvonne. Snoqualmie Pass: From Indian Trail to Interstate. (Illus.). 144p. (Orig.). 1981. pap. 6.95 (ISBN 0-89886-015-6). Mountaineers.
Pyatt, Edward. Mountains & Mountaineering Facts & Feats. (Guinness Superlatives Ser.). (Illus.). 256p. 1980. 19.95 (ISBN 0-8069-9246-8, Pub. by Guinness Superlatives England). Sterling.
Reese, Rick, ed. Montana Mountain Ranges. (Montana Geographic Series: No. 1). 100p. 1981. pap. write for info. (ISBN 0-938314-01-7). MT Mag.
A Review-Mountain Ecosystems, Nineteen Eighty. (UNEP Report Ser.: No. 2). 38p. 1980. pap. 6.00 (ISBN 0-686-70045-7, UNEP 031, UNEP). Unipub.
Rowell, Galen. High & Wild: A Mountaineer's World. LC 79-13000. (Illus.). 1979. 29.95 (ISBN 0-87156-263-4). Sierra.
St. George, George. Soviet Deserts & Mountains. (The World's Wild Places Ser.). (Illus.). 184p. 1974. 12.95 (ISBN 0-8094-2012-0). Time-Life.
Scaylea, Josef. Moods of the Mountain II. (Illus.). 64p. 1981. 24.95 (ISBN 0-87564-017-6). Superior Pub.
Tennant, Alan & Allender, Michael. The Guadalupe Mountains of Texas. (Elma Dill Russell Spencer Foundation Ser: Vol. 10). (Illus.). 167p. 1980. 29.95 (ISBN 0-292-72720-8). U of Tex Pr.
Thompson, Frances. Mountain Relics. LC 75-20605. (Illus.). 320p. 1976. 15.00 (ISBN 0-498-01774-5). A S Barnes.
Tianshan Mountains. 1980. 20.00 (ISBN 0-8351-0738-8). China Bks.
Ungnade, Herbert E. Guide to the New Mexico Mountains. enl. & rev. 2nd ed. LC 72-80752. (Illus.). 235p. 1972. 7.50 (ISBN 0-8263-0241-6); pap. 5.95 (ISBN 0-8263-0242-4). U of NM Pr.
Voldstad, Edith. Again I See the Mountains. rev. 2nd ed. LC 74-84197. 1976. soft bdg. 3.95 (ISBN 0-9603906-0-X, A735817). Voldstad Ent.
Walker, Bryce. The Great Divide. (The American Wilderness Ser.). 1973. 12.95 (ISBN 0-8094-1184-9). Time-Life.
Wheelock, Walt. Southern California Peaks. (Illus.). 1973. wrappers 1.50 (ISBN 0-910856-32-X). La Siesta.
Wheelock, Walt, ed. Desert Peaks Guide One. rev. ed. (Illus.). 1964. wrappers 1.95 (ISBN 0-910856-03-6). La Siesta.

MOUNTAINS–JUVENILE LITERATURE

A Look at the Earth Around Us: Mountains. (Wonders of Learning Kits Ser.). (gr. 3-5). 1980. incl. cassette & tchrs. guide 23.50 (ISBN 0-686-74401-2, 04965). Natl Geog.
White, Anne T. All About Mountains & Mountaineering. (Allabout Ser: No. 41). (Illus.). (gr. 5-8). 1962. PLB 5.39 (ISBN 0-394-90241-6, BYR). Random.

MOUNTAINS–GREAT BRITAIN

Hill, Howard. Freedom to Roam: The Struggle for Access to Britain's Moors & Mountains. 139p. 1980. 29.75x (ISBN 0-903485-77-X, Pub. by Moorland England). State Mutual Bk.
Pyatt, Edward C. Mountains of Britain. (Batsford Britain Ser). (Illus.). 1966. 8.95 (ISBN 0-8038-4637-1). Hastings.

MOUNTAINS–IRELAND

Pyatt, Edward C. Mountains of Britain. (Batsford Britain Ser). (Illus.). 1966. 8.95 (ISBN 0-8038-4637-1). Hastings.

MOUNTAINS IN LITERATURE

Clifford, Richard J. The Cosmic Mountain in Canaan & the Old Testament. LC 71-188968. (Semitic Monographs Ser: No. 4). (Illus.). 221p. 1972. 12.50x (ISBN 0-674-17425-9). Harvard U Pr.
Spindler, Robert. Die Alpen in der Englischen Literatur und Kunst. (Illus.). Repr. of 1932 ed. pap. 5.00 (ISBN 0-384-57080-1). Johnson Repr.

MOUNTBATTEN FAMILY

Alan. Mission with Mountbatten. 2nd ed. LC 77-4388. (Illus.). 1977. Repr. of 1972 ed. lib. bdg. 25.50x (ISBN 0-8371-9596-9, CJMM). Greenwood.
Campbell-Johnson, Alan. Mission with Mountbatten. rev. ed. 1951. pap. 2.45 (ISBN 0-88253-129-8). Ind-US Inc.

MOUNTBATTEN, LOUIS MOUNTBATTEN, EARL, 1900-1979

Hough, Richard. Mountbatten. 1981. 16.95 (ISBN 0-394-51162-X). Random.
Mountbatten: Eighty Years in Pictures. (Illus.). 1979. 16.95 (ISBN 0-670-49137-3, Studio). Viking Pr.
Ross, Josephine. Lord Mountbatten: Profiles Ser. (Illus.). 64p. (gr. 4-6). 1981. 8.95 (ISBN 0-241-10593-5, Pub. by Hamish Hamilton England). David & Charles.
Smith, Charles. Lord Mountbatten: His Butler's Story. LC 80-51787. (Illus.). 224p. 1980. 12.95 (ISBN 0-8128-2751-1). Stein & Day.
Terraine, John. The Life & Times of Lord Mountbatten. LC 79-3740. (Illus.). 288p. (Orig.). 1980. 4.95 (ISBN 0-03-056899-4). HR&W.

MOUNTFORT, WILLIAM, d. 1692

Borgman, Albert S. The Life & Death of William Mountfort. (Harvard Studies in English Ser: Vol. 15). Repr. of 1935 ed. 19.50 (ISBN 0-384-05135-9). Johnson Repr.
Mountfort, William. Plays of William Mountfort. LC 77-21660. 1977. 30.00x (ISBN 0-8201-1292-5). Schol Facsimiles.

MOURNING CUSTOMS

see also Funeral Rites and Ceremonies
Gorer, Geoffrey. Death, Grief, & Mourning. Kastenbaum, Robert, ed. LC 76-19573. (Death & Dying Ser.). (Illus.). 1977. Repr. of 1965 ed. lib. bdg. 18.00x (ISBN 0-405-09571-6). Arno.
Rosenblatt, Paul C., et al. Grief & Mourning in Cross-Cultural Perspective. LC 76-29270. (Comparative Studies Ser.). 242p. 1976. pap. 7.00x (ISBN 0-87536-334-2). HRAFP.
Stavsky, David. For Thou Art with Me: A Manual of Mourning. 1965. pap. 1.50 (ISBN 0-87306-093-8). Feldheim.
Zanca, Kenneth J. Mourning: The Healing Journey 1980. (Orig.). 1.75 (ISBN 0-914544-30-6). Living Flame Pr.
Zlotnick, Dov, tr. Tractate Mourning: Regulations Relating to Death, Burial, & Mourning. (Judaica Ser.: No. 17). 1966. 20.00x (ISBN 0-300-01069-9). Yale U Pr.

MOUSE

see Mice

MOUSSEUX

see Moso (Tribe)

MOUSSORGSKY, MODEST PETROVICH, 1839-81

Riesemann, Oskar. Moussorgsky. England, Paul, tr. 7.00 (ISBN 0-8446-4802-7). Peter Smith.
Von Riesemann, Oskar. Moussorgsky. England, Paul, tr. LC 74-121278. Repr. of 1929 ed. 14.00 (ISBN 0-404-05334-3). AMS Pr.

MOUTH

see also Jaws; Salivary Glands; Teeth; Tongue
Bosma, James F. Oral Sensation & Perception: Second Symposium. (Illus.). 580p. 1970. pap. 58.75 (ISBN 0-398-00194-4). C C Thomas.
--Symposium on Oral Sensation & Perception. (Illus.). 376p. 1967. ed. spiral bdg. 39.50photocopy (ISBN 0-398-00193-6). C C Thomas.
--Third Symposium on Oral Sensation & Perception: The Mouth of the Infant. (Illus.). 484p. 1972. 58.25 (ISBN 0-398-02238-0). C C Thomas.
Bradley. Basic Oral Physiology. Date not set. price not set (ISBN 0-8151-1183-5). Year Bk Med.
Cimasoni, Geneve. The Crevicular Fluid. (Monographs in Oral Science: Vol. 3). 121p. 1974. 33.75 (ISBN 3-8055-1699-1). S Karger.
Cole, A. S. & Eastoe, J. E. Biochemistry & Oral Biology. (Illus.). 1977. 34.95 (ISBN 0-8151-1803-1). Year Bk Med.
Emmelin, N. & Zotterman, Yngve. Oral Physiology. 311p. 1972. text ed. 75.00 (ISBN 0-08-016972-4). Pergamon.
Goldberg, Hyman J. & Ripa, Louis W. Oral Hygiene in Oral Health. (American Lecture in Dentistry). (Illus.). 408p. 1977. 28.50 (ISBN 0-398-03590-3). C C Thomas.
Goodson, J. M. & Johansen, E. L. Analysis of Human Mandibular Movement. (Monographs in Oral Science: Vol. 5). 1975. 35.50 (ISBN 3-8055-1416-6). S Karger.
Jenkins, G. Neil. The Physiology & Biochemistry of the Mouth. 4th ed. (Illus.). 508p. 1978. 42.50 (ISBN 0-632-00138-0, Blackwell). Mosby.
Kawamura, Y., ed. Physiology of Oral Tissues. (Frontiers of Oral Physiology: Vol. 2). (Illus.). 350p. 1976. 69.50 (ISBN 3-8055-1360-7). S Karger.
Kurlyandsky, V. Orthopaedic Stomatology. MIR Publishers, tr. from Rus. (Illus.). 690p. 1975. text ed. 26.00x (ISBN 0-8464-0694-2). Beekman Pubs.
Kutscher, Austin H. & Goldberg, Ivan K. Oral Care of the Aging & Dying Patient. (American Lectures in Dentistry Ser.). (Illus.). 236p. 1973. text ed. 17.50 (ISBN 0-398-02714-5). C C Thomas.
Lavelle. Applied Physiology of the Mouth. 1976. 35.00 (ISBN 0-8151-5332-5). Year Bk Med.
Massler, Maury & Schour, Isaac. Atlas of the Mouth. 2nd ed. (Illus.). 9.50 (ISBN 0-685-05572-8). Am Dental.
Myers, H. M. Reprinted Selected Top Articles Published 1977, No. 1. (Karger Highlights, Oral Science One). 1979. 9.00 (ISBN 3-8055-3028-5). S Karger.
Nguyen Thanh Nguyen & Roulf, Patty de. Your Mouth. LC 78-7180. (Illus.). 1978. 8.95 (ISBN 0-8019-6667-1). Chilton.
Nolte, William A. Oral Microbiology. 3rd ed. LC 77-1945. (Illus.). 1977. text ed. 31.95 (ISBN 0-8016-3688-4). Mosby.
Permar, Dorothy & Melfi, Rudy C. Oral Embryology and Microscopic Anatomy: A Textbook for Students in Dental Hygiene. 6th ed. LC 76-30711. (Illus.). 186p. 1977. text ed. 9.50 (ISBN 0-8121-0582-6). Lea & Febiger.
Perryman, James H., ed. Oral Physiology & Occlusion: An International Symposium. LC 78-17812. 268p. 1979. 30.00 (ISBN 0-08-023183-7). Pergamon.
Schoenberg, Bernard, et al, eds. Terminal Patient: Oral Care. LC 72-9892. 1973. 20.00x (ISBN 0-88238-701-4). Columbia U Pr.
Shaw, James H., et al. Textbook of Oral Biology. LC 76-14687. (Illus.). 1978. 39.50 (ISBN 0-7216-8182-4). Saunders.
Slavkin, Harold C. & Bavetta, Lucien A., eds. Developmental Aspects of Oral Biology. 1972. 59.50 (ISBN 0-12-648350-7). Acad Pr.
Staple, Peter H., ed. Advances in Oral Biology. Vol. 1. 1964. 56.00 (ISBN 0-12-030501-1); Vol. 2. 1966. 56.00 (ISBN 0-12-030502-X); Vol. 3. 1968. 56.00 (ISBN 0-12-030503-8); Vol. 4. 1970. 56.00 (ISBN 0-12-030504-6). Acad Pr.
Woelfel, Julian B. Permar's Outline for Dental Anatomy. 2nd ed. LC 78-31312. (Illus.). 228p. 1979. pap. 14.50 (ISBN 0-8121-0662-8). Lea & Febiger.

MOUTH–ABNORMITIES AND DEFORMITIES

Garliner, Daniel. Myofunctional Therapy. LC 75-14781. (Illus.). 450p. 1976. text ed. 39.00 (ISBN 0-7216-4055-9). Saunders.
Stewart & Prescott. Oral Facial Genetics. LC 76-21322. (Illus.). 1976. 49.50 (ISBN 0-8016-4810-6). Mosby.

MOUTH–BACTERIOLOGY
see Mouth–Microbiology
MOUTH–DISEASES
see also Gums–Diseases; Oral Manifestations of General Diseases
Application of the International Classification of Diseases to Dentistry & Stomatology (ICD-DA) (Also avail. in French & Spanish). 1973. pap. 6.40 (ISBN 92-4-154029-X). World Health.
Barrett & Hanson, Marvin L. Oral Myofunctional Disorders. 2nd ed. LC 78-7029. 1978. text ed. 37.50 (ISBN 0-8016-0497-4). Mosby.
Bhaskar, S. N. Synopsis of Oral Pathology. 5th ed. LC 77-481. (Illus.). 1977. 23.95 (ISBN 0-8016-0689-6). Mosby.
Burnett, George W. & Schuster, George. Oral Microbiology & Infectious Disease. 4th ed. (Illus.). 784p. 1976. 79.00 (ISBN 0-683-01225-8); student ed. 26.00 (ISBN 0-683-01226-6). Williams & Wilkins.
Chisholm, Derrick M., et al. Introduction to Oral Medicine. (Illus.). 1979. text ed. 18.00 (ISBN 0-7216-2593-2). Saunders.
Colby, Robert A., et al. Color Atlas of Oral Pathology. 3rd ed. LC 73-147050. (Illus.). 200p. 1971. 29.50 (ISBN 0-397-50279-6). Har-Row.
Eversole, Lewis R. Clinical Outline of Oral Pathology: Diagnosis & Treatment. LC 77-16203. (Illus.). 331p. 1978. text ed. 25.00 (ISBN 0-8121-0592-3). Lea & Febiger.
Gayford, J. J. & Haskell, R. Clinical Oral Medicine. 2nd ed. (Illus.). 1979. 35.00 (ISBN 0-8151-4185-8). Year Bk Med.
Kerr, Donald A. & Ash, M., Jr. Oral Pathology: An Introduction to General & Oral Pathology for Hygienists. 4th ed. LC 77-4902. (Illus.). 350p. 1978. text ed. 11.50 (ISBN 0-8121-0609-1). Lea & Febiger.
Kuenzel, W. & Toman, J., eds. Kinderstomatologie 2. revised ed. 1976. 56.00 (ISBN 3-8055-2407-2). S Karger.
Kurlyandsky, V. Orthopaedic Stomatology. 588p. 1977. 12.25 (ISBN 0-8285-0764-3, Pub. by Mir Pubs Russia). Imported Pubns.
Kutscher, Austin H., et al, eds. The Mouth in Critical & Terminal Illness. (Thanatology Ser.). 1978. 16.50x (ISBN 0-8422-7295-X). Irvington.
--Oral Care: The Mouth in Termminal & Critical Illness. LC 79-48046. 1980. lib. bdg. 18.00 (ISBN 0-405-12642-5). Arno.
Laskin, Daniel M. Management of Oral Emergencies. (Illus.). 128p. 1964. 7.25 (ISBN 0-398-01082-X). C C Thomas.
Lucas, R. B. Pathology of Tumours of the Oral Tissues. 3rd ed. (Illus.). 1977. text ed. 67.50 (ISBN 0-443-01397-7). Churchill.
Lynch, Malcolm, ed. Burket's Oral Medicine. 7th ed. LC 77-2752. 1977. text ed. 45.00 (ISBN 0-397-52083-2, JBL-Med-Nursing). Har-Row.
McCarthy, Philip L. & Shklar, Gerald. Diseases of the Oral Mucosa. 2nd ed. LC 80-10335. (Illus.). 579p. 1980. text ed. 47.50 (ISBN 0-8121-0641-5). Lea & Febiger.
Marsland, E. A. & Browne, R. M. Colour Atlas of Oral Histopathology. (Illus.). 1975. 39.50 (ISBN 0-8151-5774-6). Year Bk Med.
Pelton, Walter J., et al. Epidemiology of Oral Health. LC 77-88811. (Vital & Health Statistics Monographs, American Public Health Association). (Illus.). 1969. 10.00x (ISBN 0-674-25885-1). Harvard U Pr.
Pindborg. Atlas of Diseases of the Oral Mucosa. 3rd ed. LC 78-54520. 1980. 75.00 (ISBN 0-7216-7277-9). Saunders.
Pindborg, J. J. & Kramer, I. R. Histological Typing of Odontogenic Tumours, Jaw Cysts & Allied Lesions. (World Health Organization: International Histological Classification of Tumours Ser.). (Illus.). 1971. incl. slides 112.50 (ISBN 0-89189-114-5, 70-1-005-00). Am Soc Clinical.
Pullon, Peter A. & Miller, Arthur S. Oral Pathology: An Independent Learning Program. 90p. 1974. pap. text ed. 23.75 (ISBN 0-7216-9867-0); filmstrips 250.00 (ISBN 0-7216-9866-2); slides 375.00 (ISBN 0-7216-9872-7). Saunders.
Renson, C. E. Oral Disease. (Illus.). 1978. text ed. 14.50x (ISBN 0-906141-04-4, Pub. by Update Pubns England). Kluwer Boston.
Staple, Peter H., ed. Advances in Oral Biology. Vol. 1. 1964. 56.00 (ISBN 0-12-030501-1); Vol. 2. 1966. 56.00 (ISBN 0-12-030502-X); Vol. 3. 1968. 56.00 (ISBN 0-12-030503-8); Vol. 4. 1970. 56.00 (ISBN 0-12-030504-6). Acad Pr.
Stewart & Prescott. Oral Facial Genetics. LC 76-21322. (Illus.). 1976. 49.50 (ISBN 0-8016-4810-6). Mosby.
Topazian, Richard G. & Goldberg, Morton H. Management of Infections of the Oral & Maxillofacial Regions. (Illus.). 500p. 1981. text ed. write for info. (ISBN 0-7216-8879-9). Saunders.
Toto, Patrick D. Diseases of the Oral Mucosa. Gardner, Alvin F., ed. LC 77-94880. (Postgraduate Dental Handbook Ser.). 1978. cancelled (ISBN 0-88416-156-0). Wright-PSG.
Toto, Patrick D., et al. Pathology of the Oral Cavity. (Atlases of the Pathology of the Head & Neck). 1976. text & slides 76.50 (ISBN 0-89189-030-0, 15-1-018-00). Am Soc Clinical.
Wahl, Norman. Oral Signs & Symptons: A Diagnostic Handbook, a Guide to the Identification of Lesions of the Mouth. (Illus.). 332p. 1969. photocopy ed. spiral 32.75 (ISBN 0-398-01999-1). C C Thomas.
Wahl, P. N. Histological Typing of Oral & Oropharyngeal Tumours. (World Health Organization: International Histological Classification of Tumours Ser.). (Illus.). 1971. incl. slides 37.00 (ISBN 0-89189-116-1, 70-1-004-00). Am Soc Clinical.
Wood, Norman K. & Goaz, Paul W. Differential Diagnosis of Oral Lesions. LC 75-9764. (Illus.). 750p. 1975. 28.50 (ISBN 0-8016-5616-8). Mosby.
Zegarelli, Edward V., et al, eds. Diagnosis of Diseases of the Mouth & Jaws. 2nd ed. LC 77-27480. (Illus.). 600p. 1978. text ed. 42.50 (ISBN 0-8121-0605-9). Lea & Febiger.
MOUTH–DISEASES–DIAGNOSIS
Cohen, Lawrence, ed. Oral Diagnosis & Treatment Planning. (Amer. Lec. Dentistry Ser). (Illus.). 344p. 1973. 25.00 (ISBN 0-398-02568-1). C C Thomas.
Lavelle, Christopher L. & Proctor, Donald B. Clinical Pathology of the Oral Mucosa. (Illus.). 1978. text ed. 27.50x (ISBN 0-06-141519-7, Harper Medical). Har-Row.
McElroy, Donald L. Handbook of Oral Diagnosis & Treatment Planning. LC 69-14460. 230p. 1974. Repr. of 1969 ed. 9.50 (ISBN 0-88275-126-3). Krieger.
Mitchell, David F., et al. Oral Diagnosis-Oral Medicine. 3rd ed. LC 76-30670. (Illus.). 586p. 1978. text ed. 26.50 (ISBN 0-8121-0590-7). Lea & Febiger.
MOUTH–MICROBIOLOGY
Burnett, George W. & Schuster, George. Oral Microbiology & Infectious Disease. 4th ed. (Illus.). 784p. 1976. 79.00 (ISBN 0-683-01225-8); student ed. 26.00 (ISBN 0-683-01226-6). Williams & Wilkins.
Miller, W. D. The Micro-Organism of the Human Mouth: The Local & General Diseases Which Are Caused by Them. (Illus.). 1973. 38.00 (ISBN 3-8055-1614-2). S Karger.
Nolte, William A. Oral Microbiology: With Basic Microbiology & Immunology. 4th ed. (Illus.). 736p. 1982. text ed. 29.50 (ISBN 0-8016-3697-3). Mosby.
Roth, Gerald I. & Clames, Robert. Oral Biology. LC 81-11122. (Illus.). 544p. 1981. pap. text ed. 24.95 (ISBN 0-8016-4182-9). Mosby.
MOUTH–RADIOGRAPHY
Stafne, Edward C. & Gibilisco, Joseph A. Oral Roentgenographic Diagnosis. 4th ed. LC 74-9440. (Illus.). 450p. 1975. text ed. 25.00 (ISBN 0-7216-8547-1). Saunders.
MOUTH–SURGERY
see also Teeth–Extraction
Archer, W. Harry. Oral & Maxillofacial Surgery. 5th ed. LC 73-89931. (Illus.). 1859p. 1975. Vol. 1. text ed. 47.00 (ISBN 0-7216-1362-4); Vol. 2. text ed. 47.00 (ISBN 0-7216-1363-2); Set. text ed. 94.00 (ISBN 0-685-49556-6). Saunders.
Birn, Herluf & Winther, Jens E. Manual of Minor Oral Surgery: A Step by Step Atlas. LC 75-18759. (Illus.). 1976. text ed. 26.00 (ISBN 0-7216-1705-0). Saunders.
Ehrlich, Ann. Introduction to the Auxiliary's Role in Oral Surgery. (Illus.). 1978. 3.85 (ISBN 0-940012-11-1). Colwell Co.
Hayward, James R. Oral Surgery. (American Lectures in Dentistry Ser.). (Illus.). 408p. 1976. 37.50 (ISBN 0-398-03468-0). C C Thomas.
Irby, William B., ed. Current Advances in Oral Surgery, Vols. 2-3. LC 74-8602. (Illus.). Vol. 2, 1977. 50.95 (ISBN 0-8016-2341-3); Vol. 3, 1980. 50.95 (ISBN 0-8016-2342-1). Mosby.
Killey, H. C. Outline of Oral Surgery. (Illus.). Pt. 1, 1977. pap. 18.95 (ISBN 0-8151-5037-7); Pt. 2, 1976. pap. 19.95 (ISBN 0-8151-5038-5). Year Bk Med.
Kruger & Worthington. Oral Surgery in Dental Practice. 1981. write for info. (ISBN 0-931386-19-5). Quint Pub Co.
Laskin, Daniel M. Oral & Maxillofacial Surgery: The Biomedical & Clinical Basis for Surgical Practice, Vol. 1. 6th. ed. LC 79-18723. 1979. text ed. 77.00 (ISBN 0-8016-2822-9). Mosby.
Moore, J. R. Principles of Oral Surgery. 256p. 1976. 21.00x (ISBN 0-7190-0650-3, Pub. by Manchester U Pr England). State Mutual Bk.
Oakley, Janet & Parkin, S. F. A Textbook for Dental Surgery Assistants. (Illus.). 230p. (Orig.). 1973. pap. 8.95 (ISBN 0-571-10253-0, Pub. by Faber & Faber). Merrimack Bk Serv.
Starshak, Thomas J. Preprosthetic Oral & Maxillofacial Surgery. LC 80-17921. (Illus.). 351p. 1980. 49.50 (ISBN 0-8016-4757-6). Mosby.
Steiner, Robert B. & Thompson, Robert D. Oral Surgery & Anesthesia. LC 76-4251. (Illus.). 1977. text ed. 29.50 (ISBN 0-7216-8589-7). Saunders.
Thoma, Kurt H. Oral Surgery, 2 Vols. 5th ed. LC 69-15220. (Illus.). 1969. Set. 79.50 (ISBN 0-8016-4915-3). Mosby.
--Oral Surgery, 2 Vols. 5th ed. LC 69-15220. (Illus.). 1969. Set. 79.50 (ISBN 0-8016-4915-3). Mosby.
Waite, Daniel E., ed. Textbook of Practical Oral Surgery. 2nd ed. LC 77-23401. (Illus.). 600p. 1978. text ed. 34.00 (ISBN 0-8121-0615-6). Lea & Febiger.
MOUTH-ORGAN
Gindick, Jon. The Natural Blues & Country Western Harmonica. (Illus.). 128p. pap. 4.95 (ISBN 0-8256-9923-1). Music Sales.
--The Natural Blues & Country Western Harmonica. (Illus.). 130p. 1978. pap. 4.95 (ISBN 0-930948-01-7). Cross Harp.
--The Natural Blues & Country Western Harmonica. 2nd ed. LC 77-83727. (Illus.). 1978. 4.95 (ISBN 0-930948-01-7). J Gindick.
Glover, Tony. Blues Harp. (Illus., Orig.). 1973. pap. 4.95 (ISBN 0-8256-0018-9, 000018, Oak). Music Sales.
--Blues Harp Songbook. (Illus.). pap. 6.95 with recordiing (ISBN 0-8256-0157-6, Oak). Music Sales.
Harris, M. & Leschot, N. Harmonium Manual. LC 79-54823. (Illus., Orig.). Date not set. pap. cancelled (ISBN 0-89793-016-9). Hunter Hse.
How to Play the Harmonica. 1981. 2.50 (ISBN 0-88284-157-2). Alfred Pub.
Leighton, Hal. The Harmonica for Fun & Profit. 1978. pap. 4.00 (ISBN 0-87980-354-1). Wilshire.
--How to Play the Harmonica for Fun & Profit. (Orig.). 1978. 5.00 (ISBN 0-87980-213-8); pap. 3.00 (ISBN 0-685-03332-5). Borden.
MOUTRAY, JOHN
Minutes of the Proceedings at a Court Martial, Assembled for the Trial of Capt. John Moutray of His Majesty's Ship the Ramillies. LC 77-81076. (Eyewitness Accounts of the American Revolution Ser., No. 2). Repr. of 1781 ed. 10.00 (ISBN 0-405-01163-6). Arno.
MOUVEMENT REPUBLICAN POPULAIRE
Einaudi, Mario & Goguel, Francois. Christian Democracy in Italy & France. LC 69-19224. 1969. Repr. of 1952 ed. 18.50 (ISBN 0-208-00801-2, Archon). Shoe String.
MOVE GAMES
see Board Games
MOVEMENT, DISORDERS OF
see Movement Disorders
MOVEMENT, ECUMENICAL
see Ecumenical Movement
MOVEMENT, ESTHETICS OF
see also Esthetics; Movement, Psychology of; Rhythm
Aesthetics for Dancers. 1976. 5.00x (ISBN 0-685-67028-7, 243-25828). AAHPERD.
Barlin, Anne. Teaching Your Wings to Fly: The Nonspecialists Guide to Movement Activities for Young Children. LC 77-20894. (Illus.). 1979. 15.95 (ISBN 0-87620-892-8). Goodyear.
Best, David. Expression in Movement & the Arts: A Philosophical Enquiry. 12.00 (ISBN 0-8238-0200-0). Plays.
Fisher, Margaret. Palm Leaf Patterns: A New Approach to Clothing Design. LC 76-57189. (Illus.). 1977. pap. 4.95 (ISBN 0-915572-20-6). Panjandrum.
Jones, Genevieve. Seeds of Movement: Philosophy of Movement with Techniques Applied to the Beginner. (Illus.). 1971. spiral bdg. 12.00 (ISBN 0-913650-10-2). Volkwein Bros.
Laban, Rudolf. The Language of Movement: A Guidebook to Choreutics. rev. ed. LC 73-13552. Orig. Title: Choreutics. (Illus.). 1974. 14.95 (ISBN 0-8238-0159-4). Plays.
MOVEMENT, FREEDOM OF
see Freedom of Movement
MOVEMENT, NOTATION OF
Holbrook, Jennifer K. Movement Activity in Gymnastics. 1974. 9.95 (ISBN 0-8238-0158-6). Plays.
Kestenberg, Judith S. & Sossin, K. Mark. The Role of Movement Patterns in Development, Vol. II. LC 78-67319. (Illus.). 1979. pap. text ed. 7.95x (ISBN 0-932582-01-X). Dance Notation.
Redfern, H. B. Concepts in Modern Educational Dance. 10.00 (ISBN 0-8238-0247-7). Plays.
Sutton, Valerie J. Sign Writing, Sutton Movement Shorthand, the Sign Language Key, Key Five. rev. & enl. ed. (Illus.). 1978. text ed. 18.00x (ISBN 0-914336-06-1); 8 hr. audio cassette o.p. 35.00 (ISBN 0-685-93665-1); book & cassette 50.00x (ISBN 0-914336-07-X). Move Short Soc.
--The Three Bournonville Barres & Music for the Three Bournonville Barres. (Illus.). 72p. (Orig.). 1975. pap. text ed. 25.00x (ISBN 0-914336-16-9). Move Short Soc.
MOVEMENT, PSYCHOLOGY OF
see also Motion Perception (Vision); Motor Ability; Movement, Esthetics of; Rhythm; Time and Motion Study
Arnold, Peter. Meaning in Movement, Sport & Physical Education. LC 80-670037. 1980. text ed. 29.95x (ISBN 0-435-80033-7); pap. text ed. 15.95x (ISBN 0-435-80034-5). Heinemann Ed.
Bayley, Nancy. Development of Motor Abilities During the First Three Years. 1935. pap. 4.00 (ISBN 0-527-01486-9). Kraus Repr.
Best, David. Philosophy & Human Movement. (Unwin Education Bks.). 1979. text ed. 21.95x (ISBN 0-04-370088-8); pap. text ed. 7.95x (ISBN 0-04-370089-6). Allen Unwin.
Cherry, Clare. Creative Movement for the Developing Child: A Nursery School Handbook for Non-Musicians. rev. ed. LC 79-125140. (Illus.). 1971. pap. 4.95 (ISBN 0-8224-1660-3). Pitman Learning.
Christina, Robert W. & Landers, Daniel M., eds. Psychology of Motor Behavior & Sport: 1976, 2 vols. Incl. Vol. 1. (ISBN 0-931250-02-1); Vol. 2. (ISBN 0-931250-03-X). LC 78-641529. (Psychology of Motor Behavior & Sport Ser.). (Illus.). 1977. Set. pap. text ed. 16.00x (ISBN 0-931250-01-3); pap. text ed. 9.00x ea. Human Kinetics.
Complo, Jannita M. Funtactics: Movement & Speech Activities for Young Special Children. LC 78-50133. 1978. pap. 4.95 (ISBN 0-8224-3176-9). Pitman Learning.
Cratty, Bryant J. Developmental Sequences of Perceptional Motor Tasks. 1967. 3.75 (ISBN 0-914296-01-9). Activity Rec.
--Movement Behavior & Motor Learning. 3rd ed. LC 73-1938. (Health & Physical Education & Recreation Ser.). (Illus.). 512p. 1973. text ed. 11.50 (ISBN 0-8121-0425-0). Lea & Febiger.
--Some Educational Implications of Movements. LC 78-123868. (Orig.). 1971. pap. 7.00x (ISBN 0-87562-022-1). Spec Child.
Cratty, Bryant J., et al. Movement Activities, Motor Ability & the Education of Children. (Illus.). 192p. 1970. pap. 18.75 photocopy ed. spiral (ISBN 0-398-00360-2). C C Thomas.
Davis, Martha. Towards Understanding the Intrinsic in Body Movement. new ed. LC 74-7857. (Body Movement Perspectives in Research Ser). (Illus.). 192p. 1975. 23.00x (ISBN 0-405-06200-1). Arno.
Davis, Martha, ed. Psychoanalytic Perspectives of Movement: An Original Anthology. LC 74-9161. (Body Movement Perspectives in Research Ser). 164p. 1975. Repr. 22.00x (ISBN 0-405-06199-4). Arno.
Grant, Barbara M. & Hennings, Dorothy G. The Teacher Moves: An Analysis of Non-Verbal Activity. LC 71-148592. 1971. pap. text ed. 5.95x (ISBN 0-8077-1456-9). Tchrs Coll.
Harrow, Anita J. A Taxonomy of the Psychomotor Domain: A Guide for Developing Behavioral Objectives. LC 74-185136. 1979. pap. text ed. 8.95x (ISBN 0-582-28128-8, Pub. by MacKay). Longman.
Jones, Genevieve. Movement in the Right Direction. LC 79-65275. (Illus., Orig.). 1979. pap. text ed. 12.00 (ISBN 0-913650-06-4). Volkwein Bros.
Kelley, David L. Kinesiology: Fundamentals of Motion Description. LC 79-144098. (Physical Education Ser). 1971. text ed. 18.50 (ISBN 0-13-516260-2). P-H.
Legge, David & Barber, Paul J. Information & Skill. (Essential Psychology Ser.). 1976. pap. 4.50x (ISBN 0-416-84070-1). Methuen Inc.
Lewis, D. & Bartenieff, I. Body Movement: Coping with the Environment. 304p. 1980. 42.50 (ISBN 0-677-05500-5). Gordon.
Lowe, John C. & Moryadas, S. Spatial Interaction: The Geography of Movement. 1975. text ed. 21.95 (ISBN 0-395-18584-X). HM.
Mandler, George. Mind & Emotion. 296p. Date not set. Repr. of 1975 ed. lib. bdg. price not set (ISBN 0-89874-350-8). Krieger.
Moran, Joan M. & Kalakian, Leonard. Movement Experiences for the Mentally Retarded or Emotionally Disturbed Child. 2nd ed. LC 77-70931. 1977. text ed. 15.95x (ISBN 0-8087-1386-8). Burgess.
Morison, Ruth. A Movement Approach to Educational Gymnastics. 1974. 8.95 (ISBN 0-8238-0153-5). Plays.
North, Marion. Personality-Assessment Through Movement. 320p. 1980. 15.00x (ISBN 0-7121-1622-2, Pub. by Macdonald & Evans). State Mutual Bk.
North, Marion, ed. Personality Assessment Through Movement. LC 74-13127. 1975. 12.95 (ISBN 0-8238-0173-X). Plays.
Pesso, Albert. Movement in Psychotherapy: Psychomotor Techniques & Training. LC 69-19257. 1969. 15.00x (ISBN 0-8147-0340-2). NYU Pr.

Piaget, Jean. Child's Conception of Movement & Speed. LC 70-84025. 1969. 15.00x (ISBN 0-465-01082-2). Basic.
Research Approaches to Movement & Personality. LC 72-347. (Body Movement Ser.: Perspectives in Research). 290p. 1972. Repr. 18.00 (ISBN 0-405-03146-7). Arno.
Roach, Eugene & Kephart, Newell. Purdue Perceptual-Motor Survey. LC 66-14493. (To be used with The Slow Learner in the Classroom). 1966. pap. text ed. 13.95x spiral bdg. (ISBN 0-675-09797-5). Merrill.
Robbins, Arthur. Expressive Therapy: A Creative Arts Approach to Depth-Oriented Therapy. LC 80-13005. 319p. 1980. text ed. 22.95 (ISBN 0-87705-101-1). Human Sci Pr.
Roberts, Glyn C. & Newell, Karl M., eds. Psychology of Motor Behavior & Sport: Nineteen Seventy-Eight. LC 78-641529. 1979. pap. text ed. 15.95x (ISBN 0-931250-12-9). Human Kinetics.
Sinclair, Caroline B. Movement of the Young Child: Ages Two to Six. LC 72-96100. 1973. pap. text ed. 8.95 (ISBN 0-675-08975-1). Merrill.
Towe, Arnold L. & Luschei, Erich S., eds. Handbook of Behavioral Neurobiology: Motor Coordination, Vol. 5. 610p. 1981. text ed. 45.00 (ISBN 0-306-40613-6, Plenum Pr). Plenum Pub.
Warner, Francis. Physical Expression: Its Modes & Principles. (The International Scientific Ser.). 1979. Repr. of 1886 ed. lib. bdg. 30.00 (ISBN 0-8495-5741-0). Arden Lib.
Washburn, Margaret F. Movement & Mental Imagery: Outlines of a Motor Theory of the Complexer Mental Processes. LC 73-2996. (Classics in Psychology Ser). Repr. of 1916 ed. 13.00 (ISBN 0-405-05168-9). Arno.
Wethered, Audrey G. Drama & Movement in Therapy. 144p. 1980. 12.00x (ISBN 0-7121-0411-9, Pub. by Macdonald & Evans). State Mutual Bk.
Zsilka, Janos. The Dialects of the Motion Forms of Language. (Janua Linguarum, Series Minor). 1979. text ed. 30.75 (ISBN 0-686-27020-7). Mouton.

MOVEMENT CURE
see Mechanotherapy

MOVEMENT DISORDERS
see also Chorea

Carlsson, A., et al, eds. Current Topics in Extrapyramidal Disorders. (Journal of Neural Transmission Supplementum: No. 16). (Illus.). 240p. 1980. 57.90 (ISBN 0-387-81570-8). Springer-Verlag.
Cratty, Bryant J. Remedial Motor Activity for Children. LC 74-26973. (Illus.). 327p. 1975. text ed. 13.50 (ISBN 0-8121-0513-3). Lea & Febiger.
Dubowitz, Victor. Muscle Disorders in Childhood. LC 77-23997. (Major Problems in Clinical Pediatrics Ser.: Vol. 16). (Illus.). 1978. text ed. 29.00 (ISBN 0-7216-3210-6). Saunders.
Feldman. Spasticity: Disorders of Motor Control. 1980. 61.50 (ISBN 0-8151-3240-9). Year Bk Med.
Feldman, Robert G., ed. Spasticity: A Disorder of Motor Control. 1980. write for info. (ISBN 0-8151-3240-9). Symposia Special.
Gillingham, F. J. & Hitchcock, E. R., eds. Advances in Stereotezctic & Functional Neurosurgery: Proceedings. LC 77-22266. (Acta Neurochirurgica: Supplementum 24). (Illus.). 1978. 81.50 (ISBN 0-387-81422-1). Springer-Verlag.
McClenaghan, Bruce A. & Gallahue, David L. Fundamental Movement: A Developmental & Remedial Approach. LC 77-75534. (Illus.). 1978. text ed. 12.95 (ISBN 0-7216-5888-1). HR&W.
Payton, Otto, et al, eds. Scientific Bases for Neurophysiological Approaches to Therapeutic Exercise: An Anthology. LC 76-53831. 290p. 1977. pap. text ed. 10.00 (ISBN 0-8036-6795-7). Davis Co.
Smith, Janet. Play Environments for Movement Experience. (Illus.). 64p. 1980. pap. 9.50 (ISBN 0-398-04073-7). C C Thomas.
Yahr, Melvin D. & Purpura, Dominick P., eds. Neurophysiological Basis of Normal & Abnormal Motor Activities. LC 67-28247. 512p. 1967. 37.50 (ISBN 0-911216-04-9). Raven.

MOVEMENTS OF ANIMALS
see Animal Locomotion; Animal Mechanics

MOVEMENTS OF PLANTS
see Plants-Irritability and Movements

MOVIE CAMERAS
see Moving-Picture Cameras

MOVING, HOUSEHOLD

Booher, Dianna D. Help, We're Moving. LC 78-17894. (Illus.). 1978. pap. 3.25 (ISBN 0-8054-4702-4). Broadman.
Bourke, Linda. It's Your Move: Picking up, Packing up, & Settling in. LC 81-3439. (Illus.). 88p. (gr. 4-8). 1981. 8.95 (ISBN 0-201-00009-1, 0009). A-W.
Davis, Geraldine H. The Moving Experience. (Illus.). 150p. (Orig.). 1980. pap. 5.95 (ISBN 0-89865-029-1); moving calendar 2.50 (ISBN 0-89865-098-4). Donning Co.
Hennessey, James. The Nomadic Handbook: A Guide to Moving & to Finding & Adapting Your Next Home. LC 78-73962. (Illus.). 1979. pap. 5.95 (ISBN 0-394-73782-2). Pantheon.
Hullinger, Robert & Grosch, Robert. Move Yourself, & Save! 1980. pap. 3.50 (ISBN 0-915644-15-0). Clayton Pub Hse.
Lansing, John B., et al. New Homes & Poor People: A Study of Chains of Moves. LC 70-625278. 136p. 1969. pap. 5.50 (ISBN 0-87944-065-1). Inst Soc Res.
Lowry, Lois. Anastasia Again! (Illus.). (gr. 3-6). 1981. 7.95 (ISBN 0-395-31147-0). HM.
Neuman, Patricia O. Moving: The What, When, Where, & How of It. (Illus.). 132p. 1981. pap. 5.95 (ISBN 0-89651-450-1). Icarus.
Pfaltz, Marilyn & Reed, Ann. How to Move Your Family Successfully. LC 78-52272. (Illus.). 1979. pap. 4.95 (ISBN 0-89586-011-2). H P Bks.
Rossi, Peter H. Why Families Move. 2nd ed. LC 79-25370. (Illus.). 243p. 1980. 20.00 (ISBN 0-8039-1348-6); pap. 9.95 (ISBN 0-8039-1349-4). Sage.

MOVING PHOTOMICROGRAPHY
see Microcinematography

MOVING-PICTURE ACADEMY AWARDS
see Academy Awards (Moving-Pictures)

MOVING-PICTURE ACTORS AND ACTRESSES

Adams, Cindy. Lee Strasberg: The Imperfect Genius of the Actors Studio. LC 79-7191. 1980. 13.95 (ISBN 0-385-12496-1). Doubleday.
Agan, Patrick. The Decline & Fall of the Love Goddesses. (Orig.). 1979. pap. 7.95 (ISBN 0-523-40623-1). Pinnacle Bks.
Aherne, Brian. A Dreadful Man. 1979. 9.95 (ISBN 0-671-24797-2). S&S.
Anger, Kenneth. Hollywood Babylon. Date not set. pap. 3.50 (ISBN 0-440-15325-5). Dell.
--Hollywood Babylon. 1976. pap. 7.95 (ISBN 0-440-55325-3, Delta). Dell.
Arkin, Alan. Halfway Through the Door: An Actor's Journey Towards the Self. LC 78-20154. 1979. 6.95 (ISBN 0-06-010133-4, HarpT). Har-Row.
Ashley, Elizabeth & Firestone, Ross. Actress: Postcards from the Road. 1980. pap. 2.25 (ISBN 0-449-24104-1, Crest). Fawcett.
Baltake, Joe. The Films of Jack Lemmon. 1977. 14.95 (ISBN 0-8065-0560-5). Citadel Pr.
Barris, Alex. Hollywood's Other Men. LC 73-18863. (Illus.). 288p. 1975. 17.50 (ISBN 0-498-01428-2). A S Barnes.
Baxter, Anne. Intermission: A True Story. LC 75-45285. 1976. 10.00 (ISBN 0-399-11577-3). Putnam.
Berman, Connie. Leif Garrett. LC 78-64950. (Junior Bio Ser.). (Illus.). (gr. 4 up). 1979. pap. 1.95 (ISBN 0-448-17033-7, Tempo). Ace Bks.
Bermingham, Cedric O. Stars of the Screen 1931. 1976. lib. bdg. 75.00 (ISBN 0-8490-3065-X). Gordon Pr.
Bodeen, Dewitt. More from Hollywood! LC 77-3213. (Illus.). 512p. 1977. 15.00 (ISBN 0-498-01533-5). A S Barnes.
Bojarski, Richard. The Films of Bela Lugosi. 1980. 16.95 (ISBN 0-8065-5071-6). Lyle Stuart.
Brundidge, Harry. Twinkle Twinkle Movie Star. Kupelnick, Bruce S., ed. LC 76-52094. (Classics of Film Literature Ser.). 1978. lib. bdg. 18.00 (ISBN 0-8240-2868-6). Garland Pub.
Bruno, Michael. Venus in Hollywood: The Continental Enchantress from Garbo to Loren. LC 71-90838. (Illus.). 1970. 6.95 (ISBN 0-8184-0091-9). Lyle Stuart.
Carpozi, George, Jr. That's Hollywood: The Great Ladies of Hollywood, No. 4. 1978. pap. 1.95 (ISBN 0-532-19214-1). Woodhill.
--That's Hollywood: The Magnificent Entertainers, No. 3. 1978. pap. 1.95 (ISBN 0-532-19194-3). Woodhill.
--That's Hollywood: The Matinee Idols, No. 1. 1978. pap. 1.95 (ISBN 0-532-19190-0). Woodhill.
Castanza, Philip. Films of Jeannette MacDonald & Nelson Eddy. (Citadel Press Film Ser.). (Illus.). (gr. 7 up). 1978. 14.95 (ISBN 0-8065-0600-8). Citadel Pr.
Character People. (Illus.). 1979. pap. 6.95 (ISBN 0-8065-0701-2). Citadel Pr.
Cooper, Jackie & Kleiner, Dick. Please Don't Shoot My Dog: The Autobiography of Jackie Cooper with Dick Kleiner. LC 80-27834. (Illus.). 288p. 1981. 12.95 (ISBN 0-688-03659-7). Morrow.
Crawley, Tony. The Films of Sophia Loren. (Illus.). pap. 6.95 (ISBN 0-8065-0700-4). Citadel Pr.
De Beauvoir, Simone. Brigitte Bardot & the Lolita Syndrome. LC 78-169346. (Arno Press Cinema Program). (Illus.). 100p. 1972. Repr. of 1960 ed. 13.00 (ISBN 0-405-03912-3). Arno.
Dyer, Richard. Stars. (BFI Ser.). (Illus., Orig.). 1979. pap. 9.95 (ISBN 0-85170-085-3). NY Zoetrope.
Earley, Mary D. Stars of the Twenties: 125 Photographs. (Illus.). 1975. 10.00 (ISBN 0-670-66836-2, Studio). Viking Pr.
Edelson, Edward. The Funny Men of the Movies. LC 75-14817. 128p. (gr. 4-7). 1976. PLB 5.95 (ISBN 0-385-09693-3). Doubleday.
Finch, John R. & Elby, Paul A. Close-Ups. LC 74-30974. (Illus.). 1978. 25.00 (ISBN 0-498-01723-0). A S Barnes.
Fontaine, Joan. No Bed of Roses. LC 78-7003. (Illus.). 1978. 9.95 (ISBN 0-688-03344-X). Morrow.
Goetz, W. Werner Krauss. 1976. lib. bdg. 59.95 (ISBN 0-8490-2814-0). Gordon Pr.
Gordon, R., ed. Stars & Featured Players of Paramount of 1930-1931. 1976. lib. bdg. 80.00 (ISBN 0-8490-2663-6). Gordon Pr.
Halliwell, Leslie. Halliwell's Filmgoer's Companion. 788p. 1980. 39.50 (ISBN 0-684-16660-7, ScribT). Scribner.
Hanna, David. Hollywood Confidential. (Illus., Orig.). 1976. pap. 1.50 (ISBN 0-8439-0331-7, LB331DK, Leisure Bks). Nordon Pubns.
Harrison, Joel L. Bloody Wednesday: The True Story of the Ramon Navarro Murder. 1978. pap. 2.95 (ISBN 0-89041-215-4, 3215). Major Bks.
Herndon, Booton. Mary Pickford & Douglas Fairbanks: The Most Popular Couple the World Has Known. (Illus.). 1977. 9.95 (ISBN 0-393-07508-7). Norton.
Hirschhorn, Clive. The Films of James Mason. 1977. 14.95 (ISBN 0-8065-0584-2). Citadel Pr.
Houseman, John. Front & Center. 1979. 15.00 (ISBN 0-671-24328-4). S&S.
Hughes, Eleanor. Famous Stars of Filmdom: Women. 1976. lib. bdg. 59.95 (ISBN 0-8490-1805-6). Gordon Pr.
Hughes, Elinor. Famous Stars of Filmdom: Men. LC 76-107716. (Essay Index Reprint Ser). 1932. 22.00 (ISBN 0-8369-1518-6). Arno.
--Famous Stars of Filmdom: Women. LC 70-107717. (Essay Index Reprint Ser). 1931. 22.00 (ISBN 0-8369-1519-4). Arno.
Hunter, Kim. Loose in the Kitchen. LC 75-21398. (Illus.). 394p. 1975. 8.00 (ISBN 0-915392-02-X, Domina Bks). Double M Pr.
Ihering, H. Emil Jannings. 1976. lib. bdg. 70.00 (ISBN 0-8490-1760-2). Gordon Pr.
Jacobs, Jack & Braum, Myron. The Films of Norma Shearer. (Illus.). 1977. pap. 6.95 (ISBN 0-8065-0576-1). Citadel Pr.
Kanin, Garson. Together Again. LC 80-2863. (Illus.). 256p. 1981. 24.95 (ISBN 0-385-17471-3). Doubleday.
Kerr, Walter. The Silent Clowns. LC 75-8231. (Illus.). 1979. pap. 9.95 (ISBN 0-394-73450-5). Knopf.
Keyes, Evelyn. Scarlett O'Hara's Younger Sister: My Lively Life in & Out of Hollywood. 1977. 10.00 (ISBN 0-8184-0243-1). Lyle Stuart.
Kobal, John. Film-Star Portraits of the Fifties: 163 Glamor Photos. (Illus.). 164p. (Orig.). 1980. pap. 6.95 (ISBN 0-486-24008-8). Dover.
--Hollywood Glamour Portraits: 125 Photos of Stars 1926-1949. 8.00 (ISBN 0-8446-5526-0). Peter Smith.
Kobal, John, ed. Film-Star Portraits of the Fifties. (Illus.). 12.50 (ISBN 0-8446-5781-6). Peter Smith.
Kobal, John C. Hollywood Glamor Portraits: One Hundred & Fifty Photos of Stars, 1926-1949. (Illus.). 144p. (Orig.). 1976. pap. 6.00 (ISBN 0-486-23352-9). Dover.
Lake, Veronica & Bain, Donald. Veronica: The Autobiography of Veronica Lake. (Illus.). 1971. 6.95 (ISBN 0-8065-0226-6). Citadel Pr.
McBride, M. M. Constance Bennett. 1976. lib. bdg. 59.95 (ISBN 0-8490-1667-3). Gordon Pr.
McDonald, Gerald D., et al. Films of Charlie Chaplin. 1971. 12.00 (ISBN 0-8065-0241-X); pap. 6.95 (ISBN 0-685-03371-6). Citadel Pr.
Maltin, Leonard. The Great Movie Comedians. (Illus.). 1978. 12.95 (ISBN 0-517-53241-7). Crown.
Marlowe, Don. Hollywood That Was. LC 68-26007. (Illus.). 1968. 5.95 (ISBN 0-87706-001-0). Branch-Smith.
Montalban, Ricardo & Thomas, Bob. Reflections: A Life in Two Worlds. LC 77-15166. (Illus.). 1980. 8.95 (ISBN 0-385-12878-9). Doubleday.
Morella, Joe & Epstein, Edward Z. Rebels: The Rebel Hero in Films. (Illus.). 224p. 1973. 9.95 (ISBN 0-685-29241-X); pap. 6.95 (ISBN 0-8065-0360-2). Citadel Pr.
Nunn, Curtis. Marguerite Clark: America's Darling of Broadway & the Silent Screen. LC 81-4178. (Illus.). 208p. Date not set. pap. 15.00 (ISBN 0-912646-69-1). Tex Christian.
Parish, James R. Film Actors Guide: Western Europe. LC 77-22485. 1977. 28.50 (ISBN 0-8108-1044-1). Scarecrow.
--Hollywood's Great Love Teams. (Illus.). 1978. pap. 7.95 (ISBN 0-89508-004-4). Rainbow Bks.
--The RKO Gals. (Illus.). 1978. pap. 7.95 (ISBN 0-89508-005-2). Rainbow Bks.
--The Tough Guys. LC 76-16867. (Illus.). 1976. 19.95 (ISBN 0-87000-338-0). Arlington Hse.
--The Tough Guys. (Illus.). 1978. pap. 7.95 (ISBN 0-89508-007-9). Rainbow Bks.
Parish, James R. & Leonard, William T. Hollywood Players: The Thirties. (Illus.). 1978. pap. 7.95 (ISBN 0-89508-003-6). Rainbow Bks.
--Hollywood Players: The Thirties. LC 76-17647. (Illus.). 1976. 19.95 (ISBN 0-87000-365-8). Arlington Hse.
Parish, James R. & Stanke, Don E. The All-Americans. (Illus.). 1978. pap. 12.95 (ISBN 0-89508-011-7). Rainbow Bks.
--The All-Americans. 1977. 20.00 (ISBN 0-87000-363-1). Arlington Hse.
--The Glamour Girls. (Illus.). 1978. pap. 7.95 (ISBN 0-89508-002-8). Rainbow Bks.
--The Leading Ladies. (Illus.). 1978. pap. 12.95 (ISBN 0-89508-016-8). Rainbow Bks.
--The Swashbucklers. (Illus.). 1976. 19.95 (ISBN 0-87000-326-7). Arlington Hse.
--The Swashbucklers. (Illus.). 1978. pap. 7.95 (ISBN 0-89508-006-0). Rainbow Bks.
Peary, Danny, ed. Close-Ups: The Movie Star Book. LC 78-7113. 1978. 15.95 (ISBN 0-89480-044-2, IBM 2011); pap. 8.95 (ISBN 0-89480-043-4, IBM 2003). Workman Pub.
Pickard, Roy. Who Played Who in the Movies. LC 80-26546. 304p. 1981. 14.95 (ISBN 0-8052-3766-6); pap. 6.95 (ISBN 0-8052-0676-0). Schocken.
Pitts, Michael R. Horror Film Stars. LC 80-11241. (Illus.). 333p. 1981. lib. bdg. 16.95x (ISBN 0-89950-003-X); pap. 12.95x (ISBN 0-89950-004-8). McFarland & Co.
Pitts, Michael R. & Harrison, Louis H. Hollywood on Record: The Film Stars' Discography. LC 77-17144. (Illus.). 1978. 19.50 (ISBN 0-8108-1093-X). Scarecrow.
Quirk, Lawrence J. The Films of Myrna Loy. 1980. 16.95 (ISBN 0-8065-0735-7). Lyle Stuart.
--The Films of Robert Taylor. (Illus.). 1979. pap. 6.95 (ISBN 0-8065-0667-9). Citadel Pr.
--The Films of Ronald Colman. (Illus.). 1977. 14.95 (ISBN 0-8065-0562-1). Citadel Pr.
Ragan, David. Who's Who in Hollywood, 1900-1976. 1977. 30.00 (ISBN 0-87000-349-6). Arlington Hse.
Ringgold, Gene. The Films of Rita Hayworth: The Legend & Career of a Love Godess. new ed. 256p. 1974. 12.00 (ISBN 0-8065-0439-0). Citadel Pr.
Samuels, M. Screen Greats: Bogart. 1980. pap. 2.95 (ISBN 0-931064-31-7). Starlog.
--Screen Greats: Hollywood Nostalgia. 1980. pap. 2.00 (ISBN 0-931064-30-9). Starlog.
--Screen Greats: Monroe. 1980. pap. 2.95 (ISBN 0-931064-32-5). Starlog.
Scagnetti, Jack. Movie Stars in Bathtubs. LC 74-31216. (Illus.). 160p. 1975. 12.95 (ISBN 0-8246-0196-3). Jonathan David.
Shields, Brook. The Brooke Book. 1978. pap. 3.95 (ISBN 0-671-79018-8, Wallaby). PB.
Shipman, David. The Great Movie Stars: The Golden Years. rev. ed. (Illus.). 1981. 19.95 (ISBN 0-8090-5170-2). Hill & Wang.
--The Great Movie Stars: The International Years. rev. ed. (Illus.). 1981. 19.95 (ISBN 0-8090-5171-0). Hill & Wang.
Slide, Anthony. The Idols of Silence. LC 73-125. (Illus.). 1976. 15.00 (ISBN 0-498-01611-0). A S Barnes.
Spada, James. The Films of Robert Redford. 256p. 1977. 14.00 (ISBN 0-8065-0529-X). Citadel Pr.
Springer, John & Hamilton, Jack. They Had Faces Then: Annabella to Zorina: the Superstars, Stars & Starlets of the 1930s. (Illus.). 384p. 1974. 19.95 (ISBN 0-8065-0300-9). Citadel Pr.
Steinberg, Margery. The Christopher Reeve Scrapbook. 160p. (Orig.). (gr. 5 up). 1981. pap. 1.95 (ISBN 0-448-17223-2, Tempo). G&D.
Stewart, John, compiled by. Filmarama: The Formidable Years, 1893-1919, Vol. 1. LC 75-2440. 401p. 1975. 18.00 (ISBN 0-8108-0802-1). Scarecrow.
Stewart, William T., et al. International Film Necrology. LC 80-17636. (Garland Reference Library of Humanities). 350p. 1981. 35.00 (ISBN 0-8240-9552-9). Garland Pub.
Swann, Thomas B. The Heroine or the Horse: Leading Ladies in Republic's Films. LC 76-18483. (Illus.). 1978. 17.50 (ISBN 0-498-01962-4). A S Barnes.
Trotta, V. & Lewis, C. Screen Personalities of 1933. 1976. lib. bdg. 75.95 (ISBN 0-8490-2576-1). Gordon Pr.
Truitt, Evelyn M. Who Was Who on Screen. 2nd ed. LC 77-22651. 1977. 32.50 (ISBN 0-8352-0914-8). Bowker.
Valentino, Lou. The Films of Lana Turner. 256p. 1976. 14.00 (ISBN 0-8065-0553-2). Citadel Pr.

Vermilye, Jerry. The Films of Charles Bronson. (Illus.). 1980. 16.95 (ISBN 0-8065-0693-8). Citadel Pr.

Vermilye, Jerry & Ricci, Mark. The Films of Elizabeth Taylor. (Citadel Press Film Ser.). (Illus.). 1978. pap. 6.95 (ISBN 0-8065-0656-3). Citadel Pr.

Weaver, John T. Forty Years of Screen Credits Nineteen Twenty-Nine to Nineteen Sixty-Nine, 2 Vols. LC 76-12592. 1970. Set. 45.00 (ISBN 0-8108-0299-6). Scarecrow.

Weis, Elisabeth. Movie Star. 1981. pap. 12.95 (ISBN 0-14-005947-4). Penguin.

Welsch, J. R. Film Archetypes: Sisters, Mistresses, Mothers & Daughters. LC 77-22913. (Illus.). 1978. lib. bdg. 22.00x (ISBN 0-405-10757-9). Arno.

Wilkie, Jane. Confessions of an Ex-Fan Magazine Writer. LC 80-780. (Illus.). 288p. 1981. 12.95 (ISBN 0-385-15921-8). Doubleday.

Young, Christopher. The Films of Hedy Lamarr. (Illus.). 1978. 14.95 (ISBN 0-8065-0579-6). Citadel Pr.

MOVING-PICTURE ACTORS AND ACTRESSES, AFRO-AMERICAN
see Afro-American Motion Picture Actors and Actresses

MOVING-PICTURE ADAPTATIONS
see Film Adaptations

MOVING-PICTURE AUDIENCES

Handel, Leo A. Hollywood Looks at Its Audience: A Report of Film Audience Research. LC 75-22819. (America in Two Centuries Ser). 1976. Repr. of 1950 ed. 14.00x (ISBN 0-405-07691-6). Arno.

Leyda, Jay. Dianying - Electric Shadows: An Account of Films & the Film Audience in China. 272p. 1972. 15.00x (ISBN 0-262-12046-1); pap. 5.95 (ISBN 0-262-62030-8). MIT Pr.

Lynch, F. D. Clozentropy: A Technique for Studying Audience Response to Films. LC 77-22911. (Illus.). 1978. lib. bdg. 10.00x (ISBN 0-405-10754-4). Arno.

Seldes, Gilbert V. Great Audience. Repr. of 1950 ed. lib. bdg. 15.00 (ISBN 0-8371-2802-1, SEGA). Greenwood.

MOVING-PICTURE AUTHORSHIP

Brady, John. The Craft of the Screenwriter. 1981. 14.95 (ISBN 0-671-25229-1). S&S.

Bronfeld, Stewart. Writing for Film & Television. 160p. 1980. 10.95 (ISBN 0-13-970608-9, Spec); pap. 4.95 (ISBN 0-13-970590-2). P-H.

Brown, Kent R. The Screenwriter As Collaborator. Jowett, Garth S., ed. LC 79-6669. (Dissertations on Film, 1980 Ser.). 1980. lib. bdg. 24.00x (ISBN 0-405-12903-3). Arno.

Caughie, John, ed. Theories of Authorship. (B. F. I. Readers in Film Studies). (Illus.). 320p. 1981. 28.00 (ISBN 0-7100-0649-7); pap. 14.00 (ISBN 0-7100-0650-0). Routledge & Kegan.

Greenbaum, Everett. The Goldenberg Who Couldn't Dance. LC 79-3353. 168p. 1980. 8.95 (ISBN 0-15-136174-6). HarBraceJ.

Halliwell, Leslie. Halliwell's Filmgoer's Companion. 788p. 1980. 39.50 (ISBN 0-684-16660-7, ScribT). Scribner.

Hayward, Stan. Scriptwriting for Animation. (Media Manual Ser.). 1978. pap. 7.95 (ISBN 0-8038-6741-7). Hastings.

Hoyt, Robert. How to Write Educational & Technical Films. (Illus.). 1978. pap. text ed. 4.95 (ISBN 0-935056-00-9). Big Morning Pr.

Lee, Robert & Misiorowski, Robert. Script Models: A Handbook for the Media Writer. 1978. 9.50 (ISBN 0-8038-6755-7); pap. text ed. 4.50x (ISBN 0-8038-6754-9). Hastings.

Maltz, Albert & Wald, Malvin. The Naked City: A Screenplay. LC 79-10826. (Screenplay Library). (Illus.). 158p. 1979. 12.50 (ISBN 0-8093-0909-2); pap. 4.95 (ISBN 0-8093-0910-6). S Ill U Pr.

Marion, Frances. How to Write & Sell Film Scripts. Kupelnick, Bruce S., ed. LC 76-52115. (Classics of Film Literature Ser.). 1978. lib. bdg. 18.00 (ISBN 0-8240-2884-8). Garland Pub.

Miller, William. Screenwriting for Narrative Film & Television. (Communication Arts Bks.). 320p. 1980. 16.95 (ISBN 0-8038-6772-7); pap. 9.95x (ISBN 0-8038-6773-5). Hastings.

Morsberger, Robert & Thompson, Tracy, eds. American Screenwriters One & Two, 2 vols. (Dictionary of Literary Biography Ser.). (Illus.). 1981. Set. 116.00 (ISBN 0-8103-0917-3, Bruccoli Clark Book). Gale.

Rilla, Wolf. The Writer & the Screen: On Writing for Film & Television. 1974. pap. 4.95 (ISBN 0-688-05234-7). Morrow.

Root, Wells. Writing the Script: A Practical Guide for Films & Television. LC 79-1927. 252p. 12.95 (ISBN 0-03-044226-5); pap. 5.95 (ISBN 0-03-044221-4). HR&W.

Schwartz, Nancy & Schwartz, Sheila. The Hollywood Writers' Wars. LC 80-2728. (Illus.). 448p. 1981. 17.95 (ISBN 0-394-41140-4). Knopf.

Stein, Gertrude. How to Write. 1978. Repr. of 1931 ed. 3.95 (ISBN 0-9603324-1-3). Sherry Urie.

Stempel, Tom. Screenwriter: The Life & Times of Nunnally Johnson. LC 78-75339. (Illus.). 1980. 12.00 (ISBN 0-498-02362-1). A S Barnes.

Sunshine Books Editors. On Writing Quality Scripts for TV & Movies: An Advanced Manual for Professional Scriptwriters. 1980. 7.95 (ISBN 0-934606-02-1). Sunshine Bks.

MOVING-PICTURE CAMERAS
see also Kinetograph

Cermak. How to Repair Your Own 35mm Camera. 224p. 1981. 14.95 (ISBN 0-8306-9637-7); pap. 8.95 (ISBN 0-8306-1270-X, 1270). TAB Bks.

Eastman Kodak, ed. Cinematographer's Field Guide, (H-2) 3rd rev. ed. (Illus.). 100p. 1980. text ed. 6.95 (ISBN 0-87985-276-3). Eastman Kodak.

Edera, Bruno & Halas, John. Full Length Animated Feature Films. (Library of Animation Technology Ser.). (Illus.). 1977. 35.00 (ISBN 0-240-50818-1). Focal Pr.

How to Use Your 35mm Camera. 1981. 2.50 (ISBN 0-88284-140-8). Alfred Pub.

Lipton, L. Super Eight Book. 1975. 9.95 (ISBN 0-671-22082-9, Fireside). S&S.

Matzkin, Myron A. The Super Eight Film-Makers Handbook. LC 75-45778. (Illus.). 1976. 21.95 (ISBN 0-240-50755-X). Focal Pr.

Samuelson, David. Motion Picture Camera & Lighting Equipment. (Media Manuals). (Illus.). 1977. pap. 8.95 (ISBN 0-8038-4685-1). Focal Pr.

--Motion Picture Camera Data. (Media Manual Ser.): (Illus.). 1979. pap. 9.95 (ISBN 0-240-50998-6). Focal Pr.

--Motion Picture Camera Techniques. (Media Manuals). (Illus.). 1978. pap. 9.95 (ISBN 0-240-50982-X). Focal Pr.

Souto, H. Mario. The Technique of the Motion Picture Camera. 3rd., rev., enl. ed. (Illus.). 1977. 27.95 (ISBN 0-240-50917-X). Focal Pr.

MOVING-PICTURE CARTOONS
see also Animation (Cinematography); Comedy Films

Andersen, Yvonne. Make Your Own Animated Movies. (Illus.). (gr. 4 up). 1970. 7.95 (ISBN 0-316-03940-3). Little.

Bourgeois, Jacques. Animating Films Without a Camera. LC 74-82324. (Little Craft Bk.). (Illus.). 48p. (gr. 7-9). 1974. 5.95 (ISBN 0-8069-5304-7); PLB 6.69 (ISBN 0-8069-5305-5). Sterling.

Canemaker, John. The Animated Raggedy Ann & Andy: The Story Behind the Movie. LC 76-53289. (Illus.). 1977. 25.00 (ISBN 0-672-52329-9); pap. 12.95 (ISBN 0-672-52330-2). Bobbs.

Durgant, Raymond. The Crazy Mirror. 1972. pap. 2.45 (ISBN 0-440-51616-1, Delta). Dell.

Foster, Alan D. Walt Disney Animated Features & Silly Symphonies. (Illus.). 192p. 1980. 19.95 (ISBN 0-89659-120-4). Abbeville Pr.

Friedwald, Will & Beck, Jerry. The Warner Brothers Cartoons. LC 80-27839. 287p. 1981. 15.00 (ISBN 0-8108-1396-3). Scarecrow.

Grush, Byron. The Shoestring Animator: Making Animated Films with Super Eight. (Illus.). 160p. 1981. 12.95 (ISBN 0-8092-5847-1); pap. 6.95 (ISBN 0-8092-5884-6). Contemp Bks.

Havoc in Heaven, Pictures & Text from the Cartoon Film. 1979. 3.95 (ISBN 0-8351-0670-5). China Bks.

Hepworth, Cecil M. Animated Photography: The ABC of the Cinematograph. LC 73-124009. (Literature of Cinema Ser). Repr. of 1900 ed. 8.00 (ISBN 0-405-01615-8). Arno.

Lenburg, Jeff. The Encyclopedia of Animated Cartoon Series: Nineteen Hundred & Nine to Nineteen Seventy-Nine. (Illus.). 1981. 24.95 (ISBN 0-87000-441-7). Arlington Hse.

Looney Tunes Poster Book. (Illus.). 1979. pap. 7.95 (ISBN 0-517-53680-3, Dist. by Crown). Crown.

Lutz, E. G. Animated Cartoons. 1976. lib. bdg. 69.95 (ISBN 0-8490-1433-6). Gordon Pr.

Stephenson, Ralph. The Animated Film. rev. ed. LC 72-1785. (International Film Guide Ser). (Illus.). 224p. 1981. pap. 5.95 (ISBN 0-498-01202-6). A S Barnes.

MOVING-PICTURE COLLECTIONS
see Moving-Picture Film Collections

MOVING-PICTURE CRITICISM
Here are entered works dealing with the concept and technique of moving-picture reviews.
see also Moving-Picture Plays–History and Criticism; Moving-Pictures–Evaluation

Andrew, Dudley. Andre Bazin. (Illus.). 1978. 17.95 (ISBN 0-19-502165-7). Oxford U Pr.

Barry, Iris. Let's Go to the Movies. LC 79-169357. (Arno Press Cinema Program). (Illus.). 318p. 1972. Repr. of 1926 ed. 18.00 (ISBN 0-405-03911-5). Arno.

Beja, Morris. Film & Literature. 1979. pap. text ed. 11.95x (ISBN 0-582-28094-X). Longman.

Benderson, Albert E. Critical Approaches to Federico Fellini's Eight & Half, Vol. 4. LC 74-2078. (Dissertations on Film Ser.). 239p. 1974. 12.00 (ISBN 0-405-04877-7). Arno.

Blades, Joseph D., Jr. A Comparative Study of Selected American Film Critics, 1958-1974. Jowett, Garth S., ed. LC 75-21429. (Dissertations on Film Ser.). 1976. lib. bdg. 13.00x (ISBN 0-405-07532-4). Arno.

Carter, Huntly. The New Spirit in the Cinema. 59.95 (ISBN 0-8490-0724-0). Gordon Pr.

Clarens, Carlos. Crime Movies. (Illus.). 1980. 19.95 (ISBN 0-393-01262-X); pap. 8.95 (ISBN 0-393-00940-8). Norton.

Colette. Colette at the Movies: Criticism & Screenplays. Virmaux, Alain & Virmaux, Odette, eds. Smith, Sarah W., tr. from Fr. LC 79-6148. (Ungar Film Library). (Illus.). 300p. 1980. 10.95 (ISBN 0-8044-2125-0); pap. 5.95 (ISBN 0-8044-6086-8). Ungar.

Curran, Trisha. A New Note on the Film. Jowett, Garth S., ed. LC 79-6671. (Dissertations on Film, 1980 Ser.). 1980. lib. bdg. 15.00x (ISBN 0-405-12905-X). Arno.

Curtis, David. Experimental Cinema. 1972. pap. 2.45 (ISBN 0-440-52423-7, Delta). Dell.

Dawson, Jan & Wenders, Wim. Wim Wenders. (Illus., Orig.). 1977. pap. 4.50 (ISBN 0-918432-04-9). NY Zoetrope.

De Bartolo, Dick. The Return of a Mad Look at Old Movies. pap. 1.25 (ISBN 0-451-06835-1, Y6835, Sig). NAL.

Denby, David, ed. Awake in the Dark: An Anthology of American Film Criticism, 1915 to the Present. 1977. pap. 4.95 (ISBN 0-394-72194-2, Vin). Random.

--Film Seventy to Seventy-One. 1971. pap. 2.95 (ISBN 0-671-21048-3, Touchstone Bks). S&S.

Durgnat, Raymond. Durgnat on Film. (Illus.). 238p. 1976. pap. 7.95 (ISBN 0-571-10656-0, Pub. by Faber & Faber). Merrimack Bk Serv.

Eberwein, Robert T. A Viewer's Guide to Film Theory & Criticism. LC 79-9380. 243p. 1979. 13.50 (ISBN 0-8108-1237-1). Scarecrow.

Eschlach, Achim & Rader, Wendelin, eds. Semiotics of Films. 203p. 1978. 26.00 (ISBN 0-89664-080-9, Pub. by K G Saur). Gale.

Feldman, Joseph & Feldman, Harry. Dynamics of the Film. LC 73-169342. (Arno Press Cinema Program). (Illus.). 1972. Repr. of 1952 ed. 13.00 (ISBN 0-405-03917-4). Arno.

Films in Review 1950-1953, 4 vols. (Cinema Program Ser). Repr. of 1950 ed. 125.00 set (ISBN 0-405-04103-9). Arno.

French, Warren, ed. The South & Film. (Southern Quarterly Ser.). 200p. 1981. Repr. 12.50 (ISBN 0-87805-148-1). U Pr of Miss.

Friedlander, Madeline S. Leading Film Discussions. 42p. 1972. pap. 2.25 include mailing (ISBN 0-916130-00-2). LWV NYC.

Garrett, George P., et al, eds. Film Scripts Four: A Hard Day's Night, The Best Man, Darling. LC 71-135273. (Orig.). 1972. Set. 19.50x (ISBN 0-89197-162-9); pap. text ed. 8.95x ea.; instruc. manual free avail. Irvington.

Grierson, John. Grierson on the Movies. Hardy, H. Forsyth, ed. 200p. 1981. 22.00 (ISBN 0-571-11665-5, Pub. by Faber & Faber). Merrimack Bk Serv.

Halliwell, Leslie. The Filmgoer's Companion. 6th ed. 825p. 1977. 30.00 (ISBN 0-8090-4485-4). Hill & Wang.

Hammond, Paul, ed. The Shadow & Its Shadow: Surrealist Writings on Cinema. (BFI Ser). 1978. pap. 8.25 (ISBN 0-85170-074-8). NY Zoetrope.

Harley, John E. World-Wide Influences of the Cinema: A Study of Official Censorship & the International Cultural Aspects of Motion Pictures. LC 77-160234. (Moving Pictures Ser). xvi, 320p. 1971. Repr. of 1940 ed. lib. bdg. 16.95x (ISBN 0-89198-035-0). Ozer.

Heath, Stephen. Questions of Cinema. LC 81-47524. (Illus.). 272p. 1981. 22.50x (ISBN 0-253-15913-X); pap. 9.95 (ISBN 0-253-15914-8). Ind U Pr.

Hochman, Stanley, ed. American Film Directors. LC 73-92923. (Library of Film Criticism Ser.). 375p. 1974. 30.00 (ISBN 0-8044-3120-5). Ungar.

Hound & Horn: Essays on Cinema. LC 70-169344. (Arno Press Cinema Program). (Illus.). 136p. 1972. Repr. of 1971 ed. 10.00 (ISBN 0-405-03928-X). Arno.

Ideas of Order in Literature & Film: Selected Papers from the 4th Annual Florida State University Conferenceon Literature & Film. LC 80-26017. viii, 136p. (Orig.). 1981. pap. 8.00 (ISBN 0-8130-0699-6). U Presses Fla.

Jinks, William. The Celluloid Literature: Film in the Humanities. 2nd ed. LC 73-7361. (Illus.). 208p. 1974. pap. text ed. 9.95 (ISBN 0-02-474910-9, 47490). Macmillan.

Jowett, Garth S., ed. Dissertations on Film, 1980 Series, 23 bks. 1980. Set. lib. bdg. 532.00x (ISBN 0-686-71580-2). Arno.

Kael, Pauline. I Lost It at the Movies. 1965. 8.95 (ISBN 0-316-48164-5, Pub. by Atlantic Monthly Pr); pap. 5.95 (ISBN 0-316-48165-3, Pub. by Atlantic Monthly Pr). Little.

--Reeling. 512p. 1976. 12.95 (ISBN 0-316-48179-3, Pub. by Atlantic Monthly Pr.). Little.

Kauffmann, Stanley. Before My Eyes: Film Criticism & Comment. LC 78-20171. 1980. 16.95 (ISBN 0-06-012298-6, HarpT). Har-Row.

--Figures of Light: Film Criticism & Comment. LC 70-138742. 1971. 12.95 (ISBN 0-06-012274-9, HarpT). Har-Row.

Kauffmann, Stanley & Henstell, Bruce. American Film Criticism: From the Beginnings to Citizen Kane. LC 78-31669. 1979. Repr. of 1972 ed. lib. bdg. 25.00x (ISBN 0-313-21246-5, KAFI). Greenwood.

Kawin, Bruce F. Telling It Again & Again: Repetition in Literature & Film. LC 75-37753. 208p. 1972. 14.50x (ISBN 0-8014-0698-6). Cornell U Pr.

Lane, Tamar. What's Wrong with the Movies? LC 78-160237. (Moving Pictures Ser). 254p. 1971. Repr. of 1923 ed. lib. bdg. 11.95x (ISBN 0-89198-038-5). Ozer.

Lounsbury, Myron O. The Origins of American Film Criticisms, 1909-1939. LC 72-556. (Dissertations on Film Ser). 560p. 1972. Repr. of 1966 ed. 24.00 (ISBN 0-405-04099-7). Arno.

Lovell, Terry. Pictures of Reality: Aesthetics, Politics, Pleasure. (BFI Ser.). 112p. 1980. 21.95 (ISBN 0-85170-102-7); pap. 10.95 (ISBN 0-85170-103-5). NY Zoetrope.

Marcorelles, Louis. Elements Pour un Nouveau Cinema. 154p. (Orig., Fr.). 1972. pap. 5.00 (ISBN 0-685-23603-X, U218, UNESCO). Unipub.

Meyer, William R. The Making of the Great Westerns. (Illus.). 1979. 20.00 (ISBN 0-87000-431-X). Arlington Hse.

Murray, Edward. Nine American Film Critics: Study of Theory & Practice. LC 74-78444. 256p. 1975. 12.95 (ISBN 0-8044-2647-3); pap. 5.95 (ISBN 0-8044-6534-7). Ungar.

Perlman, William J., ed. The Movies on Trial: The Views & Opinions of Outstanding Personalities Anent Screen Entertainment Past & Present. LC 78-160245. (Moving Pictures Ser). 1971. Repr. of 1936 ed. lib. bdg. 14.25x (ISBN 0-89198-046-6). Ozer.

Petric, Vlada, ed. Film & Dreams: An Approach to Bergman. 1981. pap. 11.80 (ISBN 0-913178-61-6). Redgrave Pub Co.

Sherwood, Robert E. Robert E. Sherwood: Film Critic. (Illus.). 359p. 1973. 95.00 (ISBN 0-685-32337-4). Revisionist Pr.

Sitney, P. Adams, ed. The Avant-Garde Film: A Reader of Theory & Criticism. LC 78-57645. (Illus.). 1978. 29.50x (ISBN 0-8147-7793-7); pap. 14.50x (ISBN 0-8147-7794-5). NYU Pr.

Slide, Anthony & Wagenknecht, Edward. Fifty Great American Silent Films, 1912-1920: A Pictorial Survey. (Illus.). 176p. (Orig.). 1981. pap. 6.95 (ISBN 0-486-23985-3). Dover.

Walker, Alexander. Double Takes: Notes & Afterthoughts on the Movies, 1956-1976. 1978. 8.95 (ISBN 0-241-89395-X, Pub. by Hamish Hamilton England). David & Charles.

Walsh, Martin. The Brechtian Aspect of Radical Cinema. 108p. 1981. 27.95 (ISBN 0-85170-111-6, BFI); pap. 13.95 (ISBN 0-85170-112-4). NY Zoetrope.

Weiss, Elizabeth. The National Society of Film Critics on the Movie Star. 400p. 1981. pap. text ed. 12.95 (ISBN 0-14-005947-4). Penguin.

Williams, Christopher, ed. Realism & the Cinema: A Reader. (BFI Readers in Film Ser.). 320p. 1980. 25.00 (ISBN 0-7100-0477-X); pap. 11.95 (ISBN 0-7100-0478-8). Routledge & Kegan.

Wilson, Robert, ed. & pref. by. The Film Criticism of Otis Ferguson. LC 72-174660. 491p. 1971. 20.00x (ISBN 0-87722-005-0). Temple U Pr.

Wood, Robin. Personal Views - Explorations in Film. LC 76-373367. 1979. 14.50 (ISBN 0-900406-64-X, Pub. by G Fraser). Intl Schol Bk Serv.

MOVING-PICTURE DIRECTION
see Moving-Pictures–Production and Direction

MOVING-PICTURE EDITING
see Moving-Pictures–Editing

MOVING-PICTURE FILM COLLECTIONS
see also Libraries and Moving-Pictures

Bunuel, Luis. L' Age Dor: Un Chien Andalou. Bd. with Chien Andalou. LC 68-27591. (Classic Film Scripts). 1968. pap. 1.95 (ISBN 0-671-20086-0, Touchstone Bks). S&S.

Chittock, J. World Directory of Stockshot & Film Production Libraries. 1969. 32.00 (ISBN 0-08-013246-4). Pergamon.

Gidal, Peter. Structural Film Anthology. rev. ed. (BFI Ser.). (Orig.). 1977. pap. 5.75 (ISBN 0-85170-053-5). NY Zoetrope.

Harrison, Helen P. Film Library Techniques: Principles of Administration. (Studies in Media Management). 1973. 17.50 (ISBN 0-8038-2294-4). Hastings.

--Film Library Techniques: Principles of Administration. (Studies in Media Management). 1973. 16.50 (ISBN 0-240-50820-3). Focal Pr.

Library of Congress Motion Picture, Broadcasting, & Recorded Sound Division. The George Kleine Collection of Early Motion Pictures in the Library of Congress: A Catalog. Horwitz, Rita & Harrison, Harriet, eds. LC 79-607073. (Illus.). 270p. 1980. 11.00 (ISBN 0-8444-0331-8). Lib Congress.
Peterson, Sidney. The Dark of the Screen. (Anthology Film Archives Ser.: No. 4). (Illus.). 220p. 1980. 22.50x (ISBN 0-8147-6581-5); pap. 9.00x (ISBN 0-8147-6582-3). NYU Pr.
Screen Monographs One. LC 75-124020. (Literature of Cinema, Ser. 1). Repr. of 1970 ed. 5.00 (ISBN 0-405-01626-3). Arno.
Screen Monographs Two. LC 75-124020. (Literature of Cinema, Ser. 1). Repr. of 1970 ed. 7.00 (ISBN 0-405-01627-1). Arno.
Springer, John. Forgotten Films to Remember. (Illus.). 1980. 16.95 (ISBN 0-8065-0692-X). Citadel Pr.
Stern, Seymour. Index to the Films of D.W. Griffith. (Film Ser.). 1979. lib. bdg. 75.00 (ISBN 0-8490-2947-3). Gordon Pr.
Weiner, J. How to Organize & Run a Film Society. 1973. 7.95 (ISBN 0-02-625700-9). Macmillan.

MOVING-PICTURE FILM EDITING
see Moving-Pictures–Editing

MOVING-PICTURE INDUSTRY
see also Moving-Pictures–Production and Direction

Academy of Motion Picture Arts & Sciences. Annual Index to Motion Picture Credits, 1978. Ramsey, Verna, ed. LC 79-644761. 1979. lib. bdg. 150.00 (ISBN 0-313-20950-2, AN78). Greenwood.
Accounting for Motion Picture Films. 1973. pap. 3.50 (ISBN 0-685-39831-5). Am Inst CPA.
Anderson, P. D. In Its Own Image: The Cinematic Vision of Hollywood. LC 77-22903. (Dissertations on Film Ser.). 1978. lib. bdg. 18.00x (ISBN 0-405-10749-8). Arno.
Anger, Kenneth. Hollywood Babylon. Date not set. pap. 3.50 (ISBN 0-440-15325-5). Dell.
Atkins, Dick, ed. Method to the Madness: Hollywood Explained. LC 75-12118. (Illus.). 160p. 1975. 7.95 (ISBN 0-915618-09-5). Prince Pubs.
Balio, Tino. United Artists: The Company Built by the Stars. LC 75-12208. (Illus.). 344p. 1976. 22.50x (ISBN 0-299-06940-0); pap. 7.95 (ISBN 0-299-06944-3). U of Wis Pr.
Balio, Tino, ed. The American Film Industry. LC 75-32070. (Illus.). 512p. 1976. 25.00 (ISBN 0-299-07000-X); pap. 8.95 (ISBN 0-299-07004-2). U of Wis Pr.
Barr, Charles. Ealing Studios. LC 79-15033. (Illus.). 200p. 1980. 17.95 (ISBN 0-87951-101-X). Overlook Pr.
Barthes, et al. Apparatus. Cha, Theresa H., ed. 320p. 1981. 15.95 (ISBN 0-934378-22-3); pap. 7.95 (ISBN 0-934378-21-5). Tanam Pr.
Basten, Fred E. Beverly Hills: Portrait of a Fabled City. LC 75-22571. (Illus.). 384p. 1975. 23.50 (ISBN 0-913264-23-7). Douglas-West.
Biberman, Herbert. Salt of the Earth: The Story of a Film. Cortes, Carlos E., ed. LC 76-1248. (Chicano Heritage Ser.). (Illus.). 1976. Repr. of 1965 ed. 10.00x (ISBN 0-405-09486-8). Arno.
Bluem, A. William & Squire, Jason E. The Movie Business: American Film Industry Practice. (Studies in Media Management). 384p. 1972. 12.50 (ISBN 0-8038-4665-7); pap. text ed. 7.50x (ISBN 0-8038-4667-3). Hastings.
Brooks, Stanley J. Brooks' Standard Rate Book. 125p. 1980. 15.00 (ISBN 0-686-28425-9). S J Brooks.
Brownlow, Kevin. Hollywood: The Pioneers. LC 79-1197. (Illus.). 1980. 20.00 (ISBN 0-394-50851-3). Knopf.
Carpozi, George, Jr. That's Hollywood: The Magnificent Entertainers, No. 3. 1978. pap. 1.95 (ISBN 0-532-19194-3). Woodhill.
--That's Hollywood: The Matinee Idols, No. 1. 1978. pap. 1.95 (ISBN 0-532-19190-0). Woodhill.
Ceplair, Larry S. & Englund, Steven. The Inquisition in Hollywood: Politics in the Film Community, 1930-1960. LC 77-25587. (Illus.). 1980. 17.50 (ISBN 0-385-12900-9, Anchor Pr). Doubleday.
Chase, Donald. Filmmaking: The Collaborative Art. 1975. 9.95 (ISBN 0-316-13819-3). Little.
Costa, Sylvia. How to Prepare a Production Budget for Film & Video Tape. 2nd ed. LC 75-27372. 196p. 1975. 12.95 (ISBN 0-8306-5845-9, 845). TAB Bks.
Croy, Homer. How Motion Pictures Are Made. Jowett, Garth S., ed. LC 77-11373. (Aspects of Film Ser.). (Illus.). 1978. Repr. of 1918 ed. lib. bdg. 30.00x (ISBN 0-405-11129-0). Arno.
David, Saul. The Industry: Life in the Hollywood Fast Lane. Chase, Edward T., ed. LC 80-5783. 288p. 1981. 14.50 (ISBN 0-8129-0971-2). Times Bks.
Delson, Donn. The Dictionary of Marketing & Related Terms in the Motion Picture Industry. LC 79-67865. 70p. (Orig.). 1979. pap. text ed. 7.95 (ISBN 0-9603574-0-8). Bradson.
Eastman Kodak Company, ed. The Business of Filmmaking. LC 78-55882. (Illus.). 1978. pap. 6.95 (ISBN 0-87985-203-8, H-55). Eastman Kodak.
Edmonds, I. G. Big U: Universal in the Silent Days. LC 76-10874. (Illus.). 1977. 15.00 (ISBN 0-498-01809-1). A S Barnes.
Fadiman, William. Hollywood Now. 1972. 6.95 (ISBN 0-87140-556-3). Liveright.
Farber, Donald C. & Baumgarten, Paul. Producing, Financing, & Distributing Film. LC 72-87054. 1973. 15.95 (ISBN 0-910482-31-4). Drama Bk.
Gordon, R., ed. Camera: Digest of the Motion Picture Industry Anthology, 6 vols. 1976. lib. bdg. 1000.00 (ISBN 0-8490-1563-4). Gordon Pr.
--Motion Picture Trade Directory of 1928. 1976. lib. bdg. 140.00 (ISBN 0-8490-2300-9). Gordon Pr.
Gordon, R. F., ed. Motion Picture Studio Directory & Trade Annual 1919-1920. 1976. lib. bdg. 129.00 (ISBN 0-8490-2298-3). Gordon Pr.
Gregory, Mollie. Making Films Your Business. LC 79-14428. 1979. 14.50x (ISBN 0-8052-3728-3); pap. text ed. 6.95 (ISBN 0-8052-0639-6). Schocken.
Hurst, Richard M. Republic Studios: Between Poverty Row & the Majors. LC 79-19844. 1979. 14.50 (ISBN 0-8108-1254-1). Scarecrow.
Hurst, Walter E. & Hale, William Storm. Motion Picture Distribution: Business & or Racket. Date not set. 10.00 (ISBN 0-685-55910-6); pap. 5.00 (ISBN 0-685-55911-4). Borden.
Hurt, Walter E., et al. Motion Picture Distribution: Business & or Racket. (Entertainment Industry Ser.). (Illus.). 1975. 10.00 (ISBN 0-911370-23-4); pap. 10.00 (ISBN 0-911370-24-2). Seven Arts.
Jacobs, Diane. Hollywood Renaissance. 1980. pap. 6.95 (ISBN 0-440-53382-1, Delta). Dell.
Jobes, Gertrude. Motion Picture Empire. (Illus.). 1966. 25.00 (ISBN 0-208-00169-7, Archon). Shoe String.
Jones, Charles R. Breaking into the Movies. 1976. lib. bdg. 59.95 (ISBN 0-8490-1553-7). Gordon Pr.
Jowett, Garth & Linton, James M. Movies As Mass Communication. LC 80-13508. (The Sage Comtext Ser.: Vol. 4). (Illus.). 149p. 1980. 14.00 (ISBN 0-8039-1090-8); pap. 6.95 (ISBN 0-8039-1091-6). Sage.
Kemp's Directory, Nineteen Eighty to Nineteen Eighty-One, 3 vols. 1143p. 1981. Set. pap. 60.25 (ISBN 0-905255-86-0, KEMP 9, Kemps). Unipub.
Klingender, F. D. & Legg, Stuart. Money Behind the Screen. Jowett, Garth S., ed. LC 77-11378. (Aspects of Film Ser.). 1978. Repr. of 1937 ed. lib. bdg. 15.00x (ISBN 0-405-11134-7). Arno.
Kopple, Robert C. & Stiglitz, Bruce M. Taxation of the Motion Picture Industry. 290p. 1978. 35.00 (ISBN 0-87179-267-2). BNA.
Kuleshov, Lev. Kuleshov on Film: Writings by Lev Kuleshov. Levaco, Ronald, ed. & tr. LC 73-90666. (Illus.). 1975. 15.95 (ISBN 0-520-02659-4); pap. 3.45 (ISBN 0-520-03012-5). U of Cal Pr.
Leedy, David J. Motion Picture Distribution: An Accountants Perspective. 73p. (Orig.). 1980. pap. text ed. 6.95 (ISBN 0-9603574-1-6). Bradson.
Lewis, Arthur H. It Was Fun While It Lasted. new ed. 1973. 8.95 (ISBN 0-671-27106-7). Trident.
Madison Avenue Handbook. 300p. 1979. 13.00 (ISBN 0-686-62466-1). B Klein Pubns.
Mayer, Michael F. The Film Industries: Practical Business-Legal Problems in Production, Distribution & Exhibition. rev., 2nd, enl. ed. 1978. 12.50 (ISBN 0-8038-2370-3); pap. text ed. 6.75x (ISBN 0-8038-2371-1). Hastings.
Minus, Johnny & Hale, William S. Movie Industry Book: (Stories, Texts, Forms, Contracts) LC 79-121752. (Entertainment Industry Ser., Vol. 5). Orig. Title: Movie Producers First Business & Law Book. 1970. 35.00 (ISBN 0-911370-05-6). Seven Arts.
Monaco, James. American Film Now: The People, the Power, the Movies. (Illus.). 1979. pap. 7.95 (ISBN 0-452-25212-1, Z5212, Plume). NAL.
The Movies Begin: Making Movies in New Jersey 1887-1920. LC 77-73649. 1977. 13.95 (ISBN 0-87100-121-7). Newark Mus.
Parish, James R., et al. Hollywood on Hollywood. LC 78-15513. (Illus.). 1978. lib. bdg. 21.00 (ISBN 0-8108-1164-2). Scarecrow.
Powdermaker, Hortense. Hollywood: The Dream Factory; an Anthropologist Looks at the Movie-Makers. Coser, Lewis A. & Powell, Walter W., eds. LC 79-7013. (Perennial Works in Sociology Ser.). 1979. Repr. of 1950 ed. lib. bdg. 25.00x (ISBN 0-405-12112-1). Arno.
Pye, Michael & Myles, Lynda. The Movie Brats: How the Film Generation Took Over Hollywood. LC 78-11901. 1979. 12.95 (ISBN 0-03-042671-5); pap. 5.95 (ISBN 0-03-042676-6). HR&W.
Robertson, Patrick. Movie Facts & Feats. LC 80-52340. (Illus.). 272p. 1980. 17.95 (ISBN 0-8069-0204-3); lib. bdg. 15.99 (ISBN 0-8069-0205-1). Sterling.
Rosten, Leo C. Hollywood: The Movie Colony, the Movie Makers. LC 74-124036. (Literature of Cinema, Ser. 1). Repr. of 1941 ed. 23.00 (ISBN 0-405-01636-0). Arno.
Schlossberg, Julian & Yellen, Barry, eds. Inside the Movie Business. LC 79-93082. 224p. Date not set. cancelled (ISBN 0-8069-0188-8); lib. bdg. cancelled (ISBN 0-8069-0189-6). Sterling.
Seabury, William M. The Public & the Motion Picture Industry. LC 75-160247. (Moving Pictures Ser). xiv, 340p. 1971. Repr. of 1926 ed. lib. bdg. 17.50x (ISBN 0-89198-048-2). Ozer.
Silke, James R. Here's Looking at You, Kid: Fifty Years of Fighting, Working & Dreaming at Warner Brothers. (Illus.). 1976. 24.95 (ISBN 0-316-79131-8). Little.
Simonet, Thomas S. Regression Analysis of Prior Experiences of Key Production Personnel As Predictors of Revenues from High-Grossing Motion Pictures in American Release. Jowett, Garth S., ed. LC 79-6685. (Dissertations on Film, 1980 Ser.). 1980. lib. bdg. 30.00x (ISBN 0-405-12917-3). Arno.
Sinclair, Upton. Upton Sinclair Presents William Fox. LC 78-124037. (Literature of Cinema, Ser. 1). Repr. of 1933 ed. 12.00 (ISBN 0-405-01637-9). Arno.
Stanley, Robert H. The Celluloid Empire. (Illus.). 1978. 16.75 (ISBN 0-8038-1246-9); pap. 7.95x (ISBN 0-8038-1247-7). Hastings.
Steinberg, Cobbett. Film Facts. 480p. 1980. 17.95 (ISBN 0-87196-313-2). Facts on File.
U. S. House of Representatives, Committee on Education. Motion Picture Commission. Jowett, Garth S., ed. LC 77-11386. (Aspects of Film Ser.). 1978. Repr. of 1914 ed. lib. bdg. 18.00x (ISBN 0-405-11136-3). Arno.
U. S. Senate, Temporarary National Economic Committee. Investigation of Concentration of Economic Power. Jowett, Garth S., ed. LC 77-27366. (Aspects of Film Ser.). 1978. Repr. of 1941 ed. lib. bdg. 15.00x (ISBN 0-405-11127-4). Arno.
Warren, L. The Film Game. 1976. lib. bdg. 59.95 (ISBN 0-8490-1832-3). Gordon Pr.

MOVING-PICTURE INDUSTRY–BIOGRAPHY
see Moving-Pictures–Biography

MOVING-PICTURE MUSIC

Aros, Andrew A. Broadway & Hollywood Too. LC 80-67670. 60p. 1980. pap. 6.50 (ISBN 0-932352-04-9). Applause Pubns.
Bazelon, Irwin. Knowing the Score: Notes on Film Music. LC 80-24925. (Illus.). 432p. 1981. pap. 9.95 (ISBN 0-668-05132-9, 5132). Arco.
Collins, William. The Amateur Filmmaker's Handbook of Sound Sync & Scoring. LC 74-14325. (Illus.). 210p. 1974. 8.95 (ISBN 0-8306-4736-8); pap. 5.95 (ISBN 0-8306-3736-2, 736). TAB Bks.
Craig, Warren. Great Songwriters of Hollywood. LC 79-87793. 256p. 1980. 14.95 (ISBN 0-498-02439-3). A S Barnes.
Evans, Mark. Soundtrack: The Music of the Movies. (Paperback Ser.). 1979. pap. 6.95 (ISBN 0-306-80099-3). Da Capo.
Foort, Reginald. The Cinema Organ. LC 75-117943. (Illus.). 7.95 (ISBN 0-911572-05-8). Vestal.
Hofmann, Charles. Sounds for Silents. LC 74-107465. (Illus.). 1969. 10.00 (ISBN 0-910482-14-4); record incl. (ISBN 0-89676-035-9). Drama Bk.
Huntley, John. British Film Music. LC 72-169331. (Literature of Cinema, Series 2). (Illus.). 272p. 1972. Repr. of 1948 ed. 16.00 (ISBN 0-405-03897-6). Arno.
Lang, Edith & West, George. Musical Accompaniment of Moving Pictures. LC 72-124014. (Literature of Cinema, Ser. 1). Repr. of 1920 ed. 10.00 (ISBN 0-405-01620-4). Arno.
Limbacher, James L. Film Music: From Violins to Video. LC 73-16153. 1974. 25.00 (ISBN 0-8108-0651-7). Scarecrow.
--Keeping Score: Film Music Nineteen Seventy-Two to Nineteen Seventy-Nine. LC 80-26474. 510p. 1981. 22.50 (ISBN 0-8108-1390-4). Scarecrow.
London, Kurt. Film Music. LC 70-124016. (Literature of Cinema Ser). Repr. of 1936 ed. 9.50 (ISBN 0-405-01622-0). Arno.
Lustig, Milton. Music Editing for Motion Pictures. new ed. (Illus.). 160p. 1980. 15.95 (ISBN 0-8038-4729-7, Communication Arts). Hastings.
Manvell, Roger & Huntley, John. Technique of Film Music. 2nd ed. (Library of Communication Techniques Ser.). 1975. 24.95 (ISBN 0-240-50848-3). Focal Pr.
Music in Film & Television: International Catalogue, 1964-1974. 197p. 1976. pap. 9.25 (ISBN 92-3-201273-1, U396, UNESCO). Unipub.
Okun, Milton, ed. The New York Times Great Songs of the Sixties. LC 70-125482. (Illus.). 328p. 1972. 17.50 (ISBN 0-8129-0153-3); pap. 8.95 (ISBN 0-8129-6201-X). Times Bks.
Prendergast, Roy M. Film Music: A Neglected Art. (Illus.). 1978. pap. 5.95 (ISBN 0-393-00862-2, N862, Norton Lib). Norton.
--A Neglected Art: A Critical Study of Music in Films. LC 76-11713. 288p. 1977. 15.00x (ISBN 0-8147-6565-3). NYU Pr.
Rapee, Erno. Encyclopedia of Music for Pictures. LC 77-124034. (Literature of Cinema Ser). Repr. of 1925 ed. 25.00 (ISBN 0-405-01634-4). Arno.
--Motion Picture Moods for Pianists & Organists, a Rapid Reference Collection of Selected Pieces. LC 70-124035. (Literature of Cinema, Ser. 1). Repr. of 1924 ed. 33.00 (ISBN 0-405-01635-2). Arno.
Sabaneev, Leonid. Music for the Films. Jowett, Garth S., ed. Pring, S. W., tr. LC 77-11382. (Aspects of Film Ser.). 1978. Repr. of 1935 ed. lib. bdg. 15.00x (ISBN 0-405-11142-8). Arno.
Skiles, Marlin. Music Scoring for TV & Motion Pictures. LC 75-13011. (Illus.). 266p. 1976. 12.95 (ISBN 0-8306-6779-2, 779). TAB Bks.
Thomas, Tony. Harry Warren & the Hollywood Musical. (Illus.). 1975. 17.95 (ISBN 0-8065-0468-4). Citadel Pr.
--Music for the Movies. LC 72-37818. (Illus.). 284p. 1973. 14.50 (ISBN 0-498-01071-6); pap. 6.95 (ISBN 0-498-01980-2). A S Barnes.
Thomas, Tony, ed. Film Score. LC 78-75341. 1979. 14.50 (ISBN 0-498-02358-3). A S Barnes.

MOVING-PICTURE PLAYS
see also Comedy Films; Film Adaptations; Moving-Pictures–Plots, Themes, etc.

Amberg, G., intro. by. Film Society Programmes, 1925-1939. LC 77-103815. (Contemporary Art Ser). 1971. Repr. of 1925 ed. 29.00 (ISBN 0-405-00741-8). Arno.
Berryman, John. Love & Fame. 96p. 1970. 6.50 (ISBN 0-374-19233-2); pap. 3.95 (ISBN 0-374-51031-8). FS&G.
Brady, John. The Craft of the Screenwriter. 1981. 14.95 (ISBN 0-671-25229-1). S&S.
Bresson, Robert. The Complete Screenplays, Vol. I: A Prisoner Escaped. Michelson, Annette, ed. Burch, Noel, tr. 1981. 15.00 (ISBN 0-89396-033-0); pap. 7.95 (ISBN 0-89396-034-9). Urizen Bks.
Cohen, Henry, ed. The Public Enemy. LC 80-52292. (Wisconsin-Warner Bros. Screenplay Ser.). (Illus.). 224p. (Orig.). 1981. 15.00 (ISBN 0-299-08460-4); pap. 5.95 (ISBN 0-299-08464-7). U of Wis Pr.
Culbert, David, ed. Mission to Moscow. (Wisconsin - Warner Bros. Screenplay Ser.). (Illus.). 310p. 1980. 15.00 (ISBN 0-299-08380-2); pap. 5.95 (ISBN 0-299-08384-5). U of Wis Pr.
Dick, Bernard F., ed. Dark Victory. LC 81-50822. (Wisconsin-Warner Bros. Screenplay Ser.). (Illus.). 240p. (Orig.). 1981. 15.00 (ISBN 0-299-08760-3); pap. 5.95 (ISBN 0-299-08764-6). U of Wis Pr.
Esenwein, J. Berg & Leeds, Arthur. Writing the Photoplay. 425p. 1980. Repr. of 1913 ed. lib. bdg. 35.00 (ISBN 0-8495-1350-2). Arden Lib.
Field, Syd. Screenplay. 1979. pap. 5.95 (ISBN 0-440-58273-3, Delta). Dell.
Fumento, Rocco, ed. Forty-Second Street. (Wisconsin - Warner Bros. Screenplay Ser.). (Illus.). 220p. 1980. 15.00 (ISBN 0-299-08100-1); pap. 5.95 (ISBN 0-299-08104-4). U of Wis Pr.
Gassner, John & Nichols, Dudley. Best Film Plays, Nineteen Forty-Three to Forty-Four. LC 76-52102. (Classics of Film Literature Ser.: Vol. 11). (Illus.). 1977. Repr. of 1945 ed. lib. bdg. 32.00 (ISBN 0-8240-2875-9). Garland Pub.
--Twenty Best Film Plays, 2 vols. LC 76-52104. (Classics of Film Literature Ser.: Vol. 13). 1977. Repr. of 1943 ed. Set. lib. bdg. 114.00 (ISBN 0-8240-2877-5); lib. bdg. 57.00 ea. Garland Pub.
Harwell, Richard. GWTW: The Screenplay by Sidney Howard. 1980. 17.95 (ISBN 0-02-548660-8). Macmillan.
Herman, Lewis. Practical Manual of Screen Playwriting for Theater & Television Films. pap. 3.95 (ISBN 0-452-00360-1, FM360, Mer). NAL.
Herzog, Werner. Screenplays. Greenberg, Alan, tr. from Ger. 208p. 1980. 11.95 (ISBN 0-934378-02-9); pap. 5.95 (ISBN 0-934378-03-7). Tanam Pr.
Kurosawa, Akira. Seven Samurai. (Film Scripts-Modern Ser). 1970. pap. 3.45 (ISBN 0-671-20619-2, Touchstone Bks). S&S.
Lee, Donna. Magic Methods of Screenwriting. 3rd rev. ed. LC 78-56520. 1978. 12.95 (ISBN 0-89632-005-7). Del Oeste.

Lelouche, Claude. Man & A Women. (Film Scripts-Modern Ser). 1971. pap. 2.25 (ISBN 0-671-20963-9, Touchstone Bks). S&S.

Loos, Anita. San Francisco: A Screenplay. LC 78-9034. (Screenplay Library). (Illus.). 212p. 1979. 10.00 (ISBN 0-8093-0876-2); pap. 6.95 (ISBN 0-8093-0877-0). S Ill U Pr.

Lucas, George. American Graffiti. 1979. pap. 1.75 (ISBN 0-394-17072-5, B373, BC). Grove.

McCarty, Clifford. Film Composers in America: A Checklist of Their Work. LC 72-4448. (Music Ser.). 196p. 1972. Repr. of 1953 ed. lib. bdg. 19.50 (ISBN 0-306-70495-1). Da Capo.

--Published Screenplays: A Checklist. LC 73-138656. (Serif Ser.: No. 18). 1971. 9.00x (ISBN 0-87338-112-2). Kent St U Pr.

McGilligan, Patrick, ed. Yankee Doodle Dandy. LC 80-52293. (Wisconsin-Warner Bros. Screenplay Ser.). (Illus.). 192p. (Orig.). 1981. 15.00 (ISBN 0-299-08470-1); pap. 5.95 (ISBN 0-299-08474-4). U of Wis Pr.

Mungo, Raymond. Between Two Moons. 1972. 4.95 (ISBN 0-8070-6402-5, Pub. by Montana Bks); pap. 2.95 (ISBN 0-8070-6405-X). Madrona Pubs.

Myerson, Michael. Memories of Underdevelopment: The Revolutionary Films of Cuba. LC 72-93281. (Illus.). 224p. 1973. 7.95 (ISBN 0-670-46827-4, Grossman). Viking Pr.

Niver, Kemp R. D. W. Griffith's "the Battle at Elderbush Gulch". LC 72-85599. (Illus.). 1972. 7.50 (ISBN 0-913986-04-6). Locare.

--Klaw & Erlanger: Famous Plays in Pictures. LC 75-44556. (Illus.). 1976. 15.00 (ISBN 0-913986-07-0). Locare.

Noble, Lorraine. Four Star Scripts. Kupelnick, Bruce S., ed. LC 76-52117. (Classics of Film Literature Ser.). 1978. lib. bdg. 20.00 (ISBN 0-8240-2885-6). Garland Pub.

O'Connor, John E., ed. I Am a Fugitive from a Chain Gang. LC 81-50823. (Wisconsin-Warner Bros. Sceenplay Ser.). (Illus.). 224p. (Orig.). 1981. 15.00 (ISBN 0-299-08750-6); pap. 5.95 (ISBN 0-299-08754-9). U of Wis Pr.

Patterson, Frances. Motion Picture Continuities. Kupelnick, Bruce S., ed. LC 76-52120. (Classics of Film Literature Ser.). 1978. lib. bdg. 18.00 (ISBN 0-8240-2888-0). Garland Pub.

Peary, Gerald, ed. Little Caesar. LC 80-52291. (Wisconsin-Warner Bros. Screenplay Ser.). (Illus.). 200p. (Orig.). 1981. 15.00 (ISBN 0-299-08450-7); pap. 5.95 (ISBN 0-299-08454-X). U of Wis Pr.

Peary, Gerald & Shatzkin, Roger, eds. The Modern American Novel & the Movies. LC 78-4373. (Ungar Film Library). (Illus.). 1978. 15.95 (ISBN 0-8044-2682-1); pap. 6.95 (ISBN 0-8044-6649-1). Ungar.

Phillips, Gene D. The Films of Tennessee Williams. LC 76-50204. (Illus.). 336p. 1980. 22.50 (ISBN 0-87982-025-X). Art Alliance.

Phillips, Henry A. Photodrama. LC 70-124032. (Literature of Cinema, Ser. 1). Repr. of 1914 ed. 7.00 (ISBN 0-405-01632-8). Arno.

Pinter, Harold. The French Lieutenant's Woman: A Screenplay. 1981. 10.95 (ISBN 0-316-70851-8); deluxe ed. 50.00 (ISBN 0-316-70852-6). Little.

--The Proust Screenplay. LC 77-78081. 1977. pap. 3.95 (ISBN 0-394-17018-0, E690, Ever). Grove.

Prevert, Jacques & Carne, Marcel. Jour Se Leve. (Film Scripts-Classic Ser.). 1970. pap. 2.25 (ISBN 0-671-20616-8). S&S.

Schulberg, Budd. On the Waterfront: A Screenplay. Bruccoli, Matthew J., ed. LC 80-15734. (Screenplay Library). (Illus.). 166p. 12.50 (ISBN 0-8093-0956-4); pap. 5.95 (ISBN 0-8093-0957-2). S Ill U Pr.

Scriptwriting for Short Films. Orig. Title: Manual on Short Film Script Writing. 1970. pap. 2.25 (ISBN 92-3-100744-0, U593, UNESCO). Unipub.

Shawn, Wallace & Gregory, Andre. My Dinner with Andre. 240p. (Orig.). 1981. pap. 4.95 (ISBN 0-394-17948-X, Ever). Grove.

Simon, Paul. One-Trick Pony. LC 80-7636. (Illus.). 224p. 1980. 15.95 (ISBN 0-394-51381-9); pap. 8.95 (ISBN 0-394-73961-2). Knopf.

Taylor, John R. Directors & Directions: Cinema for the Seventies. 1975. 11.95 (ISBN 0-8090-3901-X); pap. 5.95 (ISBN 0-8090-1375-4). Hill & Wang.

Von Stroheim, Erich. Greed. (Film Scripts-Classic Ser.). 1970. pap. 4.95 (ISBN 0-671-20614-1). S&S.

Wertmuller, Lina. The Screenplays of Lina Wertmuller. LC 76-52816. (Illus.). 1977. 12.95 (ISBN 0-8129-0685-3). Times Bks.

Winston, Douglas G. The Screenplay As Literature. LC 72-654. 240p. 1973. 16.50 (ISBN 0-8386-1200-8). Fairleigh Dickinson.

MOVING-PICTURE PLAYS–BIBLIOGRAPHY

Dougall. War. Peace. Film Guide. pap. 1.50 (ISBN 0-8164-9240-9). Continuum.

Gerlach, John & Gerlach, Lana. The Critical Index: A Bibliography of Articles on Film in English, 1946-1973 - Arranged by Names & Topics. Milic, Louis T., ed. LC 74-1959. 1974. pap. text ed. 9.25x (ISBN 0-8077-2438-6). Tchrs Coll.

Poteet, G. Howard. Published Radio, Television & Film Scripts: A Bibliography. LC 74-18201. iii, 245p. 1975. 15.00x (ISBN 0-87875-063-0). Whitston Pub.

Samples, Gordon. The Drama Scholars' Index to Plays & Filmscripts: A Guide to Plays & Filmscripts in Selected Anthologies, Series & Periodicals, Vol. 2. LC 73-22165. 705p. 1980. 30.00 (ISBN 0-8108-1249-5). Scarecrow.

MOVING-PICTURE PLAYS–COLLECTIONS

Garrett, George P., et al, eds. Film Scripts One: Henry V, The Big Sleep, A Streetcar Named Desire. LC 71-135273. (Orig.). 1971. pap. text ed. 19.50x set (ISBN 0-89197-163-7); pap. text ed. 8.95x ea.; instructor's manual avail. (ISBN 0-8290-0137-9). Irvington.

--Film Scripts Two: High Noon, Twelve Angry Men, The Defiant Ones. LC 71-135273. (Orig.). 1971. pap. 19.50x set (ISBN 0-89197-165-3); pap. text ed. 8.95x ea.; instructor's manual free avail. (ISBN 0-8290-0137-9). Irvington.

Gassner, John & Nicholas, Dudley. Best Film Plays Nineteen Forty-Five. Kupelnick, Bruce S., ed. LC 76-52103. (Classics of Film Literature Ser.). 1978. lib. bdg. 32.00 (ISBN 0-8240-2876-7). Garland Pub.

Gordon, Raoul, ed. Films: A Catalogue of Catalogues, Eight & Sixteen Millimeter Films Available to Institutions & the General Public, 2 vols. (Film Trade List Annual Ser.). 1979. Set. lib. bdg. 200.00 (ISBN 0-8490-2919-8). Gordon Pr.

Samples, Gordon. The Drama Scholars Index to Plays & Filmscripts. LC 73-22165. 1974. 15.00 (ISBN 0-8108-0699-1). Scarecrow.

Shaw, G. B. The Collected Screenplays of Bernard Shaw. Dukore, Bernard F., ed. LC 80-13320. (Illus.). 400p. 1980. 35.00 (ISBN 0-8203-0524-3). U of Ga Pr.

MOVING-PICTURE PLAYS–HISTORY AND CRITICISM

Brittain, Joan T. Laurence Stallings. LC 74-23831. (U. S. Authors Ser.: No. 250). 1975. lib. bdg. 10.95 (ISBN 0-8057-0686-0). Twayne.

DeNitto, Dennis & Herman, William. Film & the Critical Eye. (Illus.). 480p. 1975. pap. text ed. 9.95 (ISBN 0-02-328370-X, 32837). Macmillan.

Ellis, John, intro. by. Screen Reader One: Cinema, Ideology, Politics. (Screen Ser.). 1977. pap. 15.00 (ISBN 0-900676-07-8). NY Zoetrope.

Garbicz, Adam & Klinowski, Jacek. Cinema, the Magic Vehicle-A Guide to Its Achievement-Journey One: The Cinema Through 1949. LC 75-2183. 551p. 1975. 22.50 (ISBN 0-8108-0801-3). Scarecrow.

Gerlach, John & Gerlach, Lana. The Critical Index: A Bibliography of Articles on Film in English, 1946-1973 - Arranged by Names & Topics. Milic, Louis T., ed. LC 74-1959. 1974. pap. text ed. 9.25x (ISBN 0-8077-2438-6). Tchrs Coll.

Hochman, Stanley, ed. American Film Directors. LC 73-92923. (Library of Film Criticism Ser.). 375p. 1974. 30.00 (ISBN 0-8044-3120-5). Ungar.

Huss, Roy & Silverstein, Norman. Film Experience. 1969. pap. 3.95 (ISBN 0-440-52547-0, Delta). Dell.

Jorgens, Jack J. Shakespeare on Film. LC 76-12365. (Midland Bks.: No. 234). (Illus.). 352p. 1977. 15.00x (ISBN 0-253-35196-0); pap. 6.95x (ISBN 0-253-20234-5). Ind U Pr.

Kael, Pauline. Kiss Kiss Bang Bang. 1968. pap. 4.95 (ISBN 0-316-48163-7, Pub. by Atlantic Monthly Pr). Little.

Kanin, Garson. Moviola. (gr. 11 up). 1980. pap. 2.95 (ISBN 0-671-82794-4). PB.

Kauffman, Stanley. World on Film. 1967. pap. 2.65 (ISBN 0-440-59697-1, Delta). Dell.

Kauffmann, Stanley. A World on Film. LC 73-15313. 437p. 1975. Repr. of 1966 ed. lib. bdg. 26.00x (ISBN 0-8371-7188-1, KAWF). Greenwood.

Kracauer, Siegfreid. From Caligari to Hitler: A Psychological History of the German Film. 22.50 (ISBN 0-691-08708-3); pap. 5.95 (ISBN 0-691-02505-3). Princeton U Pr.

MacCann, Richard D., ed. Cinema Examined: Selections from Cinema Journal, 1966-1976. (Illus.). 1979. pap. 9.95 (ISBN 0-525-47464-1). Dutton.

Mekas, Jonas. Movie Journal. 420p. 1972. pap. 3.50 (ISBN 0-02-012500-3, Collier). Macmillan.

Poteet, George H. Film Criticism in Popular American Periodicals, 1933-1967. (Cinema Ser). lib. bdg. 69.95 (ISBN 0-87700-240-1). Revisionist Pr.

Silver, Alain & Ursini, James. The Vampire Film. LC 74-9301. (Illus.). 192p. 1975. 12.00 (ISBN 0-498-01429-0). A S Barnes.

Taylor, John R. Directors & Directions: Cinema for the Seventies. 1975. 11.95 (ISBN 0-8090-3901-X); pap. 5.95 (ISBN 0-8090-1375-4). Hill & Wang.

Thiher, Allen. The Cinematic Muse: Critical Studies in the History of French Cinema. LC 79-1560. (Illus.). 1979. text ed. 18.00x (ISBN 0-8262-0277-2). U of Mo Pr.

Wertmuller, Lina. The Screenplays of Lina Wertmuller. LC 76-52816. (Illus.). 1977. 12.95 (ISBN 0-8129-0685-3). Times Bks.

Young, Vernon. On Film: Unpopular Essays on a Popular Art. LC 72-156335. 454p. 1972. 12.95 (ISBN 0-8129-0188-6); pap. 3.95 (1974) (ISBN 0-8129-6230-3). Times Bks.

MOVING-PICTURE PLOTS

see Moving-Pictures-Plots, Themes, etc.

MOVING-PICTURE PRODUCERS AND DIRECTORS

Art Directors Club of New York. The Fifty-Ninth Art Directors Annual. Solomon, Miriam L., ed. (Illus.). 672p. 1980. 34.95 (ISBN 0-937414-00-X). ADC Pubns.

Atkins, Thomas R. Frederick Wiseman. (Monarch Film Studies). 1975. pap. 2.95 (ISBN 0-671-08101-2). Monarch Pr.

Basinger, Jeanine, ed. Working with Kazan. (Illus.). 1973. pap. 4.00x (ISBN 0-8195-8016-3, Pub. by Wesleyan U Pr). Columbia U Pr.

Baxter, Peter. Sternberg. (BFI Ser.). (Illus.). 130p. 1980. 23.95 (ISBN 0-85170-098-5); pap. 11.95 (ISBN 0-85170-099-3). NY Zoetrope.

Berg-Pan, Renata. Leni Riefenstahl. (Theatrical Arts Ser.). 1980. lib. bdg. 13.95 (ISBN 0-8057-9275-9). Twayne.

Beveridge, James. John Grierson: Film Master. LC 77-17799. 1978. 22.95 (ISBN 0-02-510530-2). Macmillan.

Bock, Audie. Japanese Film Directors. LC 77-75968. (Illus.). 1978. 14.95 (ISBN 0-87011-304-6). Kodansha.

Bogdanovich, Peter. Allan Dwan. (A Belvedere Bk.). 220p. 1981. pap. 5.95 (ISBN 0-87754-320-8). Chelsea Hse.

Braudy, Leo & Dickstein, Morris, eds. Great Film Directors: A Critical Anthology. 1978. pap. text ed. 8.95x (ISBN 0-19-502312-9). Oxford U Pr.

Brooker, Nancy J., ed. John Schlesinger: A Guide to References & Resources. (Reference & Resource Guide Ser.). 1978. lib. bdg. 14.00 (ISBN 0-8161-8024-5). G K Hall.

Canham, Kingsley. The Hollywood Professionals, Vol. 1: Curtiz, Walsh, & Hathaway. LC 72-1786. (International Film Guide Ser.). (Illus.). 224p. 1973. pap. 4.95 (ISBN 0-498-01204-2). A S Barnes.

Cannom, Robert. Van Dyke & the Mythical City Hollywood. LC 76-52096. (Classics of Film Literature Ser.: Vol. 8). (Illus.). 1977. Repr. of 1948 ed. lib. bdg. 22.00 (ISBN 0-8240-2870-8). Garland Pub.

Casper, Joseph A. Stanley Donen & His Films. (Illus.). 288p. 1981. 19.95 (ISBN 0-498-02561-6). A S Barnes.

Cecchettini, P. & Whittlemore, D. Passport to Hollywood: Film Immigrants. 1976. pap. 13.50 (ISBN 0-07-070052-4, C); study guide 3.00 (ISBN 0-07-070051-6); 13.50 (ISBN 0-07-070053-2). McGraw.

Christie, Ian, ed. Powell Pressburger & Others. (BFI Ser.). 1979. pap. 8.25 (ISBN 0-85170-086-1). NY Zoetrope.

Cole, Lester. Hollywood Red: The Autobiography of Lester Cole. LC 81-51701. (Illus.). 450p. 1981. 12.95 (ISBN 0-87867-085-8). Ramparts.

Combs, Richard, ed. Robert Aldrich. (BFI Ser.). 1979. pap. 4.00 (ISBN 0-85170-084-5). NY Zoetrope.

Cornwell, Regina. Snow Seen: The Films & Photographs of Michael Snow. (PMA Bks.). (Illus.). 1980. 21.95 (ISBN 0-88778-197-7). NY Zoetrope.

Delmar, Rosalind. Joris Ivens. (BFI Ser.). (Orig.). 1980. pap. 10.95 (ISBN 0-85170-092-6). NY Zoetrope.

Diakite, Madubuko. Film, Culture, & the Black Filmmaker. Jowett, Garth S., ed. LC 79-6679. (Issertations on Film, 1980 Ser.). 1980. lib. bdg. 19.00x (ISBN 0-405-12907-6). Arno.

Dmytryk, Edward. It's a Hell of a Life but Not a Bad Living. LC 78-58166. 1979. 10.95 (ISBN 0-8129-0785-X). Times Bks.

Easton, Carol. The Search for Sam Goldwyn. LC 75-28167. 1976. 8.95 (ISBN 0-688-03007-6). Morrow.

Eaton, Mick, ed. Anthropology-Reality-Cinema: The Films of Jean Rouch. (BFI Ser.). (Orig.). 1979. pap. 6.50 (ISBN 0-85170-090-X). NY Zoetrope.

Edinburgh Festival. Jacques Tourneur. (EIFF Ser). 1978. pap. 4.00 (ISBN 0-918432-15-4). NY Zoetrope.

Edmonds, I. G. & Mimura, Reiko. Oscar Directors. 1980. 17.95 (ISBN 0-498-02533-0); pap. write for info. (ISBN 0-498-02444-X). A S Barnes.

--Oscar Directors. 1980. 17.95 (ISBN 0-498-02533-0); pap. write for info. (ISBN 0-498-02444-X). A S Barnes.

Epstein, Lawrence J. Samuel Goldwyn. (Theatrical Arts Ser.). 1981. lib. bdg. 14.95 (ISBN 0-8057-9282-1). Twayne.

Feineman, N. Persistence of Vision: The Films of Robert Altman. LC 77-22906. (Dissertations on Film Ser.). 1978. lib. bdg. 13.00x (ISBN 0-405-10752-8). Arno.

Feineman, Neil. Nicolas Roeg. (Theatrical Art Ser.). 1978. 12.50 (ISBN 0-8057-9258-9). Twayne.

Gaston, Georg. Karel Reisz. (Theatrical Arts Ser.). 1980. lib. bdg. 13.95 (ISBN 0-8057-9277-5). Twayne.

Gomez, Joseph A. Peter Watkins. (Theatrical Arts Ser.). 1979. lib. bdg. 10.95 (ISBN 0-8057-9267-8). Twayne.

Gordon, R., ed. Motion Picture Director Anthology. 1976. lib. bdg. 69.95 (ISBN 0-8490-2294-0). Gordon Pr.

Halliwell, Leslie. Halliwell's Filmgoer's Companion. 788p. 1980. 39.50 (ISBN 0-684-16660-7, ScribT). Scribner.

Helweg, Marianne. Carl Dreyer. (Film Ser.). 1979. lib. bdg. 59.95 (ISBN 0-8490-2880-9). Gordon Pr.

Houseman, John. Front & Center. 1981. pap. 7.95 (ISBN 0-671-41391-0, Touchstone Bks). S&S.

--Run-Through. 1981. pap. 7.95 (ISBN 0-671-41390-2, Touchstone Bks). S&S.

Huff, Theodore. An Index to the Films of Charles Chaplin. (Gordon Press Film Ser.). 1980. lib. bdg. 59.95 (ISBN 0-8490-3090-0). Gordon Pr.

International Portrait Gallery: Vol. 10, Film Directors & Producers Supplement. (Illus.). 64p. 1981. 50.00 (ISBN 0-686-69446-5, IPG-10). Gale.

Jacobs, Diane. Hollywood Renaissance. LC 76-18796. (Illus.). 1977. 12.00 (ISBN 0-498-01785-0). A S Barnes.

Johnston, Alva. The Great Goldwyn. Jowett, Garth S., ed. LC 77-11377. (Aspects of Film Ser.). (Illus.). 1978. Repr. of 1937 ed. lib. bdg. 15.00x (ISBN 0-405-11133-9). Arno.

Kass, Judith M. Robert Altman. 1978. pap. 2.25 (ISBN 0-445-04262-1). Popular Lib.

Kelly, Mary P. Martin Scorsese: The First Decade. (Illus., Orig.). 1980. pap. 9.90 (ISBN 0-913178-67-5). Redgrave Pub Co.

Kolker, Robert P. A Cinema of Loneliness: Penn, Kubrick, Coppola, Scorsese, Altman. LC 79-978. (Illus.). 1980. 15.95 (ISBN 0-19-502588-1). Oxford U Pr.

Korda, Michael. Charmed Lives. 560p. 1981. pap. 3.50 (ISBN 0-380-53017-1, 53017). Avon.

Koszarski, Richard, ed. Hollywood Directors: 1914-1940. LC 76-9262. (Illus.). 1976. 16.95 (ISBN 0-19-502085-5). Oxford U Pr.

--Hollywood Directors, 1914-1940. 1976. pap. 4.95 (ISBN 0-19-502086-3, 417, GB). Oxford U Pr.

--Hollywood Directors, 1941-1976. LC 76-51716. (Illus.). 1977. 19.95 (ISBN 0-19-502217-3). Oxford U Pr.

--Hollywood Directors, 1941-1976. LC 76-51716. (Illus.). 1977. pap. 6.95 (ISBN 0-19-502218-1, GB 509, GB). Oxford U Pr.

Kreidl, John F. Nicholas Ray. (Theatrical Arts Ser.). 1977. lib. bdg. 12.50 (ISBN 0-8057-9250-3). Twayne.

Lambray, Maureen. The American Film Directors. 1977. pap. 9.95 (ISBN 0-02-077220-3, Collier). Macmillan.

Lamster, Frederick. Souls Made Great Through Love & Adversity: The Film Work of Frank Borzage. LC 80-28441. 242p. 1981. 12.50 (ISBN 0-8108-1404-8). Scarecrow.

Lasky, Michael S. & Harris, Robert A. The Films of Alfred Hitchcock. (Illus.). pap. 7.95 (ISBN 0-8065-0619-9). Citadel Pr.

Leaming, Barbara. Grigori Kozintsey. (Theatrical Arts Ser.). 1980. lib. bdg. 14.95 (ISBN 0-8057-9276-7). Twayne.

Lehman, Peter & Luhr, William. Blake Edwards. LC 80-28440. (Illus.). xiv, 288p. 1981. 18.95x (ISBN 0-8214-0605-1); pap. 8.95 (ISBN 0-8214-0616-7). Ohio U Pr.

Leyda, Jay. An Index to the Creative Work of Alexander Dovzhenko. (Gordon Press Film Ser.). 1980. lib. bdg. 59.95 (ISBN 0-8490-3094-3). Gordon Pr.

--An Index to the Creative Work of V. I. Pudovkin. (Gordon Press Film Ser.). 1980. lib. bdg. 59.95 (ISBN 0-8490-3092-7). Gordon Pr.

McGerr, Celia. Rene Clair. (Theatrical Arts Ser.). 1980. lib. bdg. 12.95 (ISBN 0-8057-9262-7). Twayne.

Maddock, Brent. The Films of Jacques Tati. LC 77-11084. 1977. 10.00 (ISBN 0-8108-1065-4). Scarecrow.

Marx, Arthur. Goldwyn: A Biography of the Man Behind the Myth. (Illus.). 416p. 1976. 9.95 (ISBN 0-393-07497-8). Norton.

Mellen, Joan. Voices from the Japanese Cinema. (Illus.). 295p. 1975. 12.50 (ISBN 0-87140-604-7); pap. 4.95 (ISBN 0-87140-101-0). Liveright.

Mellen, Joan, ed. The World of Luis Bunuel: Essays in Criticism. (Illus.). 1978. 15.95x (ISBN 0-19-502398-6). Oxford U Pr.

Meyer, William R. The Warner Brothers Directors: The Hard-Boiled, the Comic, & the Weepers. LC 77-22194. (Illus.). 1978. 20.00 (ISBN 0-87000-397-6). Arlington Hse.
Michalczyk, John J. The French Literary Filmmakers. LC 78-75171. (Illus.). 230p. 1980. 19.50 (ISBN 0-87982-027-6). Art Alliance.
Millichap, Joseph R. Lewis Milestone. (Theatrical Arts Ser.). 1981. lib. bdg. 14.95 (ISBN 0-8057-9281-3). Twayne.
Minnelli, Vincente & Arce, Hector. I Remember It Well. 1975. pap. 1.75 (ISBN 0-425-02907-7, Medallion). Berkley Pub.
Monaco, James. The New Wave: Truffaut, Godard, Chabrol, Rohmer, Rivette. LC 75-38099. 1977. pap. 5.95 (ISBN 0-19-502246-7, GB516, GB). Oxford U Pr.
Murphy, William T., ed. Robert Flaherty: A Guide to References & Resources. (Reference & Resource Guide Ser.). 1978. lib. bdg. 18.00 (ISBN 0-8161-8022-9). G K Hall.
Noble, Peter. Anthony Asquith. (Film Ser.). 1979. lib. bdg. 6.95 (ISBN 0-8490-2866-3). Gordon Pr.
Ott, Frederick W. The Films of Fritz Lang. 1979. 17.95 (ISBN 0-8065-0435-8). Citadel Pr.
Parish, James R., et al. Film Directors Guide: Western Europe. LC 76-1891. (Illus.). 1976. 13.50 (ISBN 0-8108-0908-7). Scarecrow.
Parrish, Robert. Growing up in Hollywood. LC 77-4120. 1977. pap. 3.95 (ISBN 0-15-637315-7, Harv). HarBraceJ.
Phillips, Gene D. John Schlesinger. (Theatrical Arts Ser.). 1981. lib. bdg. 14.95 (ISBN 0-8057-9280-5). Twayne.
--Ken Russell. (Theatrical Arts Ser.). 1979. lib. bdg. 10.95 (ISBN 0-8057-9266-X). Twayne.
Poague, Leland A. The Hollywood Professionals, Vol. 7: Billy Wilder & Leo McCarey. LC 72-1786. (Illus.). 1979. 12.00 (ISBN 0-498-02181-5). A S Barnes.
Pye, Michael & Myles, Lynda. The Movie Brats: How the Film Generation Took Over Hollywood. LC 78-11901. 1979. 12.95 (ISBN 0-03-042671-5); pap. 5.95 (ISBN 0-03-042676-6). HR&W.
Queval, Jean. Marcel Carne. (Film Ser.). 1979. lib. bdg. 59.95 (ISBN 0-8490-2970-8). Gordon Pr.
Rainsberger, Todd. Eloquent Light: The Cinematography of James Wong Howe. LC 80-26542. (Illus.). 218p. 1981. 17.50 (ISBN 0-498-02405-9). A S Barnes.
Renoir, Jean. My Life & My Films. Denny, Norman, tr. from Fr. LC 74-77850. (Illus.). 320p. 1974. pap. 5.95 (ISBN 0-689-10629-7, 219). Atheneum.
Richard, Valliere I. Norman McLaren, Manipulator of Movement: The National Film Board Years, 1947-67. LC 80-53998. (Illus.). 220p. 1982. 20.00 (ISBN 0-87413-192-8). U Delaware Pr.
Rosenfeldt, Diane, ed. Ken Russell: A Guide to Reference & Resources. (Reference & Resource Guide Ser.). 1978. lib. bdg. 14.00 (ISBN 0-8161-7881-X). G K Hall.
--Richard Lester: A Guide to References & Resources. (Reference & Resource Guide Ser.). 1978. lib. bdg. 15.00 (ISBN 0-8161-8185-3). G K Hall.
Roud, Richard, ed. Cinema: A Critical Dictionary, the Major Film-Makers, 2 vols. (Illus.). 1980. Set. 75.00 (ISBN 0-670-22257-7). Viking Pr.
Rovin, Jeff. From the Land Beyond: The Films of Willis O'Brien & Ray Harryhausen. 1977. pap. 5.95 (ISBN 0-425-03506-9, Windhover). Berkley Pub.
Sadoul, Georges. Dictionnaire Des Cineastes. 256p. (Fr.). 1974. pap. 9.95 (ISBN 0-686-56798-6, F-79852). French & Eur.
--Georges Melies. (Film Ser.). 1979. lib. bdg. 59.95 (ISBN 0-8490-2925-2). Gordon Pr.
Schuster, Mel. Motion Picture Directors: A Bibliography of Magazine & Periodical Articles, 1900-1972. LC 73-780. 1973. 16.50 (ISBN 0-8108-0590-1). Scarecrow.
Schuth, H. Wayne. Mike Nichols. (Theatrical Arts Ser.). 1978. lib. bdg. 12.50 (ISBN 0-8057-9255-4). Twayne.
Sherman, Eric. Directing the Film: Film Directors on Their Art. 1976. 15.95 (ISBN 0-316-78541-5). Little.
Soren, David. Unreal Reality: The Cinema of Harry Kumel. LC 78-71774. (Illus.). 1979. pap. text ed. 9.50x (ISBN 0-87543-145-3). Lucas.
Spoto, Donald. Stanley Kramer: Film Maker. LC 78-18834. (Illus.). 1978. 12.95 (ISBN 0-399-12214-1); pap. 6.95 (ISBN 0-399-12249-4). Putnam.
Stern, Michael. Douglas Sirk. (Theatrical Arts Ser.). 1979. lib. bdg. 10.95 (ISBN 0-8057-9269-4). Twayne.
Taylor, John R. Directors & Directions: Cinema for the Seventies. 1975. 11.95 (ISBN 0-8090-3901-X); pap. 5.95 (ISBN 0-8090-1375-4). Hill & Wang.
Taylor, William R. Sydney Pollack. (Theatrical Arts Ser.). 1981. lib. bdg. 14.95 (ISBN 0-8057-9279-1). Twayne.
Thomas, Tony, et al. The Hollywood Professionals, Vol. 2: Wood, King & Milestone. LC 73-3764. (International Film Guide Ser.). 192p. 1974. pap. 4.95 (ISBN 0-498-01394-4). A S Barnes.
Tuska, Jon, et al, eds. Close up: The Contract Director. LC 76-41345. 1976. 21.00 (ISBN 0-8108-0961-3). Scarecrow.
--Close-up: The Hollywood Director. LC 77-14114. 1978. 21.00 (ISBN 0-8108-1085-9). Scarecrow.
Van Wert, William. The Film Career of Alain Robbe-Grillet. Gottesman, Ronald, ed. (Three Directors Set). 1979. pap. 7.80 (ISBN 0-913178-59-4). Redgrave Pub Co.
Vidor, King. A Tree Is a Tree. Kupelnick, Bruce S., ed. LC 76-52132. (Classics of Film Literature Ser.). 1978. lib. bdg. 18.00 (ISBN 0-8240-2896-1). Garland Pub.
Vronskaya, Jeanne. Young Soviet Film Makers. 1972. 9.50 (ISBN 0-04-791023-2); pap. 5.50 (ISBN 0-04-791024-0). Allen Unwin.
Wallis, Hal & Higham, Charles. Starmaker: The Autobiography of Hal Wallis. 304p. 1981. pap. 2.75 (ISBN 0-425-05141-2). Berkley Pub.
--Starmaker: The Autobiography of Hal Wallis. (Illus.). 256p. 1980. 13.95 (ISBN 0-02-623170-0). Macmillan.
Walsh, Gene, ed. Werner Herzog: Images at the Horizon. Ebert, Roger. (Facets Multimedia Ser.). (Illus., Orig.). 1980. pap. 4.00 (ISBN 0-918432-26-X). NY Zoetrope.
Watt, Henry. Don't Look at the Camera. 1974. 9.95 (ISBN 0-236-17717-6, Pub. by Paul Elek). Merrimack Bk Serv.
Wexman, Virginia W. & Bisplinghoff, Gretchen. Roman Polanski: A Guide to References & Resources. (Reference Bks.). 1979. lib. bdg. 15.00 (ISBN 0-8161-7906-9). G K Hall.
Willemen, Paul. Ophuls. (BFI Ser.). 1979. pap. 8.25 (ISBN 0-85170-082-9). NY Zoetrope.
Zuker, Joel. Arthur Penn: A Guide to Reference & Resources. 1979. lib. bdg. 22.50 (ISBN 0-8161-8116-0). G K Hall.

MOVING-PICTURE PRODUCTION

see Moving-Pictures-Production and Direction

MOVING-PICTURE PROJECTION

Mannino, Philip. Organizing a School Projectionist Club. pap. 0.75 (ISBN 0-685-48118-2). Sch Proj Club.
Projectionists' Programmed Primer. (Illus.). 1979. 1-19 copies 4.38 ea. (ISBN 0-9601006-0-1); 20 or more copies 3.95 ea. G T Yeamans.
Rudman, Jack. Motion Picture Operator. (Career Examination Ser.: C-501). (Cloth bdg. avail. on request). pap. 8.00 (ISBN 0-8373-0501-2). Natl Learning.

MOVING-PICTURE SERIALS

Barbour, Alan G. Cliffhanger. 1978. pap. 7.95 (ISBN 0-8065-0669-5). Citadel Pr.
--Cliffhanger. 1977. 14.95 (ISBN 0-89104-070-6). A & W Pubs.
Stedman, Raymond W. The Serials: Suspense & Drama by Installment. 2nd, rev. & enl. ed. LC 76-62516. (Illus.). 1977. 18.95 (ISBN 0-8061-1403-7). U of Okla Pr.

MOVING-PICTURE STARS

see Moving-Picture Actors and Actresses

MOVING-PICTURE THEATERS

see also Moving-Picture Projection

Aloi, R. Theatres & Auditoriums Architecture. (Illus.). 1972. 50.00 (ISBN 0-685-30575-9). Heinman.
Batschelet, Ralph J. The Flick & I. 176p. 1981. 9.00 (ISBN 0-682-49717-7). Exposition.
Grau, Robert. Stage in the Twentieth Century. LC 68-54536. (Illus.). 1912. 20.00 (ISBN 0-405-08572-9, Blom Pubns). Arno.
Hall, Ben M. The Best Remaining Seats: The Story of the Golden Age of the Movie Palace. (Illus.). 278p. 1961. 15.00 (ISBN 0-517-02057-2). Crown.
--The Golden Age of the Movie Palace: The Best Remaining Seats. (Illus.). 272p. 1975. pap. 4.95 (ISBN 0-517-52450-3, Dist. by Crown). Potter.
Hulfish, David. Motion-Picture Work. LC 71-124011. (Literature of Cinema, Ser. 1). Repr. of 1915 ed. 25.00 (ISBN 0-405-01617-4). Arno.

MOVING-PICTURE WRITING

see Moving-Picture Authorship

MOVING-PICTURES

Here are entered general works on moving-pictures. Works on organization and management in the motion picture field are entered under Moving-Picture Industry. Works on photographic processes are entered under Cinematography.

see also Afro-Americans in Motion Pictures; Animals in Moving-Pictures; Art in Moving-Pictures; Cinematography; Comedy Films; Experimental Films; Horror Films; Libraries and Moving-Pictures; Moving-Picture Projection; Politics in Motion Pictures; Religion in Motion Pictures; Sex in Moving-Pictures; Stunt Men; War Films; Western Films; Women in Moving-Pictures

Abi-Nader, Jeannette. A Creative Look at Film Arts. 88p. (Orig.). 1974. pap. text ed. 4.95 (ISBN 0-89076-002-0); pap. text ed. 3.00 5 or more (ISBN 0-685-51253-3). Educ Impact.
Academy of Motion Picture Arts & Sciences. Annual Index to Motion Picture Credits, 1978. Ramsey, Verna, ed. LC 79-644761. 1979. lib. bdg. 150.00 (ISBN 0-313-20950-2, AN78). Greenwood.
Academy of Motion Pictures Arts & Sciences. Annual Index to Motion Picture Credits, 1980. LC 79-644761. 450p. 1981. lib. bdg. 150.00 (ISBN 0-313-20952-9, AN80). Greenwood.
Amberg, G., intro. by. Film Society Programmes, 1925-1939. LC 77-103815. (Contemporary Art Ser). 1971. Repr. of 1925 ed. 29.00 (ISBN 0-405-00741-8). Arno.
American Film Institute, ed. American Film Heritage. LC 72-3813. (Illus.). 200p. 1972. pap. 7.95 (ISBN 0-87491-336-5). Acropolis.
Anderson, P. D. In Its Own Image: The Cinematic Vision of Hollywood. LC 77-22903. (Dissertations on Film Ser.). 1978. lib. bdg. 18.00x (ISBN 0-405-10749-8). Arno.
Anobile, Richard J., ed. The Official Rocky Horror Picture Show Movie Novel. LC 79-24556. 192p. 1980. pap. 6.95 (ISBN 0-89104-180-X); 15.00 (ISBN 0-89104-186-9). A & W Pubs.
Arnheim, Rudolf. Film as Art. LC 57-10496. 1957. pap. 2.95 (ISBN 0-520-00035-8, CAL 6). U of Cal Pr.
Bacon, James. Hollywood Is a Four Letter Town. 1977. pap. 1.95 (ISBN 0-380-01671-0, 33399). Avon.
Balazs, Bela. Theory of the Film: Character & Growth of a New Art. LC 77-130963. 1971. pap. 5.00 (ISBN 0-486-22685-9). Dover.
Basten, Fred E. Glorious Technicolor: The Movies' Magic Rainbow. LC 78-67469. (Illus.). 1980. 30.00 (ISBN 0-498-02317-6). A S Barnes.
Baxter, John. The Cinema of Josef von Sternberg. LC 70-159812. (International Film Guide Ser). (Illus.). 1971. pap. 4.95 (ISBN 0-498-07991-0). A S Barnes.
Bazin, Andre. What Is Cinema, Vol. 1. Gray, Hugh, tr. LC 67-18899. 1967. 14.95x (ISBN 0-520-00091-9); pap. 3.45 (ISBN 0-520-00092-7, CAL151). U of Cal Pr.
--What Is Cinema, Vol. 2. Gray, Hugh, tr. & compiled by. 1971. 14.95x (ISBN 0-520-02034-0); pap. 4.50 (ISBN 0-520-02255-6, CAL250). U of Cal Pr.
Beale, J. D. Adventurous Film Making. (Illus.). 224p. 1980. 27.95 (ISBN 0-240-51047-X). Focal Pr.
Beaton, Welford. Know Your Movies. 1976. lib. bdg. 59.95 (ISBN 0-8490-2119-7). Gordon Pr.
Beckerman, Bernard & Siegman, Howard, eds. On Stage: Selected Theater Reviews from the New York Times, 1920-1970. 514p. 1973. 12.50 (ISBN 0-8129-0363-3). Times Bks.
Behlmer, Rudy & Thomas, Tony. Hollywood's Hollywood: The Movies About the Movies. (Illus.). 384p. 1975. 19.95 (ISBN 0-8065-0491-9). Citadel Pr.
Belgrano, Giovanni. Let's Make a Movie. LC 72-90235. (Illus.). 48p. (gr. 4-9). 1973. 5.75 (ISBN 0-87592-028-4). Scroll Pr.
Benoit-Levy, Jean. Art of the Motion Picture. LC 70-112568. (Literature of Cinema Ser). Repr. of 1946 ed. 11.00 (ISBN 0-405-01603-4). Arno.
Bluestone, George. Novels into Film: The Metamorphosis of Fiction into Cinema. 1957. pap. 3.95 (ISBN 0-520-00130-3, CAL41). U of Cal Pr.
Blumenberg, Richard M. Critical Focus: An Introduction to Film. 1975. pap. text ed. 10.95x (ISBN 0-534-00417-2). Wadsworth Pub.
Bobker, Lee R. Elements of Film. 3rd ed. 302p. 1979. pap. text ed. 11.95 (ISBN 0-15-522096-9, HC). HarBraceJ.
Bordwell, David & Thompson, Kristin. Film Art: An Introduction. LC 78-18633. (Illus.). 1979. pap. text ed. 12.95 (ISBN 0-201-00566-2). A-W.
Bowser, Eileen, ed. Film Notes. LC 68-54926. 1969. spiral bdg. 5.00 (ISBN 0-87070-330-7). Museum Mod Art.
Braudy, Leo. World in a Frame: What We See in Films. LC 75-6151. 1977. pap. 3.95 (ISBN 0-385-03605-1, Anchor Pr). Doubleday.
Brode, Douglas. The Films of the Fifties. (Illus.). 288p. 1976. 14.00 (ISBN 0-8065-0510-9). Citadel Pr.
Brown, B. Talking Pictures. 1976. lib. bdg. 69.95 (ISBN 0-8490-2730-6). Gordon Pr.
Buckle, Gerard F. Mind & the Film, a Treatise on the Psychological Factors in the Film. LC 70-112573. (Literature of Cinema, Ser. 1). Repr. of 1926 ed. 9.50 (ISBN 0-405-01604-2). Arno.
Camp, A. Cinema Mexicain. 1976. lib. bdg. 59.95 (ISBN 0-8490-1634-7). Gordon Pr.
Chanan, Michael. Chilean Cinema. (BFI Ser.). 1977. pap. 5.00 (ISBN 0-85170-058-6). NY Zoetrope.
Corbett, D. J. Motion Picture & Television Film. (Focal Library Ser.). 1967. 34.95 (ISBN 0-240-50652-9). Focal Pr.
Coynik, David. Film: Real to Reel. rev. ed. (Illus., Orig.). 1976. pap. text ed. 11.50 scp (ISBN 0-06-382530-9, HarpC). Har-Row.
Dale, Edgar. Content of Motion Pictures. LC 77-124026. (Literature of Cinema Ser: Payne Fund Studies of Motion Pictures & Social Values). Repr. of 1935 ed. 12.00 (ISBN 0-405-01644-1). Arno.
--How to Appreciate Motion Pictures. LC 70-124027. (Literature of Cinema: Payne Fund Studies of Motion Pictures & Social Values). Repr. of 1937 ed. 8.50 (ISBN 0-405-01645-X). Arno.
Davy, Charles, ed. Footnotes to the Film. LC 75-124004. (Literature of Cinema, Ser. 1). Repr. of 1938 ed. 12.00 (ISBN 0-405-01610-7). Arno.
Dawson, Jan & Kluge, Alexander. Alexander Kluge. (Illus., Orig.). 1977. pap. 4.50 (ISBN 0-918432-03-0). NY Zoetrope.
DeBartolo, Dick & Davis, Jack. The Return of a Mad Look at Old Movies. (Mad Ser.). (Illus.). 1977. pap. 1.25 (ISBN 0-446-86301-7). Warner Bks.
Denby, David, ed. Awake in the Dark: An Anthology of American Film Criticism, 1915 to the Present. 1977. pap. 4.95 (ISBN 0-394-72194-2, Vin). Random.
Dick, Bernard F. The Anatomy of Film. LC 76-28140. 1978. pap. text ed. 7.95 (ISBN 0-312-03395-8). St Martin.
Durgnat, Raymond. Films & Feelings. 1971. pap. 5.95 (ISBN 0-262-54016-9). MIT Pr.
Earley, Stephen C. An Introduction to American Movies. (Illus., Orig.). (RL 10). 1978. pap. 2.25 (ISBN 0-451-61638-3, ME1638, Ment). NAL.
Eberwein, Robert T. A Viewer's Guide to Film Theory & Criticism. LC 79-9380. 243p. 1979. 13.50 (ISBN 0-8108-1237-1). Scarecrow.
Eidsvik, Charles. Cineliteracy: Film Among the Arts. 1978. pap. text ed. 11.95x (ISBN 0-394-32065-4). Random.
Eisenstein, Sergei. Film Form. LC 49-8349. 1969. pap. 3.95 (ISBN 0-15-630920-3, HB153, Harv). HarBraceJ.
--Film Sense. LC 47-6064. 1969. pap. 4.95 (ISBN 0-15-630935-1, HB154, Harv). HarBraceJ.
--Notes of a Film Director. rev. ed. Danko, X., tr. LC 69-19729. (Film Ser). 1970. pap. 4.50 (ISBN 0-486-22392-2). Dover.
Fell, John L. Film: An Introduction. LC 73-18865. (Illus.). 274p. 1975. pap. 10.95 (ISBN 0-02-758911-0). Praeger.
Films: A Quarterly of Discussion & Analysis, Nos. 1-4. LC 68-9238. (Cinema Program Ser). 1968. Repr. of 1940 ed. Set. 25.00 (ISBN 0-405-00717-5). Arno.
Finch, Christopher & Rosenkrantz, Linda. Gone Hollywood. LC 78-20026. (Illus.). 1979. 14.95 (ISBN 0-385-12808-8). Doubleday.
Freeburg, Victor O. Art of Photoplay Making. LC 72-124006. (Literature of Cinema Ser). Repr. of 1918 ed. 9.00 (ISBN 0-405-01612-3). Arno.
--Pictorial Beauty on the Screen. LC 76-124007. (Literature of Cinema, Ser. 1). Repr. of 1923 ed. 9.50 (ISBN 0-405-01613-1). Arno.
Frost, David, intro. by. The Bluffer's Guides, 6 bks. Incl. Bluff Your Way in Art. Lampitt, L; Bluff Your Way in Cinema. Wlaschin, Ken; Bluff Your Way in Literature. Seymoursmith, Martin; Bluff Your Way in Music. Gammond, Peter; Bluff Your Way in Opera. Coleman, Francis; Bluff Your Way in Wine. Clark, Wick. 64p. 1971. pap. 1.00 ea. Crown.
Gadney, Alan. How to Enter & Win Film Contests. 1981. 12.95 (ISBN 0-87196-517-8); pap. 5.95 (ISBN 0-87196-524-0). Facts on File.
Gershuny, Theodore. Soon to Be a Major Motion Picture: The Anatomy of an All-Star, Big-Budget, Multimillion-Dollar Disaster. LC 79-3433. (Illus.). 368p. 1980. 14.95 (ISBN 0-03-053591-3). HR&W.
Giannetti, Louis. Master of the American Cinema. 255p. 1981. text ed. 17.95 (ISBN 0-13-560110-X); pap. text ed. 11.95 (ISBN 0-13-560102-9). P-H.
Giannetti, Louis D. Understanding Movies. 2nd ed. (Illus.). 512p. 1976. ref. ed. o.p. 16.95 (ISBN 0-13-936302-5); pap. 12.50x (ISBN 0-13-936294-0). P-H.
Glaessner, Verina. Kung Fu: Cinema of Vengeance. (Illus.). 1975. pap. 2.95 (ISBN 0-517-51832-5). Crown.
Glazier, Lyle. Stills from a Moving Picture: Paunch No. 39. 1974. pap. 2.00 (ISBN 0-9602478-3-1). Paunch.
Godard, Jean-Luc. Godard: Three Films. LC 75-4352. (Masterworks Film Ser.). (Illus.). 1975. pap. 4.95 (ISBN 0-06-430065-X, IN-65, HarpT). Har-Row.
Goldner, Orville & Turner, George E. The Making of King Kong. LC 74-18. (Illus.). 288p. 1975. 19.95 (ISBN 0-498-01510-6). A S Barnes.
Gomez, Mesa L. Cinema. 1976. lib. bdg. 59.95 (ISBN 0-8490-1632-0). Gordon Pr.
Gordon, R. The Yiddish Film. 1977. lib. bdg. 59.95 (ISBN 0-8490-2851-5). Gordon Pr.

Gordon, R., ed. Cinegramas Anthology, 3 vols. 1976. lib. bdg. 999.75 (ISBN 0-8490-1631-2). Gordon Pr.
--Cinema Digest Anthology, 3 vols. lib. bdg. 995.00 (ISBN 0-8490-1633-9). Gordon Pr.
--Film Mercury Anthology, 6 vols. Set. lib. bdg. 950.00 (ISBN 0-8490-1835-8). Gordon Pr.
--Hollywood Filmograph Anthology, 2 vols. 1976. lib. bdg. 200.00 (ISBN 0-8490-2016-6). Gordon Pr.
--Motion Picture Classic Anthology, 6 vols. 1976. lib. bdg. 995.00 (ISBN 0-8490-2293-2). Gordon Pr.
--Motion Picture Story Magazine Anthology, 6 vols. 1976. lib. bdg. 995.00 (ISBN 0-8490-2296-7). Gordon Pr.
--Moving Picture World Anthology, 6 vols. 1976. lib. bdg. 995.00 (ISBN 0-8490-2304-1). Gordon Pr.
--Primer Plano Anthology, 6 vols. 1976. lib. bdg. 999.95 (ISBN 0-8490-2471-4). Gordon Pr.
--Revue Du Cinema Anthology. 1976. lib. bdg. 75.00 (ISBN 0-8490-2522-2). Gordon Pr.
--Shadowland Anthology, 2 vols. 1976. Set. lib. bdg. 200.00 (ISBN 0-8490-2595-8). Gordon Pr.
--Sight & Sound Anthology 1936-1955, 6 vols. 1976. lib. bdg. 950.95 (ISBN 0-8490-2603-2). Gordon Pr.
--UFA Film. 1976. lib. bdg. 100.95 (ISBN 0-8490-2781-0). Gordon Pr.
Gottesman, Ronald & Geduld, Harry M. Guidebook to Film: An Eleven in One Referenc. LC 77-167811. 1972. pap. text ed. 4.95x (ISBN 0-03-085292-7). Irvington.
Grant, Barry K., ed. Film Genre: Theory & Criticism. LC 77-8908. 1977. 12.00 (ISBN 0-8108-1059-X). Scarecrow.
Grau, Robert. Theatre of Science. LC 68-56483. (Illus.). 1914. 20.00 (ISBN 0-405-08573-7, Blom Pubns). Arno.
Gregory, Mollie. Making Films Your Business. LC 79-14428. 1979. 14.50x (ISBN 0-8052-3728-3); pap. text ed. 6.95 (ISBN 0-8052-0639-6). Schocken.
Griffith, Richard, et al. The Movies. rev. ed. (Illus.). 1981. 24.95 (ISBN 0-671-42765-2). S&S.
Halliwell, Leslie. The Filmgoer's Companion. 1978. pap. 9.95 (ISBN 0-380-00430-5, 50419). Avon.
Harryhausen, Ray. Film Fantasy Scrapbook. 2nd rev. ed. LC 74-7630. (Illus.). 144p. 1974. 17.50 (ISBN 0-498-01632-3). A S Barnes.
Hell's Angels Movie Program. pap. 1.00 (ISBN 0-913076-06-6). Beachcomber Bks.
Herdeg, Walter, ed. Film & TV Graphics, 2. (Visual Communication Bks.). (Illus.). 1976. 39.50 (ISBN 0-8038-2322-3). Hastings.
Hickman, Gail M. The Films of George Pal. LC 76-18479. (Illus.). 1977. 17.50 (ISBN 0-498-01960-8). A S Barnes.
Hirsh, Foster. The Dark Side of the Screen: Film Noir. LC 80-28955. (Illus.). 192p. 1981. 14.95 (ISBN 0-498-02234-X). A S Barnes.
Holaday, Perry W. & Stoddard, George D. Getting Ideas from the Movies. LC 78-124029. (Literature of Cinema Ser.: Payne Fund Studies of Motion Pictures & Social Values). Repr. of 1933 ed. 9.00 (ISBN 0-405-01647-6). Arno.
Holm, Bill & Quimby, George I. Edward S. Curtis in the Land of the War Canoes: A Pioneer Cinematographer in the Pacific Northwest. LC 79-56590. (Thomas Burke Memorial Washington State Museum Monograph: No. 2). (Illus.). 128p. 1980. 19.95 (ISBN 0-295-95708-5). U of Wash Pr.
Holt, Jerry. Making for the Falcon: Studies in Recent Film. 1976. pap. text ed. 7.25 (ISBN 0-8191-0017-X). U Pr of Amer.
Home Video Tape-Disc Guide: Movies & Entertainment. 1980. pap. 12.95 (ISBN 0-452-25255-5, 25255, Plume). NAL.
Hopwood, Henry V. Living Pictures: Their History, Photo-Production & Practical Working. LC 78-124010. (Literature of Cinema, Ser. 1). Repr. of 1899 ed. 10.00 (ISBN 0-405-01616-6). Arno.
Hughes, L. The Truth About the Movies. 1976. lib. bdg. 59.95 (ISBN 0-8490-2776-4). Gordon Pr.
Hulfish, David. Motion-Picture Work. LC 71-124011. (Literature of Cinema, Ser. 1). Repr. of 1915 ed. 25.00 (ISBN 0-405-01617-4). Arno.
Hunter, William. Scrutiny of Cinema. LC 70-169328. (Literature of Cinema, Series 2). (Illus.). 92p. 1972. Repr. of 1932 ed. 12.00 (ISBN 0-405-03896-8). Arno.
Hurt, J. Focus on Film & Theatre. 1974. pap. 2.95 (ISBN 0-13-314658-8, Spec). P-H.
Jacobs, Lewis. The Movies As Medium. 1973. lib. bdg. 21.00x (ISBN 0-374-94139-4). Octagon.
Jacobs, Lewis, ed. Compound Cinema: The Film Writings of Harry Alan Potamkin. LC 76-55401. 1977. text ed. 26.50 (ISBN 0-8077-1559-X). Tchrs Coll.
--Introduction to the Art of the Movies. LC 77-138945. 1970. Repr. lib. bdg. 18.00x (ISBN 0-374-94137-8). Octagon.
--The Movies As Medium. LC 71-97611. (Illus.). 352p. 1970. pap. 7.95 (ISBN 0-374-50852-6, N388). FS&G.
James, C. Rodney. Film As a National Art. Jowett, Garth S., ed. LC 76-40787. (Diss. on Film Ser.). (Illus.). 1978. Repr. of 1977 ed. lib. bdg. 43.00x (ISBN 0-405-09891-X). Arno.
Johnson, L. The Film: Space, Time, Light & Sound. LC 73-20887. 1974. text ed. 13.95 (ISBN 0-03-078050-0, HoltC). HR&W.
Johnson, Ron & Bone, Jan. Understanding the Film. LC 75-20875. (Illus.). 248p. 1976. pap. 9.25 (ISBN 0-8174-2903-4). Amphoto.
Jowett, Garth. Film: The Democratic Art. 1976. 19.95 (ISBN 0-316-47370-7). Little.
Jowett, Garth S., ed. Aspects of Film Series, 21 bks. 1978. Set. lib. bdg. 481.00x (ISBN 0-405-11125-8). Arno.
Kael, Pauline. I Lost It at the Movies. 1965. 8.95 (ISBN 0-316-48164-5, Pub. by Atlantic Monthly Pr); pap. 5.95 (ISBN 0-316-48165-3, Pub. by Atlantic Monthly Pr). Little.
Kaminsky, Stuart M. & Hodgdon, Dana. Basic Filmmaking. LC 81-613. (Illus.). 256p. 1981. 11.95 (ISBN 0-668-05148-5); pap. 7.95 (ISBN 0-668-05156-6). Arco.
Kawin, Bruce F. Faulkner & Film. LC 77-2519. (Ungar Fil Library). (Illus.). 1977. 11.00 (ISBN 0-8044-2454-3); pap. 4.95 (ISBN 0-8044-6347-6). Ungar.
Knight, Arthur. The Liveliest Art. rev ed. (RL 9). 1979. pap. 2.50 (ISBN 0-451-61743-6, ME1743, Ment). NAL.
Kracauer, Siegfried. Theory of Film: The Redemption of Physical Reality. (Illus.). 1965. pap. 6.95 (ISBN 0-19-500721-2, GB). Oxford U Pr.
Kuhns, William. Movies in America. (gr. 10-12). 1973. pap. text ed. 7.95x (ISBN 0-8278-0045-2). Pflaum-Standard.
--The Moving Picture Book. (Illus.). 320p. 1975. pap. text ed. 7.95x (ISBN 0-8278-0054-1). Pflaum-Standard.
Kuhns, William & Stanley, Robert. Exploring the Film. (gr. 9-12). 1969. pap. 5.65x (ISBN 0-8278-0050-9); teacher's manual 4.90x (ISBN 0-8278-0051-7). Pflaum-Standard.
Larsen, S. Spotlight on Films. 1976. lib. bdg. 69.95 (ISBN 0-8490-2662-8). Gordon Pr.
Lawton, Richard. A World of Movies. 1976. pap. 7.95 (ISBN 0-440-59690-4, Delta). Dell.
Lees, David & Berkowitz, Stan. The Movie Business. (Orig.). 1981. pap. 4.95 (ISBN 0-394-74666-X, V-666, Vin). Random.
Leiser, Erwin. Nazi Cinema. (Illus.). 1975. 7.95 (ISBN 0-02-570230-0). Macmillan.
Leish, Kenneth. Cinema. LC 73-89395. (World of Culture Ser.). (Illus.). 12.95 (ISBN 0-88225-109-0). Newsweek.
Lescarboura, Austin C. Behind the Motion-Picture Screen. LC 75-174878. (Illus.). Repr. of 1919 ed. 25.00 (ISBN 0-405-08742-X, Pub. by Blom). Arno.
Leyda, Jay. Dianying - Electric Shadows: An Account of Films & the Film Audience in China. 272p. 1972. 15.00x (ISBN 0-262-12046-1); pap. 5.95 (ISBN 0-262-62030-8). MIT Pr.
Limbacher, James L. Four Aspects of the Film. Jowett, Garth S., ed. LC 77-11379. (Aspects of Film Ser.). (Illus.). 1978. Repr. of 1969 ed. lib. bdg. 30.00x (ISBN 0-405-11138-X). Arno.
Lindsay, Vachel. Art of the Moving Picture. LC 75-114381. 1970. pap. 3.45 (ISBN 0-87140-004-9). Liveright.
Lipton, Lenny. Lipton on Filmmaking. 1979. 12.95 (ISBN 0-671-24427-2, Fireside); pap. 7.95 (ISBN 0-671-24791-3). S&S.
Lutz, Edwin G. Motion-Picture Cameraman. LC 76-169332. (Literature of Cinema, Series 2). (Illus.). 264p. 1972. Repr. of 1927 ed. 16.00 (ISBN 0-405-03899-2). Arno.
MacCann, Richard D. Hollywood in Transition. LC 77-5314. 1977. Repr. of 1962 ed. lib. bdg. 16.75x (ISBN 0-8371-9616-7, MAHT). Greenwood.
MacCann, Richard D., ed. Film: A Montage of Theories. pap. 3.45 (ISBN 0-525-47181-2). Dutton.
McLaughlin, Robert. Broadway & Hollywood: A History of Economic Interaction. LC 73-21606. (Dissertations on Film Ser.: Vol. 3). 322p. 1974. 16.00x (ISBN 0-405-04873-4). Arno.
MacPherson, Kenneth & Bryher, Winifred, eds. Close-Up: A Magazine Devoted to the Art of Films, Vols 1-10. LC 70-88572. (Contemporary Art Ser). Repr. of 1927 ed. Set. 245.00 (ISBN 0-405-00732-9); 27.50 ea. Arno.
Malis, Gene. The Great Movie Quiz Book. LC 80-7760. (Illus.). 256p. (Orig.). 1980. pap. 3.95 (ISBN 0-06-463518-X, EH 518, EH). Har-Row.
Maltin, Leonard. The Disney Films. 1978. pap. 2.25 (ISBN 0-445-04276-1). Popular Lib.
Manoogian, Haig P. The Film Maker's Art. LC 66-16372. 1966. 9.95x (ISBN 0-465-02398-3). Basic.
Manvell, Roger, ed. Experiment in the Film. LC 73-124017. (Literature of Cinema Ser). Repr. of 1949 ed. 13.00 (ISBN 0-405-01623-9). Arno.
Marcorelles, Louis. Living Cinema: New Directions in Contemporary Film-Making. Quigley, Isabel, tr. (Illus.). 1973. pap. 5.50 (ISBN 0-04-791026-7). Allen Unwin.
Mast, Gerald & Cohen, Marshall, eds. Film Theory & Criticism: Introductory Readings. 2nd ed. (Illus.). 1979. 26.95x (ISBN 0-19-502503-2); pap. text ed. 10.95x (ISBN 0-19-502498-2). Oxford U Pr.
Matthews, J. H. Surrealism & American Feature Films. (Theatrical Arts Ser.). 1979. lib. bdg. 10.95 (ISBN 0-8057-9265-1). Twayne.
Mayakovsky, Vladimir & Brik, Lily. Enchained in Film. Segall, Helen, tr. (Illus.). 1981. 15.00x (ISBN 0-931556-01-5); pap. 6.50 (ISBN 0-931556-03-1). Translation Pr.
Mendez-Leite, L. El Cine Norteamericano. 1976. lib. bdg. 90.00 (ISBN 0-8490-1630-4). Gordon Pr.
Metz, Christian. Film Language: A Semiotics of the Cinema. Taylor, Michael, tr. from Fr. 288p. 1974. 17.95 (ISBN 0-19-501762-5). Oxford U Pr.
Miller, Gabriel. Screening the Novel: Rediscovered American Fiction in Film. LC 79-48071. (Ungar Film Library). (Illus.). 250p. 1980. 10.95 (ISBN 0-8044-2622-8). Ungar.
Monaco, James. American Film Now: The People, the Power, the Money, the Movies. (Illus.). 1979. 19.95 (ISBN 0-19-502570-9). Oxford U Pr.
--How to Read a Film: The Art, Technology, Language, History, & Theory of Film & Media. rev. ed. (Illus.). 560p. 1981. 25.00 (ISBN 0-19-502802-3); pap. 11.95 (ISBN 0-19-502806-6). Oxford U Pr.
Munsterberg, Hugo. Film: A Psychological Study. LC 76-94325. (Film Ser). Orig. Title: Photoplay: A Psychological Study. 1969. pap. 2.50 (ISBN 0-486-22476-7). Dover.
--Photoplay: A Psychological Study. LC 79-124021. (Literature of Cinema, Ser. 1). Repr. of 1916 ed. 7.50 (ISBN 0-405-01628-X). Arno.
New York Times. Directory of the Film. 1971. 25.00 (ISBN 0-394-47419-8, Dist. by Random). Arno.
Nichols, Bill, ed. Movies & Methods. LC 74-22968. 1977. 35.00x (ISBN 0-520-02890-2); pap. 8.95 (ISBN 0-520-03151-2, CAL 339). U of Cal Pr.
Nicoll, Allardyce. Film & Theatre. LC 77-169335. (Literature of Cinema, Series 2). 272p. 1972. Repr. of 1936 ed. 12.00 (ISBN 0-405-03902-6). Arno.
Okoshi, T. Three-Dimensional Imaginary Techniques. 1976. 30.00 (ISBN 0-12-525250-1). Acad Pr.
Ongoing Dissertations on Film Series, 8 vols. 1974. write for info. (ISBN 0-405-07530-8). Arno.
Peary, Gerald & Kay, Karyn, eds. Women & the Cinema: A Critical Anthology. 1977. pap. 8.95 (ISBN 0-525-47459-5). Dutton.
Petruck, Peninah. The Camera Viewed: A Critical Anthology of Writings on Photography, 2 vols. (Illus.). 1979. Vol. I. pap. 9.95 (ISBN 0-525-47535-4); Vol. II. pap. 9.95 (ISBN 0-525-47536-2). Dutton.
Phillips, Baxter. Cut: The Unseen Cinema. (Illus.). 191p. 1975. pap. 3.95 (ISBN 0-517-52417-1). Crown.
Pickard, Roy. The Award Movies: A Complete Guide from A to Z. LC 80-54142. (Illus.). 354p. 1981. 14.95 (ISBN 0-8052-3767-4); pap. 6.95 (ISBN 0-8052-0677-9). Schocken.
Pratley, Gerald. The Cinema of Otto Preminger. LC 74-141573. (International Film Guide Ser). (Illus.). 1971. pap. 4.95 (ISBN 0-498-07860-4). A S Barnes.
Pratt, William & Bridges, Herbert. Scarlett Fever: The Ultimate Pictorial Treasury of "Gone with the Wind". (Illus.). 1977. pap. 8.95 (ISBN 0-02-012510-0, Collier). Macmillan.
Pryluck, Calvin. Sources of Meaning in Motion Pictures & Television. Lowett, Garth S., ed. LC 75-21434. (Dissertations on Film Ser.). 1976. lib. bdg. 15.00 (ISBN 0-405-07535-9). Arno.
Pudovkin, V. I. Film Technique & Film Acting. Montagu, Ivor, ed. & tr. 1970. pap. 6.95 (ISBN 0-394-17457-7, B683, BC). Grove.
Ray, Satyajit. Our Films, Their Films. LC 76-902792. 1976. 14.00x (ISBN 0-88386-861-X, Orient Longman). South Asia Bks.
Reader, Keith. Teach Yourself the Cinema. 1979. pap. 4.95 (ISBN 0-679-12056-4). McKay.
Robertson, Joseph F. Motion Picture Distribution Handbook. (Illus.). 1981. 19.95 (ISBN 0-8306-9797-7, 1115). TAB Bks.
Rosenbaum, Jonathan. Moving Places: A Life at the Movies. LC 80-7596. (Illus.). 288p. 1980. 11.95 (ISBN 0-06-013657-X, HarpT); pap. 5.95 (ISBN 0-06-090823-8, CN823). Har-Row.
Rosow, Eugene. Born to Lose: The Gangster Film in America. LC 78-4942. (Illus.). 1978. 22.50 (ISBN 0-19-502382-X). Oxford U Pr.
Ross, Murray. Stars & Strikes: Unionization in Hollywood. LC 41-24783. Repr. of 1941 ed. 17.00 (ISBN 0-404-05408-0). AMS Pr.
Rovin, Jeff. The Films of Charlton Heston. 1977. 14.95 (ISBN 0-8065-0561-3). Citadel Pr.
Salz, Kay, compiled by. Film Service Profiles. LC 80-10394. 56p. (Orig.). 1980. pap. 5.00 (ISBN 0-935654-00-3, Pub. by Ctr for Arts Info). Pub Ctr Cult Res.
Samuels, Charles T. Mastering the Film & Other Essays. Graver, Lawrence, ed. LC 77-642. 1977. 12.50x (ISBN 0-87049-209-8). U of Tenn Pr.
Sarris, Andrew. The Primal Screen: Essays on Film & Related Subjects. LC 72-90401. 1973. 9.95 (ISBN 0-671-21341-5). S&S.
The Saturday Evening Post Movie Book. LC 77-85389. (Illus.). 1977. 10.95 (ISBN 0-89387-013-7); pap. 7.95 (ISBN 0-89387-013-7). Sat Eve Post.
Scagnetti, Jack. Movie Stars in Bathtubs. LC 74-31216. (Illus.). 160p. 1975. 12.95 (ISBN 0-8246-0196-3). Jonathan David.
Schad, Tennyson & Shapiro, Ira, eds. American Showcase of Photography, Illustration, Graphic Design, TV, Film, & Video. 336p. 37.50 (ISBN 0-931144-06-X); pap. 25.00 (ISBN 0-931144-05-1). Am Showcase.
Schatz, Thomas. Hollywood Genres: Formulas, Filmmaking & the Studio System. (Illus.). 297p. 1981. 19.95 (ISBN 0-87722-222-3). Temple U Pr.
Schlossheimer, Michael. The Films You Don't See on Television. 1979. 6.95 (ISBN 0-533-03540-6). Vantage.
Scott, J. F. Film: The Medium & the Maker. LC 74-26611. 1975. text ed. 8.50 (ISBN 0-03-079445-5, HoltC). HR&W.
Seabury, William M. Motion Picture Problems. Jowett, Garth S., ed. LC 77-11383. (Aspects of Film Ser.). 1978. Repr. of 1929 ed. lib. bdg. 30.00x (ISBN 0-405-11143-6). Arno.
Seldes, Gilbert. An Hour with the Movies & the Talkies. (Cinema Program Ser). Repr. of 1929 ed. 10.00 (ISBN 0-405-04108-X). Arno.
--The Movies Come from America. Jowett, Garth S., ed. LC 77-11384. (Aspects of Film Ser.). 1978. Repr. of 1937 ed. lib. bdg. 20.00x (ISBN 0-405-11144-4). Arno.
Sheahan, Eileen. Moving Pictures. LC 78-55576. (Illus.). 1978. 9.95 (ISBN 0-498-02296-X); pap. 5.95 (ISBN 0-498-02297-8). A S Barnes.
Silet, Charles L. & Bataile, Grettchen M. The Pretend Indians: Images of Native Americans in the Movies. (Illus.). 1980. text ed. 19.95 (ISBN 0-8138-0925-8); pap. text ed. 9.95 (ISBN 0-8138-0715-8). Iowa St U Pr.
Siskà, H. W. Wunderwelt Film. 1976. lib. bdg. 105.95 (ISBN 0-8490-2823-X). Gordon Pr.
Slide, Anthony. The Big V. LC 76-21247. 1976. 10.00 (ISBN 0-8108-0967-2). Scarecrow.
Sobchack, Thomas & Sobchack, Vivian C. An Introduction to Film. (Illus.). 512p. 1980. pap. text ed. 11.95 (ISBN 0-316-80250-6); instructor's manual free (ISBN 0-316-80251-4). Little.
Sobchack, Vivian C. The Limits of Infinity: The American Science Fiction Film. LC 78-69642. (Illus.). 1980. 14.50 (ISBN 0-498-02210-2). A S Barnes.
Sontag, Susan. Duet for Cannibals. (Illus.). 144p. 1970. pap. 2.25 (ISBN 0-374-50868-2, N392). FS&G.
Speed, F. Maurice, ed. Film Review, Nineteen Seventy-Seven to Seventy-Eight. (Illus.). 1978. 15.00 (ISBN 0-491-02211-5). Transatlantic.
Spottiswoode, Raymond. A Grammar of the Film: An Analysis of Film Technique. (Illus.). 1950. pap. 2.85 (ISBN 0-520-01200-3, CAL30). U of Cal Pr.
Stauffacher, Frank, ed. Art in Cinema: A Symposium of Avant-Garde Film. LC 68-9243. (Contemporary Art Ser). (Illus.). 1968. Repr. of 1947 ed. 10.00 (ISBN 0-405-00724-8). Arno.
Stern, Seymour & Jacobs, Lewis, eds. Experimental Cinema, Nos. 1-5. LC 70-103816. (Contemporary Art Ser). (Illus.). 1971. Repr. of 1934 ed. Set. 20.00 (ISBN 0-405-00739-6). Arno.
Sutro, John. Diversion: Twenty-Two Authors on the Lively Arts. 1977. Repr. of 1950 ed. lib. bdg. 10.00 (ISBN 0-8495-4807-1). Arden Lib.
Swain, Dwight V. Film Scriptwriting: A Practical Manual. (Communication Arts Bks.). 1976. 15.95 (ISBN 0-8038-2318-5); pap. text ed. 7.50x (ISBN 0-8038-2319-3). Hastings.
Talbot, Daniel, ed. Film: An Anthology. 2nd ed. LC 59-11203. (YA) (gr. 9 up). 1966. pap. 3.95 (ISBN 0-520-01251-8, CAL117). U of Cal Pr.
Thomas, Tony. The Great Adventure Films. pap. 7.95 (ISBN 0-8065-0747-0). Lyle Stuart.
Thompson, David. Overexposures: The Crisis in American Filmmaking. LC 81-944. 333p. 1981. 13.95 (ISBN 0-688-00400-8, Quill); pap. 7.95 (ISBN 0-686-73373-8, Quill). Morrow.

Thomson, David. Movie Man. LC 67-23534. 1969. pap. 2.95 (ISBN 0-8128-1235-2). Stein & Day.
--Overexposures: The Crises in American Filmmaking. LC 81-944. 288p. 1981. 11.95 (ISBN 0-688-00400-8); pap. 6.95 (ISBN 0-688-00489-X). Morrow.
Thorp, Margaret. America at the Movies. LC 75-124039. (Literature of Cinema Series). Repr. of 1939 ed. 11.00 (ISBN 0-405-01639-5). Arno.
Thorpe, Frances, ed. International Index to Film Periodicals, 1977. 1979. 35.00x (ISBN 0-312-42247-4). St Martin.
Trelles Plazaola, Luis. El Cine Visto En Puerto Rico: 1962-1972. (UPREX, Teatro y Cine: No. 44). pap. 1.85 (ISBN 0-8477-0044-5). U of PR Pr.
Tyler, Parker. Sex, Psyche, Etcetera in the Film. LC 71-78790. 1969. 7.50 (ISBN 0-8180-0700-1). Horizon.
UNESCO. Press, Film, Radio, 3 vols, Vols. 1-5. LC 72-4683. (International Propaganda & Communications Ser.). 2114p. 1972. Repr. of 1951 ed. Set. 96.00 (ISBN 0-405-04767-3). Arno.
Unwin, Derick. Cinematica. (Sp.). 1970. pap. 1.50 (ISBN 0-06-317010-8, IntlDept). Har-Row.
Van Zile, E. S. That Marvel the Movie. 1976. lib. bdg. 59.95 (ISBN 0-8490-2738-1). Gordon Pr.
Villegas, L. A. Album De Cinelandia. 1976. lib. bdg. 105.00 (ISBN 0-8490-1408-5). Gordon Pr.
Vogel, Amos. Film As a Subversive Art. 1976. pap. 8.95 (ISBN 0-394-73207-3). Random.
Weaver, Kathleen, ed. Film Programmer's Guide to 16mm Rentals. 2nd rev. & enl. ed. LC 75-26168. 1975. 10.00 (ISBN 0-934456-01-1). Reel Res.
Weinberg, Herman G. Saint Cinema: Writings on Film; Nineteen Twenty-Nine to Nineteen Seventy. LC 79-6151. (Ungar Film Library). (Illus.). 1980. Repr. of 1973 ed. 14.95 (ISBN 0-8044-2971-5). Ungar.
--Stroheim: A Pictorial Record of His Nine Films. (Illus.). 259p. (Orig.). 1975. pap. 4.95 (ISBN 0-486-22723-5). Dover.
Weiss, Paul. Cinematics. LC 74-20933. 240p. 1975. 9.95x (ISBN 0-8093-0671-9). S Ill U Pr.
Willink, L. Film. 1976. lib. bdg. 96.00 (ISBN 0-8490-1808-0). Gordon Pr.
Willis, John. Screen World: 1977, Vol. 28. 1977. 12.95 (ISBN 0-517-52970-X). Crown.
--Screen World: 1981. (Vol. 32). (Illus.). 1981. 19.95 (ISBN 0-517-54482-2). Crown.
Willis, John, ed. Screen World-1976, Vol. 27. 1976. 12.95 (ISBN 0-517-52583-6). Crown.
Wolfe, Glenn J. Vachel Lindsay: The Poet As Film Theorist. LC 72-554. (Dissertations on Film Ser). 250p. 1972. 15.00 (ISBN 0-405-04097-0). Arno.
Wood, Michael. America in the Movies. 1976. pap. 5.95 (ISBN 0-440-50289-6, Delta). Dell.
World Communications: A Two Hundred Country Survey of Press, Radio, Television, Film. 550p. 1975. 27.50 (ISBN 0-89059-001-X). Bowker.
Wright, Basil. Use of the Film. LC 75-169356. (Arno Press Cinema Program). 76p. 1972. Repr. of 1948 ed. 7.00 (ISBN 0-405-03927-1). Arno.
Wysotsky, Michael Z. Wide-Screen Cinema & Sterophonic Sound. (Library of Image & Sound Technology). Date not set. 17.95 (ISBN 0-8038-8044-8). Hastings.

MOVING-PICTURES–ACADEMY AWARDS
see Academy Awards (Moving-Pictures)

MOVING-PICTURES–AUDIENCES
see Moving-Picture Audiences

MOVING-PICTURES–BIBLIOGRAPHY

Aceto, Vincent J., et al, eds. Film Literature Index 1974. LC 74-642396. 545p. 1975. 67.50 (ISBN 0-8352-0937-7). Bowker.
--Film Literature Index 1973. LC 74-642396. 430p. 1975. 67.50 (ISBN 0-8352-0936-9). Bowker.
--Film Literature Index 1975. LC 74-642396. 1977. 67.50 (ISBN 0-8352-0954-7). Bowker.
Aros, Andrew A. A Title Guide to the Talkies, Nineteen Sixty-Four to Nineteen Seventy-Four. LC 76-40451. 1977. 15.00 (ISBN 0-8108-0976-1). Scarecrow.
Baer, D. Richard. Movie World Almanac 1982-83. (Illus.). 360p. 1981. 19.95 (ISBN 0-913616-05-2); lib. bdg. 31.95 (ISBN 0-913616-06-0). Hollywd Film Arch.
Batty, Linda, compiled by. Retrospective Index to Film Periodicals 1930-1971. LC 74-34246. 425p. 1975. 32.50 (ISBN 0-8352-0660-2). Bowker.
Bowles, Stephen E., ed. Index to Critical Film Reviews in British & American Film Periodicals, 3 vols in 2. new ed. LC 74-12109. x, 900p. 1975. Set. 35.00 (ISBN 0-89102-040-3). B Franklin.
Brooker, Nancy J., ed. John Schlesinger: A Guide to References & Resources. (Reference & Resource Guide Ser.). 1978. lib. bdg. 14.00 (ISBN 0-8161-8024-5). G K Hall.
Bukalski, Peter, compiled by. Film Research: A Critical Bibliography with Annotations & Essay. 1972. lib. bdg. 12.50 (ISBN 0-8161-0971-0). G K Hall.
Chicorel, Marietta, ed. Chicorel Index to Film Literature, Vols. 22 & 22A. LC 75-22340. (Index Ser.). 1975. Set. 170.00 (ISBN 0-934598-29-0). Am Lib Pub Co.
Dyment, Alan R., ed. The Literature of the Film: A Bibliographical Guide to the Film As Art & Entertainment 1936-1970. 1975. 54.00 (ISBN 0-685-70659-1). Gale.
Ellis, Jack, et al. The Film Book Bibliography: 1940-1975. LC 78-4055. 1979. 31.00 (ISBN 0-8108-1127-8). Scarecrow.
Eschlach, Achim & Rader, Wendelin, eds. Semiotics of Films. 203p. 1978. 26.00 (ISBN 0-89664-080-9, Pub. by K G Saur). Gale.
Essoe, Gabe. The Offical Book of Movie Lists. (Illus.). 256p. 1981. 12.95 (ISBN 0-87000-496-4). Arlington Hse.
Film Index: A Bibliography, Vol. 1 The Film As Art. LC 41-8716. (Museum of Modern Art: Publications in Repr. Ser). (Illus.). Repr. of 1941 ed. 24.00 (ISBN 0-405-01512-7). Arno.
FilmRow Film Index. 100p. 1981. pap. price not set (ISBN 0-937874-04-3). Filmrow Pubns.
Jones, Emily S., ed. College Film Library Collection, 2 vols. (Orig.). 1971. pap. 14.95 (ISBN 0-87272-059-4). Brodart.
--College Film Library Collection--Selected Filmstrips & 8 Mm Films, Vol. 2. LC 77-16469. (Orig.). 1971. pap. 9.95 (ISBN 0-87272-021-7). Brodart.
--College Film Library Collection--16 mm Films, Vol. 1. LC 77-164678. (Orig.). 1971. pap. 7.95 (ISBN 0-87272-020-9). Brodart.
Leyda, Jay. Dianying - Electric Shadows: An Account of Films & the Film Audience in China. 272p. 1972. 15.00x (ISBN 0-262-12046-1); pap. 5.95 (ISBN 0-262-62030-8). MIT Pr.
Library of Congress. National Union Catalog: A Cumulative Author List, 1958-1962. Incl. Vol. 51. Music & Phonorecords - Authors List, Pt. 1 (ISBN 0-87471-731-0); Vol. 52. Music & Phonorecords - Subject Index, Pt. 2 (ISBN 0-87471-732-9); Vol. 53. Motion Pictures & Film Strips, Titles, Pt. 1 (ISBN 0-87471-733-7); Vol. 54. Motion Pictures & Film Strips, Pt. 2 - Subject Index (ISBN 0-87471-734-5). 40.00x ea. Rowman.
--National Union Catalog, a Cumulative Author List, 1953-57, 28 Vols. Set. 395.00x (ISBN 0-87471-728-0); vol. 27 music & phonorecords 40.00x (ISBN 0-87471-729-9); vol. 28 motion pictures & film strips 40.00 (ISBN 0-87471-730-2). Rowman.
Manchel, Frank. Film Study: A Resource Guide. LC 72-3262. 422p. 1973. 22.50 (ISBN 0-8386-1225-3). Fairleigh Dickinson.
Mental Health Materials Center, ed. Current Audiovisuals for Mental Health Education. 2nd ed. LC 78-71134. 1979. pap. 8.50 (ISBN 0-8379-5201-8). Marquis.
Minus, Johnny & Hale, William S. Films: Books of Over 1000 More Public Domain Films, Bks. 1-10. (The Film Copyright Public Domain Ser., No. 1). pap. 10.00 ea.; Bk. 1. pap. (ISBN 0-911370-11-0); Bk. 2. pap. (ISBN 0-911370-12-9); Bk. 3. pap. (ISBN 0-911370-13-7); Bk. 4. pap. (ISBN 0-911370-14-5); Bk. 5. pap. (ISBN 0-911370-15-3); Bk. 6. pap. (ISBN 0-911370-16-1); Bk. 7. pap. (ISBN 0-911370-17-X); pap. bk. 8 (isbn 0-911370-18-8); bk. 9 (isbn 0-911370-19-6); bk. 10 (isbn 0-911370-20-x. Seven Arts.
Monaco, James & Schenker, Susan. Books About Film: A Bibliographical Checklist. 1977. pap. 3.50 (ISBN 0-918432-01-4). NY Zoetrope.
Murphy, William T., ed. Robert Flaherty: A Guide to References & Resources. (Reference & Resource Guide Ser.). 1978. lib. bdg. 18.00 (ISBN 0-8161-8022-9). G K Hall.
Nicoll, Allardyce. Film & Theatre. LC 77-169335. (Literature of Cinema, Series 2). 272p. 1972. Repr. of 1936 ed. 12.00 (ISBN 0-405-03902-6). Arno.
Niver, Kemp R. Motion Pictures from the Library of Congress Paper Print Collection, 1894-1912. 1967. 65.00x (ISBN 0-520-00947-9). U of Cal Pr.
Parker, David L. & Siegel, Esther. Guide to Dance in Films: A Guide to Information Sources. LC 76-20339. (Performing Arts Information Guide Series: Vol. 3). 1978. 36.00 (ISBN 0-8103-1377-4). Gale.
Powers, Anne. Blacks in American Movies: A Selected Bibliography. LC 74-1925. 1974. 10.00 (ISBN 0-8108-0753-X). Scarecrow.
Ricci, Mark, et al. The Films of John Wayne. (Illus.). 288p. 1972. pap. 6.95 (ISBN 0-685-24206-4); pap. 6.95 (ISBN 0-8065-0296-7). Citadel Pr.
Rosenfeldt, Diane, ed. Ken Russell: A Guide to Reference & Resources. (Reference & Resource Guide Ser.). 1978. lib. bdg. 14.00 (ISBN 0-8161-7881-X). G K Hall.
--Richard Lester: A Guide to References & Resources. (Reference & Resource Guide Ser.). 1978. lib. bdg. 15.00 (ISBN 0-8161-8185-3). G K Hall.
Rovin, Jeff. Signet Book of Movie Lists. (Illus., Orig.). 1979. pap. 1.75 (ISBN 0-451-08929-4, E8929, Sig). NAL.
Salz, Kay, ed. Craft Films: An Index of International Films on Crafts. LC 79-14780. (Illus.). 156p. 1979. 19.95x (ISBN 0-918212-08-1). Neal-Schuman.
Schuster, Mel. Motion Picture Performers: A Bibliography of Magazine & Periodical Articles, Supp. No. 1, 1970-74. LC 70-154300. 1976. 32.50 (ISBN 0-8108-0879-X). Scarecrow.
Vincent, Carl, et al, eds. General Bibliography of Motion Pictures. LC 76-138689. (Cinema Program Ser). 1971. Repr. of 1953 ed. 15.00 (ISBN 0-405-00769-8). Arno.
Weaver, Kathleen, ed. Film Programmer's Guide to 16mm Rentals. 3rd ed. 1980. pap. 21.25 (ISBN 0-934456-02-X). Reel Res.
Welch, Jeffrey. Liturature & Film: An Annotated Bibliography, 1900 to 1977. LC 80-8509. 350p. 1981. lib. bdg. 40.00 (ISBN 0-8240-9478-6). Garland Pub.
Wheaton, Christopher D. & Jewell, Richard B.compiled by. Primary Cinema Resources: Index of Screen Plays, Interviews & Special Collections at the University of Southern California. 450p. 1975. lib. bdg. 21.00 (ISBN 0-8161-1198-7). G K Hall.
Zucker, Ralph, ed. Filmrow Film Index (1981-1982) 100p. 1981. pap. 29.95 (ISBN 0-686-30692-9). Filmrow Pubns.
--Filmrow Updata, Vol. I. 75p. 1982. pap. 115.00 (ISBN 0-937874-07-8). Filmrow Pubns.

MOVING-PICTURES–BIOGRAPHY
see also Moving-Picture Actors and Actresses; Moving-Picture Producers and Directors

Baxter, John. The Hollywood Exiles. LC 75-34734. (Illus.). 232p. 1976. 14.95 (ISBN 0-8008-3918-8). Taplinger.
Brakhage, Stan. Film Biographies. LC 77-82308. (New World Writing Ser.). (Illus.). 1977. 15.00 (ISBN 0-913666-03-3); pap. 7.95 (ISBN 0-913666-17-3). Turtle Isl Foun.
Burrows, Abe. Honest, Abe. (Illus.). 1980. 14.95 (ISBN 0-316-11771-4, Pub. by Atlantic-Little Brown). Little.
Castanza, Philip. The Films of Jeanette MacDonald & Nelson Eddy. (Illus.). 224p. 1981. pap. 7.95 (ISBN 0-8065-0771-3). Citadel Pr.
Ciment, Michel. Kazan on Kazan. LC 73-11978. (Cinema One Ser). (Illus.). 176p. 1974. 7.50 (ISBN 0-670-41187-6). Viking Pr.
Drinkwater, John. The Life & Adventures of Carl Laemmle. Jowett, Garth S., ed. LC 77-11374. (Aspects of Film Ser.). 1978. Repr. of 1931 ed. lib. bdg. 28.00x (ISBN 0-405-11130-4). Arno.
Dunne, Philip. Take Two: A Life in Movies & Politics. (Illus.). 1980. 14.95 (ISBN 0-07-018306-6). McGraw.
Edelson, Edward. Great Kids of the Movies. LC 78-14697. 1979. 6.95a (ISBN 0-385-14127-0); PLB (ISBN 0-385-14128-9). Doubleday.
--Tough Guys & Gals of the Movies. LC 77-17002. (gr. 4-7). 1978. PLB 5.95 (ISBN 0-385-12789-8). Doubleday.
Eyles, Allen & Billings, Pat. Hollywood Today. LC 77-141571. (International Film Guide Ser). (Illus.). 1971. pap. 4.95 (ISBN 0-498-07858-2). A S Barnes.
Farinas, Peggy, ed. Reel People, Nineteen Eighty-One. 75p. 1981. pap. 15.00 (ISBN 0-87314-080-X). Peter Glenn.
Fischer, Edward J. Bodies by Fischer. Strange, Maureen, ed. 1979. write for info. (ISBN 0-933518-05-6). Marnel Pr.
Fosterer, Selig. Seymour Stern: American Film Historian. 1980. lib. bdg. 49.75 (ISBN 0-686-59417-7). Revisionist Pr.
Fox, Charles D. Famous Film Folk. 1976. lib. bdg. 95.00 (ISBN 0-8490-1802-1). Gordon Pr.
Haas, Robert. Muybridge: Man in Motion. LC 73-78542. (Illus.). 1975. 25.00 (ISBN 0-520-02464-8). U of Cal Pr.
Johnson, Dorris & Leventhal, Ellen, eds. The Letters of Nunnally Johnson. LC 81-47522. (Illus.). 288p. 1981. 15.95 (ISBN 0-394-50672-3). Knopf.
Kerr, Walter. The Silent Clowns. LC 75-8231. (Illus.). 1979. pap. 9.95 (ISBN 0-394-73450-5). Knopf.
Korda, Michael. Charmed Lives: A Family Romance. LC 79-4762. (Illus.). 1979. 15.00 (ISBN 0-394-41954-5). Random.
Lacalamita, M. & Di Gammateo, F., eds. Filmlexicon Degli Autori E Delle Opere, 7 Vols. (Illus., It.). 1968. Set. 210.00 (ISBN 0-405-08505-2); 30.00 ea. Vol. 1 (ISBN 0-405-08506-0). Vol. 2 (ISBN 0-405-08507-9). Vol. 3 (ISBN 0-405-08508-7). Vol. 4 (ISBN 0-405-08509-5). Vol. 5. Vol. 6 (ISBN 0-405-08511-7). Vol. 7 (ISBN 0-405-08512-5). Arno.
Lamour, Dorothy. Dorothy Lamour: My Side of the Road. LC 79-26300. (Illus.). 300p. 1980. 12.95 (ISBN 0-13-218594-6). P-H.
Logan, Joshua. Movie Stars, Real People, & Me. 1978. 9.95 (ISBN 0-440-06258-6). Delacorte.
Meyers, Warren B. Who Is That? (Illus.). 1976. pap. 3.95 (ISBN 0-8065-0535-4). Citadel Pr.
O'Leary, Liam. Rex Ingram: Master of the Silent Cinema. (Illus.). 224p. 1980. 28.50 (ISBN 0-686-70951-9). B&N.
Pickard, Roy. Who Played Who in the Movies. LC 80-26546. 304p. 1981. 14.95 (ISBN 0-8052-3766-6); pap. 6.95 (ISBN 0-8052-0676-0). Schocken.
Sadoul, Georges. Dictionary of Film Makers. Morris, Peter, tr. from Fr. LC 78-136028. 1972. 27.50x (ISBN 0-520-01862-1); pap. 5.95 (ISBN 0-520-02151-7, CAL241). U of Cal Pr.
Salles Gomes, P. E. Jean Vigo. Francovich, Allan, tr. LC 72-104102. 1972. 23.75x (ISBN 0-520-01676-9); pap. 5.95 (ISBN 0-520-02332-3, CAL252). U of Cal Pr.
Sarris, Andrew. American Cinema: Directors & Directions: 1929-1968. 1969. pap. 5.50 (ISBN 0-525-47227-4). Dutton.
Thomson, David. The Biographical Dictionary of Film. 2nd, rev. ed. LC 80-20500. 700p. 1981. 15.95 (ISBN 0-688-00132-7); pap. 10.95 (ISBN 0-688-00131-9). Morrow.
--A Biographical Dictionary of the Cinema. 2nd, rev. ed. 682p. (Orig.). 1980. pap. 17.50x (ISBN 0-436-52013-3). Intl Pubns Serv.
Vermilye, Jerry. The Films of Charles Bronson. (Illus.). 256p. 1981. pap. 7.95 (ISBN 0-8065-0777-2). Citadel Pr.
Wagenknecht, Edward. The Movies in the Age of Innocence. (Illus.). 1962. pap. 6.95 (ISBN 0-8061-1297-2). U of Okla Pr.
Wagner, R. Film Folk: Closeups of Men, Women, & Children Who Make the Movies. 1976. lib. bdg. 59.95 (ISBN 0-8490-1831-5). Gordon Pr.
Winchester, Clarence, ed. World Film Encyclopedia: 1933. 95.00 (ISBN 0-87968-462-3). Gordon Pr.
Wing, Ruth. Blue Book of the Screen. lib. bdg. 75.00 (ISBN 0-87968-762-2). Gordon Pr.
Wishniac, Vance L. Theodore Huff: American Film Historian. 1980. lib. bdg. 49.75 (ISBN 0-686-59418-5). Revisionist Pr.
Zuker, J. S. Ralph Steiner: Filmmaker & Still Photographer. LC 77-22910. 1978. lib. bdg. 28.00x (ISBN 0-405-10758-7). Arno.

MOVING-PICTURES–CATALOGS

Allyn, Mildred V., ed. About Aging: A Catalog of Films, (1981 Supplement to Fourth Edition) LC 81-6693. 105p. 1981. pap. 4.25 (ISBN 0-88474-126-5). USC Andrus Geron.
American Film Institute, compiled by. American Film Institute Catalog of Motion Pictures. Incl. Feature Films 1921-1930, 2 vols. 1653p. Set. 68.50 (ISBN 0-8352-0440-5). LC 79-128587. Bowker.
Aros, Andrew A. Actor's Guide to the Talkies, Nineteen Sixty-Five to Nineteen Seventy-Four. LC 77-21589. 1977. 32.50 (ISBN 0-8108-1052-2). Scarecrow.
Boston Public Library. Cumulative Film Catalog Supplement. 1978. 2.50 (ISBN 0-685-59551-X). Boston Public Lib.
--Film Catalog. 1975. 7.50 (ISBN 0-89073-005-9). Boston Public Lib.
British Film Institute. London. Catalogue of the Book Library of the British Film Institute, 3 vols. 1975. Set. lib. bdg. 285.00 (ISBN 0-8161-0004-7). G K Hall.
Catalogue De Films Sur les Arts Du Spectacle Dans les Pays Arabes et En Asie. 172p. 1976. pap. 7.50 (ISBN 92-3-201259-6, U66, UNESCO). Unipub.
Conservation Education Association. Critical Index of Films on Man & His Environment. LC 65-23951. 32p. 1972. pap. text ed. 1.25x (ISBN 0-8134-1374-5, 1374). Interstate.
Dawson, Bonnie. Women's Films in Print: An Annotated Guide to Eight Hundred Films Made by Women. LC 74-80642. 1975. pap. 5.00x (ISBN 0-685-52346-2). Booklegger Pr.
Dimmitt, Richard B. Actor Guide to the Talkies, 1949-1964, 2 vols. LC 67-12057. 1967. Set. 45.00 (ISBN 0-8108-0000-4). Scarecrow.
--Title Guide to the Talkies, 2 Vols. LC 65-13556. 1965. Set. 60.00 (ISBN 0-8108-0171-X). Scarecrow.
FAO Film Loan Catalogue. 277p. 1980. pap. 18.75 (ISBN 0-686-61373-2, F 1869, FAO). Unipub.
Films: A Supplement 1977. 1977. pap. 4.00 (ISBN 0-87104-627-X, Branch Lib). NY Pub Lib.
Fox, Stuart, compiled by. Jewish Films in the United States: A Comprehensive Survey & Descriptive Filmography. 1976. lib. bdg. 40.00 (ISBN 0-8161-7893-3). G K Hall.
Gluski, J. Proverbs: English, French, German, Italian, Spanish, Russian. 1971. 34.25 (ISBN 0-444-40904-1). Elsevier.
Historical Film Catalog, 1894-1915. 2nd ed. 1979. pap. 2.50 (ISBN 0-913986-00-3). Locare.

Kennedy, Peter, ed. Films on Traditional Music & Dance: A First International Catalogue. (Orig.). 1970. pap. 9.50 (ISBN 92-3-100838-2, U241, UNESCO). Unipub.

Kitching, Jessie & Braun, Susan, eds. Dance & Mime Film & Videotape Catalog. rev. ed. (Orig.). 1980. pap. 10.95 (ISBN 0-914438-00-X). Dance Films.

Krafsur, Richard, ed. American Film Institute Catalog of Motion Pictures: Feature Films 1961-1970, 2 vol. LC 79-128587. 1976. 98.00 set (ISBN 0-685-88228-4). Bowker.

Lee, Walt, ed. Reference Guide to Fantastic Films, Science Fiction, Fantasy, & Horror, Vol. 3: P-Z. LC 72-88775. (Illus.). 240p. (Orig.). 1974. pap. 15.95 (ISBN 0-913974-03-X). Chelsea-Lee Bks.

--Reference Guide to Fantastic Films, Science Fiction, Fantasy, & Horror, Vol. 2: G-O. LC 72-88775. (Illus.). 240p. (Orig.). 1973. pap. 15.95 (ISBN 0-913974-02-1). Chelsea-Lee Bks.

--Reference Guide to Fantastic Films, Science Fiction, Fantasy, & Horror, Vol. 1: A-F. LC 72-88775. (Illus.). 230p. (Orig.). 1972. pap. 15.95 (ISBN 0-913974-01-3). Chelsea-Lee Bks.

--Reference Guide to Fantastic Films, Science Fiction, Fantasy, & Horror, 3 vols. LC 72-88775. (Illus.). 1974. pap. 47.85 set (ISBN 0-913974-04-8). Chelsea-Lee Bks.

Library of Congress Motion Picture, Broadcasting, & Recorded Sound Division. The George Kleine Collection of Early Motion Pictures in the Library of Congress: A Catalog. Horwitz, Rita & Harrison, Harriet, eds. LC 79-607073. (Illus.). 270p. 1980. 11.00 (ISBN 0-8444-0331-8). Lib Congress.

Limbacher, James L., ed. Feature Films on Eight Millimeter & Sixteen Millimeter & Videotape. 6th ed. 1979. 26.25 (ISBN 0-8352-1112-6). Bowker.

Minus, Johnny & Hale, William S. Film Superlist: Twenty Thousand Motion Pictures in the Public Domain. new ed. Hurst, Walter E., ed. LC 73-84212. (Entertainment Industry Ser). 1380p. 1973. 150.00 (ISBN 0-911370-10-2); lib. bdg. 95.00 (ISBN 0-685-31953-9). Seven Arts.

Motion Pictures from the Library of Congress Paper Print Collection 1894-1912. LC 66-28789. 1967. 45.00 (ISBN 0-686-77323-3, Univ. Calif. Press). Locare.

The National Union Catalog Cumulative Author List 1968-1972, 128 Vol. Set. Includes 5 Volume Music & Phonorecord Set & 4 Volume Motion Picture & Filmstrip Set. 1973. 1950.00 (ISBN 0-685-72997-4). Edwards Bros.

The National Union Catalog Cumulative Author List 1968-1972 4 Volume Motion Picture & Filmstrip Set. 1973. 140.00 (ISBN 0-685-72993-1). Edwards Bros.

The National Union Catalog Cumulative Author List 1963-67 2 Volume Motion Picture & Filmstrips Set. 1969. 85.00 (ISBN 0-685-72994-X). Edwards Bros.

Ottoson, Robert. A Reference Guide to the American Film Noir: 1940-1958. LC 80-23176. 290p. 1981. 15.00 (ISBN 0-8108-1363-7). Scarecrow.

Parish, James R. & Pitts, Michael R. The Great Science Fiction Pictures. LC 77-5426. 1977. 18.00 (ISBN 0-8108-1029-8). Scarecrow.

Parish, James R., et al. Hollywood on Hollywood. LC 78-15513. (Illus.). 1978. lib. bdg. 21.00 (ISBN 0-8108-1164-2). Scarecrow.

Parlato, Salvatore J. Films Ex Libris: Literature in Sixteen mm & Video. LC 80-10181. (Illus.). 283p. 1980. lib. bdg. 16.95x (ISBN 0-89950-006-4). McFarland & Co.

Parlato, Salvatore J., Jr. Films-Too Good for Words: A Directory of Nonnarrated 16mm Films. LC 72-12831. 192p. 1973. 16.95 (ISBN 0-8352-0618-1). Bowker.

--Superfilms: An International Guide to Award Winning Educational Films. LC 76-10801. 1976. 16.50 (ISBN 0-8108-0953-2). Scarecrow.

Schrank, Jeffrey. Teaching Human Beings: 101 Subversive Activities for the Classroom. LC 73-179154. 288p. (Orig.). 1972. 7.95 (ISBN 0-8070-3176-3); pap. 4.95x (ISBN 0-8070-3177-1, BP425). Beacon Pr.

Selected List of Catalogues for Short Films & Filmstrips. (Orig.). 1964. pap. 2.25 (ISBN 92-3-100586-3, UNESCO). Unipub.

Seltz-Petrash, Ann, compiled by. AAAS Science Film Catalog. LC 75-11536. 398p. 1975. 19.95 (ISBN 0-8352-0860-5). Bowker.

Sprecher, Daniel, ed. Guide to Free-Loan Films About Foreign Lands. 1975. pap. 9.95 (ISBN 0-685-73562-1). Serina.

--Guide to Free-Loan Films on the Urban Condition. 1976. pap. 7.95 (ISBN 0-685-73563-X). Serina.

--Guide to Free-Loan Sports Films. 2nd ed. 1975. pap. 6.95 (ISBN 0-685-73564-8). Serina.

--Guide to Free-Loan Training Films 16mm. 1975. pap. 7.95 (ISBN 0-685-73561-3). Serina.

--Guide to Government Loan Films, Vol. 2. 2nd ed. 1976. pap. 9.95 (ISBN 0-685-73565-6). Serina.

Systems Film Catalog. (Reference Ser.). 1977. 3.00 (ISBN 0-934356-17-3). Assn Syst Mgmt.

Taylor, Richard. Film Propaganda: Soviet Russia & Nazi Germany. LC 79-1399. (Illus.). 1979. text ed. 25.00x (ISBN 0-06-496778-6). B&N.

Weiss, Ken. The Movie Collector's Catalog. (Illus.). 160p. (Orig.). 1977. pap. 5.95 (ISBN 0-938350-50-1). Cummington Pub.

Willis, Donald C. Horror & Science Fiction Films: A Checklist. LC 72-3682. 1972. 21.00 (ISBN 0-8108-0508-1). Scarecrow.

MOVING-PICTURES–CENSORSHIP

Beman, Lamar T., ed. Selected Articles on Censorship of the Theater & Moving Pictures. LC 78-160229. (Moving Pictures Ser). 385p. 1971. Repr. of 1931 ed. lib. bdg. 18.75x (ISBN 0-89198-030-X). Ozer.

Bertrand, Ian. Film Censorship in Australia. (Illus.). 1978. 24.95x (ISBN 0-7022-1057-9); pap. 14.95 (ISBN 0-7022-1056-0). U of Queensland Pr.

Ernst, Morris & Lorentz, Pare. Censored: The Private Life of the Movies. LC 72-160230. (Moving Pictures Ser). xvi, 199p. 1971. Repr. of 1930 ed. lib. bdg. 11.95x (ISBN 0-89198-031-8). Ozer.

Farber, Stephen. Movie Rating Game. 1972. pap. 4.50 (ISBN 0-685-57344-3). Pub Aff Pr.

Nizer, Louis. New Courts of Industry: Self-Regulation Under the Motion Picture Code, Including an Analysis of the Code. LC 70-160243. (Moving Pictures Ser). 344p. 1971. Repr. of 1935 ed. lib. bdg. 16.95x (ISBN 0-89198-044-X). Ozer.

Phelps, Guy. Film Censorship in Britain. LC 76-352257. (Illus.). 1976. 16.50x (ISBN 0-575-01987-5). Intl Pubns Serv.

Randall, Richard S. Censorship of the Movies: The Social & Political Control of a Mass Medium. LC 68-14035. 296p. 1968. 22.50 (ISBN 0-299-04731-8); pap. 6.95x (ISBN 0-299-04734-2). U of Wis Pr.

Schumach, Murray. The Face on the Cutting Room Floor: The Story of Music & Television Censorship. LC 73-19776. (Civil Liberties in American History Ser.). (Illus.). 306p. 1974. Repr. of 1956 ed. lib. bdg. 19.50 (ISBN 0-306-70603-2). Da Capo.

--The Face on the Cutting Room Floor: The Story of Movie & Television Censorship. LC 74-23937. (Illus.). 306p. 1975. pap. 3.95 (ISBN 0-306-80009-8). Da Capo.

Short, William A. A Generation of Motion Pictures. Kupelnick, Bruce S., ed. LC 76-52129. (Classics of Film Literature Ser.). 1978. lib. bdg. 25.00 (ISBN 0-8240-2894-5). Garland Pub.

Vasudev, Aruna. Liberty & Licence in the Indian Cinema. 1978. 11.00x (ISBN 0-8364-0162-X). South Asia Bks.

Wistrich, Enid. I Don't Mind the Sex It's the Violence: Film Censorship Explored. 160p. 1978. (Pub. by M Boyars); pap. 7.95 (ISBN 0-7145-2535-9, Pub. by M Boyars). Merrimack Bk Serv.

MOVING-PICTURES–COLLECTORS AND COLLECTING

Chaneles, Sol. Collecting Movie Memorabilia. LC 76-44008. (Illus.). 1979. pap. 3.95 (ISBN 0-668-04788-7, 4788-7). Arco.

--Collecting Movie Memorabilia. LC 76-44008. (Illus.). 1977. 10.00 (ISBN 0-668-04048-3). Arco.

McKee, Gerald. Film Collecting. LC 76-50200. (Illus.). 1978. 12.00 (ISBN 0-498-01918-7). A S Barnes.

Weiss, Ken. The Movie Collector's Catalog. (Illus.). 160p. (Orig.). 1977. pap. 5.95 (ISBN 0-938350-50-1). Cummington Pub.

MOVING-PICTURES–COPYRIGHT

see Copyright–Moving-Pictures

MOVING-PICTURES–COSTUME

see Costume

MOVING-PICTURES–CRITICISM

see Moving-Picture Criticism

MOVING-PICTURES–DICTIONARIES

Appelbaum, Stanley & Cirker, Hayward. The Movies: A Picture Quiz Book. (Illus.). 128p. (Orig.). 1972. pap. 3.00 (ISBN 0-486-20222-4). Dover.

Arliss, G. Picturegoers Who's Who & Encyclopedia of the Screen. 608p. 1976. lib. bdg. 95.00 (ISBN 0-8490-0837-9). Gordon Pr.

Arnau, Frank. Universal Film Lexicon. 69.95 (ISBN 0-8490-1246-5). Gordon Pr.

Baer, D. Richard, ed. The Film Buff's Checklist of Motion Pictures (1912-1979) LC 79-14820. (Illus.). 1979. 19.95 (ISBN 0-913616-03-6); lib. bdg. 25.95 (ISBN 0-913616-04-4). Hollywd Film Arch.

Barnet, Sylvan, et al. A Dictionary of Literary, Dramatic, & Cinematic Terms. 2nd ed. 124p. 1971. pap. 4.95 (ISBN 0-316-08194-9). Little.

Bawden, Liz-Anne, ed. Oxford Companion to Film. (Illus.). 700p. 1976. 29.95 (ISBN 0-19-211541-3). Oxford U Pr.

Boyer, Pierre. Enciclopedia del Cine Amateur. 2nd ed. 416p. (Espn.). 1976. 37.50 (ISBN 84-279-4513-2, S-14382). French & Eur.

Clason, W. E. Elsevier's Dictionary of Cinema, Sound & Music. (Polyglot). 1956. 85.50 (ISBN 0-444-40117-2). Elsevier.

Daisne, Johan. Filmographic Dictionary of World Literature, 2 vols, Vol.1. (Fr, Flemish & Ger). 1971. Vol. 1. text ed. 70.00x (ISBN 0-391-01585-0); Vol. 2. text ed. 75.00x (ISBN 0-391-01586-9). Humanities.

Delson, Donn. The Dictionary of Marketing & Related Terms in the Motion Picture Industry. LC 79-67865. 70p. (Orig.). 1979. pap. text ed. 7.95 (ISBN 0-9603574-0-8). Bradson.

Dworkin, Martin S., ed. Literature of Cinema: Series Two, 15 bks. 1972. Repr. Set. 265.00 (ISBN 0-405-03887-9). Arno.

Enciclpedia Ilustrada Del Cine, 4 vols. 2nd ed. 1600p. (Espn.). 1971. Set. 260.00 (ISBN 84-335-7906-1, S-14446). French & Eur.

Farber, Manny. Movies. LC 74-76610. Orig. Title: Negative Space. (Illus.). 320p. 1975. pap. 3.95 (ISBN 0-88373-014-6). Stonehill Pub Co.

Fawcett, L'Estrange. Film Facts & Forecasts. lib. bdg. 59.95 (ISBN 0-8490-1830-7). Gordon Pr.

Grau, Wolfgang. Woerterbuch der Photo, Film und Kinotechnik. (Ger., Eng. & Fr., Dictionary of Photo, Film & Cinematechniques). 1958. pap. 28.00 (ISBN 3-8101-0021-8, M-6968). French & Eur.

Gregor, U. & Patalas, E. Geschichte Des Films, 2 vols. 560p. (Ger.). 1976. pap. 13.95 (ISBN 3-499-16193-1, M-7421). French & Eur.

Katz, Ephraim. Film Encyclopedia. LC 79-7089. 1979. 29.95 (ISBN 0-690-01204-7). T y Crowell.

La Beau, Dennis, ed. Theatre, Film, & TV Biographies Master Index. 1st ed. LC 77-2470. (Gale Biographical Index Ser.: No. 5). 1979. 52.00 (ISBN 0-8103-1081-3). Gale.

Lacalamita, M. & Di Gammateo, F., eds. Filmlexicon Degli Autori E Delle Opere, 7 Vols. (Illus., It.). 1968. Set. 210.00 (ISBN 0-405-08505-2); 30.00 ea. Vol. 1 (ISBN 0-405-08506-0). Vol. 2 (ISBN 0-405-08507-9). Vol. 3 (ISBN 0-405-08508-7). Vol. 4 (ISBN 0-405-08509-5). Vol. 5. Vol. 6 (ISBN 0-405-08511-7). Vol. 7 (ISBN 0-405-08512-5). Arno.

Quick, John & LaBau, Tom. Dictionary of Motion Picture & Video Terms. (Illus.). 1981. 14.95 (ISBN 0-89046-067-1). Herman Pub.

Romero Gualda, Maria V. Vocabulario De Cine y Television En Espana. 400p. (Espn.). 1976. pap. 23.95 (ISBN 84-313-0234-8, S-50002). French & Eur.

Sadoul, George. Dicccionario del Cine, 2 vols. 800p. (Espn.). 1977. Set. pap. 29.95 (ISBN 84-7090-082-X, S-50057). French & Eur.

Sadoul, Georges. Dictionary of Films. Morris, Peter, tr. from Fr. LC 78-136028. 1972. 27.50x (ISBN 0-520-01864-8); pap. 8.95 (ISBN 0-520-02152-5, CAL240). U of Cal Pr.

--Dictionnaire Des Films. 288p. (Fr.). 1969. pap. 8.95 (ISBN 0-686-56797-8, F-79854). French & Eur.

Spottiswoode, Raymond. The Focal Encyclopedia of Film & Television: Techniques. (Communication Arts Bks.). (Illus.). 1969. 45.00 (ISBN 0-240-50654-5). Focal Pr.

Steinbrunner, Chris & Penzler, Otto. Encyclopedia of Mystery & Detection. 1976. 24.50 (ISBN 0-07-061121-1, P&RB). McGraw.

Thomson, David. The Biographical Dictionary of Film. 2nd, rev. ed. LC 80-20500. 700p. 1981. 15.95 (ISBN 0-688-00132-7); pap. 10.95 (ISBN 0-688-00131-9). Morrow.

Wiaschin, Ken. The Illustrated Encyclopedia of the World's Greatest Movie Stars & Their Films. (Illus.). 1979. 24.95 (ISBN 0-517-53714-1, Dist. by Crown); pap. 9.95 (ISBN 0-517-53715-X). Crown.

MOVING-PICTURES–DIRECTION

see Moving-Pictures–Production and Direction

MOVING-PICTURES–DIRECTORIES

Academy of Motion Picture Arts & Sciences. Annual Index to Motion Picture Credits, 1979. Ramsay, Verna, ed. LC 79-644761. 430p. 1980. lib. bdg. 150.00 (ISBN 0-313-20951-0, AN79). Greenwood.

Ackermann, Jean M., ed. Films of a Changing World: A Critical International Guide. (Illus.). 8.00 set (ISBN 0-685-80769-X); Vol. 1 (1972) pap. 4.00 (ISBN 0-911402-03-9); Vol. 2 (1977) pap. 4.00 (ISBN 0-911402-04-7). Soc Intl Dev.

Armour, Robert A. Film: A Reference Guide. LC 79-6566. (American Popular Culture). xxiv, 251p. 1980. lib. bdg. 29.95 (ISBN 0-313-22241-X, AFR/). Greenwood.

Artel, Linda & Wengraf, Susan. Positive Images: A Guide to 400 Non-Sexist Films for Young People. LC 75-46089. 1976. pap. 6.00x (ISBN 0-685-65283-1). Booklegger Pr.

Baer, D. Richard. Film Buff's Bible of Motion Pictures (1915-1972) LC 73-153235. 1972. 12.95x (ISBN 0-913616-01-X); pap. 5.95x (ISBN 0-913616-02-8). Hollywd Film Arch.

Beaton, Welford, ed. Film Spectator Anthology. 1976. lib. bdg. 95.00 (ISBN 0-8490-1836-6). Gordon Pr.

Cowie, Peter. International Film Guide 1979. LC 64-1076. (Illus.). 1978. pap. 7.95 (ISBN 0-498-02241-2). A S Barnes.

--International Film Guide 1980. LC 64-1076. (Illus.). 1979. pap. 7.95 (ISBN 0-498-02423-7). A S Barnes.

Cowie, Peter, ed. International Film Guide Nineteen Seventy-Four. LC 64-1076. (International Film Guide Ser.). (Illus.). 600p. pap. 7.95 (ISBN 0-498-01379-0). A S Barnes.

--International Film Guide, 1975: International Film Guide Ser. 12th ed. LC 64-1076. (Illus.). 640p. 1975. pap. 7.95 (ISBN 0-498-01564-5). A S Barnes.

Dwoskin, Stephen. Film Is: The International Free Cinema. LC 75-7685. (Illus.). 272p. 1978. pap. 6.95 (ISBN 0-87951-072-2). Overlook Pr.

Educational Film Locator: Of the Consortium of University Film Centers & R. R. Bowker. 2nd ed. 2611p. 1980. 50.00 (ISBN 0-8352-1295-5). Bowker.

Emmens, Carol A. Short Stories on Film. LC 78-13488. 1978. lib. bdg. 25.00x (ISBN 0-87287-146-0). Libs Unl.

Halliwell, Leslie. Halliwell's Film Guide. 2nd ed. 1981. 36.00 (ISBN 0-684-16467-1, ScribT). Scribner.

Katz, Ephraim. Film Encyclopedia. LC 79-7089. 1979. 29.95 (ISBN 0-690-01204-7). T y Crowell.

Mehr, Linda, ed. Motion Pictures, Television & Radio. (Reference Publications Ser.). 1977. lib. bdg. 27.00 (ISBN 0-8161-8089-X). G K Hall.

Meyer, William R. The Film Buff's Catalog. 1978. 18.95 (ISBN 0-87000-417-4). Arlington Hse.

Monaco, James. Who's Who in American Film Now. 1981. 19.95 (ISBN 0-918432-34-0); pap. 7.95 (ISBN 0-17-005572-8). NY Zoetrope.

Motion Picture Studio Directory & Trade Annuals 1918-1929. 2000.00 (ISBN 0-686-66700-X). Gordon Pr.

Mueller, John. Dance Film Directory: An Annotated & Evaluative Guide to Films on Ballet & Modern Dance. LC 78-70263. (Illus.). 103p. 1979. pap. 9.95 (ISBN 0-916622-08-8). Princeton Bk Co.

Parish, James R. & Pitts, Michael R. Film Directors: A Guide to Their American Films. LC 74-17398. (Illus.). 1974. 18.50 (ISBN 0-8108-0752-1). Scarecrow.

Peyton, Patricia, ed. Reel Change: A Guide to Social Issue Films. LC 79-54657. (Film Fund Ser.). (Illus., Orig.). 1980. pap. 6.95 (ISBN 0-686-77488-4). NY Zoetrope.

Pickard, Roy. Hollywood Gold. LC 78-63445. (Illus.). 1979. 14.95 (ISBN 0-8008-3919-6); pap. 9.95 (ISBN 0-8008-3920-X). Taplinger.

Roll, Sally, ed. Annual Index to Motion Picture Credits. 1980. 150.00 (ISBN 0-313-20952-9). Acad Motion Pic.

Slide, Anthony. Early American Cinema. LC 77-119639. (International Film Guide Ser). 1970. pap. 4.95 (ISBN 0-498-07717-9). A S Barnes.

Townsend, Derek. Practical Guide to Holiday Family Movies. Date not set. 10.95x (ISBN 0-392-09401-0, SpS). Sportshelf.

Weiss, Ken & Goodgold, Ed. To Be Continued...a Complete Guide to Over Two-Hundred Twenty Motion Picture Serials with Sound Tracks. (Illus.). 1972. 12.95 (ISBN 0-517-50340-9). Crown.

Willis, John. Screen World: Nineteen Eighty, Vol. 31. (Screen World Ser.). (Illus.). 256p. 1980. 15.95 (ISBN 0-517-54140-8). Crown.

Zucker, Ralph. FilmRow Motion Picture Marketing BlackBook, Pt. I. (Los Angeles). 350p. 1981. 50.00 (ISBN 0-937874-03-5). Filmrow Pubns.

MOVING-PICTURES–EDITING

Ash, Rene L. The Motion Picture Film Editor. LC 74-4072. 1974. 10.00 (ISBN 0-8108-0718-1). Scarecrow.

Burder, J. Technique of Editing Sixteen Mm. Films. 4th ed. (Illus.). 152p. 1979. 19.95 (ISBN 0-240-51019-4). Focal Pr.

Burder, John. Sixteen Millimeter Film Cutting. (Media Manuals Ser.). (Illus.). 1975. pap. 7.95 (ISBN 0-8038-6730-1). Hastings.

Burger. Sixteen MM Film Cutting. 158p. 1975. 7.95 (ISBN 0-240-50857-2). Focal Pr.

Copestake, Timothy. Editing Super Eight. (Illus.). 288p. 1980. 19.95 (ISBN 0-240-50997-8). Focal Pr.

Daley, Ken. Basic Film Techniques. (Media Manual Series). (Illus.). 160p. 1980. pap. 9.95 (ISBN 0-240-51016-X). Focal Pr.

Dove, Bob, ed. The Movie Maker's Handbook. (Illus.). 1980. 25.00 (ISBN 0-87165-044-4). Ziff-Davis Pub.

Jenkins, Philip. Focalguide to Movie Tilting. (Focal Guide Ser.). (Illus.). 160p. 1981. pap. 7.95 (ISBN 0-240-51011-9). Focal Pr.

Reisz, Karel & Millar, Gavin. Technique of Film Editing. enl. ed. (Library of Communication Techniques Ser). (Illus., Orig.). 1968. text ed. 21.95 (ISBN 0-240-50673-1); pap. text ed. 14.95 (ISBN 0-240-50846-7). Focal Pr.

Rosenblum, Ralph & Karen, Robert. When the Shooting Stops...the Cutting Begins: A Film Editor's Story. 1980. pap. 4.95 (ISBN 0-14-005698-X). Penguin.

--When the Shooting Stops...the Cutting Begins: A Film Editor's Story. (Illus.). 1979. 12.95 (ISBN 0-670-75991-0). Viking Pr.
Rudman, Jack. Film Editor. (Career Examination Ser.: C-1286). (Cloth bdg. avail. on request). pap. 8.00 (ISBN 0-8373-1286-8). Natl Learning.
Stecker, Elinor. The Master Handbook of Still & Movie Titling for Amateur & Professional. (Illus.). 1979. 14.95 (ISBN 0-8306-9850-7); pap. 9.95 (ISBN 0-8306-1001-4, 1001). TAB Bks.
Walter, Ernst. Technique of the Film Cutting Room. rev. 2nd ed. (Library Oof Communication Techniques). (Illus.). 1973. 21.95 (ISBN 0-240-50657-X). Focal Pr.

MOVING-PICTURES–ESTHETICS

see also Esthetics

Campbell, Russell, compiled by. Photographic Theory for the Motion Picture Cameraman. (Illus.). 160p. 1981. pap. 6.95 (ISBN 0-498-07776-4). A S Barnes.
Casty, Alan. Dramatic Art of the Film. 1971. pap. text ed. 10.50 scp (ISBN 0-06-041214-3, HarpC). Har-Row.
Cavell, Stanley. The World Viewed: Reflections on the Ontology of Film. enl. ed. (Paperback Ser.: No. 151). 1980. 15.00x (ISBN 0-674-96197-8); pap. 5.95 (ISBN 0-674-96196-X). Harvard U Pr.
Cocteau, Jean, et al. Du Cinematographe. (Illus.). 205p. 1973. 12.95 (ISBN 0-686-54523-0). French & Eur.
Giannetti, Louis D. Godard & Others: Essays on Film Form. LC 73-2893. (Illus.). 184p. 1975. 14.50 (ISBN 0-8386-1291-1). Fairleigh Dickinson.
Harpole, C. H. Gradients of Depth in the Cinema Image. LC 77-22907. 1978. lib. bdg. 17.00x (ISBN 0-405-10753-6). Arno.
McConnell, Frank D. The Spoken Seen: Film & the Romantic Imagination. LC 75-11342. (Illus.). 212p. 1975. 15.00x (ISBN 0-8018-1725-0); pap. 3.95 (ISBN 0-8018-1726-9). Johns Hopkins.
Neale, Stephen. Genre. (BFI Ser.). (Orig.). 1980. pap. 7.25 (ISBN 0-85170-094-2). NY Zoetrope.
Schrader, Paul. Transcendental Style in Film: Ozu-Bresson-Dreyer. LC 73-157824. 1972. 16.95x (ISBN 0-520-02038-3). U of Cal Pr.
Wollen, Peter. Signs & Meaning in the Cinema. rev. enl. ed. LC 72-82722. (Cinema One Ser.: No. 9). (Illus.). 176p. 1973. pap. 4.95x (ISBN 0-253-18141-0). Ind U Pr.
Wollenberg, H. H. Anatomy of the Film: An Illustrated Guide to Film Appreciation. LC 71-169355. (Arno Press Cinema Program). (Illus.). 108p. 1972. Repr. of 1947 ed. 12.00 (ISBN 0-405-03926-3). Arno.

MOVING-PICTURES–EVALUATION

Allen, Robert C. Vaudeville & Film. Jowett, Garth S., ed. LC 79-6667. (Dissertations on Film, 1980 Ser.). 1980. lib. bdg. 32.00x (ISBN 0-405-12901-7). Arno.
Benderson, Albert E. Critical Approaches to Federico Fellini's Eight & Half, Vol. 4. LC 74-2078. (Dissertations on Film Ser.). 239p. 1974. 12.00 (ISBN 0-405-04877-7). Arno.
Berger, Arthur A., ed. Film in Society. LC 78-55943. 151p. 1980. 10.95 (ISBN 0-87855-245-6). Transaction Bks.
Bettetini, Gianfranco. The Language & Technique of the Film. (Approaches to Semiotics Ser: No. 28). 1973. text ed. 33.00x (ISBN 90-2792-412-0). Mouton.
Carringer, Robert, et al. Film Study Guides. 1977. pap. text ed. 3.50x (ISBN 0-87563-155-X). Stipes.
Cozyris, George A. Christian Metz & the Reality of Film. Jowett, Garth S., ed. LC 79-6670. (Dissertation on Film, 1980 Ser.). 1980. lib. bdg. 19.00x (ISBN 0-405-12904-1). Arno.
Crowther, Bosley. Reruns: Fifty Memorable Films. LC 78-6271. (Illus.). 1978. 17.50 (ISBN 0-399-12112-9); pap. 7.95 (ISBN 0-399-12230-3). Putnam.
Daly, David A. A Comparison of Exhibition & Distribution Patterns in Three Recent Feature Motion Pictures. abridged ed. Jowett, Garth S., ed. LC 79-6672. (Dissertations on Film, 1980). lib. bdg. 20.00x (ISBN 0-405-12906-8). Arno.
Dart, Peter. Pudovkin's Films & Film Theory. LC 74-986. (Dissertations on Film Ser.). 1974. 12.00 (ISBN 0-405-04874-2). Arno.
Diakite, Madubuko. Film, Culture, & the Black Filmmaker. Jowett, Garth S., ed. LC 79-6679. (Issertations on Film, 1980 Ser.). 1980. lib. bdg. 19.00x (ISBN 0-405-12907-6). Arno.
Dick, Bernard F. Anatomy of Film. LC 76-28140. (Illus.). 1978. 10.00 (ISBN 0-312-03360-5). St Martin.
Ellis, Reed. A Journey into Darkness. Jowett, Garth S., ed. LC 79-6673. (Dissertations on Film, 1980). 1980. lib. bdg. 19.00x (ISBN 0-405-12908-4). Arno.
Facey, Paul W. The Legion of Decency: A Sociological Analysis of the Emergence & Development of a Social Pressure Group. LC 73-21596. (Dissertations on Film). 1974. 11.00 (ISBN 0-405-04871-8). Arno.
Garton, Joseph W. The Film Acting of John Barrymore. Jowett, Garth S., ed. LC 79-6676. (Dissertations on Film, 1980 Ser.). 1980. lib. bdg. 22.00x (ISBN 0-405-12910-6). Arno.
Glasser, et al. Explorations in National Cinema. Lawton, Ben & Staiger, Janet, eds. (Film Studies Annual, 1977: Pt. 1). (Illus.). 1977. pap. 6.00 (ISBN 0-913178-52-7). Redgrave Pub Co.
Guzzetti, Alfred. Two or Three Things I Know About Her: Analysis of a Film by Godard. LC 80-15832. (Film Studies). (Illus.). 376p. 1981. text ed. 27.50x (ISBN 0-674-91500-3). Harvard U Pr.
Halliwell. Halliwell's Film Guide. 2nd. ed. Date not set. 36.00 (ISBN 0-684-16467-1). Scribner.
Henderson, Brian. Critique of Film Theory. 224p. 1980. 15.95 (ISBN 0-525-08740-0); pap. 8.95 (ISBN 0-525-47526-5). Dutton.
Hinton, David B. The Films of Leni Riefenstahl. LC 78-7036. 1978. 10.00 (ISBN 0-8108-1141-3). Scarecrow.
Issari, M. Ali & Paul, Doris A. What Is Cinema Verite? LC 79-20110. 216p. 1979. 11.50 (ISBN 0-8108-1253-3). Scarecrow.
Kael, Pauline. Deeper into Movies. 1980. pap. 2.95 (ISBN 0-446-93525-5). Warner Bks.
--Going Steady. 1979. pap. 2.50 (ISBN 0-446-91075-9). Warner Bks.
Kauffmann, Stanley. Figures of Light: Film Criticism & Comment. LC 70-138742. 1971. 12.95 (ISBN 0-06-012274-9, HarpT). Har-Row.
Kindem, Gorham A. Toward a Semiotic Theory of Visual Communication in the Cinema. Jowett, Garth S., ed. LC 79-6678. (Dissertations on Film, 1980 Ser.). 1980. lib. bdg. 26.00x (ISBN 0-405-12912-2). Arno.
Kreidl, John F. Nicholas Ray. (Theatrical Arts Ser.). 1977. lib. bdg. 12.50 (ISBN 0-8057-9250-3). Twayne.
Limbacher, James L. Film Sneaks Annual. 1972. 10.00 (ISBN 0-87650-027-0). Pierian.
McGuire, Jeremiah C. Cinema & Value Philosophy. LC 68-30751. 1968. 3.00 (ISBN 0-8022-2259-5). Philos Lib.
Manvell, Roger, et al, eds. The Penguin Film Review 1946-1949, 2 vols. (Illus.). 1978. Repr. of 1946 ed. Set. 49.50x (ISBN 0-8476-6029-X). Rowman.
Miller, Arthur, et al. Poetry & Film: Two Symposiums. 1972. pap. 3.50 (ISBN 0-910664-24-2). Gotham.
Moore, Barry W. Aesthetic Aspects of Recent Experimental Film. Jowett, Garth S., ed. LC 79-6680. (Dissertations on Film, 1980 Ser.). 1980. lib. bdg. 20.00x (ISBN 0-405-12913-0). Arno.
Murray, Edward. Ten Film Classics: A Re-Viewing. LC 78-4293. (Ungar Film Library). (Illus.). 1978. 12.95 (ISBN 0-8044-2650-3); pap. 5.95 (ISBN 0-8044-6535-5). Ungar.
Rehrauer, George. Short Film: An Evaluative Selection of 500 Films. 1975. 12.50 (ISBN 0-02-469530-0). Macmillan Info.
Rose, Brian G. An Examination of Narrative Structure in Four Films of Frank Capra. Jowett, Garth S., ed. LC 79-6683. (Dissertations on Film, 1980 Ser.). 1980. lib. bdg. 22.00x (ISBN 0-405-12915-7). Arno.
Rosenthal, Alan. The New Documentary in Action: A Casebook in Film Making. 1972. 16.95 (ISBN 0-520-01888-5); pap. 2.95 (ISBN 0-520-02254-8, CAL249). U of Cal Pr.
Rovin, Jeff. The Fabulous Fantasy Films. LC 76-10876. (Illus.). 1977. 19.95 (ISBN 0-498-01803-2). A S Barnes.
Salvaggio, Jerry L. A Theory of Film Language. Jowett, Garth S., ed. LC 79-6684. (Dissertations on Film, 1980 Ser.). 1980. lib. bdg. 20.00x (ISBN 0-405-12916-5). Arno.
Siska, William C. Modernism in the Narrative Cinema. Jowett, Garth S., ed. LC 79-6686. (Dissertations on Film, 1980 Ser.). 1980. lib. bdg. 15.00x (ISBN 0-405-12918-1). Arno.
Sitney, P. Adams, ed. The Avant-Garde Film: A Reader of Theory & Criticism. LC 78-57645. (Illus.). 1978. 29.50x (ISBN 0-8147-7793-7); pap. 14.50x (ISBN 0-8147-7794-5). NYU Pr.
--The Essential Cinema: Essays on Films in The Collection of Anthology Film Archives. LC 74-10371. (Anthology Film Archives Series). 380p. 1975. 20.00x (ISBN 0-8147-7767-8); pap. 12.00x (ISBN 0-8147-7768-6). NYU Pr.
Sproxton, Vernon. Watching Films. 1979. Repr. of 1948 ed. lib. bdg. 10.00 (ISBN 0-8492-8088-5). R West.
Thomas, Tony. The Films of Ronald Reagan. (Illus.). 256p. 1980. 16.95 (ISBN 0-8065-0751-9). Citadel Pr.
Wead, George & Lellis, Geore. Film: Form & Function. LC 80-82804. (Illus.). 512p. 1981. pap. text ed. 12.95 (ISBN 0-395-29740-0). HM.
Williams, Alan L. Max Ophuls & the Cinema of Desire. abridged ed. Jowett, Garth S., ed. LC 79-6693. (Dissertations on Film, 1980 Ser.). 1980. lib. bdg. 18.00x (ISBN 0-405-12924-6). Arno.

MOVING-PICTURES–FILM EDITING

see Moving-Pictures–Editing

MOVING-PICTURES–HISTORY

Agel, Jerome, ed. The Making of Kubrick's 2001. (Film Ser.). (RL 10). 1972. pap. 1.95 (ISBN 0-451-07139-5, J7139, Sig). NAL.
Allen, Don, ed. The World of Film & Filmmakers: A Visual History. (Illus.). 1979. 19.95 (ISBN 0-517-53662-5). Crown.
Anderson, John & Fulop-Miller, Rene. The American Theatre, & the Motion Picture in America. (English Literary Reference, House Ser). Repr. of 1938 ed. lib. bdg. 34.50 (ISBN 0-384-01435-6). Johnson Repr.
Andrew, J. Dudley. The Major Film Theories: An Introduction. (Illus.). 275p. (Orig.). 1976. pap. 5.95 (ISBN 0-19-501991-1, 450, GB). Oxford U Pr.
Anstel, Edgar. Shots in the Dark: Films of 1949-1951. 1976. lib. bdg. 59.95 (ISBN 0-8490-2601-6). Gordon Pr.
Appelbaum, Stanley. The Hollywood Musical: A Picture Quiz Book. (Illus., Orig.). 1974. pap. 2.50 (ISBN 0-486-23008-2). Dover.
Armes, Roy. A Critical History of British Cinema. LC 77-73893. (Illus.). 1978. 19.50 (ISBN 0-19-520043-8). Oxford U Pr.
--Film & Reality: An Historical Survey. 5.50 (ISBN 0-8446-5153-2). Peter Smith.
Balazs, Bela. Theory of the Film: Character & Growth of a New Art. 6.50 (ISBN 0-8446-0017-2). Peter Smith.
Ball, Robert H. Shakespeare on Silent Film. LC 68-14014. (Illus.). 1968. 3.10 (ISBN 0-87830-116-X). Theatre Arts.
Balshofer, Fred J. & Miller, Arthur C. One Reel a Week. LC 67-24119. (Illus.). 1968. 19.95 (ISBN 0-520-00073-0). U of Cal Pr.
Bardeche, Maurice & Brasillach, Robert. History of Motion Pictures. LC 70-112565. (Literature of Cinema Ser). Repr. of 1938 ed. 17.00 (ISBN 0-405-01602-6). Arno.
Barris, Alex. Hollywood According to Hollywood. LC 75-38435. (Illus.). 1978. 17.50 (ISBN 0-498-01748-6). A S Barnes.
Basten, Fred E. Glorious Technicolor: The Movies' Magic Rainbow. LC 78-67469. (Illus.). 1980. 30.00 (ISBN 0-498-02317-6). A S Barnes.
Baxter, John. Hollywood in the Sixties. LC 70-181065. (Hollywood Ser.). (Illus.). 192p. 1972. pap. 4.95 (ISBN 0-498-01096-1). A S Barnes.
--Hollywood in the Thirties. LC 68-24003. (Hollywood Ser.). 1968. pap. 4.95 (ISBN 0-498-06927-3). A S Barnes.
Behlmer, Rudy & Thomas, Tony. Hollywood's Hollywood: The Movies About the Movies. (Illus.). 384p. 1975. 19.95 (ISBN 0-8065-0491-9). Citadel Pr.
Bergman, Andrew. We're in the Money: Depression America & Its Films. LC 74-159533. (Illus.). 1971. cusa 14.50x (ISBN 0-8147-0964-8). NYU Pr.
Bergsten, Bebe. The Great Dane & the Great Northern Film Company. LC 72-97021. (Illus.). 1973. 8.95 (ISBN 0-913986-05-4). Locare.
Blum, Daniel. A Pictorial History of the Silent Screen. (Illus.). 1972. pap. 6.95 (ISBN 0-399-11098-4). Putnam.
Blum, Daniel & Kobal, John. A New Pictorial History of the Talkies. rev. ed. (Illus.). 384p. 1973. pap. 7.95 (ISBN 0-399-11231-6). Putnam.
Bohn, Thomas W., et al. Light & Shadows: A History of Motion Pictures. 2nd ed. LC 77-25909. 479p. 1978. pap. text ed. 11.50x (ISBN 0-88284-057-6). Alfred Pub.
Brode, Douglas. The Films of the Fifties. (Illus.). 1978. pap. 6.95 (ISBN 0-8065-0621-0). Citadel Pr.
--The Films of the Sixties. (Illus.). 1980. 16.95 (ISBN 0-8065-0694-6). Citadel Pr.
Brosnan, John. James Bond in the Cinema. 2nd rev. ed. LC 80-26573. (Illus.). 200p. 1981. 9.95 (ISBN 0-498-02546-2). A S Barnes.
Brownlow, Kevin. The Parade's Gone by. LC 75-17302. 1976. pap. 9.95 (ISBN 0-520-03068-0). U of Cal Pr.
Buscombe, et al. Film: Theoretical-Historical Speculations. Lawton, Ben & Staiger, Janet, eds. (Film Studies Annual, 1977: Pt. 2). (Orig.). 1977. pap. 6.00 (ISBN 0-913178-53-5). Redgrave Pub Co.
Carter, Huntly. New Spirit in the Cinema. LC 76-112580. (Literature in Cinema, Ser. 1). Repr. of 1930 ed. 14.00 (ISBN 0-405-01605-0). Arno.
Casty, Alan. Development of the Film: An Interpretive History. 1973. pap. text ed. 11.95 (ISBN 0-15-517622-6, HC). HarBraceJ.
Cawelti, John. Six-Gun Mystique. 148p. 1970. 7.95 (ISBN 0-87972-007-7); pap. 4.95 (ISBN 0-87972-008-5). Bowling Green Univ.
Champlin, Charles. The Movies Grow up, Nineteen Forty to Nineteen Eighty. rev. ed. LC 80-29388. Orig. Title: The Flicks; or Whatever Became of Andy Hardy? (Illus.). xii, 284p. 1981. 25.95 (ISBN 0-8040-0363-7); pap. 12.00 (ISBN 0-8040-0364-5). Swallow.
Chanan, Michael. The Dream That Kicks: The Prehistory & Early Years of Cinema in Britain. (Illus.). 1980. 32.50 (ISBN 0-7100-0319-6). Routledge & Kegan.
Character People. (Illus.). 1979. pap. 6.95 (ISBN 0-8065-0701-2). Citadel Pr.
Clarens, Carlos. Crime Movies. (Illus.). 1980. 19.95 (ISBN 0-393-01262-X); pap. 8.95 (ISBN 0-393-00940-8). Norton.
Cohn, Lawrence. Movietone Presents the 20th Century. LC 75-26177. (Illus.). 1976. 17.95 (ISBN 0-312-55055-3). St Martin.
Cook, David A. A History of Narrative Film, 1889-1979. (Illus.). 1981. pap. text ed. price not set (ISBN 0-393-09022-1). Norton.
Cook, Jim & Lewington, Mike, eds. Images of Alcoholism. (BFI Ser.). (Orig.). 1980. pap. 7.25 (ISBN 0-85170-091-8). NY Zoetrope.
Cowie, Peter, ed. Hollywood, 1920-1970. LC 73-18863. (Illus.). 288p. 1976. 25.00 (ISBN 0-498-01400-2). A S Barnes.
Crowther, Bosley. Vintage Films. LC 76-19038. (Illus.). 1977. 15.00 (ISBN 0-399-11637-0). Putnam.
Dawson, Jan. Films of Hellmuth Costard. 1979. pap. 3.50 (ISBN 0-918432-24-3). NY Zoetrope.
Deutelbaum, Marshall, ed. Image on the Art & Evolution of Film: Photographs & Articles from the Magazine of the International Museum of Photography. LC 78-94843. (Illus.). 1979. pap. 8.95 (ISBN 0-486-23777-X). Dover.
Dickinson, Thorold. A Discovery of Cinema. (Illus.). 192p. 1973. pap. 5.95 (ISBN 0-19-211440-9). Oxford U Pr.
Dooley, Roger. From Scarface to Scarlett: American Films in the 1930s. LC 80-8745. (Illus.). 700p. 1981. 25.00 (ISBN 0-15-133789-6). HarBraceJ.
Dworkin, Martin S., ed. The Literature of Cinema: Series One, 48 bks. 1970. Set. 587.00 (ISBN 0-405-01600-X). Arno.
Edelson, Edward. Great Movie Spectaculars. LC 76-56. 144p. (gr. 4-7). 1976. PLB 6.95 (ISBN 0-385-11180-0). Doubleday.
--Great Movie Spectaculars. (gr. 7-9). 1977. pap. 1.50 (ISBN 0-671-29994-8). Archway.
Edmonds, I. G. & Mimura, Reiko. Paramount Pictures & the People Who Made Them. (Illus.). 288p. 1980. 17.50 (ISBN 0-498-02322-2). A S Barnes.
Eidsvik, Charles V. Cineliteracy: Film Among the Arts. LC 77-94015. (Illus.). 1978. 14.95 (ISBN 0-8180-0708-7). Horizon.
Eisenstein, Sergei. The Battleship Potemkin. 1978. pap. 7.95 (ISBN 0-380-30460-0, 30460). Avon.
Ellis, Jack C. A History of Film. (Illus.). 1979. pap. 15.95 ref. ed. (ISBN 0-13-389460-6). P-H.
Ellis-Jones, Barrie. The Cinema. (Guided Readers Ser.). (Illus.). 1977. pap. 2.25x (ISBN 0-435-27031-1). Heinemann Ed.
Epstein, Edward Z., et al. Films of World War Two. (Illus.). 256p. 1975. pap. 6.95 (ISBN 0-8065-0482-X). Citadel Pr.
Everson, William K. American Silent Film. LC 77-25188. (Illus.). 1978. 18.95 (ISBN 0-19-502348-X). Oxford U Pr.
--Bad Guys: A Pictorial History of the Movie Villain. (Photos). 1968. pap. 6.95 (ISBN 0-8065-0198-7, C264). Citadel Pr.
--Love in the Film. (Illus.). 256p. 1981. pap. 7.95 (ISBN 0-8065-0778-0). Citadel Pr.
--Love in the Film: Seventy Years of Romantic Classics. (Illus.). 1979. 14.95 (ISBN 0-8065-0644-X). Citadel Pr.
--Pictorial History of the Western Film. (Illus.). 1971. 10.00 (ISBN 0-685-00330-2); pap. 6.95 (ISBN 0-8065-0257-6). Citadel Pr.
Farmer, James H. Celluloid Wings: The Impact of the Movies on Aviation. LC 81-3579. (Illus.). 384p. 1981. 25.00 (ISBN 0-498-02543-8). A S Barnes.
Fell, John L. Film & the Narrative Tradition. LC 73-7428. (Illus.). 400p. 1974. 16.95x (ISBN 0-8061-1127-5). U of Okla Pr.
--A History of Films. LC 78-16203. 1979. pap. text ed. 14.95 (ISBN 0-03-036316-0, HoltC). HR&W.
Fernett, Gene. Hollywood's Poverty Row. LC 73-86757. (Film History Ser). (Illus.). 178p. 1973. 9.95 (ISBN 0-914042-01-7). Coral Reef.
The First Twenty Years: A Segment of Film History. 2nd ed. LC 68-58700. (Illus.). 1979. 10.00 (ISBN 0-913986-01-1). Locare.
Fitzgerald, Michael. Universal Pictures: A Panoramic History in Words, Pictures & Filmographies. (Illus.). 1977. 35.00 (ISBN 0-87000-366-6). Arlington Hse.
Fitzgerald, Michael G. American Movies: The Forties, Vol. 1: 1940-1944. 1979. 30.00 (ISBN 0-87000-424-7). Arlington Hse.

Flamini, Roland. Scarlett, Rhett, & a Cast of Thousands. (Illus.). 368p. 1977. 13.95 (ISBN 0-02-538670-0). Macmillan.

--Scarlett, Rhett & a Cast of Thousands: The Filming of "Gone with the Wind". 1978. pap. 5.95 (ISBN 0-02-012250-0, Collier). Macmillan.

Fox, Charles D. Mirrors of Hollywood: Hollywood Studios of 1925. 1976. lib. bdg. 59.95 (ISBN 0-8490-2260-6). Gordon Pr.

Franklin, Joe. Classics of the Silent Screen. (Illus.). 1967. pap. 6.95 (ISBN 0-8065-0181-2, C255). Citadel Pr.

Fulton, A. R. Motion Pictures: The Development of an Art. rev. ed. LC 79-6711. (Illus.). 274p. 1980. 14.95x (ISBN 0-8061-1633-1). U of Okla Pr.

Gabree, John. Gangsters: From Little Caesar to the Godfather. LC 74-33233. (Film Stars Ser.). (Illus.). 5.95 (ISBN 0-88365-290-0). Brown Bk.

Garbicz, Adam & Klinowski, Jacek. Cinema, the Magic Vehicle-A Guide to Its Achievement-Journey Two: The Cinema in the Fifties. LC 75-2183. 551p. 1979. 27.50 (ISBN 0-8108-1241-X). Scarecrow.

Gordon, R. Carl Laemmle & Universal Pictures: A Tribute. 1976. lib. bdg. 69.95 (ISBN 0-8490-1579-0). Gordon Pr.

Gordon, R., ed. RKO Radio Pictures of 1931-1935. 1976. lib. bdg. 100.95 (ISBN 0-8490-2528-1). Gordon Pr.

--Universal Pictures in the Twenties & Thirties, 2 vols. 1976. lib. bdg. 200.00 (ISBN 0-8490-2787-X). Gordon Pr.

Gould, Michael. Surrealism & the Cinema. LC 74-9284. (Illus.). 192p. 1976. 9.95 (ISBN 0-498-01498-3). A S Barnes.

Gow, Gordon. Hollywood in the Fifties. LC 70-141572. (Hollywood Ser). (Illus.). 1971. pap. 4.95 (ISBN 0-498-07859-0). A S Barnes.

Gregor, U. & Patalas, E. Geschichte Des Films, 2 vols. 560p. (Ger.). 1976. pap. 13.95 (ISBN 3-499-16193-1, M-7421). French & Eur.

Griffith, Richard & Mayer, Arthur. The Movies. (Illus.). 494p. (YA) 1975. pap. 9.95 (ISBN 0-671-22142-6, Fireside). S&S.

Halliwell, Leslie. Mountain of Dreams: The Golden Years of Paramount Pictures. LC 77-71225. 224p. 1977. 14.95 (ISBN 0-88373-036-7). Stonehill Pub Co.

Hampton, Benjamin. History of the Movies. 59.95 (ISBN 0-8490-0357-1). Gordon Pr.

Hampton, Benjamin B. History of the American Film Industry from Its Beginnings to 1931. (Illus.). 11.50 (ISBN 0-8446-0677-4). Peter Smith.

--History of the American Film Industry from Its Beginnings to 1931. Griffith, Richard, ed. (Dover Film Ser.). Orig. Title: History of the Movies. (Illus.). 1970. pap. 6.50 (ISBN 0-486-22403-1). Dover.

--History of the Movies. LC 70-124008. (Literature of Cinema, Ser. 1). Repr. of 1931 ed. 24.00 (ISBN 0-405-01614-X). Arno.

Harryhausen, Ray. Film Fantasy Scrapbook. 3rd. rev. enlr. ed. LC 81-3625. (Illus.). 160p. 1981. pap. 13.95 (ISBN 0-498-02571-3). A S Barnes.

Hepworth, Thomas C. The Book of the Lantern. Jowett, Garth S., ed. LC 77-11376. (Aspects of Film Ser.). (Illus.). 1978. Repr. of 1899 ed. lib. bdg. 25.00x (ISBN 0-405-11132-0). Arno.

Herring, Robert. Films of the Year Nineteen Twenty Seven - Nineteen Twenty Eight. 69.95 (ISBN 0-8490-0165-X). Gordon Pr.

Higham, Charles. Celebrity Circus. 1979. 9.95 (ISBN 0-440-01210-4). Delacorte.

Higham, Charles & Greenberg, Joel. Hollywood in the Forty's. LC 68-24004. 192p. 1981. pap. 5.95 (ISBN 0-498-06928-1). A S Barnes.

Hinton, David B. The Films of Leni Riefenstahl. LC 78-7036. 1978. 10.00 (ISBN 0-8108-1141-3). Scarecrow.

Hirsch, Foster. The Hollywood Epic. LC 77-82674. (Illus.). 1978. 15.00 (ISBN 0-498-01747-8). A S Barnes.

Hirschorn, Clive, ed. The Warner Brother Story: The Complete History of Hollywood's Greatest Studio. (Illus.). 1979. 30.00 (ISBN 0-517-53834-2). Crown.

Hochman, Stanley, ed. From Quasimodo to Scarlett O'Hara: A National Board of Review Anthology (1920-1940) LC 81-40463. 450p. 1982. 24.95 (ISBN 0-8044-2381-4); pap. 12.95 (ISBN 0-8044-6274-7). Ungar.

Hove, Arthur & Balio, Tino, eds. Gold Diggers of Nineteen Thirty-Three. LC 79-5402. (Wisconsin-Warner Bros. Screenplay Ser.). (Illus.). 192p. 1980. 15.00 (ISBN 0-299-08080-3); pap. 5.95 (ISBN 0-299-08084-6). U of Wis Pr.

Ideas of Order in Literature & Film: Selected Papers from the 4th Annual Florida State University Conferenceon Literature & Film. LC 80-26017. viii, 136p. (Orig.). 1981. pap. 8.00 (ISBN 0-8130-0699-6). U Presses Fla.

Ifkovic, Edward. Dream Street: The American Movies & the Popular Imagination, 1889-1939, 2 vols. (Cinema Ser). (Illus.). 800p. 1977. lib. bdg. 150.00 (ISBN 0-685-75580-0). Revisionist Pr.

Isenberg, Michael T. War on Film: The American Cinema & World War 1, 1914-1941. LC 76-19835. 280p. 1981. 27.50 (ISBN 0-8386-2004-3). Fairleigh Dickinson.

--War on Films: The American Cinema & World War I, 1914-1941. LC 76-19835. 400p. 1981. 27.50 (ISBN 0-8386-2004-3). Fairleigh Dickinson.

Jackson, Clyde O. In Old Hollywood: The Movies During Their Golden Years. 1977. 6.50 (ISBN 0-682-48971-9). Exposition.

Jacobs, Diane. Hollywood Renaissance. LC 76-18796. (Illus.). 1977. 12.00 (ISBN 0-498-01785-0). A S Barnes.

Jacobs, Lewis. Rise of the American Film: A Critical History with an Essay "Experimental Cinema in America 1921-1947". LC 68-25845. (Illus.). 1968. text ed. 21.50 (ISBN 0-8077-1556-5); pap. 14.95x (ISBN 0-8077-1555-7). Tchrs Coll.

Johnson, Nora. Flashback: Nora Johnson on Nunnally Johnson. LC 78-18137. 1979. 11.95 (ISBN 0-385-13406-1). Doubleday.

Karimi, A. M. Toward a Definition of American Film Noir (1941-1949) Lowett, Garth S., ed. LC 75-21431. (Dissertations of Film Ser.). 1976. lib. bdg. 16.00x (ISBN 0-405-07534-0). Arno.

Kawin, Bruce F. Telling It Again & Again: Repetition in Literature & Film. LC 75-37753. 208p. 1972. 14.50x (ISBN 0-8014-0698-6). Cornell U Pr.

Kawin, Bruce F. & Balio, Tino, eds. To Have & Have Not. LC 79-5403. (Wisconsin-Warner Bros. Screenplay Ser.). (Illus.). 224p. 1980. 15.00 (ISBN 0-299-08090-0); pap. 5.95 (ISBN 0-299-08094-3). U of Wis Pr.

Kennedy, Joseph P., ed. The Story of Films. LC 74-160236. (Moving Pictures Ser). xxi, 377p. 1971. Repr. of 1927 ed. lib. bdg. 18.75x (ISBN 0-89198-037-7). Ozer.

Knight, Arthur. The Liveliest Art: A Panoramic History of the Movies. rev. ed. (Illus.). 1978. 19.95 (ISBN 0-02-564210-3). Macmillan.

Knowles, Eleanor. Films of Jeannette Macdonald & Nelson Eddy. LC 73-148. (Illus.). 640p. 1976. 25.00 (ISBN 0-498-01218-2). A S Barnes.

Koszarski, Richard, et al. The Rivals of D.W. Griffith: Alternate Auteurs, 1913 to 1918. (Illus.). 58p. (Orig.). 1980. pap. 4.95 (ISBN 0-918432-32-4). Ny Zoetrope.

Kreuger, Miles, ed. Souvenir Programs of Twelve Classic Movies: 1927-1941. LC 76-20162. (Illus.). 236p. 1977. pap. 6.50 (ISBN 0-486-23423-1). Dover.

--Souvenir Programs of Twelve Classics Movies, 1927-1941. 12.50 (ISBN 0-8446-5595-3). Peter Smith.

Lahue, Kalton C. Continued Next Week: A History of the Moving Picture Serial. (Illus.). 1969. Repr. of 1964 ed. 14.95x (ISBN 0-8061-0633-6). U of Okla Pr.

--World of Laughter: The Motion Picture Comedy Short 1910-1930. (Illus.). 1972. 10.95x (ISBN 0-8061-0693-X); pap. 5.95 (ISBN 0-8061-1254-9). U of Okla Pr.

Lasky, Michael S. & Harris, Robert A. The Films of Alfred Hitchcock. (Illus.). pap. 7.95 (ISBN 0-8065-0619-9). Citadel Pr.

Lee, Walt, ed. Fantastic Films: Nineteen Forty to Nineteen Forty-One. LC 78-52514. (Illus.). Date not set. 19.95 (ISBN 0-913974-05-6). Chelsea Lee Bks.

Levy, William T. & Scherle, Victor. The Films of Frank Capra. 1977. 16.95 (ISBN 0-8065-0430-7). Citadel Pr.

Liehm, Mira & Liehm, Antonin. The Most Important Art: East European Film After 1945. 1977. 28.50 (ISBN 0-520-03157-1); pap. 10.95 (ISBN 0-520-04128-3, CAL 474). U of Cal Pr.

Life Goes to the Movies. 300p. 1975. 24.95 (ISBN 0-8094-1643-3). Time-Life.

McCallum, John. Scooper. (Illus.). 1961. 8.95 (ISBN 0-8323-0191-4). Binford.

MacGowan, Kenneth. Behind the Screen. (Illus.). 1967. pap. 3.95 (ISBN 0-440-50528-3, Delta). Dell.

Madden, David. Harlequin's Stick, Charlie's Cane. (Illus.). 220p. 1975. 10.00 (ISBN 0-87972-058-1). Bowling Green Univ.

Magny, Claude-Edmonde. The Age of the American Novel: The Film Aesthetics of Fiction Between the Two Wars. Hochman, Eleanor, tr. from Fr. LC 77-178166. 256p. 1972. 11.50 (ISBN 0-8044-2586-8). Ungar.

Maltin, Leonard. The Great Movie Shorts. (Illus.). 1972. 9.95 (ISBN 0-517-50455-3). Crown.

Maltin, Leonard & Bann, Richard W. Our Gang: the Life & Times of the Little Rascals. 1979. 12.95 (ISBN 0-517-52675-1); pap. 7.95 (ISBN 0-517-53808-3). Crown.

Manvell, Roger & Jowett, Garth S., eds. The Cinema, 1950. LC 77-11380. (Aspects of Film Ser.). (Illus.). 1978. Repr. of 1950 ed. lib. bdg. 25.00x (ISBN 0-405-11139-8). Arno.

--The Cinema, 1951. LC 77-18644. (Aspects of Film Ser.). (Illus.). 1978. Repr. of 1951 ed. lib. bdg. 25.00x (ISBN 0-405-11145-2). Arno.

--The Cinema. 1952. LC 77-18645. (Aspects of Film Ser.). (Illus.). 1978. Repr. of 1952 ed. lib. bdg. 25.00x (ISBN 0-405-11146-0). Arno.

Marill, Alvin H. The Films of Anthony Quinn. 1977. pap. 6.95 (ISBN 0-8065-0570-2). Citadel Pr.

--Movies Made for Television: The Telefeature & the Mini-Series, 1964-1979. (Illus.). 1979. 30.00 (ISBN 0-87000-451-4). Arlington Hse.

Marvin, Edgar. When the Movies Began: First Film Stars. LC 78-15167. (Famous Firsts Ser.). (Illus.). 1978. lib. bdg. 7.35 (ISBN 0-686-51118-2). Silver.

Mast, Gerald. A Short History of the Movies. 3rd ed. (Illus.). 1981. 20.00 (ISBN 0-226-50982-6). U of Chicago Pr.

--A Short History of the Movies. 3rd ed. LC 80-18024. (Illus.). 516p. 1981. pap. text ed. 13.95 (ISBN 0-672-61521-5). Bobbs.

Meeker, David. Jazz in the Movies. 1978. 13.95 (ISBN 0-87000-403-4). Arlington Hse.

Meyer, William R. The Making of the Great Westerns. (Illus.). 1979. 20.00 (ISBN 0-87000-431-X). Arlington Hse.

Meyers, Richard. The World of Fantasy Films. LC 78-696400. (Illus.). 192p. 1980. 17.50 (ISBN 0-498-02213-7). A S Barnes.

Miller, Randall M., ed. The Kaleidoscopic Lens: How Hollywood Views Ethnic Groups. 1980. lib. bdg. 13.95x (ISBN 0-89198-120-9); pap. text ed. 6.95x (ISBN 0-89198-121-7). Ozer.

Montagu, Ivor. With Eisenstein in Hollywood. 356p. 1969. pap. 1.95 (ISBN 0-7178-0220-5). Intl Pub Co.

Mordden, Ethan. The Hollywood Musical. (Illus.). 256p. 1981. 15.95 (ISBN 0-312-38835-7). St Martin.

Morella, Joe, et al. The Films of World War Two. (Illus.). 256p. 1973. 12.00 (ISBN 0-8065-0365-3). Citadel Pr.

Morris, Peter. Embattled Shadows: A History of Canadian Cinema, 1895-1939. (Illus.). 1978. 19.95x (ISBN 0-7735-0322-6); pap. 7.95 (ISBN 0-7735-0323-4). McGill-Queens U Pr.

Moussinac, L. Panoramique Du Cinema. 1976. lib. bdg. 99.95 (ISBN 0-8490-2406-4). Gordon Pr.

Murphy, Michael J. The Celluloid Vampires: A History & Filmography, Eighteen Ninety-Seven to Nineteen Seventy-Nine. LC 79-84271. 1979. 14.95 (ISBN 0-87650-108-0). Pierian.

North, Joseph H. The Early Development of the Motion Picture, 1887-1909. LC 72-558. (Dissertations on Film Ser.). 316p. 1972. Repr. of 1949 ed. 18.00 (ISBN 0-405-04101-2). Arno.

Overbey, David, ed. Springtime in Italy: A Reader on Neo-Realism. 242p. 1979. 15.00 (ISBN 0-208-01824-7, Archon). Shoe String.

Parish, James R. The RKO Gals. (Illus.). 1978. pap. 7.95 (ISBN 0-89508-005-2). Rainbow Bks.

--The Tough Guys. (Illus.). 1978. pap. 7.95 (ISBN 0-89508-007-9). Rainbow Bks.

Parish, James R. & Mank, Gregory W. The Hollywood Reliables. (Illus.). 1979. 25.00 (ISBN 0-87000-430-1). Arlington Hse.

Parish, James R. & Pitts, Michael R. The Great Spy Pictures. LC 73-19509. (Illus.). 1974. 21.00 (ISBN 0-8108-0655-X). Scarecrow.

Parish, James R. & Stanke, Don E. The All-Americans. (Illus.). 1978. pap. 12.95 (ISBN 0-89508-011-7). Rainbow Bks.

--The Swashbucklers. (Illus.). 1978. pap. 7.95 (ISBN 0-89508-006-0). Rainbow Bks.

Peary, Danny. Cult Movies. 1981. pap. 12.95 (ISBN 0-440-51647-1, Delta). Dell.

Petruck, Peninah. The Camera Viewed: A Critical Anthology of Writings on Photography, 2 vols. (Illus.). 1979. Vol. I. pap. 9.95 (ISBN 0-525-47535-4); Vol. II. pap. 9.95 (ISBN 0-525-47536-2). Dutton.

Pitts, Michael R. Famous Movie Detectives. LC 79-17474. 367p. 1979. 18.50 (ISBN 0-8108-1236-3). Scarecrow.

Pye, Michael & Myles, Lynda. The Movie Brats: How the Film Generation Took Over Hollywood. LC 78-11901. 1979. 12.95 (ISBN 0-03-042671-5); pap. 5.95 (ISBN 0-03-042676-6). HR&W.

Quirk, Lawrence J. The Great Romantic Films. (Illus.). 256p. 1974. 12.00 (ISBN 0-8065-0401-3). Citadel Pr.

--The Great Romantic Films. (Illus.). 1976. pap. 7.95 (ISBN 0-8065-0539-7). Citadel Pr.

Rabkin, G. & Lauro, Al Di. Dirty Movies: An Illustrated History of the Stag Film 1915-1970. LC 76-43040. (Illus.). 160p. 1976. 15.00 (ISBN 0-87754-046-2). Chelsea Hse.

Reyes Nevares, Beatriz. The Mexican Cinema: Interviews with Thirteen Directors. Mora, Carl & Gard, Elizabeth, trs. from Span. LC 75-40835. (Illus.). 191p. 1976. 9.95x (ISBN 0-8263-0410-9); pap. 4.50x (ISBN 0-8263-0411-7). U of NM Pr.

Richards, Jeffrey. Swordsmen of the Screen: From Douglas Fairbanks to Michael York. (Cinema & Society Ser.). (Illus.). 312p. 1980. pap. 15.00 (ISBN 0-7100-0681-0). Routledge & Kegan.

Robinson, David. The History of World Cinema. rev. ed. LC 80-51767. (Illus.). 512p. 1981. 25.00 (ISBN 0-8128-2747-3). Stein & Day.

--The History of World Cinema. LC 76-187546. (Illus.). 440p. 1974. pap. 7.95 (ISBN 0-8128-1753-2). Stein & Day.

--Hollywood in the Twenties. LC 68-24002. (Hollywood Ser.). 1968. pap. 4.95 (ISBN 0-498-06926-5). A S Barnes.

Roffman, Peter & Purdy, Jim. The Hollywood Social Problem Film: Madness, Despair, & Politics from the Depression to the Fifties. LC 80-8100. (Midland Bks.: No. 261). (Illus.). 374p. 1981. 25.00x (ISBN 0-253-12707-6); pap. 12.95x (ISBN 0-253-20261-2). Ind U Pr.

Rovin, Jeff. The Fabulous Fantasy Films. LC 76-10876. (Illus.). 1977. 19.95 (ISBN 0-498-01803-2). A S Barnes.

Rubinstein, Leonard. The Great Spy Films. (Illus.). 256p. 1981. pap. 7.95 (ISBN 0-8065-0775-6). Citadel Pr.

Sands, Pierre N. A Historical Study of the Academy of Motion Picture Arts & Sciences, 1927-1947. LC 72-557. (Dissertations on Film Ser). 254p. 1972. 14.00 (ISBN 0-405-04100-4). Arno.

Sarris, Andrew. The History of the Cannes Film Festival, 1946-1979. (Illus.). 450p. Date not set. 14.95 (ISBN 0-87754-224-4). Chelsea Hse.

Saturday Evening Post Editors. The Saturday Evening Post Movie Book. LC 77-85389. (Illus.). 160p. 1977. 13.95 (ISBN 0-89387-013-7); pap. 7.95 (ISBN 0-686-30102-1). Curtis Pub Co.

Schary, Dore. Case History of a Movie. Kupelnick, Bruce S., ed. LC 76-52128. (Classics of Film Literature Ser.). 1978. lib. bdg. 18.00 (ISBN 0-8240-2893-7). Garland Pub.

Schulberg, Budd. Moving Pictures: Memories of a Hollywood Prince. LC 80-9055. 448p. 1981. 16.95 (ISBN 0-8128-2817-8). Stein & Day.

Shadoian, Jack. Dreams & Dead Ends: The American Gangster-Crime Film. 1977. pap. 6.95 (ISBN 0-262-69065-9). MIT Pr.

Shindler, Colin. Hollywood Goes to War. (Cinema & Society Ser.). (Illus.). 1979. 23.50 (ISBN 0-7100-0290-4). Routledge & Kegan.

Silver, Alain. The Samurai Film. LC 74-9299. (Illus.). 1977. 12.50 (ISBN 0-498-01349-9). A S Barnes.

Singer, Marilyn. A History of the American Avant-Garde Cinema. new ed. LC 76-3966. (Illus.). 1976. pap. text ed. 6.50 (ISBN 0-685-70896-9). Am Fed Arts.

Sitney, P. Adams. Visionary Film: The American Avant-Garde 1943-1978. 2nd ed. (Illus.). 1979. 19.95 (ISBN 0-19-502485-0). Oxford U Pr.

--Visionary Film: The American Avant-Garde 1943-1978. 2nd ed. (Illus.). 1979. pap. 7.95 (ISBN 0-19-502486-9, GB565, GB). Oxford U Pr.

Sklar, Robert. Movie-Made America: A Cultural History of American Movies. 1976. pap. 6.95 (ISBN 0-394-72120-9, Vin). Random.

Slide, Anthony. Aspects of American Film History Prior to 1920. LC 78-2912. 1978. 10.00 (ISBN 0-8108-1130-8). Scarecrow.

--Early American Cinema. LC 77-119639. (International Film Guide Ser). 1970. pap. 4.95 (ISBN 0-498-07717-9). A S Barnes.

--Films on Film History. LC 79-17662. 242p. 1979. 13.00 (ISBN 0-8108-1238-X). Scarecrow.

Solomon, Jon. The Ancient World in the Cinema. LC 77-74119. (Illus.). 1978. 19.95 (ISBN 0-498-02032-0). A S Barnes.

Solomon, Stanley J. The Film Idea. (Illus.). 403p. 1972. pap. text ed. 8.50 (ISBN 0-15-527375-2, HC). HarBraceJ.

Sorlin, Pierre. The Film in History: Restaging the Past. (Illus.). 226p. 1980. 21.50x (ISBN 0-389-20130-8). B&N.

Springer, John. Forgotten Films to Remember. (Illus.). 1980. 16.95 (ISBN 0-8065-0692-X). Citadel Pr.

Steinberg, Cobbett. Film Facts. 480p. 1980. 17.95 (ISBN 0-87196-313-2). Facts on File.

Steinbrunner, Chris & Michaels, Norman. The Films of Sherlock Holmes. (Illus.). 1978. 14.95 (ISBN 0-8065-0599-0). Citadel Pr.

Stern, Seymour & Jacobs, Lewis, eds. Experimental Cinema, Nos. 1-5. LC 70-103816. (Contemporary Art Ser). (Illus.). 1971. Repr. of 1934 ed. Set. 20.00 (ISBN 0-405-00739-6). Arno.

Stewart, John, compiled by. Filmarama: The Flaming Years, 1920-1929, Vol. 2. LC 75-2440. 1977. 30.00 (ISBN 0-8108-1008-5). Scarecrow.

Stoil, Michael J. Cinema Beyond the Danube: The Camera & Politics. LC 74-5274. 1974. 10.00 (ISBN 0-8108-0722-X). Scarecrow.

Strickland, A. W. & Ackerman, Forrest J. A Collection of Great Science Fiction Films. rev. ed. 200p. 1981. price not set (ISBN 0-89917-321-7). TIS Inc.

--Reference Guide to American Science Fiction Films: 1970-1980, Vol. IV. LC 81-51748. 400p. 1982. price not set (ISBN 0-89917-320-9). TIS Inc.
Tarbox, Charles H. Five Ages of the Cinema. (Illus.). 90p. 1980. 20.00 (ISBN 0-682-49618-9, Banner). Exposition.
Taylor, C. W. Masters & Masterpieces of the Screen. 95.00 (ISBN 0-87968-353-8). Gordon Pr.
Thomas, Tony. The Films of the Forties. (Illus.). 256p. 1975. 12.00 (ISBN 0-8065-0471-4). Citadel Pr.
--The Films of the Forties. 1977. pap. 6.95 (ISBN 0-8065-0571-0). Citadel Pr.
--The Great Adventure Films. 256p. 1976. 14.00 (ISBN 0-8065-0556-7). Citadel Pr.
--Hollywood & the American Image. (Illus.). 192p. 1981. 22.95 (ISBN 0-87000-525-1). Arlington Hse.
Thomas, Tony & Behlmer, Rudy. Hollywood's Hollywood. 1979. pap. 8.95 (ISBN 0-8065-0680-6). Citadel Pr.
Thorp, Margaret F. America at the Movies. 1946. 17.50 (ISBN 0-8482-7257-9). Norwood Edns.
Torrence, Bruce. Those Fabulous Film Factories: The History of Motion Picture Studios in California. (Illus.). 240p. Date not set. price not set (ISBN 0-87905-086-1). Peregrine Smith.
Vardac, A. Nicholas. Stage to Screen: Theatrical Method from Garrick to Griffith. LC 68-20251. (Illus.). 1968. Repr. of 1949 ed. 18.00 (ISBN 0-405-09039-0). Arno.
Vreeland, Frank. Foremost Films of 1938. lib. bdg. 95.00 (ISBN 0-87968-239-6). Gordon Pr.
Wagenknecht, Edward. The Movies in the Age of Innocence. (Illus.). 1962. pap. 6.95 (ISBN 0-8061-1297-2). U of Okla Pr.
Wald, Jerry & Macaulay, Richard. Best Motion Pictures of Nineteen Thirty-Nine to Forty: Year Book of Motion Pictures. lib. bdg. 95.00 (ISBN 0-87968-241-8). Gordon Pr.
Walker, Alexander. The Shattered Silents: How the Talkies Came to Stay. LC 79-88931. (Illus.). 1979. 10.95 (ISBN 0-688-03544-2). Morrow.
Wenden, D. J. The Birth of the Movies. 1975. pap. 5.95 (ISBN 0-525-47394-7). Dutton.
White, David M. & Averson, Richard. The Celluloid Weapon: Social Comment in the American Film. (Illus.). 288p. 1972. 14.95 (ISBN 0-8070-6170-0). Beacon Pr.
Williams, Carol T. The Dream Beside Me: The Movies & the Children of the Forties. LC 78-66858. 304p. 1980. 19.50 (ISBN 0-8386-2290-9). Fairleigh Dickinson.
Windeler, Robert. The Films of Shirley Temple. 1978. 14.95 (ISBN 0-8065-0615-6). Citadel Pr.
Wolf, William & Wolf, Lillian K. Landmark Films: The Cinema & Our Century. LC 79-14817. (Illus.). 1979. 14.95 (ISBN 0-448-23172-7). Paddington.
Zinman, David. Fifty from the 50'S. LC 78-14988. (Illus.). 1979. 25.00 (ISBN 0-87000-318-6). Arlington Hse.

MOVING-PICTURES–INDUSTRIAL APPLICATION

see Moving-Pictures in Industry

MOVING-PICTURES–JUVENILE LITERATURE

Andrews, Emma. The Films of Michael Caine. Castell, David, ed. (The Films of...Ser.). (Illus.). (gr. 7-12). 1978. Repr. of 1974 ed. PLB 5.95 (ISBN 0-912616-90-3). Greenhaven.
--The Films of Sean Connery. Castell, David, ed. (The Films of...Ser.). (Illus.). (gr. 7-12). 1978. Repr. of 1974 ed. PLB 5.95 (ISBN 0-912616-85-7). Greenhaven.
Avallone, Michael. Name That Movie: A Test Yourself Humor Book. (gr. 7 up). 1978. pap. 1.25 (ISBN 0-590-05392-2, Schol Pap). Schol Bk Serv.
Aylesworth, Thomas G. Monsters from the Movies. 160p. (gr. 4-6). 1981. pap. 1.95 (ISBN 0-553-15091-X, Skylark). Bantam.
Barsam, Richard M. In the Dark: A Primer for the Movies. (gr. 7 up). 1977. 10.00 (ISBN 0-670-39682-6). Viking Pr.
Bowskill, Derek. All About Cinema. 1976. 7.50 (ISBN 0-491-01716-2). Transatlantic.
Campbell, Joanna. The Films of Steve McQueen. Castell, David, ed. (The Films of... Ser.). (Illus.). (gr. 7-12). 1978. Repr. of 1973 ed. PLB 5.95 (ISBN 0-912616-84-9). Greenhaven.
Castell, David. The Films of Robert Redford. (The Films of... Ser.). (Illus.). (gr. 7-12). 1978. Repr. of 1973 ed. PLB 5.95 (ISBN 0-912616-77-6). Greenhaven.
D'Arcy, Susan. The Films of Liza Minelli. Castell, David, ed. (The Films of...Ser.). (Illus.). (gr. 7-12). 1978. Repr. of 1973 ed. PLB 5.95 (ISBN 0-912616-82-2). Greenhaven.
Edelson, Edward. Great Monsters of the Movies. (gr. 4-6). 1974. pap. 1.75 (ISBN 0-671-56108-1). Archway.
--Great Movie Spectaculars. (gr. 7-9). 1977. pap. 1.50 (ISBN 0-671-29994-8). Archway.
--Great Movies Spectaculars. (Illus.). (YA) (gr. 7-9). 1977. pap. 1.50 (ISBN 0-671-29994-8). PB.
Goldreich, Gloria & Goldreich, Esther. What Can She Be? A Film Producer. LC 77-8889. (What Can She Be? Ser.). (Illus.). (gr. 1-5). 1977. PLB 7.20 (ISBN 0-688-51815-X). Lothrop.
Levine, Michael L. Moviemaking: A Guide for Beginners. LC 80-19314. (Illus.). 48p. (gr. 5 up). 1980. 9.95 (ISBN 0-684-16707-7). Scribner.
Manchel, Frank. An Album of Great Science Fiction Films. (Picture Albums Ser.). (gr. 5 up). 1976. PLB 6.90 (ISBN 0-531-00345-0). Watts.
--Gangsters on the Screen. LC 78-5953. (Illus.). (gr. 6 up). 1978. PLB 7.90 s&l (ISBN 0-531-01471-1). Watts.
Newton, Sandra. Enjoying the Arts: Film. (YA) 1978. PLB 7.97 (ISBN 0-8239-0395-8). Rosen Pr.
Priest, Christopher. Your Book of Film Making. (gr. 7-9). 1974. 7.95 (ISBN 0-571-10463-0). Transatlantic.
Quackenbush, Robert. Movie Monsters & Their Masters: The Birth of the Horror Film. Tucker, Kathleen, ed. LC 79-27291. (Illus.). (gr. 3 up). 1980. 6.95g (ISBN 0-8075-5299-2). A Whitman.
--Who Threw That Pie? The Birth of Movie Comedy. Pacini, Kathy, ed. LC 78-27047. (Illus.). (gr. 3 up). 1979. 6.95g (ISBN 0-8075-9058-4). A Whitman.
Ronan, Margaret. The Dynamite Kids' Guide to the Movies. 80p. (Orig.). (gr. 3 up). 1980. pap. 3.95 (ISBN 0-590-31228-6, Schol Pap). Schol Bk Serv.
Schoen, Juliet P. Silents to Sound: A History of the Movies. LC 76-16092. (Illus.). 192p. (gr. 7 up). 1976. 7.95 (ISBN 0-590-07337-0, Four Winds). Schol Bk Serv.
Snow White & the Seven Dwarfs. (Illus.). 1979. 29.95 (ISBN 0-670-65381-0, Studio). Viking Pr.
Thurman, Judith & David, Jonathan. The Magic Lantern: How Movies Got to Move. LC 78-5197. (Illus.). (gr. 4-6). 1978. 8.95 (ISBN 0-689-30628-8). Atheneum.
Weinberg, Larry. Star Wars: The Making of the Movie. LC 80-13500. (Step-up Book: No. 32). (Illus.). 72p. (gr. 2-5). 1980. bds. 4.95 (ISBN 0-394-84493-9); PLB 4.99 (ISBN 0-394-94493-3). Random.
Weiss, Harvey. How to Make Your Own Movies. LC 72-11650. (Illus.). 96p. (gr. 5 up). 1973. PLB 8.95 (ISBN 0-201-09310-3, A-W Childrens). A-W.
Williams, John. The Films of Charlton Heston. Castell, David, ed. (The Films of...Ser.). (Illus.). (gr. 7-12). 1978. Repr. of 1974 ed. PLB 5.95 (ISBN 0-912616-80-6). Greenhaven.
--The Films of Roger Moore. Castell, David, ed. (The Films of...Ser.). (Illus.). (gr. 7-12). 1979. Repr. of 1974 ed. PLB 5.95 (ISBN 0-912616-89-X). Greenhaven.

MOVING-PICTURES–LAW

see also Copyright–Moving-Pictures

American Society of Composers, Authors & Publishers (ASCAP) Copyright Law Symposium: Proceedings. Incl. No. 4. 1952. 17.50x (ISBN 0-231-02081-3); No. 5. 1954. 17.50x (ISBN 0-231-02025-2); No. 6. 1955. 17.50x (ISBN 0-231-02091-0); No. 8. 1957. 17.50x (ISBN 0-231-02192-5); No. 9. 1958; No. 10. 1959. 17.50x (ISBN 0-231-02351-0); No. 11. 1962. 17.50x (ISBN 0-231-02528-9); No. 13. 1964; No. 14; No. 15. 1967. 17.50x (ISBN 0-231-03004-5); No. 16. 1968. 17.50x (ISBN 0-231-03167-X); No. 17. 1969. 17.50x (ISBN 0-231-03235-8); No. 18. 1970. 17.50x (ISBN 0-231-03411-3); No. 19. 1971. 17.50x (ISBN 0-231-03521-7); No. 20. 7.50x (ISBN 0-231-03636-1). LC 40-8341. Columbia U Pr.
Baumgarten, Paul A. & Leavy, Morton L. Legal & Business Problems of Financing Motion Pictures, 1979. LC 78-88389. (Patents, Copyrights, Trademarks, & Literary Property Course Handbook Ser.: 1978-1979). 1979. pap. text ed. 20.00 (ISBN 0-686-59550-5, G4-3658). PLI.
Conant, Michael. Antitrust in the Motion Picture Industry. Jowett, Garth S., ed. LC 77-11372. (Aspects of Film Ser.). (Illus.). 1978. Repr. of 1960 ed. lib. bdg. 20.00x (ISBN 0-405-11128-2). Arno.
Minus, Johnny, et al. Film-TV Law (Your Introduction to Film-TV Copyright, Contracts & Other Law) LC 73-75217. (The Entertainment Industry Ser. Vol. 7). (Illus.). 240p. 1973. 10.00 (ISBN 0-911370-09-9). Seven Arts.
Terrou, Fernand & Solal, Lucien. Legislation for Press, Film & Radio: Comparative Study of the Main Types of Regulations Governing the Information Media. LC 72-4680. (International Propaganda & Communications Ser.). 420p. 1972. Repr. of 1951 ed. 24.00 (ISBN 0-405-04764-9). Arno.
U. S. House of Representatives, Committee on Education. Federal Motion Picture Commission. Jowett, Garth S., ed. LC 77-11385. (Aspects of Film Ser.). 1978. Repr. of 1916 ed. lib. bdg. 22.00x (ISBN 0-405-11135-5). Arno.
Young, Donald R. Motion Pictures: A Study in Social Legislation. LC 79-160248. (Moving Pictures Ser). vi, 109p. 1971. Repr. of 1922 ed. lib. bdg. 7.75x (ISBN 0-89198-049-0). Ozer.

MOVING-PICTURES–MISCELLANEA

Altman, Richard. And the Envelopes Please. LC 77-26775. 1978. pap. 3.95 (ISBN 0-397-01270-5). Har-Row.
Andree, Mary. Movie Trivia! Everything You Always Knew About Movies...but Thought You Forgot. Pohl, Jude C., ed. 72p. (Orig.). 1977. pap. 4.00 (ISBN 0-939332-01-9). Pohl Assoc.
Bresson, Robert. Notes on Cinematography. Griffen, Jonathan, tr. 1977. 6.95 (ISBN 0-916354-28-8); pap. 3.50 (ISBN 0-916354-29-6). Urizen Bks.
Burt, Rob. The Illustrated Movie Quiz Book. (Illus.). 96p. 1981. 5.95 (ISBN 0-8317-6112-1, Rutledge Pr). Smith Pubs.
--Illustrated Movie Quiz Book. 96p. (YA) 1981. pap. 5.95 (ISBN 0-8317-6112-1, Mayflower Bks). Smith Pubs.
Clifton, N. Roy. The Figure in Film. LC 80-54539. 580p. 1982. 35.00 (ISBN 0-87413-189-8). U Delaware Pr.
Gardner, Gerald & Gardner, Harriet M. The Tara Treasury. (Illus.). 192p. 1980. 19.95 (ISBN 0-87000-482-4). Arlington Hse.
Glut, Donald F. Classic Movie Monsters. LC 77-16014. (Illus.). 1978. 18.00 (ISBN 0-8108-1049-2). Scarecrow.
Gordon, R., ed. Move Humor Anthology, 2 vols. 1976. lib. bdg. 200.00 (ISBN 0-8490-2301-7). Gordon Pr.
The Great TV & Movie Quiz. (Illus.). 256p. 1981. 5.95 (ISBN 0-686-31188-4, 3000). Playmore & Prestige.
Gross, Martin A. The Official Movie Trivia Quiz Book No. 2. 1978. pap. 1.50 (ISBN 0-451-07898-5, W7898, Sig). NAL.
Haun, Harry. The Movie Quote Book. LC 80-7865. 500p. 1980. 22.00 (ISBN 0-690-02000-7). Har-Row.
Haydock, Ron. Deerstalker! Holmes & Watson on the Screen. LC 77-24465. 1978. 15.00 (ISBN 0-8108-1061-1). Scarecrow.
Henkin, Bill. The Rocky Horror Picture Show Book. LC 79-63619. (Illus., Orig.). 1979. pap. 8.95 (ISBN 0-8015-6436-0, Hawthorn). Dutton.
Howard, John M. The Movie Murder Mystery Quiz Book. LC 79-25871. (Illus.). 160p. 1980. pap. 9.95 (ISBN 0-498-02522-5). A S Barnes.
Libby, Bill. They Didn't Win the Oscars. (Illus.). 256p. 1980. 18.95 (ISBN 0-87000-455-7). Arlington Hse.
Medved, Harry & Medved, Michael. The Golden Turkey Awards. x ed. 1980. pap. 6.95 (ISBN 0-399-50463-X, Perigee). Putnam.
Rovin, Jeff. The Films of Charlton Heston. (The Films of...Ser.). (Illus.). 256p. 1980. pap. 7.95 (ISBN 0-8065-0741-1). Citadel Pr.
--The UFO Movie Quiz Book. (Illus., Orig.). 1978. pap. 1.50 (ISBN 0-451-08258-3, W8258, Sig). NAL.
Schapiro, Steve & Chierichetti, David. The Movie Poster Book. (Illus.). 1980. 19.95 (ISBN 0-525-93069-8); pap. 10.95 (ISBN 0-525-47501-X). Dutton.
Steinberg, Cobbett, ed. Reel Facts: The Movie Book of Records. 1978. pap. 3.95 (ISBN 0-394-72416-X, Vin). Random.
Steinbrunner, Christopher & Michaels, Norman. The Films of Sherlock Holmes. (The Films of...Ser.). 256p. 1980. pap. 9.95 (ISBN 0-8065-0739-X). Citadel Pr.
Taylor, Derek. The Making of Raiders of the Lost Ark. 192p. 1981. pap. 2.75 (ISBN 0-345-29725-3). Ballantine.
Thomas, Tony. The Great Adventure Films. (The Films of...Ser.). (Illus.). 256p. 1980. pap. 7.95 (ISBN 0-8065-0747-0). Citadel Pr.
Trojan, Judith & Covert, Nadine, eds. Sixteen Millimeter Distribution. (Illus.). 1977. pap. 6.00 (ISBN 0-87520-000-1). EFLA.
TV & Movie Puzzles. (Illus.). 544p. 1981. pap. 7.95 (ISBN 0-686-31163-9, 2503). Playmore & Prestige.
Vance, Malcolm. The Movie Ad Book. (Illus.). 160p. 1981. 15.95 (ISBN 0-89893-503-2); pap. 9.95 (ISBN 0-89893-301-3). CDP.

MOVING-PICTURES–MONTAGE

see Moving-Pictures–Editing

MOVING-PICTURES–MORAL AND RELIGIOUS ASPECTS

see also Sex in Moving-Pictures

Adler, Mortimer J. Art & Prudence. Jowett, Garth S., ed. LC 77-11371. (Aspects of Film Ser.). 1978. Repr. of 1937 ed. lib. bdg. 45.00x (ISBN 0-405-11126-6). Arno.
Blumer, Herbert. Movies & Conduct. LC 76-124023. (Literature of Cinema Ser.: Payne Fund Studies of Motion Pictures & Social Values). Repr. of 1933 ed. 12.00 (ISBN 0-405-01640-9). Arno.
Blumer, Herbert & Hauser, Philip M. Movies, Delinquency, - Crime. LC 70-124024. (Literature of Cinema Ser.: Payne Fund Studies of Motion Pictures & Social Values). Repr. of 1933 ed. 11.00 (ISBN 0-405-01641-7). Arno.
Cinema Commission Of Inquiry. Cinema: Its Present Position & Future Possibilities. LC 78-124002. (Literature of Cinema Ser). Repr. of 1917 ed. 15.00 (ISBN 0-405-01608-5). Arno.
Dale, Edgar. Content of Motion Pictures. LC 77-124026. (Literature of Cinema Ser: Payne Fund Studies of Motion Pictures & Social Values). Repr. of 1935 ed. 12.00 (ISBN 0-405-01644-1). Arno.
Lindsay, Gordon. Should Christians Attend Movies? 0.95 (ISBN 0-89985-007-3). Christ Nations.
Martin, Olga J. Hollywood's Movie Commandments, a Handbook for Motion Picture Writers & Reviewers. LC 77-124018. (Literature of Cinema, Ser. 1). Repr. of 1937 ed. 9.00 (ISBN 0-405-01624-7). Arno.
Martin, Thomas M. Images & the Imageless: A Study in Religious Consciousness & Film. LC 79-57611. 200p. 1981. 20.00 (ISBN 0-8387-5005-2). Bucknell U Pr.
Oberholtzer, Ellis P. The Morals of the Movie. LC 74-160244. (Moving Pictures Ser). 251p. 1971. Repr. of 1922 ed. lib. bdg. 14.25x (ISBN 0-89198-045-8). Ozer.
Peters, Charles C. Motion Pictures & Standards of Morality. LC 72-124030. (Literature of Cinema Ser.: Payne Fund Studies). Repr. of 1933 ed. 9.00 (ISBN 0-405-01648-4). Arno.
Peterson, Ruth C. & Thurstone, L. L. Motion Pictures & the Social Attitudes of Children. Bd. with The Social Conduct & Attitudes of Movie Fans. Shuttleworth, Frank K. & May, Mark A.. LC 76-124031. (Literature of Cinema Ser: Payne Fund Studies). Repr. of 1933 ed. 8.00 (ISBN 0-405-01631-X). Arno.
Schumach, Murray. The Face on the Cutting Room Floor: The Story of Music & Television Censorship. LC 73-19776. (Civil Liberties in American History Ser.). (Illus.). 306p. 1974. Repr. of 1956 ed. lib. bdg. 19.50 (ISBN 0-306-70603-2). Da Capo.
Tozer, A. H. Menace of the Religious Movie. 1974. pap. 1.00 (ISBN 0-685-89800-8, 51-X). Rapids Christian.
White, John Wesley. Man from Krypton: The Gospel According to Superman. LC 78-73455. 1978. pap. 2.25 (ISBN 0-87123-384-3, 200384). Bethany Hse.

MOVING-PICTURES–MUSICAL ACCOMPANIMENT

see Moving-Picture Music

MOVING-PICTURES–PICTORIAL WORKS

Anglund, Dale & Hirsch, Janis. Gone with the Ape. 1977. pap. 3.95 (ISBN 0-425-03480-1, Windhover). Berkley Pub.
Appelbaum, Stanley & Cirker, Hayward. The Movies: A Picture Quiz Book. (Illus.). 128p. (Orig.). 1972. pap. 3.00 (ISBN 0-486-20222-4). Dover.
Blum, Daniel. A Pictorial History of the Silent Screen. (Illus.). 1972. pap. 6.95 (ISBN 0-399-11098-4). Putnam.
Blum, Daniel & Kobal, John. A New Pictorial History of the Talkies. rev. ed. (Illus.). 384p. 1973. pap. 7.95 (ISBN 0-399-11231-6). Putnam.
Franklin, Joe. Classics of the Silent Screen. (Illus.). 1967. pap. 6.95 (ISBN 0-8065-0181-2, C255). Citadel Pr.
Griffith, Richard, et al. The Movies. rev. ed. (Illus.). 1981. 24.95 (ISBN 0-671-42765-2). S&S.
Lacy, Madison S. & Morgan, Don. Leg Art: Sixty Years of Hollywood Cheesecake. (Illus.). 256p. 1981. 19.95 (ISBN 0-8065-0734-9). Citadel Pr.
Life Goes to the Movies. 300p. 1975. 24.95 (ISBN 0-8094-1643-3). Time-Life.
Pratt, William & Bridges, Herbert. Scarlett Fever: The Ultimate Pictorial Treasury of "Gone with the Wind". (Illus.). 1977. 16.95 (ISBN 0-02-598560-4). Macmillan.
Seemayer, Stephen. The Young Turks. (Illus.). 160p. (Orig.). 1981. pap. 8.00 (ISBN 0-937122-06-8). Astro Artz.
Selling Dreams. (Illus.). 84p. 1980. pap. 7.95 (ISBN 0-905171-20-9, Pub. by Welsh Art Council). Intl Schol Bk Serv.
Sherman, David G., ed. Life Goes to the Movies. 1977. pap. 8.95 (ISBN 0-671-79000-5, Wallaby). PB.
Skogsberg, Bertil. Wings on the Screen. Bisset, George, tr. from Swedish. LC 81-4790. (Illus.). 192p. 1981. 25.00 (ISBN 0-498-02495-4). A S Barnes.
Slide, Anthony & Wagenknecht, Edward. Fifty Great American Silent Films 1912-1920: A Pictorial Survey. Date not set. 12.50 (ISBN 0-8446-5813-8). Peter Smith.

Weegee, pseud. Naked Hollywood. LC 75-4767. (Photography Ser). (Illus.). 124p. 1975. lib. bdg. 16.50 (ISBN 0-306-70728-4); pap. 6.95 (ISBN 0-306-80047-0). Da Capo.
Winchester, C., ed. The Wonder Album of Filmland. 1976. lib. bdg. 150.00 (ISBN 0-8490-2837-X). Gordon Pr.

MOVING-PICTURES–PLAY-WRITING
see Moving-Picture Authorship

MOVING-PICTURES–PLOTS, THEMES, ETC.
Films on specific topics are entered under specific headings, e.g. Horror Films; War Films; Children in Motion Pictures; Death in Motion Pictures.
see also Film Adaptations

Aylesworth, Thomas G. Monsters from the Movies. LC 72-1995. (Illus.). 160p. (gr. 5-9). 1972. PLB 8.95 (ISBN 0-397-31590-2, JBL-J); pap. 3.50 (ISBN 0-397-31415-9, LSC-15). Har-Row.
Brode, Douglas. The Films of the Fifties. (Illus.). 288p. 1976. 14.00 (ISBN 0-8065-0510-9). Citadel Pr.
Butler, Ivan. Religion in the Cinema. LC 69-14897. 1969. pap. 4.95 (ISBN 0-498-07417-X). A S Barnes.
Campbell, Edward D., Jr. The Celluloid South: Hollywood & the Southern Myth. LC 81-7457. (Illus.). 256p. 1981. 17.50x (ISBN 0-87049-327-2). U of Tenn Pr.
Corliss, Richard. Talking Pictures: Screenwriters in the American Cinema. LC 72-94413. 416p. 1974. 20.00 (ISBN 0-87951-007-2). Overlook Pr.
DeFelice, James. Filmguide to Odd Man Out. LC 74-6519. (Filmguide Ser.: No. 9). 96p. 1975. 6.95x (ISBN 0-253-39317-5); pap. 1.95x (ISBN 0-253-39318-3). Ind U Pr.
Dickey, James. Deliverance. (Screenplay Library Ser.). (Illus.). 184p. 1981. price not set (ISBN 0-8093-1029-5); pap. price not set (ISBN 0-8093-1030-9). S Ill U Pr.
Everson, William K. Bad Guys: A Pictorial History of the Movie Villain. (Photos). 1968. pap. 6.95 (ISBN 0-8065-0198-7, C264). Citadel Pr.
--The Detective in Film. (Illus.). 256p. 1972. 9.95 (ISBN 0-8065-0298-3). Citadel Pr.
--The Detective in Film. (Illus.). 256p. (Orig.). 1974. pap. 6.95 (ISBN 0-8065-0448-X). Citadel Pr.
Gehring, Wes D. Leo McCarey & the Comic Anti-Hero in American Film. Jowett, Garth S., ed. LC 79-6677. (Dissertations on Film, 1980 Ser.). 1980. lib. bdg. 22.00x (ISBN 0-405-12911-4). Arno.
Gordon, R., ed. Moving Picture Stories Anthology, 6 vols. 1976. lib. bdg. 995.00 (ISBN 0-8490-2303-3). Gordon Pr.
--Picture-Play Magazine Anthology, 6 vols. 1976. lib. bdg. 995.00 (ISBN 0-8490-2440-4). Gordon Pr.
Haddad-Garcia, George. The Films of Jane Fonda. (Illus.). 256p. 1981. 16.95 (ISBN 0-8065-0752-7). Citadel Pr.
Henry, Marilyn & DeSourdis, Ron. The Films of Alan Ladd. (Illus.). 256p. 1981. 16.95 (ISBN 0-8065-0736-5). Citadel Pr.
Hill, W. Aber. Ten Million Photoplay Plots. Kupelnick, Bruce S., ed. LC 76-52108. (Classics of Film Literature Ser.). 1978. lib. bdg. 15.00 (ISBN 0-8240-2879-1). Garland Pub.
Jeavons, Clyde. A Pictorial History of War Films. (Illus.). 224p. 1974. 12.00 (ISBN 0-8065-0426-9). Citadel Pr.
Jordan, Thomas. The Anatomy of Cinematic Humor, with an Analytic Essay on the Marx Brothers. (Cinema Ser). 1974. write for info. (ISBN 0-87700-205-3); lib. bdg. 69.95 (ISBN 0-685-50723-8). Revisionist Pr.
Karpf, Stephen L. The Gangster Film: Emergence, Variation & Decay of a Genre, 1930-1940. LC 72-555. (Dissertations on Film Ser.). 306p. 1970. 18.00 (ISBN 0-405-04098-9). Arno.
Kinder, Marsha & Houston, Beverle. The Self & Cinema. 1980. pap. 12.70 (ISBN 0-913178-62-4). Redgrave Pub Co.
Look Magazine, ed. Movie Lot to Beachhead: The Motion Picture Goes to War & Prepares for the Future. LC 79-6696. 1980. Repr. of 1945 ed. lib. bdg. 26.00x (ISBN 0-405-12935-1). Arno.
McConnell, Frank. Storytelling & Mythmaking: Images from Film & Literature. LC 78-27538. (Illus.). 1979. 13.95 (ISBN 0-19-502572-5). Oxford U Pr.
Medved, Harry & Medved, Michael. The Golden Turkey Awards. 400p. 1981. Repr. pap. 3.50 (ISBN 0-425-05187-0). Berkley Pub.
Mellen, Joan. Big Bad Wolves: Masculinity in American Films. LC 77-5189. 1978. 12.95 (ISBN 0-394-49800-3). Pantheon.
Menville, Douglas. A Historical & Critical Survey of the Science Fiction Film. new ed. LC 74-16509. (Science Fiction Ser). 177p. 1975. 11.00x (ISBN 0-405-06330-X). Arno.
Neale, Stephen. Genre. (BFI Ser.). (Orig.). 1980. pap. 7.25 (ISBN 0-85170-094-2). NY Zoetrope.
O'Connor, John E. & Jackson, Martin A., eds. American History, American Film: Interpreting the Hollywood Image. LC 78-4295. (Ungar Film Library). (Illus.). 1979. 12.50 (ISBN 0-8044-2663-5); pap. 6.95 (ISBN 0-8044-6616-5). Ungar.
Ottoson, Robert. A Reference Guide to the American Film Noir: 1940-1958. LC 80-23176. 290p. 1981. 15.00 (ISBN 0-8108-1363-7). Scarecrow.
Palmer, F. Photoplay Plot Encyclopedia. 1976. lib. bdg. 59.95 (ISBN 0-8490-2437-4). Gordon Pr.
Parish, James R. & Pitts, Michael R. Great Gangster Pictures. LC 75-32402. (Illus.). 1976. 18.00 (ISBN 0-8108-0881-1). Scarecrow.
Rose, Brian G. An Examination of Narrative Structure in Four Films of Frank Capra. Jowett, Garth S., ed. LC 79-6683. (Dissertations on Film, 1980 Ser.). 1980. lib. bdg. 22.00x (ISBN 0-405-12915-7). Arno.
Rubenstein, Leonard. The Great Spy Films: A Pictorial History. (Illus.). 1979. 14.95 (ISBN 0-8065-0663-6). Citadel Pr.
Russo, Vito. The Celluloid Closet: Homosexuality in the Movies. LC 79-1682. (Illus.). 256p. 1981. 15.00 (ISBN 0-06-013704-5, HarpT); pap. 7.95 (ISBN 0-06-090871-8, CN871, HarpT). Har-Row.
Silver, Alain & Ward, Elizabeth. Film Noir: An Encyclopedic Reference to the American Style. LC 76-47092. (Illus.). 400p. 1980. 25.00 (ISBN 0-87951-055-2). Overlook Pr.
Siska, William C. Modernism in the Narrative Cinema. Jowett, Garth S., ed. LC 79-6686. (Dissertations on Film, 1980 Ser.). 1980. lib. bdg. 15.00x (ISBN 0-405-12918-1). Arno.
Tyler, Parker. A Pictorial History of Sex in Films. (Illus.). 256p. 1974. 14.95 (ISBN 0-8065-0443-9). Citadel Pr.
Williams, Alan L. Max Ophuls & the Cinema of Desire. abridged ed. Jowett, Garth S., ed. LC 79-6693. (Dissertations on Film, 1980 Ser.). 1980. lib. bdg. 18.00x (ISBN 0-405-12924-6). Arno.
Willis, Donald C. Horror & Science Fiction Films: A Checklist. LC 72-3682. 1972. 21.00 (ISBN 0-8108-0508-1). Scarecrow.

MOVING-PICTURES–PRODUCTION AND DIRECTION
see also Moving-Picture Producers and Directors

Accounting for Motion Picture Films. 1973. pap. 3.50 (ISBN 0-685-39831-5). Am Inst CPA.
Adams, William B. Handbook of Motion Picture Production. LC 76-51818. (Wiley Ser. on Human Communication). 352p. 1977. 29.50 (ISBN 0-471-00459-6, Pub. by Wiley-Interscience). Wiley.
Agel, Jerome, ed. The Making of Kubrick's 2001. (Film Ser.). (RL 10). 1972. pap. 1.95 (ISBN 0-451-07139-5, J7139, Sig). NAL.
Amberg, George, et al. Art of Cinema: Selected Essays. LC 75-124020. (Arno Press Cinema Program). (Illus.). 106p. 1972. Repr. of 1971 ed. 10.00 (ISBN 0-405-03924-7). Arno.
Anderson, Lindsay. Making a Film. LC 76-52087. (Classics of Film Literature Ser.: Vol. 1). (Illus.). 1977. Repr. of 1952 ed. lib. bdg. 18.00 (ISBN 0-8240-2863-5). Garland Pub.
Arijon, Daniel. Grammar of the Film Language. (Illus.). 650p. 1976. text ed. 35.00 (ISBN 0-240-50779-7). Focal Pr.
Arnold, Alan. Once Upon a Galaxy: A Journal of the Making of the Empire Strikes Back. 1980. pap. 2.75 (ISBN 0-345-29075-5, Del Rey Bks). Ballantine.
Bacher, L. The Mobile Mise En Scene: A Critical Analysis of the Theory & Practice of Long Take Camera Movement in the Narrative Film. LC 77-22904. (Dissertations on Film Ser.). 1978. lib. bdg. 18.00x (ISBN 0-405-10750-1). Arno.
Bare, Richard L. The Film Director: A Practical Guide to Motion Pictures & Television Techniques. LC 76-130944. (Illus.). 256p. 1973. pap. 4.95 (ISBN 0-02-012130-X, Collier). Macmillan.
Beckman, Henry. How to Sell Your Film Project. (Orig.). 1979. pap. 9.95 (ISBN 0-523-40624-X). Pinnacle Bks.
Bension, Shmuel. New York Production Manual 1979-80: The "Producer's Masterguide" for Motion Picture, Television, Commercials & Videotape Industries. 1979. pap. 35.00 (ISBN 0-935744-00-2). NY Prod Manual.
--New York Production Manual 1981: "The Producer's Masterguide" for: Motion Picture, Television, Commercials & Videotape Industries. 1000p. (Orig.). 1981. pap. 49.50 (ISBN 0-935744-01-0). NY Prod Manual.
Bobker, Lee. Making Movies: From Script to Screen. 1973. pap. text ed. 12.95 (ISBN 0-15-554630-9, HC). HarBraceJ.
Bogdanovich, Peter. Pieces of Time: Peter Bogdanovich on the Movies. LC 73-82189. 1973. 7.95 (ISBN 0-87795-069-5). Arbor Hse.
Broughton, James. Seeing the Light. LC 76-30681. 1977. pap. 3.00 (ISBN 0-87286-090-6). City Lights.
Brown, Geoff. Launder & Gilliat. (BFI Ser.). (Orig.). 1978. pap. 8.25 (ISBN 0-85170-071-3). NY Zoetrope.
Brown, Kent R. The Screenwriter As Collaborator. Jowett, Garth S., ed. LC 79-6669. (Dissertations on Film, 1980 Ser.). 1980. lib. bdg. 24.00x (ISBN 0-405-12903-3). Arno.
Burch, Noel. Theory of Film Practice. Lane, Helen R., tr. from French. LC 80-8676. (Illus.). 172p. 1981. 18.50x (ISBN 0-691-03962-3); pap. 5.95 (ISBN 0-691-00329-7). Princeton U Pr.
Callaghan, Barry. Van Nostrand Reinhold Manual of Film-Making. 1973. 9.95 (ISBN 0-442-21445-6). Van Nos Reinhold.
Ciment, Michel. Kazan on Kazan. LC 73-11978. (Cinema One Ser). (Illus.). 176p. 1974. 7.50 (ISBN 0-670-41187-6). Viking Pr.
Cornford, Adam. Shooting Scripts. (Illus.). 1979. 25.00 (ISBN 0-686-28250-7); pap. 10.00 (ISBN 0-686-28251-5). Black Stone.
Costa, Sylvia. How to Prepare a Production Budget for Film & Video Tape. 2nd ed. LC 75-27372. 196p. 1975. 12.95 (ISBN 0-8306-5845-9, 845). TAB Bks.
Croy, Homer. How Motion Pictures Are Made. Jowett, Garth S., ed. LC 77-11373. (Aspects of Film Ser.). (Illus.). 1978. Repr. of 1918 ed. lib. bdg. 30.00x (ISBN 0-405-11129-0). Arno.
--How Motion Pictures Are Made. 1978. Repr. of 1918 ed. lib. bdg. 45.00 (ISBN 0-89760-107-6, Telegraph). Dynamic Learn Corp.
Daly, David A. A Comparison of Exhibition & Distribution Patterns in Three Recent Feature Motion Pictures. abridged ed. Jowett, Garth S., ed. LC 79-6672. (Dissertations on Film, 1980). lib. bdg. 20.00x (ISBN 0-405-12906-8). Arno.
Denton, Clive & Canham, Kingsley. The Hollywood Professionals, Vol. 5: Vidor, Cromwell, & Leroy. LC 72-1786. (Illus.). 192p. 1976. pap. 4.95 (ISBN 0-498-01689-7). A S Barnes.
Eastman Kodak Company, ed. Basic Production Techniques for Motion Pictures. 2nd ed. LC 76-16716. (Illus.). 62p. (Orig.). 1976. pap. 5.00 (ISBN 0-87985-004-3, P18). Eastman Kodak.
Edmonds, Robert. Sights & Sounds of Cinema. 1982. text ed. price not set (ISBN 0-8077-2680-X); pap. text ed. price not set (ISBN 0-8077-2679-6). Tchrs Coll.
Eisenstein, S. M. Que Viva Mexico! LC 70-169341. (Arno Press Cinema Program). (Illus.). 94p. 1972. Repr. of 1951 ed. 8.00 (ISBN 0-405-03916-6). Arno.
Eisenstein, Sergei. Notes of a Film Director. (Illus.). 6.75 (ISBN 0-8446-0087-3). Peter Smith.
Ellis, Reed. A Journey into Darkness. Jowett, Garth S., ed. LC 79-6673. (Dissertations on Film, 1980). 1980. lib. bdg. 19.00x (ISBN 0-405-12908-4). Arno.
Film Daily Directors Annual & Production Guide, 1929-1937, 8 vols. 50.00 ea. Gordon Pr.
Francisco, Charles. You Must Remember This: The Filming of Casablanca. LC 80-18176. 1980. 10.00 (ISBN 0-13-977058-5). P-H.
Gehring, Wes D. Leo McCarey & the Comic Anti-Hero in American Film. Jowett, Garth S., ed. LC 79-6677. (Dissertations on Film, 1980 Ser.). 1980. lib. bdg. 22.00x (ISBN 0-405-12911-4). Arno.
Glimcher, Sumner & Johnson, Warren. Movie Making: A Guide to Film Production. new ed. LC 74-34300. (Illus.). 236p. 1975. 15.00x (ISBN 0-231-03962-X). Columbia U Pr.
Godden, Rumer. The Tale of the Tales. LC 79-166292. (Illus.). 1971. 21.95 (ISBN 0-7232-1421-2). Warne.
Goldstein, Laurence & Kaufman, Jay. Into Film, 2 vols. 1976. Set. pap. 12.95 (ISBN 0-525-47315-7). Dutton.
Gregory, Mollie. Making Films Your Business. LC 79-14428. 1979. 14.50x (ISBN 0-8052-3728-3); pap. text ed. 6.95 (ISBN 0-8052-0639-6). Schocken.
Gulliver, William C. & Gulliver, Ann W. A Guide to Creative Filmmaking. LC 73-92154. (Illus.). 144p. (Orig.). (gr. 6-12). 1974. pap. text ed. 1.45 (ISBN 0-88301-128-X). Pendulum Pr.
Hacker, Leonard. Cinematic Design. Jowett, Garth S., ed. LC 77-11375. (Aspects of Film Ser.). (Illus.). 1978. Repr. of 1931 ed. lib. bdg. 16.00x (ISBN 0-405-11131-2). Arno.
Haller, Robert A. & Haller, Robert S., eds. Brakhage Scrapbook: Collected Writings, 1964 to 1980. (Illus.). 256p. 1981. 16.95x (ISBN 0-914232-46-0); pap. 9.95x (ISBN 0-914232-45-2); ltd. signed ed. 35.00x (ISBN 0-914232-47-9). Treacle.
Harmetz, Aljean. The Making of the Wizard of Oz. 1977. 12.95 (ISBN 0-394-49350-8). Knopf.
Hitchcock, Alfred, ed. Breaking the Screen Barrier. 224p. 1976. pap. 1.95 (ISBN 0-440-14627-5). Dell.
Horvath, Joan. Filmmaking for Beginners. 1977. pap. 2.95 (ISBN 0-346-12289-9). Cornerstone.
Huettig, Mae D. Economic Control of the Motion Picture Industry: A Study in Industrial Organization. LC 70-160235. (Moving Pictures Ser). x, 163p. 1971. Repr. of 1944 ed. lib. bdg. 10.95x (ISBN 0-89198-036-9). Ozer.
Huss, Roy & Silverstein, Norman. Film Experience. 1969. pap. 3.95 (ISBN 0-440-52547-0, Delta). Dell.
Hutchison, David. Special Effects, Vol. II. 1980. pap. 7.95 (ISBN 0-931064-22-8). Starlog.
Huxley, D. Making Films in Super Eight. LC 77-84809. (Illus.). 1978. pap. 8.95x (ISBN 0-521-29300-6). Cambridge U Pr.
Johnston, Claire, ed. Edinburgh Seventy-Seven: History-Production-Memory. (EIFF Ser.). 1978. pap. 6.00 (ISBN 0-918432-17-0). NY Zoetrope.
--Edinburgh Seventy-Six: Psychoanalysis, Cinema, Avante-Garde. (EIFF Ser.). 1978. pap. 5.00 (ISBN 0-918432-16-2). NY Zoetrope.
Karp, Alan. The Films of Robert Altman. LC 80-29501. 178p. 1981. 10.00 (ISBN 0-8108-1408-0). Scarecrow.
Klein, Michael & Parker, Gillian, eds. The English Novel & the Movies. LC 80-5342. (Ungar Film Library). (Illus.). 350p. 1980. 14.50 (ISBN 0-8044-2472-1); pap. 6.95 (ISBN 0-8044-6358-1). Ungar.
Koszarski, Richard, ed. Hollywood Directors: 1914-1940. LC 76-9262. (Illus.). 1976. 16.95 (ISBN 0-19-502085-5). Oxford U Pr.
Koszarski, Richard, et al. The Rivals of D.W. Griffith: Alternate Auteurs, 1913 to 1918. (Illus.). 58p. (Orig.). 1980. pap. 4.95 (ISBN 0-918432-32-4). Ny Zoetrope.
Kozintzev, Grigori. King Lear: the Space of Tragedy: The Diary of a Film Director. Mackintosh, Mary, tr. LC 76-50248. (Illus.). 1977. 17.50 (ISBN 0-520-03392-2). U of Cal Pr.
Lambert, Gavin. GWTW: The Making of Gone with the Wind. (Illus.). 1973. 7.95 (ISBN 0-316-51284-2, Pub. by Atlantic Monthly Pr). Little.
LeGrice, Malcolm. Abstract Film & Beyond. 1977. 13.95 (ISBN 0-262-12077-1). MIT Pr.
Lerner, Alan J. The Street Where I Live. (Illus.). 1978. 12.95 (ISBN 0-393-07532-X). Norton.
Lescarboura, Austin C. Behind the Motion Picture Screen. 1978. Repr. of 1919 ed. lib. bdg. 50.00 (ISBN 0-8495-3246-9). Arden Lib.
McClain, Bebe F. Super Eight Filmaking from Scratch. (Illus.). 1978. ref. 15.95 (ISBN 0-13-876128-0); pap. 9.95 (ISBN 0-13-876110-8). P-H.
Macek, Carl. The Art of Heavy Metal: The Adult Animation Movie. (Illus.). 128p. (Orig.). 1981. pap. 9.95 (ISBN 0-918432-38-3). NY Zoetrope.
Maddux, Rachel & Silliphant, Stirling. Fiction into Film. 1972. pap. 2.45 (ISBN 0-440-52592-6, Delta). Dell.
Mascelli, Joseph V. Five C's of Cinematography. 20.00 (ISBN 0-685-07317-3). Borden.
--Five C's of Cinematography. 8th ed. LC 65-28785. 1979. Repr. of 1965 ed. buckram 20.00 (ISBN 0-9600240-0-X). Cine-Grafic.
--The Five C's of Cinematography. lib. bdg. 25.00 (ISBN 0-9600240-0-X). Calif Pubns.
Mikolas, Mark & Hoos, Gunther. Handbook of Super-Eight Production. rev., 2nd ed. LC 76-15482. (Illus.). 1978. spiral bdg 14.95 (ISBN 0-915616-07-6). United Busn.
Millerson, Gerald. The Technique of Lighting for Television & Motion Pictures. (Library of Communication Techniques Ser.). 376p. 1972. 24.95 (ISBN 0-240-50722-3). Focal Pr.
Parker, Ben & Drabik, Pat. Creative Intention. LC 73-13509. (Illus.). 1974. 14.50 (ISBN 0-88238-054-0). Law-Arts.
Phillips, Gene D. Hemingway & Film. LC 80-7563. (Ungar Film Library). (Illus.). 250p. 1980. 10.95 (ISBN 0-8044-2695-3); pap. 5.95 (ISBN 0-8044-6644-0). Ungar.
--The Movie Makers: Artists in an Industry. LC 73-75524. 1973. 21.95x (ISBN 0-911012-43-5). Nelson-Hall.
Pirie, David, ed. Anatomy of the Movies. (Illus.). 320p. 1981. 15.95 (ISBN 0-02-597540-4). Macmillan.
Prats, A. J. The Autonomous Image: Cinematic Narration & Humanism. LC 81-50182. 192p. 1981. 14.50 (ISBN 0-8131-1406-3). U Pr of Ky.
Prawer, S. S. Caligari's Children: The Film As Tale of Terror. 1980. 19.95 (ISBN 0-19-217584-X). Oxford U Pr.
Richie, Donald. Ozu: His Life & Films. (Illus.). 1974. 22.50 (ISBN 0-520-02445-1); pap. 5.95 (ISBN 0-520-03277-2). U of Cal Pr.
Roberts, Kenneth H. & Sharples, Win, Jr. Primer for Film-Making: A Complete Guide to 16mm & 35mm Film Production. LC 70-91620. (Illus.). 1971. pap. 11.95 (ISBN 0-672-63582-8). Pegasus.
Rosenthal, Stuart & Kass, Judith M. The Hollywood Professionals, Vol. 4: Browning & Siegel. LC 74-14266. (Illus.). 192p. 1976. pap. 4.95 (ISBN 0-498-01665-X). A S Barnes.

Rotha, Paul. Rotha on the Film. Kupelnick, Bruce S., ed. LC 76-52126. (Classics of Film Literature Ser.). 1978. lib. bdg. 19.00 (ISBN 0-8240-2892-9). Garland Pub.

Rowlands, Avril J. Script Continuity & the Production Secretary. (Media Manuals Ser.). (Illus.). 1977. pap. 7.95 (ISBN 0-240-50949-8). Focal Pr.

Rubin, Steven J. Combat Films: American Realism, Nineteen Forty-Five to Nineteen Seventy. LC 80-17022. (Illus.). 245p. 1981. lib. bdg. 15.95x (ISBN 0-89950-013-7); pap. 11.95x (ISBN 0-89950-014-5). McFarland & Co.

--The James Bond Films. (Illus.). 224p. 1981. 19.95 (ISBN 0-87000-523-5); pap. 11.95 (ISBN 0-87000-524-3). Arlington Hse.

Ruchti, Ulrich & Taylor, Sybil. Story into Film. 1978. pap. 1.75 (ISBN 0-440-98368-1, LFL). Dell.

Sackett, Susan & Roddenberry, Gene. The Making of Star Trek: The Motion Picture. 1980. pap. 7.95 (ISBN 0-671-79109-5). S&S.

Salles Gomes, P. E. Jean Vigo. Francovich, Allan, tr. LC 72-104102. 1972. 23.75x (ISBN 0-520-01676-9); pap. 5.95 (ISBN 0-520-02332-3, CAL252). U of Cal Pr.

Schroeppel, Tom. The Bare Bones Camera Course for Film & Video. 2nd ed. LC 79-92048. (Illus.). 89p. (Orig.). 1980. pap. 5.95 (ISBN 0-9603718-0-X). Schroeppel.

Schulberg, B. P., et al. How Talkies Are Made. 1976. lib. bdg. 69.95 (ISBN 0-8490-2020-4). Gordon Pr.

Slide, Anthony. The Kindergarten of the Movies: A History of the Fine Arts Company. LC 80-20391. 246p. 1980. 13.50 (ISBN 0-8108-1358-0). Scarecrow.

Stephenson, Ralph & Debrix, J. R. Cinema As Art. (Illus.). (YA) (gr. 9 up). 1966. pap. 4.95 (ISBN 0-14-020677-9, Pelican). Penguin.

Sulik, Boleslaw. A Change of Tack: The Making of "The Shadow Line". (BFI Ser.). (Illus., Orig.). 1977. pap. 5.50 (ISBN 0-85170-061-6). Ny Zoetrope.

Talbot, Frederick A. Moving Pictures: How They Are Made & Worked. LC 71-124038. (Literature of Cinema, Ser. 1). Repr. of 1912 ed. 14.00 (ISBN 0-405-01638-7). Arno.

Tromberg, Sheldon. Making Money Making Movies: The Independent Movie Maker's Handbook. 1979. 6.95 (ISBN 0-531-06370-4); pap. 6.95 (ISBN 0-531-06753-X). Watts.

Truffaut, Francois. Day for Night. Flores, Sam, tr. from Fr. LC 74-28585. (Illus.). 1975. pap. 3.95 (ISBN 0-394-17840-8, E658, Ever). Grove.

Tuska, Jon, et al, eds. Close-Up: The Contemporary Director. LC 80-23551. 437p. 1981. 22.50 (ISBN 0-8108-1366-1). Scarecrow.

Vendetti, James. The Theatre Student-FilmMaking. (Theatre Student Ser.). (Illus.). (gr. 7-12). PLB 12.50 (ISBN 0-8239-0386-9). Rosen Pr.

Vincent, Richard C. Financial Characteristics of Selected "B" Film Productions of Albert J. Cohen, 1951 to 1957. Jowett, Garth S., ed. LC 79-6691. (Dissertations on Film, 1980 Ser.). 1980. lib. bdg. 21.00x (ISBN 0-405-12922-X). Arno.

Wentz, Bud. Paper Movie Machines. 1975. pap. 3.50 (ISBN 0-912300-57-4, 57-4). Troubador Pr.

Wolverton, Mike. Reality on Reels: A Handbook on Radio-TV-Film Documentaries. 200p. 1981. 13.95 (ISBN 0-87201-776-1). Gulf Pub.

Zettl, Herbert. Sight, Sound, Motion: Applied Media Aesthetics. 1973. text ed. 25.95x (ISBN 0-534-00238-2). Wadsworth Pub.

MOVING-PICTURES–PSYCHOLOGICAL ASPECTS

Carroll, John M. Toward a Structural Psychology of Cinema. (Approaches to Semiotics Ser.: No. 55). 224p. 1980. 31.75 (ISBN 90-279-3447-9). Mouton.

Derry, Charles. Dark Dreams: The Horror Film from Psycho to Jaws. LC 76-10879. (Illus.). 1977. 15.00 (ISBN 0-498-01915-2). A S Barnes.

Goldberg, Albert L. The Effects of Two Types of Sound Motion Pictures on Attitudes of Adults Toward Minority Groups. LC 74-76510. 1974. Repr. of 1956 ed. soft bdg. 8.00 (ISBN 0-88247-292-5). R & E Res Assoc.

Lovell, A. Anarchist Cinema. 59.95 (ISBN 0-87968-189-6). Gordon Pr.

Metz, Christian. The Imaginary Signifier: Psychoanalysis & the Cinema. Brewster, Ben & Guzzetti, Alfred, trs. LC 81-47551. 1981. 22.50x (ISBN 0-253-33105-6). Ind U Pr.

New Jersey State Museum, et al. The Hollywood Indian: Stereotypes of Native Americans in Films. (Illus.). 80p. (Orig.). 1981. 5.95 (ISBN 0-938766-00-7). NJ State Mus.

Wolfenstein, Martha & Leites, Nathan. Movies: A Psychological Study. LC 50-7374. (Illus.). 1970. pap. text ed. 3.45x (ISBN 0-689-70252-3, 165). Atheneum.

Wright, Will. Sixguns & Society. 1975. pap. 5.95 (ISBN 0-520-03491-0). U of Cal Pr.

MOVING-PICTURES–REVIEWS

Agate, James. Around Cinemas. LC 72-169323. (Literature of the Cinema, Series 2). (Illus.). 286p. 1972. Repr. of 1946 ed. 15.00 (ISBN 0-405-03888-7). Arno.

--Around Cinemas: Second Series. LC 76-169324. (Literature of Cinema, Series 2). (Illus.). 300p. 1972. Repr. of 1948 ed. 16.00 (ISBN 0-405-03889-5). Arno.

Amberg, George, ed. The New York Times Film Reviews 1913-1970. abr. ed. LC 75-176229. 512p. 1972. 12.50 (ISBN 0-8129-0233-5). Times Bks.

Anstey, Edgar. Shots in the Dark. Kupelnick, Bruce S., ed. LC 76-52088. (Classics of Film Literature Ser.). 1978. lib. bdg. 18.00 (ISBN 0-8240-2864-3). Garland Pub.

Bowles, Stephen E. Index to Critical Film Reviews: Nineteen Seventy-Two to Nineteen Seventy-Six, Vol. IV. 1979. lib. bdg. 32.50x (ISBN 0-89102-123-X). B Franklin.

Bowles, Stephen E., ed. Index to Critical Film Reviews in British & American Film Periodicals, 3 vols in 2. new ed. LC 74-12109. x, 900p. 1975. Set. 35.00 (ISBN 0-89102-040-3). B Franklin.

Colette. Colette at the Movies: Criticism & Screenplays. Virmaux, Alain & Virmaux, Odette, eds. Smith, Sarah W., tr. from Fr. LC 79-6148. (Ungar Film Library). (Illus.). 300p. 1980. 10.95 (ISBN 0-8044-2125-0); pap. 5.95 (ISBN 0-8044-6086-8). Ungar.

Cowie, Peter, ed. International Film Guide 1981. 17th ed. LC 64-1076. (Illus.). 512p. 1981. pap. 9.95 (ISBN 0-498-02530-6). A S Barnes.

Froelich, Robert E., ed. Film Reviews in Psychiatry, Psychology, & Mental Health: A Descriptive & Evaluative Listing of Educational & Instructional Films. LC 73-78294. 1974. 12.50 (ISBN 0-87650-037-8). Pierian.

Gilliatt, Penelope. Three Quarter Face: Reports & Reflections. LC 79-20607. 1980. 12.95 (ISBN 0-698-11015-3). Coward.

Gordon, G., ed. Continental Film Review Anthology, 1953-55, 2 vols. 1976. lib. bdg. 200.00 (ISBN 0-8490-1670-3). Gordon Pr.

Greene, Graham. The Pleasure Dome: The Collected Film Criticism 1935-40. Taylor, John R., ed. (Illus.). 288p. 1980. pap. 8.95 (ISBN 0-19-281286-6, GB604, GB). Oxford U Pr.

Heinzkill, Richard. Film Criticism: An Index to Critics' Anthologies. LC 75-20159. 1975. 10.00 (ISBN 0-8108-0840-4). Scarecrow.

Kael, Pauline. When the Lights Go Down. LC 79-19067. 608p. (Orig.). 1980. 18.95 (ISBN 0-03-042511-5); pap. 9.95 (ISBN 0-03-056842-0). HR&W.

MacDonald, Dwight. On Movies. (Quality Paperbacks Ser.). 492p. 1981. pap. 9.95 (ISBN 0-306-80150-7). Da Capo.

Magill, Frank N., ed. Magill's Survey of Cinema: First Series, 4 vols. LC 80-52131. 2200p. 1980. 200.00 (ISBN 0-89356-225-4). Salem Pr.

New York Times Film Reviews, 1913-1974, 8 vols. (Illus.). Set. 507.00, incl. index, individual vols. available (ISBN 0-405-02191-7, New York Times). Arno.

Pechter, William S. Movies Plus One: Seven Years of Film Reviewing. 380p. 1981. 16.95 (ISBN 0-8180-0709-5). Horizon.

Salem, James M. A Guide to Critical Reviews, Part II: The Musical, 1909-1974. 2nd ed. LC 73-3120. 1976. 25.00 (ISBN 0-8108-0959-1). Scarecrow.

--A Guide to Critical Reviews, Part IV: The Screenplay from the Jazz Singer to Dr. Strangelove, 2 Vols. LC 66-13733. 1971. Set. 39.50 (ISBN 0-8108-0367-4). Scarecrow.

Samples, Gordon. How to Locate Reviews of Plays & Films: A Bibliography of Criticism from the Beginnings to the Present. LC 76-3509. 124p. 1976. 10.00 (ISBN 0-8108-0914-1). Scarecrow.

Taylor, John R. Graham Greene on Film: Collected Film Criticism 1935-1939. LC 72-83894. (Illus.). 1972. 12.50 (ISBN 0-671-21412-8). S&S.

Truffaut, Francois. The Films in My Life. LC 78-27054. 1979. pap. 5.95 (ISBN 0-671-24663-1, Touchstone Bks). S&S.

Walker, Alexander. Double Takes: Notes & Afterthoughts on the Movies, 1956-1976. 1978. 8.95 (ISBN 0-241-89395-X, Pub. by Hamish Hamilton England). David & Charles.

Yacowar, Maurice. I Found It at the Movies: Film Studies & Film Reviews. (Cinema Ser.). 1976. lib. bdg. 69.95 (ISBN 0-685-69713-4). Revisionist Pr.

MOVING-PICTURES–SERIALS

see Moving-Picture Serials

MOVING-PICTURES–SETTING AND SCENERY

see also Scene Painting; Television–Stage-Setting and Scenery; Theaters–Stage-Setting and Scenery

Hutchison, David. Special Effects, Vol. II. 1980. pap. 7.95 (ISBN 0-931064-22-8). Starlog.

Marner, Terence S. Film Design. LC 72-9938. (International Film Guide Ser). (Illus.). 176p. 1973. pap. 6.95 (ISBN 0-498-01326-X). A S Barnes.

Ritsko, Alan J. Lighting for Location Motion Pictures. 224p. 1980. pap. 8.95 (ISBN 0-442-23136-9). Van Nos Reinhold.

MOVING-PICTURES–SOCIAL ASPECTS

Adair, Gilbert. Vietnam on Film. (Illus.). 208p. 1981. 13.95 (ISBN 0-906071-43-7). Proteus Pub NY.

Beman, Lamar T., ed. Selected Articles on Censorship of the Theater & Moving Pictures. LC 78-160229. (Moving Pictures Ser). 385p. 1971. Repr. of 1931 ed. lib. bdg. 18.75x (ISBN 0-89198-030-X). Ozer.

Cohen, Louis H. The Cultural-Political Traditions & Development of the Soviet Cinema: 1917-1972. LC 74-2077. (Dissertations on Film Ser.: Vol. 1). 724p. 1974. 35.00x (ISBN 0-405-04876-9). Arno.

Diakite, Madubuko. Film, Culture, & the Black Filmmaker. Jowett, Garth S., ed. LC 79-6679. (Issertations on Film, 1980 Ser.). 1980. lib. bdg. 19.00x (ISBN 0-405-12907-6). Arno.

Ernst, Morris & Lorentz, Pare. Censored: The Private Life of the Movies. LC 72-160230. (Moving Pictures Ser). xvi, 199p. 1971. Repr. of 1930 ed. lib. bdg. 11.95x (ISBN 0-89198-031-8). Ozer.

Federal Council of the Churches of Christ in America. The Public Relations of the Motion Picture Industry: A Report by the Department of Research & Education. LC 76-160231. (Moving Pictures Ser). 156p. 1971. Repr. of 1931 ed. lib. bdg. 9.95x (ISBN 0-89198-032-6). Ozer.

Harley, John E. World-Wide Influences of the Cinema: A Study of Official Censorship & the International Cultural Aspects of Motion Pictures. LC 77-160234. (Moving Pictures Ser). xvi, 320p. 1971. Repr. of 1940 ed. lib. bdg. 16.95x (ISBN 0-89198-035-0). Ozer.

Huettig, Mae D. Economic Control of the Motion Picture Industry: A Study in Industrial Organization. LC 70-160235. (Moving Pictures Ser). x, 163p. 1971. Repr. of 1944 ed. lib. bdg. 10.95x (ISBN 0-89198-036-9). Ozer.

Hurley, Neil. The Reel Revolution: A Film Primer on Liberation. LC 77-17634. (Illus.). 1979. pap. 7.95 (ISBN 0-88344-433-X). Orbis Bks.

Jarvie, I. C. Movies As Social Criticism: Aspects of Their Social Psychology. LC 77-26778. 1978. 12.00 (ISBN 0-8108-1106-5). Scarecrow.

Jowett, Garth. Film: The Democratic Art. 1976. 19.95 (ISBN 0-316-47370-7). Little.

Kennedy, Joseph P., ed. The Story of Films. LC 74-160236. (Moving Pictures Ser). xxi, 377p. 1971. Repr. of 1927 ed. lib. bdg. 18.75x (ISBN 0-89198-037-7). Ozer.

Koenigil, Mark. Movies in Society. 5.95 (ISBN 0-8315-0000-X). Speller.

Lane, Tamar. What's Wrong with the Movies? LC 78-160237. (Moving Pictures Ser). 254p. 1971. Repr. of 1923 ed. lib. bdg. 11.95x (ISBN 0-89198-038-5). Ozer.

MacBean, James R. Film & Revolution. LC 75-1936. (Midland Bks.: No. 191). (Illus.). 344p. 1976. 15.00x (ISBN 0-253-32189-1); pap. 5.95x (ISBN 0-253-20191-8). Ind U Pr.

May, Lary L. Screening Out the Past: The Birth of Mass Culture & the Motion Picture Industry. LC 80-11889. (Illus.). 352p. 1980. 19.95 (ISBN 0-19-502762-0). Oxford U Pr.

Mayer, J. P. Sociology of Film: Studies & Documents. LC 73-169334. (Literature of Cinema, Series 2). (Illus.). 398p. 1972. Repr. of 1946 ed. 20.00 (ISBN 0-405-03901-8). Arno.

Mayer, Jakob P. Sociology of Film: Studies & Documents. LC 75-160239. (Moving Pictures Ser). 328p. 1971. Repr. of 1946 ed. lib. bdg. 16.95x (ISBN 0-89198-040-7). Ozer.

Mitchell, Alice M. Children & Movies. LC 70-160240. (Moving Pictures Ser). xxiv, 181p. 1971. Repr. of 1929 ed. lib. bdg. 10.95x (ISBN 0-89198-041-5). Ozer.

Moley, Raymond. The Hays Office. LC 73-160241. (Moving Pictures Ser). 266p. 1971. Repr. of 1945 ed. lib. bdg. 14.25x (ISBN 0-89198-042-3). Ozer.

National Conference on Motion Pictures, New York, 1929 & Motion Picture Producers & Distributors of America. The Community & the Motion Picture: Report. LC 77-160242. (Moving Pictures Ser). 96p. 1971. Repr. of 1929 ed. lib. bdg. 7.75x (ISBN 0-89198-043-1). Ozer.

New Jersey State Museum, et al. The Hollywood Indian: Stereotypes of Native Americans in Films. (Illus.). 80p. (Orig.). 1981. 5.95 (ISBN 0-938766-00-7). NJ State Mus.

Nichols, Bill. Ideology & the Image: Social Representation in the Cinema & Other Media. LC 80-7684. (Midland Bks.: No. 256). (Illus.). 384p. 1981. 29.95x (ISBN 0-253-18287-5); pap. 9.95x (ISBN 0-253-20256-6). Ind U Pr.

Nizer, Louis. New Courts of Industry: Self-Regulation Under the Motion Picture Code, Including an Analysis of the Code. LC 70-160243. (Moving Pictures Ser). 344p. 1971. Repr. of 1935 ed. lib. bdg. 16.95x (ISBN 0-89198-044-X). Ozer.

Oberholtzer, Ellis P. The Morals of the Movie. LC 74-160244. (Moving Pictures Ser). 251p. 1971. Repr. of 1922 ed. lib. bdg. 14.25x (ISBN 0-89198-045-8). Ozer.

Perlman, William J., ed. The Movies on Trial: The Views & Opinions of Outstanding Personalities Anent Screen Entertainment Past & Present. LC 78-160245. (Moving Pictures Ser). 1971. Repr. of 1936 ed. lib. bdg. 14.25x (ISBN 0-89198-046-6). Ozer.

Rimberg, John. The Motion Picture in the Soviet Union, 1918-1952: A Sociological Analysis. LC 72-559. (Dissertations on Film Ser.). 238p. 1972. Repr. of 1959 ed. 17.00 (ISBN 0-405-04102-0). Arno.

Robson, E. W. & Robson, M. M. Film Answers Back: An Historical Appreciation of the Cinema. LC 73-169350. (Arno Press Cinema Program). (Illus.). 402p. 1972. Repr. of 1939 ed. 20.00 (ISBN 0-405-03923-9). Arno.

Sarris, Andrew. Politics & Cinema. 1978. 15.00x (ISBN 0-231-04034-2). Columbia U Pr.

Seabury, William M. The Public & the Motion Picture Industry. LC 75-160247. (Moving Pictures Ser). xiv, 340p. 1971. Repr. of 1926 ed. lib. bdg. 17.50x (ISBN 0-89198-048-2). Ozer.

Short, Kenneth, ed. Feature Films As History. LC 80-28715. 192p. 1981. 16.50x (ISBN 0-87049-314-0). U of Tenn Pr.

Short, William A. A Generation of Motion Pictures. Kupelnick, Bruce S., ed. LC 76-52129. (Classics of Film Literature Ser.). 1978. lib. bdg. 25.00 (ISBN 0-8240-2894-5). Garland Pub.

Spoto, Donald. Camarado: Hollywood & the American Man. (Orig.). 1978. pap. 4.95 (ISBN 0-452-25186-9, Z5186, Plume). NAL.

Thomson, David. America in the Dark: Hollywood & the Gift of Unreality. LC 79-53130. 1979. pap. 4.95 (ISBN 0-688-08210-6, Quill). Morrow.

Tudor, Andre. Image & Influence: Studies in the Sociology of Film. LC 74-26212. 256p. 1975. text ed. 19.95 (ISBN 0-312-40915-X). St Martin.

Wead, George & Lellis, Geore. Film: Form & Function. LC 80-82804. (Illus.). 512p. 1981. pap. text ed. 12.95 (ISBN 0-395-29740-0). HM.

White, David M. & Averson, Richard. The Celluloid Weapon: Social Comment in the American Film. (Illus.). 288p. 1972. 14.95 (ISBN 0-8070-6170-0). Beacon Pr.

Woll, Allen L. The Latin Image in American Film. rev. ed. LC 80-620041. (Latin American Studies: Vol. 50). 1981. pap. 6.95 (ISBN 0-87903-050-X). UCLA Lat Am Ctr.

MOVING-PICTURES–SPECIAL EFFECTS

see Cinematography, Trick

MOVING-PICTURES–STUDY AND TEACHING

Balazs, Bela. Theory of the Film: Character & Growth of a New Art. LC 71-169347. (Arno Press Cinema Program). (Illus.). 312p. 1972. Repr. of 1952 ed. 18.00 (ISBN 0-405-03910-7). Arno.

Bowles, Stephen E. An Approach to Film Study: A Selected Booklist & Bibliography. (Cinema Ser.). 1974. 59.95 (ISBN 0-87700-206-1). Revisionist Pr.

Coynik, David. Film: Real to Reel. (Mass Media Ser.). (Illus.). 273p. (Orig.). (gr. 10-12). 1972. pap. text ed. 6.60 (ISBN 0-88343-304-4); tchrs'. manual 1.50 (ISBN 0-88343-305-2). McDougal-Littell.

Gordon Press Editorial Staff, ed. Directory of American Film Scholars: Who's Who in American Film Scholarship. 1977. 75.00 (ISBN 0-87968-226-4). Gordon Pr.

Lowndes, Douglas. Film Making in Schools. (Illus.). (gr. 9-12). 1969. text ed. 12.95 (ISBN 0-8230-1750-8). Watson-Guptill.

Manchel, Frank. Film Study: A Resource Guide. LC 72-3262. 422p. 1973. 22.50 (ISBN 0-8386-1225-3). Fairleigh Dickinson.

Mercer, John. The Informational Film. LC 80-54273. (Illus.). 200p. Date not set. pap. text ed. 6.00x (ISBN 0-87563-197-5). Stipes.

Phillips, Leona & Phillips, Jill. Film Appreciation: An Outline & Study Guide for Colleges & Universities. 1978. lib. bdg. 69.95 (ISBN 0-8490-1390-9). Gordon Pr.

Selby, S. A. The Study of Film As an Art Form in American Secondary Schools. LC 77-22913. 1978. lib. bdg. 16.00x (ISBN 0-405-10755-2). Arno.

MOVING-PICTURES–TITLING

see Moving-Pictures–Editing

MOVING-PICTURES–VOCATIONAL GUIDANCE

see Moving-Pictures As a Profession

MOVING-PICTURES–YEARBOOKS

Alicoate, J. Film Daily Production Guide & Directors Annual of 1934. 1976. lib. bdg. 75.00 (ISBN 0-8490-1814-5). Gordon Pr.

--Film Daily Production Guide & Directors Annual of 1935. 1976. lib. bdg. 79.50 (ISBN 0-8490-1815-3). Gordon Pr.

--Film Daily Yearbook of Motion Pictures of 1930. 1976. lib. bdg. 79.95 (ISBN 0-8490-1818-8). Gordon Pr.

--Film Daily Yearbook of Motion Pictures of 1932. 1976. lib. bdg. 79.95 (ISBN 0-8490-1819-6). Gordon Pr.

--Film Daily Yearbook of Motion Pictures of 1935. 1976. lib. bdg. 79.95 (ISBN 0-8490-1820-X). Gordon Pr.

--Film Daily Yearbook of Motion Pictures of 1936. lib. bdg. 79.95 (ISBN 0-8490-1821-8). Gordon Pr.

--Film Daily Yearbook of Motion Pictures of 1922-1923. 1976. lib. bdg. 79.95 (ISBN 0-8490-1828-5). Gordon Pr.

Alicoate, J., ed. Film Daily Directors Annual & Production Guide of 1929. 1976. lib. bdg. 75.95 (ISBN 0-8490-1810-2). Gordon Pr.

--Film Daily Directors Annual & Production Guide of 1930. lib. bdg. 75.95 (ISBN 0-8490-1811-0). Gordon Pr.

--Film Daily Directors Annual & Production Guide of 1932. 1976. lib. bdg. 75.00 (ISBN 0-8490-1812-9). Gordon Pr.

--Film Daily Production Guide & Directors Annual of 1936. 1976. lib. bdg. 79.75 (ISBN 0-8490-1816-1). Gordon Pr.

--Film Daily Production Guide & Directors Annual of 1937. 1976. lib. bdg. 79.75 (ISBN 0-8490-1817-X). Gordon Pr.

--Film Daily Yearbook of Motion Pictures of 1940. 1976. lib. bdg. 75.00 (ISBN 0-8490-1822-6). Gordon Pr.

--Film Daily Yearbook of Motion Pictures of 1934. 1976. lib. bdg. 79.95 (ISBN 0-8490-1823-4). Gordon Pr.

--Film Daily Yearbook of Motion Pictures of 1933. 1976. lib. bdg. 79.95 (ISBN 0-8490-1824-2). Gordon Pr.

--Film Daily Yearbook of Motion Pictures of 1926. 1976. lib. bdg. 79.95 (ISBN 0-8490-1825-0). Gordon Pr.

--Film Daily Yearbook of Motion Pictures of 1939. 1976. lib. bdg. 79.95 (ISBN 0-8490-1826-9). Gordon Pr.

--Film Daily Yearbook of Motion Pictures of 1937. 1976. lib. bdg. 79.95 (ISBN 0-8490-1827-7). Gordon Pr.

--Film Daily Yearbook of Motion Pictures of 1921-1922. 1976. lib. bdg. 79.95 (ISBN 0-8490-1829-3). Gordon Pr.

Blum, Daniel. Screen World, 10 vols. 1949, 1951-1959. LC 70-84068. (Illus.). 1969. Set. 165.00x (ISBN 0-8196-0255-8); 18.00x ea. Biblo.

Castell, David, ed. Cinema Seventy Nine. (Illus.). 1978. pap. 7.95 (ISBN 0-8467-0504-4, Pub. by Two Continents). Hippocrene Bks.

--Cinema '80. (Illus.). 160p. 1980. pap. 8.95 (ISBN 0-88254-547-7, Pub. by BCW Pub England). Hippocrene Bks.

Cowie, Peter. International Film Guide 1978. LC 64-1076. (Illus.). 1978. pap. 7.95 (ISBN 0-498-02106-8). A S Barnes.

Cowie, Peter, ed. International Film Guide, 1977. LC 64-1076. pap. 7.95 (ISBN 0-498-01907-1). A S Barnes.

Film Daily Directors Annual & Production Guide of 1931. 1976. lib. bdg. 75.95 (ISBN 0-8490-1813-7). Gordon Pr.

Film Daily Yearbook of Motion Pictures, 1970. LC 39-24344. (Cinema Program Ser.). 1971. 25.00 (ISBN 0-405-02550-5). Arno.

Film Daily Yearbook of Motion Pictures: Wid's Year Book, 4 vols. LC 71-167701. (Cinema Program Ser). 45.00 ea. Arno.

Film Daily Yearbook, 1918-1941, 20 vols. Set. 75.00 ea. (ISBN 0-8490-0164-1). Gordon Pr.

Gertner, Richard, ed. Motion Picture Almanac, 1981, Vol. 52. 716p. 1981. 38.00 (ISBN 0-900610-23-9). Quigley Pub Co.

Gordon, R., ed. Film Lovers Annual: 1932-1934, 3 vols. 1976. Set. lib. bdg. 300.00 (ISBN 0-8490-1834-X). Gordon Pr.

--Motion Picture News Blue Book 1929-30, 2 vols. 1976. lib. bdg. 250.00 (ISBN 0-8490-2295-9). Gordon Pr.

--Paramount Films of 1928-1929. 1976. lib. bdg. 70.00 (ISBN 0-8490-2410-2). Gordon Pr.

--Paramount Pictures of 1931-1932. 1976. lib. bdg. 100.00 (ISBN 0-8490-2411-0). Gordon Pr.

Gordon, R. F., ed. Universal Pictures of 1932-1933. 1976. lib. bdg. 78.00 (ISBN 0-8490-2788-8). Gordon Pr.

Justice, Fred C. & Smith, T. R. Who's Who in the Film World of 1914. 1976. lib. bdg. 59.95 (ISBN 0-8490-2820-5). Gordon Pr.

Kemp's Film & Television Yearbook (International) 1979-80. LC 59-47486. 1979. 65.00x (ISBN 0-905255-65-8). Intl Pubns Serv.

Motion Picture Almanac 1929-1941, 12 vols. 2100.00 (ISBN 0-8490-2292-4). Gordon Pr.

Motion Picture Studio Campaign Books 1920-1940, 20 vols. Set. 3500.00 (ISBN 0-8490-2297-5). Gordon Pr.

Mutch, William A., ed. Film Goers Annual of 1932. 1976. lib. bdg. 88.95 (ISBN 0-8490-1833-1). Gordon Pr.

Noble, Peter, ed. Screen International Film & TV Yearbook, 1980-81. 35th ed. LC 76-646393. 744p. 1980. 57.50x (ISBN 0-900925-11-6). Intl Pubns Serv.

Ozer, Jerome S., ed. Film Review Annual, 1979. 1980. lib. bdg. 66.00x (ISBN 0-89198-124-1). Ozer.

Ramsaye, Terry. Motion Picture Almanac of 1930. 1976. lib. bdg. 700.00 (ISBN 0-8490-2288-6). Gordon Pr.

--Motion Picture Almanac of 1933. 1976. lib. bdg. 79.95 (ISBN 0-8490-2289-4). Gordon Pr.

--Motion Picture Almanac of 1935-1936. 1976. lib. bdg. 99.50 (ISBN 0-8490-2290-8). Gordon Pr.

--Motion Picture Almanac of 1937-1938. 1976. lib. bdg. 120.00 (ISBN 0-8490-2291-6). Gordon Pr.

Riefenstahl, L., et al, eds. Internationaler Tonfilm & Almanach of 1931. 1976. lib. bdg. 99.95 (ISBN 0-8490-2063-8). Gordon Pr.

Sherwood, Robert E. Best Moving Pictures Nineteen Twenty Two - Nineteen Twenty Three. 95.00 (ISBN 0-87700-136-7). Revisionist Pr.

Watts, Stephen, ed. Stars & Films of 1937 & 1938, 2 vols. 1976. lib. bdg. 200.00 (ISBN 0-8490-2664-4). Gordon Pr.

Willis, John. Screen World Nineteen Seventy-Eight, Vol. 29. (Illus.). 1978. 12.95 (ISBN 0-517-53451-7). Crown.

--Screen World: 1975, Vol. 26. (Illus.). 256p. 1975. 9.95 (ISBN 0-517-52102-4). Crown.

--Screen World: 1979, Vol. 30. (Illus.). 1979. 15.95 (ISBN 0-517-53835-0). Crown.

--Screen World: 25th Anniversary Edition, Vol. 25. (Illus.). 256p. 1974. 9.95 (ISBN 0-517-51532-6). Crown.

Willis, John, ed. Screen World-1976, Vol. 27. 1976. 12.95 (ISBN 0-517-52583-6). Crown.

MOVING-PICTURES–AFRICA

Notcott, L. A. & Latham, G. C. The African & the Cinema. 1976. lib. bdg. 69.95 (ISBN 0-8490-1403-4). Gordon Pr.

Ohrn, Steven & Riley, Rebecca, eds. Africa from Real to Reel. 1976. pap. 15.00 (ISBN 0-918456-01-0). African Studies Assn.

MOVING-PICTURES–AUSTRALIA

Murray, Scott, ed. The New Australian Cinema. (Illus.). 208p. (Orig.). 1981. pap. 19.95 (ISBN 0-17-005572-8). NY Zoetrope.

Reade, Eric. Australian Silent Films: A Pictorial History, 1896-1929. 1970. 12.50 (ISBN 0-87491-368-3). Acropolis.

--History & Heartburn: The Saga of Australian Film, 1896-1978. 353p. 1980. 40.00 (ISBN 0-8386-3082-0). Fairleigh Dickinson.

Stratton, David. The Last New Wave: The Australian Film Revival. (Illus.). 356p. 1981. 19.95 (ISBN 0-8044-2842-5). Ungar.

MOVING-PICTURES–CANADA

Beattie, Eleanor. A Handbook of Canadian Film. 2nd ed. (Take One-PMA Film Ser). (Illus.). 1977. pap. 9.95 (ISBN 0-88778-131-4). NY Zoetrope.

Dictionnaire du Cinema Quebecois. (Fr.). 1979. 32.50 (ISBN 0-686-57105-3, M-6132). French & Eur.

Feldman, Seth & Nelson, Joyce, eds. The Canadian Film Reader. (Take One-PMA Film Book Ser). 1977. 19.95 (ISBN 0-88778-158-6); pap. 9.95 (ISBN 0-88778-159-4). NY Zoetrope.

Morris, Peter. Embattled Shadows: A History of Canadian Cinema, 1895-1939. (Illus.). 1978. 19.95x (ISBN 0-7735-0322-6); pap. 7.95 (ISBN 0-7735-0323-4). McGill-Queens U Pr.

MOVING-PICTURES–CHINA

Eberhard, Wolfram. The Chinese Silver Screen: Hong Kong & Taiwanese Motion Pictures in the 1960's, No. 23. (Asian Folklore & Social Life Monograph). 1972. 5.30 (ISBN 0-89986-025-7). E Langstaff.

Lu Su-Shang. History of Taiwanese Films, 1921-1950. (National Peking University & Chinese Assn. for Folklore, Folklore & Folkliterature Ser.: No. 126 & 127). (Chinese.). 18.00 (ISBN 0-89986-201-2). E Langstaff.

MOVING-PICTURES–CZECHOSLAVAKIA

Liehm, Antonin J. Closely Watched Films: The Czechoslovak Experience. Polackova, Kaca, tr. LC 72-94987. (Illus.). 1974. 20.00 (ISBN 0-87332-036-0). M E Sharpe.

Skvorecky, Josef. All the Bright Young Men & Women: A Personal History of the Czech Cinema. 2nd ed. (Take One-PMA Film Book Ser). (Illus.). 1977. 17.95 (ISBN 0-88778-056-3); pap. 8.95 (ISBN 0-88778-110-1). NY Zoetrope.

MOVING-PICTURES–EUROPE

Armes, Roy. The Ambiguous Image: Narrative Style in Modern European Cinema. LC 75-37266. (Illus.). 256p. 1976. 15.00x (ISBN 0-253-30560-8). Ind U Pr.

Diccionario Del Cine Espanol, 1896-1968. 359p. (Espn.). 1970. pap. 15.75 (ISBN 84-276-0249-9, S-50008). French & Eur.

Frayling, Christopher. Spaghetti Westerns: Cowboys & Europeans from Karl May to Sergio Leone. LC 80-40822. (Cinema & Society Ser.). (Illus.). 304p. 1981. 40.00 (ISBN 0-7100-0503-2); pap. 20.00 (ISBN 0-7100-0504-0). Routledge & Kegan.

Hibbin, Nina. Eastern Europe: A Screen Guide. LC 69-14898. (Illus.). 1969. 4.95 (ISBN 0-498-07421-8). A S Barnes.

Liehm, Mira & Liehm, Antonin. The Most Important Art: East European Film After 1945. 1977. 28.50 (ISBN 0-520-03157-1); pap. 10.95 (ISBN 0-520-04128-3, CAL 474). U of Cal Pr.

Riefenstahl, L., et al. Film Anthology (Amsterdam 1927) Frita, ed. Gordon, R., ed. 1976. lib. bdg. 200.00 (ISBN 0-8490-1809-9). Gordon Pr.

Stoil, Michael J. Cinema Beyond the Danube: The Camera & Politics. LC 74-5274. 1974. 10.00 (ISBN 0-8108-0722-X). Scarecrow.

MOVING-PICTURES–FRANCE

Armes, Roy. French Cinema Since 1946, 2 Vols. rev. enl. ed. LC 77-106379. (International Film Guide Ser). (Illus.). 1970. Vol. 1. pap. 4.95 (ISBN 0-498-07652-0); Vol. 2. pap. 4.95 (ISBN 0-498-07655-5). A S Barnes.

Bazin, Andre. French Cinema of the Occupation & Resistance: The Birth of a Critical Esthetic. Hochman, Stanley, tr. from Fr. LC 80-5343. (Ungar Film Library). (Illus.). 256p. 1981. 12.95 (ISBN 0-8044-2022-X). Ungar.

Bordwell, David. French Impressionist Cinema. Jowett, Garth S., ed. LC 79-6668. (Dissertations on Film, 1980 Ser.). 1980. lib. bdg. 30.00x (ISBN 0-405-12902-5). Arno.

Charensol, Georges. Panorama De Cinema. 1947. 35.00 (ISBN 0-685-84537-0). Norwood Edns.

Cocteau, Jean. Beauty & the Beast: Diary of a Film. (Illus.). 7.50 (ISBN 0-8446-4527-3). Peter Smith.

Glasser, et al. Explorations in National Cinema. Lawton, Ben & Staiger, Janet, eds. (Film Studies Annual, 1977: Pt. 1). (Illus.). 1977. pap. 6.00 (ISBN 0-913178-52-7). Redgrave Pub Co.

Guzzetti, Alfred. Two or Three Things I Know About Her: Analysis of a Film by Godard. LC 80-15832. (Film Studies). (Illus.). 376p. 1981. text ed. 27.50x (ISBN 0-674-91500-3). Harvard U Pr.

Harvey, Sylvia. May Sixty-Eight & Film Culture. rev. ed. (BFI Ser.). (Illus.). 168p. (Orig.). 1980. pap. 11.95 (ISBN 0-85170-104-3). NY Zoetrope.

Martin, Marcel. France: Screen Guide. LC 69-14900. (International Film Guide Ser). 1971. pap. 4.95 (ISBN 0-498-07518-4). A S Barnes.

Michalczyk, John J. The French Literary Filmmakers. LC 78-75171. (Illus.). 230p. 1980. 19.50 (ISBN 0-87982-027-6). Art Alliance.

Monaco, James. The New Wave: Truffaut, Godard, Chabrol, Rohmer, Rivette. LC 75-38099. (Illus.). 384p. 1976. 22.50 (ISBN 0-19-501992-X). Oxford U Pr.

--The New Wave: Truffaut, Godard, Chabrol, Rohmer, Rivette. LC 75-38099. 1977. pap. 5.95 (ISBN 0-19-502246-7, GB516, GB). Oxford U Pr.

Monaco, P. Cinema & Society: France & Germany During the Twenties. 1976. 12.95 (ISBN 0-444-99019-4, Pub. by Elsevier). Greenwood.

Sadoul, Georges. French Film. Manvell, Roger, ed. LC 70-169336. (National Cinema Ser). (Illus.). 176p. 1972. Repr. of 1953 ed. 15.00 (ISBN 0-405-03903-4). Arno.

Sesonske, Alexander. Jean Renoir: The French Years, 1924-1939. LC 79-17406. (Harvard Film Studies). (Illus.). 1980. text ed. 25.00x (ISBN 0-674-47355-8, HP 169); pap. text ed. 9.95 (ISBN 0-674-47360-4). Harvard U Pr.

Strebel, Elizabeth G. French Social Cinema of the Nineteen Thirties. Jowett, Garth S., ed. LC 79-6688. (Dissertations on Film, 1980 Ser.). 1980. lib. bdg. 27.00x (ISBN 0-405-12920-3). Arno.

Thiher, Allen. The Cinematic Muse: Critical Studies in the History of French Cinema. LC 79-1560. (Illus.). 1979. text ed. 18.00x (ISBN 0-8262-0277-2). U of Mo Pr.

Van Wert, W. F. The Theory & Practice of the Cine-Roman. LC 77-22912. 1978. lib. bdg. 24.00x (ISBN 0-405-10756-0). Arno.

MOVING-PICTURES–GERMANY

Bucher, Felix. Germany: Screen Guide. LC 69-14899. (Screen Guide Ser). (Illus.). 1970. pap. 4.95 (ISBN 0-498-07517-6). A S Barnes.

Eisner, Lotte. The Haunted Screen: Expressionism in the German Cinema & the Influence of Max Reinhardt. Greaves, Roger, tr. LC 68-8719. Orig. Title: Ecran Demoniaque. 1969. pap. 6.50 (ISBN 0-520-02479-6). U of Cal Pr.

Glasser, et al. Explorations in National Cinema. Lawton, Ben & Staiger, Janet, eds. (Film Studies Annual, 1977: Pt. 1). (Illus.). 1977. pap. 6.00 (ISBN 0-913178-52-7). Redgrave Pub Co.

Gordon, R. Deutschen Filmschaffenden of 1935. 1976. lib. bdg. 120.00 (ISBN 0-8490-1712-2). Gordon Pr.

Gordon, R., ed. Deutsche Filmwoche Anthology. 1976. lib. bdg. 200.00 (ISBN 0-8490-1711-4). Gordon Pr.

Hull, David S. Film in the Third Reich: A Study of the German Cinema, 1933-1945. LC 69-16739. 1969. 19.95 (ISBN 0-520-01489-8). U of Cal Pr.

Jason, A. Das Filmschaffen in Deutschland, 1935-1939. 1976. lib. bdg. 70.95 (ISBN 0-8490-1839-0). Gordon Pr.

Leiser, Erwin. Nazi Cinema. (Illus.). 1975. 7.95 (ISBN 0-02-570230-0). Macmillan.

Monaco, P. Cinema & Society: France & Germany During the Twenties. 1976. 12.95 (ISBN 0-444-99019-4, Pub. by Elsevier). Greenwood.

Petley, Julian. Capital & Culture: German Cinema Nineteen Thirty-Three to Nineteen Forty-Five. (BFI Ser.). (Orig.). 1979. pap. 10.95 (ISBN 0-85170-088-8). NY Zoetrope.

Prels, M. Kino: A Study of the German Film 1915-1919. 1976. lib. bdg. 70.00 (ISBN 0-8490-2118-9). Gordon Pr.

Sandford, John. The New German Cinema. (Illus.). 180p. 1980. 25.75x (ISBN 0-389-20015-8). B&N.

Semprun, J. La Guerre Est Finie. Seaver, Richard, tr. (Illus., Text for the film by Alain Resnais. Film editor Robert Hughes.). 5.75 (ISBN 0-8446-2906-5). Peter Smith.

Taylor, Richard. Film Propaganda: Soviet Russia & Nazi Germany. LC 79-1399. (Illus.). 1979. text ed. 25.00x (ISBN 0-06-496778-6). B&N.

Wollenberg, H. H. Fifty Years of German Film. Manvell, Roger, ed. LC 74-169337. (National Cinema Ser.). (Illus.). 68p. 1972. Repr. of 1948 ed. 12.00 (ISBN 0-405-03904-2). Arno.

MOVING-PICTURES–GREAT BRITAIN

Aldgate, Anthony. Cinema & History: British Newsreels & the Spanish Civil War. (Illus., Orig.). 1980. pap. 11.95 (ISBN 0-85967-486-X). NY Zoetrope.

Armes, Roy. A Critical History of British Cinema. LC 77-73893. (Illus.). 1978. 19.50 (ISBN 0-19-520043-8). Oxford U Pr.

Balcon, Michael, et al. Twenty Years of British Film: 1925-1945. LC 73-169326. (National Cinema Ser.). (Illus.). 120p. 1972. Repr. of 1947 ed. 13.00 (ISBN 0-405-03890-9). Arno.

Brown, Geoff. Launder & Gilliat. (BFI Ser.). (Orig.). 1978. pap. 8.25 (ISBN 0-85170-071-3). NY Zoetrope.

Brown, Geoff, ed. Walter Forde. (BFI Ser.). 1977. pap. 4.50 (ISBN 0-85170-062-4). NY Zoetrope.

Carrick, Edward, ed. Art & Design in the British Film: A Pictorial Directory of British Art Directors & Their Work. LC 76-169340. (Arno Press Cinema Program). (Illus.). 144p. 1972. Repr. of 1948 ed. 14.00 (ISBN 0-405-03913-1). Arno.

Chanan, Michael. The Dream That Kicks: The Prehistory & Early Years of Cinema in Britain. (Illus.). 1980. 32.50 (ISBN 0-7100-0319-6). Routledge & Kegan.

--Labour Power in the British Film Industry. (BFI Ser.). (Orig.). 1977. pap. 6.50 (ISBN 0-85170-050-0). NY Zoetrope.

Gifford, Denis. The Illustrated Who's Who in British Films. (Illus.). 1980. 32.00 (ISBN 0-7134-1434-0). David & Charles.

Kemp's International Film & Television Yearbook, 1980-1981, 3 pts. 1074p. 1981. 47.00 (ISBN 0-905255-81-X, KEMP8, Kemps). Unipub.

Lovell, Alan, ed. BFI Production Board. (BFI Ser.). (Orig.). 1977. pap. 3.25 (ISBN 0-85170-059-4). NY Zoetrope.

Low, Rachel. The History of the British Film, 6 vols. Incl. Vol. 1, 1896-1906. Manvell, Roger. 1973. Repr. of 1948 ed. 12.95 (ISBN 0-686-57901-1); Vol. 2, 1906-1914. 1973. Repr. of 1948 ed. 15.95 (ISBN 0-04-791008-9); Volume 3, 1914-1918. 1973. Repr. of 1949 ed. 16.95 (ISBN 0-04-791009-7); Vol. 4, 1918-1929. 1971. 21.50 (ISBN 0-04-791021-6); Vol. V. Documentary & Educational Films of the Nineteen Thirties. Low, Rachael. (Illus.). 1979. 18.50 (ISBN 0-04-791036-4); Vol. VI. Films of Comment & Persuasion of the Nineteen Thirties. Low, Rachael. 1979. 18.50 (ISBN 0-04-791037-2). LC 73-10747. (Illus., Pub by Allen & Unwin). Bowker.

Macpherson, Donald. The Traditions of Independence: British Cinema in the 30's. (BFI Ser.). (Orig.). 1980. pap. 14.50 (ISBN 0-85170-093-4). NY Zoetrope.

Mayer, J. P. British Cinemas & Their Audiences. Jowett, Garth S., ed. LC 77-11387. (Aspects of Film Ser.). (Illus.). 1978. lib. bdg. 25.00x (ISBN 0-405-11141-X). Arno.

Orbanz, Eva, et al. Journey to a Legend & Back: The British Realistic Film. 1981. pap. 11.95 (ISBN 3-920889-51-7). NY Zoetrope.
Phelps, Guy. Film Censorship in Britain. LC 76-352257. (Illus.). 1976. 16.50x (ISBN 0-575-01987-5). Intl Pubns Serv.
Sussex, Elizabeth. The Rise & Fall of British Documentary: The Story of the Film Movement Founded by John Grierson. LC 74-16719. (Illus.). 1976. 19.50 (ISBN 0-520-02869-4). U of Cal Pr.
Thorpe, Frances & Pronay, Nicholas. British Official Films in the Second World War: A Descriptive Catalog. 321p. 1980. 45.00 (ISBN 0-903450-27-5). ABC Clio.
The U. K. Cinema Today: 1980. 1981. 125.00x (ISBN 0-686-71958-1, Pub. by Euromonitor). State Mutual Bk.
Vermilye, Jerry. The Great British Films. (Illus.). 1980. pap. 6.95 (ISBN 0-8065-0699-7). Citadel Pr.
--The Great British Films. 1978. 14.95 (ISBN 0-8065-0661-X). Citadel Pr.

MOVING-PICTURES-GREECE, MODERN

Schuster, Mel. The Contemporary Greek Cinema. LC 78-20969. 1979. lib. bdg. 16.50 (ISBN 0-8108-1196-0). Scarecrow.

MOVING-PICTURES-HUNGARY

Nemeskurty, Istvan. A Short History of the Hungarian Cinema. (Illus.). 141p. (Orig.). 1981. pap. 4.95 (ISBN 963-13-1101-5). NY Zoetrope.
--Word & Image: History of the Hungarian Cinema. enl. 2nd ed. (Illus.). 252p. 1974. 8.00x (ISBN 963-13-6707-X). Intl Pubns Serv.
Petrie, Graham. History Must Answer to Man: The Contemporary Hungarian Cinema. (Illus.). 284p. (Orig.). 1978. pap. 7.50x (ISBN 963-13-0485-X). Intl Pubns Serv.
--Hungarian Cinema Today: History Must Answer to Man. (Illus.). 284p. (Orig.). 1980. pap. 8.95 (ISBN 9-6313-0485-X). NY Zoetrope.

MOVING-PICTURES-INDIA

Barnouw, Erik & Krishnaswamy, S. Indian Film. 2nd ed. (Illus.). 1980. 15.95 (ISBN 0-19-502682-9, GB 592, GB); pap. 5.95 (ISBN 0-19-502683-7). Oxford U Pr.
Das Gupta, Chidananda. The Cinema of Satyajit Ray. (Illus.). 88p. 1980. text ed. 27.50 (ISBN 0-7069-1035-4, Pub. by Vikas India). Advent NY.
--Talking About Films. 1981. 17.50x (ISBN 0-86131-229-5, Orient Longman). South Asia Bks.
Sarkar, Kobita. Indian Cinema Today. LC 75-900977. (Illus.). 1975. 7.50x (ISBN 0-8002-0321-6). Intl Pubns Serv.
--Indian Cinema Today: An Analysis. LC 75-900977. 1975. 9.00x (ISBN 0-88386-597-1). South Asia Bks.
Shah, Panna. Indian Film. LC 81-6268. (Illus.). xv, 290p. 1981. Repr. of 1950 ed. lib. bdg. 15.00 (ISBN 0-8371-3144-8, SHIF). Greenwood.
Vasudev, Aruna. Liberty & Licence in the Indian Cinema. 1978. 11.00x (ISBN 0-8364-0162-X). South Asia Bks.

MOVING-PICTURES-ITALY

Apra, Adriana & Pistagnesi, Patrizia, eds. The Fabulous Thirties: Italian Cinema Nineteen Twenty-Nine to Nineteen Forty-Four. (Illus.). 1979. pap. 12.95 (ISBN 0-8478-5306-3). Rizzoli Intl.
Glasser, et al. Explorations in National Cinema. Lawton, Ben & Staiger, Janet, eds. (Film Studies Annual, 1977: Pt. 1). (Illus.). 1977. pap. 6.00 (ISBN 0-913178-52-7). Redgrave Pub Co.
Jarratt, Vernon. Italian Cinema. Manvell, Roger, ed. LC 78-169338. (National Cinema Series). (Illus.). 152p. 1972. Repr. of 1951 ed. 15.00 (ISBN 0-405-03898-4). Arno.
Malerba, L., ed. Italian Cinema 1945-51. 1976. lib. bdg. 69.95 (ISBN 0-8490-2084-0). Gordon Pr.
Overbey, David, ed. Springtime in Italy: A Reader on Neo-Realism. 242p. 1979. 15.00 (ISBN 0-208-01824-7, Archon). Shoe String.
Prats, A. J. The Autonomous Image: Cinematic Narration & Humanism. LC 81-50182. 192p. 1981. 14.50 (ISBN 0-8131-1406-3). U Pr of Ky.
Trelles Plazaola, Luis. El Cine De Federico Fellini. (UPREX, Teatro y Cine: No. 14). pap. 1.85 (ISBN 0-8477-0014-3). U of PR Pr.

MOVING-PICTURES-JAPAN

Burch, Noel. To the Distant Observer: Form & Meaning in Japanese Cinema. LC 77-20316. 1979. 24.50x (ISBN 0-520-03605-0); pap. 9.75 (ISBN 0-520-03877-0). U of Cal Pr.
Mellen, Joan. The Waves at Genji's Door: Japan Through Its Cinema. LC 76-9592. 448p. 1976. 15.00 (ISBN 0-394-49799-6); pap. 7.95 (ISBN 0-394-73278-2). Pantheon.

MOVING-PICTURES-LATIN AMERICA

Buscombe, et al. Film: Theoretical-Historical Speculations. Lawton, Ben & Staiger, Janet, eds. (Film Studies Annual, 1977: Pt. 2). (Orig.). 1977. pap. 6.00 (ISBN 0-913178-53-5). Redgrave Pub Co.
Johnson, Randal & Stam, Robert. Brazilian Cinema. LC 80-66323. (Illus.). 260p. 1981. 20.00 (ISBN 0-8386-3078-2). Fairleigh Dickinson.

MOVING-PICTURES-NEAR EAST

Landau, Jacob M. Studies in the Arab Theatre & Cinema. LC 56-12588. 1958. 14.00x (ISBN 0-8122-7188-2). U of Pa Pr.

MOVING-PICTURES-NETHERLANDS

Cowie, Peter. Dutch Cinema. LC 79-63543. (Illus.). 1979. 12.00 (ISBN 0-498-02425-3). A S Barnes.

MOVING-PICTURES-RUSSIA

Birkos, Alexander S. Soviet Cinema: Directors & Films. (Illus., Orig.). 1976. 19.50 (ISBN 0-208-01581-7, Archon). Shoe String.
Carter, Huntly. New Theatre & Cinema of Soviet Russia. LC 74-124001. (Literature of Cinema, Ser. 1). Repr. of 1924 ed. 13.00 (ISBN 0-405-01607-7). Arno.
Cohen, Louis H. The Cultural-Political Traditions & Development of the Soviet Cinema: 1917-1972. LC 74-2077. (Dissertations on Film Ser.: Vol. 1). 724p. 1974. 35.00x (ISBN 0-405-04876-9). Arno.
Dickinson, Thorold & De La Roche, Catherine. Soviet Cinema. Manvell, Roger, ed. LC 77-169327. (National Cinema Series). (Illus.). 140p. 1972. Repr. of 1948 ed. 15.00 (ISBN 0-405-03891-7). Arno.
Rimberg, John. The Motion Picture in the Soviet Union, 1918-1952: A Sociological Analysis. LC 72-559. (Dissertations on Film Ser). 238p. 1972. Repr. of 1959 ed. 17.00 (ISBN 0-405-04102-0). Arno.
Schnitzer, Luda, et al. Cinema in Revolution. Robinson, David, tr. (Illus.). 1973. 8.95 (ISBN 0-8090-3467-0). Hill & Wang.
Taylor, R. The Politics of the Soviet Cinema: Nineteen Seventeen to Nineteen Twenty-Nine. LC 78-67809. (International Studies). 1979. 27.50 (ISBN 0-521-22290-7). Cambridge U Pr.
Taylor, Richard. Film Propaganda: Soviet Russia & Nazi Germany. LC 79-1399. (Illus.). 1979. text ed. 25.00x (ISBN 0-06-496778-6). B&N.

MOVING PICTURES-SPAIN

Martinez Torres, Augusto. Diccionario Nuevos Directores Franceses. 176p. (Espn.). 1976. pap. 3.95 (ISBN 84-245-0202-7, S-50075, French & Eur). French & Eur.
This Loving Darkness: The Cinema & Spanish Writers, 1920-1936. 194p. 1980. 39.50 (ISBN 0-19-713440-8). Oxford U Pr.

MOVING-PICTURES-SWEDEN

Cowie, Peter, ed. Sweden, 2 Vols. rev. ed. LC 69-14905. (Screen Ser.). (Illus.). 1969. 4.95 ea. Vol. 1 (ISBN 0-498-07419-6). Vol. 2 (ISBN 0-498-07447-1). A S Barnes.
Glasser, et al. Explorations in National Cinema. Lawton, Ben & Staiger, Janet, eds. (Film Studies Annual, 1977: Pt. 1). (Illus.). 1977. pap. 6.00 (ISBN 0-913178-52-7). Redgrave Pub Co.
Hardy, Forsyth. Scandinavian Film. Manvell, Roger, ed. LC 79-169330. (National Cinema Series). (Illus.). 108p. 1972. Repr. of 1952 ed. 13.00 (ISBN 0-405-03895-X). Arno.

MOVING-PICTURES, AMATEUR

see Amateur Moving-Pictures

MOVING-PICTURES, DOCUMENTARY

see also Moving-Pictures-Evaluation

Alexander, William. Film on the Left: American Documentary Film from 1931 to 1942. LC 80-8534. (Illus.). 364p. 1981. 27.50x (ISBN 0-691-04678-6); pap. 12.50x (ISBN 0-691-10111-6). Princeton U Pr.
Baddeley, W. Hugh. Technique of Documentary Film Production. rev. 4th ed. (Library of Communication Techniques Ser). 1973. 21.95 (ISBN 0-240-50918-8). Focal Pr.
Barnouw, Erik. Documentary: A History of the Non-Fiction Film. (Illus.). 1974. 15.95 (ISBN 0-19-501835-4). Oxford U Pr.
--Documentary: A History of the Non-Fiction Film. LC 74-79618. (Illus.). 336p. 1976. pap. 6.95 (ISBN 0-19-502005-7, 451, GB). Oxford U Pr.
Barsam, Richard M., ed. Nonfiction Film: Theory & Criticism. 1976. pap. 6.95 (ISBN 0-525-47425-0). Dutton.
Centre de Documentation De l'Armement, ed. Lexique des Mots-Cles, Descripteurs et Identificateurs, Francais et Anglais, a Utiliser Pour la Recherche Documentaire, 3 vols. 2001p. (Fr. & Eng., Lexicon of Key Words, Descriptions and Identification to be Used for Documentary Research, English-French). 1976. Set. pap. 95.00 (ISBN 0-686-56758-7, M-6360). French & Eur.
Edmonds, Robert. About Documentary: Anthropology on Film. LC 74-84292. 115p. 1974. text ed. 6.95x (ISBN 0-8278-0295-1); pap. text ed. 4.50x (ISBN 0-8278-0294-3). Intl Bk Co IL.
Fielding, Raymond. The American Newsreel, Nineteen Eleven to Nineteen Sixty Seven. LC 73-17734. (Illus.). 400p. 1972. 17.95 (ISBN 0-8061-1004-X). U of Okla Pr.
Hardy, Forsyth. John Grierson: A Documentary Biography. LC 79-670273. (Illus.). 270p. 1979. 21.95 (ISBN 0-571-10331-6, Pub. by Faber & Faber). Merrimack Bk Serv.
Klein, Walter J. The Sponsored Film. (Communication Arts Bks.). 1976. 13.95 (ISBN 0-8038-6734-4). Hastings.
MacCann, Richard D. The People's Films: A Political History of U. S. Government Motion Pictures. (Studies in Public Communication). 1973. pap. text ed. 7.50x (ISBN 0-8038-5796-9). Hastings.
McGuire, Jerry. How to Write, Direct & Produce Effective Business Films & Documentaries. 14.95 (ISBN 0-8306-7897-2, 897). TAB Bks.
Mamber, Stephen. Cinema Verite in America: Studies in Uncontrolled Documentary. (Illus.). 288p. 1974. 15.00x (ISBN 0-262-13092-0); pap. 5.95 (ISBN 0-262-63058-3). MIT Pr.
Mehta, Ved. The Photographs of Chachaji: The Making of a Documentary Film. (Illus.). 300p. 1980. 15.95 (ISBN 0-19-502792-2). Oxford U Pr.
Nichols, William J. Newsreel. Jowett, Garth S., ed. LC 79-6681. (Dissertations on Film, 1980). 1980. lib. bdg. 25.00x (ISBN 0-405-12914-9). Arno.
Rosenthal, Alan. The Documentary Conscience: A Casebook in Film-Making. LC 79-64487. (Illus.). 1980. 19.50 (ISBN 0-520-03932-7); pap. 8.95 (ISBN 0-520-04022-8, CAL. NO. 436). U of Cal Pr.
Snyder, Robert L. Pare Lorentz & the Documentary Film. LC 68-10301. (Illus.). 1968. 12.50x (ISBN 0-8061-0784-7). U of Okla Pr.
Starr, Cecile, ed. Ideas on Film: A Handbook for the Sixteen Millimeter Film User. facsimile ed. LC 78-134137. (Essay Index Reprint Ser). Repr. of 1951 ed. 22.00 (ISBN 0-8369-2371-5). Arno.
Strasser, Alex. The Work of the Science Film Maker. (Library of Film & Television Practice). 1972. 18.95 (ISBN 0-8038-8051-0). Hastings.
Sussex, Elizabeth. The Rise & Fall of British Documentary: The Story of the Film Movement Founded by John Grierson. LC 74-16719. (Illus.). 1976. 19.50 (ISBN 0-520-02869-4). U of Cal Pr.

MOVING-PICTURES, EXPERIMENTAL

see Experimental Films

MOVING-PICTURES, MUSICAL

see also Moving-Picture Music

Altman, Rick, ed. Genre: The Musical. (BFI Readers in Film Ser.). 180p. 1981. price not set (ISBN 0-7100-0816-3); pap. price not set (ISBN 0-7100-0817-1). Routledge & Kegan.
Appelbaum, Stanley. The Hollywood Musical: A Picture Quiz Book. (Illus., Orig.). 1974. pap. 2.50 (ISBN 0-486-23008-2). Dover.
Burton, Jack. Blue Book of Hollywood Musicals. (Burton Blue Bk). (Illus.). 1953. lib. bdg. 18.00 (ISBN 0-87282-013-0). Century Hse.
Delamater, Jerome. Dance in the Hollywood Musical. Kirkpatrick, Diane, ed. LC 81-7513. (Studies in Photography & Cinematography: No. 4). 324p. 1981. 29.95 (ISBN 0-8357-1198-6, Pub. by UMI Res Pr). Univ Microfilms.
Druxman, Michael B. The Musical: From Broadway to Hollywood. LC 79-62893. (Illus.). 1979. 17.50 (ISBN 0-498-02282-X). A S Barnes.
Gibbon, Monk. Red Shoes Ballet & the Tales of Hoffman, Vol. 14. Kupelnick, Bruce S., ed. LC 76-52106. (Classics of Film Literature Ser.). 1978. lib. bdg. 39.00 (ISBN 0-8240-2878-3). Garland Pub.
Hirschhorn, Clive. The Hollywood Musical. 456p. 1981. 30.00 (ISBN 0-517-54044-4). Crown.
Kreuger, Miles, ed. The Movie Musical from Vitaphone to 42nd Street: As Reported in a Great Fan Magazine. (Illus.). 10.00 (ISBN 0-8446-5212-1). Peter Smith.
Ringgold, Gene & Bodeen, Dewitt. Chevalier: The Films & Career of Maurice Chevalier. (Illus.). 256p. 1973. 12.00 (ISBN 0-8065-0354-8). Citadel Pr.
Sennett, Ted. Hollywood Musicals. (Illus.). 360p. 1981. 50.00 (ISBN 0-8109-1075-6). Abrams.
Woll, Allen L. Songs from Hollywood Musical Comedies, 1927 to the Present: A Dictionary. LC 75-24089. (Reference Library of the Humanities: Vol. 44). 300p. 1975. lib. bdg. 31.00 (ISBN 0-8240-9958-3). Garland Pub.

MOVING-PICTURES, SILENT

Appelbaum, Stanley. Silent Movies: A Picture Quiz Book. 1974. pap. 2.50 (ISBN 0-486-23054-6). Dover.
Berg, Charles M. An Investigation of the Motives for & Realization of Music to Accompany the American Silent Film, 1896-1927. Lowett, Garth E., ed. LC 75-21428. (Dissertations on Film Ser.). 1976. lib. bdg. 18.00x (ISBN 0-405-07531-6). Arno.
Blotnick, Elihu. Saltwater Flats: a silent film. LC 74-18166. (Illus.). 64p. 1975. pap. 9.95 (ISBN 0-915090-00-7). Calif Street.
Brownlow, Kevin. Hollywood: The Pioneers. LC 79-1197. (Illus.). 1980. 20.00 (ISBN 0-394-50851-3). Knopf.
Kerr, Walter. The Silent Clowns. 1975. 20.00 (ISBN 0-394-46907-0). Knopf.
Koszarski, Diane K. The Complete Films of William S. Hart: A Pictorial Record. LC 79-52652. (Illus., Orig.). 1980. pap. 8.95 (ISBN 0-486-23863-6). Dover.
Phillips, Leona R. Silent Cinema: An Annotated Critical Bibliography. 1977. lib. bdg. 69.95 (ISBN 0-8490-1368-2). Gordon Pr.
Pratt, George C. Spellbound in Darkness: A History of the Silent Film. LC 72-80412. (Illus.). 576p. 1973. pap. 9.95 (ISBN 0-8212-0489-0, 805769). NYGS.
Reade, Eric. Australian Silent Films: A Pictorial History, 1896-1929. 1970. 12.50 (ISBN 0-87491-368-3). Acropolis.
Slide, Anthony & Wagenknecht, Edward. Fifty Great American Silent Films, Nineteen Twelve to Nineteen Twenty: A Pictorial Survey. (Illus.). 12.50 (ISBN 0-8446-5813-8). Peter Smith.
--Fifty Great American Silent Films 1912-1920: A Pictorial Survey. Date not set. 12.50 (ISBN 0-8446-5813-8). Peter Smith.
Weaver, John T. Twenty Years of Silents, Nineteen Hundred & Eight to Nineteen Twenty-Eight. LC 73-157729. 514p. 1971. lib. bdg. 20.50 (ISBN 0-8108-0299-6). Scarecrow.

MOVING-PICTURES, TALKING

see also Video Tapes

Cameron, Evan W., ed. Sound & the Cinema: The Coming of Sound to American Film. 1979. pap. 7.40 (ISBN 0-913178-56-X). Redgrave Pub Co.
Frater, Charles. Sound Recording for Motion Pictures. LC 74-19811. (Illus.). 1979. pap. 5.95 (ISBN 0-498-01666-8). A S Barnes.
Geduld, Harry M. The Birth of the Talkies: From Edison to Jolson. LC 74-11887. 352p. 1975. 12.50x (ISBN 0-253-10743-1). Ind U Pr.
Griffith, Richard. The Talkies. LC 71-164734. (Dover Film Ser). (Orig.). 1971. pap. 6.95 (ISBN 0-486-22762-6). Dover.

MOVING-PICTURES ABOUT ART

see Art in Moving-Pictures

MOVING-PICTURES AND CHILDREN

Charters, W. W. Motion Pictures & Youth: A Summary. LC 73-124025. (Literature of Cinema Ser.: Payne Fund Studies of Motion Pictures & Social Values). Repr. of 1933 ed. 4.00 (ISBN 0-405-01642-5). Arno.
Dale, Edgar. Children's Attendance at Motion Pictures. Bd. with The Emotional Responses of Children to the Motion Picture Situation. Dysinger, Wendell S. & Ruckmick, Christian A.. LC 75-125462. (Literature of Cinema Ser.: Payne Fund Studies). Repr. of 1935 ed. 7.00 (ISBN 0-405-01643-3). Arno.
Edgar, Patricia. Children & Screen Violence. 1977. 17.95x (ISBN 0-7022-1403-5). U of Queensland Pr.
Forman, Henry J. Our Movie Made Children. LC 72-124028. (Literature of Cinema Ser: Payne Fund Studies of Motion Pictures & Social Values). Repr. of 1935 ed. 12.00 (ISBN 0-405-01646-8). Arno.
Goldstein, Ruth M. & Zornow, Edith. The Screen Image of Youth: Movies About Children & Adolescents. LC 80-14053. (Illus.). xxi, 363p. 1980. 20.00 (ISBN 0-8108-1316-5). Scarecrow.
Mitchell, Alice M. Children & Movies. LC 70-160240. (Moving Pictures Ser). xxiv, 181p. 1971. Repr. of 1929 ed. lib. bdg. 10.95x (ISBN 0-89198-041-5). Ozer.
Renshaw, Samuel, et al. Children's Sleep: A Series of Studies on the Influence of Motion Pictures. LC 76-124031. (Literature of Cinema Ser: Payne Fund Studies of Motion Pictures & Social Valves). Repr. of 1933 ed. 10.00 (ISBN 0-405-01631-X). Arno.
UNESCO. The Influence of the Cinema on Children & Adolescents. LC 74-31869. (Reports & Papers on Mass Communication Ser). 106p. 1975. Repr. of 1961 ed. lib. bdg. 15.00x (ISBN 0-8371-7944-0, UNIC). Greenwood.

MOVING-PICTURES AND DANCING

see Dancing in Moving-Pictures, Television, etc.

MOVING-PICTURES AND LIBRARIES

see Libraries and Moving-Pictures

MOVING-PICTURES AND LITERATURE

Aquino, John. Film in the Language Arts Class. 56p. 1976. pap. 2.75 (ISBN 0-686-63668-6, 1811-7-06). NEA.
Cohen. Film & Fiction. LC 79-64073. 1979. 14.50x (ISBN 0-300-02366-9). Yale U Pr.
Harrington, John. Film and-as Literature. (Illus.). 1977. pap. text ed. 11.95 (ISBN 0-13-315945-0). P-H.
McConnell, Frank. Storytelling & Mythmaking: Images from Film & Literature. LC 78-27538. (Illus.). 1979. 13.95 (ISBN 0-19-502572-5). Oxford U Pr.

Marcus, Fred H. Short Story-Short Film. (Illus.). 1977. pap. text ed. 11.95 (ISBN 0-13-809558-2). P-H.
Murray, Edward. The Cinematic Imagination: Writers & the Motion Pictures. LC 74-178168. 340p. 1972. 12.00 (ISBN 0-8044-2643-0). Ungar.
Peary, Gerald & Shatzkin, Roger, eds. The Modern American Novel & the Movies. LC 78-4373. (Ungar Film Library). (Illus.). 1978. 15.95 (ISBN 0-8044-2682-1); pap. 6.95 (ISBN 0-8044-6649-1). Ungar.
Pohle, Robert W., Jr. & Hart, Douglas C. Sherlock Holmes on the Screen. LC 76-10887. (Illus.). 1977. 19.95 (ISBN 0-498-01889-X). A S Barnes.
Spiegel, Alan. Fiction & the Camera Eye: Visual Consciousness in Film & the Modern Novel. LC 75-22353. 1976. 12.95x (ISBN 0-8139-0598-2). U Pr of Va.
Van Wert, W. F. The Theory & Practice of the Cine-Roman. LC 77-22912. 1978. lib. bdg. 24.00x (ISBN 0-405-10756-0). Arno.
Wagner, Geoffrey. The Novel & the Cinema. LC 74-20939. (Illus.). 394p. 1975. 18.00 (ISBN 0-8386-1618-6). Fairleigh Dickinson.
Winston, Douglas G. The Screenplay As Literature. LC 72-654. 240p. 1973. 16.50 (ISBN 0-8386-1200-8). Fairleigh Dickinson.

MOVING-PICTURES AND RELIGION
see Moving-Pictures–Moral and Religious Aspects

MOVING-PICTURES AND TELEVISION
see also Television Film
Englander, A. Arthur & Petzold, Paul. Filming for Television. (Communication Arts Bks.). 1976. 19.50 (ISBN 0-240-50961-7). Focal Pr.
Ewing, Sam. Don't Look at the Camera: Shortcuts to Television Photography & Filmmaking. LC 72-97218. (Illus.). 224p. 1973. 9.95 (ISBN 0-8306-3649-8, 649). TAB Bks.
Scheuer, Steven H., ed. Movies on TV: 1981-82. 816p. (Orig.). pap. 3.95 (ISBN 0-553-13815-4). Bantam.

MOVING-PICTURES AS A PROFESSION
see also Acting As a Profession
Bukalski, Peter, ed. American Film Institute Guide to College Courses in Film & Television. 7th ed. 334p. 1980. pap. 11.50 (ISBN 0-87866-158-1). Petersons Guides.
Callow, Ridgeway, et al. You Can Make It: A Insider's Guide to a Hollywood Career. (Illus.). 88p. (Orig.). 1981. pap. 7.95 (ISBN 0-9606328-0-8). You Can Make It Ent.
Goldreich, Gloria & Goldreich, Esther. What Can She Be? A Film Producer. LC 77-8889. (What Can She Be? Ser.). (Illus.). (gr. 1-5). 1977. PLB 7.20 (ISBN 0-688-51815-X). Lothrop.
Hyland, Wende & Haynes, Roberta. How to Make It in Hollywood. LC 75-17523. 250p. 1975. 15.95x (ISBN 0-88229-239-0). Nelson Hall.
London, Mel. Getting into Film. LC 77-78329. 1977. pap. 9.95 (ISBN 0-345-28977-3). Ballantine.
Photoplay Research Society. Opportunities in the Motion Picture Industry & How to Qualify for Positions in Its Many Branches. LC 73-124033. (Literature of Cinema, Ser. 1). Repr. of 1922 ed. 9.00 (ISBN 0-405-01633-6). Arno.
Shaw, William H. Presenting Entertainment Arts: Stage, Film, Television. 192p. 1980. pap. text ed. 9.95 (ISBN 0-8403-2226-7). Kendall-Hunt.
Tromberg, Sheldon. Making Money Making Movies: The Independent Movie Maker's Handbook. 1979. 6.95 (ISBN 0-531-06370-4); pap. 6.95 (ISBN 0-531-06753-X). Watts.

MOVING-PICTURES FOR CHILDREN
Here are entered works which discuss collectively fiction and non-fiction films for children.
see also Moving-Pictures and Children
Gaffney, Maureen, ed. More Films Kids Like. LC 77-12174. 1977. pap. 9.50 (ISBN 0-8389-0250-2). ALA.
Goldstein, Ruth M. & Zornow, Edith. Movies for Kids: A Guide for Parents & Teachers on the Entertainment Film for Children. rev. ed. LC 79-6149. (Illus.). 300p. 1980. 14.95 (ISBN 0-8044-2267-2); pap. 6.95 (ISBN 0-8044-6194-5). Ungar.
Great Moments from the Films of Walt Disney. 96p. 1981. 10.95 (ISBN 0-8317-3975-4, Rutledge Pr). Smith Pubs.

MOVING-PICTURES IN BUSINESS
see Moving-Pictures in Industry

MOVING-PICTURES IN EDUCATION
see also Libraries and Moving-Pictures; Moving-Pictures–Evaluation
Aquino, John. Film in the Language Arts Class. 56p. 1976. pap. 2.75 (ISBN 0-686-63668-6, 1811-7-06). NEA.
Arnspiger, Varney C. Measuring the Effectiveness of Sound Pictures As Teaching Aids. LC 71-176524. (Columbia University. Teachers College. Contributions to Education: No. 565). Repr. of 1933 ed. 17.50 (ISBN 0-404-55565-9). AMS Pr.
Beatty, LaMond F. Motion Pictures. Duane, James E., ed. LC 80-21340. (The Instructional Media Library: Vol. 8). (Illus.). 112p. 1981. 13.95 (ISBN 0-87778-168-0). Educ Tech Pubns.
Bell, Geoffrey. Eight Millimeter Film for Adult Audiences. 1968. pap. 2.25 (ISBN 92-3-100715-7, U215, UNESCO). Unipub.
Blackaby, Linda, et al. In Focus: A Guide to Using Films. (Cine Information Ser.). 1980. pap. 10.95 (ISBN 0-918432-22-7). NY Zoetrope.
Dale, Edgar, et al. Motion Pictures in Education: A Summary of the Literature. LC 71-124003. (Literature of Cinema, Ser. 1). Repr. of 1938 ed. 15.00 (ISBN 0-405-01609-3). Arno.
Diffor, John C. & Horkheimer, Mary F., eds. Educators Guide to Free Films. 40th rev. ed. LC 45-412. 1980. pap. 17.75 (ISBN 0-87708-101-8). Ed Prog.
Herman, Lewis. Educational Films: Writing, Directing, Producing for Classroom, Television & Industry. (YA) (gr. 9 up). 1965. 5.95 (ISBN 0-517-50956-3). Crown.
Hoban, Charles F. & Van Ormer, Edward B. Instructional Film Research, Nineteen Eighteen to Nineteen Fifty. LC 76-124015. (Literature of Cinema, Ser. 1). Repr. of 1950 ed. 13.00 (ISBN 0-405-01621-2). Arno.
Hodgkinson, A. W. Screen Education. (Orig.). 1964. pap. 4.00 (ISBN 92-3-100554-5, U591, UNESCO). Unipub.
Jackson, Martin A. & O'Connor, John E. Teaching History with Film. LC 74-78660. (Discussions on Teaching Ser: No. 2). (Illus.). 60p. 1974. pap. 1.50 (ISBN 0-87229-018-2). Am Hist Assn.
Knowlton, D. C. Motion Pictures in History Teaching. 1929. 24.50x (ISBN 0-685-69835-1). Elliots Bks.
Lacey, Richard A. Seeing with Feeling: Film in the Classroom. LC 77-165281. (Massachusetts Education Ser.). (Illus.). 1972. pap. 3.95 (ISBN 0-7216-5590-4). HR&W.
Marchant, James & Jowett, Garth S., eds. The Cinema in Education. LC 77-11381. (Aspects of Film Ser.). (Illus.). 1978. Repr. of 1925 ed. lib. bdg. 15.00x (ISBN 0-405-11140-1). Arno.
Maynard, Richard. Classroom Cinema. LC 77-21653. (Illus.). 1977. pap. text ed. 7.50x (ISBN 0-8077-2540-4). Tchr's Coll.
Miller, Hannah E. Films in the Classroom: A Practical Guide. LC 78-21941. 1979. lib. bdg. 13.50 (ISBN 0-8108-1184-7). Scarecrow.
Murray, Lawrence. The Celluloid Persuasion. LC 79-16764. (Orig.). 1980. pap. 6.95 (ISBN 0-8028-1813-7). Eerdmans.
Parlato, Salvatore J., Jr. Films-Too Good for Words: A Directory of Nonnarrated 16mm Films. LC 72-12831. 192p. 1973. 16.95 (ISBN 0-8352-0618-1). Bowker.
--Superfilms: An International Guide to Award Winning Educational Films. LC 76-10801. 1976. 16.50 (ISBN 0-8108-0953-2). Scarecrow.
Ross, Theodore J. Film & the Liberal Arts. LC 78-104815. 1970. pap. text ed. 8.95x (ISBN 0-03-081104-X). Irvington.
Rulon, P. J. The Sound Motion Picture in Science Teaching. (Harvard Studies in Education: Vol. 20). Repr. of 1933 ed. pap. 15.50 (ISBN 0-384-52560-1). Johnson Repr.
Schillaci, Anthony & Culkin, John M., eds. Films Deliver: Teaching Creatively with Film. LC 70-130630. (Illus., Orig.). 1970. pap. 5.95 (ISBN 0-590-09155-7, Citation). Schol Bk Serv.
Smith, P., ed. The Historian & Film. LC 75-19577. 235p. 1976. 24.95 (ISBN 0-521-20992-7). Cambridge U Pr.
Westfall, Leon H. A Study of Verbal Accompaniments to Educational Motion Pictures. LC 76-177647. (Columbia University. Teachers College. Contributions to Education: No. 617). Repr. of 1934 ed. 17.50 (ISBN 0-404-55617-5). AMS Pr.

MOVING-PICTURES IN INDUSTRY
Burder, John. Work of the Industrial Film Maker. (Library of Film & Television Practice). 1974. 16.95 (ISBN 0-8038-8053-7). Hastings.
--Work of the Industrial Film Maker. (Library of Film & Television Practice). 1974. 14.50 (ISBN 0-240-50762-2). Focal Pr.
Educational Research Council of America. Industrial Film Maker. rev. ed. Ferris, Theodore N. & Marchak, John P., eds. (Real People at Work Ser: G). (Illus.). 1976. pap. text ed. 2.25 (ISBN 0-89247-053-4). Changing Times.
The Industrial Film Guide. 1st ed. LC 75-307020. 400p. 1974. 15.00x (ISBN 0-85038-330-7). Intl Pubns Serv.
Klein, Walter J. The Sponsored Film. (Communication Arts Bks.). 1976. 13.95 (ISBN 0-8038-6734-4). Hastings.
McGuire, Jerry. How to Write, Direct & Produce Effective Business Films & Documentaries. 14.95 (ISBN 0-8306-7897-2, 897). TAB Bks.
Soft-Aware Associates, Inc. Reel Change: A Guide to Films on Appropriate Technology. LC 79-90198. 1979. pap. 3.50 (ISBN 0-913890-34-0). Friends Earth.
Systems Film Catalog. (Reference Ser.). 1977. 3.00 (ISBN 0-934356-17-3). Assn Syst Mgmt.

MOVING-PICTURES IN PSYCHOTHERAPY
see also Psychodrama

MOVING-PICTURES IN THE SOCIAL SCIENCES
see also Social Sciences–Study and Teaching
Worth, Sol & Adair, John. Through Navajo Eyes: An Exploration in Film Communication & Anthropology. LC 78-180488. (Illus.). 320p. 1973. 12.50x (ISBN 0-253-36015-3); pap. 4.50x (ISBN 0-253-36016-1). Ind U Pr.

MOVING-PICTURES ON TELEVISION
see Television Broadcasting of Films

MOWING MACHINES
see also Harvesting Machinery
Peterson, Franklyn, ed. Handbook of Landmower Repair. rev. ed. LC 77-92313. (Illus.). 1978. pap. 5.95 (ISBN 0-8015-3256-6, Hawthorn). Dutton.

MOWRY, SALOME LINCOLN, 1807-1841
Davis, Almond H. The Female Preacher: Memoir of Salome Lincoln, Afterwards the Wife of Elder Junia S. Mowry. LC 72-2599. (American Women Ser: Images & Realities). (Illus.). 168p. 1972. Repr. of 1843 ed. 9.50 (ISBN 0-405-04489-5). Arno.

MOXON, EMMA ISOLA, 1809-1891
Ross, Ernest C. Charles Lamb & Emma Isola. 1950. lib. bdg. 10.00 (ISBN 0-8414-2579-5). Folcroft.

MOYLAN, STEPHEN, 1734-1811
Griffin, Marvin I. General Stephen Moylan, Muster-Master General, Secretary & Aide-De-Camp to General Washington. 1972. Repr. of 1909 ed. 18.50x (ISBN 0-8422-8062-6). Irvington.

MOZAMBIQUE
Barnard, F. L. Three Years' Cruize in the Mozambique Channel: For the Suppression of the Slave Trade. facs. ed. LC 79-149863. (Black Heritage Library Collection Ser). 1848. 17.25 (ISBN 0-8369-8745-4). Arno.
Elkiss, T. H. The Quest for an African Eldorado: Sofala, Southern Zambezia, & the Portuguese, 1500-1865. (Illus.). 124p. 1981. write for info. (ISBN 0-918456-41-X). Crossroads MA.
Hardy, Ronald. Rivers of Darkness. LC 78-11788. 1979. 10.95 (ISBN 0-399-12266-4). Putnam.
Henriksen, Thomas H. Mozambique: A History. (Illus.). 276p. 1979. 25.75x (ISBN 0-8476-2291-6). Rowman.
Isaacman, Allen. The Tradition of Resistance in Mozambique: The Zambesi Valley. LC 75-17292. 1977. 25.00x (ISBN 0-520-03065-6). U of Cal Pr.
Lappe, Frances M. & Beccar-Varela, Adele. Mozambique & Tanzania: Asking the Big Questions. (Illus.). 128p. 1980. pap. 4.75 (ISBN 0-935028-05-6). Inst Food & Develop.
Martins, Elisio. Colonialism & Imperialism in Mozambique. 206p. 1974. pap. 4.95 (ISBN 0-88289-097-2). Pelican.
Mittelman, James H. Underdevelopment & the Transition to Socialism: Mozambique & Tanzania. LC 81-2728. (Studies in Social Discontinuity Ser.). 1981. 27.50 (ISBN 0-12-500660-8). Acad Pr.
Mondlane, Eduardo. The Struggle for Mozambique. 256p. 1981. Repr. of 1969 ed. 35.00 (ISBN 0-86232-011-9, Pub. by Zed Pr). Lawrence Hill.
Peters, Karl. Eladorado of the Ancients. LC 70-88445. (Illus.). Repr. of 1902 ed. 31.00x (ISBN 0-8371-1905-7, Pub. by Negro U Pr). Greenwood.
Searle, Chris. We're Building the New School! Diary of a Teacher in Mozambique, 1977-1978. (Illus.). 240p. (Orig.). 1981. 18.00 (ISBN 0-905762-87-8, Pub. by Zed Pr); pap. cancelled (ISBN 0-905762-88-6). Lawrence Hill.
Serapiao, Luis B. & El-Khawas, Mohamed A. Mozambique in the Twentieth Century: From Colonialism to Independence. LC 79-64964. 1979. pap. text ed. 12.00 (ISBN 0-8191-0502-3). U Pr of Amer.
Theal, George M. Portuguese in South Africa. LC 73-82020. Repr. of 1896 ed. 15.25x (ISBN 0-8371-1570-1). Greenwood.
Vail, Leroy & White, Landeg. Capitalism & Colonialism in Mozambique: A Study of the Quelimane District. LC 80-22702. (Illus.). 424p. 1981. 45.00x (ISBN 0-8166-1039-8). U of Minn Pr.

MOZART, JOHANN CHRYSOSTOM WOLFGANG AMADEUS, 1756-1791
Badura-Skoda, Eva & Badura-Skoda, Paul. Interpreting Mozart on the Keyboard. 1957. 17.00 (ISBN 0-312-42525-2); pap. 4.95 (ISBN 0-312-42490-6). St Martin.
Benn, Frederick C. Mozart on the Stage. LC 74-24041. Repr. of 1946 ed. 18.00 (ISBN 0-404-12864-5). AMS Pr.
Berlioz, Hector. Mozart, Weber & Wagner. 1976. Repr. of 1918 ed. lib. bdg. 35.00 (ISBN 0-403-08963-8). Scholarly.
Biancolli, Louis, ed. The Mozart Handbook: A Guide to the Man & His Music. LC 75-32504. (Illus.). 629p. 1976. Repr. of 1954 ed. lib. bdg. 35.50x (ISBN 0-8371-8496-7, BIMH). Greenwood.
Blom, Eric. Mozart. rev. ed. (Master Musicians Ser.: No. M155). (Illus.). 388p. 1978. pap. 7.95 (ISBN 0-8226-0700-X). Littlefield.
--Mozart. rev. ed. (Master Musicians Ser). (Illus.). 400p. 1976. Repr. of 1974 ed. 13.50x (ISBN 0-460-03157-0, Pub. by J. M. Dent England). Biblio Dist.
Broder, Nathan. Great Operas of Mozart. 1962. 9.95 (ISBN 0-02-870440-1). Schirmer Bks.
Buchner, Alexander. Mozart & Prague. LC 73-181118. 22.00 (ISBN 0-403-01517-0). Scholarly.
Davenport, Marcia. Mozart. 1979. pap. 3.50 (ISBN 0-380-45534-X, 45534, Discus). Avon.
--Mozart. (Illus.). 1956. lib. rep. ed. 20.00 (ISBN 0-684-14504-9, ScribT). Scribner.
Deutsch, Otto E. Mozart: A Documentary Biography. 1966. 22.50x (ISBN 0-8047-0233-0). Stanford U Pr.
De Wyzewa, T. & De Saint-Foix, G. Mozart: Sa Vie Musicale & Son Oeuvre, 2 vols. (Music Reprint 1980 Ser.). 2274p. 1980. Repr. of 1936 ed. Set. lib. bdg. 95.00 (ISBN 0-306-79561-2). Da Capo.
Dickinson, Alan E. A Study of Mozart's Last Three Symphonies. LC 73-181142. 1927. Repr. 29.00 (ISBN 0-403-01543-X). Scholarly.
Dunhill, Thomas F. Mozart's String Quartets. LC 77-104260. Repr. of 1927 ed. lib. bdg. 15.00x (ISBN 0-8371-3919-8, DUMQ). Greenwood.
Einstein, Alfred. Mozart: His Character, His Work. (Orig.). 1945. 29.95x (ISBN 0-19-500538-4). Oxford U Pr.
--Mozart: His Character, His Work. 1965. pap. 9.95 (ISBN 0-19-500732-8, GB). Oxford U Pr.
Farmer, Henry G. & Smith, Herbert. New Mozartiana. LC 74-24077. (Illus.). Repr. of 1935 ed. 19.50 (ISBN 0-404-12906-4). AMS Pr.
Gehring, Franz E. Mozart. facsimile ed. LC 78-37881. (Select Bibliographies Reprint Ser). Repr. of 1883 ed. 14.00 (ISBN 0-8369-6718-6). Arno.
Gianturco, Carolyn. Mozart's Early Operas. (Illus.). 192p. 1981. 35.00 (ISBN 0-7134-2240-8, Pub. by Batsford England). David & Charles.
Girdlestone, Cuthbert. Mozart & His Piano Concertos. 10.00 (ISBN 0-8446-2131-5). Peter Smith.
Gounod, Charles F. Mozart's Don Giovanni: A Commentary. LC 78-125050. (Music Ser). 1970. Repr. of 1895 ed. lib. bdg. 17.50 (ISBN 0-306-70015-8). Da Capo.
Haldane, Charlotte. Mozart. LC 75-3733. (Illus.). 1976. Repr. of 1960 ed. lib. bdg. 14.00x (ISBN 0-8371-8062-7, HAMOZ). Greenwood.
Hildesheimer, Wolfgang. Mozart. (Suhrkamp Taschenbuecher: No. 598). 432p. 1980. pap. text ed. 6.50 (ISBN 3-518-37098-7, Pub. by Suhrkamp Verlag Germany). Suhrkamp.
--Mozart. Faber, Marion, tr. from Ger. (Illus.). 1981. 20.00 (ISBN 0-374-21483-2). FS&G.
Hitchcock, Thomas. Unhappy Loves of Men of Genius: Gibbon, Johnson, Goethe, Mozart & Irving. 1979. Repr. of 1892 ed. lib. bdg. 25.00 (ISBN 0-8492-5322-5). R West.
Holmes, Edward. The Life of Mozart. (Music Reprint Ser.). 1979. Repr. of 1845 ed. lib. bdg. 29.50 (ISBN 0-306-79560-4). Da Capo.
--The Life of Mozart. LC 79-25356. 303p. 1980. Repr. of 1912 ed. lib. bdg. 24.25x (ISBN 0-313-22283-5, HOLM). Greenwood.
Hughes, Spike. Famous Mozart Operas. rev. ed. 256p. 1972. pap. 3.00 (ISBN 0-486-22858-4). Dover.
--Famous Mozart Operas: An Analytical Guide for the Opera-Goer & Armchair Listener. 2nd rev. ed. (Illus.). 6.00 (ISBN 0-8446-4559-1). Peter Smith.
Hussey, Dyneley. Wolfgang Amade Mozart. LC 70-104288. (Illus.). 1971. Repr. of 1928 ed. lib. bdg. 16.00x (ISBN 0-8371-3957-0, HUWM). Greenwood.
--Wolfgang Amade Mozart. LC 73-94272. (Select Bibliographies Reprint Ser). 1928. 24.00 (ISBN 0-8369-5046-1). Arno.
Hutchings, Arthur. Companion to Mozart's Piano Concertos. 2nd ed. 1950. 14.95x (ISBN 0-19-318404-4). Oxford U Pr.
--Mozart: the Man - the Musician. LC 75-13790. 1976. 45.00 (ISBN 0-02-871140-8). Schirmer Bks.
--Mozart: the Man - the Musician. LC 75-13790. 1976. 45.00 (ISBN 0-02-871140-8). Schirmer Bks.
Jahn, Otto. Life of Mozart, 3 Vols. Townsend, Pauline D., ed. LC 78-125917. (Illus.). 1970. Repr. of 1891 ed. lib. bdg. 57.50x (ISBN 0-8154-0343-7). Cooper Sq.

Kenyon, Max. Mozart in Salzburg. LC 78-13863. (Encore Music Editions Ser.). (Illus.). 1979. Repr. of 1953 ed. 22.50 (ISBN 0-88355-803-3). Hyperion Conn.
Kerst, Friedrich. Mozart: The Man & the Artist As Revealed in His Own Words. Krehbiel, Henry E., tr. 1926. pap. 2.25 (ISBN 0-486-21316-1). Dover.
Keys, Ivor. Mozart, His Music in His Life. LC 79-19028. (Illus.). 1980. text ed. 24.50x (ISBN 0-8419-0576-2). Holmes & Meier.
King, A. Hyatt. Mozart Chamber Music. LC 79-80512. (BBC Music Guides Ser.: No. 4). (Illus.). 68p. 1969. pap. 2.95 (ISBN 0-295-95018-8, BBC4). U of Wash Pr.
King, Alec H. Mozart Wind & String Concertos. LC 75-27957. (BBC Music Guides: No. 35). (Illus.). 64p. (Orig.). 1978. pap. 2.95 (ISBN 0-295-95478-7). U of Wash Pr.
King, Alec H., ed. Mozart: A Biography, with a Survey of Books, Editions, & Recordings. (Concertgoer's Companion Ser). 1970. 13.50 (ISBN 0-208-00887-X, Archon). Shoe String.
King, Alexander. Mozart in Retrospect. LC 76-1016. 278p. 1976. Repr. of 1970 ed. lib. bdg. 18.50x (ISBN 0-8371-8760-5, KIMR). Greenwood.
Kolb, Annette. Mozart. LC 74-29634. (Illus.). 299p. 1975. Repr. of 1956 ed. lib. bdg. 18.50x (ISBN 0-8371-7977-7, KOMO). Greenwood.
Landon, H. Robbins & Mitchell, Donald, eds. Mozart Companion. 1969. pap. 5.95 (ISBN 0-393-00499-6, Norton Lib). Norton.
--Mozart Companion. 1969. pap. 5.95 (ISBN 0-393-00499-6, Norton Lib). Norton.
Lang, Paul H., ed. Creative World of Mozart. (Illus.). 1963. pap. 3.95 (ISBN 0-393-00218-7, Norton Lib). Norton.
Levey, Michael. Life & Death of Mozart. LC 70-163451. 1972. pap. 3.95 (ISBN 0-8128-1530-0). Stein & Day.
Liebner, Janos. Mozart on the Stage. 1980. pap. 4.95 (ISBN 0-7145-1070-X). Riverrun NY.
Lievense, W. De Familie Mozart Op Bezoek in Nederland: Een Reisverslag. 1965. 22.50 (ISBN 90-6027-019-3, Pub. by Frits Knuf Netherlands). Pendragon NY.
Lingg, Ann M. Mozart: Genius of Harmony. LC 75-154714. 331p. 1973. Repr. of 1946 ed. 17.00 (ISBN 0-8046-1743-0). Kennikat.
Lusington, Vernon. Mozart: A Commemorative Address. 1976. Repr. of 1883 ed. lib. bdg. 19.00 (ISBN 0-403-03806-5). Scholarly.
Luthy, W. Mozart und Die Tonarten-Characteristik. (Sammlung Mw.Abh. Ser.). iv, 94p. 24.50 (ISBN 90-6027-291-9, Pub. by Frits Knuf Netherlands). Pendragon NY.
Mann, William. The Operas of Mozart. LC 76-9279. (Illus.). 1977. 35.00 (ISBN 0-19-519891-3). Oxford U Pr.
Marks, F. Helena. The Sonata, Its Form & Meaning As Exemplified in the Piano Sonatas by Mozart: A Descriptive Analysis with Musical Examples. LC 78-66911. (Encore Music Editions Ser.). (Illus.). 1980. Repr. of 1921 ed. 19.50 (ISBN 0-88355-751-7). Hyperion Conn.
Mersmann, Hans, ed. Letters of Wolfgang Amadeus Mozart. Bozman, M. M., tr. (Illus.). 6.75 (ISBN 0-8446-4587-7). Peter Smith.
Milnes, John, et al. The Magic Flute: Mozart. Beasch, Anthony & Besch, Anthony, trs. 1980. pap. 4.95 (ISBN 0-7145-3768-3). Riverrun NY.
Mozart: Der Schauspieldirektor. facsimile ed. 1976. in slipcase 65.00 (ISBN 0-685-65615-2, Oxford U Pr); pap. 25.00 (ISBN 0-87598-055-4). Pierpont Morgan.
Mozart, Wolfgang A. Eine Kleine Nachtmusik: Reproduction of the Autograph Manuscript. 525p. 8.00 (ISBN 0-8446-0812-2). Peter Smith.
--Man & the Artist Revealed in His Own Words. Krehbiel, tr. & ed. 5.50 (ISBN 0-8446-2626-0). Peter Smith.
Nettl, Paul. Mozart & Masonry. LC 78-114564. (Music Ser). 1957. Repr. of 1957 ed. lib. bdg. 17.50 (ISBN 0-306-71922-3). Da Capo.
Niemtschek, Franz X. Life of Mozart. Mautner, Helen, tr. LC 78-66914. (Encore Music Editions Ser.). 1979. Repr. of 1956 ed. 12.50 (ISBN 0-88355-754-1). Hyperion Conn.
--Life of Mozart. LC 74-181224. 87p. 1956. Repr. 18.00 (ISBN 0-403-01751-3). Scholarly.
Osborne, Charles. The Complete Operas of Mozart. LC 78-55623. 1978. 14.95 (ISBN 0-689-10886-9). Atheneum.
Ottaway, Hugh. Mozart. (Illus.). 208p. 1980. 19.95 (ISBN 0-8143-1657-3). Wayne St U Pr.
Pohl, C. F. Mozart & Haydn in London, 2 vols. in 1. LC 70-125059. (Music Ser). 1970. Repr. of 1867 ed. lib. bdg. 35.00 (ISBN 0-306-70024-7). Da Capo.
Radcliffe, Philip. Mozart Piano Concertos. LC 75-27958. (BBC Music Guides: No. 34). (Illus.). 64p. (Orig.). 1978. pap. 2.95 (ISBN 0-295-95477-9). U of Wash Pr.
Roseberry, Eric. W. A. Mozart. LC 60-3144. (Great Masters Ser.). 1960. pap. 3.00 (ISBN 0-913932-20-5). Boosey & Hawkes.
Rosen, Charles. The Classical Style: Haydn, Mozart, Beethoven. LC 72-8920. (Illus.). 464p. 1972. pap. 6.95 (ISBN 0-393-00653-0, Norton Lib). Norton.
Sachs, David. Mozart. (Illus.). 128p. 1980. pap. text ed. 5.95 (ISBN 0-8256-3159-9). Music Sales.
Sadie, Stanley. Mozart. LC 70-94089. (Illus.). 192p. 1970. pap. 7.50x (ISBN 0-670-49198-5). Vienna Hse.
Singer, Irving. Mozart & Beethoven: The Concept of Love in Their Operas. LC 77-4551. 1977. text ed. 12.00x (ISBN 0-8018-1987-3). Johns Hopkins.
Sitwell, Sacheverell. Mozart. facsimile ed. LC 71-114896. (Select Bibliographies Reprint Ser). 1932. 15.00 (ISBN 0-8369-5300-2). Arno.
--Mozart. Repr. of 1932 ed. lib. bdg. 15.00 (ISBN 0-8371-4022-6, SIMO). Greenwood.
Stendhal. Vie de Haydn, de Mozart et de Metastase. 48.00 (ISBN 0-686-55083-8). French & Eur.
Stendhal, et al. Haydn, Mozart et Metatase. (Illus.). 9.95 (ISBN 0-686-55061-7). French & Eur.
Thomson, Katharine. The Masonic Thread in Mozart. (Illus.). 1977. text ed. 13.50x (ISBN 0-85315-381-7). Humanities.
Tobin, Joseph R. Mozart & the Sonata Form. LC 76-125063. (Music Ser). 1971. Repr. of 1916 ed. lib. bdg. 15.00 (ISBN 0-306-70027-1). Da Capo.
--Mozart & the Sonata Form: A Companion Book to Any Edition of Mozart's Piano Sonatas-Including an Analysis of the Form of Each Movement. LC 76-109867. 1971. Repr. of 1916 ed. lib. bdg. 15.00x (ISBN 0-8371-4358-6, TOMS). Greenwood.
Turner, Walter J. Mozart: The Man & His Works. LC 78-20497. (Encore Music Editions Ser.). 1981. Repr. of 1938 ed. 28.50 (ISBN 0-88355-873-4). Hyperion Conn.
--Mozart: The Man & His Works. LC 78-60148. 1979. Repr. of 1938 ed. lib. bdg. 27.50x (ISBN 0-313-20550-7, TUMO). Greenwood.
Von Kochel, Ludwig R. Chronologischthematisches Verzeichnis Saemtlicher Tonwerke Wolfgang Amadeus Mozarts. (Tr, from Ger). 1971. Repr. of 1862 ed. 79.00 (ISBN 0-403-01060-8). Scholarly.
Woodford, Peggy. Mozart: His Life & Times. expanded ed. (Life & Times Ser.). (Illus.). 192p. 1981. Repr. of 1977 ed. 19.95 (ISBN 0-87666-643-8, Z-42). Paganiniana Pubns.
--Mozart: His Life & Times. (Illustrated Lives & Times of the Composers). (Illus.). 1978. 16.95 (ISBN 0-8467-0419-6, Pub. by Two Continents); pap. 9.95 (ISBN 0-8467-0420-X). Hippocrene Bks.
Wyzewa, Th. & Saint-Foix, G. W. A. Mozart: Sa Vie Musicale et Son Oeuvre, 2 vols. (Music Reprint Ser.). 1980. Repr. of 1946 ed. Set. 95.00 (ISBN 0-306-79561-2). Da Capo.
Young, Percy M. Mozart. (Illus.). (gr. 7 up). 1966. 3.50 (ISBN 0-87250-223-6); PLB 3.27 (ISBN 0-87250-423-9). D White.

MOZART, JOHANN CHRYSOSTOM WOLFGANG AMADEUS, 1756-1791-JUVENILE LITERATURE

Seroff, Victor. Wolfgang Amadeus Mozart. (Illus.). (gr. 7 up). 1965. 8.95g (ISBN 0-02-781870-5). Macmillan.

MOZART, JOHANN CHRYSOSTOM WOLFGANG AMADEUS, 1756-1791-THEMATIC CATALOGUES

Hill, George R. & Gould, Murray. A Thematic Locator for Mozart's Works, As Listed in Koechel's Chronologischen Thematisches Verzeichnis. 6th ed. (Music Indexes & Bibliographies: No. 1). 1970. pap. 6.75 (ISBN 0-913574-01-5). Eur-Am Music.
Hutchings, Arthur. Companion to Mozart's Piano Concertos. 2nd ed. 1950. 14.95x (ISBN 0-19-318404-4). Oxford U Pr.

MPANGWE

see Fan (African People)

MU MESONS

see Muons

MUCHA, ALPHONSE MARIE, 1860-1939

Bowers, Q. David & Martin, Mary L. The Postcards of Alphonse Mucha. (Illus.). 120p. 1980. 9.95 (ISBN 0-911572-18-X). Vestal.
Bridges, Ann, ed. Alphonse Mucha: The Graphic Works. (Illus.). 192p. 1980. 30.00 (ISBN 0-517-54189-0, Harmony). Crown.
Mucha, Alphonse. The Art Nouveau Style Book of Alphonse Mucha. (Illus.). 15.00 (ISBN 0-8446-5795-6). Peter Smith.
--The Art Nouveau Style Book of Alphonse Mucha. (Illus.). 80p. 1980. pap. 7.95 (ISBN 0-486-24044-4). Dover.
--Posters of Mucha: A Collection of Posters by Alphonse Mucha. (Illus.). 48p. 1975. pap. 7.95 (ISBN 0-517-52043-5, Dist. by Crown). Crown.
Mucha, Alphonse M. Drawings of Mucha: Seventy Works. 8.75 (ISBN 0-8446-5796-4). Peter Smith.
--Drawings of Mucha: Seventy Works. 1978. pap. 4.00 (ISBN 0-486-23672-2). Dover.
Mucha, Jiri & Henderson, Marina. Alphonse Mucha. rev. & enl. ed. LC 73-90408. (Illus.). 1974. 25.00 (ISBN 0-312-55160-6). St Martin.
--The Graphic Work of Alphonse Mucha. LC 73-89209. (Illus.). 1974. 40.00 (ISBN 0-312-34440-6). St Martin.

MUCILAGE

see also Adhesives

MUCK

see Humus

MUCORALES

Benjamin, Richard K. The Merosporangiferous Mucorales. (Bibl. Myco.). (Illus.). 1967. Repr. of 1965 ed. 30.00 (ISBN 3-7682-0514-2). Lubrecht & Cramer.
Zycha, H. & Siepmann, R. Mucorales. (Illus.). 50.00 (ISBN 3-7682-0145-7). Lubrecht & Cramer.

MUCORINEAE

Blakeslee, A. F. Sexual Reproduction in the Mucorinaeae. (Biblioteca Mycologica Ser: No. 48). 1976. Repr. of 1904 ed. text ed. 20.00 (ISBN 3-7682-1064-2). Lubrecht & Cramer.

MUCOUS MEMBRANE

see also Endometrium; Gastric Mucosa

Brain, et al. Respiratory Defense Mechanisms, Pt. 1. (Lung Biology in Health & Disease: Vol. 5). 1977. 49.75 (ISBN 0-8247-6381-5). Dekker.
Demetrious, Rafla S. Mucous & Salivary Gland Tumours. (American Lecture Radiation Therapy). (Illus.). 296p. 1970. pap. 29.75 (ISBN 0-398-01537-6). C C Thomas.
Milton, G. W. Malignant Melanoma of the Skin & Mucous Membrane. LC 76-30318. (Illus.). 1977. text ed. 43.75 (ISBN 0-443-01422-1). Churchill.
Nasemann, Theodor. Viral Diseases of the Skin, Mucous Membranes & Genitals: Clinical Features, Differential Diagnosis & Therapy, with Basic Principles of Virology. Frosch, Peter J., tr. LC 75-25271. (Illus.). 1977. text ed. 29.95 (ISBN 0-7216-6655-8). Saunders.
O'Connor, Richard C., ed. Immunologic Diseases of the Mucous Membranes: Pathology, Diagnosis, & Treatment. LC 80-82050. (Illus.). 176p. 1980. 29.50x (ISBN 0-89352-102-7). Masson Pub.
Strassburg, M. & Knolie, G. Disease of the Oral Mucosa: A Color Atlas. (Illus.). 270p. 1972. 58.00 (ISBN 0-686-29192-1). Quint Pub Co.

MUCOVISCIDOSIS

see Cystic Fibrosis

MUCUS

Ciba Foundation. CIBA Foundation Symposium 54: Respiratory Tract Mucus. 1978. 40.00 (ISBN 0-444-90016-0, Excerpta Medica). Elsevier.
Forstner, G. G., ed. Mucus Secretions & Cystic Fibrosis. (Modern Problems in Paediatrics: Vol. 19). (Illus.). 1977. 66.50 (ISBN 3-8055-2678-4). S Karger.
Parke, Dennis V. & Parke, eds. Mucus in Health & Disease. LC 77-22376. (Advances in Experimental Medicine & Biology: Vol. 89). 558p. 1977. 45.00 (ISBN 0-306-32689-2, Plenum Pr). Plenum Pub.

MUD-LADEN FLUIDS

see Drilling Muds

MUD LUMPS

Morgan, James P., et al. Mudlumps at the Mouth of South Pass, Mississippi River: Sedimentology, Paleontology, Structure, Origin, & Relation to Deltaic Processes. LC 63-22268. (Coastal Studies Ser.: Vol. 10). (Illus.). 1963. pap. 4.00x (ISBN 0-8071-0624-0). La State U Pr.

MUDDIMAN, HENRY, 1629-1692

Muddiman, Joseph G. King's Journalist 1659-1689: Studies in the Reign of Charles Second. LC 74-125774. (English Book Trade). (Illus.). Repr. of 1923 ed. 15.00x (ISBN 0-678-00729-2). Kelley.

MUDEJARES

Here are entered works on Muslims living in Spain under Christian protection before 1492 who did not convert to Christianity. Works on Muslims in Spain after about 1492 who were converted to Christianity by decree are entered under the heading Moriscos. Works including both Mudejares and Moriscos are entered under Moriscos.

see also Moriscos

MUDLUMPS

see Mud Lumps

MUDRA

see Gesture

MUDS, DRILLING

see Drilling Muds

MUELLER, FRIEDRICH MAX, 1823-1900

Mueller, Friedrich M. The Life & Letters of the Right Honourable Friedrich Max Mueller, 2 vols. LC 73-18820. (Illus.). Repr. of 1902 ed. 57.50 set (ISBN 0-404-11445-8). AMS Pr.
Neufeldt, Ronald. F. Max Muller & the Rg-Veda. 1980. 16.00x (ISBN 0-8364-0040-2). South Asia Bks.

MUELLER, GEORGE, 1805-1898

Bailey, Faith C. George Mueller. 160p. 1980. pap. 2.50 (ISBN 0-8024-0031-0). Moody.
Miller, Basil. George Mueller: Man of Faith. 160p. 1972. pap. 2.25 (ISBN 0-87123-182-4, 200182). Bethany Hse.
Muller, George. Autobiography of George Muller. Wayland, H. Lincoln, ed. (Giant Summit Books Ser.). 490p. 1981. pap. 8.95 (ISBN 0-8010-6105-9). Baker Bk.
Pierson, Arthur T. George Muller of Bristol. 1971. 10.95 (ISBN 0-8007-0106-2). Revell.
Steer, Roger. George Mueller: Delighted in God. LC 75-33488. 1979. pap. 5.95 (ISBN 0-87788-303-3). Shaw Pubs.
--George Muller: Delighted in God! rev. ed. 351p. 1981. pap. 3.50 (ISBN 0-87788-304-1, 304-1). Shaw Pubs.

MUGGERIDGE, MALCOLM, 1903-

Hunter, Ian. Malcolm Muggeridge: A Life. 1980. 13.95 (ISBN 0-8407-4084-0). Nelson.
Muggeridge, Malcolm. A Twentieth Century Testimony. LC 78-15925. 1978. 12.50 (ISBN 0-8407-5143-5). Nelson.

MUGHAL EMPIRE

see Mogul Empire

MUHAMMAD 2ND, SULTAN OF TURKEY, 1430 (ca.)-1481

Kritoboulos. History of Mehmed the Conqueror. Riggs, Charles T., tr. Repr. of 1954 ed. lib. bdg. 15.00x (ISBN 0-8371-3119-7, KRHM). Greenwood.
Tursun, Beg. The History of Mehmed the Conqueror. LC 77-89803. 1978. 30.00x (ISBN 0-88297-018-6). Bibliotheca.

MUHAMMAD, AHMAD, CALLING HIMSELF AL MAHDI, 1848-1885

Duckworth, George E. Foreshadowing & Suspense. (Studies in Comparative Literature, No. 35). 1970. pap. 12.95 (ISBN 0-8383-0021-9). Haskell.

MUHAMMAD, SAIYID

Khan, Abdul M. Transition in Bengal, 1756-1775: A Study of Saiyid Muhammed Reza Khan. LC 69-29329. (South Asian Studies Ser.: No. 7). (Illus.). 1969. 34.95 (ISBN 0-521-07124-0). Cambridge U Pr.

MUHAMMAD 'ABD ALLAH, CALLED THE MAD MULLAH, d. 1920

Jardine, Douglas J. Mad Mullah of Somaliland. LC 75-89036. Repr. of 1923 ed. 17.00x (ISBN 0-8371-1762-3, Pub. by Negro U Pr). Greenwood.

MUHAMMAD 'ABDUH, 1848-1905

Adams, Charles C. Islam & Modernism in Egypt: A Study of the Modern Reform Movement Inaugurated by Muhammed 'Abduh. LC 68-25061. 1968. Repr. of 1933 ed. 18.00 (ISBN 0-8462-1218-8). Russell.

MUHAMMAD ALI, 1942-

Atyeo & Dennis. The Holy Warrior: Muhammad Ali. 112p. 1975. pap. 2.95 (ISBN 0-671-22201-5, Fireside). S&S.
Bortstein, Larry, ed. Ali. (gr. 7-12). 1976. pap. 1.25 (ISBN 0-590-10261-3, Schol Pap). Schol Bk Serv.
Burchard, Marshall. Sports Hero: Muhammad Ali. (Sports Hero Ser.). (Illus.). 96p. (gr. 3-5). 1975. PLB 6.29 (ISBN 0-399-61013-8). Putnam.
Butler, Frank. Muhammad Ali. (Profiles Ser.). (Illus.). 64p. (gr. 4-6). 1981. 8.95 (ISBN 0-241-10600-1, Pub. by Hamish Hamilton England). David & Charles.
Edwards, A. & Wohl, G. The Picture Life of Muhammad Ali. 1977. pap. 1.75 (ISBN 0-380-01904-3, 51623, Camelot). Avon.
Edwards, Audrey & Wohl, Gary. Muhammad Ali: The Peoples Champ. LC 77-4719. (Illus.). (gr. 7-12). 1977. 8.95 (ISBN 0-316-21172-9). Little.
Eldred, Patricia M. Boxing's World Champion: Muhammad Ali. (The Allstars Ser.). (Illus.). (gr. 2-6). 1977. PLB 5.95 (ISBN 0-87191-586-3); pap. 2.95 (ISBN 0-89812-198-1). Creative Ed.
Hahn, James & Hahn, Lynn. Ali! The Sports Career of Muhammad Ali. Schroeder, Howard, ed. (Sports Lgends Ser.). (Illus.). 48p. (gr. 3 up). 1981. PLB 6.95 (ISBN 0-89686-130-9); pap. text ed. 3.25 (ISBN 0-89686-145-7). Crestwood Hse.
Hano, Arnold. Muhammad Ali: The Champion. LC 76-50101. (Putnam Sports Shelf). (Illus.). (gr. 6-8). 1977. PLB 6.29 (ISBN 0-399-61091-X). Putnam.
Hoskins, Robert. Muhammad Ali. (Illus.). 96p. (Orig.). 1980. pap. 1.25 (ISBN 0-87067-313-0). Holloway.
Korn, Henry J. Muhammad Ali Retrospective. 96p. 1976. pap. 4.95 (ISBN 0-685-56013-9). Assembling Pr.
Lardner, Rex. Ali. pap. 1.50 (ISBN 0-685-56295-6, 7443, Tempo). Ace Bks.
Lipsyte, Robert. Free to Be Muhammad Ali. LC 77-25640. (Ursula Nordstrom Bk.). (gr. 5 up). 1978. 8.79 (ISBN 0-06-023901-8, HarpJ); PLB 7.89 (ISBN 0-06-023902-6). Har-Row.
--Free to Be Muhammed Ali. (gr. 7 up). 1979. pap. 1.95 (ISBN 0-553-14165-1, Y 14165-1). Bantam.
Mailer, Norman. The Fight. LC 75-15824. 1975. 7.95 (ISBN 0-316-54416-7). Little.

Rudeen, Kenneth. Muhammad Ali. LC 76-12093. (Biography Ser.). (Illus.). 40p. (gr. 1-4). 1976. 8.79 (ISBN 0-690-01128-8, TYC-J). Har-Row.
Schmitz, Dorothy C. Muhammad Ali: The Greatest. LC 77-70893. (Pros Ser.). (Illus.). (gr. 2). 1977. PLB 6.95 (ISBN 0-913940-60-7). Crestwood Hse.
Thomas, Linda. Muhammad Ali. LC 75-28194. (Creative Superstars Ser.). 1975. PLB 5.95 (ISBN 0-87191-262-7); pap. 2.95 (ISBN 0-89812-188-4). Creative Ed.

MUHAMMAD 'ALI, KHEDIVE OF EGYPT, 1769-1849

Dodwell, Henry H. The Founder of Modern Egypt. LC 74-15029. (BCL Ser. II). Repr. of 1931 ed. 22.50 (ISBN 0-404-12036-9). AMS Pr.
Tugay, Emine F. Three Centuries: Family Chronicles of Turkey & Egypt. LC 73-19304. (Illus.). 324p. 1974. Repr. of 1963 ed. lib. bdg. 22.50x (ISBN 0-8371-7117-2, TUTC). Greenwood.

MUHAMMAD IBN-'ABDULLAH IBN-BATTUTAH, 1304-1377

Ibn Batuta. The Travels of Ibn Batuta. LC 74-172523. (Oriental Translation Fund, Publications: No. 1). Repr. of 1829 ed. 18.50 (ISBN 0-8337-2051-1). B Franklin.
McDonald, Lucile. The Arab Marco Polo: Ibn Battuta. LC 75-4651. (Illus.). 160p. (gr. 6 up). 1975. 7.95 (ISBN 0-525-66441-6). Elsevier-Nelson.

MUHAMMAD RAFI', 1713-1781

Russell, Ralph & Islam, Khurshidul. Three Mughal Poets: Mir, Sauda, Mir Hasan. LC 68-15643. 1968. 15.00x (ISBN 0-674-88980-0). Harvard U Pr.

MUHAMMAD RASHID RIDA

Adams, Charles C. Islam & Modernism in Egypt: A Study of the Modern Reform Movement Inaugurated by Muhammed 'Abduh. LC 68-25061. 1968. Repr. of 1933 ed. 18.00 (ISBN 0-8462-1218-8). Russell.

MUHAMMAD TAKI, called MIR, d. 1810

Russell, Ralph & Islam, Khurshidul. Three Mughal Poets: Mir, Sauda, Mir Hasan. LC 68-15643. 1968. 15.00x (ISBN 0-674-88980-0). Harvard U Pr.

MUHAMMAD THE PROPHET

see Mohammed, the Prophet, 570-632

MUHAMMADANISM

see Islam

MUHAMMADANS

see Muslims

MUHLENBERG FAMILY

Wallace, Paul A. Muhlenbergs of Pennsylvania. facs. ed. LC 75-124264. (Select Bibliographies Reprint Ser). 1950. 21.00 (ISBN 0-8369-5452-1). Arno.

MUI TSAI

see Slavery

MUIR, EDWIN, 1887-

Butter, Peter H. Edwin Muir: Man & Poet. LC 76-11018. 1977. Repr. of 1966 ed. lib. bdg. 22.50 (ISBN 0-8371-8169-0, BUEM). Greenwood.
Hoy, Peter C. & Mellown, Elgin W. Checklist of Writings About Edwin Muir. LC 70-150336. 1971. 7.50x (ISBN 0-87875-012-6). Whitston Pub.
Knight, Roger. Edwin Muir: An Introduction to His Work. LC 79-42832. (Illus.). 210p. 1980. text ed. 21.00x (ISBN 0-582-48901-6); pap. text ed. 11.95x (ISBN 0-582-48906-7). Longman.
Mellown, E. W. Bibliography of the Writings of Edwin Muir: Bibliography & Supplement Bound Together. 174p. 1970. 10.75x (ISBN 0-8173-9511-3). U of Ala Pr.
Mellown, Elgin W. Bibliography of the Writings of Edwin Muir. LC 64-8393. 144p. 1964. 9.75x (ISBN 0-8173-9507-5). U of Ala Pr.
--Edwin Muir. (English Authors Ser.: No. 248). 1979. lib. bdg. 12.95 (ISBN 0-8057-6687-1). Twayne.
--Edwin Muir. (Twayne English Authors Ser.). 1979. lib. bdg. 11.50 (ISBN 0-8057-6687-1). G K Hall.
--Supplement to Bibliography of the Writings of Edwin Muir. 30p. 1970. pap. 2.50 (ISBN 0-8173-9510-5). U of Ala Pr.
Noble, Andrew, ed. Edwin Muir: Uncollected Scottish Criticism. (Barnes & Noble Critical Studies). 208p. 1981. 28.50x (ISBN 0-389-20202-9). B&N.
Phillips, Michael J. Edwin Muir: A Master of Modern Poetry. LC 78-67103. 1978. 19.50 (ISBN 0-915144-54-9). Hackett Pub.

MUIR, JOHN, 1838-1914

Bade, William F. Life & Letters of John Muir, 2 Vols. LC 77-153302. (BCL Ser.: No. I). Repr. of 1924 ed. Set. 45.00 (ISBN 0-404-00444-X); 23.50 ea. Vol. 1 (ISBN 0-404-08001-4). Vol. 2 (ISBN 0-404-08002-2). AMS Pr.
Clarke, James M. The Life & Adventures of John Muir. LC 79-64178. (Sierra Club Paperback Library Ser.). (Illus.). 326p. 1980. pap. 7.95 (ISBN 0-87156-241-3). Sierra.
--The Life & Adventures of John Muir. new ed. LC 79-64178. (Illus.). 1979. 14.95 (ISBN 0-932238-01-7). Word Shop.
Dannen, Kent & Country Beautiful Editors, eds. The American Wilderness in the Words of John Muir. LC 73-84624. (Illus.). 192p. 1973. 19.95 (ISBN 0-87294-049-7). Country Beautiful.
Engberg, Robert & Wesling, Donald. John Muir-to Yosemite & Beyond: Writings from the Years 1863-1875. (Illus.). 178p. 1980. 17.50 (ISBN 0-299-08270-9); pap. 5.95 (ISBN 0-299-08274-1). U of Wis Pr.
Fox, Stephen R. John Muir & His Legacy: The American Conservation Movement. (Illus.). 416p. 1981. 17.50 (ISBN 0-316-29110-2). Little.
Lyon, Thomas J. John Muir. LC 72-619587. (Western Writers Ser: No. 3). (Illus.). 48p. (Orig.). 1972. pap. 2.00 (ISBN 0-88430-002-1). Boise St Univ.
Melham, Tom. John Muir's Wild America. LC 76-687. (Special Publications Ser: No. 11). (Illus.). 200p. 1976. 6.95 (ISBN 0-87044-186-8); lib. bdg. 8.50 (ISBN 0-685-66422-8). Natl Geog.
Muir, John. Letters to a Friend. new ed. LC 15-5890. 194p. 1973. 12.00 (ISBN 0-910220-48-4). Larlin Corp.
--My First Summer in the Sierra. 1979. pap. 7.95 (ISBN 0-395-28521-6). HM.
--Rambles of a Botanist Among the Plants & Climates of California. Kimes, William F., intro. by. (Illus.). 44p. 1974. 7.50 (ISBN 0-87093-301-9). Dawsons.
--The Story of My Boyhood & Youth. new ed. LC 13-5573. (Illus.). 301p. 1975. pap. 18.00 (ISBN 0-910220-70-0). Larlin Corp.
--Travels in Alaska. LC 77-19358. 1979. pap. 5.95 (ISBN 0-395-28522-4). HM.
Smith, Herbert F. John Muir. (Twayne's United States Authors Ser). 1964. pap. 3.45 (ISBN 0-8084-0186-6, T73, Twayne). Coll & U Pr.
Watkins, T. H. John Muir's America. (Illus.). 160p. 1981. pap. 12.95 (ISBN 0-912856-64-5). Graphic Arts Ctr.
Wolfe, Linnie M. Son of the Wilderness: The Life of John Muir. LC 78-53294. 398p. 1978. 20.00 (ISBN 0-299-07730-6); pap. 6.95 (ISBN 0-299-07734-9). U of Wis Pr.
Young, S. Hall. Alaska Days with John Muir. LC 74-174351. (Illus.). Repr. of 1915 ed. 15.00 (ISBN 0-405-09110-9). Arno.

MUIR WOODS NATIONAL MONUMENT

Morley, Jim. Muir Woods. LC 68-29407. (Illus.). pap. 2.50 (ISBN 0-8310-6005-0). Howell-North.

MULATTOES

Berry, Brewton. Almost White. 1969. pap. 1.25 (ISBN 0-02-095250-3, Collier). Macmillan.
Johnson, James W. Autobiography of an Ex-Coloured Man. 1933. 8.95 (ISBN 0-394-41582-5). Knopf.
Mencke, John G. Mulattoes & Race Mixture: American Attitudes & Images, 1865-1918. Berkhofer, Robert, ed. LC 78-27611. (Studies in American History & Culture: No. 4). 1979. 29.95 (ISBN 0-8357-0984-1, Pub. by UMI Res Pr). Univ Microfilms.
Reuter, Edward B. Mulatto in the United States. LC 70-100495. (Studies in Black History & Culture, No. 54). 1970. 54.95 (ISBN 0-8383-1216-0). Haskell.
--Mulatto in the United States. LC 69-16569. Repr. of 1918 ed. 17.50x (ISBN 0-8371-0938-8, Pub. by Negro U Pr). Greenwood.
--The Mulatto in the United States: Including a Study of the Role of Mixed Blood Races Throughout the World. (Basic Afro-American Reprint Ser.). 1970. Repr. of 1918 ed. 19.50 (ISBN 0-384-50330-6). Johnson Repr.
--Race Mixtures: Studies in Intermarriage & Miscegenation. LC 71-94486. Repr. of 1931 ed. 100.75x (ISBN 0-8371-2375-5). Greenwood.
Williamson, Joel. New People: Miscegenation & Mulattoes in the United States. LC 80-65201. 1980. 16.95 (ISBN 0-02-934790-4). Free Pr.

MULCASTER, RICHARD, 1530-1611

Benndorf, Cornelie. Die Englische Padagogik Im 16. Jahrhundert. Repr. of 1905 ed. pap. 10.00 (ISBN 0-384-03895-6). Johnson Repr.

MULCHING

Alth, Max. How to Farm Your Backyard the Mulch Organic Way. (Illus.). 1977. 9.95 (ISBN 0-07-001128-1, P&RB). McGraw.
Mulches. 1.95 (ISBN 0-686-21125-1). Bklyn Botanic.
Mulching Effects on Plant Climate & Yield: WMO 388. (Technical Note Ser: No. 136). 92p. 1975. pap. 20.00 (ISBN 92-63-10388-7, WMO). Unipub.
Organic Gardening & Farming Magazine Editors. Organic Way to Mulching. LC 70-170280. 208p. 1972. 8.95 (ISBN 0-87857-009-8). Rodale Pr Inc.
Plastic Mulches for Vegetable Production. 1981. 12.00x (ISBN 0-686-75423-9, Pub. by Grower Bks). State Mutual Bk.
Stout, Ruth. Gardening Without Work. 1974. pap. 1.95 (ISBN 0-346-12158-2). Cornerstone.

MULE DEER

Bare, Coleen S. Mule Deer. (A Skylight Bk.). (Illus.). 64p. (gr. 3-5). 1981. PLB 6.95 (ISBN 0-396-07971-7). Dodd.
Wallmo, Olof C., ed. Mule & Black-tailed Deer of North America. LC 80-20128. (Illus.). xviii, 650p. 1981. 29.95 (ISBN 0-8032-4715-X). U of Nebr Pr.

MULES

Ferris, Bill. Ray Lum: Mule Trader -- an Essay. Friedman, Jack, ed. LC 76-53834. (Illus.). 1977. 2.50 (ISBN 0-89267-003-7); film transcript 2.50 (ISBN 0-89267-001-0); record transcript 2.50 (ISBN 0-89267-002-9). Ctr South Folklore.
Helmstrom, J. G. Scientific Horse, Mule & Ox Shoeing. (Illus.). 117p. pap. 11.50 (ISBN 0-8466-6029-6, SJU29). Shorey.
Telleen, Maurice. Draft Horse Primer. LC 77-898. 1977. 10.95 (ISBN 0-87857-161-2). Rodale Pr Inc.

MULLENDORE, E. C., 1937-1970

Kwitny, Jonathan. The Mullendore Murder Case. LC 74-14650. (Illus.). 336p. 1974. 11.95 (ISBN 0-374-21599-5). FS&G.

MULLER, FRIEDRICH MAX, 1823-1900

see Mueller, Friedrich Max, 1823-1900

MULLER, GEORGE

see Mueller, George, 1805-1898

MULLER, HERMANN JOSEPH, 1890-1967

Carlson, Elof Axel. Genes, Radiation & Society: The Life and Work of H. J. Muller. LC 81-5486. (Illus.). 496p. 1981. 29.95 (ISBN 0-8014-1304-4). Cornell U Pr.
Muller, Hermann J. Man's Future Birthright: Essays on Science & Humanity. Carlson, Elof A., ed. LC 79-171215. 200p. 1973. 12.00 (ISBN 0-87395-097-6); microfiche 12.00 (ISBN 0-87395-197-2). State U NY Pr.
--The Modern Concept of Nature. Carlson, Elof A., ed. LC 74-170884. (Illus.). 200p. 1973. 19.50 (ISBN 0-87395-096-8); microfiche 19.50 (ISBN 0-87395-196-4). State U NY Pr.

MULTI-AGE GROUPING

see Nongraded Schools

MULTICOMPONENT FLOW

see Multiphase Flow

MULTI-FAMILY HOUSING

see Apartment Houses

MULTILATERAL TREATY FOR THE RENUNCIATION OF WAR, PARIS

see Renunciation of War Treaty, Paris, Aug. 27, 1928

MULTILINGUALISM

see also Bilingualism

Fishman, J. A., ed. Advances in the Study of Societal Multilingualism. (Contributions to the Sociology of Language Ser.: No. 9). 1978. 103.00x (ISBN 90-279-7742-9). Mouton.
Savard, J. G. & Vigneault, R., eds. Multilingual Political Systems: Problems & Solutions. (Travaux Du Centre International De Recherche Sur le Bilinguisme). 591p. (Orig.). 1976. pap. 27.50x (ISBN 2-7637-6738-9, Pub. by Laval). Intl Schol Bk Serv.
Tabory, Mala. International Multilingual Documents: Selected Problems. 1979. 18.00x (ISBN 965-20-0019-1, Pub. by Turtledove Pub Ltd Israel). Intl Schol Bk Serv.
--Multilingualism in International Law & Institutions. LC 80-51742. 304p. 1980. 32.50x (ISBN 90-286-0210-0). Sijthoff & Noordhoff.
Teller, Virginia & White, Sheila J., eds. Studies in Child Language & Multilingualism. LC 80-16810. (Annals of the New York Academy of Sciences: Vol. 345). 187p. 1980. 28.00x (ISBN 0-89766-078-1); pap. 28.00x (ISBN 0-89766-079-X). NY Acad Sci.

MULTIMACHINE ASSIGNMENTS

see Methods Engineering

MULTINATIONAL CORPORATIONS

see International Business Enterprises

MULTIPHASE FLOW

see also Two-Phase Flow

Bajura, R. A., ed. Polyphase Flow & Transport Technology. 270p. 1980. 40.00 (ISBN 0-686-69858-4, H00158). ASME.
Cooper, Paul, ed. Polyphase Flow in Turbomachinery. 1978. 40.00 (ISBN 0-685-66809-6, H00123). ASME.
Govier, George W. & Aziz, Khalid. The Flow Properties of Complex Mixutre in Pipes. LC 77-2591. 842p. 1977. Repr. of 1972 ed. 41.50 (ISBN 0-88275-547-1). Krieger.
Hammitt, Frederick G. Cavitation & Multiphase Flow Phenomena. 448p. 1980. text ed. 48.00 (ISBN 0-07-025907-0). McGraw.
Hetsroni, G. Handbook of Multiphase Systems. 1024p. 1981. 64.50 (ISBN 0-07-028460-1, P&RB). McGraw.
Multi-Phase Flow & Heat Transfer Symposium-Workshop, 2nd, Miami Beach, Apr. 16-18, 1979. Multiphase Transport: Fundamentals, Reactor Safety, Applications: Proceedings, 5 vols. Veziroglu, T. Nejat, ed. LC 80-11157. 3500p. 1980. Set. text ed. 350.00 (ISBN 0-89116-159-7). Hemisphere Pub.
Stock, D. E., ed. Measurements in Polyphase Flows. 1978. 20.00 (ISBN 0-685-66803-7, H00121). ASME.
Waid, Robert L. Cavitation & Polyphase Flow Forum - 1979: Book No. G00143. 26p. 1979. pap. text ed. 4.00 (ISBN 0-685-81925-6). ASME.

MULTI-PHASE MATERIALS

see Composite Materials

MULTIPLE EMPLOYMENT

see Supplementary Employment

MULTIPLE HEMORRHAGIC SARCOMA

see Kaposi's Sarcoma

MULTIPLE INTEGRALS

see Integrals, Multiple

MULTIPLE LINE INSURANCE

see Insurance, Multiple Line

MULTIPLE SCLEROSIS

Adams, C. W. Research on Multiple Sclerosis. (Amer. Lec. Living Chemistry Ser.). (Illus.). 192p. 1972. 18.75 (ISBN 0-398-02214-3). C C Thomas.
Adams, John M. Multiple Sclerosis--Scars of Childhood: New Horizons & Hope. (Illus.). 96p. 1977. pap. 11.50 (ISBN 0-398-03595-4). C C Thomas.
Bauer, H. J., ed. Progress in Multiple Sclerosis Research. (Illus.). 630p. 1980. 46.60 (ISBN 0-387-09867-4). Springer-Verlag.
Birrer, Cynthia. Multiple Sclerosis: A Personal View. (Illus.). 304p. 1979. text ed. 24.75 (ISBN 0-398-03864-3); pap. text ed. 18.75 (ISBN 0-398-03886-4). C C Thomas.
Boese, A., ed. Search for the Cause of Multiple Sclerosis & Other Chronic Diseases of the Central Nervous System. (Illus.). 516p. (Orig.). pap. text ed. 55.00 (ISBN 3-527-25875-2). Verlag Chemie.
Brenneman, Helen G. Learning to Cope. LC 75-32724. 88p. 1976. pap. 1.65 (ISBN 0-8361-1782-4). Herald Pr.
Capusan, I., et al. Systemic Sclerosis: Current Research, Vol. 2. 1974. text ed. 29.50x (ISBN 0-8422-7203-8). Irvington.
Davis, Marcella Z. Living with Multiple Sclerosis: A Social Psychological Analysis. 80p. 1973. 9.50 (ISBN 0-398-02850-8). C C Thomas.
Davison, A. N. & Cuzner, M. L., eds. The Suppression of Experimental Allergic Encephalomyelitis & Multiple Sclerosis. LC 79-41796. 1980. 39.50 (ISBN 0-12-206660-X). Acad Pr.
Deutsche Gesellschaft Fuer Neurochirurgie, 25th, Bochum, Germany, September 1974. Proceedings. Klug, W., et al, eds. LC 75-8941. (Advances in Neurosurgery Ser.: Vol. 2). (Illus.). 500p. 1975. pap. 44.20 (ISBN 0-387-07237-3). Springer-Verlag.
Field, E. J. Multiple Sclerosis: A Critical Conspectus. 1977. 29.50 (ISBN 0-8391-1132-0). Univ Park.
--Multiple Sclerosis in Childhood: Diagnosis & Prophylaxis. (Illus.). 144p. 1980. text ed. 12.75 (ISBN 0-398-03919-4). C C Thomas.
Field, E. J., et al. Multiple Sclerosis: Progress in Research. (Clinical Studies Ser.: Vol. 3). 1972. 30.25 (ISBN 0-444-10344-9, North-Holland). Elsevier.
Forsythe, Elizabeth. Living with Multiple Sclerosis. 144p. 1979. 11.95 (ISBN 0-571-11293-5, Pub. by Faber & Faber); pap. 6.95 (ISBN 0-571-11294-3). Merrimack Bk Serv.
Ginther, John R. But You Look So Well! LC 77-26009. 1978. 13.95 (ISBN 0-88229-399-0). Nelson-Hall.
Greenblatt, M. H. Multiple Sclerosis & Me. (Illus.). 86p. 1972. 8.75 (ISBN 0-398-02300-X). C C Thomas.
Hanig, Martin. Catheter Center. 141p. (Orig.). 1973. pap. 2.95 (ISBN 0-910286-32-9). Boxwood.
Hess, George H. Living at Your Best with Multiple Sclerosis. rev. ed. (Illus.). 128p. 1972. pap. 11.75 photocopy ed., spiral (ISBN 0-398-02621-1). C C Thomas.
Hirsch, Ernest A. Starting Over. 1977. 6.95 (ISBN 0-8158-0350-8). Chris Mass.
Joint Conference Held by the Medical Research Council & the Multiple Sclerosis Society of Great Britain & Northern Ireland. Multiple Sclerosis Research: Proceedings. Davison, A. N., et al, eds. 1976. 57.00 (ISBN 0-444-99847-0, North Holland). Elsevier.
Kuroiwa, Y., ed. Multiple Sclerosis in Asia. 1976. 49.50 (ISBN 0-8391-0948-2). Univ Park.
Leibowitz, Uri. Multiple Sclerosis: Clues to Its Cause. 1973. 39.00 (ISBN 0-444-10433-X, North-Holland). Elsevier.
Leibowitz, Uri, ed. Progress in Multiple Sclerosis: Research & Treatment. 1973. 38.00 (ISBN 0-12-441350-1). Acad Pr.
Matthews, Bryan. Multiple Sclerosis: The Facts. (Illus.). 120p. 1981. pap. 4.95 (ISBN 0-19-520275-9, GB 656, GB). Oxford U Pr.
Matthews, W. Bryan. Multiple Sclerosis: The Facts. (Illus.). 1978. text ed. 11.95 (ISBN 0-19-261139-9). Oxford U Pr.
Michael, Peter P. Multiple Sclerosis: A Dragon with a Hundred Heads. 1981. 10.95 (ISBN 0-87949-170-1). Ashley Bks.

Millar, J. H. Multiple Sclerosis: A Disease Acquired in Childhood. (American Lecture Living Chemistry Ser.). (Illus.). 120p. 1971. text ed. 10.75 (ISBN 0-398-01307-1). C C Thomas.
Ogilvie, J. C. Overcoming Multiple Sclerosis. 4.50 (ISBN 0-686-29841-1). Cancer Bk Hse.
Ottenberg, Miriam. The Pursuit of Hope. LC 78-54041. 1978. 9.95 (ISBN 0-89256-069-X). Rawson Wade.
Poser, S. Multiple Sclerosis: An Analysis of 812 Cases by Means of Electronic Data Processing. (Neurology Ser.: Vol. 20). (Illus.). 1978. 20.80 (ISBN 0-387-08644-7). Springer-Verlag.
Riekkinen, Paavo, et al. The Nature of Multiple Sclerosis. (Illus.). 220p. 1973. text ed. 29.50x (ISBN 0-8422-7070-1). Irvington.
Russell, W. R. Multiple Sclerosis: Control of the Disease. 1976. 15.00 (ISBN 0-08-021003-1); pap. 10.00 (ISBN 0-08-021002-3). Pergamon.
Simmons, Robert A. Leadership for the New Frontier. 1977. 6.50 (ISBN 0-8158-0348-6). Chris Mass.
Swank, Roy L. & Pullen, Mary-Helen. The Multiple Sclerosis Diet Book: A Low-Fat Diet for the Treatment of M.S. Heartdisease & Stroke. LC 76-24215. 1977. 9.95 (ISBN 0-385-12092-3). Doubleday.
Winkelmann, Richard K., et al, eds. Systemic Sclerosis: Current Research, Vol. 1. 212p. 1974. text ed. 28.50x (ISBN 0-8422-7202-X). Irvington.
Wolfgram, Frederick, ed. Multiple Sclerosis. (Illus.). 1972. 26.50 (ISBN 0-12-761950-X). Acad Pr.

MULTIPLICATION

Burkes, Joyce M. The Math Machine Book: Multiplication. LC 79-93267. 64p. (gr. 7-11). 1980. wire-o bdg. 4.95 (ISBN 0-89709-017-9). Liberty Pub.
Clark, Clara E. & Lytle, Gretchen B. Beginning Multiplication & Division. (The Basic Skills in Math Ser.). (Illus.). 1975. tchr's manual 3.25 (ISBN 0-89170-007-2). Laurel Pub.
Hughes, Susan. The Kid's Multiplication Book. 1977. pap. 0.95 (ISBN 0-448-14291-0, Tempo). Ace Bks.
Hunt, R. Multiplication & Division. LC 78-730962. 1978. pap. text ed. 135.00 (ISBN 0-89290-093-8, A509-SATC). Soc for Visual.
Laycock, Mary & McLean, Peggy. Skateboard Practice: Multiplication & Division. (Illus.). (gr. 3-6). 1979. pap. text ed. 4.95 (ISBN 0-918932-65-3). Activity Resources.
Learning Achievement Corporation. Multiplication & Energy & Construction: Division & Medicine. Zak, Therese A., ed. (MATCH Ser.). (Illus.). 144p. 1981. text ed. 5.28 (ISBN 0-07-037112-1, G). McGraw.
LeBlanc, John F., et al. Mathematics-Methods Program: Multiplication & Division. (Mathematics Ser.). (Illus.). 1976. 3.95 (ISBN 0-201-14610-X); instr's man. 1.50 (ISBN 0-201-14611-8). A-W.
Madell, Robert. Picturing Multiplication & Division. 1979. 6.95 (ISBN 0-88488-122-9). Creative Pubns.
Mathews, Louise. Bunches & Bunches of Bunnies. (Illus.). 32p. 1980. Repr. pap. 1.95 (ISBN 0-590-31536-6, Schol Pap). Schol Bk Serv.
Mick, Beverly J. Multiplication Facts & Basic Fractions. (gr. 5-12). 1981. Set. 8.50 (ISBN 0-932786-01-4); Bk. 1. 4.25 (ISBN 0-932786-02-2); Bk. 2. 4.25 (ISBN 0-932786-03-0). Bellefontaine.
--Multiplication Facts, Decimals, & Percents, 2 bks. (gr. 5-12). 1981. Set. 8.50 (ISBN 0-932786-04-9); Bk. 1. 4.25 (ISBN 0-932786-05-7); Bk. 2. 4.25 (ISBN 0-932786-06-5). Bellefontaine.
Multiplication Book. (Basic Activity Bks.). 1976. 1.25 (ISBN 0-448-12171-9). G&D.
The Old-Fashioned Multiplication Table Book. (Orig.). (gr. 1-12). 1975. pap. 1.50 (ISBN 0-8431-0402-3). Price Stern.
Peppe, Rodney. Humphrey the Number Horse: Fun with Counting & Multiplication. LC 77-18782. (Illus.). (gr. k-3). 1978. 7.95 (ISBN 0-670-38666-9). Viking Pr.
Quinn, Daniel & Mills, Richard G. Multiplication Learning Module. 1975. pap. text ed. 330.00 (ISBN 0-89290-133-0). Soc for Visual.
Slater, Barbara. Old Fashioned Drill Sheets. 128p. (Orig.). 1981. pap. 7.00 (ISBN 0-87879-267-8). Acad Therapy.
Thornton, Carol A. Look into the Facts: Multiplication & Division. Gregory, John, ed. (Illus.). (gr. 2-6). 1977. wkbk. set of 5 8.50 (ISBN 0-88488-063-X); wkbk. set of 30 40.00 (ISBN 0-88488-156-3); tchr's ed. 4.95 (ISBN 0-88488-075-3). Creative Pubns.
Wehrli, Kitty. Michigan Arithmetic Program,Multiplication, Level 2: Consuable Edition. (gr. 3). 1975. 7.00x (ISBN 0-89039-132-7). Ann Arbor Pubs.
--Multiplication,Level 1: Consumable Edition. (Michigan Arithmetic Program Ser.). (gr. 3). 1975. Repr. wkbk 7.00x (ISBN 0-89039-094-0). Ann Arbor Pubs.

MULTIPLIER (ECONOMICS)

see also Circular Velocity of Money

Hegeland, Hugo. Multiplier Theory. LC 66-23018. (Illus.). Repr. of 1954 ed. 15.00x (ISBN 0-678-00162-6). Kelley.
Larsen, Ronald. Introduction to the Theory of Multipliers. LC 78-134023. (Grundlehren der Mathematischen Wissenschaften: Vol. 175). 1971. 48.80 (ISBN 0-387-05120-1). Springer-Verlag.

MULTIVARIATE ANALYSIS

see also Cluster Analysis

Aaker, David A. Multivariate Analysis in Marketing. 2nd ed. 1980. pap. text ed. 13.50x (ISBN 0-89426-029-4). Scientific Pr.
Afifi, A. A. & Azen, Stanley P. Statistical Analysis: A Computer Oriented Approach. 2nd ed. 1979. 19.50 (ISBN 0-12-044460-7). Acad Pr.
Aitchison, J. & Dunsmore, I. R. Statistical Prediction Analysis. (Illus.). 284p. 1980. pap. 14.95x (ISBN 0-521-29858-X). Cambridge U Pr.
Anderson, T. W. & Sclove, Stanley L. An Introduction to the Statistical Analysis of Data. LC 77-78890. (Illus.). 1978. text ed. 18.50 (ISBN 0-395-15045-0); sol. manual 0.75 (ISBN 0-395-15046-9). HM.
Anderson, T. W., et al. A Bibliography of Multivariate Statistical Analysis. LC 76-54249. 1977. Repr. of 1972 ed. lib. bdg. 32.50 (ISBN 0-88275-477-7). Krieger.
Andrews, Frank M. & Messenger, Robert C. Multivariate Nominal Scale Analysis: A Report on a New Analysis Technique & a Computer Program. LC 72-629721. 114p. 1973. cloth 8.00 (ISBN 0-87944-135-6); pap. 5.00 (ISBN 0-87944-134-8). Inst Soc Res.
Andrews, Frank M., et al. Multiple Classification Analysis: A Report on a Computer Program for Multiple Regression Using Categorical Predictors. rev. ed. LC 73-620206. 105p. 1973. cloth 9.00 (ISBN 0-87944-148-8); pap. 5.50 (ISBN 0-87944-055-4). Inst Soc Res.
Armstrong. ORACLS: A Design System for Linear Multivariable Control. (Control & Systems Theory Ser.: Vol. 10). 256p. 1980. 35.00 (ISBN 0-8247-1239-0). Dekker.
Arnold, Steven F. The Theory of Linear Models & Multivariate Analysis. LC 80-23017. (Wiley Ser. in Probability & Math Statistics). 475p. 1981. 34.95 (ISBN 0-471-05065-2). Wiley.
Atchley, W. R. & Bryant, E. H. Multivariate Statistical Methods: Among-Groups Covariation. LC 75-9893. (Benchmark Papers in Systematic & Evolutionary Biology: Vol. 1). 480p. 1975. 50.00 (ISBN 0-12-786085-1). Acad Pr.
Bevington, Philip R. Data Reduction & Error Analysis for the Physical Sciences. LC 69-16942. 1969. pap. text ed. 12.95 (ISBN 0-07-005135-6, C). McGraw.
Bishop, Yvonne, et al. Discrete Multivariate Analysis: Theory & Practice. 1974. text ed. 45.00x (ISBN 0-262-02113-7); pap. 16.50x (ISBN 0-262-52040-0). MIT Pr.
Blackith, R. E. & Reyment, R. A. Multivariate Morphometrics. 1972. 65.00 (ISBN 0-12-103150-0). Acad Pr.
Bock, Darrell. Multivariate Statistical Methods in Behavioral Research. LC 74-8618. (Psychology Ser.). (Illus.). 640p. 1975. text ed. 25.00 (ISBN 0-07-006305-2, C). McGraw.
Chou, E. Statistical Analysis. 2nd ed. 1975. 24.95 (ISBN 0-686-70998-5). Dryden Pr.
Christiensen, Ronald, ed. Entropy Minimax Sourcebook. (Entropy Minimax Sourcebook Ser.: Vol. IV). 1981. lib. bdg. 59.50 (ISBN 0-938876-07-4). Entropy Ltd.
Committee on National Statistics, National Research Council. Estimating Population & Income of Small Areas. 1980. pap. text ed. 13.75 (ISBN 0-309-03096-X). Natl Acad Pr.
Cooley, William W. & Lohnes, Paul R. Multivariate Data Analysis. LC 70-127661. (Illus.). 1971. 24.95 (ISBN 0-471-17060-7). Wiley.
Farrell, R. H. Techniques of Multivariate Calculation. (Lecture Notes in Mathematics: Vol. 520). 1976. pap. 16.40 (ISBN 0-387-07695-6). Springer-Verlag.
Ferguson, George A. Statistical Analysis in Psychology & Education. 5th, rev. ed. (Psychology Ser.). (Illus.). 560p. 1981. text ed. 21.00x (ISBN 0-07-020482-9, C); instructor's manual 4.95 (ISBN 0-07-020483-7). McGraw.
Fienberg, Stephen. The Analysis of Cross-Classified Categorical Data. 2nd ed. 1980. text ed. 14.00x (ISBN 0-262-06071-X). MIT Pr.
Finn, J. General Model for Multivariate Analysis. LC 74-8629. 1974. text ed. 24.95 (ISBN 0-03-083239-X, HoltC). HR&W.
Finn, Jeremy D. Multivariance Six: Univariate & Multivariate Analysis of Variance, Covariance, Regression & Repeated Measures. pap. 9.75 (ISBN 0-89498-003-3). Natl Ed Res.
Finn, Jeremy D. & Mattsson, Ingrid. Multivariate Analysis in Educational Research. pap. 12.50 (ISBN 0-89498-001-7). Natl Ed Res.
Gnanadesikan, Ramanathan. Methods for Statistical Data Analysis of Multivariate Observations. LC 76-14994. (Probability & Mathematical Statics Ser.). 1977. 31.00x (ISBN 0-471-30845-5, Pub. by Wiley-Interscience). Wiley.
Goodman, Leo A. Analyzing Qualitative Categorical Data: Log-Linear Models & Latent-Strucutre Analysis. Magidson, Jay, ed. 1978. text ed. 25.00 (ISBN 0-89011-513-3). Abt Assoc.
Gordon, A. D. Classification: Methods for the Exploratory Analysis of Multivariate Data. 1981. 26.00x (ISBN 0-412-22850-5, Pub. by Chapman & Hall). Methuen Inc.
Green, P. & Barban. Analyzing Multivariate Data. 1978. 28.95 (ISBN 0-03-020786-X). Dryden Pr.
Green, Paul E. & Carroll, Douglas. Mathematical Tools for Applied Multivariate Analysis: Student Edition. 1978. 20.00 (ISBN 0-12-297552-9). Acad Pr.
Green, Paul E., ed. Mathematical Tools for Applied Multivariate Analysis. 1976. 46.50 (ISBN 0-12-297550-2). Acad Pr.
Hair, Joseph F., et al. Multivariate Data Analysis. 1979. 20.95 (ISBN 0-87814-077-8). Pennwell Pub.
Harnett, D. L. & Murphy, J. L. Introductory Statistical Analysis. 2nd ed. 1980. 19.95 (ISBN 0-201-02758-5); student's wkbk. 5.95 (ISBN 0-201-02859-X); instructor's manual 2.95 (ISBN 0-201-02759-3). A-W.
Harris, Richard J. A Primer of Multivariate Statistics. 1974. text ed. 22.95 (ISBN 0-12-327250-5). Acad Pr.
Hawkins, Clark A. & Weber, Jean E. Statistical Analysis: Applications to Business & Economics. (Illus.). 1980. text ed. 24.50 scp (ISBN 0-06-042723-X, HarpC); scp solution manual 22.95 (ISBN 0-06-362687-X). Har-Row.
Helwig, Jane T. SAS Introductory Guide. 1978. pap. 4.95 (ISBN 0-917382-07-2). SAS Inst.
Hilton, Gordon. Intermediate Politometrics. LC 75-43733. 336p. 1976. 17.00x (ISBN 0-231-03783-X). Columbia U Pr.
Hope, K. Methods of Multivariate Analysis. 1970. 44.00 (ISBN 0-677-61360-1). Gordon.
IFIP TC Four Working Conference. Decision Making & Medical Care: Proceedings. De Dombal, E. T. & Gremy, F., eds. 1976. 68.50 (ISBN 0-7204-0464-9, North-Holland). Elsevier.
International Symposium, Fourth, Wright State University, June, 1975 & Krishnaiah, P. R. Multivariate Analysis 4: Proceedings. 1977. 61.00 (ISBN 0-7204-0520-3, North-Holland). Elsevier.
Johnston, R. J. Multivariate Statistical Analysis in Geography: A Primer of the General Linear Model. (Illus.). 1980. pap. text ed. 11.95x (ISBN 0-582-30034-7). Longman.
Kendall, Maurice. Multivariate Analysis. 2nd ed. (Griffin Statistical Monograph). 1980. 29.95 (ISBN 0-02-847570-4). Macmillan.
Krishnaiah. Multivariate Analysis: Proceedings of Third International Symposium. 1973. 63.00 (ISBN 0-12-426653-3). Acad Pr.
Krishnaiah, P., ed. Multivariate Analysis. 1969. 73.00 (ISBN 0-12-426652-5). Acad Pr.
Kshirsagar, A. M. Multivariate Analysis. (Statistics Textbks & Monographs: Vol. 2). 1972. 32.50 (ISBN 0-8247-1386-9). Dekker.
Lawlis, G. Frank & Chatfield, Douglas. Multivariate Approaches for the Behavioral Sciences: A Brief Text. (Illus., Orig.). 1974. pap. text ed. 5.00 (ISBN 0-89672-051-9). Tex Tech Pr.
Lindeman, Richard, et al. Introduction to Bivariate & Multivariate Statistics. 1980. text ed. 19.95x (ISBN 0-673-15099-2). Scott F.
Looking at Multivariate Data-Conference. Interpreting Multivariate Data: Proceedings. Barnett, ed. (Wiley Ser. in Probability & Mathematical Statistics). 360p. 1981. 25.00 (ISBN 0-471-28039-9, Pub. by Wiley Interscience). Wiley.
McCollough, Celeste. Introduction to Statistical Analysis: A Semiprogrammed Approach. (Illus.). 400p. (Prog. Bk.). 1974. text ed. 13.95 (ISBN 0-07-044805-1, C); pap. text ed. 10.95 (ISBN 0-07-044804-3). McGraw.
MacFarlane, A. G. Complex Variable Methods for Linear Multivariate Feedback Systems. 1981. 39.50x (ISBN 0-85066-197-8, Pub. by Taylor & Francis). Methuen Inc.
Mardia, K. V., et al. Multivariate Analysis. LC 79-40922. (Probability and Mathematical Statistics Ser.). 1980. 63.00 (ISBN 0-12-471250-9); pap. 35.50 (ISBN 0-12-471252-5). Acad Pr.
Maxwell, A. E. Multivariate Analysis in Behavioral Research: For Medical & Social Science Students. 2nd ed. 1978. 13.95x (ISBN 0-412-15580-X, Pub. by Chapman & Hall). Methuen Inc.
Morrison, D. F. Multivariate Statistical Methods. 2nd ed. 1976. 19.95 (ISBN 0-07-043186-8, C). McGraw.
Namboodri, Krishman, et al. Applied Multivariate Analysis & Experimental Design. (Illus.). 600p. 1975. text ed. 27.50 (ISBN 0-07-045865-0, C). McGraw.
O'Muircheartaigh, Colm A. & Payne, Clive. The Analysis of Survey Data, 2 vols. LC 76-951. 1977. Vol. 1 Exploring Data Structures. 45.50 (ISBN 0-471-01706-X); Vol. 2 Model Fitting. 45.50 (ISBN 0-471-99426-X); 91.00 set (ISBN 0-471-99466-9, Pub. by Wiley-Interscience). Wiley.
Orloci, L., et al, eds. Multivariate Methods in Ecological Work. (Statistical Ecology Ser.: Vol. 7). 580p. 1980. 50.00 (ISBN 0-89974-004-9). Intl Co-Op.
Overall, John E. & Klett, C. James. Applied Multivariate Analysis. 522p. 1981. Repr. of 1972 ed. lib. bdg. write for info. (ISBN 0-89874-325-7). Krieger.
--Applied Multivariate Analysis. (Psychology Ser.). (Illus.). 528p. 1971. text ed. 30.00 (ISBN 0-07-047935-6, C). McGraw.
Parsons, Robert. Statistical Analysis: A Decision Making Approach. 2nd ed. 1978. text ed. 24.50 scp (ISBN 0-06-045016-9, HarpC); scp student solutions manual 8.50 (ISBN 0-06-045017-7). Har-Row.
Press, S. James. Applied Multivariate Analysis. LC 80-26922. Date not set. Repr. of 1981 ed. price not set (ISBN 0-88275-976-0). Krieger.
Research Seminar on Multivariate Statistical Inference, Dalhousie U., Halifax, N.S., March 1972. Multivariate Statistical Inference: Proceedings. Kabe, D. G. & Gupta, R. P., eds. 264p. 1973. 29.50 (ISBN 0-444-10532-8, North-Holland). Elsevier.
Roberts, Harry V. Interactive Data Analysis. Date not set. text ed. write for info (ISBN 0-8162-7206-9). Holden-Day.
Royce, Joseph R., ed. Multivariate Analysis & Psychological Theory. 1973. 84.00 (ISBN 0-12-600750-0). Acad Pr.
Sheth, J. Multivariate Methods for Market & Survey Research. LC 76-39893. 388p. 1977. 20.00 (ISBN 0-87757-081-7). Am Mktg.
Srivastava, M. S. & Khatri, C. G. An Introduction to Multivariate Statistics. LC 78-21491. 1979. 19.50 (ISBN 0-444-00302-9, North Holland). Elsevier.
Tatsuoka, Maurice M. Multivariate Analysis: Techniques for Educational & Psychological Research. LC 78-151729. 310p. 1971. 23.95 (ISBN 0-471-84590-6). Wiley.
Tong, Y. L. Probability Inequalities in Multivariate Distribution. LC 79-27077. (Probability & Mathematical Statistics Ser.). 1980. 29.50 (ISBN 0-12-694950-6). Acad Pr.
Wang, Peter C., ed. Graphical Representation of Multivariate Data. 1978. 23.50 (ISBN 0-12-734750-X). Acad Pr.
Zeller, K. & Schempp, W., eds. Multivariate Approximation Theory. (Internationale Schriftenreihe zur Numerischen Mathematik: No. 51). (Illus.). 455p. 1979. pap. text ed. 38.00 (ISBN 3-7643-1102-9). Birkhauser.

MUMFORD, GEDDES, 1925-1944

Mumford, Lewis. Green Memories: The Story of Geddes Mumford. LC 73-6213. (Illus.). 342p. 1973. Repr. of 1947 ed. lib. bdg. 17.50x (ISBN 0-8371-6892-9, MUGM). Greenwood.

MUMMIES

Aliki. Mummies Made in Egypt. LC 77-26603. (Illus.). (gr. 2-6). 1979. 8.95 (ISBN 0-690-03858-5, TYC-J); PLB 9.89 (ISBN 0-690-03859-3). Har-Row.
Budge, E. A. Mummy. 2nd ed. LC 64-13391. (Illus.). 1894. 15.00x (ISBN 0-8196-0139-X). Biblo.
--The Mummy. (Illus.). 424p. 1972. pap. 5.95 (ISBN 0-02-030760-8, Collier). Macmillan.
David, A. R., ed. The Manchester Museum Mummy Project: Multi-Disciplinary Research on Ancient Egyptian Mummified Remains. 168p. 1979. 65.00x (ISBN 0-7190-1293-7, Pub. by Manchester U Pr England). State Mutual Bk.
David, Rosalie, ed. Mysteries of the Mummies. (Illus.). 1979. 14.95 (ISBN 0-684-16171-0, ScribT). Scribner.
Davisson, Emmett D. Art & Mysteries in Tombs, Mummies & Catacombs. (Illus.). 1980. deluxe ed. 51.50 deluxe binding (ISBN 0-930582-63-2). Gloucester Art.
Drerup, Heinrich. Die Datierung der Mumienportrats. 1933. pap. 5.50 (ISBN 0-384-12835-1). Johnson Repr.
Glubok, Shirley & Tamarin, Alfred. The Mummy of Ramose. LC 76-21392. (Illus.). 1978. 8.95 (ISBN 0-06-022039-2, HarpJ); PLB 9.89 (ISBN 0-06-022042-2). Har-Row.
Hamilton-Paterson, James & Andrews, Carol. Mummies: Death & Life in Ancient Egypt. LC 79-9856. (Illus.). (gr. 7 up). 1979. 9.95 (ISBN 0-670-49512-3). Viking Pr.
Harris, James E. & Weeks, Kent R. X-Raying the Pharaohs. LC 72-1180. (Encore Edition). (Illus.). 265p. 1973. pap. 2.95 (ISBN 0-684-16899-5, SL 535, ScribT). Scribner.

McHargue, Georgess. Mummies. LC 72-2324. (Illus.). 160p. (gr. 5-9). 1972. 8.95 (ISBN 0-397-31516-3, JBL-J). Har-Row.
Mummies in Fact & Fiction. (gr. 5 up). 1980. PLB 7.90 (ISBN 0-531-04154-9). Watts.
Pace, Mildred M. Wrapped for Eternity: The Story of the Egyptian Mummies. (Illus.). 192p. (gr. 5 up). 1974. 6.95 (ISBN 0-07-048053-2, GB). McGraw.
Pronzini, Bill. Mummy! A Chrestomathy of Crypt-ology. LC 80-66496. 1980. 10.95 (ISBN 0-87795-271-X). Arbor Hse.
Spiegelberg, W., ed. Inscriptiones Nominvm Graecorvm et Aegyptiacorvm Aetatis Romanae, Incisae Sivescriptae in Tabellis, (Mummy Labels) 1978. 25.00 (ISBN 0-89005-244-1). Ares.

MUMMING

Brody, Alan. English Mummers & Their Plays: Traces of Ancient Mystery. LC 77-92855. (Folklore & Folklife Ser). (Illus.). 1971. 14.00x (ISBN 0-8122-7611-6). U of Pa Pr.
Glassie, Henry. All Silver & No Brass: An Irish Christmas Mumming. LC 75-9132. (Illus.). 224p. 1976. 12.50x (ISBN 0-253-30470-9). Ind U Pr.
Sumberg, Samuel L. Nuremberg Schembart Carnival. (Columbia University. Germanic Studies, New Ser.: No. 12). Repr. of 1941 ed. 22.50 (ISBN 0-404-50462-0). AMS Pr.
Tiddy, Reginald J. Mummers' Play. LC 72-8091. 1923. lib. bdg. 30.00 (ISBN 0-88305-652-6). Norwood Edns.

MUMPS–JUVENILE LITERATURE

Lerner, Marguerite R. Dear Little Mumps Child. LC 59-15145. (Medical Bks. for Children). (Illus.). (gr. k-5). 1959. PLB 3.95 (ISBN 0-8225-0003-5). Lerner Pubns.

MUNBY, ARTHUR JOSEPH, 1828-1910

Hudson, Derek, ed. Munby, Man of Two Worlds. LC 72-83706. (Illus.). 461p. 1972. 12.50 (ISBN 0-87645-066-4). Gambit.

MUNBY, J. ALFRED, fl. 19TH CENTURY

Hudson, Derek, ed. Munby, Man of Two Worlds. LC 72-83706. (Illus.). 461p. 1972. 12.50 (ISBN 0-87645-066-4). Gambit.

MUNCH, EDVARD, 1863-1944

Dunlop, Ian. Edvard Munch. LC 77-71078. (Art for All Ser.). 1977. pap. 5.95 (ISBN 0-312-23822-3). St Martin.
Elderfield, John & Eggum, Arne. The Masterworks of Edvard Munch. (Illus.). 1979. pap. 6.95 (ISBN 0-87070-492-3). Museum Mod Art.
Hodin, J. P. Edvard Munch. (World of Art Ser.). (Illus.). 1972. pap. text ed. 9.95 (ISBN 0-19-519936-7). Oxford U Pr.
Lieberman, William S. Edvard Munch: A Selection of His Prints from American Collections. LC 79-169306. (Museum of Modern Art Publications in Reprint). (Illus.). 42p. Repr. of 1957 ed. 15.00 (ISBN 0-405-01565-8). Arno.
Munch, Edvard. Graphic Works of Edvard Munch. (Illus.). 1979. pap. 5.00 (ISBN 0-486-23765-6). Dover.
Selz, Jean. Edvard Munch. (Q L P Art Ser.). (Illus.). 96p. 1974. 6.95 (ISBN 0-517-51571-7). Crown.
Stang, N. Munch, Edvard. (Tanum of Norway Tokens Ser.). (Illus.). 302p. (Orig.). 1972. pap. 20.00x (ISBN 8-2518-0010-2, N518). Vanous.
Stang, N. C. Edvard Munch. Knudsen, Carol J., tr. (Tokens of Norway Ser). (Illus.). 305p. (Orig.). 1972. pap. 15.00x (ISBN 82-518-0010-2). Intl Pubns Serv.
Stang, Ragna. Edvard Munch: The Man & His Art. Culverwell, Geoffrey, tr. LC 78-31813. (Illus.). 1979. 55.00 (ISBN 0-89659-025-9). Abbeville Pr.
Wingfield, Digby C. Meaning & Symbol in Three Modern Artists: Edward Munch, Henry Moore, Paul Nash. LC 55-2585. 204p. 1955. Repr. 20.00 (ISBN 0-403-04167-8). Somerset Pub.

MUNCHHAUSEN, KARL FRIEDRICH HIERONYMUS FREIHERR VON, 1720-1797

Von Munchhausen, Angelita. The Real Munchhausen: Baron of Bodenwerder. (Illus.). 224p. (gr. 6 up). 1960. 6.00 (ISBN 0-8159-6701-2). Devin.

MUNDAS

Griffiths, Walter G. The Kol Tribe of Central India. LC 76-44727. (Asiatic Society, Calcutta. Monograph Ser.: Vol. 2). (Illus.). Repr. of 1946 ed. 31.50 (ISBN 0-404-15864-1). AMS Pr.
Sachchidananda. The Changing Munda. 316p. 1979. 20.00 (ISBN 0-8002-2308-X). Intl Pubns Serv.
--The Changing Munda. 1979. text ed. 25.00x (ISBN 0-391-01932-5). Humanities.

MUNDT, THEODORE, 1808-1861

Draeger, O. Theodor Mundt und Seine Beziehungen Zum Jungen Deutschland. 1909. pap. 7.00 (ISBN 0-384-12605-7). Johnson Repr.

MUNICH

Hanser, Richard. A Noble Treason: The Revolt of the Munich Students Against Hitler. LC 78-20832. (Illus.). 1979. 12.50 (ISBN 0-399-12041-6). Putnam.
Keetman, Peter. Munich: A Picture Book. 4th ed. Goepel, E., ed. 1965. 8.75x (ISBN 0-8002-1314-9). Intl Pubns Serv.
Kirsch, Peter. Munich in the Middle East. LC 78-63081. 1978. 10.00 (ISBN 0-88400-062-1). Shengold.
Levine-Meyer, Rosa. Levine the Spartacist. 1978. pap. 6.95 (ISBN 0-86033-062-1). Gordon-Cremonesi.
Munich. (Polyglott Travel Ser.). 1981. pap. 3.95 (ISBN 0-686-71866-6, Pub. by Langenscheidt Germany). Hippocrene Bks.
Munich. (Panorama Bks.). (Illus., Fr.). 3.95 (ISBN 0-685-11409-0). French & Eur.
Paley, Alan L. Munich & the Sudeten Crisis. Rahmas, D. Steve, ed. LC 72-89217. (Events of Our Times Ser.: No. 8). 32p. 1973. lib. bdg. 2.95 incl. catalog cards (ISBN 0-87157-703-8); pap. 1.50 vinyl laminated covers (ISBN 0-87157-203-6). SamHar Pr.
Time-Life Books Editors & Bailey, George. Munich. (The Great Cities Ser.). (Illus.). 200p. 1981. 14.95 (ISBN 0-8094-3120-3). Time-Life.

MUNICH–PINAKOTHER, ALTE

Ragghianti, Carlo L. Pinakothek: Munich. LC 69-19062. (Great Museums of the World Ser.). (Illus.). 1968. 16.95 (ISBN 0-88225-235-6). Newsweek.

MUNICH, UNIVERSITY OF

Scholl, Inge. Students Against Tyranny: The Resistance of the White Rose, Munich, 1942-1943. rev. ed. Schultz, Arthur R., tr. from Ger. LC 73-105504. Orig. Title: Weisse Rose. (Illus.). 1970. 12.50x (ISBN 0-8195-4021-8, Pub. by Wesleyan U Pr). Columbia U Pr.

MUNICH FOUR-POWER AGREEMENT, 1938

Douglas, Roy. In the Year of Munich. LC 77-82823. (Illus.). 1978. 18.95 (ISBN 0-312-41179-0). St Martin.
Kennan, George F. From Prague After Munich: Diplomatic Papers, 1938-1939. LC 66-26587. 1968. 20.00 (ISBN 0-691-05620-X); pap. 7.95 (ISBN 0-691-01063-3). Princeton U Pr.
Lammers, Donald N. Explaining Munich: The Search for Motive in British Policy. LC 65-26304. (Studies: No. 16). 1966. pap. 3.95 (ISBN 0-8179-3162-7). Hoover Inst Pr.
Ripka, Herbert. Munich, Before & After. LC 68-9630. 1969. Repr. of 1939 ed. 22.50 (ISBN 0-86527-133-X). Fertig.
Werth, Alexander. France & Munich. LC 68-9632. 1969. Repr. of 1939 ed. 27.50 (ISBN 0-86527-071-6). Fertig.

MUNICIPAL ADMINISTRATION

see Municipal Government

MUNICIPAL AND INTERNATIONAL LAW

see International and Municipal Law

MUNICIPAL ART

see Art, Municipal

MUNICIPAL BONDS

see also School Bonds

Amdursky, Robert S., ed. Basics for Municipal Bond Lawyers: Course Handbook. LC 80-82474. (Nineteen Seventy-Nine to Nineteen Eighty Corporate Law & Practice Course Handbook Ser.). 887p. 1980. pap. 25.00 (ISBN 0-686-69164-4, B4-6551). PLI.
Anderson, Kay. Municipal Disclosure Standards Sourcebook, Vol. 7. (Municipal Securities Regulation Ser.). 1978. pap. text ed. 60.00x (ISBN 0-916450-18-X). Coun on Municipal.
Chadbourne, et al. Federal Legislative Background & Four Legal Memoranda, Vols. 5 & 6. (Municipal Securites Regulation Ser.). 1978. Set. pap. text ed. 65.00 (ISBN 0-916450-35-X). Vol. 5 (ISBN 0-916450-12-0). Vol. 6 (ISBN 0-916450-13-9). Coun on Municipal.
--State Laws, Vol. 8. (Municipal Securities Regulation Ser.). 1978. pap. text ed. 50.00x (ISBN 0-916450-19-8). Coun on Municipal.
Complete Set of Monthly Bond Values for Invoicing Municipal Bonds. rental 50.00 (ISBN 0-685-59983-3). Finan Pub.
Donheiser, Alan. Creating Investor Confidence in Municipal Bonds. 1977. pap. 1.00 (ISBN 0-686-22982-7). Lincoln Inst Land.
Fincher, Cameron. Atlanta Studies Its Bond Issue: A Survey of Public Opinion. LC 63-63299. (Research Monograph: No. 25). 1963. spiral bdg. 5.00 (ISBN 0-88406-041-1). Ga St U Busn Pub.
A Guide for Developing Municipal Bond Credit Files. 1968. 4.00 (ISBN 0-89982-084-0, 270300). Am Bankers.
Hillhouse, Albert M. Municipal Bonds: A Century of Experience. facsimile ed. LC 75-2640. (Wall Street & the Security Market Ser.). 1975. Repr. of 1936 ed. 35.00x (ISBN 0-405-06965-0). Arno.
Kaufman, George G. Efficiency in the Municipal Bond Market: The Use of Tax Exempt Financing for "Private" Purposes, Vol. 30. Altman, Edward I. & Walter, Ingo, eds. LC 80-82481. (Contemporary Studies in Economic & Financial Analysis). 275p. 1981. 29.50 (ISBN 0-89232-168-7). Jai Pr.
Lamb, Robert & Rappaport, Stephen. Municipal Bonds: The Comprehensive Review of Tax-Exempt Securities & Municipal Finance. (Illus.). 384p. 1980. 14.95 (ISBN 0-07-036082-0, P&RB). McGraw.
Mussa, Michael L. & Kormendi, Roger G. Taxation of Municipal Bonds: An Economic Appraisal. 1979. pap. 7.25 (ISBN 0-8447-3331-8). Am Enterprise.
Public Securities Assoc. Fundamentals of Municipal Bonds. (Illus.). 1980. cancelled (ISBN 0-89490-048-X). Enslow Pubs.
Public Securities Association. Fundamentals of Municipal Bonds. (Illus.). 208p. 1981. text ed. 14.95 (ISBN 0-686-29692-3). Pub Securities.
Rousmaniere, Peter F. Selling Your City, No. M-1. (Practitioner Manuals Ser.). 1978. pap. text ed. 8.00x (ISBN 0-916450-22-8). Coun on Municipal.
Steiss, Alan W. Local Government Finance: Capital Facilities Planning & Debt Administration in Local Government. 288p. 1975. 21.95 (ISBN 0-669-00126-0). Lexington Bks.
Twentieth Century Fund, Inc. Building a Broader Market: Report of the Twentieth Century Fund Task Force on the Municipal Bond Market. LC 76-28368. 1976. 7.95 (ISBN 0-07-065629-0, P&RB). McGraw.
Twentieth Century Fund. Task Force on Municipal Bond Credit Ratings & Petersen, John E. The Rating Game: Report of the Twentieth Century Fund Task Force on Municipal Bond Credit Ratings: Background Paper. LC 77-4987. 1977. pap. 7.00 (ISBN 0-527-02780-4). Kraus Repr.
White, Anthony G. Municipal Bonding & Taxation. LC 78-68296. (Reference Library of Social Sciences Ser.). 1979. lib. bdg. 20.00 (ISBN 0-8240-9761-0). Garland Pub.

MUNICIPAL BUDGETS

Hammond, Thomas H. & Knott, Jack H. A Zero-Based Look at Zero-Base Budgeting. LC 79-65228. 145p. 1980. 14.95 (ISBN 0-87855-365-7). Transaction Bks.
Henderson, Thomas A. & Foster, John L. Urban Policy Game: A Simulation of Urban Politics. LC 78-17118. 1978. pap. text ed. 10.95 (ISBN 0-471-03398-7). Wiley.
Kimmel, Wayne A., et al. Municipal Management & Budget Methods: An Evaluation of Policy Related Research. 1974. pap. 7.50 (ISBN 0-87766-135-9, 96000). Urban Inst.
Kramer, Fred A. Contemporary Approaches to Public Budgeting. (Illus.). 1979. pap. text ed. 7.95 (ISBN 0-87626-168-3). Winthrop.
Lynch, Thomas, ed. Contemporary Public Budgeting. LC 79-67062. 224p. 1981. pap. text ed. 7.95 (ISBN 0-87855-722-9). Transaction Bks.
Metropolitan Futures, Inc. A Model Operating Budget for a Medium-Sized Town. LC 74-4517. (Operating Budget Handbook, Series A). (Illus.). 150p. (Orig.). 1975. pap. 12.00 (ISBN 0-915218-00-3). Metro Futures.
Steiss, Alan W. Local Government Finance: Capital Facilities Planning & Debt Administration in Local Government. 288p. 1975. 21.95 (ISBN 0-669-00126-0). Lexington Bks.
Wacht, Richard F. A New Approach to Capital Budgeting for City & County Governments. LC 80-13336. (Research Monograph: No. 87). 1980. pap. 29.00 (ISBN 0-88406-140-X). Ga St U Busn Pub.
Ward, T. S. & Nelid, R. R. The Measurement & Reform of Budgetary Policy. 1978. pap. text ed. 18.50x (ISBN 0-435-84880-1). Heinemann Ed.
Worthley, John A. & Ludwin, William G., eds. Zero-Base Budgeting in State & Local Government: Current Experiences & Cases. LC 79-10162. 1979. 20.95 (ISBN 0-03-049121-5). Praeger.

MUNICIPAL BUILDING

see Public Buildings

MUNICIPAL CIVIL SERVICE

see Municipal Officials and Employees

MUNICIPAL CONTRACTS

see Public Contracts

MUNICIPAL CORPORATIONS

see also Mayors; Metropolitan Government; Municipal Finance; Municipal Government; Parishes; Police Power; Special Assessments; Tort Liability of Municipal Corporations

McGoldrick, Joseph D. Law & Practice of Municipal Home Rule, 1916-1930. LC 33-22314. Repr. of 1933 ed. 22.45 (ISBN 0-404-04128-0). AMS Pr.
Maddox, Russell W. Extraterritorial Powers of Municipalities in the United States. (Studies in Political Science Ser: No. 2). 1955. pap. 3.95 (ISBN 0-87071-092-3). Oreg St U Pr.
Mandelker, Daniel R. Managing Our Urban Environment. 2nd ed. (Contemporary Legal Education Ser). 1971. 21.00 (ISBN 0-672-81707-1, Bobbs-Merrill Law). Michie-Bobbs.
Reed, P. W. The Economics of Public Enterprise. 1974. 19.50x (ISBN 0-8448-0884-9). Crane-Russak Co.
Yokley, E. C. Municipal Corporations, 4 vols. 3rd ed. 1956. with 1980 cum. suppl. 175.00 (ISBN 0-87215-063-1); 1980 cum suppl seperately 90.00 (ISBN 0-87215-340-1). Michie-Bobbs.

MUNICIPAL COURTS

Criminal Courts in New York State. facsimile ed. LC 74-3841. (Criminal Justice in America Ser.). 1974. Repr. of 1909 ed. 35.00x (ISBN 0-405-06141-2). Arno.
Jacob, Herbert. Urban Justice: Law & Order in American Cities. 160p. 1973. pap. 7.95 ref. ed. (ISBN 0-13-938944-X). P-H.
Marks, Edward. Acme's Uniform City Court Practice. 35.00 (ISBN 0-685-05156-0). Acme Law.

MUNICIPAL ELECTIONS

see Elections

MUNICIPAL EMPLOYEES

see Municipal Officials and Employees

MUNICIPAL ENGINEERING

see also Bridges; City Planning; Drainage; Housing; Parks; Public Buildings; Refuse and Refuse Disposal; Sanitary Engineering; Sewerage; Shore Protection; Street Cleaning; Streets; Water-Supply

Equipment Management Manual, Pt. 1. 1975. 15.00 (ISBN 0-917084-02-0). Am Public Works.
Streetscape Equipment Sourcebook I. 1976. 15.00 (ISBN 0-917084-04-7). Am Public Works.

MUNICIPAL FINANCE

see also Finance, Public; Licenses; Local Finance; Local Taxation; Municipal Bonds; Municipal Budgets

Auletta, Ken. The Streets Were Paved with Gold. LC 78-21838. 1979. 12.95 (ISBN 0-394-50019-9). Random.
Bahl, Roy W. & Vogt, Walter. Fiscal Centralization & Tax Burdens: State and Regional Finance of City Services. LC 75-31649. 192p. 1976. text ed. 19.50 (ISBN 0-88410-423-0). Ballinger Pub.
Bierwag, G. O. The Primary Market for Municipal Debt: Bidding Rules & the Cost of Long-Term Borrowing, Vol. 29. Altman, Edward I. & Walter, Ingo, eds. LC 80-82480. (Contemporary Studies in Economic & Financial Analysis). 300p. 1981. 32.50 (ISBN 0-89232-167-9). Jai Pr.
Burton, John C. A Revised Financial Reporting Model for Municipalities, No. 6-7. (Government Auditing Ser.). 1980. pap. 6.00 (ISBN 0-686-70150-X). Coun on Municipal.
Chadbourne, et al. Summary of Publications & Hearings, Vol. 4. (Municipal Securities Regulation Ser.). 1977. pap. text ed. 70.00 (ISBN 0-916450-11-2). Coun on Municipal.
Cleveland, Frederick A. Chapters Municipal Administration & Accounting. Brief, Richard P., ed. LC 80-1479. (Dimensions of Accounting Theory & Practice Ser.). 1981. Repr. of 1909 ed. lib. bdg. 35.00x (ISBN 0-405-13509-2). Arno.
Colman, William G. Cities, Suburbs & States: Governing & Financing Urban America. LC 75-2810. (Illus.). 1975. 17.95 (ISBN 0-02-906490-2). Free Pr.
Duke Law Journal, ed. Municipal Finance: The Duke Law Journal Symposium. LC 77-15994. 1977. 19.50 (ISBN 0-88410-662-4). Ballinger Pub.
Financing America's States & Cities. 1970. 3.00 (ISBN 0-89982-101-4, 182900). Am Bankers.
Fisher, Glenn W. & Fairbanks, Robert P. Illinois Municipal Finance: A Political & Economic Analysis. LC 67-21852. (Illus.). 1968. 14.95 (ISBN 0-252-72373-2). U of Ill Pr.
Foster, C. D., et al. Local Government Finance in a Unitary State. (Illus.). 640p. 1980. text ed. 60.00x (ISBN 0-04-336066-1). Allen Unwin.
Friedman, Lewis. City Budgets. 35p. 1974. write for info. (ISBN 0-916450-04-X). Coun on Municipal.
Harrison, Bennet. Urban Economic Development: Suburbanization, Minority Opportunity, and the Condition of the Central City. 1974. 10.00 (ISBN 0-87766-098-0, 48000); pap. 4.50 (ISBN 0-87766-102-2, 51000). Urban Inst.
Heilbrun, James. Urban Economics & Public Policy. 384p. 1973. text ed. 14.95 (ISBN 0-312-83440-3). St Martin.
Hillhouse, Albert M. Municipal Bonds: A Century of Experience. facsimile ed. LC 75-2640. (Wall Street & the Security Market Ser.). 1975. Repr. of 1936 ed. 35.00x (ISBN 0-405-06965-0). Arno.
Hirsch, Werner Z., et al. Fiscal Pressures on the Central City: The Impact of Commuters, Nonwhites & Overlapping Governments. LC 70-170272. (Special Studies in U.S. Economic, Social & Political Issues). 1971. 28.00x (ISBN 0-89197-759-7). Irvington.

Hordon, Harris E. Introduction to Urban Economics: Analysis & Policy. 1973. pap. text ed. 14.95 (ISBN 0-13-499491-4). P-H.
Hudson, Joseph L., Jr. The Urban Crisis: A Call for Corporate Action. (William K. McInally Memorial Lecture Ser.: 3rd). 1968. pap. 1.00 (ISBN 0-87712-147-8). U Mich Busn Div Res.
Hutchinson, Ruth G. State-Administered Locally-Shared Taxes. LC 68-58593. (Columbia University. Studies in the Social Sciences: No. 355). Repr. of 1931 ed. 16.50 (ISBN 0-404-51355-7). AMS Pr.
Introduction & Certain Legal Considerations, 2 vols, Vols. 1&2. (Municipal Securities Regulation Ser.). 1977. Vol. 1. pap. text ed. 50.00 (ISBN 0-916450-08-2); Vol. 2. pap. text ed. (ISBN 0-916450-09-0). Coun on Municipal.
Kohler, Heinz. Economics & Urban Problems. 1973. pap. text ed. 8.95x (ISBN 0-669-84566-3). Heath.
Laird, Melvin, et al. Financial Crisis of Our Cities. 1976. pap. 3.75 (ISBN 0-8447-2077-1). Am Enterprise.
Margolis, Julius, ed. The Public Economy of Urban Communities: Papers Presented at the 2nd Conference on Urban Public Expenditures, Feb. 21-22, 1964. LC 77-86404. (Resources for the Future, Inc. Publications). Repr. of 1965 ed. 32.50 (ISBN 0-404-60339-4). AMS Pr.
Mathewson, Kent & Neenan, William B., eds. Financing the Metropolis. 352p. 1980. 29.95 (ISBN 0-03-056886-2). Praeger.
Meltsner, Arnold J. The Politics of City Revenue. LC 70-129610. (Oakland Project). 1971. 21.50x (ISBN 0-520-01812-5); pap. 6.95x (ISBN 0-520-02773-6). U of Cal Pr.
Municipal Accounting & Auditing: Where We Are Now, Where We Should Be Going, No. 17. (COMP Papers Ser.). 170p. 1980. pap. 18.00 (ISBN 0-916450-41-4). Coun on Municipal.
Perlman, Mark, et al, eds. Spatial Regional & Population Economics. 1972. 68.75 (ISBN 0-677-15020-2). Gordon.
Rogers, David. Can Business Management Save the Cities? The Case of New York. LC 77-18594. 1978. 13.95 (ISBN 0-02-926730-7). Free Pr.
Rosewater, Victor. Special Assessments: A Study in Municipal Finance. LC 68-56686. (Columbia University. Studies in the Social Sciences: No. 7). Repr. of 1898 ed. 16.50 (ISBN 0-404-51007-8). AMS Pr.
Rousmaniere, Peter F. Self-Regulation: Is It Working, Vol. 3. (Municipal Securities Regulation Ser.). 1977. pap. text ed. 40.00 (ISBN 0-916450-10-4). Coun on Municipal.
--State Level Disclosure Guidelines, Vol. 9. (Municipal Securities Regulation Ser.). 233p. 1980. pap. 40.00 (ISBN 0-916450-20-1). Coun on Municipal.
--The Way Back: Toward Accountability in America's Cities, Vol. 10. (Municipal Securities Regulation Ser.). 231p. 1979. pap. 25.00x (ISBN 0-916450-21-X). Coun on Municipal.
Sackrey, Charles. The Political Economy of Urban Poverty. 172p. 1972. pap. 4.95x (ISBN 0-393-09410-3, NortonC). Norton.
Schaller, Howard G., ed. Public Expenditure Decisions in the Urban Community. (Resources for the Future Ser). (Illus.). 208p. 1963. pap. 3.50x (ISBN 0-8018-0576-7). Johns Hopkins.
Securities Regulation Series, 10 vols. Incl. Vol. 1. An Introduction. Marlin, John T. & Rousmaniere, Peter F. 36p; Vol. 2. Certain Legal Considerations. Chadbourne, et al. 129p. (Vols. 1 & 2 bound together) (ISBN 0-916450-09-0); Vol. 3. Self Regulation: Is It Working? Rousmaniere, Peter F. 148p (ISBN 0-916450-10-4); Vol. 4. Summary of Publications & Hearings. Chadbourne, et al. 264p; Vol. 5. Federal Legislative Background. Chadbourne, et al.; Vol. 6. Four Legal Memoranda. Chadbourne, et al. (Vols. 5 & 6 bound together, 122p.) (ISBN 0-916450-13-9); Vol. 7. Municipal Disclosure Standards Sourcebook. Anderson, Kay. 199p (ISBN 0-916450-18-X); Vol. 8. State Laws. Chadbourne, et al. 204p (ISBN 0-916450-19-8); State Level Disclosure Guidelines. Rousmaniere, Peter F. 233p (ISBN 0-916450-20-1); Vol. 10. The Way Back: Toward Accountability in America's Cities. Rousmaniere, Peter F. 231p (ISBN 0-916450-21-X). 1977-80. Set. 300.00 (ISBN 0-686-70181-X). Coun on Municipal.
Seward, Samuel M., et al. Municipal Resource Allocation: Minimizing the Cost of Fire Protection. 1976. 2.50 (ISBN 0-686-64193-0). U CO Busn Res Div.
Stokes, Howard K. The Finances & Administration of Providence. LC 78-64270. (Johns Hopkins University. Studies in the Social Sciences. Extra Volumes: 25). Repr. of 1903 ed. 34.50 (ISBN 0-404-61372-1). AMS Pr.
U. S. House Committee on Banking, Currency & Housing. The New York City Fiscal Crisis. LC 77-74954. (American Federalism-the Urban Dimension). (Illus.). 1978. Repr. of 1975 ed. lib. bdg. 20.00x (ISBN 0-405-10498-7). Arno.
Upson, Lent D. Sources of Municipal Revenue in Illinois. (Illus.). Repr. of 1912 ed. 9.50 (ISBN 0-384-63300-5). Johnson Repr.
Walker, Mabel L. Business Enterprise & the City. 1976. Repr. of 1957 ed. pap. 7.00 (ISBN 0-527-93960-9). Kraus Repr.
--Municipal Expenditures. LC 78-64283. (Johns Hopkins University. Studies in the Social Sciences. Extra Volumes.: 13). Repr. of 1930 ed. 19.50 (ISBN 0-404-61383-7). AMS Pr.
Walzer, Norman & Fisher, Glen W. Cities, Suburbs & Property Taxes. 256p. 1981. text ed. 22.50 (ISBN 0-89946-110-7). Oelgeschlager.

MUNICIPAL FINANCE–ACCOUNTING
see Finance, Public–Accounting

MUNICIPAL FRANCHISES
see also Public Service Commissions; Public Utilities

Arent, Leonora. Electric Franchises in New York City. LC 70-77999. (Columbia University Studies in the Social Sciences: No. 201). Repr. of 1919 ed. 17.50 (ISBN 0-404-51201-1). AMS Pr.
Carman, Harry J. Street Surface Railway Franchises of New York City. LC 76-77998. (Columbia University Studies in the Social Sciences: No. 200). Repr. of 1919 ed. 20.00 (ISBN 0-404-51200-3). AMS Pr.
Myers, Gustavus. History of Public Franchises in New York City: Manhattan, Bronx, March, 1900. LC 73-19163. (Politics & People Ser.). 136p. 1974. Repr. 7.00x (ISBN 0-405-05885-3). Arno.

MUNICIPAL GOVERNMENT
see also Boroughs; Elections; Local Government; Mayors; Metropolitan Finance; Metropolitan Government; Municipal Corporations; Municipal Finance; Municipal Home Rule; Municipal Officials and Employees; Municipal Reports; Municipal Research; Public Administration
also subdivision Politics and Government under names of cities, e.g. San Francisco–Politics and Government

Academy of Political Science. Municipal Income Taxes: Proceedings, Vol. 28, No. 4. Connery, R. H., ed. 6.00 (ISBN 0-8446-1887-X). Peter Smith.
Addams, Jane. Newer Ideals of Peace. LC 71-137523. (Peace Movement in America Ser). xviii, 243p. 1972. Repr. of 1907 ed. lib. bdg. 14.25x (ISBN 0-89198-050-4). Ozer.
--Newer Ideals of Peace. Repr. of 1911 ed. 20.00 (ISBN 0-685-72767-X). Norwood Edns.
Allen, Robert S., ed. Our Fair City. LC 73-19124. (Politics & People Ser.). 396p. 1974. Repr. 20.00x (ISBN 0-405-05851-9). Arno.
American Academy of Political & Social Science. Education for Urban Administration. LC 72-94416. (Monograph: No. 16). 1973. pap. 6.00 (ISBN 0-87761-164-5). Am Acad Pol Soc Sci.
Anderson, Wayne F., et al, eds. Managing Human Services. LC 77-2464. (Municipal Management Ser.). (Illus.). 1977. text ed. 25.00 (ISBN 0-87326-017-1). Intl City Mgt.
Arkes, Hadley. The Philosopher in the City: The Moral Dimensions of Urban Politics. LC 80-8536. 496p. 1981. 27.50x (ISBN 0-691-09356-3); pap. 6.95x (ISBN 0-691-02822-2). Princeton U Pr.
Banfield, Edward C. Big City Politics: A Comparative Guide to the Political Systems of Nine American Cities. 1965. pap. text ed. 3.40x (ISBN 0-394-30848-4). Phila Bk Co.
--Political Influence. LC 60-12182. 1965. pap. text ed. 7.95 (ISBN 0-02-901590-1). Free Pr.
Banfield, Edward C. & Wilson, James Q. City Politics. LC 63-19134. (Joint Center for Urban Studies Publications Ser). (Illus.). 1963. 18.00x (ISBN 0-674-13250-5). Harvard U Pr.
--City Politics. 1966. pap. 1.95 (ISBN 0-394-70335-9, V335, Vin). Random.
Banfield, Edward C., ed. Urban Government: Reader in Administration & Politics. 2nd ed. LC 69-11169. 1969. text ed. 15.95 (ISBN 0-02-901690-8). Free Pr.
Beard, Charles A. American City Government: A Survey of Newer Tendencies. LC 70-112522. (Rise of Urban America). (Illus.). 1970. Repr. of 1912 ed. 20.00 (ISBN 0-405-02435-5). Arno.
Bent, Alan E. & Rossum, Ralph A., eds. Urban Administration: Management, Politics & Change. 1976. 18.50 (ISBN 0-8046-7106-0); pap. 8.95 (ISBN 0-8046-7109-5). Kennikat.
Berkowitz, Marvin. The Social Costs of Human Underdevelopment: Case Study of Seven New York City Neighborhoods. LC 73-19440. (Special Studies in U.S. Economic, Social & Political Issues). 1974. 28.50x (ISBN 0-275-28821-8). Irvington.
Bhattacharya, Mohit. Municipal Government: Problems & Prospects. LC 74-901159. 124p. 1974. 9.50x (ISBN 0-8002-0055-1). Intl Pubns Serv.
Bish, Robert L. & Ostrom, Vincent. Understanding Urban Government: Metropolitan Reform Reconsidered. 1973. pap. 5.25 (ISBN 0-8447-3120-X). Am Enterprise.
Bollens, John C. Appointed Executive Local Government: The California Experience. LC 52-12988. (Illus.). xi, 233p. Repr. of 1952 ed. lib. bdg. 15.00x (ISBN 0-8371-8068-6, BOAE). Greenwood.
Brecher, Charles & Horton, Raymond D., eds. Setting Municipal Priorities, Nineteen Eighty Two. LC 81-66978. (Illus.). 390p. 1981. text ed. 32.50x (ISBN 0-87154-137-8). Russell Sage.
--Setting Municipal Priorities, 1981. LC 80-67392. 212p. 1981. text ed. 25.00 (ISBN 0-86598-010-1). Allanheld.
Bromage, Arthur W. Councilmen at Work. 1954. 1.75x (ISBN 0-685-21779-5). Wahr.
--Introduction to Municipal Government & Administration. 2nd ed. LC 57-7072. (Illus.). 1957. 29.50x (ISBN 0-89197-243-9). Irvington.
Brooks, Robert C. Bibliography of Municipal Problems & City Conditions. LC 78-112527. (Rise of Urban America). 1970. Repr. of 1901 ed. 17.00 (ISBN 0-405-02439-8). Arno.
Brosz, Allyn & Morgan, David R. Improving Municipal Productivity: A Handbook for Local Officials. 1978. 3.50 (ISBN 0-686-22969-X). Univ OK Gov Res.
Brownell, Blaine A. & Stickle, Warren E., eds. Bosses & Reformers: Urban Politics in America, 1880-1920. LC 72-4798. (New Perspectives in History Ser.). 250p. (Orig.). 1973. pap. text ed. 7.25 (ISBN 0-395-14050-1, 3-41025). HM.
Caraley, Demetrios. City Governments & Urban Problems: A New Introduction to Urban Politics. LC 76-28327. (Illus.). 1977. 17.95 (ISBN 0-13-134973-2). P-H.
Carr, T. R. & Colston, Stephanie. State & Urban Policy Analysis: An Annotated Bibliography. 1975. 3.50 (ISBN 0-686-18643-5). Univ OK Gov Res.
Clark, Terry N., ed. Citizen Preferences & Urban Public Policy: Models, Measures, Uses. LC 76-53963. (Sage Contemporary Social: Vol. 34). (Illus.). 142p. 1976. pap. 5.95 (ISBN 0-8039-0749-4). Sage.
Cleveland, Frederick A. Chapters Municipal Administration & Accounting. Brief, Richard P., ed. LC 80-1479. (Dimensions of Accounting Theory & Practice Ser.). 1981. Repr. of 1909 ed. lib. bdg. 35.00x (ISBN 0-405-13509-2). Arno.
Coleman, James S. Community Conflict. 1957. pap. text ed. 2.95 (ISBN 0-02-906480-5). Free Pr.
Colman, William G. Cities, Suburbs & States: Governing & Financing Urban America. LC 75-2810. (Illus.). 1975. 17.95 (ISBN 0-02-906490-2). Free Pr.
Cook, Edward M., Jr. The Fathers of the Towns: Leadership & Community Structure in Eighteenth Century New England. LC 75-36937. (Studies in Historical & Political Science). 1978. pap. 4.95 (ISBN 0-8018-2149-5). Johns Hopkins.
--The Fathers of the Towns: Leadership & Community Structure in Eighteenth Century New England. LC 75-36937. (Studies in Historical & Political Sciences: Ninety-Fourth Series NO.2 (1976)). (Illus.). 296p. 1976. 18.50x (ISBN 0-8018-1741-2). Johns Hopkins.
Cox, H. & Morgan, D. City Politics & the Press. LC 72-96678. (Illus.). 200p. 1973. 23.95 (ISBN 0-521-20162-4). Cambridge U Pr.
Crawford, Clan, Jr. Strategy & Tactics in Municipal Zoning. (Illus.). 1979. 24.95 (ISBN 0-13-850990-5, Busn). P-H.
Crew, Michael A., ed. Problems in Public-Utility Economics & Regulation. 192p. 1979. 17.95 (ISBN 0-669-02775-8). Lexington Bks.
Dahl, Robert A. Who Governs: Democracy & Power in an American City. LC 61-16913. (Studies in Political Science: No. 4). (Illus.). 1961. 27.50x (ISBN 0-300-00395-1); pap. 5.95x (ISBN 0-300-00051-0, Y73). Yale U Pr.
Daland, Robert T., ed. Comparative Urban Research. LC 69-18751. 368p. 1969. 20.00 (ISBN 0-8039-0012-0). Sage.
David, Stephen M. & Peterson, Paul E. Urban Politics & Public Policy: The City in Crisis. 2nd ed. LC 75-45450. 351p. (Orig.). 1976. pap. text ed. 7.95 (ISBN 0-03-036131-1, HoltC). HR&W.
Dearlove, J. The Politics of Policy in Local Government. LC 73-77179. (Illus.). 300p. 1973. 27.50 (ISBN 0-521-20244-2). Cambridge U Pr.
De Toledano, Ralph. The Municipal Doomsday Machine. LC 75-19174. 192p. 1976. pap. 1.95 (ISBN 0-916054-31-4, Caroline Hse Inc). Green Hill.
Dimond, Paul R. Dilemma of Local Government: Discrimination in the Provision of Public Services. LC 78-57187. (Illus.). 1978. 21.95 (ISBN 0-669-02372-8). Lexington Bks.
Dorsett, Lyle W. Franklin D. Roosevelt & the City Bosses. (National University Publications Interdisciplinary Urban Ser.). 1977. 12.50 (ISBN 0-8046-9186-X). Kennikat.
Elles, Neil. Community Law Through the Cases. 1973. 18.50 (ISBN 0-685-32576-8). Bender.
Eulau, Heinz & Prewitt, Kenneth. Labyrinths of Democracy: Adaptations, Linkages, Representation, and Policies in Urban Politics. LC 72-77129. 1973. 28.50x (ISBN 0-672-51155-X); pap. text ed. 12.95x (ISBN 0-89197-821-6). Irvington.
Fainstein, Norman I. & Fainstein, Susan S. Urban Political Movements: The Search for Power by Minority Groups in American Cities. LC 73-21876. 352p. 1974. ref. ed. 11.95 (ISBN 0-13-939330-7); pap. 9.95 ref. ed. (ISBN 0-13-939322-6). P-H.
Feldman, Lionel D. & Graham, Katherine A. Bargaining for Cities, Municipalities & Intergovernmental Relations: An Assessment. 143p. 1979. pap. text ed. 10.95x (ISBN 0-920380-21-2, Pub. by Inst Res Pub Canada). Renouf.
Fischer, John. Vital Signs, U. S. A. LC 74-15823. 210p. 1975. 10.00 (ISBN 0-06-011247-6, HarpT). Har-Row.
Five-Step Workplan for Municipal Services Planning with Full Accountability. 2nd ed. 1974. 29.95 (ISBN 0-934752-02-8). Eckman Ctr.
Fowler, Floyd J. Citizen Attitudes Toward Local Government, Services & Taxes. LC 74-9976. 180p. 1974. text ed. 20.00 (ISBN 0-88410-408-7). Ballinger Pub.
Fox, Kenneth P. Better City Government: Innovation in American Urban Politics, 1850-1937. LC 77-71957. 1977. 29.50x (ISBN 0-87722-099-9). Temple U Pr.
Fried, Robert C. & Rabinovitz, Frances F. Comparative Urban Politics: A Performance Approach. 240p. 1980. pap. text ed. 10.95 (ISBN 0-13-154351-2). P-H.
Friesema, Harry P. Metropolitan Political Structure: Intergovernmental Relations & Political Integration in the Quad Cities. LC 73-147925. (Illus.). 1971. 7.95x (ISBN 0-87745-020-X). U of Iowa Pr.
Gardiner, John A. & Olson, David J., eds. Theft of the City: Readings on Corruption in Urban America. LC 73-16519. 448p. 1974. 15.00x (ISBN 0-253-35860-4); pap. 4.95x (ISBN 0-253-35861-2). Ind U Pr.
Gilbert, William H., ed. Public Relations in Local Government. LC 75-29400. (Municipal Management Ser.). 1975. text ed. 24.00 (ISBN 0-87326-012-0). Intl City Mgt.
Goodman, Jay S. The Dynamics of Urban Government & Politics. 2nd ed. (Illus.). 1980. pap. text ed. 11.95 (ISBN 0-02-344830-X). Macmillan.
Goodnow, Frank J. City Government in the United States. LC 73-11903. (Metropolitan America Ser.). 330p. 1974. Repr. 16.00x (ISBN 0-405-05394-0). Arno.
Gotherman, John E. Ohio Municipal Law: Procedure & Forms, 3 vols. 2nd rev. ed. (Baldwin's Ohio Practice Ser.). 1975. Set. 150.00 (ISBN 0-685-92079-8). Banks-Baldwin.
Greer, Ann L. The Mayor's Mandate: Municipal Statecraft & Political Trust. 200p. 1974. pap. 5.95 (ISBN 0-87073-165-3). Schenkman.
Greer, Scott. The Urbane View: Life & Politics in Metropolitan America. (Illus.). 352p. 1972. 14.95 (ISBN 0-19-501544-4). Oxford U Pr.
Greer, Scott, et al, eds. Accountability in Urban Society: Public Agencies Under Fire. LC 78-17295. (Urban Affairs Annual Reviews: Vol. 15). 304p. 1978. 22.50 (ISBN 0-8039-1081-9); pap. 9.95 (ISBN 0-8039-1082-7). Sage.
Griffith, Ernest S. History of American City Government. LC 72-3615. (Law, Politics & History Ser.). Repr. of 1938 ed. lib. bdg. 42.50 (ISBN 0-306-70526-5). Da Capo.
Haeger, John & Weber, Michael. The Bosses. rev. ed. LC 78-73266. 1979. pap. text ed. 4.95x (ISBN 0-88273-103-3). Forum Pr MO.
Hahn, Harlan & Levine, Charles, eds. Urban Politics: Past, Present & Future. (Orig.). 1980. pap. text ed. 11.95x (ISBN 0-582-28166-0). Longman.
Harrigan. Political Change in the Metropolis. 2nd ed. 1981. pap. text ed. 11.95 (ISBN 0-316-34744-2); training manual free (ISBN 0-316-34745-0). Little.
Harrigan, John J. Political Change in the Metropolis. 1976. pap. 11.95 (ISBN 0-316-34741-8). Little.
Harris, George M. Local Government in Many Lands. LC 74-110907. 1970. Repr. of 1933 ed. 17.00 (ISBN 0-8046-0889-X). Kennikat.
Hatry, Harry P., et al. Measuring the Effectiveness of Basic Municipal Services: Initial Report. 118p. 1974. pap. 4.00 (ISBN 0-685-99466-X, 74000). Urban Inst.
--How Effective Are Your Community Services: Procedures for Monitoring the Effectiveness of Municipal Services. 1977. pap. 10.00 (ISBN 0-87766-206-1, 19500). Urban Inst.

Hawkins, Brett W. Politics & Urban Policy. 144p. pap. text ed. 4.95x (ISBN 0-8290-0331-2). Irvington.

Hawley, W. D. & Lipsky, M. Theoretical Perspectives on Urban Politics. 1976. 18.95 (ISBN 0-13-913202-3). P-H.

Hogan, James B. The Chief Administrative Officer: An Alternative to Council-Manager Government. LC 75-26477. (Institute of Government Research Ser.). 1976. pap. text ed. 3.50x (ISBN 0-8165-0545-4). U of Ariz Pr.

Horton, Raymond D. & Brecher, Charles, eds. Setting Municipal Priorities. LC 79-88261. 224p. 1979. text ed. 24.00 (ISBN 0-916672-37-9). Allanheld.

Howe, Frederic C. City: The Hope of Democracy. LC 68-1361. (American Library Ser: No. 1). 350p. 1967. Repr. of 1905 ed. 11.50 (ISBN 0-295-97858-9). U of Wash Pr.

Ingebritsen, Karl J. Reston Home Owners Association: A Case Study in New Community Management. Ader-Brin, Dianne, ed. 1977. pap. text ed. 11.50 (ISBN 0-912104-26-0). Inst Real Estate.

International City Management Association. Municipal Year Book. LC 34-27121. 1979. 27.50 (ISBN 0-87326-954-3). Intl City Mgt.

Jacobson, Robert E. Municipal Control of Cable Communications. LC 77-7815. (Praeger Special Studies). 1977. text ed. 22.95 (ISBN 0-03-021831-4). Praeger.

Janowitz, Morris & Wright, D. Public Administration & the Public - Perspectives Toward Government in a Metropolitan Community. LC 76-49866. (Michigan Governmental Studies, University of Michigan: No. 36). 1977. Repr. of 1958 ed. lib. bdg. 15.00x (ISBN 0-8371-9396-6, JAPU). Greenwood.

Kraemer, Kenneth L., et al. The Municipal Information Systems Directory. LC 75-22891. (Illus.). 1976. 41.95 (ISBN 0-669-00469-3). Lexington Bks.

League of Women Voters Education Fund. Supercity, Hometown U. S. A. Prospects for Two-Tier Government. 138p. 1974. pap. 1.95, 5-15 copies 1.50 ea. (ISBN 0-89959-086-1, 477, Pub. by Proeger). LWV US.

Lee, Kaiman. Integrated Municipal Information System. LC 74-184835. 52p. 1974. 12.00 (ISBN 0-915250-12-8). Environ Design.

Levy, Frank S., et al. Urban Outcomes: Schools, Streets, & Libraries. (The Oakland Project). 1974. 24.50x (ISBN 0-520-02546-6); pap. 7.95x (ISBN 0-520-03045-1). U of Cal Pr.

Liebert, Roland J. Disintegration & Political Action: The Changing Functions of City Governments in America. 1976. 22.00 (ISBN 0-12-449650-4). Acad Pr.

Lineberry, Robert L. Equality & Urban Policy: The Distribution of Municipal Public Services. LC 76-53962. (Sage Library of Social Research: Vol. 39). 205p. 1977. 20.00x (ISBN 0-8039-0742-7); pap. 9.95 (ISBN 0-8039-0743-5). Sage.

Lineberry, Robert L. & Sharkansky, Ira. Urban Politics & Public Policy. 3rd ed. 1978. pap. text ed. 15.50 scp (ISBN 0-06-044029-5, HarpC). Har-Row.

Lutzin, Sidney G., ed. Managing Municipal Leisure Services. LC 80-17378. (Municipal Management). 1980. pap. text ed. 15.00 (ISBN 0-87326-023-6). Intl City Mgt.

McGoldrick, Joseph D. Law & Practice of Municipal Home Rule, 1916-1930. LC 33-22314. Repr. of 1933 ed. 22.45 (ISBN 0-404-04128-0). AMS Pr.

Madgwick, P. J. American City Politics. (Library of Political Studies). 1970. 8.95x (ISBN 0-7100-6807-7). Routledge & Kegan.

Margolis, Julius, ed. The Public Economy of Urban Communities: Papers Presented at the 2nd Conference on Urban Public Expenditures, Feb. 21-22, 1964. LC 77-86404. (Resources for the Future, Inc. Publications). Repr. of 1965 ed. 32.50 (ISBN 0-404-60339-4). AMS Pr.

Masotti, Louis H. & Lineberry, Robert L. The New Urban Politics. LC 76-5869. 1976. text ed. 15.00 (ISBN 0-88410-422-2); pap. 9.95 (ISBN 0-88410-472-9). Ballinger Pub.

Mikulecky, Thomas J., ed. Small Cities Management Training Program. LC 75-27076. 1975. text ed. 40.00 (ISBN 0-87326-011-2). Intl City Mgt.

Miller, Zane L. Boss Cox's Cincinnati: Urban Politics in the Progressive Era. LC 79-21545. 1980. pap. 6.95 (ISBN 0-226-52598-8, P873, Phoen). U of Chicago Pr.

Mishra, S. N. Politics & Leadership in Municipal Government. 1979. text ed. 9.00x (ISBN 0-391-01845-0). Humanities.

Morgan, David R. & Kirkpatrick, Samuel A. Urban Political Analysis. LC 74-156838. 1972. 15.95 (ISBN 0-02-922060-2). Free Pr.

Morgan, David R., ed. Urban Management. LC 72-8662. 183p. 1973. text ed. 29.75x (ISBN 0-8422-5065-4); pap. text ed. 8.95x (ISBN 0-8422-0249-8). Irvington.

Morris, Margaret F. & West, Elliott, eds. Essays on Urban America. LC 74-31058. (Walter Prescott Webb Memorial Lectures: No. 9). 147p. 1975. 9.95x (ISBN 0-292-72011-4). U of Tex Pr.

Moses, Bernard. The Establishment of Municipal Government in San Francisco. LC 78-63787. (Johns Hopkins University. Studies in the Social Sciences. Seventh Ser. 1889: 2-3). Repr. of 1889 ed. 11.50 (ISBN 0-404-61052-8). AMS Pr.

Murphy, Thomas P., ed. Urban Politics: A Guide to Information Sources. LC 78-54117. (Urban Studies Information Guide: Vol. 1). 1978. 36.00 (ISBN 0-8103-1395-2). Gale.

Mushkin, Selma J. & Sandifer, Frank H. Personnel Management & Productivity in City Government. (Illus.). 1979. 19.95 (ISBN 0-669-02805-3). Lexington Bks.

National Municipal League, Committee on Metropolitan Government. The Government of Metropolitan Areas in the United States. (Metropolitan America Ser.). 408p. 1974. Repr. 21.00x (ISBN 0-405-05405-X). Arno.

Orr, Larry L. Income, Employment & Urban Residential Location. (Institute for Research on Poverty Monograph Ser). 1975. 12.00 (ISBN 0-12-528440-3). Acad Pr.

Ostrom, Elinor, ed. The Delivery of Urban Services: Outcomes of Change. LC 75-11133. (Urban Affairs Annual Reviews Ser.: Vol. 10). (Illus.). 320p. 1976. 20.00x (ISBN 0-8039-0469-X); pap. 9.95x (ISBN 0-8039-0679-X). Sage.

Ostrom, Vincent & Bish, Frances P., eds. Comparing Urban Service Delivery Systems: Structure & Performance. LC 76-6312. (Urban Affairs Annual Reviews: Vol. 12). (Illus.). 304p. 1977. 22.50 (ISBN 0-8039-0470-3); pap. 9.95 (ISBN 0-8039-0680-3). Sage.

Patterson, Ernest. Black City Politics. 308p. (Orig.). 1974. pap. text ed. 11.50 scp (ISBN 0-06-045058-4, HarpC). Har-Row.

Perloff, Harvey S. & Wingo, Lowdon, Jr., eds. Issues in Urban Economics. LC 68-15454. (Resources for the Future). (Illus.). 668p. (Orig.). 1968. 24.50x (ISBN 0-8018-0528-7); pap. 6.50x (ISBN 0-8018-0529-5). Johns Hopkins.

Petit-Dutaillis, C., ed. The French Communes in the Middle Ages. (Europe in the Middle Ages Selected Studies: Vol. 6). 1978. 31.75 (ISBN 0-7204-0550-5, North-Holland). Elsevier.

Polsby, Nelson W. Community Power & Political Theory: A Further Look at Problems of Evidence & Inference. 2nd rev. ed. LC 79-22966. 1980. text ed. 25.00 (ISBN 0-300-02445-2); pap. 6.95x (ISBN 0-300-02528-9). Yale U Pr.

Poole, Robert, Jr. Cutting Back City Hall. LC 79-6411. 224p. 1981. pap. 5.95 (ISBN 0-87663-557-5). Universe.

Powers, Stanley P., et al, eds. Developing the Municipal Organization. LC 74-79125. (Municipal Management Ser.). 1974. text ed. 24.00 (ISBN 0-87326-001-5). Intl City Mgt.

Rabinovitz, Francine F. City Politics & Planning. LC 69-19454. 1970. 18.95x (ISBN 0-202-24091-6). Aldine Pub.

Rapp, B. & Patitucci, F. Managing Local Government for Improved Performance: A Practical Approach. LC 76-25240. 1977. lib. bdg. 36.25x (ISBN 0-89158-121-9); pap. 14.50x (ISBN 0-89158-412-9). Westview.

Rice, Bradley R. Progressive Cities: The Commission Government Movement in America, 1901-1920. 180p. 1977. 10.95x (ISBN 0-292-76441-3). U of Tex Pr.

Roeseler, W. G. Public Intervention & Pseudo Government in Urban Areas. LC 78-16981. 1977. pap. 1.24 (ISBN 0-930308-03-4). EMR Pubns.

Rowe, Roger M. Telecommunications & Municipal Management. 1974. pap. 2.50x (ISBN 0-89011-465-X, TEC-105). Abt Assoc.

Russell, John R. Cases in Urban Management. 552p. 1974. text ed. 24.00x (ISBN 0-262-18066-9). MIT Pr.

Schaller, Howard G., ed. Public Expenditure Decisions in the Urban Community. (Resources for the Future Ser). (Illus.). 208p. 1963. pap. 3.50x (ISBN 0-8018-0576-7). Johns Hopkins.

Schiesl, Martin. The Politics of Efficiency: Municipal Administration & Reform in America, 1880-1920. LC 75-17285. 1977. 23.75x (ISBN 0-520-03067-2); pap. 7.95x (ISBN 0-520-04086-4). U of Cal Pr.

Schultze, William. Urban & Community Politics. 1974. 7.95x (ISBN 0-87872-063-4). Duxbury Pr.

Seminar, Izmir, May-June 1972. Aspects of Urban Management: Proceedings. Thornley, Jennifer R. & McLoughlin, J. Brian, eds. 97p. 1974. 3.25x (ISBN 92-64-11169-7). OECD.

Sentell, R. Perry. The Law of Municipal Tort Liability in Georgia. 3rd ed. LC 79-24276. 184p. 1980. pap. text ed. 15.00x (ISBN 0-89854-053-4). U of GA Inst Govt.

Shank, Alan. Political Power & the Urban Crisis. 3rd ed. 570p. 1976. pap. text ed. 12.95 (ISBN 0-205-05491-9, 765491X). Allyn.

Shapley, Rufus E. Solid for Mulhooly: A Political Satire. LC 76-112572. (Rise of Urban America). (Illus.). 1970. Repr. of 1889 ed. 16.00 (ISBN 0-405-02475-4). Arno.

Shavley, Rufus. Solid for Mulhooly..."I'm Fur 'im". LC 76-96894. Repr. of 1881 ed. lib. bdg. 14.00x (ISBN 0-8398-1855-6). Irvington.

Smith, Hans & Herzog, Peter E. The Law of the European Economic Community. 1976. 500.000 set (ISBN 0-685-32577-6). Bender.

Sonenblum, Sidney, et al. How Cities Provide Services: An Evaluation of Alternative Delivery Structures. LC 77-2313. 1977. 17.50 (ISBN 0-88410-439-7). Ballinger Pub.

Spector, Samuel I. Municipal & County Zoning in a Changing Urban Environment. LC 71-28934. 1970. pap. 3.95 (ISBN 0-88406-014-4). Ga St U Busn Pub.

Stedman, Murray S., Jr. Urban Politics. 2nd ed. 1975. ref. ed. 11.00 (ISBN 0-87626-903-X); pap. text ed. 9.95 (ISBN 0-87626-902-1). Winthrop.

Steffens, Lincoln. Shame of the Cities. 1959. 7.50 (ISBN 0-8446-3001-2). Peter Smith.

--Shame of the Cities. 1957. pap. 3.95 (ISBN 0-8090-0008-3, AmCen). Hill & Wang.

Steggert, Frank X. Community Action Groups & City Governments. LC 75-5912. 128p. 1975. text ed. 16.50 (ISBN 0-88410-415-X). Ballinger Pub.

Sternlieb, George S. & Beaton, W. Patrick. The Zone of Emergence: A Case Study of an Older Suburb. LC 78-186710. 1972. 14.95x (ISBN 0-87855-035-6). Transaction Bks.

Stewart, Frank M. A Half-Century of Municipal Reform. LC 74-168967. 289p. 1972. Repr. of 1950 ed. lib. bdg. 15.25x (ISBN 0-8371-6240-8, STHC). Greenwood.

Stone, C., et al. Urban Policy & Politics in a Bureaucratic Age. pap. 12.95 (ISBN 0-13-939538-5). P-H.

Story, Russell M. The American Municipal Executive. Repr. of 1918 ed. 15.50 (ISBN 0-384-58510-8). Johnson Repr.

Swanson, B. E. & Swanson, E. Discovering the Community: Comparative Analysis of Social, Political & Economic Change. LC 76-30488. 1977. 22.50 (ISBN 0-470-99060-0). Halsted Pr.

Teaford, Jon C. City & Suburb: The Political Fragmentation of Metropolitan Areas, 1850-1970. LC 78-20519. 1979. text ed. 15.00x (ISBN 0-8018-2202-5). Johns Hopkins.

--The Municipal Revolution in America: Origins of Modern Urban Government, 1650-1825. LC 74-33512. 160p. 1975. lib. bdg. 9.75x (ISBN 0-226-79165-3). U of Chicago Pr.

Tees, David W. & Douthit, Lee I. Beyond Good Intentions: A Program for Encouraging Effective Human Action in Advisory Committee Work. 1979. 150.00 (ISBN 0-686-28255-8). Inst Urban Studies.

Tees, David W. & Hawk, Curtis E. Municipal Personnel Systems Training Program, 6 modules. 1979. Set. 55.00 (ISBN 0-686-28254-X). Inst Urban Studies.

Upson, Lent D. Practice of Municipal Administration. LC 73-11912. (Metropolitan America Ser.). 604p. 1974. Repr. 28.00x (ISBN 0-405-05432-7). Arno.

Urban Government: Supplementary Report of the Urbanism Committee to the National Resources Committee, Vol. 1. LC 77-74951. (American Federalism-the Urban Dimension). (Illus.). 1978. Repr. of 1939 ed. lib. bdg. 18.00x (ISBN 0-405-10509-6). Arno.

Walker, Jacilyn G. & DeHaven, Martha L. Texas Conservation Guide for Municipal Services. 1977. 6.00 (ISBN 0-686-28253-1). Inst Urban Studies.

Wallace, Schuyler C. State Administrative Supervision Over Cities in the United States. LC 68-58633. (Columbia University. Studies in the Social Sciences: No. 304). Repr. of 1928 ed. 22.50 (ISBN 0-404-51304-2). AMS Pr.

Washnis, George J. Municipal Decentralization & Neighborhood Resources: Case Studies of Twelve Cities. LC 72-80467. (Special Studies in U.S. Economic, Social & Political Issues). 1972. 29.50x (ISBN 0-685-70540-4); pap. text ed. 14.50x (ISBN 0-89197-860-7). Irvington.

Webb, Beatrice. Beatrice Webb's American Diary, Eighteen Ninety-Eight. Shannon, David, ed. (Illus.). 198p. 1963. 17.50 (ISBN 0-299-02851-8). U of Wis Pr.

White, Anthony G. Reforming Metropolitan Governments: A Bibliography. LC 75-7832. (Garland Ref. Lib. of Humanities). 1979. lib. bdg. 21.00 (ISBN 0-8240-9994-X). Garland Pub.

White, Leonard D. City Manager. LC 72-160135. Repr. of 1927 ed. 16.00 (ISBN 0-404-06931-2). AMS Pr.

--City Manager. LC 68-57647. (Illus.). 1969. Repr. of 1927 ed. lib. bdg. 17.75x (ISBN 0-8371-0750-4, WHCM). Greenwood.

Whitlock, Brand. On the Enforcement of Law in Cities. LC 69-14952. (Criminology, Law Enforcement, & Social Problems Ser.: No. 74). 1969. Repr. of 1913 ed. 6.50 (ISBN 0-87585-074-X). Patterson Smith.

Wilcox, Delos F. Great Cities in America: Their Problems & Their Government. LC 73-11907. (Metropolitan America Ser.). 442p. 1974. Repr. 21.00x (ISBN 0-405-05435-1). Arno.

--Municipal Government in Michigan & Ohio: A Study in the Relations of City & Commonwealth. LC 68-56697. (Columbia University. Studies in the Social Sciences: No. 15). Repr. of 1896 ed. 16.50 (ISBN 0-404-51015-9). AMS Pr.

--Municipal Government in Michigan & Ohio: A Study in the Relations of City & Commonwealth. LC 68-56697. (Columbia University. Studies in the Social Sciences: No. 15). Repr. of 1896 ed. 16.50 (ISBN 0-404-51015-9). AMS Pr.

Williams, Oliver P. & Adrian, Charles R. Four Cities: A Study in Comparative Policy Making. LC 63-7853. 1963. 10.00x (ISBN 0-8122-7381-8). U of Pa Pr.

Wingo, Lowdon, ed. Reform As Reorganization. LC 73-19348. (The Governance of Metropolitan Regions Ser: No. 4). (Illus.). 140p. (Orig.). 1974. pap. 4.00x (ISBN 0-8018-1544-4). Johns Hopkins.

Yates, Douglas. The Ungovernable City: The Politics of Urban Problems & Policy Making. 1977. text ed. 17.50x (ISBN 0-262-24020-3); pap. 5.95 (ISBN 0-262-74013-3). MIT Pr.

Yin, Robert K. & Yates, Douglas. Street-Level Governments. 192p. 1975. 16.00x (ISBN 0-669-00076-0). Lexington Bks.

Young, Ken, ed. Essays on the Study of Urban Politics. xi, 208p. (Orig.). 1975. 17.50 (ISBN 0-208-01400-4, Archon). Shoe String.

Zimmerman, Joseph F. The Federated City: Community in Large Cities. 128p. 1972. text ed. 14.95 (ISBN 0-312-28595-7); pap. text ed. 4.95 (ISBN 0-312-28560-4). St Martin.

Zink, Harold. City Bosses in the United States. LC 74-182729. 1930. 29.50 (ISBN 0-404-07076-0). AMS Pr.

Zueblin, Charles. American Municipal Progress. LC 73-11931. (Metropolitan America Ser.). (Illus.). 606p. 1974. Repr. 29.00x (ISBN 0-405-05436-X). Arno.

MUNICIPAL GOVERNMENT–BIBLIOGRAPHY

American Library Association, Government Documents Round Table & Hernon, Peter, eds. Municipal Government Reference Sources: Publications & Collections. 1978. 21.75 (ISBN 0-8352-1003-0). Bowker.

Goehlert, Robert. Municipal Government: A Selected Bibliography of Journal Literature. (Public Administration Ser.: P 176). 1979. pap. 7.50 (ISBN 0-686-24636-5). Vance Biblios.

Ross, Bernard H., ed. Urban Management: A Guide to Information Sources. LC 78-10310. (The Urban Studies Information Guide Ser.: Vol. 8). 1979. 36.00 (ISBN 0-8103-1430-4). Gale.

MUNICIPAL GOVERNMENT–JUVENILE LITERATURE

Benson, Christopher. Careers with the City. LC 73-22158. (Early Career Bks). (Illus.). 36p. (gr. 2-5). 1974. PLB 4.95 (ISBN 0-8225-0319-0). Lerner Pubns.

Hildebrandt, illus. Who Runs the City? LC 77-82832. (A Pandaback Book). (Illus.). (gr. 1-3). 1978. pap. 0.95 (ISBN 0-448-49602-X). Platt.

MUNICIPAL GOVERNMENT–CANADA

Budden, Sandra & Ernst, Joseph. Movable Airport. LC 73-88115. (Case Studies in Community Action). 167p. 1973. 12.00 (ISBN 0-88866-538-5); pap. 4.95 (ISBN 0-88866-539-3). Samuel Stevens.

Crawford, Kenneth G. Canadian Municipal Government. LC 55-3. (Canadian Government Ser.). 1954. 15.00x (ISBN 0-8020-5022-0). U of Toronto Pr.

MUNICIPAL GOVERNMENT–GREAT BRITAIN

Fraser, Derek. Power & Authority in the Victorian City. LC 79-10895. 1979. 18.50x (ISBN 0-312-63366-1). St Martin.

--Urban Politics in Victorian England: The Structure of Politics in Victorian Cities. 320p. 1976. text ed. 30.00x (ISBN 0-7185-1145-X, Leicester). Humanities.

Glassberg, Andrew D. Representation & Urban Community. 200p. 1982. 19.50x (ISBN 0-8448-1408-3). Crane-Russak Co.

Laski, Harold J., et al. A Century of Municipal Progress, 1835-1935. Laski, H. J. & Jennings, W. Ivor, eds. LC 75-41171. Repr. of 1935 ed. 29.50 (ISBN 0-685-14561-1). AMS Pr.

Laski, Harold J., et al, eds. A Century of Municipal Progress, 1835-1935. LC 77-27362. 1978. Repr. of 1935 ed. lib. bdg. 33.75x (ISBN 0-313-20192-7, LACE). Greenwood.

Stephenson, Carl. Borough & Town: A Study of Urban Origins in England. 1964. Repr. of 1933 ed. 12.00 (ISBN 0-910956-08-1). Medieval Acad.

Thomas, James H. Town Government in the Sixteenth Century. LC 70-81148. (Illus.). Repr. of 1933 ed. 13.50x (ISBN 0-678-00508-7). Kelley.

Thompson, James. Essay on English Municipal History. LC 72-158774. (Research & Source Works Ser.: No. 733). 1971. Repr. of 1867 ed. lib. bdg. 15.00 (ISBN 0-8337-4447-X). B Franklin.

MUNICIPAL GOVERNMENT–INDIA

Bhagwan, Vishnoo. Municipal Government & Politics in Haryana: A Case Study of Rohtak City. (Illus.). 356p. 1975. text ed. 12.00x (ISBN 0-8426-0767-6). Verry.

Bhattacharya, Mohit. Management of Urban Government in India. LC 76-902905. 1976. 12.50x (ISBN 0-88386-864-4). South Asia Bks.

Jangam, R. T. Leadership in Urban Government. 1972. 7.50x (ISBN 0-8002-1644-X). Intl Pubns Serv.

Oldenburg, Philip. Big City Government in India: Councilor, Administrator, & Citizen in Delhi. LC 76-4426. (Association for Asian Studies Monograph: No.31). 1976. 9.50x (ISBN 0-8165-0554-3); pap. 4.95x (ISBN 0-8165-0553-5). U of Ariz Pr.

Rosenthal, Donald, ed. The City in Indian Politics. LC 76-900868. 1976. 14.00x (ISBN 0-88386-859-8). South Asia Bks.

MUNICIPAL GOVERNMENT–PERU

Moore, John P. Cabildo in Peru Under the Bourbons: A Study in the Decline & Resurgence of Local Government in the Audiencia of Lima, 1700-1824. LC 66-22590. 1966. 16.50 (ISBN 0-8223-0116-4). Duke.

MUNICIPAL GOVERNMENT–ROME

Abbott, Frank F. & Johnson, Allan C. Municipal Administration in the Roman Empire. LC 68-25670. 1968. Repr. of 1926 ed. 35.00 (ISBN 0-8462-1159-9). Russell.

MUNICIPAL GOVERNMENT BY CITY MANAGERS

Bollens, John C. Appointed Executive Local Government: The California Experience. LC 52-12988. (Illus.). xi, 233p. Repr. of 1952 ed. lib. bdg. 15.00x (ISBN 0-8371-8068-6, BOAE). Greenwood.

Harlow, LeRoy F. Without Fear or Favor. LC 76-40172. (Illus.). 1977. 1.25 (ISBN 0-8425-1461-9); pap. 0.95 (ISBN 0-8425-1458-9). Brigham.

Harlow, LeRoy F., ed. Servants of All: Professional Management of City Government. LC 80-39899. 387p. 1981. 19.95 (ISBN 0-8425-1892-4). Brigham.

ICMA. The Municipal Year Book 1981. LC 34-37121. (Illus.). 416p. 1981. text ed. 42.00x (ISBN 0-87326-956-X). Intl City Mgt.

Kammerer, Gladys, et al. City Managers in Politics: An Analysis of Manager Tenure & Termination. LC 62-63138. (U of Fla. Social Sciences Monographs: No. 13). 1962. pap. 2.95 (ISBN 0-8130-0126-9). U Presses Fla.

OECD. Training for Urban Management. (Urban Management Studies No. 2). 204p. (Orig.). 1979. pap. 12.50x (ISBN 92-64-11914-0). OECD.

Stillman, Richard J. The Rise of the City Manager: A Public Professional in Local Government. LC 74-80742. 170p. 1979. pap. 7.50 (ISBN 0-8263-0508-3). U of NM Pr.

Toulmin, Harry A., Jr. The City Manager: A New Profession. LC 73-11936. (Metropolitan America Ser.). 328p. 1974. Repr. 16.00x (ISBN 0-405-05428-9). Arno.

White, Leonard D. City Manager. LC 72-160135. Repr. of 1927 ed. 16.00 (ISBN 0-404-06931-2). AMS Pr.

--City Manager. LC 68-57647. (Illus.). 1969. Repr. of 1927 ed. lib. bdg. 17.75x (ISBN 0-8371-0750-4, WHCM). Greenwood.

MUNICIPAL HOME RULE

Ashford, Douglas E. National Resources & Urban Policy. LC 77-94185. (Illus.). 320p. 1980. text ed. 27.50 (ISBN 0-416-60181-2). Methuen Inc.

McGoldrick, Joseph D. Law & Practice of Municipal Home Rule, 1916-1930. LC 33-22314. Repr. of 1933 ed. 22.45 (ISBN 0-404-04128-0). AMS Pr.

Vaubel, George D. Municipal Home Rule in Ohio. LC 78-52029. 1978. Repr. of 1975 ed. lib. bdg. 27.50 (ISBN 0-930342-58-5). W S Hein.

Wilcox, Delos F. Municipal Government in Michigan & Ohio: A Study in the Relations of City & Commonwealth. LC 68-56697. (Columbia University. Studies in the Social Sciences: No. 15). Repr. of 1896 ed. 16.50 (ISBN 0-404-51015-9). AMS Pr.

MUNICIPAL INCOME TAX

see Income Tax, Municipal

MUNICIPAL INCORPORATION

Miller, Gary J. Cities by Contract: The Politics of Municipal Incorporation. 256p. 1981. text ed. 19.95x (ISBN 0-262-13164-1). MIT Pr.

MUNICIPAL JUNIOR COLLEGES

see Community Colleges

MUNICIPAL LAW (MUNICIPAL CORPORATION)

see Municipal Corporations

MUNICIPAL LIGHTING

see also Lighting; Lighting, Architectural and Decorative

MUNICIPAL OFFICIALS AND EMPLOYEES

Cook, Edward M., Jr. The Fathers of the Towns: Leadership & Community Structure in Eighteenth Century New England. LC 75-36937. (Studies in Historical & Political Science). 1978. pap. 4.95 (ISBN 0-8018-2149-5). Johns Hopkins.

--The Fathers of the Towns: Leadership & Community Structure in Eighteenth Century New England. LC 75-36937. (Studies in Historical & Political Sciences: Ninety-Fourth Series N0.2 (1976)). (Illus.). 296p. 1976. 18.50x (ISBN 0-8018-1741-2). Johns Hopkins.

Gross, Ernest, et al. New Jersey Police & Fire Arbitration Databook, 1980, 2 vols. 2000p. 1980. Set. 100.00 (ISBN 0-686-29000-3). Inst Mgmt & Labor.

Hayes, Frederick O. Productivity in Local Government. LC 76-20400. 1977. 24.95 (ISBN 0-669-00883-4). Lexington Bks.

International City Management Assoc. Municipal Year Book. LC 34-27121. 1980. 36.00 (ISBN 0-87326-955-1). Intl City Mgt.

Intl City Management Assn. Effective Supervisory Practices. LC 77-28712. (Municipal Management Ser.). 1978. pap. text ed. 21.50 (ISBN 0-87326-019-8). Intl City Mgt.

Jangam, R. T. Leadership in Urban Government. 1972. 7.50x (ISBN 0-8002-1644-X). Intl Pubns Serv.

Langer, Steven & Lutz, Carl F., eds. Municipal Personnel Report. 1979. pap. 75.00 (ISBN 0-916506-42-8). Abbott Langer Assocs.

Mushkin, Selma J. & Sandifer, Frank H. Personnel Management & Productivity in City Government. (Illus.). 1979. 19.95 (ISBN 0-669-02805-3). Lexington Bks.

Rudman, Jack. City Comptroller. (Career Examination Ser.: C-1746). (Cloth bdg. avail. on request). 1977. pap. 10.00 (ISBN 0-8373-1746-0). Natl Learning.

--Deputy Town Clerk. (Career Examination Ser.: C-1855). (Cloth bdg. avail. on request). 1977. pap. 8.00 (ISBN 0-8373-1855-6). Natl Learning.

MUNICIPAL OFFICIALS AND EMPLOYEES–GREAT BRITAIN

Hennock, E. P. Fit & Proper Persons: Ideal & Reality in Nineteenth-Century Urban Government. (Studies in Urban History: No. 2). (Illus.). 416p. 1973. 22.00x (ISBN 0-7735-0154-1). McGill-Queens U Pr.

MUNICIPAL OWNERSHIP

Pond, Oscar L. Municipal Control of Public Utilities: A Study of the Attitudes of Our Courts Toward an Increase of the Sphere of Municipal Activity. LC 79-76676. (Columbia University, Studies in the Social Sciences Ser., No. 65). Repr. of 1906 ed. 16.50 (ISBN 0-404-51065-5). AMS Pr.

Speirs, Frederic W. The Street Railway System of Philadelphia: Its History & Present Condition. Repr. of 1897 ed. pap. 10.00 (ISBN 0-384-57013-5). Johnson Repr.

MUNICIPAL POWER AND SERVICE BEYOND CORPORATE LIMITS

see also Special Districts

Costikyan, Edward N. & Lehman, Maxwell. New Strategies for Regional Cooperation: A Model for the Tri-State New York-New Jersey-Connecticut Area. LC 73-9388. (Special Studies in U.S. Economic, Social & Political Issues). 1973. 27.50x (ISBN 0-275-28777-7). Irvington.

MUNICIPAL REPORTS

Cox, C. Robinson. Criminal Justice: Improving Police Report Writing. 1977. pap. text ed. 8.95xstudent manual (ISBN 0-8134-1902-6, 1902); instructor's manual 1.75x (ISBN 0-8134-1906-9, 1906). Interstate.

MUNICIPAL RESEARCH

Berry, B. J. City Classification Handbook: Methods & Applications. LC 71-171911. (Urban Research Ser.). 394p. 1972. 41.95 (ISBN 0-471-07115-3, Pub. by Wiley-Interscience). Wiley.

Betters, Paul V. Federal Services to Municipal Governments. LC 77-749330. (American Federalism-the Urban Dimension). 1977. Repr. of 1931 ed. lib. bdg. 12.00x (ISBN 0-405-10479-0). Arno.

Committee On Urban Technology - Division Of Engineering. Long-Range Planning for Urban Research & Development: Technological Considerations. (Illus., Orig.). 1969. pap. 4.75 (ISBN 0-309-01729-7). Natl Acad Pr.

Knobbe, Mary L. Planning & Urban Affairs Library Manual. 3rd ed. 1975. 15.00 (ISBN 0-87326-015-5). Intl City Mgt.

Markusen, James R. & Scheffman, David T. Speculation & Monopoly in Urban Development: Analytical Foundations with Evidence for Toronto. (Ontario Economic Council Research Studies). 1977. pap. 12.50 (ISBN 0-8020-3348-2). U of Toronto Pr.

Perloff, Harvey S. A National Program of Research in Housing & Urban Development: The Major Requirements & a Suggested Approach. LC 77-86406. (A Resources for the Future Staff Study). Repr. of 1961 ed. 12.00 (ISBN 0-404-60341-6). AMS Pr.

Portes, Alejandro & Browning, Harley L., eds. Current Perspectives in Latin American Urban Research. LC 75-620107. (Institute of Latin American Studies Special Pubn. Ser.). 191p. 1976. 9.95x (ISBN 0-292-71036-4); pap. 4.95x (ISBN 0-292-71037-2). U of Tex Pr.

Schwartz, Gail G. Advanced Industrialization & the Inner Cities. LC 79-3744. 192p. 1981. 19.95x (ISBN 0-669-03512-2). Lexington Bks.

Ward, Edith, et al, eds. Urban Affairs Subject Headings. LC 75-33026. vi, 34p. (Orig.). 1975. lib. bdg. 15.00 (ISBN 0-8371-8537-8, ICSH). Greenwood.

Wolf, C. P. Urban Impact Assessment: A Preliminary Bibliography. (Public Administration Ser.: P 251). 1979. pap. 6.50 (ISBN 0-686-25114-8). Vance Biblios.

MUNICIPAL SERVICES WITHIN CORPORATE LIMITS

see Municipal Government

MUNICIPAL TAXATION

see Local Taxation

MUNICIPAL TRANSIT

see Local Transit

MUNICIPAL TRANSPORTATION

see Urban Transportation

MUNICIPAL UNIVERSITIES AND COLLEGES

Armytage, W. H. Civil Universities: Aspects of a British Tradition. LC 76-55207. (The Academic Profession Ser.). (Illus.). 1977. Repr. of 1955 ed. lib. bdg. 19.00x (ISBN 0-405-10031-0). Arno.

Bender, Louis W. The States, Communities, & Control of the Community Colleges. 60p. 1975. pap. 1.50 (ISBN 0-87117-083-3). Am Assn Comm Jr Coll.

Fein & Gatner. University & Community: The New Partnership. LC 75-165286. 1971. 15.00 (ISBN 0-913252-03-4); pap. 8.50 (ISBN 0-913252-04-2). LIU Univ.

Gilbaugh, John W. Plea for Sanity in the Public Colleges & Universities. 1966. pap. 2.00 (ISBN 0-686-00735-2). Modern Ed.

Lombardi, John. Black Studies in the Community Colleges. (ERIC Monographs Ser.). 68p. 1971. pap. 2.00 (ISBN 0-87117-006-X). Am Assn Comm Jr Coll.

Pray, Francis C. A New Look at Community College Boards of Trustees & Presidents & Their Relationships: Suggestions for Change. 41p. 1975. pap. 1.50 (ISBN 0-87117-072-8). Am Assn Comm Jr Coll.

Thurston, Alice, et al. The Chief Student Personnel Administrator in the Public Two-Year College. (ERIC Monographs Ser). 80p. 1972. pap. 3.00 (ISBN 0-87117-050-7). Am Assn Comm Jr Coll.

MUNICIPAL UTILITIES

see Public Utilities

MUNICIPALITIES

see Cities and Towns; Municipal Government

MUNICIPALITY OF METROPOLITAN TORONTO

Kaplan, Harold. Urban Political Systems: A Functional Analysis of Metro Toronto. LC 67-29577. (Metropolitan Politics Ser.). 320p. 1967. 20.00x (ISBN 0-231-02982-9). Columbia U Pr.

MUNITIONS

see also Armaments; Firearms Industry and Trade; Weapons Systems

Adams, R. J. Arms & the Wizard: Lloyd George & the Ministry of Munitions, 1915-1916. LC 77-16694. 272p. 1978. 13.50x (ISBN 0-89096-045-3). Tex A&M Univ Pr.

Barnet, Richard J. Economy of Death. LC 72-97133. 1969. pap. text ed. 3.45x (ISBN 0-689-70264-7, 171). Atheneum.

Brown, James K. & Stothoff, George S. The Defense Industry: Some Perspectives from the Financial Community. LC 76-22015. (Report Ser.: No. 693). 1976. pap. 30.00 (ISBN 0-8237-0127-1). Conference Bd.

Cox, John. Overkill: Weapons of the Nuclear Age. LC 77-27663. (Illus.). (gr. 7 up). 1978. 7.95 (ISBN 0-690-03856-9, TYC-J); PLB 7.89 (ISBN 0-690-03857-7). Har-Row.

Cromwell, Giles. The Virginia Manufactory of Arms. LC 74-8802. 1975. 20.00 (ISBN 0-8139-0573-7). U Pr of Va.

Dornan, James E., Jr. The U.S. War Machine. (Illus.). 1978. 17.95 (ISBN 0-517-53543-2). Crown.

Farley, Philip J., et al. Arms Across the Sea. LC 77-91804. 1978. 9.95 (ISBN 0-8157-2746-1); pap. 3.95 (ISBN 0-8157-2745-3). Brookings.

Glackin, James J. Improvised Munitions Systems. LC 76-13258. 60p. 1976. pap. 5.00 (ISBN 0-87364-057-8). Paladin Ent.

Gorgol, John Francis. The Military-Industrial Firm: A Practical Theory & Model. LC 75-170024. (Special Studies in U.S. Economic, Social, & Political Issues). 1972. 26.50x (ISBN 0-275-28229-5); pap. text ed. 12.50x (ISBN 0-89197-848-8). Irvington.

Hanifhen, Frank C. & Engelbrecht, Helmuth C. Merchants of Death: A Study of the International Armaments Industry. LC 79-147546. (Library of War & Peace; Control & Limitation of Arms). lib. bdg. 38.00 (ISBN 0-8240-0327-6). Garland Pub.

Harkavy, Robert E. The Arms Trade & International Systems. LC 74-14844. 300p. 1975. text ed. 18.50 (ISBN 0-88410-021-9). Ballinger Pub.

Hart, Guy. Challenge of War: Britain's Scientific & Engineering Contributions to World War Two. LC 70-106910. 1970. 10.95 (ISBN 0-8008-1431-2). Taplinger.

Lusar, Rudolph. German Weapons of the Second World War. 1959. 10.00 (ISBN 0-8022-1005-8). Philos Lib.

Noel-Baker, Philip. The Private Manufacture of Armaments. LC 78-145399. 1971. pap. 6.00 (ISBN 0-486-22736-7). Dover.

Ra'Anan, Uri, et al. Arms Transfer to the Third World: Problems & Policies. LC 77-17949. (Westview Special Studies in International Relations & U.S. Foreign Policy). 1978. lib. bdg. 38.75x (ISBN 0-89158-092-1). Westview.

Stockholm International Peace Research Institute (SIPRI) The Arms Trade Registers. LC 75-868. 186p. 1975. text ed. 18.00x (ISBN 0-262-19138-5). MIT Pr.

Stockholm International Peace Research Institute. Arms Trade with the 3rd World. rev. ed. LC 75-15746. 362p. 1975. 29.50x (ISBN 0-8419-0213-5). Holmes & Meier.

Swearengen, Thomas F. Tear Gas Munitions: An Analysis of Commercial Riot Gas Guns, Tear Gas Projectiles, Grenades, Small Arms Ammunition & Related Tear Gas Devices. (Illus.). 596p. 1966. 59.75 (ISBN 0-398-01888-X). C C Thomas.

Tunis, Edwin. Weapons: A Pictorial History. LC 76-29699. (Illus.). (gr. 6 up). 1977. 14.95 (ISBN 0-690-01340-X, TYC-J). Har-Row.

MUNITIONS–LAW AND LEGISLATION

see also Firearms–Laws and Regulations

Cullin, William H. How to Conduct Foreign Military Sales: The Eighty-One United States Guide with Fy '81 Update. 1980. loose-leaf 95.00 (ISBN 0-87179-315-6). BNA.

MUNOZ-MARIN, LUIS, 1898-

Norris, Marianna. Father & Son for Freedom. LC 67-26145. (Illus.). (gr. 7 up). 1968. 4.95 (ISBN 0-396-05661-X). Dodd.

MUNOZ-RIVERA, LUIS

Norris, Marianna. Father & Son for Freedom. LC 67-26145. (Illus.). (gr. 7 up). 1968. 4.95 (ISBN 0-396-05661-X). Dodd.

Reynolds, Mack. Puerto Rican Patriot: The Life of Luis Munoz Rivera. LC 73-81548. (Illus.). (gr. 5 up). 1969. 8.95 (ISBN 0-02-776160-6, CCPr). Macmillan.

MUNRO, HECTOR HUGH, 1870-1916

Gillen, Charles H. H. H. Munro (Saki) (English Authors Ser.: No. 102). lib. bdg. 9.95 (ISBN 0-8057-1408-1). Twayne.

Langguth, A. J. Saki: A Life of Hector Hugh Munro with Six Short Stories Never Before Collected. 1981. 14.95 (ISBN 0-671-24715-8). S&S.

Munro, Hector H. Novels & Plays of Saki. LC 71-145199. 1971. Repr. of 1945 ed. 25.00 (ISBN 0-403-01123-X). Scholarly.

MUNSEE LANGUAGE

see also Delaware Language

MUNSELL, JOEL, 1808-1880

Edelstein, David S. Joel Munsell: Printer & Antiquarian. LC 75-164751. (Columbia University. Studies in the Social Sciences: No. 560). Repr. of 1950 ed. 24.50 (ISBN 0-404-51560-6). AMS Pr.

MUNSEY, FRANK ANDREW, 1854-1925

Britt, George. Forty Years - Forty Millions. LC 72-153203. 1971. Repr. of 1935 ed. 15.00 (ISBN 0-8046-1513-6). Kennikat.

MUNSI

see Tivi (African People)

MUNSTERBERG, HUGO, 1863-1916

Hale, Matthew, Jr. Human Science & Social Order: Hugo Munsterberg & the Origins of Applied Psychology. 1980. 17.50 (ISBN 0-87722-154-5). Temple U Pr.

MUONS

see also Mesons

Ache, Hans J., ed. Positronium & Muonium Chemistry. LC 79-11709. (Advances in Chemistry Ser.: No. 175). 1979. 41.00 (ISBN 0-8412-0417-9). Am Chemical.

Hughes, Vernon & Wu, C. S., eds. Muon Physics. Incl. Vol. 1. 54.00 (ISBN 0-12-360601-2); Vol. 2. Weak Interactions. 92.50 (ISBN 0-12-360602-0); Vol. 3. Chemistry & Solids. 66.50 (ISBN 0-12-360603-9). 1975. 172.50 set (ISBN 0-685-72444-1). Acad Pr.

Massey, Harrie, et al. Electronic & Ionic Impact Phenomena: Slow Position & Muon Collisions - & Notes on Recent Advances, Vol. 5. (International Ser. of Monographs on Physics). (Illus.). 596p. 1974. 89.00x (ISBN 0-19-851283-X). Oxford U Pr.
Morita, Masato. Beta Decay & Muon Capture. 380p. 1973. text ed. 23.50 (ISBN 0-8053-7152-4, Adv Bk Prog). Benjamin-Cummings.
Weissenberg, A. O. Muons. 1968. 49.00 (ISBN 0-444-10306-6, North-Holland). Elsevier.

MURAL PAINTING AND DECORATION
see also Cave-Drawings; Mosaics
Allen, Edward D. Early American Wall Paintings. Wood, Serry, ed. (Visual Art Classics Ser). (Illus.). 1969. pap. text ed. 3.95 (ISBN 0-87282-002-5). Century Hse.
Alpatov, M. V., intro. by. Frescoes of the Church of the Assumption at Volotovo. Friedman, V. S., tr. Date not set. 25.00 (ISBN 0-89893-040-5). CDP.
Anthony, Edgar W. Romanesque Frescoes. LC 76-112320. (Illus.). 208p. Repr. of 1951 ed. lib. bdg. 26.25x (ISBN 0-8371-4707-7, ANRF). Greenwood.
Bacon, Richard M. The Art & Craft of Wall Stenciling. LC 76-41361. (Funk & W Bk.). 1977. 9.95 (ISBN 0-308-10274-6). T Y Crowell.
Baillie, Sheila & Skjelver, Mabel R. Graphics for Interior Space. LC 79-64692. (Illus.). 1979. pap. 9.50x (ISBN 0-8032-6054-7). U of Nebr Pr.
Barnett, Alan W. Murals of Prokat. LC 79-21552. (Illus.). 400p. 1981. 35.00 (ISBN 0-87982-030-6). Art Alliance.
--Murals of Protest. LC 79-21552. (Illus.). 600p. 1982. 60.00 (ISBN 0-8453-4731-4). Cornwall Bks.
Berman, Greta. The Lost Years: Mural Painting in New York City Under the Works Progress Administration's Federal Art Project 1935-1943. LC 77-94687. (Outstanding Dissertations in the Fine Arts Ser.). 1978. lib. bdg. 45.00 (ISBN 0-8240-3216-0). Garland Pub.
Borsook, Eve. The Mural Painters of Tuscany: From Cimabue to Andrea Del Sarto. (Oxford Studies in the History of Art & Architecture Ser.). (Illus.). 400p. 1981. 150.00 (ISBN 0-19-817301-6). Oxford U Pr.
Carmean, E. A., ed. Robert Motherwell's "Reconcilliation Elegy". A Journal of Collaboration. LC 80-51574. (Illus.). 90p. 1980. 30.00 (ISBN 0-8478-0337-6); pap. 14.95 (ISBN 0-8478-0336-8). Rizzoli Intl.
Carnegie Institution of Washington. Ancient Maya Paintings of Bonampak Mexico. LC 55-12545. (Illus.). 1955. pap. 5.50 (ISBN 0-87279-945-X, S46). Carnegie Inst.
Charlot, Jean. The Mexican Mural Renaissance Nineteen Twenty to Nineteen Twenty-Five. LC 79-83880. (Illus.). 1979. Repr. of 1962 ed. lib. bdg. 35.00 (ISBN 0-87817-251-3). Hacker.
Christian, John. The Oxford Union Murals. LC 79-23664. (Illus.). 84p. 1981. incl. fiche 24.00 (ISBN 0-226-68922-0). U of Chicago Pr.
Clark, Yoko, et al. California Murals. (Lancaster-Miller Art Ser.). (Illus.). 1980. 8.95 (ISBN 0-89581-016-6). Lancaster-Miller.
Cockcroft, Eva, et al. Toward a People's Art. 1977. pap. 7.95 (ISBN 0-525-47426-9). Dutton.
Edwards, Emily & Alvarez, Bravo M. Painted Walls of Mexico: From Prehistoric Times Until Today. (Spencer Foundation Ser.: No. 3). (Illus.). 330p. 1966. 35.00 (ISBN 0-292-73624-X). U of Tex Pr.
Environmental Communications. Big Art: Megamurals & Supergraphics. Teacher, Stuart, et al, eds. LC 77-14043. (Illus.). 1977. lib. bdg. 19.80 (ISBN 0-89471-007-9); pap. 7.95 (ISBN 0-89471-006-0). Running Pr.
Fairbank, Wilma. Adventures in Retrieval: Han Murals & Shang Bronze Molds. LC 79-173410. (Harvard-Yenching Institute Studies: No. 28). 187p. 1972. pap. 8.50x (ISBN 0-674-00575-9). Harvard U Pr.
Hale, Gardner. Technique of Fresco Painting. (Illus.). 6.00 (ISBN 0-8446-2184-6). Peter Smith.
Howe, Eunice D. The Hospital of Santo Spirito & Pope Sixtus IV. (Outstanding Dissertations in the Fine Arts Ser.). (Illus.). 1978. lib. bdg. 43.00x (ISBN 0-8240-3230-6). Garland Pub.
Kalokyris, Konstantin. The Byzantine Wall Paintings of Crete. Hionides, Harry, ed. Contos, Leonidas, tr. from Gr. LC 73-85747. (Illus.). 186p. 1973. 25.00 (ISBN 0-87376-023-9). Red Dust.
Leveen, Jacob. The Hebrew Bible in Art. LC 74-78239. (Illus.). 208p. 1974. Repr. 14.50 (ISBN 0-87203-045-8). Hermon.
Little, Alan. Roman Bridal Drama. 1978. 6.50 (ISBN 0-89679-009-6). Moretus Pr.
Marhoefer, Barbara, et al. Early American Wall Stencils in Color. (Illus.). 144p. 1982. 25.75 (ISBN 0-525-93214-3); pap. 16.50 (ISBN 0-525-47683-0). Dutton.
Merrifield, Mary. The Art of Fresco Painting. 1971. 10.00- (ISBN 0-85458-918-X). Transatlantic.
Moretti, Mario. New Monuments of Etruscan Painting. LC 68-8548. (Illus.). 1970. 89.50x (ISBN 0-271-00079-1). Pa St U Pr.
Mueller, Mary K. & Pollack, Ted G. Murals: Creating an Environment. LC 78-72194. (Illus.). 1979. 11.95 (ISBN 0-87192-106-5). Davis Mass.
Munteanu, Voichita. The Cycle of Frescoes of the Chapel of Le Liget. LC 77-94712. (Outstanding Dissertations in the Fine Arts Ser.). 1978. lib. bdg. 31.00x (ISBN 0-8240-3244-6). Garland Pub.
Murals from the Han to the Tang Dynesties. 1974. 35.00 (ISBN 0-8351-0161-4). China Bks.
Oxford Union Murals. John Christian. 1980. 22.50 (ISBN 0-226-68922-0). U of Chicago Pr.
Panayotova, Dora. Bulgarian Mural Paintings of the 14th Century. Alexieva, Marguerite & Athanassova, Theodora, trs. (Illus.). 32.50x (ISBN 0-8057-5003-7). Irvington.
Pasztory, Esther. The Murals of Tepantitla, Teotihaucan. LC 75-23806. (Outstanding Dissertations in the Fine Arts - Native American Arts). (Illus.). 1976. lib. bdg. 45.00 (ISBN 0-8240-2000-6). Garland Pub.
Schulz, Juergen. Venetian Painted Ceilings of the Renaissance. (California Studies in the History of Art: No. VIII). (Illus.). 1968. 67.50x (ISBN 0-520-01154-6). U of Cal Pr.
Sessions, Keith. Vanner's How-to Guide to Murals, Painting & Pinstriping. (Illus.). 1978. 8.95 (ISBN 0-8306-9888-4); pap. 5.95 (ISBN 0-8306-1032-4, 1032). TAB Bks.
Sjostrom, Ingrid. Quadratura: Studies in Italian Ceiling Painting. (Stockholm Studies in the History of Art: No. 30). (Illus.). 1978. pap. text ed. 22.00x (ISBN 91-22-00176-X). Humanities.
Southard, Edna C. The Frescoes in Siena's Palazzo Pubblico, Twelve Eighty-Nine to Fifteen Thirty-Nine: Studies in Imagery & Relations to Other Communal Palaces in Tuscany. LC 78-74381. (Fine Arts Dissertations, Fourth Ser.). (Illus.). 1980. lib. bdg. 66.00 (ISBN 0-8240-3967-X). Garland Pub.
Underwood, Paul A. Kariye Djami, 4 vols. LC 65-10404. (Bollingen Ser.: Vol. 70). (Illus.). 1966. Vols. 1-3. boxed set 85.00 (ISBN 0-691-09777-1); Vol. 4, 1975. 60.00 (ISBN 0-691-09778-X); Vols. 1-4. boxed set 125.00 (ISBN 0-686-57571-7). Princeton U Pr.
Ward, James. Fresco Painting: Its Art & Technique. LC 77-94626. 1979. Repr. of 1909 ed. lib. bdg. 10.00 (ISBN 0-89341-230-9). Longwood Pr.

MURATHEE LANGUAGE
see Marathi Language

MURCH, WALTER
Robbins, Daniel. Walter Murch. LC 66-29132. (Illus.). 1966. 1.75 (ISBN 0-686-00768-9). Mus of Art RI.

MURCIA, SPAIN (PROVINCE)–DESCRIPTION AND TRAVEL
Castillo-Puche, J. L. Costa Blanca & Costa De La Luz. LC 67-130. (Spanish Guide Ser). (Illus.). 1964. 4.50x (ISBN 0-8002-0728-9). Intl Pubns Serv.

MURDER
see also Assassination; Homicide; Infanticide; Poisoning; Trials (Murder)
Bolitho, William. Murder for Profit. 332p. 1981. Repr. of 1926 ed. lib. bdg. 25.00 (ISBN 0-8495-0467-8). Arden Lib.
Borowitz, Albert. The Woman Who Murdered Black Satin: The Bermondsey Horror. LC 80-39756. 347p. 1981. 17.50 (ISBN 0-8142-0320-5). Ohio St U Pr.
Bradlee, Ben, Jr. The Ambush Murders: The True Account of the Killing of Two California Policemen. LC 79-10418. (Illus.). 1979. 12.95 (ISBN 0-396-07624-6). Dodd.
Brearley, H. C. Homicide in the United States. LC 69-14913. (Criminology, Law Enforcement, & Social Problems Ser.: No. 36). 1969. Repr. of 1932 ed. 15.00 (ISBN 0-87585-036-7). Patterson Smith.
Buchanan, Edna. Carr: Three Years of Murder. 1979. 10.95 (ISBN 0-525-07657-3, Thomas Congdon Book). Dutton.
Bugliosi, Vincent & Gentry, Curt. Helter Skelter. (Illus.). 704p. 1975. pap. 2.50 (ISBN 0-553-13162-1). Bantam.
--Helter Skelter: The True Story of the Manson Murders. (Illus.). 502p. 1974. 15.00 (ISBN 0-393-08700-X). Norton.
Bugliosi, Vincent & Hurwitz, Ken. Till Death Us Do Part: A True Murder Mystery. 1979. pap. 2.75 (ISBN 0-553-12500-1). Bantam.
Buglioso, Vincent & Hurwitz, Ken. Till Death Us Do Part: A True Murder Mystery. 1978. 12.95 (ISBN 0-393-08821-9). Norton.
Capote, Truman. In Cold Blood. 1971. pap. 2.95 (ISBN 0-451-09958-3, E9958, Sig). NAL.
--In Cold Blood. 1966. 12.95 (ISBN 0-394-43023-9). Random.
Carpozi, George, Jr. Great Crimes of the Century: Murderers Leave Clues, No. 8. (Orig.). 1980. pap. 1.95 (ISBN 0-532-23130-9). Woodhill.
--Great Crimes of the Century: The Savage Killers, No. 7. (Orig.). 1980. pap. 1.95 (ISBN 0-532-23129-5). Woodhill.
Crump, David & Jacobs, George. Capital Murder. (Illus.). 1977. 11.95 (ISBN 0-87244-046-X). Texian.
Donoghue, Mary A. Assassination: Murder in Politics. LC 75-18442. (Illus.). 192p. (Orig.). 1975. pap. 1.25 (ISBN 0-89041-012-7, 3012). Major Bks.
Frank, Gerold. Boston Strangler. 1971. pap. 1.50 (ISBN 0-451-05957-3, W5957, Sig). NAL.
Gardiner, Muriel. The Deadly Innocents: Portraits of Children Who Kill. LC 75-36379. 192p. 1976. 13.95x (ISBN 0-465-01583-2). Basic.
--The Deadly Innocents: Portraits of Children Who Kill. LC 75-36379. 192p. 1976. 13.95x (ISBN 0-465-01583-2). Basic.
Gaute, J. H. & Odell, Robin. The Murderer's Who's Who. LC 78-64828. (Illus.). 1979. 17.95x (ISBN 0-416-00201-3). Methuen Inc.
Giese, Donald J. Carol Thompson Murder Case. 1969. pap. 1.00 (ISBN 0-87542-290-X). Llewellyn Pubns.
Hartman, Mary S. Victorian Murderesses: A True History of Thirteen Respectable French & English Women Accused of Unspeakable Crimes. LC 75-34877. (Illus.). 1979. pap. 6.95 (ISBN 0-8052-0627-2). Schocken.
--Victorian Murderesses: A True History of Thirteen Respectable French & English Women Accused of Unspeakable Crimes. LC 75-34877. (Studies in the Life of Women). (Illus.). 1976. 15.00x (ISBN 0-8052-3608-2). Schocken.
Hirsch, Richard. Crimes That Shook the World. facs. ed. LC 77-148217. (Biography Index Reprint Ser.). 1949. 19.00 (ISBN 0-8369-8064-6). Arno.
Jayewardene, C. H. Penalty of Death: The Canadian Experiment. LC 77-167. (Illus.). 1977. 15.95 (ISBN 0-669-01464-8). Lexington Bks.
Jones, Ann. Women Who Kill. LC 80-12329. 420p. 1980. 15.95 (ISBN 0-03-040711-7). HR&W.
Kunstler, William M. The Hall-Mills Murder Case: The Minister & the Choir Singer. 350p. 1980. pap. 6.95 (ISBN 0-8135-0912-2). Rutgers U Pr.
Kutash, Irwin L., et al. Violence: Perspectives on Murder & Aggression. LC 78-62555. (Social & Behavioral Science Ser.). (Illus.). 1978. text ed. 26.95x (ISBN 0-87589-388-0). Jossey-Bass.
Lester, David & Lester, Gene. Crime of Passion: Murder & the Murderer. LC 74-20788. 308p. 1975. 17.95x (ISBN 0-88229-139-4). Nelson-Hall.
Levitt, Leonard. The Healer: A True Story of Medicine & Murder. 276p. 1980. 12.95 (ISBN 0-670-36442-8). Viking Pr.
Lunde, Donald T. Murder & Madness. 1979. pap. 3.95 (ISBN 0-393-00954-8). Norton.
--Murder & Madness. LC 75-45416. (Portable Stanford Ser.). 1976. pap. 4.95 (ISBN 0-913374-33-4). SF Bk Co.
Lundsgaarde, Henry. Murder in Space City: A Cultural Analysis of Houston Homicidal Patterns. LC 76-9229. (Illus.). 1977. 12.95 (ISBN 0-19-502100-2). Oxford U Pr.
Lundsgaarde, Henry P. Murder in Space City: A Cultural Analysis of Houston Homicide Patterns. (Illus.). 288p. 1981. pap. text ed. 6.95x (ISBN 0-19-502984-4). Oxford U Pr.
McComas, J. Francis. Graveside Companion. 1962. 8.95 (ISBN 0-8392-1040-X). Astor-Honor.
Mars, Florence. Witness in Philadelphia. LC 76-50660. 1977. 10.00 (ISBN 0-8071-0265-2). La State U Pr.
Mewshaw, Michael. Life for Death. LC 79-6747. 1980. 10.00 (ISBN 0-385-14505-5). Doubleday.
Moore, B. F. From Darkness to Light. 1980. 4.95 (ISBN 0-8062-1189-X). Carlton.
Pearson, Edmund. More Studies in Murder. 317p. 1980. Repr. of 1936 ed. lib. bdg. 30.00 (ISBN 0-89760-715-5). Telegraph Bks.
--Murder at Smutty Nose & Other Murders. Repr. of 1926 ed. lib. bdg. 25.00 (ISBN 0-8495-4329-0). Arden Lib.
Phillips, Steven. No Heroes, No Villains: The Story of a Murder. 1978. pap. 2.45 (ISBN 0-394-72531-X, Vin). Random.
Simpson, Keith. Forty Years of Murder. (Illus.). 398p. 1981. pap. 5.95 (ISBN 0-586-05038-8, Pub. by Granada England). Academy Chi Ltd.
--Forty Years of Murder. (Illus.). 1979. 12.95 (ISBN 0-684-16334-9, ScribT). Scribner.
Swigert, Victoria & Farrell, Ronald A. Murder, Inequality, & the Law: Differential Treatment & the Legal Process. LC 76-22222. 1976. 15.95 (ISBN 0-669-00881-8). Lexington Bks.
Trenerry, Walter N. Murder in Minnesota: A Collection of True Cases. LC 62-63717. (Illus.). 252p. 1962. 6.95 (ISBN 0-87351-018-6). Minn Hist.
Trilling, Diana. Mrs. Harris: The Death of the Scarsdale Diet Doctor. 1981. 14.95 (ISBN 0-686-74856-5). HarBraceJ.
Wallace, William S. Murders & Mysteries: A Canadian Series. LC 74-10432. (Classics of Crime & Criminology Ser.). 333p. 1975. Repr. of 1931 ed. 16.50 (ISBN 0-88355-199-3). Hyperion Conn.
Wellman, Manly W. Dead & Gone. 1955. 7.50 (ISBN 0-8078-0666-8); pap. 4.95 (ISBN 0-8078-4072-6). U of NC Pr.
Wertham, Frederic. Show of Violence. Repr. of 1949 ed. lib. bdg. 14.00x (ISBN 0-8371-1040-8, WESV); pap. 5.95x (ISBN 0-8371-8945-4, WES). Greenwood.
West, Donald J. Murder Followed by Suicide. LC 66-2706. 1965. 10.00x (ISBN 0-674-58850-9). Harvard U Pr.
Whittington, Stephen N. The Psychology of Murder & of Murderers. (Illus.). 1980. deluxe ed. 39.85 (ISBN 0-89920-004-4). Am Inst Psych.
Wille, Warren S. Citizens Who Commit Murder: A Psychiatric Study. LC 73-376. (Illus.). 280p. 1975. 12.50 (ISBN 0-87527-128-6). Green.

MURDER–AFRICA
Bohannan, Paul, ed. African Homicide & Suicide. LC 59-13873. 1967. pap. text ed. 2.95x (ISBN 0-689-70018-0, 109). Atheneum.
Guttmacher, Manfred S. Mind of the Murderer. LC 72-10849. (Select Bibliographies Reprint Ser.). 1973. Repr. of 1960 ed. 17.00 (ISBN 0-8369-7111-6). Arno.

MURDER–GREAT BRITAIN
Altick, Richard D. Victorian Studies in Scarlet. LC 70-103962. 1970. 7.95 (ISBN 0-393-08605-4). Norton.
Roughead, William. Classic Crimes. 1977. pap. 4.95 (ISBN 0-394-71648-5, Vin). Random.
--Classic Crimes: A Selection from Works of William Roughead Made by W. N. Roughead. LC 74-10431. (Classics in Crime & Criminology Ser.). 449p. 1975. Repr. of 1951 ed. 17.50 (ISBN 0-88355-198-5). Hyperion Conn.
Warning for Fair Women. LC 70-133757. (Tudor Facsimile Texts. Old English Plays: No. 84). Repr. of 1912 ed. 31.50 (ISBN 0-404-53384-1). AMS Pr.
Williamson, Hugh R. Historical Enigmas. 1974. 8.95 (ISBN 0-312-37380-5). St Martin.

MURDER, RITUAL
see Blood Accusation

MURDER TRIALS
see Trials (Murder)

MURDOCH, IRIS, 1919-
Baldanza, Frank. Iris Murdoch. (English Authors Ser.: No. 169). 169p. 1974. lib. bdg. 10.95 (ISBN 0-8057-1410-3). Twayne.
Gerstenberger, Donna. Iris Murdoch. LC 74-126290. (Irish Writers Ser.). 85p. 1975. 4.50 (ISBN 0-8387-7774-0); pap. 1.95 (ISBN 0-8387-7731-7). Bucknell U Pr.
Rabinovitz, Rubin. Iris Murdoch. LC 68-19756. (Columbia Essays on Modern Writers Ser.: No. 34). (Orig.). (gr. 9 up). 1968. pap. 2.00 (ISBN 0-231-03000-2). Columbia U Pr.
Todd, Richard. Iris Murdoch: The Shakespearian Interest. (Critical Studies Ser.). 1979. 22.50x (ISBN 0-06-496935-5). B&N.
Tominaga, Thomas T. & Schneidermeyer, Wilma. Iris Murdoch & Muriel Spark: A Bibliography. LC 76-909. (Author Bibliographies Ser.: No. 27). 253p. 1976. 12.00 (ISBN 0-8108-0907-9). Scarecrow.

MURE FAMILY
Mure, William. Selections from the Family Papers Preserved at Caldwell, 2 pts. in 3 vols. LC 70-173006. (Maitland Club, Glasgow. Publications: No. 71). Repr. of 1854 ed. Set. 105.00 (ISBN 0-404-53091-5). AMS Pr.

MURFREE, MARY NOAILLES, 1850-1922
Cary, Richard. Mary N. Murfree. (Twayne's United States Authors Ser). 1967. pap. 3.45 (ISBN 0-8084-0216-1, T121, Twayne). Coll & U Pr.
--Mary N. Murfree. LC 67-24762. (United States Authors Ser.). 1967. lib. bdg. 8.95x (ISBN 0-89197-839-9); pap. text ed. 2.95x (ISBN 0-89197-990-5). Irvington.
Parks, Edd W. Charles Egbert Craddock. LC 75-159098. 1971. Repr. of 1941 ed. 14.50 (ISBN 0-8046-1641-8). Kennikat.

MURIA
Elwin, Verrier. Kingdom of the Young. abr. ed. Orig. Title: Muria & Their Ghotul. 1968. 8.50x (ISBN 0-19-690368-8). Oxford U Pr.

MURIATIC ACID
see Hydrochloric Acid

MURNAU, F. W. 1889-1931
Huff, Theodore. An Index to the Films of F. W. Murnau. 1976. lib. bdg. 59.95 (ISBN 0-8490-2049-2). Gordon Pr.

MURPHY, ARTHUR, 1727-1805
Dunbar, H. H. Dramatic Career of Arthur Murphy. 1946. pap. 20.00 (ISBN 0-527-25600-5). Kraus Repr.
Spector, Robert D. Arthur Murphy. (English Authors Ser.: No. 258). 1979. lib. bdg. 13.50 (ISBN 0-8057-6751-7). Twayne.

MURPHY, CHARLES FRANCIS, 1858-1924
Weiss, Nancy. Charles Francis Murphy, Eighteen Fifty-Eight-Nineteen Twenty-Four: Respectability & Responsibility in Tammany Politics. LC 67-21037. (Edwin H. Land Prize Essays). 1968. 2.00 (ISBN 0-87391-012-5). Smith Coll.
MURPHY, EDGAR GARDNER, 1869-1913
Bailey, Hugh C. Edgar Gardner Murphy: Gentle Progressive. LC 68-29705. (Illus.). 1968. 10.95x (ISBN 0-87024-093-5). U of Miami Pr.
MURPHY, FRANK, 1893-1949
Fine, Sidney. Frank Murphy: The Detroit Years. LC 74-25945. (Illus.). 1975. 20.00 (ISBN 0-472-32949-9). U of Mich Pr.
--Frank Murphy: The New Deal Years. LC 74-25945. 1979. lib. bdg. 42.00x (ISBN 0-226-24934-4). U of Chicago Pr.
Howard, J. Woodford, Jr. Mister Justice Murphy: A Political Biography. LC 68-11444. 1968. 32.00 (ISBN 0-691-09213-3). Princeton U Pr.
MURPHY, GERALD, 1888-1964
Tompkins, Calvin. Living Well Is the Best Revenge. 1978. pap. 1.95 (ISBN 0-380-01939-6, 37887). Avon.
MURPHY, SARA
Tompkins, Calvin. Living Well Is the Best Revenge. 1978. pap. 1.95 (ISBN 0-380-01939-6, 37887). Avon.
MURRAY, ANDREW, 1828-1917
Douglas, W. M. Andrew Murray & His Message. (Christian Biography Ser.). 336p. Date not set. pap. 3.95 (ISBN 0-8010-2908-2). Baker Bk.
MURRAY, GILBERT, 1866-1957
Essays on Honor of Gilbert Murray. 308p. 1981. Repr. of 1936 ed. lib. bdg. 30.00 (ISBN 0-8495-1354-5). Arden Lib.
MURRAY RIVER, AUSTRALIA
Davis, Peter S. Man & the Murray. LC 78-60244. (Illus.). 1979. text ed. 15.95 (ISBN 0-909465-76-2, 5029). Bks Australia.
MURRIETA, JOAQUIN, 1832-1853
Latta, Frank F. Joaquin Murrieta & His Horse Gangs. (Illus.). 1980. 24.95 (ISBN 0-686-26705-2). Bear State.
MURROW, EDWARD R.
Lichello, Robert. Edward R. Murrow: Broadcaster of Courage. Rahmas, D. Steve, ed. LC 75-185660. (Outstanding Personalities Ser.: No. 4). 32p. (Orig.). (gr. 7-12). 1972. lib. bdg. 2.95 incl. catalog cards (ISBN 0-87157-504-3); pap. 1.50 vinyl laminated covers (ISBN 0-87157-004-1). SamHar Pr.
Smith, R. Franklin. Edward R. Murrow: The War Years. (Orig.). 1978. pap. 5.95 (ISBN 0-932826-04-0). New Issues MI.
MURRY, JOHN MIDDLETON, 1889-1957
Griffin, Ernest G. John Middleton Murray. LC 68-24284. (English Authors Ser.). 1969. lib. bdg. 8.95x (ISBN 0-89197-812-7); pap. text ed. 4.95x (ISBN 0-89197-998-0). Irvington.
Heppenstall, Rayner. Four Absentees: Eric Gill, George Orwell, Dylan Thomas and J. Middleton Murry. 1979. Repr. of 1960 ed. lib. bdg. 30.00 (ISBN 0-8495-2277-3). Arden Lib.
Lilley, George P. Bibliography of John Middleton Murry, Eighteen Eighty-Nine to Nineteen Fifty-Seven. LC 74-22293. 1975. 35.00x (ISBN 0-8020-2184-0). U of Toronto Pr.
Smiles, S. A Publisher (John Murray) & His Friends, 2 vols. 1891. Repr. 75.00 (ISBN 0-8274-3226-7). R West.
MUSAR MOVEMENT
Eckman, Lester. The History of the Musar Movement 1840-1945. LC 75-2649. 1975. 8.95 (ISBN 0-88400-041-9). Shengold.
MUSCLE
see also Contractility (Biology); Heart-Muscle; Myoneural Junction; Neuromuscular Transmission
Adams, Raymond D. Diseases of Muscle: A Study in Pathology. 3rd ed. (Illus.). 1975. 52.00x (ISBN 0-06-140056-4, Harper Medical). Har-Row.
American Alliance for Health, Physical Education & Recreation. Kinesiology, Four. 1974. pap. 2.25x (ISBN 0-685-42012-4, 245-25548). AAHPERD.
--Kinesiology, Three. 1973. pap. 2.25x (ISBN 0-685-42013-2, 245-25440). AAHPERD.
Biro. Symposium on the Muscle. 1976. 11.50 (ISBN 0-9960001-9-4, Pub. by Kaido Hungary). Heyden.
Biro, E & Garamvolgyi, N., eds. Symposium on the Muscle. 1977. 12.50x (ISBN 963-05-1006-5). Intl Pubns Serv.
Bourne, Geoffrey H. The Structure & Function of Muscle. 2nd ed. Vol. 1, 1972. 76.50 (ISBN 0-12-119101-X); Vol. 2, 1973. 83.00 (ISBN 0-12-119102-8); Vol. 3, 1973. 76.50 (ISBN 0-12-119103-6); Vol. 4, 1974. 76.50 (ISBN 0-12-119104-4); 255.00 set (ISBN 0-685-36103-9). Acad Pr.
Briskey, Ernest J., et al, eds. Physiology & Biochemistry of Muscle As a Food: Proceedings, 1965, 2 vols. (Illus.). 1966. Vol. 1. 35.00x (ISBN 0-299-04110-7); Vol. 2. 50.00 (ISBN 0-299-05680-5). U of Wis Pr.
Bulbring, E. & Shuba, M. F., eds. Physiology of Smooth Muscle. LC 75-14566. 440p. 1976. 41.50 (ISBN 0-89004-051-6). Raven.
Casteels, R., et al, eds. Excitation Contraction Coupling in Smooth Muscle. 1977. 74.75 (ISBN 0-444-80017-4, Biomedical Pr). Elsevier.
Ciba Foundation. CIBA Foundation Symposium 56: Cerebral Vascular Smooth Muscle & Its Control. 1978. 40.00 (ISBN 0-444-90026-8, Excerpta Medica). Elsevier.
Daniel, Edwine & Paton, David M. Methods in Pharmacology: Vol. 3, Smooth Muscle. (Illus.). 731p. 1975. 49.50 (ISBN 0-306-35263-X, Plenum Pr). Plenum Pub.
De Villafranca, George W. Driving Force: Muscle. LC 72-189425. (Katharine Asher Engel Lecture for 1971). (Illus.). 1972. pap. 1.50 (ISBN 0-87391-010-9). Smith Coll.
Dowben, R. M. & Shay, J. W., eds. Cell & Muscle Motility, Vol. 1. 350p. 1981. 39.50 (ISBN 0-306-40703-5, Plenum Pr). Plenum Pub.
Dowben, Robert M. & Shay, Jerry W., eds. Cell & Muscle Motility, Vol. 2. 300p. 1982. text ed. price not set (ISBN 0-306-40798-1, Plenum Pr). Plenum Pub.
Ebashi, S., et al, eds. Muscle Contraction: Its Regulatory Mechanism. 549p. 1981. 64.00 (ISBN 0-387-10411-9). Springer-Verlag.
Forrest, John C., et al. Principles of Meat Science. LC 75-8543. (Food & Nutrition Ser.). (Illus.). 1975. text ed. 26.95x (ISBN 0-7167-0743-8). W H Freeman.
Grinnell, Alan D., et al, eds. The Regulation of Muscle Contraction: Excitation-Contraction Coupling. LC 81-4362. (UCLA Forum in Medical Sciences: Vol. 22). 1981. 30.00 (ISBN 0-12-303780-8). Acad Pr.
Gutmann, Ernest, ed. Denervated Muscle. 486p. 1962. 50.00 (ISBN 0-306-10653-1, Consultants). Plenum Pub.
Harrington, William F. Theories of Muscle Contraction. Head, J. J., ed. LC 77-94953. (Oxford-Carolina Biology Readers). 32p. (gr. 11-12). pap. 2.50 (ISBN 0-89278-314-1, 45-9714). Carolina Biological.
Hill, A. V. First & Last Experiments in Muscle Mechanics. LC 73-96092. (Illus.). 1970. 34.95 (ISBN 0-521-07664-1). Cambridge U Pr.
Huddart, Henry. Comparative Structure & Function of Muscle. 1975. text ed. 56.00 (ISBN 0-08-017845-6). Pergamon.
Kaldor, George & DiBattista, William J., eds. Aging: Aging in Muscle, Vol. 6. LC 78-4356. 244p. 1978. 22.00 (ISBN 0-89004-097-4). Raven.
Keith, Arthur. Menders of the Maimed: The Anatomical & Physiological Principles Underlying the Treatment of Injuries to Muscles, Nerves, Bones & Joints. LC 75-19489. 352p. 1975. Repr. of 1919 ed. 17.50 (ISBN 0-88275-341-X). Krieger.
Keul, J., et al. Energy Metabolism of Human Muscle. Skinner, James B., tr. from Ger. (Medicine & Sport Ser.: Vol. 7). (Illus.). 1972. 39.50 (ISBN 0-8391-0604-1, Pub by Karger). Univ Park.
McGeachie, J. Smooth Muscle Regeneration: A Review & Experimental Study. (Monographs in Developmental Biology: Vol. 9). (Illus.). vii, 90p. 1975. 33.00 (ISBN 3-8055-2058-1). S Karger.
Needham, Dorothy M. Machina Carnis: The Biochemistry of Muscular Contraction in Its Historical Development. (Illus.). 1972. 99.50 (ISBN 0-521-07974-8). Cambridge U Pr.
Peachey, L. D. Muscle & Motility. (Biocore Ser: Unit 18). 1974. 17.50 (ISBN 0-07-005349-9, C). McGraw.
Reuben, John P., et al, eds. Electrobiology of Nerve, Synapse & Muscle. LC 75-14587. 405p. 1976. 34.50 (ISBN 0-89004-030-3). Raven.
Roy, P. E. & Dhalla, N. S., eds. The Sarcolemma. (Recent Advances in Studies on Cardiac Structure & Metabolism Ser.: Vol. 9). (Illus.). 600p. 1976. 39.50 (ISBN 0-8391-0669-6). Univ Park.
Roy, P. E. & Rona, G., eds. The Metabolism of Contraction. (Recent Advances in Studies on Cardiac Structure & Metabolism Ser.: Vol. 10). (Illus.). 600p. 1975. 39.50 (ISBN 0-8391-0670-X). Univ Park.
Sanadi, D. Rao, ed. Chemical Mechanisms in Bioenergetics. LC 76-26707. (ACS Monograph: 172). 1976. 33.00 (ISBN 0-8412-0274-5). Am Chemical.
Smith, David S. Muscle. (Ultrastructure of Cells & Organisms Monographs). 1972. 19.50 (ISBN 0-12-454145-3). Acad Pr.
Stephens, N. L., ed. Biochemistry of Smooth Muscle. (Illus.). 1977. 44.50 (ISBN 0-8391-0848-6). Univ Park.
Stuart, Harold C. Growth of Bone, Muscle & Overlying Tissues. 1940. pap. 13.00 (ISBN 0-527-01515-6). Kraus Repr.
Svendgaard, N. A., et al. Regenerative Properties of Central Monoamine Neurons: Studies in the Adult Rat Using Cerebral Iris Implants As Targets. (Advances in Anatomy, Embroyology, & Cell Biology Ser.: Vol. 51, Pt. 4). (Illus.). 70p. (Orig.). 1975. pap. 34.30 (ISBN 0-387-07299-3). Springer-Verlag.
Tonomura, Y. Muscle Proteins, Muscle Contraction & Cation Transport. (Illus.). 1976. 34.50 (ISBN 0-8391-0739-0). Univ Park.
Tribe, M. A. & Eraut, M. R. Nerves & Muscle. LC 76-55511. (Basic Biology Course Ser.: Bk. 10). (Illus.). 1977. 32.50 (ISBN 0-521-21369-X); pap. 11.95x (ISBN 0-521-21368-1). Cambridge U Pr.
U. S.-Japan Cooperative Symposium. Molecular & Cellular Aspects of Vasecular Smooth Muscle in Health & Disease: Proceedings. Bohr, D. F. & Takenha, F., eds. (Blood Vessels: Vol. 15, No. 1-3). (Illus.). 1978. 52.25 (ISBN 3-8055-2857-4). S Karger.
Urbanowski, Ferris. Yoga for New Parents. LC 75-9355. (Illus.). 160p. 1975. pap. 6.95 (ISBN 0-06-128300-2, TD232). Har-Row.
Usherwood, P. N. Insect Muscle. 1975. 97.00 (ISBN 0-12-709450-4). Acad Pr.
Varga, E., et al, eds. Molecular & Cellular Aspects of Muscle Function: Proceedings of the 28th International Congress of Physiological Sciences, Budapest 1980 (Including Proceedings of the Satellite Symposium on Membrane Control of Skeletal Muscle Function) LC 80-42101. (Advances in Physiological Sciences: Vol. 5). (Illus.). 320p. 1981. 40.00 (ISBN 0-08-026817-X). Pergamon.
Von Euler, Ulf S. & Pernow, Bengt, eds. Substance P. LC 76-52600. (Nobel Symposium Ser: No. 37). 360p. 1977. 31.50 (ISBN 0-89004-100-8). Raven.
Zachar, Jozef. Electrogenesis & Contractility in Skeletal Muscle Cells. (Illus.). 1972. 44.50 (ISBN 0-8391-0587-8). Univ Park.
MUSCLE RELAXANTS
see also Anticonvulsants
Clarke, J. F. & McChesney, M. Dynamics of Relaxing Gases. 2nd ed. 1976. 54.95 (ISBN 0-408-70667-8). Butterworth.
MUSCLE STRENGTH
Hettinger, Theodor. Physiology of Strength. (Illus.). 96p. 1961. photocopy ed. spiral 11.50 (ISBN 0-398-04281-0). C C Thomas.
Knight, Virgil. The Florida Edge: Strength Training, Conditioning & Rehabilitation. LC 81-80787. (Fitness America Ser.). (Illus.). 208p. (Orig.). 1981. pap. 5.95 (ISBN 0-918438-80-2). Leisure Pr.
Pickering, R. J. Strength Training for Athletics. Date not set. pap. 3.95x (ISBN 0-392-08944-0, SpS). Sportshelf.
Schwarzenegger, Arnold & Hall, Douglas K. Arnold: The Education of a Body Builder. (Illus.). 1977. 14.95 (ISBN 0-671-22879-X). S&S.
Weider, Joe. The Best of Joe Weider's Muscle & Fitness Training Tips & Routines. (Illus.). 1981. 12.95 (ISBN 0-8092-5911-7); pap. 5.95 (ISBN 0-8092-5910-9). Contemp Bks.
--The Best of Joe Weider's Muscle & Fitness: The Worlds's Leading Bodybuilders Answer Your Questions. (Illus.). 1981. 12.95 (ISBN 0-8092-5914-1); pap. 5.95 (ISBN 0-8092-5912-5). Contemp Bks.
Wong, Harry. Dynamic Tension. LC 80-53545. (Illus.). 144p. 1980. pap. 5.95 (ISBN 0-86568-013-2). Unique Pubns.
MUSCLE TISSUE
see Muscle
MUSCLES
Here are entered works on the gross anatomy and movements of muscles. Works on the histology and physiological properties of muscular tissue are entered under the heading Muscle.
see also Animal Locomotion; Eye-Muscles; Ligaments; Muscle Strength; Neuromuscular Transmission; Tendons;
also names of muscles
Aguayo, A. G. & Karpati, G., eds. Current Topics in Nerve & Muscle Research. LC 79-13037. (International Congress Ser.: No. 455). 328p. 1979. 58.75 (ISBN 0-444-90057-8, North Holland). Elsevier.
Arronet, N. I. Motile Muscle & Cell Models. LC 72-88884. (Studies in Soviet Science - Life Sciences). 192p. 1973. 35.00 (ISBN 0-306-10877-1, Consultants). Plenum Pub.
Barham, Jerry N. & Thomas, William L. Anatomical Kinesiology: A Programmed Text. (Illus., Prog. Bk.). 1969. pap. text ed. 10.50 (ISBN 0-02-306010-7, 30601). Macmillan.
Barreto, Delia. Muscles: A Study Aid for Students of the Allied Health Professions. (Illus.). 48p. 1974. pap. 2.75 (ISBN 0-87936-005-4). Scholium Intl.
Basmajian. Muscles Alive. 4th ed. (Illus.). 1979. 36.00 (ISBN 0-683-00413-1). Williams & Wilkins.
Betz, E., ed. Ionic Actions on Vascular Smooth Muscle. (Illus.). 1976. soft cover 15.30 (ISBN 0-387-07836-3). Springer-Verlag.
Bradley, W. D., ed. Recent Advances in Myology. (International Congress Ser: No. 360). 630p. 1976. 111.75 (ISBN 0-444-15130-3, North-Holland). Elsevier.
Bratzler, L. J., ed. Cross Sectional Muscle Nomenclature of the Beef Carcass. (Illus.). 1952. pap. text ed. 3.50x (ISBN 0-87013-001-3). Mich St U Pr.
Broer, Marion R. & Houtz, Sara J. Patterns of Muscular Activity in Selected Sport Skills: An Electromyographic Study. (Illus.). 96p. 1967. ed. spiral bdg. 12.75photocopy (ISBN 0-398-00229-0). C C Thomas.
Bulbring, Edith, et al, eds. Smooth Muscle. (Illus.). 1981. text ed. 95.00x (ISBN 0-292-77569-5). U of Tex Pr.
Carlsoo, Sven. How Man Moves: Kinesiological Methods & Studies. (Eng.). 1972. 13.00x (ISBN 0-434-90215-2). Intl Pubns Serv.
Cosgrove, Margaret. Your Muscles & Ways to Exercise Them. LC 79-22936. (Illus.). (gr. 3-6). 1980. PLB 6.95 (ISBN 0-396-07787-0). Dodd.
Crass, Maurice, ed. Vascular Smooth Muscle. Barnes, Charles. (Research Topics in Physiology Ser.). 1982. price not set (ISBN 0-12-195220-7). Acad Pr.
Daniels, Lucille & Worthingham, Catherine. Muscle Testing: Techniques of Manual Examination. 4th ed. LC 79-67302. (Illus.). 191p. 1980. 11.95 (ISBN 0-7216-2877-X). Saunders.
Darden, Ellington. How Your Muscles Work: Featuring Nautilus Training Equipment. Darden, Ellington, ed. LC 77-75757. (Physical Fitness & Sports Medicine Ser.). (Illus.). 1977. pap. 3.95 (ISBN 0-89305-010-5). Anna Pub.
Freilinger, G., et al, eds. Muscle Transplantation. (Illus.). 320p. 1981. 69.10 (ISBN 0-387-81636-4). Springer-Verlag.
George, J. C. & Berger, Andrew J. Avian Myology. 1966. 56.00 (ISBN 0-12-280150-4). Acad Pr.
Goldspink, D. F., ed. The Development & Specialisation of Skeletal Muscle. (Society for Experimental Biology Seminar Ser.: No. 7). (Illus.). 200p. 1981. 45.00 (ISBN 0-521-23317-8); pap. 19.95 (ISBN 0-521-29907-1). Cambridge U Pr.
Granit, Ragnar. Basis of Motor Control. 1970. 55.00 (ISBN 0-12-295350-9). Acad Pr.
Green, Robert M. Galvani: Commentary on the Effect of Electricity & Muscular Motion. 98p. 1953. 6.50 (ISBN 0-686-65362-9). Krieger.
Greenblatt, Gordon M. Cat Musculature: A Photographic Atlas. 2nd ed. LC 80-25610. (Illus.). 32p. 1981. pap. 4.00 (ISBN 0-226-30656-9). U of Chicago Pr.
Guba, F., et al, eds. Mechanism of Muscle Adaptation to Functional Requirements: Proceedings of a Satellite Symposium of the 28th International Congress of Physiological Sciences, Szeged, Hungary, 1980. LC 80-42250. (Advances in Physiological Sciences Ser.: Vol. 24). (Illus.). 500p. 1981. 60.00 (ISBN 0-08-027345-9). Pergamon.
Jacobson, Edmund. Progressive Relaxation: A Physiological & Clinical Investigation of Muscular States & Their Significance in Psychology & Medical Practice. 3rd rev ed. LC 38-13310. (Midway Reprint Ser). xvii, 494p. 1974. pap. 20.00x (ISBN 0-226-39059-4). U of Chicago Pr.
Junge, Douglas. Nerve & Muscle Excitation. 2nd ed. LC 80-18158. (Illus.). 230p. 1981. pap. text ed. 12.95x (ISBN 0-87893-410-3). Sinauer Assoc.
Kendall, Henry O., et al. Muscles: Testing & Function. 2nd ed. (Illus.). 294p. 1971. 29.95 (ISBN 0-683-04574-1). Williams & Wilkins.
Knott, Margaret & Voss, Dorothy E. Proprioceptive Neuromuscular Facilitation: Patterns & Techniques. 2nd ed. (Illus.). 1968. 28.50 (ISBN 0-06-141441-7, Harper Medical). Har-Row.
Krejci, Vladimir & Koch, Peter. Muscle & Tendon Injuries in Athletes. (Illus.). 1979. pap. 9.95 (ISBN 0-8151-5195-0). Year Bk Med.
Lockhart, R. D. Living Anatomy. 96p. 1974. pap. 6.95 (ISBN 0-571-09177-6, Pub. by Faber & Faber). Merrimack Bk Serv.
McGraw, Myrtle B. Neuromuscular Maturation of the Human Infant. (Illus.). 1963. Repr. of 1945 ed. 10.75 (ISBN 0-02-849080-0). Hafner.
Mathes, Stephen J. & Nahai, Foad. Clinical Applications for Muscle & Musculocutanious Flaps. 2nd ed. (Illus.). 550p. 1981. text ed. 12.95 (ISBN 0-8016-3164-5). Mosby.
--Clinical Atlas of Muscle & Musculocutaneous Flaps. LC 79-10739. (Illus.). 1979. text ed. 44.50 (ISBN 0-8016-3141-6). Mosby.
Matzen, Peter-Friedrich & Fleissner, Horst K. Orthopedic Roentgen Atlas. Michaelis, L. S., tr. (Illus.). 300p. 1970. 95.00 (ISBN 0-8089-0634-8). Grune.
Mitchell, Laura. Simple Relaxation. LC 78-73069. 1979. 8.95 (ISBN 0-689-10961-X). Atheneum.
Pearson, Carl M. & Mostofi, F. K., eds. The Striated Muscle. LC 73-6903. 518p. 1973. 38.50 (ISBN 0-683-06811-3). Krieger.

Pernow, Bengt & Saltin, Bengt, eds. Muscle Metabolism During Exercise. LC 71-148821. (Advances in Experimental Medicine & Biology Ser: Vol. 11). 588p. 1971. 42.50 (ISBN 0-306-39011-6, Plenum Pr). Plenum Pub.

Pette, D., ed. Plasticity of Muscle. 1979. 100.00x (ISBN 3-1100-7961-5). De Gruyter.

Rahn, Joan E. Grocery Store Zoology: Bones & Muscles. LC 76-26599. (Illus.). (gr. 5-9). 1977. 6.95 (ISBN 0-689-30560-5). Atheneum.

Royce, Joseph. Surface Anatomy. (Illus.). 280p. 1973. pap. text ed. 11.00 (ISBN 0-8036-7641-7). Davis Co.

Serafini, Anthony. The Muscle Book. LC 81-4654. (Illus.). 160p. 1981. lib. bdg. 9.95 (ISBN 0-668-05088-8); pap. 6.95 (ISBN 0-668-05092-6). Arco.

Squire, John. The Structural Analysis of Muscular Contraction. 685p. 1981. 55.00 (ISBN 0-306-40582-2). Plenum Pub.

--The Structural Basis of Muscular Contraction. 685p. 1981. 55.00 (ISBN 0-306-40582-2, Plenum Pr). Plenum Pub.

Taylor, A., ed. Muscle Receptors & Movement. Prochazka, A. 464p. 1981. text ed. 50.00x (ISBN 0-19-520280-5). Oxford U Pr.

Thompson, Clem W. Manual of Structural Kinesiology. 8th ed. LC 76-46400. (Illus.). 1977. pap. text ed. 11.95 (ISBN 0-8016-4939-0). Mosby.

Warfel, John H. The Extremities. 4th ed. LC 73-7977. (Illus.). 124p. 1974. text ed. 5.25 (ISBN 0-8121-0457-9). Lea & Febiger.

White, D. C. & Thorson, John. The Kinetics of Muscle Contraction. 1975. pap. text ed. 11.25 (ISBN 0-08-018149-X). Pergamon.

Wiesendanger, M. Pathophysiology of Muscle Tone. LC 72-189294. (Neurology Series: Vol. 9). (Illus.). 52p. 1972. 20.10 (ISBN 0-387-05761-7). Springer-Verlag.

Wright, Wilhelmine G. Muscle Function. (Illus.). 1962. Repr. of 1928 ed. 15.25 (ISBN 0-02-855000-5). Hafner.

MUSCLES–DISEASES

see also Myotonia; Neuromuscular Diseases

Bethlem, Jaap. Myopathies. LC 77-80955. (Illus.). 1977. 28.00 (ISBN 0-397-58227-7, JBL-Med-Nursing). Har-Row.

Dreyfus, Jean-Claude & Schapira, Georges. Biochemistry of Hereditary Myopathies. (American Lecture Living Chemistry). (Illus.). 160p. 1962. ed. spiral bdg. 15.50photocopy (ISBN 0-398-00475-7). C C Thomas.

Dubowitz, Victor. Muscle Disorders in Childhood. LC 77-23997. (Major Problems in Clinical Pediatrics Ser.: Vol. 16). (Illus.). 1978. text ed. 29.00 (ISBN 0-7216-3210-6). Saunders.

Harris, John B., ed. Muscular Dystrophy & Other Inherited Diseases of Skeletal Muscle in Animals, Vol. 317. LC 78-27609. (Annals of the New York Academy of Science Ser.). 716p. 1979. pap. 80.00x (ISBN 0-89766-005-6). NY Acad Sci.

Hughes, J. Trevor. Pathology of Muscle. LC 73-89178. (Major Problems in Pathology Ser.: No. 4). (Illus.). 225p. 1974. text ed. 14.00 (ISBN 0-7216-4827-4). Saunders.

International Congress on Muscle Disease, 2nd, 1971. Muscle Diseases Part I, Basic Research in Myology: Proceedings. Kakulas, B. A., ed. (International Congress Ser.: No. 294). 700p. 1974. 96.75 (ISBN 90-219-0163-3, Excerpta Medica). Elsevier.

International Congress on Muscle Diseases, 2nd, 1971. Muscle Diseases Part 2, Clinical Studies in Myology: Proceedings. Kakulas, B. A., ed. (International Congress Ser.: No. 295). 700p. 1974. 94.25 (ISBN 0-444-15102-8, Excerpta Medica); with part I 151.25 (ISBN 0-686-66903-7). Elsevier.

Kark, Pieter, et al, eds. The Inherited Ataxias: Biochemical, Viral, & Pathological Studies. LC 77-92490. (Advances in Neurology Ser.: Vol. 21). 444p. 1978. 45.50 (ISBN 0-89004-268-3). Raven.

Mair, W. G. & Tome, F. M. Atlas of the Ultrastructure of Diseased Human Muscle. (Illus.). 1972. 20.75x (ISBN 0-443-00831-0). Churchill.

Mauro, Alexander, ed. Muscle Regeneration. 576p. 1979. text ed. 59.50 (ISBN 0-89004-284-5). Raven.

Murphy, E. G. The Chemistry & Therapy of Disorders of Voluntary Muscles. (American Lecture Living Chemistry). (Illus.). 140p. 1964. photocopy ed. spiral 13.75 (ISBN 0-398-01374-8). C C Thomas.

Walton, J. A. Disorders of Voluntary Muscle. 4th ed. (Illus.). 1080p. 1981. text ed. 120.00 (ISBN 0-443-01847-2). Churchill.

Walton, J. N. Disorders of Voluntary Muscle. 3rd ed. (Illus.). 1000p. 1977. text ed. 79.00 (ISBN 0-443-01077-3). Churchill.

Wyman, Dorothy. Bruce. LC 78-23504. (Orion Ser). 1979. pap. 1.95 (ISBN 0-8127-0217-4). Review & Herald.

MUSCLES–JUVENILE LITERATURE

Silverstein, Alvin & Silverstein, Virginia B. Muscular System: How Living Creatures Move. (gr. 1-4). 1972. PLB 4.95 (ISBN 0-13-606947-9). P-H.

MUSCONETCONG VALLEY, NEW JERSEY

Wacker, Peter O. The Musconetcong Valley of New Jersey: A Historical Geography. LC 68-18694. (Illus.). 1968. 15.00 (ISBN 0-8135-0575-5). Rutgers U Pr.

MUSCULAR COORDINATION

see Motor Ability

MUSCULAR DYSTROPHY

Bonsett, Charles A. Studies of Pseudohypertrophic Muscular Dystrophy. (American Lecture Living Chemistry). (Illus.). 168p. 1969. ed. spiral bdg. 18.75photocopy (ISBN 0-398-00188-X). C C Thomas.

Experimental Myopathies & Muscular Dystrophy. (Neurology Ser.: Vol. 16). 115p. 1975. 25.00 (ISBN 0-387-07376-0). Springer-Verlag.

Franks, Hugh. Will to Live. 1979. 14.00 (ISBN 0-7100-0181-9). Routledge & Kegan.

Harris, John B., ed. Muscular Dystrophy & Other Inherited Diseases of Skeletal Muscle in Animals, Vol. 317. LC 78-27609. (Annals of the New York Academy of Science Ser.). 716p. 1979. pap. 80.00x (ISBN 0-89766-005-6). NY Acad Sci.

Milhorat, A. T., ed. Exploratory Concepts in Muscular Dystrophy. LC 74-84458. (International Congress Ser: No. 333). 664p. 1975. 91.25 (ISBN 0-444-15055-2, Excerpta Medica). Elsevier.

Symposium on Muscular Dystrophy, Jerusalem 1976. Muscular Dystrophy 1976: Proceedings. Robin, Gordon C. & Falewski de Leon, George, eds. (Illus.). 1977. 29.50 (ISBN 3-8055-2680-6). S Karger.

MUSCULAR SENSE

see also Movement, Psychology Of

Huxley, Andrew. Reflections on Muscle. LC 79-5480. (Illus.). 120p. 1980. 17.50 (ISBN 0-691-08255-3). Princeton U Pr.

MUSCULOSKELETAL SYSTEM

see also Bones; Connective Tissues; Muscles

Albright, James A. & Brand, Richard A., eds. The Scientific Basis of Orthopedics. (Illus.). 448p. 1979. 32.00 (ISBN 0-8385-8503-5). ACC.

Evans, F. Gaynor. Biomechanical Studies of the Musculo-Skeletal System. 232p. 1961. pap. 22.50 photocopy ed. spiral (ISBN 0-398-04102-4). C C Thomas.

Hessler, Robert R. Cephalocarida: Comparative Skeletomusculature. (Connecticut Academy of Arts & Sciences Memoirs: Vol. 16). 1964. pap. 12.50 (ISBN 0-208-00711-3). Shoe String.

Lewis, D. H., ed. Induced Skeletal Muscle Ischemia in Man. (Illus.). viii, 200p. 1982. pap. 70.75 (ISBN 3-8055-3427-2). S Karger.

Poland, James L., et al. Musculoskeletal System. 1981. pap. write for info. (ISBN 0-87488-667-8). Med Exam.

Roberts, T. D. M. Neurophysiology of Postural Mechanisms. 2nd ed. 1978. text ed. 99.95 (ISBN 0-408-70808-5). Butterworth.

Rosse, Cornelius & Clawson, D. Kay. Introduction to the Musculoskeletal System. (Illus.). 1970. 15.50x (ISBN 0-06-142285-1, Harper Medical). Har-Row.

Sokoloff, Leon & Bland, John H. Musculoskeletal System. LC 74-30473. 180p. 1975. 18.00 (ISBN 0-683-07888-7). Krieger.

Trindade, C. The Musculo-Skeletal System. (Penguin Library of Nursing Ser.). (Illus.). Date not set. pap. text ed. write for info. (ISBN 0-443-01611-9). Churchill.

Wilson, Frank C. The Musculoskeletal System. LC 75-22187. (Illus.). 288p. 1975. text ed. 20.75 (ISBN 0-397-52071-9). Lippincott.

Zohn, David A. & Mennell, John M. Musculoskeletal Pain: Principles of Physical Diagnosis & Physical Treatment. 1976. 19.95 (ISBN 0-316-98893-6). Little.

MUSCULOSKELETAL SYSTEM–DISEASES

see also Torticollis

Abramson, D. I. & Miller, D. S. Vascular Problems in Musculoskeletal Disorders of the Limbs. (Illus.). 404p. 1981. 39.50 (ISBN 0-387-90524-3). Springer-Verlag.

Committee on Prosthetics Research & Development. Comprehensive Management of Musculoskeletal Disorders in Hemophilia. (Illus.). 200p. 1973. pap. 8.75 (ISBN 0-309-02139-1). Natl Acad Pr.

D'Ambrosia, Robert D., ed. Musculoskeletal Disorders: Regional Examination & Differential Diagnosis. LC 77-8562. 1977. 49.75 (ISBN 0-397-50373-3). Har-Row.

Gozna, Eric R. & Harrington, Ian J. Biomechanics of Musculoskeletal Injury. 150p. 1981. lib. bdg. 19.95 (ISBN 0-683-03728-5). Williams & Wilkins.

Rosse, Cornelius & Clawson, Kay. The Musculoskeletal System in Health & Disease. (Illus.). 425p. 1980. text ed. 35.00 (ISBN 0-686-74087-4, Harper Medical). Har-Row.

Salter, Robert B. Textbook of Disorders & Injuries of the Musculoskeletal System. 1970. 29.95 (ISBN 0-683-07497-0). Williams & Wilkins.

Sokoloff, Leon & Bland, John H. Musculoskeletal System. LC 74-30473. 180p. 1975. 18.00 (ISBN 0-683-07888-7). Krieger.

Steinbrocker, Otto & Neustadt, David H. Aspiration & Injection Therapy in Arthritis & Musculoskeletal Disorders: A Handbook on Technique & Management. (Illus.). 1972. 12.00x (ISBN 0-06-142497-8, Harper Medical). Har-Row.

Wilder, Mary H. & Wilson, Rondel W. Prevalence of Chronic Skin & Musculoskeletal Conditions, U. S. 1969. LC 74-6262. (Data from the Health Interview Survey Ser. 10: No. 92). 61p. 1974. pap. 1.70 (ISBN 0-8406-0019-4). Natl Ctr Health Stats.

MUSEOLOGY

see Museum Techniques

MUSETTE

see Bagpipe

MUSEUM CURATORSHIP AS A PROFESSION

see Museum Work As a Profession

MUSEUM OF FINE ARTS, BOSTON

Ragghianti, Ca Rlo L. Museum of Fine Arts: Boston. LC 69-19065. (Great Museums of the World Ser.). (Illus.). 1968. 16.95 (ISBN 0-88225-230-5). Newsweek.

Whitehill, Walter M. Museum of Fine Arts, Boston: A Centennial History, 2 vols. LC 70-102674. 1970. Set. 30.00x (ISBN 0-674-58875-4, Belknap Pr). Harvard U Pr.

MUSEUM OF MODERN ART, NEW YORK CITY

Barr, Alfred H. Painting and Sculpture in the Museum of Modern Art, 1929-1967. LC 68-54923. (Illus.). 1977. 40.00 (ISBN 0-87070-540-7). Museum Mod Art.

Museum of Modern Art, New York. Catalog of the Library of the Museum of Modern Art, New York, 14 vols. 1976. Set. lib. bdg. 1140.00 (ISBN 0-8161-0015-2). G K Hall.

MUSEUM TECHNIQUES

Baxi, Smita J. Modern Museum: Organization & Practice in India. LC 73-903725. (Illus.). 208p. 1973. 13.50x (ISBN 0-8002-0933-8). Intl Pubns Serv.

Chenhall, Robert G. Nomenclature for Museum Cataloging: A System for Classifying Man-Made Objects. LC 77-20097. (Illus.). 1978. 25.00 (ISBN 0-910050-30-9). AASLH.

Dexter, Kerry. The Display Book. (Illus.). 1977. pap. 5.25 (ISBN 0-8192-1226-1). Morehouse.

Ezell, Mancil. Making Nonprojected Visuals & Displays. new ed. LC 74-21565. 64p. 1975. pap. 2.95 (ISBN 0-8054-3419-4). Broadman.

Harris, Karyn J. Costume Display Techniques. LC 77-5404. 1977. pap. 5.75 (ISBN 0-910050-27-9). AASLH.

Hoving, Thomas. King of the Confessors. 1981. 16.95 (ISBN 0-671-43388-1). S&S.

Neal, Arminta. Exhibits for the Small Museum: A Handbook. LC 76-21812. (Illus.). 1976. pap. 8.00 (ISBN 0-910050-23-6). AASLH.

The Organization of Museums: Practical Advice. (Illus.). 1960. pap. 15.00 (ISBN 92-3-100441-7, U441, UNESCO). Unipub.

Price, James E. Analysis of a Middle Mississippian House in Butler County, Missouri. LC 70-628940. (Museum Brief: No. 1). (Illus.). 1969. pap. 1.60x (ISBN 0-913134-00-7). Mus Anthro Mo.

Quimby, Ian M. Material Culture & the Study of American Life. (A Winterthur Bk.). (Illus.). 1978. 12.95x (ISBN 0-393-05661-9); pap. 5.95x (ISBN 0-393-09037-X). Norton.

Ripley, S. Dillon, 2nd. Cabinets Lost & Found. (Connecticut Academy of Arts & Sciences: Transaction: Vol. 46, Pp. 1-12). 11p. 1975. pap. 3.50 (ISBN 0-208-01559-0, Archon). Shoe String.

Schneider, Mary Jane. Cataloguing & Care of Collections for Small Museums. LC 72-612235. (Museum Brief: No. 8). 30p. 1971. pap. 2.00x (ISBN 0-913134-07-4). Mus Anthro Mo.

Temporary & Travelling Exhibitions. 1963. pap. 6.25 (ISBN 92-3-100507-3, UNESCO). Unipub.

Thomson. Museum Environment: Control for Preservation. LC 78-40366. 1978. 39.95 (ISBN 0-408-70792-5). Butterworth.

MUSEUM WORK AS A PROFESSION

Burcaw, G. Ellis. Introduction to Museum Work. LC 74-32248. (Illus.). 200p. 1975. pap. text ed. 6.75x (ISBN 0-910050-14-7). AASLH.

Burns, William. Your Future in Museums. LC 67-15470. (Careers in Depth Ser). (gr. 8-12). 1967. PLB 5.97 (ISBN 0-8239-0053-3). Rosen Pr.

Girouard, Mark. Alfred Waterhouse & the Natural History Museum. LC 80-53742. (Illus.). 1981. 12.95x (ISBN 0-300-02578-5). Yale U Pr.

Hoachlander, Marjorie. Profile of a Museum Registrar. 120p. (Orig.). 1980. pap. 3.00 (ISBN 0-89492-038-3). Acad Educ Dev.

Rudman, Jack. Museum Director. (Career Examination Ser.: C-2372). (Cloth bdg. avail. on request). pap. 10.00 (ISBN 0-8373-2372-X). Natl Learning.

--Principal Museum Curator. (Career Examination Ser.: C-2375). (Cloth bdg. avail. on request). pap. 12.00 (ISBN 0-8373-2375-4). Natl Learning.

--Senior Museum Curator. (Career Examination Ser.: C-2374). (Cloth bdg. avail. on request). pap. 10.00 (ISBN 0-8373-2374-6). Natl Learning.

Williams, Patricia M. Museums of Natural History & the People Who Work in Them. LC 72-93926. 128p. 1973. 5.95 (ISBN 0-312-56105-9). St Martin.

MUSEUMS

see also Art Museums; Historical Museums; Industrial Museums; Museum Techniques; Museum Work As a Profession; Naval Museums; Zoological Specimens–Collection and Preservation also subdivision Galleries and Museums under names of cities, e.g. new york (City)–Galleries and Museums; names of individual museums; and subdivision Collection and Preservation under Insect, Zoological Specimens and similar headings

Albin, Edgar A., et al. Selections from the Permanent Collection of the Springfield Art Museum. Landwehr, William C., ed. LC 80-53333. 100p. (Orig.). 1980. pap. text ed. 9.95 (ISBN 0-934306-03-6). Springfield.

Alegre, Mitchell R. Guide to Museum Villages. LC 77-72399. (Illus.). 1978. pap. 5.95 (ISBN 0-8069-8370-1, 025995). Sterling.

Aloi, R. Museums: Architecture, Technics. (Illus.). 1962. 50.00 (ISBN 0-685-12032-5). Heinman.

Althea. Visiting a Museum. 1980. pap. 1.60 ea.; pap. in 5 pk. avail. (ISBN 0-85122-200-5, Pub. by Dinosaur Pubns). Merrimack Bk Serv.

American Association of Museums. A Statistical Survey of Museums in the United States & Canada. LC 75-21957. (America in Two Centuries Ser). 1976. Repr. of 1965 ed. 9.50x (ISBN 0-405-07735-1). Arno.

Amon Carter Museum. Amon Carter Museum: Nineteen Sixty-One to Nineteen Seventy-Seven. LC 77-81806. (Illus.). 47p. 1977. pap. 3.50 (ISBN 0-88360-028-5). Amon Carter.

Anderson, John & Sperberg, Diana. Public Media Manual for Museums. Collins, Jerome, ed. LC 79-22531. (Orig.). 1979. pap. text ed. 7.00 (ISBN 0-935260-00-5). Tex Assn Mus.

Arey, June B. The Purpose, Financing & Governance of Museums: Three Conferences on Present & Future Issues. 1978. pap. text ed. 2.50 (ISBN 0-932676-01-4). Spring Hill.

Audience Studies of the Performing Arts & Museums: A Critical Review Report No.9, No. 9. (National Endowment for the Arts Research Division Reports). 106p. (Orig.). 1978. pap. 3.00x (ISBN 0-89062-092-X, Pub. by Natl Endow Arts). Pub Ctr Cult Res.

Bernice Pauahi Bishop Museum, Honolulu. Museum of Polynesian Ethnology & Natural History: Honolulu Bulletins, Nos. 1-12, 14-223. 1922-1961. 2826.00 set (ISBN 0-527-02103-2). Kraus Repr.

Celebrate! The Story of the Museum of International Folk Art. (Illus.). 1979. pap. 3.95 (ISBN 0-89013-119-8). Museum NM Pr.

Driver, Clive E. A Selection from Our Shelves: Books, Manuscripts & Drawings from the Rosenbach Foundation Museum. 1972. pap. 12.50 (ISBN 0-939084-08-2). Rosenbach Mus and Lib.

Eis, Ruth. Torah Binders of the Judah L. Magnes Museum. LC 79-83877. 80p. 1979. pap. 18.00 (ISBN 0-686-30820-4). Magnes Museum.

Finkelstein, Irving L. Prints of the High Museum: Image & Process. Morris, Kelly, ed. LC 78-61741. (Illus.). 72p. (Orig.). 1978. pap. 4.00 (ISBN 0-939802-06-6). High Mus Art.

Flower, William H. Essays on Museums. LC 72-6793. (Essay Index Reprint Ser). 1972. Repr. of 1898 ed. 18.75 (ISBN 0-8369-7255-4). Arno.

Girouard, Mark. Alfred Waterhouse & the Natural History Museum. (Illus.). 64p. 1981. pap. 4.50x (ISBN 0-565-00831-5, Pub. by Brit Mus Nat Hist England). Sabbot-Natural Hist Bks.

--Alfred Waterhouse & the Natural History Museum. LC 80-53742. (Illus.). 1981. 12.95x (ISBN 0-300-02578-5). Yale U Pr.

Greene, Richard L. & Wheeling, Kenneth E. A Pictorial History of the Shelburne Museum. (Illus., Orig.). 1972. pap. 6.00 (ISBN 0-939384-04-3). Shelburne.

Greenfield, Kent R. The Museum, Its First Half Century: Annual I. (Illus.). 1968. pap. 4.00 (ISBN 0-912298-25-1). Baltimore Mus.

The Guarding of Cultural Property: Protection of the Cultural Heritage - Technical Handbooks for Museums & Monuments. (Illus.). 40p. 1978. pap. 4.75 (ISBN 92-3-101429-3, U813, UNESCO). Unipub.

Harrison, Molly. Museums & Galleries. (Local Search Ser). (Illus.). 1973. 7.50 (ISBN 0-7100-7588-X). Routledge & Kegan.

Hartman, Hedy A. Funding Sources & Technical Assistance for Museums & Historical Agencies. (Orig.). 1979. pap. text ed. 10.00 (ISBN 0-910050-40-6). AASLH.
Harvey, Emily D. & Friedberg, Bernard, eds. A Museum for the People. LC 78-155728. 1971. 5.95 (ISBN 0-405-02568-8). Arno.
Hodge, G. Stuart. Flint Institute of Arts: Highlights from the Collections. (Illus.). 84p. (Orig.). 1979. pap. 5.00 (ISBN 0-939896-01-X). Flint Inst Arts.
Hudson, Kenneth. Museums for the Nineteen Hundred & Eighties: A Survey of World Trends. LC 77-24930. 1978. text ed. 49.50x (ISBN 0-8419-0327-1). Holmes & Meier.
--A Social History of Museums. 150p. 1975. text ed. 15.00x (ISBN 0-391-00402-6). Humanities.
Hunt, David C. Guide to Oklahoma Museums. LC 80-5939. (Illus.). 256p. 1981. 17.50 (ISBN 0-8061-1567-X); pap. 9.95 (ISBN 0-8061-1752-4). U of Okla Pr.
James, Betsy. A Museum Sketchbook. (Illus.). 1976. pap. 2.25 (ISBN 0-89013-087-6). Museum NM Pr.
Keck, Caroline K. A Primer on Museum Security. pap. 2.50 (ISBN 0-686-26191-7). Fenimore Bk.
Krakel, Dean. Adventures in Western Art. LC 76-21136. (Illus.). 1977. 11.95 (ISBN 0-913504-35-1). Lowell Pr.
Kuehnemund, Terry M., ed. Treasure House: Museums of the Empire State. LC 79-53226. (Illus.). 1979. pap. 10.00 (ISBN 0-89062-042-3). Pub Ctr Cult Res.
Learner, Howard. White Paper on Science Museums. (Orig.). 1979. pap. 4.00 (ISBN 0-89329-025-4). Ctr Sci Public.
Martin, John H., ed. The Corning Flood: Museum Under Water. LC 77-73627. (Illus.). 1977. pap. 6.00 (ISBN 0-87290-063-0). Corning.
Masterpieces of the Peabody Museum. LC 78-67472. 1978. pap. 3.50 (ISBN 0-87365-797-7). Peabody Harvard.
Migne, J. P., ed. Dictionnaire des Muses ou Description des Principaux Musees d'Europe... Suivi Notions sur la Photographie par X. (Troisieme et Derniere Encyclopedie Theologique Ser.: Vol. 4). 740p. (Fr.). Date not set. Repr. of 1855 ed. lib. bdg. 95.00x (ISBN 0-89241-291-7). Caratzas Bros.
Museum Assoc., ed. Museums Yearbook, 1979. 1980. 50.00x (ISBN 0-686-75466-2, Pub. by Mus Assn England). State Mutual Bk.
Museum Council of Philadelphia, ed. Guide to Museums in the Delaware Valley. (Illus.). 122p. pap. 2.95 (ISBN 0-87982-021-7). Art Alliance.
Museums & Children. 195p. 1980. pap. 10.50 (ISBN 92-3-101692-X, U 969, UNESCO). Unipub.
Museums for the 1980's: A Survey of World Trends. (Illus.). 1978. 49.50 (ISBN 92-3-101435-8, U-807, UNESCO). Unipub.
Museums Yearbook, 1980. 1980. 75.00x (ISBN 0-686-75467-0, Pub. by Mus Assn England). State Mutual Bk.
Neal, Arminta. Help! for the Small Museum. LC 70-75438. (Illus.). 1969. pap. 9.95 (ISBN 0-87108-138-5). Pruett.
The Organization of Museums: Practical Advice. (Illus.). 1960. pap. 15.00 (ISBN 92-3-100441-7, U441, UNESCO). Unipub.
Perry, Kenneth, ed. The Museum Forms Book. 390p. (Orig.). 1980. pap. text ed. 10.00 (ISBN 0-935260-01-3). Tex Assn Mus.
Protection of Museum Collections: 2eight Hundred & Nine Hundred Ser. 1974. pap. 2.50 (ISBN 0-685-58198-5, 911). Natl Fire Prot.
Ragghianti, C. L. Treasures of the Egyptian Museum-Cairo. LC 69-19066. (Illus.). 1978. pap. 9.95 (ISBN 0-88225-262-3). Newsweek.
Ripley, S. Dillon. The Sacred Grove: Essays on Museums. LC 78-10785. 1979. pap. 4.50 (ISBN 0-87474-809-7). Smithsonian.
Roat, Evelyn C. The Museum of Northern Arizona. (MNA Special Publication Ser.: No. 8). 1968. 4.00 (ISBN 0-89734-016-7); pap. 0.60 (ISBN 0-89734-015-9). Mus Northern Ariz.
Rose, Roger G. A Museum to Instruct & Delight. LC 80-69203. (Special Publication Ser.: No. 68). (Illus.). 96p. 1980. pap. 6.50 (ISBN 0-910240-28-0). Bishop Mus.
Rudman, Jack. Museum Attendant. (Career Examination Ser.: C-1374). (Cloth bdg. avail. on request). pap. 8.00 (ISBN 0-8373-1374-0). Natl Learning.
--Museum Curator. (Career Examination Ser.: C-1375). (Cloth bdg. avail. on request). pap. 10.00 (ISBN 0-8373-1375-9). Natl Learning.
--Museum Instructor. (Career Examination Ser.: C-1705). (Cloth bdg. avail. on request). pap. 10.00 (ISBN 0-8373-1705-3). Natl Learning.
--Museum Intern. (Career Examination Ser.: C-1376). (Cloth bdg. avail. on request). pap. 8.00 (ISBN 0-8373-1376-7). Natl Learning.
--Museum Laboratory Technician. (Career Examination Ser.: C-1377). (Cloth bdg. avail. on request). pap. 8.00 (ISBN 0-8373-1377-5). Natl Learning.
--Museum Technician. (Career Examination Ser.: C-522). (Cloth bdg. avail. on request). pap. 8.00 (ISBN 0-8373-0522-5). Natl Learning.
--Senior Museum Instructor. (Career Examination Ser.: C-1016). (Cloth bdg. avail. on request). pap. 10.00 (ISBN 0-8373-1016-4). Natl Learning.
--Supervising Museum Instructor. (Career Examination Ser.: C-1048). (Cloth bdg. avail. on request). pap. 10.00 (ISBN 0-8373-1048-2). Natl Learning.
Sellers, Charles C. Mr. Peale's Museum: Charles Willson Peale & the First Popular Museum of Natural Science. (Barra Bks.). (Illus.). 1980. 14.95 (ISBN 0-393-05700-3). Norton.
Shishkin, J. K. The New Museum Is a Wonder. (Illus.). 1968. pap. 0.50 (ISBN 0-89013-033-7). Museum NM Pr.
Sloan, Blanche C. & Swinburne, Bruce R. Campus Art Museums & Galleries: A Profile. LC 80-23418. 64p. (Orig.). 1981. pap. 9.95 (ISBN 0-8093-1005-8). S Ill U Pr.
Smith, Watson. The Story of the Museum of Northern Arizona. (MNA Special Publication Ser.). 1969. pap. 0.75 (ISBN 0-89734-014-0). Mus Northern Ariz.
Springfield Museum of Fine Arts. The Gloucester Years. (Illus.). 1980. 8.00 (ISBN 0-686-30581-7). Springfield Lib & Mus.
Toledo Museum of Art Staff. Toledo Museum of Art, European Paintings. LC 76-24500. (Illus.). 396p. 1976. lib. bdg. 22.50 (ISBN 0-271-01249-8); pap. 12.95 (ISBN 0-271-01248-X). Toledo Mus Art.
Torres, Heloisa A. Museums of Brazil. 1976. lib. bdg. 59.95 (ISBN 0-8490-0680-5). Gordon Pr.
Wasserman, Paul, ed. Catalog of Museum Publications & Media. 2nd ed. LC 79-22633. 1980. 148.00 (ISBN 0-8103-0388-4). Gale.
White, Anne. Visiting Museums. (Illus.). 1968. 7.50x (ISBN 0-571-08741-8). Intl Pubns Serv.
Whitehill, Walter M. Cabinet of Curiosities: Five Episodes in the Evolution of American Museums. LC 67-21660. (Illus.). 1967. 8.95x (ISBN 0-8139-0238-X). U Pr of Va.
Zelger, Franz. The Oskar Reinhart Collections. Dembo, Margot, tr. LC 81-50896. (Museums Discovered Ser.). (Illus.). 208p. 1981. 22.50 (ISBN 0-686-75687-8, Woodbine Bks); leather binding 27.50 (ISBN 0-934516-39-1). Shorewood Fine Art.

MUSEUMS–BIBLIOGRAPHY

International Council of Museums. International Museological Bibliography-Bibliographie Museologique Internationale. 1968 ed. 1970 5.00x (ISBN 0-8002-0836-6); 1970 ed. 1973 5.00x (ISBN 0-8002-0837-4); 1972-73 ed. 1974 8.00x (ISBN 0-8002-0518-9). Intl Pubns Serv.
Museums of the World. rev. 3rd ed. (Handbook of International Documentation & Information Ser.). 623p. 1981. 185.00 (ISBN 0-686-76770-5). Gale.
Roulstone, Michael, ed. The Bibliography of Museum & Art Gallery Publications & Audio-Visual Aids in Great Britain & Ireland, 1979-80. LC 80-15709. 560p. 1980. 89.50x (ISBN 0-930466-23-3). Meckler Bks.

MUSEUMS–DATA PROCESSING

Chenhall, Robert G. Museum Cataloging in the Computer Age. LC 74-16439. (Illus.). viii, 261p. 1975. 17.50 (ISBN 0-910050-12-0). AASLH.
Computers & Their Potential Applications in Museums. LC 68-58185. Repr. of 1968 ed. 12.50 (ISBN 0-405-00014-6). Arno.
Orna, Elizabeth. Information Retrieval for Museums. 1980. text ed. 12.00 (ISBN 0-89664-440-5). K G Saur.

MUSEUMS–DIRECTORIES

Allen, Jon. Aviation & Space Museums of America. LC 73-91258. (Illus.). 192p. 1975. 12.00 (ISBN 0-668-03426-2); pap. 6.95 (ISBN 0-668-03631-1). Arco.
Hanauer, Gary. Small Museums of the West. Vandenburgh, Jane, ed. LC 80-67476. (Illus.). 288p. (Orig.). Date not set. pap. 9.95 (ISBN 0-89395-051-3). Cal Living Bks.
Handbook of Museums. 2nd ed. 750p. 1981. 175.00 (ISBN 0-686-72833-5, Pub. by K G Saur). Gale.
Harnik, Tema. Wherewithal: A Guide to Resources for Museums & Historical Societies. 120p. (Orig.). 1981. pap. write for info. (ISBN 0-935654-01-1, Pub. by Ctr for Arts Info). Pub Ctr Cult Res.
Hodupp, Shelley, compiled by. Second Shopper's Guide to Museum Stores. LC 78-52191. (Illus.). 1978. pap. 7.95 (ISBN 0-87663-983-X). Universe.
--The Shopper's Guide to Museum Stores. LC 76-41662. (Illus.). 1977. pap. 6.95 (ISBN 0-87663-935-X). Universe.
Hudson, Kenneth & Nicholls, Ann. The Directory of World Museums. 2nd ed. LC 80-21695. 681p. 1981. 75.00 (ISBN 0-87196-468-6). Facts on File.
--Directory of World Museums. 1974. 75.00x (ISBN 0-685-49917-0, 0-231-3907-7). Columbia U Pr.
Mueller, Kimberly J., ed. California Museum Directory. LC 78-78310. (California Information Guides Ser.). 1980. pap. 15.00x (ISBN 0-912102-41-1). Cal Inst Public.
Museums & Art Galleries in Great Britain and Ireland 1980. LC 58-46943. (Illus.). 108p. (Orig.). 1980. pap. 4.50x (ISBN 0-900486-27-9). Intl Pubns Serv.
Museums of the World. 3rd ed. 1981. 195.00 (ISBN 0-686-69416-3, Dist. by Gale Research). K G Saur.
National Register Publishing Co. The Official Museum Directory. LC 79-144805. 1981. 53.35 (ISBN 0-87217-005-5). Natl Register.
Official Museum Products & Services Directory. 1981. 27.00 (ISBN 0-686-75086-1). Natl Register.
Old Slave Mart Museum & Library. Catalog of the Old Slave Mart Museum & Library. 1978. lib. bdg. 125.00 (ISBN 0-8161-0073-X). G K Hall.
Rubin, Cynthia & Rubin, Jerome. Guide to Massachusetts Museums, Historic Houses & Points of Interest. new ed. 126p. (Orig.). 1972. pap. 1.95 (ISBN 0-88278-004-2). Emporium Pubns.

MUSEUMS–JUVENILE LITERATURE

Adams, P., illus. The Child's Play Museum. (Illus.). 1977. text ed. 4.50 (ISBN 0-85953-094-9, Pub. by Childs's Play England). Playspaces.
Burns, William A. Enjoying the Arts: Museums. (YA) 1977. PLB 7.97 (ISBN 0-8239-0389-3). Rosen Pr.
Sandak, Cass R. Museums: What They Are and How They Work. (First Bks.). (Illus.). 72p. (gr. 4 up). 1981. lib. bdg. 7.40 (ISBN 0-531-04348-7). Watts.
Weisgard, Leonard. Treasures to See: A Museum Picture-Book. LC 56-10739. (Illus.). (gr. k-3). 1956. 6.95 (ISBN 0-15-290337-2, HJ). HarBraceJ.
White, Anne. Visiting Museums. (Illus.). 1968. 7.50x (ISBN 0-571-08741-8). Intl Pubns Serv.

MUSEUMS–EGYPT

Boardman, John & Vollenweider, Marie-Louise. Catalogue of the Engraved Gems & Finger Rings in the Ashmoleaw Museum, Vol. I: Green & Etruscan. (Illus.). 1978. 79.00 (ISBN 0-19-813195-X). Oxford U Pr.

MUSEUMS–FRANCE

Etoffes Merveilleuses Du Musee Historique Des Tissus, Lyon. Incl. Vol. I. France - 17th & 18th Century (ISBN 0-8120-5211-0); Vol. II. France - 19th & 20th Century (ISBN 0-8120-5212-9); Vol. III. Spain, Italy & Orient (ISBN 0-8120-5213-7). (Illus.). 1977. 395.00 ea. Barron.
Tresors des Musees de Province, 5 tomes. Set. 209.95 (ISBN 0-685-35924-7). French & Eur.

MUSEUMS–GREAT BRITAIN

Abse, Joan. The Art Galleries of Britain & Ireland: A Guide to Their Collections. LC 75-24944. (Illus.). 248p. 1975. 15.00 (ISBN 0-8386-1850-2). Fairleigh Dickinson.
Greater London Council. Survey of London, Vol. 38: The Museum Area of South Kensington & Westminster. (Illus.). 480p. 1975. text ed. 83.25x (ISBN 0-485-48238-X, Athlone Pr). Humanities.
Museums & Galleries in Great Britain & Ireland 1979. LC 58-46943. (British Historic Guides Ser). (Illus.). 1979. 3.50x (ISBN 0-900486-24-4). Intl Pubns Serv.
Museums & Galleries of Great Britain & Ireland. pap. 3.00 (ISBN 0-8277-0375-9). British Bk Ctr.
Roulstone, Michael, ed. The Bibliography of Museum & Art Gallery Publications & Audio-Visual Aids in Great Britain & Ireland, 1979-80. LC 80-15709. 560p. 1980. 89.50x (ISBN 0-930466-23-3). Meckler Bks.
Winstanley, Barbara. Children & Museums. (Illus.). 1967. 5.00x (ISBN 0-8002-0718-1). Intl Pubns Serv.

MUSEUMS–GREECE

Andronicus, M., et al. The Greek Museums. 1981. 90.00x (ISBN 0-686-75404-2). State Mutual Bk.
Andronikos, M., et al. Greek Museums. (Illus.). 420p. 1975. 65.00 (ISBN 0-89241-005-1). Caratzas Bros.
--The Greek Museums. Incl. Acropolis. soft bd. 7.50 (ISBN 0-685-83206-6); Benaki. soft bd. 7.50 (ISBN 0-685-83207-4); Byzantine. soft bd. 7.50 (ISBN 0-685-83208-2); Cyprus. soft bd. 7.50 (ISBN 0-685-83209-0); Delphi. oft bd. 7.50 (ISBN 0-685-83210-4); Herakleion. soft bd. 7.50 (ISBN 0-685-83211-2); National. soft bd. 9.00 (ISBN 0-685-83212-0); Olympia. soft bd. 7.50 (ISBN 0-685-83213-9); Pella. soft bd. 7.50 (ISBN 0-685-83214-7); Thessalonike. soft bd. 7.50 (ISBN 0-685-83215-5). (Illus.). 1977. Caratzas Bros.
Andronikos, Manolis. Herakleion Museum & Archaeological Sites of Crete. new ed. Lidell, Robert, tr. from Gr. (The Greek Museum Ser). (Illus.). 56p. (Orig.). 1975. pap. 7.50 (ISBN 0-89241-012-4). Caratzas Bros.
--National Museum. Jongh, Brian De, tr. from Gr. (Greek Museums Ser.). (Illus.). 114p. 1975. pap. 9.00 (ISBN 0-89241-007-8). Caratzas Bros.
--Olympia. new ed. Cicellis, Kay, tr. from Gr. (The Greek Museums Ser). (Illus.). 52p. 1975. pap. 7.50 (ISBN 0-89241-009-4). Caratzas Bros.
--Pella Museum. Cicellis, Kay, tr. from Gr. (The Greek Museums Ser). (Illus.). 28p. (Orig.). 1975. pap. 7.50 (ISBN 0-89241-010-8). Caratzas Bros.
--Thessalonike Archaeological Museum. Cicellis, Kay, tr. (The Greek Museums Ser). (Illus.). 32p. (Orig.). 1975. pap. 7.50 (ISBN 0-89241-013-2). Caratzas Bros.
Chatzidakis, Manolis. Benaki Museum. Cicellis, Kay, tr. from Gr. (Greek Museums Ser.). (Illus.). 48p. 1975. pap. 7.50 (ISBN 0-89241-015-9). Caratzas Bros.
--Byzantine Museum. Jonas, Brian De, tr. from Gr. (Greek Museums Ser.). (Illus.). 44p. 1975. pap. 7.50 (ISBN 0-89241-014-0). Caratzas Bros.
Karageorghis, Vassos. Cyprus Museum & Archaeological Sites of Cyprus. Cicellis, Kay, tr. from Gr. (The Greek Museums Ser). (Illus.). 56p. 1975. pap. 7.50 (ISBN 0-89241-011-6). Caratzas Bros.
Karouzou, Semni. The National Museum. (Illustrated Travel Guides Ser.). (Illus.). 1979. pap. 9.95 (ISBN 0-89241-100-7). Caratzas Bros.
Papahatzis, Nicos. Ancient Corinth: The Museums of Corinth, Isthmia & Sicyon. (Illustrated Travel Guides Ser.). (Illus.). 1979. pap. 9.95 (ISBN 0-89241-103-1). Caratzas Bros.
Sakellarakis, J. A. Herakleion Museum. (Illustrated Travel Guides Ser.). (Illus.). 1979. pap. 9.95 (ISBN 0-89241-101-5). Caratzas Bros.

MUSEUMS–HUNGARY

Fulep, Ferenc, ed. The Hungarian National Museum. Hoch, Elizabeth, tr. Date not set. 15.95 (ISBN 0-89893-161-4). CDP.
Garas, Klara, intro. by. Paintings in the Budapest Museum of Fine Arts. Halapy, Lili, tr. Date not set. 15.95 (ISBN 0-89893-160-6). CDP.
The Hungarian National Museum. Hoch, Elisabeth, tr. from Hungarian. (Illus.). 1978. 12.50x (ISBN 963-13-0268-7). Intl Pubns Serv.
Kisdegi-Kirimi, Iren, intro. by. Still-Lifes in the Hungarian National Gallery. Halapy, Lily, tr. Date not set. 15.95 (ISBN 0-89893-162-2). CDP.
Solymar, Istvan, ed. Collections of the Hungarian National Gallery. Bodoczky, Caroline & Bodoczky, Istvan, trs. Date not set. 15.95 (ISBN 0-89893-159-2). CDP.
Supka, Magdolna B., intro. by. Genre Painting in the Hungarian National Gallery. Compton, Agnes, tr. Date not set. 15.95 (ISBN 0-89893-154-1). CDP.

MUSEUMS–JAPAN

Roberts, Laurance O. Roberts' Guide to Japanese Museums. LC 77-75965. 348p. 1978. 12.50 (ISBN 0-87011-306-2). Kodansha.

MUSEUMS–PUERTO RICO

Gordon, Raoul, ed. The Museums of Puerto Rico. 1976. lib. bdg. 59.95 (ISBN 0-8490-0681-3). Gordon Pr.

MUSEUMS–RUSSIA

Derzhavina, M. Central V. I. Lenin Museum. 3.50 (ISBN 0-8285-1790-8, Pub by Progress Pubs Russia). Imported Pubns.
Kozhina, Elena, intro. by. The Hermitage: Western European Painting of the 13th to 18th Centuries. Date not set. 19.95 (ISBN 0-89893-002-2). CDP.
Linnik, I., compiled by. The Hermitage: Western European Painting. Pamfilov, Yu. & Nemetsky, Yu., trs. Date not set. 24.95 (ISBN 0-89893-001-4). CDP.
Piotrovsky, Boris, intro. by. The Hermitage Picture Gallery. Date not set. 24.95 (ISBN 0-686-31466-2). CDP.

MUSEUMS–SPAIN

Mercader, Gasper. El Prado De Valencia. Repr. of 1907 ed. 26.00 (ISBN 0-384-38150-2). Johnson Repr.

MUSEUMS-YUGOSLAVIA

Srejovic, Dragoslav. Museums of Yugoslavia. La Farge, Henry, ed. LC 76-56055. (Great Museums of the World Ser.). (Illus.). 1977. 16.95 (ISBN 0-88225-240-2). Newsweek.

MUSEUMS AND SCHOOLS

Thomas, Minor W., Jr. Springfield Armory Museum, Springfield, Massachusetts: Proposals for Academic Museum Curricula. (Consultant Service Grant Report). (Illus.). 1974. pap. 2.00 (ISBN 0-89133-025-9). Preservation Pr.

Zetterberg, Hans L. Museums & Adult Education. LC 70-95622. (Illus.). 1969. lib. bdg. 10.00x (ISBN 0-678-07753-3). Kelley.

MUSGRAVE, JAMES E.

Fletcher, Jesse C. Search for Blonnye Foreman. LC 69-17895. 1969. 3.25 (ISBN 0-8054-7209-6). Broadman.

MUSHROOM CULTURE

Chang, S. T. & Hayes, W. A., eds. The Biology & Cultivation of Edible Mushrooms. LC 77-6591. 1978. 77.50 (ISBN 0-12-168050-9). Acad Pr.

Duggar, B. M. Cultivation of Mushrooms. facs. ed. Repr. of 1904 ed. pap. 3.95 (ISBN 0-8466-6038-5, SJU38). Shorey.

Genders, Roy. Growing Mushrooms. 108p. 1976. 6.95 (ISBN 0-7207-0903-2, Pub. by Michael Joseph). Merrimack Bk Serv.

--Mushroom Growing for Everyone. 1970. 11.50 (ISBN 0-571-08992-5). Transatlantic.

Harris, Bob. Growing Wild Mushrooms. (Illus.). pap. 4.95 (ISBN 0-914728-17-2). Wingbow Pr.

Lincoff, Gary H. The Audubon Society Field Guide to North American Mushrooms. LC 81-80827. (Illus.). 864p. 1981. 11.95 (ISBN 0-394-51992-2). Knopf.

Mueller, Jo. Growing Your Own Mushrooms: Cultivating, Cooking & Preserving. (Illus.). 176p. 1976. o. p. 8.95 (ISBN 0-88266-090-X); pap. 6.95 (ISBN 0-88266-089-6). Garden Way Pub.

Petersen, R. H. A Monograph of Ramaria Subgenus Echinoramaria. (Bibliotheca Mycologica). (Illus.). 150p. 1981. lib. bdg. 30.00x (ISBN 3-7682-1290-4). Lubrecht & Cramer.

Pollock, Steven H. Magic Mushroom Cultivation. (Illus.). 1981. pap. 6.00 (ISBN 0-930074-01-7). Herbal Med.

Watling, Roy. How to Identify Mushrooms to Genus V. Using Cultural & Developmental Features. 1981. pap. 6.95 (ISBN 0-916422-17-8). Mad River.

MUSHROOMS

see also Cookery (Mushrooms); Fungi; Mushroom Culture; Truffles

Arora, David. Mushrooms Demystified. LC 79-8513. (Illus.). 680p. 1979. 18.95 (ISBN 0-89815-010-8); pap. 11.95 (ISBN 0-89815-009-4). Ten Speed Pr.

Atkinson, G. F. Studies of American Fungi: Mushrooms, Edible, Poisonous, Etc. (Illus.). 1961. Repr. of 1903 ed. 21.75 (ISBN 0-02-840600-1). Hafner.

Barr, M. E. Diaporthales in North America with Emphasis on Gnomonia and Its Segregates. (Mycologia Memoirs: No. 7). (Illus.). 1977. lib. bdg. 40.00 (ISBN 3-7682-1189-4). Lubrecht & Cramer.

Big D Unlimited. A Guidebook to the Psilocybin Mushrooms of Mexico. (Illus., Orig.). 1976. pap. 2.50x (ISBN 0-934600-01-5). Mother Duck Pr.

Bigelow, Howard E. Mushroom Pocket Field Guide. (Illus.). 1979. pap. 4.95 (ISBN 0-02-062200-7, Collier). Macmillan.

Charles, Vera K. Introduction to Mushroom Hunting. (Illus.). 3.50 (ISBN 0-8446-5015-3). Peter Smith.

Christensen, Clyde M. Common Fleshy Fungi. 3rd ed. LC 65-11818. 1965. spiral bdg. 10.95x (ISBN 0-8087-0312-9). Burgess.

--Molds, Mushrooms, & Mycotoxins. LC 74-21808. (Illus.). 292p. 1975. 15.00x (ISBN 0-8166-0743-5). U of Minn Pr.

Coker, William C. The Club & Coral Mushrooms (Clavarias) of the United States & Canada. (Illus.). 8.00 (ISBN 0-8446-5171-0). Peter Smith.

Coker, William C. & Beers, Alma. The Boleti of North Carolina. (Illus.). 163p. 1974. pap. 4.50 (ISBN 0-486-20377-8). Dover.

Dickerman, Alexandra. The Mushroom Growing & Cooking Book. LC 77-87212. (Illus., Orig.). 1978. pap. 3.95 (ISBN 0-912800-45-3). Woodbridge Pr.

Dickinson, Colin & Lucas, John. The Encyclopedia of Mushrooms. LC 77-14635. (Illus.). 1979. 25.00 (ISBN 0-399-12104-8). Putnam.

Farlow, W. G. Some Edible & Poisonous Fungi. facs. ed. 17p. Repr. of 1897 ed. pap. 3.50 (ISBN 0-8466-6001-6, SJU1). Shorey.

Findlay, W. P. Observer's Book of Mushrooms, Toadstools, & Other Common Fungi. (Observer Bks.). (Illus.). 1977. 3.95 (ISBN 0-684-15201-0, ScribT). Scribner.

Froman, Robert. Mushrooms & Molds. LC 71-187936. (A Let's-Read-&-Find-Out Science Book). (Illus.). (gr. k-3). 1972. PLB 8.79 (ISBN 0-690-56603-4, TYC-J). Har-Row.

Glick, Phyllis. The Mushroom Trail Guide. LC 78-18424. (Illus.). 1979. 9.95 (ISBN 0-03-018306-5); pap. 5.95 (ISBN 0-03-018301-4). HR&W.

Graham, Verne O. Mushrooms of the Great Lakes Region. (Illus.). 9.00 (ISBN 0-8446-0656-1). Peter Smith.

--Mushrooms of the Great Lakes Region. (Illus.). 1970. pap. 5.00 (ISBN 0-486-22538-0). Dover.

Guild, Ben. Alaskan Mushroom Hunter's Guide. LC 76-29729. (Illus.). 1977. pap. 13.95 (ISBN 0-88240-064-9). Alaska Northwest.

Haard, Richard & Haard, Karen. Poisonous & Hallucinogenic Mushrooms. 2nd ed. (Illus.). 164p. 1980. pap. 7.95 (ISBN 0-930180-05-4). Homestead Bk.

Hard, Miron E. Mushrooms, Edible & Otherwise: Habitat & Time of Growth. 12.50 (ISBN 0-8446-5452-3). Peter Smith.

Hesler, L. R. Entoloma (Rhodophyllus) in Southeastern North America. 1967. pap. 40.00 (ISBN 3-7682-5423-2). Lubrecht & Cramer.

--Mushrooms of the Great Smokies: A Field Guide to Some Mushrooms & Their Relatives. LC 60-12221. (Illus.). 1960. 9.95 (ISBN 0-87049-028-1). U of Tenn Pr.

Jackson, H. A. Mr. Jackson's Mushrooms. Cazort, Mimi, intro. by. (Illus.). 1979. 35.00 (ISBN 0-88884-364-X, 56430-4, Pub. by Natl Gallery Canada). U of Chicago Pr.

Jenkins, D. T. Taxonomic & Nomenclatural Study of the Genus Amanita Section Amanita for North America. (Bibliotheca Mycologica Ser.: No. 57). (Illus.). 1977. lib. bdg. 30.00x (ISBN 3-7682-1132-0). Lubrecht & Cramer.

Jenkins, David T. A Taxonomic & Nomenclatural Study of the Genus Amanita Section Amanita for North America. (Bibliotheca Mycologica: Band 57). (Illus.). 1978. pap. 25.00x (ISBN 3-7682-1132-0, Pub. by J Cramer). Intl Schol Bk Serv.

Kavaler, Lucy. Mushrooms, Moulds & Miracles: The Strange World of Fungi. 5.95 (ISBN 0-686-05401-6). British Am Bks.

Kibby, Geoffrey. Mushrooms & Toadstools: A Field Guide. (Illus.). 256p. 1979. text ed. 23.00x (ISBN 0-19-217688-9). Oxford U Pr.

Kreisel, H. Die Phytopathogehen Grosspilze Deutschlands (Basidiomycetes mit Ausschluss der Rost-und Brandpilze) (Illus.). 1979. Repr. of 1961 ed. lib. bdg. 25.00x (ISBN 3-7682-1228-9). Lubrecht & Cramer.

Krieger, L. C. Mushroom Handbook. (Illus.). 10.00 (ISBN 0-8446-2404-7). Peter Smith.

Krieger, Louis C. Mushroom Handbook. (Illus.). 1967. pap. 5.00 (ISBN 0-486-21861-9). Dover.

Largent, David. How to Identify Mushrooms (to Genus I) Macroscopic Features. 2nd ed. (Illus.). 86p. 1977. pap. 4.85x (ISBN 0-916422-00-3). Mad River.

Largent, David, et al. How to Identify Mushrooms (to Genus III) Microscopic Features. (Illus.). 148p. 1977. pap. 8.25x (ISBN 0-916422-09-7). Mad River.

Largent, David L. & Thiers, H. How to Identify Mushrooms (to Genus II): Field Identification of Genera. (Illus.). 32p. 1977. pap. 3.50x (ISBN 0-916422-08-9). Mad River.

Lincoff, Gary. S&S Guide to Mushrooms. 1981. 22.50 (ISBN 0-671-42798-9, Fireside); pap. 9.95 (ISBN 0-671-42849-7). S&S.

McIlvaine, Charles & MacAdam, Robert. One Thousand American Fungi. (Illus.). 729p. 1973. pap. 6.95 (ISBN 0-486-22782-0). Dover.

McKenny, Margaret. The Savory Wild Mushroom. rev. ed. Stuntz, Daniel E., ed. LC 78-160288. (Illus.). 296p. 1971. 15.95 (ISBN 0-295-95155-9); pap. 8.95 (ISBN 0-295-95156-7). U of Wash Pr.

Major, Alan. Collecting & Studying Mushrooms, Toadstools, & Fungi. (Illus.). 1975. 12.00 (ISBN 0-668-03725-3). Arco.

Marteka, Vincent. Mushrooms - Wild & Edible: A Seasonal Guide to the Most Easily Recognized Mushrooms. (Illus.). 1980. 19.95 (ISBN 0-393-01356-1). Norton.

Matsumoto, Kosai. The Mysterious Reishi Mushroom: Its Amazing Medicinal Uses. LC 78-71030. (Lifeline Bks.). (Illus.). 1979. pap. 2.95 (ISBN 0-912800-52-6). Woodbridge Pr.

Menser, Gary. Hallucinogenic & Poisonous Mushroom Field Guide. LC 77-89431. (Illus.). 1977. pap. 5.95 (ISBN 0-915904-28-4). And-or Pr.

Miller, Orson K., et al. Multi-Purpose Mushroom Calendar: 1982. (Illus.). 12p. (Orig.). 1981. pap. 8.80 without mailer (ISBN 0-686-73525-0); pap. text ed. 9.95 with mailer (ISBN 0-686-73526-9). Mad River.

Miller, Orson K., Jr. Mushrooms of North America. rev. ed. 1979. 16.95 (ISBN 0-525-16166-X); pap. 10.95 (ISBN 0-525-47482-X). Dutton.

Miller, Richard A. & Tatelman, David. Magical Mushroom Handbook. 2nd rev. ed. (Illus.). 1977. pap. 2.95 (ISBN 0-930180-01-1). Homestead Bk.

Mori, Kisaku. Mushrooms As Health Foods. Orig. Title: Mushrooms & Molds-Nutritional & Medicinal Benefits. (Illus.). 112p. (Orig.). 1974. pap. 3.25 (ISBN 0-87040-332-X). Japan Pubns.

Myer, Donna. Answers to Your Mushroom Questions Plus Recipes. LC 77-87780. (Illus.). 1977. pap. 3.95x (ISBN 0-9601516-1-3). Mushroom Cave.

Neuner, Andreas. Mushrooms & Fungi. LC 78-316610. (Nature Guides Ser.). (Illus.). 144p. 1979. pap. 5.95 (ISBN 0-7011-2328-1, Pub. by Chatto Bodley Jonathan). Merrimack Bk Serv.

Norland, Richard H. Mushroom Classification Bibliography to What's in a Mushroom: Nutritional & Medical Mushrooms, Pt. 1. 1977. pap. text ed. 5.95 (ISBN 0-918578-02-7). Pear Tree.

--Psilocybin Bibliography: Companion to What's in a Mushroom, Pt. 3. 1977. pap. text ed. 5.95x (ISBN 0-918578-06-X). Pear Tree.

--Toxic Mushroom Bibliography: Companion to What's in a Mushroom, 426 Toxic Mushrooms, Pt. 2. pap. 5.95 (ISBN 0-918578-04-3). Pear Tree.

--What's in a Mushroom, 3 pts. Incl. Pt. 1. Nutritional & Medical Mushrooms. 13.95 (ISBN 0-918578-12-4); pap. 9.95 (ISBN 0-918578-01-9); Pt. 2. Four Hundred Twenty-Six Toxic Mushrooms. 11.95 (ISBN 0-918578-14-0); pap. 7.95 (ISBN 0-918578-03-5); Pt. 3. Psycho-Active Mushrooms. 9.95 (ISBN 0-918578-16-7); pap. 5.95 (ISBN 0-918578-05-1). (Illus.). 1977. 29.95 (ISBN 0-918578-11-6). Pear Tree.

Ola'h, Gyorgy M. Le Pleurote Quebecois: Comment Cultiver Ce Champignon et Comment le Cuisiner. (Illus.). 1976. pap. 5.95 (ISBN 0-7746-6767-2, Pub. by Laval). Intl Schol Bk Serv.

Orr, Robert T. & Orr, Dorothy B. Mushrooms & Other Common Fungi of Southern California. (California Natural History Guides: No. 22). (Illus.). 1968. pap. 1.75 (ISBN 0-520-00978-9). U of Cal Pr.

--Mushrooms of Western North America. LC 77-93468. (Illus.). 1980. 12.95 (ISBN 0-520-03656-5). U of Cal Pr.

Ott, Jonathan & Bigwood, Jeremy, eds. Teonanacatl: Hallucinogenic Mushrooms of North America. LC 78-14794. 1978. 14.50x (ISBN 0-914842-32-3); pap. 8.95 (ISBN 0-914842-29-3). Madrona Pubs.

Parker, Loni & Jenkins, David T. Mushrooms: A Separate Kingdom. LC 79-88459. (Illus.). 1979. 16.95 (ISBN 0-8487-0501-7). Oxmoor Hse.

Rattan, S. S. & Khurana, I. P. S. The Clavaria of the Sikkim Himalayas. (Bibliotheca Mycologica Ser.: No. 66). (Illus.). 1978. pap. text ed. 12.50x (ISBN 3-7682-1212-2). Lubrecht & Cramer.

Rayner, Ronald. Mushrooms & Toadstools. (Illus.). 128p. 1980. 8.95 (ISBN 0-600-36283-3). Transatlantic.

Rice, Miriam C. How to Use Mushrooms for Color. rev. ed. (Illus.). 145p. 1980. pap. 8.10 (ISBN 0-916422-19-4). Mad River.

Rinaldi, Augusto & Tyndalo, Vassili. The Complete Book of Mushrooms: Over 1,000 Species & Varieties of American, European, & Asiatic Mushrooms. (Illus.). 330p. 1974. 17.95 (ISBN 0-517-51493-1). Crown.

Savonius, Moira. All Color Book of Mushrooms & Fungi. (Bounty Bks.). (Illus.). 72p. 1974. pap. 2.95 (ISBN 0-517-51410-9). Crown.

Singer, R. Boletinae of Florida with Notes on Extralimital Species: 4 Parts in One Vol. (Bibliotheca Mycologica Ser.: No. 58). (Illus.). 1977. lib. bdg. 30.00x (ISBN 3-7682-1145-2). Lubrecht & Cramer.

Singer, Rolf. Boletes & Related Groups in South America. (Illus.). pap. 8.00 (ISBN 3-7682-0212-7). Lubrecht & Cramer.

Sivanesan, A. Taxonomy & Pathology of Venturia Species. (Bibliotheca Mycologica Ser.: No. 59). 1977. lib. bdg. 20.00x (ISBN 3-7682-1167-3). Lubrecht & Cramer.

Smith, Alexander, et al. How to Know the Non-Gilled Mushrooms. 2nd ed. 1981. write for info. wire coil (ISBN 0-697-04778-4). Wm C Brown.

Smith, Alexander H. A Field Guide to Western Mushrooms. LC 74-25949. (Illus.). 1975. 16.50 (ISBN 0-472-85599-9). U of Mich Pr.

Smith, Alexander H. & Weber, Nancy. The Mushroom Hunter's Field Guide: All Color & Enlarged. (Illus.). 336p. 1980. 14.95 (ISBN 0-472-85610-3). U of Mich Pr.

Smith, Helen V., et al. How to Know the Gilled Mushrooms. (Pictured Key Nature Ser.). 400p. 1979. write for info. (ISBN 0-697-04772-5); write for info. wire coil (ISBN 0-697-04773-3). Wm C Brown.

Snell, W. H. & Dick, E. A. The Boleti of Northeastern North America. (Illus.). 1970. 125.00 (ISBN 3-7682-0681-5). Lubrecht & Cramer.

Stamets, Paul. Psilocybe Mushrooms & Their Allies. Harris, Bob, ed. LC 77-26546. (Illus.). 1978. pap. 9.95 (ISBN 0-930180-03-8). Homestead Bk.

Stevens & Gee. How to Grow & Identify Psilocybin Mushrooms. (Illus.). 1978. perfect bdg. 5.95 (ISBN 0-686-26205-0). Pacific Pipeline.

Stuntz, Daniel. How to Identify Mushrooms (to Genus IV) Keys to Families & Genera. (Illus.). 94p. 1977. pap. 5.50x (ISBN 0-916422-10-0). Mad River.

Thiers, Harry. California Mushrooms: A Field Guide to the Boletes. LC 74-11002. (Illus.). 1974. text ed. 17.50 (ISBN 0-02-853410-7). Hafner.

Thiers, Harry D. Mushrooms of California I: The Genus Amanita. (Illus.). 60p. (Orig.). 1982. pap. price not set (ISBN 0-916422-24-0). Mad River.

Thomas, William S. Field Book of Common Mushrooms. rev ed. (Putnam's Nature Field Bks.). (Illus.). 1948. 6.95 (ISBN 0-399-10285-X). Putnam.

Tosco, Umberto. World of Mushrooms. (World of Nature Ser.). 1973. 4.98 (ISBN 0-517-12039-9, Bounty Books). Crown.

Wasson, R. Gordon. The Wonderous Mushroom: Mycolatry in Mesoamerica. LC 79-26895. (Illus.). 178p. 1980. 14.95 (ISBN 0-07-068441-3); deluxe ed. 435.00 (ISBN 0-07-068442-1); pap. 10.95 (ISBN 0-07-068443-X). McGraw.

Watling, Roy, ed. A Literature Guide to the Identification of Mushrooms. 120p. (Orig.). 1980. pap. 6.95 (ISBN 0-916422-18-6). Mad River.

Wells, M. H. & Mitchel, D. H. Colorado Mushrooms. 1966. pap. 2.60 (ISBN 0-916278-44-1). Denver Mus Natl Hist.

Zeitmayr, Linus. Wild Mushrooms: An Illustrated Handbook. Gregory, Otto, tr. from Ger. (Illus.). 138p. 1976. 9.75 (ISBN 0-584-10324-7). Transatlantic.

MUSHROOMS-CULTURE

see Mushroom Culture

MUSHROOMS, EDIBLE

see also Mushroom Culture

Charles, Vera K. Introduction to Mushroom Hunting. LC 73-85355. (Illus.). 1974. Repr. of 1931 ed. 1.35 (ISBN 0-486-20667-X). Dover.

Christensen, Clyde M. Edible Mushrooms. 2nd, rev. ed. (Illus.). 136p. 1981. 12.95 (ISBN 0-8166-1049-5); pap. 6.95 (ISBN 0-8166-1050-9). U of Minn Pr.

Devignes, Antoine & Pepin, Jacques. How to Recognize 30 Edible Mushrooms. Geldart, G. W., tr. from Fr. 1977. pap. text ed. 5.95 (ISBN 0-8120-0790-5). Barron.

Faubion, Nina L. Some Edible Mushrooms & How to Cook Them. LC 62-15309. (Illus.). 1972. 8.95 (ISBN 0-8323-0119-1). Binford.

Gray, William D. The Use of Fungi As Food & in Food Processing, Pt. 1. (Monotopic Reprint Ser.). 1971. 11.95 (ISBN 0-87819-104-6). CRC Pr.

Haard, Karen & Haard, Richard. Foraging for Edible Wild Mushrooms. rev. ed. (Illus.). 1978. lib. bdg. 11.95 (ISBN 0-88930-015-1, Pub. by Cloudburst Canada); pap. 5.95 (ISBN 0-88930-017-8). Madrona Pubs.

McIlvaine, Charles & MacAdam, Robert. One Thousand American Fungi. (Illus.). 729p. 1973. pap. 6.95 (ISBN 0-486-22782-0). Dover.

McIlvaine, Charles & MacAdam, Robert K. One Thousand American Fungi. LC 72-91857. (Illus.). 1973. 30.00 (ISBN 0-87110-093-2); pap. 10.00 (ISBN 0-87110-094-0). Ultramarine Pub.

Marteka, Vincent. Mushrooms - Wild & Edible: A Seasonal Guide to the Most Easily Recognized Mushrooms. (Illus.). 1980. 19.95 (ISBN 0-393-01356-1). Norton.

Mushroom Terms: Polyglot on Research & Cultivation of Edible Fungi. 312p. 1981. pap. 83.00 (ISBN 90-220-0673-5, PDC 211, Pudoc). Unipub.

Recommended International Standard for Canned Mushrooms. (Codex Alimentarius Commission Reports Ser.). 16p. (Orig.). 1975. pap. 4.50 (ISBN 0-685-53177-5, F596, FAO). Unipub.

Recommended International Standard for Dessicated Coconut & Dehydrated Fruits & Vegetables Including Edible Fungi. 1972. pap. 3.00 (ISBN 0-685-36290-6, FAO). Unipub.

Recommended International Standard for Dried Edible Fungi. 1970. pap. 4.50 (ISBN 0-685-36293-0, F645, FAO). Unipub.

Recommended International Standard for Edible Fungi & Fungus Products. 1970. pap. 4.50 (ISBN 0-685-36344-9, F644, FAO). Unipub.

Schmitz, Helga. Untersuchungen Zur Konservierung der Frucht Koerper des Speisepilzes Pleurotus ostreatus (Jacqu. ex Fr.) Kummer in der Partiellen Autlyse von Pilzzellwaenden. (Bibliothaca Mycologica: No. 77). (Illus.). 85p. (Ger.). 1980. pap. text ed. 15.00x (ISBN 3-7682-1278-5). Lubrecht & Cramer.

Stubbs, Ansel H. Wild Mushrooms Worth Knowing. LC 76-107330. Orig. Title: Wild Mushrooms of the Central Midwest. (Illus.). 160p. 1980. pap. 7.95 (ISBN 0-913504-58-0). Lowell Pr.

MUSIAL, STANLEY FRANK, 1920-

Broeg, Bob. The Man Stan: Musial, Then & Now. new ed. (Illus.). 1977. 8.95 (ISBN 0-8272-2313-7); pap. 3.95 (ISBN 0-8272-2312-9). Bethany Pr.

MUSIC

see also Arrangement (Music); Chamber Music; Choral Music; Christmas Music; Church Music; Composition (Music); Computer Music; Concerts; Conservatories of Music; Counterpoint; Dance Music; Dance Orchestras; Easter Music; Electronic Music; Folk Dance Music; Folk Music; Folk-Songs; Funeral Music; Harmony; Harmony (Esthetics); Impressionism (Music); Improvisation (Music); Instrumental Music; Instrumentation and Orchestration; Jazz Music; Kindergarten–Music; Melodrama; Melody; Military Music; Moving-Picture Music; National Music; National Songs; Opera; Operetta; Orchestral Music; Passion-Music; Program Music; Romanticism in Music; School Music; Singing; Songs; Sound; Street Music and Musicians; Symbolism in Music; Symphony Orchestras; Television Music; Transposition (Music); Vocal Music; Voice; Waits also subdivision Songs and Music under specific subjects, classes of persons, names of individuals, institutions, societies, etc; also other headings beginning with the words Music and Musical

Adriaenssen, Emanuel. Pratum Musicum Longe Amoenissimum. xvi, 180p. Repr. of 1576 ed. 67.50 (ISBN 90-6027-157-2, Pub. by Frits Knuf Netherlands); wrappers 52.50 (ISBN 90-6027-155-6). Pendragon NY.

Allgemeine Musikalische Zeitung, Leipziger: 1. Jahrgang-17. Jahrgang Redigirt von Selmar Bagge. 8660p. 1969. Repr. of 1882 ed. 1000.00 (ISBN 90-6027-135-1, Pub. by Frits Knuf Netherlands). Pendragon NY.

Allgemeine Musikalische Zeitung, Neue Folge: 1. Jahrgang - 3. Jahrgang Redigirt von Selmar Bagge. 1360p. 1969. Repr. of 1865 ed. 200.00 (ISBN 90-6027-134-3, Pub. by Frits Knuf Netherlands). Pendragon NY.

Allgemeine Musikalische Zeitung: 1. Jahrgang - 50. Jahrgang und Index. 24000p. 1966. Repr. of 1848 ed. 3750.00 (ISBN 90-6027-079-7, Pub. by Frits Knuf Netherlands). Pendragon NY.

Arlin, M., et al. Music Sources: A Collection of Excerpts & Complete Movements. 1979. pap. 17.95 (ISBN 0-13-607168-6). P-H.

Bachelder, Louise, ed. The Gift of Music. 1975. 2.95 (ISBN 0-442-82556-0). Peter Pauper.

Ballentine, George K. Your Voice in Speech or Song. 1978. 5.95 (ISBN 0-533-03378-0). Vantage.

Bamberger, Jeanne S. & Brofsky, Howard. The Art of Listening: Developing Musical Perception. 4th ed. LC 78-20837. 1979. pap. text ed. 16.50 scp (ISBN 0-06-040943-6, HarpC); inst. manual free (ISBN 0-06-360966-5); Set Of 5 Records. scp 26.50 (ISBN 0-06-040981-9). Har-Row.

Barnes-Ostrander, Marilyn. Music: Reflections in Sound. 1976. scp 16.50 (ISBN 0-06-371056-0, HarpC). Har-Row.

Bayne, Pauline S., ed. Basic Music Library. LC 78-11997. 1978. pap. text ed. 5.00 (ISBN 0-8389-0281-2). ALA.

Beach, Scott. Musicdotes. LC 76-30883. (Illus.). 1977. 9.00 (ISBN 0-913668-78-8); pap. 4.00 (ISBN 0-913668-64-8). Ten Speed Pr.

Beer, Alice S. & Graham, Richard. Teaching Music to the Exceptional Child: A Handbook for Mainstreaming. (Illus.). 1980. text ed. 15.95 (ISBN 0-13-893982-9); pap. text ed. 10.95 (ISBN 0-13-893974-8). P-H.

Behague, Gerard. The Beginnings of Musical Nationalism in Brazil. LC 79-174730. (Detroit Monographs in Musicology: No. 1). 43p. 1971. pap. 2.00 (ISBN 0-911772-50-2). Info Coord.

Bennett, R. Form & Design. (Cambridge Assignment in Music Ser.). (Illus.). 72p. Date not set. pap. 3.95 (ISBN 0-521-29812-1). Cambridge U Pr.

Bentley, Arnold. Music in Education: A Point View. (General Ser.). 125p. 1975. pap. text ed. 10.00x (ISBN 0-85633-066-3, NFER). Humanities.

Benton, Rita. Ignace Pleyel: A Thematic Catalogue of His Compositions. (Thematic Catalogue Ser.: No. 2). 1977. lib. bdg. 48.00 (ISBN 0-918728-04-5). Pendragon NY.

Benward, Bruce. Music in Theory & Practice, Vol. 1. 2nd ed. 400p. 1981. write for info. wkbk. (ISBN 0-697-03445-3); instrs.' manual avail. (ISBN 0-697-03423-2); plastic comb. avail. (ISBN 0-697-03447-X). Wm C Brown.

Beranek, Leo L. Music, Acoustics & Architecture. Stone, Geraldine, ed. LC 78-27324. (Illus.). 598p. 1979. Repr. of 1962 ed. lib. bdg. 33.00 (ISBN 0-88275-851-9). Krieger.

Bernonis Augiensis Abbatis De Arta Musica Disputationes Traditae pars A Bernonis Augiensis De Mensurando Monochordo. (DMA Ser. A: Vol. VIa). (Illus.). 120p. 1978. wrappers 35.00 (ISBN 0-686-30878-6, Pub. by Frits Knuf Netherlands). Pendragon NY.

Bisgaard, Erling & Aaron, Tossi. In Canon. 1978. pap. 5.00 (ISBN 0-918812-03-8). Magnamusic.

Bisgaard, Erling & Stehouwer, Gulle. Musicbook 0: Pulse, Pitch, Rhythm, Form, Dynamics. Aaron, Tossi, ed. 1976. pap. 6.00 (ISBN 0-918812-04-6). Magnamusic.

Blom, Eric. Classics: Major & Minor. LC 74-166098. 212p. 1972. Repr. of 1958 ed. lib. bdg. 19.50 (ISBN 0-306-70293-2). Da Capo.

Blume, Friedrich. Classic & Romantic Music. Norton, M. D., tr. LC 78-77390. 1970. pap. 5.95x (ISBN 0-393-09868-0). Norton.

Bontrager, Ernest J. & Bontrager, Ida, eds. Rudiments of Music. 1968. pap. 1.00x (ISBN 0-87813-102-7). Park View.

Boughton, Rutland. The Reality of Music. LC 72-80495. Repr. of 1934 ed. 14.00 (ISBN 0-405-08294-0, Blom Pubns). Arno.

Brody, Elaine & Brook, Claire. The Music Guide to Italy. LC 78-6846. (Music Guides Ser.). 1978. 10.00 (ISBN 0-396-07436-7). Dodd.

Broekema, Andrew J. The Music Listener. 1978. text ed. write for info. (ISBN 0-697-03400-3); pap. instrs.' resource man. & test items avail. (ISBN 0-685-84643-1); 8 records avail. (ISBN 0-697-03416-X); student study guide avail. (ISBN 0-697-03415-1). Wm C Brown.

Brook, Barry S. Thematic Catalogues in Music: An Annotated Bibliography. (RILM Retrospectives Ser,: No. 1). 1972. lib. bdg. 25.00 (ISBN 0-918728-02-9). Pendragon NY.

Bruckner-Bigenwald, Martha. Die Anfange der Liepzieger Allgemeinen Musiualischen Zeitung. 1965. Repr. of 1938 ed. wrappers 20.00 (ISBN 90-6027-018-5, Pub. by Frits Knuf Netherlands). Pendragon NY.

Buck, Dudley. Prouncing Musical Art. lib. bdg. 19.00 (ISBN 0-685-95460-9). Scholarly.

Buck, Percy C. Scope of Music. facsimile ed. LC 70-93321. (Essay Index Reprint Ser). 1924. 12.00 (ISBN 0-8369-1276-4). Arno.

Burnett, Millie & Cummins, Mary Ann. Texas Tales & Tunes: A Suite for Speech, Voices, & Orff Instruments. 1977. pap. 3.50 (ISBN 0-918812-00-3). Magnamusic.

Cage, John. Empty Words. LC 78-27212. 1979. 17.50x (ISBN 0-8195-5032-9, Pub. by Wesleyan U Pr). Columbia U Pr.

Carlton, Joseph R. Carlton's Complete Reference Book of Music. LC 44-181. (Illus.). 729p. 1980. PLB 40.00 (ISBN 0-937348-00-7). Carlton Pubns CA.

Charteris, Richard. John Coprario: A Thematic Catalogue of His Music. (Thematic Catalogue Ser.: No. 3). 1977. lib. bdg. 15.50 (ISBN 0-918728-05-3). Pendragon NY.

Christ, William, et al. Materials & Structures of Music, Vol. 1. 3rd ed. 1980. text ed. 16.95 (ISBN 0-13-540417-7); wkbk. 7.95 (ISBN 0-13-560425-7). P-H.

Clementi, Muzio. Collected Works, 13 vols in 5. LC 70-75299. (Music Reprint Ser). 1973. 65.00 ea.; Set. 300.00 (ISBN 0-306-77260-4). Da Capo.

Clinkscale, Edward & Brook, Claire, eds. A Musical Offering: Essays in Honor of Martin Bernstein. (Festschrift Ser.: No. 1). lib. bdg. 25.00 (ISBN 0-918728-03-7). Pendragon NY.

Codex Oxoniensis Bibl. Bodl. Rawl. C Two Seventy Pars a "De Vocum Consonantiis" ac 'De Re Musica Osberni Cantuariensis. (Divitiae Musicae Artis DMA Ser. a: Vol. Xa). (Illus.). 67p. 1979. wrappers 22.00 (ISBN 90-6027-204-8, Pub. by Frits Knuf Netherlands). Pendragon NY.

Cone, Edward T. The Composer's Voice. LC 73-80830. (Illus.). 1974. 18.95x (ISBN 0-520-02508-3). U of Cal Pr.

Copland, Aaron. Copland on Music. 1963. pap. 5.95 (ISBN 0-393-00198-9, Norton Lib). Norton.

--Copland on Music. LC 76-13512. 1976. Repr. of 1960 ed. lib. bdg. 25.00 (ISBN 0-306-70775-6). Da Capo.

Cunningham, William P. The Music Locator. 2nd ed. 400p. 1980. 49.95 (ISBN 0-89390-020-6); pap. 39.95 (ISBN 0-89390-012-5). Resource Pubns.

Daniels, A. & Wagner, L. Music. LC 74-30827. 1975. text ed. 13.95 (ISBN 0-03-012681-9, HoltC); instructor's manual avail., write for info. (ISBN 0-03-014956-8). HR&W.

Darling, James S., ed. A Jefferson Music Book. LC 76-30510. 1977. pap. 2.95 (ISBN 0-87935-044-X). Williamsburg.

Davies, Laurence. Paths to Modern Music. LC 79-155057. 1971. pap. text ed. 3.95x (ISBN 0-684-12790-3, ScribC). Scribner.

Davis, Stephen & Simon, Peter. Reggae Bloodlines. LC 76-42428. 1977. pap. 8.95 (ISBN 0-385-12330-2, Anch). Doubleday.

Dearling, Robert, et al. Music Facts & Feats. rev. ed. (Illus.). 288p. 1981. 19.95 (ISBN 0-8069-9250-6, Pub. by Guinness Superlatives England). Sterling.

Debussy, Claude. Debussy Prelude. Austin, William W., ed. (Critical Score Ser). 1970. pap. 5.95x (ISBN 0-393-09939-3). Norton.

De Cande, R. La Musique. 550p. (Fr.). 42.50 (ISBN 0-686-56978-4, M-6105). French & Eur.

De Lafontaine, Henry C. The King's Musick: A Transcript of Records Relative to Music & Musicians. LC 70-169648. 522p. 1973. Repr. of 1909 ed. lib. bdg. 39.50 (ISBN 0-306-70269-X). Da Capo.

De Souza, Chris. Looking at Music. 48p. 1980. 8.95 (ISBN 0-442-24337-5). Van Nos Reinhold.

Dinn, Freda. The Observer's Book of Music. rev. ed. (Illus.). 1979. 3.95 (ISBN 0-684-16590-2, ScribT). Scribner.

Dorian, Frederick. Musical Workshop. LC 77-138109. (Illus.). 1971. Repr. of 1947 ed. lib. bdg. 17.75x (ISBN 0-8371-5685-8, DOMW). Greenwood.

Downes, Edward. The Guide to Symphonic Music. LC 76-13813. Orig. Title: The New York Philharmonic Guide to the Symphony. (Illus.). 1058p. pap. 14.95 (ISBN 0-8027-7177-7). Walker & Co.

Elley, Derek. International Music Guide 1979. LC 76-4626. (Illus.). 1978. pap. 7.95 (ISBN 0-498-02242-0). A S Barnes.

Elley, Derek, ed. International Music Guide, 1981. LC 75-21259. (Illus.). 1981. pap. 8.95 (ISBN 0-686-69099-0). A S Barnes.

Ernst, David. Musique Concrete. LC 72-87761. 1973. pap. 3.00 (ISBN 0-8008-5457-8, Crescendo). Taplinger.

The Evils of Music Management. LC 75-10070. 1975. 10.00 (ISBN 0-686-12008-6). La Car Pub.

Ferraro, Louis & Adams, Sam. Music: Imaginative Listening. 1969. 8.00x (ISBN 0-685-00424-4). Claitors.

Fisher, Renee. Heroes of Music. LC 79-161375. (Heroes of Ser.). (Illus.). 128p. (gr. 9 up). 1973. 6.95 (ISBN 0-8303-0101-1). Fleet.

French Language Dissertations in Music: An Annotated Index. (RILM Retrospectives Ser.: No. 2). 1979. lib. bdg. 27.50 (ISBN 0-918728-09-6). Pendragon NY.

Frost, David, intro. by. The Bluffer's Guides, 6 bks. Incl. Bluff Your Way in Art. Lampitt, L; Bluff Your Way in Cinema. Wlaschin, Ken; Bluff Your Way in Literature. Seymoursmith, Martin; Bluff Your Way in Music. Gammond, Peter; Bluff Your Way in Opera. Coleman, Francis; Bluff Your Way in Wine. Clark, Wick. 64p. 1971. pap. 1.00 ea. Crown.

Fundamentals of Music. 2nd, rev. enl. ed. (Illus.). 1981. pap. text ed. 5.95 (ISBN 0-910648-04-2). Gamut Music.

Furtwangler, Wilhelm. Concerning Music. L. J., Lawrence, tr. from German. LC 76-57174. (Illus.). 1977. Repr. of 1953 ed. lib. bdg. 15.00x (ISBN 0-8371-8665-X, FUCM). Greenwood.

Gaburo, K. The Beauty of Irrelevant Music. (Paperplay Ser.: Vol. 1). (Illus.). 22p. 1976. softcover 2.75 (ISBN 0-939044-01-3). Lingua Pr.

Glennon, James. Understanding Music. 1980. 15.00 (ISBN 0-312-83144-7). St Martin.

Gordon, L. Music & Modern Media of Transmission. 1975. lib. bdg. 75.00 (ISBN 0-87968-328-7). Gordon Pr.

Gordon, Roderick D. The World of Musical Sound. 1979. pap. text ed. 10.95 (ISBN 0-8403-2078-7). Kendall-Hunt.

Gould & Fredericks. Official Price Guide to Music Collectibles. (Collector Ser.). (Illus.). 400p. 1980. pap. 9.95 (ISBN 0-87637-010-5, 010-05). Hse of Collectibles.

Grunfeld, Frederic V. Music. (World of Culture Ser.). (Illus.). 192p. 1974. 12.95 (ISBN 0-88225-101-5). Newsweek.

Guicciardini, Franceso. Ricordi: Italian Text with English Translation. Thomson, Ninian H., tr. 1949. 7.50x (ISBN 0-913298-41-7). S F Vanni.

Haggin, B. H. Thirty Five Years of Music. 1974. 10.00 (ISBN 0-8180-1213-7). Horizon.

Haggin, Bernard H. Music in the Nation. facsimile ed. LC 71-167350. (Essay Index Reprint Ser). Repr. of 1949 ed. 21.00 (ISBN 0-8369-2503-3). Arno.

Handel. Handel's "Messiah". The Conducting Score. 460p. 1979. Repr. of 1974 ed. 75.00x (ISBN 0-85967-158-5, Pub. by Scolar Pr England). Biblio Dist.

Hardy, Donna D. Music Mixtures. LC 77-92092. 1977. pap. 8.50 (ISBN 0-913650-04-8). Volkwein Bros.

Hart, Muriel. Music in the Primary School. 1973. pap. text ed. 4.50x (ISBN 0-435-80606-8). Heinemann Ed.

Hays, William. Twentieth Century Views of Musical History. 1972. lib. rep. ed. 22.50x (ISBN 0-684-15149-9, ScribT). Scribner.

Hegyi, Erzsebet. Solfege According to the Kodaly Concept, Vol. 2. Ittzes, Kata, tr. from Hungarian. (Illus.). 563p. 1979. 36.00 (ISBN 963-330-274-9, Pub. by Editio Musica Budapest Hungary). Boosey & Hawkes.

Heline, Corinne. Music: The Keynote of Human Evolution. pap. 5.95 (ISBN 0-87613-084-8). New Age.

Herndon, Marcia & McLeod, Norman. Music & Culture. 2nd ed. 217p. 1981. lib. bdg. 22.50 (ISBN 0-8482-4476-1). Norwood Edns.

Hoffer, Charles & Hoffer, Marjorie. Basic Musicianship for Classroom Teachers. 1976. pap. text ed. 13.95x (ISBN 0-534-00394-X). Wadsworth Pub.

Homewood, Inez V. Music in Further Education. (Student's Music Library Ser). 1958. 6.95 (ISBN 0-234-77217-4). Dufour.

Hopkins, Antony. Understanding Music. (Illus.). 255p. 1980. Repr. of 1979 ed. 17.50x (ISBN 0-460-04376-5, Pub. by J. M. Dent England). Biblio Dist.

Howes, Frank. The Music of William Walton. 2nd ed. (Illus.). 1973. 37.50 (ISBN 0-19-315431-5). Oxford U Pr.

Howes, Frank S. Man, Mind & Music. facsimile ed. LC 70-128878. (Select Bibliographies Reprint Ser). Repr. of 1948 ed. 15.00 (ISBN 0-8369-5498-X). Arno.

Hull, Arthur E. Music: Classical, Romantic & Modern. facsimile ed. (Select Bibliographies Reprint Ser). Repr. of 1927 ed. 25.00 (ISBN 0-8369-5803-9). Arno.

Hurd, Michael, ed. The Oxford Junior Companion to Music. new ed. (Illus.). 1980. 25.00 (ISBN 0-19-314302-X). Oxford U Pr.

Jeans, James. Science & Music. LC 68-24652. 1968. lib. bdg. 10.50 (ISBN 0-88307-617-9). Gannon.

Johnson, Frances H. Musical Memories of Hartford. LC 70-136370. Repr. of 1931 ed. 25.50 (ISBN 0-404-07224-0). AMS Pr.

Johnson, Roger, commentary by. Scores: An Anthology of New Music. LC 80-53302. (Illus.). 450p. 1981. pap. text ed. 15.95 (ISBN 0-02-871190-4). Schirmer Bks.

Jousse, John. Catechism of Music. 1891. pap. 2.25 (ISBN 0-02-871180-7). Schirmer Bks.

Kamien, Roger. Norton Scores: An Anthology for Listening, 2 Vols. LC 78-95537. 1970. Vol. 1. pap. 5.95x (ISBN 0-393-09909-1); Vol. 2. pap. 6.95x (ISBN 0-393-09920-2). Norton.

Kamien, Roger, ed. Norton Scores: Standard Edition. rev. ed. 1972. 20.00x (ISBN 0-393-02167-X); pap. 7.50x (ISBN 0-393-09386-7); of 9 records 14.95x set (ISBN 0-393-09960-1). Norton.

Katz, Adele T. Challenge to Musical Tradition. LC 79-180046. 408p. 1972. Repr. of 1945 ed. lib. bdg. 32.50 (ISBN 0-306-70428-5). Da Capo.

Kirby, F. E. Introduction to Western Music. LC 69-15248. 1970. text ed. 12.95 (ISBN 0-02-917360-4). Free Pr.

Klerk, M. Muziek-Karikaturen: Music-Caricatures. (Haags Gemeentemuseum, Kijkboekjes Ser.: Vol. 2). 60p. 1981. wrappers 15.00 (ISBN 90-6027-282-X, Pub. by Frits Knuf Netherlands). Pendragon NY.

Knuth, Alice & Knuth, William E. Basic Resources in Learning Music. 2nd ed. 1973. pap. 13.95x (ISBN 0-534-00236-6). Wadsworth Pub.

Kolodin, Irving. In Quest of Music. LC 78-22336. (Illus.). 360p. 1980. 14.95 (ISBN 0-385-13061-9). Doubleday.

Komar, Arthur J. Music & Human Experience. LC 79-7479. (Illus.). 1980. text ed. 14.95 (ISBN 0-02-871070-3); record pkg. 12.95 (ISBN 0-02-871840-2). Schirmer Bks.

Krohn, Ernst C. Missouri Music. LC 65-23398. (Music Ser.). xlvi, 380p. 1971. Repr. of 1924 ed. lib. bdg. 37.50 (ISBN 0-306-70932-5). Da Capo.

Kusel, George. The Marching Drummer's Companion. 2nd ed. 52p. 1981. pap. 4.95 (ISBN 0-9604476-0-1). Kusel.

Lanier, S. Music & Poetry. LC 68-25292. (Studies in Poetry, No. 38). 1969. Repr. of 1898 ed. lib. bdg. 27.95 (ISBN 0-8383-0306-4). Haskell.

Lanier, Sidney. Music & Poetry. 1973. lib. bdg. 69.95 (ISBN 0-87968-028-8). Gordon Pr.

--Music & Poetry: Essays Upon Some Aspects & Interrelations of the Two Arts. Repr. of 1898 ed. lib. bdg. 15.00x (ISBN 0-8371-1001-7, LAMP). Greenwood.

Laskowski, Larry. Heinrich Schenker: An Annotated Index to His Analyses of Musical Works. (Annotated Reference Tools in Music Ser.: No. 1). 1978. lib. bdg. 21.00 (ISBN 0-918728-06-1). Pendragon NY.

Leyerle, Anne & Leyerle, William D. Song Anthology One. rev. 2nd ed. LC 79-90829. 144p. (gr. 9 up). 1980. pap. 8.95 plastic comb. (ISBN 0-9602296-1-2). W D Leyerle.

Lynn, Theodore A. Introductory Musicianship: A Workbook. 246p. 1979. pap. 12.95 text-wkbk. (ISBN 0-15-543551-5, HC). HarBraceJ.

McDonald, Dorothy T. Music in Our Lives: The Early Years. LC 79-51509. 1979. pap. text ed. 2.50 (ISBN 0-912674-65-2). Natl Assn Child Ed.

Machlis, Joseph. The Enjoyment of Music. 4th ed. LC 76-62482. (Illus.). 1977. 16.95x (ISBN 0-393-09118-X); shorter 14.95x (ISBN 0-393-09125-2); workbk 4.95x (ISBN 0-393-09122-8). Norton.

McNair, Joseph. An Odyssey: Poetry & Music. LC 76-7152. (Illus.). 1976. pap. 4.25 (ISBN 0-916692-06-X). Black River.

Manoff, Tom. The Music Kit. 1976. pap. text ed. 16.95x (ISBN 0-393-09179-1); tchrs. manual avail. (ISBN 0-393-09157-0). Norton.

Martin, Gary M. Basic Concepts in Music. 2nd ed. 288p. 1980. pap. text ed. 13.95x (ISBN 0-534-00761-9). Wadsworth Pub.

Mason, Daniel G., ed. The Art of Music, 14 vols. LC 74-26067. Repr. of 1917 ed. Set. 525.00 (ISBN 0-404-13020-8); 37.50 ea. AMS Pr.

Meyer, Kathi. Bedeutung und Wesen der Musik: Der Bedeutungswandel der Musik. (Samml. Mw.Abh. Ser). 267p. 40.00 (ISBN 90-6027-379-6, Pub. by Frits Knuf Netherlands). Pendragon NY.

Monuments of Music & Music Literature in Facsimile: Series One. Incl. Orpheus Britannicus. Purcell, Henry. 1965. 52.50x (ISBN 0-8450-2001-3); Vol. 2. Amphion Anglicus. Blow, John. 1965. 42.50x (ISBN 0-8450-2002-1); Vol. 3. Les Pieces De Clavessin. De Chambonnieres, Jacques Champion. 1967. 27.50x (ISBN 0-8450-2003-X); Vol. 4. Pieces de clavecin (Livre Premier) D'Anglebert, Jean Henry. 1965. 27.50x (ISBN 0-8450-2004-8); Vol. 5. Pieces de Clavecin. Mattheson, Johann. 1965. 30.00x (ISBN 0-8450-2005-6); Vol. 6. Musical Entertainer; Bickham's Musical Entertainer. Bickham, George. 1965. 85.00x (ISBN 0-8450-2006-4); Vol. 7. Pieces De Clavessin. Rameau, Jean-Philippe. 1967. 25.00x (ISBN 0-8450-2007-2); Vol. 8. Componimenti Musicali. Muffat, Gottlieb. 1967. 32.50x (ISBN 0-8450-2008-0); Vol. 9. Pieces de Clavecin: Premier, Second, Troisieme et Quatrieme Livres. Couperin, Francois. 1974. 75.00x (ISBN 0-8450-2009-9); Vol. 10. Harmonice Musices Odhecaton A. Petrucci, Ottaviano. 1973. 40.00x (ISBN 0-8450-2010-2); Vol. 11. Parthenia, or the Maydenhead of the first musicke that ever was printed for the Virginalls. Byrd, William, et al. 1972. 27.50x (ISBN 0-8450-2011-0); Vol. 12. Recerchari, Motetti, Canzoni, Libro Primo. Cavazzoni, Marco Antonio. 1974. 25.00x (ISBN 0-8450-2012-9); Vol. 13. Nouvelles Suites de Pieces de Clavecin. Rameau, Jean-Philippe. 1967. 25.00x (ISBN 0-8450-2013-7); Vol. 14. L'art du Violon. Cartier, Jean-Baptiste. 1973. 60.00x (ISBN 0-8450-2014-5); Vol. 15. New Instructions for Playing the Harpsichord, Piano-forte or Spinnet. 1967. 22.50x (ISBN 0-8450-2015-3); Vol. 16. The Preceptor for Piano-forte, the Organ or Harpsichord. 1967. 22.50x (ISBN 0-8450-2016-1); Vol. 18. Seventy-Two Versetl Sammt Twelve Toccaten. Muffat, Gottlieb. 1967. 35.00x (ISBN 0-8450-2018-8); Vol. 19. Sonate (12) D'intavolatura per L'organo E' L'cemba. Martini, Giovanni Battista. 1977. 32.50x (ISBN 0-8450-2019-6); Vol. 20. Tabulatur Buch. Schmid, Bernhard. 1967. 45.00x (ISBN 0-8450-2020-X); Vol. 22. Musical Century. Carey, Henry. 1976. 45.00x (ISBN 0-8450-2022-6); Vol. 23. Canti B Numero Cinquanta. Petrucci, Ottaviano. 1975. 37.50x (ISBN 0-8450-2023-4); Vol. 25. Canti C No Cento Cinquanta. Petrucci, Ottaviano. 1977. 47.50x (ISBN 0-8450-2025-0); Vol. 26. A Choice Collection of Lessons for the Harpsichord or Spinnet. Purcell, Henry. 1978. 25.00x (ISBN 0-8450-2026-9); Vol. 27. Eight Suits of Lessons for the Harpsichord or Spinnet in Most of the Keys. Roseningrave, Thomas. 1967. 30.00x (ISBN 0-8450-2027-7); Vol. 29. Le Musiche, Sopra L'euridice. Peri, Jacopo. 1973. 30.00x (ISBN 0-8450-2028-5); Vol. 30. Le Nuove Musiche. Caccini, Guilio. 1973. 30.00x (ISBN 0-8450-2029-3). (Illus.). Repr. Broude.

Monuments of Music & Music Literature in Facsimile: Series Two-Part 2, 21 vols. Incl. Vol. 32. Treatise of the Natural Grounds & Principles of Harmony. Holder, William. 1967. 27.50x (ISBN 0-8450-2232-6); Vol. 33. Anfangsgruende der Theoretischen Musik. Marpurg, Friedrich W. 1966. 27.50x (ISBN 0-8450-2233-4); Vol. 34. Rudimenta Musices. Agricola, Martin. 1966. 22.50x (ISBN 0-8450-2234-2); Vol. 35. Templum Musicum: or the Musical Synopsis. Alsted, Johann H. 1967. 25.00x (ISBN 0-8450-2235-0); Vol. 36. Versuch Einer Anleitung zur Heroisch-Musikalischen Trompeter und Pauker-Kunst. Altenburg, Johann E. 1966. 32.50x (ISBN 0-8450-2236-9); Vol. 38. Dialogue sur la Musique des Anciens. De C. Chateauneuf, Francois. 1966. 25.00x (ISBN 0-8450-2238-5); Vol. 39. Rerum Musicarum. Frosch, Johann. 1967. 32.50x (ISBN 0-8450-2239-3); Vol. 40. A Musical Dictionary. Grassineau, James. 1966. 30.00x (ISBN 0-8450-2240-7); Vol. 41. Memoire sur la Musique des Anciens. Roussier, Pierre J. 1966. 30.00x (ISBN 0-8450-2241-5); Vol. 42. Llave de la Modulacion, y Antiguedades de la Musica. Soler, Antonio. 1967. 32.50x (ISBN 0-8450-2242-3); Vol. 44. Phonurgia Nova. Kircher, Athanasius. 1966. 42.50x (ISBN 0-8450-2244-X); Vol. 45. Le Maitre a Danser. Rameau, Pierre. 1967. 30.00x (ISBN 0-8450-2245-8); Vol. 46. Il Ballarino. Caroso, Marco F. 1967. 40.00x (ISBN 0-8450-2246-6); Vol. 47. Lettres sur la Danse et sur les Ballets. Noverre, Jean-Georges. 1967. 27.50x (ISBN 0-8450-2247-4); Vol. 48. A Treatise on the Art of Dancing. Gallini, Giovanni A. B. 1967. 35.00x (ISBN 0-8450-2248-2); Vol. 51, Antiquae Musicae Auctores Septem, Marcus Meilbom, 1977. 80.00x (ISBN 0-8450-2251-2); Vol. 52. Essais sur les Principes de l'Harmonie. Serre, Jean-Adam. 1967. 27.50x (ISBN 0-8450-2252-0); Vol. 53. Observations sur les Principes de l'Harmonie. Serre, Jean-Adam. 1967. 30.00x (ISBN 0-8450-2253-9); Vol. 54. Observations sur Notre Instinct pour la Musique. Rameau, Jean-Philippe. 1967. 25.00x (ISBN 0-8450-2254-7); Vol. 55. An Essay on Musical Expression. Avison, Charles. 1967. 30.00x (ISBN 0-8450-2255-5). (Illus.). Repr. Broude.

Monuments of Music & Music Literature in Facsimile: Series Two-Part 4. Incl. Vol. 90. Tentamen Novae Theoriae Musicae. Euler, Leonhard. 1968. 37.50x (ISBN 0-8450-2290-3); Vol. 93. Musica Theorica. Fogliani, Lodovico. 1969. 32.50x (ISBN 0-8450-2293-8); Vol. 102. Methode Simple pour Apprendre a Preluder. Gretry, Andre. 1968. 25.00x (ISBN 0-8450-2302-0); Vol. 110. Anleitung zum Clavierspielen. Marpurg, Friedrich W. 1969. 27.50x (ISBN 0-8450-2310-1); Vol. 117. The Present State of Music in Germany, the Netherlands, & United Provinces, 2 vols. Burney, Charles. 1969. 55.00x set (ISBN 0-8450-2317-9); Vol. 101. Conclusioni nel Suono dell'Organo. Banchieri, Adriano. 1975. 30.00x (ISBN 0-8450-2301-2); Vol. 115. Breve E Facile Maniera. Conforto, Giovanni. 1978. 22.50x (ISBN 0-8450-2315-2). Broude. (Illus.). Repr. Broude.

Monuments of Music & Music Literature in Facsimile: Series Two-Part 5, 10 vols. Incl. Vol. 130. Choregraphie ou l'art de decrire la dance; Recueil de dances, composees par M. Feuillet; Recueil de Dances, composees, par M. Pecour. Feuillet, Raoul-Auger. 1968. 32.50x (ISBN 0-8450-2330-6); Vol. 133. Opinioni de'Cantori Antichi, e Moderni. Tosi, Pietro F. 1968. 25.00x (ISBN 0-8450-2333-0); Vol. 135. Recueil de Contredances. Feuillet, Raoul-Auger. 1968. 25.00x (ISBN 0-8450-2335-7); Vol. 136. Libellus de Rudimentis Musices. Rossetti, Biagio. 1968. 27.50x (ISBN 0-8450-2336-5); Vol. 137. Erreurs sur la Musique dans l'encyclopedie. Rameau, Jean-Philippe. 1969. 25.00x (ISBN 0-8450-2337-3); Vol. 138. Nouvelle Reflexions ...sur sa Demonstration du Principe de l'harmonie. Rameau, Jean-Philippe. 1969. 25.00x (ISBN 0-8450-2338-1); Vol. 139. De Arte Canendi, ac Vero Signorum in Cantibus Usu. Heyden, Sebald. 1969. 27.50x (ISBN 0-8450-2339-X); Vol. 141. Le Gratie d'Amore. Negri, Cesare. 1969. 40.00x (ISBN 0-8450-2341-1); Vol. 127. Sound Anatomiz'd. Turner, William. 1974. 25.00x (ISBN 0-8450-2327-6). (Illus.). Repr. Broude.

Moon, John C., ed. Slow Marches. LC 75-19259. (Music of Fifes & Drums Ser.: Vol. 2). 1977. pap. 2.50 (ISBN 0-87935-046-6). Williamsburg.

Morley, Thomas. A Plain & Easy Introduction to Practical Music. Harmon, R. Alec, ed. (Norton Library Ser., N682). (Illus.). 352p. 1973. pap. 6.95 (ISBN 0-393-00682-4). Norton.

Mumford, Lewis, et al. Arts in Renewal. facs. ed. LC 70-84296. (Essay Index Reprint Ser). 1951. 14.50 (ISBN 0-8369-1121-0). Arno.

Munford, Gregory. Munford's Simple Guide to Classical Music. 1979. pap. 4.95 (ISBN 0-9602760-0-9). Chicago Review.

Music Educators National Conference. Power of Music. LC 72-88397. (Illus.). 1972. pap. 6.00x (ISBN 0-940796-14-7). Music Ed.

National Institute for Food Service Industry & Kotschevar, Lendal H. Management by Menu. 381p. 1981. text ed. write for info. (ISBN 0-915452-20-0); instrs.' manual avail. (ISBN 0-915452-21-9); students manual avail. (ISBN 0-915452-22-7); home study bk avail. (ISBN 0-915452-23-5). Wm C Brown.

Naylor, Edward W. The Poets & Music. LC 78-66913. (Encore Music Editions Ser.). (Illus.). 1979. Repr. of 1929 ed. 19.00 (ISBN 0-88355-753-3). Hyperion Conn.

Nielsen, Patricia H. & Sucher, Floyd. Mockingbird Flight: Music Book & Records. (Kindergarten Keys Ser.). (Illus.). 1975. pap. text ed. 10.80 (ISBN 0-87892-660-7); record set 49.50 (ISBN 0-87892-666-6). Economy Co.

Nitze, William A. Arthurian Romance & Modern Poetry & Music. LC 72-105816. 1970. Repr. of 1940 ed. 10.00 (ISBN 0-8046-1049-5). Kennikat.

Nye, Robert E. & Bergethon, Bjorner. Basic Music: Functional Musicianship for the Non-Music Major. 5th ed. (Illus.). 240p. 1981. pap. text ed. 11.95 (ISBN 0-13-065672-0). P-H.

Olson, Robert G. Music Dictation: A Stereo Taped Series. (Orig.). 1970. pap. 9.95x (ISBN 0-534-00671-X); stereo taped s 195.00x (ISBN 0-534-00672-8). Wadsworth Pub.

Ostrow, Laurence. The Folk Musician's Handbook. Date not set. 17.50 (ISBN 0-312-29704-1); pap. 8.95 (ISBN 0-312-29705-X). St Martin.

Owen, Barbara, intro. by. The American Musical Directory. (Music Reprint Ser.). (Illus.). 260p. 1980. Repr. of 1861 ed. lib. bdg. 22.50 (ISBN 0-306-76037-1). Da Capo.

Palisca, Claude. The Norton Anthology of Western Music. 1980. pap. text ed. 17.95x (ISBN 0-393-95155-3). Norton.

Pars B Quae ratio est inter tria opera de arte musica Bernonis Augiensis. (DMA Ser. A: Vol. VIb). (Illus.). 82p. 1979. wrappers 24.00 (ISBN 0-686-30879-4, Pub. by Frits Knuf Netherlands). Pendragon NY.

Partch, Harry. The Genesis of a Music. 2nd ed. LC 73-4333. (Music Reprint Ser.). 1974. lib. bdg. 29.50 (ISBN 0-306-71597-X); pap. 9.50 (ISBN 0-306-80106-X). Da Capo.

Perle, George. Twelve-Tone Tonality. LC 76-50258. 1978. 20.00x (ISBN 0-520-03387-6). U of Cal Pr.

Pleasants, Henry. Serious Music & All That Jazz. LC 69-12093. 1971. pap. 2.95 (ISBN 0-671-21072-6, Fireside). S&S.

Politaske, Daniel. Music. 2nd ed. 1979. 17.95 (ISBN 0-13-607556-8); study guide & workbook 5.95 (ISBN 0-13-607564-9); records set 16.95 (ISBN 0-13-607580-0). P-H.

Rachlin, Harvey. The Encyclopedia of the Music Business. LC 81-47235. (Illus.). 480p. 1981. 17.75 (ISBN 0-06-014913-2, HarpT). Har-Row.

Randolph, David. This Is Music. 1979. pap. 3.95 (ISBN 0-346-12387-9). Cornerstone.

Rau, Albert G. & David, Hans T. Catalogue of Music by American Moravians, 1742-1842. LC 76-134283. Repr. of 1938 ed. 14.00 (ISBN 0-404-07206-2). AMS Pr.

Ravenscroft, Thomas. A Briefe Discourse of the true (but neglected) use of Charact'ring the Degrees... (Monuments of Music and Music Literature in Facsimile: Series II, Vol. 22). 1977. Repr. of 1614 ed. 32.50x (ISBN 0-8450-2222-9). Broude.

Reinecke, Hans P. Cents Frequency Period: Umrechnungstabellen fuer musikalische Akustik und Musikethnologie. (Ger. & Eng.). 1970. 11.25x (ISBN 3-11-006397-2). De Gruyter.

Reis, Claire. Composers, Conductors, & Critics. LC 74-75896. (Detroit Reprints in Music Ser.). 1974. Repr. of 1955 ed. 5.00 (ISBN 0-911772-63-4). Info Coord.

Reynolds, Malvina. There's Music in the Air. LC 76-19261. (Illus.). 96p. (gr. 1-12). 1976. pap. 5.00 (ISBN 0-915620-05-7). Schroder Music.

Rimbault, E. F. London Eighteen Seventy-Seven. (Auction Catalogues of Music Ser.: Vol. 6). 1975. wrappers 42.50 (ISBN 90-6027-330-3, Pub. by Frits Knuf Netherlands). Pendragon NY.

Romano, Eustachio. Musica Duorum, Vol. 6. (Monuments of Renaissance Music Ser.). 1975. 27.50x (ISBN 0-226-22646-8). U of Chicago Pr.

Rossi, Nick. Hearing Music: An Introduction. 508p. 1981. pap. text ed. 16.95 (ISBN 0-15-535597-X). HarBraceJ.

Rudman, Jack. Music. (Undergraduate Program Field Test Ser.: UPFT-16). (Cloth bdg. avail. on request). pap. 9.95 (ISBN 0-8373-6016-1). Natl Learning.

Saint-Saens, Camille. Outspoken Essays on Music. facs. ed. Rothwell, F., tr. LC 71-84335. (Essay Index Reprint Ser). 1922. 12.75 (ISBN 0-8369-1105-9). Arno.

Salzer, Feliz, ed. The Music Forum, Vol. V. 384p. 1980. 27.50x (ISBN 0-231-04720-7). Columbia U Pr.

Schoenberg, Arnold. Style & Idea: Selected Writings of Arnold Schoenberg. Stein, Leonard, ed. LC 72-85510. 1975. 45.00 (ISBN 0-312-77420-6). St Martin.

Scholes, Percy A. Everyman & His Music. facs. ed. LC 72-76914. (Essay Index Reprint Ser). 1917. 15.00 (ISBN 0-8369-0029-4). Arno.

Schumann, Robert. Music & Musicians, 2 vols. in one. LC 77-87622. 1977. Repr. of 1880 ed. lib. bdg. 40.00 (ISBN 0-89341-075-6). Longwood Pr.

Scott, Cyril. Music: Its Secret Influence Throughout the Ages. LC 79-16380. 208p. 1973. pap. 4.95 (ISBN 0-87728-336-2). Weiser.

Scriabin, Alexander. The Complete Preludes & Etudes for Pianoforte Solo. Igumnov, K. N. & Mil' shteyn, Y. I., eds. 7.50 (ISBN 0-8446-4813-2). Peter Smith.

Seligson-Rose, Bonnie. Advanced Placement Music: Comprehensive Review of Theory & History of Music. LC 79-16113. 1979. pap. text ed. 4.95 (ISBN 0-668-04743-7, 4743-7). Arco.

Sessions, Roger. Questions About Music. LC 72-102672. (Charles Eliot Norton Lectures Ser: 1968-1969). 1970. 9.00x (ISBN 0-674-74350-4). Harvard U Pr.

Sheean, Vincent. First & Last Love. LC 78-26964. 1979. Repr. of 1956 ed. lib. bdg. 21.00x (ISBN 0-313-20549-3, SHFL). Greenwood.

Shemel, Sidney & Krasilovsky, M. William. More About This Business of Music. rev. ed. (Illus.). 204p. 1974. 12.95 (ISBN 0-8230-7566-4, Billboard Pub). Watson-Guptill.

--This Business of Music. rev. ed. (Illus.). 1977. 18.50 (ISBN 0-8230-7752-7). Watson-Guptill.

Shinn, Duane. How to Sell Music by Mail. 1975. pap. 3.95 (ISBN 0-912732-17-2). Duane Shinn.

Slim, H. Colin, ed. A Gift of Madrigals & Motets. LC 73-172799. (Illus.). 1973. Set Of 2 Vols. 37.50x (ISBN 0-226-76271-8); Vol. 2. pap. 8.75x (ISBN 0-226-76272-6). U of Chicago Pr.

Slonimsky, Nicolas. The Road to Music. rev. ed. (Illus.). 1966. 6.00 (ISBN 0-8446-0260-4). Peter Smith.

--A Thing or Two About Music. LC 72-156213. 304p. Repr. of 1948 ed. lib. bdg. 15.00x (ISBN 0-8371-6163-0, SLAM). Greenwood.

Smith, F. J., ed. In Search of Musical Method. 1976. 21.00x (ISBN 0-677-12640-9). Gordon.

Sonneck, Oscar G. Suum Cuique. facs. ed. LC 70-76916. (Essay Index Reprint Ser). 1916. 16.00 (ISBN 0-8369-0031-6). Arno.

Spano, Salvatore P. Fundamentals Limited: A Combined Text & Workbook Designed for Developing Skills in Fundamentals of Music. 2nd ed. 1978. pap. text ed. 8.95 (ISBN 0-8403-1538-4). Kendall-Hunt.

Spencer, Herbert. Literary Style & Music. LC 78-91057. 1970. Repr. of 1951 ed. 10.00 (ISBN 0-8046-0667-6). Kennikat.

Stravinsky, Igor. Poetics of Music in the Form of Six Lessons. LC 79-99520. (Charles Eliot Norton Lectures Ser: 1939-1940). (Fr. & Eng.). 1970. 9.00x (ISBN 0-674-67855-9); pap. 2.95 (ISBN 0-674-67856-7). Harvard U Pr.

Taubman, Howard. Music on My Beat: An Intimate Volume of Shop Talk. LC 76-57173. 1977. Repr. of 1943 ed. lib. bdg. 17.00x (ISBN 0-8371-9433-4, TAMU). Greenwood.

Taylor, Charles. Sounds of Music. (Illus.). 1978. 15.95 (ISBN 0-684-15476-5, ScribT). Scribner.

Taylor, Deems. Of Men & Music. LC 80-2305. Repr. of 1937 ed. 36.00 (ISBN 0-404-18873-7). AMS Pr.

--The Well Tempered Listener. LC 70-138190. 333p. 1972. Repr. of 1940 ed. lib. bdg. 15.75x (ISBN 0-8371-5647-5, TAWT). Greenwood.

Thompson, Oscar. How to Understand Music. 347p. 1980. Repr. of 1935 ed. lib. bdg. 30.00 (ISBN 0-89984-453-7). Century Bookbindery.

Tompkins, Flora. Ashland Collegiate Institute & Musical Academy. (Illus.). 1979. pap. 4.50 (ISBN 0-686-65490-0). Hope Farm.

Tremblay, George. The Definitive Cycle of the Twelve Tone Row. LC 72-97808. 1974. cancelled (ISBN 0-685-41684-4). Criterion Mus.

Verster, J. F. XL Muzikale Boekmerken Met Een Opgave Van Meer Dan CCC Spreuken, Die Op Dit Soort Van Boekmerken Voorkomen. wrappers 30.00 (ISBN 90-6027-362-1, Pub. by Frits Knuf Netherlands). Pendragon NY.

Waller, Adrian. Adrian Waller's Guide to Music. (Quality Paperback: No. 296). (Illus.). 156p. (Orig.). 1975. pap. 2.95 (ISBN 0-8226-0296-2). Littlefield.

Walters, Raymond. Bethlehem Bach Choir: An Historical & Interpretive Sketch. LC 77-135726. (No. 248). Repr. of 1918 ed. 24.50 (ISBN 0-404-07200-3). AMS Pr.

Weber, Max. Rational & Social Foundations of Music. Martindale, Don, et al, trs. LC 56-12134. 198p. 1958. Repr. lib. bdg. 12.95x (ISBN 0-8093-0015-X). S Ill U Pr.
Webern, Anton. The Path to the New Music. Reich, Willi, ed. Black, Leo, tr. from Ger. pap. 3.95 (ISBN 3-7024-0030-3, 47-12947). Eur-Am Music.
Wedge, George A. The Gist of Music. 1936. 3.00 (ISBN 0-02-872780-0). Schirmer Bks.
Whitehall Company. Basic Music. LC 73-168633. pap. 2.95x (ISBN 0-87655-524-5). Whitehall Co.
Winckel, Fritz. Music, Sound & Sensation: A Modern Exposition. 7.50 (ISBN 0-8446-3192-2). Peter Smith.
Wooley, Rebecca. Musical Book for Children & Adult. new ed. 1978. write for info (ISBN 0-9601654-1-X). R S Wooley.
Yannatos, James. Explorations in Musical Materials: A Working Approach to Making Music. (Illus.). 1978. pap. text ed. 14.50 (ISBN 0-13-295956-9). P-H.
Young, Percy M. Great Ideas in Music. Pringle, Patrick, ed. LC 68-56098. (Great Ideas Ser). (gr. 12 up). 1970. 4.95 (ISBN 0-87250-212-0). D White.
Zonis, Ella. Classical Persian Music: An Introduction. LC 76-188350. (Illus.). 288p. 1973. 16.50x (ISBN 0-674-13435-4). Harvard U Pr.
Zorn, Jay & Hanshumaker, James. Fundammentals Learning Through Making Music. Feldstein, Sandy, ed. LC 79-25768. 1980. pap. 13.50 (ISBN 0-88284-105-X). Alfred Pub.
Zuckerland, Victor. Sound & Symbol, 2 vols. Incl. Vol. 1. Music & the External World. Trask, W. R., tr. 1956. 25.00 (ISBN 0-691-09828-X); pap. 6.95 (ISBN 0-691-01759-X, 183); Vol. 2. Man the Musician. Guterman, Norbert, tr. 450p. 1973. 25.00 (ISBN 0-691-09925-1); pap. 7.95 (ISBN 0-691-01812-X). LC 55-11489. (Bollingen Ser.: Vol. 44). Set. 42.50 (ISBN 0-686-64022-5). Princeton U Pr.

MUSIC–ACOUSTICS AND PHYSICS

see also Electro-Acoustics; Musical Intervals and Scales; Musical Temperament; Sound

Appelman, D. Ralph. Science of Vocal Pedagogy: Theory & Application. LC 67-10107. (Illus.). 448p. 1967. 25.00x (ISBN 0-253-35110-3); of 3 tapes 15.00 set (ISBN 0-253-35115-4); Tape 1. 15.00 (ISBN 0-253-35112-X); Tape 2. 15.00 (ISBN 0-253-35113-8); Tape 3. 5.95 (ISBN 0-253-35114-6). Ind U Pr.
Backus, John. Acoustical Foundations of Music. 2nd ed. LC 68-54957. (Illus.). 1977. 14.95x (ISBN 0-393-09096-5, NortonC). Norton.
Bartholomew, Wilmer T. Acoustics of Music. LC 79-17650. (Illus.). 1980. Repr. of 1942 ed. lib. bdg. 19.50x (ISBN 0-313-22087-5, BAAC). Greenwood.
Benade, A. H. Fundamentals of Musical Acoustics. (Illus.). 608p. 1976. text ed. 16.95x (ISBN 0-19-502030-8). Oxford U Pr.
Benade, Arthur H. Horns, Strings, & Harmony. LC 78-25707. (Illus.). 1979. Repr. of 1960 ed. lib. bdg. 19.75x (ISBN 0-313-20771-2, BEHO). Greenwood.
Broadhouse, John. Musical Acoustics: Or the Phenomena of Sound As Connected with Music. LC 72-181115. 425p. 1926. Repr. 35.00 (ISBN 0-403-01630-4). Scholarly.
--Musical Acoustics: Student's Helmholtz. LC 77-81653. 1977. Repr. of 1926 ed. lib. bdg. 20.00 (ISBN 0-89341-073-X). Longwood Pr.
Bullock, Theodore H., ed. Recognition of Complex Acoustic Signals, LSRR 5. (Dahlem Workshop Reports Ser.). 1977. pap. 37.70 (ISBN 0-89573-089-8). Verlag Chemie.
Culver, Charles A. Musical Acoustics. 4th ed. 1956. text ed. 23.00 (ISBN 0-07-014904-6). McGraw.
Diamond, Dorothy & Tiffin, Robert. Musical Instruments. LC 77-82979. (Teaching Primary Science Ser.). (Illus.). 1977. pap. text ed. 7.95 (ISBN 0-356-05077-7). Raintree Child.
Erickson, Robert. Sound Structure in Music. LC 72-9352. (Illus.). 1975. 18.50x (ISBN 0-520-02376-5). U of Cal Pr.
Fletcher, Neville. The Physics of Music. (The Fundamentals of Senior Physics Ser.: Textbook 2). 1976. pap. text ed. 4.95x (ISBN 0-686-65411-0, 00509); cassette 6.95x (ISBN 0-686-65412-9, 00510). Heinemann Ed.
Hall, Donald E. Musical Acoustics: An Introduction. 528p. 1979. text ed. 21.95x (ISBN 0-534-00758-9). Wadsworth Pub.
Helmholtz, Hermann L. On the Sensations of Tone. 1954. pap. 7.50 (ISBN 0-486-60753-4). Dover.
Hutchins, Carleen M., ed. Musical Acoustics: Violin Family Functions, 2 pts. (Benchmark Papers in Acoustics Ser.: No. 5). 1975-76. Pt. 1. 55.50 (ISBN 0-12-786691-4); Pt. 2. 55.50 (ISBN 0-12-786692-2); Set. 96.90 (ISBN 0-686-77107-9). Acad Pr.
Jeans, James. Science & Music. (Illus.). 1968. pap. 3.50 (ISBN 0-486-61964-8). Dover.
Levarie, Siegmund & Levy, Ernst. Tone: A Study in Musical Acoustics. 2nd ed. LC 80-29383. (Illus.). xvii, 256p. 1981. Repr. of 1980 ed. lib. bdg. 27.50x (ISBN 0-313-22499-4, LETO). Greenwood.
--Tone: A Study in Musical Acoustics. rev. ed. LC 80-16794. (Illus.). 280p. 1980. pap. 6.75x (ISBN 0-87338-250-1). Kent St U Pr.
Lloyd, Llewelyn S. Music & Sound. LC 70-107815. (Select Bibliographies Reprint Ser). 1937. 16.00 (ISBN 0-8369-5188-3). Arno.
--Music & Sound. Repr. of 1937 ed. lib. bdg. 15.00x (ISBN 0-8371-4260-1, LLMS). Greenwood.
Lowery, H. Guide to Musical Acoustics. 1956. 6.95 (ISBN 0-234-77220-4). Dufour.
Mason, Warren P. & Thurston, Robert N., eds. Physical Acoustics: Principles & Methods, Vol. 15. 1981. 45.00 (ISBN 0-12-477915-8). Acad Pr.
Miller, Dayton C. The Science of Musical Sounds. 2nd ed. LC 76-181211. 286p. 1926. Repr. 25.00 (ISBN 0-403-01622-3). Scholarly.
Morgan, Joseph. The Physical Basis of Musical Sound. (Illus.). 168p. (Orig.). 1980. lib. bdg. 9.50 (ISBN 0-88275-656-7). Krieger.
Olson, Harry F. Music, Physics, & Engineering. rev. & enl. ed. Orig. Title: Musical Engineering. (Illus.). 1966. pap. 6.00 (ISBN 0-486-21769-8). Dover.
Rettinger, M. Studio Acoustics. 1981. 35.00 (ISBN 0-8206-0283-3). Chem Pub.
Rigden, John S. Physics & the Sound of Music. LC 77-5638. 1977. 17.50 (ISBN 0-471-02433-3). Wiley.
Roederer, J. Introduction to the Physics & Psychophysics of Music. 2nd ed. (Heidelberg Science Library). (Illus.). 202p. 1980. pap. 9.00 (ISBN 0-387-90116-7). Springer-Verlag.
Rosberger, Paul. The Theory of Total Consonance. LC 71-92560. (Illus.). 108p. 1970. 12.00 (ISBN 0-8386-7570-0). Fairleigh Dickinson.
Rossing, Thomas D. Science of Sound: Musical, Electronic, Environmental. LC 80-12028. (Chemistry Ser.). (Illus.). 512p. 1981. text ed. price not set (ISBN 0-201-06505-3). A-W.
Sabine, Wallace C. Collected Papers on Acoustics. 8.50 (ISBN 0-8446-2849-2). Peter Smith.
Savage, William R. Problems for Musical Acoustics. 1977. pap. text ed. 5.95x (ISBN 0-19-502251-3). Oxford U Pr.
Schafer, R. Murray. The Tuning of the World. 1977. 12.95 (ISBN 0-394-40966-3). Knopf.
Strong, William J. & Plitnik, George R. Music, Speech, & High Fidelity: A Descriptive Acoustics Workbook. (Illus.). 1977. pap. 12.95x (ISBN 0-8425-0797-3). Brigham.
Swenson, Christian N. & Holdsworth, Eugene I. Physics of Sound for Musicians. LC 80-80008. (Illus.). 208p. (Orig.). 1980. pap. 15.00x (ISBN 0-916030-05-9). Bethany Coll Ks.
Taylor, Sedley. Sound & Music: A Non-Mathematical Treatise on the Physical Constitution of Musical Sounds & Harmony. (Illus.). Repr. of 1873 ed. 16.00 (ISBN 0-384-59641-X). Johnson Repr.
Wagner, Michael. Introductory Musical Acoustics. (Illus.). 1978. pap. text ed. 10.00 (ISBN 0-89892-025-6). Contemp Pub Co of Raleigh.
Winckel, Fritz. Music, Sound & Sensation: A Modern Exposition. Binkley, Thomas, tr. (Illus.). 1967. pap. text ed. 3.50 (ISBN 0-486-21764-7). Dover.
Wood, Alexander. The Physics of Music. 7th ed. Bowsher, J. M., ed. LC 80-20967. (Illus.). xiv, 258p. 1981. Repr. of 1975 ed. lib. bdg. 28.50x (ISBN 0-313-22644-X, WOPM). Greenwood.
Wood, Alexander, ed. The Physics of Music. 7th ed. Bowsher, J. M. LC 74-4025. 258p. 1975. pap. text ed. 12.95x (ISBN 0-412-21140-8, Pub. by Chapman & Hall England). Methuen Inc.

MUSIC–ADDRESSES, ESSAYS, LECTURES

Abraham, Gerald. Tradition of Western Music. LC 72-97738. (Ernest Bloch Lectures Ser). 1974. 15.75x (ISBN 0-520-02414-1); pap. 6.50x (ISBN 0-520-02615-2). U of Cal Pr.
Aldrich, Richard. Musical Discourse, from the New York Times. facsimile ed. LC 67-28740. (Essay Index Reprint Ser). 1928. 16.00 (ISBN 0-8369-0144-4). Arno.
Apthorp, William F. Musicians & Music-Lovers: And Other Essays. LC 74-39633. (Essay Index Reprint Ser.). Repr. of 1894 ed. 20.00 (ISBN 0-8369-2736-2). Arno.
--Musicians & Music-Lovers & Other Essays. 1979. Repr. of 1894 ed. lib. bdg. 30.00 (ISBN 0-8492-0095-4). R West.
Bacon, Ernst. Words on Music. LC 73-427. 183p. 1973. Repr. of 1960 ed. lib. bdg. 15.00 (ISBN 0-8371-6768-X, BAWM). Greenwood.
Berlioz, Hector. Hector Berlioz: Selections from His Letters, and Aesthetic, Humorous & Satirical Writings. Apthorp, William F., ed. & tr. from French. LC 76-22325. 1976. Repr. of 1879 ed. lib. bdg. 40.00 (ISBN 0-89341-018-7). Longwood Pr.
Bernstein, Leonard. The Unanswered Question: Six Talks at Harvard. (The Charles Eliot Norton Lectures). 1976. slipcased with 3 records 25.00 (ISBN 0-674-81065-1); pap. 12.50 (ISBN 0-674-92001-5). Harvard U Pr.
Blok, Alexander. The Spirit of Music. Freiman, I., tr. from Rus. LC 72-14050. (Soviet Literature in English Translation Ser.). (Illus.). 70p. 1973. Repr. of 1946 ed. 8.50 (ISBN 0-88355-001-6). Hyperion Conn.
Blom, Eric. Stepchildren of Music. facs. ed. LC 67-28731. (Essay Index Reprint Ser). 1926. 18.00 (ISBN 0-8369-0217-3). Arno.
Bonavia, Ferruccio, ed. Musicians on Music. LC 78-66892. (Encore Music Editions Ser.). 1979. Repr. of 1956 ed. 21.50 (ISBN 0-88355-725-8). Hyperion Conn.
Borroff, Edith. Notations & Editions. (Music Reprint Series). 1977. Repr. of 1974 ed. lib. bdg. 25.00 (ISBN 0-306-70867-1). Da Capo.
Brown, Malcolm H., ed. Papers of the Yugoslav-American Seminar on Music. 1970. 7.95 (ISBN 0-89357-007-9); pap. 4.95 (ISBN 0-89357-006-0). Slavica.
Buck, Percy C. Scope of Music. facsimile ed. LC 70-93321. (Essay Index Reprint Ser). 1924. 12.00 (ISBN 0-8369-1276-4). Arno.
Cage, John. Silence: Lectures & Writings. LC 61-14238. 1961. pap. 7.95 (ISBN 0-8195-6028-6, Pub. by Wesleyan U Pr). Columbia U Pr.
Cairns, David. Responses. (Music Ser.). 1980. Repr. of 1973 ed. 25.00 (ISBN 0-306-76047-9). Da Capo.
Cardus, Neville. Talking of Music. LC 74-14112. 320p. 1975. Repr. of 1957 ed. lib. bdg. 16.25x (ISBN 0-8371-7786-3, CAMU). Greenwood.
Carner, Mosco. Major & Minor. LC 79-27481. (Illus.). 1980. text ed. 41.50x (ISBN 0-8419-0600-9). Holmes & Meier.
CISM (International Center for Mechanical Sciences), Dept. of Automation & Information, Univ of Geneva, 1971. Controlled & Conditioned Invariance. Basile, G., ed. (CISM Pubns. Ser.: No. 109). (Illus.). 51p. 1972. pap. 7.50 (ISBN 0-387-81132-X). Springer-Verlag.
Colles, Henry C. Essays & Lectures. facs. ed. LC 73-128225. (Essay Index Reprint Ser). 1945. 16.80 (ISBN 0-8369-1910-6). Arno.
Crawford, Richard. American Studies & American Musicology: A Point of View & a Case in Point. LC 75-874. (I. S. A. M. Monograph Ser: No. 4). 34p. 1975. pap. 3.00 (ISBN 0-914678-03-5). Inst Am Music.
Damrosch, Walter J. My Musical Life. LC 71-109725. (Illus.). 376p. 1972. Repr. of 1923 ed. lib. bdg. 17.00x (ISBN 0-8371-4215-6, DAML). Greenwood.
De Falla, Manuel. On Music & Musicians. 136p. 1979. 14.95 (ISBN 0-7145-2600-2, Pub. by M Boyars); pap. 7.95 (ISBN 0-7145-2735-1). Merrimack Bk Serv.
De Lerma, Dominique-Rene, et al. Reflections on Afro-American Music. LC 72-619703. 350p. 1973. 14.00x (ISBN 0-87338-135-1). Kent St U Pr.
Dyson, George. New Music. (Select Bibliographies Reprint Ser). 1924. 15.00 (ISBN 0-8369-5231-6). Arno.
--Progress of Music. LC 79-93334. (Essay Index Reprint Ser). 1932. 16.00 (ISBN 0-8369-1287-X). Arno.
Einstein, Alfred. Essays on Music. 1962. pap. 5.95 (ISBN 0-393-00177-6, Norton Lib). Norton.
Engel, Carl. Discords Mingled: Essays on Music. facs. ed. LC 67-28752. (Essay Index Reprint Ser). 1931. 16.00 (ISBN 0-8369-0417-6). Arno.
--Musical Myths & Facts, 2 vols. in one. LC 76-25760. 1976. Repr. of 1876 ed. lib. bdg. 50.00 (ISBN 0-89341-026-8). Longwood Pr.
Finck, Henry T. Chopin, & Other Musical Essays. facsimile ed. LC 78-37471. (Essay Index Reprint Ser). Repr. of 1889 ed. 17.00 (ISBN 0-8369-2548-3). Arno.
Flothius, Marius. Notes on Notes: Selected Essays. (Illus.). 178p. 1974. 35.00 (ISBN 90-6027-227-7, Pub. by Frits Knuf Netherlands); wrappers 20.00 (ISBN 90-6027-226-9, Pub. by Frits Knuf Netherlands). Pendragon NY.
Fox-Strangways, Arthur H. Music Observed: The Selection Made by Steuart Wilson. facs. ed. LC 68-16931. (Essay Index Reprint Ser). 1936. 15.00 (ISBN 0-8369-0452-4). Arno.
Fraser, Andrew A. Essays on Music. facs. ed. LC 68-16932. (Essay Index Reprint Ser). 1930. 13.00 (ISBN 0-8369-0454-0). Arno.
Gerboth, Walter, et al, eds. Introduction to Music: Selected Readings. rev ed (Orig.). 1969. pap. text ed. 5.95x (ISBN 0-393-09790-0, NortonC). Norton.
Gilman, Lawrence. Music of To-Morrow & Other Studies. facs. ed. LC 71-128246. (Essay Index Reprint Ser). 1907. 12.00 (ISBN 0-8369-1830-4). Arno.
--Music of To-Morrow & Other Studies. LC 73-153249. (Essay & General Literature Index Reprint Ser). 1971. Repr. of 1907 ed. 12.75 (ISBN 0-8046-1502-0). Kennikat.
--Phases of Modern Music. facs. ed. LC 68-22915. (Essay Index Reprint Ser). 1904. 13.00 (ISBN 0-8369-0476-1). Arno.
Grace, Harvey. Musician at Large. LC 78-107703. (Essay Index Reprint Ser). 1928. 16.00 (ISBN 0-8369-1506-2). Arno.
Gray, Cecil. Contingencies & Other Essays. facs. ed. LC 75-134084. (Essay Index Reprint Ser). 1947. 15.00 (ISBN 0-8369-2159-3). Arno.
--A Survey of Contemporary Music. 2nd ed. LC 78-163551. 266p. 1972. Repr. of 1927 ed. lib. bdg. 15.00x (ISBN 0-8371-6211-4, GRCM). Greenwood.
Grey, Robin. Studies in Music. LC 74-24092. Repr. of 1901 ed. 27.50 (ISBN 0-404-12937-4). AMS Pr.
Hadow, William H. Collected Essays. facs. ed. LC 68-20305. (Essay Index Reprint Ser). 1928. 18.00 (ISBN 0-8369-0505-9). Arno.
High Fidelity Editors. High Fidelity's Silver Anniversary Treasury. LC 76-42077. 1976. 9.95 (ISBN 0-911656-01-4). Wyeth Pr.
Huneker, James G. Bedouins. LC 72-6579. (Illus.). Repr. of 1920 ed. 21.50 (ISBN 0-404-10526-2). AMS Pr.
--Old Fogy, His Musical Opinions & Grotesques. LC 78-13862. (Encore Music Editions Ser.). 1979. Repr. of 1913 ed. 17.50 (ISBN 0-88355-799-1). Hyperion Conn.
--Unicorns. LC 72-6581. Repr. of 1917 ed. 22.50 (ISBN 0-404-10529-7). AMS Pr.
Inserra, Lorraine. The Music of Henry Ainsworth's Psalter (Amsterdam 1612) Hitchcock, H. Wiley, ed. LC 81-81547. (Monograph: No. 15). 128p. (Orig.). 1981. pap. 9.00 (ISBN 0-914678-15-9). Inst Am Music.
Ives, Charles. Essays Before a Sonata, the Majority, & Other Writings. Boatwright, Howard, ed. 1970. pap. 4.95 (ISBN 0-393-00528-3, Norton Lib). Norton.
Kirby, F. E. Music in the Classic Period: An Anthology with Commentary. LC 77-84939. 1979. pap. text ed. 14.95 (ISBN 0-02-870710-9). Schirmer Bks.
Krehbiel, Henry E. Music & Manners in the Classical Period. LC 76-22336. 1976. Repr. of 1898 ed. lib. bdg. 30.00 (ISBN 0-89341-014-4). Longwood Pr.
Krenek, Ernst. Exploring Music. 1968. 8.50 (ISBN 0-8079-0047-8); pap. 2.95 (ISBN 0-8079-0048-6). October.
Lang, Paul H., ed. Problems of Modern Music. 1962. pap. 2.95 (ISBN 0-393-00115-6, Norton Lib). Norton.
Lowens, Irving, pref. by. Lectures on the History & Art of Music: The Louis Charles Elson Memorial Lectures at the Library of Congress 1946-1965. LC 68-55319. (Music Ser.). 1968. Repr. of 1963 ed. lib. bdg. 22.50 (ISBN 0-306-71193-1). Da Capo.
McCue, George, ed. Music in American Society 1776-1976. LC 76-24527. (Illus.). 1976. text ed. 14.95 (ISBN 0-87855-209-X); pap. text ed. 3.95 (ISBN 0-87855-634-6). Transaction Bks.
MacDougall & Duncan, eds. The Bond of Music: An Anthology. 1978. Repr. lib. bdg. 17.50 (ISBN 0-8495-3507-7). Arden Lib.
MacDowell, Edward. Critical & Historical Essays. 2nd ed. LC 69-11289. 1969. Repr. of 1912 ed. lib. bdg. 25.00 (ISBN 0-306-71098-6). Da Capo.
Mason, Daniel G. Dilemma of American Music, & Other Essays. Repr. of 1928 ed. lib. bdg. 14.50x (ISBN 0-8371-1155-2, MAAM). Greenwood.
Mathews, William S. Music: Its Ideals & Methods, a Collection of Essays for Young Teachers, Amateurs, & Students. LC 70-173057. Repr. of 1897 ed. 20.50 (ISBN 0-404-07211-9). AMS Pr.
May, Elizabeth, ed. Musics of Many Cultures: An Introduction. LC 76-50251. 1981. 38.50x (ISBN 0-520-03393-0). U of Cal Pr.
Meyer, Leonard B. Explaining Music: Essays & Explorations. LC 77-90968. 1978. pap. 8.95 (ISBN 0-226-52142-7, P769, Phoen). U of Chicago Pr.
Moore, Jerrold N., annotations by. Music & Friends: Letters to Adrian Boult. (Illus.). 224p. 1979. 19.95 (ISBN 0-241-10178-6, Pub. by Hamish Hamilton England). David & Charles.
Newman, Ernest. Essays from the World of Music. LC 77-17326. (Music Reprint Ser.: 1978). (Illus.). 1978. Repr. of 1956 ed. lib. bdg. 27.50 (ISBN 0-306-77519-0). Da Capo.
--More Essays from the World of Music. LC 77-17332. (Music Reprint Ser.: 1978). (Illus.). 1978. Repr. of 1958 ed. lib. bdg. 27.50 (ISBN 0-306-77520-4). Da Capo.
--A Musical Motley. LC 76-10332. (Music Reprint Ser.). 1976. lib. bdg. 25.00 (ISBN 0-306-70784-5). Da Capo.
Noblitt, Thomas, ed. Music East & West: Essays in Honor of Walter Kaufman. (Festschrift Ser.: No. 3). (Illus.). x, 386p. 1981. lib. bdg. 36.00 (ISBN 0-918728-15-0). Pendragon NY.

Olleson, Edward, ed. Modern Musical Scholarship: Studies in Musical History. (Illus.). 1980. write for info. (ISBN 0-85362-180-2, Oriel). Routledge & Kegan.

Pound, Ezra. Ezra Pound & Music: The Complete Criticism. Schafer, R. Murray, ed. LC 77-9609. 1977. 42.00 (ISBN 0-8112-0668-8). New Directions.

Reich, Steve. Writings About Music. 1974. pap. 7.00 (ISBN 0-686-67541-X, 50-26921). Eur-Am Music.

Rosenfeld, Paul. By Way of Art: Criticisms of Music, Literature, Painting, Sculpture & the Dance. facs. ed. LC 67-30230. (Essay Index Reprint Ser). 1928. 16.00 (ISBN 0-8369-0835-X). Arno.

--Discoveries of a Music Critic. LC 79-183510. 402p. 1972. Repr. of 1936 ed. 20.00x (ISBN 0-8443-0064-0). Vienna Hse.

--Musical Chronicle, 1917-1923. LC 77-175877. 17.00 (ISBN 0-685-26463-7). Arno.

--Musical Impressions: Selections from Paul Rosenfeld's Criticism. Leibowitz, Herbert A., ed. LC 76-75252. 334p. 1969. 7.95 (ISBN 0-8090-7172-X). Hill & Wang.

Rosenstrauch, Henrietta. Essays on Rhythm, Music, Movement. LC 73-77959. 1973. spiral bdg. 5.00 (ISBN 0-913650-01-3). Volkwein Bros.

Saint-Saens, C. Musical Memories. Rich, Edwin G., tr. LC 79-137288. Repr. of 1919 ed. 12.50 (ISBN 0-404-05502-8). AMS Pr.

Saint-Saens, Camille. Musical Memories. LC 70-93980. (Music Reprint Ser). 1969. Repr. of 1919 ed. lib. bdg. 29.50 (ISBN 0-306-71821-9). Da Capo.

--Outspoken Essays on Music. Rothwell, Fred, tr. Repr. of 1922 ed. lib. bdg. 15.00x (ISBN 0-8371-4010-2, SAES). Greenwood.

--Outspoken Essays on Music. LC 75-181243. 186p. 1922. Repr. 19.00 (ISBN 0-403-01668-1). Scholarly.

Schnabel, Arthur. Reflections on Music, Betrachtungen Ueber Musik: A Lecture. LC 70-181247. 31p. 1933. Repr. 8.00 (ISBN 0-403-01672-X). Scholarly.

Scholes, Percy A. Crotchets: A Few Short Musical Notes. facs. ed. LC 67-22115. (Essay Index Reprint Ser). 1924. 16.00 (ISBN 0-8369-0855-4). Arno.

Simon, Robert E., ed. Be Your Own Music Critic. facsimile ed. LC 70-134135. (Essay Index Reprint Ser). 1941. 18.00 (ISBN 0-8369-2095-3). Arno.

Smits Van Waesberghe, J. Dia-Pason: Ausgewahlte Aufsatze Von Joseph Smits Van Waesberghe. 200p. 1976. 32.50 (ISBN 90-6027-345-1, Pub. by Frits Knuf Netherlands). Pendragon NY.

Sonneck, Oscar G. Miscellaneous Studies in History of Music. LC 70-127897. Repr. of 1921 ed. 24.00 (ISBN 0-404-06155-9). AMS Pr.

--Miscellaneous Studies in the History of Music. LC 68-9192. (Music Reprint Ser). 1968. Repr. of 1921 ed. lib. bdg. 35.00 (ISBN 0-306-71163-X). Da Capo.

Sorabji, Kaikhosru S. Around Music. LC 78-66925. (Encore Music Editions Ser.). (Illus.). 1979. Repr. of 1932 ed. 19.50 (ISBN 0-88355-764-9). Hyperion Conn.

Spaeth, Sigmund. Fifty Years with Music. LC 77-13488. 1977. Repr. of 1959 ed. lib. bdg. 22.25x (ISBN 0-8371-9862-3, SPFY). Greenwood.

--Importance of Music. LC 62-20701. (Illus.). 1963. 8.95 (ISBN 0-8303-0022-8). Fleet.

Spangenberg, Wolfhart. Saemtliche Werke, Vol. 1: Von der Musica. Singschul, Vol. 1. Tarnai, A. & Vizkelety, A., eds. 173p. 1971. 46.25x (ISBN 3-11-001846-2). De Gruyter.

Stanford, Charles V. Studies & Memories. LC 76-22352. (Illus.). 1976. Repr. of 1908 ed. lib. bdg. 25.00 (ISBN 0-89341-023-3). Longwood Pr.

Stasov, Vladimir. Selected Essays in Music. Jonas, Florence, tr. (Music Reprint 1980 Ser.). (Illus.). 200p. 1980. Repr. of 1968 ed. lib. bdg. 22.50 (ISBN 0-306-76033-9). Da Capo.

Stein, Erwin. Orpheus in New Guises. Keller, Hans, tr. LC 78-66921. (Encore Music Editions Ser.). (Illus.). 1980. Repr. of 1953 ed. 18.50 (ISBN 0-88355-765-7). Hyperion Conn.

Suchoff, Benjamin, ed. B'ela Bart'ok: Essays. LC 76-5202. (Illus.). 1976. 75.00 (ISBN 0-312-07350-X). St Martin.

Surette, Thomas W. Music & Life. 1965. pap. 5.00 (ISBN 0-911318-04-6). E C Schirmer.

Taylor, H., ed. Edward J. Dent: Selected Essays. LC 78-62111. (Illus.). 1979. 34.50 (ISBN 0-521-22174-9). Cambridge U Pr.

Terry, Richard R. Voodooism in Music, & Other Essays. facs. ed. LC 68-16978. (Essay Index Reprint Ser). 1934. 15.00 (ISBN 0-8369-0930-5). Arno.

Thomson, Virgil. A Virgil Thomson Reader. 576p. 1981. 25.00 (ISBN 0-395-31330-9). HM.

Tovey, Donald F. Musical Articles from the Encyclopedia Britannica. LC 79-181279. 251p. 1944. Repr. 21.00 (ISBN 0-403-01702-5). Scholarly.

Van Dieren, Bernard. Down Among the Dead Men & Other Essays. facs. ed. LC 67-26732. (Essay Index Reprint Ser). 1935. 16.00 (ISBN 0-8369-0374-9). Arno.

Vaughan Williams, Ralph. The Making of Music. LC 76-1009. (Illus.). 61p. 1976. Repr. of 1955 ed. lib. bdg. 15.00 (ISBN 0-8371-8771-0, WIMM). Greenwood.

--Some Thoughts on Beethoven's Choral Symphony, with Writings on Other Musical Subjects. LC 81-2079. (Illus.). 172p. 1981. Repr. of 1953 ed. lib. bdg. 22.50x (ISBN 0-313-23049-8, VWST). Greenwood.

Vinton, John. Essays After a Dictionary: Music & Culture at the Close of Western Civilization. 170p. 1977. 12.50 (ISBN 0-8387-1898-1). Bucknell U Pr.

Westrup, Jack A. Sharps & Flats. LC 79-134156. (Essay Index Reprint Ser). 1940. 16.00 (ISBN 0-8369-1937-8). Arno.

Whiteside, Abby. Mastering the Chopin Etudes & Other Essays. LC 79-85263. 1969. 12.50 (ISBN 0-684-10654-X, ScribT). Scribner.

Whittaker, William G. Collected Essays. LC 73-111873. (Essay Index Reprint Ser). 1940. 16.00 (ISBN 0-8369-1636-0). Arno.

Whone, Herbert. The Hidden Face of Music. rev. ed. LC 78-11098. (Illus.). 1979. pap. 4.95 (ISBN 0-932934-00-5). Garden Studio.

Widdess, D. R. & Wolpert, R. F., eds. Music & Tradition: Essays on Asian & Other Musics. LC 78-73235. (Illus.). 1981. 59.50 (ISBN 0-521-22400-4). Cambridge U Pr.

MUSIC–ANALYSIS, APPRECIATION

see also Music–Interpretation (Phrasing, Dynamics, Etc.)

Apicella, Anthony J., et al. Simplicity in Music Appreciation. 2nd ed. 1974. 13.95 (ISBN 0-13-810150-7). P-H.

Apthorp, William F. Musicians & Music-Lovers & Other Essays. LC 78-58194. 1978. Repr. of 1894 ed. lib. bdg. 35.00 (ISBN 0-89341-433-6). Longwood Pr.

Bacharach, A. L., ed. New Musical Companion. 1964. 7.50x (ISBN 0-575-00496-7). Intl Pubns Serv.

--New Musical Companion. 22nd rev. ed. 1957. 5.50x (ISBN 0-8426-1131-2). Verry.

Baker, Richard. Richard Baker's Music Guide. LC 79-52366. (Illus.). 144p. 1980. 11.95 (ISBN 0-7153-7782-5). David & Charles.

Barlow, Wayne. Foundations of Music. LC 53-8987. (Illus.). 1953. 28.50x (ISBN 0-89197-176-9); pap. text ed. 16.50x (ISBN 0-8290-0678-8). Irvington.

Barry, Wallace. Structural Functions in Music. (Illus.). 512p. 1976. 21.95 (ISBN 0-13-853903-0). P-H.

Benward, Bruce. Ear Training: A Technique for Listening. 1978. wire coil avail. (ISBN 0-697-03550-6); 14 tapes avail. (ISBN 0-697-03552-2); instrs.' man. avail. (ISBN 0-697-03551-4). Wm C Brown.

--Music in Theory & Practice, 2 vols. Incl. Vol. 1. (ISBN 0-697-03595-6); Wkbk. (ISBN 0-697-03597-2); Vol. 2. (ISBN 0-697-03596-4); Wkbk. (ISBN 0-697-03598-0). 1977. plastic comb 13.95 ea.; wkbk. 7.95 ea.; Vols. 1 & 2. pap. instr's resource man. 3.00x (ISBN 0-685-93541-8). Wm C Brown.

Bernstein, Martin & Picker, Martin. Introduction to Music. 4th ed. LC 77-178158. (Illus.). 1972. text ed. 19.95 (ISBN 0-13-489559-2). P-H.

Birkenshaw, Lois. Music for Fun, Music for Learning. 2nd ed. 1978. text ed. 15.95 (ISBN 0-03-022446-2, HoltC). HR&W.

Bockmon, Guy A. & Starr, William J. Scored for Listening: A Guide to Music. 2nd ed. (Illus., Orig.). 1972. pap. text ed. 12.95 (ISBN 0-15-579055-2, HC). HarBraceJ.

Braunstein, Joseph. Musica Aeterna: Program Notes, 1961-1967. LC 72-8420. (Music Ser). 332p. 1973. Repr. of 1968 ed. lib. bdg. 32.50 (ISBN 0-306-70554-0). Da Capo.

Busoni, Ferruccio B. The Essence of Music & Other Papers. Ley, Rossmund, tr. LC 78-66899. (Encore Music Editions Ser.). (Illus.). 1979. Repr. of 1957 ed. 19.00 (ISBN 0-88355-728-2). Hyperion Conn.

Cohn, Arthur. Twentieth-Century Music in Western Europe: The Compositions & Recordings. LC 70-39297. 510p. 1972. Repr. of 1965 ed. lib. bdg. 37.50 (ISBN 0-306-70460-9). Da Capo.

Copland, Aaron. What to Listen for in Music. rev. ed. (Illus.). 1957. 9.95 (ISBN 0-07-013089-2, GB). McGraw.

--What to Listen for in Music. rev. ed. (RL 9). 1964. pap. 1.95 (ISBN 0-451-61882-3, MJ1882, Ment). NAL.

Courtney, Elise & Celeste, Emily. How to Find Music Easily for Good Times in Harmony. LC 80-51888. (Illus.). 317p. (Orig.). 1980. pap. 6.00 (ISBN 0-686-28899-8). Merk.

Dallin, Leon. Listener's Guide to Musical Understanding. 5th ed. 464p. 1982. pap. text ed. price not set (ISBN 0-697-03487-9); price not set wkbk. (ISBN 0-697-03521-2); price not set recordings (ISBN 0-697-03520-4); instructor's manual avail. Wm C Brown.

--Listeners Guide to Musical Understanding. 4th ed. 416p. 1977. pap. text ed. write for info. (ISBN 0-697-03437-2); wkbk. avail. (ISBN 0-697-03438-0); recordings avail. (ISBN 0-697-03439-9); tchrs.' manual & key avail. (ISBN 0-686-67596-7). Wm C Brown.

Debussy, Claude. Debussy on Music. Lesure, Francois, ed. Smith, Richard L., tr. 1977. 15.00 (ISBN 0-394-48120-8). Knopf.

Debussy, Claude, et al. Three Classics in the Aesthetic of Music. 1962. lib. bdg. 10.50x (ISBN 0-88307-071-5). Gannon.

DeLone, R. P. Music: Patterns & Style. 1971. 15.95 (ISBN 0-201-01489-0). A-W.

Dickinson, Edward. The Spirit of Music: How to Find It & How to Share It. (Select Bibliographies Reprint Ser.). Repr. of 1925 ed. 16.00 (ISBN 0-8369-6683-X). Arno.

Dolmetsch, Arnold. Interpretation of the Music of the Seventeenth & Eighteenth Centuries. LC 76-75611. (Illus.). 512p. 1969. pap. 7.95 (ISBN 0-295-78578-0, WP51); 2 lp records 13.50 (ISBN 0-295-75007-3). U of Wash Pr.

Dorian, Frederick. History of Music in Performance. (Illus.). 1966. pap. 2.95 (ISBN 0-393-00369-8, Norton Lib). Norton.

Downes, Olin. Olin Downes on Music: A Selection from His Writings During the Half-Century 1906-1955. Downes, Irene, ed. LC 69-13886. Repr. of 1957 ed. lib. bdg. 20.00x (ISBN 0-8371-0390-8, DOOD). Greenwood.

Dwyer, Terence. Teaching Musical Appreciation. 1967. 8.00x (ISBN 0-19-317409-X). Oxford U Pr.

Erickson, Robert. The Structure of Music: a Listener's Guide: A Study of Music in Terms of Melody & Counterpoint. LC 75-31361. 1977. Repr. of 1955 ed. lib. bdg. 18.25x (ISBN 0-8371-8519-X, ERSM). Greenwood.

Ewen, David. Complete Book of Classical Music. 1965. 24.95 (ISBN 0-13-156042-5). P-H.

--World of Twentieth Century Music. LC 68-11358. 1968. 19.95 (ISBN 0-13-968776-9). P-H.

Fenton, William N. Sioux Music. lib. bdg. 29.00 (ISBN 0-403-08975-1). Scholarly.

Ferguson, Donald N. A History of Musical Thought. LC 73-5265. 675p. 1975. Repr. of 1959 ed. lib. bdg. 38.75x (ISBN 0-8371-6882-1, FEMT). Greenwood.

Fiske, Roger. Beethoven's Missa Solemnis. (Illus.). 1979. 14.95 (ISBN 0-684-16228-8, ScribT). Scribner.

Forcucci, Samuel L. Let There Be Music. new ed. (gr. 9-12). 1973. text ed. 14.40 (ISBN 0-205-03768-2, 5837685); tchrs'. guide 2.40 (ISBN 0-205-03794-1, 5837944). Allyn.

Forte, Allen. The Structure of Atonal Music. LC 72-91295. 1977. pap. 18.50x (ISBN 0-300-01610-7); pap. 7.95 (ISBN 0-300-02120-8). Yale U Pr.

Fuller-Maitland, John A. Spell of Music: An Attempt to Analyse the Enjoyment of Music. LC 76-102239. (Select Bibliographies Reprint Ser). 1926. 13.00 (ISBN 0-8369-5124-7). Arno.

Gafurius, Franchinus. Monuments of Music & Music Literature in Facisimile: Series Two Pt.4, Vol. 96. Apologia. 1979. 25.00x (ISBN 0-8450-2296-2). Broude.

--Monuments of Music & Music Literature in Facsimile: Series Two Pt.4, Vol. 99. (Practica Musice). 1979. 42.50x (ISBN 0-8450-2299-7). Broude.

Gelineau, P. Experiences in Music. 2nd ed. 1975. text ed. 15.50 (ISBN 0-07-023092-7, C). McGraw.

Geminiani, Francesco. Treatise on Good Taste in the Art of Musick. 2nd ed. LC 68-16233. (Music Reprint Ser). 1969. Repr. of 1749 ed. lib. bdg. 17.50 (ISBN 0-306-70985-6). Da Capo.

Gilbert, Jean. Musical Activities with Young Children. LC 75-332407. (Illus.). 1975. 10.00x (ISBN 0-7062-3462-6). Intl Pubns Serv.

Goodrich, A. J. Complete Musical Analysis. 1976. Repr. of 1889 ed. lib. bdg. 27.00 (ISBN 0-403-03565-1). Scholarly.

Haggin, B. H. The New Listener's Companion & Record Guide. 5th ed. LC 77-77128. 1978. 15.00 (ISBN 0-8180-1216-1); pap. 6.95 (ISBN 0-8180-1217-X). Horizon.

Hansen, Peter S. An Introduction to Twentieth Century Music. 4th ed. 1978. pap. text ed. 17.95 (ISBN 0-205-05921-X). Allyn.

Hardy, Gordon & Fish, Arnold. Music Literature: A Workbook for Analysis, 2 vols. (Orig.). 1963-66. Vol. 1. pap. text ed. 14.50 scp (ISBN 0-06-042633-0, HarpC); Vol. 2. pap. text ed. 15.50 scp (ISBN 0-06-042634-9). Har-Row.

Hickok, Robert. Exploring Music. 3rd ed. LC 78-62545. (Illus.). 1979. text ed. 15.95 (ISBN 0-201-02929-4); instructor's manual 3.00 (ISBN 0-201-02932-4); student's wkbk. 4.95 (ISBN 0-201-02933-2); record 21.95 (ISBN 0-201-02934-0). A-W.

Hines, Robert S., ed. The Composer's Point of View: Essays on Twentieth-Century Choral Music by Those Who Wrote It. LC 80-12636. (Illus.). xiv, 342p. 1980. Repr. of 1963 ed. lib. bdg. 28.50x (ISBN 0-313-22461-7, HICM). Greenwood.

Hoffer, Charles R. The Understanding of Music. 4th ed. 544p. 1981. text ed. 16.95x (ISBN 0-534-00915-8); wkbk. 6.95x (ISBN 0-534-00916-6); record album 24.95x (ISBN 0-686-74671-6). Wadsworth Pub.

Hughes, Charles W. Human Side of Music. LC 70-107871. (Music Ser). 1970. Repr. of 1948 ed. lib. bdg. 32.50 (ISBN 0-306-71895-2). Da Capo.

Hunter, Stanley A., ed. Music & Religion. LC 72-1615. Repr. of 1930 ed. 19.00 (ISBN 0-404-08316-1). AMS Pr.

Jenkins, David & Visocchi, Mark. Portraits in Music I. 66p. 1980. 6.00 (ISBN 0-19-321400-8). Oxford U Pr.

Johnson, Dale R. Yuarn Music Dramas: Studies in Prosody & Structure & a Complete Catalogue of Northern Arias in the Dramatic Style. LC 80-25372. (Michigan Papers in Chinese Studies: No. 40). 400p. (Orig.). 1980. pap. 8.00 (ISBN 0-89264-040-5). U of Mich Ctr Chinese.

Johnson, Frances H. Musical Memories of Hartford. LC 70-136370. Repr. of 1931 ed. 25.50 (ISBN 0-404-07224-0). AMS Pr.

Kaufmann, Helen. You Can Enjoy Music. (New Reprints in Essay & General Literature Index Ser.). 1975. Repr. of 1940 ed. 21.75 (ISBN 0-518-10203-3, 10203). Arno.

Kelly, Robert. Aural & Visual Recognition: A Musical Eartraining Series. LC 73-83550. 1972. instructor's manual 0.95x (ISBN 0-252-00028-5); chromatic student quiz book 2.95x (ISBN 0-252-00098-6); diatonic student quiz book 2.95x (ISBN 0-252-00099-4); 6 cassettes for diatonic ser 42.00x (ISBN 0-252-00070-6); 6 cassettes for chromatic ser 42.00x (ISBN 0-252-00071-4); 3 cassettes for student practice 22.95x (ISBN 0-252-00072-2); complete ser 90.00x (ISBN 0-252-00073-0). U of Ill Pr.

Kraft, Leo. Gradus-an Integrated Approach to Harmony, Counterpoint, & Analysis: Gradus One (Text & Anthology) Incl. Gradus One (Text & Anthology) 360p. pap. text ed. 5.50x (ISBN 0-393-09180-5); Anthology. pap. text ed. 5.50x (ISBN 0-393-09185-6). Combined Ed (ISBN 0-685-62589-3). 1976. Vol. 1. 15.95x set (ISBN 0-393-09154-6); Vol. 2. 19.95x (ISBN 0-393-09148-1). Norton.

Krehbiel, Henry E. How to Listen to Music. LC 77-90800. 1978. Repr. of 1896 ed. lib. bdg. 35.00 (ISBN 0-89341-417-4). Longwood Pr.

--How to Listen to Music: (Hints & Suggestions to Untaught Lovers of the Art) 1978. Repr. of 1927 ed. lib. bdg. 20.00 (ISBN 0-685-01671-4). Norwood Edns.

--How to Listen to Music: Hints & Suggestions to Untaught Lovers of the Art. 1979. Repr. of 1910 ed. lib. bdg. 20.00 (ISBN 0-8495-3035-0). Arden Lib.

Krenek, Ernst. Exploring Music. 1980. pap. 4.95 (ISBN 0-7145-0226-X). Riverrun NY.

La Rue, Jan. Guidelines for Style Analysis. LC 73-77409. (Illus.). 1971. 9.95x (ISBN 0-393-09946-6). Norton.

Machlis, Joseph. Enjoyment of Music. 3rd ed. LC 77-90980. (Illus.). 1970. 10.95x (ISBN 0-393-09929-6, NortonC); instructor's manual free (ISBN 0-393-09951-2); album 1 12.95x (ISBN 0-393-09406-5). Norton.

--Enjoyment of Music. 3rd shr. ed. 1970. 9.95x (ISBN 0-393-09940-7, NortonC); teachers' manual, free (ISBN 0-393-09129-5); album 1 18.95x (ISBN 0-393-09121-X); album 2 18.95x (ISBN 0-393-09115-5). Norton.

--The Enjoyment of Music. 4th ed. LC 76-62482. (Illus.). 1977. 16.95x (ISBN 0-393-09118-X); shorter 14.95x (ISBN 0-393-09125-2); workbk 4.95x (ISBN 0-393-09122-8). Norton.

--Introduction to Contemporary Music. 2nd ed. (Illus.). 1979. text ed. 17.95x (ISBN 0-393-09026-4); instructor's guide free (ISBN 0-393-95023-9). Norton.

Mathews, William S. Masters & Their Music. LC 78-153364. Repr. of 1898 ed. 19.75 (ISBN 0-404-07209-7). AMS Pr.

Miller, Hugh M. Introduction to Music. (Illus., Orig.). 1978. pap. 4.50 (ISBN 0-06-460177-3, CO 177, COS). Har-Row.

Moore, Douglas. Guide to Musical Styles: From Madrigal to Modern Music. (Illus.). 1963. pap. 5.95 (ISBN 0-393-00200-4, Norton Lib.). Norton.

--Listening to Music. rev. ed. (Illus.). 1963. pap. 5.45 (ISBN 0-393-00130-X, Norton Lib). Norton.

Mozart, Wolfgang A. Seventeen Divertimenti for Various Instruments. 256p. 1979. pap. 6.95 (ISBN 0-486-23862-8). Dover.
Nadeau, Roland & Tesson, William. Listen: A Guide to the Pleasures of Music. 3rd ed. LC 80-84110. 544p. 1980. pap. text ed. 14.95 (ISBN 0-8403-2332-8). Kendall-Hunt.
Narmour, Eugene. Beyond Schenkerism: The Need for Alternatives in Music Analysis. LC 76-25632. xii, 238p. 1980. pap. 7.50 (ISBN 0-226-56848-2, P893, Phoen). U of Chicago Pr.
--Beyond Schenkerism: The Need for Alternatives in Music Analysis. LC 76-25632. 1977. lib. bdg. 20.00x (ISBN 0-226-56847-4). U of Chicago Pr.
Nelson, Alice D. People & Music. new ed. (gr. 9-12). 1973. text ed. 14.80 (ISBN 0-205-03292-3, 5832926); tchrs'. guide 2.40 (ISBN 0-205-03646-5, 5836468). Allyn.
Nyman, Michael. Experimental Music: Cage & Beyond. LC 81-1166. (Illus.). 154p. 1981. pap. 8.95 (ISBN 0-02-871660-4). Schirmer Bks.
Parry, Charles H. Style in Musical Art. LC 78-13864. (Encore Music Editions Ser.). 1979. Repr. of 1924 ed. 29.50 (ISBN 0-88355-807-6). Hyperion Conn.
Phillips, Lois. Lieder Line by Line. 1980. 35.00 (ISBN 0-684-16442-6, ScribT). Scribner.
Pink, Heinz-Guenther. Pink's Shortcuts in Music Theory & Compositions from Life. 1974. pap. 4.95 (ISBN 0-915946-05-X, A592432). Pink Hse Pub.
Porter, Andrew. Music of Three Seasons 1974-1977. 672p. 1978. 20.00 (ISBN 0-374-21646-0). FS&G.
Ratner, Leonard G. Music: The Listener's Art. 3rd ed. LC 76-23395. 1977. text ed. 13.95 (ISBN 0-07-051221-3, C); instructor's manual 2.95 (ISBN 0-07-051222-1). McGraw.
Reimer, B., Jr. & Evans, E. Developing the Experience of Music: Listening Charts. 1973. wkbk. 10.95 (ISBN 0-13-294876-1). P-H.
--The Experience of Music. 1973. text ed. 18.95 (ISBN 0-13-294553-3). P-H.
--Library for Developing the Experience of Music. 1973. 14 record set 139.95 (ISBN 0-13-294892-3). P-H.
--Listening for the Experience of Music. 1973. student's 7 record set 19.95 (ISBN 0-13-294900-8). P-H.
Reimer, Bennett & Evans, Edward. The Experience of Music. (Illus.). 384p. 1973. text ed. 18.95 (ISBN 0-13-294553-3); wkbk. 9.95 (ISBN 0-13-294876-1); records 18.95 (ISBN 0-13-294900-8); library of records 110.50 (ISBN 0-13-294892-3); demonstration record 129.95 (ISBN 0-686-76953-8). P-H.
Reti, Rudolph R. The Thematic Process in Music. LC 77-13622. 1978. Repr. of 1951 ed. lib. bdg. 26.50x (ISBN 0-8371-9875-5, RETH). Greenwood.
Russell, Anthony. Blacks, Whites & Blues. LC 78-120109. 112p. 2.95 (ISBN 0-8128-1320-0). Stein & Day.
Sacher, Jack & Eversole, James. The Art of Sound: An Introduction to Music. 2nd ed. (Illus.). 1977. pap. text ed. 13.95 (ISBN 0-13-048744-9); records 8.95 (ISBN 0-13-048660-4). P-H.
Samaroff Stokowski, Olga S. The Listener's Music Book. rev. ed. LC 72-164473. 293p. Repr. of 1947 ed. lib. bdg. 14.00x (ISBN 0-8371-6217-3, STLM). Greenwood.
Sargeant, Winthrop. Listening to Music. LC 76-58564. (Illus.). 1977. Repr. of 1958 ed. lib. bdg. 19.25x (ISBN 0-8371-9461-X, SALM). Greenwood.
Schauffler, Robert H. Musical Amateur: A Book on the Human Side of Music. LC 74-167411. (Essay Index Reprint Ser.). Repr. of 1911 ed. 18.00 (ISBN 0-8369-2858-X). Arno.
Scholes, Percy A. Complete Book of the Great Musicians, 3 Vols in One. (Illus.). 1949. 13.95x (ISBN 0-19-314101-9). Oxford U Pr.
--Listener's Guide to Music: With a Concert-Goer's Glossary. 10th ed. (Illus.). (YA) (gr. 9 up). 1961. pap. 4.95x (ISBN 0-19-284002-9). Oxford U Pr.
Schonberg, Harold C. Facing the Music. 1981. 17.95 (ISBN 0-671-25406-5). Summit Bks.
Seashore, Carl E. In Search of Beauty in Music: A Scientific Approach to Musical Esthetics. LC 80-25447. (Illus.). xvi, 389p. 1981. Repr. of 1947 ed. lib. bdg. 29.50x (ISBN 0-313-22758-6, SEIS). Greenwood.
Seyer, Philip & Harmon, Paul. What Makes Music Work? Novick, Allan, ed. LC 81-4930. (Wiley Self-Teaching Guide Ser.). 300p. 1981. pap. text ed. 9.85 (ISBN 0-471-35192-X). Wiley.
Shaw, Bernard. How to Become a Musical Critic. Laurence, Dan H., ed. LC 77-26653. (Music Reprint Ser., 1978). 1978. Repr. of 1961 ed. lib. bdg. 27.50 (ISBN 0-306-77569-7). Da Capo.
Sherman, Robert W. & Knight, Morris H. Aural Comprehension in Music, 2 vols. (Illus.). 672p. (Orig.). 1972. wkbk. 13.95 ea. (C). Vol. 1 (ISBN 0-07-056569-4). Vol. 2 O.p (ISBN 0-07-056570-8). instructor's manual 3.95 (ISBN 0-07-056573-2); test manual 3.95 (ISBN 0-07-056574-0). McGraw.
Siegmeister, Elie. Invitation to Music. LC 61-15658. (Illus.). (gr. 8-12). 1961. PLB 6.27 (ISBN 0-8178-3182-7). Harvey.
Silbermann, Alphons. The Sociology of Music. Stewart, Corbet, tr. from German. LC 76-58565. 1977. Repr. of 1963 ed. lib. bdg. 18.50 (ISBN 0-8371-9455-5, SISM). Greenwood.
Smith, Robert. Harmonics; or, the Philosophy of Musical Sounds. LC 65-23394. (Music Ser.). 1966. Repr. of 1749 ed. lib. bdg. 25.00 (ISBN 0-306-70916-3). Da Capo.
Smyth, Ethel. Impressions That Remained. (Music Ser.). (Illus.). 558p. 1981. Repr. of 1919 ed. lib. bdg. 42.50 (ISBN 0-306-76107-6). Da Capo.
Spaeth, Sigmund G. At Home with Music. facs. ed. LC 77-128313. (Essay Index Reprint Ser). 1945. 25.00 (ISBN 0-8369-2076-7). Arno.
--The Common Sense of Music. LC 74-163550. (Illus.). 375p. 1972. Repr. of 1924 ed. lib. bdg. 16.75x (ISBN 0-8371-6210-6, SPSM). Greenwood.
Spalding, Walter R. Music: An Art & a Language. LC 78-58201. 1978. Repr. of 1920 ed. lib. bdg. 35.00 (ISBN 0-89341-434-4). Longwood Pr.
Spence, Keith & Swayne, Giles. How Music Works. LC 81-5998. (Illus.). 416p. 1981. 17.95 (ISBN 0-02-612870-5). Macmillan.
Steinitz, Paul. Bach's Passions. (Illus.). 1979. 14.95 (ISBN 0-684-16229-6, ScribT). Scribner.
Stevens, Denis. Musicology: A Practical Guide. (The Yehudi Menuhin Music Guides Ser.). (Illus.). 250p. 1981. 17.95 (ISBN 0-02-872530-1); pap. 8.95 (ISBN 0-02-872540-9). Schirmer Bks.
Stravinsky, Igor & Craft, Robert. Expositions & Developments. (Orig.). 1981. pap. 4.95 (ISBN 0-520-04403-7, CAL 503). U of Cal Pr.
--Memories & Commentaries. (Orig.). 1981. pap. 4.95 (ISBN 0-520-04402-9, CAL 502). U of Cal Pr.
Thompson, Oscar. How to Understand Music. 1979. Repr. of 1936 ed. lib. bdg. 25.00 (ISBN 0-8492-2747-X). R West.
--How to Understand Music. LC 72-275. (Essay Index Reprint Ser.). Repr. of 1935 ed. 23.00 (ISBN 0-8369-2829-6). Arno.
Thompson, William. Music for Listeners. (Illus.). 1978. text ed. 17.95 (ISBN 0-13-608026-X); records 17.95 (ISBN 0-13-608018-9). P-H.
Thomson, Virgil. Art of Judging Music. LC 69-14114. 1969. Repr. of 1948 ed. lib. bdg. 20.50x (ISBN 0-8371-0683-4, THJM). Greenwood.
--Music, Right & Left. LC 68-55327. (Illus.). 1968. Repr. of 1951 ed. lib. bdg. 15.00x (ISBN 0-8371-0685-0, THMU). Greenwood.
--Musical Scene. Repr. of 1945 ed. lib. bdg. 15.75x (ISBN 0-8371-0684-2, THMS). Greenwood.
Ulrich, Homer. The Education of a Concert-Goer. LC 77-13817. (Illus.). 1978. lib. bdg. 24.25x (ISBN 0-8371-9872-0, ULEC). Greenwood.
Van Ess, Donald H. Heritage of Musical Style. LC 73-101138. (Illus.). text ed. 16.95x (ISBN 0-03-081241-0); listener's guide 3.95x (ISBN 0-03-081242-9). Irvington.
Vista, Isabel D. & Faurot, Albert. Culture Currents of World Music. 1978. pap. 6.75x (ISBN 0-686-23911-3, Pub. by New Day Pub). Cellar.
Wade, Graham. The Shape of Music: An Introduction to Musical Form. 96p. 1981. 11.95 (ISBN 0-8052-8109-6, Pub. by Allison & Busby England); pap. 5.95 (ISBN 0-8052-8110-X). Schocken.
Walton, Charles W. Basic Forms in Music. LC 73-81046. 218p. 1974. text ed. 9.95x (ISBN 0-88284-010-X). Alfred Pub.
Webern, Anton. The Path to the New Music. Reich, Willi, ed. Black, Leo, tr. from Ger. pap. 3.95 (ISBN 3-7024-0030-3, 47-12947). Eur-Am Music.
White, John D. Analysis of Music. 1976. 15.95 (ISBN 0-13-033233-X). P-H.
Wink, Richard L. & Williams, Lois. Invitation to Listening. 2nd ed. LC 75-31007. (Illus.). 352p. 1976. text ed. 14.95 (ISBN 0-395-18651-X); instructor's manual 1.25 (ISBN 0-395-18778-8); of six LP records 18.75 set (ISBN 0-395-19372-9). HM.
Zabrack, Harold. Creative Musical Encounters. LC 78-95127. 1978. 4.25 (ISBN 0-934286-04-3). Kenyon.
Zarlino, Gioseffo. Monuments of Music & Music Literature in Facsimile: Series Two Part I, Vol. 15. (Illus., Sopplimenti musicali). 1979. 47.50x (ISBN 0-8450-2215-6). Broude.
Zuckerkandl, Victor. Sense of Music. rev. ed. (Illus.). 1970. 17.50x (ISBN 0-691-09102-1); pap. 5.95 (ISBN 0-691-02700-5, 89); reel to reel tapes 52.50 (ISBN 0-691-03838-4); cassette tapes 40.00 (ISBN 0-691-09128-5). Princeton U Pr.

MUSIC-ANALYSIS, APPRECIATION-AUDIO-VISUAL AIDS

Bernstein, Leonard. The Joy of Music. 1963. pap. 3.95 (ISBN 0-671-39721-4, Fireside). S&S.
Gaburo, Virginia. Notation. LC 77-75432. (Illus.). 176p. 1977. soft-cover 14.45 (ISBN 0-939044-16-1). Lingua Pr.
Kamien, Roger. Music: An Appreciation. 1976. text ed. 15.95 (ISBN 0-07-033266-5, C); instructor's manual 3.95 (ISBN 0-07-033269-X); record package 17.95 (ISBN 0-07-033270-3). McGraw.
Mathews, William S. How to Understand Music: A Concise Course in Musical Culture by Object Lessons & Essays, 2 Vols. 5th ed. LC 75-144657. Repr. of 1901 ed. Set. 34.75 (ISBN 0-404-07213-5). Vol. 1 (ISBN 0-404-07214-3). Vol. 2 (ISBN 0-404-07215-1). AMS Pr.

MUSIC-ANALYTICAL GUIDES

Caluori, Eleanor. The Cantatas of Luigi Rossi: Analysis & Thematic Index, 2 vols. Buelow, George, ed. LC 81-4749. (Studies in Musicology: No. 41). 1981. Set. 75.00 (ISBN 0-8357-1171-4, Pub. by UMI Res Pr). Vol. 1 (ISBN 0-8357-1191-9). Vol. 2 (ISBN 0-8357-1192-7). Univ Microfilms.
Mitchell, William J. & Salzer, Felix, eds. Music Forum, 3 vols. LC 67-16204. 1967-73. Vol. 3. 22.50x (ISBN 0-231-03522-5); Vol. 4. 22.50x (ISBN 0-231-03153-X); Vol. 5. 22.50x (ISBN 0-231-03522-5). Columbia U Pr.
Muller-Reuter, Theodor. Lexikon der Deutschen Konzertliteratur, 2 Vols. LC 70-171079. (Music Ser). 1972. Repr. of 1921 ed. lib. bdg. 95.00 (ISBN 0-306-70274-6). Da Capo.
Piston, Walter. Principles of Harmonic Analysis. 1933. pap. 7.50 (ISBN 0-911318-05-4). E C Schirmer.
Reimer, B., Jr. & Evans, E. Developing the Experience of Music: Listening Charts. 1973. wkbk. 10.95 (ISBN 0-13-294876-1). P-H.
Tovey, Donald F. Essays in Musical Analysis, 6 vols. Incl. Vol. 1. Symphonies 1. 1935. pap. 6.95 (ISBN 0-19-315137-5); Vol. 2. Symphonies 2, Variations & Orchestral Polyphony. 1935. pap. 8.95x (ISBN 0-19-315138-3);; Vol. 3. Concertos. 1936. 7.50x (ISBN 0-19-315129-4); pap. 6.95 (ISBN 0-19-315139-1); Vol. 4. Illustrative Music. 1936. pap. 9.95 (ISBN 0-19-315140-5); Vol. 5. Vocal Music. 1937. pap. 6.95 (ISBN 0-19-315141-3); Vol. 6. Miscellaneous Notes, Glossary, Index. 1939. pap. 6.95 (ISBN 0-19-315142-1). Oxford U Pr.
--Essays in Musical Analysis: Chamber Music. 1944 (ISBN 0-19-315126-X). pap. 6.95 (ISBN 0-19-315136-7). Oxford U Pr.

MUSIC-APPRECIATION

see Music-Analysis, Appreciation

MUSIC-BIBLIOGRAPHY

see also Music-Discography; Music-Manuscripts; Music Libraries

Allen, W. D. Philosophies of Music History: A Study of General Histories of Music, 1600-1960. 9.50 (ISBN 0-8446-1529-3). Peter Smith.
Allen, Warren D. Philosophies of Music History: A Study of General Histories of Music, 1600-1960. (Illus.). 1962. pap. 5.00 (ISBN 0-486-20282-8). Dover.
Aros, Andrew A. Broadway & Hollywood Too. LC 80-67670. 60p. 1980. pap. 6.50 (ISBN 0-932352-04-9). Applause Pubns.
Bartlett, Hazel & Gregory, Julia. Catalogue of Early Books on Music (Before 1800) LC 69-12684. (Music Ser). 1969. Repr. of 1913 ed. lib. bdg. 32.50 (ISBN 0-306-71223-7). Da Capo.
Bell, Doris L. Contemporary Art Trends, Nineteen Sixty to Nineteen Eighty: A Guide to Sources. LC 81-5668. 183p. 1981. 11.00 (ISBN 0-8108-1445-5). Scarecrow.
Berkowitz, Freda P. Popular Titles & Subtitles of Musical Compositions. 2nd ed. LC 75-4751. 217p. 1975. 10.00 (ISBN 0-8108-0806-4). Scarecrow.
Bibliographic Guide to Music, 1975. 1976. lib. bdg. 70.00 (ISBN 0-8161-6817-2). G K Hall.
Bibliographic Guide to Music: 1976. (Bibliographic Guides Ser.). 1976. lib. bdg. 70.00 (ISBN 0-8161-6829-6). G K Hall.
Blom, Eric. A General Index to Modern Musical Literature in the English Language: Including Periodicals for the Years 1915-1926. LC 71-108736. (Music Ser). 1970. Repr. of 1927 ed. lib. bdg. 17.50 (ISBN 0-306-71898-7). Da Capo.
Bookspan, Martin. One Hundred One Masterpieces of Music & Their Composers. rev. ed. LC 72-84961. 480p. 1973. pap. 4.95 (ISBN 0-385-05721-0, Dolp). Doubleday.
Boonin, Joseph M. An Index to the Solo Songs of Robert Franz. (Music Indexes & Bibliographies: No. 4). 1970. pap. 1.50 (ISBN 0-913574-04-X). Eur-Am Music.
Boston Public Library. Dictionary Catalog of the Music Collection, Boston Public Library, 20 vols. 15617p. 1972. Set. lib. bdg. 1700.00 (ISBN 0-8161-0956-7); lib. bdg. 310.00 1st suppl., 4 vols. 1977 (ISBN 0-8161-1014-X). G K Hall.
--Dictionary Catalog of the Music Collection, Boston Public Library, 20 vols. 15617p. 1972. Set. lib. bdg. 1700.00 (ISBN 0-8161-0956-7); lib. bdg. 310.00 1st suppl., 4 vols. 1977 (ISBN 0-8161-1014-X). G K Hall.
Brown, Rae L. Music, Printed & Manuscript, in the James Weldon Johnson Memorial Collection of Negro Arts & Letters, Yale University: An Annotated Catalog. 1981. lib. bdg. 30.00 (ISBN 0-8240-9319-4). Garland Pub.
Bryant, E. T. Music. 1965. 4.95 (ISBN 0-8022-0190-3). Philos Lib.
Cahoon, H., ed. The Mary Flagler Cary Music Collection. 1970. 17.50 (ISBN 0-87598-030-9); pap. 10.50 (ISBN 0-87598-009-0). Pierpont Morgan.
Catalogue of Printed Music in the British Museum. 444p. 1980. 90.00x (ISBN 0-7141-0116-8, Pub. by Brit Lib England). State Mutual Bk.
Catalogue of Printed Music in the British Library to 1980, 62 vols. 1980. Set. 13,700.00 (ISBN 0-85157-900-0, Dist. by Gale Research Co.). K G Saur.
Charbon, M. H. Historische en theoretische werken tot Eighteen Hundred: Catalogus van de muziekbibliotheek van het Haags Gemeentemuseum, 2 vols. (Haags Gemeente-Museum Ser.). 1973. 45.00 (ISBN 90-6027-073-8, Pub. by Frits Knuf Netherlands). Pendragon NY.
Charles, Sydney R. Handbook of Music & Music Literature: In Sets & Series. LC 71-143502. 1972. 17.95 (ISBN 0-02-905400-1). Free Pr.
Chase, Gilbert, ed. Guide to the Music of Latin America. 2nd rev. & enl. ed. LC 70-18910. (BCL Ser.: No. II). Repr. of 1962 ed. 22.50 (ISBN 0-404-08306-4). AMS Pr.
Chicorel, Marietta, ed. Chicorel Bibliography to Books on Music & Musicians, Vol. 10. LC 74-161012. (Chicorel Index Ser). 500p. 1974. 85.00 (ISBN 0-934598-18-5). Am Lib Pub Co.
Christian Heinrich Postel 1658-1705: Bibliographie. (Beschreihende Bibliographien: Vol. 4). 92p. (Ger.). 1976. pap. text ed. 20.00x (ISBN 90-6203-081-5). Humanities.
Cohn, Albert & Miller, Leta E. Music in the Paris Academy of Sciences. LC 78-70025. (Detroit Studies in Music Bibliography Ser.: No. 43). 1979. 8.50 (ISBN 0-911772-96-0). Info Coord.
Davies, J. H. Musicalia: Sources of Information in Music. 2nd ed. 1969. 12.25 (ISBN 0-08-006357-8); pap. 7.00 (ISBN 0-08-006356-X). Pergamon.
De Coussemaker, C. E. Catalogue des livres, manuscripts et instruments de musique. (Auction Catalogues of Music Ser.: Vol. 4). 1976. Repr. of 1877 ed. wrappers 45.00 (ISBN 90-6027-198-X, Pub. by Frits Knuf Netherlands). Pendragon NY.
Dichter, H. Handbook of American Sheet Music. (Illus.). pap. 4.00x (ISBN 0-87556-077-6). Saifer.
Duckles, Vincent. Music Reference & Research Materials: An Annotated Bibliography. 3rd ed. LC 73-10697. 1974. text ed. 14.95 (ISBN 0-02-907700-1). Free Pr.
Eagon, Angelo. Catalog of Published Concert Music by American Composers. LC 68-9327. (2nd suppl. to 2nd ed.). 1974. 10.00 (ISBN 0-8108-0728-9). Scarecrow.
Ecorcheville, Jules A. Catalogue Du Fonds De Musique Ancienne De la Bibliotheque Nationale, 4 vols. LC 79-166103. (Music Ser). (Illus.). 1973. Repr. of 1914 ed. Set. lib. bdg. 165.00 (ISBN 0-306-70280-0). Da Capo.
Engel, Carl. The Literature of National Music. LC 77-75201. 1977. Repr. of 1879 ed. lib. bdg. 12.50 (ISBN 0-89341-103-5). Longwood Pr.
Evans, May G. Music & Edgar Allan Poe: A Bibliographical Study. LC 68-54418. (Illus.). 1968. Repr. of 1939 ed. lib. bdg. 15.00x (ISBN 0-8371-0410-6, EVMP). Greenwood.
Feather, Leonard. Encyclopedia of Jazz in the Sixties. 1967. 20.00 (ISBN 0-8180-1205-6). Horizon.
Flanders, Peter. A Thematic Index to the Works of Benedetto Pallavicino. (Music Indexes & Bibliographies: No. 11). 1974. pap. 8.00 (ISBN 0-913574-11-2). Eur-Am Music.
Fuld, James J. Book of World-Famous Music: Classical, Folk, & Popular. rev. ed. 1971. 15.00 (ISBN 0-517-50298-4). Crown.
Gilder, Eric & Port, June. A Dictionary of Composers & Their Music: Every Listener's Companion Arranged Chronologically & Alphabetically. LC 77-15998. 1978. 12.95 (ISBN 0-448-22364-3). Paddington.

Goodman, A. Harold. Instrumental Music Guide. LC 77-7923. 1977. pap. 2.40 (ISBN 0-8425-1525-9). Brigham.

Goovaerts, A. Histoire et Bibliographie de la Typographie Musicale dans les Pays-Bas. 1963. Repr. of 1880 ed. 62.50 (ISBN 90-6027-002-9, Pub. by Frits Knuf Netherlands). Pendragon NY.

Gregoir, Edouard G. Bibliographie musicale: Histoire de l'Orgue. 2nd ed. (Bibliotheca Organologica Ser.: Vol. 15). 1972. Repr. of 1865 ed. 47.50 (ISBN 90-6027-231-5, Pub. by Frits Knuf Netherlands). Pendragon NY.

Harris, Ernest E., ed. Music Education: A Guide to Information Sources. LC 74-11560. (Education Information Guide Ser.: Vol. 1). 1978. 36.00 (ISBN 0-8103-1309-X). Gale.

Hill, George R. A Preliminary Checklist of Research on the Classic Symphony & Concerto to the Time of Beethoven (Excluding Haydn & Mozart) (Music Indexes & Bibliographies: No. 2). pap. 4.50 (ISBN 0-913574-02-3). Eur-Am Music.

Hill, George R. & Gould, Murray. A Thematic Locator for Mozart's Works, As Listed in Koechel's Chronologisch Thematisches Verzeichnis. 6th ed. (Music Indexes & Bibliographies: No. 1). 1970. pap. 6.75 (ISBN 0-913574-01-5). Eur-Am Music.

Hilton, Ruth B. An Index to Early Music in Selected Anthologies. (Music Indexes & Bibliographies: No. 13). 1978. 25.00 (ISBN 0-913574-13-9). Eur-Am Music.

Hopkinson, Cecil. Bibliography of the Works of Giacomo Puccini, 1858-1924. (Illus.). 78p. 1968. 30.00x (ISBN 0-8450-7002-9). Broude.

Horn, David. Literature of American Music in Books & Folk Music Collections: A Fully Annotated Bibliography. LC 76-13160. 1977. 24.00 (ISBN 0-8108-0996-6). Scarecrow.

Hughes-Hughes, A. Catalogue of Manuscript Music in the British Museum: Instrumental Music, Treatises Etc, Vol. 3. 568p. 1981. 40.00x (ISBN 0-7141-0427-2, Pub. by Brit Lib England). State Mutual Bk.

--Catalogue of Manuscript Music in the British Museum: Sacred Vocal Music, Vol. 1. 644p. 1981. 40.00x (ISBN 0-7141-0425-6, Pub. by Brit Lib England). State Mutual Bk.

--Catalogue of Manuscript Music in the British Museum: Secular Vocal Music, Vol. 2. 988p. 1981. 45.00x (ISBN 0-7141-0426-4, Pub. by Brit Lib England). State Mutual Bk.

International Association of Music Libraries. Guide for Dating Early Published Music: A Manual of Bibliographical Practices. Krummel, Don W., ed. (Illus.). 1974. 25.00 (ISBN 0-913574-25-2). Eur-Am Music.

Jackson, Richard. United States Music: Sources of Bibliography & Collective Biography. LC 73-80637. (I. S. A. M. Monograph Ser: No. 1). 80p. (Orig.). 1973. pap. 5.00 (ISBN 0-914678-00-0). Inst Am Music.

Jarman, Lynne, ed. Canadian Music: A Selected Checklist, 1950-1973. LC 76-55840. 1976. 15.00x (ISBN 0-8020-5327-0). U of Toronto Pr.

Kenneson, Claude. Bibliography of Cello Ensemble Music. LC 73-79444. (Detroit Studies in Music Bibliography Ser.: No. 31). 1974. pap. 2.00 (ISBN 0-911772-60-X). Info Coord.

Kidson, Frank. British Music Publishers, Printers & Engravers. LC 67-23861. 1967. Repr. of 1900 ed. 12.75 (ISBN 0-405-08701-2, Blom Pubns). Arno.

Kimmey, John A. Arnold Schoenberg - Hans Nachod Collection. LC 78-70020. (Detroit Studies in Music Bibliography Ser.: No. 41). 1979. 20.00 (ISBN 0-911772-88-X). Info Coord.

Krummel, Donald W. Bibliotheca Bolduaniana: A Renaissance Music Bibliography. LC 71-175176. (Detroit Studies in Music Bibliography Ser.: No. 22). 1972. 5.00 (ISBN 0-911772-46-4); pap. 2.00 (ISBN 0-89990-006-2). Info Coord.

Lee, Douglas A. The Works of Christoph Nichelmann: A Thematic Index. LC 71-151301. (Detroit Studies in Music Bibliography Ser.: No. 19). 1971. pap. 2.00 (ISBN 0-911772-41-3). Info Coord.

Library of Congress. National Union Catalog: A Cumulative Author List, 1958-1962. Incl. Vol. 51. Music & Phonorecords - Authors List, Pt. 1 (ISBN 0-87471-731-0); Vol. 52. Music & Phonorecords - Subject Index, Pt. 2 (ISBN 0-87471-732-9); Vol. 53. Motion Pictures & Film Strips, Titles, Pt. 1 (ISBN 0-87471-733-7); Vol. 54. Motion Pictures & Film Strips, Pt. 2 - Subject Index (ISBN 0-87471-734-5). 40.00x ea. Rowman.

--National Union Catalog, a Cumulative Author List, 1953-57, 28 Vols. Set. 395.00x (ISBN 0-87471-728-0); vol. 27 music & phonorecords 40.00x (ISBN 0-87471-729-9); vol. 28 motion pictures & film strips 40.00 (ISBN 0-87471-730-2). Rowman.

Lyons, David B. Lute, Vihuela, Guitar to Nineteen Hundred: A Bibliography. LC 78-6302. (Detroit Studies in Music Bibliography Ser.: No. 40). 1978. 12.50 (ISBN 0-911772-93-6). Info Coord.

McLean, Mervyn. Oceanic Music & Dance: An Annotated Bibliography. 1977. pap. text ed. 11.00x (ISBN 0-8248-0589-5). U Pr of Hawaii.

Marco, Guy, et al. Information on Music: A Handbook of Reference Sources in European Languages, Vol. 2, The Americas. LC 74-32132. 1977. lib. bdg. 22.50x (ISBN 0-87287-141-X). Libs Unl.

Marco, Guy A. Information on Music: A Handbook of Reference Sources in European Languages Vol. 1, Basic & Universal Sources. LC 74-32132. 1975. lib. bdg. 17.50x (ISBN 0-87287-096-0). Libs Unl.

Markewich, Reese. Definitive Bibliography of Harmonically Sophisticated Tonal Music. LC 77-104898. 1970. pap. 4.95 (ISBN 0-9600160-2-3). Markewich.

Mathiesen, Thomas J. A Bibliography of Sources for the Study of Ancient Greek Music. (Music Indexes & Bibliographies: No. 10). 1974. pap. 4.50 (ISBN 0-913574-10-4). Eur-Am Music.

Mead, Rita H. Doctoral Dissertations in American Music: A Classified Bibliography. LC 74-18893. (I. S. A. M. Monograph Ser: No. 3). 155p. (Orig.). 1974. pap. 5.00 (ISBN 0-914678-02-7). Inst Am Music.

Meggett, Joan M. Music Periodical Literature: An Annotated Bibliography of Indexes & Bibliographies. LC 77-19120. 1978. 10.00 (ISBN 0-8108-1109-X). Scarecrow.

Meggett, Joan M., compiled by. Keyboard Music by Women Composers: A Catalog & Bibliography. LC 81-4130. (Illus.). 232p. 1981. lib. bdg. 29.95 (ISBN 0-313-22833-7, MKM/). Greenwood.

Miller, Dayton C. Catalogue of Books & Literary Material Relating to the Flute & Other Musical Instruments, with Annotations. LC 72-181210. 19.00 (ISBN 0-403-01621-5). Scholarly.

Mixter, Keith E. General Bibliography for Music Research. 2nd ed. LC 72-174731. (Detroit Studies in Music Bibliography Ser.: No. 33). 135p. 1975. 7.00 (ISBN 0-911772-75-8). Info Coord.

Music Educators National Conference. Selective Music Lists - 1979: Instrumental Solos & Ensembles. LC 72-75840. 1979. pap. 5.00x (ISBN 0-940796-17-1). Music Ed.

--Selective Music Lists-1974: Vocal Solos & Ensembles. LC 74-81894. 1974. pap. 4.50x (ISBN 0-940796-18-X). Music Ed.

Nardone, Thomas R., ed. Choral Music in Print: Supplement 1976. LC 73-87918. (Music in Print Ser.). 419p. 1976. lib. bdg. 75.00 (ISBN 0-88478-007-4). Musicdata.

New York Public Library & Library of Congress. Bibliographic Guide to Music: 1977. 1977. lib. bdg. 70.00 (ISBN 0-8161-6842-3). G K Hall.

--Bibliographic Guide to Music: 1979. 1979. lib. bdg. 85.00 (ISBN 0-8161-6875-X). G K Hall.

Newberry Library. Bibliographical Inventory to the Early Music in the Newberry Library, Chicago, Illinois. Krummel, D. W., ed. 1977. lib. bdg. 75.00 (ISBN 0-8161-0042-X). G K Hall.

Newman, Joel & Rikko, Fritz. A Thematic Index to the Works of Salamon Rossi. (Music Indexes & Bibliographies: No. 6). 1972. pap. 11.00 (ISBN 0-913574-06-6). Eur-Am Music.

Parkinson, John A. An Index to the Vocal Works of Thomas Augustine Arne & Michael Arne. LC 78-175175. (Detroit Studies in Music Bibliography Ser.: No. 21). (Orig.). 1972. pap. 2.00 (ISBN 0-911772-45-6). Info Coord.

Pazdirek, Franz. Universal-Handbuch der Musikliteratur Aller Zeiten und Volker, 34 vols. in 12. ccxxxiv, 11973p. 1967. Set. 1237.50 (ISBN 90-6027-034-7, Pub. by Frits Knuf Netherlands). Pendragon NY.

Pruett, James & Rigsby, Lee. Selective Music Bibliography from the Period 1663-1763. (Illus.). 1962. pap. 1.00 (ISBN 0-86526-109-1). NC Archives.

Reddick, William J. Standard Musical Repertoire with Accurate Timings. Repr. of 1947 ed. lib. bdg. 15.00x (ISBN 0-8371-2692-4, REMR). Greenwood.

Research Libraries of the New York Public Library & the Library of Congress. Bibliographic Guide to Music: Nineteen Seventy Eight. (Library Catalogs-Bib. Guides). 1979. lib. bdg. 85.00 (ISBN 0-8161-6858-X). G K Hall.

--Bibliographic Guide to Music: 1980. (Libraries Catalogs-Bib. Guides Sew.). 1981. lib. bdg. 90.00 (ISBN 0-8161-6891-1). G K Hall.

Rezits, Joseph & Deatsman, Gerald. The Pianist's Resource Guide. 2nd ed. Bd. with Piano Music in Print & Literature on the Pianistic Art. LC 77-79564. 1280p. 1978. pap. 65.00, 5 sections in 1 vol. (ISBN 0-8497-7800-X, PM7, Pub. by Pallma). Kjos.

Ripin, Edwin M. The Instrument Catalogs of Leopoldo Franciolini. (Music Indexes & Bibliographies: No. 9). 1974. pap. 15.00 (ISBN 0-913574-09-0). Eur-Am Music.

Roberts, Kenneth. A Checklist of Twentieth-Century Choral Music for Male Voices. (Detroit Studies in Music Bibliography Ser.: No. 17). 1970. pap. 2.00 (ISBN 0-911772-39-1). Info Coord.

Rust, Brian. Brian Rust's Guide to Discography. LC 79-6827. (Discographies: No. 4). (Illus.). x, 133p. 1980. lib. bdg. 19.95 (ISBN 0-313-22086-7, RGD/). Greenwood.

Saylor, Bruce. The Writings of Henry Cowell: A Descriptive Bibliography. LC 77-81276. (ISAM Monograph: No. 7). 1977. pap. 4.00 (ISBN 0-914678-07-8). Inst Am Music.

Scholes, Percy A. A List of Books About Music in the English Language: Prepared As an Appendix to the Oxford Companion to Music. LC 75-181251. 64p. 1940. Repr. 19.00 (ISBN 0-403-01754-8). Scholarly.

Showalter, Grace I. The Music Books of Ruebush & Kieffer, 1866-1942: A Bibliography. (Illus.). 56p. 1975. pap. 2.00x (ISBN 0-88490-066-5, Virginia State Library). U Pr of Va.

Skowronski, JoAnn. Women in American Music: A Bibliography. LC 77-26611. 1978. 10.00 (ISBN 0-8108-1105-7). Scarecrow.

Sollinger, C. String Class Publications in the United States, 1851-1951. LC 73-87276. (Detroit Studies in Music Bibliography Ser.: No. 30). 1974. 5.00 (ISBN 0-911772-61-8). Info Coord.

Sonneck, Oscar G. Bibliography of Early Secular American Music: Eighteenth Century. 3rd ed. LC 64-18992. (Music Ser). 1964. Repr. of 1945 ed. lib. bdg. 45.00 (ISBN 0-306-70902-3). Da Capo.

Sowinski, A. Musiciens Polonais & Slaves. LC 77-155149. (Music Ser). 1971. Repr. of 1857 ed. lib. bdg. 55.00 (ISBN 0-306-70166-9). Da Capo.

Spiess, L. & Stanford, T. An Introduction to Certain Mexican Musical Archives. (Detroit Studies in Music Bibliography Ser.: No. 15). 1969. pap. 2.00 (ISBN 0-911772-37-5). Info Coord.

Stahl, Dorothy. Selected Discography of Solo Song: A Cumulation Through 1971. LC 72-90432. (Detroit Studies in Music Bibliography Ser.: No. 24). 1972. 5.00 (ISBN 0-911772-35-9); pap. 2.00 (ISBN 0-89990-009-7). Info Coord.

Stellfeld, J. A. Bibliographie Des Editions Musicales Platiniennes. (Acad. Royale, Mem. Ser.: Vol. 3). (Illus.). 248p. wrappers 35.00 (ISBN 90-6027-353-2, Pub. by Frits Knuf Netherlands). Pendragon NY.

Sturgis, Russell & Krehbiel, Henry E. Annotated Bibliography of Fine Art. Iles, George, ed. LC 76-27528. 1976. Repr. of 1897 ed. lib. bdg. 15.00 (ISBN 0-89341-053-5). Longwood Pr.

Swanson, Gerald, ed. Music Book Guide: 1974. 200p. 1975. lib. bdg. 60.00 (ISBN 0-8161-6808-3). G K Hall.

Tischler, Alice. Karel Boleslov Jirak: A Catalog of His Works. LC 74-33792. (Detroit Studies in Music Bibliography Ser.: No. 32). 85p. 1975. 5.00 (ISBN 0-911772-75-8). Info Coord.

Turk, D. E. Verzeichniss der Musikalischen und Andern Bucher. (Auction Catalogues of Music Ser.: Vol. 3). Date not set. Repr. of 1973 ed. wrappers 25.00 (ISBN 90-6027-361-3, Pub. by Frits Knuf Netherlands). Pendragon NY.

Tyrrell, John. Music Congress Reports. LC 77-83364. (Library of Humanities Reference Bks.: No. 118). lib. bdg. 38.50 (ISBN 0-8240-9839-0). Garland Pub.

United States Library of Congress. Music Division. African Music: A Brief Annotated Bibliography. Thieme, Darius L., ed. LC 78-17849. 1978. Repr. of 1964 ed. lib. bdg. 16.75 (ISBN 0-313-20543-4, USAM). Greenwood.

Weichlein, William J. A Checklist of American Music Periodicals, 1850-1900. LC 74-15083. (Detroit Studies in Music Bibliography Ser.: No. 16). 1970. pap. 2.00 (ISBN 0-911772-38-3). Info Coord.

Whistling, Carl F. & Hofmeister, Friedrich. Handbuch der Musikalischen Litteratur (the 1817 Edition & the Ten Supplements, 1818-27) Ratliff, Neil, intro. by. & intro. by. LC 74-23416. (Reference Library of the Humanities: No. 21). 1427p. 1975. lib. bdg. 150.00 (ISBN 0-8240-1064-7). Garland Pub.

Wolfe, Richard J. Early American Music Engraving & Printing: A History of Music Publishing in America from 1787 to 1825 with Commentary on Earlier & Later Practices. 321p. 1980. 24.95 (ISBN 0-686-31067-5). Biblio Soc Am.

Wood, David A. Music in the Harvard Libraries: A Catalogue of Early Printed Music & Books on Music in the Houghton Library & the Eda Kuhn Loeb Music Library. (Illus.). 1979. 50.00x (ISBN 0-674-59125-9). Harvard U Pr.

MUSIC–BIO-BIBLIOGRAPHY

ASCAP Biographical Dictionary. 4th ed. 589p. 1980. 41.95 (ISBN 0-8352-1283-1). Bowker.

Bingley, William. Musical Biography, Two Vols. LC 70-127286. (Music Ser). 1971. Repr. of 1834 ed. Set. lib. bdg. 65.00 (ISBN 0-306-70032-8). Da Capo.

Bone, Philip J. The Guitar & Mandolin: Biographies of Celebrated Players & Composers. LC 78-166222. 388p. 1954. Repr. 49.00 (ISBN 0-403-01349-6). Scholarly.

Bookspan, Martin. One Hundred One Masterpieces of Music & Their Composers. rev. ed. LC 72-84961. 480p. 1973. pap. 4.95 (ISBN 0-385-05721-0, Dolp). Doubleday.

Brown, James D. & Stratton, Stephen S. British Musical Biography: A Dictionary of Musical Artists, Authors & Composers, Born in Britain & Its Colonies. LC 76-139197. (Music Ser). 1971. Repr. of 1897 ed. lib. bdg. 42.50 (ISBN 0-306-70076-X). Da Capo.

Cobbett, Walter W., ed. Cyclopedic Survey of Chamber Music, 3 Vols. 2nd ed. 1963. Set. 98.00x (ISBN 0-19-318306-4); Vol. 1. 45.00x (ISBN 0-19-318303-X); Vol. 2. 45.00x (ISBN 0-19-318304-8); Vol. 3. 23.00x (ISBN 0-19-318305-6). Oxford U Pr.

Dunstan, Ralph. A Cyclopaedic Dictionary of Music. LC 72-14060. 642p. 1973. Repr. of 1925 ed. lib. bdg. 52.50 (ISBN 0-306-70559-1). Da Capo.

Ellinwood, L. & Porter, K. Bio-Biographical Index of Musicians in the United States of America Since Colonial Times. LC 76-159677. (Music Ser). 1971. Repr. of 1956 ed. lib. bdg. 35.00 (ISBN 0-306-70183-9). Da Capo.

Ewen, David, ed. Great Composers: Thirteen Hundred-Nineteen Hundred. (Illus.). 1966. 15.00 (ISBN 0-8242-0018-7). Wilson.

Feather, Leonard & Gitler, Ira. The Encyclopedia of Jazz in the Seventies. LC 76-21196. (Illus.). 1976. 20.00 (ISBN 0-8180-1215-3). Horizon.

Fetis, Francois J. Biographie Universelle Des Musiciens, 10 Vols. 1964. Repr. of 1873 ed. Set. lea. bdg. 418.00 (ISBN 0-685-05184-6). Adler.

Gammond, Peter, ed. An Illustrated Guide to Composers of Classical Music. LC 81-66318. (Illus.). 240p. 1981. 9.95 (ISBN 0-668-05315-1, 5315). Arco.

Hixon, Don L. & Hennessee, Don. Women in Music: A Biobibliography. LC 75-23075. 358p. 1975. 15.00 (ISBN 0-8108-0869-2). Scarecrow.

Kay, Ernest, ed. International Who's Who in Music & Musician's Directory. 7th ed. 1348p. 1975. 45.00x (ISBN 0-686-27156-4, Pub. by Intl. Biog). Biblio Dist.

Matthew, James E. Literature of Music. LC 69-12688. (Music Ser). 1969. Repr. of 1896 ed. lib. bdg. 27.50 (ISBN 0-306-71227-X). Da Capo.

Moore, John W. Complete Encyclopedia of Music. LC 72-1713. Repr. of 1880 ed. 45.00 (ISBN 0-404-09916-5). AMS Pr.

Osborne, Charles, ed. The Dictionary of Composers. LC 78-58291. (Illus.). 1978. 14.95 (ISBN 0-8008-2194-7, Crescendo). Taplinger.

Panassie, Hugues & Gautier, Madeleine. Guide to Jazz. Gurwitch, A. A., ed. Flower, Desmond, tr. from Fr. LC 73-435. (Illus.). 312p. 1973. Repr. of 1956 ed. lib. bdg. 20.50x (ISBN 0-8371-6766-3, PAGJ). Greenwood.

Pedigo, Alan. International Encyclopedia of Violin-Keyboard Sonatas & Composer Biographies. LC 79-84899. (Illus.). 1979. 22.50 (ISBN 0-686-27237-4). Arriaga Pubns.

Riemann, Hugo. Dictionary of Music. LC 75-125060. (Music Ser). 1970. Repr. of 1908 ed. lib. bdg. 65.00 (ISBN 0-306-70025-5). Da Capo.

--Dictionary of Music. LC 74-166256. 925p. 1893. Repr. 48.00 (ISBN 0-403-01383-6). Scholarly.

Rogal, Samuel J. Sisters of Sacred Song: Selected Listing of Women Hymnodists in Great Britain & America. LC 80-8482. 180p. 1981. lib. bdg. 22.00 (ISBN 0-8240-9482-4). Garland Pub.

Roxon, Lillian. Rock Encyclopedia. 1971. pap. 9.95 (ISBN 0-448-14572-3, UL). G&D.

Scholes, Percy A. Oxford Companion to Music. 10th ed. Ward, John O., ed. 1970. 35.00 (ISBN 0-19-311306-6). Oxford U Pr.

Stern, Susan. Women Composers: A Handbook. LC 78-5505. 1978. 10.00 (ISBN 0-8108-1138-3). Scarecrow.

Thompson, Kenneth. St. Martin's Dictionary of Twentieth-Century Composers: Nineteen-Ten to Nineteen Seventy-One. LC 78-175526. 1973. 30.00 (ISBN 0-312-75460-4). St Martin.

Thompson, Oscar. International Cyclopedia of Music & Musicians. 10th, rev. ed. Bohle, Bruce, ed. LC 64-23285. (Illus.). 2600p. 1975. 49.95 (ISBN 0-396-07005-1). Dodd.

Westrup, J. A. & Harrison, F. L. The New College Encyclopedia of Music. rev. ed. (Illus.). 1976. 19.95 (ISBN 0-393-02191-2). Norton.

Westrup, J. A. & Harrison, F. L., eds. New College Encyclopedia of Music. 1960. 15.00 (ISBN 0-393-02109-2); pap. 7.95 (ISBN 0-393-00273-X, Norton Lib). Norton.

Young, Percy M. A Critical Dictionary of Composers & Their Music. LC 78-66927. (Encore Music Editions Ser.). 1981. Repr. of 1954 ed. 27.50 (ISBN 0-88355-771-1). Hyperion Conn.

MUSIC-BIOGRAPHY

see Composers; Conductors (Music); Music-Bio-Bibliography; Music Teachers; Musicians; Pianists; Singers

MUSIC-CLASSIFICATION

see Classification-Music

MUSIC-COMPOSITION

see Composition (Music)

MUSIC-CONSERVATORIES

see Conservatories of Music

MUSIC-DICTIONARIES

see also Music-Terminology

American History & Encyclopedia of Music, 10 vols. 1908. Repr. Set. 175.00 (ISBN 0-403-03303-9). Somerset Pub.

Ammer, Christine. Harper's Dictionary of Music. LC 77-134280. (Illus.). 1972. 18.95 (ISBN 0-06-010113-X, HarpT). Har-Row.

--Harper's Dictionary of Music. LC 77-134280. (Illus.). 1972. 18.95 (ISBN 0-06-010113-X, HarpT). Har-Row.

Apel & Daniel. Harvard Brief Dictionary of Music. pap. 2.95 (ISBN 0-671-41448-8). PB.

Apel, Willi. Harvard Dictionary of Music. rev., enl. ed. LC 68-21970. (Illus.). 1969. 25.00 (ISBN 0-674-37501-7, Belknap Pr). Harvard U Pr.

Baker, Th. Dictionary of Musical Terms: Containing an English-Italian Vocabulary for Composers & Students. 22.50 (ISBN 0-87557-053-4, 053-4). Saphrograph.

Baker, Theodore. Dictionary of Musical Terms. LC 75-124595. 1970. Repr. of 1923 ed. 8.00 (ISBN 0-404-00468-7). AMS Pr.

Benet, William R., ed. Reader's Encyclopedia. 2nd ed. LC 65-12510. (Illus.). 1965. 15.95 (ISBN 0-690-67128-8); thumb indexed 17.95 (ISBN 0-690-67129-6). T Y Crowell.

Blom, Eric. Everyman's Dictionary of Music. 816p. (RL 10). 1973. pap. 5.95 (ISBN 0-452-25193-1, 25193, Plume). NAL.

Blom, Eric & Westrub, Sir Jackcompiled by. Everyman's Dictionary of Music. LC 70-173562. 800p. 1972. 15.00 (ISBN 0-312-27230-8). St Martin.

Brenet, Michel. Diccionario De la Musica: Historico y Tecnico. 3rd ed. 566p. (Espn.). 1976. 50.00 (ISBN 84-7082-139-3, S-16685). French & Eur.

Buck, Dudley. Musical Pronouncing Dictionary. Repr. lib. bdg. 19.00 (ISBN 0-403-03787-5). Scholarly.

--Pronouncing Musical Dictionary. 1976. lib. bdg. 19.00 (ISBN 0-403-03787-5). Scholarly.

Champlin, John. Cyclopedia of Music & Musicians, 3 vols. Set. 350.00 (ISBN 0-87968-985-4). Gordon Pr.

Clarke, Hugh A. Pronouncing Dictionary of Musical Terms, Giving the Meaning Derivation & Pronunciation of Italian, German, French & Other Words. 1977. Repr. 15.00 (ISBN 0-403-07492-4). Scholarly.

Clason, W. E. Elsevier's Dictionary of Cinema, Sound & Music. (Polyglot). 1956. 85.50 (ISBN 0-444-40117-2). Elsevier.

Cooke, George W., et al, eds. Pronouncing Dictionary of Musical Terms & Composer's Names. LC 76-2985. (Illus.). 1976. pap. 2.50 (ISBN 0-87824-127-2). Univ Soc.

Dahlhaus, Carl & Eggebrecht, Hans H. Brockhaus Riemann Musiklexikon, Vol. 1, A-K. (Ger.). 1978. 99.50 (ISBN 3-7653-0303-8). Eur-Am Music.

De Brossard, Sebastien. Dictionaire de Musique, contenant une explication des Termes Grecs, Latins, Italiens, & Francois, les plus usitez dans la Musique. 2nd ed. (Dictionarium Musicum: Vol. 1). 1965. Repr. of 1705 ed. 62.50 (ISBN 90-6027-377-X, Pub. by Frits Knuf Netherlands); wrappers 47.50 (ISBN 90-6027-015-0, Pub. by Frits Knuf Netherlands). Pendragon NY.

Demantius, J. C. Isagoge Artis Musicae. (Dictionarium Musicum Ser.: Vol. 3). 1975. Repr. of 1607 ed. wrappers 35.00 (ISBN 90-6027-209-9, Pub. by Frits Knuf Netherlands). Pendragon NY.

Dexter, Harry & Tobin, Raymond, eds. Pocket Encyclopedia of Music. 2.75 (ISBN 0-8022-0390-6). Philos Lib.

Diccionario De Celebridades Musicales. 600p. (Espn.). 19.95 (ISBN 0-686-57361-7, S-50141). French & Eur.

Dunstan, Ralph. A Cyclopaedic Dictionary of Music. LC 72-181147. 632p. 1925. Repr. 34.00 (ISBN 0-403-01353-4). Scholarly.

--A Cyclopaedic Dictionary of Music. LC 72-14060. 642p. 1973. Repr. of 1925 ed. lib. bdg. 52.50 (ISBN 0-306-70559-1). Da Capo.

Eaglefield-Hull, A., ed. Dictionary of Modern Music & Musicians. LC 78-139192. (Music Ser). 1971. Repr. of 1924 ed. lib. bdg. 45.00 (ISBN 0-306-70086-7). Da Capo.

Elson, Louis C. Elson's Music Dictionary. LC 70-173097. xii, 306p. 1972. Repr. of 1905 ed. 24.00 (ISBN 0-8103-3268-X). Gale.

Emery, Frederic B. The Violinist's Encyclopedic Dictionary. LC 77-75206. 1979. Repr. of 1928 ed. lib. bdg. 35.00 (ISBN 0-89341-105-1). Longwood Pr.

Encyclopedia Britannica. The Britannica Book of Music. Hadley, Benjamin, et al, eds. LC 79-7195. (Illus.). 1980. 24.95 (ISBN 0-385-14191-2). Doubleday.

Encyclopedie de la Musique Sacree, 2 tomes. Set. 135.00 (ISBN 0-685-35925-5). French & Eur.

Fotine, Larry. Contemporary Musician's Handbook & Dictionary. (Illus.). 1981. softcover 10.00 (ISBN 0-933830-03-3). Poly Tone.

Framery, Nicolas E., et al. Encyclopedie Methodique: Musique, 2 vols. LC 73-125049. (Music Ser.). 1971. Repr. of 1791 ed. Vols. 1 & 2. lib. bdg. 125.00 (ISBN 0-306-70014-X). Da Capo.

Gaster, Adrian, ed. International Who's Who in Music & Musician's Directory. 9th ed. LC 73-91185. 1000p. 1980. 90.00 (ISBN 0-8103-0427-9). Gale.

Gilder, Eric & Port, June. A Dictionary of Composers & Their Music: Every Listener's Companion Arranged Chronologically & Alphabetically. LC 77-15998. 1978. 12.95 (ISBN 0-448-22364-3). Paddington.

Grigg, Carolyn D., compiled by. Music Translation Dictionary: An English-Czech-Danish-Dutch-French-German-Hungarian-Italian-Polish-Portuguese-Russian-Spanish-Swedish Vocabulary of Music. LC 78-60526. 1978. lib. bdg. 25.00x (ISBN 0-313-20559-0, GMT/). Greenwood.

Gurlitt, W. & Eggebrecht, H. Riemann Musiklexikon. 108p. (Ger.). 1967. 135.00 (ISBN 3-7957-0031-0, M-7602, Pub. by Schatt's Soehne). French & Eur.

Hamel, Fred. Enciclppedia De la Musica, 3 vols. 7th ed. 1100p. (Espn.). 1979. Set. 70.00 (ISBN 84-253-0246-3, S-50533). French & Eur.

Hodgson, Julian. Music Titles in Translation: A Checklist of Musical Compositions. 400p. 1976. 19.50 (ISBN 0-208-01520-5, Linnet). Shoe String.

Hoeweler, Casper. Enciclopedia De la Musica: Guia Del Melomano y Del Discofilo. 7th ed. 536p. (Espn.). 1978. 26.95 (ISBN 84-279-4503-5, S-16711). French & Eur.

Honegger, M. Dictionnaire de la Musique: Science de la Musique, 2 vols. 1216p. (Fr.). 1976. Set. 125.00 (ISBN 2-04-005140-6, M-6318). French & Eur.

Honegger, Marc, ed. Dictionnaire de la Musique, Vol. 1. 1232p. (Fr.). 1970. 65.00 (ISBN 0-686-56821-4, M-6599). French & Eur.

Hoyle, John. Dictionarium Musica, Being a Complete Dictionary, or, Treasury of Music. (Monuments of Music and Music Literature in Facsimile: Series II, Vol. 83). 1977. Repr. of 1770 ed. 27.50x (ISBN 0-8450-2283-0). Broude.

Hubbard, W. L. Dictionary of Music. 1976. lib. bdg. 39.00 (ISBN 0-403-03818-9). Scholarly.

Hull, Arthur E., ed. Dictionary of Modern Music & Musicians. LC 72-1619, Repr. of 1924 ed. 27.50 (ISBN 0-404-08315-3). AMS Pr.

--A Dictionary of Modern Music & Musicians. LC 77-166238. 543p. 1924. Repr. 35.00 (ISBN 0-403-01365-8). Scholarly.

Illing, Robert. Dictionary of Musicians & Music, 2 Vols. 1, Music & 2, Musicians. 1976. Vol. 2, Musicians. 15.00 (ISBN 0-686-67515-0); pap. 6.50 ea. (ISBN 0-08-010337-5). Pergamon.

--Pergamon Dictionary of Musicians & Music: Vols. 1 & 2. Incl. Vol. 1. Musicians. pap. text ed. 5.00 (ISBN 0-08-009963-7); Vol. 2. Music. text ed. 11.50 (ISBN 0-08-010338-3); pap. text ed. 5.00 (ISBN 0-08-010337-5). 1963. Pergamon.

International Association of Music Libraries & International Musicological Society. Terminorum Musicae Index Septen Linguis Redactus. Leuchtmann, Horst, ed. (Illus.). 1978. 89.50 (ISBN 3-7618-0553-5). Eur-Am Music.

Jacobs, Arthur. Diccionario de Musica. 392p. (Span.). 1966. 15.95 (ISBN 0-686-56715-3, S-33050). French & Eur.

--New Dictionary of Music. (Reference Ser.). (Orig.). (YA) (gr. 9 up). 1958. pap. 3.95 (ISBN 0-14-051012-5). Penguin.

Janowka, T. B. Clavis ad Thesaurum Magnae Artis Musicae. (Dictionarium Musicum Ser.: Vol. 2). 1973. Repr. of 1701 ed. wrappers 37.50 (ISBN 90-6027-270-6, Pub. by Frits Knuf Netherlands). Pendragon NY.

Jones, F. O., ed. Handbook of American Music & Musicians. LC 76-155355. (Music Ser). 1971. Repr. of 1886 ed. lib. bdg. 19.50 (ISBN 0-306-70163-4). Da Capo.

Karp, Theodore. Dictionary of Music. (Orig.). 1973. pap. 2.25 (ISBN 0-440-32013-5, LE). Dell.

Kennedy, Michael, ed. The Concise Oxford Dictionary of Music. 3rd ed. (Illus.). 736p. 1981. 19.95 (ISBN 0-19-311315-5); pap. 9.95 (ISBN 0-19-311320-1). Oxford U Pr.

Lawrence, John T. A Dictionary of Musical Biography. 1976. lib. bdg. 75.00 (ISBN 0-8490-1720-3). Gordon Pr.

Leuchtmann, Horst. Woerterbuch Musik. (Ger. - Eng., Dictionary of Terms in Music). 1977. 38.00 (ISBN 3-7940-3186-5, M-6911). French & Eur.

Lindlar, H. Rororo Musikhandbuch, 2 vols. (Ger.). 1976. pap. 12.95 (ISBN 3-499-16167-2, M-7605, Pub. by Rowohlt). French & Eur.

Lovelock, William. A Student's Dictionary of Music. (Illus.). 1964. 8.50 (ISBN 0-8044-0340-6). Ungar.

Mathews, William S. & Liebling, Emil. Pronouncing & Defining Dictionary of Music. LC 78-173059. Repr. of 1896 ed. 20.50 (ISBN 0-404-07210-0). AMS Pr.

Moore, John W. Complete Encyclopaedia of Music: Elementary, Technical, Historical, Biographical, Vocal, & Instrumental, 2 vols. LC 70-166247. 1004p. 1854. Repr. 43.00 (ISBN 0-403-01624-X). Scholarly.

--Complete Encyclopedia of Music. LC 72-1713. Repr. of 1880 ed. 45.00 (ISBN 0-404-09916-5). AMS Pr.

--Dictionary of Musical Information. LC 76-143644. (Bibliography & Reference Ser.: No. 418). 1971. Repr. of 1876 ed. lib. bdg. 21.50 (ISBN 0-8337-2449-5). B Franklin.

--A Dictionary of Musical Information. LC 72-1714. Repr. of 1876 ed. 15.00 (ISBN 0-404-09915-7). AMS Pr.

Pulver, Jeffrey. A Bibliographical Dictionary of Old English Music: Old English Music & Musical Instruments. LC 73-80260. 1970. Repr. of 1927 ed. 22.50 (ISBN 0-8337-2867-9). B Franklin.

--A Dictionary of Old English Music & Musical Instruments. 75.00 (ISBN 0-8490-0042-4). Gordon Pr.

Quarry, W. Edmund. Dictionary of Musical Compositions & Composers. 1976. lib. bdg. 25.00 (ISBN 0-403-03576-7). Scholarly.

Queval, Jean. Lexique de la Musique. 130p. 1968. 5.95 (ISBN 0-686-57289-0, F-11890). French & Eur.

Randel, Don M. Harvard Concise Dictionary of Music. LC 78-5948. (Illus.). 1978. 15.00 (ISBN 0-674-37471-1, Belknap Pr); pap. text ed. 6.95 (ISBN 0-674-37470-3, Belknap Pr). Harvard U Pr.

Reichenbach, Barbara. Hermann Heiss eine Dokumentation. 100p. (Ger.). 1975. pap. 15.95 (ISBN 3-7957-1572-5, M-7464, Pub. by Schott). French & Eur.

Research Libraries of the New York Public Library. Dictionary Catalog of the Music Collection, Supplement 1974. 1976. lib. bdg. 80.00 (ISBN 0-8161-0059-4). G K Hall.

Ricart Matas, Juan. Diccionario Biografico de la Musica. 2nd ed. 1144p. (Espn.). 1966. 60.00 (ISBN 84-7082-140-7, S-12347). French & Eur.

Riemann, Hugo. Dictionary of Music. LC 75-125060. (Music Ser). 1970. Repr. of 1908 ed. lib. bdg. 65.00 (ISBN 0-306-70025-5). Da Capo.

--Dictionary of Music. LC 74-166256. 925p. 1893. Repr. 48.00 (ISBN 0-403-01383-6). Scholarly.

Roche, Jerome & Roche, Elizabeth. A Dictionary of Early Music. (Illus.). 208p. 1981. 15.95 (ISBN 0-19-520255-4). Oxford U Pr.

Rousseau, Jean J. A Complete Dictionary of Music. LC 72-1664. Repr. of 1779 ed. 30.00 (ISBN 0-404-08335-8). AMS Pr.

--Dictionnaire De Musique. (Fr). Repr. of 1768 ed. 37.50 (ISBN 0-384-52200-9). Johnson Repr.

Sadie, Stanley, ed. The New Grove Dictionary of Music & Musicians, 20 vols. 1980. 1900.00 (ISBN 0-333-23111-2). Groves Dict Music.

Salter, Lionel. The Illustrated Encyclopedia of Classical Music. (Illus.). 1978. 17.95 (ISBN 0-517-53476-2); pap. 8.95 (ISBN 0-517-53477-0). Crown.

Scholes, Percy A. Oxford Companion to Music. 10th ed. Ward, John O., ed. 1970. 35.00 (ISBN 0-19-311306-6). Oxford U Pr.

Stainer, J. & Barrett, W. A. A Dictionary of Musical Terms. 35.00 (ISBN 0-8490-0041-6). Gordon Pr.

Stainer, John & Barrett, W. A. Dictionary of Musical Terms. LC 71-166266. 464p. 1898. Repr. 45.00 (ISBN 0-403-01690-8). Scholarly.

Thompson, Kenneth. St. Martin's Dictionary of Twentieth-Century Composers: Nineteen-Ten to Nineteen Seventy-One. LC 78-175526. 1973. 30.00 (ISBN 0-312-75460-4). St Martin.

Thompson, Oscar. International Cyclopedia of Music & Musicians. 10th, rev. ed. Bohle, Bruce, ed. LC 64-23285. (Illus.). 2600p. 1975. 49.95 (ISBN 0-396-07005-1). Dodd.

Vinton, John. Dictionary of Contemporary Music. 1974. 25.00 (ISBN 0-525-09125-4). Dutton.

Walther, Johann. Musikalisches Lexikon. 3rd ed. (Ger.). 1967. pap. 48.00 (ISBN 3-7618-0229-3, M-7565, Pub. by Baerenreiter). French & Eur.

Westrup, J. A. & Harrison, F. L. The New College Encyclopedia of Music. (Illus.). 768p. 1981. pap. 9.95 (ISBN 0-393-00074-5). Norton.

--The New College Encyclopedia of Music. rev. ed. (Illus.). 1976. 19.95 (ISBN 0-393-02191-2). Norton.

Westrup, J. A. & Harrison, F. L., eds. New College Encyclopedia of Music. 1960. 15.00 (ISBN 0-393-02109-2); pap. 7.95 (ISBN 0-393-00273-X, Norton Lib). Norton.

Young, Percy M. A Critical Dictionary of Composers & Their Music. LC 78-66927. (Encore Music Editions Ser.). 1981. Repr. of 1954 ed. 27.50 (ISBN 0-88355-771-1). Hyperion Conn.

MUSIC-DISCOGRAPHY

see also Phonorecord Libraries

Allen, Daniel. Bibliography of Discographies: Jazz, Vol. II. 200p. 1981. 35.00 (ISBN 0-8352-1342-0). Bowker.

Angoff, Charles. Fathers of Classical Music. facs. ed. LC 73-84294. (Essay Index Reprint Ser). 1947. 16.00 (ISBN 0-8369-1119-9). Arno.

Barbour, Harriot B. & Freeman, Warren S. Story of Music. rev. ed. (Illus.). (gr. 7-9). text ed. 11.00 (ISBN 0-87487-033-X). Summy.

Barry, Ron. All American Elvis. (Illus.). 1976. pap. 7.95 (ISBN 0-686-22760-3). Maxigraphics.

Bennett, John R., compiled by. Melodiya: A Soviet Russian L. P. Discography. LC 81-4247. (Discographies Ser.: No. 6). (Illus.). xxii, 832p. 1981. lib. bdg. 75.00 (ISBN 0-313-22596-6, BME/). Greenwood.

Brunet, Jacques, ed. Oriental Music: A Selected Discography. (Occasional Publication). 1971. pap. 3.00 (ISBN 0-89192-148-6). Interbk Inc.

Clough, Francis F., ed. World's Encyclopedia of Recorded Music, 3 vols. LC 71-100214. Repr. of 1966 ed. Set. lib. bdg. 103.50x (ISBN 0-8371-3003-4, CLRM). Greenwood.

Cross, Milton & Ewen, David. Milton Cross New Encyclopedia of the Great Composers & Their Music, 2 Vols. LC 70-87097. two-volume, boxed set 24.95 (ISBN 0-385-03635-3). Doubleday.

Croucher, Trevor. Discography of Early Music, 2 vols. 1981. pap. text ed. write for info. (ISBN 0-85365-613-4, Pub. by Lib Assn England). Oryx Pr.

East Suffolk (Eng.) Country Library. Gramophone Record Catalogue. LC 77-28824. 1978. Repr. of 1969 ed. lib. bdg. 19.75x (ISBN 0-313-20282-6, ESGR). Greenwood.

Finney, Theodore M. A History of Music. LC 73-17926. (Illus.). 720p. 1976. Repr. of 1947 ed. lib. bdg. 40.75x (ISBN 0-8371-7270-5, FIHM). Greenwood.

Foreman, Lewis. Systematic Discography. 176p. 1974. 14.50 (ISBN 0-208-01197-8, Linnet). Shoe String.

Gammond, Peter & Burnett, James. Music on Record: A Critical Guide, 4 vols. Incl. Vol. 1 & 2. Orchestral Music; Vol. 3. Chamber & Instrumental Music; Vol. 4. Opera & Vocal Music. LC 78-8183. 1978. Repr. of 1962 ed. Set. lib. bdg. 69.50x (ISBN 0-313-20514-0, GAMR). Greenwood.

George, B. & Defoe, M., eds. Volume International Discography of the New Wave. 264p. (Orig.). (YA) 1980. pap. 7.95 (ISBN 0-9605778-0-7). One Ten Records.

Gibson, Gerald O. & Gray, Michael H., eds. A Bibliography of Discographies: Volume I Classical Music, 1925-1975. LC 77-22661. 1977. 21.95 (ISBN 0-8352-1023-5). Bowker.

Gramophone Shop Inc. - New York. Gramophone Shop Encyclopedia of Recorded Music. Reid, Robert H., ed. Repr. of 1948 ed. lib. bdg. 33.75x (ISBN 0-8371-3718-7, GRSE). Greenwood.

Greenfield, Edward. Penguin Guide to Bargain Records. LC 70-873233. 607p. 1970. 5.00x (ISBN 0-901143-01-4). Intl Pubns Serv.

The Guide to Long-Playing Records, 3 vols. 1978. Repr. of 1955 ed. lib. bdg. 61.50x (ISBN 0-313-20298-2, GULP). Greenwood.

Haggin, B. H. The New Listener's Companion & Record Guide. 5th ed. LC 77-77128. 1978. 15.00 (ISBN 0-8180-1216-1); pap. 6.95 (ISBN 0-8180-1217-X). Horizon.

Halsey, Richard S. Classical Music Recordings for Home & Library. LC 75-40205. 1976. text ed. 15.00 (ISBN 0-8389-0188-3). ALA.

Howard, John T. This Modern Music. facs. ed. LC 68-58796. (Essay Index Reprint Ser). 1942. 16.00 (ISBN 0-8369-0018-9). Arno.

Kolodin, Irving. Orchestral Music. LC 78-95. (The Guide to Long-Playing Records: Vol. 1). 1978. Repr. of 1955 ed. lib. bdg. 19.00x (ISBN 0-313-20297-4, GULP01). Greenwood.

A Label Discography of Long-Playing Records Series 2--H.M.V. (Red Label) Oct. 1952 - Dec. 1962. (Voices of the Past). 90p. 1975. pap. 5.00x (ISBN 0-85361-178-5). Intl Pubns Serv.

Leibowitz, Alan. The Record Collector's Record Books. Adler, Roger & Adler, Andrew, eds. 1979. pap. 5.95x (ISBN 0-916844-07-2). Turtle Pr.

Locke, Alain. Negro & His Music. Bd. with Negro Art: Past & Present. LC 69-18592. (American Negro-His History & Literature Ser., No.2). 1969. Repr. of 1936 ed. 8.00 (ISBN 0-405-01879-7). Arno.

Maleady, Antoinette O. Index to Record & Tape Reviews: A Classical Music Buying Guide 1980. LC 72-3355. (Annual Ser.). 1981. 55.00x (ISBN 0-917600-06-1). Chulainn Press.

--Index to Record & Tape Reviews: A Classical Music Buying Guide, 1977. LC 72-3355. 1978. 42.50 (ISBN 0-917600-03-7). Chulainn Press.

--Index to Record & Tape Reviews: A Classical Music Buying Guide, 1976. LC 72-3355. 1977. 37.50 (ISBN 0-917600-02-9). Chulainn Press.

Marco, Guy A. Information on Music: A Handbook of Reference Sources in European Languages Vol. 1, Basic & Universal Sources. LC 74-32132. 1975. lib. bdg. 17.50x (ISBN 0-87287-096-0). Libs Unl.

Meyers, Betty & Fellers, Frederick P., eds. Discographies of Commercial Recordings of the Cleveland Orchestra (1924-1977) and the Cincinnati Symphony Orchestra (1917-1977) LC 78-3122. 1978. lib. bdg. 22.50x (ISBN 0-313-20375-X, MDI/). Greenwood.

Moses, Julian M. Collector's Guide to American Recordings: 1895-1925. (Illus.). 200p. 1977. pap. 3.50 (ISBN 0-486-23448-7). Dover.

Mukes, Martin J. & Miles, Daniel J. Miles Chart Display of Popular Music, Vol. 3. 400p. 1981. lib. bdg. 40.00 (ISBN 0-913920-04-5). Convex Indus.

New York Public Library, Research Libraries. Dictionary Catalog of the Music Collection, Supplement II, 10 vols. 1973. Set. lib. bdg. 1300.00 (ISBN 0-8161-0760-2). G K Hall.

Poulton, Alan J. A Label Discography of Long-Playing Records Series 1-- Columbia (Blue & Green Labels) Oct. 1952 - Dec. 1962. (Voices of the Past). 90p. 1975. pap. 5.00x (ISBN 0-85361-177-7). Intl Pubns Serv.

Rezits, Joseph. Guitar Music in Print. LC 80-84548. 500p. (Orig.). 1981. pap. 65.00 (ISBN 0-8497-7802-6, PM9, Pub. by Palma). Kjos.

Ruppli, Michel. The Savoy Label: A Discography. LC 79-7727. (Discographies: No. 2). (Illus.). 1980. lib. bdg. 29.95 (ISBN 0-313-21199-X, RUS/). Greenwood.

Rust, Brian. The American Record Label Book: From the 19th Century Through 1942. (Illus.). 1978. 20.00 (ISBN 0-87000-414-X). Arlington Hse.

--Brian Rust's Guide to Discography. LC 79-6827. (Discographies: No. 4). (Illus.). x, 133p. 1980. lib. bdg. 19.95 (ISBN 0-313-22086-7, RGD/). Greenwood.

Sablosky, Irving L. American Music. LC 79-78094. (Chicago History of American Civilization Ser). 1969. 10.00x (ISBN 0-226-73324-6); pap. 3.95 (ISBN 0-226-73325-4, CHAC24). U of Chicago Pr.

Sackville-West, Edward & Shawe-Taylor, Desmond. The Record Guide, 2 vols. LC 78-5028. 1978. Repr. of 1955 ed. lib. bdg. 58.75x inc. suppl. (ISBN 0-313-20404-7, SWRG). Greenwood.

Sarian, John. Record Guide. LC 79-63060. 1979. pap. 3.00 (ISBN 0-933706-05-7). Ararat Pr.

Schleman, Hilton R. Rhythm on Record. LC 77-28303. (Illus.). 1978. Repr. of 1936 ed. lib. bdg. 22.25x (ISBN 0-313-20257-5, SCRR). Greenwood.

Schonberg, Harold C. Chamber & Solo Instrument Music. LC 78-96. (The Guide to Long-Playing Records: Vol. 3). 1978. Repr. of 1955 ed. lib. bdg. 19.50x (ISBN 0-313-20296-6, GULP03). Greenwood.

Sears, Richard S. V-Discs: A History & Discography. LC 80-1022. (Discographies: No. 5). (Illus.). xciii, 1166p. 1980. lib. bdg. 67.50 (ISBN 0-313-22207-X, SHD/). Greenwood.

Simosko, Vladimir & Tepperman, Barry. Eric Dolphy: A Musical Biography & Discography. LC 79-15117. (Da Capo Quality Paperback Ser.). (Illus.). 132p. 1979. pap. 5.95 (ISBN 0-306-80107-8). Da Capo.

Sir Thomas Beecham Society. Sir Thomas Beecham Discography. LC 78-2261. 1978. Repr. of 1975 ed. lib. bdg. 15.25x (ISBN 0-313-20367-9, STBD). Greenwood.

Sublette, Ned, ed. A Discography of Hispanic Music in the Fine Arts Library of the University of New Mexico: Sources, No. One. LC 77-28293. 1978. Repr. of 1973 ed. lib. bdg. 15.00x (ISBN 0-313-20238-9, SUDH). Greenwood.

Tudor, Dean & Biesenthal, Linda. Popular Music Periodicals Index, 1976. LC 74-11578. 1977. 12.00 (ISBN 0-8108-1079-4). Scarecrow.

Tudor, Dean, et al. Annual Index to Popular Music Record Reviews 1976. LC 73-8909. 1977. 25.00 (ISBN 0-8108-1070-0). Scarecrow.

Whitburn, Joel. Top Country & Western Records, 1974. 40p. (Orig.). 1975. pap. text ed. 10.00 (ISBN 0-89820-017-2). Record Research.

--Top Country & Western Records, 1975. 40p. (Orig.). 1976. pap. text ed. 10.00 (ISBN 0-89820-018-0). Record Research.

--Top Country & Western Records, 1976. 40p. (Orig.). pap. text ed. 10.00 (ISBN 0-89820-019-9). Record Research.

--Top Country & Western Records, 1977. 40p. (Orig.). 1978. pap. text ed. 10.00 (ISBN 0-89820-020-2). Record Research.

--Top Easy Listening Records, 1975. 28p. (Orig.). 1976. pap. text ed. 10.00 (ISBN 0-89820-022-9). Record Research.

--Top Easy Listening Records, 1976. 28p. (Orig.). 1977. pap. text ed. 10.00 (ISBN 0-89820-023-7). Record Research.

--Top Easy Listening Records, 1977. 24p. (Orig.). 1978. pap. text ed. 10.00 (ISBN 0-89820-024-5). Record Research.

--Top Easy Listening Records, 1978. 24p. (Orig.). 1979. pap. text ed. 10.00 (ISBN 0-89820-034-2). Record Research.

--Top LP's 1973. 32p. (Orig.). 1974. pap. text ed. 10.00 (ISBN 0-89820-010-5). Record Research.

--Top LP's, 1974. 32p. (Orig.). 1975. pap. text ed. 10.00 (ISBN 0-89820-011-3). Record Research.

--Top LP's, 1975. 36p. (Orig.). 1976. pap. text ed. 10.00 (ISBN 0-89820-012-1). Record Research.

--Top LP's, 1976. 32p. (Orig.). 1977. pap. text ed. 10.00 (ISBN 0-89820-013-X). Record Research.

--Top LP's 1977. 32p. (Orig.). 1978. pap. text ed. 10.00 (ISBN 0-89820-014-8). Record Research.

--Top LP's, 1978. 32p. (Orig.). 1979. pap. text ed. 10.00 (ISBN 0-89820-032-6). Record Research.

Wilson, W. J. The Stereo Index: A Complete Catalogue of Every Recommended Stereo Disc. LC 78-6968. 1978. Repr. of 1970 ed. lib. bdg. 27.75x (ISBN 0-313-20512-4, WITS). Greenwood.

MUSIC–DYNAMICS, PHRASING

see Music–Interpretation (Phrasing, Dynamics, etc.)

MUSIC–ECONOMIC ASPECTS

see also Music Trade

Biederman, Donald E. Legal & Business Aspects of the Music Industry: Music, Videocassettes & Records, Course Handbook. LC 80-81531. (Patents, Copyrights, Trademarks & Literary Property 1979-80 Course Handbook Ser.). 736p. 1980. pap. text ed. 25.00 (ISBN 0-686-68825-2, G4-3676). PLI.

Carpenter, Paul S. Music, an Art & a Business. 1950. 11.95x (ISBN 0-8061-0202-0). U of Okla Pr.

Hurst, Walter E. & Hale, Walter S. U. S. Master Producers & British Music Scene Book: Stories, Text, Forms, Contracts. LC 68-4500. (Entertainment Industry Ser., No. 4). (Illus.). 1968. 25.00 (ISBN 0-911370-04-8). Seven Arts.

Hurst, Walter E. & Hale, William S. Music Publishers Office Manual: How to Do Your Paperwork in the Music Publishing Industry. LC 66-19600. (Entertainment Industry Ser., Vol. 3). 1966. 25.00 (ISBN 0-911370-03-X). Seven Arts.

Rogers, Kenny & Epand, Len. Making It with Music: Kenny Rogers' Guide to the Music Business. LC 78-2164. (Illus.). 1978. 12.95 (ISBN 0-06-013598-0, HarpT). Har-Row.

Shemel, Sidney & Krasilovsky, M. William. This Business of Music. 4th ed. 18.50 (ISBN 0-8230-7753-5, Billboard Pub). Watson-Guptill.

Shinn, Duane. How People Make Money in Music. 40p. 1971. pap. 6.95 (ISBN 0-912732-01-6). Duane Shinn.

MUSIC–EDITING

Borroff, Edith. Notations & Editions. (Music Reprint Series). 1977. Repr. of 1974 ed. lib. bdg. 25.00 (ISBN 0-306-70867-1). Da Capo.

Dart, Thurston, et al. Editing Early Music: Notes on the Preparation of Printer's Copy. 1963. 1.00x (ISBN 0-19-323200-6). Oxford U Pr.

Donato, Anthony. Preparing Music Manuscript. LC 77-4024. (Illus.). 1977. Repr. of 1963 ed. lib. bdg. 16.75x (ISBN 0-8371-9587-X, DOPM). Greenwood.

Lustig, Milton. Music Editing for Motion Pictures. new ed. (Illus.). 160p. 1980. 15.95 (ISBN 0-8038-4729-7, Communication Arts). Hastings.

MUSIC–ESTHETICS

see Music–Philosophy and Esthetics

MUSIC–EXAMINATIONS, QUESTIONS, ETC.

see also Musical Ability–Testing

Baily, Ben E. Constructing Class Room Tests in Music. LC 71-126990. pap. 2.95x (ISBN 0-87655-520-2). Whitehall Co.

Gordon, Edwin. Musical Aptitude Profile. write for info. (ISBN 0-395-09344-9). HM.

Lovelock, William. Rudiments of Music. LC 71-145436. (Illus.). 1971. pap. 5.95 (ISBN 0-312-69545-4, R91000). St Martin.

Murphy, James F. Music: Advanced Test for the G. R. E. LC 73-83716. (Orig.). 1974. pap. 3.95 (ISBN 0-668-01471-7). Arco.

Rudman, Jack. Music. (Graduate Record Examination Ser.: GRE-13). 14.95 (ISBN 0-8373-5263-0); pap. 9.95 (ISBN 0-8373-5213-4). Natl Learning.

--Music - Jr. H.S. (Teachers License Examination Ser.: T-42). (Cloth bdg. avail. on request). pap. 10.00 (ISBN 0-8373-8042-1). Natl Learning.

--Music - Sr. H.S. (Teachers License Examination Ser.: T-43). (Cloth bdg. avail. on request). pap. 10.00 (ISBN 0-8373-8043-X). Natl Learning.

--Music Education. (National Teachers Examination Ser.: NT-11). (Cloth bdg. avail. on request). pap. 9.95 (ISBN 0-8373-8421-4). Natl Learning.

--Musical Supervisor. (Career Examination Ser.: C-525). (Cloth bdg. avail. on request). pap. 10.00 (ISBN 0-8373-0525-X). Natl Learning.

MUSIC–HISTORIOGRAPHY

see also Musical Criticism; Musicology

MUSIC–HISTORY AND CRITICISM

Abbey, Lester & Glen R. A History of Music for Those Who Don't Want to Know Too Much About Music History. LC 80-124026. (Illus.). 278p. 1981. 9.00 (ISBN 0-939400-01-4); pap. 3.00 (ISBN 0-939400-00-6). RWS Bks.

Abraham, Gerald. The Concise Oxford History of Music. (Illus.). 1980. 39.95 (ISBN 0-19-311319-8). Oxford U Pr.

--Hundred Years of Music. 4th ed. 333p. 1974. 40.50x (ISBN 0-7156-1006-6, Pub. by Duckworth England); pap. 13.50x (ISBN 0-7156-0704-9, Pub. by Duckworth England). Biblio Dist.

Abraham, Gerald, ed. The History of Music in Sound, Vols. 1-3. Incl. Vol. 1. Ancient & Oriental Music. Wellesz, Egon, ed. (Illus.). 42p. 1957 (ISBN 0-19-323100-X); Vol. 2. Early Medieval Music up to 1300. Hughes, Dom A., ed. 70p. 1953 (ISBN 0-19-323101-8); Vol. 3. Ars Nova & the Renaissance, - C. 1300-1540. Westrup, J. A., ed. 70p. 1954 (ISBN 0-19-323102-6). 6.00 ea. Oxford U Pr.

--The History of Music in Sound, Vols. 4-10. Incl. Vol 4. The Age of Humanism, 1540-1630. Westrup, J. A., ed. 1954 (ISBN 0-19-323103-4); Vol 5. Opera & Church Music, 1630-1750. Westrup, J. A., ed. 1954 (ISBN 0-19-323104-2); Vol 6. The Growth of Instrumental Music 1630-1750. Westrup, J. A., ed. 1954 (ISBN 0-19-323105-0); Vol 7. Symphonic Outlook, 1750-90. Wellesz, Egon, ed. 1957 (ISBN 0-19-323106-9); Vol. 8. The Age of Beethoven, 1790-1830. Abraham, Gerald, ed. 1958 (ISBN 0-19-323107-7); Vol. 9. Romanticism, 1830-90. Abraham, Gerald, ed. 1958 (ISBN 0-19-323108-5); Vol. 10. Modern Music, 1890-1950. Abraham, Gerald, ed. 1959 (ISBN 0-19-323109-3). 6.00 ea. Oxford U Pr.

Abraham, Gerald, et al, eds. New Oxford History of Music. Incl. Vol. 1. Ancient & Oriental Music. Wellesz, Egon, ed. (15 plates). 1957. 44.00 (ISBN 0-19-316301-2); Vol. 2. Early Medieval Music up to 1300. Hughes, Dom Anselm, ed. 1954. 49.95 (ISBN 0-19-316302-0); Vol 3. Ars Nova & the Renaissance, 1300-1540. Hughes, Dom Anselm & Abraham, Gerald, eds. 1960. 49.95 (ISBN 0-19-316303-9); Vol. 4. The Age of Humanism, 1540-1630. Abraham, Gerald, ed. (Illus.). 1968. 44.00x (ISBN 0-19-316304-7); Vol. 7. The Age of Enlightenment, 1745-1790. Wellesz, Egon & Sternfeld, Frederick, eds. (Illus.). 1973. 49.95 (ISBN 0-19-316307-1); Vol. 10. Modern Age, 1890-1960. Cooper, Martin, ed. 1974. 49.95x (ISBN 0-19-316310-1). Oxford U Pr.

Adriaansz, Willem. Introduction to Shamisen Kumiuta: History, Analysis & Anthology. (Source Materials & Studies in Ethnomusicology Ser.: Vol. 10). 1978. 47.50 (ISBN 90-6027-149-1, Pub. by Frits Knuf Netherlands); wrappers 35.00 (ISBN 0-686-30875-1, Pub. by Frits Knuf Netherlands). Pendragon NY.

Apel, Willi. The History of Keyboard Music to 1700. Tischler, Hans, tr. LC 79-135015. 896p. 1972. 30.00x (ISBN 0-253-32795-4). Ind U Pr.

Armitage, Andrew D. & Tudor, Dean. Annual Index to Popular Music Record Reviews 1972. LC 73-8909. 1973. 16.50 (ISBN 0-8108-0636-3). Scarecrow.

Artz, Frederick B. From the Renaissance to Romanticism: Trends in Style in Art, Literature, & Music 1300-1830. LC 62-20021. 1962. 12.50x (ISBN 0-226-02837-2). U of Chicago Pr.

--From the Renaissance to Romanticism: Trends in Style, in Art, Literature & Music, 1300-1830. LC 62-20021. 1962. pap. 3.95 (ISBN 0-226-02838-0, P186, Phoen). U of Chicago Pr.

Bacharach, A. L., ed. New Musical Companion. 1964. 7.50x (ISBN 0-575-00496-7). Intl Pubns Serv.

--New Musical Companion. 22nd rev. ed. 1957. 5.50x (ISBN 0-8426-1131-2). Verry.

Baraka, Imamu A. Black Music. LC 80-15439. (Illus.). 221p. 1980. Repr. of 1967 ed. lib. bdg. 19.25x (ISBN 0-313-22518-4, JOBK). Greenwood.

Barne, Kitty. Listening to the Orchestra. LC 72-13098. (Essay Index Reprint Ser.). Repr. of 1946 ed. 18.50 (ISBN 0-8369-8146-4). Arno.

Barzun, Jacques, ed. Pleasures of Music: An Anthology of Writings About Music & Musicians from Cellini to Bernard Shaw. abr. ed. 1977. 15.00x (ISBN 0-226-03856-4); pap. 4.95 (ISBN 0-226-03854-8, P727, Phoen). U of Chicago Pr.

Bekker, Paul. Story of Music: An Historical Sketch of the Changes in Musical Form. LC 74-124592. (BCL Ser. I). (Illus.). 1970. Repr. of 1927 ed. 22.50 (ISBN 0-404-00729-5). AMS Pr.

Blacking, John & Kealiinohomoku, Joann W., eds. The Performing Arts: Music & Dance. (World Anthropology Ser.). 1979. text ed. 44.00x (ISBN 90-279-7870-0). Mouton.

Bontinck, Irmgard, ed. New Patterns of Musical Behaviour of the Young Generation in Industrial Societies. 1974. 27.00 (ISBN 3-7024-0057-5, 51-26246). Eur-Am Music.

Borroff, Edith. Music in Europe & the United States: A History. (Illus.). 1971. text ed. 21.95 (ISBN 0-13-608083-9). P-H.

Boulez, Pierre. Boulez on Music Today. Bradshaw, Susan & Bennett, Richard R., trs. 144p. 1979. 5.95 (ISBN 0-571-09420-1, Pub. by Faber & Faber); pap. 3.95 (ISBN 0-571-10587-4). Merrimack Bk Serv.

Boyer, Bathyah. Material Relics of Music in Ancient Palestine and Its Environs. LC 64-251. 1963. pap. 6.50 (ISBN 0-913932-33-7). Boosey & Hawkes.

Brandt, William, et al. The Comprehensive Study of Music: Anthology of Music from Beethoven Through Wagner. 1977. pap. text ed. 11.50 scp (ISBN 0-06-161422-X, HarpC). Har-Row.

--The Comprehensive Study of Music: Anthology of Music from Debussy Through Stockhausen. 1976. pap. text ed. 11.50 scp (ISBN 0-06-161420-3, HarpC). Har-Row.

--The Comprehensive Study of Music: Anthology of Music from Monteverdi Through Mozart. 1977. pap. text ed. 11.50 scp (ISBN 0-06-161417-3, HarpC). Har-Row.

Brown, Irving, ed. The New York Times Nostalgic Years in Song. LC 73-89470. (Illus.). 255p. 1974. spiral bdg. 12.50 (ISBN 0-8129-0448-6); pap. 7.95 (ISBN 0-8129-6262-1). Times Bks.

Buck, Percy C. The Scope of Music. LC 77-18119. Repr. of 1938 ed. 9.50 (ISBN 0-685-34509-2). Scholarly.

Busby, Thomas. General History of Music from the Earliest Times, 2 Vols. LC 68-21091. (Music Ser). 1968. Repr. of 1819 ed. 55.00 (ISBN 0-306-71063-3). Da Capo.

Butor, Michel. Dialogue avec 33 Variations de Ludwig van Beethoven sur une Valse de Diabelli. (Coll. le Chemin). pap. 8.95 (ISBN 0-685-37245-6). French & Eur.

Cage, John. M: Writings '67-'72. LC 72-11051. (Illus.). 224p. 1973. pap. 7.95 (ISBN 0-8195-6035-9, Pub. by Wesleyan U Pr). Columbia U Pr.

Calvocoressi, Michel D. The Principles & Methods of Musical Criticism. LC 78-66887. (Encore Music Editions Ser.). (Illus.). 1979. Repr. of 1931 ed. 17.50 (ISBN 0-88355-729-0). Hyperion Conn.

Cannon, Beekman C., et al. Art of Music: A Short History of Musical Styles & Ideas. (Illus.). 1960. text ed. 22.50 scp (ISBN 0-690-10254-2, HarpC). Har-Row.

Chadwick, George W. Judith: Lyric Drama for Soli, Chorus, & Orchestra. LC 70-169727. (Earlier American Music Ser.: Vol. 3). 176p. 1972. Repr. of 1901 ed. lib. bdg. 22.50 (ISBN 0-306-77303-1). Da Capo.

--Symphony No. Two: In B Flat, Opus 21. facsimile ed. LC 71-170930. (Earlier American Music Ser.: No. 4). 216p. 1972. Repr. of 1888 ed. 22.50 (ISBN 0-306-77304-X). Da Capo.

Chailley, Jacques. Forty Thousand Years of Music: Man in Search of Music. Myers, Rollo, tr. from Fr. LC 74-31227. (Music Reprint Ser). (Illus.). xiv, 229p. 1975. Repr. of 1964 ed. lib. bdg. 25.00 (ISBN 0-306-70661-X). Da Capo.

Clark, J. Bunker. Transposition in Seventeenth Century English Organ Accompaniments & the Transposing Organ. LC 72-96873. (Detroit Monographs in Musicology: No. 4). 1974. 5.00 (ISBN 0-911772-56-1). Info Coord.

Cleaver, Dale G. & Eddins, John M. Art & Music: An Introduction. (Illus., Orig.). 1977. pap. text ed. 14.95 (ISBN 0-15-503437-5, HC); record 5.95 (ISBN 0-15-503438-3). HarBraceJ.

Clendenin, William R. History of Music. (Quality Paperback: No. 272). (Illus.). 464p. 1974. pap. 4.95 (ISBN 0-8226-0272-5). Littlefield.

Colles, H. C. The Growth of Music. 4th ed. 1978. 12.95x (ISBN 0-19-316116-8). Oxford U Pr.

--Symphony & Drama 1850-1900. LC 72-97077. (Oxford History of Music Ser). 1973. Repr. of 1934 ed. lib. bdg. 22.50x (ISBN 0-8154-0475-1). Cooper Sq.
Cooke, J. F. Standard History of Music. 59.95 (ISBN 0-8490-1120-5). Gordon Pr.
Corner, Philip. Ear Journeys: Water. (Illus.). 1979. box 7.00 (ISBN 0-914162-30-6). Printed Edns.
Crowest, Frederick J. The Story of the Art of Music. 1979. Repr. of 1904 ed. lib. bdg. 25.00 (ISBN 0-8495-0921-1). Arden Lib.
Davidson, Audrey. Substance & Manner: Studies in Music & the Other Arts. (Illus.). 1977. lib. bdg. 12.95 (ISBN 0-930276-01-9); pap. 4.95 (ISBN 0-930276-00-0). Hiawatha Pr.
Davis, Thomas. National & Historical Ballads, Songs, & Poems. (Folklore Ser.). 1869. 20.00 (ISBN 0-685-43837-6). Norwood Edns.
Davison, Archibald T. & Apel, Willi, eds. Historical Anthology of Music, 2 vols. Incl. Vol. 1. Oriental, Medieval, & Renaissance Music. rev. ed. (Illus.). 258p. 1949 (ISBN 0-674-39300-7); Vol. 2. Baroque, Rococo, & Pre-Classical Music. (Illus.). 303p. 1950 (ISBN 0-674-39301-5). LC 49-4339. 15.00 ea. Harvard U Pr.
De la Halle, Adam. Oeuvres completes du trouvere Adam de la Halle Poesies et musique. De Coussemaker, Edmond, ed. (Illus.). 516p. (Fr.). 1964. Repr. of 1872 ed. 60.00x (ISBN 0-8450-1003-4). Broude.
Demuth, Norman. An Anthology of Musical Criticism. LC 72-138219. 397p. 1972. Repr. of 1947 ed. lib. bdg. 26.75x (ISBN 0-8371-5576-2, DEMC). Greenwood.
Detheridge, Joseph, compiled by. Chronology of Music Composers, 2 vols. LC 77-166270. (Illus.). 311p. 1972. Repr. of 1936 ed. Set. 35.00 (ISBN 0-403-01390-9). Scholarly.
Diamond, Harold J. Music Criticism: An Annotated Guide to the Literature. LC 79-22279. 326p. 1979. 17.50 (ISBN 0-8108-1268-1). Scarecrow.
Dickinson, Edward. The Spirit of Music. 59.95 (ISBN 0-8490-1111-6). Gordon Pr.
--The Study of the History of Music. 59.95 (ISBN 0-8490-1155-8). Gordon Pr.
Dorian, Frederick. The History of Music in Performance: The Art of Musical Interpretation from the Renaissance to Our Day. LC 80-28028. (Illus.). 387p. 1981. Repr. of 1971 ed. lib. bdg. 29.75x (ISBN 0-313-22893-0, DOHM). Greenwood.
Dufourcq, N., ed. Musique, 2 Vols. (Illus., Fr.). 62.50x ea. Vol. 1 (ISBN 2-03-014110-0). Vol. 2 (ISBN 2-03-014120-8). Larousse.
Duke, Vernon. Listen Here. 1963. 7.95 (ISBN 0-685-06621-5); pap. 4.50 (ISBN 0-8392-5010-X). Astor-Honor.
Dyson, George. Progress of Music. LC 79-93334. (Essay Index Reprint Ser). 1932. 16.00 (ISBN 0-8369-1287-X). Arno.
Eastcott, R. Sketches of the Origin, Process & Effects of Music. LC 70-159680. (Music Ser). 1971. Repr. of 1793 ed. lib. bdg. 27.50 (ISBN 0-306-70184-7). Da Capo.
Eaton, Quaintance. Opera Caravan. LC 78-9128. (Music Reprint 1978 Ser.). (Illus.). 1978. lib. bdg. 29.50 (ISBN 0-306-77596-4); pap. 6.95 (ISBN 0-306-80089-6). Da Capo.
Edmunds, John A. Williamsburg Songbook. LC 64-20095. (Colonial Williamsburg). (Illus.). 137p. 1964. 5.95x (ISBN 0-8139-0321-1). U Pr of Va.
Edwards, George T. Music & Musicians of Maine. LC 74-135736. Repr. of 1928 ed. 23.00 (ISBN 0-404-07231-3). AMS Pr.
Ehlert, Louis. From the Tone World: A Series of Essays. Tretbar, Helen D., tr. from Ger. LC 72-13099. (Essay Index Reprint Ser.). Repr. of 1885 ed. 16.25 (ISBN 0-8369-8156-1). Arno.
Eimert, Herbert & Stockhausen, Karlheinz, eds. Musical Craftsmanship. Cardew, Cornelius & Black, Leo, trs. from Ger. (Die Reihe: No. 3). 1959. pap. 10.00 (ISBN 0-900938-11-0, 47-26103). Eur-Am Music.
--Reports, Analyses. Black, Leo & Koenig, Ruth, trs. from Ger. (Die Reihe: No. 5). 1961. pap. 10.00 (ISBN 0-900938-13-7, 47-26105). Eur-Am Music.
--Retrospective. Cardew, Cornelius & Koenig, Ruth, trs. (Die Reihe: No. 8). 1968. pap. 4.50 (ISBN 3-7024-0152-0, 50-26108). Eur-Am Music.
Einstein, Alfred. Greatness in Music. LC 70-87527. 1972. Repr. of 1941 ed. lib. bdg. 25.00 (ISBN 0-306-71441-8). Da Capo.
--Greatness in Music. LC 75-181148. 287p. 1941. Repr. 29.00 (ISBN 0-403-01549-9). Scholarly.
--Short History of Music. 1954. pap. 2.45 (ISBN 0-394-70004-X, Vin, V4). Random.
Eisler, Paul E. World Chronology of Music History, 5 vols. plus index. LC 73-4354. (Illus.). 512p. 1976. lib. bdg. 45.00 ea. (ISBN 0-379-16080-3). Oceana.
Eisler, Paul E., compiled by. World Chronology of Music History, Vol. 5. LC 72-4345. 1978. text ed. 45.00x (ISBN 0-379-16085-4). Oceana.
Ellis, William A. Richard Wagner to Mathilde Wesendonck. LC 76-86960. (Reprints Ser). (Illus.). 1970. Repr. of 1905 ed. lib. bdg. 25.00 (ISBN 0-87821-020-2). Milford Hse.
Elson, Louis. Curiosities of Music. 59.95 (ISBN 0-87968-978-1). Gordon Pr.
Elson, Louis C. Curiosities of Music. LC 77-90801. 1978. Repr. of 1908 ed. lib. bdg. 35.00 (ISBN 0-89341-418-2). Longwood Pr.
--European Reminiscences Musical & Otherwise. LC 72-125046. (Music Ser). (Illus.). 301p. 1972. Repr. of 1896 ed. lib. bdg. 29.50 (ISBN 0-306-70011-5). Da Capo.
--History of American Music. (Illus.). 1971. Repr. 29.00 (ISBN 0-8337-1055-9). B Franklin.
Ewen, David. Pioneers in Music. LC 72-6816. (Essay Index Reprint Ser). 1972. Repr. of 1940 ed. 25.00 (ISBN 0-8369-7262-7). Arno.
Ewen, David, ed. From Bach to Stravinsky: The History of Music by Its Foremost Critics. LC 79-124770. Repr. of 1933 ed. 12.50 (ISBN 0-404-02359-2). AMS Pr.
--From Bach to Stravinsky: The History of Music by Its Foremost Critics. LC 68-54419. (Illus.). 1968. Repr. of 1933 ed. lib. bdg. 14.75x (ISBN 0-8371-0411-4, EWBS). Greenwood.
Fallet, E. M. La Vie Musicale au Pays de Neuchatel du XIIIe a la fin du XVIIIe siecle: Contribution a l'histoire de la Musique en Suisse. (Sammlung Mw. Abh. 20-1936 Ser.). xx, 322p. 47.50 (ISBN 90-6027-222-6, Pub. by Frits Knuf Netherlads). Pendragon NY.
Ferguson, Donald N. A History of Musical Thought. LC 73-5265. 675p. 1975. Repr. of 1959 ed. lib. bdg. 38.75x (ISBN 0-8371-6882-1, FEMT). Greenwood.
--A Short History of Music. LC 73-5266. (Illus.). 500p. 1974. Repr. of 1946 ed. lib. bdg. 22.50x (ISBN 0-8371-6881-3, FEHM). Greenwood.
Finck, H. T. My Adventures in the Golden Age of Music. LC 70-87496. (Music Ser.). 462p. 1971. Repr. of 1926 ed. lib. bdg. 39.50 (ISBN 0-306-71448-5). Da Capo.
Finck, Henry T. Songs & Song Writers. LC 78-31290. 1979. Repr. of 1902 ed. lib. bdg. 25.00 (ISBN 0-89341-439-5). Longwood Pr.
Finney, Theodore M. A History of Music. LC 73-17926. (Illus.). 720p. 1976. Repr. of 1947 ed. lib. bdg. 40.75x (ISBN 0-8371-7270-5, FIHM). Greenwood.
Forbes, Elliot, ed. Beethoven: Symphony No. Five in C Minor. LC 73-98890. (Critical Score Ser). 1971. 10.00 (ISBN 0-393-02151-3); pap. 5.95x (ISBN 0-393-09893-1). Norton.
Foss, Hubert J. & Fellowes, E. H. Heritage of Music, Vol. 2. facsimile ed. LC 73-156642. (Essay Index Reprint Ser). Repr. of 1934 ed. 17.00 (ISBN 0-8369-2356-1). Arno.
Foss, Hubert J., ed. Heritage of Music. LC 73-93338. (Essay Index Reprint Ser). 1927. 17.00 (ISBN 0-8369-1292-6). Arno.
Foster, Stephen. The Social Orchestra: A Collection of Popular Melodies Arranged As Duets, Trios, & Quartets. Hitchcock, H. Wiley, ed. LC 79-169645. (Earlier American Music Ser: Vol. 13). (Illus.). 96p. 1973. Repr. of 1854 ed. lib. bdg. 19.50 (ISBN 0-306-77313-9). Da Capo.
Gafurius, Franchinus. Monuments of Music & Music Literature in Facisimile: Series Two Pt.4, Vol. 96, Apologia. 1979. 25.00x (ISBN 0-8450-2296-2). Broude.
--Monuments of Music & Music Literature in Facsimile: Series Two Pt.4, Vol. 99. (Practica Musicae). 1979. 42.50x (ISBN 0-8450-2299-7). Broude.
Gelatt, Roland. Music Makers: Some Outstanding Musical Performers of Our Day. LC 72-2334. (Music Ser.). Repr. of 1953 ed. lib. bdg. 25.00 (ISBN 0-306-70519-2). Da Capo.
Gerboth, Walter, et al, eds. Introduction to Music: Selected Readings. rev ed. (Orig.). 1969. pap. text ed. 5.95x (ISBN 0-393-09790-0, NortonC). Norton.
Gleason, Harold & Becker, Warren. Chamber Music: Haydn to Bartok. 2nd ed. (Music Literature Outlines: Ser. V). 1980. pap. text ed. 10.95 (ISBN 0-89917-267-9, Frangipani Press). TIS Inc.
--Early American Music. 2nd ed. (Music Literature Outlines Ser. III). 1981. write for info. (ISBN 0-89917-265-2, Frangipani Pr). TIS Inc.
Gleich, C. C. von. Die Bedeutung der Allgemeinen Musikalischen Zeitung: 1798-1848 & 1863-1882. 1969. wrappers 15.00 (ISBN 90-6027-072-X, Pub. by Frits Knuf Netherlands). Pendragon NY.
Gohler, Karl A. Die Messkataloge im Dienste der musikalischen Geschichtsforschung: Verzeichnis der in den Frankfurter und Leipziger Messkatalogen der Jahre 1564 bis 1759 angezeigten Musikalien, 2 vols. 1965. Repr. Set. wrappers 32.50 (ISBN 0-686-30880-8, Pub. by Frits Knuf Netherlands). Vol. 1 (ISBN 90-6027-013-4). Vol. 2 (ISBN 90-6027-014-2). Pendragon NY.
Goovaerts, A. Histoire et Bibliographie de la Typographie Musicale dans les Pays-Bas. 1963. Repr. of 1880 ed. 62.50 (ISBN 90-6027-002-9, Pub. by Frits Knuf Netherlands). Pendragon NY.
Gray, Cecil. A History of Music. 2nd ed. (History of Civilization Ser.). 1931. 7.95 (ISBN 0-7100-6105-6). Routledge & Kegan.
--The History of Music. LC 78-10335. 1979. Repr. of 1935 ed. lib. bdg. 19.50x (ISBN 0-313-20655-4, GRHM). Greenwood.
Groia, Philip. They All Sang on the Corner. (Illus.). 1973. pap. 4.95 (ISBN 0-912954-08-6). Edmond Pub Co.
Grout, Donald J. A History of Western Music. 3rd, shorter ed. (Illus.). 1980. write for info. (ISBN 0-393-01411-8); pap. 16.95x (ISBN 0-393-95142-1). Norton.
--A History of Western Music. 3rd ed. 1980. text ed. 18.95x (ISBN 0-393-95136-7). Norton.
--History of Western Music. rev. ed. (Illus.). 1973. text ed. 18.95x (ISBN 0-393-09416-2). Norton.
--History of Western Music. rev. ed. (Illus.). 540p. 1973. pap. text ed. 15.95x (ISBN 0-393-09358-1). Norton.
Grunfeld, Frederic V. Music. (World of Culture Ser.). (Illus.). 192p. 1974. 12.95 (ISBN 0-88225-101-5). Newsweek.
Hadow, William H. English Music. LC 74-38356. (Select Bibliographies Reprint Ser.). Repr. of 1931 ed. 15.00 (ISBN 0-8369-6773-9). Arno.
--Music. LC 72-137238. Repr. of 1925 ed. 20.00 (ISBN 0-404-03021-1). AMS Pr.
Hadow, William H., ed. The Oxford History of Music, 8 vols. 2nd, rev. ed. Incl. Introductory Volume. Buck, P. 1929. 12.50x (ISBN 0-8154-0482-4); Polyphonic Period I, 330-1400. Wooldridge, H. E. 17.50x (ISBN 0-8154-0470-0); Polyphonic Period II, 1400-1600. Wooldridge, H. E. 24.50x (ISBN 0-8154-0470-0); The Age of Bach & Handel. Fuller-Maitland, J. A. 22.50x (ISBN 0-8154-0472-7); The Music of the Seventeenth Century. Parry, Hubert H. 22.50x (ISBN 0-8154-0471-9); The Viennese Period. Hadow, William H. 17.50x (ISBN 0-8154-0473-5); The Romantic Period. Dannreuther, E. 17.50x (ISBN 0-8154-0474-3); Symphony & Drama, 1850-1900. Colles, H. C. 22.50x (ISBN 0-8154-0475-1). 1973. Cooper Sq.
Haggin, B. H. A Decade of Music. 256p. 1973. 10.00 (ISBN 0-8180-1210-2). Horizon.
Hale, Philip L. Great Concert Music. lib. bdg. 16.00 (ISBN 0-403-08980-8). Scholarly.
Hamel, Peter M. Through Music to the Self: How to Appreciate & Experience Music Anew. Lemesurier, Peter, tr. from Ger. LC 78-70774. (Illus.). 1979. pap. 6.95 (ISBN 0-394-73681-8). Shambhala Pubns.
Hamm, Charles. Yesterdays: Popular Song in America. (Illus.). 1979. 24.95 (ISBN 0-393-01257-3). Norton.
Harmen, Alec & Mellers, Wilfrid. Man & His Music, 3 vols. LC 74-166272. 1962. Repr. Set. 89.00 (ISBN 0-403-01391-7). Scholarly.
Harter, Jim. Music: A Pictorial Archive of Woodcuts & Engravings. (Pictorial Archive Ser.). (Illus.). 155p. (Orig.). 1981. pap. 6.00 (ISBN 0-486-24002-9). Dover.
Haydon, Glen. Evolution of the Six-Four Chord: A Chapter in the History of Dissonant Treatment. LC 75-125052. (Music Ser). 1971. Repr. of 1933 ed. lib. bdg. 19.50 (ISBN 0-306-70017-4). Da Capo.
Hayes, Gerald R. King's Music: An Anthology. LC 78-66906. (Encore Music Editions Ser.). (Illus.). 1981. Repr. of 1937 ed. 14.00 (ISBN 0-88355-746-0). Hyperion Conn.
Hays, William. Twentieth Century Views of Musical History. 1972. lib. rep. ed. 22.50x (ISBN 0-684-15149-9, ScribT). Scribner.
Headington, Christopher. The History of Western Music. LC 76-20883. 1977. 12.95 (ISBN 0-02-871090-8); pap. text ed. 8.95 (ISBN 0-02-871080-0). Schirmer Bks.
Hegar, E. Die Anfange der neueren Musikgeschichtsschreibung um 1770 bei Gerbert, Burney und Hawkins. (Sammlung MW Abh. 7-1933 Ser.). vi, 90p. 25.00 (ISBN 90-6027-254-4, Pub. by Frits Knuf Netherlands). Pendragon NY.
Heritte-Viardot, Louise. Memories & Adventures. LC 77-22220. (Music Reprint Ser.). (Illus.). 1978. Repr. of 1913 ed. lib. bdg. 25.00 (ISBN 0-306-77515-8). Da Capo.
Herndon, Marcia & McLeod, Norma. Music As Culture. 1979. lib. bdg. 17.50 (ISBN 0-8482-4479-6). Norwood Edns.
Hervey, Arthur. Masters of French Music. LC 72-13993. (Essay Index Reprint Ser.). (Illus.). Repr. of 1894 ed. 24.00 (ISBN 0-518-10014-6). Arno.
Hilton, John. Catch That Catch Can. LC 75-87492. (Music Ser). 1970. Repr. of 1652 ed. lib. bdg. 17.50 (ISBN 0-306-71498-1). Da Capo.
Hitchcock, H. Wiley. Marc-Antoine Charpentier's Pestis Mediolanensis: (the Plague of Milan) LC 79-320. (Early Musical Masterworks-Critical Editions & Commentaries Ser.). 1979. 19.00x (ISBN 0-8078-1365-6). U of NC Pr.
Hogarth, George. Musical History, Biography, & Criticism. LC 69-12685. (Music Reprint Ser). 1969. Repr. of 1848 ed. lib. bdg. 22.50 (ISBN 0-306-71234-2). Da Capo.
Hogwood, Christopher. Music at Court. (Illus.). 1981. text ed. 18.75x (ISBN 0-575-02877-7). Verry.
Horn, David. Literature of American Music in Books & Folk Music Collections: A Fully Annotated Bibliography. LC 76-13160. 1977. 24.00 (ISBN 0-8108-0996-6). Scarecrow.
Horton, John. Scandinavian Music: A Short History. LC 73-7673. (Illus.). 180p. 1975. Repr. of 1963 ed. lib. bdg. 14.50x (ISBN 0-8371-6944-5, HOSM). Greenwood.
Howes, Frank S. Man, Mind & Music. LC 70-181179. 184p. 1948. Repr. 12.00 (ISBN 0-403-01582-0). Scholarly.
Huneker, James G. Mezzotints in Modern Music: Brahms, Tchaikovsky, Chopin, Richard Strauss, Liszt & Wagner. LC 79-181181. 318p. 1905. Repr. 24.00 (ISBN 0-403-01586-3). Scholarly.
Hurry, Jamieson B. Sumer Is Icumen in. LC 77-75217. 1977. Repr. of 1914 ed. lib. bdg. 15.00 (ISBN 0-89341-117-5). Longwood Pr.
Ingman, Nicholas. The Story of Music. LC 76-8999. (Illus.). 1980. pap. 8.95 (ISBN 0-8008-7463-3, Crescendo). Taplinger.
Jacobs, Arthur. A Short History of Western Music. (Orig.). 1972. pap. 2.95 (ISBN 0-14-021421-6, Pelican). Penguin.
--Short History of Western Music. 16.95 (ISBN 0-7153-5743-3). David & Charles.
Janson, H. & Kerman, Joseph. History of Art & Music. 1969. pap. text ed. 13.95 (ISBN 0-13-389312-X). P-H.
Johnson, H. Earle. Musical Interludes in Boston, 1795-1830. LC 43-11010. Repr. of 1943 ed. 14.00 (ISBN 0-404-03588-4). AMS Pr.
Kamien, Roger, ed. The Norton Scores. 3rd ed. 1000p. (Orig.). 1977. pap. text ed. 15.95x standard ed. (ISBN 0-393-09111-2). Norton.
Kendall, Alan. Music: Its Story in the West. LC 79-27607. (Illus.). 256p. 1980. 17.95 (ISBN 0-668-04931-6, 4931-6). Arco.
Kiesewetter, Raphael G. History of the Modern Music of Western Europe: From the First Century of the Christian Era to the Present Day. LC 74-140375. (Music Ser). 354p. 1973. Repr. of 1848 ed. lib. bdg. 25.00 (ISBN 0-306-70089-1). Da Capo.
Kirby, F. E. Short History of Keyboard Music. LC 66-23081. 1966. 17.95 (ISBN 0-02-917330-2). Free Pr.
Kivy, Peter. The Corded Shell: Reflections on Musical Expression. LC 80-7539. (Princeton Essays on the Arts: No. 9). 176p. 1980. 15.00 (ISBN 0-691-07258-2); pap. 6.95 (ISBN 0-691-02014-0). Princeton U Pr.
Knight, William F. St. Augustine's De Musica: A Synopsis. LC 78-13795. (Encore Music Editions Ser.). 1979. Repr. of 1949 ed. 13.00 (ISBN 0-88355-737-1). Hyperion Conn.
Kolodin, Irving, ed. Critical Composer. LC 72-93351. (Essay Index Reprint Ser). 1940. 18.00 (ISBN 0-8369-1358-2). Arno.
Kottick, Edward. The Collegium: A Handbook. 1978. 15.00 (ISBN 0-8079-0189-X). October.
Krebs, Carl. Dittersdorfiana. LC 72-166092. (Music Ser.). 1972. Repr. of 1900 ed. lib. bdg. 19.50 (ISBN 0-306-70259-2). Da Capo.
Krehbiel, Henry E. Music & Manners: From Pergolese to Beethoven. facsimile ed. LC 72-154156. (Select Bibliographies Reprint Ser). Repr. of 1898 ed. 17.00 (ISBN 0-8369-5772-5). Arno.
Kresky, Jeffrey. Tonal Music: Twelve Analytic Studies. LC 77-74447. (Illus.). 192p. 1978. 12.50x (ISBN 0-253-37011-6). Ind U Pr.
Krohn, Ernst C. The History of Music. LC 65-23398. (Music Reprint Ser.). 1973. Repr. of 1958 ed. lib. bdg. 27.50 (ISBN 0-306-70595-8). Da Capo.
Kruger, L. Die Hamburgische Musikorganisation Im XVII. (Sammlung Mw. Abh. Ser.). viii, 276p. 35.00 (ISBN 90-6027-286-2, Pub. by Frits Knuf Netherlands). Pendragon NY.
Lambert, Barbara, ed. Music in Colonial Massachusetts, Sixteen Thirty to Eighteen Twenty: Music in Public Places, Vol. 1. LC 80-66188. (Illus.). 404p. 1981. 25.00x (ISBN 0-8139-0914-7, Colonial Soc MA). U Pr of Va.
Landowska, Wanda. Music of the Past. LC 75-181199. 184p. 1924. Repr. 19.00 (ISBN 0-403-01609-6). Scholarly.
Lang, Paul H. & Bettmann, Otto L. Pictorial History of Music. (Illus.). (gr. 9 up). 1960. 19.95 (ISBN 0-393-02107-6). Norton.
Lang, Paul H., ed. Music in Western Civilization. (Illus.). 1940. 34.95x (ISBN 0-393-09428-6, NortonC). Norton.

Laurence, Dan H., ed. Shaw's Music: The Complete Musical Criticism, 3 vols. LC 80-1113. 1981. Boxed Set. 150.00 (ISBN 0-396-07967-9). Vol. 1 (ISBN 0-396-07960-1). Vol. 2 (ISBN 0-396-07961-X). Vol. 3 (ISBN 0-396-07962-8). Dodd.

Leichtentritt, Hugo. Music, History, & Ideas. LC 38-17551. 1938. 16.50x (ISBN 0-674-58950-5). Harvard U Pr.

Lengyel, Cornel, ed. History of Music in San Francisco, 7 Vols. Repr. of 1942 ed. Set. 220.00 (ISBN 0-404-07240-2); sep. vols. avail. (ISBN 0-685-05824-7). AMS Pr.

Lerner, Edward R. Study Scores of Musical Styles. 1968. pap. text ed. 13.95 (ISBN 0-07-037211-X, C). McGraw.

Loft, Abram. Violin & Keyboard: The Duo Repertoire, 2 vols. Incl. Vol. 1. From the Seventeenth Century to Mozart. Vol. 1. 20.00 (ISBN 0-670-74701-7); Vol. 2. From Beethoven to the Present. Vol. 2. 20.00 (ISBN 0-670-74702-5). LC 72-93279. (Illus.). 832p. 1973. Set. 40.00 (ISBN 0-670-74700-9, Grossman). Viking Pr.

Lowe, Claude E. A Chronological Cyclopedia of Musicians & Musical Events from A. D. 320 to 1896. 1976. lib. bdg. 75.00 (ISBN 0-8490-1623-1). Gordon Pr.

McClain, Ernest G. The Myth of Invariance: The Origin of the Gods, Mathematics & Music from the Rg Veda to Plato. LC 76-28411. 1976. 10.00 (ISBN 0-89254-003-6). Nicolas-Hays.

McCusker, Honor. Fifty Years of Music in Boston. 3.00 (ISBN 0-686-70271-9). Boston Public Lib.

MacDonald, Donald. Collection of the Ancient Martial Music of Caledonia. 1975. 21.00x (ISBN 0-8464-0255-6). Beekman Pubs.

McGowan, James A. Hear Today, Gone Tomorrow: A Personal History of Rhythm & Blues. (Illus.). 1981. 7.50 (ISBN 0-87164-141-0). William-F.

Mackinley, Malcolm S. Garcia the Centenarian & His Times. LC 75-40206. (Music Reprint Ser.). 1975. Repr. of 1908 ed. lib. bdg. 29.50 (ISBN 0-306-70671-7). Da Capo.

McLin, Lena. Pulse: A History of Music. LC 77-75478. (Illus.). (gr. 6-12). 1977. pap. 4.95 (ISBN 0-8497-5600-6, WE 3, Pub by Kjos West). Kjos.

Madeira, Louis C., compiled by. Music in Philadelphia & History of the Musical Fund Society. LC 78-169650. (Music Reprint Ser.). (Illus.). 234p. 1973. Repr. of 1896 ed. lib. bdg. 25.00 (ISBN 0-306-70260-6). Da Capo.

Marothy. Music & the Bourgeois, Music & the Proletarian. 1974. 36.00 (ISBN 0-9960013-1-X, Pub. by Kaido Hungary). Heyden.

Marshall, Robert L., ed. Studies in Renaissance & Baroque Music in Honor of Arthur Mendel. 1974. 35.00 (ISBN 0-913574-26-0). Eur-Am Music.

Mason, Daniel G. From Grieg to Brahms. new & enl. ed. LC 79-149689. Repr. of 1927 ed. 20.50 (ISBN 0-404-04199-X). AMS Pr.

Mason, Dorothy E. Music in Elizabethan England. LC 59-1448. (Folger Guides to the Age of Shakespeare). 1958. pap. 3.95 (ISBN 0-918016-21-5). Folger Bks.

Mathews, William S. Popular History of the Art of Music from the Earliest Times Until the Present. rev. ed. LC 74-173058. Repr. of 1915 ed. 37.50 (ISBN 0-404-07212-7). AMS Pr.

Mattheson, Johann. Critica Musica, D.I. Grundrichtige Untersuch- und Beurtheilung: So in Alten und Neuen, Gedruckten und Ungedruckten, Musicalischen Schrifften Zu Finden. 784p. 100.00 (ISBN 90-6027-005-3, Pub. by Frits Knuf Netherlands). Pendragon NY.

Matthews, Denis, ed. Keyboard Music. LC 78-58317. (Illus.). 1978. 12.50 (ISBN 0-8008-4455-6, Crescendo); pap. 7.95 (ISBN 0-8008-4456-4, Crescendo). Taplinger.

Menuhin, Yehudi & Davis, Curtis W. The Music of Man. (Illus.). 1979. 24.95 (ISBN 0-416-00101-7). Methuen Inc.

Meyer, Ernst. English Chamber Music. LC 71-127181. (Music Ser). (Illus.). 1971. Repr. of 1946 ed. lib. bdg. 27.50 (ISBN 0-306-70037-9). Da Capo.

Miller, Hugh M. History of Music. 4th ed. LC 72-81476. (Illus.). 247p. 1973. 10.00x (ISBN 0-06-480580-8). B&N.

Millet, Jean. La Belle Methode Ou l'Art De Bien Chanter. LC 71-126600. (Music Ser). 76p. 1973. Repr. of 1666 ed. lib. bdg. 18.50 (ISBN 0-306-70044-1). Da Capo.

Mitchell, W. J. Ludwig Beethoven: Sonata for Violoncello & Pianoforte Opus 69, 1st Movement: Facsimile of the Autograph. LC 74-120289. 6.00x (ISBN 0-231-03417-2). Columbia U Pr.

Monuments of Music & Music Literature in Facsimile: Series Two-Part 3. Incl. Vol. 60. Harmonicorum Libri Tres. Ptolemaeus, Claudius. 1977. 40.00 (ISBN 0-8450-2260-1); Vol. 63, Neder-Landtsche Gedenck-Clanck, Adrianus Valerius, 1974. 42.50 (ISBN 0-8450-2263-6); Vol. 64. De 'Principj dell'Armonia Musicale. Tartini, Giuseppe. 1967. 25.00x (ISBN 0-8450-2264-4); Vol. 65. Dodecachordon. Glareanus, Henricus. 1967. 57.50x (ISBN 0-8450-2265-2); Vol. 66. Compendiolo di Molti Dubbi, segreti et sentenze intorno canto fermo, et figurato. Aaron, Pietro. 1974. 27.50x (ISBN 0-8450-2266-0); Vol. 67. Libri tres de institutione harmonica. Aaron, Pietro. 1975. 27.50x (ISBN 0-8450-2267-9); Vol. 68, Lucidario In Musica Di Alcune Oppenioni Antiche, Et Moderne, Pietro Aaron, 1978. 27.50x (ISBN 0-8450-2268-7); Vol. 69, Thoscanello De La Musica, Pietro Aaron, 1969. 35.00x (ISBN 0-8450-2269-5); Vol. 70. The Present State of Music in France & Italy. Burney, Charles. 1969. 30.00x (ISBN 0-8450-2270-9); Vol. 75. L'art du Chant. Berard, Jean-Baptiste. 1967. 27.50x (ISBN 0-8450-2275-X); Vol. 77. Regula Musice Plane. Brescia, Bonarventura Da. 20.00x (ISBN 0-8450-2277-6); Vol. 78. Musico Prattico. Bononcini, Giovanni Maria. 1969. 27.50x (ISBN 0-8450-2278-4); Vol. 81. Institution Harmonique. Caus, Salomon de. 1969. 47.50x (ISBN 0-8450-2281-4); Vol. 83. Dictionarium Musica. Hoyle, John. 1977. 27.50x (ISBN 0-8450-2283-0); Vol. 84. Dictionnaire de Danse. Compan, Charles. 1974. 37.50x (ISBN 0-8450-2284-9); Vol. 86. Methode de Harpe. Cousineau, Jacques Georges. 1968. 27.50x (ISBN 0-8450-2286-5); Vol. 87. Musicae Compendium. Descartes, Rene. 1968. 25.00x (ISBN 0-8450-2287-3). (Illus.). Repr. Broude.

Morgenstern, Sam. Composers in Music: From Palestrina to Copland. LC 55-10283. 1975. pap. 5.95 (ISBN 0-394-73040-2). Pantheon.

Morgenstern, Sam, ed. Composers on Music: An Anthology of Composers Writings from Palestrino to Copland. Repr. of 1956 ed. lib. bdg. 24.50x (ISBN 0-8371-1147-1, MOCO). Greenwood.

Morphy, Guillermo. Les Luthistes espagnols du XVIe siecle, 2 vols in 1. (Illus.). 306p. (Ger., Fr.). 1969. Repr. of 1902 ed. 75.00x (ISBN 0-8450-1008-5). Broude.

Morse, Constance. Music & Music-Makers. facs. ed. LC 68-54363. (Essay Index Reprint Ser). 1926. 18.25 (ISBN 0-8369-0724-8). Arno.

Mueller, John H. The American Symphony Orchestra: A Social History of Musical Taste. LC 76-8875. (Illus.). 1976. Repr. of 1951 ed. lib. bdg. 27.25x (ISBN 0-8371-8915-2, MUAS). Greenwood.

Muller, Joseph. The Star Spangled Banner: Words & Music Issued Between 1814-1864. LC 79-169653. (Music Ser). (Illus.). 1973. Repr. of 1935 ed. lib. bdg. 25.00 (ISBN 0-306-70263-0). Da Capo.

Music & Western Man. (Canadian Broadcasting Corporation Ser.). 11.50 (ISBN 0-685-27210-9). Dufour.

Mussulman, Joseph A. Music in the Cultured Generation: Musical Life in America, 1870-1900. LC 77-149920. (Pi Kappa Lambda Studies in American Music). 1971. 12.95x (ISBN 0-8101-0350-8). Northwestern U Pr.

Nelson, Alice D. People & Music. new ed. (gr. 9-12). 1973. text ed. 14.80 (ISBN 0-205-03292-3, 5832926); tchrs'. guide 2.40 (ISBN 0-205-03646-5, 5836468). Allyn.

Nettl, Bruno & Foltin, Bela. Daramad of Chahargah: A Study in the Performance Practice of Persian Music. LC 74-175174. (Detroit Monographs in Musicology: No. 2). 84p. 1972. pap. 2.00 (ISBN 0-911772-51-0). Info Coord.

North, Roger. Memoirs of Musick. Rimbault, Edward F., ed. LC 74-24169. Repr. of 1846 ed. 25.00 (ISBN 0-404-13073-9). AMS Pr.

Paine, John K. History of Music to the Death of Schubert. LC 78-127280. (Music Ser). (Illus.). 1971. Repr. of 1907 ed. lib. bdg. 27.50 (ISBN 0-306-70038-7). Da Capo.

Palisca, Claude, ed. The Norton Anthology of Western Music. 600p. (Orig.). 1980. Vol. I. pap. text ed. 12.95x (ISBN 0-393-95143-X); Vol. II. pap. text ed. 12.95x (ISBN 0-393-95151-0). Norton.

Parrish, Carl. Treasury of Early Music. (Illus.). 1964. pap. 6.95x (ISBN 0-393-09444-8, NortonC). records avail. Norton.

Parrish, Carl & Ohl, John F. Masterpieces of Music Before 1750. (Illus.). 1950. 9.95x (ISBN 0-393-09739-0, NortonC). Norton.

Parry, Charles H. Evolution of the Art of Music. Colles, Henry C., ed. Repr. of 1930 ed. lib. bdg. 17.25x (ISBN 0-8371-0609-5, PAEM). Greenwood.

Pedrell, Felipe, ed. Hispaniae Schola Musica Sacra, 8 vols. in 4. Repr. of 1894 ed. per double vol. 30.00 (ISBN 0-384-45635-9); 110.00 set (ISBN 0-384-45635-9); pap. 25.00 per double vol. (ISBN 0-686-57641-1); pap. 90.00 set (ISBN 0-685-31549-5). Johnson Repr.

Perrin, H., et al. New Approach to Music. (Winston Mine Editions). Pts. 1-3. 1970. text ed. 6.53 (ISBN 0-685-33351-5, HoltC); Pts. 4-6. 1972. text ed. 8.14 (ISBN 0-685-33352-3). HR&W.

Phipson, T. L. Voice & Violin. LC 77-92440. 1978. Repr. of 1898 ed. lib. bdg. 25.00 (ISBN 0-89341-425-5). Longwood Pr.

Pichierei, L. Music in New Hampshire, 1623-1800. LC 60-13940. 297p. 1960. 20.00x (ISBN 0-231-02377-4). Columbia U Pr.

Plantinga, Leon B. Schumann As Critic. LC 76-7599. (Music Reprint Ser.). 1976. Repr. of 1967 ed. pap. 27.50 (ISBN 0-306-70785-3). Da Capo.

Porte, John F. Edward MacDowell: A Great American Tone Poet His Life & Music. LC 78-16529. 1978. Repr. of 1922 ed. lib. bdg. 20.00 (ISBN 0-89341-435-2). Longwood Pr.

Pound, Ezra. Antheil & the Treatise on Harmony. 2nd ed. LC 68-27463. (Music Ser). (gr. 9 up). 1968. Repr. of 1927 ed. lib. bdg. 17.50 (ISBN 0-306-70981-3). Da Capo.

Powers, Harold, ed. Studies in Music History: Essays for Oliver Strunk. LC 80-14086. (Illus.). x, 527p. 1980. Repr. of 1968 ed. lib. bdg. 39.75x (ISBN 0-313-22501-X, POSM). Greenwood.

Price, Kingsley, ed. On Criticizing Music: Five Philosophical Perspectives. LC 81-47597. (Illus.). 128p. 1981. text ed. 12.00x (ISBN 0-8018-2613-6). Johns Hopkins.

Prizer, William F. Courtly Pastimes: The Frottole of Marchetto Cara. Buelow, George, ed. LC 80-22519. (Studies in Musicology: No. 33). 440p. 1980. 42.95 (ISBN 0-8357-0996-5). Univ Microfilms.

Prunieres, Henry. A New History of Music: The Middle Ages to Mozart. LC 79-166276. 413p. 1943. Repr. 32.00 (ISBN 0-403-01652-5). Scholarly.

--A New History of Music: The Middle Ages to Mozart. Lockspeiser, Edward, ed. LC 75-183327. 413p. 1972. Repr. of 1943 ed. 35.00x (ISBN 0-8443-0029-2). Vienna Hse.

Pulver, Jeffrey. A Dictionary of Old English Music & Musical Instruments. 75.00 (ISBN 0-8490-0042-4). Gordon Pr.

Raynor, Henry. A Social History of Music: From the Middle Ages to Beethoven & Music & Society Since 1815. LC 78-58318. 1978. pap. 7.95 (ISBN 0-8008-7238-X, Crescendo). Taplinger.

Restout, Denise & Hawkins, Robert, eds. Landowska on Music. LC 64-22698. 1969. pap. 8.95 (ISBN 0-8128-1233-6). Stein & Day.

Richardson, Alfred M. The Medieval Modes: Their Melody & Harmony for the Use of the Modern Composer. LC 78-66918. (Encore Music Editions Ser.). (Illus.). 1979. Repr. of 1933 ed. 11.50 (ISBN 0-88355-758-4). Hyperion Conn.

Rickward, Edell. Scrutinies by Various Writers, Vol. 1. LC 76-23140. 1928. lib. bdg. 20.00 (ISBN 0-8414-7239-4). Folcroft.

Riemann, Hugo. Handbuch der Musikgeschichte, 2 vols. in 4. 2189p. Repr. of 1920 ed. Set. 115.00 (ISBN 0-384-50833-2). Johnson Repr.

Rimbault, Edward F., ed. The Old Cheque-Book, or Book of Rememberance of the Chapel Royal from 1561. LC 65-23407. (Music Ser.). 1966. Repr. of 1872 ed. lib. bdg. 25.00 (ISBN 0-306-70911-2). Da Capo.

Rockstro, William S. A General History of Music from the Infancy of the Greek Drama to the Present Period. LC 78-16042. 1978. Repr. of 1886 ed. lib. bdg. 55.00 (ISBN 0-89341-436-0). Longwood Pr.

Roland-Manuel. Histoire de la Musique, 2 vols. (Historique Ser.). Vol. 1. 69.95 (ISBN 0-686-56457-X); Vol. 2. 65.50 (ISBN 0-686-56458-8). French & Eur.

--Histoire de la Musique, Vol. 2. (Historique Ser.). 1894p. 65.50 (ISBN 0-686-56459-6). French & Eur.

Rosen, Charles. The Classical Style: Haydn, Mozart, Beethoven. LC 79-83250. (Illus.). 1971. 12.50 (ISBN 0-670-22510-X). Viking Pr.

Rossi, Nick & Rafferty, Sadie. Music Through the Centuries. LC 80-9066. (Illus.). 760p. 1981. lib. bdg. 27.00 (ISBN 0-8191-1498-7); pap. text ed. 16.75 (ISBN 0-8191-1499-5). U Pr of Amer.

Rothschild, Fritz. The Lost Tradition in Music: Rhythm & Tempo in J. S. Bach's Time. LC 78-19565. (Encore Music Editions Ser.). (Illus.). 1979. Repr. of 1953 ed. 25.00 (ISBN 0-88355-760-6). Hyperion Conn.

Rowbotham, John F. A History of Music to the Time of the Troubadours, 3 vols. LC 77-75196. 1978. Repr. of 1893 ed. Set. lib. bdg. 95.00 (ISBN 0-89341-096-9). Longwood Pr.

Saam, Joseph. Zur Geschichte Des Klavierquartetts Bis In Die Romantik. 174p. 35.00 (ISBN 90-6027-335-4, Pub. by Frits Knuf Netherlands). Pendragon NY.

Sachs, Curt. Our Musical Heritage: A Short History of Music. LC 78-3636. (Illus.). 1978. Repr. of 1955 ed. lib. bdg. 31.50x (ISBN 0-313-20374-1, SAOM). Greenwood.

Saint-Saens, Camille. Outspoken Essays on Music. facs. ed. Rothwell, F., tr. LC 71-84335. (Essay Index Reprint Ser). 1922. 12.75 (ISBN 0-8369-1105-9). Arno.

Schafer, R. Murray. The Public of the Music Theatre--Louis Riel: A Case Study. 1972. pap. 5.75 (ISBN 0-685-93739-9, 51-26702). Eur-Am Music.

Scherchen, Hermann. The Nature of Music. LC 76-181246. 193p. 1950. Repr. 15.00 (ISBN 0-403-01671-1). Scholarly.

Schumann, Robert. Music & Musicians: Essays & Criticisms. Ritter, Fanny R., ed. LC 72-8379. (Select Bibliographies Reprint Ser). (Second series). 1972. Repr. of 1880 ed. 28.00 (ISBN 0-8369-6998-7). Arno.

Scott, Cyril. Music, Its Secret Influence Throughout the Ages. 59.95 (ISBN 0-8490-0676-7). Gordon Pr.

Seay, Albert, ed. Quart Livre. (Transcriptions Ser.: No. 6). v, 48p. 1981. 4.00 (ISBN 0-933894-09-0). Colo Coll Music.

Seeger, Charles. Studies in Musicology, 1935-1975. LC 76-19668. 1977. 30.00x (ISBN 0-520-02000-6). U of Cal Pr.

Sessions, Roger. Questions About Music. 1971. pap. 3.95 (ISBN 0-393-00571-2). Norton.

Shapiro, Nat, ed. An Encyclopedia of Quotations About Music. (Da Capo Quality Paperbacks Ser.). 1981. pap. 7.95 (ISBN 0-306-80138-8). Da Capo.

Shaw, Arnold. The Rockin' Fifties. (Illus.). 256p. 1974. 13.50 (ISBN 0-8015-6432-8, Hawthorn); pap. 4.95 (ISBN 0-8015-6434-4, Hawthorn). Dutton.

Shawn, Ted. One Thousand & One Night Stands. (Paperbacks Ser.). 1979. pap. 6.95 (ISBN 0-306-80095-0). Da Capo.

Sheppard, John T. Music at Belmont: And Other Essays & Addresses. LC 72-152214. (Essay Index Reprint Ser.). Repr. of 1951 ed. 15.00 (ISBN 0-8369-2860-1). Arno.

Silet, Charles L. The Writings of Paul Rosenfeld: An Annotated Bibliography. LC 79-7931. 250p. 1981. lib. bdg. 35.00 (ISBN 0-8240-9532-4). Garland Pub.

Sparks, Edgar H. Cantus Firmus in Mass & Motet Fourteen Twenty to Fifteen Twenty. LC 74-31190. (Music Reprint Ser). (Illus.). xi, 504p. 1975. Repr. of 1963 ed. lib. bdg. 42.50 (ISBN 0-306-70720-9). Da Capo.

Spohr, Louis. Musical Journeys of Louis Spohr. Pleasants, Henry, ed. (Illus.). 1961. 10.95x (ISBN 0-8061-0492-9). U of Okla Pr.

Starr, William J. & Devine, George F., eds. Music Scores Omnibus, Vol. 1. 2nd ed. 430p. 1974. pap. text ed. 19.95 (ISBN 0-13-608349-8). P-H.

Stein, Leon. Structure & Style. rev. enlarged ed. LC 78-15541. (Illus.). xx, 297p. (Orig.). (gr. 9 up). 1979. pap. text ed. 12.90 (ISBN 0-87487-164-6). Summy.

Stevens, J. E., ed. Music & Poetry in the Early Tudor Court. LC 77-90180. (Cambridge Studies in Music). (Illus.). 1979. 69.50 (ISBN 0-521-22030-0); pap. 17.95 (ISBN 0-521-29417-7). Cambridge U Pr.

Stevenson, Robert. Music Before the Classic Era, an Introductory Guide. LC 73-9131. 215p. 1973. Repr. of 1958 ed. lib. bdg. 15.00x (ISBN 0-8371-6986-0, STCE). Greenwood.

Streatfeild, Richard A. Masters of Italian Music. LC 72-3381. (Essay Index Reprint Ser.). Repr. of 1895 ed. 25.00 (ISBN 0-8369-2929-2). Arno.

Strunk, Oliver. Essays on Music in the Western World. (Illus.). 200p. 1974. 8.95 (ISBN 0-393-02178-5). Norton.

Strunk, Oliver, ed. Source Readings in Music History, 5 vols. Incl. Vol. 1. Antiquity & the Middle Ages. pap. 4.95x (ISBN 0-393-09680-7); Vol. 2. The Renaissance Era. pap. 4.95x (ISBN 0-393-09681-5); Vol. 3. Baroque Era. pap. 4.95x (ISBN 0-393-09682-3); Vol. 4. Classic Era. pap. 4.95x (ISBN 0-393-09683-1); Vol. 5. Romantic Era. pap. 4.95x (ISBN 0-393-09684-X). 1950. one vol. ed 24.95x (ISBN 0-393-09742-0, NortonC). Norton.

Swan, Howard. Music in the Southwest, 1825-1950. LC 77-5421. (Music Reprint Ser.). 1977. Repr. of 1952 ed. lib. bdg. 29.50 (ISBN 0-306-77418-6). Da Capo.

Tarasti, Eero. Myth & Music: A Semiotic Approach to the Aesthetics of Myth in Music... (Approaches to Semiotics Ser.: No. 51). 1979. pap. text ed. 35.25x (ISBN 90-279-7918-9). Mouton.

Thompson, Oscar. Practical Musical Criticism. (Music Reprint Ser.: 1979). 1979. Repr. of 1934 ed. lib. bdg. 19.50 (ISBN 0-306-79514-0). Da Capo.

Tudor, Dean & Tudor, Nancy. Grass Roots Music. LC 78-31686. (American Popular Music on Elpee). 1979. lib. bdg. 25.00x (ISBN 0-87287-133-9). Libs Unl.

Turner, Walter J. Music: A Short History. 2nd ed. LC 71-181285. 105p. 1949. Repr. 19.00 (ISBN 0-403-01708-4). Scholarly.

Ulanov, Barry. A History of Jazz in America. LC 74-37324. 382p. 1972. Repr. of 1955 ed. lib. bdg. 25.00 (ISBN 0-306-70427-7). Da Capo.

U. S. George Washington Bicentennial Commission. The Music of George Washington's Time. Howard, John T., ed. LC 74-24120. Repr. of 1931 ed. 22.50 (ISBN 0-404-12976-5). AMS Pr.

Van Ess, Donald H. The Heritage of Musical Style. LC 80-6235. 384p. 1981. lib. bdg. 28.75 (ISBN 0-8191-1667-X); pap. text ed. 18.50 (ISBN 0-8191-1668-8). U Pr of Amer.

Wade, Bonnie. Music in India: The Classical Traditions. 1979. 14.95 (ISBN 0-13-607036-1); pap. 10.95 (ISBN 0-13-607028-0). P-H.

Wagner, Richard. In Paris & Dresden. (Vol. 7). 1967. Repr. of 1898 ed. 22.50x (ISBN 0-8450-2107-9). Broude.

Wakefield, A. M., ed. Ruskin on Music. 158p. 1981. Repr. of 1894 ed. lib. bdg. 40.00 (ISBN 0-8495-5660-0). Arden Lib.

Walton, Charles. Music Literature for Analysis & Study. 1972. pap. 13.95x (ISBN 0-534-00163-7). Wadsworth Pub.

Weingartner, Felix. The Symphony Since Beethoven. 59.95 (ISBN 0-8490-1169-8). Gordon Pr.

Weisstein, Ulrich, ed. Essence of Opera. 1969. pap. 5.95 (ISBN 0-393-00498-8, Norton Lib). Norton.

Werner, Eric. Three Ages of Musical Thought: Essays on Ethics & Aesthetics. (Music Reprint Ser.). iv, 368p. 1981. Repr. of 1965 ed. 35.00 (ISBN 0-306-76032-0). Da Capo.

Westerby, Herbert. History of Pianoforte Music. LC 78-87624. (Music Ser). 1970. Repr. of 1924 ed. lib. bdg. 29.50 (ISBN 0-306-71809-X). Da Capo.

Whitwell, David. A New History of Wind Music. 1980. pap. 9.00 (ISBN 0-686-15899-7). Instrumental Co.

Willeby, Charles. Masters of English Music. LC 72-5561. (Essay Index Reprint Ser.). Repr. of 1893 ed. 25.00 (ISBN 0-8369-7280-5). Arno.

Williams, Leonard. The Dancing Chimpanzee. LC 80-40598. 128p. 1980. 11.95 (ISBN 0-8052-8057-X, Pub. by Allison & Busby England); pap. 5.95 (ISBN 0-8052-8056-1). Schocken.

Wiora, Walter. Four Ages of Music. Norton, M. Herter, tr. (Illus.). 1967. pap. 4.95 (ISBN 0-393-00427-9, Norton Lib). Norton.

Wold, Milo & Cykler, Edmund. An Introduction to Music & Art in the Western World. 6th ed. 380p. 1980. pap. text ed. write for info. (ISBN 0-697-03119-5); instrs.' man. avail. (ISBN 0-697-03120-9). Wm C Brown.

--An Outline History of Music. 5th ed. 336p. 1981. pap. text ed. price not set (ISBN 0-697-03489-5). Wm C Brown.

--An Outline History of Music. 4th ed. 330p. 1977. pap. text ed. write for info. (ISBN 0-697-03529-8). Wm C Brown.

Wolf, Johannes, ed. Music of Earlier Times, vocal & instrumental examples. 158p. 1946. pap. text ed. 3.75x (ISBN 0-8450-2576-7). Broude.

Woodfill, Walter L. Musicians in English Society from Elizabeth to Charles First. LC 69-12694. (Music Ser). (Illus.). 1969. Repr. of 1953 ed. lib. bdg. 29.50 (ISBN 0-306-71225-3). Da Capo.

Wooldridge, H. E. Polyphonic Period, 2 pts. LC 72-97072. (Oxford History of Music Ser.). (330-1400 pt. 1, 1400-1600 pt. 2). 1973. Repr. of 1929 ed. Pt. 1. 17.50x (ISBN 0-8154-0470-0); Pt. 2. 24.00x (ISBN 0-8154-0470-0). Cooper Sq.

Worner, Karl H. The History of Music: A Book for Study & Reference. 5th ed. Wager, Willis, tr. LC 72-90547. 1973. 25.00 (ISBN 0-02-935500-1). Free Pr.

Young, P. Great Ideas in Music. 6.25 (ISBN 0-08-007072-8). Pergamon.

Zarlino, Gioseffo. Monuments of Music & Music Literature in Facsimile: Series Two Part I, Vol. 15. (Illus., Sopplimenti musicali). 1979. 47.50x (ISBN 0-8450-2215-6). Broude.

Zuck, Barbara A. A History of Musical Americanism. Buelow, George, ed. (Studies in Musicology: No. 19). 412p. 1980. 34.95 (ISBN 0-8357-1109-9, Pub. by UMI Res Pr). Univ Microfilms.

MUSIC–HISTORY AND CRITICISM–METHODS

see Musical Criticism

MUSIC–HISTORY AND CRITICISM–SOURCES

Da Brescia, Bonaventura. Regula Musice Plane. (Monuments of Music & Music Literature in Facsimile Series II: Vol. 77). (Illus.). 46p. (It.). 1975. Repr. of 1497 ed. 20.00x (ISBN 0-8450-2277-6). Broude.

MacClintock, Carol, ed. Readings in the History of Music in Performance. LC 78-9511. (Illus.). 448p. 1979. 19.50x (ISBN 0-253-14495-7). Ind U Pr.

Nettl, Paul. Book of Musical Documents. 1948. lib. bdg. 17.25x (ISBN 0-8371-2116-7, NEMD). Greenwood.

Petrucci, Ottaviano. Canti B Numero Cinquanta. (Monuments of Music & Music Literature in Facsimile: Series I, Vol. 23). (Illus.). 119p. (Lat, Fr.). 1975. Repr. of 1502 ed. 37.50x (ISBN 0-8450-2023-4). Broude.

Reese, Gustave. Fourscore Classics of Music Literature. LC 78-87616. (Music Reprint Ser). 1969. Repr. of 1957 ed. lib. bdg. 17.50 (ISBN 0-306-71620-8). Da Capo.

Rowen, R. Music Through Sources & Documents. 1979. pap. 15.95 (ISBN 0-13-608331-5). P-H.

Starr, William J. & Devine, George F., eds. Music Scores Omnibus. Incl. Pt. 2. Romantic & Impressionist Music. 1964. pap. text ed. 19.95 (ISBN 0-13-608216-5). 1964. P-H.

Strunk, Oliver, ed. Source Readings in Music History, 5 vols. Incl. Vol. 1. Antiquity & the Middle Ages. pap. 4.95x (ISBN 0-393-09680-7); Vol. 2. The Renaissance Era. pap. 4.95x (ISBN 0-393-09681-5); Vol. 3. Baroque Era. pap. 4.95x (ISBN 0-393-09682-3); Vol. 4. Classic Era. pap. 4.95x (ISBN 0-393-09683-1); Vol. 5. Romantic Era. pap. 4.95x (ISBN 0-393-09684-X). 1950. one vol. ed 24.95x (ISBN 0-393-09742-0, NortonC). Norton.

MUSIC–HISTORY AND CRITICISM–THEORY, ETC.

see Musical Criticism

MUSIC–HISTORY AND CRITICISM–TO 400

see also Bible–Music; Music, Greek and Roman; Music, Jewish

Engel, Carl. Music of the Most Ancient Nations, Particularly of the Assyrians, Egyptians, & Hebrews, with Special Reference to Recent Discoveries in Western Asia & in Egypt. LC 73-114875. (Select Bibliographies Reprint Ser). 1909. 20.00 (ISBN 0-8369-5279-0). Arno.

Galpin, Francis W. Music of the Sumerians & Their Immediate Successors, the Babylonians & Assyrians. Repr. of 1937 ed. lib. bdg. 22.75x (ISBN 0-8371-3928-7, GAMS). Greenwood.

Gleason, Harold & Becker, Warren. Examples of Music Before Fourteen Hundred. 2nd ed. 1982. pap. text ed. write for info. (ISBN 0-89917-035-8, Frangipani Press). TIS Inc.

Mathiesen, Thomas J. A Bibliography of Sources for the Study of Ancient Greek Music. (Music Indexes & Bibliographies: No. 10). 1974. pap. 4.50 (ISBN 0-913574-10-4). Eur-Am Music.

Polin, Claire C. Music of the Ancient Near East. LC 73-20879. (Illus.). 138p. 1974. Repr. of 1954 ed. lib. bdg. 14.50x (ISBN 0-8371-5796-X, PONE). Greenwood.

--Music of the Ancient Near East. LC 73-20879. (Illus.). 138p. 1974. Repr. of 1954 ed. lib. bdg. 14.50x (ISBN 0-8371-5796-X, PONE). Greenwood.

Ptolomaeus, Claudius. Harmonicorum Libri Tres. Wallis, John, ed. & tr. (Monuments of Music and Music Literature in Facsimile: Series II, Vol. 60). (Illus.). 1977. Repr. of 1682 ed. 40.00x (ISBN 0-8450-2260-1). Broude.

Sendrey, Alfred. Music in the Social & Religious Life of Antiquity. LC 72-160458. 489p. 1971. 40.00 (ISBN 0-8386-1003-X). Fairleigh Dickinson.

MUSIC–HISTORY AND CRITICISM–400-1500

see also Chants (Plain, Gregorian, etc.)–History and Criticism; Madrigal; Motet

Aubry, Pierre. Trouveres & Troubadours: A Popular Treatise. Aveling, Claude, tr. LC 68-59029. Repr. of 1914 ed. 11.00x (ISBN 0-8154-0265-1). Cooper Sq.

Aubry, Pierre, et al. Melanges de musicologie critique, 4 vols. Incl. Vol. 1. La Musicologie Medievale, Histoire et Methodes. pap. 32.50x (ISBN 0-8450-2511-2); Vol. 2. Adam De Saint-Victor, les Proses Texte et Musique. pap. 42.50x (ISBN 0-8450-2512-0); Vol. 3. Lais et Descorts Francais du XIIIe Siecle, texte et musique. pap. 35.00x (ISBN 0-8450-2513-9); Vol. 4. Les Plus Anciens Monuments de la Musique Francaise. pap. 32.50x (ISBN 0-8450-2514-7). (Illus., Repr. of 1900-1905 ed). 1969. pap. 142.50x set (ISBN 0-8450-2510-4). Broude.

Brown, Howard M. Music in the Renaissance. (History of Music Ser.). (Illus.). 368p. 1976. pap. text ed. 12.95x (ISBN 0-13-608497-4). P-H.

Bukofzer, Manfred F. Studies in Medieval & Renaissance Music. (Illus.). 1964. pap. 5.95 (ISBN 0-393-00241-1, Norton Lib.). Norton.

Bullock-Davies, C. Menestrellorum Multitudo: Minstrels at a Royal Feast. 1978. text ed. 32.50x (ISBN 0-7083-0656-X). Verry.

Caldwell, John. Medieval Music. LC 77-94060. (Illus.). 304p. 1978. 18.95x (ISBN 0-253-33731-3). Ind U Pr.

Carpenter, Nan Cooke. Music in the Medieval & Renaissance Universities. LC 70-171380. (Music Ser). (Illus.). 394p. 1972. Repr. of 1958 ed. lib. bdg. 29.50 (ISBN 0-306-70453-6). Da Capo.

Chambonnieres, Jacques C. Oeuvres completes. Brunold, Paul & Tessier, Andre, eds. Restout, Denise, tr. (Illus.). 170p. 1967. Repr. of 1925 ed. 37.50x (ISBN 0-8450-1001-8). Broude.

Coover, James & Colvig, Richard. Medieval & Renaissance Music on Long-Playing Records: Supplement 1962-1971. (Detroit Studies in Music Bibliography: No. 26). 1973. 5.00 (ISBN 0-911772-44-8); pap. 2.00 (ISBN 0-89990-008-9). Info Coord.

Crocker, Richard L. The Early Medieval Sequence. LC 74-84143. 1977. 42.50x (ISBN 0-520-02847-3). U of Cal Pr.

Da Brescia, Bonaventura. Brevis Collectio Artis Musicae. Seay, Albert, ed. (Critical Texts Ser.: No. 11). (Illus.). vi, 93p. 1981. pap. text ed. 6.00 (ISBN 0-933894-01-5). Colo Coll Music.

De Coussemaker, Edmond. L'art harmonique aux XIIe et XIIIe Siecles. (Illus.). 550p. (Fr.). 1964. Repr. of 1865 ed. 55.00x (ISBN 0-8450-2501-5). Broude.

Farmer, Henry G. Historical Facts for the Arabian Musical Influence. LC 75-173164. 21.00 (ISBN 0-405-08496-X, Blom Pubns). Arno.

Fenlon, Iain, ed. Music in Medieval & Early Modern Europe: Patronage, Sources & Texts. LC 80-40490. (Illus.). 290p. 1981. 57.50 (ISBN 0-521-23328-3). Cambridge U Pr.

Gafurius, Franchinus. Practica Musice. (Monuments of Music & Music Literature in Facsimile, Ser. II: Vol. 99). 1979. Repr. of 1496 ed. 42.50 (ISBN 0-8450-2299-7). Broude.

Gerold, T. Histoire De la Musique Des Origines a la Fin Du 14th Siecle. LC 78-162869. (Music Ser). (Fr). 1971. Repr. of 1936 ed. lib. bdg. 49.50 (ISBN 0-306-70196-0). Da Capo.

Gleason, Harold & Becker, Warren. Examples of Music Before Fourteen Hundred. 2nd ed. 1982. pap. text ed. write for info. (ISBN 0-89917-035-8, Frangipani Press). TIS Inc.

--Medieval & Renaissance Music. 3rd ed. (Music Literature Outlines: Ser. I). 1981. pap. text ed. write for info. (ISBN 0-89917-034-X, Frangipani Pr). TIS Inc.

Greenberg, Noah & Maynard, Paul, eds. Anthology of Early Renaissance Music. new ed. 304p. 1975. 20.00x (ISBN 0-393-02182-3). Norton.

Gysin, H. P. Studien zum Vokabular der Musiktheorie Im Mittelalter: Eine linguistische Analyse. 1972. Repr. of 1959 ed. wrappers 22.50 (ISBN 90-6027-250-1, Pub. by Frits Knuf Netherlands). Pendragon NY.

Harman, Alec. Medieval & Early Renaissance Music. LC 70-75742. (Man & His Music Ser.: Vol. 1). 1969. pap. 3.95 (ISBN 0-8052-0261-7). Schocken.

Hoppin, Richard H. Medieval Music. (Introduction to Music History Ser.). (Illus.). 1978. 14.95x (ISBN 0-393-09090-6). Norton.

Hoppin, Richard H., ed. Anthology of Medieval Music. (Norton Introduction to Music Ser.). 1978. 12.95x (ISBN 0-393-02202-1); pap. 6.95x (ISBN 0-393-09080-9). Norton.

Hughes, Andrew. Medieval Manuscripts for Mass & Office: A Guide to Their Organization & Terminology. 496p. 1981. 45.00x (ISBN 0-8020-5467-6). U of Toronto Pr.

--Medieval Music: The Sixth Liberal Art. 2nd ed. (Toronto Medieval Bibliographies Ser.). 1980. 25.00x (ISBN 0-8020-2358-4). U of Toronto Pr.

LaRue, Jan, ed. Aspects of Medieval & Renaissance Music: A Birthday Offering to Gustave Reese. (Festschrift Ser.: No. 2). 1978. lib. bdg. 45.00 (ISBN 0-918728-07-X). Pendragon NY.

Lowinsky, Edward E. Secret Chromatic Art in the Netherlands Motet. Buchman, Carl, tr. LC 66-27120. (Illus.). 1967. Repr. of 1946 ed. 10.00 (ISBN 0-8462-0847-4). Russell.

Magistri Domni Heinrici Augustensis Musica (A.D. 1050) (DMA Ser. A: Vol. VII). (Illus.). 72p. 1976. wrappers 21.00 (ISBN 90-6027-204-8, Pub. by Frits Knuf Netherlands). Pendragon NY.

Marix, Jenne, ed. Les Musiciens de la Cour de Bourgogne au XVe Siecle, 1420-1467. LC 76-4478. (Illus.). Repr. of 1937 ed. 37.50 (ISBN 0-404-56627-8). AMS Pr.

Marrocco, W. Thomas & Sandon, Nicholas, eds. Medieval Music. (Oxford Anthology of Music Ser.). 1977. text ed. 15.50x (ISBN 0-19-323207-3). Oxford U Pr.

Minor, Andrew C. Music in Medieval & Renaissance Life: Anthology of Vocal & Instrumental Music, 1200-1614. 1964. 9.50x (ISBN 0-8262-0026-5). U of Mo Pr.

Nemerov, Howard. Figures of Thought: Speculations on the Meaning of Poetry & Other Essays. LC 77-78361. 1978. 15.00 (ISBN 0-87923-212-9). Godine.

Parrish, Carl. The Notation of Medieval Music. James, intro. by. 1978. lib. bdg. 18.00 (ISBN 0-918728-08-8). Pendragon NY.

Picker, Martin. The Chanson Albums of Marguerite of Austria. 1965. 62.50x (ISBN 0-520-01009-4). U of Cal Pr.

Plamenac, D., intro. by. Dijon: Bibliotheque Publique, Ms. 517. (Veroffentlichungen Mittelalterlicher Musikhandschriften - Publications of Medieval Musical Manuscr Ipts Ser.). 1972. 32.30 (ISBN 0-912024-12-7). Inst Mediaeval Mus.

Pope, Isabel & Kanazawa, Masakata, eds. The Musical Manuscript Montecassino 871: A Neapolitan Repertory of Sacred & Secular Music. (Illus.). 1979. 79.00x (ISBN 0-19-816132-8). Oxford U Pr.

Reese, Gustave. Music in the Middle Ages. (Illus.). 1940. 24.95x (ISBN 0-393-09750-1, NortonC). Norton.

--Music in the Renaissance. rev. ed. (Illus.). 1959. 29.95x (ISBN 0-393-09530-4, NortonC). Norton.

Ribera y Tarrago, Julian. Historia De la Musica Arabe Medieval y Su Influencia En la Espanola. LC 78-178587. Repr. of 1927 ed. 24.50 (ISBN 0-404-56664-2). AMS Pr.

--La Musica Andaluza Medieval En las Canciones De Trovadores, Troveros y Minnesinger, 3 vols. in 1. LC 71-178588. Repr. of 1925 ed. 24.50 (ISBN 0-404-56665-0). AMS Pr.

Rosenberg, Samuel N. & Tischler, Hans, eds. Chanter M'estuet: Songs of the Trouveres. LC 80-8383. 608p. 1981. 32.50x (ISBN 0-253-14942-8). Ind U Pr.

Sargent, B. Minstrels II. LC 73-80470. (Resources of Music Ser.). (Illus.). 1979. 4.95 (ISBN 0-521-21551-X). Cambridge U Pr.

Seay, Albert. Music in the Medieval World. 2nd ed. (Illus.). 202p. 1975. pap. text ed. 10.95 (ISBN 0-13-608125-8). P-H.

Self, George. Make a New Sound. 1976. pap. 9.75 (ISBN 0-900938-46-3, 50-26909). Eur-Am Music.

Stainer, J. F. & Stainer, C. Dufay & His Contemporaries: Fifty Compositions (Ranging from About A.D. Fourteen Hundred to Fourteen Hundred & Forty. 1966. Repr. of 1898 ed. 50.00 (ISBN 90-6027-003-7, Pub. by Frits Knuf Netherlands). Pendragon NY.

Stevens, J. E., ed. Music & Poetry in the Early Tudor Court. LC 77-90180. (Cambridge Studies in Music). (Illus.). 1979. 69.50 (ISBN 0-521-22030-0); pap. 17.95 (ISBN 0-521-29417-7). Cambridge U Pr.

Wright, O. The Modal System of Arab & Persian Music A.D. 1250-1300. (Illus.). 292p. 1976. 95.00x (ISBN 0-19-713575-7). Oxford U Pr.

MUSIC–HISTORY AND CRITICISM–16TH CENTURY

Aaron, Pietro. Trattato...di Canto Figurato. (Monuments of Music & Music Literature, Ser. II: Vol. 129). 1979. Repr. of 1525 ed. 30.00x (ISBN 0-8450-2329-2). Broude.

Arnold, Denis. Giovanni Gabrieli & the High Renaissance. (Illus.). 334p. 1979. text ed. 65.00x (ISBN 0-19-315232-0). Oxford U Pr.

Blume, Friedrich. Renaissance & Baroque Music, a Comprehensive Survey. Norton, M. Herter, tr. (Illus., Orig.). 1967. pap. 4.95x (ISBN 0-393-09710-2, NortonC). Norton.

Boyd, Morrison C. Elizabethan Music & Musical Criticism. LC 73-1837. (Illus.). 363p. 1973. Repr. of 1962 ed. lib. bdg. 24.25x (ISBN 0-8371-6805-8, BOEL). Greenwood.

Brown, Howard M. Embellishing Sixteenth-Century Music. (Early Music Ser.). 1976. pap. 10.95x (ISBN 0-19-323175-1). Oxford U Pr.

--Music in the Renaissance. (History of Music Ser.). (Illus.). 368p. 1976. pap. text ed. 12.95x (ISBN 0-13-608497-4). P-H.

Bukofzer, Manfred F. Music in the Baroque Era. (Illus.). 1947. 14.95x (ISBN 0-393-09745-5, NortonC). Norton.

--Studies in Medieval & Renaissance Music. (Illus.). 1964. pap. 5.95 (ISBN 0-393-00241-1, Norton Lib.). Norton.

De Robeck, Nesta. Music of the Italian Renaissance. LC 69-12689. (Music Ser). 1969. Repr. of 1928 ed. lib. bdg. 10.00 (ISBN 0-306-71232-6). Da Capo.

De Ronsard, Pierre, et al. La Fleur des musiciens de P. de Ronsard. Expert, Henry, ed. (Illus.). 116p. (Fr.). 1965. pap. 25.00x (ISBN 0-8450-1245-2). Broude.

Fenlon, Iain, ed. Music & Patronage in Sixteenth Century Mantua. LC 79-41377. (Cambridge Studies in Music). (Illus.). 350p. 1981. 57.50 (ISBN 0-521-22905-7). Cambridge U Pr.

Gafurius, Franchinus. Apologia Franchini Gafurii. (Monuments of Music & Music Literature in Facsimile, Ser. II: Vol. 96). 1979. Repr. of 1520 ed. 25.00x (ISBN 0-8450-2296-2). Broude.

--De Harmonia Musicorum Instrumentorum Opus. (Monuments of Music & Music Literature in Facsimile, Ser. II: Vol. 97). 1979. Repr. of 1518 ed. 42.50x (ISBN 0-8450-2297-0). Broude.

Harman, Alec. Medieval & Early Renaissance Music. LC 70-75742. (Man & His Music Ser.: Vol. 1). 1969. pap. 3.95 (ISBN 0-8052-0261-7). Schocken.
Hayes, Gerald R. Musical Instruments & Their Music: 1500-1750, 2 vols. in 1. LC 74-26053. Repr. of 1930 ed. 24.50 (ISBN 0-404-12958-7). AMS Pr.
Jeppesen, Knud. Style of Palestrina & the Dissonance. 1970. pap. 4.50 (ISBN 0-486-22386-8). Dover.
Lowinsky, Edward E., ed. Josquin Des Prez. (Illus.). 1977. incl. 3 seven inch discs 74.00x (ISBN 0-19-315229-0). Oxford U Pr.
Maniates, Maria R. Mannerism in Italian Music & Culture, Fifteen Thirty to Sixteen Thirty. LC 78-11236. (Illus.). 1979. 29.50x (ISBN 0-8078-1319-2). U of NC Pr.
Minor, Andrew C. Music in Medieval & Renaissance Life: Anthology of Vocal & Instrumental Music, 1200-1614. 1964. 9.50x (ISBN 0-8262-0026-5). U of Mo Pr.
Morris, Reginald O. Contrapuntal Technique in the Sixteenth Century. (Illus.). 1975. pap. 11.75x (ISBN 0-19-321468-7). Oxford U Pr.
Naylor, Edward W. Shakespeare & Music. 2nd ed. LC 65-16244. (Illus.). Repr. of 1931 ed. 10.00 (ISBN 0-405-08814-0). Arno.
--Shakespeare & Music. LC 65-16244. (Music Ser). 1965. Repr. of 1931 ed. lib. bdg. 18.50 (ISBN 0-306-70908-2). Da Capo.
Newcomb, Anthony. Madrigal at Ferrara, Fifteen Seventy-Nine to Fifteen Ninety-Seven, 2 vols. LC 78-573. (Studies in Music: No. 7). 1979. Set. 60.00x (ISBN 0-691-09125-0). Princeton U Pr.
Pattison, Bruce. Music & Poetry of the English Renaissance. LC 70-127278. (Music Ser). (Illus.). 1970. Repr. of 1948 ed. lib. bdg. 22.50 (ISBN 0-306-71298-9). Da Capo.
--Music & Poetry of the English Renaissance. LC 72-193387. 1948. lib. bdg. 20.00 (ISBN 0-685-10372-2). Folcroft.
Pirie, Peter J. The English Musical Renaissance. 1980. 16.95 (ISBN 0-312-25435-0). St Martin.
Price, D. C. Patrons & Musicians of the English Renaissance. LC 80-40054. (Cambridge Studies in Music). (Illus.). 250p. 1981. 55.00 (ISBN 0-521-22806-9). Cambridge U Pr.
Reese, Gustave. Music in the Renaissance. rev. ed. (Illus.). 1959. 29.95x (ISBN 0-393-09530-4, NortonC). Norton.
Ripin, Edwin M., ed. Keyboard Instruments: Studies in Keyboard Organology, 1500-1800. 6.50 (ISBN 0-8446-5605-4). Peter Smith.
Seay, Albert, ed. Cinquiesme Livre. (Transcriptions Ser.: No. 5). iii, 72p. 1980. pap. 4.00 (ISBN 0-933894-10-4, Pub. by Moderne)). Colo Coll Music.
--Dixseptiesme Livre. (Transcriptions Ser.: No. 2). iii, 64p. 1979. pap. 4.00 (ISBN 0-933894-04-X, Pub. by Attaingnant). Colo Coll Music.
--Second Livre. (Transcriptions Ser.: No. 3). ii, 64p. 1980. pap. 4.00 (ISBN 0-933894-05-8, Pub. by Attaingnant). Colo Coll Music.
--Vingt Deuxiesme Livre. (Transcriptions Ser.: No. 4). iii, 67p. 1981. pap. 4.00 (ISBN 0-933894-07-4, Pub. by Attaingnant). Colo Coll Music.
Shire, Helena M. Song, Dance & Poetry of the Court of Scotland Under King James Sixth. LC 69-13793. (Illus.). 1969. 49.50 (ISBN 0-521-07181-X). Cambridge U Pr.
Spataro, Giovanni. Tractato di Musica. (Monuments of Music & Music Literature in Facsimile, Ser. II: Vol. 88). 1980. Repr. of 1531 ed. 30.00x (ISBN 0-8450-2288-1). Broude.
Stevens, J. E., ed. Music & Poetry in the Early Tudor Court. LC 77-90180. (Cambridge Studies in Music). (Illus.). 1979. 69.50 (ISBN 0-521-22030-0); pap. 17.95 (ISBN 0-521-29417-7). Cambridge U Pr.
Stevenson, Robert. Spanish Cathedral Music in the Golden Age. LC 76-1013. (Illus.). 523p. 1976. Repr. of 1961 ed. lib. bdg. 39.50x (ISBN 0-8371-8744-3, STSP). Greenwood.
Zarlino, Gioseffo. Sopplimenti Musicali. (Monuments of Music & Literature in Facsimile, Ser. II: Vol. 15). (Illus.). 1979. Repr. of 1588 ed. 52.50x (ISBN 0-8450-2215-6). Broude.

MUSIC-HISTORY AND CRITICISM-17TH CENTURY

Arnold, Denis. Giovanni Gabrieli & the High Renaissance. (Illus.). 334p. 1979. text ed. 65.00x (ISBN 0-19-315232-0). Oxford U Pr.
Blume, Friedrich. Renaissance & Baroque Music, a Comprehensive Survey. Norton, M. Herter, tr. (Illus., Orig.). 1967. pap. 4.95x (ISBN 0-393-09710-2, NortonC). Norton.
Bonini, Don Severo. Severo Bonini's Discorsi e Regole: A Bilingual Edition. Bonino, MaryAnn, ed. & tr. from Italian. LC 77-18514. (Illus.). 1979. text ed. 24.95x (ISBN 0-8425-0997-6). Brigham.
Brevia musicae rudimenta Latino Belgicae ex prolixioribus musicorum praeceptis excerpta Corte onderwysinghe van de musike... Leyden Sixteen Hundred & Five. (Early Music Theory in the Low Countries Ser.: Vol. 3). 24p. 1973. Repr. of 1591 ed. wrappers 20.00 (ISBN 90-6027-177-7, Pub. by Frits Knuf Netherlands). Pendragon NY.
Bukofzer, Manfred F. Music in the Baroque Era. (Illus.). 1947. 14.95x (ISBN 0-393-09745-5, NortonC). Norton.
Caswell, Austin B. Music at the Court of Louis XIV. 1976. pap. text ed. 4.50 scp (ISBN 0-06-161007-0, HarpC). Har-Row.
Dolmetsch, Arnold. The Interpretation of the Music of the Seventeenth & Eighteenth Centuries Revealed by Contemporary Evidence. LC 77-181143. 493p. 1946. Repr. 59.00 (ISBN 0-403-01544-8). Scholarly.
Fuller-Maitland, J. A. The Age of Bach & Handel. LC 72-97074. (Oxford History of Music Ser.). 1973. Repr. of 1931 ed. lib. bdg. 22.50x (ISBN 0-8154-0472-7). Cooper Sq.
Hayes, Gerald R. Musical Instruments & Their Music: 1500-1750, 2 vols. in 1. LC 74-26053. Repr. of 1930 ed. 24.50 (ISBN 0-404-12958-7). AMS Pr.
Hudson, Richard. Passacaglio & Ciaccona: From Guitar Music to Italian Keyboard Variations in the 17th Century. LC 81-25. (Studies in Musicology: No. 37). 1980. 54.95 (ISBN 0-8357-1161-7, Pub. by UMI Res Pr). Univ Microfilms.
Isherwood, Robert M. Music in the Service of the King: France in the Seventeenth Century. LC 72-3842. (Illus.). 422p. 1973. 30.00x (ISBN 0-8014-0734-6). Cornell U Pr.
Marais, Marin. Pieces a une et a deux Violes. Hsu, John & McDowell, Bonney, eds. (The Instrumental Works: Vol. 1). (Illus.). 1977. 67.50x (ISBN 0-8450-7201-3). Broude.
Naylor, Edward W. Shakespeare & Music. LC 65-16244. (Music Ser). 1965. Repr. of 1931 ed. lib. bdg. 18.50 (ISBN 0-306-70908-2). Da Capo.
Neumann, F. Ornamentation in Baroque & Post-Baroque Music: With Special Emphasis on J. S. Bach. LC 77-72130. (Illus.). 1978. 60.00 (ISBN 0-691-09123-4). Princeton U Pr.
Parry, C. Hubert. The Music of the Seventeenth Century. LC 72-97073. (Oxford History of Music Ser.). 1973. Repr. of 1938 ed. lib. bdg. 22.50x (ISBN 0-8154-0471-9). Cooper Sq.
Pirie, Peter J. The English Musical Renaissance. 1980. 16.95 (ISBN 0-312-25435-0). St Martin.
Playford, John. The English Dancing Master (Sixteen Fifty-One) Dean-Smith, Margaret, ed. 1957. 13.75 (ISBN 0-901938-44-0, 75-A11316). Eur-Am Music.
Price, D. C. Patrons & Musicians of the English Renaissance. LC 80-40054. (Cambridge Studies in Music). (Illus.). 250p. 1981. 55.00 (ISBN 0-521-22806-9). Cambridge U Pr.
Ripin, Edwin M., ed. Keyboard Instruments: Studies in Keyboard Organology, 1500-1800. 6.50 (ISBN 0-8446-5605-4). Peter Smith.
Salter, Lionel. The Illustrated Encyclopedia of Classical Music. (Illus.). 1978. 17.95 (ISBN 0-517-53476-2); pap. 8.95 (ISBN 0-517-53477-0). Crown.
Valerius, Adrianus. Neder-Landtsche Gedenck-Clanck. (Monuments of Music & Music Literature in Facsimile: Series II, Vol. 63). (Illus.). 314p. (Dutch.). 1974. Repr. of 1626 ed. 42.50x (ISBN 0-8450-2263-6). Broude.

MUSIC-HISTORY AND CRITICISM-18TH CENTURY

see also Classicism in Music

Adson, John. Courtly Masquing Ayres, to 5 & 6 Parts, for Violins, Consorts, & Cornets. LC 77-6842. (English Experience Ser.: No. 838). 1977. Repr. of 1621 ed. lib. bdg. 16.00 (ISBN 90-221-0838-4). Walter J Johnson.
Brand, Oscar. Songs of Seventy Six: A Folksinger's History of the Revolution. LC 72-83733. (Illus.). 176p. 1972. 10.00 (ISBN 0-87131-092-9); pap. 4.95 (ISBN 0-87131-170-4). M Evans.
Bukofzer, Manfred F. Music in the Baroque Era. (Illus.). 1947. 14.95x (ISBN 0-393-09745-5, NortonC). Norton.
Campardon, Emile. L'academie Royale de Musique au 18 Siecle, 2 Vols. LC 73-141152. (Music Ser). 1971. Repr. of 1884 ed. lib. bdg. 95.00 (ISBN 0-306-70090-5). Da Capo.
Capri, Antonio. Il Settecento Musicale in Europa. LC 77-5523. (Music Reprint Ser). 1977. Repr. of 1936 ed. lib. bdg. 35.00 (ISBN 0-306-77413-5). Da Capo.
Cohen, Albert. Music in the French Royal Academy of Sciences: A Study in the Evolution of Musical Thought. LC 81-47118. (Illus.). 168p. 1981. 14.00x (ISBN 0-691-09127-7). Princeton U Pr.
Crawford, Thomas. Society & the Lyric: A Study of the Song Culture of Eighteenth-Century Scotland. 208p. 1980. 13.50 (ISBN 0-7073-0227-7, Pub. by Scottish Academic Pr). Columbia U Pr.
Dolmetsch, Arnold. The Interpretation of the Music of the Seventeenth & Eighteenth Centuries Revealed by Contemporary Evidence. LC 77-181143. 493p. 1946. Repr. 59.00 (ISBN 0-403-01544-8). Scholarly.
Donakowski, Conrad L. A Muse for the Masses: Ritual & Music in an Age of Democratic Revolution, 1770-1870. LC 77-6228. 1977. lib. bdg. 25.00x (ISBN 0-226-15621-4). U of Chicago Pr.
Dunning, Albert. Count Unico Wilhelm van Wassenaar, Sixteen Ninety-Two to Seventeen Sixty-Six: A Master Unmasked or the Pergolesi-Ricciotti Puzzle Solved. Rimmer, Joan, tr. from Dutch. (Illus.). 210p. 65.00 (ISBN 90-6027-400-8, Pub. by Frits Knuf Netherlands); wrappers 47.50 (ISBN 90-6027-399-0, Pub. by Frits Knuf Netherlands). Pendragon NY.
Freystatter, Wilhelm. Die Musikalischen Zeitschriften seit ihrer Entstenhung bis zur Gegenwart Seventeen Twenty-Two to Eighteen Eighty-Four. 1971. Repr. of 1884 ed. wrappers 20.00 (ISBN 90-6027-139-4, Pub. by Frits Knuf Netherlands). Pendragon NY.
Gretry, Andre. Memoires, Ou Essais Sur la Musique, 3 Vols. LC 73-160852. (Music Ser). (Fr., Fr). 1971. Repr. of 1789 ed. Set. lib. bdg. 182.50 (ISBN 0-306-70194-4). Da Capo.
Hadow, William H., ed. The Viennese Period. 2nd, rev. ed. LC 72-97075. (Oxford History of Music Ser). 1973. Repr. lib. bdg. 17.50x (ISBN 0-8154-0473-5). Cooper Sq.
Harriss, Ernest C. Johann Mattheson's der Vollkommene Capellmeister: A Revised Translation with Critical Commentary. Buelow, George, ed. (Studies in Musicology: No. 21). 932p. 1981. 69.95 (ISBN 0-8357-1134-X, Pub. by UMI Res Pr). Univ Microfilms.
Hayes, Gerald R. Musical Instruments & Their Music: 1500-1750, 2 vols. in 1. LC 74-26053. Repr. of 1930 ed. 24.50 (ISBN 0-404-12958-7). AMS Pr.
Hosler, Bellamy. Changing Aesthetic Views of Instrumental Music in Eighteenth Century Germany. Buelow, George, ed. LC 81-4754. (Studies in Musicology: No. 42). 1981. 39.95 (ISBN 0-8357-1172-2, Pub. by UMI Res Pr). Univ Microfilms.
Kirby, F. E. Music in the Classic Period: An Anthology with Commentary. LC 77-84939. 1979. pap. text ed. 14.95 (ISBN 0-02-870710-9). Schirmer Bks.
Landon, Robbins H. & Chapman, Roger. Studies in Eighteenth Century Music: A Tribute to Karl Geiringer on His 70th Birthday. (Music Reprint Ser.). 1979. Repr. of 1970 ed. lib. bdg. 35.00 (ISBN 0-306-79519-1). Da Capo.
Larsen, Jens P., et al, eds. Haydn Studies. 1981. 35.00x (ISBN 0-393-01454-1). Norton.
Lee, Vernon & Paget, Violet. Studies of the Eighteenth Century in Italy. LC 77-17466. (Music Reprint Ser.: 1978). 1978. Repr. of 1887 ed. lib. bdg. 27.50 (ISBN 0-306-77517-4). Da Capo.
Lowens, Irving. Bibliography of Songsters Printed in America Before Eighteen Twenty-One. LC 75-5021. 1976. 19.95x (ISBN 0-912296-05-4, Dist. by U Pr of Va). Am Antiquarian.
McHose, Allen I. Contrapuntal Harmonic Technique of the Eighteenth Century. 1947. 20.95 (ISBN 0-13-171843-6). P-H.
Mason, Daniel G. Beethoven & His Forerunners. new ed. LC 70-119653. Repr. of 1930 ed. 24.75 (ISBN 0-404-04197-3). AMS Pr.
Menke, Werner. History of the Trumpet of Bach & Handel. 1981. Repr. lib. bdg. 19.00 (ISBN 0-403-01620-7). Scholarly.
Nettl, Paul. Other Casanova: A Contribution to Eighteenth-Century Music & Manners. LC 73-107872. (Music Ser). (Illus.). 1970. Repr. of 1951 ed. lib. bdg. 29.50 (ISBN 0-306-71896-0). Da Capo.
Neumann, F. Ornamentation in Baroque & Post-Baroque Music: With Special Emphasis on J. S. Bach. LC 77-72130. (Illus.). 1978. 60.00 (ISBN 0-691-09123-4). Princeton U Pr.
Niedt, F. E. Musicalische Handleitung: Hamburg 1700-1721, 3 vols in one. (Bibliotheca Organologica: Vol. 32). 1976. 75.00 (ISBN 90-6027-306-0, Pub. by Frits Knuf Netherlands). Pendragon NY.
Pauly, Reinhard G. Music in the Classic Period. 2nd ed. (History of Music Ser). 224p. 1973. pap. text ed. 10.95 (ISBN 0-13-607630-0). P-H.
Rich, Allan. Listerners Guide to Classical Music. 1980. 9.95 (ISBN 0-671-25440-5). S&S.
Ripin, Edwin M., ed. Keyboard Instruments: Studies in Keyboard Organology, 1500-1800. 6.50 (ISBN 0-8446-5605-4). Peter Smith.
Rolland, Romain. Musical Tour Through the Land of the Past. facs. ed. Miall, B., tr. LC 67-30229. (Essay Index Reprint Ser). 1922. 15.00 (ISBN 0-8369-0830-9). Arno.
--Voyage Musical Aux Pays du Passe. facsimile ed. (Illus.). 271p. 1976. 22.50 (ISBN 0-686-55282-2). French & Eur.
Salter, Lionel. The Illustrated Encyclopedia of Classical Music. (Illus.). 1978. 17.95 (ISBN 0-517-53476-2); pap. 8.95 (ISBN 0-517-53477-0). Crown.
Sonneck, O. G. Early Concert Life in America: 1731-1800. 338p. Repr. of 1907 ed. 68.60 (ISBN 3-500-20500-3). Adler.
Turner, William. Sound Anatomiz'd. (Monuments of Music & Music Literature in Facsimile Series II: Vol. 127). (Illus.). 103p. 1974. Repr. of 1724 ed. 25.00x (ISBN 0-8450-2327-6). Broude.
Whittaker, W. Gillies. The Cantatas of Johann Sebastian Bach, Sacred & Secular, 2 vols. 1978. pap. 21.00x (ISBN 0-19-315238-X). Oxford U Pr.
Wright, Josephine R., ed. Ignatius Sancho, an Early African Composer in England, 1729 to 1780: The Collected Editions of His Music in Facsimile. LC 80-8525. 130p. 1981. lib. bdg. 20.00 (ISBN 0-8240-9459-X). Garland Pub.

MUSIC-HISTORY AND CRITICISM-19TH CENTURY

see also Romanticism in Music

Bekker, Paul. Richard Wagner: His Life in His Work. facsimile ed. Bozman, M. M., tr. LC 70-107792. (Select Bibliographies Reprint Ser). 1931. 29.00 (ISBN 0-8369-5176-X). Arno.
Crowest, Frederick J. The Great Tone Poets. LC 77-94566. 1978. Repr. of 1874 ed. lib. bdg. 40.00 (ISBN 0-89341-404-2). Longwood Pr.
Dahlhaus, Carl. Between Romanticism & Modernism: Four Studies in the Music of the Later Nineteenth Century. Whittall, Mary, tr. from Ger. LC 78-54793. (California Studies in 19th Century Music). 100p. 1980. 11.50x (ISBN 0-520-03679-4). U of Cal Pr.
Dannreuther, E. The Romantic Period. 2nd, rev. ed. LC 72-97076. (Oxford History of Music Ser). 1973. Repr. of 1932 ed. lib. bdg. 17.50x (ISBN 0-8154-0474-3). Cooper Sq.
Davis, Ronald L. A History of Music in American Life, Vol. 2: The Gilded Years, 1865-1920. LC 79-25359. 314p. 1980. lib. bdg. 14.25 (ISBN 0-89874-003-7). Krieger.
Donakowski, Conrad L. A Muse for the Masses: Ritual & Music in an Age of Democratic Revolution, 1770-1870. LC 77-6228. 1977. lib. bdg. 25.00x (ISBN 0-226-15621-4). U of Chicago Pr.
Einstein, Alfred. Music in the Romantic Era. (Illus.). 1947. 11.95x (ISBN 0-393-09733-1, NortonC). Norton.
Epstein, David. Beyond Orpheus: Studies in Musical Structure. 1979. 24.95x (ISBN 0-262-05016-1). MIT Pr.
Freystatter, Wilhelm. Die Musikalischen Zeitschriften seit ihrer Entstenhung bis zur Gegenwart Seventeen Twenty-Two to Eighteen Eighty-Four. 1971. Repr. of 1884 ed. wrappers 20.00 (ISBN 90-6027-139-4, Pub. by Frits Knuf Netherlands). Pendragon NY.
Gray, Cecil. A Survey of Contemporary Music. 2nd ed. LC 78-163551. 266p. 1972. Repr. of 1927 ed. lib. bdg. 15.00x (ISBN 0-8371-6211-4, GRCM). Greenwood.
Hatcher, Danny, ed. Proceedings of the Eighteen Ninety Convention of Local Phonograph Companies. 210p. 1974. pap. 6.95 (ISBN 0-915608-03-0). Country Music Found.
Hermann, Klein. Thirty Years of Musical Life in London 1870-1900. 1980. Repr. of 1903 ed. lib. bdg. 50.00 (ISBN 0-89341-442-5). Longwood Pr.
Hutchings, A. Church Music in the Nineteenth Century. (Illus.). 166p. 1967. 22.00 (ISBN 90-6027-266-8, Pub. by Frits Knuf Netherlands). Pendragon NY.
Laforet, Claude. La Vie Musicale Au Temps Romantique. LC 77-4153. (Music Reprint Ser., 1977). 1977. Repr. of 1929 ed. lib. bdg. 19.50 (ISBN 0-306-70890-6). Da Capo.
Locke, Arthur W. Music & the Romantic Movement in France. LC 72-83508. Repr. of 1920 ed. 15.00 (ISBN 0-405-08751-9, Pub. by Blom). Arno.
Longyear, Rey M. Nineteenth Century Romanticism in Music. 2nd ed. LC 72-3962. (History of Music Ser). (Illus.). 304p. 1973. pap. text ed. 10.95 (ISBN 0-13-622647-7). P-H.
Mason, Daniel G. Great Modern Composers: Biographical Sections by M. L. Mason, Appreciation of Music Vol. 2. facs. ed. LC 68-20319. (Essay Index Reprint Ser). 1916. 14.75 (ISBN 0-8369-0690-X). Arno.
Mussulman, Joseph A. Music in the Cultured Generation: Musical Life in America, 1870-1900. LC 77-149920. (Pi Kappa Lambda Studies in American Music). 1971. 12.95x (ISBN 0-8101-0350-8). Northwestern U Pr.
Raynor, Henry. Music & Society Since Eighteen Fifteen. LC 76-1377. 1976. 15.00x (ISBN 0-8052-3626-0). Schocken.
Reich, Steve. Writings About Music. LC 73-87481. (The Nova Scotia Ser). (Illus.). 82p. 1974. pap. 8.00x (ISBN 0-8147-7357-5). NYU Pr.

Ripin, Edwin M., ed. Keyboard Instruments: Studies in Keyboard Organology, 1500-1800. 6.50 (ISBN 0-8446-5605-4). Peter Smith.
Rosenfeld, Paul. Musical Impressions: Selections from Paul Rosenfeld's Criticism. Leibowitz, Herbert A., ed. LC 76-75252. 334p. 1969. 7.95 (ISBN 0-8090-7172-X). Hill & Wang.
--Musical Portraits: Interpretations of Twenty Modern Composers. facs. ed. LC 68-29243. (Essay Index Reprint Ser). 1920. 16.00 (ISBN 0-8369-0837-6). Arno.
Salazar, Adolfo. Music in Our Time: Trends in Music Since the Romantic Era. Pope, Isabel, tr. Repr. of 1946 ed. lib. bdg. 14.50x (ISBN 0-8371-3014-X, SAMT). Greenwood.
Stumpf, Carl. Tonpsychologie: Leipzig 1883-1890, 2 vols. Repr. of 1965 ed. 80.00 (ISBN 90-6027-020-7, Pub. by Frits Knuf Netherlands). Pendragon NY.
Wenk, Arthur B. Nineteenth Century Music. LC 78-20700. (Illus.). 1981. 12.95 (ISBN 0-8008-5576-0, Crescendo). Taplinger.

MUSIC–HISTORY AND CRITICISM–20TH CENTURY

see also Jazz Music

Aldrich, Richard. Concert Life in New York, Nineteen Hundred to Nineteen Twenty-Three. facsimile ed. Johnson, Harold, ed. LC 78-156603. (Essay Index Reprint Ser). Repr. of 1941 ed. 36.00 (ISBN 0-8369-2263-8). Arno.
Austin, William. Music in the Twentieth Century. (Illus.). 1966. 19.95x (ISBN 0-393-09704-8, NortonC). Norton.
Bauer, Marion. Twentieth Century Music: How It Developed, How to Listen to It. (Music Ser.). 354p. 1978. Repr. of 1933 ed. lib. bdg. 24.50 (ISBN 0-306-79503-5). Da Capo.
Benjamin, Thomas, et al. Music for Analysis: Examples from the Common Practice Period & the Twentieth Century. LC 77-78237. 1978. pap. text ed. 12.95 (ISBN 0-395-25507-4). HM.
Boretz, Benjamin & Cone, Edward T., eds. Perspectives on American Composers. 1971. pap. 5.95 (ISBN 0-393-00549-6, Norton Lib). Norton.
--Perspectives on Contemporary Music Theory. 304p. (Orig.). 1972. pap. 4.95 (ISBN 0-393-00548-8, Norton Lib). Norton.
Brindle, Reginald S. The New Music. (Illus.). 200p. 1975. pap. 8.75x (ISBN 0-19-315424-2). Oxford U Pr.
Chavez, Carlos. Toward a New Music: Music & Electricity. Weinstock, Herbert, tr. from Span. LC 74-28308. (Illus.). 180p. 1975. Repr. of 1937 ed. lib. bdg. 19.50 (ISBN 0-306-70719-5). Da Capo.
Cohn, Arthur. The Collector's Twentieth-Century Music in the Western Hemisphere. LC 74-167848. (Music Ser.). 1972. Repr. of 1961 ed. 25.00 (ISBN 0-306-70404-8). Da Capo.
Cone, Edward T., ed. Roger Sessions on Music: Collected Essays. LC 78-51190. 1979. 27.00 (ISBN 0-691-09126-9); pap. 8.95 limited paperback ed. (ISBN 0-691-10074-8). Princeton U Pr.
Copland, Aaron. Music & Imagination. LC 52-9385. (Charles Eliot Norton Lectures Ser: 1951-1952). 1952. pap. 2.95 (ISBN 0-674-58915-7). Harvard U Pr.
--New Music: 1900-1960. rev. ed. LC 68-10878. 1968 7.50 (ISBN 0-393-02060-6); pap. 4.95, 1969 (ISBN 0-393-00239-X). Norton.
Dallin, Leon. Techniques of Twentieth Century Composition: A Guide to the Materials of Modern Music. 3rd ed. 260p. 1974. text ed. write for info. (ISBN 0-697-03614-6). Wm C Brown.
Davis, Ronald L. A History of Music in American Life, Vol. 2: The Gilded Years, 1865-1920. LC 79-25359. 314p. 1980. lib. bdg. 14.25 (ISBN 0-89874-003-7). Krieger.
--A History of Music in American Life, Vol. 3: The Modern Era, 1920 to the Present. LC 79-25359. 522p. 1981. lib. bdg. 23.50 (ISBN 0-89874-004-5); lib. bdg. 49.50 (ISBN 0-686-66036-6). Krieger.
Delone, Richard, et al. Aspects of Twentieth-Century Music. (Illus.). 541p. 1974. 21.95x (ISBN 0-13-049346-5). P-H.
Demuth, Norman. Musical Trends in the Twentieth Century. LC 73-6258. (Illus.). 359p. 1975. Repr. of 1952 ed. lib. bdg. 30.75x (ISBN 0-8371-6896-1, DEMT). Greenwood.
Deri, Otto. Exploring Twentieth-Century Music. LC 68-18408. 1968. text ed. 14.95 (ISBN 0-03-066895-6, HoltC). HR&W.
Dunn, David. Sky Drift. LC 80-80806. (Illus.). 90p. 1979. soft wrap-around cover 13.50 (ISBN 0-939044-16-1). Lingua Pr.
Dyson, George. New Music. (Select Bibliographies Reprint Ser). 1924. 15.00 (ISBN 0-8369-5231-6). Arno.
Edwards, Allen. Flawed Words & Stubborn Sounds: A Conversation with Elliott Carter. LC 77-152660. 1972. 7.95x (ISBN 0-393-02159-9). Norton.
Eschman, Karl. Changing Forms in Modern Music. 2nd ed. LC 67-26898. (Illus.). 213p. 1967. 5.00 (ISBN 0-911318-01-1). E C Schirmer.
Ewen, David. Composers of Tomorrow's Music: A Non-Technical Introduction to the Musical Avant-Garde Movement. LC 79-18514. (Illus.). 1980. Repr. of 1971 ed. lib. bdg. 17.75x (ISBN 0-313-22107-3, EWCT). Greenwood.
--Twentieth Century Composers. facs. ed. LC 68-16930. (Essay Index Reprint Ser). 1937. 22.00 (ISBN 0-8369-0434-6). Arno.
--World of Twentieth Century Music. LC 68-11358. 1968. 19.95 (ISBN 0-13-968776-9). P-H.
Fink, Robert R. & Ricci, Robert. The Language of Twentieth-Century Music. LC 74-13308. 1975. 12.95 (ISBN 0-02-870600-5). Schirmer Bks.
Gaburo, Virginia. Who Is Bruce Simonds. 44p. 1978. saddle-stitced 13.95, soft cover, lP recording (ISBN 0-939044-22-6). Lingua Pr.
Gleason, Harold & Becker, Warren. Twentieth Century American Music. 2nd ed. (Music Literature Outlines: Series IV). 1980. 10.95 (ISBN 0-89917-266-0, Frangipani Press). TIS Inc.
Graf, Max. Modern Music: Composers & Music of Our Time. Maier, Beatrice R., tr. LC 77-27613. 1978. Repr. of 1946 ed. lib. bdg. 25.50x (ISBN 0-313-20185-4, GRMM). Greenwood.
Graves, Charles L. Post-Victorian Music. LC 71-102838. 1970. Repr. of 1911 ed. 15.00 (ISBN 0-8046-0754-0). Kennikat.
Gray, Cecil. Predicaments, or Music & the Future: An Essay in Constructive Criticism. LC 79-103652. (Select Bibliographies Reprint Ser). 1936. 22.00 (ISBN 0-8369-5152-2). Arno.
--Survey of Contemporary Music. LC 75-93341. (Essay Index Reprint Ser). 1924. 17.00 (ISBN 0-8369-1294-2). Arno.
Griffiths, Paul. Concise History of Avant Garde Music: From Debussy to Boulez. LC 77-25056. (World of Art Ser.). (Illus.). 1978. pap. 9.95 (ISBN 0-19-520045-4). Oxford U Pr.
--Modern Music: The Avant Garde Since 1945. (Illus.). 332p. 1981. 35.00x (ISBN 0-460-04365-X, Pub. by J. M. Dent England). Biblio Dist.
--Modern Music: The Avant Garde Since 1945. LC 81-10123. (Illus.). 331p. 1981. pap. 10.95 (ISBN 0-8076-1018-6). Braziller.
Hansen, Peter S. An Introduction to Twentieth Century Music. 4th ed. 1978. pap. text ed. 17.95 (ISBN 0-205-05921-X). Allyn.
Hanson, Howard. Harmonic Materials of Modern Music: Resources of the Tempered Scale. LC 58-8138. (Eastman School of Music Ser.). (Illus.). 1960. 34.00x (ISBN 0-89197-207-2); pap. text ed. 18.50x (ISBN 0-89197-208-0). Irvington.
Hines, Robert S., ed. The Composer's Point of View: Essays on Twentieth-Century Choral Music by Those Who Wrote It. LC 80-12636. (Illus.). xiv, 342p. 1980. Repr. of 1963 ed. lib. bdg. 28.50x (ISBN 0-313-22461-7, HICM). Greenwood.
Hodeir, Andre. Since Debussy: A View of Contemporary Music. Burch, Noel, tr. LC 74-28310. (Illus.). 256p. 1975. Repr. of 1961 ed. lib. bdg. 22.50 (ISBN 0-306-70662-8). Da Capo.
Howard, John T. This Modern Music. facs. ed. LC 68-58796. (Essay Index Reprint Ser). 1942. 16.00 (ISBN 0-8369-0018-9). Arno.
Howard, John T. & Lyons, James. Modern Music: A Popular Guide to Greater Musical Enjoyment. LC 78-60139. 1978. Repr. of 1957 ed. lib. bdg. 16.25x (ISBN 0-313-20556-6, HOMU). Greenwood.
Kofsky, Frank. Black Nationalism & the Revolution in Music. LC 77-108716. (Illus.). 1970. 14.00 (ISBN 0-87348-149-6); pap. 4.95 (ISBN 0-87348-129-1). Path Pr NY.
Krenek, Ernst. Horizons Circled: Reflections on My Music. LC 72-89790. (Illus.). 1975. 17.50x (ISBN 0-520-02338-2). U of Cal Pr.
Lambert, Constant. Music Ho. 1967. 7.95 (ISBN 0-8079-0086-9). October.
Landau, Anneliese. The Lied: The Unfolding of Its Style. LC 79-6725. 1980. text ed. 15.00 (ISBN 0-8191-0935-5); pap. text ed. 7.50 (ISBN 0-8191-0936-3). U Pr of Amer.
Lang, Paul H., ed. Problems of Modern Music. 1962. pap. 2.95 (ISBN 0-393-00115-6, Norton Lib). Norton.
Leibowitz, Rene. Schoenberg & His School: The Contemporary Stage of the Language of Music. Newlin, Dika, tr. from Fr. LC 75-115338. (Music Ser). 1970. Repr. of 1949 ed. lib. bdg. 27.50 (ISBN 0-306-71930-4). Da Capo.
--Schoenberg & His School: The Contemporary Stage of the Language of Music. LC 75-14128. (Music Ser.). 1975. pap. 5.95 (ISBN 0-306-80020-9). Da Capo.
Lipman, Samuel. Music After Modernism. LC 78-73768. 1979. 12.95 (ISBN 0-465-04740-8). Basic.
Machlis, Joseph. Introduction to Contemporary Music. 2nd ed. (Illus.). 1979. text ed. 17.95x (ISBN 0-393-09026-4); instructor's guide free (ISBN 0-393-95023-9). Norton.
Martin, William R. & Drossin, Julius. Music of the Twentieth Century. (Illus.). 1980. text ed. 15.95 (ISBN 0-13-608927-5). P-H.
Mason, Daniel G. Dilemma of American Music, & Other Essays. Repr. of 1928 ed. lib. bdg. 14.50x (ISBN 0-8371-1155-2, MAAM). Greenwood.
Matthew, James E. Manual of Musical History. 462p. 1981. Repr. of 1892 ed. lib. bdg. 85.00 (ISBN 0-89987-568-8). Darby Bks.
Mellers, Wilfrid. Caliban Reborn: Renewal in Twentieth-Century Music. (Music Reprint Ser.). 1979. Repr. of 1967 ed. lib. bdg. 22.50 (ISBN 0-306-79569-8). Da Capo.
Mellers, Wilfrid H. Studies in Contemporary Music. LC 74-24153. Repr. of 1947 ed. 17.50 (ISBN 0-404-13046-1). AMS Pr.
Mellquist, Jerome & Wiese, Lucie. Paul Rosenfeld, Voyager in the Arts. 1978. Repr. of 1948 ed. lib. bdg. 15.50z (ISBN 0-374-95561-1). Octagon.
Mencken, H. L. H. L. Mencken on Music. Cheslock, Louis, ed. LC 61-13949. 1975. pap. 3.95 (ISBN 0-02-871550-0). Schirmer Bks.
Meyer, Leonard B. Music, the Arts, & Ideas. LC 67-25515. 1967. 12.50x (ISBN 0-226-52140-0). U of Chicago Pr.
--Music, the Arts, & Ideas. LC 67-25515. 1969. pap. 6.95 (ISBN 0-226-52141-9, P336, Phoen). U of Chicago Pr.
Morey, Arthur. The Sixties. Weiss, Jeffrey, ed. LC 76-50481. (Illus., Orig.). 1977. pap. 6.95 (ISBN 0-8256-4196-9, Consolidated). Music Sales.
Moscheles, Ignatz. Recent Music & Musicians As Described in the Diaries & Correspondence of Ignatz Moscheles. LC 73-125057. (Music Ser). 1970. Repr. of 1873 ed. lib. bdg. 32.50 (ISBN 0-306-70022-0). Da Capo.
Nettl, Bruno, et al. Contemporary Music & Music Cultures. 304p. 1974. 14.95 (ISBN 0-13-170175-4). P-H.
New York Times Great Songs of Broadway. LC 72-85051. (Illus.). 1973. 14.95 (ISBN 0-8129-0288-2). Times Bks.
Nyman, Michael. Experimental Music: Cage & Beyond. LC 74-4848. (Illus.). 1975. Repr. of 1974 ed. 15.00 (ISBN 0-02-871200-5). Schirmer Bks.
Palmer, Robert. A Tale of Two Cities: Memphis Rock, New Orleans Roll. (I.S.A.M. Monograph: No. 12). (Illus.). 1979. pap. 5.00 (ISBN 0-914678-12-4). Inst Am Music.
Pannain, Guido. Modern Composers. LC 76-99644. (Essay Index Reprint Ser). 1932. 19.50 (ISBN 0-8369-1715-4). Arno.
Perlis, Vivian, et al. Two Men for Modern Music. (ISAM Monograph: No. 9). (Illus.). 1978. pap. 5.00 (ISBN 0-914678-09-4). Inst Am Music.
Peyser, Joan. Boulez. LC 76-20884. (Illus.). 1978. pap. 5.95 (ISBN 0-02-871810-0). Schirmer Bks.
Pleasants, Henry. Agony of Modern Music. 1962. pap. 2.95 (ISBN 0-671-01401-3, Touchstone Bks). S&S.
Porter, Andrew. Music of Three More Seasons: 1977-1980. 20.00 (ISBN 0-394-51813-6). Knopf.
--Music of Three Seasons 1974-1977. 672p. 1978. 20.00 (ISBN 0-374-21646-0). FS&G.
Radcliffe, Joe. This Business of Disco. 192p. 1980. 14.50 (ISBN 0-8230-7756-X). Watson-Guptill.
Raynor, Henry. Music & Society Since Eighteen Fifteen. LC 76-1377. 1976. 15.00x (ISBN 0-8052-3626-0). Schocken.
Reck, David. Music of the Whole Earth. LC 76-12493. 1977. 19.95 (ISBN 0-684-14631-2, ScribT); pap. 15.95 (ISBN 0-684-14633-9, SL648, ScribT). Scribner.
Rosenfeld, Paul. Discoveries of a Music Critic. LC 79-183510. 402p. 1972. Repr. of 1936 ed. 20.00x (ISBN 0-8443-0064-0). Vienna Hse.
--Musical Chronicle, 1917-1923. LC 77-175877. 17.00 (ISBN 0-685-26463-7). Arno.
--Musical Impressions: Selections from Paul Rosenfeld's Criticism. Leibowitz, Herbert A., ed. LC 76-75252. 334p. 1969. 7.95 (ISBN 0-8090-7172-X). Hill & Wang.
--Musical Portraits: Interpretations of Twenty Modern Composers. facs. ed. LC 68-29243. (Essay Index Reprint Ser). 1920. 16.00 (ISBN 0-8369-0837-6). Arno.
Rostand, Claude. French Music Today. LC 73-4333. 146p. 1973. Repr. of 1955 ed. lib. bdg. 18.50 (ISBN 0-306-70578-8). Da Capo.
Salazar, Adolfo. Music in Our Time: Trends in Music Since the Romantic Era. Pope, Isabel, tr. Repr. of 1946 ed. lib. bdg. 14.50x (ISBN 0-8371-3014-X, SAMT). Greenwood.
Saminsky, Lazare. Music of Our Day. LC 78-117838. (Essay Index Reprint Ser). 1939. 19.50 (ISBN 0-8369-1682-4). Arno.
Schwartz, Elliot & Childs, Barney, eds. Contemporary Composers on Contemporary Music. (Music Reprint Ser., 1978). 1978. Repr. of 1967 ed. lib. bdg. 32.50 (ISBN 0-306-77587-5). Da Capo.
Scott, Michael. The Record of Singing. LC 79-28332. (Illus.). 1980. text ed. 49.50x (ISBN 0-8419-0599-1). Holmes & Meier.
Shead, Richard. Music in the Nineteen Twenties. LC 77-82644. 1977. 14.95x (ISBN 0-312-55482-6). St Martin.
Slonimsky, Nicholas. Music Since 1900. 4th ed. LC 70-114929. 1971. 49.50 (ISBN 0-684-10550-0, ScribT). Scribner.
Solzman, E. Twentieth Century Music: An Introduction. 2nd ed. 1974. pap. 10.95 (ISBN 0-13-935007-1). P-H.
Stone, Else & Stone, Kurt, eds. The Writings of Elliott Carter: An American Composer Looks at Modern Music. LC 76-48539. (Illus.). 416p. 1977. 18.50x (ISBN 0-253-36720-4). Ind U Pr.
Stuckenschmidt, H. H. Twentieth Century Music. 1969. pap. 3.95 (ISBN 0-07-062213-2, SP). McGraw.
Swan, Alfred J. Music: Nineteen Hundred to Nineteen Thirty. LC 77-181273. 86p. 1929. Repr. 19.00 (ISBN 0-403-01696-7). Scholarly.
Thompson, Ellen. Teaching & Understanding Contemporary Piano Music. LC 76-24574. 1976. pap. 9.95 (ISBN 0-910842-06-X, WP30, Pub by Kjos West). Kjos.
Thomson, Virgil. American Music Since Nineteen Ten. (Illus.). 1971. pap. 2.95 (ISBN 0-03-091484-1). HR&W.
Weissmann, Adolf. The Problems of Modern Music. LC 78-66930. (Encore Music Editions Ser.). (Illus.). 1979. Repr. of 1925 ed. 22.50 (ISBN 0-88355-768-1). Hyperion Conn.
Wennerstrom, Mary H. Anthology of Twentieth Century Music. 1969. pap. 18.95 (ISBN 0-13-038489-5). P-H.
Whittal, Arnold. Music Since the First World War. LC 77-1650. 1977. 15.95x (ISBN 0-312-55492-3). St Martin.
Witmark, Isidore & Goldberg, Isaac. Story of the House of Witmark: From Ragtime to Swingtime. LC 76-20707. (Roots of Jazz Ser.). 1975. Repr. of 1939 ed. lib. bdg. 29.50 (ISBN 0-306-70686-5). Da Capo.
Woodworth, George W. World of Music. LC 64-13432. 1964. 10.00x (ISBN 0-674-96135-8, Belknap Pr). Harvard U Pr.
Xenakis, Iannis. Formalized Music: Thought & Mathematics in Composition. LC 76-135017. (Illus.). 288p. 1971. 15.00x (ISBN 0-253-32378-9). Ind U Pr.
Yates, Peter. Twentieth Century Music: Its Evolution from the End of the Harmonic Era into the Present Era of Sound. LC 80-23310. xv, 367p. 1981. Repr. of 1967 ed. lib. bdg. 28.75x (ISBN 0-313-22516-8, YATC). Greenwood.

MUSIC–INSTRUCTION AND STUDY

see also Chromatic Alteration (Music); Composition (Music); Conducting; Conservatories of Music; Counterpoint; Ear Training; Embellishment (Music); Harmony; Instrumental Music–Instruction and Study; Instrumentation and Orchestration; Kindergarten–Music; Music–Analytical Guides; Music–Interpretation (Phrasing, Dynamics, etc.); Music–Manuals, Text-Books, Etc.; Music in Universities and Colleges; Music Teachers; Musical Accompaniment; Musical Form; Sight-Reading (Music); Singing–Instruction and Study; Thorough Bass; Transposition (Music)

also subdivision Instruction and Study under names of musical instruments, e.g. Piano–Instruction and Study

All Standards for All Organs, 4 vols. pap. 2.95 ea. Peer-Southern.
Allen, Margaret. Guides to Creative Motion Musicianship. 136p. 1979. 6.95 (ISBN 0-8059-2616-X). Dorrance.
Andress, Barbara. Music Experiences in Early Childhood. LC 79-26605. 198p. (Orig.). 1980. pap. text ed. 12.95 (ISBN 0-03-021771-7, HoltC). HR&W.
Andress, Barbara L. Music in Early Childhood. LC 73-84863. (Orig.). 1973. pap. 3.50x (ISBN 0-940796-09-0). Music Ed.
Aronoff, Frances W. Music & Young Children: Expanded Edition. LC 72-75917. 224p. 1979. pap. text ed. 7.95 (ISBN 0-9602590-0-7). Turning Wheel Pr.
Athey, Margaret & Hotchkiss, Gwen. A Galaxy of Games for the Music Class. 1975. 11.95 (ISBN 0-13-346064-9, Parker). P-H.
Austin, Virginia. Learning Fundamental Concepts of Music: An Activities Approach. 2nd ed. 1977. pap. text ed. 8.95 (ISBN 0-8403-1769-7). Kendall-Hunt.
Bailey, Phillip. They Can Make Music. (Illus.). 160p. 1973. 9.95x (ISBN 0-19-311913-7). Oxford U Pr.
Barbour, Harriot B. & Freeman, Warren S. Story of Music. rev. ed. (Illus.). (gr. 7-9). text ed. 11.00 (ISBN 0-87487-033-X). Summy.

Barnes, R. A. Fundamentals of Music: A Program for Self-Instruction. 1964. pap. text ed. 8.95 (ISBN 0-07-003771-X, C). McGraw.
Batcheller, John M. Music in Early Childhood. (Classroom Music Enrichment Units Ser.). (Illus.). 1974. pap. 5.95x (ISBN 0-87628-212-5). Ctr Appl Res.
Beatty, Eleanor & Schnitger, Carol. Center in on Music: Individualized Learning Centers in the Elementary Classroom. LC 77-76865. (Illus.). 1977. pap. 9.95 (ISBN 0-916656-06-3); material packet 11.95 (ISBN 0-916656-07-1). Mark Foster Mus.
Bellaman, Henry. A Music Teacher's Notebook. 59.95 (ISBN 0-8490-0683-X). Gordon Pr.
Benjamin, Thomas E., et al. Techniques & Materials of Tonal Music: With an Introduction to Twentieth Century Techniques. 2nd ed. LC 78-69578. (Illus.). 1979. text ed. 16.25 (ISBN 0-395-27066-9). HM.
Benward, Bruce. Workbook in Advanced Ear Training. 175p. 1974. wire coil avail. (ISBN 0-697-03589-1); tchrs.' dictation avail. (ISBN 0-697-03590-5); 10 tapes avail. (ISBN 0-697-03696-0). Wm C Brown.
Bernstein, Seymour. With Your Own Two Hands: Self-Discovery Through Music. (Illus.). 320p. 1981. 14.95 (ISBN 0-02-870310-3). Schirmer Bks.
Boehnlein, Frank. Handbook of Musicianship in the Contemporary Classroom. 1977. pap. text ed. 9.00 (ISBN 0-8191-0340-3). U Pr of Amer.
Borisoff, Alexander. How to Write a Melody. 119p. 1980. pap. 9.95 (ISBN 0-938170-01-5). Wimbledon Music.
Borroff, Edith & Irvin, Marjory. Music in Perspective. (Illus., Orig.). 1976. pap. text ed. 13.95 (ISBN 0-15-564883-7, HC); 6 record set 15.95 (ISBN 0-15-564884-5). HarBraceJ.
Bradley, Jack. How to Read & Write Music: Including Professional Chord Symbol Method. LC 78-54969. 1978. pap. 9.95 (ISBN 0-931856-01-9). Quest WV.
Bramscher, Cynthia S. Treasury of Musical Motivators for the Elementary Classroom. (Illus.). 1979. 13.95 (ISBN 0-13-930610-2, Parker). P-H.
Brandt, William, et al. The Comprehensive Study of Music: Anthology of Music from Plainchant Through Gabrieli. 1979. pap. text ed. 11.50 scp (ISBN 0-06-161411-4, HarpC). Har-Row.
Bukofzer, Manfred, et al, eds. The Place of Musicology in American Institutions of Higher Learning, 2 vols. in one. Incl. Some Aspects of Musicology. LC 77-4226. (Music Reprint Ser.). 1977. Repr. of 1957 ed. lib. bdg. 19.50 (ISBN 0-306-77407-0). Da Capo.
Burnett, Michael & Lawrence, Ian, eds. Music Education Review, Vol. 2. 226p. 1980. pap. text ed. 15.00x (ISBN 0-85633-196-1, NFER). Humanities.
Burnett, Millie. Melody Movement & Language: A Teacher's Guide of Music in Game Form for the Pre-School & Primary Grades. LC 73-80728. tchr's guide 5.00 (ISBN 0-88247-236-4). R & E Res Assoc.
Burton, Leon & Hughes, William. Music Play--Learning Activities for Young Children. (gr. k-6). 1980. pap. text ed. 12.25 (ISBN 0-201-00883-1, Sch Div). A-W.
Carlsen, James C. Melodic Perception: A Program for Self-Instruction. 1965. text ed. 10.95 (ISBN 0-07-009975-8, C); instructor's manual 3.95 (ISBN 0-07-009977-4); 150.00 (ISBN 0-07-009976-6). McGraw.
Carlton, Malcolm. Music in Education. (New Education Ser.). Date not set. 18.50x (ISBN 0-7130-0155-0, Woburn Pr England). Biblio Dist.
Chacksfield, K. M., et al. Music & Language with Young Children. (Illus.). 190p. 1975. 18.50x (ISBN 0-631-15330-6, Pub. by Basil Blackwell). Biblio Dist.
Choate, Robert A., ed. Documentary Report of the Tanglewood Symposium. LC 68-57058. (Orig.). 1968. pap. 10.00x (ISBN 0-940796-02-3). Music Ed.
Christiansen, Nels W. The Relation of Supervision & Other Factors to Certain Phases of Musical Achievement in the Rural Schools of Utah. LC 79-176699. (Columbia University. Teachers College. Contributions to Education: No. 934). Repr. of 1948 ed. 17.50 (ISBN 0-404-55934-4). AMS Pr.
Clark, Frances & Goss, Louise. Teaching the Music Tree: A Handbook for Teachers. (Frances Clark Library for Piano Students). 1973. pap. text ed. 3.85 (ISBN 0-87487-124-7). Summy.
Colwell, Richard & Colwell, Ruth. Concepts for a Musical Foundation. LC 73-4749. (Illus.). 320p. 1974. pap. text ed. 15.95 (ISBN 0-13-166298-8). P-H.
Cooper, Grosvenor. Learning to Listen: A Handbook for Music. LC 57-8579. 1962. pap. 3.75 (ISBN 0-226-11519-4, P79, Phoen). U of Chicago Pr.
Cradock, Eveline. Musical Appreciation in an Infant School. (Illus.). 50p. (Orig.). 1977. pap. text ed. 6.75 (ISBN 0-19-321055-X). Oxford U Pr.
Crews, Katherine. Music & Perceptual Motor Development. (Classroom Music Enrichment Units Ser.). (Illus.). 1974. pap. 5.95x (ISBN 0-87628-213-3). Ctr Appl Res.
Daniel, Katinka S. Kodaly Approach, Method Book One. 2nd ed. LC 79-53162. 204p. 1979. wire 20.00 (ISBN 0-916656-13-6); materials for transparencies 20.00 (ISBN 0-916656-14-4). Mark Foster Mus.
Day, Thomas. Monarch College Outline on Music. pap. 4.95 (ISBN 0-671-08048-2). Monarch Pr.
Dee, Margaret. Face the Music, Bk. I. 1955. 1.00 (ISBN 0-913650-36-6). Volkwein Bros.
--Face the Music, Bk. II. 1955. 0.75 (ISBN 0-913650-37-4). Volkwein Bros.
--On We Go, Bk. II. 1953. 1.75 (ISBN 0-913650-33-1). Volkwein Bros.
Dennis, Brian. Experimental Music in Schools: Towards a New World of Sound. 1970. pap. 4.75 (ISBN 0-19-323195-6); materials 1-20 3.25 (ISBN 0-19-323196-4). Oxford U Pr.
Dickinson, Edward. Music & the Higher Education. (Educational Ser.). Repr. 20.00 (ISBN 0-685-43008-1). Norwood Edns.
Duckworth, William. A Creative Approach to Music Fundamentals. 320p. 1981. pap. text ed. 14.95x (ISBN 0-534-00891-7). Wadsworth Pub.
Dwyer, Terence. Teaching Musical Appreciation. 1967. 8.00x (ISBN 0-19-317409-X). Oxford U Pr.
Edelstein, Stefan, et al. Creating Curriculum in Music. (gr. k-12). 1980. tchrs'. materials 13.50 (ISBN 0-201-01587-0, Sch Div). A-W.
Edwards, Ruth. Complete Music Teacher: For Teachers, Parents & Students. LC 79-109368. 1970. 5.95 (ISBN 0-87672-106-4). Geron-X.
Eimert, Herbert & Stockhausen, Karlheinz, eds. Speech & Music. Shenfield, Margaret & Koenig, Ruth, trs. from Ger. (Die Reihe: No. 6). 1964. pap. 4.50 (ISBN 0-900938-14-5, 50-26106). Eur-Am Music.
Eisenkramer, Henry E. Classroom Music. LC 78-60416. (Illus.). 1978. pap. 9.95 (ISBN 0-916656-11-X). Mark Foster Mus.
Evans, David. Sharing Sounds: Musical Experiences with Young Children. (Early Childhood Education Ser). 1977. text ed. 12.95x (ISBN 0-582-25006-4); pap. text ed. 6.95x (ISBN 0-582-25008-0). Longman.
Fay, Amy. Music Study in Germany. (Music Reprint Ser.: 1979). 1979. Repr. of 1880 ed. lib. bdg. 29.50 (ISBN 0-306-79541-8). Da Capo.
Fortunato, Connie. Music Is for Children. LC 78-50962. 1978. pap. 1.50 (ISBN 0-89191-128-6). Cook.
Franco, Eloise & Franco, Johan. Making Music. (Illus.). (gr. 1-5). 1976. pap. 4.25 (ISBN 0-87516-212-6). De Vorss.
Funes, Donald J. & Munson, Kenneth. Musical Involvement: A Guide to Perceptive Listening. (Illus.). 178p. (Orig.). 1975. pap. text ed. 12.95 (ISBN 0-15-564950-7, HC); boxed set of six records 16.95 (ISBN 0-15-564951-5). HarBraceJ.
Gary, Charles L. & Landis, Beth. Comprehensive Music Program. 12p. (Orig.). pap. 1.00x (ISBN 0-940796-01-5). Music Ed.
Gilbert, Jean. Musical Activities with Young Children. LC 75-332407. (Illus.). 1975. 10.00x (ISBN 0-7062-3462-6). Intl Pubns Serv.
Gillett, Dorothy. Comprehensive Musicianship Through Classroom Music: Zone 3, Book A. Burton, Leon & Thomson, William, eds. (University of Hawaii Music Project). (gr. 3). 1974. pap. text ed. 6.84 (ISBN 0-201-00858-0, Sch Div); tchr's ed. 11.48 (ISBN 0-201-00859-9). A-W.
Glaser, Victoria. Training for Musicianship. 17.95x (ISBN 0-8008-7829-9, Crescendo). Taplinger.
Glynne-Jones, Marjorie. Music: Schooling in the Middle Years. (Basic Books in Education Ser.). 1974. 14.00 (ISBN 0-208-01390-3). Shoe String.
Gordon, Edwin. Psychology of Music Teaching. (Contemporary Perspectives in Music Education Ser). (Illus.). 1971. ref. ed. 11.95 (ISBN 0-13-736215-3). P-H.
Gordon, Edwin, ed. Experimental Research in the Psychology of Music, Vols. 6-9. Incl. Vol. 6. LC 73-632181. 1970. 4.75x (ISBN 0-87745-018-8); Vol. 7. LC 73-632181. 1971. 6.95x (ISBN 0-87745-024-2); Vol. 8. LC 73-632181. 1972. 7.95x (ISBN 0-87745-034-X); Vol. 9. LC 73-632181. 1974. text ed. 15.00x (ISBN 0-87745-048-X). (Studies in the Psychology of Music Ser). U of Iowa Pr.
Gordon, Edwin E. Learning Sequences in Music(Skill, Content, & Patterns) 289p. 1980. 16.95 (ISBN 0-686-28115-2). GIA Pubns.
Greenberg, Marvin. Your Children Need Music: A Guide for Parents & Teachers of Young Children. (Illus.). 1979. text ed. 16.95 (ISBN 0-13-977116-6, Spec); pap. 8.95 (ISBN 0-13-977108-5). P-H.
Greenleaf, E. E. Basic Music Work & Play. 1964. pap. 0.85x (ISBN 0-685-08144-3). Claitors.
Greer, Douglas. Design for Music Learning. LC 79-21117. 1980. pap. text ed. 12.95x (ISBN 0-8077-2573-0). Tchrs Coll.
Hackett, Patricia, et al. The Musical Classroom: Models, Skills, & Backgrounds for Elementary Teaching. 1979. pap. 16.95 ref. (ISBN 0-13-608356-0). P-H.
Haines, B. Joan & Gerber, Linda L. Guiding Young Children to Music: A Resource Book for Teachers. (Early Childhood Education Ser.: No. C24). 288p. 1980. pap. text ed. 13.95 spiral bdg. (ISBN 0-675-08161-0). Merrill.
Harris, Ernest E., ed. Music Education: A Guide to Information Sources. LC 74-11560. (Education Information Guide Ser.: Vol. 1). 1978. 36.00 (ISBN 0-8103-1309-X). Gale.
Hewitt, Helen, ed. Petrucci's Harmnica Musices Odhecation-A. LC 77-25989. (Music Reprint Ser., 1978). 1978. Repr. of 1942 ed. lib. bdg. 42.50 (ISBN 0-306-77562-X). Da Capo.
Hill, Frank W. & Searight, Roland. Study Outline & Workbook in the Elements of Music. 7th ed. 154p. 1980. write for info. wire coil (ISBN 0-697-03441-0); tchrs'. manual avail. (ISBN 0-697-03482-8). Wm C Brown.
Hindemith, Paul. Elementary Training for Musicians. 1946. pap. 7.50 (ISBN 0-901938-16-5). Eur-Am Music.
Hochheimer, Laura. A Sequential Sourcebook for Elementary School Music. 2nd ed. 1980. pap. 12.95 (ISBN 0-918812-12-7). Magnamusic.
Hoffer, Charles. A Concise Introduction to Music Listening. 2nd. ed. 1979. pap. 13.95x (ISBN 0-534-00627-2); study guide 6.95x (ISBN 0-534-00705-8); records 19.95x (ISBN 0-534-00692-2). Wadsworth Pub.
Holt, John. Never Too Late. 1978. 10.00 (ISBN 0-440-06641-7, Sey Lawr). Delacorte.
How to Read Music . . . in One Evening. 1971. pap. 6.95 (ISBN 0-912732-00-8). Duane Shinn.
Hughes, William. General Music: A Comprehensive Approach-Zone 4, Book A. new ed. (University of Hawaii Music Project Ser.). (gr. 7-9). 1975. pap. text ed. 9.72 (ISBN 0-201-00817-3, Sch Div); tchr's ed. 11.48 (ISBN 0-201-00818-1). A-W.
Hunt, Norman J. Brass Ensemble Method: Beginning Class Instruction. 3rd ed. 176p. 1974. write for info. plastic comb. (ISBN 0-697-03498-4). Wm C Brown.
Hunter, Hilda. Grammar of Music. (Student's Music Library Ser). 1952. 6.95 (ISBN 0-234-77208-5). Dufour.
International Directory of Music Education Institutions. 1968. pap. 4.00 (ISBN 92-3-000711-0, 323, UNESCO). Unipub.
Jaques-Dalcroze, Emile. Eurhythmics, Art & Education. LC 78-180927. Repr. of 1930 ed. 18.00 (ISBN 0-405-08665-2, Blom Pubns). Arno.
--Rhythm, Music & Education. LC 77-187829. (Illus.). Repr. of 1921 ed. 18.00 (ISBN 0-405-08666-0, Blom Pubns). Arno.
Jones, Rod. How to Play Harmonica, Autoharp, Kazoo & Half-a-Dozen Other Low-Cost Musical Instruments. 32p. 1975. pap. 6.95 (ISBN 0-912732-14-8). Duane Shinn.
Juilliard School of Music - New York. Juilliard Report on Teaching the Literature & Materials of Music. Repr. of 1953 ed. lib. bdg. 15.00x (ISBN 0-8371-3008-5, JURT). Greenwood.
Karolyi, Otto. Introducing Music. (Orig.). (YA) (gr. 11 up). 1965. pap. 2.95 (ISBN 0-14-020659-0, Pelican). Penguin.
Keene, James A. A History of Music Education in the United States. LC 81-51610. 500p. 1982. text ed. 25.00 (ISBN 0-87451-212-3). U Pr of New Eng.
Keetman, Gunild. Elementaria, First Acquaintance with Orff-Schulwerk. LC 75-1152. (Illus.). 1974. 12.00 (ISBN 0-901938-04-1). Eur-Am Music.
Keller, Wilhelm. Introduction to Music for Children. Kennedy, Susan, tr. from Ger. (Orff-Schulwerk). 1974. pap. 5.00 (ISBN 0-930448-10-3, 70-00271). Eur-Am Music.
Kenneson, Claude. A Cellist's Guide to the New Approach. LC 73-86546. 1974. 4.50 (ISBN 0-682-47819-9, University). Exposition.
Kidd, Eleanor. Threshold to Music, Level 1. 2nd ed. (gr. 2-4). 1974. pap. 10.00 teacher's resources book (ISBN 0-8224-9062-5); experience charts 53.00 (ISBN 0-8224-9063-3). Pitman Learning.
--Threshold to Music, Level 2. 2nd ed. (gr. 4-7). 1975. pap. 10.00 teacher's resource book (ISBN 0-8224-9064-1); experience charts 53.00 (ISBN 0-8224-9065-X). Pitman Learning.
--Threshold to Music: Early Childhood. 2nd ed. (gr. k-2). 1974. pap. 8.00 teacher's resource book (ISBN 0-8224-9060-9); experience charts 44.00 (ISBN 0-8224-9061-7). Pitman Learning.
--Threshold to Music: Higher Grades. 2nd ed. (gr. 3-5). 1978. tchr's. resource book 10.00 (ISBN 0-8224-9068-4); experience charts 53.00 (ISBN 0-8224-9069-2). Pitman Learning.
Kinyon, John. The Teacher on the Podium. LC 75-4891. (Illus.). 250p. 1975. pap. text ed. 9.95x spiral bdg. (ISBN 0-88284-028-2). Alfred Pub.
Kliewer, Vernon L. Music Reading: A Comprehensive Approach, Vol. 1. LC 72-3870. (Illus.). 352p. 1973. pap. text ed. 12.95 (ISBN 0-13-607903-2). P-H.
Kreter, L. Sight & Sound: A Manual of Aural Musicianship, 2 vols. 1976. Vol. 1. pap. 12.95 (ISBN 0-13-809905-7); Vol. 2. pap. 13.50 (ISBN 0-13-809913-8); Tapes Vols. 1 & 2. 150.00 (ISBN 0-13-809921-9). P-H.
Kromer, Marcin. De Musica Figurata. Seay, Albert, ed. (Texts-Translations Ser.: No. 3). 35p. 1980. pap. 5.00 (ISBN 0-933894-08-2). Colo Coll Music.
Labuta, J. Guide to Accountability in Music Instruction. 1973. 11.95 (ISBN 0-13-367953-5, Parker). P-H.
Lament, Marylee M. Music in Elementary Education: Enjoy Experience & Learn. (Illus.). 416p. 1976. text ed. 15.95 (ISBN 0-02-367340-0). Macmillan.
Landis, Beth & Carder, Polly. Eclectic Curriculum in American Music Education: Contributions of Dalcroze, Kodaly, & Orff. LC 72-83395. (Illus.). 1972. pap. 8.00x (ISBN 0-940796-03-1). Music Ed.
Lawrence, Ian. Composers & the Nature of Music Education. 240p. 1979. 19.95 (ISBN 0-85967-401-0, Pub. by Scolar Pr England). Biblio Dist.
--Music & the Teacher. 112p. 1975. 12.95x (ISBN 0-8464-0658-6). Beekman Pubs.
Leonhard, Charles & House, Robert W. Foundations & Principles of Music Education. 2nd ed. 448p. 1971. text ed. 14.95 (ISBN 0-07-037199-7, C). McGraw.
Levine, Arthur D. The Nashville Number System: A Practical Music Technic for Musicians & Songwriters Who Play Music by Ear. rev. ed. LC 81-81410. (Illus.). 64p. 1981. 9.95 (ISBN 0-9606284-1-X); pap. 6.95 (ISBN 0-9606284-0-1). Gibraltar.
Logier, Johann B. Logier's Comprehensive Course in Music: Harmony & Practical Composition. LC 76-15186. (Music Reprint Ser.). 1976. Repr. of 1888 ed. lib. bdg. 32.50 (ISBN 0-306-70794-2). Da Capo.
Lovelock, William. Common Sense in Music Teaching. (Illus.). 1968. Repr. of 1965 ed. 6.95 (ISBN 0-7135-0682-2). Dufour.
Luck, James T. Creative Music for the Classroom Teacher. 1970. pap. text ed. 6.95x (ISBN 0-394-30369-5). Phila Bk Co.
Mabus, Eileen L. Music for Tiny Tots: A Teacher's Manual for Group Teaching of Four-&-Five-Year-Olds. 1977. 8.00 (ISBN 0-682-48719-8). Exposition.
McDonald, Gerald. Training & Careers for the Professional Musician. 112p. 1979. 15.00x (ISBN 0-905418-03-4, Pub. by Grehsham England). State Mutual Bk.
McDowell, Bonney & Steele, Janet. Elementary Musicianship. 1981. pap. text ed. 14.95 (ISBN 0-394-32369-6). Knopf.
Mack, Glenn. Adventures in Modes & Keys. 32p. (gr. 3-12). 1973. pap. text ed. 4.50 (ISBN 0-87487-625-7). Summy.
Mackinnon, Lillias. Music by Heart. LC 80-26551. xi, 141p. 1981. Repr. of 1954 ed. lib. bdg. 17.50x (ISBN 0-313-22810-8, MAMB). Greenwood.
Madison, Thurber H., ed. Basic Concepts of Music Education. LC 58-5681. (National Society for the Study of Education Yearbooks Ser: No. 57, Pt. 1). 1958. 6.50x (ISBN 0-226-60044-0). U of Chicago Pr.
Madsen, Clifford K. & Kuhn, Terry L. Contemporary Music Education. LC 77-90672. (Illus.). 1978. pap. text ed. 7.50x (ISBN 0-88295-350-8). Harlan Davidson.
Mark, Michael L. Contemporary Music Education. LC 77-80230. 1979. text ed. 15.95 (ISBN 0-02-871640-X). Schirmer Bks.
Mattson, Donald E. & Walz, Louis D. Old Fort Snelling Instruction Book for Fife, with Music of Early America. 2nd ed. LC 74-7298. (Minnesota Historic Sites Pamphlet Ser: No. 11). 112p. 1976. pap. 5.50 (ISBN 0-87351-090-9). Minn Hist.
Mears, Caroline. Music for Today. 1978. 12.00 (ISBN 0-19-570082-1). Oxford U Pr.
MENC National Committee on Instruction, ed. Selected Instructional Programs in Music. 1977. pap. 2.00x (ISBN 0-940796-16-3). Music Ed.
Metaxa, George. Music for Children's Eurythmy & Dance. 1973. pap. 3.00 (ISBN 0-916786-11-0, Pub by Waldorf School Monographs). St George Bk Serv.

Metz, Donald E. Teaching Music in Grades Six to Nine. (Secondary Education Ser.: No. C28). 192p. 1980. pap. text ed. 11.95 spiral bdg. (ISBN 0-675-08176-9). Merrill.
Meyer, Leonard B. Explaining Music: Essays & Explorations. LC 73-187749. (Illus.). 1973. 18.50x (ISBN 0-520-02216-5). U of Cal Pr.
Meyer-Denkmann, Gertrud. Experiments in Sound: New Directions in Musical Education for Young Children. Paynter, Elizabeth & Paynter, John, eds. LC 50-26923. 1977. pap. 8.75 (ISBN 0-900938-49-8). Eur-Am Music.
Miller, Hugh M. Introduction to Music. (Illus., Orig.). 1978. pap. 4.50 (ISBN 0-06-460177-3, CO 177, COS). Har-Row.
Mills, Elizabeth & Murphy, Sr. Therese, eds. Suzuki Method, or Suzuki Concept: An Introduction to a Successful Method for Early Music Education. (Illus.). 220p. 1973. 6.95 (ISBN 0-87297-002-7); pap. 5.95 (ISBN 0-87297-003-5). Diablo.
Monsour, Sally. Music in Open Education. (Classroom Music Enrichment Units Ser.). (Illus.). 1974. pap. 5.95x (ISBN 0-87628-214-1). Ctr Appl Res.
Music Education National Conference. Study of Music in the Elementary School: A Conceptual Approach. Evenson, Flavis & Gary, Charles L., eds. LC 67-31352. (Orig.). 1967. pap. 5.50x (ISBN 0-940796-19-8). Music Ed.
Music Educators Journal Indexes, 2 bks. Incl. Bk. 1. Vol. 46-51, Sep. 1959-Jun 1965. 20p (ISBN 0-940796-06-6, 321-10194); Bk. 2. Vol. 52-56, Sep 1965-May 1970. 22p (ISBN 0-940796-07-4, 321-10402). pap. 1.00x ea. Music Ed.
Nallin, W. E. Musical Idea: A Consideration of Music & Its Ways. 1968. text ed. 13.95x (ISBN 0-02-385900-8). Macmillan.
Newman, Ernest. Musical Studies. 2nd ed. LC 70-181220. 319p. 1910. Repr. 19.00 (ISBN 0-403-01631-2). Scholarly.
Newman, Grant. Teaching Children Music: Fundamentals of Music & Method. 300p. 1979. write for info. (ISBN 0-697-03418-6); study guide & wkbk avail. (ISBN 0-697-03420-8); answer key avail. (ISBN 0-685-91881-5). Wm C Brown.
Nielsen, Floraine & Folstrom, Roger. Music Fundamentals: A Creative Activities Approach. (Illus., Orig.). 1969. 13.95 (ISBN 0-201-05250-4). A-W.
Nye, Vernice T. Music for Young Children. 2nd ed. 307p. 1979. pap. text ed. write for info. (ISBN 0-697-03419-4). Wm C Brown.
Orff, Carl. The Schulwerk, Vol. 3. Murray, Margaret, tr. from Ger. (Carl Orff Documentation Ser.). 1978. pap. 14.95 (ISBN 0-930448-06-5, 70-00065). Eur-Am Music.
Peters, David & Miller, Robert. Music Teaching & Learning. (Music Ser.). 1981. pap. text ed. 12.95x (ISBN 0-582-28142-3). Longman.
Phelps, Roger P. A Guide to Research in Music Education. 2nd ed. LC 80-12107. 400p. 1980. 16.00 (ISBN 0-8108-1303-3). Scarecrow.
Preas, Jerry L. Instruction: Guitar, Voice, Keyboard & Bass. (Illus.). 60p. (Orig.). 1981. pap. 2.95 (ISBN 0-935622-03-9). Texan-Am Pub.
Puopolo, Vito. Music Fundamentals. LC 75-4316. (Illus.). 1976. pap. text ed. 8.95 (ISBN 0-02-871890-9). Schirmer Bks.
Raebeck, Lois & Wheeler, Lawrence. New Approaches to Music in the Elementary School. 4th ed. 300p. 1980. pap. text ed. write for info. plastic comb (ISBN 0-697-03421-6). Wm C Brown.
Rainbow, Bernarr. Music in the Classroom. 2nd ed. 1971. text ed. 11.50x (ISBN 0-435-81746-9). Heinemann Ed.
Regelski, Thomas A. Teaching General Music: Action Learning for Middle & Secondary Schools. LC 80-5561. (Illus.). 448p. 1981. text ed. 12.95 (ISBN 0-02-872070-9). Schirmer Bks.
Regner, Hermann, ed. Music for Children. (Orff-Schulwerk: Vol. 2). 1977. pap. 17.50 (ISBN 0-930448-00-6). Eur-Am Music.
Reimer, Bennett. Philosophy of Music Education. (Contemporary Perspectives in Music Education Ser). 1970. pap. text ed. 10.95 (ISBN 0-13-663872-4). P-H.
Reynolds, Jane L. Music Lessons You Can Teach. 1980. pap. 6.95 (ISBN 0-13-607978-4). P-H.
Rivera, A. Ramon & Gruenbaum, Thelma. To Music & Children with Love! Reflections for Parents & Teachers. 133p. 1979. pap. 6.95 (ISBN 0-936190-03-5). ExPressAll.
Rosen, Charles. Arnold Shoenberg. LC 80-8773. 113p. (Orig.). 1981. pap. 4.95 (ISBN 0-691-02706-4). Princeton U Pr.
Schafer, Murray. Creative Music Education. LC 75-30286. (Illus.). 1976. pap. text ed. 9.95 (ISBN 0-02-872330-9). Schirmer Bks.
Schafer, R. Murray. The Rhinoceros in the Classroom. 1975. pap. 5.00 (ISBN 0-900938-44-7, 50-26922). Eur-Am Music.
Schmitt, Cecilia. Rapport & Success: Human Relations in Music Education. 1976. 4.95 (ISBN 0-8059-2293-8). Dorrance.
Seay, Albert, ed. Quart Livre. (Transcriptions Ser.: No. 6). v, 48p. 1981. 4.00 (ISBN 0-933894-09-0). Colo Coll Music.
Seyer, Phil, et al. What Makes Music Work? (Self-Teaching Guides). 1981. pap. text ed. write for info (ISBN 0-471-35192-X). Wiley.
Shanet, Howard. Learn to Read Music. rev. ed. 1971. pap. 3.95 (ISBN 0-671-21027-0, Fireside). S&S.
Sheehy, Emma D. Children Discover Music & Dance. LC 68-24571. 1968. pap. text ed. 7.25x (ISBN 0-8077-2150-6). Tchrs Coll.
Sheftel, Paul. The Keyboard: Explorations & Discoveries. 288p. (Orig.). 1980. pap. text ed. 10.95 (ISBN 0-03-043091-7, HoltC). HR&W.
Shinn, Duane. How to Teach Yourself All About Chords. 40p. 1973. pap. 6.95 (ISBN 0-912732-11-3). Duane Shinn.
Slonimsky, Nicolas. The Road to Music. (Music Reprint Ser.). 1979. Repr. of 1966 ed. lib. bdg. 17.95 (ISBN 0-306-79566-3). Da Capo.
Spalding, Walter R. Music at Harvard: A Historical Review of Men & Events. LC 76-58921. (Music Reprint Series). 1977. Repr. of 1935 ed. lib. bdg. 27.50 (ISBN 0-306-70871-X). Da Capo.
Spencer, Ruth A. Early Childhood Music Kit: The First Year. (Illus.). 120p. 1980. tchr's ed, cassettes included 40.00 (ISBN 0-89824-008-5). Trillium Pr.
--Early Childhood Music Kit: The Second Year. (Illus.). 150p. 1980. tchrs' ed, cassettes included 40.00 (ISBN 0-89824-011-5). Trillium Pr.
Stanislaw, Richard J. A Checklist of Four-Shape Shape-Note Tunebooks. LC 78-61291. (ISAM Monograph: No. 10). 61p. 1978. pap. 6.00 (ISBN 0-914678-10-8). Inst Am Music.
Stevens, Denis. Musicology: A Practical Guide. (The Yehudi Menuhin Music Guides Ser.). (Illus.). 250p. 1981. 17.95 (ISBN 0-02-872530-1); pap. 8.95 (ISBN 0-02-872540-9). Schirmer Bks.
Surplus, Robert W. Alphabet of Music. LC 62-20799. (Musical Books for Young People Ser). (gr. 5-11). 1963. PLB 3.95g (ISBN 0-8225-0058-2). Lerner Pubns.
Suzuki, Shinichi. Nurtured by Love: A New Approach to Education. Suzuki, Waltraud, tr. LC 79-82726. 1969. 7.95 (ISBN 0-682-47518-1, University). Exposition.
Swanson, Bessie R. Music in the Education of Children. 4th ed. 448p. 1980. text ed. 19.95x (ISBN 0-534-00880-1). Wadsworth Pub.
Swanwick, Keith. A Basis for Music Education. (Orig.). 1979. pap. text ed. 13.25x (ISBN 0-85633-180-5). Humanities.
Taylor, J. F., et al. Introduction to Literature & the Fine Arts. (Illus.). 418p. 1950. text ed. 10.00x (ISBN 0-87013-037-4). Mich St U Pr.
Tottle, Jack. Bluegrass Mandolin. LC 74-77692. (Illus.). 120p. (Orig.). 1975. pap. 6.95 with recording (ISBN 0-8256-0154-1, Oak). Music Sales.
Travis, John W. Let's Tune Up. Rathman, R. Annabel, ed. LC 68-14025. (Illus.). 1968. 17.50x (ISBN 0-9600394-2-2); pap. 15.50x (ISBN 0-9600394-3-0). Travis.
Trubitt, Allen R. & Hines, Robert S. Ear Training & Sight-Singing: An Integrated Approach, Book 1. LC 77-5214. 1979. pap. text ed. 12.95 (ISBN 0-02-870810-5); tapes 49.50 (ISBN 0-02-870770-2). Schirmer Bks.
University of Hawaii Music Project & Burton, Leon. Comprehensive Musicianship Through Classroom Music: Zone 2, Hawaii. (gr. 2-3). 1972. Bk. A. text ed. 4.88 (ISBN 0-201-00785-1, Sch Div); Bk. B. text ed. 6.20 (ISBN 0-201-00856-4); tchr's bk. for bk. A 11.48 (ISBN 0-201-00788-6); tchr's bk. for bk. B 11.48 (ISBN 0-201-00857-2). A-W.
Van Vactor, David & Moore, Katherine D. Every Child May Hear. LC 80-12222. 1960. pap. 5.00x (ISBN 0-87049-030-3). U of Tenn Pr.
Vulliamy, Graham & Lee, Ed, eds. Pop Music in School. 2nd ed. LC 79-7708. (The Resources of Music Ser.: No. 13). (Illus.). 1980. 22.95 (ISBN 0-521-22930-8); pap. 8.95x (ISBN 0-521-29727-3). Cambridge U Pr.
Weidensee, Victor. Instrumental Music in the Public Schools: Organization & Administration. LC 72-77169. 6.50 (ISBN 0-8008-4193-X, Crescendo). Taplinger.
White, John D. Guidelines for College Teaching of Music Theory. LC 81-8985. 190p. 1981. 12.50 (ISBN 0-8108-1456-0). Scarecrow.
Williamson, Robin. The Penny Whistle Book. LC 76-41141. (Illus.). 64p. (Orig.). 1977. pap. 4.95 (ISBN 0-8256-0190-8, Oak). Music Sales.
Wilt, Michele. Music Experiences for Young Children. 1981. comb-bound 17.95x (ISBN 0-87628-588-4). Ctr Appl Res.
Winslow, Robert W. & Dallin, Leon. Music Skills for Classroom Teachers. 5th ed. 325p. 1979. write for info. plastic comb. (ISBN 0-697-03474-7). Wm C Brown.
Wisbey, Audrey A. Music As the Source of Learning. 165p. 1981. text ed. 19.50 (ISBN 0-8391-1648-9). Univ Park.
Wittlich, Gary & Humphries, Lee. Ear Training: An Approach Through Music Literature. 384p. (Orig.). 1974. pap. text ed. 13.95 (ISBN 0-15-518707-4, HC); 2-record set 8.95 (ISBN 0-15-518709-0); tapes 100.00 (ISBN 0-15-518708-2); cassettes 75.00 (ISBN 0-15-518710-4). HarBraceJ.
Yarbrough, Cornelia & Madsen, Clifford K. Competency-Based Music Education. (Illus.). 1980. text ed. 12.95 (ISBN 0-13-154963-4); pap. text ed. 6.95 (ISBN 0-13-154955-3). P-H.
Yost, Gaylord. The Key to the Mastery of Double Stopping. 1941. 3.00 (ISBN 0-913650-20-X). Volkwein Bros.
Zemke, Lorna & Daniel, Katinka S. Kodaly Thirty-Five Lesson Plans and Folk Song Supplement. 2nd ed. LC 76-39689. 1976. pap. text ed. 8.95 (ISBN 0-916656-04-7). Mark Foster Mus.
Zimmer, Lowell J. Music Handbook for the Child in Special Education. 1976. pap. 3.95 (ISBN 0-913574-99-6, 01260). Eur-Am Music.
Zimmerman, Marilyn P. Musical Characteristics of Children. LC 73-176274. (From Research to the Music Classroom Ser). 32p. (Orig.). 1971. pap. 2.00x (ISBN 0-940796-10-4). Music Ed.
Zorn, J. D. Brass Ensemble Methods for Music Educators. 1977. pap. text ed. 14.95x (ISBN 0-534-00503-9). Wadsworth Pub.

MUSIC–INSTRUCTION AND STUDY–AUDIO-VISUAL AIDS

Baird, Jo Ann. Using Media in the Music Program. (Classroom Music Enrichment Units Ser.). 1974. pap. 5.95x (ISBN 0-87628-211-7). Ctr Appl Res.
Charlie Parker Omnibook: Recorded Solos for B Flat Instruments. 1981. 9.95 (ISBN 0-686-75119-1, Atlantic Music Corp.). Criterion Mus.
Charlie Parker Omnibook: Recorded Solos for "C" Instruments. 9.95 (ISBN 0-686-75118-3, Atlantic Music Corp.). Criterion Mus.
Dallin, Leon. Basic Music Skills: A Supplementary Program for Self-Instruction. 108p. 1971. pap. text ed. write for info. (ISBN 0-697-03464-X). Wm C Brown.
Gell, Heather. Music, Movement, & the Young Child. rev. ed. (Illus.). 1973. 10.50 (ISBN 0-900882-06-9). Volkwein Bros.

MUSIC–INTERPRETATION (PHRASING, DYNAMICS, ETC.)

see also Music–Analysis, Appreciation

Cone, Edward T. Musical Form & Musical Performance. LC 68-11157. (Illus.). 1968. pap. 4.95x (ISBN 0-393-09767-6). Norton.
Dart, Thurston. Interpretation of Music. pap. 3.50 (ISBN 0-06-090025-3, CN25, CN). Har-Row.
--Interpretation of Music. 1975. Repr. of 1967 ed. pap. text ed. 9.25x (ISBN 0-09-031683-5, Hutchinson U Lib). Humanities.
Fuller-Maitland, J. A. The Consort of Music: A Study of Interpretation & Emsemble. LC 72-83279. Repr. of 1915 ed. 12.50 (ISBN 0-405-08541-9, Blom Pubns). Arno.
Haydon, Glen. Evolution of the Six-Four Chord: A Chapter in the History of Dissonant Treatment. LC 75-125052. (Music Ser). 1971. Repr. of 1933 ed. lib. bdg. 19.50 (ISBN 0-306-70017-4). Da Capo.
Hutcheson, Jere T. Musical Form & Analysis, 2 vols. pap. 11.95x ea. (Crescendo); Vol. 1. (ISBN 0-8008-5454-3); Vol. 2. (ISBN 0-8008-5455-1). Taplinger.
Keller, Hermann. Phrasing & Articulation: A Contribution to a Rhetoric of Music. Gerdine, Leigh, tr. (Illus.). 128p. 1973. pap. 4.95 (ISBN 0-393-00681-6, N681, Norton Lib). Norton.
Korn, Richard. Orchestral Accents. facsimile ed. LC 79-156673. (Essay Index Reprint Ser). Repr. of 1956 ed. 18.00 (ISBN 0-8369-2320-0). Arno.
Matthay, Tobias. Musical Interpretation Its Laws & Principles. lib. bdg. 7.95 (ISBN 0-686-30014-9). Boston Music.
Matthay, Tobias A. Musical Interpretation, Its Laws & Principles, & Their Application in Teaching & Performing. LC 70-107820. (Select Bibliographies Reprint Ser). 1913. 13.50 (ISBN 0-8369-5191-3). Arno.
--Musical Interpretation, Its Laws & Principles, & Their Application in Teaching & Performing. Repr. of 1913 ed. lib. bdg. 15.00 (ISBN 0-8371-4277-6, MAMU). Greenwood.
Wilkinson, Charles W. How to Play Bach's 48 Preludes & Fuges. 1976. lib. bdg. 19.00 (ISBN 0-403-03814-6). Scholarly.

MUSIC–JEWS

see Bible–Music; Chants (Jewish); Jews–Liturgy and Ritual; Music, Jewish

MUSIC–JUVENILE LITERATURE

see also Composers–Juvenile Literature; Musical Instruments–Juvenile Literature; Musicians–Juvenile Literature

Boy Scouts Of America. Music & Bugling. LC 19-600. (Illus.). 48p. (gr. 6-12). 1968. pap. 0.70x (ISBN 0-8395-3336-5, 3336). BSA.
Brace, G. & Burton, I. Listen! Music & Nature. (Illus.). (gr. 5-8). 1976. pap. 5.95 (ISBN 0-521-20706-1). Cambridge U Pr.
Burkes, Joyce M. The Music Machine: Level I. LC 79-92121. (The Music Machine Bks.). (Orig.). 1981. pap. 6.95 (ISBN 0-931218-07-1). Joybug.
--The Music Machine: Level 2. LC 79-92121. (The Music Machine Bks.). (Orig.). 1981. pap. 6.95 (ISBN 0-931218-08-X). Joybug.
--The Music Machine: Primer. LC 79-92121. (The Music Machine Bks.). 20p. (Orig.). 1981. pap. 6.95 (ISBN 0-931218-06-3). Joybug.
Crane, Walter. The Baby's Opera. Date not set. 6.95 (ISBN 0-671-42551-X). Windmill Bks.
Crane, William. Oom-Pah. LC 80-18404. 204p. (gr. 5-8). 1981. PLB 9.95 (ISBN 0-689-30804-3). Atheneum.
Davis, May & Davis, Anita. All About Music. (gr. 7-10). 1977. pap. 5.25 (ISBN 0-19-314919-2). Oxford U Pr.
Edmunds, Alice. Who Puts the Grooves in the Record? LC 76-1021. (Adventures in the World of Work Ser). (Illus.). (gr. 5 up). 1977. pap. 2.50 (ISBN 0-394-83281-7, BYR). Random.
Hawkinson, John & Faulhaber, Martha. Rhythms, Music & Instruments to Make. LC 70-91737. (Activity Bks. - Music Involvement Ser.: No. 2). (Illus.). (gr. 3 up). 1970. 6.50g (ISBN 0-8075-6958-5). A Whitman.
Haywood, Carolyn. Eddie Makes Music. (Illus.). (gr. 3-7). 1957. PLB 8.40 (ISBN 0-688-31256-X). Morrow.
Kettelkamp, Larry. Drums, Rattles, & Bells. (Illus.). (gr. 3-7). 1960. PLB 7.44 (ISBN 0-688-31247-0). Morrow.
Mitchell, Don. Music Train Activity Book. (gr. k-8). 1979. 5.95 (ISBN 0-916456-58-7, GA124). Good Apple.
Moore, John Travers. Story of Silent Night. LC 65-19252. (gr. 2-3). 1965. 5.50 (ISBN 0-570-03430-2, 56-1056). Concordia.
Morse, Constance. Music & Music-Makers. facs. ed. LC 68-54363. (Essay Index Reprint Ser). 1926. 18.25 (ISBN 0-8369-0724-8). Arno.
Nelson, Esther L. Musical Games for Children of All Ages. LC 76-19804. (Illus.). (gr. 3 up). 1976. 8.95 (ISBN 0-8069-4540-0); PLB 8.29 (ISBN 0-8069-4541-9); pap. 6.95 (ISBN 0-686-77162-1). Sterling.
Preucil, Doris. Viola Part, Vol. 1. (Suzuki Viola School Ser.). 32p. (gr. k-12). 1981. pap. text ed. price not set. Summy.
--Viola Part, Vol. 2. (Suzuki Viola School Ser.). 32p. (gr. k-12). 1981. pap. text ed. price not set (ISBN 0-87487-242-1). Summy.
Pugmire, M. C. Experiences in Music for Young Children. LC 76-4304. (gr. 10-12). 1977. pap. text ed. 10.00 (ISBN 0-8273-0567-2); instructor's guide 2.00 (ISBN 0-8273-0568-0); tape cassette 5.75 (ISBN 0-8273-0566-4). Delmar.
Rattner. Enjoying the Arts: Music. LC 75-19258. (gr. 7-12). 1975. PLB 7.97 (ISBN 0-8239-0332-X). Rosen Pr.
Reeves, Harriet R. Music Today & Everyday: One Hundred & One Quick & Easy Lessons for the Elementary Classroom. LC 80-29363. 240p. 1981. 14.95 (ISBN 0-13-608273-4, Parker). P-H.
Siegmeister, Elie. Invitation to Music. LC 61-15658. (Illus.). (gr. 8-12). 1961. PLB 6.27 (ISBN 0-8178-3182-7). Harvey.
Spence, Keith. Living Music. (Illus.). (gr. 12 up). 1979. 10.95 (ISBN 0-531-03415-1). Watts.
Spencer, Cornelia. How Art & Music Speak to Us. rev. ed. LC 63-1234. (Illus.). (gr. 5-8). 1968. 7.95 (ISBN 0-381-99698-0, A35460, JD-J). Har-Row.
Surplus, Robert W. Story of Musical Organizations. LC 62-20805. (Musical Books for Young People Ser). (Illus.). (gr. 5-11). 1963. PLB 3.95 (ISBN 0-8225-0060-4). Lerner Pubns.
Tobin, J. Raymond. Inside Music: Answers to 1001 Questions. LC 68-55601. Orig. Title: Music Box One Thousand One Answers on Music. (Illus.). (gr. 9 up). 1969. 9.95 (ISBN 0-87523-170-5). Emerson.
Weissman, Jackie. All About Me: Picture Song by Miss Jackie. (Illus., Orig.). (ps-3). 1981. pap. 3.00 (ISBN 0-686-30103-X). Miss Jackie.
—Let's Be Friends: Picture Song by Miss Jackie. (Illus., Orig.). (ps-3). 1981. pap. 3.00 (ISBN 0-686-30104-8). Miss Jackie.
Wessells, K. T. The Golden Songbook. (Special Ser.). (Illus.). 48p. (ps up). 1981. 4.95 (ISBN 0-307-15811-X, Golden Pr); PLB 12.23 (ISBN 0-307-65811-2). Western Pub.
Willson, Robina B. The Voice of Music. LC 77-3225. (Illus.). 224p. (gr. 7 up). 1977. 8.95 (ISBN 0-689-50096-3, McElderry Bk). Atheneum.
Young, Percy M. A Concise History of Music. (Illus.). 210p. (gr. 7 up). 1973. 8.95 (ISBN 0-87250-445-X). D White.
Zanderbergen, Geo. Made for Music. LC 76-24208. (Spotlight Ser.). (Illus.). (gr. 4). 1976. PLB 6.45 (ISBN 0-913940-51-8). Crestwood Hse.

MUSIC–KINDERGARTEN

see Kindergarten–Music

MUSIC–MANUALS, TEXT-BOOKS, ETC.

Anderson, Paul G. Brass Solo & Study Guide. 15.00 (ISBN 0-686-15889-X). Instrumental Co.

Barbour, Harriot B. & Freeman, Warren S. Story of Music. rev. ed. (Illus.). (gr. 7-9). text ed. 11.00 (ISBN 0-87487-033-X). Summy.

Beall, Gretchen H. Music As Experience: Structure & Sequence for the Elementary School. 403p. 1980. plastic comb bdg. (ISBN 0-697-03444-5). Wm C Brown.

Bockmon, Guy A. & Starr, William J. Scored for Listening: A Guide to Music. 2nd ed. (Illus., Orig.). 1972. pap. text ed. 12.95 (ISBN 0-15-579055-2, HC). HarBraceJ.

Busby, Thomas. A Grammar of Music. LC 76-20711. (Music Reprint Ser). 1976. Repr. of 1818 ed. lib. bdg. 35.00 (ISBN 0-306-70789-6). Da Capo.

Cooper, Grosvenor. Learning to Listen: A Handbook for Music. LC 57-8579. 1962. pap. 3.75 (ISBN 0-226-11519-4, P79, Phoen). U of Chicago Pr.

Csida, Joseph. The Music-Record Career Handbook. rev. ed. 360p. 1980. 16.95 (ISBN 0-8230-7581-8). Watson-Guptill.

Dallin, Leon. Listeners Guide to Musical Understanding. 4th ed. 416p. 1977. pap. text ed. write for info. (ISBN 0-697-03437-2); wkbk. avail. (ISBN 0-697-03438-0); recordings avail. (ISBN 0-697-03439-9); tchrs.' manual & key avail. (ISBN 0-686-67596-7). Wm C Brown.

Darazs, Arpad & Jay, Stephen. Sight & Sound: Teachers' Manual. LC 64-25360. 1965. 6.50 (ISBN 0-913932-02-7). Boosey & Hawkes.

De Vito, Albert. Fake It for All Keyboard Instruments. LC 75-40687. 1976. 5.00 (ISBN 0-934286-05-1). Kenyon.

--Playing the Chord Organ & Learning to Read Music. 1974. 3.95 (ISBN 0-934286-08-6). Kenyon.

--Pocket Dictionary of Music Terms. LC 65-8450. 1965. 1.00 (ISBN 0-934286-09-4). Kenyon.

Forcucci, Samuel L. Let There Be Music. new ed. (gr. 9-12). 1973. text ed. 14.40 (ISBN 0-205-03768-2, 5837685); tchrs'. guide 2.40 (ISBN 0-205-03794-1, 5837944). Allyn.

Fotine, Larry. Contemporary Musician's Handbook & Dictionary. (Illus.). 1981. softcover 10.00 (ISBN 0-933830-03-3). Poly Tone.

Horacek, Leo & Lefkoff, Gerald. Programed Ear Training. Incl. Vol. 1. Intervals. 146p. pap. text ed. 6.95 (ISBN 0-15-572015-5, HC); 18 tapes 100.00 (ISBN 0-15-572019-8, HC); Vol. 2. Melody & Rhythm. 392p. pap. text ed. 9.50 (ISBN 0-15-572016-3, HC); 25 tapes 125.00 (ISBN 0-15-572020-1, HC); Vol. 3. Chords, Part 1. 276p. pap. text ed. 7.50 (ISBN 0-15-572017-1, HC); 14 tapes 75.00 (ISBN 0-685-24342-7, HC); Vol. 4. Chords, Part 2. 392p. pap. text ed. 8.95 (ISBN 0-15-572018-X, HC); 18 tapes 100.00 (ISBN 0-15-572022-8, HC). (Prog. Bk.). 1970. instructors' manual avail. (ISBN 0-15-572023-6, HC); tests avail. (ISBN 0-15-572024-4, HC). HarBraceJ.

Ivey, Donald. Sound Pleasure: A Prelude to Active Listening. LC 75-30287. (Illus., Orig.). 1977. pap. text ed. 12.95 (ISBN 0-02-870900-4); record package 12.95 (ISBN 0-02-870870-9). Schirmer Bks.

Janes, William H. Masonic Musical Manual. 1969. pap. 3.00 (ISBN 0-685-88799-5, M-44). Macoy Pub.

John, Robert W. & Nordholm, Harriet. Learning Music: Musicianship for the Elementary Classroom Teacher. LC 70-91237. 1970. pap. text ed. 10.95 (ISBN 0-13-527085-5). P-H.

Kohs, Ellis B. Music Theory: A Syllabus for Teacher & Student, 2 Vols. 1961. pap. 6.95x ea. Vol. 1 (ISBN 0-19-500935-5). Vol. 2 (ISBN 0-19-500936-3). Oxford U Pr.

Lindsay, Charles, Jr. Music Blank Book. 112p. 1981. pap. 4.95 (ISBN 0-8256-3254-4, Quick Fox). Music Sales.

Longy-Miquelle, Renee. Principles of Musical Theory. 1925. 5.00 (ISBN 0-911318-06-2). E C Schirmer.

Note: A Handbook of Classroom Ideas to Motivate the Teaching of Elementary Music. (The Spice Ser). 1973. 6.50 (ISBN 0-89273-113-3). Educ Serv.

Nye, Robert E. & Nye, Vernice T. Essentials of Teaching Elementary School Music. (Illus.). 288p. 1974. 16.95 (ISBN 0-13-289280-4); pap. 12.95 (ISBN 0-13-289272-3). P-H.

Osbeck, Kenneth W. My Music Workbook. 120p. 1981. pap. 4.95 (ISBN 0-8254-3415-7). Kregel.

Playford, John & Purcell, Henry. An Introduction to the Skill of Musick. LC 67-27551. (Music Reprint Ser.). 282p. 1972. Repr. of 1694 ed. lib. bdg. 29.50 (ISBN 0-306-70937-6). Da Capo.

Swan, Alfred J. The Music Director's Guide to Musical Literature for Voices & Instruments. LC 70-181274. 164p. 1941. Repr. 19.00 (ISBN 0-403-01697-5). Scholarly.

Whitlock, John B. Music Handbook. LC 72-6832. 183p. 1972. text ed. 29.50x (ISBN 0-8422-5023-9); pap. text ed. 12.50x (ISBN 0-8422-0247-1). Irvington.

Whittall, Arnold. Schoenberg Chamber Music. LC 72-549. (BBC Music Guide Ser.: No. 21). (Illus.). 64p. (Orig.). 1972. pap. 1.95 (ISBN 0-295-95248-2). U of Wash Pr.

Wingell. Experiencing Music. LC 80-26637. 476p. 1981. 15.95 (ISBN 0-88284-116-5); instr's. manual free (ISBN 0-88284-131-9); wkbk. 4.95 (ISBN 0-88284-117-3); record set 30.00 (ISBN 0-88284-132-7). Alfred Pub.

Wink, Richard. Fundamentals of Music. LC 76-20867. (Illus.). 1977. pap. text ed. 14.50 (ISBN 0-395-20598-0). HM.

MUSIC–MANUSCRIPTS

Baxter, James H. An Old St. Andrews Music Book. facsimile ed. LC 70-178515. Repr. of 1931 ed. 27.50 (ISBN 0-404-56525-5). AMS Pr.

Beck, Jean & Beck, Louise, eds. Les Chansonniers des Troubadours et des Trouveres publies par Jean Beck, 4 vols. Incl. Chansonnier Cange, 2 vols. Repr. of 1927 ed (ISBN 0-8450-0002-0); Manuscrit du Roi, 2 vols. Repr. of 1938 ed (ISBN 0-8450-0003-9). (Illus., Fr.). 1964. 370.00x set (ISBN 0-8450-0005-5); 185.00x ea. Broude.

Beethoven, Ludwig Von. Complete String Quartets & Grosse Fuge: From the Breitkopf & Hartel Complete Works Edition. 10.00 (ISBN 0-8446-0028-8). Peter Smith.

--Piano Sonata No. 32 in C Minor, Op. III: Reproduction of the Autograph Manuscript. 7.50 (ISBN 0-8446-0482-8). Peter Smith.

Catalog of Printed Music in the British Museum: Music in the Hirsch Library. 1976. Repr. of 1951 ed. lib. bdg. 49.00 (ISBN 0-403-03789-1). Scholarly.

Catalogue of Printed Music in the British Library to 1980, 62 vols. 1980. Set. 13,700.00 (ISBN 0-85157-900-0, Dist. by Gale Research Co.). K G Saur.

Chansonnier D'Arras, Reproduction En Phototypie. 1925. 28.00 (ISBN 0-384-08465-6); pap. 23.00 (ISBN 0-384-08475-3). Johnson Repr.

De Coussemaker, C. E. Catalogue des livres, manuscrits et instruments de musique. (Auction Catalogues of Music Ser.: Vol. 4). 1976. Repr. of 1877 ed. wrappers 45.00 (ISBN 90-6027-198-X, Pub. by Frits Knuf Netherlands). Pendragon NY.

De La Fage, Adrien. Essais de Diptherographie musicale ou notices, descriptions, analyses, extraits et reproductions de manuscrits relatifs a la pratique, a la theorie et a l'histoire de la musique. 1964. Repr. of 1864 ed. 62.50 (ISBN 90-6027-006-1, Pub. by Frits Knuf Netherlands). Pendragon NY.

Duckles, Vincent & Elmer, Minnie. Thematic Catalog of a Manuscript Collection of Eighteenth-Century Italian Instrumental Music in the University of California, Berkeley, Music Library. LC 63-16571. 1963. 28.75x (ISBN 0-520-00361-6). U of Cal Pr.

Eckhard, Jacob. Jacob Eckhard's Choirmaster's Book of 1809. Williams, George W., ed. LC 72-149489. (Illus.). 1971. 27.50x (ISBN 0-87249-215-X). U of SC Pr.

Eitner, Robert. Das Deutsche Lied Des XV und XVI Jahrhunderts, 2 vols. in 1. LC 71-178529. Repr. of 1876 ed. 37.50 (ISBN 0-404-56542-5). AMS Pr.

Fraenkel, G. S. Decorative Music Title Pages: 201 Examples from 1500 to 1800. (Illus.). 8.00 (ISBN 0-8446-2079-3). Peter Smith.

Gostling, John, compiled by. Gostling Manuscript. LC 77-1563. 442p. 1977. text ed. 35.00x (ISBN 0-292-72713-5). U of Tex Pr.

Haberlen, John & Rosolack, Stephen. Elizabethan Madrigal Dinners: Scripts, with Music for Singers, Players, & Dancers. LC 78-70082. 1978. pap. 15.95 (ISBN 0-916656-09-8); wire bdg. 16.95 (ISBN 0-916656-12-8). Mark Foster Mus.

Hammerich, Angul. Mediaeval Musical Relics of Denmark. LC 74-24104. Repr. of 1912 ed. 24.50 (ISBN 0-404-12952-8). AMS Pr.

Handlist of Music Manuscripts Acquired Nineteen-Eight - Nineteen Sixty-Seven. 1981. 12.00x (ISBN 0-7141-0463-9, Pub. by Brit Lib England). State Mutual Bk.

Kirkpatrick, Ralph, ed. Domenico Scarlatti, 18 vols. 2684p. 1971. 385.00 set (ISBN 0-384-29519-3); per volume 23.00 (ISBN 0-686-66721-2). Johnson Repr.

Lowinsky, Edward, ed. Medici Codex of 1518. LC 67-13810. (Monuments of Renaissance Music Ser: Vols. 1, 2 & 3). 1968. Vol. 1, No. 3. 37.00x (ISBN 0-226-49480-2); Vol. 2, No. 4. 47.00x (ISBN 0-226-49481-0); Vol. 3, No. 5. 37.00x (ISBN 0-226-49482-9). U of Chicago Pr.

Mozart, Wolfgang A. Eine Kleine Nachtmusik: Reproduction of the Autograph Manuscript. 525p. 8.00 (ISBN 0-8446-0812-2). Peter Smith.

Petrucci, Ottaviano. Canti C No Cento Cinquanta. (Monuments of Music & Music Literature in Facsimile Ser I: Vol. 25). (Illus.). 1977. Repr. of 1504 ed. 47.50x (ISBN 0-8450-2025-0). Broude.

Pope, Isabel & Kanazawa, Masakata, eds. The Musical Manuscript Montecassino 871: A Neapolitan Repertory of Sacred & Secular Music. (Illus.). 1979. 79.00x (ISBN 0-19-816132-8). Oxford U Pr.

Riano, J. F. Critical & Biographical Notes on Early Spanish Music. LC 79-158958. (Music Ser). 1971. Repr. of 1887 ed. lib. bdg. 19.50 (ISBN 0-306-70193-6). Da Capo.

Silbiger, Alexander. Italian Manuscript Sources of Seventeenth Century Keyboard Music. Buelow, George, ed. (Studies in Musicology: No. 18). 1980. 34.95x (ISBN 0-8357-1075-0, Pub. by UMI Res Pr). Univ Microfilms.

Williams, Ken J. Music Preparation: A Guide to Music Copying. LC 79-56140. (Illus.). 149p. 1980. pap. text ed. 16.75 (ISBN 0-9603742-0-5). K J Williams Pubns.

Young, Phillip. The Look of Music: Vancouver Centennial Museum. pap. 16.95 (ISBN 0-686-75604-5). U of Wash Pr.

MUSIC–MISCELLANEA

Cage, John. For the Birds. 320p. 1981. 20.00 (ISBN 0-7145-2690-8, Pub. by M. Boyars). Merrimack Bk Serv.

Carter, Roy. Classical Music Quiz with Richard Baker. LC 80-67581. 128p. 1980. 11.95 (ISBN 0-7153-7819-8). David & Charles.

Chapman, Gary & Bryant, Steven, eds. Melodic Index to Haydn's Instrumental Music: A Thematic Locator for the Hoboken Thematisch-Bibliographisches Werkverzeichnis, Vols. I & II. 120p. 1981. lib. bdg. price not set (ISBN 0-918728-19-3). Pendragon NY.

Great Rock, Pop & Soul Quiz. (Illus.). 256p. 1981. 5.95 (ISBN 0-686-31190-6, 3002). Playmore & Prestige.

Jacobs, Ben, ed. Musica: The First Guide to Classical Music on U. S. & Canadian Radio Stations. LC 76-18472. 1978. pap. 4.95 (ISBN 0-9600964-3-4). Musica.

Murphy, James F. Music: Advanced Test for the G. R. E. LC 73-83716. (Orig.). 1974. pap. 3.95 (ISBN 0-668-01471-7). Arco.

Nelson, Esther L. Musical Games for Children of All Ages. (Illus.). 72p. (gr. k-6). 1981. pap. 6.95 spiral (ISBN 0-8069-7520-2). Sterling.

Ray, Robin. Robin Ray's Music Quiz. 1978. 13.50 (ISBN 0-7134-1492-8, Pub. by Batsford England). David & Charles.

Tobin, J. Raymond. Inside Music: Answers to 1001 Questions. LC 68-55601. Orig. Title: Music Box One Thousand One Answers on Music. (Illus.). (gr. 9 up). 1969. 9.95 (ISBN 0-87523-170-5). Emerson.

Tudor, Dean, et al. Annual Index to Popular Music Record Reviews 1976. LC 73-8909. 1977. 25.00 (ISBN 0-8108-1070-0). Scarecrow.

MUSIC–MODES

see Musical Intervals and Scales

MUSIC–NOTATION

see Musical Notation

MUSIC–NURSERY SCHOOLS

see Nursery Schools–Music

MUSIC–PERFORMANCE

see also Concerts; Conducting; Dance Orchestras; Improvisation (Music); Music–Interpretation (Phrasing, Dynamics, etc.)

Boretz, Benjamin & Cone, Edward T., eds. Perspectives on Notation & Performance. (Illus.). 1976. 10.00x (ISBN 0-393-02190-4, Norton Lib); pap. 3.95 (ISBN 0-393-00809-6). Norton.

Crocker, Richard L. History of Musical Style. (Music Ser). 1966. text ed. 19.95 (ISBN 0-07-013850-8, C). McGraw.

Daniels, Elva S. Performing for Others. (Classroom Music Enrichment Units Ser.). 1974. pap. 5.95x (ISBN 0-87628-215-X). Ctr Appl Res.

Dart, Thurston. Interpretation of Music. pap. 3.50 (ISBN 0-06-090025-3, CN25, CN). Har-Row.

--Interpretation of Music. 1975. Repr. of 1967 ed. pap. text ed. 9.25x (ISBN 0-09-031683-5, Hutchinson U Lib). Humanities.

Donington, Robert. The Interpretation of Early Music. rev. ed. LC 73-81205. 1974. 39.95 (ISBN 0-312-42420-5). St Martin.

--A Performer's Guide to Baroque Music. LC 72-3659. (Illus.). 320p. 1974. 20.00 (ISBN 0-684-13155-2, ScribT). Scribner.

Dorian, Frederick. History of Music in Performance. (Illus.). 1966. pap. 2.95 (ISBN 0-393-00369-8, Norton Lib). Norton.

Grosbayne, Benjamin. Techniques of Modern Orchestral Conducting. rev. ed. LC 78-184105. (Illus.). 215p. 1973. 18.50x (ISBN 0-674-87226-6). Harvard U Pr.

Johnson, H. Earle. First Performances in America to Nineteen Hundred. LC 75-23554. (Bibliographies in American Music: No. 4). 1979. 20.00 (ISBN 0-911772-64-2). Info Coord.

Liggett, Clayton E. Theatre Student: Concert Theatre. LC 72-104705. (Illus.). (gr. 9 up). 1970. PLB 7.97 (ISBN 0-8239-0194-7). Rosen Pr.

MacClintock, Carol, ed. Readings in the History of Music in Performance. LC 78-9511. (Illus.). 448p. 1979. 19.50x (ISBN 0-253-14495-7). Ind U Pr.

McLeod, Norman & Herndon, Marcia. The Ethnography of Musical Performance. 212p. 1980. lib. bdg. 18.50 (ISBN 0-8482-4416-8). Norwood Edns.

Nettl, Bruno & Foltin, Bela. Daramad of Chahargah: A Study in the Performance Practice of Persian Music. LC 74-175174. (Detroit Monographs in Musicology: No. 2). 84p. 1972. pap. 2.00 (ISBN 0-911772-51-0). Info Coord.

Ottman, Robert W. & Mainous, Frank D. Rudiments of Music. 1970. pap. text ed. 15.95 (ISBN 0-13-783662-7). P-H.

Schnabel, Artur. Music & the Line of Most Resistance. LC 69-12690. (Music Ser). 1969. Repr. of 1942 ed. lib. bdg. 15.00 (ISBN 0-306-71224-5). Da Capo.

MUSIC–PERIODICALS

Dwight, John S. Dwight's Journal of Music, 21 Vols. 1852-1881. Set. 850.00 (ISBN 0-384-13545-5). Johnson Repr.

Negro Music Journal. Negro Music Journal: Devoted to the Education Interest of the Negro in Music, Vol. 1-2. 1902-1903. Repr. 33.00x (ISBN 0-8371-9118-1, Pub. by Negro U Pr). Greenwood.

Tovey, Donald F. Musical Articles from the Encyclopedia Britannica. LC 79-181279. 251p. 1944. Repr. 21.00 (ISBN 0-403-01702-5). Scholarly.

MUSIC–PERIODICALS–INDEXES

Blom, Eric. A General Index to Modern Musical Literature in the English Language: Including Periodicals for the Years 1915-1926. LC 71-108736. (Music Ser). 1970. Repr. of 1927 ed. lib. bdg. 17.50 (ISBN 0-306-71898-7). Da Capo.

Farish, Margaret K., ed. String Music in Print. 2nd ed. LC 80-18425. (Music in Print Ser.: Vol. 6). 464p. 1980. Repr. lib. bdg. 69.00 (ISBN 0-88478-011-2). Musicdata.

Goodkind, Herbert K., compiled by. Cumulative Index 1915-1959 to the Musical Quarterly. LC 16-24484. 1960. pap. 40.00x (ISBN 0-9600498-2-7); pap. 50.00x with 1960-64 supplement (ISBN 0-9600498-3-5). H K Goodkind.

Tudor, Dean & Armitage, Andrew. Popular Music Periodicals Index, 1974. LC 74-11578. 1975. 18.00 (ISBN 0-8108-0867-6). Scarecrow.

MUSIC–PHILOSOPHY AND ESTHETICS

see also Classicism in Music; Romanticism in Music; Style, Musical; Symbolism in Music

Adorno, Theodor W. Philosophy of Modern Music. rev. ed. 233p. 1980. pap. 7.95 (ISBN 0-8164-9012-0). Continuum.

Aristotle. On the Art of Poetry. Bywater, Ingram, tr. 1920. pap. 4.50 (ISBN 0-19-814110-6). Oxford U Pr.

Barford, Philip. Keyboard Music of C.P.E. Bach. 1966. 10.00 (ISBN 0-8079-0072-9). October.

Bekker, Paul. Richard Wagner: His Life in His Work. facsimile ed. Bozman, M. M., tr. LC 70-107792. (Select Bibliographies Reprint Ser). 1931. 29.00 (ISBN 0-8369-5176-X). Arno.

Blom, Eric. The Limitations of Music: A Study in Aesthetics. LC 72-80139. Repr. of 1928 ed. 12.00 (ISBN 0-405-08275-4, Blom Pubns). Arno.

--The Limitations of Music: A Study of Aesthetics. 1976. Repr. of 1928 ed. 25.00 (ISBN 0-685-71323-7, Regency). Scholarly.

Chastellux, Francois J. Essay on Public Happiness, 2 Vols. LC 67-29497. Repr. of 1774 ed. Set. 37.50x (ISBN 0-678-00557-5). Kelley.

Coker, W. Music & Meaning. LC 72-142358. 1972. 12.95 (ISBN 0-02-906350-7). Free Pr.

Cone, Edward T. Musical Form & Musical Performance. LC 68-11157. (Illus.). 1968. pap. 4.95x (ISBN 0-393-09767-6). Norton.

Cooke, Deryck. Language of Music. 1959. pap. 11.50x (ISBN 0-19-284004-5, OPB). Oxford U Pr.

Corner, Philip. I Can Walk Through the World As Music, Pt. 1. 1980. 19.95 (ISBN 0-914162-18-7); pap. 4.00 (ISBN 0-914162-19-5). Printed Edns.

Debussy, Claude, et al. Three Classics in the Aesthetic of Music. pap. 3.25 (ISBN 0-486-20320-4). Dover.

Dent, E. J. The Future of Music. 1966. pap. 5.75 (ISBN 0-08-011354-0). Pergamon.

Donington, Robert. Wagner's 'Ring' & Its Symbols. 3rd ed. (Illus.). 342p. 1974. pap. 8.95 (ISBN 0-571-04818-8, Pub. by Faber & Faber). Merrimack Bk Serv.

Dunwell, Wilfred. Music & European Mind. lib. bdg. 25.00 (ISBN 0-685-95456-0). Scholarly.

Einstein, Alfred. Greatness in Music. LC 76-6984. 1976. pap. 6.95 (ISBN 0-306-80046-2). Da Capo.

Ferguson, Donald N. Music As Metaphor: The Elements of Expression. LC 73-9210. (Illus.). 198p. 1973. Repr. of 1960 ed. lib. bdg. 15.00x (ISBN 0-8371-6981-X, FEMM). Greenwood.
Graf, Max. From Beethoven to Shostakovich: The Psychology of the Composing Process. LC 73-94607. Repr. of 1947 ed. lib. bdg. 17.25x (ISBN 0-8371-2452-2, GRBS). Greenwood.
Hadow, W. H. Studies in Modern Music, 2 Vols. LC 75-102839. (Illus.). 1970. Repr. of 1926 ed. Set. 27.50 (ISBN 0-8046-0755-9). Kennikat.
Hand, Ferdinand. Aesthetics of Musical Art. 1976. lib. bdg. 25.00 (ISBN 0-403-03769-7). Scholarly.
Hanslick, Eduard. The Beautiful in Music: A Contribution to the Revisal of Musical Aesthetics. rev. ed. Cohen, Gustav, tr. LC 74-1362. (Music Ser.). 174p. 1974. Repr. of 1891 ed. lib. bdg. 19.50 (ISBN 0-306-70649-0). Da Capo.
Hastings, Thomas. Dissertation on Musical Taste. LC 6-18360. (American Studies). 1968. Repr. of 1853 ed. 19.50 (ISBN 0-384-21750-8). Johnson Repr.
--Dissertation on Musical Taste. LC 68-16237. (Music Ser.). 228p. 1974. Repr. of 1822 ed. lib. bdg. 22.50 (ISBN 0-306-71085-4). Da Capo.
Henderson, William J. What Is Good Music? LC 72-2485. (Select Bibliography Reprint Ser). 1972. Repr. of 1898 ed. 16.00 (ISBN 0-8369-6857-3). Arno.
Hughes, Charles W. Human Side of Music. LC 70-107871. (Music Ser). 1970. Repr. of 1948 ed. lib. bdg. 32.50 (ISBN 0-306-71895-2). Da Capo.
Lambert, Constant. Music Ho. 1967. 7.95 (ISBN 0-8079-0086-9). October.
Le Huray, Peter & Day, James. Music & Aesthetics in the Eighteenth & Early Nineteenth Centuries. (Cambridge Studies in Music: Readings in the Literature of Music). (Illus.). 700p. Date not set. 69.50 (ISBN 0-521-23426-3). Cambridge U Pr.
Lippman, Edward A. A Humanistic Philosophy of Music. LC 76-44573. 1977. 21.50x (ISBN 0-8147-4973-9). NYU Pr.
McClain, Ernest G. The Myth of Invariance: The Origin of the Gods, Mathematics & Music from the Rg Veda to Plato. LC 76-28411. 1976. 10.00 (ISBN 0-89254-003-6). Nicolas-Hays.
Meyer, Leonard B. Emotion & Meaning in Music. LC 56-9130. 1961. pap. 4.50 (ISBN 0-226-52139-7, P56, Phoen). U of Chicago Pr.
--Music, the Arts, & Ideas. LC 67-25515. 1967. 12.50x (ISBN 0-226-52140-0). U of Chicago Pr.
--Music, the Arts, & Ideas. LC 67-25515. 1969. pap. 6.95 (ISBN 0-226-52141-9, P336, Phoen). U of Chicago Pr.
Nietzsche, Friedrich. The Birth of Tragedy. Kaufmann, Walter, tr. Bd. with The Case of Wagner. (Orig.). 1967. pap. 2.95 (ISBN 0-394-70369-3, Vin). Random.
Opper, Jacob. Science & the Arts: A Study in Relationships from 1600-1900. LC 70-178042. 226p. 1973. 12.00 (ISBN 0-8386-1054-4). Fairleigh Dickinson.
Pelmont, R. A. Paul Valery et les Beaux-Arts. 1949. pap. 12.00 (ISBN 0-527-01121-5). Kraus Repr.
Perry, Rosalie S. Charles Ives & the American Mind. LC 74-620003. (Illus.). 200p. 1974. 9.50x (ISBN 0-87338-152-1). Kent St U Pr.
Portnoy, Julius. Music in the Life of Man. LC 73-9265. (Illus.). 300p. 1973. Repr. of 1963 ed. lib. bdg. 18.25x (ISBN 0-8371-7000-1, POMU). Greenwood.
--The Philosopher & Music. (Music Reprint Ser.: 1980). 1980. Repr. of 1954 ed. lib. bdg. 25.00 (ISBN 0-306-76006-1). Da Capo.
Reimer, Bennett. Philosophy of Music Education. (Contemporary Perspectives in Music Education Ser). 1970. pap. text ed. 10.95 (ISBN 0-13-663872-4). P-H.
Schafer, R. Murray. The Tuning of the World. 1977. 12.95 (ISBN 0-394-40966-3). Knopf.
Schnabel, Artur. Music & the Line of Most Resistance. LC 69-12690. (Music Ser). 1969. Repr. of 1942 ed. lib. bdg. 15.00 (ISBN 0-306-71224-5). Da Capo.
Singer, Irving. Mozart & Beethoven: The Concept of Love in Their Operas. LC 77-4551. 1977. text ed. 12.00x (ISBN 0-8018-1987-3). Johns Hopkins.
Weber, Max. Rational & Social Foundations of Music. Martindale, Don, et al, trs. LC 56-12134. (Arcturus Books Paperbacks). 1969. pap. 6.95 (ISBN 0-8093-0355-8). S Ill U Pr.
Xenakis, Iannis. Formalized Music: Thought & Mathematics in Composition. LC 76-135017. (Illus.). 288p. 1971. 15.00x (ISBN 0-253-32378-9). Ind U Pr.

MUSIC–PHRASING, DYNAMICS, ETC.
see Music–Interpretation (Phrasing, Dynamics, etc.)

MUSIC–PHYSIOLOGICAL ASPECTS
see also Hearing; Music, Influence Of; Music Therapy; Voice
Benade, Arthur H. Horns, Strings, & Harmony. LC 78-25707. (Illus.). 1979. Repr. of 1960 ed. lib. bdg. 19.75x (ISBN 0-313-20771-2, BEHO). Greenwood.
Christianson, Helen M. Bodily Rhythmic Movements of Young Children in Relation to Rhythm in Music. LC 74-176644. (Columbia University. Teachers College. Contributions to Education: No. 736). Repr. of 1938 ed. 17.50 (ISBN 0-404-55736-8). AMS Pr.
Critchley, Macdonald & Henson, R. A. Music & the Brain: Studies in the Neurology of Music. (Illus.). 476p. 1977. 37.50 (ISBN 0-398-03653-5). C C Thomas.
Gutheil, Emil. Music & Your Emotions. new ed. LC 75-131283. 1970. pap. 4.95 (ISBN 0-87140-529-6). Liveright.
Helmholtz, Hermann L. On the Sensations of Tone. 1954. pap. 7.50 (ISBN 0-486-60753-4). Dover.
Howes, Frank S. Man, Mind & Music. LC 70-181179. 184p. 1948. Repr. 12.00 (ISBN 0-403-01582-0). Scholarly.
Retallack, Dorothy. The Sound of Music & Plants. (Illus.). 96p. 1973. pap. 3.00 (ISBN 0-87516-170-7). De Vorss.
Stebbing, L. Music & Healing. 1973. lib. bdg. 59.95 (ISBN 0-87968-555-7). Krishna Pr.

MUSIC–POETRY
Anderson, Erland. Harmonious Madness: A Study of Musical Metaphors in the Poetry of Coleridge, Shelley & Keats. (Salzburg Studies in English Literature, Romantic Reassessment Ser.: No. 12). 321p. 1975. pap. text ed. 25.00x (ISBN 0-391-01299-1). Humanities.
Brun, Herbert & Gaburo, Kenneth. Collaboration One. 24p. 1976. soft cover saddle-stitched 15.00 (ISBN 0-939044-10-2). Lingua Pr.
Naylor, Edward W. The Poets & Music. (Music Ser.). 1980. Repr. of 1928 ed. 19.50 (ISBN 0-306-76038-X). Da Capo.
Stravinsky, Igor. Poetics of Music in the Form of Six Lessons. LC 79-99520. (Charles Eliot Norton Lectures Ser: 1939-1940). (Fr. & Eng.). 1970. 9.00x (ISBN 0-674-67855-9); pap. 2.95 (ISBN 0-674-67856-7). Harvard U Pr.

MUSIC–PROGRAMMED INSTRUCTION
Ashford, Theodore H. A Programmed Introduction to the Fundamentals of Music. 3rd ed. 1980. pap. text ed. write for info. (ISBN 0-697-03440-2). Wm C Brown.
Ottman, Robert & Mainous, Frank. Programmed Rudiments of Music. 1979. pap. 15.95 (ISBN 0-13-729962-1). P-H.
Regelski, Thomas A. Principles & Problems of Music Education. (Illus.). 328p. 1975. ref. ed. o.p. 16.95 (ISBN 0-13-709840-5); pap. 14.95 ref. ed. (ISBN 0-13-709832-4). P-H.
Wingell. Experiencing Music. LC 80-26637. 476p. 1981. 15.95 (ISBN 0-88284-116-5); instr's. manual free (ISBN 0-88284-131-9); wkbk. 4.95 (ISBN 0-88284-117-3); record set 30.00 (ISBN 0-88284-132-7). Alfred Pub.
Worthing, Michelle G. Elements of Music: A Programmed Approach. 250p. 1978. pap. text ed. write for info. plastic comb (ISBN 0-697-03414-3). Wm C Brown.

MUSIC–PSYCHOLOGY
see also Musical Ability–Testing; Music Therapy; Symbolism in Music; Time Perception
Bayless, Kathleen M. & Ramsey, Marjorie E. Music: A Way of Life for the Young Child. LC 77-14310. (Illus.). 1978. pap. text ed. 12.95 (ISBN 0-8016-0515-6). Mosby.
Buck, Percy C. Psychology for Musicians. 1944. pap. 8.75x (ISBN 0-19-311914-5). Oxford U Pr.
Critchley, Macdonald & Henson, R. A. Music & the Brain: Studies in the Neurology of Music. (Illus.). 476p. 1977. 37.50 (ISBN 0-398-03653-5). C C Thomas.
Davies, John B. The Psychology of Music. LC 77-92339. (Illus.). 1978. 13.95x (ISBN 0-8047-0980-7); pap. 4.95 (ISBN 0-8047-1057-0, SP-158). Stanford U Pr.
Dorian, Frederick. Musical Workshop. LC 77-138109. (Illus.). 1971. Repr. of 1947 ed. lib. bdg. 17.75x (ISBN 0-8371-5685-8, DOMW). Greenwood.
Farnsworth, Paul R. Social Psychology of Music. 2nd ed. 1969. 12.95x (ISBN 0-8138-1547-9). Iowa St U Pr.
Gordon, Edwin, ed. & intro. by. Experimental Research in the Psychology of Music. LC 73-632181. (Studies in the Psychology of Music Ser.: Vol. 10). (Illus.). 192p. 1975. text ed. 15.00x (ISBN 0-87745-052-8). U of Iowa Pr.
Gordon, Edwin, ed. Experimental Research in the Psychology of Music, Vols. 6-9. Incl. Vol. 6. LC 73-632181. 1970. 4.75x (ISBN 0-87745-018-8); Vol. 7. LC 73-632181. 1971. 6.95x (ISBN 0-87745-024-2); Vol. 8. LC 73-632181. 1972. 7.95x (ISBN 0-87745-034-X); Vol. 9. LC 73-632181. 1974. text ed. 15.00x (ISBN 0-87745-048-X). (Studies in the Psychology of Music Ser). U of Iowa Pr.
Graf, Max. From Beethoven to Shostakovich: The Psychology of the Composing Process. LC 73-94607. Repr. of 1947 ed. lib. bdg. 17.25x (ISBN 0-8371-2452-2, GRBS). Greenwood.
Lipps, Theodor. Psychological Studies. 2nd ed. LC 73-2972. (Classics in Psychology Ser.). Repr. of 1926 ed. 17.00 (ISBN 0-405-05145-X). Arno.
Lundin, Robert W. An Objective Psychology of Music. 2nd ed. 1967. 17.95x (ISBN 0-8260-5600-8). Wiley.
Mackinnon, Lillias. Music by Heart. LC 80-26551. xi, 141p. 1981. Repr. of 1954 ed. lib. bdg. 17.50x (ISBN 0-313-22810-8, MAMB). Greenwood.
Meyer, Leonard B. Emotion & Meaning in Music. LC 56-9130. 1961. pap. 4.50 (ISBN 0-226-52139-7, P56, Phoen). U of Chicago Pr.
Moog, Helmut. The Musical Experience of the Pre-School Child. Clarke, Claudia, tr. from Ger. 1976. pap. 7.00 (ISBN 0-901938-06-8, 75-A11154). Eur-Am Music.
Mursell, James. Psychology of Music. lib. bdg. 15.00 (ISBN 0-403-01750-5). Scholarly.
Mursell, James L. The Psychology of Music. LC 37-28429. (Music - Practice & Theory Ser). 1970. Repr. of 1937 ed. 21.00 (ISBN 0-384-40680-7). Johnson Repr.
--The Psychology of Music. LC 77-110274. (Illus.). 389p. Repr. of 1937 ed. lib. bdg. 29.75x (ISBN 0-8371-4500-7, MUPM). Greenwood.
Radocy, Rudolf E. & Boyle, J. David. Psychological Foundations of Musical Behavior. (Illus.). 360p. 1979. text ed. 25.75 (ISBN 0-398-03841-4). C C Thomas.
Revesz, Geza. The Psychology of a Musical Prodigy. (Psychology Ser). 1970. Repr. of 1925 ed. 15.50 (ISBN 0-384-50360-8). Johnson Repr.
--Psychology of a Musical Prodigy. Repr. of 1925 ed. lib. bdg. 15.00x (ISBN 0-8371-4004-8, REMP). Greenwood.
--The Psychology of a Musical Prodigy. LC 77-173178. (Illus.). Repr. of 1925 ed. 12.75 (ISBN 0-405-08879-5). Arno.
Schoen, Max. The Psychology of Music: A Survey for Teacher & Musician. LC 73-181248. 258p. 1940. Repr. 23.00 (ISBN 0-403-01673-8). Scholarly.
Schoen, Max, ed. Effects of Music: A Series of Essays: International Lib. of Psychology, Philosophy, & Scientific Method. facs. ed. LC 68-20330. (Essay Index Reprint Ser). 1927. 18.00 (ISBN 0-8369-0854-6). Arno.
Seashore, Carl E. In Search of Beauty in Music: A Scientific Approach to Musical Esthetics. LC 80-25447. (Illus.). xvi, 389p. 1981. Repr. of 1947 ed. lib. bdg. 29.50x (ISBN 0-313-22758-6, SEIS). Greenwood.
--Psychology of Music. (Illus.). 9.00 (ISBN 0-8446-2898-0). Peter Smith.
--Psychology of Music. pap. 5.00 (ISBN 0-486-21851-1). Dover.
Sessions, Roger. Musical Experience of Composer, Performer, Listener. 1971. 12.50x (ISBN 0-691-09116-1); pap. 4.95 (ISBN 0-691-02703-X). Princeton U Pr.
Sudnow, David. Talk's Body: A Meditation Between Two Keyboards. 128p. 1980. pap. 3.95 (ISBN 0-14-005700-5). Penguin.
Van Alstyn, E. Dorothy & Osborne, E. Rhythmic Response of Negro & White Children Two to Six. (SRCD: Vol. 2, No.4). 1937. pap. 4.00 (ISBN 0-527-01497-4). Kraus Repr.
Watkins, John G. Objective Measurement of Instrumental Performance. LC 77-177658. (Columbia University. Teachers College. Contributions to Education: No. 860). Repr. of 1942 ed. 17.50 (ISBN 0-404-55860-7). AMS Pr.
Wheelwright, Lorin F. An Experimental Study of the Perceptibility & Spacing of Musical Symbols. LC 79-177645. (Columbia University. Teachers College. Contributions to Education: No. 775). Repr. of 1939 ed. 17.50 (ISBN 0-404-55775-9). AMS Pr.

MUSIC–READING
see Score Reading and Playing

MUSIC–SOCIETIES, ETC.
see also Choral Societies
Am. School Band Dir. Assoc., ed. ASBDA Curriculum Guide. 1974. 15.00 (ISBN 0-913650-19-6). Volkwein Bros.
Johnson, H. Earle. Hallelujah, Amen! The Story of the Handel & Haydn Society of Boston. (Music Ser.). (Illus.). 256p. 1981. Repr. of 1965 ed. lib. bdg. 22.50 (ISBN 0-306-79598-1). Da Capo.

MUSIC–STUDY AND TEACHING
see Music–Instruction and Study

MUSIC–SUNDAY-SCHOOLS
see Sunday-Schools–Hymns

MUSIC–TERMINOLOGY
Ammer, Christine. Musician's Handbook of Foreign Terms. 1971. pap. 4.95 (ISBN 0-02-870100-3). Schirmer Bks.
Baker, Theodore. Dictionary of Musical Terms. 1923. 10.95 (ISBN 0-02-870200-X). Schirmer Bks.
--Schirmer Pronouncing Pocket Manual of Musical Terms. 4th ed. LC 77-5236. 1978. pap. 3.50 (ISBN 0-02-870250-6). Schirmer Bks.
Berkman, Al. Singers Glossary of Show Business Jargon. 1961. 3.00 (ISBN 0-934972-06-0). Melrose Pub Co.
Buck, Dudley. Musical Pronouncing Dictionary. Repr. lib. bdg. 19.00 (ISBN 0-403-03787-5). Scholarly.
Busby, Thomas. A Musical Manual, or Technical Directory. LC 76-20708. (Music Reprint Ser). 1976. Repr. of 1828 ed. lib. bdg. 22.50 (ISBN 0-306-70788-8). Da Capo.
Delara, Adelina. Finale. LC 78-181138. 222p. 1955. Repr. 19.00 (ISBN 0-403-01539-1). Scholarly.
Dictionary of Terms in Music: English-German - German-English. 2nd ed. 500p. 1981. 38.00 (ISBN 3-598-10338-7, Pub. by K G Saur). Shoe String.
Grant, W. Parks. Handbook of Music Terms. LC 67-10187. 1967. 22.50 (ISBN 0-8108-0054-3). Scarecrow.
Grigg, Carolyn D., compiled by. Music Translation Dictionary: An English-Czech-Danish-Dutch-French-German-Hungarian-Italian-Polish-Portuguese-Russian-Spanish-Swedish Vocabulary of Music. LC 78-60526. 1978. lib. bdg. 25.00x (ISBN 0-313-20559-0, GMT/). Greenwood.
Headington, Christopher. Illustrated Dictionary of Musical Terms. LC 79-48042. (Illus.). 160p. 1980. 12.95 (ISBN 0-06-011819-9, HarpT). Har-Row.
Hopkins, Anthony. The Downbeat Guide to Music. (Illus.). 1977. 5.95x (ISBN 0-19-311322-8). Oxford U Pr.
Leach, R. Musical Thesaurus: A Dictionary of Musical Language. LC 78-51565. 1978. 10.00 (ISBN 0-912728-21-3). Newbury Bks.
Leuchtmann, Horst. Woerterbuch Musik. (Ger. - Eng., Dictionary of Terms in Music). 1977. 38.00 (ISBN 3-7940-3186-5, M-6911). French & Eur.
Levarie, Siegmund & Levy, Ernst. A Dictionary of Musical Morphology. (Wissenschaftliche Abhandlungen-Musicological Studies: Vol. 29). viii, 400p. 1980. lib. bdg. 132.00 (ISBN 0-912024-32-1). Inst Mediaeval Mus.
Padelford, Frederick M. Old English Musical Terms. LC 76-22346. 1976. Repr. of 1899 ed. lib. bdg. 15.00 (ISBN 0-89341-012-8). Longwood Pr.
Picerno, Vincent J. Dictionary of Musical Terms. LC 76-14903. (Studies in Music: NO. 42). 1976. lib. bdg. 39.95 (ISBN 0-8383-2119-4). Haskell.
Stainer, John & Barrett, W. A. Dictionary of Musical Terms. LC 71-166266. 464p. 1898. Repr. 45.00 (ISBN 0-403-01690-8). Scholarly.
Tinctoris, Johannes. Dictionary of Musical Terms. Parrish, Carl, tr. (Music Reprint Ser.). 1978. lib. bdg. 17.50 (ISBN 0-306-77560-3). Da Capo.
Wotton, Tom S. A Dictionary of Foreign Musical Terms & Handbook of Orchestral Instruments. LC 79-166268. 226p. 1907. Repr. 19.00 (ISBN 0-403-01389-5). Scholarly.

MUSIC–THEMATIC CATALOGS
Flanders, Peter. A Thematic Index to the Works of Benedetto Pallavicino. (Music Indexes & Bibliographies: No. 11). 1974. pap. 8.00 (ISBN 0-913574-11-2). Eur-Am Music.
Hill, George R. A Thematic Catalog of the Instrumental Music of Florian Leopold Gassmann. (Music Indexes & Bibliographies: No. 12). 1976. 25.00 (ISBN 0-913574-12-0). Eur-Am Music.
Newman, Joel & Rikko, Fritz. A Thematic Index to the Works of Salamon Rossi. (Music Indexes & Bibliographies: No. 6). 1972. pap. 11.00 (ISBN 0-913574-06-6). Eur-Am Music.
Steelman, Robert, ed. Catalog of the Lititz Congregation Collection. LC 80-27511. 670p. 1981. 40.00x (ISBN 0-8078-1477-6). U of NC Pr.
Taylor, Thomas F. Thematic Catalog of the Works of Jeremiah Clarke. LC 75-23551. (Detroit Studies in Music Bibliography Ser.: No. 35). 1977. 12.00 (ISBN 0-911772-84-7). Info Coord.

MUSIC–THEORY
see also Chromatic Alteration (Music); Composition (Music); Counterpoint; Harmony; Instrumentation and Orchestration; Melody; Music–Acoustics and Physics; Music–Philosophy and Esthetics; Musical Form; Musical Intervals and Scales; Musical Meter and Rhythm; Musical Temperament; Thorough Bass; Transposition (Music); Twelve-Tone System
Andrews, J. Austin & Wardian, Jeanne. Introduction to Music Fundamentals. 4th ed. 1978. pap. text ed. 14.95 (ISBN 0-13-489575-4). P-H.
Ban, Ioan A. Zang-Bloemzel...(Theoretical Parts) & Kort Sangh-Bericht... (Early Music Theory in the Low Countries Ser.: Vol. 1). wrappers 20.00 (ISBN 90-6027-077-0, Pub. by Frits Knuf Netherlands). Pendragon NY.

Benward, Bruce. Music in Theory & Practice, 2 vols. Incl. Vol. 1. (ISBN 0-697-03595-6); Wkbk. (ISBN 0-697-03597-2); Vol. 2. (ISBN 0-697-03596-4); Wkbk. (ISBN 0-697-03598-0). 1977. plastic comb 13.95 ea.; wkbk. 7.95 ea.; Vols. 1 & 2. pap. instr's resource man. 3.00x (ISBN 0-685-93541-8). Wm C Brown.

--Music in Theory & Practice, Vol. 1. 2nd ed. 400p. 1981. write for info. wkbk. (ISBN 0-697-03445-3); instrs.' manual avail. (ISBN 0-697-03423-2); plastic comb. avail. (ISBN 0-697-03447-X). Wm C Brown.

Benward, Bruce & Jackson, Barbara G. Practical Beginning Theory. 4th ed. 1980. plastic comb avail. (ISBN 0-697-03600-6); tchr's man. 3.00 (ISBN 0-686-60779-1); 3 cassettes 30.00 (ISBN 0-697-03698-7). Wm C Brown.

Billingham, Richard & Goodkin, Marie. First Steps to Musicianship. 256p. 1980. pap. text ed. 10.95x (ISBN 0-917974-38-7). Waveland Pr.

Blankenburg, Quirinus Van. Elementa Musica...'s. (Early Music Theory in the Low Countries Ser.: Vol. 4). 1973. Repr. of 1739 ed. wrappers 37.50 (ISBN 0-686-30910-3, Pub. by Frits Knuf Netherlands). Pendragon NY.

Boatwright, Howard. Introduction to the Theory of Music. (Illus.). 1956. 16.95x (ISBN 0-393-02057-6, NortonC). Norton.

Boretz, Benjamin & Cone, Edward T., eds. Perspectives on Contemporary Music Theory. 304p. (Orig.). 1972. pap. 4.95 (ISBN 0-393-00548-8, Norton Lib). Norton.

Brandt, William, et al. The Comprehensive Study of Music: Basic Principles of Music Theory, Vol. II. 1980. scp 16.95 (ISBN 0-06-040921-5, HarpC). Har-Row.

Browne, Richmond, ed. Music Theory: Special Topics. LC 80-70592. 1981. write for info. (ISBN 0-12-138080-7). Acad Pr.

Brye, Joseph. Basic Principles of Music Theory. (Illus.). 1965. 21.50 (ISBN 0-8260-1460-7). Wiley.

Bukofzer, M. Geschichte des emglischen Diskants und des Fauxbourdons nach den Theoretischen Quellen. (Sammlung Mw. Abh. 21-1936 Ser.). 184p. 35.00 (ISBN 90-6027-178-5, Pub. by Frits Knuf Netherlands). Pendragon NY.

Carlsen, James C. Melodic Perception: A Program for Self-Instruction. 1965. text ed. 10.95 (ISBN 0-07-009975-8, C); instructor's manual 3.95 (ISBN 0-07-009977-4); 150.00 (ISBN 0-07-009976-6). McGraw.

Cass, Jeannette. Rudiments of Music: A Detailed Study in Music Essentials. (Illus., Orig.). 1956. pap. text ed. 14.95 (ISBN 0-13-783654-6). P-H.

Castellini, John. Rudiments of Music. (Illus.). 1962. 15.95x (ISBN 0-393-09573-8, NortonC). Norton.

Cavaille-Coll, A. Complete Theoretical Works. Huybens, G., ed. (Bibliotheca Organologica Ser.: Vol. 45). (Illus.). xiii, 218p. (Fr.). 1980. 50.00 (ISBN 90-6027-192-0, Pub. by Frits Knuf Netherlands). Pendragon NY.

Chastek, Winifred K. Keyboard Skills: Sight Reading, Transposition, Harmonization, Improvisation. 1967. 12.95x (ISBN 0-534-00666-3). Wadsworth Pub.

Christ, William & Delone, Richard P. Introduction to Materials & Structure of Music. (Illus.). 390p. 1975. pap. text ed. 14.95 (ISBN 0-13-485532-9). P-H.

Christ, William, et al. Materials & Structure of Music, Vol. 2. 2nd ed. (Illus.). 512p. 1973. ref. ed. 17.95 (ISBN 0-13-560367-6); wkbk. 9.95 (ISBN 0-13-560383-8). P-H.

Christ, William B., et al. Materials & Structure of Music, Vol. 2. 3rd ed. 480p. 1981. text ed. 17.95 (ISBN 0-13-560433-8); pap. text ed. 10.95 wkbk. (ISBN 0-686-77609-7). P-H.

Cogan, Robert & Escot, Pozzi. Sonic Design: The Nature of Sound & Music. (Illus.). 544p. 1976. 19.95 (ISBN 0-13-822726-8). P-H.

Cooper, Paul. Perspectives in Music Theory: An Historical-Analytical Approach. 2nd ed. LC 78-26448. 1980. text ed. 16.50 scp (ISBN 0-06-041373-5, HarpC); Vol. 1. wkbk. scp 10.50 (ISBN 0-06-041374-3); Vol. 2. wkbk. scp 10.50 (ISBN 0-06-041375-1). Har-Row.

Cope, David. New Music Composition. LC 76-21376. 1977. pap. text ed. 10.95 (ISBN 0-02-870630-7). Schirmer Bks.

Copley, R. Evan. Harmony: Baroque to Contemporary, Pt. 1. 198p. 1978. pap. text ed. 9.80x (ISBN 0-87563-158-4). Stipes.

Cossaboom, Sterling P. Fundamentals of Music Theory. LC 72-87760. 1973. pap. 2.50 (ISBN 0-8008-3102-0, Crescendo). Taplinger.

Dallin, Leon. Foundations in Music Theory. 2nd ed. 1967. pap. 13.95x (ISBN 0-534-00659-0). Wadsworth Pub.

Denis, Jean. Traite De L'accord De L'Espinette. 2nd ed. LC 68-16229. (Music Ser.). 1969. Repr. of 1650 ed. 15.00 (ISBN 0-306-70950-3). Da Capo.

Diller, Angela. First Theory Book. 1921. pap. 7.95 (ISBN 0-02-870720-6). Schirmer Bks.

Douglas, Charles H. Basic Music Theory. McKenzie, Wesley M., ed. 1970. pap. 2.25 (ISBN 0-910842-01-9, GE11, Pub. by GWM). Kjos.

Douwes, Klaas. Grondig ondersoek van de Toonen der Musyk. (Early Music Theory in the Low Countries Ser.: Vol. 2). 1971. Repr. of 1699 ed. wrappers 25.00 (ISBN 90-6027-142-4, Pub. by Frits Knuf Netherlands). Pendragon NY.

Duckworth, William. A Creative Approach to Music Fundamentals. 320p. 1981. pap. text ed. 14.95x (ISBN 0-534-00891-7). Wadsworth Pub.

Duckworth, William & Brown, Edward. Theoretical Foundations of Music. 1978. text ed. 17.95x (ISBN 0-534-00526-8). Wadsworth Pub.

During, Ingemar. Ptolemaios und Porphyrios Uber Die Musik. LC 78-20290. (Ancient Philosophy Ser.). 293p. 1980. lib. bdg. 28.50 (ISBN 0-8240-9599-5). Garland Pub.

Elliott, Raymond. Fundamentals of Music. 3rd ed. LC 76-139599. (Illus.). 1971. pap. text ed. 12.95 (ISBN 0-13-341305-5). P-H.

Erickson, Robert. The Structure of Music: a Listener's Guide: A Study of Music in Terms of Melody & Counterpoint. LC 75-31361. 1977. Repr. of 1955 ed. lib. bdg. 18.25x (ISBN 0-8371-8519-X, ERSM). Greenwood.

Faulhaber, Martha & Underhill, Janet. Music: Invent Your Own. LC 74-13315. (Music Involvement Ser). (Illus.). 48p. (gr. 3 up). 1974. 6.95g (ISBN 0-8075-5355-7). A Whitman.

Ferguson, Donald N. A History of Musical Thought. LC 73-5265. 675p. 1975. Repr. of 1959 ed. lib. bdg. 38.75x (ISBN 0-8371-6882-1, FEMT). Greenwood.

Ghezzo, Marta A. Solfege, Ear Training, Rhythm, Dictation, & Music Theory: A Comprehensive Course. LC 78-16047. 268p. 1980. 21.75x (ISBN 0-8173-6403-X). U of Ala Pr.

Goetschius, Percy. Structure of Music. LC 72-109736. Repr. of 1934 ed. lib. bdg. 15.00x (ISBN 0-8371-4226-1, GOSM). Greenwood.

Green, Douglass M. Form in Tonal Music: An Introduction to Analysis. 2nd ed. LC 78-27072. 1979. text ed. 18.95 (ISBN 0-03-020286-8, HoltC). HR&W.

Gysin, H. P. Studien zum Vokabular der Musiktheorie Im Mittelalter: Eine linguistische Analyse. 1972. Repr. of 1959 ed. wrappers 22.50 (ISBN 90-6027-250-1, Pub. by Frits Knuf Netherlands). Pendragon NY.

Hanson, John. Music Fundamentals Workbook. 1979. pap. text ed. 13.95x (ISBN 0-582-28111-3). Longman.

Helmholtz, Hermann. On the Sensations of Tone As a Physiological Basis for the Theory of Music. 12.50 (ISBN 0-8446-2238-9). Peter Smith.

Holst, Imogen. ABC of Music: A Short Practical Guide to the Basic Essentials of Rudiments, Harmony, & Form. (Orig.). 1963. 8.95x (ISBN 0-19-317103-1). Oxford U Pr.

Howard, Bertrand. Fundamentals of Music Theory: A Program. 2nd ed. 256p. (Orig.). 1975. pap. text ed. 13.95 (ISBN 0-15-529461-X, HC). HarBraceJ.

Jones, George T. Music Theory. (Illus.). 288p. (Orig.). 1974. pap. 3.95 (ISBN 0-06-460137-4, CO 137, COS). Har-Row.

Katz, Adele T. Challenge to Musical Tradition. LC 79-180046. 408p. 1972. Repr. of 1945 ed. lib. bdg. 32.50 (ISBN 0-306-70428-5). Da Capo.

Kiely, Dennis K. Essentials of Music for New Musicians. (Illus.). 192p. 1975. pap. text ed. 11.50 (ISBN 0-13-286492-4). P-H.

Kohs, Ellis B. Music Theory: A Syllabus for Teacher & Student, 2 Vols. 1961. pap. 6.95x ea. Vol. 1 (ISBN 0-19-500935-5). Vol. 2 (ISBN 0-19-500936-3). Oxford U Pr.

Kraft, Leo. Gradus-an Integrated Approach to Harmony, Counterpoint, & Analysis: Gradus One (Text & Anthology) Incl. Gradus One (Text & Anthology) 360p. pap. text ed. 5.50x (ISBN 0-393-09180-5); Anthology. pap. text ed. 5.50x (ISBN 0-393-09185-6). Combined Ed (ISBN 0-685-62589-3). 1976. Vol. 1. 15.95x set (ISBN 0-393-09154-6); Vol. 2. 19.95x (ISBN 0-393-09148-1). Norton.

Land, Lois R. & Vaughan, Mary Ann. Music in Today's Classroom. 2nd ed. 1978. pap. text ed. 13.95 (ISBN 0-15-564895-0, HC); 4 records 9.95 (ISBN 0-15-564894-2). HarBraceJ.

Lilienfeld, Robert. Learning to Read Music. 136p. 1979. pap. 3.95 (ISBN 0-06-463495-7, EH 495, EH). Har-Row.

Livre Plaisant et Tresutile Pour Apprendre a Faire et Ordonner Toutes Tabulatures Hors le Discant. (Early Music Theory in the Low Countries Ser.: Vol. 9). 1973. Repr. of 1568 ed. 25.00wrappers (ISBN 90-6027-289-7, Pub. by Frits Knuf Netherlands). Pendragon NY.

Longy-Miquelle, Renee. Principles of Musical Theory. 1925. 5.00 (ISBN 0-911318-06-2). E C Schirmer.

Lovelock, William. Rudiments of Music. LC 71-145436. (Illus.). 1971. pap. 5.95 (ISBN 0-312-69545-4, R91000). St Martin.

Luck, James T. Creative Music for the Classroom Teacher. 1970. pap. text ed. 6.95x (ISBN 0-394-30369-5). Phila Bk Co.

Mankin, Linda R., et al. Prelude to Musicianship: Fundamental Concepts & Skills. LC 78-2196. 1979. pap. 16.95 (ISBN 0-03-011036-X, HoltC). HR&W.

Marquis, G. Welton. Twentieth-Century Music Idioms. LC 81-4197. xvi, 269p. 1981. Repr. of 1964 ed. lib. bdg. 27.50x (ISBN 0-313-22624-5, MATC). Greenwood.

Maue, Kenneth. Water in the Lake: Real Events for the Imagination. LC 78-4737. 1979. pap. 4.95 (ISBN 0-06-090670-7, CN-670, CN). Har-Row.

--Water in the Lake: Real Events for the Imagination. LC 78-4737. 1979. 11.95 (ISBN 0-06-012952-2, HarpT). Har-Row.

Meibom, Marcus. Antiquae Musicae Auctores Septem Graece et latine, 2 vols. (Monuments of Music & Music Literature in Facsimile: Series 2, Vol. 51). (Illus.). Repr. of 1652 ed. 80.00x (ISBN 0-8450-2251-2). Broude.

Mitchell, William J. & Salzer, Felix, eds. Music Forum, 3 vols. LC 67-16204. 1967-73. Vol. 3. 22.50x (ISBN 0-231-03522-5); Vol. 4. 22.50x (ISBN 0-231-03153-X); Vol. 5. 22.50x (ISBN 0-231-03522-5). Columbia U Pr.

Narmour, Eugene. Beyond Schenkerism: The Need for Alternatives in Music Analysis. LC 76-25632. 1977. lib. bdg. 20.00x (ISBN 0-226-56847-4). U of Chicago Pr.

National Institute for Food Service Industry & Kotschevar, Lendal H. Management by Menu. 381p. 1981. text ed. write for info. (ISBN 0-915452-20-0); instrs.' manual avail. (ISBN 0-915452-21-9); students manual avail. (ISBN 0-915452-22-7); home study bk avail. (ISBN 0-915452-23-5). Wm C Brown.

Oswald, Jonas. Introduction to the Theory of Heinrich Schenker. Rothgeb, John, tr. (Music Ser.). 1981. text ed. 14.95x (ISBN 0-582-28227-6). Longman.

Parrott, Ian. Guide to Musical Thought. (Student's Music Library Ser). 1955. 6.95 (ISBN 0-234-77309-X). Dufour.

Peters, Charles S. & Yoder, Paul. Master Theory, 6 bks. Incl. Bk. 1. Beginning Theory. 1963 (ISBN 0-8497-0154-6, L173); Bk. 2. Intermediate Theory. 1964 (ISBN 0-8497-0155-4, L174); Bk. 3. Advanced Theory. 1965 (ISBN 0-8497-0156-2, L175); Bk. 4. Elementary Harmony. 1966 (ISBN 0-8497-0157-0, L179); Bk. 5. Intermediate Harmony. 1967 (ISBN 0-8497-0158-9, L181); Bk. 6. Advanced Harmony & Arranging. 1968 (ISBN 0-8497-0159-7, L185). (Master Theory Ser.). pap. text ed. 2.45 ea. Kjos.

Ratner, Leonard. Classic Music: Expression, Form, & Style. LC 76-57808. (Illus.). 1980. 35.00 (ISBN 0-02-872020-2). Schirmer Bks.

Reti, Rudolph R. The Thematic Process in Music. LC 77-13622. 1978. Repr. of 1951 ed. lib. bdg. 26.50x (ISBN 0-8371-9875-5, RETH). Greenwood.

--Tonality, Atonality, Pantonality: A Study of Some Trends in Twentieth Century Music. LC 78-6162. (Illus.). 1978. Repr. of 1958 ed. lib. bdg. 19.50x (ISBN 0-313-20478-0, RETO). Greenwood.

Robinson, Helene. Basic Piano for Adults. 1967. pap. 9.95x (ISBN 0-534-00065-7). Wadsworth Pub.

--Intermediate Piano for Adults, Vol. 1. 1970. pap. 10.95x (ISBN 0-534-00210-2). Wadsworth Pub.

Robitzek, Klara C. Peter in the Land of Musical Theory. 1977. 4.95 (ISBN 0-8008-6284-8, Crescendo). Taplinger.

Rosberger, Paul. The Theory of Total Consonance. LC 71-92560. (Illus.). 108p. 1970. 12.00 (ISBN 0-8386-7570-0). Fairleigh Dickinson.

Rosen, Charles. The Classical Style: Haydn, Mozart, Beethoven. LC 79-83250. (Illus.). 1971. 12.50 (ISBN 0-670-22510-X). Viking Pr.

Salzer, Felix. Structural Hearing: Tonal Coherence in Music, 2 Vols. (Illus.). 1952. text ed. 7.50 ea.; Vol. 1. text ed. (ISBN 0-486-22275-6); Vol. 2. text ed. (ISBN 0-486-22276-4). Dover.

Seligson-Rose, Bonnie. Advanced Placement Music: Comprehensive Review of Theory & History of Music. LC 79-16113. 1979. pap. text ed. 4.95 (ISBN 0-668-04743-7, 4743-7). Arco.

Swanson. Music Fund Through Folksong. 1977. 12.95x (ISBN 0-534-00505-5). Wadsworth Pub.

Symons, Arthur. Plays, Acting & Music: A Book of Theory. 1978. Repr. of 1928 ed. lib. bdg. 20.00 (ISBN 0-8492-8077-X). R West.

Thomson, W. Introduction to Music As Structure. 1970. pap. 10.32 (ISBN 0-201-07498-2); teacher's guide 2.52 (ISBN 0-201-07499-0). A-W.

Toch, Ernst. Shaping Forces in Music. 1948. 11.95 (ISBN 0-685-02533-0). Criterion Mus.

--The Shaping Forces in Music: An Inquiry into the Nature of Harmony, Melody, Counterpoint & Form. 7.00 (ISBN 0-8446-5615-1). Peter Smith.

--The Shaping Forces in Music: An Inquiry into the Nature of Harmony, Melody, Counterpoint, Form. 1977. pap. text ed. 3.50 (ISBN 0-486-23346-4). Dover.

Verrall, John W., ed. Outline & Syllabus for Music Theory. (Orig.). 1965. pap. 1.95x (ISBN 0-87015-132-0). Pacific Bks.

Wachhaus, Gustav & Kuhn, Terry L. Fundamental Classroom Music Skills: Theory & Performing Techniques. LC 78-13476. 1979. pap. text ed. 14.95 (ISBN 0-03-041775-9, HoltC). HR&W.

Warfield, Gerald. Layer Analysis: A Primer of Elementary Tonal Structures. (Music Ser.). 1978. pap. text ed. 12.95x (ISBN 0-582-28069-9). Longman.

Weber, Max. Rational & Social Foundations of Music. Martindale, Don, et al, trs. LC 56-12134. (Arcturus Books Paperbacks). 1969. pap. 6.95 (ISBN 0-8093-0355-8). S Ill U Pr.

Westergaard, Peter. Introduction to Tonal Theory. 448p. 1976. pap. text ed. 16.00x (ISBN 0-393-09342-5). Norton.

Whitney, Maurice. Backgrounds in Music Theory. 1954. pap. 5.95 (ISBN 0-02-872870-X). Schirmer Bks.

Williams, David R. Bibliography of the History of Music Theory. 2nd ed. 1971. pap. 8.00 (ISBN 0-918194-08-3). Accura.

Wink, Richard. Fundamentals of Music. LC 76-20867. (Illus.). 1977. pap. text ed. 14.50 (ISBN 0-395-20598-0). HM.

Winold, A. & Rehm, J. Introduction to Music Theory. 2nd ed. 1979. pap. 16.95 (ISBN 0-13-489666-1). P-H.

Wolff, E. G. Grundlagen Einer Autonomen Musikasthetik, 2 vols. (Illus.). 150p. 65.00 (ISBN 90-6027-371-0, Pub. by Frits Knuf Netherlands). Pendragon NY.

Yeston, Maury, ed. Readings in Schenker Analysis & Other Approaches. LC 76-40140. 1977. 20.00x (ISBN 0-300-02032-5); pap. text ed. 8.95x (ISBN 0-300-02114-3). Yale U Pr.

Zuckerkandl, Victor. Sense of Music. rev. ed. (Illus.). 1970. 17.50x (ISBN 0-691-09102-1); pap. 5.95 (ISBN 0-691-02700-5, 89); reel to reel tapes 52.50 (ISBN 0-691-03838-4); cassette tapes 40.00 (ISBN 0-691-09128-5). Princeton U Pr.

MUSIC-THEORY-PROGRAMMED INSTRUCTION

Harder. Harmonic Materials in Tonal Music: A Programed Course, Pts. 1 & 2. 4th ed. 320p. 1980. pap. 15.95 (ISBN 0-686-77803-0, 5869250). Pt. 1 (ISBN 0-205-06925-8). Pt. 2 (ISBN 0-205-06945-2, 5869455). Allyn.

Harder, Paul. Basic Materials in Music Theory: A Programmed Course. 4th ed. 1978. pap. text ed. 14.95 (ISBN 0-205-06045-5). Allyn.

Martin, Gary M. Musical Beginnings: For Teachers & Their Students. 1975. pap. text ed. 13.95x (ISBN 0-534-00385-0). Wadsworth Pub.

Toutant, William H. Fundamental Concepts of Music. 336p. 1979. pap. text ed. 15.95x (ISBN 0-534-00743-0). Wadsworth Pub.

Verrall, John W. Basic Theory of Music: Programmed Instruction in Intervals, Scales, & Modes. (Prog. Bk.). 1970. pap. text ed. 3.95x (ISBN 0-87015-183-5). Pacific Bks.

MUSIC-THEORY-TO 400

see also Music, Greek and Roman

MUSIC-THEORY-400-1500

see also Organum

Hammerich, Angul. Mediaeval Musical Relics of Denmark. LC 74-24104. Repr. of 1912 ed. 24.50 (ISBN 0-404-12952-8). AMS Pr.

Palisca, Claude V., ed. Hucbald, Guido & John on Music: Three Medieval Treatises. Babb, Warren, tr. LC 77-1331. (Music Theory Translation Ser). (Illus.). 1978. 20.00x (ISBN 0-300-02040-6). Yale U Pr.

Tinctoris, Johannes. Dictionary of Musical Terms. Parrish, Carl, tr. (Music Reprint Ser.). 1978. lib. bdg. 17.50 (ISBN 0-306-77560-3). Da Capo.

Ultan, Lloyd. Music Theory: Problems & Practices in the Middle Ages & Renaissance. LC 77-75597. 1977. text ed. 13.95x (ISBN 0-8166-0802-4); wkbk. 8.95x (ISBN 0-8166-0803-2). U of Minn Pr.

Young, Irwin, tr. Practica Musicae of Franchinus Gafurius. (Illus.). 1969. 25.00 (ISBN 0-299-05180-3). U of Wis Pr.

MUSIC-THEORY-16TH-17TH CENTURIES

Aaron, Pietro. Libri Tres de Institutione Harmonica. (Monuments of Music & Music Literature in Facsimile, Ser. II: Vol. 67). 134p. (Lat.). 1975. Repr. of 1516 ed. 27.50x (ISBN 0-8450-2267-9). Broude.

Berger, Karol. Theories of Chromatic & Enharmonic Music in Late Sixteenth Century Italy. (Studies in Musicology: No. 10). 1980. 31.95 (ISBN 0-8357-1065-3, Pub. by UMI Res Pub). Univ Microfilms.

Bonini, Don Severo. Severo Bonini's Discorsi e Regole: A Bilingual Edition. Bonino, MaryAnn, ed. & tr. from Italian. LC 77-18514. (Illus.). 1979. text ed. 24.95x (ISBN 0-8425-0997-6). Brigham.

Butler, Charles. Principles of Musik, in Singing & Setting. LC 68-13273. (Music Ser). 1970. Repr. of 1636 ed. lib. bdg. 17.50 (ISBN 0-306-70939-2). Da Capo.

--The Principles of Musik, in Singing & Setting. LC 74-25439. (English Experience Ser.: No. 284). 136p. 1971. Repr. of 1636 ed. 14.00 (ISBN 90-221-0284-X). Walter J Johnson.

Dolmetsch, Arnold. Interpretation of the Music of the Seventeenth & Eighteenth Centuries. LC 76-75611. (Illus.). 512p. 1969. pap. 7.95 (ISBN 0-295-78578-0, WP51); 2 lp records 13.50 (ISBN 0-295-75007-3). U of Wash Pr.

Garside, Charles, Jr. The Origins of Calvin's Theology of Music: Fifteen Thirty-Six to Fifteen Forty-Three. LC 78-73171. (Transactions Ser.: Vol. 69, Pt. 4). 1979. 7.00 (ISBN 0-87169-694-0). Am Philos.

Merritt, Arthur T. Sixteenth Century Polyphony: A Basis for the Study of Counterpoint. LC 39-25128. 1939. 10.00x (ISBN 0-674-81060-0). Harvard U Pr.

Morley, Thomas. A Plaine & Easie Introduction to Practicall Musicke. LC 72-222. (English Experience Ser.: No. 207). 1969. Repr. of 1597 ed. 42.00 (ISBN 90-221-0207-6). Walter J Johnson.

Ornithoparchus, Andreas. A. Ornithoparcus His Micrologus, or Introduction: Containing the Art of Singing. Douland, J., tr. LC 75-25884. (English Experience Ser.: No. 160). 90p. 1969. Repr. of 1609 ed. 21.00 (ISBN 90-221-0160-6). Walter J Johnson.

Rivera, Benito V. German Music Theory in the Early Seventeenth Century: The Treatises of Johannes Lippius. Buelow, George, ed. (Studies in Musicology: No. 17). 1980. 34.95x (ISBN 0-8357-1074-2, Pub. by UMI Res Pr). Univ Microfilms.

MUSIC-THEORY-18TH CENTURY

Dolmetsch, Arnold. Interpretation of the Music of the Seventeenth & Eighteenth Centuries. LC 76-75611. (Illus.). 512p. 1969. pap. 7.95 (ISBN 0-295-78578-0, WP51); 2 lp records 13.50 (ISBN 0-295-75007-3). U of Wash Pr.

Harder. Harmonic Materials in Tonal Music: A Programed Course, Pts. 1 & 2. 4th ed. 320p. 1980. pap. 15.95 (ISBN 0-686-77803-0, 5869250). Pt. 1 (ISBN 0-205-06925-8). Pt. 2 (ISBN 0-205-06945-2, 5869455). Allyn.

Malcolm, A. Treatise of Musick, Speculative, Practical & Historical. LC 69-16676. (Music Ser). 1970. Repr. of 1721 ed. lib. bdg. 49.50 (ISBN 0-306-71099-4). Da Capo.

MUSIC-THERAPEUTIC USE

see Music Therapy

MUSIC-VOCATIONAL GUIDANCE

Beverly Hills Bar Association Barristers Committee for the Arts. The Musician's Manual: A Practical Career Guide. Halloran, Mark, ed. 288p. 1981. 17.95 (ISBN 0-8015-5204-4, Hawthorn, Hawthorn). Dutton.

Boye, Henry. How to Make Money Selling the Songs You Write. rev. ed. LC 75-124473. 192p. 1975. pap. 4.95 (ISBN 0-8119-0381-8). Fell.

Cooke, Frank E. Write That Song! LC 81-90107. (Illus.). 134p. (Orig.). 1981. pap. 9.95 (ISBN 0-940076-00-4, RB101). Fiesta City.

Cornell, Richard. Your Career in Music. LC 77-13361. (Arco Career Guidance Ser.). 1979. pap. 3.95 (ISBN 0-668-04459-4); pap. 3.50 (ISBN 0-668-04461-6). Arco.

Csida, Joseph. The Music-Record Career Handbook. 376p. 1975. 14.95 (ISBN 0-8230-7580-X, Billboard Pub). Watson-Guptill.

Curtis, Robert E. Your Future in Music. LC 62-11574. (Careers in Depth Ser.). (gr. 7 up). 1976. PLB 5.97 (ISBN 0-8239-0054-1). Rosen Pr.

Dutton, Phyl. Music Clubs, Festivals & Concerts: How to Organize Them. 128p. 1980. softcover 25.00x (ISBN 0-905418-86-7, Pub. by Gresham England). State Mutual Bk.

Edmunds, Alice. Who Puts the Grooves in the Record? LC 76-1021. (Adventures in the World of Work Ser). (Illus.). (gr. 5 up). 1977. pap. 2.50 (ISBN 0-394-83281-7, BYR). Random.

Goldreich, Gloria & Goldreich, Esther. What Can She Be? A Musician. LC 74-28461. (What Can She Be? Ser.). (Illus.). 48p. (gr. k-5). 1975. 7.50 (ISBN 0-688-41701-9); PLB 7.20 (ISBN 0-688-51701-3). Lothrop.

Hurst, Walter E. & Hale, William S. Music-Record Business & Law: Your Introduction to Music-Record Copyright, Contracts & Other Business & Law. new ed. (The Entertainment Industry Ser.). (Illus.). 234p. (gr. 12). 1974. 10.00 (ISBN 0-911370-21-8); pap. 10.00 (ISBN 0-911370-22-6). Seven Arts.

McDonald, Gerald. Training & Careers for the Professional Musician. 112p. 1979. 15.00x (ISBN 0-905418-03-4, Pub. by Grehsham England). State Mutual Bk.

Mitz, Rick. Aim for a Job in the Record Business. (Aim High Vocational Ser). (YA) 1977. PLB 5.97 (ISBN 0-8239-0384-2). Rosen Pr.

Parker, Horatio W., ed. Music & Public Entertainment. LC 74-24180. (Illus.). Repr. of 1911 ed. 32.50 (ISBN 0-404-13082-8). AMS Pr.

Rappaport, Victor. Making It in Music. 1979. 12.95 (ISBN 0-13-547612-7, Spec); pap. 5.95 (ISBN 0-13-547604-6, Spec). P-H.

Stearns, Betty & Degen, Clara, eds. Careers in Music. rev. ed. LC 76-150516. (Illus.). 1980. pap. text ed. 2.00 (ISBN 0-918196-00-0). American Music.

Taubman, Joseph. The Business & Law of Music. 199p. 1965. 8.50 (ISBN 0-87945-009-6). Fed Legal Pubn.

Thomson, Virgil. The State of Music. LC 73-17658. 250p. 1974. Repr. of 1939 ed. lib. bdg. 15.00x (ISBN 0-8371-7258-6, THSM). Greenwood.

Weismann, Dick. The Music Business: Career Opportunities & Self Defense. 1979. 11.95 (ISBN 0-517-53433-9); pap. 6.95 (ISBN 0-517-53689-7). Crown.

MUSIC-YEARBOOKS

Elley, Derek. International Music Guide Nineteen Eighty. LC 76-4626. (Illus.). 1979. pap. 7.95 (ISBN 0-498-02424-5). A S Barnes.

--International Music Guide 1978. LC 76-4626. (Illus.). 1978. pap. 7.95 (ISBN 0-498-02107-6). A S Barnes.

Elley, Derek, ed. International Music Guide. LC 76-4626. 1977. pap. 7.95 (ISBN 0-498-01913-6). A S Barnes.

Jacobs, Artur & Barton, Marianne, eds. British Music Yearbook, 1981. 7th ed. 555p. 1981. pap. 24.50x (ISBN 0-8476-3722-0). Rowman.

Kemps International Music & Recording Industry Year Book 1981. 405p. 1981. pap. 30.50 (ISBN 0-905255-92-5, KEMP 010, Kemps). Unipub.

Kemps International Music & Recording Industry Year Book 1980. (Illus.). 408p. (Orig.). 1979. pap. 32.50x (ISBN 0-905255-68-2). Intl Pubns Serv.

Marchbank, Pearce & Miles. The Illustrated Rock Almanac. LC 76-57167. (Illus.). 1977. pap. 3.99 (ISBN 0-448-22675-8). Paddington.

Musician's Guide. 6th ed. LC 54-14954. 990p. 1980. 59.50 (ISBN 0-8379-5601-3, 031095). Marquis.

Pierre Key's Music Year Book. The Standard Music Annual from Nineteen Twenty-Four to Nineteen Thirty-Eight, 6 vols. LC 70-181231. 1928-35. Repr. 23.00 ea.; Set. 135.00 (ISBN 0-403-01645-2). Scholarly.

Stearns, Betty & Bjorneberg, Paul, eds. Music U. S. A., 1981. rev. ed. (Illus.). 1981. pap. text ed. 3.50 (ISBN 0-686-73042-9). American Music.

MUSIC, AFRICAN

African Music. (Illus.). 154p. (Orig.). 1973. pap. 27.50 (ISBN 0-685-31875-3, UM31, UNESCO). Unipub.

Akpabot, Samuel E. Ibibi Music in Nigerian Culture. (Illus.). 140p. 1975. 7.50x (ISBN 0-87013-193-1). Mich St U Pr.

Ames, David W. & King, Anthony V. Glossary of Hausa Music & Its Social Contexts. LC 76-164884. 1971. 11.95x (ISBN 0-8101-0361-3). Northwestern U Pr.

Bebey, Francis. African Music: A People's Art. Bennett, Josephine, tr. from French. LC 74-9348. (Illus.). 192p. 1975. 12.95 (ISBN 0-88208-051-2); pap. 8.95 (ISBN 0-88208-050-4). Lawrence Hill.

Brandel, R. Music of Central Africa: An Ethnomusicological Study. (Illus.). 1973. pap. 35.00 (ISBN 9-0247-0634-3). Heinman.

Chernoff, John M. African Rhythm & African Sensibility: Aesthetics & Social Action in African Musical Idioms. LC 79-189. xviii, 262p. 1981. including cassette tape 9.95 (ISBN 0-226-10345-5, 10346-3, Phoen). U of Chicago Pr.

--African Rhythm & African Sensibility. LC 79-189. 1980. 20.00 (ISBN 0-226-10344-7). U of Chicago Pr.

International African Institute. Select Bibliography of Music in Africa. LC 66-36908. (African Bibliography Ser.). 1965. 16.50x (ISBN 0-85302-031-0). Intl Pubns Serv.

Jones, A. M. Studies in African Music, 2 Vols. 1959. 49.00x (ISBN 0-19-713512-9). Oxford U Pr.

Kaufman, Fredrick & Guckin, John P. The African Roots of Jazz. LC 78-8470. 148p. 1979. 14.95 (ISBN 0-88284-065-7); pap. 7.95 (ISBN 0-686-64874-9). Alfred Pub.

Keil, Charles. Tiv Song. LC 78-3178. 1979. lib. bdg. 26.00x (ISBN 0-226-42962-8). U of Chicago Pr.

Legum, Colin, ed. Africa Contemporary Record: Annual Survey & Documents. Incl. Vol. 1. 1968-69. 904p (ISBN 0-8419-0150-3); Vol. 2. 1969-70. 1213p (ISBN 0-8419-0151-1); Vol. 3. 1970-71. 1065p (ISBN 0-8419-0152-X); Vol. 4. 1971-1972. 1100p (ISBN 0-8419-0153-8); Vol. 5. 1972-73. Legum, Colin, ed (ISBN 0-8419-0154-6). LC 70-7957. 125.00 ea. (Africana). Holmes & Meier.

Merriam, Alan P. African Music in Perspective. 1981. lib. bdg. 45.00 (ISBN 0-8240-9461-1). Garland Pub.

Nketia, Joseph H. The Music of Africa. (Illus.). 278p. 1974. pap. 6.95x (ISBN 0-393-09249-6). Norton.

Southern, Eileen. Biographical Dictionary of Afro-American & African Musicians. LC 81-2586. (The Greenwood Encyclopedia of Black Music Ser.). 496p. 1981. lib. bdg. 49.95 (ISBN 0-313-21339-9, SOD/). Greenwood.

Tracey, Hugh. Chopi Musicians. (Illus.). 1970. Repr. of 1948 ed. 36.00x (ISBN 0-19-724182-4). Oxford U Pr.

United States Library of Congress. Music Division. African Music: A Brief Annotated Bibliography. Thieme, Darius L., ed. LC 78-17849. 1978. Repr. of 1964 ed. lib. bdg. 16.75 (ISBN 0-313-20543-4, USAM). Greenwood.

Walker, Wyatt T. Somebody's Calling My Name. LC 79-14155. 1979. 10.00 (ISBN 0-8170-0849-7). Judson.

Wright, Josephine R., ed. Ignatius Sancho, an Early African Composer in England, 1729 to 1780: The Collected Editions of His Music in Facsimile. LC 80-8525. 130p. 1981. lib. bdg. 20.00 (ISBN 0-8240-9459-X). Garland Pub.

Zemp, Hugo. Musique Dan: La Musique D'une Societe Africaine. (Cahiers De L'homme, Novelle Serie: No. 11). (Illus.). 1971. pap. 35.50x (ISBN 90-2796-913-2). Mouton.

MUSIC, AFRO-AMERICAN

see Afro-American Music

MUSIC, AMERICAN

see also Afro-American Songs

Anderson, Sherwood. Mid-American Chants. 82p. 1980. Repr. of 1923 ed. lib. bdg. 15.00 (ISBN 0-8482-0047-0). Norwood Edns.

Armsby, Leonora W. Musicians Talk. facsimile ed. LC 76-99679. (Essay Index Reprint Ser). 1935. 17.00 (ISBN 0-8369-1338-8). Arno.

Ayars, Christine M. Contributions to the Art of Music in America by the Music Industries of Boston: 1640-1936. 23.00 (ISBN 0-384-02825-X). Johnson Repr.

Barker, John N. & Bray, John. The Indian Princess, 2 vols in 1. LC 77-169587. (Earlier American Music Ser.: No. 11). Repr. of 1808 ed. 19.50 (ISBN 0-306-77311-2). Da Capo.

Belcher, Supply. The Harmony of Maine. Hitchcock, H. Wiley, ed. LC 77-169607. (Earlier American Music Ser: Vol. 6). 104p. 1972. Repr. of 1794 ed. lib. bdg. 18.50 (ISBN 0-306-77306-6). Da Capo.

Billings, William. The Psalm Singer's Amusement. LC 73-5100. (Earlier American Music Ser.: Vol. 20). 104p. 1974. Repr. of 1781 ed. lib. bdg. 22.50 (ISBN 0-306-70587-7). Da Capo.

Blair, John. The Illustrated Discography of Surf Music: 1959-1965. 1978. pap. 4.50 (ISBN 0-9601880-0-2). J Bee Prods.

Bond, Carrie J. Old Melodies of the South. 59.95 (ISBN 0-8490-0760-7). Gordon Pr.

Bristow, George. Rip Van Winkle. (Early American Music Ser.: No. 25). 297p. 1981. 39.50 (ISBN 0-306-76124-6). Da Capo.

Broderick, Richard, ed. The New York Times One Hundred Great Country Songs. LC 73-79907. 1974. spiral bdg. 14.95 (ISBN 0-8129-0376-5); pap. 7.95 (ISBN 0-8129-6239-7). Times Bks.

Brooks, Henry M. Olden-Time Music. LC 70-39537. Repr. of 1888 ed. 21.00 (ISBN 0-404-09919-X). AMS Pr.

Buerkle, Jack V. & Barker, Danny. Bourbon Street Black: The New Orleans Black Jazzman. LC 73-77926. (Illus.). 254p. 1974. pap. 4.95 (ISBN 0-19-501832-X, GB415, GB). Oxford U Pr.

Burton, Frederick R. American Primitive Music, with Special Attention to Songs of the Highways. 1977. lib. bdg. 59.95 (ISBN 0-8490-1416-6). Gordon Pr.

Cage, John. For the Birds. 320p. 1981. 20.00 (ISBN 0-7145-2690-8, Pub. by M. Boyars). Merrimack Bk Serv.

Carney, George O. The Sounds of People & Places: Readings in the Geography of Music. 1978. pap. text ed. 11.25 (ISBN 0-8191-0394-2). U Pr of Amer.

Carr, Benjamin. Musical Miscellany. (Early American Music Ser.). 1981. Repr. of 1825 ed. 47.50 (ISBN 0-306-79547-7). Da Capo.

Casurella, Frank. Twentieth Century Country Music Stars, & the Hall of Fame. new ed. LC 73-86073. (Illus.). 350p. 1974. pap. text ed. write for info. (ISBN 0-685-50219-8). Charlotte Pubs.

Chadwick, George W. Judith: Lyric Drama for Soli, Chorus, & Orchestra. LC 70-169727. (Earlier American Music Ser.: Vol. 3). 176p. 1972. Repr. of 1901 ed. lib. bdg. 22.50 (ISBN 0-306-77303-1). Da Capo.

Chase, Gilbert. America's Music, from the Pilgrims to the Present. 2nd rev. ed. LC 80-28027. (Illus.). xxi, 759p. 1981. Repr. of 1966 ed. lib. bdg. 45.00x (ISBN 0-313-22391-2, CHAM). Greenwood.

Clarke, Garry E. Essays on American Music. LC 76-52606. (Contributions in American History: No. 62). (Illus.). 1977. lib. bdg. 16.95x (ISBN 0-8371-9484-9, CAM/). Greenwood.

Cowell, Henry, ed. American Composers on American Music: A Symposium. LC 62-9681. 1962. pap. 4.95 (ISBN 0-8044-6088-4). Ungar.

Crawford, Richard. A Historian's Introduction to Early American Music. (Illus.). 1980. pap. 4.00 (ISBN 0-912296-44-5, Dist. by U Pr of Va). Am Antiquarian.

Cumnock, Frances, ed. Catalog of the Salem Congregation Music. LC 79-15173. (Illus.). 682p. 1980. 30.00x (ISBN 0-8078-1398-2). U of NC Pr.

Daniel, Ralph T. The Anthem in New England Before Eighteen Hundred. (Music Reprint Ser.). 1979. Repr. of 1966 ed. 27.50 (ISBN 0-306-79511-6). Da Capo.

Darling, J. S., ed. Colonial Keyboard Tunes. LC 80-12691. 1980. pap. 1.50 (ISBN 0-87935-055-5). Williamsburg.

David, Hans T. Music of the Moravians in America from the Archives of the Moravian Church at Bethlehem Pa, 2 vols. Incl. Vol. 1. Ten Sacred Songs. Dencke, J., et al.; Vol. 2. Six Quintets. Peter, John F. write to C. F. Peters Corp., NY for prices (ISBN 0-685-22862-2). NY Pub Lib.

Davis, Ronald L. A History of Music in American Life, Vol. 1: The Formative Years, 1620-1865. LC 79-25359. 386p. 1981. lib. bdg. 17.50 (ISBN 0-89874-002-9). Krieger.

Davis, Ronald L., ed. A History of Music in American Life. LC 79-25359. Set. 49.50 (ISBN 0-89874-080-0). Krieger.

Drummond, Robert R. Early German Music in Philadelphia. LC 74-125068. (Music Ser). 1970. Repr. of 1910 ed. lib. bdg. 14.50 (ISBN 0-306-70005-0). Da Capo.

Duke, Vernon. Listen Here. 1963. 7.95 (ISBN 0-685-06621-5); pap. 4.50 (ISBN 0-8392-5010-X). Astor-Honor.

Edwards, George T. Music & Musicians of Maine. LC 74-135736. Repr. of 1928 ed. 23.00 (ISBN 0-404-07231-3). AMS Pr.

Eisen, Jonathan, ed. Age of Rock: Sounds of the American Cultural Revolution. LC 70-117675. 1970. pap. 3.45 (ISBN 0-394-70535-1, Vin). Random.

Elson, Louis. History of American Music. 59.95 (ISBN 0-8490-0316-4). Gordon Pr.

Elson, Louis C. History of American Music. (Illus.). 1971. Repr. 29.00 (ISBN 0-8337-1055-9). B Franklin.

--The National Music of America & Its Sources. LC 70-159950. (Illus.). 1975. Repr. of 1911 ed. 24.00 (ISBN 0-8103-4039-9). Gale.

Encyclopedia of American Art & Music. lib. bdg. 75.00 (ISBN 0-403-08974-3). Scholarly.

Engel, Carl & Strunk, W. Oliver, eds. Music from the Days of George Washington. LC 73-36418. Repr. of 1931 ed. 19.50 (ISBN 0-404-07230-5). AMS Pr.

Erskine, John. My Life in Music. LC 73-8158. (Illus.). 283p. 1973. Repr. of 1950 ed. lib. bdg. 14.25x (ISBN 0-8371-6950-X, ERLM). Greenwood.

Ffrench, Florence, compiled by. Music & Musicians in Chicago. LC 74-24082. Repr. of 1899 ed. 32.50 (ISBN 0-404-12910-2). AMS Pr.

Ffrench, Florence F. Music & Musicians in Chicago. (Music Reprint Ser.). 1979. Repr. of 1899 ed. lib. bdg. 27.50 (ISBN 0-306-79542-6). Da Capo.

Fife Record: The Sounds of Ancient Fifes & Drums Music of the American Revolution, Vol. 3. 1975. 5.00x (ISBN 0-686-26757-5). Conn Hist Soc.

Finck, H. T. My Adventures in the Golden Age of Music. LC 70-87496. (Music Ser.). 462p. 1971. Repr. of 1926 ed. lib. bdg. 39.50 (ISBN 0-306-71448-5). Da Capo.

Fisher, William A. Notes on Music in Old Boston. LC 74-27340. Repr. of 1918 ed. 15.00 (ISBN 0-404-12914-5). AMS Pr.

--One Hundred & Fifty Years of Music Publishing in the U. S. 1783--1933. 1981. Repr. lib. bdg. cancelled (ISBN 0-686-71937-9). Scholarly.

Foote, Arthur. Suite in E, Serenade in E. (Early American Music Ser.: No. 60). 60p. 1981. 18.50 (ISBN 0-686-70214-X). Da Capo.

Ford, Ira W. Traditional Music of America. (Music Reprint Ser., 1978). 1978. Repr. of 1940 ed. lib. bdg. 35.00 (ISBN 0-306-77588-3). Da Capo.

Gerson, Robert A. Music in Philadelphia. LC 76-95121. Repr. of 1940 ed. lib. bdg. 19.25x (ISBN 0-8371-3930-9, GEMP). Greenwood.
Gleason, Harold & Becker, Warren. Twentieth Century American Music. 2nd ed. (Music Literature Outlines: Series IV). 1980. 10.95 (ISBN 0-89917-266-0, Frangipani Press). TIS Inc.
Goldberg, Isaac. Tin Pan Alley. LC 60-63364. (Illus.). 1961. pap. 5.95 (ISBN 0-8044-6196-1). Ungar.
Goldman, Richard F. Richard Franko Goldman: Selected Essays & Reviews, 1948-1968. Klotzman, Dorothy, ed. LC 79-56152. (I.S.A.M. Monograph: No. 13). 262p. 1980. pap. 10.00 (ISBN 0-914678-13-2). Inst Am Music.
Goldman, Richard F., ed. Landmarks of Early American Music 1760-1800. LC 72-1631. Repr. of 1943 ed. 14.50 (ISBN 0-404-08309-9). AMS Pr.
Heinrich, Anthony P. The Dawning of Music in Kentucky, The Western Minstrel. LC 79-39732. (Earlier American Music Ser: Vol. 10). 297p. 1973. Repr. of 1820 ed. lib. bdg. 29.50 (ISBN 0-306-77310-4). Da Capo.
Herndon, Marcia. Native American Music. new ed. 233p. 1980. lib. bdg. 20.00 (ISBN 0-8482-4475-3). Norwood Edns.
Hitchcock, H. Wiley. Music in the United States: A Historical Introduction. 2nd ed. (Illus.). 288p. 1974. text ed. 13.50 (ISBN 0-13-608398-6); pap. text ed. 11.95 (ISBN 0-13-608380-3). P-H.
Hood, George. History of Music in New England, with Biographical Sketches of Reformers & Psalmists. (American Studies). 1970. Repr. of 1846 ed. 15.50 (ISBN 0-384-24140-9). Johnson Repr.
Hoogerwerf, Frank W., ed. Music in Georgia. (Music Ser.). (Illus.). 328p. 1981. lib. bdg. 32.50 (ISBN 0-306-76096-7). Da Capo.
Howard, John T. & Bellows, George K. Short History of Music in America. (Apollo Eds.). (Orig.). (YA) (gr. 9-12). pap. 3.95 (ISBN 0-8152-0162-1, A162). T Y Crowell.
Hubbard, William L., ed. History of American Music. LC 72-1617. Repr. of 1908 ed. 27.50 (ISBN 0-404-08314-5). AMS Pr.
Hughes, Rupert. American Composers. LC 72-1618. Repr. of 1914 ed. 37.50 (ISBN 0-404-09905-X). AMS Pr.
Ingalls, Jeremiah. The Christian Harmony. (Earlier American Music Ser.: Vol. 22). 230p. 1980. Repr. of 1805 ed. lib. bdg. 22.50 (ISBN 0-306-79617-1). Da Capo.
Inter-American Conference on Ethnomusicology, 2nd & Inter-American Composers Seminar, 1st. Music in the Americas. List, George & Orrego-Salas, Juan, eds. LC 67-64444. (International American Music Monograph Ser: Vol. 1). (Orig.). 1967. pap. text ed. 12.00x (ISBN 0-87750-140-8). Res Ctr Lang Semiotic.
Jablonski, Edward. Encyclopedia of American Music. LC 77-16925. 648p. 1981. 24.95 (ISBN 0-385-08088-3). Doubleday.
Jones, F. O., ed. Handbook of American Music & Musicians. LC 76-155355. (Music Ser). 1971. Repr. of 1886 ed. lib. bdg. 19.50 (ISBN 0-306-70163-4). Da Capo.
Kaufman, Charles H. Music in New Jersey, 1655-1860. LC 78-75180. 304p. 1981. 35.00 (ISBN 0-8386-2270-4); 65.00 (ISBN 0-8386-2270-4). Fairleigh Dickinson.
Kaufmann, Helen L. From Jehovah to Jazz. LC 72-86028. (Essay & General Literature Index Reprint Ser). 1969. Repr. of 1937 ed. 12.75 (ISBN 0-8046-0565-3). Kennikat.
--From Jehovah to Jazz: Music in America from Psalmody to the Present Day. facs. ed. LC 68-54352. (Essay Index Reprint Ser). 1968. Repr. of 1937 ed. 18.00 (ISBN 0-8369-0585-7). Arno.
Kingman, Daniel. American Music: A Panorama. LC 78-22782. 1979. pap. text ed. 10.95 (ISBN 0-02-871260-9). Schirmer Bks.
Klein, Herman. Unmusical New York: A Brief Criticism of Triumphs, Failures, & Abuses. (Music Reprint Ser.). 1979. Repr. of 1910 ed. lib. bdg. 19.50 (ISBN 0-306-79517-5). Da Capo.
Kmen, Henry A. Music in New Orleans: The Formative Years, 1791-1841. LC 66-25723. (Illus.). 1966. 22.50x (ISBN 0-8071-0548-1). La State U Pr.
Krummel, D. W., et al, eds. Resources of American Music History: A Directory of Source Materials from Colonial Times to World War II. LC 80-14873. (Music in American Life Ser.). 500p. 1981. lib. bdg. 70.00 (ISBN 0-252-00828-6). U of Ill Pr.
Lahee, Henry C. Annals of Music in America. LC 78-97889. Repr. of 1922 ed. 14.75 (ISBN 0-404-03801-8). AMS Pr.
--Annals of Music in America. LC 72-107810. (Select Bibliographies Reprint Ser). 1922. 19.00 (ISBN 0-8369-5185-9). Arno.
Lambert, Barbara, ed. Music in Colonial Massachusetts, Sixteen Thirty to Eighteen Twenty: Music in Public Places, Vol. 1. LC 80-66188. (Illus.). 404p. 1981. 25.00x (ISBN 0-8139-0914-7, Colonial Soc MA). U Pr of Va.
Leichtentritt, Hugo. Serge Koussevitsky, the Boston Symphony Orchestra & the New American Music. LC 75-41172. Repr. of 1946 ed. 16.45 (ISBN 0-404-14680-5). AMS Pr.
Lowens, Irving. Music & Musicians in Early America. (Illus.). 1964. 12.95x (ISBN 0-393-09743-9, NortonC). Norton.
MacDougall, Hamilton C. Early New England Psalmody: An Historical Appreciation, 1620-1820. LC 79-87398. (Music Reprint Ser). 1969. Repr. of 1940 ed. lib. bdg. 19.50 (ISBN 0-306-71542-2). Da Capo.
McLin, Lena. Pulse: A History of Music. LC 77-75478. (Illus.). (gr. 6-12). 1977. pap. 4.95 (ISBN 0-8497-5600-6, WE 3, Pub by Kjos West). Kjos.
Malone, Bill C. Country Music, U.S.A. A Fifty-Year History. LC 68-66367. (American Folklore Society Memoir Ser.: No. 54). (Illus.). 438p. 1969. 15.95 (ISBN 0-292-78377-9); pap. 4.95 (ISBN 0-292-71029-1). U of Tex Pr.
--Southern Music American Music. Roland, Charles P., ed. LC 79-4005. (New Perspectives on the South Ser.). (Illus.). 224p. 1979. 14.00 (ISBN 0-8131-0300-2). U Pr of Ky.
Marcuse, Maxwell F. Tin Pan Alley in Gaslight. LC 58-59691. (Illus.). 1959. 15.00 (ISBN 0-87282-084-X). Century Hse.
Marks, Edward B. They All Had Glamour: From the Swedish Nightingale to the Naked Lady. (Illus.). 448p. 1972. Repr. of 1944 ed. lib. bdg. 22.50x (ISBN 0-8371-6075-8, MATA). Greenwood.
Marrocco, W. Thomas & Gleason, Harold. Music in America: An Anthology from the Landing of the Pilgrims to the Close of the Civil War 1620-1865. (Illus.). 384p. 1974. pap. 12.95x (ISBN 0-393-09296-8). Norton.
Mason, Daniel G. Dilemma of American Music, & Other Essays. Repr. of 1928 ed. lib. bdg. 14.50x (ISBN 0-8371-1155-2, MAAM). Greenwood.
--Tune in, America. LC 72-90664. (Essay Index Reprint Ser). 1931. 15.00 (ISBN 0-8369-1228-4). Arno.
--Tune in America! A Study of Our Coming Musical Independence. LC 72-1720. Repr. of 1931 ed. 16.45 (ISBN 0-404-08328-5). AMS Pr.
Mathews, William S., ed. Hundred Years of Music in America. LC 73-135725. Repr. of 1889 ed. 42.50 (ISBN 0-404-04259-7). AMS Pr.
Mead, Rita. Henry Cowell's New Music, Nineteen Twenty-Five to Nineteen Thirty-Six: The Society, the Music Editions, & the Recordings. Buelow, George, ed. (Studies in Musicology: No. 40). 1981. 69.95 (ISBN 0-8357-1170-6, Pub. by UMI Res Pr). Univ Microfilms.
Mellers, Wilfrid. Music in a New Found Land: Two Hundred Years of American Music. LC 64-17706. (Illus.). 1975. pap. 5.95 (ISBN 0-88373-023-5). Stonehill Pub Co.
Meyer, Hazel. The Gold in Tin Pan Alley. LC 77-7039. 1977. Repr. of 1958 ed. lib. bdg. 18.00x (ISBN 0-8371-9694-9, MEGO). Greenwood.
Molnar, John W. Songs from the Williamsburg Theatre: A Selection of Fifty Songs Performed on the Stage in Williamsburg in the Eighteenth Century. LC 78-165363. (Colonial Williamsburg Publications Ser). (Illus.). 250p. 1972. 15.00x (ISBN 0-8139-0381-5). U Pr of Va.
Moses, Julian M. & DeLuca, G. Collector's Guide to American Recordings: 1895-1925. 7.50 (ISBN 0-8446-5598-8). Peter Smith.
Music Educators National Conference. Perspectives in Music Education. Kowall, Bonnie C., ed. LC 66-25659. 1966. 8.00x (ISBN 0-940796-12-0). Music Ed.
National Society of Colonial Dames of America. Church Music & Musical Life in Pennsylvania in the Eighteenth Century, 3 vols. in 4 pts. LC 79-38037. (Illus.). Repr. of 1926 ed. Set. 135.00 (ISBN 0-404-08090-1); Vol. 1. 33.00 (ISBN 0-404-08091-X); Vol. 2. 37.50 (ISBN 0-404-08092-8); Vol. 3, Pt. 1. 30.00 (ISBN 0-404-08093-6); Vol. 3, Pt. 2. 37.50 (ISBN 0-404-08094-4). AMS Pr.
--Church Music & Musical Life in Pennsylvania in the Eighteenth Century, 3 vols. in 4 pts. LC 79-38037. (Illus.). Repr. of 1926 ed. Set. 135.00 (ISBN 0-404-08090-1); Vol. 1. 33.00 (ISBN 0-404-08091-X); Vol. 2. 37.50 (ISBN 0-404-08092-8); Vol. 3, Pt. 1. 30.00 (ISBN 0-404-08093-6); Vol. 3, Pt. 2. 37.50 (ISBN 0-404-08094-4). AMS Pr.
Nevell. A Time to Dance. (Illus.). 272p. 1980. pap. 6.95 (ISBN 0-312-80523-3). St Martin.
Offenbach, Jacques. Orpheus in America: Offenbach's Diary of His Journey to the New World. MacClintock, Lander, tr. (Illus.). Repr. of 1957 ed. lib. bdg. 15.00 (ISBN 0-8371-0598-6, OFOA). Greenwood.
Owen, Barbara, intro. by. The American Musical Directory. (Music Reprint Ser.). (Illus.). 260p. 1980. Repr. of 1861 ed. lib. bdg. 22.50 (ISBN 0-306-76037-1). Da Capo.
Pavlakis, Christopher. The American Music Handbook. LC 73-2127. 1974. 25.00 (ISBN 0-02-925180-X). Free Pr.
Ritter, Frederic L. Music in America. LC 4-11739. 1971. Repr. of 1890 ed. 23.00 (ISBN 0-384-50990-8). Johnson Repr.
Roberts, John S. The Latin Tinge: The Impact of Latin American Music on the United States. LC 78-26534. (Illus.). 1979. 14.95 (ISBN 0-19-502564-4). Oxford U Pr.
Robinette, Richard. Historical Perspectives in Popular Music: A Historical Outline. (Orig.). 1980. pap. text ed. 10.95 (ISBN 0-8403-2161-9). Kendall-Hunt.
Rodriguez, Jose, ed. Music & Dance in California. LC 78-166257. 467p. 1940. Repr. 39.00 (ISBN 0-403-01384-4). Scholarly.
Rohrer, Gertrude M. Music & Musicians of Pennsylvania. LC 71-124996. (Keystone Historical Publications Ser). 1970. 9.00 (ISBN 0-87198-512-8). Friedman.
Rosenfeld, Paul. American Music. LC 78-19563. (Encore Music Editions Ser.). 1979. Repr. of 1929 ed. 16.50 (ISBN 0-88355-759-2). Hyperion Conn.
Rublowsky, John. Popular Music. LC 67-28387. (Culture & Discovery Ser). (Illus.). (gr. 9 up). 1967. 9.50x (ISBN 0-465-06024-2). Basic.
Sablosky, Irving L. American Music. LC 79-78094. (Chicago History of American Civilization Ser). 1969. 10.00x (ISBN 0-226-73324-6); pap. 3.95 (ISBN 0-226-73325-4, CHAC24). U of Chicago Pr.
Saunders, Richard D., ed. Music & Dance in the Central States. LC 70-166260. 173p. 1952. Repr. 25.00 (ISBN 0-403-01386-0). Scholarly.
Schickel, Richard. The World of Carnegie Hall. LC 73-7674. (Illus.). 438p. 1973. Repr. of 1960 ed. lib. bdg. 20.75x (ISBN 0-8371-6946-1, SCWC). Greenwood.
Smith, Cecil. Worlds of Music. LC 73-7312. 328p. 1973. Repr. of 1952 ed. lib. bdg. 15.25x (ISBN 0-8371-6925-9, SMWM). Greenwood.
Sonneck, O. G. Early Concert-Life in America: 1731-1800. LC 78-2580. (Music Reprint, 1978 Ser.). 1978. Repr. of 1907 ed. lib. bdg. 29.50 (ISBN 0-306-77591-3). Da Capo.
Sonneck, Oscar G. Francis Hopkinson, the First American Poet-Composer, & James Lyon, Patriot, Preacher, Psalmodist. 2nd ed. LC 65-23393. (Music Ser). 1966. Repr. of 1905 ed. lib. bdg. 19.50 (ISBN 0-306-70918-X). Da Capo.
Spalding, Walter R. Music at Harvard: A Historical Review of Men & Events. LC 76-58921. (Music Reprint Series). 1977. Repr. of 1935 ed. lib. bdg. 27.50 (ISBN 0-306-70871-X). Da Capo.
Spell, Lota M. Music in Texas. LC 72-1675. Repr. of 1936 ed. 16.50 (ISBN 0-404-09907-6). AMS Pr.
Stoutamire, Albert. Music of the Old South: Colony to Confederacy. LC 74-149827. (Illus.). 349p. 1972. 18.00 (ISBN 0-8386-7910-2). Fairleigh Dickinson.
Swan, John C. Music in Boston: Readings from the First Three Centuries. 1977. write for info. (ISBN 0-89073-052-0). Boston Public Lib.
Tawa, Nicholas. Sweet Songs for Gentle Americans. LC 78-71394. 1980. 21.95 (ISBN 0-87972-130-8); pap. 10.95 (ISBN 0-87972-157-X). Bowling Green Univ.
Vernon, Grenville. Yankee Doodle-Doo: A Collection of Songs of the Early American Stage. LC 73-78662. 1972. Repr. of 1927 ed. 24.00 (ISBN 0-8103-3872-6). Gale.
Watson, Herbert. A Rollick of Recorders or Other Instruments: Thirteen Popular Colonial Tunes Set for Trio. LC 75-12728. (Orig.). 1975. pap. 1.50 (ISBN 0-87935-029-6). Williamsburg.
Wetzel, Richard D. Frontier Musicians on the Connoquenessing, Wabash & Ohio: A History of the Music & Musicians of George Rapp's Harmony Society (1805-1906) LC 74-80809. (Illus.). 293p. 1976. 16.00x (ISBN 0-8214-0208-0). Ohio U Pr.
Wickes, George. Americans in Paris. (Illus.). xvi, 302p. 1980. pap. 6.95 (ISBN 0-306-80127-2). Da Capo.
Wiggin, Frances T. Maine Composers & Their Music. 1976. pap. 4.00 (ISBN 0-915592-26-6). Maine Hist.
Williams, Martin, ed. The Art of Jazz: Ragtime to Bebop. (Da Capo Quality Paperbacks Ser.). 248p. 1981. pap. 6.95 (ISBN 0-306-80134-5). Da Capo.
Wise, Arthur & Lord, Francis A. Bands & Drummer Boys of the Civil War. (Music Reprint Ser.). 1979. Repr. of 1966 ed. 27.50 (ISBN 0-306-79571-X). Da Capo.
Wootton, Richard. Honky Tonkin' A Travel Guide to American Music. LC 80-503. (Illus.). 192p. 1980. pap. 6.95 (ISBN 0-914788-26-4). East Woods.
Work, Henry C. Songs. LC 73-5099. (Earlier American Music Ser.: Vol. 19). (Illus.). 180p. 1974. Repr. of 1884 ed. lib. bdg. 25.00 (ISBN 0-306-70586-9). Da Capo.

MUSIC, AMERICAN–BIBLIOGRAPHY

Board of Music Trade of the USA. Complete Catalogue of Sheet Music & Musical Works. LC 69-1666. 575p. 1973. Repr. of 1871 ed. lib. bdg. 55.00 (ISBN 0-306-71401-9). Da Capo.
Davis, Elizabeth A. Index to the New World Recorded Anthology of American Music. 224p. 1981. pap. text ed. write for info. (ISBN 0-393-95172-3). Norton.
Dichter, Harry & Shapiro, Elliot. Early American Sheet Music 1768-1889. LC 77-70454. (Illus.). 1977. pap. 6.95 (ISBN 0-486-23364-2). Dover.
Eagon, Angelo. Catalog of Published Concert Music by American Composers. LC 68-9327. (Suppl. to 2nd ed.). 1971. 10.00 (ISBN 0-8108-0387-9). Scarecrow.
Epstein, Dena J. Music Publishing in Chicago Before 1871: The Firm of Root & Cady, 1858-1871. (Detroit Studies in Music Bibliography Ser.: No. 14). 1969. pap. 2.00 (ISBN 0-911772-36-7). Info Coord.
Hitchcock, H. Wiley, pref. by. American Music Before 1865 in Print & on Records: A Biblio-Discography. LC 76-23559. (I. S. A. M. Monograph: No. 6). 114p. (Orig.). 1976. pap. 6.50 (ISBN 0-914678-05-1). Inst Am Music.
Jackson, Richard. U. S. Bicentennial Music I. LC 77-66. (I.S.A.M. Special Publications: No. 1). (Orig.). 1977. pap. 1.50 (ISBN 0-914678-06-X). Inst Am Music.
Priest, Daniel. American Sheet Music: A Guide to Collectible Sheet Music from 1775-1975 with Prices. (Illus.). 1978. 7.95 (ISBN 0-87069-205-4). Wallace-Homestead.
Rowell, Lois. American Organ Music on Records. (Bibliotheca Organologica: Vol. 71). 17.50 (ISBN 90-6027-333-8, Pub. by Frits Knuf Netherlands). Pendragon NY.
Thomson, Virgil. American Music Since Nineteen Ten. (Illus.). 1971. pap. 2.95 (ISBN 0-03-091484-1). HR&W.

MUSIC, ANCIENT

see Music–History and Criticism–To 400

MUSIC, APPRECIATION OF

see Music–Analysis, Appreciation

MUSIC, ARABIC

Al Faruqi, Lois I., ed. An Annotated Glossary of Arabic Musical Terms. LC 81-4129. 536p. 1981. lib. bdg. 45.00 (ISBN 0-313-20554-X, AFM/). Greenwood.
Bulos, Afif. Handbook of Arabic Music. pap. 6.95x (ISBN 0-86685-006-6). Intl Bk Ctr.
Farmer, Henry G. Historical Facts for the Arabian Musical Influence. LC 75-173164. 21.00 (ISBN 0-405-08496-X, Blom Pubns). Arno.
Ribera, Julian. Music in Ancient Arabia & Spain: Being La Musica De las Cantigas. LC 70-87614. (Music Ser). 1970. Repr. of 1929 ed. lib. bdg. 25.00 (ISBN 0-306-71622-4). Da Capo.
Ribera y Tarrago, Julian. Historia De la Musica Arabe Medieval y Su Influencia En la Espanola. LC 78-178587. Repr. of 1927 ed. 24.50 (ISBN 0-404-56664-2). AMS Pr.
Salvador-Daniel, Francesco. The Music & Musical Instruments of the Arab. Farmer, Henry G., ed. & tr. from French. LC 76-22349. (Illus.). 1976. Repr. of 1915 ed. lib. bdg. 30.00 (ISBN 0-89341-008-X). Longwood Pr.
Wright, O. The Modal System of Arab & Persian Music A.D. 1250-1300. (Illus.). 292p. 1976. 95.00x (ISBN 0-19-713575-7). Oxford U Pr.

MUSIC, ASIAN

Beliaev, V. M. Central Asian Music: Essays in the History of the Music of the People of the U.S.S.R. Slobin, Mark, ed. Slobin, Greta N., tr. from Rus. LC 74-5913. 360p. 1975. 35.00x (ISBN 0-8195-4083-8, Pub. by Wesleyan U Pr). Columbia U Pr.
Blaukopf, Kurt & Desmont, Mark, eds. The Cultural Behaviour of Youth: Towards a Cross-Cultural Survey in Europe & Asia. 1976. pap. 17.00 (ISBN 3-7024-0114-8, 51-26247). Eur-Am Music.
Kunst, Jaap. The Cultural Background of Indonesian Music. LC 77-86978. Repr. of 1949 ed. 16.00 (ISBN 0-404-16753-5). AMS Pr.
--Music in Flores: A Study of the Vocal & Instrumental Music Among Tribes Living in Flores. Van Loo, Emile, tr. LC 77-86964. (Illus.). Repr. of 1942 ed. 35.00 (ISBN 0-404-16754-3). AMS Pr.
McPhee, Colin. Music in Bali. LC 76-4979. (Music Reprint Ser.). 1976. Repr. of 1966 ed. lib. bdg. 45.00 (ISBN 0-306-70778-0). Da Capo.
Morton, David. The Traditional Music of Thailand. LC 70-142048. 1976. 32.50x (ISBN 0-520-01876-1). U of Cal Pr.

Pham Duy. The Musics of Vietnam. Whiteside, Dale R., ed. LC 74-17249. 182p. 1975. 8.95x (ISBN 0-8093-0644-1). S Ill U Pr.
Picken, Laurence, ed. Musica Asiatica I. (Illus.). 1978. pap. 19.95x (ISBN 0-19-323234-0). Oxford U Pr.
--Musica Asiatica Two. (Illus.). 195p. 1980. pap. 32.00x (ISBN 0-19-323235-9). Oxford U Pr.
Polin, Claire C. Music of the Ancient Near East. LC 73-20879. (Illus.). 138p. 1974. Repr. of 1954 ed. lib. bdg. 14.50x (ISBN 0-8371-5796-X, PONE). Greenwood.
Slobin, Mark. Kirgiz Instrumental Music. LC 70-93475. (D (Monographs), No. 2). (Illus.). xiv, 158p. (Orig.). 1969. pap. text ed. 6.00x (ISBN 0-913360-01-5). Asian Music Pub.
--Music in the Culture of Northern Afghanistan. LC 74-31998. (Viking Fund Publications in Anthropology: No. 54). 1976. pap. 5.95x (ISBN 0-8165-0498-9). U of Ariz Pr.
Song, Bang-Song. An Annotated Bibliography of Korean Music. LC 75-163013. (A (Bibliographies), No. 2). xiv, 251p. (Orig.). 1971. pap. text ed. 11.75x (ISBN 0-913360-04-X). Asian Music Pub.
Widdess, D. R. & Wolpert, R. F., eds. Music & Tradition: Essays on Asian & Other Musics. LC 78-73235. (Illus.). 1981. 59.50 (ISBN 0-521-22400-4). Cambridge U Pr.
Zainnuddin. Songs of Indonesia. 1970. pap. text ed. 3.50x (ISBN 0-686-65419-6, 00508). Heinemann Ed.

MUSIC, ASSYRO-BABYLONIAN

Galpin, Francis W. Music of the Sumerians. LC 78-87458. (Music Reprint Ser). 1970. Repr. of 1937 ed. lib. bdg. 25.00 (ISBN 0-306-71462-0). Da Capo.
--Music of the Sumerians & Their Immediate Successors, the Babylonians and Assyrians. LC 73-109625. (Select Bibliographies Reprint Ser). 1936. 16.00 (ISBN 0-8369-5234-0). Arno.

MUSIC, AUSTRALIAN

Callaway, Frank, ed. Australian Composition in the Twentieth Century. Tunley, David. 1979. 42.00x (ISBN 0-19-550522-0). Oxford U Pr.
Chenoweth, Vida. The Usarufas & Their Music. (Museum of Anthropology Publications: No. 5). 458p. 1979. 14.90x (ISBN 0-88312-154-9); microfiche 3.40 (ISBN 0-88312-242-1). Summer Inst Ling.
Orchard, William A. Music in Australia. LC 74-24174. Repr. of 1952 ed. 14.50 (ISBN 0-404-13078-X). AMS Pr.

MUSIC, AUSTRIAN

Brody, Elaine & Brook, Claire. The Music Guide to Austria & Germany. LC 75-30822. (Music Guides Ser.). 350p. 1976. 10.00 (ISBN 0-396-07217-8). Dodd.
Chorley, Henry F. Modern German Music: Recollections & Criticisms, 2 vols. LC 79-110994. (Music Reprint Ser.). 1973. Repr. of 1854 ed. 57.50 (ISBN 0-306-71911-8). Da Capo.
Gartenberg, Egon. Vienna: Its Musical Heritage. LC 67-27110. (Illus.). 1968. 15.95 (ISBN 0-271-73131-1). Pa St U Pr.
Graf, Max. Legend of a Musical City. LC 71-90515. Repr. of 1945 ed. lib. bdg. 14.25x (ISBN 0-8371-2128-0, GRLM). Greenwood.
Graf-Khittel, G., ed. Austria: Music & Theatre. 2nd ed. (Illus.). 132p. 1969. 10.00x (ISBN 0-8002-0666-5). Intl Pubns Serv.
Hanslick, Eduard. Vienna's Golden Years of Music, 1850-1900. facs. ed. Pleasants, Henry, ed. LC 69-18928. (Essay Index Reprint Ser). 1950. 20.00 (ISBN 0-8369-0043-X). Arno.
Kobald, Karl. Franz Schubert & His Times. Marshall, Beatrice, tr. from Ger. LC 70-102840. (Illus.). 1970. Repr. of 1928 ed. 13.75 (ISBN 0-8046-0756-7). Kennikat.
Landon, H. C. Chronicle & Works, 5 vols. Incl. Vol. 1 Haydn: the Early Years, 1732-1765. 656p. 1981. 85.00x (ISBN 0-253-37001-9); Vol. 2. Haydn at Eszterhaza; 1766-1790. 820p. 1978. 60.00x (ISBN 0-253-37002-7); Vol. 3. Haydn in England, 1791-1795. 640p. 1976. 70.00x (ISBN 0-253-37003-5); Vol. 4. Haydn: the Years of "the Creation" 1796-1800. 640p. 1976. 55.00x (ISBN 0-253-37004-3); Vol. 5. Haydn: the Late Years, 1801-1809. 496p. 1977. 55.00x (ISBN 0-253-37005-1). Set. 260.00x (ISBN 0-686-70203-4). Ind U Pr.
Lanner, Josef. Saemtliche Werke fuer Klavier von Josef Lanner, 8 vols. Kremser, Eduard, ed. Incl. Vol. 1. Walzer, 1-30 (ISBN 0-8450-1011-5); Vol. 2. Walzer, 31-51 (ISBN 0-8450-1012-3); Vol. 3. Walzer, 52-70 (ISBN 0-8450-1013-1); Vol. 4. Walzer, 71-93 (ISBN 0-8450-1014-X); Vol. 5. Walzer, 94-106; Anhang (ISBN 0-8450-1015-8); Vol. 6. Laendler, Polkas und Mazurkas (ISBN 0-8450-1016-6); Vol. 7. Galoppe (ISBN 0-8450-1017-4); Vol. 8. Quadrillen, Maersche und andere Werke (ISBN 0-8450-1018-2). (Repr. of 1889-1891 ed.). 1973. pap. 325.00x (ISBN 0-8450-1010-7); pap. 55.00x ea. Broude.
Mozart, Wolfgang A. Der Schauspieldirektor (the Impressario) A Comedy with Music in One Act. (Illus., Facsimile of the Autographed Manuscript in the Mary Flagercary Music Collection, the Pierpont Morgan Library). 1976. 65.00 (ISBN 0-19-323301-0). Oxford U Pr.
Rickett, Richard. Music & Musicians in Vienna. (Illus.). 1973. 15.00 (ISBN 3-85367-019-9). Heinman.

MUSIC, BALINESE

Lentz, Donald A. Gamelan Music of Java & Bali: An Artistic Anomaly Complementary to Primary Tonal Theoretical Systems. LC 65-10545. 1965. 5.95x (ISBN 0-8032-0103-6). U of Nebr Pr.

MUSIC, BAROQUE

Agay, Denes. The Baroque Period: Masters of the 17th & 18th Centuries. (An Anthology of Piano Music Ser.: Vol. 1). 232p. 1981. pap. 9.95 (ISBN 0-8256-8041-7). Music Sales.
Anthony, James R. French Baroque Music. 468p. 1981. pap. 8.95 (ISBN 0-393-00967-X). Norton.
--French Baroque Music. (Illus.). 1973. 20.00x (ISBN 0-393-02173-4). Norton.
--French Baroque Music: From Beaujoyeulx to Rameau. 1978. 22.50x (ISBN 0-393-02198-X). Norton.
Bedbrook, Gerald S. Keyboard Music from the Middle Ages to the Beginnings of the Baroque. 2nd ed. LC 69-15605. (Music Ser). (Illus.). 1973. Repr. of 1949 ed. 19.50 (ISBN 0-306-71056-0). Da Capo.
Blume, Friedrich. Renaissance & Baroque Music, a Comprehensive Survey. Norton, M. Herter, tr. (Illus., Orig.). 1967. pap. 4.95x (ISBN 0-393-09710-2, NortonC). Norton.
Borroff, Edith. The Music of the Baroque. LC 77-17401. (Music Reprint Ser.: 1978). (Illus.). 1978. Repr. of 1970 ed. lib. bdg. 20.00 (ISBN 0-306-77438-0). Da Capo.
Clercx, Suzanne. Le Baroque et la musique: Essai d'esthetique musicale. LC 76-43910. Repr. of 1948 ed. 21.00 (ISBN 0-404-60153-7). AMS Pr.
Donington, Robert. String Playing in Baroque Music. LC 76-15291. 1977. 25.00 (ISBN 0-684-14928-1, ScribT); encore ed. 9.95 (ISBN 0-686-77273-3). Scribner.
Dubois, P. Le Baroque. new ed. (Collection themes et textes). 256p. (Orig., Fr.). 1973. pap. 5.95 (ISBN 2-03-035016-8). Larousse.
Fortune, Nigel & Lewis, Anthony, eds. New Oxford History of Music, Vol. 5: Opera & Church Music 1630-1750. (Illus.). 800p. 1975. 49.95x (ISBN 0-19-316305-5). Oxford U Pr.
Gleason, Harold & Becker, Warren. Music in the Baroque. 3rd ed. (Music Literature Outlines: Ser. II). 1979. pap. 10.95 (ISBN 0-89917-016-1, Frangipani Pr). TIS Inc.
Hutchings, Arthur J. The Baroque Concerto. (Illus.). 1979. 17.50 (ISBN 0-684-16059-5, ScribT). Scribner.
Klenz, William. Giovanni Maria Bononcini of Modena: A Chapter in Baroque Instrumental Music. LC 62-20213. 1962. 24.50 (ISBN 0-8223-0098-2). Duke.
Marshall, Robert L., ed. Studies in Renaissance & Baroque Music in Honor of Arthur Mendel. 1974. 35.00 (ISBN 0-913574-26-0). Eur-Am Music.
Neumann, F. Ornamentation in Baroque & Post-Baroque Music: With Special Emphasis on J. S. Bach. LC 77-72130. (Illus.). 1978. 60.00 (ISBN 0-691-09123-4). Princeton U Pr.
Newman, William S. Sonata in the Baroque Era. 3rd ed. 1972. pap. 6.95 (ISBN 0-393-00622-0, Norton Lib). Norton.
Palisca, Claude. Baroque Music. 2nd ed. (P-H History of Music Ser.). (Illus.). 1980. text ed. 15.95 (ISBN 0-13-055954-7); pap. text ed. 11.50 (ISBN 0-13-055947-4). P-H.
Rangel-Ribeiro, Victor. Baroque Music: A Practical Guide for the Performer. LC 80-5222. (Illus.). 260p. 1981. 20.00 (ISBN 0-02-871980-8). Schirmer Bks.

MUSIC, BELGIAN

Ban, Ioan A. Zang-Bloemzel...(Theoretical Parts) & Kort Sangh-Bericht... (Early Music Theory in the Low Countries Ser.: Vol. 1). wrappers 20.00 (ISBN 90-6027-077-0, Pub. by Frits Knuf Netherlands). Pendragon NY.
Blankenburg, Quirinus Van. Elementa Musica...'s. (Early Music Theory in the Low Countries Ser.: Vol. 4). 1973. Repr. of 1739 ed. wrappers 37.50 (ISBN 0-686-30910-3, Pub. by Frits Knuf Netherlands). Pendragon NY.
Boone, Hubert. De Hommel in de Lage Landen: L'epinette aus Pays Bas. (Illus.). 188p. 1976. 37.50 (ISBN 90-6027-174-2, Pub. by Frits Knuf Netherlands); wrappers 25.00 (ISBN 90-6027-173-4, Pub. by Frits Knuf Netherlands). Pendragon NY.
Brevia musicae rudimenta Latino Belgicae ex prolixioribus musicorum praeceptis excerpta Corte onderwysinghe van de musike... Leyden Sixteen Hundred & Five. (Early Music Theory in the Low Countries Ser.: Vol. 3). 24p. 1973. Repr. of 1591 ed. wrappers 20.00 (ISBN 90-6027-177-7, Pub. by Frits Knuf Netherlands). Pendragon NY.
Brody, Elaine & Brook, Claire. The Music Guide to Belgium, Luxembourg, Holland & Switzerland. LC 77-6446. (Music Guides Ser.). (Illus.). 1977. 10.00 (ISBN 0-396-07437-5). Dodd.
Douwes, Klaas. Grondig ondersoek van de Toonen der Musyk. (Early Music Theory in the Low Countries Ser.: Vol. 2). 1971. Repr. of 1699 ed. wrappers 25.00 (ISBN 90-6027-142-4, Pub. by Frits Knuf Netherlands). Pendragon NY.
Gleich, C. C. Von. Pianofortes uit de Lage Landen. (Haags Gemeentemuseum, Kijkboekjes Ser.: Vol. 4). (Illus.). 72p. (Dutch & Eng.). 1981. wrappers 15.00 (ISBN 0-686-30911-1, Pub. by Frits Knuf Netherlands). Pendragon NY.
Goovaerts, A. Histoire et Bibliographie de la Typographie Musicale dans les Pays-Bas. 1963. Repr. of 1880 ed. 62.50 (ISBN 90-6027-002-9, Pub. by Frits Knuf Netherlands). Pendragon NY.
Haine, Malou & Keyser, Ignace de. Catalogue des Instruments Sax au Musee Instrumental de Bruxelles: Suivi de la liste de 400 instruments Sax conserves dans des collections publiques et privees. (Illus.). vi, 280p. 1980. 40.00 (ISBN 90-6027-397-4, Pub. by Frits Knuf Netherlands). Pendragon NY.
Livre Plaisant et Tresutile Pour Apprendre a Faire et Ordonner Toutes Tabulatures Hors le Discant. (Early Music Theory in the Low Countries Ser.: Vol. 9). 1973. Repr. of 1568 ed. 25.00wrappers (ISBN 90-6027-289-7, Pub. by Frits Knuf Netherlands). Pendragon NY.
Mahillon, Victor C. Catalogue Descriptif et Analytique Du Musee Instrumental De Conservatoire Royal De Musique De Bruxelles(1893-1922, 5 vols. 1978. 162.50 (ISBN 90-6027-295-1, Pub. by Frits Knuf Netherlands). Pendragon NY.

MUSIC, BOHEMIAN

see Music, Czech

MUSIC, BRITISH

see also Music, English

Agate, James. Immoment Toys. LC 77-86884. Repr. of 1945 ed. 12.00 (ISBN 0-405-08189-8, Pub. by Blom). Arno.
Boyd, Malcolm. Grace Williams. (Composers of Wales Ser.: No. 4). 98p. 1980. pap. text ed. 10.00 (ISBN 0-7083-0762-0). Verry.
Brody, Elaine & Brook, Claire. The Music Guide to Great Britain. LC 75-30809. (Music Guides Ser.). 350p. 1976. 10.00 (ISBN 0-396-06955-X). Dodd.
Bruce, John C. & Stokoe, John. Northumbrian Minstrelsy: A Collection of the Ballads, Melodies, & Small-Pipe Tunes of Northumbria. LC 65-4143. xxxiv, 197p. 1965. Repr. of 1882 ed. 10.00 (ISBN 0-8103-5042-4). Gale.
Cheney, David R. & Hunt, Leigh. Musical Evenings: Or Selections, Vocal & Instrumental. LC 64-12876. 1964. 4.50x (ISBN 0-8262-0033-8). U of Mo Pr.
Fennell, Frederick. Basic Band Repertory: British Band Classics from the Conductor's Point of View. 1980. pap. 6.00 (ISBN 0-686-29444-0). Instrumental Co.
Jacobs, Arthur, ed. British Music Yearbook, 1980. 6th ed. 637p. 1980. pap. 24.50x (ISBN 0-8476-6255-1). Rowman.
Jacobs, Artur & Barton, Marianne, eds. British Music Yearbook, 1981. 7th ed. 555p. 1981. pap. 24.50x (ISBN 0-8476-3722-0). Rowman.
Lawrence, William J. Elizabethan Playhouse & Other Studies, 2 vols. in 1. LC 63-15167. (Illus., 1963. Repr. of 1912-13 eds). 25.00 (ISBN 0-8462-0360-X). Russell.
Lee, Lorraine A. An Elizabethan Songbook: With Arrangements for Appalachian Dulcimer. LC 77-81693. (American Music Ser.). (Illus.). 1977. pap. 4.95 (ISBN 0-89461-004-X). Comm Pr Inc.
Mackenzie-Grieve, Averil. Clara Novello. (Music Reprint Ser.). 1980. Repr. of 1955 ed. lib. bdg. 29.50 (ISBN 0-306-76009-6). Da Capo.
Norris, Gerald. Musical Gazetteer of Great Britain & Ireland. LC 81-65957. (Illus.). 352p. 1981. 36.00 (ISBN 0-7153-7845-7). David & Charles.
Palmer, Russell. British Music. LC 78-166249. 283p. 1948. Repr. 26.00 (ISBN 0-403-01641-X). Scholarly.
Pearsall, Ronald. Victorian Sheet Music Covers. LC 72-6422. (Illus.). 116p. 1972. 16.00 (ISBN 0-8103-2001-0). Gale.
Senelick, Laurence, et al. British Music Hall 1840-1923: A Bibliography & Guide to Sources with a Supplement on European Music-Hall. LC 81-4996. (Archon Books on Popular Entertainments Ser.). 1981. 37.50 (ISBN 0-208-01840-9, Archon). Shoe String.
Wienpahl, Robert W. Music at the Inns of Court: During the Reigns of Elizabeth, James, & Charles. LC 79-14881. (Orig.). 1979. pap. 20.75 (ISBN 0-8357-0417-3, SS-00103). Univ Microfilms.

MUSIC, BRITISH–HISTORY AND CRITICISM

Borren, Charles V. Sources of Keyboard Music in England. Matthew, James E., tr. LC 78-106714. Repr. of 1914 ed. lib. bdg. 16.25x (ISBN 0-8371-3444-7, BOKM). Greenwood.
Burney, Charles. An Account of the Musical Performances in Westminster Abbey. (Music Reprint Ser.). 1979. Repr. of 1785 ed. 29.50 (ISBN 0-306-79524-8). Da Capo.
Crowest, Frederick J. The Story of British Music: From the Earliest Times to the Tudor Period. LC 76-22328. (Illus.). 1976. Repr. of 1896 ed. lib. bdg. 40.00 (ISBN 0-89341-024-1). Longwood Pr.
Davey, Henry. History of English Music. 3rd ed. LC 69-15620. (Music Ser). 1969. Repr. of 1921 ed. lib. bdg. 35.00 (ISBN 0-306-71133-8). Da Capo.
Elbourne, Roger. Music & Tradition in Early Industrial Lancashire: Seventeen Eighty to Eighteen Forty. (Folklore Society Mistletoe Ser.). 177p. 1980. 26.00x (ISBN 0-8476-6244-6). Rowman.
Fuller-Maitland, J. A. English Music in the Nineteenth Century. LC 76-22334. 1976. Repr. of 1902 ed. lib. bdg. 30.00 (ISBN 0-89341-019-5). Longwood Pr.
Harrison, Frank L. Music in Medieval Britain. 4th ed. (Illus.). xx, 491p. 1980. 45.00 (ISBN 90-6027-252-8, Pub. by Frits Knuf Netherlands); wrappers 35.00 (ISBN 90-6027-251-X). Pendragon NY.
Holborne, Anthony. Complete Works, 2 vols. Kanazawa, Masakata, ed. Incl. Vol. 1. Music for Lute & Bandora. (Illus.). 1967. pap. 17.50x (ISBN 0-674-15500-9); Vol. 2. Music for Cittern. 1974. pap. 15.95x (ISBN 0-674-15512-2). LC 67-14341. (Publications in Music Ser: No. 1, 5). Harvard U Pr.
Hueffer, Francis. Half a Century of Music in England 1837-1887: Essays Towards a History. LC 76-22335. 1976. Repr. of 1889 ed. lib. bdg. 25.00 (ISBN 0-89341-025-X). Longwood Pr.
Jackson, Vincent. English Melodies from the Thirteenth to the Eighteenth Century. LC 71-153330. Repr. of 1910 ed. 21.50 (ISBN 0-404-08030-8). AMS Pr.
Kassler, Jamie C. The Science of Music in Britain, 1714-1830: A Catalogue of Writings, Lectures & Inventions, 2 vols. LC 76-52675. (Reference Library of the Humanities: Vol. 79). 1977. Set. lib. bdg. 115.00 (ISBN 0-8240-9894-3). Garland Pub.
Knight, Frida. Cambridge Music: From the Middle Ages to Modern Times. (Cambridge Town, Gown & Country Ser.: Vol. 29). (Illus.). 1980. 22.50 (ISBN 0-900891-51-3). Oleander Pr.
Le Huray, P. Music & the Reformation in England: Fifteen Forty-Nine to Sixteen Sixty. LC 77-87383. (Studies in Music). (Illus.). 1978. 64.50 (ISBN 0-521-21958-2); pap. 14.95x (ISBN 0-521-29418-5). Cambridge U Pr.
Padelford, Frederick M. Old English Musical Terms. LC 76-22346. 1976. Repr. of 1899 ed. lib. bdg. 15.00 (ISBN 0-89341-012-8). Longwood Pr.
Pattison, Bruce. Music & Poetry of the English Renaissance. 220p. 1980. Repr. of 1948 ed. lib. bdg. 30.00 (ISBN 0-8495-4368-1). Arden Lib.
--Music & Poetry of the English Renaissance. LC 72-193387. 1948. lib. bdg. 20.00 (ISBN 0-685-10372-2). Folcroft.
Price, Curtis A. Music in the Restoration Theatre: With a Catalogue of Instrumental Music in the Plays, 1665-1713. LC 79-11742. (Studies in Musicology: No. 4). 1979. 29.95 (ISBN 0-8357-0998-1). Univ Microfilms.
Price, D. C. Patrons & Musicians of the English Renaissance. LC 80-40054. (Cambridge Studies in Music). (Illus.). 250p. 1981. 55.00 (ISBN 0-521-22806-9). Cambridge U Pr.
Scholes, Percy A. Mirror of Music, 1844-1944, 2 Vols. facs. ed. LC 71-124255. (Select Bibliographies Reprint Ser). 1947. Set. 75.00 (ISBN 0-8369-5443-2). Arno.
Thorp, Willard. Songs from the Restoration Theatre. LC 76-102003. (Music Ser). 1970. Repr. of 1934 ed. lib. bdg. 17.50 (ISBN 0-306-71867-7). Da Capo.

MUSIC, BYZANTINE

Hatherly, S. G. Treatise on Byzantine Music. LC 77-75226. 1977. Repr. of 1892 ed. lib. bdg. 20.00 (ISBN 0-89341-071-3). Longwood Pr.

Strunk, Oliver. Essays on Music in the Byzantine World. (Illus.). 1977. 22.95x (ISBN 0-393-02183-1). Norton.
Tillyard, Henry J. Byzantine Music & Hymnography. LC 74-24242. Repr. of 1923 ed. 11.50 (ISBN 0-404-13116-6). AMS Pr.
Wellesz, Egon. History of Byzantine Music & Hymnography. 2nd ed. 1961. 49.95x (ISBN 0-19-816111-5). Oxford U Pr.

MUSIC, CANADIAN

Canadian Broadcasting Corporation. Thirty-Four Biographies of Canadian Composers. LC 75-166224. 1964. Repr. 19.00 (ISBN 0-403-01351-8). Scholarly.
Cherney, Brian. Harry Somers. LC 75-15845. (Canadian Composers Ser.). (Illus.). 1975. 20.00x (ISBN 0-8020-5325-4). U of Toronto Pr.
Fowke, Edith F. Traditional Singers & Songs from Ontario. LC 65-26777. (Illus.). x, 210p. Repr. of 1965 ed. 22.00 (ISBN 0-8103-5011-4). Gale.
Jarman, Lynne, ed. Canadian Music: A Selected Checklist, 1950-1973. LC 76-55840. 1976. 15.00x (ISBN 0-8020-5327-0). U of Toronto Pr.
Kallmann, Helmut, ed. Catalogue of Canadian Composers. LC 75-166240. 1972. Repr. of 1952 ed. 21.00 (ISBN 0-403-01375-5). Scholarly.
Kallmann, Helmut, et al, eds. Encyclopedia of Music in Canada. 1100p. 1981. 65.00 (ISBN 0-8020-5509-5). U of Toronto Pr.
Macmillan, Ernest, ed. Music in Canada. LC 77-18206. 232p. 1955. Repr. 21.00 (ISBN 0-403-01616-9). Scholarly.
Proctor, George A. Canadian Music of the Twentieth Century. 1980. 27.50x (ISBN 0-8020-5419-6). U of Toronto Pr.

MUSIC, CHINESE

Chao, Mei-Po. The Yellow Bell: A Brief Sketch of the History of Chinese Music. lib. bdg. 69.95 (ISBN 0-87968-135-7). Krishna Pr.
Clack, Robert W. Celestial Symphonies: A History of Chinese Music. 1975. lib. bdg. 69.95 (ISBN 0-87968-447-X). Gordon Pr.
Crump, J. I., ed. Chinese & Japanese Music-Dramas. Malm, William P. (Michigan Papers in Chinese Studies Ser.: No. 19). (Illus.). 255p. 1975. pap. 2.00 (ISBN 0-89264-019-7). U of Mich Ctr Chinese.
Hsu, Princeton S. A Study of the Bronze Drums of South China. (Asian Folklore & Social Life Monographs: Vol. 95). 1977. 5.50 (ISBN 0-89986-327-2). E Langstaff.
Johnson, Dale R. Yuarn Music Dramas: Studies in Prosody & Structure & a Complete Catalogue of Northern Arias in the Dramatic Style. LC 80-25372. (Michigan Papers in Chinese Studies: No. 40). 400p. (Orig.). 1980. pap. 8.00 (ISBN 0-89264-040-5). U of Mich Ctr Chinese.
Kaufmann, Walter. Musical References in the Chinese Classics. LC 74-75914. (Detroit Monographs in Musicology: No. 5). 1976. 15.00 (ISBN 0-911772-68-5). Info Coord.
Lieberman, Fredric. Chinese Music: An Annotated Bibliography. 2nd ed. LC 76-24755. (Reference Library of the Humanities Ser.: Vol. 75). 1976. lib. bdg. 31.00 (ISBN 0-8240-9922-2). Garland Pub.
Pian, Rulan C. Sonq Dynasty Musical Sources & Their Interpretation. LC 65-22046. (Harvard-Yenching Institute Monograph Ser: No. 16). (Illus.). 1967. 12.50x (ISBN 0-674-82095-9). Harvard U Pr.
Van Gulik, R. H. Hsi K'ang & His Poetical Essay on the Lute. LC 68-58913. 1969. 15.00 (ISBN 0-8048-0868-6). C E Tuttle.

MUSIC, CHORAL

see Choral Music

MUSIC, COMMUNITY

see Community Music

MUSIC, CZECH

Newmarch, Rosa. The Music of Czechoslovakia. LC 77-26269. (Music Reprint Ser., 1978). 1978. Repr. of 1942 ed. lib. bdg. 22.50 (ISBN 0-306-77563-8). Da Capo.
Service, Robert W. Ballads of a Bohemian. 220p. 1981. pap. write for info. (ISBN 0-86649-069-8). Twentieth Century.

MUSIC, DANISH

Hammerich, Angul. Mediaeval Musical Relics of Denmark. LC 74-24104. Repr. of 1912 ed. 24.50 (ISBN 0-404-12952-8). AMS Pr.
Kappel, Vagn. Contemporary Danish Composers Against the Background of Danish Musical Life & History. LC 70-181195. 1948. Repr. 19.00 (ISBN 0-403-01602-9). Scholarly.

MUSIC, DRAMATIC

see Ballad Opera; Music in Theaters; Musical Revue, Comedy, Etc.; Opera; Operetta

MUSIC, DUTCH

Ban, Ioan A. Zang-Bloemzel...(Theoretical Parts) & Kort Sangh-Bericht... (Early Music Theory in the Low Countries Ser.: Vol. 1). wrappers 20.00 (ISBN 90-6027-077-0, Pub. by Frits Knuf Netherlands). Pendragon NY.
Blankenburg, Quirinus Van. Elementa Musica...'s. (Early Music Theory in the Low Countries Ser.: Vol. 4). 1973. Repr. of 1739 ed. wrappers 37.50 (ISBN 0-686-30910-3, Pub. by Frits Knuf Netherlands). Pendragon NY.
Bols, Jan. Hondred Vlaamsche Liederen, met woorden en zangwijzen, voor de eerste maal aan het licht gebracht. (Facsimile of Dutch Songbks.: Vol. 5). 1979. Repr. of 1897 ed. 36.00 (ISBN 90-6027-171-8, Pub. by Frits Knuf Netherlands); wrappers 24.00 (ISBN 90-6027-170-X, Pub. by Frtis Knuf Netherlands). Pendragon NY.
Boone, Hubert. De Hommel in de Lage Landen: L'epinette aus Pays Bas. (Illus.). 188p. 1976. 37.50 (ISBN 90-6027-174-2, Pub. by Frits Knuf Netherlands); wrappers 25.00 (ISBN 90-6027-173-4, Pub. by Frits Knuf Netherlands). Pendragon NY.
Brody, Elaine & Brook, Claire. The Music Guide to Belgium, Luxembourg, Holland & Switzerland. LC 77-6446. (Music Guides Ser.). (Illus.). 1977. 10.00 (ISBN 0-396-07437-5). Dodd.
Cavaille-Coll, A. Devis d'un grand orgue a trois claviers et un pedalier complets projete pour la vieille Eglise Lutherienne Evangelique a Amsterdam. (Bibliotheca Organologica Ser.: Vol. 45). 52p. 1980. Repr. of 1881 ed. wrappers 17.50 (ISBN 90-6027-193-9, Pub. by Frits Knuf Netherlands). Pendragon NY.
Douwes, Klaas. Grondig ondersoek van de Toonen der Musyk. (Early Music Theory in the Low Countries Ser.: Vol. 2). 1971. Repr. of 1699 ed. wrappers 25.00 (ISBN 90-6027-142-4, Pub. by Frits Knuf Netherlands). Pendragon NY.
Dunning, Albert. Count Unico Wilhelm van Wassenaar, Sixteen Ninety-Two to Seventeen Sixty-Six: A Master Unmasked or the Pergolesi-Ricciotti Puzzle Solved. Rimmer, Joan, tr. from Dutch. (Illus.). 210p. 65.00 (ISBN 90-6027-400-8, Pub. by Frits Knuf Netherlands); wrappers 47.50 (ISBN 90-6027-399-0, Pub. by Frits Knuf Netherlands). Pendragon NY.
Duyse, Florimond van. De Melodie van het Nederlandsche Lied en hare rhytmische vormen. (Facsimile of Dutch Songbks. Ser.: Vol. 6). 1979. Repr. of 1902 ed. 45.00 (ISBN 90-6027-216-1, Pub. by Frits Knuf Netherlands); wrappers 30.00 (ISBN 90-6027-215-3, Pub. by Frits Knuf Netherlands). Pendragon NY.
Eck, G. H. van, Jr. Handboek der Nederlandsche Muzieklitteratuur, 2 pts. in 1. (Dictionarium Musicum Ser.: Vol. 4). 1978. Repr. of 1890 ed. Set. 45.00 (ISBN 90-6027-218-8, Pub. by Frits Knuf Netherlands); Set. wrappers 30.00 (ISBN 90-6027-217-X, Pub. by Frits Knuf Netherlands). Pendragon NY.
Gleich, C. C. Von. Pianofortes uit de Lage Landen. (Haags Gemeentemuseum, Kijkboekjes Ser.: Vol. 4). (Illus.). 72p. (Dutch & Eng.). 1981. wrappers 15.00 (ISBN 0-686-30911-1, Pub. by Frits Knuf Netherlands). Pendragon NY.
Goovaerts, A. Histoire et Bibliographie de la Typographie Musicale dans les Pays-Bas. 1963. Repr. of 1880 ed. 62.50 (ISBN 90-6027-002-9, Pub. by Frits Knuf Netherlands). Pendragon NY.
Huybens, Gilbert. Het geestelijk em wereldijk Volksliedboek van de Zuidelijke Nederlanden, 6e - 18e eeuw - Gedrukte bronnen. (Facsimile of Dutch Songbks. Ser.: Vol. 7). 1981. write for info. (ISBN 90-6027-267-6, Pub. by Frits Knuf Netherlands). Pendragon NY.
Huys, Bernard, intro. by. Occo Codex. (Facsimilia Musica Neerlandica Ser.: Vol. 1). xxix, 154p. 1979. 72.50 (ISBN 90-6027-308-7, Pub. by Frits Knuf Netherlands). Pendragon NY.
Hymni. Ofte Loff-Sangen op de Christelijcke Feest-Dagen ende Ander-Sins. (Facsimile of Dutch Songbks. Ser.: Vol. 1). 1967. Repr. of 1615 ed. wrappers 20.00 (ISBN 90-6027-047-9, Pub. by Frits Knuf Netherlands). Pendragon NY.
Livre Plaisant et Tresutile Pour Apprendre a Faire et Ordonner Toutes Tabulatures Hors le Discant. (Early Music Theory in the Low Countries Ser.: Vol. 9). 1973. Repr. of 1568 ed. 25.00wrappers (ISBN 90-6027-289-7, Pub. by Frits Knuf Netherlands). Pendragon NY.
Lowinsky, Edward E. Secret Chromatic Art in the Netherlands Motet. Buchman, Carl, tr. LC 66-27120. (Illus.). 1967. Repr. of 1946 ed. 10.00 (ISBN 0-8462-0847-4). Russell.
Mahaut, A. Maandelyks Musikaels Tydverdryf: Bestaende in Nieuwe Hollandsche Canzonetten of Zang-Liederen Op D'italiaensche Trant In't Musiek Gebragt. 1979. 57.50 (ISBN 90-6027-294-3, Pub. by Frits Knuf Netherlands); complete in 12 issues 37.50 (ISBN 90-6027-293-5). Pendragon NY.
Muzikaal Nederland 1850-1910: Bio-Bibliografisch Woordenboek Van Nederlandsche Tookunstenaars En Tookunstenaressen, Alsmede Van Schrijvers En Schrijfsters Op Muziekliteraturisch Gebied. (Dictionarium Musicum: Vol. 6). 1981. Repr. of 1913 ed. 45.00 (ISBN 90-6027-387-7, Pub. by Frits Knuf Netherlands); 32.50 (ISBN 90-6027-386-9). Pendragon NY.
Sollitt, Edna R. Dufay to Sweelinck, Netherlands Masters of Music. Repr. of 1933 ed. lib. bdg. 15.00 (ISBN 0-8371-4028-5, SODS). Greenwood.
Souter, Liedekens. Ghemaect Ter Eeren Gods, Op Alle Dye Psalmen Van David: Tot Stichtinghe, En Een Gheestelijcke Vermakinghe Van Alle Christe Mensche. (Facs. of Dutch Songbooks: Vol. 2). 1982. Set. 50.00 (ISBN 0-686-30870-0, Pub. by Frits Knuf Netherlands). Vol. 1 (ISBN 90-6027-348-6). Vol. 2 Intro., Notes, Commentary & Bibliography (ISBN 90-6027-349-4). Pendragon NY.

MUSIC, EFFECT OF

see Music, Influence of; Music Therapy

MUSIC, ELECTRONIC

see Electronic Music

MUSIC, ENGLISH

see also Music, British

Blom, Eric. Music in England. LC 71-181112. 220p. 1942. Repr. 19.00 (ISBN 0-403-01511-1). Scholarly.
Boyd, Morrison C. Elizabethan Music & Musical Criticism. LC 73-1837. (Illus.). 363p. 1973. Repr. of 1962 ed. lib. bdg. 24.25x (ISBN 0-8371-6805-8, BOEL). Greenwood.
Calvocoressi, Michel D. Music & Ballet. LC 74-24053. Repr. of 1934 ed. 24.50 (ISBN 0-404-12877-7). AMS Pr.
Chappell, William. Popular Music of the Olden Time, 2 Vols. (Illus.). Set. 11.00 (ISBN 0-8446-1839-X). Peter Smith.
Cowling, George H. Music on the Shakespearian Stage. LC 74-24063. Repr. of 1913 ed. 10.00 (ISBN 0-404-12889-0). AMS Pr.
Dutka, JoAnna. Music in the English Mystery Plays. (Early Drama, Art, & Music Ser.). (Illus.). 171p. 1980. 18.80 (ISBN 0-918720-10-9); pap. 11.80 (ISBN 0-918720-11-7). Medieval Inst.
Evans, Peter. The Music of Benjamin Britten. 1979. 29.50x (ISBN 0-8166-0836-9). U of Minn Pr.
Graves, Charles L. Post-Victorian Music. LC 71-102838. 1970. Repr. of 1911 ed. 15.00 (ISBN 0-8046-0754-0). Kennikat.
Holland, Arthur K. Henry Purcell: The English Musical Tradition. facs. ed. LC 70-107807. (Select Bibliographies Reprint Ser). 1932. 17.00 (ISBN 0-8369-5183-2). Arno.
Hughes, H. V., ed. Early English Harmony from the 10th to the 15th Century, 2 vols. LC 74-26041. (Illus.). Repr. of 1913 ed. Set. 37.50 (ISBN 0-404-12925-0); Vol. 1. (ISBN 0-404-12926-9); Vol. 2. (ISBN 0-404-12927-7). AMS Pr.
Klein, Hermann. Thirty Years of Musical Life in London. LC 78-2565. (Music Reprint Ser., 1978). (Illus.). 1978. Repr. of 1903 ed. lib. bdg. 32.50 (ISBN 0-306-77586-7). Da Capo.
Mackerness, Eric D. A Social History of English Music. LC 75-40994. (Illus.). 307p. 1976. Repr. of 1964 ed. lib. bdg. 18.25x (ISBN 0-8371-8705-2, MAHEM). Greenwood.
Mason, Dorothy E. Music in Elizabethan England. LC 59-1448. (Folger Guides to the Age of Shakespeare). 1958. pap. 3.95 (ISBN 0-918016-21-5). Folger Bks.
Mazzaro, Jerome. Transformations in the Renaissance English Lyric. LC 74-124726. 228p. 1970. 20.00x (ISBN 0-8014-0587-4). Cornell U Pr.
Meyer, Ernst. English Chamber Music. LC 71-127181. (Music Ser). (Illus.). 1971. Repr. of 1946 ed. lib. bdg. 27.50 (ISBN 0-306-70037-9). Da Capo.
Moore, Arthur W., ed. Manx Ballads & Music. LC 78-72642. (Celtic Language & Literature: Goidelic & Brythonic). Repr. of 1896 ed. 26.00 (ISBN 0-404-17575-9). AMS Pr.
Nettel, Reginald. The Orchestra in England: A Social History. LC 75-181219. 272p. 1956. Repr. 17.00 (ISBN 0-403-01630-4). Scholarly.
Ottaway, Hugh. Vaughan Williams Symphonies. LC 72-6084. (BBC Music Guides Ser.: No. 28). (Illus.). 64p. (Orig.). 1973. pap. 1.95 (ISBN 0-295-95233-4). U of Wash Pr.
Palmer, Roy. A Ballad History of England: From Fifteen Eighty-Eight to the Present Day. (Illus.). 192p. 1979. 27.00 (ISBN 0-686-74070-X, Pub. by Batsford England). David & Charles.
Parke, W. T. Musical Memoirs, Comprising an Account of the General State of Music in England. 2 Vols. in 1. LC 77-125058. (Music Ser). 1970. Repr. of 1830 ed. lib. bdg. 55.00 (ISBN 0-306-70023-9). Da Capo.
Pattison, Bruce. Music & Poetry of the English Renaissance. LC 70-127278. (Music Ser). (Illus.). 1970. Repr. of 1948 ed. lib. bdg. 22.50 (ISBN 0-306-71298-9). Da Capo.
Pearsall, Ronald. Edwardian Popular Music. LC 75-10734. (Illus.). 207p. 12.00 (ISBN 0-8386-1781-6). Fairleigh Dickinson.
Pirie, Peter J. The English Musical Renaissance. 1980. 16.95 (ISBN 0-312-25435-0). St Martin.
Pohl, C. F. Mozart & Haydn in London, 2 vols. in 1. LC 70-125059. (Music Ser). 1970. Repr. of 1867 ed. lib. bdg. 35.00 (ISBN 0-306-70024-7). Da Capo.
Pulver, Jeffrey. A Bibliographical Dictionary of Old English Music: Old English Music & Musical Instruments. LC 73-80260. 1970. Repr. of 1927 ed. 22.50 (ISBN 0-8337-2867-9). B Franklin.
Ravenscroft, Thomas. A Briefe Discourse of the True Use of Charact'ring the Degrees in Measurable Musicke, 2 pts. LC 70-171785. (English Experience Ser.: No. 409). 108p. 1971. Repr. of 1614 ed. Set. 9.50 (ISBN 90-221-0409-5). Walter J Johnson.
The Rounds, Catches & Carons of England: A Collection of Specimens of the Sixteenth, Seventeenth, & Eighteenth Centuries Adopted to Modern Use. LC 76-21067. (Music Reprint Ser.). 208p. 1976. 25.00 (ISBN 0-306-70823-X). Da Capo.
Shaw, Bernard. How to Become a Musical Critic. Laurence, Dan H., ed. LC 77-26653. (Music Reprint Ser., 1978). 1978. Repr. of 1961 ed. lib. bdg. 27.50 (ISBN 0-306-77569-7). Da Capo.
Shaw, George B. Collected Music Criticism of Bernard Shaw, 4 vols. Incl. Music in London 1890-1894, 3 vols. Vol. 1 (ISBN 0-8443-0059-4). Vol. 2 (ISBN 0-8443-0060-8). Vol. 3 (ISBN 0-8443-0061-6); London Music in 1888-1889 As Heard by Corno Di Bassetto (Bernard Shaw) Repr. of 1937 ed (ISBN 0-8443-0058-6). 1973. Set. in slipcase 75.00 (ISBN 0-8443-0063-2). Vienna Hse.
--Music in London: Eighteen Ninety to Eighteen Ninety-Four, 3 vols. LC 77-181257. 1956. Repr. 69.00 (ISBN 0-403-01680-0). Scholarly.
Stanford, Charles V. Studies & Memories. LC 76-22352. (Illus.). 1976. Repr. of 1908 ed. lib. bdg. 25.00 (ISBN 0-89341-023-3). Longwood Pr.
Stevens, J. E., ed. Music & Poetry in the Early Tudor Court. LC 77-90180. (Cambridge Studies in Music). (Illus.). 1979. 69.50 (ISBN 0-521-22030-0); pap. 17.95 (ISBN 0-521-29417-7). Cambridge U Pr.
Trefusis, Mary, ed. Songs, Ballads & Instrumental Pieces Composed by King Henry the Eighth. LC 74-26054. Repr. of 1912 ed. 32.50 (ISBN 0-404-12962-5). AMS Pr.
Van Den Borren, Charles. The Sources of Keyboard Music in England. Matthew, J. E., tr. LC 77-75227. 1977. Repr. of 1914 ed. lib. bdg. 20.00 (ISBN 0-89341-131-0). Longwood Pr.
Walker, Ernest. A History of Music in England. 3rd ed. Westrup, J. A., ed. LC 78-4596. (Music Reprint 1978 Ser.). 1978. Repr. of 1952 ed. lib. bdg. 35.00 (ISBN 0-306-77570-0). Da Capo.
Willeby, Charles. Masters of English Music. LC 77-23963. 1977. Repr. of 1893 ed. lib. bdg. 30.00 (ISBN 0-89341-132-9). Longwood Pr.

MUSIC, ETHIOPIC

Powne, Michael. Ethiopian Music, an Introduction: A Survey of Ecclesiastical & Secular Ethiopian Music & Instruments. LC 80-14087. (Illus.). xix, 160p. 1980. Repr. of 1966 ed. lib. bdg. 19.00x (ISBN 0-313-22161-8, POEM). Greenwood.

MUSIC, EUROPEAN

Blaukopf, Kurt & Desmont, Mark, eds. The Cultural Behaviour of Youth: Towards a Cross-Cultural Survey in Europe & Asia. 1976. pap. 17.00 (ISBN 3-7024-0114-8, 51-26247). Eur-Am Music.
Borroff, Edith. Music in Europe & the United States: A History. (Illus.). 1971. text ed. 21.95 (ISBN 0-13-608083-9). P-H.
Brody, Elaine & Brook, Claire. The Music Guide to Belgium, Luxembourg, Holland & Switzerland. LC 77-6446. (Music Guides Ser.). (Illus.). 1977. 10.00 (ISBN 0-396-07437-5). Dodd.
Burney, Charles. Dr. Charles Burney's Continental Travels. LC 76-26048. Repr. of 1927 ed. 21.50 (ISBN 0-404-12920-X). AMS Pr.
Capri, Antonio. Il Settecento Musicale in Europa. LC 77-5523. (Music Reprint Ser). 1977. Repr. of 1936 ed. lib. bdg. 35.00 (ISBN 0-306-77413-5). Da Capo.
Cohn, Arthur. Twentieth-Century Music in Western Europe: The Compositions & Recordings. LC 70-39297. 510p. 1972. Repr. of 1965 ed. lib. bdg. 37.50 (ISBN 0-306-70460-9). Da Capo.

Dr. Burney's Musical Tours in Europe, 2 vols. Incl. An Eighteenth Century Musical Tour in France & Italy: Being Dr. Charles Burney's Account of His Musical Experiences As It Appears in His Published Volume with Which Are Incorporated His Travel Experiences According to His Original Intention. Vol. 1. (ISBN 0-313-21106-X); An Eighteenth-Century Musical Tour in Central Europe & the Netherlands: Being Dr. Charles Burney's Account of His Musical Experiences. Vol. 2. (ISBN 0-313-21107-8). 1979. Repr. of 1959 ed. Set. lib. bdg. 55.00x (ISBN 0-313-21105-1, BUMT). Greenwood.

Hartog, Howard, ed. European Music in the Twentieth Century. LC 75-45461. 341p. 1976. Repr. of 1957 ed. lib. bdg. 20.50x (ISBN 0-8371-8680-3, HAEMT). Greenwood.

Hughes, David G. History of European Music. (Illus.). 512p. 1974. text ed. 17.95 (ISBN 0-07-031105-6, C). McGraw.

Mee, John. The Oldest Music Room in Europe. 1978. Repr. of 1899 ed. lib. bdg. 19.95 (ISBN 0-89761-004-0). Dunn & Webster.

Peyser, Joan. Twentieth-Century Music: The Sense Behind the Sound. LC 79-57286. (Illus.). 1980. pap. 5.95 (ISBN 0-02-871880-1). Schirmer Bks.

Van Der Straeten, Edmond. Musique Aux Pays Bas Avant le Neuvieme Siecle, 4 Vols. 1968. Repr. 15.00 ea.; Vol. 1. (ISBN 0-486-21585-7); Vol. 2. (ISBN 0-486-21586-5); Vol. 3. (ISBN 0-486-21587-3); Vol. 4. (ISBN 0-486-21588-1). Dover.

MUSIC, FRENCH

Anthony, James R. French Baroque Music. (Illus.). 1973. 20.00x (ISBN 0-393-02173-4). Norton.

--French Baroque Music: From Beaujoyeulx to Rameau. 1978. 22.50x (ISBN 0-393-02198-X). Norton.

Blaze, Francois H. L' Academie Imperiale De Musique: Histoire Litteraire, Musicale, Politique et Galant De Ce Theatre, De 1645 a 1855, 2 vols. LC 80-2258. Repr. of 1855 ed. 95.00 (ISBN 0-404-18804-4). AMS Pr.

Blunt, Anthony & Lockspeiser, Edward. French Art & Music Since Fifteen Hundred. 1974. pap. text ed. 3.95x (ISBN 0-416-81650-9). Methuen Inc.

Bollioud-Mermet, Louis. De la corruption du goust dans la musique francaise. LC 76-43907. (Music & Theatre in France in the 17th & 18th Centuries). Repr. of 1746 ed. 11.50 (ISBN 0-404-60150-2). AMS Pr.

Borrel, Eugene. L' Interpretation de la musique francaise: De Lully a la revolution. LC 76-43908. (Music & Theatre in France in the 17th & 18th Centuries). Repr. of 1934 ed. 20.00 (ISBN 0-404-60151-0). AMS Pr.

Brenet, Michel. Les Concerts en France Sous l'Ancien Regime. LC 68-16224. (Music Ser). 1970. Repr. of 1900 ed. lib. bdg. 39.50 (ISBN 0-306-71061-7). Da Capo.

Burney, Charles. The Present State of Music in France & Italy. 2nd corr. ed. LC 74-24263. 1976. Repr. of 1773 ed. 27.50 (ISBN 0-404-12875-0). AMS Pr.

Calvocoressi, Michel D. Music & Ballet. LC 74-24053. Repr. of 1934 ed. 24.50 (ISBN 0-404-12877-7). AMS Pr.

Chouquet, Gustave. Histoire De la Musique Dramatique En France Depuis Ses Origines Jusqu'a Nos Jours. LC 80-2265. Repr. of 1873 ed. 45.00 (ISBN 0-404-18818-4). AMS Pr.

Clercx, Suzanne. Gretry: 1741-1813. LC 76-43911. (Music & Theatre in France in the 17th & 18th Centuries). (Fr.). Repr. of 1944 ed. 16.50 (ISBN 0-404-60154-5). AMS Pr.

Cooper, Martin. French Music: From the Death of Berlioz to the Death of Faure. 1951. pap. 8.95x (ISBN 0-19-316202-4). Oxford U Pr.

Cortot, Alfred. French Piano Music. Andrews, Hilda, tr. from Fr. LC 77-4108. (Music Reprint, 1977 Ser.). 1977. Repr. of 1932 ed. 19.50 (ISBN 0-306-70896-5). Da Capo.

Crozet, Felix. Revue De la Musique Dramatique En France. Bd. with Supplement a la Revue De la Musique Dramatique En France. LC 80-2270. 1981. Repr. of 1866 ed. 48.50 (ISBN 0-404-18833-8). AMS Pr.

Crussard, Claude. Un Musicien francais oublie, Marc-Antoine Charpentier, 1634-1704. LC 76-43912. (Music & Theatre in France in the 17th & 18th Centuries). Repr. of 1945 ed. 14.00 (ISBN 0-404-60155-3). AMS Pr.

Cucuel, G. La Poupliniere et la Musique De Chambre Au Xv111 Siecle. LC 70-158961. (Music Ser). 1971. Repr. of 1913 ed. lib. bdg. 49.50 (ISBN 0-306-70186-3). Da Capo.

De Laborde, Jean B. Essai sur la musique ancienne et moderne, 4 vols. LC 76-43922. (Music & Theatre in France in the 17th & 18th Centuries). Repr. of 1780 ed. Set. 175.00 (ISBN 0-404-60180-4). AMS Pr.

De la Laurencie, Lionel. Lully. 2nd ed. LC 76-43923. (Music & Theatre in France in the 17th & 18th Centuries). (Fr.). Repr. of 1919 ed. 19.50 (ISBN 0-404-60167-7). AMS Pr.

De Meude-Monpas, Jean J. Dictionnaire de musique dans lequel on simplifie les expressions et les definitions mathematiques et physiques qui ont rapport a cet art. LC 76-43927. (Music & Theatre in France in the 17th & 18th Centuries). Repr. of 1787 ed. 22.50 (ISBN 0-404-60175-8). AMS Pr.

De Monte, Philippe. The Complete Works of Philippe de Monte, 31 vols, Vols. 1-29. Van den Borren, Charles & Van Nuffel, Julius, eds. Incl. Vol. 1. Missa "Inclina cor meum" (ISBN 0-8450-1501-X); Vol. 2. Motettum "O bone Jesu," tripartitum. Van Doorslaer, George & Nuffel, Julius Van, eds. (ISBN 0-8450-1502-8); Vol. 3. Missa Sine nomine, 2a (ISBN 0-8450-1503-6); Vol. 4. Missa "O altitudo divitiarum" (ISBN 0-8450-1504-4); Vol. 5. Missa "Ultimi miei sospiri" (ISBN 0-8450-1505-2); Vol. 6. Madrigalium Spiritualium cum sex vocibus: Liber Primus. Van Doorslaer, George, ed (ISBN 0-8450-1506-0); Vol. 7. Missa sine nomine (ISBN 0-8450-1507-9); Vol. 8. Missa "Ancor che col partire" (ISBN 0-8450-1508-7); Vol. 9. Missa "Reviens Vers moi" (ISBN 0-8450-1509-5); Vol. 10. Missa "Nasce la pena mia" (ISBN 0-8450-1510-9); Vol. 11. Missa Sine nomine, Ia (ISBN 0-8450-1511-7); Vol. 12. Canticum Magnificat (ISBN 0-8450-1512-5); Vol. 13. Missa de "Requiem" (ISBN 0-8450-1513-3); Vol. 14. Missa "la dolce vista" (ISBN 0-8450-1514-1); Vol. 15. Collectio decem Motettorum 5-6-7 et 8 vocum (ISBN 0-8450-1515-X); Vol. 16. Missa quaternis vocibus (ISBN 0-8450-1516-8); Vol. 17. Liber Septimus Motettorum cum quinque vocibus (ISBN 0-8450-1517-6); Vol. 18. Missa Sex vocum (ISBN 0-8450-1518-4); Vol. 19. Liber quartus Madrigalium quatuor vocum (ISBN 0-8450-1519-2); Vol. 20. Collectio Decem Carminum Gallicorum, Alias Chansons Francaises 4-5 Vocum (ISBN 0-8450-1520-6); Vol. 21. Missa super "Cara la vita mia" (ISBN 0-8450-1521-4); Vol. 22. Liber quartus Motettorum quinque vocum (ISBN 0-8450-1522-2); Vol. 23. Missa "Quando lieta sperai" (ISBN 0-8450-1523-0); Vol. 24. Missa "Cum sit omnipotens rector Olympi" (ISBN 0-8450-1524-9); Vol. 25. Cantiones (ISBN 0-8450-1525-7); Vol. 26. Missa "Aspice Domine" (ISBN 0-8450-1526-5); Vol. 27. Missa "Quomodo dilexi" (ISBN 0-8450-1527-3); Vol. 28. Missa "Sine nomine" (ISBN 0-8450-1528-1); Vol. 29. Missa "Sine nomine" (ISBN 0-8450-1529-X). 2808p. (Repr. of 1927-39 ed.). 1966. pap. 525.00x set of 31 (ISBN 0-8450-1500-1); pap. 22.50x ea. Broude.

Dubos, Jean B. Critical Reflections on Poetry, Painting & Music, 3 vols. LC 78-3659. (Music & Theatre in France in the 17th & 18th Centuries). Repr. of 1748 ed. Set. 74.50 (ISBN 0-404-60170-7). AMS Pr.

Durey De Noinville, Jacques B. Histoire Du Theatre De l'Academie Royale De Musique En France, Depuis Son Etablissement Jusqu' a Present, 2 vols. in 1. 2nd ed. LC 80-2273. Repr. of 1757 ed. 47.50 (ISBN 0-404-18838-9). AMS Pr.

Ecorcheville, Jules A. Catalogue Du Fonds De Musique Ancienne De la Bibliotheque Nationale, 4 vols. LC 79-166103. (Music Ser). (Illus.). 1973. Repr. of 1914 ed. Set. lib. bdg. 165.00 (ISBN 0-306-70280-0). Da Capo.

Expert, Henry, ed. Maitres Musiciens de la Renaissance Francaise, 23 vols. Incl. Vol. 1. Premier fascicule des Melanges. De Lassus, Orlando (ISBN 0-8450-1201-0); Vol. 2. Premier Fascicule des 150 Psaumes. Goudimel, Claude (ISBN 0-8450-1202-9); Vol. 3. Musique, Premier Fascicule. Costeley, Guillaume (ISBN 0-8450-1203-7); Vol. 4. Deuxieme Fascicule des 150 Psaumes. Goudimel, Claude (ISBN 0-8450-1204-5); Vol. 5. Trente et une Chansons musicales: Claude de Sermisy, Clement Janequin et al (ISBN 0-8450-1205-3); Vol. 6. Troisieme Fascicule des 150 Psaumes. Goudimel, Claude (ISBN 0-8450-1206-1); Vol. 7. Chansons Attaingnant. Janequin, Clement (ISBN 0-8450-1207-X); Vol. 8. Missa "de beata virgine", Missa "Ave Maria". Brumel, Antoine & De La Rue, Pierre. (ISBN 0-8450-1208-8); Vol. 9. Missa "Alma redemptoris - Missa "Mente Tota". Mouton, J. & Fevin, A. de. (ISBN 0-8450-1209-6); Vol. 10. Chansonnettes mesurees de Ian-Antoine de Baif. Mauduit, Jacques (ISBN 0-8450-1210-X); Vol. 11. Dodecacorde, Premier Fascicule. LeJeune, Claude (ISBN 0-8450-1211-8); Vol. 12. Le Printemps, Premier Fascicule. LeJeune, Claude (ISBN 0-8450-1212-6); Vol. 13. Le Printemps, Deuxieme Fascicule. LeJeune, Claude (ISBN 0-8450-1213-4); Vol. 14. Le Printemps, Troisieme Fascicule. LeJeune, Claude (ISBN 0-8450-1214-2); Vol. 15. Poesies de P. de Ronsard et Autres Poetes. Regnard, Francois (ISBN 0-8450-1215-0); Vol. 16. Melanges Premier Fascicule. LeJeune, Claude (ISBN 0-8450-1216-9); Vol. 17. Melanges, Premier Fascicule. Du Caurroy, Eustache (ISBN 0-8450-1217-7); Vol. 18. Musique, Deuxieme Fascicule. Costeley, Guillaume (ISBN 0-8450-1218-5); Vol. 19. Musique, Troiseme Fascicule. Costeley, Guillaume (ISBN 0-8450-1219-3); Vol. 20. Pseaumes En Vers Mezurez, Premier Fascicule. LeJeune, Claude (ISBN 0-8450-1220-7); Vol. 21. Pseaumes en vers mezurez. LeJeune, Claude (ISBN 0-8450-1221-5); Vol. 22. Pseaumes en vers mezurez, Troisieme Fascicule. LeJeune, Claude (ISBN 0-8450-1222-3); Vol. 23. Danceries, Premier Volume. Gervaise, Claude & Du Terte, Estienne. (ISBN 0-8450-1223-1). (Illus., Repr. of 1894-1908 ed). 1964. pap. 525.00x set (ISBN 0-8450-1200-2); pap. 25.00x ea. Broude.

--Monuments de la musique francaise au temps de la Renaissance, 10 vols. Incl. Vol. I. Octonaires de la vanite et inconstance du monde (I-VIII) LeJeune, Claude (ISBN 0-8450-1231-2); Vol. II. Messes a quatre voix. Certon, Pierre (ISBN 0-8450-1232-0); Vol. III. Airs de plusiers musiciens reduits a quatre parties. Le Blanc, Didier (ISBN 0-8450-1233-9); Vol. IV. Premier Livre Des Amours De Pierre De Ronsard, (I-XIX) De Bertrand, Anthoine (ISBN 0-8450-1234-7); Vol. V. Premier livre des Amours de Pierre de Ronsard, (XX-XXXV) De Bertrand, Anthoine (ISBN 0-8450-1235-5); Vol. VI. Second livre des Amours de Pierre de Ronsard (ISBN 0-8450-1236-3); Vol. VII. Troisieme livre de chansons. De Bertrand, Anthoine (ISBN 0-8450-1237-1); Vol. VIII. Octonaires de la vanite et inconstance du monde, (IX-XII; Pseaumes des Meslanges de 1612; Dialoque e a sept parties. LeJeune, Claude (ISBN 0-8450-1238-X); Vol. IX. Messes a quatre voix. Goudimel, Claude (ISBN 0-8450-1239-8); Vol. X. Premier livre des Octonaires de la vanite du Monde. De l'Estocart, Paschal (ISBN 0-8450-1240-1). (Illus.). 1952. pap. 275.00x set (ISBN 0-8450-1230-4); pap. 35.00x ea. Broude.

Favre, Georges. La Musique francaise de piano avant 1830. LC 76-43917. (Music & Theatre in France in the 17th & 18th Centuries). Repr. of 1953 ed. 19.50 (ISBN 0-404-60158-8). AMS Pr.

Gaudefroy-Demombynes, Jean. Les Jugements allemands sur la musique francaise au XVIIIe siecle. LC 76-43918. (Music & Theatre in France in the 17th & 18th Centuries). Repr. of 1941 ed. 30.00 (ISBN 0-404-60159-6). AMS Pr.

Grace, Harvey. French Organ Music, Past & Present. LC 77-94581. 1979. Repr. of 1919 ed. lib. bdg. 25.00 (ISBN 0-89341-409-3). Longwood Pr.

Gretry, Andre E. Reflexions d'un solitaire, 4 vols. Solvay, Lucien & Closson, Ernest, eds. LC 76-43920. (Music & Theatre in France in the 17th & 18th Centuries). Repr. of 1922 ed. Set. 105.00 (ISBN 0-404-60190-1). AMS Pr.

Grimarest, Jean L. Traite du recitatif dans la lecture, dans l'action publique, dans la declamation, et dans le chant. LC 76-43921. (Music & Theatre in France in the 17th & 18th Centuries). 1977. Repr. of 1760 ed. 17.50 (ISBN 0-404-60164-2). AMS Pr.

Grubb, Thomas. Singing in French: A Manual of French Diction & French Vocal Repertoire. LC 77-18473. 1979. pap. text ed. 9.95 (ISBN 0-02-870790-7). Schirmer Bks.

Hale, Philip, ed. French Art Songs of the Nineteenth Century: 39 Works from Berlioz to Debussy. 10.00 (ISBN 0-8446-5767-0). Peter Smith.

Hervey, Arthur. French Music in the XIXth Century. LC 74-24113. Repr. of 1903 ed. 18.50 (ISBN 0-404-12965-X). AMS Pr.

--Masters of French Music. LC 77-75214. 1977. Repr. of 1903 ed. lib. bdg. 25.00 (ISBN 0-89341-114-0). Longwood Pr.

Hill, Edward B. Modern French Music. Repr. of 1924 ed. lib. bdg. 17.50x (ISBN 0-8371-3942-2, HIMF). Greenwood.

--Modern French Music. LC 71-87491. (Music Reprint Ser). 1969. Repr. of 1924 ed. lib. bdg. 27.50 (ISBN 0-306-71497-3). Da Capo.

Isherwood, Robert M. Music in the Service of the King: France in the Seventeenth Century. LC 72-3842. (Illus.). 422p. 1973. 30.00x (ISBN 0-8014-0734-6). Cornell U Pr.

Jean-Aubry, Georges. French Music of Today. Evans, Edwin, tr. (Select Bibliographies Reprint Ser.). 1973. Repr. of 1919 ed. 19.00 (ISBN 0-8369-7113-2). Arno.

Jeppesen, Knud & Brondal, Viggo, eds. The Copenhagen Chansonnier. (Illus.). 276p. (Ger.). 1965. Repr. of 1927 ed. 50.00x (ISBN 0-8450-0004-7). Broude.

Leppert, Richard D. Arcadia at Versailles: Noble Amateur Musicians & Their Musettes & Hurdy-Gurdies at the French Court (C. 1660-1789), a Visual Study. 138p. 1978. pap. text ed. 32.50 (ISBN 90-265-0246-X, Pub. by Swets Pub Serv Holland). Swets North Am.

Locke, Arthur W. Music & the Romantic Movement in France. LC 72-83508. Repr. of 1920 ed. 15.00 (ISBN 0-405-08751-9, Pub. by Blom). Arno.

Lully, Jean Baptiste. Oeuvres Completes de Jean-Baptiste Lully, 11 vols. Prunieres, Henry, et al, eds. Incl. Les ballets, 1654-1657 (ISBN 0-8450-1261-4); Les ballets tome 2, 1658-1660 (ISBN 0-8450-1262-2); Les comedies-ballets, tome 1, 1664-1665 (ISBN 0-8450-1263-0); Les comedies-ballets, tome 2, 1666-1668 (ISBN 0-8450-1264-9); Les comedies-ballets, tome 3, 1669-1670 (ISBN 0-8450-1265-7); Les motets, tome 1, 1664: Miserere mei Deus (ISBN 0-8450-1266-5); Les motets, tome 2: Plaude, laetare, Gallia; Te Deum Laudamus; Dies Irae; Dies Illa; 1668-1677 (ISBN 0-8450-1267-3); Les motets, tome 3: De profundis; Ave coeli munus supernum; Omnes gentes; Domine salvum fac regem (ISBN 0-8450-1268-1); Les Operas, tome 1: Cadmus et Hermione (ISBN 0-8450-1269-X); Les Operas, tome 2: Alceste (ISBN 0-8450-1270-3); Les Operas, tome 3: Amadis, 1684 (ISBN 0-8450-1271-1). (Illus.). 1930-1972. pap. 660.00x set (ISBN 0-8450-1260-6); pap. 60.00x ea. Broude.

Mather, Betty B. Interpretation of French Music from 1675-1775 for Woodwind & Other Performers. 1973. 12.00 (ISBN 0-686-31346-1). McGinnis & Marx.

Music & Theatre in France in the 17th & 18th Centuries - le Grand Siecle: Basic Collection for Musical, Theatrical, Literary & Cultural Historians, 37 titles in 48 vols. Repr. 1275.00 (ISBN 0-404-60100-6). AMS Pr.

Noske, Frits R. French Song from Berlioz to DuParc: The Origins & Development of the Melodie. Benton, Rita, tr. LC 68-11171. (Illus.). 1970. pap. 6.95 (ISBN 0-486-22104-0). Dover.

Parfaict, Francois & Parfaict, Claude. Memoires pour servir a l'histoire des spectacles de la foire, 2 vols. in 1. LC 76-43933. (Music & Theatre in France in the 17th & 18th Centuries). Repr. of 1743 ed. 37.50 (ISBN 0-404-60179-0). AMS Pr.

Prunieres, Henry. La Vie illustre et libertine de Jean-Baptiste Lully. LC 76-43934. (Music & Theatre in France in the 17th & 18th Centuries). Repr. of 1929 ed. 22.00 (ISBN 0-685-83142-6). AMS Pr.

Rolland, Romain. Musicians of To-Day. facs. ed. Blaiklock, M., tr. LC 72-86777. (Essay Index Reprint Ser). 1915. 17.00 (ISBN 0-8369-1188-1). Arno.

Rosenberg, Samuel N. & Tischler, Hans, eds. Chanter M'estuet: Songs of the Trouveres. LC 80-8383. 608p. 1981. 32.50x (ISBN 0-253-14942-8). Ind U Pr.

Rostand, Claude. French Music Today. LC 73-4333. 146p. 1973. Repr. of 1955 ed. lib. bdg. 18.50 (ISBN 0-306-70578-8). Da Capo.

Schwan, Eduard. Altfranzosischen Liederhandschriften Ihr Verhaltniss: Ihre Entstehung und Ihre Bestimmung. LC 80-2169. Repr. of 1886 ed. 39.50 (ISBN 0-404-19033-2). AMS Pr.

Schwartz, Boris. French Instrumental Music Between the Revolutions. (Music Reprint Ser.). 350p. 1981. 29.50 (ISBN 0-306-79545-0). Da Capo.

Sonnette, Jean-Jacques, pseud. Le Brigandage de la musique italienne. LC 76-43941. (Music & Theatre in France in the 17th & 18th Centuries). Repr. of 1777 ed. 16.50 (ISBN 0-404-60196-0). AMS Pr.

Spanke, Hans, ed. Eine Altfranzosische Liedersammlung, Deranonyme Teil der Liederhandschriften Knpx. LC 80-2161. Repr. of 1925 ed. 54.50 (ISBN 0-404-19025-1). AMS Pr.
Striffling, Louis. Esquisse d'une histoire du gout musical en France au XVIIIe siecle. LC 76-4392. (Music & Theatre in France in the 17th & 18th Centuries). Repr. of 1912 ed. 21.50 (ISBN 0-404-60198-7). AMS Pr.
Van Duesen, Nancy. Music at Nevers Cathedral: Principal Sources of Mediaeval Chant. (Musicological Studies). 430p. 1980. lib. bdg. 55.00 pt. 1 (ISBN 0-912024-34-8); lib. bdg. 55.00 pt. 2 (ISBN 0-912024-33-X). Inst Mediaeval.
Vian, Boris. Derriere la Zizique: Textes de Pochettes de Disquesde de Jazz et de Varietes. 176p. 1976. 8.95 (ISBN 0-686-55690-9). French & Eur.
--En Avant la Zizique. 185p. 1971. 4.95 (ISBN 0-686-55694-1). French & Eur.

MUSIC, GERMAN

Adorno, Theodor. In Search of Wagner. 160p. 1981. 14.50 (ISBN 0-8052-7087-6, Pub. by NLB England). Schocken.
Baker, Theodore. Uber Die Musik der Nordamerikanischen Wilden. LC 71-38496. Repr. of 1882 ed. 15.00 (ISBN 0-404-08337-4). AMS Pr.
Blume, F., ed. Musik in Geschichte und Gegenwart: Allegemeine Enzyklopaedie der Musik, 16 vols. 2380.20 set (ISBN 3-7618-0641-8); 1 index vol. incl. Adler.
Brahms, Johannes. Complete Concerti in Full Score. Orig. Title: Johannes Brahms, Samtliche Werke. 352p. 1981. pap. price not set (ISBN 0-486-24170-X). Dover.
Brody, Elaine & Brook, Claire. The Music Guide to Austria & Germany. LC 75-30822. (Music Guides Ser.). 350p. 1976. 10.00 (ISBN 0-396-07217-8). Dodd.
Chorley, Henry F. Modern German Music: Recollections & Criticisms, 2 vols. LC 79-110994. (Music Reprint Ser.). 1973. Repr. of 1854 ed. 57.50 (ISBN 0-306-71911-8). Da Capo.
Cooke, Deryck. Gustav Mahler: An Introduction to His Music. 1980. 19.95 (ISBN 0-521-23175-2); pap. 5.95 (ISBN 0-521-29847-4). Cambridge U Pr.
De Lafontaine, Henry C. The King's Musick: A Transcript of Records Relative to Music & Musicians. LC 70-169648. 522p. 1973. Repr. of 1909 ed. lib. bdg. 39.50 (ISBN 0-306-70269-X). Da Capo.
Drummond, Pippa. The German Concerto: Five Eighteenth Century Studies. (Oxford Monographs on Music). (Illus.). 1980. 69.00x (ISBN 0-19-816122-0). Oxford U Pr.
Drummond, Robert R. Early German Music in Philadelphia. LC 72-1596. Repr. of 1910 ed. 11.50 (ISBN 0-404-09917-3). AMS Pr.
--Early German Music in Philadelphia. LC 74-125068. (Music Ser). 1970. Repr. of 1910 ed. lib. bdg. 14.50 (ISBN 0-306-70005-0). Da Capo.
Fischer, Johann K. Saemtliche Werke fuer Klavier und Orgel. Werra, Ernst Von, ed. 142p. (Ger.). 1966. pap. 27.50x (ISBN 0-8450-1007-7). Broude.
Fuller-Maitland, J. A. Masters of German Music. LC 77-20818. 1977. Repr. of 1894 ed. lib. bdg. 25.00 (ISBN 0-89341-133-7). Longwood Pr.
Gohler, Karl A. Die Messkataloge im Dienste der musikalischen Geschichtsforschung: Verzeichnis der in den Frankfurter und Leipziger Messkatalogen der Jahre 1564 bis 1759 angezeigten Musikalien, 2 vols. 1965. Repr. Set. wrappers 32.50 (ISBN 0-686-30880-8, Pub. by Frits Knuf Netherlands). Vol. 1 (ISBN 90-6027-013-4). Vol. 2 (ISBN 90-6027-014-2). Pendragon NY.
Handel, George F. Complete Concerti Grossi in Full Score. Orig. Title: Georg Friedrich Handel's Werke. 272p. 1981. pap. price not set (ISBN 0-486-24164-5). Dover.
Holmes, Edward. Ramble Among the Musicians of Germany. 2nd ed. LC 68-16239. 1969. Repr. of 1828 ed. lib. bdg. 29.50 (ISBN 0-306-71086-2). Da Capo.
Hosler, Bellamy. Changing Aesthetic Views of Instrumental Music in Eighteenth Century Germany. Buelow, George, ed. LC 81-4754. (Studies in Musicology: No. 42). 1981. 39.95 (ISBN 0-8357-1172-2, Pub. by UMI Res Pr). Univ Microfilms.
Mason, Lowell. Musical Letters from Abroad. 2nd ed. LC 67-13035. (Music Ser). 1967. Repr. of 1854 ed. lib. bdg. 25.00 (ISBN 0-306-70940-6). Da Capo.
Muller-Reuter, Theodor. Lexikon der Deutschen Konzertliteratur, 2 Vols. LC 70-171079. (Music Ser). 1972. Repr. of 1921 ed. lib. bdg. 95.00 (ISBN 0-306-70274-6). Da Capo.
Niedt, F. E. Musicalische Handleitung: Hamburg 1700-1721, 3 vols in one. (Bibliotheca Organologica: Vol. 32). 1976. 75.00 (ISBN 90-6027-306-0, Pub. by Frits Knuf Netherlands). Pendragon NY.
O'Brien, Grace. The Golden Age of German Music & Its Origins. LC 78-20485. (Encore Music Editions Ser.). 1980. Repr. of 1953 ed. 22.00 (ISBN 0-88355-861-0). Hyperion Conn.
Peake, A. S., et al. Germany in the Nineteenth Century: Second Ser. Manchester Univ. Pubns. Historical Ser. No. 24. facs. ed. LC 67-30189. (Essay Index Reprint Ser). 1915. 13.00 (ISBN 0-8369-0472-9). Arno.
Perle, George. Serial Compositon & Atonality: An Introduction to the Music of Schoenberg, Berg, & Webern. 5th ed. 1981. 17.95 (ISBN 0-520-04365-0). U of Cal Pr.
Pinthus, G. Das Konzertleben in Deutschland. (Sammlung Mw.Abh. Ser.). 160p. 35.00 (ISBN 90-6027-322-2, Pub. by Frits Knuf Netherlands). Pendragon NY.
Rolland, Romain. Musicians of To-Day. facs. ed. Blaiklock, M., tr. LC 72-86777. (Essay Index Reprint Ser). 1915. 17.00 (ISBN 0-8369-1188-1). Arno.
Schiedermair, Ludwig. Die Deutche Oper: Grundzuge Ihres Werdens & Wesens. LC 80-2299. Repr. of 1930 ed. 38.50 (ISBN 0-404-18868-0). AMS Pr.
Schulze, Walter. Die Quellen der Hamburger Oper Sixteen Seventy Eight to Seventeen Thirty Eight. LC 80-2300. 1981. Repr. of 1938 ed. 25.50 (ISBN 0-404-18869-9). AMS Pr.
Schumann, Elisabeth. German Song. LC 79-4136. (Illus.). 1980. Repr. of 1948 ed. lib. bdg. 14.50x (ISBN 0-313-20999-5, SCGE). Greenwood.
Schumann, Robert. Selected Songs for Solo Voice & Piano. Appelbaum, Stanley, tr. Orig. Title: Robert Schumann's Werke. 256p. (Repr. of 1882-87 eds.). 1981. pap. price not set (ISBN 0-486-24202-1). Dover.
Strauss, Richard. Salome in Full Score. 352p. 1981. pap. price not set (ISBN 0-486-24208-0). Dover.
Tyson, Alan. Beethoven String Quartet Opus Fifty-Nine, No. Two: Second "Razumovsky" Quartet, in E Minor. 82p. 1981. 175.00x (ISBN 0-85967-547-5, Pub. by Scolar Pr England). Biblio Dist.
Tyson, Alan, ed. Beethoven String Quartet Opus Fifty-Nine, No. One: First "Razumovsky" Quartet in F Major. (Scolar Press Music Manuscripts in Facsimile Ser.). 104p. 1981. 185.00x (ISBN 0-85967-546-7, Pub. by Scolar Pr England). Biblio Dist.
Unger, Max. Muzio Clementis Leben. LC 72-158959. (Music Ser). 1971. Repr. of 1914 ed. lib. bdg. 27.50 (ISBN 0-306-70192-8). Da Capo.
Wagner, Richard. Prose Works, 8 vols. 1981. Repr. Set. lib. bdg. 360.00 (ISBN 0-403-00255-9). Scholarly.

MUSIC, GOSPEL

see Gospel Music

Kruger, L. Die Hamburgische Musikorganisation Im XVII. (Sammlung Mw. Abh. Ser.). viii, 276p. 35.00 (ISBN 90-6027-286-2, Pub. by Frits Knuf Netherlands). Pendragon NY.

MUSIC, GREEK AND ROMAN

see also Music, Byzantine

Georgiades, Thrasybulos. Greek Music, Verse & Dance. LC 73-4336. 156p. 1973. Repr. of 1955 ed. lib. bdg. 17.50 (ISBN 0-306-70561-3). Da Capo.
Hipkins, Alfred J. Greek Music. LC 77-75215. 1977. Repr. of 1930 ed. lib. bdg. 15.00 (ISBN 0-89341-115-9). Longwood Pr.
Holst, Gail. The Theodorakis Myth & Modern Greek Music. 262p. 1981. pap. text ed. 19.25x (ISBN 90-256-0795-0, Pub. by Hakkert). Humanities.
Lippman, Edward A. Musical Thought in Ancient Greece. LC 74-23415. (Music Reprint Ser.). 1975. Repr. of 1964 ed. lib. bdg. 22.50 (ISBN 0-306-70669-5). Da Capo.
Mathiesen, Thomas J. A Bibliography of Sources for the Study of Ancient Greek Music. (Music Indexes & Bibliographies: No. 10). 1974. pap. 4.50 (ISBN 0-913574-10-4). Eur-Am Music.
Michaelides, Solon. The Music of Ancient Greece: An Encyclopedia. (Illus.). 382p. 1978. 39.00 (ISBN 0-571-10021-X, Pub. by Faber & Faber). Merrimack Bk Serv.
Stanley, Albert A. Greek Themes in Modern Musical Settings. Repr. of 1924 ed. 31.00 (ISBN 0-384-38815-9). Johnson Repr.
Theon Of Smyrna. Theon of Smyrna: Mathematics Useful for Understanding Plato or, Pythagorean Arithmetic, Music, Astronomy, Spiritual Disciplines. Lawlor, Robert, tr. from Greek. LC 77-73716. (Secret Doctrine Reference Ser.). (Illus.). 1979. 11.95 (ISBN 0-913510-24-6). Wizards.
Wellesz, Egon. History of Byzantine Music & Hymnography. 2nd ed. 1961. 49.95x (ISBN 0-19-816111-5). Oxford U Pr.
Williams, Charles F. Music of the Ancient Greek Drama. LC 77-75203. 1977. Repr. of 1921 ed. lib. bdg. 10.00 (ISBN 0-89341-099-3). Longwood Pr.
Wright, Frederick A. Arts in Greece. LC 75-101054. 1969. Repr. of 1923 ed. 9.50 (ISBN 0-8046-0719-2). Kennikat.

MUSIC, HAWAIIAN

Burlingame, Burl & Kasher, Robert K. Da Kine Sound: Conversations with People Who Create Hawaiian Music. Poole-Burlingame, Mary, ed. LC 78-17556. 1978. pap. 5.95 (ISBN 0-916630-08-0). Pr Pacifica.
Emerson, Nathaniel B. Unwritten Literature of Hawaii; the Sacred Songs of the Hula. Repr. of 1909 ed. 35.00 (ISBN 0-403-03720-4). Scholarly.
Johnson, Rubellite K. Kumulipo: The Hawaiian Hymn of Creation. Holt, John D., ed. (Illus.). 1981. text ed. 35.00 (ISBN 0-914916-53-X); leather 100.00 (ISBN 0-914916-59-9). Topgallant.
Kahananui, Dorothy M. Music of Ancient Hawaii: A Brief Survey. (Illus.). 1978. pap. 2.95 (ISBN 0-912180-36-6). Petroglyph.
Kanahele, George S., ed. Hawaiian Music & Musicians: An Illustrated History. LC 79-14233. (Illus.). 1979. 25.00 (ISBN 0-8248-0578-X). U Pr of Hawaii.
Roberts, H. H. Ancient Hawaiian Music. Repr. of 1926 ed. pap. 35.00 (ISBN 0-527-02132-6). Kraus Repr.
Roberts, Helen H. Ancient Hawaiian Music. 12.50 (ISBN 0-8446-2816-6). Peter Smith.

MUSIC, HEBREW

see Music, Jewish

MUSIC, HINDUSTANI

Fox Strangeways, A. H. The Music of Hindustan. LC 75-905015. 1975. 20.00x (ISBN 0-88386-638-2). South Asia Bks.
Tabla - A Rhythmic Introduction to Indian Music. (Illus.). pap. 5.00 (ISBN 0-686-09081-0). Peer-Southern.
Van Der Meer, Wim. Hindustani: Music in the Twentieth Century. 272p. 1980. lib. bdg. 58.00 (ISBN 90-247-2066-4, Pub. by Martinus Nijhoff Netherlands). Kluwer Boston.

MUSIC, HUNGARIAN

Barbedette, Hippolyte. Stephen Heller: His Life & Works. LC 74-75886. (Detroit Reprints in Music). 132p. 1974. Repr. of 1877 ed. 5.00 (ISBN 0-911772-69-3). Info Coord.
Bartok, Bela. Hungarian Folk Music. Calvocoressi, M. D., tr. LC 78-62328. (Encore Music Editions). (Illus.). 1979. Repr. of 1931 ed. 27.50 (ISBN 0-88355-722-3). Hyperion Conn.
Forrai, Katalin, et al. Music Education in Hungary. 3rd, enl. ed. Macnicol, Fred, tr. from Hungarian. LC 80-123375. 310p. 1975. 12.00 (ISBN 0-85162-025-6). Boosey & Hawkes.
Kaldy, Gyula. History of Hungarian Music. 1971. Repr. of 1902 ed. 17.00 (ISBN 0-403-00646-5). Scholarly.
--History of Hungarian Music. LC 68-25291. (Studies in Music, No. 42). 1969. Repr. of 1902 ed. lib. bdg. 24.95 (ISBN 0-8383-0305-6). Haskell.

MUSIC, INCA

see Incas–Music

MUSIC, INDIC

Bandyopadhyaya, S. The Origin of Raga. 1978. 7.50x (ISBN 0-8364-0255-3). South Asia Bks.
Bhattacharya, Arun. A Treatise on Ancient Indian Music. 1978. 12.00x (ISBN 0-8364-0051-8). South Asia Bks.
Bhattacharya, Bhabani. Music for Mohini. 2nd ed. 1976. pap. 2.75 (ISBN 0-89253-071-5). Ind-US Inc.
Clements, E. Introduction to the Study of Indian Music. LC 77-75213. 1977. Repr. of 1913 ed. lib. bdg. 20.00 (ISBN 0-89341-113-2). Longwood Pr.
Deshpande, Vamanrao H. Indian Musical Traditions: An Aesthetic Study of the Gharanas in Hindustani Music. (Illus.). 117p. 1973. 7.00x (ISBN 0-8002-1544-3). Intl Pubns Serv.
Deva, B. Chaitanya. The Music of India: A Scientific Study. 278p. 1981. text ed. 18.00x (ISBN 0-391-02419-1, Pub. by Munshiram Manoharlal India). Humanities.
Deva, B. Chitanya. Musical Instruments of India. (Illus.). 1978. 21.00x (ISBN 0-8364-0231-6). South Asia Bks.
Ganguly, Anil B. Fine Arts in Ancient India. 1980. 16.00x (ISBN 0-8364-0581-1, Pub. by Abhinav India). South Asia Bks.
Gautam, M. R. Musical Heritage of India. 138p. 1981. text ed. 30.00x (ISBN 0-391-02237-7, Pub. by Abhinav India). Humanities.
Holroyde, Peggy. Indian Music: A Vast Ocean of Promise. 1972. 21.00 (ISBN 0-04-780020-8). Allen Unwin.
Howard, Wayne. Samavedic Chant. LC 76-49854. (Illus.). 1977. 35.00x (ISBN 0-300-01956-4). Yale U Pr.
Joshi, Baburao. Understanding Indian Music. LC 73-15055. 102p. 1974. Repr. of 1963 ed. lib. bdg. 15.00x (ISBN 0-8371-7156-3, JOIM). Greenwood.
Joshi, Baburao & Lobo, Antsher. Introducing Indian Music. 1965. 7.50x (ISBN 0-8002-1583-4). Intl Pubns Serv.
Kaufmann, Walter. The Ragas of South India: A Catalogue of Scalar Material. LC 75-1941. (Oriental Ser.). 832p. 1976. 25.00x (ISBN 0-253-39508-9). Ind U Pr.
Krishnaswami, S. Musical Instruments of India. (Illus.). 1967. 2.50x (ISBN 0-88253-378-9); pap. 1.00x (ISBN 0-88253-915-9). Ind-US Inc.
Krishnaswamy, S. Musical Instruments of India. 1970. pap. 2.95 (ISBN 0-8008-5461-6, Crescendo). Taplinger.
Kuppuswamy, Gowry, ed. Indian Music: A Perspective. 1980. 32.50x (ISBN 0-8364-0629-X, Pub. by Sundeep). South Asia Bks.
Massey, Reginald & Massey, Jamila. The Music of India. (Illus.). 1977. 10.00 (ISBN 0-87597-108-3, Crescendo). Taplinger.
Menon, R. R. Discovering Indian Music. 1973. 6.75x (ISBN 0-8002-0577-4). Intl Pubns Serv.
Neuman, Daniel M. The Life of Music in North India: The Organization of an Artistic Tradition. LC 79-16889. (Illus.). 1979. 16.95x (ISBN 0-8143-1632-8). Wayne St U Pr.
Prajnanananda, Swami. Historical Development of Indian Music. 2nd. rev. ed. (Illus.). 495p. 1973. 15.00x (ISBN 0-88386-344-8). South Asia Bks.
Prajnancinanda, Swami. The Music of the Nations. 216p. 1973. 10.50x (ISBN 0-8002-1738-1). Intl Pubns Serv.
Ray, Sukumar. Music of Eastern India. LC 73-906837. 264p. 1973. 12.50x (ISBN 0-88386-261-1). South Asia Bks.
Rosenthall, Ethel. Story of Indian Music & Its Instruments. 1980. Repr. lib. bdg. 25.00 (ISBN 0-403-03852-9). Scholarly.
Sarangadeva. Sangita Ratnakara of Sarngadeva, Vol. 1. Shringy, R. K., tr. from Sanskrit. 1978. 22.95 (ISBN 0-89684-009-3, Pub. by Motilal Banarsidass India). Orient Bk Dist.
Sarmadee, Shahab, ed. Ghunyat-Ul-Munya: The Earliest Known Persian Work on Indian Music. (Persian.). 1979. text ed. 12.95x (ISBN 0-210-40611-9). Asia.
Shirali, Vishnudas. Sargam: an Introduction to Indian Music. 1978. 37.00x (ISBN 0-88386-830-X). South Asia Bks.
Sorrell, Neil. Indian Music in Performance. 212p. 1981. 70.00x (ISBN 0-686-73060-7, Pub. by Manchester U Pr England). State Mutual Bk.
--What Happens in Indian Music: A Practical Introduction. (Illus.). 1980. pap. 32.50x (ISBN 0-8147-7815-1). NYU Pr.
Tagore, Sourindo M. The Musical Scales of the Hindus. LC 74-24225. Repr. of 1884 ed. 21.50 (ISBN 0-404-12837-8). AMS Pr.
Tagore, Sourindo M., compiled by. Hindu Music, from Various Authors. 2nd ed. LC 74-24223. 1977. Repr. of 1882 ed. 35.00 (ISBN 0-404-12835-1). AMS Pr.
Theaker, Drachen. Eastern Rhythms. LC 79-89945. (Orig.). Date not set. pap. cancelled (ISBN 0-89793-017-7). Hunter Hse.
Vedas. Der Rig-Veda, 4 pts. Ingalls, Daniel H., ed. LC 54-10046. (Oriental Ser: No. 33-36). Pts. 1-3. 1952 50.00x (ISBN 0-674-76965-1); Pt. 4. 1957 12.50x (ISBN 0-674-76967-8). Harvard U Pr.
Wade, Bonnie. Music in India: The Classical Traditions. 1979. 14.95 (ISBN 0-13-607036-1); pap. 10.95 (ISBN 0-13-607028-0). P-H.
White, Emmons E. Appreciating India's Music: An Introduction, with an Emphasis on the Music of South India. 1971. 6.00 (ISBN 0-8008-0278-0, Crescendo). Taplinger.

MUSIC, INFLUENCE OF

see also Music Therapy

Portnoy, Julius. Music in the Life of Man. LC 73-9265. (Illus.). 300p. 1973. Repr. of 1963 ed. lib. bdg. 18.25x (ISBN 0-8371-7000-1, POMU). Greenwood.
Scott, Cyril. Music: Its Secret Influence Throughout the Ages. LC 79-16380. 208p. 1973. pap. 4.95 (ISBN 0-87728-336-2). Weiser.

MUSIC, INSTRUMENTAL

see Instrumental Music

MUSIC, IRISH

Flood, Wm. H. A History of Irish Music. 1979. Repr. of 1905 ed. lib. bdg. 85.00 (ISBN 0-8495-1639-0). Arden Lib.
--Introductory Sketch of Irish Musical History. LC 77-75229. 1977. Repr. of 1921 ed. lib. bdg. 15.00 (ISBN 0-89341-085-3). Longwood Pr.
Graves, Alfred P. Irish Literary & Musical Studies. facs. ed. LC 67-23224. (Essay Index Reprint Ser). 1914. 16.00 (ISBN 0-8369-0494-X). Arno.
Hogan, I. M. Anglo-Irish Music, Seventeen Eighty to Eighteen Thirty. (Illus.). 1966. 6.50x (ISBN 0-8426-1306-4). Verry.
Moore, Thomas. Moore's Irish Melodies with Symphonies & Accompaniments. 1981. 35.00x (ISBN 0-89453-259-6). M Glazier.
Norris, Gerald. Musical Gazetteer of Great Britain & Ireland. LC 81-65957. (Illus.). 352p. 1981. 36.00 (ISBN 0-7153-7845-7). David & Charles.
O Canainn, Tomas. Traditional Music in Ireland. (Illus.). 1978. pap. 10.00 (ISBN 0-7100-0021-9). Routledge & Kegan.
O'Neill, Francis. Irish Minstrels & Musicians. LC 75-40336. 1975. Repr. of 1913 ed. lib. bdg. 25.00 (ISBN 0-8414-6532-0). Folcroft.

MUSIC, ISLAMIC

Gerson-Kiwi, Edith. The Persian Doctrine of Dastga-Composition. LC 64-252. 46p. 1963. pap. 9.00 (ISBN 0-913932-28-0). Boosey & Hawkes.

MUSIC, ITALIAN

Arnold, Denis. Giovanni Gabrieli & the High Renaissance. (Illus.). 334p. 1979. text ed. 65.00x (ISBN 0-19-315232-0). Oxford U Pr.

Barbezieux, Rigaut De. Le Canzoni: Testi E Commento a Cura Di Mauro Braccini. LC 80-2188. Repr. of 1960 ed. 26.00 (ISBN 0-404-19017-0). AMS Pr.

Bonini, Don Severo. Severo Bonini's Discorsi e Regole: A Bilingual Edition. Bonino, MaryAnn, ed. & tr. from Italian. LC 77-18514. (Illus.). 1979. text ed. 24.95x (ISBN 0-8425-0997-6). Brigham.

Burney, Charles. The Present State of Music in France & Italy. 2nd corr. ed. LC 74-24263. 1976. Repr. of 1773 ed. 27.50 (ISBN 0-404-12875-0). AMS Pr.

Bussi, F. Catalogo del Fondo Musicale dell'Archivio del Duomo di Piacenza. 1967. wrappers 31.00 (ISBN 90-6027-191-2, Pub. by Frits Knuf Netherlands). Pendragon NY.

--Umanita e Arte di Gerolamo Parabosco: Madrigalista, Organista e Poligrafo, 2 vols. (Illus.). 278p. 1961. 34.00 (ISBN 90-6027-190-4, Pub. by Frits Knuf Netherlands). Pendragon NY.

Corte, Andrea D., ed. Canto E Bel Canto P.F. Tosi: Opinioni De Cantori Antchi E Moderni 1723. LC 80-2268. Repr. of 1933 ed. 31.50 (ISBN 0-404-18823-0). AMS Pr.

Einstein, A. Italian Madrigal, 3 vols. 1971. Set. 85.00x (ISBN 0-691-09112-9). Princeton U Pr.

Hagopian, Viola L. Italian Ars Nova Music: A Bibliographic Guide to Modern Editions & Related Literature. 2nd, rev. ed. LC 70-187748. 1973. 20.00x (ISBN 0-520-02223-8). U of Cal Pr.

Joyce, John J. The Monodies of Sigismondo d'India. Buelow, George, ed. LC 81-7541. (Studies in Musicology: No. 47). 1981. 41.95 (ISBN 0-8357-1190-0, Pub. by UMI Res Pr). Univ Microfilms.

Klenz, William. Giovanni Maria Bononcini of Modena: A Chapter in Baroque Instrumental Music. LC 62-20213. 1962. 24.50 (ISBN 0-8223-0098-2). Duke.

Lee, Vernon & Paget, Violet. Studies of the Eighteenth Century in Italy. LC 77-17466. (Music Reprint Ser.: 1978). 1978. Repr. of 1887 ed. lib. bdg. 27.50 (ISBN 0-306-77517-4). Da Capo.

Levarie, Siegmund. Musical Italy Revisited. LC 73-7196. (Illus.). 212p. 1973. Repr. of 1963 ed. lib. bdg. 14.00x (ISBN 0-8371-6916-X, LEMU). Greenwood.

Liuzzi, Fernando. La Lauda e i Primordi Della Melodia Italiana, 2 vols. LC 80-2238. 1981. Repr. of 1935 ed. 185.00 (ISBN 0-404-19037-5). AMS Pr.

Lowinsky, Edward, ed. Medici Codex of 1518. LC 67-13810. (Monuments of Renaissance Music Ser: Vols. 1, 2 & 3). 1968. Vol. 1, No. 3. 37.00x (ISBN 0-226-49480-2); Vol. 2, No. 4. 47.00x (ISBN 0-226-49481-0); Vol. 3, No. 5. 37.00x (ISBN 0-226-49482-9). U of Chicago Pr.

Maniates, Maria R. Mannerism in Italian Music & Culture, Fifteen Thirty to Sixteen Thirty. LC 78-11236. (Illus.). 1979. 29.50x (ISBN 0-8078-1319-2). U of NC Pr.

Newcomb, Anthony. Madrigal at Ferrara, Fifteen Seventy-Nine to Fifteen Ninety-Seven, 2 vols. LC 78-573. (Studies in Music: No. 7). 1979. Set. 60.00x (ISBN 0-691-09125-0). Princeton U Pr.

O'Brien, Grace. The Golden Age of Italian Music. LC 78-20486. (Encore Music Editions Ser.). 1980. Repr. of 1918 ed. 21.00 (ISBN 0-88355-862-9). Hyperion Conn.

Silbiger, Alexander. Italian Manuscript Sources of Seventeenth Century Keyboard Music. Buelow, George, ed. (Studies in Musicology: No. 18). 1980. 34.95x (ISBN 0-8357-1075-0, Pub. by UMI Res Pr). Univ Microfilms.

MUSIC, JAPANESE

Crihfield, Liza. Ko-Uta: Little Songs of the Geisha World. LC 78-66085. (Illus.). 1979. 8.50 (ISBN 0-8048-1292-6). C E Tuttle.

Crump, J. I., ed. Chinese & Japanese Music-Dramas. Malm, William P. (Michigan Papers in Chinese Studies Ser.: No. 19). (Illus.). 255p. 1975. pap. 2.00 (ISBN 0-89264-019-7). U of Mich Ctr Chinese.

Garfias, Robert. Music of One Thousand Autumns: The Togaku Style of Japanese Courtly Music. LC 75-13865. 1976. 39.75x (ISBN 0-520-01977-6). U of Cal Pr.

Harich-Schneider, Eta. A History of Japanese Music. (Illus.). 1973. 69.00x (ISBN 0-19-316203-2). Oxford U Pr.

Hatano, Tano. Note on the Japanese Moonharp Guitar Music. (Asian Folklore & Social Life Monographs: Vol. 98). 1977. 5.50 (ISBN 0-89986-324-8). E Langstaff.

Klerk, M. & Mensink, O. Japanese Preten Met Muziek: Japanese Woodcuts with Music. (Haags Gemeentemuseum, Kijkboekjes Ser.: Vol. 1). 1976. wrappers 15.00 (ISBN 90-6027-281-1, Pub. by Frits Knuf Netherlands). Pendragon NY.

Malm, William P. Japanese Music & Musical Instruments. LC 59-10411. (Illus.). 1959. 32.50 (ISBN 0-8048-0308-0). C E Tuttle.

--Nagauta: The Heart of Kabuki Music. LC 73-6260. (Illus.). 344p. 1973. Repr. of 1963 ed. lib. bdg. 24.25 (ISBN 0-8371-6900-3, MANA). Greenwood.

Mensink, O. Traditionele Muziekinstrumenten Van Japan: Traditional Musical Instruments of Japan. (Haags Gemeentemuseum, Kijkboekjes: Vol. 3). (Illus.). 64p. 1979. 15.00 (ISBN 90-6027-301-X, Pub. by Frits Knuf Netherlands). Pendragon NY.

Piggott, F. T. The Music & Musical Instruments of Japan. LC 70-155234. (Music Ser). 1971. Repr. of 1909 ed. lib. bdg. 22.50 (ISBN 0-306-70160-X). Da Capo.

Wade, Bonnie C. Tegotomono: Music for Japanese Koto. LC 75-5265. (Contributions in Intercultural & Comparative Studies: No. 2). 1976. lib. bdg. 19.95 (ISBN 0-8371-8908-X, WTM/). Greenwood.

MUSIC, JAVANESE

Becker, Judith. Traditional Music in Modern Java. LC 80-19180. (Illus.). 1980. text ed. 30.00x (ISBN 0-8248-0563-1). U Pr of Hawaii.

Hood, Mantle. The Nuclear Theme As a Determinant of Patet in Javanese Music. LC 77-5680. (Music Reprint Ser.). 1977. Repr. of 1954 ed. lib. bdg. 32.50 (ISBN 0-306-77419-4). Da Capo.

Kunst, J. Music in Java: Its History, Its Theory & Its Technique, 2 vols. 3rd, enl ed. (Illus.). 1973. Set. 115.00 (ISBN 9-0247-1519-9). Heinman.

Lentz, Donald A. Gamelan Music of Java & Bali: An Artistic Anomaly Complementary to Primary Tonal Theoretical Systems. LC 65-10545. 1965. 5.95x (ISBN 0-8032-0103-6). U of Nebr Pr.

MUSIC, JEWISH

Binder, Abraham W. Studies in Jewish Music: The Collected Writings of the Noted Musicologist. Heskes, Irene, ed. LC 72-136423. 1971. 10.00 (ISBN 0-8197-0272-2). Bloch.

Concise Encyclopedia of Jewish Music. Date not set. 9.95 (ISBN 0-686-76494-3). Feldheim.

Eisikovits, Max. Songs of the Martyrs: Hassidic Melodies of Maramures. LC 79-67624. 1980. pap. 7.50 (ISBN 0-87203-089-X). Hermon.

Fromm, Herbert. Herbert Fromm on Jewish Music: A Composers View. LC 78-60716. 1979. 7.95 (ISBN 0-8197-0465-2). Bloch.

Gradenwitz, Peter. Music & Musicians in Israel. LC 75-166232. 226p. 1959. Repr. 24.00 (ISBN 0-403-01568-5). Scholarly.

Holde, Artur & Heskes, Irene, eds. Jews in Music: From the Age of Enlightenment to the Mid-Twentieth Century. rev. ed. LC 74-83942. 364p. 1974. 7.95 (ISBN 0-8197-0372-9). Bloch.

Idelsohn, A. Z. Jewish Music: In Its Historical Development. LC 67-25236. 1967. pap. 8.95 (ISBN 0-8052-0165-3). Schocken.

Idelsohn, Abraham Z. Thesaurus of Hebrew Oriental Melodies, 10 vols. in 4. 100.00x (ISBN 0-87068-201-6). Ktav.

Marks, Paul F. Bibliography of Literature Concerning Yemenite-Jewish Music. LC 72-90431. (Detroit Studies in Music Bibliography Ser.: No. 27). 1973. pap. 2.00 (ISBN 0-911772-57-X). Info Coord.

Ravina, Menasha. Organum & the Samaritans. LC 64-254. 1963. pap. 10.00 (ISBN 0-913932-35-3). Boosey & Hawkes.

Rothmuller, A. M. The Music of the Jews: An Historical Appreciation. 8.50 (ISBN 0-8446-5870-7). Peter Smith.

Rothmuller, Aron M. The Music of the Jews. rev. ed. LC 65-14229. (Illus.). 288p. 1975. pap. 4.95 (ISBN 0-498-04096-8). A S Barnes.

Sendrey, A., ed. Bibliography of Jewish Music. Repr. of 1951 ed. 26.00 (ISBN 0-527-81400-8). Kraus Repr.

Stainer, John. Music of the Bible. LC 74-100657. (Music Ser). (Illus.). 1970. Repr. of 1914 ed. lib. bdg. 22.50 (ISBN 0-306-71862-6). Da Capo.

Stevens, Joel & Olizky, Kerry M. An Index to the Sound Recordings Collection of the American Jewish Archives. Date not set. 7.50x (ISBN 0-87820-009-6). Ktav.

Werner, Eric. A Voice Still Heard: The Sacred Songs of the Ashkenazic Jews. LC 75-26522. 1976. 22.50 (ISBN 0-271-01167-X). Pa St U Pr.

Werner, Eric, ed. Contributions to a Historical Study of Jewish Music. 1972. 25.00x (ISBN 0-87068-183-4). Ktav.

MUSIC, LATIN-AMERICAN

Aros, Andrew A. The Latin Music Handbook. LC 78-59987. (Illus.). 1978. pap. 6.50 (ISBN 0-932352-00-6). Applause Pubns.

--The Latin Music Yearbook: 1980. (Vinyl Gold Ser.: No. 2). (Orig.). 1980. pap. 6.50 (ISBN 0-932352-02-2). Applause Pubns.

Behague, Gerard. Music in Latin America: an Introduction. (History of Music Ser.). (Illus.). 1979. text ed. 16.95 (ISBN 0-13-608919-4); pap. text ed. 11.95 (ISBN 0-13-608901-1). P-H.

Canino, Marcelino J. El Cantar Folklorico De Puerto Rico: Estudio y Florilegio. pap. 5.00 (ISBN 0-8477-0501-3). U of PR Pr.

Chase, Gilbert. Music of Spain. 2nd ed. (Illus.). 1960. pap. 5.00 (ISBN 0-486-20549-5). Dover.

Chase, Gilbert, ed. Guide to the Music of Latin America. 2nd rev. & enl. ed. LC 70-18910. (BCL Ser.: No. II). Repr. of 1962 ed. 22.50 (ISBN 0-404-08306-4). AMS Pr.

Cruz, Lopez. La Musica Folklorica De Puerto Rico. 1967. 19.95 (ISBN 0-87751-008-3, Pub by Troutman Press). E Torres & Sons.

Girard, Sharon. Funeral Music & Customs in Venezuela. (Special Studies: No. 22). 99p. 1980. pap. text ed. 8.95 (ISBN 0-87918-050-1). ASU Lat Am St.

--Funeral Music & Customs in Venezuela. (Special Studies: No. 22). (Illus.). 1981. pap. 8.95 (ISBN 0-87918-050-1). ASU Lat Am St.

Gordon, Raoul, ed. Puerto Rican Music. 1976. lib. bdg. 59.95 (ISBN 0-8490-0918-9). Gordon Pr.

Inter-American Conference on Ethnomusicology, 2nd & Inter-American Composers Seminar, 1st. Music in the Americas. List, George & Orrego-Salas, Juan, eds. LC 67-64444. (International American Music Monograph Ser: Vol. 1). (Orig.). 1967. pap. text ed. 12.00x (ISBN 0-87750-140-8). Res Ctr Lang Semiotic.

Jimenez, Francisco G. Carlos Gardel & His Epoch. (Latin American Music Ser.). 1980. lib. bdg. 75.00 (ISBN 0-8490-3058-7). Gordon Pr.

Luce, Allena, ed. Popular & Traditional Songs of Puerto Rico, Cuba, Mexico & Spain. (Latin American Music Ser.). 1979. lib. bdg. 59.95 (ISBN 0-8490-2985-6). Gordon Pr.

Morena, Miguel A. The Artistic History of Carlos Gardel: A Chronological Study with Filmography & Discography. (Latin American Music Ser.). 1980. lib. bdg. 75.00 (ISBN 0-8490-3059-5). Gordon Pr.

Munoz. La Musica En Puerto Rico. 1966. 12.95 (ISBN 0-87751-012-1, Pub by Troutman Press). E Torres & Sons.

Olleros, Angel Rodriguez. Canto a la Raza: Composicion Sangvinea De Estudiantes De la Universidad De Puerto Rico. 2.50 (ISBN 0-8477-2314-3). U of PR Pr.

Ribera Chevremont, Evaristo. Canto De Mi Tierra. 2.50 (ISBN 0-8477-3213-4). U of PR Pr.

Roberts, John S. The Latin Tinge: The Impact of Latin American Music on the United States. LC 78-26534. (Illus.). 1979. 14.95 (ISBN 0-19-502564-4). Oxford U Pr.

Slonimsky, Nicolas. Music of Latin America. LC 69-11288. (Music Ser). (Illus.). 374p. 1972. Repr. of 1949 ed. lib. bdg. 25.00 (ISBN 0-306-71188-5). Da Capo.

MUSIC, MAORI

Andersen, Johannes C. Maori Music, with Its Polynesian Background. LC 75-35222. Repr. of 1934 ed. 42.00 (ISBN 0-404-14401-2). AMS Pr.

Barrow, T. Music of the Maori. 50p. 1965. 3.95x (ISBN 0-85467-034-3, Pub. by Viking New Zealand). Intl Schol Bk Serv.

Burrows, E. G. Songs of Urea & Futuna. Repr. of 1945 ed. pap. 14.00 (ISBN 0-527-02291-8). Kraus Repr.

Viking Seven Seas Ltd., ed. Maori Music. 70p. 1979. pap. 3.25x (ISBN 0-85467-038-6, Pub. by Viking New Zealand). Intl Schol Bk Serv.

MUSIC, MEDIEVAL

see Music-History and Criticism-400-1500; Music-Theory-400-1500

MUSIC, MILITARY

see Military Music

MUSIC, MONGOLIAN

Haslund-Christensen, Henning & Cmshevner, Ernst. Music of the Mongols: Eastern Mongolia. LC 79-125045. (Music Ser). 1971. Repr. of 1943 ed. lib. bdg. 25.00 (ISBN 0-306-70009-3). Da Capo.

MUSIC, MUSLIM

see Music, Islamic

MUSIC, NATIONAL

see National Music

MUSIC, NORWEGIAN

Blom, Jan P., et al, eds. Norwegian Folk Music: Series One: Slattar for the Harding Fiddle. Vol. VI, Springar in 3/4 Time. 1979. 36.00x (ISBN 82-00-08794-8, Dist. by Columbia U. Pr.). Universitet.

Grinde, Nils. Contemporary Norwegian Music Nineteen Twenty to Nineteen Eighty. 125p. 1981. 20.00 (ISBN 82-00-05693-7). Universitet.

Lange, Kristian. Norwegian Music: A Survey. (Tokens of Norway Ser). (Illus., Orig.). 1971. pap. 6.50x (ISBN 82-518-0012-9). Intl Pubns Serv.

Qvamme, Borre. Norwegian Music & Composers. 1980. Repr. of 1949 ed. lib. bdg. 10.00 (ISBN 0-89341-445-X). Longwood Pr.

MUSIC, ORIENTAL

Brunet, Jacques, ed. Oriental Music: A Selected Discography. (Occasional Publication). 1971. pap. 3.00 (ISBN 0-89192-148-6). Interbk Inc.

Dauvillier, Jean. Le Mariage En Droit Canonique Oriental. LC 80-2357. Repr. of 1936 ed. 35.00 (ISBN 0-404-18905-9). AMS Pr.

Kaufmann, Walter. Musical Notations of the Orient. (Illus.). 15.00 (ISBN 0-8446-4018-2). Peter Smith.

Malm, William P. Music Cultures of the Pacific, the Near East & Asia. 2nd ed. (Illus.). 1977. text ed. 13.95 (ISBN 0-13-608000-6); pap. text ed. 10.95 (ISBN 0-13-607994-6). P-H.

MUSIC, PHYSICAL EFFECT OF

see Music Therapy

MUSIC, POLISH

Houghtby, Natalie. The Music of Szymanowski. LC 80-51747. 120p. 1981. 11.95 (ISBN 0-8008-7539-7, Crescendo). Taplinger.

MUSIC, POLYNESIAN

Burrows, E. G. Native Music of the Tuamotus. Repr. of 1933 ed. pap. 12.00 (ISBN 0-527-02215-2). Kraus Repr.

Handy, E. S. & Winne, J. L. Music in the Marquesas Islands. Repr. of 1925 ed. pap. 6.00 (ISBN 0-527-02120-2). Kraus Repr.

Kunst, Jaap. Music in New Guinea: Three Studies. (Illus.). 1967. 30.00x (ISBN 0-8002-1289-4). Intl Pubns Serv.

Viking Seven Seas Ltd., ed. Polynesian Music. 85p. 1966. pap. 3.25x (ISBN 0-85467-052-1, Pub. by Viking New Zealand). Intl Schol Bk Serv.

MUSIC, POPULAR (SONGS, ETC.)

see also Country Music; Gospel Music; Rock Music

Alvarenga, Oneyda. Musica Popular Brasileira. 1976. lib. bdg. 59.95 (ISBN 0-8490-2308-4). Gordon Pr.

Applebaum, Stanley, ed. Show Songs from the Black Crook to the Red Mill: Original Sheet Music for 60 Songs from 50 Shows, 1866-1906. (Illus.). 11.50 (ISBN 0-8446-5152-4). Peter Smith.

Armitage, Andrew D. & Tudor, Dean. Annual Index to Popular Music Record Reviews 1975. LC 73-8909. 1976. 24.00 (ISBN 0-8108-0934-6). Scarecrow.

Baker, Glenn A. & Cope, Stuart. The New Music. (Illus.). 1981. 14.95 (ISBN 0-517-54503-9, Harmony); pap. 6.95 (ISBN 0-517-54504-7, Harmony). Crown.

Boot, Adrian & Thomas, Michael. Jamaica: Babylon on a Thin Wire. LC 76-41756. (Illus.). 1977. pap. 6.95 (ISBN 0-8052-0556-X). Schocken.

Burton, J. Index American Popular Song. 1981. 17.00 (ISBN 0-686-30431-4). Cent Hse Americana.

Carvainis, Maria & Lax, Roger. The Moustache Book. 1978. pap. 6.95 (ISBN 0-8256-3144-0, Quick Fox). Music Sales.

Cohen, Leonard. Songs of Leonard Cohen. (Illus.). 1969. pap. 3.95 (ISBN 0-02-060290-1, Collier). Macmillan.

Colbert, W. Who Wrote That Song: Popular Songs in America & Their Composers. 1974. lib. bdg. 69.95 (ISBN 0-87700-216-9). Revisionist Pr.

Creedence Clearwater Revival. 5.95 (ISBN 0-671-21265-6, Fireside). S&S.

Denisoff, R. Serge. Solid Gold: The Popular Record Industry. 504p. 1981. pap. text ed. 8.95 (ISBN 0-87855-586-2). Transaction Bks.

Dylan, Bob. The Songs of Bob Dylan. LC 77-18965. 1978. pap. 11.95 (ISBN 0-394-73523-4). Knopf.

Eldred, Patricia M. Diana Ross. (Rock 'n Pop Stars Ser.). (Illus.). (gr. 4-12). 1975. PLB 5.95 (ISBN 0-87191-462-X); pap. 2.75 o. p. (ISBN 0-89812-112-4). Creative Ed.

Ewen, David, ed. Songs of America: A Cavalcade of Popular Songs with Commentaries. LC 77-26155. (Illus.). 1978. Repr. of 1947 ed. lib. bdg. 24.25x (ISBN 0-313-20166-8, EWSA). Greenwood.

Fuld, James J. Book of World-Famous Music: Classical, Folk, & Popular. rev. ed. 1971. 15.00 (ISBN 0-517-50298-4). Crown.

Gammond, Peter & Clayton, Peter. Dictionary of Popular Music. LC 73-166229. 274p. 1961. Repr. 24.50 (ISBN 0-403-01563-4). Scholarly.

Gilbert & Sullivan. The Authentic Gilbert & Sullivan Songbook: 92 Unabridged Selections from All 14 Operas. Binney, M. & Lavender, P., eds. 12.50 (ISBN 0-8446-5576-7). Peter Smith.

Gilman, Lawrence. Phrases of Modern Music. 59.95 (ISBN 0-8490-0832-8). Gordon Pr.

Gordon, Raoul, ed. Salsa. 1976. lib. bdg. 59.95 (ISBN 0-8490-0989-8). Gordon Pr.

Green, Jonathon, compiled by. Famous Last Words. 1979. pap. 4.95 (ISBN 0-8256-3930-1, Quick Fox). Music Sales.

Grinde, Nils. Contemporary Norwegian Music Nineteen Twenty to Nineteen Eighty. 125p. 1981. 20.00 (ISBN 82-00-05693-7). Universitet.

Hamburger, Robert & Stern, Susan. The Thirties. Weiss, Jeffrey, ed. LC 75-16985. (Illus.). 144p. 1975. pap. 4.95 (ISBN 0-8256-4194-2, Quick Fox). Music Sales.

Hammerstein, Oscar. Songs of Oscar Hammerstein II. LC 74-21637. (Illus.). 1975. 14.95 (ISBN 0-02-871020-7); pap. 8.95 (ISBN 0-02-871010-X). Schirmer Bks.

Kinkle, Roger D. The Complete Encyclopedia of Popular Music & Jazz 1900-1950, 4 vols. 1974. 75.00 (ISBN 0-87000-229-5). Arlington Hse.

Lee, Edward. Music of the People: A Study of Popular Music in Great Britain. 274p. 1972. text ed. 13.25x (ISBN 0-214-66067-2). Humanities.

Lydon, Michael. Rock Folk. 1973. pap. 2.45 (ISBN 0-440-57402-1, Delta). Dell.

McCartney, Paul. Wings Complete. (MPL Communications, Inc. Bks.). (Illus.). 1977. pap. 9.95 (ISBN 0-394-73503-X). Random.

McGreane, Meagon. On Stage with John Denver. (gr. 6-12). 1975. PLB 5.95 (ISBN 0-87191-483-2); pap. 2.95 (ISBN 0-89812-104-3). Creative Ed.

Mainous, Frank. Melodies to Harmonize with. (Illus.). 1978. pap. 12.95 ref. ed. (ISBN 0-13-574277-3). P-H.

Meyer, Hazel. The Gold in Tin Pan Alley. LC 77-7039. 1977. Repr. of 1958 ed. lib. bdg. 18.00x (ISBN 0-8371-9694-9, MEGO). Greenwood.

Nanry, Charles, ed. American Music: From Storyville to Woodstock. LC 71-164978. (Culture & Society Ser.). 1975. 12.95 (ISBN 0-87855-007-0); pap. text ed. 4.95x (ISBN 0-87855-506-4). Transaction Bks.

New York Times Great Songs of Broadway. LC 72-85051. (Illus.). 1973. 14.95 (ISBN 0-8129-0288-2). Times Bks.

Norback, Peter & Norback, Craig, eds. Great Songs of "Madison Avenue". LC 75-37374. 224p. (Orig.). 1976. pap. 7.95 (ISBN 0-8129-0626-8). Times Bks.

Okun, Milton, ed. The New York Times Great Songs of Lennon & McCartney. LC 73-82491. (Illus.). 320p. 1973. spiral bdg. 14.95 (ISBN 0-8129-0400-1); pap. 9.95 (ISBN 0-8129-0509-1). Times Bks.

--The New York Times Great Songs of the Seventies. LC 77-79037. 1978. spiral binding 19.95 (ISBN 0-8129-0727-2). Times Bks.

--The New York Times Great Songs of the Sixties. LC 70-125482. (Illus.). 328p. 1972. 17.50 (ISBN 0-8129-0153-3); pap. 8.95 (ISBN 0-8129-6201-X). Times Bks.

--The New York Times Great Songs of the Sixties - 2. LC 70-125482. 286p. 1975. pap. 8.95 (ISBN 0-8129-6271-0). Times Bks.

Omar, Adisa M., pseud. Nineteen Sixty to Nineteen Eighty: Songs for the Black Struggle. (Illus., Orig.). 1981. pap. 4.95 (ISBN 0-939366-00-2). AKU Pr.

Reynolds, Malvina. Not in Ourselves, nor in Our Stars Either. 40p. 1975. pap. 1.00 (ISBN 0-915620-03-0). Schroder Music.

Rodgers, Richard & Hart, Lorenz. The Rodgers & Hart Song Book. 1977. pap. 6.95 (ISBN 0-671-22421-2, Fireside). S&S.

Rodgers, Richard. One Hundred Best Songs from the Twenties & the Thirties. (Illus.). 450p. 1973. hidden spiral bd. 9.95 (ISBN 0-517-52411-2). Crown.

Rossi, Nick & Choate, Robert. Music of Our Time. LC 69-16933. 1970. 12.50 (ISBN 0-8008-5456-X, Crescendo). Taplinger.

Roxon, Lillian. Rock Encyclopedia. 1971. pap. 9.95 (ISBN 0-448-14572-3, UL). G&D.

Saxton, Martha. The Fifties. Weiss, Jeffrey, ed. (Illus.). 144p. 1975. pap. 4.95 (ISBN 0-8256-4195-0, Quick Fox). Music Sales.

--The Twenties. Weiss, Jeffrey, ed. LC 75-32890. (Illus.). 144p. (Orig.). 1976. pap. 5.95 (ISBN 0-8256-4197-7, Quick Fox). Music Sales.

Simon, Paul. The Songs of Paul Simon. 1972. pap. 9.95 (ISBN 0-394-70783-4). Knopf.

Spaeth, Sigmund. Weep Some More, My Lady. (Music Reprint 1980 Ser.). (Illus.). xv, 268p. 1980. Repr. of 1927 ed. lib. bdg. 22.50 (ISBN 0-306-76003-7). Da Capo.

Stecheson, Anne & Stecheson, Anthony. Stecheson Classified Song Directory: With Supplement Thru 1978. 1961. 40.00 (ISBN 0-685-02531-4). Criterion Mus.

Taupin, Bernie. The One Who Writes the Words for Elton John. 1976. 6.95 (ISBN 0-394-40506-4). Knopf.

Taylor, Paula. Carole King. (Rock 'n Pop Stars Ser.). (Illus.). (gr. 4-12). 1976. PLB 5.95 (ISBN 0-87191-465-4); pap. 2.95 (ISBN 0-89812-111-6). Creative Ed.

--On Stage with the Jackson Five. (gr. 6-12). 1975. PLB 5.95 (ISBN 0-87191-484-0); pap. 2.95 (ISBN 0-89812-144-2). Creative Ed.

Thomas, Tony. Harry Warren & the Hollywood Musical. (Illus.). 1975. 17.95 (ISBN 0-8065-0468-4). Citadel Pr.

Tudor, Dean & Tudor, Nancy. Black Music. LC 78-15563. (American Popular Music on Elpee Ser). 1979. lib. bdg. 22.50x (ISBN 0-87287-147-9). Libs Unl.

Vulliamy, Graham & Lee, Ed, eds. Pop Music in School. 2nd ed. LC 79-7708. (The Resources of Music Ser.: No. 13). (Illus.). 1980. 22.95 (ISBN 0-521-22930-8); pap. 8.95x (ISBN 0-521-29727-3). Cambridge U Pr.

Walton, Ortiz. Music: Black, White & Blue. (Illus.). 182p. 1972. pap. 4.95 (ISBN 0-688-05025-5). Morrow.

Westburg, John E., ed. The Popular Songs of Bruce Kingery. 56p. pap. 3.00 (ISBN 0-87423-014-4). Westburg.

Whitburn, Joel. Top Pop Records Nineteen Seventy-Nine. (Record Research Ser.). 55p. (Orig.). 1980. pap. text ed. 10.00 (ISBN 0-89820-038-5). Record Research.

White, John I. Git Along Little Dogies: Songs & Songmakers of the American West. LC 75-6704. (Music in American Life Ser). (Illus.). 224p. 1975. 11.95 (ISBN 0-252-00327-6). U of Ill Pr.

Wilder, Alec. American Popular Song: The Great Innovators, 1900-1950. (Illus.). 512p. 1972. 20.00 (ISBN 0-19-501445-6). Oxford U Pr.

Zalkind, Ronald. Contemporary Music Almanac: 1980-1981. (Illus.). 1980. 15.95 (ISBN 0-02-872960-9); pap. 9.95 (ISBN 0-02-872970-6). Schirmer Bks.

MUSIC, POPULAR (SONGS, ETC.)–BIBLIOGRAPHY

Burton, Jack. Blue Book of Tin Pan Alley, 2 Vols. LC 62-16426. Set. 25.00 (ISBN 0-686-66390-X); Vol. 1. (ISBN 0-87282-014-9); Vol. 2. (ISBN 0-87282-015-7). Century Hse.

Craig, Warren. Sweet & Lowdown: America's Popular Song Writers. LC 77-20223. 1978. 30.00 (ISBN 0-8108-1089-1). Scarecrow.

Emerson, Lucy. Gold Record. LC 76-23396. 1978. pap. 4.95 (ISBN 0-916184-04-8). Fountain Pub Co NY.

Ewen, David, ed. American Popular Songs from the Revolutionary War to the Present. 1966. 17.50 (ISBN 0-394-41705-4). Random.

Shapiro, Nat, ed. Popular Music, an Annotated Index of American Popular Songs, 6 vols, Vols. 1-6. Incl. Vol. 1. 1950-1959. 1964 (ISBN 0-910024-01-4); Vol. 2. 1940-1949. 1965 (ISBN 0-910024-02-2); Vol. 3. 1960-1964. 1967 (ISBN 0-910024-03-0); Vol. 4. 1930-1939. 1968 (ISBN 0-910024-04-9); Vol. 5. 1920-1929. 1969 (ISBN 0-910024-05-7); Vol. 6, 1965-1969. 1973 (ISBN 0-910024-06-5). LC 64-23761. Vols. 1, 2, & 5. 16.00 ea.; Vol. 3, 4, & 6. 18.50 ea. Adrian.

Stambler, Irwin. Encyclopedia of Pop, Rock & Soul. LC 65-20817. (Illus.). 1975. 19.95 (ISBN 0-312-24990-X). St Martin.

Stecheson, Anthony & Stecheson, Anne. Classified Song Directory. 1961. 25.00 (ISBN 0-685-21904-6). Wehman.

Tudor, Dean & Tudor, Nancy. Popular Music Periodicals Index: 1973. LC 74-11578. 1974. 14.50 (ISBN 0-8108-0763-7). Scarecrow.

Tudor, Dean & Armitage, Andrew D., eds. Popular Music Periodicals Index, 1975. LC 74-11578. 376p. 1976. 18.00 (ISBN 0-8108-0927-3). Scarecrow.

MUSIC, POPULAR (SONGS, ETC.)–DISCOGRAPHY

Armitage, Andrew D. & Tudor, Dean. Annual Index to Popular Music Record Reviews 1973. LC 73-8909. 1974. 24.00 (ISBN 0-8108-0774-2). Scarecrow.

Burton, Jack. Blue Book of Tin Pan Alley, 2 Vols. LC 62-16426. Set. 25.00 (ISBN 0-686-66390-X); Vol. 1. (ISBN 0-87282-014-9); Vol. 2. (ISBN 0-87282-015-7). Century Hse.

Malone, Bill C. Country Music, U.S.A. A Fifty-Year History. LC 68-66367. (American Folklore Society Memoir Ser.: No. 54). (Illus.). 438p. 1969. 15.95 (ISBN 0-292-78377-9); pap. 4.95 (ISBN 0-292-71029-1). U of Tex Pr.

Propes, Steve. Golden Goodies: A Guide to 50's & 60's Popular Rock & Roll Record Collecting. 208p. 1975. 7.95 (ISBN 0-8019-6220-X); pap. 3.50 o. p. (ISBN 0-8019-6221-8). Chilton.

Rust, Brian. The American Dance Band Discography 1917-1942, 2 vols. 1976. 35.00 (ISBN 0-87000-248-1). Arlington Hse.

Rust, Brian A. & Debus, Allen G. The Complete Entertainment Discography: From the Mid - 1897 to 1942. 1000p. 1973. 14.95 (ISBN 0-87000-150-7). Arlington Hse.

Soderbergh, Peter A. Seventy-Eight RPM & Price Guide. 1977. softbound 5.95 (ISBN 0-87069-169-4). Wallace-Homestead.

Tudor, Dean & Tudor, Nancy. Contemporary Popular Music. LC 78-32124. (American Popular Music on Elpee). 1979. lib. bdg. 22.50x (ISBN 0-87287-191-6). Libs Unl.

Whitburn, Joel. Pop Annual, Nineteen Fifty-Five to Nineteen Seventy-Seven. new ed. LC 78-60195. (Record Research Ser.). 623p. (Orig.). 1978. text ed. 50.00 (ISBN 0-89820-001-6); pap. text ed. 40.00 (ISBN 0-89820-002-4). Record Research.

--Top Easy Listening Records, Nineteen Sixty-One to Nineteen Seventy-Four. new ed. LC 75-10541. (Record Research Ser.). (Illus., Orig.). 1975. softcover 25.00 (ISBN 0-89820-021-0). Record Research.

--Top LP's, Nineteen Forty-Five to Nineteen Seventy-Two. new ed. LC 74-75179. (Record Research Ser.). (Illus.). 224p. (Orig.). 1973. pap. text ed. 30.00 (ISBN 0-89820-009-1). Record Research.

--Top LP's, 1974. 40p. (Orig.). 1975. pap. text ed. 10.00 (ISBN 0-89820-005-9). Record Research.

--Top Pop Artists & Singles Nineteen Fifty Five to Nineteen Seventy Eight. LC 79-67484. (Record Research Ser.). (Illus.). 662p. (Orig.). 1979. text ed. 60.00 (ISBN 0-89820-039-3); pap. text ed. 50.00 (ISBN 0-89820-037-7). Record Research.

--Top Pop Records Nineteen Eighty. (Record Research Ser.). 56p. (Orig.). 1981. pap. text ed. 10.00 (ISBN 0-89820-044-X). Record Research.

--Top Pop Records, Nineteen Forty to Nineteen Fifty-Five. new ed. LC 73-76719. (Record Research Ser.). 88p. (Orig.). pap. text ed. 20.00 (ISBN 0-89820-003-2). Record Research.

--Top Pop Records, Nineteen Seventy-Eight. new ed. (Record Research Ser.). 1979. pap. text ed. 10.00 (ISBN 0-89820-031-8). Record Research.

MUSIC, POPULAR (SONGS, ETC.)–HISTORY AND CRITICISM

Armitage, Andrew D. & Tudor, Dean. Annual Index to Popular Music Record Reviews 1974. LC 73-8909. 1976. 24.00 (ISBN 0-8108-0865-X). Scarecrow.

Bell, Doris L. Contemporary Art Trends, Nineteen Sixty to Nineteen Eighty: A Guide to Sources. LC 81-5668. 183p. 1981. 11.00 (ISBN 0-8108-1445-5). Scarecrow.

Belz, Carl. The Story of Rock. 2nd ed. (Illus.). 304p. 1972. 13.95 (ISBN 0-19-501554-1). Oxford U Pr.

Burton, Jack. Blue Book of Tin Pan Alley, 2 Vols. LC 62-16426. Set. 25.00 (ISBN 0-686-66390-X); Vol. 1. (ISBN 0-87282-014-9); Vol. 2. (ISBN 0-87282-015-7). Century Hse.

Ewen, David. All the Years of American Popular Music. LC 77-6733. 1977. 24.95 (ISBN 0-13-022442-1). P-H.

Ewen, David, ed. Songs of America: A Cavalcade of Popular Songs with Commentaries. LC 77-26155. (Illus.). 1978. Repr. of 1947 ed. lib. bdg. 24.25x (ISBN 0-313-20166-8, EWSA). Greenwood.

Fong-Torres, Ben, ed. Rolling Stone Interviews: 1967-1980. (Illus.). 400p. 1981. 24.95 (ISBN 0-312-68954-3); pap. 12.95 (ISBN 0-312-68955-1). St Martin.

Gilbert, Douglas. Lost Chords: The Diverting Story of American Popular Songs. LC 74-139203. 1971. Repr. of 1942 ed. lib. bdg. 15.00x (ISBN 0-8154-0370-4). Cooper Sq.

Goldberg, Isaac. Tin Pan Alley. LC 60-63364. (Illus.). 1961. pap. 5.95 (ISBN 0-8044-6196-1). Ungar.

Hamm, Charles. Yesterdays: Popular Song in America. (Illus.). 1979. 24.95 (ISBN 0-393-01257-3). Norton.

Harker, Dave. One for the Money: Politics & Popular Song. 301p. 1981. text ed. 25.00x (ISBN 0-09-140730-3, Hutchinson U Lib). Humanities.

Jahn, Mike. Rock: From Elvis Presley to the Rolling Stones. LC 72-90449. (Illus.). 384p. 1975. 9.95 (ISBN 0-8129-0314-5); pap. 4.95 (ISBN 0-8129-6263-X). Times Bks.

Levy, Lester S. Give Me Yesterday: American History in Song, 1890-1920. 1975. 27.50 (ISBN 0-8061-1241-7). U of Okla Pr.

Mabey, Richard. Pop Process. 1969. 7.50x (ISBN 0-09-098870-1). Intl Pubns Serv.

Malone, Bill C. Country Music, U.S.A. A Fifty-Year History. LC 68-66367. (American Folklore Society Memoir Ser.: No. 54). (Illus.). 438p. 1969. 15.95 (ISBN 0-292-78377-9); pap. 4.95 (ISBN 0-292-71029-1). U of Tex Pr.

Marcuse, Maxwell F. Tin Pan Alley in Gaslight. LC 58-59691. (Illus.). 1959. 15.00 (ISBN 0-87282-084-X). Century Hse.

Marple, Hugo D. Background & Approaches to Junior High School Music. 512p. 1975. text ed. write for info. (ISBN 0-697-03411-9). Wm C Brown.

Mellers, Wilfred. Twilight of the Gods: The Beatles in Retrospect. LC 73-3508. (Richard Seaver Books). (Illus.). 288p. 1974. 7.95 (ISBN 0-670-73598-1). Viking Pr.

Miles, Betty T., et al. Miles Chart Display of Popular Music: Vol 1: Top 100, 1955-1970. 3rd ed. (Illus.). 1979. Repr. lib. bdg. 95.00 (ISBN 0-913920-03-7). Convex Indus.

Oster, Harry. Living Country Blues. LC 69-20397. (Illus.). 1969. 22.00 (ISBN 0-8103-5026-2). Gale.

O'Toole, J. Watts & Woodstock: Identity & Culture in the United States & South Africa. LC 72-85483. (Case Studies in Cultural Anthropology). 1973. pap. text ed. 4.95 (ISBN 0-03-000936-7, HoltC). HR&W.

Pavletich, Aida. Rock-A-Bye Baby. LC 76-23709. (Illus.). 1980. 14.95 (ISBN 0-385-11207-6). Doubleday.

Pearsall, Ronald. Popular Music of the Twenties. (Illus.). 176p. 1976. 13.75x (ISBN 0-87471-747-7). Rowman.

--Victorian Popular Music. (Illus.). 250p. 1973. 15.00 (ISBN 0-8103-2002-9). Gale.

Propes, Stephen. Those Oldies but Goodies: A Guide to 50's Record Collecting. 160p. 1973. pap. 1.95 (ISBN 0-02-061430-6). Macmillan.

Roberts, John S. The Latin Tinge: The Impact of Latin American Music on the United States. LC 78-26534. (Illus.). 1979. 14.95 (ISBN 0-19-502564-4). Oxford U Pr.

Robinette, Richard. Historical Perspectives in Popular Music: A Historical Outline. (Orig.). 1980. pap. text ed. 10.95 (ISBN 0-8403-2161-9). Kendall-Hunt.

Rublowsky, John. Popular Music. LC 67-28387. (Culture & Discovery Ser). (Illus.). (gr. 9 up). 1967. 9.50x (ISBN 0-465-06024-2). Basic.

Stambler, Irwin. Encyclopedia of Pop, Rock & Soul. LC 73-87393. (Illus.). 1977. pap. 6.95 (ISBN 0-312-25025-8). St Martin.

Storemen, Win. Jazz Piano: Ragtime to Rock Jazz. LC 75-7888. 1975. pap. 3.95 (ISBN 0-668-03828-4). Arco.

Trow, Mike. The Pulse of '64: The Mersey Beat. 1978. 4.95 (ISBN 0-533-03396-9). Vantage.

Tudor, Dean & Biesenthal, Linda. Annual Index to Popular Music Record Reviews 1977. LC 73-8909. 604p. 1979. 25.00 (ISBN 0-8108-1217-7). Scarecrow.

Whitburn, Joel. Pop Annual, Nineteen Fifty-Five to Nineteen Seventy-Seven. new ed. LC 78-60195. (Record Research Ser.). 623p. (Orig.). 1978. text ed. 50.00 (ISBN 0-89820-001-6); pap. text ed. 40.00 (ISBN 0-89820-002-4). Record Research.

--Top Easy Listening Records, Nineteen Sixty-One to Nineteen Seventy-Four. new ed. LC 75-10541. (Record Research Ser.). (Illus., Orig.). 1975. softcover 25.00 (ISBN 0-89820-021-0). Record Research.

--Top LP's, Nineteen Forty-Five to Nineteen Seventy-Two. new ed. LC 74-75179. (Record Research Ser.). (Illus.). 224p. (Orig.). 1973. pap. text ed. 30.00 (ISBN 0-89820-009-1). Record Research.

--Top Pop Records, Nineteen Forty to Nineteen Fifty-Five. new ed. LC 73-76719. (Record Research Ser.). 88p. (Orig.). pap. text ed. 20.00 (ISBN 0-89820-003-2). Record Research.

Williams, John R. This Was Your Hit Parade: 1935-1950. 210p. 1973. 6.95 (ISBN 0-913954-09-8). Courier of Maine.

Wolman, Baron, et al. Festival: The Book of American Music Celebrations. 1970. pap. 3.95 (ISBN 0-02-061950-2, Collier). Macmillan.

MUSIC, POPULAR (SONGS, ETC.)–WRITING AND PUBLISHING

Boyce, Tommy. How to Write a Hit Song & Sell It. 1974. pap. 7.00 (ISBN 0-87980-291-X). Wilshire.

Boye, Henry. How to Make Money Selling the Songs You Write. rev. ed. LC 75-124473. 192p. 1975. pap. 4.95 (ISBN 0-8119-0381-8). Fell.

Dranov, Paula. Inside the Music Publishing Industry. LC 80-13304. (Communications Library Ser.). 185p. 1980. 24.95x (ISBN 0-914236-40-7). Knowledge Indus.

Fisher, W. One Hundred Years of Music Publishing in the U. S. 59.95 (ISBN 0-8490-0768-2). Gordon Pr.

Fong-Torres, Ben, ed. Rolling Stone Interviews: 1967-1980. (Illus.). 400p. 1981. 24.95 (ISBN 0-312-68954-3); pap. 12.95 (ISBN 0-312-68955-1). St Martin.

Frankel, Aaron. Writing the Broadway Musical. LC 76-58925. 1977. pap. text ed. 10.00x (ISBN 0-910482-82-9). Drama Bk.

Glaser, Hy. How to Write Lyrics That Make Sense & Dollars. 1977. 9.95 (ISBN 0-682-48764-3, Banner). Exposition.

Herscher, Lou. Successful Songwriting. 2nd ed. Mills, Paul, ed. LC 66-6554. (Orig.). 1966. pap. 4.95 (ISBN 0-913754-01-3). Solo.

Kasha, Al & Hirschhorn, Joel. If They Ask You, You Can Write a Song. 1979. 12.95 (ISBN 0-671-24149-4). S&S.

Kosser, Michael. How to Become a Successful Nashville Songwriter. Brown, H. Jackson, Jr., ed. LC 81-82498. (Illus.). 100p. 1981. pap. 4.95 (ISBN 0-9606550-0-X). Porch Swing.

Pincus, Lee. The Songwriters' Success Manual. LC 77-352498. (Illus.). 1976. pap. 6.95 (ISBN 0-918318-01-7). Music Pr.

Pollock, Bruce. In Their Own Words: Lyrics & Lyricists, 1955-74. 224p. 1975. 10.95 (ISBN 0-02-597950-7). Macmillan.
Rachlin, Harvey. The Songwriter's Handbook. LC 77-2946. (Funk & W Bk.). (Illus.). 1977. 10.95 (ISBN 0-308-10321-1). T Y Crowell.
Whitfield, Jane. Songwriters Rhyming Dictionary. 1974. pap. 5.00 (ISBN 0-87980-293-6). Wilshire.
Wilbur, L. Perry. How to Write Songs That Sell. LC 76-55653. 1977. 8.95 (ISBN 0-8092-7861-8); pap. 5.95 o. p. (ISBN 0-8092-7846-4). Contemp Bks.
Wolfe, Richard J. Early American Music Engraving & Printing: A History of Music Publishing in America from 1787 to 1825 with Commentary on Earlier & Later Practices. LC 79-12955. (Music in Amerecian Life Ser.). (Illus.). 340p. 1980. 24.95 (ISBN 0-252-00726-3). U of Ill Pr.

MUSIC, PORTUGUESE

Chase, Gilbert. Music of Spain. 2nd ed. (Illus.). 1960. pap. 5.00 (ISBN 0-486-20549-5). Dover.

MUSIC, PRIMITIVE

see also Songs, Australian (Aboriginal); Ethnomusicology; Indians of North America-Music; Musical Instruments, Primitive

Boughton, Rutland. The Reality of Music. LC 72-80495. Repr. of 1934 ed. 14.00 (ISBN 0-405-08294-0, Blom Pubns). Arno.
Harrison, F. Time, Place & Music: An Anthology of Ethnomusicological Observation, C. 1550 to C. 1800. (Illus.). 1973. pap. 45.00 (ISBN 0-685-79105-X). Heinman.
Hood, Mantle. The Nuclear Theme As a Determinant of Patet in Javanese Music. LC 77-5680. (Music Reprint Ser.). 1977. Repr. of 1954 ed. lib. bdg. 32.50 (ISBN 0-306-77419-4). Da Capo.
Jones, A. M. Studies in African Music, 2 Vols. 1959. 49.00x (ISBN 0-19-713512-9). Oxford U Pr.
Nettl, Bruno. Folk & Traditional Music of the Western Continents. 2nd ed. (Illus.). 272p. 1973. pap. 10.95 (ISBN 0-13-322933-5). P-H.
--Music in Primitive Culture. LC 56-8551. 1956. 12.50x (ISBN 0-674-59000-7). Harvard U Pr.
Schaeffner, Andre. Origine Des Instruments De Musique. Repr. of 1936 ed. 14.00 (ISBN 0-384-53500-3); pap. 10.00 (ISBN 0-685-13544-6). Johnson Repr.
Tracey, Hugh. Chopi Musicians. (Illus.). 1970. Repr. of 1948 ed. 36.00x (ISBN 0-19-724182-4). Oxford U Pr.
Walleschek, Richard. Primitive Music. LC 72-125062. (Music Ser). 1970. Repr. of 1893 ed. lib. bdg. 25.00 (ISBN 0-306-70028-X). Da Capo.
Williams, Leonard. The Dancing Chimpanzee. LC 80-40598. 128p. 1980. 11.95 (ISBN 0-8052-8057-X, Pub. by Allison & Busby England); pap. 5.95 (ISBN 0-8052-8056-1). Schocken.

MUSIC, PRINTING OF

see Music Printing

MUSIC, PUERTO RICAN

Callejo, Fernando. Music & Musicians of Puerto Rico. (Puerto Rico Ser.). 1979. lib. bdg. 59.95 (ISBN 0-8490-2974-0). Gordon Pr.

MUSIC, RELIGIOUS

see Church Music

MUSIC, ROMAN

see Music, Greek and Roman

MUSIC, RUSSIAN

Abraham, Gerald. On Russian Music. 1976. lib. bdg. 13.00 (ISBN 0-403-03757-3). Scholarly.
--Studies in Russian Music. 1976. Repr. of 1935 ed. lib. bdg. 25.00 (ISBN 0-403-03700-X). Scholarly.
Abraham, Gerald E. Eight Soviet Composers. LC 71-106679. Repr. of 1943 ed. lib. bdg. 15.00 (ISBN 0-8371-3350-5, ABSC). Greenwood.
--On Russian Music: Critical & Historical Studies of Glinka's Operas. LC 39-32448. (Music Ser.: Practice & Theory). Repr. of 1939 ed. 17.00 (ISBN 0-384-00150-5). Johnson Repr.
--Studies in Russian Music. facs. ed. LC 68-20285. (Essay Index Reprint Ser). 1936. 15.25 (ISBN 0-8369-0133-9). Arno.
Bakst, James. A History of Russian-Soviet Music. LC 76-55406. (Illus.). 1977. Repr. of 1966 ed. lib. bdg. 28.75 (ISBN 0-8371-9422-9, BARS). Greenwood.
Bennett, John R., compiled by. Melodiya: A Soviet Russian L. P. Discography. LC 81-4247. (Discographies Ser.: No. 6). (Illus.). xxii, 832p. 1981. lib. bdg. 75.00 (ISBN 0-313-22596-6, BME/). Greenwood.
Calvocoressi, M. D. A Survey of Russian Music. LC 73-6208. (Illus.). 142p. 1974. Repr. of 1944 ed. lib. bdg. 15.00x (ISBN 0-8371-6888-0, CARM). Greenwood.
Ginsburg, Lev. Ysaye. Paradise, ed. (Illus.). 576p. 1980. text ed. 20.00 (ISBN 0-87666-619-5, Z-31). Paganiniana Pubns.
Houghton, Norris. Moscow Rehearsals. 1973. lib. bdg. 16.00x (ISBN 0-374-93981-0). Octagon.
Leonard, Richard A. A History of Russian Music. LC 77-6760. 1977. Repr. of 1957 ed. lib. bdg. 31.00x (ISBN 0-8371-9658-2, LERM). Greenwood.
Miliukov, Paul. Architecture, Painting, & Music in Russia. (Part III). pap. text ed. 3.95 (ISBN 0-498-04008-9, Prpta). A S Barnes.
--Architecture, Painting, & Music in Russia. (Outlines of Russian Culture, Vol. 3). 6.00 (ISBN 0-8446-2585-X). Peter Smith.
Montagu-Nathan, M. History of Russian Music. LC 76-82815. 1918. 12.00x (ISBN 0-8196-0251-5). Biblo.
--A History of Russian Music. LC 77-8740. 1977. Repr. of 1914 ed. lib. bdg. 25.00 (ISBN 0-89341-129-9). Longwood Pr.
Olkhovsky, Andrey. Music Under the Soviets: The Agony of an Art. LC 74-20341. (Studies of the Research Program of the U.S.S.R.: No. 11). 427p. 1975. Repr. of 1955 ed. lib. bdg. 22.75x (ISBN 0-8371-7856-8, OLMS). Greenwood.
--Music Under the Soviets: The Agony of an Art. LC 74-20341. (Studies of the Research Program of the U.S.S.R.: No. 11). 427p. 1975. Repr. of 1955 ed. lib. bdg. 22.75x (ISBN 0-8371-7856-8, OLMS). Greenwood.
Poliakova, Liudmila V. Soviet Music. Shartse, Olga, ed. Danko, Xena, tr. LC 78-66920. (Encore Music Editions Ser.). (Illus.). 1980. Repr. of 1961 ed. cancelled (ISBN 0-88355-757-6). Hyperion Conn.
Ridenour, Robert C. Nationalism, Modernism, & Personal Rivalry in Nineteenth-Century Russian Music. Brown, Malcolm, ed. LC 81-76. (Russian Music Studies). 1981. 34.95 (ISBN 0-8357-1162-5, Pub. by UMI Res Pr). Univ Microfilms.
Sabaneev, Leonid L. Modern Russian Composers. facs. ed. Joffe, J. A., tr. LC 67-23270. (Essay Index Reprint Ser). 1927. 18.00 (ISBN 0-8369-0847-3). Arno.
Werth, Alexander. Musical Uproar in Moscow. LC 73-5211. 103p. 1973. Repr. of 1949 ed. lib. bdg. 15.00 (ISBN 0-8371-6864-3, WEMU). Greenwood.
Zetlin, Mikhael. The Five: The Evolution of the Russian School of Music. Panin, George, ed. & tr. from Rus. LC 73-1439. (Illus.). 344p. 1975. Repr. of 1959 ed. lib. bdg. 19.25x (ISBN 0-8371-6797-3, ZETF). Greenwood.

MUSIC, SACRED

see Church Music

MUSIC, SCOTTISH

see also Bagpipe

Collinson, Francis. The Traditional & National Music of Scotland. (Illus.). 1970. Repr. of 1966 ed. 25.00 (ISBN 0-7100-1213-6). Routledge & Kegan.
Crawford, Thomas. Society & the Lyric: A Study of the Song Culture of Eighteenth-Century Scotland. 208p. 1980. 13.50 (ISBN 0-7073-0227-7, Pub. by Scottish Academic Pr). Columbia U Pr.
Dalyell, John G. Musical Memoirs of Scotland with Historical Annotations. LC 72-6979. 1972. lib. bdg. 35.00 (ISBN 0-88305-152-4). Norwood Edns.
Dalyell, Sir John G. Musical Memoirs of Scotland. 300p. 1980. Repr. of 1849 ed. lib. bdg. 35.00 (ISBN 0-8492-4214-2). R West.
Emmerson, George S. Rantin' Pipe & Tremblin' String: A History of Scottish Dance Music. (Illus.). 1971. 14.50 (ISBN 0-7735-0116-9). McGill-Queens U Pr.
Farmer, Henry G. History of Music in Scotland. LC 70-100613. (Music Ser). (Illus.). 1970. Repr. of 1947 ed. lib. bdg. 29.50 (ISBN 0-306-71865-0). Da Capo.
MacDonald, Donald. Collection of the Ancient Martial Music of Caledonia. 1975. 21.00x (ISBN 0-8464-0255-6). Beekman Pubs.
MacDonell, Margaret. The Emigrant Experience: Songs of Highland Emigrants in North America. 208p. 1981. 18.95 (ISBN 0-8020-5469-2). U of Toronto Pr.
MacKay, Angus. A Collection of Ancient Piobaireachd or Highland Pipe Music. LC 73-12948. (Norwood Folklore Ser.). 15.00 (ISBN 0-88305-418-3). Norwood Edns.
--A Collection of Ancient Piobaireache or Highland Pipe Music. 171p. 1980. Repr. of 1838 ed. lib. bdg. 20.00 (ISBN 0-8414-6427-8). Folcroft.
Shire, Helena M. Song, Dance & Poetry of the Court of Scotland Under King James Sixth. LC 69-13793. (Illus.). 1969. 49.50 (ISBN 0-521-07181-X). Cambridge U Pr.

MUSIC, SLAVIC

Kolar, Walter W. Croatian Musical Folklore: An Introduction. (Illus.). 85p. (Orig.). 1981. pap. 5.00 (ISBN 0-936922-02-8). Tamburitza.

MUSIC, SPANISH

Arce de Vazquez, Margot. Garcilaso De la Vega: Contribucion Al Estudio De la Lirica Espanola Del Siglo XVI. 4th ed. (UPREX, E. Literarios: No. 43). pap. 1.85 (ISBN 0-8477-0043-7). U of PR Pr.
--Garcilaso De la Vega: Contribucion Al Estudio De la Lirica Espanola Del Siglo XVI. 3rd ed. 2.50 (ISBN 0-8477-3105-7). U of PR Pr.
Barcelona, Biblioteca Central, Seccion De Musica. La Musica De las Cantigas De Santa Maria Del Rey Alfonso el Sabio, 4 pts. in 3 vols. LC 80-2193. 1981. Set. 375.00 (ISBN 0-404-19046-4). Vol. 1 (ISBN 0-404-19047-2). Vol. 2 (ISBN 0-404-19048-0). Vol. 3 (ISBN 0-404-19049-9). AMS Pr.
Broderick, Richard, ed. The New York Times Great Latin Songs. LC 73-90174. (Illus.). 288p. 1974. 14.95 (ISBN 0-8129-0377-3); pap. 7.95 (ISBN 0-8129-6238-9). Times Bks.
Chase, Gilbert. Music of Spain. 2nd ed. (Illus.). 1960. pap. 5.00 (ISBN 0-486-20549-5). Dover.
Cistercian Abbey of las Huelgas, Burgos, Spain. El Codex Musical de las Huelgas, 3 vols. LC 71-178510. (Publications del Departament de Musica, Biblioteca de Catalunya: No. 6). (Illus.). Repr. of 1931 ed. Set. 195.00 (ISBN 0-404-56504-2); Vol. 1. (ISBN 0-404-56505-0); Vol. 2. (ISBN 0-404-56506-9); Vol. 3. (ISBN 0-404-56507-7). AMS Pr.
Fuenllana, Miguel De. Orphenica Lyra (Seville, 1554) Jacobs, Charles, ed. (Illus.). 1978. 98.00x (ISBN 0-19-816128-X). Oxford U Pr.
Hamilton, M. N. Music in Eighteenth Century Spain. LC 74-162868. (Music Ser). 1971. Repr. of 1937 ed. lib. bdg. 25.00 (ISBN 0-306-70279-7). Da Capo.
Livermore, Ann. A Short History of Spanish Music. LC 72-86597. 262p. 1972. 12.50x (ISBN 0-8443-0077-2). Vienna Hse.
--A Short History of Spanish Music. 262p. 1972. 40.50x (ISBN 0-7156-0634-4, Pub. by Duckworth England); pap. 13.50x (ISBN 0-7156-0886-X). Biblio Dist.
Morley, S. Griswold & Hills, E. C. Modern Spanish Lyric. 59.95 (ISBN 0-8490-0652-X). Gordon Pr.
Powell, Linton E. A History of Spanish Piano Music. LC 79-3761. 224p. 1980. 17.50x (ISBN 0-253-18114-3). Ind U Pr.
Riano, J. F. Critical & Biographical Notes on Early Spanish Music. LC 79-158958. (Music Ser). 1971. Repr. of 1887 ed. lib. bdg. 19.50 (ISBN 0-306-70193-6). Da Capo.
Ribera, Julian. Music in Ancient Arabia & Spain: Being La Musica De las Cantigas. LC 70-87614. (Music Ser). 1970. Repr. of 1929 ed. lib. bdg. 25.00 (ISBN 0-306-71622-4). Da Capo.
Ribera y Tarrago, Julian. Historia De la Musica Arabe Medieval y Su Influencia En la Espanola. LC 78-178587. Repr. of 1927 ed. 24.50 (ISBN 0-404-56664-2). AMS Pr.
Snow, Robert J. The Extant Music of Rodrigo De Ceballos & Its Sources. LC 78-70024. (Detroit Studies in Music Bibliography Ser.: No. 44). 1980. 17.50 (ISBN 0-89990-001-1). Info Coord.
--The Sixteen-Thirteen Print of Juan Esquivel Barahona. LC 78-70021. (Detroit Monographs in Musicology: No. 7). 1978. 11.00 (ISBN 0-911772-92-8). Info Coord.
Stevenson, Robert. Spanish Music in the Age of Columbus. LC 78-20496. (Encore Music Editions Ser.). 1981. Repr. of 1960 ed. 29.50 (ISBN 0-88355-872-6). Hyperion Conn.
Subira, Jose. Historia De la Musica Teatral en Espana. LC 80-2304. Repr. of 1945 ed. 27.50 (ISBN 0-404-18871-0). AMS Pr.
Tinnell, Roger D. An Annotated Discography of Music in Spain Before 1650. 146p. 1980. 12.00 (ISBN 0-686-29367-3). Hispanic Seminary.
Trend, John B. Manuel de Falla & Spanish Music. LC 74-181283. 184p. 1934. Repr. 19.00 (ISBN 0-403-01706-8). Scholarly.
--Music of Spanish History to Sixteen Hundred. 1926. 15.00 (ISBN 0-527-90780-4). Kraus Repr.

MUSIC, SUMERIAN

Galpin, Francis W. Music of the Sumerians. LC 78-87458. (Music Reprint Ser). 1970. Repr. of 1937 ed. lib. bdg. 25.00 (ISBN 0-306-71462-0). Da Capo.
--Music of the Sumerians & Their Immediate Successors, the Babylonians and Assyrians. LC 73-109625. (Select Bibliographies Reprint Ser). 1936. 16.00 (ISBN 0-8369-5234-0). Arno.
--Music of the Sumerians & Their Immediate Successors, the Babylonians & Assyrians. Repr. of 1937 ed. lib. bdg. 22.75x (ISBN 0-8371-3928-7, GAMS). Greenwood.
--The Music of the Sumerians & Their Immediate Successors, the Babylonians & Assyrians. 2nd ed. (Illus.). 1955. 15.00x (ISBN 3-87320-533-5). Intl Pubns Serv.

MUSIC, THEATRICAL

see Ballad Opera; Music in Theaters; Musical Revue, Comedy, etc.; Opera; Operetta

MUSIC, VOCAL

see Vocal Music

MUSIC, YIDDISH

see Music, Jewish

MUSIC AND ART

see Art and Music

MUSIC AND LITERATURE

see also Music-Poetry; Musical Fiction

Aaron, Pietro. Lucidario in Musica di Alcune oppenioni Antiche et Moderne. (Monuments of Music & Music Literature in Facsimile: Ser. II, Vol. 68). (Illus.). 1978. Repr. of 1545 ed. 27.50 (ISBN 0-8450-2268-7). Broude.
Aronson, Alex. Music & the Novel: A Study in Twentieth Century Fiction. 267p. 1980. 22.50x (ISBN 0-8476-6170-9). Rowman.
Brown, Calvin S. Music & Literature: A Comparison of the Arts. LC 78-8071. 287p. 1948. 12.50x (ISBN 0-8203-0128-0). U of Ga Pr.
--Tones into Words: Musical Compositions as Subjects of Poetry. LC 53-11755. 171p. 1953. 10.00x (ISBN 0-8203-0187-6). U of Ga Pr.
Chan, Mary. Music in the Theatre of Ben Jonson. (Illus.). 344p. 1980. 69.00x (ISBN 0-19-812632-8). Oxford U Pr.
Cheney, David R. & Hunt, Leigh. Musical Evenings: Or Selections, Vocal & Instrumental. LC 64-12876. 1964. 4.50x (ISBN 0-8262-0033-8). U of Mo Pr.
Conforto, Giovanni. Breve e Facile Maniera. (Monuments of Music Literature in Facsimile: Ser. II, Vol. 115). 1978. Repr. of 1593 ed. 22.50x (ISBN 0-8450-2315-2). Broude.
Day, James. Literary Background of Bach's Cantatas. (Student's Music Library-Historical & Critical Studies Ser). (Illus.). 1961. 10.95 (ISBN 0-234-77522-X). Dufour.
Finney, Gretchen L. Musical Backgrounds for English Literature 1580-1650. LC 75-35024. 292p. 1976. Repr. of 1962 ed. lib. bdg. 20.25x (ISBN 0-8371-8572-6, FIMB). Greenwood.
Freedman, William. Laurence Sterne & the Origins of the Musical Novel. LC 77-7082. 232p. 1978. 15.00 (ISBN 0-8203-0429-8). U of Ga Pr.
Frye, Northrop, ed. Sound & Poetry. LC 57-11003. (Essays of the English Institute). 1957. 12.50x (ISBN 0-231-02209-3). Columbia U Pr.
Gooch, Bryan N. & Thatcher, David S. Musical Settings of Late Victorian & Modern British Literature. LC 75-24085. (Garland Ref. Lib. of Humanities). 1979. lib. bdg. 120.00 (ISBN 0-8240-9981-8). Garland Pub.
Kelly, James W. The Faust Legend in Music. LC 74-75893. (Detroit Reprints in Music). 1976. 10.00 (ISBN 0-911772-81-2). Info Coord.
Lanier, S. Music & Poetry. LC 68-25292. (Studies in Poetry, No. 38). 1969. Repr. of 1898 ed. lib. bdg. 27.95 (ISBN 0-8383-0306-4). Haskell.
Lanier, Sidney. Music & Poetry. LC 74-171656. Repr. of 1898 ed. 5.00 (ISBN 0-404-03874-3). AMS Pr.
--Music & Poetry: Essays Upon Some Aspects & Interrelations of the Two Arts. Repr. of 1898 ed. lib. bdg. 15.00x (ISBN 0-8371-1001-7, LAMP). Greenwood.
Louis, Louise. The Dervish Dance. 40p. 1971. Repr. of 1958 ed. text ed. 4.95 (ISBN 0-686-29406-8). Pen-Art.
Manifold, John S. The Music in English Drama from Shakespeare to Purcell. LC 70-181207. 208p. 1956. Repr. 19.00 (ISBN 0-403-01617-7). Scholarly.
Mazzaro, Jerome. Transformations in the Renaissance English Lyric. LC 74-124726. 228p. 1970. 20.00x (ISBN 0-8014-0587-4). Cornell U Pr.
Modern Language Association. Bibliography on the Relations of Literature & the Other Arts. LC 68-58407. Repr. of 1967 ed. 18.00 (ISBN 0-404-04348-8). AMS Pr.
Neumann, Alfred R. Literature & the Other Arts. LC 77-14281. 1977. Repr. lib. bdg. 5.50 (ISBN 0-8414-6302-6). Folcroft.
Nitze, William A. Arthurian Romance & Modern Poetry & Music. LC 76-122995. (Arthurian Legend & Literature Ser., No. 1). 1970. Repr. of 1940 ed. lib. bdg. 27.95 (ISBN 0-8383-1128-8). Haskell.
--Arthurian Romance & Modern Poetry & Music. LC 72-105816. 1970. Repr. of 1940 ed. 10.00 (ISBN 0-8046-1049-5). Kennikat.
--Arthurian Romance & Modern Poetry & Music. LC 74-23623. 1974. Repr. of 1940 ed. lib. bdg. 17.50 (ISBN 0-8414-6282-8). Folcroft.
Pattison, Bruce. Music & Poetry of the English Renaissance. LC 70-127278. (Music Ser). (Illus.). 1970. Repr. of 1948 ed. lib. bdg. 22.50 (ISBN 0-306-71298-9). Da Capo.
--Music & Poetry of the English Renaissance. LC 72-193387. 1948. lib. bdg. 20.00 (ISBN 0-685-10372-2). Folcroft.
Ross, Martin. Music & James Joyce. LC 73-11054. 1936. lib. bdg. 6.00 (ISBN 0-8414-2587-6). Folcroft.
Rubsamen, Walter H. Literary Sources of Secular Music in Italy: 1500. LC 72-4482. (Music Ser.). 82p. 1972. Repr. of 1943 ed. lib. bdg. 15.00 (ISBN 0-306-70496-X). Da Capo.
Schoolfield, George C. Figure of the Musician in German Literature. LC 56-63563. (North Carolina. University. Studies in the Germanic Languages & Literatures: No. 19). 18.50 (ISBN 0-404-50919-3). AMS Pr.

Smith, Patrick J. Tenth Muse: A Historical Study of the Opera Libretto. LC 73-111254. (Illus.). 1970. 12.95 (ISBN 0-394-44822-7). Knopf.
Stein, Jack M. Poem & Music in the German Lied from Gluck to Hugo Wolf. LC 70-152772. 1971. 12.50x (ISBN 0-674-67451-0). Harvard U Pr.
--Richard Wagner & the Synthesis of the Arts. LC 73-1840. (Illus.). 229p. 1973. Repr. of 1960 ed. lib. bdg. 17.25x (ISBN 0-8371-6806-6, STRX). Greenwood.
Tooze, Ruth & Krone, Beatrice P. Literature & Music As Resources for Social Studies. LC 73-21289. (Illus.). 457p. 1974. Repr. of 1955 ed. lib. bdg. 23.50x (ISBN 0-8371-6153-3, TOLM). Greenwood.
Wilson, Christopher. Shakespeare & Music. LC 76-58560. (Music Reprint Series). 1977. Repr. of 1922 ed. lib. bdg. 17.50 (ISBN 0-306-70868-X). Da Capo.
Winn, James A. Unsuspected Eloquence: A History of the Relations Between Poetry & Music. LC 80-27055. 384p. 1981. 18.95x (ISBN 0-300-02615-3). Yale U Pr.

MUSIC AND MAGIC
see also Music, Primitive

MUSIC AND MORALS
Lawhead, Steve. Rock Reconsidered: A Christian Looks at Contemporary Music. LC 81-8129. 156p. (Orig.). 1981. pap. 4.25 (ISBN 0-87784-812-2). Inter-Varsity.

MUSIC AND RELIGION
see Religion and Music

MUSIC AND ROMANTICISM
see Romanticism in Music

MUSIC AND SOCIETY
see also Music–Economic Aspects
Adorno, Theodor W. Introduction to the Sociology of Music. Ashton, E. B., tr. from Ger. LC 75-33883. 1976. 12.95 (ISBN 0-8164-9266-2). Continuum.
Allen, Warren D. Our Marching Civilization. LC 77-25408. (Music Reprint Ser., 1978). 1978. Repr. of 1943 ed. lib. bdg. 16.95 (ISBN 0-306-77568-9). Da Capo.
Denisoff, R. Serge. Great Day Coming: Folk Music & the American Left. LC 74-155498. (Music in American Life Ser). (Illus.). 1971. 12.50 (ISBN 0-252-00179-6). U of Ill Pr.
Etzkorn, K. Peter. Music & Society: The Later Writings of Paul Honigsheim. LC 78-21234. 350p. 1979. Repr. of 1973 ed. 21.50 (ISBN 0-88275-831-4). Krieger.
Finkelstein, Sidney. How Music Expresses Ideas. rev. ed. LC 70-115168. 1970. pap. 1.95 (ISBN 0-7178-0095-4). Intl Pub Co.
Gaburo, Kenneth. Beauty of Irrelevant Music. (Paperplay Mini-Bks.: Vol. 1). (Illus.). 22p. 1976. saddle stitched 2.75 (ISBN 0-939044-04-8). Lingua Pr.
Mackerness, Eric D. A Social History of English Music. LC 75-40994. (Illus.). 307p. 1976. Repr. of 1964 ed. lib. bdg. 18.25x (ISBN 0-8371-8705-2, MAHEM). Greenwood.
Mussulman, Joseph A. Music in the Cultured Generation: Musical Life in America, 1870-1900. LC 77-149920. (Pi Kappa Lambda Studies in American Music). 1971. 12.95x (ISBN 0-8101-0350-8). Northwestern U Pr.
Nanry, Charles, ed. American Music: From Storyville to Woodstock. LC 71-164978. (Culture & Society Ser.). 1975. 12.95 (ISBN 0-87855-007-0); pap. text ed. 4.95x (ISBN 0-87855-506-4). Transaction Bks.
Pichaske, David. A Generation in Motion: Popular Music & Culture in the 1960's. LC 78-63033. (Illus.). 1979. 15.00 (ISBN 0-02-871860-7); pap. 5.95 (ISBN 0-02-871850-X). Schirmer Bks.
Schauffler, Robert H. The Musical Amateur: A Book on the Human Side of Music. LC 79-181244. 261p. 1911. Repr. 14.00 (ISBN 0-403-01670-3). Scholarly.
Schuessler, Karl F. Musical Taste & Socio-Economic Background. Zuckerman, Harriet & Merton, Robert K., eds. LC 79-9024. (Dissertations on Sociology Ser.). 1980. lib. bdg. 11.00x (ISBN 0-405-12990-4). Arno.
Shepherd, John, et al. Whose Music? A Sociology of Musical Language. 300p. 1980. 19.95 (ISBN 0-87855-384-3); pap. text ed. 7.95 (ISBN 0-87855-815-2). Transaction Bks.
Siegmeister, Elie. Music & Society. LC 74-2318. (Studies in Music, No. 42). 1974. lib. bdg. 49.95 (ISBN 0-8383-2050-3). Haskell.
Silbermann, Alphons. The Sociology of Music. Stewart, Corbet, tr. from German. LC 76-58565. 1977. Repr. of 1963 ed. lib. bdg. 18.50 (ISBN 0-8371-9455-5, SISM). Greenwood.
Small, Christopher. Music, Society, Education. LC 77-81648. (Illus.). 1977. 12.95 (ISBN 0-02-872440-2). Schirmer Bks.
Tooze, Ruth & Krone, Beatrice P. Literature & Music As Resources for Social Studies. LC 73-21289. (Illus.). 457p. 1974. Repr. of 1955 ed. lib. bdg. 23.50x (ISBN 0-8371-6153-3, TOLM). Greenwood.
Wildman, Louis. Studies in the Sociology of Music. (Orig.). 1981. pap. text ed. 6.00 (ISBN 0-939630-08-7). Inst Qual Hum Life.

MUSIC AND STATE
see also State Encouragement of Science, Literature, and Art
Backus, Rob. Fire Music: A Political History of Jazz. (Illus.). 104p. (Orig.). 1977. pap. 3.95 (ISBN 0-917702-00-X). Vanguard Bks.
Harker, Dave. One for the Money: Politics & Popular Song. 301p. 1981. text ed. 25.00x (ISBN 0-09-140730-3, Hutchinson U Lib). Humanities.
Werth, Alexander. Musical Uproar in Moscow. LC 73-5211. 103p. 1973. Repr. of 1949 ed. lib. bdg. 15.00 (ISBN 0-8371-6864-3, WEMU). Greenwood.

MUSIC AS RECREATION
Batcheller, John M. & Monsour, Sally. Music in Recreation & Leisure. 200p. 1972. plastic comb avail. (ISBN 0-697-03486-0). Wm C Brown.
Cooke, Charles. Playing the Piano for Pleasure. 1960. pap. 1.95 (ISBN 0-671-57801-4, Fireside). S&S.
Shera, Frank H. Amateur in Music. facsimile ed. LC 74-114894. (Select Bibliographies Reprint Ser). 1939. 11.00 (ISBN 0-8369-5298-7). Arno.

MUSIC BOX
Chapuis, Alfred. History of the Musical Box & of Mechanical Music. Fitch, Howard M. & Fitch, Helen F., eds. Roesch, Joseph E., tr. from Fr. LC 80-12449. (Illus.). xvi, 304p. 1980. 27.50 (ISBN 0-915000-01-6). Musical Box Soc.
Ord-Hume, Arthur W. The Musical Box. (Illus.). 1980. 55.00 (ISBN 0-04-789007-X). Allen Unwin.
--Restoring Musical Boxes. (Illus.). 1980. 34.00 (ISBN 0-04-789006-1). Allen Unwin.

MUSIC CLUBS
see Music–Societies, Etc.

MUSIC CONDUCTORS
see Conductors (Music)

MUSIC CONSERVATORIES
see Conservatories of Music

MUSIC FESTIVALS
see also Concerts; Hymn Festivals
Dutton, Phyl. Music Clubs, Festivals & Concerts: How to Organize Them. 128p. 1980. softcover 25.00x (ISBN 0-905418-86-7, Pub. by Gresham England). State Mutual Bk.
Edgcumbe, Richard. Musical Reminiscences of the Earl of Mount Edgcumbe. LC 76-125071. 294p. 1973. Repr. of 1834 ed. lib. bdg. 27.50 (ISBN 0-306-70008-5). Da Capo.
International Guide to Music Festivals. (Illus.). 1980. pap. 6.95 (ISBN 0-8256-3165-3). Music Sales.
Kupferberg, Herbert. Tanglewood. LC 76-11772. 1976. pap. 9.95 (ISBN 0-07-035644-0, GB). McGraw.
Mason, Lowell. Musical Letters from Abroad. 2nd ed. LC 67-13035. (Music Ser). 1967. Repr. of 1854 ed. lib. bdg. 25.00 (ISBN 0-306-70940-6). Da Capo.
Rabin, Carol. Guide to Music Festivals in North America. rev., enl. ed. LC 78-74201. 260p. 1981. 6.95 (ISBN 0-912944-67-6). Berkshire Traveller.
Rabin, Carol P. A Guide to Music Festivals in Europe. LC 79-55709. (Illus.). 1980. pap. 5.95 (ISBN 0-912944-59-5). Berkshire Traveller.
Wolman, Baron, et al. Festival: The Book of American Music Celebrations. 1970. pap. 3.95 (ISBN 0-02-061950-2, Collier). Macmillan.

MUSIC-HALLS
see also Theaters
Aloi, R. Theatres & Auditoriums Architecture. (Illus.). 1972. 50.00 (ISBN 0-685-30575-9). Heinman.
Johnson, H. Earle. Symphony Hall, Boston. (Music Reprint Ser.). 1979. Repr. of 1950 ed. lib. bdg. 32.50 (ISBN 0-306-79518-3). Da Capo.
Lerner, Sharon. Places of Musical Fame. LC 62-20803. (Musical Books for Young People Ser). (gr. 5-11). 1962. PLB 3.95 (ISBN 0-8225-0055-8). Lerner Pubns.
Senelick, Laurence, et al. British Music Hall 1840-1923: A Bibliography & Guide to Sources with a Supplement on European Music-Hall. LC 81-4996. (Archon Books on Popular Entertainments Ser.). 1981. 37.50 (ISBN 0-208-01840-9, Archon). Shoe String.

MUSIC-HALLS (VARIETY-THEATERS, CABARETS, ETC.)
see also Burlesque (Theater); Vaudeville
Allen, Mearle L. Welcome to the Stork Club. LC 79-5424. 300p. 1980. 14.95 (ISBN 0-498-02395-8). A S Barnes.
Cheshire, D. F. Music Hall in Britain. LC 74-2581. (Illus.). 112p. 1974. 12.00 (ISBN 0-8386-1563-5). Fairleigh Dickinson.
Watters, Eugene & Murtagh, Matthew. Infinite Variety: Dan Lowery's Music Hall 1879-1897. (Illus.). 1975. 12.95 (ISBN 0-7171-0711-6). Irish Bk Ctr.

MUSIC IN ART
see also Art and Music
Beck, Sydney & Roth, Elizabeth. Music in Prints: Fifty Two Prints Illustrating Musical Instruments from the 15th Century to the Present. LC 65-13045. (Illus.). 1965. 12.00 (ISBN 0-87104-124-3). NY Pub Lib.
Brown, Howard M. & Lascelle, Joan. Musical Iconography: A Manual for Cataloguing Musical Subjects in Western Art Before 1800. LC 76-180151. (Illus.). 224p. 1972. 12.50x (ISBN 0-674-59220-4). Harvard U Pr.
Celender, Donald. Musical Instruments in Art. LC 65-29037. (Fine Art Books). (Illus.). (gr. 5-11). 1966. PLB 4.95 (ISBN 0-8225-0160-0). Lerner Pubns.
Fischer, Pieter. Music in Paintings of the Low Countries in the 16th & 17th Centuries. 112p. pap. text ed. 15.50 (ISBN 90-265-0185-4, Pub. by Swets Pub Serv Holland). Swets North Am.
Kinksy, Georg. A History of Music in Pictures. LC 71-166274. 363p. 1934. Repr. 75.00 (ISBN 0-403-01606-1). Scholarly.
Lang, Paul H. & Bettmann, Otto L. Pictorial History of Music. (Illus.). (gr. 9 up). 1960. 19.95 (ISBN 0-393-02107-6). Norton.
Langley, Patrick P. The Intimate Connection Between Music & Art. 132p. 1980. 39.65 (ISBN 0-89266-256-5). Am Classical Coll Pr.

MUSIC IN CHURCHES
see also Church Music; Psalmody; Religion and Music
Bay, Bill. The Liturgical Guitarist. 360p. 1980. spiral bdg. 9.95 (ISBN 0-89228-055-7). Impact Bks MO.
Flint, Tommy & Griffin, Neil. Gospel Guitar. 48p. 1976. wkbk 2.95 (ISBN 0-89228-018-2). Impact Bks MO.
Kurfees, M. C. Instrumental Music in Worship. 9.00 (ISBN 0-89225-106-9). Gospel Advocate.
Lovelace, Austin C. & Rice, William C. Music & Worship in the Church. rev. & enl. ed. LC 76-13524. 1976. 12.95 (ISBN 0-687-27358-7). Abingdon.
Lutkin, Peter C. Music in the Church. LC 72-135722. Repr. of 1910 ed. 21.45 (ISBN 0-404-04069-1). AMS Pr.
Routley, Erik. Church Music & the Christian & Faith. LC 78-110219. 1979. 8.95 (ISBN 0-916642-11-9, Agape). Hope Pub.
Scholes, Percy A. Puritans & Music in England & New England: A Contribution to the Cultural History of 2 Nations. 1934. 36.00x (ISBN 0-19-816117-4). Oxford U Pr.

MUSIC IN RELIGION
see Religion and Music

MUSIC IN SYNAGOGUES
see also Music, Jewish; Religion and Music

MUSIC IN THE HOME
see also Music As Recreation
Johnson, Gerald W. A Little Night-Music. LC 70-108844. x, 125p. Repr. of 1937 ed. lib. bdg. 15.00x (ISBN 0-8371-3733-0, JONM). Greenwood.
--A Little Night Music. 8.00 (ISBN 0-403-08984-0). Scholarly.
Shera, Frank H. Amateur in Music. facsimile ed. LC 74-114894. (Select Bibliographies Reprint Ser). 1939. 11.00 (ISBN 0-8369-5298-7). Arno.

MUSIC IN THEATERS
Here are entered works on music as an adjunct to theatrical productions.
Appin, Adolphe. Music & Bit of the Theatre. Hewitt, Barnard, ed. LC 62-20172. (Bks. in the Theatre: No. 3). 1962. 14.95 (ISBN 0-87024-018-8). U of Miami Pr.
Chouquet, Gustave. Histoire De la Musique Dramatique En France Depuis Ses Origines Jusqu'a Nos Jours. LC 80-2265. Repr. of 1873 ed. 45.00 (ISBN 0-404-18818-4). AMS Pr.
Crump, J. I., ed. Chinese & Japanese Music-Dramas. Malm, William P. (Michigan Papers in Chinese Studies Ser.: No. 19). (Illus.). 255p. 1975. pap. 2.00 (ISBN 0-89264-019-7). U of Mich Ctr Chinese.
Dutka, JoAnna. Music in the English Mystery Plays. (Early Drama, Art, & Music Ser.). (Illus.). 171p. 1980. 18.80 (ISBN 0-918720-10-9); pap. 11.80 (ISBN 0-918720-11-7). Medieval Inst.
Gaburo, K. Music in Beckett's: Play. (Paperplay Ser.: Vol. 6). 12p. 1976. softcover 2.75 (ISBN 0-939044-06-4). Lingua Pr.
Hummel, David. The Collector's Guide to the American Musical Theater: Supplement One to the Second Edition. 1979. 9.00 (ISBN 0-934628-02-5). D H Ent.
Maillot, Antoine L. La Musique au Theatre. LC 80-2288. Date not set. Repr. of 1863 ed. 44.00 (ISBN 0-404-18856-7). AMS Pr.
Price, Curtis A. Music in the Restoration Theatre: With a Catalogue of Instrumental Music in the Plays, 1665-1713. LC 79-11742. (Studies in Musicology: No. 4). 1979. 29.95 (ISBN 0-8357-0998-1). Univ Microfilms.
Settle, Ronald. Music in the Theatre. LC 70-181255. 96p. 1957. Repr. 18.00 (ISBN 0-403-03652-6). Scholarly.

MUSIC IN UNIVERSITIES AND COLLEGES
see also Students' Songs
Buckton, La Verne. College & University Bands, Their Organization & Administration. LC 75-176612. (Columbia University. Teachers College. Contributions to Education: No. 374). Repr. of 1929 ed. 17.50 (ISBN 0-404-55374-5). AMS Pr.
Gordon, Philip. The Availability of Contemporary American Music for Performing Groups in High Schools & Colleges. LC 72-176815. (Columbia U. Teachers College Contributions to Education Ser.: No. 961). Repr. of 1950 ed. 17.50 (ISBN 0-404-55961-1). AMS Pr.
Kaho, Elizabeth. Analysis of the Study of Music Literature in Selected American Colleges. LC 78-176925. (Columbia University. Teachers College. Contributions to Education: No. 971). Repr. of 1950 ed. 17.50 (ISBN 0-404-55971-9). AMS Pr.

MUSIC INTERVALS AND SCALES
see also Twelve-Tone System

MUSIC LIBRARIES
Auction of the Library of Vincent Novello. (Auction Catalogues of Music Ser.: Vol. 5). 1975. wrappers 25.00 (ISBN 90-6027-307-9, Pub. by Frits Knuf Netherlands). Pendragon NY.
Bayne, Pauline S., ed. Basic Music Library. LC 78-11997. 1978. pap. text ed. 5.00 (ISBN 0-8389-0281-2). ALA.
Bradley, Carol J., ed. Reader in Music Librarianship. LC 73-82994. (Reader Ser. in Library & Information Science: Vol. 12). 1973. 20.00 (ISBN 0-910972-23-0). IHS-PDS.
Burney, Charles. Catalogue of the Valuable Collection of Music. (Auction Catalogues of Music Ser.: Vol. 2). 1973. Repr. of 1814 ed. 22.50 (ISBN 90-6027-188-2, Pub. by Frits Knuf Netherlands). Pendragon NY.
Catalogue of Printed Music in the British Library to 1980, 62 vols. 1980. Set. 13,700.00 (ISBN 0-85157-900-0, Dist. by Gale Research Co.). K G Saur.
Charbon, M. H. Historische en theoretische werken tot Eighteen Hundred: Catalogus van de muziekbibliotheek van het Haags Gemeentemuseum, 2 vols. (Haags Gemeente-Museum Ser.). 1973. 45.00 (ISBN 90-6027-073-8, Pub. by Frits Knuf Netherlands). Pendragon NY.
Jones, Malcolm. Music Librarianship. 370p. 1979. 12.00 (ISBN 0-85157-274-X, Pub. by Bingley England). Shoe String.
King, Alec H. Printed Music in the British Museum: A Guide to the Catalogues & Their Construction. 208p. 1979. 31.50 (ISBN 0-85157-287-1, Pub. by Bingley England). Shoe String.
Mizler, Lorenz C. Neu Eroffnete Musikalische Bibliothek Oder Grundliche Nachricht Nebst Unpartheyischem Urteil Von Alten und Neuen Musikalischen Schriften und Buchern: Leipzig 1739-1754, 3 vols. 2250p. 1966. 200.00 set (ISBN 90-6027-029-0, Pub. by Frits Knuf Netherlands). Pendragon NY.
Moor, Arthur P. The Library-Museum of Music & Dance: A Study of Needs & Resources, Leading to Suggestions for an Educational Program. LC 76-177079. (Columbia University. Teachers College. Contributions to Education: No. 750). Repr. of 1938 ed. 17.50 (ISBN 0-404-55750-3). AMS Pr.
New York Public Library, Research Libraries. Dictionary Catalog of the Music Collection, 33 Vols. 1964. Set. lib. bdg. 2400.00 (ISBN 0-8161-0709-2). G K Hall.
Penney, B., ed. Music in British Libraries: A Directory of Resources. 3rd ed. 1981. pap. 34.50 (ISBN 0-85365-981-8, Pub. by Lib Assn England). Oryx Pr.
Redfern, Brian. Organising Music in Libraries: Vol. Two Cataloguing. 2nd ed. 151p. 1979. 14.50 (ISBN 0-208-01678-3, Linnet). Shoe String.
--Organizing Music in Libraries, 2nd Edition: Vol. One, Arrangement & Classification. 1978. 12.50 (ISBN 0-208-01544-2, Linnet). Shoe String.
Selfoh, Nicolaas. Catalogue D'une Tres Belle Bibliotheque De Livres De Musique, Ainsi Qu'une Collection De Toutes Sortes D'instruments. (Auction Catalogues of Music Ser.: Vol. 1). 1973. wrappers 50.00 (ISBN 90-6027-341-9, Pub. by Frits Knuf Netherlands). Pendragon NY.

MUSIC OF THE SPHERES
see Harmony of the Spheres

MUSIC PRINTING
see also Music, Popular (Songs, etc.)–Writing and Publishing
Ayars, Christine M. Contributions to the Art of Music in America by the Music Industries of Boston: 1640-1936. 23.00 (ISBN 0-384-02825-X). Johnson Repr.
Barksdale, A. Beverly. The Printed Note: Five Hundred Years of Music Printing & Engraving. (Music Ser.). (Illus.). 145p. 1981. Repr. of 1957 ed. lib. bdg. 18.50 (ISBN 0-306-76087-8). Da Capo.

Dichter, H. Handbook of American Sheet Music. (Illus.). pap. 4.00x (ISBN 0-87556-077-6). Saifer.
Epstein, Dena J. Music Publishing in Chicago Before 1871: The Firm of Root & Cady, 1858-1871. (Detroit Studies in Music Bibliography Ser.: No. 14). 1969. pap. 2.00 (ISBN 0-911772-36-7). Info Coord.
Farish, Margaret K., ed. String Music in Print. 2nd ed. LC 80-18425. (Music in Print Ser.: Vol. 6). 464p. 1980. Repr. lib. bdg. 69.00 (ISBN 0-88478-011-2). Musicdata.
Gamble, W. Music Engraving & Printing: Historical & Technical Treatise. LC 70-155576. (Music Ser). 1971. Repr. of 1923 ed. lib. bdg. 25.00 (ISBN 0-306-70168-5). Da Capo.
Gamble, William. Music Engraving & Printing: Historical & Technical Treatise. LC 72-173166. (Illus.). Repr. of 1923 ed. 20.00 (ISBN 0-405-08549-4, Blom Pubns). Arno.
His Maiesties Gracious Grant & Privilege to William Braithwaite, for the Sole Printing & Publishing Musicke, His Way. LC 73-6105. (English Experience Ser.: No. 573). 1973. Repr. of 1636 ed. 3.50 (ISBN 90-221-0573-3). Walter J Johnson.
International Association of Music Libraries. Guide for Dating Early Published Music: A Manual of Bibliographical Practices. Krummel, Don W., ed. (Illus.). 1974. 25.00 (ISBN 0-913574-25-2). Eur-Am Music.
Kidson, Frank. British Music Publishers, Printers & Engravers. LC 67-23861. 1967. Repr. of 1900 ed. 12.75 (ISBN 0-405-08701-2, Blom Pubns). Arno.
Krohn, Ernst C. Music Publishing in the Middle Western States Before the Civil War. LC 70-175173. (Detroit Studies in Music Bibliography Ser.: No. 23). 1972. pap. 2.00 (ISBN 0-911772-47-2). Info Coord.
Krummel, D. W. English Music Printing, Fifteen Fifty-Three to Seventeen Hundred. (Illus.). 1976. 20.00x (ISBN 0-19-721788-5). Oxford U Pr.
Littleton, Alfred H. A Catalogue of One Hundred Works Illustrating the History of Music Pointing from the 15 to the End of the 17 Century in the Library of Alfred H. Littleton. LC 79-181201. 32p. 1911. Repr. 19.00 (ISBN 0-403-01612-6). Scholarly.
Spiegel, Irwin O. & Cooper, Jay L., eds. Record & Music Publishing Forms of Agreement in Current Use. LC 72-144789. 859p. 1971. looseleaf 42.50 (ISBN 0-88238-028-1). Law-Arts.
Steele, Robert. The Earliest English Music Printing. LC 78-181268. 102p. 1903. Repr. 18.00 (ISBN 0-403-01691-6). Scholarly.
Wolfe, Richard J. Early American Music Engraving & Printing: A History of Music Publishing in America from 1787 to 1825 with Commentary on Earlier & Later Practices. LC 79-12955. (Music in Ameerican Life Ser.). (Illus.). 340p. 1980. 24.95 (ISBN 0-252-00726-3). U of Ill Pr.

MUSIC PUBLISHERS
see Publishers and Publishing

MUSIC READING
see Score Reading and Playing; Sight-Reading (Music)

MUSIC ROOMS AND EQUIPMENT
Anderton, Craig. Home Recording for Musicians. (Illus.). 300p. pap. 9.95 (ISBN 0-89122-019-4). Music Sales.
Geerdes, Harold P. Planning & Equipping Educational Music Facilities. LC 75-15271. (Illus.). 83p. (Orig.). 1975. pap. 7.00x (ISBN 0-940796-13-9). Music Ed.
Miller, Fred. Studio Recording for Musicians. (Illus.). 144p. pap. 15.95 (ISBN 0-8256-4204-3). Music Sales.

MUSIC SCHOOLS
see Conservatories of Music

MUSIC SOCIETIES
see Music-Societies, Etc.

MUSIC TEACHERS
Lawrence, Ian. Music & the Teacher. 112p. 1975. 12.95x (ISBN 0-8464-0658-6). Beekman Pubs.
Lovelock, William. Common Sense in Music Teaching. (Illus.). 1968. Repr. of 1965 ed. 6.95 (ISBN 0-7135-0682-2). Dufour.
McEachern, Edna. A Survey & Evaluation of the Education of School Music Teachers in the United States. LC 78-177023. (Columbia University. Teachers College. Contributions to Education: No. 701). Repr. of 1937 ed. 17.50 (ISBN 0-404-55701-5). AMS Pr.
Marchesi, Mathilde. Marchesi & Music: Passages from the Life of a Famous Singing-Teacher. LC 77-27354. (Music Reprint Ser., 1978). 1978. Repr. of 1898 ed. lib. bdg. 27.50 (ISBN 0-306-77577-8). Da Capo.
Mason, Lowell. The Pestalozzian Music Teacher. 1977. lib. bdg. 59.95 (ISBN 0-8490-2425-0). Gordon Pr.
Watson, Jack M. The Education of School Music Teachers for Community Music Leadership. LC 76-177655. (Columbia University. Teachers College. Contributions to Education: No. 948). Repr. of 1948 ed. 17.50 (ISBN 0-404-55948-4). AMS Pr.

MUSIC THERAPY
Allen, Walter C., ed. Studies in Jazz Discography: No. 1. LC 78-5037. 1978. Repr. of 1971 ed. lib. bdg. 17.75 (ISBN 0-313-20407-1, ALJD). Greenwood.
Alvin, Juliette. Music for the Handicapped Child. 1976. pap. 9.95x (ISBN 0-19-314920-6). Oxford U Pr.
--Music Therapy. LC 74-25290. 1975. 12.50x (ISBN 0-465-04743-2). Basic.
--Music Therapy for the Autistic Child. 1979. pap. 9.95x (ISBN 0-19-317414-6). Oxford U Pr.
Beavers, Stacie V. Music Therapy: A Practice. 1978. 6.50 (ISBN 0-533-03740-9). Vantage.
Benenzon, Rolando O. Music Therapy Manual. (Illus.). 178p. 1981. 16.75 (ISBN 0-398-04502-X). C C Thomas.
Bernstein, Seymour. With Your Own Two Hands: Self-Discovery Through Music. (Illus.). 320p. 1981. 14.95 (ISBN 0-02-870310-3). Schirmer Bks.
Bull, Inez. Retarded Child. LC 72-94851. 1973. 5.00 (ISBN 0-682-47652-8). Exposition.
Clark, Cynthia & Chadwick, Donnacompiled by. Clinically Adapted Instruments for the Multiply Handicapped: A Sourcebook. rev. ed. 1980. Repr. of 1979 ed. 12.95 (ISBN 0-918812-13-5). Magnamusic.
Gaston, E. Thayer. Music in Therapy. (Illus.). 1968. text ed. 18.95 (ISBN 0-02-340700-X, 34070). Macmillan.
Gutheil, Emil. Music & Your Emotions. new ed. LC 75-131283. 1970. pap. 4.95 (ISBN 0-87140-529-6). Liveright.
Hall, Manly P. Therapeutic Value of Music. pap. 1.75 (ISBN 0-89314-364-2). Philos Res.
Harbert, Wilhelmina K. Opening Doors Through Music: A Practical Guide for Teachers, Therapists, Students, Parents. Ellsworth, Mrs. Nancy H. & Keniston, Rachel P., eds. (Illus.). 160p. 1974. pap. 16.25 spiral (ISBN 0-398-02593-2). C C Thomas.
Heline, Corinne. Healing & Regeneration Through Music. 11th ed. pap. 1.75 (ISBN 0-87613-010-4). New Age.
Michel, Donald E. Music Therapy: An Introduction to Therapy & Special Education Through Music. (Illus.). 152p. 1979. 12.75 (ISBN 0-398-03518-0). C C Thomas.
Nordoff, Paul & Robbins, Clive. Creative Music Therapy: Individualized Treatment for the Handicapped Child. LC 75-6898. (John Day Bk.). 1977. 30.00 (ISBN 0-381-97100-7). T Y Crowell.
--Music Therapy in Special. 256p. 1980. 21.00x (ISBN 0-7121-1371-1, Pub. by Macdonald & Evans). State Mutual Bk.
--Therapy in Music for Handicapped Children. 1971. text ed. 4.25x (ISBN 0-575-00755-9). Humanities.
Nordoff, Paul & Robbins, Clive E. Music Therapy in Special Education. LC 70-89312. (John Day Bk.). 1971. 10.95 (ISBN 0-381-97031-0, A52100). T Y Crowell.
Plach, Tom. The Creative Use of Music in Group Therapy. (Illus.). 92p. 1981. 14.75 (ISBN 0-398-04156-3). C C Thomas.
Purvis, Jennie & Samet, Shelly. Music in Developmental Therapy. (Illus.). 300p. 1976. pap. 13.95 (ISBN 0-8391-0895-8). Univ Park.
Robbins, Arthur. Expressive Therapy: A Creative Arts Approach to Depth-Oriented Therapy. LC 80-13005. 319p. 1980. text ed. 22.95 (ISBN 0-87705-101-1). Human Sci Pr.
Robbins, Carol & Robbins, Clive. Music for the Hearing Impaired. 1980. pap. 29.50 (ISBN 0-918812-11-9). Magnamusic.
Ruud, Even. Music Therapy & Its Relationship to Current Treatment Theories. rev ed. 1980. pap. 6.50 (ISBN 0-918812-14-3). Magnamusic.
Schulberg, Cecilia. The Music Therapy Sourcebook. 296p. 1981. text ed. 19.95x (ISBN 0-89885-007-X). Human Sci Pr.
--The Music Therapy Sourcebook: A Collection of Activities Categorized & Analyzed. 1981. 19.95 (ISBN 0-89885-007-X). Human Sci Pr.
Schullian, Dorothy M. & Schoen, Max. Music & Medicine. facsimile ed. LC 78-142693. (Essay Index Reprint Ser). 1948. 25.00 (ISBN 0-8369-2132-1). Arno.
Tomat, Jean H. & Krutzky, Carmel D. Learning Through Music for Special Children & Their Teachers. LC 75-25031. 82p. (Orig.). 1975. pap. 5.00 (ISBN 0-914562-02-9). Merriam-Eddy.
Ward, David. Hearts & Hands & Voices: Music in the Education of Slow Learners. (Illus.). 1976. pap. 5.95x (ISBN 0-19-314921-4). Oxford U Pr.
--Sing a Rainbow: Musical Activities with Mentally Handicapped Children. (Illus.). 64p. (Orig.). 1979. pap. text ed. 8.95x (ISBN 0-19-317416-2). Oxford U Pr.

MUSIC TRADE
see also Music-Economic Aspects
Ayars, Christine M. Contributions to the Art of Music in America by the Music Industries of Boston: 1640-1936. 23.00 (ISBN 0-384-02825-X). Johnson Repr.
Biederman, Donald E. Legal & Business Aspects of the Music Industry: Music, Videocassettes & Records, Course Handbook. LC 80-81531. (Patents, Copyrights, Trademarks & Literary Property 1979-80 Course Handbook Ser.). 736p. 1980. pap. text ed. 25.00 (ISBN 0-686-68825-2, G4-3676). PLI.
Carpenter, Paul S. Music, an Art & a Business. 1950. 11.95x (ISBN 0-8061-0202-0). U of Okla Pr.
Eliason, Robert E. Graves & Company: Musical Instrument Makers. new ed. (Illus.). 24p. 1975. pap. text ed. 2.00 (ISBN 0-685-56427-4). Brass Pr.
Garofalo, Reebee & Chapple, Steve. Rock 'n' Roll Is Here to Pay: The History & Politics of the Music Industry. LC 77-10488. 1978. 20.95x (ISBN 0-88229-395-8); pap. 11.95x (ISBN 0-88229-437-7). Nelson-Hall.
Gelly, David. The Facts About a Rock Group: Featuring Wings. (Illus.). 1977. 4.95 (ISBN 0-517-52983-1, Harmony). Crown.
The Guitars Friend: Mail Order Guide to Musical Instruments & Supplies. LC 76-8072. (Orig.). 1977. pap. 4.95 (ISBN 0-8256-3072-X, Quick Fox). Music Sales.
Kemps Music & Recording Industry Yearbook International, 1979. 1979. pap. 29.75 (ISBN 0-905255-52-6, KEMP004, Kemps). Unipub.
Kuroff, B., ed. Songwriter's Market, 1981. 1981. 11.95 (ISBN 0-89879-028-X). Writers Digest.
Laurie, David. Reminiscences of a Fiddle Dealer. (Illus.). 1977. Repr. of 1924 ed. text ed. 14.00 (ISBN 0-918624-01-0). Virtuoso.
Meggs, Brown. Aria. LC 77-5188. 1978. 10.95 (ISBN 0-689-10832-X). Atheneum.
Rogers, Kenny & Epand, Len. Making It with Music: Kenny Rogers' Guide to the Music Business. LC 78-2164. (Illus.). 1978. 12.95 (ISBN 0-06-013598-0, HarpT). Har-Row.
Sadler, Barry. Everything You Want to Know About the Record Industry. 1978. 4.95 (ISBN 0-87695-227-9). Aurora Pubs.
Stein, Howard & Zalkind, Ronald. Promoting Rock Concerts: A Practical Guide. LC 79-63032. 1979. 10.95 (ISBN 0-02-872490-9); pap. 6.95 (ISBN 0-02-872470-4). Schirmer Bks.
Van Ryzin, Lani. Cutting a Record in Nashville, No. 3. (Hi Lo Ser.). 96p. (YA) (gr. 6 up). 1981. pap. 1.50 (ISBN 0-553-14620-3). Bantam.
Weismann, Dick. The Music Business: Career Opportunities & Self Defense. 1979. 11.95 (ISBN 0-517-53433-9); pap. 6.95 (ISBN 0-517-53689-7). Crown.
Young, Jean & Young, Jim. Succeeding in the Big World of Music. 1977. pap. 6.95 (ISBN 0-316-97709-8). Little.
Zalkind, Ronald. Getting Ahead in the Music Business. LC 79-7366. 1979. 15.00 (ISBN 0-02-872990-0); pap. 6.95 (ISBN 0-02-873000-3). Schirmer Bks.

MUSIC WEEK
see also Community Music

MUSICA FICTA
see also Chromatic Alteration (Music)

MUSICAL ABILITY
Blacking, John. How Musical Is Man? LC 72-6710. (John Danz Lecture Ser). (Illus.). 132p. 1973. 9.50 (ISBN 0-295-95218-0, WP72); pap. 5.95 (ISBN 0-295-95338-1); tapes 17.50 (ISBN 0-295-75510-5); c-60 cassette 17.50 (ISBN 0-295-75517-2). U of Wash Pr.

MUSICAL ABILITY-TESTING
Aliferis, James. Aliferis Music Achievement Test: College Entrance Level. specimen set 4.75 (ISBN 0-8166-0091-0); manual 4.00 ea., test booklets 20 for 4.00, 2 or more packets 3.50 ea, scoring template 0.75 ea, tape recording 10.50 ea. U of Minn Pr.
Aliferis, James & Stecklein, John E. Aliferis-Stecklein Music Achievement Test: College Midpoint Level. specimen set 4.75 (ISBN 0-8166-0272-7); manual 4.00 ea., test booklets 20 for 4.00, 2 or more packets 3.50 ea, scoring template 0.75 ea, tape recordings 10.50 ea. U of Minn Pr.
Bently, Arnold. Musical Ability in Children & Its Measurement. 1966. 7.95 (ISBN 0-8079-0187-3). October.
Gordon, Edwin. A Three-Year Longitudinal Predictive Validity Study of the Musical Aptitude Profile. (Studies in the Psychology of Music Ser: Vol. 5). 1967. pap. 3.95x (ISBN 0-87745-009-9). U of Iowa Pr.
--Tonal & Rhythm Patterns. LC 76-7947. 1976. 18.00 (ISBN 0-87395-354-1). State U NY Pr.
Watkins, John G. Objective Measurement of Instrumental Performance. LC 77-177658. (Columbia University. Teachers College. Contributions to Education: No. 860). Repr. of 1942 ed. 17.50 (ISBN 0-404-55860-7). AMS Pr.
Wing, Herbert. Tests of Musical Ability & Appreciation. LC 68-23919. 98p. 1968. Repr. text ed. 6.50x (ISBN 0-521-07251-4). U of Iowa Pr.

MUSICAL ACCOMPANIMENT
see also Hymns-Accompaniment; Moving-Picture Music; Transposition (Music)
Abe & Malka. One Hundred Guitar Accompaniment Patterns. LC 73-92398. (Orig.). 1974. pap. 7.95 (ISBN 0-8256-2812-1, Amsco Music). Music Sales.
Adler, K. The Art of Accompanying & Coaching. LC 79-147128. (Music Ser.). 260p. 1971. lib. bdg. 27.50 (ISBN 0-306-70360-2); pap. 7.95 (ISBN 0-306-80027-6). Da Capo.
--The Art of Accompanying & Coaching. LC 79-147128. (Music Ser.). 260p. 1971. lib. bdg. 27.50 (ISBN 0-306-70360-2); pap. 7.95 (ISBN 0-306-80027-6). Da Capo.
Bach, Carl P. Essay on the True Art of Playing Keyboard Instruments. Mitchell, William J., ed. (Illus.). 1948. 16.95x (ISBN 0-393-09716-1, NortonC). Norton.
Buck, Dudley. Illustrations in Choir Accompaniment. LC 79-137316. Repr. of 1892 ed. 18.00 (ISBN 0-404-01145-4). AMS Pr.
Fetis, F. J. Treatise on Accompaniment from Score. 1976. lib. bdg. 25.00 (ISBN 0-403-03715-8). Scholarly.
Lang, Edith & West, George. Musical Accompaniment of Moving Pictures. LC 72-124014. (Literature of Cinema, Ser. 1). Repr. of 1920 ed. 10.00 (ISBN 0-405-01620-4). Arno.
Lishka, Gerald R. A Handbook for the Ballet Accompanist. LC 78-2051. (Illus.). 256p. 1979. 15.00x (ISBN 0-253-32704-0). Ind U Pr.
Moore, Thomas. Moore's Irish Melodies with Symphonies & Accompaniments. 1981. 35.00x (ISBN 0-89453-259-6). M Glazier.
Pelz, William. Basic Keyboard Skills: An Introduction to Accompaniment Improvisation, Transposition & Modulation, with an Appendix on Sight Reading. LC 80-22820. vii, 173p. 1981. Repr. of 1963 ed. PLB 23.50x (ISBN 0-313-22882-5, PEBK). Greenwood.
Quantz, Johann J. On Playing the Flute. Reilly, Edward R., tr. LC 75-10986. (Illus.). 1975. 19.95 (ISBN 0-02-871940-9); pap. 8.95 (ISBN 0-02-871930-1). Schirmer Bks.
Rapee, Erno. Motion Picture Moods for Pianists & Organists, a Rapid Reference Collection of Selected Pieces. LC 70-124035. (Literature of Cinema, Ser. 1). Repr. of 1924 ed. 33.00 (ISBN 0-405-01635-2). Arno.
Taussig, Harry. Folk Style Autoharp. LC 67-27260. (Illus., Orig.). 1967. pap. 5.95 (ISBN 0-8256-0021-9, Oak). Music Sales.
Williams, P. Figured Bass Accompaniment, 20 vols. 1971. Vol. 1. 7.00x (ISBN 0-85224-054-6, Pub. by Edinburgh U Pr Scotland); Vol. 2. 7.50x (ISBN 0-85224-055-4). Columbia U Pr.

MUSICAL BOX
see Music Box

MUSICAL CLUBS
see Music-Societies, Etc.

MUSICAL COMEDIES
see Musical Revues, Comedies, etc.

MUSICAL COMEDY
see Musical Revue, Comedy, Etc.

MUSICAL COMPOSITION
see Composition (Music)

MUSICAL CRITICISM
Cairns, David. Responses. (Music Ser.). 1980. Repr. of 1973 ed. 25.00 (ISBN 0-306-76047-9). Da Capo.
Calvocoressi, M. D. The Principles & Methods of Musical Criticism. (Music Reprint Ser.). 1979. Repr. of 1931 ed. 20.00 (ISBN 0-306-79557-4). Da Capo.
Cowart, Georgia. The Origins of Modern Musical Criticism: French & Italian Music, 1600-1750. Buelow, George, ed. LC 81-641. (Studies in Musicology: No. 38). 1981. 39.95 (ISBN 0-8357-1166-8, Pub. by UMI Res Pr). Univ Microfilms.
Diamond, Harold J. Music Criticism: An Annotated Guide to the Literature. LC 79-22279. 326p. 1979. 17.50 (ISBN 0-8108-1268-1). Scarecrow.
Fiske, Roger. Beethoven's Missa Solemnis. (Illus.). 1979. 14.95 (ISBN 0-684-16228-8, ScribT). Scribner.
Kolodin, Irving, ed. Critical Composer. LC 72-93351. (Essay Index Reprint Ser). 1940. 18.00 (ISBN 0-8369-1358-2). Arno.
Meisner, Maurice & Murphy, Rhoads. The Mozartian Historian: Essays on the Works of Joseph R. Levenson. LC 74-82849. 250p. 1976. 18.00x (ISBN 0-520-02826-0). U of Cal Pr.
Meyer, Leonard B. Explaining Music: Essays & Explorations. LC 77-90968. 1978. pap. 8.95 (ISBN 0-226-52142-7, P769, Phoen). U of Chicago Pr.
Rosenfeld, Paul. Discoveries of a Music Critic. LC 76-181238. 402p. 1936. Repr. 19.00 (ISBN 0-403-01662-2). Scholarly.

Schnabel, Artur. Music & the Line of Most Resistance. LC 69-12690. (Music Ser). 1969. Repr. of 1942 ed. lib. bdg. 15.00 (ISBN 0-306-71224-5). Da Capo.
Shaw, Bernard. How to Become a Musical Critic. Laurence, Dan H., ed. LC 77-26653. (Music Reprint Ser., 1978). 1978. Repr. of 1961 ed. lib. bdg. 27.50 (ISBN 0-306-77569-7). Da Capo.
Simon, Robert E., ed. Be Your Own Music Critic. facsimile ed. LC 70-134135. (Essay Index Reprint Ser). 1941. 18.00 (ISBN 0-8369-2095-3). Arno.
Slonimsky, Nicolas. Lexicon of Musical Invective: Critical Assaults on Composers Since Beethoven's Time. 2nd ed. LC 65-26270. 331p. 1969. pap. 7.95 (ISBN 0-295-78579-9, WP52). U of Wash Pr.
Steinitz, Paul. Bach's Passions. (Illus.). 1979. 14.95 (ISBN 0-684-16229-6, ScribT). Scribner.

MUSICAL DECLAMATION

see Singing–Diction

MUSICAL DICTATION

see also Ear Training

McHose, Allen I. Teachers Dictation Manual. (Eastman School of Music Ser.). text ed. 16.00x (ISBN 0-89197-437-7); pap. text ed. 7.95x (ISBN 0-89197-960-3). Irvington.
McHose, Allen I. & White, Donald F. Keyboard & Dictation Manual. (Eastman School of Music Ser.). 1949. 29.50x (ISBN 0-89197-255-2); pap. text ed. 18.50x (ISBN 0-89197-819-4). Irvington.
Thomson, William & De Lone, Richard P. Introduction to Ear Training. 1967. 13.95x (ISBN 0-534-00664-7). Wadsworth Pub.

MUSICAL EDUCATION

see Music–Instruction and Study

MUSICAL FESTIVALS

see Music Festivals

MUSICAL FICTION

Huneker, James G. Melomaniacs. Repr. of 1902 ed. 14.00 (ISBN 0-404-03388-1). AMS Pr.

MUSICAL FORM

see also names of particular musical forms, e.g. Fugue; Motet; Opera; Sonata

Applebaum, Samuel & Roth, Henry. The Way They Play, Bk. 7. (Illus.). 288p. 1980. 9.95 (ISBN 0-87666-620-9, Z-33). Paganiniana Pubns.
Bairstow, Edward C. The Evolution of Musical Form. LC 72-80135. 119p. 1972. Repr. of 1943 ed. lib. bdg. 8.50x (ISBN 0-8154-0427-1). Cooper Sq.
Berry, Wallace. Form in Music: An Examination of Traditional Techniques of Musical Structure & Their Application in Historical & Contemporary Styles. 1966. text ed. 21.95 (ISBN 0-13-329201-0). P-H.
Burkhart, Charles. Anthology for Musical Analysis. 3rd ed. LC 78-15566. 1979. pap. text ed. 18.95 (ISBN 0-03-018866-0, HoltC). HR&W.
Cone, Edward T. Musical Form & Musical Performance. LC 68-11157. (Illus.). 1968. pap. 4.95x (ISBN 0-393-09767-6). Norton.
Davie, Cedric T. Musical Structure & Design. (Illus.). 1966. pap. 3.25 (ISBN 0-486-21629-2). Dover.
De Stwolinski, Gail. Form & Content in Instrumental Music. 1977. text ed. 13.95 (ISBN 0-697-03412-7). Wm C Brown.
Eimert, Herbert & Stockhausen, Karlheinz, eds. Form--Space. Cardew, Cornelius, tr. from Ger. (Die Reihe: No. 7). 1965. pap. 10.00 (ISBN 3-7024-0142-3, 47-26107). Eur-Am Music.
Fiske, Roger. Score Reading, 4 vols. Incl. Vol. 1. Orchestration. 1958. 5.75 (ISBN 0-19-321301-X); Vol. 2. Musical Form. 1958. 5.75 (ISBN 0-19-321302-8); Vol. 3. Concertos. 1960. 5.75 (ISBN 0-19-321303-6); Vol. 4. Oratorios. 1955. 5.75 (ISBN 0-19-321304-4). (YA) (gr. 9up). Oxford U Pr.
Fontaine, P. Basic Formal Structures in Music. 1967. text ed. 18.95 (ISBN 0-13-061416-5). P-H.
Goetschius, Percy. Homophonic Forms of Musical Composition. LC 70-122594. Repr. of 1898 ed. 20.00 (ISBN 0-404-02853-5). AMS Pr.
--Lessons in Music Form. LC 79-109735. Repr. of 1904 ed. lib. bdg. 15.00x (ISBN 0-8371-4225-3, GOMF). Greenwood.
--Lessons in Music Form. lib. bdg. 19.00 (ISBN 0-403-08978-6). Scholarly.
Hadow, W. H. Studies in Modern Music, 2 Vols. LC 75-102839. (Illus.). 1970. Repr. of 1926 ed. Set. 27.50 (ISBN 0-8046-0755-9). Kennikat.
Hutcheson, Jere T. Musical Form & Analysis, 2 vols. pap. 11.95x ea. (Crescendo); Vol. 1. (ISBN 0-8008-5454-3); Vol. 2. (ISBN 0-8008-5455-1). Taplinger.
Kohs, Ellis B. Musical Form: Studies in Analysis & Synthesis. 1976. text ed. 19.95 (ISBN 0-395-18613-7). HM.
Leichtentritt, Hugo. Musical Form. LC 51-11139. (Illus.). 1951. 22.50x (ISBN 0-674-59201-8). Harvard U Pr.
Lucas, Clarence. The Story of Musical Form. LC 77-75191. 1977. Repr. of 1908 ed. lib. bdg. 25.00 (ISBN 0-89341-102-7). Longwood Pr.
Moore, Douglas. Guide to Musical Styles: From Madrigal to Modern Music. (Illus.). 1963. pap. 5.95 (ISBN 0-393-00200-4, Norton Lib.). Norton.
Morris, Reginald O. Structure of Music: An Outline for Students. 1935. 6.75 (ISBN 0-19-317310-7). Oxford U Pr.
Nadeau, Roland & Tesson, William. Form in Music: Process & Procedure. LC 74-12772. 1974. pap. 3.00x (ISBN 0-8008-2969-7, Crescendo). Taplinger.
Nallin, W. E. Musical Idea: A Consideration of Music & Its Ways. 1968. text ed. 13.95x (ISBN 0-02-385900-8). Macmillan.
Prout, Ebenezer. Applied Forms: A Sequel to Musical Form. LC 77-10853. 1971. Repr. of 1895 ed. 7.00 (ISBN 0-403-00329-6). Scholarly.
--Applied Forms: A Sequel to Musical Form. 3rd ed. LC 71-155615. Repr. of 1895 ed. 8.00 (ISBN 0-404-05138-3). AMS Pr.
--Musical Form. LC 70-137280. Repr. of 1893 ed. 12.00 (ISBN 0-404-05145-6). AMS Pr.
--Musical Form. LC 70-137280. Repr. of 1893 ed. 12.00 (ISBN 0-404-05145-6). AMS Pr.
--Musical Form. LC 78-108526. 1970. Repr. of 1893 ed. 6.50 (ISBN 0-403-00327-X). Scholarly.
Scholes, Percy A. Listener's Guide to Music: With a Concert-Goer's Glossary. 10th ed. (Illus.). (YA) (gr. 9 up). 1961. pap. 4.95x (ISBN 0-19-284002-9). Oxford U Pr.
Stein, Leon. Anthology of Musical Forms. 1962. pap. text ed. 12.50 (ISBN 0-87487-044-5). Summy.
Tyndall, Robert E. Musical Form. LC 77-399. 1977. Repr. of 1964 ed. lib. bdg. 20.25x (ISBN 0-8371-9493-8, TYMF). Greenwood.
Ward - Steinman, David & Ward - Steinman, Susan L. Comparative Anthology of Musical Forms, 2 vols. 1976. pap. text ed. 15.95x ea. (ISBN 0-685-69709-6); Vol. 1. (ISBN 0-534-00439-3); Vol. 2. (ISBN 0-534-00459-8). Wadsworth Pub.
Wennerstrom, Mary H. Anthology of Musical Structure & Style. 550p. 1982. pap. 17.95 (ISBN 0-686-76584-2). P-H.

MUSICAL INSTRUCTION

see Music–Instruction and Study

MUSICAL INSTRUMENTS

see also Instrumental Music–History and Criticism; Instrumentation and Orchestration; Musical Instruments, Electronic; Orchestra; Tuning;
also groups of instruments, e.g. Stringed Instruments; also names of individual musical instruments, e.g. Piano, Violin

Andersson, Otto E. The Bowed Harp, a Study in the History of Early Musical Instruments. rev. ed. Schlesinger, Kathleen, ed. Stenback, Mary, tr. Repr. of 1930 ed. 24.50 (ISBN 0-404-56503-4). AMS Pr.
Anoyianakis, Phoibos. Greek Folk Musical Instruments. (Illus.). 400p. 1979. 80.00x (ISBN 0-89241-082-5, Pub by Natl. Bank of Greece). Caratzas Bros.
Ayars, Christine M. Contributions to the Art of Music in America by the Music Industries of Boston: 1640-1936. 23.00 (ISBN 0-384-02825-X). Johnson Repr.
Baines, Anthony, ed. Musical Instruments. (YA) (gr. 9 up). 1962. pap. 3.95 (ISBN 0-14-020347-8, Pelican). Penguin.
--Musical Instruments Through the Ages. LC 66-22505. (Illus.). 352p. 1975. 15.00 (ISBN 0-8027-0469-7). Walker & Co.
Barrett, Henry. The Viola: Complete Guide for Teachers & Students. 2nd ed. LC 70-169498. 1978. 17.95 (ISBN 0-8173-6402-1). U of Ala Pr.
Bechler, Leo & Rahm, B. Die Oboe und die Ihr Verwandten Istrumente, Nebst Biographischen Skizzen der Bedeutendsten Ihrer Meister: Ph. Losch, Musikliteratur fur Oboe. 1978. Repr. of 1914 ed. 35.00 (ISBN 90-6027-165-3, Pub. by Frits Knuf Netherlands); wrappers 22.50 (ISBN 90-6027-164-5, Pub. by Frits Knuf Netherlands). Pendragon NY.
Beck, Sydney & Roth, Elizabeth. Music in Prints: Fifty Two Prints Illustrating Musical Instruments from the 15th Century to the Present. LC 65-13045. (Illus.). 1965. 12.00 (ISBN 0-87104-124-3). NY Pub Lib.
Benade, Arthur H. Horns, Strings, & Harmony. LC 78-25707. (Illus.). 1979. Repr. of 1960 ed. lib. bdg. 19.75x (ISBN 0-313-20771-2, BEHO). Greenwood.
Bonanni, Filippo. Antique Musical Instruments & Their Players. rev. ed. (Illus.). 1923. pap. 4.00 (ISBN 0-486-21179-7). Dover.
Bowers, Q. David. Encyclopedia of Automatic Musical Instruments. LC 78-187497. (Illus.). 37.00 (ISBN 0-911572-08-2). Vestal.
Broadhead, G. F. Orchestral & Band Instruments. 1976. lib. bdg. 19.00 (ISBN 0-403-03788-3). Scholarly.
Carrington, John F. Talking Drums of Africa. LC 70-77195. (Illus.). Repr. of 1949 ed. 10.50x (ISBN 0-8371-1292-3, Pub. by Negro U Pr). Greenwood.
Chelebi, Ewliya. Turkish Instruments of Music in the Seventeenth Century. Farmer, Henry G., ed. LC 76-42034. 1977. Repr. of 1937 ed. lib. bdg. 12.50 (ISBN 0-89341-068-3). Longwood Pr.
Clark, Cynthia & Chadwick, Donnacompiled by. Clinically Adapted Instruments for the Multiply Handicapped: A Sourcebook. rev. ed. 1980. Repr. of 1979 ed. 12.95 (ISBN 0-918812-13-5). Magnamusic.
Common, Alfred. How to Repair Violins & Other Musical Instruments. 1977. lib. bdg. 59.95 (ISBN 0-8490-2023-9). Gordon Pr.
Crane, Frederick. Extant Medieval Musical Instruments: A Provisional Catalogue by Types. LC 72-185993. (Illus.). 144p. 1972. text ed. 6.95x (ISBN 0-87745-022-6). U of Iowa Pr.
Curtis, Tony, ed. Musical Instruments. (Illus.). 1978. 3.95 (ISBN 0-902921-50-9). Apollo.
Dalyell, John G. Musical Memoirs of Scotland with Historical Annotations. LC 72-6979. 1972. lib. bdg. 35.00 (ISBN 0-88305-152-4). Norwood Edns.
De Coussemaker, C. E. Catalogue des livres, manuscripts et instruments de musique. (Auction Catalogues of Music Ser.: Vol. 4). 1976. Repr. of 1877 ed. wrappers 45.00 (ISBN 90-6027-198-X, Pub. by Frits Knuf Netherlands). Pendragon NY.
Densmore, Frances. Handbook of the Collection of Musical Instruments in the United States National Museum. LC 79-155231. (Music Ser). 1971. Repr. of 1927 ed. lib. bdg. 25.00 (ISBN 0-306-70167-7). Da Capo.
Deva, B. Chitanya. Musical Instruments of India. (Illus.). 1978. 21.00x (ISBN 0-8364-0231-6). South Asia Bks.
Diagram Group. Musical Instruments of the World: An Illustrated Encyclopedia. (Illus.). 320p. 1978. 24.95 (ISBN 0-87196-320-5). Facts on File.
--Musical Instruments of the World: An Illustrated Encyclopedia. LC 76-21722. (Illus.). 1976. 17.95 (ISBN 0-448-23301-0). Paddington.
Educational Research Council of America. Instrument Repairer. Ferris, Theodore N. & Marchak, John P., eds. (Real People at Work: Series O). (Illus., Orig.). (gr. 5). 1976. pap. text ed. 2.25 (ISBN 0-89247-110-7). Changing Times.
Engel, Carl. Musical Instruments. LC 77-75199. 1977. Repr. of 1875 ed. lib. bdg. 17.50 (ISBN 0-89341-095-0). Longwood Pr.
Farmer, Henry G. Studies in Oriental Musical Instruments: First & Second Ser, 2 vols. in 1. LC 77-75185. 1977. Repr. of 1939 ed. lib. bdg. 30.00 (ISBN 0-89341-056-X). Longwood Pr.
Felix, John H., et al. The Ukulele: A Portuguese Gift to Hawaii. LC 80-66299. (Illus.). 75p. (Orig.). (gr. 4-12). 1980. pap. 4.95 (ISBN 0-9604190-0-4). Nunes.
Gabry, G. Old Musical Instruments. (Illus.). 1978. 6.50 (ISBN 0-912728-85-X). Newbury Bks.
Gabry, Gyorgy. Old Musical Instruments. 2nd rev. ed. (Illus.). 1969. 7.50x (ISBN 0-568-00087-0). Intl Pubns Serv.
Galpin, Frances W. A Textbook of European Musical Instruments. LC 75-36509. (Illus.). 256p. 1976. Repr. of 1956 ed. lib. bdg. 16.50x (ISBN 0-8371-8648-X, GAEM). Greenwood.
Galpin, Francis W. Old English Instruments of Music: Their History & Character. 3rd rev. ed. LC 74-181161. 327p. 1932. Repr. 35.00 (ISBN 0-403-01562-6). Scholarly.
--A Textbook of European Musical Instruments. 1977. lib. bdg. 59.95 (ISBN 0-8490-2737-3). Gordon Pr.
Geiringer, Karl. Instruments in the History of Western Music. 3rd ed. 1978. 22.50 (ISBN 0-19-520057-8). Oxford U Pr.
Germann, Sheridan & Guglietti, Paul. Early Keyboard Instruments: A Bibliography of Published Works on Harpsichords, Clavichords, Early Pianos, & Related Instruments. 1981. lib. bdg. 20.00 (ISBN 0-8240-9312-7). Garland Pub.
Haine, Malou. Adolphe Sax: Sa vie, son oeuvre, ses instruments de musique. (Illus.). 283p. 1980. 37.50 (ISBN 90-6027-235-8, Pub. by Frits Knuf Netherlands); wrappers 25.00 (ISBN 90-6027-234-X, Pub. by Frits Knuf Netherlands). Pendragon NY.
Haine, Malou & Keyser, Ignace de. Catalogue des Instruments Sax au Musee Instrumental de Bruxelles: Suivi de la liste de 400 instruments Sax conserves dans des collections publiques et privees. (Illus.). vi, 280p. 1980. 40.00 (ISBN 90-6027-397-4, Pub. by Frits Knuf Netherlands). Pendragon NY.
Haslund-Christensen, Henning & Cmshevner, Ernst. Music of the Mongols: Eastern Mongolia. LC 79-125045. (Music Ser). 1971. Repr. of 1943 ed. lib. bdg. 25.00 (ISBN 0-306-70009-3). Da Capo.
Hayes, Gerald. The Viols & Other Bowed Instruments. (Illus.). 278p. 1970. Repr. of 1930 ed. 15.00x (ISBN 0-8450-2581-3). Broude.
Hayes, Gerald R. Musical Instruments & Their Music: 1500-1750, 2 vols. in 1. LC 74-26053. Repr. of 1930 ed. 24.50 (ISBN 0-404-12958-7). AMS Pr.
Hill, Jackson. The Harold E. Cook Collection of Musical Instruments: An Illustrated Catalogue. (Illus.). 102p. 1976. 12.50 (ISBN 0-8387-1574-5). Bucknell U Pr.
Hosier, John. Instruments of the Orchestra. 1977. pap. 4.75 (ISBN 0-19-321351-6); 4 records & book boxed 14.25x (ISBN 0-19-321352-4). Oxford U Pr.
Hutchins, Carleen M., intro. by. The Physics of Music: Readings from Scientific American. LC 77-28461. (Illus.). 1978. pap. 7.95x (ISBN 0-7167-0095-6). W H Freeman.
Ingman, Nicholas. What Instrument Shall I Play? LC 76-8998. (Illus.). (YA) (gr. 7 up). 1976. 9.95 (ISBN 0-8008-8169-9). Taplinger.
Jenkins, J. International Directory of Musical Instrument Collections. 1978. 35.00 (ISBN 90-6027-378-8, Pub. by Frits Knuf Netherlands); wrappers 22.00 (ISBN 90-6027-276-5, Pub. by Frits Knuf Netherlands). Pendragon NY.
Jenkins, Jean, ed. International Directory of Musical Instrument Collections. 1977. pap. 25.00 (ISBN 0-685-01107-0). Heinman.
Jones, Rod. How to Play Harmonica, Autoharp, Kazoo & Half-a-Dozen Other Low-Cost Musical Instruments. 32p. 1975. pap. 6.95 (ISBN 0-912732-14-8). Duane Shinn.
Kelly, Edgar S. Musical Instruments. 1980. Repr. of 1925 ed. lib. bdg. 25.00 (ISBN 0-89341-444-1). Longwood Pr.
Kjeldsberg, P. A. Musikinstrumenter Ved Ringve Museum: The Collection of Musical Instruments of the Ringve Museum. 1976. wrappers 17.50 (ISBN 90-6027-280-3, Pub. by Frits Knuf Netherlands). Pendragon NY.
Krishnaswami, S. Musical Instruments of India. (Illus.). 1967. 2.50x (ISBN 0-88253-378-9); pap. 1.00x (ISBN 0-88253-915-9). Ind-US Inc.
Kunst, J. Music in Java: Its History, Its Theory & Its Technique, 2 vols. 3rd, enl ed. (Illus.). 1973. Set. 115.00 (ISBN 9-0247-1519-9). Heinman.
Lang, Paul H. & Bettmann, Otto L. Pictorial History of Music. (Illus.). (gr. 9 up). 1960. 19.95 (ISBN 0-393-02107-6). Norton.
Lichtenwanger, W. A Survey of Musical Instrument Collections in the United States & Canada. 1974. 22.00 (ISBN 90-6027-288-9, Pub. by Frits Knuf Netherlands). Pendragon NY.
Luttrell, Guy. The Instruments of Music. LC 77-11968. (Illus.). (gr. 6 up). 1978. Repr. 6.95 (ISBN 0-525-66559-5). Elsevier-Nelson.
Malm, William P. Japanese Music & Musical Instruments. LC 59-10411. (Illus.). 1959. 32.50 (ISBN 0-8048-0308-0). C E Tuttle.
Manniche, Lise. Musical Instruments from the Tomb of Tut'Ankhamun. (Tut'Ankhamun's Tomb Ser.: Vol. VI). (Illus.). 1977. 14.50x (ISBN 0-900416-05-X, Pub. by Aris & Phillips). Intl Schol Bk Serv.
Marcuse, Sibyl. Musical Instruments: A Comprehensive Dictionary. 656p. 1975. pap. 7.95 (ISBN 0-393-00758-8, Norton Lib). Norton.
--A Survey of Musical Instruments. LC 72-9135. (Illus.). 878p. 1975. 24.95 (ISBN 0-06-012776-7, HarpT). Har-Row.
Mason, Daniel G. Orchestral Instruments & What They Do: A Primer for Concert-Goers. LC 75-109785. (Illus.). 1971. Repr. of 1909 ed. lib. bdg. 15.00 (ISBN 0-8371-4275-X, MAOI). Greenwood.
Mensink, O. Traditionele Muziekinstrumenten Van Japan: Traditional Musical Instruments of Japan. (Haags Gemeentemuseum, Kijkboekjes: Vol. 3). (Illus.). 64p. 1979. 15.00 (ISBN 90-6027-301-X, Pub. by Frits Knuf Netherlands). Pendragon NY.
Meyer, R. F. The Band Director's Guide to Instrument Repair. LC 72-96638. (Illus.). 150p. 1973. pap. text ed. 7.95 (ISBN 0-88284-002-9). Alfred Pub.
Montagu, Jeremy. The World of Baroque & Classical Musical Instruments. LC 78-65227. (Instrument Ser.). (Illus.). 136p. 1979. 27.95 (ISBN 0-87951-089-7). Overlook Pr.
--The World of Medieval & Renaissance Musical Instruments. LC 76-5987. (Illus.). 136p. 1976. 27.95 (ISBN 0-87951-045-5). Overlook Pr.
--The World of Romantic & Modern Musical Instruments. LC 80-26106. (Musical Instruments Ser.). (Illus.). 136p. 1981. 27.95 (ISBN 0-87951-126-5). Overlook Pr.
Munrow, David. Instruments of the Middle Ages & Renaissance. 1977. pap. 12.95 (ISBN 0-19-321321-4). Oxford U Pr.
Nederveen, Cornelis J. Acoustical Aspects of Woodwind Instruments. 1969. 45.00 (ISBN 90-6027-078-9, Pub. by Frits Knuf Netherlands); 30.00 (ISBN 90-6027-305-2). Pendragon NY.

Olson, Harry F. Music, Physics, & Engineering. rev. & enl. ed. Orig. Title: Musical Engineering. (Illus.). 1966. pap. 6.00 (ISBN 0-486-21769-8). Dover.
Panum, Hortense. Stringed Instruments of the Middle Ages. Repr. lib. bdg. 19.00 (ISBN 0-403-03850-2). Scholarly.
Picken, Lawrence. Folk Musical Instruments of Turkey. (Illus.). 656p. 1975. 108.00x (ISBN 0-19-318102-9). Oxford U Pr.
Piggott, F. T. The Music & Musical Instruments of Japan. LC 70-155234. (Music Ser). 1971. Repr. of 1909 ed. lib. bdg. 22.50 (ISBN 0-306-70160-X). Da Capo.
Price, Christine. Talking Drums of Africa. LC 73-6405. (Illus.). 48p. (gr. 3-7). 1973. reinforced bdg. 5.95 (ISBN 0-684-13492-6, ScribJ). Scribner.
Pulver, Jeffrey. A Bibliographical Dictionary of Old English Music: Old English Music & Musical Instruments. LC 73-80260. 1970. Repr. of 1927 ed. 22.50 (ISBN 0-8337-2867-9). B Franklin.
Read, Gardner. Thesaurus of Orchestral Devices. Repr. of 1953 ed. lib. bdg. 45.00x (ISBN 0-8371-1884-0, REOD). Greenwood.
Remnant, Mary. Musical Instruments of the West. LC 77-20880. 1978. 18.50x (ISBN 0-312-55583-0). St Martin.
Ripin, Edwin M. The Instrument Catalogs of Leopoldo Franciolini. (Music Indexes & Bibliographies: No. 9). 1974. pap. 15.00 (ISBN 0-913574-09-0). Eur-Am Music.
Robitzek, Klara C. Peter in the Land of Musical Instruments. 1977. 4.95 (ISBN 0-8008-6283-X, Crescendo). Taplinger.
Rosenthall, Ethel. Story of Indian Music & Its Instruments. 1980. Repr. lib. bdg. 25.00 (ISBN 0-403-03852-9). Scholarly.
Ruckers Colloquium. Restauratieproblemen Van Antwerpse Klavecimbels: Lectures in English, French, German & Dutch by Ripin, Schutze, Skowroneck. (Keyboard Studies: Vol. 3). 85p. 1971. wrappers 20.00 (ISBN 90-6027-334-6, Pub. by Frits Knuf Netherlands). Pendragon NY.
Ruckers Colloquium 1977. Antwerpen, Museum Vleeshuis. (Brussels Museum of Musical Instruments Bulletin Ser.: Vol. 7). (Illus.). 130p. wrappers 20.00 (ISBN 90-6027-184-X, Pub. by Frits Knuf Netherlands). Pendragon NY.
The Russell Collection: & Other Early Keyboard Instruments in Saint Cecilia's Hall. (Keyboard Studies: Vol. 7). (Illus.). xi, 80p. 1968. wrappers 15.00 (ISBN 90-6027-388-5, Pub. by Frits Knuf Netherlands). Pendragon NY.
Sachs, Curt. Geist und Werden Des Musikinstrumente. 1975. 35.00 (ISBN 90-6027-336-2, Pub. by Frits Knuf Netherlands); wrappers 22.50 (ISBN 90-6027-023-1). Pendragon NY.
--History of Musical Instruments. (Illus.). 1940. 17.50x (ISBN 0-393-02068-1, NortonC). Norton.
Salvador-Daniel, Francesco. The Music & Musical Instruments of the Arab. Farmer, Henry G., ed. & tr. from French. LC 76-22349. (Illus.). 1976. Repr. of 1915 ed. lib. bdg. 30.00 (ISBN 0-89341-008-X). Longwood Pr.
Schaeffner, Andre. Origine Des Instruments De Musique. Repr. of 1936 ed. 14.00 (ISBN 0-384-53500-3); pap. 10.00 (ISBN 0-685-13544-6). Johnson Repr.
--Origine Des Instruments De Musique: Introduction Ethnologique a L'histoire De la Musique Instrumentale. (Reeditions Ser.: No. 3). (Illus.). 1968. 27.75x (ISBN 90-2796-085-2); pap. 23.50 (ISBN 0-686-21788-8). Mouton.
Schlessinger, Kathleen. A Bibliography of Musical Instruments & Archeology. LC 76-22350. (Illus.). 1978. Repr. of 1912 ed. lib. bdg. 12.50 (ISBN 0-89341-010-1). Longwood Pr.
Schwartz, Harry W. Story of Musical Instruments, from Shepherd's Pipe to Symphony. facsimile ed. LC 70-114893. (Select Bibliographies Reprint Ser). 1938. 32.00 (ISBN 0-8369-5297-9). Arno.
Selfoh, Nicolaas. Catalogue D'une Tres Belle Bibliotheque De Livres De Musique, Ainsi Qu'une Collection De Toutes Sortes D'instruments. (Auction Catalogues of Music Ser.: Vol. 1). 1973. wrappers 50.00 (ISBN 90-6027-341-9, Pub. by Frits Knuf Netherlands). Pendragon NY.
Sloane, Irving. Making Musical Instruments. 1978. 18.95 (ISBN 0-87690-293-X). Dutton.
Smalle, P. W. Instruments & Art of the Orchestra. 1976. lib. bdg. 19.00 (ISBN 0-403-03782-4). Scholarly.
Snethlage, Emil H. Musikinstrumente der Indianer Des Guaporegebietes. 1939. 18.50 (ISBN 0-384-56350-3). Johnson Repr.
Stainer, John. Music of the Bible. LC 74-100657. (Music Ser). (Illus.). 1970. Repr. of 1914 ed. lib. bdg. 22.50 (ISBN 0-306-71862-6). Da Capo.
Stanley, Burton, ed. Instrument Repair for the Music Teacher. LC 78-11832. 154p. (Orig.). 1978. pap. 9.95x (ISBN 0-88284-075-4); pap. text ed. 9.95x (ISBN 0-686-64875-7). Alfred Pub.
Steel, Grizelle. With Lute & Lyre: History of Instruments. 1977. lib. bdg. 34.95 (ISBN 0-8490-2829-9). Gordon Pr.
Tagore, Sourindro M. Yantra Kosha. LC 74-24227. 1976. Repr. of 1875 ed. 27.50 (ISBN 0-404-12839-4). AMS Pr.
Tiede, Clayton H. Practical Band Instrument Repair Manual. 3rd ed. 160p. 1976. write for info. wire coil (ISBN 0-697-03678-2). Wm C Brown.
Ullyot, Marianne W. The First Book of Musical Instruments. (Illus.). 16p. (ps-4). 1973. pap. 2.95 (ISBN 0-913514-00-4). Am Natl Pub.
Unger-Hamilton, Clive. Keyboard Instruments. (Illus.). 128p. 1981. 15.95 (ISBN 0-89893-505-9); pap. 10.95 (ISBN 0-89893-303-X). CDP.
Van Leeuwen Bookmkamp, C. & Van der Meer, J. H. The Carl Van Leeuwen Boomkamp Collection of Musical Instruments. (Haags Gemeente Museum Ser.). 1971. 25.00 (ISBN 90-6027-150-5, Pub. by Frits Knuf Netherlands). Pendragon NY.
Walls, Jerry G. Conchs, Tibias, & Harps. (Illus.). 192p. 1980. 9.95 (ISBN 0-87666-629-2, S-103). TFH Pubns.
Wieschoff, Heinrich A. Die Afrikanischen Trommeln und Ihre Ausserafrikanischen Beziehungen. pap. 15.50 (ISBN 0-384-68373-8). Johnson Repr.
Willcutt, J. Robert & Ball, Kenneth R. The Musical Instrument Collector. Brines, Steven F., ed. LC 78-68088. (Illus.). pap. 8.95 (ISBN 0-933224-00-1). Bold Strummer Ltd.
Winternitz, Emanuel. Musical Instruments & Their Symbolism in Western Art. (Illus.). 1979. 30.00x (ISBN 0-300-02324-3); pap. 10.95 (ISBN 0-300-02376-6). Yale U Pr.
Young, Phillip T. Twenty-Five Hundred Historical Woodwind Instruments: An Inventory of the Major Collections. (Illus.). 1981. lib. bdg. write for info. (ISBN 0-918728-17-7). Pendragon NY.

MUSICAL INSTRUMENTS–CONSTRUCTION

Banek, Reinhold & Scoville, Jon. Sound Designs: A Handbook of Musical Instrument Building. (Illus., Orig.). 1980. pap. 6.95 (ISBN 0-89815-011-6). Ten Speed Pr.
Cline, Dallas. Homemade Instruments. LC 76-8073. 1976. pap. 3.95 (ISBN 0-8256-0186-X, Oak). Music Sales.
Dalby, Stuart. Make Your Own Musical Instruments. 1978. 19.95 (ISBN 0-7134-0545-7, Pub. by Batsford England). David & Charles.
DePaule, Andy. Country Instruments: Makin' Your Own. 1979. pap. 7.95 (ISBN 0-442-26117-9). Van Nos Reinhold.
Farrell, Susan C. Directory of Contemporary American Musical Instrument Makers. LC 80-24924. 320p. 1981. text ed. 24.00x (ISBN 0-8262-0322-1). U of Mo Pr.
Fichter, George S. American Indian Music & Musical Instruments. (gr. 5-10). 1978. 7.95 (ISBN 0-679-20443-1). McKay.
Ford, Charles, ed. Making Musical Instruments: Strings & Keyboard. LC 77-88774. (Illus.). 1979. 15.00 (ISBN 0-394-49210-2); pap. 7.95 (ISBN 0-394-73561-7). Pantheon.
Giltay, J. W. Bow Instruments: Their Form & Construction. LC 75-181164. 129p. 1923. Repr. 19.00 (ISBN 0-403-01566-9). Scholarly.
Hayes, Phyllis. Musical Instruments You Can Make. (Easy-Read Activity Bks.). (Illus.). 32p. (gr. 1-3). 1981. lib. bdg. 8.90 (ISBN 0-531-04310-X). Watts.
Hunter, Ilene & Judson, Marilyn. Simple Folk Instruments to Make & Play. LC 76-50091. 1977. 10.95 (ISBN 0-671-22446-8). S&S.
--Simple Folk Instruments to Make & to Play. 1980. 4.95 (ISBN 0-671-25432-4). S&S.
Mandell, Muriel & Wood, Robert E. Make Your Own Musical Instruments. rev. ed. LC 57-11535. (Illus.). (gr. 3-8). 1959. 6.95 (ISBN 0-8069-5022-6); PLB 7.49 (ISBN 0-8069-5023-4). Sterling.
Sawyer, David. Vibrations. LC 76-11499. (The Resources of Music Series). (Illus.). 1978. 9.95 (ISBN 0-521-20812-2). Cambridge U Pr.
Sloane, Irving. Classic Guitar Construction. 1966. 10.95 (ISBN 0-525-08200-X). Dutton.
Walther, Tom. Make Mine Music: How to Make & Play Instruments & Why They Work. (Brown Paper School Ser.). (Illus.). 128p. (Orig.). (gr. 3 up). 1981. 9.95 (ISBN 0-316-92111-4); pap. 5.95 (ISBN 0-316-92112-2). Little.
Waring, Dennis. Making Folk Instruments in Wood. LC 81-50985. (Illus.). 160p. (Orig.). 1981. pap. 7.95 (ISBN 0-8069-7540-7). Sterling.
Young, Thomas C. Making of Musical Instruments. LC 79-90698. (Essay Index Reprint Ser). 1939. 18.00 (ISBN 0-8369-1317-5). Arno.

MUSICAL INSTRUMENTS–INDUSTRY AND TRADE

see Music Trade

MUSICAL INSTRUMENTS–INSTRUCTION AND STUDY

see Instrumental Music–Instruction and Study

MUSICAL INSTRUMENTS–JUVENILE LITERATURE

see also Rhythm Bands and Orchestras

Anders, Rebecca. Making Musical Instruments. LC 74-33533. (Early Craft Bks). (Illus.). 32p. (gr. 1-4). 1975. PLB 3.95 (ISBN 0-8225-0868-0). Lerner Pubns.
Bonner, Mary G. Wonders of Musical Instruments. (Illus.). (gr. 4-10). 1963. PLB 6.19 (ISBN 0-8313-0009-4). Lantern.
Craig, Jean. Heart of the Orchestra: The Story of the Violin & Other Strings. LC 62-20802. (Musical Books for Young People Ser). (Illus.). (gr. 5-11). 1962. PLB 3.95 (ISBN 0-8225-0053-1). Lerner Pubns.
Darlow, Denys. Musical Instruments. (Junior Ref. Ser). (Illus.). (gr. 7-9). 1962. 7.95 (ISBN 0-7136-2043-9). Dufour.
Dietz, Betty W. & Olatunji, M. Babatunde. Musical Instruments of Africa: Their Nature, Use & Place in the Life of a Deeply Musical People. LC 65-13733. (Illus.). (gr. 7 up). 1965. 15.00 (ISBN 0-381-97013-2, A52200, JD-J). Har-Row.
Etkin, Ruth. The Rhythm Band Book. LC 78-57886. (Illus.). (gr. 2 up). 1978. 8.95 (ISBN 0-8069-4570-2); PLB 8.29 (ISBN 0-8069-4571-0). Sterling.
Fichter, George S. American Indian Music & Musical Instruments. (gr. 5-10). 1978. 7.95 (ISBN 0-679-20443-1). McKay.
Gilbert, Jean. Musical Activities with Young Children. LC 75-332407. (Illus.). 1975. 10.00x (ISBN 0-7062-3462-6). Intl Pubns Serv.
Gilmore, Lee. Folk Instruments. LC 62-18816. (Musical Books for Young People Ser). (gr. 5-11). 1962. PLB 3.95 (ISBN 0-8225-0051-5). Lerner Pubns.
Ingman, Nicholas. What Instrument Shall I Play? LC 76-8998. (Illus.). (YA) (gr. 7 up). 1976. 9.95 (ISBN 0-8008-8169-9). Taplinger.
Isadora, Rachel. Ben's Trumpet. LC 78-12885. (Illus.). (gr. k-3). 1979. 7.50 (ISBN 0-688-80194-3). Greenwillow.
Lacey, Marion. Picture Book of Musical Instruments. (Illus.). (gr. 4-6). 1942. PLB 7.44 (ISBN 0-688-51396-4). Lothrop.
Montgomery, Elizabeth R. The Story Behind Musical Instruments. LC 53-9527. (Illus.). (gr. 7-9). 1953. 4.50 (ISBN 0-396-03522-1). Dodd.
Rudoff, Harvey. Practically Complete Guide to Almost Real Musical Instruments for Nearly Everyone. LC 64-25637. (General Juvenile Bks.). (Illus.). (gr. k-5). 1964. PLB 3.95 (ISBN 0-8225-0252-6). Lerner Pubns.
Walther, Tom. Make Mine Music: How to Make & Play Instruments & Why They Work. (Brown Paper School Ser.). (Illus.). 128p. (Orig.). (gr. 3 up). 1981. 9.95 (ISBN 0-316-92111-4); pap. 5.95 (ISBN 0-316-92112-2). Little.
Wiseman, Ann. Making Musical Things. (Illus.). 64p. (gr. 2 up). 1979. 8.95 (ISBN 0-684-16114-1). Scribner.

MUSICAL INSTRUMENTS (MECHANICAL)

see also Automata; Music Box; Musical Instruments, Electronic; Player-Piano

Association For Recorded Sound Collections. Preliminary Directory of Sound Recordings Collections in the United States & Canada. LC 67-31297. 1967. pap. 5.00 (ISBN 0-87104-144-8). NY Pub Lib.
Buchner, Alexander. Mechanical Muscial Instruments. LC 78-5429. (Illus.). 1978. Repr. of 1959 ed. lib. bdg. 46.00x (ISBN 0-313-20440-3, BUMM). Greenwood.
De Waard, Romke. From Music Boxes to Street Organs. LC 67-27808. (Illus.). 1967. 9.95 (ISBN 0-911572-04-X). Vestal.
Ord-Hume, Arthur W. Clockwork Music: An Illustrated History of Mechanical Musical Instruments from the Musical Box: to the Pianola, from Automaton Lady Virginal Players to Orchestration. (Illus.). 334p. 1973. 21.00 (ISBN 0-04-789004-5). Allen Unwin.
Roehl, Harvey N. Player Pianos & Music Boxes: Keys to a Musical Past. LC 68-59054. (Illus.). 3.00 (ISBN 0-911572-06-6). Vestal.

MUSICAL INSTRUMENTS, ELECTRONIC

see also Electro-Acoustics; Electronic Organ

Chavez, Carlos. Toward a New Music: Music & Electricity. Weinstock, Herbert, tr. from Span. LC 74-28308. (Illus.). 180p. 1975. Repr. of 1937 ed. lib. bdg. 19.50 (ISBN 0-306-70719-5). Da Capo.
Crowhurst, Norman. Electronic Musical Instruments. LC 70-133801. (Illus.). 1971. 8.95 (ISBN 0-8306-1546-6); pap. 5.95 (ISBN 0-8306-0546-0, 546). TAB Bks.
Devarahi, pseud. The Complete Guide to Synthesizers. (Illus.). 272p. 1982. pap. 13.95 (ISBN 0-13-160630-1). P-H.
Douglas, Alan. The Electronic Musical Instrument Manual. 1977. lib. bdg. 59.95 (ISBN 0-8490-1755-6). Gordon Pr.
--The Electronic Musical Instrument Manual. LC 76-15887. 9.95 (ISBN 0-8306-6832-2); pap. 6.95 (ISBN 0-8306-5832-7, 832). TAB Bks.
Douglas, Alan L. The Electronic Musical Instrument Manual: A Guide to Theory & Design. 4th ed. LC 74-181145. 491p. 1942. Repr. 39.00 (ISBN 0-403-01546-4). Scholarly.
Horn, Delton T. Electronic Music Synthesizers. (Illus.). 168p. 1980. 10.95 (ISBN 0-8306-9722-5); pap. 6.95 (ISBN 0-8306-1167-3, 1167). TAB Bks.
Jenkins, John & Smith, Jon. Electric Music: A Practical Manual. LC 75-18233. (Midland Bks.: No. 195). (Illus.). 176p. 1976. 10.00x (ISBN 0-253-31944-7). Ind U Pr.
Master Electronics in Music. (gr. 10 up). 1977. pap. 6.95 (ISBN 0-8104-0842-2). Hayden.

MUSICAL INSTRUMENTS, PRIMITIVE

see also Music, Primitive

Balfour, Henry. Natural History of the Musical Bow. LC 76-22326. (Illus.). 1976. Repr. of 1899 ed. lib. bdg. 12.50 (ISBN 0-89341-006-3). Longwood Pr.
Carrington, John F. Talking Drums of Africa. LC 70-77195. (Illus.). Repr. of 1949 ed. 10.50x (ISBN 0-8371-1292-3, Pub. by Negro U Pr). Greenwood.
International African Institute. Select Bibliography of Music in Africa. LC 66-36908. (African Bibliography Ser.). 1965. 16.50x (ISBN 0-85302-031-0). Intl Pubns Serv.
Schaeffner, Andre. Origine Des Instruments De Musique. Repr. of 1936 ed. 14.00 (ISBN 0-384-53500-3); pap. 10.00 (ISBN 0-685-13544-6). Johnson Repr.
--Origine Des Instruments De Musique: Introduction Ethnologique a L'histoire De la Musique Instrumentale. (Reeditions Ser.: No. 3). (Illus.). 1968. 27.75x (ISBN 90-2796-085-2); pap. 23.50 (ISBN 0-686-21788-8). Mouton.
Tracey, Hugh. Chopi Musicians. (Illus.). 1970. Repr. of 1948 ed. 36.00x (ISBN 0-19-724182-4). Oxford U Pr.
Wieschoff, Heinrich A. Die Afrikanischen Trommeln und Ihre Ausserafrikanischen Beziehungen. pap. 15.50 (ISBN 0-384-68373-8). Johnson Repr.
Young, Phillip. The Look of Music: Rare Musical Instruments, 1500-1900. (Illus.). 240p. 1980. 35.00 (ISBN 0-295-95784-0); pap. 16.95 (ISBN 0-295-95785-9). U of Wash Pr.

MUSICAL INTERPRETATION

see Music–Interpretation (Phrasing, Dynamics, etc.)

MUSICAL INTERVALS AND SCALES

see also Tonality

Brindle, Reginald S. Serial Composition. (YA) (gr. 9 up). 1966. 8.50x (ISBN 0-19-311906-4). Oxford U Pr.
Clough, John. Scales, Intervals, Keys & Triads: A Self-Instruction Program. (Orig., Prog. Bk.). 1964. pap. 6.95x (ISBN 0-393-09625-4, NortonC). Norton.
Lloyd, Llewelyn. Intervals, Scales & Temperaments. rev ed. Boyle, Hugh, ed. LC 78-7124. 1979. 15.00 (ISBN 0-312-42533-3). St Martin.
Signell, Karl. Makam: Modal Practice in Turkish Art Music. LC 74-76787. (D Monographs: No. 4). 1976. pap. text ed. 9.00x (ISBN 0-913360-07-4). Asian Music Pub.
Slonimsky, Nicholas. Thesaurus of Scales & Melodic Patterns. 1947. 27.50 (ISBN 0-684-10551-9, ScribT). Scribner.
Tagore, Sourindo M. The Musical Scales of the Hindus. LC 74-24225. Repr. of 1884 ed. 21.50 (ISBN 0-404-12837-8). AMS Pr.
Whitlock, Robert R. & Whitlock, Linda J. The Sunnyside of Chords: An Encyclopedia of Chord & Scale Diagrams for Fingerboard Instruments. LC 78-71087. (Illus.). 240p. 1979. pap. 22.00 (ISBN 0-9602178-0-0). Pattecky Music.
Yost, Gaylord. Scale & Arpeggio Studies. 2.50 (ISBN 0-913650-52-8). Volkwein Bros.

MUSICAL METER AND RHYTHM

see also Chants (Plain, Gregorian, etc.)–Instruction and Study; Musical Notation

Cooper, Grosvenor & Meyer, Leonard B. Rhythmic Structure of Music. LC 60-14068. 1960. pap. 3.95 (ISBN 0-226-11522-4, P118, Phoen). U of Chicago Pr.
Findlay, Elsa. Rhythm & Movement: Applications of Dalcroze Eurhythmics. LC 71-169706. 1971. pap. 9.95 (ISBN 0-87487-078-X). Summy.
Hendren, Joseph W. Study of Ballad Rhythm with Special Reference to Ballad Music. LC 66-29463. (Princeton Studies in English: No. 14). 1966. Repr. of 1936 ed. 8.50 (ISBN 0-87752-052-6). Gordian.
Jaques-Dalcroze, Emile. Eurhythmics, Art & Education. LC 78-180927. Repr. of 1930 ed. 18.00 (ISBN 0-405-08665-2, Blom Pubns). Arno.

--Rhythm, Music & Education. LC 77-187829. (Illus.). Repr. of 1921 ed. 18.00 (ISBN 0-405-08666-0, Blom Pubns). Arno.

Read, Gardner. Modern Rhythmic Notation. LC 77-9860. 288p. 1978. 22.50x (ISBN 0-253-33867-0). Ind U Pr.

Rosenstrauch, Henrietta. Essays on Rhythm, Music, Movement. LC 73-77959. 1973. spiral bdg. 5.00 (ISBN 0-913650-01-3). Volkwein Bros.

Sachs, Curt. The Wellsprings of Music. Kunst, Jaap, ed. LC 77-23410. 1977. pap. 4.95 (ISBN 0-306-80073-X). Da Capo.

Schillinger, Joseph. Encyclopedia of Rhythms: Instrumental Forms of Harmony. LC 76-10326. (Music Rerint Ser.). 1976. Repr. of 1966 ed. lib. bdg. 35.00 (ISBN 0-306-70782-9). Da Capo.

Williams, C. Abdy. The Aristoxenian Theory of Musical Rhythm. LC 77-75224. 1977. Repr. lib. bdg. 25.00 (ISBN 0-89341-123-X). Longwood Pr.

--The Rhythm of Song. LC 77-75202. 1977. Repr. of 1925 ed. lib. bdg. 20.00 (ISBN 0-89341-100-0). Longwood Pr.

Wilson, Katharine M. Sound & Meaning in English Poetry. LC 76-113352. 1970. Repr. of 1930 ed. 13.50 (ISBN 0-8046-1060-6). Kennikat.

Yeston, Maury. The Stratification of Musical Rhythm. LC 75-18189. 176p. 1976. 15.00x (ISBN 0-300-01884-3). Yale U Pr.

MUSICAL MODES

see Musical Intervals and Scales

MUSICAL MOVING PICTURES

see Moving-Pictures, Musical

MUSICAL NOTATION

see also Embellishment (Music)

Apel, Willi. Notation of Polyphonic Music, 900-1600. 5th ed. 1961. 14.00 (ISBN 0-910956-15-4). Medieval Acad.

Boehm, Laszlo. Modern Music Notation. 1961. pap. 7.95 (ISBN 0-02-870490-8). Schirmer Bks.

Boretz, Benjamin & Cone, Edward T., eds. Perspectives on Notation & Performance. (Illus.). 1976. 10.00x (ISBN 0-393-02190-4, Norton Lib); pap. 3.95 (ISBN 0-393-00809-6). Norton.

Boustead, Alan. Writing Down Music. (Illus.). 1976. pap. 15.00 (ISBN 0-19-317104-X). Oxford U Pr.

Cole, Hugo. Sounds & signs: Aspects of Musical Notation. 200p. 1973. pap. 6.00x (ISBN 0-19-317105-8). Oxford U Pr.

Cope, David. New Music Notation. LC 75-32585. 1976. perfect bdg. 4.95 (ISBN 0-8403-1315-2). Kendall-Hunt.

Craig, Jean. Story of Musical Notes. LC 62-11819. (Musical Books for Young People Ser). (Illus.). (gr. 5-11). 1962. PLB 3.95 (ISBN 0-8225-0052-3). Lerner Pubns.

Donato, Anthony. Preparing Music Manuscript. LC 77-4024. (Illus.). 1977. Repr. of 1963 ed. lib. bdg. 16.75x (ISBN 0-8371-9587-X, DOPM). Greenwood.

Epperson, Gordon. Musical Symbol. 1967. pap. 11.40 facsimile ed (ISBN 0-8138-2390-0). Iowa St U Pr.

Gibson, Jon. Melody III, Book II. pap. 10.00 (ISBN 0-89439-003-1). Printed Matter.

Jacob, Archibald. Musical Handwriting. (Music Reprint Ser.). 1979. Repr. of 1947 ed. lib. bdg. 13.50 (ISBN 0-306-79578-7). Da Capo.

Karkoschka, Erhard. Notation in New Music: A Critical Guide to Interpretation & Realisation. Koenig, Rush, tr. from Ger. LC 75-134522. Orig. Title: Das Schriftbild der Neuen Musik. 1972. 31.25 (ISBN 0-900938-28-5, 50-26902). Eur-Am Music.

Lefkoff, Gerald. Reading & Writing Intervals: A Self-Instruction Book. 130p. 1980. pap. text ed. 12.50 (ISBN 0-935964-01-0). Glyphic Pr.

Lilienfeld, Robert. Learning to Read Music. 136p. 1979. pap. 3.95 (ISBN 0-06-463495-7, EH 495, EH). Har-Row.

Long, John, Jr., et al. Tune in to Early Math: Songs You Can Count on. 1976. pap. 5.00x (ISBN 0-87076-323-7). Stanwix.

Read, Gardner. Modern Rhythmic Notation. LC 77-9860. 288p. 1978. 22.50x (ISBN 0-253-33867-0). Ind U Pr.

--Music Notation. LC 68-54213. (Illus.). 1979. pap. 9.95 (ISBN 0-8008-5453-5, Crescendo). Taplinger.

--Music Notation: A Manuel of Modern Practice. LC 68-54213. 1972. 13.95 (ISBN 0-8008-5459-4, Crescendo). Taplinger.

Risatti, Howard. New Music Vocabulary: A Guide to Notational Signs for Contemporary Music. LC 73-81565. (Illus.). 144p. 1975. pap. 5.45 (ISBN 0-252-00406-X). U of Ill Pr.

Rosecrans, Glen. A Music Notation Primer. 1979. 3.95 (ISBN 0-8256-9149-4). Music Sales.

Rosecrans, Glen R. A Music Notation Primer. 2nd ed. (Illus.). 1976. pap. 3.95 (ISBN 0-9601430-1-7). Music Sales.

Sabbe, Herman, et al, eds. Report on the International Conference on New Musical Notation Organized by the Index of New Musical Notation (New York) & the Seminar of Musicology (Ghent) 120p. 1975. pap. text ed. 25.50 (ISBN 90-265-0221-4, Pub. by Swets Pub Serv Holland). Swets North Am.

Scholes, Percy A. Crotchets: A Few Short Musical Notes. LC 71-181250. 292p. 1924. Repr. 12.00 (ISBN 0-403-01675-4). Scholarly.

Smith, Norman & Stoutamire, Albert. Band Music Notes. LC 79-91984. 1979. pap. 17.95 (ISBN 0-8497-5401-1, WB42, Pub. by Kjos West). Kjos.

Stone, Kurt. Music Notation in the Twentieth Century: A Practical Guidebook. (Illus.). 1981. text ed. 29.95x (ISBN 0-393-95053-0). Norton.

Tillyard, Henry J. Byzantine Music & Hymnography. LC 74-24242. Repr. of 1923 ed. 11.50 (ISBN 0-404-13116-6). AMS Pr.

Virtue, Constance. Notagraph: Design for Music Notation. 1980. text ed. 10.00 (ISBN 0-914596-01-2). Virtue Notagraph.

--Virtue Notagraph Manual. 1974. 6.00 (ISBN 0-914596-01-2). Virtue Notagraph.

Warfield, Gerald. How to Write Music Manuscript (in Pencil) A Workbook in the Basics of Music Notation. LC 76-58400. (Music Ser.). 1977. pap. text ed. 10.95x (ISBN 0-679-30332-4, Pub. by MacKay). Longman.

Williams, C. Abdy. Story of Notation. LC 69-16797. 1968. Repr. of 1903 ed. 18.00 (ISBN 0-8103-3557-3). Gale.

--The Story of Notation. LC 77-90803. 1978. Repr. of 1903 ed. lib. bdg. 25.00 (ISBN 0-89341-420-4). Longwood Pr.

Williams, Charles. Story of Notation. LC 68-25306. (Studies in Music, No. 42). (Illus.). 1969. Repr. of 1903 ed. lib. bdg. 47.95 (ISBN 0-8383-0317-X). Haskell.

Williams, Charles F. Story of Notation. LC 68-57648. (Illus.). 1969. Repr. of 1903 ed. lib. bdg. 15.00x (ISBN 0-8371-1622-8, WINO). Greenwood.

Williams, Ken J. Music Preparation: A Guide to Music Copying. LC 79-56140. (Illus.). 149p. 1980. pap. text ed. 16.75 (ISBN 0-9603742-0-5). K J Williams Pubns.

MUSICAL NOVELS

see Musical Fiction

MUSICAL PERFORMANCE

see Music-Performance

MUSICAL RESEARCH

see Musicology

MUSICAL REVUE, COMEDY, ETC.

For descriptive or historical material. Scores are entered under the heading Musical, Revues, Comedies, etc.

Appelbaum, Stanley & Camner, James. Stars of the American Musical Theater in Historic Photographs: 361 Portraits from the 1860s to 1950. (Illus.). 1981. pap. price not set (ISBN 0-486-24209-9). Dover.

Baral, Robert. Revue. LC 62-7579. (Illus.). 1970. 14.00 (ISBN 0-8303-0091-0). Fleet.

Chouquet, Gustave. Histoire De la Musique Dramatique En France Depuis Ses Origines Jusqu'a Nos Jours. LC 80-2265. Repr. of 1873 ed. 45.00 (ISBN 0-404-18818-4). AMS Pr.

Craig, Warren. Great Songwriters of Hollywood. LC 79-87793. 256p. 1980. 14.95 (ISBN 0-498-02439-3). A S Barnes.

Eddins, Martha, et al. There's More to Musicals Than Music. (Illus.). 72p. 1980. pap. 4.95 (ISBN 0-916642-13-5, 566). Somerset Pr IL.

Engel, Lehman. The American Musical Theater. rev. ed. 240p. 1975. pap. 5.95 (ISBN 0-02-012280-2, Collier). Macmillan.

--The Making of a Musical. 1977. 10.95 (ISBN 0-02-536070-1). Macmillan.

Engle, Gary D. This Grotesque Essence: Plays from the American Minstrel Stage. LC 77-16617. 1978. 14.95x (ISBN 0-8071-0370-5). La State U Pr.

Fuchs, Peter P., ed. The Music Theater of Walter Felsenstein. (Illus.). 1975. 10.95x (ISBN 0-393-02186-6). Norton.

Green, Stanley. The Broadway Musical: A Picture Quiz Book. (Picture Quiz Book Ser). (Illus.). 128p. 1977. pap. 3.50 (ISBN 0-486-23403-7). Dover.

--Encyclopedia of the Musical Theatre. (Illus.). 1980. pap. 8.95 (ISBN 0-306-80113-2). Da Capo.

--Encyclopedia of the Musical Theatre. LC 76-21069. 1976. 17.50 (ISBN 0-396-07221-6). Dodd.

--The World of Musical Comedy. 4th, rev. ed. LC 80-16915. 448p. 1980. 19.95 (ISBN 0-498-02344-3). A S Barnes.

Harding, James. Folies De Paris: The Rise & Fall of the French Operetta. 1979. 11.50 (ISBN 0-903443-28-7, Pub by Hamish Hamilton). David & Charles.

Kreuger, Miles. The Movie Musical from Vitaphone to "42nd Street" As Reported in a Great Fan Magazine. LC 74-76739. (Illus.). 367p. (Orig.). 1975. pap. 7.95 (ISBN 0-486-23154-2). Dover.

--Show Boat: The Story of a Classic American Musical. LC 76-51717. (Illus.). 1977. 25.00 (ISBN 0-19-502275-0). Oxford U Pr.

Laufe, Abe. Broadway's Greatest Musicals: The New Illustrated Edition. 3rd ed. LC 72-7574. (Funk & W Bk.). (Illus.). 481p. 1977. 14.95 (ISBN 0-308-10317-3). T Y Crowell.

Lerner, Alan J. The Street Where I Live. (Illus.). 336p. 1980. pap. 5.95 (ISBN 0-393-00970-X). Norton.

Mander, Raymond & Mitchenson, Joe. Musical Comedy: A Story in Pictures. LC 70-94125. 1970. 12.00 (ISBN 0-8008-5460-8). Taplinger.

--Revue: A Story in Pictures. LC 76-163477. (Illus.). 1971. 10.95 (ISBN 0-8008-6789-0). Taplinger.

Mates, Julian. The American Musical Stage Before 1800. 1962. 20.00 (ISBN 0-8135-0393-0). Rutgers U Pr.

Mordden, Ethan. Better Foot Forward: The History of American Musical Theater. (Illus.). 352p. 1976. 15.00 (ISBN 0-670-15974-3, Grossman). Viking Pr.

O'Hara, Mary. Musical in the Making. 3.95 (ISBN 0-685-02674-4, Pub. by Markane). Taplinger.

Richards, Stanley, ed. Great Musicals of the American Theatre, Vol. 2. 1976. 17.95 (ISBN 0-8019-6177-7). Chilton.

Rodgers, Richard. Musical Stages. 1978. pap. 2.95 (ISBN 0-515-04647-7). Jove Pubns.

Root, Deane L. American Popular Stage Music, 1860-1880. Buelow, George, ed. (Studies in Musicology: No. 44). 1981. 39.95 (ISBN 0-8357-1174-9). Univ Microfilms.

Sampson, Henry T. Blacks in Blackface: A Source Book on Early Black Musical Shows. LC 80-15048. 562p. 1980. 27.50 (ISBN 0-8108-1318-1). Scarecrow.

Smith, Cecil & Litton, Glenn. Musical Comedy in America: From the Black Crook Through Sweeney Todd. LC 80-51638. (Illus.). 1981. pap. 14.95 (ISBN 0-87830-564-5). Theatre Arts.

Toll, Robert C. Blacking up: The Minstrel Show in Nineteenth-Century America. 1974. 15.95 (ISBN 0-19-501820-6). Oxford U Pr.

--Blacking up: The Minstrel Show in Nineteenth-Century America. LC 74-83992. (Illus.). 1977. pap. 5.95 (ISBN 0-19-502172-X, 489, GB). Oxford U Pr.

Utley, Francis L. & Toll, Robert C., eds. Old Slack's Reminiscences & Pocket History of the Colored Profession. LC 73-78159. 150p. 1973. lib. bdg. 7.95 (ISBN 0-87972-057-3). Bowling Green Univ.

Wilson, Sandy. I Could Be Happy. LC 75-12729. (Illus.). 282p. 1975. 25.00x (ISBN 0-8128-1843-1). Stein & Day.

MUSICAL REVUES, COMEDIES, ETC.

Bernstein, Leonard, et al. Candide: The Complete Words & Music of the Drama Critics Award Winning Broadway Musical. LC 75-43171. (Illus.). 1976. 35.00 (ISBN 0-02-870450-9); pap. 25.00 (ISBN 0-02-870460-6). Schirmer Bks.

Burton, Jack. Blue Book of Broadway Musicals. rev. ed. LC 69-55070. (Burton Blue Book Ser). (Illus.). 344p. 1974. lib. bdg. 18.00 (ISBN 0-87282-012-2). Century Hse.

Coward, Noel. The Lyrics of Noel Coward. LC 73-77884. 432p. 1978. pap. 6.95 (ISBN 0-87951-061-7). Overlook Pr.

Engel, Lehman. The Musical Theater Workshop. (Sound Seminars Ser). bk., tapes, listening guide 350.00x (ISBN 0-88432-066-9, 11500). J Norton Pubs.

--Words with Music. 300p. 6.95 (ISBN 0-02-870370-7). Macmillan.

--Words with Music: The Broadway Musical Libretto. LC 80-15412. 1981. pap. 8.95 (ISBN 0-02-870370-7). Schirmer Bks.

Foster, Steven. Minstrel-Show Songs. (Early American Music Ser.). 1980. Repr. of 1863 ed. lib. bdg. 18.50 (ISBN 0-306-77314-7). Da Capo.

Frankel, Aaron. Writing the Broadway Musical. LC 76-58925. 1977. pap. text ed. 10.00x (ISBN 0-910482-82-9). Drama Bk.

Gottfried, Martin. Broadway Musicals. (Illus.). 1979. 50.00 (ISBN 0-8109-0664-3). Abrams.

Hodgins, Gordon W. The Broadway Musical: A Complete LP Discography. LC 80-18911. 188p. 1980. 10.00 (ISBN 0-8108-1343-2). Scarecrow.

Jackson, Arthur. The Best Musicals--from Show Boat to a Chorus Line: Broadway, Off-Broadway, London. (Illus.). 1977. 15.95 (ISBN 0-517-53122-4). Crown.

MacQueen-Pope, W. Knights of Gladness: The Story of Musical Plays. 268p. 1980. Repr. lib. bdg. 30.00 (ISBN 0-8492-6752-8). R West.

Okun, Milton, ed. The New York Times Great Songs of the Sixties. LC 70-125482. (Illus.). 328p. 1972. 17.50 (ISBN 0-8129-0153-3); pap. 8.95 (ISBN 0-8129-6201-X). Times Bks.

Powers, Bill. Behind the Scenes of a Broadway Musical. (Illus.). 96p. 1981. 10.95 (ISBN 0-517-54466-0). Crown.

Richards, Stanleu. Great Rock Musicals. 1978. 19.95 (ISBN 0-8128-2509-8). Stein & Day.

Toll, Robert C. Blacking up: The Minstrel Show in Nineteenth-Century America. 1974. 15.95 (ISBN 0-19-501820-6). Oxford U Pr.

Tumbusch, Tom. Theatre Student: Guide to Broadway Musical Theatre. LC 72-153811. (Theatre Student Ser). (Illus.). (gr. 7-12). 1972. PLB 12.50 (ISBN 0-8239-0243-9). Rosen Pr.

Wittke, Carl F. Tambo & Bones: A History of the American Minstrel Stage. LC 69-10174. 1968. Repr. of 1930 ed. lib. bdg. 19.75x (ISBN 0-8371-0276-6, WIAM). Greenwood.

MUSICAL REVUES, COMEDIES, ETC.-BIBLIOGRAPHY

Drone, Jeanette M. Index to Opera, Operetta & Musical Comedy Synopses in Collections & Periodicals. LC 77-25822. 1978. 10.00 (ISBN 0-8108-1100-6). Scarecrow.

Hummel, David. The Collector's Guide to the American Musical Theater: Supplement One to the Second Edition. 1979. 9.00 (ISBN 0-934628-02-5). D H Ent.

Raymond, Jack. Show Music on Record: From the 1890's to the 1980's. LC 81-40471. 260p. 1981. 16.95 (ISBN 0-8044-5774-3); pap. 9.95 (ISBN 0-8044-6672-6). Ungar.

MUSICAL REVUES, COMEDIES, ETC.-LIBRETTOS

see also Operas-Librettos

Bernstein, Leonard, et al. West Side Story. 1958. 8.95 (ISBN 0-394-40788-1). Random.

Comden, Betty, et al. On the Twentieth Century. LC 79-28365. (Illus.). 1981. 8.95 (ISBN 0-89676-033-2). Drama Bk.

Darion, Joe & Wasserman, Dale. Man of la Mancha. 1966. 9.95 (ISBN 0-394-40621-4); pap. 3.95 (ISBN 0-394-40619-2). Random.

Gibson, William & Odets, Clifford. Golden Boy. LC 74-77624. 1965. 3.95 (ISBN 0-689-10217-8). Atheneum.

Gilbert, W. S. Gilbert Before Sullivan: Six Comic Plays. Stedman, Jane W., ed. LC 67-16778. (Illus.). 1967. 10.00x (ISBN 0-226-77160-1). U of Chicago Pr.

Herman, Jerry, et al. Mame. 1967. 7.95 (ISBN 0-394-40627-3). Random.

Lerner, Alan J. My Fair Lady. (RL 9). pap. 1.25 (ISBN 0-451-08006-8, Y8006, Sig). NAL.

Lerner, Alan J. & Loewe, Frederick. Camelot. 1961. 7.95 (ISBN 0-394-40521-8). Random.

Rodgers & Hammerstein. Sound of Music. 1960. 7.95 (ISBN 0-394-40724-5). Random.

Rodgers, Richard & Hammerstein, Oscar. Six Plays. 1959. 3.95 (ISBN 0-394-60200-5, M200). Modern Lib.

Schmidt, Harvey & Jones, Tom. Fantasticks. 1968. pap. 2.50 (ISBN 0-380-00915-3, 54007, Bard). Avon.

Stone, Peter & Edwards, Sherman. Seventeen Seventy-Six: A Musical Play. (Illus.). 1976. pap. 2.95 (ISBN 0-14-048139-7). Penguin.

Wheeler, Hugh & Sondheim, Stephen. Sweeney Todd, The Demon Barber of Fleet Street. LC 79-18468. (Illus.). 1979. 7.95 (ISBN 0-396-07776-5). Dodd.

MUSICAL REVUES, COMEDIES, ETC.-STAGE GUIDES

Tumbusch, Tom. Theatre Student: Complete Production Guide to Modern Musical Theatre. LC 79-75380. (Illus.). (gr. 9 up). 1969. PLB 7.97 (ISBN 0-8239-0149-1). Rosen Pr.

MUSICAL REVUES, COMEDIES, ETC.-STORIES, PLOTS, ETC.

Dunn, Donald H. The Making of 'No, No, Nanette' (Illus.). 284p. 1972. 7.95 (ISBN 0-8065-0265-7). Citadel Pr.

Laufe, Abe. Broadway's Greatest Musicals: The New Illustrated Edition. 3rd ed. LC 72-7574. (Funk & W Bk.). (Illus.). 481p. 1977. 14.95 (ISBN 0-308-10317-3). T Y Crowell.

MUSICAL SOCIETIES

see Music-Societies, Etc.

MUSICAL STYLE

see Style, Musical

MUSICAL TALENT

see Musical Ability

MUSICAL TEMPERAMENT

Barbour, James Murray. Tuning & Temperament: A Historical Survey. LC 74-37288. (Illus.). 228p. 1972. Repr. of 1951 ed. lib. bdg. 21.50 (ISBN 0-306-70422-6). Da Capo.

Lloyd, Llewelyn. Intervals, Scales & Temperaments. rev ed. Boyle, Hugh, ed. LC 78-7124. 1979. 15.00 (ISBN 0-312-42533-3). St Martin.

MUSICAL THERAPY

see Music Therapy

MUSICAL TIMES, LONDON

Scholes, Percy A. Mirror of Music, 1844-1944, 2 Vols. facs. ed. LC 71-124255. (Select Bibliographies Reprint Ser). 1947. Set. 75.00 (ISBN 0-8369-5443-2). Arno.

MUSICAL VARIATION

see Variation (Music)

MUSICIANS

see also Children As Musicians; Composers; Conductors (Music); Country Musicians; Jazz Musicians; Librettists; Music–Bio-Bibliography; Music Teachers; Pianists; Rock Musicians; Singers; Street Music and Musicians; Women Musicians

Allen, George. Life of Philidor: Musician & Chess-Player. LC 70-139198. (Music Ser). 1971. Repr. of 1863 ed. 19.50 (ISBN 0-306-70075-1). Da Capo.

Applebaum, Samuel & Roth, Henry. The Way They Play, Bk. 7. (Illus.). 288p. 1980. 9.95 (ISBN 0-87666-620-9, Z-33). Paganiniana Pubns.

Apthorp, W. F. Musicians & Music Lovers. 59.95 (ISBN 0-8490-0684-8). Gordon Pr.

Apthorp, William F. Musicians & Music-Lovers: And Other Essays. LC 74-39633. (Essay Index Reprint Ser.). Repr. of 1894 ed. 20.00 (ISBN 0-8369-2736-2). Arno.

Arnold, Ign F. Gallerie der beruhmtesten Tonkunstler des Eighteen und Nineteen Jahrhunderts: Biographien, Anekdoten, und Darstellung ihrer Werke. (Facsimiles of Early Biographies Ser.: Vol. 7). 1981. Repr. of 1810 ed. 70.00 (ISBN 90-6027-140-8, Pub. by Frits Knuf Netherlands). Pendragon NY.

Ayeroff, Stan. Charlie Christian. 72p. pap. 5.95 (ISBN 0-686-75680-0). Music Sales.

--Django Reinhardt. 72p. pap. 5.95 (ISBN 0-8256-4083-0). Music Sales.

Baker-Carr, Janet. Evening at Symphony. 1977. 10.95 (ISBN 0-395-25697-6). HM.

Baral, Robert. Revue. LC 62-7579. (Illus.). 1970. 14.00 (ISBN 0-8303-0091-0). Fleet.

Bego, Mark. Barry Manilow. (Junior Bio Ser.). 1979. pap. 1.95 (ISBN 0-448-17035-3, Tempo). Ace Bks.

Belza, Igor F. Handbook of Soviet Musicians. Bush, Alan, ed. LC 74-114468. (Illus.). 1971. Repr. of 1943 ed. lib. bdg. 15.00 (ISBN 0-8371-4764-6, BOSM). Greenwood.

Bingley, William. Musical Biography, Two Vols. LC 70-127286. (Music Ser). 1971. Repr. of 1834 ed. Set. lib. bdg. 65.00 (ISBN 0-306-70032-8). Da Capo.

Blades, James. Drum Roll: A Professional Adventure from the Circus to the Concert Hall. (Illus.). 272p. 1977. 24.00 (ISBN 0-571-10107-0, Pub. by Faber & Faber). Merrimack Bk Serv.

Boise, Otis B. Music & Its Masters. LC 73-39464. (Illus.). Repr. of 1902 ed. 14.00 (ISBN 0-404-08367-6). AMS Pr.

Bone, Philip J. The Guitar & Mandolin, Biographies of Celebrated Players & Composers. LC 75-329. (Illus.). 1972. 25.00 (ISBN 0-901938-02-5). Eur-Am Music.

Bookspan, Martin. One Hundred One Masterpieces of Music & Their Composers. rev. ed. LC 72-84961. 480p. 1973. pap. 4.95 (ISBN 0-385-05721-0, Dolp). Doubleday.

Brockway, Wallace & Weinstock, Herbert. Men of Music. rev. ed. 1958. pap. 3.95 (ISBN 0-671-46510-4, Fireside). S&S.

Brown, James D. & Stratton, Stephen S. British Musical Biography: A Dictionary of Musical Artists, Authors & Composers, Born in Britain & Its Colonies. LC 76-139197. (Music Ser). 1971. Repr. of 1897 ed. lib. bdg. 42.50 (ISBN 0-306-70076-X). Da Capo.

Burney, Charles. The Present State of Music in France & Italy. 2nd corr. ed. LC 74-24263. 1976. Repr. of 1773 ed. 27.50 (ISBN 0-404-12875-0). AMS Pr.

Burton, Gary. A Musician's Guide to the Road. 154p. 1981. pap. 7.95 (ISBN 0-8230-7583-4, Billboard Pub). Watson-Guptill.

Cande, Roland de. Dictionnaire Des Musiciens. 288p. (Fr.). 1974. pap. 8.95 (ISBN 0-686-56882-6, F-17742). French & Eur.

Carey, Hugh. Duet for Two Voices. LC 78-62115. (Illus.). 1980. 24.95 (ISBN 0-521-22312-1). Cambridge U Pr.

Chappell, Paul. Dr. S. S. Wesley 1810-1976: Portrait of a Victorian Musician. (Illus.). 1977. pap. text ed. 13.50x (ISBN 0-85597-198-3). Attic Pr.

Claghorn, Charles E. Biographical Dictionary of American Music. 1973. 13.95 (ISBN 0-13-076331-4). P-H.

Cocteau, Jean. Jean Marais. (Illus.). 136p. 1975. 12.50 (ISBN 0-686-54533-8). French & Eur.

Collin, Laure. Histoire Abregee De la Musique et Des Musiciens. (Music Reprint Series). (Fr.). 1977. Repr. of 1897 ed. lib. bdg. 29.50 (ISBN 0-306-70875-2). Da Capo.

Cooke, J. F. Great Men & Famous Musicians. 59.95 (ISBN 0-8490-0259-1). Gordon Pr.

--Music Masters Old & New. 59.95 (ISBN 0-8490-0682-1). Gordon Pr.

Crowest, Frederick J. Musicians' Wit, Humour, & Anecdote. LC 72-78131. (Illus.). 1971. Repr. of 1902 ed. 30.00 (ISBN 0-8103-3729-0). Gale.

Curcio, Louise. The Musician's Handbook. 1968. pap. 1.50 (ISBN 0-915282-03-8). J Patelson Mus.

Douglass, Fenner. Cavaille-Coll & the Musicians. (Illus.). 1600p. 78.00 (ISBN 0-915548-09-7). Sunbury Pr.

Dunstan, Ralph. A Cyclopaedic Dictionary of Music. LC 72-181147. 632p. 1925. Repr. 34.00 (ISBN 0-403-01353-4). Scholarly.

Eaglefield-Hull, A., ed. Dictionary of Modern Music & Musicians. LC 78-139192. (Music Ser). 1971. Repr. of 1924 ed. lib. bdg. 45.00 (ISBN 0-306-70086-7). Da Capo.

Edwards, George T. Music & Musicians of Maine. LC 74-135736. Repr. of 1928 ed. 23.00 (ISBN 0-404-07231-3). AMS Pr.

--Music and Musicians of Maine. (Illus.). 542p. 1928. 15.00 (ISBN 0-686-05799-6). O'brien.

Eichborn, Hermann L. Girolamo Fantini: Ein Virtuos Des Siebzehnten Jahrhunderts and seine Trompeten-Schule. LC 76-40234. (Brass Research Ser: No. 5). (Illus., German.). 1976. pap. text ed. 2.50 (ISBN 0-914282-18-2). Brass Pr.

Eliot, Marc. Death of a Rebel: Phil Ochs & a Small Circle of Friends. LC 77-25586. 1979. pap. 4.95 (ISBN 0-385-13610-2, Anch). Doubleday.

Elson, Louis. Woman in Music. 69.95 (ISBN 0-87968-459-3). Gordon Pr.

Emery, Frederic B. Violin Concerto. LC 75-93979. (Music Ser). 1969. Repr. of 1928 ed. lib. bdg. 45.00 (ISBN 0-306-71822-7). Da Capo.

Ewen, David. Men of Popular Music. LC 72-6818. (Essay Index Reprint Ser). 1972. Repr. of 1944 ed. 19.00 (ISBN 0-8369-7263-5). Arno.

Ewen, David, ed. From Bach to Stravinsky: The History of Music by Its Foremost Critics. LC 79-124770. Repr. of 1933 ed. 12.50 (ISBN 0-404-02359-2). AMS Pr.

--From Bach to Stravinsky: The History of Music by Its Foremost Critics. LC 68-54419. (Illus.). 1968. Repr. of 1933 ed. lib. bdg. 14.75x (ISBN 0-8371-0411-4, EWBS). Greenwood.

--Musicians Since Nineteen Hundred. 1978. 35.00 (ISBN 0-8242-0565-0). Wilson.

Fawcett, Anthony. John Lennon: One Day at a Time. A Personal Biography. 2nd ed. LC 76-14557. (Illus.). 192p. 1980. pap. 8.95 (ISBN 0-394-17754-1, E772, Ever). Grove.

Fenelon, Fania. Playing for Time. 1979. pap. 2.50 (ISBN 0-425-04199-9). Berkley Pub.

Ffrench, Florence, compiled by. Music & Musicians in Chicago. LC 74-24082. Repr. of 1899 ed. 32.50 (ISBN 0-404-12910-2). AMS Pr.

Ffrench, Florence F. Music & Musicians in Chicago. (Music Reprint Ser.). 1979. Repr. of 1899 ed. lib. bdg. 27.50 (ISBN 0-306-79542-6). Da Capo.

Floren, Myron & Floren, Randee. Accordion Man. (Illus.). 256p. 1981. 12.95 (ISBN 0-8289-0400-6). Greene.

Fowler, Lana N. Willie Nelson Family Album. LC 80-80523. (Illus.). 160p. (Orig.). 1980. pap. 10.00 (ISBN 0-936318-00-7); 19.95 (ISBN 0-936318-01-5). Poirot & Co.

Fuller-Maitland & Alexander, John. Joseph Joachim. 1978. Repr. of 1905 ed. lib. bdg. 12.95 (ISBN 0-89761-000-8). Dunn & Webster.

Fuller-Maitland, J. A. Masters of German Music. LC 77-20818. 1977. Repr. of 1894 ed. lib. bdg. 25.00 (ISBN 0-89341-133-7). Longwood Pr.

Gaisberg, Frederick W. The Music Goes Round. Farkas, Andrew, ed. LC 76-29936. (Opera Biographies). (Illus.). 1977. Repr. of 1942 ed. lib. bdg. 20.00x (ISBN 0-405-09678-X). Arno.

Gaster, Adrian, ed. International Who's Who in Music & Musician's Directory. 9th ed. LC 73-91185. 1000p. 1980. 90.00 (ISBN 0-8103-0427-9). Gale.

Gerald Moore, 1899- Am I Too Loud? (Illus.). 1979. 22.50 (ISBN 0-241-90019-0, Pub. by Hamish Hamilton England). David & Charles.

Hadow, W. H. Studies in Modern Music, 2 Vols. LC 75-102839. (Illus.). 1970. Repr. of 1926 ed. Set. 27.50 (ISBN 0-8046-0755-9). Kennikat.

Hall, Ruth K. A Place of Her Own: The Story of Elizabeth Garrett. (Illus.). 1976. pap. 5.95 (ISBN 0-913270-68-7). Sunstone Pr.

Heinsheimer, Hans W. Menagerie in F Sharp. LC 78-12062. 1979. Repr. of 1947 ed. lib. bdg. 19.75x (ISBN 0-313-21004-7, HEME). Greenwood.

Hill, Edward B. Modern French Music. LC 71-87491. (Music Reprint Ser). 1969. Repr. of 1924 ed. lib. bdg. 27.50 (ISBN 0-306-71497-3). Da Capo.

Holde, Artur & Heskes, Irene, eds. Jews in Music: From the Age of Enlightenment to the Mid-Twentieth Century. rev. ed. LC 74-83942. 364p. 1974. 7.95 (ISBN 0-8197-0372-9). Bloch.

Hughes, Rupert. The Biographical Dictionary of Musicians. Taylor, Deems & Kerr, Russell, eds. LC 73-166237. 481p. 1972. Repr. of 1940 ed. 18.00 (ISBN 0-403-01364-X). Scholarly.

Hull, Arthur E., ed. Dictionary of Modern Music & Musicians. LC 72-1619. Repr. of 1924 ed. 27.50 (ISBN 0-404-08315-3). AMS Pr.

--A Dictionary of Modern Music & Musicians. LC 77-166238. 543p. 1924. Repr. 35.00 (ISBN 0-403-01365-8). Scholarly.

Illing, Robert. Dictionary of Musicians & Music, 2 Vols. 1, Music & 2, Musicians. 1976. Vol. 2, Musicians. 15.00 (ISBN 0-686-67515-0); pap. 6.50 ea. (ISBN 0-08-010337-5). Pergamon.

--Pergamon Dictionary of Musicians & Music: Vols. 1 & 2. Incl. Vol. 1. Musicians. pap. text ed. 5.00 (ISBN 0-08-009963-7); Vol. 2. Music. text ed. 11.50 (ISBN 0-08-010338-3); pap. text ed. 5.00 (ISBN 0-08-010337-5). 1963. Pergamon.

International Who's Who in Music & Musicians Directory. 6th ed. 25.00x (ISBN 0-900332-44-1, Pub by Intl Biog). Biblio Dist.

Itzkoff, Seymour W. Emanuel Feuermann, Virtuoso. LC 78-11827. (Illus.). 272p. 1979. 18.95 (ISBN 0-8173-6450-1). U of Ala Pr.

Jacobson, Robert. Reverberations: Interviews with the World's Leading Musicians. LC 74-13946. 224p. 1974. 8.95 (ISBN 0-688-02875-6). Morrow.

--Reverberations: Interviews with the World's Leading Musicians. LC 74-13946. 224p. 1976. pap. 3.95 (ISBN 0-688-07875-3). Morrow.

Jean-Aubry, Georges. French Music of Today. Evans, Edwin, tr. (Select Bibliographies Reprint Ser.). 1973. Repr. of 1919 ed. 19.00 (ISBN 0-8369-7113-2). Arno.

Jimenez, Francisco G. Carlos Gardel & His Epoch. (Latin American Music Ser.). 1980. lib. bdg. 75.00 (ISBN 0-8490-3058-7). Gordon Pr.

Johnson, Frances H. Musical Memories of Hartford. LC 70-136370. Repr. of 1931 ed. 25.50 (ISBN 0-404-07224-0). AMS Pr.

Kahl, Willi. Selbstbiographien Deutscher Musiker Des XVIII. (Facsimiles of Early Biographies Ser.: Vol. 5). 1972. Repr. of 1948 ed. 37.50 (ISBN 90-6027-277-3, Pub. by Frits Knuf Netherlands); wrappers 25.00 (ISBN 90-6027-133-5). Pendragon NY.

Kallmann, Helmut, ed. Catalogue of Canadian Composers. LC 75-166240. 1972. Repr. of 1952 ed. 21.00 (ISBN 0-403-01375-5). Scholarly.

Klein, Hermann. Musicians & Mummers. LC 80-2284. (Illus.). Repr. of 1925 ed. 38.50 (ISBN 0-404-18850-8). AMS Pr.

Krohn, Ernst C. Missouri Music. LC 65-23398. (Music Ser.). xlvi, 380p. 1971. Repr. of 1924 ed. lib. bdg. 37.50 (ISBN 0-306-70932-5). Da Capo.

Leiter, Robert D. The Musicians & Petrillo. 202p. 1975. Repr. of 1953 ed. lib. bdg. 13.50x (ISBN 0-374-94923-9). Octagon.

Lightwood, James T. Samuel Wesley, Musician: The Story of His Life. LC 72-83745. Repr. of 1937 ed. 12.50 (ISBN 0-405-08748-9). Arno.

Lloyd, Frederick E., ed. Lloyd's Church Musicians Directory. LC 72-1733. Repr. of 1910 ed. 14.75 (ISBN 0-404-08319-6). AMS Pr.

Mangler, J. E. Rhode Island Music & Musicians, 1733-1850. (Detroit Studies in Music Bibliography Ser.: No. 7). 1965. pap. 2.00 (ISBN 0-911772-27-8). Info Coord.

Mathews, William S., ed. Hundred Years of Music in America. LC 73-135725. Repr. of 1889 ed. 42.50 (ISBN 0-404-04259-7). AMS Pr.

Mathis, Sharon B. Ray Charles. LC 72-7552. (Biography Ser.). (Illus.). (gr. 1-5). 1973. 8.95 (ISBN 0-690-67065-6, TYC-J). Har-Row.

Matthews, David. Michael Tippett: A Introductory Story. (Illus.). 112p. 1980. 16.95 (ISBN 0-571-10954-3, Pub. by Faber & Faber); pap. 7.95 (ISBN 0-571-11527-6, Pub. by Faber & Faber). Merrimack Bk Serv.

Metcalf, Frank J. American Writers & Compilers of Sacred Music. LC 66-24731. (Illus.). 1967. Repr. of 1925 ed. 10.00 (ISBN 0-8462-0876-8). Russell.

Moore, Elizabeth C. An Almanac for Music Lovers. LC 70-167078. (Tower Bks). xiv, 382p. 1972. Repr. of 1940 ed. 28.00 (ISBN 0-8103-3940-4). Gale.

Morena, Miguel A. The Artistic History of Carlos Gardel: A Chronological Study with Filmography & Discography. (Latin American Music Ser.). 1980. lib. bdg. 75.00 (ISBN 0-8490-3059-5). Gordon Pr.

Moscheles, Ignatz. Recent Music & Musicians As Described in the Diaries & Correspondence of Ignatz Moscheles. LC 73-125057. (Music Ser). 1970. Repr. of 1873 ed. lib. bdg. 32.50 (ISBN 0-306-70022-0). Da Capo.

Moscheles, Ignaz. Life of Ignaz Moscheles: With Selections from His Diaries & Correspondence, 2 vols. Moscheles, Charlotte, ed. Coleridge, A. D., tr. LC 77-94605. 1979. Repr. of 1873 ed. Set. lib. bdg. 60.00 (ISBN 0-89341-413-1). Longwood Pr.

Murphy, Agnes. Melba: A Biography. LC 77-8029. (Music Reprint Ser.). (Illus.). 1977. Repr. of 1909 ed. lib. bdg. 32.50 (ISBN 0-306-77428-3). Da Capo.

Nettl, Paul. Forgotten Musicians. Repr. of 1951 ed. lib. bdg. 14.25x (ISBN 0-8371-2463-8, NEFM). Greenwood.

North Carolina Federation of Music Clubs. North Carolina Musicians. LC 74-166248. 82p. 1956. Repr. 25.00 (ISBN 0-403-01638-X). Scholarly.

O'Connell, Charles. The Other Side of the Record. LC 70-110835. xi, 332p. Repr. of 1947 ed. lib. bdg. 15.00x (ISBN 0-8371-2626-6, OCOS). Greenwood.

Ossoli, Margaret F. Papers on Literature & Art, 2 pts. in 1. LC 76-144668. 1846. 24.75 (ISBN 0-404-04836-6). AMS Pr.

Ouzer, Louis & Crociata, Francis. Contemporary Musicians in Photographs. (Illus.). 1980. pap. 6.00 (ISBN 0-486-23859-8). Dover.

--Contemporary Musicians in Photographs: Taken at the Eastman School of Music. 12.50 (ISBN 0-8446-5800-6). Peter Smith.

Parker, Henry T. Eighth Notes: Voices & Figures of Music & the Dance. facs. ed. LC 68-29236. (Essay Index Reprint Ser). 1922. 15.00 (ISBN 0-8369-0768-X). Arno.

Parker, John R. A Musical Biography. LC 74-75895. (Detroit Reprints in Music). 260p. 1975. Repr. of 1825 ed. 10.50 (ISBN 0-911772-73-1). Info Coord.

Phillips, O. S. Isaac Nathan: Jewish Musician & Friend of Byron. 1976. lib. bdg. 34.95 (ISBN 0-8490-2078-6). Gordon Pr.

Pincherle, Marc. World of the Virtuoso. (Illus.). 1963. 7.95x (ISBN 0-393-02115-7). Norton.

Porte, J. F. Sir Charles V Stanford. LC 76-12570. (Music Reprint Ser.). 1976. Repr. of 1921 ed. lib. bdg. 18.50 (ISBN 0-306-70790-X). Da Capo.

Porte, John F. Edward MacDowell: A Great American Tone Poet His Life & Music. LC 78-16529. 1978. Repr. of 1922 ed. lib. bdg. 20.00 (ISBN 0-89341-435-2). Longwood Pr.

Rennert, Jonathan. George Thalben-Ball. (Illus.). 1979. 17.95 (ISBN 0-7153-7863-5). David & Charles.

Rohrer, Gertrude M. Music & Musicians of Pennsylvania. LC 71-124996. (Keystone Historical Publications Ser). 1970. 9.00 (ISBN 0-87198-512-8). Friedman.

Rolland, Romain. Some Musicians of Former Days. facs. ed. LC 68-8490. (Essay Index Reprint Ser). 1915. 19.00 (ISBN 0-8369-0831-7). Arno.

--Some Musicians of Former Days. LC 76-177517. Repr. of 1915 ed. 18.00 (ISBN 0-405-08897-3, Blom Pubns). Arno.

Rowlands, Walter. Among the Great Masters of Music. LC 77-90805. 1978. lib. bdg. 30.00 (ISBN 0-89341-422-0). Longwood Pr.

Sachs, Joel. Kapellmeister Hummel in England & France. LC 75-23550. (Detroit Monographs in Musicology: No. 6). 1977. 10.50 (ISBN 0-911772-82-0). Info Coord.

Sadie, Stanley, ed. The New Grove Dictionary of Music & Musicians, 20 vols. 1980. 1900.00 (ISBN 0-333-23111-2). Groves Dict Music.

Safane, Clifford J. Bud Powell. 40p. pap. 5.95 (ISBN 0-8256-4082-2). Music Sales.

Sainsbury, John S. Dictionary of Musicians from the Earliest Times. 1976. Repr. of 1825 ed. lib. bdg. 59.00 (ISBN 0-403-03815-4). Scholarly.

Sainsbury, John S., ed. A Dictionary of Musicians: From the Earliest Times. LC 65-23396. (Music Reprint Ser.). 963p. 1966. Repr. of 1825 ed. 55.00 (ISBN 0-306-70931-7). Da Capo.

Schalit, Michael. Heinrich Schalit: The Man & His Music. 1979. 15.00 (ISBN 0-9604630-0-3). M Schalit.

Schlick, Arnolt. Spiegel der Orgelmacher un(D) Organisten. (Bibliotheca Organologica: Vol. 63). 1981. 60.00 (ISBN 90-6027-395-8, Pub. by Frits Knuf Netherlands); wrappers 47.50 (ISBN 90-6027-338-9). Pendragon NY.

Scholes, Percy A. Complete Book of the Great Musicians, 3 Vols in One. (Illus.). 1949. 13.95x (ISBN 0-19-314101-9). Oxford U Pr.

Schubert, Franz. Complete Works. Mandyczewski, E., ed. (B. & H. Ser. 20). 466p. 7.50 ea. Vol. 18 O.p (ISBN 0-486-21340-4). Vol. 19 (ISBN 0-486-21341-2). Dover.

Scobie, Stephen. Leonard Cohen. (Studies in Canadian Literature). 294p. (Orig.). 1978. pap. 4.95 (ISBN 0-295-95686-0, Pub. by Douglas & McIntyre Canada). U of Wash Pr.

Shaw, Bernard. The Great Composers: Reviews & Bombardments. Crompton, Louis, ed. LC 76-14311. (Cal. Ser.: No. 351). 1978. 35.00x (ISBN 0-520-03253-5); pap. 6.95 (ISBN 0-520-03266-7). U of Cal Pr.

Simosko, Vladimir & Tepperman, Barry. Eric Dolphy: A Musical Biography & Discography. LC 79-15117. (Da Capo Quality Paperback Ser.). (Illus.). 132p. 1979. pap. 5.95 (ISBN 0-306-80107-8). Da Capo.

Slattery, Thomas C. Percy Grainger: The Inveterate Innovator. (Illus.). 12.50 (ISBN 0-686-15893-8). Instrumental Co.

Slonimsky, Nicolas. Music of Latin America. LC 69-11288. (Music Ser). (Illus.). 374p. 1972. Repr. of 1949 ed. lib. bdg. 25.00 (ISBN 0-306-71188-5). Da Capo.

Slonimsky, Nicolas, ed. Baker's Biographical Dictionary of Musicians. 6th ed. LC 78-17324. 1978. 85.00 (ISBN 0-02-870240-9). Schirmer Bks.

Snow, Robert J. The Extant Music of Rodrigo De Ceballos & Its Sources. LC 78-70024. (Detroit Studies in Music Bibliography Ser.: No. 44). 1980. 17.50 (ISBN 0-89990-001-1). Info Coord.

--The Sixteen-Thirteen Print of Juan Esquivel Barahona. LC 78-70021. (Detroit Monographs in Musicology: No. 7). 1978. 11.00 (ISBN 0-911772-92-8). Info Coord.

Sollitt, Edna R. Dufay to Sweelinck, Netherlands Masters of Music. Repr. of 1933 ed. lib. bdg. 15.00 (ISBN 0-8371-4028-5, SODS). Greenwood.

Sowinski, A. Musiciens Polonais & Slaves. LC 77-155149. (Music Ser). 1971. Repr. of 1857 ed. lib. bdg. 55.00 (ISBN 0-306-70166-9). Da Capo.

Stanford, Charles V. Studies & Memories. LC 76-22352. (Illus.). 1976. Repr. of 1908 ed. lib. bdg. 25.00 (ISBN 0-89341-023-3). Longwood Pr.

Stucky, Steven. Lutoslawski & His Music. 225p. 1981. 44.50 (ISBN 0-521-22799-2). Cambridge U Pr.

Tauber, Diana-Napier. Richard Tauber. (Music Ser.). 1980. Repr. of 1949 ed. 22.50 (ISBN 0-306-76049-5). Da Capo.

Taubman, Howard. Music on My Beat: An Intimate Volume of Shop Talk. LC 76-57173. 1977. Repr. of 1943 ed. lib. bdg. 17.00x (ISBN 0-8371-9433-4, TAMU). Greenwood.

Teetgen, Ada B. Waltz Kings of Old Vienna. facsimile ed. LC 78-107833. (Select Bibliographies Reprint Ser). 1939. 20.00 (ISBN 0-8369-5198-0). Arno.

Tertis, Lionel. My Viola & I: A Complete Biography. 1975. 8.75 (ISBN 0-8008-5462-4, Crescendo). Taplinger.

Thomson, John M. Recorder Profiles. 1972. pap. 4.25 (ISBN 0-901938-09-2, 75-A11330). Eur-Am Music.

Tomlin, Pinky. The Object of My Affection: An Autobiography. LC 80-5938. (Illus.). 300p. 1981. 12.50 (ISBN 0-8061-1719-2). U of Okla Pr.

Townsend, Charles. San Antonio Rose: The Life & Music of Bob Wills. LC 75-45431. (Music in American Life Ser.). (Illus.). 470p. 1976. 15.00 (ISBN 0-252-00470-1). U of Ill Pr.

Van Vechten, Carl. Excavations: A Book of Advocacies. facsimile ed. LC 71-156726. (Essay Index Reprint Ser). Repr. of 1926 ed. 19.00 (ISBN 0-8369-2336-7). Arno.

Vodarsky-Shiraeff, Alexandria, ed. Russian Composers & Musicians: A Bibliographical Dictionary. Repr. of 1940 ed. lib. bdg. 15.00 (ISBN 0-8371-2561-8, VORC). Greenwood.

Vodorsky-Shiraeff, Alexandria, ed. Russian Composers & Musicians: A Biographical Dictionary. LC 71-76422. (Music Ser.). 1969. Repr. of 1940 ed. lib. bdg. 19.50 (ISBN 0-306-71321-7). Da Capo.

White, John I. Git Along Little Dogies: Songs & Songmakers of the American West. LC 75-6704. (Music in American Life Ser.). (Illus.). 224p. 1975. 11.95 (ISBN 0-252-00327-6). U of Ill Pr.

Who's Who in Music & Musicians' International Directory. LC 79-181295. 1935. Repr. 22.00 (ISBN 0-403-01719-X). Scholarly.

Young, Percy M. George Grove-Eighteen Twenty to Nineteen Hundred: A Biography. 1980. 35.00 (ISBN 0-333-19602-3). Groves Dict Music.

MUSICIANS–BIBLIOGRAPHY

Brown, Peter A. Carlos d'Ordonez (1754-1786) LC 78-61024. (Detroit Studies in Music Bibliography Ser.: No.39). 1978. pap. 15.50 (ISBN 0-911772-89-8). Info Coord.

Champlin, John. Cyclopedia of Music & Musicians, 3 vols. Set. 350.00 (ISBN 0-87968-985-4). Gordon Pr.

Gordon, Raoul, ed. Bio-Bibliographical Index of Musicians in the United States of America. 1976. lib. bdg. 134.75 (ISBN 0-8490-1505-7). Gordon Pr.

Grove, George. Life & Letters of Sir George Grove. Graves, Charles L., ed. LC 77-75177. 1977. Repr. of 1903 ed. lib. bdg. 50.00 (ISBN 0-89341-059-4). Longwood Pr.

Hamilton, David. Listener's Guide to Great Instrumentalists. 1982. 11.95 (ISBN 0-87196-568-2). Facts on File.

Historical Records Survey. Bio-Bibliographical Index of Musicians in the United States of America Since Colonial Times. 2nd ed. Porter, Keyes, ed. LC 76-39375. Repr. of 1956 ed. 27.50 (ISBN 0-404-08075-8). AMS Pr.

Kay, Ernest, ed. International Who's Who in Music & Musician's Directory. 7th ed. 1348p. 1975. 45.00x (ISBN 0-686-27156-4, Pub. by Intl. Biog). Biblio Dist.

Rinzler, Alan. Bob Dylan: The Illustrated Record. (Illus.). 1978. 15.00 (ISBN 0-517-53354-5, Dist. by Crown); pap. 8.95 (ISBN 0-517-53355-3). Crown.

MUSICIANS–CORRESPONDENCE, REMINISCENCES, ETC.

Adami, Giuseppe, ed. Letters of Giacomo Puccini. Makin, Ena, tr. from It. LC 74-183316. (Illus.). 352p. 1973. pap. 7.50x (ISBN 0-8443-0036-5). Vienna Hse.

Alda, Frances. Men, Women & Tenors. LC 75-149653. Repr. of 1937 ed. 18.00 (ISBN 0-404-00306-0). AMS Pr.

--Men, Women & Tenors. facsimile ed. LC 72-107790. (Select Bibliographies Reprint Ser). 1937. 24.00 (ISBN 0-8369-5174-3). Arno.

Arblay, Frances D' Memoirs of Dr. Burney, Arranged from His Own Manuscripts, from Family Papers, & from Personal Recollections, 3 vols. LC 78-37680. Repr. of 1832 ed. Set. 74.50 (ISBN 0-404-56704-5). AMS Pr.

Armsby, Leonora W. Musicians Talk. facsimile ed. LC 76-99679. (Essay Index Reprint Ser). 1935. 17.00 (ISBN 0-8369-1338-8). Arno.

Baez, Joan. And Then I Wrote... (Illus.). 352p. 1980. pap. 14.95 (ISBN 0-671-44849-8). Summit Bks.

Bailey, Pearl. Raw Pearl. LC 67-11963. 1968. 9.50 (ISBN 0-15-175930-8). HarBraceJ.

--Talking to Myself. LC 78-153679. 233p. 1971. 7.95 (ISBN 0-15-187990-7). HarBraceJ.

Barkan, Hans, ed. Johannes Brahms & Theodor Billroth: Letters from a Musical Friendship. LC 77-798. 1977. Repr. of 1957 ed. lib. bdg. 21.00x (ISBN 0-8371-9500-4, BRJB). Greenwood.

Bauer, Harold. Harold Bauer: His Book. LC 76-94577. Repr. of 1948 ed. lib. bdg. 15.00 (ISBN 0-8371-2489-1, BAHB). Greenwood.

Bax, Arnold E. Farewell My Youth. LC 78-100221. Repr. of 1943 ed. lib. bdg. 15.00 (ISBN 0-8371-3246-0, BAMY). Greenwood.

Bechet, Sidney. Treat It Gentle: An Autobiography. LC 74-23412. (Roots of Jazz Ser). (Illus.). vi, 245p. 1975. lib. bdg. 22.50 (ISBN 0-306-70657-1); pap. 5.95 (ISBN 0-686-77055-2). Da Capo.

Beethoven, Ludwig Van. Beethoven: Letters, Journals & Conversations. Hamburger, Michael, ed. LC 77-13799. 1978. Repr. of 1966 ed. lib. bdg. 24.50 (ISBN 0-8371-9899-2, BELJ). Greenwood.

--Think of Me Kindly: Quotations from the Letters of Ludwig Van Beethoven. Schutz, Susan P. & Sandpiper Studios, eds. LC 78-59096. (Illus., Orig.). 1978. pap. 3.95 (ISBN 0-88396-031-1). Blue Mtn Pr CO.

Benton, Joseph. Oklahoma Tenor: Musical Memories of Giuseppe Bentonelli. LC 73-19393. (Illus.). 160p. (Orig.). 1973. pap. 4.95x (ISBN 0-8061-1179-8). U of Okla Pr.

Berlioz, Hector. Evenings with the Orchestra. Barzun, Jacques, ed. & tr. from Fr. LC 72-95224. 1973. pap. 5.95 (ISBN 0-226-04375-4, P499, Phoen). U of Chicago Pr.

--Memoirs of Hector Berlioz. new ed. Cairns, David, tr. from Fr. (Illus.). 672p. 1975. pap. 8.95 (ISBN 0-393-00698-0, Norton Lib). Norton.

--New Letters of Berlioz, 1830-1868. Barzun, Jacques, tr. & intro. by. LC 75-100144. xxix, 322p. Repr. of 1954 ed. lib. bdg. 16.75x (ISBN 0-8371-3251-7, BENL). Greenwood.

Bickley, Nora, ed. Letters from & to Joseph Joachim. LC 70-183496. 470p. 1972. Repr. of 1914 ed. 45.00x (ISBN 0-8443-0043-8). Vienna Hse.

Boone, Pat. A New Song. 192p. 1981. pap. 5.95 (ISBN 0-86608-003-1). Impact Tenn.

Brahms, Johannes. Johannes Brahms: The Herzogenberg Correspondence. Kalbeck, Max, ed. Bryant, Hannah, tr. LC 78-163787. 425p. 1972. Repr. of 1909 ed. 50.00x (ISBN 0-8443-0011-X). Vienna Hse.

Brendel, Alfred. Musical Thoughts & Afterthoughts. LC 76-3267. (Princeton Essays on the Arts: No. 4). (Illus.). 1977. 17.50 (ISBN 0-691-09122-6); pap. 6.95 (ISBN 0-691-02705-6). Princeton U Pr.

Bryant, Anita & Green, Bob. Fishers of Men. 1976. Repr. lib. bdg. 10.95 (ISBN 0-8161-6237-9, Large Print Bks). G K Hall.

Bulow, Hans Von. Letters of Hans Von Bulow to Richard Wagner & Others. Goddard, Scott, ed. LC 78-31972. (Music Reprint Ser.). 470p. 1979. Repr. of 1931 ed. 35.00 (ISBN 0-306-79539-6). Da Capo.

Burstow, Henry. Reminiscences of Horsham. LC 75-19030. 1975. Repr. of 1911 ed. lib. bdg. 22.50 (ISBN 0-8414-3125-6). Folcroft.

Busch, Fritz. Pages from a Musician's Life. Strachey, Marjorie, tr. LC 71-106715. (Illus.). 223p. Repr. of 1953 ed. lib. bdg. 15.00 (ISBN 0-8371-3445-5, BUML). Greenwood.

--Pages from a Musician's Life. LC 71-181120. 223p. 1953. Repr. 11.00 (ISBN 0-403-01519-7). Scholarly.

Busoni, Ferruccio. Letters to His Wife. Ley, Rosamond, tr. LC 74-34378. (Music Reprint Ser). (Illus.). 319p. 1975. Repr. of 1938 ed. lib. bdg. 25.00 (ISBN 0-306-70732-2). Da Capo.

Cahn, Sammy. I Should Care: The Sammy Cahn Story. LC 74-80708. (Illus.). 1974. 8.95 (ISBN 0-87795-090-3). Arbor Hse.

Campbell, Archie & Byrd, Ben. Archie Campbell: His Story. (Illus.). 144p. 1981. 9.95 (ISBN 0-87870-205-9). Memphis St Univ.

Carmichael, Hoagy. Stardust Road. LC 79-94603. Repr. of 1948 ed. lib. bdg. 14.25x (ISBN 0-8371-2451-4, CASR). Greenwood.

Carmichael, Hoagy & Longstreet, Stephen. Sometimes I Wonder. LC 76-7577. (Roots of Jazz Ser.). 1976. Repr. of 1965 ed. lib. bdg. 22.50 (ISBN 0-306-70809-4). Da Capo.

Casella, Alfredo. Music in My Time: The Memoirs of Alfredo Casella. Norton, Spencer, ed. (Illus.). 1955. 12.50x (ISBN 0-8061-0311-6). U of Okla Pr.

Chopin, Frederick. Chopin's Letters. Opienski, Henry K., ed. Voynich, E. L., tr. LC 79-163798. 424p. 1972. 45.00x (ISBN 0-8443-0020-9); pap. 15.00x (ISBN 0-8443-0090-X). Vienna Hse.

Coleridge, Arthur. Arthur Coleridge Reminiscences. Fuller-Maitland, J. A., ed. LC 77-75179. 1977. Repr. of 1921 ed. lib. bdg. 25.00 (ISBN 0-89341-055-1). Longwood Pr.

Condon, Eddie. We Called It Music: A Generation of Jazz. LC 76-110823. Repr. of 1947 ed. lib. bdg. 20.50x (ISBN 0-8371-3223-1, CWCI). Greenwood.

Cooke, James F. Great Singers on the Art of Singing. LC 74-27333. Repr. of 1921 ed. 24.50 (ISBN 0-404-12886-6). AMS Pr.

Crowest, Fred K. J. Musician's Wit, Humor & Anecdote. 1975. Repr. of 1902 ed. 14.75 (ISBN 0-8274-4069-3). R West.

Dickinson, Edward. The Education of a Music Lover. 59.95 (ISBN 0-8490-0088-2). Gordon Pr.

Ellington, Duke. Music Is My Mistress. LC 73-83189. 544p. 1973. 12.95 (ISBN 0-385-02235-2). Doubleday.

--Music Is My Mistress. LC 75-31665. 1976. pap. 7.95 (ISBN 0-306-80033-0). Da Capo.

Erskine, John. My Life in Music. LC 73-8158. (Illus.). 283p. 1973. Repr. of 1950 ed. lib. bdg. 14.25x (ISBN 0-8371-6950-X, ERLM). Greenwood.

Ewen, David, ed. Composers Since Nineteen Hundred. (Illus.). 639p. 1969. 20.00 (ISBN 0-8242-0400-X). Wilson.

Fanshawe, David. African Sanctus: A Story of Travel & Music. LC 75-2038. (Illus.). 208p. 1975. 12.50 (ISBN 0-8129-0560-1). Times Bks.

Farrar, Geraldine. Such Sweet Compulsion: The Autobiography of Geraldine Farrar. LC 72-107802. (Select Bibliographies Reprint Ser). 1938. 23.00 (ISBN 0-8369-5205-7). Arno.

--Such Sweet Compulsion, the Autobiography of Geraldine Farrar. LC 70-100656. (Music Ser). 1970. Repr. of 1938 ed. lib. bdg. 25.00 (ISBN 0-306-71863-4). Da Capo.

Farrenc, Louise. Trio in E Minor: Opus Forty Five for Piano, Flute, (Violin) & Cello. (Women Composers Ser.). 1979. Repr. of 1862 ed. 16.95 (ISBN 0-306-79553-1). Da Capo.

Fawcett, Anthony. John Lennon: One Day at a Time. A Personal Biography. 2nd ed. LC 76-14557. (Illus.). 192p. 1980. pap. 8.95 (ISBN 0-394-17754-1, E772, Ever). Grove.

Finck, H. T. My Adventures in the Golden Age of Music. LC 70-87496. (Music Ser.). 462p. 1971. Repr. of 1926 ed. lib. bdg. 39.50 (ISBN 0-306-71448-5). Da Capo.

Finck, Henry T. Musical Laughs: Jokes, Tittle-Tattle, & Anecdotes, Mostly Humorous, About Musical Celebrities. LC 79-159955. 1971. Repr. of 1924 ed. 22.00 (ISBN 0-8103-3397-X). Gale.

Flesch, Carl. The Memoirs of Carl Flesch. (Music Reprint Ser.). 1979. Repr. of 1957 ed. lib. bdg. 29.50 (ISBN 0-306-77574-3). Da Capo.

Foote, Arthur. Arthur Foote, 1853-1937: An Autobiography. LC 78-2021. (Music Reprint Ser.,1978). (Illus.). 1978. Repr. of 1946 ed. lib. bdg. 25.00 (ISBN 0-306-77531-X). Da Capo.

Foster, George M. Pops Foster: The Autobiography of a New Orleans Jazzman. Stoddard, Tom, as told to. LC 75-132414. 1971. 16.95 (ISBN 0-520-01826-5); pap. 3.45 (ISBN 0-520-02355-2). U of Cal Pr.

Fotine, Larry. Musicians & Other Noisemakers. LC 79-93016. (Illus.). 142p. 1980. pap. 4.95 (ISBN 0-933830-05-X). Poly Tone.

Freedomways Editors, ed. Paul Robeson: The Great Forerunner. LC 78-7917. (Illus.). 1978. 12.95 (ISBN 0-396-07545-2). Dodd.

Freeman, Bud. You Don't Look Like a Musician. LC 73-89352. 135p. 1974. 5.95 (ISBN 0-913642-05-3). Balamp Pub.

Friedheim, Arthur. Life & Liszt. Bullock, Theodore L., ed. LC 61-15656. (Illus.). 1961. 6.00 (ISBN 0-685-20505-3). Taplinger.

Fromm, Herbert. Key of See: Travel Journals of a Composer. 1967. 4.00 (ISBN 0-87368-061-8). Plowshare.

Gal, Hans, ed. The Musician's World: Letters of the Great Composers. 1978. pap. 7.95 (ISBN 0-500-27130-5). Thames Hudson.

Gambaccini, Paul. Paul McCartney: In His Own Words. LC 76-8068. 1976. pap. 5.95 (ISBN 0-8256-3910-7, Quick Fox). Music Sales.

Gambaccini, Peter. Bill Joel: A Photo Biography. 192p. (Orig.). 1980. pap. 2.50 (ISBN 0-515-05317-1). Jove Pubns.

Gatti-Casazza, Giulio. Memories of the Opera. Taubman, Howard, ed. LC 71-183334. (Illus.). 326p. 1973. Repr. of 1941 ed. 25.00 (ISBN 0-8443-0022-5). Vienna Hse.

Geissmar, Berta. Two Worlds of Music. LC 74-28326. Orig. Title: The Baton & the Jackboot. (Illus.). 327p. 1975. Repr. of 1946 ed. lib. bdg. 27.50 (ISBN 0-306-70664-4). Da Capo.

Gerald Moore, 1899- Farewell Recital: Further Memoirs. LC 78-54694. (Illus.). 1978. 10.95 (ISBN 0-8008-2599-3, Crescendo). Taplinger.

Gerhardt, Elena. Recital. LC 78-181162. 1953. Repr. 19.00 (ISBN 0-403-01564-2). Scholarly.

Gielow, Fred C., Jr. Laughter, Love, & a Barbershop Song. LC 80-65128. 1980. 9.75 (ISBN 0-9603938-0-3). Gielow.

Gillis, Frank J. & Miner, John W., eds. Oh, Didn't He Ramble: The Life Story of Lee Collins As Told to Mary Collins. LC 73-85485. (Music in American Life Ser.). (Illus.). 159p. 1974. 12.50 (ISBN 0-252-00234-2). U of Ill Pr.

Goossens, Eugene. Overture & Beginners: A Musical Autobiography. LC 71-138240. (Illus.). 327p. 1972. Repr. of 1951 ed. lib. bdg. 19.50x (ISBN 0-8371-5597-5, GOOB). Greenwood.

Gottschalk, Louis M. Notes of a Pianist. (Music Reprint Ser.). 1979. Repr. of 1964 ed. 32.50 (ISBN 0-306-79508-6). Da Capo.

Gounod, Charles. Autobiographical Reminiscences: With Family Letters & Notes on Music. LC 68-16235. (Music Ser). 1970. Repr. of 1896 ed. lib. bdg. 25.00 (ISBN 0-306-71081-1). Da Capo.

Graffman, Gary. I Really Should Be Practicing. LC 80-1119. 288p. 1980. 14.95 (ISBN 0-385-15559-X). Doubleday.

Gray, Cecil. Musical Chairs, or Between Two Stools: Being the Life & Memoirs of Cecil Gray. LC 72-181166. 324p. 1948. Repr. 21.00 (ISBN 0-403-01569-3). Scholarly.

Guralnick, Peter. Lost Highway. LC 79-52636. (Illus.). 1979. 18.95 (ISBN 0-87923-293-5); pap. 8.95 (ISBN 0-87923-294-3). Godine.

Guthrie, Woody. Bound for Glory. (RL 10). 1976. pap. 1.95 (ISBN 0-451-07119-0, J7119, Sig). NAL.

Hammond, Joan. Voice, a Life. (Illus.). 1970. 11.25x (ISBN 0-575-00503-3). Intl Pubns Serv.

Hauptmann, Moritz. The Letters of a Leipzig Cantor, 2 vols. Schoene, Alfred & Hiller, Ferdinand, eds. Coleridge, A. D., tr. LC 75-163789. 1972. Repr. of 1892 ed. Set. 50.00x (ISBN 0-8443-0102-7). Vienna Hse.

Hawes, Hampton & Asher, Don. Raise up off Me: A Portrait of Hampton Hawes. 180p. 1979. pap. 5.95 (ISBN 0-686-68925-9). Da Capo.

Henschel, George. Musings & Memories of a Musician. (Music Reprint Ser.). 1979. Repr. of 1919 ed. lib. bdg. 32.50 (ISBN 0-306-79540-X). Da Capo.

Hoffman, Richard. Some Musical Recollections of Fifty Years. LC 74-75890. (Detroit Reprints in Music). 1976. 9.50 (ISBN 0-911772-79-0). Info Coord.

Hueffer, Francis, ed. Correspondence of Wagner & Liszt. LC 73-86923. (Composers' Letters Ser.: No. 5). (Illus.). 752p. 1973. pap. 15.00x (ISBN 0-8443-0099-3). Vienna Hse.

Ives, Charles E. Charles E. Ives: Memos. Kirkpatrick, John E., ed. (Illus.). 1972. 15.00x (ISBN 0-393-02153-X). Norton.

Joplin, Scott. The Collected Works of Scott Joplin. Lawrence, Vera Brodsky, ed. Incl. Vol. 1. Works for Piano. Blesh, Rudi, intro. by. 305p. 30.00 (ISBN 0-87104-231-2); Vol. 2. Works for Voice. Blesh, Rudi, intro. by. 30.00 (ISBN 0-87104-232-0). LC 78-164697. (Americana Collection Music Ser., No. 1). (Illus.). 1972. Set. 50.00 (ISBN 0-87104-238-X). NY Pub Lib.

Kelly, Michael. Reminiscences of Michael Kelly. Hook, Theodore E., ed. LC 72-88491. Repr. of 1826 ed. 18.00 (ISBN 0-405-08688-1, Pub. by Blom). Arno.

--Reminiscences of Michael Kelly of the King's Theatre & Theatre Royal Drury Lane 2 Vols. 2nd ed. LC 68-16243. (Music Ser). 1968. Repr. of 1826 ed. lib. bdg. 45.00 (ISBN 0-306-71094-3). Da Capo.

Laing, Dilys. Buddy Holly. 1972. pap. 1.95 (ISBN 0-02-061100-5, Collier). Macmillan.

Lehmann, Lotte. Midway in My Song, the Autobiography of Lotte Lehmann. LC 73-107813. (Select Bibliographies Reprint Ser). 1938. 22.00 (ISBN 0-8369-5186-7). Arno.

--Midway in My Song, the Autobiography of Lotte Lehmann. Repr. of 1938 ed. lib. bdg. 15.00x (ISBN 0-8371-4255-5, LEMI). Greenwood.

--My Many Lives. Holden, Frances, tr. from Ger. LC 74-3689. (Illus.). 262p. 1974. Repr. of 1948 ed. lib. bdg. 15.00x (ISBN 0-8371-7361-2, LEML). Greenwood.

Leinsdorf, Erich. Cadenza: A Musical Career. 1976. 10.95 (ISBN 0-395-24401-3). HM.

Liszt, Franz. Letters of Franz Liszt, 2 Vols. LC 68-25294. (Studies in Music, No. 42). 1969. Repr. of 1894 ed. lib. bdg. 74.95 (ISBN 0-8383-0307-2). Haskell.
--The Letters of Franz Liszt to Olga von Meyendorff, 1871-1886, in the Mildred Bliss Collection at Dumbarton Oaks. Tyler, William R., tr. (Illus.). 553p. 1979. text ed. 30.00x (ISBN 0-88402-078-9). Harvard U Pr.
Litvinne, Felia. Ma Vie et Mon Art Souvenirs. Farkas, Andrew, ed. LC 76-29950. (Opera Biographies). (Illus., Fr.). 1977. Repr. of 1933 ed. lib. bdg. 19.00x (ISBN 0-405-09691-7). Arno.
Litzmann, Berthold, ed. Letters of Clara Schumann & Johannes Brahms, 2 vols. LC 77-163792. 1972. Repr. of 1927 ed. Set. 50.00x (ISBN 0-8443-0116-7). Vienna Hse.
--Letters of Clara Schumann & Johannes Brahms, 2 vols. LC 77-163792. (Composers' Letters Ser.: No. 7). 640p. 1974. Set. pap. 15.00x (ISBN 0-8443-0056-X). Vienna Hse.
Luening, Otto. The Odyssey of an American Composer. (Illus.). 1980. 22.50 (ISBN 0-684-16496-5, ScribT). Scribner.
McCormack, John. John McCormack: His Own Life Story. Key, Pierre V., as told to. LC 72-93828. (Illus.). 443p. 1973. Repr. of 1918 ed. 16.50x (ISBN 0-8443-0092-6). Vienna Hse.
Mahler, Alma. Gustav Mahler: Memories & Letters. 3rd ed. Mitchell, Donald & Martner, Knud, eds. LC 74-26502. (Illus.). 409p. 1968. pap. 7.95 (ISBN 0-295-95378-0). U of Wash Pr.
Maltese, John A., ed. The Accompanist: Autobiograpgy of Andre Benoist. (Illus.). 384p. 1978. 14.95 (ISBN 0-87666-614-4, Z-26). Paganiniana Pubns.
Mannes, David. Music Is My Faith: An Autobiography. (Music Reprint, 1978 Ser.). (Illus.). 1978. Repr. of 1938 ed. lib. bdg. 27.50 (ISBN 0-306-77595-6). Da Capo.
Maretzek, Max. Crochets & Quavers: Or Revelations of an Opera Manager in America. 2nd ed. LC 65-23397. (Music Ser). 1966. Repr. of 1855 ed. lib. bdg. 27.50 (ISBN 0-306-70915-5). Da Capo.
Marks, Edward B. They All Had Glamour: From the Swedish Nightingale to the Naked Lady. (Illus.). 448p. 1972. Repr. of 1944 ed. lib. bdg. 22.50x (ISBN 0-8371-6075-8, MATA). Greenwood.
Mason, Daniel G. Music in My Time & Other Reminiscences. LC 71-107818. (Select Bibliographies Reprint Ser). 1938. 30.00 (ISBN 0-8369-5189-1). Arno.
--Music in My Time & Other Reminiscences. Repr. of 1938 ed. lib. bdg. 22.25x (ISBN 0-8371-4274-1, MAMT). Greenwood.
Mason, William. Memories of a Musical Life. LC 70-133825. Repr. of 1901 ed. 21.45 (ISBN 0-404-07216-X). AMS Pr.
--Memories of a Musical Life. LC 70-125056. (Music Ser). 1970. Repr. of 1901 ed. lib. bdg. 32.50 (ISBN 0-306-70021-2). Da Capo.
Massenet, Jules E. My Recollections. Barnett, H. Villiers, tr. LC 75-107819. (Select Bibliographies Reprint Ser). 1919. 22.00 (ISBN 0-8369-5190-5). Arno.
--My Recollections, Eighteen Forty Eight-Nineteen Twelve. LC 70-137259. Repr. of 1919 ed. 11.25 (ISBN 0-404-04229-5). AMS Pr.
Maurel, Victor. Dix Ans De Carriere, 1887-1897: Ten Years of My Career,1887-1897. Farkas, Andrew, ed. LC 76-29954. (Opera Biographies). (Illus., Fr.). 1977. Repr. of 1897 ed. lib. bdg. 25.00x (ISBN 0-405-09695-X). Arno.
Mayer, Dorothy M. The Forgotten Master: The Life & Times of Louis Spohr. LC 80-27659. (Music Reprint Ser.). 208p. 1981. Repr. of 1959 ed. 22.50 (ISBN 0-686-73810-1). Da Capo.
Melba, Nellie. Melodies & Memories. LC 71-126694. Repr. of 1926 ed. 17.00 (ISBN 0-404-04287-2). AMS Pr.
--Melodies & Memories. LC 73-107821. (Select Bibliographies Reprint Ser). 1926. 24.00 (ISBN 0-8369-5192-1). Arno.
Mendelssohn, Felix. Letters of Felix Mendelssohn Bartholdy from Italy & Switzerland. Wallace, Grace, tr. LC 77-2022. 1978. Repr. of 1869 ed. lib. bdg. 30.00 (ISBN 0-89341-429-8). Longwood Pr.
--Letters of Felix Mendelssohn Bartholdy from 1833 to 1847. Bartholdy-Mendelssohn, ed. Wallace, Grace, tr. LC 77-92441. 1978. Repr. of 1868 ed. lib. bdg. 30.00 (ISBN 0-685-86665-3). Longwood Pr.
Mendelssohn-Bartholdy, F. Letters. Selden-Goth, G., ed. LC 45-5930. Repr. of 1945 ed. 18.00 (ISBN 0-527-63150-7). Kraus Repr.
Milhaud, Darius. Notes Without Music. LC 72-87419. (Music Ser). (Illus.). 1970. Repr. of 1953 ed. lib. bdg. 35.00 (ISBN 0-306-71565-1). Da Capo.
Moscheles, Ignatz. Recent Music & Musicians As Described in the Diaries & Correspondence of Ignatz Moscheles. LC 73-125057. (Music Ser). 1970. Repr. of 1873 ed. lib. bdg. 32.50 (ISBN 0-306-70022-0). Da Capo.
Moscheles, Ignaz. Fragments of an Autobiography. LC 77-94606. 1979. Repr. of 1899 ed. lib. bdg. 40.00 (ISBN 0-89341-412-3). Longwood Pr.
Mozart, Wolfgang A. Man & the Artist Revealed in His Own Words. Krehbiel, tr. & ed. 5.50 (ISBN 0-8446-2626-0). Peter Smith.
Nabokov, Nicolas. Old Friends & New Music. LC 74-7776. 294p. 1974. Repr. of 1951 ed. lib. bdg. 15.75x (ISBN 0-8371-7594-1, NAOF). Greenwood.
Norman, Gertrude & Shrifte, Mirian L., eds. Letters of Composers: An Anthology 1603-1945. LC 78-14483. 1979. Repr. of 1946 ed. lib. bdg. 27.75x (ISBN 0-313-20664-3, NOLC). Greenwood.
Palmegiani, Francesco. Matta Battistini: Il Re Dei Baritoni. Farkas, Andrew, ed. LC 76-29960. (Opera Biographies). (Illus., It.). 1977. Repr. of 1949 ed. lib. bdg. 16.00x (ISBN 0-405-09700-X). Arno.
Pepper, Art & Pepper, Laurie. Straight Life: The Story of Art Pepper. LC 79-7363. (Illus.). 1979. 12.95 (ISBN 0-02-871820-8). Schirmer Bks.
Planche, James R. Recollections & Reflections. (Music Reprint, 1978 Ser.). (Illus.). 1978. Repr. of 1901 ed. lib. bdg. 42.50 (ISBN 0-306-79501-9). Da Capo.
Previn, Dory. Bog-Trotter. LC 78-20094. (Illus.). 1980. 12.00 (ISBN 0-385-14708-2). Doubleday.
Primrose, William. Walk on the North Side: Memoirs of a Violist. LC 78-4952. (Illus.). 1978. 15.95x (ISBN 0-8425-1264-0); pap. 12.95x (ISBN 0-8425-1313-2). Brigham.
Puccini, Giacomo. Letters of Giacomo Puccini. Makin, Ena, ed. LC 71-140038. Repr. of 1931 ed. 24.50 (ISBN 0-404-05149-9). AMS Pr.
Rachmaninoff, Sergei. Rachmaninoff's Recollections Told to Oskar Von Riesemann. LC 74-111100. (Select Bibliographies Reprint Ser). 1934. 19.00 (ISBN 0-8369-5232-4). Arno.
Riddle, Almeda. Singer & Her Songs: Almeda Riddle's Book of Ballads. Abrahams, Roger D., ed. LC 77-122352. (Illus.). 1971. 13.95 (ISBN 0-8071-0021-8). La State U Pr.
Rimsky-Korsakov, Nikolai A. My Musical Life. Joffe, Judah A., tr. Van Vechten, Carl, ed. LC 74-183332. 480p. 1972. Repr. of 1942 ed. 40.00 (ISBN 0-8443-0024-1). Vienna Hse.
Robeson, Paul. Here I Stand. LC 70-159847. 1971. pap. 4.95 (ISBN 0-8070-6407-6, BP410). Beacon Pr.
Rodgers, Richard. Musical Stages: An Autobiography. (Illus.). 320p. 1975. 12.50 (ISBN 0-394-47596-8). Random.
Rubinstein, A. Autobiography, 1829-1889. LC 68-25303. (Studies in Music, No. 42). 1969. Repr. of 1890 ed. lib. bdg. 44.95 (ISBN 0-8383-0315-3). Haskell.
Rubinstein, Arthur. My Young Years. 512p. 1974. pap. 2.95 (ISBN 0-445-08296-8). Popular Lib.
Ruffo, Titta. La Mia Parabola, Memorie. Farkas, Andrew, ed. LC 76-29966. (Opera Biographies). (Illus., It.). 1977. Repr. of 1937 ed. lib. bdg. 27.00x (ISBN 0-405-09705-0). Arno.
Ryan, Thomas. Recollections of an Old Musician. (Music Reprint Ser.). 1979. Repr. of 1899 ed. lib. bdg. 29.50 (ISBN 0-306-79521-3). Da Capo.
Saint-Saens, C. Musical Memories. Rich, Edwin G., tr. LC 79-137288. Repr. of 1919 ed. 12.50 (ISBN 0-404-05502-8). AMS Pr.
Saint-Saens, Camille. Musical Memories. LC 70-93980. (Music Reprint Ser). 1969. Repr. of 1919 ed. lib. bdg. 29.50 (ISBN 0-306-71821-9). Da Capo.
--Musical Memories. LC 71-181242. 282p. 1919. Repr. 20.00 (ISBN 0-403-01667-3). Scholarly.
Schang, F. C. Visiting Cards of Pianists. LC 79-88628. (Illus.). 1979. 9.95 (ISBN 0-915282-06-2). J Patelson Mus.
Schoen-Rene, Anna E. America's Musical Inheritance: Memories & Reminiscences. LC 77-181249. 244p. 1941. Repr. 23.00 (ISBN 0-403-01674-6). Scholarly.
Schubert, Franz P. Franz Schubert's Letters & Other Writings. Deutsch, Otto E., ed. Savile, Venetia, tr. LC 76-109840. (Illus.). xx, 143p. Repr. of 1928 ed. lib. bdg. 15.00x (ISBN 0-8371-4331-4, SCLE). Greenwood.
Schumann, Clara. Clara Schumann: An Artist's Life from Diaries & Letters, 2 vols. Litzmann, Berthold, ed. Hadow, Grace E., tr. LC 70-163793. 1972. Repr. of 1913 ed. 50.00x set (ISBN 0-8443-0115-9). Vienna Hse.
Schumann, Clara J. A Passionate Friendship: Clara Schumann & Brahms. Alley, Margureite & Alley, Jean, eds. LC 79-181252. 214p. 1956. Repr. 19.00 (ISBN 0-403-01676-2). Scholarly.
Searle, Humphrey, ed. Hector Berlioz: A Selection from His Letters. LC 73-87555. (Composers' Letters Ser.: No. 8). (Illus.). 1973. pap. 10.00x (ISBN 0-8443-0114-0). Vienna Hse.
Selden-Goth, G., ed. Felix Mendelssohn: Letters. LC 73-86922. (Composers' Letters Ser.: No. 2). (Illus.). 400p. 1973. pap. 10.00x (ISBN 0-8443-0108-6). Vienna Hse.
Shaliapin, Fedor I. Man & Mask: Forty Years in the Life of a Singer. Megroz, Phyllis, tr. from Fr. LC 70-109841. (Illus.). xxvi, 358p. Repr. of 1932 ed. lib. bdg. 17.25x (ISBN 0-8371-4332-2, SHMM). Greenwood.
--Man & Mask: Forty Years in the Life of a Singer. LC 73-181256. 358p. 1932. Repr. 16.00 (ISBN 0-403-01679-7). Scholarly.
Shapiro, Nat & Hentoff, N. Hear Me Talkin to Ya. 10.00 (ISBN 0-8446-2928-6). Peter Smith.
Shaw, Artie. The Trouble with Cinderella. (Paperback Ser.). 1979. pap. 6.95 (ISBN 0-306-80091-8). Da Capo.
Smart, George. Leaves from the Journals of Sir George Smart. Cox, Bertram & Cox, C. L., eds. LC 72-154696. (Music Ser). 1971. Repr. of 1907 ed. lib. bdg. 37.50 (ISBN 0-306-70164-2). Da Capo.
Smith, Willie & Hoefer, George. Music on My Mind: The Memoirs of an American Pianist. LC 78-17246. (Da Capo Paperback Ser.). 1978. pap. 6.95 (ISBN 0-306-80087-X). Da Capo.
--Music on My Mind: The Memoirs of an American Pianist. LC 74-23406. (Roots of Jazz Ser). xvi, 318p. 1975. Repr. of 1964 ed. lib. bdg. 25.00 (ISBN 0-306-70684-9). Da Capo.
Soderstrom, Elisabeth. In My Own Key. (Illus.). 102p. 1980. 16.95 (ISBN 0-241-10318-5, Pub. by Hamish Hamilton England). David & Charles.
Spaeth, Sigmund. Fifty Years with Music. LC 77-13488. 1977. Repr. of 1959 ed. lib. bdg. 22.25x (ISBN 0-8371-9862-3, SPFY). Greenwood.
Spark, William. Musical Memories. 1976. lib. bdg. 19.00 (ISBN 0-403-03759-X). Scholarly.
Spaulding, Albert. Rise to Follow: An Autobiography. LC 74-181267. 328p. 1943. Repr. 25.00 (ISBN 0-403-01755-6). Scholarly.
Spohr, Louis. Autobiography, 2 vols. LC 69-12693. (Music Ser). (Ger). 1969. Repr. of 1878 ed. lib. bdg. 39.50 (ISBN 0-306-71222-9). Da Capo.
Stagno Bellincioni, Bianca & Bellincioni, Gemma. Roberto Stagno E Gemma Bellincioni Intimi, 2 vols. in 1. Farkas, Andrew, ed. LC 76-29969. (Opera Biographies). (Illus., It.). 1977. Repr. of 1920 ed. lib. bdg. 22.00x (ISBN 0-405-09708-5). Arno.
Strauss, Richard. Recollections & Reflections. Schuh, Willi, ed. Lawrence, L. J., tr. LC 74-72. (Illus.). 173p. 1974. Repr. of 1953 ed. lib. bdg. 15.00x (ISBN 0-8371-7366-3, STRF). Greenwood.
Sullivan, Tom & Gill, Derek. If You Could See What I Hear. (YA) (RL 9). 1976. pap. 1.95 (ISBN 0-451-09376-3, J9376, Sig). NAL.
Szigeti, Joseph. With Strings Attached: Reminiscences & Reflections. (Music Reprint Ser.). 1979. Repr. of 1947 ed. lib. bdg. 29.50 (ISBN 0-306-79567-1). Da Capo.
Thomas, Theodore. Theodore Thomas: A Musical Autobiography, 2 vols. LC 75-181278. 1905. Repr. 33.00 (ISBN 0-403-01701-7). Scholarly.
Tovey, Donald F. A Musician Talks, 2 vols. in 1. LC 73-181280. 1946. Repr. 41.00 (ISBN 0-403-01703-3). Scholarly.
Trapp, Maria A. Sound of Music: Story of the Trapp Family Singers. 1966. pap. 1.95 (ISBN 0-440-99032-7, LFL). Dell.
--Story of the Trapp Family Singers. (Illus.). (gr. 7-9). 1949. 10.00 (ISBN 0-397-00018-9). Lippincott.
Trapp, Maria Augusta. Story of the Trapp Family Singers. 1957. pap. 2.95 (ISBN 0-385-02896-2, D46, Im). Doubleday.
Upton, George P., ed. Theodore Thomas: A Musical Autobiography. 2nd ed. LC 64-18990. (Music Reprint Ser). 1964. Repr. of 1905 ed. lib. bdg. 35.00 (ISBN 0-306-70904-X). Da Capo.
Vaughan Williams, Ralph & Holst, Gustav. Heirs & Rebels: Letters Written to Each Other & Occasional Writings on Music. Vaughan Williams, Ursula & Holst, Imogen, eds. LC 80-12245. (Illus.). xiii, 111p. 1980. Repr. of 1959 ed. lib. bdg. 16.50x (ISBN 0-313-22384-X, VWHR). Greenwood.
Verdi, Guiseppe. Verdi: The Man in His Letters. LC 76-181289. 469p. 1942. Repr. 59.00 (ISBN 0-403-01712-2). Scholarly.
Von Buelow, Hans. Hans Von Buelow: The Early Correspondence. Von Buelow, Marie, ed. Bache, Constance, tr. LC 72-183503. 266p. 1972. Repr. of 1896 ed. 40.00x (ISBN 0-8443-0009-8). Vienna Hse.
--Letters of Hans Von Buelow. Eckart, Richard, ed. Waller, Hannah, tr. LC 72-183503. 434p. 1972. 45.00x (ISBN 0-8443-0051-9). Vienna Hse.
Von Dittersdorf, Karl D. Autobiography of Karl Von Dittersdorf. Coleridge, A. D., tr. LC 77-100655. (Music Ser). (Ger). 1970. Repr. of 1896 ed. lib. bdg. 22.50 (ISBN 0-306-71864-2). Da Capo.
Wagner, Richard. Family Letters of Richard Wagner. Ellis, W. Ashton, tr. LC 71-163796. 307p. 1972. Repr. of 1911 ed. 35.00x (ISBN 0-8443-0014-4). Vienna Hse.
--Letters of Richard Wagner to Mathilde Wesendonck. Ellis, W. Ashton, tr. LC 74-163794. 386p. 1972. Repr. of 1905 ed. 40.00x (ISBN 0-8443-0010-1). Vienna Hse.
--Letters of Richard Wagner to Minna Wagner, 2 vols. Ellis, W. Ashton, tr. LC 75-163797. 1972. Repr. of 1909 ed. Set. 50.00 (ISBN 0-685-32743-4). Vienna Hse.
--My Life, 2 vols. new ed. LC 78-181292. 911p. 1936. Repr. 59.00 (ISBN 0-403-01715-7). Scholarly.
--Richard Wagner: The Bayreuth Letters. Kerr, Caroline V., tr. LC 72-93825. 364p. 1972. Repr. of 1912 ed. 40.00x (ISBN 0-685-32742-6). Vienna Hse.
--Richard Wagner's Letters to His Dresden Friends. Shedlock, J. S., tr. LC 72-163800. 512p. 1972. Repr. of 1890 ed. 35.00x (ISBN 0-8443-0006-3). Vienna Hse.
Wagner, Richard & Liszt, Franz. Correspondence of Wagner & Liszt, 2 Vols. rev. ed. Ellis, W. Ashton, ed. Hueffer, Francis, tr. LC 68-25304. (Studies in Music, No. 42). 1968. Repr. of 1897 ed. lib. bdg. 64.95 (ISBN 0-8383-0316-1). Haskell.
Wallace, Grace, ed. Beethoven's Letters (1790-1826, 2 vols. in 1. Wallace, Grace, tr. from German. LC 76-22344. 1976. Repr. of 1867 ed. lib. bdg. 50.00 (ISBN 0-89341-022-5). Longwood Pr.
Webern, Anton. Letters to Hildegard Jone & Josef Humplik. Polnauer, Josef, ed. Cardew, Cornelius, tr. Orig. Title: Briefe an Hildegard Jone und Josef Humplik. 1967. pap. 5.00 (ISBN 3-7024-0031-1). Eur-Am Music.
Wechsberg, Joseph. Looking for a Bluebird. LC 73-16801. (Illus.). 210p. 1974. Repr. of 1945 ed. lib. bdg. 19.75x (ISBN 0-8371-7234-9, WELO). Greenwood.
Williams, Ralph V. & Holst, Gustav. Heirs & Rebels: Letters Between Ralph Vaughn Williams & Gustav Holst. Williams, Ursala V. & Holst, Gustav, eds. LC 73-86441. (Illus.). xii, 111p. 1974. Repr. of 1959 ed. lib. bdg. 9.00x (ISBN 0-8154-0487-5). Cooper Sq.
Willson, Meredith. And There I Stood with My Piccolo. LC 75-26870. 255p. 1976. Repr. of 1949 ed. lib. bdg. 14.75x (ISBN 0-8371-8486-X, WIMP). Greenwood.
Wood, Henry J. My Life of Music. facsimile ed. LC 72-157359. (Select Bibliographies Reprint Ser). Repr. of 1938 ed. 20.00 (ISBN 0-8369-5820-9). Arno.
Ysaye, Antoine & Ratcliffe, Betram. Ysaye: His Life, Work & Influence. LC 70-181298. 1947. Repr. 25.00 (ISBN 0-403-01723-8). Scholarly.
Zimmer, Norma. Norma. (Illus.). 1977. pap. 2.95 (ISBN 0-89066-001-8). World Wide Pubs.
--Norma. 1976. with cassette o.p. 8.95 (ISBN 0-685-80877-7); pap. 2.95 (ISBN 0-685-80878-5). Tyndale.

MUSICIANS–JUVENILE LITERATURE

see also Composers–Juvenile Literature

Barclay, Pamela. Charley Pride. LC 74-14659. (Rock'n Pop Stars Ser.). (Illus.). 32p. (gr. 4-12). 1974. PLB 5.95 (ISBN 0-87191-397-6); pap. 2.95 (ISBN 0-89812-108-6). Creative Ed.
Famous American Musicians. (Famous American Heroes & Leaders Ser.). 80p. (gr. 5-9). PLB 3.50 (ISBN 0-513-01166-8). Denison.
Hasegawa, Sam. Stevie Wonder. LC 74-147456. (Rock'n Pop Stars Ser.). (Illus.). 32p. (gr. 3-6). 1974. PLB 5.95 (ISBN 0-87191-395-X); pap. 2.95 (ISBN 0-89812-099-3). Creative Ed.
Jacobs, Linda. Cher: Simply Cher. LC 75-15552. (Women Behind the Bright Lights Ser.). (Illus.). 40p. (gr. 4 up). 1975. PLB 5.95 (ISBN 0-88436-186-1); pap. 3.50 (ISBN 0-88436-187-X). EMC.
--Elton John: Reginald Dwight & Company. LC 75-26990. (Men Behind the Bright Lights Ser.). (Illus.). 40p. (gr. 4 up). 1975. PLB 5.95 (ISBN 0-88436-213-2); pap. 3.50 (ISBN 0-88436-214-0). EMC.
--Jim Croce: The Feeling Lives on. LC 75-26984. (Men Behind the Bright Lights Ser.). (Illus.). 40p. (gr. 4 up). 1975. PLB 5.95 (ISBN 0-88436-215-9); pap. 3.50 (ISBN 0-88436-216-7). EMC.
--John Denver: A Natural High. LC 75-26649. (Men Behind the Bright Lights). (Illus.). 40p. (gr. 4 up). 1975. PLB 5.95 (ISBN 0-88436-211-6); pap. 3.50 (ISBN 0-88436-212-4). EMC.

--Olivia Newton John: Sunshine Supergirl. LC 75-15757. (Women Behind the Bright Lights). (Illus.). 40p. (gr. 4 up). 1975. PLB 5.95 (ISBN 0-88436-184-5); pap. 3.50 (ISBN 0-88436-185-3). EMC.
--Roberta Flack: Sound of Velvet Melting. LC 75-15627. (Women Behind the Bright Lights). (Illus.). 40p. (gr. 4 up). 1975. PLB 5.95 (ISBN 0-88436-188-8); pap. 3.50 (ISBN 0-88436-189-6). EMC.
Morse, Charles & Morse, Ann. Carly Simon. LC 74-14550. (Rock'n Pop Stars Ser.). 32p. (gr. 4-12). 1974. PLB 5.95 (ISBN 0-87191-393-3); pap. 2.95 (ISBN 0-89812-101-9). Creative Ed.
--John Denver. LC 74-14551. (Rock'n Pop Stars Ser.). (Illus.). 32p. (gr. 3-6). 1974. PLB 5.95 (ISBN 0-87191-392-5); pap. 2.95 (ISBN 0-89812-104-3). Creative Ed.
--Roberta Flack. LC 74-13938. (Rock'n Pop Stars Ser.). (Illus.). 32p. (gr. 3-6). 1974. PLB 5.95 (ISBN 0-87191-396-8); pap. 2.75 o. p. (ISBN 0-89812-105-1). Creative Ed.
Morse, Constance. Music & Music-Makers. facs. ed. LC 68-54363. (Essay Index Reprint Ser). 1926. 18.25 (ISBN 0-8369-0724-8). Arno.
Olsen, James T. Aretha Franklin. LC 74-14672. (Rock'n Pop Stars Ser.). (Illus.). 32p. (gr. 4-12). 1974. PLB 5.95 (ISBN 0-87191-390-9); pap. 2.75 o. p. (ISBN 0-89812-100-0). Creative Ed.
O'Regan, Susan K. Neil Diamond. (Rock 'n Pop Stars Ser.). (Illus.). (gr. 3-6). 1975. PLB 5.95 (ISBN 0-87191-464-6); pap. 2.95 (ISBN 0-89812-115-9). Creative Ed.
Paige, David. A Day in the Life of a Rock Musician. LC 78-68808. (Illus.). 32p. (gr. 4-8). 1980. PLB 6.89 (ISBN 0-89375-225-8); pap. 2.50 (ISBN 0-89375-229-0). Troll Assocs.
Taylor, Paula. Elvis Presley. LC 74-14546. (Rock'n Pop Stars Ser.). (Illus.). 32p. (gr. 3-6). 1974. PLB 5.95 (ISBN 0-87191-394-1); pap. 2.95 (ISBN 0-89812-103-5). Creative Ed.

MUSICIANS–POETRY
see Music–Poetry

MUSICIANS–PORTRAITS
Bellaigue, Camille. Portraits & Silhouettes of Musicians. Orr, Ellen, tr. LC 77-90807. 1978. Repr. of 1898 ed. lib. bdg. 35.00 (ISBN 0-89341-424-7). Longwood Pr.
Camner, James. The Great Instrumentalists in Historic Photographs: 275 Portraits from 1850 to 1950. (Illus.). 1980. pap. 6.95 (ISBN 0-486-23907-1). Dover.
Camner, James, ed. The Great Instrumentalists in Historic Photographs: 274 Portraits from 1850 to 1950. (Illus.). 15.00 (ISBN 0-8446-5741-7). Peter Smith.
Gordon, Max. Live at the Village Vanguard. 192p. 1980. 12.95 (ISBN 0-312-48879-3). St Martin.
Hedley, Arthur. Chopin. rev. ed. (The Master Musicians Ser). (Illus.). 224p. 1974. 11.00x (ISBN 0-460-03154-6, Pub. by J. M. Dent England). Biblio Dist.
Hentoff, Nat. Jazz Is. 1978. pap. 2.25 (ISBN 0-380-01858-6, 36558, Discus). Avon.
Jefferson, Alan. Delius. (Master Musicians Ser). (Illus.). 189p. 1972. 7.95x (ISBN 0-460-03131-7, Pub. by J. M. Dent England). Biblio Dist.
Lang, Paul H. & Bettmann, Otto L. Pictorial History of Music. (Illus.). (gr. 9 up). 1960. 19.95 (ISBN 0-393-02107-6). Norton.
McCartney, Linda. Linda's Pictures. (Illus.). 1976. 25.00 (ISBN 0-394-49959-X). Knopf.
Parrott, Ian. Elgar. (Master Musicians Ser). (Illus.). 154p. 1977. Repr. of 1971 ed. 11.00x (ISBN 0-460-03109-0, Pub. by J. M. Dent England). Biblio Dist.
Polonsky, Bruce. Hearing Music. (Illus.). 96p. (Orig.). 1981. pap. 14.95 (ISBN 0-9606112-0-7). Private Bks.
Robertson, Alec. Dvorak. rev. ed. (Master Musicians Ser). (Illus.). 243p. 1969. Repr. of 1964 ed. 11.00x (ISBN 0-460-03116-3, Pub. by J. M. Dent England). Biblio Dist.
Rosenberg, Bernard & Rosenberg, Deena. The Music Makers. 1979. 17.50x (ISBN 0-231-03953-0). Columbia U Pr.
Simon, George T. The Best of the Music Makers. LC 78-22358. (Illus.). 1979. 17.50 (ISBN 0-385-14380-X). Doubleday.
Walley, David. No Commercial Potential: The Saga of Frank Zappa Then & Now. (Illus.). 192p. 1980. pap. 6.95 (ISBN 0-525-93153-8). Dutton.
Wilmer, Valerie. The Face of Black Music. LC 76-18115. (Photography Ser.). 1976. lib. bdg. 18.50 (ISBN 0-306-70756-X); pap. 7.95 (ISBN 0-306-80039-X). Da Capo.

MUSICIANS–SALARIES, PENSIONS, ETC.
see also Music–Economic Aspects
Beverly Hills Bar Association Barristers Committee for the Arts. The Musician's Manual: A Practical Career Guide. Halloran, Mark, ed. 288p. 1981. 17.95 (ISBN 0-8015-5204-4, Hawthorn, Hawthorn). Dutton.

MUSICIANS, AFRO-AMERICAN
see Afro-American Musicians

MUSICIANS, STREET
see Street Music and Musicians

MUSICIANS, WOMEN
see Women Musicians

MUSICIANS AS AUTHORS
Chase, Gilbert, ed. American Composer Speaks: A Historical Anthology, 1770-1965. LC 66-11661. 1966. 22.50x (ISBN 0-8071-0347-0). La State U Pr.
Grew, Eva & Grew, Sydney. Bach. (Master Musicians Ser.). (Illus.). 230p. 1977. Repr. of 1947 ed. 11.00x (ISBN 0-460-02113-3, Pub. by J. M. Dent England). Biblio Dist.
Morgenstern, Sam. Composers in Music: From Palestrina to Copland. LC 55-10283. 1975. pap. 5.95 (ISBN 0-394-73040-2). Pantheon.
Morgenstern, Sam, ed. Composers on Music: An Anthology of Composers Writings from Palestrino to Copland. Repr. of 1956 ed. lib. bdg. 24.50x (ISBN 0-8371-1147-1, MOCO). Greenwood.

MUSICIANS IN LITERATURE
see also Music and Literature

MUSICO-CALLISTHENICS
Evans, Ruth & Battis, Emma. Childhood Rhythms. 1954. 4.50 (ISBN 0-910354-01-4). Chartwell.
Gray, Vera & Percival, Rachel. Music, Movement & Mime for Children. (Illus.). (gr. 1-6). 1962. 7.95x (ISBN 0-19-317102-3). Oxford U Pr.
Hood, Marguerite V. Learning Music Through Rhythm. LC 74-13151. (Illus.). xi, 180p. Repr. of 1949 ed. lib. bdg. 15.00 (ISBN 0-8371-5608-4, HOMT). Greenwood.
Stoll, Sharon K. Dance Aerobics Manual. LC 81-51637. (Health Ser.). 100p. (Orig.). 1981. pap. text ed. 5.95 (ISBN 0-89301-081-2). U Pr of Idaho.

MUSICOLOGY
see also Ethnomusicology; Music–Editing; Musical Criticism
Allen, W. D. Philosophies of Music History: A Study of General Histories of Music, 1600-1960. 9.50 (ISBN 0-8446-1529-3). Peter Smith.
Allen, Warren D. Philosophies of Music History: A Study of General Histories of Music, 1600-1960. (Illus.). 1962. pap. 5.00 (ISBN 0-486-20282-8). Dover.
Block, Adrienne F. The Early French Parody Noel. Buelow, George, ed. (Studies in Musicology: No. 36). 430p. 1981. 39.95 (ISBN 0-8357-1123-4, Pub. by UMI Res Pr). Univ Microfilms.
Brook, Barry S., et al, eds. Perspectives in Musicology. 400p. 1975. pap. 5.95 (ISBN 0-393-00784-7, N784, Norton Lib). Norton.
Cardamone, Donna G. The Canzone Villanesca Alla Napolitana & Related Genres, 1537-1570, 2 vols. Buelow, George, ed. LC 81-4750. (Studies in Musicology: No. 45). 616p. 1981. Set. 75.00 (ISBN 0-8357-1184-6, Pub. by UMI Res Pr). Vol. 1 (ISBN 0-8357-1203-6). Vol. 2 (ISBN 0-8357-1204-4). Univ Microfilms.
Grubbs, John W., ed. Current Thought in Musicology. LC 75-29245. (Symposia in the Arts & the Humanities Ser.: No. 4). (Illus.). 329p. 1976. 20.00x (ISBN 0-292-71017-8). U of Tex Pr.
Harrison, Frank L. Musicology. LC 73-21288. (The Princeton Studies). (Illus.). 337p. 1974. Repr. of 1963 ed. lib. bdg. 23.00x (ISBN 0-8371-6144-4, HAMU). Greenwood.
Haydon, Glen. Introduction to Musicology; a Survey of the Fields, Systematic & Historical, of Musical Knowledge. LC 78-5427. xiii, 329p. 1978. Repr. of 1941 ed. lib. bdg. 25.25 (ISBN 0-313-20429-2, HAIM). Greenwood.
Holmes, William. La Statira by Pietro Ottobuni & Allesandro Scarlatti: The Textual Sources, with a Documentary Postscript. (The Pendragon Monographs in Musicology: No. 1). 120p. 1980. lib. bdg. 12.50x (ISBN 0-918728-18-5). Pendragon NY.
Irvine, Demar. Writing About Music: A Style Book for Reports & Theses. rev. enl. ed. LC 56-13245. (Illus.). 220p. 1968. pap. 7.95 (ISBN 0-295-78558-6). U of Wash Pr.
Kassler, Jamie C. The Science of Music in Britain, 1714-1830: A Catalogue of Writings, Lectures & Inventions, 2 vols. LC 76-52675. (Reference Library of the Humanities: Vol. 79). 1977. Set. lib. bdg. 115.00 (ISBN 0-8240-9894-3). Garland Pub.
Laske, Otto E. Music, Memory, & Thought: Explorations in Cognitive Musicology. LC 77-9207. 1977. pap. 21.50 (ISBN 0-8357-0265-0, SS-00037). Univ Microfilms.
Madsen, Clifford K. & Madsen, Charles H., Jr. Experimental Research in Music. (Illus.). pap. text ed. 5.95 (ISBN 0-89892-018-3). Contemp Pub Co of Raleigh.
Madsen, Clifford K. & Moore, Randall S. Experimental Research in Music - Workbook in Design & Statistical Tests. rev. ed. 7.50 (ISBN 0-89892-017-5). Contemp Pub Co of Raleigh.
Mitchell, William J. & Salzer, Felix, eds. Music Forum, 3 vols. LC 67-16204. 1967-73. Vol. 3. 22.50x (ISBN 0-231-03522-5); Vol. 4. 22.50x (ISBN 0-231-03153-X); Vol. 5. 22.50x (ISBN 0-231-03522-5). Columbia U Pr.
Moore, James H. Vespers at St. Mark's: Music of Alessandro Grandi, Giovanni Rovetta & Francesco Cavalli, 2 vols. Buelow, George, ed. (Studies in Musicology: No. 30). 1981. Set. 84.95 (ISBN 0-8357-1143-9, Pub. by UMI Res Pr); Vol. 1. (ISBN 0-8357-1144-7); Vol. 2. (ISBN 0-8357-1145-5). Univ Microfilms.
Pruett, James W., compiled by. Studies in Musicology: Essays in History, Style and Bibliography of Music in Memory of Glenn Haydon. LC 76-7574. (Illus.). 1976. Repr. of 1969 ed. lib. bdg. 18.50x (ISBN 0-8371-8883-0, PRSM). Greenwood.
Reese, Gustave & Snow, Robert J., eds. Essays in Musicology: In Honor of Dragan Plamenac on His 70th Birthday. LC 77-8220. (Music Reprint, 1978 Ser.). (Illus.). 1977. Repr. of 1969 ed. lib. bdg. 32.50 (ISBN 0-306-77408-9). Da Capo.
Schnoebelen, Anne. Padre Martini's Collection of Letters: In the Civico Museo Bibliografico Musicale in Bologna: an Annotated Index. (Reference Tools in Music Ser.: No. 2). 1979. lib. bdg. 60.00 (ISBN 0-918728-11-8). Pendragon NY.
Schumann, Robert. Dichterliebe. rev. ed. Komar, Arthur, ed. (Norton Critical Scores). (Illus.). 136p. 1971. pap. text ed. 5.95x (ISBN 0-393-09904-0). Norton.
Skei, A. Musicology & Other Delights. (Paperplay Ser.: Vol. 9). 8p. 1978. softcover 2.00 (ISBN 0-939044-15-3). Lingua Pr.
Smith, F. J. The Experiencing of Musical Sound Prelude to a Phenomenology of Music. (Monographs on Musicology: Vol. 1). 256p. 1979. 18.75 (ISBN 0-677-04430-5). Gordon.
Spiess, Lincoln B. Historical Musicology: A Reference Manual for Research in Music. LC 78-60147. (Musicological Studies: No. 4). xiii, 294p. 1980. Repr. of 1963 ed. lib. bdg. 35.00x (ISBN 0-313-20548-5, SPHM). Greenwood.
Watanabe, Ruth T. Introduction to Music Research. 1967. 15.95 (ISBN 0-13-489641-6). P-H.

MUSIL, ROBERT, 1880-1942
Appignanesi, Lisa. Femininity & the Creative Imagination: A Study of Henry James, Robert Musil & Marcel Proust. 1973. 12.95x (ISBN 0-8464-0407-9). Beekman Pubs.
Luft, David S. Robert Musil & the Crisis of European Culture, 1880-1942. LC 78-66008. 336p. 1980. 20.00x (ISBN 0-520-03852-5). U of Cal Pr.
Peters, Frederick G. Robert Musil, Master of the Hovering Life: A Study of the Major Fiction. LC 78-5158. 286p. 1978. 17.50x (ISBN 0-231-04476-3). Columbia U Pr.

MUSK OX
Matthiessen, Peter. Oomingmak: The Expedition to the Musk Ox Island in the Bering Sea. (Illus.). (gr. 6-9). 1967. 6.95 (ISBN 0-8038-5351-3). Hastings.
Rau, Margaret. Musk Oxen: Bearded Ones of the Arctic. LC 75-26538. (Illus.). 40p. (gr. 3-7). 1976. PLB 8.79 (ISBN 0-690-01040-0, TYC-J). Har-Row.
Reynolds, S. H. Pleistocene Ovibos. Repr. of 1934 ed. pap. 8.00 (ISBN 0-384-50430-2). Johnson Repr.

MUSKELLUNGE FISHING
Schara, Ron. Muskie Mania. (Illus.). 1977. 7.95 (ISBN 0-8092-7997-5). Contemp Bks.
--Muskie Mania. LC 77-91230. 1978. pap. 4.95 (ISBN 0-8092-7525-2). Contemp Bks.

MUSKRATS
Dailey, E. J. Practical Muskrat Raising. (Illus.). 136p. pap. 3.00 (ISBN 0-936622-17-2). A R Harding Pub.
Errington, Paul L. Muskrats & Marsh Management. LC 77-14177. (Illus.). x, 183p. 1978. 13.50x (ISBN 0-8032-0975-4); pap. 3.25 (ISBN 0-8032-5892-5, BB 664, Bison). U. of Nebr Pr.

MUSLIM ARCHITECTURE
see Architecture, Islamic

MUSLIM ART
see Art, Islamic

MUSLIM CALENDAR
see Calendar, Islamic

MUSLIM CITIES AND TOWNS
see Cities and Towns, Islamic

MUSLIM CIVILIZATION
see Civilization, Islamic

MUSLIM COINS
see Coins, Islamic

MUSLIM CONVERTS TO CHRISTIANITY
see Converts From Islam

MUSLIM COUNTRIES
see Islamic Countries

MUSLIM DECORATION AND ORNAMENT
see Decoration and Ornament, Islamic

MUSLIM EMPIRE
see Islamic Empire

MUSLIM ETHICS
see Islamic Ethics

MUSLIM LEARNING AND SCHOLARSHIP
see Islamic Learning and Scholarship

MUSLIM LEGENDS
see Legends, Islamic

MUSLIM LITERATURE
see Islamic Literature

MUSLIM MYSTICISM
see Mysticism–Islam

MUSLIM PAINTING
see Painting, Islamic

MUSLIM PHILOSOPHY
see Philosophy, Islamic

MUSLIM POTTERY
see Pottery, Islamic

MUSLIM SECTS
see Islamic Sects

MUSLIM SOCIOLOGY
see Sociology, Islamic

MUSLIM TEXTILE FABRICS
see Textile Fabrics, Islamic

MUSLIM THEOLOGY
see Islamic Theology

MUSLIM WOMEN
see Women, Muslim

MUSLIMISM
see Islam

MUSLIMS
see also Islamic Learning and Scholarship; Missions to Muslims
Ahmad Ibn Yahya, Al-Baladuri. Origins of the Islamic State, 2 vols. Incl. Vol. 1. Hitti, Philip K., tr. Repr. of 1916 ed (ISBN 0-404-51694-7); Vol. 2. Murgotten, Francis C., tr. Repr. of 1924 ed (ISBN 0-404-51695-5). LC 76-82247. (Columbia University Studies in the Social Sciences: No. 163 & No. 163a). Set. 49.50 (ISBN 0-404-51163-5). AMS Pr.
Austin, Allan D. African Muslims in the New World: A Sourcebook for Cultural Historians. 1981. lib. bdg. 40.00 (ISBN 0-8240-9317-8). Garland Pub.
Azzam, Salem, frwd. by. The Muslim World & the Future Economic Order. 383p. 1980. 29.95x (ISBN 0-906041-10-4, Pub. by Islamic Council of Europe England); pap. 14.95x (ISBN 0-906041-09-0). Intl Schol Bk Serv.
Bennigsen, Alexandre A. & Wimbush, S. Enders. Muslim National Communism in the Soviet Union: A Revolutionary Strategy for the Colonial World. LC 78-8608. (Publications of the Center for Middle Eastern Studies Ser.: No. 11). 1979. lib. bdg. 20.00x (ISBN 0-226-04235-9). U. of Chicago Pr.
Brown, Marguerite. Magnificent Muslims. 1981. 6.00 (ISBN 0-911026-10-X). New World Press NY.
Dayton, Edward & Wagner, C. Peter. Unreached Peoples '80. LC 79-57522. 1980. pap. 6.95 (ISBN 0-89191-837-X). Cook.
DeLamotte, Roy C. Jalaluddin Rumi: Songbird of Sufism. LC 80-5884. 187p. 1980. lib. bdg. 16.75 (ISBN 0-8191-1286-0); pap. text ed. 8.75 (ISBN 0-8191-1287-9). U Pr of Amer.
Diara, Agadem L. Islam & Pan-Africanism. LC 72-91318. (Illus.). 120p. 1973. pap. 2.50 (ISBN 0-913358-04-5). Shabazz Pr.
Donia, Robert J. Islam Under the Double Eagle: The Muslims of Bosnia & Hercegovina, 1878-1914. (East European Monographs: No. 78). 256p. 1981. 17.50x (ISBN 0-914710-72-9). East Eur Quarterly.
Goldziher, Ignac. Muslim Studies, 2 vols. Stern, S. M., ed. & tr. Incl. Vol. 1. Muhammedanische Studien. LC 67-20745. 1967. 19.00 (ISBN 0-87395-234-0); Vol. 2. Hadith: The 'Traditions', Ascribed to Muhammed. LC 72-11731. 1972. 27.00 (ISBN 0-87395-235-9). State U NY Pr.
Hayes, K. H. A. Stories of Great Muslims. 3.95 (ISBN 0-686-18389-4). Kazi Pubns.
Irving, J. B. Had You Been Born a Muslim. pap. 1.00 (ISBN 0-686-18471-8). Kazi Pubns.
Jeffery, Patricia. Migrants and Refugees. LC 75-25428. (Illus.). 200p. 1976. 19.95 (ISBN 0-521-21070-4). Cambridge U Pr.
Kabir, Humayun. Muslim Politics, Nineteen Six to Nineteen Forty-Seven. 1969. 5.50x (ISBN 0-8426-1328-5). Verry.
Khan, Gazanfar A. & Sparroy, Wilfred. With the Pilgrims to Mecca: The Great Pilgrimage of A.H. 1319, A.D. 1902. LC 77-876447. Repr. of 1905 ed. 24.50 (ISBN 0-404-16417-X). AMS Pr.
Khan, M. Z. & Saleem, M. Umar the-Great (Al-Farqu, 2 vols. 1970. Vol. 1. 8.50x (ISBN 0-87902-171-3); 8.50x (ISBN 0-685-33011-7). Orientalia.
Kohn, Hans. Nationalism & Imperialism in the Hither East. 1932. 25.00 (ISBN 0-86527-139-9). Fertig.
Kyani, A. S. Islam & Muslims in Red Regimes. pap. 3.50 (ISBN 0-686-18575-7). Kazi Pubns.
Lockwood, William G. European Moslems: Economy & Ethnicity in Western Bosnia. (Studies in Anthropology Ser.). 1975. 35.00 (ISBN 0-12-454650-1). Acad Pr.
Massey, Kundan. Tide of the Supernatural: A Call to Love for the Muslim World. Baker, Barbara, ed. 184p. (Orig.). 1980. pap. 4.95 (ISBN 0-918956-70-6). Campus Crusade.

Nadawi, Abul H. Madha Khasira al-Alam bi-Inhtat al-Muslimin. 4th ed. 432p. (Orig., Arabic.). 1978. pap. 8.50x (ISBN 0-939830-14-0, Pub. by IIFSO Kuwait). New Era Pubns MI.
North Africa Mission. Reaching Muslims Today. 1978. pap. 1.50 (ISBN 0-87552-347-1). Presby & Reformed.
Qazi, M. A. What's in a Muslim Name? pap. 3.00 (ISBN 0-686-18582-X). Kazi Pubns.
Sardar, Ziauddin & Badawi, M. Zaki, eds. Hajj Studies, Vol. 1. (Illus.). 168p. 1978. 22.00x (ISBN 0-85664-681-4, Pub. by Croom Helm Ltd England). Biblio Dist.
Siddiqui, A. H. Muslim Generals. pap. 3.50 (ISBN 0-686-18314-2). Kazi Pubns.
Wilson, S. G. Modern Movements Among Moslems. LC 74-83190. (Islam & Mideast Ser.). 1976. Repr. of 1916 ed. 21.00 (ISBN 0-8420-1753-4). Scholarly Res Inc.
--Modern Movements Among Moslems. 1977. lib. bdg. 59.95 (ISBN 0-8490-2270-3). Gordon Pr.
Zenkovsky, Serge A. Pan-Turkism & Islam in Russia. LC 60-5399. (Russian Research Center Studies: No. 36). 1960. 17.50x (ISBN 0-674-65350-5). Harvard U Pr.

MUSLIMS-WOMEN
see Women, Muslim

MUSLIMS IN AFRICA
Gbadamosi, T. G. The Growth of Islam Among the Yoruba: 1841-1908. (Ibadan History Ser.). (Illus.). 1978. text ed. 23.00x (ISBN 0-391-00834-X). Humanities.
Klein, Martin A. Islam & Imperialism in Senegal: Sine-Saloum, 1847-1914. 1968. 15.00x (ISBN 0-8047-0621-2). Stanford U Pr.
Trimingham, John S. Islam in West Africa. 1959. 29.95x (ISBN 0-19-826511-5). Oxford U Pr.

MUSLIMS IN ASIA
Ahmed, Rafiuddin. The Bengal Muslims, Eighteen Seventy-One to Nineteen Hundred & Six: A Quest for Identity. (Illus.). 320p. 1981. 21.00x (ISBN 0-19-561260-4). Oxford U Pr.
Benningsen, Alexandre A. & Wimbush, S. Enders. Muslim National Communism in the Soviet Union: A Revolutionary Strategy for the Colonial World. LC 78-8608. xxii, 268p. 1980. pap. 7.95 (ISBN 0-226-04236-7, P915, Phoen). U of Chicago Pr.
Gowing, Peter G. Muslim Filipinos: Heritage & Horizon. (Illus.). 1979. pap. 12.25x (ISBN 0-686-25217-9, Pub. by New Day Pub). Cellar.
Long, David E. The Hajj Today: A Survey of the Contemporary Pilgrimage to Makkah. (Illus.). 1979. 19.00 (ISBN 0-87395-382-7). State U NY Pr.
Rywkin, Michael. Moscow's Muslim Challenge: Soviet Central Asia. (Illus.). 228p. 1981. 20.00 (ISBN 0-87332-196-0); pap. 6.95 (ISBN 0-87332-203-7). M E Sharpe.
Yegar, Moshe. Muslims of Burma: A Study of a Minority Group. 1972. 27.50x (ISBN 3-447-01357-5). Intl Pubns Serv.

MUSLIMS IN CHINA
Chu, Wen-Djang. Moslem Rebellion in Northwest China, 1862-1878. (Central Asiatic Studies: No. 5). 1966. pap. text ed. 48.75x (ISBN 90-2790-017-5). Mouton.
Israeli, Raphael. Muslims in China: A Study in Cultural Confrontation. (Scandinavian Institute of Asian Studies: No. 29). 272p. 1981. pap. text ed. 14.50x (ISBN 0-391-00718-1, Pub. by Curzon Pr England). Humanities.
--Muslims in China: A Study in Cultural Confrontation. (Scandinavian Institute of Asian Studies Monographs: No. 29). 224p. 1979. pap. text ed. 10.00x (ISBN 0-391-00718-1). Humanities.

MUSLIMS IN INDIA
Ahmad, Imtiaz. Muslim Political Behaviour: A Study of the Muslim Stratagem in Indian Electoral Politics. 1982. 14.00x (ISBN 0-88386-756-7). South Asia Bks.
Ahmad, Imtiaz, ed. Family, Kinship, & Marriage Among the Muslims. LC 77-74484. 1977. 17.50x (ISBN 0-88386-757-5). South Asia Bks.
--Modernization & Social Change Among Muslims in India. 1982. 17.50x (ISBN 0-88386-892-X). South Asia Bks.
--Religion & Rituals Among Muslims in India. 1982. 14.00x (ISBN 0-685-74912-6). South Asia Bks.
Ahmed, Sufia. Muslim Community in Bengal, 1884-1912. 1976. 16.00x (ISBN 0-19-576022-0). Oxford U Pr.
Aziz, Ahmad, ed. Muslim Self-Statement in India & Pakistan 1857-1968. 1970. 60.00x (ISBN 3-447-00072-4). Intl Pubns Serv.
Baig, M. R. Muslim Dilemma in India. 1974. 7.50 (ISBN 0-7069-0311-0). Intl Bk Dist.
Broomfield, J. H. Elite Conflict in a Plural Society: Twentieth-Century Bengal. LC 68-13822. 1968. 21.50x (ISBN 0-520-00179-6). U of Cal Pr.
Datta, V. N. & Gleghorn, B. E., eds. A Nationalist Muslim & Indian Politics. LC 75-902114. 352p. 1974. 14.00 (ISBN 0-333-90023-5). South Asia Bks.
Hardy, P. Muslims of British India. LC 77-184772. (South Asian Studies: No. 13). (Illus.). 300p. 1973. 39.50 (ISBN 0-521-08488-1); pap. 11.50x (ISBN 0-521-09783-5). Cambridge U Pr.
Hardy, Peter. Partners in Freedom & True Muslims: The Political Thought of Some Muslim Scholars in British India, 1912-1947. LC 80-13115. (Scandinavian Institute of Asian Studies, Monograph Ser.: No. 5). 63p. 1980. Repr. of 1971 ed. lib. bdg. 15.00x (ISBN 0-313-22424-2, HAPN). Greenwood.
Iqbal, Afzal. The Life & Times of Mohamed Ali: An Analysis of the Hopes, Fears, & Aspirations of Muslim India from 1778-1931. LC 75-930033. 1974. 12.50x (ISBN 0-88386-630-7). South Asia Bks.
Jain, N. K., ed. Muslims in India: A Biographical Dictionary, 1857-1976. 1980. 38.00x (ISBN 0-88386-886-5). South Asia Bks.
Karandikar, Maheshwar A. Islam in India's Transition to Modernity. 1972. lib. bdg. 16.00 (ISBN 0-8371-2337-2, KAI/). Greenwood.
Kaura, Uma. Muslims & Indian Nationalism, 1828-40. LC 77-74487. 1977. 11.50x (ISBN 0-88386-888-1). South Asia Bks.
Lal, K. S. Growth of Muslim Population in Medieval India (A.D. 1000-1800) (Illus.). 272p. 1973. 12.00x (ISBN 0-8002-1475-7). Intl Pubns Serv.
Lal, Kishori S. Growth of Muslim Population in Medieval India. LC 73-902800. vi, 272p. 1973. 12.00x (ISBN 0-88386-298-0). South Asia Bks.
Mathur, Y. B. Muslims & Changing India. 295p. 1973. text ed. 10.50x (ISBN 0-8426-0405-7). Verry.
Miller, Roland. Mapilla Muslims of Kerala: A Study of Islamic Trends. LC 76-901758. 1976. 14.00x (ISBN 0-88386-080-5). South Asia Bks.
Shakir, Moin. Secularization of Muslim Behavior. (Illus.). 129p. 1974. 7.50x (ISBN 0-8002-1961-9). Intl Pubns Serv.
Shibany, Roy. Status of Muslim Women in North India. 1979. 21.00x (ISBN 0-8364-0353-3). South Asia Bks.
Siddiqui, Nafis A. Population Geography of Muslims in India. 200p. 1976. text ed. 10.50x (ISBN 0-8426-0871-0). Verry.
Smith, Wilfred C. Modern Islam in India: A Social Analysis. rev. ed. LC 78-188163. (Illus., With bibliography from the 1943 ed.). 1972. Repr. of 1946 ed. 20.00 (ISBN 0-8462-1652-3). Russell.
--Modern Islam in India: A Social Analysis. LC 70-179243. Repr. of 1946 ed. 17.00 (ISBN 0-404-54869-5). AMS Pr.
Srinivasau, Nirmala. Identity Crisis of Muslims: Profiles of Lucknow Youth. 140p. 1981. text ed. 11.25x (ISBN 0-391-02279-2, Pub. by Concept India). Humanities.
Sri Ram Sharma. The Religious Policy of the Mughal Emperors. 3rd ed. 258p. 1973. lib. bdg. 8.95x (ISBN 0-210-33935-7). Asia.

MUSLIMS IN SPAIN
see Arabs in Spain

MUSLIMS IN THE UNITED STATES
Elkholy, Abdo A. The Arab Moslems in the United States. 1966. 5.00x (ISBN 0-8084-0052-5); pap. 1.95 (ISBN 0-8084-0053-3, B39). Coll & U Pr.
Richardson, E. Allen. Islamic Cultures in North America. 64p. (Orig.). 1981. pap. 3.95 (ISBN 0-8298-0449-8). Pilgrim NY.

MUSORGSKII, MODESTE PETROVICH, 1839-1881
Calvocoressi, M. D. Mussorgsky. rev. ed. Abraham, Gerald, ed. (Master Musicians Ser.: No. M141). (Illus.). 216p. 1974. pap. 7.95 (ISBN 0-8226-0718-2). Littlefield.
--Mussorgsky. rev. ed. (Master Musicians Ser). (Illus.). 1974. 7.95x (ISBN 0-460-03152-X, Pub. by J. M. Dent England). Biblio Dist.
Leyda, Jay & Bertensson, Sergei, eds. Mussorgsky Reader: A Life of Modeste Petrovich Mussorgsky in Letters & Documents. LC 70-87393. (Music Ser). (Illus.). 1970. Repr. of 1947 ed. lib. bdg. 32.50 (ISBN 0-306-71534-1). Da Capo.
Montagu-Nathan. Moussorgsky. LC 74-24157. Repr. of 1917 ed. 11.50 (ISBN 0-404-13050-X). AMS Pr.
Seroff, Victor I. Mighty Five. facs. ed. LC 77-126256. (Select Bibliographies Reprint Ser). 1948. 19.00 (ISBN 0-8369-5483-1). Arno.
Von Riesemann, Oskar. Moussorgsky. England, Paul, tr. LC 74-121278. Repr. of 1929 ed. 14.00 (ISBN 0-404-05334-3). AMS Pr.
--Moussorgsky. England, Paul, tr. from Ger. LC 71-100833. ix, 412p. Repr. of 1929 ed. lib. bdg. 18.00x (ISBN 0-8371-4007-2, RIMO). Greenwood.

MUSSELMEN
see Muslims

MUSSET, ALFRED DE, 1810-1857
Affron, Charles. Stage for Poets: Studies in the Theatre of Hugo & Musset. LC 75-153847. (Princeton Essays in Literature Ser.). 1972. 18.00 (ISBN 0-691-06201-3). Princeton U Pr.
Barine, Arvede. The Life of Alfred De Mussett. Hayden, Charles C., tr. 1978. Repr. of 1906 ed. lib. bdg. 30.00 (ISBN 0-8414-0277-9). Folcroft.
De Musset, Alfred. The Biography of Alfred De Musset. Preston, Harriet W., tr. 1877. lib. bdg. 20.00 (ISBN 0-8414-2464-0). Folcroft.
Haldane, Charlotte. Alfred: The Passionate Life of Alfred de Musset. 1978. Repr. of 1960 ed. lib. bdg. 30.00 (ISBN 0-8492-5207-5). R West.
Musset, Alfred de. Correspondance: 1827-1857. facsimile ed. 300p. Repr. of 1907 ed. 25.00 (ISBN 0-686-55545-7). French & Eur.
--Correspondance: 1827-1857. 293p. 1977. 50.00 (ISBN 0-686-55546-5). French & Eur.
Rees, Margaret A. Alfred de Musset. LC 73-120495. (World Authors Ser.). 1971. lib. bdg. 12.95x (ISBN 0-8057-2646-2). Irvington.
Sedgwick, Henry D. Alfred De Musset (1810-1857) 1978. Repr. of 1931 ed. lib. bdg. 30.00 (ISBN 0-8414-7890-2). Folcroft.
Sices, David. Theater of Solitude: The Drama of Alfred de Musset. LC 73-89268. (Illus.). 278p. 1974. text ed. 15.00x (ISBN 0-87451-083-X). U Pr of New Eng.
Tilley, Arthur A. Three French Dramatists: Racine, Marivaux, Musset. LC 66-27169. 1967. Repr. of 1933 ed. 8.50 (ISBN 0-8462-0964-0). Russell.

MUSSOLINI, BENITO, 1883-1945
Borghi, Armando. Mussolini: Red & Black. LC 73-20389. (Studies in Political Science, No. 94). 1974. lib. bdg. 32.95 (ISBN 0-8383-1765-0). Haskell.
Box, Pelham H. Three Master Builders, & Another: Studies in Modern Revolutionary & Liberal Statesmanship. facs. ed. LC 68-22904. (Essay Index Reprint Ser). 1925. 18.00 (ISBN 0-8369-0234-3). Arno.
Bradford, Gamaliel. Quick & the Dead. LC 70-85991. (Essay & General Literature Index Reprint Ser). 1969. Repr. of 1931 ed. 13.50 (ISBN 0-8046-0544-0). Kennikat.
Creighton, Warren S. The Contributions of Mussolini to the Civilization of Mankind. (Illus.). 137p. 1981. 51.55 (ISBN 0-89266-282-4). Am Classical Coll Pr.
Dabrowski, Roman. Mussolini, Twilight & Fall. LC 78-20460. 1980. Repr. of 1956 ed. 21.00 (ISBN 0-88355-839-4). Hyperion Conn.
De Fiori, Vittorio E. Mussolini, the Man of Destiny. Pei, Mario A., tr. LC 78-63673. (Studies in Fascism: Ideology & Practice). Repr. of 1928 ed. 23.50 (ISBN 0-404-16933-3). AMS Pr.
Diggins, John P. Mussolini & Fascism: The View from America. LC 78-153845. (Illus.). 1972. 22.00x (ISBN 0-691-04604-2); pap. 7.95 (ISBN 0-691-00581-8). Princeton U Pr.
Fermi, Laura. Mussolini. LC 61-17075. (Illus.). 1961. 20.00x (ISBN 0-226-24374-5). U of Chicago Pr.
--Mussolini. LC 61-17075. 1966. pap. 8.00x (ISBN 0-226-24375-3, P216, Phoen). U of Chicago Pr.
Fornari, Harry. Mussolini's Gadfly, Roberto Farinacci. LC 70-138986. (Illus.). 1971. 8.95 (ISBN 0-8265-1167-8). Vanderbilt U Pr.
Godden, G. M. Mussolini: The Birth of the New Democracy. 1979. lib. bdg. 69.95 (ISBN 0-685-96407-8). Revisionist Pr.
Godden, Gertrude M. Mussolini: The Birth of the New Democracy. 1977. lib. bdg. 59.95 (ISBN 0-8490-2309-2). Gordon Pr.
Gourlay, Jack. Monarch Notes on Mussolini's Biography. (Orig.). pap. 1.50 (ISBN 0-671-00895-1). Monarch Pr.
Gregor, A. James. Young Mussolini & the Intellectual Origins of Fascism. LC 78-64470. 1979. 20.00x (ISBN 0-520-03799-5). U of Cal Pr.
Kirkpatrick, Ivone. Mussolini, a Study in Power. LC 75-26215. (Illus.). 726p. 1976. Repr. of 1964 ed. lib. bdg. 40.25x (ISBN 0-8371-8400-2, KIMU). Greenwood.
Ludwig, Emil. Three Portraits: Hitler, Mussolini, Stalin. LC 78-63689. (Studies in Fascism: Ideology & Practice). Repr. of 1940 ed. 19.50 (ISBN 0-404-16905-8). AMS Pr.
Lussu, Emilio. Enter Mussolini: Observations & Adventures of an Anti-Fascist. Rawson, Marion, tr. from Ital. LC 78-63690. (Studies in Fascism: Ideology & Practice). Repr. of 1936 ed. 24.00 (ISBN 0-404-16952-X). AMS Pr.
Mussolini, Benito. Mussolini As Revealed in His Political Speeches: November 1914-August 1923. Quaranta Di San Severino, B., ed. LC 75-16288. xxviii, 375p. 1977. Repr. of 1923 ed. 27.50 (ISBN 0-86527-134-8). Fertig.
--Talks with Mussolini. Paul, Eden & Paul, Cedar, trs. LC 78-63699. (Studies in Fascism: Ideology & Practice). Repr. of 1933 ed. 16.00 (ISBN 0-404-16968-6). AMS Pr.
Paley, Alan L. Benito Mussolini, Fascist Dictator of Italy. new ed. Rahmus, D. Steve, ed. (Outstanding Personalities Ser.). 32p. 1975. lib. bdg. 2.95 incl. catalog cards (ISBN 0-686-11488-4); pap. 1.50 vinyl laminated covers (ISBN 0-686-11489-2). SamHar Pr.
Price, G. Ward. I Know These Dictators. LC 75-112817. 1970. Repr. of 1937 ed. 12.00 (ISBN 0-8046-1084-3). Kennikat.
Ray, John. Hitler & Mussolini. 1970. pap. text ed. 3.95x (ISBN 0-435-31755-5). Heinemann Ed.
Robertson, Esmonde M. Mussolini As Empire-Builder: Europe & Africa, 1932-36. LC 77-79016. (The Making of the 20th Century Ser.). 1978. 18.95x (ISBN 0-312-55589-X). St Martin.
Roy, P. Mussolini & the Cult of Italian Youth. 59.95 (ISBN 0-8490-0685-6). Gordon Pr.
Sarfatti, Margheritta. Life of Benito Mussolini. 59.95 (ISBN 0-8490-0527-2). Gordon Pr.
Skipper, G. C. Mussolini: A Dictator Dies. LC 80-25345. (World at War Ser.). (Illus.). 48p. (gr. 3-8). 1981. PLB 8.65 (ISBN 0-516-04790-6); pap. 2.95 (ISBN 0-516-44790-4). Childrens.
Smith, Denis M. Mussolini's Roman Empire. 1977. pap. 3.95 (ISBN 0-14-003849-3). Penguin.
Villari, Luigi. Italian Foreign Policy Under Mussolini. 1956. 7.95 (ISBN 0-8159-5820-X). Devin.

MUSSU
see Moso (Tribe)

MUSSULMANISM
see Islam

MUSTANG
Amaral, Anthony. Mustang: Life & Legends of Nevada's Wild Horses. LC 76-53821. (Lancehead Ser.). (Illus.). xiv, 156p. 1977. 9.00 (ISBN 0-87417-046-X). U of Nev Pr.
Dobie, J. Frank. The Mustangs. (Illus.). 1952. pap. 5.95 (ISBN 0-316-18798-4). Little.

MUSTANG-JUVENILE LITERATURE
Kreuger, Bob. The Wild Mustangs. (Illus.). (gr. 4-7). 1980. 6.95 (ISBN 0-679-21054-7). McKay.

MUSTANG (FIGHTER PLANES)
Feist, Uwe & Maloney, Edward T. North American P-51 Mustang. LC 67-21487. (Aero Ser.: Vol. 15). 1967. pap. 3.00 (ISBN 0-8168-0556-3). Aero.
Grinsell, Robert B. P 51 Mustang, Bk. 4. (Crown's World War II Fighter Planes Ser.). 1981. 15.95 (ISBN 0-517-54257-9). Crown.
Gruenhagen, Robert W. Mustang: Story of the P-Fifty-One Fighter. LC 75-30278. (Illus.). 1980. pap. 9.95 (ISBN 0-668-04884-0). Arco.
Hardy, M. J. The North American Mustang: Story of the Perfect Pursuit Plane, P 51. LC 77-17154. (Illus.). 1979. 11.95 (ISBN 0-668-04524-8). Arco.
Mikesh, Robert C. Excalibur III: Story of a P-51 Mustang. LC 78-606028. (Famous Aircraft of the National Air & Space Museum Ser.: No. 1). (Illus.). 76p. 1978. pap. 5.95 (ISBN 0-87474-635-3). Smithsonian.
Morgan, Len. The P-Fifty-One Mustang. LC 63-14945. (Famous Aircraft Ser.). (Illus.). 1979. pap. 4.95 (ISBN 0-8168-5647-8). Aero.
Rice, Michael S. Pilot's Manual for the F-82 Twin Mustang. (Illus.). 1976. pap. 5.95 (ISBN 0-87994-035-2). Aviation.
Shores, Christopher F. & Ward, Richard. North American Mustang Mk. 1-4. LC 73-88967. (Arco-Aircam Aviation Ser., No. 3). (Illus., Orig.). 1968. lib. bdg. 5.00 o. p. (ISBN 0-668-02098-9); pap. 2.95 (ISBN 0-668-02097-0). Arco.
Ward, Richard & McDowell, Ernest R. North American P-51BC Mustang. LC 71-93927. (Arco-Aircam Aviation Ser., No. 5). 1969. pap. 2.95 (ISBN 0-668-02101-2). Arco.

MUSTANG AUTOMOBILE
see Automobiles-Types-Mustang

MUSTERING OUT PAY
see Bounties, Military-United States

MUSU (ASIATIC TRIBE)
see Moso (Tribe)

MUTAGENESIS
Burnet, Macfarlane. Intrinsic Mutagenesis: A Genetic Approach to Aging. LC 74-6978. 236p. 1974. 42.50 (ISBN 0-471-12440-0, Pub. by Wiley Med). Wiley.
Butterworth, Byron E. Strategies for Short-Term Testing for Mutagens-Carcinogens. 1979. 49.95 (ISBN 0-8493-5661-X). CRC Pr.
De Serres, Frederick J. & Hollaender, A., eds. Chemical Mutagens: Principles & Methods for Their Detection, Vol. 6. (Illus.). 485p. 1980. 49.50 (ISBN 0-306-40364-1, Plenum Pr). Plenum Pub.
De Serres, Frederick J. & Hollaender, Alexander, eds. Chemical Mutagens: Principles & Methods for Their Detection, Vol. 7. 430p. 1981. text ed. 49.50 (ISBN 0-306-40771-X, Plenum Pr). Plenum Pub.
Drake, J. W. & Koch, R. E., eds. Mutagenesis. LC 75-43761. (Benchmark Papers in Genetics Ser: Vol. 4). 384p. 1976. 44.50 (ISBN 0-12-786375-3). Acad Pr.
Fishbein, L. Potential Industrial Carcinogens & Mutagens. (Studies in Environmental Science: Vol. 4). 1979. 73.25 (ISBN 0-444-41777-X). Elsevier.

Generoso, W. M., et al, eds. DNA Repair & Mutagenesis in Eukaryotes. (Basic Life Sciences Ser.: Vol. 15). 450p. 1980. 47.50 (ISBN 0-306-40552-0, Plenum Pr). Plenum Pub.
Hollaender, Alexander & De Serres, Frederick J., eds. Chemical Mutagens: Principles & Methods for Their Detection, 5 vols. Incl. Vol. 1. 310p. 1971. 27.50 (ISBN 0-306-37101-4); Vol. 2. 300p. 1971. 27.50 (ISBN 0-306-37102-2); Vol. 3. 304p. 1973. 27.50 (ISBN 0-306-37103-0); Vol. 4. 364p. 1976. 35.00 (ISBN 0-306-37104-9); Vol. 5. 348p. 1978. 27.50 (ISBN 0-306-37105-7). LC 73-128505. (Illus., Plenum Pr). Plenum Pub.
Hsie, Abraham W., et al, eds. Mammalian Cell Mutagenesis: The Maturation of Test Systems. LC 79-21186. (Banbury Report Ser.: No. 2). (Illus.). 504p. 1979. 45.00x (ISBN 0-87969-201-4). Cold Spring Harbor.
Kilbey, B. J., et al, eds. Handbook of Mutagenicity Test Procedures. 1977. 79.00 (ISBN 0-444-41338-3, North Holland). Elsevier.
Mehlman, Myron A., et al. Carcinogenesis & Mutagenesis. (Illus.). 388p. 1978. text ed. 23.00x (ISBN 0-930376-02-1). Pathotox Pubs.
Mutagens & Carcinogens. (Landmark Ser.). 1979. lib. bdg. 20.00x (ISBN 0-8422-4119-1). Arno.
Paget, G. E. Mutagenesis in Sub-Mammalian Systems. 231p. text ed. 29.50 (ISBN 0-8391-1367-6). Univ Park.
Prakash, Louise, et al, eds. Molecular & Environmental Aspects of Mutagenesis. (Illus.). 296p. 1975. 31.75 (ISBN 0-398-03137-1). C C Thomas.
Sutton, H. Eldon. Mutagenic Effects of Environmental Contaminants. (Environmental Science Ser.). 1972. 28.50 (ISBN 0-12-677950-3). Acad Pr.
Vinyl-Chloride Mutagenesis. (Landmark Ser.). 1979. 22.50x (ISBN 0-8422-4120-5). Irvington.
Vogel, F. & Roehrborn, G., eds. Chemical Mutagenesis in Mammals & Man: Proceedings. LC 79-121062. (Illus.). 1970. 80.00 (ISBN 0-387-05063-9). Springer-Verlag.
WHO Scientific Group. Geneva, 1971. Evaluation & Testing of Drugs for Mutagenicity; Principles & Problems: Report. (Technical Report Ser.: No. 482). (Also avail. in French & Spanish). 1971. pap. 1.20 (ISBN 92-4-120482-6). World Health.

MUTATION (BIOLOGY)
see also Chromosome Abnormalities; Evolution; Origin of Species; Variation (Biology)
Auerbach, Charlotte. Mutation Research: Problems, Results & Perspectives. LC 75-17592. 504p. 1976. text ed. 30.00x (ISBN 0-412-11280-9, Pub. by Chapman & Hall England). Methuen Inc.
Cold Spring Harbor Symposia on Quantitative Biology: Genes & Mutations, Vol. 16. LC 34-8174. (Illus.). 537p. 1952. 30.00 (ISBN 0-87969-015-1). Cold Spring Harbor.
Drake, John W. Molecular Basis of Mutation. LC 73-86859. (Illus.). 1970. text ed. 20.00x (ISBN 0-8162-2450-1). Holden-Day.
Hsie, Abraham W., et al, eds. Mammalian Cell Mutagenesis: The Maturation of Test Systems. LC 79-21186. (Banbury Report Ser.: No. 2). (Illus.). 504p. 1979. 45.00x (ISBN 0-87969-201-4). Cold Spring Harbor.
Induced Mutations Against Plant Diseases. (Proceedings Ser). (Illus.). 1978. pap. 61.75 (ISBN 92-0-010277-8, ISP462, IAEA). Unipub.
Induced Mutations & Plant Improvement. (Illus.). 554p. (Orig., Eng. & Span.). 1972. pap. 42.25 (ISBN 92-0-011072-X, ISP297, IAEA). Unipub.
Induced Mutations in Cross-Breeding. (STI-PUB-447). (Illus.). 1977. pap. 26.00 (ISBN 92-0-111676-4, ISP447, IAEA). Unipub.
Induced Mutations in Plants. (Illus., Orig., Eng., Fr. & Span.). 1969. pap. 48.75 (ISBN 92-0-010369-3, ISP231, IAEA). Unipub.
Manual on Mutation Breeding. 2nd ed. (Illus.). 1977. pap. 32.00 (ISBN 92-0-115077-6, IDC119, IAEA). Unipub.
Mutations in Plant Breeding. 1966. pap. 16.25 (ISBN 92-0-011066-5, IAEA). Unipub.
Mutations in Plant Breeding - 2. 1968. pap. 19.50 (ISBN 92-0-111368-4, IAEA). Unipub.
Ohno, S. Evolution by Gene Duplication. LC 78-112882. (Illus.). 1970. 23.60 (ISBN 0-387-05225-9). Springer-Verlag.
Rice Breeding with Induced Mutations. (Technical Reports: No. 86). 1968. pap. 11.75 (ISBN 92-0-115068-7, IDC86, IAEA). Unipub.
Sutton, H. Eldon. Mutagenic Effects of Environmental Contaminants. (Environmental Science Ser.). 1972. 28.50 (ISBN 0-12-677950-3). Acad Pr.
Walcher, Dwain N., et al, eds. Mutations: Biology & Society. Barnett, Henry L. & Kretchmer, Norman. LC 78-63411. (Illus.). 432p. 1978. 31.50x (ISBN 0-89352-020-9). Masson Pub.
Willis, John C. The Course of Evolution. LC 74-11016. 1974. 12.00 (ISBN 0-02-854860-4). Hafner.

MUTAZILITES
see Motazilites

MUTILATION
see also Tattooing
Albers, Michael D. The Terror. (Orig.). 1980. pap. 2.25 (ISBN 0-532-23311-5). Woodhill.
Haj, Fareed. Disability in Antiquity. LC 70-92087. 1970. 6.50 (ISBN 0-8022-2316-8). Philos Lib.
Ross, Robert R. & McKay, Hugh B. Self-Mutilation. (Illus.). 1979. 21.00 (ISBN 0-669-02116-4). Lexington Bks.
Summers, Ian & Kagan, Dan. Cattle Mutilations. 288p. (Orig.). 1981. pap. 2.95 (ISBN 0-686-69713-8). Bantam.

MUTINY
see also the names of particular Mutinies
Anthony, Irvin. Revolt at Sea: A Narration of Many Mutinies. Repr. of 1937 ed. 25.00 (ISBN 0-686-19878-6). Ridgeway Bks.
Barrow, Sir John. Mutiny of the Bounty. Kennedy, Gavin, ed. LC 80-66459. (Illus.). 208p. 1980. 19.95 (ISBN 0-87923-343-5). Godine.
Bligh, William. A Narrative of the Mutiny: From Tofoa, One of the Friendly Islands to Timor, a Dutch Settlement in the East Indies. 1976. Repr. of 1790 ed. 25.00 (ISBN 0-685-71284-2, Regency). Scholarly.
Fitchett, W. H. The Tale of the Great Mutiny. Repr. of 1909 ed. 25.00 (ISBN 0-686-19880-8). Ridgeway Bks.
Hadfield, Robert L. Mutiny at Sea. (Seafaring Men: Their Ships & Times Ser.). (Illus.). 1980. Repr. of 1938 ed. text ed. 22.50 (ISBN 0-930576-27-6). E M Coleman Ent.

MUTISM
Here are entered works on the inability to speak whether from any functional or physical cause other than deafness. Works on the lack of sense of hearing, including the lack combined with the inability to speak, i.e. deaf-mutism, are entered under Deafness.
Kratochwill, Thomas R. Selective Mutism: Implications for Research & Treatment. LC 80-18631. 208p. 1981. text ed. 19.95 (ISBN 0-89859-064-7). L Erlbaum Assocs.
Silverman, F. Communication for the Speechless. 1980. 18.95 (ISBN 0-13-153361-4). P-H.

MUTSUN LANGUAGE
Arroyo De La Cuesta, Felipe. Grammar of the Mutsun Language Spoken at the Mission of San Juan Bautista Alta California. LC 76-158278. (Library of American Linguistics: Vol. 4). Repr. of 1861 ed. 10.00 (ISBN 0-404-50984-3). AMS Pr.
--Vocabulary or Phrase Book of the Mutsun Language of Alta California. (Library of American Linguistics: Vol. 8). (Catalan.). Repr. of 1862 ed. 17.50 (ISBN 0-404-50988-6). AMS Pr.

MUTUAL BENEFIT ASSOCIATIONS
see Friendly Societies

MUTUAL DEFENSE ASSISTANCE PROGRAM
see Military Assistance, American

MUTUAL FUNDS
see Investment Trusts

MUTUAL HOUSING
see Housing, Cooperative

MUTUAL INSURANCE
see Insurance

MUTUAL LIFE INSURANCE COMPANY OF NEW YORK
Clough, Shepard B. Century of American Life Insurance: A History of the Mutual Life Insurance Company of New York, 1843-1943. LC 78-100150. Repr. of 1946 ed. lib. bdg. 17.25x (ISBN 0-8371-3713-6, CLAL). Greenwood.

MUTUAL SECURITY PROGRAMS, 1951-
see also Economic Assistance, American; Military Assistance, American; Technical Assistance, American
Swartz, Clarence L. What Is Mutualism. 69.95 (ISBN 0-8490-1286-4). Gordon Pr.

MY LAI (4), VIETNAM-MASSACRE, 1968
Goldstein, Joseph, et al. The My Lai Massacre & Its Cover-up: Beyond the Reach of Law? LC 75-38298. 1976. 14.95 (ISBN 0-02-912230-9); pap. 2.95 (ISBN 0-02-912240-6). Free Pr.
Kurland, Gerald. The My Lai Massacre. Rahmas, D. Steve, ed. (Events of Our Times Ser.: No. 3). 32p. 1973. lib. bdg. 2.95 incl. catalog cards (ISBN 0-87157-708-9); pap. 1.50 vinyl laminated covers (ISBN 0-87157-208-7). SamHar Pr.
Peers, W. R. The My Lai Inquiry. 1979. 14.95 (ISBN 0-393-01184-4). Norton.

MYASKOVSKY, NICKOLAI YAKOVLEVICH, 1881-
Ikonnikov, Aleksei A. Myaskovsky: His Life & Work. Repr. of 1946 ed. lib. bdg. 15.00x (ISBN 0-8371-2158-2, IKM). Greenwood.

MYASTHENIA GRAVIS
Dau, P. C. Plasmapheresis & the Immunobiology of Myasthenia Gravis. 371p. 1979. 50.00 (ISBN 0-471-09477-3, Pub. by Wiley Med). Wiley.
Dau, Peter C. Plasmapheresis & the Immunobiology of Myasthenia Gravis. (Illus.). 1979. 50.00 (ISBN 0-471-09477-3, Pub. by Wiley Med). Wiley.
Grob, David, ed. Myasthenia Gravis, Vol. 274. (Annals of the New York Academy of Sciences). 682p. 1976. 78.50x (ISBN 0-89072-053-3). NY Acad Sci.
Hermann, Christian, Jr., et al. Myasthenia Gravis. (Illus.). 220p. 1973. text ed. 29.50x (ISBN 0-8422-7074-4). Irvington.
Josephson, Emanuel. The Thymus Manganese, & Myasthenia Gravis. (Natural Health Ser.). 124p. 12.00 (ISBN 0-686-29293-6, Pub. by Chedney); pap. 6.00 (ISBN 0-686-29294-4). Alpine Ent.
Josephson, Emanuel M. The Thymus, Myasthenia Gravis & Manganese. 1979. write for info. (ISBN 0-685-96470-1). Revisionist Pr.
Kempton, Jean W. Living with Myasthenia Gravis: A Bright New Tomorrow. (Illus.). 112p. 1972. 9.75 (ISBN 0-398-02329-8). C C Thomas.
Kuhlman, Kathryn. How Big Is God? LC 74-12775. 96p. (Orig.). 1974. pap. 1.95 (ISBN 0-87123-222-7, 200222). Bethany Hse.

MYCENA
Smith, A. H. North American Species of Mycena. (Bibl. Myco.: Vol. 31). 1971. Repr. of 1947 ed. 60.00 (ISBN 3-7682-0699-8). Lubrecht & Cramer.

MYCENAE
Chadwick, John. Mycenae Tablets Three. (Transactions Ser.: Vol. 52, Pt. 7). (Illus.). 1963. pap. 1.50 (ISBN 0-87169-527-8). Am Philos.
Iakovidis, S. E. Mycenae-Epidaurus: Argos-Tiryns-Nauplion. (Illustrated Travel Guides Ser.). (Illus.). 1979. pap. 9.95 (ISBN 0-89241-102-3). Caratzas Bros.
International Colloquium For Mycenaean Studies - 3rd - Wingspread - 1961. Mycenaean Studies, Proceedings. Bennett, Emmett L., Jr., ed. (Illus.). 294p. 1964. 17.50x (ISBN 0-299-03180-2). U of Wis Pr.
Mylonas, G. Mycenae's Last Century of Greatness. 1968. pap. 4.00x (ISBN 0-424-05810-3, Pub. by Sydney U Pr). Intl Schol Bk Serv.
Mylonas, George E. Mycenae & the Mycenaean Age. 1966. 45.00 (ISBN 0-691-03523-7). Princeton U Pr.
Palmer, L. R. & Chadwick, J., eds. Proceedings. (Cambridge Colloquium on Mycenaen Studies). 42.00 (ISBN 0-521-07105-4). Cambridge U Pr.
Sargent, Michael. Mycenae. (Aspects of Greek Life). (Illus.). 1972. pap. text ed. 2.95x (ISBN 0-582-34401-8). Longman.
Schleimann, Henry. Mycenae: A Narrative of Researches & Discoveries at Myceneae & Tiryns. 1979. Repr. of 1878 ed. lib. bdg. 150.00 (ISBN 0-8495-4906-X). Arden Lib.
Schliemann, Heinrich. Mycenae. LC 66-29424. (Illus.). 1967. Repr. of 1880 ed. 28.00 (ISBN 0-405-08931-7, Pub. by Blom). Arno.
Schuchardt, C. Schliemann's Excavations: An Archaeological & Historical Study. LC 74-173145. (Illus.). Repr. of 1891 ed. 25.00 (ISBN 0-405-08938-4). Arno.
Schuchhardt, Carl. Schliemanns Excavations. Sellers, Eugenie, tr. LC 74-77893. (Illus.). 419p. 1975. 15.00 (ISBN 0-89005-034-1). Ares.

MYCENAEAN ART
see Art, Mycenaean

MYCENAEAN CIVILIZATION
see Civilization, Mycenaean

MYCENAEAN INSCRIPTIONS
see Inscriptions, Linear B

MYCENAEAN POTTERY
see Pottery, Greek

MYCETOZOA
see Myxomycetes

MYCOBACTERIUM
Chapman, John S. The Atypical Mycobacteria & Human Mycobacteriosis. LC 77-1824. (Topics in Infectious Diseases Ser.). (Illus.). 200p. 1977. 27.50 (ISBN 0-306-30997-1, Plenum Pr). Plenum Pub.
Juhasz, Stephen E. & Plummer, Gordon. Host-Virus Relationships in Mycobacterium, Nocardia & Actinomyces: Proceedings. (Illus.). 248p. 1970. photocopy ed. spiral 24.75 (ISBN 0-398-00953-8). C C Thomas.

MYCOGENETICS
see Fungi–Genetics

MYCOLOGY
see also Fungi; Medical Mycology
Ainsworth, G. C. Introduction to the History of Mycology. LC 75-21036. (Illus.). 350p. 1976. 47.50 (ISBN 0-521-21013-5). Cambridge U Pr.
Alexopoulos, Constantine J. & Mims, Charles W. Introductory Mycology. 3rd ed. LC 79-12514. 632p. 1979. text ed. 29.95 (ISBN 0-471-02214-4). Wiley.
Burnett, J. H. Fundamentals of Mycology. 688p. 1980. pap. text ed. 34.50 (ISBN 0-7131-2778-3). Univ Park.
--Fundamentals of Mycology. 2nd ed. LC 77-71624. 1977. 79.50x (ISBN 0-8448-1093-2). Crane-Russak Co.
Conant, Norman F., et al. Manual of Clinical Mycology. 3rd ed. LC 76-135321. (Illus.). 1971. 17.50 (ISBN 0-7216-2646-7). Saunders.
Deacon, J. W. Introduction to Modern Mycology. LC 80-11513. (Basic Microbiology Ser.: Vol. 7). 208p. 1980. pap. text ed. 19.95x (ISBN 0-470-26948-0). Halsted Pr.
Dennis, R. W. British Ascomycetes. rev. & enl. ed. (Illus.). 1979. 90.00 (ISBN 3-7682-0552-5, Pub. by J Cramer). Intl Schol Bk Serv.
Dennis, R. W. & Orton, P. D. New Check List of British Agarics & Boleti. (Bibliotheca Mycologica: Vol. 42). 1977. Repr. of 1960 ed. 16.00x (ISBN 3-7682-0935-0, Pub. by J. Cramer). Intl Schol Bk Serv.
Ehrenberg, C. G. Silvae Mycologicae Berolinensis. 1972. Repr. of 1818 ed. 22.50 (ISBN 90-6123-253-8). Lubrecht & Cramer.
Fuckel, K. Leopold. Symbolae Mycologicae. (Illus.). Repr. of 1877 ed. 77.00 (ISBN 0-384-17190-7). Johnson Repr.
Fuckel, L. Symbolae Mycologicae & Supplements. (Illus.). 1966. Repr. of 1877 ed. 100.00 (ISBN 3-7682-0358-1). Lubrecht & Cramer.
Gareth Jones, E. B. Recent Advances in Aquatic Mycology. LC 74-27179. 1976. 71.95 (ISBN 0-470-29176-1). Halsted Pr.
Hanlin, Richard T. & Ulloa, Miguel. Atlas of Introductory Mycology. LC 78-65422. (Illus.). 188p. 1979. pap. text ed. 9.95x (ISBN 0-89459-043-X). Hunter NC.
Hoehnel, F. Fragmente Zur Mykologie, 2vols. 1966. 150.00 (ISBN 3-7682-0467-7). Lubrecht & Cramer.
Karsten, P. A. Symbolae Ad Mycologiam Fennicam. 1966. Repr. of 1895 ed. 80.00 (ISBN 3-7682-0352-2). Lubrecht & Cramer.
Kohlmeyer, J. Index Alphabecticus Klotzschii & Rabenhorstii Herbarii Mycologici. 1962. pap. 20.00 (ISBN 3-7682-5404-6). Lubrecht & Cramer.
Kohlmeyer, Jan & Kohlmeyer, Ericka. Marine Mycology: The Higher Fungi. LC 79-14703. 1979. 65.00 (ISBN 0-12-418350-6). Acad Pr.
Krogh, P., ed. Control of Mycotoxins: Proceedings of a Symposium, Goteborg, Sweden, 1972. 116p. 1976. 23.00 (ISBN 0-08-020749-9). Pergamon.
Larone, Davise H. Medically Important Fungi: A Guide to Identification. (Illus.). 1976. pap. 13.75x (ISBN 0-06-141513-8, Harper Medical). Har-Row.
Laursen, Gary A. & Ammirati, Joseph F. Arctic & Alpine Mycology: The First International Symposium on Arcto-Alpine Mycology. LC 81-51281. 502p. 1981. 45.00 (ISBN 0-295-95856-1). U of Wash Pr.
Lemke, P. A. Viruses & Plasmids in Fungi. (Mycology Ser.: Vol. 1). 1979. 59.75 (ISBN 0-8247-6916-3). Dekker.
Mazzer, S. J. A Monographic Study of the Genus Pouzarella: A New Genus in the Rhodophyllaceae, Agaricales, Basidiomycetes. (Bibliotheca Mycologica: Vol. 46). (Illus.). 1976. pap. 17.50x (ISBN 3-7682-1054-5, Pub. by J. Cramer). Intl Schol Bk Serv.
Moore-Landecker, Elizabeth. Fundamentals of the Fungi. (Biological Ser). (Illus.). 1972. ref. ed. 24.95x (ISBN 0-13-339267-8). P-H.
Mycology Guidebook Committee, Mycological Society of America. Mycology Guidebook. rev. ed. Stevens, Russell B., ed. LC 73-17079. (Illus.). 728p. 1981. 35.00 (ISBN 0-295-95841-3). U of Wash Pr.
New York Botanical Garden. Mycologia Index: Volumes 1-58, 1909-1966. LC 57-51730. (Mycologia Ser). 1968. 20.00 (ISBN 0-89327-215-9). NY Botanical.
Persoon, Christiaan H. Observationes Mycologicae, Pt. 1. 1966. Repr. of 1796 ed. 8.00 (ISBN 0-384-45821-1). Johnson Repr.
Petersen, Ronald H. B & C: Mycological Association of M. J. Berkeley & M. A. Curtis. (Bibliotheca Mycologica: 72). (Illus.). 120p. 1980. pap. text ed. 15.00 (ISBN 3-7682-1258-0). Lubrecht & Cramer.
Ramsbottom, J. Fungi: An Introduction to Mycology. 1979. Repr. of 1929 ed. lib. bdg. 12.50 (ISBN 0-8495-4608-7). Arden Lib.
Rhodes, Martha E. Food Mycology. (Medical Bks.). 1979. lib. bdg. 28.00 (ISBN 0-8161-2136-2, Hall Medical). G K Hall.
Robinson, Peter M. Practical Fungal Physiology. LC 78-4243. 1978. pap. 13.25 (ISBN 0-471-99656-4, Pub. by Wiley-Interscience). Wiley.
Saccardo, P. A., ed. Michelia Commentarium Mycologicum: 1879-1882, 2vols. 1969. 126.00 (ISBN 90-6123-106-X). Lubrecht & Cramer.
Sharp, Robert F. Investigative Mycology. LC 79-670321. 1978. text ed. 19.95x (ISBN 0-435-60750-2); pap. text ed. 8.95x (ISBN 0-435-60751-0). Heinemann Ed.
Snell, Walter & Dick, Esther A. Glossary of Mycology. 2nd ed. LC 77-134946. 1971. 12.50x (ISBN 0-674-35451-6). Harvard U Pr.

Stevenson, J. An Account of Fungus Exiccati Containing Material from the Americas. 1971. 100.00 (ISBN 3-7682-5436-4). Lubrecht & Cramer.

Strathern, Jeffrey N., et al, eds. The Molecular Biology of the Yeast Saccharomyces, 2 bk. set. LC 81-68203. (Cold Spring Harbor Laboratory Monograph: Vol. 11 a & B). 1200p. 1981. 75.00 (ISBN 0-87969-139-5); price not set. Cold Spring Harbor.

Vanbreuseghem, R., et al. Practical Guide to Medical & Veterinary Mycology. LC 77-94829. (Illus.). 288p. 1978. text ed. 47.75x (ISBN 0-89352-018-7). Masson Pub.

MYCOPLASMATACEAE

Barile, M. F., et al, eds. The Mycoplasmas Vol. 2: Human & Animal Mycoplasmas. LC 78-20895. 1979. 48.00 (ISBN 0-12-078402-5). Acad Pr.

--The Mycoplasmas Vol. 3: Plant & Insect Mycoplasmas. 1979. 40.00 (ISBN 0-12-078403-3). Acad Pr.

Berile, M. F., et al, eds. The Mycoplasmas Vol. 1: Cell Biology. LC 78-20895. 1979. 50.00 (ISBN 0-12-078401-7). Acad Pr.

Ciba Foundation. Pathogenic Mycoplasmas. (Ciba Foundation Symposium: No. 6). 1972. 30.50 (ISBN 0-444-10383-X, Excerpta Medica). Elsevier.

Daniels, M. J. & Markham, P. G. Plant & Insect Mycoplasma Techniques. 384p. 1982. 49.95 (ISBN 0-470-27262-7). Halsted Pr.

Krudy, E. S & Shiers, D, eds. Mycoplasma: A Bibliography. 180p. 24.00 (ISBN 0-904147-06-1). Info Retrieval.

Madoff, Sarabelle. Mycoplasma & the L Forms of Bacteria. (Illus.). 116p. 1971. 24.75x (ISBN 0-677-14790-2). Gordon.

Sharp, John T. The Role of Mycoplasmas & Forms of Bacteria in Disease. (Illus.). 400p. 1970. photocopy ed. spiral 39.50 (ISBN 0-398-01733-6). C C Thomas.

Smith, Paul F. Biology of Mycoplasmas. (Cell Biology Ser). 1971. 42.00 (ISBN 0-12-652050-X). Acad Pr.

Sproessig, M. & Witzleb, M., eds. Mycloplasma Diseases of Man: Proceedings of an International Symposium, Reinhardsbrunn Castle, Oct. 1968. (Illus.). 1976. pap. 25.00 (ISBN 0-685-87209-2). Adler.

MYCOSIS

see also Fungi, Pathogenic

Annual Oholo Biological Conference, 21st, Israel, March 1976. Host-Parasite Relationships in Systemic Mycoses: Proceedings. Beemer, A. M., et al, eds. Incl. Methodology, Pathology & Immunology, Pt. I. (Contributions to Microbiology & Immunology: Vol. 3) (ISBN 3-8055-2443-9); Specific Diseases & Therapy, Pt. II. (Contributions to Microbiology & Immunology: Vol. 4) (ISBN 3-8055-2444-7). (Illus.). 1978. pap. 46.75 ea. S Karger.

Baker, Roger D., et al. Human Infection with Fungi, Actinomycetes & Algae. LC 72-160588. (Illus.). 1971. 230.60 (ISBN 0-387-05378-6). Springer-Verlag.

--Pathologic Anatomy of Mycoses. LC 25-11247. (Handbuch der Speziellen Pathologischen Anatomie: Vol. 3, Pt. 5). (Illus.). 1971. 318.60 (ISBN 0-387-05140-6). Springer-Verlag.

Chandler. Color Atlas & Textbook of the Histopathology of Mycotic Diseases. 1980. 79.50 (ISBN 0-8151-1637-3). Year Bk Med.

Dolan, C. Terrence, ed. Subcutaneous Mycoses. LC 80-720448. (Atlases of Clinical Mycology: 5). 1976. text & slides 78.00 (ISBN 0-89189-043-2, 15-7-009-00); microfiche ed. 22.00 (ISBN 0-89189-091-2, 17-7-009-00). Am Soc Clinical.

--Superficial Mycoses. LC 80-720449. (Atlases of Clinical Mycology: 4). 1975. text & slides 78.00 (ISBN 0-89189-042-4, 15-7-005-00); microfiche ed. 22.00 (ISBN 0-89189-090-4, 17-7-005-00). Am Soc Clinical.

--Systemic Mycoses: Deep Seated. LC 75-736235. (Atlases of Clinical Mycology: 2). (Illus.). 1975. text & slides 78.00 (ISBN 0-89189-040-8, 15-7-003-00); microfiche ed. 22.00 (ISBN 0-89189-088-2, 17-7-003-00). Am Soc Clinical.

--Systemic Mycoses: Opportunistic Pathogens. LC 75-736236. (Atlases of Clinical Mycology: 3). 1975. text & slides 78.00 (ISBN 0-89189-041-6, 15-7-004-00); microfiche ed. 22.00 (ISBN 0-89189-089-0, 17-7-004-00). Am Soc Clinical.

--Systemic Mycoses: Saprobic Fungi. LC 80-720450. (Atlases of Clinical Mycology: 6). (Illus.). 1976. text & slides 78.00 (ISBN 0-89189-044-0, 15-7-010-00); microfiche ed. 22.00 (ISBN 0-89189-092-0, 17-7-010-00). Am Soc Clinical.

--Systemic Mycoses: Yeasts. LC 75-736234. (Atlases of Clinical Mycology: 1). (Illus.). 1975. text & slides 78.00 (ISBN 0-89189-039-4, 15-7-002-00); microfiche ed. 22.00 (ISBN 0-89189-087-4, 17-7-002-00). Am Soc Clinical.

Palmer, Dan F., et al. Serodiagnosis of Mycotic Diseases. (Amer. Lec. Clinical Microbiology Ser.). (Illus.). 208p. 1978. 26.25 (ISBN 0-398-03592-X). C C Thomas.

Raab, W. The Treatment of Mycosis with Imidazole Derivatives. (Illus.). 180p. 1980. pap. 16.60 (ISBN 0-387-09800-3). Springer-Verlag.

Salfelder, Karlhanns. Atlas of Deep Mycoses. LC 79-67221. (Illus.). 140p. 1980. text ed. 47.50 (ISBN 0-7216-7898-X). Saunders.

Towse, G., ed. The Role of Intravenous Miconazole in the Treatment of Systemic Mycoses. (Royal Society of Medicine International Congress & Symposium Ser.: No. 45). 1981. write for info. (ISBN 0-8089-1399-9). Grune.

Wyllie, Thomas & Morehouse, Lawrence G., eds. Mycotoxic Fungi, Mycotoxins, Mycotoxicoses: An Encyclopedic Handbook, Vol. 1. 1977. 75.00 (ISBN 0-8247-6550-8). Dekker.

MYCOTOXINS

Board on Renewable Resources. Interactions of Mycotoxins in Animal Production. 1979. pap. 9.25 (ISBN 0-309-02876-0). Natl Acad Pr.

Christensen, Clyde M. Molds, Mushrooms, & Mycotoxins. LC 74-21808. (Illus.). 292p. 1975. 15.00x (ISBN 0-8166-0743-5). U of Minn Pr.

Cole, Richard J. & Cox, Richard H., eds. Handbook of Toxic Fungal Metabolites. 1981. 79.00 (ISBN 0-12-179760-0). Acad Pr.

Hayes, A. Wallace. Mycotoxin Teratogenicity & Mutagenicity. 160p. 1981. 59.95 (ISBN 0-8493-5651-2). CRC Pr.

Perspective on Mycotoxins. (FAO Food & Nutrition Paper Ser.: No. 13). 171p. 1980. pap. 11.25 (ISBN 92-5-100870-1, F1957, FAO). Unipub.

Purchase, I. F., ed. Mycotoxins. 443p. 1975. 108.00 (ISBN 0-444-41254-9, North Holland). Elsevier.

Rodricks, Joseph V., ed. Mycotoxins & Other Fungal Related Food Problems. LC 76-4547. (Advances in Chemistry Ser.: No. 149). 1976. 39.00 (ISBN 0-8412-0222-2). Am Chemical.

Shank, Ronald C. Mycotoxins & N-Nitroso Compounds: Enviornmental Risks, 2 vols. 1981. Vol. I, 272p. 74.95 (ISBN 0-8493-5307-6); Vol. II, 272 Pgs. 74.95 (ISBN 0-686-73488-2). CRC Pr.

Steyn, P. S., ed. The Biosynthesis of Mycotoxins: A Study in Secondary Metabolism. LC 80-12013. 1980. 44.00 (ISBN 0-12-670650-6). Acad Pr.

Uraguchi, Kenji & Yamazaki, Mikio, eds. Toxicology, Biochemistry & Pathology of Mycotoxins. LC 78-8992. 1978. 38.95 (ISBN 0-470-26423-3). Halsted Pr.

MYELIN

Diseases of Myelin. Defendini, Richard, ed. LC 78-720192. (Neuropathology Ser.: An Illustrated Course). 1978. 100.00 (ISBN 0-8036-2916-8). Davis Co.

Hashim, George, ed. Myelin: Chemistry & Biology. LC 80-22305. (Progress in Clinical & Biological Research: Vol. 49). 136p. 1980. 18.00 (ISBN 0-8451-0049-1). A R Liss.

Morell, Pierre, ed. Myelin. LC 76-30867. (Illus.). 531p. 1977. 45.00 (ISBN 0-306-30965-3, Plenum Pr). Plenum Pub.

MYELOGRAPHY

see Spine–Radiography

MYELOMA

Bunch, Wilton H., et al. Modern Management of Myelomeningocele. LC 75-161035. (Illus.). 320p. 1972. 22.50 (ISBN 0-87527-097-2). Green.

Kyle, Robert A. & Bayrd, Edwin A. The Monoclonal Gammopathies: Multiple Myeloma & Related Plasma-Cell Disorders. (Amer. Lec. Living Chemistry Ser.). (Illus.). 432p. 1976. 48.75 (ISBN 0-398-03545-8). C C Thomas.

Penn, Gerald M., ed. Identification of Myeloma Proteins. Davis, Ted. Davis, Ted, ed. LC 75-10803. (Illus.). 1975. pap. text ed. 17.00 perfect bdg. (ISBN 0-89189-027-0, 45-A-002-00). Am Soc Clinical.

MYELOMATOSIS

Snapper, Isidore & Kahn, Alvin. Myelomatosis: Fundamentals & Clinical Features. (Illus.). 1971. 24.50 (ISBN 0-8391-0588-6, Pub. by Karger). Univ Park.

MYERS, FREDERICK WILLIAM HENRY, 1843-1901

Gauld, Alan. The Founders of Psychical Research. LC 68-13562. 1968. 10.00x (ISBN 0-8052-3076-9). Schocken.

MYERSON, EMILE

Lalumia, Joseph. Ways of Reason: A Critical Study of the Ideas of Emile Myerson. 1966. text ed. 6.00x (ISBN 0-391-00663-0). Humanities.

MYNAHS

Bates, Henry & Busenbark, Robert. Guide to Mynahs. (Orig.). 2.95 (ISBN 0-87666-425-7, PS633). TFH Pubns.

Weil, Martin. Mynahs. (Illus.). 96p. 1981. 2.95 (ISBN 0-87666-890-2, KW-120). TFH Pubns.

MYODYNAMICS

see Muscles

MYOGLOBIN

Antonini, E. & Brunori, M. Hemoglobin & Myoglobin in Their Reactions with Ligands. (Frontiers of Biology Ser. Vol. 21). 1971. 85.50 (ISBN 0-444-10096-2, North-Holland). Elsevier.

Kagen, Lawrence J. Myoglobin: Biochemical, Physiological & Clinical Aspects. LC 73-5658. (Molecular Biology Ser.). 151p. 1973. text ed. 17.50x (ISBN 0-231-03421-0). Columbia U Pr.

MYOHEMOGLOBIN

see Myoglobin

MYOLOGY

see Muscles

MYONEURAL JUNCTION

see also Muscle; Nerves

Goldberg, Alan M. & Hanin, Israel, eds. Biology of Cholinergic Function. LC 74-14473. 730p. 1976. 48.00 (ISBN 0-911216-98-7). Raven.

Vrbova, G., et al. Nerve-Muscle Interaction. LC 78-13416. 233p. 1978. text ed. 43.00x (ISBN 0-412-15720-9, Pub. by Chapman & Hall England). Methuen Inc.

Zacks, Sumner I. The Motor Endplate. rev. ed. LC 73-84420. 508p. 1973. Repr. of 1964 ed. 27.50 (ISBN 0-88275-113-1). Krieger.

Zaimis, E., ed. Neuromuscular Junction. (Handbk of Experimental Pharmacology: Vol. 42). (Illus.). 500p. 1976. 152.60 (ISBN 0-387-07499-6). Springer-Verlag.

MYOPATHY

see Muscles–Diseases

MYOPIA

Josephson, Emanuel M. Nearsightedness Is Preventable. 1979. write for info. Revisionist Pr.

Rehm, Donald S. The Myopia Myth: The Truth About Nearsightedness & How to Prevent It. 1979. 12.50 (ISBN 0-8283-1731-3). Branden.

MYOTONIA

Adams, Raymond D. Diseases of Muscle: A Study in Pathology. 3rd ed. (Illus.). 1975. 52.00x (ISBN 0-06-140056-4, Harper Medical). Har-Row.

Caughey, J. E. & Myrianthopoulos, N. C. Dystrophia Myotonica & Related Disorders. (Illus.). 300p. 1963. ed. spiral bdg. 24.75photocopy (ISBN 0-398-00297-5). C C Thomas.

Mair, W. G. & Tome, F. M. Atlas of the Ultrastructure of Diseased Human Muscle. (Illus.). 1972. 20.75x (ISBN 0-443-00831-0). Churchill.

MYRIAPODA

see also Centipedes

Camatini, Marina, ed. Myriapod Biology. LC 79-41559. 1980. 76.50 (ISBN 0-12-155750-2). Acad Pr.

Morris, S. F. Catalogue of Type & Figured Fossil Crustacea (Exc. Ostracoda), Chelicerata & Myriapoda in the British Museum (Natural History) (Illus.). 56p. 1980. pap. 13.00x (ISBN 0-565-00828-5). Sabbot-Natural Hist Bks.

MYRIONEMA

Sauvageau, C. Sur Quelques Myrionemacees. 1897. Repr. 20.00 (ISBN 3-7682-0705-6). Lubrecht & Cramer.

MYRISTICACEAE

Landrum, Leslie R. Myrceugenia (Myrtaceae) (Flora Neotropica Monograph 29). (Illus.). 1981. pap. write for info. (ISBN 0-89327-236-1). NY Botanical.

MYSORE

Beals, Alan R. & Siegel, Bernard J. Divisiveness & Social Conflict: An Anthropological Approach. 1966. 12.50x (ISBN 0-8047-0302-7). Stanford U Pr.

Ramachandriah, N. S. Mysore. (India, Land & People Ser). (Illus.). 193p. 1973. text ed. 3.75x (ISBN 0-8426-0510-X). Verry.

MYSTERIES (DRAMATIC)

see Mysteries and Miracle-Plays

MYSTERIES, RELIGIOUS

see also Cultus; Eleusinian Mysteries; Fertility Cults; Mother-Goddesses; Oracles; Rites and Ceremonies

Allan, John. Mysteries. (Book of Beliefs). 1981. 12.95 (ISBN 0-89191-477-3, 54775). Cook.

Angus, S. The Mystery Religions & Christianity. 1977. lib. bdg. 59.95 (ISBN 0-8490-2314-9). Gordon Pr.

Angus, Samuel. Mystery Religions. 1967. 10.00 (ISBN 0-8216-0123-7). Univ Bks.

Brumfield, Allaire C. The Attic Festivals of Demeter & Their Relation to the Agricultural Year. Connor, W. R., ed. LC 80-2643. (Monographs in Classical Studies). 1981. lib. bdg. 29.00 (ISBN 0-405-14031-2). Arno.

Douhet, J. Dictionnaire des Mysteres. Migne, J. P., ed. (Nouvelle Encyclopedie Theologique Ser.: Vol. 43). 788p. (Fr.). Date not set. Repr. of 1854 ed. lib. bdg. 100.00x (ISBN 0-89241-282-8). Caratzas Bros.

Eliade, Mircea. Myths, Dreams & Mysteries: The Encounter Between Contemporary Faiths & Archaic Realities. pap. 4.95x (ISBN 0-06-131943-0, TB 1943, Torch). Har-Row.

Grant, James. The Mysteries of All Nations. LC 79-150243. 1971. Repr. of 1880 ed. 43.00 (ISBN 0-8103-3391-0). Gale.

Hall, Manly P. Lectures on Ancient Philosophy. 10.75 (ISBN 0-89314-512-2). Philos Res.

Harrison, Jane E. Prolegomena to the Study of Greek Religion. facsimile ed. LC 75-10639. (Ancient Religion & Mythology Ser.). (Illus.). 1976. Repr. of 1922 ed. 43.00x (ISBN 0-405-07018-7). Arno.

Jones, Gladys V. The Greek Love Mysteries. 1975. 6.95 (ISBN 0-87613-037-6). New Age.

Nilsson, Martin P. The Dionysiac Mysteries of the Hellenistic & Roman Age. facsimile ed. LC 75-10643. (Ancient Religion & Mythology Ser.). (Illus.). 1976. Repr. of 1957 ed. 9.00x (ISBN 0-405-07261-9). Arno.

Reitzenstein, Richard. The Hellenistic Mystery-Religions. Steely, John E., tr. from Ger. LC 77-12980. (Pittsburgh Theological Monographs: No. 15). Orig. Title: Die Hellenistischen Mysterienreligionen Nach Ihren Arundgedanken und Wirkungen. 1978. pap. text ed. 13.95 (ISBN 0-915138-20-4). Pickwick.

Steiner, Rudolf. Christianity As Mystical Fact & the Mysteries of Antiquity. 1972. pap. 7.95 (ISBN 0-910142-04-1). Anthroposophic.

Wind, Edgar. Pagan Mysteries in the Renaissance. rev. ed. (Illus.). 1969. pap. 6.95 (ISBN 0-393-00475-9, Norton Lib). Norton.

MYSTERIES AND MIRACLE-PLAYS

see also Bible Plays; Drama, Medieval; Liturgical Drama; Moralities

Block, K. S., ed. Ludus Coventriae, Or, the Place Called Corpus Christi. (Early English Text Society Ser.). 1922. 19.50x (ISBN 0-19-722560-8). Oxford U Pr.

Browne, E. Martin, ed. Religious Drama, Vol. 2: 21 Medieval Mystery & Morality Plays. 8.00 (ISBN 0-8446-2793-3). Peter Smith.

Cawley, A. C., ed. The Wakefield Pageants in the Towneley Cycle. (Old & Middle English Texts). 1958. Repr. of 1975 ed. pap. 11.50x (ISBN 0-06-491013-X). B&N.

Christie, Agatha. The Mirror Crack'd. 1980. pap. 2.50 (ISBN 0-671-41357-0). PB.

Davidson, Charles. Studies in the English Mystery Plays. LC 68-752. (Studies in Drama, No. 39). 1969. Repr. of 1892 ed. lib. bdg. 32.95 (ISBN 0-8383-0536-9). Haskell.

Davidson, Clifford. Drama & Art: An Introduction to the Use of Evidence from the Visual Arts for the Study of Early Drama. (Early Drama, Art, & Music Ser.). (Illus.). 1977. pap. 4.95 (ISBN 0-918720-00-1). Medieval Inst.

Fournier, Edouard, ed. Theatre Francais Avant La Renaissance, 1430-1550. 1965. Repr. of 1872 ed. 32.00 (ISBN 0-8337-1225-X). B Franklin.

Franklin, Alexander. Seven Miracle Plays. 1963. pap. 6.95x (ISBN 0-19-831391-8). Oxford U Pr.

Halverson, Marvin, ed. Religious Drama, Vol. 1: Five Plays. 8.00 (ISBN 0-8446-2792-5). Peter Smith.

--Religious Drama, Vol. 3. 8.00 (ISBN 0-8446-2794-1). Peter Smith.

Happe, Peter, ed. English Mystery Plays. (English Library). 714p. 1980. pap. 4.95 (ISBN 0-14-043093-8). Penguin.

Hein, Norvin. The Miracle Plays of Mathura. LC 75-99826. (Illus.). 292p. 1972. 25.00x (ISBN 0-300-01197-0). Yale U Pr.

Hone, William. Ancient Mysteries Described. LC 67-23905. (Illus.). 1969. Repr. of 1823 ed. 19.00 (ISBN 0-8103-3444-5). Gale.

Hopper, Vincent F. & Lahey, Gerald B., eds. Medieval Mysteries, Moralities & Interludes. LC 61-18362. (gr. 10 up). 1962. pap. text ed. 3.95 (ISBN 0-8120-0135-4). Barron.

Loomis, Roger S. & Wells, Henry W., eds. Representative Medieval & Tudor Plays. LC 77-111109. (Play Anthology Reprint Ser). 1942. 20.50 (ISBN 0-8369-8202-9). Arno.

Manly, John M. Specimens of the Pre-Shakespearean Drama, 2 Vols. LC 67-18432. 1897. 20.00x (ISBN 0-8196-0200-0). Biblo.

Mysteres Provencaux Du XVe Siecle. Repr. of 1893 ed. 29.00 (ISBN 0-384-40753-6). Johnson Repr.

Roane, Philip, Jr. Cherokee. 1982. 8.95 (ISBN 0-533-05083-9). Vantage.

Rose, Martial, ed. Wakefield Mystery Plays. 1969. pap. 6.95 (ISBN 0-393-00483-X, Norton Lib). Norton.

Smith, Lucy T., ed. York Plays: The Plays Performed on the Day of Corpus Christi in the 14th, 15th, & 16th Centuries. LC 63-15180. (Illus.). 1963. Repr. of 1885 ed. 21.00 (ISBN 0-8462-0313-8). Russell.

Spivack, Bernard. Shakespeare & the Allegory of Evil: The History of a Metaphor in Relation to His Major Villains. LC 57-12758. 1958. 25.00x (ISBN 0-231-01912-2). Columbia U Pr.

MYSTERIES AND MIRACLE-PLAYS–BIBLIOGRAPHY

Coleman, Edward D. Bible in English Drama: An Annotated Bibliography. rev. ed. 1969. 25.00x (ISBN 0-87068-034-X). Ktav.

--Bible in English Drama: An Annotated List of Plays. 1969. 6.95 (ISBN 0-87104-021-2, Co-Pub by Ktav). NY Pub Lib.

MYSTERIES AND MIRACLE-PLAYS–HISTORY AND CRITICISM

Cargill, Oscar. Drama & Liturgy. LC 73-86272. 1969. Repr. of 1930 ed. lib. bdg. 13.50x (ISBN 0-374-91292-0). Octagon.

Carnahan, David H. Prologue in the Old French & Provencal Mystery. LC 68-55160. (Studies in French Literature, No. 45). 1969. Repr. of 1905 ed. lib. bdg. 46.95 (ISBN 0-8383-0519-9). Haskell.

Frank, Grace. Medieval French Drama. 1954. 29.50x (ISBN 0-19-815317-1). Oxford U Pr.

Gardiner, Harold C. Mysteries' End: An Investigation of the Last Days of the Medieval Religious Stage. (Yale Studies in English Ser.: No. 103). 1967. Repr. of 1946 ed. 14.50 (ISBN 0-208-00385-1, Archon). Shoe String.

Hone, William. Ancient Mysteries Described. LC 67-23905. (Illus.). 1969. Repr. of 1823 ed. 19.00 (ISBN 0-8103-3444-5). Gale.

--Ancient Mysteries Described. 59.95 (ISBN 0-8490-1426-3). Gordon Pr.

McKean, Sr. M. Faith. Interplay of Realistic & Flamboyant Art Elements in the French Mysteres. LC 74-94196. (Catholic University of America Studies in Romance Languages & Literatures Ser: No. 60). Repr. of 1959 ed. 17.50 (ISBN 0-404-50360-8). AMS Pr.

Mathews, Godfrey W. Chester Mystery Plays. LC 77-4728. 1925. lib. bdg. 7.50 (ISBN 0-8414-6159-7). Folcroft.

Moore, E. Hamilton. English Miracle Plays & Moralities. LC 77-100517. Repr. of 1907 ed. 17.25 (ISBN 0-404-00598-5). AMS Pr.

Prosser, Eleanor. Drama & Religion in the English Mystery Plays: A Re-Evaluation. 1961. 12.50x (ISBN 0-8047-0060-5). Stanford U Pr.

MYSTERIES AND MIRACLE-PLAYS, ENGLISH

Craig, Hardin. English Religious Drama of the Middle Ages. LC 78-6893. 1978. Repr. of 1968 ed. lib. bdg. 32.50x (ISBN 0-313-20496-9, CRER). Greenwood.

Davidson, Clifford, ed. A Middle English Treatise on the Playing of Miracles. LC 81-40028. 93p. 1981. lib. bdg. 14.75 (ISBN 0-8191-1514-2); pap. text ed. 6.75 (ISBN 0-8191-1515-0). U Pr of Amer.

Davis, Norman, ed. Non-Cycle Plays & Fragments. (Early English Text Society Ser.). 1970. 19.50x (ISBN 0-19-722401-6). Oxford U Pr.

Dutka, JoAnna. Music in the English Mystery Plays. (Early Drama, Art, & Music Ser.). (Illus.). 171p. 1980. 18.80 (ISBN 0-918720-10-9); pap. 11.80 (ISBN 0-918720-11-7). Medieval Inst.

Harrison, Tony. The Passion: Selected from the Fifteenth Century Cycle of York Mystery Plays in a Version by the Company with Tony Harrison. 1978. pap. 5.00x (ISBN 0-8476-3131-1). Rowman.

Lumiansky, R. M., ed. The Chester Mystery Cycle. LC 78-84499. 300p. 1980. pap. 25.00 (ISBN 0-686-74467-5). Huntington Lib.

Woolf, Rosemary. The English Mystery Plays. 1980. pap. 7.95 (ISBN 0-520-04081-3). U of Cal Pr.

MYSTERY

Ferrars, E. X. In at the Kill. 192p. 1980. pap. 2.50 (ISBN 0-14-005644-0). Penguin.

Lowe, Walter J. Mystery & the Unconscious: A Study in the Thought of Paul Ricoeur. LC 76-44865. (ATLA Monograph: No. 9). 1977. 10.00 (ISBN 0-8108-0989-3). Scarecrow.

Moore, Lilian. The Duport Mystery. pap. 4.50 (ISBN 0-384-39987-8). Johnson Repr.

Rubin, Arnold P. True Great Mysteries. 128p. (Orig.). (gr. 7 up). pap. 1.25 (ISBN 0-590-31338-X, Schol Pap). Schol Bk Serv.

Sheridan, James F. Mystery Delight: An Unnatural Philosophy. 1980. pap. text ed. 8.75 (ISBN 0-8191-1089-2). U Pr of Amer.

MYSTERY STORIES

see Adventure and Adventurers; Detective and Mystery Stories

MYSTIC SEAPORT, MYSTIC CONNETICUT

Ansel, Willits D. Restoration of the Smack Emma C. Berry. LC 72-95937. (Illus.). 94p. 1973. pap. 7.00 (ISBN 0-913372-08-0). Mystic Seaport.

Busch, Briton C., ed. Master of Desolation: The Reminiscences of Capt. Joseph J. Fuller. (American Maritime Library: Vol. 9). 349p. 1980. 24.00 (ISBN 0-913372-21-8). Mystic Seaport.

Cutler, Carl C. Mystic: The Story of a Small New England Seaport. (Illus.). 56p. 1980. pap. 5.00 (ISBN 0-913372-14-5). Mystic Seaport.

MYSTICAL BODY OF CHRIST

see Jesus Christ–Mystical Body

MYSTICAL THEOLOGY

see Mysticism; Mysticism–Catholic Church; Mysticism–Orthodox Eastern Church

MYSTICAL UNION

Here are entered works dealing with the indwelling of the Triune God, or of any person of the trinity, in the hearts of believers and conversely, works dealing with the union between man and the Triune God, especially between man and Jesus Christ. Works dealing with the church as the mystical body of Christ are entered under the heading Jesus Christ–Mystical Body.

see also Contemplation

Applewhite, Barry. Feeling Good About God. 120p. 1981. pap. 3.95 (ISBN 0-88207-339-7). Victor Bks.

Baker, Robert J. I'm Listening Lord, Keep Talking. 200p. 1981. pap. 6.95 (ISBN 0-8361-1953-3). Herald Pr.

Beringer, Joan E. God's Gifts. (Illus.). 1981. 6.95 (ISBN 0-87510-160-7). Chr Science.

Bernard de Clairvaux, St. On Loving God: Selections from Sermons by St. Bernard of Clairvaux. Martin, Hugh, ed. LC 79-8706. (A Treasury of Christian Books). 125p. 1981. Repr. of 1959 ed. lib. bdg. 17.50x (ISBN 0-313-20787-9, BEOL). Greenwood.

Blumenthal, Warren B. The Creator & Man. LC 80-5843. 139p. 1980. lib. bdg. 15.75 (ISBN 0-8191-1340-9); pap. text ed. 7.50 (ISBN 0-8191-1341-7). U Pr of Amer.

Branson, Robert. God's Word in Man's Language. 83p. (Orig.). 1980. pap. 2.75 (ISBN 0-8341-0659-0). Beacon Hill.

Bright, Bill. How to Be Filled with the Spirit. (Transferable Concepts Ser.). 58p. 1981. pap. 1.25 (ISBN 0-918956-90-0). Campus Crusade.

Camp, Norman. Pensando Con Dios. 128p. (Span.). 1981. pap. 1.95 (ISBN 0-8024-6593-5). Moody.

Coakley, Mary L. Not Alone: For the Lord Is Nigh. 192p. (Orig.). 1981. pap. 8.95 (ISBN 0-8164-2324-5). Seabury.

Collin, Rodney. The Mirror of Light. 90p. 1981. 20.00x (ISBN 0-7224-0159-0, Pub. by Watkins England). State Mutual Bk.

Dalrymple, John. Toward the Heart of God. 108p. (Orig.). 1981. pap. 4.95 (ISBN 0-86683-602-0). Winston Pr.

Dobson, James. Dr. Dobson Fala Sobre Amor, Ira. (Portugese Bks.). (Port.). 1979. 1.80 (ISBN 0-8297-0674-7). Life Pubs Intl.

Dueland, Joy V. Filled Up Full. (Illus.). 32p. (gr. k-2). 1980. pap. 2.50 (ISBN 0-87510-151-8). Chr Science.

Fandel, John. God's Breath in Man. LC 77-76604. 1977. pap. 1.50 (ISBN 0-87957-005-9). Roth Pub.

Foglio, Frank. Ei, Deus. (Portuguese Bks.). 1979. 1.25 (ISBN 0-8297-0791-3). Life Pubs Intl.

--Oye Dios. (Spanish Bks.). (Span.). 1978. 1.65 (ISBN 0-8297-0588-0). Life Pubs Intl.

Guyon, Madame. Union with God. Edwards, Gene, ed. 50p. 1981. pap. 2.95 (ISBN 0-940232-05-7). Christian Bks.

Harper, Michael. Live by the Spirit: How to Grow in Your Relationship with God. 154p. 1980. pap. 2.25 (ISBN 0-89283-094-8). Servant.

Haught, John F. Religion & Self-Acceptance: A Study of the Relationship Between Belief in God & the Desire to Know. LC 80-5872. 195p. 1980. lib. bdg. 17.00 (ISBN 0-8191-1296-8); pap. text ed. 8.75 (ISBN 0-8191-1297-6). U Pr of Amer.

Kasimow, Harold. Divine-Human Encounter: A Study of Abraham Joshua Heschel. LC 79-63562. 1979. pap. text ed. 7.75 (ISBN 0-8191-0731-X). U Pr of Amer.

Kuhlman, Kathryn, tr. Dios Quiere Sanarte y Revolucionar Tu Vida. (Spanish Bks.). (Span.). 1977. 2.25 (ISBN 0-8297-0751-4). Life Pubs Intl.

Lane, Dermot A. The Experience of God: An Invitation to Do Theology. LC 81-80873. 96p. (Orig.). 1981. pap. 3.95 (ISBN 0-8091-2394-0). Paulist Pr.

Larsen, Norma C. Our Father Cares. LC 81-80956. 150p. 1981. 7.95 (ISBN 0-88290-182-6, 1062). Horizon Utah.

Maclennan, David A. He Restoreth. (Contempo Ser.). pap. 0.95 (ISBN 0-8010-6100-8). Baker Bk.

Malz, Betty. Prayers That Are Answered. 1981. pap. 1.95 (ISBN 0-451-11094-3, AJ1094, Sig). NAL.

Mary Of Agreda. The City of God, 4 vols. Set. 35.00 (ISBN 0-686-74594-9). Prow Bks-Franciscan.

Matthews, Anna M. God Answers Prayers. 96p. 1981. 8.95 (ISBN 0-89962-215-1). Todd & Honeywell.

Murray, Andrew. La Palabra Irresistible. (Spanish Bks.). (Span.). 1979. 1.95 (ISBN 0-8297-0520-1). Life Pubs Intl.

Ogilvie, Lloyd. Congratulations - God Believes in You. 128p. 1980. 5.95 (ISBN 0-8499-0197-9). Word Bks.

O'Sullivan, Eugene. In His Presence. 161p. (Orig.). Date not set. pap. 6.95 (ISBN 0-89453-184-0, Pub. by Dominican Pubns Ireland). M Glazier.

Palms, Roger C. Dios Guia Tu Futuro. (Spanish Bks.). (Span.). 1977. 1.60 (ISBN 0-8297-0767-0). Life Pubs Intl.

Parrott, Bob W. Ontology of Humor. LC 81-80239. 1981. 10.95 (ISBN 0-8022-2387-7). Philos Lib.

Pentecost, D. Dieu Repond-Problemes-Hommes. (French Bks.). (Fr.). 1979. 1.40 (ISBN 0-8297-0911-8). Life Pubs Intl.

Porter, Alan. You've Really Got Me, God! (Direction Bks.). pap. 1.45 (ISBN 0-8010-7019-8). Baker Bk.

Reeves, Enos C. My Personal Experiences from Hell to Heaven. 1980. 6.95 (ISBN 0-533-04617-3). Vantage.

Richards, Larry. Our Life Together: A Woman's Workshop on Fellowship. (Woman's Workshop Ser.). 160p. (Orig.). 1981. pap. 3.95 (ISBN 0-310-43451-3). Zondervan.

Richards, Lawrence O. How I Can Experience God. (Answers for Youth Ser.). 1980. pap. 2.95 (ISBN 0-310-38991-7). Zondervan.

Sales, Lorenzo. Jesus Appeals to the World. 1955. 4.95 (ISBN 0-8189-0069-5). Alba.

Stibbs, A. M. & Packer, J. I. Spirit Within You. (Canterbury Bks). pap. 2.50 (ISBN 0-8010-8142-4). Baker Bk.

Streitfeld, Harold. God's Plan: The Complete Guide to the Future. LC 81-80768. (Illus.). 160p. (Orig.). 1981. pap. 6.25 (ISBN 0-9605926-0-1). Raja Pr CA.

Talmadge, Virginia. Dear God Little Prayers to a Big God. 1981. cloth 2.95 (ISBN 0-86544-016-6). Salvation Army.

Thompson, Walter C. Repent? of What? 1982. 7.95 (ISBN 0-533-05037-5). Vantage.

Van Zweden, J. God's Sovereignty in the Lives of Twin Brothers. pap. 1.95 (ISBN 0-686-70365-0). Reiner.

Weatherhead, Leslie D. Time for God. (Festival Ser.). 1981. pap. 1.75 (ISBN 0-687-42113-6). Abingdon.

Wholeness from God. (Aglow Bible Study Bk. E-1). 64p. 1.95 (ISBN 0-930756-45-2, 4220-E1). Women's Aglow.

Wilkerson, Gwen. En Su Fuerza. (Spanish Bks.). (Span.). 1979. 1.90 (ISBN 0-8297-0910-X). Life Pubs Intl.

Woods, Richard. Mysterion: An Approach to Mystical Spirituality. 372p. 1981. 14.95 (ISBN 0-88347-127-2). Thomas More.

MYSTICISM

see also Cabala; Christian Art and Symbolism; Contemplation; Devotion; Enthusiasm; Illuminati; Immanence of God; Perfection; Private Revelations; Rosicrucians; Symbolism of Numbers; Tantrism

Abraham, Karl. Dreams & Myths: A Study in Race Psychology. White, William A., tr. (Nervous & Mental Disease Monographs: No. 15). 15.50 (ISBN 0-384-00160-2). Johnson Repr.

Addison, Charles M. The Theory & Practice of Mysticism. 1977. lib. bdg. 59.95 (ISBN 0-8490-2742-X). Gordon Pr.

Aivanhov, Omraam M. The Second Birth. (Complete Works of O. M. Aivanhov: Vol. 1). 210p. 1981. pap. 6.95 (ISBN 0-87516-418-8). De Vorss.

Andrea, Raymond. Technique of the Disciple. 5th ed. 187p. 1980. pap. 6.25 (ISBN 0-686-27981-6). AMORC.

Aristotelian Society For The Systematic Study Of Philosophy. Relativity, Logic & Mysticism: Proceedings, Supplementary Vol. 3. Repr. of 1923 ed. 12.00 (ISBN 0-384-50269-5); pap. 7.00 (ISBN 0-384-48086-1). Johnson Repr.

Arseniew, Nicholas. Mysticism & the Eastern Church. 1977. lib. bdg. 59.95 (ISBN 0-8490-2319-X). Gordon Pr.

Aude, Sapere, ed. The Chaldean Oracles. LC 78-58111. 1978. 10.00 (ISBN 0-935214-02-X). Heptangle.

Bacik, James J. Apologetics & the Eclipse of Mystery: Mystagogy According to Karl Rahner. LC 80-123. 192p. pap. text ed. 5.95 (ISBN 0-268-00593-1, NDP-261). U of Notre Dame Pr.

Bailey, Alice A. From Intellect to Intuition. 1972. 7.50 (ISBN 0-85330-008-9); pap. 4.25 (ISBN 0-85330-108-5). Lucis.

Balthasar, Hans Urs Von. A First Glance at Adrienne Von Speyr. Lawry, Antje & Englund, Sergia, Sr., trs. from Ger. LC 79-91933. Orig. Title: Erster Blick Auf Adrienne Von Speyr. 220p. (Orig.). 1981. pap. 6.95 (ISBN 0-89870-003-5). Ignatius Pr.

Bancroft, Ann. Modern Mystics & Sages. (Illus.). 256p. 1981. pap. 5.95 (ISBN 0-586-08256-5, Pub. by Granada England). Academy Chi Ltd.

Baring-Gould, Sabine. Freaks of Fanaticism & Other Strange Events. LC 68-21754. 1968. Repr. of 1891 ed. 22.00 (ISBN 0-8103-3503-4). Gale.

Benedict, Clare M. St. Sharbel, Mystic of the East. 1977. 6.95 (ISBN 0-911218-11-4); pap. 2.95 (ISBN 0-911218-12-2). Ravengate Pr.

Bennett, John G. Creation. 1978. 4.95 (ISBN 0-900306-41-6, Pub. by Coombe Springs Pr). Claymont Comm.

Bernard, Raymond. Messages from the Celestial Sanctum. AMORC, tr. from Fr. 354p. (Orig.). 1980. pap. 6.25 (ISBN 0-686-00405-1). AMORC.

Besant, Annie. Esoteric Christianity. 8th ed. 1966. 6.25 (ISBN 0-8356-7052-X). Theos Pub Hse.

Bharati, Agehananda. The Light at the Center: Context & Pretext of Modern Mysticism. 1976. lib. bdg. 11.95 (ISBN 0-915520-03-6); pap. 6.95 (ISBN 0-915520-04-4). Ross-Erikson.

Bjerregaard, C. H. The Inner Life. Incl. The Tao-Teh-King. 1977. lib. bdg. 49.00 (ISBN 0-8490-2061-1). Gordon Pr.

--Lectures on Mysticism & Nature Worship. 1977. lib. bdg. 59.95 (ISBN 0-8490-2138-3). Gordon Pr.

Boehme, Jacob. Jacob Boehme's "The Way to Christ". Stoudt, John J., tr. LC 78-13976. 1979. Repr. of 1947 ed. lib. bdg. 19.75x (ISBN 0-313-21075-6, BOTW). Greenwood.

--Six Theosophic Points & Other Writings. 1958. pap. 3.95 (ISBN 0-472-06017-1, 17, AA). U of Mich Pr.

Bolle, Kees W. Freedom of Man in Myth. LC 68-8564. 1968. 5.00 (ISBN 0-8265-1125-2). Vanderbilt U Pr.

Bonaventura, Saint The Mind's Road to God. Boas, George, tr. 1953. pap. 2.50 (ISBN 0-672-60195-8, LLA32). Bobbs.

Bower, Mathew J. Encyclopedia of Mystical Terminology. LC 78-69675. (Illus.). 1979. 12.00 (ISBN 0-498-02262-5). A S Barnes.

Bowman, Mary A., compiled by. Western Mysticism: A Guide to the Basic Sources. LC 78-18311. 1978. pap. 8.00 (ISBN 0-8389-0266-9). ALA.

Bulka, Reuven P., ed. Mystics & Medics: A Comparison of Mystical & Psychotherapeutic Encounters. 120p. 1979. pap. 8.95 (ISBN 0-87705-377-4). Human Sci Pr.

Butler, C. Western Mysticism: Neglected Chapters in the History of Religion. 69.95 (ISBN 0-87968-244-2). Gordon Pr.

Campbell, Joseph, ed. Papers from Eranos Yearbooks, 6 vols. Manheim, R. & Hull, R. F., trs. Incl. Vol. 1. Spirit & Nature. (Illus.). 1954; Vol. 2. The Mysteries. 1955. 24.00 (ISBN 0-691-09734-8); pap. 5.95 (ISBN 0-691-01823-5); Vol. 3. Man & Time. (Illus.). 1957. 22.50 (ISBN 0-691-09732-1); Vol. 4. Spirtual Disciplines. (Illus.). 1960. 27.50 (ISBN 0-691-09737-2); Vol. 5. Man & Transformation. (Illus.). 1964. 25.00 (ISBN 0-691-09733-X); pap. 5.95 (ISBN 0-691-01834-0); Vol. 6. Mystic Vision. 1969. 30.00 (ISBN 0-691-09735-6). (Bollingen Ser.: No. 30). Set. Princeton U Pr.

Capps, Walter H. & Wright, Wendy M., eds. Silent Fire. LC 78-3366. (Forum Bk.). 1978. pap. 6.95 (ISBN 0-06-061314-9, RD 290, HarpR). Har-Row.

Capra, Fritjof. The Tao of Physics. 1977. Repr. pap. 3.95 (ISBN 0-553-14206-2). Bantam.

Carty, Charles M. Who Is Teresa Neumann? 1974. pap. 1.00 (ISBN 0-89555-093-8, 156). TAN Bks Pubs.

Chaney, Robert. Mysticism: The Journey Within. LC 79-52959. 1979. softcover 12.50 (ISBN 0-918936-06-3). Astara.

Cheney, Sheldon. Men Who Have Walked with God. 1974. pap. 3.45 (ISBN 0-440-55596-5, Delta). Dell.

Clark, A. Cosmic Mysteries of the Universe. 1974. pap. 3.45 (ISBN 0-13-179192-3, Reward). P-H.

Coleman, Thomas W. English Mystics of the Fourteenth Century. LC 74-109723. 1971. Repr. of 1938 ed. lib. bdg. 15.00x (ISBN 0-8371-4213-X, COEM). Greenwood.

Connolly, J. L. John Gerson: Reformer & Mystic. (Medieval Studies Ser.). (Illus.). Repr. of 1928 ed. lib. bdg. 26.00x (ISBN 0-697-00031-1). Irvington.

Corbin, Henri. Avicenna & the Visionary Recital. Task, Willard R., tr. from French. 320p. 1980. pap. text ed. 13.50 (ISBN 0-88214-213-5). Spring Pubns.

Coward, Harold & Penelhum, Terence, eds. Mystics & Scholars: The Calgary Conference on Mysticism 1976. 121p. 1977. pap. text ed. 5.75 (ISBN 0-919812-04-X, Pub. by Laurier U Pr Canada). Humanities.

Crawfod, Shirley O. Is God Dead Within You? 112p. 1981. 6.50 (ISBN 0-682-49789-4). Exposition.

Cronk, Walter. Golden Light. 3rd ed. LC 64-15645. (Illus.). 1973. Repr. of 1964 ed. 4.95 (ISBN 0-87516-018-2). De Vorss.

D'Arcy, Martin C. The Meeting of Love & Knowledge: Perennial Wisdom. LC 78-23621. 1979. Repr. of 1957 ed. lib. bdg. 14.50x (ISBN 0-313-21145-0, DAME). Greenwood.

Davison, William T. Mystics & Poets. 167p. 1980. Repr. of 1936 ed. lib. bdg. 25.00 (ISBN 0-8482-0639-8). Norwood Edns.

Dean, Stanley R. Psychiatry & Mysticism. LC 75-8771. (Illus.). 446p. 1975. 24.95x (ISBN 0-88229-189-0); pap. 13.95 (ISBN 0-88229-657-4). Nelson-Hall.

De Jaegher, Paul, ed. An Anthology of Christian Mysticism. 1977. 7.95 (ISBN 0-87243-073-1). Templegate.
De Riencourt, Amaury. The Eye of Shiva: Eastern Mysticism & Science. LC 80-22032. 221p. 1981. 8.95 (ISBN 0-688-00036-3); pap. 4.95 (ISBN 0-688-00038-X). Morrow.
Dunlap, Knight. Mysticism, Freudianism & Scientific Psychology. facsimile ed. (Select Bibliographies Reprint Ser). Repr. of 1920 ed. 16.00 (ISBN 0-8369-5838-1). Arno.
Dupre, Louis. The Deeper Life: A Meditation on Christian Mysticism. 128p. (Orig.). 1981. pap. 4.95 (ISBN 0-8245-0007-5). Crossroad NY.
--The Deeper Life: A Meditation on Christian Mysticism. 96p. 1981. pap. 4.95 (ISBN 0-8245-0007-5). Crossroad NY.
Du Prel, Carl. The Philosophy of Mysticism, 2vols. in 1. Massey, C. C., tr. LC 75-36838. (Occult Ser.). 1976. Repr. of 1889 ed. 38.00x (ISBN 0-405-07951-6). Arno.
--The Philosophy of Mysticism, 2 vols. 1977. lib. bdg. 250.00 (ISBN 0-8490-2434-X). Gordon Pr.
Dyson, W. H. Studies in Christian Mysticism. 1977. lib. bdg. 69.95 (ISBN 0-8490-2702-0). Gordon Pr.
Elliot, Pierre. Inaugural Address to the Claymont Third Basic Course. 1978. 2.95 (ISBN 0-686-11130-3). Claymont Comm.
Ellwood, Robert S., Jr. Mysticism & Religion. 1980. text ed. 10.95 (ISBN 0-13-608810-4); pap. text ed. 8.95 (ISBN 0-13-608802-3). P-H.
Eustace, Cecil J. Infinity of Questions. facs. ed. LC 70-84356. (Essay Index Reprint Ser). 1946. 14.50 (ISBN 0-8369-1080-X). Arno.
Fairweather, William. Among the Mystics. facs. ed. LC 68-20298. (Essay Index Reprint Ser.). 1936. 12.00 (ISBN 0-8369-0437-0). Arno.
Ferguson, John. An Illustrated Encyclopedia of Mysticism & the Mystery Religions. LC 76-55812. (Illus.). 1976. 14.95 (ISBN 0-8164-9310-3). Continuum.
Fisher, J. M. Mystic Gnosis. 1977. lib. bdg. 59.95 (ISBN 0-8490-2316-5). Gordon Pr.
Flammonde, Paris. Mystic Healers. LC 73-91856. 1975. pap. 2.45 (ISBN 0-8128-1858-X). Stein & Day.
Franklin, James C. Mystical Transformations: The Imagery of Liquids in the Work of Mechthild Von Magdeburg. LC 75-5248. 192p. 1976. 12.00 (ISBN 0-8386-1738-7). Fairleigh Dickinson.
Furse, Margaret L. Mysticism - Window on a World View: Introduction to Mysticism As a Pattern of Thought & Practice. LC 76-56816. (Orig.). 1977. pap. 3.95 (ISBN 0-687-27674-8). Abingdon.
GAP Committee on Psychiatry & Religion. Mysticism: Spiritual Quest or Psychic Disorder, Vol. 9. LC 76-45931. (Report: No. 97). 1976. pap. 4.00 (ISBN 0-87318-134-4, Pub. by Adv Psychiatry). Mental Health.
Gardner, Edmund G. Dante & the Mystics. LC 68-25542. 1968. Repr. of 1913 ed. lib. bdg. 18.50x (ISBN 0-374-93002-3). Octagon.
--Dante & the Mystics: A Study of the Mystical Aspect of the Divina Commedia. LC 68-24952. (Studies in Italian Literature, No. 46). 1969. Repr. of 1913 ed. lib. bdg. 27.95 (ISBN 0-8383-0271-8). Haskell.
Gaynor, Frank. Dictionary of Mysticism. 211p. 1973. pap. 2.45 (ISBN 0-8065-0172-3). Citadel Pr.
Ghose, S. K. Mystics & Society. 5.00x (ISBN 0-210-98132-6). Asia.
Ghose, Sisirkumar. The Mystic As a Force for Change. rev. ed. LC 80-53954. 144p. 1980. pap. 4.75 (ISBN 0-8356-0547-7, Quest). Theos Pub Hse.
Golas, Thaddeus. The Lazy Man's Guide to Enlightenment. 96p. 1980. pap. 2.25 (ISBN 0-553-20440-8). Bantam.
--The Lazy Man's Guide to Enlightenment. 96p. 1980. pap. 2.25 (ISBN 0-553-20440-8). Bantam.
Goldsmith, Joel S. Awakening Mystical Consciousness. Sinkler, Lorraine, ed. LC 79-3601. 176p. 1980. 8.95 (ISBN 0-06-063174-0). Har-Row.
--Our Spiritual Resources. LC 62-7965. 1978. 7.95 (ISBN 0-06-063211-9, HarpR). Har-Row.
--Parenthesis in Eternity. LC 64-10368. 1963. 9.95 (ISBN 0-06-063230-5, HarpR). Har-Row.
--Practicing the Presence. LC 58-7474. 1958. 7.95 (ISBN 0-06-063250-X, HarpR). Har-Row.
Graef, H. C. The Way of the Mystics. 1977. lib. bdg. 59.95 (ISBN 0-8490-2811-6). Gordon Pr.
Graham, R. B. A Brazilian Mystic: Life & Miracles of Antonio Conselheiro. 1976. lib. bdg. 59.95 (ISBN 0-87968-786-X). Gordon Pr.
Grierson, Francis. Modern Mysticism. LC 77-102570. 1970. Repr. of 1899 ed. 12.50 (ISBN 0-8046-0730-3). Kennikat.
--Modern Mysticism. 1977. lib. bdg. 59.95 (ISBN 0-8490-2271-1). Gordon Pr.
Guerry, Herbert, ed. Philosophy & Mysticism. pap. 2.95 (ISBN 0-685-61376-3). Dell.
Hall, Manly P. Mystical Christ. 8.50 (ISBN 0-89314-514-9). Philos Res.
Hanson, Virginia, ed. The Silent Encounter. LC 74-4168. 240p. (Orig.). 1974. pap. 2.75 (ISBN 0-8356-0448-9, Quest). Theos Pub Hse.
Happold, Frank C. Mysticism. (Orig.). 1963. pap. 3.95 (ISBN 0-14-020568-3, Pelican). Penguin.
Harkness, Georgia. Mysticism: Its Meaning & Message. LC 72-10070. 192p. 1976. pap. 3.95 (ISBN 0-687-27667-5). Abingdon.
Haywood, Harryl. Christian Mysticism. 59.95 (ISBN 0-87968-862-9). Gordon Pr.
Heline, Corinne. Mystic Masonry & the Bible. pap. 3.95 (ISBN 0-87613-017-1). New Age.
Herman, E. The Meaning & Value of Mysticism. 3rd facsimile ed. LC 72-164607. (Select Bibliographies Reprint Ser). Repr. of 1922 ed. 22.00 (ISBN 0-8369-5891-8). Arno.
--The Meaning & Value of Mysticism. 1977. lib. bdg. 59.95 (ISBN 0-8490-2216-9). Gordon Pr.
Hodgson, Geraldine E. The Sanity of Mysticism. LC 76-11826. 1976. Repr. of 1926 ed. lib. bdg. 20.00 (ISBN 0-8414-4845-0). Folcroft.
Hopkins, Emma C. Class Lessons, Eighteen Eighty Eight. Bogart, Elizabeth, ed. 1977. 9.50 (ISBN 0-87516-219-3). De Vorss.
--High Mysticism. 368p. 1974. Repr. pap. 7.95 (ISBN 0-87516-198-7). De Vorss.
Hopkinson, Arthur W. Mysticism: Old & New. LC 77-118528. 1971. Repr. of 1946 ed. 11.25 (ISBN 0-8046-1151-3). Kennikat.
Horne, James R. Beyond Mysticism. 158p. 1978. pap. text ed. 6.75 (ISBN 0-919812-08-2, Pub. by Laurier U Pr Canada). Humanities.
Hugel, F. von. Mystical Element of Religion As Studied in St. Catherine of Genoa and Her Friends, 2 vols. 2nd ed. 1961. Repr. of 1923 ed. 37.50 set (ISBN 0-227-67535-5). Attic Pr.
Hunter, Irene, ed. American Mystical Verse. LC 79-116407. (Granger Index Reprint Ser). 1925. 14.50 (ISBN 0-8369-6148-X). Arno.
Inge, William R. Mysticism in Religion. LC 76-15407. 1976. Repr. of 1948 ed. lib. bdg. 14.75x (ISBN 0-8371-8953-5, INMR). Greenwood.
--Studies of English Mystics. facs. ed. LC 69-17578. (Essay Index Reprint Ser). 1906. 15.00 (ISBN 0-8369-0081-2). Arno.
Jae Jah Noh. Do You See What I See. LC 77-5255. (Orig.). 1977. pap. 3.95 (ISBN 0-8356-0499-3, Quest). Theos Pub Hse.
James, Joseph. The Way of Mysticism: An Anthology. 1977. lib. bdg. 59.95 (ISBN 0-8490-2810-8). Gordon Pr.
Johnston, Wiliam. The Inner Eye of Love: Mysticism & Religion. LC 78-4428. 1978. 9.95 (ISBN 0-06-064195-9, HarpR). Har-Row.
Johnston, William. Still Point: Reflections on Zen & Christian Mysticism. LC 75-95713. 1980. pap. 8.00 (ISBN 0-8232-0861-3). Fordham.
Jones, Rufus M. Mysticism & Democracy in the English Commonwealth. 1965. lib. bdg. 12.50x (ISBN 0-374-94313-3). Octagon.
--New Studies in Mystical Religion. 69.95 (ISBN 0-87968-102-0). Gordon Pr.
--Spiritual Reformers of the Sixteenth & Seventeenth Centuries. 1959. 7.25 (ISBN 0-8446-0161-6). Peter Smith.
Kalisch, Isidor. The Sepher Yezirah. Date not set. price not set (ISBN 0-686-21219-3). Heptangle.
Katz, Steven T. Mysticism & Philosophical Analysis. 1978. 15.95 (ISBN 0-19-520010-1); pap. 4.95 (ISBN 0-19-520011-X, GB 538). Oxford U Pr.
Kim, Hee-Jin. Dogen Kigen - Mystical Realist. LC 74-33725. (Association for Asian Studies Monograph: No. 29). 1975. pap. text ed. 5.95x (ISBN 0-8165-0513-6). U of Ariz Pr.
King, Thomas M. Teilhard's Mysticism of Knowing. 192p. 1981. 14.95 (ISBN 0-8164-0491-7). Seabury.
King, Ursula. Towards a New Mysticism: Teilhard de Chardin & Eastern Religions. 320p. 1980. 14.95 (ISBN 0-8164-0475-5); pap. 8.95 (ISBN 0-686-77524-4). Seabury.
Krishnamurti, J. Exploration into Insight. LC 79-6651. 192p. (Orig.). 1980. pap. 5.95 (ISBN 0-06-064811-2, RD 326). Har-Row.
Kueshana, Eklal. The Ultimate Frontier. rev., expanded ed. (Illus., Forty percent discount on 6-24 copies, fifty on 25 or more). pap. 2.25 (ISBN 0-9600308-1-6). Stelle.
Lambek, Ruth. Teaching of the Mystic. 1976. pap. 2.95 (ISBN 0-87516-213-4). De Vorss.
Landrum, Eli, Jr. Along Life's Way. 1981. pap. 4.95 (ISBN 0-8054-5183-8). Broadman.
Lang, Andrew. Magic & Religion. 59.95 (ISBN 0-8490-0576-0). Gordon Pr.
Laurence, Theodor. The Parker Lifetime Treasury of Mystic & Occult Powers. (Illus.). 1978. 9.95 (ISBN 0-13-650754-9, Parker). P-H.
Lee, Jung Y. Cosmic Religion. LC 73-82163. 128p. 1973. 4.50 (ISBN 0-8022-2125-4). Philos Lib.
Leeming, David A. Flights: Readings in Magic, Mysticism, Fantasy & Myth. 384p. (Orig.). 1974. pap. text ed. 8.95 (ISBN 0-15-527556-9, HC). HarBraceJ.
Lejeune, Abbe P. An Introduction to the Mystical Life. 1977. lib. bdg. 59.95 (ISBN 0-8490-2070-0). Gordon Pr.
LePak, Roy C. A Theology of Christian Mystical Experience. 1977. pap. text ed. 12.00 (ISBN 0-8191-0148-6). U Pr of Amer.
Lethaby, William. Architecture, Mysticism & Myth. LC 74-25316. (Illus.). 280p. 1975. 10.00 (ISBN 0-8076-0783-5). Braziller.
Leuba, James H. The Psychology of Religious Mysticism. 1972. 24.00 (ISBN 0-7100-7317-8). Routledge & Kegan.
L'Heureux, Mother Aloysius G. Mystical Vocabulary of Venerable Mere Marie De L'Incarnation & Its Problems. LC 72-94190. (Catholic University of America Studies in Romance Languages & Literatures Ser: No. 53). (Fr). Repr. of 1956 ed. 18.75 (ISBN 0-404-50353-5). AMS Pr.
Lopez, Barry H. Desert Notes: Reflections in the Eye of a Raven. (Illus.). 96p. 1976. 6.95 (ISBN 0-8362-0661-4). Andrews & McMeel.
Macfarlane, Claire. The Mystic Experience & Other Essays, 2 vols. LC 80-84935. 373p. 1981. Set. 12.95 (ISBN 0-936632-07-0); Vol. 1. 6.50 (ISBN 0-936632-08-9); Vol. 2. 6.50 (ISBN 0-936632-09-7). Mann Pubs.
MacLagan, E. R. & Russell, A. G., eds. The Prophetic Books of William Blake: Jerusalem. 1979. Repr. of 1904 ed. lib. bdg. 30.00 (ISBN 0-8495-3510-7). Arden Lib.
Mahadevan, T. M. P., ed. Spiritual Perspectives: Essays in Mysticism & Metaphysics. 303p. 1975. lib. bdg. 15.00 (ISBN 0-89253-021-9). Ind-US Inc.
Malfitano, Gilbert J. The Seven Steps on How to Become a Mystic & Enjoy the Most Exhilirating Pleasure Available to Man on This Earth. (Illus.). 1979. deluxe ed. 37.50 (ISBN 0-930582-37-3). Gloucester Art.
Marechal, Joseph. Studies in the Psychology of the Mystics. LC 65-1694. 1964. lib. bdg. 12.00x (ISBN 0-87343-044-1); pap. 6.00x (ISBN 0-87343-014-X). Magi Bks.
Massey, C. C. Thoughts of a Modern Mystic. 59.95 (ISBN 0-8490-1209-0). Gordon Pr.
Merton, Thomas. Mystics & Zen Masters. 1969. pap. 5.95 (ISBN 0-440-56263-5, Delta). Dell.
Murray, Paul. The Mysticism Debate. 1978. 0.75 (ISBN 0-8199-0722-7). Franciscan Herald.
Needleman, Jacob. The New Religions. 1977. pap. 3.50 (ISBN 0-525-47449-8). Dutton.
Newell, William L. Struggle & Submission: R. C. Zaehner on Mysticisms. LC 80-6295. 402p. 1981. lib. bdg. 21.75 (ISBN 0-8191-1696-3); pap. text ed. 12.75 (ISBN 0-8191-1697-1). U Pr of Amer.
Nicholson, D. H. The Mysticism of St. Francis of Assissi. 1977. lib. bdg. 59.95 (ISBN 0-8490-2319-X). Gordon Pr.
Nordberg, Robert. Teenager & the New Mysticism. LC 72-92837. (Personal Guidance & Social Adjustment). (gr. 7-12). 1973. PLB 5.97 (ISBN 0-8239-0278-1). Rosen Pr.
Norvell. Amazing Secrets of the Mystic East. 1980. 10.95 (ISBN 0-13-023754-X, Parker). P-H.
Orr, W. G. Sixteenth Century Indian Mystic. 1968. 4.00 (ISBN 0-685-06599-5). Assoc Bk.
Overman, Wilis H. Truth or Dare. 1980. 4.95 (ISBN 0-533-04250-X). Vantage.
Packull, Werner O. Mysticism & the Early South German-Austrian Anabaptist 1525-1531. LC 76-46557. (Studies in the Anabaptist & Mennonite History: No. 19). 1977. 17.95x (ISBN 0-8361-1130-3). Herald Pr.
Palacios, Miguel A. The Mystical Philosophy of Ibn Masarra & His Followers. Douglas, E. H. & Yoder, H. W., trs. from Span. 1978. text ed. 34.25x (ISBN 90-04-05749-8). Humanities.
Parrinder, Geoffrey. Mysticism in the World's Religions. LC 76-40554. 1977. 11.95 (ISBN 0-19-502184-3). Oxford U Pr.
--Mysticism in the World's Religions. 1976. pap. text ed. 4.95 (ISBN 0-19-502185-1, 497, GB). Oxford U Pr.
Pascher, Josef. Der Konigsweg Zu Wiedergeburt und Vergottung Bei Philon Von Alexandreia. Repr. of 1931 ed. pap. 18.50 (ISBN 0-384-45050-4). Johnson Repr.
Passmore, John. Perfectability of Man. LC 77-129625. 1970. 20.00x (ISBN 0-684-15521-4, ScribT). Scribner.
Peck, George. The Triple Way. LC 77-79824. 321p. (Orig.). 1977. pap. 0.95x (ISBN 0-87574-213-0). Pendle Hill.
Peers, E. Allison. The Mystics of Spain. 1977. lib. bdg. 59.95 (ISBN 0-8490-2322-X). Gordon Pr.
Peterkiewicz, Jerzy. The Third Adam: The Mariavite Experiment in Mystical Marriage. (Illus.). 256p. 1975. 27.50x (ISBN 0-19-212198-7). Oxford U Pr.
Prabhavananda, Swami. Yoga & Mysticism. 1969. pap. 1.50 (ISBN 0-87481-020-5). Vedanta Pr.
Ramacharaka, Yogi. Mystic Christianity. 7.00 (ISBN 0-911662-08-1). Yoga.
Ramm, Bernard H. Questions About the Spirit. pap. 3.50 (ISBN 0-87680-810-0, 98108). Word Bks.
Rampa, T. Lobsang. Twilight, 1977. pap. 2.95 (ISBN 0-685-91303-1). Weiser.
Redgrove, H. Stanley. Magic & Mysticism: Studies in Bygone Beliefs. 1970. 7.95 (ISBN 0-8216-0111-3). Univ Bks.
Reinhold, H. A. The Soul Afire: Revelations of the Mystics. 1977. Repr. of 1944 ed. 30.00 (ISBN 0-89984-099-X). Century Bookbindery.
Reinhold, H. A., ed. Soul Afire: Revelations of the Mystics. 5.75 (ISBN 0-8446-2791-7). Peter Smith.
--The Soul Afire: Revelations of the Mystics. 440p. 1973. pap. 2.95 (ISBN 0-385-01489-9, Im). Doubleday.
Riccardo, Martin V. Mystical Consciousness: Exploring an Extraordinary State of Awareness. 1977. pap. 3.50 (ISBN 0-686-19170-6). MVR Bks.
Riley, Isaac H. The Meaning of Mysticism. LC 75-26512. 1975. lib. bdg. 20.00 (ISBN 0-8414-7227-0). Folcroft.
Rivet, Mother Mary M. Influence of the Spanish Mystics on the Works of Saint Francis De Sales. LC 79-115355. (Catholic University of America. Studies in Romance Languages & Literatures: No. 22). Repr. of 1941 ed. 15.00 (ISBN 0-404-50322-5). AMS Pr.
Rowlands, Henry. Mona Antiqua Restaurata. Feldman, Burton & Richardson, Robert D., eds. LC 78-60894. (Myth & Romanticism Ser.: Vol. 21). 399p. 1979. lib. bdg. 60.00 (ISBN 0-8240-3570-4). Garland Pub.
Rufus, Jones M. Studies in Mystical Religion. 1978. Repr. of 1919 ed. lib. bdg. 45.00 (ISBN 0-8492-1257-X). R West.
Russell, Bertrand. Mysticism & Logic & Other Essays. 2nd ed. 168p. 1981. pap. 5.95x (ISBN 0-389-20135-9). B&N.
Savage, D. S. Mysticism & Aldous Huxley. LC 77-23247. 1947. lib. bdg. 7.50 (ISBN 0-8414-7805-8). Folcroft.
Sayre, Kenneth M. Starburst. LC 76-30423. 1977. 17.50 (ISBN 0-268-01690-9, IS-00024, Pub. by Univ. of Notre Dame Pr). Univ Microfilms.
Schutz, Albert. Call Adonoi: Manual of Practical Cabalah & Gestalt Mysticism. 114p. 1980. pap. 8.95 (ISBN 0-936596-00-7). Ross-Erikson.
Schwarz, Jack. Human Energy Systems. (Illus.). 1980. pap. 6.95 (ISBN 0-525-47556-7). Dutton.
Sheiner, Ben. Intellectual Mysticism. LC 78-50531. 1978. 7.50 (ISBN 0-8022-2228-5). Philos Lib.
Shirley, Ralph. Occultists & Mystics of All Ages. 176p. 1974. pap. 2.95 (ISBN 0-8065-0419-6). Citadel Pr.
Silberer, H. Problems of Mysticism & Its Symbolism. LC 70-142498. 10.00 (ISBN 0-87728-038-X). Weiser.
Smith, Margaret. An Early Mystic of Baghdad: A Study of the Life & Teaching of Harith b. Asad al-Muhasibi, A.D. 781-A.D. 857. LC 76-180379. Repr. of 1935 ed. 16.50 (ISBN 0-404-56324-4). AMS Pr.
--An Introduction to Mysticism. 1977. pap. 5.95 (ISBN 0-19-519956-1). Oxford U Pr.
--An Introduction to the History of Mysticism. 69.95 (ISBN 0-87968-437-2). Gordon Pr.
--The Way of the Mystics: The Early Christian Mystics & the Rise of the Sufis. 1978. pap. 4.95 (ISBN 0-19-519967-7, GB541, GB). Oxford U Pr.
--The Way of the Mystics: The Early Christian Mystics & the Rise of the Sufis. 1979. 14.95 (ISBN 0-19-520039-X). Oxford U Pr.
Spencer, Sidney. Mysticism in World Religion. 8.00 (ISBN 0-8446-0927-7). Peter Smith.
Sprietsma, Cargill. We Imperialists: Notes on Ernest Seilliere's "Philosophy of Imperialism". LC 70-176005. Repr. of 1931 ed. 16.50 (ISBN 0-404-06198-2). AMS Pr.
Staal, Frits. Exploring Mysticism: A Methodological. LC 74-76391. 1975. 27.50x (ISBN 0-520-02726-4); pap. 4.95 (ISBN 0-520-03119-9, CAL 313). U of Cal Pr.
Starcke, Walter. This Double Thread. 1969. 6.00 (ISBN 0-227-67738-2). Attic Pr.
Stavropoulos, C. Partakers of Divine Nature. 1976. pap. 3.50 (ISBN 0-937032-09-3). Light&Life Pub Co MN.
Steiner, Johannes. The Visions of Therese Newmann. LC 75-34182. 245p. 1976. pap. 5.95 (ISBN 0-8189-0318-X). Alba.
Steiner, Rudolf. Mysticism at the Dawn of the Modern Age. 2nd ed. Allen, Paul M., ed. Zimmer, Karl E., tr. from Ger. LC 60-15703. (The Major Writings of Rudolf Steiner in English Translation Ser.: The Centennial Edition). 256p. 1981. 12.00x (ISBN 0-8334-0721-X, Steinerbooks); pap. 7.50 (ISBN 0-8334-1721-5). Multimedia.
--Mysticism at the Dawn of the Modern Age. LC 60-15703. (Spiritual Science Library). 256p. 1980. 12.00x (ISBN 0-8334-0721-X); pap. 6.95 (ISBN 0-8334-1786-X). Steinerbks.
Stevens, Edward. An Introduction to Oriental Mysticism. 1974. pap. 2.95 (ISBN 0-8091-1798-3). Paulist Pr.
Studies in Mysticism & Religion. Date not set. 27.50 (ISBN 0-686-76265-7). Feldheim.

Stutfield, Hugh E. Mysticism & Catholicism. 1977. lib. bdg. 59.95 (ISBN 0-8490-2318-1). Gordon Pr.

Suzuki, Daisetz T. Mysticism: Christian & Buddhist. LC 75-31442. 214p. 1976. Repr. of 1957 ed. lib. bdg. 21.00x (ISBN 0-8371-8516-5, SUMY). Greenwood.

Talbot, Michael. Mysticism & the New Physics. 224p. (Orig.). 1981. pap. 3.50 (ISBN 0-553-11908-7). Bantam.

Tavard, George H. The Inner Life: Foundations of Christian Mysticism. LC 75-32858. 112p. (Orig.). 1976. pap. 1.95 (ISBN 0-8091-1927-7, Deus). Paulist Pr.

The Mother. Conversations. 1979. pap. 2.00 (ISBN 0-89744-935-5). Auromere.

Tuckwell, James H. Religion & Reality. LC 77-118552. 1971. Repr. of 1915 ed. 13.00 (ISBN 0-8046-1177-7). Kennikat.

Underhill, Evelyn. The Essentials of Mysticism & Other Essays. LC 75-41277. Repr. of 1920 ed. 18.00 (ISBN 0-404-14620-1). AMS Pr.

--Mixed Pasture. facs. ed. LC 68-8501. (Essay Index Reprint Ser). 1933. 15.00 (ISBN 0-8369-0958-5). Arno.

--The Mystic Way. 395p. 1980. Repr. of 1913 ed. lib. bdg. 35.00 (ISBN 0-8482-2755-7). Norwood Edns.

--The Mystic Way. LC 75-34166. 1975. Repr. of 1913 ed. lib. bdg. 35.00 (ISBN 0-8414-8854-1). Folcroft.

--Mysticism. 1961. pap. 6.75 (ISBN 0-525-47073-5). Dutton.

--Mysticism. 1955. pap. 5.95 (ISBN 0-452-00495-0, F495, Mer). NAL.

--Mysticism: A Study in the Nature & Development of Man's Spiritual Consciousness. 576p. 1977. Repr. of 1911 ed. 29.50x (ISBN 0-87471-883-X). Rowman.

--Mystics of the Church. 1975. 10.00 (ISBN 0-227-67820-6). Attic Pr.

--Practical Mysticism. 1960. pap. 3.50 (ISBN 0-525-47049-2). Dutton.

Upward, Allen. The Divine Mystery. LC 76-27214. 384p. 1976. lib. bdg. 12.95 (ISBN 0-915520-02-8); pap. 5.95 (ISBN 0-915520-01-X). Ross-Erikson.

Valiuddin, Mir. Love of God. (Orig.). 1979. pap. 2.45 (ISBN 0-900217-02-2, Pub. by Sufi Pub Co England). Hunter Hse.

Valla, Mary. The Mystical Way of Life. LC 74-14058. 176p. 1975. pap. 4.95 (ISBN 0-685-52237-7). De Vorss.

Veysey, Laurence. The Communal Experience: Anarchist & Mystical Communities in Twentieth Century America. LC 78-55045. 1978. pap. 7.95 (ISBN 0-226-85458-2, P786, Phoen). U of Chicago Pr.

Voillaume, Rene, ed. Silent Pilgrimage to God: The Spirituality of Charles deFoucauld. Moiser, Jeremy, tr. from Fr. LC 74-32516. 1977. pap. 3.95 (ISBN 0-88344-461-5). Orbis Bks.

Waite, Arthur E. Raymund Lully: Christian Mystic. 69.95 (ISBN 0-87968-100-4). Gordon Pr.

Walker, David. God Is a Sea: The Dynamics of Christian Living. LC 81-8072. 144p. (Orig.). 1981. pap. 4.95 (ISBN 0-686-73666-4, Pub. by Alba Bks). Alba.

Walker, Kenneth W. Mystic Mind. 1965. 7.95 (ISBN 0-87523-153-5). Emerson.

Walsh, James, ed. Pre-Reformation English Spirituality. LC 65-12885. 1966. 20.00 (ISBN 0-8232-0655-6). Fordham.

Warren, John, ed. Highest State of Consciousness. LC 70-171340. 1972. pap. 3.50 (ISBN 0-385-04532-8, Anch). Doubleday.

Waters, Frank. Mexico Mystique: The Coming Sixth World of Consciousness. LC 74-18579. (Illus.). 326p. 1975. 15.95 (ISBN 0-8040-0663-6, SB). Swallow.

Watkin, Edward I. Poets & Mystics. facs. ed. LC 68-55862. (Essay Index Reprint Ser). 1953. 17.00 (ISBN 0-8369-0979-8). Arno.

Watts, Alan W. This Is It. 1972. pap. 1.95 (ISBN 0-394-71904-2, Vin). Random.

The Way to the Kingdom. 2nd ed. 345p. 1972. pap. 6.00 (ISBN 0-87516-164-2). De Vorss.

Webb, James, ed. A Quest Anthology. LC 75-36916. (Occult Ser.). 1976. Repr. of 1976 ed. 35.00x (ISBN 0-405-07971-0). Arno.

Wetherbee, Winthrop, ed. & tr. The Cosmographia of Bernardus Silvestris. (Records of Civilization, Sources & Studies: Sources & Studies). 176p. 1973. 15.00x (ISBN 0-231-03673-6). Columbia U Pr.

White, Helen C. Mysticism of William Blake. LC 64-10715. 1964. Repr. of 1927 ed. 18.00 (ISBN 0-8462-0490-8). Russell.

Wilcox, Laird M., compiled by. Bibliography on Astrology, Mysticism, & the Occult. 1981. pap. text ed. 9.95 (ISBN 0-933592-25-6). Edit Res Serv.

Wolters, Clifton, tr. The Cloud of Unknowing & Other Works. (Classics Ser). 1978. pap. 2.95 (ISBN 0-14-044385-1). Penguin.

Woods, Richard. Understanding Mysticism. LC 78-22743. 1980. pap. 7.95 (ISBN 0-385-15117-9, Im). Doubleday.

Wright, J. Stafford. La Mente y lo Desconocido. Gilchrist, James S., tr. from Eng. LC 76-9906. 228p. (Orig., Span.). 1976. pap. 3.50 (ISBN 0-89922-070-3). Edit Caribe.

Yeats, William B. Vision. 1956. pap. 5.95 (ISBN 0-02-055600-4). Macmillan.

Younghusband, Francis. Modern Mystics. 322p. 1970. 7.95 (ISBN 0-8216-0118-0). Univ Bks.

Younghusband, Francis E. Modern Mystics. facs. ed. LC 67-28774. (Essay Index Reprint Ser). 1935. 15.75 (ISBN 0-8369-1015-X). Arno.

Zaehner, Robert C. Mysticism: Sacred & Profane. 1961. pap. 4.95x (ISBN 0-19-500229-6, GB56). Oxford U Pr.

MYSTICISM–MIDDLE AGES, 600-1500

Gebhart, E. Mystics & Heretics in Italy at the End of the Middle Ages. 1977. lib. bdg. 59.95 (ISBN 0-8490-2321-1). Gordon Pr.

Glasscoe, Marion, ed. The Medieval Mystical Tradition in England. 249p. 1981. pap. 12.00x (ISBN 0-686-69801-0, Pub. by U Exeter, England). Humanities.

Herbert, Kevin. Hugh of Saint Victor: Soliloquy on the Earnest Money of the Soul. (Medieval Philosophical Texts in Translation: No. 9). 1956. pap. 5.95 (ISBN 0-87462-209-3). Marquette.

Hopper, Vincent F. Medieval Number Symbolism: Its Sources, Meaning & Influence on Thought & Expression. LC 70-85372. 241p. 1969. Repr. of 1938 ed. 22.50x (ISBN 0-8154-0305-4). Cooper Sq.

Molinari, Paul. Julian of Norwich: The Teaching of a 14th Century English Mystic. 1978. lib. bdg. 30.00 (ISBN 0-8495-3737-1). Arden Lib.

Ozment, Steven E. Mysticism & Dissent: Religious Ideology & Social Protest in the Sixteenth Century. LC 72-91316. 272p. 1973. 25.00x (ISBN 0-300-01576-3). Yale U Pr.

Petry, Ray C., ed. Late Medieval Mysticism. (Library of Christian Classics). 1980. pap. 9.95 (ISBN 0-664-24163-8). Westminster.

Progoff, Ira. Cloud of Unknowing. 1963. 5.00 (ISBN 0-517-52768-5). Crown.

Richard Of St. Victor, et al. Cell of Self-Knowledge. Gardner, E. G., ed. LC 66-25702. (Medieval Library). Repr. of 1926 ed. 7.50x (ISBN 0-8154-0188-4). Cooper Sq.

Riehle, Wofgang. The Middle English Mystics. 256p. 1981. 32.50 (ISBN 0-7100-0612-8). Routledge & Kegan.

Tuma, George W. The Fourteenth Century English Mystics, Vol. 2. (Salzburg Studies in English Literature; Elizabethan & Renaissance Studies: No.62). 1977. pap. text ed. 25.00x (ISBN 0-391-01548-6). Humanities.

MYSTICISM–BUDDHISM

Blofeld, John. Beyond the Gods: Taoist & Buddhist Mysticism. 1974. o. p. 9.25 (ISBN 0-04-294084-2); pap. 6.95 (ISBN 0-04-294085-0). Allen Unwin.

Govinda, L. Anagarika. Foundations of Tibetan Mysticism. (Illus.). 1970. pap. 4.95 (ISBN 0-87728-064-9). Weiser.

MYSTICISM–CATHOLIC CHURCH

Arintero, John G. Mystical Evolution, 2 vols. Aumann, Jordan, tr. from Sp. LC 78-62254. Orig. Title: La Evolucion Mistica. 1979. Set. pap. 16.00 (ISBN 0-89555-073-3). TAN Bks Pubs.

Bessieres, Albert. Wife, Mother & Mystic. Newton, Douglas, ed. Rigby, Stephen, tr. from Fr. (Eng.). 1977. pap. 3.50 (ISBN 0-89555-058-X, 108). TAN Bks Pubs.

Bonaventure, St. The Mind's Journey to God (Itinerarium Mentis Ad Deum) Cunningham, Lawrence S., tr. 1979. 6.95 (ISBN 0-8199-0765-0). Franciscan Herald.

Clissold, Stephen. The Wisdom of the Spanish Mystics. LC 77-7650. (New Directions Wisdon Ser.). 1977. 7.50 (ISBN 0-8112-0663-7); pap. 2.95 (ISBN 0-8112-0664-5, NDP442). New Directions.

De Caussade, Jean-Pierre. Abandonment to Divine Providence. LC 74-2827. 120p. 1975. pap. 2.50 (ISBN 0-385-02544-0, Im). Doubleday.

Godwin, George. The Great Mystics. LC 74-2430. (St. Paul, Plotinus, St. Augustine, St. Francis, St. Teresa, Martin Luther, Jacob Boehme, George Fox, Emanuel Swedenborg, William Blake). 1945. lib. bdg. 10.00 (ISBN 0-8414-4499-4). Folcroft.

John of the Cross, St. Dark Night of the Soul. 1959. pap. 2.45 (ISBN 0-385-02930-6, D78, Im). Doubleday.

--Living Flame of Love. 1971. pap. 3.50 (ISBN 0-385-07547-2, Im). Doubleday.

McNamara, William. Mystical Passion: Spirituality for a Bored Society. 1977. pap. 5.95 (ISBN 0-8091-2053-4). Paulist Pr.

Mallory, Marilyn M. Christian Mysticism: Transcending Techniques. a Theological Reflection on the Empirical Testing of the Teaching of St. John of the Cross. 1977. pap. text ed. 34.25x (ISBN 90-232-1535-4). Humanities.

O'Connell, Patrick & Carty, Charles. The Holy Shroud & Four Visions: The Holy Shroud New Evidence Compared with the Visions of St. Bridget of Sweden, Maria d'Agrenda, Catherine Emmerick, & Teresa Neumann. (Illus.). 1974. pap. 1.00 (ISBN 0-89555-102-0, 164). TAN Bks Pubs.

Rolt-Wheeler, F. Mystic Gleams from the Holy Grail. 59.95 (ISBN 0-8490-0694-5). Gordon Pr.

Teilhard De Chardin, Pierre. Hymn of the Universe. LC 65-10375. 1969. pap. 4.95x (ISBN 0-06-131910-4, TB1910, Torch). Har-Row.

--Hymne De L'univers. 1966. 13.95 (ISBN 0-685-11240-3). French & Eur.

Watkin, Edward I. Poets & Mystics. facs. ed. LC 68-55862. (Essay Index Reprint Ser). 1953. 17.00 (ISBN 0-8369-0979-8). Arno.

MYSTICISM–HINDUISM

see also Samadhi

Bhaktivedanta, Swami A. C. Easy Journey to Other Planets. LC 70-118080. (Illus.). 1970. pap. 1.50 (ISBN 0-912776-10-2). Bhaktivedanta.

Dasgupta, S. N. Hindu Mysticism. LC 58-11626. 1960. pap. 3.95 (ISBN 0-8044-6110-4). Ungar.

--Hindu Mysticism. 1977. 6.50 (ISBN 0-8426-0929-6). Orient Bk Dist.

--Hindu Mysticism. 1977. text ed. 7.50x (ISBN 0-8426-0929-6). Verry.

Jyotir Maya Nanda, Swami. Mysticism of Hindu Gods & Goddesses. (Illus.). 1974. pap. 3.99 (ISBN 0-934664-08-0). Yoga Res Foun.

Masson, J. Moussaieff. The Oceanic Feeling: The Origins of Religious Sentiment in Ancient India. (Studies of Classical India: No. 3). 228p. 1980. lib. bdg. 34.00 (ISBN 90-277-1050-3, Pub. by Reidel Holland). Kluwer Boston.

Menen, Aubrey. The Mystics. (Illus.). 1974. 15.00 (ISBN 0-8037-6204-6). Dial.

MYSTICISM–HISTORY

Bridges, Hal. American Mysticism: From William James to Zen. LC 76-55054. 1977. pap. 3.95 (ISBN 0-87707-191-8). CSA Pr.

Eckhart, Meister. Meister Eckhart: A Modern Translation. pap. 4.95x (ISBN 0-06-130008-X, TB8, Torch). Har-Row.

Fairweather, William. Among the Mystics: The Development of Mysticism from Its Rise in the East. 161p. Repr. of 1936 ed. text ed. 4.50 (ISBN 0-567-02104-1). Attic Pr.

Gall, E. Mysticism Through the Ages. 59.95 (ISBN 0-8490-0697-X). Gordon Pr.

Jones, Rufus M. Studies in Mystical Religion. LC 79-102509. 1970. Repr. of 1909 ed. 16.00 (ISBN 0-8462-1468-7). Russell.

Katsaros, Thomas & Kaplan, Nathaniel. The Western Mystical Tradition: An Intellectual History of Western Civilization, Vol. 1. 1969. 7.50x (ISBN 0-8084-0316-8); pap. 4.95 (ISBN 0-8084-0317-6, H4). Coll & U Pr.

Louth, Andrew. The Origins of the Christian Mystical Tradition: From Plato to Denys. 240p. 1981. 29.95 (ISBN 0-19-826655-3). Oxford U Pr.

Twenty-Five Days with Great Christian Mystics: A Journey into Practical Christianity. pap. 2.50 (ISBN 0-686-13933-X). Rorge Pub Co.

Walsh, James, ed. Spirituality Through the Centuries. 1964. 5.50 (ISBN 0-02-838940-9, 83894). Kenedy.

MYSTICISM–ISLAM

see also Sufism

Archer, John C. Mystical Elements in Mohammed. LC 78-63554. (Yale Oriental Ser. Researches: No. 11 Pt. 1; All Published). Repr. of 1924 ed. 22.50 (ISBN 0-404-60281-9). AMS Pr.

Attar, Farid Al-Din. Muslim Saints & Mystics: Episodes from the Tadhkirat al-Auliya-Memorial of the Saints. (Persian Heritage Ser). 1973. 14.75 (ISBN 0-7100-1033-8). Routledge & Kegan.

Boewering, Gerhard. The Mystical Vision of Existence in Islam Classical. (Studien zur Sprache, Geschichte und Kultur desislamischen Orients, Beihefte zur "der Islam"). 296p. 1979. text ed. 79.00x (ISBN 3-11-007546-6). De Gruyter.

Hall, Manly P. Mystics of Islam. pap. 3.75 (ISBN 0-89314-532-7). Philos Res.

Morewedge, Parviz, ed. Islamic Philosophy & Mysticism. LC 80-14364. (Studies in Islamic Philosophy & Science). 1981. write for info. (ISBN 0-88206-302-2). Caravan Bks.

Mulla Sadra. The Wisdom of the Throne: An Introduction to the Philosophy of Mulla Sadra. Morris, James W., tr. from Arabic. LC 81-47153. (Princeton Library of Asian Translations). 300p. 1981. 22.50x (ISBN 0-691-06493-8). Princeton U Pr.

Nasr, Seyyed H. Sadr al-Din Shirazi & His Transcendent Theosophy. LC 78-62006. 1979. 9.50 (ISBN 0-87773-734-7). Great Eastern.

Nicholson, R. A. Mystics of Islam. 1975. pap. 7.95 (ISBN 0-7100-8015-8). Routledge & Kegan.

--Studies in Islamic Mysticism. LC 78-73958. 1979. 42.00 (ISBN 0-521-05836-8); pap. 12.50x (ISBN 0-521-29546-7). Cambridge U Pr.

Palacios, Miguel A. The Mystical Philosophy of Ibn Masarra & His Followers. Douglas, E. H. & Yoder, H. W., trs. from Span. 1978. text ed. 34.25x (ISBN 90-04-05749-8). Humanities.

Rumi the Persian Mystic. 1970. 6.50x (ISBN 0-87902-185-3). Orientalia.

Smith, Margaret. An Early Mystic of Baghdad: A Study of the Life & Teaching of Harith b. Asad al-Muhasibi, A.D. 781-A.D. 857. LC 76-180379. Repr. of 1935 ed. 16.50 (ISBN 0-404-56324-4). AMS Pr.

Zaehner, Robert C. Hindu & Muslim Mysticism. LC 74-83675. 1969. pap. 4.50 (ISBN 0-8052-0237-4). Schocken.

MYSTICISM–JUDAISM

Altmann, Alexander. Studies in Religious Philosophy & Mysticism. (New Reprints in Essay & General Literature Index Ser.). 1975. Repr. of 1969 ed. 21.75 (ISBN 0-518-10194-0). Arno.

Aptowitzer, V. & Schwarz, A. Z. Abhandlungen zur Erinnerung an Hirsch Perez Chajes. LC 7-7163. (Jewish Philosophy, Mysticism & History of Ideas Ser.). 1980. Repr. of 1933 ed. lib. bdg. 52.00x (ISBN 0-405-12237-3). Arno.

Ben Zion, Raphael, tr. from Hebrew. Anthology of Jewish Mysticism. 5.00 (ISBN 0-686-13334-X). Yesod Pubs.

Blumenthal, D. R. Understanding Jewish Mysticism: A Source Reader. (Library of Judaic Learning). 12.50x (ISBN 0-87068-334-9). Ktav.

Bokser, Ben Zion. The Jewish Mystical Tradition. 1980. 15.00 (ISBN 0-88482-922-7); pap. 6.95 (ISBN 0-88482-923-5). Hebrew Pub.

Buber, Martin. I & Thou. Kaufman, Walter, tr. LC 72-123845. 1970. 12.50 (ISBN 0-684-15575-3, ScribT); pap. 2.95 (ISBN 0-684-71725-5, SL243, ScribT). Scribner.

Greene, William B. The Blazing Star, with an Appendix Treating of the Jewish Kabbala. 1977. lib. bdg. 59.95 (ISBN 0-8490-1516-2). Gordon Pr.

Jacobs, Louis. Jewish Ethics, Philosophy & Mysticism. LC 71-80005. (Chain of Tradition Ser). 1969. pap. 3.95x (ISBN 0-87441-012-6). Behrman.

--Jewish Mystical Testimonies. LC 76-46644. 1977. pap. 7.95 (ISBN 0-8052-0585-3). Schocken.

Jellinek, Adolph. Beitrage zur Geschichte der Kabbala. Katz, Steven, ed. LC 79-7138. (Jewish Philosophy, Mysticism, & History of Ideas Ser.). 1980. Repr. of 1852 ed. lib. bdg. 14.00x (ISBN 0-405-12264-0). Arno.

Katz, Steven, ed. Studies by Samuel Horodezky: An Original Anthology. LC 79-51391. (Jewish Philosophy, Mysticism & History of Ideas Ser.). 1980. lib. bdg. 15.00x (ISBN 0-405-12233-0). Arno.

Katz, Steven T., ed. Jewish Philosophy, Mysticism & History of Ideas Series, 50 bks. (Illus.). 1980. Set. lib. bdg. 2073.00x (ISBN 0-405-12229-2). Arno.

Kaufman, William E. Journeys: An Introductory Guide to Jewish Mysticism. LC 80-69017. 1980. 12.50 (ISBN 0-8197-0482-2); pap. 7.95 (ISBN 0-686-77548-1). Bloch.

Muller, Ernst & Simon, Maurice. History of Jewish Mysticism. 4.00 (ISBN 0-686-13336-6). Yesod Pubs.

Scholem, Gersham G. Jewish Gnosticism, Merkabah Mysticism & Talmudic Tradition. 1960. 10.00x (ISBN 0-685-31427-8, Pub. by Jewish Theol Seminary). Ktav.

Scholem, Gershom. Major Trends in Jewish Mysticism. 3rd ed. LC 61-8991. 1961. pap. 7.95 (ISBN 0-8052-0005-3). Schocken.

--On Jews & Judaism in Crisis: Selected Essays. Dannhauser, Werner J., ed. LC 75-37010. 1978. 16.50 (ISBN 0-8052-3613-9); pap. 7.95 (ISBN 0-8052-0588-8). Schocken.

Singer, Isaac Bashevis & Moskowitz, Ira. A Little Boy in Search of God: Mysticism in a Personal Light. LC 75-6078. 224p. 1976. 17.95 (ISBN 0-385-06653-8); Limited Edition 50.00 (ISBN 0-385-11668-3). Doubleday.

The Way of the Faithful Anthology of Jewish Mysticism. 28.50 (ISBN 0-87559-080-2). Shalom.

MYSTICISM–ORTHODOX EASTERN CHURCH

see also Hesychasm

Arseniev, Nicholas. Mysticism & the Eastern Church. 173p. 1979. pap. 6.95 (ISBN 0-913836-55-9). St Vladimirs.

Isaac, St. Mystical Treatises of St. Isaac the Syrian, Bishop of Nineveh, 2 vols. Wensinck, A. J., tr. pap. 17.50 set (ISBN 0-686-05657-4). Eastern Orthodox.

Isaac The Syrian. Mystical Writings of St. Isaac the Syrian. Wensinck, A. J., tr. from Syriac. 1977. pap. 2.45 (ISBN 0-686-19231-1). Eastern Orthodox.

Lossky, Vladimir. The Mystical Theology of the Eastern Church. LC 76-25448. Orig. Title: Essai sur la theologie mystique de L'eglise d'orient. 252p. 1976. pap. 7.95 (ISBN 0-913836-31-1). St Vladimirs.
Macarius, Saint Fifty Spiritual Homilies. 1974. Repr. of 1921 ed. 6.50 (ISBN 0-686-10200-2). Eastern Orthodox.
Monk of the Eastern Church. Orthodox Spirituality: An Outline of the Orthodox Ascetical & Mystical Tradition. 111p. 1978. pap. 3.95 (ISBN 0-913836-51-6). St Vladimirs.
Rahner, Hugo. Greek Myths & Christian Mystery. LC 79-156736. (Illus.). 1971. Repr. of 1963 ed. 17.50x (ISBN 0-8196-0270-1). Biblo.
Wisdom of the Desert Fathers. 1979. pap. 3.95 (ISBN 0-686-25228-4). Eastern Orthodox.

MYSTICISM–GERMANY

Boehme, Jakob. The Confessions. 69.95 (ISBN 0-87968-258-2). Gordon Pr.
Clark, James M. Great German Mystics: Eckhart, Tauler & Suso. LC 73-81493. 1970. Repr. of 1949 ed. 15.00 (ISBN 0-8462-1351-6). Russell.

MYSTICISM–GREAT BRITAIN

Bradley, Ritamary & Lagorio, Valerie M. The Fourteenth Century English Mystics: A Comprehensive Annotated Bibliography. LC 79-7922. (Garland Reference Library of the Humanities). 300p. 1981. lib. bdg. 30.00 (ISBN 0-8240-9535-9). Garland Pub.
Cholmeley, Katharine. Margery Kempe, Genius & Mystic. LC 78-7811. 1978. Repr. of 1947 ed. lib. bdg. 17.50 (ISBN 0-8414-0296-5). Folcroft.
Exeter University Press, ed. The Medieval Mystical Tradition in England. 249p. 1980. 20.00x (ISBN 0-85989-141-0, Pub. by Exeter Univ England). State Mutual Bk.
Glasscoe, Marion, ed. The Medieval Mystical Tradition in England. 249p. 1981. pap. 12.00x (ISBN 0-686-69801-0, Pub. by U Exeter, England). Humanities.
Hodgson, Geraldine E. English Mystics. LC 73-13663. 1973. lib. bdg. 20.00 (ISBN 0-8414-4756-X). Folcroft.
--English Mystics. 1977. lib. bdg. 59.95 (ISBN 0-8490-1777-7). Gordon Pr.
Hollingworth, G. E. English Mystics. 1973. lib. bdg. 15.00 (ISBN 0-8414-5096-X). Folcroft.
Kempe, Margery, et al. The Cell of Self Knowledge: Seven Early English Mystical Treatises. Griffiths, John, ed. LC 81-126. (The Spiritual Classics Ser.). 128p. 1981. 8.95 (ISBN 0-8245-0082-2). Crossroad NY.
Molinari, Paolo. Julian of Norwich. LC 74-13160. 1974. Repr. of 1958 ed. lib. bdg. 27.50 (ISBN 0-8414-6168-6). Folcroft.
Roberts, Anthony. Atlantean Traditions in Ancient Britain. 1977. pap. 6.95 (ISBN 0-09-128751-0, Pub. by Hutchinson). Merrimack Bk Serv.
Sawyer, Michael E., compiled by. A Bibliographical Index of Five English Mystics. LC 73-110788. (Bibliographia Tripotamopolitana: No. 10). 1978. 10.00 (ISBN 0-931222-09-5). C E Barbour.
Spurgeon, Caroline F. Mysticism in English Literature. LC 74-105838. 1970. Repr. of 1913 ed. 11.00 (ISBN 0-8046-0981-0). Kennikat.
Way, Robert, ed. The Wisdom of the English Mystics. LC 78-6435. 1978. pap. 3.75 (ISBN 0-8112-0700-5, NDP466). New Directions.

MYSTICISM–INDIA

see also Mandala

Balse, Mayah. Mystics & Men of Miracles in India. (Illus.). 1976. 4.50 (ISBN 0-913244-10-4). Hapi Pr.
Choudhary, K. P. Modern Indian Mysticism. 1981. 17.00x (ISBN 0-8364-0744-X, Pub. by Motilal Banarsidass). South Asia Bks.
McGill, Ormond. Hypnotism & Mysticism of India. 2nd ed. (Illus.). Date not set. Repr. of 1977 ed. text ed. 10.00 (ISBN 0-930298-01-2). Westwood Pub Co.
Masson, J. Moussaieff. The Oceanic Feeling: The Origins of Religious Sentiment in Ancient India. (Studies of Classical India: No. 3). 228p. 1980. lib. bdg. 34.00 (ISBN 90-277-1050-3, Pub. by Reidel Holland). Kluwer Boston.
Sen, K. Medieval Mysticism of India. 1974. 12.50x (ISBN 0-8426-0631-9). Verry.
Sircar, M. N. Mysticism in the Bhagavad-Gita. 1977. 12.00x (ISBN 0-686-22667-4). Intl Bk Dist.
Van Over, Raymond. Eastern Mysticism: The Near East & India, Vol.1. 1977. pap. 2.50 (ISBN 0-451-61575-1, ME1575, Ment). NAL.
Vaudeville, Charlotte. Kabir, Vol. 1. 344p. 1974. text ed. 45.00x (ISBN 0-19-826526-3). Oxford U Pr.

MYSTICISM–IRAN

Palmer, Edward Henry, ed. Oriental Mysticism: A Treatise on the Sufiistic & Unitarian Theosophy of the Persians. 84p. 1969. Repr. 24.00x (ISBN 0-7146-2576-0, F Cass Co). Biblio Dist.

MYSTICISM–RUSSIA

Allen, Paul M. & Vladimir, Soloviev. Russian Mystic. LC 72-81592. (Spiritual Science Library). (Illus.). 544p. 1978. 15.00x (ISBN 0-8334-0709-0). Multimedia.

MYSTICISM–SPAIN

Clissold, Stephen. The Wisdom of the Spanish Mystics. LC 77-7650. (New Directions Wisdon Ser.). 1977. 7.50 (ISBN 0-8112-0663-7); pap. 2.95 (ISBN 0-8112-0664-5, NDP442). New Directions.
Peers, E. A. Studies of the Spanish Mystics, 3 vols. 1977. lib. bdg. 300.00 (ISBN 0-8490-2706-3). Gordon Pr.

MYSTICISM IN LITERATURE

see also Occultism in Literature

Bose, Abinash C. Three Mystic Poets: A Study of W. B. Yeats, A. E. & Rabindrath Tagore. LC 72-187263. 1945. lib. bdg. 10.00 (ISBN 0-8414-2534-5). Folcroft.
Broers, B. C. Mysticism in the Neo-Romanticists. LC 68-767. (Studies in Comparative Literature, No. 35). 1969. Repr. of 1923 ed. lib. bdg. 49.95 (ISBN 0-8383-0514-8). Haskell.
Cummins, Walter M., et al. The Other Sides of Reality: Myths, Visions & Fantasies. LC 75-182677. 400p. 1972. pap. 7.95x (ISBN 0-87835-038-1). Boyd & Fraser.
Davison, William T. Mystics & Poets. LC 77-924. 1977. lib. bdg. 25.00 (ISBN 0-8414-3680-0). Folcroft.
Hunter, Irene, ed. American Mystical Verse. LC 79-116407. (Granger Index Reprint Ser). 1925. 14.50 (ISBN 0-8369-6148-X). Arno.
Inge, William R. Studies of English Mystics. facs. ed. LC 69-17578. (Essay Index Reprint Ser). 1906. 15.00 (ISBN 0-8369-0081-2). Arno.
Itrat-Husain. Mystical Element in the Metaphysical Poets of the Seventeenth Century. LC 66-23522. 1948. 12.00x (ISBN 0-8196-0177-2). Biblo.
Jones, Rufus M. Mysticism in Robert Browning. 1924. Repr. 10.00 (ISBN 0-8274-2784-0). R West.
Jusserand, Jean A. Piers Plowman: A Contribution to the History of English Mysticism. Richards, Marion & Richards, Elise, trs. LC 65-13959. (Illus.). 1965. Repr. of 1894 ed. 10.00 (ISBN 0-8462-0548-3). Russell.
Kortelling, Jacomina. Mysticism in Blake & Wordsworth. LC 68-2111. (Studies in Poetry, No. 38). 1969. Repr. of 1928 ed. lib. bdg. 33.95 (ISBN 0-8383-0577-6). Haskell.
Osmond, Percy H. Mystical Poets of the English Church. LC 72-5166. 1919. lib. bdg. 30.00 (ISBN 0-8414-6542-8). Folcroft.
Saurat, Denis, et al. Gods of the People. LC 77-23247. 1947. lib. bdg. 12.50 (ISBN 0-685-10073-1). Folcroft.
Spurgeon, Caroline F. Mysticism in English Literature. LC 74-105838. 1970. Repr. of 1913 ed. 11.00 (ISBN 0-8046-0981-0). Kennikat.
Tuma, George W. The Fourteenth Century English Mystics: A Comparative Analysis, Vol. 1. (Salzburg Studies in English Literature: Elizabethan & Renaissance Studies: Vol. 61). (Orig.). 1977. pap. text ed. 22.75x (ISBN 0-391-01547-8). Humanities.
Wiese, Gunther. Untersuchungen Zu Den Prosaschriften Henry Vaughans. (Salburg Studies in English Literature, Elizabethan & Renaissance: No. 72). 1978. pap. text ed. 25.00x (ISBN 0-391-01568-0). Humanities.
Wright, Luella M. Literary Life of the Early Friends, 1650-1725. LC 32-25426. Repr. of 1932 ed. 19.50 (ISBN 0-404-07046-9). AMS Pr.

MYTH

see also Demythologization; Mythology

Bolle, Kees W. Freedom of Man in Myth. LC 68-8564. 1968. 5.00 (ISBN 0-8265-1125-2). Vanderbilt U Pr.
Bryant, Jacob. A New System, or, an Analysis of Ancient Mythology, 3 vols. Feldman, Burton & Richardson, Robert, eds. LC 78-60881. (Myth & Romanticism Ser.: Vol. 5). (Illus.). 1980. Set. lib. bdg. 198.00 (ISBN 0-8240-3554-2); lib. bdg. 66.00 ea. Garland Pub.
Campbell, Joseph, ed. Myths, Dreams, & Religion. 1970. pap. 4.25 (ISBN 0-525-47255-X). Dutton.
Carrabino, Victor, ed. The Power of Myth in Literature & Film. LC 80-21998. (A Florida State University Bk.). 136p. 1980. 12.25 (ISBN 0-8130-0673-2, IS-00116, Pub. by U Presses Fla). Univ Microfilms.
Cassirer, Ernst. Language & Myth. 6.75 (ISBN 0-8446-1820-9). Peter Smith.
--Language & Myth. Langer, Susanne K., tr. 1946. pap. 2.00 (ISBN 0-486-20051-5). Dover.
--Myth of the State. 1961. pap. 5.95 (ISBN 0-300-00036-7, y33). Yale U Pr.
Colloquium on Myth in Literature, Bucknell & Susquehanna Universities, Mar. 21-2, 1974. The Binding of Proteus, Perspectives on Myth & the Literary Process: Proceedings. McCune, Marjorie W. & Orbison, T. Tucker, eds. LC 76-49774. 352p. 1978. 22.50 (ISBN 0-8387-1708-X). Bucknell U Pr.
De Santillana, Giorgio & Von Dechend, Hertha. Hamlet's Mill: An Essay on Myth & the Frame of Time. LC 69-13267. (Illus.). 1969. 15.00 (ISBN 0-87645-008-7). Gambit.
Detienne, Marcel. Dionysos Slain. Muellner, M. & Muellner, L., trs. LC 78-20518. 1979. 10.95x (ISBN 0-8018-2210-6). Johns Hopkins.
Ehrenreich, Paul. Die Allgemeine Mythologie und Ihre Ethnologischen Grundlagen. Bolle, Kees W., ed. LC 77-79125. (Mythology Ser.). 1978. Repr. of 1915 ed. lib. bdg. 25.00x (ISBN 0-405-10536-3). Arno.
El Guindi, Fadwa. Religion in Culture. (Elements in Anthropology). 80p. 1977. pap. text ed. write for info. (ISBN 0-697-07549-4). Wm C Brown.
Eliade, Mircea. Myth & Reality. pap. 3.95 (ISBN 0-06-090466-6, CN466, CN). Har-Row.
--Myths, Rites, Symbols: A Mircea Eliade Reader, 2 vols. Beane, Wendell C. & Doty, William G., eds. 1976. Vol. 1. pap. 5.95x (ISBN 0-06-131955-4, TB 1955, CN); Vol. 2. pap. 4.95 (ISBN 0-06-090511-5, CN511). Har-Row.
Frost, William P. Visions of the Divine. 1977. pap. text ed. 6.50 (ISBN 0-8191-0310-1). U Pr of Amer.
Geertz, Clifford, ed. Myth, Symbol & Culture. (Daedalus Ser., 1973). 224p. 1974. 8.50x (ISBN 0-393-04254-5); pap. 4.95x (ISBN 0-393-09409-X). Norton.
Goulder, Michael, ed. Incarnation & Myth: The Debate Continued. LC 79-16509. 1979. pap. 5.95 (ISBN 0-8028-1199-X). Eerdmans.
Guerber, H. A. The Book of Myths. 1913. Repr. lib. bdg. 25.00 (ISBN 0-8414-4697-0). Folcroft.
Hoffman, Daniel. Barbarous Knowledge: Myth in the Poetry of Yeats, Graves, & Muir. LC 67-10341. 1970. pap. 4.95 (ISBN 0-19-500801-4, 307, GB). Oxford U Pr.
Kelsey, Morton. Myth, History & Faith: The Re-Mythologizing of Christianity. LC 73-94216. 1974. pap. 4.95 (ISBN 0-8091-1827-0). Paulist Pr.
Kris, Ernst & Kurz, Otto. Legend, Myth, & Magic in the Image of the Artist: A Historical Experiment. LC 78-24024. (Illus.). 175p. 1981. pap. 5.95 (ISBN 0-300-02669-2, Y-386). Yale U Pr.
Larsen, Stephen. The Shaman's Doorway. 1977. pap. 4.95 (ISBN 0-06-090547-6, CN 547, CN). Har-Row.
Leeming, David A. Flights: Readings in Magic, Mysticism, Fantasy & Myth. 384p. (Orig.). 1974. pap. text ed. 8.95 (ISBN 0-15-527556-9, HC). HarBraceJ.
Liebert, Arthur. Mythus und Kultur: Myth & Culture. Bolle, Kees W., ed. (Mythology Ser.). (Ger.). 1978. Repr. of 1925 ed. lib. bdg. 12.00x (ISBN 0-405-10549-5). Arno.
Little, Alan M. Myth & Society in Attic Drama. 1967. lib. bdg. 8.50x (ISBN 0-374-95054-7). Octagon.
Lowry, Shirley. Familiar Mysteries: The Truth in Myth. LC 80-27792. (Illus.). 352p. 1982. 15.95 (ISBN 0-19-502925-9). Oxford U Pr.
McLean, George F., ed. Myth & Philosophy. LC 72-184483. (Proceedings of the American Catholic Philosophical Association: Vol. 45). 1971. pap. 8.00 (ISBN 0-918090-05-9). Am Cath Philo.
Malinowski, Bronislaw. Myth in Primitive Psychology. LC 79-152394. 94p. 1972. Repr. of 1926 ed. lib. bdg. 10.00x (ISBN 0-8371-5954-7, Pub. by Negro U Pr). Greenwood.
Richardson, Robert D., Jr. Myth & Literature in the American Renaissance. LC 77-22638. 320p. 1978. 15.00x (ISBN 0-253-33965-0). Ind U Pr.
Righter, William. Myth & Literature. (Concepts of Literature Ser.). 1975. 12.50x (ISBN 0-7100-8137-5). Routledge & Kegan.
Steinberg, Stephen. The Ethnic Myth: Race, Ethnicity & Class in America. LC 80-69377. 1981. 14.95 (ISBN 0-689-11151-7). Atheneum.
Vignoli, Tito. Myth & Science: An Essay. Bolle, Kees W., ed. LC 77-79156. (Mythology Ser.). 1978. Repr. of 1882 ed. lib. bdg. 19.00x (ISBN 0-405-10565-7). Arno.
Weisinger, Herbert. Agony & the Triumph: Papers on the Use & Abuse of Myth. x, 283p. 1964. 5.00 (ISBN 0-87013-081-1). Mich St U Pr.

MYTHICAL ANIMALS

see Animals, Mythical

MYTHOLOGY

see also Animals, Mythical; Argonauts; Art and Mythology; Cultus; Demythologization; Fire (In Religion, Folk-Lore, etc.); Folk-Lore; Geographical Myths; Gods; Heroes; Mother-Goddesses; Myth; Religion, Primitive; Symbolism; Totemism

also Bull (Cats, Death, Kings and Rulers, Moon) (In Religion, Folk-Lore, etc.); and similar headings as listed in references under Religion, Primitive; also subdivision Religion, Primitive; also subdivision Religion and Mythology under Indians, Indians of North America (South America, etc.)

Ares, Jacques d' Encyclopedie de l'Esoterisme, 1: Mythologies. 232p. (Fr.). 1975. pap. 19.95 (ISBN 0-686-56898-2, M-6008). French & Eur.
Banier, Antoine. The Mythology & Fables of the Ancients, Explain'd from History, 4 vols. LC 75-27885. (Renaissance & the Gods Ser.: Vol. 40). (Illus.). 1976. Repr. of 1740 ed. Set. lib. bdg. 292.00 (ISBN 0-8240-2089-8); lib. bdg. 73.00 ea. Garland Pub.
Baring-Gould, S. Curious Myths of the Middle Ages. 69.95 (ISBN 0-87968-261-2). Gordon Pr.
Baring-Gould, Sabine. Curious Myths of the Middle Ages. 1976. Repr. of 1867 ed. 27.00 (ISBN 0-403-06309-4, Regency). Scholarly.
Barnard, Mary. Mythmakers. LC 66-20061. 213p. 1979. 12.95 (ISBN 0-8214-0024-X); pap. 5.50 (ISBN 0-8214-0562-4). Ohio U Pr.
Barthes, Roland. The Eiffel Tower & Other Mythologies. Howard, Richard, tr. 152p. 1979. 9.95 (ISBN 0-8090-4115-4); pap. 4.95 (ISBN 0-8090-1391-6). Hill & Wang.
Boas, Franz. Tsimshian Mythology Based on Texts Recorded by Henry W. Tate. (Landmarks in Anthropology). (Illus.). Repr. of 1916 ed. 54.00 (ISBN 0-384-04880-3). Johnson Repr.
Bolle, Kees W., ed. Mythology Series, 39 vols. (Illus.). 1978. Vols. 1-29. lib. bdg. 731.00 (ISBN 0-405-10529-0); Vols. 20-39. lib. bdg. 669.00 (ISBN 0-405-18984-2). Arno.
--Reading in Mythology: An Original Anthology. LC 77-139. (Mythology Ser.). (Ger., Fr.). 1978. lib. bdg. 12.00x (ISBN 0-405-10573-8). Arno.
--Studies of A. J. Wensinck: An Original Arno Press Anthology. LC 77-82275. (Mythology Ser.). 1978. lib. bdg. 15.00x (ISBN 0-405-10567-3). Arno.
Brenneman, Walter L., Jr. Spirals: A Study in Symbol, Myth & Ritual. LC 77-26365. 1978. pap. text ed. 7.50 (ISBN 0-8191-0463-9). U Pr of Amer.
Brinton, Daniel G. Religions of Primitive Peoples. LC 79-88423. Repr. of 1897 ed. 13.25x (ISBN 0-8371-1763-1). Greenwood.
Bulfinch, Thomas. Age of Fable. (Classics Ser). (gr. 8 up). pap. 1.95 (ISBN 0-8049-0080-9, CL-80). Airmont.
--Bulfinch's Mythology. 2nd rev. ed. LC 69-11314. (Illus.). 1970. 11.95 (ISBN 0-690-57260-3). T Y Crowell.
--Bulfinch's Mythology. abr. ed. Fuller, Edmund, ed. 1959. pap. 2.75 (ISBN 0-440-30845-3, LE). Dell.
--Bulfinch's Mythology, 3 vols. Incl. Vol. 1. The Age of Fable. pap. 1.95 (ISBN 0-451-61767-3, MJ1767); Vols 2 & 3. The Age of Chivalry & Legends of Charlemagne. pap. 2.25 (ISBN 0-451-61791-6, ME1791). (RL 7, Ment). NAL.
--Bulfinch's Mythology: The Greek & Roman Fables Illustrated. Holme, Bryan, ed. (Illus.). 1979. 15.95 (ISBN 0-670-19464-6, Studio). Viking Pr.
Burkert, Walter. Lore & Science in Ancient Pythagoreanism. Minar, Edwin L., Jr., tr. from Ger. LC 70-162856. (Illus.). 512p. 1972. 25.00x (ISBN 0-674-53918-4). Harvard U Pr.
Campbell, J. F. & Henderson, George. The Celtic Dragon Myth. (The Newcastle Mythology Library: Vol. 4). 1981. pap. 5.95 (ISBN 0-87877-048-8). Newcastle Pub.
Campbell, Joseph. The Flight of the Wild Gander. LC 70-183820. 256p. 1972. pap. 3.95 (ISBN 0-89526-914-7). Regnery-Gateway.
--Hero with a Thousand Faces. rev. ed. LC 49-8590. (Bollingen Ser.: No. 17). (Illus.). 1968. 25.00 (ISBN 0-691-09743-7); pap. 5.95 (ISBN 0-691-01784-0). Princeton U Pr.
--The Masks of God: Creative Mythology. (Illus.). 1970. pap. 5.95 (ISBN 0-14-004307-1). Penguin.
--The Masks of God: Occidental Mythology. (Illus.). 1976. pap. 4.95 (ISBN 0-14-004306-3). Penguin.
--The Masks of God: Oriental Mythology. (Illus.). 1970. pap. 4.95 (ISBN 0-14-004305-5). Penguin.
--The Masks of God: Primitive Mythology. (Illus.). 1976. pap. 4.95 (ISBN 0-14-004304-7). Penguin.
--The Masks of God 1: Primitive Mythology. 1959. 15.00 (ISBN 0-670-46012-5). Viking Pr.
--The Masks of God 4: Creative Mythology. 1968. 15.00 (ISBN 0-670-46111-3). Viking Pr.
--The Mythic Image. LC 79-166363. (Bollingen Ser, No. 100). (Illus.). 516p. 1975. 60.00 (ISBN 0-691-09869-7). Princeton U Pr.
Campbell, Joseph & Abadie, M. J. The Mythic Image. LC 79-166363. (Bollingen Series C). (Illus.). 560p. 1981. pap. 14.95x (ISBN 0-691-01839-1). Princeton U Pr.

Cassirer, Ernst. Philosophy of Symbolic Forms, Vol. 2, Mythical Thought. Manheim, Ralph, tr. 1955. 22.50x (ISBN 0-300-00354-4); pap. 5.95 1965 (ISBN 0-300-00038-3, Y147). Yale U Pr.
Cha, Theresa H. Dictee. 96p. 1981. 10.95 (ISBN 0-934378-10-X); pap. 4.95 (ISBN 0-934378-09-6). Tanam Pr.
Chase, Richard V. Quest for Myth. LC 77-90483. Repr. of 1949 ed. lib. bdg. 15.00x (ISBN 0-8371-2150-7, CHQM); pap. 4.95 (ISBN 0-8371-8985-3, CHQ). Greenwood.
Clark, Glenn. God's Voice in the Folklore. 3.50 (ISBN 0-910924-06-6). Macalester.
Clodd, Edward. Myths & Dreams. LC 70-159918. 1971. Repr. of 1891 ed. 22.00 (ISBN 0-8103-3776-2). Gale.
Conacher, D. J. Aeschylus' "Prometheus Bound". A Literary Commentary. 128p. 1980. 20.00x (ISBN 0-8020-2391-6); pap. 7.50 (ISBN 0-8020-6416-7). U of Toronto Pr.
Connor, W. R., ed. Ancient Religion & Mythology, 32 vols. (Illus.). 1976. Set. 765.00x (ISBN 0-405-07001-2). Arno.
Cox, G. W. An Introduction to the Science of Comparative Mythology & Folklore. 69.95 (ISBN 0-8490-0420-9). Gordon Pr.
Cox, George W. Introduction to the Science of Comparative Mythology & Folklore. LC 68-20124. 1968. Repr. of 1883 ed. 22.00 (ISBN 0-8103-3425-9). Gale.
--An Introduction to the Science of Comparative Mythology & Folklore. 1976. lib. bdg. 59.95 (ISBN 0-8490-2071-9). Gordon Pr.
--A Manual of Mythology. LC 77-94556. 1979. Repr. of 1867 ed. lib. bdg. 30.00 (ISBN 0-89341-307-0). Longwood Pr.
--Tales of the Gods & Heroes. LC 77-94564. 1979. Repr. of 1895 ed. lib. bdg. 25.00 (ISBN 0-89341-309-7). Longwood Pr.
Creation Myths: Man's Introduction to the World. Maclagan, David. (Illus.). 1977. pap. 8.95 (ISBN 0-500-81010-9). Thames Hudson.
Creighton, David. Deeds of Gods & Heroes. (Illus.). (gr. 9-10). 1967. text ed. 6.95 (ISBN 0-312-19075-1). St Martin.
Creuzer, Georg F. Symbolik und Mythologie der Alten Volker Besonders der Griechen, 6 vols. Bolle, Kees W., ed. LC 77-79119. (Mythology Ser.). (Illus., Ger.). 1978. Repr. of 1823 ed. lib. bdg. 252.00x (ISBN 0-405-10531-2). Arno.
Cruse, Amy. The Book of Myths. 1925. lib. bdg. 30.00 (ISBN 0-8414-9140-2). Folcroft.
Daniels, Cora L. & Stevans, C. M., eds. Encyclopedia of Superstitions, Folklore & the Occult Sciences of the World, 3 Vols. LC 70-141151. 1971. Repr. of 1903 ed. 80.00 (ISBN 0-8103-3286-8). Gale.
Davis, Hubert J. Myths & Legends of the Great Dismal Swamp. (Illus.). 112p. 1981. 7.50 (ISBN 0-930230-42-6). Johnson NC.
Davison, Peter, et al, eds. Content & Taste: Religion & Myth. LC 77-90615. (Literary Taste, Culture & Mass Communication: Vol. 7). 1978. lib. bdg. 47.00x (ISBN 0-914146-50-5). Somerset Hse.
De Civrieux, Marc. Watunna: An Orinoco Creation Cycle. Guss, David, ed. LC 80-82440. (Illus.). 216p. 1980. 17.50 (ISBN 0-86547-002-2); pap. 8.50 (ISBN 0-86547-003-0). N Point Pr.
Dumezil, Georges. Destiny of a King. Hiltebeitel, Alf, tr. 1973. 10.00x (ISBN 0-226-16975-8). U of Chicago Pr.
Eliade, Mircea. Myth & Reality. pap. 3.95 (ISBN 0-06-090466-6, CN466, CN). Har-Row.
--Myths, Dreams & Mysteries: The Encounter Between Contemporary Faiths & Archaic Realities. pap. 4.95x (ISBN 0-06-131943-0, TB 1943, Torch). Har-Row.
Fahs, Sophia L. & Cobb, Alice. Old Tales for a New Day: Early Answers to Life's Eternal Questions. LC 80-84076. (Library of Liberal Religion). (gr. 3-9). 1981. 9.95 (ISBN 0-87975-138-X); tchr's manual 7.95 (ISBN 0-87975-131-2). Prometheus Bks.
Feldman, Burton & Richardson, Robert D. The Rise of Modern Mythology, Sixteen Eighty to Eighteen Sixty. LC 71-135005. (Midland Bks.: No. 188). 592p. 1972. 15.00x (ISBN 0-253-35012-3); pap. 5.95x (ISBN 0-253-20188-8). Ind U Pr.
Fiske, John. Myths & Myth-Makers: Old Tales & Superstitions Interpreted by Comparative Mythology. LC 77-85618. 1977. Repr. of 1890 ed. lib. bdg. 30.00 (ISBN 0-89341-304-6). Longwood Pr.
Fortune, Dion. Winged Bull. pap. 6.95 (ISBN 0-87728-501-2). Weiser.
Frazer, James. The New Golden Bough. rev. ed. Gaster, Theodore, ed. 832p. 1975. pap. 3.95 (ISBN 0-451-61926-9, ME1926, Ment). NAL.
Frazer, James G. Aftermath: A Supplement to The Golden Bough. LC 75-41104. Repr. of 1937 ed. 34.00 (ISBN 0-404-14543-4). AMS Pr.
--Golden Bough. abr ed. 19.95 (ISBN 0-02-095560-X); pap. 8.95 (ISBN 0-685-15196-4). Macmillan.
--New Golden Bough. abridged ed. Gaster, Theodor H., ed. LC 59-6125. 1959. 19.95 (ISBN 0-87599-036-3). S G Phillips.
Garcia, Emilio F. Hombres De Maiz: Unidad y Sentido a Traves De Sus Simbolos Mitologicos. LC 78-57694. 1978. pap. 5.95 (ISBN 0-89729-183-2). Ediciones.
Gaster, Theodor H. Thespis: Ritual, Myth, & Drama in the Ancient Near East. 1977. Repr. of 1961 ed. pap. 5.95 (ISBN 0-393-00863-0, N863, Norton Lib). Norton.
Gentles, Frederick & Steinfield, Melvin. Hangups from Way Back: Historical Myths & Canons, Vol. 1. 2nd ed. LC 74-1191. 416p. 1974. pap. text ed. 11.95 scp (ISBN 0-06-382785-9, HarpC). Har-Row.
Goldsmith, Elisabeth E. Ancient Pagan Symbols. LC 68-18025. (Illus.). xxxix, 220p. 1976. Repr. of 1929 ed. 19.00 (ISBN 0-8103-4140-9). Gale.
Goldsmith, Elizabeth E. Ancient Pagan Symbols. (Illus.). Repr. of 1929 ed. 10.00 (ISBN 0-404-02861-6). AMS Pr.
Goodrich, Norma L. Ancient Myths. (RL 9). pap. 1.75 (ISBN 0-451-61714-2, ME 1714, Ment). NAL.
--Medieval Myths. rev. ed. (RL 9). 1977. pap. 2.25 (ISBN 0-451-61770-3, ME1770, Ment). NAL.
Goulder, Michael, ed. Incarnation & Myth: The Debate Continued. LC 79-16509. 1979. pap. 5.95 (ISBN 0-8028-1199-X). Eerdmans.
Graves, Robert. The White Goddess: A Historical Grammar of Poetic Myth. rev. & enl. ed. 511p. 1966. pap. 7.95 (ISBN 0-374-50493-8, N295). FS&G.
--The White Goddess: A Historical Grammar of Poetic Myth. 1972. lib. bdg. 20.00x (ISBN 0-374-93239-5). Octagon.
Gray, Louis H. Index to Mythology of All Races. (Mythology of All Races Ser). Repr. of 1932 ed. 20.00x (ISBN 0-8154-0088-8). Cooper Sq.
Greenway, John. The Primitive Reader: An Anthology of Myths, Tales, Songs, Riddles, & Proverbs of Aboriginal Peoples Around the World. LC 65-21986. viii, 211p. Repr. of 1965 ed. 19.00 (ISBN 0-8103-5014-9). Gale.
Gruffydd, W. J. Folklore & Myth in the Mabinogion. LC 75-34083. 1958. lib. bdg. 6.50 (ISBN 0-8414-4522-2). Folcroft.
Guerber, H. A. Myths of Norsemen. 69.95 (ISBN 0-87968-280-9). Gordon Pr.
--Myths of Northern Lands. 319p. 1980. Repr. of 1895 ed. lib. bdg. 25.00 (ISBN 0-8495-2041-X). Arden Lib.
Guerber, Helene A. Myths & Legends of the Middle Ages: Their Origin & Influence on Literature & Art. LC 72-2464. (Illus.). xvi, 405p. 1974. Repr. of 1909 ed. 22.00 (ISBN 0-8103-3873-4). Gale.
--Myths of Northern Lands: Narrated with Special Reference to Literature & Art. 1970. Repr. 24.00 (ISBN 0-8103-3862-9). Gale.
Hamilton. Mythology. 4.95 (ISBN 0-448-00093-8). G&D.
Harney, B. & Elkin, A. P. Songs of the Songmen - Aboriginal Myths Retold. rev. ed. (Illus.). 1968. 6.50x (ISBN 0-8426-1295-5). Verry.
Hartland, Edwin S. Mythology & Folktales: Their Relation & Interpretation. LC 75-144519. (Popular Studies in Mythology, Romance & Folklore: No. 7). Repr. of 1900 ed. 5.50 (ISBN 0-404-53507-0). AMS Pr.
Head, James G. & MacLea, Linda. Myth & Meaning. Littell, Joy, ed. (Special Literature Ser.). 1976. pap. text ed. 5.72 (ISBN 0-88343-299-4); tchrs'. manual 1.50 (ISBN 0-88343-301-X). McDougal-Littell.
Henderson, George. Thhe Celtic Dragon Myth. (Newcastle Mythology Library: Vol. 4). 160p. 1981. Repr. lib. bdg. 12.95 (ISBN 0-89370-648-5). Borgo Pr.
Hendricks, Rhoda A. Mythologies of the World: A Concise Encyclopedia. Shapiro, Max S., ed. (McGraw-Hill Paperbacks Ser.). 240p. 1981. pap. 4.95 (ISBN 0-07-056421-3). McGraw.
Hewitt, J. F. History & Chronology of the Myth-Making Age. LC 76-27523. (Illus.). 1976. Repr. of 1901 ed. lib. bdg. 60.00 (ISBN 0-89341-036-5). Longwood Pr.
Higginson, Thomas W. Tales of Atlantis & the Enchanted Islands. LC 80-19670. (Newcastle Mythology Library Ser.: Vol. 3). 259p. 1980. Repr. of 1977 ed. lib. bdg. 10.95x (ISBN 0-89370-642-6). Borgo Pr.
Hodges, Margaret. Persephone & the Springtime. (Illus.). 32p. (gr. k up). 1973. 5.95g (ISBN 0-316-36786-9). Little.
Hopkins, E. Washburn. Epic Mythology. 1974. Repr. 7.50 (ISBN 0-8426-0560-6). Orient Bk Dist.
Hunderfund, Richard. Magic, Myths & Medicine. (Illus.). 1980. 13.95x (ISBN 0-89863-036-3). Star Pub CA.
Hungerford, Edward B. Shores of Darkness. 7.00 (ISBN 0-8446-2285-0). Peter Smith.
Jensen, Adolf E. & Bolle, Kees W., eds. Myth, Mensch & Umwelt. LC 77-79134. (Mythology Ser.). (Illus., Ger.). 1978. Repr. of 1950 ed. lib. bdg. 27.00x (ISBN 0-405-10544-4). Arno.
Kauffman, Friedrich. Northern Mythology. LC 76-5464. 1976. Repr. of 1903 ed. lib. bdg. 12.50 (ISBN 0-8414-5524-4). Folcroft.
Kellett, Ernst E. Story of Myths. (Folklore & Society Ser). 1969. Repr. of 1927 ed. 15.50 (ISBN 0-384-29025-6). Johnson Repr.
Kelly, Walter K. Curiosities of Indo-European Tradition & Folk-Lore. LC 68-22032. 1969. Repr. of 1863 ed. 22.00 (ISBN 0-8103-3837-8). Gale.
Kerenyi, Karl. Goddesses of Sun & Moon: Circe, Aphrodite, Medea, Niobe, & Dunquin. (Dunquin Ser.). 1979. pap. text ed. 7.00 (ISBN 0-88214-211-9). Spring Pubns.
Kirk, G. S. Myth: Its Meaning & Functions in Ancient & Other Cultures. LC 72-628267. (Sather Classical Lectures: No. 40). 1970. 20.00x (ISBN 0-520-01651-3); pap. 7.95x (ISBN 0-520-02389-7). U of Cal Pr.
Kitigawa, Joseph M., et al, eds. Myths & Symbols: Studies in Honor of Mircea Eliade. LC 69-12132. 1969. 19.00x (ISBN 0-226-43827-9). U of Chicago Pr.
Kramer, Samuel Noah, ed. Mythologies of the Ancient World. LC 60-13538. 1961. pap. 2.95 (ISBN 0-385-09567-8, A229, Anch). Doubleday.
Krappe, Alexandre H. Mythologie universelle: Universal Mythology. Bolle, Kees W., ed. LC 77-79135. (Mythology Ser.). 1978. Repr. of 1930 ed. lib. bdg. 27.00x (ISBN 0-405-10545-2). Arno.
Kroeber, Alfred L. & Gifford, E. W. Karok Myths. Buzaljko, Grace, ed. LC 78-66022. 450p. 1980. 25.00 (ISBN 0-520-03870-3). U of Cal Pr.
Lang, Andrew. Custom & Myth. 2nd rev. ed. LC 68-59267. Repr. of 1885 ed. 11.00 (ISBN 0-404-03817-4). AMS Pr.
--Custom & Myth. (Illus.). 1977. Repr. of 1885 ed. 14.95x (ISBN 0-85409-969-7). Charles River Bks.
--Magic & Religion. LC 76-137255. Repr. of 1901 ed. 12.50 (ISBN 0-404-03857-3). AMS Pr.
--Magic & Religion. Repr. of 1901 ed. lib. bdg. 15.00x (ISBN 0-8371-0933-7, LAMR). Greenwood.
--Modern Mythology. LC 68-54279. Repr. of 1897 ed. 16.75 (ISBN 0-404-03852-2). AMS Pr.
--Myth, Ritual & Religion, 2 Vols in 1. LC 68-54280. Repr. of 1906 ed. 35.00 (ISBN 0-404-03868-9). AMS Pr.
Langer, Fritz. Intellektualmythologie: Betrachtungen Uber das Wesen das Mythus und Die Mythologische Methode. Bolle, Kees W., ed. LC 77-79136. (Mythology Ser.). (Ger.). 1978. Repr. of 1916 ed. lib. bdg. 16.00x (ISBN 0-405-10546-0). Arno.
Larsen, Stephen. The Shaman's Doorway. 1977. pap. 4.95 (ISBN 0-06-090547-6, CN 547, CN). Har-Row.
Larue, Gerald A. Ancient Myth & Modern Man. LC 74-9527. 320p. (Orig.). 1975. 11.95 (ISBN 0-13-035493-7); pap. 10.50 (ISBN 0-13-035485-6). P-H.
Leach, Edmund, ed. Structural Study of Myth & Totemism. (Orig.). 1968. pap. 8.95x (ISBN 0-422-72530-7, 44). Methuen Inc.
Leeming, David. Mythology. LC 75-2276. (World of Culture Ser.). (Illus.). 192p. 1976. 12.95 (ISBN 0-88225-135-X). Newsweek.
Leeming, David A. Mythology: The Voyage of the Hero. 2nd ed. (Illus.). 370p. 1980. pap. text ed. 10.50 scp (ISBN 0-06-043942-4, HarpC); instr's manual avail. (ISBN 0-06-363950-5). Har-Row.
Lengyel, Jozsef. From Beginning to End & the Spell. 14.95x (ISBN 0-8464-0432-X). Beekman Pubs.
Lessa, William A. More Tales from Ulithi Atoll. (U. C. Publications in Folklore & Mythology Studies: Vol. 32). 1980. pap. 16.50x (ISBN 0-520-09615-0). U of Cal Pr.
Levi-Strauss, Claude. Myth & Meaning. LC 78-25833. 1979. 8.95x (ISBN 0-8052-3710-0); pap. 2.95 (ISBN 0-8052-0622-1). Schocken.
--The Origin of Table Manners. LC 77-11810. 1979. pap. 6.95 (ISBN 0-06-090698-7, CN-698, CN). Har-Row.
--The Raw & the Cooked. (Science of Mythology Ser.). 1979. Repr. of 1970 ed. lib. bdg. 25.00x (ISBN 0-374-94953-0). Octagon.
--Raw & the Cooked: An Introduction to a Science of Mythology, Vol. 1. 1970. pap. 4.95 (ISBN 0-06-090441-0, CN441, CN). Har-Row.
Levy-Bruhl, J. Primitives & the Supernatural. LC 73-4358. (Studies in Comparative Literature, No. 35). 1972. Repr. of 1935 ed. lib. bdg. 43.95 (ISBN 0-8383-1589-5). Haskell.
Lipps, Gottlob F. Mythenbildung und Erkenntnis: Eine Abhandlung Uber Die Grundlagen der Philosophie. Bolle, Kees W., ed. LC 77-79141. (Mythology Ser.). 1978. lib. bdg. 20.00x (ISBN 0-405-10550-9). Arno.
Lockhart, John G. Curses, Lucks & Talismans. LC 70-132016. (Illus.). 1971. Repr. of 1938 ed. 24.00 (ISBN 0-8103-3376-7). Gale.
London, Herbert I. & Weeks, Albert. Myths That Rule America. LC 80-5866. 176p. 1981. lib. bdg. 13.50 (ISBN 0-8191-1446-4); pap. text ed. 6.95 (ISBN 0-8191-1447-2). U Pr of Amer.
Long, Haniel. Notes for a New Mythology: Pittsburgh Memoranda, 2 Vols. in 1. 1971. Repr. of 1926 ed. 19.50 (ISBN 0-384-33540-3). Johnson Repr.
Lopez, Barry H. Giving Birth to Thunder, Sleeping with His Daughter: Coyote Builds North America. 1978. 8.95 (ISBN 0-8362-0726-2). Andrews & McMeel.
MacCulloch, John A., et al, eds. Mythology of All Races, 13 Vols. LC 17-26477. (Illus.). Repr. of 1932 ed. 304.00x set (ISBN 0-8154-0144-2). Cooper Sq.
MacDonald, James. Religion & Myth. LC 74-82059. Repr. of 1893 ed. 13.00x (ISBN 0-8371-1550-7). Greenwood.
Mackenzie, D. Myths of Pre-Columbian America. 75.00 (ISBN 0-8490-0701-1). Gordon Pr.
Malville, J. McKim. The Fermenting Universe: Myths of Eternal Change. 128p. (Orig.). 1981. pap. 5.95 (ISBN 0-8164-2345-8). Seabury.
Mannhardt, Wilhelm. Mythologische Forschungen Aus Dem Nachlasse, 2 vols. in 1. Bolle, Kees W., ed. LC 77-79142. (Mythology Ser.). (Ger.). 1978. Repr. of 1868 ed. lib. bdg. 29.00x (ISBN 0-405-10551-7). Arno.
Massey, G. Ancient Egypt, the Light of the World, 2 Vols. LC 79-138084. Boxed Set. 50.00 (ISBN 0-87728-029-0). Weiser.
Massey, Gerald. The Natural Genesis, 2 vols. LC 73-92166. 1974. Repr. of 1883 ed. Set. 50.00 (ISBN 0-87728-248-X). Weiser.
Mayerson, Philip. Classical Mythology in Literature, Art, & Music. 1971. text ed. 22.95 (ISBN 0-471-00365-4). Wiley.
Mehta, Rustam. Konarak: The Sun-Temple of Love. (Illus.). 1969. 7.50x (ISBN 0-8002-1635-0). Intl Pubns Serv.
Merry, Eleanor. I Am. 59.95 (ISBN 0-8490-0380-6). Gordon Pr.
Middleton, John, ed. Gods & Rituals: Readings in Religious Beliefs & Practices. LC 75-44032. (Texas Press Sourcebooks in Anthropology: No. 6). 480p. 1976. pap. 7.95x (ISBN 0-292-72708-9). U of Tex Pr.
--Myths & Cosmos: Readings in Mythology & Symbolism. LC 75-43817. (Texas Press Sourcebooks in Anthropology: No. 5). 382p. 1976. pap. 7.95x (ISBN 0-292-75030-7). U of Tex Pr.
Miller, David L. The New Polytheism. 144p. (Orig.). 1981. pap. 8.50 (ISBN 0-88214-314-X). Spring Pubns.
Monarch Notes on Mythology. (Orig.). pap. 2.50 (ISBN 0-671-00523-5). Monarch Pr.
Moncrieff, A. R. Romance of Chivalry. LC 80-23872. (Newcastle Mythology Library: Vol. 2). 439p. 1980. Repr. of 1976 ed. lib. bdg. 11.95x (ISBN 0-89370-638-8). Borgo Pr.
Mueller, Friedrich M. Selected Essays on Language, Mythology & Religion, 2 vols. LC 73-18814. Repr. of 1881 ed. 67.50 set (ISBN 0-404-11456-3). AMS Pr.
Muller, Friedrich Max. Comparative Mythology: An Essay. rev. ed. Dorson, Richard M., ed. LC 77-70612. (International Folklore Ser.). 1977. Repr. of 1909 ed. lib. bdg. 16.00x (ISBN 0-405-10111-2). Arno.
Muller, Karl O. Introduction to a Scientific System of Mythology. Bolle, Kees W., ed. LC 77-79144. (Mythology Ser.). 1978. Repr. of 1844 ed. lib. bdg. 22.00x (ISBN 0-405-10553-3). Arno.
Munz, Peter. When the Golden Bough Breaks: Structuralism or Typology? 158p. 1973. 14.00 (ISBN 0-7100-7650-9). Routledge & Kegan.
Mus, Paul. Barabundur: Esquisse d'une histoire du bouddhisme fondee sur la critique archeologique des textes, 2 vols. in 1. Bolle, Kees W., ed. LC 77-79146. (Mythology Ser.). (Fr.). 1978. Repr. of 1935 ed. lib. bdg. 63.00x (ISBN 0-405-10555-X). Arno.
Noel, Ruth S. The Mythology of Middle Earth. 1977. 7.95 (ISBN 0-395-25006-4). HM.
Nuttall, Zelia. Fundamental Principles of Old & New World Civilization. 1901. pap. 35.00 (ISBN 0-527-01190-8). Kraus Repr.
Otto, Walter F. Gestez Urbild und Mythos. Bolle, Kees W., ed. LC 77-82281. (Mytholoy Ser.). (Ger.). 1978. Repr. of 1951 ed. lib. bdg. 12.00x (ISBN 0-405-10572-X). Arno.
Palsson, Hermann, tr. Hrafinkel's Saga. (Classics Ser). 1971. pap. 2.95 (ISBN 0-14-044238-3). Penguin.
Perry, John W. Roots of Renewal in Myth & Madness: The Meaning of Psychotic Episodes. LC 76-19500. (Social & Behavioral Science Ser.). 1976. 16.95x (ISBN 0-87589-297-3). Jossey-Bass.
Pettazzoni, Raffaele & Bolle, Kees W., eds. Miti E Leggende: Myths & Legends, 4 vols. in 1. LC 77-79151. (Mythology Ser.). (Italian.). 1978. Repr. of 1959 ed. lib. bdg. 146.00x (ISBN 0-405-10560-6). Arno.
Popular Studies in Mythology, Romance & Folklore, 15 vols. Repr. of 1908 ed. Set. 88.00 (ISBN 0-404-53500-3). AMS Pr.

Porteous, A. Forest Folklore, Mythology & Romance. 1977. lib. bdg. 59.95 (ISBN 0-8490-1858-7). Gordon Pr.

Prescott, Frederick C. Poetry & Myth. LC 67-27635. Repr. of 1927 ed. 11.00 (ISBN 0-8046-0372-3). Kennikat.

Punke, Harold H. Mythology in American Education. 480p. 1981. pap. 14.75x (ISBN 0-8134-2136-5). Interstate.

Radin, Paul. Literary Aspects of North American Mythology. 1979. Repr. of 1915 ed. lib. bdg. 10.00 (ISBN 0-8414-7304-8). Folcroft.

Raglan, FitzRoy. The Hero: A Study in Tradition, Myth, & Drama. LC 75-23424. 296p. 1975. Repr. of 1956 ed. lib. bdg. 19.25x (ISBN 0-8371-8138-0, RATH). Greenwood.

Rank, Otto. Myth of the Birth of the Hero & Other Essays. Freund, Philip, ed. 1959. pap. 2.95 (ISBN 0-394-70070-8, Vin). Random.

Reid, Doris F., ed. A Treasury of Edith Hamilton. LC 70-90989. 1969. 5.00 (ISBN 0-393-04313-4). Norton.

Robinson, H. S. & Wilson, K. The Encyclopedia of Myths & Legends of All Nations. rev. ed. Picard, Barbara L., ed. 1978. Repr. of 1974 ed. text ed. 19.50x (ISBN 0-7182-0561-8, LTB). Sportshelf.

Robinson, Herbert S. & Wilson, Knox. Myths & Legends of All Nations. (Quality Paperback Ser.: No. 319). 1978. pap. 4.95 (ISBN 0-8226-0319-5). Littlefield.

Ross, Harriet, compiled by. Myths & Legends of Many Lands. new ed. LC 60-8670. (Illus.). 160p. (YA) (gr. 5 up). 1981. PLB 6.87 (ISBN 0-87460-214-9). Lion Bks.

Schneiderman, Leo. The Psychology of Myth, Folklore & Religion. LC 81-9471. 232p. 1981. text ed. 18.95x (ISBN 0-88229-659-0); pap. text ed. 8.95x (ISBN 0-88229-783-X). Nelson-Hall.

Schwab, Gustav. Gods & Heroes. LC 47-873. 1977. pap. 6.95 (ISBN 0-394-73402-5). Pantheon.

Sebeok, Thomas A., ed. Myth: A Symposium. LC 65-29803. (Midland Bks.: No. 83). 192p. (Orig.). 1955. pap. 3.50x (ISBN 0-253-20083-0). Ind U Pr.

Sewell, H. & Bulfinch, T. Book of Myths. 1969. 9.95 (ISBN 0-02-782280-X). Macmillan.

Siecke, Ernst. Drachenkampfe: Untersuchungen Sagenkunde, Vol. 1-pt. 1. Bolle, Kees W., ed. LC 77-79155. (Mythology Ser.). (Ger.). 1978. Repr. of 1907 ed. lib. bdg. 12.00x (ISBN 0-405-10564-9). Arno.

Spence, L. The Gods of Mexico. 34.95 (ISBN 0-8490-0243-5). Gordon Pr.

Spence, Lewis. The Outlines of Mythology. LC 77-3223. 1977. Repr. of 1944 ed. lib. bdg. 15.00 (ISBN 0-8414-7803-1). Folcroft.

Sproul, Barbara C. Primal Myths: Creating the World. LC 78-4429. 1979. pap. 8.95 (ISBN 0-06-067501-2, HarpR, RD 230, HarpR). Har-Row.

Stanley, John J. Eikaaos. 1979. 6.95 (ISBN 0-533-03920-7). Vantage.

Steiner, Rudolf. Ancient Myths: Their Meaning & Connection with Evolution. Cotterell, M., tr. from Ger. 1978. pap. 4.50 (ISBN 0-919924-07-7). Anthroposophic.

Toy, Crawford H. Introduction to the History of Religions. LC 76-126655. Repr. of 1913 ed. 27.50 (ISBN 0-404-06498-1). AMS Pr.

Tripp, Edward, ed. Meridian Handbook of Classical Mythology. pap. 5.95 (ISBN 0-452-00420-9, F420, Mer). NAL.

V. Haussig, Hans. Woerterbuch der Mythologie, Vol. 1. (Ger.). 1965. 123.00 (ISBN 3-12-909810-0, M-6980). French & Eur.

--Woerterbuch der Mythologie, Vol. 2. (Ger.). 1973. 175.00 (ISBN 3-12-909820-8, M-6979). French & Eur.

Vignoli, Tito. Myth & Science. 1976. lib. bdg. 59.95 (ISBN 0-8490-2323-8). Gordon Pr.

Watts, Alan W. Myth & Ritual in Christianity. (Illus.). 1968. pap. 5.95 (ISBN 0-8070-1375-7, BP301). Beacon Pr.

Watts, Alan W., ed. Patterns of Myth Series. Incl. Lord of the Four Quarters. Perry, John W. 6.95 (ISBN 0-685-25102-0); The Two Hands of God. Watts, Alan W; The Wisdom of the Serpent. Henderson, Joseph L. & Oakes, Maud.. Braziller.

Weigel, James, Jr. Mythology. 210p. 1973. pap. 2.95 (ISBN 0-8220-0865-3). Cliffs.

Welsch, Roger L. Omaha Tribal Myths & Tricksters Tales. LC 80-22636. x, 285p. 1981. 21.95 (ISBN 0-8040-0700-4). Swallow.

Wright, Thomas. Essays on Subjects Connected with the Literature, Popular Superstitions, & History of England in the Middle Ages, 2 vols. LC 70-80262. (Research & Source Works Ser.: No. 404). 1970. Repr. of 1846 ed. lib. bdg. 36.00 (ISBN 0-8337-3889-5). B Franklin.

Ziegler, Leopold. Gestaltwander der Gotter. Bolle, Kees W., ed. LC 77-79163. (Mythology Ser.). (Ger.). 1977. Repr. of 1920 ed. lib. bdg. 32.00x (ISBN 0-405-10571-1). Arno.

MYTHOLOGY-BIBLIOGRAPHY

Law, Helen H. Bibliography of Greek Myth in English Poetry. LC 77-9519. 1955. lib. bdg. 5.00 (ISBN 0-8414-5827-8). Folcroft.

MYTHOLOGY-DICTIONARIES

Aubert, Henri. Diccionario de Mitologia. 238p. (Span.). 1961. 14.95 (ISBN 0-686-56710-2, S-33055). French & Eur.

Bell, Robert E. Dictionary of Classical Mythology: Symbols, Attributes, & Associations. Schlachter, Gail, ed. (No. 1). 1981. 47.50 (ISBN 0-87436-305-5). ABC Clio.

Bonnerjea, Biren. Dictionary of Superstitions & Mythology. LC 69-17755. 1969. Repr. of 1927 ed. 24.00 (ISBN 0-8103-3572-7). Gale.

Bray, F. C. The World of Myths, a Dictionary of Universal Mythology. 75.00 (ISBN 0-8490-1335-6). Gordon Pr.

Cavendish, Richard & Ling, Trevor, eds. Mythology: An Illustrated Encyclopedia. LC 79-92600. (Illus.). 304p. 1980. 35.00 (ISBN 0-8478-0286-8). Rizzoli Intl.

Cooper, William R. Archaic Dictionary. LC 73-76018. 1969. Repr. of 1876 ed. 47.00 (ISBN 0-8103-3885-8). Gale.

Cotterell, Arthur. A Dictionary of World Mythology. LC 79-65889. (Illus.). 1980. 12.95 (ISBN 0-399-12464-0). Putnam.

Diccionario de la Mitologia Mundial. 383p. (Espn.). 1971. 12.25 (ISBN 84-7166-165-9, S-12258). French & Eur.

Eastman, Mary H. Index to Fairy Tales, Myths & Legends. 2nd rev. enl. ed. (The Useful Reference Ser. of Library Bks: Vol. 28). 1926. lib. bdg. 14.00x (ISBN 0-87305-028-2). Faxon.

--Index to Fairy Tales, Myths & Legends, Suppl. 1. (The Useful Reference Ser. of Library Bks: Vol. 61). 1937. lib. bdg. 12.00x (ISBN 0-87305-061-4). Faxon.

--Index to Fairy Tales, Myths & Legends, Suppl. 2. (The Useful Reference Ser. of Library Bks: Vol. 82). 1952. lib. bdg. 11.00x (ISBN 0-87305-082-7). Faxon.

Gaytan, C. Diccionario Mitologico. 3.75 (ISBN 0-686-56651-3, S-25775). French & Eur.

Gottschalk, Herbert. Lexikon der Mythologie der Eurpaeischen Voelker. (Ger.). 42.00 (ISBN 3-7934-1184-2, M-7246). French & Eur.

Howe, George & Harrer, G. A. Handbook of Classical Mythology. LC 77-121209. 1970. Repr. of 1947 ed. 19.00 (ISBN 0-8103-3290-6). Gale.

Jobes, Gertrude. Dictionary of Mythology, Folklore & Symbols, 2 Vols. LC 61-860. 1961. Set. 50.00 (ISBN 0-8108-0034-9). Scarecrow.

Kravitz, David. Who's Who in Greek & Roman Mythology. 1977. 10.00 (ISBN 0-517-52746-4); pap. 3.95 (ISBN 0-517-52747-2). Potter.

Leach, ed. Funk & Wagnalls Standard Dictionary of Folklore, Mythology & Legend. LC 72-78268. (Funk & W Bk.). 22.95 (ISBN 0-308-40090-9). T Y Crowell.

Lelama, Homero. Diccionario de Mitologia. 364p. (Span.). 1974. 39.95 (ISBN 0-686-56670-X, S-33075). French & Eur.

Migne, J. P., ed. Dictionnaire de Mythologie. (Troisieme et Derniere Encyclopedie Theologique Ser.: Vol. 10). 760p. (Fr.). Date not set. Repr. of 1855 ed. lib. bdg. 96.50x (ISBN 0-89241-294-1). Caratzas Bros.

Perez Rioja, Jose A. Diccionario de Simbolos y Mitos: Las Ciencias y las Artes en Su Expresion Figurada. 2nd ed. 434p. (Espn.). 1971. 15.50 (ISBN 84-309-0310-0, S-12344). French & Eur.

Pernety, Antoine J. Le Dictionnaire Mytho-Hermetique. (Fr.). pap. 25.00 (ISBN 0-686-57069-3, M-6441). French & Eur.

Schmidt, J. Dictionnaire mythologie grecque et romaine. (Illus., Fr.). pap. 8.50 (ISBN 2-03-075408-0, 3728). Larousse.

Sedgwick, Paulita. Mythological Creatures: A Pictorial Dictionary. LC 74-8004. (Illus.). 128p. (gr. 5 up). 1974. reinforced bdg. 6.95 (ISBN 0-03-012946-X). HR&W.

Shapiro, Max S. & Hendricks, Rhoda A., eds. Mythologies of the World: A Concise Encyclopedia. LC 78-1221. 1979. 10.00 (ISBN 0-385-13667-6). Doubleday.

Stephanus, Charles. Dictionarium Historicum, Geographicum, Poeticum. LC 75-27859. (Renaissance & the Gods Ser.: Vol. 16). (Illus.). 1976. Repr. of 1596 ed. lib. bdg. 73.00 (ISBN 0-8240-2065-0). Garland Pub.

Sykes, Egerton. Everyman's Dictionary of Non-Classical Mythology. rev. ed. (Everyman's Reference Library). 298p. 1977. Repr. of 1968 ed. 13.50x (ISBN 0-460-03010-8, Pub. by J. M. Dent England). Biblio Dist.

Thomas, Joseph. Universal Pronouncing Dictionary of Biography & Mythology, 2 Vols. 5th ed. LC 76-137298. Repr. of 1930 ed. Set. 225.00 (ISBN 0-404-06386-1). AMS Pr.

Woodcock, P. G., ed. Short Dictionary of Mythology. 3.75 (ISBN 0-8022-1927-6). Philos Lib.

Zimmerman, John E. Dictionary of Classical Mythology. (YA) 1964. 16.95 (ISBN 0-06-007740-9, HarpT). Har-Row.

MYTHOLOGY-JUVENILE LITERATURE

see also subdivision Juvenile Literature under Mythology, Classical, Mythology, Greek, and similar headings.

Barber, Richard. A Companion to World Mythology. LC 79-16843. (Illus.). (gr. 4 up). 1980. 14.95 (ISBN 0-440-00750-X). Delacorte.

Benson, Sally. Stories of the Gods & Heroes. (gr. 4-6). 1979. pap. 1.75 (ISBN 0-440-98291-X, LFL). Dell.

Bernstein, Margery & Kobrin, Janet. The Summer Maker: An Ojibway Indian Myth. LC 76-14875. (Myths You Can Read by Yourself). 48p. (gr. 1-3). 1977. binding 5.95reinforced (ISBN 0-684-14716-5, ScribJ). Scribner.

Espeland, Pamela. The Story of Baucis & Philemon. LC 80-27674. (A Myth for Modern Children Ser.). (Illus.). 32p. (gr. 1-4). 1981. PLB 5.95 (ISBN 0-87614-140-8). Carolrhoda Bks.

--Theseus & the Road to Athens. LC 80-27713. (Myths for Modern Children Ser.). (Illus.). 32p. (gr. 1-4). 1981. PLB 6.95 (ISBN 0-87614-141-6). Carolrhoda Bks.

Evslin, Bernard, et al. The Greek Gods. (gr. 7-12). 1972. pap. 1.25 (ISBN 0-590-06350-2, Schol Pap). Schol Bk Serv.

Hamilton, Edith. Mythology. (Illus.). (gr. 7 up). 1942. 10.95 (ISBN 0-316-34114-2). Little.

Komaroff, Katherine. Sky Gods: The Sun & Moon in Art & Myth. LC 73-80052. (Illus.). 86p. (YA) 1976. pap. 6.95 (ISBN 0-87663-952-X). Universe.

Mabie, Hamilton W. Myths That Every Child Should Know. Repr. of 1905 ed. 20.00 (ISBN 0-89987-175-5). Darby Bks.

Naden, C. J., adapted by. Jason & the Golden Fleece. new ed. LC 80-50068. (Illus.). 32p. (gr. 4-8). 1980. PLB 6.89 (ISBN 0-89375-360-2); pap. 2.50 (ISBN 0-89375-364-5). Troll Assocs.

--Pegasus, the Winged Horse. new ed. LC 80-50069. (Illus.). 32p. (gr. 4-8). 1980. PLB 6.89 (ISBN 0-89375-361-0); pap. 2.50 (ISBN 0-89375-365-3). Troll Assocs.

--Perseus & Medusa. new ed. LC 80-50083. (Illus.). 32p. (gr. 4-8). 1980. PLB 6.89 (ISBN 0-89375-362-9); pap. 2.50 (ISBN 0-89375-366-1). Troll Assocs.

--Theseus & the Minotaur. new ed. LC 80-50067. (Illus.). 32p. (gr. 4-8). 1980. PLB 6.89 (ISBN 0-89375-363-7); pap. 2.50 (ISBN 0-89375-367-X). Troll Assocs.

Ross, Harriet, compiled by. Heroes & Heroines of Many Lands. (Illus.). 160p. 1981. PLB 7.95 (ISBN 0-87460-214-9). Lion Bks.

Zimmerman. Dictionary of Classical Mythology. (gr. 9 up). pap. 2.75 (ISBN 0-553-14483-9). Bantam.

MYTHOLOGY, AFRICAN

Abrahamsson, Hans. The Origin of Death: Studies in African Mythology. Kastenbaum, Robert, ed. LC 76-19555. (Death and Dying Ser.). 1977. Repr. of 1951 ed. lib. bdg. 17.00x (ISBN 0-405-09551-1). Arno.

Ananikian, Mardiros H. Armenian Mythology & African Mythology. (Mythology of All Races Ser.: Vol. VII). Repr. of 1932 ed. 23.50 (ISBN 0-8154-0011-X). Cooper Sq.

Beier, Ulli. The Origin of Life & Death. (African Writers Ser.). 1966. pap. text ed. 2.50x (ISBN 0-435-90023-4). Heinemann Ed.

Knappert, Jan. Myths & Legends of the Congo. (African Writers Ser.). 1971. pap. text ed. 4.50x (ISBN 0-435-90083-8). Heinemann Ed.

--Myths & Legends of the Swahili. (African Writers Ser.). 1970. pap. text ed. 4.00x (ISBN 0-435-90075-7). Heinemann Ed.

Luomala, K. Oceanic, American Indian, & African Myths of Snaring the Sun. Repr. of 1940 ed. pap. 7.00 (ISBN 0-527-02276-4). Kraus Repr.

Pelton, Robert D. The Trickster in West Africa: A Study of Mythic Irony & Sacred Delight. LC 77-75396. (Hermeneutics: Studies in the History of Religions). 1980. 29.50x (ISBN 0-520-03477-5). U of Cal Pr.

Werner, Alice. Myths & Legends of Bantu. 289p. 1968. Repr. of 1933 ed. 28.50x (ISBN 0-7146-1735-0, F Cass Co). Biblio Dist.

--Myths & Legends of the Bantu. LC 78-63237. (The Folktale). (Illus.). Repr. of 1933 ed. 34.00 (ISBN 0-404-16176-6). AMS Pr.

MYTHOLOGY, ARMENIAN

Ananikian, Mardiros H. Armenian Mythology & African Mythology. (Mythology of All Races Ser.: Vol. VII). Repr. of 1932 ed. 23.50 (ISBN 0-8154-0011-X). Cooper Sq.

Sandalgian, Joseph. Histoire documentaire de l'Armenie, 2 Vols. LC 79-175431. 1917. Repr. of 1917 ed. Set. 55.00 (ISBN 0-404-05557-5). AMS Pr.

MYTHOLOGY, ASSYRO-BABYLONIAN

Enuma, Elish. Le Poeme Babylonien de la Creation. LC 78-72734. (Ancient Mesopotamian Texts & Studies). Repr. of 1935 ed. 24.50 (ISBN 0-404-18173-2). AMS Pr.

Gaster, Theodor H., ed. Oldest Stories in the World. 1958. pap. 4.95x (ISBN 0-8070-5787-8, BP66). Beacon Pr.

Goetze, Albrecht. Old Babylonian Omen Texts. LC 79-3537. (Yale Oriental Ser.: No. 10). Repr. of 1966 ed. 32.50 (ISBN 0-404-60265-7). AMS Pr.

King, Leonard W. Babylonian Religion & Mythology. LC 73-18854. (Illus.). Repr. of 1899 ed. 18.45 (ISBN 0-404-11352-4). AMS Pr.

--Babylonian Religion & Mythology. LC 77-94592. 1978. Repr. of 1899 ed. lib. bdg. 25.00 (ISBN 0-89341-311-9). Longwood Pr.

--Legends of Babylonia & Egypt in Relation to the Hebrew Tradition. LC 77-94593. 1979. Repr. of 1918 ed. lib. bdg. 20.00 (ISBN 0-89341-310-0). Longwood Pr.

Kinnier-Wilson, J. V. & Vanstiphout, Herman. The Rebel Lands: An Investigation into the Origins of Early Mesopotamian Mythology. LC 77-1272. (Oriental Publications Ser.: No. 29). (Illus.). 1979. 36.00 (ISBN 0-521-21469-6). Cambridge U Pr.

MacKenzie, Donald A. Myths of Babylonia & Assyria. LC 77-94601. 1978. Repr. of 1915 ed. lib. bdg. 60.00 (ISBN 0-89341-315-1). Longwood Pr.

Radau, Hugo. Ninib, the Determiner of Fates from the Temple Library of Nippur. (Publications of the Babylonian Section, Ser. D: Vol. 5-2). (Illus.). 73p. 1910. soft bound 2.00 (ISBN 0-686-11919-3). Univ Mus of U PA.

Spence, Lewis. Myths & Legends of Babylonia & Assyria. LC 77-167199. (Illus.). 414p. 1975. Repr. of 1916 ed. 32.00 (ISBN 0-8103-4089-5). Gale.

MYTHOLOGY, AUSTRALIAN

Lawrie, Margaret, ed. Myths & Legends of the Torres Strait. LC 73-163219. (Illus.). 1972. 25.00 (ISBN 0-8008-5464-0). Taplinger.

Leenhardt, Maurice. Do Kamo: La Personne et le Mythe Dans le Monde Melanesien. Bolle, Kees W., ed. LC 77-79137. (Mythology Ser.). (Fr.). 1978. Repr. of 1971 ed. lib. bdg. 18.00x (ISBN 0-405-10547-9). Arno.

Reed, A. W. Myths & Legends of Australia. LC 72-779. (Illus.). 1973. 7.50 (ISBN 0-8008-5463-2). Taplinger.

Wagner, Roy. Lethal Speech: Daribi Myth As Symbolic Obviation. LC 78-58049. (Symbol, Myth, & Ritual Ser). (Illus.). 1978. 25.00x (ISBN 0-8014-1193-9). Cornell U Pr.

Wirz, Paul. Die Marind-Anim Von Hollandischsud-Neu-Guinea, 2 vols. in 1. Bolle, Kees W., ed. (Mythology Ser.). (Ger.). 1978. Repr. of 1922 ed. lib. bdg. 49.00x (ISBN 0-405-10569-X). Arno.

MYTHOLOGY, AUSTRALIAN (ABORIGINAL)

Eliade, Mircea. Australian Religions: An Introduction. Turner, Victor, ed. LC 72-6473. (Symbol, Myth, & Ritual Ser.). 205p. 1973. 22.50x (ISBN 0-8014-0729-X). Cornell U Pr.

Hiatt, L. R., ed. Australian Aboriginal Mythology: Essays in Honour of W. E. H. Stanner. (AIAS Social Anthropology Ser.: No. 9). (Illus.). 1975. pap. text ed. 9.50x (ISBN 0-85575-044-8). Humanities.

Reed, A. W. Aboriginal Myths: Tales of the Dreamtime. 1979. pap. 5.95 (ISBN 0-589-50017-1, Pub. by Reed Books Australia). C E Tuttle.

MYTHOLOGY, BABYLONIAN

see Mythology, Assyro-Babylonian

MYTHOLOGY, BRAHMAN

see Mythology, Hindu; Vedas

MYTHOLOGY, BRITISH

see also Mythology, Welsh

Bett, Henry. English Myths & Traditions. (Illus.). 144p. 1980. Repr. of 1952 ed. lib. bdg. 17.50 (ISBN 0-8414-2921-9). Folcroft.

Folklore, Myths & Legends of Britain. (Automobile Association of England Ser.). 1979. 22.95 (ISBN 0-393-01231-X). Norton.

Gayley, Charles M. The Classic Myths in English Literature & Art. LC 77-6986. 1977. Repr. of 1911 ed. lib. bdg. 45.00 (ISBN 0-89341-163-9). Longwood Pr.

Jung, Emma & Von Franz, Marie-Louise. The Grail Legend. write for info. (ISBN 0-938434-07-1); pap. write for info. (ISBN 0-938434-08-X). Sigo Pr.

Spence, Lewis. The Minor Traditions of British Mythology. LC 72-84001. Repr. of 1948 ed. 24.00 (ISBN 0-405-08989-9). Arno.

Squire, Charles. The Mythology of Ancient Britain & Ireland. LC 73-13769. 1974. Repr. of 1909 ed. lib. bdg. 15.00 (ISBN 0-8414-7650-0). Folcroft.

--The Mythology of Ancient Britain & Ireland. 1977. Repr. of 1906 ed. 12.50 (ISBN 0-685-82797-6). Sharon Hill.

--Mythology of the British Islands. LC 77-94622. 1979. Repr. of 1905 ed. lib. bdg. 45.00 (ISBN 0-89341-306-2). Longwood Pr.

MYTHOLOGY, BUDDHIST

Halder, J. R. Early Buddhist Mythology. 1977. 12.00x (ISBN 0-88386-998-5). South Asia Bks.

MYTHOLOGY, CANAANITE

Gaster, Theodor H., ed. Oldest Stories in the World. 1958. pap. 4.95x (ISBN 0-8070-5787-8, BP66). Beacon Pr.

Gibson, John C. Canaanite Myths and Legends. 2nd ed. 208p. 1978. text ed. 34.00x (ISBN 0-567-02351-6). Attic Pr.

L'Heureux, Conrad E. Rank Among the Canaanite Gods: El, Baal, & the Raphaim. LC 79-15582. (Harvard Semitic Monographs: No. 21). 1979. 10.50 (ISBN 0-89130-326-X, 040021). Scholars Pr Ca.

MYTHOLOGY, CELTIC

Arbois De Jubainville, Henri D' The Irish Mythological Cycle & Celtic Mythology. LC 70-112679. 1970. Repr. of 1903 ed. text ed. 10.00x (ISBN 0-87696-006-9). Humanities.

Davies, Edward. Celtic Researches, on the Origin, Traditions & Language, of the Ancient Britons. Feldman, Burton & Richardson, Robert D., eds. LC 78-60902. (Myth & Romanticism Ser.: Vol. 8). (Illus.). 1979. lib. bdg. 66.00 (ISBN 0-8240-3557-7). Garland Pub.

Loomis, Roger S. Celtic Myth & Arthurian Romance. LC 67-31638. (Arthurian Legend & Literature Ser., No. 1). 1969. Repr. of 1927 ed. lib. bdg. 37.95 (ISBN 0-8383-0586-5). Haskell.

McBain, Alexander. Celtic Mythology & Religion. LC 76-1877. 1976. Repr. of 1917 ed. lib. bdg. 17.50 (ISBN 0-8414-6043-4). Folcroft.

MacCulloch, John A. Celtic Mythology. Bd. with Slavic Mythology. Machal, Jan. LC 63-19088. (Mythology of All Races Ser.: Vol. 3). (Illus.). 477p. Repr. of 1964 ed. 23.50x (ISBN 0-8154-0142-6). Cooper Sq.

--The Religion of the Ancient Celts. LC 77-4127. 1977. lib. bdg. 40.00 (ISBN 0-8414-5998-3). Folcroft.

Plummer, Charles. Vitae Sanctorum Hiberniae, 2 Vols. 1910. 48.00x set (ISBN 0-19-821390-5). Oxford U Pr.

Squire, Charles. Celtic Myth & Legend. new ed. LC 74-26575. (Newcastle Mythology Library: Vol. 1). 450p. 1975. pap. 5.95 (ISBN 0-87877-030-5). Newcastle Pub.

--Celtic Myth & Legend, Poetry & Romance. LC 80-53343. (Newcastle Mythology Library: Vol. 1). 450p. 1980. Repr. of 1975 ed. lib. bdg. 12.95x (ISBN 0-89370-630-2). Borgo Pr.

--Celtic Myth & Legend, Poetry and Romance. LC 77-6985. 1977. Repr. of 1910 ed. lib. bdg. 45.00 (ISBN 0-89341-164-7). Longwood Pr.

--The Mythology of Ancient Britain & Ireland. 1977. Repr. of 1906 ed. 12.50 (ISBN 0-685-82797-6). Sharon Hill.

MYTHOLOGY, CHINESE

Chung Ching-Wen. Myths & Legends in the Ch'u Tz'u. (Folklore Series of National Sun Yat-Sen University: No. 11). (Chinese.). 5.50 (ISBN 0-89986-081-8). E Langstaff.

Collection of Myths About the Snake & Pagoda. (National Peking University & Chinese Assn. for Folklore, Folklore & Folkliterature Ser.: No. 135). (Chinese.). 6.00 (ISBN 0-89986-209-8). E Langstaff.

Hsuan-Chu. Studies on Chinese Myths. (National Peking University & Chinese Assn. for Folklore, Folklore & Folkliterature Ser.: Nos. 48 & 49). (Chinese.). 12.00 (ISBN 0-89986-140-7). E Langstaff.

Huang Chih-Kang. Chinese Water Gods & Goddesses. (National Peking University & Chinese Assn. for Folklore, Folklore & Folkliterature Ser.: No. 92). (Chinese.). 7.00 (ISBN 0-89986-172-5). E Langstaff.

Lou Tsu-Kuang. Essays on Myths. (National Peking University & Chinese Assn. for Folklore, Folklore & Folkliterature Ser.: No. 15). (Chinese.). 6.50 (ISBN 0-89986-115-6). E Langstaff.

--Myths & Legends. (National Peking University & Chinese Assn. for Folklore, Folklore & Folkliterature Ser.: No. 13). (Chinese.). 6.00 (ISBN 0-89986-113-X). E Langstaff.

Mackenzie, Donald A. The Myths of China & Japan. LC 77-6878. 1977. Repr. of 1923 ed. lib. bdg. 45.00 (ISBN 0-89341-149-3). Longwood Pr.

Mayers, W. E. The Chinese Reader's Manual: A Handbook of Biographical, Historical, Mythological, & General Literary Reference. 70.00 (ISBN 0-87968-855-6). Gordon Pr.

Schneider, Laurence A. A Madman of Ch'u: The Chinese Myth of Loyalty & Dissent. LC 78-54800. 1980. 21.75x (ISBN 0-520-03685-9). U of Cal Pr.

Siou, Lily. Chi-Kung: The Art of Mastering the Unseen Life Force. LC 75-32212. 1975. 16.50 (ISBN 0-8048-1169-5). C E Tuttle.

Wei Yin-Ch'i. Study of Gods & Goddesses from Fu-Chien. (Folklore Series of National Sun Yat-Sen University: No. 28). (Chinese.). 5.50 (ISBN 0-89986-096-6). E Langstaff.

Werner, E. T. A Dictionary of Chinese Mythology. LC 76-27521. 1976. Repr. of 1932 ed. lib. bdg. 60.00 (ISBN 0-89341-034-9). Longwood Pr.

--Myths & Legends of China. LC 71-172541. (Illus.). Repr. of 1922 ed. 25.00 (ISBN 0-405-09059-5, Pub. by Blom). Arno.

Wu Yu-Ch'eng. Studies of the Myths of Southern Kuang-Tung. (National Peking University & Chinese Assn. for Folklore, Folklore & Folkliterature Ser.: No. 116). (Chinese.). 6.00 (ISBN 0-89986-193-8). E Langstaff.

Yen Ping. Studies in Chinese Mythology. (National Peking University & Chinese Assn. for Folklore, Folkliterature Ser.: No. 91). (Chinese.). 7.00 (ISBN 0-89986-170-9). E Langstaff.

MYTHOLOGY, CLASSICAL

see also Argonauts; Gods; Heroes; Mythology, Greek; Mythology, Roman

also names of mythological persons and objects

Albricus. Allegoriae Poeticae, Repr. Of 1520 Ed. Incl. Theologia Mythologica. Pictorius, Georg. Repr. of 1532 ed; Apotheoseos Tam Exterarum Gentium Quam Romanorum Deorum. Pictorius, Georg. Repr. of 1558 ed. LC 75-27845. (Renaissance & the Gods Ser.: Vol. 4). (Illus.). 1976. lib. bdg. 73.00 (ISBN 0-8240-2053-7). Garland Pub.

Alciati, Andrea. Emblematum Libellus Cum Commentariis. LC 75-27869. (Renaissance & the Gods Ser.: Vol. 25). (Illus.). 1977. Repr. of 1621 ed. lib. bdg. 73.00 (ISBN 0-8240-2074-X). Garland Pub.

Alvarez, Octavio. The Celestial Brides: A Study in Mythology & Archaeology. LC 77-91208. (Illus.). 1978. 30.00 (ISBN 0-9601520-0-8). H Reichner.

Aycock, Wendell M. & Klein, Theodore M., eds. Classical Mythology in Twentieth-Century Thought & Literature. (Proceedings of the Comparative Literature Symposium). (Illus.). 221p. (Orig.). 1980. pap. 12.00 (ISBN 0-89672-079-9). Tex Tech Pr.

Bacon, Francis. De Sapientia Veterum, Repr. Of 1609 Ed. Bd. with The Wisedome of the Ancients, Gorges, Arthur, tr. Repr. of 1619 ed. LC 75-27863. (Renaissance & the Gods Ser.: Vol. 20). (Illus.). 1976. lib. bdg. 73.00 (ISBN 0-8240-2068-5). Garland Pub.

Baldini, Baccio. Discorso Sopra la Mascherata Della Genealogia Delg'Iddei, Repr. Of 1565 Ed. Bd. with Discorso Sopra Li Dei De'Gentili. Zucchi, Jacopo. Repr. of 1602 ed. LC 75-27852. (Renaissance & the Gods Ser.: Vol. 10). (Illus.). 1976. lib. bdg. 73.00 (ISBN 0-8240-2059-6). Garland Pub.

Barthell, Edward E., Jr. Gods & Goddesses of Ancient Greece. LC 72-129664. 1981. 49.50 (ISBN 0-87024-165-6). U of Miami Pr.

Batman, Stephen. The Golden Booke of the Leaden Gods, Repr. Of 1577 Ed. Bd. with The Third Part of the Countess of Pembroke's Yvychurch. Fraunce, Abraham. Repr. of 1592 ed; The Fountaine of Ancient Fiction. Lynche, Richard. Repr. of 1599 ed. LC 75-27856. (Renaissance & the Gods Ser.: Vol. 13). (Illus.). 1976. lib. bdg. 73.00 (ISBN 0-8240-2062-6). Garland Pub.

Baudouin, Jean. Mythologie, 2 vols. LC 75-27871. (Renaissance & the Gods Ser.: Vol. 26). (Illus.). 1976. Repr. of 1627 ed. Set. lib. bdg. 146.00 (ISBN 0-8240-2075-8); lib. bdg. 73.00 ea. Garland Pub.

Berens, E. M. The Myths & Legends of Ancient Greece & Rome. LC 77-91528. 1977. Repr. of 1880 ed. lib. bdg. 30.00 (ISBN 0-89341-029-2). Longwood Pr.

Blackwell, Thomas. Letters Concerning Mythology. LC 75-27887. (Renaissance & the Gods Ser.: Vol. 42). (Illus.). 1976. Repr. of 1748 ed. lib. bdg. 73.00 (ISBN 0-8240-2091-X). Garland Pub.

Boccaccio, Giovanni. Genealogia. LC 75-27843. (Renaissance & the Gods Ser.: Vol. 2). (Illus.). 1976. Repr. of 1494 ed. lib. bdg. 73.00 (ISBN 0-8240-2051-0). Garland Pub.

--Genealogie. LC 75-27847. (Renaissance & the Gods Ser.: Vol. 5). (Illus., Fr.). 1976. Repr. of 1531 ed. lib. bdg. 73.00 (ISBN 0-8240-2054-5). Garland Pub.

Boswell, Fred & Boswell, Jeanetta. What Men or Gods Are These? A Genealogical Approach to Classical Mythology. LC 80-13780. 324p. 1980. 19.50 (ISBN 0-8108-1314-9). Scarecrow.

Cartari, Vincenzo. The Fountaine of Ancient Fiction. Linche, Richard, tr. from It. LC 73-6109. (English Experience Ser.: No. 577). 206p. 1973. Repr. of 1599 ed. 20.00 (ISBN 90-221-0577-6). Walter J Johnson.

--Le Imagini...Degli Dei. LC 75-27855. (Renaissance & the Gods Ser.: Vol. 12). (Illus.). 1976. Repr. of 1571 ed. lib. bdg. 73.00 (ISBN 0-8240-2061-8). Garland Pub.

Chryssafis, G. A Textual & Stylistic Commentary on Theocritus' Idyll Twenty Five. (London Studies in Classical Philology Ser.: Vol. I). 289p. 1981. pap. text ed. 51.50x (ISBN 90-70265-21-4, Pub. by Gieben Holland). Humanities.

Comes, Natalis. Mythologiae. LC 75-27853. (Renaissance & the Gods Ser.: Vol. 11). (Illus.). 1976. Repr. of 1567 ed. lib. bdg. 73.00 (ISBN 0-8240-2060-X). Garland Pub.

Dall, Caroline H. Margaret & Her Friends; or, Ten Conversations with Margaret Fuller Upon the Mythology of the Greeks & Its Expression in Art. LC 72-4961. (The Romantic Tradition in American Literature Ser.). 166p. 1972. Repr. of 1895 ed. 13.00 (ISBN 0-405-04633-2). Arno.

De Montfaucon, Bernard. The Supplement to Antiquity Explained. Humphreys, David, tr. LC 75-27882. (Renaissance & the Gods Ser.: Vol. 37). (Illus.). 1976. Repr. of 1725 ed. lib. bdg. 73.00 (ISBN 0-8240-2086-3). Garland Pub.

Drake, W. Raymond. Gods & Spacemen of Greece & Rome. (Orig.). (RL 9). 1977. pap. 1.50 (ISBN 0-451-07620-6, W7620, Sig). NAL.

Du Choul, Guillaume. Discours De la Religion Des Anciens Romains Illustre. LC 75-27851. (Renaissance & the Gods Ser.: Vol. 9). (Illus.). 1976. Repr. of 1556 ed. lib. bdg. 73.00 (ISBN 0-8240-2058-8). Garland Pub.

Feder, Lillian. Ancient Myth in Modern Poetry. LC 70-154994. 1972. 24.00x (ISBN 0-691-06207-2); pap. 7.95 (ISBN 0-691-01336-5). Princeton U Pr.

Fflokes, Michael. Fflokes' Cartoon Companion to Classic Mythology. LC 78-15270. (Illus.). 1978. 10.50 (ISBN 0-7153-7585-7). David & Charles.

Fox, William S. Greek & Roman Mythology. LC 63-19086. (Mythology of All Races Ser). (Illus.). Repr. of 1932 ed. 25.00x (ISBN 0-8154-0073-X). Cooper Sq.

Gautruche, Pierre. The Poetical Histories, Repr. Of 1671 Ed. D'Assigny, Marius, tr. Bd. with Appendix De Diis et Heroibus Poeticis. Jouvency, Joseph de. Repr. of 1705 ed. LC 75-27877. (Renaissance & the Gods Ser.: Vol. 32). (Illus.). 1976. lib. bdg. 73.00 (ISBN 0-8240-2081-2). Garland Pub.

Gayley, Charles M. Classic Myths in English Literature & in Art. rev. & enlarged ed. 1939. 19.50 (ISBN 0-471-00191-0). Wiley.

Giraldi, Lilio G. De Deis Gentium. LC 75-27850. (Renaissance & the Gods Ser.: Vol. 8). (Illus.). 1976. Repr. of 1548 ed. lib. bdg. 73.00 (ISBN 0-8240-2057-X). Garland Pub.

Grand, M. & Hazel, J. Teach Yourself Who's Who in Classical Mythology. (Teach Yourself Books). (Orig.). 1980. pap. 5.95 (ISBN 0-679-12550-7). McKay.

Grant, Michael. Myths of the Greeks & Romans. (Illus.). 1964. pap. 2.50 (ISBN 0-451-61634-0, ME1634, Ment). NAL.

Harrison, Jane E. Myths of Greece & Rome. LC 76-46570. 1976. Repr. of 1927 ed. lib. bdg. 10.00 (ISBN 0-8414-4907-4). Folcroft.

Hendricks, Rhoda A., tr. from Gr. & Lat. Classical Gods & Heroes: Myths As Told by Ancient Authors. LC 74-163140. 336p. 1972. 17.00 (ISBN 0-8044-2376-8). Ungar.

Hendricks, Rhoda A., tr. & intro. by. Classical Gods & Heroes: Myths As Told by the Ancient Authors. 1974. pap. 6.95 (ISBN 0-688-05279-7). Morrow.

Henley, W. E., ed. The Golden Ass of Apuleius. Aldington, William, tr. from Lat. 249p. 1981. Repr. of 1893 ed. lib. bdg. 50.00 (ISBN 0-89984-233-X). Century Bookbindery.

Hope-Moncrieff, Ascott R. Classic Myth & Legend. LC 77-85616. 1977. Repr. of 1912 ed. lib. bdg. 45.00 (ISBN 0-89341-317-8). Longwood Pr.

Hough, Edith L. Sicily: The Fabulous Island. (Illus.). 1949. 4.00 (ISBN 0-8338-0027-2). M Jones.

Hyginus, et al. Fabularum Liber. LC 75-27848. (Renaissance & the Gods Ser.: Vol. 6). 1976. Repr. of 1535 ed. lib. bdg. 73.00 (ISBN 0-8240-2055-3). Garland Pub.

Jacqueny, Mona G. The Golden Age Society & Other Studies. LC 77-87939. 1978. 10.00 (ISBN 0-8022-2219-6). Philos Lib.

Keightley, Thomas. Classical Mythology: The Myths of Ancient Greece & Italy. 25.00 (ISBN 0-89005-189-5). Ares.

King, William. Historical Account of Heathen Gods & Heroes: Necessary for the Understanding of Ancient Poets. LC 64-18550. (Centaur Classics Ser.). (Illus.). 290p. 1965. 15.00x (ISBN 0-8093-0150-4). S Ill U Pr.

Kirkwood, G. M. Short Guide to Classical Mythology. 1960. pap. text ed. 7.50 (ISBN 0-03-008865-8, HoltC). HR&W.

Lemmi, Charles W. Classic Deities in Bacon. LC 70-120639. 1970. Repr. lib. bdg. 14.00x (ISBN 0-374-94929-8). Octagon.

Lotspeich, Henry G. Classical Mythology in the Poetry of Edmund Spenser. 1965. lib. bdg. 12.00x (ISBN 0-374-95112-8). Octagon.

Marolles, Michel de. Tableaux Du Temple Des Muses, Repr. Of 1655 Ed. Bd. with Iconologia or Moral Problems. Ripa, Cesare. Repr. of 1709 ed. LC 75-27876. (Renaissance & the Gods Ser.: Vol. 31). (Illus.). 1976. lib. bdg. 73.00 (ISBN 0-8240-2080-4). Garland Pub.

Montfaucon, Bernard de. Antiquity Explained & Represented in Sculptures, 2 vols. Humphreys, David, tr. LC 75-27881. (Renaissance & the Gods Ser.: Vol. 36). (Illus.). 1977. Repr. of 1722 ed. Set. lib. bdg. 146.00 (ISBN 0-8240-2085-5); lib. bdg. 73.00 ea. Garland Pub.

Morford, Mark P. & Lenardon, Robert J. Classical Mythology. 2nd ed. 1977. pap. text ed. 12.95x (ISBN 0-582-28004-4). Longman.

Nichols, Marianne. Man, Myth & Monument. (Illus.). 384p. 1976. pap. 5.95 (ISBN 0-688-07943-1). Morrow.

Osgood, Charles G. Classical Mythology of Milton's English Poems. LC 64-8180. 1964. Repr. of 1900 ed. 8.50 (ISBN 0-87752-080-1). Gordian.

--Classical Mythology of Milton's English Poems. LC 65-15902. (Studies in Comparative Literature, No. 35). 1969. Repr. of 1900 ed. lib. bdg. 49.95 (ISBN 0-8383-0603-9). Haskell.

Ovid. Metamorphoseon. Pontanus, Jacobus, ed. LC 75-27868. (Renaissance & the Gods Ser.: Vol. 24). (Illus.). 1977. Repr. of 1618 ed. lib. bdg. 73.00 (ISBN 0-8240-2073-1). Garland Pub.

--Metamorphoses. Garth, et al, trs. LC 75-27884. (Renaissance & the Gods Ser.: Vol. 39). (Illus.). 1976. Repr. of 1732 ed. lib. bdg. 73.00 (ISBN 0-8240-2088-X). Garland Pub.

Pater, Walter. Cupid & Psyche. (Illus.). 48p. 1977. 9.95 (ISBN 0-571-11115-7, Pub. by Faber & Faber). Merrimack Bk Serv.

Philostratus. Les Images. De Vigenere, Blaise, tr. LC 75-27866. (Renaissance & the Gods Ser.: Vol. 22). (Illus., Fr.). 1977. Repr. of 1614 ed. lib. bdg. 73.00 (ISBN 0-8240-2071-5). Garland Pub.

Pomey, Antoine. The Pantheon. LC 75-27879. (Renaissance & the Gods Ser.: Vol. 34). (Illus.). 1976. Repr. of 1694 ed. lib. bdg. 73.00 (ISBN 0-8240-2083-9). Garland Pub.

Randall, Alice E. Sources of Spenser's Classical Mythology. 1896. Repr. 5.75 (ISBN 0-8274-3476-6). R West.

Reinhold, Meyer. Past & Present: The Continuity of Classical Myth. LC 72-78016. (Illus.). 415p. 1972. text ed. 15.00 (ISBN 0-88866-508-3); pap. text ed. 6.95 (ISBN 0-88866-509-1). Samuel Stevens.

Ripa, Cesare. Iconologie. Baudouin, Jean, tr. LC 75-27874. (Renaissance & the Gods Ser.: Vol. 29). (Illus., Fr.). 1976. Repr. of 1644 ed. lib. bdg. 73.00 (ISBN 0-8240-2078-2). Garland Pub.

Ross, Alexander. Mystagogus Poeticus, or the Muses Interpreter. 2nd ed. Orgel, Stephen, ed. LC 75-27875. (Renaissance & the Gods Ser.: Vol. 30). (Illus.). 1976. Repr. of 1648 ed. lib. bdg. 73.00 (ISBN 0-8240-2079-0). Garland Pub.

Sahlins, Marshall. Historical Metaphors & Mythical Realities: Structure in the Early History of the Sandwich Islands Kingdom. LC 80-28649. 96p. 1981. pap. text ed. 5.95x (ISBN 0-472-02721-2). U of Mich Pr.

Schmidt, J. Dictionnaire mythologie grecque et romaine. (Illus., Fr.). pap. 8.50 (ISBN 2-03-075408-0, 3728). Larousse.

Seznec, Jean. The Survival of the Pagan Gods: The Mythological Tradition & Its Place in Renaissance Humanism & Art. Sessions, Barbara, tr. (Bollingen Ser.: Vol. 38). (Illus.). 108p. 1972. 22.50 (ISBN 0-691-09829-8); pap. 6.95 (ISBN 0-691-01783-2). Princeton U Pr.

Spence, Joseph. Polymetis. LC 75-27886. (Renaissance & the Gods Ser.: Vol. 41). (Illus.). 1976. Repr. of 1747 ed. lib. bdg. 73.00 (ISBN 0-8240-2090-1). Garland Pub.

Starnes, DeWitt T. & Talbert, Ernest W. Classical Myth & Legend in Renaissance Dictionaries. LC 73-11753. (Illus.). 517p. 1973. Repr. of 1955 ed. lib. bdg. 39.75x (ISBN 0-8371-7086-9, STCM). Greenwood.

Suhr, Elmer G. Before Olympos: A Study of the Aniconic Origins of Poseidon, Hermes & Eros. LC 67-19630. (Illus.). 1967. 5.95 (ISBN 0-87037-018-9). Helios.

Tabeling, Ernst. Mater Larum: Zum Wesen der Larenreligion. facsimile ed. LC 75-10657. (Ancient Religion & Mythology Ser.). (Ger.). 1976. Repr. of 1932 ed. 8.00x (ISBN 0-405-07265-1). Arno.

Tooke, Andrew. The Pantheon. LC 75-27880. (Renaissance & the Gods Ser.: Vol. 35). (Illus.). 1976. Repr. of 1713 ed. lib. bdg. 73.00 (ISBN 0-8240-2084-7). Garland Pub.

Van Aken, A. Encyclopedia of Classical Mythology. 1965. pap. 2.45 (ISBN 0-13-275362-6, S97, Spec). P-H.

Vossius, Gerardus. De Theologia Gentili, 3 vols. LC 75-27872. (Renaissance & the Gods Ser.: Vol. 28). (Illus.). 1977. Repr. of 1641 ed. Set. lib. bdg. 219.00 (ISBN 0-8240-2077-4). Garland Pub.

Wheeler, Charles F. Classical Mythology in the Plays, Masques, & Poems of Ben Jonson. LC 71-114234. 1970. Repr. of 1938 ed. 11.50 (ISBN 0-8046-1038-X). Kennikat.

Whetstone, George. Promus & Cassandra, Pts. 1 & 2. (Tudor Facsimile Texts. Old English Plays: No. 52). Repr. of 1910 ed. 31.50 (ISBN 0-404-53352-3). AMS Pr.
Winckelmann, J. J. Versuch Einer Allegorie, Repr. Of 1766 Ed. Bd. with De L'Allegorie. Winckelmann, J. J. Repr. of 1799 ed. LC 75-27890. (Renaissance & the Gods Ser.: Vol. 44). (Illus.). 1976. lib. bdg. 73.00 (ISBN 0-8240-2093-6). Garland Pub.
Wolverton, Robert E. Outline of Classical Mythology. (Quality Paperback: No. 97). (Orig.). 1975. pap. 2.95 (ISBN 0-8226-0097-8). Littlefield.

MYTHOLOGY, CLASSICAL-DICTIONARIES
see Mythology-Dictionaries

MYTHOLOGY, CLASSICAL-JUVENILE LITERATURE
Benson, Sally. Stories of the Gods & Heroes. (gr. 4-6). 1940. 7.95 (ISBN 0-8037-8291-8). Dial.
Hawthorne, Nathaniel. Tanglewood Tales. (Classics Ser). (Illus.). (gr. 7 up). 1968. pap. 1.25 (ISBN 0-8049-0175-9, CL-175). Airmont.
--Tanglewood Tales. (Companion Lib.). (Illus.). (gr. 4-9). 1967. 2.95 (ISBN 0-448-05486-8). G&D.
--Wonder Book. (Classics Ser). (gr. 5 up). pap. 1.25 (ISBN 0-8049-0118-X, CL-118). Airmont.
Proddow, Penelope. Art Tells a Story: Greek & Roman Myths. LC 76-18364. (Illus.). 1979. 7.95a (ISBN 0-385-11111-8); PLB (ISBN 0-385-11112-6). Doubleday.

MYTHOLOGY, DANISH
see Mythology, Norse

MYTHOLOGY, EGYPTIAN
Boylan, P. Thoth - the Hermes of Egypt. 215p. 1979. 12.50 (ISBN 0-89005-280-8). Ares.
Budge, E. A. Gods of the Egyptians: Or Studies in Egyptian Mythology, 2 Vols. (Illus.). Set. 25.00 (ISBN 0-8446-0520-4). Peter Smith.
--The Gods of the Egyptians: Studies in Egyptian Mythology, 2 Vols. LC 67-28633. (Illus.). 1969. pap. 8.00 ea.; Vol. 1. pap. (ISBN 0-486-22055-9); Vol. 2. pap. (ISBN 0-486-22056-7). Dover.
Budge, E. Wallis. From Fetish to God in Ancient Egypt. LC 72-82206. (Illus.). Repr. of 1934 ed. 30.00 (ISBN 0-405-08317-3, Blom Pubns). Arno.
Clymer, R. S. Los Misterios De Osiris. 1976. pap. 6.95 (ISBN 0-686-10460-9). Philos Pub.
David, Rosalie. Cult of the Sun: Myth & Magic in Ancient Egypt. (Illus.). 208p. 1980. 24.50x (ISBN 0-460-04284-X, Pub. by J M Dent England). Biblio Dist.
Hasbroeck, J. Trade & Politics in Ancient Greece. Fraser, L. M., et al, trs. 1978. 15.00 (ISBN 0-89005-240-9). Ares.
Hooke, Samuel H. Middle Eastern Mythology. (Orig.). 1963. pap. 3.95 (ISBN 0-14-020546-2, Pelican). Penguin.
Lanzone, R. V. Dizionario Di Mitologia Egizia. 1312p. 1974. 350.00 (ISBN 90-272-0931-6). Benjamins North Am.
--Dizzionario Di Mitologia Egizia, 3 vols. xv, 205p. 1975. Repr. of 1881 ed. 73.00 (ISBN 90-272-0934-0). Benjamins North Am.
Mackenzie, Donald A. Egyptian Myth & Legend. LC 76-27520. (Illus.). 1976. Repr. of 1907 ed. lib. bdg. 45.00 (ISBN 0-89341-033-0). Longwood Pr.
Massey, Gerald. The Natural Genesis, 2 vols. LC 73-92166. 1974. Repr. of 1883 ed. Set. 50.00 (ISBN 0-87728-248-X). Weiser.
Mercatante, Anthony. Who's Who in Egyptian Mythology. 1978. 14.95 (ISBN 0-517-53445-2, Dist. by Crown); pap. 5.95 (ISBN 0-517-53446-0). Potter.
Mitchnik, Helen. Egyptian & Sudanese Folk-Tales. (Oxford Myths & Legends Ser.). (Illus.). (gr. 6-12). 1978. 10.95 (ISBN 0-19-274122-5). Oxford U Pr.
Muller, W. Max. Egyptian Mythology. Bd. with Indochinese Mythology. Scott, James G. LC 63-19097. (Mythology of All Races Ser.: Vol. 12). (Illus.). Repr. of 1932 ed. 22.50x (ISBN 0-8154-0160-4). Cooper Sq.
Roche, Richard. Egyptian Myths & the Ra Ta Story: Based on the Edgar Cayce Readings. 1975. pap. 1.95 (ISBN 0-87604-084-9). ARE Pr.
Shorter, A. W. The Egyptian Gods: A Handbook. 1978. 12.00 (ISBN 0-7100-0037-5). Routledge & Kegan.
Steiner, Rudolf. Egyptian Myths & Mysteries. Macbeth, Norman, tr. from Ger. 1971. 9.95 (ISBN 0-910142-09-2); pap. 5.50 (ISBN 0-910142-10-6). Anthroposophic.

MYTHOLOGY, ESKIMO
Paul, Frances L. Kahtahah. LC 76-17804. (Illus., Orig.). (ps-8). 1976. pap. 5.95 (ISBN 0-88240-058-4). Alaska Northwest.

MYTHOLOGY, ESTONIAN
see Mythology, Finno-Ugrian

MYTHOLOGY, FINNO-UGRIAN
Holmberg, Uno. Finno-Ugric, Siberian Mythology. (Mythology of All Races Ser: Vol. Iv). (Illus.). Repr. of 1932 ed. 25.00x (ISBN 0-8154-0116-7). Cooper Sq.

MYTHOLOGY, GERMANIC
see also Mythology, Norse
Davidson, H. Ellis. Gods & Myths of Northern Europe. (Orig.). 1965. pap. 2.95 (ISBN 0-14-020670-1, Pelican). Penguin.
De La Saussaye, P. Chantepie. The Religion of the Teutons. LC 76-27519. 1976. Repr. of 1902 ed. lib. bdg. 50.00 (ISBN 0-89341-030-6). Longwood Pr.
Grimm, Jacob. Teutonic Mythology, 4 Vols. 4th ed. Stallybrass, James S., tr. Set. 50.00 (ISBN 0-8446-2168-4). Peter Smith.
Kauffmann, Friedrich. Northern Mythology. 1978. Repr. of 1903 ed. lib. bdg. 15.00 (ISBN 0-8495-3022-9). Arden Lib.
Lettsom, William N. The Nibelungenlied. LC 77-13811. 1977. lib. bdg. 45.00 (ISBN 0-8414-5830-8). Folcroft.
MacKenzie, Donald A. Teutonic Myth & Legend. LC 77-91530. 1978. Repr. of 1912 ed. lib. bdg. 50.00 (ISBN 0-89341-313-5). Longwood Pr.
Maurer, Friedrich, ed. Gottfried Von Strassburg Tristan & Isolde. 4th ed. 1977. 6.25x (ISBN 3-11-006841-9). De Gruyter.
Meyer, Richard M. Altgermanische Religionsgeschichte: History of Ancient Germanic Religion. Bolle, Kees W., ed. LC 77-79143. (Mythology Ser.). (Ger.). 1978. Repr. of 1910 ed. lib. bdg. 38.00x (ISBN 0-405-10552-5). Arno.
Phillippson, Ernst A. Germanisches Heidentum Bei Den Angelsachsen. Repr. of 1929 ed. pap. 17.00 (ISBN 0-384-46310-X). Johnson Repr.
Poser, Hans. Philosophie und Mythos. 1979. text ed. 52.00x (ISBN 3-11-007601-2). De Gruyter.
Sawyer, W. C. Teutonic Legends in the Nibelungen Lied & the Nibelungen Ring. 1976. lib. bdg. 59.95 (ISBN 0-8490-2736-5). Gordon Pr.
Stern, Herman I. The Gods of Our Fathers: A Study of Saxon Mythology. LC 77-85623. 1977. Repr. of 1898 ed. lib. bdg. 30.00 (ISBN 0-89341-303-8). Longwood Pr.
Wakefield, Ray M. Nibelungen Prosody. (De Proprietatibus Litterarum Ser.: No. 112). 1976. pap. 25.00x (ISBN 0-686-22366-7). Mouton.
Weston, Jessie L. The Legends of the Wagner Drama. LC 74-24255. Repr. of 1896 ed. 24.00 (ISBN 0-404-13132-8). AMS Pr.

MYTHOLOGY, GREEK
see also Cultus, Greek
Aldrich, Keith, tr. Apollodorus: The Library of Greek Mythology. 298p. 1975. 12.50x (ISBN 0-87291-072-5). Coronado Pr.
Apollodorus. Library, 2 Vols. (Loeb Classical Library: No. 121, 122). 11.00x ea. Vol. 1, Bks. 1-3 (ISBN 0-674-99135-4). Vol. 2 (ISBN 0-674-99136-2). Harvard U Pr.
Bacon, Frances. Wisedome of the Ancients. Gorges, A., tr. LC 68-54614. (English Experince Ser.: No. 1). 176p. 1968. Repr. of 1619 ed. 13.00 (ISBN 90-221-0001-4). Walter J Johnson.
Berens, E. M. The Myths & Legends of Ancient Greece & Rome. LC 77-91528. 1977. Repr. of 1880 ed. lib. bdg. 30.00 (ISBN 0-89341-029-2). Longwood Pr.
Bespaloff, R. On the Iliad. (Bollingen Ser.: No. 19). 1970. 10.00 (ISBN 0-691-09710-0). Princeton U Pr.
Boer, Charles, tr. from Gr. The Homeric Hymns. rev. ed. (Dunquin Ser.). 1979. pap. text ed. 8.50 (ISBN 0-88214-210-0). Spring Pubns.
Brown, R. Semitic Influence in Hellenic Mythology. xvi, 228p. Date not set. Repr. of 1898 ed. lib. bdg. 35.00x (ISBN 0-89241-206-2). Caratzas Bros.
Brown, Robert. Semetic Influence in Hellenic Mythology. LC 65-27053. (Library of Religious & Philosophical Thought). Repr. of 1898 ed. lib. bdg. 12.50x (ISBN 0-678-09952-9, Reference Bk Pubs). Kelley.
Brown, Robert F. Schelling's Treatise on "the Deities of Samothrace". A Translation & an Interpretation. LC 76-42239. (American Academy of Religion. Studies in Religion). 1977. pap. 7.50x (ISBN 0-89130-087-2, 010012). Scholars Pr Ca.
Bulfinch, Thomas. Myths of Greece & Rome. 288p. 1981. pap. 10.95 (ISBN 0-14-005643-2). Penguin.
Burkert, Walter. Structure & History in Greek Mythology & Ritual. LC 78-62856. (Sather Classical Lectures: Vol. 47). 1980. 18.50x (ISBN 0-520-03771-5). U of Cal Pr.
Butterworth, E. A. Some Traces of the Pre-Olympian World in Greek Literature & Myth. (Illus.). 1966. 29.50x (ISBN 3-11-005010-2). De Gruyter.
Cambridge School Classics Project Foundation Course. Gods of Olympus. Forrest, M., ed. (Roman World Ser.). (Illus.). 1973. text ed. 12.50x (ISBN 0-521-08469-5). Cambridge U Pr.
Carpenter, Thomas H. & Gula, Robert J. Mythology: Greek & Roman. (Illus.). (gr. 10). 1977. pap. text ed. 4.95 (ISBN 0-88334-089-5). Ind Sch Pr.
Collignon, M. Manual of Mythology in Relation to Greek Art. Harrison, J. E., tr. xvi, 335p. Date not set. Repr. of 1899 ed. lib. bdg. 47.50x (ISBN 0-89241-141-4). Caratzas Bros.
Dall, Caroline H. Margaret & Her Friends; or, Ten Conversations with Margaret Fuller Upon the Mythology of the Greeks & Its Expression in Art. LC 72-4961. (The Romantic Tradition in American Literature Ser.). 166p. 1972. Repr. of 1895 ed. 13.00 (ISBN 0-405-04633-2). Arno.
D'alulaire & D'alulaire & D'Alulaire, Edgar P. D'alulaires' Book of Greek Myths. Date not set. pap. 5.95 (ISBN 0-385-15787-8). Doubleday.
D'Aulaire, Ingri & D'Aulaire, Edgar. D'Aulaire's Book of Greek Myths. (Illus.). 1980. pap. 5.95 (ISBN 0-385-15787-8, Zephyr). Doubleday.
Diel, Paul. Symbolism in Greek Mythology: Human Desire & Its Transformations. Stuart, Vincent, et al, trs. from Fr. LC 79-67696. 240p. 1980. 15.00 (ISBN 0-394-51083-6), Shambhala Pubns.
Dietrich, B. C. Death, Fate & the Gods: Development of a Religious Idea in Greek Popular Belief & in Homer. (University of London Classical Studies: No. 3). 390p. 1967. Repr. text ed. 41.00x (ISBN 0-686-74103-X, Pub. by Aris England). Humanities.
Downing, Christine. The Goddess: Mythological Images of the Feminine. 250p. 12.95 (ISBN 0-8245-0091-1). Crossroad NY.
Duthie, Alexander. The Greek Mythology: A Reader's Handbook. 2nd ed. LC 78-12988. 1979. Repr. of 1949 ed. lib. bdg. 16.00x (ISBN 0-313-21077-2, DUGM). Greenwood.
Espeland, Pamela. The Story of Cadmus. LC 80-66795. (Myths for Modern Children Ser.). (Illus.). 32p. (gr. 1-4). 1980. PLB 5.95g (ISBN 0-87614-128-9). Carolrhoda Bks.
--The Story of King Midas. LC 80-66794. (Myths for Modern Children Ser.). (Illus.). 32p. (gr. 1-4). 1980. PLB 5.95g (ISBN 0-87614-129-7). Carolrhoda Bks.
Evslin, Bernard, et al. Heroes & Monsters of Greek Myths. (gr. 7-9). 1970. pap. 1.25 (ISBN 0-590-01555-9, Schol Pap). Schol Bk Serv.
Flint, William W. Use of Myth to Create Suspense. (Studies in Comparative Literature, No. 35). 1970. pap. 12.95 (ISBN 0-8383-0030-8). Haskell.
Fontenrose, Joseph. Orion: The Myth of the Hunter & the Huntress. (U. C. Publications in Classical Studies: Vol. 23). 230p. 1981. 14.50x (ISBN 0-520-09632-0). U of Cal Pr.
--Python: A Study of Delphic Myth & Its Origins. 637p. 1981. 30.00x (ISBN 0-520-04106-2); pap. 8.95 (ISBN 0-520-04091-0, CAL 449). U of Cal Pr.
Fortune, Dion. Goat-Foot God. pap. 7.95 (ISBN 0-87728-500-4). Weiser.
Gibson, Michael. Gods, Men & Monsters from the Greek Myths. (Illus.). 1978. 12.95 (ISBN 0-85654-027-7, Pub. by Two Continents). Hippocrene Bks.
Gordon, R. L., ed. Myth, Religion & Society: Structuralist Essays by M. Detienne, L. Gernet, J. P. Vernant & P. Vidal-Naquet. (Illus.). 250p. Date not set. text ed. price not set (ISBN 0-521-22780-1); pap. text ed. price not set (ISBN 0-521-29640-4). Cambridge U Pr.
Graves, Robert. Greek Myths, 2 Vols. (Orig.). (YA) (gr. 9 up). 1955. Vol. 1. pap. 2.95 (ISBN 0-14-020508-X, Pelican); Vol. 2. pap. 2.95 (ISBN 0-14-020509-8). Penguin.
Green, R. L. The Tale of Thebes. LC 76-22979. (Illus.). 1977. 14.95 (ISBN 0-521-21410-6); pap. 5.50 (ISBN 0-521-21411-4). Cambridge U Pr.
Grigson, Geoffrey. Goddess of Love. LC 76-6845. 1977. 12.95 (ISBN 0-8128-2069-X). Stein & Day.
Grimal, Pierre. Dictionnaire de la Mythologie Grecque et Romaine. 5th ed. 612p. (Fr.). 1969. 59.95 (ISBN 0-686-57316-1, M-6299). French & Eur.
Hamilton, Edith. Mythology. (RL 7). 1971. pap. 2.50 (ISBN 0-451-61944-7, ME1944, Ment). NAL.
Harnsberger, Caroline T. Gods & Heroes: A Quick Guide to the Occupations, Associations & Experiences of the Greek & Roman Gods & Heroes. LC 76-21470. 1977. 20.00x (ISBN 0-87875-125-4). Whitston Pub.
Harrison, Jane E. Prolegomena to the Study of Greek Religion. facsimile ed. LC 75-10639. (Ancient Religion & Mythology Ser.). (Illus.). 1976. Repr. of 1922 ed. 43.00x (ISBN 0-405-07018-7). Arno.
Hathorn, Richmond. Greek Mythology. 1977. 22.00x (ISBN 0-8156-6048-0, Am U Beirut). Syracuse U Pr.
Herberger, Charles F. The Riddle of the Sphinx: Calendric Symbolism in Myth & Icon. 1979. 8.50 (ISBN 0-533-03500-7). Vantage.
Higginson, Thomas W. Tales of Atlantis & the Enchanted Islands. (Newcastle Mythology Library: Vol. 3). (Illus.). 1977. pap. 3.95 (ISBN 0-87877-042-9, M-42). Newcastle Pub.
Hollinghurst, Hugh. Gods & Heroes of Ancient Greece. 1973. pap. text ed. 6.00x (ISBN 0-435-36405-7). Heinemann Ed.
Hunger, H. Lexikon der Griechischen und Roemischen Mythologie. 452p. (Ger.). 1974. pap. 7.95 (ISBN 3-499-16178-8, M-7252). French & Eur.
Keightley, Thomas. Classical Mythology: The Myths of Ancient Greece & Italy. 25.00 (ISBN 0-89005-189-5). Ares.
Kerenyi, C. The Gods of the Greeks. (Illus.). 1980. pap. 7.95 (ISBN 0-500-27048-1). Thames Hudson.
Kerenyi, Karl. Athene. Stein, Murray, tr. from Ger. (Orig.). 1978. pap. text ed. 7.00 (ISBN 0-88214-209-7). Spring Pubns.
Kingsley, Charles. The Heroes; or, Greek Fairy Tales. Repr. of 1882 ed. 20.00 (ISBN 0-686-20097-7). Quality Lib.
Kirk, G. S. The Nature of Greek Myths. LC 74-21683. 336p. 1975. 15.00 (ISBN 0-87951-031-5). Overlook Pr.
--Nature of Greek Myths. 1975. pap. 3.95 (ISBN 0-14-021783-5, Pelican). Penguin.
Kupfer, Grace H. Legends of Greece & Rome. 1911. 20.00 (ISBN 0-686-20105-1). Quality Lib.
Lines, Kathleen, ed. Faber Book of Greek Legends. 268p. 1973. 9.95 (ISBN 0-571-09830-4, Pub. by Faber & Faber). Merrimack Bk Serv.
Lloyd-Jones, Hugh. Myths of the Zodiac. LC 78-69955. 1978. 14.50x (ISBN 0-312-55870-8). St Martin.
Lopez-Pedraza, Rafael. Hermes & His Children. (Seminar Ser.). (Orig.). 1978. pap. 8.00 (ISBN 0-88214-113-9). Spring Pubns.
MacKenzie, Donald A. Myths of Crete & Pre-Hellenic Europe. LC 76-27522. (Illus.). 1976. Repr. of 1918 ed. lib. bdg. 45.00 (ISBN 0-89341-035-7). Longwood Pr.
Nilsson, Martin P. Greek Folk Religion. (Illus.). 8.50 (ISBN 0-8446-0218-3). Peter Smith.
--History of Greek Religion. 2nd ed. (Orig.). 1964. pap. 4.45 (ISBN 0-393-00287-X, Norton Lib). Norton.
--The Mycenaean Origin of Greek Mythology. enl ed. LC 70-181440. (Sather Classical Lectures: Vol. 8). 258p. 1973. 17.50x (ISBN 0-520-01951-2). U of Cal Pr.
Otto, Walter F. The Homeric Gods. 1978. Repr. of 1954 ed. lib. bdg. 18.50x (ISBN 0-374-96151-4). Octagon.
Page, Denys. Folktales in Homer's Odyssey. LC 73-75056. (Carl Newell Jackson Lectures Ser). 144p. 1973. text ed. 8.95x (ISBN 0-674-30720-8). Harvard U Pr.
Patrick, Richard. All Color Book of Greek Mythology. (Bounty Bks.). (Illus.). 72p. 1974. pap. 2.95 (ISBN 0-517-51411-7). Crown.
Powell, B. Athenian Mythology: Erichthonius & the Three Daughters of Cecrops. (Illus.). 1977. 10.00 (ISBN 0-89005-121-6). Ares.
Preller, Ludwig. Griechische Mythology. Bolle, Kees W., ed. LC 77-79153. (Mythology Ser.). (Ger.). 1978. lib. bdg. 56.00x (ISBN 0-405-10562-2). Arno.
Rahner, Hugo. Greek Myths & Christian Mystery. LC 79-156736. (Illus.). 1971. Repr. of 1963 ed. 17.50x (ISBN 0-8196-0270-1). Biblo.
Robert, Carl. Bild und Lied: Archaologische Beitrage Zur Geschichte der Griechischen Heldensage. facsimile ed. LC 75-10653. (Ancient Religion & Mythology Ser.). (Illus., Ger.). 1976. Repr. of 1881 ed. 15.00x (ISBN 0-405-07277-5). Arno.
Rose, Herbert J. Gods & Heroes of the Greeks. (Orig.). 1958. pap. 3.95 (ISBN 0-452-00454-3, F454, Mer). NAL.
--Handbook of Greek Mythology. 1959. pap. 4.95 (ISBN 0-525-47041-7). Dutton.
Rose, Herbert J., ed. Gods & Heroes of the Greeks: An Introduction to Greek Mythology. 8.50 (ISBN 0-8446-5113-3). Peter Smith.
Ross, Harriet, compiled by. Myths of Ancient Greece. (Illus.). 160p. 1981. PLB 7.95 (ISBN 0-87460-383-8). Lion Bks.
Rouse, W. H. Gods, Heroes & Men of Ancient Greece. (RL 5). 1971. pap. 1.95 (ISBN 0-451-61989-7, MJ1989, Ment). NAL.
Ruskin, John. The Queen of the Air: A Study of the Greek Myths of Cloud & Storm. LC 78-58190. 1978. Repr. of 1869 ed. lib. bdg. 25.00 (ISBN 0-89341-322-4). Longwood Pr.
Schmidt, Joel. Larousse Greek & Roman Mythology. LC 80-15046. (Illus.). 320p. 1980. 16.95 (ISBN 0-07-055342-4). McGraw.
Simpson, Michael, tr. Gods & Heroes of the Greeks: The Library of Apollodorus. LC 75-32489. (Illus.). 320p. 1976. 17.50x (ISBN 0-87023-205-3); pap. 7.50x (ISBN 0-87023-206-1). U of Mass Pr.
Slater, Philip E. Glory of Hera: Greek Mythology & the Greek Family. 1971. pap. 7.95 (ISBN 0-8070-5795-9, BP387). Beacon Pr.

Spretnak, Charlene. Lost Goddesses of Early Greece: A Collection of Pre-Hellenic Mythology. LC 80-68169. (Illus.). 132p. 1981. pap. 5.95 (ISBN 0-8070-3239-5, BP 617). Beacon Pr.
--Lost Goddesses of Early Greece: A Collection of Pre-Hellenic Mythology. (Illus.). 1978. pap. 4.95 (ISBN 0-931452-00-7). Moon Bks.
Warner, Rex. The Stories of the Greeks. 480p. 1978. 15.00 (ISBN 0-374-27056-2); pap. 7.95 (ISBN 0-374-50728-7). FS&G.
--Vengeance of the Gods. 192p. 1955. 3.50 (ISBN 0-87013-009-9). Mich St U Pr.
Weston, Jessie L. The Legends of the Wagner Drama: Studies in Mythology & Romance. LC 76-22354. 1976. Repr. of 1903 ed. lib. bdg. 35.00 (ISBN 0-89341-003-9). Longwood Pr.
Wittkowski, Wolfgang. Heinrich Von Kleist: Amphithryon Materialien Zur Rezeption und Interpretation. 1978. 47.75x (ISBN 3-11-006988-1). De Gruyter.

MYTHOLOGY, GREEK–JUVENILE LITERATURE

Asimov, Isaac. Words from the Myths. (Illus.). (gr. 5-10). 1961. 9.95 (ISBN 0-395-06568-2). HM.
--Words from the Myths. (Illus.). (RL 6). 1969. pap. 1.50 (ISBN 0-451-09362-3, W9362, Sig). NAL.
Coolidge, Olivia. Greek Myths. (Illus.). (gr. 7 up). 1949. 8.95 (ISBN 0-395-06721-9). HM.
D'Aulaire, Ingri & D'Aulaire, Edgar Parin. D'Aulaires' Book of Greek Myths. LC 62-15877. 1962. 10.95a (ISBN 0-385-01583-6); PLB (ISBN 0-385-07108-6). Doubleday.
Dolch, Edward W. & Dolch, M. P. Greek Stories. (Pleasure Reading Ser). (gr. 3-12). 1955. PLB 6.57 (ISBN 0-8116-2607-5). Garrard.
Evslin, Bernard. Greeks Bearing Gifts: The Epics of Achilles & Ulysses. LC 76-16039. (Illus.). 336p. (YA) 1976. 9.95 (ISBN 0-590-17431-2, Four Winds). Schol Bk Serv.
Gates, Doris. Two Queens of Heaven: Aphrodite & Demeter. (Greek Myths Ser). (Illus.). 96p. (gr. 4-6). 1974. PLB 7.95 (ISBN 0-670-73680-5). Viking Pr.
Green, R. L. The Tale of Thebes. LC 76-22979. (Illus.). 1977. 14.95 (ISBN 0-521-21410-6); pap. 5.50 (ISBN 0-521-21411-4). Cambridge U Pr.
Green, Roger L. Tales of Greek Heroes. (Orig.). (gr. 5-7). 1974. pap. 2.50 (ISBN 0-14-030119-4, Puffin). Penguin.
Kingsley, Charles. The Heroes. (Facsimilie Classics Ser.). (Illus.). 224p. (gr. 3 up). 1980. 8.95 (ISBN 0-8317-4448-0, Mayflower Bks). Smith Pubs.
--The Heroes of Greek Fairy Tales for My Children. 1889. Repr. lib. bdg. 15.00 (ISBN 0-8414-5578-3). Folcroft.
McDermott, Gerald. Sun Flight. LC 79-5067. (Illus.). 40p. 1980. 10.95 (ISBN 0-590-07632-9, Four Winds). Schol Bk Serv.
McLean, Mollie & Wiseman, Anne. Adventures of Greek Heroes. (Merit Ser.). (gr. 6). 1961. 7.95 (ISBN 0-395-06913-0). HM.
Proctor, Percy M. Star Myths & Stories: From Andromeda to Virgo. 1972. 8.50 (ISBN 0-682-47470-3, Banner). Exposition.
Silverthorne, Elizabeth. I, Heracles. LC 78-1811. (Illus.). (gr. 3-7). 1978. 5.95 (ISBN 0-687-18459-2). Abingdon.
Swinburne, Laurence & Swinburne, Irene. Ancient Myths: The First Science Fiction. LC 77-10915. (Myth, Magic & Superstition Ser.). (Illus.). (gr. 4-5). 1977. PLB 10.65 (ISBN 0-8172-1042-3). Raintree Pubs.
Wise, William. Monster Myths of Ancient Greece. (Illus.). 48p. (gr. 7-11). 1981. PLB 6.99 (ISBN 0-399-61143-6). Putnam.
Witting, Alisoun. Treasury of Greek Mythology. LC 65-24973. (Illus.). (gr. 5-8). 1966. PLB 6.29 (ISBN 0-8178-3692-6). Harvey.

MYTHOLOGY, HAWAIIAN

Beckwith, Martha W. Hawaiian Mythology. LC 70-97998. 1977. pap. 7.95 (ISBN 0-8248-0514-3). U Pr of Hawaii.
Emerson, Nathaniel B. Pele & Hiiaka: A Myth from Hawaii. LC 75-35190. Repr. of 1915 ed. 22.50 (ISBN 0-404-14218-4). AMS Pr.
McBride, L. R. Kahuna: Versatile Mystics of Old Hawaii. pap. 4.25 (ISBN 0-912180-18-8). Petroglyph.
Melville, Leinani. Children of the Rainbow: The Religions, Legends & Gods of Pre-Christian Hawaii. LC 69-17715. (Illus.). 1969. pap. 1.95 (ISBN 0-8356-0002-5, Quest). Theos Pub Hse.
Westervelt, W. D. Legends of Gods & Ghosts from Hawaiian Mythology. 1977. lib. bdg. 59.95 (ISBN 0-8490-2147-2). Gordon Pr.

MYTHOLOGY, HEBREW

see Mythology, Jewish

MYTHOLOGY, HINDU

see also Symbolism of Numbers

Bhaktivedanta, Swami A. C. Easy Journey to Other Planets. LC 70-118080. (Illus.). 1970. pap. 1.50 (ISBN 0-912776-10-2). Bhaktivedanta.
--Prahlad, Picture & Story Book. LC 72-2032. (Illus.). (gr. 2-6). 1973. pap. 1.95 (ISBN 0-685-47513-1). Bhaktivedanta.
--Teachings of Lord Caitanya. LC 75-2060. (Illus.). 1974. 7.95 (ISBN 0-912776-08-0); pap. 2.95 (ISBN 0-912776-07-2). Bhaktivedanta.
Coomaraswamy, A. K. & Noble, M. E. Myths of the Hindus & Buddhists. (Illus.). 9.00 (ISBN 0-8446-1896-9). Peter Smith.
Coomaraswamy, Ananda K. & Nivedita, Sr. Myths of the Hindus & Buddhists. (Illus.). (gr. 4-8). pap. 4.50 (ISBN 0-486-21759-0). Dover.
Dasi, Krsnastuta. Agha the Terrible Demon. LC 77-10612. (gr. 1-4). 1977. PLB 5.95 (ISBN 0-89213-007-5). Bala Bks.
Devata (an Essay on Indian Mythology), by a Recluse of Vindhyachala. LC 73-3811. (Sacred Books of the Hindus: No. 19). Repr. of 1917 ed. 22.50 (ISBN 0-404-57819-5). AMS Pr.
Dimmitt, Cornelia & Van Buitenen, J. A., trs. Classical Hindu Mythology: A Reader in the Sanskrit Puranas. LC 77-92643. 1978. 19.50x (ISBN 0-87722-117-0); pap. 12.95x (ISBN 0-87722-122-7). Temple U Pr.
Dumezil, Georges. Deesses Latines et Mythes Vediques. Bolle, Kees W., ed. LC 77-79121. (Mythology Ser.). (Fr.). 1978. Repr. of 1956 ed. lib. bdg. 12.00x (ISBN 0-405-10533-9). Arno.
Henry, Victor. La Magie dans L'Inde Antique: Paris, 1904. LC 78-74261. (Oriental Religions Ser.: Vol. 5). 325p. 1980. lib. bdg. 33.00 (ISBN 0-8240-3903-3). Garland Pub.
Hillebrandt, Alfred. Vedic Mythology, Vol. I. rev. 2nd ed. Sarma, Sreeramula R., tr. from Ger. 472p. 1980. text ed. 24.00 (ISBN 0-89684-098-0, Pub. by Motilal Banarsidass India). Orient Bk Dist.
Hopkins, E. Washburn. Epic Mythology. rev. ed. LC 76-75358. 1968. Repr. of 1915 ed. 16.00x (ISBN 0-8196-0228-0). Biblo.
The Kaliya Serpent. LC 79-4669. (Childhood Pastimes of Krishna). (Illus.). (gr. 3-6). pap. 2.95 (ISBN 0-89647-009-1). Bala Bks.
MacDonell, Arthur A. Vedic Mythology. 69.95 (ISBN 0-87968-153-5). Gordon Pr.
MacFie, J. M. Myths & Legends of India: An Introduction to the Study of Hinduism. 357p. Repr. of 1924 ed. pap. text ed. 5.95 (ISBN 0-567-22181-4). Attic Pr.
O'Flaherty, Wendy, tr. Hindu Myths. (Classics Ser). 360p. 1975. pap. 3.50 (ISBN 0-14-044306-1). Penguin.
O'Flaherty, Wendy D. Asceticism & Eroticism in the Mythology of Siva. (Illus.). 401p. 1973. 36.00x (ISBN 0-19-713573-0). Oxford U Pr.
Shulman, David D. Tamil Temple Myths: Sacrifice & Divine Marriage in the South Indian Saiva Tradition. LC 79-17051. 1980. 30.00 (ISBN 0-691-06415-6). Princeton U Pr.
Ward, William. View of the History, Literature, & Mythology of the Hindoos, 3 Vols. LC 71-115207. 1971. Repr. of 1882 ed. Set. 75.00x (ISBN 0-8046-1100-9). Kennikat.
Wilkins, R. J. Hindu Mythology. 1972. 10.75x (ISBN 0-8364-0410-6). South Asia Bks.

MYTHOLOGY, HITTITE

Gaster, Theodor H., ed. Oldest Stories in the World. 1958. pap. 4.95x (ISBN 0-8070-5787-8, BP66). Beacon Pr.

MYTHOLOGY, HUNGARIAN

see Mythology, Finno-Ugrian

MYTHOLOGY, INDIAN (AMERICAN INDIAN)

see Indians–Religion and Mythology; Indians of Central America–Religion and Mythology; Indians of Mexico–Religion and Mythology; Indians of North America–Religion and Mythology; Indians of South America–Religion and Mythology

MYTHOLOGY, INDIC

Imam, S. M. Scenes from Indian Mythology. 2nd ed. 1975. pap. 1.50 (ISBN 0-89684-347-5). Orient Bk Dist.
Jha, Akhileshwar. Sexual Designs in Indian Culture. 1979. text ed. 12.50x (ISBN 0-7069-0744-2). Humanities.
Macdonell, A. A. Vedic Mythology. 1974. Repr. 9.00 (ISBN 0-8426-0674-2). Orient Bk Dist.
Nivedita, Sr. Siva & Buddha. pap. 0.50 (ISBN 0-87481-116-3). Vedanta Pr.
O'Flaherty, Wendy D. Women, Androgynes, & Other Mythical Beasts. LC 79-16128. 1980. lib. bdg. 27.50x (ISBN 0-226-61849-8). U of Chicago Pr.
Oppert, Gustav. On the Original Inhabitants of Bharatavarsa or India. Bolle, Kees W., ed. (Mythology Ser.). 1978. Repr. of 1893 ed. lib. bdg. 42.00x (ISBN 0-405-10557-6). Arno.
Reid, Dorothy M. Tales of Nanabozho. 128p. (Orig.). 1979. pap. text ed. 3.95x (ISBN 0-19-540322-3). Oxford U Pr.
Rungachary, Santha. Tales for All Times. (Nehru Library for Children). (Illus.). (gr. 1-9). 1979. pap. 1.50 (ISBN 0-89744-187-7). Auromere.
Shastri, J. L., ed. Bhagavata Purana: Part 5. (Ancient Indian Tradition & Mythology Ser.: Vol. 11). (Contains index for vols. 1-5). 1979. text ed. 18.00x (ISBN 0-8426-1105-3). Verry.
--Garuda Purana, Pt. 1. (Ancient Indian Tradition & Mythology Ser.: Vol. 12). 1979. text ed. 18.00x (ISBN 0-8426-1106-1). Verry.
Shastri, J. L., tr. Ancient Indian Tradition & Mythology Series. Incl. Vols. 1-4. Siva Purana. 72.00x set (ISBN 0-8426-0563-0); Vols. 5-6. Linga Purana. 36.00x set (ISBN 0-8426-0578-9). 1965. Verry.
Thomas, P. Epics, Myths & Legends of India. 13th ed. (Illus.). 163p. 1973. 32.50x (ISBN 0-8002-1401-3). Intl Pubns Serv.
Venkatacharaya, T., ed. Sriharicarita Mahakavya of Srihari Padmanabhasastrin. 11.50 (ISBN 0-8356-7322-7). Theos Pub Hse.
Vidyarthi, L. P. The Sacred Complex in Hindu Gaya. 2nd ed. 264p. 1980. pap. text ed. 11.25x (ISBN 0-391-02214-8). Humanities.

MYTHOLOGY, INDO-CHINESE

David-Neel, Alexandra & Yongden, Lama. The Superhuman Life of Gesar of Ling. Bolle, Kees W., ed. LC 77-79120. (Mythology Ser.). 1978. Repr. of 1934 ed. lib. bdg. 25.00x (ISBN 0-405-10532-0). Arno.

MYTHOLOGY, INDO-EUROPEAN

see also Soma

Cox, George W. Mythology of the Aryan Nations, 2 Vols. LC 68-8202. 1969. Repr. of 1870 ed. 35.00x (ISBN 0-8046-0091-0). Kennikat.
Dumezil, Georges. Horace et les Curiaces. Bolle, Kees W., ed. (Mythology Ser.). (Fr.). 1978. Repr. of 1942 ed. lib. bdg. 12.00x (ISBN 0-405-10534-7). Arno.
Gubernatis, Angelo De. Zoological Mythology, 2 Vols. LC 68-58904. 1968. Repr. of 1872 ed. Set. 39.00 (ISBN 0-8103-3527-1). Gale.
Larson, Gerald J., et al, eds. Myth & Indo-European Antiquity. LC 72-93522. 1974. 24.00x (ISBN 0-520-02378-1). U of Cal Pr.
Tilcomb, Sarah E. Arvan Sun-Myths: The Origin of Religions. LC 78-31508. 1979. Repr. of 1889 ed. lib. bdg. 20.00 (ISBN 0-89341-323-2). Longwood Pr.
Titcom, Sarah E. Aryan Sun-Myths: The Origin of Religions. 1977. lib. bdg. 59.95 (ISBN 0-8490-1456-5). Gordon Pr.

MYTHOLOGY, INDONESIAN

Knappert, Jan. Myths & Legends of Indonesia. (Writing in Asia Ser.). 1977. pap. text ed. 5.50x (ISBN 0-686-60453-9, 00213). Heinemann Ed.

MYTHOLOGY, IRISH

Cousins, H. James. Irish Mythology. 59.95 (ISBN 0-8490-0425-X). Gordon Pr.
Gantz, Jeffrey. Old Irish Myths & Sagas. (Pengiun Classic Ser.). 1982. pap. 3.95 (ISBN 0-14-044397-5). Penguin.
Kavanagh, Peter. Irish Mythology: A Dictionary. (Illus.). 50p. (Hand Set & Printed). 100.00 (ISBN 0-914612-00-X). Kavanagh.
Squire, Charles. The Mythology of Ancient Britain & Ireland. LC 73-13769. 1974. Repr. of 1909 ed. lib. bdg. 15.00 (ISBN 0-8414-7650-0). Folcroft.

MYTHOLOGY, JAPANESE

Anderson, Benedict R. Mythology & the Tolerance of the Javanese. 3rd ed. 77p. Repr. of 1965 ed. 5.00 (ISBN 0-686-62726-1). Cornell Mod Indo.
Aston, William G. Nihongi: Chronicles of Japan from the Earliest Times to A.D. 697. LC 70-152110. (Illus.). 1971. pap. 10.50 (ISBN 0-8048-0984-4). C E Tuttle.
Davis, F. Hadland. Myths and Legends of Japan. 1978. Repr. of 1912 ed. lib. bdg. 45.00 (ISBN 0-8495-1008-2). Arden Lib.
Ferguson, John C. Chinese Mythology. Bd. with Japanese Mythology. Anesaki, Masaharu. LC 63-19093. (Mythology of All Races Ser.: Vol. 8). (Illus.). Repr. of 1932 ed. 23.50x (ISBN 0-8154-0068-3). Cooper Sq.
Mackenzie, Donald A. The Myths of China & Japan. LC 77-6878. 1977. Repr. of 1923 ed. lib. bdg. 45.00 (ISBN 0-89341-149-3). Longwood Pr.
Shikibu, Murasaki. The Tale of the Genji. Seidensticker, Edward G., tr. 1976. 25.00 (ISBN 0-394-48328-6). Knopf.

MYTHOLOGY, JEWISH

Cohn, Norman. Warrent for Genocide. LC 80-21733. pap. 14.00 (ISBN 0-89130-423-1, 14 00 23). Scholars Pr CA.
Goldziher, Ignaz. Mythology Among the Hebrews & Its Historical Development. Martineau, Russell, tr. LC 66-2396. Repr. of 1877 ed. 18.50x (ISBN 0-8154-0082-9). Cooper Sq.
Graves, Robert & Patai, Raphael. Hebrew Myths. 1966. pap. 4.95 (ISBN 0-07-024125-2, SP). McGraw.
Neugroschel, Joachim. Yenne Velt: The Great Works of Jewish Fantasy & Occult. 1978. pap. 6.95 (ISBN 0-671-79006-4, Wallaby). PB.

MYTHOLOGY, LAPPISH

see Mythology, Finno-Ugrian

MYTHOLOGY, MAGYAR

see Mythology, Finno-Ugrian

MYTHOLOGY, MAORI

see Mythology, Polynesian

MYTHOLOGY, MAYA

see Mayas–Religion and Mythology

MYTHOLOGY, NEAR EASTERN

see Mythology, Oriental

MYTHOLOGY, NORSE

Anderson, R. B. Norse Mythology or the Religion of Our Forefathers. LC 77-6879. 1977. Repr. of 1891 ed. lib. bdg. 25.00 (ISBN 0-89341-147-7). Longwood Pr.
Anderson, Rasmuus B. Norse Mythology: The Religion of Our Forefathers, Containing All the Myths of the Eddas, Systematized & Interpreted. 1976. Repr. of 1876 ed. 60.00 (ISBN 0-403-05987-9, Regency). Scholarly.
Branston, Brian. Gods, & Heroes from Viking Mythology. (Illus.). 1978. 12.95 (ISBN 0-85654-029-3, Pub. by Two Continents). Hippocrene Bks.
--Gods of the North. (Illus.). 1980. pap. 7.95 (ISBN 0-500-27177-1). Thames Hudson.
Bugge, Sophus. Home of the Eddic Poems. Schofield, William H., tr. LC 74-144524. (Grimm Library: No. 11). Repr. of 1899 ed. 21.00 (ISBN 0-404-53554-2). AMS Pr.
Craigie, William A. Religion of Ancient Scandinavia. facsimile ed. LC 74-99657. (Select Bibliographies Reprint Ser). 1906. 12.50 (ISBN 0-8369-5086-0). Arno.
Crossley-Holland, Kevin. The Norse Myths. 1981. pap. 6.95 (ISBN 0-394-74846-8). Pantheon.
Crossley-Holland, Kevin, retold by. The Norse Myths. 1980. 14.95 (ISBN 0-394-50048-2). Pantheon.
Davidson, H. Ellis. Gods & Myths of Northern Europe. (Orig.). 1965. pap. 2.95 (ISBN 0-14-020670-1, Pelican). Penguin.
De La Saussaye, P. Chantepie. The Religion of the Teutons. LC 76-27519. 1976. Repr. of 1902 ed. lib. bdg. 50.00 (ISBN 0-89341-030-6). Longwood Pr.
Dumezil, Georges. Gods of the Ancient Northmen. Haugen, Einar, ed. & tr. (Study of Comparative Folklore & Mythology, No. 3). 1974. 21.50x (ISBN 0-520-02044-8); CAL 371. pap. 3.95 (ISBN 0-520-03507-0). U of Cal Pr.
Ellis, Hilda R. Road to Hel: A Study of the Conception of the Dead in Old Norse Literature. LC 68-23286. (Illus.). 1968. Repr. of 1943 ed. lib. bdg. 15.00 (ISBN 0-8371-0070-4, ELRH). Greenwood.
Faraday, Lucy W. Edda I: The Divine Mythology of the North 2: The Heroic Mythology of the North, 2 Vols. in 1. (Popular Studies in Mythology, Romance & Folklore: Nos. 12 & 13). Repr. of 1902 ed. 11.00 (ISBN 0-404-53512-7). AMS Pr.
Gayley, Charles M. Classic Myths in English Literature & in Art. rev. & enlarged ed. 1939. 19.50 (ISBN 0-471-00191-0). Wiley.
Grimm, Jacob. Teutonic Mythology, 4 Vols. 4th ed. Stallybrass, James S., tr. Set. 50.00 (ISBN 0-8446-2168-4). Peter Smith.
Hveberg, Harald. Of Gods & Giants: Norse Mythology. 4th ed. LC 79-433620. (Norwegian Guides Ser). (Orig.). 1969. pap. 6.50x (ISBN 82-518-0083-8). Intl Pubns Serv.
Kauffmann, Friedrich. Northern Mythology. 106p. 1980. Repr. of 1903 ed. lib. bdg. 15.00 (ISBN 0-89987-450-9). Darby Bks.
--Northern Mythology. 1978. Repr. of 1903 ed. lib. bdg. 15.00 (ISBN 0-8495-3022-9). Arden Lib.
Lindow, John. Myths & Legends of the Vikings. (Illus.). 1980. pap. 2.95 (ISBN 0-88388-071-7). Bellerophon Bks.
MacCulloch, John A. Eddic Mythology. LC 63-19087. (Mythology of All Races Ser.: Vol. 2). (Illus.). Repr. of 1932 ed. 23.50x (ISBN 0-8154-0143-4). Cooper Sq.
Munch, Peter A. Norse Mythology, Legends of Gods & Heroes. Hustvedt, Sigurd B., tr. LC 74-112002. 1970. Repr. of 1926 ed. 23.75 (ISBN 0-404-04538-3). AMS Pr.
Munch, Peter A. & Olsen, Magnus, eds. Norse Mythology: Legends of Gods & Heroes. rev. ed. Hustuedt, Sigurd B., tr. LC 68-31092. (Illus.). 1968. Repr. of 1926 ed. 22.00 (ISBN 0-8103-3454-2). Gale.
Pigott, Grenville. A Manual of Scandinavian Mythology: Containing a Popular Account of the Two Eddas & of the Religion of Odin. Bolle, Kees W., ed. LC 77-79152. (Mythology Ser.). 1978. Repr. of 1839 ed. lib. bdg. 25.00x (ISBN 0-405-10561-4). Arno.
Sturluson, Snorri. Heimskringla: From the Sagas of the Norse Kings. Monsen, Erling, tr. 398p. 1980. 32.50 (ISBN 0-906191-39-4, Pub. by Findhorn-Thule Scotland). Hydra Bk.
--The Prose Edda of Snorri Sturluson: Tales from Norse Mythology. Young, Jean I., tr. 1964. pap. 4.95x (ISBN 0-520-01232-1, CAMPUS55). U of Cal Pr.
Thompson, Lawrence S., ed. Norse Mythology: The Elder Edda in Prose Translation. 136p. (Orig.). 1974. 12.50 (ISBN 0-208-01394-6, Archon). Shoe String.
Turville-Petre, E. O. Myth & Religion of the North. LC 75-5003. (Illus.). 340p. 1975. Repr. of 1964 ed. lib. bdg. 25.50x (ISBN 0-8371-7420-1, TUMR). Greenwood.

Wagner, W. Asgard & the Gods: Tales & Traditions of Our Northern Ancestors. (Folklore Ser.). 1882. 40.00 (ISBN 0-685-43826-0). Norwood Edns.

MYTHOLOGY, NORSE–JUVENILE LITERATURE

Colum, Padraic. The Children of Odin. 1920. 12.50 (ISBN 0-686-18157-3). Havertown Bks.

Coolidge, Olivia. Legends of the North. (Illus.). (gr. 7 up). 1951. 7.95 (ISBN 0-395-06726-X). HM.

D'Aulaire, Ingri & D'Aulaire, Edgar Parin. Norse Gods & Giants. LC 67-19109. (gr. 3-7). 1967. 9.95a (ISBN 0-385-04908-0); PLB (ISBN 0-385-07235-X). Doubleday.

MYTHOLOGY, ORIENTAL

see also Mythology, Semitic

Cadet, J. M. Ramakien: The Thai Epic. LC 70-128685. (Illus.). 256p. 1970. 29.50 (ISBN 0-87011-134-5). Kodansha.

Campbell, Joseph. The Masks of God 2: Oriental Mythology. (Illus.). 1962. 15.00 (ISBN 0-670-46045-1). Viking Pr.

Christesen, Barbara. Myths of the Orient. LC 77-22199. (Myth, Magic & Superstition Ser.). (Illus.). (gr. 4-5). 1977. PLB 10.65 (ISBN 0-8172-1043-1). Raintree Pubs.

Gorres, Joseph. Mythengeschichte der Asiatischen Welt: Mit einen Anhang: Beitrage aus den Heidelberger Jahrbuchern. Bolle, Kees W., ed. (Mythology Ser.). (Ger.). 1978. Repr. of 1935 ed. lib. bdg. 41.00x (ISBN 0-405-10538-X). Arno.

Inst. of Ethnology, Taikoru Imperial Univ. The Myths & Traditions of the Formosan Tribes 1935. 1976. 50.00 (ISBN 0-89986-314-0). E Langstaff.

Keith, A. Berriedale. Indian Mythology. Bd. with Iranian Mythology. Carnoy, Albert J. LC 63-19091. (Mythology of All Races Ser.: Vol. 6). (Illus.). Repr. of 1932 ed. 25.00x (ISBN 0-8154-0126-4). Cooper Sq.

Picano, Felice. An Asian Minor: The True Story of Ganymede. (Illus.). 80p. 1981. 19.95 (ISBN 0-933322-07-0); pap. 5.95 (ISBN 0-933322-06-2). Sea Horse.

MYTHOLOGY, POLYNESIAN

Andersen, Johannes C. The Maori Tohunga & His Spirit World. LC 75-35224. Repr. of 1948 ed. 15.00 (ISBN 0-404-14403-9). AMS Pr.

--Myths & Legends of the Polynesians. LC 75-35170. (Illus.). Repr. of 1931 ed. 43.50 (ISBN 0-404-14200-1). AMS Pr.

Anderson, Johannes E. Myths & Legends of the Polynesians. LC 69-13509. (Illus.). (gr. 9 up). 1969. Repr. of 1928 ed. 15.00 (ISBN 0-8048-0414-1). C E Tuttle.

Best, Elsdon. Maori Religion & Mythology. LC 75-35236. Repr. of 1924 ed. 37.50 (ISBN 0-404-14412-8). AMS Pr.

Buck, Peter H. Anthropology & Religion. LC 72-121753. 1970. Repr. of 1939 ed. 12.50 (ISBN 0-208-00950-7, Archon). Shoe String.

Dixon, Roland B. Oceanic Mythology, Vol. 9. LC 63-19094. (Mythology of All Races Ser). (Illus.). 1964. Repr. of 1932 ed. 22.50x (ISBN 0-8154-0059-4). Cooper Sq.

Gifford, E. W. Tongan Myths & Tales. Repr. of 1924 ed. pap. 17.00 (ISBN 0-527-02111-3, BMB, NO. 8). Kraus Repr.

Gill, William W. Myths & Songs from the South Pacific. Dorson, Richard M., ed. LC 77-70596. (International Folklore Ser.). 1977. Repr. of 1876 ed. lib. bdg. 19.00x (ISBN 0-405-10095-7). Arno.

Grant, Michael. Roman Myths. LC 75-162749. (Illus.). 1972. pap. 3.50 (ISBN 0-684-13237-0, SL 413, ScribT). Scribner.

Grey, George. Polynesian Mythology & Ancient Traditional History of the New Zealanders As Furnished by Their Priests & Chiefs. LC 75-35253. Repr. of 1906 ed. 20.50 (ISBN 0-404-14425-X). AMS Pr.

Reed, A. W. Maori Myth: The Supernatural World of the Maori. 1977. 8.95 (ISBN 0-589-01019-0, Pub. by Reed Books Australia). C E Tuttle.

--Myths & Legends of Maoriland. (Illus.). 1946. 8.25 (ISBN 0-589-00232-5, Pub. by Reed Books Australia). C E Tuttle.

Shortland, Edward. Maori Religion & Mythology. LC 75-35268. Repr. of 1882 ed. 14.00 (ISBN 0-404-14437-3). AMS Pr.

Williamson, Robert W. Religion & Social Organization in Central Polynesia. Piddington, Ralph, ed. LC 75-35218. Repr. of 1937 ed. 27.50 (ISBN 0-404-14241-9). AMS Pr.

--Religious & Cosmic Beliefs of Central Polynesia, 2 vols. LC 75-35220. Repr. of 1933 ed. Set. 72.00 (ISBN 0-404-14300-8). AMS Pr.

Yearbury, Pauline K. Children of Rangi & Papa: The Maori Story of Creation. 1976. 43.75x (ISBN 0-7233-0449-1). Intl Pubns Serv.

MYTHOLOGY, ROMAN

Berens, E. M. The Myths & Legends of Ancient Greece & Rome. LC 77-91528. 1977. Repr. of 1880 ed. lib. bdg. 30.00 (ISBN 0-89341-029-2). Longwood Pr.

Bulfinch, Thomas. Myths of Greece & Rome. 288p. 1981. pap. 10.95 (ISBN 0-14-005643-2). Penguin.

Carpenter, Thomas H. & Gula, Robert J. Mythology: Greek & Roman. (Illus.). (gr. 10). 1977. pap. text ed. 4.95 (ISBN 0-88334-089-5). Ind Sch Pr.

Dumezil, Georges. Deesses Latines et Mythes Vediques. Bolle, Kees W., ed. LC 77-79121. (Mythology Ser.). (Fr.). 1978. Repr. of 1956 ed. lib. bdg. 12.00x (ISBN 0-405-10533-9). Arno.

Grimal, Pierre. Dictionnaire de la Mythologie Grecque et Romaine. 5th ed. 612p. (Fr.). 1969. 59.95 (ISBN 0-686-57316-1, M-6299). French & Eur.

Harnsberger, Caroline T. Gods & Heroes: A Quick Guide to the Occupations, Associations & Experiences of the Greek & Roman Gods & Heroes. LC 76-21470. 1977. 20.00x (ISBN 0-87875-125-4). Whitston Pub.

Keightley, Thomas. Classical Mythology: The Myths of Ancient Greece & Italy. 25.00 (ISBN 0-89005-189-5). Ares.

Kupfer, Grace H. Legends of Greece & Rome. 1911. 20.00 (ISBN 0-686-20105-1). Quality Lib.

Preller, Ludwig. Romische Mythologie: Roman Mythology. Bolle, Kees W., ed. LC 77-79154. (Mythology Ser.). (Ger.). 1978. Repr. of 1865 ed. lib. bdg. 48.00x (ISBN 0-405-10563-0). Arno.

Roscher, Wilhelm & Hillman, James, eds. Pan & the Nightmare: Two Studies. (Dunquin Ser.). 1979. pap. text ed. 7.50 (ISBN 0-88214-204-6). Spring Pubns.

Sanders, Henry A., ed. Roman History & Mythology. Repr. of 1910 ed. pap. 31.00 (ISBN 0-384-38804-3). Johnson Repr.

Schmidt, Joel. Larousse Greek & Roman Mythology. LC 80-15046. (Illus.). 320p. 1980. 16.95 (ISBN 0-07-055342-4). McGraw.

MYTHOLOGY, SCANDINAVIAN

see Mythology, Norse

MYTHOLOGY, SEMITIC

see also Mythology, Assyro-Babylonian; Mythology, Jewish

Graves, Robert & Patai, Raphael. Hebrew Myths. 1966. pap. 4.95 (ISBN 0-07-024125-2, SP). McGraw.

Hooke, Samuel H. Middle Eastern Mythology. (Orig.). 1963. pap. 3.95 (ISBN 0-14-020546-2, Pelican). Penguin.

Langdon, Stephen H. Semitic Mythology. LC 63-19090. (Mythology of All Races Ser.: Vol. 5). (Illus.). Repr. of 1932 ed. 22.50x (ISBN 0-8154-0133-7). Cooper Sq.

MYTHOLOGY, SIBERIAN

Holmberg, Uno. Finno-Ugric, Siberian Mythology. (Mythology of All Races Ser: Vol. Iv). (Illus.). Repr. of 1932 ed. 25.00x (ISBN 0-8154-0116-7). Cooper Sq.

Sartakov, S. Siberian Stories. 607p. 1979. 8.40 (ISBN 0-8285-1621-9, 182171, Pub. by Progress Pubs Russia). Imported Pubns.

Shoolbraid, G. M. The Oral Epic of Siberia & Central Asia. (Uralic & Altaic Ser.: No. 111). 176p. 1975. pap. text ed. 12.00x (ISBN 0-87750-182-3). Res Ctr Lang Semiotic.

MYTHOLOGY, SLAVIC

Ralston, W. R. Songs of the Russian People: As Illustrative of Slavonic Mythology & Russian Social Life. LC 77-132444. (Studies in Music, No. 42). 1970. Repr. of 1872 ed. lib. bdg. 59.95 (ISBN 0-8383-1224-1). Haskell.

MYTHOLOGY, SUMERIAN

Kinnier-Wilson, J. V. & Vanstiphout, Herman. The Rebel Lands: An Investigation into the Origins of Early Mesopotamian Mythology. LC 77-1272. (Oriental Publications Ser.: No. 29). (Illus.). 1979. 36.00 (ISBN 0-521-21469-6). Cambridge U Pr.

Kramer, Samuel N. Sumerian Mythology. (Illus.). 1972. pap. 5.95x (ISBN 0-8122-1047-6, Pa Paperbks). U of Pa Pr.

MYTHOLOGY, SWEDISH

see Mythology, Norse

MYTHOLOGY, VEDIC

see Mythology, Hindu; Vedas

MYTHOLOGY, VOGUL

see Mythology, Finno-Ugrian

MYTHOLOGY, WELSH

Goetinck, Glenys. Peredur, a Study of Welsh Tradition in the Grail Legends. 336p. 1975. 21.00x (ISBN 0-7083-0580-6). Verry.

Guest, Charlotte. Mabinogion. (Illus.). 1978. 22.50 (ISBN 0-902375-34-2); pap. 9.95 (ISBN 0-89733-000-5). Academy Chi Ltd.

Newstead, Helaine. Bran the Blessed in Arthurian Romance. LC 40-4360. Repr. of 1939 ed. 14.50 (ISBN 0-404-04687-8). AMS Pr.

Owen, William. The Cambrian Biography; or Historical Notices of Celebrated Men Among the Ancient Britons. Feldman, Burton & Richardson, Robert, eds. LC 78-60896. (Myth & Romanticism Ser.: Vol. 20). (Illus.). 1980. lib. bdg. 66.00 (ISBN 0-8240-3569-0). Garland Pub.

MYTHOLOGY IN ART

see Art and Mythology

MYTHOLOGY IN LITERATURE

Bush, Douglas. Mythology & the Renaissance Tradition in English Poetry. rev. ed. 1963. pap. 3.45x (ISBN 0-393-00187-3, Norton Lib). Norton.

--Mythology & the Romantic Tradition in English Poetry. rev. ed. LC 72-85071. 1969. 25.00x (ISBN 0-674-59825-3). Harvard U Pr.

--Pagan Myth & Christian Tradition in English Poetry. LC 68-8639. (Memoirs Ser.: Vol. 72). 1968. 3.50 (ISBN 0-87169-072-1). Am Philos.

Cook, Albert. Myth & Language. LC 79-84259. 352p. 1980. 22.50x (ISBN 0-253-14027-7). Ind U Pr.

Euripides. Hippolytus in Drama & Myth. Sutherland, Donald, tr. LC 60-13112. 1960. pap. 3.50x (ISBN 0-8032-5195-5, BB 103, Bison). U of Nebr Pr.

Feder, Lillian. Ancient Myth in Modern Poetry. LC 70-154994. 1972. 24.00x (ISBN 0-691-06207-2); pap. 7.95 (ISBN 0-691-01336-5). Princeton U Pr.

Franklin, H. Bruce. The Wake of the Gods: Melville's Mythology. 1963. 12.50x (ISBN 0-8047-0137-7). Stanford U Pr.

Gould, Eric. Mythical Intentions in Modern Literature. LC 81-47132. 304p. 1981. 20.00x (ISBN 0-691-06482-2). Princeton U Pr.

Greenway, John L. The Golden Horns: Mythic Imagination & the Nordic Past. LC 74-30676. 248p. 1977. 15.00x (ISBN 0-8203-0384-4). U of Ga Pr.

Hunger, H. Lexikon der Griechischen und Roemischen Mythologie. 452p. (Ger.). 1974. pap. 7.95 (ISBN 3-499-16178-8, M-7252). French & Eur.

Lapp, John C. The Brazen Tower: Essays on Mythological Imagery in French Renaissance & Baroque, 1550-1670. (Stanford French & Italian Studies: No. 7). 1978. pap. 20.00 (ISBN 0-915838-35-4). Anma Libri.

Lemmi, Charles W. Classic Deities in Bacon. LC 70-120639. 1970. Repr. lib. bdg. 14.00x (ISBN 0-374-94929-8). Octagon.

Lucente, Gregory L. The Narrative of Realism & Myth: Verga, Lawrence, Faulkner, Pavese. LC 81-2084. 208p. 1981. text ed. 14.00x (ISBN 0-8018-2609-8). Johns Hopkins.

Moorman, Charles. Arthurian Triptych: Mythical Materials in Charles Williams, C. S. Lewis & T. S. Eliot. LC 72-85002. ix, 163p. 1973. Repr. of 1960 ed. 13.00 (ISBN 0-8462-1716-3). Russell.

Noel, Ruth S. Mythology of Middle-Earth. 1978. pap. 3.95 (ISBN 0-395-27208-4). HM.

--The Mythology of Middle Earth. 1977. 7.95 (ISBN 0-395-25006-4). HM.

Norton, Daniel S. & Rushton, Peters. Classical Myths in English Literature. Repr. of 1952 ed. lib. bdg. 25.25x (ISBN 0-8371-2440-9, NOCM). Greenwood.

Osgood, C. G. The Classical Mythology of Milton's English Poems. (Reprints in History). Repr. of 1900 ed. lib. bdg. 22.50x (ISBN 0-697-00014-1). Irvington.

Ruthven, K. K. Myth. LC 76-17221. (Critical Idiom Ser.: Vol. 31). 96p. 1976. text ed. 8.50x (ISBN 0-416-78990-0); pap. 5.50x (ISBN 0-416-79000-3). Methuen Inc.

Schafer, Edward H. The Divine Woman: Dragon Ladies & Rain Maidens in T'ang Literature. LC 73-78543. 1973. 12.50x (ISBN 0-520-02465-6). U of Cal Pr.

Sharpless, F. Parvin. Symbol & Myth in Modern Literature. (Humanities Ser.). (Illus.). 272p. 1976. pap. 6.19x (ISBN 0-8104-5071-2). Hayden.

Slochower, Harry. Mythopoesis: Mythic Patterns in the Literary Classics. LC 96-11337. (Waynebooks Ser: No. 35). 1970. 14.95x (ISBN 0-8143-1395-7); pap. text ed. 4.95x (ISBN 0-8143-1511-9). Wayne St U Pr.

Stillman, Peter R. Introduction to Myth. (Literature Ser.). (gr. 10 up). 1977. pap. text ed. 6.95x (ISBN 0-8104-5890-X). Hayden.

Strelka, Joseph P., ed. Literary Criticism & Myth. LC 79-15111. (Yearbook of Comparative Criticism Ser.: Vol. IX). 1980. text ed. 16.75x (ISBN 0-271-00225-5). Pa St U Pr.

Tarrant, Desmond. James Branch Cabell: The Dream & the Reality. (Illus.). 1967. 15.95x (ISBN 0-8061-0755-3). U of Okla Pr.

Vickery, John B., ed. Myth & Literature: Contemporary Theory & Practice. LC 65-11563. 1969. pap. 4.50x (ISBN 0-8032-5208-0, BB 500, Bison). U of Nebr Pr.

Vickery, John B. & Sellery, J'nan M, eds. Scapegoat: Ritual & Literature. LC 70-166472. (Myth & Dramatic Form Ser). (Orig.). 1972. pap. text ed. 8.50 (ISBN 0-395-11256-7, 3-57680). HM.

Waddington, Raymond B. The Mind's Empire: Myth & Form in George Chapman's Narrative Poems. LC 74-6841. (Illus.). 231p. 1975. 16.00x (ISBN 0-8018-1566-5). Johns Hopkins.

Wetzels, Walter D., ed. Myth & Reason: A Symposium. LC 72-3096. (Germanic Languages Symposium Ser). 206p. 1973. 9.95x (ISBN 0-292-75003-X). U of Tex Pr.

White, John J. Mythology in the Modern Novel: A Study of Prefigurative Techniques. LC 71-155004. 1972. 18.00x (ISBN 0-691-06210-2). Princeton U Pr.

Whitman, Cedric H. Euripides & the Full Circle of Myth. LC 74-81676. (Loeb Classical Monographs Ser). 176p. 1974. text ed. 9.00x (ISBN 0-674-26920-9). Harvard U Pr.

MYTHS

see Mythology

MYXEDEMA

see also Graves' Disease

Aikawa, Jerry K. Myxedema. 116p. 1961. ed. spiral bdg. 12.75photocopy (ISBN 0-398-04185-7). C C Thomas.

DeGroot, Leslie J. & Stanbury, John B. The Thyroid & Its Diseases. 4th ed. LC 73-17916. 840p. 1975. 51.95 (ISBN 0-471-20530-3). Krieger.

MYXOMATOSIS CUNICULI

Fenner, Frank & Ratcliffe, F. N. Myxomatosis. 1966. 65.00 (ISBN 0-521-04991-1). Cambridge U Pr.

MYXOMYCETES

Cappucinelli, P. & Ashworth, J., eds. Developments & Differentiation in the Cellular Slime Molds. 1977. 38.75 (ISBN 0-444-41608-0, Biomedical Pr). Elsevier.

Fullmer, E. L. The Slime Molds of Ohio. 1921. 1.50 (ISBN 0-686-30285-0). Ohio Bio Survey.

Lister, Arthur L. Monograph of the Mycetozoa. 3rd ed. (Illus.). Repr. of 1925 ed. 38.50 (ISBN 0-384-32930-6). Johnson Repr.

Martin, G. W. & Alexopoulos, C. J. Myxomycetes. LC 77-88357. (Illus.). 1969. 45.00x (ISBN 0-87745-000-5). U of Iowa Pr.

Olive, Lindsay S. The Mycetozoans. 1975. 36.50 (ISBN 0-12-526250-7). Acad Pr.

--The Mycetozoans. 1975. 36.50 (ISBN 0-12-526250-7). Acad Pr.

Singer, Rolf. Mycoflora Australis. 1969. pap. 80.00 (ISBN 3-7682-5429-1). Lubrecht & Cramer.

Tilden, J. The Myxophyceae of North America & Adjacent Regions. (Bibl. Phyco.: Vol. 4). (Illus.). 1968. pap. 40.00 (ISBN 3-7682-0546-0). Lubrecht & Cramer.

MYXOSPORIDIA

Kudo, Roksabro. Studies on Myxosporidia. (Illus.). 1920. Repr. of 1920 ed. 18.50 (ISBN 0-384-30620-9). Johnson Repr.

MYXOVIRUSES

Kilbourne, Edwin D., ed. The Influenza Viruses & Influenza. 1975. 60.50 (ISBN 0-12-407050-7). Acad Pr.

N

N-WAY ALGEBRA

see Algebra, Universal

NAAMAN (BIBLICAL CHARACTER)

Diamond, Lucy. Naaman & the Little Maid. (Ladybird Ser). (Illus.). 1959. bds. 1.49 (ISBN 0-87508-852-X). Chr Lit.

Scheck, Joann. Man Who Took Seven Baths. (Arch Bks, Set 7). (Illus., Orig.). (ps-3). 1970. pap. 0.79 (ISBN 0-570-06048-6, 59-1164). Concordia.

NAAMAN'S CREEK, DELAWARE

Cresson, H. T. Report Upon Pile-Structures in Naaman's Creek, Near Claymont, Delaware. (Harvard University Peabody Museum of Archaeology & Ethnology Papers Ser: HU. PMP Vol. 1, No. 4). Repr. of 1892 ed. pap. 4.00 (ISBN 0-527-01186-X). Kraus Repr.

NABATAEANS

Glueck, Nelson. Deities & Dolphins: The Story of the Nabataeans. (Illus.). 650p. 1965. 15.00 (ISBN 0-374-13668-8). FS&G.

Hammond, Philip C. The Nabataeans--Their History, Culture & Archaeology. (Studies in Mediterranean Archaeology Ser.: No. XXXVII). 1973. pap. text ed. 28.00x (ISBN 91-85058-57-2). Humanities.

Lawlor, John I. The Nabataeans in Historical Perspective. (Baker Studies in Biblical Archaeology Ser.). (Orig.). 1973. pap. 3.95 (ISBN 0-8010-5536-9). Baker Bk.

NABOKOV, VLADIMIR VLADIMIROVICH, 1899-1977

Albright, Daniel. Representation & the Imagination: Beckett, Kafka, Nabokov, & Schoenberg. LC 80-26975. (Chicago Originals Ser.). 256p. 1981. lib. bdg. 20.00x (ISBN 0-226-01252-2). U of Chicago Pr.

Appel, Alfred. Nabokov's Dark Cinema. (Illus.). 334p. 1974. 19.95 (ISBN 0-19-501834-6). Oxford U Pr.

Field, Andrew. Nabokov: A Bibliography. LC 72-10473. 276p. 1973. 15.00 (ISBN 0-07-020680-5, GB). McGraw.

--Nabokov: His Life in Part. LC 76-47042. 1977. 15.00 (ISBN 0-670-50367-3). Viking Pr.

Fowler, Douglas. Reading Nabokov. LC 73-20798. 224p. 1974. trim-size ed. 17.50x (ISBN 0-8014-0828-8). Cornell U Pr.

Grabes, H. Fictitious Biographies: Vladimir Nabokov's English Novels. 1977. 21.25x (ISBN 90-279-3345-6). Mouton.
Grayson, Jane. Nabokov Translated: A Comparison of Nabokov's Russian & English Prose. (Oxford Modern Languages & Literature Monographs). 1977. 36.00x (ISBN 0-19-815527-1). Oxford U Pr.
Hyde, G. M. Vladimir Nabokkov. LC 78-307708. 240p. 1979. pap. 7.95 (ISBN 0-7145-2574-X, Pub. by M Boyars). Merrimack Bk Serv.
Hyde, George. Vladimir Nabokov: America's Russian Novelist. (Critical Appraisals Ser.). 1977. text ed. 18.25x (ISBN 0-391-00763-7). Humanities.
Karlinsky, Simon, ed. The Nabokov-Wilson Letters: Correspondence Between Vladimir Nabokov & Edmund Wilson, 1940-1971. LC 78-69627. 1979. 15.00 (ISBN 0-06-012262-5, HarpT). Har-Row.
--The Nabokov-Wilson Letters Nineteen Forty to Nineteen Seventy-One. LC 78-69627. 1980. pap. 6.95 (ISBN 0-06-090753-3, CN 753, CN). Har-Row.
Lee, L. L. Vladimir Nabokov. (U. S. Authors Ser.: No. 266). 1976. lib. bdg. 12.50 (ISBN 0-8057-7166-2). Twayne.
Mason, Bobbie A. Nabokov's Garden: A Study of Ada. (Illus.). 180p. 1974. 10.00 (ISBN 0-88233-052-7); pap. 3.25 (ISBN 0-88233-053-5). Ardis Pubs.
Morton, Donald E. Vladimir Nabokov. LC 74-76128. (Modern Literature Ser.). 176p. 1974. 10.95 (ISBN 0-8044-2638-4). Ungar.
Moynahan, Julian. Vladimir Nabokov. (Pamphlets on American Writers Ser: No. 96). (Orig.). 1971. pap. 1.25x (ISBN 0-8166-0600-5, MPAW96). U of Minn Pr.
Nabokov, Vladimir. Drugie Beraga. (Rus.). 1978. 15.00 (ISBN 0-88233-325-9); pap. 7.00 (ISBN 0-88233-326-7). Ardis Pubs.
--Look at the Harlequins. (McGraw-Hill Paperback Ser.). 1981. pap. 5.95 (ISBN 0-07-045717-4). McGraw.
--Speak Memory: An Autobiography Revisted. (Illus.). 1978. 10.00 (ISBN 0-399-10763-0). Putnam.
--Strong Opinions. (McGraw-Hill Paperbacks Ser.). 348p. 1981. pap. 6.95 (ISBN 0-07-045725-5). McGraw.
Nakhimovsky, A. D. & Paperno, V. A. An English-Russian Dictionary of Nabokov's "Lolita". (Rus. & Eng.). 1981. 16.50x (ISBN 0-88233-443-3); pap. 7.50x (ISBN 0-88233-444-1). Ardis Pubs.
Naumann, Marina Turkevich. Blue Evenings in Berlin: Nabokov's Short Stories of the 1920s. LC 77-82751. (New York University Studies in Comparative Literature: Vol. 9). 254p. 1978. 20.00x (ISBN 0-8147-5753-7). NYU Pr.
Paine, Sylvia. Beckett, Nabokov, Nin: Motives & Modernism. (Literary Criticism Ser.). 1981. 15.00 (ISBN 0-8046-9288-2). Kennikat.
Pifer, Ellen. Nabokov & the Novel. LC 80-16197. 1980. text ed. 12.50x (ISBN 0-674-59840-7). Harvard U Pr.
Proffer, Carl R., ed. A Book of Things About Vladimir Nabokov. (Illus.). 230p. 1974. 12.95 (ISBN 0-88233-054-3); pap. 4.50 (ISBN 0-88233-055-1). Ardis Pubs.
Quennell, Peter, ed. Vladimir Nabokov: A Tribute. LC 80-10081. (Illus.). 150p. 1981. 8.95 (ISBN 0-688-03637-6); pap. 5.95 (ISBN 0-688-00470-9). Morrow.
--Vladimir Nabokov: A Tribute. LC 80-10081. (Illus.). 150p. 1980. 8.95 (ISBN 0-688-03637-6). Morrow.
Rowe, W. Woodin. Nabokov's Spectral Dimension. 1981. 15.00 (ISBN 0-88233-641-X); pap. 7.50 (ISBN 0-686-77777-8). Ardis Pubs.
Rowe, William Woodin. Nabokov's Deceptive World. LC 76-158968. 1971. 18.50x (ISBN 0-8147-7353-2). NYU Pr.
Schuman, Samuel. Vladimir Nabokov: A Reference Guide. 1979. lib. bdg. 24.00 (ISBN 0-8161-8134-9). G K Hall.
Stark, John O. The Literature of Exhaustion: Borges, Nabokov & Barth. LC 73-92536. 1974. 12.75 (ISBN 0-8223-0316-7). Duke.
Stuart, Dabney. Nabokov: The Dimensions of Parody. LC 77-20870. 1978. 15.00x (ISBN 0-8071-0384-5). La State U Pr.

NABUCO, JOAQUIM, 1849-1910

Nabuco, Carolina. Life of Joaquim Nabuco. Hilton, Ronald, et al, eds. LC 69-10140. 1969. Repr. of 1950 ed. lib. bdg. 20.25x (ISBN 0-8371-0181-6, NAJN). Greenwood.

NACHTWACHEN

see Bonaventura, Pseud. Nachtwachen

NADAPADA

Guenther, Herbert V., ed. Life & Teaching of Naropa: Translated from the Original Tibetan with Philosophical Commentary Based on the Oral Transmission. 1971. pap. text ed. 5.95 (ISBN 0-19-501473-1, GB362, GB). Oxford U Pr.

NADARS

Hardgrave, Robert L., Jr. The Nadars of Tamilnad: The Political Culture of a Community in Change. LC 69-13726. (Center for South & Southeast Asia Studies, UC Berkeley). (Illus.). 1969. 24.00x (ISBN 0-520-01471-5). U of Cal Pr.

NADELMAN, ELIE, 1885-1946

Kirstein, Lincoln. Elie Nadelman. LC 72-85651. (Illus.). 358p. 1973. 85.00x (ISBN 0-87130-034-6). Eakins.
Kirstein, Lincoln, ed. Elie Nadelman Drawings. LC 74-116359. (Illus.). 1970. Repr. of 1949 ed. buckram 20.00 (ISBN 0-87817-045-6). Hacker.

NADER, RALPH, 1934-

Brown, Stephen D. Ralph's Nadir: What Went Wrong with the Nader Congress Project. (Illus.). 1976. 8.95 (ISBN 0-686-16898-4). Bookhaus.
Holsworth, Robert D. Public Interest Liberalism, & the Crisis of Affluence. 320p. 1981. pap. text ed. 8.95x (ISBN 0-87073-061-4). Schenkman.
Whiteside, Thomas. The Investigation of Ralph Nader. LC 72-79452. Orig. Title: Ralph Nader. 1972. 7.95 (ISBN 0-87795-034-2). Arbor Hse.

NADER SHAH, SHAH OF IRAN, 1688-1747

Lockhart, Laurence. Nadir Shah: A Critical Study Based Mainly Upon Contemporary Sources. LC 78-180358. Repr. of 1938 ed. 28.45 (ISBN 0-404-56290-6). AMS Pr.

NAGA-ED-DER, EGYPT

Reisner, George A. A Provincial Cemetary of the Pyramid Age Naga-Ed-der, Pt. 3. (U. C. Publ. in Egyptain Archaeology: Vol. 6). 1932. 80.00x (ISBN 0-520-01060-4). U of Cal Pr.

NAGAI, KAFU, 1879-1959

Seidensticker, Edward. Kafu the Scribbler: The Life & Writings of Nagai Kafu, 1879-1959. (Illus.). 1965. 15.00x (ISBN 0-8047-0267-5). Stanford U Pr.

NAGALAND, INDIA

Anand, V. K. Conflict in Nagaland. 1981. 18.50x (ISBN 0-8364-0683-4, Pub. by Chanakya India). South Asia Bks.
--Nagaland in Transition. 1971. 6.00x (ISBN 0-8426-1120-7). Verry.
--Nagaland in Transition. 1968. 10.50 (ISBN 0-686-20277-5). Intl Bk Dist.
Aram, M. Peace in Nagaland: Eight Year Story, 1964-72. LC 74-902035. 335p. 1974. 13.00x (ISBN 0-88386-527-0). South Asia Bks.
Gundevia, Y. D. War & Peace in Nagaland. LC 75-908123. 1975. 12.50x (ISBN 0-88386-580-7). South Asia Bks.
Maxwell, Neville. India & the Nagas. (Minority Rights Group: No. 17). 1973. pap. 2.50 (ISBN 0-89192-103-6). Interbk Inc.
Singh, Prakash. Nagaland. (India, Land & People Ser). (Illus.). 233p. 1973. 3.75x (ISBN 0-8426-0523-1). Verry.

NAGANA

see Trypanosomiasis

NAGARJUNA, SIDDHA

Johnston, E. H. & Kunst, Arnold. The Dialectical Method of Nagarjuna. Bhattacharya, Kamaleswar, tr. 1978. 7.95 (ISBN 0-89684-046-8, Pub. by Motilal Banarsidass India). Orient Bk Dist.
Ramanan, K. Venkata. Nagarjuna's Philosophy. 1978. 12.50 (ISBN 0-89684-283-5, Pub. by Molital Banarsidass India). Orient Bk Dist.

NAGAS

Fuerer-Haimendorf, Christoph von. Return to the Naked Naga. (Illus.). 270p. 1976. 14.00x (ISBN 0-8002-1921-X). Intl Pubns Serv.
Fuerer-Haimendorf, Christopher V. The Naked Nagas: Head-Hunters of Assam in Peace & War. LC 76-44720. Repr. of 1946 ed. 24.50 (ISBN 0-404-15924-9). AMS Pr.
Horam, M. Naga Polity. LC 75-907212. 1975. 12.50x (ISBN 0-88386-699-4). South Asia Bks.
Maxwell, Neville. India & the Nagas. (Minority Rights Group: No. 17). 1973. pap. 2.50 (ISBN 0-89192-103-6). Interbk Inc.
Mills, James P. The Lhota Nagas. LC 76-44760. Repr. of 1922 ed. 32.50 (ISBN 0-404-15869-2). AMS Pr.
--The Rengma Nagas. LC 76-44761. Repr. of 1937 ed. 34.50 (ISBN 0-404-15870-6). AMS Pr.
Yonuo, A. Rising Nagas: A Historical & Political Study. 1974. 24.00x (ISBN 0-8426-0761-7). Verry.

NAGPUR, INDIA (RESIDENCY)

Sinha, R. M. Bhonslas of Nagpur: The Last Phase-1818-54. 1967. 7.00x (ISBN 0-8426-1542-3). Verry.

NAHUAS

Leon-Portilla, Miguel. Aztec Thought & Culture: A Study of the Ancient Nahuatl Mind. Davis, Jack E., tr. (Civilization of the American Indian Ser.: Vol. 67). (Illus.). 1978. Repr. of 1963 ed. 12.50 (ISBN 0-8061-0569-0). U of Okla Pr.

NAHUATL LANGUAGE

see Aztec Language

NAHUATL LITERATURE

see Aztec Literature

NAHUATLECAS

see Nahuas

NAIDU, SAROJINI, 1879-1949

Naravane, V. S. Sarojini Naidu: An Introduction to Her Life, Work & Poetry. 1981. 17.50x (ISBN 0-8364-0736-9, Orient Longman). South Asia Bks.

NAILS (ANATOMY)

De Nicola, P., et al. Nail Diseases in Internal Medicine. (Illus.). 128p. 1974. 14.75 (ISBN 0-398-03178-9). C C Thomas.
Hyde, Judy. Nail Biter's Handbook. (Illus.). 24p. (Orig.). 1980. pap. 2.95 (ISBN 0-930380-11-8). Quail Run.
Lerner, Marguerite R. Horns, Hoofs, Nails. LC 65-29040. (Medical Bks for Children). (Illus.). (gr. 3-9). 1965. PLB 3.95 (ISBN 0-8225-0015-9). Lerner Pubns.
Pardo-Castello, V. & Pardo, Osvaldo A. Diseases of the Nails. 3rd ed. (Illus.). 320p. 1960. photocopy ed. spiral 32.00 (ISBN 0-398-01446-9). C C Thomas.
Samman, Peter D. The Nails in Disease. 3rd ed. (Illus.). 1979. 33.95 (ISBN 0-8151-7531-0). Year Bk Med.
Smith, Frederick H. Nail-Biting: The Beatable Habit. LC 80-11687. (Illus., Orig.). 1980. pap. 7.95 (ISBN 0-8425-1806-1). Brigham.
Taylor-Moore, Suzanne. Nail Biters Anonymous. 48p. 1981. pap. 3.00 (ISBN 0-686-28092-X). MTM Pub Co.
Zaias, Nardo. The Nail. LC 78-18238. (Illus.). 272p. 1980. text ed. 60.00 (ISBN 0-89335-066-4). Spectrum Pub.

NAILS AND SPIKES

Wiswell, Glenn & Evans, John. Date Nails Complete. LC 76-27156. 352p. 1976. deluxe ed. 22.00 (ISBN 0-686-17795-9); spiral bdg. 15.00 (ISBN 0-686-17796-7); pap. 7.00 (ISBN 0-686-28596-4). Wesis Pubns.

NAIMY, MIKHAIL, 1889-

Naimy, Nadeem N. Mikhail Naimy, an Introduction. 1967. pap. 15.95x (ISBN 0-8156-6028-6, Am U Beirut). Syracuse U Pr.

NAIPALI LANGUAGE

see Nepali Language

NAIPAUL, VIDIADHAR SURAJPRASAD, 1932-

Hamner, Robert D. Critical Perspectives on V. S. Naipaul, Vol. 2. LC 77-71683. (Illus., Orig.). 1977. 20.00x (ISBN 0-914478-17-6); pap. 10.00x (ISBN 0-914478-18-4). Three Continents.
--V. S. Naipaul. (World Authors Ser.: West Indies: No. 258). 1973. lib. bdg. 10.95 (ISBN 0-8057-2647-0). Twayne.
Morris, Robert K. Paradoxes of Order: Some Perspectives on the Fiction of V. S. Naipaul. LC 74-23752. (Literary Frontiers Ser). 128p. 1975. pap. 5.00 (ISBN 0-8262-0172-5). U of Mo Pr.

NAIROBI

Hake, Andrew. African Metropolis. LC 75-4266. 1977. 22.50 (ISBN 0-312-00980-1). St Martin.
Jackson, J. H. Nairobi: A Joke, a Junket, or a Journey? LC 76-27046. 1976. 5.50 (ISBN 0-935990-03-8). Townsend Pr.
Ross, Marc H. Grass Roots in an African City: Political Behavior in Nairobi. LC 74-34263. 192p. 1975. text ed. 22.50x (ISBN 0-262-18074-X). MIT Pr.
Werlin, Herbert. Governing an African City: A Study of Nairobi. LC 73-84989. 275p. 1974. text ed. 29.50x (ISBN 0-8419-0139-2, Africana). Holmes & Meier.

NA-KHI

see Moso (Tribe)

NAMAQUALAND–SOCIAL CONDITIONS

Carstens, W. Peter. The Social Structure of a Cape Coloured Reserve. LC 75-3985. (Illus.). 264p. 1975. Repr. of 1966 ed. lib. bdg. 16.00x (ISBN 0-8371-7431-7, CACR). Greenwood.

NAMATH, JOE WILLIE, 1943-

Namath, Joe & Oates, Bob, Jr. A Matter of Style. (Illus.). 1973. 12.50 (ISBN 0-316-59690-6). Little.
Olsen, James. Joe Namath. LC 76-16187. 1974. PLB 5.95 (ISBN 0-87191-265-1); pap. 2.95 (ISBN 0-89812-165-5). Creative Ed.

NAMES

see also Code Names; Names, Geographical; Names, Personal; Terms and Phrases

Algeo, John. On Defining the Proper Name. LC 73-9849. (U of Fla. Humanities Monograph Ser.: No. 41). 94p. 1973. pap. 3.50 (ISBN 0-8130-0410-1). U Presses Fla.
Clodd, Edward. Magic in Names & Other Things. 59.95 (ISBN 0-8490-0577-9). Gordon Pr.
Devitt, Michael. Designation. LC 80-26471. 304p. 1981. 26.00x (ISBN 0-231-05126-3). Columbia U Pr.
Hargrave, Basil. Origins & Meanings of Popular Phrases & Names. LC 68-23164. 1968. Repr. of 1925 ed. 26.00 (ISBN 0-8103-3089-X). Gale.
Hazen, Barbara S. Last, First, Middle & Nick: All About Names. (Illus.). (gr. 1-4). 1979. 7.95 (ISBN 0-13-523944-3). P-H.
Linsky, Leonard. Names & Descriptions. LC 76-8093. 1980. pap. 4.50 (ISBN 0-226-48442-4, P871, Phoen). U of Chicago Pr.
--Names & Descriptions. LC 76-8093. 1977. lib. bdg. 13.50x (ISBN 0-226-48441-6). U of Chicago Pr.
Long, Harry A. Personal & Family Names. LC 68-26584. 1968. Repr. of 1883 ed. 22.00 (ISBN 0-8103-3128-4). Gale.
Marshall, Martha L. Pronouncing Dictionary of California Names in English & Spanish. facs. ed. Repr. of 1925 ed. pap. 6.00 (ISBN 0-8466-0155-9, SJS155). Shorey.
Mencken, H. L. The American Language. 1977. pap. 8.95 (ISBN 0-394-73315-0). Knopf.
Mencken, Henry L. The American Language, 3 vols. 4th ed. Incl. Vol. 1. The American Language. 1936. 25.00 (ISBN 0-394-40075-5); Vol. 2. The American Language, Supplement One. 1945. 25.00 (ISBN 0-394-40076-3); Vol. 3. The American Language, Supplement Two. 1948. 20.00 (ISBN 0-394-40077-1). Knopf.
--American Language: An Inquiry into the Development of English in the United States. abr. 4th ed. McDavid, Raven I., Jr., ed. 1963. 20.00 (ISBN 0-394-40081-X). Knopf.
Name Authority Control for Card Catalogs in the General Libraries. (Contributions to Librarianship Ser.: No. 5). 1981. pap. 10.00 (ISBN 0-930214-07-2). U TX Austin Gen Libs.
Neuffer, Claude. The Name Game: From Oyster Point to Keowee. LC 72-76383. (Illus.). 1979. 5.50 (ISBN 0-87844-009-7). C H Neuffer.
Rajec, E. M. The Study of Names in Literature: A Bibliography. 261p. 1978. 50.00 (ISBN 0-89664-000-0, Pub. by K G Saur). Gale.
Sager, J. C., ed. Standardization of Nomenclature: International Journal of the Sociology of Language, No. 23. 1980. pap. text ed. 21.95x (ISBN 90-279-3028-7). Mouton.
Schwartz, Stephen P., ed. Naming, Necessity, & Natural Kinds. LC 76-28021. (Illus.). 1977. 20.00x (ISBN 0-8014-1049-5); pap. 8.95x (ISBN 0-8014-9861-9). Cornell U Pr.
Taggart, Jean E. Motorboat, Yacht or Canoe - You Name It. LC 73-14607. 1974. 10.00 (ISBN 0-8108-0661-4). Scarecrow.
Taylor, Isaac. Names & Their Histories. 1896. Repr. 35.00 (ISBN 0-8274-3009-4). R West.
Wagner, Leopold. More About Names. LC 68-17937. 1968. Repr. of 1893 ed. 24.00 (ISBN 0-8103-3099-7). Gale.
--Names & Their Meaning. 1893. Repr. 35.00 (ISBN 0-8274-3010-8). R West.
--Names & Their Meanings, a Book for the Curious. LC 68-22060. 1968. Repr. of 1893 ed. 22.00 (ISBN 0-8103-3098-9). Gale.
--The Significance of Names. 1893. Repr. 35.00 (ISBN 0-8274-3412-X). R West.

NAMES–DICTIONARIES

Browder, Sue. The New Age Baby Name Book. 272p. 1974. pap. 2.50 (ISBN 0-446-91323-5). Warner Bks.
Duden-Woerterbuch Geographischer Namen: Europa. (Ger.). 28.95 (ISBN 3-411-00926-8, M-7345, Pub. by Bibliographisches Institut). French & Eur.
Dunne, William P. Is It a Saint's Name? 1977. pap. 1.00 (ISBN 0-89555-024-5, 189). TAN Bks Pubs.
Fletcher, Barbara R., ed. Don't Blame the Stork! - the Cyclopedia of Unusual Names. LC 81-90191. (Illus.). 304p. (Orig.). 1981. pap. 7.95 (ISBN 0-940364-00-X). Rainbow WA.
Foreign Versions of English Names: And Foreign Equivalents of United States Military & Civilian Titles. 227p. (Document No. M-131). 1980. Repr. of 1973 ed. 22.00 (ISBN 0-8103-1015-5). Gale.
Hakim, Dawud. Arabic Names & Other African Names & Their Meanings. pap. 1.50 (ISBN 0-686-10009-3). Hakims Pubs.
Haydn, Joseph T. Dictionary of Names & Universal Information. Repr. 69.00 (ISBN 0-403-00083-1). Scholarly.
Johnson, Rossiter, ed. A Dictionary of Famous Names in Fiction, Drama, Poetry, History & Art. LC 75-167012. 1974. Repr. of 1908 ed. 32.00 (ISBN 0-8103-3875-0). Gale.
Mackey, Mary S. & Mackey, Maryette G., eds. The Pronunciation of Ten Thousand Proper Names. 1979. Repr. of 1922 ed. 38.00 (ISBN 0-8103-4137-9). Gale.
Mawson, C. O. International Book of Names. 308p. 1981. Repr. of 1934 ed. lib. bdg. 40.00 (ISBN 0-8495-3927-7). Arden Lib.
Merriam Webster Pocket Dictionary of Proper Names. pap. 2.50 (ISBN 0-671-80624-6). PB.
Mossman, Jennifer, ed. Pseudonyms & Nicknames Dictionary. LC 80-13274. 700p. 1980. 64.00 (ISBN 0-8103-0549-6). Gale.
Sager, J. C., ed. Standardization of Nomenclature: International Journal of the Sociology of Language, No. 23. 1980. pap. text ed. 21.95x (ISBN 90-279-3028-7). Mouton.
Stewart, George R. American Given Names: Their Origin & History in the Context of the English Language. 1979. 14.95 (ISBN 0-19-502465-6). Oxford U Pr.

Vroonen, Eugene. Encyclopedie Des Noms Personnes. 496p. (Fr.). 1967. 95.00 (ISBN 0-686-57253-X, M-6562). French & Eur.

Wright, F. A., ed. Lempriere's Classical Dictionary. new rev. ed. 1969. Repr. of 1788 ed. 21.00 (ISBN 0-7100-1734-0). Routledge & Kegan.

NAMES, BIBLICAL

see Bible–Names

NAMES, CHINESE

Mayers, William F. Chinese Reader's Manual. LC 68-30660. 1968. Repr. of 1910 ed. 24.00 (ISBN 0-8103-3335-X). Gale.

NAMES, CHRISTIAN

see Names, Personal

NAMES, CLASSICAL

Bailey, D. R. Two Studies in Roman Nomenclature. (American Philological Association, American Classical Studies). 1976. pap. 6.00 (ISBN 0-89130-243-3, 400403). Scholars Pr Ca.

Swanson, Donald C. Names in Roman Verse: A Lexicon & Reverse Index of All Proper Names of History, Mythology & Geography Found in the Classical Roman Poets. 446p. 1967. 30.00x (ISBN 0-299-04560-9). U of Wis Pr.

NAMES, CODE

see Code Names

NAMES, ENGLISH

see also English Language–Etymology–Names

Ackerman, Robert W. Index of the Arthurian Names in Middle English. LC 78-158222. (Stanford University, Stanford Studies in Language & Literature: No. 10). Repr. of 1952 ed. 18.00 (ISBN 0-404-51820-6). AMS Pr.

Chapman, Coolidge O. An Index of Names in Pearl, Purity, Patience & Gawain. LC 77-29259. 1978. Repr. of 1951 ed. lib. bdg. 15.00x (ISBN 0-313-20213-3, CHIN). Greenwood.

Gelling, Margaret. Signposts to the Past: Place-Names & the History of England. (Illus.). 256p. 1978. 15.75x (ISBN 0-460-04264-5, J M Dent England). Biblio Dist.

NAMES, FICTICIOUS

see Anonyms and Pseudonyms

NAMES, GEOGRAPHICAL

see also Street Names

Alotta, Robert I. Old Names & New Places. LC 78-20915. 1979. 8.95 (ISBN 0-664-32647-1). Westminster.

Asimov, Isaac. Words on the Map. (Illus.). (gr. 7 up). 1962. 9.95 (ISBN 0-395-06569-0). HM.

Aurousseau, Marcel. The Rendering of Geographical Names. LC 73-21258. (Illus.). 148p. 1975. Repr. of 1957 ed. lib. bdg. 15.00 (ISBN 0-8371-6133-9, AUGN). Greenwood.

Blackie, C. Geographical Etymology: A Dictionary of Place-Names Giving Their Derivations. LC 68-17916. 1968. Repr. of 1887 ed. 19.00 (ISBN 0-8103-3882-3). Gale.

Blenner-Hassett, Roland. Study of the Place-Names in Lawman's Brut. LC 50-4808. (Stanford University. Stanford Studies in Language & Literature: No. 1). Repr. of 1950 ed. 14.50 (ISBN 0-404-51817-6). AMS Pr.

Dorion, Henri & Poirier, Jean. Lexique Des Termes Utiles a L'etude Des Noms De Lieux. 162p. (Fr.). 1975. pap. 12.95 (ISBN 0-686-57121-5, M-6168). French & Eur.

--Lexique des Terms Utiles a l'Etude des Noms de Lieux. (Choronoma Ser.). (Fr.). 1976. pap. 12.00 (ISBN 2-7637-6741-9, Pub. by Laval). Intl Schol Bk Serv.

Efveraren, C. J. Names of Places in the Transferred Sense in English: Asematological Study. 59.95 (ISBN 0-8490-0703-8). Gordon Pr.

Egli, J. J. Geschichte der Geographischen Namenkunde: Mit Probe Einer Toponomastischen Karte. (Ger.). 1886. pap. text ed. 21.25x (ISBN 90-6041-015-7). Humanities.

Egli, Johann J. Geschichte der Geographischen Namenkunde, 2 vols. 1962. Repr. of 1886 ed. 32.50 (ISBN 0-8337-1025-7). B Franklin.

Engeln, Oscar D. Von & Urquhart, Jane M. Story Key to Geographic Names. LC 72-113299. 1970. Repr. of 1924 ed. 13.50 (ISBN 0-8046-1330-3). Kennikat.

Engeln, Oscar Dedrich Von & Urquhart, Jane M. The Story Key to Geographic Names. LC 74-13855. 279p. 1976. Repr. of 1924 ed. 24.00 (ISBN 0-8103-4062-3). Gale.

Field, John. Discovering Place-Names: Their Origins & Meanings. 2nd ed. (Discovering Ser.). 55p. 1978. pap. 2.50 (ISBN 0-913714-18-6). Legacy Bks.

Fuson, Robert H. Fundamental Place-Name Geography. 4th ed. 120p. 1978. pap. text ed. write for info. (ISBN 0-697-05206-0). Wm C Brown.

Gilbert, Allan H. Geographical Dictionary of Milton. LC 68-10922. 1968. Repr. of 1919 ed. 9.50 (ISBN 0-8462-1105-X). Russell.

--A Geographical Dictionary of Milton. 1979. Repr. of 1919 ed. lib. bdg. 35.00 (ISBN 0-8495-2014-2). Arden Lib.

Knox, Alexander. Glossary of Geographical & Topographical Terms. LC 68-30592. 1968. Repr. of 1904 ed. 19.00 (ISBN 0-8103-3236-1). Gale.

Names of Countries-& of Their Capital Cities Including Adjectives of Nationality. (Terminology Bulletin Ser.: No. 20, Rev. 4). 1978. pap. 7.50 (ISBN 92-5-000604-7, F1481, FAO). Unipub.

Peddie, Robert A. Place-Names in Imprints: An Index to the Latin & Other Forms Used on Title-Pages. LC 68-30594. 1968. Repr. of 1932 ed. 19.00 (ISBN 0-8103-3239-6). Gale.

Phillips, James W. Washington State Place Names. rev. ed. LC 73-159435. (Illus.). 186p. 1971. 11.50 (ISBN 0-295-95158-3); pap. 6.95 (ISBN 0-295-95498-1). U of Wash Pr.

Poirier, Jean. Toponymie, Methode D'Enquete. (Fr). 1965. pap. 3.25x (ISBN 2-7637-6112-7, Pub. by Laval). Intl Schol Bk Serv.

Sager, J. C., ed. Standardization of Nomenclature: International Journal of the Sociology of Language, No. 23. 1980. pap. text ed. 21.95x (ISBN 90-279-3028-7). Mouton.

Sharp, Harold S. Handbook of Geographical Nicknames. LC 79-26860. 153p. 1980. lib. bdg. 10.00 (ISBN 0-8108-1280-0). Scarecrow.

Simons, Howard. Simons' List Book. LC 77-1845. 1977. pap. 5.95 (ISBN 0-671-22605-3). S&S.

Stendhal. Tables Alphabetiques des Noms Cites, 4 vols. Set. 195.00 (ISBN 0-686-55082-X). French & Eur.

Stewart, George R. Names on the Globe. 416p. 1975. 17.50 (ISBN 0-19-501895-8). Oxford U Pr.

Sugden, Edward H. Topographical Dictionary to the Works of Shakespeare & His Fellow Dramatists. 1969. Repr. of 1925 ed. 66.75 (ISBN 3-4870-2702-X). Adler.

Taylor, Isaac. Names & Their Histories. LC 68-17936. 1969. Repr. of 1898 ed. 26.00 (ISBN 0-8103-4217-0). Gale.

--Words & Places, or Etymological Illustrations of History, Ethnology, & Geography. 4th ed. 1968. Repr. of 1909 ed. 24.00 (ISBN 0-8103-3240-X). Gale.

United States Geographic Board. Sixth Report of the United States Geographic Board: 1890-1932. LC 67-8571. 1967. Repr. of 1933 ed. 28.00 (ISBN 0-685-11676-X). Gale.

Weisberg, David B. Texts from the Time of Nebuchadnezzar. LC 79-16038. (Yale Oriental Ser. Babylonian Texts: Vol. XVII). 288p. 1980. text ed. 35.00x (ISBN 0-300-02338-3). Yale U Pr.

NAMES, GEOGRAPHICAL–ASIA

Shuppansha, Times. Manual of Chinese-Manchurian Place Names. 1943. 4.95x (ISBN 0-685-21794-9). Wahr.

NAMES, GEOGRAPHICAL–CANADA

Boas, Franz. Geographical Names of the Kwakiutl Indians. LC 77-82361. (Columbia Univ. Contributions to Anthropology Ser.: No. 20). 1969. Repr. of 1934 ed. 25.00 (ISBN 0-404-50570-8). AMS Pr.

Canada: Third United Nations Conference on the Standardization of Geographical Names, United Nations, Athens, 1977. 1979. pap. 9.25 (ISBN 0-660-50066-3, SSC123, SSC). Unipub.

Frame, Elizabeth. A List of Micmac Names of Places, Rivers, Etc., in Nova Scotia. 1978. Repr. of 1892 ed. 10.00 (ISBN 0-8492-4606-7). R West.

Seary, E. R. Place Names of the Avalon Peninsula of the Island of Newfoundland. LC 73-151390. 1971. 22.50x (ISBN 0-8020-3243-5). U of Toronto Pr.

NAMES, GEOGRAPHICAL–FRANCE

Dauzat, Albert, et al. Dictionnaire Etymologique des Noms de Rivieres et de Montagnes en France. (Fr.). 1978. pap. 35.00 (ISBN 0-686-56974-1, M-6101). French & Eur.

Longnon, Auguste H. Les Noms De Lieu De la France: Leur Origine Leur Signification, Leurs Transformation. LC 75-140989. 1973. Repr. of 1920 ed. lib. bdg. 49.00 (ISBN 0-8337-2142-9). B Franklin.

NAMES, GEOGRAPHICAL–GREAT BRITAIN

Davies, Stella & Levitt, John. What's in a Name. 1970. 12.95 (ISBN 0-7100-6753-4). Transatlantic.

Efvergren, Carl J. Names of Places in a Transferred Sense in English: A Sematological Study. LC 68-17922. 1969. Repr. of 1909 ed. 19.00 (ISBN 0-8103-3233-7). Gale.

Ekwall, Eilert. Concise Oxford Dictionary of English Place-Names. 4th ed. 1960. 29.00x (ISBN 0-19-869103-3). Oxford U Pr.

Field, John. Place-Names of Great Britain & Ireland. (Illus.). 208p. 1980. 15.00x (ISBN 0-389-20154-5). B&N.

Harrison, Michael. The London That Was Rome. 1971. 10.50 (ISBN 0-04-913011-0). Allen Unwin.

Hope, Robert C. Glossary of Dialectal Place-Nomenclature. LC 68-58761. 1968. Repr. of 1883 ed. 19.00 (ISBN 0-8103-3530-1). Gale.

Lower, Mark A. Contributions to Literature: Historical, Antiquarian, & Metrical. LC 72-4578. (Essay Index Reprint Ser.). Repr. of 1854 ed. 18.00 (ISBN 0-8369-2959-4). Arno.

Moorman, Frederic W. The Placenames of the West Riding of Yorkshire. pap. 28.00 (ISBN 0-384-40020-5). Johnson Repr.

Orton, Harold & Wright, Nathalia. A Word Geography of England. 1975. 48.50 (ISBN 0-12-785608-0). Acad Pr.

Reaney, P. H. The Origin of English Place-Names. 1969. Repr. of 1960 ed. 20.00 (ISBN 0-7100-2010-4). Routledge & Kegan.

Watson, Godfrey. Goodwife Hot & Others: Northumberland's Past As Shown in Its Place Names. 1970. 10.50 (ISBN 0-85362-090-3, Oriel). Routledge & Kegan.

Whatmore, Arthur W. Insulae Britannicae. LC 72-118508. 1971. Repr. of 1913 ed. 15.00 (ISBN 0-8046-1256-0). Kennikat.

NAMES, GEOGRAPHICAL–HUNGARY

Kalman, Bela. The World of Names: A Study in Hungarian Onomatology. LC 79-300962. 1978. 15.00x (ISBN 963-05-1399-4). Intl Pubns Serv.

NAMES, GEOGRAPHICAL–INDIAN

see Indians of North America–Names

NAMES, GEOGRAPHICAL–IRELAND

Field, John. Place-Names of Great Britain & Ireland. (Illus.). 208p. 1980. 15.00x (ISBN 0-389-20154-5). B&N.

NAMES, GEOGRAPHICAL–UNITED STATES

Abernathy, Elton. Directing Speech Activities. 1970. text ed. 3.95 (ISBN 0-8418-4672-3). University Pr.

Arnold, Pauline & White, Percival. How We Named Our States. LC 65-24208. (Illus.). (gr. 5-9). 1965. 10.95 (ISBN 0-200-71911-4, 339010, AbS-J). Har-Row.

Baker, Ronald L. & Carmony, Marvin. Indiana Place Names. LC 74-17915. 224p. 1976. pap. 3.95x (ISBN 0-253-28340-X). Ind U Pr.

Bloodworth, Bertha E. & Morris, Alton C. Places in the Sun: The History & Romance of Fla. Place-Names. LC 77-13754. 1979. 12.50 (ISBN 0-8130-0544-2). U Presses Fla.

Carlson, Helen S. Nevada Place Names: A Geographical Dictionary. LC 74-13877. xiv, 282p. 1974. 15.00 (ISBN 0-87417-041-9). U of Nev Pr.

Cassidy, F. G. The Place-Names of Dane County, Wisconsin. (Publications of the American Dialect Society Ser., No. 7). 255p. 1947. pap. 7.50x (ISBN 0-8173-0607-2). U of Ala Pr.

Chadbourne, Ava H. Maine Place Names & the Peopling of Its Towns: Hancock County. Wheelwright, Thea, ed. LC 77-115159. (Illus.). 1970. pap. 1.95 (ISBN 0-87027-112-1). Wheelwright.

--Maine Place Names & the Peopling of Its Towns: Lincoln County. Wheelwright, Thea, ed. LC 77-115159. 1970. pap. 1.95 (ISBN 0-87027-113-X). Wheelwright.

Dunlap, A. R. Dutch & Swedish Place-Names in Delaware. LC 57-62613. 66p. pap. 2.50 (ISBN 0-87413-110-3). U Delaware Pr.

Espenshade, A. Howry. Pennsylvania Place Names. LC 71-112824. (Pennsylvania State College History & Political Science Ser: No. 1). 1970. Repr. of 1925 ed. 18.50 (ISBN 0-8063-0416-2). Genealog Pub.

Espenshade, Abraham H. Pennsylvania Place Names. LC 68-30591. 1969. Repr. of 1925 ed. 22.00 (ISBN 0-8103-3234-5). Gale.

Espy, Willard R. Omak Me Yours Tonight or Ilwaco Million Miles for One of Your Smiles. (Illus.). 72p. (Orig.). 1975. pap. 3.95 (ISBN 0-915112-00-0). Seattle Bk.

Finnie, W. Bruce. Topographic Terms in the Ohio Valley 1748-1800. (Publications of the American Dialect Society: No. 53). 144p. 1970. pap. 8.00x (ISBN 0-8173-0653-6). U of Ala Pr.

Fitzpatrick, Lilian L. Nebraska Place-Names. Fairclough, G. Thomas, ed. LC 60-15471. 1960. pap. 3.50 (ISBN 0-8032-5060-6, BB 107, Bison). U of Nebr Pr.

Foscue, Virginia O. The Place Names of Sumter County, Alabama. Hartman, James W., ed. (Publication of the American Dialect Society: No. 65). (Illus.). 1978. pap. 5.35x (ISBN 0-8173-0663-3). U of Ala Pr.

Gannett, Henry. Origin of Certain Place Names in the United States. LC 68-23159. 1971. Repr. of 1902 ed. 19.00 (ISBN 0-8103-3382-1). Gale.

--The Origin of Certain Place Names in the United States. 2nd ed. LC 72-11709. 1977. 15.00 (ISBN 0-8063-0544-4). Genealog Pub.

Goff, John H. Placenames of Georgia: Essays of John H. Goff. Utley, Francis L. & Hemperley, Marion R., eds. LC 73-86366. (Illus.). 534p. 1975. 18.50 (ISBN 0-8203-0342-9). U of Ga Pr.

Granger, Byrd H. Arizona Place Names. 2nd ed. LC 59-63657. 1960. 17.95 (ISBN 0-8165-0009-6). U of Ariz Pr.

Gudde, Erwin G. California Place Names: The Origin & Etymology of Current Geographical Names. LC 68-26529. 1969. 25.00 (ISBN 0-520-01574-6). U of Cal Pr.

--One Thousand California Place Names: Their Origin & Meaning. 3rd rev. ed. 1969. pap. 2.95 (ISBN 0-520-01432-4). U of Cal Pr.

Harder, Kelsie B. Illustrated Dictionary of American Place Names: United States & Canada. 1975. 19.95 (ISBN 0-442-23069-9). Van Nos Reinhold.

Hiden, Martha W. How Justice Grew - Virginia Counties: An Abstract of Their Formation. (Illus.). 1957. pap. 1.95x (ISBN 0-8139-0143-X). U Pr of Va.

Hixson. Place Names of the White Mtns. 446p. 1980. pap. 8.95 (ISBN 0-89272-069-7). Down East.

Holt, Alfred H. American Place Names. LC 68-26574. 1969. Repr. of 1938 ed. 19.00 (ISBN 0-8103-3235-3). Gale.

Huden, John C. Indian Place Names of New England, Vol. 18. LC 62-18399. (Contributions Ser.). 1962. soft cover 7.50 (ISBN 0-934490-18-X). Mus Am Ind.

Krakow, Kenneth K. Georgia Place Names. 1975. 12.50 (ISBN 0-915430-00-2); pap. 8.00 (ISBN 0-915430-01-0). Winship Pr.

Lederer, Richard M., Jr. Place Names of Westchester County, New York. LC 78-13727. (Illus.). 1978. 9.75 (ISBN 0-916346-30-7). Harbor Hill Bks.

McNamara, John. History in Asphalt: The Origin of Bronx Street & Place Names. LC 78-13741. (Illus.). 1978. 19.75 (ISBN 0-916346-31-5). Harbor Hill Bks.

Marinacci, Barbara & Marinacci, Rudy. California's Spanish Place-Names: What They Mean & How They Got There. LC 80-11381. (Illus.). 1980. pap. 6.95 (ISBN 0-89141-102-X). Presidio Pr.

Morgan, L. H. League of the Iroquois. (Illus.). 11.50 (ISBN 0-8446-2612-0). Peter Smith.

Morris, Allen. Florida Place Names. LC 74-13949. 160p. 1974. 7.95 (ISBN 0-87024-256-3). U of Miami Pr.

Newton, Charles H. The Reasons Why Place Names in Arizona Are So Named. 48p. pap. 1.95 (ISBN 0-915030-25-X). Tecolote Pr.

Parkerson, Codman. Those Strange Louisiana Names. 1969. pap. 1.25 (ISBN 0-685-08223-7). Claitors.

Pearce, T. M. New Mexico Place Names: A Geographical Dictionary. LC 64-17808. 1980. pap. 5.95 (ISBN 0-8263-0082-0). U of NM Pr.

Pizer, Vernon. Ink, Ark., & All That: How American Places Got Their Names. LC 76-13176. (Illus.). (gr. 6-8). 1976. 8.95 (ISBN 0-399-20532-2). Putnam.

Pukui, Mary K., et al. Place Names of Hawaii. 2nd ed. LC 73-85582. 320p. 1974 (ISBN 0-8248-0208-X). pap. 5.95 (ISBN 0-8248-0524-0). U Pr of Hawaii.

Ramsay, R. L. The Place Names of Boone County, Missouri. (Publications of the American Dialect Society: No. 18). 52p. 1952. pap. 1.50x (ISBN 0-8173-0618-8). U of Ala Pr.

Ramsay, Robert L. Our Storehouse of Missouri Place Names. LC 73-79512. 1952. pap. 4.00x (ISBN 0-8262-0586-0). U of Mo Pr.

Rudolph, Robert S. Wood County Place Names. 1970. 3.95x (ISBN 0-299-05703-8). U of Wis Pr.

Rydjord, John. Kansas Place-Names. LC 78-177346. (Illus.). 400p. 1972. 29.50 (ISBN 0-8061-0994-7). U of Okla Pr.

Sanchez, Nellie. Spanish & Indian Place Names of California: Their Meaning & Their Romance. Cortes, Carlos E., ed. LC 76-1573. (Chicano Heritage Ser.). (Illus.). 1976. Repr. of 1930 ed. 23.00x (ISBN 0-405-09523-6). Arno.

Shankle, George E. American Nicknames. 2nd ed. 1955. 15.00 (ISBN 0-8242-0004-7). Wilson.

--State Names, Flags, Seals, Songs, Birds, Flowers, & Other Symbols: A Study Based on Historical Documents. 1971. Repr. of 1938 ed. 59.00 (ISBN 0-403-00784-4). Scholarly.

--State Names, Flags, Seals, Songs, Birds, Flowers, & Other Symbols. rev. ed. LC 73-109842. (Illus.). 522p. Repr. of 1938 ed. lib. bdg. 23.50x (ISBN 0-8371-4333-0, SHSN). Greenwood.

Stein, Lou. San Diego County Place-Names. LC 75-23831. 170p. 1975. 9.95 (ISBN 0-914488-06-6); pap. 4.95 (ISBN 0-914488-07-4). Rand-Tofua.

Stewart, George R. American Place-Names: A Concise & Selective Dictionary for the Continental United States of America. LC 72-83018. 1970. 19.95 (ISBN 0-19-500121-4). Oxford U Pr.

Swift, Esther M. Vermont Place-Names, Footprints of History. LC 76-13815. 1977. 35.00 (ISBN 0-8289-0291-7). Greene.

Tooker, William W. The Indian Place-Names on Long Island & Islands Adjacent with Their Probable Significations. Chamberlain, Alexander, ed. LC 62-13522. (Empire State Historical Publications). 1975. 12.50 (ISBN 0-8046-8006-X). Kennikat.

Trumbull, J. Hammond. Indian Names in Connecticut. xii, 93p. (Facsimile of 1881 ed.). 1974. 11.50 (ISBN 0-208-01415-2, Archon). Shoe String.
Upham, Warren. Minnesota Geographic Names: Their Origin & Historic Significance. LC 71-95570. 788p. 1969. Repr. of 1920 ed. 12.50 (ISBN 0-87351-144-1). Minn Hist.
Urbanek, Mae. Wyoming Place Names. 3rd ed. 236p. 1979. 7.50x (ISBN 0-940514-09-5); pap. 5.00 (ISBN 0-940514-10-9). Urbanek.
Vogel, Virgil J. Indian Place Names in Illinois. 1963. pap. 2.00 (ISBN 0-912226-01-3). Ill St Hist Soc.
Wolk, Alan. The Naming of America: How Continents, Countries, States, Counties, Cities, Towns, Villages, Hamlets, & Post Offices Came by Their Names. LC 77-31833. (gr. 7 up). 1978. 8.95 (ISBN 0-525-66562-5). Elsevier-Nelson.
Wolk, Allan. The Naming of America. 196p. 1980. pap. 3.95 (ISBN 0-346-12434-4). Cornerstone.
Wood, Bryce. San Juan Island: Coastal Place Names & Cartographic Nomenclature. LC 80-17728. (Sponsor Ser.). 280p. (Orig.). 1980. pap. 20.75 (ISBN 0-8357-0526-9, SS-00132). Univ Microfilms.
Work Projects Administration in the State of South Carolina, ed. Palmetto Place Names. LC 74-34408. (Illus.). 160p. 1975. Repr. of 1941 ed. 13.50 (ISBN 0-87152-191-1). Reprint.

NAMES, GERMANIC

Gottschald, Max. Deutsche Namenkunde: Unsere Familiennamen nach ihrer Entstehung und Bedeutung. 4th ed. (Ger). 1971. 48.75x (ISBN 3-11-006467-7). De Gruyter.

NAMES, HUNGARIAN

Kalman, Bela. The World of Names: A Study in Hungarian Onomatology. LC 79-300962. 1978. 15.00x (ISBN 963-05-1399-4). Intl Pubns Serv.

NAMES, INDIAN

see Indians of North America–Names

NAMES, PERSONAL

see also Anonyms and Pseudonyms; Christian Patron Saints; Nicknames;
also Name under names of persons, Jesus Christ–Name

Algeo, John. On Defining the Proper Name. LC 73-9849. (U of Fla. Humanities Monograph Ser.: No. 41). 94p. 1973. pap. 3.50 (ISBN 0-8130-0410-1). U Presses Fla.
Ames, Winthrop. What Shall We Name the Baby? 1977. pap. 2.50 (ISBN 0-671-42217-0). PB.
Ames, Winthrop, ed. What Shall We Name the Baby. (Illus.). 1959. pap. 1.95 (ISBN 0-671-81210-6, Fireside). S&S.
Arthur, William. Etymological Dictionary of Family & Christian Names. LC 68-17911. 1969. Repr. of 1857 ed. 26.00 (ISBN 0-8103-3107-1). Gale.
Attwater, Donald. Names & Name-Days: A Dictionary of Catholic Christian Names in Alphabetical Order with Origins & Meanings. LC 68-30595. 1968. Repr. of 1939 ed. 22.00 (ISBN 0-8103-3108-X). Gale.
Bander, Edward J. Change of Name & Law of Names. LC 73-11060. (Legal Almanac Ser.: No. 34). 128p. 1973. lib. bdg. 5.95 (ISBN 0-379-11088-1). Oceana.
Baring-Gould, Sabine. Family Names & Their Story. LC 68-23136. 1969. Repr. of 1910 ed. 19.00 (ISBN 0-8103-0151-2). Gale.
--Family Names & Their Story. LC 68-54868. 1968. Repr. of 1910 ed. 18.50 (ISBN 0-8063-0023-X). Genealog Pub.
Bowman, William D. Story of Surnames. LC 68-8906. 1968. Repr. of 1932 ed. 21.00 (ISBN 0-8103-3110-1). Gale.
Browder, Sue. The New Age Baby Name Book. LC 77-18435. 1978. pap. 3.95 (ISBN 0-89480-029-9). Workman Pub.
Chuks-Orji, Ogonna. Names from Africa. 1972. pap. 4.95 (ISBN 0-87485-046-0). Johnson Chi.
Dillard, J. L. Black Names. Fishman, Joshua A., ed. (Contributions to the Sociology of Language Ser.: No. 13). 1976. pap. text ed. 15.75x (ISBN 90-2797-602-3). Mouton.
Falk, Bryon A. & Falk, Valerie. Personal Name Index to the New York Times Index: Eighteen Fifty One to Nineteen Seventy Four, Vol.15. 417p. 1980. lib. bdg. 38.25 (ISBN 0-89902-115-8). Roxbury Data.
Falk, Byron A. & Falk, Valerie R. Personal Name Index to the New York Times Index, Vols. 13 & 14: Eighteen Fifty-One to Nineteen Seventy-Four. LC 76-12217. 1980. lib. bdg. 52.50 ea. Vol. 13 (ISBN 0-89902-113-1). Vol. 14 (ISBN 0-89902-114-X). Roxbury Data.
--Personal Name Index to the New Youk Times Index: Eighteen Fifty One to Nineteen Seventy Four, Vol.16. 624p. 1980. lib. bdg. 50.50 (ISBN 0-89902-116-6). Roxbury Data.
Falk, Byron A., Jr. & Falk, Valerie R. Personal Name Index to the New York Times Index: Eighteen Fifty One to Nineteen Seventy Four, Vol. 17. 659p. 1981. lib. bdg. 62.00 (ISBN 0-89902-117-4). Roxbury Data.
--Personal Name Index to the New York Times Index: Eighteen Fifty-One to Nineteen Seventy-Four, Vol. 18. 600p. 1981. lib. bdg. 57.50 (ISBN 0-89902-118-2). Roxbury Data.
Francis, Linda, et al. What's in a Name? (Orig.). 1976. pap. 3.50 (ISBN 0-934400-06-7). Landmark Bks.
Freeman, J. W. Discovering Surnames: Their Origins & Meanings. 4th ed. (Discovering Ser.). 72p. (gr. 6 up). 1979. pap. 2.50 (ISBN 0-913714-36-4). Legacy Bks.
Homer. Signing off: How to Have Fun with Names. 140p. 1980. pap. 3.95 (ISBN 0-936944-00-5). Comm Creat.
Know & Claim Your African Name. 40p. 1976. pap. 3.50 (ISBN 0-686-14428-7). Rucker Pr.
Kolatch. The Jonathan David Dictionary of First Names. 1980. 19.95 (ISBN 0-8246-0234-X). Jonathan David.
Kolatch, Alfred J. The Name Dictionary. rev. ed. LC 66-25122. 432p. 1973. 10.00 (ISBN 0-8246-0060-6). Jonathan David.
Lansky, Bruce & Lansky, Vicki, eds. The Best Baby Name Book in the Whole Wide World. (Illus.). 130p. 1979. pap. 2.95 (ISBN 0-915658-17-8). Meadowbrook Pr.
Lee, Mary P. Your Name: All About It. LC 79-22145. 1980. 9.95 (ISBN 0-664-32656-0). Westminster.
Let's Name the Baby. 1977. pap. 2.50 (ISBN 0-8378-5099-1). Gibson.
Loeb. How to Change Your Name. 2nd ed. 1979. pap. 7.95 (ISBN 0-917316-12-6). Nolo Pr.
Long, Harry A. Personal & Family Names. LC 68-26584. 1968. Repr. of 1883 ed. 22.00 (ISBN 0-8103-3128-4). Gale.
Loughead, Flora H. Dictionary of Given Names. 1966. 12.50 (ISBN 0-87062-048-7). A H Clark.
McCue, Marion. How to Pick the Right Name for Your Baby. 1977. pap. 2.95 (ISBN 0-448-12977-9). G&D.
MacWethy, Lou D. Book of Names Especially Relating to the Early Palatines & the First Settlers in the Mohawk Valley. LC 69-17132. (Illus.). 1969. Repr. of 1933 ed. 12.50 (ISBN 0-8063-0231-3). Genealog Pub.
Moody, Sophy. What Is Your Name: A Popular Account of the Meaning & Derivations of Christian Names. LC 73-5523. 1975. Repr. of 1863 ed. 30.00 (ISBN 0-8103-4250-2). Gale.
Nevins, Albert J. A Saint for Your Name: Saints for Boys. LC 79-92504. (Illus.). 120p. (YA) (gr. 7 up). 1980. 7.95 (ISBN 0-87973-330-6, 330); pap. 4.95 (ISBN 0-87973-320-9, 320). Our Sunday Visitor.
--A Saint for Your Name: Saints for Girls. LC 79-92502. (Illus.). 104p. (YA) (gr. 7 up). 1980. 7.95 (ISBN 0-87973-331-4, 331); pap. 4.95 (ISBN 0-87973-321-7, 321). Our Sunday Visitor.
Nurnberg, Maxwell & Rosenblum, Morris. What to Name Your Baby. Orig. Title: Your Baby's Name. 1962. pap. 2.50 (ISBN 0-02-081020-2, Collier). Macmillan.
Page, Andre. Babies Names A to Z. LC 78-9402. 1979. pap. 1.75 (ISBN 0-668-04603-1, 4603). Arco.
Phillimore, William P. & Fry, E. A. Index to Changes of Name, LC 68-54685. 1968. Repr. of 1905 ed. 17.50 (ISBN 0-8063-0276-3). Genealog Pub.
Pierradrd, Pierre. Larousse Des Prenoms et Des Saints. 256p. (Fr.). 1976. 42.50 (ISBN 0-686-57079-0, M-6454). French & Eur.
Rashed, Leon H. A Change-of-Name Guide for Bilalians. (Illus.). 1979. 4.00 (ISBN 0-682-49330-9). Exposition.
Rule, Lareina. Name Your Baby. 224p. (Orig.). 1980. pap. 2.50 (ISBN 0-553-20406-8). Bantam.
Sager, J. C., ed. Standardization of Nomenclature: International Journal of the Sociology of Language, No. 23. 1980. pap. text ed. 21.95x (ISBN 90-279-3028-7). Mouton.
Salvador, Salazar G. Nombres Para el Bebe. LC 78-2535. (Sp.). 1978. pap. 2.50 (ISBN 0-668-04614-7, 4614). Arco.
Sleigh, Linwood & Johnson, Charles. Apollo Book of Girls' Names. (Apollo Eds.). 1971. pap. 3.50 (ISBN 0-8152-0302-0, A302, TYC-T). T Y Crowell.
Smith, Elsdon C. The Book of Smith. LC 79-10098. (Illus.). 1979. pap. 4.95 (ISBN 0-399-50393-5, Perigee). Putnam.
--The Book of Smith. LC 78-2765. 1978. 9.95 (ISBN 0-8424-0119-9). Nellen Pub.
--Personal Names: A Bibliography. LC 66-31855. 1965. Repr. of 1952 ed. 19.00 (ISBN 0-8103-3134-9). Gale.
--Story of Our Names. LC 71-109181. 1970. Repr. of 1950 ed. 18.00 (ISBN 0-8103-3858-0). Gale.
Stephens, Ferris J. Personal Names from Cuneiform Inscriptions of Cappadocia. (Yale Oriental Researches Ser.: No. XIII). 1928. pap. 22.50x (ISBN 0-685-69868-8). Elliots Bks.
Swan, H. Girls' Christian Names. 69.95 (ISBN 0-87968-345-7). Gordon Pr.
Swan, Helena. Girls' Christian Names: Their History, Meaning & Association. LC 74-109419. 1970. bds. 5.50 (ISBN 0-8048-0899-6). C E Tuttle.
--Girls' Christian Names, Their History, Meaning & Association. LC 68-17935. 1968. Repr. of 1900 ed. 24.00 (ISBN 0-8103-3135-7). Gale.
Taylor, Isaac. Names & Their Histories. 59.95 (ISBN 0-8490-0702-X). Gordon Pr.
Thomson, Christine C. Boy or Girl? Names for Every Child. 1969. pap. 1.50 (ISBN 0-668-00858-X). Arco.
Three Thousand Five Hundred Names for Baby. (Purse Books). 1967. pap. 0.69 (ISBN 0-440-68859-0). Dell.
Train, John. Remarkable Names of Real People. (Illus.). 1977. 5.95 (ISBN 0-517-53130-5). Potter.
Wagner, Leopold. More About Names. 1893. Repr. 35.00 (ISBN 0-8274-2762-X). R West.
Weekley, Ernest. Jack & Jill: A Study in Our Christian Names. 1939. Repr. 25.00 (ISBN 0-8274-2593-7). R West.
--Surnames. LC 74-6099. 1973. lib. bdg. 45.00 (ISBN 0-8414-9521-1). Folcroft.
Weidenhan, Joseph L. Baptismal Names. 4th ed. LC 68-26618. 1968. Repr. of 1931 ed. 26.00 (ISBN 0-8103-3136-5). Gale.
Wells, Evelyn. What to Name the Baby. 1953. 7.95 (ISBN 0-385-00183-5). Doubleday.
Wells, Jane & Adkins, Cheryl L. The Name for Your Baby. (Illus.). 1972. pap. 1.95 (ISBN 0-517-51797-3). Barre.
What to Name the Baby. 1980. pap. 2.50 (ISBN 0-671-82739-1). PB.
Yonge, Charlotte M. History of Christian Names. 1966. Repr. of 1884 ed. 26.00 (ISBN 0-8103-3139-X). Gale.
--History of Christian Names. 75.00 (ISBN 0-87968-368-6). Gordon Pr.

NAMES, PERSONAL–AMORITE

Huffmon, Herbert B. Amorite Personal Names in the Mari Texts: A Structural and Lexical Study. 320p. 1965. 22.50x (ISBN 0-8018-0283-0). Johns Hopkins.

NAMES, PERSONAL–ASSYRO-BABYLONIAN

Chiera, E. Lists of Personal Names from the Temple School of Nippur: A Syllabary of Personal Names. (Publications of the Babylonian Section: Vol. 11-1). (Illus.). 88p. 1916. soft bound 7.00 (ISBN 0-686-11923-1). Univ Mus of U PA.
--Lists of Personal Names from the Temple School of Nippur: Lists of Akkadian Personal Names. (Publications of the Babylonian Section: Vol. 11-2). (Illus.). 85p. 1916. soft bound 7.00 (ISBN 0-686-11924-X). Univ Mus of U PA.
Ranke, Hermann. Early Babylonian Personal Names from the Published Tablets of the So-Called Hammurabi Dynasty 2000 B. C. (Publications of the Babylonian Section, Ser. D: Vol. 3). 255p. 1905. soft bound 3.00 (ISBN 0-686-11916-9). Univ Mus of U PA.
Weisberg, David B. Texts from the Time of Nebuchadnezzar. LC 79-16038. (Yale Oriental Ser. Babylonian Texts: Vol. XVII). 288p. 1980. text ed. 35.00x (ISBN 0-300-02338-3). Yale U Pr.

NAMES, PERSONAL–CELTIC

Evans, D. Ellis. Gaulish Personal Names: A Study of Some Continental Celtic Formations. 1967. 44.00x (ISBN 0-19-811930-5). Oxford U Pr.

NAMES, PERSONAL–ENGLISH

Addison, William. Understanding English Surnames. 1978. 19.95 (ISBN 0-7134-0295-4). David & Charles.
Barber, Henry. British Family Names. 2nd ed. LC 68-17914. 1968. Repr. of 1903 ed. 22.00 (ISBN 0-8103-3109-8). Gale.
--British Family Names. 2nd enl ed. LC 68-54867. 1968. Repr. of 1903 ed. 17.50 (ISBN 0-8063-0021-3). Genealog Pub.
Bardsley, Charles W. Curiosities of Puritan Nomenclature. LC 76-140409. 1971. Repr. of 1897 ed. 19.00 (ISBN 0-8103-3715-0). Gale.
Baring-Gould, Sabine. Family Names & Their Story. LC 68-23136. 1969. Repr. of 1910 ed. 19.00 (ISBN 0-8103-0151-2). Gale.
--Family Names & Their Story. LC 68-54868. 1968. Repr. of 1910 ed. 18.50 (ISBN 0-8063-0023-X). Genealog Pub.
Camden, William. Britannia, 4 vols. 2nd ed. LC 73-113571. (Illus.). Repr. of 1806 ed. Set. 145.00 (ISBN 0-404-01370-8). Vol. 1 (ISBN 0-404-01371-6). Vol. 2 (ISBN 0-404-01372-4). Vol. 3 (ISBN 0-404-01373-2). Vol. 4 (ISBN 0-404-01374-0). AMS Pr.
--Remaines Concerning Britain. LC 77-113572. (Illus.). Repr. of 1657 ed. 46.50 (ISBN 0-404-01367-8). AMS Pr.
Charnock, Richard S. Ludus Patronymicus: Or, the Etymology of Curious Surnames. LC 68-23141. 1968. Repr. of 1868 ed. 19.00 (ISBN 0-8103-3122-5). Gale.
Ewen, Cecil. A Guide to the Origin of British Surnames. 59.95 (ISBN 0-8490-0273-7). Gordon Pr.
--A History of Surnames of the British Isles. 59.95 (ISBN 0-8490-0349-0). Gordon Pr.
Ewen, Cecil H. Guide to the Origin of British Surnames. LC 68-30596. 1969. Repr. of 1938 ed. 22.00 (ISBN 0-8103-3123-3). Gale.
--History of Surnames of the British Isles: A Concise Account of Their Origin, Evolution, Etymology & Legal Status. LC 68-30597. 1968. Repr. of 1931 ed. 24.00 (ISBN 0-8103-3124-1). Gale.
--History of Surnames of the British Isles. LC 68-54687. 1968. Repr. of 1931 ed. 20.00 (ISBN 0-8063-0106-6). Genealog Pub.
Hutson, Arthur E. British Personal Names in the Historia Regun Britanniae. LC 75-19158. 1974. Repr. of 1940 ed. lib. bdg. 25.00 (ISBN 0-8414-4891-4). Folcroft.
Lower, M. A. English Surnames. 59.95 (ISBN 0-8490-0119-6). Gordon Pr.
Lower, Mark A. English Surnames, 2 Vols. 4th ed. LC 68-22037. 1968. Repr. of 1875 ed. Set. 24.00 (ISBN 0-8103-3129-2). Gale.
Meier, Arnold. Alttestamentliche Namengebung in England. pap. 6.00 (ISBN 0-685-13337-0). Johnson Repr.
Phillimore, W. P. & Fry, E. A. Index to Changes of Name. LC 68-27180. 1969. Repr. of 1905 ed. 22.00 (ISBN 0-8103-3132-2). Gale.
Phillimore, William P. & Fry, E. A. Index to Changes of Name, LC 68-54685. 1968. Repr. of 1905 ed. 17.50 (ISBN 0-8063-0276-3). Genealog Pub.
Reaney, P. H. A Dictionary of British Surnames. 2nd ed. 1976. 42.00 (ISBN 0-7100-8106-5). Routledge & Kegan.
--The Origin of English Surnames. 1980. pap. 8.95 (ISBN 0-7100-0353-6). Routledge & Kegan.
--The Origin of English Surnames. 1967. 25.00 (ISBN 0-7100-2885-7). Routledge & Kegan.
Tolman, Albert H. Views About Hamlet & Other Essays. LC 78-177468. Repr. of 1904 ed. 16.00 (ISBN 0-404-06477-9). AMS Pr.
Weekley, Ernest. Jack & Jill: A Study in Our Christian Names. LC 74-148925. 1974. Repr. of 1939 ed. 19.00 (ISBN 0-8103-3649-9). Gale.
--Words & Names. facsimile ed. LC 73-164634. (Select Bibliographies Reprint Ser.). Repr. of 1932 ed. 17.00 (ISBN 0-8369-5918-3). Arno.
Withycombe, E. G. The Oxford Dictionary of English Christian Names. 3rd ed. 344p. 1977. 14.50x (ISBN 0-19-869124-6). Oxford U Pr.
--The Oxford Dictionary of English Christian Names. 3rd ed. 1977. pap. 4.95 (ISBN 0-19-281213-0, GB511, GB). Oxford U Pr.

NAMES, PERSONAL–FRENCH

Blanche, Claude-Pierre. Dictionnaire et Armorial des Noms de Famille de France. 312p. (Fr.). 1974. pap. 33.50 (ISBN 0-686-56922-9, M-6038). French & Eur.
Dauzat, A. Dictionnaire des noms de famille et prenoms de France. (Fr). 23.50 (ISBN 2-03-020260-6, 3615). Larousse.
Losique, Serge. Dictionnaire Etymologique des Noms de Pays et de Peuples. 243p. (Fr.). 1971. pap. 22.50 (ISBN 0-686-57294-7, F-35990). French & Eur.

NAMES, PERSONAL–FRENCH-CANADIAN

Dionne, Narcisse-Eutrope. Canadiens-Francais: Origine Des Familles Emigrees De France D'Espagne, De Suisse Etc. LC 73-76767. 1969. Repr. of 1914 ed. 22.50 (ISBN 0-8063-0095-7). Genealog Pub.

NAMES, PERSONAL–IRISH

Kelly, Patrick. Irish Family Names. LC 68-26580. 1975. Repr. of 1939 ed. 26.00 (ISBN 0-8103-4146-8). Gale.
MacLysaght, Edward. The Surnames of Ireland. 3rd ed. 336p. 1978. 15.00x (ISBN 0-7165-2164-4, Pub. by Irish Academic Pr Ireland); pap. 6.00x (ISBN 0-7165-2291-8). Biblio Dist.
Woulfe, Patrick. Irish Names for Children. rev. & enlarged ed. 1974. pap. 2.25 (ISBN 0-7171-0697-7). Irish Bk Ctr.

NAMES, PERSONAL–JAPANESE

Hearn, Lafcadio. Shadowings. LC 77-138070. (Illus.). 1971. pap. 5.75 (ISBN 0-8048-0967-4). C E Tuttle.
Koop, Albert J. & Inada, Hogitaro. Japanese Names & How to Read Them: A Manual for Art-Collectors & Students. 1972. 75.00 (ISBN 0-7100-1707-3). Routledge & Kegan.
O'Neill, P. G. Japanese Names: A Comprehensive Index by Characters & Readings. LC 70-157274. 376p. 1972. 27.50 (ISBN 0-8348-0060-8). Weatherhill.

NAMES, PERSONAL–JEWISH

Kaganoff, Benzion C. A Dictionary of Jewish Names & Their History. LC 77-70227. 1977. 10.95 (ISBN 0-8052-3660-0). Schocken.
Singerman, Robert. Jewish & Hebrew Onomastics: A Bibliography. (Reference Library of the Humanities: Vol. 92). (LC 76-052684). 1977. lib. bdg. 19.50 (ISBN 0-8240-9881-1). Garland Pub.

NAMES, PERSONAL–ROMAN
Jones, A. H., et al, eds. Prosopography of the Later Roman Empire, Vol. 1. A. D. 260-395. LC 77-118859. (Illus.). 1971. 140.00 (ISBN 0-521-07233-6). Cambridge U Pr.
NAMES, PERSONAL–RUSSIAN
Benson, Morton, ed. Dictionary of Russian Personal Names. LC 64-19386. 1964. 14.00x (ISBN 0-8122-7452-0). U of Pa Pr.
NAMES, PERSONAL–SCOTTISH
Black, George F. Surnames of Scotland: Their Origin, Meaning & History. new, rev. ed. LC 47-1716. 1975. Repr. of 1946 ed. 17.50 (ISBN 0-87104-172-3). NY Pub Lib.
NAMES, PERSONAL–SPANISH
Woods, Richard D. & Alvarez-Altman, Grace, eds. Spanish Surnames in the Southwestern United States: A Dictionary. (Reference Publications). 1978. lib. bdg. 18.00 (ISBN 0-8161-8145-4). G K Hall.
NAMES, PERSONAL–UNITED STATES
American Council of Learned Societies, Committee on Linguistics & National Stocks. Surnames in the United States Census of 1790. LC 68-56110. (American Historical Association Annual Report Ser). 1971. Repr. of 1932 ed. 15.00 (ISBN 0-8063-0004-3). Genealog Pub.
Holmes, Frank R. Directory of the Ancestral Heads of New England Families, 1620-1700. LC 64-19755. 1974. Repr. of 1923 ed. 15.00 (ISBN 0-8063-0182-1). Genealog Pub.
Mencken, Henry L. The American Language, 3 vols. 4th ed. Incl. Vol. 1. The American Language. 1936. 25.00 (ISBN 0-394-40075-5); Vol. 2. The American Language, Supplement One. 1945. 25.00 (ISBN 0-394-40076-3); Vol. 3. The American Language, Supplement Two. 1948. 20.00 (ISBN 0-394-40077-1). Knopf.
Parkerson, Codman. Those Strange Louisiana Names. 1969. pap. 1.25 (ISBN 0-685-08223-7). Claitors.
Rupp, Israel D. A Collection of Upwards of Thirty Thousand Names of German, Swiss, Dutch, French & Other Immigrants in Pennsylvania from 1727 to 1776. 2nd ed. LC 65-26916. (Illus.). 583p. 1980. Repr. of 1876 ed. 20.00 (ISBN 0-8063-0302-6). Genealog Pub.
Shankle, George E. American Nicknames. 2nd ed. 1955. 15.00 (ISBN 0-8242-0004-7). Wilson.
Smith, Elsdon C. The New Dictionary of Family Names. LC 72-79693. 512p. 1973. 17.50 (ISBN 0-06-013933-1, HarpT). Har-Row.
Stewart, George R. American Given Names: Their Origin & History in the Context of the English Language. 1979. 14.95 (ISBN 0-19-502465-6). Oxford U Pr.
Woods, Richard D. & Alvarez-Altman, Grace, eds. Spanish Surnames in the Southwestern United States: A Dictionary. (Reference Publications). 1978. lib. bdg. 18.00 (ISBN 0-8161-8145-4). G K Hall.
NAMIBIA
Aydelotte, William O. Bismarck & British Colonial Policy: The Problem of South West Africa, 1883-1885. LC 71-111563. 1937. Repr. of 1937 ed. 10.25x (ISBN 0-8371-4584-8, Pub. by Negro U Pr). Greenwood.
Bannister, Anthony & Johnson, Peter. Namibia: Africa's Harsh Paradise. Gordon, Rene, ed. LC 79-10312. (Illus.). 240p. 1979. 37.50 (ISBN 0-89196-060-0, Domus Bks). Quality Bks IL.
Calvert, Albert F. South-West Africa, During the German Occupation, 1884-1914. LC 70-97418. Repr. of 1915 ed. 21.50x (ISBN 0-8371-2721-1, Pub. by Negro U Pr). Greenwood.
Fraenkel, Peter. Namibians of Southwest Africa. (Minority Rights Group: No. 19). 1974. pap. 2.50 (ISBN 0-89192-105-2). Interbk Inc.
Hahn, C. H., et al. Native Tribes of South West Africa. (Illus.). 211p. 1966. 27.50x (ISBN 0-7146-1670-2, F Cass Co). Biblio Dist.
Kerina, Mbrumba. Namibia. (Illus.). 336p. 1980. 19.95 (ISBN 0-916728-39-0). Bks in Focus.
NAMIBIA–DESCRIPTION AND TRAVEL
Alexander, James E. An Expedition of Discovery into the Interior of Africa, 2 Vols. (Illus.). Set. 44.00 (ISBN 0-384-00690-6). Johnson Repr.
Cubitt, G. S. & Richter, J. South West. 1976. text ed. 16.50x (ISBN 0-86977-075-6). Verry.
NAMIBIA–HISTORY
Barron, L. Smythe. The Nazis in Africa: Lost Documents on the Third Reich, Vol. 3. 1978. 24.95 (ISBN 0-89712-076-0). Documentary Pubns.
First, Ruth. South West Africa. 8.00 (ISBN 0-8446-2061-0). Peter Smith.
Freislich, R. Last Tribal War: A History of the Bondelswarth Uprising Which Took Place in South West Africa in 1922. 1964. 5.00x (ISBN 0-8426-1263-7). Verry.
Goldblatt, I. History of South West Africa from the Beginning of the 19th Century. (Illus.). 290p. 1971. 20.00x (ISBN 0-8002-1506-0). Intl Pubns Serv.
--History of South West Africa from the Beginning of the 19th Century. (Illus.). 290p. 1971. 20.00x (ISBN 0-8002-1506-0). Intl Pubns Serv.
Nabudere, Dan. The Political Economy of Imperialism. 2nd ed. 304p. 1980. 15.00 (ISBN 0-905762-03-7, Pub. by Zed Pr); pap. 7.95 (ISBN 0-905762-02-9). Lawrence Hill.
To Be Born a Nation: The Struggle of the Namibian People. 360p. 1981. pap. 9.95 (ISBN 0-905762-73-8, Pub. by Zed Pr England). Lawrence Hill.
Vedder, Heinrich. South West Africa in Early Times. Hall, C. G., tr. (Illus.). 525p. 1966. 32.50x (ISBN 0-7146-1733-4, F Cass Co). Biblio Dist.
NAMIBIA–POLITICS AND GOVERNMENT
Braum, Robert Love, ed. Southwest Africa Under Mandate. 1976. lib. bdg. 24.95 (ISBN 0-89712-017-5). Documentary Pubns.
Carroll, Faye. South West Africa & the United Nations. LC 75-3984. 123p. 1975. Repr. of 1967 ed. lib. bdg. 15.00 (ISBN 0-8371-7441-4, CASWA). Greenwood.
DeKiewiet, C. W. History of South Africa, Social & Economic. 1941. pap. 14.95x (ISBN 0-19-821638-6). Oxford U Pr.
Namibia: SWAPO Fights for Freedom. 2.95 (ISBN 0-919914-27-6). LSM Pr.
Sohn, Louis B., ed. Basic Documents of African Regional Organizations, 4 vols. LC 72-141326. 1973. 47.50 ea. (ISBN 0-379-00361-9). Oceana.
To Be Born a Nation: The Struggle of the Namibian People. 360p. 1981. pap. 9.95 (ISBN 0-905762-73-8, Pub. by Zed Pr England). Lawrence Hill.
Ya-Otto, John, et al. Battlefront Namibia. 188p. 1981. 12.95 (ISBN 0-88208-132-2); pap. 6.95 (ISBN 0-88208-133-0). Lawrence Hill.
NAMIBIA–RACE QUESTION
Dewaldt, Franz, ed. Native Uprisings in Southwest Africa. 1976. 24.95 (ISBN 0-89712-019-1). Documentary Pubns.
Molnar, Thomas. South West Africa. LC 66-26807. (Illus.). 1966. 6.95 (ISBN 0-8303-0029-5). Fleet.
NANAK, 1ST GURU OF THE SIKHS, 1469-1538
McLeod, W. H. Guru Nanak & the Sikh Religion. 1968. pap. text ed. 9.95x (ISBN 0-19-560806-2). Oxford U Pr.
Singh, Harbans. Guru Nanak & the Origins of Sikh Faith. 1970. 10.00x (ISBN 0-210-22311-1). Asia.
Singh, Khushwant, ed. & tr. Hymns of Guru Nanak. 1978. Repr. of 1969 ed. 4.00x (ISBN 0-8364-0302-9, Orient Longman). South Asia Bks.
Singh, Mala. The Story of Guru Nanak. (Illus.). (gr. 2-9). 1979. 5.50 (ISBN 0-89744-138-9). Auromere.
NANDI (AFRICAN TRIBE)
Hollis, Alfred C. Nandi: Their Language & Folk-Lore. LC 71-76481. (Illus.). Repr. of 1909 ed. 20.00x (ISBN 0-8371-1515-9, Pub. by Negro U Pr). Greenwood.
NANGATU LANGUAGE
see Tupi Language
NANSEN, FRIDTJOF, 1861-1930
Acker, Helen. Four Sons of Norway. facsimile ed. LC 72-117318. (Biography Index Reprint Ser). 1948. 20.00 (ISBN 0-8369-8010-7). Arno.
NANTASKET BEACH, MASSACHUSETTS
Bergan, William M. Old Nantasket. rev. ed. LC 72-78036. (Illus.). 1969. 6.00 (ISBN 0-8158-0022-3); pap. 3.95 (ISBN 0-8158-0286-2). Chris Mass.
NANTES, EDICT OF
see Edict of Nantes
NANTUCKET, MASSACHUSETTS
Burroughs, Polly. Guide to Nantucket. LC 74-76535. (Illus., Orig.). 1980. pap. 4.95 (ISBN 0-87106-144-9). Globe Pequot.
Chamberlain, Barbara B. These Fragile Outposts. 352p. 1981. pap. 9.95 (ISBN 0-940160-12-9). Parnassus Imprints.
Dreyer, Peter & Stackpole, Edouard. Nantucket in Color. (Profiles of America Ser). (Illus.). 1974. 7.95 (ISBN 0-8038-5030-1). Hastings.
Gambee, Robert. Nantucket Island. rev., 3rd ed. (Illus.). 192p. 1981. 15.00 (ISBN 0-8038-5077-8); pap. 10.95 (ISBN 0-8038-5078-6). Hastings.
Hare, Lloyd C. Thomas Mayhew, Patriarch to the Indians, 1593-1682. LC 76-104347. (Illus.). Repr. of 1932 ed. 20.00 (ISBN 0-404-03108-0). AMS Pr.
Lancaster, Clay. Nantucket in the Nineteenth Century. LC 77-75512. (Illus.). 1979. pap. 6.95 (ISBN 0-486-23747-8). Dover.
McCalley, John. Nantucket Yesterday & Today. (Illus.). 176p. (Orig.). 1981. pap. 8.95 (ISBN 0-486-24059-2). Dover.
Mackay, Dick. Nantucket! Nantucket! Nantucket! An Insider's Guide. LC 81-52145. (Illus.). 144p. (Orig.). 1981. pap. 8.95 (ISBN 0-9609926-0-X). Sankaty Head.
Macy, Obed. History of Nantucket. 2nd ed. LC 72-140546. Repr. of 1880 ed. lib. bdg. 15.00x (ISBN 0-678-00832-9). Kelley.
Mooney, Robert F. & Sigourney, Andre R. The Nantucket Way. LC 78-20086. (Illus.). 1980. 12.95 (ISBN 0-385-14372-9). Doubleday.
Seeler, Katherine & Seeler, Edgar. Nantucket Lightship Baskets. 2nd ed. LC 76-53378. (Illus.). 1976. 10.00 (ISBN 0-9600596-2-8); 5 or more 6.00 (ISBN 0-686-77313-6). Deermouse.
Stackpole, Edouard A. & Summerfield, Melvin B. Nantucket Doorways: Thresholds to the Past. (Illus.). 1974. 8.95 (ISBN 0-8038-5038-7). Hastings.
Starbuck, Alexander. The History of Nantucket: County, Island & Town. LC 69-13507. (Illus.). 1969. 29.50 (ISBN 0-8048-0250-5). C E Tuttle.
Sterling, Dorothy. The Outer Lands: A Natural History Guide to Cape Cod, Martha's Vineyard, Nantucket, Block Island, & Long Island. (Illus.). 1978. 10.95 (ISBN 0-393-06438-7); pap. 5.95 (ISBN 0-393-06441-7). Norton.
Stevens, William O. Nantucket: The Far-Away Island. LC 81-3297. 1981. pap. 4.95 (ISBN 0-396-07947-4). Dodd.
Wetherbee, David K., et al. Time-Lapse Ecology, Muskegat Island, Nantucket, Massachusetts. 1972. pap. text ed. 14.50x (ISBN 0-8422-0185-8). Irvington.
Whipple, A. B. Vintage Nantucket. LC 78-7107. (Illus.). 1978. 8.95 (ISBN 0-396-07517-7). Dodd.
NANTUCKET, MASSACHUSETTS–HISTORY
Brenizer, Meredith M. & Curtis, Mary T., eds. The First Nantucket Tea Party. LC 78-62476. (Illus.). 1978. pap. 3.95 (ISBN 0-88492-022-4). W S Sullwold.
Hinchman, Lydia S., compiled by. The Early Settlers of Nantucket: Sixteen Fifty-Nine to Eighteen Fifty. LC 80-54078. (Illus.). 346p. 1981. Repr. of 1926 ed. 35.00 (ISBN 0-8048-1354-X). C E Tuttle.
Macy, Obed. History of Nantucket. 2nd ed. LC 72-140546. Repr. of 1880 ed. lib. bdg. 15.00x (ISBN 0-678-00832-9). Kelley.
Williams, Winston. Nantucket: Then and Now. (Illus.). (gr. 7 up). 1977. 5.95 (ISBN 0-396-07411-1). Dodd.
NAOROJI, DADABHAI, 1825-1917
Naoroji, Dadabhai. Dadabhai Naoroji Correspondence, 2 pts, Vol. 2. Patwardhan, R. P., ed. 1978. 37.50x ea. Pt. 1 (ISBN 0-8364-0219-7). Pt. 2 (ISBN 0-8364-0220-0). South Asia Bks.
NAPLES
Bernier, Olivier. Pleasure & Privilege: Life in France, Naples & America. LC 79-6174. (Illus.). 304p. 1981. 14.95 (ISBN 0-385-15780-0). Doubleday.
Bonechi, Edoardo. How to Visit the Beauties of Naples. (Illus.). 142p. 1973. pap. 6.00x (ISBN 0-8002-0830-7). Intl Pubns Serv.
Clay, Edith. Lady Blessington at Naples. 1979. 12.50 (ISBN 0-241-89975-3, Pub. by Hamish Hamilton England). David & Charles.
Davis, John A. Merchants, Monopolists, & Contractors: A Study of Economic Activity & Society in Bourbon Naples 1815-1860. Bruchey, Stuart, ed. LC 80-2802. (Dissertations in European Economic History II). (Illus.). 1981. lib. bdg. 32.00x (ISBN 0-405-13986-1). Arno.
De Franciscis, Alfonso, et al, eds. Naples & Its Environs: Italian Regions. (Illus.). 1979. 100.00 (ISBN 0-8478-5236-9). Rizzoli Intl.
Fernandez, Dominique. The Mother Sea: Travels in South Italy, Sardinia & Sicily. Callum, Michael, tr. 236p. 1967. 5.95 (ISBN 0-8090-7100-2). Hill & Wang.
--Porporino, or the Secrets of Naples. 1977. 10.95 (ISBN 0-688-03058-0). Morrow.
Lewis, Norman. Naples '44. LC 78-13060. 1979. 8.95 (ISBN 0-394-50354-6). Pantheon.
Menen, Aubrey. Four Days of Naples. 320p. 1980. pap. 2.50 (ISBN 0-345-28906-4). Ballantine.
Pereira, Anthony. Naples, Pompeii & Southern Italy. 1977. 24.00 (ISBN 0-7134-0815-4, Pub. by Batsford England). David & Charles.
Rea, Domenico. All Naples & Pompeii. (Italia Artistica Ser). (Illus.). 64p. 1972. 7.50x (ISBN 0-8002-0653-3). Intl Pubns Serv.
Stendhal. Rome, Naples et Florence, 3 vols. facsimile ed. Set. 100.00 (ISBN 0-686-55081-1). French & Eur.
Unterkircher, F., intro. by. King Rene's Book of Love. LC 75-7957. (Illus.). 48p. 1975. slipcase 17.50 (ISBN 0-8076-0788-6). Braziller.
Wrubel, Arno. Gulf of Naples. (Panorama Bks.). (Illus., Fr.). 1962. 3.95 (ISBN 0-685-11228-4). French & Eur.
NAPLES (KINGDOM)
Croce, Benedetto. The History of the Kingdom of Naples. Hughes, H. Stuart, ed. Frenaye, Frances, tr. from It. LC 71-113253. (Classic European Historians Ser). xxiv, 260p. 1972. pap. 2.95 (ISBN 0-226-12081-3, P377, Phoen). U of Chicago Pr.
--History of the Kingdom of Naples. LC 71-113253. 1970. 11.00x (ISBN 0-226-12080-5). U of Chicago Pr.
Johnston, Robert M. The Napoleonic Empire in Southern Italy & the Rise of the Secret Societies, 2 vols. LC 77-156852. (Europe 1815-1945 Ser). 640p. 1973. Repr. of 1904 ed. lib. bdg. 49.50 (ISBN 0-306-70558-3). Da Capo.
Jordan, Edouard. Origines De la Domination Angevine En Italie, 2 Vols. 1967. Repr. of 1909 ed. 50.50 (ISBN 0-8337-1875-4). B Franklin.
Romani, George T. The Neopolitan Revolution of Eighteen Twenty to Eighteen Twenty-One. LC 78-6235. (Illus.). 1978. Repr. of 1950 ed. lib. bdg. 18.75x (ISBN 0-313-20395-4, RONE). Greenwood.
Ryder, Alan. The Kingdom of Naples Under Alfonso the Magnanimous: The Making of a Modern State. 1976. 67.50x (ISBN 0-19-822535-0). Oxford U Pr.
NAPOLEON 1ST, EMPEROR OF THE FRENCH, 1769-1821
Adams, Henry. Historical Essays. Repr. of 1891 ed. 39.50 (ISBN 3-4870-4645-8). Adler.
Alger, John G. Napoleon's British Visitors & Captives, 1801-1815. LC 71-113541. Repr. of 1904 ed. 19.50 (ISBN 0-404-00324-9). AMS Pr.
Arnold, Eric A. Fouche, Napoleon, & the General Police. LC 79-62894. 1979. pap. text ed. 9.50 (ISBN 0-8191-0716-6). U Pr of Amer.
Ballard, Colin R. Napoleon: An Outline. facsimile ed. LC 76-179503. (Select Bibliographies Reprint Ser). Repr. of 1924 ed. 19.00 (ISBN 0-8369-6632-5). Arno.
Balmain, Aleksandr. Napoleon in Captivity: Reports of Count Balmain Russian Commissioner on the Island of St. Helena 1816-1820. facsimile ed. Park, Julian, ed. & tr. LC 72-160955. (Select Bibliographies Reprint Ser). Repr. of 1927 ed. 21.00 (ISBN 0-8369-5822-5). Arno.
Barnett, Correlli. Bonaparte. (Illus.). 224p. 1978. 19.95 (ISBN 0-8090-3049-7). Hill & Wang.
Burton, June. Napoleon & Clio: Historical Writing, Teaching, & Thinking During the First Empire. LC 77-88659. 1979. 11.95 (ISBN 0-89089-077-3). Carolina Acad Pr.
Butterfield, Herbert. Napoleon. 1962. pap. 1.95 (ISBN 0-02-001870-3, Collier). Macmillan.
--The Peace Tactics of Napoleon, 1806-1808. LC 70-159170. viii, 395p. 1972. Repr. of 1929 ed. lib. bdg. 22.50x (ISBN 0-374-91130-4). Octagon.
Caulaincourt, Armand. No Peace with Napoleon. Hanoteau, Jean, ed. Libaire, George, tr. LC 74-29631. 286p. 1975. Repr. of 1936 ed. lib. bdg. 16.00x (ISBN 0-8371-7984-X, CANP). Greenwood.
Caulaincourt, Armand A. With Napolean in Russia: The Memoirs of General De Caulaincourt, Duke of Vicenza. Hanoteau, Jean & Libaire, George, eds. LC 75-40914. 1976. Repr. of 1935 ed. lib. bdg. 31.50x (ISBN 0-8371-8689-7, CAWN). Greenwood.
Chaplin, Arnold. The Illness & Death of Napoleon Bonaparte: A Medical Criticism. 1977. lib. bdg. 59.95 (ISBN 0-8490-2033-6). Gordon Pr.
Charles-Roux, Francois. Bonaparte: Governor of Egypt. Dickes, E. W., tr. LC 80-1932. (Illus., Fr.). Repr. of 1937 ed. 47.50 (ISBN 0-404-18958-X). AMS Pr.
Chateaubriand, Rene de. Napoleon. 1969. 7.95 (ISBN 0-686-54372-6). French & Eur.
Collins, Irene. Napoleon & His Parliaments, Eighteen Hundred to Eighteen Fifteen. 1979. 22.50x (ISBN 0-312-55892-9). St Martin.
Connelly, Owen. The Epoch of Napoleon. LC 77-13473. 208p. 1978. pap. text ed. 6.25 (ISBN 0-88275-622-2). Krieger.
Constant, Benjamin. Memoires Sur les Cent Jours. 348p. 14.95 (ISBN 0-686-54614-8). French & Eur.
Currie, Laurence. The Baton in the Knapsack. 224p. 1980. Repr. lib. bdg. 25.00 (ISBN 0-8495-0850-9). Arden Lib.
Delery, Simone De La Souchere. Napoleon's Soldiers in America. LC 74-186543. (Illus.). 224p. 1972. 10.00 (ISBN 0-911116-58-3). Pelican.
Deutsch, Harold C. The Genesis of Napoleonic Imperialism. LC 75-25811. (Perspectives in European Hist. Ser.: No. 4). 460p. Repr. of 1938 ed. lib. bdg. 25.00x (ISBN 0-87991-611-7). Porcupine Pr.

Dodge, Theodore A. Napoleon: A History of the Art of War, 4 Vols. Repr. of 1907 ed. Set. 140.00 (ISBN 0-404-02160-3); 35.00 ea. Vol. 1 (ISBN 0-404-02161-1). Vol. 2 (ISBN 0-404-02162-X). Vol. 3 (ISBN 0-404-02163-8). Vol. 4 (ISBN 0-404-02164-6). AMS Pr.

Dowd, D. L. Napoleon: Was He the Heir of the Revolution? 60p. 1957. pap. 1.50 (ISBN 0-03-008285-4). Krieger.

Draper, John E., ed. Napoleon's Thoughts on History, Politics & the Management of Men. (Illus.). 1980. deluxe ed. 39.75 (ISBN 0-89266-232-8). Am Classical Coll Pr.

Dunn-Pattison, R. P. Napoleon's Marshals. (Illus.). 373p. 1977. Repr. of 1909 ed. 26.50x (ISBN 0-8476-6060-5). Rowman.

Durant, Will & Durant, Ariel. The Age of Napoleon. LC 75-6888. (Illus.). 1975. 24.95 (ISBN 0-671-21988-X). S&S.

Ebeyer, Paul P. Revelations Concerning Napoleon's Escape from St. Helena. 1947. 10.00 (ISBN 0-911116-75-3). Pelican.

Emerson, R. W. Napoleon: Or, the Man of the World. Davidson, F., ed. 1947. pap. 5.00 (ISBN 0-527-27150-0). Kraus Repr.

Esposito, Vincent J. & Elting, John R. Military History & Atlas of the Napoleonic Wars. LC 77-14708. Repr. of 1968 ed. 49.50 (ISBN 0-404-16950-3). AMS Pr.

Fisher, Herbert. Napoleon. 1978. Repr. of 1913 ed. lib. bdg. 12.50 (ISBN 0-8414-4310-6). Folcroft.

Gray, Daniel S. In the Words of Napoleon. LC 77-71468. 1977. pap. 8.50x (ISBN 0-916624-07-2). TSU Pr.

Hazen, Charles D. The French Revolution & Napoleon. 1979. Repr. of 1917 ed. lib. bdg. 25.00 (ISBN 0-8482-4482-6). Norwood Edns.

Holtman, Robert B. Napoleonic Propaganda. Repr. of 1950 ed. lib. bdg. 15.00 (ISBN 0-8371-2140-X, HONA). Greenwood.

Horne, Alistair. Napoleon: Master of Europe. LC 79-1981. (Illus.). 1979. 17.95 (ISBN 0-688-03500-0). Morrow.

Hugo, V. Napoleon the Little. 75.00 (ISBN 0-8490-0705-4). Gordon Pr.

Jaunez-Sponville, Pierre-Ignace & Bugnet, Nicolas. La Philosophie de Ruravebohni, 2 vols. (Utopias in the Enlightenment Ser.). 575p. (Fr.). 1974. Repr. of 1809 ed. Set. lib. bdg. 154.00x (ISBN 0-8287-0462-7). Clearwater Pub.

Jones, R. Ben. Napoleon: Man & Myth. LC 78-15801. 1977. text ed. 17.50x (ISBN 0-8419-0440-5); pap. text ed. 8.75x (ISBN 0-8419-6204-9). Holmes & Meier.

Jonge, Alex De, tr. from Fr. Napoleon's Last Will & Testament. LC 77-6665. (Illus.). 1977. pap. 4.95 (ISBN 0-448-22186-1). Paddington.

Kemble, James. Saint Helena During Napoleon's Exile: Gorrequer's Diary. (Illus.). 1969. 19.50 (ISBN 0-208-00981-7, Archon). Shoe String.

Kircheisen, F. M. Napoleon. St. Lawrence, Henry, tr. LC 72-8400. (Select Bibliographies Reprint Ser). 1972. Repr. of 1932 ed. 58.00 (ISBN 0-8369-6981-2). Arno.

Korngold, Ralph. The Last Years of Napoleon. LC 74-12578. (Illus.). 429p. 1974. Repr. of 1959 ed. lib. bdg. 24.50x (ISBN 0-8371-7725-1, KONA). Greenwood.

Lacey, Robert. The Rise of Napoleon. (Jackdaw Ser: No. 71). 1971. 6.95 (ISBN 0-670-59910-7, Grossman). Viking Pr.

Lacour-Gayet, G. Napoleon: Sa Vie Son Oeuvre, Son Temps. 1977. Repr. of 1921 ed. lib. bdg. 75.00 (ISBN 0-8414-5847-2). Folcroft.

Lanfrey, Pierre. History of Napoleon First, 4 Vols. 2nd ed. LC 77-171654. Repr. of 1886 ed. Set. 130.00 (ISBN 0-404-07340-9); 32.50 ea. Vol. 1 (ISBN 0-404-07341-7). Vol. 2 (ISBN 0-404-07342-5). Vol. 3 (ISBN 0-404-07343-3). Vol. 4 (ISBN 0-404-07344-1). AMS Pr.

Larned, Josephus N. Study of Greatness in Men. facsimile ed. LC 73-156677. (Essay Index Reprint Ser). Repr. of 1911 ed. 18.00 (ISBN 0-8369-2557-2). Arno.

Lefebvre, Georges. Napoleon: From Tilsit to Waterloo, 1807-1815. Anderson, J. E., tr. LC 74-79193. 414p. 1969. 20.00x (ISBN 0-231-03313-3). Columbia U Pr.

Lewis, Michael. Napolean & His British Captives. Date not set. 19.95x (ISBN 0-392-13304-0, SpS). Sportshelf.

Liddell Hart, Basil H. The Ghost of Napoleon. LC 79-23039. 1980. Repr. of 1933 ed. lib. bdg. 19.75x (ISBN 0-313-22172-3, LHGN). Greenwood.

Ludwig, Emil. Napoleon. 1979. Repr. of 1926 ed. lib. bdg. 30.00 (ISBN 0-8495-4016-X). Arden Lib.

Markham, Felix. Napoleon & the Awakening of Europe. 1965. pap. 2.95 (ISBN 0-02-034510-0, Collier). Macmillan.

Markham, Felix M. Napoleon. (Illus.). pap. 2.25 (ISBN 0-451-61725-8, ME1725, Ment). NAL.

--Napoleon & the Awakening of Europe. (Men & Their Times Ser). 1972. Repr. of 1954 ed. 6.00x (ISBN 0-340-08366-2). Verry.

Martineau, Gilbert. Napoleon's Last Journey. Partridge, Frances, tr. (Illus.). 1977. 15.00 (ISBN 0-7195-3293-0). Transatlantic.

Melvin, Frank E. Napoleon's Navigation System. LC 79-135721. Repr. of 1919 ed. 26.75 (ISBN 0-404-04288-0). AMS Pr.

Morton, J. B. Brumaire: The Rise of Bonaparte. (Select Bibliographies Reprint Ser.). Repr. of 1948 ed. 20.75 (ISBN 0-518-19075-7). Arno.

Mowat, Robert B. Diplomacy of Napoleon. LC 76-139931. 1971. Repr. of 1924 ed. 14.50 (ISBN 0-8462-1539-X). Russell.

Napoleon I. Correspondance De Napoleon Ier Publiee Par Ordre De L'empereur Napoleon Iii, 32 vols. Incl. Set. 1280.00 (ISBN 0-404-07400-6); 40.00 ea.; Vol. 1. (ISBN 0-404-07401-4); Vol. 2. (ISBN 0-404-07402-2); Vol. 3. (ISBN 0-404-07403-0); Vol. 4. (ISBN 0-404-07404-9); Vol. 5. (ISBN 0-404-07405-7); Vol. 6. (ISBN 0-404-07406-5); Vol. 7. (ISBN 0-404-07407-3); Vol. 8. (ISBN 0-404-07408-1); (ISBN 0-404-07409-X, VOL. 9); Vol. 10. (ISBN 0-404-07410-3); Vol. 11. (ISBN 0-404-07411-1); Vol. 12. (ISBN 0-404-07412-X); Vol. 13. (ISBN 0-404-07413-8); Vol. 14. (ISBN 0-404-07414-6); Vol. 15. (ISBN 0-404-07415-4); Vol. 16. (ISBN 0-404-07416-2); Vol. 17. (ISBN 0-404-07417-0); Vol. 18. (ISBN 0-404-07418-9); Vol. 19. (ISBN 0-404-07419-7); Vol. 20. (ISBN 0-404-07420-0); Vol. 21. (ISBN 0-404-07421-9); Vol. 22. (ISBN 0-404-07422-7); Vol. 23. (ISBN 0-404-07423-5); Vol. 24. (ISBN 0-404-07424-3); Vol. 25. (ISBN 0-404-07425-1). Repr. of 1870 ed. Vol. 26. (ISBN 0-404-07426-X); Vol. 27. (ISBN 0-404-07427-8); Vol. 28. (ISBN 0-404-07428-6); Vol. 29. (ISBN 0-404-07429-4); Vol. 30. (ISBN 0-404-07430-8); Vol. 31. (ISBN 0-404-07431-6); Vol. 32. (ISBN 0-404-07432-4). AMS Pr.

Niven, Alexander C. Napoleon & Alexander I: A Study in Franco-Russian Relations, 1807-1812. LC 78-60628. 1978. pap. text ed. 6.50 (ISBN 0-8191-0561-9). U Pr of Amer.

Norman, Barbara. Napoleon & Talleyrand: The Last Two Weeks. LC 75-11823. (Illus.). 256p. 1976. 35.00 (ISBN 0-8128-1830-X). Stein & Day.

O'Meara, Barry E. Napoleon in Exile, 2 Vols. LC 74-106520. Repr. of 1853 ed. Set. 47.50 (ISBN 0-404-00610-8). Vol. 1 (ISBN 0-404-00611-6). Vol. 2 (ISBN 0-404-00612-4). AMS Pr.

Pinkney, David H., ed. Napoleon: Historical Enigma. LC 77-76609. (Problems in Civilization Ser). 1978. pap. text ed. 3.95x (ISBN 0-88273-403-2). Forum Pr MO.

Ragsdale, Hugh. Detente in the Napoleonic Era: Bonaparte & the Russians. LC 79-28494. (Illus.). 196p. 1980. 17.50x (ISBN 0-7006-0201-1). Regents Pr KS.

Roseberry, Lord. Napoleon the Last Phase. 1900. Repr. 20.00 (ISBN 0-685-43305-6). Norwood Edns.

Saunders, Edith. Hundred Days. (Illus.). 1964. 6.00x (ISBN 0-393-07332-7). Norton.

Shulim, Joseph I. Old Dominion & Napoleon Bonaparte. LC 68-59263. (Columbia University. Studies in the Social Sciences: No. 572). Repr. of 1952 ed. 18.50 (ISBN 0-404-51572-X). AMS Pr.

Sloane, William M. The Life of Napoleon Bonaparte, 4 vols. 1980. Repr. of 1910 ed. Set. lib. bdg. 125.00 (ISBN 0-8492-8128-8). R West.

--Life of Napoleon Bonaparte, 4 Vols. (Illus.). Repr. of 1910 ed. Set. 130.00 (ISBN 0-404-06100-1); 32.50 ea. Vol. 1 (ISBN 0-404-06101-X). Vol. 2 (ISBN 0-404-06102-8). Vol. 3 (ISBN 0-404-06103-6). Vol. 4 (ISBN 0-404-06104-4). AMS Pr.

Stendhal, pseud. A Life of Napoleon. LC 76-13154. 1977. Repr. of 1956 ed. 18.50 (ISBN 0-86527-272-7). Fertig.

Stendhal. Napoleon, 2 vols. Abravanel, Ernest & Del Litto, Victor, eds. (Illus.). 1970. 9.95 ea. French & Eur.

--Napoleon, 2 vols. facsimile ed. Set. 100.00 (ISBN 0-686-55074-9). French & Eur.

Stendhal, pseud. Vie de Napoleon. (Petite Bibliotheque Payot). pap. 5.95 (ISBN 0-685-35023-1). French & Eur.

Sutherland, Christine. Maria Walewska: Napoleon's Great Love. (Illus.). 1979. 9.95 (ISBN 0-670-28473-4, The Vendome Pr). Viking Pr.

Tames, Richard. Napoleon. Yapp, Malcolm & Killingray, Margaret, eds. (World History Ser.). (Illus.). (gr. 10). 1980. Repr. of 1977 ed. lib. bdg. 5.95 (ISBN 0-89908-044-8); pap. text ed. 1.95 (ISBN 0-89908-019-7). Greenhaven.

Tarle, Eugene. Napoleon's Invasion of Russia in 1812. LC 77-120670. 1970. Repr. lib. bdg. 24.00x (ISBN 0-374-97758-5). Octagon.

Whitcomb, Edward A. Napoleon's Diplomatic Service. LC 78-74846. (Illus.). 1979. 14.75 (ISBN 0-8223-0421-X). Duke.

Wilson, R. McNair. Napoleon the Man, 2 vols. lib. bdg. 250.00 (ISBN 0-87968-357-0). Gordon Pr.

--Napoleon's Love Story. 75.00 (ISBN 0-8490-0706-2). Gordon Pr.

--Napoleon's Mother. 75.00 (ISBN 0-8490-0707-0). Gordon Pr.

Wyndham, Roger P. The Secret Love Story of Napoleon & Madame Walewska. (An Essential Knowledge Library Bk). 1979. 24.00 (ISBN 0-89266-169-0). Am Classical Coll Pr.

Zeldin, Theodore. Political System of Napoleon 3rd. (Illus.). 1971. pap. 4.95x (ISBN 0-393-00580-1, Norton Lib). Norton.

NAPOLEON 1ST, EMPEROR OF THE FRENCH, 1769-1821–BIBLIOGRAPHY

Horward, Donald D. The French Revolution & Napoleon Collection at Florida State University: A Bibliographical Guide. LC 72-89895. 450p. 1972. 12.50 (ISBN 0-686-02405-2). Friends Fla St.

Kircheisen, Friederich M. Bibliographie Du Temps De Napoleon Comprenant L'Histoire Des Etats-Unis, 2 vols in 1. LC 68-57910. (Bibliography & Reference Ser.: No. 236). (Fr). 1968. Repr. of 1908 ed. 40.50 (ISBN 0-8337-1928-9). B Franklin.

Sloane, William M. Life of Napoleon Bonaparte, 4 Vols. (Illus.). Repr. of 1910 ed. Set. 130.00 (ISBN 0-404-06100-1); 32.50 ea. Vol. 1 (ISBN 0-404-06101-X). Vol. 2 (ISBN 0-404-06102-8). Vol. 3 (ISBN 0-404-06103-6). Vol. 4 (ISBN 0-404-06104-4). AMS Pr.

NAPOLEON 1ST, EMPEROR OF THE FRENCH, 1769-1821–CAMPAIGNS

see also Austerlitz, Battle of, 1805; Waterloo, Battle of, 1815

Bourgogne. The Memoirs of Sergeant Bourgogne: 1812-1813. LC 78-72010. (Illus.). 1979. 14.95 (ISBN 0-88254-474-8). Hippocrene Bks.

Chandler, David. The Campaigns of Napoleon: The Mind & Method of History's Greatest Soldier. 1216p. 1973. 35.00 (ISBN 0-02-523660-1). Macmillan.

Clausewitz, Karl Von. The Campaign of Eighteen Hundred & Twelve in Russia. LC 79-84266. (Illus.). 1977. Repr. of 1843 ed. lib. bdg. 25.00x (ISBN 0-8371-5004-3, CLCA). Greenwood.

Delderfield, R. F. Imperial Sunset. LC 79-31696. (Illus.). 320p. 1980. pap. 6.95 (ISBN 0-8128-6056-X). Stein & Day.

Denon, Vivant. Travels in Upper & Lower Egypt, 3 vols. in 1. LC 73-6275. (The Middle East Ser.). Repr. of 1803 ed. 65.00 (ISBN 0-405-05331-2). Arno.

Ellis, Geoffrey. Napoleon's Continental Blockade: The Case of Alsace. (Oxford Historical Monographs). (Illus.). 368p. 1981. 49.95 (ISBN 0-19-821881-8). Oxford U Pr.

Glover, Michael. The Napoleonic Wars: An Illustrated History 1792-1815. LC 78-74016. (Illus.). 1979. 22.50 (ISBN 0-88254-473-X). Hippocrene Bks.

Lacey, Robert. Retreat from Moscow 1812. (Jackdaw Ser: No. 73). 1971. 6.95 (ISBN 0-670-59566-7, Grossman). Viking Pr.

Lefebvre, Georges. Napoleon: From Eighteen Brumaire to Tilsit, 1799-1807. Stockhold, Henry F., tr. LC 68-29160. 337p. 1969. 20.00x (ISBN 0-231-02558-0). Columbia U Pr.

Petre, F. Loraine. Napoleon at Bay, 1814. LC 77-77986. 1978. 14.95 (ISBN 0-88254-447-0). Hippocrene Bks.

--Napoleon's Conquest of Prussia, 1806. LC 77-72679. 1977. 14.95 (ISBN 0-88254-435-7). Hippocrene Bks.

--Napoleon's Last Campaign in Germany, 1813. LC 74-78176. (Illus.). 1976. 14.95 (ISBN 0-88254-264-8). Hippocrene Bks.

Segur, Philippe P. Napoleon's Russian Campaign. Townsend, J. David, tr. from Fr. LC 75-27657. (Illus.). 306p. 1976. Repr. of 1958 ed. lib. bdg. 20.75 (ISBN 0-8371-8443-6, SENR). Greenwood.

Thornton, Michael J. Napoleon After Waterloo: England & the St. Helena Decision. LC 68-26782. 1968. 10.00x (ISBN 0-8047-0672-7). Stanford U Pr.

Von Clausewitz, Carl. Campaign of Eighteen Hundred & Twelve in Russia. (Russian Ser.: Vol. 26). 1843. 15.00 (ISBN 0-87569-014-9). Academic Intl.

Warner, Richard. Napoleon's Enemies. (Illus.). 1977. 14.95 (ISBN 0-85045-172-8). Hippocrene Bks.

NAPOLEON 1ST, EMPEROR OF THE FRENCH, 1769-1821–CARTOONS, SATIRE, ETC.

Ashton, John. English Caricature & Satire on Napoleon 1st. LC 68-25953. (Illus.). 1968. Repr. of 1888 ed. 22.00 (ISBN 0-405-08222-3, Pub. by Blom). Arno.

--English Caricature & Satire on Napoleon 1st. LC 67-24349. (Social History Reference Ser). 1968. Repr. of 1888 ed. 22.00 (ISBN 0-8103-3248-5). Gale.

Bainville, Jacques. Napoleon. Miles, Hamish, tr. LC 74-112794. 1970. Repr. of 1932 ed. 15.00 (ISBN 0-8046-1061-4). Kennikat.

NAPOLEON 1ST, EMPEROR OF THE FRENCH, 1769-1821–FICTION

Evans, Henry. The Napoleon Myth. 59.95 (ISBN 0-8490-0704-6). Gordon Pr.

Tolstoy, Leo. War & Peace. 1931. 5.95 (ISBN 0-394-60701-5, G1). Modern Lib.

--War & Peace. Dunnigan, Ann, tr. (Orig.). 1968. pap. 3.95 (ISBN 0-451-51513-7, CE1513, Sig Classics). NAL.

--War & Peace. 14.95 (ISBN 0-19-250898-9). Oxford U Pr.

--War & Peace. abr ed. Simmons, Ernest J., ed. (Orig.). (gr. 10 up). pap. 3.95 (ISBN 0-671-41893-9). WSP.

NAPOLEON 1ST, EMPEROR OF THE FRENCH, 1769-1821–JUVENILE LITERATURE

Robbins, Ruth. L' Empereur et le Tambour. LC 62-15686. (Illus., Fr.). (gr. 2-6). 4.95 (ISBN 0-87466-076-9). Parnassus.

--The Emperor & the Drummer Boy. (Illus.). (gr. 2-6). 1962. 4.95 (ISBN 0-87466-043-2); PLB 5.38 (ISBN 0-87466-011-4). Parnassus.

Wheeler, Thomas G. Fanfare for the Stalwart. LC 67-22813. (gr. 8 up). 1967. 9.95 (ISBN 0-87599-139-4). S G Phillips.

NAPOLEON 1ST, EMPEROR OF THE FRENCH, 1769-1821–SATIRE

see Napoleon 1st, Emperor of the French, 1769-1821–Cartoons, Satire, etc.

NAPOLEON 2ND

see Bonaparte, Francois Charles Joseph, Herzog Von Reichstadt, Called Napoleon 2nd, 1811-1832

NAPOLEON 3RD, EMPEROR OF THE FRENCH, 1808-1873

Bainville, Jacques. Napoleon. Miles, Hamish, tr. LC 74-112794. 1970. Repr. of 1932 ed. 15.00 (ISBN 0-8046-1061-4). Kennikat.

Bush, John W. Venetia Redeemed: Franco-Italian Relations, 1864-1866. LC 67-26918. 1967. 12.00x (ISBN 0-8156-2111-6). Syracuse U Pr.

Cadogan, Edward. Makers of Modern History. LC 75-112797. 1970. Repr. of 1905 ed. 10.50 (ISBN 0-8046-1064-9). Kennikat.

Corley, Thomas A. Democratic Despot: A Life a Napoleon III. LC 74-8651. (Illus.). 402p. 1974. Repr. of 1961 ed. lib. bdg. 20.75x (ISBN 0-8371-7587-9, CODC). Greenwood.

Forbes, Archibald. Life of Napoleon the Third. LC 70-112802. 1970. Repr. of 1898 ed. 14.50 (ISBN 0-8046-1068-1). Kennikat.

Gooch, Brison D., ed. Napoleon III - Man of Destiny: Enlightened Statesman or Proto-Fascist? LC 75-12666. (European Problem Studies). 128p. 1976. pap. 5.50 (ISBN 0-88275-323-1). Krieger.

Gooch, George P. The Second Empire. LC 75-1151. (Illus.). 324p. 1975. Repr. of 1960 ed. lib. bdg. 19.75x (ISBN 0-8371-7985-8, GOSE). Greenwood.

Guerard, Albert L. Napolean Third: A Great Life in Brief. LC 78-13974. 1979. Repr. of 1966 ed. lib. bdg. 17.00x (ISBN 0-313-21062-4, GUNA). Greenwood.

Hallberg, Charles W. Franz Joseph & Napoleon Third, 1852-1864: A Study of Austro-French Relations. 1972. lib. bdg. 22.50x (ISBN 0-374-93380-4). Octagon.

Hugo, Victor. Les Chatiments. 3.95 (ISBN 0-686-54061-1). French & Eur.

Mange, Alyce E. The Near Eastern Policy of the Emperor Napoleon III. LC 74-12762. (Illinois Studies in the Social Sciences Ser). 150p. 1975. Repr. of 1940 ed. lib. bdg. 15.00 (ISBN 0-8371-7742-1, MAEN). Greenwood.

Marx, Karl. The Eighteenth Brumaire of Louis Bonaparte. 132p. 1972. pap. 0.75 (ISBN 0-8285-0025-8, Pub. by Progress Pubs Russia). Imported Pubns.

--Eighteenth Brumaire of Louis Bonaparte. 1978. pap. 1.95 (ISBN 0-8351-0578-4). China Bks.

Oncken, Hermann. Napoleon Third & the Rhine: The Origin of the War of 1870-1871. Zeydel, Edwin H., tr. LC 66-24743. 1967. Repr. of 1928 ed. 8.00 (ISBN 0-8462-0966-7). Russell.

Palm, Franklin C. England & Napoleon Three, a Study of the Rise of a Utopian Dictator. (Perspectives in European History Ser: No. 23). (Illus.). Repr. of 1948 ed. lib. bdg. 15.00x (ISBN 0-87991-630-3). Porcupine Pr.

Pottinger, Evelyn A. Napoleon Third & the German Crisis, 1865-1866. LC 66-18253. (Historical Studies: No. 75). 1966. 12.50x (ISBN 0-674-60050-9). Harvard U Pr.

Ridley, Jasper. Napoleon III & Eugenie. (Illus.). 784p. 1980. 25.00 (ISBN 0-670-50428-9). Viking Pr.

Rothney, John. Bonapartism After Sedan. LC 68-9752. (Illus.). 360p. 1969. 22.50x (ISBN 0-8014-0473-8). Cornell U Pr.

Sencourt, Robert. Napoleon III: The Modern Emperor. LC 71-38366. (Select Bibliographies Reprint Ser.). Repr. of 1933 ed. 22.00 (ISBN 0-8369-6783-6). Arno.

Simpson, Frederick A. Louis Napoleon & the Recovery of France. LC 75-8490. (Illus.). 400p. 1975. Repr. of 1951 ed. lib. bdg. 21.75x (ISBN 0-8371-8153-4, SILN). Greenwood.

Thompson, James M. Louis Napoleon & the Second Empire. (Illus.). 1967. pap. 2.95 (ISBN 0-393-00403-1, Norton Lib). Norton.
Williams, Roger L. Mortal Napoleon Third. LC 75-155005. (Illus.). 1971. 16.00x (ISBN 0-691-05192-5). Princeton U Pr.

NAPOLEON, JOSEPH CHARLES PAUL BONAPARTE, PRINCE, 1822-1891

Ferri-Pisani, Camille F. Prince Napoleon in America, 1861: Letters from His Aide-De-Camp. Joyaux, Georges J., tr. from Fr. LC 72-85279. (Illus.). 1973. Repr. of 1959 ed. 14.50 (ISBN 0-8046-1695-7). Kennikat.
Henderson, Ernest F. Blucher & the Uprising of Prussia Against Napoleon: 1806-15. LC 73-14448. (Heroes of the Nations Series). (Illus.). Repr. of 1911 ed. 30.00 (ISBN 0-404-58266-4). AMS Pr.
Morris, William O. Napoleon. LC 73-14458. (Heroes of the Nations Series). Repr. of 1893 ed. 30.00 (ISBN 0-404-58276-1). AMS Pr.

NAPOLEON, LOUIS, 1914-

Simpson, F. A. Rise of Louis Napoleon. (Illus.). 400p. 1968. Repr. of 1925 ed. 24.00x (ISBN 0-7146-1359-2, F Cass Co). Biblio Dist.
Williams, Roger. Manners & Murders in the World of Louis-Napoleon. LC 75-15938. (Illus.). 220p. 1975. 12.50 (ISBN 0-295-95431-0). U of Wash Pr.

NAPOLEON, CONTINENTAL SYSTEM OF

see Continental System of Napoleon

NAPOLEONIC WARS

see Europe–History–1789-1815; France–History–Revolution, 1789-1799; France–History–Consulate and Empire, 1799-1815; Peninsular War, 1807-1814

NARAYAN, R. K., 1907-

Holmstrom, Lakshmi. The Novels of R. K. Narayan. (Writers Workshop Greybird Ser.). 130p. 1975. 15.00 (ISBN 0-88253-584-6); pap. text ed. 8.00 (ISBN 0-88253-583-8). Ind-US Inc.

NARBONNE–HISTORY

Emery, Richard W. Heresy & Inquisition in Narbonne. LC 75-166031. (Columbia University Studies in the Social Sciences: No. 480). 17.50 (ISBN 0-404-51480-4). AMS Pr.

NARCISSISM

Chessick, Richard. Intensive Psychotherapy of the Borderline Patient. LC 76-22867. 1977. 25.00x (ISBN 0-87668-254-9, 25494). Aronson.
Goldberg, Carl. In Defense of Narcissism: The Creative Self in Search of Meaning. 224p. 1980. text ed. 21.95x (ISBN 0-89876-005-4). Gardner Pr.
Grunberger, Bela. Narcissism: Psychoanalytic Essays. Diamanti, Joyce, tr. from Fr. LC 77-92104. 1979. text ed. 22.50 (ISBN 0-8236-3491-4). Intl Univs Pr.
Hutcheon, Linda. Narcissistic Narrative: The Metafictional Paradox, Vol. 5. Dimic, Milan V., ed. (Library of the Canadian Review of Comparative Literature). 168p. 1980. text ed. 10.75 (ISBN 0-88920-102-1, Pub. by Laurier U Pr Canada). Humanities.
Kernberg, Otto. Borderline Conditions & Pathological Narcissism. LC 75-5606. 368p. 1975. 25.00x (ISBN 0-87668-205-0). Aronson.
Kohut, Heinz. The Analysis of Self: A Systematic Approach to the Psychoanalytic Treatment of Narcissistic Personality Disorders. LC 70-143392. (Psychoanalytic Study of the Child Monographs: No. 4). 1971. text ed. 22.50 (ISBN 0-8236-0145-5). Intl Univs Pr.
Lasch, Christopher. The Culture of Narcissism: American Life in an Age of Diminishing Expectations. 1979. 14.95x (ISBN 0-393-01177-1). Norton.
Mandell, Dale. Early Feminine Development: Current Psychoanalytic Views. 303p. 1981. text ed. 25.00 (ISBN 0-89335-135-0). Spectrum Pub.
Masterson, James F. The Narcissistic & Borderline Disorders: An Integrated Developmental Approach. 250p. 1981. 20.00 (ISBN 0-87630-292-4). Brunner-Mazel.
Mecke, Gunter. Hair, or, the Ligurinus Shock: On a Narcissistic Crisis in Puberty & Its Recurrence in the Man of Fifty. LC 74-82753. 1975. 5.00 (ISBN 0-87212-044-9). Libra.
Nelson, Marie. The Narcissistic Condition: A Fact of Our Lives & Times, Vol. 1. LC 76-20724. (Self in Process Ser.). 1977. text ed. 24.95 (ISBN 0-87705-250-6). Human Sci Pr.
Rochlin, Gregory. Man's Aggression: The Defense of the Self. LC 73-144339. 299p. 1973. 9.95 (ISBN 0-87645-068-0). Gambit.
Rothstein, Arnold. Narcissistic Pursuit of Perfection. 1980. 22.50 (ISBN 0-8236-3493-0). Intl Univs Pr.
Schall, Maxine. Limits: A Search for New Values. Southern, Carol, ed. 352p. 1981. 12.95 (ISBN 0-517-54143-2). Potter.
Spotnitz, Hyman & Meadow, Phyllis W. Treatment of the Narcissistic Neuroses. LC 76-6716. 256p. 1976. 18.00x (ISBN 0-916850-01-3). Ctr Mod Psych Stud.

NARCOTIC ADDICTION

see Narcotic Habit

Bellis, David J. Heroin & Politicians: The Failure of Public Policy to Control Addiction in America. LC 80-21373. (Contributions in Political Science Ser.: No. 58). (Illus.). 256p. 1981. lib. bdg. 27.50 (ISBN 0-313-22557-5, BHP/). Greenwood.

NARCOTIC ADDICTS

see also Narcotics, Control of

Bates, William & Crowther, Betty. Toward a Typology of Opiate Users. 160p. 1974. pap. text ed. 5.50 (ISBN 0-87073-960-3). Schenkman.
Becker, Howard S. Outsiders: Studies in the Sociology of Deviance. LC 63-8413. 1963. 12.95 (ISBN 0-02-902200-2); pap. 3.95 (ISBN 0-02-902140-5). Free Pr.
Bejerot, Nils. Addiction & Society. (Illus.). 272p. 1970. ed. spiral bdg. 27.50photocopy (ISBN 0-398-00126-X). C C Thomas.
Caplovitz, David. The Working Addict. LC 77-94070. 1978. 17.50 (ISBN 0-87332-116-2). M E Sharpe.
Crowley, Aleister. Diary of a Drug Fiend. LC 79-142495. 1981. pap. 5.95 (ISBN 0-87728-146-7). Weiser.
Cuskey, Walter R., et al. Drug-Trip Abroad: American Drug-Refugees in Amsterdam & London. LC 73-182497. (Orig.). 1972. 10.00x (ISBN 0-8122-7653-1); pap. 4.95 (ISBN 0-8122-1041-7, Pa Paperbks). U of Pa Pr.
Franchi, Eda. The Long Road Back. (Orig.). 1975. pap. 1.50 (ISBN 0-451-06360-0, W6360, Sig). NAL.
Macmartin, D. F. Thirty Years in Hell: Or, the Confessions of a Drug Fiend. Grob, Gerald N., ed. LC 80-1256. (Addiction in America Ser.). 1981. Repr. of 1921 ed. lib. bdg. 25.00x (ISBN 0-405-13606-4). Arno.
Maurer, David W. & Vogel, Victor H. Narcotics & Narcotic Addiction. 4th ed. (American Lectures in Public Protection). (Illus.). 496p. 1973. 24.75 (ISBN 0-398-02906-7). C C Thomas.
Plant, Martin A. Drugtakers in an English Town. (Illus.). 1975. 25.00x (ISBN 0-422-74650-9, Pub. by Tavistock England). Methuen Inc.
Platt, Jerome & Labate, Christina. Heroin Addiction: Theory, Research, & Treatment. LC 76-5794. (Personality Processes Ser.). 417p. 1976. 32.95 (ISBN 0-471-69114-3, Pub. by Wiley-Interscience). Wiley.
Pratt, Arthur. How to Help & Understand the Alcoholic or Drug Addict. LC 80-82964. 127p. 1981. lib. bdg. 14.95 (ISBN 0-915216-62-0); pap. 4.95 (ISBN 0-915216-63-9). Love Street.
Rudman, Jack. Addiction Counselor. (Career Examination Ser.: C-2150). (Cloth bdg. avail. on request). 1976. pap. 10.00 (ISBN 0-8373-2150-6). Natl Learning.
--Supervising Addiction Specialist. (Career Examination Ser.: C-1501). (Cloth bdg. avail. on request). pap. 10.00 (ISBN 0-8373-1501-8). Natl Learning.
Schmidt, J. E. Narcotics: Lingo & Lore. 216p. 1959. 7.50 (ISBN 0-398-01671-2). C C Thomas.
Schur, Edwin M. Crimes Without Victims - Deviant Behavior & Public Policy: Abortion, Homosexuality, Drug Addiction. (Orig.). 1965. pap. 3.95 (ISBN 0-13-192930-5, S111, Spec). P-H.
Simmons, Luiz R. & Gold, Martin B., eds. Discrimination & the Addict. LC 72-98048. (International Yearbooks of Drug Addiction & Society: Vol. 1). 320p. 1973. 22.50 (ISBN 0-8039-0203-4). Sage.
Singer, K. The Prognosis of Narcotic Addiction. 1975. 9.95 (ISBN 0-407-00021-6). Butterworth.
Torres, Victor & Wilkerson, Don. Son of Evil Street. LC 73-10828. 1977. pap. 1.95 (ISBN 0-87123-516-1, 200516). Bethany Hse.
Wisnie, H. A. The Impulsive Personality. LC 77-23464. (Illus.). 208p. 1977. 18.95 (ISBN 0-306-30973-4, Plenum Pr). Plenum Pub.

NARCOTIC ADDICTS–REHABILITATION

Brill, Leon. The De-Addiction Process: Studies in the De-Addiction of Confirmed Heroin Addicts. 180p. 1972. 18.75 (ISBN 0-398-02532-0). C C Thomas.
Burns, John. Answer to Addiction. (Rudolf Steiner Publications). 232p. 1980. 7.95x (ISBN 0-8334-0712-0). Multimedia.
Cannon, Sharol. Social Functioning Patterns in Families of Offspring Receiving Treatment for Drug Abuse. LC 75-42602. 1975. 6.95 (ISBN 0-87212-040-6). Libra.
Coombs, Robert H., ed. Junkies & Straights. LC 75-27250. (Illus.). 240p. 1975. 19.95 (ISBN 0-669-00320-4). Lexington Bks.
De Leon, George, ed. Phoenix House: Studies in a Therapeutic Community (1968-1973) 214p. 1974. text ed. 29.75x (ISBN 0-8422-7238-0). Irvington.
Harms, E., ed. Drugs & Youth: The Challenge of Today. 1973. text ed. 21.00 (ISBN 0-08-017063-3). Pergamon.
Marshall, Shelly, ed. Young, Sober, & Free. 1978. 4.95 (ISBN 0-89486-055-0). Hazelden.
Nelkin, Dorothy. Methadone Maintenance: A Technological Fix. LC 72-96071. (Science, Technology & Society Ser). 192p. 1973. pap. 1.95 (ISBN 0-8076-0680-4). Braziller.
Nyswander, Marie. Drug Addict As a Patient. LC 55-12227. 192p. 1956. 29.75 (ISBN 0-8089-0351-9). Grune.
Rehabilitating the Narcotic Addict. LC 68-31058. (Illus.). 1968. Repr. of 1966 ed. 6.95 (ISBN 0-405-00056-1). Arno.
Rudman, Jack. Addiction Specialist. (Career Examination Ser.: C-1075). (Cloth bdg. avail. on request). pap. 10.00 (ISBN 0-8373-1075-X). Natl Learning.
Sells, Saul B. The Effectiveness of Drug Abuse Treatment: Evaluation of Treatment Outcomes for 1972-1973 Darp Admission Cohort, Vol. 5. LC 74-1069. 1976. 25.00 (ISBN 0-88410-039-1). Ballinger Pub.
Turner, David. Addiction Specialist: All Grades; Senior, Supervising, Principal. 256p. 1973. pap. 8.00 (ISBN 0-668-03351-7). Arco.
Wilmarth, S. S. & Avram, A. Therapeutic Effectiveness of Methadone Maintenance Programs in the USA. (Offset Pub.: No. 3). (Also avail. in French). 1974. pap. 6.80 (ISBN 92-4-170003-3). World Health.
Zarcone, Vincent P. Drug Addicts in a Therapeutic Community. LC 75-15875. (Illus.). 256p. 1975. 14.00x (ISBN 0-912752-06-8). York Pr.

NARCOTIC HABIT

see also Narcotic Addicts; Narcotics and Crime; Narcotics and Youth; Opium Habit

Adams, Winstead. Psychoanalysis of Drug Dependence. 1978. 34.50 (ISBN 0-8089-1148-1). Grune.
Anslinger, H. J. & Tompkins, William F. The Traffic in Narcotics. Grob, Gerald N., ed. LC 80-1211. (Addiction in America Ser.). 1981. Repr. of 1953 ed. lib. bdg. 30.00x (ISBN 0-405-13567-X). Arno.
Ausubel, David P. Drug Addiction: Physiological, Psychological, & Sociological Aspects. (Orig.). 1958. pap. text ed. 4.95 (ISBN 0-394-30877-8, RanC). Random.
Bayer Symposium, 4th. Psychic Dependence: Definition, Assessment in Animals & Man, Theoretical and Clinical Implications. Hoffmeister, F. & Goldberg, L., eds. LC 73-13497. (Illus.). 244p. 1974. 39.50 (ISBN 0-387-06478-8). Springer-Verlag.
Bishop, Ernest S. The Narcotic Drug Problem. LC 75-17204. (Social Problems & Social Policy Ser.). 1976. Repr. of 1920 ed. 10.00x (ISBN 0-405-07476-X). Arno.
Blachly, Paul H. Seduction: A Conceptual Model in Drug Dependencies & Other Contagious Ills. (Illus.). 96p. 1973. 9.00 (ISBN 0-398-00160-X). C C Thomas.
Burkhalter, Pamela K. Nursing Care of the Alcoholic & Drug Abuser. (Illus.). 384p. 1975. pap. text ed. 9.95 (ISBN 0-07-009051-3, HP). McGraw.
Charles, St. Narcotics Menace. 3.00 (ISBN 0-685-07390-4). Borden.
Craig, Robert J. & Baker, Stewart L. Drug Dependent Patients: Treatment & Research. (Illus.). 384p. 1981. price not set (ISBN 0-398-04562-3). C C Thomas.
Edwards, Gabrielle. The Student Biologist Explores Drug Abuse. LC 73-93545. (Student Scientist Ser.). (Illus.). (gr. 7-12). 1975. PLB 7.97 (ISBN 0-8239-0298-6). Rosen Pr.
Grob, Gerald N. The Medical Professions & Drug Addiction: Six Studies, 1882 to 1932, An Original Anthology. LC 80-1206. (Addiction in America Ser.). 1981. lib. bdg. 32.00x (ISBN 0-405-13560-2). Arno.
Grob, Gerald N., ed. Public Policy & the Problem of Addiction: Four Studies, 1914 to 1924, An Original Anthology. LC 70-1208. (Addiction in America Ser.). 1981. lib. bdg. 15.00x (ISBN 0-405-13564-5). Arno.
Hatterer, Lawrence J. The Pleasure Addicts. LC 79-50769. 392p. 1981. Repr. of 1980 ed. 12.00 (ISBN 0-498-02285-4). A S Barnes.
Hesse, Erich. Narcotics & Drug Addiction. 1946. 25.00 (ISBN 0-8274-4219-X). R West.
Hofmann, Frederick G. & Hofmann, Adele D. A Handbook on Drug & Alcohol Abuse: The Biomedical Aspects. (Illus.). 336p. 1975. pap. text ed. 9.95x (ISBN 0-19-501922-9). Oxford U Pr.
Hubbard, Fred H. The Opium Habit & Alcoholism. Grob, Gerald N., ed. LC 80-1232. (Addiction in America Ser.). 1981. Repr. of 1881 ed. lib. bdg. 25.00x (ISBN 0-405-13591-2). Arno.
Hyde, Margaret O. Mind Drugs. 3rd ed. 192p. (gr. 9 up). 1974. PLB 6.95 (ISBN 0-07-031634-1, GB). McGraw.
Kaplan, Eugene H. & Wieder, Herbert. Drugs Don't Take People, People Take Drugs. 1974. 8.00 (ISBN 0-8184-0154-0). Lyle Stuart.
Kerr, Norman. Inebriety or Narcomania: Its Etiology, Pathology, Treatment & Jurispruben. Grob, Gerald N., ed. LC 80-1238. (Addiction in America Ser.). 1981. Repr. of 1894 ed. lib. bdg. 55.00x (ISBN 0-405-13598-X). Arno.
Keup, Wolfram, ed. Drug Abuse: Current Concepts & Research. (Illus.). 496p. 1972. 27.50 (ISBN 0-398-02331-X). C C Thomas.
Krystal, Henry & Raskin, Herbert A. Drug Dependence: Aspects of Ego Functions. LC 76-121920. 1970. text ed. 8.95x (ISBN 0-8143-1419-8). Wayne St U Pr.
Leech, Kenneth & Jordan, Brenda. Drugs for Young People: Their Use & Misuse. 2nd ed. 1974. 3.85 (ISBN 0-08-017938-X). Pergamon.
Lefebure, Molly. Samuel Taylor Coleridge: A Bondage of Opium. LC 74-80899. 544p. 1974. 15.00 (ISBN 0-8128-1711-7). Stein & Day.
Light, Arthur, et al. Opiate Addiction. Grob, Gerald N., ed. LC 80-1257. (Addiction in America Ser.). 1981. Repr. of 1929 ed. lib. bdg. 12.00 (ISBN 0-405-13604-8). Arno.
Marks, Jeanette. Genius & Disaster: Studies in Drugs & Genius. LC 68-26299. 1968. Repr. of 1926 ed. 12.00 (ISBN 0-8046-0301-4). Kennikat.
Martin, W. R., ed. Drug Addiction I: Morphine, Sedative-Hypnotic & Alcohol Dependence. (Handbook of Experimental Pharmacology: Vol. 45, Pt. 1). (Illus.). 1977. 131.60 (ISBN 0-387-08170-4). Springer-Verlag.
Newman, R. G. Methadone Treatment in Narcotic Addiction: Program Management,Findings, & Prospects for the Future. 1977. 33.50 (ISBN 0-12-517050-5). Acad Pr.
Peele, Stanton & Brodsky, Archie. Love & Addiction. 1976. pap. 2.25 (ISBN 0-451-06985-4, E6985, Sig). NAL.
Pettey, George E. The Narcotic Drug Diseases & Allied Ailments: Pathology, Pathogenesis, & Treatment. Grob, Gerald N., ed. LC 80-1246. (Addiction in America Ser.). (Illus.). 1981. Repr. of 1913 ed. lib. bdg. 45.00x (ISBN 0-405-13616-1). Arno.
Podolsky, Edward. Management of Addictions. 1955. 7.50 (ISBN 0-8022-1993-4). Philos Lib.
Richter, Derek, ed. Addiction & Brain Damage. 320p. 1980. 45.00x (ISBN 0-686-69917-3, Pub. by Croom Helm England). State Mutual Bk.
Rudman, Jack. Principal Addiction Specialist. (Career Examination Ser.: C-1398). (Cloth bdg. avail. on request). pap. 10.00 (ISBN 0-8373-2167-0). Natl Learning.
Sapira, J. D. & Cherubin, C. E. Drug Abuse: A Guide for the Clinician. 1976. 102.00 (ISBN 0-444-16711-0, Excerpta Medica). Elsevier.
Schur, Edwin M. Narcotic Addiction in Britain & America: The Impact of Public Policy. LC 75-22646. 1977. Repr. of 1962 ed. lib. bdg. 19.75x (ISBN 0-8371-8360-X, SCNA). Greenwood.
Shaffer, Howard & Burglass, Milton E., eds. Classic Contributions in the Addictions. LC 80-39589. 544p. 1981. 35.00 (ISBN 0-87630-260-6). Brunner-Mazel.
Swinson, Richard P. & Eaves, Derek. Alcoholism & Addiction. 360p. 1980. 15.00x (ISBN 0-7121-0161-6, Pub. by Macdonald & Evans). State Mutual Bk.
Tarshis, Maurice S. The LSD Controversy: An Overview. (Illus.). 96p. 1972. 9.75 (ISBN 0-398-02523-1). C C Thomas.
Weil, Andrew. The Natural Mind: A New Way of Looking at Drugs & the Higher Consciousness. 1972. 9.95 (ISBN 0-395-13936-8); pap. 4.95 (ISBN 0-395-16612-8). HM.
Wolfe, Tom. The Electric Kool-Aid Acid Test. LC 68-13008. 416p. 1968. 10.00 (ISBN 0-374-14704-3). FS&G.
Woods, Geraldine. Drug Use & Drug Abuse. (First Bks.). (Illus.). (gr. 4 up). 1979. s&l 6.90 (ISBN 0-531-02941-7). Watts.

NARCOTIC LAWS

see also Drugs–Laws and Legislation; Narcotics, Control of; Opium Habit; Pharmacy–Laws and Legislation

Anslinger, H. J. & Tompkins, William F. The Traffic in Narcotics. Grob, Gerald N., ed. LC 80-1211. (Addiction in America Ser.). 1981. Repr. of 1953 ed. lib. bdg. 30.00x (ISBN 0-405-13567-X). Arno.
Bailey, F. Lee & Rothblatt, Henry B. Handling Narcotic & Drug Cases. LC 72-84855. (Criminal Law Library). 652p. 1972. 47.50 (ISBN 0-686-05452-0). Lawyers Co-Op.
Bogomolny, R. L., et al. A Handbook on the 1970 Federal Drug Act: Shifting the Perspective. (Illus.). 192p. 1975. 17.25 (ISBN 0-398-03190-8). C C Thomas.
Danaceau, Paul. Pot Luck in Texas: Changing a Marijuana Law. LC 74-20154. (Special Studies Ser). 1974. 1.25 (ISBN 0-686-09381-X). Drug Abuse.
Eldridge, William B. Narcotics & the Law. 2nd ed. LC 67-25528. 1967. 15.00x (ISBN 0-226-20315-8). U of Chicago Pr.
Grob, Gerald N., ed. Public Policy & the Problem of Addiction: Four Studies, 1914 to 1924, An Original Anthology. LC 70-1208. (Addiction in America Ser.). 1981. lib. bdg. 15.00x (ISBN 0-405-13564-5). Arno.

Levine, Harvey R. Legal Dimensions of Drug Abuse in the United States. (Criminal Law Education & Research Center Ser.). 208p. 1974. 13.75 (ISBN 0-398-02876-1). C C Thomas.
Levine, Samuel M. Narcotics & Drug Abuse. (Criminal Justice Text Ser). 1973. pap. 12.00 (ISBN 0-87084-521-7). Anderson Pub Co.
Messick, Hank. Of Grass & Snow. LC 78-31553. (Illus.). 1979. 9.95 (ISBN 0-13-630558-X). P-H.
Rudman, Jack. Narcotics Security Assistant. (Career Examination Ser.: C-1378). (Cloth bdg. avail. on request). pap. 10.00 (ISBN 0-8373-1378-3). Natl Learning.

NARCOTIC TRADE
see Narcotics, Control of

NARCOTICS
see also Hashish; Heroin; Morphine; Opium; Sedatives; Stimulants

Adler, M. W., et al, eds. Factors Affecting the Action of Narcotics. LC 78-2999. (Monographs of the Mario Negri Institute for Pharmacological Research). 1978. 49.00 (ISBN 0-89004-272-1). Raven.
Austrian, Geoffrey. Truth About Drugs. LC 70-103729. 1971. 5.95 (ISBN 0-385-02329-4). Doubleday.
Bates, William & Crowther, Betty. Toward a Typology of Opiate Users. 160p. 1974. pap. text ed. 5.50 (ISBN 0-87073-960-3). Schenkman.
Blum, K., ed. Alcohol & Opiates: Neurochemical & Behavioral Mechanisms. 1977. 34.50 (ISBN 0-12-108450-7). Acad Pr.
Bradley, P. B. & Costa, E., eds. Studies of Narcotic Drugs: 26th International Congress of Physiological Sciences, New Delhi, October 1974. 1976. pap. text ed. 14.50 (ISBN 0-08-020565-8). Pergamon.
Braude, M. C., et al, eds. Narcotic Antagonists. LC 73-84113. (Advances in Biochemical Psychopharmacology Ser.: Vol. 8). (Illus.). 580p. 1974. 48.00 (ISBN 0-911216-55-3). Raven.
Brown, James W., et al. Narcotics, Knowledge & Nonsense: Program Disaster Versus a Scientific Model. LC 74-1237. 184p. 1974. text ed. 17.50 (ISBN 0-88410-016-2). Ballinger Pub.
Child Study Association of America. You, Your Child & Drugs. LC 77-122013. 1971. pap. 1.50 (ISBN 0-87183-239-9). Child Study.
Comparative Statement of Estimates & Statistics on Narcotic Drugs for 1978. 42p. 1980. pap. 4.00 (ISBN 0-686-68946-1, UN80/6/5, UN). Unipub.
Ehrenpreis, S. & Neidel, A. eds. Methods in Narcotics Research. (Modern Pharmacology-Toxicology Ser.: Vol.5). 424p. 1975. 43.50 (ISBN 0-8247-6308-4). Dekker.
Emboden, William. Narcotic Plants. enlarged ed. 1979. 19.95 (ISBN 0-02-535480-9). Macmillan.
Estimated World Requirements of Narcotic Drugs in 1980. 60p. 1980. pap. 6.00 (ISBN 0-686-68954-2, UN80/11/1, UN). Unipub.
Faber, Stuart J., et al. Angel Dust: What Everyone Should Know About PLP. 1979. pap. 5.95 (ISBN 0-89074-066-6). Lega Bks.
Fazey, C. The Aetiology of Psychoactive Substance Use: A Report & Critically Annotated Bibliography on Research into the Aetiology of Alcohol, Nicotine, Opiate & Other Psychoactive Substance Use. 1978. pap. 18.00 (ISBN 92-3-101508-7, U776, UNESCO). Unipub.
Fisher, S. & Freedman, A. M., eds. Opiate Addiction: Origins & Treatment. LC 73-19073. (Series in General Psychiatry). 264p. 1974. 11.95 (ISBN 0-470-26153-6). Halsted Pr.
Goldstein, Avram, ed. The Opiate Narcotics: Neurochemical Mechanisms of Analgesia & Dependence. 270p. 1976. text ed. 30.00 (ISBN 0-08-019869-4). Pergamon.
Herz, Albert. Developments in Opiate Research. (Pharmacology-Toxicology Ser.: Vol. 14). 1978. 43.50 (ISBN 0-8247-6762-4). Dekker.
Institute of Medicine. Sleeping Pills, Insomnia, & Medical Practice. 1979. pap. text ed. 6.00 (ISBN 0-309-02881-7). Natl Acad Pr.
Kitahata, Luke M. Narcotic Analgesics in Anesthesiology. (Illus.). 209p. 1981. lib. bdg. 25.00 (ISBN 0-683-04619-5). Williams & Wilkins.
Kosterlitz, H., ed. Opiates & Endogenous Opioid Peptides. 1976. 61.00 (ISBN 0-7204-0599-8, North-Holland). Elsevier.
Michaux, Henri. The Major Ordeals of the Mind & the Countless Minor Ones. Howard, Richard, tr. from Fr. LC 73-16237. Orig. Title: Les Grandes Epreuves De L'esprit. 192p. 1974. pap. 2.95 (ISBN 0-15-655250-7, HB267, Harv). HarBraceJ.
Paribok, V. P. Narcotics & Cell Narcosis in Chemotherapy. LC 62-12855. 52p. 1962. 25.00 (ISBN 0-306-10553-5, Consultants). Plenum Pub.
Report of the International Narcotics Board for 1979. 39p. 1980. pap. 5.00 (ISBN 0-686-68968-2, UN80/XI/2, UN). Unipub.
Rudman, Jack. Narcotics Education Assistant. (Career Examination Ser.: C-2503). (Cloth bdg. avail. on request). pap. 10.00 (ISBN 0-8373-2503-X). Natl Learning.
Schleiffer, Hedwig. Narcotic Plants of the Old World, Used in Rituals & Everyday Life: An Anthology of Texts from Ancient Times to the Present. (Illus., Orig.). 1979. lib. bdg. 12.50x (ISBN 0-934454-01-9); pap. text ed. 7.95x (ISBN 0-934454-00-0). Lubrecht & Cramer.
Statistics on Narcotic Drugs for 1978. 99p. 1980. pap. 9.00 (ISBN 0-686-68974-7, UN80/11/4, UN). Unipub.
Sumner, Robert L. Menace of Narcotics. 72p. 1971. pap. 1.95 (ISBN 0-87398-558-3, Pub. by Bibl Evang Pr). Sword of Lord.
Way, E. Leong, ed. Endogenous & Exogenous Opiate Agonists & Antagonists: Proceedings of the International Narcotic Club Conference, 11-15 June 1979, North Falmouth, Massachusetts, USA. (Book Supplement to Pergamon Journal Life Sciences). (Illus.). 600p. 1980. 66.00 (ISBN 0-08-025488-8). Pergamon.
Weston, Paul B., et al. Narcotics, U. S. A. Weston, Paul, ed. 319p. 1981. Repr. lib. bdg. 40.00 (ISBN 0-89987-864-4). Darby Bks.
WHO Expert Committee. Geneva, 1969, 17th. WHO Expert Committee on Drug Dependence: Report. (Technical Report Ser.: No. 437). (Also avail. in French, Russian & Spanish). 1970. pap. 2.00 (ISBN 92-4-120437-0). World Health.
WHO Expert Committee. Geneva, 1970, 18th. WHO Expert Committee on Drug Dependence: Report. (Technical Report Ser.: No. 460). (Also avail. in French, Russian & Spanish). 1970. pap. 2.00 (ISBN 92-4-120460-5). World Health.
WHO Expert Committee. Geneva, 1972, 19th. WHO Expert Committee on Drug Dependence: Report. (Technical Report Ser.: No. 526). (Also avail. in French & Spanish). 1973. pap. 1.60 (ISBN 92-4-120526-1). World Health.
WHO Expert Committee. Geneva, 1973, 20th. Who Expert Committee on Drug Dependence: Report. (Technical Report Ser.: No. 551). (Also avail. in French & Spanish). 1974. pap. 2.80 (ISBN 92-4-120551-2). World Health.
WHO Scientific Group. Geneva, 1971. Opiates & Their Alternates for Pain & Cough Relief: Report. (Technical Report Ser.: No. 495). (Also avail. in Spanish). 1972. pap. 1.20 (ISBN 92-4-120495-8). World Health.
Zimmermann, E. & George, R., eds. Narcotics & the Hypothalamus. LC 74-83453. 286p. 1974. 27.00 (ISBN 0-911216-87-1). Raven.

NARCOTICS, CONTROL OF
see also Narcotic Addicts; Narcotic Habit; Narcotic Laws

Anslinger, H. J. & Tompkins, William F. The Traffic in Narcotics. Grob, Gerald N., ed. LC 80-1211. (Addiction in America Ser.). 1981. Repr. of 1953 ed. lib. bdg. 30.00x (ISBN 0-405-13567-X). Arno.
Bailey, F. Lee & Rothblatt, Henry B. Handling Narcotic & Drug Cases. LC 72-84855. (Criminal Law Library). 652p. 1972. 47.50 (ISBN 0-686-05452-0). Lawyers Co-Op.
Blake, John B., ed. Safeguarding the Public: Historical Aspects of Medicinal Drug Control. LC 76-84651. (Josiah Macy Foundation Ser). (Illus.). 211p. 1970. 14.00x (ISBN 0-8018-1054-X). Johns Hopkins.
Bruun, Kettil, et al. The Gentlemen's Club: International Control of Drugs & Alcohol. LC 74-21343. (Studies in Crime & Justice Ser). xiv, 338p. 1975. 17.50x (ISBN 0-226-07777-2, Phoen); pap. 5.95 (ISBN 0-226-07778-0). U of Chicago Pr.
Eisenlohr, L. E. International Narcotics Control. Grob, Gerald N., ed. LC 80-1226. (Addiction in America Ser.). 1981. Repr. of 1934 ed. lib. bdg. 25.00x (ISBN 0-405-13584-X). Arno.
Fooner, Michael. Smuggling Drugs: The World-Wide Connection. (Illus.). 48p. 1977. PLB 5.59 (ISBN 0-698-30664-3). Coward.
Fuqua, Paul. Drug Abuse: Investigation & Control. LC 77-5809. (Illus.). 1977. text ed. 13.95 (ISBN 0-07-022665-2, G); teacher's manual & key 3.50 (ISBN 0-07-022666-0). McGraw.
Harney, Malachi L. & Cross, John C. The Narcotic Officer's Notebook. 2nd ed. (Illus.). 396p. 1975. 21.75 (ISBN 0-398-02310-7). C C Thomas.
Helbrant, Maurice. Narcotic Agent. Grob, Gerald N., ed. LC 80-1230. (Addiction in America Ser.). 1981. Repr. of 1941 ed. lib. bdg. 28.00x (ISBN 0-405-13589-0). Arno.
Kunnes, Richard. The American Heroin Empire: Power, Profits & Politics. LC 72-3930. 250p. 1973. 5.95 (ISBN 0-396-06697-6). Dodd.
Kupperstein, Lenore, et al, eds. Drugs & Social Policy. LC 74-84800. (Annals Ser: No. 417). 250p. 1975. 7.50 (ISBN 0-87761-184-X); pap. 6.00 (ISBN 0-87761-185-8). Am Acad Pol Soc Sci.
Lentini, Joseph. Vice & Narcotics Control. 1977. text ed. 10.50x (ISBN 0-02-475480-3). Glencoe.
Levine, Samuel M. Narcotics & Drug Abuse. (Criminal Justice Text Ser). 1973. pap. 12.00 (ISBN 0-87084-521-7). Anderson Pub Co.
Lowes, Peter D. The Genesis of International Narcotics Control. Grob, Gerald N., ed. LC 80-1267. (Additionn in America Ser.). 1981. Repr. of 1966 ed. lib. bdg. 20.00x (ISBN 0-405-13605-6). Arno.
McCoy, Alfred W. The Politics of Heroin in Southeast Asia. 325p. 1973. pap. 7.95x (ISBN 0-06-131942-2, TB 1942, Torch). Har-Row.
McKinney, Wilson. Carrasco! (Illus.). Date not set. 9.95 (ISBN 0-913206-06-7). Heidelberg Pub.
--Fred Carrasco: The Heroin Merchant. new ed. LC 75-16126. (Illus.). 1975. 9.95 (ISBN 0-913206-06-7). Heidelberg Pubs.
Moore. Buy & Bust. LC 73-11665. (Illus.). 1977. 19.95 (ISBN 0-669-88179-1). Lexington Bks.
Musto, David. The American Disease: Origins of Narcotic Control. LC 72-75024. (Illus.). 350p. 1973. 22.50x (ISBN 0-300-01537-2). Yale U Pr.
Platt, Jerome & Wicks, Robert. Drug Abuse: A Criminal Justice Primer. 1977. pap. text ed. 6.95x (ISBN 0-02-477200-3). Macmillan.
Rosenberg, Philip. The Spivey Assignment. LC 79-10085. 320p. 1979. 10.95 (ISBN 0-03-044371-7). HR&W.
Rudman, Jack. Narcotics Investigator. (Career Examination Ser.: C-1600). (Cloth bdg. avail. on request). pap. 10.00 (ISBN 0-685-60520-5). Natl Learning.
--Narcotics Security Assistant. (Career Examination Ser.: C-1378). (Cloth bdg. avail. on request). pap. 10.00 (ISBN 0-8373-1378-3). Natl Learning.
--Senior Community Narcotic Education Representative. (Career Examination Ser.: C-1942). (Cloth bdg. avail. on request). pap. 10.00 (ISBN 0-8373-1942-0). Natl Learning.
--Senior Narcotics Investigator. (Career Examination Ser.: C-2531). (Cloth bdg. avail. on request). pap. 12.00 (ISBN 0-8373-2531-5). Natl Learning.
Shafer. Drug Use in America: Problem in Perspective & Report of National Commission on Marijuana & Drug Abuse. 1975. text ed. 25.00x (ISBN 0-8422-7239-9). Irvington.
Spillard, William J. Needle in a Haystack: The Exciting Adventures of a Federal Narcotic Agent. Grob, Gerald N., ed. LC 80-1263. (Addiction in America Ser.). 1981. Repr. of 1945 ed. lib. bdg. 18.00x (ISBN 0-405-13618-8). Arno.
Taylor, Arnold H. American Diplomacy & the Narcotics Traffic, 1900-1939: A Study in International Humanitarian Reform. LC 77-86482. 1969. 14.75 (ISBN 0-8223-0219-5). Duke.
U. S. Government. D.E.A. Narcotics Investigator's Manual. 300p. 1981. pap. 50.00 (ISBN 0-87364-235-X). Paladin Ent.
Ware, Mitchell. Operational Handbook for Narcotic Law Enforcement Officers. 128p. 1975. 16.75 (ISBN 0-398-03349-8). C C Thomas.

NARCOTICS AND CRIME
see also Narcotic Laws

Lentini, Joseph. Vice & Narcotics Control. 1977. text ed. 10.50x (ISBN 0-02-475480-3). Glencoe.
Trebach, Arnold S., ed. Drugs, Crime, & Politics. LC 78-5735. (Praeger Special Studies). 1978. 23.95 (ISBN 0-03-042286-8). Praeger.

NARCOTICS AND YOUTH

Blum, Richard H., et al. Drug Education: Results & Recommendations. LC 75-45821. (Illus.). 1976. 21.50 (ISBN 0-669-00575-4). Lexington Bks.
Bowker, Lee H. Drug Use at a Small Liberal Arts College. LC 75-38309. 1976. softbound 9.00 (ISBN 0-88247-398-0). R & E Res Assoc.
Coles, Robert, et al. Drugs & Youth. LC 72-114383. 8.95x (ISBN 0-87140-501-6, 1970); pap. 3.95 (ISBN 0-87140-039-1). Liveright.
Deschin, Celia. The Teenager in a Drugged Society. LC 72-190581. (Personal Guidance, Social Adjustment Ser). (gr. 7 up). 1972. PLB 5.97 (ISBN 0-8239-0226-9). Rosen Pr.
Donlan, Joan. I Never Saw the Sun Rise: The Private Diary of a 15 Year Old Recovering from Drugs & Alcohol. LC 77-87738. (Illus.). 1977. pap. 5.95 (ISBN 0-89638-007-6). CompCare.
Du Toit, Brian M. Drug Use & South African Students. LC 78-21910. (Papers in International Studies: Africa: No. 35). (Illus.). 1978. pap. 7.50 (ISBN 0-89680-076-8). Ohio U Ctr Intl.
Etons, Ursula. Angel Dusted: A Family's Nightmare. 1981. 8.95 (ISBN 0-02-002600-5); pap. 4.95 (ISBN 0-02-002600-5). Macmillan.
Flender, Harold, as told to. We Were Hooked. (gr. 6 up). 1972. PLB 4.99 (ISBN 0-394-92376-6). Random.
Larkin, Ralph W. Suburban Youth in Cultural Crisis. LC 78-10742. 1979. text ed. 14.95 (ISBN 0-19-502522-9); pap. text ed. 4.95x (ISBN 0-19-502523-7). Oxford U Pr.
Love, Harold D. Youth & the Drug Problem: A Guide for Parents & Teachers. 116p. 1971. photocopy ed. spiral 12.00 (ISBN 0-398-01152-4). C C Thomas.
Marin, Peter & Cohen, Allen Y. Understanding Drug Use: An Adult's Guide to Drugs & the Young. LC 69-15318. 1971. 10.95 (ISBN 0-06-012768-6, HarpT). Har-Row.
Reinherz, Helen, et al. The Arlington Youth Consultation Center: A Community's Response to Drug Abuse. LC 75-36556. 1976. softbound 9.00 (ISBN 0-88247-405-7). R & E Res Assoc.
Scott, Edward M. The Adolescent Gap: Research Findings on Drug Using & Non-Drug Using Teens. (Illus.). 160p. 1972. 9.75 (ISBN 0-398-02403-0). C C Thomas.
U. S. Congress - Senate Committee on the Judiciary. Juvenile Delinquency: Treatment & Rehabilitation of Juvenile Drug Addicts. LC 68-55116. (Illus.). 1968. Repr. of 1957 ed. lib. bdg. 17.75x (ISBN 0-8371-2335-6, JUDT). Greenwood.

NAROPA
see Nadapada

NARRAGANSETT BAY-DESCRIPTION

Hale, Stu. Narragansett Bay: A Friend's Perspective. LC 80-52813. (Marine Bulletin Ser.: No. 42). 7.00 (ISBN 0-938412-19-1). URI MAS.
Olsen, Steve, et al. An Interpretive Atlas of Narragansett Bay. (Marine Bulletin Ser.: No. 40). 1980. 2.00 (ISBN 0-938412-16-7). URI MAS.

NARRAGANSETT PIER RAILROAD

Henwood, James. Short Haul to the Bay: Narragansett Pier RR. LC 70-76525. (Shortline Railroad Ser.). (Illus., Orig.). (gr. 7 up). 1969. pap. 3.95 (ISBN 0-8289-0284-4). Greene.

NARRATION (RHETORIC)

Banfield, Ann. Unspeakable Sentences: Narration & Representation in the Language of Fiction. 304p. 1982. price not set (ISBN 0-7100-0905-4). Routledge & Kegan.
Barton, Jim T. Eighter from Decatur: Growing up in North Texas. LC 79-5279. (Illus.). 172p. 1980. 12.95 (ISBN 0-89096-089-5). Tex A&M Univ Pr.
Bentley, Phyllis. Some Observations on the Art of Narrative. LC 73-16136. 1946. lib. bdg. 6.50 (ISBN 0-8414-9881-4). Folcroft.
Bentley, Phyllis E. Some Observations on the Art of Narrative. 1978. Repr. of 1946 ed. lib. bdg. 6.50 (ISBN 0-8495-0444-9). Arden Lib.
Berne, Stanley & Zekowski, Arlene. A First Book of the Neo-Narrative. 1954. 75.00 (ISBN 0-913844-09-8). Am Canadian.
Borges, Jorge L. & Casares, Adolfo B. Extraordinary Tales. 1977. 6.50 (ISBN 0-285-64712-1, Pub. by Souvenir Pr). Intl Schol Bk Serv.
Chatman, Seymour. Story & Discourse: Narrative Structure in Fiction & Film. 1978. 19.50x (ISBN 0-8014-1131-9); pap. 5.95 (ISBN 0-8014-9186-X). Cornell U Pr.
Dowling, William C. Language & Logos in Boswell's Life of Johnson. LC 80-8545. 232p. 1981. 16.00x (ISBN 0-691-06455-5). Princeton U Pr.
Genette, Gerard. Narrative Discourse: An Essay in Method. Lewin, Jane E., tr. from Fr. LC 79-13499. (Illus.). 1979. 18.50x (ISBN 0-8014-1099-1). Cornell U Pr.
Hardy, Barbara. Tellers & Listeners: The Narrative Imagination. 279p. 1976. text ed. 27.50x (ISBN 0-485-11153-5, Athlone Pr). Humanities.
Holloway, John. Narrative & Structure: Exploratory Essays. LC 78-20826. 1979. 19.95 (ISBN 0-521-22574-4). Cambridge U Pr.
Hutcheon, Linda. Narcissistic Narrative: The Metafictional Paradox, Vol. 5. Dimic, Milan V., ed. (Library of the Canadian Review of Comparative Literature). 168p. 1980. text ed. 10.75 (ISBN 0-88920-102-1, Pub. by Laurier U Pr Canada). Humanities.
Kermode, Frank. The Genesis of Secrecy: On the Interpretation of Narrative. LC 78-23403. (Charles Elliot Norton Lectures Ser.). 1979. text ed. 10.00x (ISBN 0-674-34525-8); pap. 3.95 (ISBN 0-674-34525-8). Harvard U Pr.
Nineteenth-Century Fiction. Narrative Endings: Narrative Endings. (Cal Ser.: No. 410). 1978. pap. 3.95 (ISBN 0-520-03783-9). U of Cal Pr.
Olmstead, John. The Design of the Narrative. new ed. Buell, Lawrence, ed. LC 73-75456. 74p. (gr. 7-12). 1973. pap. text ed. 1.45 (ISBN 0-88301-079-8). Pendulum Pr.

Palmer, Michael. Notes for Echo Lake. LC 80-28436. 112p. 1981. 12.50 (ISBN 0-86547-023-5); pap. 6.00 (ISBN 0-86547-024-3). N Point Pr.

Parshall, Linda B. The Art of Narration in Wolfram's "Parzival" & Albrecht's "Jungerer Titurel". LC 79-21146. (Anglica Germanica Ser.: No. 2). 380p. Date not set. price not set (ISBN 0-521-22237-0). Cambridge U Pr.

Plaks, Andrew H., ed. Chinese Narrative: Critical & Theoretical Essays. LC 76-45907. 1977. text ed. 30.00 (ISBN 0-691-06328-1). Princeton U Pr.

Rabkin, Eric S. Narrative Suspense: 'When Slim Turned Sidways...' LC 72-93403. (Illus.). 216p. 1973. 7.95 (ISBN 0-472-75400-9). U of Mich Pr.

Romberg, Bertil. Studies in the Narrative Technique of the First Person Novel. 377p. 1980. Repr. of 1962 ed. lib. bdg. 40.00 (ISBN 0-8495-4632-X). Arden Lib.

Ryding, William W. Structure in Medieval Narrative. LC 72-154531. (De Proprietatibus Litterarum, Ser. Major: No. 12). 177p. 1971. text ed. 25.00x (ISBN 90-2791-795-7). Mouton.

Smitten, Jeffrey R. & Daghistany, Ann, eds. Spatial Form in Narrative. LC 81-3244. (Illus.). 304p. 1981. 19.50x (ISBN 0-8014-1375-3). Cornell U Pr.

Stein, Gertrude. Narration: Four Lectures. LC 36-27069. (Illus.). 1969. Repr. of 1935 ed. lib. bdg. 15.00x (ISBN 0-8371-0939-6, STFL). Greenwood.

Stepto, Robert B. From Behind the Veil: A Study of Afro-American Narrative. LC 79-11283. 1979. 12.50 (ISBN 0-252-00752-2). U of Ill Pr.

Todorov, Tzvetan. The Poetics of Prose. Howard, Richard, tr. LC 76-28124. 1977. 22.50x (ISBN 0-8014-0857-1); pap. 6.95 (ISBN 0-8014-9165-7). Cornell U Pr.

NARRATIVE PAINTING

Sitwell, Sacheverell. Narrative Pictures: A Survey of English Genre & Its Painters. LC 72-180039. Repr. of 1937 ed. 22.00 (ISBN 0-405-08978-3). Arno.

NARRATIVE POETRY

see also Epic Poetry

Blegvad, Lenore. Moon-Watch Summer. LC 74-187855. (Illus.). 63p. (gr. 2-5). 1972. 4.75 (ISBN 0-15-255350-9, HJ). HarBraceJ.

Ferris, Helen, compiled by. Love's Enchantment: Story Poems & Ballads. LC 73-86796. (Granger Index Reprint Ser). 1944. 16.00 (ISBN 0-8369-6076-9). Arno.

Kennedy, Richard. Delta Baby & Two Sea Songs. LC 78-6895. (Illus.). (gr. 3 up). 1979. PLB 5.95 (ISBN 0-201-03598-7, A-W Childrens). A-W.

Loane, George. Longer Narrative Poems. 1977. Repr. of 1930 ed. 15.00 (ISBN 0-89984-048-5). Century Bookbindery.

MacCallum, M. & Holme, E. English Narrative Poems from the Renaissance. 1977. Repr. of 1909 ed. 15.00 (ISBN 0-89984-055-8). Century Bookbindery.

Phillips, Nigel. Sijobang: Sung Narrative Poetry of West Sumatra. LC 80-42227. (Cambridge Studies in Oral & Literate Culture: No. 1). (Illus.). 248p. Date not set. price not set (ISBN 0-521-23737-8). Cambridge U Pr.

Power, C. J. A Selection of Narrative Verse. 1977. Repr. of 1931 ed. 15.00 (ISBN 0-89984-093-0). Century Bookbindery.

Seward, S. S. Narrative & Lyric Poems for Students. 1909. lib. bdg. 10.00 (ISBN 0-8414-8120-2). Folcroft.

Tupper, James. Narrative & Lyric Poetry. Repr. of 1927 ed. 25.00 (ISBN 0-686-18776-8). Scholars Ref Lib.

--Narrative & Lyric Poetry. 1977. Repr. of 1927 ed. 20.00 (ISBN 0-89984-131-7). Century Bookbindery.

Van Deinse, Howard A. Exploring Narrative Poetry. (Illus.). 88p. (Orig.). (gr. 7-9). 1971. pap. text ed. 2.60 (ISBN 0-88489-010-4); tchr's ed. 3.30 (ISBN 0-88489-079-1). St Marys.

NARRATIVE POETRY–HISTORY AND CRITICISM

Doorn, Willem V. Theory & Practice of English Narrative Verse Since Eighteen Thirty-Three. 253p. 1980. Repr. of 1833 ed. lib. bdg. 25.00 (ISBN 0-8492-4220-7). R West.

Keach, William. Elizabethan Erotic Narratives: Irony & Pathos in the Ovidian Poetry of Shakespeare, Marlowe, & Their Contemporaries. 1977. 19.50 (ISBN 0-8135-0830-4). Rutgers U Pr.

Kroeber, Karl. Romantic Narrative Art. (Illus.). 238p. 1960. pap. 7.50x (ISBN 0-299-02244-7). U of Wis Pr.

NARRATIVE WRITING

see Narration (Rhetoric)

NARROW-GAGE RAILROADS

see Railroads, Narrow-Gage

NARVAEZ, PANFILO DE, d. 1528

Nunez Cabeza de Vaca, Alvar. The Journey of Alvar Nunez Cabeza de Vaca & His Companions from Florida to the Pacific, 1528-1536. Bandelier, A. F., ed. Bandelier, Fanny, tr. LC 72-2822. (American Explorers Ser.). Repr. of 1922 ed. 20.00 (ISBN 0-404-54915-2). AMS Pr.

NASA

see United States–National Aeronautics and Space Administration

NASBY, PETROLEUM V.

see Locke, David Ross, 1833-1888

NASCIMENTO, EDSON ARANTES DO, 1940-

Bodo, Peter & Hishey, David. Pele's New World. (Illus.). 1977. 8.95 (ISBN 0-393-08758-1). Norton.

Burchard, S. H. Sports Star: Pele. LC 75-33707. (Sports Star Ser). (Illus.). (gr. 1-5). 1976. pap. 2.50 (ISBN 0-15-278032-7, VoyB). HarBraceJ.

Hahn, James & Hahn, Lynn. Pele'! Edson do Nascimento. Schroeder, Howard, ed. (Sports Legends Ser.). (Illus.). 48p. (Orig.). (gr. 3-5). 1981. PLB 6.95 (ISBN 0-89686-125-2); pap. text ed. 3.25 (ISBN 0-89686-140-6). Crestwood Hse.

Kowet, Don. Pele. LC 75-38344. (YA) (gr. 9 up). 1976. 6.95 (ISBN 0-689-10713-7). Atheneum.

Pele & Fish, Robert L. My Life & the Beautiful Game. (Illus.). 1978. pap. 2.50 (ISBN 0-446-81639-6). Warner Bks.

Sabin, Louis. Pele: Soccer Superstar. (Putnam Sports Shelf). (Illus.). (gr. 5 up). 1976. PLB 6.29 (ISBN 0-399-61034-0). Putnam.

NASH, JOHN, 1752-1835

Summerson, John. The Life & Work of John Nash, Architect. (Illus.). 288p. 1980. text ed. 35.00x (ISBN 0-262-19190-3). MIT Pr.

Summerson, John N. John Nash: Architect to King George the Fourth. LC 35-10833. 295p. 1935. Repr. 19.00 (ISBN 0-403-03876-6). Somerset Pub.

Temple, Nigel. John Nash & the Village Picturesque. (Illus.). 172p. 1980. text ed. 31.25x (ISBN 0-904387-24-0). Humanities.

NASH, PAUL, 1889-1946

Causey, Andrew. Paul Nash. (Illus.). 532p. 1980. 98.00x (ISBN 0-19-817348-2). Oxford U Pr.

--Paul Nash: Paintings & Watercolours. (Tate Gallery Art Ser.). (Illus.). 1977. Barron.

Wingfield, Digby C. Meaning & Symbol in Three Modern Artists: Edward Munch, Henry Moore, Paul Nash. LC 55-2585. 204p. 1955. Repr. 20.00 (ISBN 0-403-04167-8). Somerset Pub.

NASH, RICHARD, 1674-1762

Sitwell, Edith. Bath. LC 78-24153. 1980. Repr. of 1932 ed. lib. bdg. 21.75x (ISBN 0-313-20815-8, SIBT). Greenwood.

NASH, THOMAS, 1567-1601

Harman, Edward G. Gabriel Harvey & Thomas Nashe. LC 74-2009. 1932. Repr. lib. bdg. 30.00 (ISBN 0-8414-4809-4). Folcroft.

Howarth, R. G. Two Elizabethan Writers of Fiction: Thomas Nashe & Thomas Deloney. LC 77-3511. 1956. lib. bdg. 7.50 (ISBN 0-8414-4711-X). Folcroft.

McGinn, Donald J. Thomas Nashe. (English Authors Ser.: No. 317). 12.95 (ISBN 0-8057-6804-1). Twayne.

NASH-HEALEY (AUTOMOBILE)

see Automobiles, Foreign–Types–Healey

NASHIS

see Moso (Tribe)

NASHVILLE, BATTLE OF, 1864

Horn, Stanley F. Decisive Battle of Nashville. LC 56-12173. (Illus.). 1968. Repr. of 1956 ed. 8.50 (ISBN 0-87049-087-7). U of Tenn Pr.

NASHVILLE METROPOLITAN AREA

Adams, G. Rollie & Christian, Ralph J. Nashville: A Pictorial History. LC 80-20196. (Illus.). 1980. 16.95 (ISBN 0-89865-013-5); ltd. ed. 24.95 (ISBN 0-89865-000-3). Donning Co.

Blumstein, James F. & Walter, Benjamin, eds. Growing Metropolis: Aspects of Development in Nashville. LC 74-32320. 357p. 1975. 12.95x (ISBN 0-8265-1200-3). Vanderbilt U Pr.

Hall, Tom T. The Storyteller's Nashville. LC 78-22632. (Illus.). 1979. 9.95 (ISBN 0-385-14690-6). Doubleday.

Hawkins, Brett W. Nashville Metro: The Politics of City-County Consolidation. LC 66-20048. 1966. 5.00 (ISBN 0-8265-1088-4). Vanderbilt U Pr.

Hoss, E. E. & Reese, William B. A History of Nashville, Tennessee. Woolridge, J., ed. (Illus.). 1970. Repr. of 1890 ed. 40.00 (ISBN 0-918450-01-2). C Elder.

Thomas, Jane H. & Ramsey, J. G. Old Days in Nashville & Historical Sketch of 1854. (Illus.). 190p. 1980. Repr. of 1897 ed. 10.00 (ISBN 0-918450-15-2). C Elder.

Tipps, H. T., et al. Seven Early Churches of Nashville. (Illus.). 1972. 9.95 (ISBN 0-918450-07-1). C Elder.

Zibart, Carl. Yesterday's Nashville. LC 75-44475. (Historic Cities Ser.: No. 16). (Illus.). 1976. 9.95 (ISBN 0-912458-57-7). E A Seemann.

NASOPHARYNX

Dodd, Gerald D. & Jing, Bao-Shan. Radiology of the Nose, Paranasal Sinuses & Nasopharynx. (Golden's Diagnostic Radiology Ser.: Section 2). 264p. 1977. 46.00 (ISBN 0-683-02602-X). Williams & Wilkins.

Lederman, M. Cancer of the Nasopharynx: Its Natural History & Treatment. (American Lecture Rediation Therapy). (Illus.). 128p. 1961. photocopy ed. spiral 12.75 (ISBN 0-398-04330-2). C C Thomas.

Mancuso, Anthony. Computed Tomography of the Larynx & Nasopharynx. (Illus.). 438p. 1981. lib. bdg. 30.00 (ISBN 0-683-05475-9). Williams & Wilkins.

NASORAEANS

see Mandaeans

NASSAU, BAHAMAS

Bacon, Edgar M. Notes on Nassau: The Capital of the Bahamas. 1976. lib. bdg. 59.95 (ISBN 0-8490-2358-0). Gordon Pr.

Michael, Julia W. Native Nassau. 1977. lib. bdg. 59.95 (ISBN 0-8490-2331-9). Gordon Pr.

Nassau. (Panorama Bks.). (Illus., Fr.). 3.95 (ISBN 0-685-11413-9). French & Eur.

Northcroft, G. J. Sketches of Summerland: Nassau & the Bahama Islands. 1976. lib. bdg. 59.95 (ISBN 0-8490-2614-8). Gordon Pr.

NASSAU COUNTY, NEW YORK

Gates, Arnold. Nassau County in the Civil War. Date not set. pap. 1.25 (ISBN 0-686-24668-3). Basin Pub.

Gonzalez, Arturo. Eugene H. Nickerson: Statesman of a New Society. (Future Maker Ser). (Illus.). 1964. 3.95 (ISBN 0-685-11955-6). Heineman.

Smits, Edward J. Nassau: Suburbia, U. S. A. LC 74-16383. (Illus.). 256p. 1974. 12.95 (ISBN 0-385-08902-3). Doubleday.

Weidman, Bette S. & Martin, Linda B. Nassau County, Long Island, in Early Photographs, 1869-1940. (Illus.). 144p. (Orig.). 1981. pap. 7.95 (ISBN 0-486-24136-X). Dover.

NASSER, GAMAL ABDEL, PRES. UNITED ARAB REPUBLIC, 1918-1970

Dubois, Shirley G. Gamal Abdel Nasser: Son of the Nile. (Illus.). 250p. 1972. 10.00 (ISBN 0-89388-048-5). Okpaku Communications.

Joesten, Joachim. Nasser, the Rise to Power. LC 74-3752. (Illus.). 224p. 1974. Repr. of 1960 ed. lib. bdg. 15.00x (ISBN 0-8371-7471-6, JONA). Greenwood.

--Nasser, the Rise to Power. LC 74-3752. (Illus.). 224p. 1974. Repr. of 1960 ed. lib. bdg. 15.00x (ISBN 0-8371-7471-6, JONA). Greenwood.

Shivanandan, Mary. Nasser, Modern Leader of Egypt. new ed. Rahmas, D. Steve, ed. LC 73-87627. (Outstanding Personalities Ser.: No. 64). 32p. (Orig.). (gr. 7-12). 1973. lib. bdg. 2.95 incl. catalog cards (ISBN 0-87157-064-5); pap. 1.50 vinyl laminated covers (ISBN 0-686-05481-4). SamHar Pr.

Vatikiotis, P. J. Nasser & His Generation. LC 78-9765. 1978. 22.50x (ISBN 0-312-55938-0). St Martin.

NAST, THOMAS, 1840-1902

Keller, Morton. The Art & Politics of Thomas Nast. LC 68-19762. (Illus.). 365p. 1975. pap. 9.95 (ISBN 0-19-501929-6, GB437, GB). Oxford U Pr.

Nast, Thomas. Cartoons & Illustrations of Thomas Nast. 1974. 8.50 (ISBN 0-486-23067-8); pap. 5.50 (ISBN 0-486-22983-1). Dover.

--Thomas Nast's Christmas Drawings. (Illus.). 1978. pap. 3.50 (ISBN 0-486-23660-9). Dover.

Paine, Albert B. Th. Nast: His Period & His Pictures. LC 78-177504. (Illus.). Repr. of 1904 ed. 25.00 (ISBN 0-405-08831-0). Arno.

--Thomas Nast: His Period & His Pictures. LC 80-20105. (American Men & Women of Letters Ser.). (Illus.). 624p. 1981. pap. 8.95 (ISBN 0-87754-169-8). Chelsea Hse.

--Thomas Nast: His Period & Pictures. (Illus.). 1904. 9.50 (ISBN 0-8446-1339-8). Peter Smith.

NAT TURNER'S INSURRECTION

see Southampton Insurrection, 1831

NATAL

Bleek, W. H. Natal Diaries, Eighteen Fifty-Five to Eighteen Fifty-Six. Spohr, O. H., ed. (Illus.). 1965. 6.00x (ISBN 0-8426-1169-X). Verry.

Botha, Colin G. Public Archives of South Africa, Sixteen Fifty-Two to Nineteen Hundred & Ten. LC 70-82015. 1969. Repr. of 1928 ed. lib. bdg. 19.50 (ISBN 0-8337-0340-4). B Franklin.

Braby's Natal Directory: Including Zululand, East Griqualand & Pondoland. 73rd ed. 1976. 17.50x (ISBN 0-8002-1358-0). Intl Pubns Serv.

Brookes, Edgar H. & Webb, C. D. History of Natal. (Illus.). 1965. 20.00x (ISBN 0-8426-0437-5). Verry.

Broome, Mary A. Life in South Africa. LC 70-97379. Repr. of 1877 ed. 10.00x (ISBN 0-8371-2441-7, Pub. by Negro U Pr). Greenwood.

Cowles, Raymond B. Zulu Journal: Field Notes of a Naturalist in South Africa. LC 59-8760. 1959. 20.00x (ISBN 0-520-00274-1); pap. 1.95 (ISBN 0-520-00276-8, CAL73). U of Cal Pr.

Deane, Dee S. Black South Africans - A Who's Who: Profiles of Natal's Leading Blacks. (Illus.). 1978. text ed. 17.50x (ISBN 0-19-570148-8). Oxford U Pr.

Hilliard, O. M. Compositae in Natal. (Illus.). 1977. text ed. 47.50x (ISBN 0-86980-088-4). Verry.

Konczacki, Zbigniew A. Public Finance & Economic Development of Natal, 1893-1910. LC 67-23301. 1967. 13.75 (ISBN 0-8223-0101-6). Duke.

Merrett, C. E. A Selected Bibliography of Natal Maps. 1979. lib. bdg. 42.50 (ISBN 0-8161-8276-0). G K Hall.

Pietermaritzburg-University of Natal-Department of Sociology & Social Work. Small Towns of Natal, a Socioeconomic Sample Survey. LC 71-97410. (Illus.). Repr. of 1953 ed. 11.25x (ISBN 0-8371-2653-3). Greenwood.

Shooter, Joseph. Kafirs of Natal & the Zulu Country. LC 77-82073. (Illus.). Repr. of 1857 ed. 19.25x (ISBN 0-8371-1538-8, Pub. by Negro U Pr). Greenwood.

NATAL–HISTORY

Palmer, Mabel A. The History of the Indians in Natal. LC 77-1599. (Natal Regional Survey: Vol. 10). 1977. Repr. of 1957 ed. 21.75x (ISBN 0-8371-9555-1, PAHI). Greenwood.

Ross, Louisa G. Life at Natal a Hundred Years Ago (by a Lady) 134p. 1972. 9.00x (ISBN 0-86977-012-8). Verry.

NATCHEZ, MISSISSIPPI

Butler, Pierce. Laurel Hill & Later: The Record of a Teacher. (Illus.). 5.00 (ISBN 0-685-08694-1). Crager.

Gandy, Joan W. & Gandy, Thomas H. Norman's Natchez: An Early Photographer & His Town. LC 78-15570. (Illus.). 1978. 25.00 (ISBN 0-87805-078-7). U Pr of Miss.

Ingraham, Joseph H. South-West, 2 Vols. LC 68-55895. 1835. 29.00x (ISBN 0-8371-0493-9, Pub. by Negro U Pr). Greenwood.

NATCHEZ INDIANS

see Indians of North America–Eastern States

NATCHEZ TRACE

Coates, Robert M. The Outlaw Years: The History of the Land Pirates of the Natchez Trace. LC 74-1087. (Illus.). 307p. 1974. Repr. of 1930 ed. 28.00 (ISBN 0-8103-3961-7). Gale.

--The Outlaw Years: The History of the Land Pirates of The Natchez Trace. 1979. Repr. of 1930 ed. lib. bdg. 25.00 (ISBN 0-8495-0929-7). Arden Lib.

NATH LANGUAGE

see Nuer Language

NATHAN, GEORGE JEAN, 1882-1958

Goldberg, Isaac. Theatre of George Jean Nathan. LC 68-54272. (BCL Ser.: I). Repr. of 1926 ed. 21.50 (ISBN 0-404-02859-4). AMS Pr.

Irwin, Constance. Dramatic Criticism of George Jean Nathan. LC 70-153213. 1971. Repr. of 1943 ed. 12.50 (ISBN 0-8046-1523-3). Kennikat.

NATHAN, ROBERT, 1894-

Sandelin, Clarence K. Robert Nathan. (U. S. Authors Ser.: No. 148). 12.50 (ISBN 0-8057-0548-1). Twayne.

NATIC LANGUAGE

see Massachuset Language

NATION (NEW YORK)

Grimes, Alan P. The Political Liberation of the New York "Nation", 1865-1932. (James Sprunt Study in History & Political Science: No. 34). (Orig.). 1953. pap. text ed. 4.00x (ISBN 0-8078-5034-9). U of NC Pr.

NATION OF ISLAM

see Black Muslims

NATION-STATE

see National State

NATIONAL ACADEMY OF SCIENCES, UNITED STATES

Biographical Memoirs, Vol. 48. (Biographical Memoirs Ser.). 1976. 10.00 (ISBN 0-309-02349-1). Natl Acad Pr.

True, Frederick & Cohen, I. Bernard, eds. The Semi-Centennial Anniversary of the National Academy of Sciences: & a History of the First Half-Century of the National Academy of Sciences, 2 vols. 1863-1913. LC 79-7977. (Three Centuries of Science in America Ser.). (Illus.). 1980. Repr. of 1913 ed. Set. lib. bdg. 42.00x (ISBN 0-405-12560-7). Arno.

NATIONAL ACCOUNTING

see National Income–Accounting

NATIONAL AGRICULTURAL WHEEL

Morgan, W. Scott. History of the Wheel & Alliance & the Impending Revolution. LC 68-56745. (Research & Source Works Ser: No. 225). (Illus.). 1968. Repr. of 1891 ed. 39.00 (ISBN 0-8337-2462-2). B Franklin.

NATIONAL ANTARCTIC EXPEDITION, 1901-1904

Scott, Robert F. Voyage of the Discovery, 2 Vols. LC 68-55218. (Illus.). 1969. Repr. of 1905 ed. Set. lib. bdg. 57.00x (ISBN 0-8371-1334-2, SCDI). Greenwood.

Scott, Robert S. Voyage of the 'Discovery' (Illus.). 1951. 15.00 (ISBN 0-685-20649-1). Transatlantic.

Wilson, Edward. Diary of the Discovery Expedition to the Antarctic Regions, 1901-1904. 1967. text ed. 25.00x (ISBN 0-7137-0431-4). Humanities.

NATIONAL ANTHEMS

see National Songs

NATIONAL ASSOCIATION FOR STOCK CAR RACING

Benyo, Richard. Superspeedway: The Story of NASCAR Grand National Racing. 1977. 8.95 (ISBN 0-442-80391-5); pap. 7.95 (ISBN 0-442-80564-0). Van Nos Reinhold.

NATIONAL ASSOCIATION FOR THE ADVANCEMENT OF COLORED PEOPLE

Finch, Minnie. The NAACP: It's Fight for Justice. LC 81-5324. 285p. 1981. 15.00 (ISBN 0-8108-1436-6). Scarecrow.

Kellogg, Charles Flint. NAACP-A History of the National Association for the Advancement of Colored People, Vol. 1: 1909-1920. LC 66-28507. 360p. 1967. pap. 4.95 (ISBN 0-8018-1554-1). Johns Hopkins.

Meier, August, ed. Papers of the NAACP: Meetings of the Board of Directors, Conferences, Speeches, & Special Reports. 1981. 1040.00 (ISBN 0-89093-397-9, Altheia). U Pubns Amer.

Ovington, Mary W. The Walls Came Tumbling Down. LC 68-17687. 1970. pap. 2.45 (ISBN 0-8052-0251-X). Schocken.

--Walls Came Tumbling Down. LC 69-18543. (American Negro: His History & Literature Ser., No. 2). 1969. Repr. of 1947 ed. 11.00 (ISBN 0-405-01884-3). Arno.

Record, Wilson. Race & Radicalism: The NAACP & the Communist Party in Conflict. 237p. 1966. pap. 3.95 (ISBN 0-8014-9035-9, CP35). Cornell U Pr.

Ross, B. Joyce. J. E. Spingarn & the Rise of the NAACP. LC 78-139326. (Studies in American Negro Life). 1972. 10.00 (ISBN 0-689-10531-2); pap. text ed. 3.95x (ISBN 0-689-70337-6, NL32). Atheneum.

St. James, Warren. NAACP: Triumphs of a Pressure Group 1909-1980. (Illus.). 288p. 1980. 11.95 (ISBN 0-682-49605-7, University). Exposition.

Vose, Clement E. Caucasians Only: The Supreme Court, the NAACP, & the Restrictive Covenant Cases. LC 59-8758. 1959. 22.75x (ISBN 0-520-01308-5); pap. 5.95x (ISBN 0-520-01309-3, CAMPUS1). U of Cal Pr.

Zangrando, Robert L. The Naacp Crusade Against Lynching, 1909 to 1950. 320p. 1980. 22.95x (ISBN 0-87722-174-X). Temple U Pr.

NATIONAL ASSOCIATION OF BLUE SHIELD PLANS

Eilers, Robert D. Regulation of Blue Cross & Blue Shield Plans. 1963. 9.00x (ISBN 0-256-00644-X). Irwin.

NATIONAL ASSOCIATION OF MANUFACTURERS OF THE U. S. A.

Taylor, Albion G. Labor Policies of the National Association of Manufacturers. LC 73-2536. (Big Business; Economic Power in a Free Society Ser.). Repr. of 1928 ed. 10.00 (ISBN 0-405-05114-X). Arno.

NATIONAL ASSOCIATION OF SECURITIES DEALERS

Commerce Clearing House. National Association of Securities Dealers, Inc. Reprint of the Manual As of May, 1981. 1981. 7.50 (ISBN 0-686-75920-6). Commerce.

NATIONAL BASEBALL HALL OF FAME AND MUSEUM

see Cooperstown, New York, National Baseball Hall of Fame and Museum

NATIONAL BASKETBALL ASSOCIATION

Armstrong, Robert. The Coaches. (Stars of the NBA Ser.). (Illus.). (gr. 4-12). 1977. PLB 7.95 (ISBN 0-87191-566-9). Creative Ed.

NATIONAL BIBLIOGRAPHY

see Bibliography, National

NATIONAL CEMETERIES–UNITED STATES

Singletary, Milly. Punchbowl: National Memorial Cemetery of the Pacific. (Illus.). 32p. 1977. pap. 1.95 (ISBN 0-9601256-2-0). Singletary.

NATIONAL CHARACTERISTICS

see also Ethnopsychology

Aylesworth, Thomas G. & Aylesworth, Virginia. If You Don't Invade My Intimate Zone or Clean up My Water Hole... LC 77-93999. 1978. pap. 2.25 (ISBN 0-89516-026-9). Condor Pub Co.

Barker, Sir Ernest. National Character & the Factors in Its Formation. LC 78-59002. 1979. Repr. of 1948 ed. 21.00 (ISBN 0-88355-678-2). Hyperion Conn.

Clark, Cumberland. Shakespeare & National Character. LC 76-181002. (Studies in Shakespeare, No. 24). 308p. 1972. Repr. of 1932 ed. lib. bdg. 41.95 (ISBN 0-8383-1371-X). Haskell.

De Madariaga, Salvador. Portrait of Europe. LC 67-12943. 1967. 13.75 (ISBN 0-8173-6602-4). U of Ala Pr.

Fyfe, H. The Illusion of National Character. 1977. lib. bdg. 59.95 (ISBN 0-8490-2035-2). Gordon Pr.

Herman, Marguerite S. & Herman, Lewis. Foreign Dialects. LC 58-10332. 1943. 14.95 (ISBN 0-87830-048-1). Theatre Arts.

Kurz, Harry. European Characters in French Drama of the Eighteenth Century. LC 72-1018. (Columbia University. Studies in Romance Philology & Literature: No. 17). Repr. of 1916 ed. 19.50 (ISBN 0-404-50617-8). AMS Pr.

Lambert, Wallace E. & Klineberg, Otto. Children's Views of Foreign People: A Cross-National Study. LC 66-24057. (Century Psychology Ser.). (Illus.). 1967. 18.00x (ISBN 0-89197-076-2); pap. text ed. 6.95x (ISBN 0-89197-077-0). Irvington.

Lynn, R. Personality & National Character. 1971. 27.00 (ISBN 0-08-016516-8). Pergamon.

Maquet, Jacques. Africanity: The Cultural Unity of Black Africa. Rayfield, Joan R., tr. (Illus.). 200p. 1972. pap. 4.95 (ISBN 0-19-519700-3, 380, GB). Oxford U Pr.

Park, Robert E. & Miller, Herbert A. Old World Traits Transplanted. LC 69-18788. (American Immigration Collection Ser., No. 1). (Illus.). 1969. Repr. of 1921 ed. 9.50 (ISBN 0-405-00536-9). Arno.

Platt, Washington. National Character in Action: Intelligence Factors in Foreign Relations. 1961. 17.50x (ISBN 0-8135-0382-5). Rutgers U Pr.

Rummel, R. J. National Attributes & Behavior. LC 76-50501. (Dimensions of Nations Ser.: Vol. 3). 472p. 1979. 27.50 (ISBN 0-8039-0392-8). Sage.

Schollianos, Alva. Call to Greatness: Essays on National Purpose. 1975. 7.00 (ISBN 0-87164-018-X). William-F.

NATIONAL CHARACTERISTICS, AMERICAN

Adams, Henry. United States in Eighteen Hundred. (YA) 1955. pap. 2.95 (ISBN 0-8014-9014-6). Cornell U Pr.

Adams, James T. Our Business Civilization: Some Aspects of Our American Culture. LC 75-92608. Repr. of 1929 ed. 17.50 (ISBN 0-404-00288-9). AMS Pr.

Allen, Frederick L. Big Change, America Transforms Itself, Nineteen Hundred - Nineteen Fifty. 1969. pap. 1.95 (ISBN 0-06-080150-6, P150, PL). Har-Row.

Barbe, Wren, ed. Young Japan Views Uncle Sam: A Collection of Opinions on America. LC 65-13413. (gr. 7 up). 1965. 4.15 (ISBN 0-8048-0641-1). C E Tuttle.

Barzun, Jacques. God's Country & Mine. LC 73-3919. 344p. 1973. Repr. of 1954 ed. lib. bdg. 15.75x (ISBN 0-8371-6860-0, BAGC). Greenwood.

Basso, Hamilton. Mainstream. facsimile ed. LC 73-106406. (Essay Index Reprint Ser). 1943. 17.00 (ISBN 0-8369-1444-9). Arno.

Beck, Earl R. Germany Rediscovers America. LC 68-54592. 1968. 12.00 (ISBN 0-8130-0424-1). U Presses Fla.

Belloc, Hilaire. The Contrast: Foreign Travelers in America, 1810-1935 Ser. LC 73-13117. 278p. 1974. Repr. of 1924 ed. 16.00x (ISBN 0-405-05442-4). Arno.

Blair, Walter. Native American Humor. 1960. pap. text ed. 9.50 scp (ISBN 0-8102-0044-9, HarpC). Har-Row.

Boorstin, Daniel. The Exploring Spirit: America & the World, Then & Now. LC 77-4454. 1977. pap. 2.45 (ISBN 0-394-72423-2, V-423, Vin). Random.

Boorstin, Daniel J. America & the Image of Europe: Reflections on American Thought. 7.50 (ISBN 0-8446-1703-2). Peter Smith.

--Image: A Guide to Pseudo-Events in America. LC 62-7936. Orig. Title: Image, or What Happened to the American Dream. 1962. pap. 4.95 (ISBN 0-689-70280-9, 173). Atheneum.

Bridge, James H. Uncle Sam at Home. LC 73-13153. (Foreign Travelers in America, 1810-1935 Ser.). (Illus.). 248p. 1974. Repr. 13.00x (ISBN 0-405-05446-7). Arno.

Brogan, D. W. American Character. 6.75 (ISBN 0-8446-1746-6). Peter Smith.

Brooks, Van Wyck. The Wine of the Puritans: A Study of Present Day America. 1978. Repr. of 1908 ed. lib. bdg. 20.00 (ISBN 0-8495-0446-5). Arden Lib.

Brown, Elijah. The Real America. LC 73-13124. (Foreign Travelers in America, 1810-1935 Ser.). 308p. 1974. Repr. 18.00x (ISBN 0-405-05447-5). Arno.

Burns, Edward M. The American Idea of Mission: Concepts of National Purpose & Destiny. LC 72-11302. (Illus.). 385p. 1973. Repr. of 1957 ed. lib. bdg. 23.00x (ISBN 0-8371-6648-9, BUAI). Greenwood.

Burt, Maxwell S. Other Side. facsimile ed. LC 70-134064. (Essay Index Reprint Ser). Repr. of 1928 ed. 18.00 (ISBN 0-8369-2218-2). Arno.

Chase, Stuart. American Credos. LC 75-8835. 216p. 1975. Repr. of 1962 ed. lib. bdg. 15.00x (ISBN 0-8371-8108-9, CHAC). Greenwood.

Clark, John P. America, Their America. LC 79-80851. 1969. pap. 6.50x (ISBN 0-8419-0012-4, Africana). Holmes & Meier.

Cobden, Richard. American Diaries. Cawley, Elizabeth H., ed. LC 75-90488. Repr. of 1952 ed. lib. bdg. 15.00x (ISBN 0-8371-2261-9, COAD). Greenwood.

Cocteau, Jean. Lettre Aux Americains. 102p. 1949. 8.95 (ISBN 0-686-54536-2). French & Eur.

Commager, Henry S. The American Mind: An Interpretation of American Thought & Character Since the 1800's. 1950. 30.00x (ISBN 0-300-00377-3); pap. 7.95x (ISBN 0-300-00046-4, Y7). Yale U Pr.

Craven, Wesley F. Legend of the Founding Fathers. 22p. (YA) (gr. 9-12). 1965. pap. 3.95 (ISBN 0-8014-9087-1, CP87). Cornell U Pr.

De Tocqueville, Alexis, et al. Bitch-Goddess Success. LC 68-15189. 1968. 5.95x (ISBN 0-87130-000-1). Eakins.

Eaton, Clement. Mind of the Old South. rev. ed. LC 67-11648. (Walter Lynwood Fleming Lectures). (Illus.). 1967. 25.00x (ISBN 0-8071-0443-4); pap. text ed. 8.95 (ISBN 0-8071-0120-6). La State U Pr.

Eaton, Clement, ed. Leaven of Democracy: The Growth of the Democratic Spirit in the Time of Jackson. LC 63-17877. (American Epochs Ser). pap. 7.95 (ISBN 0-8076-0394-5). Braziller.

Epstein, Joseph. Familiar Territory: Observations on American Life. 1979. 13.95 (ISBN 0-19-502604-7). Oxford U Pr.

Fay, Bernard. American Experiment. 1969. Repr. of 1929 ed. 12.50 (ISBN 0-8046-0142-9). Kennikat.

Frank, Waldo D. Our America. LC 73-105512. Repr. of 1919 ed. 18.50 (ISBN 0-404-02547-1). AMS Pr.

Frohock, W. M. Strangers to This Ground: Cultural Diversity in Contemporary American Writing. LC 61-17183. 1961. 4.95 (ISBN 0-87074-055-5). SMU Press.

Fulton, Maurice G., ed. National Ideals & Problems. facs. ed. LC 68-54346. (Essay Index Reprint Ser). 1918. 18.00 (ISBN 0-8369-0113-4). Arno.

Gilhooley, Leonard. Contradiction & Dilemma: Orestes Brownson & the American Idea. LC 78-158738. xvi, 231p. 1972. 20.00 (ISBN 0-8232-0930-X). Fordham.

Gorer, Geoffrey. American People, a Study in National Character. rev. ed. 1964. pap. 3.25x (ISBN 0-393-00262-4, Norton Lib). Norton.

Griffith, Thomas. The Waist-High Culture. LC 72-10978. 275p. 1973. Repr. of 1959 ed. lib. bdg. 15.00x (ISBN 0-8371-6645-4, GRWC). Greenwood.

Gurko, Leo. Heroes, Highbrows & the Popular Mind. facs. ed. LC 73-134089. (Essay Index Reprint Ser). 1953. 18.00 (ISBN 0-8369-2160-7). Arno.

Howard, Leon. Literature & the American Tradition. LC 78-180985. 354p. 1972. Repr. of 1960 ed. text ed. 12.00 (ISBN 0-87752-156-5). Gordian.

Kallen, Horace M. Culture & Democracy in the United States: Studies in the Group Psychology of the American Peoples. LC 72-129404. (American Immigration Collection, Ser. 2). 1970. Repr. of 1924 ed. 16.00 (ISBN 0-405-00557-1). Arno.

Karon, Bertram P. Black Scars: A Rigorous Investigation of the Effects of Discrimination, New Edition of the Negro Personality. LC 74-79412. 220p. 1975. 10.95 (ISBN 0-8261-1540-3). Springer Pub.

Kemp, Jack. American Renaissance: A Strategy for the Nineteen Eighty's. LC 78-19825. 1979. 8.95 (ISBN 0-06-012283-8, HarpT). Har-Row.

Klapp, Orrin E. Heroes, Villains, & Fools: The Changing American Character. 1979. write for info. Aegis Pub Co.

Knoles, George H. Jazz Age Revisited: British Criticism of American Civilization During the 1920's. LC 68-54276. (Stanford University. Stanford Studies in History, Economics, & Political Science: No. 11). Repr. of 1955 ed. 17.50 (ISBN 0-404-50974-6). AMS Pr.

Lacour-Gayet, Robert. Everyday Life in the United States Before the Civil War, 1830-60. Ilford, Mary, tr. LC 70-81571. (gr. 9-12). 1969. 12.50 (ISBN 0-8044-1500-5). Ungar.

LaPiere, Richard T. The Freudian Ethic. LC 74-6710. 299p. 1974. Repr. of 1959 ed. lib. bdg. 15.75x (ISBN 0-8371-7543-7, LAFE). Greenwood.

Lemelin, Robert. Pathway to the National Character, 1830-1861. LC 74-80589. 1974. 12.50 (ISBN 0-8046-9087-1, Natl U). Kennikat.

Lerner, Max. America As a Civilization, 2 vols. Incl. Vol. 1. Culture & Personality. 1967 (ISBN 0-671-20161-1); Vol. 2. The/Basic Frame (ISBN 0-671-20162-X). 1967. pap. 6.95 ea (Touchstone Bks). S&S.

Lynn, Kenneth S. The Dream of Success: A Study of the Modern American Imagination. LC 73-176134. 269p. 1972. Repr. of 1955 ed. lib. bdg. 19.75x (ISBN 0-8371-6269-6, LYDS). Greenwood.

McConnell, Donald. Economic Virtues in the United States. LC 73-2520. (Big Business; Economic Power in a Free Society Ser.). Repr. of 1930 ed. 8.00 (ISBN 0-405-05100-X). Arno.

McDermott, John J. The Culture of Experience: Philosophical Essays in the American Grain. LC 76-5962. 237p. 1976. 20.00x (ISBN 0-8147-5406-6); pap. 9.50x (ISBN 0-8147-5424-4). NYU Pr.

McFarland, C. K. Readings in Intellectual History. 473p. 1970. pap. 9.50 (ISBN 0-03-081298-4, Pub. by HR&W). Krieger.

McGiffert, Michael, ed. The Character of Americans: A Book of Readings. rev. ed. (Orig.). 1970. pap. text ed. 10.50x (ISBN 0-256-01138-9). Dorsey.

Mann, Arthur. The One & the Many: Reflections on the American Identity. LC 78-27849. 1979. 12.95 (ISBN 0-226-50337-2). U of Chicago Pr.

Mead, Margaret. And Keep Your Powder Dry: An Anthropologist Looks at America. facsimile ed. LC 77-156694. (Essay Index Reprint Ser). Repr. of 1942 ed. 18.00 (ISBN 0-8369-2416-9). Arno.

Messerschmidt, Donald A., ed. Anthropologists at Home in North America: Methods & Issues in the Study of One's Own Society. LC 81-3873. (Illus.). 336p. Date not set. price not set (ISBN 0-521-24067-0); pap. price not set (ISBN 0-521-28419-8). Cambridge U Pr.

Muirhead, James F. America the Land of Contrasts: A Briton's View of His American Kin. LC 74-87430. (American Scene Ser). Orig. Title: Bodley Head. 1970. Repr. of 1902 ed. lib. bdg. 32.50 (ISBN 0-306-71576-7). Da Capo.

Munsterberg, Hugo. American Problems, from the Point of View of a Psychologist. facs. ed. LC 75-84328. (Essay Index Reprint Ser.). 1910. 14.75 (ISBN 0-8369-1098-2). Arno.

Nathan, George J. & Mencken, H. L. The American Credo: A Contribution Toward the Interpretation of the National Mind. 1976. Repr. of 1920 ed. lib. bdg. 13.50x (ISBN 0-374-96036-4). Octagon.

Nevins, Allan, ed. American Social History As Recorded by British Travellers. LC 68-9764. Repr. of 1923 ed. 19.50x (ISBN 0-678-00464-1). Kelley.

Nye, Russell B. Society & Culture in America: 1830-1860. LC 73-14277. (New American Nation Ser.). (Illus.). 416p. (YA) 1974. 15.00x (ISBN 0-06-013229-9, HarpT). Har-Row.

People of Destiny: Americans at Home & Abroad. LC 73-13132. (Foreign Travelers in America,1810-1935 Ser.). (Illus.). 216p. 1974. Repr. 11.00x (ISBN 0-405-05454-8). Arno.

Perry, Bliss. American Mind. 1968. Repr. of 1912 ed. 12.50 (ISBN 0-8046-0361-8). Kennikat.

Perry, Ralph B. Characteristically American. facs. ed. LC 73-134125. (Essay Index Reprint Ser). 1949. 16.00 (ISBN 0-8369-2013-9). Arno.

Potter, David. History & American Society: The Essays of David Potter. Fehrenbacher, Don E., ed. 448p. 1973. 15.95 (ISBN 0-19-501628-9). Oxford U Pr.

Potter, David M. Freedom & Its Limitations in American Life. Fehrenbacher, Don E., ed. LC 76-17786. 112p. 1976. 6.50x (ISBN 0-8047-0933-5); pap. 2.95 (ISBN 0-8047-1009-0, SP147). Stanford U Pr.

--People of Plenty: Economic Abundance & the American Character. LC 54-12797. 1954. 12.00x (ISBN 0-226-67632-3). U of Chicago Pr.

--People of Plenty: Economic Abundance & the American Character. (Walgreen Foundation Lecutre Ser). 1954. pap. 2.95 (ISBN 0-226-67633-1; P28, Phoen). U of Chicago Pr.

Putney, Snell & Putney, Gail. The Adjusted American: Normal Neuroses in the Individual & Society. pap. 2.75 (ISBN 0-06-090095-4, CN95, CN). Har-Row.

Riesman, David, et al. Lonely Crowd: A Study of the Changing American Character. abr. ed. (Studies in National Policy Ser.: No. 3). 1973. 25.00x (ISBN 0-300-01767-7); pap. 5.95 (ISBN 0-300-00193-2, Y41). Yale U Pr.

Royster, Charles. A Revolutionary People at War: The Continental Army & American Character, 1775-1783. (Illus.). 512p. 1981. pap. text ed. 7.95x (ISBN 0-393-95173-1). Norton.

Sellers, Charles G., Jr., ed. Southerner As American. 1960. 16.00x (ISBN 0-8078-0791-5). U of NC Pr.

Shukair, Ali A. The American Way of Life. LC 72-82793. 144p. 1972. 6.00 (ISBN 0-685-27908-1). Philos Lib.
Sloane, Eric. Spirits of Seventeen Seventy-Six. 1976. pap. 2.95 (ISBN 0-345-24875-9). Ballantine.
Spencer, Benjamin T. Quest for Nationality: An American Literary Campaign. LC 57-12017. 1957. 12.95x (ISBN 0-8156-2020-9). Syracuse U Pr.
Spiller, Robert E. & Larrabee, Eric, eds. American Perspectives: The National Self-Image in the Twentieth Century. LC 61-8841. (The Library of Congress Ser. in American Civilization). 1961. 12.50x (ISBN 0-674-02700-0). Harvard U Pr.
Strunsky, Simeon. Rediscovery of Jones, Studies in the Obvious. facs. ed. LC 67-22064. (Essay Index Reprint Ser). 1931. 15.00 (ISBN 0-8369-0911-9). Arno.
Wells, H. G. The Future in America. LC 73-13156. (Foreign Travelers in America, 1810-1935 Ser.). (Illus.). 320p. 1974. Repr. 16.00x (ISBN 0-405-05469-6). Arno.
Wyllie, Irvin G. Self-Made Man in America. 1966. pap. text ed. 7.95 (ISBN 0-02-935670-9). Free Pr.
Youmans, Edward L., ed. Herbert Spencer on the Americans: And the Americans on Herbert Spencer. LC 73-2542. (Big Business; Economic Power in a Free Society Ser.). Repr. of 1883 ed. 8.00 (ISBN 0-405-05122-0). Arno.

NATIONAL CHARACTERISTICS, ARGENTINE
Fillol, Tomas R. Social Factors in Economic Development: The Argentine Case. LC 75-28498. (M.I.T. Research Monograph). 118p. 1975. Repr. of 1961 ed. lib. bdg. 15.00x (ISBN 0-8371-8432-0, FISF). Greenwood.
Martinez Estrada, Ezequiel. X-Ray of the Pampa. Swietlicki, Alain, tr. LC 70-165913. (Texas Pan American Ser). 429p. 1971. 17.50x (ISBN 0-292-70140-3); pap. 9.95x (ISBN 0-292-79500-9). U of Tex Pr.

NATIONAL CHARACTERISTICS, AUSTRALIAN
Hiatt, L. R. Australian Aboriginal Concepts. LC 78-58302. 1978. text ed. 17.00x (ISBN 0-391-00887-0); pap. text ed. 10.00x (ISBN 0-391-00888-9). Humanities.
Learmonth, Nancy. The Australians: How They Live & Work. LC 72-89452. 166p. 1973. text ed. 8.95 (ISBN 0-03-029571-8, HoltC). HR&W.

NATIONAL CHARACTERISTICS, BRAZILIAN
Behague, Gerard. The Beginnings of Musical Nationalism in Brazil. LC 79-174730. (Detroit Monographs in Musicology: No. 1). 43p. 1971. pap. 2.00 (ISBN 0-911772-50-2). Info Coord.

NATIONAL CHARACTERISTICS, BRITISH
see also National Characteristics, English
Barbu, Zevedei. Problems of Historical Psychology. LC 75-28659. 1976. Repr. of 1960 ed. lib. bdg. 19.75 (ISBN 0-8371-8476-2, BAHP). Greenwood.

NATIONAL CHARACTERISTICS, CANADIAN
Berger, Carl. Sense of Power: Studies in the Ideas of Canadian Imperialism, 1867-1914. LC 79-470040. 1970. 17.50x (ISBN 0-8020-1669-3); pap. 6.50 (ISBN 0-8020-6113-3). U of Toronto Pr.
Graham & Rolland. Dear Enemies. 1965. 4.50 (ISBN 0-8159-5300-3). Devin.

NATIONAL CHARACTERISTICS, CHINESE
Heiliger, Wilhelm S. Soviet & Chinese Personalities. LC 80-1383. 221p. 1980. lib. bdg. 17.75 (ISBN 0-8191-1213-5); pap. text ed. 9.50 (ISBN 0-8191-1214-3). U Pr of Amer.
Hu Shih & Lin Yu-Tang. China's Own Critics. LC 72-77386. 1969. 8.50 (ISBN 0-8188-0047-X). Paragon.
Smith, A. H. Chinese Characteristics. (Illus.). 344p. 1972. Repr. of 1900 ed. 29.00x (ISBN 0-7165-2043-5, Pub. by Irish Academic Pr Ireland). Biblio Dist.
Smith, Arthur H. Chinese Characteristics. LC 78-115206. 1971. Repr. of 1894 ed. 14.50 (ISBN 0-8046-1099-1). Kennikat.

NATIONAL CHARACTERISTICS, COLOMBIAN
Reichel-Dolmatoff, Gerardo & De Reichel, Alicia D. People of Aritama. LC 60-14234. (Illus.). 1962. 15.00x (ISBN 0-226-70791-1). U of Chicago Pr.

NATIONAL CHARACTERISTICS, EAST-INDIAN
Carstairs, G. Morris. The Twice - Born: A Study of a Community of High-Caste Hindus. LC 58-9003. (Midland Bks.: No. 108). 344p. 1957. pap. 3.95x (ISBN 0-253-20108-X). Ind U Pr.

NATIONAL CHARACTERISTICS, ENGLISH
see also National Characteristics, British
Ashley, Robert, tr. A Comparison of the English & Spanish Nation: Composed by a French Gentleman Against Those of the League. LC 72-38141. (English Experience Ser.: No. 467). 52p. 1972. Repr. of 1589 ed. 8.00 (ISBN 90-221-0467-2). Walter J Johnson.
Belloc, Hilaire. The Contrast: Foreign Travelers in America, 1810-1935 Ser. LC 73-13117. 278p. 1974. Repr. of 1924 ed. 16.00x (ISBN 0-405-05442-4). Arno.
Bradley, R. N. Racial Origins of English Character. LC 72-118461. 1971. Repr. of 1926 ed. 10.50 (ISBN 0-8046-1210-2). Kennikat.
Inge, William R. English Genius: A Survey of the English Achievement. facsimile ed. Lunn, Hugh K., ed. LC 73-167380. (Essay Index Reprint Ser). Repr. of 1938 ed. 18.00 (ISBN 0-8369-2435-5). Arno.
Kelly, John A. England & the Englishman in German Literature of the Eighteenth Century. LC 21-7048. (Columbia University. Germanic Studies, Old Ser.: No. 24). Repr. of 1921 ed. 17.50 (ISBN 0-404-50424-8). AMS Pr.
Knowler, John. Trust an Englishman. 1980. pap. 3.95 (ISBN 0-14-005662-9). Penguin.
Larned, Josephus N., et al. English Leadership. LC 70-93353. (Essay Index Reprint Ser). 1918. 22.00 (ISBN 0-8369-1416-3). Arno.
Mikes, George. How to Be an Alien: England. (Illus.). 1946. 9.75 (ISBN 0-233-95500-3). Transatlantic.
Notestein, Wallace. English Folk. LC 72-99643. (Essay Index Reprint Ser). 1938. 25.00 (ISBN 0-8369-1475-9). Arno.
Orwell, George. The English People. LC 74-7022. (British History Ser., No. 30). 1974. lib. bdg. 32.95 (ISBN 0-8383-1897-5). Haskell.
Raleigh, Walter. Shakespeare & England. 1918. lib. bdg. 6.50 (ISBN 0-8414-7264-5). Folcroft.
Raleigh, Walter, et al, eds. Shakespeare's England: An Account of the Life & Manners of His Age, 2 Vols. (Illus.). 1916. 59.00x (ISBN 0-19-821252-6). Oxford U Pr.
Spinley, B. M. The Deprived & the Privileged. LC 72-11337. 208p. 1973. Repr. of 1953 ed. lib. bdg. 19.75 (ISBN 0-8371-6663-2, SPDP). Greenwood.
Wallace, Malcolm W. English Character & the English Literary Tradition. LC 72-194457. 1952. lib. bdg. 8.50 (ISBN 0-8414-9678-1). Folcroft.
Weymouth, Anthony, ed. English Spirit. facsimile ed. LC 70-167437. (Essay Index Reprint Ser). Repr. of 1942 ed. 15.00 (ISBN 0-8369-2677-3). Arno.

NATIONAL CHARACTERISTICS, FRENCH
Leites, Nathan. Rules of the Game in Paris. Coltman, Derek, tr. LC 69-19276. 1969. 14.50x (ISBN 0-226-47145-4). U of Chicago Pr.
Maugham, W. Somerset. France at War. LC 75-25373. (Works of W. Somerset Maugham Ser.). 1977. Repr. of 1940 ed. 15.00x (ISBN 0-405-07835-8). Arno.
Romains, Jules. Examen de Conscience des Francais. 168p. 1954. 3.95 (ISBN 0-686-55306-3). French & Eur.
Stein, Gertrude. Paris, France. new ed. LC 76-131286. (Illus.). 1970. pap. 3.95 (ISBN 0-87140-031-6). Liveright.
Wiley, William L. Formal French. LC 67-17322. (Illus.). 1967. 15.00x (ISBN 0-674-30900-6). Harvard U Pr.

NATIONAL CHARACTERISTICS, GERMAN
Eich, Hermann. The Germans. LC 79-6750. (Illus.). 272p. 1980. pap. 5.95 (ISBN 0-8128-6057-8). Stein & Day.
Gottlieb, Fichte J. Addresses to the German Nation. Jones, R. F. & Turnbull, G. H., eds. LC 78-12431. 1979. Repr. of 1922 ed. lib. bdg. 20.00x (ISBN 0-313-21207-4, FIAG). Greenwood.
Kulski, W. W., ed. Thus Speaks Germany. LC 72-180394. Repr. of 1941 ed. 26.50 (ISBN 0-404-56115-2). AMS Pr.
Mayer, Milton. They Thought They Were Free: The Germans 1933-45. 2nd ed. LC 55-5137. 1966. pap. 5.95 (ISBN 0-226-51192-8, P222, Phoen). U of Chicago Pr.
Mitscherlich, Alexander & Mitscherlich, Margarete. The Inability to Mourn: Principles of Collective Behavior. 1975. pap. 22.00 (ISBN 0-686-51232-4, ST00020). Grove.
Remak, Joachim. Gentle Critic: Theodor Fontane & German Politics, 1848-1898. LC 64-16920. 1964. 10.95x (ISBN 0-8156-2064-0). Syracuse U Pr.
Stael, de. De l'Allemagne, 5 vols. (Grands Escrivains de France). 350p. 1967. 15.95 ea. French & Eur.
--De l'Allemagne, Vol. 1. Balaye, Simone, ed. 1959. pap. 4.50 (ISBN 0-686-54923-6). French & Eur.

NATIONAL CHARACTERISTICS, GREEK
see National Characteristics, Greek (Modern)

NATIONAL CHARACTERISTICS, GREEK (MODERN)
Hutton, Maurice. Greek Point of View. LC 72-105840. (Classics Ser). 1971. Repr. of 1926 ed. 12.00 (ISBN 0-8046-1200-5). Kennikat.
Stephanides, Marios. The Greeks in Detroit: Authoritarianism - a Critical Analysis of Greek Culture, Personality, Attitudes & Behavior. LC 75-18134. 1975. soft bdg. 9.00 (ISBN 0-685-64834-6). R & E Res Assoc.

NATIONAL CHARACTERISTICS, HINDU
Hamilton, Walter. Geographical, Statistical & Historical Description of Hindustan & Adjacent Countries, 2 vols. LC 73-926702. 1971. Repr. of 1820 ed. Set. 50.00x (ISBN 0-8002-1454-4). Intl Pubns Serv.

NATIONAL CHARACTERISTICS, INDONESIAN
Koentjaraningrat, R. M. Introduction to the Peoples & Cultures of Indonesia & Malaysia. LC 75-4078. 1975. pap. 6.95 (ISBN 0-8465-1670-5). Benjamin-Cummings.

NATIONAL CHARACTERISTICS, IRISH
Bulwer-Lytton, Edward. England & the English, 2 vols. 723p. 1971. Repr. of 1833 ed. 45.00x (ISBN 0-7165-1592-X, Pub. by Irish Academic Pr Ireland). Biblio Dist.
Green, Alice S. Irish Nationality. 1977. Repr. lib. bdg. 12.50 (ISBN 0-8492-0911-0). R West.
Gwynn, Stephen L. Irish Books & Irish People. facs. ed. LC 74-86756. (Essay Index Reprint Ser.). 1920. 12.00 (ISBN 0-8369-1136-9). Arno.
Ussher, Arland. The Face & Mind of Ireland. 1979. pap. 5.95 (ISBN 0-8159-5517-0). Devin.

NATIONAL CHARACTERISTICS, ISRAELI
Dicks, Brian. The Israelis: How They Live & Work. LC 74-30350. 156p. 1975. text ed. 8.95 (ISBN 0-03-029706-0, HoltC). HR&W.
Gonen, Jay Y. A Psychohistory of Zionism. 384p. 1976. pap. 3.95 (ISBN 0-452-00441-1, F441, Mer). NAL.

NATIONAL CHARACTERISTICS, ITALIAN
Barzini, Luigi. The Italians. LC 63-17858. 1977. pap. 6.95 (ISBN 0-689-70540-9, 225). Atheneum.
Bryant, Andrew. The Italians: How They Live & Work. LC 75-27493. 164p. 1976. text ed. 8.95 (ISBN 0-03-028511-9, HoltC). HR&W.
Sforza, Carlo. Real Italians: A Study of European Psychology. LC 42-14340. Repr. of 1942 ed. 14.50 (ISBN 0-404-05758-6). AMS Pr.

NATIONAL CHARACTERISTICS, JAPANESE
see also Bushido
Kawasaki, Ichiro. Japan Unmasked. LC 69-13500. (Illus.). 1969. pap. 5.50 (ISBN 0-8048-0277-7). C E Tuttle.
Lifton, Robert J. Six Lives-Six Deaths. 1979. 22.50x (ISBN 0-300-02266-2). Yale U Pr.
Mainichi Newspapers. Japan & the Japanese. new ed. LC 72-95973. 240p. 1974. 7.50 (ISBN 0-87040-223-4); pap. 4.95 (ISBN 0-87040-227-7). Japan Pubns.
Minami, Hiroshi. Psychology of the Japanese People. LC 72-75736. 210p. 1972. 15.00x (ISBN 0-8020-1881-5). U of Toronto Pr.
Moloney, James C. Understanding the Japanese Mind. LC 68-23316. 1968. Repr. of 1954 ed. lib. bdg. 15.75x (ISBN 0-8371-0172-7, MOJM). Greenwood.
Nitobe, Inazo. The Japanese Nation. LC 72-82103. (Japan Library Ser.). (Illus.). 1973. Repr. of 1912 ed. lib. bdg. 21.00 (ISBN 0-8420-1396-2). Scholarly Res Inc.
Riesman, David & Riesman, Evelyn T. Conversations in Japan: Modernization, Politics, & Culture. (Midway Reprint Ser.). 1967. pap. 13.00x (ISBN 0-226-71739-9). U of Chicago Pr.
Seward, Jack. Japanese in Action: Useful & Amusing Language Book. LC 68-55570. 224p. 1969. pap. 5.95 (ISBN 0-8348-0033-0). Weatherhill.
Singer, Kurt. Mirror, Sword & Jewel. LC 72-92831. 180p. 1973. 7.95 (ISBN 0-8076-0670-7). Braziller.
Sinha, S. Aspects of Japan. 6.25x (ISBN 0-210-98193-8). Asia.

NATIONAL CHARACTERISTICS, MEXICAN
Diaz-Guerrero, R. Psychology of the Mexican: Culture & Personality. LC 74-23309. (Texas Pan American Ser). 193p. 1975. 12.50x (ISBN 0-292-77512-1); pap. 5.95x (ISBN 0-292-76430-8). U of Tex Pr.
Paz, Octavio. The Labyrinth of Solitude: Life & Thought in Mexico. Kemp, Lysander, tr. from Span. (YA) (gr. 9 up). 1962. pap. 3.95 (ISBN 0-394-17242-6, E359, Ever). Grove.
Ramos, Samuel. Profile of Man & Culture in Mexico. Earle, Peter G., tr. LC 62-9792. (Texas Pan American Ser.). 220p. 1962. 12.50x (ISBN 0-292-73340-2); pap. 4.95x (ISBN 0-292-70072-5). U of Tex Pr.

NATIONAL CHARACTERISTICS, NIGERIAN
LeVine, Robert Alan. Dreams & Deeds: Achievement Motivation in Nigeria. LC 66-20580. 1966. 6.00x (ISBN 0-226-47571-9). U of Chicago Pr.

NATIONAL CHARACTERISTICS, ORIENTAL
Michaux, Henri. Barbarian in Asia. Beach, Sylvia, tr. LC 49-8940. 1949. 6.50 (ISBN 0-8112-0315-8). New Directions.
Nakamura, Hajime. Ways of Thinking of Eastern Peoples: India, China, Tibet, Japan. rev. ed. Wiener, Philip P., ed. 1964. (Eastwest Ctr); pap. text ed. 7.95x (ISBN 0-8248-0078-8). U Pr of Hawaii.

NATIONAL CHARACTERISTICS, RUSSIAN
Barghoorn, Frederick C. Soviet Russian Nationalism. LC 76-6861. 1976. Repr. of 1956 ed. lib. bdg. 21.50x (ISBN 0-8371-8429-0, BASRN). Greenwood.
Heiliger, Wilhelm S. Soviet & Chinese Personalities. LC 80-1383. 221p. 1980. lib. bdg. 17.75 (ISBN 0-8191-1213-5); pap. text ed. 9.50 (ISBN 0-8191-1214-3). U Pr of Amer.
Hingley, Ronald. The Russian Mind. LC 77-7286. 1977. encore ed. 4.95 (ISBN 0-684-16357-8, ScribT). Scribner.
Kovalevskii, Maxime. Modern Customs & Ancient Laws of Russia: Being the Ilchester Lectures 1889-90. LC 78-130599. (Research & Source Works Ser: No. 542). 1970. Repr. of 1891 ed. 22.50 (ISBN 0-8337-1952-1). B Franklin.
Lawrence, Louise D. Another Winter, Another Spring: A Love Remembered. LC 76-19094. 1977. 8.95 (ISBN 0-07-036722-1, GB). McGraw.
Mead, Margaret. Soviet Attitudes Toward Authority: An Interdisciplinary Approach to Problems of Soviet Character. LC 78-10846. 1979. Repr. of 1951 ed. lib. bdg. 14.50x (ISBN 0-313-21081-0, MESO). Greenwood.
Pitcher, H. J. Understanding the Russians. 1964. 7.50x (ISBN 0-8002-2118-4). Intl Pubns Serv.
Smirnov, Georgi. Soviet Man: The Making of a Socialist Type of Personality. 306p. 1975. 15.00x (ISBN 0-8464-0873-2). Beekman Pubs.

NATIONAL CHARACTERISTICS, SCOTTISH
McIntyre, J. A. & Waterston, Elizabeth. Passionate Canadians: Essays on Scots in Canada. 176p. 1981. pap. text ed. 12.95 (ISBN 0-8403-2433-2). Kendall-Hunt.
Notestein, Wallace. The Scot in History. LC 76-104225. xvii, 371p. Repr. of 1946 ed. lib. bdg. 16.25x (ISBN 0-8371-3342-4, NOSH). Greenwood.

NATIONAL CHARACTERISTICS, SPANISH
Ashley, Robert, tr. A Comparison of the English & Spanish Nation: Composed by a French Gentleman Against Those of the League. LC 72-38141. (English Experience Ser.: No. 467). 52p. 1972. Repr. of 1589 ed. 8.00 (ISBN 90-221-0467-2). Walter J Johnson.
Crow, John A. Spain: The Root & the Flower. rev. ed. LC 74-1802. (Illus.). 490p. (YA) 1975. 16.95 (ISBN 0-06-010919-X, HarpT). Harrow.
Daunce, Edward. A Briefe Discourse of the Spanish State, with a Dialogue Intituled Philobasilis. LC 72-6281. (English Experience Ser.: No. 73). 52p. 1968. Repr. of 1590 ed. 7.00 (ISBN 90-221-0073-1). Walter J Johnson.
Ganivet, Angel. Spain: An Interpretation. LC 75-41109. 1976. Repr. of 1946 ed. 15.50 (ISBN 0-404-14755-0). AMS Pr.
Menendez Pidal, Ramon. Spaniards & Their History. Starkie, Walter, tr. 1966. pap. 3.95x (ISBN 0-393-00353-1, Norton Lib). Norton.
Pritchett, V. S. The Spanish Temper. LC 76-7943. 1976. Repr. of 1954 ed. lib. bdg. 19.00x (ISBN 0-8371-8862-8, PRSP). Greenwood.
Williamson, Rene D. Culture & Policy: The United States & the Hispanic World. 1949. 5.00x (ISBN 0-87049-004-4). U of Tenn Pr.

NATIONAL CIVIC FEDERATION
Green, Marguerite. The National Civic Federation & the American Labor Movement. LC 73-9337. 537p. 1973. Repr. of 1956 ed. lib. bdg. 23.00x (ISBN 0-8371-7007-9, GRCF). Greenwood.

NATIONAL DANCES
see Folk Dance Music; Folk Dancing

NATIONAL DATA CENTER
Computer & Invasion of Privacy, U. S. Government Hearings on the Proposed National Data Center. LC 66-62406. Repr. of 1966 ed. 4.95 (ISBN 0-405-00016-2). Arno.

NATIONAL DEBTS
see Debts, Public

NATIONAL EDUCATION ASSOCIATION OF THE UNITED STATES
Carr, William G. The Continuing Education of William Carr: An Autobiography. 442p. 1978. pap. 10.50 (ISBN 0-686-63680-5, 1399-9-06). NEA.
NEA Representative Assembly. Proceedings: 1979. 1979. pap. 12.00 (ISBN 0-686-63695-3, 1207-0-16). NEA.
Nea Representative Assembly, Minneapolis, Mn., ed. Proceedings, Vol. 115. 1977. pap. 6.00 (ISBN 0-8106-1205-4). NEA.
Schultz, Michael J., Jr. National Education Association & the Black Teacher: The Integration of a Professional Organization. LC 70-121684. 1970. 9.95x (ISBN 0-87024-162-1). U of Miami Pr.
Selle, Erwin S. The Organization & Activities of the National Education Association: A Case Study in Educational Sociology. LC 70-177797. (Columbia University. Teachers College. Contributions to Education: No. 513). Repr. of 1932 ed. 17.50 (ISBN 0-404-55513-6). AMS Pr.

West, Allan M. The National Education Association: The Power Base for Education. LC 80-66130. 1980. 15.95 (ISBN 0-02-934880-3). Free Pr.

NATIONAL EMBLEMS

see Emblems

NATIONAL FARMERS' ALLIANCE AND INDUSTRIAL UNION

Blood, F. G., ed. Handbook & History of the National Farmers' Alliance & Industrial Union. 1976. Repr. of 1893 ed. 25.00 (ISBN 0-685-71317-2, Regency). Scholarly.

Jelley, Symmes. Voice of Labor. LC 72-114813. (Research & Source Works: No. 428). 1970. Repr. of 1888 ed. text ed. 24.00 (ISBN 0-8337-1835-5). B Franklin.

Leopold, Vincent, illus. The Alliance & Labor Songster. facsimile ed. LC 74-30660. (American Farmers & the Rise of Agribusiness Ser.). 1975. Repr. of 1891 ed. 9.50x (ISBN 0-405-06837-9). Arno.

McMath, Robert C. Populist Vanguard: A History of the Southern Farmers' Alliance. 1977. pap. 3.95x (ISBN 0-393-00869-X, N869, Norton Lib). Norton.

Morgan, W. Scott. History of the Wheel & Alliance & the Impending Revolution. LC 68-56745. (Research & Source Works Ser: No. 225). (Illus.). 1968. Repr. of 1891 ed. 39.00 (ISBN 0-8337-2462-2). B Franklin.

Schwartz, Michael. Radical Protest & Social Structure: The Southern Farmer's Alliance & Cotton Tenancy, 1880-1890. (Studies in Social Discontinuity Ser.). 1976. 30.00 (ISBN 0-12-632850-1). Acad Pr.

NATIONAL FARMERS' HOLIDAY ASSOCIATION

Shover, John L. Cornbelt Rebellion: The Farmers' Holiday Association. LC 65-11738. (Illus.). 1965. 15.00 (ISBN 0-252-72363-5). U of Ill Pr.

NATIONAL FARMERS ORGANIZATION

Brandsberg, George. Two Sides in N F O's Battle. 1964. 4.50x (ISBN 0-8138-1705-6). Iowa St U Pr.

Campbell, Christiana M. The Farm Bureau & the New Deal: A Study of the Making of National Farm Policy, Nineteen Thirty-Three to Nineteen Forty. LC 62-13210. 1962. 12.50 (ISBN 0-252-72410-0). U of Ill Pr.

NATIONAL FLOWERS

see also State Flowers

NATIONAL FOOTBALL LEAGUE

Berger, Phil. More Championship Teams of the NFL. LC 74-4199. (NFL Punt, Pass & Kick Library). (Illus.). 160p. (gr. 5 up). 1974. PLB 3.69 (ISBN 0-394-92767-2, BYR). Random.

Gutman, Bill. Gamebreakers of the NFL. (NFL Punt, Pass & Kick Library: No. 18). (Illus.). (gr. 5 up). 1973. (BYR); PLB 3.69 (ISBN 0-394-92501-7). Random.

Libby, Bill. Star Quarterbacks of the NFL. LC 70-117548. (NFL Punt, Pass & Kick Library: No. 13). (Illus.). (gr. 5-9). 1970. PLB 3.69 (ISBN 0-394-90155-X, BYR). Random.

May, Julian. Los Angeles Rams. (The NFL Today). (Illus.). (gr. 3-6). 1977. PLB 6.45 (ISBN 0-87191-596-0); pap. 2.95 (ISBN 0-686-67473-1). Creative Ed.

--Minnesota Vikings. (The NFL Today). (Illus.). (gr. 3-6). 1977. PLB 6.45 (ISBN 0-87191-594-4); pap. 2.95 (ISBN 0-686-67477-4). Creative Ed.

--New York Giants. (The NFL Today). (Illus.). (gr. 3-6). 1977. PLB 6.45 (ISBN 0-87191-598-7); pap. 2.95 (ISBN 0-686-67476-6). Creative Ed.

--Oakland Raiders. (The NFL Today). (Illus.). (gr. 3-6). 1977. PLB 6.45 (ISBN 0-87191-595-2); pap. 2.95 (ISBN 0-686-67475-8). Creative Ed.

--San Francisco Forty Nine'ers. (The NFL Today). (Illus.). (gr. 3-6). 1977. PLB 6.45 (ISBN 0-87191-599-5); pap. 2.95 (ISBN 0-686-67474-X). Creative Ed.

--Washington Redskins. (The NFL Today). (Illus.). (gr. 3-6). 1977. PLB 6.45 (ISBN 0-87191-597-9); pap. 2.95 (ISBN 0-686-67472-3). Creative Ed.

NFL Public Relations Dept. NFL Nineteen Eighty-One Media Information Book. (Illus.). 130p. 1981. pap. 7.95 (ISBN 0-89480-148-1). Workman Pub.

Rathet, Mike. The Rutledge Book of Football. 128p. 1981. 10.95 (ISBN 0-8317-7597-1, Rutledge Pr). Smith Pubs.

Rollow, Cooper. Cooper Rollow's Bears 1977 Football Book. LC 77-77329. (Orig.). 1977. pap. 1.95 (ISBN 0-916054-49-7). Green Hill.

Rubin, Bob. All-Stars of the NFL. LC 76-8133. (Punt Pass & Kick Library Ser.: No. 24). (Illus.). (gr. 5 up). 1976. (BYR); PLB 3.69 (ISBN 0-394-93258-7). Random.

NATIONAL FORESTS

see Forest Reserves

NATIONAL GALLERY, LONDON

Potterton, Homan. The National Gallery London. (Illus.). 1978. pap. 8.95 (ISBN 0-500-20161-7). Thames Hudson.

NATIONAL GALLERY OF ART, WASHINGTON, D. C.

Carmean, E. A., ed. Robert Motherwell's "Reconcilliation Elegy". A Journal of Collaboration. LC 80-51574. (Illus.). 90p. 1980. 30.00 (ISBN 0-8478-0337-6); pap. 14.95 (ISBN 0-8478-0336-8). Rizzoli Intl.

Finley, David E. A Standard of Excellence: Andrew W. Mellon Founds the National Gallery of Art at Washington, D. C. LC 73-5676. (Illus.). 200p. 1975. 9.95x (ISBN 0-87474-132-7). Smithsonian.

King, Marian. Adventures in Art. LC 77-20926. (Illus.). 1978. 15.95 (ISBN 0-8109-1769-6); pap. 7.95 (ISBN 0-8109-2167-7). Abrams.

Ragghianti, C Arlo L. National Gallery: Washington. LC 68-20027. (Great Museums of the World Ser.). (Illus.). 1968. 16.95 (ISBN 0-88225-232-1). Newsweek.

Walker, John. The National Gallery of Art: Washington, D.C. LC 74-10716. (Illus.). 1976. 50.00 (ISBN 0-8109-0336-9). Abrams.

Walker, John, commentaries by. National Gallery of Art. concise ed. (Illus.). 1979. 20.00 (ISBN 0-8109-1364-X); pap. 9.95 (ISBN 0-8109-2185-5). Abrams.

NATIONAL GEOGRAPHIC MAGAZINE

Allen, Thomas B., ed. Images of the World: Photography at the National Geographic. (Illus.). 396p. 1981. 18.95 (ISBN 0-87044-394-1). Natl Geog.

Buxbaum, Edwin C. Collector's Guide to the National Geographic Magazine. 3rd ed. 1971. 26.25 (ISBN 0-9600494-0-1). Buxbaum.

Buxbaum, Edwin C., ed. Collector's Guide to the National Geographic Magazine: 35th Anniversary. (Illus.). 1971. deluxe ed. 125.00 (ISBN 0-9600494-1-X). Buxbaum.

National Geographic Picture Atlas of Our World. 312p. 1979. lib. bdg. 16.95 (ISBN 0-87044-312-7); 14.95 (ISBN 0-87044-311-9). Natl Geog.

NATIONAL GERMAN-AMERICAN ALLIANCE

Child, Clifton J. German-Americans in Politics, 1914-1917. LC 70-129394. (American Immigration Collection, Ser. 2). (Illus.). 1970. Repr. of 1939 ed. 8.50 (ISBN 0-405-00549-0). Arno.

NATIONAL GILDS

see Gild Socialism

NATIONAL GREENBACK PARTY

see also Greenbacks

NATIONAL GUARD (U. S.)

see United States–National Guard

NATIONAL GUARD ASSOCIATION OF THE UNITED STATES

Derthick, Martha A. National Guard in Politics. LC 65-11588. (Political Studies Ser). 1965. 12.50x (ISBN 0-674-60200-5). Harvard U Pr.

NATIONAL HEALTH SERVICE, GREAT BRITAIN

see Great Britain–National Health Service

NATIONAL HOCKEY LEAGUE

Thorne, Ian. The Great Defensemen. (Stars of the NHL Ser.). (Illus.). (gr. 4-12). 1976. PLB 7.95 (ISBN 0-87191-493-X). Creative Ed.

NATIONAL HOLIDAYS

see Holidays

NATIONAL HOLINESS ASSOCIATION

Rose, Delbert R. Vital Holiness: A Theology of Christian Experience. Orig. Title: A Theology of Christian Experience. 336p. 1965. pap. 3.95 (ISBN 0-87123-539-0). Bethany Hse.

NATIONAL HONOR SOCIETY

National Association of Secondary School Principals. National Honor Society Handbook. rev. ed. 1978. pap. 3.00 (ISBN 0-88210-051-3). Natl Assn Principals.

--National Junior Honor Society Handbook. rev. ed. 1978. pap. 3.00 (ISBN 0-88210-058-0). Natl Assn Principals.

NATIONAL HYSTERIA

see Hysteria (Social Psychology)

NATIONAL IMAGES

see National Characteristics

NATIONAL INCOME

see also Gross National Product; Multiplier (Economics)

Beckerman, Wilfred. An Introduction to National Income Analysis. 3rd ed. (Illus.). 326p. 1981. pap. text ed. 17.50x (ISBN 0-297-77726-2, Pub. by Weidenfeld & Nicolson England). Biblio Dist.

Hansen, Alvin H. Business Cycles & National Income. expanded ed. 1964. 14.95x (ISBN 0-393-09726-9, NortonC). Norton.

Kendrick, John W. The National Wealth of the United States: By Major Sectors & Industry. LC 76-41080. (Report Ser: No. 698). (Illus., Orig.). 1976. pap. 30.00 (ISBN 0-8237-0132-8). Conference Bd.

King, Willford I., et al. The National Economic Accounts of the United States. Mitchell, Wesley C., ed. LC 75-19734. (National Bureau of Economic Research Ser.). (Illus.). 1975. Repr. 15.00x (ISBN 0-405-07611-8). Arno.

Kuznets, Simon. National Income: A Summary of Findings. LC 75-19719. (National Bureau of Economic Research Ser.). (Illus.). 1975. Repr. 12.00x (ISBN 0-405-07598-7). Arno.

--National Income & Capital Formation, 1919-1935: A Preliminary Report. LC 75-19720. (National Bureau of Economic Research Ser.). (Illus.). 1975. Repr. 9.00x (ISBN 0-405-07599-5). Arno.

Machlup, Fritz. International Trade & the National Income Multiplier. LC 65-18335. Repr. of 1943 ed. 15.00x (ISBN 0-678-00083-2). Kelley.

Marchal, J. & Ducros, Bernard, eds. Distribution of National Income. (International Economic Assn. Ser). 1969. 27.50 (ISBN 0-312-21350-6). St Martin.

Martin, Robert F. National Income in the United States, 1799-1938. LC 75-22827. (America in Two Centuries Ser). 1976. Repr. of 1939 ed. 11.00x (ISBN 0-405-07699-1). Arno.

OECD Staff. National Accounts of OECD Countries 1950-1979, Vol. 1. 89p. (Orig.). 1981. pap. text ed. 7.50x (ISBN 92-64-02117-5, 30-81-01-3). OECD.

Peterson, Wallace C. Income, Employment & Economic Growth. 3rd ed. (Illus.). 500p. 1974. text ed. 10.95x (ISBN 0-393-09279-8). Norton.

Relative National Accounts: A Statistical Basebook-1976 Edition. LC 77-70217. (Report Ser.: No. 708). (Illus., Orig.). 1977. 30.00 (ISBN 0-8237-0142-5). Conference Bd.

U. S. Board Of Governors Of The Federal Reserve System. Flow of Funds in the United States, 1939-1953. LC 69-10163. 1969. Repr. of 1955 ed. lib. bdg. 19.75x (ISBN 0-8371-0254-5, USFR). Greenwood.

Usher, Dan. The Price Mechanism & the Meaning of National Income Statistics. LC 79-11629. (Illus.). 1979. Repr. of 1968 ed. lib. bdg. 18.50x (ISBN 0-313-21466-2, USPR). Greenwood.

NATIONAL INCOME–ACCOUNTING

Alexander, Sidney S., et al. Five Monographs on Business Income. LC 73-84377. 1973. Repr. of 1950 ed. text ed. 13.00 (ISBN 0-914348-00-0). Scholars Bk.

Arya, P. L. Social Accounting for Developing Countries. 1976. 11.00x (ISBN 0-333-90092-8). South Asia Bks.

Correa, Hector. Integrated Economic Accounting: Theory & Applications to National, Real, & Financial Economic Planning. LC 76-17445. 1976. 26.95 (ISBN 0-669-00779-X). Lexington Bks.

Dernburg, Thomas F. & McDougall, Duncan. Macroeconomics. 5th ed. 1976. text ed. 16.95 (ISBN 0-07-016526-2, C). McGraw.

Downing, Richard I. National Income & Social Accounts: An Australian Study. 12th ed. 1970. pap. 4.50x (ISBN 0-522-83953-3, Pub. by Melbourne U Pr). Intl Schol Bk Serv.

Edey, Harold C. & Peacock, Alan. National Income & Social Accounting. 1966. text ed. 5.50x (ISBN 0-09-036763-4, Hutchinson U Lib); (Hutchinson U Lib). Humanities.

Gambling, Trevor. Societal Accounting. 1974. text ed. 17.95x (ISBN 0-04-330242-4). Allen Unwin.

Goldsmith, Raymond W., et al. Studies in the National Balance Sheet of the United States, 2 Vols. (Studies in Capital Formation & Financing Ser.: No. 11). 1963. Set. 27.50 (ISBN 0-691-04180-6, Dist. by Princeton U Pr); Vol. 1. 15.00 (ISBN 0-686-66494-9); Vol. 2. 15.00 (ISBN 0-686-66495-7). Natl Bur Econ Res.

Juster, F. Thomas & Land, Kenneth C., eds. Social Accounting Systems: Essays on the State of the Art. (Studies in Population). 1981. price not set (ISBN 0-12-392550-9). Acad Pr.

Maison des Sciences de l'Homme Symposium, Paris, 1971. Political Economy of Environment: Problems of Method. (Environment & Social Sciences Ser: No. 2). 1972. pap. text ed. 17.75x (ISBN 90-2796-995-7). Mouton.

Nardone, M. A. Income Tax Nineteen Seventy-Nine - Nineteen Eighty. 192p. 1980. 19.75x (ISBN 0-906501-08-3, Pub. by Keenan England). State Mutual Bk.

Pyatt, G., et al. Social Accounting for Development Planning with Special Reference to Sri Lanka. LC 76-53523. 1978. 34.50 (ISBN 0-521-21578-1). Cambridge U Pr.

Ruggles, Nancy & Ruggles, Richard. Design of Economic Accounts. (General Ser.: No. 89). 1970. text ed. 12.50x (ISBN 0-87014-204-6, Dist. by Columbia U Pr). Natl Bur Econ Res.

Yanovsky, M. Anatomy of Social Accounting Systems. 237p. 1969. pap. text ed. 5.95x (ISBN 0-412-20690-0, Pub. by Chapman & Hall England). Methuen Inc.

NATIONAL INCOME–STUDY AND TEACHING

Scott, Robert H. Problems in National Income Analysis & Forecasting. rev. ed. 1972. pap. 6.95x (ISBN 0-673-07793-4). Scott F.

NATIONAL INCOME–GREAT BRITAIN

Bowers, J. The Anatomy of Regional Activity Rates. Bd. with Regional Social Accounts for the U.K. Woodward, V. H. (Economic & Social Research Ser: No. 1). 1971. 13.95 (ISBN 0-521-07719-2). Cambridge U Pr.

Clark, Colin. National Income Nineteen Twenty-Four to Nineteen Thirty-One. LC 67-33571. Repr. of 1932 ed. 24.00x (ISBN 0-678-05161-5). Kelley.

--National Income, 1924-1931. 180p. 1965. Repr. 26.00x (ISBN 0-7146-1215-4, F Cass Co). Biblio Dist.

Feinstein, C. H. National Income, Expenditure & Output of the United Kingdom, 1855-1965. LC 71-163055. (Studies in the National Income & Expenditure of the United Kingdom: Vol. 6). (Illus.). 1972. 71.50 (ISBN 0-521-07230-1). Cambridge U Pr.

--Statistical Tables of National Income Expenditure & Output of the UK 1855-1965. LC 76-19627. 1976. limp bdg. 21.50x (ISBN 0-521-21396-7). Cambridge U Pr.

Welham, Philip J. Monetary Circulation in the United Kingdom. LC 78-92500. 1969. 11.50x (ISBN 0-678-06251-X). Kelley.

NATIONAL INCOME–RUSSIA

Becker, Abraham S. Soviet National Income, 1958-1964: National Accounts of the USSR in the Seven Year Plan Period. LC 70-77483. (Illus.). 1969. 40.00x (ISBN 0-520-01437-5). U of Cal Pr.

Bergson, Abram. Soviet National Income & Product in 1937. LC 75-104222. Repr. of 1953 ed. lib. bdg. 15.00x (ISBN 0-8371-3332-7, BESO). Greenwood.

NATIONAL INDUSTRIAL RECOVERY ACT, 1933

Berle, A. A., Jr., et al. America's Recovery Program. facs. ed. Wilcox, C., et al, eds. LC 76-104990. (Essay Index Reprint Ser). 1934. 18.00 (ISBN 0-8369-1591-7). Arno.

Brown, Douglas V., et al. The Economics of the Recovery Program. LC 70-163644. (FDR & the Era of the New Deal Ser). 1971. Repr. of 1934 ed. lib. bdg. 22.50 (ISBN 0-306-70197-9). Da Capo.

Roos, C. F. NRA Economic Planning. LC 72-171693. (Fdr & the Era of the New Deal Ser.). 596p. 1972. Repr. of 1937 ed. lib. bdg. 55.00 (ISBN 0-306-70396-3). Da Capo.

NATIONAL LABOR RELATIONS BOARD

see United States–National Labor Relations Board

NATIONAL LEAGUE OF PROFESSIONAL BASEBALL CLUBS

Dickey, Glenn. History of National League Baseball. LC 78-24076. (Illus.). 1979. 12.95 (ISBN 0-8128-2577-2). Stein & Day.

Economics of the Recovery Program. facs. ed. LC 68-29202. (Essay Index Reprint Ser). 1968. Repr. of 1934 ed. 10.25 (ISBN 0-8369-0400-1). Arno.

NATIONAL LIBRARIES

see Libraries, National

NATIONAL MARITIME UNION OF AMERICA

Rubin, Charles. The Log of Rubin the Sailor. LC 73-77809. 336p. 1973. pap. 2.25 (ISBN 0-7178-0387-2). Intl Pub Co.

NATIONAL MUSIC

see also Folk Dancing; Folk Music; Folk-Songs; National Songs

Elson, Louis. The National Music of America. 59.95 (ISBN 0-8490-0712-7). Gordon Pr.

Engel, Carl. An Introduction to the Study of National Music: Comprising Researches into Popular Songs, Traditions & Customs. LC 74-24075. Repr. of 1866 ed. 29.50 (ISBN 0-404-12904-8). AMS Pr.

--The Literature of National Music. LC 74-24076. Repr. of 1879 ed. 11.00 (ISBN 0-404-12905-6). AMS Pr.

Sonneck, Oscar G. Report On' The Star-Spangled Banner,' 'Hail Columbia,' 'America,' 'Yankee Doodle' 6.00 (ISBN 0-8446-4606-7). Peter Smith.

NATIONAL OBSERVER

Mockler, Robert J. Circulation Planning & Development for the National Observer. LC 68-64354. (Research Monograph: No. 39). 1967. spiral bdg. 5.00 (ISBN 0-88406-053-5). Ga St U Busn Pub.

NATIONAL NONPARTISAN LEAGUE

Gaston, Herbert E. The Nonpartisan League. LC 75-316. (The Radical Tradition in America Ser.). 325p. 1975. Repr. of 1920 ed. 22.50 (ISBN 0-88355-219-1). Hyperion Conn.

McCurry, Dan C. & Rubenstein, Richard E., eds. The National Nonpartisan League Debate: An Original Anthology. LC 74-30645. (American Farmers & the Rise of Agribusiness Ser.). (Illus.). 1975. 20.00x (ISBN 0-405-06815-8). Arno.

Morlan, Robert L. Political Prairie Fire: The Nonpartisan League,1915-1922. LC 74-9275. (Illus.). 408p. 1974. Repr. of 1955 ed. lib. bdg. 24.75 (ISBN 0-8371-7639-5, MOPF). Greenwood.

Russell, Charles E. The Story of the Nonpartisan League: A Chapter in American Evolution. facsimile ed. McCurry, Dan C. & Rubenstein, Richard E., eds. LC 74-30651. (American Farmers & the Rise of Agribusiness Ser.). (Illus.). 1975. Repr. of 1920 ed. 24.00x (ISBN 0-405-06823-9). Arno.

NATIONAL PARKS AND RESERVES

see also Forest Reserves; Marine Parks and Reserves; Natural Monuments; United States–National Park Service; Wilderness Areas; also names of national parks, e.g. Yellowstone National Park

Albright, Horace M. & Taylor, Frank J. Oh, Ranger! rev. 14th ed. Jones, William R., ed. (Illus.). 176p. pap. 6.95 (ISBN 0-89646-068-1). Outbooks.

Allen, E. F. Guide to the National Parks of America. 59.95 (ISBN 0-8490-0272-9). Gordon Pr.

AMC Maine Mountain Guidebook Committee, ed. AMC Trail Guide to Mount Desert Island & Acadia National Park. 2nd ed. (Illus.). 1975. pap. 2.50 (ISBN -0910146-04-7). Appalach Mtn.

American Heritage. Natural Wonders of America. pap. 6.95 (ISBN 0-671-24712-3, Fireside). S&S.

America's Great Outdoors. 32.00 (ISBN 0-87827-250-X). Ency Brit Ed.

Barker, Ballard M. & Jameson, William C. Platt National Park. LC 74-15909. 1975. 6.95 (ISBN 0-8061-1256-5). U of Okla Pr.

--Platt National Park. (Illus.). 1979. pap. 2.95 (ISBN 0-8061-1540-8). U of Okla Pr.

Belknap, Bill & Belknap, Buzz. Canyonlands River Guide: Westwater, Lake Powell, Canyonlands National Park. LC 74-80876. (Illus.). 64p. 1974. waterproof 8.95 (ISBN 0-916370-08-9); pap. 5.95 (ISBN 0-916370-07-0). Westwater.

Bennett, Ross S., ed. The New America's Wonderlands: Our National Parks. rev. ed. LC 80-12579. 464p. 1980. 12.95 (ISBN 0-686-61302-3). Natl Geog.

Brockman, C. Frank & Merriam, Lawrence C., Jr. Recreational Use of Wildlands. 2nd ed. (American Forestry Ser.). (Illus.). 336p. 1972. text ed. 17.00 (ISBN 0-07-007981-1, C). McGraw.

Brooks, Maurice. Life of the Mountains. (Our Living World of Nature Ser). (Illus.). (gr. 7 up). 1968. 9.95 (ISBN 0-07-008075-5, P&RB); by subscription. 3.95 (ISBN 0-07-046010-8). McGraw.

Butcher, Devereux. Exploring Our National Parks & Monuments. 7th ed. rev. ed. LC 76-12323. (Illus.). 1976. pap. 7.95 (ISBN 0-87645-094-X). Gambit.

Cahn, Robert. American Photographers & the National Parks. Ketchum, Robert, ed. LC 81-918. (Illus.). 180p. 1981. slipcased 75.00 (ISBN 0-670-41778-5, Studio). Viking Pr.

Cameron, Jenks. The National Park Service: Its History, Activities & Organization. LC 72-3024. (Brookings Institution. Institute for Government Research. Service Monographs of the U.S. Government: No. 11). Repr. of 1922 ed. 19.50 (ISBN 0-404-57111-5). AMS Pr.

Clary, Raymond. The Making of Golden Gate Park: The Early Years, 1865-1906. LC 79-51159. (Illus.). 224p. 1980. 25.00 (ISBN 0-89395-024-6); pap. 10.95 (ISBN 0-89395-025-4). Cal Living Bks.

Collier & Helfrich. Mount Desert Island & Acadia National Park. (Illus.). 1978. 9.95 (ISBN 0-89272-078-6); pap. 6.95 (ISBN 0-89272-044-1). Down East.

Conservation Foundation. National Parks for the Future. LC 89-567. 254p. 1974. pap. 7.00 (ISBN 0-89164-009-6). Conservation Foun.

Country Beautiful Editors. One Hundred One Wonders of America. LC 73-77091. (Illus.). 296p. 1973. 25.00 (ISBN 0-87294-036-5). Country Beautiful.

Country Beautiful Editors, ed. America's Great National Forests. (Home Library Ser). (Illus.). Date not set. price not set (ISBN 0-87294-106-X). Country Beautiful.

--National Parks of America. 3rd rev. ed. (Illus.). Date not set. price not set (ISBN 0-87294-105-1). Country Beautiful.

Culhane, Paul J. Public Lands Politics: Interest Group Influences on the Forest Service & the Bureau of Land Management Resources for the Future. LC 80-8776. 376p. 1981. text ed. 29.50x (ISBN 0-8018-2598-9); pap. text ed. 11.95x (ISBN 0-8018-2599-7). Johns Hopkins.

Cutter, John M. Cutter's Official Guide to Hot Springs, Arkansas: 1917. (Illus.). 1979. pap. 3.95 (ISBN 0-89646-057-6). Outbooks.

Daniel, Glenda. Dune Country: A Guide for Hikers & Naturalists. LC 77-78782. (Illus.). 167p. 1977. pap. 6.95 (ISBN 0-8040-0757-8). Swallow.

An Ecological Survey of the Proposed Volcan Baru National Park, Republic of Panama. (Illus.). 1973. pap. 8.50x (ISBN 2-88032-039-9, IUCN21, IUCN). Unipub.

Frome, Michael. National Park Guide, 1981. LC 77-4075. 1981. pap. 7.95 (ISBN 0-528-84544-6). Rand.

--The National Parks. rev.. ed. (Illus.). 160p. (Orig.). 1981. 35.00 (ISBN 0-528-81055-3); pap. 9.95 (ISBN 0-528-88045-4). Rand.

Hakola, John W. Legacy of a Lifetime: The Story of Baxter State Park in Maine. (Illus.). 448p. 1981. 16.00 (ISBN 0-931474-18-3). TBW Bks.

Harris, Ann G. Geology of National Parks. 2nd ed. LC 74-25041. (Illus.). 1977. pap. text ed. 12.95 (ISBN 0-8403-1092-7). Kendall-Hunt.

Harris, D. V. The Geologic Story of the National Parks & Monuments. 3rd ed. 344p. 1980. pap. 19.95 (ISBN 0-471-09764-0, Pub. by Wiley Med). Wiley.

Hjelte, George. Footprints in the Parks. 12.95 (ISBN 0-686-14611-5). Public Serv Pubns.

Hoard, Dorothy. A Hiker's Guide to Bandelier National Monument. (Illus.). 1979. pap. 3.50 (ISBN 0-933004-01-X). Adobe Pr.

Holt-Jensen, Arild. The Norwegian Wilderness: National Parks & Protected Areas. LC 79-321366. (Tokens of Norway Ser.). (Illus.). 78p. (Orig.). 1978. pap. 10.50x (ISBN 82-518-0719-0). Intl Pubns Serv.

Hornby, George, ed. Your National Parks: A Photographic Guide to the National Parks System of the U.S. (Illus.). 1979. 19.95 (ISBN 0-517-53370-7). Crown.

Ise, John. Our National Park Policy: A Critical History. Bruchey, Stuart, ed. LC 78-53548. (Development of Public Land Law in the U. S. Ser.). 1979. Repr. of 1961 ed. lib. bdg. 42.00x (ISBN 0-405-11377-3). Arno.

Jackson, Earl. Your National Park System in the Southwest. 4th ed. LC 67-26925. (Popular Ser.: No. 11). (Illus.). 1978. pap. 3.50 (ISBN 0-911408-50-9). SW Pks Mnmts.

James, Harlean. Romance of the National Parks. LC 72-2847. (Use & Abuse of America's Natural Resources Ser). (Illus.). 258p. 1972. Repr. of 1939 ed. 18.00 (ISBN 0-405-04513-1). Arno.

Ketchum, Richard M. The American Heritage Book of Great Historic Places. LC 57-11274. (Illus.). 288p. 1973. 24.95 (ISBN 0-8281-0280-5, Dist. by Scribner). Am Heritage.

Lewis, William J. Interpreting for Park Visitors. (Illus.). 158p. Date not set. pap. 1.95 (ISBN 0-915992-11-6). Eastern Acorn.

Lindsay, Diana E. Our Historic Desert. Puurade, Richard F., ed. LC 73-11878. (Illus.). 160p. 1973. 14.50 (ISBN 0-913938-15-7). Copley Bks.

A Manual for Planning Interpretive Programmes in National Parks. (Illus.). 22p. 1976. pap. 2.00 (ISBN 0-685-68961-1, FAO). Unipub.

Matthews, William H., III. A Guide to the National Parks, Their Landscape - Geology. 1968. 6.95 (ISBN 0-385-06298-2). Natural Hist.

Milley, John. Treasures of Independence. (Illus.). 224p. 1980. 25.00 (ISBN 0-8317-8593-4, Mayflower Bks). Smith Pubs.

Muir, John. Our National Parks. LC 80-53957. 300p. 1981. 25.00x (ISBN 0-299-02590-X); pap. 6.95x (ISBN 0-299-08604-6). U of Wis Pr.

--Our National Parks. LC 70-120568. Repr. of 1901 ed. 11.50 (ISBN 0-404-04516-2). AMS Pr.

--Our National Parks. LC 1-26282. 1901. 9.00 (ISBN 0-403-00194-3). Scholarly.

--A Rival of the Yosemite: The Canon of the South Fork of King's River, California. Jones, William R., ed. (Illus.). 24p. 1977. Repr. of 1891 ed. pap. 2.00 (ISBN 0-89646-010-X). Outbooks.

Murfin, Jim. National Parks of the USA. (Illus.). 288p. 1981. 24.95 (ISBN 0-8317-6325-6, Pub. by Mayflower Bks). Smith Pubs.

National Parks Planning. 42p. 1976. pap. 7.50 (ISBN 92-5-100077-8, F1031, FAO). Unipub.

Norton, Boyd. Alaska: Wilderness Frontier. (Illus.). 1977. pap. 10.00 (ISBN 0-88349-136-2). Readers Digest Pr.

Peterson, Charles S. Look to the Mountains: Southeastern Utah & the La Sal National Forest. LC 74-18031. 260p. 1975. 0.90 (ISBN 0-8425-0152-5). Brigham.

Planning for Man & Nature in National Parks: Reconciling Perpetuation & Use. (Illus.). 1973. pap. 6.50x (ISBN 2-88032-035-6, IUCN54, IUCN). Unipub.

Pollock, George F. Skyland: The Heart of the Shenandoah National Park. Brown, Stuart E., Jr., ed. LC 60-16567. (Illus.). 283p. 1960. 10.00 (ISBN 0-685-65073-1); pap. 3.50 (ISBN 0-685-65074-X). Va Bk.

Radlauer, Ruth. Haleakala National Park. LC 79-10500. (Parks for People Ser.). (Illus.). (gr. 3 up). 1979. 3.95 (ISBN 0-516-17499-1, Elk Grove Bks); PLB 10.00 (ISBN 0-516-07499-7). Childrens.

Radlauer, Ruth S. Grand Canyon National Park. LC 76-58525. (Parks for People Ser.). (Illus.). (gr. 3 up). 1977. 3.95 (ISBN 0-516-17492-4, Elk Grove Bks); PLB 10.00 (ISBN 0-516-07492-X). Childrens.

Rich, Pamela E. & Tussing, Arlon R. The National Park System in Alaska: An Economic Impact Study. LC 73-620004. (Joint Institute of Social & Economic Research Ser.: No. 35). 96p. 1972. pap. 5.00 (ISBN 0-295-95302-0). U of Wash Pr.

--The National Park System in Alaska: An Economic Impact Study. LC 73-620004. (Illus.). 88p. 1973. pap. 2.00 (ISBN 0-88353-008-2). U Alaska Inst Res.

Riley, Laura & Riley, William. Guide to the National Wildlife Refuges. LC 78-60300. 1979. 17.95 (ISBN 0-385-14014-2, Anchor Pr). Doubleday.

Rowe, Royle C. Geology of Our Western National Parks & Monuments. LC 73-13278. (Illus.). 1976. pap. 4.95 (ISBN 0-8323-0237-6). Binford.

Runte, Alfred. National Parks: The American Experience. LC 79-1431. (Illus.). xvi, 240p. 1979. 16.50 (ISBN 0-8032-3852-5). U of Nebr Pr.

Sax, Joseph L. Mountains Without Handrails: Reflections on the National Parks. 160p. 1980. 10.00x (ISBN 0-472-09324-X); pap. 5.95 (ISBN 0-472-06324-3). U of Mich Pr.

Scott, David L. & Scott, Kay W. Traveling & Camping in the National Park Areas: Eastern States. LC 78-69951. (Illus.). 1979. pap. 4.95 (ISBN 0-87106-001-9). Globe Pequot.

--Traveling & Camping in the National Park Areas: Mid-America. LC 78-69951. (Illus.). 1978. pap. 4.95 (ISBN 0-87106-000-0). Globe Pequot.

--Traveling & Camping in the National Park Areas: Western States. LC 78-69951. (Illus.). 1978. pap. 4.95 (ISBN 0-87106-099-X). Globe Pequot.

Second World Conference on National Parks. (Illus.). 1974. 27.50x (ISBN 2-88032-036-4, IUCN13, IUCN). Unipub.

Shands, William E. Federal Resource Lands & Their Neighbors. LC 79-55692. 98p. 1979. pap. 5.00 (ISBN 0-89164-060-6). Conservation Foun.

Sharpe, Grant W. Interpreting the Environment. 2nd ed. 600p. 1982. text ed. 23.95 (ISBN 0-471-09007-7). Wiley.

Spring & Manning. National Parks of the Northwest. LC 76-6935. (Illus.). 184p. 1976. 14.95 (ISBN 0-87564-015-X). Superior Pub.

Sterling, E. M. The South Cascades: The Gifford Pinchot National Forest. LC 75-14526. (Illus.). 96p. (Orig.). 1975. pap. 4.95 (ISBN 0-916890-37-6). Mountaineers.

Sunset Editors. National Parks of the West. LC 79-90339. (Illus.). 256p. 1980. pap. 8.95 (ISBN 0-376-05583-9, Sunset Bks). Sunset-Lane.

Swain, Donald C. Wilderness Defender: Horace M. Albright & Conservation. LC 70-93057. (Illus.). 1970. 15.00x (ISBN 0-226-78292-1). U of Chicago Pr.

Tilden, Freeman. National Parks. rev. ed. 1968. pap. 7.95 (ISBN 0-394-43764-0). Knopf.

Udall, Stewart L. The National Parks of America. rev. ed. Country Beautiful Editors, ed. LC 72-8646. (Illus.). 226p. 1972. 22.50 (ISBN 0-87294-030-6). Country Beautiful.

Umhoefer, Jim. Guide to Wisconsin's State Parks, Forests, & Trails. (Illus.). 160p. (Orig.). Date not set. cancelled (ISBN 0-915024-26-8). Tamarack Pr.

United Nations List of National Parks & Equivalent Reserves: 1980 Edition. 121p. 1980. pap. 10.75 (ISBN 2-88032-406-8, IUCN 80, IUCN). Unipub.

Van Name, Willard G. Vanishing Forest Reserves. Bruchey, Stuart, ed. LC 78-56688. (Management of Public Lands in the U. S. Ser.). 1979. Repr. of 1929 ed. lib. bdg. 15.00x (ISBN 0-405-11356-0). Arno.

Villagran, M. C. Vegetationsgeschichtliche und Pflanzensoziologische Untersuchungen Im Vicente Perez Nationalpark: Chile. (Dissertationes Botanicae: No. 54). (Illus.). 166p. (Ger.). 1981. pap. text ed. 25.00x (ISBN 3-7682-1265-3). Lubrecht & Cramer.

World Directory of National Parks & Other Protected Areas, 2 vols. 1979. 85.00 set (ISBN 0-686-58176-8, IUCN 75, IUCN). Unipub.

NATIONAL PARKS AND RESERVES–JUVENILE LITERATURE

Colby, C. B. America's Natural Wonders: Strange Forests, Mysterious Caverns, & Amazing Formations. (Illus.). (gr. 4-7). 1956. PLB 5.29 (ISBN 0-698-30009-2). Coward.

Radlauer, Ruth. Acadia National Park. LC 77-18056. (Parks for People Ser.). (Illus.). (gr. 3 up). 1978. PLB 10.00 (ISBN 0-516-07495-4, Elk Grove Bks). Childrens.

--Denali National Park. (Parks for People Ser.). (Illus.). (gr. 3 up). 1981. PLB 10.00 (ISBN 0-516-07743-0). Childrens.

--Mesa Verde National Park. LC 76-27350. (Parks for People Ser.). (Illus.). (gr. 3 up). 1977. 3.95 (ISBN 0-516-17490-8, Elk Grove Bks); PLB 10.00 (ISBN 0-516-07490-3). Childrens.

--Virgin Islands National Park. (Parks for People Ser.). (Illus.). (gr. 3 up). 1981. PLB 10.00 (ISBN 0-516-07741-4). Childrens.

Radlauer, Ruth S. Glacier National Park. LC 76-48993. (Parks for People Ser). (Illus.). (gr. 3 up). 1977. 3.95 (ISBN 0-516-17491-6, Elk Grove Bks); PLB 10.00 (ISBN 0-516-07491-1). Childrens.

--Rocky Mountain National Park. LC 77-2585. (Parks for People Ser.). (Illus.). (gr. 3 up). 1977. 3.95 (ISBN 0-516-17493-2, Elk Grove Bks); PLB 10.00 (ISBN 0-516-07493-8). Childrens.

NATIONAL PARKS AND RESERVES–AFRICA

Proceedings of a Regional Meeting on the Creation of a Coordinated System of National Parks & Reserves in Eastern Africa. (New Publications Ser.: Supp. Paper No. 45). (Illus.). 1977. pap. text ed. 16.00 (ISBN 2-88032-040-2, IUCN 68, IUCN). Unipub.

NATIONAL PARKS AND RESERVES–GREAT BRITAIN

Bell, Mervyn, ed. Britain's National Parks. LC 74-20450. (Illus.). 160p. 1975. 17.95 (ISBN 0-7153-6792-7). David & Charles.

MacEwen, Ann & MacEwan, Malcolm. National Parks: Conservation or Cosmetics. (The Resource Management Ser.). write for info. Allen Unwin.

Waugh, Mary. The Shell Book of Country Parks. LC 80-68695. (Illus.). 224p. 1981. 19.95 (ISBN 0-7153-7963-1). David & Charles.

NATIONAL PLANNING

see Economic Policy; Social Policy

NATIONAL PRODUCT, GROSS

see Gross National Product

NATIONAL PSYCHOLOGY

see Ethnopsychology; National Characteristics

NATIONAL REPUBLICAN PARTY

see also Whig Party

NATIONAL RESEARCH COUNCIL, CANADA

Thistle, Mel W. Inner Ring: The Early History of the National Research Council of Canada. LC 66-8418. 1966. 25.00x (ISBN 0-8020-3156-0). U of Toronto Pr.

NATIONAL RESEARCH COUNCIL, UNITED STATES

Howell, W. H., frwd. by. National Research Council: A History of the National Research Council, 1919-1933. LC 72-94322. (The American Scientific Community, 1790-1920). 1973. Repr. of 1933 ed. lib. bdg. 9.00 (ISBN 0-8420-1663-5). Scholarly Res Inc.

Physics Survey Committee. Physics in Perspective: The Nature of Physics and the Subfields of Physics (Student Edition) (Illus.). 368p. 1973. pap. 7.00x (ISBN 0-309-02118-9). Natl Acad Pr.

NATIONAL RESOURCES

see also Natural Resources; also subdivision Economic Conditions under names of countries, regions, etc. e.g. United States–Economic Conditions

Clawson, Marion. New Deal Planning: The National Resources Planning Board. LC 80-8777. 376p. 1981. 32.50 (ISBN 0-8018-2595-4). Johns Hopkins.

Hirschman, Albert O. National Power & the Structure of Foreign Trade. (California Library Reprint Ser.: No. 105). 1980. 16.50 (ISBN 0-520-04084-8); pap. 5.95x (ISBN 0-520-04082-1, CAMPUS 254). U of Cal Pr.

Thompson, Dennis. Politics, Policy & Natural Resources. LC 76-143506. 1972. 14.95 (ISBN 0-02-932580-3). Free Pr.

NATIONAL SELF-DETERMINATION

see Self-Determination, National

NATIONAL SOCIALISM

see also Anti-Nazi Movement; Fascism; Fascism–Germany; Jews in Germany; Socialism; Totalitarianism; World War, 1939-1945–Causes

Allen, William S. Nazi Seizure of Power: The Experience of a Single German Town, 1930-1935. (Illus.). 1965. pap. 6.95 (ISBN 0-531-06439-5). Watts.

Angebert, Jean-Michel. The Occult & the Third Reich: The Mystical Origins of Nazism & the Search for the Holy Grail. (McGraw-Hill Paperbacks Ser.). 336p. 1975. pap. 3.95 (ISBN 0-07-001850-2, SP). McGraw.

Askenasy, Hans. Are We All Nazis? 1978. 8.95 (ISBN 0-8184-0248-2). Lyle Stuart.

Beradt, Charlotte. The Third Reich of Dreams. 1972. 4.95 (ISBN 0-8129-0047-2). Times Bks.

Bird, Keith W. Weimar, the German Naval Officer Corps & the Rise of National Socialism. 1977. pap. text ed. 34.25x (ISBN 90-6032-094-8). Humanities.

Butler, Rohan D. The Roots of National Socialism 1783-1933. LC 78-63657. (Studies in Fascism: Ideology & Practice). Repr. of 1941 ed. 27.00 (ISBN 0-404-16917-1). AMS Pr.

Chesterton, Gilbert K. End of the Armistice. facs. ed. LC 78-117767. (Essay Index Reprint Ser.). 1940. 15.00 (ISBN 0-8369-1644-1). Arno.

Dewey, John. German Philosophy & Politics. facs. ed. (Select Bibliographies Reprint Ser). 1915. 12.50 (ISBN 0-8369-5552-8). Arno.

Diamond, Sander A. The Nazi Movement in the United States, Nineteen Twenty-Four to Nineteen Forty-One. LC 73-16654. 380p. 1973. 25.00x (ISBN 0-8014-0788-5). Cornell U Pr.

Dunlap, J., et al. Nazis Will Rule the World. 1979. 8.95 (ISBN 0-686-14563-1). World Intl.

Dunlap, James & Koken, Nickolas. World Nazism Grows. 1978. 8.95 (ISBN 0-686-20931-1). World Intl.

Dutch, Oswald, pseud. Hitler's Twelve Apostles. facsimile ed. LC 75-93333. (Essay Index Reprint Ser). 1940. 17.00 (ISBN 0-8369-1286-1). Arno.

Florinsky, Michael T. Fascism & National Socialism: A Study of the Economic & Social Policies of the Totalitarian State. LC 78-63667. (Studies in Fascism: Ideology & Practice). Repr. of 1936 ed. 24.50 (ISBN 0-404-16934-1). AMS Pr.

Flynn, John T. As We Go Marching. LC 79-172212. (Right Wing Individualist Tradition in America Ser). 1972. Repr. of 1944 ed. 15.00 (ISBN 0-405-00421-4). Arno.

Forman, James. Nazism. (gr. 7-12). 1980. pap. 1.50 (ISBN 0-440-95772-9, LFL). Dell.

Forman, James D. Nazism. (gr. 6 up). 1978. PLB 6.90 s&l (ISBN 0-531-01473-8). Watts.

Fraenkel, Ernst. Dual State. LC 78-86276. 1969. Repr. of 1941 ed. lib. bdg. 14.00x (ISBN 0-374-92831-2). Octagon.

Freyer, Hans. Revolution von Rechts. LC 78-63670. (Studies in Fascism: Ideology & Practice). Repr. of 1931 ed. 12.50 (ISBN 0-404-16527-3). AMS Pr.

Gasman, Daniel. The Scientific Origins of National Socialism: Social Darwinism in Ernst Haeckel & the German Monist League. LC 77-132637. 1971. lib. bdg. 15.00 (ISBN 0-685-52449-3). N Watson.

Gilbert, G. M. The Psychology of Dictatorship: Based on an Examination of the Leaders of Nazi Germany. LC 79-15335. (Illus.). 1979. Repr. of 1950 ed. lib. bdg. 19.75x (ISBN 0-313-21975-3, GIPD). Greenwood.

Hartshorne, Edward Y. The German Universities & National Socialism. LC 78-63679. (Studies in Fascism: Ideology & Practice). Repr. of 1937 ed. 18.00 (ISBN 0-404-16943-0). AMS Pr.

Hitler, Adolph. My New Order. De Roussy De Sales, Raoul, ed. LC 73-3444. 1008p. 1973. Repr. of 1941 ed. lib. bdg. 40.00x (ISBN 0-374-93918-7). Octagon.

Jaworski, Leon. After Fifteen Years. (Illus.). 167p. 1961. 7.95 (ISBN 0-87201-017-1). Gulf Pub.

Katz, William L. An Album of Nazism. LC 78-12723. (Picture Album Ser.). (Illus.). (gr. 5 up). 1979. PLB 8.40 s&l (ISBN 0-531-01500-9). Watts.

Knoop, Hans. The Menten Affair. 1979. 12.95 (ISBN 0-02-564500-5). Macmillan.

Lane, Barbara M. & Rupp, Leila J., trs. from Ger. Nazi Ideology before 1933: A Documentation. 208p. 1978. 12.95x (ISBN 0-292-75512-0). U of Tex Pr.

Lewis, Wyndham. Hitler. LC 72-82189. 1972. Repr. of 1931 ed. lib. bdg. 75.00 (ISBN 0-87968-005-9). Gordon Pr.

--The Hitler Cult. LC 72-82187. 1972. Repr. of 1939 ed. lib. bdg. 75.00 (ISBN 0-87968-006-7). Gordon Pr.

Lloyd, Roger B. Revolutionary Religion: Christianity, Fascism, & Communism. LC 78-63686. (Studies in Fascism: Ideology & Practice). Repr. of 1938 ed. 18.50 (ISBN 0-404-16903-1). AMS Pr.

Mann, Thomas. Order of the Day. facs. ed. LC 79-80389. (Essay Index Reprint Ser). 1942. 16.75 (ISBN 0-8369-1060-5). Arno.

Marinoff, Irene. The Heresy of National Socialism. 1976. lib. bdg. 59.95 (ISBN 0-8490-1945-1). Gordon Pr.

Mayer, Milton. They Thought They Were Free: The Germans 1933-45. 2nd ed. LC 55-5137. 1966. pap. 5.95 (ISBN 0-226-51192-8, P222, Phoen). U of Chicago Pr.

Merkl, Peter H. Political Violence Under the Swastika: 581 Early Nazis. 1975. 47.50 (ISBN 0-691-07561-1); pap. 16.50 (ISBN 0-691-10028-4). Princeton U Pr.

Micklem, Nathaniel. National Socialism & the Roman Catholic Church. LC 78-63696. (Studies in Fascism: Ideology & Practice). Repr. of 1939 ed. 24.50 (ISBN 0-404-16957-0). AMS Pr.

Mosse, George L. Nazism: A Historical & Comparative Analysis of National Socialism. LC 77-80873. 134p. 1978. text ed. 5.95 (ISBN 0-87855-236-7); pap. text ed. 2.95 (ISBN 0-87855-661-3). Transaction Bks.

Neumann, Franz L. Behemoth: The Structure & Practice of National Socialism, 1933-1944. 2nd ed. 1963. lib. bdg. 40.00x (ISBN 0-374-96080-1). Octagon.

Noakes, Jeremy & Pridham, Geoffrey, eds. Documents on Nazism: 1919-1945. LC 74-5514. 704p. 1975. 20.00 (ISBN 0-670-27584-0). Viking Pr.

--Documents on Nazism: 1919-1945. LC 74-5514. 704p. 1975. 20.00 (ISBN 0-670-27584-0). Viking Pr.

Pauley, Bruce. Hitler & the Forgotten Nazis. LC 80-17006. xvi, 292p. 1981. 19.00x (ISBN 0-8078-1456-3). U of NC Pr.

Pauley, Bruce F. Hitler & the Forgotten Nazis. LC 80-17006. 294p. 1981. 19.00 (ISBN 0-8078-1456-3). U of NC Pr.

Raab, Earl. The Anatomy of Nazism. rev. ed. (Illus.). 1.50 (ISBN 0-686-74928-6). ADL.

Rauschning, Hermann. Men of Chaos. facsimile ed. LC 71-167405. (Essay Index Reprint Ser). Repr. of 1942 ed. 21.00 (ISBN 0-8369-2471-1). Arno.

Rector, Frank. The Nazi Extermination of Homosexuals. LC 79-3708. (Illus.). 256p. 1980. 12.95 (ISBN 0-8128-2729-5). Stein & Day.

Reitlinger, Gerald. SS: Alibi of a Nation. LC 79-21727. Repr. of 1957 ed. 19.50 (ISBN 0-89201-087-8). Zenger Pub.

Remak, Joachim, ed. Nazi Years: A Documentary History. LC 69-11359. 1969. pap. text ed. 3.95 (ISBN 0-13-610535-1, S195, Spec). P-H.

Snell, John L. Nazi Revolution: Hitler's Dictatorship & the German Nation. 2nd ed. Mitchell, Allan, rev. by. (Problems in European Civilization Ser). 1973. pap. text ed. 4.95x (ISBN 0-669-81752-X). Heath.

Snyder, Louis. Encyclopedia of the Third Reich. (Illus.). 1976. 26.50 (ISBN 0-07-059525-9, P&RB). McGraw.

Staudinger, Hans. The Inner Nazi: A Critical Analysis of Mein Kampe. Rutkoff, Peter M. & Scott, William B., eds. LC 81-7277. 152p. 1981. text ed. 14.95x (ISBN 0-8071-0882-0). La State U Pr.

Stephenson, Jill. The Nazi Organisation of Women. 246p. 1981. 23.50x (ISBN 0-389-20113-8). B&N.

Tenenbaum, Joseph. Race & Reich: The Story of an Epoch. LC 76-8503. (Illus.). 1976. Repr. of 1956 ed. lib. bdg. 35.25x (ISBN 0-8371-8857-1, TERR). Greenwood.

The Third Reich in Perspective: A Resource Unit on Nazism. 24p. 0.35 (ISBN 0-686-74936-7). ADL.

U. S. Department of State, Division of European Affairs. National Socialism. Murphy, Raymond E., et al, eds. LC 75-35378. (U.S. Government Documents Program Ser.). (Illus.). 510p. 1976. Repr. of 1943 ed. lib. bdg. 27.25x (ISBN 0-8371-8601-3, USNS). Greenwood.

University Of Colorado Department Of Philosophy. Readings on Fascism & National Socialism. 112p. (Orig.). 1952. pap. 4.95x (ISBN 0-8040-0259-2). Swallow.

Vermeil, Edmond. Germany's Three Reichs. LC 68-9638. 1969. Repr. of 1944 ed. 28.50 (ISBN 0-86527-086-4). Fertig.

Wagner, Jonathan F. Brothers Beyond the Sea: (National Socialism in Canada) 322p. 1981. text ed. 14.75x (ISBN 0-88920-096-3, Pub. by Laurier U Pr). Humanities.

Waite, R. Hitler & Nazi Germany. LC 65-19350. 1969. pap. text ed. 8.95 (ISBN 0-03-082797-3, HoltC). HR&W.

Waite, Robert G. Vanguard of Nazism: The Free Corps Movement in Postwar Germany, 1918-1923. LC 52-5045. (Harvard Historical Studies Ser: No. 60). 1952. 16.50x (ISBN 0-674-93142-4). Harvard U Pr.

Weinstein, Fred. The Dynamics of Nazism: Leadership, Ideology & the Holocaust. LC 80-514. (Studies in Social Discontinuity Ser.). 1980. 13.50 (ISBN 0-12-742480-6). Acad Pr.

Wiener Library. On the Track of Tyranny. facs. ed. Beloff, M., ed. LC 70-134159. (Essay Index Reprint Ser). 1960. 16.00 (ISBN 0-8369-2090-2). Arno.

Zabel, James A. Nazism & the Pastors. LC 75-30607. (American Academy of Religion. Dissertation Ser.: No. 14). 1976. pap. 7.50 (ISBN 0-89130-040-6, 010114). Scholars Pr Ca.

Zeman, Z. A. Nazi Propaganda. 2nd ed. (Illus.). 265p. 1973. pap. 3.95 (ISBN 0-19-285060-1, GB394, GB). Oxford U Pr.

Ziemer, Gregor. Education for Death, the Making of the Nazi. 1972. lib. bdg. 13.00x (ISBN 0-374-98905-2). Octagon.

NATIONAL SOCIALIST WORKERS PARTY

see Nationalsozialistische Deutsche Arbeiter-Partei

NATIONAL SOCIETY OF THE COLONIAL DAMES OF AMERICA

Browning, Charles H. Some Colonial Dames of Royal Descent: Pedigrees Showing Lineal Descent from Kings of Some Members of the National Society of the Colonial Dames of America, & of the Order of the Crown. LC 76-81187. 1969. Repr. of 1900 ed. 17.50 (ISBN 0-8063-0057-4). Genealog Pub.

National Society of the Colonial Dames of America. American War Songs. LC 73-156922. 1974. Repr. of 1925 ed. 22.00 (ISBN 0-8103-3722-3). Gale.

NATIONAL SONGS

see also Folk-Songs; Patriotic Poetry; Political Ballads and Songs

also names of national songs, e.g. Star Spangled Banner

Browne, C. A. Story of Our National Ballads. rev. ed. Heaps, Willard A., ed. LC 60-15255. (gr. 5 up). 1960. 12.95 (ISBN 0-690-77707-8, TYC-J). Har-Row.

Lyons, John H. Stories of Our American Patriotic Songs. LC 42-24375. (Illus.). (gr. 5-12). 7.95 (ISBN 0-8149-0354-1). Vanguard.

Moore, Frank & Decker, Peter, eds. Songs & Ballads of the American Revolution. LC 79-76562. (Eyewitness Accounts of the American Revolution Ser., No. 2). (Illus.). 1969. Repr. of 1856 ed. 19.50 (ISBN 0-405-01164-4). Arno.

Morris, Christopher. The Oxford Book of Tudor Anthems. 1978. pap. 10.00 (ISBN 0-19-353325-1). Oxford U Pr.

National Anthems of the American Nations. facsimile ed. (Eng., Span., Fr. & Port.). 5.00 (ISBN 0-8270-4385-6). OAS.

Shaw, Martin, et al, eds. National Anthems of the World. 5th ed. LC 75-13887. (Illus.). 480p. 1975. 24.95 (ISBN 0-668-04496-9). Arco.

NATIONAL STATE

Banks, Arthur S. Cross-Polity Time-Series Data. 328p. 1971. 50.00 (ISBN 0-262-02071-8). MIT Pr.

Barnes, Harry E. The Making of a Nation. 69.95 (ISBN 0-87700-032-8). Revisionist Pr.

Eldridge, Albert F., ed. Legislatures in Plural Societies: The Search for Cohesion in National Development. LC 76-28916. 1977. 14.75 (ISBN 0-8223-0373-6). Duke.

Fallers, Lloyd A. Social Anthropology of the Nation-State. LC 74-76548. 192p. 1974. 19.95x (ISBN 0-202-01128-3). Aldine Pub.

Halle, L. J. Men & Nations. 1962. pap. 6.95 (ISBN 0-691-01954-1). Princeton U Pr.

Meinecke, Friedrich. Cosmopolitanism & the National State: Welburgertum Und Nationalstaat. Kimber, Robert B., tr. LC 65-17150. 1970. 25.00 (ISBN 0-691-05177-1). Princeton U Pr.

Pullum, Thomas W. Measuring Occupational Inheritance. LC 74-10262. (Progress in Mathematical Social Sciences Ser: Vol. 5). 176p. 1975. 15.95 (ISBN 0-444-41260-3). Elsevier.

Pulparampil, John K. Models of Nation Building. LC 75-903375. 124p. 1975. 9.00x (ISBN 0-8002-0929-X). Intl Pubns Serv.

Tivey, Leonard. The Nation-State. 224p. 1981. 27.50x (ISBN 0-312-55941-0). St Martin.

Van Nieuwenhuijze, C. A. Nation & the Ideal City: Three Studies in Social Identity. (Orig.). 1966. pap. text ed. 13.50x (ISBN 0-686-22449-3). Mouton.

NATIONAL TEACHER EXAMINATIONS

Arco Editorial Board. Education in the Elementary School: Teaching Area Exam for the National Teacher Examination. LC 79-130295. (Orig.). 1967. pap. 8.00 (ISBN 0-668-01318-4). Arco.

--National Teacher Examination. 5th ed. LC 79-148866. 1974. pap. 6.75 (ISBN 0-668-00823-7). Arco.

Bobrow, Jerry, et al. NTE (National Teacher Examinations) Preparation Guide. (Cliffs Test Preparation Ser.). (Illus.). 534p. (Orig.). 1981. pap. text ed. 9.95 (ISBN 0-8220-2017-3). Cliffs.

Lorentz, Moses L. How to Prepare for the National Teacher Examination (NTE) Common Examinations. 1980. pap. 5.95 (ISBN 0-07-038745-1). McGraw.

Rudman, Jack. Audiology. (National Teachers Examination Ser.: NT-34). (Cloth bdg. avail. on request). pap. 9.95 (ISBN 0-8373-8444-3). Natl Learning.

--Computer Technician. (Teachers License Examination Ser.: T-67). (Cloth bdg. avail. on request). pap. 10.00 (ISBN 0-8373-8087-1). Natl Learning.

--Early Childhood Education - Kindergarten-Grade 3. (National Teachers Examination Ser.: NT-2). (Cloth bdg. avail. on request). pap. 9.95 (ISBN 0-8373-8412-5). Natl Learning.

--Education in an Urban Setting. (National Teachers Examination Ser.: NT-31). (Cloth bdg. avail. on request). pap. 9.95 (ISBN 0-8373-8441-9). Natl Learning.

--Education in the Elementary School - Grades 3-8. (National Teachers Examination Ser.: NT-1). (Cloth bdg. avail. on request). pap. 9.95 (ISBN 0-8373-8411-7). Natl Learning.

--German. (National Teachers Examination Ser.: NT-32). (Cloth bdg. avail. on request). pap. 9.95 (ISBN 0-8373-8442-7). Natl Learning.

--Media Specialist - Library & Audio-Visual Services. (National Teachers Examination Ser.: NT-29). (Cloth bdg. avail. on request). pap. 9.95 (ISBN 0-8373-8439-7). Natl Learning.

--Men's Physical Education. (National Teachers Examination Ser.: NT-36). (Cloth bdg. avail. on request). pap. 9.95 (ISBN 0-8373-8446-X). Natl Learning.

--National Teacher Examination - Common Examination (NTE) (Admission Test Ser.: ATS-15). 300p. (Cloth bdg. avail. on request). pap. 13.95 (ISBN 0-8373-5015-8). Natl Learning.

--National Teacher Examination Passbook Series. (Entire Series). (Cloth bdg. avail. on request). pap. write for info. (ISBN 0-8373-8400-1). Natl Learning.

--Playgrounds (Health Education) Women. (Teachers License Examination Ser.: T-47b). (Cloth bdg. avail. on request). pap. 10.00 (ISBN 0-8373-8047-2). Natl Learning.

--Reading Specialist. (National Teachers Examination Ser.: NT-30). (Cloth bdg. avail. on request). pap. 9.95 (ISBN 0-8373-8440-0). Natl Learning.

--Speech Communication & Theatre. (National Teachers Examination Ser.: NT-35). (Cloth bdg. avail. on request). pap. 9.95 (ISBN 0-8373-8445-1). Natl Learning.

--Speech Pathology. (National Teachers Examination Ser.: NT-33). (Cloth bdg. avail. on request). pap. 9.95 (ISBN 0-8373-8443-5). Natl Learning.

--Teachers License Examination Passbook Series. (Entire Series). (Cloth bdg. avail. on request). pap. write for info. (ISBN 0-8373-8000-6). Natl Learning.

--Texas Government. (National Teachers Examination Ser.: NT-38). (Cloth bdg. avail. on request). pap. 9.95 (ISBN 0-8373-8448-6). Natl Learning.

--Women's Physical Education. (Teachers License Examination Ser.: NT-37). (Cloth bdg. avail. on request). pap. 9.95 (ISBN 0-8373-1632-4). Natl Learning.

Weinlander, Albertina A. Barron's How to Prepare for the National Teachers Examination - Common Examination. LC 68-56408. (Orig.). 1971. pap. 5.50 (ISBN 0-8120-0352-7). Barron.

--Barron's How to Prepare for the National Teachers Examinations-Area Examination: Education in the Elementary School. LC 70-110468. 1971. pap. 5.50 (ISBN 0-8120-0348-9). Barron.

NATIONAL TERRITORY

see Territory, National

NATIONAL TRAINING LABORATORIES

Bradford, Leland P., et al, eds. T-Group Theory & Laboratory Method: Innovation in Re-Education. LC 64-11499. 1964. 28.00 (ISBN 0-471-09510-9). Wiley.

NATIONAL TRUST FOR PLACES OF HISTORIC INTEREST OR NATURAL BEAUTY

Fedden, Robin, ed. Treasures of the National Trust. (Illus.). 1976. 24.00 (ISBN 0-224-01241-X). Transatlantic.

Jackson-Stops, Gervase, ed. National Trust Studies Nineteen Seventy-Nine. (Illus.). 184p. 1978. 27.50x (ISBN 0-85667-051-0, Pub. by Sotheby Parke Bernet England). Biblio Dist.

--National Trust Studies, 1980. (Illus.). 175p. 1979. 27.50x (ISBN 0-85667-065-0, Pub. by Sotheby Parke Bernet England). Biblio Dist.

--National Trust Studies 1981. (Illus.). 160p. 1980. 32.50x (ISBN 0-85667-110-X, Pub. by Sotheby Parke Bernet England). Biblio Dist.

Laws, Peter. A Guide to the National Trust in Devon & Cornwall. LC 77-91765. (Illus.). 1978. 14.95 (ISBN 0-7153-7581-4). David & Charles.

Mulloy, Elizabeth D. The History of the National Trust for Historic Preservation, 1963-1973. LC 65-4705. (Illus.). 192p. 1976. 9.95 (ISBN 0-89133-033-X). Preservation Pr.

NATIONAL UNION OF TEACHERS

Bourne, Richard & MacArthur, Brian. Struggle for Education. LC 79-136012. 1971. 20.00 (ISBN 0-8022-2041-X). Philos Lib.

Thompson, Donna F. Professional Solidarity Among the Teachers of England. LC 68-57584. (Columbia University Studies in the Social Sciences: No. 228). Repr. of 1927 ed. 24.50 (ISBN 0-404-51288-7). AMS Pr.

NATIONAL WOMEN'S TRADE UNION LEAGUE OF AMERICA

Boone, Gladys. Women's Trade Union Leagues in Great Britain & United States of America. LC 68-58549. (Columbia University Studies in the Social Sciences: No. 489). Repr. of 1942 ed. 21.00 (ISBN 0-404-51489-8). AMS Pr.

NATIONALDEMOKRATISCHE PARTEI DEUTSCHLANDS–GERMANY (FEDERAL REPUBLIC, 1949-)

Infield, Glenn B. Secrets of the SS. LC 80-5434. 304p. 1981. 14.95 (ISBN 0-8128-2790-2). Stein & Day.

Mosse, George L. Nazi Culture. LC 80-26608. 432p. 1981. pap. 8.95 (ISBN 0-8052-0668-X). Schocken.

NATIONALISM

see also Cargo Movement; Ethnocentrism; Internationalism; Languages–Political Aspects; Minorities; National Characteristics; National State; Nationalism and Socialism; Nativistic Movements; Patriotism; Regionalism; Self-Determination, National

Apter, David E., ed. Ideology & Discontent. LC 64-20305. 1964. 17.95 (ISBN 0-02-900760-7). Free Pr.
Bagehot, Walter. Physics & Politics. LC 73-716. 164p. 1973. Repr. of 1956 ed. lib. bdg. 15.00 (ISBN 0-8371-6781-7, BAPO). Greenwood.
Barnes, Harry E. History & Social Intelligence. 75.00 (ISBN 0-87700-030-1). Revisionist Pr.
Benda, Julien. Treason of the Intellectuals. Aldington, Richard, tr. 1969. pap. 5.95 (ISBN 0-393-00470-8, Norton Lib). Norton.
Bertelsen, Judy S., ed. Non-State Nations in International Politics: Comparative System Analyses. LC 75-36404. 1978. text ed. 29.95 (ISBN 0-275-56320-0). Praeger.
Brutents. National Liberation Revolutions Today, 2 vols. 555p. 1977. 6.90 (ISBN 0-8285-3218-4, Pub. by Progress Pubs Russia). Imported Pubns.
Carr, Edward H. Nationalism & After. 1945. 9.95 (ISBN 0-312-56000-1). St Martin.
Chertijin, V., et al. America Latina: Nacionalismo, Democracia y Revolucion. 188p. (Span.). 1978. pap. 3.75 (ISBN 0-8285-1675-8, Pub. by Progress Pubs Russia). Imported Pubns.
Daly, D. J. & Globerman, S. Tariff & Science Policies: Applications of a Model of Nationalism. LC 76-24911. (Ontario Economic Council Ser). (Illus.). 1976. pap. 7.50 (ISBN 0-8020-3338-5). U of Toronto Pr.
Davis, Horace B. Toward a Marxist Theory of Nationalism. 1980. pap. 7.50 (ISBN 0-85345-516-3, PB5163). Monthly Rev.
Deutsch, Karl W. Nationalism & Social Communication: An Inquiry into the Foundations of Nationality. (Illus.). 1953. pap. 8.95x (ISBN 0-262-54001-0). MIT Pr.
Doob, Leonard W. Patriotism & Nationalism: Their Psychological Foundations. LC 76-42309. (Illus.). 1976. Repr. of 1964 ed. lib. bdg. 22.00x (ISBN 0-8371-8978-0, DOPN). Greenwood.
Earle, Edward M., ed. Nationalism & Internationalism: Essays Inscribed to Carlton J. H. Hayes. LC 74-4429. xvii, 508p. 1974. Repr. of 1951 ed. lib. bdg. 25.00x (ISBN 0-374-92447-3). Octagon.
Farmer, Kenneth C. Ukrainian Nationalism in the Post-Stalin Era: Myth, Symbols & Ideology in Soviet Nationalities Policy. (Studies in Contemporary History: Vol. 4). 253p. 1980. lib. bdg. 36.50 (ISBN 90-247-2401-5, Pub. by Martinus Nijhoff). Kluwer Boston.
Fisher, Herbert A. Common Weal. facs. ed. LC 68-22911. (Essay Index Reprint Ser). 1924. 16.00 (ISBN 0-8369-0440-0). Arno.
Fishman, Joshua A. Language & Nationalism. LC 72-149036. 1973. pap. 11.95 (ISBN 0-912066-15-6). Newbury Hse.
Freud, Arthur. Of Human Sovereignty. LC 65-10993. 1965. 6.00 (ISBN 0-8022-0539-9). Philos Lib.
Fuller, John F. War & Western Civilization, 1832-1932. LC 72-102238. (Select Bibliographies Reprint Ser). 1932. 22.00 (ISBN 0-8369-5123-9). Arno.
Groth, Alexander J. Major Ideologies: An Interpretative Survey of Democracy, Socialism & Nationalism. LC 74-168636. 244p. 1971. pap. 9.50 (ISBN 0-471-32895-2). Krieger.
Hayes, Carlton J. Essays on Nationalism. LC 66-27097. 1966. Repr. of 1926 ed. 13.00 (ISBN 0-8462-0802-4). Russell.
--Historical Evolution of Modern Nationalism. LC 68-15128. 1968. Repr. of 1931 ed. 19.00 (ISBN 0-8462-1147-5). Russell.
Jessup, Phillip C. Birth of Nations. LC 73-15515. (Illus.). 361p. 1974. 17.50x (ISBN 0-231-03721-X). Columbia U Pr.
Joseph, Bernard. Nationality: Its Nature & Problems. 1923. 37.50x (ISBN 0-686-51422-X). Elliots Bks.
Kamenka, Eugene, ed. Nationalism. LC 76-15051. 1976. 15.95x (ISBN 0-312-55965-8). St Martin.
Kayser, Elmer L. Grand Social Enterprise: A Study of Jeremy Bentham in His Relation to Liberal Nationalism. LC 32-31698. (Columbia University Studies in the Social Sciences: No. 377). Repr. of 1932 ed. 12.50 (ISBN 0-404-51377-8). AMS Pr.
Kedourie, E. Nationalism. 3rd ed. 1979. pap. text ed. 6.50x (ISBN 0-391-02077-3, Hutchinson U Lib). Humanities.
Kohn, H. Nationalism & Realism: 1852-1879. 4.75 (ISBN 0-8446-2396-2). Peter Smith.
Kohn, Hans. Idea of Nationalism. 1961. pap. 3.95 (ISBN 0-02-073660-6, Collier). Macmillan.
--Nationalism & Realism: 1852-1879. (Anvil Ser.). 191p. 1968. pap. 4.95 (ISBN 0-442-00096-0, Pub. by Van Nos Reinhold). Krieger.
--Nationalism: Its Meaning & History. rev. ed. (Orig.). 1965. pap. 5.95x (ISBN 0-442-00008-1, 8, Anv). Van Nos Reinhold.
--Prophets & People: Studies in Nineteenth Century Nationalism. LC 75-4697. v, 213p. 1975. Repr. of 1946 ed. lib. bdg. 15.50x (ISBN 0-374-94613-2). Octagon.
--Revolutions & Dictatorships. facs. ed. LC 75-80388. (Essay Index Reprint Ser). 1939. 23.00 (ISBN 0-8369-1145-8). Arno.
Kushner, David. The Rise of Turkish Nationalism 1876-1908. 126p. 1977. 25.00x (ISBN 0-7146-3075-6, F Cass Co). Biblio Dist.
Leakey, Louis S. Defeating Mau Mau. LC 74-15061. Repr. of 1954 ed. 14.00 (ISBN 0-404-12102-0). AMS Pr.
Lenin, Vladimir I. Lenin on the National & Colonial Questions. 1967. pap. 0.75 (ISBN 0-8351-0129-0). China Bks.
Leone, Bruno, ed. Nationalism: Opposing Viewpoints. (ISMS Ser.). (Illus.). (gr. 9-12). 1978. 8.95 (ISBN 0-912616-57-1); pap. 3.95 (ISBN 0-912616-56-3). Greenhaven.
Luxemburg, Rosa. The National Question: Selected Writings by Rosa Luxembourg. Davis, Horace B., ed. LC 74-2148. (Illus.). 320p. 1981. pap. 7.00 (ISBN 0-85345-577-5). Monthly Rev.
Luza, Radomir. Austro-German Relations in the Anschluss Era. 432p. 1975. 31.50x (ISBN 0-691-07568-9). Princeton U Pr.
Macartney, Carlile A. National States & National Minorities. 2nd ed. LC 68-15136. (With a new intro. & epilogue). 1968. Repr. of 1934 ed. 18.50 (ISBN 0-8462-1266-8). Russell.
McCoy, Duke. Brave Words & Bloody Knuckles: How to Start Your Own White Nationalist Party. 1981. pap. 8.95 (ISBN 0-686-30638-4). Loompanics.
McCully, Bruce T. English Education & the Origins of Indian Nationalism. 1966. 7.50 (ISBN 0-8446-1308-8). Peter Smith.
Marcu, E. D. Nationalism in the Sixteenth Century. LC 75-39172. 1975. 8.50 (ISBN 0-913870-08-0). Abaris Bks.
Merritt, Richard L. Symbols of American Community, 1735-1775. LC 76-23442. (Yale Studies in Political Science Ser: No. 16). (Illus.). 279p. 1976. Repr. of 1966 ed. lib. bdg. 19.00x (ISBN 0-8371-9012-6, MESY). Greenwood.
Mitchison, Rosalind. The Roots of Nationalism: Studies in Northern Europe. 175p. 1980. text ed. 31.25x (ISBN 0-85976-058-8). Humanities.
Mosse, George L. The Nationalization of the Masses: Political Symbolism & Mass Movements in Germany from the Napoleonic Wars Through the Third Reich. 1977. pap. 4.95 (ISBN 0-452-00464-0, F464, Mer). NAL.
Muir, Ramsay. Interdependent World & Its Problems. LC 76-137953. (Economic Thought, History & Challenge Ser). 1971. Repr. of 1933 ed. 13.50 (ISBN 0-8046-1455-5). Kennikat.
Oinas, Felix J., ed. Folklore Nationalism & Politics. 1977. pap. 9.95 (ISBN 0-89357-043-5). Slavica.
Palumbo, Michael & Shanahan, William O., eds. Nationalism: Essays in Honor of Louis L. Snyder. LC 81-6501. (Contributions in Political Science Ser.: No. 65). 232p. 1981. lib. bdg. 27.50 (ISBN 0-313-23176-1, PNA/). Greenwood.
--Nationalism: Essays in Honor of Louis L. Snyder. 1981. 19.95 (ISBN 0-935764-02-X). Ark Hse NY.
Peake, Cyrus H. Nationalism & Education in Modern China. LC 72-80580. 1970. Repr. of 1932 ed. 21.00 (ISBN 0-86527-138-0). Fertig.
Pundt, Alfred G. Arndt & the Nationalist Awakening in Germany. LC 68-54287. (Columbia University. Studies in the Social Sciences: No. 413). Repr. of 1935 ed. 14.00 (ISBN 0-404-51413-8). AMS Pr.
Ramadhan, S. Islam & Nationalism. pap. 1.00 (ISBN 0-686-18586-2). Kazi Pubns.
Richards, Leyton. Realistic Pacifism: The Ethics of War & the Politics of Peace. LC 79-147676. (Library of War & Peace; Relig. & Ethical Positions on War). lib. bdg. 38.00 (ISBN 0-8240-0433-7). Garland Pub.
Rocker, Rudolf. Nationalism & Culture. Chase, Ray E., tr. from Ger. LC 78-5960. 1978. 15.00 (ISBN 0-9602574-1-1). M E Coughlin.
--Nationalism & Culture. 50.00 (ISBN 0-87700-076-X). Revisionist Pr.
Rokkan, Stein, et al. Nation-Building: A Review of Recent Comparative Research & a Select Bibliography of Analytical Studies. (Current Sociology-la Sociologie Contemporaine: No. 19-3). 1973. pap. 10.00x (ISBN 90-2797-220-6). Mouton.
Royal Institute Of International Affairs. Nationalism. LC 66-31536. Repr. of 1939 ed. 25.00x (ISBN 0-678-05194-1). Kelley.
Sarbadhikari, Pradip. New Nationalism & International Society. LC 74-900392. 211p. 1973. 7.50x (ISBN 0-8002-0937-0). Intl Pubns Serv.
Seton-Watson, H. Nationalism: Old & New. 1965. pap. 2.00x (ISBN 0-424-05070-6, Pub. by Sydney U Pr). Intl Schol Bk Serv.
Seton-Watson, Hugh. Nations & States: An Enquiry into the Origins of Nations & the Politics of Nationalism. 563p. lib. bdg. 33.75 (ISBN 0-89158-227-4); pap. text ed. 15.00 (ISBN 0-89158-227-4). Westview.
Seton-Watson, R. W. War & Democracy. Wilson, Dover, ed. LC 70-110922. 1970. Repr. of 1915 ed. 14.50 (ISBN 0-8046-0904-7). Kennikat.
Shafer, Boyd C. Faces of Nationalism: New Realities & Old Myths. LC 74-6068. 560p. 1974. pap. 5.45 (ISBN 0-15-629800-7, HB296, Harv). HarBraceJ.
--Nationalism & Internationalism: Belonging in Human Experience. 1981. pap. 4.95 (ISBN 0-89874-260-9). Krieger.
Siegfried, Andre. America Comes of Age: A French Analysis. 2nd ed. Hemming, Doris & Hemming, H. H., trs. LC 68-16244. (American Scene Ser.). 368p. 1974. Repr. of 1927 ed. lib. bdg. 32.50 (ISBN 0-306-71025-0). Da Capo.
Smith, Anthony D. Nationalism: A Trend Report & Bibliography Prepared for the International Sociological Association Under the Auspices of the International Committee for Social Sciences Documentation. (Current Sociology-la Sociologie Contemporaine: Vol. XXI, 3). 1975. pap. 19.50x (ISBN 0-686-21792-6). Mouton.
--Nationalism in the Twentieth Century. LC 78-71404. 1979. cusa 20.00x (ISBN 0-8147-7799-6); pap. 9.00x cusa (ISBN 0-8147-7803-8). NYU Pr.
--Nationalist Movements. LC 77-75680. 1977. 16.95x (ISBN 0-312-56012-5). St Martin.
Snyder, Louis L. Meaning of Nationalism. LC 68-8338. (Illus.). 1968. Repr. of 1954 ed. lib. bdg. 19.25x (ISBN 0-8371-0233-2, SNMN). Greenwood.
--New Nationalism. LC 68-16391. (gr. 11-12). 1968. 25.00x (ISBN 0-8014-0401-0). Cornell U Pr.
--Varieties of Nationalism. LC 73-2097. 1976. text ed. 9.95 (ISBN 0-03-079420-X, HoltC). HR&W.
Stubbs, W. Historical Introductions to the Rolls Series. LC 68-25267. (British History Ser., No. 30). 1969. Repr. of 1902 ed. lib. bdg. 45.95 (ISBN 0-8383-0243-2). Haskell.
Symmons-Symonolewicz, Konstantin. Modern Nationalism: Towards a Consensus in Theory. 1968. pap. text ed. 3.50x (ISBN 0-914048-01-5). Maplewood.
--Nationalist Movements: A Comparative View. 1970. text ed. 6.50x (ISBN 0-914048-03-1); pap. text ed. 4.50x (ISBN 0-914048-02-3). Maplewood.
Tagore, Rabindranath. Nationalism. 159p. 1973. Repr. of 1917 ed. lib. bdg. 15.00x (ISBN 0-8371-6571-7, TANA). Greenwood.
Thomas, R. Hinton. Liberalism, Nationalism & the German Intellectuals, 1822-1847. LC 75-11803. 148p. 1975. Repr. of 1951 ed. lib. bdg. 15.00x (ISBN 0-8371-8140-2, THLI). Greenwood.
Thornton, A. P. Imperialism in the Twentieth Century. LC 77-81211. 1978. 22.50x (ISBN 0-8166-0820-2). U of Minn Pr.
Ulyanovsky, R. National Liberation. 397p. 1978. 7.25 (ISBN 0-8285-1498-4, Pub. by Progress Pubs Russia). Imported Pubns.
Ward, Barbara. Five Ideas That Change the World. 1959. pap. 5.95x (ISBN 0-393-09438-3, NortonC). Norton.
Yapp, Malcolm. Nationalism. Killingray, Margaret & O'Connor, Edmund, eds. (World History Ser.). (Illus.). 32p. (gr. 10). 1980. Repr. of 1977 ed. lib. bdg. 5.95 (ISBN 0-89908-227-0); pap. text ed. 1.95 (ISBN 0-89908-202-5). Greenhaven.
Zimmern, Alfred E. America & Europe & Other Essays. facs. ed. LC 78-84350. (Essay Index Reprint Ser). 1929. 14.50 (ISBN 0-8369-1117-2). Arno.
--Prospects of Democracy & Other Essays. facs. ed. LC 68-8506. (Essay Index Reprint Ser). 1929. 17.00 (ISBN 0-8369-1017-6). Arno.
Znaniecki, Florian. Modern Nationalities. LC 72-7875. 196p. 1973. Repr. of 1952 ed. lib. bdg. 15.75x (ISBN 0-8371-6549-0, ZNMN). Greenwood.

NATIONALISM–AFRICA

Akintoye, S. A. Emergent African States: Topics in Twentieth Century African History. 1977. pap. text ed. 6.50x (ISBN 0-582-60127-4). Longman.
Al-Fasi, Alal. Independence Movements in Arab North Africa. LC 70-96201. 1969. Repr. of 1954 ed. lib. bdg. 22.50x (ISBN 0-374-90095-7). Octagon.
Andrews, William G. French Politics & Algeria: The Process of Policy Formation 1954-1962. LC 62-15310. (Orig.). 1962. pap. text ed. 9.95x (ISBN 0-89197-179-3). Irvington.
Ayandele, E. A. Holy Johnson: Pioneer of African Nationalism, 1836-1917. (Africana Modern Library: No. 13). 1970. text ed. 12.75x (ISBN 0-391-00041-1). Humanities.
Azikiwe, Nnamdi. Renascent Africa. LC 79-94488. Repr. of 1937 ed. 12.25x (ISBN 0-8371-2365-8). Greenwood.
Chilcote, Ronald H., compiled by. Emerging Nationalism in Portuguese Africa: A Bibliography of Documentary Ephemera Through 1965. LC 71-155299. (Bibliographical Ser.: No. 39). 114p. 1969. 9.95 (ISBN 0-8179-2391-8); pap. 5.95 (ISBN 0-8179-2392-6). Hoover Inst Pr.
Hall, Richard. The High Price of Principles: Kaunda & the White South. LC 74-106642. 1970. 17.50x (ISBN 0-8419-0038-8, Africana). Holmes & Meier.
Hodgkin, Thomas. Nationalism in Colonial Africa. LC 57-8133. (Orig.). 1957. 10.00x (ISBN 0-8147-0190-6); pap. 7.00x (ISBN 0-8147-0191-4). NYU Pr.
Kedourie, Elie, ed. Nationalism in Asia & Africa. 1970. pap. 4.95 (ISBN 0-452-00271-0, F271, Mer). NAL.
Kesteloot, Lilyan. Intellectual Origins of the African Revolution. Mboukou, Alexandre, tr. from Fr. LC 70-172329. Orig. Title: Negritude et Situation Coloniale. 120p. 1972. 8.50 (ISBN 0-87953-003-0, BO). Inscape Corp.
Kohn, Hans & Sokolsky, Wallace. African Nationalism in the Twentieth Century. (Orig.). 1965. pap. 4.95x (ISBN 0-442-00079-0, 79, Anv). Van Nos Reinhold.
Legum, Colin. Southern Africa: Year of the Whirlwind. LC 77-6264. (Current Affairs Ser.). 1977. pap. text ed. 6.95x (ISBN 0-8419-0318-2, Africana). Holmes & Meier.
Marcum, John A. Angolan Revolution Vol. 1: The Anatomy of an Explosion, 1950-1962. (Studies in Communism, Revisionism & Revolution). 1969. 30.00x (ISBN 0-262-13048-3). MIT Pr.
Mazrui, Ali A. Towards a Pax Africana: A Study of Ideology & Ambition. LC 67-12232. (Nature of Human Society Ser). 1967. 12.50x (ISBN 0-226-51427-7). U of Chicago Pr.
Padmore, George. Africa: Britain's Third Empire. LC 75-92754. Repr. of 1949 ed. 13.25x (ISBN 0-8371-2182-5, Pub. by Negro U Pr). Greenwood.
Panikkar, K. Madhu. Revolution in Africa. LC 74-27428. 202p. 1975. Repr. of 1961 ed. lib. bdg. 15.00x (ISBN 0-8371-7901-7, PARA). Greenwood.
Quigg, Philip W., ed. Africa: A Foreign Affairs Reader. LC 75-40999. 1977. Repr. of 1964 ed. lib. bdg. 19.75x (ISBN 0-8371-8713-3, QUAF). Greenwood.
Ritner, Peter V. Death of Africa. 1960. 4.95 (ISBN 0-02-603540-5). Macmillan.
Rotberg, Robert I. Rise of Nationalism in Central Africa: The Making of Malawi & Zambia, 1873-1964. LC 65-19829. (Center for International Affairs Ser). (Illus.). 1965. 16.50x (ISBN 0-674-77190-7); pap. 4.95x (ISBN 0-674-77191-5, HP39). Harvard U Pr.
Sithole, Ndabaningi. African Nationalism. 2nd ed. LC 68-133467. (Illus.). 1968. 10.50x (ISBN 0-19-215631-4); pap. 3.95x (ISBN 0-19-501053-1). Oxford U Pr.
Stockholm International Peace Research Institute. Southern Africa: The Escalation of a Conflict. LC 76-4518. (Special Studies). 400p. 1976. text ed. 32.50 (ISBN 0-275-56840-7). Praeger.
Thwaite, Daniel. Seething African Pot, a Study of Black Nationalism, 1882-1935. Repr. of 1936 ed. 13.50x (ISBN 0-8371-3757-8). Greenwood.
Walshe, Peter. The Rise of African Nationalism in South Africa: The African National Congress, 1912-1952. (Perspectives on Southern Africa: No. 3). 1971. 35.00x (ISBN 0-520-01810-9). U of Cal Pr.
Weinstein, Brian. Gabon: Nation-Building on the Ogooue. (Illus.). 1967. 17.00x (ISBN 0-262-23023-2). MIT Pr.
Wilson, Henry S., ed. Origins of West African Nationalism. LC 73-88171. 1970. pap. 7.50 (ISBN 0-312-58905-0). St Martin.

NATIONALISM–ARAB COUNTRIES

Abraham, A. J. Lebanon at Mid-Century: Maronite-Druze Relations in Lebanon 1840-1860; a Prelude to Arab Nationalism. LC 80-6253. 156p. 1981. lib. bdg. 17.50 (ISBN 0-8191-1536-3); pap. text ed. 8.50 (ISBN 0-8191-1537-1). U Pr of Amer.
Clements, Frank. The Emergence of Arab Nationalism. LC 76-5160. 1976. 16.00 (ISBN 0-8420-2096-9). Scholarly Res Inc.
Cleveland, William L. Making of an Arab Nationalist: Ottomanism & Arabism in the Life & Thought of Sati' Al-Husri. LC 78-155961. 1972. 16.00 (ISBN 0-691-03088-X). Princeton U Pr.
Cottam, Richard W. Nationalism in Iran: Updated Through 1978. LC 78-12302. 1979. 15.95 (ISBN 0-8229-3396-9); pap. 6.95 (ISBN 0-8229-5299-8). U of Pittsburgh Pr.
Dawn, C. Ernest. From Ottomanism to Arabism: Essays on the Origins of Arab Nationalism. LC 72-88953. 212p. 1973. 12.50 (ISBN 0-252-00202-4). U of Ill Pr.
Ismael, Tareq Y. Arab Left. LC 76-48136. 1976. 15.00x (ISBN 0-8156-0124-7); pap. 6.95x (ISBN 0-8156-0125-5). Syracuse U Pr.
Katibah, Habeeb I. The New Spirit in Arab Lands. LC 76-180352. Repr. of 1940 ed. 23.45 (ISBN 0-404-56284-1). AMS Pr.

Tibi, Bassam, ed. Arab Nationalism: A Critical Inquiry. 1980. 20.00 (ISBN 0-312-04716-9). St Martin.

Tutsch, Hans E. Facets of Arab Nationalism. LC 65-12128. (Waynebooks Ser: No. 16). (Orig.). 1965. 6.95x (ISBN 0-8143-1258-6); pap. 4.95x (ISBN 0-8143-1259-4). Wayne St U Pr.

NATIONALISM–ASIA

Anderson, Benedict R. Java in a Time of Revolution. LC 74-174891. 512p. 1972. 27.50x (ISBN 0-8014-0687-0). Cornell U Pr.

Brown, D. M. Nationalist Movement: Indian Political Thought from Ranade to Bhave. 1962. 5.00 (ISBN 0-8446-1753-9). Peter Smith.

Croizier, Ralph C. Koxinga & Chinese Nationalism: History, Myth & the Hero. (East Asian Monographs Ser: No. 66). 150p. 1977. pap. 9.00x (ISBN 0-674-50566-2). Harvard U Pr.

De Francis, John. Nationalism & Language Reform in China. LC 74-187315. xii, 306p. 1972. Repr. of 1950 ed. lib. bdg. 18.00x (ISBN 0-374-92095-8). Octagon.

Ghose, Sankar. Renaissance to Militant Nationalism in India. 1969. 8.50x (ISBN 0-8188-1042-4). Paragon.

Graebner, Norman. Nationalism & Communism in Asia: The American Response. (Problems in American Civilization Ser.). 1976. pap. text ed. 4.95x (ISBN 0-669-00683-1). Heath.

Haithcox, John P. Communism & Nationalism in India: M. N. Roy & Comintern Policy, 1920-1939. LC 79-120755. (Research Institute of Communist Affairs Ser). 1971. 28.00x (ISBN 0-691-08722-9). Princeton U Pr.

Harrison, Selig S. The Widening Gulf: Asian Nationalism & American Policy. LC 76-57881. (Illus.). 1979. pap. text ed. 8.95 (ISBN 0-02-914090-0). Free Pr.

--The Widening Gulf: Asian Nationalism & American Policy. LC 76-57881. (Illus.). 1978. 17.95 (ISBN 0-02-914080-3). Free Pr.

Holland, William L., ed. Asian Nationalism & the West. LC 73-8327. 1973. Repr. of 1953 ed. lib. bdg. 25.00x (ISBN 0-374-93924-1). Octagon.

Johnson, Chalmers A. Peasant Nationalism & Communist Power: The Emergence of Revolutionary China, 1937-1945. 1962. 12.50x (ISBN 0-8047-0073-7); pap. 4.95 (ISBN 0-8047-0074-5). Stanford U Pr.

Kahin, George M. Nationalism & Revolution in Indonesia. (Illus.). 506p. 1970. pap. 7.95 (ISBN 0-8014-9108-8, CP108). Cornell U Pr.

Kedourie, Elie, ed. Nationalism in Asia & Africa. 1970. pap. 4.95 (ISBN 0-452-00271-0, F271, Mer). NAL.

Kennedy, Joseph. Asian Nationalism in the Twentieth Century. (Illus.). 1968. text ed. 14.95 (ISBN 0-312-05635-4). St Martin.

Kohn, Hans. History of Nationalism in the East. (BCL History Reprint Ser). 1929. 19.00 (ISBN 0-403-00079-3). Scholarly.

--Nationalism & Imperialism in the Hither East. 1932. 25.00 (ISBN 0-86527-139-9). Fertig.

Lenin, V. I. The National Liberation Movement in the East. 363p. 1969. 2.50 (ISBN 0-8285-0141-6, Pub. by Progress Pubs Russia). Imported Pubns.

Rakowska-Harmstone, Teresa. Russia & Nationalism in Central Asia: The Case of Tadzhikistan. LC 69-13722. 325p. 1970. 22.50x (ISBN 0-8018-1021-3). Johns Hopkins.

Ray, Niharranjan. Nationalism in India: An Historical Analysis of Its Stresses & Strains. LC 73-906984. 180p. 1973. 7.50x (ISBN 0-8002-1292-4). Intl Pubns Serv.

Schneider, Laurence A. Ku Chieh-kang & China's New History: Nationalism & the Quest for Alternative Traditions. LC 73-129608. (Center for Chinese Studies, UC Berkeley). 1971. 28.75x (ISBN 0-520-01804-4). U of Cal Pr.

Seal, Anil. Emergence of Indian Nationalism. (Political Change in Modern Asia: No. 1). (Illus.). 1968. 39.95 (ISBN 0-521-06274-8); pap. 11.50x (ISBN 0-521-09652-9). Cambridge U Pr.

Soekarno. Nationalism, Islam & Marxism. (Translation Ser). (Orig.). 1970. pap. 3.00 (ISBN 0-685-08665-8, A139054). Cornell Mod Indo.

Tsang Chiu-Sam. Nationalism in School Education in China. 2nd ed. 1967. 6.00x (ISBN 0-685-19331-4). Paragon.

Vella, Walter F. & Vella, Dorothy. Chaiyo! King Vajiravudh & the Development of Thai Nationalism. LC 78-1060. 1978. text ed. 20.00x (ISBN 0-8248-0493-7). U Pr of Hawaii.

NATIONALISM–CANADA

Berger, Carl. Sense of Power: Studies in the Ideas of Canadian Imperialism, 1867-1914. LC 79-470040. 1970. 17.50x (ISBN 0-8020-1669-3); pap. 6.50 (ISBN 0-8020-6113-3). U of Toronto Pr.

Cook, Ramsay, ed. Constitutionalism & Nationalism in Lower Canada. LC 23-16213. (Canadian Historical Readings Ser.: No. 5). 1969. pap. 2.50x (ISBN 0-8020-1615-4). U of Toronto Pr.

Esman, Milton J. Ethnic Conflict in the Western World. LC 76-28012. 1977. 22.50x (ISBN 0-8014-1016-9). Cornell U Pr.

Graham & Rolland. Dear Enemies. 1965. 4.50 (ISBN 0-8159-5300-3). Devin.

Quinn, Herbert F. The Union Nationale: Quebec Nationalism from Duplessis to Levesque. rev ed. 1980. 22.50x (ISBN 0-8020-2318-5); pap. 8.95 (ISBN 0-8020-6347-0). U of Toronto Pr.

Schwartz, Mildred A. Public Opinion & Canadian Identity. LC 67-17693. 1967. 24.50x (ISBN 0-520-01156-2). U of Cal Pr.

NATIONALISM–EUROPE

Allworth, Edward, ed. Nationality Group Survival in Multi-Ethnic States: Shifting Support Patterns in the Soviet Baltic Region. LC 77-4952. 1977. text ed. 30.95 (ISBN 0-275-24040-1). Praeger.

Anderson, Eugene N. Nationalism & Cultural Crisis in Prussia, 1806-1815. 1967. lib. bdg. 18.50x (ISBN 0-374-90228-3). Octagon.

Armstrong, John A. Ukranian Nationalism. 2nd ed. LC 79-25529. 361p. 1980. Repr. of 1963 ed. 30.00x (ISBN 0-87287-193-2). Libs Unl.

Ashkenasi, Abraham. Modern German Nationalism. LC 75-33702. 222p. 1976. 14.95 (ISBN 0-470-03492-0). Halsted Pr.

Azrael, Jeremy R., ed. Soviet Nationality Policies & Practices. LC 77-83478. 1978. 35.95 (ISBN 0-03-041476-8). Praeger.

Banac, Ivo, et al, eds. Nation & Ideology. (East European Monographs: No. 95). 450p. 1981. 24.00x (ISBN 0-914710-89-3). East Eur Quarterly.

Binkley, Robert C. Realism & Nationalism: 1852-1871. (Rise of Modern Europe Ser.). 1935. pap. 6.95x (ISBN 0-06-133038-8, TB3038, Torch). Har-Row.

Buthman, W. C. The Rise of Integral Nationalism in France with Special Reference to the Ideas & Activities of Charles Maurras. LC 78-120239. 1970. Repr. lib. bdg. 20.00x (ISBN 0-374-91128-2). Octagon.

Campbell, John C. French Influence & the Rise of Roumanian Nationalism, Generation of 1848: 1830-1857. LC 73-135839. (Eastern Europe Collection Ser). 1970. Repr. of 1940 ed. 19.00 (ISBN 0-405-02781-8). Arno.

Chadwick, H. Munro. The Nationalities of Europe & the Growth of National Ideologies. LC 72-88264. (Illus.). viii, 209p. 1973. Repr. of 1945 ed. lib. bdg. 11.00x (ISBN 0-8154-0446-8). Cooper Sq.

Clough, Shepard B. History of the Flemish Movement in Belgium. 1967. lib. bdg. 16.00x (ISBN 0-374-91767-1). Octagon.

Ergang, Robert R. Herder & the Foundations of German Nationalism. 1967. lib. bdg. 18.00x (ISBN 0-374-92622-0). Octagon.

Esman, Milton J. Ethnic Conflict in the Western World. LC 76-28012. 1977. 22.50x (ISBN 0-8014-1016-9). Cornell U Pr.

Falnes, Oscar J. National Romanticism in Norway. LC 68-54263. (Columbia University. Studies in the Social Sciences: No. 386). Repr. of 1933 ed. 21.50 (ISBN 0-404-51386-7). AMS Pr.

Greenfield, Kent R. Economics & Liberalism in the Risorgimento: A Study of Nationalism in Lombardy, 1814-1848. LC 78-17674. 1978. Repr. of 1965 ed. lib. bdg. 22.25x (ISBN 0-313-20510-8, GREL). Greenwood.

Hagen, William W. Germans, Poles, & Jews: The Nationality Conflict in the Prussian East, 1772-1914. LC 80-10557. (Illus.). 1980. lib. bdg. 17.50x (ISBN 0-226-31242-9). U of Chicago Pr.

Hertz, Frederick. The German Public Mind, in the Nineteenth Century: A Social History of German Political Sentiments, Aspirations & Ideas. Eyck, Frank, ed. Northcott, Eric, tr. 422p. 1975. 22.50x (ISBN 0-87471-580-6). Rowman.

Hyslop, Beatrice F. French Nationalism in 1789 According to the General Cahiers. 1968. Repr. lib. bdg. 15.50 (ISBN 0-374-94085-1). Octagon.

Jaszi, Oscar. Dissolution of the Habsburg Monarchy. LC 29-22812. 1961. pap. 3.45 (ISBN 0-226-39568-5, P70, Phoen). U of Chicago Pr.

Kann, Robert A. Multinational Empire: Nationalism & National Reform in the Habsburg Monarchy, 1848-1918, 2 Vols. 1964. lib. bdg. 42.50x (ISBN 0-374-94503-9). Octagon.

Kennedy, Paul & Nicholls, Anthony, eds. Nationalist & Racialist Movements in Britain & Germany Before 1914. 204p. 1981. 16.50x (ISBN 0-8448-1395-8). Crane-Russak Co.

Klein, George & Reban, Milan J., eds. The Politics of Ethnicity in Eastern Europe. (East European Monographs: No. 93). 288p. 1981. 20.00x (ISBN 0-914710-87-7). East Eur Quarterly.

Knapp, W. Unity & Nationalism in Europe Since 1945. 1969. pap. 5.75 (ISBN 0-08-013439-4). Pergamon.

Kohn, Hans. Nationalism & Liberty: The Swiss Example. LC 77-28360. 1978. Repr. of 1956 ed. lib. bdg. 14.50x (ISBN 0-313-20233-8, KONL). Greenwood.

Ladas, Stephen P. The Exchange of Minorities: Bulgaria, Greece & Turkey. LC 77-87521. (Illus.). Repr. of 1932 ed. 56.00 (ISBN 0-404-16596-6). AMS Pr.

Lamb, Margaret. Nationalism. (History Monographs: Bk. 8). 1974. pap. text ed. 4.50x (ISBN 0-435-31530-7). Heinemann Ed.

Lasic-Vasojevic, Milija M. Enemies on All Sides: The Fall of Yugoslavia. LC 76-41596. (Illus.). 300p. 1976. 10.00 (ISBN 0-88265-010-6). North Am Intl.

Link, Werner & Feld, Werner J., eds. The New Nationalism: Implications for Transatlantic Relations. new ed. LC 78-17144. (Pergamon Policy Studies). 1979. text ed. 19.25 (ISBN 0-08-023370-8); pap. text ed. 7.95 (ISBN 0-08-023369-4). Pergamon.

Meinecke, Friedrich. Cosmopolitanism & the National State: Welburgertum Und Nationalstaat. Kimber, Robert B., tr. LC 65-17150. 1970. 25.00 (ISBN 0-691-05177-1). Princeton U Pr.

Mosse, George L. Masses & Man: Nationalist & Fascist Perceptions of Reality. LC 80-15399. xi, 362p. 1980. 25.00 (ISBN 0-86527-334-0). Fertig.

Mosse, W. E. European Powers & the German Question, 1848-1871. LC 74-76002. 1969. Repr. of 1958 ed. lib. bdg. 30.00x (ISBN 0-374-95928-5). Octagon.

Noether, Emiliana P. Seeds of Italian Nationalism, 1700-1815. LC 79-94926. (Columbia Univ. Social Science Ser.: No. 570). Repr. of 1951 ed. 14.00 (ISBN 0-404-51570-3). AMS Pr.

Palmer, Stephen E., Jr. & King, Robert. Yugoslav Communism & the Macedonian Question. LC 79-116904. (Illus.). 1971. 18.50 (ISBN 0-208-00821-7, Archon). Shoe String.

Pinson, Koppel S. Pietism As a Factor in the Rise of German Nationalism. 1967. lib. bdg. 14.00x (ISBN 0-374-96460-2). Octagon.

Pundt, Alfred G. Arndt & the Nationalist Awakening in Germany. LC 68-54287. (Columbia University. Studies in the Social Sciences: No. 413). Repr. of 1935 ed. 14.00 (ISBN 0-404-51413-8). AMS Pr.

Riasanovsky, Nicholas V. Nicholas I & Official Nationality in Russia, 1825-1855. (Russian & East European Studies). 1959. 23.50x (ISBN 0-520-01064-7); pap. 6.95x (ISBN 0-520-01065-5, CAMPUS 120). U of Cal Pr.

Rogger, Hans J. National Consciousness in Eighteenth-Century Russia. LC 60-8450. (Russian Research Center Studies: No. 38). 1960. 16.50x (ISBN 0-674-60150-5). Harvard U Pr.

Rossinyol, Jaume. Le Probleme National Catalan. (Illus.). 1974. pap. 47.50x (ISBN 90-2797-258-3). Mouton.

Salvadori, M. Cavour & the Unification of Italy. (Anvil Ser.). 191p. 1961. pap. 4.95 (ISBN 0-685-91059-8, Pub. by Van Nostrand Reinhold). Krieger.

Skendi, Stavro. Albanian National Awakening, Eighteen Seventy-Eight - Nineteen Twelve. 1967. 25.00 (ISBN 0-691-05100-3). Princeton U Pr.

Smal-Stocki, Roman. The Captive Nations: Nationalism of the Non-Russian Nations in the Soviet Union. 1960. pap. 1.45 (ISBN 0-8084-0068-1, B9). Coll & U Pr.

Snyder, Louis L. Roots of German Nationalism. LC 77-74437. (Illus.). 320p. 1978. 17.50x (ISBN 0-253-35026-3). Ind U Pr.

Thaden, Edward C. Conservative Nationalism in Nineteenth-Century Russia. LC 64-20490. 283p. 1964. 11.50 (ISBN 0-295-73753-0). U of Wash Pr.

Tipton, C., ed. Nationalism in the Middle Ages. (European Problem Ser.). 128p. 1972. pap. 5.50 (ISBN 0-03-084157-7, Pub. by HR&W). Krieger.

Tudjman, Franjo. Nationalism in Contemporary Europe. (East European Monographs: No. 76). 352p. 1981. 21.50x (ISBN 0-914710-70-2). East Eur Quarterly.

Van Deusen, Glyndon G. Sieyes: His Life & His Nationalism. LC 68-58632. (Columbia University. Studies in the Social Sciences: No. 362). Repr. of 1932 ed. 16.50 (ISBN 0-404-51362-X). AMS Pr.

Weber, Eugen. The Nationalist Revival in France. (California Library Reprint Series: No. 7). 1968. 25.75x (ISBN 0-520-01321-2). U of Cal Pr.

Wilson, William A. Folklore & Nationalism in Modern Finland. LC 75-23895. (Illus.). 288p. 1976. 10.00x (ISBN 0-253-32327-4). Ind U Pr.

Zeman, Z. A. The Break-up of the Habsburg Empire 1914-1918: A Study in National & Social Revolution. 1977. Repr. of 1961 ed. lib. bdg. 16.50x (ISBN 0-374-98847-1). Octagon.

Ziemer, Gregor. Education for Death, the Making of the Nazi. 1972. lib. bdg. 13.00x (ISBN 0-374-98905-2). Octagon.

Zinner, Paul E., ed. National Communism & Popular Revolt in Eastern Europe: A Selection of Documents on Events in Poland & Hungary Feb. - Nov., 1956. LC 57-13560. (Orig.). 1956. pap. 10.00x (ISBN 0-231-02200-X). Columbia U Pr.

NATIONALISM–GREAT BRITAIN

Knight, G. Wilson. Olive & the Sword. 1944. lib. bdg. 15.00 (ISBN 0-8414-5591-0). Folcroft.

NATIONALISM–INDIA

Ambedkar, Bhimrao R. Pakistan or Partition of India. LC 77-179171. (South & Southeast Asia Studies). Repr. of 1945 ed. 32.50 (ISBN 0-404-54801-6). AMS Pr.

Bose, Nemai S. The Indian National Movement: An Outline. 2nd ed. 1974. lib. bdg. 8.00x (ISBN 0-88386-559-9). South Asia Bks.

Choudhary, Sukhbir. Growth of Nationalism in India, 1857-1929, 2 vols. 640p. 1974. text ed. 45.00x (ISBN 0-8426-0729-3). Verry.

Dasgupta, Biplab. The Naxalite Movement. (Centre for the Study of Developing Countries, Monograph No. One). 282p. 1974. 12.00x (ISBN 0-85655-158-9). Intl Pubns Serv.

Lovett, V. History of the Indian Nationalist Movement. 303p. 1968. 25.00x (ISBN 0-7146-2016-5, F Cass Co). Biblio Dist.

Lovett, Verney. A History of the Indian Nationalist Movement. LC 79-94540. 303p. 1972. Repr. of 1972 ed. 10.00x (ISBN 0-8002-0910-9). Intl Pubns Serv.

McLane, John R. Indian Nationalism & the Early Congress. LC 77-72127. 1977. 32.00x (ISBN 0-691-03113-4); pap. 12.50 (ISBN 0-691-10056-X). Princeton U Pr.

Mulraj, R. B. Beginnings of Punjab Nationalism: Autobiography of R. B. Mulraj. 1976. 8.00x (ISBN 0-88386-775-3). South Asia Bks.

Nanda, B. R. Gokhale, Gandhi & the Nehrus: Studies in Indian Nationalism. LC 74-76991. 200p. 1974. 19.95 (ISBN 0-312-33145-2). St Martin.

Sarkadi, Ajit S. Nationalisms in India. LC 74-904108. 312p. 1975. 13.00x (ISBN 0-8002-0940-0). Intl Pubns Serv.

Singh, Diwakar P. American Attitude Towards Indian Nationalist Movement. xvi, 352p. 1974. 15.00x (ISBN 0-88386-335-9). South Asia Bks.

Smith, William R. Nationalism & Reform in India. LC 72-85314. 496p. 1973. Repr. of 1938 ed. 18.50 (ISBN 0-8046-1716-3). Kennikat.

Srivastava, Nagendra. Growth of Nationalism in India: Effects of International Events. 207p. 1973. 11.25x (ISBN 0-8002-1478-1). Intl Pubns Serv.

Tucker, Richard P. Ranade & the Roots of Indian Nationalism. (Midway Reprint Ser.). pap. 11.00x (ISBN 0-226-81532-3). U of Chicago Pr.

NATIONALISM–IRELAND

Strauss, Eric. Irish Nationalism & British Democracy. LC 75-8727. 307p. 1975. Repr. of 1951 ed. lib. bdg. 16.50x (ISBN 0-8371-8046-5, STINA). Greenwood.

NATIONALISM–JAPAN

Narasimha-Murthy, P. A. The Rise of Modern Nationalism in Japan: A Historical Study of the Role of Education in the Making of Modern Japan. 518p. 1973. 22.50x (ISBN 0-8002-1926-0). Intl Pubns Serv.

NATIONALISM–JEWS

see also Zionism

Jacobs, Louis. Jewish Thought Today. LC 73-116679. (Chain of Tradition Ser). 1970. pap. 3.95x (ISBN 0-87441-014-2). Behrman.

Janowsky, Oscar I. Jews & Minority Rights, 1898-1919. LC 33-31678. (Columbia University. Studies in the Social Sciences: No. 384). Repr. of 1933 ed. 24.50 (ISBN 0-404-51384-0). AMS Pr.

Pilzer, Jay. Anti-Semitism & Jewish Nationalism. LC 79-11650. 1980. pap. 5.95 (ISBN 0-915442-89-2, Unilaw). Donning Co.

Simon, Leon. Studies in Jewish Nationalism. LC 75-6458. (The Rise of Jewish Nationalism & the Middle East Ser.). xi, 174p. 1975. Repr. of 1920 ed. 18.00 (ISBN 0-88355-343-0). Hyperion Conn.

The Twenty-Eighth Zionist Congress, 1971. Incl. Vol. 1. Reports; Vol. 2. Minutes. 1977. write for info. (ISBN 0-686-18946-9). Inst Palestine.

NATIONALISM–LATIN AMERICA

Baily, Samuel L. Labor, Nationalism, & Politics in Argentina. 1967. 16.00 (ISBN 0-8135-0556-9). Rutgers U Pr.

Bell, Wendell. Jamaican Leaders: Political Attitudes in a New Nation. LC 64-19447. 1964. 22.50x (ISBN 0-520-00103-6). U of Cal Pr.

Smith, Robert F. The United States & Revolutionary Nationalism in Mexico, 1916-1932. LC 73-182872. 1972. 15.00x (ISBN 0-226-76506-7). U of Chicago Pr.

Solberg, Carl. Immigration & Nationalism: Argentina & Chile, 1890-1914. (Latin American Monographs: No. 18). 238p. 1970. 10.00x (ISBN 0-292-70020-2). U of Tex Pr.

NATIONALISM–MOROCCO
Halstead, John P. Rebirth of a Nation: Origins & Rise of Moroccan Nationalism, 1912-1944. LC 67-31566. (Middle Eastern Monographs Ser: No. 18). (Orig.). 1967. pap. 7.95x (ISBN 0-674-75000-4). Harvard U Pr.
NATIONALISM–NEAR EAST
Banac, Ivo, et al, eds. Nation & Ideology. (East European Monographs: No. 95). 450p. 1981. 24.00x (ISBN 0-914710-89-3). East Eur Quarterly.
Haddad, William W. & Ochsenwald, William L., eds. Nationalism in a Non-National State: The Dissolution of the Ottoman Empire. LC 77-1253. 1977. 15.00x (ISBN 0-8142-0191-1). Ohio St U Pr.
Kohn, Hans. History of Nationalism in the East. (BCL History Reprint Ser). 1929. 19.00 (ISBN 0-403-00079-3). Scholarly.
Nalbandian, Louise Z. The Armenian Revolutionary Movement: The Development of Armenian Political Parties Through the Nineteenth Century. (Near Eastern Center, UCLA). 1963. 18.50x (ISBN 0-520-00914-2). U of Cal Pr.
NATIONALISM–RHODESIA AND NYASALAND
Franck, Thomas M. Race & Nationalism: The Struggle for Power in Rhodesia-Nyasaland. LC 73-11853. 369p. 1973. Repr. of 1960 ed. lib. bdg. 18.00x (ISBN 0-8371-7074-5, FRRN). Greenwood.
NATIONALISM–SCOTLAND
Greenberg, William. Scottish Nationalism, on the Celtic Fringe. 3.95 (ISBN 0-686-10857-4). British Am Bks.
Harvie, Christopher. Scotland & Nationalism: Scottish Society & Politics, 1707-1977. (Illus.). 1977. text ed. 21.00x (ISBN 0-04-941006-7); pap. text ed. 9.95x (ISBN 0-04-941007-5). Allen Unwin.
MacLean, Colin, ed. The Crown & the Thistle. 224p. 1980. text ed. 10.50x (ISBN 0-7073-0249-8, Pub. by Scottish Academic Pr). Columbia U Pr.
Webb, Keith. Growth of Nationalism in Scotland. LC 77-372254. (Scotland in Perspective Ser.). 1977. 12.50x (ISBN 0-904002-17-9). Intl Pubns Serv.
NATIONALISM–TUNISIA
Ziadeh, Nicola. Origins of Nationalism in Tunsia. (Arab Background Ser.). Repr. of 1969 ed. 8.00x (ISBN 0-685-77110-5). Intl Bk Ctr.
NATIONALISM–UNITED STATES
Babcock, K. W. Rise of American Nationality 1811-1819. LC 68-24970. (American History & Americana Ser., No. 47). 1969. Repr. of 1906 ed. lib. bdg. 43.95 (ISBN 0-8383-0910-0). Haskell.
Berens, John F. Providence & Patriotism in Early America, Sixteen Forty to Eighteen Fifteen. LC 78-5889. 1978. 9.75x (ISBN 0-8139-0779-9). U Pr of Va.
Bowers, David F., ed. Foreign Influences in American Life: Essays & Critical Biographies. (Studies in American Civilization: Vol. 2). 1944. pap. 7.95 (ISBN 0-691-02802-8). Princeton U Pr.
Dalzell, Robert F., Jr. Daniel Webster & the Trial of American Nationalism, 1843-1852. 384p. 1978. 14.95x (ISBN 0-393-07524-9, N782, Norton Lib); pap. 4.95x (ISBN 0-393-00782-0). Norton.
Dangerfield, George. Awakening of American Nationalism, 1815-1828. (New American Nation Ser). (Illus.). 1965. 15.00x (ISBN 0-06-010945-9, HarpT). Har-Row.
--Awakening of American Nationalism, 1815-1828. (New American Nation Ser.). pap. 4.95x (ISBN 0-06-133061-2, TB3061, Torch). Har-Row.
Davidson, Donald. The Attack on Leviathan: Regionalism & Nationalism in the United States. 8.50 (ISBN 0-8446-1149-2). Peter Smith.
Davis, Jerome. Citizens of One World. (Orig.). 1961. pap. 1.95 (ISBN 0-8065-0185-5, X-68). Citadel Pr.
Kohn, Hans. American Nationalism: An Interpretative Essay. LC 79-24317. xi, 272p. 1980. Repr. of 1957 ed. lib. bdg. 22.50x (ISBN 0-313-22231-2, KOAM). Greenwood.
Nackman, Mark E. A Nation Within a Nation: The Rise of Texas Nationalism. (American Studies Ser.). 183p. 1975. 15.00 (ISBN 0-8046-9131-2, Natl U). Kennikat.
Preas, Jerry L. Be Proud. (Illus.). 90p. pap. 3.95 (ISBN 0-935622-02-0). Texan-Am Pub.
Shafer, Boyd C. Nationalism: Its Nature & Interpreters. 4th ed. LC 76-15045. (AHA Pamphlets: No. 701). 1976. pap. text ed. 1.50 (ISBN 0-87229-020-4). Am Hist Assn.
Small, Albion W. The Beginnings of American Nationality. LC 78-63792. (Johns Hopkins University. Studies in the Social Sciences. Eighth Ser. 1890: 1-2). Repr. of 1890 ed. 11.50 (ISBN 0-404-61057-9). AMS Pr.
Spencer, Benjamin T. Quest for Nationality: An American Literary Campaign. LC 57-12017. 1957. 12.95x (ISBN 0-8156-2020-9). Syracuse U Pr.
Weaver, Robert B. Our Flag & Other Symbols of Americanism. 76p. (gr. 7-8). 1972. pap. 0.50 (ISBN 0-912530-09-X); test 0.10 (ISBN 0-686-77026-9). Patriotic Educ.
NATIONALISM AND RELIGION
see also Buddhism and State; Church and State; Jews–Election, Doctrine of; Islam and State; Religion and Language; Religion and State; War and Religion
Baron, Salo W. Modern Nationalism & Religion. facs. ed. LC 79-134050. (Essay Index Reprint Ser). 1947. 19.50 (ISBN 0-8369-2142-9). Arno.
Christensen, Duane L. Transformations of the War Oracle in Old Testament Prophecy. LC 75-34264. (Harvard Dissertations in Religion Ser.). 1975. pap. 9.00 (ISBN 0-89130-064-3, 020103). Scholars Pr Ca.
Cogan, Morton. Imperialism & Religion: Assyria, Judah and Israel in the Eighth and Seventh Centuries B.C.E. LC 73-83723. (Society of Biblical Literature. Monograph). 1974. 9.00 (ISBN 0-89130-330-8, 060019); pap. 7.50 (ISBN 0-89130-331-6). Scholars Pr Ca.
Guterman, Simeon L. Religious Toleration & Persecution in Ancient Rome. LC 70-104269. 160p. Repr. of 1951 ed. lib. bdg. 15.00x (ISBN 0-8371-3936-8, GURT). Greenwood.
Holtom, D. C. Modern Japan & Shinto Nationalism. 2nd ed. 1963. 14.00 (ISBN 0-8188-0042-9). Paragon.
Hudson, Winthrop S. Nationalism & Religion in America: Concepts of American Identity & Mission. 8.00 (ISBN 0-8446-0711-8). Peter Smith.
Marx, Victor. Catholicism, Judaism & the Effort at World Domination, 2 vols. in one. (Institute for Economic & Political World Strategic Studies). (Illus.). 191p. 1975. Set. 65.00 (ISBN 0-913314-61-7). Am Classical Coll Pr.
Schoffeleers, Matthews & Meijers, Daniel. Religion, Nationalism & Economic Action Critical Questions on Durkheim & Weber. 1978. pap. text ed. 9.25x (ISBN 90-232-1614-8). Humanities.
Smith, Donald E. Religion & Politics in Burma. 1965. 24.00 (ISBN 0-691-03054-5). Princeton U Pr.
Smith, Wilfred C. Modern Islam in India: A Social Analysis. rev. ed. LC 78-188163. (Illus., With bibliography from the 1943 ed.). 1972. Repr. of 1946 ed. 20.00 (ISBN 0-8462-1652-3). Russell.
--Modern Islam in India: A Social Analysis. LC 70-179243. Repr. of 1946 ed. 17.00 (ISBN 0-404-54869-5). AMS Pr.
Von Der Mehden, Fred R. Religion & Nationalism in Southeast Asia: Burma, Indonesia, & the Philippines. (Illus.). 272p. 1963. pap. 6.95 (ISBN 0-299-02944-1). U of Wis Pr.
NATIONALISM AND SOCIALISM
Bennigsen, Alexandre A. & Wimbush, S. Enders. Muslim National Communism in the Soviet Union: A Revolutionary Strategy for the Colonial World. LC 78-8608. (Publications of the Center for Middle Eastern Studies Ser.: No. 11). 1979. lib. bdg. 20.00x (ISBN 0-226-04235-9). U of Chicago Pr.
Davis, Horace B. Nationalism & Socialism: Marxist & Labor Theories of Nationalism to 1917. LC 67-19255. 1967. pap. 3.95 (ISBN 0-85345-293-8, PB2938). Monthly Rev.
Kamenetsky, Ihor. Nationalism and Human Rights: Processes of Modernization in the USSR. LC 77-1257. (Series in Issues Studies (Ussr & East Europe): No. 1). 1977. lib. bdg. 18.50x (ISBN 0-87287-143-6). Libs Unl.
Talmon, J. L. The Myth of the Nation & the Vision of Revolution: The Origins of Ideological Polarization in the Twentieth Century. 700p. 1981. 35.00x (ISBN 0-520-04449-5). U of Cal Pr.
Vajda, Mihaly. The State & Socialism. (Allison & Busby Motive Ser.). 160p. 1981. pap. 8.95 (ISBN 0-8052-8070-7, Pub. by Allison & Busby England). Schocken.
NATIONALISM IN LITERATURE
Lewald, H. Ernest, ed. The Cry of Home: Cultural Nationalism & the Modern Writer. LC 76-173656. 1972. 17.50 (ISBN 0-87049-135-0). Lib Soc Sci.
--The Cry of Home: Cultural Nationalism & the Modern Writer. LC 76-173656. 412p. 1972. 15.50x (ISBN 0-87049-135-0). U of Tenn Pr.
NATIONALITY (CITIZENSHIP)
see Citizenship
NATIONALITY, DUAL
see Dual Nationality
NATIONALIZATION
see Government Ownership
NATIONALIZATION OF ALIEN PROPERTY
see Eminent Domain (International Law)
NATIONALIZATION OF LAND
see Land, Nationalization of
NATIONALIZATION OF RAILROADS
see Railroads and State
NATIONALSOZIALISTISCHE DEUTSCHE ARBEITER-PARTEI
see also Denazification
Allen. The Nazi Seizure of Power: The Experience of a Single German Town, 1930-1935. 2nd ed. 1980. 12.50 (ISBN 0-531-09935-0, EE22); pap. 6.95 (ISBN 0-531-05633-3, EE27). Watts.
Bayles, William D. Caesars in Goose Step. LC 68-2622. 1968. Repr. of 1940 ed. 12.50 (ISBN 0-8046-0021-X). Kennikat.
Bischoff, Ralph F. Nazi Conquest Through German Culture. LC 78-63651. (Studies in Fascism: Ideology & Practice). Repr. of 1942 ed. 22.00 (ISBN 0-404-16906-6). AMS Pr.
Bormann, Martin. The Bormann Letters. Trevor-Roper, H. R., ed. Stevens, R. H., tr. LC 78-63655. (Studies in Fascism: Ideology & Practice). (Illus.). 232p. Repr. of 1954 ed. 24.50 (ISBN 0-404-16908-2). AMS Pr.
Cunningham, Charles. Germany Today & Tomorrow. LC 70-180396. Repr. of 1936 ed. 19.00 (ISBN 0-404-56117-9). AMS Pr.
Davidson, Basil. Scenes from the Anti-Nazi War. LC 81-81696. 1981. 16.00 (ISBN 0-686-31613-4); pap. 8.65 (ISBN 0-686-31614-2). Monthly Rev.
Dutch, Oswald, pseud. Hitler's Twelve Apostles. facsimile ed. LC 75-93333. (Essay Index Reprint Ser). 1940. 17.00 (ISBN 0-8369-1286-1). Arno.
Gangulee, N., ed. The Mind & Face of Nazi Germany: An Anthology. LC 78-63671. (Studies in Fascism: Ideology & Practice). 1979. Repr. of 1942 ed. 17.50 (ISBN 0-404-16528-1). AMS Pr.
Germany Speaks. LC 70-180400. Repr. of 1938 ed. 28.00 (ISBN 0-404-56124-1). AMS Pr.
Gurian, Waldemar. Hitler & the Christians. Peeler, E. F., tr. LC 78-63675. (Studies in Fascism: Ideology & Practice). 184p. Repr. of 1936 ed. 22.00 (ISBN 0-404-16937-6). AMS Pr.
Hamburger, Ludwig. How Nazi Germany Has Controlled Business. LC 78-63678. (Studies in Fascism: Ideology & Practice). Repr. of 1943 ed. 12.50 (ISBN 0-404-16939-2). AMS Pr.
Hamlin, David. The Nazi - Skokie Conflict: A Civil Liberties Battle. LC 80-67091. 192p. 1981. pap. 5.95 (ISBN 0-8070-3231-X, BP 624). Beacon Pr.
Heberle, Rudolf. From Democracy to Nazism: A Regional Case Study on Political Parties in Germany. LC 72-80556. 1970. Repr. 17.50 (ISBN 0-86527-076-7). Fertig.
Heiden, Konrad. Hitler: A Biography. Ray, Winifred, tr. LC 79-18065. Repr. of 1936 ed. 24.50 (ISBN 0-404-56401-1). AMS Pr.
Hertzstein, Robert. The Nazis. Time-Life Bks, ed. (World War II Ser.). (Illus.). 208p. 1980. 14.95 (ISBN 0-8094-2534-3). Time-Life.
Hitler, Adolf. Mein Kampf. Manheim, Ralph, tr. 15.95 (ISBN 0-395-07801-6); pap. 8.95 (ISBN 0-686-57537-7). HM.
--Mein Kampf. 1962. pap. 8.95 (ISBN 0-395-08362-1, 13, SenEd). HM.
--Table Talk, Nineteen Forty-One to Nineteen Forty-Four. Cameron, Norman & Stevens, R. H., trs. LC 78-63681. (Studies in Fascism: Ideology & Practice). 1979. Repr. of 1953 ed. 49.50 (ISBN 0-404-16946-5). AMS Pr.
Kele, Max H. Nazis & Workers: National Socialist Appeals to German Labor, 1919-1933. LC 77-174786. 288p. 1972. 16.50x (ISBN 0-8078-1184-X). U of NC Pr.
Kirk, Robert. Women in Hitler's Germany: The Limits of Misogyny. Date not set. lib. bdg. 12.50 (ISBN 0-89733-016-1); pap. 5.95 (ISBN 0-89733-031-5). Academy Chi Ltd.
Kirkpatrick, Clifford. Nazi Germany: Its Women & Family Life. LC 78-63684. (Studies in Fascism: Ideology & Practice). Repr. of 1938 ed. 37.50 (ISBN 0-404-16949-X). AMS Pr.
Koch, H. W. The Hitler Youth. LC 75-34399. (Illus.). 352p. 1976. 35.00 (ISBN 0-8128-1904-7). Stein & Day.
Lichtenberger, Henri. Third Reich. Pinson, Koppel S., tr. LC 73-102249. (Select Bibliographies Reprint Ser). 1937. 29.00 (ISBN 0-8369-5134-4). Arno.
Mayer, S. L., ed. Signal: The Years of Triumph. (Illus.). 1978. 12.95 (ISBN 0-13-810010-1). P-H.
Merkl, Peter H. The Making of a Stormtrooper. LC 79-3223. 1980. 16.50 (ISBN 0-691-07620-0). Princeton U Pr.
--Political Violence Under the Swastika: 581 Early Nazis. 1975. 47.50 (ISBN 0-691-07561-1); pap. 16.50 (ISBN 0-691-10028-4). Princeton U Pr.
Mitchell, Otis, ed. Nazism & the Common Man: Essays in German History (1929-1939) 2nd ed. LC 80-6284. 163p. 1981. lib. bdg. 17.75 (ISBN 0-8191-1546-0); pap. text ed. 8.75 (ISBN 0-8191-1547-9). U Pr of Amer.
The Nazi Conspiracy in Spain. LC 77-180418. Repr. of 1937 ed. 16.50 (ISBN 0-404-56193-4). AMS Pr.
Nyomarkay, Joseph. Charisma & Factionalism in the Nazi Party. LC 67-21015. 1967. 7.50x (ISBN 0-8166-0429-0). U of Minn Pr.
O'Neill, Robert J. German Army & the Nazi Party, 1933-39. (Illus.). 1967. 8.50 (ISBN 0-685-11957-2). Heineman.
Orlow, Dietrich. The History of the Nazi Party, 1919-1933. LC 69-20026. 1969. 17.95 (ISBN 0-8229-3183-4). U of Pittsburgh Pr.
--The History of the Nazi Party, 1933-1945. LC 72-81795. 1973. 17.95 (ISBN 0-8229-3253-9). U of Pittsburgh Pr.
Pool, James & Pool, Suzanne. Who Financed Hitler? The Secret Funding of Hitler's Rise to Power 1919-1933. (Illus.). 1978. 10.95 (ISBN 0-8037-9039-2). Dial.
Rauschning, Hermann. The Revolution of Nihilism: Warning to the West. Dickes, E. W., tr. LC 72-180666. Repr. of 1939 ed. 16.00 (ISBN 0-404-56402-X). AMS Pr.
--The Revolution of Nihilism: Warning to the West. LC 72-4291. (World Affairs Ser.: National & International Viewpoints). 318p. 1972. Repr. of 1939 ed. 15.00 (ISBN 0-405-04583-2). Arno.
Rhodes, James M. The Hitler Movement: A Modern Millenarian Revolution. LC 78-70391. (Publications Ser.: 213). 263p. 1980. 15.95 (ISBN 0-8179-7131-9). Hoover Inst Pr.
Rosenberg, Alfred. Der Mythus des 20 Jahrhunderts. LC 78-63710. (Studies in Fascism: Ideology & Practice). Repr. of 1935 ed. 49.50 (ISBN 0-404-16983-X). AMS Pr.
Rubin, Arnold P. Evil That Men Do: The Story of the Nazis. LC 77-2272. 224p. (YA) (gr. 7 up). 1981. PLB 10.79 (ISBN 0-671-32852-2). Messner.
Stachura, Peter D. Nazi Youth in the Weimar Republic. LC 74-14196. (Studies in International & Comparative Politics: No. 5). 301p. 1975. text ed. 21.50 (ISBN 0-87436-198-2); pap. text ed. 11.75 (ISBN 0-87436-199-0). ABC-Clio.
Strasser, Otto. Hitler & I. David, Gwenda & Mosbacher, Eric, trs. LC 78-63724. (Studies in Fascism: Ideology & Practice). Repr. of 1940 ed. 24.50 (ISBN 0-404-16997-X). AMS Pr.
Strasser, Otto & Stern, Michael. Flight from Terror. LC 78-63723. (Studies in Fascism: Ideology & Practice). Repr. of 1943 ed. 30.00 (ISBN 0-404-16996-1). AMS Pr.
Thyssen, Fritz. I Paid Hitler. LC 71-153243. 1971. Repr. of 1941 ed. 14.00 (ISBN 0-8046-1553-5). Kennikat.
Turrou, Leon G. Nazi Spy Conspiracy in America. LC 72-1433. (Select Bibliographies Reprint Ser.). 1972. Repr. of 1939 ed. 20.00 (ISBN 0-8369-6838-7). Arno.
Wilkinson, Ellen C. & Conze, Edward. Why Fascism? LC 78-177843. Repr. of 1934 ed. 18.00 (ISBN 0-404-56169-1). AMS Pr.
Wolfe, Burton H. Hitler & the Nazis. (gr. 7 up). 1970. PLB 5.49 (ISBN 0-399-60261-5). Putnam.
Woolston, Maxine Y. Structure of the Nazi Economy. LC 68-10957. (Illus.). 1968. Repr. of 1941 ed. 10.00 (ISBN 0-8462-1088-6). Russell.
World Committee For The Relief Of The Victims Of German Fascism. The Reichstag Fire Trial: The Second Brown Book of the Hitler Terror. LC 68-9605. 1969. Repr. of 1934 ed. 22.50 (ISBN 0-86527-165-8). Fertig.
NATIONALSOZIALISTISCHE DEUTSCHE ARBEITER-PARTEI, SCHUTZSTAFFEL
Kogon, Eugene. The Theory & Practice of Hell. LC 73-1055. 307p. 1972. Repr. of 1950 ed. lib. bdg. 18.50x (ISBN 0-374-94610-8). Octagon.
Mollo, Andrew. A Pictorial History of the S. S. LC 76-49044. (Illus.). 1977. 35.00 (ISBN 0-8128-2174-2). Stein & Day.
Neumann, Peter. The Black March! The Personal Story of an SS Man. 1981. pap. 2.50 (ISBN 0-553-20125-5). Bantam.
Reider, Frederic. Hitler's S.S. (Illus.). 256p. 1981. 24.95 (ISBN 0-89404-061-8). Aztex.
Speer, Albert. Infiltration: The SS & German Armament. Neugroschel, Joachim, tr. 604p. 1981. 15.95 (ISBN 0-02-612800-4). Macmillan.
Stein, George H. Waffen SS: Hitler's Elite Guard at War, 1939-1945. LC 66-1104. 330p. 1966. 24.50x (ISBN 0-8014-0407-X). Cornell U Pr.
U. S. Department of State, Division of European Affairs. National Socialism. Murphy, Raymond E., et al, eds. LC 75-35378. (U.S. Government Documents Program Ser.). (Illus.). 510p. 1976. Repr. of 1943 ed. lib. bdg. 27.25x (ISBN 0-8371-8601-3, USNS). Greenwood.
NATIONS, LAW OF
see International Law
NATIONS, MIGRATIONS OF
see Migrations of Nations
NATIONS, SMALL
see States, Small
NATIVE AMERICAN CHURCH OF NORTH AMERICA
Slotkin, J. S. The Peyote Religion. 195p. 1975. Repr. of 1956 ed. lib. bdg. 13.50x (ISBN 0-374-97480-2). Octagon.

NATIVE AMERICAN PARTY
see American Party

NATIVE RACES
see also Ethnology; Indians of North America-Government Relations;
also subdivision Native Races under names of continents, countries, etc. e.g. Africa-Native Races

Adas, Michael. Prophets of Rebellion: Millenarian Protest Movements Against the European Colonial Order. LC 78-26775. xxix, 243p. 1979. 19.00x (ISBN 0-8078-1353-2). U of NC Pr.

Bennett, Gordon. Aboriginal Rights in International Law. (RAI Occasional Papers: No. 37). 1978. pap. text ed. 8.25x (ISBN 0-391-01109-X). Humanities.

Greaves, Ida C. Modern Production Among Backward Peoples. LC 68-9759. Repr. of 1935 ed. 13.50x (ISBN 0-678-00419-6). Kelley.

Harris, John. Century of Emancipation. LC 72-122864. 1971. Repr. of 1933 ed. 13.50 (ISBN 0-8046-1369-9). Kennikat.

Harris, John H. Slavery or Sacred Trust? LC 72-90116. Repr. of 1926 ed. 13.25x (ISBN 0-8371-2032-2). Greenwood.

Howitt, William. Colonization & Christianity: A Popular History of the Treatment of the Natives by the Europeans in All Their Colonies. LC 70-76856. Repr. of 1838 ed. 22.75x (ISBN 0-8371-1162-5, Pub. by Negro U Pr). Greenwood.

Huffer, Virginia, et al. The Sweetness of the Fig: Aboriginal Women in Transition. LC 80-21658. (Illus.). 244p. 1981. 15.00 (ISBN 0-295-95790-5). U of Wash Pr.

Indigenous Peoples. (Studies & Reports, New Ser.: No. 35). 628p. 1953. 13.70 (ISBN 92-2-100933-5). Intl Labour Office.

Lindley, Mark F. Acquisition & Government of Backward Territory in International Law. LC 77-78770. Repr. of 1926 ed. 18.50x (ISBN 0-8371-1401-2, Pub. by Negro U Pr). Greenwood.

MacDonald, Allan J. Trade, Politics & Christianity in Africa & the East. LC 77-89007. Repr. of 1916 ed. 14.50x (ISBN 0-8371-1755-0). Greenwood.

Snow, Alpheus H. The Question of Aborigines in the Law & Practice of Nations. LC 79-99409. 218p. 1972. Repr. of 1919 ed. lib. bdg. 14.50 (ISBN 0-8411-0082-9). Metro Bks.

Verrill, Alpheus H. Strange Customs, Manners & Beliefs. facs. ed. LC 75-86791. (Essay Index Reprint Ser). 1946. 18.00 (ISBN 0-8369-1199-7). Arno.

NATIVISM
see also American Party; Ku Klux Klan

Beals, Carleton. Brass-Knuckle Crusade. (American Procession Ser). 1960. 9.95 (ISBN 0-8038-0703-1). Hastings.

Fell, Marie L. The Foundations of Nativism in American Textbooks, 1783-1860. LC 76-145480. (The American Immigration Library). ix, 259p. 1971. Repr. of 1941 ed. lib. bdg. 13.95x (ISBN 0-89198-011-3). Ozer.

Hughes, John & Breckinridge, John. Discussion on Civil & Religious Liberty. LC 76-122167. (Civil Liberties in American History Ser). 1970. Repr. of 1836 ed. lib. bdg. 55.00 (ISBN 0-306-71979-7). Da Capo.

Leonard, Ira M. & Parmet, Robert D. American Nativism. 1971. pap. 4.95x (ISBN 0-442-30110-3, 110, Anv). Van Nos Reinhold.

--American Nativism, Eighteen Thirty to Eighteen Sixty. LC 79-4301. (Anvil Ser.). 192p. 1979. pap. 4.95 (ISBN 0-88275-901-9). Krieger.

Peterson, Richard H. Manifest Destiny in the Mines: A Cultural Interpretation of Anti-Mexican Nativism in Califofnia, 1848-1853. LC 75-5334. 1975. soft bdg. 9.00 (ISBN 0-88247-365-4). R & E Res Assoc.

Schultz, Alfred P. Race or Mongrel: History of the Rise & Fall of the Ancient Races of Earth. Grob, Gerald, ed. LC 76-46103. (Anti-Movements in America). 1977. Repr. of 1908 ed. lib. bdg. 21.00x (ISBN 0-405-09974-6). Arno.

Scisco, Louis D. Political Nativism in New York State. LC 79-76668. (Columbia University. Studies in the Social Sciences: No. 35). 1968. Repr. of 1901 ed. 16.50 (ISBN 0-404-51035-3). AMS Pr.

NATIVISTIC MOVEMENTS
see also Cargo Movement; Ghost Dance

Clarebout, David, ed. Ethnic Group Adjustment in America. new ed. 1980. lib. bdg. 9.95 (ISBN 0-915574-19-5). Soc Sci & Soc Res.

Daneel, M. L. Zionism & Faith-Healing in Rhodesia: Aspects of African Independent Churches. V. A. February Communications, tr. from Dutch. (Illus.). 1970. pap. 8.35x (ISBN 90-2796-278-2). Mouton.

Desroche, Henri, et al. Dieux D'hommes: Dictionnaire Des Messianismes & Millenarismes De L'ere Chretienne. 1969. 42.25x (ISBN 90-2796-415-7). Mouton.

Fuchs, Stephen. Rebellious Prophets: A Study of Messianic Movements in Indian Religions. 1965. 8.95x (ISBN 0-210-27136-1). Asia.

How to Respond to the Cults. 1977. 1.25 (ISBN 0-570-07682-X, 12-2654). Concordia.

Sanchez, Julio. La Religion De los Orichas (Creencias y Ceremonias De un Culto Afro-Caribeno) 1978. pap. 12.95 (ISBN 0-685-60704-6). Ediciones.

Williams, Francis E. The Vailala Madness & the Destruction of Native Ceremonies in the Gulf Division. LC 75-35166. (Territory of Papua. Anthropological Report: No. 4). Repr. of 1923 ed. 12.00 (ISBN 0-404-14180-3). AMS Pr.

Wrede, William. Messianic Secret. Greig, J. C., tr. 1972. 20.00 (ISBN 0-227-67717-X). Attic Pr.

NATIVITY OF CHRIST
see Jesus Christ-Nativity

NATO
see North Atlantic Treaty Organization

NATRONA COUNTY, WYOMING

Mokler, Alfred J. History of Natrona County, Wyoming, 1888-1922. LC 65-27181. 560p. Repr. of 1923 ed. 22.50 (ISBN 0-405-03679-5). Arno.

NATURAL BOUNDARIES
see Boundaries

NATURAL CALAMITIES
see Natural Disasters

NATURAL CHILDBIRTH

Atlee, H. B. Natural Childbirth. (American Lecture Ynecology & Obstetrics). (Illus.). 96p. 1956. pap. 9.75 spiral bdg. (ISBN 0-398-04195-4). C C Thomas.

Baldwin, Rahima. Special Delivery. LC 78-61611. (Illus.). 1979. pap. 9.95 (ISBN 0-89087-934-6). Les Femmes Pub.

Dick-Read, Grantly. Childbirth Without Fear. rev. 4th ed. LC 77-181616. (Illus.). 1979. pap. 2.95 (ISBN 0-06-080490-4, P 490, PL). Har-Row.

Ewy, Donna & Ewy, Rodger. Preparation for Childbirth. 224p. 1974. pap. 2.25 (ISBN 0-451-08774-7, E8774, Sig). NAL.

--Preparation for Childbirth: A Lamaze Guide. rev. ed. (Illus.). 1976. pap. 5.95 (ISBN 0-87108-508-9). Pruett.

Hartman, Rhondda E. Exercises for True Natural Childbirth. LC 74-1814. (Illus.). 160p. 1975. 10.95 (ISBN 0-06-011766-4, HarpT). Har-Row.

Heardman, Helen. Relaxation & Exercise for Natural Childbirth. 4th ed. Ebner, Maria, ed. LC 74-29077. (Illus.). 1975. pap. 1.25x (ISBN 0-443-01249-0). Churchill.

--A Way to Natural Childbirth: A Manual for Physiotherapists & Parents-to-Be. 3rd ed. Ebner, Maria, ed. LC 73-85388. (Illus.). 100p. 1974. pap. text ed. 3.25 (ISBN 0-443-01061-7). Churchill.

Holt, Kenneth S. Developmental Pediatrics. (Postgraduate Pediatric Ser.). 304p. 1977. 14.95 (ISBN 0-407-00065-8). Butterworth.

Joseph, Lou & Cucco, Ulisse. A Doctor Discusses Prepared Childbirth. 1980. pap. 2.50 (ISBN 0-910304-21-1). Budlong.

Karmel, Marjorie. Thank You Dr. Lamaze. rev. ed. LC 80-8372. 192p. 1981. 10.95 (ISBN 0-06-014831-4, HarpT). Har-Row.

--Thank You, Doctor Lamaze. pap. 2.95 (ISBN 0-385-03752-X, C458, Dolp). Doubleday.

Kitzinger, Sheila. Birth at Home. (Illus.). 1979. 13.95x (ISBN 0-19-261160-7). Oxford U Pr.

Lamaze, Fernand. Painless Childbirth. 1977. pap. 2.75 (ISBN 0-671-80400-6). PB.

--Painless Childbirth: The Lamaze Method. LC 74-126152. 1970. 8.95 (ISBN 0-8092-9640-3). Contemp Bks.

Leshan, Eda J. Natural Parenthood. 1970. pap. 1.25 (ISBN 0-685-57126-2, Pub. by NAL). Formur Intl.

Marilus, Esther. Natural Childbirth the Swiss Way: The New Program for a More Comfortable Pregnancy & Easier Childbirth. 1979. 9.95 (ISBN 0-13-610055-4); pap. 4.95 (ISBN 0-13-610048-1). P-H.

Mitchell, Ingrid. Giving Birth Together: The Modern Parents' Home Program of Natural Childbirth Exercises. LC 75-12938. (Illus.). 192p. 1975. 8.95 (ISBN 0-8164-9223-9). Continuum.

Parvati, Jeannine & Medvin, O'Brien. Prenatal Yoga & Natural Birth. LC 74-19553. (Illus.). 1978. pap. text ed. 5.00 (ISBN 0-913512-52-4). Freestone Pub Co.

Smith, Lynette. The Natural Childbirth Book. 1981. pap. 4.95 (ISBN 0-686-76165-0). Bethany Hse.

Stewart, David & Stewart, Lee. Safe Alternatives in Childbirth. 3rd ed. LC 76-19336. 1978. pap. 5.75 (ISBN 0-917314-06-9). NAPSAC.

--Twenty-First Century Obstetrics Now, 2 vols. 2nd ed. LC 77-72854. (Illus.). 1978. Set. pap. 12.25 set (ISBN 0-917314-09-3); pap. 7.25 ea. Vol. 1 (ISBN 0-917314-07-7). Vol. 2 (ISBN 0-917314-08-5). NAPSAC.

Tanzer, Deborah & Block, Jean L. Why Natural Childbirth? A Psychologist's Report on the Benefits to Mothers, Fathers, & Babies. LC 75-36495. 308p. 1976. pap. 5.50 (ISBN 0-8052-0518-7). Schocken.

Wessel, Helen. The Joy of Natural Childbirth. LC 76-9978. 352p. 1976. pap. 4.95 (ISBN 0-06-069314-2, RD 321, HarpR). Har-Row.

--Natural Childbirth & the Family. rev. ed. LC 73-4136. (Illus.). 358p. 1974. 10.95 (ISBN 0-06-014542-0, HarpT). Har-Row.

Young, Joy. Christian Home Birth: A Preparation for Spirit, Soul & Body. (Illus.). 208p. (Orig.). 1980. pap. 6.00x (ISBN 0-686-28082-2). J Young.

NATURAL DISASTERS
see also Avalanches; Earth Movements; Floods; Forest Fires; Storms; Tsunamis; Volcanism

Annual Summary of Information on Natural Disasters, 1969. (Illus., Orig.). 1971. pap. 4.00 (ISBN 0-685-02042-8, U25, UNESCO). Unipub.

Annual Summary of Information on Natural Disasters, 1967. (Illus., Orig.). 1970. pap. 5.25 (ISBN 0-685-04903-5, U23, UNESCO). Unipub.

Annual Summary of Information on Natural Disasters, 1968. (Illus., Orig.). 1970. pap. 4.00 (ISBN 0-685-04904-3, U24, UNESCO). Unipub.

Annual Summary of Information on Natural Disasters 1970. (Illus.). 64p. (Orig.). 1973. pap. 5.25 (ISBN 0-685-31672-6, U26, UNESCO). Unipub.

Annual Summary of Information on Natural Disasters, 1971, No. 6. LC 72-83612. 82p. 1973. pap. 5.25 (ISBN 92-3-101042-5, U27, UNESCO). Unipub.

Annual Summary of Information on Natural Disasters, 1979, No. 10. 1975. pap. 9.25 (ISBN 92-3-001636-5, U914, UNESCO). Unipub.

Annual Summary of Information on Natural Disasters 1966: No. 1. (Illus., Orig.). 1970. pap. 5.25 (ISBN 0-685-20804-4, U26, UNESCO). Unipub.

Asimov, Isaac. A Choice of Catastrophes. 1979. 11.95 (ISBN 0-671-22701-7). S&S.

Bolt, B. A., et al. Geological Hazards. LC 74-32049. (Illus.). 450p. 1977. 22.90 (ISBN 0-387-90254-6). Springer-Verlag.

Bulter, J. R. & Doessel, D. P. The Economics of Natural Disaster Relief in Australia. LC 79-50570. (Centre for Research on Federal Financial Relations - Research Monograph: No. 27). 147p. (Orig.). 1980. pap. text ed. 14.95 (ISBN 0-7081-1073-8, 0565). Bks Australia.

Butler, John E. Natural Disasters. 1976. pap. text ed. 7.95x (ISBN 0-435-34068-9). Heinemann Ed.

Cohen, Stephen P. & Raghavulu, C. V. The Andhra Cyclone of Nineteen Seventy-Seven: Individual & Institutional Responses to Mass Death. 1979. 15.00x (ISBN 0-7069-0765-5, Pub. by Vikas India). Advent NY.

Frazier, Kendrick. The Violent Face of Nature. LC 79-16073. (Illus.). 1979. 12.95 (ISBN 0-688-03528-0). Morrow.

Holford, Ingrid. British Weather Disasters. LC 76-20117. 1976. 6.50 (ISBN 0-7153-7276-9). David & Charles.

International Conference Held in Bangkok, Jan. 7-9, 1980 & Karasudhi, Pisidhi. Engineering for Protection from Natural Disasters: Proceedings. Kanok-Nukulchai, Worsak, ed. LC 80-4169. 1981. 101.00 (ISBN 0-471-27895-5, Pub. by Wiley-Interscience). Wiley.

Pickup, Geoffrey & Minor, Joseph E. Assessment of Research & Practice in Australian Natural Hazards Management. (North Australi Research Bulletin: No. 6). 207p. 1980. pap. text ed. 11.00 (ISBN 0-909596-51-4, 0555, Pub. by ANUP Australia). Bks Australia.

Richner, Mark E. A Bibliographic Guide to Recent Research in Environmental Geology & Natural Hazards. (Public Administration Ser.: Bibliography P-707). 1981. pap. text ed. 18.00 (ISBN 0-686-30146-3). Vance Biblios.

Sweeney, Karen O. Nature Runs Wild: True Disaster Stories. (Illus.). (gr. 5-8). 1979. PLB 7.45 s&l (ISBN 0-531-02220-X). Watts.

Tufty, Barbara. One Thousand and One Questions Answered About Earthquakes, Avalanches, Floods & Other Natural Disasters. Date not set. 8.75 (ISBN 0-8446-5826-X). Peter Smith.

--One Thousand & One Questions Answered About Earthquakes, Avalanches, Floods & Other Natural Disasters. (Illus.). 1978. pap. 4.00 (ISBN 0-486-23646-3). Dover.

Verschuur, Gerrit L. Cosmic Catastrophes. LC 77-92164. (Illus.). 1978. 9.95 (ISBN 0-201-08098-2); pap. 4.95 (ISBN 0-201-08099-0). A-W.

Whittow, John. Disasters: The Anatomy of Environmental Hazards. LC 79-5236. (Illus.). 405p. 1981. pap. 9.95 (ISBN 0-8203-0542-1). U of Ga Pr.

Wright, James D., et al. After the Clean-Up: Long Range Effects of Natural Disasters. LC 79-15768. (Contemporary Evaluation Research: Vol. 2). (Illus.). 230p. 1979. 20.00 (ISBN 0-8039-1194-7); pap. 9.95 (ISBN 0-8039-1195-5). Sage.

NATURAL FOOD
see Food, Natural

NATURAL FOOD COOKERY
see Cookery (Natural Foods)

NATURAL GARDENING
see Organic Gardening

NATURAL GAS
see Gas, Natural

NATURAL HISTORY
see also Animal Lore; Aquariums; Biology; Botany; Desert Biology; Geographical Distribution of Animals and Plants; Geology; Marine Biology; Mineralogy; Paleontology; Plant Lore; Soil Biology; Zoology

Agassiz, Louis. The Primitive Diversity & Number of Animals in Geological Times. 1976. Repr. of 1854 ed. 25.00 (ISBN 0-685-71153-6, Regency). Scholarly.

Anderson, Edgar. Landscape Papers. Callahan, Bob, ed. LC 73-43625. (New World Writing Ser). 1976. 10.00 (ISBN 0-913666-15-7); pap. 4.00 (ISBN 0-913666-11-4). Turtle Isl Foun.

Bates, Marston. Jungle in the House: Essays in Natural & Unnatural History. LC 70-103375. 1970. 7.50 (ISBN 0-8027-0159-0). Walker & Co.

Bateson, William. Scientific Papers of William Bateson, 2 Vols. Punnett, R. C., ed. Repr. of 1928 ed. Set. 69.50 (ISBN 0-384-03533-7). Johnson Repr.

Borland, Hal. The Golden Circle: A Book of Months. LC 77-23560. (Illus.). (gr. 5 up). 1977. 10.95 (ISBN 0-690-03803-8, TYC-J). Har-Row.

Brimley, Herbert H. North Carolina Naturalist, H. H. Brimley. facs. ed. Odum, Eugene P., ed. LC 78-134058. (Essay Index Reprint Ser). 1949. 18.00 (ISBN 0-8369-2145-3). Arno.

British Museum (Natural History) Nature Stored, Nature Studied: Collections, Conservation & Allied Research at the British Museum (Natural History) (Illus.). 64p. 1981. pap. 5.00x (ISBN 0-565-00835-8, Pub. by Brit Mus Nat Hist England). Sabbot-Natural Hist Bks.

Brown, Vinson. The Amateur Naturalists's Handbook. (Illus.). 448p. 1980. 15.95 (ISBN 0-13-023739-6, Spec); pap. 6.95 (ISBN 0-13-023721-3). P-H.

Buchanan, Handasyde. Nature into Art: A Treasury of Great Natural History Books. LC 79-12481. (Illus.). 1980. 25.00 (ISBN 0-8317-6337-X, Mayflower Bks). Smith Pubs.

Buckland, Francis T. Curiosities of Natural History. (Illus.). 318p. Repr. of 1858 ed. 16.95x (ISBN 0-8464-0307-2). Beekman Pubs.

Buffon, Georges L. The Natural History of Oviparous Quadrupeds & Serpents: Arranged & Published from the Papers & Collections of the Count De Buffon, 4 vols. in one. Sterling, Keir B., ed. Kerr, Robert, tr. LC 77-81119. (Biologists & Their World Ser.). (Illus.). 1978. Repr. of 1802 ed. Set. lib. bdg. 100.00x (ISBN 0-405-10710-2); lib. bdg. 50.00x ea. Vol. 1 (ISBN 0-405-10711-0). Vol. 2 (ISBN 0-405-10712-9). Arno.

Campbell, Bruce, ed. Countryman Wild Life Book. LC 76-85490. (Illus.). 1969. 6.50 (ISBN 0-8008-1965-9). Taplinger.

Cecchettini, Philip A. CLEP: Introduction to Natural Science. 1979. pap. text ed. 5.95 (ISBN 0-07-010309-7, C). McGraw.

Chalmers-Hunt, J. M., ed. Natural History Auctions, Seventeen Hundred to Nineteen Seventy-Two: A Register of Sales in the British Isles. 192p. 1976. 45.00x (ISBN 0-85667-021-9, Pub. by Sotheby Parke Bernet England). Biblio Dist.

Clark, Ann N. Along Sandy Trails. (37 Color Photos, 32p). (gr. 4-6). 1969. PLB 5.95 (ISBN 0-670-11485-5). Viking Pr.

Copeland, Herbert F. Classification of Lower Organisms. LC 56-7944. (Illus.). 1956. 14.95x (ISBN 0-87015-059-6). Pacific Bks.

Cornell, James, Jr. Strange Sudden & Unexpected. (gr. 7-12). 1972. pap. 1.25 (ISBN 0-590-09380-0, Schol Pap). Schol Bk Serv.

Daehnhardt, Alfred O., ed. Natursagen, 4 vols. 1971. Repr. of 1907 ed. lib. bdg. 110.00 (ISBN 0-8337-0760-4). B Franklin.

Darwin, Charles. The Collected Papers of Charles Darwin, Vols. I & II. Barrett, Paul H., ed. LC 76-606. (Illus.). 1977. lib. bdg. 40.00x set (ISBN 0-226-13657-4). U of Chicago Pr.

--Journal of Researches into the Natural History & Geology of the Countries Visited During the Voyage of H. M. S. "Beagle" Round the World, Under the Command of Capt. Fitz Roy, R. A. 1977. Repr. of 1892 ed. lib. bdg. 25.00 (ISBN 0-8482-0544-8). Norwood Edns.

--Voyage of the Beagle. LC 62-2990. 1962. 3.95 (ISBN 0-385-02767-2, Anchor). Natural Hist.

Darwin, Charles R. Journal of Researches into the Geology & Natural History of the Various Countries Visited by H. M. S. Beagle Under the Command of Captain Fitzroy, R. N. from 1832 to 1836. (Illus.). 636p. 1969. Repr. of 1839 ed. 65.00x (ISBN 0-8002-1621-0). Intl Pubns Serv.

Darwin, Francis. Rustic Sounds & Other Studies in Literature & Natural History. facs. ed. LC 69-17572. (Essay Index Reprint Ser). 1917. 15.00 (ISBN 0-8369-0069-3). Arno.

De Grazia, Alfred. Chaos & Creation: An Introduction to Quantavolution in Human & Natural History. (Quantavolution Ser.). (Illus.). xiii, 336p. 1981. 21.00 (ISBN 0-940268-00-0). Metron Pubns.

Douglas, Charles. Natural History Notebook, No. 3. (Illus.). iv, 54p. 1980. pap. 2.50 (ISBN 0-660-10341-9, 56444-4, Pub. by Natl Mus Canada). U of Chicago Pr.

--Natural History Notebook, No. 4. (National Museum of Natural Science Ser.). (Illus.). iv, 56p. 1981. pap. 2.50 (ISBN 0-660-10321-4, 56445-2, Pub. by Natl Mus Canada). U of Chicago Pr.

--Natural History Notebook Number Four, No. 4. (Illus.). 56p. 1981. pap. 2.50 (ISBN 0-226-56445-2). U of Chicago Pr.

Durrell, Gerald, frwd. by. The Encyclopedia of Natural History. (Octopus Book). (Illus.). 1978. 16.95 (ISBN 0-7064-0676-1, Mayflower Bks). Smith Pubs.

Egerton, Frank N., ed. Natural History, General & Particular: An Original Anthology, 2 vols. LC 77-74206. (History of Ecology Ser.). (Illus.). 1978. lib. bdg. 76.00x (ISBN 0-405-10376-X). Arno.

Fuentes, Carlos. Where the Air Is Clear. Hileman, Sam, tr. 1971. pap. 7.95 (ISBN 0-374-50919-0, N405). FS&G.

Godman, John D. American Natural History: Mastogogy & Rambles of a Naturalist, Part No. 1, 3 vols. in one. LC 73-17821. (Natural Sciences in America Ser.). (Illus.). 1079p. 1974. Repr. 56.00x (ISBN 0-405-05737-7). Arno.

Gould, Stephen J. Ever Since Darwin: Reflections in Natural History. 1979. pap. 4.95 (ISBN 0-393-00917-3). Norton.

--The Panda's Thumb: More Reflections in Natural History. (Illus.). 1980. 12.95 (ISBN 0-393-01380-4). Norton.

Grant, May B. Wildly Speaking. LC 75-122574. (Popular Ser.: No. 10). 1972. pap. 2.00 (ISBN 0-87768-005-1). Denver Mus Natl Hist.

Gribbin, John. Genesis: The Origins of Man & Universe. (Illus.). 384p. 1981. 13.95 (ISBN 0-440-02832-9). Delacorte.

Grinnell, Joseph. Joseph Grinnell's Philosophy of Nature: Selected Writings of a Western Naturalist. facs. ed. LC 68-20304. (Essay Index Reprint Ser). 1943. 19.50 (ISBN 0-8369-0499-0). Arno.

Hafslund, Per. Little Wonders of Nature. (Illus.). (gr. 7 up). 1964. 4.00 (ISBN 0-8184-0051-X). Lyle Stuart.

Halbritter, Kurt. Halbritter's Plant-&-Animal World. Turnbull, Joanne & Githens, John, trs. from Ger. LC 81-2277. Orig. Title: Halbritters Tier-und Pflanzenwelt. (Illus.). 160p. 1981. 14.95 (ISBN 0-394-51805-5). Seaver Bks.

Hobson, E. W. The Domain of Natural Science. 6.00 (ISBN 0-8446-2260-5). Peter Smith.

Hobson, Ernest W. The Domain of Natural Science. LC 77-27210. (Gifford Lectures: 1921-22). Repr. of 1923 ed. 24.50 (ISBN 0-404-60467-6). AMS Pr.

Hudson, William H. Book of a Naturalist. Repr. of 1923 ed. 21.50 (ISBN 0-404-03410-1). AMS Pr.

--Hind in Richmond Park. Repr. of 1923 ed. 21.50 (ISBN 0-404-03413-6). AMS Pr.

--Nature in Downland. Repr. of 1923 ed. 21.50 (ISBN 0-404-03398-9). AMS Pr.

Jordan, David S. Science Sketches. new & enl. ed. (Essay Index Reprint Ser.). Repr. of 1896 ed. 18.00 (ISBN 0-518-10181-9). Arno.

Kessel, Edward L., ed. A Century of Progress in the Natural Sciences, 1853-1953. LC 73-17827. (Natural Sciences in America Ser.). (Illus.). 824p. 1974. Repr. 41.00x (ISBN 0-405-05745-8). Arno.

Knight, David M. Natural Science Books in English, Sixteen Hundred to Nineteen Hundred. 1972. 60.00 (ISBN 0-7134-0728-X, Pub. by Batsford England). David & Charles.

Kolisko, Eugen. Natural History. 1980. pap. 3.25x (ISBN 0-906492-21-1, Pub. by Kolisko Archives). St George Bk Serv.

Lankester, Edwin R. Diversions of a Naturalist. LC 77-105024. (Essay Index Reprint Ser). 1915. 24.00 (ISBN 0-8369-1471-6). Arno.

--Science from an Easy Chair, First Series. facs. ed. LC 79-152185. (Essay Index Reprint Ser). 1910. 22.00 (ISBN 0-8369-2194-1). Arno.

--Secrets of Earth & Sea. LC 76-93352. (Essay Index Reprint Ser). 1920. 17.00 (ISBN 0-8369-1301-9). Arno.

Leopold, Luna B., ed. Round River: From the Journals of Aldo Leopold. (Illus.). 188p. 1972. pap. 3.95 (ISBN 0-19-501563-0, 372, GB). Oxford U Pr.

Linnaeus, Carl. Miscellaneous Tracts Relating to Natural History, Husbandry, & Physick: Calender of Flora Is Added. Egerton, Frank N., 3rd, ed. LC 77-74237. (History of Ecology Ser.). 1978. Repr. of 1762 ed. lib. bdg. 21.00x (ISBN 0-405-10406-5). Arno.

Lyon, John & Sloan, Philip. From Natural History to the History of Nature: Readings from Buffon & His Critics. LC 81-1320. 432p. 1981. text ed. 19.95 (ISBN 0-268-00955-4). U of Notre Dame Pr.

Madson, John. John Madson: Out Home. McIntosh, Michael, ed. (Illus.). 1979. 11.95 (ISBN 0-87691-285-4). Winchester Pr.

Mandahl-Barth, G. Woodland Life. (European Ecology Ser.). (Illus.). 1966. 9.95 (ISBN 0-7137-0417-9, Pub by Blandford Pr England). Sterling.

Le Monde de la nature. (Illus.). 1978. text ed. 26.95x (ISBN 2-03-019112-4). Larousse.

Moscovici, Serge. The Human History of Nature. (European Ideas Ser.). 1977. text ed. 16.25x (ISBN 0-391-01080-8). Humanities.

Moseley, Henry N. Notes by a Naturalist. new & rev. ed. LC 72-1710. Orig. Title: Notes by a Naturalist on the Challenger. (Illus.). Repr. of 1892 ed. 36.45 (ISBN 0-404-08159-2). AMS Pr.

Muir, John. Wilderness Essays. (Literature of the American Wilderness Ser.). 288p. 1980. pap. 3.75 (ISBN 0-87905-072-1). Peregrine Smith.

Myers, George, Jr. Natural History. LC 81-80891. (Illus.). 80p. (Orig.). 1981. pap. 3.50 (ISBN 0-9602424-6-5). Paycock Pr.

Olson, Sigurd F. Listening Point. (Illus.). 1958. 10.95 (ISBN 0-394-43358-0). Knopf.

Pain, Nesta. Grassblade Jungle. 1979. 12.50x (ISBN 0-86025-805-X, Pub. by Ian Henry Pubns England). State Mutual Bk.

Palmer, E. Lawrence & Fowler, H. Seymour. Fieldbook of Natural History. 1975. 19.95 (ISBN 0-07-048425-2, GB); PLB 21.50 (ISBN 0-07-048196-2). McGraw.

Pliny. Natural History, Vols. 1-5 Of 11. Warmington, E. H., ed. (Loeb Classical Library: No. 330, 352-353, 370-371). 11.00x ea. Vol. 1 (ISBN 0-674-99364-0). Vol. 2 (ISBN 0-674-99388-8). Vol. 3 (ISBN 0-674-99389-6). Vol. 4 (ISBN 0-674-99408-6). Vol. 5 (ISBN 0-674-99409-4). Harvard U Pr.

--Natural History, Vols. 6-10 Of 11. (Loeb Classical Library: No. 392-394, 418-419). 11.00x ea. Vol. 6 (ISBN 0-674-99431-0). Vol. 7 (ISBN 0-674-99432-9). Vol. 8 (ISBN 0-674-99460-4). Vol. 9 (ISBN 0-674-99433-7). Vol. 10 (ISBN 0-674-99461-2). Harvard U Pr.

Roe, Shirley A. & Cohen, I. Bernard, eds. The Natural Philosophy of Albrecht Von Haller. LC 80-2109. (Development of Science Ser.). (Illus.). 1981. lib. bdg. 40.00x (ISBN 0-405-13874-1). Arno.

Rood, Ronald. Who Wakes the Groundhog? (Illus.). 192p. 1973. 6.95 (ISBN 0-393-08524-4). Norton.

Roth, Charles. Then There Were None. LC 77-4400. (Illus.). 1977. 6.95 (ISBN 0-201-06539-8, A-W Childrens). A-W.

Scandone, Thomas. Emphasis: Natural History. 1979. coil binging 12.95 (ISBN 0-88252-098-9). Paladin Hse.

Schopf, J. William. Cradle of Life. 1981. price not set (ISBN 0-87735-339-5). Freeman C.

Smellie, William. The Philosophy of Natural History, 2 vols. LC 78-67541. Repr. 125.00 set (ISBN 0-404-17230-X). AMS Pr.

Smithsonian Institution. Magnificent Foragers: Smithsonian Explorations in the Natural Sciences. LC 78-61066. 223p. (Orig.). 1978. 16.95 (ISBN 0-89599-001-6). Smithsonian Exposition.

Storer, Tracy I. & Usinger, Robert L. Sierra Nevada Natural History: An Illustrated Handbook. (Illus.). 1963. pap. 6.95 (ISBN 0-520-01227-5). U of Cal Pr.

Swain, Roger. Earthly Pleasures. (Illus.). 192p. 1981. 10.95 (ISBN 0-684-16657-7, ScribT). Scribner.

Teale, Edwin W. A Walk Through the Year. LC 78-9786. (Illus.). 1978. 15.00 (ISBN 0-396-07621-1). Dodd.

Thoreau, Henry D. The Natural History Essays. (Literature of the American Wilderness Ser.). 288p. (Orig.). 1980. pap. 3.75 (ISBN 0-87905-071-3). Peregrine Smith.

Tyler, Waldo R. Waldo Tyler's World: A Naturalist's Year. 230p. 1973. 15.00 (ISBN 0-913954-09-8). Courier of Maine.

White, Gilbert. Natural History of Selborne. 1980. 20.00x (ISBN 0-905418-22-0, Pub. by Gresham England). State Mutual Bk.

Wilson, David S. In the Presence of Nature. LC 77-90733. (Illus.). 1978. 15.00x (ISBN 0-87023-020-4). U of Mass Pr.

NATURAL HISTORY–BIBLIOGRAPHY

Bridson, Gavin D., et al, eds. Natural History Manuscript Resources in the British Isles. LC 79-92886. 6000p. 1980. 245.00 (ISBN 0-8352-1281-5). Bowker.

Brightman, Frank, ed. Natural History Book Reviews: An International Biography. 1981. 35.00x (ISBN 0-686-72935-8, Pub by A B Academic England). State Mutual Bk.

Dryander, Jonas. Catalogus Bibliothecae Historico-Naturalis Josephi Banks, 5 vols. 1966. Set. 200.00 (ISBN 90-6123-003-9). Lubrecht & Cramer.

Freeman, R. B. The Works of Charles Darwin: An Annotated Bibliographical Handlist. rev. & 2nd ed. LC 76-30002. 235p. 1977. 22.50x (ISBN 0-7129-0740-8, Pub. by St. Pauls Biblios England). U Pr of Va.

Munz, Lucile T. & Slauson, Nedra. Index to Illustrations of Living Things Outside of North America: Where to Find Pictures of Flora & Fauna. 452p. 1981. 49.50 (ISBN 0-208-01857-3, Archon). Shoe String.

Research Catalog of the Library of the American Museum of Natural History: Classed Catalog. 1978. 1010.00 (ISBN 0-8161-0238-4). G K Hall.

NATURAL HISTORY–DICTIONARIES

Brockhaus der Naturwissenschaften und der Technik. 832p. (Ger.). 35.00 (ISBN 3-7653-0019-5, M-7314, Pub. by Wiesbaden). French & Eur.

Habibi, B. Deutsch - Persisches Fachwoerterbuch Fuer Naturwissenschaft, Medezin und Landwirtschaft. 240p. (Ger.). 1964. pap. 17.50 (ISBN 3-447-00354-5, M-7331, Pub. by Harrassowitz). French & Eur.

Harmer, S. F. & Shipley, A. E., eds. Cambridge Natural History, 10 vols. 1960. 120.00 set (ISBN 0-934454-19-1). Lubrecht & Cramer.

Historia Natural, 4 vols. 11th ed. 1984p. (Espn.). 1976. Set. leather 215.00 (ISBN 84-85009-42-8, S-50569). French & Eur.

Jehan, L. F. Dictionnaire d'Anthropologie ou Histoire Naturelle del'Homme et des Races Humaines. Migne, J. P., ed. (Nouvelle Encyclopedie Theologique Ser.: Vol. 42). 800p. (Fr.). Date not set. Repr. of 1853 ed. lib. bdg. 101.50x (ISBN 0-89241-281-X). Caratzas Bros.

--Dictionnaire Historique des Sciences Physiques et Naturelles. Migne, J. P., ed. (Troisieme et Derniere Encyclopedie Theologique Ser.: Vol. 30). 654p. (Fr.). Date not set. Repr. of 1857 ed. lib. bdg. 85.00x (ISBN 0-89241-309-3). Caratzas Bros.

Khatib, Ahmad. Dictionary of the Natural Environment: English-Arabic. 1979. pap. 7.95 (ISBN 0-86685-073-2). Intl Bk Ctr.

Lewis, Walter H. Ecology Field Glossary: A Naturalist's Vocabulary. LC 77-71856. 1977. lib. bdg. 15.00x (ISBN 0-8371-9547-0, LEF/). Greenwood.

Seager, Herbert W. Natural History in Shakespeare's Time. LC 79-160134. Repr. of 1896 ed. 24.00 (ISBN 0-404-05667-9). AMS Pr.

NATURAL HISTORY–JUVENILE LITERATURE

see also Botany–Juvenile Literature; Geology–Juvenile Literature; Zoology–Juvenile Literature; also Animals–Juvenile Literature; birds–Juvenile Literature, and similar headings; also names of individual animals, birds, etc.

Allison, Linda. The Sierra Club Summer Book. LC 76-57681. (Sierra Club-Scribner Juvenile Ser.). (Illus.). (gr. 3 up). 1977. 7.95 (ISBN 0-684-15014-X); pap. 4.95 (ISBN 0-684-15015-8). Sierra.

Bale, Robert O. What on Earth. (Illus.). 1969. pap. 3.95 (ISBN 0-87603-000-2). Am Camping.

Boreman, Thomas, ed. A Description of Three Hundred Animals. (Illus.). Repr. of 1786 ed. 14.50 (ISBN 0-384-05125-1). Johnson Repr.

Borland, Hal. The Golden Circle: A Book of Months. LC 77-23560. (Illus.). (gr. 5 up). 1977. 10.95 (ISBN 0-690-03803-8, TYC-J). Har-Row.

Boy Scouts Of America. Nature. LC 19-600. (Illus.). 48p. (gr. 6-12). 1973. pap. 0.70x (ISBN 0-8395-3285-7, 3285). BSA.

Burton, Virginia L. Life Story. (Illus.). (gr. k-3). 1962. reinforced bdg. 8.95 (ISBN 0-395-16030-8). HM.

Caras, Roger. Mysteries of Nature: Explained & Unexplained. (Illus.). (gr. 5 up). 1979. 5.95 (ISBN 0-15-256346-6, HJ). HarBraceJ.

Comenius, John A. Orbis Pictus of John Amos Comenius. Bardeen, Charles W., ed. LC 67-23933. (Illus., Eng. & Lat.). 1968. Repr. of 1887 ed. 22.00 (ISBN 0-8103-3476-3). Gale.

Crosby, Alexander L. Pond Life. LC 64-12627. (Junior Science Books Ser). (Illus.). (gr. 2-5). 1964. PLB 6.09 (ISBN 0-8116-6169-5). Garrard.

Facklam, Margery. Frozen Snakes & Dinosaur Bones: Exploring a Natural History Museum. LC 75-41394. (Illus.). 128p. (gr. 3-7). 1976. 6.95 (ISBN 0-15-230275-1, HJ). HarBraceJ.

Hawkinson, John. Collect, Print & Paint from Nature. LC 63-13330. (Illus.). (gr. 3 up). 1963. 6.95g (ISBN 0-8075-1272-9). A Whitman.

Herford, Oliver. Child's Primer of Natural History. (Illus.). (gr. 1-6). 1966. pap. 2.00 (ISBN 0-486-21647-0). Dover.

Howitt, Mary B. Sketches of Natural History. (Early Children's Bks). 1970. Repr. of 1851 ed. 14.50 (ISBN 0-384-24510-2). Johnson Repr.

Knight, David C. Bees Can't Fly, but They Do: Things That Are Still a Mystery to Science. LC 76-8491. 48p. (gr. 3 up). 1976. 7.95 (ISBN 0-02-750860-9, 75086). Macmillan.

McPhee Gribble Publishers. Exploring: Getting to Know Your World. (Practical Puffins Ser.). (Illus.). (gr. 2-7). 1978. pap. 1.50 (ISBN 0-14-049152-X, Puffin). Penguin.

Mari, Lela. Eat & Be Eaten. (Illus.). (gr. k-6). 1980. 5.95 (ISBN 0-8120-5396-6). Barron.

May, Julian. Wildlife in the City. Publication Associates, ed. LC 70-104927. (gr. 2-4). 1970. PLB 6.95 (ISBN 0-87191-040-3). Creative Ed.

Moore, John A. Wonder of Life. (Illus.). (gr. 4-6). 1960. PLB 6.95 (ISBN 0-87396-016-5). Stravon.

Moser, Don. The Snake River Country. LC 74-80283. (American Wilderness). (Illus.). (gr. 6 up). 1974. PLB 11.97 (ISBN 0-8094-1242-X, Pub. by Time-Life). Silver.

National Geographical Society, ed. Books for Young Explorers, 4 vols, Set 1. Incl. Dinosaurs. LC 72-91418; Treasures in the Sea. LC 72-91421; Dogs Working for People. LC 72-91419; Lion Cubs. LC 72-91420. (ps-3). 1972. Set. 7.95, avail. only from Natl. Geog. (ISBN 0-87044-125-6). Natl Geog.

Pringle, Laurence P., ed. Discovering Nature Indoors: A Nature & Science Guide to Investigations with Small Animals. LC 70-103134. (gr. 4-7). 1970. 4.95 (ISBN 0-385-01000-1). Natural Hist.

Richards, John. Hidden Country: Nature on Your Doorstep. LC 72-12745. (Illus.). 144p. (gr. 5-8). 1973. PLB 9.95 (ISBN 0-87599-195-5). S G Phillips.

Schulz, Charles M. Charlie Brown's Second Super Book of Questions & Answers: About the Earth & Space from Plants to Planets. LC 77-74455. (Illus.). (gr. 3-6). 1977. 7.95 (ISBN 0-394-83491-7, BYR); PLB 8.99 (ISBN 0-394-93491-1). Random.

Sommer, Robert & Becker, Harriet. Sidewalk Fossils. LC 75-10056. (Illus.). 48p. (gr. 1-4). 1976. 5.95 (ISBN 0-8027-6228-X); PLB 5.85 (ISBN 0-8027-6233-6). Walker & Co.

Tanner, Ogden. Urban Wilds. (American Wilderness). (Illus.). (gr. 6 up). 1975. PLB 11.97 (ISBN 0-8094-1335-3, Pub. by Time-Life). Silver.

Waitley, Douglas. My Backyard: A Living World of Nature. LC 69-10443. 1970. 6.95 (ISBN 0-87250-224-4). D White.

Williams, Patricia M. Museums of Natural History & the People Who Work in Them. LC 72-93926. 128p. 1973. 5.95 (ISBN 0-312-56105-9). St Martin.

Zim, Herbert S. How Things Grow. (Illus.). (gr. 3-7). 1960. PLB 6.00 (ISBN 0-688-31409-0). Morrow.

NATURAL HISTORY–NOMENCLATURES

see also Botany–Nomenclature

Kessel, Edward L., ed. A Century of Progress in the Natural Sciences, 1853-1953. LC 73-17827. (Natural Sciences in America Ser.). (Illus.). 824p. 1974. Repr. 41.00x (ISBN 0-405-05745-8). Arno.

NATURAL HISTORY–OUTDOOR BOOKS

Barrus, Clara, ed. The Heart of Burrough's Journals. 1979. Repr. of 1928 ed. lib. bdg. 30.00 (ISBN 0-8495-0504-6). Arden Lib.

Bedichek, Roy. Adventures with a Texas Naturalist. (Illus.). 360p. 1961. pap. 7.95 (ISBN 0-292-70311-2). U of Tex Pr.

Borland, Hal. Hal Borland's Book of Days. 1976. 10.95 (ISBN 0-394-40187-5). Knopf.

Burroughs, John. Winter Sunshine. 1879. lib. bdg. 15.00 (ISBN 0-8414-1605-2). Folcroft.

--A Year in the Fields. 1901. lib. bdg. 15.00 (ISBN 0-8414-1607-9). Folcroft.

Cooper, Elizabeth K. Science in Your Own Back Yard. LC 58-5705. (Illus.). (gr. 4-7). 1958. 6.95 (ISBN 0-15-270664-X, HJ). HarBraceJ.

Cooper, Susan F. Rural Hours. LC 68-29419. (York State Books). (Illus.). 1968. Repr. of 1887 ed. 8.95 (ISBN 0-8156-0065-8). Syracuse U Pr.

Errington, Paul L. The Red Gods Call. (Illus.). 127p. 1973. 6.95 (ISBN 0-8138-1340-9). Iowa St U Pr.

Fuller, Raymond T. Now That We Have to Walk: Exploring the Out-of-Doors. facsimile ed. LC 72-37921. (Essay Index Reprint Ser). Repr. of 1943 ed. 17.00 (ISBN 0-8369-2590-4). Arno.

Godfrey, Michael A. A Sierra Club Naturalist's Guide to the Piedmont. LC 79-22328. (Naturalists Guide Ser.). (Illus.). 1980. 19.95 (ISBN 0-87156-268-5); pap. 9.95 (ISBN 0-87156-269-3). Sierra.

Halle, Louis J. Spring in Washington. LC 42-30273. (Illus.). 1963. pap. 1.25 (ISBN 0-689-70084-9, 22). Atheneum.

Hanenkrat, Frank T. Wildlife Watcher's Handbook. (Illus.). 1979. 10.00 (ISBN 0-87691-245-5); pap. 7.95 (ISBN 0-87691-306-0). Winchester Pr.

Jefferies, Richard. Old House at Coate. LC 70-111840. (Essay Index Reprint Ser). 1948. 16.00 (ISBN 0-8369-1664-6). Arno.

Kieran, John F. Nature Notes. facs. ed. LC 77-84315. (Essay Index Reprint Ser). 1941. 14.50 (ISBN 0-8369-1087-7). Arno.
Leopold, Aldo. Sand County Almanac Illustrated. new ed. LC 77-22656. 1977. 25.00 (ISBN 0-915024-15-2). Tamarack Pr.
--Sand County Almanac: With Other Essays on Conservation from Round River. (Illus.). 1966. 15.95 (ISBN 0-19-500619-4). Oxford U Pr.
Olson, Sigurd F. Listening Point. (Illus.). 1958. 10.95 (ISBN 0-394-43358-0). Knopf.
--Open Horizons. (Illus.). (YA) 1969. 10.95 (ISBN 0-394-43934-1). Knopf.
--Sigurd F. Olson's Wilderness Days. (Illus.). 1972. 17.95 (ISBN 0-394-47155-5). Knopf.
Pearson, Haydn S. Sea Flavor. facs. ed. LC 68-58809. (Essay Index Reprint Ser). 1948. 15.00 (ISBN 0-8369-0051-0). Arno.
Rowlands, John J. Cache Lake Country. (Illus.). (gr. 7 up). 1959. 12.95 (ISBN 0-393-08468-X). Norton.
Sharp, Dallas L. Face of the Fields. facs. ed. LC 67-26782. (Essay Index Reprint Ser). 1911. 15.00 (ISBN 0-8369-0870-8). Arno.
--Sanctuary! Sanctuary! facs. ed. LC 73-128312. (Essay Index Reprint Ser). 1926. 10.00 (ISBN 0-8369-2134-8). Arno.
Sharp, William. Where the Forest Murmurs. LC 73-111865. (Essay Index Reprint Ser). 1906. 19.50 (ISBN 0-8369-1627-1). Arno.
Shepard, Odell. Harvest of a Quiet Eye: A Book of Digressions. facsimile ed. LC 77-117843. (Essay Index Reprint Ser). Repr. of 1927 ed. 19.50 (ISBN 0-8369-2428-2). Arno.
Teale, Edwin W. American Seasons, 4 Vols. (Illus.). 1966. Set. 40.00 (ISBN 0-396-05399-8); 10.00 ea. Dodd.
--Autumn Across America. LC 56-10059. (Illus.). 1956. 10.00 (ISBN 0-396-03888-3). Dodd.
--North with the Spring. LC 51-13966. (Illus.). 1951. 10.00 (ISBN 0-396-03325-3). Dodd.
Wiley, Farida, ed. John Burrough's America. (American Naturalists Ser.). (Illus.). 220p. (gr. 9 up). 7.50 (ISBN 0-8159-5109-4); pap. 5.25 (ISBN 0-8159-5114-0). Devin.

NATURAL HISTORY–PICTORIAL WORKS

see also Animal Pictures; Botany–Pictorial Works; Nature Photography; Zoology–Pictorial Works

Archer, Mildred. Natural History Drawings in the India Office Library. (Illus.). 116p. 1962. 22.50x (ISBN 0-85667-082-0, Pub. by Sotheby Parke Bernet England). Biblio Dist.
Blacklock, Les & Russell, Andy. The High West. (Illus.). 1977. pap. 6.95 (ISBN 0-14-004425-6). Penguin.
Ewan, Joseph. William Bartram: Botanical & Zoological Drawings, 1756-88. LC 68-8640. (Memoirs Ser.: Vol. 74). (Illus.). 1968. 40.00 (ISBN 0-87169-074-8). Am Philos.
Kipping, John. Jungle Coloring Album. (Natural Science Ser.). 1975. pap. 3.50 (ISBN 0-912300-61-2, 61-2). Troubador Pr.
Krasemann, S. J. & Outdoor World Editors. Diary of a Country Year: Thoreau Revisited. LC 73-79343. (Illus.). 160p. 1973. 15.95 (ISBN 0-87294-045-4). Country Beautiful.
Strache, Wolf. Forms & Patterns in Nature. LC 73-3468. 1973. 10.00 (ISBN 0-394-42541-3); pap. 5.95 (ISBN 0-394-70974-8). Pantheon.
Sutton, Ann & Sutton, Myron. The Wild Places: A Photographic Celebration of Unspoiled America. LC 73-1075. (Illus.). 258p. 1973. 35.00 (ISBN 0-06-014176-X, HarpT). Harper-Row.
Tanner, Ogden. The New England Wilds. LC 73-92887. (American Wilderness). (Illus.). (gr. 6 up). 1974. PLB 11.97 (ISBN 0-8094-1230-6, Pub. by Time-Life). Silver.
Teale, Edwin W. Photographs of American Nature. LC 72-5876. (Illus.). 1972. 17.50 (ISBN 0-396-06713-1). Dodd.
Thompson, John W., compiled by. Index to Illustrations of the Natural World: Where to Find Pictures of the Living Things of North America. Slauson, Nedra, ed. 29.95 (ISBN 0-915794-12-8). Gaylord Prof Pubns.

NATURAL HISTORY–PRE-LINNEAN WORKS

Bacon, Francis. De Sapientia Veterum, Repr. Of 1609 Ed. Bd. with The Wisedome of the Ancients. Gorges, Arthur, tr. Repr. of 1619 ed. LC 75-27863. (Renaissance & the Gods Ser.: Vol. 20). (Illus.). 1976. lib. bdg. 73.00 (ISBN 0-8240-2068-5). Garland Pub.
Derham, William. Physico-Theology: A Demonstration of the Being & Attributes of God, from His Works of Creation. Egerton, Frank N., 3rd, ed. LC 77-74212. (History of Ecology Ser.). 1978. Repr. of 1716 ed. lib. bdg. 28.00 (ISBN 0-405-10383-2). Arno.

NATURAL HISTORY–STORIES

see Nature Stories

NATURAL HISTORY–STUDY AND TEACHING

see also Nature Study

Agassiz, Louis. Methods of Study in Natural History. LC 72-125728. (American Environmental Studies). 1970. Repr. of 1863 ed. 15.00 (ISBN 0-405-02653-6). Arno.
--Methods of Study in Natural History. 1976. Repr. of 1863 ed. 42.00 (ISBN 0-403-05824-4, Regency). Scholarly.
Arnspiger, Varney C. Measuring the Effectiveness of Sound Pictures As Teaching Aids. LC 71-176524. (Columbia University. Teachers College. Contributions to Education: No. 565). Repr. of 1933 ed. 17.50 (ISBN 0-404-55565-9). AMS Pr.
Gross, Phyllis P. & Railton, Esther P. Teaching Science in an Outdoor Environment: Handbook for Students, Parents, Teachers, & Camp Leaders. LC 73-173903. (California Natural History Guides: No. 30). (Illus.). 175p. 1972. 14.95x (ISBN 0-520-03092-3); pap. 3.95 (ISBN 0-520-02148-7). U of Cal Pr.
Hughes-Evans, ed. Environmental Education - Key Issues of the Future: Proceedings of the Conference Held at the College of Technology, Farnborough, England. LC 77-827. 1977. pap. text ed. 12.00 (ISBN 0-08-021490-8). Pergamon.
Sharpe, Grant W. Interpreting the Environment. 2nd ed. 600p. 1982. text ed. 23.95 (ISBN 0-471-09007-7). Wiley.

NATURAL HISTORY–TECHNIQUE

see also Aquariums; Insects–Collection and Preservation; Microscope and Microscopy–Technique; Nature Photography; Plants–Collection and Preservation; Stains and Staining (Microscopy); Taxidermy; Zoological Specimens–Collection and Preservation

Hillcourt, William. New Field Book of Nature Activities & Hobbies. rev. ed. LC 78-96211. (Putnam's Nature Field Bks.). (Illus.). 1970. 6.95 (ISBN 0-399-10290-6). Putnam.
Hussey, Lois J. & Pessino, Catherine. Collecting for the City Naturalist. LC 73-17293. (Illus.). 96p. (gr. 5 up). 1975. 8.95 (ISBN 0-690-00317-X, TYC-J). Har-Row.

NATURAL HISTORY–AFRICA

Brown, Leslie. Africa: A Natural History. (Illus.). 1965. 25.00 (ISBN 0-394-41449-7). Random.
--East African Mountains & Lakes. (Illus.). 122p. 1971. 12.50x (ISBN 0-8002-0566-9). Intl Pubns Serv.
--The Life of the African Plains. (Our Living World of Nature Ser). (Illus.). 1972. 9.95 (ISBN 0-07-008245-6, P&RB); by subscription 3.95 (ISBN 0-07-046013-2). McGraw.
Drummond, Henry. Tropical Africa. LC 69-18651. (Illus.). Repr. of 1890 ed. 10.00x (ISBN 0-8371-2266-X). Greenwood.
Du Chaillu, Paul B. Explorations & Adventures in Equatorial Africa. rev. & enl. ed. Repr. of 1871 ed. 27.00 (ISBN 0-384-13180-8). Johnson Repr.
--A Journey to Ashango-Land & Further Penetration into Equatorial Africa. LC 5-9143. 1971. Repr. of 1867 ed. 23.00 (ISBN 0-384-13185-9). Johnson Repr.
Johnston, Harry H. British Central Africa. LC 78-88439. Repr. of 1897 ed. 51.00x (ISBN 0-8371-1910-3, Pub. by Negro U Pr). Greenwood.
Kolb, Peter. The Present State of the Cape of Good-Hope: Or, a Particular Account of the Several Nations of the Hottentots, 2 vols. (Anthropology Ser.). 1969. Repr. of 1731 ed. Vol. 1. 27.00 (ISBN 0-384-30100-2); Vol. 2. 34.50 (ISBN 0-685-13553-5). Johnson Repr.
Norton, Boyd. Alaska: Wilderness Frontier. (Illus.). 1977. pap. 10.00 (ISBN 0-88349-136-2). Readers Digest Pr.
Rogers, Dilwyn J., ed. A Bibliography of African Ecology: A Geographically & Topically Classified List of Books & Articles. LC 78-19935. (Special Bibliographic Ser: No. 6). 1979. lib. bdg. 37.50 (ISBN 0-313-20552-3, RAE/). Greenwood.
Schaller, George B. Year of the Gorilla. LC 64-13946. (Illus.). 1964. 15.00x (ISBN 0-226-73637-7); pap. 5.50 (ISBN 0-226-73638-5, P209, Phoen). U of Chicago Pr.
Smith, Arthur D. Through Unknown African Countries: The Expedition from Somaliland to Lake Lamu. LC 68-55221. (Illus.). 1968. Repr. of 1897 ed. lib. bdg. 29.75x (ISBN 0-8371-1722-4, SMUC). Greenwood.
Sweeney, Charles. Naturalist in the Sudan. LC 73-17778. (Illus.). 256p. 1974. 8.50 (ISBN 0-8008-5466-7). Taplinger.
Willock, Colin. Africa's Rift Valley. (The World's Wild Places Ser). (Illus.). 184p. 1974. 12.95 (ISBN 0-8094-2009-0). Time-Life.

NATURAL HISTORY–ALASKA

Brown, Dale. Wild Alaska. (The American Wilderness Ser.). (Illus.). 1972. 12.95 (ISBN 0-8094-1152-0). Time-Life.
Murie, Margaret E. Two in the Far North. 2nd ed. LC 78-16407. (Illus.). 1978. pap. 6.95 (ISBN 0-88240-111-4). Alaska Northwest.

NATURAL HISTORY–AMERICA

Abbey, Edward. Down the River with Henry David Thoreau & Friends. (Illus.). 244p. 1982. 13.50 (ISBN 0-525-09524-1); pap. 7.25 (ISBN 0-525-47676-8). Dutton.
Barber, Lynn. The Heyday of Natural History. LC 79-6533. (Illus.). 320p. 1981. 17.95 (ISBN 0-385-12574-7). Doubleday.
Chambers, Kenneth. The Country Lover's Guide to Wildlife: Mammals, Amphibians, & Reptiles of the Northeastern United States. LC 79-4338. (Illus.). 1979. 14.95 (ISBN 0-8018-2207-6). Johns Hopkins.
Sterling, Keir B., ed. Natural Sciences in America, 58 vols. 1974. 1800.00x set (ISBN 0-405-05700-8). Arno.

NATURAL HISTORY–ANTARCTIC REGIONS

Adrian, Mary. Wildlife in the Antarctic. LC 78-7256. (Illus.). 64p. (gr. 3-5). 1978. PLB 6.97 (ISBN 0-671-32946-4). Messner.
Halle, Louis J. The Sea & the Ice: A Naturalist in Antarctica. 1973. 10.95 (ISBN 0-395-15470-7). HM.
Lewis, C. P. & Jorgensen, A. A. The Great Steam Trek. LC 79-4027. (Illus.). 1979. 24.95 (ISBN 0-8317-4018-3, Mayflower Bks). Smith Pubs.
Llano, George A., ed. Antarctic Terrestrial Biology. LC 72-92709. (Antarctic Research Ser.: Vol. 20). (Illus.). 1972. 30.00 (ISBN 0-87590-120-4). Am Geophysical.
Lowry, James K. Soft Bottom Macrobenthic Community of Arthur Harbor, Antarctica: Paper 1 in Biology of the Antarctic Seas V. Pawson, David L., ed. LC 75-22056. (Antarctic Research Ser: Vol. 23). (Illus.). 1975. pap. 4.00 (ISBN 0-87590-123-9). Am Geophysical.

NATURAL HISTORY–ARCTIC REGIONS

Ross, John. Narrative of a Second Voyage in Search of a North-West Passage, & of a Residence in the Arctic Regions During the Years 1829, 1830,1831, 1833, 2 Vols. LC 68-55217. 1968. Repr. of 1835 ed. Set. lib. bdg. 56.25x (ISBN 0-8371-3860-4, RONP). Greenwood.

NATURAL HISTORY–ASIA

Archer, Mildred. Natural History Drawings in the India Office Library. (Illus.). 116p. 1962. 22.50x (ISBN 0-85667-082-0, Pub. by Sotheby Parke Bernet England). Biblio Dist.
Griffith, William. Icones Plantrum Asiaticarum, 8 vols. (Illus.). 1978. Repr. of 1849 ed. Set. 844.00x (ISBN 0-89955-284-6, Pub. by Intl Bk Dist). Intl Schol Bk Serv.
Matthiessen, Peter. The Snow Leopard. 1978. 12.95 (ISBN 0-670-65374-8). Viking Pr.

NATURAL HISTORY–AUSTRALIA

Bedford, Roger B. Guide to Native Australian Orchids. (Illus.). 1969. 16.00x (ISBN 0-8426-1149-5). Verry.
Breeden, Stanley & Breeden, Kay. Australia's North. (A Natural History of Australia Ser.: No. 3). 208p. 1980. 34.95x (ISBN 0-00-211441-0, Pub. by W Collins Australia). Intl Schol Bk Serv.
--Wildlife of Eastern Australia. (Illus.). 260p. 1974. 12.95 (ISBN 0-8008-8332-2). Taplinger.
Child, John. Australian Alpine Life. (Periwinkle Colour Ser.). (Illus.). (gr. 9 up). 1969. pap. 6.50x (ISBN 0-392-01184-0, ABC). Sportshelf.
Huxley, Thomas H. & Huxley, Julian S. Diary of the Voyage of H. M. S. Rattlesnake. Repr. of 1936 ed. 18.00 (ISBN 0-527-43860-X). Kraus Repr.
Kangaroos & Other Creatures from Down Under. LC 77-87164. (Wild, Wild World of Animals Ser.). (Illus.). 1978. lib. bdg. 11.97 (ISBN 0-686-51172-7). Silver.
Leeper, Geoffrey W. Evolution of Living Organisms. 1962. 27.50x (ISBN 0-522-83657-7, Pub. by Melbourne U Pr). Intl Schol Bk Serv.
Morcombe, Michael K. Wild Australia. LC 70-179495. (Illus.). 112p. (YA) 1972. 7.95 (ISBN 0-8008-8322-5). Taplinger.
Slater, Peter, et al. Field Guide to Australian Birds: Non-Passerines. LC 78-140167. (Illus.). 1971. 15.00 (ISBN 0-87098-036-X). Livingston.
Spencer, Baldwin. Wanderings in Wild Australia, 2 Vols. (Illus.). Repr. of 1928 ed. Set. 92.50 (ISBN 0-384-57023-2). Johnson Repr.
Stephenson, W. Outdoor Studies on Living Animals in Queensland. rev. 2nd ed. (Illus.). 1966. pap. 9.95x (ISBN 0-7022-0722-5). U of Queensland Pr.
Sturt, Charles. Narrative of an Expedition into Central Australia, Performed During the Years 1844-1846, 2 Vols. LC 68-55225. 1968. Repr. of 1849 ed. Set. lib. bdg. 34.00x (ISBN 0-8371-3868-X, STCA). Greenwood.

NATURAL HISTORY–BAHAMAS

Catesby, Mark. Natural History of Carolina, Florida & the Bahama Islands, Catalogue Volume. (Illus.). 50.00 (ISBN 0-685-88560-7). Johnson Repr.
Osborn, Henry F., ed. Naturalist in the Bahamas: October 12, 1861 - June 25, 1891. LC 10-13587. 1910. 10.00 (ISBN 0-404-04794-7). AMS Pr.

NATURAL HISTORY–BARBADOS

Schomburgk, Robert H. History of Barbados. LC 68-21443. Repr. of 1848 ed. 35.00x (ISBN 0-678-05003-1). Kelley.

NATURAL HISTORY–CANADA

Boily, Lise & Blanchette, Jean-Francois. The Bread Ovens of Quebec. (Illus.). 1979. pap. 8.95 (ISBN 0-660-00120-9, 56284-0, Pub. by Natl Mus Canada). U of Chicago Pr.
Denys, Nicolas. Description - Natural History of the Coasts of North America. Ganong, William F., ed. LC 68-28597. 1968. Repr. of 1908 ed. lib. bdg. 42.25x (ISBN 0-8371-3873-6, DEDH). Greenwood.
Douglas, Charles. Natural History Notebook, 2 bks. (Illus.). 1977. No. 1. pap. 2.50 (ISBN 0-660-00092-X, 56440-1, Pub. by Natl Mus Canada); No. 2. pap. 2.00 (ISBN 0-660-00094-6, 56442-8). U of Chicago Pr.
Edey, Maitland A. The Northeast Coast. (The American Wilderness Ser.). (Illus.). 184p. 1972. 12.95 (ISBN 0-8094-1148-2). Time-Life.
Hearne, Samuel. Journey from Prince of Wale's Fort in Hudson's Bay to the Northern Ocean. LC 78-133870. (Illus.). 1971. 19.25 (ISBN 0-8048-1007-9). C E Tuttle.
--Journey from Prince of Wales's Fort in Hudson's Bay to the Northern Ocean in the Years 1769-1772. LC 68-28601. (Illus.). 1968. Repr. of 1911 ed. lib. bdg. 32.75x (ISBN 0-8371-5045-0, HEJP). Greenwood.
Janes, Robert. The Great Canadian Outback. (Illus.). 1979. 19.95 (ISBN 0-295-95678-X, Pub. by Douglas & McIntyre Canada). U of Wash Pr.
Judd, W. W. & Speirs, J. Murray, eds. Naturalist's Guide to Ontario. LC 65-3239. (Canadian University Paperbooks). (Illus.). 1964. pap. 6.50 (ISBN 0-8020-6039-0). U of Toronto Pr.
Knauth, Percy. The North Woods. (The American Wilderness Ser.). (Illus.). 1972. 12.95 (ISBN 0-8094-1164-4). Time-Life.
Laird, M. Bibliography of the Natural History of Newfoundland & Labrador. 1980. 66.50 (ISBN 0-12-434050-4). Acad Pr.
Lawrence, R. D. Paddy: A Naturalist's Story of an Orphan Beaver. 1977. 10.95 (ISBN 0-394-40403-3). Knopf.
Russell, Frank. Explorations in the Far North. LC 74-5873. Repr. of 1898 ed. 25.00 (ISBN 0-404-11682-5). AMS Pr.

NATURAL HISTORY–CARIBBEAN AREA

Philibosian, Richard & Yntema, John A. Annotated Checklist of the Birds, Mammals, Reptiles, & Amphibians of the Virgin Islands & Puerto Rico. LC 77-670077. (Illus.). 48p. 1977. pap. 3.50 (ISBN 0-9601490-0-7). Info Services.

NATURAL HISTORY–CHINA

Schafer, Edward H. The Vermilion Bird: T'ang Images of the South. LC 67-10463. 1967. 26.75x (ISBN 0-520-01145-7). U of Cal Pr.
Whitehead, P. S. & Edwards, P. I. Chinese Natural History Drawings: Selected from the Reeves Collection in the British Museum. (Illus.). portfolio ed. 500.00x (ISBN 0-565-00721-1, Pub. by Brit Mus Nat Hist). Sabbot-Natural Hist Bks.
Wilson, Ernest H. A Naturalist in Western China, 2 vols. LC 76-46620. 1977. Repr. of 1913 ed. write for info (ISBN 0-913728-17-9). Theophrastus.

NATURAL HISTORY–EUROPE

Hudson, William H. Afoot in England. Repr. of 1923 ed. 21.50 (ISBN 0-404-03405-5). AMS Pr.
Pitard, J. & Proust, L. Les Iles Canaries, Flore de L'archipel. 1973. Repr. of 1908 ed. lib. bdg. 75.00x (ISBN 3-87429-050-6). Lubrecht & Cramer.
Steffens, H. Beitrage zur Inneren Naturgeschichte der Erde: Erster Theil. (Ger.). 1801. text ed. 18.75x (ISBN 90-6041-085-8). Humanities.

NATURAL HISTORY–GALAPAGOS ISLANDS

Harris, Lester E. Galapagos. LC 76-23727. (Crown Ser.). 128p. (gr. 8 up). 1976. pap. 4.50 (ISBN 0-8127-0125-9). Review & Herald.

NATURAL HISTORY–GAMBIA

Reeve, Henry F. Gambia, Its History. LC 75-79275. (Illus.). Repr. of 1912 ed. 23.25x (ISBN 0-8371-1449-7, Pub. by Negro U Pr). Greenwood.

NATURAL HISTORY–GREAT BRITAIN

Aubrey, John. Natural History of Wiltshire. LC 69-17617. Repr. of 1847 ed. 15.00x (ISBN 0-678-05542-4). Kelley.
Bridson, Gavin D., et al, eds. Natural History Manuscript Resources in the British Isles. LC 79-92886. 6000p. 1980. 245.00 (ISBN 0-8352-1281-5). Bowker.
Burrows, Roger. The Naturalist in Devon & Cornwall. (Regional Naturalist Ser.). (Illus.). 304p. 1971. 14.95 (ISBN 0-7153-5360-8). David & Charles.
Dennis, Eve. Everyman's Nature Reserve: Ideas for Action. (Illus.). 256p. 1973. 7.50 (ISBN 0-7153-5918-5). David & Charles.
Freeman, R. B. British Natural History Books from Fourteen Ninety-Five to Nineteen Hundred: A Handlist. 437p. 1980. 39.50 (ISBN 0-686-62545-5, Archon). Shoe String.

--British Natural History Books, 1495 to 1900: A Handlist. 400p. 1981. 90.00x (ISBN 0-7129-0971-0, Pub. by Dawson). State Mutual Bk.
Garrad, Larch S. The Naturalist in the Isle of Man. (Naturalist in...Ser.). (Illus.). 232p. 1973. 5.95 (ISBN 0-7153-5628-3). David & Charles.
Hardy, Eric. The Naturalist in Lakeland. (Regional Naturalist Ser.). (Illus.). 1973. 2.95 (ISBN 0-7153-5745-X). David & Charles.
Hoeniger, F. D. & Hoeniger, J. F. Development of Natural History in Tudor England. LC 69-19336. (Folger Guides to the Age of Shakespeare). 1969. pap. 3.95 (ISBN 0-918016-14-2). Folger Bks.
--Growth of Natural History in Stuart England: From Gerard to the Royal Society. LC 69-17335. (Folger Guides to the Age of Shakespeare). 1969. pap. 3.95 (ISBN 0-8139-0264-9). Folger Bks.
Hudson, William H. Land's End. Repr. of 1923 ed. 21.50 (ISBN 0-404-03404-7). AMS Pr.
Janovy, John, Jr. Keith County Journal. 1980. pap. 4.95 (ISBN 0-312-45124-5). St Martin.
Jones, Derek. Derek Jones' Country Book. LC 74-33155. (Illus.). 128p. 1975. 4.95 (ISBN 0-7153-6963-6). David & Charles.
Manning, S. A. The Naturalist in South East England. (Regional Naturalist Ser.). (Illus.). 1973. 7.50 (ISBN 0-7153-6109-0). David & Charles.
Simms, Eric. A Natural History of Britian & Ireland. (Illus.). 258p. 1979. 15.75x (ISBN 0-460-04372-2, Pub. by J. M. Dent England). Biblio Dist.
White, Gilbert. Natural History of Selborne: In the County of Southampton. (World's Classics Ser: No. 22). 6.95 (ISBN 0-19-250022-8). Oxford U Pr.

NATURAL HISTORY–GUYANA

Beebe, William. Edge of the Jungle. 1921. 20.00 (ISBN 0-8482-7358-3). Norwood Edns.
Rodway, James. In the Guiana Forest: Studies of Nature in Relations to the Struggle for Life. LC 69-18997. (Illus.). Repr. of 1894 ed. 15.50x (ISBN 0-8371-1027-0). Greenwood.
Waterton, Charles. Wanderings in South America, the Northwest of the United States, & the Antilles in the Years Eighteen Twelve, Eighteen Sixteen, Eighteen Twenty, & Eighteen Twenty-Four. 341p. 1968. Repr. of 1828 ed. 25.00 (ISBN 0-8398-2157-3). Parnassus Imprints.

NATURAL HISTORY–HAWAII

Kay, E. Alison, ed. Natural History of the Hawaiian Islands: Selected Readings. (Illus.). 665p. 1972. pap. 10.00x (ISBN 0-8248-0203-9). U Pr of Hawaii.
Merlin, Mark D. Hawaiian Coastal Plants: And Scenic Shorelines. LC 77-86156. (Illus.). 1978. pap. 4.00 (ISBN 0-932596-02-9, Pub. by Oriental). Intl Schol Bk Serv.
--Hawaiian Forest Plants. LC 76-36304. (Illus.). 1978. pap. 4.00 (ISBN 0-932596-00-2, Pub. by Oriental). Intl Schol Bk Serv.

NATURAL HISTORY–ICELAND

Oddsson, Gisli. Annalium in Islandia Farrago, & De Mirabilibus Islandiae. Hermannsson, Halldor, ed. (Islandica Ser.: Vol. 10). 1917. pap. 8.00 (ISBN 0-527-00340-9). Kraus Repr.

NATURAL HISTORY–ISLANDS OF THE PACIFIC

Baltazar, Clare R. & Salazar, Nelia P. Philippine Insects: An Introduction. (Illus.). 1980. text ed. 17.00x (ISBN 0-8248-0675-1, Pub. by U of Philippines Pr); pap. text ed. 12.00x (ISBN 0-8248-0676-X). U Pr of Hawaii.
Hudson, William H. Idle Days in Patagonia. Repr. of 1923 ed. 21.50 (ISBN 0-404-03395-4). AMS Pr.

NATURAL HISTORY–LATIN AMERICA

De Acosta, Joseph. The Natural & Moral History of the Indies, 2 Vols. Markham, Clements R., ed. LC 75-134715. (Hakluyt Society Ser.: No. 60-61). 1970. Set. lib. bdg. 60.50 (ISBN 0-8337-0798-1). B Franklin.
Kerr, John G. Naturalist in the Gran Chaco. LC 68-55200. (Illus.). 1968. Repr. of 1950 ed. lib. bdg. 16.75x (ISBN 0-8371-0511-0, KEGC). Greenwood.
Roosevelt, Theodore. Theodore Roosevelt's America: American Naturalists Ser. Wiley, Farida, ed. (Illus.). 1955. 10.00 (ISBN 0-8159-6714-4). Devin.
Rumphius. The Poison Tree: Selected Writings of Rumphius on the Natural History of the Indies. Beekman, E. M., tr. from Dutch & Lat. LC 81-7605. (Library of the Indies). (Illus.). 256p. 1981. lib. bdg. 20.00x (ISBN 0-87023-329-7). U of Mass Pr.

NATURAL HISTORY–LIBERIA

Harvard African Expedition. African Republic of Liberia & the Belgian Congo, Based on the Observations Made & Material Collected During the Harvard African Expediton, 1926-1927, 2 Vols. Strong, Richard P., ed. Repr. of 1930 ed. Set. lib. bdg. 86.50x (ISBN 0-8371-2480-8, HAAE). Greenwood.
Johnston, Harry H. Liberia, 2 Vols. LC 71-78372. (Illus.). Repr. of 1906 ed. 76.00x (ISBN 0-8371-3897-3, Pub. by Negro U Pr). Greenwood.

NATURAL HISTORY–MADAGASCAR

Shaw, George A. Madagascar & France, with Some Account of the Island, Its People, Its Resources & Development. LC 73-82072. (Illus.). Repr. of 1885 ed. 17.00x (ISBN 0-8371-1562-0, Pub. by Negro U Pr). Greenwood.

NATURAL HISTORY–MALAY ARCHIPELAGO

Stein, Norbert. Coniferen Im Westlichen: Malayischen Archipel. (Biogeographica Ser: No. 11). 1978. lib. bdg. 31.50 (ISBN 90-6193-212-2, Pub. by Junk Pubs Netherlands). Kluwer Boston.

NATURAL HISTORY–MEDITERRANEAN REGION

Parrack, James D. The Naturalist in Majorca. (Regional Naturalist Ser). (Illus.). 208p. 1973. 2.95 (ISBN 0-7153-5948-7). David & Charles.

NATURAL HISTORY–MELANESIA

Huxley, Thomas H. & Huxley, Julian S. Diary of the Voyage of H. M. S. Rattlesnake. Repr. of 1936 ed. 18.00 (ISBN 0-527-43860-X). Kraus Repr.

NATURAL HISTORY–MEXICO

De Sahagun, Bernardino. Florentine Codex, General History of the Things of New Spain, 12 bks. Anderson, Arthur J. & Dibble, Charles E., trs. Incl. Bk. 1. Gods. 15.00x (ISBN 0-87480-000-5); Bk. 2. Ceremonies. 40.00x (ISBN 0-87480-194-X); Bk. 3. Origin of the Gods. 15.00x (ISBN 0-87480-002-1); Bks. 4 & 5. The Soothsayers, the Omens. 40.00x (ISBN 0-87480-003-X); Bk. 6. Rhetoric & Moral Philosophy. 40.00x (ISBN 0-87480-010-2); Bk. 7. Sun, Moon & Stars, & the Binding of the Years. 15.00x (ISBN 0-87480-004-8); Bk. 8. Kings & Lords. 20.00x (ISBN 0-87480-005-6); Bk. 9. Merchants. 15.00x (ISBN 0-87480-006-4); Bk. 10. People. 30.00x (ISBN 0-87480-007-2); Bk. 11. Earthly Things. 45.00x (ISBN 0-87480-008-0); Bk. 12. Conquest of Mexico. 25.00x (ISBN 0-87480-096-X). U of Utah Pr.
Johnson, William W. Baja California. (The American Wilderness Ser.). (Illus.). 1972. 12.95 (ISBN 0-8094-1160-1). Time-Life.
Nelson, Edward W. Lower California & Its Natural Resources. LC 66-24189. (Illus.). 1966. 49.50x (ISBN 0-910950-00-8). Manessier.
Sutton, George M. At a Bend in a Mexican River. LC 72-83709. (Illus.). 184p. 1972. 14.95 (ISBN 0-8397-0780-0). Eriksson.
Tinker, Ben. Mexican Wilderness & Wildlife. LC 77-14030. (Illus.). 143p. 1978. 9.95 (ISBN 0-292-75037-4). U of Tex Pr.

NATURAL HISTORY–NEAR EAST

Goor, Asaph & Nurock, Max. The Fruits of the Holy Land. (Illus.). 1978. 16.95 (ISBN 0-89955-235-8, Pub. by IPST). Intl Schol Bk Serv.
Jennings, Michael C. Birds of the Arabian Gulf. (The Natural History of the Arabian Gulf Ser.). (Illus.). 176p. 1981. text ed. 25.00x (ISBN 0-04-598009-8). Allen Unwin.
Meadow, Richard H. & Zeder, Melinda A., eds. Approaches to Faunal Analysis in the Middle East. LC 78-50908. (Peabody Museum Bulletin: No. 27). 1978. pap. text ed. 10.00x (ISBN 0-87365-951-1). Peabody Harvard.

NATURAL HISTORY–NEPAL

Bhatt, Dibya D. Natural History & Economic Botany of Nepal. 248p. 1981. 15.00x (ISBN 0-86125-412-0, Pub. by Orient Longman India). State Mutual Bk.
Matthiessen, Peter. The Snow Leopard. 1979. pap. 3.50 (ISBN 0-553-12343-2). Bantam.

NATURAL HISTORY–NEW ZEALAND

Buick, Thomas L. The Mystery of the Moa, New Zealand's Avian Giant. LC 75-35244. (Illus.). Repr. of 1931 ed. 30.00 (ISBN 0-404-14418-7). AMS Pr.
Clark, Andrew H. Invasion of New Zealand by People, Plants & Animals: The South Island. LC 71-100249. Repr. of 1949 ed. lib. bdg. 18.50x (ISBN 0-8371-2982-6, CLIN). Greenwood.
Harvey, Norman B. New Zealand Botanical Paintings. 30.00x (ISBN 0-8426-1297-1). Verry.

NATURAL HISTORY–NORTH AMERICA

Clark, Champ. The Badlands. LC 74-18063. (American Wilderness). (Illus.). (gr. 6 up). 1974. PLB 11.97 (ISBN 0-8094-1209-8, Pub. by Time-Life). Silver.
Clement, Roland. Nature Atlas of America. 2nd ed. (Illus.). 256p. 1976. 19.95 (ISBN 0-8437-3513-9); pap. 9.95 (ISBN 0-8437-3512-0). Hammond Inc.
Eisen, G. Enchytroids. Bd. with Tubicolous Annelids. Bush, K. J. (Harriman Alaska Expedition, 1899). (Illus.). 1904. 28.00 (ISBN 0-527-38172-1). Kraus Repr.
Errington, Paul L. Of Men & Marshes. fasc. ed. (Illus.). 1957. pap. 9.45x (ISBN 0-8138-2350-1). Iowa St U Pr.
Kozloff, Eugene N. Plants & Animals of the Pacific Northwest: An Illustrated Guide to the Natural History of Western Oregon, Washington, & British Columbia. LC 75-40875. (Illus.). 280p. 1976. 20.00 (ISBN 0-295-95449-3); pap. 9.95 (ISBN 0-295-95597-X). U of Wash Pr.
Ogburn, Charlton, Jr. The Winter Beach. (Illus.). 1966. 7.95 (ISBN 0-688-02785-7). Morrow.
Olson, Sigurd F. Open Horizons. (Illus.). (YA) 1969. 10.95 (ISBN 0-394-43934-1). Knopf.
Osgood, Wilfred H. Natural History of the Queen Charlotte Islands, British Columbia & Cooks Inlet, Alaska. (North American Fauna Ser, No. 21). (Illus.). Repr. of 1901 ed. pap. 10.50 (ISBN 0-8466-0260-1, SJS260). Shorey.
Our Continent: A Natural History of North America. LC 76-26633. (Natural Science Library). (Illus.). 1976. 14.95 (ISBN 0-87044-153-1); deluxe ed. 26.90 in deluxe slipcase with Wild Animals of North America (ISBN 0-686-68032-4). Natl Geog.
Platt, Rutherford. Wilderness, the Discovery of a Continent of Wonder. LC 72-9919. (Illus.). 310p. 1973. Repr. of 1961 ed. lib. bdg. 16.00x (ISBN 0-8371-6608-X, PLWI). Greenwood.
Rowlands, John J. Cache Lake Country. (Illus.). (gr. 7 up). 1959. 12.95 (ISBN 0-393-08468-X). Norton.
Selected Works by Eighteenth Century Naturalists & Travelers. LC 73-17840. (Natural Sciences in America Ser.). 266p. 1974. Repr. 14.00x (ISBN 0-405-05762-8). Arno.
Tanner, Ogden. The New England Wilds. LC 73-92887. (American Wilderness). (Illus.). (gr. 6 up). 1974. PLB 11.97 (ISBN 0-8094-1230-6, Pub. by Time-Life). Silver.
Thompson, John W. & Slauson, Nedra, eds. Index to Illustrations of the Natural World: Where to Find Pictures of the Living Things of North America. 265p. 1981. Repr. of 1980 ed. 29.95 (ISBN 0-208-01911-1, Lib Prof Pubns). Shoe String.
Yocom, Charles & Dasmann, Raymond. Pacific Coastal Wildlife Region. rev. ed. (American Wildlife Region Ser.: Vol. 3). (Illus.). (gr. 4 up). 1965. 7.95 (ISBN 0-911010-05-X); pap. 3.95 (ISBN 0-911010-04-1). Naturegraph.

NATURAL HISTORY–OCEANICA

Spoehr, Florence M. White Falcon: The House of Godeffroy & Its Commercial & Scientific Role in the Pacific. LC 63-18693. (Illus.). 1963. 7.95 (ISBN 0-87015-119-3). Pacific Bks.

NATURAL HISTORY–PANAMA

Wafer, Lionel. New Voyage & Description of the Isthmus of America. Winship, George P., ed. LC 79-114820. 1970. Repr. of 1903 ed. 18.50 (ISBN 0-8337-3663-9). B Franklin.

NATURAL HISTORY–POLAR REGIONS

Cousteau, Jacques. The Whitecaps. LC 74-23941. (Ocean World of Jacques Cousteau Ser.: Vol. 16). (Illus.). 144p. 1975. 9.95 (ISBN 0-8109-0590-6). Abrams.

NATURAL HISTORY–RUSSIA

Omelyanovsky, M. E. Lenin & Modern Natural Science. 422p. 1978. 5.75 (ISBN 0-8285-0198-X, Pub. by Progress Pubs Russia). Imported Pubns.

NATURAL HISTORY–SCOTLAND

Darling, F. F. Naturalist on Rona: Essays of a Biologist in Isolation. LC 42-5414. Repr. of 1939 ed. 10.00 (ISBN 0-527-21400-0). Kraus Repr.
Maxwell, Gavin. Ring of Bright Water. (gr. 8 up). 1965. pap. 5.95 (ISBN 0-525-47174-X). Dutton.

NATURAL HISTORY–SOUTH AMERICA

Fitz-Roy, Robert, et al. Narrative of the Surveying Voyages of His Majesty's Ships Adventure & Beagle, 3 Vols. in 4 Pts. Repr. of 1839 ed. Set. 170.00 (ISBN 0-404-09900-9); 43.00 ea. Vol. 1 (ISBN 0-404-09901-7). Vol. 2 Pt. 1 (ISBN 0-404-09902-5). Vol. 2 Pt. 2 (ISBN 0-404-09903-3). Vol. 3 (ISBN 0-404-09904-1). AMS Pr.
Hudson, W. H. Idle Days in Patagonia. (Illus.). 1979. pap. 5.95 (ISBN 0-916870-25-1). Creative Arts.
Hudson, William H. Purple Land. Repr. of 1922 ed. 21.50 (ISBN 0-404-03391-1). AMS Pr.
Humboldt, Alexander Von. Personal Narrative of Travels to the Equinoctial Regions of America During the Years 1799-1804, 3 Vols. Ross, Thomasina, tr. LC 69-13241. 1969. Repr. of 1851 ed. 60.00 (ISBN 0-405-08642-3, Blom Pubns). Arno.
Miller, Robert R. For Science & National Glory: The Spanish Scientfic Expedition to America 1862-1866. LC 68-15676. (American Exploration & Travel Ser: No. 55). (Illus.). 1968. 10.95x (ISBN 0-8061-0802-9). U of Okla Pr.
Morrison, Tony. Land Above the Clouds: Wildlife in the Andes. (Illus.). 244p. 1974. 12.50x (ISBN 0-87663-203-7). Universe.
Normas Ecologicas Para el Desarrollo Del Tropico Humedo Americano. (Sp.). 1975. pap. 3.00x (ISBN 2-88032-006-2, IUCN57, IUCN). Unipub.
Von Humboldt, Alexander & Bonpland, Aime. Personal Narrative of Travels to the Equinoctial Regions of America During the Years 1799-1804, 7 Vols. in 6 Pts. Williams, Helen M., tr. LC 1-20782. Repr. of 1829 ed. Set. 215.00 (ISBN 0-404-03440-3). AMS Pr.
Wallace, Alfred R. Narrative of Travels on Amazon & Rio Negro. LC 68-25280. (World History Ser., No. 48). 1969. Repr. of 1889 ed. lib. bdg. 37.95 (ISBN 0-8383-0251-3). Haskell.

NATURAL HISTORY–TROPICS

Lewis, W. M., Jr. Zooplankton Community Analysis Studies on a Tropical System. (Illus.). 1979. 26.00 (ISBN 0-387-90434-4). Springer-Verlag.
Wallace, Alfred R. Tropical Nature, & Other Essays. LC 72-1663. Repr. of 1878 ed. 27.00 (ISBN 0-404-08187-8). AMS Pr.

NATURAL HISTORY–UNITED STATES

Abbey, Edward. Cactus Country. (American Wilderness Ser.). (Illus.). 1973. 12.95 (ISBN 0-8094-1168-7). Time-Life.
Abbott, Henry. Birch Bark Books of Henry Abbott: Sporting Adventures & Nature Observations in the Adirondacks in the Early 1900s. LC 80-11071. (Illus., Repr. of 1914 & 1932 eds.). 1980. 19.95 (ISBN 0-916346-40-4). Harbor Hill Bks.
Agassiz, Jean L. Contributions to the Natural History of the United States of America, 4 vols. in two. Sterling, Keir B., ed. LC 77-81094. (Biologists & Their World Ser.). (Illus.). 1978. Repr. of 1862 ed. Set. lib. bdg. 90.00x (ISBN 0-405-10675-0); 45.00x ea. Vol. 1 (ISBN 0-405-10676-9). Vol. 2 (ISBN 0-405-10677-7). Arno.
Agassiz, Louis. Contributions to the Natural History of the United States of America. 1976. Repr. of 1857 ed. 195.00 (ISBN 0-403-05820-1, Regency). Scholarly.
Aitchison, Stewart W. Oak Creek Canyon & the Red Rock Country of Arizona. LC 78-53385. (Illus., Orig.). 1978. pap. 5.95 (ISBN 0-933762-01-1). Stillwater Canyon Pr.
Allen, Durward L. Life of Prairies & Plains. (Our Living World of Nature Ser). 1967. 9.95 (ISBN 0-07-001099-4, P&RB); by subscription 3.95 (ISBN 0-07-046005-1). McGraw.
Anderson, Walter. A Place of Power: The American Episode in Human Evolution. LC 76-12809. 1976. text ed. 15.95 (ISBN 0-87620-080-3); pap. text ed. 11.95 (ISBN 0-87620-079-X). Goodyear.
Austin, Mary. The Land of Little Rain. LC 74-84233. (Zia Bks). (Illus.). 171p. 1974. pap. 4.95 (ISBN 0-686-67074-4). U of NM Pr.
Bakker, Elna. An Island Called California: An Ecological Introduction to Its Natural Communities. LC 70-107657. (Illus.). 1971. 15.95 (ISBN 0-520-01682-3); pap. 4.95 (ISBN 0-520-02159-2, CAL244). U of Cal Pr.
Bartram, John & Bartram, William. John & William Bartram's America: American Naturalists Ser. Cruickshank, Helen G., ed. (Illus.). 10.00 (ISBN 0-8159-5101-9). Devin.
Bedichek, Roy. Adventures with a Texas Naturalist. (Illus.). 360p. 1961. pap. 7.95 (ISBN 0-292-70311-2). U of Tex Pr.
--Karankaway Country. 2nd ed. LC 74-3537. 318p. 1974. 12.50 (ISBN 0-292-74300-9); pap. 7.95 (ISBN 0-292-74304-1). U of Tex Pr.
Beston, Henry. The Outermost House. 1976. pap. 2.95 (ISBN 0-14-004315-2). Penguin.
Blacklock, Les & Russell, Andy. The High West. (Illus.). 1977. pap. 6.95 (ISBN 0-14-004425-6). Penguin.
Borland, Hal. The History of Wildlife in America. Bourne, Russell & MacConomy, Alma D., eds. LC 75-15494. (Illus.). 208p. 1975. 14.95 (ISBN 0-912186-20-8). Natl Wildlife.
Brickell, John. Natural History of North Carolina. (Illus.). 1968. Repr. of 1737 ed. 12.00 (ISBN 0-930230-17-5). Johnson NC.
--The Natural History of North Carolina. (American Studies). (Illus.). Repr. of 1737 ed. lib. bdg. 31.00 (ISBN 0-384-05740-3). Johnson Repr.
Brimley, Herbert H. North Carolina Naturalist, H. H. Brimley. facs. ed. Odum, Eugene P., ed. LC 78-134058. (Essay Index Reprint Ser). 1949. 18.00 (ISBN 0-8369-2145-3). Arno.
Brooks, Maurice G. Appalachians. (Illus.). 1965. 11.95 (ISBN 0-395-07458-4). HM.
Brown, Vinson & Hoover, David. California Wildlife Map Book. (Illus.). (gr. 4 up). 1967. 8.95 (ISBN 0-911010-29-7); pap. 4.95 (ISBN 0-911010-28-9). Naturegraph.
Brown, Vinson & Lawrence, George. The Californian Wildlife Region. (American Wildlife Region Ser.: Vol. 1). (Illus.). 128p. (gr. 4 up). 1965. 7.95 (ISBN 0-911010-01-7); pap. 3.95 (ISBN 0-911010-00-9). Naturegraph.
Brown, Vinson & Livezey, Robert. The Sierra Nevadan Wildlife Region. 2nd rev. ed. (American Wildlife Region Ser.: Vol. 2). (Illus.). (gr. 4 up). 1962. 7.50 (ISBN 0-911010-03-3); pap. 3.50 (ISBN 0-911010-02-5). Naturegraph.

Brown, Vinson, et al. Wildlife of the Intermountain West. (American Wildlife Region Ser.: Vol. 4). (Illus.). (gr. 4 up). 1968. 8.50 (ISBN 0-911010-15-7); pap. 4.50 (ISBN 0-911010-14-9). Naturegraph.
Burnaby, Andrew. Travels Through the Middle Settlements of North America. 3rd ed. LC 68-55496. Repr. of 1914 ed. 15.00x (ISBN 0-678-00682-2). Kelley.
Burroughs, John. Camping & Tramping with Roosevelt. LC 71-125733. (American Environmental Studies). 1970. Repr. of 1906 ed. 9.50 (ISBN 0-405-02658-7). Arno.
Carr, Archie. The Everglades. (The American Wilderness Ser). (Illus.). 1973. 12.95 (ISBN 0-8094-1172-5). Time-Life.
Catesby, Mark. Natural History of Carolina, Florida & the Bahama Islands, Catalogue Volume. (Illus.). 50.00 (ISBN 0-685-88560-7). Johnson Repr.
Chapman, Frank M. Frank M. Chapman in Florida: His Journals & Letters. Austin, Elizabeth S., ed. LC 66-30436. (Illus.). 1967. 7.95 (ISBN 0-8130-0045-9). U Presses Fla.
Clark, Champ. The Badlands. (The American Wilderness Ser.). (Illus.). 1975. 12.95 (ISBN 0-8094-1208-X). Time-Life.
Coleman, Edmund T. Mountaineering on the Pacific in 1868. Jones, William R., ed. (Illus.). 24p. 1977. Repr. of 1869 ed. pap. 2.00 (ISBN 0-89646-014-2). Outbooks.
Contributions to the History of American Natural History. LC 73-17809. (Natural Sciences of America Ser.). (Illus.). 876p. 1974. Repr. 50.00x (ISBN 0-405-05726-1). Arno.
Dannen, Kent & Country Beautiful Editors, eds. The American Wilderness in the Words of John Muir. LC 73-84624. (Illus.). 192p. 1973. 19.95 (ISBN 0-87294-049-7). Country Beautiful.
DeKay, James E. Anniversary Address on the Progress of the Natural Sciences of the United States. LC 76-125737. (American Environmental Studies). 1970. Repr. of 1826 ed. 9.50 (ISBN 0-405-02662-5). Arno.
Doolittle, Jerome. Canyons & Mesas. LC 74-77772. (American Wilderness). (Illus.). (gr. 6 up). 1974. PLB 11.97 (ISBN 0-8094-1238-1, Pub. by Time-Life). Silver.
Ewan, Joseph & Ewan, Nesta. John Banister & His Natural History of Virginia, 1678-1692. LC 77-94395. (Illus.). 1970. 25.00 (ISBN 0-252-00075-7). U of Ill Pr.
Fenton, Carroll L. & Fenton, Mildred. Mountains. facs. ed. LC 70-84305. (Essay Index Reprint Ser). 1942. 20.00 (ISBN 0-8369-1129-6). Arno.
Flanner, Hildegarde. A Vanishing Land. 60p. (Orig.). 1980. pap. 6.00 (ISBN 0-931832-15-2). No Dead Lines.
Gantz, Charlotte O. A Naturalist in Southern Florida. LC 74-126195. (Illus.). 1971. 9.95 (ISBN 0-87024-172-9). U of Miami Pr.
Geiser, Samuel W. Naturalists of the Frontier. rev. ed. LC 48-7357. (Illus.). 1948. 5.95 (ISBN 0-87074-059-8). SMU Press.
Gillette, Elizabeth, ed. Action for Wilderness. LC 79-189967. (Battlebook Ser.). 224p. (Orig.). 1972. pap. 2.25 (ISBN 0-87156-062-3). Sierra.
Gordon, Burton L. Monterey Bay Area: Natural History & Cultural Imprints. 2nd ed. LC 74-13912. (Illus.). 192p. 1977. pap. text ed. 5.95 (ISBN 0-910286-37-X). Boxwood.
Gordon, Robert B. The Natural Vegetation of Ohio in Pioneer Days. 1973. Repr. of 1969 ed. 4.00 (ISBN 0-686-30325-3). Ohio Bio Survey.
Grossman, Mary L. & Hamlet, John N. Our Vanishing Wilderness. 1969. 10.95 (ISBN 0-448-01208-1, MSP). G&D.
Halle, Louis J. Spring in Washington. LC 42-30273. (Illus.). 1963. pap. 1.25 (ISBN 0-689-70084-9, 22). Atheneum.
Hanley, Wayne & Massachusetts Audobon Society. Natural History in America: From Mark Catesby to Rachel Carson. LC 76-9704. (Illus.). 1977. 14.95 (ISBN 0-8129-0643-8, Demeter). Times Bks.
Hay, John. The Run. (Illus.). 1979. 9.95 (ISBN 0-393-01269-7); pap. 3.95 (ISBN 0-393-00946-7). Norton.
--Sandy Shore. LC 68-18991. (Illus.). 1968. 4.95 (ISBN 0-85699-006-X). Chatham Pr.
Heckman, Hazel. Island Year. LC 74-178701. (Illus.). 269p. 1972. 8.95 (ISBN 0-295-95171-0). U of Wash Pr.
Holt, Perry C., et al, eds. The Distributional History of the Biota of the Southern Appalachians, 3 vols. Incl. Pt. 1. Invertebrates. 1969. pap. 4.95x (ISBN 0-8139-0538-9); Pt 2. Flora. 1970. pap. 5.95x (ISBN 0-8139-0539-7); Pt 3. Vertebrates. 1971; Pt. 4, Algae & Fungi. Parker, Bruce C. & Roane, Martha K., eds. LC 75-636021. 1977. 20.00x (ISBN 0-8139-0660-1). U Pr of Va.
Hoover, Helen. Place in the Woods. (Illus.). (YA) 1969. 10.95 (ISBN 0-394-44065-X). Knopf.
--Years of the Forest. 1973. 10.95 (ISBN 0-394-47538-0). Knopf.
Hudson, Bess. Windows to Nature. LC 78-65090. (Illus.). 1978. 4.50 (ISBN 0-89301-059-6). U Pr of Idaho.
Jackson, Earl. Natural History Story of Chiricahua National Monument. LC 74-75812. (Orig.). 1970. pap. 1.00 (ISBN 0-911408-20-7). Sw Pks Mnmts.
Jaeger, Edmund C. & Smith, Arthur C. Introduction to the Natural History of Southern California. (Califonia Natural History Guides: No. 13). (Illus., Orig.). 1966. 14.95x (ISBN 0-520-03245-4); pap. 3.25 (ISBN 0-520-00601-1). U of Cal Pr.
Jorgensen, Neil. Sierra Club Naturalist's Guide to Southern New England. LC 77-28543. (Naturalist's Guide Ser.). (Illus.). 1978. 15.00 (ISBN 0-87156-190-5); pap. 9.95 (ISBN 0-87156-183-2). Sierra.
Keasey, Merritt S. Gasden's Silent Observers: An Introduction to Natural History of Southern Arizona. LC 75-103353. (Wild & Woolly West Ser.: No. 42). (Illus.). 56p. 1974. 7.00 (ISBN 0-910584-38-9); pap. 2.50 (ISBN 0-910584-68-0). Filter.
Kelley, Don G. Edge of a Continent: The Pacific Coast from Alaska to Baja. LC 78-119004. (Great West Ser). (Illus.). 1971. 17.50 (ISBN 0-910118-19-1). Am West.
Kinkead, Eugene. A Concrete Look at Nature: Central Park (& Other) Glimpses. LC 74-77936. (Illus.). 256p. 1974. 7.95 (ISBN 0-8129-0471-0). Times Bks.
Kirk, Ruth. Desert: The American Southwest. (Naturalist's America Ser.: Vol. 3). (Illus.). 1973. 10.00 (ISBN 0-395-17209-8). HM.
Koch, Albert C. Journey Through a Part of the United States of North America in the Years 1844-1846. Stadler, Ernst A., ed. & tr. LC 76-188701. (Travels on the Western Waters Ser). (Illus.). 243p. 1972. 12.50x (ISBN 0-8093-0581-X). S Ill U Pr.
Lafferty, Michael B., ed. Ohio's Natural Heritage. LC 78-60505. 1979. 23.95 (ISBN 0-933128-01-0). Ohio Acad Sci.
Lawson, John. New Voyage to Carolina. Lefler, Hugh T., ed. 1967. 14.95 (ISBN 0-8078-1042-8); limited ed. 25.00 (ISBN 0-8078-1041-X). U of NC Pr.
Leonard, Jonathan N. Atlantic Beaches. LC 72-79775. (The American Wilderness Ser.). (Illus.). 1972. 12.95 (ISBN 0-8094-1156-3). Time-Life.
Leopold, Aldo. Sand County Almanac Illustrated. new ed. LC 77-22656. 1977. 25.00 (ISBN 0-915024-15-2). Tamarack Pr.
--Sand County Almanac: With Other Essays on Conservation from Round River. (Illus.). 1966. 15.95 (ISBN 0-19-500619-4). Oxford U Pr.
Literary & Philosophical Society of New York, May, 1814 & Clinton, Dewitt. An Introductory Discourse: Proceedings. Albritton, Claude C., ed. LC 77-6515. (History of Geology Ser.). 1978. Repr. of 1815 ed. lib. bdg. 12.00x (ISBN 0-405-10437-5). Arno.
McLachlan, Dan H. & Ayres, Jak. The Fieldbook of Pacific Northwest Sea Creatures. LC 79-9769. (Illus.). 1979. 13.95 (ISBN 0-87961-069-7); pap. 9.95 (ISBN 0-87961-068-9). Naturegraph.
McPherson, Alan & McPherson, Sue. Wild Food Plants of Indiana & Adjacent States. LC 76-48528. (Illus.). 192p. 1977. 12.50x (ISBN 0-253-19039-8); pap. 4.95x (ISBN 0-253-28925-4). Ind U Pr.
Mahr, August C. The Visit of the Rurik to San Francisco in 1816. LC 78-155606. (Stanford University. Stanford Studies in History, Economics, & Political Science: Vol. 2, Pt. 2). (Illus.). Repr. of 1932 ed. 18.75 (ISBN 0-404-50964-9). AMS Pr.
Marcy, Randolph B. & McClellan, G. B. Adventure on Red River: A Report on the Exploration of the Headwaters of the Red River. Foreman, Grant, ed. (American Exploration & Travel Ser.: Vol. 1). (Illus.). 1968. Repr. of 1938 ed. 8.95 (ISBN 0-8061-0067-2). U of Okla Pr.
Marshall, Mel. Sierra Summer. LC 79-4174. (Illus.). 225p. 1979. 10.50 (ISBN 0-87417-053-2). U of Nev Pr.
Moser, Don. The Snake River Country. (The American Wilderness Ser.). (Illus.). 1974. 12.95 (ISBN 0-8094-1241-1). Time-Life.
Murphy, Robert C. Fish-Shape Paumanok. LC 63-22603. (Memoirs Ser.: Vol. 58). (Illus.). 1964. 5.00 (ISBN 0-87169-058-6). Am Philos.
Pearson, Haydn S. Sea Flavor. facs. ed. LC 68-58809. (Essay Index Reprint Ser). 1948. 15.00 (ISBN 0-8369-0051-0). Arno.
Philbrick, Ralph N., ed. Symposium on the Biology of the California Islands: Proceedings. (Illus.). 1967. 12.50 (ISBN 0-916436-01-2). Santa Barb Botanic.
Power, Dennis M., ed. The California Islands: Proceedings of a Multidisciplinary Symposium. LC 80-463. 787p. (Orig.). 1980. pap. text ed. 20.00 (ISBN 0-936494-01-8). Santa Barbara Mus Nat Hist.
Pritchard, Peter C., ed. Rare & Endangered Biota of Florida. Incl. Vol. One. Mammals. Layne, James N., ed. 53p. 1979. pap. 5.00 (ISBN 0-8130-0617-1); Vol. Two. Birds. Kale, Herbert W., ed. xix, 121p. 1979. pap. 7.00 (ISBN 0-8130-0618-X); Vol. Three. Amphibians & Reptiles. McDiarmid, Roy W., ed. xxiv, 74p. 1979. pap. 5.50 (ISBN 0-8130-0619-8); Vol. Four. Fishes. Gilbert, Carter R., ed. xviii, 58p. 1979. pap. 5.00 (ISBN 0-8130-0620-1); Vol. 5. Plants. Ward, Daniel B., ed. 1980. pap. 10.50 (ISBN 0-8130-0638-4). LC 78-12121. U Presses Fla.
Rabkin, Richard & Rabkin, Jacob. Nature Guide to Florida. (Illus.). 1978. pap. 7.95 (ISBN 0-916224-44-9). Banyan Bks.
Radford, Albert E., et al. Natural Heritage: Classification, Inventory, & Information. LC 80-23087. xii, 485p. 1981. 25.00x (ISBN 0-8078-1463-6). U of NC Pr.
Robertson, William B., Jr. Everglades - the Park Story. (Illus.). 1959. pap. 2.95 (ISBN 0-87024-006-4). U of Miami Pr.
Rose, Hilary & Rose, Steven. Ideology of-in the Natural Sciences. 363p. 1980. pap. text ed. 11.25x (ISBN 0-87073-881-X). Schenkman.
Sanger, Marjory B. World of the Great White Heron. LC 67-18236. (Illus.). 1967. 10.00 (ISBN 0-8159-7214-8). Devin.
Shoman, J. Nature Realms Across America. Date not set. 8.00 (ISBN 0-686-26727-3, 29). Am Forestry.
Smallwood, William M. & Smallwood, Mabel S. Natural History & the American Mind. LC 41-16864. Repr. of 1941 ed. 14.00 (ISBN 0-404-06116-8). AMS Pr.
Smith, Arthur C. Introduction to the Natural History of the San Francisco Bay Region. (California Natural History Guides: No. 1). (Illus.). 1959. 14.95x (ISBN 0-520-03099-0); pap. 3.95 (ISBN 0-520-01185-6). U of Cal Pr.
Smith, J. Lawrence. Potomac Naturalist. 1968. 8.00 (ISBN 0-87012-023-9). McClain.
Sprunt, Alexander & Dick, John H. Carolina Low Country Impressions. (Illus.). 1964. 10.00 (ISBN 0-8159-5201-5). Devin.
Sterling, Keir B., ed. The Cabinet of Natural History & American Rural Sports, 3 vols. in one. LC 77-81115. (Biologists & Their World Ser.). (Illus.). 1978. Repr. of 1833 ed. lib. bdg. 53.00x (ISBN 0-405-10704-8). Arno.
--Early Herpetological Studies & Surveys in the Eastern United States: Original Anthology. LC 77-81101. (Biologists & Their World Ser.). (Illus.). 1978. lib. bdg. 40.00x (ISBN 0-405-10685-8). Arno.
Tanner, Ogden. The New England Wilds. (The American Wilderness Ser.). (Illus.). 184p. 1974. 12.95 (ISBN 0-8094-1229-2). Time-Life.
Teale, Edwin W. American Seasons, 4 Vols. (Illus.). 1966. Set. 40.00 (ISBN 0-396-05399-8); 10.00 ea. Dodd.
--The American Seasons. LC 76-11794. (Illus.). 1976. 17.50 (ISBN 0-396-07353-0). Dodd.
--Autumn Across America. LC 56-10059. (Illus.). 1956. 10.00 (ISBN 0-396-03888-3). Dodd.
--A Naturalist Buys an Old Farm. LC 74-3779. (Illus.). 275p. 1974. 10.00 (ISBN 0-396-06974-6). Dodd.
--North with the Spring. LC 51-13966. (Illus.). 1951. 10.00 (ISBN 0-396-03325-3). Dodd.
Thompson, Zadock. Natural History of Vermont. LC 77-152112. (Illus.). 1971. Repr. pap. 3.85 (ISBN 0-8048-0983-6). C E Tuttle.
Thomson, Betty F. The Changing Face of New England. LC 77-4476. 1977. pap. 3.95 (ISBN 0-395-25725-5). HM.
Trautman, Milton B. The Ohio Country from 1750-1977--a Naturalist's View. 1977. 2.50 (ISBN 0-686-30341-5). Ohio Bio Survey.
Wallace, David R. The Dark Range: A Naturalist's Night Notebook. LC 78-1452. (Illus.). 1978. 15.00 (ISBN 0-87156-212-X); pap. 8.95 (ISBN 0-87156-251-0). Sierra.
Watkins, T. H. John Muir's America. (Illus.). 160p. 1981. pap. 12.95 (ISBN 0-912856-64-5). Graphic Arts Ctr.
White, George. Statistics of the State of Georgia. LC 71-187392. 701p. 1972. Repr. of 1849 ed. 27.00 (ISBN 0-87152-087-7). Reprint.
Wiley, Farida, ed. John Burrough's America. (American Naturalists Ser.). (Illus.). 220p. (gr. 9 up). 7.50 (ISBN 0-8159-5109-4); pap. 5.25 (ISBN 0-8159-5114-0). Devin.
Yocom, Charles & Dasmann, Raymond. Pacific Coastal Wildlife Region. rev. ed. (American Wildlife Region Ser.: Vol. 3). (Illus.). (gr. 4 up). 1965. 7.95 (ISBN 0-911010-05-X); pap. 3.95 (ISBN 0-911010-04-1). Naturegraph.
Zwinger, Ann. Wind in the Rock: A Naturalist Explores the Canyon Country of the Southwest. LC 78-2176. (Illus.). 1978. 15.00 (ISBN 0-06-014209-X, HarpT). Har-Row.

NATURAL HISTORY, BIBLICAL

see Bible-Natural History

NATURAL LAW

see also Ethics; International Law; Jurisprudence; Law-Philosophy; Liberty; Political Ethics

Battaglia, Anthony. Toward a Reformulation of Natural Law. 1981. 14.95 (ISBN 0-8164-0490-9). Seabury.
Becker, Carl. Declaration of Independence. 6.75 (ISBN 0-8446-1619-2). Peter Smith.
Becker, Carl L. Declaration of Independence: A Study in the History of Political Ideas. 1958. pap. 2.45 (ISBN 0-394-70060-0, V-60, Vin). Random.
Burlamaqui, Jean J. The Principles of Natural & Politic Law. 5th ed. Nugent, Thomas, tr. LC 70-38249. (The Evolution of Capitalism Ser.). 500p. 1972. Repr. of 1807 ed. 29.00 (ISBN 0-405-04114-4). Arno.
Center for the Study of Democratic Institutions. Natural Law & Modern Society. facsimile ed. LC 73-156626. (Essay Index Reprint Ser). Repr. of 1963 ed. 17.00 (ISBN 0-8369-2388-X). Arno.
Del Vecchio, Giorgio. Man & Nature: Selected Essays. Newman, Ralph A., ed. Campbell, A. H., tr. LC 72-75156. 1969. 9.00x (ISBN 0-268-00316-5). U of Notre Dame Pr.
D'Entreves, A. P. Natural Law: An Introduction to Legal Philosophy. 2nd rev. ed. 1964. text ed. 14.50x (ISBN 0-09-102600-8, Hutchinson U Lib); pap. text ed. 8.50x (ISBN 0-09-102601-6, Hutchinson U Lib). Humanities.
D'Holbach, Paul H. Nature & Her Laws. 59.95 (ISBN 0-8490-0714-3). Gordon Pr.
A Dissertation on the Law of Nature, the Law of Nations, & the Civil Law in General. Together with Some Observations on the Roman Civil Law in Particular: To Which Is Added, by Way of Appendix, a Curious Catalogue of Books, Very Useful to the Students of These Several Laws, Together with the Canon Law. iv, 132p. 1980. Repr. of 1723 ed. lib. bdg. 20.00x (ISBN 0-8377-0510-X). Rothman.
Edwards, Charles S. Hugo Grotius, the Miracle of Holland: A Study of Political & Legal Thought. LC 81-4592. 288p. 1981. text ed. 19.95x (ISBN 0-88229-624-8). Nelson-Hall.
Escherny, Francois L. De. De L'egalite Ou Principes Generaux Sur les Institutions Civiles, Politiques et Religieuses. (Rousseauism, 1788-1797). 1978. Repr. lib. bdg. 244.00x (ISBN 0-8287-0317-5). Clearwater Pub.
Gin, Pierre C. Des Causes De Nos Maux, De Leurs Proges et Des Moyens D'y Remedier. (Rousseauism, 1788-1797). 1978. Repr. lib. bdg. 20.50x (ISBN 0-8287-0378-7). Clearwater Pub.
Haines, Charles G. Revival of Natural Law Concepts. LC 65-13943. 1965. Repr. of 1930 ed. 9.50 (ISBN 0-8462-0535-1). Russell.
Hegel, G. W. Natural Law. Knox, T. M., tr. from Ger. LC 75-10123. 1975. pap. 4.95x (ISBN 0-8122-1083-2, Pa Paperbks). U of Pa Pr.
--Philosophy of Right. Knox, T. M., tr. 1942. 42.00x (ISBN 0-19-824128-3); pap. 6.95x (ISBN 0-19-500276-8). Oxford U Pr.
Kant, Immanuel. Philosophy of Law. Hastie, W., tr. LC 77-146882. 265p. Repr. of 1887 ed. lib. bdg. 15.00x (ISBN 0-678-01152-4). Kelley.
Kaplan, Morton A. Justice, Human Nature, & Political Obligation. LC 76-8145. 1976. 16.95 (ISBN 0-02-916890-2). Free Pr.
Kelsen, Hans. General Theory of Law & State. Wedberg, Anders, tr. LC 61-12122. 1961. Repr. of 1945 ed. 25.00 (ISBN 0-8462-0215-8). Russell.
Krieger, Leonard. Politics of Discretion. LC 65-14428. 1965. 15.00x (ISBN 0-226-45359-6). U of Chicago Pr.
Labadie, Laurance. On Natural Law & Punishment. (Men & Movements in the History & Philosophy of Anarchism Ser.). 1979. lib. bdg. 59.95 (ISBN 0-685-96408-6). Revisionist Pr.
Lemos, Ramon M. Hobbes & Locke: Power & Consent. LC 77-7482. 190p. 1978. 13.50x (ISBN 0-8203-0428-X). U of Ga Pr.
McPherson, Thomas. Political Obligation. (Library of Political Studies). 1967. pap. text ed. 2.25x (ISBN 0-7100-3159-9). Humanities.
Marechal, Sylvain. Dame Nature a la Barre De L'assemblee Nationale. Repr. of 1791 ed. 9.50 (ISBN 0-8287-0578-X). Clearwater Pub.
Maritain, Jacques. Rights of Man & Natural Law. LC 74-150416. 1971. Repr. of 1943 ed. text ed. 7.50 (ISBN 0-87752-146-8). Gordian.
Melden, A. I. Rights & Persons. LC 77-80180. 1978. 22.75x (ISBN 0-520-03528-3); pap. 5.95 (ISBN 0-520-03839-8). U of Cal Pr.
Mullett, Charles F. Fundamental Law & the American Revolution, 1760-1776. 1966. lib. bdg. 14.50x (ISBN 0-374-96023-2). Octagon.
Pound, Roscoe. Law & Morals. LC 70-96339. Repr. of 1924 ed. 9.00x (ISBN 0-678-04532-1). Kelley.
Robson, William A. Civilization & the Growth of Law: Study of Relations Between Men's Ideas About the Universe & the Institutions of Law & Government. LC 74-25779. (European Sociology Ser.). 374p. 1975. Repr. 21.00x (ISBN 0-405-06532-9). Arno.

Rousseau, Jean-Jacques. Discours sur les Sciences et les Arts: Avec: Discours sur l'Origine et l'Inegalite. 510p. 1955. 3.95 (ISBN 0-686-55341-1). French & Eur.
--Discours Sur Les Sciences et Les Arts. Havens, G. R., ed. 1946. pap. 16.00 (ISBN 0-527-77300-X). Kraus Repr.
--Discours sur l'origine de l'inegalite. (Nouveaux Classiques Larousse). (Fr). pap. 2.95 (ISBN 0-685-13891-7, 293). Larousse.
--Discours sur l'Origine et les Fondements de l'Inegalite Parmi les Hommes: Avec: La Reine Fantastique. 192p. 1973. 15.00 (ISBN 0-686-55342-X); pap. 4.95 (ISBN 0-686-55343-8). French & Eur.
--First & Second Discourses. Masters, Roger D., ed. 1964. pap. 5.95 (ISBN 0-312-69440-7). St Martin.
Schwarz-Liebermann Von Wahlendorf, H. A. Relexions Sur la Nature Des Choses et la Logique Du Droit: Contribution a L'ontologie & a L'epistemologie Juridiques. 1973. 32.50x (ISBN 90-2797-168-4). Mouton.
--Vom Primat Des Rechts: Drei Vortrage. 1972. pap. 12.50x (ISBN 90-2797-027-0). Mouton.
Shuman, Samuel I. Legal Positivism: Its Scope & Limitations. LC 62-14874. 1963. 11.95x (ISBN 0-8143-1213-6). Wayne St U Pr.
Simon, Yves. Tradition of Natural Law: A Philosopher's Reflections. Kuic, Vukan, ed. LC 64-24756. 1965. 15.00 (ISBN 0-8232-0640-8). Fordham.
Singh, N. Human Rights & International Co-Operation. LC 70-904156. 1969. 12.50x (ISBN 0-8002-0907-9). Intl Pubns Serv.
Spooner, Lysander. Let's Abolish Government: An Original Arno Press Compilation. LC 73-172232. (Right Wing Individualist Tradition in America Ser). 1971. Repr. of 1898 ed. 22.00 (ISBN 0-405-00441-9). Arno.
Stanlis, Peter J. Edmund Burke & the Natural Law. 1958. pap. 2.25 (ISBN 0-472-06106-2, 106, AA). U of Mich Pr.
Stone, Julius. Human Law & Human Justice. 1965. 18.75x (ISBN 0-8047-0215-2). Stanford U Pr.
Strauss, Leo. Natural Right & History. 1965. pap. 5.95 (ISBN 0-226-77694-8, P195, Phoen). U of Chicago Pr.
Tuck, Richard. Natural Rights Theories. LC 78-73819. 1980. 29.95 (ISBN 0-521-22512-4). Cambridge U Pr.
Waddell, Elizabeth G. Edge of a Kingdom. LC 79-66934. 1981. 5.95 (ISBN 0-533-04419-7). Vantage.
Weiss, Paul. Our Public Life. LC 59-9852. 256p. 1966. 10.95x (ISBN 0-8093-0219-5). S Ill U Pr.
--Our Public Life. LC 59-9852. (Arcturus Books Paperbacks). 256p. 1966. pap. 7.95 (ISBN 0-8093-0220-9). S Ill U Pr.
Wild, John. Plato's Modern Enemies & the Theory of Natural Law. LC 53-2434. 1953. 9.50x (ISBN 0-226-89738-9). U of Chicago Pr.
Willey, Basil. Eighteenth Century Background: Studies on the Idea of Nature in the Thought of the Period. LC 40-31307. 1941. 20.00x (ISBN 0-231-01234-9). Columbia U Pr.
Windolph, Francis L. Leviathan & Natural Law. Repr. of 1951 ed. lib. bdg. 15.00x (ISBN 0-8371-2520-0, WILL). Greenwood.
Wu, John C. Fountain of Justice: A Study of the Natural Law. 287p. 1980. 3.95 (ISBN 0-89955-183-1, Pub. by Mei Ya China). Intl Schol Bk Serv.

NATURAL MONUMENTS

see also Forest Reserves; National Parks and Reserves; Wilderness Areas; Wildlife Refuges

American Heritage. Natural Wonders of America. pap. 6.95 (ISBN 0-671-24712-3, Fireside). S&S.
Clark, Champ. The Badlands. (The American Wilderness Ser.). (Illus.). 1975. 12.95 (ISBN 0-8094-1208-X). Time-Life.
--The Badlands. LC 74-18063. (American Wilderness). (Illus.). (gr. 6 up). 1974. PLB 11.97 (ISBN 0-8094-1209-8, Pub. by Time-Life). Silver.
Colby, C. B. Wildlife in Our National Parks: Birds, Reptiles & Mammals. (Illus.). (gr. 4-7). 1965. PLB 5.29 (ISBN 0-698-30410-1). Coward.
Janus, Horst. Nature As Architect. LC 57-7666. (Illus.). 12.00 (ISBN 0-8044-5514-7). Ungar.
Schull, Diantha D. Landmarks of Otsego County. (Illus.). 288p. 1980. 18.95 (ISBN 0-8156-0157-3); pap. 9.95 (ISBN 0-8156-0158-1). Syracuse U Pr.
Ziegler, Arthur P. & Kidney, Walter C. Historic Preservation in Small Towns. (Illus.). 146p. (Orig.). 1980. pap. text ed. 8.95 (ISBN 0-910050-43-0). AASLH.

NATURAL RELIGION

see Natural Theology

NATURAL RESOURCES

see also Aquatic Resources; Commercial Products; Conservation of Natural Resources; Fisheries; Forests and Forestry; Geothermal Resources; Marine Resources; Mines and Mineral Resources; Power Resources; Reclamation of Land; Water-Power; Water Resources Development; Water-Supply; Wind Power

Alexandersson, Gunnar & Kleverbring, Bjorn. World Resources: Energy & Minerals, Vol. 1. 1978. 21.25x (ISBN 3-11-006577-0). De Gruyter.
Ali, S. A. Resources for Future Economic Growth. 1979. text ed. 10.50x (ISBN 0-7069-0746-9, Pub. by Vikas India). Advent NY.
Apsimon, John. The Total Synthesis of Natural Products, Vol. 4. LC 72-4075. (The Total Synthesis of Natural Products Ser.). 610p. 1981. 60.00 (ISBN 0-471-05460-7, Pub. by Wiley-Interscience). Wiley.
Aviel, Joanne F. Resource Shortages & World Politics. 162p. 1977. pap. text ed. 8.00 (ISBN 0-8191-0263-6). U Pr of Amer.
Backstrand, G. Resources, Society & Future. 1980. 40.00 (ISBN 0-08-023266-3); pap. 18.00 (ISBN 0-08-023267-1). Pergamon.
Banks, Ferdinand E. The Economics of Natural Resources. LC 76-25583. (Illus.). 267p. 1976. 24.50 (ISBN 0-306-30926-2, Plenum Pr). Plenum Pub.
Barnett, Harold J. & Morse, Chandler. Scarcity & Growth: The Economics of Natural Resource Availability. (Resources for the Future Ser). (Illus.). 304p. 1963. 19.50x (ISBN 0-8018-0056-0); pap. 4.50x (ISBN 0-8018-0057-9). Johns Hopkins.
Blinder, Alan S. & Friedman, Philip, eds. Natural Resources, Uncertainty, Dynamics & Trade: Essays in Honor of Rafael Lusky. (Economic Theory & Mathematical Economics Ser.). 1977. 37.50 (ISBN 0-12-106150-7). Acad Pr.
Bliss, Christopher. Economic Growth & Resources: Natural Resources, Vol III. LC 79-4430. 1979. 37.50x (ISBN 0-312-23316-7). St Martin.
Board on Agriculture and Renewable Resources, National Research Council. Renewable Resources for Industrial Materials. LC 76-44604. 1976. pap. 8.25 (ISBN 0-309-02528-1). Natl Acad Pr.
Boyd, K., ed. The Ethics of Resource Allocations. 128p. 1980. text ed. 12.00x (ISBN 0-85224-368-5, Pub. by Edinburgh U Pr Scotland). Columbia U Pr.
Brooks, David B., ed. Resource Economics: Selected Works of Orris C. Herfindahl. LC 74-6814. (Resources for the Future Research Report Ser). (Illus.). 346p. 1974. 24.00x (ISBN 0-8018-1645-9). Johns Hopkins.
Burton, Ian & Kates, Robert W., eds. Readings in Resource Management & Conservation. LC 65-14427. 1965. 12.50x (ISBN 0-226-08237-7). U of Chicago Pr.
Butlin, John A. Economics & Resources Policy. (Illus.). 1981. pap. text ed. 15.95x (ISBN 0-582-45074-8). Longman.
Cambridge Information & Research Services, Ltd. World Directory of Energy Information, Vol. I: Western Europe. 1981. 85.00 (ISBN 0-87196-563-1). Facts on File.
Campos-Lopez, Enrique, ed. Renewable Resources: A Systematic Approach. 1980. 29.50 (ISBN 0-12-158350-3). Acad Pr.
Clark, Robert M. & Gillean, James I. Resource Recovery Planning & Management. 1981. text ed. 24.00 (ISBN 0-250-40298-X). Ann Arbor Science.
The Concept of Compensation in the Field of Trade & Environment: (EPLP 4) 1973. pap. 7.50x (ISBN 2-88032-074-7, IUCN30, IUCN). Unipub.
Conference Internationale Sur la Conservation De la Nature & De Ses Ressources a Madagascar. (Illus.). 1972. pap. 15.00x (ISBN 2-88032-046-1, IUCN32, IUCN). Unipub.
Cottle, R. W. & Krarup, J., eds. Optimization Methods for Resource Allocation. LC 72-96097. 448p. 1974. 49.50x (ISBN 0-8448-0162-3). Crane-Russak Co.
Crout, D. H. Chemistry of Natural Products. 1982. price not set (ISBN 0-87735-213-5). Freeman C.
Deju, Raul, et al. The Environment & Its Resources. 1972. 44.00x (ISBN 0-677-14120-3). Gordon.
Dorner, Peter & El-Shafie, Mahmoud A., eds. Resources & Development: Natural Resource Policies & Economic Development in an Interdependent World. 506p. 1980. 25.00 (ISBN 0-299-08250-4). U of Wis Pr.
Ehrlich, Paul R. & Erlich, Anne H. The End of Affluence. 307p. 1975. lib. bdg. 16.60x (ISBN 0-89190-862-5). Am Repr-Rivercity Pr.
Ehrlich, Paul R. & Ehrlich, Anne H. The End of Affluence: A Blueprint for Your Future. 320p. 1974. pap. 2.50 (ISBN 0-345-29049-6). Ballantine.
Environmental Studies & Natural Resource Management. 159p. 1980. pap. 20.00 (ISBN 0-89059-007-9, SC001). Unipub.
Firey, Walter. Man, Mind, & Land: A Theory of Resource Use. LC 77-12902. 1977. Repr. of 1960 ed. lib. bdg. 21.00x (ISBN 0-8371-9834-8, FIMM). Greenwood.
Fisher, Anthony C. Resource & Environmental Economics: Natural Resources & the Environment in Economics. LC 81-9951. (Cambridge Surveys of Economic Literature Ser.). 256p. Date not set. price not set (ISBN 0-521-24306-8); pap. price not set (ISBN 0-521-28594-1). Cambridge U Pr.
Goldsmith, M., et al, eds. A Strategy for Resources. 1977. 34.25 (ISBN 0-7204-0438-X, North-Holland). Elsevier.
Gopalakrishnan, Chennat. Natural Resources & Energy: Theory & Policy. (Illus.). 120p. 1980. 12.50 (ISBN 0-250-40385-4). Ann Arbor Science.
Herfindahl, Orris C. Natural Resource Information for Economic Development. LC 69-15762. (Resources for Future Ser). (Illus.). 227p. 1969. 14.50x (ISBN 0-8018-1026-4). Johns Hopkins.
Hicks, C. S. Man & Natural Resources: An Agricultural Perspective. 250p. 1980. 29.00x (ISBN 0-686-69934-3, Pub. by Croom Helm England). State Mutual Bk.
Hicks, Cedric S. Man & Natural Resources: An Agricultural Perspective. LC 75-15274. 130p. 1975. 18.95 (ISBN 0-312-51065-9). St Martin.
Hinckley, A. D. Renewable Resources in Our Future. (Environmental Sciences & Applications: Vol. 8). 1980. 13.50 (ISBN 0-686-66168-0); pap. 6.75 (ISBN 0-08-023433-X). Pergamon.
Howe, Charles W. Natural Resource Economics: Issues Analysis & Policy. LC 78-24174. 1979. text ed. 25.95x (ISBN 0-471-04527-6). Wiley.
Jarrett, Henry, et al. Science & Resources: Prospects & Implications of Technological Advance. LC 77-23132. (Resources for the Future, Inc.). (Illus.). 1977. Repr. of 1959 ed. lib. bdg. 17.00x (ISBN 0-8371-9470-9, JASR). Greenwood.
Keyes, Dale L. Land Development & the Natural Environment: Estimating Impacts. (Land Development Impact Ser.). 128p. 1976. pap. 4.95 (ISBN 0-685-99523-2, 13500). Urban Inst.
Krutilla, John V. & Fisher, Anthony C. The Economics of Natural Environments: Studies in the Valuation of Commodity and Amenity Resources. LC 74-24400. (Resources for the Future Ser). (Illus.). 320p. 1975. 18.50x (ISBN 0-8018-1699-8); pap. 4.50x (ISBN 0-8018-1752-8). Johns Hopkins.
Land Water Classification. (Ecological Land Classification Ser.: No. 5). 1979. pap. 7.00 (ISBN 0-660-10039-8, SSC124, SSC). Unipub.
Lecomber, Richard. Economics of Natural Resources. LC 78-23595. 247p. 1979. 27.95 (ISBN 0-470-26546-9). Halsted Pr.
Leiter, Robert D. & Friedlander, Stanley L., eds. Economics of Resources. (Illus.). 250p. 1976. text ed. 18.00x (ISBN 0-8290-0396-7). Irvington.
--Economics of Resources: Annual Volume of the City College Department of Economics, Vol. 3. 300p. 1976. 21.95 (ISBN 0-915326-04-3). Cyrco Pr.
Little, Dennis L., et al, eds. Renewable Natural Resources: A Management Handbook for the Eighties. (Special Studies in Natural Resources & Energy Management). 375p. (Orig.). 1981. 26.25x (ISBN 0-89158-665-2); lib. bdg. 12.50x (ISBN 0-686-77772-7). Westview.
Macfarlane, A. Resources & Population. LC 75-13448. (Cambridge Studies in Social Anthropology: No. 12). (Illus.). 352p. 1976. 44.50 (ISBN 0-521-20913-7). Cambridge U Pr.
McMains, Harvey & Wilcox, Lyle, eds. Alternatives for Growth: The Engineering & Economics of Natural Resources Development. LC 77-11870. (Published for the National Bureau of Economic Research). 1978. 16.50 (ISBN 0-88410-480-X). Ballinger Pub.
Maczak, Antoni & Parker, Wm. N., eds. Natural Resources in European History: A Conference Report. LC 78-24688. (Resources for the Future Ser.). 1979. 6.75x (ISBN 0-8018-2237-8). Johns Hopkins.
Manthy, Robert S. Natural Resource Commodities: A Century of Statistics, Prices, Output, Consumotion, Foreign Trade & Employment in the U.S., 1870-1973. LC 78-8429. (Resources for the Future Ser). 1978. text ed. 25.00x (ISBN 0-8018-2142-8). Johns Hopkins.
Marsh, George P. Earth As Modified by Human Action. LC 74-106906. 1970. Repr. of 1878 ed. 24.00 (ISBN 0-403-00198-6). Scholarly.
Meier, Richard L. Planning for an Urban World: The Design of Resource-Conserving Cities. 1975. 30.00x (ISBN 0-262-13112-9). MIT Pr.
--Science & Economic Development: New Patterns of Living. 2nd ed. 1966. 14.00x (ISBN 0-262-13024-6). MIT Pr.
Mezerik, Avrahm G., ed. Natural Resources: Restrictions, Regulations, Agreements. 1964. pap. 15.00 (ISBN 0-685-13207-2, 80). Intl Review.
Mikdashi, Zuhayr. The International Politics of Natural Resources. LC 75-38002. 1976. 22.50x (ISBN 0-8014-1001-0). Cornell U Pr.
Mouzon, Olin T. International Resources & National Policy. LC 77-26194. (Illus.). 1978. Repr. of 1959 ed. lib. bdg. 55.50x (ISBN 0-313-20069-6, MOIR). Greenwood.
Natural Resources & the Human Enviroment for Food & Agriculture. (FAO Environment Paper Ser.: No. 1). 62p. 1980. pap. 7.50 (ISBN 92-5-100967-8, F2132, FAO). Unipub.
Nature Conservation in the Pacific. (Illus.). 1973. pap. 18.50x (ISBN 2-88032-051-8, IUCN37, IUCN). Unipub.
Novick, David. A World of Scarcities: Critical Issues in Public Policy. LC 75-42278. 1976. 30.95 (ISBN 0-470-15002-5). Halsted Pr.
Orr, David W. & Soroos, Marvin S., eds. The Global Predicament: Ecological Perspectives on World Order. LC 78-10207. 1979. 19.00 (ISBN 0-8078-1346-X); pap. 9.00x (ISBN 0-8078-1349-4). U of NC Pr.
Report of the Ad Hoc Advisory Committee Meeting on the Programme on the Use & Management of Natural Resources. 14p. 1979. pap. 5.00 (ISBN 0-686-61492-5, TUNU 002, UNU). Unipub.
Report of the Expert Panel Meetings on the Programme on the Use & Management of Natural Resources. 51p. 1980. pap. 5.00 (ISBN 0-686-61493-3, TUNU 003, UNU). Unipub.
Research Group on Living & Surviving. Inhabiting the Earth As a Finite World. 1979. lib. bdg. 28.00 (ISBN 0-89838-018-9, Pub. by Martinus Nijhoff Netherlands). Kluwer Boston.
Reynolds, John E., et al. Readings in Natural Resource Economics. Redfern, J. Martin & Shulstad, Robert N., eds. 199p. 1974. text ed. 29.00x (ISBN 0-685-50581-2); pap. text ed. 8.95x (ISBN 0-8422-0449-0). Irvington.
Ridgeway, James. Who Owns the Earth? 1980. 15.95 (ISBN 0-02-603300-3); pap. 8.95 (ISBN 0-02-081220-5). Macmillan.
Ridker, Ronald G. & Watson, William D., Jr. To Choose a Future. LC 79-3643. (Resources for the Future Ser.). 1980. 33.50x (ISBN 0-8018-2354-4). Johns Hopkins.
Robinson, Harry. Population & Resources. 1981. 22.00x (ISBN 0-312-63120-0). St Martin.
Rodgers, William H., Jr. Cases & Materials on Energy & Natural Resources Law. LC 78-31515. (American Casebook Ser.). 995p. 1979. text ed. 23.95 (ISBN 0-8299-2029-3). West Pub.
Schachter, Oscar. Sharing the World's Resources. LC 76-28422. 1977. 12.50x (ISBN 0-231-04110-1). Columbia U Pr.
Shaler, Nathaniel S. Man & the Earth. Repr. of 1905 ed. 14.50 (ISBN 0-384-54960-8). Johnson Repr.
Siebert, Horst. Economics of the Environment. LC 80-7442. 1981. 24.95x (ISBN 0-669-03693-5). Lexington Bks.
Simmons, Ian. The Ecology of Natural Resources. LC 74-4812. 424p. 1974. pap. text ed. 14.95 (ISBN 0-470-79194-2). Halsted Pr.
Skinner, B. Earth Resources. 2nd ed. 1976. pap. 8.95 (ISBN 0-13-223008-9). P-H.
Smith, V. L., ed. Economics of Natural & Environmental Resources. 1977. 36.25x (ISBN 0-677-15040-7). Gordon.
Spooner, Henry J. Wealth from Waste: Elimination of Waste a World Problem. LC 73-8599. (Management History Ser.: No. 60). 332p. 1973. Repr. of 1918 ed. 17.50 (ISBN 0-87960-063-2). Hive Pub.
Stamp, Laurence D. & Wooldridge, Sidney W. London Essays in Geography. facs. ed. LC 76-80399. (Essay Index Reprint Ser). 1951. 21.25 (ISBN 0-8369-1050-8). Arno.
Stoltenberg, Carl, et al. Planning Research for Resource Decisions. facsimile ed. LC 76-103839. (Illus.). 1970. pap. 8.20x (ISBN 0-8138-2260-2). Iowa St U Pr.
Stone, A. Harris. Last Free Bird. (Illus.). (ps-3). 1967. PLB 5.95 (ISBN 0-13-523993-1); pap. 1.50 (ISBN 0-13-523985-0). P-H.
Townsend, Colin R. & Calow, Peter, eds. Physiological Ecology: An Evolutionary Approach to Resource Use. (Illus.). 480p. 1981. text ed. price not set (ISBN 0-87893-827-3); pap. text ed. price not set (ISBN 0-87893-828-1). Sinauer Assoc.
U. S. Congress - House Committee of Interior & Insular Affairs. Physical & Economic Foundation of Natural Resources. 1952-1953. lib. bdg. 36.25x (ISBN 0-8371-2900-1, PHEF). Greenwood.
Wilson, Charles M. Middle America. facs. ed. LC 75-128334. (Essay Index Reprint Ser). 1944. 23.00 (ISBN 0-8369-2092-9). Arno.

Wilson, Kenneth D., ed. Prospects for Growth: Changing Expectations for the Future. LC 77-14567. (Praeger Special Studies). 1977. 24.95 (ISBN 0-03-041446-6); pap. 11.95 (ISBN 0-03-041441-5). Praeger.

NATURAL RESOURCES–BIBLIOGRAPHY

Hoadley, Irene B., ed. Natural Resources Bibliography. LC 76-63420. 242p. 1970. 5.00 (ISBN 0-88215-014-6). Ohio St U Lib.

NATURAL RESOURCES–JUVENILE LITERATURE

Pringle, Laurence. Our Hungry Earth: The World Food Crisis. LC 76-10828. (Science for Survival Ser.). 128p. (gr. 7 up). 1976. 7.95 (ISBN 0-02-775290-9, 77529). Macmillan.

NATURAL RESOURCES–LAW AND LEGISLATION

see also Forestry Law and Legislation; Water–Laws and Legislation; Wildlife Conservation–Law and Legislation

Arsanjani, Mahnoush H. International Regulation of Internal Resources: A Study of Law & Policy. LC 80-21169. 1981. write for info. (ISBN 0-8139-0879-5). U Pr of Va.

Elian, G. The Principle of Sovereignty Over Natural Resources. 250p. 1979. 42.50x (ISBN 90-286-0049-3). Sijthoff & Noordhoff.

Fawcett, J. E. & Parry, Audrey. Law & International Resource Conflicts. 250p. 1981. 55.00 (ISBN 0-19-825359-1). Oxford U Pr.

Financing Environmental Measures in Developing Countries: The Principle of Additionality (EPLP 6) 1974. pap. 7.50x (ISBN 2-88032-076-3, IUCN52, IUCN). Unipub.

Fiscal Measures for Environmental Protection: Two Divergent Views, (EPLP 11) (Illus.). 1976. pap. 8.50x (ISBN 2-88032-081-X, IUCN63, IUCN). Unipub.

Hershman, Marc, et al. Under New Management: Port Growth & Emerging Coastal Management Programs. LC 78-66066. (Washington Sea Grant). (Illus.). 244p. 1979. pap. 12.50 (ISBN 0-295-95659-3). U of Wash Pr.

A Legal & Institutional Framework for Natural Resources Management. (Legislative Studies Ser.: No. 9). 44p. 1975. pap. 7.50 (ISBN 0-685-61957-5, F1022, Fao). Unipub.

Martz, Clyde O. Cases & Materials on the Law of Natural Resources. Bruchey, Stuart, ed. LC 78-53553. (Development of Public Lands Law in the U. S. Ser.). 1979. Repr. of 1951 ed. lib. bdg. 65.00x (ISBN 0-405-11379-X). Arno.

Rajan, M. S. Sovereignty Over Natural Resources. 1978. text ed. 10.00x (ISBN 0-391-00869-2). Humanities.

Rodgers, William H., Jr. Cases & Materials on Energy & Natural Resources Law. LC 78-31515. (American Casebook Ser.). 995p. 1979. text ed. 23.95 (ISBN 0-8299-2029-3). West Pub.

Sullivan, Thomas F., ed. Resource Conservation & Recovery Act: A Compliance Analysis. LC 78-78342. 162p. 1978. pap. text ed. 22.50 (ISBN 0-86587-077-2). Gov Insts.

NATURAL RESOURCES–STUDY AND TEACHING

Conservation Education Association. Education: Key to Conservation. Incl. Bk. 1. Important Characteristics of a Good Local Program. (Illus.). 8p. 1965; Bk. 2. Planning a State Program in Conservation Education. (Illus.). 16p. 1965. pap. text ed. 0.30 (ISBN 0-8134-0870-9, 870); Bk. 3. Twenty-Five Key Guides for Preparing Conservation Education Publications & Visual Aids. (Illus.). 16p. 1965. pap. text ed. 0.30 (ISBN 0-8134-0871-7, 871); Bk. 5. A Selected List of Filmstrips on the Conservation of Natural Resources. (Illus.). 48p. 1968. pap. text ed. 0.50 (ISBN 0-8134-1040-1, 1040). LC 65-23951. Interstate.

Emanuelson, Clifford E. & Emanuelson, Virginia, eds. Conservation Quickies. LC 66-22432. (Illus.). pap. text ed. 1.25x (ISBN 0-8134-6875-2, 6875). Interstate.

NATURAL RESOURCES–AFRICA

Ecological Guidelines for the Use of Natural Resources in the Middle East & South West Asia. (IUCN Publications New Ser: No. 34). 1978. pap. 15.00 (ISBN 0-685-65229-7, IUCN 73, IUCN). Unipub.

FAO-Danida Regional Seminar on Small-Scale Water Resources Development in Africa (West) Report. 29p. 1978. pap. 7.50 (ISBN 92-5-100449-8, F1320, FAO). Unipub.

Management of Natural Resources in Africa: Traditional Strategies & Modern Decision Making. (MAB Technical Note Ser.: No. 9). 1979. pap. 10.00 (ISBN 92-3-101587-7, U867, UNESCO). Unipub.

NATURAL RESOURCES–ALASKA

Cooley, Richard A. Alaska: A Challenge in Conservation. (Illus.). 186p. (YA) (gr. 9-12). 1966. pap. 4.00x (ISBN 0-299-04024-0). U of Wis Pr.

Harrison, Gordon S., ed. Alaska Public Policy. 2nd ed. LC 73-620050. 332p. 1973. pap. 5.00 (ISBN 0-88353-901-2). U Alaska Inst Res.

Leopold, A. Starker & Darling, F. Fraser. Wildlife in Alaska, an Ecological Reconnaissance. LC 72-6927. 129p. 1973. Repr. of 1953 ed. lib. bdg. 15.00x (ISBN 0-8371-6509-1, LEWI). Greenwood.

Young, Oran. Resource Management at the International Level. 1977. 17.50 (ISBN 0-89397-027-1). Nichols Pub.

NATURAL RESOURCES–ASIA

Ecological Guidelines for the Use of Natural Resources in the Middle East & South West Asia. (IUCN Publications New Ser: No. 34). 1978. pap. 15.00 (ISBN 0-685-65229-7, IUCN 73, IUCN). Unipub.

Natural Resources of Humid Tropical Asia. (Natural Resources Research Ser., No. 12). (Illus.). 456p. (Orig.). 1974. 44.75 (ISBN 92-3-101055-7, U407, UNESCO). Unipub.

The Use of Ecological Guidelines for Development in Tropical Forest Areas of South East Asia. (Illus.). 1975. pap. 17.50x (ISBN 2-88032-005-4, IUCN64, IUCN). Unipub.

NATURAL RESOURCES–CANADA

Barker, Mary L. Natural Resources of British Columbia & the Yukon Territory. (Illus.). 166p. 1977. 14.95 (ISBN 0-295-95561-9). U of Wash Pr.

Beigie, Carl E. & Hero, Alfred O., Jr., eds. Natural Resources in U. S. - Canadian Relations: Patterns & Trends in Resource Supplies & Policies, Vol. 2. 1980. lib. bdg. 28.75x (ISBN 0-89158-555-9); pap. text ed. 12.00x (ISBN 0-89158-878-7). Westview.

--Natural Resources in U. S. - Canadian Relations: The Evolution of Policies & Issues, Vol. 1. (Illus.). 362p. 1980. 26.25x (ISBN 0-89158-554-0); pap. text ed. 10.00x (ISBN 0-89158-877-9). Westview.

The Legal Aspects of Ecological Reserve Creation & Management in Canada: (EPLP 9) 1975. pap. 9.50x (ISBN 2-88032-079-8, IUCN12, IUCN). Unipub.

Nelles, H. V. The Politics of Development: Forests, Mines & Hydro-Electro Power in Ontario, 1849-1941. 565p. 1974. 25.00 (ISBN 0-208-01450-0, Archon). Shoe String.

NATURAL RESOURCES–GREAT BRITAIN

Stamp, L. Dudley & Beaver, S. H. The British Isles. 6th ed. LC 70-17425. (Geographies for Advanced Studies). 1972. 35.00 (ISBN 0-312-10325-5). St Martin.

NATURAL RESOURCES–LATIN AMERICA

Actas De la Reunion Centroamericana Sobre Manejo De Recursos Naturales y Culturales, San Jose, Costa Rica, Nine to Fourteen, Diciembre, Nineteen Seventy-Four. 1976. pap. 12.50x (ISBN 0-686-53039-X, IUCN50, IUCN). Unipub.

Grunwald, Joseph & Musgrove, Philip. Natural Resources in Latin American Development. LC 77-108381. (Resources for the Future Ser). 511p. 1970. 30.00x (ISBN 0-8018-1145-7). Johns Hopkins.

Rippy, James F. Latin America & the Industrial Age. 2nd ed. LC 70-136082. (Illus.). 1971. Repr. of 1947 ed. lib. bdg. 17.50x (ISBN 0-8371-5232-1, RIAM). Greenwood.

Uranium Deposits in Latin America: Geology & Exploration. (Panel Proceedings Ser.). 624p. 1981. pap. 78.00 (ISBN 92-0-041081-2, ISP505, IAEA). Unipub.

Wilgus, A. Curtis, ed. Caribbean: Natural Resources. LC 51-12532. (Caribbean Conference Ser: Vol. 9). (Illus.). 1959. 9.00 (ISBN 0-8130-0249-4). U Presses Fla.

NATURAL RESOURCES–RUSSIA

Gerasimov, I. P., et al, eds. Natural Resources of the Soviet Union: Their Use & Renewal, English Edition. LC 74-138667. (Illus.). 1971. text ed. 31.95x (ISBN 0-7167-0248-7). W H Freeman.

Gustafson, Thane. Reform in Soviet Politics: The Lessons of Recent Policies on Land & Water. LC 80-24286. (Illus.). 224p. Date not set. price not set (ISBN 0-521-23377-1). Cambridge U Pr.

Shabad, Theodore & Mote, Victor L. Gateway to Siberian Resources: The BAM. (Scripta Series in Geography). 1977. 15.95 (ISBN 0-470-99040-6). Halsted Pr.

Young, Oran. Resource Management at the International Level. 1977. 17.50 (ISBN 0-89397-027-1). Nichols Pub.

NATURAL RESOURCES–UNITED STATES

Allen, Shirley W. & Leonard, J. W. Conserving Natural Resources. 3rd ed. 1966. 17.50 (ISBN 0-07-001081-1, C). McGraw.

Avery, T. E. Natural Resources Measurements. 2nd ed. (The American Forestry Ser). 1975. 19.95 (ISBN 0-07-002502-9, C). McGraw.

Beigie, Carl E. & Hero, Alfred O., Jr., eds. Natural Resources in U. S. - Canadian Relations: Patterns & Trends in Resource Supplies & Policies, Vol. 2. 1980. lib. bdg. 28.75x (ISBN 0-89158-555-9); pap. text ed. 12.00x (ISBN 0-89158-878-7). Westview.

--Natural Resources in U. S. - Canadian Relations: The Evolution of Policies & Issues, Vol. 1. (Illus.). 362p. 1980. 26.25x (ISBN 0-89158-554-0); pap. text ed. 10.00x (ISBN 0-89158-877-9). Westview.

Chase, Stuart. Rich Land, Poor Land. LC 70-92612. (Illus.). Repr. of 1936 ed. 26.50 (ISBN 0-404-01478-X). AMS Pr.

Coyle, David C. Roads to a New America. facsimile ed. LC 77-103649. (Select Bibliographies Reprint Ser). 1938. 29.00 (ISBN 0-8369-5149-2). Arno.

Eckes, Alfred E. The United States & the Global Struggle for Minerals. LC 78-11082. 365p. 1979. text ed. 18.95x (ISBN 0-292-78506-2); pap. 8.95x (ISBN 0-292-78511-9). U of Tex Pr.

Ely, Richard T., et al, eds. Foundations of National Prosperity: Studies in the Conservation of Permanent National Resources. LC 19-1787. 1971. Repr. of 1918 ed. 23.00 (ISBN 0-384-16495-1, D055). Johnson Repr.

Finley, Robert W. Characteristics & Natural Resources of Lands in Wisconsin & Michigan. (Library of American Indian Affairs). 60p. 1974. lib. bdg. 27.00 (ISBN 0-8287-0968-8). Clearwater Pub.

Hays, Samuel P. Conservation & the Gospel of Efficiency: The Progressive Conservation Movement, 1890-1920. LC 59-9274. 1969. pap. text ed. 4.95x (ISBN 0-689-70091-1, 139). Atheneum.

Hershman, Marc, et al. Under New Management: Port Growth & Emerging Coastal Management Programs. LC 78-66066. (Washington Sea Grant). (Illus.). 244p. 1979. pap. 12.50 (ISBN 0-295-95659-3). U of Wash Pr.

Highsmith, Richard M., Jr. & Jensen, J. Granville, eds. Conservation in the United States. LC 78-6195. (Illus.). 1978. Repr. of 1969 ed. lib. bdg. 46.50x (ISBN 0-313-20511-6, HICU). Greenwood.

Hill, James J. Highways of Progress. LC 73-2512. (Big Business; Economic Power in a Free Society Ser.). Repr. of 1910 ed. 18.00 (ISBN 0-405-05093-3). Arno.

Hitch, Allen S. & Sorenson, Marian. Conservation & You. 1964. 5.95 (ISBN 0-442-03418-0). Van Nos Reinhold.

Huth, Hans. Nature & the American: Three Centuries of Changing Attitudes. LC 57-12393. (Illus.). xvii, 250p. 1972. 15.95x (ISBN 0-8032-0926-6); pap. 7.50x (ISBN 0-8032-5761-9, BB 554, Bison). U of Nebr Pr.

Krutilla, John V. & Fisher, Anthony C. The Economics of Natural Environments: Studies in the Valuation of Commodity and Amenity Resources. LC 74-24400. (Resources for the Future Ser). (Illus.). 320p. 1975. 18.50x (ISBN 0-8018-1699-8); pap. 4.50x (ISBN 0-8018-1752-8). Johns Hopkins.

Landsberg, Hans H., et al. Resources in America's Future: Patterns of Requirements and Availabilities, 1960-2000. (Resources for the Future Ser). (Illus.). 1963. 35.00x (ISBN 0-8018-0357-8). Johns Hopkins.

Levinson, Alfred L. Energy & Materials in Three Sectors of the Economy: A Dynamic Model with Technological Change As an Endogenous Variable. LC 78-75010. (Outstanding Dissertations on Energy Ser.). 1979. lib. bdg. 15.50 (ISBN 0-8240-3983-1). Garland Pub.

Mattison, Charles W. & Alvarez, Joseph. Man & His Resources. LC 66-25119. (In Todays World Ser). (Illus.). (gr. 4-8). 1967. PLB 7.95 (ISBN 0-87191-001-2). Creative Ed.

Mouzon, Olin T. Resources & Industries of the United States. LC 66-19968. (Illus.). 1966. 24.50x (ISBN 0-89197-381-8); pap. text ed. 8.95x (ISBN 0-89197-382-6). Irvington.

Petulla, Joseph M. American Environmental History: The Exploitation & Conservation of Natural Resources. LC 75-4870. (Illus.). 1977. 18.00x (ISBN 0-87835-058-6); pap. text ed. 10.95x (ISBN 0-87835-055-1). Boyd & Fraser.

Potter, Neal & Christy, Francis T., Jr. Trends in Natural Resource Commodities: Statistics of Prices, Output, Consumption, Foreign Trade & Employment in the United States, 1870-1959. (Resources for the Future Ser). 608p. 1962. 35.00x (ISBN 0-8018-0536-8). Johns Hopkins.

Resources for the Future, Inc. The Nation Looks at Its Resources: Report of the Mid-Century Conference of Resources for the Future. Washington, D.C., Dec. 2-4, 1953. LC 77-86410. 1977. Repr. of 1954 ed. 47.50 (ISBN 0-404-60343-2). AMS Pr.

Richardson, Elmo. Dams, Parks & Politics: Resource Development & Preservation in the Truman-Eisenhower Era. LC 72-91670. (Illus.). 256p. 1973. 16.00x (ISBN 0-8131-1284-2). U Pr of Ky.

Schurr, Sam, et al. Energy in America's Future: The Choices Before Us. LC 79-2195. (Resources for the Future Ser.). 1979. 30.00x (ISBN 0-8018-2280-7); pap. 10.95 (ISBN 0-686-65565-6). Johns Hopkins.

Smith, Kerry V. Scarcity & Growth Reconsidered. LC 78-27236. (Resources for the Future Ser.). 1979. text ed. 18.50x (ISBN 0-8018-2232-7); pap. text ed. 6.95x (ISBN 0-8018-2233-5). Johns Hopkins.

Supplementary Report of the Land Planning Committee to the National Resources Board, 1935-1942. LC 72-2851. (Use & Abuse of America's Natural Resources). (Illus.). 1058p. 1972. Repr. of 1935 ed. 60.00 (ISBN 0-405-04535-2). Arno.

Texas University. Texas Looks Ahead, Vol. 1. The Resources Of Texas. facs. ed. Drummond, Lorena, ed. LC 68-58814. (Essay Index Reprint Ser). 1944. 22.00 (ISBN 0-8369-0093-6). Arno.

Twentieth Century Fund. America's Needs & Resources: A New Survey. 1955. 12.00 (ISBN 0-527-02837-1). Kraus Repr.

United States National Resources Committee. The Structure of the American Economy, 2 vols. in 1. LC 78-173418. (FDR & the Era of the New Deal Ser). 1972. Repr. of 1939 ed. lib. bdg. 45.00 (ISBN 0-306-70388-2). Da Capo.

U. S. National Resources Planning Board. Industrial Location & National Resources. LC 43-53694. 1943. 22.00 (ISBN 0-527-92000-2). Kraus Repr.

The Use of Ecological Guidelines for Development in the American Humid Tropics. (Illus.). 1975. pap. 25.00x (ISBN 2-88032-004-6, IUCN62, IUCN). Unipub.

El Uso De Normas Ecologicas Para el Desarrollo En el Tropico Huedo American. (Illus.). 1976. pap. 25.00x (ISBN 2-88032-007-0, IUCN15, IUCN). Unipub.

Warken, Philip W. A History of the National Resources Planning Board, 1933-1943. Freidel, Frank, ed. LC 78-66882. (Modern American History Ser.: Vol. 19). 1979. lib. bdg. 24.00 (ISBN 0-8240-3642-5). Garland Pub.

Weidenbaum, Murray L. Prospects for Reallocating Public Resources: A Study in Federal-State Fiscal Relations. 1967. pap. 4.25 (ISBN 0-8447-3059-9). Am Enterprise.

Wengert, Norman. Administration of Natural Resources: The American Experience. 3.00x (ISBN 0-210-33801-6). Asia.

Western Resources Conference, 3rd, Colorado State University, 1961. Land & Water: Planning for Economic Growth: Proceedings. Amoss, Harold L. & McNickle, Roma K., eds. LC 76-44432. (Illus.). 1976. Repr. of 1962 ed. lib. bdg. 16.25x (ISBN 0-8371-9037-1, AMLW). Greenwood.

Whitaker, J. Russell & Ackerman, Edward A. American Resources: Their Management & Conservation. LC 72-2874. (Use & Abuse of America's Natural Resources Ser). 514p. 1972. Repr. of 1951 ed. 25.00 (ISBN 0-405-04542-5). Arno.

NATURAL RESOURCES–UNITED STATES–ECONOMIC CONDITIONS

Banks, Ferdinand E. Scarcity, Energy and Economic Progress. LC 77-4630. 1977. 21.00 (ISBN 0-669-01781-7). Lexington Bks.

Clawson, Marion, ed. Natural Resources & International Development. LC 77-86392. (Resources for the Future, Inc. Publications). Repr. of 1964 ed. 32.50 (ISBN 0-404-60330-0). AMS Pr.

Dasgupta, P. S. & Heal, G. M. Economic Theory & Exhaustible Resources. LC 79-51749. (Cambridge Economic Handbooks Ser.). 1980. 42.50 (ISBN 0-521-22991-X); pap. 16.95x (ISBN 0-521-29761-3). Cambridge U Pr.

Pine, Wilfred H. Natural Resources Economics. 1977. pap. 4.00 (ISBN 0-686-00368-3). AG Pr.

Simon, Julian L. The Ultimate Resource. LC 80-8575. 336p. 1981. 14.50x (ISBN 0-691-09389-X). Princeton U Pr.

Spengler, Joseph J., ed. Natural Resources & Economic Growth: Papers Presented at a Conference, Ann Arbor, Michigan, April 7-9, 1960. LC 77-86411. (Resources for the Future, Inc. Publications). Repr. of 1961 ed. 34.50 (ISBN 0-404-60344-0). AMS Pr.

NATURAL RESOURCES–WEST INDIES

Wilgus, A. Curtis, ed. Caribbean: Natural Resources. LC 51-12532. (Caribbean Conference Ser: Vol. 9). (Illus.). 1959. 9.00 (ISBN 0-8130-0249-4). U Presses Fla.

NATURAL RIGHTS

see Natural Law

NATURAL SCENERY

see Landscape; Views

NATURAL SCIENCE

see Natural History; Physics; Science

NATURAL SELECTION

see also Evolution; Heredity; Origin of Species

Bajema, Carl J., ed. Natural Selection in Human Populations: The Measurement of Ongoing Genetic Evolution in Contemporary Societies. LC 76-50639. (Illus.). 416p. 1977. Repr. of 1971 ed. lib. bdg. 13.50 (ISBN 0-88275-476-9). Krieger.

Berry, R. J. Inheritance & Natural History. (The New Natural Ser.). (Illus.). 1978. 14.95 (ISBN 0-8008-4195-6). Taplinger.

Campbell, Bernard. Sexual Selection & the Descent of Man. LC 70-169510. 1972. 34.95x (ISBN 0-202-02005-3). Aldine Pub.
Darwin, Charles. The Descent of Man & Selection in Relation to Sex. LC 80-8679. (Illus.). 935p. 1981. 30.00x (ISBN 0-691-08278-2); pap. 8.95 (ISBN 0-691-02369-7). Princeton U Pr.
--Natural Selection. Stauffer, R. C., ed. LC 72-95406. (Illus.). 1975. 105.00 (ISBN 0-521-20163-2). Cambridge U Pr.
--Origin of Species. 1962. pap. 2.95 (ISBN 0-02-092120-9, Collier). Macmillan.
--Origin of Species. pap. 2.95 (ISBN 0-451-61928-5, ME1928, Ment). NAL.
--The Origin of the Species. (Rowman & Littlefield University Library). 488p. 1972. 15.00x (ISBN 0-87471-662-4); pap. 6.75x (ISBN 0-87471-663-2). Rowman.
Darwin, Charles R. The Descent of Man & Selection in Relation to Sex, 2 vols. 916p. 1971. Repr. of 1871 ed. Set. 87.50x (ISBN 0-8002-0149-3). Intl Pubns Serv.
--Foundations of the Origin of Species. Darwin, Francis, ed. LC 10-1422. 1909. 13.00 (ISBN 0-527-21610-0). Kraus Repr.
--Origin of Species. Burrow, J. W., ed. (Classics Ser). (YA) (gr. 9 up). 1968. pap. 2.50 (ISBN 0-14-040001-X, Pelican). Penguin.
Darwin, Charles R. & Wallace, Alfred R. Evolution by Natural Selection. LC 58-14868. 1971. Repr. of 1958 ed. 23.00 (ISBN 0-384-10875-X, B132). Johnson Repr.
Fisher, Ronald. The Genetical Theory of Natural Selection. 2nd ed. 1958. pap. 4.50 (ISBN 0-486-60466-7). Dover.
Ford, E. B. Ecological Genetics. 4th ed. 442p. 1979. text ed. 29.95x (ISBN 0-412-14130-2, Pub. by Chapman & Hall England). Methuen Inc.
Gause, G. F. Struggle for Existence. (Illus.). 1969. Repr. of 1934 ed. 9.75 (ISBN 0-02-845200-3). Hafner.
Gilpin, Michael. Group Selection in Predator-Prey Communities. (Monographs in Population Biology: No. 9). 120p. 1974. 14.00x (ISBN 0-691-08157-3); pap. 5.95x (ISBN 0-691-08161-1). Princeton U Pr.
Gould, Stephen J. Ever Since Darwin: Reflections in Natural History. (Illus.). 1977. 12.95 (ISBN 0-393-06425-5). Norton.
Huntington, Ellsworth. The Character of Races: Influenced by Physical Environment, Natural Selection & Historical Development. Grob, Gerald, ed. LC 76-46082. (Anti-Movements in America). 1977. lib. bdg. 23.00x (ISBN 0-405-09955-X). Arno.
Johnson, C. Introduction to Natural Selection. 1976. 12.50 (ISBN 0-8391-0936-9). Univ Park.
Kraus, Gerhard. Homo Sapiens in Decline: A Reappraisal of Natural Selection. 189p. 1973. text ed. 8.00x (ISBN 0-7121-5601-1). Humanities.
Montagu, Ashley. Darwin: Competition & Cooperation. LC 72-11332. 148p. 1973. Repr. of 1952 ed. lib. bdg. 15.00 (ISBN 0-8371-6657-8, MODC). Greenwood.
O'Donald, Peter. Genetic Models of Sexual Selection. LC 78-73249. (Illus.). 1980. 32.50 (ISBN 0-521-22533-7). Cambridge U Pr.
Ohguchi, Osamu. Prey Density and Selection Against Oddity by Three-Spined Sticklebacks. (Advances in Ethology Ser.: Vol. 23). (Illus.). 80p. (Orig.). 1981. pap. text ed. 22.00 (ISBN 0-686-30706-2). Parey Sci Pubs.
Russett, Cynthia E. Darwin in America: The Intellectual Response, 1865-1912. LC 75-40476. (Illus.). 1976. pap. text ed. 4.95x (ISBN 0-7167-0563-X). W H Freeman.
Shahshahani, S. A New Mathematical Framework for the Study of Linkage & Selection. LC 78-23487. (Memoirs: No. 211). 1979. 7.60 (ISBN 0-8218-2211-X). Am Math.
Sheppard, Philip M. Natural Selection & Heredity. 4th ed. 1975. text ed. 10.75x (ISBN 0-09-036801-0, Hutchinson U Lib); pap. text ed. 7.50x (ISBN 0-09-036802-9). Humanities.
Smith, J. M. & Holliday, R. The Evolution of Adaptation by Natural Selection. (Royal Society of London Discussion Ser.). 170p. 1980. Repr. text ed. 26.00x (ISBN 0-85403-118-9, Pub. by Royal Soc England). Scholium Intl.
Wallace, Alfred R. Contributions to the Theory of Natural Selection. LC 72-1670. Repr. of 1870 ed. 26.50 (ISBN 0-404-08181-9). AMS Pr.
Wallace, Alfred-Russel. La Selection Naturelle, Essais. Repr. of 1872 ed. 121.00 (ISBN 0-8287-0878-9). Clearwater Pub.
Williams, George C. Adaptation & Natural Selection: A Critique of Some Current Evolutionary Thought. 1966. 22.50x (ISBN 0-691-07900-5); pap. 6.95 (ISBN 0-691-02357-3). Princeton U Pr.
Wilson, D. S. The Natural Selection of Population & Communities. 1980. 16.95 (ISBN 0-8053-9560-1). A-W.
Wilson, David S. The Natural Selection of Populations & Communities. 1979. 12.95 (ISBN 0-8053-9560-1). Benjamin-Cummings.

NATURAL THEOLOGY
see also Analogy (Religion); Creation; Philosophy of Nature; Religion and Science; Teleology; Theodicy
Anderson, James A. Natural Theology: The Metaphysics of God. 1962. 3.95 (ISBN 0-02-810200-2). Glencoe.
Banks, Natalie N. Golden Thread. 1979. pap. 2.75 (ISBN 0-85330-127-1). Lucis.
Bushnell, Horace. Nature & the Supernatural As Together Constituting the One System of God. LC 70-39569. Repr. of 1858 ed. 29.50 (ISBN 0-404-01246-9). AMS Pr.
Currey, Cecil B. Reason & Revelation: John Duns Scotus on Natural Theology. LC 77-9614. (Synthesis Ser.). 1977. pap. 0.65 (ISBN 0-8199-0717-0). Franciscan Herald.
Derham, William. Physico-Theology: A Demonstration of the Being & Attributes of God, from His Works of Creation. Egerton, Frank N., 3rd, ed. LC 77-74212. (History of Ecology Ser.). 1978. Repr. of 1716 ed. lib. bdg. 28.00 (ISBN 0-405-10383-2). Arno.
D'Holbach, Paul T. & Diderot, eds. The System of Nature or, Laws of the Moral & Physical World, 2 Vols. in 1. Robinson, H. D., tr. LC 79-143669. (Research & Source Works Ser.: No. 618). 1971. Repr. of 1836 ed. lib. bdg. 29.50 (ISBN 0-8337-0753-1). B Franklin.
Greene, John C. Darwin & the Modern World View. LC 61-15489. (Rockwell Lectures Ser.). 152p. 1973. pap. text ed. 4.95x (ISBN 0-8071-0062-5). La State U Pr.
Haldane, J. R. With All Thy Mind. 1968. 4.00x (ISBN 0-900391-10-3). Intl Pubns Serv.
Hartshorne, Charles. A Natural Theology for Our Time. LC 66-14722. 145p. 1967. 12.95 (ISBN 0-87548-238-4); pap. 3.95 (ISBN 0-87548-239-2). Open Court.
Holloway, Maurice R. Introduction to Natural Theology. LC 59-6522. 1959. text ed. 14.95x (ISBN 0-89197-244-7). Irvington.
Hume, David. Dialogues Concerning Natural Religion. Smith, Norman K., ed. 1947. pap. 5.95 (ISBN 0-672-60404-3, LLA174). Bobbs.
--Dialogues Concerning Natural Religion. Aiken, Henry D., ed. (Library of Classics Ser: No. 5). pap. text ed. 3.25 (ISBN 0-02-846180-0). Hafner.
--Dialogues Concerning Natural Religion: Text & Critical Essays. Pike, Nelson, ed. LC 77-132933. (Text & Critical Essays Ser). (Orig.). 1970. pap. 6.50 (ISBN 0-672-61119-8, TC6). Bobbs.
--The Natural History of Religion & Dialogues Concerning Natural Religion. Colver, A. Wayne & Price, Vladimir, eds. 1976. 45.00x (ISBN 0-19-824379-0). Oxford U Pr.
--A Treatise of Human Nature, 2 vols. Green, T. H. & Grose, T. H., eds. 1025p. 1981. Repr. of 1898 ed. lib. bdg. 200.00 (ISBN 0-89987-377-4). Darby Bks.
Joyce, George H. Principles of Natural Theology. LC 79-170829. Repr. of 1923 ed. 37.45 (ISBN 0-404-03609-0). AMS Pr.
Klubertanz, George P. & Holloway, Maurice R. Being & God: Introduction to the Philosophy of Being & to Natural Theology. LC 63-15359. 1963. 29.00x (ISBN 0-89197-045-2); pap. text ed. 16.50x (ISBN 0-89197-674-4). Irvington.
LeMahieu, D. L. The Mind of William Paley: A Philosopher & His Age. LC 75-22547. xiv, 215p. 1976. 14.95x (ISBN 0-8032-0865-0). U of Nebr Pr.
Lincoln, Bruce. Priests, Warriors & Cattle: A Study in the Ecology of Religions. LC 78-68826. (Hermeneutics: Studies in the History of Religions). 240p. 1981. 32.50 (ISBN 0-520-03880-0). U of Cal Pr.
McCormick, John F. Natural Theology. 1931. text ed. 2.90 (ISBN 0-8294-0091-5). Loyola.
Mahan, Asa. The Science of Natural Theology. LC 75-3273. Repr. of 1867 ed. 27.50 (ISBN 0-404-59261-9). AMS Pr.
Mather, Cotton. Christian Philosopher: A Collection of the Best Discoveries in Nature, with Religious Improvements. LC 68-29082. 1968. Repr. of 1721 ed. 33.00x (ISBN 0-8201-1033-7). Schol Facsimiles.
Morriss, Frank. Forgotten Revelation. 1964. 2.95 (ISBN 0-8199-0023-0, L38171). Franciscan Herald.
Mueller, Friedrich M. Natural Religion. LC 73-18810. (Gifford Lectures: 1888). Repr. of 1889 ed. 34.50 (ISBN 0-404-11450-4). AMS Pr.
--Physical Religion. LC 73-18811. (Gifford Lectures: 1890). Repr. of 1891 ed. 27.50 (ISBN 0-404-11451-2). AMS Pr.
Ray, John. The Wisdom of God Manifested in the Works of the Creation: Heavenly Bodies, Elements, Meteors, Fossils, Vegetables, Animals. Egerton, Frank N., 3rd, ed. LC 77-74250. (History of Ecology Ser.). 1978. Repr. of 1717 ed. lib. bdg. 30.00x (ISBN 0-405-10419-7). Arno.
Robb, J. Wesley. The Reverent Skeptic. LC 79-83609. 1979. 12.50 (ISBN 0-8022-2245-5). Philos Lib.
Royce, Josiah. World & the Individual, 2 Vols. (Series 1 & series 2). Set. 17.00 (ISBN 0-8446-2842-5). Peter Smith.
Sinnott, Edmund W. Matter, Mind & Man: The Biology of Human Nature. LC 56-13282. 1962. pap. text ed. 2.75x (ISBN 0-689-70182-9, 9). Atheneum.
Smart, Ninian. Yogi & the Devotee: The Interplay Between the Upanishads & Catholic Theology. 1968. text ed. 5.50x (ISBN 0-391-02072-2). Humanities.
Smithline, Arnold. Natural Religion in American Literature. 1966. 6.00 (ISBN 0-8084-0227-7); pap. 2.25 (ISBN 0-8084-0228-5, L19). Coll & U Pr.
Stokes, George G. Natural Theology. LC 77-27232. (Gifford Lectures: 1891). Repr. of 1891 ed. 24.50 (ISBN 0-404-60452-8). AMS Pr.
Taylor, Alfred E. Faith of a Moralist, 2 Vols. in 1. LC 37-23815. (Gifford Lectures 1926-1928). 1968. Repr. of 1937 ed. 34.00 (ISBN 0-527-89062-6). Kraus Repr.
Temple, William. Nature, Man & God. LC 77-27190. (Gifford Lectures: 1932-33, 1933-34). 1979. Repr. of 1935 ed. 40.00 (ISBN 0-404-60493-5). AMS Pr.
Tholen, Gerald. Massism Vs. Natural Religion. 1980. pap. 3.00 (ISBN 0-686-70316-2). Am Atheist.
Tindal, Matthew. Christianity As Old Creation or the Gospel. Wellek, Rene, ed. LC 75-11256. (British Philosophers & Theologians of the 17th & 18th Centuries Ser.). 1978. lib. bdg. 42.00 (ISBN 0-8240-1806-0). Garland Pub.
Torrance, Thomas F. The Ground & Grammar of Theology. LC 79-21429. 1980. 9.95x (ISBN 0-8139-0819-1). U Pr of Va.
Wallace, Robert. Various Prospects of Mankind, Nature & Providence. LC 69-19550. Repr. of 1761 ed. 19.50x (ISBN 0-678-00491-9). Kelley.
Ward, J. Naturalism & Agnosticism: The Gifford Lectures Delivered Before the University of Aberdeen in 1896-1898, 2 Vols. in 1. 4th ed. Repr. of 1899 ed. 30.00 (ISBN 0-527-94500-5). Kraus Repr.
Wilkins, John. Of the Principles & Duties of Natural Religion: Two Books. Repr. of 1693 ed. 31.00 (ISBN 0-384-68500-5). Johnson Repr.
Willey, Basil. Eighteenth Century Background: Studies on the Idea of Nature in the Thought of the Period. LC 40-31307. 1941. 20.00x (ISBN 0-231-01234-9). Columbia U Pr.
--Religion of Nature. LC 76-40105. 1957. lib. bdg. 8.50 (ISBN 0-8414-9506-8). Folcroft.
Wollaston, William. The Religion of Nature Delineated. Wellek, Rene, ed. LC 75-11267. (British Philosophers & Theologians of the 17th & 18th Centuries Ser.). 1978. Repr. of 1722 ed. lib. bdg. 42.00 (ISBN 0-8240-1816-8). Garland Pub.

NATURAL WATER CHEMISTRY
see Water Chemistry

NATURALISM
see also Mechanism (Philosophy)
Adams, Elie M. Ethical Naturalism & the Modern World-View. LC 73-3019. 229p. 1973. Repr. of 1960 ed. lib. bdg. 15.00 (ISBN 0-8371-6820-1, ADEN). Greenwood.
Boller, Paul F., Jr. American Thought in Transition: The Impact of Evolutionary Naturalism, 1865-1900. LC 80-6210. 285p. 1981. lib. bdg. 19.25 (ISBN 0-8191-1550-9); pap. text ed. 10.50 (ISBN 0-8191-1551-7). U Pr of Amer.
Brown, Vinson. The Amateur Naturalists's Handbook. (Illus.). 448p. 1980. 15.95 (ISBN 0-13-023739-6, Spec); pap. 6.95 (ISBN 0-13-023721-3). P-H.
Butler, J. Donald. Four Philosophies & Their Practice in Education & Religion. 3rd ed. 1968. text ed. 22.50 scp (ISBN 0-06-041108-2, HarpC). Har-Row.
Delaney, Cornelius F. Mind & Nature: A Study in the Naturalistic Philosophies of Cohen, Woodbridge & Sellars. LC 70-75150. 1969. 9.95x (ISBN 0-268-00313-0). U of Notre Dame Pr.
Dennes, William R. Some Dilemmas of Naturalism. facs. ed. (Select Bibliographies Reprint Ser). 1960. 12.50 (ISBN 0-8369-5551-X). Arno.
Eames, S. Morris. Pragmatic Naturalism: An Introduction. LC 76-58441. 256p. 1977. pap. 7.95x (ISBN 0-8093-0803-7). S Ill U Pr.
Farber, Marvin. Naturalism & Subjectivism. LC 59-11896. 1959. pap. 11.00 (ISBN 0-87395-036-4). State U NY Pr.
Goodsell, Willystine. Conflict of Naturalism & Humanism. LC 74-176814. (Columbia University. Teachers College. Contributions to Education: No. 33). Repr. of 1910 ed. 17.50 (ISBN 0-404-55033-9). AMS Pr.
Johnson, Glen. Some Ethical Implications of a Naturalistic Philosophy of Education. LC 70-176912. (Columbia University. Teachers College. Contributions to Education: No. 930). Repr. of 1947 ed. 17.50 (ISBN 0-404-55930-1). AMS Pr.
Krikorian, Yervant H., ed. Naturalism & the Human Spirit. LC 44-2760. 397p. 1944. 20.00x (ISBN 0-231-01424-4). Columbia U Pr.
Lamprecht, Sterling P. Metaphysics of Naturalism. LC 67-18049. (Century Philosophy Ser.). 1967. 24.00x (ISBN 0-89197-302-8). Irvington.
Ouden, Bernard D. The Fusion of Naturalism & Humanism. LC 79-5348. 1979. pap. text ed. 9.00 (ISBN 0-8191-0869-3). U Pr of Amer.
Pratt, James B. Naturalism. LC 72-85424. 192p. 1973. Repr. of 1939 ed. 11.00 (ISBN 0-8046-1729-5). Kennikat.
Punzo, V. C. Reflective Naturalism. 1969. 15.95 (ISBN 0-02-397000-6). Macmillan.
Randall, John H. Nature & Historical Experience: Essays in Naturalism & the Theory of History. LC 57-11694. 1958. 22.50x (ISBN 0-231-02161-5); pap. 9.00x (ISBN 0-231-08537-0). Columbia U Pr.
Skutch, Alexander. A Naturalist on a Tropical Farm. (Illus.). 408p. 1981. pap. 7.95 (ISBN 0-520-04149-6, CAL 461). U of Cal Pr.
Stromberg, Roland N., ed. Realism, Naturalism & Symbolism. (Documentary History of Western Civilization Ser). 1968. 15.00 (ISBN 0-8027-2018-8). Walker & Co.
Wallace, James D. Virtues & Vices. LC 77-90912. (Contemporary Philosophy Ser.). 1978. 18.50x (ISBN 0-8014-1142-4). Cornell U Pr.
Warren, W. Preston. Roy Wood Sellars. LC 74-30132. (World Leaders Ser: No. 45). 1975. lib. bdg. 9.95 (ISBN 0-8057-3719-7). Twayne.

NATURALISM IN ART
see also Idealism in Art; Realism in Art; Romanticism in Art
Nochlin, Linda. Realism & Tradition in Art, Eighteen Forty-Eight - Nineteen Hundred: Sources & Documents. (Orig.). 1966. pap. 11.95 ref. ed. (ISBN 0-13-766584-9). P-H.

NATURALISM IN LITERATURE
see also Idealism in Literature; Realism in Literature; Romanticism
Block, Haskell M. Naturalistic Triptych: The Fictive & the Real in Zola, Mann & Dreiser. 1970. pap. text ed. 2.95 (ISBN 0-685-19749-2). Phila Bk Co.
Dircks, Henry. Naturalistic Poetry. 1872. lib. bdg. 20.00 (ISBN 0-8414-2472-1). Folcroft.
Furst, Lillian R. & Skrine, Peter N. Naturalism. (Critical Idiom Ser.). 1971. pap. text ed. 5.50x (ISBN 0-416-65670-6). Methuen Inc.
Madsen, Borge G. Strindberg's Naturalistic Theatre: Its Relation to French Naturalism. LC 73-76919. 192p. 1973. Repr. of 1962 ed. 12.00 (ISBN 0-8462-1729-5). Russell.
Mathur, D. C. Naturalistic Philosophies of Experience. LC 79-117613. 192p. 1971. 12.00 (ISBN 0-87527-052-2). Fireside Bks.
Maurer, Warren R. The Naturalist Image of German Literature: A Study of the German Naturalists - Appraisal of Their Literary Heritage. 269p. 1972. bds. 36.70 (ISBN 3-7705-0726-6). Adler.
Osborne, John. Naturalist Drama in Germany. 185p. 1971. 12.50x (ISBN 0-87471-027-8). Rowman.
Pizer, Donald. Realism & Naturalism in Nineteenth-Century American Literature. LC 75-29942. 176p. 1976. Repr. of 1966 ed. 20.00 (ISBN 0-8462-1794-5). Russell.
Root, Winthrop H. German Criticism of Zola, 1875-1893, with Special Reference to the Rougon-Macquart Cycle & the Roman Experimental. LC 31-32036. (Columbia University. Germanic Studies, Old Ser.: No. 35). Repr. of 1931 ed. 15.00 (ISBN 0-404-50435-3). AMS Pr.
Steinhauer, Harry, ed. Das Deutsche Drama, Vol. 2. 1939. 6.95x (ISBN 0-393-09435-9, NortonC). Norton.
Walcutt, Charles C. American Literary Naturalism, a Divided Stream. LC 73-10584. 332p. 1973. Repr. of 1956 ed. lib. bdg. 20.50 (ISBN 0-8371-7017-6, WALN); pap. 5.95x (ISBN 0-8371-8989-6, WAL). Greenwood.
Walcutt, Charles C., ed. Seven Novelists in the American Naturalist Tradition: An Introduction. LC 74-14209. (Library on American Writers: Vol. 8). 336p. 1974. 13.95x (ISBN 0-8166-0730-3). U of Minn Pr.
Willey, Basil. Eighteenth Century Background: Studies on the Idea of Nature in the Thought of the Period. LC 40-31307. 1941. 20.00x (ISBN 0-231-01234-9). Columbia U Pr.

NATURALISTIC ETHICS
see Ethics, Evolutionary

NATURALISTS
see also Biologists; Botanists; Ecologists; Geologists; Ornithologists; Paleontologists; Scientists; Zoologists
Agassiz, Louis. Louis Agassiz: His Life & Correspondence, 2 vols. LC 72-78637. 1885. Set. 49.00 (ISBN 0-403-01992-3). Somerset Pub.

Aldington, Richard. Four English Portraits: Eighteen Hundred & One to Eighteen Fifty-One. LC 79-51232. (Essay Index in Reprint Ser.). (Illus.). Date not set. Repr. of 1948 ed. 19.75x (ISBN 0-8486-3033-5). Core Collection.
Bartram, John & Bartram, William. John & William Bartram's America: American Naturalists Ser. Cruickshank, Helen G., ed. (Illus.). 10.00 (ISBN 0-8159-5101-9). Devin.
Belt, Thomas. The Naturalist in Nicaragua: A Narraitive of a Residence at the Gold Mines of Chontales; Journeys in the Savannahs & Forests; with Obervations on Animals & Plants in Reference to the Theory of Evolution of Living Forms. 1976. Repr. of 1888 ed. 54.00 (ISBN 0-403-06615-8, Regency). Scholarly.
Berra, Tim M. William Beebe (1877-1962) An Annotated Bibliography. (Illus.). 1977. 19.50 (ISBN 0-208-01608-2, Archon). Shoe String.
Beston, Henry. The Outermost House. 1976. pap. 2.95 (ISBN 0-14-004315-2). Penguin.
Bond, Mary W. To James Bond with Love. LC 80-17134. (Illus.). 224p. 1980. 10.95 (ISBN 0-915010-28-3). Sutter House.
Brooks, Paul. Speaking for Nature: How Our Literary Naturalists Have Shaped America. (Illus.). 288p. 1980. 12.95 (ISBN 0-395-29610-2). HM.
Burton, John. The Naturalist in London. LC 74-78247. (Regional Naturalist). (Illus.). 168p. 5.95 (ISBN 0-7153-6215-1). David & Charles.
Carr, Archie. The Windward Road: Adventures of a Naturalist on Remote Carribean Shores. (Illus.). xxx, 258p. 1980. pap. 6.95 (ISBN 0-8130-0639-2). U Presses Fla.
Channing, William E. Thoreau the Poet-Naturalist: With Memorial Verses. LC 80-2680. Repr. of 1873 ed. 37.50 (ISBN 0-404-19073-1). AMS Pr.
Clodd, Edward. Thomas Henry Huxley. LC 75-30018. Repr. of 1902 ed. 14.50 (ISBN 0-404-14023-8). AMS Pr.
Coan, Eugene. James Graham Cooper: Pioneer Western Naturalist. LC 80-52313. (GEM Books-Historical & Natural History Ser.). (Illus.). 210p. (Orig.). 1981. pap. 11.95 (ISBN 0-89301-071-5). U Pr of Idaho.
Coates, Ruth A. Great American Naturalists. LC 73-21989. (Pull Ahead Bks). Orig. Title: Famous Great American Naturalists. (Illus.). 104p. (gr. 5-10). 1974. PLB 4.95 (ISBN 0-8225-0467-7). Lerner Pubns.
Collett, Rosemary K. My Orphans of the Wild: Rescue & Home Care of Native Wildlife. LC 74-1111. (Illus.). 1974. 9.95 (ISBN 0-397-01021-4). Har-Row.
Colp, Ralph, Jr. To Be an Invalid: The Illnes of Charles Darwin. LC 76-17698. 1977. 17.50 (ISBN 0-226-11401-5). U of Chicago Pr.
Cummings, Jean. They Call Him the Buffalo Doctor. LC 73-147172. 320p. 1980. Repr. of 1971 ed. 7.00 (ISBN 0-8187-0035-1). Harlo Pr.
Cutright, Paul R. Great Naturalists Explore South America. facs. ed. LC 68-8454. (Essay Index Reprint Ser). 1940. 24.00 (ISBN 0-8369-0357-9). Arno.
Cutright, Paul R. & Brodhead, Michael J. Elliott Coues: Naturalist & Frontier Historian. LC 80-12424. (Illus.). 510p. 1981. 28.50 (ISBN 0-252-00802-2). U of Ill Pr.
Darwin, Charles. The Collected Papers of Charles Darwin, Vols. I & II. Barrett, Paul H., ed. LC 76-606. (Illus.). 1977. lib. bdg. 40.00x set (ISBN 0-226-13657-4). U of Chicago Pr.
--The Voyage of Charles Darwin. Ralling, Christopher, ed. LC 79-916. (Illus.). 1980. 12.50 (ISBN 0-8317-9212-4, Mayflower Bks). Smith Pubs.
Dick, John H. Other Edens: The Sketchbook of an Artist-Naturalist. LC 79-67270. (Illus.). 1979. 19.95 (ISBN 0-8159-6412-9). Devin.
Eiseley, Loren. The Night Country. LC 78-162747. (Illus.). 1971. pap. 3.95 (ISBN 0-684-13224-9, SL 412, ScribT). Scribner.
Elman, Robert. First in the Field: America's Pioneering Naturalists. 1979. pap. 5.95 (ISBN 0-442-21565-7). Van Nos Reinhold.
Furnell, Dennis L. The Country Book of the Year. LC 79-56061. (Illus.). 192p. 1980. 22.50 (ISBN 0-7153-7878-3). David & Charles.
Geiser, Samuel W. Naturalists of the Frontier. rev. ed. LC 48-7357. (Illus.). 1948. 5.95 (ISBN 0-87074-059-8). SMU Press.
Gillham, Mary. A Naturalist in New Zealand. Date not set. 14.50 (ISBN 0-392-14176-0, SpS). Sportshelf.
Haines, John. Other Days. (Illus.). 52p. 1981. 40.00x (ISBN 0-915308-29-0); pap. 16.00x (ISBN 0-915308-30-4). Graywolf.
Hanley, Wayne & Massachusetts Audubon Society. Natural History in America: From Mark Catesby to Rachel Carson. LC 76-9704. (Illus.). 1977. 14.95 (ISBN 0-8129-0643-8, Demeter). Times Bks.
Holden, Edith. The Country Diary of an Edwardian Lady. LC 77-71359. (Illus.). 1977. 16.95 (ISBN 0-03-021026-7). HR&W.
Hutchins, Ross E. Trails to Nature's Mysteries: The Life of a Working Materialist. LC 76-50554. (Illus.). (gr. 7 up). 1977. 6.95 (ISBN 0-396-07401-4). Dodd.
Jefferies, Richard. Landscape & Labour. Pearson, John, ed. (Illus.). 1979. text ed. 15.00x (ISBN 0-239-00188-5). Humanities.
Jenkins, Alan C. The Naturalists. (Illus.). 1978. 14.50 (ISBN 0-8317-6330-2, Mayflower Bks). Smith Pubs.
Kastner, Joseph. A Species of Eternity. LC 77-74983. 1977. 15.00 (ISBN 0-394-49033-9). Knopf.
Keynes, Darwin R., ed. The Beagle Record. LC 77-82500. (Illus.). 1979. 79.00 (ISBN 0-521-21822-5). Cambridge U Pr.
LaBastille, Anne. Woodswoman. LC 75-34071. 1976. 10.95 (ISBN 0-525-23715-1); pap. 4.50 (ISBN 0-525-47504-4). Dutton.
Lawrence, Gale. The Beginning Naturalist. LC 79-89171. (Illus.). xii, 209p. (Orig.). 1979. pap. 6.95 (ISBN 0-933050-02-X). New Eng Pr VT.
Leslie, Robert L. Miracle at Square Top Mountain. (Illus.). 1979. 10.95 (ISBN 0-525-15595-3). Dutton.
Miall, L. C. Early Naturalists, Their Lives & Work, 1530-1789. 1969. Repr. of 1912 ed. 19.25 (ISBN 0-02-849220-X). Hafner.
Mitchell, John. The Curious Naturalist. 1980. 15.95 (ISBN 0-13-195412-1, Spec); pap. 9.95 (ISBN 0-13-195404-0, Spec). P-H.
Naturalists' Directory (International) 42nd ed. LC 5-5997. 1975. pap. 7.95 (ISBN 0-686-10195-2). World Natural Hist.
Osborn, Henry F. Cope: Master Naturalist: Life & Letters of Edward Drinker Cope, with a Bibliography of His Writings. LC 77-81135. (Biologists & Their World Ser.). (Illus.). 1978. Repr. of 1931 ed. lib. bdg. 45.00x (ISBN 0-405-10735-8). Arno.
Peterson, Houston. Huxley, Prophet of Science. LC 75-30039. Repr. of 1932 ed. 26.00 (ISBN 0-404-14040-8). AMS Pr.
Pliny. The Elizabethan Zoo. Byrne, M. St. Clare, ed. Holland, Philemon & Topsell, Edward, trs. LC 79-88477. (Illus.). 192p. 1979. 17.50 (ISBN 0-87923-300-1, Nonpareil Bks.); pap. 7.95 (ISBN 0-87923-299-4). Godine.
Poole, Lynn & Poole, Gray. Scientists Who Work Outdoors. LC 63-15473. (Illus.). 1963. 3.50 (ISBN 0-396-04804-8). Dodd.
Raven, Charles E. English Naturalists from Neckam to Ray: A Study of the Making of the Modern World. LC 47-12381. 1968. Repr. of 1947 ed. 22.00 (ISBN 0-527-74100-0). Kraus Repr.
Rudman, Jack. Naturalist. (Career Examination Ser.: C-1379). (Cloth bdg. avail. on request). pap. 8.00 (ISBN 0-8373-1379-1). Natl Learning.
Savage, Henry, Jr. Discovering America, Seventeen Hundred to Eighteen Seventy-Five. Morris, Richard B. & Commager, Henry S., eds. LC 78-20113. (New American Nation Ser.). (Illus.). 1979. 17.95 (ISBN 0-06-013782-7, HarpT). Har-Row.
Seward, Mark, et al, eds. A Handbook for Naturalists. 1981. 15.00x (ISBN 0-09-462390-2, Pub. by Constable Pubs England). State Mutual Bk.
Shapiro, Irwin. Darwin & the Enchanted Isles. LC 77-7544. (Science Discovery Bks.). (Illus.). (gr. 3-6). 1977. PLB 5.99 (ISBN 0-698-30679-1). Coward.
Simpson, Charles T. Out of Doors in Florida: The Adventures of a Naturalist. Repr. of 1923 ed. lib. bdg. 35.00 (ISBN 0-8495-5001-7). Arden Lib.
Smith, Gary. Windsinger. (Illus.). 176p. 1978. pap. 5.95 (ISBN 0-345-25677-8). Ballantine.
Smith, James E. A Selection of the Correspondence of Linnaeus & Other Naturalists: From Original Manuscripts, 2 vols. Sterling, Keir B., ed. LC 77-81132. (Biologists & Their World Ser.). (Illus.). 1978. Repr. of 1821 ed. Set. lib. bdg. 74.00x (ISBN 0-405-10730-7); lib. bdg. 37.00x ea. Vol. 1 (ISBN 0-405-10731-5). Vol. 2 (ISBN 0-405-10732-3). Arno.
Spoehr, Florence M. White Falcon: The House of Godeffroy & Its Commercial & Scientific Role in the Pacific. LC 63-18693. (Illus.). 1963. 7.95 (ISBN 0-87015-119-3). Pacific Bks.
Sterling, Keir B. Last of the Naturalists: The Career of C. Hart Merriam. LC 73-17847. (Natural Sciences in America Ser.). (Illus.). 500p. 1974. Repr. 23.00x (ISBN 0-405-05770-9). Arno.
Stoddard, Herbert L. Memoirs of a Naturalist. LC 69-16713. (Illus.). 303p. (Orig.). 1969. 16.95 (ISBN 0-8061-0857-6); pap. 7.95 (ISBN 0-8061-1167-4). U of Okla Pr.
Swinton, A. Instructions to Young Naturalists: Fossils. 12.50x (ISBN 0-392-03503-0, SpS). Sportshelf.
Van Leeuwenhoek, Antoni. The Collected Letters of Antoni van Leeuwenhoek, 10 vols. Incl. Vol. 1. 454p. 1939; Vol. 2. 506p. 1941 (ISBN 90-265-0041-6); Vol. 3. 560p. 1948; Vol. 4. 383p. 1952 (ISBN 90-265-0043-2); Vol. 5. 457p. 1958 (ISBN 90-265-0044-0); Vol. 6. 425p. 1961 (ISBN 90-265-0045-9); Vol. 7. 427p. 1965 (ISBN 90-265-0046-7); Vol. 8. 383p. 1967 (ISBN 90-265-0047-5); Vol. 9. 482p. 1976 (ISBN 90-265-0220-6); Vol. 10. 362p. 1979 (ISBN 90-265-0285-0). (Illus., Dutch & Eng.). text ed. 105.00 ea. (Pub. by Swets Serv Holland). Swets North Am.
Wayne, Bennett, ed. & commentary by. They Loved the Land. LC 74-915. (Target Bks). (Illus.). 168p. (gr. 5-12). 1974. PLB 7.29 (ISBN 0-8116-4908-3). Garrard.
Weiss, Harry B. & Ziegler, Grace M. Thomas Say: Early American Naturalist. Sterling, Keir B., ed. LC 77-81137. (Biologists & Their World Ser.). (Illus.). 1978. Repr. of 1931 ed. lib. bdg. 18.00x (ISBN 0-405-10737-4). Arno.
White, Gilbert. Gilbert White's Journals. LC 73-105555. 1970. 15.00 (ISBN 0-8008-3263-9). Taplinger.

NATURALISTS–DIRECTORIES
see Scientists–Directories

NATURALIZATION
see also Aliens; Allegiance; Citizenship

Fragomen, Austin T., Jr., ed. Tenth Annual Immigration & Naturalization Institute. LC 79-53161. 1979. text ed. 35.00 (ISBN 0-686-58199-7, H2-2947). PLI.
Franklin, Frank G. Legislative History of Naturalization in the United States from the Revolutionary War to 1861. LC 75-119538. Repr. of 1906 ed. 8.50x (ISBN 0-678-00689-X). Kelley.
--Legislative History of Naturalization in the United States: From the Revolutionary War to 1861. LC 69-18776. (American Immigration Collection Ser., No. 1). 1969. Repr. of 1906 ed. 9.00 (ISBN 0-405-00524-5). Arno.
Kettner, James H. Development of American Citizenship, Sixteen Hundred Eight to Eighteen Seventy. LC 78-954. (Institute of Early American History & Culture Ser.). 1978. 20.00x (ISBN 0-8078-1326-5). U of NC Pr.
Morse, Samuel F. Imminent Dangers to the Free Institutions of the United States Through Foreign Immigration & the Present State of the Naturalization Laws. LC 69-18785. (American Immigration Collection Ser., No. 1). 1969. Repr. of 1835 ed. 7.00 (ISBN 0-405-00533-4). Arno.
Smith, Darrell H. The Bureau of Naturalization: Its History, Activities & Organization. LC 72-3059. (Brookings Institution. Institute for Government Research. Service Monographs of the U.S. Government: No. 43). Repr. of 1926 ed. 16.50 (ISBN 0-404-57143-3). AMS Pr.
Webster, Prentiss. Law of Naturalization in the United States of America & of Other Countries. xx, 403p. 1981. Repr. of 1895 ed. lib. bdg. 32.50x (ISBN 0-8377-1309-9). Rothman.
Wiener, Solomon. Questions & Answers on American Citizenship. new rev. ed. (gr. 9 up). 1970. pap. text ed. 2.75 (ISBN 0-88345-136-0, 17862). Regents Pub.

NATURE
see also Landscape; Man-Influence on Nature

Abraitys, Vincent. The Backyard Wilderness: From the Canadian Maritimes to the Florida Keys. LC 74-80236. (Illus.). 208p. 1975. 10.95 (ISBN 0-914366-02-5). Columbia Pub.
Adams, Richard. Nature Day & Night. (Illus.). 112p. 1980. pap. 7.95 (ISBN 0-14-005345-X). Penguin.
Angier, Bradford. Wilderness Neighbors. LC 76-26303. 228p. 1981. pap. 5.95 (ISBN 0-8128-6100-0). Stein & Day.
Arthur, Elizabeth. Island Sojourn. LC 79-2611. (Illus.). 1980. 9.95 (ISBN 0-06-010156-3, HarpT). Har-Row.
Atkeson, Mira, photos by. The World of Mira Atkeson. LC 77-77012. (Illus.). 120p. (Text by Luella O'Conner). 1977. 19.50 (ISBN 0-912856-36-X). Graphic Arts Ctr.
Bate, John. The Mysterys of Nature & Art: In Foure Tretises. LC 77-6850. (English Experience Ser.: No. 845). 1977. Repr. of 1634 ed. lib. bdg. 20.00 (ISBN 90-221-0845-7). Walter J Johnson.
Bellamy, David. Forces of Life. (Illus.). 1979. 15.95 (ISBN 0-517-53529-7). Crown.
Biese, Alfred. The Development of the Feeling for Nature in the Middle Ages and Modern Times. 1964. Repr. of 1905 ed. 26.50 (ISBN 0-8337-0276-9). B Franklin.
Boker, Dea. Alike - but Unalike. 1974. pap. text ed. 0.50 (ISBN 0-8134-1635-3, 1635). Interstate.
Burton, Maurice. Maurice Burton's Daily Telegraph Nature Book. LC 75-10701. (Illus.). 128p. 1975. 5.95 (ISBN 0-7153-7078-2). David & Charles.
Burton, Robert. Nature by the Roadside. (Countryside Leisure Ser.). (Illus.). 1978. 9.95 (ISBN 0-7158-0471-5). Charles River Bks.
Cannon, Barrie R. & Cannon, George W. Coming into the Light: An Invitation. (Illus.). 1979. pap. 12.95 (ISBN 0-9603020-0-X). Voyager Pubns.
Collingwood, Robin G. Idea of Nature. 1960. pap. 4.95 (ISBN 0-19-500217-2, GB). Oxford U Pr.
Collis, John S. Worm Forgives the Plough. LC 73-92678. (Illus.). 160p. 1975. 7.95 (ISBN 0-8076-0745-2). Braziller.
Commoner, Barry. Closing Circle. 1971. 12.50 (ISBN 0-394-42350-X). Knopf.
Cottrell, Alan. Portrait of Nature. LC 75-837. (Illus.). 1975. pap. 1.95 encore ed. (ISBN 0-684-16370-5, SL725, ScribT). Scribner.
Danforth, Edward J. Song of the White-Throat. LC 77-70657. (Illus.). 1977. pap. 3.00 (ISBN 0-9601174-1-5). E J Danforth.
Dillard, Annie. Pilgrim at Tinker Creek. LC 73-18655. 232p. 1974. 10.00 (ISBN 0-06-121980-0). Har-Row.
--Pilgrim at Tinker Creek. 288p. 1975. pap. 2.95 (ISBN 0-553-13706-9). Bantam.
Economou, George D. The Goddess Natura in Medieval Literature. LC 72-75405. 240p. 1972. 10.00x (ISBN 0-674-35535-0). Harvard U Pr.
Embry, Joan. My Wild World. Date not set. pap. 2.95 (ISBN 0-440-15941-5). Dell.
Emerson, Ralph W. Collected Works of Ralph Waldo Emerson: Nature, Addresses, & Lectures, Vol. 1. Ferguson, Alfred E., et al, eds. 1979. 18.50x (ISBN 0-674-13970-4); pap. 7.95x (ISBN 0-674-60476-8). Harvard U Pr.
Fowles, John. The Tree. 1980. 24.95 (ISBN 0-316-28957-4). Little.
Friends of the Earth. The Last Wildlands 1981. (Orig.). 1980. pap. 5.95 (ISBN 0-671-41216-7, Fireside). S&S.
Gabriel, Richard A. & Cohen, Sylvan H. The Environment: Critical Factors in Strategy Development. LC 73-13651. 1973. 32.50x (ISBN 0-8422-5131-6); pap. text ed. 8.95x (ISBN 0-8422-0355-9). Irvington.
Gardner, Judith K. & Gardner, Howard, eds. Factors Determining Intellectual Attainment: An Original Anthology. LC 74-21406. (Classics in Child Development Ser). 204p. 1975. Repr. 14.00x (ISBN 0-405-06458-6). Arno.
Grant, Allen. Flashlights on Nature: A Popular Account of the Life Histories of Some Familiar Insects, Birds, Plants, Etc. 1978. Repr. of 1898 ed. lib. bdg. 25.00 (ISBN 0-8492-0088-1). R West.
Graves, John. From a Limestone Ledge. LC 80-7641. (Illus.). 256p. 1980. 11.95 (ISBN 0-394-51238-3). Knopf.
Grigoryev, V. & Myakishev, G. Forces of Nature. (Illus.). 346p. 1975. 14.95x (ISBN 0-8464-1099-0). Beekman Pubs.
--The Forces of Nature. 346p. 1971. 4.50 (ISBN 0-8285-0820-8, Pub. by Mir Pubs Russia). Imported Pubns.
Haines, John. Other Days. (Illus.). 52p. 1981. 40.00x (ISBN 0-915308-29-0); pap. 16.00x (ISBN 0-915308-30-4). Graywolf.
Hamerstrom, Frances. Walk When the Moon Is Full. LC 75-33878. (Illus.). 64p. (gr. 3-8). 1975. 6.95 (ISBN 0-912278-69-2); pap. 3.95 (ISBN 0-912278-84-6). Crossing Pr.
Head, W. S. The California Chaparral: An Elfin Forest. LC 75-24239. (gr. 4 up). 1972. 7.50 (ISBN 0-87961-003-4); pap. 3.50 (ISBN 0-87961-002-6). Naturegraph.
Headstrom, Richard. Nature Discoveries with a Hand Lens. (Illus.). 425p. 1981. pap. 6.00 (ISBN 0-486-24077-0). Dover.
Henderson, Lawrence J. Order of Nature. facs. ed. LC 70-150186. (Select Bibliographies Reprint Ser). 1917. 16.00 (ISBN 0-8369-5699-0). Arno.
Henderson, M. A. The Survival Resource Book. (Illus.). 180p. 1981. pap. 8.95 (ISBN 0-312-77951-8). St Martin.
Hillman, Ruth E. Life Along the Fencerow. LC 74-10859. (Illus.). 88p. 1974. 4.95 (ISBN 0-8361-1746-8). Herald Pr.
Janovy, John, Jr. Keith County Journal. LC 78-3986. 1978. 8.95 (ISBN 0-312-45123-7). St Martin.
John The Scot. Periphyseon: On the Division of Nature. Uhlfelder, Myra, ed. & tr. LC 75-16475. (LLA Ser: No. 157). 408p. 1976. pap. 7.95 (ISBN 0-672-60377-2). Bobbs.
Kaufmann, Paul. Paddling the Gate. LC 77-18272. (Illus.). 1978. 6.00 (ISBN 0-87787-007-1). Mara.
Kinkead, Eugene. A Concrete Look at Nature. (Illus.). 242p. 1974. 6.00 (ISBN 0-8129-0471-0). E Kinkead.
--Wildness Is All Around Us. (Illus.). 178p. 1978. 10.00x (ISBN 0-87690-277-8). E Kinkead.
Koenigsberger, Dorothy. Renaissance Man & Creative Thinking: A History of Concepts of Harmony 1400-1700. LC 78-956. 1979. text ed. 27.50x (ISBN 0-391-00851-X). Humanities.
Krutch, Joseph. Twelve Seasons. LC 72-134106. (Essay Index Reprint Ser). 1949. 16.00 (ISBN 0-8369-1970-X). Arno.

Lawrence, Gale. The Beginning Naturalist. LC 79-89171. (Illus.). xii, 209p. (Orig.). 1979. pap. 6.95 (ISBN 0-933050-02-X). New Eng Pr VT.

Life Nature Library, 24 vols. Spanish Version. 12.50 ea.; French Version. 19.95 ea. French & Eur.

The Living World of Nature. 1980. pap. 2.50 (ISBN 0-425-04720-2). Berkley Pub.

Mabie, Hamilton W. Nature & Culture. 1973. lib. bdg. 12.50 (ISBN 0-8414-6380-8). Folcroft.

MacConomy, Alma D., ed. Wildlife's Holiday Album. LC 78-56861. (Illus.). 1978. 11.95 (ISBN 0-912186-27-5). Natl Wildlife.

McKain, David W., ed. Whole Earth: Essays in Appreciation, Anger, & Hope. 384p. 1971. pap. text ed. 6.95 (ISBN 0-312-87045-0). St Martin.

Macmillan. The Wonders of Nature. (Illus.). 240p. 1981. 29.95 (ISBN 0-02-619550-X). Macmillan.

McMillan, Vicky & McMillan, Bill. Nature Quizzes for Canadians. pap. 6.50 (ISBN 0-88894-109-9, Pub. by Douglas & McIntyre). Intl Schol Bk Serv.

Martin, Bill, tr. Little Woodland Books. (10 books & 10 cassettes). 119.00 (ISBN 0-87827-322-0). Ency Brit Ed.

Martin, Bill, Jr. Little Nature Books. Incl. Poppies Afield; Frogs in a Pond; Butterflies Becoming; Germanation; Ants Underground; A Mushroom Is Growing; A Hydro Goes Walking; Moon Cycle; Messenger Bee; June Bugs. (Illus.). (gr. 1-6). 1975. 119.00 (ISBN 0-87827-196-1); tchr's guide incl. (ISBN 0-685-55948-3); recordings incl. Ency Brit Ed.

Marx, Leo. Machine in the Garden: Technology & the Pastoral Ideal in America. (Illus.). 1967. pap. 6.95 (ISBN 0-19-500738-7, GB). Oxford U Pr.

Mason, Frances B. Great Design: Order & Progress in Nature. facsimile ed. LC 72-156690. (Essay Index Reprint Ser). Repr. of 1934 ed. 19.00 (ISBN 0-8369-2562-9). Arno.

Mill, John S. Three Essays on Religion. LC 76-130995. Repr. of 1874 ed. 23.45 (ISBN 0-404-04325-9). AMS Pr.

--Three Essays on Religion. Repr. of 1874 ed. lib. bdg. 16.25x (ISBN 0-8371-1986-3, MIER). Greenwood.

Moon, Jan. Living with Nature in Hawaii. rev. ed. 136p. 1979. pap. 6.50 (ISBN 0-912180-06-4). Petroglyph.

Moore, Leonard. Enciclopedia Juvenil De la Naturaleza. 256p. (Espn.). 1976. 37.50 (ISBN 84-272-5930-1, S-50476). French & Eur.

Mueser, Annie. Bugs, Snakes & Creepy Things. (Pal Paperbacks, - Pal Skills II Ser.). (Illus.). (gr. 5-12). 1980. pap. 1.25 (ISBN 0-8374-6803-5). Xerox Ed Pubns.

Muir, John. Stickeen. 90p. 1981. pap. 3.95 (ISBN 0-930588-05-3). Heyday Bks.

Myers, Jack, ed. Nature's Wonderful Family. (Highlights Handbooks Ser.). (gr. 2-6). 1971. pap. 1.95 (ISBN 0-87534-146-2). Highlights.

Nasr, Seyyed H. Man & Nature. (Mandala Books). 1976. pap. 4.50 (ISBN 0-04-109013-6). Allen Unwin.

Nature Thoughts. 1966. 2.95 (ISBN 0-442-82351-7). Peter Pauper.

Nearing, Helen & Nearing, Scott. The Maple Sugar Book: Together with Remarks on Pioneering As a way of Living in the Twentieth Century. LC 73-148417. (Illus.). 1971. 8.95 (ISBN 0-8052-3400-4); pap. 4.95 (ISBN 0-8052-0308-7). Schocken.

Neilson, Francis. Our Garden: Reflections on Nature. 59.95 (ISBN 0-87700-015-8). Revisionist Pr.

Nicholls, Richard, ed. The Audubon Notebook: An Illustrated Journal with Space for Notes. (Illus.). 96p. (Orig.). 1981. lib. bdg. 12.90 (ISBN 0-89471-149-0); pap. 4.95 (ISBN 0-89471-148-2). Running Pr.

North, Marianne. A Vision of Eden. LC 80-14882. (Illus.). 224p. 1980. 22.95 (ISBN 0-03-057453-6). HR&W.

Nygaard, Anita. Earthclock. 1977. pap. 4.95 (ISBN 0-8065-0567-2). Citadel Pr.

Olson, Sigurd F. Reflections from the North Country. 1976. 10.95 (ISBN 0-394-40265-0). Knopf.

--Sigurd F. Olson's Wilderness Days. (Illus.). 1972. 17.95 (ISBN 0-394-47155-5). Knopf.

Outdoor World Editors. The Beauty of Outdoor World. LC 73-79043. (Illus.). 160p. 1973. 9.95 (ISBN 0-87294-038-1). Country Beautiful.

Pennington, Eunice. Master of the Mountain. 1971. 4.50 (ISBN 0-685-47078-4); pap. 2.50 (ISBN 0-685-47079-2). Pennington.

Prishvin, Mikhail M. Jen Sheng: The Root of Life. Walton, George & Gibbons, Philip, trs. from Rus. LC 72-90307. (Soviet Literature in English Translation Ser). (Illus.). 177p. 1973. Repr. of 1936 ed. 16.50 (ISBN 0-88355-018-0). Hyperion Conn.

Quinn, John R. Nature's World Records. (gr. k-3). 1978. pap. 1.25 (ISBN 0-590-05393-0, Schol Pap). Schol Bk Serv.

Risser, Paul G. & Cornelison, Kathy D. Man & the Biosphere. LC 79-4953. (Illus.). 109p. 1979. pap. 7.95 (ISBN 0-8061-1610-2). U of Okla Pr.

Rood, Ronald. Elephant Bones & Lonelyhearts. LC 77-79291. 1977. 7.95 (ISBN 0-8289-0317-4). Greene.

Russell, Andy. Trails of a Wilderness Wanderer. LC 75-118715. (YA) 1970. 10.95 (ISBN 0-394-44938-X). Knopf.

Russell, Terry & Russell, Renny. On the Loose. LC 79-15243. (Sierra Club Paperback Library). (Illus.). 1979. pap. 6.95 (ISBN 0-87156-264-2). Sierra.

Rusten, Philip. On the Growing Edge. (Illus.). 96p. 1981. 22.00 (ISBN 0-686-29722-9). Way of Seeing.

Rutstrum, Calvin. Greenhorns in the Southwest. LC 79-4936. (Illus.). 1979. pap. 6.95 (ISBN 0-8263-0512-1). U of NM Pr.

Smith, Don I. Sagebrush Seed. LC 77-4347. (Illus.). 1977. 5.95 (ISBN 0-687-36746-8). Abingdon.

Smith, Gary. Windsinger. (Illus.). 176p. 1978. pap. 5.95 (ISBN 0-345-25677-8). Ballantine.

Smithe, Frank B. Naturalist's Color Guide, 2 pts. Incl. Part I. binder 9.00 (ISBN 0-913424-03-X); Part II. pap. 5.00 (ISBN 0-913424-04-8). LC 75-320672. 1975. Am Mus Natl Hist.

Stephens, Wilson, ed. The Third Field Bedside Book. (Illus.). 252p. 1973. 4.95 (ISBN 0-7153-5865-0). David & Charles.

Stevens, Peter S. Patterns in Nature. LC 73-19720. (Illus.). 256p. 1974. 12.50 (ISBN 0-316-81328-1, Pub. by Atlantic Monthly Pr); pap. 6.95 (ISBN 0-316-81331-1). Little.

Stevenson, L. W. The Secret Place. (Illus.). 133p. (Orig.). 1981. lib. bdg. 11.95 (ISBN 0-686-72344-9); pap. 5.95 (ISBN 0-89733-042-0). Academy Chi Ltd.

Sturges, Patricia P. The Endless Chain of Nature: Experiment at Hubbard Brook. LC 76-15962. (Illus.). 1976. 7.95 (ISBN 0-664-32597-1). Westminster.

Sun Bear. At Home in the Wilderness. (Illus.). (gr. 4 up). 1970. pap. 3.50 (ISBN 0-87961-004-2). Naturegraph.

Szczelkun, Stefan A. Survival Scrapbook 2: Food. LC 73-82211. (Illus.). 90p. 1973. pap. 3.45 (ISBN 0-8052-0412-1). Schocken.

Thomson, John A. The System of Animate Nature, 2 vols. LC 77-27212. (Gifford Lectures: 1915-16). Repr. of 1920 ed. Set. 49.50 (ISBN 0-404-60520-6). AMS Pr.

Watkins, William J. Suburban Wilderness. (Illus.). 192p. 1981. 9.95 (ISBN 0-399-12552-3). Putnam.

White, William M., ed. All Nature Is My Bride: Selections from Thoreau. LC 74-27954. (Illus.). 1975. 6.95 (ISBN 0-85699-113-9). Chatham Pr.

Whitehead, Alfred N. Concept of Nature. 32.95 (ISBN 0-521-06787-1); pap. 8.95x (ISBN 0-521-09245-0). Cambridge U Pr.

Wilson, David A. Nature's Pantry. (Illus., Orig.). 1972. pap. 3.00 (ISBN 0-934852-08-1, LH-8). Lorien Hse.

Young, Richard B., et al. Three Studies in the Renaissance: Sidney, Jonson, Milton. LC 69-15695. (Yale Studies in English Ser.: No. 138). 1969. Repr. of 1958 ed. 19.50 (ISBN 0-208-00780-6, Archon). Shoe String.

Zim, Herbert, et al. The Golden Guide Nature Center. (Golden Guide Ser.). 160p. (gr. 7 up). 10.95 (ISBN 0-307-23950-0, Golden Pr). Western Pub.

NATURE-PHILOSOPHY

see Philosophy of Nature

NATURE-POETRY

Burroughs, John. Birds & Poets. 1877. lib. bdg. 15.00 (ISBN 0-8414-2547-7). Folcroft.

--Songs of Nature. 1901. lib. bdg. 15.00 (ISBN 0-8414-1604-4). Folcroft.

Burroughs, John, ed. Songs of Nature. facsimile ed. LC 79-98077. (Granger Index Reprint Ser). 1901. 19.00 (ISBN 0-8369-6070-X). Arno.

Claxton, William J. A Book of Nature Poetry. 1978. Repr. of 1912 ed. lib. bdg. 20.00 (ISBN 0-8495-0767-7). Arden Lib.

Feroe, Paul, ed. Silent Voices: Recent American Poems on Nature. LC 78-54317. 1978. 6.50 (ISBN 0-915408-18-X); pap. 2.95 (ISBN 0-915408-17-1). Ally Pr.

Grover, Edwin O., ed. The Nature Lover's Knapsack. enlarged ed. LC 78-73488. (Granger Poetry Library). 1979. Repr. of 1947 ed. 22.75x (ISBN 0-89609-114-7). Granger Bk.

Johnson, E. D., ed. The Poetry of Earth: A Collection of English Nature Writings. LC 65-23661. 1974. pap. text ed. 4.25x (ISBN 0-689-70514-X, 205). Atheneum.

Lockyer, Joseph N. & Lockyer, Winifred L., eds. Tennyson As a Student & Poet of Nature. LC 70-184233. 1972. Repr. of 1910 ed. 14.50 (ISBN 0-8462-1644-2). Russell.

Lovejoy, Mary I., ed. Nature in Verse. LC 78-73490. (Granger Poetry Library). (Illus.). 1979. Repr. of 1895 ed. 24.50x (ISBN 0-89609-116-3). Granger Bk.

Mizumura, Kazue. Flower Moon Snow: A Book of Haiku. LC 76-41180. (Illus.). (gr. k-4). 1977. 7.95 (ISBN 0-690-01291-8, TYC-J); PLB 7.89 (ISBN 0-690-01290-X). Har-Row.

Peake, Charles, ed. Poetry of the Landscape & the Night: Two Eighteenth-Century Traditions. LC 79-116474. (English Library). (Orig.). 1970. pap. 3.95x (ISBN 0-87249-161-7). U of SC Pr.

Reynolds, Myra. The Treatment of Nature in English Poetry Between Pope & Wordsworth. 2nd ed. LC 76-170847. (Ces 3: No. 3). Repr. of 1909 ed. 27.50 (ISBN 0-404-50263-6). AMS Pr.

Van Dyke, Henry. The Poetry of Nature. 1909. Repr. 20.00 (ISBN 0-8274-3176-7). R West.

NATURE-RELIGIOUS INTERPRETATIONS

Beers, Gil. Cats & Bats & Things Like That. 32p. (gr. 1-3). 1972. 4.95 (ISBN 0-8024-1211-4). Moody.

Belgum, Harold J. Family Vacation Idea Book. LC 66-21173. (Orig.). 1966. pap. 2.50 (ISBN 0-570-03063-3, 6-1116). Concordia.

Dannen, Kent. Listen to the Sparrow's Song. LC 79-10169. (God Speaks Today Ser.: No. 1). (Illus.). 1979. pap. 3.00 (ISBN 0-8272-2116-9). Bethany Pr.

Glacken, Clarence J. Traces on the Rhodian Shore: Nature & Culture in Western Thought from Ancient Times to the End of the Eighteenth Century. LC 67-10970. 1967. pap. 12.95x (ISBN 0-520-03216-0, CAMPUS 170). U of Cal Pr.

Gray, Wm. G. The Simplified Guide to the Holy Tree of Life. White, Nelson H., ed. (Illus.). 63p. (Orig.). 1973. pap. 4.00 (ISBN 0-939856-01-8, Magick Circle). Tech Group.

Hendry, George S. Theology of Nature. LC 79-27375. 1980. pap. 12.95 (ISBN 0-664-24305-3). Westminster.

Nature - the Mirror of God. (Franciscan Educational Conferences Ser). 1955. pap. 3.50 (ISBN 0-685-77540-2). Franciscan Herald.

Robertson, Josephine. Garden Meditations. LC 77-23316. (Illus.). 1977. 5.95 (ISBN 0-687-14000-5). Abingdon.

Schaeffer, Francis. Pollution & the Death of Man. pap. 2.95 (ISBN 0-8423-4840-9). Tyndale.

Schofield, Joseph A., Jr. Object Lessons from Nature. (Object Lessons Ser.). 1971. pap. 2.50 (ISBN 0-8010-8016-9). Baker Bk.

Shewell-Cooper, W. E. Plants, Flowers & Herbs of the Bible. LC 76-58772. (Illus.). 180p. 1977. 7.95 (ISBN 0-87983-166-9); pap. 3.95 (ISBN 0-87983-147-2). Keats.

Walker, Raymond B. Beside Still Waters. LC 75-32601. (Illus.). 1975. 12.50 (ISBN 0-8323-0264-3). Binford.

Wollaston, William. The Religion of Nature Delineated, 1724 & Related Commentaries. LC 74-1469. 1974. 33.00x (ISBN 0-8201-1127-9). Schol Facsimiles.

NATURE-STORIES

see Nature Stories

NATURE (ESTHETICS)

see also Landscape

Anesaki, Masaharu. Art, Life & Nature in Japan. LC 77-109705. (Illus.). 1971. Repr. of 1933 ed. lib. bdg. 15.00 (ISBN 0-8371-4196-6, ANNJ). Greenwood.

Avebury. The Dread & the Love of Nature. (Illus.). 1980. Repr. of 1909 ed. deluxe ed. 30.75 deluxe binding (ISBN 0-89901-012-1). Found Class Reprints.

The Beautiful Naturecraft Book. (Illus.). 1979. 16.95 (ISBN 0-8069-5388-8); lib. bdg. 13.99 (ISBN 0-8069-5389-6). Sterling.

Behrens, Roy R. Art & Camouflage: Concealment & Deception in Nature, Art & War. (Orig.). 1981. pap. 10.95 (ISBN 0-915996-07-3). North Am Rev.

Brandt, Bill & Haworth-Booth, Mark, eds. The Land: Twentieth Century Landscape Photographs. LC 75-30640. 1976. 15.00 (ISBN 0-306-70753-5); pap. 7.95 (ISBN 0-306-80026-8). Da Capo.

Buchanan, Handasyde. Nature into Art: A Treasury of Great Natural History Books. LC 79-12481. (Illus.). 1980. 25.00 (ISBN 0-8317-6337-X, Mayflower Bks). Smith Pubs.

Carli, Enzo. The Landscape in Art: From Three Thousand B.C. to Today. Cinotti, Mia, ed. Fitton, Mary, tr. from Ital. LC 80-81667. Orig. Title: Il Paesaggio. (Illus.). 320p. 1980. 35.00 (ISBN 0-688-03678-3). Morrow.

D'Arbeloff, Natalie. Designing with Natural Forms. LC 72-6451. (Illus.). 150p. 1973. 10.95 (ISBN 0-8230-1318-9). Watson-Guptill.

Day, Lewis F. Nature & Ornament: Nature the Raw Material of Design. LC 74-137355. (Illus.). 1971. Repr. of 1930 ed. 22.00 (ISBN 0-8103-3328-7). Gale.

--Nature in Ornament. LC 70-159852. (Illus.). 1971. Repr. of 1898 ed. 22.00 (ISBN 0-8103-3207-8). Gale.

--Nature in Ornament. LC 76-17768. (Aesthetic Movement Ser.: Vol. 23). (Illus.). 1977. Repr. of 1892 ed. lib. bdg. 44.00 (ISBN 0-8240-2472-9). Garland Pub.

Dendel, Esther W. Designing from Nature: A Source Book for Artists & Craftsmen. LC 77-92756. 1978. 10.95 (ISBN 0-8008-2173-4); pap. 5.95 (ISBN 0-8008-2174-2). Taplinger.

Fairclough, Henry R. Love of Nature Among the Greeks & Romans. LC 63-10298. (Our Debt to Greece & Rome Ser). (Illus.). Repr. of 1930 ed. 7.50x (ISBN 0-8154-0063-2). Cooper Sq.

Fielding, Newton. How to Sketch from Nature. (Illus.). 1980. deluxe ed. 36.45 (ISBN 0-930582-66-7). Gloucester Art.

The Germ, 4 nos. in 1 vol. LC 78-88238. Repr. of 1901 ed. 12.50 (ISBN 0-404-08897-X). AMS Pr.

Haeckel, Ernst. Art Forms in Nature. (Illus.). 112p. 1974. pap. 5.00 (ISBN 0-486-22987-4). Dover.

--Art Forms in Nature. (Illus.). 10.00 (ISBN 0-8446-5043-9). Peter Smith.

Knoepflmacher, U. C. & Tennyson, G. B., eds. Nature & the Victorian Imagination. LC 76-7761. 1978. 27.50 (ISBN 0-520-03229-2). U of Cal Pr.

Manwaring, Elizabeth W. Italian Landscape in Eighteenth Century England. LC 66-10419. (Illus.). 1965. Repr. of 1925 ed. 10.00 (ISBN 0-8462-0705-2). Russell.

Manwaring, Elizabeth Wheeler. Italian Landscape in Eighteenth Century England. (Illus.). 243p. 1965. Repr. 25.00x (ISBN 0-7146-2069-6, F Cass Co). Biblio Dist.

Pearce, Peter. Structure in Nature Is a Strategy for Design. LC 77-26866. 1978. 45.00x (ISBN 0-262-16064-1); pap. 12.50 (ISBN 0-262-66045-8). MIT Pr.

Peterson, Willis. Glory of Nature's Form. Shangle, Robert D., ed. LC 79-12418. (Illus.). 160p. 1979. 27.50 (ISBN 0-89802-001-8). Beautiful Am.

Steadman, P. The Evolution of Designs. LC 78-18255. (Cambridge Urban & Architectural Studies: No. 5). 32.50 (ISBN 0-521-22302-4). Cambridge U Pr.

Tunnard, Christopher. A World with a View: An Inquiry into the Nature of Scenic Values. LC 77-13729. (Illus.). 1978. 19.50x (ISBN 0-300-02157-7). Yale U Pr.

Westmorland Gazette, ed. Welsh Mountain Drawings. 1981. 40.00x (ISBN 0-686-75521-9, Pub. by Westmorland Gazette). State Mutual Bk.

NATURE (IN RELIGION, FOLK-LORE, ETC.)

see also Animal Lore; Geographical Myths; Nature Worship; Plant Lore; Weather Lore

Glacken, Clarence J. Traces on the Rhodian Shore: Nature & Culture in Western Thought from Ancient Times to the End of the Eighteenth Century. LC 67-10970. 1967. pap. 12.95x (ISBN 0-520-03216-0, CAMPUS 170). U of Cal Pr.

NATURE, EFFECT OF MAN ON

see Man-Influence on Nature

NATURE, HEALING POWER OF

see also Naturopathy

Neuburger, Max. The Doctrine of the Healing Power of Nature: Through the Course of Time. Boyd, Linn J., tr. (Historia Medicinae). Repr. of 1932 ed. lib. bdg. 15.00x (ISBN 0-87991-710-5). Porcupine Pr.

NATURE, LAW OF

see Natural Law

NATURE, PHILOSOPHY OF

see Philosophy of Nature

NATURE, UNIFORMITY OF

see Uniformity of Nature

NATURE CONSERVATION

see also Natural Monuments; Wildlife Conservation

Arbib, Robert S., Jr. Lord's Woods. LC 73-139373. 1971. 6.95 (ISBN 0-393-08639-9). Norton.

Baldwin, D. N. The Quiet Revolution. LC 72-90480. 1973. 9.95 (ISBN 0-87108-062-1). Pruett.

Bertram, G. L. Conservation of Sirenia: Current Status & Perspectives for Action. 1974. pap. 7.50x (ISBN 2-88032-023-2, IUCN35, IUCN). Unipub.

Blake, Peter. God's Own Junkyard. LC 63-22178. (Illus.). 1979. 12.95 (ISBN 0-03-047431-0); pap. 5.95 (ISBN 0-03-047436-1). HR&W.

Brazee, Edward, ed. Index to the Sierra Club Bulletin, 1950-1976. (Bibliographic Ser.: No. 16). 1978. pap. 5.00 (ISBN 0-87071-136-9). Oreg St U Pr.

Bryant, Jeannette, ed. Conservation Directory. 1979. 4.00 (ISBN 0-912186-28-3). Natl Wildlife.

Clark, John. Rookery Bay: Ecological Constraints on Coastal Development. (Illus.). 91p. 1975. pap. 7.50 (ISBN 0-89164-019-3). Conservation Foun.

Cohen, Stan. The Tree Army: A Pictorial History of the Civilian Conservation Corps 1933-1943. LC 80-81071. 172p. 1980. 11.95 (ISBN 0-933126-11-5); pap. 7.95 (ISBN 0-933126-10-7). Pictorial Hist.

Conference Internationale Sur la Conservation De la Nature & De Ses Ressources a Madagascar. (Illus.). 1972. pap. 15.00x (ISBN 2-88032-046-1, IUCN32, IUCN). Unipub.
Curry-Lindahl, Kai. Conservation for Survival: An Ecological Strategy. 1972. 7.95 (ISBN 0-688-00018-5). Morrow.
Dennis, Eve. Everyman's Nature Reserve: Ideas for Action. (Illus.). 256p. 1973. 7.50 (ISBN 0-7153-5918-5). David & Charles.
The Easement As a Conservation Technique: (EPLP 1) 1972. pap. 7.50x (ISBN 2-88032-071-2, IUCN18, IUCN). Unipub.
Ehrenfeld, David. Conserving Life on Earth. (Illus.). 325p. 1972. 16.95 (ISBN 0-19-501598-3). Oxford U Pr.
Ermentrout, Robert A. Forgotten Men: The Civilian Conservation Corps. 112p. 1981. 6.50 (ISBN 0-682-49805-X). Exposition.
Frankel, O. H. & Soule, M. E. Conservation & Evolution. LC 80-40528. (Illus.). 300p. 1981. 49.50 (ISBN 0-521-23275-9); pap. 17.95 (ISBN 0-521-29889-X). Cambridge U Pr.
Gifford, John C. On Preserving Tropical Florida. LC 78-126196. (Illus.). 1972. 9.95 (ISBN 0-916224-21-X). Banyan Bks.
Gunter, A. Y. Big Thicket: A Challenge for Conservation. LC 73-184310. 1972. 14.95 (ISBN 0-8363-0120-X); pap. 8.50 (ISBN 0-685-02984-0). Jenkins.
Harrison, Jeffery & Grant, Peter. The Thames Transformed: London's River & Its Waterflow. (Illus.). 1977. 15.00 (ISBN 0-233-96840-7). Transatlantic.
Huth, Hans. Nature & the American: Three Centuries of Changing Attitudes. LC 57-12393. (Illus.). xvii, 250p. 1972. 15.95x (ISBN 0-8032-0926-6); pap. 7.50x (ISBN 0-8032-5761-9, BB 554, Bison). U of Nebr Pr.
International Convention for the Protection of New Varieties of Plants & Additional Act. 1976. pap. 3.00x (ISBN 0-686-53008-X, WIPO20, WIPO). Unipub.
Krutilla, John V., ed. Natural Environments: Studies in Theoretical & Applied Analysis. LC 72-4441. (Resources for the Future Ser.). 360p. 1973. 20.00x (ISBN 0-8018-1446-4). Johns Hopkins.
Leopold, Aldo. Sand County Almanac Illustrated. new ed. LC 77-22656. 1977. 25.00 (ISBN 0-915024-15-2). Tamarack Pr.
May, Allan. A Voice in the Wilderness. LC 77-28519. (Illus.). 1978. 14.95x (ISBN 0-88229-309-5); pap. 7.95 (ISBN 0-88229-605-1). Nelson-Hall.
Muir, John. A Rival of the Yosemite: The Canon of the South Fork of King's River, California. Jones, William R., ed. (Illus.). 24p. 1977. Repr. of 1891 ed. pap. 2.00 (ISBN 0-89646-010-X). Outbooks.
Myers, Phyllis. Slow Start in Paradise. 34p. 1974. pap. 1.50 (ISBN 0-89164-015-0). Conservation Foun.
Parker, Bruce C., ed. Conservation Problems in Antarctica. LC 72-85836. 1972. 20.00x (ISBN 0-8139-0840-X). U Pr of Va.
Proposals for Nature Conservation in Northern Greece. (Illus.). 1971. pap. 7.50x (ISBN 2-88032-052-6, IUCN42, IUCN). Unipub.
Propositions Pour la Creation du Parc National Ivoirien De Tai. (Illus.). 1973. pap. 7.50x (ISBN 2-88032-041-0, IUCN58, IUCN). Unipub.
Ratcliffe, D. A., ed. A Nature Conservation, 2 vols. Incl. Vol. 1. 115.00 (ISBN 0-521-21159-X); Vol. 2. 90.00 (ISBN 0-521-21403-3). LC 76-11065. (Illus.). 1977. Cambridge U Pr.
Reiger, John F. American Sportsmen & the Origins of Conservation. (Illus.). 352p. 1975. 11.95 (ISBN 0-87691-173-4). Winchester Pr.
Stermer, Dugald. Vanishing Creatures: A Series of Portraits. (Illus.). 80p. 1980. 15.95 (ISBN 0-89581-019-0); pap. 8.95 (ISBN 0-89581-021-2). Lancaster-Miller.
Usher, M. Biological Management & Conservation. LC 72-6457. 394p. 1973. text ed. 29.95x (ISBN 0-412-11330-9, Pub. by Chapman & Hall England). Methuen Inc.
Weston, Harold. Freedom in the Wilds: A Saga of the Adirondacks. LC 79-160118. (Illus.). 232p. 1972. 9.95 (ISBN 0-9600450-0-7); pap. 4.95 (ISBN 0-685-25194-2). Adirondack Trail.

NATURE IN ART
see Nature (Esthetics)

NATURE IN LITERATURE
see also Birds in Literature; Mountains in Literature; Pastoral Poetry; Sea in Literature
Alcorn, John. The Nature Novel from Hardy to Lawrence. LC 76-17552. 139p. 1977. 16.00x (ISBN 0-231-04122-5). Columbia U Pr.
Andersson, Theodore M. Early Epic Scenery: Homer, Virgil, & the Medieval Legacy. LC 76-12593. 1976. 19.50x (ISBN 0-8014-1013-4). Cornell U Pr.
Batt, Max. The Treatment of Nature in German Literature from Guenther to Goethe's Werner. 1976. lib. bdg. 59.95 (ISBN 0-8490-2764-0). Gordon Pr.
--Treatment of Nature in German Literature from Gunther to the Appearance of Goethe's Werther. LC 72-91034. 1969. Repr. of 1902 ed. 9.50 (ISBN 0-8046-0644-7). Kennikat.
Berndt, Elsa. Dame Nature in der Englishen Literatur. (Ger). Repr. of 1923 ed. 14.00 (ISBN 0-384-04033-0); pap. 11.00 (ISBN 0-685-02221-8). Johnson Repr.
Biese, Alfred. The Development of the Feeling for Nature in the Middle Ages and Modern Times. 1964. Repr. of 1905 ed. 26.50 (ISBN 0-8337-0276-9). B Franklin.
Blunden, Edmund. Nature in English Literature. LC 74-113330. 1970. Repr. of 1929 ed. 10.00 (ISBN 0-8046-0941-1). Kennikat.
Brentano, Sr. Mary B. Nature in the Works of Fray Luis De Granada. LC 75-94164. (Catholic University. Studies in Romance Languages & Literatures: No. 15). Repr. of 1936 ed. 16.50 (ISBN 0-404-50315-2). AMS Pr.
Bryan, John T. The Interpretation of Nature in English Poetry. LC 72-194748. 1973. Repr. of 1932 ed. lib. bdg. 25.00 (ISBN 0-8414-2514-0). Folcroft.
Danton, George H. Nature Sense in the Writings of Ludwig Tieck. LC 78-163673. (Columbia University. Germanic Studies, Old Ser.: No. 9). Repr. of 1907 ed. 15.00 (ISBN 0-404-50409-4). AMS Pr.
Drabble, Margaret. A Writer's Britain: Landscape in Literature. LC 79-2117. (Illus.). 1979. 22.50 (ISBN 0-394-50819-X). Knopf.
Edgar, Pelham. Study of Shelley. LC 70-116792. (Studies in Shelley, No. 25). 1970. Repr. of 1899 ed. lib. bdg. 29.95 (ISBN 0-8383-1034-6). Haskell.
Fairclough, Henry R. Love of Nature Among the Greeks & Romans. LC 63-10298. (Our Debt to Greece & Rome Ser). (Illus.). Repr. of 1930 ed. 7.50x (ISBN 0-8154-0063-2). Cooper Sq.
Fardwell, Francis V. Landscape in the Works of Marcel Proust. LC 76-168004. (Catholic University of America. Studies in Romance Languages & Literatures: No. 35). Repr. of 1948 ed. 22.00 (ISBN 0-404-50335-7). AMS Pr.
Foerster, Norman. Nature in American Literature. LC 58-12864. 1958. Repr. of 1923 ed. 13.00 (ISBN 0-8462-0184-4). Russell.
Friedman, Clarence W. Prefigurations in Meistergesang. LC 75-140020. (Catholic University of America Studies in German Ser.: No. 18). Repr. of 1943 ed. 17.00 (ISBN 0-404-50238-5). AMS Pr.
Geikie, Archibald. Types of Scenery & Their Influence on Literature. LC 72-113335. 1970. Repr. of 1898 ed. 9.50 (ISBN 0-8046-0954-3). Kennikat.
The Germ, 4 nos. in 1 vol. LC 78-88238. Repr. of 1901 ed. 12.50 (ISBN 0-404-08897-X). AMS Pr.
Graham, P. Anderson. Nature in Books. 1891. Repr. 25.00 (ISBN 0-8274-3014-0). R West.
Hargrove, Nancy D. Landscape As Symbol in the Poetry of T. S. Eliot. LC 78-9270. (Illus.). 1978. 15.00x (ISBN 0-87805-077-9). U Pr of Miss.
Hornaday, Clifford L. Nature in the German Novel of the Late Eighteenth Century. LC 40-31490. (Columbia University. Germanic Studies, New Ser.: No. 10). Repr. of 1940 ed. 19.00 (ISBN 0-404-50460-4). AMS Pr.
Huscher, Herbert. Ueber Eigenart und Ursprung Des Englischen Naturgefuehls. 1967. Repr. of 1929 ed. pap. 6.00 (ISBN 0-384-25040-8). Johnson Repr.
Hutman, Norma L. Machado: A Dialogue with Time: Nature As an Expression of Temporality in the Poetry of Antonio Machado. LC 70-78554. 207p. 1969. text ed. 21.50x (ISBN 0-8290-0186-7). Irvington.
Kline, Marcia. Beyond the Land Itself: Views of Nature in Canada & the United States. LC 77-114407. (Essays in History & Literature). 1970. pap. 2.00x (ISBN 0-674-06915-3). Harvard U Pr.
Knoepflmacher, U. C. & Tennyson, G. B., eds. Nature & the Victorian Imagination. LC 76-7761. 1978. 27.50 (ISBN 0-520-03229-2). U of Cal Pr.
Kuse, James A. The Beauty of Winter. (Illus.). 1979. pap. 4.95 (ISBN 0-89542-073-2). Ideals.
Leach, Eleanor W. Vergil's Eclogues: Landscapes of Experience. LC 73-17699. 288p. 1974. 22.50x (ISBN 0-8014-0820-2). Cornell U Pr.
Lovell, Ernest J., Jr. Byron: The Record of a Quest, Studies in a Poet's Concept & Treatment of Nature. 1966. Repr. of 1949 ed. 19.50 (ISBN 0-208-00251-0, Archon). Shoe String.
Miles, Josephine. Pathetic Fallacy in the Nineteenth Century. 1965. lib. bdg. 14.00x (ISBN 0-374-95662-6). Octagon.
Moore, John C. Country Men. facs. ed. LC 69-17585. (Essay Index Reprint Ser). 1935. 16.00 (ISBN 0-8369-0088-X). Arno.
Palgrave, F. T. Landscape in Poetry from Homer to Tennyson. 59.95 (ISBN 0-8490-0484-5). Gordon Pr.
Palgrave, Francis T. Landscape in Poetry from Homer to Tennyson. LC 76-40039. 1897. lib. bdg. 15.00 (ISBN 0-8414-6768-4). Folcroft.
Reynolds, Myra. Treatment of Nature in English Poetry Between Pope & Wordsworth. LC 66-29468. 1966. Repr. of 1909 ed. 8.50 (ISBN 0-87752-091-7). Gordian.
--The Treatment of Nature in English Poetry Between Pope & Wordsworth. 2nd ed. LC 76-170847. (Ces 3: No. 3). Repr. of 1909 ed. 27.50 (ISBN 0-404-50263-6). AMS Pr.
Rice, Richard A. Rousseau & the Poetry of Nature in Eighteenth Century France. LC 74-9920. 1925. 10.00 (ISBN 0-8414-7313-7). Folcroft.
Roper, Alan. Arnold's Poetic Landscapes. LC 70-86097. (Illus.). 268p. 1969. 17.00x (ISBN 0-8018-1050-7). Johns Hopkins.
Sandford, John. Landscape & Landscape Imagery in R. M. Rilke. 40.00x (ISBN 0-85457-096-9, Pub. by Inst Germanic Stud England). State Mutual Bk.
Shairp, J. C. Poetic Interpretation of Nature. LC 72-187951. 1878. lib. bdg. 13.50 (ISBN 0-8414-0570-0). Folcroft.
Soutar, George. Nature in Greek Poetry, Studies Partly Comparative. Repr. of 1939 ed. 23.00 (ISBN 0-384-56750-9). Johnson Repr.
Strong, Archibald T. Three Studies in Shelley & an Essay on Nature in Wordsworth & Meredith. 1968. Repr. of 1921 ed. 16.50 (ISBN 0-208-00665-6, Archon). Shoe String.
Tichi, Cecelia. New World, New Earth. LC 78-15809. 1979. 20.00x (ISBN 0-300-02287-5). Yale U Pr.
Turner, James G. The Politics of Landscape: Rural Scenery & Society in English Poetry, 1630-1660. LC 78-11027. (Illus.). 1979. text ed. 14.50 (ISBN 0-674-68930-5). Harvard U Pr.
Wagman, Frederick H. Magic & Natural Science in German Baroque Literature. LC 42-9041. (Coulmbia University. Germanic Studies, New Ser.: No. 13). Repr. of 1942 ed. 19.00 (ISBN 0-404-50463-9). AMS Pr.
Woods, M. J. The Poet & the Natural World in the Age of Gongora. (Modern Languages & Literature Monographs). 1978. 37.50x (ISBN 0-19-815533-6). Oxford U Pr.

NATURE IN MUSIC
see Program Music

NATURE IN ORNAMENT
see Decoration and Ornament; Design, Decorative-Animal Forms; Design, Decorative-Plant Forms

NATURE IN POETRY
see Nature in Literature

NATURE PHOTOGRAPHY
see also Photography of Animals; Photography of Birds; Photography of Insects; Photography of Plants
Allen, Rodney F., et al, eds. The Work of Thy Hands. LC 72-95647. (Illus.). 89p. (Orig.). 1973. pap. 3.25 (ISBN 0-88489-051-1). St Marys.
Angel, Heather. Nature Photography: Its Art & Techniques. (Illus.). 222p. 1972. 22.50x (ISBN 0-85242-670-4). Intl Pubns Serv.
Bauer, Erwin A. Outdoor Photography. 2nd rev. ed. (Illus.). 1980. 12.95 (ISBN 0-525-93094-9); pap. 4.95 (ISBN 0-525-93081-7). Dutton.
Bennett, Edna. Nature Photography Simplified. (Illus.). 96p. 1975. pap. 4.95 (ISBN 0-8174-0184-9); Spanish Ed. pap. 6.95 (ISBN 0-8174-0312-4). Amphoto.
Blaker, Alfred A. Field Photography: Beginning & Advanced Techniques. LC 75-33382. (Illus.). 1976. text ed. 26.95x (ISBN 0-7167-0518-4); field supplement incl. W H Freeman.
Brodatz, Phil. Land, Sea & Sky: A Photographic Album for Artists & Designers. 7.50 (ISBN 0-8446-5453-1). Peter Smith.
Cahn, Robert. American Photographers & the National Parks. Ketchum, Robert, ed. LC 81-918. (Illus.). 180p. 1981. slipcased 75.00 (ISBN 0-670-41778-5, Studio). Viking Pr.
Emerson, Peter H. Naturalistic Photography for Students of the Art. LC 72-9195. (The Literature of Photography Ser.). Repr. of 1889 ed. 17.00 (ISBN 0-405-04905-6). Arno.
--Naturalistic Photography for Students of the Art. 3rd ed. Incl. The Death of Naturalistic Photography. LC 72-9197. (The Literature of Photography Ser.). 16.00 (ISBN 0-405-04906-4); pap. 4.95 (ISBN 0-685-32644-6). Arno.
Feininger, Andreas. The Anatomy of Nature. (Illus.). 1979. pap. 7.95 (ISBN 0-486-23840-7). Dover.
--Nature Close Up: A Fantastic Journey into Reality. rev. ed. (Illus.). 160p. 1981. pap. 8.95 (ISBN 0-486-24102-5). Dover.
Freeman, Michael. The Complete Book of Wildlife & Nature Photography. (Illus.). 1981. 24.95 (ISBN 0-671-41255-8). S&S.
Gilpin, Arthur. Nature Photography. (Countryside Leisure Ser.). (Illus.). 1978. 9.95 (ISBN 0-7158-0614-9). Charles River Bks.
Guggisberg, C. A. Early Wildlife Photographers. LC 76-54404. (Illus.). 1977. 9.95 (ISBN 0-8008-2352-4). Taplinger.
Guyler, Vivan V. Design in Nature. LC 76-93119. (gr. 9-12). 1970. 12.95 (ISBN 0-87192-031-X). Davis Mass.
Hoban, Tana. Look Again. LC 72-127469. (Illus.). (gr. k-2). 1971. 8.95 (ISBN 0-02-744050-8). Macmillan.
Holmarau, Ingmar. Nature Photography. 1981. pap. 9.95 (ISBN 0-87165-109-2). Ziff-Davis Pub.
Holzman, Richard W. Impact of Nature Photography. (Illus.). 1979. 17.95 (ISBN 0-8174-2476-8); pap. 9.95 (ISBN 0-8174-2147-5). Amphoto.
Hopkins, Lee B., ed. To Look at Any Thing. LC 77-88962. (Illus.). (gr. 1 up). 1978. 6.95 (ISBN 0-15-289083-1, HJ). HarBraceJ.
Kaufman, Kenneth. Of Trees, Leaves, & Ponds: Studies in Photo-Impressionism. 64p. 1981. 20.75 (ISBN 0-525-93210-0); pap. 11.50 (ISBN 0-525-47678-4). Dutton.
Kinne, Russ. The Complete Book of Nature Photography. 3rd ed. (Illus.). 1979. 15.95 (ISBN 0-8174-2470-9). Amphoto.
Macmillan. The Wonders of Nature. (Illus.). 240p. 1981. 29.95 (ISBN 0-02-619550-X). Macmillan.
Marchington, John. Your Book of Photographing Wild Life. (gr. 7 up). 1973. 4.95 (ISBN 0-571-09601-8). Transatlantic.
Marshall, Alexandra. Still Waters: The Life of a Pond. LC 78-18723. (Illus.). 14.95 (ISBN 0-688-03342-3). Morrow.
Maye, Patricia. Fieldbook of Nature Photography. LC 73-86880. (Totebook Ser.). (Illus.). 210p. 1974. pap. 7.95 (ISBN 0-87156-085-2). Sierra.
Moon, G. J. Photographing Nature. LC 70-118605. (Illus.). (gr. 9 up). 1970. 10.00 (ISBN 0-8048-0921-6). C E Tuttle.
Norton, Boyd. Wilderness Photography. (Illus.). pap. 6.95 (ISBN 0-88349-115-X). Readers Digest Pr.
Nuridsany, C. & Perrennou, M. Photographing Nature: From the Magnifying Glass to the Microscope. Steward, J. W., tr. LC 76-9256. (Illus.). 1976. 27.50 (ISBN 0-19-519885-9). Oxford U Pr.
Osolinski, Stanley. Nature Photography: A Guide to Better Outdoor Pictures. (Illus.). 192p. 1981. 29.95 (ISBN 0-13-610428-2); pap. 14.95 (ISBN 0-13-610410-X). P-H.
Peterson, Willis. A Guide to Better Nature Photography. Shangle, Robert D., ed. LC 79-16569. 1979. pap. 1.95 (ISBN 0-89802-086-7). Beautiful Am.
Pfeiffer, C. Boyd. Field Guide to Outdoor Photography. LC 76-55380. (Illus.). 224p. 1977. pap. 5.95 (ISBN 0-8117-2261-9). Stackpole.
Photographing Nature. (Life Library of Photography). (Illus.). 1971. 14.95 (ISBN 0-8094-1044-3). Time-Life.
Porter, Eliot. In Wildness Is the Preservation of the World. LC 62-20527. (Exhibit Format Ser.). (Illus.). 168p. 1962. 32.50 (ISBN 0-87156-000-3). Sierra.
--Intimate Landscapes. (Illus.). 1979. 35.00 (ISBN 0-525-13443-3). Dutton.
Price, William L. A Manual of Photographic Manipulation Treating of the Practice of the Art; & Its Various Applications to Nature. 2nd ed. LC 72-9223. (The Literature of Photography Ser.). Repr. of 1868 ed. 18.00 (ISBN 0-405-04930-7). Arno.
Strache, Wolf. Forms & Patterns in Nature. LC 73-3468. 1973. 10.00 (ISBN 0-394-42541-3); pap. 5.95 (ISBN 0-394-70974-8). Pantheon.
Thompson, John W. & Slauson, Nedra, eds. Index to Illustrations of the Natural World: Where to Find Pictures of the Living Things of North America. 265p. 1981. Repr. of 1980 ed. 29.95 (ISBN 0-208-01911-1, Lib Prof Pubns). Shoe String.
Turner Ettlinger, D. M., ed. Natural History Photography. 1975. 47.00 (ISBN 0-12-703950-3). Acad Pr.
Walker, Theodore D. Nature's Design: A Photographic Essay. (Illus.). 103p. 1980. 12.00 (ISBN 0-914886-09-6). PDA Pubs.
Wootters, John & Smith, Jerry T. Wildlife Images: A Complete Guide to Outdoor Photography. (Illus.). 200p. 1981. 17.95 (ISBN 0-8227-3020-0). Petersen Pub.
Young, Catherine M. To See Our World. LC 79-65448. (Illus.). 1979. 29.95 (ISBN 0-688-03540-X). Morrow.

NATURE PROTECTION
see Nature Conservation

NATURE SOUNDS
see also Animal Sounds; Bird-Song; Sound Production by Animals

NATURE STORIES
Baker, Doug. River Place. LC 79-27119. 176p. 1980. pap. 8.50 (ISBN 0-917304-57-8, Pub. by Timber Pr). Intl Schol Bk Serv.
Burgess, Thornton W. Mother West Wind's Children. new ed. (Nature Story Bks). (Illus.). (gr. 1-3). 1962. 8.95 (ISBN 0-316-11645-9). Little.

Cornell, James C., Jr. Nature at Its Strangest: True Stories from the Files of the Smithsonian Institution's Center for Short-Lived Phenomena. LC 74-82336. (Illus.). 128p. (gr. 3 up). 1974. 6.95 (ISBN 0-8069-3924-9); PLB 6.69 (ISBN 0-8069-3925-7). Sterling.
Favorite Nature Stories from the Reader's Digest. (Illus.). 144p. (Orig.). 1976. pap. 1.25 (ISBN 0-916544-07-9). Natural Sci Youth.
Heady, Ray A. Hard Head I & Other Outdoor Stories. LC 80-83551. (Illus.). 312p. 1980. 12.95 (ISBN 0-913504-59-9). Lowell Pr.
Hoover, Helen. Years of the Forest. 1973. 10.95 (ISBN 0-394-47538-0). Knopf.
Lewis, Roger. Darndest Things Happen to an Outdoorsman. 1980. 5.75 (ISBN 0-8062-1378-7). Carlton.
Ramblings of a Sportsman-Naturalists "BB". (Illus.). 192p. 1980. 13.50 (ISBN 0-7181-1815-4, Pub. by Michael Joseph). Merrimack Bk Serv.
Scott, J. Robertson. A Century of Nature Stories. 25.00 (ISBN 0-686-18761-X). Scholars Ref Lib.
--A Century of Nature Stories. lib. bdg. 20.00 (ISBN 0-8414-8154-7). Folcroft.
Skutch, Alexander. A Naturalist on a Tropical Farm. LC 78-64474. (Illus.). 1980. 18.95 (ISBN 0-686-77795-6); pap. 7.95 (ISBN 0-520-04149-6, CAL 461). U of Cal Pr.
Uttley, Alison. From Spring to Spring: Stories of the 4 Seasons. Lines, Kathleen, ed. (Illus.). 128p. 1978. 9.95 (ISBN 0-571-11144-0, Pub. by Faber & Faber). Merrimack Bk Serv.
Woolner, Frank. My New England. LC 72-87870. (Illus.). 176p. 1972. 10.00 (ISBN 0-913276-01-4). Stone Wall Pr.
Young, F. M. Man Meets Grizzly: Encounters in the Wild from Lewis & Clark to Modern Times. Beyers, Coralie M., ed. 1980. 12.95 (ISBN 0-395-29194-1). HM.

NATURE STUDY

see also Animals, Habits and Behavior of; Animals, Legends and Stories Of; Biology; Botany; Natural History-Outdoor Books; Natural History-Study and Teaching; Nature Photography; Zoology

Allaby, Michael. A Year in the Life of a Field. LC 80-68681. (Illus.). 192p. 1981. 24.00 (ISBN 0-7153-7889-9). David & Charles.
Barrus, Clara, ed. The Heart of Burrough's Journals. 1979. Repr. of 1928 ed. lib. bdg. 30.00 (ISBN 0-8495-0504-6). Arden Lib.
Bartram, William. The Travels of William Bartram. Peck, Robert M., ed. & intro. by. (Literature of the American Wilderness). 332p. 1980. pap. 3.95 (ISBN 0-87905-079-9). Peregrine Smith.
Bazalgette, Leon. Henry Thoreau Bachelor of Nature. Brooks, Wyck Van, tr. LC 80-2679. Repr. of 1924 ed. 37.50 (ISBN 0-404-19076-6). AMS Pr.
Blincoe, Edith. Nature Walks with Edith Blincoe. (Illus.). 128p. (Orig.). Date not set. 9.50 (ISBN 0-938492-02-0). Journal Herald.
Borland, Barbara D., ed. Hal Borland's Twelve Moons of the Year. LC 79-2164. (Illus.). 1979. 12.50 (ISBN 0-394-50496-8). Knopf.
Broome, Harvey. Faces of the Wilderness. LC 72-78038. (Illus.). 271p. 1972. 7.95 (ISBN 0-87842-027-4). Mountain Pr.
Brown, Erik. Seat in a Wild Place. (Illus.). 128p. 1981. 8.95 (ISBN 0-87233-059-1). Bauhan.
Burroughs, John. Return of the Birds: Selected Nature Essays of John Burroughs, Vol. 1. Bergon, Frank, ed. (Literature of the American Wilderness). 320p. Date not set. pap. 4.45 (ISBN 0-87905-081-0). Peregrine Smith.
--A Sharp Lookout: Nature Essays of John Burroughs, Vol. II. Bergone, Frank, ed. (Literature of the American Wilderness). 320p. Date not set. pap. 4.45 (ISBN 0-87905-082-9). Peregrine Smith.
--Signs & Seasons. LC 80-8403. (Nature Library Ser.). 300p. 1981. pap. 5.95 (ISBN 0-06-090840-8, CN 840, CN). Har-Row.
Burton, John. The Naturalist in London. LC 74-78247. (Regional Naturalist). (Illus.). 168p. 5.95 (ISBN 0-7153-6215-1). David & Charles.
Bystrom, Robert. Nature's Special Moments. Batts, H. Lewis, ed. & illus. (Illus.). 80p. 1975. 7.50 (ISBN 0-939294-01-X). Beech Leaf.
Campbell, A. C. The Larousse Guide to the Seashore & Shallow Seas of Britain & Europe. LC 80-82755. (Larousse Nature Guides Ser.). (Illus.). 320p. (Orig.). 1981. 10.95 (ISBN 0-88332-251-X, 8068). Larousse.
Carson, Rachel. The Sense of Wonder. 1965. 12.95 (ISBN 0-06-010645-X, HarpT); PLB 10.87 (ISBN 0-06-010646-8). Har-Row.
Carter, W. Horace. Creatures & Chronicles from Cross Creek. (Illus.). 286p. (Orig.). 1981. pap. text ed. 5.95 (ISBN 0-937866-02-4). Atlantic Pub Co.
Chinery, Michael. Enjoying Nature with Your Family: Learn, Look & Conserve. (Illus.). 1977. 12.95 (ISBN 0-517-53007-4). Crown.
Clapper, Ronald. The Development of Walden: A Genetic Text. LC 80-2503. 1981. 75.00 (ISBN 0-404-19051-0). AMS Pr.
Cohen, Michael J. Our Classroom Is Wild America. LC 74-76019. (Illus.). 1978. pap. 6.00 (ISBN 0-89166-011-9). Cobblesmith.
Collier, Richard. Eagle Day: New Illustrated Edition. 1980. 12.95 (ISBN 0-525-09650-7). Dutton.
Comstock, Anna B. Handbook of Nature Study. 24th ed. (HANH Ser.). (Illus.). 957p. (gr. 7 up). 1939. 24.95 (ISBN 0-8014-0081-3); text ed. 15.00x (ISBN 0-8014-0082-1). Comstock.
Cornell, Joseph B. Sharing Nature with Children. LC 78-74650. (Illus.). 143p. 1979. pap. 4.95 (ISBN 0-916124-14-2). Ananda.
De Lubicz, R. A. Nature-World. Lawlor, Deborah, tr. from Fr. 144p. 1981. 9.95 (ISBN 0-89281-036-X). Inner Tradit.
Dorward, Douglas. Wild Australia. (Illus.). 128p. 1980. 20.95x (ISBN 0-00-211446-1, Pub. by W Collins Australia). Intl Schol Bk Serv.
Feininger, Andreas. The Anatomy of Nature. 12.50 (ISBN 0-8446-5760-3). Peter Smith.
Fiedler, Judith. Field Research: A Manual for Logistics & Management of Scientific Studies in Natural Settings. LC 78-62562. (Social & Behavioral Science Ser.). (Illus.). 1978. text ed. 14.95x (ISBN 0-87589-381-3). Jossey-Bass.
Freethy, Ron. The Making of the British Countryside. LC 80-68688. (Illus.). 192p. 1981. 24.00 (ISBN 0-7153-8012-5). David & Charles.
Gardner, John F. Book of Nature Activities. (gr. 4-8). 1967. pap. text ed. 0.50x (ISBN 0-8134-1009-6, 1009). Interstate.
--The Naturalist's Almanac & Environmentalist's Companion. 5th ed. (Illus.). 1976. 4.95 (ISBN 0-916544-13-3). Natural Sci Youth.
--The Northeast Edition of the Naturalist's Almanac & Environmentalist's Companion: 1975-76. (Naturalist's Almanac Ser). (Illus., Orig.). 1975. pap. 1.95 (ISBN 0-916544-05-2). Natural Sci Youth.
Hamlet, John N. & Carter, W. Horace. Land That I Love. (Illus.). 295p. 1980. 10.95 (ISBN 0-937866-00-8). Atlantic Pub Co.
Headstrom, Richard. Adventures with a Hand Lens. 1976. pap. 3.00 (ISBN 0-486-23330-8). Dover.
Herzog, Werner. Of Walking in Ice. Greenberg, Alan, tr. from Ger. 96p. 1980. 9.95 (ISBN 0-934378-14-2); pap. 4.95 (ISBN 0-934378-01-0). Tanam Pr.
Hillcourt, William. New Field Book of Nature Activities & Hobbies. rev. ed. LC 78-96211. (Putnam's Nature Field Bks.). (Illus.). 1970. 6.95 (ISBN 0-399-10290-6). Putnam.
--The New Field Book of Nature Activities & Hobbies. LC 78-96211. (Putnam's Nature Field Bks.). (Illus.). 1978. pap. 3.95 (ISBN 0-399-12158-7). Putnam.
Home, Lord. Reflections on Field & Stream. (Illus.). 112p. 1980. 12.50 (ISBN 0-316-37196-3). Little.
Hoy, Ken. On Nature's Trail. LC 78-65673. 1979. 14.95 (ISBN 0-89479-039-0). A & W Pubs.
Huggler, Thomas E. Westwind Woods. LC 78-106385. (Illus.). 1978. pap. 2.95 (ISBN 0-933112-00-9). Mich United Conserv.
Karlin, Sol. A. Introduction to the Living World. 1974. pap. text ed. 10.95 (ISBN 0-917962-33-8); lab manual 4.50 (ISBN 0-917962-29-X). Peek Pubns.
Karstad, Aleta. Wild Habitats. (Illus.). 1979. 12.95 (ISBN 0-684-16236-9, ScribT). Scribner.
Keasey, Merritt S. The Saquaro Book. 72p. 1981. pap. text ed. 4.95 (ISBN 0-8403-2392-1). Kendall-Hunt.
Kidney, Dorothy B. Wilderness Journey. (Illus.). 200p. (Orig.). 1980. pap. 7.95 (ISBN 0-930096-10-X). G Gannett.
Kilham, Lawrence. A Naturalist's Field Guide. (Illus.). 274p. 1981. 13.95 (ISBN 0-8117-1012-2). Stackpole.
Lawrence, Louise D. To Whom the Wilderness Speaks. (Illus.). 208p. 1980. 14.95 (ISBN 0-07-092400-7, GB). McGraw.
Lawrence, R. D. The Study of Life: A Naturalist's View. (Illus.). 43p. 1980. pap. 1.50 (ISBN 0-913098-37-X). Myrin Institute.
Lehmberg, Paul. In the Strong Woods. 160p. 1981. pap. 4.95 (ISBN 0-312-41173-1). St Martin.
Levy, Wilbert J. Man Studies the World Around Him. (gr. 10-12). 1973. pap. text ed. 3.83 (ISBN 0-87720-372-5). AMSCO Sch.
Link, Michael. Nature's Classroom: A Manual for Teaching Outdoor Education. (Illus.). 1978. 4.25 (ISBN 0-930698-01-0). Natl Audubon.
--Outdoor Education: A Manual for Teaching in Nature's Classroom. 224p. 1981. 15.95 (ISBN 0-13-645028-8); pap. 6.95 (ISBN 0-13-645010-5). P-H.
McDonald, Ralph J. A Down-Home Gallery of American Wildlife. (Illus.). 101p. 1980. 39.95 (ISBN 0-9605428-1-7); signed numbered ed. 95.00 (ISBN 0-9605428-0-9). Countryside Studio.
Milne, Lururus J. & Milne, Margery J. The World of Night. LC 80-8404. (Nature Library Ser.). (Illus.). 248p. (Orig.). 1981. pap. 5.95 (ISBN 0-06-090839-4, CN 839, CN). Har-Row.
National Geographic Society, ed. Books for Young Explorers, 4 vols, Set 2. Incl. Honeybees. LC 73-7111; How Animals Hide. LC 73-7112; Namu. LC 73-7113; Pandas. LC 73-7114. (ps-3). 1973. Set. 7.95, avail. only from Natl Geog (ISBN 0-87044-145-0). Natl Geog.
Natural Science Centers Conference 1974, Nashville, Tennessee. Proceedings. Gardner, John F., ed. (Illus., Orig.). 1975. 5.00 (ISBN 0-916544-04-4). Natural Sci Youth.
Nelson, Wendell. Earth Singers & Their Songs: A Companion to American Nature Writing. (Illus.). 1981. 14.50 (ISBN 0-933474-19-9, Gabriel Bks). Minn Scholarly.
Nickelsburg, Janet. Nature Program for Early Childhood. new ed. 1976. pap. text ed. 9.75 (ISBN 0-201-05097-8, Sch Div). A-W.
Ogburn, Charlton. The Winter Beach. LC 66-23350. (Illus.). 1979. pap. 4.95 (ISBN 0-688-07785-4, Quill). Morrow.
Olsen, Don. Nature's Candles. LC 74-30730. (Illus.). 1976. 9.95 (ISBN 0-498-01669-2). A S Barnes.
Pedretti, Carlo. Leonardo Da Vinci Nature Studies from the Royal Library at Windsor Castle. (Illus.). 95p. (Orig.). 1980. pap. 10.00 (ISBN 0-384-32298-0). J P Getty Mus.
Pyle, Robert M. The Audubon Society Field Guide to North American Butterflies. LC 80-84240. (Illus.). 864p. 1981. 11.95 (ISBN 0-394-51914-0). Knopf.
Raphael, Ray. An Everyday History of Somewhere. (Illus.). 192p. 1980. pap. 8.00 (ISBN 0-933280-11-4). Island CA.
Rifkin, Natalie, ed. USSR - Land of the Russian Bear. LC 78-730222. (National Wildlife Challenge Kit Ser.). (gr. 3-6). 1978. 35.00 (ISBN 0-912186-26-7). Natl Wildlife.
Rood, Ronald. Laska: Adventures with a Wolfdog. 1980. 10.95 (ISBN 0-393-01360-X). Norton.
--The Loon in My Bathtub. LC 64-23363. (Illus.). 192p. 1974. pap. 3.95 (ISBN 0-8289-0229-1). Greene.
Rowlands, John J. Cache Lake Country: Life in the North Woods. (Illus.). 1978. pap. 5.95 (ISBN 0-393-00908-4). Norton.
Russell, Franklin. Watchers at the Pond. LC 80-83963. 1981. pap. 7.95 (ISBN 0-87923-390-7). Godine.
Russell, Ian. Ponds & Streams. LC 80-85505. (Wildlife Ser.). (Illus.). 52p. 1981. pap. 5.95 (ISBN 0-7153-8162-8). David & Charles.
Sharpe, Grant W. Interpreting the Environment. 2nd ed. 600p. 1982. text ed. 23.95 (ISBN 0-471-09007-7). Wiley.
Shomon, Joseph J. Nature Centers in America. (Illus.). 1980. 20.00 (ISBN 0-8424-0122-9). Nellen Pub.
Smith, V. Kerry & Krutilla, John V. Structure & Properties of a Wilderness Travel Simulator: An Application to the Spanish Peaks Area. LC 75-33766. (Resources for the Future Ser). 188p. 1976. 14.00x (ISBN 0-8018-1808-7). Johns Hopkins.
Spawls, Stephen. Sun, Sand & Snakes. LC 79-89260. (Illus.). 1980. 12.95 (ISBN 0-688-03572-8). Morrow.
The Spotter's Handbook to Wildflowers, Trees & Birds or North America. LC 79-10397. (Spotter's Guides). (Illus.). 1980. 5.95 (ISBN 0-8317-7953-5, Mayflower Bks); pap. 3.95 (ISBN 0-8317-7954-3). Smith Pubs.
Stokes, Donald W. A Guide to Nature in Winter: Northeast & North Central North America. (Illus.). 1976. 8.95 (ISBN 0-316-81720-1); pap. 6.95 (ISBN 0-316-81723-6). Little.
Stone, R. H. A Basic Biology for the Tropics, 2 vols. (Illus.). (gr. 9). 1973. text ed. 6.95 ea. Vol. 1 (ISBN 0-521-08233-1). Vol. 2 (ISBN 0-521-08612-4). Cambridge U Pr.
Thompson, David. In the Shining Mountains. 272p. 1981. pap. 3.95 (ISBN 0-553-14821-4). Bantam.
Thoreau, Henry D. Ktaadn. 96p. 1980. 9.95 (ISBN 0-934378-15-0); pap. 4.95 (ISBN 0-934378-16-9). Tanam Pr.
Van Dieren, W. & Hummelinck, M. W. Nature Is Price: The Economics of Mother Earth. (Ideas in Progress Ser). 224p. 1979. 15.00 (ISBN 0-7145-2663-0, Pub. by M Boyars); pap. 6.95 (ISBN 0-7145-2664-9). Merrimack Bk Serv.
Walker, N. W. Back to the Land. (Illus.). pap. 4.50 (ISBN 0-89019-063-1, Norwalk Pr). O'Sullivan Woodside.
Wilson, Andrew. Nature by the Month. LC 75-21181. 1976. pap. text ed. 2.95x (ISBN 0-8134-1757-0, 1757). Interstate.
Wunderlich, Klaus & Gloede, Wolfgang. Nature As Constructor. Varecha, Vladimir, tr. from Ger. LC 80-18311. (Illus.). 196p. 1979. 40.00x (ISBN 0-8002-2424-8). Intl Pubns Serv.
Zwinger, Ann. Beyond the Aspen Grove. LC 80-8407. (Nature Library). (Illus.). 384p. (Orig.). 1981. pap. 5.95 (ISBN 0-06-090842-4, CN 842, CN). Har-Row.

NATURE STUDY–JUVENILE LITERATURE

Adrian, Mary. A Day & a Night in a Tide Pool. LC 72-4743. (Balance in Nature Ser). (Illus.). 64p. (gr. 2-5). 1972. 5.95g (ISBN 0-8038-1549-2). Hastings.
Allison, Linda. The Reasons for Seasons: The Great Cosmic Megagalactic Trip Without Moving from Your Chair. (A Brown Paper School Book). (Illus.). 128p. (gr. 4 up). 1975. 8.95 (ISBN 0-316-03439-8); pap. 5.95 (ISBN 0-316-03440-1). Little.
Arnosky, Jim. Outdoors on Foot. (Illus.). (ps-1). 1978. PLB 4.97 (ISBN 0-698-30684-8). Coward.
Barlowe, Dot & Barlowe, Sy. Who Lives Here? LC 79-27494. (Picturebacks Ser.). (Illus.). 32p. (ps-3). 1980. PLB 4.99 (ISBN 0-394-93740-6); pap. 1.25 (ISBN 0-394-83740-1). Random.
Bartholin, Rasmus. Erasmi Bartholini: De Naturae Mirabilibus quaestiones academicae. 207p. 1981. Repr. of 1674 ed. lib. bdg. 90.00 (ISBN 0-8287-1452-5). Clearwater Pub.
Berenstain, Stan & Berenstain, Janice. The Bears' Nature Guide. LC 75-8070. (Now I Know! Ser). (Illus.). 72p. (ps-3). 1975. 4.95 (ISBN 0-394-83125-X, BYR); PLB 5.99 (ISBN 0-394-93125-4). Random.
Burroughs, John. Far & Near. 1904. lib. bdg. 15.00 (ISBN 0-8414-2548-5). Folcroft.
--Fresh Fields. 1884. lib. bdg. 15.00 (ISBN 0-8414-2549-3). Folcroft.
--Prepacton. 1881. lib. bdg. 15.00 (ISBN 0-8414-1601-X). Folcroft.
--Sings & Seasons. 1886. lib. bdg. 15.00 (ISBN 0-8414-1602-8). Folcroft.
Carpenter, Mimi G. What the Sea Left Behind. LC 81-66251. (Illus.). 32p. (gr. 2-3). 1981. pap. 7.95 (ISBN 0-89272-123-5). Down East.
Cassell, Sylvia. Nature Games & Activities. LC 56-5150. (Illus.). (gr. 2-6). 1956. PLB 7.89 (ISBN 0-06-021156-3, HarpJ). Har-Row.
Clery, Val. A Day in the Woods. (Illus.). 1979. 3.95 (ISBN 0-8120-5329-X). Barron.
Creative Editors. Forces of Nature. LC 73-140636. (Our Changing Environment Ser). (Illus.). (gr. 4-9). 1971. PLB 6.95 (ISBN 0-87191-075-6). Creative Ed.
--Our Natural Environment. LC 79-140640. (Our Changing Environment Ser). (Illus.). (gr. 4-9). 1971. PLB 6.95 (ISBN 0-87191-071-3). Creative Ed.
Cutler, Katherine N. From Petals to Pinecones: A Nature Art & Craft Book. LC 70-81753. (Illus.). (gr. 4 up). 1969. PLB 7.92 (ISBN 0-688-51594-0). Lothrop.
De Jonge, Joanne. Bats & Bugs & Snakes & Slugs. (Voyager Ser.). 64p. (Orig.). 1981. pap. 2.50 (ISBN 0-8010-2914-7). Baker Bk.
Fegus, Meryl. Discovering Out of Doors. Self, Margaret M., ed. (Illus.). 24p. (Orig.). (ps-5). 1974. 2.75 (ISBN 0-8307-0307-1, 56-004-05). Regal.
Guerra, Mario. The Naturalist's Handbook -- Collecting & Preparing Animals, Plants & Minerals. LC 79-91396. (Illus.). 96p. (gr. 10 up). Date not set. cancelled (ISBN 0-8069-3114-0); PLB 9.29 (ISBN 0-8069-3115-9). Sterling.
Hawkinson, John. Let Me Take You on a Trail. LC 71-188428. (Activity Bks.). (Illus.). 48p. (gr. 5 up). 1972. 6.95g (ISBN 0-8075-4452-3). A Whitman.
Hutchins, Ross E. Nature Invented It First. LC 79-23791. (Illus.). (gr. 5 up). 1980. 5.95 (ISBN 0-396-07788-9). Dodd.
Inouye, Carol. Naturecraft. LC 74-33681. 64p. (gr. 4-7). 1975. PLB 5.95 (ISBN 0-385-01190-3). Doubleday.
Jones, Elizabeth, ed. Ranger Rick's Surprise Book. LC 79-88095. (Illus.). (gr. 2-7). 1979. 7.95 (ISBN 0-912186-32-1). Natl Wildlife.
Jones, Elizabeth G., ed. Ranger Rick's Holiday Book. LC 80-81621. (Illus.). 96p. (gr. 2-7). 1980. 8.95 (ISBN 0-912186-38-0). Natl Wildlife.
Moore, Leonard. Enciclopedia Juvenil De la Naturaleza. 256p. (Espn.). 1976. 37.50 (ISBN 84-272-5930-1, S-50476). French & Eur.
National Geographic Society, ed. Books for Young Explorers, 4 vols, Set 4. Incl. Cowboys. LC 75-6067; A Day in the Woods. LC 75-6068; Tricks Animals Play. LC 75-6066; The Wild Ponies of Assategue Island. LC 75-6065. 7.95 set (ISBN 0-87044-170-1, 00170). Natl Geog.
--Books for Young Explorers, 4 vols, Set 5. Incl. Camping Adventures. LC 76-2116; Wonders of the Desert World. LC 76-2221; The Playful Dolphins. LC 76-2118; Animals That Build Their Homes. LC 76-2117. 7.95 set (ISBN 0-87044-200-7, 00200). Natl Geog.
--Books for Young Explorers, 4 vols, Set 6. Incl. Creatures of the Night. LC 77-76968; The Blue Whale. LC 77-76971; Let's Go to the Moon. LC 77-76972; What Happens in the Spring. LC 77-76970. 7.95 set (ISBN 0-87044-245-7, 00245); PLB 9.95 set (ISBN 0-685-88096-6, 00250). Natl Geog.

Nero, Robert W. The Great Gray Owl: Phantom of the Northern Forest. LC 80-607110. (Illus.). 168p. 1980. 17.50 (ISBN 0-87474-672-8). Smithsonian.
Overbeck, Cynthia. Monkeys. LC 81-1961. (Lerner Natural Science Bks.). (Illus.). (gr. 4-10). 1981. PLB 7.95 (ISBN 0-8225-1464-8, AACRZ). Lerner Pubns.
Patent, Dorothy H. Sizes & Shapes in Nature: What They Mean. LC 78-12554. (Illus.). (gr. 6 up). 1979. 7.95 (ISBN 0-8234-0340-8). Holiday.
Pringle, Laurence. The Hidden World: Life Under a Rock. LC 76-47641. (Exploring an Ecosystem Ser.). (Illus.). (gr. 3-7). 1977. 8.95 (ISBN 0-02-775340-9, 77534). Macmillan.
Rahn, Joan E. Traps & Lures in the Living World. LC 79-22699. (Illus.). (gr. 4-6). 1980. 8.95 (ISBN 0-689-30766-7). Atheneum.
Richey, David. A Child's Introduction to the Outdoors. 192p. 1975. 8.95 (ISBN 0-919364-99-3, ADON 3555). Pagurian.
Rights, Mollie & Solga, Tim. Beastly Neighbors: Or Why Earwigs Make Good Mothers. (Brown Paper School Ser.). (Illus.). 128p. (Orig.). (gr. 3 up). 1981. 9.95 (ISBN 0-316-74576-6); pap. 5.95 (ISBN 0-316-74577-4). Little.
Samson, John G. The Pond. (YA) 1979. 7.95 (ISBN 0-394-83714-2); PLB 7.99 (ISBN 0-394-93714-7). Knopf.
Schulz, Charles M. Snoopy's Facts & Fun Book About Farms. LC 79-22307. (Snoopy's Facts & Fun Bks.). (Illus.). 40p. (ps-1). 1980. bds. 2.95 (ISBN 0-394-84300-2); PLB 3.99 (ISBN 0-394-94300-7). Random.
--Snoopy's Facts & Fun Book About Nature. LC 79-22307. (Snoopy's Facts & Fun Bks.). (Illus.). 40p. (ps-1). 1980. bds. 2.95 (ISBN 0-394-84299-5); PLB 3.99 (ISBN 0-394-94299-X). Random.
Selsam, Millicent E. How to Be a Nature Detective. LC 66-15947. (Illus.). (gr. 1-5). PLB 9.89 (ISBN 0-06-025301-0, HarpJ). Har-Row.
Sheehan, Angela, ed. Discovering Nature. LC 77-6206. (Illus.). (gr. 3-12). 1977. PLB 17.85 (ISBN 0-8393-0025-5). Raintree Child.
Silverstein, Alvin & Silverstein, Virginia. Nature's Champions: The Biggest, the Fastest, the Best. LC 79-20698. (Illus.). 72p. (gr. 4-7). 1980. bds. 5.95 (ISBN 0-394-84191-3); PLB 5.99 (ISBN 0-394-94191-8). Random.
Stone, R. H. A Basic Biology for the Tropics, 2 vols. (Illus.). (gr. 9). 1973. text ed. 6.95 ea. Vol. 1 (ISBN 0-521-08233-1). Vol. 2 (ISBN 0-521-08612-4). Cambridge U Pr.
Waters, Udell. Mother O'Possum's Problem. 1980. 4.95 (ISBN 0-8062-1494-5). Carlton.
Welch, Martha M. Close Looks in a Spring Woods. (Illus.). 64p. (gr. 2-5). 1981. PLB 7.95 (ISBN 0-396-07998-9). Dodd.

NATURE WORSHIP
see also Anthropomorphism; Phallicism; Sun-Worship
Bjerregaard, C. H. Lectures on Mysticism & Nature Worship. 1977. lib. bdg. 59.95 (ISBN 0-8490-2138-3). Gordon Pr.
Frazer, James G. The Worship of Nature. LC 73-21271. (Gifford Lectures: 1924-25). Repr. of 1926 ed. 41.50 (ISBN 0-404-11427-X). AMS Pr.
Hopkins, Edward W. Origin & Evolution of Religion. LC 76-79199. 370p. 1969. Repr. of 1923 ed. 15.00x (ISBN 0-8154-0294-5). Cooper Sq.
Willoughby, William C. Nature-Worship & Taboo: Further Studies in "The Soul of the Bantu". LC 74-15105. Repr. of 1932 ed. 24.50 (ISBN 0-404-12153-5). AMS Pr.

NATUROPATHY
Bragg, Paul C. & Bragg, Patricia. Nature's Way to Health. 10th ed. pap. 1.75 (ISBN 0-87790-019-1). Health Sci.
Bricklin, Mark. The Practical Encyclopedia of Natural Healing. LC 76-26864. 1976. 19.95 (ISBN 0-87857-136-1). Rodale Pr Inc.
Carroll, David. The Complete Book of Natural Medicines. LC 80-11332. (Illus.). 416p. 1980. 17.95 (ISBN 0-671-24418-3); pap. 7.95 (ISBN 0-671-41623-5). Summit Bks.
Clark, Linda. Get Well Naturally. LC 65-18927. 1968. pap. 2.75 (ISBN 0-668-01762-7). Arco.
--Get Well Naturally. 1974. Repr. of 1965 ed. 5.95 (ISBN 0-8159-5605-3). Devin.
--Handbook of Natural Remedies for Common Ailments. LC 75-13349. 256p. 1976. 9.95 (ISBN 0-8159-5710-6). Devin.
D'Adamo, James. One Man's Food: Is Someone Else's Poison. 320p. 1980. 10.95 (ISBN 0-399-90092-6). Marek.
Davis, Ben. Rapid Healing Foods. LC 79-22770. 1980. 10.95 (ISBN 0-13-753137-0, Parker). P-H.
Garten, M. O. Natural & Drugless Way for Better Health. LC 72-135619. (Illus.). 1971. pap. 1.65 (ISBN 0-668-02412-7). Arco.
Granger, B. Noice. Health Without Drugs: A Practical Nature Cure. 1975. lib. bdg. 69.95 (ISBN 0-685-51373-4). Revisionist Pr.
Homola, Samuel. Secrets of Naturally Youthful Health & Vitality. LC 70-152523. (Illus.). 1971. 10.95 (ISBN 0-13-797514-7, Parker). P-H.
Liss, Joseph. Victory Over Heart Attacks. 144p. 1977. 5.95 (ISBN 0-8059-2367-5). Dorrance.
Lust, Benedict. Only Nature Cures. 1976. pap. 2.95 (ISBN 0-87904-014-9). Lust.
Roth, Julius A. Health Purifiers & Their Enemies: A Study of the Natural Health Movement in the United States with a Comparison to Its Counterpart in Germany. LC 77-2210. 1977. 15.00 (ISBN 0-88202-117-6); pap. 5.95 (ISBN 0-686-67897-4). N Watson.
Schneider, L. L. & Stone, Robert B. Old Fashioned Health Remedies That Work Best. 1977. 12.95 (ISBN 0-13-633701-5, Parker). P-H.
Thomson, Robert. The Grosset Encyclopedia of Natural Medicine. LC 79-56186. (Illus.). 1980. pap. 9.95 (ISBN 0-448-14897-8). G&D.

NATZLER, OTTO
Norman-Wilcox, Gregor, intro. by. Natzler Ceramics. LC 68-57263. (Orig.). 1968. pap. 12.50 (ISBN 0-87587-034-1). LA Co Art Mus.

NAUDE, GABRIEL, 1600-1653
Clarke, Jack. Gabriel Naude, 1600-1653. 1970. 16.50 (ISBN 0-208-00971-X, Archon). Shoe String.
Rice, James. Gabriel Naude, 1600-1653. (Johns Hopkins University Studies in Romance Literatures & Languages: Vol. 35). 134p. Repr. of 1939 ed. pap. 11.50 (ISBN 0-384-50720-4). Johnson Repr.

NAURU
Petit-Skinner, Solange. The Nauruans. (Illus.). 315p. 1981. 22.80 (ISBN 0-9606272-0-0). MacDuff Pr.

NAUTICAL ALMANACS
see also Ephemerides
Ingram-Brown, R., ed. Brown's Nautical Almanac, 1981. 104th ed. (Illus.). 1981. 37.50x (ISBN 0-8002-2780-8). Intl Pubns Serv.

NAUTICAL ASTRONOMY
see also Longitude; Navigation; Time
Bensaude, J. L'astronomie Nautique Au Portugal a L'epoque des Grandes Decouvertes. (Fr.). 1912. text ed. 21.25x (ISBN 90-6041-002-5). Humanities.
Birney, A. A. Noon Sight Navigation: Simplified Celestial. LC 72-88042. (Illus.). 1972. pap. 5.00 (ISBN 0-87033-171-X). Cornell Maritime.
Blewitt, Mary. Celestial Navigation for Yachtsmen. LC 67-25097. 1967. 7.95 (ISBN 0-8286-0028-7). De Graff.
Bowditch, Nathaniel. The Marine Sextant. 1976. 7.95 (ISBN 0-679-50653-5); pap. 4.95 (ISBN 0-679-50668-3). McKay.
Campbell, Stafford. The Yachtsman Guide to Celestial Navigation. (Illus.). 1979. 8.95 (ISBN 0-87165-019-3, Yachting-Zd). Ziff-Davis Pub.
Cotter, Charles H. The Elements of Navigation & Nautical Astronomy. 1981. 75.00x (ISBN 0-85174-270-X, Pub. by Nautical England). State Mutual Bk.
Craine, Eric R. Problems in Celestial Navigation. (The Astronomy Quarterly Library: Vol. 3). 1981. pap. text ed. 14.95 (ISBN 0-912918-08-X). Pachart Pub Hse.
Davies, Thomas D. Star Sight Reduction Tables for Forty-Two Stars: Assumed Altitude Method of Celestial Navigation. LC 79-7464. 1980. 28.50x (ISBN 0-87033-250-3). Cornell Maritime.
Hobbs, Richard R. Marine Navigation Two: Celestial & Electronic. 2nd ed. LC 81-75837. 344p. 1981. text ed. 14.95x (ISBN 0-87021-363-6). Naval Inst Pr.
Howell, Susan P. Practical Celestial Navigation. 1979. pap. 10.00 (ISBN 0-9603076-0-5). S P Howell.
Kittredge, Robert Y. Self-Taught Navigation. LC 73-121015. (Illus.). 1970. 5.95 (ISBN 0-87358-049-4). Northland.
Linton, Anthony. Newes of the Complement of the Art of Navigation & of the Mightie Empire of Cataia. LC 72-215. (English Experience Ser.: No. 204). 1969. Repr. of 1609 ed. 8.00 (ISBN 90-221-0204-1). Walter J Johnson.
Norville, Warren. Celestial Navigation Step by Step. LC 72-95225. 168p. 1973. 17.50 (ISBN 0-87742-028-9). Intl Marine.
Schlereth, Hewitt. Commonsense Celestial Navigation. 1979. pap. 6.95 (ISBN 0-8092-7219-9). Contemp Bks.
Thompson. Celestial Navigation. 1981. 12.50 (ISBN 0-679-50965-8). McKay.
Toghill, Jeff. Celestial Navigation for Beginners. (Orig.). 1980. pap. 10.00x (ISBN 0-8464-0998-4). Beekman Pubs.
Wright, Edward. Certaine Errors in Navigation (the Voyage of George Earl of Cumberland to the Azores) LC 74-80224. (English Experience Ser.: No. 703). 1974. Repr. of 1599 ed. 29.00 (ISBN 90-221-0703-5). Walter J Johnson.
Wright, Frances W. Celestial Navigation. LC 70-76202. (Illus.). 1969. 7.50 (ISBN 0-87033-000-4). Cornell Maritime.

NAUTICAL CHARTS
Burton, S. M. & Cunningham, G. F. Burton's Nautical Tables. 8th ed. 362p. 1974. 17.50x (ISBN 0-540-07380-6). Sheridan.
Motte, G. A. Chartwork & Marine Navigation: For Fisherman & Boat Operations. LC 77-21925. (Illus.). 1977. 7.50 (ISBN 0-87033-242-2). Cornell Maritime.
Winlund, Edmond. ChartGuide for Southern California 1981-83. rev. ed. LC 74-29812. (Illus.). 72p. (Orig.). 1981. pap. 25.00 (ISBN 0-938206-04-4). ChartGuide.

NAUTICAL INSTRUMENTS
see also Gyroscopic Instruments; Inertial Navigation Systems
also names of nautical instruments, e.g. Compass
American Neptune Pictorial Supplements: Instruments of Navigation, Vol. 17. (Illus.). 1975. pap. 3.25 (ISBN 0-87577-104-1). Peabody Mus Salem.
Barlow, William. The Navigators Supply. LC 76-38150. (English Experience Ser.: No. 430). 100p. Repr. of 1597 ed. 16.00 (ISBN 90-221-0430-3). Walter J Johnson.
Bedwell, C., ed. Developments in Electronics for Offshore Fields, Vol. 1. (Illus.). 1978. text ed. 42.60x (ISBN 0-85334-753-0, Pub. by Applied Science). Burgess-Intl Ideas.
Horsley, John. Tools of the Maritime Trades. (Illus.). 316p. 1978. 35.00 (ISBN 0-7153-5280-6). David & Charles.
Roy, G. J. Notes on Instrumentation & Control. (Marine Engineering Ser.). 144p. 1978. pap. 9.50x (ISBN 0-540-07344-X). Sheridan.
Shufeldt, H. H. & Newcomer, Kenneth. The Calculator Afloat: A Mariner's Guide to the Electronic Calculator. LC 80-81091. 256p. 1980. 16.95 (ISBN 0-87021-116-1). Naval Inst Pr.
Tobin, Wallace E., III. Mariner's Pocket Companion Nineteen Eighty-One. LC 75-21689. 224p. 1980. pap. 6.95 (ISBN 0-87021-381-4). Naval Inst Pr.

NAUTICAL MUSEUMS
see Naval Museums

NAUTICAL SURVEYING
see Hydrographic Surveying

NAUTICAL TERMS
see Naval Art and Science–Dictionaries; Naval Art and Science–Terminology

NAUVOO, ILLINOIS
Federal Writers Project, Illinois. Nauvoo Guide. LC 73-3616. (American Guide Ser.). Repr. of 1939 ed. 14.00 (ISBN 0-404-57919-1). AMS Pr.
Flack, Dora B. Testimony in Bronze: The Story of Florence P. Hanson & the Nauvoo Monument to Women. 1980. pap. 5.95 (ISBN 0-913420-84-0). Olympus Pub Co.
Flanders, Robert B. Nauvoo: Kingdom on the Mississippi. LC 65-19110. (Illus.). 374p. 1975. pap. 6.95 (ISBN 0-252-00561-9). U of Ill Pr.

NAVAHO INDIAN RESERVATION
Goodman, James M. The Navaho Atlas: Environments, Resources, People, & History of the Dine Bikeyah. LC 81-40287. (The Civilization of the American Indian Ser.: Vol. 157). (Illus.). 144p. 1981. 14.95 (ISBN 0-8061-1621-8). U of Okla Pr.
New Mexico People & Energy Collective, et al. Red Ribbons for Emma. LC 80-83883. (Illus.). 48p. (Orig.). (gr. 3 up). 1981. 5.00 (ISBN 0-938678-07-8). New Seed.
Scudder, Thayer, et al. No Place to Go: Effects of Compulsory Relocation on Navajos. LC 81-6723. (Developments Anthropology Monographs). (Illus.). 208p. 1981. text ed. 17.50x (ISBN 0-89727-029-0). Inst Study Human.

NAVAHO INDIANS
see Indians of North America–Southwest, New

NAVAHO LANGUAGE
Franciscans, Saint Michaels, Arizona. An Ethnologic Dictionary of the Navaho Language. LC 76-43710. Repr. of 1910 ed. 31.00 (ISBN 0-404-15766-1). AMS Pr.
Goossen, Irvy W. Navajo Made Easier. 7th ed. LC 68-1360. 6.95 (ISBN 0-87358-023-0). Northland.
Haile, Berard. A Stem Vocabulary of the Navaho Language, 2 vols. LC 73-15403. Repr. of 1951 ed. Set. 49.50 (ISBN 0-404-11241-2). AMS Pr.
Kari, James M. Navajo Verb Prefix Phonology. LC 75-25117. (American Indian Linguistics Ser.). 1976. lib. bdg. 42.00 (ISBN 0-8240-1968-7). Garland Pub.
Schauber, Ellen. The Syntax & Semantics of Questions in Navajo. Hankamer, Jorge, ed. LC 78-66568. (Outstanding Dissertations in Linguistics Ser.). 1979. lib. bdg. 35.00 (ISBN 0-8240-9676-2). Garland Pub.
Witherspoon, Gary. Language & Art in the Navajo Universe. (Illus.). 1977. text ed. 16.00x (ISBN 0-472-08965-X); pap. text ed. 8.95x (ISBN 0-472-08966-8). U of Mich Pr.
Young, Robert W. & Morgan, William. The Navaho Language. 1976. 11.95 (ISBN 0-87747-491-5). Deseret Bk.
--The Navajo Language: A Grammar & Colloquial Dictionary. LC 79-56812. 1980. 35.00x (ISBN 0-8263-0536-9). U of NM Pr.

NAVAHO LANGUAGE-TEXTS
Sapir, Edward. Navaho Texts. LC 73-15405. Repr. of 1942 ed. 35.00 (ISBN 0-404-11246-3). AMS Pr.

NAVAHO SAND DRAWINGS
see Sandpaintings

NAVAL ADMINISTRATION
see Naval Art and Science; United States–Navy

NAVAL AERONAUTICS
see Aeronautics, Military

NAVAL ARCHITECTURE
see also Boat-Building; Electricity on Ships; Marine Engineering; Ship-Building; Ship Propulsion; Ships, Iron and Steel; Ships, Wooden; Stability of Ships; Trim (Of Ships); Warships; Yacht-Building;
also types of vessels, e.g. Motor-Boats
Baxter, B. Naval Architecture: Examples & Theory. 240p. 1977. pap. text ed. 29.75x (ISBN 0-85264-179-6, Pub. by Charles Griffin & Co Ltd England). Lubrecht & Cramer.
--Naval Architecture: Examples & Theory. 450p. 1978. 39.95x (ISBN 0-85264-179-6, Pub. by Griffin England). State Mutual Bk.
Beebe, Robert P. Voyaging Under Power. 1978. 12.50 (ISBN 0-685-56451-7). Seven Seas.
Benford, Harry & Mathes, J. C. Your Future in Naval Architecture. Rosen, Ruth C., ed. LC 68-12156. (Careers in Depth Ser.). (Illus., Photos). (YA) 1968. PLB 5.97 (ISBN 0-8239-0056-8). Rosen Pr.
Bishop, R. E. & Price, W. G. Hydroelasticity of Ships. LC 78-67297. 1980. 90.00 (ISBN 0-521-22328-8). Cambridge U Pr.
Buxton, Ian. Big Gun Monitors: The History of the Design, Construction & Operation of the Royal Navy's Monitors. LC 80-81901. (Illus.). 215p. 1980. 21.95 (ISBN 0-87021-104-8). Naval Inst Pr.
Fincham, John. A History of Naval Architecture. (Scolar Maritime Library). (Illus.). 607p. 1979. Repr. of 1851 ed. 65.00x (ISBN 0-85967-569-6, Pub. by Scolar Pr England). Biblio Dist.
Garden, William. Yacht Designs. LC 76-8772. (Illus.). 1977. 20.00 (ISBN 0-87742-066-1). Intl Marine.
Gillmer, Thomas C. Modern Ship Design. 2nd ed. LC 74-25031. (Illus.). 355p. 1975. text ed. 18.95x (ISBN 0-87021-388-1). Naval Inst Pr.
Hutchinson, William. A Treatise on Naval Architecture. 303p. 1980. 49.95x (ISBN 0-85177-002-9, Pub. by Conway Maritime England). State Mutual Bk.
Jacobsson, A., et al, eds. Computer Applications in the Automation of Shipyard Operation & Ship Design II: Proceedings of the IFIP-IFAC Conference, June 8-11, 1976. (Computer Applications in Shipping & Shipbuilding: Vol. 4). 1977. 73.25 (ISBN 0-7204-0530-0, North-Holland). Elsevier.
Kinney, Francis S. You Are First: The Story of Olin & Rod Stephens of Sparkman & Stephens, Inc. LC 78-8148. (Illus.). 1978. 17.95 (ISBN 0-396-07567-3). Dodd.
Landstrom, Bjorn. Ship. LC 61-14718. 1967. 20.00 (ISBN 0-385-09823-5). Doubleday.
Leather, John. Colin Archer & the Seaworthy Double-Ender. LC 78-55782. (Illus.). 1979. 20.00 (ISBN 0-87742-086-6). Intl Marine.
Munro-Smith, R. Elements of Ship Design. 145p. 1976. pap. 13.50x (ISBN 0-900976-39-X, Pub. by Inst Marine Eng). Intl Schol Bk Serv.
--Ships & Naval Architecture (S. I. Units) (Illus.). 1977. pap. 22.50 (ISBN 0-900976-68-3, Pub. by Inst Marine Eng). Intl Schol Bk Serv.
Rabl, S. S. Ship & Aircraft Fairing & Development: For Draftsman & Loftsmen & Sheet Metal Workers. (Illus.). 1941. pap. 6.00x spiral bdg. (ISBN 0-87033-096-9). Cornell Maritime.
The Society of Naval Architects & Marine Engineers: Transactions, Vol. 87. 412p. 1980. text ed. 35.00 (ISBN 0-9603048-1-9). Soc Naval Archh.
The Work of Thomas W. Nason, N. A. (Illus.). 1976. 65.00 (ISBN 0-89073-012-1). Boston Public Lib.

NAVAL ART AND SCIENCE
see also Camouflage (Military Science); Imaginary Wars and Battles; Logistics; Marine Engineering; Military Art and Science; Naval Strategy; Navies; Navigation; Navy-Yards and Naval Stations; Privateering; Sea-Power; Seamanship; Seamen; Ship-Building; Signals and Signaling; Submarine Warfare; Torpedoes; Warships
Angelucci, Enzo & Cucari, Attilio. Ships. LC 77-5067. (Illus.). 1977. 24.95 (ISBN 0-07-001809-X, GB). McGraw.
AUFS Reports: 1952-1970, 63 vols. 750.00 (ISBN 0-910116-84-9). Am U Field.
Brodie, Bernard. A Guide to Naval Strategy. LC 77-22392. (Illus.). 1977. Repr. of 1958 ed. lib. bdg. 22.50x (ISBN 0-8371-9735-X, BRGN). Greenwood.
--Sea Power in the Machine Age. LC 69-13840. Repr. of 1943 ed. lib. bdg. 18.50x (ISBN 0-8371-1445-4, BRSP). Greenwood.

Carlisle, Rodney P. Sovereignty for Sale. LC 81-607020. 336p. 1981. 19.95 (ISBN 0-87021-668-6). Naval Inst Pr.

Cornell, F. M. & Hoffman, A. C. American Merchant Seamans Manual. 6th ed. Hayler, William B., ed. LC 56-12402. (Illus.). 1981. 22.50x (ISBN 0-87033-267-8). Cornell Maritime.

Couhat, Jean L. Combat Fleets of the World Nineteen Eighty & Eighty-One: Their Ships, Aircraft, & Armament. LC 78-50192. (Illus.). 808p. 1980. 64.95x (ISBN 0-87021-123-4). Naval Inst Pr.

Crenshaw, R. S., Jr. Naval Shiphandling. 4th ed. LC 74-26360. (Illus.). 496p. 1975. 19.95x (ISBN 0-87021-474-8). Naval Inst Pr.

Crichton, Tom. Naval Warfare. LC 77-430997. (Pegasus Books: No. 22). (Illus.). 1969. 10.50x (ISBN 0-234-77184-4). Intl Pubns Serv.

Deutermann, P. T. OPS Officer's Manual. LC 79-89179. (Illus.). 216p. 1980. 14.95x (ISBN 0-87021-505-1). Naval Inst Pr.

Dietel, Werner. Seefahrts-Worterbuch: Dictionary of Nautical Terms. 2nd ed. LC 66-56741. (Ger. Eng.). 1964. 32.00x (ISBN 3-7637-0028-5). Intl Pubns Serv.

Dorwart, Jeffery M. The Office of Naval Intelligence: Birth of America's First Intelligence Agency, 1882-1918. LC 79-84925. 1979. 15.95x (ISBN 0-87021-498-5). Naval Inst Pr.

Fioravanzo, Guiseppe. A History of Naval Tactical Thought. LC 78-70966. (Illus.). 1979. 16.95x (ISBN 0-87021-271-0). Naval Inst Pr.

Fire Terms: A Guide to Their Meaning & Use. (Illus.). 224p. 1980. 10.00 (ISBN 0-686-71646-9, SPP-60). Natl Fire Prot.

Griffiths, Maurice. The Hidden Menace. 160p. 1980. 20.75x (ISBN 0-85177-186-6, Pub. by Conway Maritime England). State Mutual Bk.

Harbeck, Charles T. Contribution to the Bibliography of the History of the United States Navy. LC 76-132677. (Bibliography & Reference Ser: No. 368). 1970. Repr. of 1906 ed. lib. bdg. 22.50 (ISBN 0-8337-1567-4). B Franklin.

Hezlet, Arthur. Electronics & Sea Power. LC 75-29410. (Illus.). 300p. 1975. 35.00x (ISBN 0-8128-1811-3). Stein & Day.

Hobbs, Richard R. Marine Navigation 1: Piloting. LC 74-75837. (Fundamentals of Naval Science Ser: No. 4). (Illus.). 1974. text ed. 12.95x (ISBN 0-87021-204-4). Naval Inst Pr.

Holley, Ben. The True Sex Life & Adventures of a Country Boy. 1981. 5.95 (ISBN 0-8062-1784-7). Carlton.

Jacobson, Kenneth C. The Watch Officer's Guide. 11th ed. LC 79-87470. 1979. 11.50x (ISBN 0-87021-749-6). Naval Inst Pr.

Koopman, Bernard O. Search & Screening: General Principles with Historical Applications. LC 79-16909. (Illus.). 400p. 1980. 50.00 (ISBN 0-08-023136-5); pap. 21.00 (ISBN 0-08-023135-7). Pergamon.

La Dage, John H. & Van Gemert, Lee. Stability & Trim for the Ship's Officer. 2nd ed. LC 56-6885. 1956. 11.00x (ISBN 0-87033-167-1). Cornell Maritime.

Lord, Lindsay. Nautical Etiquette & Customs. LC 76-44659. 1976. pap. 3.00 (ISBN 0-87033-225-2). Cornell Maritime.

Minikin, R. R. Winds, Waves & Maritime Structures. 295p. 1963. 29.75x (ISBN 0-85264-091-9, Pub. by Griffin England). State Mutual Bk.

Morrison, John S. & Williams, R. T. Greek Oared Ships, Nine Hundred - Three Hundred Twenty-Two B.C. LC 67-19504. (Illus.). 1968. 72.00 (ISBN 0-521-05770-1). Cambridge U Pr.

Naval Science Dept., U. S. Naval Academy, ed. Naval Operations Analysis. 2nd ed. LC 77-73342. 1977. 16.95x (ISBN 0-87021-440-3). Naval Inst Pr.

Navies & Men Series, 25 bks. 1980. Repr. Set. lib. bdg. 706.00x (ISBN 0-405-13030-9). Arno.

Office of the Chief of Naval Operations, Dept. of the Navy. Soviet Naval Developments, 1981-82. 4th ed. (Illus.). 132p. 1981. 14.50 (ISBN 0-933852-24-X). Nautical & Aviaation.

Prokop, Jan, ed. Computers in the Navy. LC 76-27260. 1976. text ed. 12.95x (ISBN 0-87021-128-5). Naval Inst Pr.

Richmond, Herbert W. Sea Power in the Modern World. LC 72-4293. (World Affairs Ser.: National & International Viewpoints). 318p. 1972. Repr. of 1934 ed. 16.00 (ISBN 0-405-04585-9). Arno.

Robison, Samuel S. A History of Naval Tactics from 1530-1930: The Evolution of Tactical Maxims. LC 75-41234. Repr. of 1942 ed. 52.50 (ISBN 0-404-14698-8). AMS Pr.

Rodgers, William L. Greek & Roman Naval Warfare. LC 79-121795. (Illus.). 1964. Repr. of 1937 ed. 13.95 (ISBN 0-87021-226-5). Naval Inst Pr.

--Naval Warfare Under Oars Fourth to Sixteenth Centuries. LC 75-121794. (Illus.). 1967. Repr. of 1940 ed. 13.95 (ISBN 0-87021-487-X). Naval Inst Pr.

Sansom, R. G. Language of the Navy in English. (English for Careers Ser). (Illus.). (gr. 10 up). 1978. pap. text ed. 3.50 (ISBN 0-88345-274-X). Regents Pub.

Sundt, Wilbur. Naval Science, Vol. 4. LC 78-56424. 1979. text ed. 15.00x (ISBN 0-87021-483-7). Naval Inst Pr.

Sundt, Wilbur A. Naval Science, Vol. 1. LC 78-56425. (Illus.). 320p. 1980. 8.50x (ISBN 0-87021-489-6). Naval Inst Pr.

--Naval Science, Vol. 3. LC 78-56425. 1978. text ed. 12.25x (ISBN 0-87021-479-9). Naval Inst Pr.

--Naval Science Two. (Illus.). 360p. 1981. 7.95 (ISBN 0-87021-457-8). Naval Inst Pr.

Transactions, Vol. 88. (Illus.). 450p. 1981. 35.00 (ISBN 0-9603048-2-7). Soc Naval Arch.

Uhlig, Frank, ed. Naval Review. LC 62-21028. 1975. 10.00x (ISBN 0-87021-472-1). Naval Inst Pr.

Uhlig, Frank J., ed. Naval Review Nineteen Eighty. LC 62-21028. (Illus.). 264p. 1980. 11.00x (ISBN 0-87021-490-X). Naval Inst Pr.

Uhlig, Frank, Jr., ed. Naval Review, Nineteen Eighty-One. (Illus.). 256p. 1981. 11.00 (ISBN 0-87021-496-9). Naval Inst Pr.

White, Lawrence A. The Coast Guardsman's Manual. 6th ed. LC 76-5558. 1976. pap. text ed. 9.50x (ISBN 0-87021-120-X). Naval Inst Pr.

Williams, Robert H. The Old Corps. (Illus.). 160p. Date not set. 25.95 (ISBN 0-87021-504-3). Naval Inst Pr.

Winters, David D. The Boat Officer's Handbook. LC 81-607042. 112p. 1981. pap. 8.95x (ISBN 0-87021-102-1). Naval Inst Pr.

NAVAL ART AND SCIENCE–BIBLIOGRAPHY

Naval Observatory Library. Washington D.C. Catalog of the Naval Observatory Library, Washington, D,C, 6 vols. 1976. Set. lib. bdg. 490.00 (ISBN 0-8161-0031-4). G K Hall.

NAVAL ART AND SCIENCE–DICTIONARIES

Bachman, G. Bryant. Definitions: Some Nautical-Some Naughtycal. (Illus.). 1979. 6.95 (ISBN 0-533-03572-4). Vantage.

Blackburn, Graham. The Overlook Illustrated Dictionary of Nautical Terms. LC 80-39640. (Illus.). 368p. 1981. 19.95 (ISBN 0-87951-124-9). Overlook Pr.

Cazzaroli, Gianni. Dictionnaire De la Navication. 392p. (Fr.). 1973. 23.50 (ISBN 0-686-56803-6, M-4650). French & Eur.

Dluhy, Robert. Maritime Dictionary: Covering Shipbuilding, Shipping, Marine Engineering & Related Fields, 2 vols. 3rd enl. ed. Incl. Vol. 1. (Ger. -Eng.). 1967. 75.00x (ISBN 0-8002-1299-1); Vol. 2. (Eng. -Ger.). 1968. LC 74-357050. 75.00x (ISBN 0-8002-1300-9). Intl Pubns Serv.

Falconer, William. Universal Dictionary of the Marine. LC 72-87321. (Illus.). Repr. of 1780 ed. lib. bdg. 24.50x (ISBN 0-678-05655-2). Kelley.

Gaynor, Frank, ed. New Military & Naval Dictionary. Repr. of 1951 ed. lib. bdg. 14.25x (ISBN 0-8371-2129-9, GAMN). Greenwood.

Jal, Augustin. Nouveau Glossaire Nautique, 2 lettre. 1848 ed. Lettre A, 1970. pap. 16.00 (ISBN 90-2796-442-4); Lettre B,1972. pap. 20.00x (ISBN 90-2797-028-9). Mouton.

--Nouveau Glossaire Nautique, Lettre C: Revision De L'edition Publiee En 1848. (Fr.). 1978. pap. 57.00x (ISBN 90-279-7538-8). Mouton.

Kemp, P. K. The Oxford Companion to Ships & the Sea. (Illus.). 1976. 39.95 (ISBN 0-19-211553-7). Oxford U Pr.

MacEwen, W. A. & Lewis, A. H. Encyclopedia of Nautical Knowledge. LC 53-9685. 1953. 15.00 (ISBN 0-87033-010-1). Cornell Maritime.

Naval Encyclopaedia. LC 73-155740. 1971. Repr. of 1884 ed. 54.00 (ISBN 0-8103-3389-9). Gale.

Nobel, John V. Naval Terms Dictionary. 1977. lib. bdg. 75.00 (ISBN 0-8490-2332-7). Gordon Pr.

Noel, John V., Jr. The VNR Dictionary of Ships & the Sea. 400p. 1980. text ed. 19.95 (ISBN 0-442-25631-0). Van Nos Reinhold.

Palmer, Joseph, compiled by. Jane's Dictionary of Naval Terms. 1976. 11.95 (ISBN 0-356-08258-X). Hippocrene Bks.

Smyth, W. H. Sailor's Word Book: An Alphabetical Digest of Nautical Terms & an Authoritative Encyclopedia of Naval Science & Nomenclature. 1977. pap. 75.00 (ISBN 0-8490-2555-9). Gordon Pr.

Standard Marine Navigational Vocabulary. 44p. 1977. pap. 8.25 (ISBN 0-686-64013-6, IMCO 38, IMCO). Unipub.

Tver, David F. Ocean & Marine Dictionary. LC 79-1529. 1979. 18.50 (ISBN 0-87033-246-5). Cornell Maritime.

Wedertz, Bill, ed. Dictionary of Naval Abbreviations. 2nd ed. LC 77-77336. 1977. 11.95x (ISBN 0-87021-154-4). Naval Inst Pr.

NAVAL ART AND SCIENCE–EXAMINATIONS, QUESTIONS, ETC.

Rudman, Jack. Officer Candidate School Admission Test (OCS) (Admission Test Ser.: ATS-53). (Cloth bdg. avail. on request). pap. 13.95 (ISBN 0-8373-5053-0). Natl Learning.

NAVAL ART AND SCIENCE–STUDY AND TEACHING

see Naval Education

NAVAL ART AND SCIENCE–TERMINOLOGY

Blackburn, Graham. The Overlook Illustrated Dictionary of Nautical Terms. LC 80-39640. (Illus.). 368p. 1981. 19.95 (ISBN 0-87951-124-9). Overlook Pr.

Colcord, Joanna C. Sea Language Comes Ashore. Dorsen, Richard M., ed. (International Folklore Ser.). 1977. Repr. of 1945 ed. lib. bdg. 12.00x (ISBN 0-405-10089-2). Arno.

Layton, C. W. Dictionary of Nautical Words & Terms. 1981. 60.00x (ISBN 0-85174-324-2, Pub. by Nautical England). State Mutual Bk.

NAVAL ARTILLERY

see Artillery

NAVAL ATTACHES

see Military Attaches

NAVAL AVIATION

see Aeronautics, Military

NAVAL BASES

see Navy-Yards and Naval Stations

NAVAL BATTLES

see also Battles; Naval History;
also subdivision History, Naval under names of countries, e.g. Great Britain–History, Naval; also names of naval battles

Chatterton, E. Keble. Battles by Sea. (Illus.). 271p. 1975. Repr. of 1925 ed. 13.50x (ISBN 0-87471-619-5). Rowman.

Cross, Wilbur. Naval Battles & Heroes. LC 60-13854. (American Heritage Junior Library). 154p. (YA) (gr. 7 up). 1960. 9.95 (ISBN 0-06-021375-2, HarpJ); PLB 12.89 (ISBN 0-06-021376-0). Har-Row.

Frere-Cook, Gervis & Macksey, Kenneth. History of Sea Warfare. (Illus.). 245p. 1980. 14.95 (ISBN 0-8069-9214-X, Pub by Guinness Superlatives England). Sterling.

Green, Fitzhugh & Frost, Holloway. Some Famous Sea Fights. facs. ed. LC 68-58792. (Essay Index Reprint Ser). 1927. 21.00 (ISBN 0-8369-0075-8). Arno.

Grishanov, V. M., ed. Man and Sea Warfare. 226p. 1978. 3.90 (ISBN 0-686-74552-3, Pub. by Progress Pubs Russia). Imported Pubns.

Howarth, David. Famous Sea Battles. 1981. 22.50 (ISBN 0-316-37480-6). Little.

Kennedy, Ludovic. The Death of the Tirpitz. (Illus.). 176p. 1980. 14.95 (ISBN 0-316-48905-0). Little.

Pack, S. W. C. The Battle of Sirte. LC 74-31677. (Sea Battles in Close-up Ser.: No. 14). 1975. 7.50 (ISBN 0-87021-813-1). Naval Inst Pr.

Padfield, Peter. Tide of Empires: Decisive Naval Campaigns in the Rise of the West, Vol. 1. (Illus.). 268p. 1979. 18.95 (ISBN 0-7100-0150-9). Routledge & Kegan.

Sanderson, Michael. Sea Battles: A Reference Guide. LC 74-21917. (Illus.). 216p. 1975. 14.95x (ISBN 0-8195-4080-3, Pub. by Wesleyan U Pr). Columbia U Pr.

Y'Blood, William T. Red Sun Setting: The Battle of the Philippine Sea. LC 80-84062. 208p. 1981. 18.95 (ISBN 0-87021-532-9). Naval Inst Pr.

NAVAL BIOGRAPHY

see Admirals; Seamen; Naval History;
also subdivision Biography under Navies e.g. United States–Navy–Biography

NAVAL CONSTRUCTION

see Naval Architecture; Ship-Building

NAVAL COOKERY

see Cookery, Marine

NAVAL EDUCATION

Nash, Ray. Navy at Dartmouth. (Illus.). 111p. 1946. text ed. 5.00x (ISBN 0-87451-009-0). U Pr of New Eng.

NAVAL ENGINEERING

see Marine Engineering

NAVAL GUNNERY

see also Ballistics

Hodges, Peter. The Big Gun: Battleship Main Armament, 1860-1945. LC 80-84051. 160p. 1981. 21.95 (ISBN 0-87021-917-0). Naval Inst Pr.

Smith, John. A Sea Grammar. LC 68-54664. (English Experience Ser.: No. 5). 76p. 1968. Repr. of 1627 ed. 16.00 (ISBN 90-221-0005-7). Walter J Johnson.

NAVAL HEALTH AND HYGIENE

see also Medicine, Naval;
also subdivision Medical and Sanitary Affairs under wars and campaigns, e.g. World War, 1939-1945–Medical and Sanitary Affairs

NAVAL HISTORY

Albion, Robert G. Naval & Maritime History: An Annotated Bibliography. 4th rev. ed. LC 73-186863. 370p. 1972. 10.00 (ISBN 0-913372-05-6); pap. 5.00 (ISBN 0-913372-06-4). Mystic Seaport.

Cable, James. Gunboat Diplomacy. 260p. 1981. 25.00 (ISBN 0-312-35346-4). St Martin.

Chatterton, E. Keble. King's Cutters & Smugglers, 1700-1855. LC 79-173106. (Illus.). Repr. of 1912 ed. 22.00 (ISBN 0-405-08351-3, Blom Pubns). Arno.

Coletta, Paolo E. French Ensor Chadwick: Scholarly Warrior. LC 80-67240. 264p. 1980. lib. bdg. 18.75 (ISBN 0-8191-1153-8); pap. text ed. 10.75 (ISBN 0-8191-1154-6). U Pr of Amer.

Coletta, Paolo E., ed. A Bibliography of American Naval History. LC 80-24864. 453p. 1981. 15.95x (ISBN 0-87021-105-6). Naval Inst Pr.

Courtemanche, Regis A. No Need of Glory. LC 76-56069. 1977. 13.95x (ISBN 0-87021-493-4). Naval Inst Pr.

Cranwell, John P. Spoilers of the Sea. facsimile ed. LC 78-93331. (Essay Index Reprint Ser). 1941. 25.00 (ISBN 0-8369-1563-1). Arno.

Creswell, John. British Admirals of the Eighteenth Century: Tactics in Battle. 460p. 1972. 18.50 (ISBN 0-208-01223-0, Archon). Shoe String.

Doenhoff, Richard A., ed. Versatile Guardian: Research in Naval History. LC 79-15678. 1979. 17.50 (ISBN 0-88258-078-7). Howard U Pr.

Fiske, Bradley A. The Navy As a Fighting Machine. 1977. lib. bdg. 59.95 (ISBN 0-8490-2333-5). Gordon Pr.

Fox, Frank. Great Ships: The Battlefleet of King Charles the Second. 208p. 1980. 69.75x (ISBN 0-85177-166-1, Pub. by Conway Maritime England). State Mutual Bk.

Frothingham, Jessie P. Sea Fighters from Drake to Farragut. facs. ed. LC 67-26743. (Essay Index Reprint Ser). 1902. 17.00 (ISBN 0-8369-0461-3). Arno.

Gibson, Charles Dana. The Ordeal of Convoy Ny 119. LC 73-83176. (Illus.). 178p. 1973. 10.00 (ISBN 0-913344-15-X). South St Sea Mus.

Gill, Conrad. Merchants & Mariners of the Eighteenth Century. LC 78-5810. (Illus.). 1978. Repr. of 1961 ed. lib. bdg. 15.75x (ISBN 0-313-20386-5, GIMM). Greenwood.

Goodrich, Frank B. History of the Sea: From the Ark to the Present Time. 1977. lib. bdg. 75.00 (ISBN 0-8490-2006-9). Gordon Pr.

Gorshkov, S. G. Red Star Rising at Sea. LC 74-82031. 200p. 1974. 15.00 (ISBN 0-87021-223-0). Naval Inst Pr.

Green, Fitzhugh. Our Naval Heritage. 1977. lib. bdg. 69.95 (ISBN 0-8490-2390-4). Gordon Pr.

Haas, Irvin. America's Historic Ships: Replicas & Restorations. LC 74-30893. (Illus.). 1975. 8.95 (ISBN 0-668-03768-7). Arco.

Hough, Richard. Man O' War: The Fighting Ship in History. (Illus.). 1979. 14.95 (ISBN 0-684-16189-3, ScribT). Scribner.

Howarth, D. Men-of-War. Time-Life Books, ed. (The Seafarers). (Illus.). 1979. 14.95 (ISBN 0-8094-2666-8). Time-Life.

Kelley, J. D. Our Navy, Its Growth & Achievements. 1977. lib. bdg. 99.95 (ISBN 0-8490-2391-2). Gordon Pr.

Kemp, P. K. The Oxford Companion to Ships & the Sea. (Illus.). 1976. 39.95 (ISBN 0-19-211553-7). Oxford U Pr.

Lewis, Archibald R. Naval Power & Trade in the Mediterranean: A.D. 500-1100. (Princeton Studies in History: Vol. 5). 1970. Repr. of 1951 ed. 18.50 (ISBN 0-384-32470-3). Johnson Repr.

Lewis, Charles L. Famous Old-World Sea Fighters. LC 70-99708. (Essay Index Reprint Ser). 1929. 25.00 (ISBN 0-8369-1419-8). Arno.

Lewis, Charles Lee. Famous Sea Fighters: Outstanding Naval Engagements Over 23 Centuries of Sea History with a Bibliography of 102 Works. 1977. lib. bdg. 75.00 (ISBN 0-8490-1804-8). Gordon Pr.

Lloyd, Christopher. Atlas of Maritime History. LC 74-32634. (Illus.). 1975. Repr. 35.00 (ISBN 0-668-03779-2). Arco.

Lott, Arnold S. Brave Ship, Brave Men. LC 78-50823. 1978. pap. 1.95 (ISBN 0-89559-020-4). Dale Books Inc.

Love, Robert W., ed. Changing Interpretations & New Sources in Naval History. LC 80-5. (Papers from the Third United States Naval Academy History Symposium). 500p. 1980. lib. bdg. 44.00 (ISBN 0-8240-9517-0). Garland Pub.

Mahan, A. & Preston, A. Influence of Seapower in History. 29.95 (ISBN 0-13-464537-5). P-H.

Mahan, A. T. Influence of Sea Power Upon History. 12.50 (ISBN 0-8446-2510-8). Peter Smith.

Mahan, Alfred T. The Influence of Sea-Power Upon History, 1660-1783. (Illus.). 1890. 10.00 (ISBN 0-316-54382-9). Little.

--The Influence of Seapower Upon History. 1957. pap. 7.95 (ISBN 0-8090-0010-5, AmCen). Hill & Wang.

Pemsel, Helmut. A History of War at Sea: An Atlas & Chronology of Conflict at Sea from 480 B. C. to the Present. LC 76-45237. Orig. Title: Atlas of Naval Warfare 480 BC - 1975 AD. 1977. 17.95 (ISBN 0-87021-803-4). Naval Inst Pr.

Pope, Dudley. Life in Nelson's Navy. LC 80-82726. 296p. 1981. 14.95 (ISBN 0-87021-346-6). Naval Inst Pr.

Ranft, Bryan, ed. Technical Change & British Naval Policy, 1860-1939. 1977. text ed. 24.50x (ISBN 0-8419-6207-3). Holmes & Meier.

Raven, Alan & Roberts, John. Man O'war. Incl. No. 1. County Class Cruisers. 1978 (ISBN 0-933514-01-8); No. 2. V&W Class Destroyers. 1979 (ISBN 0-933514-02-6); No. 3. Rodney & Nelson. 1979 (ISBN 0-933514-03-4). (Illus.). pap. 6.95 ea. RSV Pub.

Reynolds, Clark G. Command of the Sea: The History & Strategy of Maritime Empires. (Illus.). 1974. 15.00 (ISBN 0-688-00267-6). Morrow.

--The Fast Carriers: The Forging of an Air Navy. LC 77-10914. 522p. 1978. Repr. of 1968 ed. 24.00 (ISBN 0-88275-608-7). Krieger.

Robison, Samuel S. A History of Naval Tactics from 1530-1930: The Evolution of Tactical Maxims. LC 75-41234. Repr. of 1942 ed. 52.50 (ISBN 0-404-14698-8). AMS Pr.

Rose, J. Holland. Indecisiveness of Modern War. LC 68-15834. 1968. Repr. of 1927 ed. 11.00 (ISBN 0-8046-0392-8). Kennikat.

Scammell, G. V. The World Encompassed: The First European Maritime Empires. LC 80-6319. (Illus.). 536p. 1981. 35.00 (ISBN 0-520-04422-3); pre-Jan. 29.95 (ISBN 0-686-76230-4). U of Cal Pr.

Smith, Philip C., et al. East India Marine Hall: 1824-1974. (Illus.). 1974. pap. 3.25 (ISBN 0-87577-050-9). Peabody Mus Salem.

Spiers, George. The Wavertree: An Ocean Wanderer. (Illus.). 134p. 1969. 4.50 (ISBN 0-913344-01-X). South St Sea Mus.

Symonds, Craig L., ed. New Aspects of Naval History. LC 81-4987. 1981. text ed. 32.95x (ISBN 0-87021-495-0). Naval Inst Pr.

Towers, Edwin L. Operation Thunderhead: Hope for Freedom. LC 81-80291. 205p. pap. text ed. 2.95 (ISBN 0-89882-010-3). Lane & Assoc.

Van Duyn, John & Southworth. War at Sea, 4 vols. Incl. Bk. 1. The Ancient Fleets: The Story of Naval Warfare Under Oars, 2600 B.C. - 1597 A.D. LC 67-16200. 370p; Bk. 2. The Age of Sails: The Story of Naval Warfare Under Sail, 1213 A.D. - 1853 A.D. LC 68-17224. 468p. (H-589); Bk. 3. The Age of Steam, Pt. 1: 1783-1936. (H-590); Bk. 4. The Age of Steam, Pt. 2: The Story of Engine-Powered Naval Warfare, 1936-1972. LC 67-16200. 443p. (H-591). (Illus.). 7.50 ea. Hippocrene Bks.

Von Pivka, Otto. Navies of the Napoleonic Era. (Illus.). 273p. 1980. 24.95 (ISBN 0-88254-505-1, Pub by David & Charles England). Hippocrene Bks.

Warner, Oliver. Great Naval Actions. LC 76-28568. 1976. 13.50x (ISBN 0-8448-1015-0). Crane-Russak Co.

Wede, Karl. The Ship's Bell. (Illus.). 60p. 1972. 1.00 (ISBN 0-913344-10-9). South St Sea Mus.

White, Elsberry V. The First Iron-Clad Naval Engagement in the World: The Merrimac & the Monitor. (Illus.). 1906. wrappers 12.50 (ISBN 0-686-17397-X). R S Barnes.

Wilson, Herbert W. Battleships in Action, 2 Vols. 1968. Repr. of 1926 ed. Set. 39.00 (ISBN 0-403-00046-7). Scholarly.

NAVAL HISTORY–BIBLIOGRAPHY

Great Britain Ministry Of Defence - London. Author & Subject Catalogues of the Naval Library, Ministry of Defence, 5 Vols. 1967. Set. lib. bdg. 395.00 (ISBN 0-8161-0755-6). G K Hall.

NAVAL HISTORY, ANCIENT

Casson, Lionel. Ancient Mariners. 1959. 9.95 (ISBN 0-02-522830-7). Macmillan.

Guilmartin, J. F., Jr. Gunpowder & Galleys. LC 73-83109. (Early Modern History Studies). (Illus.). 380p. 1975. 46.50 (ISBN 0-521-20272-8). Cambridge U Pr.

NAVAL LAW

see also Courts-Martial and Courts of Inquiry; Maritime Law; Military Law; War, Maritime (International Law)

Office of the Chief of Engineers, U.S. Army, ed. Laws of the United States Relating to the Improvement of Rivers & Harbors from August 11, 1790 to June 29, 1938, 3 vols. LC 73-5434. Repr. of 1940 ed. Set. 125.00 (ISBN 0-404-11190-4); Vol. 1. (ISBN 0-404-11191-2); Vol. 2. (ISBN 0-404-11192-0); Vol. 3. (ISBN 0-404-11193-9). AMS Pr.

NAVAL LOGISTICS

see Logistics

NAVAL MEDICINE

see Medicine, Naval

NAVAL MUSEUMS

see also Museums

Mystic Seaport Museum, Inc. International Congress of Maritime Museums, 3rd Conference: Proceedings, 1978. LC 79-26650. 306p. (Orig.). 1979. pap. 20.00 (ISBN 0-913372-22-6, IS-00103, Pub. by Mystic Seaport). Univ Microfilms.

Stammers, M. K. Discovering Maritime Museums & Historic Ships. (Discovering Ser.). (Illus.). 84p. (Orig.). 1978. pap. 2.50 (ISBN 0-913714-37-2). Legacy Bks.

NAVAL OFFENSES

see also Mutiny

NAVAL PENSIONS

see Pensions, Military

NAVAL POLICY

see Sea-Power;

also subdivision Defenses under names of countries, e.g. United States–Defense; also Great Britain–Navy; United States–Navy and similar headings

NAVAL PRINTS

Mariners Museum Library - Newport News - Virginia. Catalog of Marine Prints & Paintings, 3 Vols. 1964. Set. lib. bdg. 235.00 (ISBN 0-8161-0684-3). G K Hall.

NAVAL SCHOOLS

see Naval Education

NAVAL SCIENCE

see Naval Art and Science

NAVAL SHIPS

see Warships

NAVAL SHIPYARDS

see Navy-Yards and Naval Stations

NAVAL SIGNALING

see Signals and Signaling

NAVAL STATIONS

see Navy-Yards and Naval Stations

NAVAL STORES

Malone, Joseph J. Pine Trees & Politics. Bruchey, Stuart, ed. LC 78-53552. (Development of Public Land Law in the U. S. Ser.). 1979. Repr. of 1964 ed. lib. bdg. 15.00x (ISBN 0-405-11380-3). Arno.

NAVAL STRATEGY

see also Sea-Power

Corbett, Julian S. Naval Operations, 1914-1918, 5 vols. Incl. Vol. 1, Pt. 1 (ISBN 0-404-09281-0); Vol. 1, Pt. 2 (ISBN 0-404-09282-9); Vol. 2 (ISBN 0-404-09283-7); Vol. 3, Pt. 1 (ISBN 0-404-09284-5); Vol. 3, Pt. 2 (ISBN 0-404-09285-3); Vol. 4, Pt. 1 (ISBN 0-404-09286-1); Vol. 4, Pt. 2 (ISBN 0-404-09287-X); Vol. 5, Pt. 1 (ISBN 0-404-09288-8); Vol. 5, Pt. 2 (ISBN 0-404-09289-6). (Illus.). Repr. of 1931 ed. Set. 420.00 (ISBN 0-404-09280-2). AMS Pr.

--Some Principles of Maritime Strategy. LC 76-154122. (BCL Ser. II). Repr. of 1911 ed. 10.00 (ISBN 0-404-09227-6). AMS Pr.

Fioravanzo, Guiseppe. A History of Naval Tactical Thought. LC 78-70966. (Illus.). 1979. 16.95x (ISBN 0-87021-271-0). Naval Inst Pr.

Jordan, Gerald, ed. Naval Warfare in the Twentieth Century: A Festschrift in Honour of Professor Arthur J. Marder. LC 76-28613. 1977. 24.50x (ISBN 0-8448-1001-0). Crane-Russak Co.

Leutze, James R. Bargaining for Supremacy: Anglo-American Naval Collaboration, 1937-1941. LC 77-669. 1977. 22.50 (ISBN 0-8078-1305-2). U of NC Pr.

Mahan, Alfred T. Naval Strategy. LC 74-14359. (Illus.). 475p. 1975. Repr. of 1911 ed. lib. bdg. 34.25x (ISBN 0-8371-7802-9, MANS). Greenwood.

NAVAL WARFARE

see Naval Art and Science; Naval Battles; War, Maritime (International Law)

NAVARRE (KINGDOM)

Hamilton, Earl J. Money, Prices, & Wages in Valencia, Aragon & Navarre 1351-1500. LC 75-25653. (Perspectives in European Hist. Ser.: No. 6). (Illus.). xxviii, 310p. Repr. of 1936 ed. lib. bdg. 17.50x (ISBN 0-87991-613-3). Porcupine Pr.

Marguerite De Valois. Memoires et Lettres De Marguerite De Valois. Gessard, M. F., ed. 35.50 (ISBN 0-384-35398-3); pap. 31.00 (ISBN 0-384-35388-6). Johnson Repr.

NAVIES

see also Armies; Disarmament; Naval Art and Science; Sea-Power; Seamen; Warships; also Great Britain–Navy; United States–Navy; and similar headings

Blechman, Barry M. Guide to Far Eastern Navies. LC 77-87942. 1978. 32.95 (ISBN 0-87021-235-4). Naval Inst Pr.

Booth, Ken. Navies & Foreign Policies. LC 79-2254. 1979. text ed. 23.50x (ISBN 0-8419-0518-5). Holmes & Meier.

Brodie, Bernard. Sea Power in the Machine Age. LC 69-13840. Repr. of 1943 ed. lib. bdg. 18.50x (ISBN 0-8371-1445-4, BRSP). Greenwood.

Davis, George T. A Navy Second to None: The Development of Modern American Naval Policy. LC 77-110826. (Illus.). xiii, 508p. Repr. of 1940 ed. lib. bdg. 20.25x (ISBN 0-8371-3226-6, DANS). Greenwood.

Jane, Fred T., ed. All the World's Fighting Ships, Eighteen Ninety-Eight. LC 69-14519. (Illus.). Repr. of 1898 ed. 14.95x (ISBN 0-685-06494-8, Pub by Arco). Biblo.

Nitz, Paul H., et al. Securing the Seas: The Soviet Naval Challenge & Western Alliance Options. (Illus.). 1979. lib. bdg. 30.75 (ISBN 0-89158-359-9); pap. text ed. 14.50x (ISBN 0-89158-360-2). Westview.

Teitler, G. The Genesis of the Professional Officers' Corps. LC 77-23307. (Sage Series on Armed Forces & Society: Vol. 11). 246p. 1977. 20.00 (ISBN 0-8039-0841-5). Sage.

Woodward, E. L. Great Britain & German Navy. 524p. 1964. 32.50x (ISBN 0-7146-1528-5, F Cass Co). Biblio Dist.

NAVIES–MEDICAL SERVICE

see Medicine, Naval

NAVIGATION

see also Aids to Navigation; Coastwise Navigation; Electronics in Navigation; Harbors; Hydrographic Surveying; Inland Navigation; Knots and Splices; Lighthouses; Log Books; Longitude; Nautical Almanacs; Nautical Astronomy; Nautical Charts; Nautical Instruments; Naval Art and Science; Navigation (Astronautics); Ocean Currents; Pilot Guides; Pilots and Pilotage; Rule of the Road at Sea; Seamanship; Ship-Building; Shipwrecks; Signals and Signaling; Steam-Navigation; Stowage; Submarine Topography; Submarines; Tides; Traverse Tables; Winds; Yachts and Yachting also names of nautical instruments, e.g. Compass, Gyroscope

Anderson, E. W. The Principles of Navigation. LC 66-70107. (Illus.). 654p. 1979. 25.00 (ISBN 0-370-00311-X, Pub. by Chatto Bodley Jonathan). Merrimack Bk Serv.

Appleyard, S. F. Marine Electronic Navigation. (Illus.). 256p. 1980. 34.50 (ISBN 0-7100-0533-4). Routledge & Kegan.

Bayless, A. Compact Sight Reduction Table. LC 80-15129. (Illus.). 1980. 4.50 (ISBN 0-87033-269-4). Cornell Maritime.

Blair, Carvel H. Seamanship: A Handbook for Oceanographers. LC 76-56349. (Illus.). 1977. 9.00x (ISBN 0-87033-228-7). Cornell Maritime.

Blewitt, Mary. Celestial Navigation for Yachtsmen. LC 67-25097. 1967. 7.95 (ISBN 0-8286-0028-7). De Graff.

--Celestial Navigation for Yachtsmen. 5th ed. (Illus.). 66p. 1971. 12.00x (ISBN 0-8464-0236-X). Beekman Pubs.

--Navigation for Yachtsmen. 3rd ed. (Illus.). 101p. 1974. 12.95x (ISBN 0-8464-0668-3). Beekman Pubs.

Bowditch, Nathaniel. The American Pratical Navigator; Being an Epitome of Navigation, 2 vols. 1976. Repr. 65.00 (ISBN 0-403-08994-8, Regency). Scholarly.

--Bowditch for Yachtsmen: Piloting. abridged ed. (Illus.). 270p. 1976. 9.95 (ISBN 0-679-50603-9). McKay.

--Bowditch's Coastal Navigation. LC 78-5232. (Illus.). 1979. pap. 9.95 (ISBN 0-668-04460-8). Arco.

Buchanek & Bergin. Piloting-Navigation with the Pocket Calculator. LC 76-23228. (Illus.). 1976. 14.95 (ISBN 0-8306-6853-5); pap. 8.95 (ISBN 0-8306-5853-X, 853). TAB Bks.

Budlong, John P. Shoreline & Sextant: Practical Coastline Navigation. 224p. 1980. pap. text ed. 12.95 (ISBN 0-442-21928-8). Van Nos Reinhold.

--Shoreline & Sextant: Practical Coastline Navigation. 1977. 9.95 (ISBN 0-442-21142-2). Van Nos Reinhold.

Campbell, John F. History & Bibliography of the New American Practical Navigator & the American Coast Pilot. LC 64-15742. (Illus.). 1964. 10.00 (ISBN 0-87577-006-1). Peabody Mus Salem.

Campbell, Stafford. Yachtsman's Guide to Calculator Navigation. 1980. 8.95 (ISBN 0-87165-035-5). Ziff-Davis Pub.

Cohen, Phillip M. Bathymetric Navigation & Charting. LC 79-6107. (Navies & Men Ser.). (Illus.). 1980. Repr. of 1970 ed. lib. bdg. 12.00x (ISBN 0-405-13036-8). Arno.

Congleton, Carol A. Navigational Applications of Plane & Spherical Trigonometry. LC 79-9431. (Illus.). 1980. pap. 8.50x (ISBN 0-87033-256-2). Cornell Maritime.

Cotter, Charles H. The Elements of Navigation & Nautical Astronomy. 1981. 75.00x (ISBN 0-85174-270-X, Pub. by Nautical England). State Mutual Bk.

Davies, Thomas D. Star Sight Reduction Tables for Forty-Two Stars: Assumed Altitude Method of Celestial Navigation. LC 79-7464. 1980. 28.50x (ISBN 0-87033-250-3). Cornell Maritime.

Davis, John. Voyages & Works of John Davis the Navigator. Markham, Albert H., ed. & intro. by. LC 71-134714. (Hakluyt Society, First Ser.: No. 59). (Illus.). 1970. Repr. of 1880 ed. lib. bdg. 32.00 (ISBN 0-8337-2241-7). B Franklin.

Derrick, David. Navigation for Offshore & Ocean Sailors. LC 81-67008. (Illus.). 160p. 1981. 22.00 (ISBN 0-7153-8086-9). David & Charles.

Devereux, Frederick L., Jr. Practical Navigation for the Yachtsman. (Illus.). 316p. 1972. 19.95 (ISBN 0-393-03171-3). Norton.

Dixon, Conrad. Basic Coastal Navigation. (Illus.). 96p. 1973. 6.95x (ISBN 0-8464-0174-6). Beekman Pubs.

--Basic Coastal Navigation. (Illus.). 1979. 5.95 (ISBN 0-229-97364-7, ScribT). Scribner.

--Navigation by Pocket Calculator. (Illus.). 1979. 7.95 (ISBN 0-229-11618-3, ScribT). Scribner.

--Start to Navigate. (Illus.). 120p. 1977. 9.95x (ISBN 0-8464-1139-3). Beekman Pubs.

--Start to Navigate. (Illus.). 1979. 6.95 (ISBN 0-229-11573-X, ScribT). Scribner.

Dodge, D. O. & Kyriss, S. E. Seamanship: Fundamentals for the Deck Officer. 2nd ed. LC 80-81089. (Fundamentals of Naval Science: Vol. 2). 272p. 1981. text ed. 16.95x (ISBN 0-87021-613-9). Naval Inst Pr.

Dunlap, G. D. & Shufeldt, Captain H. H. Piloting & Dead Reckoning. LC 78-123789. (Illus., Orig.). 1970. flexible bdg. 9.95 (ISBN 0-87021-511-6). Naval Inst Pr.

Fifield, L. W. Navigation for Watchkeepers. (Illus.). 416p. 1980. text ed. 32.50x (ISBN 0-686-77794-8). Sheridan.

Frost, A. The Principles & Practice of Navigation. 1981. 40.00x (ISBN 0-85174-310-2, Pub. by Nautical England). State Mutual Bk.

Graves, Frederick. Piloting. LC 80-84742. (Illus.). 256p. 1981. 24.95 (ISBN 0-87742-116-1). Intl Marine.

Guzzwell, John. Trekka Round the World. (Illus.). 1979. 9.95 (ISBN 0-8286-0084-8). De Graff.

Hart, M. R. How to Navigate Today. 5th ed. LC 68-23169. (Illus.). 1970. pap. 4.00 (ISBN 0-87033-035-7). Cornell Maritime.

Hay, David & Hay, Joan. Cruising in Strange Waters. (Illus.). 253p. 1970. 14.95x (ISBN 0-8464-0306-4). Beekman Pubs.

Hobbs, Richard R. Marine Navigation One: Piloting. 2nd ed. LC 81-75837. 320p. 1981. text ed. 14.95x (ISBN 0-87021-358-X). Naval Inst Pr.

--Marine Navigation 2: Celestial & Electronic. LC 74-75837. (Fundamental of Naval Science Ser: No. 5). (Illus.). 1974. text ed. 12.95x (ISBN 0-87021-365-2). Naval Inst Pr.

Howell, F. S. Navigation Primer for Fishermen. 1978. 25.00 (ISBN 0-685-63443-4). State Mutual Bk.

Hutson, A. B. The Navigator's Art. (Illus.). 192p. 1975. 9.95 (ISBN 0-263-05592-2). Transatlantic.

James, Richard & Plant, Richard M. The Multiple Choice Examinations for Chief Mate & Master: Study Guide. LC 76-48096. (Illus.). 1976. 25.00x (ISBN 0-87033-232-5). Cornell Maritime.

--The Multiple Choice Examinations for Third & Second Mates: Study Guide. 3rd ed. LC 79-1735. 1979. pap. 20.00x (ISBN 0-87033-252-X). Cornell Maritime.

Kane, G. R. Instant Navigation. (Illus.). 1977. pap. 7.95 (ISBN 0-87799-081-6). Aztex.

Kemp, John F. Ocean Navigator (Reed's) 1977. 3rd ed. (Illus.). 1978. 45.00 (ISBN 0-900335-47-5). Heinman.

Lane, Carl D. & Montgomery, John. Navigation the Easy Way. (Illus.). 1949. 14.95 (ISBN 0-393-03134-9). Norton.

Layton, C. W. Harbord's Glossary of Navigation. 1981. 50.00x (ISBN 0-85174-277-7, Pub. by Nautical England). State Mutual Bk.

Letcher, John. Self-Contained Celestial Navigation with H.O. 208. LC 76-8782. (Illus.). 1977. 17.50 (ISBN 0-87742-082-3). Intl Marine.

Lewis, David. The Voyaging Stars. (Illus.). 1978. 10.95 (ISBN 0-393-03226-4). Norton.

MacEwen, W. A. Blue Book of Questions & Answers for Second Mate, Chief Mate & Master. LC 62-15957. (Illus.). 320p. 1969. pap. 8.50x (ISBN 0-87033-007-1). Cornell Maritime.

Madden, Anne, ed. Best of Sail Navigation. (Illus.). 1980. 13.95 (ISBN 0-914814-27-3). Sail Bks.

Maloney, Albert S. Dutton's Navigation & Piloting. 13th ed. LC 77-87943. 1978. 26.95 (ISBN 0-87021-164-1). Naval Inst Pr.

Milligan, John E. Celestial Navigation by H. O. 249. LC 74-1464. (Illus.). 1974. pap. 6.00 (ISBN 0-87033-191-4). Cornell Maritime.

Mills, H. R. Positional Astronomy & Astro-Navigation Made Easy: A New Approach Using the Pocket Calculator. LC 77-13142. 1978. 36.95x (ISBN 0-470-99324-3). Halsted Pr.

Moeller, Jan & Moeller, Bill. The Intracoastal Waterway. (Illus.). Date not set. pap. 7.95 (ISBN 0-915160-23-4). Seven Seas.

Moody, Alton B. Navigation Afloat: A Manual for the Seaman. 768p. 1981. 35.00 (ISBN 0-442-25488-1). Van Nos Reinhold.

Motte, G. A. Chartwork & Marine Navigation: For Fisherman & Boat Operations. LC 77-21925. (Illus.). 1977. 7.50 (ISBN 0-87033-242-2). Cornell Maritime.
Motte, R. Weather Routeing of Ships. 1972. 15.00 (ISBN 0-540-00382-4). Heinman.
Navigation. (Library of Boating Ser.). (Illus.). 176p. 1975. 16.95 (ISBN 0-8094-2112-7). Time-Life.
Navigation Primer. (Illus.). 1978. pap. 21.75 (ISBN 0-85238-081-X, FN27, FNB). Unipub.
Nordenskiold, Nils A. Periplus: An Essay on the Early History of Charts & Sailing Directions. Bather, Francis A., tr. from Swed. (Illus.). 1897. 189.00 (ISBN 0-8337-2572-6). B Franklin.
Offshore. (Library of Boating Ser.). (Illus.). 1976. 16.95 (ISBN 0-8094-2136-4). Time-Life.
Plant, Richard M. Formulae for the Mariner. LC 78-21543. (Illus.). 1978. spiral bdg. 7.00x (ISBN 0-87033-251-1). Cornell Maritime.
Randier, Jean. Marine Navigation Instruments. (Illus.). 219p. 1980. text ed. 47.50x (ISBN 0-7195-3733-9). Humanities.
Recommendation on Basic Principles & Operational Guidance Relating to Navigational Watchkeeping. 12p. 1974. pap. 7.75 (ISBN 92-801-1032-2, IMCO 62, IMCO). Unipub.
Rogoff, Mortimer. Calculator Navigation. (Illus.). 1980. 29.95 (ISBN 0-393-03192-6). Norton.
Royal Yachting Association. Navigation: An RYA Manual. (Illus.). 168p. 1981. 19.95 (ISBN 0-7153-8246-2). David & Charles.
Schlereth, Hewitt. Commonsense Coastal Navigation. (Illus.). 1981. 18.95 (ISBN 0-393-03224-8). Norton.
Shufeldt, H. H. & Dunlap, G. D. Piloting & Dead Reckoning. 2nd ed. LC 80-606921. 164p. 1981. pap. 11.95 (ISBN 0-87021-512-4). Naval Inst Pr.
Simonsen, S. Simonsen's Navigation. LC 72-8426. 1973. 12.95 (ISBN 0-13-809970-7). P-H.
Singleton, Robert R. You'll Never Get Lost Again. (Illus.). 1979. 9.95 (ISBN 0-87691-294-3); pap. 6.95 (ISBN 0-87691-295-1). Winchester Pr.
Slocum, Jonah. Celestial Navigation with a Pocket Calculator. 1980. softbound 14.95 (ISBN 0-917410-03-3). Basic Sci Pr.
Smith, I. & Mulroney, R. A. Parallel Indexing Techniques. 1979. pap. 6.50x (ISBN 0-540-07353-9). Sheridan.
Tobin, Wallace E., III. Mariner's Pocket Companion Nineteen Eighty-One. LC 75-21689. 224p. 1980. pap. 6.95 (ISBN 0-87021-381-4). Naval Inst Pr.
Toghill, Jeff. Celestial Navigation for Beginners. (Illus.). 112p. (Orig.). 1978. pap. 6.75 (ISBN 0-589-50042-2, Pub. by Reed Books Australia). C E Tuttle.
--Coastal Navigation for Beginners. (Illus.). 1976. pap. 5.25 (ISBN 0-589-07191-2, Pub. by Reed Books Australia). C E Tuttle.
--Navigating with Chart & Compass. (Illus.). 96p. (Orig.). 1980. pap. 8.25 (ISBN 0-589-50183-6, Pub. by Reed Bks Australia). C E Tuttle.
Toghill, Jeff E. The Yachtsman's Navigation Manual. LC 76-24492. 1976. 12.50 (ISBN 0-8286-0077-5). De Graff.
Townsend, Sallie & Ericson, Virginia. The Amateur Navigator's Handbook. LC 73-15985. (Illus.). 256p. 1974. 11.95 (ISBN 0-690-00192-4). T Y Crowell.
U.S. Naval Academy. Navigation & Operations. LC 72-75502. (Fundamentals of Naval Science Ser: No. 3). 1972. 11.50x (ISBN 0-87021-491-8). Naval Inst Pr.
U.S. Naval Training Command. Navigation. (Nautical Ser.). (Illus.). 1977. pap. 6.95 (ISBN 0-679-50775-2). McKay.
Van Der Ree, Frieda. Exploring the Coast by Boat. LC 79-63559. (Illus.). 240p. 1979. pap. 8.95 (ISBN 0-916076-09-1). Writing.
Waters, D. W., ed. Rutters of the Sea: The Sailing Directions of Pierre Gracie - a Study of the First English & French Printed Sailing Directions. (Illus.). 1967. 45.00x (ISBN 0-300-01028-1). Yale U Pr.
Whitaker, S. F. Night Sailing. (Illus.). 94p. 1974. 12.50x (ISBN 0-8464-1115-6). Beekman Pubs.
Wilensky, Julius M. Yachtsman's Guide to the Windward Islands. 2nd, rev. ed. Van Ost, John R., ed. LC 78-65702. (Illus.). 1978. 15.75 (ISBN 0-918752-01-9). Wescott Cove.
Willan, T. S. River Navigation in England: 1600-1750. 2nd ed. 163p. 1964. 24.00x (ISBN 0-7146-1383-5, F Cass Co). Biblio Dist.
Wright, Frances W. Celestial Navigation. LC 70-76202. (Illus.). 1969. 7.50 (ISBN 0-87033-000-4). Cornell Maritime.
--Particularized Navigation: How to Prevent Navigational Emergencies. LC 73-10239. (Illus.). 1973. 5.00 (ISBN 0-87033-188-4). Cornell Maritime.
Wright, John. Dead Reckoning Navigation. (Illus.). 164p. 1973. 15.95x (ISBN 0-8464-0315-3). Beekman Pubs.

NAVIGATION–DICTIONARIES
see Naval Art and Science–Dictionaries

NAVIGATION–EARLY WORKS TO 1800
Aspley, John. Speculum Nauticum: A Looking Glasse, for Sea-Men. LC 77-6849. (English Experience Ser: No. 844). 1977. Repr. of 1624 ed. lib. bdg. 9.50 (ISBN 90-221-0844-9). Walter J Johnson.
Barlow, William. The Navigators Supply. LC 76-38150. (English Experience Ser.: No. 430). 100p. Repr. of 1597 ed. 16.00 (ISBN 90-221-0430-3). Walter J Johnson.
Cuningham, William. The Cosmographical Glasse, Conteinyng the Principles of Cosmographie, Etc. LC 68-54632. (English Experience Ser.: No. 44). 1968. Repr. of 1559 ed. 49.00 (ISBN 90-221-0044-8). Walter J Johnson.
Dee, John. General & Rare Memorials Pertayning to Perfecte Arte of Navigation. LC 68-54635. (English Experience Ser.: No. 62). 82p. 1968. Repr. of 1577 ed. 28.00 (ISBN 90-221-0062-6). Walter J Johnson.
Galilei, Galileo. Galileo Galilei: Operations of the Geometric & Military Compass. Drake, Stillman, tr. from Ital. & intro. by. LC 78-2433. (Illus.). 1978. pap. text ed. 5.95 (ISBN 0-87474-383-4). Smithsonian.
Linton, Anthony. Newes of the Complement of the Art of Navigation & of the Mightie Empire of Cataia. LC 72-215. (English Experience Ser.: No. 204). 1969. Repr. of 1609 ed. 8.00 (ISBN 90-221-0204-1). Walter J Johnson.
Norwood, Richard. The Sea-Mans Practice. LC 74-28877. (English Experience Ser.: No. 755). 1975. Repr. of 1637 ed. 13.00 (ISBN 90-221-0755-8). Walter J Johnson.
--Trigonometrie, or the Doctrine of Triangles, 2 pts. LC 78-171779. (English Experience Ser.: No. 404). 362p. 1971. Repr. of 1631 ed. 53.00 (ISBN 90-221-0404-4). Walter J Johnson.
Tanner, Robert. A Briefe Treatise for the Ready Use of the Sphere. LC 73-6164. (English Experience Ser.: No. 627). 110p. 1973. Repr. of 1592 ed. 9.50 (ISBN 90-221-0627-6). Walter J Johnson.
Wright, Edward. Certaine Errors in Navigation (the Voyage of George Earl of Cumberland to the Azores) LC 74-80224. (English Experience Ser.: No. 703). 1974. Repr. of 1599 ed. 29.00 (ISBN 90-221-0703-5). Walter J Johnson.

NAVIGATION–HISTORY
Angelucci, Enzo & Cucari, Attilio. Ships. LC 77-5067. (Illus.). 1977. 24.95 (ISBN 0-07-001809-X, GB). McGraw.
Casson, Lionel. Ancient Mariners. 1959. 9.95 (ISBN 0-02-522830-7). Macmillan.
Finney, Ben R., compiled by. Pacific Navigation & Voyaging. (Illus.). 1976. text ed. 12.50x (ISBN 0-8248-0584-4). U Pr of Hawaii.
Fire Terms: A Guide to Their Meaning & Use. (Illus.). 224p. 1980. 10.00 (ISBN 0-686-71646-9, SPP-60). Natl Fire Prot.
Morgan, Bryan. Navigation. (Jackdaw Ser: No. 107). 1974. 6.95 (ISBN 0-670-50527-7, Grossman). Viking Pr.
Nadvi, S. Arab Navigation. 5.50 (ISBN 0-686-18335-5). Kazi Pubns.
Taylor, E. G. The Haven-Finding Art. 1971. 14.00 (ISBN 0-444-19608-0). Elsevier.
Whall, W. B. The Romance of Navigation. LC 72-83272. (Illus.). Repr. of 1930 ed. 15.00 (ISBN 0-405-09061-7). Arno.

NAVIGATION–JUVENILE LITERATURE
Navigation. LC 75-13778. (Library of Boating Ser.). (Illus.). (gr. 6 up). 1975. PLB 13.95 (ISBN 0-8094-2113-5, Pub. by Time-Life). Silver.

NAVIGATION–SAFETY MEASURES
see also Radio in Navigation
Dixon, Conrad. Start to Navigate. (Illus.). 1979. 6.95 (ISBN 0-229-11573-X, ScribT). Scribner.
International Conference on Maritime Search & Rescue, 1979. 38p. 1979. 9.25 (ISBN 0-686-70812-1, IMCO). Unipub.
International Conference on Revision of the International Regulations for Preventing Collisions at Sea. 128p. 1974. 12.50 (ISBN 0-686-70770-2, IMCO). Unipub.
International Conference on Safety of Fishing Vessels. 204p. 1977. 18.00 (ISBN 0-686-70767-2, IMCO). Unipub.
International Conference on Safety of Life at Sea Nineteen Seventy-Four (Solas Nineteen Seventy-Four) 320p. 1975. pap. 20.75 (ISBN 0-686-64011-X, IMCO 4, IMCO). Unipub.
International Conference on Tanker Safety & Pollution Prevention. 106p. 1978. 18.00 (ISBN 0-686-70803-2, IMCO). Unipub.
Marine Publications Intl. Ltd., ed. International Manual of Maritime Safety. 1981. 125.00x (ISBN 0-906314-00-3, Pub. by Marine Pubns Intl England). State Mutual Bk.
--Marine Personnel Safety Manual. 1981. 38.00x (ISBN 0-906314-08-9, Pub. by Marine Pubns Intl England). State Mutual Bk.
--Ships Firefighting Manual. 1981. 50.00x (ISBN 0-906314-03-8, Pub. by Marine Pubns Intl England). State Mutual Bk.
--Ships Operational Safety Manual. 1981. 150.00x (ISBN 0-906314-09-7, Pub. by Marine Pubns Intl England). State Mutual Bk.
National Safety Council. Motor Fleet Safety Manual. 2nd ed. 420p. 1972. 14.50 (ISBN 0-87912-046-0, 221.02). Natl Safety Coun.
--Small Fleet Guide. LC 80-85327. 96p. 1971. pap. 8.50 (ISBN 0-87912-055-X, 221.20). Natl Safety Coun.

NAVIGATION–TABLES
see also Traverse Tables
Gibbs, Tony, ed. Pilot's Work Book. 1979. pap. 4.00 (ISBN 0-915160-03-X). Seven Seas.
Moeller, Jan & Moeller, Bill. The Intracoastal Waterway. (Illus.). Date not set. pap. 7.95 (ISBN 0-915160-23-4). Seven Seas.
Nichols, Daniel E. Distance off Tables. 2nd ed. LC 43-15657. 1943. 4.00x (ISBN 0-87033-020-9). Cornell Maritime.
Norwood, Richard. Trigonometrie, or the Doctrine of Triangles, 2 pts. LC 78-171779. (English Experience Ser.: No. 404). 362p. 1971. Repr. of 1631 ed. 53.00 (ISBN 90-221-0404-4). Walter J Johnson.

NAVIGATION, AERIAL
see Navigation (Aeronautics)

NAVIGATION (AERONAUTICS)
see also Airplanes–Piloting; Electronics in Aeronautics; Guidance Systems (Flight); Inertial Navigation (Aeronautics)
AGARD-NATO. Radar Techniques for Detection Tracking & Navigation. (Agardographs Ser.: No. 100). (Illus.). 1966. 128.75x (ISBN 0-677-11030-8). Gordon.
Downie, Don. Cockpit Navigation Guide. 1962. 8.95 (ISBN 0-8306-9939-2); pap. 4.95 (ISBN 0-8306-2208-X, 2208). TAB Bks.
Garrison, P. Cockpit Computers & Navigation Avionics. 1982. price not set (ISBN 0-07-022893-0). McGraw.
Harbold, Norris B. The Log of Air Navigation. 1970. pap. 8.00 (ISBN 0-89126-085-4); pap. 8.00 (ISBN 0-686-63601-5). MA-AH Pub.
Hoyt, John R. As the Pro Flies. (Illus.). 1959. 8.95 (ISBN 0-07-030610-9, GB). McGraw.
Practical Air Navigation. 3rd ed. 336p. 1978. pap. text ed. 8.95 (ISBN 0-88487-053-7, JS314136). Jeppesen Sanderson.
Reithmaier, Larry. Flight Planning Guide for Pilots. LC 71-94967. (Pilot Guides). 1970. pap. 1.50 (ISBN 0-8168-7204-X). Aero.
Sabin, Arthur J. Pilot Training: You Can Learn to Fly. LC 78-24387. (Illus.). 200p. 1979. pap. 4.95 (ISBN 0-89037-171-7). Anderson World.
Smith, Robert. Instrument Flying Guide. 1964. pap. 5.95 (ISBN 0-8306-2217-9, 2217). TAB Bks.
Stremming, Ken & Holmes, Harold J., eds. Where Am I, VOR Course, 3 bks. 1976. Set. 9.95 (ISBN 0-911720-27-8, Pub. by Haldon Bks). Aviation.
Technical Regulations: Meteorological Service for International Air Navigation, Vol. 2. (Basic Documents Ser: No. 2). (Illus.). 70p. 1977. pap. 16.00 (ISBN 0-685-76012-X, WMO). Unipub.
Wassenbergh, H. A. Aspects of Air Law & Civil Air Policy in the Seventies. LC 79-538221. 1970. 30.00x (ISBN 90-247-5003-2). Intl Pubns Serv.

NAVIGATION (ASTRONAUTICS)
see also Space Flight; Space Vehicles
Dixon, Conrad. Basic Astro Navigation. (Illus.). 119p. 1973. 9.95x (ISBN 0-8464-0173-8). Beekman Pubs.
--Basic Astronavigation. (Illus.). 1979. 8.95 (ISBN 0-229-98579-3, ScribT). Scribner.
--Navigation by Pocket Calculator. (Illus.). 1979. 7.95 (ISBN 0-229-11618-3, ScribT). Scribner.
Mieville, A. D. Astronomical Navigation Without Mathematics. (Illus.). 1945. pap. text ed. 1.00 (ISBN 0-911090-17-7). Pacific Bk Supply.

NAVIGATION, ELECTRONICS IN
see Electronics in Navigation

NAVIGATION, INLAND
see Inland Navigation

NAVIGATION, PRIMITIVE
see also Indians of North America–Boats
Lewis, David. We, the Navigators: The Ancient Art of Landfinding in the Pacific. LC 72-82139. (Illus.). 368p. 1975. pap. 5.95 (ISBN 0-8248-0394-9). U Pr of Hawaii.

NAVIGATION, RADAR IN
see Radar in Navigation

NAVIGATION ACTS, 1649-1696
Dickerson, O. M. The Navigation Acts & the American Revolution. LC 71-120248. xv, 344p. 1974. Repr. of 1951 ed. lib. bdg. 21.00x (ISBN 0-374-92162-8). Octagon.
Harper, Lawrence A. English Navigation Laws. 1964. lib. bdg. 30.00x (ISBN 0-374-93667-6). Octagon.

NAVIGATION BY BIRDS
see Bird Navigation

NAVIGATION CHARTS
see Nautical Charts

NAVIGATION LAWS
see Inland Navigation; Maritime Law

NAVIGATORS
see Discoveries (In Geography); Explorers; Seamen

NAVY
see Naval Art and Science; Navies; Sea-Power; also subdivision Navy under names of countries, e.g. United States–Navy

NAVY WIVES
Ebbert, Jean. The Sailor's Wife. 3rd ed. LC 77-73598. 1977. pap. 5.95 (ISBN 0-87021-589-2). Naval Inst Pr.
Hoffman, Mary A. & Sitler, Filomena. Parent's Guide to Navy Life. LC 81-81666. 1981. pap. 14.95x (ISBN 0-87021-513-2). Naval Inst Pr.

NAVY-YARDS AND NAVAL STATIONS
Chen, Gideon. Tso Tsung T'ang: Pioneer Promoter of the Modern Dockyard & the Woolen Mill in China. LC 67-31401. (Illus.). 1961. pap. 4.00 (ISBN 0-8188-0018-6). Paragon.
Revere, Joseph W. Naval Duty in California. (California Heritage Ser.: Vol. 11). 18.00 (ISBN 0-686-12797-8). Sullivan Bks.
Simpson, William K. Papyrus Reisner II: Accounts of the Dockyard Workshop at This in the Reign of Sesostris I. (Illus.). 1965. 35.00 (ISBN 0-87846-031-4). Mus Fine Arts Boston.
Tompkins, Tom. Yokosuka: Base of an Empire. (Illus.). 192p. 1981. pap. 12.95 (ISBN 0-89141-088-0). Presidio Pr.

NAZI MOVEMENT
see Germany–Politics and Government–1933-1945

NAZI PARTY
see Nationalsozialistische Deutsche Arbeiter-Partei

NAZISM
see National Socialism

NDANI (NEW GUINEA PEOPLE)
see Dani (New Guinea People)

NDEBELE
see Matabele

NDEMBU (AFRICAN TRIBE)
Turner, V. W. Schism & Continuity in an African Society. 1972. pap. text ed. 13.95x (ISBN 0-7190-1038-1). Humanities.
Turner, Victor. The Forest of Symbols: Aspects of Ndembu Ritual. LC 67-12308. (Illus.). 405p. 1967. 28.50x (ISBN 0-8014-0432-0); pap. 7.95 (ISBN 0-8014-9101-0, CP101). Cornell U Pr.
--Revelation & Divination in Ndembu Ritual. LC 75-1623. (Symbol, Myth & Ritual Ser). (Illus.). 352p. 1975. 25.00x (ISBN 0-8014-0863-6); pap. 6.95 (ISBN 0-8014-9158-4). Cornell U Pr.

NEAL, JOHN, 1793-1876
Lease, Benjamin. That Wild Fellow John Neal & the American Literary Revolution. 1973. 10.00x (ISBN 0-226-46969-7). U of Chicago Pr.
Lough, Arthur G. Influence of John Mason Neale. 1962. text ed. 10.00x (ISBN 0-8401-1430-3). Allenson-Breckinridge.
Sears, Donald A. John Neal. (United States Authors Ser.). 1978. lib. bdg. 12.50 (ISBN 0-8057-7230-8). Twayne.

NEAR EAST
see also Arab Countries; Eastern Question; Levant;
also names of specific countries, cities, geographic areas, etc. in the Near East, e.g. Iraq; Mesopotamia; Jerusalem
Alexander, Yonah & Kittrie, Nicholas N. F., eds. Crescent & Star: Arab & Israeli Perspectives on the Middle East Conflict. LC 72-5797. (AMS Studies in Modern Society: Political & Social Issues). 30.00 (ISBN 0-404-10522-X); pap. 11.95 (ISBN 0-404-10523-8). AMS Pr.
Anshen, Ruth N., ed. Mid-East - World Center: Yesterday, Today & Tomorrow. LC 78-20183. (Science & Culture Ser.). xiv, 386p. 1975. Repr. of 1956 ed. lib. bdg. 17.50x (ISBN 0-8154-0508-1). Cooper Sq.
Ben-Meir, Alon. The Middle East Imperatives & Choices. LC 75-26110. (Illus.). 1975. 7.95x (ISBN 0-915474-01-8, Decalogue). Effective Learn.
Bloomfield, B. C., ed. Middle East Studies & Libraries: A Felicitation Volume for J. D. Pearson. 244p. 1981. text ed. 47.30 (ISBN 0-7201-1512-4, Pub. by Mansell England). Merrimack Bk Serv.
Brown, L. Carl & Itzkowitz, Norman, eds. Psychological Dimensions of Near Eastern Studies. LC 75-43499. 382p. 1977. 9.95x (ISBN 0-87850-028-6). Darwin Pr.
Cattan, Henry. The Garden of Joys. 11.95 (ISBN 0-7043-2219-6, Pub. by Quartet England). Charles River Bks.
Chaffetz, David & Rapoport, Mitchell, eds. The Middle East: Issues & Events of 1978 from The New York Times Information Bank. LC 78-32140. (News in Print Ser.). 1979. lib. bdg. 24.95x (ISBN 0-405-12875-4). Arno.
Clarke, J. I. & Fisher, W. B. Populations of the Middle East & North Africa: A Geographical Approach. LC 72-80410. 432p. 1972. text ed. 39.50x (ISBN 0-8419-0125-2). Holmes & Meier.
Cleveland, Ray L. Middle East & South Asia 1979. 11th ed. (Illus.). 1977. pap. 2.75 (ISBN 0-686-23397-2). Stryker-Post.

Clouston, William A. Flowers from a Persian Garden & Other Papers. Dorsen, Richard M., ed. LC 77-70584. (International Ser.). Repr. of 1890 ed. lib. bdg. 21.00x (ISBN 0-405-10088-4). Arno.
Congressional Quarterly Inc. Middle East. 5th ed. 250p. (Orig.). 1981. pap. text ed. 8.95 (ISBN 0-87187-211-0). Congr Quarterly.
Coon, C. S. Caravan: The Story of the Middle East. rev. ed. LC 75-45344. 390p. 1976. Repr. of 1958 ed. 15.50 (ISBN 0-88275-393-2). Krieger.
Dishon, Daniel, ed. Middle East Record, 6 vols. Incl. Vol. 1. 1960; Vol. 2. 826p. 1961 (ISBN 0-87855-165-4); Vol. 3. 668p. 1967 (ISBN 0-87855-166-2); Vol. 4. 920p. 1968 (ISBN 0-87855-167-0). vols. 2-4 69.95 ea.; Set. casebound 200.00 (ISBN 0-87855-223-5). Transaction Bks.
Fisher, W. B. The Oil States. (Illus.). 72p. (gr. 9-12). 1980. 14.95 (ISBN 0-7134-2477-X, Pub. by Batsford England). David & Charles.
Gobineau, Conte D. Romances of the East. LC 73-6282. (The Middle East Ser.). Repr. of 1878 ed. 18.00 (ISBN 0-405-05340-1). Arno.
Greenman, Joseph & Joachim, Ann, eds. Educational Film Guide for Middle Eastern Studies. xxxvii, 126p. 1980. pap. text ed. 6.00 (ISBN 0-932098-16-9). Ctr for NE & North African Stud.
Hamalian, Leo. Burn After Reading. LC 78-67678. 1979. 8.95 (ISBN 0-933706-02-2); pap. 4.95 (ISBN 0-933706-03-0). Ararat Pr.
Heravi, Mehdi, ed. Concise Encyclopedia of the Middle East. 1973. 12.00 (ISBN 0-8183-0130-9). Pub Aff Pr.
Hirschmann, Maria A. Will the East Wind Blow? Hansi Reports on the Middle East. LC 78-71319. (Illus.). 160p. (Orig.). 1979. pap. text ed. 2.50 (ISBN 0-932878-04-0, HB-04). Hansi.
International Law & the Middle East Crisis: A Symposium, Vol. 4. 1957. 5.00 (ISBN 0-930598-03-2). Tulane Stud Pol.
Jackson, Abraham V. From Constantinople to the Home of Omar Khayyam. LC 74-149389. (Illus.). Repr. of 1911 ed. 33.75 (ISBN 0-404-09012-5). AMS Pr.
Keddie, Nikki. The Middle East & Beyond. 1981. 29.50x (ISBN 0-7146-3151-5, F Cass Co). Biblio Dist.
Kedourie, Elie. Chatham House Version & Other Middle-Eastern Studies. 488p. 1970. 32.50x (ISBN 0-7146-3044-6, F Cass Co). Biblio Dist.
Kerr, Stanley E. The Lions of Marash: Personal Experiences with American Near East Relief, 1919-1922. LC 75-38001. 122p. 1973. 23.00 (ISBN 0-87395-200-6); microfiche 23.00 (ISBN 0-87395-201-4). State U NY Pr.
King, Condon, ed. Middle East, 4 bks. rev ed. (Culture Studies Program). (gr. 7-12). 1979. tchr's. manual 2.76 (ISBN 0-201-42672-2, Sch Div); text ed. 6.04 (ISBN 0-201-42671-4). A-W.
Kublin, Hyman. The Middle East: Selected Readings. rev ed. LC 72-12182. (World Regional Studies). (Illus.). 246p. (gr. 9-12). 1973. pap. text ed. 6.60 (ISBN 0-395-13932-5, 2-31076). HM.
Kublin, Hyman, et al. Middle East: Regional Study. rev. ed. (World Regional Studies). (gr. 9-12). 1973. pap. text ed. 6.60 (ISBN 0-395-13931-7). HM.
Landau, Jacob M. Middle Eastern Themes: Papers in History & Politics. 309p. 1973. 29.50x (ISBN 0-7146-2969-3, F Cass Co). Biblio Dist.
Legum, Colin & Shaked, Haim, eds. Arab Relations in the Middle East. LC 78-20888. (Middle Affairs Ser.: No. 1). 1978. pap. text ed. 8.50x (ISBN 0-8419-0447-2). Holmes & Meier.
Longrigg, Stephen H. Middle East. 2nd ed. LC 75-91722. 1970. lib. bdg. 21.95x (ISBN 0-202-10008-1). Aldine Pub.
Magnus, Ralph H., ed. Documents on the Middle East. 1969. pap. 7.25 (ISBN 0-8447-3066-1). Am Enterprise.
Michaud, Jacob-Black. Cohesive Force: Feud in the Middle East. LC 74-83518. 272p. 1975. 22.50 (ISBN 0-312-14700-7). St Martin.
Mid-East Studies, 55 titles in 67 vols. Repr. of 1954 ed. Set. write for info (ISBN 0-404-56200-0). AMS Pr.
The Middle East & North Africa 1978-1979. 936p. 1979. 60.00 (ISBN 0-905118-23-5, EUR 7, Pub. by Europa). Unipub.
The Middle East & North Africa 1979-1980. 1979. 70.00 (ISBN 0-686-61267-1, EUR 13, Pub. by Europa). Unipub.
Middle East & North Africa 1980-1981. 27th ed. LC 48-3250. (Illus.). 1000p. 1980. 80.00 (ISBN 0-905118-50-2, Pub. by Europa England). Gale.
Middle East & North Africa, 1981 to 1982. (Illus.). 1000p. 1981. 80.00 (ISBN 0-686-72831-9, Pub. by Europa England). Gale.
The Middle East & North Africa 1981-82. 28th ed. LC 48-3250. (Illus.). 970p. 1981. 90.00x (ISBN 0-905118-65-0). Intl Pubns Serv.
Middle East Contemporary Survey, Vol. 1. (Illus.). 1978. 115.00x (ISBN 0-8419-0323-9). Holmes & Meier.
Middle East Yearbook, 1980. 1980. 25.00 (ISBN 0-531-03919-6). Watts.
Newlon, Clarke. The Middle East & Why. LC 76-53443. (Illus.). (gr. 7 up). 1977. 6.95 (ISBN 0-396-07425-1). Dodd.
Parr, Leland W. Introduction to the Anthropology of the Near East in Ancient & Recent Times, with a Chapter on Near Eastern Bloodgroups. 1980. lib. bdg. 59.95 (ISBN 0-8490-3164-8). Gordon Pr.
Peretz, Don. The Middle East Today. 3rd ed. LC 78-2441. 1978. text ed. 18.95 (ISBN 0-03-021576-5, HoltC). HR&W.
Polk, William R. & Chambers, Richard L., eds. Beginnings of Modernization in the Middle East: The Nineteenth Century. LC 68-16712. (Publications of the Center for Middle Eastern Studies Ser). 1968. 14.00x (ISBN 0-226-67425-8). U of Chicago Pr.
Proceedings of a Technical Meeting on Wetland Conservation. (Illus.). 1968. pap. 18.00x (ISBN 2-88032-031-3, IUCN11, IUCN). Unipub.
Rowland, John. A History of Sino-Indian Relations: Hostile Co-Existence. 304p. 1966. pap. 8.50 (ISBN 0-442-07085-3, Pub. by Van Nos Reinhold). Krieger.
Sachar, Howard M. Emergence of the Middle East. (Illus.). Repr. of 1969 ed. 15.00 (ISBN 0-394-44754-9). Knopf.
Said, Edward W. Orientalism. LC 78-51803. 1978. 15.00 (ISBN 0-394-42814-5). Pantheon.
Stickley, Thomas S., et al, eds. Man, Food & Agriculture in the Middle East. 20.00x (ISBN 0-8156-6015-4, Am U Beirut). Syracuse U Pr.
Sweet, Louise E., ed. The Central Middle East: A Handbook of Anthropology & Published Research. LC 70-148003. (Area Survey Ser.). xii, 324p. 1971. 15.00x (ISBN 0-87536-107-2); pap. 7.50x (ISBN 0-87536-108-0). HRAFP.
Tikku, Girdhari L., ed. Islam & Its Cultural Divergence. LC 75-126522. 1971. 15.00 (ISBN 0-252-00127-3). U of Ill Pr.
Trevelyan, Humphrey. Middle East in Revolution. LC 70-121353. 1971. 7.95 (ISBN 0-87645-033-8). Gambit.
Udovitch, A. L. The Middle East: Oil, Conflict & Hope, Vol. 10. LC 75-44728. (Critical Choices for Americans Ser.). 1976. 25.95 (ISBN 0-669-00424-3). Lexington Bks.
Vatikiotis, P. J. Conflict in the Middle East. (Illus.). 1971. text ed. 27.50x (ISBN 0-04-327036-0). Allen Unwin.
Warriner, Doreen. Land Reform & Development in the Middle East. LC 75-31476. (Illus.). 238p. 1976. Repr. of 1962 ed. lib. bdg. 15.25x (ISBN 0-8371-8530-0, WALR). Greenwood.
Wevers, J. W. & Redford, D. B., eds. Essays on the Ancient Semitic World. LC 79-151397. 1971. 15.00x (ISBN 0-8020-1603-0). U of Toronto Pr.
Winston, Henry. Black Americans & the Middle East Conflict. 1970. pap. 0.25 (ISBN 0-87898-058-X). New Outlook.
Woods, John E., et al, eds. The Middle East, 39 bks. 1973. Set. 994.00 (ISBN 0-405-05310-X). Arno.
Wright, Quincy. Middle East: Prospects for Peace. Shapiro, Issac, ed. LC 72-102936. (Hammarskjold Forum Ser). 1969. 10.00 (ISBN 0-379-11813-0). Oceana.
Yale Near Eastern Researches, Vols. 1-3. Repr. of 1968 ed. Set. 69.00 (ISBN 0-404-60260-6). AMS Pr.

NEAR EAST–ANTIQUITIES

Avi-Yonah, Michael, ed. The Encyclopedia of Archaeological Excavations in the Holy Land, Vol. 2. LC 76-14997. (Illus.). 400p. 1975. 25.00 (ISBN 0-13-275123-2). P-H.
Bates, Daniel G. Nomads & Farmers: A Study of the Yordk of Southeastern Turkey. (Anthropological Papers: No. 52). (Illus.). 1973. pap. 5.00x (ISBN 0-932206-50-6). U Mich Mus Anthro.
Buccellati, Giorgio & Kelly-Buccellati, M. Terqa Preliminary Report: The Fourth Season, Introduction & the Stratigraphic Record. (Bibliotheca Mesopotamica Ser.: Vol. 10). (Illus.). 96p. 1979. 23.50 (ISBN 0-89003-042-1); pap. 19.50 (ISBN 0-89003-043-X). Undena Pubns.
Burney, C. A. The Ancient Near East. LC 76-55483. (Archaeology & Civilization Ser.). (Illus.). 1977. 22.50 (ISBN 0-8014-1080-0). Cornell U Pr.
Carleton, Patrick. Buried Empires: The Earliest Civilizations of The Middle East. LC 78-14110. (Illus.). 1979. Repr. of 1939 ed. 26.50 (ISBN 0-88355-782-7). Hyperion Conn.
Coon, Carleton S. The Seven Caves: Archaeological Explorations in the Middle East. LC 80-24503. (Illus.). xx, 354p. 1981. Repr. of 1957 ed. lib. bdg. 31.50x (ISBN 0-313-22824-8, COSCA). Greenwood.
Eichler, Barry L. Indenture at Nuzi: The Personal Tidennutu Contracts & Its Mesopotamian Analogues. LC 73-77148. 180p. 1973. 17.50x (ISBN 0-300-01467-8). Yale U Pr.
Finegan, Jack. Archaeological History of the Ancient Middle East. (Illus.). 1979. lib. bdg. 36.25 (ISBN 0-89158-164-2, Dawson). Westview.
Goedicke, Hans & Roberts, J. J. M., eds. Unity & Diversity: Essays in the History, Literature, & Religion of the Ancient Near East. LC 74-24376. (Near Eastern Studies). (Illus.). 240p. 1975. 16.00x (ISBN 0-8018-1638-6). Johns Hopkins.
Gordon, Cyrus H. Adventures in the Nearest East. 1957. 6.95 (ISBN 0-911566-10-4). Ventnor.
Jones, Wilbur D. Venus & Sothis: How the Ancient Near East Was Rediscovered. 200p. 1981. text ed. 18.95x (ISBN 0-88229-691-4); pap. text ed. 8.95x (ISBN 0-88229-780-5). Nelson-Hall.
Laroche, Lucienne. The Middle East. Nannicini, Giuliana & Bowman, John, eds. Mondadori, tr. from It. LC 72-79616. (Monuments of Civilization Ser). (Illus.). 192p. 1974. 25.00 (ISBN 0-448-02021-1, Msp). G&D.
Mellaart, James. The Neolithic of the Near East. LC 75-15209. (Illus.). 320p. 1976. pap. 4.95 (ISBN 0-684-14484-0, SL616, ScribT). Scribner.
Noveck, Madeline. The Mark of Ancient Man: Ancient Near Eastern Stamp Seals & Cylinder Seals: the Gorelick Collection. LC 75-10584. (Illus.). 96p. (Orig.). 1975. pap. 4.95 (ISBN 0-87273-002-6). Bklyn Mus.
Obrink, Ulla. Hala Sultan Tekke Five. (Studies in Mediterranean Archaeology XLV: No. 5). (Orig.). 1979. pap. text ed. 42.00x (ISBN 91-85058-91-2). Humanities.
Oriental Institute. The Nineteen Nineteen-Nineteen Twenty Breasted Expedition to the Near East. LC 77-2731. 1977. 2 black & white fiches incl. 14.00 (ISBN 0-226-69473-9, Chicago Visual Lib). U of Chicago Pr.
Orlin, Louis L. Assyrian Colonies in Cappadocia. (Orig.). 1970. pap. text ed. 55.00x (ISBN 0-686-22408-6). Mouton.
Pearson, H. F., et al. Preliminary Report on the Synagogue at Dura-Europos. (Illus.). 1936. pap. 32.50x (ISBN 0-686-51290-1). Elliots Bks.
Phillips, Jill M. Archaeology of the Collective East: Greece, Asia Minor, Egypt, Lebanon, Mesopatamia, Syria, Palestine, an Annotated Bibliography. 1977. lib. bdg. 69.95 (ISBN 0-8490-1362-3). Gordon Pr.
Pritchard, James B., ed. The Ancient Near East. Incl. Vol. I. An Anthology of Texts & Pictures. 1958. 17.50x (ISBN 0-691-03501-6); pap. 6.95 (ISBN 0-691-00200-2); Vol. II. A New Anthology of Texts & Pictures. LC 72-11944. (Princeton Studies on the Near East Ser.). 1973. 17.50x (ISBN 0-691-03549-0); pap. 6.95 (ISBN 0-691-00209-6). Princeton U Pr.
--Ancient Near East in Pictures with Supplement. 2nd ed. Incl. Ancient Near Eastern Texts Relating to the Old Testament with Supplement. 3rd ed. Set. 50.00 ea. (ISBN 0-691-03503-2); 90.00 (ISBN 0-686-76919-8). 1969. deluxe ed. 46.50x ea. (ISBN 0-691-03502-4); Set. 82.50x (ISBN 0-686-66606-2). Princeton U Pr.
Richmond, Diana. Antar & IAbla: A Bedouin Romance. 9.95 (ISBN 0-7043-2162-9, Pub. by Quartet England). Charles River Bks.
Sasson, Jack M. Dated Texts from Mari: A Tabulation. LC 80-53524. (Aids & Research Tools in Near Eastern Studies: Vol. 13). 154p. (Orig.). 1981. pap. write for info. (ISBN 0-89003-066-9). Undena Pubns.
Solecki, Rose L. An Early Village Site at Zawi Chemi Shanidar. (Bibliotheca Mesopotamia: Vol. 13). (Illus.). xi, 102p. 1981. write for info. (ISBN 0-89003-067-7); pap. write for info. (ISBN 0-89003-068-5). Undena Pubns.
Stewart, James R. Tell el Ajjul: The Middle Eastern Bronze Age Remains. (Studies in Mediterranean Archaeology Ser.: No. XXXVIII). (Illus.). 1974. pap. text ed. 28.00x (ISBN 91-85058-56-4). Humanities.

NEAR EAST–BIBLIOGRAPHY

Atiyeh, George N., compiled by. The Contemporary Middle East, 1948-1973: An Annotated & Selective Bibliography. (Series Seventy). 775p. 1975. lib. bdg. 49.00 (ISBN 0-8161-1085-9). G K Hall.
B. D'Herbelot de Molainville, et al. Bibliotheque Orientale, ou Dictionnaire universel, contenant generalment tout ce qui regarde la connaissance des peuples del 'orient, 4 vols. 2864p. (Fr.). 1981. Repr. of 1782 ed. lib. bdg. 525.00x (ISBN 0-89241-342-5). Caratzas Bros.
Bevis, Richard, ed. Bibliotheca Cisorientalia: An Annotated Checklist of Early Travel Books on the Near & Middle East. 1973. lib. bdg. 29.50 (ISBN 0-8161-0969-9). G K Hall.
Ettinghausen, Richard. Selected & Annotated Bibliography of Books & Periodicals in Western Languages Dealing with the Near & Middle East, with Special Emphasis on Medieval & Modern Times. LC 70-180337. Repr. of 1954 ed. 24.50 (ISBN 0-404-56249-3). AMS Pr.
Grimwood-Jones, Diana, ed. Middle East & Islam: A Bibliographical Introduction. 2nd rev. & enl. ed. LC 72-85349. 429p. 1979. 50.00x (ISBN 3-85750-032-8). Intl Pubns Serv.
Grimwood-Jones, Diana, et al, eds. Arab-Islamic Bibliography: Based on Giuseppe Gabrieli's Manvale Di Bibliografia Muselmana. 1977. text ed. 52.00x (ISBN 0-391-00691-6). Humanities.
Institute Of Asian Economic Affairs, ed. Union Catalogue of the Documentary Materials on Middle East, 1965. 1965. 20.00 (ISBN 0-379-00281-7). Oceana.
Matthews, Noel & Wainwrights, Doreen M., eds. A Guide to Manuscrpits & Documents in the British Isles Relating to the Middle East & North Africa. 500p. 1980. 148.00x (ISBN 0-19-713598-6). Oxford U Pr.
Rossi, Peter M. & White, Wayne E., eds. Articles on the Middle East, 1947-1971: A Cumulation of Bibliographies from the Middle East Journal, 4 vols. 1980. Set. 160.00 (ISBN 0-87650-030-0). Pierian.
U. S. Department of State-Division of Library & Reference Services. Point Four, Near East & Africa: A Selected Bibliography of Studies on Economically Underdeveloped Countries. LC 65-55124. (Illus.). 1968. Repr. of 1951 ed. lib. bdg. 15.00x (ISBN 0-8371-1732-1, ROFO). Greenwood.
Univ. of the State of New York, Foreign Area Materials Center. Middle East & North Africa: A Bibliography for Undergraduate Libraries. Howard, Harry N., ed. LC 72-151801. (Occasional Publications Ser: No. 14). 80p. 1971. 8.95 (ISBN 0-87272-018-7). Brodart.
Zuwiyya, Jalal. The Near East(South-West Asia & North Africa) A Bibliographic Study. LC 72-13364. 1973. 13.50 (ISBN 0-8108-0583-9). Scarecrow.

NEAR EAST–CIVILIZATION

Bagnole, John W. Cultures of the Islamic Middle East. (America-Mideast Educational & Training Servies, Inc. - Occasional Paper: No. 4). 86p. (Orig.). 1978. pap. text ed. 4.00 (ISBN 0-89192-296-2). Interbk Inc.
Brown, L. Carl, ed. From Madina to Metropolis: Heritage & Change in the Near Eastern City. LC 76-161054. (Illus.). 343p. 1973. 16.95 (ISBN 0-87850-006-5). Darwin Pr.
Covensky, Milton. The Ancient Near Eastern Tradition. (Orig.). 1966. pap. text ed. 10.50 scp (ISBN 0-06-041365-4, HarpC). Har-Row.
Ellis, Maria, ed. Essays on the Ancient Near East in Memory of Jacob Joel Finkelstein. (Connecticut Academy of Arts & Science Memoir: Vol. XIX). 1977. 17.50 (ISBN 0-208-01714-3). Shoe String.
Gaube, Heinz. Iranian Cities. LC 77-25748. (Hagop Kevorkian Series on Near Eastern Art & Civilization). (Illus.). 1979. 25.00x (ISBN 0-8147-2971-1). NYU Pr.
Hawkes, Jacquetta. First Great Civilizations. 1973. 15.95 (ISBN 0-394-46161-4). Knopf.
Jurji, Edward J. The Middle East, Its Religion & Culture. LC 72-9809. 159p. 1973. Repr. of 1956 ed. lib. bdg. 13.00x (ISBN 0-8371-6597-0, JUME). Greenwood.
Laroche, Lucienne. The Middle East. Nannicini, Giuliana & Bowman, John, eds. Mondadori, tr. from It. LC 72-79616. (Monuments of Civilization Ser). (Illus.). 192p. 1974. 25.00 (ISBN 0-448-02021-1, Msp). G&D.
Morton, H. V. In Search of the Holy Land. (Illus.). 1979. 15.00 (ISBN 0-396-07691-2). Dodd.
Redman, Charles L. The Rise of Civilization: From Early Farmers to Urban Society in the Ancient Near East. LC 78-1493. (Illus.). 1978. text ed. 24.95x (ISBN 0-7167-0056-5); pap. text ed. 14.95x (ISBN 0-7167-0055-7). W H Freeman.
Solecki, Rose L. An Early Village Site at Zawi Chemi Shanidar. (Bibliotheca Mesopotamia: Vol. 13). (Illus.). xi, 102p. 1981. write for info. (ISBN 0-89003-067-7); pap. write for info. (ISBN 0-89003-068-5). Undena Pubns.
Starr, Chester G. Early Man: Prehistory & the Civilizations of the Ancient Near East. (Illus.). 224p. 1973. 15.95 (ISBN 0-19-501641-6); pap. 8.95x (ISBN 0-19-501640-8). Oxford U Pr.
Stephens, John L. Incidents of Travel in Egypt, Arabia Petraea & the Holy Land. (Illus.). 1970. 24.95 (ISBN 0-8061-0886-X). U of Okla Pr.
Traditional Rural Institutions & Their Implications for Development Planning: Studies from Hamadan Province or Iran. 14p. 1981. pap. 5.00 (ISBN 92-808-0148-1, TUNU 115, UNU). Unipub.

Van Nieuwenhuijze, C., ed. Sociology of the Middle East: A Stocktaking & Interpretation. (Social, Economic & Political Studies of the Middle East: Vol. 1). (Illus.). 819p. 1971. text ed. 128.25x (ISBN 90-040-2564-2). Humanities.

Woolley, C. Leonard. Forgotten Kingdom. (Illus.). 1968. pap. 1.95x (ISBN 0-393-00450-3, Norton Lib). Norton.

NEAR EAST–COMMERCE

Kilmarx & Alexander. Business & the Middle East. (Pergamon Policy Studies). 250p. Date not set. text ed. price not set (ISBN 0-08-025992-8). Pergamon.

Maclean, Ian. Statistical Review of Middle East Markets. 1976. 62.50 (ISBN 0-85038-321-8, Kogan Pg). Nichols Pub.

Martin, Esmond B. & Martin, Chryssee P. Cargoes of the East: The Ports, Trade & Culture of the Arabian Seas & Western Indian Ocean. 1979. 35.00 (ISBN 0-241-89855-2, Pub by Hamish Hamilton). David & Charles.

NEAR EAST–DESCRIPTION AND TRAVEL

Barnes, Marjorie H. Midwest Meets Mideast. 1979. 4.50 (ISBN 0-682-49319-8). Exposition.

Beaumont, Peter, et al. The Middle East: A Georgraphical Study. LC 74-28284. 614p. 1976. 50.50 (ISBN 0-471-06117-4, Pub. by Wiley-Interscience); pap. 23.25 (ISBN 0-471-06119-0). Wiley.

Browne, John R. Yusef: The Journey of the Frangi; a Crusade in the East. Davis, Moshe, ed. LC 77-70686. (America & the Holy Land Ser.). (Illus.). 1977. Repr. of 1853 ed. lib. bdg. 24.00x (ISBN 0-405-10232-1). Arno.

Davis, Moshe, ed. Holy Land Missions & Missionaries: An Original Anthology. LC 77-70703. (America & the Holy Land Ser.). (Illus.). 1977. lib. bdg. 15.00x (ISBN 0-405-10259-3). Arno.

Drower, Ethel S. By Tigris & Euphrates. LC 77-87642. (Illus.). Repr. of 1923 ed. 29.50 (ISBN 0-404-16424-2). AMS Pr.

Ethridge, Willie S. There's Yeast in the Middle East. LC 62-19853. 1962. 7.95 (ISBN 0-8149-0091-7). Vanguard.

Field, Michael, ed. Middle East Annual Review, 1981. 7th ed. pap. 24.95 (ISBN 0-528-84519-5). Rand.

Finnie, David H. Pioneers East: The Early American Experience in the Middle East. LC 67-20875. (Middle Eastern Studies: No. 13). (Illus.). 1967. 16.50x (ISBN 0-674-66900-2). Harvard U Pr.

Fisher, W. B. The Middle East: A Physical, Social, & Regional Geography. 7th ed. (Illus.). 1978. text ed. 45.95x (ISBN 0-416-71510-9); pap. 25.00x (ISBN 0-416-71520-6). Methuen Inc.

Harvard Student Agencies. Let's Go, Greece, Israel & Europe: The Budget Guide 1981 to 1982 Edition. (Illus.). 352p. 1981. pap. 5.95 (ISBN 0-525-93146-5). Dutton.

Lewis, Wyndham. Filibusters in Barbary. LC 72-2114. (English Literature Ser., No. 33). 1972. Repr. of 1932 ed. lib. bdg. 42.95 (ISBN 0-8383-1477-5). Haskell.

Makki, M. S. Medina, Saudi Arabia: A Geographic Analysis of the City & the Region. 1981. 75.00x (ISBN 0-86127-301-X, Pub. by Avebury Pub England). State Mutual Bk.

Mallowan, Agatha C. Come Tell Me How You Live. (Illus.). 226p. 1976. 8.95 (ISBN 0-396-07320-4). Dodd.

Morton, H. V. In Search of the Holy Land. (Illus.). 1979. 15.00 (ISBN 0-396-07691-2). Dodd.

Paddington Press. Middle East Business Travel Guide. 288p. 1981. 19.95 (ISBN 0-87196-343-4); pap. 11.95 (ISBN 0-87196-323-X). Facts on File.

Patterson, Harriet-Louise H. Come with Me to the Holy Land. rev. ed. 1969. 5.95 (ISBN 0-8170-0301-0). Judson.

Payne, Robert. The Splendor of the Holy Land: Egypt, Jordon, Israel, Lebanon. LC 76-5523. (Illus.). (YA) 1976. 12.50 (ISBN 0-06-013294-9, HarpT). Har-Row.

Rotherberg, Beno & Weyer, Helfried. Sinai. LC 78-53350. (Illus.). 1980. 55.00 (ISBN 0-89674-002-1). J J Binns.

Rutstein, Harry & Kroll, Joanne. In the Footsteps of Marco Polo: A Twentieth-Century Odyssey. LC 80-5369. (Illus.). 128p. 1980. 14.95 (ISBN 0-670-39683-4, Studio). Viking Pr.

Schiffer, Michael. Lessons of the Road. 1980. 10.95 (ISBN 0-671-25380-8). S&S.

Sitwell, Sacheverell. Arabesque & Honeycomb. facsimile ed. LC 78-37124. (Essay Index Reprint Ser). Repr. of 1957 ed. 25.00 (ISBN 0-8369-2522-X). Arno.

Stark, Freya. Journey's Echo. 16.95 (ISBN 0-7195-1336-7). Transatlantic.

Sterling Editors, ed. The Middle East-The Arab States-In Pictures. (Illus.). (gr. 5 up). 1978. 17.95 (ISBN 0-8069-0156-X); PLB 15.99 (ISBN 0-8069-0157-8). Sterling.

Taylor, Baynard. The Lands of the Saracen: Pictures of Palestine, Asia Monor, Sicily & Spain. Davis, Moshe, ed. LC 77-70749. (America & the Holy Land Ser.). 1977. Repr. of 1855 ed. lib. bdg. 26.00x (ISBN 0-405-10294-1). Arno.

Traveller's Guide to the Middle East. 1981. pap. 8.45 (ISBN 0-531-03965-X). Watts.

Trowbridge, Catherine. Car Trek. LC 81-50914. 184p. 1981. 10.95 (ISBN 0-938232-03-7); pap. 7.95 (ISBN 0-938232-04-5). Winston-Derek.

Walker, Jane & Ambrose, Mark, eds. The Paddington Business Traveller's Handbook: A Guide to the Middle East. LC 79-21688. (The Paddington Business Traveller's Handbook Ser.). (Illus.). 1980. 13.95 (ISBN 0-448-22123-3). Paddington.

NEAR EAST–ECONOMIC CONDITIONS

Abbott, Carl. Boosters & Businessmen: Popular Economic Thought & Urban Growth in the Antebellum Middle West. LC 80-1795. (Contributions in American Studies: No. 53). (Illus.). xii, 266p. 1981. lib. bdg. 27.50 (ISBN 0-313-22562-1, ABB/). Greenwood.

Amirie, Abbas, ed. The Persian Gulf & Indian Ocean in International Politics. 1975. 15.00x (ISBN 0-8139-0846-9); pap. 7.50x (ISBN 0-685-88513-5). U Pr of Va.

Askari, Hossein & Cummings, John T. Middle East Economies in the 1970's: A Comparative Approach. (Illus.). 1976. text ed. 46.95 (ISBN 0-275-23130-5). Praeger.

Badr, Albirt Y. & Siksek, Simon G. Manpower & Oil in Arab Countries. LC 79-2850. (Illus.). 270p. 1981. Repr. of 1959 ed. 22.50 (ISBN 0-8305-0026-X). Hyperion Conn.

Becker, Abraham S., et al. The Economics & Politics of the Middle East. LC 74-14466. (Middle East Ser.). 131p. 1975. 16.95 (ISBN 0-444-00149-2, North Holland). Elsevier.

Bonne, Alfred. The Economic Development of the Middle East: An Outline of Planned Reconstruction After the War. LC 79-51856. 1981. Repr. of 1945 ed. 17.50 (ISBN 0-88355-949-8). Hyperion Conn.

Clerin, Rose M. Taxation Planning for Middle East Operations. 1978. pap. 19.00 (ISBN 90-200-0515-4, Pub. by Kluwer Law Netherlands). Kluwer Boston.

Cook, M. A., ed. Studies in the Economic History of the Middle East: From the Rise of Islam to the Present Day. 1970. 32.00x (ISBN 0-19-713561-7). Oxford U Pr.

Coppock, Joseph. Foreign Trade of the Middle East: Instability & Growth, 1946-1962. 1966. pap. 11.95x (ISBN 0-8156-6022-7, Am U Beirut). Syracuse U Pr.

Ellis, Howard S. Private Enterprise & Socialism in the Middle East. 1970. pap. 5.25 (ISBN 0-8447-1040-7). Am Enterprise.

El-Mallakh, Ragaei, et al. Capital Investment in the Middle East: The Use of Surplus Funds for Regional Development. LC 77-7806. (Praeger Special Studies). 1977. text ed. 25.95 (ISBN 0-03-021986-8). Praeger.

Fallon, N. Middle East Oil Money & Its Future Expenditure. 239p. 1976. 19.00x (ISBN 0-86010-024-3, Pub. by Graham & Trotman England). State Mutual Bk.

--Winning Business in Saudi Arabia. 61p. 1976. 65.00x (ISBN 0-86010-043-X, Pub. by Graham & Trotman England). State Mutual Bk.

Grunwald, Kurt & Ronall, Joachim O. Industrialization in the Middle East. Shwadran, Benjamin, ed. LC 75-16486. (Illus.). 394p. 1975. Repr. of 1960 ed. lib. bdg. 21.25x (ISBN 0-8371-8192-5, GRIME). Greenwood.

The Gulf Telephone Directory 1980. 1980. 95.00x (ISBN 0-686-69890-8, Pub. by Parrish-Rogers England). State Mutual Bk.

Hamad, M. F. Fundamentals of Engineering Economy. 2nd. ed. 300p. (Arabic.). 1981. pap. 13.00 (ISBN 0-471-06325-8). Wiley.

Hindus, Maurice G. In Search of a Future: Persia, Egypt, Iraq, & Palestine. LC 79-3072. 270p. 1980. Repr. of 1949 ed. 22.50 (ISBN 0-8305-0035-9). Hyperion Conn.

Issawi, Charles, ed. Economic History of the Middle East: A Book of Readings. LC 66-11883. (Midway Reprints Ser). 1976. pap. 18.00x (ISBN 0-226-38609-0). U of Chicago Pr.

The Jeddah Commercial Directory 1980. 1980. 95.00x (ISBN 0-686-69891-6, Pub. by Parrish-Rogers England). State Mutual Bk.

Kapoor, Ashok, ed. International Business in the Middle East: Case Studies. (Special Studies in International Economics & Business). 1979. lib. bdg. 20.00x (ISBN 0-89158-257-6). Westview.

Karam, N. H., tr. Tax Laws of Kuwait. 50p. 1979. 22.00x (ISBN 0-86010-140-1, Pub. by Graham & Trotman). State Mutual Bk.

Kedourie, Elie, ed. The Middle Eastern Economy: Studies in Economics & Economic History. 185p. 1976. 26.00x (ISBN 0-7146-3074-8, F Cass Co). Biblio Dist.

Kerr, Malcolm H. & Yassin, El Sayed, eds. Rich & Poor Nations in the Middle East. (Special Studies on the Middle East). 500p. (Orig.). 1981. lib. bdg. 35.00 (ISBN 0-86531-275-3); pap. 16.00 (ISBN 0-86531-276-1). Westview.

Legum, Colin & Shaked, Haim, eds. Middle East Contemporary Survey, Vol. 2. LC 78-648245. (Illus.). 1979. 115.00x (ISBN 0-8419-0398-0). Holmes & Meier.

--Middle East Contemporary Survey: Volume 4, 1979-1980. LC 78-648245. (Illus.). 850p. 1981. text ed. 125.00x (ISBN 0-8419-0609-2). Holmes & Meier.

Mallakh, Ragaei El, et al. Implications of Regional Development in the Middle East for U.S. Trade, Capital Flows, & Balance of Payments. LC 77-73035. 1977. pap. 5.00x (ISBN 0-918714-01-X). Intl Res Ctr Energy.

Mansfield, Peter. The Middle East: A Political & Economic Survey. (Illus.). 1980. 29.95 (ISBN 0-19-215851-1). Oxford U Pr.

May, Brian. The Third World Calamity. (Illus.). 272p. 1981. 19.95 (ISBN 0-7100-0764-7). Routledge & Kegan.

Middle East & North Africa 1980-81. 985p. 1981. 80.00 (ISBN 0-905118-50-2, EUR 23, Europa). Unipub.

The Middle East & North Africa 1980-81. 27th ed. LC 48-3250. (Illus.). 1005p. 1980. 80.00x (ISBN 0-905118-50-2). Intl Pubns Serv.

Middle East Economic Papers. 1969. pap. 10.00x (ISBN 0-8156-6017-0, Am U Beirut). Syracuse U Pr.

The Middle East: Life & Work for the Civil Engineer. 85p. 1980. 29.00x (ISBN 0-7277-0064-2, Pub. by Telford England). State Mutual Bk.

Nicholas, David. The Middle East: Its Oil, Economies, & Investment Policies: A Guide to Sources of Financial Information. LC 80-28555. xxiv, 201p. 1981. lib. bdg. 39.95 (ISBN 0-313-22986-4, NME/). Greenwood.

Owen, Roger. Middle East in the World Economy, 1800-1914. 1981. 45.00x (ISBN 0-416-14270-2). Methuen Inc.

Preston, Lee E. Trade Patterns in the Middle East. 1970. pap. 4.25 (ISBN 0-8447-1042-3). Am Enterprise.

A Selected & Annotated Bibliography of Economic Literature in the Arabic Countries of the Middle East, 2 vols. Vol. 1, 1938-1952. pap. 10.00x (ISBN 0-8156-6020-0, Am U Beirut); Vol. 2, 1953-1965. pap. 14.95x (ISBN 0-8156-6021-9). Syracuse U Pr.

Shilling, N. A. Doing Business in Saudi Arabia & the Arab Gulf States. LC 75-37251. (Doing Business in the Middle East Ser.). 185.00 (ISBN 0-916400-01-8); supplement o.p. 65.00 (ISBN 0-685-83461-1). Inter-Crescent.

Tames, Richard. The Arab World Today. (Today Ser.). (Illus.). 96p. 1980. text ed. 15.95x (ISBN 0-7182-0461-1, SpS). Sportshelf.

Trado Asian-African Directory of Exporters-Importers & Manufacturers, 1980. 25th ed. LC 60-41792. 1640p. 1980. 50.00x (ISBN 0-8002-2736-0). Intl Pubns Serv.

Turner, Louis & Bedore, James. Middle East Industrialisation: A Study of Saudi & Iranian Downstream Investment. LC 79-89599. (Praeger Special Studies). (Illus.). 230p. 1980. 29.95 (ISBN 0-03-053381-3). Praeger.

Warriner, Doreen. Land & Poverty in the Middle East. LC 79-1596. 1981. Repr. of 1948 ed. 16.00 (ISBN 0-88355-901-3). Hyperion Conn.

Waterbury, John & Mallakh, Ragaei E. The Middle East in the Coming Decade: From Wellhead to Well-Being. (Council on Foreign Relations 1980's Project Ser.). 1978. text ed. 9.95x (ISBN 0-07-068445-6, P&RB); pap. 5.95 (ISBN 0-07-068446-4). McGraw.

Wilson, Rodney. The Economies of the Middle East. LC 78-13792. 1979. text ed. 39.50x (ISBN 0-8419-0446-4). Holmes & Meier.

--Trade & Investment in the Middle East. LC 77-8841. 1977. text ed. 26.00x (ISBN 0-8419-0328-X). Holmes & Meier.

Winning Business in Arab Markets: Proceedings of the 1975 Graham & Trotman Conference. 162p. 1975. 77.00x (ISBN 0-86010-044-8, Pub. by Graham & Trotman England). State Mutual Bk.

NEAR EAST–FOREIGN RELATIONS

Abu-Jaber, Faiz S. Middle East Issues. 200p. 1977. pap. text ed. 7.50 (ISBN 0-8191-0044-7). U Pr of Amer.

Al-Marayati, Abid A., ed. International Relations of the Middle East & North Africa. 400p. 1982. text ed. 22.50x (ISBN 0-87073-824-0). Schenkman.

Amirie, Abbas, ed. The Persian Gulf & Indian Ocean in International Politics. 1975. 15.00x (ISBN 0-8139-0846-9); pap. 7.50x (ISBN 0-685-88513-5). U Pr of Va.

Ayoob, Mohammed, ed. The Middle East in World Politics. LC 80-22312. 224p. 1981. write for info. (ISBN 0-312-53184-2). St Martin.

Bagnole, John W. Cultures of the Islamic Middle East. (America-Mideast Educational & Training Servies, Inc. - Occasional Paper: No. 4). 86p. (Orig.). 1978. pap. text ed. 4.00 (ISBN 0-89192-296-2). Interbk Inc.

Campbell, John C. The Middle East in the Muted Cold War. (Monograph Ser. in World Affairs, Vol. 2: 1964-65 Ser., Pt. A). 4.00 (ISBN 0-87940-003-X). U of Denver Intl.

Cattan, Henry. Palestine: The Road to Peace. (Illus., Orig.). 1971. pap. 3.00x (ISBN 0-582-78022-5). Intl Pubns Serv.

Chakmakjian, Hagop A. In Quest of Justice & Peace in the Middle East. 1980. 8.95 (ISBN 0-533-04539-8). Vantage.

Duigan, Peter & Gann, L. H. The Middle East & North Africa: The Challenge to Western Security. 160p. 1981. pap. 9.95 (ISBN 0-8179-7392-3). Hoover Inst Pr.

Field, James A., Jr. America & the Mediterranean World, 1776-1882. LC 68-11440. 1969. 28.50x (ISBN 0-691-04590-9); pap. 5.95 (ISBN 0-691-00586-9). Princeton U Pr.

Hitti, Philp K. Islam & the West: A Historical Cultural Survey. LC 78-10793. (Anvil Ser.). 192p. 1979. pap. 4.95 (ISBN 0-88275-787-3). Krieger.

Hurewitz, J. C., ed. The Middle East & North Africa in World Politics: A Documentary Record. 2nd ed. LC 74-83525. 672p. 1975. Vol. 1: European Expansion, 1535-1914. 40.00x (ISBN 0-300-01294-2); Vol. 2: British-french Supremacy, 1914-1945. text ed. 60.00 (ISBN 0-300-02203-4). Yale U Pr.

Ismael, Tareq Y. The Middle East in World Politics: A Study in Contemporary International Relations. LC 73-16637. 330p. 1974. 6.95x (ISBN 0-8156-0101-8). Syracuse U Pr.

Jureidini, Paul & McLaurin, R. D. Beyond Camp David: Emerging Alignments & Leaders in the Middle East. LC 80-27406. (Contemporary Issues in the Middle East Ser.). 232p. 1981. text ed. 18.00x (ISBN 0-8156-2235-X); pap. text ed. 8.95x (ISBN 0-8156-2236-8). Syracuse U Pr.

Khadduri, Majid. Major Middle Eastern Problems in International Law. 1972. pap. 5.25 (ISBN 0-8447-3080-7). Am Enterprise.

Kilmarx & Alexander. Business & the Middle East. (Pergamon Policy Studies). 250p. Date not set. text ed. price not set (ISBN 0-08-025992-8). Pergamon.

Kurland, Gerald. The Arab-Israeli Conflict. Rahmas, D. Steve, ed. LC 72-89221. (Topics of Our Times Ser.: No. 2). 32p. 1973. lib. bdg. 2.95 incl. catalog cards (ISBN 0-87157-802-6); pap. 1.50 vinyl laminated covers (ISBN 0-87157-302-4). SamHar Pr.

Leitenberg, Milton & Sheffer, Gabriel, eds. Great Power Intervention in the Middle East. LC 79-341. (Pergamon Policy Studies). 400p. 1979. 28.00 (ISBN 0-08-023867-X). Pergamon.

Lewis, Bernard. The Middle East & the West. 7.50 (ISBN 0-8446-5856-1). Peter Smith.

--Middle East & the West. 1968. pap. 3.50x (ISBN 0-06-131274-6, TB1274, Torch). Har-Row.

Lozoya, Jorge A. & Cuadra, Hector, eds. Africa, the Middle East & the New International Economic Order. LC 80-14688. (Pergamon Policy Studies). 170p. 1980. 20.00 (ISBN 0-08-025117-X). Pergamon.

McLaurin, R. D., et al. Foreign Policy Making in the Middle East: Domestic Influences on Policy in Egypt, Iraq, Israel, & Syria. LC 76-24360. (Special Studies). 1977. text ed. 29.95 (ISBN 0-275-23870-9); pap. 10.95 (ISBN 0-275-65010-3). Praeger.

Mehdi, Mohammad T. Kennedy & Sirhan, Why. LC 68-57262. (Illus., Orig.). pap. 4.00 (ISBN 0-911026-04-5, KSW). New World Press NY.

The Middle East & the Attempt at World Economic Hegemony. 1976. 44.75 (ISBN 0-685-85009-9). Inst Econ Finan.

Middle East Negotiations: A Conversation with Joseph Sisco. 1980. pap. 3.25 (ISBN 0-8447-3394-6). Am Enterprise.

Schulz, Ann T., ed. International & Regional Politics in the Middle East & North Africa: A Guide to Information Sources. LC 74-11568. (International Relations Information Guide Ser.: Vol. 6). 1977. 36.00 (ISBN 0-8103-1326-X). Gale.

Shichor, Y. The Middle East in China's Foreign Policy: 1949-1977. LC 78-58801. (International Studies). (Illus.). 1979. 29.95 (ISBN 0-521-22214-1). Cambridge U Pr.

Wilmington, Martin W. Middle East Supply Centre. Evans, Laurence, ed. LC 70-136278. 1971. 19.00 (ISBN 0-87395-081-X); microfiche 19.00 (ISBN 0-87395-181-6). State U NY Pr.

NEAR EAST–FOREIGN RELATIONS–FRANCE

Nevakivi, Jukka. Britain, France & the Arab Middle East 1914-1920. (Univ. of London Historical Studies: No. 23). 1969. text ed. 26.00x (ISBN 0-485-13123-4, Athlone Pr). Humanities.

Zeine, Zeine N. The Struggle for Arab Independence. 2nd ed. LC 77-5149. 280p. 1977. lib. bdg. 25.00x (ISBN 0-88206-002-3). Caravan Bks.

NEAR EAST–FOREIGN RELATIONS–GREAT BRITAIN

Busch, Briton C. Mudros to Lausanne: Britain's Frontier in West Asia, 1918-1923, Vol. 3. LC 76-21641. 1976. 34.00 (ISBN 0-87395-265-0). State U NY Pr.

Darwin, John. Britain, Egypt & the Middle East. LC 80-14718. 1980. write for info. (ISBN 0-312-09736-0). St Martin.

Kedourie, E. In the Anglo-Arab Labyrinth. LC 75-3975. (Studies in the History & Theory of Politics). (Illus.). 370p. 1976. 44.95 (ISBN 0-521-20826-2). Cambridge U Pr.

Nevakivi, Jukka. Britain, France & the Arab Middle East 1914-1920. (Univ. of London Historical Studies: No. 23). 1969. text ed. 26.00x (ISBN 0-485-13123-4, Athlone Pr). Humanities.

Zeine, Zeine N. The Struggle for Arab Independence. 2nd ed. LC 77-5149. 280p. 1977. lib. bdg. 25.00x (ISBN 0-88206-002-3). Caravan Bks.

NEAR EAST–FOREIGN RELATIONS–RUSSIA

Confino, M. & Shamir, S., eds. USSR & the Middle East. 450p. 1973. casebound 21.95 (ISBN 0-87855-160-3). Transaction Bks.

Glassman, Jon D. Arms for the Arabs: The Soviet Union & War in the Middle East. LC 75-29254. (Illus.). 254p. 1976. 17.00x (ISBN 0-8018-1747-1). Johns Hopkins.

Laqueur, Walter Z., ed. Middle East in Transition: Studies in Contemporary History. facsimile ed. LC 70-156676. (Essay Index Reprint Ser). Repr. of 1958 ed. 26.00 (ISBN 0-8369-2367-7). Arno.

McLane, Charles B. Soviet-Third World Relations: Soviet-Middle East Relations, Vol. 1. 126p. 1973. 17.50x (ISBN 0-903424-06-1). Columbia U Pr.

NEAR EAST–FOREIGN RELATIONS–UNITED STATES

Baram, Phillip J. The Department of State in the Middle East, 1919-1945. LC 77-20302. 1978. 30.00x (ISBN 0-8122-7743-0). U of Pa Pr.

Bryson, Thomas A. American Diplomatic Relations with the Middle East, 1784-1975: A Survey. LC 76-44344. 1977. 21.00 (ISBN 0-8108-0988-5). Scarecrow.

Childs, J. Rives. Foreign Service Farewell. LC 71-76185. (Illus.). 208p. 1969. 7.50x (ISBN 0-8139-0261-4). U Pr of Va.

Churba, Joseph. Politics of Defeat: America's Decline in the Middle-East. LC 77-75992. 1978. 10.00 (ISBN 0-685-80285-X). Cyrco Pr.

Congressional Quarterly. Middle East: U. S. Policy, Israel, Oil & the Arabs. 4th ed. 1979. pap. text ed. 7.95 (ISBN 0-87187-176-9). Congr Quarterly.

Grabill, Joseph L. Protestant Diplomacy & the Near East: Missionary Influence in American Policy, 1810-1927. LC 70-5750. (Illus.). 1971. 15.00x (ISBN 0-8166-0575-0). U of Minn Pr.

Hart, Parker T. America & the Middle East. new ed. Lambert, Richard D., ed. LC 72-78294. (Annals Ser.: 401). 300p. 1972. pap. 6.00 (ISBN 0-87761-148-3). Am Acad Pol Soc Sci.

Hurewitz, Jacob C. Middle East Dilemmas: The Background of United States Policy. LC 72-90566. (Illus.). xiv, 273p. 1973. Repr. of 1953 ed. 16.00 (ISBN 0-8462-1713-9). Russell.

Kennedy, William J., ed. Secret History of the Oil Companies in the Middle East, 2 vols. new ed. 1979. 40.00 set (ISBN 0-89712-078-7). Documentary Pubns.

McDonald, John & Burleson, Clyde. Flight from Dhahran: The True Experiences of an American Businessman Held Hostage in Saudi Arabia. 256p. 1981. 12.95 (ISBN 0-13-322453-8). P-H.

Marx, Victor. The Betrayal of the State of Israel & the Foreign Policy of the United States: A Blueprint for Peace in the Middle East. new ed. (Illus.). 1977. 47.50 (ISBN 0-89266-059-7). Am Classical Coll Pr.

Ramazani, R. K. Beyond the Arab-Israeli Settlement: New Directions for U. S. Policy in the Middle East. LC 77-87564. (Foreign Policy Reports Ser.). 69p. 1977. 5.00 (ISBN 0-89549-006-4). Inst Foreign Policy Anal.

Stevens, Gergiana G., ed. The United States & the Middle East. LC 64-14027. 1963. 5.95 (ISBN 0-936904-05-4); pap. 1.95 (ISBN 0-936904-30-5). Am Assembly.

U. S. Department Of State. United States Policy in the Middle East, September 1956-June 1957: Documents. LC 68-55122. (Illus.). 1968. Repr. of 1957 ed. lib. bdg. 18.75x (ISBN 0-8371-0707-5, USPM). Greenwood.

NEAR EAST–HISTORICAL GEOGRAPHY

Curtis, Michael, ed. People & Politics in the Middle East. LC 72-140617. 325p. 1971. 12.95 (ISBN 0-87855-000-3). Transaction Bks.

NEAR EAST–HISTORIOGRAPHY

Binder, Leonard. The Study of the Middle East: Research & Scholarship in the Humanities & Social Sciences. LC 76-7408. 648p. 1976. 43.50 (ISBN 0-471-07304-0, Pub. by Wiley-Interscience). Wiley.

Jones, Wilbur D. Venus & Sothis: How the Ancient Near East Was Rediscovered. 200p. 1981. text ed. 18.95x (ISBN 0-88229-691-4); pap. text ed. 8.95x (ISBN 0-88229-780-5). Nelson-Hall.

Rosenthal, Franz. History of Muslim Historiography. 1968. text ed. 93.50x (ISBN 90-04019-06-5). Humanities.

NEAR EAST–HISTORY

see also Islamic Empire

Allfree, P. S. Warlords of Oman. LC 68-29860. (Illus.). 1968. 5.00 (ISBN 0-498-06845-5). A S Barnes.

Armajani, Yahya. Middle East-Past & Present. (Illus.). 1969. text ed. 18.95x (ISBN 0-13-581579-7). P-H.

Arnakis, George & Vucinish. History of the Near East in Modern Times, 3 vols. Incl. Vol. 1. The Ottoman Empire & the Balkan States to 1900. (Illus.). 452p (ISBN 0-8363-0046-7); Vol. 2. Forty Crucial Years: 1900-1940 (ISBN 0-8363-0047-5). 15.00 ea. Jenkins.

Ashtor, E. Social & Economic History of the Near East in the Middle Ages. LC 74-29800. 1976. 28.50x (ISBN 0-520-02962-3). U of Cal Pr.

Asimov, Isaac. Land of Canaan. LC 70-155557. (Illus.). (gr. 7 up). 1971. 5.95 (ISBN 0-395-12572-3). HM.

--Near East: 10,000 Years of History. (Illus.). (gr. 7 up). 1968. 4.95 (ISBN 0-395-06562-3). HM.

Atiya, Aziz S. The Copts & Christian Civilization. (The University of Utah William Frederick Reynolds Lecture Ser.: No. 42). (Orig.). 1979. 5.00 (ISBN 0-87480-145-1). U of Utah Pr.

Bacharach, Jere L. A Near East Studies Handbook. rev. ed. LC 76-56610. (Illus.). 166p. 1977. 15.00 (ISBN 0-295-95549-X); pap. 5.95 (ISBN 0-295-95551-1). U of Wash Pr.

Baillie, Alexander F. Kurrachee: Past, Present & Future. (Illus.). 290p. 1975. 20.75x (ISBN 0-19-577211-3). Oxford U Pr.

Bernstein, Burton. Sinai: The Great & Terrible Wilderness. (Illus.). 1979. 13.95 (ISBN 0-670-34837-6). Viking Pr.

Bulliet, Richard W. The Camel & the Wheel. LC 75-571. 352p. 1975. text ed. 18.50x (ISBN 0-674-09130-2). Harvard U Pr.

Busch, Briton C. Mudros to Lausanne: Britain's Frontier in West Asia, 1918-1923, Vol. 3. LC 76-21641. 1976. 34.00 (ISBN 0-87395-265-0). State U NY Pr.

Byrne, Janet, ed. The Middle East: Issues & Events of 1979. LC 80-1718. (News in Print Ser.). (Illus.). 1980. lib. bdg. 24.95x (ISBN 0-405-12878-9). Arno.

Chaffetz, David & Rapoport, Mitchell, eds. The Middle East: Issues & Events of 1978. LC 78-32140. (News in Print Ser.). 300p. 1979. lib. bdg. 21.95 (ISBN 0-405-12875-4). Arno.

Chouraqui, Andre. Letter to an Arab Friend. Gugli, William V., tr. LC 72-77573. 284p. 1973. 12.50x (ISBN 0-87023-108-1). U of Mass Pr.

Clarke, J. I. & Bowen-Jones, H. Change & Development in the Middle East: Essays in Honour of W. B. Fisher. 1981. 47.00x (ISBN 0-416-71080-8). Methuen Inc.

Dennis, A. L. Eastern Problems at the Close of the Eighteenth Century. 277p. Repr. of 1901 ed. lib. bdg. 19.50x (ISBN 0-87991-092-5). Porcupine Pr.

Dishon, Daniel, ed. Middle East Record, 1969-70, 2 vols in one, Vol. 5-6. 1414p. text ed. 89.95 (ISBN 0-87855-218-9). Transaction Bks.

Elgood, Percival G. Transit of Egypt. LC 68-27055. (Illus.). 1969. Repr. of 1928 ed. 11.00 (ISBN 0-8462-1275-7). Russell.

Finegan, Jack. Archaeological History of the Ancient Middle East. 1979. lib. bdg. 36.25 (ISBN 0-89158-164-2, Dawson). Westview.

Fisher, Sydney N. Middle East: A History. rev. ed. (Illus.). 1968. text ed. 16.95 (ISBN 0-394-30197-8, KnopfC). Knopf.

--The Middle East: A History. 3rd ed. 1978. text ed. 20.95x (ISBN 0-394-32098-0). Knopf.

Fraser, T. G. The Middle East: 1914-1979. 1980. 19.95 (ISBN 0-312-53181-8). St Martin.

Frye, Richard N. Islamic Iran & Central Asia (7th-12th Centuries) 380p. 1980. 75.00x (ISBN 0-86078-044-9, Pub. by Variorum England). State Mutual Bk.

Goedicke, Hans & Roberts, J. J. M., eds. Unity & Diversity: Essays in the History, Literature, & Religion of the Ancient Near East. LC 74-24376. (Near Eastern Studies). (Illus.). 240p. 1975. 16.00x (ISBN 0-8018-1638-6). Johns Hopkins.

Goldschmidt, Arthur, Jr. A Concise History of the Middle East. 1979. lib. bdg. 29.75x (ISBN 0-89158-251-7); pap. text ed. 11.50x (ISBN 0-89158-289-4). Westview.

Habib, John S. Ibn Sa'ud's Warriors of Islam: The Ikhwan of Nadjd & Their Role in the Creation of Sa'udi Kingdom 1910-1930. (Social Economic & Political Studies of the Middle East: No. 27). (Illus.). 1978. text ed. 33.00x (ISBN 90-040-5757-9). Humanities.

Haddad, William W. & Ochsenwald, William L., eds. Nationalism in a Non-National State: The Dissolution of the Ottoman Empire. LC 77-1253. 1977. 15.00x (ISBN 0-8142-0191-1). Ohio St U Pr.

Hallo, William W. & Simpson, William K. The Ancient Near East: A History. LC 71-155560. 319p. 1971. pap. text ed. 9.95 (ISBN 0-15-502755-7, HC). HarBraceJ.

Harkness, Georgia & Kraft, Charles F. The Biblical Backgrounds of the Middle East Conflict. LC 76-22644. (Illus.). 1976. 3.95 (ISBN 0-687-03435-3). Abingdon.

Heravi, Mehdi. Concise Encyclopedia of the Middle East. 1979. 12.00 (ISBN 0-8183-0130-9); pap. 6.50 (ISBN 0-8183-0260-7). Pub Aff Pr.

Hinz, Walther. The Lost World of Elam: Re-creation of a Vanished Civilization. Barnes, Jennifer, tr. (Illus.). 192p. 1972. 16.50x (ISBN 0-8147-3365-4). NYU Pr.

Holt, P. M. Studies in the History of the Near East. (Illus.). 261p. 1973. 30.00x (ISBN 0-7146-2984-7, F Cass Co). Biblio Dist.

Jones, Wilbur D. Venus & Sothis: How the Ancient Near East Was Rediscovered. 200p. 1981. text ed. 18.95x (ISBN 0-88229-691-4); pap. text ed. 8.95x (ISBN 0-88229-780-5). Nelson-Hall.

Khaldun, Ibn. Ibn Khaldun - the Maqaddimah: An Introduction to History, 3 vols. 2nd ed. Rosenthal, Franz, tr. from Arabic. (Bollingen Ser.: No. 43). (Illus.). 1700p. 1967. 110.00x (ISBN 0-691-09797-6). Princeton U Pr.

--Ibn Khaldun - the Muqaddimah: An Introduction to History. abridged ed. Dawood, N. J., ed. Rosenthal, Franz, tr. from Arabic. (Bollingen Ser.: No. 43). (Illus.). 480p. 1967. pap. 8.50 (ISBN 0-691-01754-9). Princeton U Pr.

Kimche, Jon. Seven Fallen Pillars. LC 76-6848. (The Middle East in the 20th Century). 1976. Repr. of 1950 ed. lib. bdg. 39.50 (ISBN 0-306-70820-5). Da Capo.

Kouymjian, Dickran K. & Bacharach, Jere L., eds. Near Eastern Numismatics, Iconography, Epigraphy & History: Studies in Honor of George C. Miles. 1974. 55.00x (ISBN 0-8156-6041-3, Am U Beirut). Syracuse U Pr.

Kuntz, J. Kenneth. The People of Ancient Israel: An Introduction to the Old Testament Literature, History & Thought. (Illus.). 1974. pap. text ed. 15.50 scp (ISBN 0-06-043822-3, HarpC). Har-Row.

Lamberg-Karlovsky, C. C. & Sabloff, Jeremy A. Ancient Civilizations: The Near East & Mesoamerica. 1979. pap. text ed. 12.95 (ISBN 0-8053-5672-X). Benjamin-Cummings.

Landau, Jacob M. Jews in Nineteenth-Century Egypt. LC 69-18282. (Studies in Near Eastern Civilization: No. 2). (Illus.). 1969. 16.00x (ISBN 0-8147-0248-1). NYU Pr.

Landen, Robert G. Emergence of the Modern Middle East: Selected Readings. 1970. pap. text ed. 8.95x (ISBN 0-442-23155-5). Van Nos Reinhold.

Lassner, Jacob. The Shaping of 'Abbasid Rule. LC 79-84000. (Princeton Studies in the Near East). (Illus.). 1980. 25.00x (ISBN 0-691-05281-6). Princeton U Pr.

Lawless, Richard. The Middle East in the Twentieth Century. (Illus.). 96p. 1980. 14.95 (ISBN 0-7134-2494-X, Pub. by Batsford England). David & Charles.

Legum, Colin & Shaked, Haim, eds. Arab Relations in the Middle East. LC 78-20888. (Middle Affairs Ser.: No. 1). 1978. pap. text ed. 8.50x (ISBN 0-8419-0447-2). Holmes & Meier.

Leitenberg, Milton & Sheffer, Gabriel, eds. Great Power Intervention in the Middle East. LC 79-341. (Pergamon Policy Studies). 400p. 1979. 28.00 (ISBN 0-08-023867-X). Pergamon.

Lilienthal, Alfred M. The Zionist Connection: What Price Peace? LC 78-10556. 1978. 19.95 (ISBN 0-396-07564-9). Dodd.

Mangold, Peter. Superpower Intervention in the Middle East. LC 77-9237. 1978. 18.95x (ISBN 0-312-77668-3). St Martin.

Mansfield, Peter. The Ottoman Empire & Its Successors. LC 73-86362. (Making of the Twentieth Century Ser). 224p. 1973. text ed. 15.95 (ISBN 0-312-59010-5); pap. 5.95 (ISBN 0-312-58975-1). St Martin.

Mansoor, Menahem. Political and Diplomatic History of the Arab World: A Biographical Dictionary. LC 73-94313. 1974. 55.00 (ISBN 0-910972-41-9). IHS-PDS.

Mitchell, Richard P. An Annotated Bibliography on the Modern History of the Near East. 38p. 1980. pap. text ed. 2.00 (ISBN 0-932098-17-7). Ctr for NE & North African Stud.

Mobley, Jonathan H. The Elusive Peace: The Middle East, Oil & the Economic & Political Future of the World. (The Major Currents in Contemprary World History Lib.). (Illus.). 144p. 1981. 67.75 (ISBN 0-930008-79-0). Inst Econ Pol.

Noeldeke, Theodor. Sketches from Eastern History. LC 78-15077. (Studies in Islamic History: No. 12). 288p. Repr. of 1892 ed. lib. bdg. 19.50x (ISBN 0-87991-461-0). Porcupine Pr.

O'Ballance, Edgar. The Electronic War in the Middle East 1968-70. (Illus.). 142p. 1974. 15.00 (ISBN 0-208-01469-1, Archon). Shoe String.

O'Brien, Edna. Arabian Days. 15.95 (ISBN 0-7043-2150-5, Pub. by Quartet England). Charles River Bks.

Parry, V. J. & Yapp, M. E. War, Technology, & Society in the Middle East. (Illus.). 464p. 1975. 33.00x (ISBN 0-19-713581-1). Oxford U Pr.

Polk, William R. The Elusive Peace: The Middle East in the Twentieth Century. LC 79-16393. 1979. 14.50x (ISBN 0-312-24383-9). St Martin.

Polk, William R., ed. The Developmental Revolution: North Africa, the Middle East & South Asia. 1963. 4.00 (ISBN 0-916808-03-3). Mid East Inst.

Prawer, Joshua. Crusader Institutions. (Illus.). 536p. 1980. 89.00x (ISBN 0-19-822536-9). Oxford U Pr.

Rossi, Peter M. & White, Wayne E., eds. Articles on the Middle East, 1947-1971: A Cumulation of Bibliographies from the Middle East Journal, 4 vols. 1980. Set. 160.00 (ISBN 0-87650-030-0). Pierian.

Sachar, Howard M. Europe Leaves the Middle East: Nineteen Thirty-Six to Nineteen Fifty-Four. LC 76-79349. 1972. 15.00 (ISBN 0-394-46064-2, 4754). Knopf.

Schwantes, Siegfried J. Short History of the Ancient Near East. (Illus.). 1965. pap. 4.95 (ISBN 0-8010-8026-6). Baker Bk.

Shwadran, Benjamin. Middle East Oil: Issues & Problems. LC 77-2982. 122p. 1977. text ed. 13.25x (ISBN 0-87073-597-7); pap. text ed. 7.95x (ISBN 0-87073-598-5). Schenkman.

Spuler, Bertold. The Muslim World: A Historical Survey, Vol. 4. 1981. text ed. write for info. (ISBN 0-391-01209-6). Humanities.

Stern, S. M. Documents from Islamic Chanceries. LC 74-93306. (Oriental Studies: No. 3). (Illus.). 1970. 19.50x (ISBN 0-87249-178-1). U of SC Pr.

Stowasser, Barbara F. & Manalo, Kathleen H. Twenty-Year Cumulative Index to the Middle East Journal, 1947-1966. LC 79-92823. 1972. text ed. 25.00 (ISBN 0-916808-10-6). Mid East Inst.

Sykes, Cristopher. Orde Wingate. (Return to Zion Ser.). 575p. Repr. lib. bdg. 35.00x (ISBN 0-87991-146-8). Porcupine Pr.

Thomas, Lewis V. A Study of Naima. Itzkowitz, Norman, ed. LC 71-189129. 163p. 1972. 12.50x (ISBN 0-8147-8150-0). NYU Pr.

Tibawi, A. L. Arabic & Islamic Themes: Historical, Education & Literary Studies. 1976. text ed. 27.00x (ISBN 0-7189-0164-9). Verry.

Tuma, Elias H., ed. Food & Population in the Middle East. LC 76-57917. 83p. 1976. pap. 5.00 (ISBN 0-934484-08-2). Inst Mid East & North Africa.

Walz, Jay. Middle East. LC 65-27595. (New York Times Byline Books). (Orig.). 1965. 3.95 (ISBN 0-689-10279-8); pap. 1.95 (ISBN 0-689-10280-1). Atheneum.

Winstone, H. V. Captain Shakespear. 9.95 (ISBN 0-7043-2201-3, Pub. by Quartet England). Charles River Bks.

Woods, John E. The Aqquyunlu: Clan, Confederation, & Empire. LC 74-27613. (Studies in Middle Eastern History: No. 3). 1976. 27.50x (ISBN 0-88297-011-9). Bibliotheca.

Yale, William. Near East: A Modern History. rev. & enl. ed. LC 68-29269. (History of the Modern World Ser). 1968. 10.00 (ISBN 0-472-07021-5). U of Mich Pr.

Yapp, Malcolm. The Ancient Near East. Killingray, Margaret, et al, eds. (World History Ser.). (Illus.). 32p. (gr. 10). 1980. Repr. of 1977 ed. lib. bdg. 5.95 (ISBN 0-89908-025-1); pap. text ed. 1.95 (ISBN 0-89908-000-6). Greenhaven.

Young, Ezra. Lands of the Unexpected: Memoirs of the Middle East. new ed. Smith, James C., Jr., ed. LC 78-75083. (Illus.). 1979. pap. 7.95 (ISBN 0-913270-77-6). Sunstone Pr.

Zeine, Zeine N. The Struggle for Arab Independence. 2nd ed. LC 77-5149. 280p. 1977. lib. bdg. 25.00x (ISBN 0-88206-002-3). Caravan Bks.

NEAR EAST–HISTORY–SOURCES

Hansen, Henny H. Investigations in a Shi'a Village in Bahrain. (Ethnographical Ser.: No. 12). (Illus.). 1968. pap. text ed. 28.75x (ISBN 87-480-7202-8). Humanities.

Matthews, Noel & Wainwrights, Doreen M., eds. A Guide to Manuscrpits & Documents in the British Isles Relating to the Middle East & North Africa. 500p. 1980. 148.00x (ISBN 0-19-713598-6). Oxford U Pr.

Vanbery, Armin. Scenes from the East: Through the Eyes of a European Traveller in the 1860's. Kortvelyessy, Eniko & Gaster, Bertha, trs. from Hungarian. (Illus.). 418p. (Orig.). 1979. pap. 8.50 (ISBN 963-13-0832-4). Intl Pubns Serv.

NEAR EAST–HISTORY–STUDY AND TEACHING

Hodgkin, E. C. The Arabs. (Jackdaw Ser: No. 142). (gr. 7 up). 1975. 6.95 (ISBN 0-670-13010-9). Viking Pr.

Kenworthy, Leonard S. Studying the Middle East in Elementary & Secondary Schools. rev. ed. LC 65-19213. (Orig.). 1965. pap. text ed. 3.50x (ISBN 0-8077-1611-1). Tchrs Coll.

NEAR EAST–JUVENILE LITERATURE

Newlon, Clarke. The Middle East & Why. LC 76-53443. (Illus.). (gr. 7 up). 1977. 6.95 (ISBN 0-396-07425-1). Dodd.

Rice, Edward. Babylon, Next to Nineveh: Where the World Began. LC 79-12809. (Illus.). 192p. (gr. 7 up). 1979. 8.95 (ISBN 0-590-07438-5, Four Winds). Schol Bk Serv.

Stephens, Anne C. Signpost-Middle East. (Orig.). (gr. 4-6). 1979. pap. 2.50 (ISBN 0-377-00087-6). Friend Pr.

NEAR EAST–MAPS

Carta. Map of the Middle East. rev. ed. (Illus.). 1978. pap. 6.95 (ISBN 0-930038-09-6). Arbit.

Tarasar, Constance J. New Friends-New Places. (Orig.). (gr. 1-3). 1979. pap. 2.50 (ISBN 0-377-00088-4). Friend Pr.

NEAR EAST–POLITICS AND GOVERNMENT

Allen, Richard. Imperialism & Nationalism in the Fertile Crescent: Sources & Prospects of the Arab-Israeli Conflict. (Illus.). 1974. pap. 9.95x (ISBN 0-19-501781-1). Oxford U Pr.

Amirie, Abbas, ed. The Persian Gulf & Indian Ocean in International Politics. 1975. 15.00x (ISBN 0-8139-0846-9); pap. 7.50x (ISBN 0-685-88513-5). U Pr of Va.

Anderson, M. S., ed. Great Powers & the Near East. (Documents of Modern History Ser). 1971. 17.95 (ISBN 0-312-34650-6). St Martin.

Anthony, John D. The Middle East: Oil, Politics & Development. LC 75-29689. (Conference Proceedings Ser). 1975. 12.25 (ISBN 0-8447-2067-4); pap. 5.25 (ISBN 0-8447-2066-6). Am Enterprise.

The Arabian Gulf Government & Public Services Directory 1980-81. 1980. 175.00x (ISBN 0-686-69888-6, Pub. by Parrish-Rogers England). State Mutual Bk.

Ayoob, Mohammed, ed. The Middle East in World Politics. LC 80-22312. 224p. 1981. write for info. (ISBN 0-312-53184-2). St Martin.

Barnds, William J., ed. The Two Koreas in East Asian Affairs. LC 75-27379. 216p. 1976. 15.00x (ISBN 0-8147-0988-5). NYU Pr.

Becker, Abraham S., et al. The Economics & Politics of the Middle East. LC 74-14466. (Middle East Ser.). 131p. 1975. 16.95 (ISBN 0-444-00149-2, North Holland). Elsevier.

Ben-Dor, Gabriel. The Druzes in Israel: A Political Study: Political Innovation & Integration in a Middle Eastern Minority. 287p. 1981. lib. bdg. 31.25x (ISBN 0-686-64555-3, Pub. by Magnes Pr). Westview.

Bernstein, Burton. Sinai: The Great & Terrible Wilderness. (Illus.). 1979. 13.95 (ISBN 0-670-34837-6). Viking Pr.

Bill, James A. & Leiden, Carl. Politics in the Middle East. 1979. 9.95 (ISBN 0-316-09505-2). Little.

Borthwick, Bruce M. Comparative Politics of the Middle East: An Introduction. 1980. pap. text ed. 10.95 (ISBN 0-13-154088-2). P-H.

Bowman, David H. Conflict of Community: A Guide to the Middle East Mosaic. (Orig.). 1979. pap. 2.75 (ISBN 0-377-00085-X). Friend Pr.

Brown, William R. The Last Crusade: A Negotiator's Middle East Handbook. LC 79-18462. 1980. text ed. 22.95x (ISBN 0-88229-554-3); pap. 11.95x (ISBN 0-88229-738-4). Nelson-Hall.

Butler, Grant C. Beyond Arabian Sands. (Illus.). 1964. 5.95 (ISBN 0-8159-5105-1). Devin.

Cantori, Louis J. & Harik, Iliya, eds. Local Politics & Development in the Middle East. (Special Studies on the Middle East). 350p. 1981. lib. bdg. 25.75x (ISBN 0-86531-169-2). Westview.

Chubin, Shahram, ed. Domestic Political Factors. LC 81-572. (Security in the Persian Gulf Ser.: Vol. 1). 104p. 1981. pap. text ed. 10.00 (ISBN 0-86598-044-6). Allanheld.

--The Role of Outside Powers. LC 80-28314. (Security in the Persian Gulf Ser.: Vol. 4). 100p. 1981. text ed. 10.00 (ISBN 0-86598-047-0). Allanheld.

Clarke, Thurston. By Blood & Fire. 288p. 1981. 13.95 (ISBN 0-399-12605-8). Putnam.

Cohen, Amnon. Political Parties in the West Bank Under the Jordanian Regime, 1949-1967. 280p. 1981. 19.50x (ISBN 0-8014-1321-4). Cornell U Pr.

Curtis, Michael, ed. Religion & Politics in the Middle East. 300p. 1981. lib. bdg. 25.25x (ISBN 0-86531-065-3). Westview.

Davis, Helen C., ed. Constitutions, Electoral Laws, Treaties of States in the Near & Middle East. LC 79-99886. Repr. of 1953 ed. 27.50 (ISBN 0-404-01995-1). AMS Pr.

Dawn, C. Ernest. From Ottomanism to Arabism: Essays on the Origins of Arab Nationalism. LC 72-88953. 212p. 1973. 12.50 (ISBN 0-252-00202-4). U of Ill Pr.

Drabek, Anne G. & Knapp, Wilfred. The Politics of African & Middle Eastern States: An Annotated Bibliography. LC 76-26649. 1977. text ed. 26.00 (ISBN 0-08-020584-4); pap. text ed. 11.50 (ISBN 0-08-020583-6). Pergamon.

Duignan, Peter & Gann, L. H. The Middle East & North Africa: The Challenge to Western Security. (Publication Ser.: No.239). 180p. 1981. pap. 9.95 (ISBN 0-8179-7392-3). Hoover Inst Pr.

Duker, Abraham G. & Ben Hurin, Meir. Emancipation & Counter Emancipation. LC 70-147927. 420p. 1974. text ed. 20.00x (ISBN 0-87068-160-5). Ktav.

El-Hakim, Ali A. The Middle Eastern States & the Law of the Sea. (Illus.). 310p. 1979. 30.00x (ISBN 0-8156-2217-1). Syracuse U Pr.

El-Khawas, Mohamed A. Qaddafi's Ideology: The Theory & the Practice. Nyang, Sulayman S., ed. (Third World Monograph). 58p. (Orig.). 1981. pap. 1.50x (ISBN 0-931494-12-5). Brunswick Pub.

Fitzsimons, Matthew A. Empire by Treaty: Britain & the Middle East in the Twentieth Century. (International Studies Ser). 1964. 9.95x (ISBN 0-268-00088-3). U of Notre Dame Pr.

Forrest, A. C. The Unholy Land. (Illus.). 1972. pap. 4.95 (ISBN 0-8159-7006-4). Devin.

Frankel, Dave. Self-Determination in the Mideast: A Debate. 1974. pap. 0.60 (ISBN 0-87348-335-9). Path Pr NY.

Gordon, Murray, ed. Conflict in the Persian Gulf. (Checkmark Book Ser.). 200p. 1981. lib. bdg. 17.50 (ISBN 0-87196-158-X). Facts on File.

Haddad, George M. Revolutions & Military Rule in the Middle East: Egypt, Sudan, Yemen, Vol. 3. 12.50 (ISBN 0-8315-0061-1). Speller.

--Revolutions & Military Rule in the Middle East: The Arab States, Vol. 2. 12.50 (ISBN 0-8315-0060-3). Speller.

--Revolutions & Military Rule in the Middle East: The Northern Tier, Vol. 1. 10.00 (ISBN 0-8315-0059-X). Speller.

Halderman, John W., ed. Middle East Crisis: Test of International Law. LC 69-19795. (Law & Contemporary Problems Ser. No. 11). 1969. 10.00 (ISBN 0-379-11511-5). Oceana.

Halpern, Manfred. Politics of Social Change in the Middle East & North Africa. (Rand Corporation Research Studies). 1963. 26.00x (ISBN 0-691-03051-0); pap. 8.95 (ISBN 0-691-00006-9). Princeton U Pr.

Hammond, P. Y. Political Dynamics in the Middle East. (Middle East Ser.). 1972. 24.95 (ISBN 0-444-00110-7, North Holland). Elsevier.

Harris, William W. Taking Root: Israeli Settlement in the West Bank, the Golan & Gaza-Sinai, 1967-1980. LC 80-40953. (Geographical Research Studies). 223p. 1980. 49.50 (ISBN 0-471-27863-7, Pub. by Wiley-Interscience). Wiley.

Helms, Christine M. The Cohesion of Saudi Arabia: Evolution of Political Identity. LC 80-8026. (Illus.). 320p. 1981. text ed. 28.00x (ISBN 0-8018-2475-3). Johns Hopkins.

Henkin, Louis. World Politics & the Jewish Condition. LC 70-190130. 1972. 9.95 (ISBN 0-8129-0265-3). Times Bks.

Henry, Clement M. Politics & International Relations in the Middle East: An Annotated Bibliography. 107p. (Orig.). 1980. pap. 4.00 (ISBN 0-932098-18-5). Ctr for NE & North Aafrican Stud.

Heravi, Mehdi. Concise Encyclopedia of the Middle East. 1979. 12.00 (ISBN 0-8183-0130-9); pap. 6.50 (ISBN 0-8183-0260-7). Pub Aff Pr.

Hourani, Albert. The Emergence of the Modern Middle East. 1981. 30.00x (ISBN 0-520-03862-2). U of Cal Pr.

Hurewitz, J. C. Middle East Politics: The Military Dimension. xviii, 553p. 1974. Repr. lib. bdg. 25.00x (ISBN 0-374-94059-2). Octagon.

Jones, Rodney W. Nuclear Proliferation: Islam, the Bomb & South Asia. LC 81-1685. (The Washington Papers Ser.: Vol. IX, No. 82). (Illus.). 80p. 1981. pap. 4.00 (ISBN 0-8039-1609-4). Sage.

Jureidini, Paul & McLaurin, R. D. Beyond Camp David: Emerging Alignments & Leaders in the Middle East. LC 80-27406. (Contemporary Issues in the Middle East Ser.). 232p. 1981. text ed. 18.00x (ISBN 0-8156-2235-X); pap. text ed. 8.95x (ISBN 0-8156-2236-8). Syracuse U Pr.

Kirk, George E. The Middle East: 1945-1950. 1954. 50.00 (ISBN 0-384-29490-1); pap. 45.00 (ISBN 0-685-13514-4). Johnson Repr.

Klieman, Aaron S. Israel, Jordan, Palestine: The Search for a Durable Peace. (The Washington Papers Ser.: Vol. 84). 88p. 1981. 4.00 (ISBN 0-8039-1684-1). Sage.

Koury, Enver M. The Middle East & North Africa: Definition & Analysis of Regional Balances of Power. LC 74-84755. 132p. 1974. pap. 6.00 (ISBN 0-934484-06-6). Inst Mid East & North Africa.

Landau, Jacob M., et al, eds. Electoral Politics in the Middle East: Issues, Voters & Elites. (Publication Ser.: No. 241). 400p. 1980. 29.95 (ISBN 0-8179-7411-3). Hoover Inst Pr.

Laqueur, Walter. Confrontation: The Middle East & World Politics. LC 74-79438. 1974. 8.95 (ISBN 0-8129-0454-0). Times Bks.

Laqueur, Walter Z., ed. Middle East in Transition: Studies in Contemporary History. facsimile ed. LC 70-156676. (Essay Index Reprint Ser). Repr. of 1958 ed. 26.00 (ISBN 0-8369-2367-7). Arno.

Legum, Colin & Shaked, Haim, eds. Middle East Contemporary Survey, Vol. 2. LC 78-648245. (Illus.). 1979. 115.00x (ISBN 0-8419-0398-0). Holmes & Meier.

--Middle East Contemporary Survey: 1978-1979, Vol. 3. LC 78-648245. (Illus.). 1980. text ed. 125.00x (ISBN 0-8419-0514-2). Holmes & Meier.

Lenczowski, George. The Middle East in World Affairs. 4th ed. LC 79-17059. (Illus.). 1980. 32.50x (ISBN 0-8014-1273-0); pap. 16.95x (ISBN 0-8014-9872-4). Cornell U Pr.

Lenczowski, George, ed. Political Elites in the Middle East. LC 75-10898. 1975. 15.25 (ISBN 0-8447-3164-1); pap. 7.25 (ISBN 0-8447-3163-3). Am Enterprise.

Lewis, Bernard. Middle East & the West. 1968. pap. 3.50x (ISBN 0-06-131274-6, TB1274, Torch). Har-Row.

Long, David E. & Reich, Bernard, eds. The Government & Politics of the Middle East & North Africa. 465p. 1980. text ed. 31.25x (ISBN 0-89158-593-1); pap. text ed. 13.50x (ISBN 0-89158-871-X). Westview.

Lumer, Hyman. Middle East Crisis. 1967. pap. 0.25 (ISBN 0-87898-023-7). New Outlook.

McDonald, John & Burleson, Clyde. Flight from Dhahran: The True Experiences of an American Businessman Held Hostage in Saudi Arabia. 256p. 1981. 12.95 (ISBN 0-13-322453-8). P-H.

McLaurin, R. D., ed. The Political Role of Minorities in the Middle East. LC 79-20588. (Praeger Special Studies). 328p. 1979. 27.95 (ISBN 0-03-052596-9). Praeger.

Mansfield, Peter. The Middle East: A Political & Economic Survey. (Illus.). 1980. 29.95 (ISBN 0-19-215851-1). Oxford U Pr.

Mari on Mushkat. Violence & Peace Building in the Middle East: Proceedings of a Symposium Held by the Israeli Institute for the Study of International Affairs. iv, 320p. 1981. 21.00 (ISBN 3-598-10355-7, Pub. by K G Saur). Shoe String.

Marx, Victor. The Betrayal of the State of Israel & the Foreign Policy of the United States: A Blueprint for Peace in the Middle East. new ed. (Illus.). 1977. 47.50 (ISBN 0-89266-059-7). Am Classical Coll Pr.

--The Middle East & the Attempt at World Economic Hegemony. (Illus.). 1977. 47.75 (ISBN 0-89266-047-3). Am Classical Coll Pr.

--The Middle East Conspiracy & the Survival of the Human Race. 1978. deluxe ed. 47.50 (ISBN 0-930008-17-0). Inst Econ Pol.

--The Middle East Conspiracy & the Survival of the Human Race. (Illus.). 235p. 1976. 47.50 (ISBN 0-89266-007-4). Am Classical Coll Pr.

May, Brian. The Third World Calamity. (Illus.). 272p. 1981. 19.95 (ISBN 0-7100-0764-7). Routledge & Kegan.

Merlin, Samuel, ed. Big Powers & the Present Crisis in the Middle East. LC 68-8864. 201p. 1968. 12.00 (ISBN 0-8386-7349-X). Fairleigh Dickinson.

Mezerik, Avrahm G., ed. Middle East Crisis. 1958. pap. 15.00 (ISBN 0-685-13206-4, 45). Intl Review.

Middle East & North Africa 1980-81. 985p. 1981. 80.00 (ISBN 0-905118-50-2, EUR 23, Europa). Unipub.

The Middle East & North Africa 1980-81. 27th ed. LC 48-3250. (Illus.). 1005p. 1980. 80.00x (ISBN 0-905118-50-2). Intl Pubns Serv.

Mobley, Jonathan H. The Elusive Peace: The Middle East, Oil & the Economic & Political Future of the World. (The Major Currents in Contemprary World History Lib.). (Illus.). 144p. 1981. 67.75 (ISBN 0-930008-79-0). Inst Econ Pol.

Mroz, John E. Beyond Security: Private Perceptions Among Arabs & Israelis. (Illus.). 230p. 1981. 19.50 (ISBN 0-08-027517-6); pap. 8.95 (ISBN 0-08-027516-8). Pergamon.

Naff, Thomas, ed. The Middle East Challenge: Nineteen Eighty to Nineteen Eighty-Five. LC 81-5651. 176p. (Orig.). 1981. pap. write for info. (ISBN 0-8093-1042-2). S Ill U Pr.

Narayan, B. K. Oman & Gulf-Security. 300p. 1980. text ed. 24.00x (ISBN 0-8426-1660-8). Verry.

Neilson, Francis. Unrest in the Middle East. 1979. lib. bdg. 39.95 (ISBN 0-685-96646-1). Revisionist Pr.

Petras, James, et al. Class, State & Power in the Third World: With Case Studies on Class Conflict in Latin America. 285p. 1981. text ed. 19.95 (ISBN 0-86598-018-7); pap. text ed. 8.95 (ISBN 0-86598-056-X). Allanheld.

Plascov, Avi, ed. Modernization, Political Development & Stability. LC 80-28387. (Security in the Persian Gulf Ser.: Vol. 3). 100p. 1981. pap. text ed. 10.00 (ISBN 0-86598-046-2). Allanheld.

Poliak, A. N. Geopolitics of Israel & the Middle East. 1978. lib. bdg. 49.95 (ISBN 0-685-62294-0). Revisionist Pr.

Poliak, Abraham N. Feudalism in Egypt, Syria, Palestine & Lebanon 1250-1900: With Two Additional Articles. LC 77-10729. (Studies in Islamic History: No. 13). 125p. Repr. of 1939 ed. lib. bdg. 12.50x (ISBN 0-87991-462-9). Porcupine Pr.

Polk, William R. The Elusive Peace: The Middle East in the Twentieth Century. LC 79-16393. 1979. 14.50x (ISBN 0-312-24383-9). St Martin.

Price, David L. Oil & Middle East Security. LC 76-54450. (The Washington Papers: No. 41). 1977. 4.00 (ISBN 0-8039-0791-5). Sage.

Prittie, Terrence. Whose Jerusalem? 224p. 1981. 45.00x (ISBN 0-584-10440-5, Pub. by Muller Ltd). State Mutual Bk.

Rabinovich, I. & Shaked, H., eds. From June to October: The Middle East Between 1967 & 1973. LC 76-45942. 550p. 1977. text ed. 19.95 (ISBN 0-87855-230-8). Transaction Bks.

Ramazani, R. K. Beyond the Arab-Israeli Settlement: New Directions for U. S. Policy in the Middle East. LC 77-87564. (Foreign Policy Reports Ser.). 69p. 1977. 5.00 (ISBN 0-89549-006-4). Inst Foreign Policy Anal.

Roberts, Hugh. An Urban Profile of the Middle East. LC 78-27185. 1979. 32.50x (ISBN 0-312-83467-5). St Martin.

Roosevelt, Kermit. Arabs, Oil & History. LC 75-79311. 1969. Repr. of 1949 ed. 12.00 (ISBN 0-8046-0532-7). Kennikat.

Safran, Nadav. From War to War: The Arab-Israeli Confrontation, 1948-1967. LC 69-27991. (Illus.). 464p. 1969. text ed. 24.50x (ISBN 0-8290-0173-5). Irvington.

--From War to War: The Arab-Israeli Confrontation 1948-1967. LC 68-27991. 1969. pap. 9.95 (ISBN 0-672-63540-2). Pegasus.

Seibert, Robert F. & Anderson, Roy R. Politics & Change in the Middle East: Sources of Conflict & Accommodation. 352p. 1982. pap. 11.95 (ISBN 0-13-685057-X). P-H.

Shaked, Haim, et al, eds. Political Dictionary of the Middle East in the Twentieth Century. rev. ed. LC 74-78998. 512p. 1974. 15.00 (ISBN 0-8129-0482-6). Times Bks.

Sid-Ahmed, Mohamed. After the Guns Fall Silent. LC 76-24997. 1976. 19.95 (ISBN 0-312-01155-5). St Martin.

Sinai, Anne & Pollack, Allen, eds. The Hashemite Kingdom of Jordan & the West Bank. 1977. pap. text ed. 6.95 (ISBN 0-917158-01-6). AAAPME.

Sobel, Lester. Peacemaking in the Middle East. (Checkmark Bk.). 200p. 1980. lib. bdg. 17.50 (ISBN 0-87196-267-5). Facts on File.

Soloway, Arnold, et al. Truth & Peace in the Middle East: A Critical Analysis of the Quaker Report. 112p. pap. 1.25 (ISBN 0-686-74978-2). ADL.

Stoddard, Philip, et al, eds. Change & the Muslim World. (Contemporary Issues in the Middle East Ser.). 224p. 1981. pap. text ed. 12.95x (ISBN 0-8156-2251-1). Syracuse U Pr.

Stowasser, Barbara F. & Manalo, Kathleen H. Twenty-Year Cumulative Index to the Middle East Journal, 1947-1966. LC 79-92823. 1972. text ed. 25.00 (ISBN 0-916808-10-6). Mid East Inst.

Sutton, Hilton & Levitt, Zola. The Mid-East Peace Puzzle. 1979. pap. 2.95 (ISBN 0-8407-5703-4). Nelson.

Tachau, Frank, ed. Political Elites & Political Development in the Middle East. LC 74-20507. 1975. text ed. 18.95 (ISBN 0-470-84314-4); pap. 8.95x (ISBN 0-470-84315-2). Halsted Pr.

Tames, Richard. The Arab World Today. (Today Ser.). (Illus.). 96p. 1980. text ed. 15.95x (ISBN 0-7182-0461-1, SpS). Sportshelf.

Thayer, Philip W. Tensions in the Middle East. LC 78-6231. 1978. Repr. of 1958 ed. lib. bdg. 21.75x (ISBN 0-313-20505-1, THTE). Greenwood.

Thompson, Jack H. & Reischauer, Robert D. Modernization of the Arab World. (New Perspectives in Political Science Ser: No. 11). (Orig.). 1966. pap. 4.95x (ISBN 0-442-08483-8, NP11). Van Nos Reinhold.

Toward Peace in the Middle East: Report of a Study Group. 1975. pap. 2.00 (ISBN 0-8157-9751-6). Brookings.

Towle, Philip, ed. Estimating Foreign Military Power. 270p. 1981. text ed. 27.00x (ISBN 0-8419-0736-6). Holmes & Meier.

Treverton, Gregory, ed. Crisis Management & the Super-Powers in the Middle East. LC 80-67837. (Adelphi Library: Vol. 5). 192p. 1981. text ed. 28.50 (ISBN 0-916672-73-5). Allanheld.

Von Pivka, Otto. Armies of the Middle East. LC 79-13223. (Illus.). 1979. 12.95 (ISBN 0-8317-0443-8, Mayflower Bks). Smith Pubs.

Waterbury, John & Mallakh, Ragaei E. The Middle East in the Coming Decade: From Wellhead to Well-Being. (Council on Foreign Relations 1980's Project Ser.). 1978. text ed. 9.95x (ISBN 0-07-068445-6, P&RB); pap. 5.95 (ISBN 0-07-068446-4). McGraw.

Whetten, L. L. The Canal War: Four-Power Conflict in the Middle East. 1974. 25.00x (ISBN 0-262-23069-0). MIT Pr.

Wise, George S. & Issawi, Charles, eds. Middle East Perspectives: The Next Twenty Years. LC 81-2562. 246p. 1981. 19.95 (ISBN 0-87850-037-5). Darwin Pr.

Wolpin, Miles D. Militarism & Social Revolution in the Third World. LC 81-65014. 256p. 1981. text ed. 19.95 (ISBN 0-86598-021-7). Allanheld.

Young, Ezra. Lands of the Unexpected: Memoirs of the Middle East. new ed. Smith, James C., Jr., ed. LC 78-75083. (Illus.). 1979. pap. 7.95 (ISBN 0-913270-77-6). Sunstone Pr.

Zelter, Moshe. Aspects of Near East Society. 1962. 8.50x (ISBN 0-8084-0390-7); pap. 2.45 (ISBN 0-8084-0391-5, B12). Coll & U Pr.

NEAR EAST-RELATIONS (GENERAL) WITH GREAT BRITAIN

Bray, N. N. Shifting Sands. LC 70-180321. Repr. of 1934 ed. 16.00 (ISBN 0-404-56216-7). AMS Pr.

NEAR EAST-RELATIONS (GENERAL) WITH THE UNITED STATES

American Assembly & Stevens, G. G. The United States & the Middle East. (New Reprints in Essay & General Literature Index Ser.). 1975. Repr. of 1964 ed. 18.25 (ISBN 0-518-10195-9, 10195). Arno.

Daniel, Robert L. American Philanthropy in the Near East, 1820-1960. LC 74-81451. xii, 322p. 1970. 15.00x (ISBN 0-8214-0063-0). Ohio U Pr.

De Novo, John A. American Interests & Policies in the Middle East 1900-1939. LC 63-21129. (Illus.). 1963. 19.50x (ISBN 0-8166-0302-2). U of Minn Pr.

NEAR EAST-RELIGION

Arberry, Arthur J. Religion in the Middle East, 2 Vols. LC 68-21187. (Illus.). 1969. Set. 88.00 (ISBN 0-521-07400-2); 54.00 ea.; Vol. 1. (ISBN 0-521-20543-3); Vol. 2. (ISBN 0-521-20544-1). Cambridge U Pr.

Chakmakjian, Hagop A. In Quest of Justice & Peace in the Middle East. 1980. 8.95 (ISBN 0-533-04539-8). Vantage.

Curtis, Michael, ed. Religion & Politics in the Middle East. 300p. 1981. lib. bdg. 25.25x (ISBN 0-86531-065-3). Westview.

Dunn, Jean, ed. Seeds of Consciousness: The Wisdom of Sri Nisargadatta Maharaj. 192p. (Orig.). 1981. pap. 12.50 (ISBN 0-394-17939-0, Ever). Grove.

It Is No Dream. LC 78-51766. 1978. pap. 3.95 (ISBN 0-915540-21-5). Friends Israel-Spearhead Pr.

Jurji, Edward J. The Middle East, Its Religion & Culture. LC 72-9809. 159p. 1973. Repr. of 1956 ed. lib. bdg. 13.00x (ISBN 0-8371-6597-0, JUME). Greenwood.

Teixidor, Javier. The Pagan God: Popular Religion in the Greco-Roman Near East. LC 76-24300. 1977. text ed. 14.50 (ISBN 0-691-07220-5). Princeton U Pr.

NEAR EAST-SOCIAL CONDITIONS

The Arabian Gulf Government & Public Services Directory 1980-81. 1980. 175.00x (ISBN 0-686-69888-6, Pub. by Parrish-Rogers England). State Mutual Bk.

Baer, Gabriel. Fellah & Townsman in the Middle East: Studies in Social History. 1981. 30.00x (ISBN 0-7146-3126-4, F Cass Co). Biblio Dist.

--Population & Society in the Arab East. Szoke, Hanna, tr. LC 76-16835. (Illus.). 1976. Repr. of 1964 ed. lib. bdg. 21.25x (ISBN 0-8371-8963-2, BAPSA). Greenwood.

Bedouins, Wealth, & Change: A Study of Rural Development in the United Arab Emirates & the Sultanate of Oman. 64p. 1980. pap. 11.75 (ISBN 9-2808-0143-0, TUNU 086, UNU). Unipub.

Bowman, David H. Conflict of Community: A Guide to the Middle East Mosaic. (Orig.). 1979. pap. 2.75 (ISBN 0-377-00085-X). Friend Pr.

Clarke, J. I. & Fisher, W. B. Populations of the Middle East & North Africa: A Geographical Approach. LC 72-80410. 432p. 1972. text ed. 39.50x (ISBN 0-8419-0125-2). Holmes & Meier.

Clarke, Thurston. By Blood & Fire. 288p. 1981. 13.95 (ISBN 0-399-12605-8). Putnam.

Costello, V. F. Urbanization in the Middle East. LC 76-11075. (Urbanization in Developing Countries Ser.). (Illus.). 1977. 19.95 (ISBN 0-521-21324-X); pap. 6.95x (ISBN 0-521-29110-0). Cambridge U Pr.

Dodd, Stuart C. Social Relations in the Near East. 2nd, rev. & enl. ed. LC 75-180333. Repr. of 1940 ed. 62.50 (ISBN 0-404-56239-6). AMS Pr.

Fisher, Sydney N., ed. Social Forces in the Middle East. LC 68-23289. (Illus.). 1968. Repr. of 1955 ed. lib. bdg. 20.00x (ISBN 0-8371-0074-7, FIME). Greenwood.

Golan, Galia. Yom Kippur & After. LC 76-2278. (Soviet & East European Studies). 1977. 38.50 (ISBN 0-521-21090-9). Cambridge U Pr.

Halpern, Manfred. Politics of Social Change in the Middle East & North Africa. (Rand Corporation Research Studies). 1963. 26.00x (ISBN 0-691-03051-0); pap. 8.95 (ISBN 0-691-00006-9). Princeton U Pr.

Hindus, Maurice G. In Search of a Future: Persia, Egypt, Iraq, & Palestine. LC 79-3072. 270p. 1980. Repr. of 1949 ed. 22.50 (ISBN 0-8305-0035-9). Hyperion Conn.

Laqueur, Walter Z., ed. Middle East in Transition: Studies in Contemporary History. facsimile ed. LC 70-156676. (Essay Index Reprint Ser). Repr. of 1958 ed. 26.00 (ISBN 0-8369-2367-7). Arno.

Middle East & North Africa 1980-81. 985p. 1981. 80.00 (ISBN 0-905118-50-2, EUR 23, Europa). Unipub.

Mroz, John E. Beyond Security: Private Perceptions Among Arabs & Israelis. (Illus.). 230p. 1981. 19.50 (ISBN 0-08-027517-6); pap. 8.95 (ISBN 0-08-027516-8). Pergamon.

Nassif, R. E. & Thaddeus, J. D., eds. Education for Health Manpower in the Middle East. 1967. pap. 12.95x (ISBN 0-8156-6006-5, Am U Beirut). Syracuse U Pr.

Pratt, et al. Peace, Justice & Reconciliation in the Arab-Israeli Conflict: A Christian Perspective. (Orig.). 1979. pap. 2.75 (ISBN 0-377-00090-6). Friend Pr.

Stoddard, Philip, et al, eds. Change & the Muslim World. (Contemporary Issues in the Middle East Ser.). 224p. 1981. pap. text ed. 12.95x (ISBN 0-8156-2251-1). Syracuse U Pr.

Tames, Richard. The Arab World Today. (Today Ser.). (Illus.). 96p. 1980. text ed. 15.95x (ISBN 0-7182-0461-1, SpS). Sportshelf.

Traditional Rural Institutions & Their Implications for Development Planning: Studies from Hamadan Province or Iran. 14p. 1981. pap. 5.00 (ISBN 92-808-0148-1, TUNU 115, UNU). Unipub.

Tuma, Elias H., ed. Food & Population in the Middle East. LC 76-57917. 83p. 1976. pap. 5.00 (ISBN 0-934484-08-2). Inst Mid East & North Africa.

Vanbery, Armin. Scenes from the East: Through the Eyes of a European Traveller in the 1860's. Kortvelyessy, Eniko & Gaster, Bertha, trs. from Hungarian. (Illus.). 418p. (Orig.). 1979. pap. 8.50 (ISBN 963-13-0832-4). Intl Pubns Serv.

Van Nieuwenhuijze, C., ed. Sociology of the Middle East: A Stocktaking & Interpretation. (Social, Economic & Political Studies of the Middle East: Vol. 1). (Illus.). 819p. 1971. text ed. 128.25x (ISBN 90-040-2564-2). Humanities.

Wolpin, Miles D. Militarism & Social Revolution in the Third World. LC 81-65014. 256p. 1981. text ed. 19.95 (ISBN 0-86598-021-7). Allanheld.

Woodsmall, Ruth F. Moslem Women Enter a New World. LC 75-180309. Repr. of 1936 ed. 31.50 (ISBN 0-404-56334-1). AMS Pr.

NEAR EAST-SOCIAL LIFE AND CUSTOMS

Bagnole, John W. Cultures of the Islamic Middle East. (America-Mideast Educational & Training Servies, Inc. - Occasional Paper: No. 4). 86p. (Orig.). 1978. pap. text ed. 4.00 (ISBN 0-89192-296-2). Interbk Inc.

Bowman, David H. Conflict of Community: A Guide to the Middle East Mosaic. (Orig.). 1979. pap. 2.75 (ISBN 0-377-00085-X). Friend Pr.

Eickelman, Dale F. The Middle East: An Anthropological Approach. (Ser. in Anthropology). (Illus.). 368p. 1981. text ed. 11.95 (ISBN 0-13-581629-7). P-H.

Hansen, Henny H. Investigations in a Shi'a Village in Bahrain. (Ethnographical Ser.: No. 12). (Illus.). 1968. pap. text ed. 28.75x (ISBN 87-480-7202-8). Humanities.

Patal, Raphael. Society, Culture & Change in the Middle East. LC 70-84742. Orig. Title: Golden River to Golden Road. (Illus.). 1971. pap. 9.95x (ISBN 0-8122-1009-3, Pa Paperbks). U of Pa Pr.

Pierce, Joe E. Understanding the Middle East. LC 70-172002. 1971. 6.25 (ISBN 0-8048-0670-5). C E Tuttle.

Pillai, K. C. Light Through an Eastern Window. 4.95 (ISBN 0-8315-0057-3). Speller.

Rosenfeld, Erwin & Geller, Harriet. El Medio Oriente y Africa Del Norte. Casares, Angel & Casasnovas, Sonia, trs. from Eng. LC 75-33319. (Afro Asian Culture Studies: Unit 3). (Illus., Span.). (gr. 9-12). 1976. pap. text ed. 3.25 (ISBN 0-8120-0600-3). Barron.

Zartman, I. William, ed. Elites in the Middle East. 270p. 1980. 24.95 (ISBN 0-03-055961-8). Praeger.

Zelter, Moshe. Aspects of Near East Society. 1962. 8.50x (ISBN 0-8084-0390-7); pap. 2.45 (ISBN 0-8084-0391-5, B12). Coll & U Pr.

NEAR EASTERN ARCHITECTURE

see Architecture–Near East

NEAR EASTERN ART

see Art, Near Eastern

NEARING, SCOTT, 1883-

Nearing, Helen & Nearing, Scott. Continuing the Good Life: Half a Century of Homesteading. LC 78-21151. (Illus.). 208p. 1980. pap. 4.95 (ISBN 0-8052-0642-6). Schocken.

Whitfield, Stephen J. Scott Nearing: Apostle of American Radicalism. 1974. 15.00x (ISBN 0-231-03816-X). Columbia U Pr.

Witmer, Lightner. Nearing Case: Limitation of Academic Freedom at the Univ. of Penn. by Act of the Board of Trustees, June 14, 1915. LC 71-122163. (Civil Liberties in American Liberty Ser.). 123p. 1974. Repr. of 1915 ed. lib. bdg. 17.50 (ISBN 0-306-71978-9). Da Capo.

--The Nearing Case: The Limitation of Academic Freedom at the University of Pennsylvania by Act of the Board of Trustees June 14, 1915. 144p. 1972. pap. 6.95x (ISBN 0-8377-2726-X). Rothman.

NEARSIGHTEDNESS

see Myopia

NEBRASKA

see also names of cities, counties, towns, etc. in Nebraska

Bailey, Bernadine. Picture Book of Nebraska. rev. ed. LC 56-7756. (Illus.). (gr. 3-5). 1966. 5.50g (ISBN 0-8075-9530-6). A Whitman.

Bare, Charles L. Nebraska Economic Projections II, 1980-2000. Keefe, Jean, ed. (Nebraska Economic & Business Report Ser.: No. 19). 1978. 7.50 (ISBN 0-686-28409-7). Bur Busn Res U Nebr.

--Nebraska Gross State Product Nineteen Sixty to Ninety Seventy-Six. (Nebraska Economic & Business Report: No. 22). 1978. 5.00 (ISBN 0-686-28411-9). Bur Busn Res U Nebr.

Bentley, A. F. Condition of the Western Farmer As Illustrated by the Economic History of a Nebraska Township. pap. 8.00 (ISBN 0-384-03938-3). Johnson Repr.

Carlson, Gayle F. Archeological Investigations at Fort Atkinson: Washington County, Nebraska 1956-1971. (Publications in Anthropology: No. 8). 1979. 8.95 (ISBN 0-686-27209-9). Nebraska Hist.

Carpenter, Allan. Nebraska. LC 78-10480. (New Enchantment of America State Bks). (Illus.). (gr. 4 up). 1979. PLB 10.60 (ISBN 0-516-04127-4). Childrens.

Comer, John C. & Johnson, James B., eds. Nonpartisanship in the Legislative Process: Essays on the Nebraska Legislature. LC 78-69835. 1978. pap. text ed. 7.50 (ISBN 0-8191-0579-1). U Pr of Amer.

Deichert, Jerome A., et al. Migration Patterns of Young Adults in Nebaska. (Nebraska Economic & Business Report: No. 25). 1978. 5.00 (ISBN 0-686-28413-5). Bur Busn Res U Nebr.

Diller, Robert. Farm Ownership, Tenancy, & Land Use in the Nebraska Community. Bruchey, Stuart, ed. LC 78-56629. (Management of Public Lands in the U. S. Ser.). 1979. Repr. of 1932 ed. lib. bdg. 15.00x (ISBN 0-405-11339-0). Arno.

Faulkner, Virginia, ed. Roundup: A Nebraska Reader. LC 57-8597. (Illus.). 1975. pap. 4.95 (ISBN 0-8032-5807-0, BB 593, Bison). U of Nebr Pr.

Federal Writers' Project. Nebraska: A Guide to the Cornhusker State. 424p. 1939. Repr. 39.00 (ISBN 0-403-02177-4). Somerset Pub.

Federal Writers' Project of the Works Progress Administration. Nebraska: A Guide to the Cornhusker State. LC 78-26756. (Illus.). xxiv, 424p. 1979. 21.50x (ISBN 0-8032-1953-9); pap. 5.50 (ISBN 0-8032-6851-3, BB 690, Bison). U of Nebr Pr.

Fitzpatrick, Lilian L. Nebraska Place-Names. Fairclough, G. Thomas, ed. LC 60-15471. 1960. pap. 3.50 (ISBN 0-8032-5060-6, BB 107, Bison). U of Nebr Pr.

Fradin, Dennis. Nebraska: In Words & Pictures. LC 79-19456. (Young People's Stories of Our States Ser.). (Illus.). 48p. (gr. 2-5). 1980. PLB 9.65 (ISBN 0-516-03927-X). Childrens.

Hackmann, Duane. Nebraska Subcounty Population Estimates. Keefe, Jean, ed. (Nebraska Economic & Business Report: No. 18). 1977. 5.00 (ISBN 0-686-10884-1). Bur Busn Res U Nebr.

Hale, Edward E. Kansas & Nebraska. facsimile ed. LC 75-37595. (Black Heritage Library Collection). Repr. of 1854 ed. 17.75 (ISBN 0-8369-8971-6). Arno.

Hart, Herbert M. Tour Guide to Old Forts of Texas, Kansas, Nebraska, Oklahoma, Vol. 4. (Illus.). 65p. (Orig.). 1981. pap. 3.95 (ISBN 0-87108-583-6). Pruett.

Lawson, Merlin P., et al. Climatic Atlas of Nebraska. LC 77-6643. (Nebraska Atlas Project Ser.). (Illus.). 1977. 14.95 (ISBN 0-8032-0924-X). U of Nebr Pr.

Lentz, Donald A. & Olsen, Walter R. Gleanings from the First Century of Nebraska Bands. (Illus.). 1979. 12.50 (ISBN 0-918626-12-9). Word Serv.

Lonsdale, Richard E., ed. Economic Atlas of Nebraska. LC 76-30887. (Nebraska Atlas Project). (Illus.). 1977. 16.95 (ISBN 0-8032-0911-8). U of Nebr Pr.

Luebke, Frederick C. Immigrants & Politics: The Germans of Nebraska, 1880-1900. LC 69-15924. (Illus.). 1969. 14.95x (ISBN 0-8032-0107-9). U of Nebr Pr.

Manley, Robert N. Nebraska: Our Pioneer Heritage. (Illus.). 197p. (gr. 4-5). 1981. text ed. 12.50x (ISBN 0-939644-00-2). Media Prods & Mktg.

--Nebraska: Our Pioneer Heritage. 76p. (gr. 4-5). 1981. write for info. tchr's guide. (ISBN 0-939644-01-0). Media Prods & Mktg.

Nebraska. 28.00 (ISBN 0-89770-103-8). Curriculum Info Ctr.

Paul, Justus F. Senator Hugh Butler & Nebraska Republicanism. LC 76-42167. (Nebraska State Historical Society Miscellaneous Ser.: No. 1). 1976. 15.50 (ISBN 0-8357-0185-9, IS-00014, Pub. by Nebraska State Historical Society). Univ Microfilms.

Pursell, Donald E. Nebraska Retail Sales, 1968-1975: Nebraska Economic & Business Report Ser. Keefe, Jean, ed. (No. 15). 1977. 7.50 (ISBN 0-686-10883-3). Bur Busn Res U Nebr.

Richards, Bartlett, Jr. & Van Ackeren, Ruth. Bartlett Richards: Nebraska Sandhills Cattleman. (Illus.). 289p. (Orig.). 1980. 12.00 (ISBN 0-686-31143-4). Nebraska Hist.

Starck, Robert & Dance, Lynn. Nebraska Photographic Documentary Project, 1975-1977. LC 77-72782. (Illus.). 1977. pap. 12.95 (ISBN 0-8032-5864-X). U of Nebr Pr.

State Industrial Directories. Nebraska State Industrial Directory, 1980. 1980. pap. 20.00 (ISBN 0-89910-005-8). State Indus Dir.

Stepp, Vicki S. Nebraska Population Counts-Revised 1970. Keefe, Jean, ed. (Nebraska Economic & Business Report: No. 17). 1977. 5.00 (ISBN 0-686-10885-X). Bur Busn Res U Nebr.

--Nebraska Population Estimates. Keefe, Jean, ed. (Nebraska Economic & Business Report: No. 16). 1977. 5.00 (ISBN 0-686-10886-8). Bur Busn Res U Nebr.

--A Review of Population Estimates & Projections for Nebraska Cities. (Nebraska Economic & Business Report: No. 21). 1978. 5.00 (ISBN 0-686-28412-7). Bur Busn Res U Nrbr.

NEBRASKA-GENEALOGY

Abbott, Othman A. & Sheldon, Addison E. Recollections of a Pioneer Lawyer: A Special Publication of the Nebraska State Historical Society. (Illus.). 1929. write for info. Nebraska Hist.

Jackson, Ronald V. & Teeples, Gary R. Nebraska Census Index Eighteen Sixty. (Illus.). Date not set. lib. bdg. price not set (ISBN 0-89593-216-4). Accelerated Index.

NEBRASKA-HISTORY

Agenbroad, Larry D. The Hudson-Meng Site: An Alberta Bison Kill in the Nebraska High Plains. LC 78-57606. (Illus.). 1978. pap. text ed. 10.00 (ISBN 0-8191-0530-9). U Pr of Amer.

Bartels, Michael M., et al. A Railfan's Guide to Nebraska. 48p. 1975. pap. 1.75 (ISBN 0-685-57652-3). J-B Pubs.

Bentley, Arthur F. The Condition of the Western Farmer As Illustrated by the Economic History of a Nebraska Township. LC 78-63821. (Johns Hopkins University. Studies in the Social Sciences. Eleventh Ser. 1893: 7-8). Repr. of 1893 ed. 11.50 (ISBN 0-404-61083-8). AMS Pr.

Beranek, Susan K. & Rapp, William F. An Industrial Archaeology of Nebraska. (Illus.). 50p. 1981. pap. write for info (ISBN 0-916170-00-4). J-B Pubs.
Butcher, Solomon D. Pioneer History of Custer County. 12.00 (ISBN 0-931068-05-3). Purcells.
Carlson, Gayle F. Archeological Investigations at Fort Atkinson: Washington County, Nebraska 1956-1971. (Publications in Anthropology: No. 8). 1979. 8.95 (ISBN 0-686-27209-9). Nebraska Hist.
Carlson, Gayle F. & Jensen, Richard E. Archeological Salvage & Survey in Nebraska. (Publications in Anthropology: No. 5). 1973. pap. 6.00 (ISBN 0-686-20018-7). Nebraska Hist.
Cherny, Robert W. Populism, Progressivism, & the Transformation of Nebraska Politics: 1885-1915. LC 80-11151. (Illus.). xviii, 227p. 1981. 17.50x (ISBN 0-8032-1407-3). U of Nebr Pr.
Chrisman, Berna H. When You & I Were Young, Nebraska. Chrisman, Harry E. & Blasingame, Clara, eds. (Illus.). 1971. 9.00 (ISBN 0-931068-04-5). Purcells.
Creigh, Dorothy W. Nebraska: A History. (States & the Nation Ser.). (Illus.). 1977. 12.95 (ISBN 0-393-05598-1, Co-Pub. by Aaslh). Norton.
Dick, Everett. Conquering the Great American Desert: Nebraska. LC 74-17591. (Nebraska State Historical Publications Ser.: Vol. 27). 1975. 10.95 (ISBN 0-686-18150-6). Nebraska Hist.
Gradwohl, David M. Prehistoric Villages in Eastern Nebraska. (Publications in Anthropology: No. 4). 1970. pap. 6.00 (ISBN 0-686-20021-7). Nebraska Hist.
Grange, Roger T., Jr. Pawnee & Lower Loup Pottery. (Publications in Anthropology: No. 3). 1968. pap. 6.00 (ISBN 0-686-20020-9). Nebraska Hist.
Hansen, Charles, Jr. The Northwest Gun. (Publications in Anthropology: No. 2). 1976. pap. 6.00 (ISBN 0-686-20019-5). Nebraska Hist.
Jackson, Franklin C. Echoes from the Sandhills. LC 77-77333. (Illus.). 1977. 10.00 (ISBN 0-918626-00-5). Word Serv.
Johnson, George E., II. The Nebraskan. 240p. 1981. write for info. (ISBN 0-89305-036-9). Anna Pub.
Johnson, Harrison. Johnson's History of Nebraska. facsimile ed. LC 75-106. (Mid American Frontier Ser.). (Illus.). 1975. Repr. of 1880 ed. 32.00x (ISBN 0-405-06873-5). Arno.
Kivett, Marvin F. Woodland Sites in Nebraska, Vol. 1. (Publications in Anthropology: No. 1). 1970. pap. 6.00 (ISBN 0-686-20023-3). Nebraska Hist.
McKee, James L. & Duerschner, Arthur E. Lincoln: A Photographic History. LC 75-36000. (Illus.). 200p. (Orig.). 1980. pap. 10.95 (ISBN 0-934904-03-0). J & L Lee.
Malin, J. C. The Nebraska Question, 1852-1854. 7.50 (ISBN 0-8446-2517-5). Peter Smith.
Martin, Aquinata. The Catholic Church on the Nebraska Frontier: 1854-1885. LC 73-3580. (Catholic University of America. Studies in American Church History: No. 26). Repr. of 1937 ed. 19.50 (ISBN 0-404-57776-8). AMS Pr.
Mattes, Merrill J. The Great Platte River Road: The Covered Wagon Mainline Via Fort Kearny to Fort Laramie. 2nd ed. LC 79-627916. (Nebraska State Historical Society Publications Ser.: Vol. 25). (Illus.). 1979. pap. 8.95 (ISBN 0-686-26254-9). Nebraska Hist.
Moss, Ira. Their Chosen Land. (Illus.). 1978. 12.50 (ISBN 0-918626-06-4). Word Serv.
Neuman, Robert W. The Sonota Complex & Associated Sites on the Northern Great Plains. (Publications in Anthropology: No. 6). 1975. pap. 6.00 (ISBN 0-686-20022-5). Nebraska Hist.
Nicoll, Bruce H. & Savery, Gilbert M., eds. Nebraska: A Pictorial History. bicentennial ed. LC 75-3570. (Illus.). 240p. 1975. 15.95 (ISBN 0-8032-0863-4); pap. 8.95 (ISBN 0-8032-5825-9). U of Nebr Pr.
Okada, Yasue. Public Lands & Pioneer Farmers, Gage County, Nebraska, 1850-1900. Bruchey, Stuart, ed. LC 78-56687. (Management of Public Lands in the U.S. Ser.). (Illus.). 1979. Repr. of 1971 ed. lib. bdg. 14.00x (ISBN 0-405-11348-X). Arno.
Olson, James C. History of Nebraska. 2nd ed. LC 54-8444. (Illus.). xiv, 427p. 1966. 14.95x (ISBN 0-8032-0135-4); pap. 9.95 (ISBN 0-8032-5790-2, BB 579, Bison). U of Nebr Pr.
Phillips, E. Bryant. Nebraska Street & Interurban Railways. 1975. pap. 3.75 (ISBN 0-685-52986-X). J-B Pubs.
Rapp, William F. Nebraska C. B. & Q. Stations. 46p. 1975. pap. 3.75 (ISBN 0-685-57651-5). J-B Pubs.
Shippey, Melda H. Nebraska Pioneer. 1975. 15.00 (ISBN 0-686-20883-8). Polyanthos.
Smith, Philip R. Improved Surface Transportation & Nebraska's Population Distribution, 1860-1960. Bruchey, Stuart, ed. LC 80-1289. (Railroads Ser.). (Illus.). 1981. lib. bdg. 30.00x (ISBN 0-405-13760-5). Arno.
Switzer, Colleen. The Settlement of Loup & Blaine Counties. (Illus.). 1977. 10.00 (ISBN 0-931068-12-6). Purcells.
Walton, Gerome. A History of Nebraska Banking & Paper Money. LC 76-12825. (Illus.). 674p. (Orig.). 1979. lib. bdg. 74.50 (ISBN 0-934904-06-5); pap. 48.50 (ISBN 0-934904-05-7). J & L Lee.
Watkins, Albert, ed. Collections of the Nebraska State Historical Society, Vol. XVI. 1911. write for info. Nebraska Hist.
--Publications of the Nebraska State Historical Society, Vol. XX. 1922. write for info. Nebraska Hist.
White, John B. Nebraska State Historical Society: Published Sources on Territorial Nebraska - An Essay & Bibliography, Vol. XXIII. 1956. write for info. Nebraska Hist.
Workers of the Writer's Program. The Italians of Omaha. LC 74-17940. (Italian American Experience Ser). (Illus.). 138p. 1975. Repr. 12.00x (ISBN 0-405-06411-X). Arno.

NEBRASKA-IMPRINTS

Historical Records Survey: Check List of Nebraska Non-Documentary Imprints, 1847-1876. 1942. pap. 12.00 (ISBN 0-527-01921-6). Kraus Repr.

NEBULAE

see also Galaxies; Planetary Nebulae

Gehrels, T., ed. Planets, Stars & Nebulae Studied With Photopolarimetry. LC 73-86446. 720p. 1974. 27.50x (ISBN 0-8165-0428-8). U of Ariz Pr.
Glasby, John S. The Nebular Variables. LC 74-3354. 220p. 1974. text ed. 42.00 (ISBN 0-08-017949-5). Pergamon.
Iau Symposium, No. 46 Jodrell Bank, England, August 5-7, 1970. The Crab Nebula: Proceedings. Davies, R. D. & Smith, F. G., eds. LC 73-154735. (IAU Symposia: No. 46). 470p. 1971. 50.00 (ISBN 90-277-0183-0, Pub. by Reidel Holland). Kluwer Boston.
Kaufmann, William J., III. Stars & Nebulas. LC 78-17544. (Illus.). 1978. pap. text ed. 8.95x (ISBN 0-7167-0085-9). W H Freeman.
Menzel, Donald H., ed. Selected Papers on Physical Processes in Ionized Plasmas. (Orig.). 1962. pap. text ed. 5.00 (ISBN 0-486-60060-2). Dover.
Middlehurst, Barbara M. & Aller, Lawrence H., eds. Nebulae & Interstellar Matter. LC 66-13879. (Stars & Stellar Systems Ser.: Vol. 7). (Illus.). 1968. 43.00x (ISBN 0-226-45959-4). U of Chicago Pr.
Mitton, Simon. The Crab Nebula. (Illus.). 1979. 16.95 (ISBN 0-684-16077-3, ScribT). Scribner.

NEBULAR HYPOTHESIS

see also Cosmogony; Creation

Kant, Immanuel. Kant's Cosmogony. Hastie, W., ed. 1971. Repr. 19.50 (ISBN 0-384-28575-9). Johnson Repr.
Numbers, Ronald L. Creation by Natural Law: Laplace's Nebular Hypothesis in American Thought. LC 76-45810. 196p. 1977. 16.95 (ISBN 0-295-95439-6). U of Wash Pr.

NECESSITY (LAW)

see also Self-Defense (Law)

Kass, Louis A. Necessary Elements. 1979 ed. 59p. 1979. 4.50 (ISBN 0-87526-242-2). Gould.
Springborg, Patricia. The Problem of Human Needs & the Critique of Civilization. 320p. 1981. text ed. 28.50x (ISBN 0-04-301133-0). Allen Unwin.

NECESSITY (PHILOSOPHY)

see also Causation; Chance; Fate and Fatalism; Free Will and Determinism; Ontology; Predestination; Teleology; Truth

Bisogno, Paolo & Forti, Augusto. Research & Human Needs: A Search for a New Development Paradigm. (Illus.). 176p. 1981. 32.51 (ISBN 0-08-027417-X). Pergamon.
Bramhall, John. Castigations of Mr. Hobbes. Wellek, Rene, ed. LC 75-11199. (British Philosophers & Theologians of the 17th & 18th Centuries: Vol. 6). 1976. Repr. of 1658 ed. lib. bdg. 42.00 (ISBN 0-8240-1755-2). Garland Pub.
--A Defence of True Liberty from Ante-Cedent & Extrinsical Necessity. an Answer to Hobbes' a Treatise of Liberty & Necessity. Wellek, Rene, ed. LC 75-11200. (British Philosophers & Theologians of the 17th & 18th Centuries: Vol. 7). 1976. Repr. of 1655 ed. lib. bdg. 42.00 (ISBN 0-8240-1756-0). Garland Pub.
Chiari, Joseph. The Necessity of Being. LC 73-3338. 168p. 1973. 9.00 (ISBN 0-87752-167-0). Gordian.
Harre, Romano & Madden, E. H. Causal Powers: A Theory of Natural Necessity. 191p. 1975. 18.50x (ISBN 0-87471-624-1). Rowman.
Knowledge of Necessity. 1970. 17.95 (ISBN 0-312-45920-3). St Martin.
Schwartz, Stephen P., ed. Naming, Necessity, & Natural Kinds. LC 76-28021. (Illus.). 1977. 20.00x (ISBN 0-8014-1049-5); pap. 8.95x (ISBN 0-8014-9861-9). Cornell U Pr.
Skyrms, Brian. Causal Necessity: A Pragmatic Investigation of the Necessity of Laws. LC 79-22983. (Illus.). 1980. 25.00x (ISBN 0-300-02339-1). Yale U Pr.

NECHAEV, SERGEI GENNADIEVICH, 1847-1882

Pomper, Philip. Sergei Nechaev. (Illus.). 1979. 19.50 (ISBN 0-8135-0867-3). Rutgers U Pr.

NECK

Bateman, James E. The Shoulder & Neck. 2nd ed. LC 77-84658. (Illus.). 1978. text ed. 55.00 (ISBN 0-7216-1571-6). Saunders.
Cailliet, Rene. Neck & Arm Pain. 2nd ed. LC 80-17352. (The Pain Ser.). (Illus.). 158p. 1981. pap. text ed. 8.95 (ISBN 0-8036-1609-0). Davis Co.
Cohn, Sidney A. & Gottlieb, Marvin I. Head & Neck Anatomy Review. (Basic Science Review Bks.). 1976. spiral bdg. 8.50 (ISBN 0-87488-222-2). Med Exam.
Conley, John. Regional Flaps of the Head & Neck. LC 76-11603. (Illus.). 1976. text ed. 70.00 (ISBN 0-7216-2647-5). Saunders.
De Gravelles, William D. & Kelley, John H. Injuries Following Rear-End Automobile Collisions. (Illus.). 256p. 1969. photocopy ed. spiral 22.75 (ISBN 0-398-00414-5). C C Thomas.
Fisk, James W. A Practical Guide to Management of the Painful Neck & Back: Diagnosis, Manipulation, Exercises, Prevention. (Illus.). 248p. 1977. 22.50 (ISBN 0-398-03640-3). C C Thomas.
Fried, Lawerence A. Anatomy of the Head, Neck, Face, & Jaws. 2nd ed. LC 80-16800. (Illus.). 299p. 1980. text ed. 17.50 (ISBN 0-8121-0717-9). Lea & Febiger.
Gerrick, David J. Surface Anatomy: The Neck. (Illus.). 1978. 20.00 (ISBN 0-916750-62-0). Dayton Labs.
Gurdjian, E. S. & Thomas, L. M. Neckache & Backache: Proceedings. (Illus.). 296p. 1970. 14.50 (ISBN 0-398-00747-0). C C Thomas.
Hiatt, James L. & Gartner, Leslie P. Textbook of Head & Neck Anatomy. 416p. 1982. 24.50 (ISBN 0-8385-8876-X). ACC.
Macnab, Ian. Neck & Shoulder Pain. (Illus.). 300p. Date not set. lib. bdg. price not set (ISBN 0-683-05354-X). Williams & Wilkins.
Montgomery, Royce L. Head & Neck Anatomy: With Clinical Correlations. (Illus.). 352p. 1981. text ed. 25.00 (ISBN 0-07-042853-0). McGraw.
Paff, George H. Anatomy of the Head & Neck. LC 72-93117. (Illus.). 235p. 1973. text ed. 19.95 (ISBN 0-7216-7041-5). Saunders.
Palacios, Enrique, et al. Multiplanar Anatomy of the Head & Neck: For Computed Tomography. LC 80-11368. 206p. 1980. 160.00 (ISBN 0-471-05820-3, Pub. by WileyMed). Wiley.
Pernkoph, Eduard. Atlas of Topographical & Applied Human Anatomy: Head & Neck, Vol. 1. rev. 2nd ed. Ferner, Helmut, ed. Monsen, Harry, tr. from Ger. LC 79-25264. Orig. Title: Atlas der Topographischen und Angewamdten Anatomie Des Menschen. (Illus.). 308p. 1980. Repr. of 1963 ed. text ed. 98.00 (ISBN 0-7216-7198-5). Saunders.
Reed, Gretchen M. & Sheppard, Vincent F. Basic Structures of the Head & Neck: A Programmed Instruction in Clinical Anatomy for Dental Professionals. LC 75-298. (Illus.). 640p. 1976. pap. text ed. 24.50 (ISBN 0-7216-7516-6). Saunders.
Riviere, Holliston L. Anatomy & Embryology of the Head & Neck. 1981. text ed. 22.95 (ISBN 0-8359-0211-0). Reston.
Seltzer, Samuel. Pain Control in Dentistry. LC 78-8053. 1978. 19.95 (ISBN 0-397-50396-2). Lippincott.
Sicher, Harry & DuBrul, E. Lloyd. Oral Anatomy. 6th ed. LC 74-20890. 1975. text ed. 24.50 (ISBN 0-8016-4604-9). Mosby.

NECK-DISEASES

see also Torticollis

Anderson, Robin & Hoopes, John, eds. Symposium on Malignancies of the Head & Neck, Vol. 11. LC 74-22108. 1975. 45.00 (ISBN 0-8016-0183-5). Mosby.
Gelb, Harold. Clinical Management of Head, Neck & TMJ Pain & Dysfunction: A Multi-Disciplinary Approach to Diagnosis & Treatment. LC 76-50148. (Illus.). 1977. text ed. 49.50 (ISBN 0-7216-4072-9). Saunders.
Gorlin, R. V., et al. Syndromes of the Head & Neck. 2nd ed. (Illus.). 1976. text ed. 48.00 (ISBN 0-07-023790-5, HP). McGraw.
Jeffreys, T. E., et al. Disorders of the Cervical Spine. (Illus.). 1980. text ed. 73.95 (ISBN 0-407-00158-1). Butterworth.
Pendergrass, Eugene P., et al. The Head & Neck in Roentgen Diagnosis, 2 vols. 2nd ed. (Illus.). 1880p. 1956. photocopy ed. spiral 188.00 (ISBN 0-398-01473-6). C C Thomas.

NECK-SURGERY

Bernstein, Leslie, ed. Third International Symposium in Plastic & Reconstructive Surgery of the Head & Neck: Aesthetic Surgery, Vol. 1. 1981. price not set (ISBN 0-8089-1372-7). Grune.
--Third International Symposium in Plastic & Reconstructive Surgery of the Head & Neck: Rehabilitative Surgery, Vol.2. 1981. price not set (ISBN 0-8089-1373-5). Grune.
Conley, John. Complications of Head & Neck Surgery. LC 79-416. (Illus.). 1979. text ed. 39.00 (ISBN 0-7216-2649-1). Saunders.
--Concepts in Head & Neck Surgery. (Illus.). 300p. 1970. 98.25 (ISBN 0-8089-0631-3). Grune.
Freund, H. R. Principles of Head & Neck Surgery. 2nd ed. (Illus.). 459p. 1979. 45.50 (ISBN 0-8385-7922-1). ACC.
Hollinshead, W. Henry. Anatomy for Surgeons Vol. 1: The Head & the Neck. 2nd ed. (Illus.). 1968. 37.00x (ISBN 0-06-141241-4, Harper Medical). Har-Row.
Lesavoy, Malcolm A. Reconstruction of the Head & Neck. (Illus.). 258p. 1981. 43.00 (ISBN 0-683-04949-6). Williams & Wilkins.
Naumann, H. H. Head & Neck Surgery, 2 vols. LC 79-3798. (Illus.). 1980. Vol. 1, 473 Pp. text ed. 97.50 (ISBN 0-7216-6663-9); Vol. 2, 475 Pp. 97.50 (ISBN 0-7216-6664-7). Saunders.
Stell, P. M. & Maran, A. G. Head & Neck Surgery. 2nd ed. LC 78-66407. 1979. 35.00 (ISBN 0-397-58241-2). Lippincott.
Wilson, John S. Head & Neck: Volumes 1 & 2. (Operative Surgery Ser.). 1981. Set. text ed. price not set (ISBN 0-407-00624-9). Vol. 1 (ISBN 0-407-00622-2). Vol. 2 (ISBN 0-407-00623-0). Butterworth.
Wise, Robert A. & Baker, Harvey W. Surgery of the Head & Neck. 3rd ed. (Handbook of Operative Surgery Ser). (Illus.). 1968. 27.50 (ISBN 0-8151-9335-1). Year Bk Med.

NECK-TUMORS

Barbosa, Jorge F. Surgical Treatment of Head & Neck Tumors. Von Becker Froon, Rosemarie, tr. from Portuguese. LC 74-3460. (Illus.). 416p. 1974. 67.75 (ISBN 0-8089-0811-1). Grune.
Batsakis, John G. Tumors of the Head & Neck: Clinical & Pathological Considerations. 2nd ed. (Illus.). 584p. 1979. 53.50 (ISBN 0-683-00476-X). Williams & Wilkins.
Chambers, R. G., et al. Cancer of the Head & Neck: Proceedings of the International Symposium, Switzerland, 1976. (International Congress Ser.: No. 365). 1975. 72.25 (ISBN 0-444-15190-7, Excerpta Medica). Elsevier.
Pollack, R. S. Tumor Surgery of the Head & Neck. (Illus.). x, 206p. 1975. 43.75 (ISBN 3-8055-2092-1). S Karger.
Zacarian, Setrag A. Cryosurgical Advances in Dermatology & Tumors of the Head & Neck. (Illus.). 296p. 1977. 41.75 (ISBN 0-398-03597-0). C C Thomas.

NECKAM, ALEXANDER, 1157-1217

Holmes, Urban T., Jr. Daily Living in the Twelfth Century: Based on the Observations of Alexander Neckam in London & Paris. (Illus.). 1952. pap. 7.95x (ISBN 0-299-00854-1). U of Wis Pr.

NECKER, JACQUES, 1732-1804

Carre, Antonio. Necker et la question des grains a la fin du XVIIIe siecle. LC 79-147152. 220p. 1973. Repr. of 1903 ed. 21.00 (ISBN 0-8337-0481-8). B Franklin.
Gomel, Charles. Causes Financieres De la Revolution Francaise, 2 vols. 1892-93. Set. 55.00 (ISBN 0-8337-1374-4); 30.00 ea. (ISBN 0-8337-1374-4). B Franklin.
Harris, Robert D. Necker: Reform Statesman of the Ancien Regime. LC 77-93464. 1979. 23.75x (ISBN 0-520-03647-6). U of Cal Pr.

NECROMANCY

see Magic

NECROPSY

see Autopsy

NECROSIS

see also Gangrene

Bohrer, Stanley P., ed. Bone Infarction in Sickle Cell Disease. (Illus.). 400p. 1981. 44.50 (ISBN 0-87527-188-X). Green.
Davidson, J. K. Aseptic Necrosis of Bone. 1976. 96.75 (ISBN 0-444-16714-5, Excerpta Medica). Elsevier.
Ficat, R. Paul, et al. Ischemic & Necroses of Bone. 200p. 1980. lib. bdg. 32.95 (ISBN 0-683-03199-6). Williams & Wilkins.
Laszlo, F. A. Renal Cortical Necrosis. (Contributions to Nephrology Ser.: Vol. 28). (Illus.). viii, 216p. 1981. pap. 45.00 (ISBN 3-8055-2109-X). S Karger.

NECTURUS

Chiasson, Robert B. Laboratory Anatomy of Necturus. 3rd ed. (Laboratory Anatomy Ser). 72p. 1976. wire coil avail. (ISBN 0-697-04623-0). Wm C Brown.
Gilbert, Stephen G. Pictorial Anatomy of the Necturus. LC 78-152332. (Illus.). 54p. (Orig.). 1973. pap. text ed. 6.95 (ISBN 0-295-95149-4). U of Wash Pr.

NEDERLANDSCHE OOST-INDISCHE CAMPAGNIE
Marsden, Peter. The Wreck of the Amsterdam. LC 74-24329. (Illus.). 300p. 1975. 35.00x (ISBN 0-8128-1760-5). Stein & Day.
NEEDLEPOINT CANVAS WORK
see Canvas Embroidery
NEEDLEPOINT EMBROIDERY
see Canvas Embroidery
NEEDLES
see Pins and Needles
NEEDLEWORK
see also Applique; Dressmaking; Embroidery; Fabric Pictures; Fancy Work; Lace and Lace Making; Netting; Patchwork; Quilting; Samplers; Sewing; Tapestry
Aber, Ita. The Art of Judaic Needlework: Traditional & Contemporary Designs. (Illus.). 1979. 17.50 (ISBN 0-684-16239-3, ScribT). Scribner.
Alford, M. Needlework As Art. (Illus.). 620p. 1975. Repr. of 1886 ed. 25.95x (ISBN 0-8464-0669-1). Beekman Pubs.
American School of Needlework. The Great Afghan Book. LC 80-68389. (Illus.). 160p. 1981. 14.99 (ISBN 0-8069-5445-0, Columbia Hse). Sterling.
Amir, Ziv. Arabesque: Decorative Needlework from the Holy Land. (Illus.). 1977. 12.95 (ISBN 0-442-20290-3). Van Nos Reinhold.
Baker, Muriel, et al. Needlepoint: Design Your Own. 1977. pap. 10.95 (ISBN 0-684-14867-6, ScribT). Scribner.
Bakke, Karen. Sewing Machine As a Creative Tool. (Illus.). 128p. 1976 (ISBN 0-13-807255-8, Spec). pap. 4.95 (ISBN 0-13-807248-5). P-H.
Ballarian, Anna. Fabric Collage. Horn, George F., ed. LC 76-29553. (Books in Art Education). (Illus.). 1977. 10.95 (ISBN 0-87192-089-1). Davis Mass.
The Bantam Step by Step Book of Needlecraft. 512p. 1980. pap. 14.95 (ISBN 0-553-01221-5). Bantam.
Belfer, Nancy. Designing in Stitching & Applique. LC 76-57240. (Creative Handicrafts Series). (Illus.). 160p. 1977. pap. 7.95 (ISBN 0-13-202010-6, Spec). P-H.
Bengtsson, Gerda. Flower Designs in Cross Stitch. (Illus.). 80p. 1973. pap. 7.95 (ISBN 0-442-29987-7); pap. 6.95 (ISBN 0-442-29988-5). Van Nos Reinhold.
Better Homes & Gardens Books Editors, ed. Better Homes & Gardens Needlepoint. (Illus.). 1978. 5.95 (ISBN 0-696-00475-5). Meredith Corp.
Borssuck, B. One Thousand One Designs for Needlepoint & Cross Stitch. LC 77-1701. (Illus.). 1979. pap. 8.95 (ISBN 0-668-04222-2). Arco.
Borssuck, B. & Jackson, Ann. Picture Your Dog in Needlework. LC 79-25446. (Illus.). 128p. 1981. pap. 8.95 (ISBN 0-668-05084-5, 5084). Arco.
--Picture Your Dog in Needlework. LC 79-25446. (Illus.). 128p. 1980. 11.95 (ISBN 0-668-04850-6). Arco.
Boyles, Margaret. The Margaret Boyles Book of Needle Art. LC 77-73064. (Illus.). 1978. pap. 9.95 (ISBN 0-15-657964-2, Harv). HarBraceJ.
--Margaret Boyles' Needlework Gifts for Special Occasions. (Illus.). 1981. 15.95 (ISBN 0-671-25322-0). S&S.
Bridgeman, Harriet & Drury, Elizabeth, eds. Needlework: An Illustrated History. LC 78-7238. (Illus.). 1978. 24.95 (ISBN 0-448-22066-0). Paddington.
Burchette, Dorothy. Needlework Blocking & Finishing. 1981. pap. 8.95 (ISBN 0-684-16939-8, ScribT). Scribner.
Burns, Hildy P. & Thorne-Thomsen, Kathleen. American Cross-Stitch. (Illus.). 104p. 1974. 9.95 (ISBN 0-442-28514-0). Van Nos Reinhold.
Caulfeild, S. F. & Saward, Blanche C. Encyclopedia of Victorian Needlework, 2 vols. 1972. pap. 6.00 ea. Vol. 1 (ISBN 0-486-22800-2). Vol. 2 (ISBN 0-486-22801-0). Dover.
Caulfield, S. F. & Saward, Blanche C. The Dictionary of Needlework: An Encyclopedia of Artistic, Plain & Fancy Needlework. 1972. 6.98 (ISBN 0-517-50002-7); pap. 2.98 (ISBN 0-517-50003-5). Crown.
--Encyclopedia of Victorian Needlework, 2 vols. Orig. Title: Dictionary of Needlework. (Illus.). Set. 25.00 (ISBN 0-8446-0299-X); Vol. 1. (ISBN 0-8446-0300-7); Vol. 2. (ISBN 0-8446-0301-5). Peter Smith.
Caulfield, Sophia F. & Saward, Blanche C. Dictionary of Needlework. LC 75-172439. (Illus.). 1971. Repr. of 1882 ed. 63.00 (ISBN 0-8103-3404-6). Gale.
Chicago, Judy & Hill, Susan. Embroidering Our Heritage: The Dinner Party Needlework. (Illus.). 1980. pap. 15.95 (ISBN 0-385-14569-1, Anch). Doubleday.
--Embroidering Our Heritage: The Dinner Party Needlework. LC 79-6645. (Illus.). 288p. 1980. 34.95 (ISBN 0-385-14568-3, Anchor Pr). Doubleday.
Cirker, Blanche, ed. Needlework Alphabets & Designs. LC 74-21222. 1975. lib. bdg. 9.50x (ISBN 0-88307-599-7). Gannon.
--Needlework Alphabets & Designs. pap. 2.25 (ISBN 0-486-23159-3). Dover.
Coleman, Anne. Fabrics & Threads for Schools. 1977. 17.95 (ISBN 0-7134-0187-7, Pub. by Batsford England). David & Charles.
Cordello, B. Needlework Classics: Nostalgic Designs from Butterick. 13.95 (ISBN 0-685-70730-X). Wehman.
Cornelius, Rosemary, et al. Teaching Needlecraft. 1979. pap. 13.95 (ISBN 0-442-22167-3). Van Nos Reinhold.
Cust, M. M. Needlework As Art. Stansky, Peter & Shewan, Rodney, eds. LC 76-17770. (Aesthetic Movement & the Arts & Crafts Movement Ser.). 1978. Repr. of 1886 ed. lib. bdg. 44.00x (ISBN 0-8240-2474-5). Garland Pub.
Danish Handcraft Guild. Book of Danish Stiitchery. 136p. 1980. pap. 9.95 (ISBN 0-442-20179-6). Van Nos Reinhold.
Davies, Rhiannon. Needlework Notebook. 1968. pap. text ed. 5.50x (ISBN 0-435-42830-6). Heinemann Ed.
Day, Lewis F. & Buckle, Mary. Art in Needlework. Stansky, Peter & Shewan, Rodney, eds. LC 76-17769. (Aesthetic Movement & the Arts & Crafts Movement Ser.). 1977. Repr. of 1900 ed. lib. bdg. 44.00x (ISBN 0-8240-2473-7). Garland Pub.
De Dillmont, Th. The Complete Encyclopedia of Needlework. LC 78-72286. (Illus.). 787p. 1972. lib. bdg. 12.90 (ISBN 0-914294-36-9); pap. 7.95 (ISBN 0-914294-00-8). Running Pr.
De Dillmont, Therese. Encyclopedia of Needlework. (Illus., Eng. span. ger. fr.). 12.75 (ISBN 0-685-20554-1). Toggitt.
DuBane, Janet & Friend, Diane, eds. Needlework Plus. new ed. (Illus.). 96p. 1980. pap. 2.00 (ISBN 0-918178-18-5). Simplicity.
Dudley, Taimi. Strip Patchwork: Quick & Easy Patchwork Using the Seminole Technique. 112p. 1980. 16.95 (ISBN 0-442-20400-0). Van Nos Reinhold.
Duncan, Ida R. The Complete Book of Needlecraft. LC 61-15020. (Illus.). 1972. pap. 3.95 (ISBN 0-87140-944-5). Liveright.
Editors of Time-Life Books. Traditional Favorites. LC 73-94381. (The Art of Sewing). (Illus.). (gr. 6 up). 1974. PLB 11.97 (ISBN 0-8094-1715-4, Pub. by Time-Life). Silver.
Edmonds, Mary J. Geometric Designs in Needlepoint. 131p. 1981. pap. 8.95 (ISBN 0-442-21260-7). Van Nos Reinhold.
Fanning, Robbie. Open Chain's Selected Annotated Bibliography of Self-Study in the Needlearts. (Illus.). 1978. 2.00 (ISBN 0-932086-01-2). Fibar Designs.
Feldman, Annette. Annette Feldman's Needlework for the Home. LC 78-10690. 1979. 14.95 (ISBN 0-13-036897-0). P-H.
--The Big Book of Small Needlework Gifts. 160p. 1980. 7.95 (ISBN 0-8437-3360-8). Hammond Inc.
Finley, Ruth E. Old Patchwork Quilts. (Illus.). 1971. 8.95 (ISBN 0-8231-5025-9). Branford.
Foose, Sandra L. More Scrap Savers Stitchery. LC 80-2740. 1981. 12.95 (ISBN 0-385-17526-4). Doubleday.
Foose, Sandy. Scrap Saver's Stitchery Book: A Farm Journal Book. 1978. 10.95 (ISBN 0-385-13437-1). Doubleday.
Golden Book of Hand & Needle Arts. (Illus.). 1977. 10.95 (ISBN 0-307-49125-0, Golden Pr); PLB 15.31 (ISBN 0-307-69125-X). Western Pub.
Gorham, Georgia & Warth, Jeanne. Charted Designs for Holidays & Special Occasions: Over 224 Motifs for Counted Cross-Stitch & Other Needlecrafts. (Illus.). 48p. (Orig.). 1981. pap. price not set (ISBN 0-486-24192-0). Dover.
Grow, Judith. Classic Needlework: Contemporary Designs Inspired by the American Past. (Illus.). 1976. 14.95 (ISBN 0-442-22881-3). Van Nos Reinhold.
Guild, Vera P. Good Housekeeping New Complete Book of Needlecraft. LC 76-137519. (Illus.). 560p. 1971. 14.95 (ISBN 0-87851-002-8). Hearst Bks.
Harayda, Marel. Needlework Magic with Two Basic Stitches. (gr. 7 up). 1980. pap. 2.95 (ISBN 0-679-20825-9). McKay.
Harding, Mary & Coughtrie, Margo, eds. Make It Yourself: The Complete Step by Step Library of Needlework & Crafts, 20 vols. rev. ed. LC 77-23734. (Illus.). 1977. Repr. of 1975 ed. Set. lib. bdg. 199.50 set (ISBN 0-8393-6012-6). Purnell Ref Bks.
Hodgson, Mary Anne & Paine, Josephine Ruth. Fast & Easy Needlepoint. LC 76-56302. (gr. 3-7). 1978. PLB 6.95 (ISBN 0-385-12432-5). Doubleday.
Houck, Carter & Miller, Myron. The Boat Buff's Book of Embroidery: Needlepoint, Crewel, Applique. (Encore Edition). (Illus.). 1979. pap. 8.95 (ISBN 0-684-16052-8); pap. 4.95 (ISBN 0-684-16904-5). Scribner.
Houck, Carter, ed. White Work: Techniques & 180 Designs. (Needlework Ser.). (Illus.). 1979. pap. 2.00 (ISBN 0-486-23695-1). Dover.
Howard, Constance. The Constance Howard Book of Stitches. (Illus.). 144p. 1980. 13.75 (ISBN 0-7134-1005-1). Branford.
Illes, Robert. Men in Stitches. (Illus.). 1975. 13.95 (ISBN 0-442-23630-1). Van Nos Reinhold.
J. & P. Coats, J. & P. Ltd. Fifty Needlepoint Stitches. (Illus.). 1977. pap. 2.95 (ISBN 0-684-14786-6, ScribT). Scribner.
Jarnow, Jill. The Complete Book of Pillow Stitchery. 1979. 12.95 (ISBN 0-671-22538-3). S&S.
John, Edith. Creative Stitches. (Illus.). 4.75 (ISBN 0-8446-5050-1). Peter Smith.
--New Stitches for Needlecraft. (Illus.). 96p. 1973. Repr. of 1968 ed. 3.00 (ISBN 0-486-22971-8). Dover.
--New Stitches for Needlecraft. (Illus.). 4.75 (ISBN 0-8446-5051-X). Peter Smith.
Kaestner, Dorothy. Designs for Needlepoint & Latch Hook Rugs. LC 76-50111. (Illus.). 1978. encore ed. 5.95 (ISBN 0-684-16359-4, ScribT). Scribner.
Kalina, Judith S. Bible Stitchery. LC 79-8934. (Illus.). 112p. 1980. pap. 8.95 (ISBN 0-385-14966-2, Galilee). Doubleday.
Kerimov, Lyatif. Folk Designs from the Caucasus for Weaving & Needlework. LC 73-80558. (Illus.). 128p. 1974. pap. 3.50 (ISBN 0-486-23014-7). Dover.
--Folk Designs from the Caucasus for Weaving & Needlework. (Illus.). 6.75 (ISBN 0-8446-5054-4). Peter Smith.
--Persian Rug Motifs for Needlepoint. LC 75-3650. 1975. lib. bdg. 9.50x (ISBN 0-88307-608-X). Gannon.
Kliot, Jules. Sprang: Language & Techniques. 2nd ed. 16p. 1974. pap. 2.95 (ISBN 0-916896-03-X). Lacis Pubns.
Kurten, Nancy N. Needlepoint: Stitch by Stitch. (Illus.). 1977. pap. 1.95 (ISBN 0-684-15291-6, ScribT). Scribner.
Lane, Rose W. Woman's Day Book of American Needlework. Woman's Day Editors, ed. 1977. pap. 8.95 (ISBN 0-671-22786-6, Fireside). S&S.
Laury, Jean R. A Treasury of Needlecraft Gifts for the New Baby. LC 76-12186. (Illus.). 192p. 1976. 12.95 (ISBN 0-8008-7858-2). Taplinger.
McCall's Needlework, ed. The McCall's Book of Afghans. 1976. 9.95 (ISBN 0-671-22224-4, 22224). S&S.
McCall's Publishing Company. The McCall's Needlework Treasury. 1977. pap. 9.95 (ISBN 0-394-73399-1). Random.
McKim, Ruby S. One Hundred & One Patchwork Patterns. (Illus.). 8.50 (ISBN 0-8446-1711-3). Peter Smith.
--One Hundred & One Patchwork Patterns. rev. ed. (Illus.). 1962. pap. 3.25 (ISBN 0-486-20773-0). Dover.
Mayorcas, M. J. English Needlework Carpets, 16th-19th Centuries. (Illus.). 1963. 33.50 (ISBN 0-87245-210-7). Textile Bk.
Meilach, Dona A. & Menagh, Dee. Exotic Needlework with Ethnic Patterns, Techniques, Inspirations. (Illus.). 1978. 14.95 (ISBN 0-517-52953-X); pap. 9.95 (ISBN 0-517-52954-8). Crown.
Merrill, Virginia & Jessop, Jean. Needlework in Miniature. (Illus.). 1978. 10.95 (ISBN 0-517-52824-X); pap. 6.95 (ISBN 0-517-52825-8). Crown.
Merrill, Virginia & Richardson, Susan M. Reproducing Period Furniture & Accessories in Miniature. Aymar, Brant, ed. 320p. 1981. 25.00 (ISBN 0-517-53816-4). Crown.
Miller, Heather S. A Needleworker's Botany. LC 78-59803. (Illus.). 1978. 6.95 (ISBN 0-912274-81-6). NH Pub Co.
Miniature Needlepoint & Sewing Projects for Dollhouses. (Illus.). 1979. (Hawthorn); pap. 7.95 (ISBN 0-8015-5073-4). Dutton.
Morocco Embroideries. 34p. 6.85 (ISBN 0-685-26798-9, 8228). Toggitt.
Murayama, Misako. Cross Stitch Patterns Two. new ed. (Ondori Needlework Ser.). (Illus.). 1978. pap. 4.50 (ISBN 0-87040-427-X). Japan Pubns.
Norton, Maggie Jo. Crochet Designs from Simple Motifs. 1978. 19.95 (ISBN 0-7134-1238-0). David & Charles.
Oleson, Karen E. Floral Patterns for Needlecraft & the Decorative Arts. 1978. pap. 10.95 (ISBN 0-442-26282-5). Van Nos Reinhold.
Olsen, Mary P. For the Greater Glory: A Church Needlepoint Handbook. (Illus.). 192p. 1980. 17.50 (ISBN 0-8164-0476-3). Seabury.
Parolini-Ruffini, Elvira. Charted Swiss Folk Designs. LC 77-87356. (Needlework Ser.). (Illus.). 1978. pap. 1.50 (ISBN 0-486-23574-2). Dover.
Purdy, A. T. Needle-Punching. 69.00x (ISBN 0-686-63775-5). State Mutual Bk.
Riley, Patricia. Needlecraft Projects. 1978. 14.95 (ISBN 0-7134-0745-X). David & Charles.
Ring, Betty, ed. Needlework: An Historical Survey. LC 75-10933. (Illus.). 176p. 1975. 12.95x (ISBN 0-87663-251-7). Universe.
Rockland, Mae S. The Work of Our Hands: Jewish Needlecraft for Today. LC 72-91608. (Illus.). 250p. 1973. 10.00 (ISBN 0-8052-3502-7); pap. 5.95 (ISBN 0-8052-0489-X). Schocken.
Ryan, Mildred G. The Complete Encyclopedia of Stitchery. 1981. pap. 8.95 (ISBN 0-452-25264-4, Z5264, Plume). NAL.
--The Complete Encyclopedia of Stitchery: More Than 1400 Illustrations & 1000 Entries. LC 77-16942. (Illus.). 1979. 14.95 (ISBN 0-385-12385-X). Doubleday.
Scharf, Bella. Butterick's Fast & Easy Needlecrafts: Over Fifty Fashion & Decorating Projects You Can Make in Less Than a Day. Speiser, W., ed. LC 76-56596. (Illus.). 1977. 9.95 (ISBN 0-8329-0211-X). New Century.
Schiffer, Margaret B. Historical Needlework of Pennsylvania. (Illus.). 160p. 10.00 (ISBN 0-685-78508-4). Schiffer.
Schoenfeld, Susan & Bendiner, Winifred. Pattern Design for Needlepoint & Patchwork. 200p. Date not set. pap. 9.95 (ISBN 0-442-20671-2). Van Nos Reinhold.
Schraffenberger, Nancy, ed. Woman's Day Decorative Needlework for the Home. (Illus.). 176p. 1981. 15.95 (ISBN 0-8069-5442-6, Columbia Hse). Sterling.
--Woman's Day Decorative Needlework for the Home. (Illus.). 176p. 1981. 13.99 (ISBN 0-8069-5443-4, Columbia Hse). Sterling.
Sibmacher, Johan, illus. Baroque Charted Designs for Needlework. LC 75-2820. Orig. Title: Kreuzstich-Muster, 36 Tafeln. (Illus.). 48p. 1975. pap. 1.75 (ISBN 0-486-23186-0). Dover.
Siegler, Susan. Needlework Patterns from the Metropolitan Museum of Art. LC 76-10097. (Illus.). 1976. 17.50 (ISBN 0-8212-0639-7, 599700). NYGS.
--Needlework Patterns from the Metropolitan Museum of Art. LC 76-10097. (Illus.). 1978. pap. 10.95 (ISBN 0-8212-0736-9, 599719). NYGS.
Silverstein, Mira. International Needlework Designs. LC 77-21189. (Encore Edition). (Illus.). 1978. 8.95 (ISBN 0-684-16925-8, ScribT). Scribner.
Stone, Patricia. Portuguese Needlework Rugs: The Time-Honored Art of Arraiolos Rugs Adapted for the Modern Handcrafter. (Illus.). 128p. 1981. 22.50 (ISBN 0-914440-49-7). EPM Pubns.
Swan, Susan B. A Winterthur Guide to American Needlework. (Winterthur Ser.). (Illus.). 1976. 6.95 (ISBN 0-517-52785-5). Crown.
Swedish Handcraft Guild. Counted Cross Stitch Patterns & Designs. (Illus.). 72p. 1981. pap. 9.95 (ISBN 0-684-16950-9, ScribT). Scribner.
Thorne-Thomsen, Kathleen. Mother Goose in Stitches. LC 75-21486. 1976. 9.95 (ISBN 0-03-015201-1). HR&W.
Warren & Pullman. Treasures in Needlework. (Illus.). 1976. pap. 3.95 (ISBN 0-425-03108-X, Windhover). Berkley Pub.
Warren, Geoffrey. A Stitch in Time: Victorian & Edwardian Needlecraft. LC 76-12187. (Illus.). 1976. 9.95 (ISBN 0-8008-7435-8). Taplinger.
Weiss, Rita. Needlepoint Designs After Illustrations by Beatrix Potter. LC 75-9177. (Illus.). 32p. (Orig.). 1976. pap. 1.50 (ISBN 0-486-20218-6). Dover.
Whiting, Gertrude. Old-Time Tools & Toys of Needlework. 1970. pap. 6.00 (ISBN 0-486-22517-8). Dover.
--Old-Time Tools & Toys of Needlework. (Illus.). 8.00 (ISBN 0-8446-0292-2). Peter Smith.
Williams, Elsa S. Creative Canvas Work. (Illus.). 1975. pap. 5.95 (ISBN 0-442-29484-0). Van Nos Reinhold.
--The Joy of Stitching. 1978. 8.95 (ISBN 0-442-29465-4). Van Nos Reinhold.
Wilson, Erica. The Animal Kingdom. (Illus.). 1978. pap. 2.50 (ISBN 0-684-15902-3, ScribT). Scribner.
--Say It with Stitches. (Illus.). 1978. pap. 2.50 (ISBN 0-684-15901-5, ScribT). Scribner.
Winter, Adalee. Needlecraft Kingdom. LC 75-32265. (Family Guidebooks Ser). (Illus.). 60p. 1976. pap. 4.95 (ISBN 0-8487-0413-4). Oxmoor Hse.
--Needlecraft Patterns. (Family Guidebook Ser). (Illus.). 1970. pap. 4.95 (ISBN 0-8487-0241-7). Oxmoor Hse.
--A Needlecraft Treasury from Adalee Winter. LC 79-83708. (Illus.). 1979. 14.95 (ISBN 0-8487-0499-1). Oxmoor Hse.
--Religious Designs for Needlework. LC 77-74196. (Family Guidebooks). (Illus.). 1977. pap. 3.95 (ISBN 0-8487-0470-3). Oxmoor Hse.
--Wildflower Designs for Needlework. LC 79-83710. (Family Guidebooks). (Illus.). 1979. pap. 5.95 (ISBN 0-8487-0498-3). Oxmoor Hse.

Zimiles, Martha R. Iron-on Transfers from a Treasury of Needlework Designs: Ready-to-Use Patterns for Needlepoint & Embroidery. 96p. 1981. pap. 9.95 (ISBN 0-442-23119-9). Van Nos Reinhold.

NEENAH, WISCONSIN

Glaab, Charles N. & Larsen, Lawrence H. Factories in the Valley: Neenah-Menasha 1870-1915. LC 69-63012. (Illus.). 1969. 10.00 (ISBN 0-87020-106-9). State Hist Soc Wis.

Smith, Alice E. Millstone & Saw: The Origins of Neenah-Menasha. LC 67-63002. (Illus.). 1967. 5.50 (ISBN 0-87020-096-8). State Hist Soc Wis.

NEFERTETE, QUEEN OF EGYPT, 14TH CENTURY B.C.

Holmes, Burnham. Nefertiti: The Mystery Queen. LC 77-10445. (Great Unsolved Mysteries Ser.). (Illus.). (gr. 4-5). 1977. PLB 10.65 (ISBN 0-8172-1056-3). Raintree Pubs.

NEGATION (LOGIC)

Buck-Morss, Susan. The Origin of Negative Dialectics: Theodor W. Adorno, Walter Benjamin, & the Frankfurt Institute. LC 76-55103. 1979. pap. text ed. 7.95 (ISBN 0-02-905150-9). Free Pr.

Englebretsen, G. Logical Negation. 72p. 1981. pap. text ed. 5.75x (ISBN 90-232-1814-0, Pub. by Van Gorcum Holland). Humanities.

Matilal, Bimal K. Navya-Nyaya Doctrine of Negation. LC 67-27088. (Oriental Ser: No. 46). 1968. 10.00x (ISBN 0-674-60650-7). Harvard U Pr.

Rooks, George. The Book of Losers. 160p. 1980. 8.95 (ISBN 0-312-08956-2). St Martin.

NEGATIVE INCOME TAX

Browning, Edgar K. Redistribution & the Welfare System. LC 75-15155. (Orig.). 1975. pap. 5.25 (ISBN 0-8447-3170-6). Am Enterprise.

Golloday, Frederick L. & Haveman, Robert H. The Economic Impacts of Tax-Transfer Policy: Regional & Distributional Effects. 1976. 18.50 (ISBN 0-12-288850-2). Acad Pr.

Organization for Economic Cooperation & Development. Negative Income Tax: An Approach to the Co-Ordination of Taxation and Social Welfare Policies. 56p. 1974. 2.50x (ISBN 92-64-11220-0). OECD.

Pechman, Joseph A. Work Incentives & Income Guarantees: The New Jersey Negative Income Tax Experiment. Timpane, P. Michael, ed. (Studies in Social Experimentation). 232p. 1975. 11.95 (ISBN 0-8157-6976-8); pap. 4.95 (ISBN 0-8157-6975-X). Brookings.

NEGATIVE IONS

see Anions

NEGATIVE PROPOSITIONS

see Negation (Logic)

NEGATIVES

see Photography-Negatives

NEGEB

Evenari, Michael, et al. Negev: The Challenge of a Desert. LC 75-119073. (Illus.). 1971. 17.50x (ISBN 0-674-60670-1). Harvard U Pr.

Musil, Alois. Northern Negd: A Topographical Itinerary. LC 77-87090. (American Geographical Society. Oriental Explorations & Studies: No. 5). Repr. of 1928 ed. 35.00 (ISBN 0-404-60235-5). AMS Pr.

NEGLIGENCE

see also Accident Law; Damages; Employers' Liability; Liability for Condition and Use of Land; Occupations, Dangerous; Proximate Cause (Law); Tort Liability of Municipal Corporations; Torts

Erenius, Gillis. Criminal Negligence & Individuality. (Institutet for Rattsvetenskaplig Forskning: No. 85). 1976. pap. text ed. 20.00x (ISBN 91-1-767071-3). Rothman.

Mirabel & Levy. Law of Negligence. 30.00 (ISBN 0-685-05162-5). Acme Law.

Roady, Thomas G., Jr. & Andersen, William R., eds. Professional Negligence. LC 60-8216. 1960. 11.50 (ISBN 0-8265-1055-8). Vanderbilt U Pr.

Schwartz, Victor E. Comparative Negligence. 1974. text ed. 42.50 including 1981 suppl. (ISBN 0-87473-075-9). A Smith Co.

--Comparative Negligence: 1981. 1981. 18.00 (ISBN 0-685-59627-3). A Smith Co.

Woods, Henry. The Negligence Case: Comparative Fault, Vol. 1. LC 78-51108. 1978. 47.50 (ISBN 0-686-29237-5). Lawyers Co-Op.

NEGOTIABLE INSTRUMENTS

see also Acceptances; Bills of Exchange; Bonds; Checks; Letters of Credit

Baxter, Nevins D. Commercial Paper Market. LC 65-29170. 1966. 10.00 (ISBN 0-87267-000-7). Bankers.

Bills & Notes. 75p. 1980. 5.00 (ISBN 0-87526-194-9). Gould.

Bills & Notes. 1979 ed. 75p. 1978. 5.00 (ISBN 0-685-54963-1). Gould.

Brannan, Joseph D. & Beutel, Frederick K. Beutel's Brannan Negotiable Instruments Law. 7th ed. LC 74-92297. 1971. Repr. of 1948 ed. Set. lib. bdg. 58.75x (ISBN 0-8371-3076-X, BRNI). Greenwood.

Co-Op East Law Outlines: Commercial Paper. LC 76-23087. (Orig.). 1976. 3.00 (ISBN 0-88408-049-8). Sterling Swift.

Coppola, Andrew J. The Law of Commercial Paper. rev. ed. LC 69-14862. (Quality Paperback: No. 232). 1977. pap. 4.95 (ISBN 0-8226-0232-6). Littlefield.

Crane, Dwight D. & Riley, Michael J. NOW Accounts. LC 77-6580. 1978. 18.95 (ISBN 0-669-01612-8). Lexington Bks.

Foulke, Roy A. The Commercial Paper Market. Bruchey, Stuart, ed. LC 80-1148. (The Rise of Commercial Banking Ser.). (Illus.). 1981. Repr. of 1931 ed. lib. bdg. 24.00x (ISBN 0-405-13651-X). Arno.

Greef, Albert O. The Commercial Paper House in the United States. facsimile ed. LC 75-2637. (Wall Street & the Security Market Ser.). 1975. Repr. of 1938 ed. 32.00x (ISBN 0-405-06962-6). Arno.

Hawkland, William & Bailey, Henry J. Commercial Paper. 2nd ed. (Sum & Substance Ser.). 1979. 10.95 (ISBN 0-686-18192-1). Center Creative Ed.

Negotiable Instruments & the Payments Mechanism. 1976. 13.00 (ISBN 0-89982-069-7, 057100). Am Bankers.

Negotiable Instruments Under U.C.C. 1981. 5.50 (ISBN 0-87526-183-3). Gould.

Peters. Negotiable Instruments Primer. 2nd ed. 1974. pap. 5.00 (ISBN 0-672-81994-5, Bobbs-Merrill Law). Michie-Bobbs.

Santiago Romero, Basilio. Tratado De Instrumentos Negociables. 2nd, enl.,rev. ed. LC 79-22321. (Illus.). 1980. write for info. (ISBN 0-8477-2636-3). U of PR Pr.

Whaley. Problems & Materials on Negotiable Instruments. Date not set. text ed. price not set (ISBN 0-316-93214-0). Little.

Zola, Paul. Bills & Notes. 31p. 1964. pap. 1.75x (ISBN 0-87526-006-3). Gould.

NEGOTIABLE INSTRUMENTS–TAXATION

see Taxation of Bonds, Securities, etc.

NEGOTIATION

see also Arbitration, Industrial; Arbitration, International; Collective Bargaining; Treaties

Bacharach, Samuel B. & Lawler, Edward J. Bargaining: Power, Tactics & Outcomes. LC 81-8197. (Social & Behavioral Science Ser.). 1981. text ed. price not set (ISBN 0-87589-498-4). Jossey-Bass.

Bartos, Otomar. The Process & Outcome of Negotiations. LC 73-12473. 451p. 1974. 27.00x (ISBN 0-231-03242-0). Columbia U Pr.

Beckmann, Neal W. Negotiations, Understanding the Bargaining Process. 1980. 16.50 (ISBN 0-87527-242-8). Green.

--Student Guide for Negotiations: Understanding the Bargaining Process. Date not set. write for info. (ISBN 0-87527-241-X). Green.

Bellow, Gary & Moulton, Bea. The Lawyering Process: Negotiation. LC 81-67776. (University Casebook Ser.). 299p. 1981. pap. text ed. write for info. (ISBN 0-88277-039-X). Foundation Pr.

Calero, Henry H. Winning the Negotiation. LC 79-84208. 1979. 10.95 (ISBN 0-8015-3680-4, Hawthorn). Dutton.

Coffin, Royce A. The Negotiator: A Manual for Winners. LC 73-75768. (Illus.). 1973. 10.95 (ISBN 0-8144-5327-9). Am Mgmt.

Cohen, Herb. You Can Negotiate Anything. 1980. 12.00 (ISBN 0-8184-0305-5). Lyle Stuart.

Druckman, Daniel, ed. Negotiations: Social-Psychological Perspectives. LC 76-58353. (Illus.). 416p. 1977. 37.50x (ISBN 0-8039-0829-6). Sage.

Fisher, Roger & Ury, William. Getting to Yes: Negotiating Agreement Without Giving in. 160p. 1981. 10.95 (ISBN 0-395-31757-6). HM.

Greenburger, Francis & Kiernan, Thomas. How to Ask for More and Get It: The Art of Creative Negotiations. 1980. pap. 4.95 (ISBN 0-8092-7050-1). Contemp Bks.

--How to Ask for More, & Get It: The Art of Creative Negotiation. LC 77-80889. 1978. 7.95 (ISBN 0-385-12495-3). Doubleday.

Gulliver, Philip H. Disputes & Negotiations: A Cross-Cultural Perspective. LC 79-22735. (Studies on Law & Social Control). 1979. 19.00 (ISBN 0-12-305550-4). Acad Pr.

Hanan, Mack, et al. Sales Negotiation Strategies: Building the Win-Win Customer Relationship. LC 76-44021. 1977. 11.95 (ISBN 0-8144-5431-3). Am Mgmt.

Harnett, D. L. & Cummings, L. L. Bargaining Behavior: An International Study. LC 79-67421. (Illus.). 307p. 1980. text ed. 20.95x (ISBN 0-931920-14-0). Dame Pubns.

Ilich, John. Art & Skill of Successful Negotiation. 1973. 10.95 (ISBN 0-13-046805-3). P-H.

Ilich, John & Jones, Barbara S. Successful Negotiating Skills for Women. LC 80-12476. 130p. 1980. text ed. 8.95 (ISBN 0-201-03148-5). A-W.

Karrass, Chester L. Give & Take: The Complete Guide to Negotiating Strategies & Tactics. LC 74-4360. 1974. 9.95 (ISBN 0-690-00566-0). T Y Crowell.

--Negotiating Game: How to Get What You Want. LC 74-1440. 1970. 9.95 (ISBN 0-690-00359-5). T Y Crowell.

Kennedy, Marilyn M. Salary Strategies: Everything You Need to Know to Get the Salary You Want. 1982. 12.95 (ISBN 0-686-30973-1). Rawson Wade.

Kent, George. Effects of Threats. LC 67-63352. (Illus., Orig.). 1967. pap. 2.00 (ISBN 0-8142-0072-9). Ohio St U Pr.

Kniveton, Bromley & Towers, Brian. Training for Negotiating. 213p. 1978. text ed. 21.00x (ISBN 0-220-66347-5, Pub. by Busn Bks England). Renouf.

Kriesberg, Louis. Social Conflicts. 2nd ed. (Prentice Hall Ser. in Sociology). (Illus.). 352p. 1982. pap. text ed. 15.95 (ISBN 0-13-815589-5). P-H.

Lall, Sanjaya, ed. Conflict & Bargaining. 1976. pap. text ed. 16.25 (ISBN 0-08-021060-0). Pergamon.

Nierenberg, Gerard I. Art of Negotiating. (Illus.). 1971. pap. 4.95 (ISBN 0-346-12272-4). Cornerstone.

--Art of Negotiating. LC 68-30720. 1968. 9.95 (ISBN 0-8015-0408-2, Hawthorn). Dutton.

--Fundamentals of Negotiating. new ed. 1977. 14.95 (ISBN 0-8015-2868-2, Hawthorn); pap. 6.50 (ISBN 0-8015-2869-0, Hawthorn). Dutton.

Nothdurft, K. H. The Complete Guide to Successful Business Negotiation. LC 73-77703. 224p. 1972. 9.00x (ISBN 0-900537-16-7, Dist. by Hippocrene Books Inc.). Leviathan Hse.

Pruitt, Dean G. Negotiation Behavior. (Organizational & Occupational Psychology Ser.). 1981. price not set (ISBN 0-12-566250-5). Acad Pr.

Roth, A. E. Axiomatic Models of Bargaining. (Lecture Notes in Economics & Mathematical Systems: Vol. 170). 1979. pap. 9.50 (ISBN 0-387-09540-3). Springer-Verlag.

Schatzki, Michael & Coffey, Wayne R. Negotiation: The Art of Getting What You Want. (Orig.). 1981. pap. 2.95 (ISBN 0-686-77452-3, AE11224, Sig). NAL.

Schelling, Thomas C. Strategy of Conflict. LC 60-11560. (Illus.). 1960. 15.00x (ISBN 0-674-84030-5); pap. text ed. 6.95x (ISBN 0-674-84031-3). Harvard U Pr.

Scott, W. P. The Skills of Negotiating. LC 81-6472. 244p. 1981. 21.95 (ISBN 0-470-27219-8). Halsted Pr.

Seltz, David D. & Modica, Alfred J. Negotiate Your Way to Success. 1981. pap. 2.95 (ISBN 0-451-62018-6, ME2018, Ment). NAL.

Siegel, Sidney & Fouraker, Lawrence E. Bargaining & Group Decision Making: Experiments in Bilateral Monopoly. LC 77-14561. 1977. Repr. of 1960 ed. lib. bdg. 14.00x (ISBN 0-8371-9837-2, SIBG). Greenwood.

Strauss, Anselm. Negotiations: Varieties, Contexts, Processes & Social Order. LC 78-1156. (Social & Behavioral Science Ser.). 1978. text ed. 16.95x (ISBN 0-87589-369-4). Jossey-Bass.

Swingle, Paul G., ed. Structure of Conflict. (Social Psychology Ser). 1970. 37.50 (ISBN 0-12-679160-0). Acad Pr.

Walton, Richard E. Interpersonal Peacemaking: Confrontations & Third Party Consultation. (Organization Development Ser). (Orig.). 1969. pap. text ed. 6.50 (ISBN 0-201-08435-X). A-W.

Warschaw, Tessa A. Negotiating to Win. 1980. 9.95 (ISBN 0-07-000780-2). McGraw.

--Winning by Negotiation. 320p. 1981. pap. 2.95 (ISBN 0-425-05094-7). Berkley Pub.

Young, Oran R., ed. Bargaining: Formal Theories of Negotiation. LC 72-75493. 420p. 1975. 21.00 (ISBN 0-252-00273-3). U of Ill Pr.

Zartman, I. William, ed. The Negotiation Process: Theories & Applications. LC 78-19536. 240p. 1978. 22.50 (ISBN 0-8039-1141-6); pap. 9.95 (ISBN 0-8039-1034-7). Sage.

NEGOTIATIONS IN INTERNATIONAL DISPUTES

see Diplomatic Negotiations in International Disputes

NEGRILLOS

see also Bambute

Vanden Bergh, Leonard J. On the Trail of Pigmies: An Anthropological Exploration Under the Cooperation of the American Museum of Natural History & American Universities. LC 77-79822. (Illus.). Repr. of 1921 ed. 21.50x (ISBN 0-8371-1470-5). Greenwood.

NEGRITOS

see also Negrillos

NEGRO ACTORS AND ACTRESSES

This heading discontinued January 1976. See Afro-American Actors for later materials.

see also Negro Moving-Picture Actors and Actresses

Abdul, Raoul, ed. Famous Black Entertainers of Today. LC 73-7096. (Famous Biographies Ser.). (Illus.). 192p. (gr. 7 up). 1974. 5.95 (ISBN 0-396-06849-9). Dodd.

Johnson, James W. Black Manhattan. LC 68-29003. (American Negro: His History & Literature, Ser. No. 1). 1968. Repr. of 1940 ed. 15.00 (ISBN 0-405-01822-3). Arno.

Mills, Earl. Dorothy Dandridge: A Portrait in Black. (Orig.). 1970. pap. 1.95 (ISBN 0-87067-643-1, BH643). Holloway.

NEGRO ART

This heading discontinued January 1976. See Afro-American Art for later materials.

see also Negro Artists; Negroes in Art

Brawley, Benjamin G. Negro Genius. LC 66-17517. 1966. Repr. of 1937 ed. 10.50x (ISBN 0-8196-0184-5). Biblo.

Colloquium on Negro Art, Dakar, 1966. World Festival of Negro Arts. LC 75-477146. 1968. 13.50x (ISBN 0-8002-0618-5). Intl Pubns Serv.

Fax, Elton C. Seventeen Black Artists. LC 72-165671. (Illus.). 1971. 7.95 (ISBN 0-396-06391-8). Dodd.

Harmon Foundation, Inc. Negro Artists. facsimile ed. LC 72-161262. (Black Heritage Library Collection). (Illus.). Repr. of 1935 ed. 16.00 (ISBN 0-8369-8821-3). Arno.

Huggins, Nathan I. Harlem Renaissance. 258p. 1973. pap. 5.95 (ISBN 0-19-501665-3, GB). Oxford U Pr.

Locke, Alain. Negro & His Music. Bd. with Negro Art: Past & Present. LC 69-18592. (American Negro-His History & Literature Ser., No.2). 1969. Repr. of 1936 ed. 8.00 (ISBN 0-405-01879-7). Arno.

--Negro in Art: A Pictorial Record of the Negro Artist & the Negro Theme in Art. LC 79-99389. 1969. Repr. of 1940 ed. lib. bdg. 24.50 (ISBN 0-8411-0060-8). Metro Bks.

Locke, Alain, ed. Negro in Art: A Pictorial Record of the Negro Artist & of the Negro Theme in Art. LC 68-9006. (Illus.). 1971. Repr. of 1940 ed. lib. bdg. 25.00 buckram (ISBN 0-87817-013-8). Hacker.

Mount, Marshall W. African Art: The Years Since 1920. LC 73-75401. (Illus.). 256p. 1973. 15.00x (ISBN 0-253-10056-9). Ind U Pr.

National Art Education Association. Black Art: A Bibliography. 1970. pap. 1.00 (ISBN 0-686-00140-0, 061-02180). Natl Art Ed.

Parry, Ellwood. The Image of the Indian & the Black Man in American Art, 1590-1900. new ed. LC 73-79606. (Illus.). 180p. 1974. 12.50 (ISBN 0-8076-0706-1). Braziller.

Porter, James A. Modern Negro Art. LC 69-18593. (American Negro: His History & Literature Ser., No. 2). 1969. Repr. of 1943 ed. 12.00 (ISBN 0-405-01889-4). Arno.

Stokes, Olivia P. Beauty of Being Black: Folktales, Poems & Art from Africa. Crane, Louise, ed. (Orig.). (gr. 4-6). 1971. pap. 2.50 (ISBN 0-377-11611-4). Friend Pr.

NEGRO ARTISTS

This heading discontinued January 1976. See Afro-American Artists for later materials.

see also Negro Art; Negroes in Art

Bailey, Leaonead P., ed. Broadside Authors & Artists. 1974. pap. 9.95 (ISBN 0-685-42549-5). Broadside.

Brawley, Benjamin G. Negro in Literature & Art in the United States. 3rd ed. LC 75-144586. (BCL Ser. I). Repr. of 1930 ed. 14.50 (ISBN 0-404-00139-4). AMS Pr.

Cederholm, Theresa. Afro-American Artists: A Bio-Bibliographical Directory. 1973. 10.00 (ISBN 0-89073-007-5). Boston Public Lib.

Du Bois, W. E. B. The Negro Artisan. (Atlanta Univ. Publ. Ser.: No. 7). (Orig.). 1902. Repr. pap. 6.00 (ISBN 0-527-03110-0). Kraus Repr.

Locke, Alain, ed. Negro in Art: A Pictorial Record of the Negro Artist & of the Negro Theme in Art. LC 68-9006. (Illus.). 1971. Repr. of 1940 ed. lib. bdg. 25.00 buckram (ISBN 0-87817-013-8). Hacker.

Porter, James A. Modern Negro Art. LC 69-18593. (American Negro: His History & Literature Ser., No. 2). 1969. Repr. of 1943 ed. 12.00 (ISBN 0-405-01889-4). Arno.

NEGRO ATHLETES

This heading discontinued January 1976. See Afro-American Athletes for later materials.

Behee, John R. Hail to the Victors. LC 74-75995. 140p. 1974. pap. 4.95 (ISBN 0-914464-01-9). J & J Bks.

Edwards, Harry. Revolt of the Black Athlete. LC 70-85475. 1970. pap. 3.95 (ISBN 0-02-909030-X). Free Pr.

Foreman, Thomas E. Discrimination Against the Negro in American Athletics. LC 74-76466. 1975. soft bdg. 8.00 (ISBN 0-88247-340-9). R & E Res Assoc.

Orr, Jack. Black Athlete: His Story in American History. (gr. 6 up). 1969. PLB 8.95 (ISBN 0-87460-104-5). Lion Bks.

Robinson, Louis, Jr. Arthur Ashe, Tennis Champion. LC 67-1917. (gr. 5-9). 1970. 5.95 (ISBN 0-385-06284-2). Doubleday.

Schwartz, Bert. Great Black Athletes. new ed. (Illus.). 191p. (Orig.). (gr. 9-12). 1971. pap. 0.75 (ISBN 0-88301-108-5). Pendulum Pr.

Young, A. S. Negro Firsts in Sports. 1963. 4.95 (ISBN 0-87485-006-1). Johnson Chi.

NEGRO AUTHORS
This heading discontinued January 1976. See Afro-American Authors for later materials.
Adams, William, et al, eds. Afro-American Authors. LC 74-160035. (Multi-Ethnic Literature Ser.). (Illus.). 165p. (gr. 10-12). 1971. pap. text ed. 5.32 (ISBN 0-395-12700-9, 2-40591); inst guide 5.84 (ISBN 0-395-24042-5). HM.
Bailey, Leaonead P., ed. Broadside Authors & Artists. 1974. pap. 9.95 (ISBN 0-685-42549-5). Broadside.
Beier, Ulli, ed. Black Writing from New Guinea. (Asian & Pacific Writing Ser.). 1973. 14.95x (ISBN 0-7022-0835-3); pap. 8.50x (ISBN 0-7022-0846-9). U of Queensland Pr.
Brawley, Benjamin. Early American Negro Writers. Foner, Philip S., ed. (Black Rediscovery Ser). 1970. pap. 5.00 (ISBN 0-486-22623-9). Dover.
Brawley, Benjamin G. Early Negro American Writers. facs. ed. LC 68-25601. (Essay Index Reprint Ser). 1968. Repr. of 1935 ed. 22.00 (ISBN 0-8369-0246-7). Arno.
--Negro Genius. LC 66-17517. 1966. Repr. of 1937 ed. 10.50x (ISBN 0-8196-0184-5). Biblo.
--Negro in Literature & Art in the United States. 3rd ed. LC 75-144586. (BCL Ser. I). Repr. of 1930 ed. 14.50 (ISBN 0-404-00139-4). AMS Pr.
Brown, Lloyd W., ed. Black Writer in Africa & the Americas. LC 70-188989. (University of Southern California Studies in Comparative Literature Ser: No. 6). 1973. pap. 7.95x (ISBN 0-912158-51-4). Hennessey.
Butterfield, Stephen. Black Autobiography in America. LC 73-93178. 320p. 1974. pap. 7.95x (ISBN 0-87023-162-6). U of Mass Pr.
Davis, Arthur P. From the Dark Tower: Afro-American Writers from 1900 to 1960. LC 73-88969. 352p. 1974. 10.95x (ISBN 0-88258-004-3). Howard U Pr.
Gibson, Donald B., ed. Five Black Writers: Essays on Wright, Ellison, Baldwin, Hughes & LeRoi Jones. LC 70-114760. (The Gotham Library). 304p. 1970. 20.00x (ISBN 0-8147-0462-X); pap. 9.50x (ISBN 0-8147-0490-5). NYU Pr.
Hallie Q. Brown Memorial Library. Index to Periodical Articles by & About Negroes, Annuals, 1960-1969. 1971. lib. bdg. 15.00 ea. G K Hall.
Higginson, Thomas W. Letters & Journals of Thomas Wentworth Higginson: 1846-1906. Higginson, Mary T., ed. LC 73-88435. (Illus.). 358p. 1921. Repr. 17.25x (ISBN 0-8371-1843-3, Pub. by Negro U Pr). Greenwood.
Hughes, Carl M. Negro Novelist 1940-1950. 1970. pap. 3.95 (ISBN 0-8065-0006-9). Citadel Pr.
Miller, Wayne Charles, ed. A Gathering of Ghetto Writers: Irish, Italian, Jewish, Black, & Puerto Rican. LC 76-189130. (Gotham Library). 440p. 1972. 20.00x (ISBN 0-8147-5360-4); pap. 4.95x (ISBN 0-8147-5358-2). NYU Pr.
Mitchell, Loften. Voices of the Black Theatre. LC 74-30081. (Illus.). 1975. 12.50 (ISBN 0-88371-006-4). J T White.
Noble, Enrique, ed. Literatura Afro-Hispano Americana: Poesia y prosa de ficcion. LC 77-189125. 216p. 1973. pap. text ed. 9.95x (ISBN 0-471-00757-9). Wiley.
Rollins, Charlemae. Famous American Negro Poets. LC 65-11811. (Illus.). (gr. 7-9). 1965. 5.95 (ISBN 0-396-05129-4). Dodd.
Rush, Theressa G., et al. Black American Writers Past & Present: A Biographical & Bibliographical Dictionary, 2 vols. LC 74-28400. 1975. Set. 35.00 (ISBN 0-8108-0785-8). Scarecrow.
Turner, Darwin T. In a Minor Chord: Three Afro-American Writers & Their Search for Identity. LC 72-132491. (Crosscurrents-Modern Critiques Ser.). 175p. 1971. 6.95 (ISBN 0-8093-0481-3). S Ill U Pr.
Wayland, Edward M., ed. Howard A. Kester Papers, 1923-1972. 277p. 1973. pap. 50.00 (ISBN 0-667-00535-8). Microfilming Corp.

NEGRO BUSINESSMEN
This heading discontinued January 1976. See Afro-Americans in Business for later materials.
Bates, Timothy M. Black Capitalism: A Quantitative Analysis. LC 73-9060. (Special Studies in U.S. Economic,Social & Political Issues). 1973. 29.50x (ISBN 0-89197-680-9). Irvington.
Carter, Wilmoth A. The Urban Negro in the South. LC 72-94979. (Illus.). 272p. 1973. Repr. of 1962 ed. 17.00 (ISBN 0-8462-1721-X). Russell.
Coles, Flournoy A., Jr. Black Economic Development. LC 74-30495. 232p. 1975. 17.95x (ISBN 0-88229-176-9). Nelson-Hall.
Cross, Theodore L. Black Capitalism: Strategy for Business in the Ghetto. LC 72-80268. 1971. pap. 3.95 (ISBN 0-689-70266-3, 174). Atheneum.
Dubois, William E. Negro in Business. LC 70-153098. Repr. of 1899 ed. 12.50 (ISBN 0-404-00153-X). AMS Pr.
Fernandez, John P. Black Managers in White Corporations. LC 75-6820. 308p. 1975. 31.50 (ISBN 0-471-25764-8, Pub. by Wiley-Interscience). Wiley.
Gelber, Steven M. Black Men & Businessman: The Growing Awareness of a Social Responsibility. LC 74-77654. 320p. 1974. 17.50 (ISBN 0-8046-9062-6, Natl U). Kennikat.
Harris, Abram L. Negro As Capitalist. LC 73-117597. (Studies in Negro History & Culture, No. 54). 1970. Repr. of 1936 ed. lib. bdg. 33.95 (ISBN 0-8383-1030-3). Haskell.
--The Negro As Capitalist: A Study of Banking & Business Among American Negroes. 7.50 (ISBN 0-8446-0680-4). Peter Smith.
--Negro As Capitalist: Study of Banking and Business Among American Negroes. LC 77-97425. Repr. of 1936 ed. 10.00x (ISBN 0-8371-2731-9, Pub. by Negro U Pr). Greenwood.
Haynes, George E. Negro at Work in New York City. LC 77-76709. (Columbia University, Studies in the Social Sciences Ser.: No. 124). Repr. of 1912 ed. 5.50 (ISBN 0-404-51124-4). AMS Pr.
Lee, Roy F. Setting for Black Business Development: A Study in Sociology & Political Economy. LC 72-619630. 1973. pap. 7.00 (ISBN 0-87546-039-9); pap. 10.00 special hard bdg (ISBN 0-87546-275-8). NY Sch Indus Rel.
Oak, Vishnu V. Negro's Adventure in General Business. LC 79-100311. Repr. of 1949 ed. 12.25x (ISBN 0-8371-4983-5, Pub. by Negro U Pr). Greenwood.
Ofari, Earl. Myth of Black Capitalism. LC 70-105313. 1970. pap. 3.25 (ISBN 0-85345-163-X, PB-163X). Monthly Rev.
Pierce, Joseph A. Negro Business & Business Education. LC 71-138015. (Illus.). 1971. Repr. of 1947 ed. text ed. 16.25x (ISBN 0-8371-5662-9, Pub. by Negro U Pr). Greenwood.
Seder, John & Burrell, Berkeley G. Getting It Together: Black Businessmen in America. LC 70-142096. 1971. 6.95 (ISBN 0-15-135275-5). HarBraceJ.
Washington, Booker T. The Negro in Business. Repr. of 1907 ed. 19.50 (ISBN 0-384-65980-2). Johnson Repr.
--Negro in Business. LC 72-99418. 1969. Repr. of 1907 ed. lib. bdg. 17.50 (ISBN 0-8411-0092-6). Metro Bks.
Washington, Booker T. & Dubois, W. E. Negro in Business. LC 71-144699. (Illus.). Repr. of 1907 ed. 12.50 (ISBN 0-404-00237-4). AMS Pr.
--Negro in Business. LC 71-144699. (Illus.). Repr. of 1907 ed. 12.50 (ISBN 0-404-00237-4). AMS Pr.

NEGRO CHILDREN
This heading discontinued January 1976. See Afro-American Children for later materials.
Coles, Robert. Children of Crisis. 1968. pap. 3.95 (ISBN 0-440-51235-2, Delta). Dell.
--Children of Crisis, Vol. 1: A Study of Courage & Fear. (Children of Crisis Ser.). (Illus.). 1967. 16.95 (ISBN 0-316-15159-9, Pub. by Atlantic Monthly Pr); pap. 6.95 (ISBN 0-316-15154-8). Little.
Cottie, Thomas J. Black Children, White Dreams. 208p. 1975. pap. 2.75 (ISBN 0-440-54453-X, Delta). Dell.
Daniel, Robert P. Psychological Study of Delinquent & Non-Delinquent Negro Boys. LC 75-176718. (Columbia University. Teachers College. Contributions to Education: No. 546). Repr. of 1932 ed. 17.50 (ISBN 0-404-55546-2). AMS Pr.
Goff, Regina M. Problems & Emotional Difficulties of Negro Children As Studied in Selected Communities & Attributed by Parents - Children to the Fact That They Are Negro. LC 76-476808. (Columbia University. Teachers College. Contributions to Education: No. 960). Repr. of 1949 ed. 17.50 (ISBN 0-404-55960-3). AMS Pr.
Porter, Judith D. Black Child, White Child: The Development of Racial Attitudes. LC 76-133213. 1971. 14.00x (ISBN 0-674-07610-9); pap. 4.50x (ISBN 0-674-07611-7). Harvard U Pr.
Salkman, Victoria. There Is a Child for You. 1972. 6.50 (ISBN 0-671-21443-8). S&S.

NEGRO CHILDREN'S WRITINGS
This heading discontinued January 1976. See Afro-American Children's Writings for later materials.
Dee, Ruby, ed. Glowchild & Other Poems. LC 72-77858. 112p. (gr. 7 up). 1972. 5.95 (ISBN 0-89388-040-X). Okpaku Communications.

NEGRO CLERGY
This heading discontinued January 1976. See Afro-American Clergy for later materials.
Asher, Jeremiah. Incidents in the Life of the Rev. J. Asher. facsimile ed. LC 74-168506. (Black Heritage Library Collection). Repr. of 1850 ed. 10.00 (ISBN 0-8369-8860-4). Arno.
Early, Sarah J. Life & Labors of Rev. Jordan W. Early. One of the Pioneers of African Methodism in the West & South. facsimile ed. LC 72-164386. (Black Heritage Library Collection). Repr. of 1894 ed. 14.00 (ISBN 0-8369-8845-0). Arno.
Nelsen, Hart M., et al, eds. Black Church in America. LC 79-147014. 1971. text ed. 10.75x (ISBN 0-465-00691-4). Basic.
Tucker, David M. Black Pastors & Leaders: The Memphis Clergy, 1819-1972. LC 75-1248. 176p. 1975. 9.95x (ISBN 0-87870-024-2). Memphis St Univ.
Williams, Ethel L. Biographical Directory of Negro Ministers. 3rd ed. (Reference Bks.). 578p. 1975. lib. bdg. 28.00 (ISBN 0-8161-1183-9). G K Hall.

NEGRO CONSUMERS
This heading discontinued January 1976. See Afro-Americans As Consumers for later materials.
Andreasen, Alan R. The Disadvantaged Consumer. LC 75-2805. (Illus.). 1975. 16.95 (ISBN 0-02-900690-2). Free Pr.
Edwards, Paul K. The Southern Urban Negro As a Consumer. LC 32-6325. (Basic Afro-American Reprint Library). 1970. Repr. of 1932 ed. 15.50 (ISBN 0-384-13875-6). Johnson Repr.
--Southern Urban Negro As a Consumer. LC 73-89022. (Illus.). Repr. of 1932 ed. 16.50x (ISBN 0-8371-1891-3, Pub. by Negro U Pr). Greenwood.
Joyce, George & Govoni, Norman A., eds. Black Consumer, Dimensions of Power & Strategy. 1971. pap. text ed. 5.95x (ISBN 0-394-31130-2). Phila Bk Co.

NEGRO CRIMINALS
This heading discontinued January 1976. See Afro-American Criminals for later materials.
Du Bois, W. E. B. Some Notes on Negro Crime Particularly in Georgia. (Atlanta Univ. Publ. Ser.: No. 9). (Orig.). 1904. Repr. pap. 4.00 (ISBN 0-527-03111-9). Kraus Repr.
Raper, Arthur F. Tragedy of Lynching. LC 72-90191. (Mass Violence in America Ser). Repr. of 1933 ed. 17.00 (ISBN 0-405-01334-5). Arno.
--Tragedy of Lynching. LC 69-16568. (Illus.). Repr. of 1933 ed. 20.75x (ISBN 0-8371-1145-5). Greenwood.

NEGRO ENGINEERS
This heading discontinued January 1976. See Afro-American Engineers for later materials.
Ho, James K. K., ed. Black Engineers in the United States: A Directory. LC 73-84956. 308p. 1974. 18.00x (ISBN 0-88258-000-0). Howard U Pr.

NEGRO FAMILIES
This heading discontinued January 1976. See Afro-American Families for later materials.
Billingsley, Andrew. Black Families in White America. LC 68-54602. 1968. pap. 2.95 (ISBN 0-13-077453-7, Spec). P-H.
Du Bois, W. E., ed. Negro American Family. LC 68-55882. (Illus.). Repr. of 1908 ed. 13.75x (ISBN 0-8371-1342-3, Pub. by Negro U Pr). Greenwood.
Du Bois, W. E. B. The Negro American Family. (Atlanta Univ. Publ. Ser.: No. 13). (Orig.). 1908. Repr. of 1908 ed. pap. 5.00 (ISBN 0-527-03114-3). Kraus Repr.
Frazier, E. Franklin. Free Negro Family: A Study of Family Origins Before the Civil War. LC 68-28996. (American Negro: His History & Literature Ser.,No. 1). 1968. Repr. of 1932 ed. 10.00 (ISBN 0-405-01815-0). Arno.
--Negro Family in the United States. rev. & abr ed. LC 66-13868. 1966. pap. 2.95 (ISBN 0-226-26141-7, P205, Phoen). U of Chicago Pr.
Heiss, Jerold. The Case of the Black Family: A Sociological Inquiry. new ed. LC 74-34418. 246p. 1975. 17.50x (ISBN 0-231-03782-1). Columbia U Pr.
Rodman, Hyman. Lower-Class Families: The Culture of Poverty in Negro Trinidad. 256p. 1971. pap. 4.50x (ISBN 0-19-501378-6). Oxford U Pr.
Stack, Carol B. All Our Kin: Strategies for Survival in a Black Community. 1975. pap. 3.95 (ISBN 0-06-090424-0, CN424, CN). Har-Row.
Thomas, George B. Young Black Adults: Liberation & Family Attitudes. 1974. pap. 1.95 (ISBN 0-377-00002-7). Friend Pr.
Thompson, Daniel C. Sociology of the Black Experience. LC 73-20974. (Contributions in Sociology: No. 14). 261p. 1974. lib. bdg. 15.75 (ISBN 0-8371-7336-1, TBE/); pap. 4.95 (ISBN 0-8371-8928-4, TBE). Greenwood.
Willie, Charles V. Family Life of Black People. LC 79-127082. 1970. pap. text ed. 6.50x (ISBN 0-675-09297-3). Merrill.
Woods, Sr. Frances J. Marginality & Identity: A Colored Creole Family Through Ten Generations. LC 72-79342. 432p. 1972. 25.00x (ISBN 0-8071-0241-5). La State U Pr.

NEGRO FARMERS
This heading discontinued January 1976. See Afro-American Farmers for later materials.
Farm Tenancy: Black & White, Two Reports. LC 79-137166. (Poverty U.S.A. Historical Record Ser). 1971. Repr. of 1935 ed. 12.00 (ISBN 0-405-03134-3). Arno.
Marshall, F. Ray & Godwin, Lamond. Cooperatives & Rural Poverty in the South. LC 70-135534. (Policy Studies in Employment and Welfare: No.7). (Illus.). 128p. 1971. 8.50x (ISBN 0-8018-1232-1); pap. 2.95x (ISBN 0-8018-1233-X). Johns Hopkins.

NEGRO JEWISH RELATIONS
This heading discontinued January 1976. See Afro-Americans-Relations With Jews for later materials.
Laboritz, Sherman. Attitudes Toward Blacks Among Jews: Historical Antecedents & Current Concerns. LC 75-5365. 1975. soft bdg. 9.00 (ISBN 0-88247-358-1). R & E Res Assoc.
Weisbord, Robert G. & Stein, Arthur. Bittersweet Encounter: The Afro-American & the American Jew. LC 72-127828. (Contributions in Afro-American & African Studies: No. 5). 1970. 14.75 (ISBN 0-8371-5093-0, Pub. by Negro U Pr). Greenwood.

NEGRO LAWYERS
This heading discontinued January 1976. See Afro-American Lawyers for later materials.
Woodson, Carter G. Negro Professional Man & the Community, with Special Emphasis on the Physician & the Lawyer. Repr. of 1934 ed. 18.50 (ISBN 0-384-69208-7). Johnson Repr.
--Negro Professional Man & the Community, with Special Emphasis on the Physician & the Lawyer. LC 74-89025. Repr. of 1934 ed. 18.75x (ISBN 0-8371-1896-4, Pub. by Negro U Pr). Greenwood.

NEGRO LIBRARIANS
This heading discontinued January 1976. See Afro-American Librarians for later materials.
Josey, E. J. What Black Librarians Are Saying. LC 72-5372. 1972. 10.00 (ISBN 0-8108-0530-8). Scarecrow.
Josey, E. J., ed. & intro. by. Black Librarian in America. LC 79-17850. 1970. 10.00 (ISBN 0-8108-0362-3). Scarecrow.

NEGRO LITERATURE
This heading discontinued January 1976. See American Literature-Afro-American Authors for later materials.
see also Negroes in Literature
Abrash, Barbara, ed. Black African Literature in English Since 1952. LC 67-29100. Repr. pap. 6.00 (ISBN 0-384-00201-3). Johnson Repr.
Adams, William, et al, eds. Afro-American Literature: Drama. (Afro-American Literature Ser). (gr. 9-12). 1970. pap. 5.32 (ISBN 0-395-01973-7, 2-00200). HM.
--Afro-American Literature: Nonfiction. (Afro-American Literature Ser). (gr. 9-12). 1970. pap. 5.32 (ISBN 0-395-01979-6, 2-00206). HM.
Baraka, Amiri & Neal, Roy, eds. Black Fire: An Anthology of Afro-American Writing. 1968. pap. 5.95 (ISBN 0-688-26984-2). Morrow.
Brooks, Gwendolyn. Family Pictures. 5.00 (ISBN 0-910296-43-X); pap. 1.00 (ISBN 0-910296-67-7); tape 5.00 (ISBN 0-685-24799-6). Broadside.
Brown, Lloyd W., ed. Black Writer in Africa & the Americas. LC 70-188989. (University of Southern California Studies in Comparative Literature Ser: No. 6). 1973. pap. 7.95x (ISBN 0-912158-51-4). Hennessey.
Carrington, Harold. Drive Suite. (Heritage Ser). 1970. pap. 2.50x (ISBN 0-685-26074-7). Broadside.
Clack, ed. Black Literature Resources. (Library & Information Science Ser.: Vol.16). 224p. 1975. 25.75 (ISBN 0-8247-6307-6). Dekker.
The Crisis - a Record of the Darker Races 1910-60: Journal of the National Association for the Advancement of Colored People, 50 vols. LC 70-84750. Set. 1450.00 (ISBN 0-405-01001-X). Arno.
Culp, Daniel W., ed. Twentieth Century Negro Literature. facs. ed. LC 73-89416. (Black Heritage Library Collection Ser). 1902. 21.50 (ISBN 0-8369-8551-6). Arno.
Dodson, Owen. The Confession Stone. (Heritage Ser). 1970. pap. 2.50x (ISBN 0-685-26075-5). Broadside.
Durem, Ray. Take No Prisoners. (Heritage Ser). 1971. pap. 2.50x (ISBN 0-685-26076-3). Broadside.
Harris, Joel C. Nights with Uncle Remus: Myths & Legends of the Old Plantation. LC 70-164329. 1971. Repr. of 1883 ed. 28.00 (ISBN 0-8103-3866-1). Gale.
Howard University Libraries, Washington, D.C. Dictionary Catalog of the Arthur B. Spingarn Collection of Negro Authors, 2 vols. 1970. lib. bdg. 165.00 (ISBN 0-8161-0872-2). G K Hall.
Redmond, Eugene, ed. Sides of the River: A Mini-Anthology of Black Writings. 1969. pap. 1.50 (ISBN 0-916692-01-9). Black River.

Turner, Darwin T. Black American Literature: Essays, Poetry, Fiction, Drama. 1970. pap. text ed. 12.95x (ISBN 0-675-09278-7). Merrill.
Washington, William D. & Beckoff, Samuel, eds. Black Literature: An Anthology of Black Writers. pap. 3.95 (ISBN 0-671-18701-5). Monarch Pr.
Whitlow, Roger. Black American Literature: A Critical History. LC 73-75525. 303p. 1973. 17.95x (ISBN 0-88229-100-9). Nelson-Hall.

NEGRO LITERATURE–HISTORY AND CRITICISM
This heading discontinued January 1976. See American Literature–Afro-American Authors–History and Criticism for later materials.
McIntosh, Maria J. Two Pictures. facsimile ed. LC 72-39094. (Black Heritage Library Collection). Repr. of 1863 ed. 23.50 (ISBN 0-8369-9032-3). Arno.
Mays, Benjamin E. Negro's God As Reflected in His Literature. LC 69-16578. (Illus.). Repr. of 1938 ed. 16.50x (ISBN 0-8371-1139-0, Pub. by Negro U Pr). Greenwood.
Turner. Black American Literature: Essays. 1969. pap. text ed. 4.95 (ISBN 0-675-09503-4). Merrill.

NEGRO MOVING-PICTURE ACTORS AND ACTRESSES
This heading discontinued January 1976. See Afro-American Motion Picture Actors and Actresses for later materials.
Mapp, Edward. Blacks in American Films: Today & Yesterday. LC 72-172946. (Illus.). 1972. 10.00 (ISBN 0-8108-0458-1). Scarecrow.
Noble, Peter. Negro in Films. LC 72-124022, (Literature of Cinema, Ser. 1). Repr. of 1949 ed. 15.00 (ISBN 0-405-01629-8). Arno.

NEGRO MUSIC
This heading discontinued January 1976. See Afro-American Music for later materials.
Baraka, Amiri, pseud. Black Music. 1967. pap. 3.95 (ISBN 0-688-24344-4). Morrow.
--Blues People: Negro Music in White America. 1963. pap. 4.95 (ISBN 0-688-18474-X). Morrow.
Courlander, Harold. Negro Folk Music, U.S.A. LC 63-18019. 324p. 1963. 20.00x (ISBN 0-231-02365-0); pap. 7.50x (ISBN 0-231-08634-2). Columbia U Pr.
Cuney-Hare, Maud. Negro Musicians & Their Music. LC 74-4108. (Music Reprint Ser.). 1974. Repr. of 1936 ed. 35.00 (ISBN 0-306-70652-0). Da Capo.
Davis, Ronald L. A History of Music in American Life, Vol. 1: The Formative Years, 1620-1865. LC 79-25359. 386p. 1981. lib. bdg. 17.50 (ISBN 0-89874-002-9). Krieger.
Howard University Libraries, Washington, D.C. Dictionary Catalog of the Arthur B. Spingarn Collection of Negro Authors, 2 vols. 1970. lib. bdg. 165.00 (ISBN 0-8161-0872-2). G K Hall.
Keil, Charles. Urban Blues. LC 66-13876. (Illus.). 1966. 10.00x (ISBN 0-226-42959-8). U of Chicago Pr.
--Urban Blues. LC 66-13876. (Illus.). 1968. pap. 2.45 (ISBN 0-226-42960-1, P291, Phoen). U of Chicago Pr.
Roberts, John S. Black Music of Two Worlds. 1974. pap. 3.95 (ISBN 0-688-24344-4). Morrow.
Southern, Eileen. Music of Black Americans: A History. (Illus.). 1971. text ed. 19.95x (ISBN 0-393-02156-4); pap. text ed. 6.95x (ISBN 0-393-09899-0). Norton.
Thomas, Will H. Some Current Folksongs of the Negro. 1912. pap. 1.00 (ISBN 0-87074-114-4). SMU Press.

NEGRO MUSICIANS
This heading discontinued January 1976. See Afro-American Musicians for later materials.
Baraka, Amiri, pseud. Black Music. 1967. pap. 3.95 (ISBN 0-688-24344-4). Morrow.
Brawley, Benjamin G. Negro Genius. LC 66-17517. 1966. Repr. of 1937 ed. 10.50x (ISBN 0-8196-0184-5). Biblo.
Cuney-Hare, Maud. Negro Musicians & Their Music. LC 74-4108. (Music Reprint Ser.). 1974. Repr. of 1936 ed. 35.00 (ISBN 0-306-70652-0). Da Capo.
Jones, Hettie. Big Star Fallin' Mama: Five Women in Black Music. (Illus.). 152p. (gr. 7 up). 1974. 7.95 (ISBN 0-670-16408-9). Viking Pr.
Keil, Charles. Urban Blues. LC 66-13876. (Illus.). 1966. 10.00x (ISBN 0-226-42959-8). U of Chicago Pr.
Kimball, Robert & Bolcom, William. Reminiscing with Sissle & Blake. (Illus.). 1973. 12.95 (ISBN 0-670-59388-5). Viking Pr.
Kofsky, Frank. Black Nationalism & the Revolution in Music. LC 77-108716. (Illus.). 1970. 14.00 (ISBN 0-87348-149-6); pap. 4.95 (ISBN 0-87348-129-1). Path Pr NY.
Locke, Alain. Negro & His Music. Bd. with Negro Art: Past & Present. LC 69-18592. (American Negro-His History & Literature Ser., No.2). 1969. Repr. of 1936 ed. 8.00 (ISBN 0-405-01879-7). Arno.
Marsh, J. B. Story of the Jubilee Singers with Their Songs. rev. ed. LC 72-165509. (Illus.). Repr. of 1880 ed. 14.00 (ISBN 0-404-04189-2). AMS Pr.
--Story of the Jubilee Singers, with Their Songs. rev. ed. LC 79-78583. (Illus.). Repr. of 1881 ed. 15.75x (ISBN 0-8371-1424-1, Pub. by Negro U Pr). Greenwood.
Negro Music Journal. Negro Music Journal: Devoted to the Education Interest of the Negro in Music, Vol. 1-2. 1902-1903. Repr. 33.00x (ISBN 0-8371-9118-1, Pub. by Negro U Pr). Greenwood.
Ramsey, Frederic & Smith, Charles E., eds. Jazzmen. LC 78-181233. 360p. 1939. Repr. 27.00 (ISBN 0-403-01654-1). Scholarly.
Spellman, A. B. Black Music: Four Lives. LC 66-10410. 1971. pap. 3.95 (ISBN 0-8052-0281-1). Schocken.
Trotter, James M. Music & Some Highly Musical People. LC 71-99415. 1969. Repr. of 1880 ed. lib. bdg. 21.50 (ISBN 0-8411-0088-8). Metro Bks.
--Music & Some Highly Musical People. (Basic Afro-American Reprint Library). Repr. of 1881 ed. 23.00 (ISBN 0-384-61720-4). Johnson Repr.

NEGRO NEWSPAPERS (AMERICAN)
This heading discontinued January 1976. See Afro-American Press for later materials.
Oak, Vishnu V. Negro Newspaper. LC 70-135605. (Illus.). Repr. of 1948 ed. 12.75x (ISBN 0-8371-5180-5, Pub. by Negro U Pr). Greenwood.

NEGRO ORATORS
This heading discontinued January 1976. See Afro-American Orators for later materials.
Woodson, Carter G., ed. Negro Orators & Their Orations. LC 69-14223. 1969. Repr. of 1925 ed. 25.00 (ISBN 0-8462-1316-8). Russell.

NEGRO PHYSICIANS
This heading discontinued January 1976. See Afro-American Physicians for later materials.
Poindexter, Hildrus A. My World of Reality. LC 72-85752. (Illus.). 349p. 1973. 9.95 (ISBN 0-913642-03-7). Balamp Pub.
Still, James. Early Recollections & Life of Doctor James Still. LC 72-107522. Repr. of 1877 ed. 12.75x (ISBN 0-8371-3769-1, Pub. by Negro U Pr). Greenwood.
--Early Recollections & Life of Dr. James Still, 1812-1885. (Illus.). 288p. 1973. Repr. 19.50 (ISBN 0-8135-0769-3). Rutgers U Pr.
Woodson, Carter G. Negro Professional Man & the Community, with Special Emphasis on the Physician & the Lawyer. Repr. of 1934 ed. 18.50 (ISBN 0-384-69208-7). Johnson Repr.
--Negro Professional Man & the Community, with Special Emphasis on the Physician & the Lawyer. LC 74-89025. Repr. of 1934 ed. 18.75x (ISBN 0-8371-1896-4, Pub. by Negro U Pr). Greenwood.

NEGRO POETRY
This heading discontinued January 1976. See American poetry–Afro-American Authors for later materials.
Adoff, Arnold, ed. The Poetry of Black America: Anthology of the Twentieth Century. LC 72-76518. 576p. (gr. 7 up). 1973. 20.00 (ISBN 0-06-020089-8, HarpJ); PLB 18.79 (ISBN 0-06-020090-1). Har-Row.
Alhamsi, Ahmed & Wangara, Harun K., eds. Black Arts: An Anthology of Black Creations. 1969. pap. 3.50 (ISBN 0-685-07539-7). Broadside.
Bell, Bernard. Folk Roots of Afro-American Poetry. 1974. 5.00 (ISBN 0-910296-93-6); pap. 2.75 (ISBN 0-910296-98-7). Broadside.
Brooks, Gwendolyn, et al. A Capsule Course in Black Poetry Writing. 64p. 1975. pap. 5.00 (ISBN 0-685-57551-9). Broadside.
Cartey, Wilfred. Black Images. LC 75-113096. 1970. pap. 7.75x (ISBN 0-8077-1144-6). Tchrs Coll.
Chapman, Dorothy H. Index to Black Poetry. 250p. 1974. lib. bdg. 25.00 (ISBN 0-8161-1143-X). G K Hall.
Hughes, Langston, ed. Poems from Black Africa. LC 62-8972. (Poetry Ser. Poetry Paperback: No. 30). 160p. 1963. 6.50x (ISBN 0-253-16490-7). Ind U Pr.
Hughes, Langston & Bontemps, Arna, eds. Poetry of the Negro, Seventeen Forty-Six-Nineteen Seventy. 1970. Doubleday.
Randall, James. Cities & Other Disasters. 1973. pap. 1.50 (ISBN 0-910296-81-2). Broadside.
Rivers, Conrad K. The Wright Poems-Essay by Ronald Fair. (Heritage Ser). 1971. pap. 2.50x (ISBN 0-685-26077-1). Broadside.

NEGRO POLICEMEN
This heading discontinued January 1976. See Afro-American Police for later materials.
Friedman, Ina. Black Cop: A Biography of Tilmon O'Bryant. LC 73-20142. (Illus.). (gr. 6 up). 1974. 5.95 (ISBN 0-664-32546-7). Westminster.
--Black Cop: A Biography of Tilmon O'Bryant. LC 73-20142. (Illus.). (gr. 6 up). 1974. 5.95 (ISBN 0-664-32546-7). Westminster.

NEGRO PRESS
This heading discontinued January 1976. See Afro-American Press for later materials.
La Brie, Henry G. The Black Press in America: A Bibliography. 1974. pap. 3.50 (ISBN 0-89080-003-0). Mercer Hse.
Penn, I. Garland. Afro-American Press & Its Editors. LC 69-18574. (American Negro-His History & Literature, Series No. 2). 1969. Repr. of 1891 ed. 21.00 (ISBN 0-405-01887-8). Arno.
Wolseley, Roland E. The Black Press, U.S.A. facsimile ed. (Illus.). 352p. 1971. pap. 15.15x (ISBN 0-8138-2355-2). Iowa St U Pr.

NEGRO RACE
see Black Race

NEGRO SEAMEN
This heading discontinued January 1976. See Afro-American Seamen for later materials.
Mulzac, Hugh. A Star to Steer by. 1972. pap. 1.50 (ISBN 0-7178-0352-X). Intl Pub Co.

NEGRO SOLDIERS
This heading discontinued January 1976. See Afro-American Soldiers for later materials.
Black, Lowell-Dwight. The Negro Volunteer Militia Units of the Ohio National Guard, 1870-1954: The Struggle for Military Recognition & Equality in the State of Ohio. 1976. pap. text ed. 35.00x (ISBN 0-89126-031-5). MA-AH Pub.
Black Women in the Armed Forces: A Pictoral History. LC 74-24961. 125p. 1975. 10.00 (ISBN 0-915044-11-0); pap. 4.00 (ISBN 0-915044-12-9). Carver Pub.
Brown, Earl L. & Leighton, George R. Negro & the War. LC 75-172045. Repr. of 1942 ed. 11.50 (ISBN 0-404-00194-7). AMS Pr.
Carroll, John M., ed. The Black Military Experience in the American West. 1974. pap. 3.95 (ISBN 0-87140-085-5). Liveright.
Cornish, Dudley T. Sable Arm: Negro Troops in the Union Army, 1861-1865. 1966. pap. 5.95 (ISBN 0-393-00334-5, Norton Lib). Norton.
Delsarte, Walter W. Negro, Democracy & the War. LC 71-155386. Repr. of 1919 ed. 9.25x (ISBN 0-8371-3666-0, Pub. by Negro U Pr). Greenwood.
Fletcher, Marvin E. The Black Soldier & Officer in the United States Army, 1891-1917. LC 73-93640. 1974. 12.50x (ISBN 0-8262-0161-X). U of Mo Pr.
Fowler, Arlen L. The Black Infantry in the West, 1869-1891. LC 78-105985. (Contributions in Afro-American & African Studies: No. 6). (Illus.). 1971. 13.50x (ISBN 0-8371-3313-0, Pub. by Negro U Pr). Greenwood.
Greene, Robert E. Black Defenders of America, 1775-1973. LC 73-15607. (Illus.). 432p. 1974. 17.95 (ISBN 0-87485-053-3). Johnson Chi.
Guthrie, James M. Camp-Fires of the Afro-American: Or the Colored Man As a Patriot, Soldier, Sailor, & Hero, in the Cause of Free America. Repr. of 1899 ed. 42.50 (ISBN 0-384-20484-8). Johnson Repr.
Higginson, Thomas W. Army Life in a Black Regiment. 296p. 1971. Repr. of 1870 ed. 9.00 (ISBN 0-87928-022-0). Corner Hse.
The Negro Soldier: A Select Compilation. 1861-1919. Repr. 10.25x (ISBN 0-8371-1870-0, Pub. by Negro U Pr). Greenwood.
Sweeney, W. Allison. History of the American Negro in the Great World War: His Splendid Record in the Battle Zones of Europe Including a Resume of His Past Services to His Country. LC 72-92764. (Illus.). 307p. 1919. Repr. 24.00x (ISBN 0-8371-2199-X, Pub. by Negro U Pr). Greenwood.
Wilkes, Laura E. Missing Pages in American History: Revealing the Services of Negroes in the Early Wars in the United States of America, 1641-1815. LC 72-7728. Repr. of 1919 ed. 11.50 (ISBN 0-404-06948-7). AMS Pr.

NEGRO SPIRTUALS
see Spirituals (Songs)

NEGRO STUDENTS
This heading discontinued January 1976. See Afro-American Students for later materials.
Caliver, Ambrose. Personnel Study of Negro College Students: A Study of the Relations Between Certain Background Factors of Negro College Studens & Their Subsequent Careers in College. LC 73-107470. Repr. of 1931 ed. 10.75x (ISBN 0-8371-3749-7). Greenwood.
--A Personnel Study of Negro College Students: A Study of the Relations Between Certain Background Factors of Negro College Students & Their Subsequent Careers in College. LC 76-176623. (Columbia University. Teachers College. Contributions to Education: No. 484). Repr. of 1931 ed. 8.75 (ISBN 0-404-55484-9). AMS Pr.
Daniel, Walter G. Reading Interests & Needs of Negro College Freshmen Regarding Social Science Materials. LC 79-176719. (Columbia University. Teachers College. Contributions to Education: No. 862). Repr. of 1942 ed. 17.50 (ISBN 0-404-55862-3). AMS Pr.
Ginzberg, Eli, et al. The Middle-Class Negro in the White Man's World. LC 67-26364. 1967. 15.00x (ISBN 0-231-03096-7); pap. 5.00x (ISBN 0-231-08596-6). Columbia U Pr.
Harper. Black Student, White Campus. 72p. 1975. pap. 7.50 (ISBN 0-686-11207-5). Am Personnel.
Miller, LaMar P., ed. The Testing of Black Students. LC 74-6237. 128p. 1974. 16.95 (ISBN 0-13-911966-3). P-H.
Petroni, Frank A. & Hirsch, Ernest A. Two, Four, Six, Eight, When You Gonna Integrate? 1971. pap. 2.75 (ISBN 0-87140-041-3). Liveright.

NEGRO TALES
This heading discontinued January 1976. See Afro-American Tales for later materials.
Brewer, J. Mason. Dog Ghosts & Other Negro Folk Tales. Bd. with The Word on the Brazos: Negro Preacher Tales from the Brazos Bottoms of Texas. 268p. 1976. pap. 4.95 (ISBN 0-292-71512-9). U of Tex Pr.
Cotter, Joseph S. Negro Tales. facs. ed. LC 75-83923. (Black Heritage Library Collection Ser). 1912. 10.00 (ISBN 0-8369-8548-6). Arno.
Dorson, Richard M. Negro Folktales in Michigan. LC 73-21099. (Illus.). 245p. 1974. Repr. of 1956 ed. lib. bdg. 15.50x (ISBN 0-8371-5989-X, DONF). Greenwood.
--Negro Tales from Pine Bluff, Arkansas & Calvin, Michigan. LC 58-63484. (Indiana University Folklore Ser: No. 12). 1958. 16.00 (ISBN 0-527-24650-6). Kraus Repr.
Owen, Mary A. Voodoo Tales As Told Among the Negroes of the Southwest. facs. ed. LC 70-149874. (Black Heritage Library Collection Ser). 1893. 15.00 (ISBN 0-8369-8754-3). Arno.
Short, Sam. Tis So: Negro Folk Tales. 1972. 3.50 (ISBN 0-685-27205-2); pap. 1.95 (ISBN 0-685-27206-0). Claitors.

NEGRO TEACHERS
This heading discontinued January 1976. See Afro-American Teachers for later materials.
Browne, Rose B. & English, James W. Love My Children. LC 74-80406. 250p. 1974. pap. 1.95 (ISBN 0-912692-43-X). Cook.
Caliver, Ambrose. Education of Negro Teachers. LC 70-82090. Repr. of 1933 ed. 14.25x (ISBN 0-8371-3206-1, Pub. by Negro U Pr). Greenwood.
Clark, Felton G. The Control of State-Supported Teacher-Training Programs for Negroes. LC 75-176647. (Columbia University. Teachers College. Contributions to Education: No. 605). Repr. of 1934 ed. 17.50 (ISBN 0-404-55605-1). AMS Pr.
Colson, Edna M. The Analysis of the Specific References to Negroes in Selected Curricula for the Education of Teachers. LC 75-17663. (Columbia University. Teachers College. Contributions to Education: No. 822). Repr. of 1940 ed. 17.50 (ISBN 0-404-55822-4). AMS Pr.
Harris, Ruth M. Teachers' Social Knowledge & Its Relation to Pupils' Responses: A Study of Four St. Louis Negro Elementary Schools. LC 77-176843. (Columbia University. Teachers College. Contributions to Education: No. 816). Repr. of 1941 ed. 17.50 (ISBN 0-404-55816-X). AMS Pr.
McAllister, Jane E. The Training of Negro Teachers in Louisiana. LC 71-177016. (Columbia University. Teachers College. Contributions to Education: No. 364). Repr. of 1929 ed. 17.50 (ISBN 0-404-55364-8). AMS Pr.
Moore, William, Jr. & Wagstaff, Lonnie H. Black Educators in White Colleges: Progress & Prospect. LC 73-12066. (Higher Education Ser). 224p. 1974. 15.95x (ISBN 0-87589-206-X). Jossey-Bass.
Silver, Catherine B. Black Teachers in Urban Schools: The Case of Washington D.C. LC 72-92467. (Special Studies in U.S. Economic, Social, & Political Issues). 1973. 26.00x (ISBN 0-8290-0456-4); pap. text ed. 12.50x (ISBN 0-89197-682-5). Irvington.
Two Black Teachers During the Civil War. LC 73-92243. (The American Negro: His History & Literature Ser. 3). 1969. Repr. of 1864 ed. 6.50 (ISBN 0-405-01931-9). Arno.

NEGRO UNIVERSITIES AND COLLEGES
This heading discontinued January 1976. See Afro-American Universities and Colleges for later materials.
Gallagher, Buell G. American Caste & the Negro College. LC 66-29471. 1966. Repr. of 1938 ed. 10.00 (ISBN 0-87752-041-0). Gordian.
Holmes, Dwight O. Evolution of the Negro College. LC 74-128993. (Columbia University. Teachers College. Contributions to Education: No. 609). Repr. of 1934 ed. 8.50 (ISBN 0-404-00172-6). AMS Pr.
--Evolution of the Negro College. LC 69-18570. (American Negro: His History & Literature Ser. No. 2). 1969. Repr. of 1934 ed. 9.50 (ISBN 0-405-01871-1). Arno.

Thompson, Daniel C. Private Black Colleges at the Crossroads. LC 72-841. (Contributions in Afro-American & African Studies: No. 13). 1973. lib. bdg. 15.95 (ISBN 0-8371-6410-9, TBC/). Greenwood.

Wolters, Raymond. The New Negro on Campus: Black College Rebellions of the 1920's. 324p. 1975. 26.00x (ISBN 0-691-04628-X). Princeton U Pr.

NEGRO WIT AND HUMOR

This heading discontinued January 1976. See Afro-American Wit and Humor for later materials.

Corrothers, James D. Black Cat Club: Negro Humor & Folk-Lore. LC 72-1047. (Illus.). Repr. of 1902 ed. 18.00 (ISBN 0-404-00023-1). AMS Pr.

Johnson, Charles. Black Humor. (Illus.). 1970. pap. 3.95 (ISBN 0-87485-036-3). Johnson Chi.

Pickens, William. American Aesop: Negro & Other Humor. LC 76-99888. Repr. of 1926 ed. 17.50 (ISBN 0-404-00206-4). AMS Pr.

Scott, Flo H. That Passing Laughter: Stories of the Southland. 1966. pap. 4.95 (ISBN 0-87651-004-7). Southern U Pr.

NEGROES

This heading discontinued January 1976. See Afro-Americans for later materials on the permanent residents of the United States. See Blacks for later materials on persons outside the United States.

Ahmann, Mathew H. New Negro. LC 73-77031. 1969. Repr. of 1961 ed. 9.50x (ISBN 0-8196-0232-9). Biblo.

Albert, Octavia V. The House of Bondage. facsimile ed. LC 70-37580. (Black Heritage Library Collections). Repr. of 1890 ed. 14.50 (ISBN 0-8369-8956-2). Arno.

Alexander, William T. History of the Colored Race in America, Containing Also Their Ancient & Modern Life in Africa, the Origin & Development of Slavery, the Civil War. 2nd ed. LC 68-55867. (Illus.). Repr. of 1887 ed. 28.00x (ISBN 0-8371-0283-9, Pub. by Negro U Pr). Greenwood.

American Academy of Political & Social Science. American Negro. Young, Donald R., ed. LC 28-29716. Repr. of 1928 ed. 19.00 (ISBN 0-527-02100-8). Kraus Repr.

American Academy Of Political And Social Science. Negro's Progress in Fifty Years. LC 71-92737. Repr. of 1913 ed. 12.00x (ISBN 0-8371-2187-6, Pub. by Negro U Pr). Greenwood.

American Negro Academy. American Negro Academy Occasional Papers Nos. 1-22. LC 77-94134. (The American Negro: His History & Literatrue, Ser. No. 3). 1970. 24.00 (ISBN 0-405-01913-0). Arno.

Aptheker, Herbert. American Negro Slave Revolts. 1969. pap. 3.75 (ISBN 0-7178-0003-2). Intl Pub Co.

Archer, William. Through Afro-America; an English Reading on the Race Problem. LC 76-132074. Repr. of 1910 ed. 15.25x (ISBN 0-8371-0429-7). Greenwood.

Armistead, W. S. Negro Is a Man. facs. ed. LC 74-89427. (Black Heritage Library Collection Ser). 1903. 18.25 (ISBN 0-8369-8505-2). Arno.

Armistead, Wilson. Tribute for the Negro. facs. ed. (Black Heritage Library Collection Ser). 1848. 25.00 (ISBN 0-8369-8503-6). Arno.

Atkinson, J. Edward, ed. Black Dimensions in Contemporary American Art. 3.95 (ISBN 0-452-25041-2, Z5041, Plume). NAL.

Baker, Ross K., ed. Afro-American Readings. 1970. pap. 8.50x (ISBN 0-442-00505-9). Van Nos Reinhold.

Baldwin, James. Fire Next Time. 1970. pap. 1.50 (ISBN 0-440-32542-0). Dell.

--Nobody Knows My Name. 1961. 7.95 (ISBN 0-8037-6435-9). Dial.

Baraka, Amiri, pseud. Black Music. 1967. pap. 3.95 (ISBN 0-688-24344-4). Morrow.

--Blues People: Negro Music in White America. 1963. pap. 4.95 (ISBN 0-688-18474-X). Morrow.

Barbour, Floyd B., ed. Black Seventies. LC 74-133967. (Extending Horizons Ser). 1970. pap. 2.95 (ISBN 0-87558-059-9). Porter Sargent.

Bell, Howard H. Survey of the Negro Convention Movement. LC 74-94129. (American Negro: His History & Literature, Ser. No. 3). 1970. Repr. of 1953 ed. 14.00 (ISBN 0-405-01915-7). Arno.

Bell, Howard H., ed. Minutes of the Proceedings of the National Negro Conventions 1830-1864. LC 72-105552. (American Negro: His History & Literature, Ser. No. 3). 1970. Repr. of 1969 ed. 19.50 (ISBN 0-405-01916-5). Arno.

Bennett, Lerone, Jr. Before the Mayflower. (YA) (gr. 9 up). 1966. pap. 3.95 (ISBN 0-14-020856-9, Pelican). Penguin.

--The Challenge of Blackness. 330p. 1972. 6.95 (ISBN 0-87485-054-1). Johnson Chi.

--Negro Mood. 1964. 3.95 (ISBN 0-87485-012-6). Johnson Chi.

Bettany, G. T. Dark Peoples of the Land of Sunshine. facs. ed. LC 73-89424. (Black Heritage Library Collection Ser). 1890. 12.25 (ISBN 0-8369-8510-9). Arno.

Black Pilgrimage in America Kits: As Seen in Christian Perspective. 1970. 3.75 (ISBN 0-687-03592-9). Abingdon.

Blauner, Robert. Racial Oppression in America. 1972. pap. text ed. 11.50 scp (ISBN 0-06-040771-9, HarpC). Har-Row.

Bontemps, Arna. One Hundred Years of Negro Freedom. LC 61-11716. (Illus.). (gr. 9 up). 1961. pap. 2.95 (ISBN 0-396-05520-6). Dodd.

Bracey, John H., et al. Black Nationalism in America. LC 79-99161. 1970. pap. 10.95 (ISBN 0-672-60150-8, AHS89). Bobbs.

Brawley, Benjamin G. Social History of the American Negro: Being a History of the Negro Problem in the United States. (Basic Afro-American Reprint Library). Repr. of 1921 ed. 19.50 (ISBN 0-384-05580-X). Johnson Repr.

Breitman, George. How a Minority Can Change Society: The Real Potential of the Afro-American Struggle. pap. 0.50 (ISBN 0-87348-050-3). Path Pr NY.

Breitman, George, et al. Marxism & the Negro Struggle. 2nd ed. 1968. pap. 0.75 (ISBN 0-87348-072-4). Path Pr. NY.

Brooks, Gwendolyn, ed. The Black Position. No. 1, 1971. 1.00 (ISBN 0-685-42543-6); No. 2, 1972. 1.50 (ISBN 0-685-42544-4); No. 3, 1973. 3.00 (ISBN 0-685-42545-2); No. 4. 2.50 (ISBN 0-685-42546-0). Broadside.

Brotherhood Of Liberty. Justice & Jurisprudence: An Inquiry Concerning the Constitutional Limitations of the Thirteenth, Fourteenth & Fifteenth Amendments. LC 75-77191. Repr. of 1889 ed. 22.75x (ISBN 0-8371-1301-6, Pub. by Negro U Pr). Greenwood.

Brown, Earl L. & Leighton, George R. Negro & the War. LC 75-172045. Repr. of 1942 ed. 11.50 (ISBN 0-404-00194-7). AMS Pr.

Brown, William W. Rising Son: The Antecedents & Advancement of the Colored Race. facs. ed. LC 79-79008. (Black Heritage Library Collection Ser). 1874. 20.50 (ISBN 0-8369-8519-2). Arno.

--The Rising Sun or the Antecedents & Advancement of the Colored Race. (Basic Afro-American Reprint Library). 1970. Repr. of 1874 ed. lib. bdg. 25.50 (ISBN 0-384-05995-3). Johnson Repr.

Bruce, Philip A. The Plantation Negro As a Freeman: Observations on His Character, Condition & Prospects in Virginia. LC 79-99354. ix, 262p. 1972. Repr. of 1889 ed. lib. bdg. 14.75 (ISBN 0-8411-0025-X). Metro Bks.

Butcher, Margaret J. The Negro in American Culture. 2nd ed. 1972. 10.95 (ISBN 0-394-47943-2). Knopf.

Cable, George W. Silent South: Including the Freedman's Case in Equity, the Convict Lease System & to Which Has Been Added Eight Hitherto Uncollected Essays by Cable on Prison & Asylum Reform & an Essay on Cable by Arlin Turner. LC 69-14915. (Criminology, Law Enforcement, & Social Problems Ser.: No. 57). 1969. 10.00 (ISBN 0-87585-057-X). Patterson Smith.

Carter, Edward R. The Black Side. facsimile ed. LC 78-170692. (Black Heritage Library Collection). Repr. of 1894 ed. 30.75 (ISBN 0-8369-8882-5). Arno.

Chametzky, Jules & Kaplan, Sidney, eds. Black & White in American Culture: An Anthology from the Massachusetts Review. LC 74-76045. (Illus.). 1969. 16.50x (ISBN 0-87023-046-8). U of Mass Pr.

Child, Lydia M. Freedmen's Book. LC 68-28989. (American Negro: His History & Literature Ser., No. 1). (Illus.). 1968. Repr. of 1865 ed. 13.00 (ISBN 0-405-01809-6). Arno.

Clowes, William L. Black America: A Study of the Ex - Slave - His Late Master. LC 78-109322. Repr. of 1891 ed. 13.50x (ISBN 0-8371-3588-5, Pub. by Negro U Pr). Greenwood.

Conference On Jewish Social Studies. Negro-Jewish Relations in the United States. 1966. pap. 1.50 (ISBN 0-8065-0092-1, 218). Citadel Pr.

Coombs, Orde, ed. Do You See My Love for You Growing? LC 72-1538. 750p. 1972. 6.95 (ISBN 0-396-06518-X). Dodd.

Cooper, Anna J. Voice from the South. LC 77-78762. Repr. of 1892 ed. 19.75x (ISBN 0-8371-1384-9). Greenwood.

Crogman, William H. Talks for the Times. facs. ed. LC 78-152919. (Black Heritage Library Collection Ser). 1896. 18.25 (ISBN 0-8369-8763-2). Arno.

Cromwell, John W. The Negro in American History: Men & Women Eminent in the Evolution of the American of African Descent. (Basic Afro-American Reprint Library). 1969. Repr. of 1914 ed. 13.00 (ISBN 0-384-10215-8). Johnson Repr.

Crummell, Alexander. Africa & America: Addresses & Discourses. LC 70-77198. Repr. of 1891 ed. 20.50x (ISBN 0-8371-1291-5, Pub. by Negro U Pr). Greenwood.

Cruse, Harold. The Crisis of the Negro Intellectual. 1967. pap. 7.95 (ISBN 0-688-25224-9). Morrow.

--Rebellion or Revolution. 1972. pap. 3.95 (ISBN 0-688-06047-1). Morrow.

Cunnard, Nancy. Negro Anthology. LC 69-16589. (Illus.). Repr. of 1934 ed. 110.00 (ISBN 0-8371-1952-9, Pub. by Negro U Pr). Greenwood.

Curtis, James C. & Gould, Lewis L., eds. The Black Experience in America: Selected Essays. 209p. 1970. pap. 5.00x (ISBN 0-292-70096-2). U of Tex Pr.

Damned. Lessons from the Damned: Class Struggle in the Black Community. LC 72-95287. (Illus.). 160p. (Orig.). 1973. 7.95 (ISBN 0-87810-523-9); pap. 3.25 (ISBN 0-87810-023-7). Times Change.

Delange, Jacqueline. The Art & Peoples of Black Africa. (Illus.). 1974. pap. 7.95 (ISBN 0-525-47364-5). Dutton.

Delany, Martin R. Condition, Elevation, Emigration & Destiny of the Colored People of the U.S. Politically Considered. LC 68-28993. (American Negro: His History & Literature, Ser. No. 1). 1968. Repr. of 1852 ed. 8.00 (ISBN 0-405-01812-6). Arno.

Dowd, Jerome. Negro in American Life. LC 68-56331. Repr. of 1926 ed. 29.00x (ISBN 0-8371-0389-4, Pub. by Negro U Pr). Greenwood.

DuBois, W. Burghardt. Negro. 1970. pap. 4.95 (ISBN 0-19-501262-3, 333, GB). Oxford U Pr.

Du Bois, W. E. Black Reconstruction in America, 1860-1880. LC 68-1237. 1956. Repr. of 1935 ed. 30.00 (ISBN 0-8462-0172-0). Russell.

--Burghardt Souls of Black Folk. (Great Illustrated Classics). (gr. 7 up). 1979. 8.95 (ISBN 0-396-07757-9). Dodd.

Du Bois, W. E. B. Black Folk Then & Now: An Essay. LC 75-28300. 1975. Repr. of 1939 ed. 18.00 (ISBN 0-527-25275-1). Kraus Repr.

--The Negro. LC 74-7274. 1975. Repr. of 1915 ed. 14.00 (ISBN 0-527-25315-4). Kraus Repr.

Du Bois, William E. A B C of Color. (Orig.). 1970. pap. 1.35 (ISBN 0-7178-0000-8). Intl Pub Co.

Dubois, William E. Darkwater: Voices from Within the Veil. LC 70-91785. Repr. of 1920 ed. 12.50 (ISBN 0-404-00151-3). AMS Pr.

Du Bois, William E. Darkwater: Voices from Within the Veil. LC 69-19627. (Sourcebooks in Negro History Ser). 1969. pap. 3.75 (ISBN 0-8052-0212-9). Schocken.

--Souls of Black Folk. 4.50 (ISBN 0-8446-1999-X). Peter Smith.

--Souls of Black Folk. (Classic Ser). (Orig.). 1969. pap. 1.95 (ISBN 0-451-51458-0, CJ1458, Sig Classics). NAL.

Embree, Edwin R. Brown Americans. LC 78-122075. Repr. of 1945 ed. 13.50x (ISBN 0-678-03153-3). Kelley.

Ferris, William H. The African Abroad, or, His Evolution in Western Civilization, 2 Vols. (Basic Afro-American Reprint Library). 1969. Repr. of 1913 ed. Set. 46.00 (ISBN 0-384-15530-8). Johnson Repr.

Fortune, T. Thomas. Black & White: Land, Labor & Politics in the South. LC 79-102978. (Ebony Classics Ser). 1970. 3.50 (ISBN 0-87485-030-4). Johnson Chi.

Fortune, Timothy T. Black & White: Land, Labor & Politics in the South. LC 68-28995. (American Negro: His History & Literature, Ser. No. 1). 1968. Repr. of 1884 ed. 11.00 (ISBN 0-405-01814-2). Arno.

Foster, William Z. Negro People in American History. 1970. 8.50 (ISBN 0-7178-0275-2); pap. 3.45 (ISBN 0-7178-0276-0). Intl Pub Co.

Franklin, John H., ed. Three Negro Classics. Incl. Up from Slavery. Washington, Booker T; The Souls of Black Folk. Du Bois, William E; The Autobiography of an Ex-Colored Man. Johnson, James W. 1965. pap. 3.50 (ISBN 0-380-01581-1, 51409, Discus). Avon.

Frazier, E. Franklin. Black Bourgeoisie. 1965. pap. text ed. 6.95 (ISBN 0-02-910580-3). Free Pr.

--Black Bourgeoisie: The Rise of a New Middle Class in the United States. (Orig.). 1962. pap. 1.95 (ISBN 0-02-095600-2, Collier). Macmillan.

--E. Franklin Frazier on Race Relations. Edwards, G. Franklin, ed. LC 68-8586. (Heritage of Sociology Ser.). 1968. 15.00x (ISBN 0-226-18743-8). U of Chicago Pr.

--E. Franklin Frazier on Race Relations. Edwards, G. Franklin, ed. LC 68-8586. (Heritage of Sociology Ser). (Orig.). 1968. pap. 3.95 (ISBN 0-226-18744-6, P324, Phoen). U of Chicago Pr.

Free People of Color: On the Condition of the Free People of Color in the United States(Present Condition of the Free Colored People in the United States. LC 75-92232. (American Negro: His History & Literature, Ser. No. 3). 1970. Repr. of 1853 ed. 7.50 (ISBN 0-405-01928-9). Arno.

Frobenius, Leo & Fox, Douglas C. African Genesis. LC 66-29780. (Illus.). 1937. 15.00 (ISBN 0-405-08539-7, Blom Pubns). Arno.

Gaines, Wesley J. Negro & the White Man. LC 75-88430. Repr. of 1897 ed. 12.25x (ISBN 0-8371-1889-1, Pub. by Negro U Pr). Greenwood.

Gallagher, Buell G. American Caste & the Negro College. LC 66-29471. 1966. Repr. of 1938 ed. 10.00 (ISBN 0-87752-041-0). Gordian.

Garrett, Romeo B. Famous First Facts About Negroes. LC 75-172613. 224p. 1972. 10.00 (ISBN 0-405-01987-4). Arno.

Garvey, Marcus. Philosophy & Opinions of Marcus Garvey. Jacques-Garvey, Amy, ed. LC 69-15523. (Studies in American Negro Life Ser). 1969. pap. text ed. 7.95x (ISBN 0-689-70079-2, NL14). Atheneum.

Gerlach, Luther P. & Hine, Virginia H. People, Power, Change: Movements of Social Transformation. LC 70-109434. 1970. pap. 6.50 (ISBN 0-672-60613-5). Bobbs.

Gibson, J. W. & Crogman, W. H. Progress of a Race: Or, Remarkable Advancement of the American Negro. facs. ed. LC 79-81118. (Black Heritage Library Collection Ser). 1902. 28.25 (ISBN 0-8369-8578-8). Arno.

Gilligan, Francis J. Morality of the Color Line. LC 71-94478. Repr. of 1928 ed. 12.25x (ISBN 0-8371-2353-4, Pub. by Negro U Pr). Greenwood.

Graham, Stephen. Children of the Slaves. (Basic Afro-American Reprint Library Ser). 1970. Repr. of 1920 ed. 14.50 (ISBN 0-384-19620-9). Johnson Repr.

--Soul of John Brown. LC 70-109915. Repr. of 1920 ed. 25.00 (ISBN 0-404-00162-9). AMS Pr.

Hall, Charles E. Negroes in the United States, 1920-1932. LC 69-18629. (American Negro: His History & Literature Ser., No. 2). 1969. Repr. of 1935 ed. 29.00 (ISBN 0-405-01866-5). Arno.

Harris, Joel C. Mingo & Other Sketches in Black & White. facs. ed. LC 70-83911. (Black Heritage Library Collection Ser). 1884. 14.50 (ISBN 0-8369-8696-2). Arno.

Herskovits, Melville J. Anthropometry of the American Negro. LC 73-121370. (Studies in Black History & Culture, No. 54). 1970. Repr of 1930 ed. lib. bdg. 52.95 (ISBN 0-8383-1116-4). Haskell.

--Anthropometry of the American Negro. LC 76-82369. (Columbia University. Contributions to Anthropology: No. 11). Repr. of 1930 ed. 21.00 (ISBN 0-404-50561-9). AMS Pr.

Hesslink, G. K. Black Neighbors: Negroes in a Northern Rural Community. 2nd ed. LC 73-8915. 345p. 1974. 8.95 (ISBN 0-672-51522-9). Bobbs.

Hoffman, Frederick L. Race Traits & Tendencies of the American Negro. LC 70-169474. Repr. of 1896 ed. 24.50 (ISBN 0-404-00065-7). AMS Pr.

Horton, David, ed. Freedom & Equality: Addresses by Harry S. Truman. LC 60-12645. 1960. 8.00x (ISBN 0-8262-0003-6). U of Mo Pr.

Hough, Joseph C., Jr. Black Power & White Protestants: A Christian Response to the New Negro Pluralism. 1968. 11.95 (ISBN 0-19-501178-3). Oxford U Pr.

--Black Power & White Protestants: A Christian Response to the New Negro Pluralism. (Orig.). (YA) (gr. 9-12). 1968. pap. 4.95 (ISBN 0-19-500765-4, GB). Oxford U Pr.

Imbert, Dennis. The Colored Gentleman: A Product of Modern Civilization. LC 73-18581. Repr. of 1931 ed. 14.00 (ISBN 0-404-11392-3). AMS Pr.

Inquiry into the Condition & Prospects of the African Race in the United States. facs. ed. LC 70-154079. (Black Heritage Library Collection Ser). 1839. 15.00 (ISBN 0-8369-8790-X). Arno.

Jervey, Theodore D. Slave Trade: Slavery & Color. LC 73-84688. Repr. of 1925 ed. 14.25x (ISBN 0-8371-1649-X). Greenwood.

Johnson, Charles S. Negro in American Civilization: A Study of Negro Life & Race Relations in the Light of Social Research. LC 30-15942. (Basic Afro-American Reprint Library Ser). 1970. Repr. of 1930 ed. 23.50 (ISBN 0-384-27650-4). Johnson Repr.

Johnson, Charles S., ed. Ebony & Topaz. facsimile ed. LC 70-161264. (Black Heritage Library Collection). Repr. of 1927 ed. 21.50 (ISBN 0-8369-8823-X). Arno.

Johnson, Edward A. Light Ahead for the Negro. LC 74-170817. Repr. of 1904 ed. 14.75 (ISBN 0-404-00074-6). AMS Pr.

Johnson, James W. Autobiography of an Ex-Coloured Man. 1933. 8.95 (ISBN 0-394-41582-5). Knopf.
--Negro Americans, What Now. LC 72-155618. Repr. of 1938 ed. 12.00 (ISBN 0-404-00075-4). AMS Pr.
Jones, James M. Struggle for Survival. 192p. (Orig.). 1972. pap. 1.50 (ISBN 0-87067-428-5, BH428). Holloway.
Keil, Charles. Urban Blues. LC 66-13876. (Illus.). 1966. 10.00x (ISBN 0-226-42959-8). U of Chicago Pr.
--Urban Blues. LC 66-13876. (Illus.). 1968. pap. 2.45 (ISBN 0-226-42960-1, P291, Phoen). U of Chicago Pr.
Kerlin, Robert T. Voice of the Negro, 1919. LC 68-54163. (American Negro: His History & Literature Ser., No. 1). 1968. Repr. of 1920 ed. 9.00 (ISBN 0-405-01825-8). Arno.
Kletzing, Henry F. & Crogman, William H. Progress of a Race: Or the Remarkable Advancement of the Afro-American from the Bondage of Slavery, Ignorance & Poverty to the Freedom of Citizenship, Intelligence Affluence, Honor & Trust. LC 70-76489. (Illus.). Repr. of 1897 ed. 28.00x (ISBN 0-8371-1382-2). Greenwood.
Lawson, Jesse. How to Solve the Race Problem: The Proceedings of the Washington Conference on the Race Problem in the United States. LC 75-99388. 1969. Repr. of 1904 ed. lib. bdg. 12.50 (ISBN 0-8411-0059-4). Metro Bks.
Lewis, Edward E. The Mobility of the Negro. LC 68-58603. (Columbia University. Studies in the Social Sciences: No. 342). Repr. of 1931 ed. 12.50 (ISBN 0-404-51342-5). AMS Pr.
Litwack, Leon F. North of Slavery: The Negro in the Free States, 1790-1860. LC 61-10869. 1961. 14.00x (ISBN 0-226-48585-4). U of Chicago Pr.
--North of Slavery: The Negro in the Free States, 1790-1860. LC 61-10869. 1965. pap. 4.95 (ISBN 0-226-48586-2, P179, Phoen). U of Chicago Pr.
Livermore, George. Historical Research Respecting the Opinion of Founders of the Republic on Negroes As Slaves, Citizens & As Soldiers. 4th ed. LC 68-57124. (Research & Source Works Ser.: No. 131). 1969. Repr. of 1863 ed. 16.50 (ISBN 0-8337-2125-9). B Franklin.
--Historical Research Respecting the Opinion of the Founders of the Republic on Negroes As Slaves, As Citizens & As Soldiers. LC 68-18599. Repr. of 1863 ed. 7.50x (ISBN 0-678-00547-8). Kelley.
--Historical Research Respecting the Opinions of the Founders of the Republic on Negroes As Slaves, As Citizens, & As Soldiers. LC 69-18541. (American Negro: His History & Literature Ser., No. 2). 1969. Repr. of 1863 ed. 8.00 (ISBN 0-405-01878-9). Arno.
Locke, A., ed. The New Negro: An Interpretation. 59.95 (ISBN 0-8490-0723-2). Gordon Pr.
Locke, Alain, ed. The New Negro. LC 68-55749. (Studies in American Negro Life). (Illus.). 1968. pap. text ed. 5.95x (ISBN 0-689-70128-4, NL10). Atheneum.
--New Negro: An Interpretation. LC 68-29008. (American Negro: His History & Literature Ser., No. 1). 1968. Repr. of 1925 ed. 13.00 (ISBN 0-405-01826-6). Arno.
Locke, Alain L., ed. The New Negro: An Interpretation. 1968. Repr. of 1925 ed. 14.00 (ISBN 0-384-33280-3). Johnson Repr.
Loescher, Frank S. The Protestant Church & the Negro, a Pattern of Segregation. LC 76-135601. 159p. 1972. Repr. of 1948 ed. text ed. 11.75x (ISBN 0-8371-5193-7). Greenwood.
Logan, Rayford W., ed. & intro. by. What the Negro Wants. LC 77-76847. 1969. Repr. 12.00x (ISBN 0-87586-013-3). Agathon.
McKinley, Carlyle. Appeal to Pharoah: The Negro Problem, & Its Radical Solution. LC 79-107477. Repr. of 1907 ed. 12.25x (ISBN 0-8371-3756-X, Pub. by Negro U Pr). Greenwood.
Merriam, George S. Negro & the Nation. LC 75-95441. (Studies in Black History & Culture, No. 54). 1970. Repr. of 1906 ed. lib. bdg. 52.95 (ISBN 0-8383-0994-1). Haskell.
--Negro & the Nation: A History of American Slavery & Enfranchisement. LC 70-77207. Repr. of 1906 ed. 15.50x (ISBN 0-8371-1311-3, Pub. by Negro U Pr). Greenwood.
Mezu. Leopold Sedar Senghor et la defense et illustration de la civilisation noire. 19.50 (ISBN 0-685-36567-0). French & Eur.
Miller, Kelly. Appeal to Conscience: America's Code of Caste a Disgrace to Democracy. LC 69-18553. (American Negro: His History & Literature, Ser. No. 2). 1969. Repr. of 1918 ed. 8.75 (ISBN 0-405-01881-9). Arno.
--Out of the House of Bondage. LC 69-18554. (American Negro: His History & Literature Ser., No. 2). 1969. Repr. of 1914 ed. 7.50 (ISBN 0-405-01882-7). Arno.
--Race Adjustment. Incl. Essays on the Negro in America; Everlasting Stain. LC 68-29012. (American Negro-His History & Literatur Ser., No. 1). 688p. 1968. Repr. of 1924 ed. 24.00 (ISBN 0-405-01831-2). Arno.
--Race Adjustment: Essays on the Negro in America. facs. ed. LC 77-89389. (Black Heritage Library Collection Ser). 1908. 20.50 (ISBN 0-8369-8634-2). Arno.
--Race Adjustment: Essays on the Negro in America. pap. 2.95 (ISBN 0-685-16796-8, N210P). Mnemosyne.
Mohonk Conference on the Negro Question. First & Second. 1890-1891. Repr. 14.00x (ISBN 0-8371-2001-2, Pub. by Negro U Pr). Greenwood.
Moon, Bucklin. High Cost of Prejudice. LC 70-111584. Repr. of 1947 ed. 10.50x (ISBN 0-8371-4608-9, Pub. by Negro U Pr). Greenwood.
Morel, Edmund D. The Black Man's Burden. LC 75-99396. 241p. 1972. Repr. of 1920 ed. lib. bdg. 11.00 (ISBN 0-8411-0067-5). Metro Bks.
Muse, Benjamin. American Negro Revolution. 1970. pap. 2.95 (ISBN 0-8065-0003-4). Citadel Pr.
Myrdal, Gunnar. American Dilemma. 20th anniv. ed. LC 62-19706. 1962. 25.00x (ISBN 0-06-034590-X, HarpT). Har-Row.
--An American Dilemma, Vols. 1 & 2. LC 74-18494. 1975. pap. 5.95 ea.; Vol. 1. pap. (ISBN 0-394-73042-9); Vol. 2. pap. (ISBN 0-394-73043-7). Pantheon.
National Interracial Conference. Toward Interracial Cooperation. LC 73-97408. Repr. of 1926 ed. 10.50x (ISBN 0-8371-2658-4). Greenwood.
National Negro Conference - 1909. Proceedings. LC 69-18544. (American Negro: His History & Literature Ser., No. 2). 1969. Repr. of 1909 ed. 8.50 (ISBN 0-405-01890-8). Arno.
Nearing, Scott. Black America. LC 29-26477. (Basic Afro-American Reprint Library Ser). 1970. Repr. of 1929 ed. 12.50 (ISBN 0-384-41035-9). Johnson Repr.
Nell, William C. Colored Patriots of the American Revolution. LC 68-29013. (American Negro: His History & Literature, Ser. No. 1). 1968. Repr. of 1855 ed. 16.00 (ISBN 0-405-01832-0). Arno.
Nelson, John H. Negro Character in American Literature. LC 73-128982. Repr. of 1926 ed. 11.50 (ISBN 0-404-00203-X). AMS Pr.
Odum, Howard W. Race & Rumors of Race: Challenge to American Crisis. LC 77-97433. Repr. of 1943 ed. 13.75x (ISBN 0-8371-2715-7). Greenwood.
Olivier, Sydney H. White Capital & Coloured Labour. LC 74-132079. Repr. of 1910 ed. 10.75x (ISBN 0-8371-4681-X). Greenwood.
Oppenheimer, Martin. Urban Guerrilla. (Orig.). 1972. 5.50 (ISBN 0-8129-0105-3, QP 219); pap. 2.95 (ISBN 0-8129-6112-9). Times Bks.
Owen, R. D. Wrong of Slavery, the Right of Emancipation & the Future of the African Race in the United States. LC 12-4240. 1864. 12.00 (ISBN 0-527-68870-3). Kraus Repr.
Owens, Don B., Jr. Dark Valor. 4.98 (ISBN 0-911734-02-3). Black Hope Found.
--The Most Controversial American. 4.98 (ISBN 0-685-72448-4). Black Hope Found.
--Most Controversial American & Why the Negro Lacks Unity. LC 63-14707. 1963. pap. 3.98 (ISBN 0-911734-25-2). Commonsense.
Page, Thomas N. The Negro: The Southerner's Problem. LC 4-34917. (American Studies). 1970. Repr. of 1904 ed. 15.50 (ISBN 0-384-44490-3). Johnson Repr.
Park, Robert E. Race & Culture. 1964. pap. text ed. 5.95 (ISBN 0-02-923790-4). Free Pr.
Parks, Gordon. Born Black. LC 78-146692. (Illus.). 1971. 10.00 (ISBN 0-397-00690-X). Har-Row.
Patterson, Raymond. The Negro & His Needs. facsimile ed. LC 74-178480. (Black Heritage Library Collection). Repr. of 1911 ed. 14.50 (ISBN 0-8369-8929-5). Arno.
Pennington, James. Textbook of the Origin & History of the Colored People. LC 77-92437. 1841. 17.00 (ISBN 0-403-00169-2). Scholarly.
Pickens, William. New Negro, His Political, Civil & Mental Status & Related Essays. LC 71-89051. Repr. of 1916 ed. 11.00x (ISBN 0-8371-1937-5, Pub. by Negro U Pr). Greenwood.
Pickett, William P. Negro Problem: Abraham Lincoln's Solution. LC 76-92757. Repr. of 1909 ed. 24.75x (ISBN 0-8371-2200-7, Pub. by Negro U Pr). Greenwood.
Pipkin, J. J. The Story of a Rising Race. facsimile ed. LC 70-173609. (Black Heritage Library Collection). Repr. of 1902 ed. 36.00 (ISBN 0-8369-8901-5). Arno.
Pollard, Edward A. Lost Cause Regained. facs. ed. LC 78-117889. (Select Bibliographies Reprint Ser). 1868. 16.00 (ISBN 0-8369-5342-8). Arno.
Porter, Dorothy, et al, eds. Negro Protest Pamphlets: A Compendium. LC 79-75853. (American Negro: His History & Literature Ser., No. 2). 1969. Repr. of 1837 ed. 9.00 (ISBN 0-405-01888-6). Arno.
Possibilities of the Negro in Symposium. LC 75-89052. Repr. of 1904 ed. 8.50x (ISBN 0-8371-1948-0). Greenwood.
The Possibilities of the Negro in Symposium. facsimile ed. LC 75-173610. (Black Heritage Library Collection). Repr. of 1904 ed. 14.00 (ISBN 0-8369-8902-3). Arno.
Pullen-Burry, Bessie. Ethiopia in Exile: Jamaica Revisited. facs. ed. LC 76-157376. (Black Heritage Library Collection Ser). 1905. 16.75 (ISBN 0-8369-8814-0). Arno.
Rainwater, Lee & Yancey, William L. Moynihan Report & the Politics of Controversy. (Illus.). 1967. pap. 9.95x (ISBN 0-262-68009-2). MIT Pr.
Record, Wilson. Race & Radicalism: The NAACP & the Communist Party in Conflict. 237p. 1966. pap. 3.95 (ISBN 0-8014-9035-9, CP35). Cornell U Pr.
Reid, Ira D. In a Minor Key: Negro Youth in Story & Fact. LC 73-160450. (Illus.). 134p. Repr. of 1940 ed. lib. bdg. 14.75x (ISBN 0-8371-3346-7, RENY). Greenwood.
--Negro Immigrant: His Background, Characteristics & Social Adjustment, 1899-1937. LC 68-58615. (Columbia University. Studies in the Social Sciences: No. 449). Repr. of 1939 ed. write for info. (ISBN 0-404-51449-9). AMS Pr.
--Negro Immigrant: His Background, Characteristics and Social Adjustment, 1899-1937. LC 69-18771. (American Immigration Collection, Ser., No. 1). 1969. Repr. of 1939 ed. 12.00 (ISBN 0-405-00537-7). Arno.
Reimers, D. M., ed. Racism in the United States: An American Dilemma? 121p. 1972. pap. text ed. 5.50 (ISBN 0-03-080091-9, Pub. by HR&W). Krieger.
Reuter, Edward B. Race Mixtures: Studies in Intermarriage & Miscegenation. LC 71-94486. Repr. of 1931 ed. 100.75x (ISBN 0-8371-2375-5). Greenwood.
Richings, G. F. Evidences of Progress Among Colored People. LC 73-99402. 1969. Repr. of 1900 ed. lib. bdg. 19.50 (ISBN 0-8411-0073-X). Metro Bks.
Riley, Benjamin F. White Man's Burden. LC 76-89055. Repr. of 1910 ed. 12.75x (ISBN 0-8371-1945-6). Greenwood.
Robert, Charles E. Negro Civilization in the South. facsimile ed. LC 70-173614. (Black Heritage Library Collection). Repr. of 1880 ed. 14.25 (ISBN 0-8369-8906-6). Arno.
Roman, Charles V. American Civilization & the Negro. facsimile ed. LC 74-37316. (Black Heritage Library Collection). Repr. of 1916 ed. 32.00 (ISBN 0-8369-8953-8). Arno.
--American Civilization & the Negro: The Afro-American in Relation to National Progress. LC 75-187910. (Illus.). xii, 434p. 1972. Repr. of 1916 ed. 18.50 (ISBN 0-8411-0100-0). Metro Bks.
Rose, Arnold. Negro in America: The Condensed Version of Gunnar Myrdal's an American Dilemma. 7.50 (ISBN 0-8446-2828-X). Peter Smith.
Rose, Harold M. & McConnell, Harold, eds. Geography of the Ghetto: Perceptions, Problems, & Alternatives. LC 72-1388. (Perspectives in Geography Ser., Vol. 2). (Illus.). 273p. 1972. 17.50x (ISBN 0-87580-031-9). N Ill U Pr.
Rose, Peter I., et al, eds. Through Different Eyes: Black & White Perspectives on American Race Relations. 1974. pap. 5.95 (ISBN 0-19-501594-0, 385, GB). Oxford U Pr.
Roucek, Joseph S. & Kiernan, Thomas. Negro Impact on Western Civilization. LC 72-86509. 1970. 15.00 (ISBN 0-8022-2329-X). Philos Lib.
Rudwick, Elliot. W. E. B. Du Bois: Propagandist of the Negro Protest. LC 68-16418. (Studies in American Negro Life). 1968. pap. text ed. 6.95x (ISBN 0-689-70169-1, NL6). Atheneum.
Schoolcraft, Mary H. Plantation Life: The Narratives of Mrs. Henry Rowe Schoolcraft. LC 68-55926. 1852-1860. Repr. 23.75x (ISBN 0-8371-2084-5). Greenwood.
Scott, Emmett J. Negro Migration During the War. LC 69-18555. (American Negro: His History & Literature Ser., No 2). 1969. Repr. of 1920 ed. 9.50 (ISBN 0-405-01891-6). Arno.
Shannon, Alexander H. Racial Integrity & Other Features of the Negro Problem. facsimile ed. LC 70-38024. (Black Heritage Library Collection). Repr. of 1907 ed. 17.25 (ISBN 0-8369-8990-2). Arno.
Silberman, Charles. Crisis in Black & White. 1964. pap. 1.95 (ISBN 0-394-70279-4, Vin). Random.
Silberman, Charles E. Crisis in Black & White. 1964. 12.95 (ISBN 0-394-42075-6). Random.
Skinner, Thomas. Black & Free. (Illus.). 1970. pap. 2.75 (ISBN 0-310-32812-8). Zondervan.
Smith, Fred T. Experiment in Modifying Attitudes Toward the Negro. LC 76-177777. (Columbia University. Teachers College. Contributions to Education: No. 887). Repr. of 1943 ed. 17.50 (ISBN 0-404-55887-9). AMS Pr.
Smith, William B. Color Line: A Brief in Behalf of the Unborn. LC 75-78775. Repr. of 1905 ed. 12.00x (ISBN 0-8371-1396-2, Pub. by Negro U Pr). Greenwood.
Spencer, Samuel R., Jr. Booker T. Washington & the Negro's Place in American Life. (The Library of American Biography). 212p. 1965. pap. 4.95 (ISBN 0-316-80621-8). Little.
Steward, T. G. Colored Regulars in the United States Army. LC 69-18558. (American Negro: His History & Literature, Ser. No. 2). 1969. Repr. of 1904 ed. 12.00 (ISBN 0-405-01896-7). Arno.
Stone, Alfred H. Studies in the American Race Problem. LC 79-92763. Repr. of 1908 ed. 24.00x (ISBN 0-8371-2185-X, Pub. by Negro U Pr). Greenwood.
Sweeney, W. Allison. History of the American Negro in the Great World War. LC 19-10990. (Basic Afro-American Reprint Library). Repr. of 1919 ed. 18.50 (ISBN 0-384-59080-2). Johnson Repr.
Thomas, William H. American Negro: What He Was, What He Is, & What He May Become. LC 79-78776. Repr. of 1901 ed. 20.00x (ISBN 0-8371-1397-0, Pub. by Negro U Pr). Greenwood.
Thompson, Edgar T., ed. Race Relations & the Race Problem, a Definition & an Analysis. LC 68-29750. (Illus.). 1968. Repr. of 1939 ed. lib. bdg. 16.75x (ISBN 0-8371-0249-9, THR&). Greenwood.
U. S. Bureau Of The Census, ed. Negro Population, Seventeen Ninety-Nineteen Fifteen. LC 18-26864. Repr. of 1918 ed. 45.00 (ISBN 0-527-91820-2). Kraus Repr.
U. S. Bureau Of The Census. Negroes in the United States. LC 74-106827. Repr. of 1904 ed. 26.00x (ISBN 0-8371-3410-2, Pub. by Negro U Pr). Greenwood.
U. S. Bureau Of The Census, ed. Negroes in the United States, Nineteen Twenty to Nineteen Thirty Two. large quarto ed. LC 35-26735. Repr. of 1935 ed. 45.00 (ISBN 0-527-91800-8). Kraus Repr.
U. S. Department Of Labor - Division Of Negro Economics. Negro Migration in 1916-1917 - Reports. LC 78-78580. Repr. of 1919 ed. 9.75x (ISBN 0-8371-1417-9, Pub. by Negro U Pr). Greenwood.
Van Evrie, John H. Negroes & Negro Slavery: The First an Inferior Race, the Latter Its Normal Condition. facs. ed. LC 73-83881. (Black Heritage Library Collection Ser). 1863. 14.75 (ISBN 0-8369-8674-1). Arno.
--White Supremacy & Negro Subordination: Or, Negroes, a Subordinate Race & So-Called Slavery Its Normal Condition. LC 78-88455. Repr. of 1868 ed. 18.50x (ISBN 0-8371-1904-9). Greenwood.
Vincent, Theodore G., ed. Voices of a Black Nation: Political Journalism in the Harlem Renaissance. LC 72-85094. 1973. 10.00 (ISBN 0-87867-034-3); pap. 4.95 (ISBN 0-87867-035-1). Ramparts.
Walker, Anne K. Tuskegee & the Black Belt. 1945. 3.00 (ISBN 0-685-09016-7). Dietz.
Washington, Booker T. Black-Belt Diamonds. LC 78-88420. Repr. of 1898 ed. 10.00x (ISBN 0-8371-1838-7, Pub. by Negro U Pr). Greenwood.
--Future of the American Negro. LC 79-99417. 1969. Repr. of 1899 ed. lib. bdg. 11.00 (ISBN 0-8411-0091-8). Metro Bks.
--Future of the American Negro. Repr. of 1899 ed. lib. bdg. 15.00 (ISBN 0-8371-0905-1, WAA). Greenwood.
--My Larger Education. pap. 3.50 (ISBN 0-685-16791-7, N285P). Mnemosyne.
Washington, Booker T., et al. Negro Problem. 1970. Repr. of 1903 ed. 11.50 (ISBN 0-404-00238-2). AMS Pr.
--Negro Problem: A Series of Articles by Representative American Negroes of Today. LC 69-18560. (American Negro: His History & Literature Ser., No. 2). 1969. Repr. of 1903 ed. 9.50 (ISBN 0-405-01903-3). Arno.
--New Negro for a New Century. LC 74-172759. Repr. of 1900 ed. 10.00 (ISBN 0-404-00197-1). AMS Pr.
Wattenberg, William W., ed. All Men Are Created Equal. LC 66-10937. (Leo M. Franklin Memorial Lectures in Human Relations Ser: Vol. 14). 1966. 5.95x (ISBN 0-8143-1278-0). Wayne St U Pr.
White, Walter F. Man Called White. LC 69-18561. (American Negro: His History & Literature Ser., No. 2). 1969. Repr. of 1948 ed. 17.00 (ISBN 0-405-01906-8). Arno.
--Rope & Faggot: Biography of Judge Lynch. LC 69-18545. (American Negro: His History & Literature Ser. No. 2). 1969. Repr. of 1929 ed. 12.00 (ISBN 0-405-01907-6). Arno.

Whitman, Albery A. Not a Man, & Yet a Man. facs. ed. LC 79-83896. (Black Heritage Library Collection Ser). 1877. 12.50 (ISBN 0-8369-8688-1). Arno.
Williams, Chancellor. The Destruction of Black Civilization. 1974. 10.00 (ISBN 0-88378-030-5); pap. 6.95 (ISBN 0-88378-077-1). Third World.
Wood, Forrest G. Black Scare: The Racist Response to Emancipation & Reconstruction. 1968. 24.50x (ISBN 0-520-01361-1); pap. 2.45 (ISBN 0-520-01664-5, CAL190). U of Cal Pr.
Wood, Norman B. White Side of a Black Subject. rev. ed. LC 70-78589. (Illus.). Repr. of 1896 ed. 20.00x (ISBN 0-8371-1421-7). Greenwood.
Wood, Peter H. Black Majority. 1974. 12.95 (ISBN 0-394-48396-0). Knopf.
Woodson, Carter G. African Background Outlined: Or, Handbook for the Study of the Negro. LC 68-55922. (Illus.). Repr. of 1936 ed. 16.50x (ISBN 0-8371-0760-1, Pub. by Negro U Pr). Greenwood.
--Century of Negro Migration. LC 70-108768. Repr. of 1918 ed. 8.00 (ISBN 0-404-00241-2). AMS Pr.
--Century of Negro Migration. LC 69-16770. (Illus.). 1969. Repr. of 1918 ed. 9.00 (ISBN 0-8462-1319-2). Russell.
Woofter, Thomas J. Basis of Racial Adjustment. facsimile ed. (Select Bibliographies Reprint Ser). 1925. 20.00 (ISBN 0-8369-5105-0). Arno.
--Negro Migration: Changes in Rural Organization & Population of the Cotton Belt. LC 70-144705. Repr. of 1920 ed. 7.50 (ISBN 0-404-00243-9). AMS Pr.
--Negro Migration, Changes in Rural Organization & Population of the Cotton Belt. LC 76-89063. Repr. of 1920 ed. 10.00x (ISBN 0-8371-1943-X, Pub. by Negro U Pr). Greenwood.
World Encyclopedia of Black Peoples, Vol. 1-3. 1975. lib. bdg. 59.00 (ISBN 0-403-01796-3). Scholarly.

NEGROES–BIBLIOGRAPHY

This heading discontinued January 1976. See Afro-Americans and Blacks for later materials.

Atlanta University. Atlanta University Publications. LC 68-28985. (The American Negro: History & Literature, Ser. No. 3). 1970. Repr. of 1898 ed. No. 3. 5. 6. 7. 10. 12. 19. 20. 37.00 (ISBN 0-405-01914-9). Arno.
The Chicago Afro-American Union Analytic Catalog: An Index to Materials on the Afro American in the Principal Libraries of Chicago, 5 vols. 1972. lib. bdg. 475.00 (ISBN 0-8161-0978-8). G K Hall.
Du Bois, W. E. B., ed. A Select Bibliography of the Negro American. (Atlanta Univ. Publ. Ser.: No. 10). (Orig.). 1905. Repr. pap. 4.00 (ISBN 0-527-03112-7). Kraus Repr.
Ferris, William R., Jr. Mississippi Black Folklore: A Research Bibliography & Discography. LC 70-158331. 61p. 1971. pap. 2.50x (ISBN 0-87805-001-9). U Pr of Miss.
Fisk University Library (Nashville) Dictionary Catalog of the Negro Collection of the Fisk University Library, 6 vols. (Library Catalogs Ser.). 1974. Set. lib. bdg. 490.00 (ISBN 0-8161-1055-7). G K Hall.
Hallie Q. Brown Memorial Library. Index to Periodical Articles by & About Negroes, Annuals, 1960-1969. 1971. lib. bdg. 15.00 ea. G K Hall.
--Index to Periodical Articles by & About Negroes, Decennial Cumulation, 1950-1959. 1962. 45.00 (ISBN 0-8161-0503-0). G K Hall.
--Index to Periodicals Articles by & About Negroes, Annual, 1971. lib. bdg. 42.00 (ISBN 0-8161-0869-2). G K Hall.
Howard University Libraries, Washington, D.C, Dictionary Catalog of the Jesse E. Moorland Collection of Negro Life & History, 9 vols. 1970. Set. lib. bdg. 725.00 (ISBN 0-8161-0871-4). G K Hall.
Matthews, Geraldine O., et al, eds. Black American Writers: 1773-1949, a Bibliography & Union List. (Series Seventy). xv, 230p. 1975. lib. bdg. 16.95 (ISBN 0-8161-1164-2). G K Hall.
Miller, Elizabeth W. & Fisher, Mary, eds. Negro in America: A Bibliography. rev. ed. LC 71-120319. (gr. 10-12). 1970. 17.50x (ISBN 0-674-60703-1); pap. 5.95x (ISBN 0-674-60702-3). Harvard U Pr.
Ross, Frank A. Bibliography of Negro Migration. LC 78-80745. (Bibliography & Reference Ser.: No. 370). 1969. Repr. of 1934 ed. 21.00 (ISBN 0-8337-3057-6). B Franklin.
Thompson, E. T. & Thompson, Alma M., eds. Race & Region. Repr. of 1949 ed. 14.00 (ISBN 0-527-89750-7). Kraus Repr.
Universite Federale de Cameroun, ed. Bibliographic Guide to the Negro World, Vol. 1, 2 Pts. 229p. (Orig.). 1971. pap. 55.00x (ISBN 0-8002-1232-0). Intl Pubns Serv.
Welsch, Erwin K. The Negro in the United States: A Research Guide. LC 65-23085. 160p. (Orig.). 1965. pap. 2.25x (ISBN 0-253-34001-2). Ind U Pr.

NEGROES–BIOGRAPHY

This heading discontinued January 1976. See Afro-Americans and Blacks for later materials.

Alexander, Rae P., ed. Young & Black in America. LC 70-117005. (Illus.). (gr. 6 up). 1970. 3.95 (ISBN 0-394-80482-1, BYR); PLB 4.99 (ISBN 0-394-90482-6). Random.
Allen, Harold C. Great Black Americans. new ed. (Illus.). 126p. (Orig.). 1971. pap. 0.75 (ISBN 0-88301-107-7). Pendulum Pr.
Allen, James E. The Negro in New York. 1964. 5.00 (ISBN 0-682-42082-4). Exposition.
Baird, William. General Wauchope. LC 72-4077. (Black Heritage Library Collection Ser.). Repr. of 1901 ed. 17.00 (ISBN 0-8369-9094-3). Arno.
Bontemps, Arna. One Hundred Years of Negro Freedom. LC 61-11716. (Illus.). (gr. 9 up). 1961. pap. 2.95 (ISBN 0-396-05520-6). Dodd.
--We Have Tomorrow. (gr. 9 up). 1945. 6.95 (ISBN 0-395-06646-8). HM.
Borcherds, Petrus B. Autobiographical Memoir of Petrus Borchardus Borcherds. LC 72-5526. (Black Heritage Library Collection). 1972. Repr. of 1861 ed. 26.25 (ISBN 0-8369-9135-4). Arno.
Boston City Council. Memorial of Crispus Attucks, Samuel Maverick, James Caldwell, Samuel Gray & Patrick Carr, from the City of Boston. facs. ed. LC 71-79022. (Black Heritage Library Collection Ser). 1889. 8.75 (ISBN 0-8369-8515-X). Arno.
Botkin, Benjamin A., ed. Lay My Burden Down: A Folk History of Slavery. LC 45-5576. (Illus.). 1958. pap. 2.95 (ISBN 0-226-06723-8, P24, Phoen). U of Chicago Pr.
Brawley, Benjamin. Negro Builders & Heroes. 1937. 12.50 (ISBN 0-8078-0241-7). U of NC Pr.
Brignano, Russell C. Black Americans in Autobiography: An Annotated Bibliography of Autobiographies & Autobiographical Books Written Since the Civil War. LC 73-92535. 1974. 9.75 (ISBN 0-8223-0317-5). Duke.
Brown, W. W. Black Man, His Antecedents, His Genius and His Achievements. 1865. 14.00 (ISBN 0-527-12100-2). Kraus Repr.
Brown, William W. Black Man, His Antecedents, His Genius, & His Achievements. LC 77-82179. (Anti-Slavery Crusade in America Ser). 1969. Repr. of 1863 ed. 14.00 (ISBN 0-405-00618-7). Arno.
--The Black Man: His Antecedents, His Genius & His Achievements. 2nd ed. (Basic Afro-American Reprint Library Ser). 1969. Repr. of 1863 ed. 13.00 (ISBN 0-384-05975-9). Johnson Repr.
--Black Man, His Antecedents, His Genius, & His Achievements. pap. 2.95 (ISBN 0-685-16779-8, N189P). Mnemosyne.
--Rising Son, Or, the Antecedents & Advancement of the Colored Race. LC 75-100258. Repr. of 1874 ed. 18.25x (ISBN 0-8371-2856-0). Greenwood.
--The Rising Sun or the Antecedents & Advancement of the Colored Race. (Basic Afro-American Reprint Library). 1970. Repr. of 1874 ed. lib. bdg. 25.50 (ISBN 0-384-05995-3). Johnson Repr.
Bryant, Lawrence C. Negro Lawmakers in the South Carolina Legislature, 1868-1902. 1968. pap. 10.00 (ISBN 0-686-05563-2). L C Bryant.
--Negro Legislators in South Carolina, 1865-1894. 1966. 15.00 (ISBN 0-686-05568-3); pap. 10.00 (ISBN 0-686-05569-1). L C Bryant.
--Negro Legislators in South Carolina, 1868-1902. 1967. 15.00 (ISBN 0-686-05564-0); pap. 10.00 (ISBN 0-686-05565-9). L C Bryant.
--Negro Senators & Representatives in the South Carolina Legislature. 1968. 15.00 (ISBN 0-686-05566-7); pap. 10.00 (ISBN 0-686-05567-5). L C Bryant.
--South Carolina Negro Legislators: A Glorious Success. 1974. 15.00 (ISBN 0-686-05553-5); pap. 10.00 (ISBN 0-686-05554-3). L C Bryant.
Bullock, Ralph W. In Spite of Handicaps: Brief Biographical Sketches with Discussion Outlines of Outstanding Negroes Now Living Who Are Achieving Distinction in Various Lines of Endeavor. facs. ed. LC 68-25602. (Essay Index Reprint Ser). 1927. 16.00 (ISBN 0-8369-0264-5). Arno.
Child, Lydia M. Freedmen's Book. LC 68-28989. (American Negro: His History & Literature Ser., No. 1). (Illus.). 1968. Repr. of 1865 ed. 13.00 (ISBN 0-405-01809-6). Arno.
Christopher, Maurine. America's Black Congressman. LC 76-8943. (Apollo Eds.). (Illus.). 288p. 1975. pap. 3.95 (ISBN 0-8152-0376-4, A-376). T Y Crowell.
Cohen, Robert C. Black Crusader: A Biography of Robert Franklin Williams. 1972. 10.00 (ISBN 0-8184-0015-3). Lyle Stuart.
Cromwell, John W. The Negro in American History: Men & Women Eminent in the Evolution of the American of African Descent. (Basic Afro-American Reprint Library). 1969. Repr. of 1914 ed. 13.00 (ISBN 0-384-10215-8). Johnson Repr.
David, Jay & Crane, Elaine. Living Black in White America. LC 75-142400. 1971. pap. 2.95 (ISBN 0-688-06044-7). Morrow.
Drotning, Philip T. & South, Wesley. Up from the Ghetto. LC 70-90066. (Illus.). 1969. 5.95 (ISBN 0-8092-9224-6). Contemp Bks.
Ebony Editors. Ebony Success Library, Vols. 1-3. Incl. Vol. 1. One Thousand Successful Black (ISBN 0-87485-060-6); Vol. 2. Famous Blacks Give Secrets of Success (ISBN 0-87485-061-4); Vol. 3. Career Guide: Opportunities and Resources for You (ISBN 0-87485-062-2). (Illus.). 960p. 1973. Set. 27.95 (ISBN 0-87485-058-4). Johnson Chi.
Elmore, Inez K. The Story of a Great Pioneer in Black Education: Bennie Carl Elmore, 1909-1973. 1975. 5.00 (ISBN 0-682-48194-7). Exposition.
Griffiths, Julia, ed. Autographs for Freedom, 2 Vols. facs. ed. LC 71-83965. (Black Heritage Library Collection Ser). 1854. 25.00 (ISBN 0-8369-8583-4). Arno.
Langston, J. M. From the Virginia Plantation to the National Capitol; or First & Only Negro Representative in Congress from the Old Dominion. 1894. 24.00 (ISBN 0-527-54450-7). Kraus Repr.
Lotz, Philip H., ed. Rising Above Color. facsimile ed. LC 78-152190. (Essay Index Reprints - Creative Personalities Ser.: Vol. 5). Repr. of 1943 ed. 12.00 (ISBN 0-8369-2605-6). Arno.
Lynch, Hollis R. Edward Wilmot Blyden: Pan-Negro Patriot, 1832-1912. (West African History Ser). (Illus.). 1970. pap. 4.95 (ISBN 0-19-501268-2, GB). Oxford U Pr.
Marrs, Elijah P. Life & History of the Rev. Elijah P. Marrs. facs. ed. LC 70-89395. (Black Heritage Library Collection Ser). 1885. 12.25 (ISBN 0-8369-8625-3). Arno.
Memoirs of Elleanore Eldridge. (Negro Heritage Ser). 4.95 (ISBN 0-8363-0067-X). Jenkins.
Morrow, E. Frederic. Way Down South, Up North. LC 72-13451. 1973. 6.95 (ISBN 0-8298-0246-0). Pilgrim NY.
Murray, Lindley. Narratives of Colored Americans. facsimile ed. LC 70-170702. (Black Heritage Library Collection). Repr. of 1877 ed. 16.75 (ISBN 0-8369-8892-2). Arno.
Nichols, Charles H. Many Thousand Gone. 1963. 42.00 (ISBN 0-685-05259-1). Adler.
O'Connor, Ellen M., ed. Myrtilla Miner. facs. ed. LC 79-89384. (Black Heritage Library Collection Ser). 1885. 8.75 (ISBN 0-8369-8640-7). Arno.
Osofsky, Gilbert, ed. Puttin' on Ole Massa: The Slave Narratives of Henry Bibb, William W. Brown, & Solomon Northrup. 1969. pap. 7.50x (ISBN 0-06-131432-3, TB1432, Torch). Har-Row.
Penn, I. Garland. Afro-American Press & Its Editors. LC 69-18574. (American Negro-His History & Literature, Series No. 2). 1969. Repr. of 1891 ed. 21.00 (ISBN 0-405-01887-8). Arno.
Peters, Margaret W. The Ebony Book of Black Achievement. rev. ed. LC 79-128544. (Illus.). 128p. (gr. 4-8). 1974. Repr. 5.50 (ISBN 0-87485-040-1). Johnson Chi.
Richardson, Clement. National Cyclopedia of the Colored Race. 75.00 (ISBN 0-8490-0711-9). Gordon Pr.
Seder, John & Burrell, Berkeley G. Getting It Together: Black Businessmen in America. LC 70-142096. 1971. 6.95 (ISBN 0-15-135275-5). HarBraceJ.
Simmons, William J. Men of Mark: Eminent, Progressive & Rising. LC 68-29017. (American Negro: His History & Literature Ser., No. 1). 1968. Repr. of 1887 ed. 44.00 (ISBN 0-405-01836-3). Arno.
Smith, Sidonie. Where I'm Bound. new ed. LC 73-20973. 194p. 1974. lib. bdg. 15.00 (ISBN 0-8371-7337-X, SPS/). Greenwood.
Social Science Institute Fisk Univ. Unwritten History of Slavery. LC 68-58168. 1968. 13.00 (ISBN 0-910972-66-4). IHS-PDS.
Spencer, Chauncey E. Who Is Chauncey Spencer? 1975. 7.95 (ISBN 0-685-52218-0). Broadside.
Stevens, Charles E. Anthony Burns: A History. 232p. 1973. Repr. of 1854 ed. 9.50 (ISBN 0-87928-027-1). Corner Hse.
Turner, Morrie & Turner, Letha. Famous Black Americans. pap. 0.95 (ISBN 0-8170-0591-9). Judson.

NEGROES–BIOGRAPHY–JUVENILE LITERATURE

This heading discontinued January 1976. See Afro-Americans and Blacks for later materials.

Haber, Louis. Black Pioneers of Science & Invention. LC 77-109090. (Curriculum Related Bks.). (Illus.). (gr. 5 up). 1970. 6.75 (ISBN 0-15-208565-3, HJ). HarBraceJ.
Peters, Margaret W. The Ebony Book of Black Achievement. rev. ed. LC 79-128544. (Illus.). 128p. (gr. 4-8). 1974. Repr. 5.50 (ISBN 0-87485-040-1). Johnson Chi.
Rollins, Charlemae H. They Showed the Way: Forty American Negro Leaders. LC 64-20692. (gr. 4 up). 1964. 10.95 (ISBN 0-690-81612-X, TYC-J). Har-Row.
Sterne, Emma G. I Have a Dream. (Illus.). (gr. 5 up). 1965. PLB 5.99 (ISBN 0-394-91234-9). Knopf.
Streeter, James. Home Is Over the Mountains: The Journey of Five Black Children. LC 70-181763. (Regional American Stories). (Illus.). 64p. (gr. 3-6). 1972. PLB 6.09 (ISBN 0-8116-4256-9). Garrard.
Wayne, Bennett, ed. & commentary by. Black Crusaders for Freedom. LC 74-3154. (Target Bks). (Illus.). 168p. (gr. 5-12). 1974. PLB 7.29 (ISBN 0-8116-4910-5). Garrard.

NEGROES–CIVIL RIGHTS

This heading discontinued January 1976. See Afro-Americans–Civil Rights and Blacks–Civil Rights for later materials.

Allen, Gary. Communist Revolution in the Streets. LC 66-28922. (Illus.). 1967. 5.00 (ISBN 0-88279-212-1). Western Islands.
Angeles, Peter A. Possible Dream: Toward Understanding the Black Experience. (Orig.). 1971. pap. 1.95 (ISBN 0-377-01211-4). Friend Pr.
Baraka, Imamu A., pseud. It's Nation Time. 1970. pap. 0.50 (ISBN 0-88378-008-9). Third World.
Barbour, Floyd B., ed. Black Power Revolt. LC 67-31432. (Extending Horizons Ser). 1968. 5.95 (ISBN 0-87558-038-6). Porter Sargent.
Berry, M. Black Resistance - White Law: A History of Institutional Racism in America. 1971. pap. text ed. 11.95 (ISBN 0-13-077735-8). P-H.
Blaustein, Albert P. & Zangrando, Robert L., eds. Civil Rights & the American Negro. 1968. 7.95 (ISBN 0-671-27014-1). Trident.
Boggs, James. American Revolution: Pages from a Negro Worker's Notebook. LC 63-20103. (Orig.). 1963. pap. 2.95 (ISBN 0-85345-015-3, PB0153). Monthly Rev.
--Racism & the Class Struggle: Further Pages from a Black Worker's Notebook. LC 74-105314. 1970. 6.00 (ISBN 0-85345-126-5, CL-1265); pap. 5.95 (ISBN 0-85345-164-8, PB-1648). Monthly Rev.
Bond, Julian. A Time to Speak, A Time to Act. 1972. pap. 1.95 (ISBN 0-671-21345-8, Touchstone Bks). S&S.
Bosmajian, Haig A. & Bosmajian, Hamida. Rhetoric of the Civil Rights Movement. 1969. pap. text ed. 2.95 (ISBN 0-685-19763-8). Phila Bk Co.
Broderick, Francis, et al, eds. Black Protest Thought in the Twentieth Century. 2nd ed. LC 79-119007. (American Heritage Ser). 1971. pap. 10.95 (ISBN 0-672-61178-3, AHS-56R). Bobbs.
Butwin, Miriam & Pirmantgen, Pat. Protest II. LC 76-128798. (Real World: Crisis & Conflict Bks). (Illus.). (gr. 5-11). 1972. PLB 4.95 (ISBN 0-8225-0626-2). Lerner Pubns.
Carmichael, Stokely S. & Hamilton, Charles V. Black Power: The Politics of Liberation in America. 1967. pap. 2.95 (ISBN 0-394-70033-3, V33, Vin). Random.
Cox, Archibald, et al. Civil Rights, the Constitution & the Courts. LC 67-20874. 1967. 5.50x (ISBN 0-674-13300-5). Harvard U Pr.
Cox, John H. & Cox, Lawanda. Politics, Principle & Prejudice 1865-1866: Dilemma of Reconstruction in America. LC 63-10647. (Studies in American Negro Life). 1969. pap. 4.95 (ISBN 0-689-70053-9, NL18). Atheneum.
Delsarte, Walter W. Negro, Democracy & the War. LC 71-155386. Repr. of 1919 ed. 9.25x (ISBN 0-8371-3666-0, Pub. by Negro U Pr). Greenwood.
Ebony Editors. White Problem in America. 1966. 3.50 (ISBN 0-87485-020-7). Johnson Chi.
Gilligan, Francis J. Morality of the Color Line. LC 71-94478. Repr. of 1928 ed. 12.25x (ISBN 0-8371-2353-4, Pub. by Negro U Pr). Greenwood.
Grant, Joann E., ed. Black Protest: History, Documents & Analyses from Sixteen Nineteen to the Present. (Political Perspectives Ser). 1979. pap. 2.25 (ISBN 0-449-30841-3, Prem). Fawcett.
Greenberg, Jack. Race Relations & American Law. LC 59-11179. 481p. 1959. 17.50x (ISBN 0-231-02313-8). Columbia U Pr.
Greenberg, Jack & Lambert, Richard D., eds. Blacks & the Law. new ed. LC 72-93252. (Annals of the American Academy of Political & Social Science: No. 407). 250p. 1973. 7.50 (ISBN 0-87761-163-7); pap. 6.00 (ISBN 0-87761-162-9). Am Acad Pol Soc Sci.
Greenidge, Edwin & Pantell, Dora. If Not Now, When: The Many Meanings of Black Power. 1970. 5.95 (ISBN 0-440-03970-3). Delacorte.
Gregory, Dick. No More Lies: The Myth & the Reality of American History. McGraw, James, ed. pap. 2.95 (ISBN 0-06-080236-7, P236, PL). Har-Row.
--Up from Nigger. McGraw, James R., ed. LC 75-12817. (Illus.). 256p. 1976. 8.95 (ISBN 0-8128-1832-6). Stein & Day.

Harvey, James C. Black Civil Rights During the Johnson Administration. LC 73-80241. 256p. 1973. pap. 5.95x (ISBN 0-87805-021-3). U Pr of Miss.
Johnson, James W. Negro Americans, What Now. LC 72-155618. Repr. of 1938 ed. 12.00 (ISBN 0-404-00075-4). AMS Pr.
--Negro Americans, What Now? LC 72-8355. 103p. 1973. Repr. of 1934 ed. lib. bdg. 12.50 (ISBN 0-306-70531-1). Da Capo.
Kalven, Harry, Jr. Negro & the First Amendment. LC 66-29115. 1966. pap. 2.45 (ISBN 0-226-42315-8, P240, Phoen). U of Chicago Pr.
King, Martin L., Jr. Where Do We Go from Here? Chaos or Community. pap. 4.95 (ISBN 0-8070-0571-1, BP285). Beacon Pr.
--Where Do We Go from Here: Chaos or Community. 1967. 11.95 (ISBN 0-06-012394-X, HarpT). Har-Row.
--Why We Can't Wait. 1964. 11.95 (ISBN 0-06-012395-8, HarpT). Har-Row.
--Why We Can't Wait. (Illus.). (RL 7). pap. 2.50 (ISBN 0-451-62019-4, ME2019, Ment). NAL.
Lester, Julius. Look Out Whitey! Black Power's Gon' Get Your Mama! 1969. pap. 1.95 (ISBN 0-394-17139-X, B197, BC). Grove.
Levitan, Sar A., et al. Still a Dream: The Changing Status of Blacks Since 1960. LC 74-16539. 1975. 18.50x (ISBN 0-674-83855-6); pap. 7.95x (ISBN 0-674-83856-4). Harvard U Pr.
McClellan, Grant S., ed. Civil Rights. (Reference Shelf Ser: Vol. 36, No. 6). 1964. 6.25 (ISBN 0-8242-0083-7). Wilson.
McPherson, James M. The Abolitionist Legacy: From Reconstruction to the NAACP. LC 75-22101. 1976. Limited Ed. 31.00 (ISBN 0-691-04637-9); pap. 11.50 (ISBN 0-691-10039-X). Princeton U Pr.
Malcolm X. By Any Means Necessary. Breitman, George, ed. LC 74-108718. (Illus.). 1970. 12.00 (ISBN 0-87348-145-3); pap. 3.45 (ISBN 0-87348-150-X). Path Pr NY.
--Two Speeches by Malcolm X. (Orig.). pap. 0.75 (ISBN 0-87348-087-2). Path Pr NY.
Meier, August & Rudick, Elliott. CORE: A Study in the Civil Rights Movement, 1942-1968. 448p. 1973. 24.95 (ISBN 0-19-501627-0). Oxford U Pr.
Meier, August & Rudwick, Elliott. CORE: A Study in the Civil Rights Movement, 1942-1968. LC 72-92294. 580p. 1975. pap. 7.95 (ISBN 0-252-00567-8). U of Ill Pr.
National Conference Of Colored Men Of The United States - Nashville Tennessee - 1879. Proceedings. LC 70-110004. Repr. of 1879 ed. 9.50x (ISBN 0-8371-4140-0). Greenwood.
The Negro Problem: A Series of Articles by Representative American Negroes of To-Day. LC 75-79015. (Black Heritage Library Collection). Repr. of 1903 ed. 9.50 (ISBN 0-8369-8636-9). Arno.
Negro Story, a Magazine for All Americans, Vols. 1-2. 1944-1946. Repr. 54.00x (ISBN 0-8371-9119-X, Pub. by Negro U Pr). Greenwood.
Paul, Arnold M., ed. Black Americans & the Supreme Court. (American Problem Studies). 140p. 1972. pap. text ed. 5.50 (ISBN 0-03-084009-0, Pub. by HR&W). Krieger.
Pettigrew, Thomas F., ed. Racial Discrimination in the United States. (Readers in Social Problems Ser.). 429p. 1975. pap. text ed. 11.50 scp (ISBN 0-06-045183-1, HarpC). Har-Row.
Poinsett, Alex. Black Power Gary Style: The Making of Mayor Richard Gordon Hatcher. LC 72-128545. 1970. 6.95 (ISBN 0-87485-042-8). Johnson Chi.
Police & the Blacks: U. S. Civil Rights Commission Hearings. LC 76-154591. (Police in America Ser). 1971. Repr. of 1960 ed. 16.00 (ISBN 0-405-03381-8). Arno.
Randall, Dudley. Cities Burning. 1966. pap. 1.00 (ISBN 0-910296-10-3). Broadside.
Rodgers, Harrell R. & Bullock, Charles S. Law & Social Change: Civil Rights Laws & Their Consequences. (Illus.). 160p. 1972. pap. text ed. 7.95 (ISBN 0-07-053378-4, C). McGraw.
Stang, Alan. It's Very Simple: True Story of Civil Rights. LC 65-23268. (Illus.). 1965. 5.00 (ISBN 0-88279-207-5); pap. 0.75 pocketsize (ISBN 0-88279-007-2). Western Islands.
Stephenson, Gilbert T. Race Distinctions in American Law. LC 70-99889. Repr. of 1910 ed. 16.00 (ISBN 0-404-00215-3). AMS Pr.
--Race Distinctions in American Law. LC 76-84694. Repr. of 1910 ed. 21.75x (ISBN 0-8371-1669-4). Greenwood.
Synnestvedt, Sig. The White Response to Black Emancipation: Second-Class Citizenship in the United States Since Reconstruction. 288p. 1972. pap. text ed. 6.50x (ISBN 0-02-418750-X). Macmillan.
Warren, Robert P. Who Speaks for the Negro. (gr. 6 up). 1965. 12.95 (ISBN 0-394-45183-X). Random.
Warsoff, Louis A. Equality & the Law. LC 75-136089. 324p. 1975. Repr. of 1938 ed. lib. bdg. 15.00x (ISBN 0-8371-5239-9, WAEL). Greenwood.
Weale, B. L. Conflict of Colour: Threatened Upheaval Throughout the World. facs. ed. LC 70-89431. (Black Heritage Library Collection Ser). 1910. 14.25 (ISBN 0-8369-8680-6). Arno.
Wolk, Allan. Presidency & Black Civil Rights: Eisenhower to Nixon. LC 70-135029. 276p. 1971. 16.50 (ISBN 0-8386-7805-X). Fairleigh Dickinson.

NEGROES–CIVIL RIGHTS–JUVENILE LITERATURE

This heading discontinued January 1976. See Afro-Americans–Civil Rights and Blacks–Civil Rights for later materials.

Sterling, Dorothy. Tear Down the Walls: A History of the American Civil Rights Movement. LC 68-14212. (gr. 7 up). 1968. PLB 6.95 (ISBN 0-385-09436-1). Doubleday.
Sterne, Emma G. I Have a Dream. (Illus.). (gr. 5 up). 1965. PLB 5.99 (ISBN 0-394-91234-9). Knopf.
Stevens, Leonard A. Equal! The Case of Integration vs Jim Crow, the Fourteenth Amendment. LC 75-25646. (Great Constitutional Issues Ser.). 228p. (gr. 7 up). 1975. PLB 6.59 (ISBN 0-698-30597-3). Coward.

NEGROES–COLONIZATION

This heading discontinued January 1976. See Afro-Americans–Colonization for later materials.

Alexander, Archibald. History of Colonization of the Western Coast of Africa. 2nd facs. ed. LC 71-149861. (Black Heritage Library Collection Ser). 1849. 27.25 (ISBN 0-8369-8743-8). Arno.
--History of Colonization on the Western Coast of Africa. LC 70-82319. Repr. of 1846 ed. 28.00x (ISBN 0-8371-1652-X, Pub. by Negro U Pr). Greenwood.
American Colonization Society. Annual Reports: First to Ninety First, Ninety Third. LC 77-90128. (Illus.). 1818-1910. Repr. 180.00x (ISBN 0-8371-2476-X, Pub. by Negro U Pr). Greenwood.
Brown, Isaac V. Biography of the Reverend Robert Finley. LC 73-82178. (Anti-Slavery Crusade in America Ser). 1969. Repr. of 1857 ed. 16.00 (ISBN 0-405-00617-9). Arno.
Campbell, Penelope. Maryland in Africa: The Maryland State Colonization Society, 1831-1857. LC 75-131058. 1971. 14.95 (ISBN 0-252-00133-8). U of Ill Pr.
Christy, David. Ethiopia: Her Gloom & Glory. LC 73-75550. Repr. of 1857 ed. 13.00x (ISBN 0-8371-1016-5, Pub. by Negro U Pr). Greenwood.
Crummell, Alexander. Africa & America: Addresses & Discourses. LC 70-77198. Repr. of 1891 ed. 20.50x (ISBN 0-8371-1291-5, Pub. by Negro U Pr). Greenwood.
Delany, M. R. & Campbell, Robert. Search for a Place: Black Separatism & Africa, 1860. Bell, Howard, ed. 1971. pap. 2.25 (ISBN 0-472-06179-8, AA). U of Mich Pr.
Dewees, Jacob. Great Future of America & Africa. facs. ed. LC 75-154075. (Black Heritage Library Collection Ser). 1854. 13.25 (ISBN 0-8369-8786-1). Arno.
--Great Future of America & Africa. LC 72-92425. 1854. 12.00 (ISBN 0-403-00158-7). Scholarly.
Dick, Robert C. Black Protest: Issues & Tactics. LC 72-794. 320p. 1974. lib. bdg. 16.95 (ISBN 0-8371-6366-8, DNA/); pap. 5.95 (ISBN 0-8371-8922-5). Greenwood.
Fox, Early L. American Colonization Society, 1817-1840. Repr. of 1919 ed. 14.00 (ISBN 0-404-00159-9). AMS Pr.
Freeman, Frederick. Africa's Redemption, the Salvation of Our Country. LC 76-106873. Repr. of 1852 ed. 19.75x (ISBN 0-8371-3290-8, Pub. by Negro U Pr). Greenwood.
--Africa's Redemption, the Salvation of Our Country. LC 70-92427. 1852. 16.00 (ISBN 0-403-00160-9). Scholarly.
--Yaradee: A Plea for Africa. LC 70-79807. Repr. of 1836 ed. 17.75x (ISBN 0-8371-1505-1). Greenwood.
Garrison, William L. Thoughts on African Colonization. LC 68-28997. (American Negro: His History & Literature Ser., No. 1). (Illus.). 1968. Repr. of 1832 ed. 12.00 (ISBN 0-405-01816-9). Arno.
Garvey, Marcus. Aims & Objects of Movement for Solution of Negro Problem: A Nation of Their Own in Africa. 1924. pap. 1.50 (ISBN 0-685-20858-3). Univ Place.
Griffith, Cyril E. The African Dream: Martin R. Delany & the Emergence of Pan-African Thought. LC 74-20559. 176p. 1975. 12.95x (ISBN 0-271-01181-5). Pa St U Pr.
Gurley, Ralph R. Life of Jehudi Ashmun. facs. ed. LC 73-149867. (Black Heritage Library Collection Ser). 1835. 20.50 (ISBN 0-8369-8749-7). Arno.
--Life of Jehudi Ashmun, Late Colonial Agent in Liberia. LC 76-75532. Repr. of 1835 ed. 21.00x (ISBN 0-8371-1101-3, Pub. by Negro U Pr). Greenwood.
Innes, William, ed. Liberia: Or, Early History & Signal Preservation of the American Colony of Free Negroes on the Coast of Africa. facs. ed. LC 76-154078. (Black Heritage Library Collection Ser). 1831. 14.00 (ISBN 0-8369-8789-6). Arno.
Jay, William. Inquiry into the Character & Tendency of the American Colonization & American Anti-Slavery Societies. facs. ed. LC 74-83947. (Black Heritage Library Collection Ser). 1835. 12.75 (ISBN 0-8369-8611-3). Arno.
McKinley, Carlyle. Appeal to Pharoah: The Negro Problem, & Its Radical Solution. LC 79-107477. Repr. of 1907 ed. 12.25x (ISBN 0-8371-3756-X, Pub. by Negro U Pr). Greenwood.
Mallison, George. Color at Home & Abroad. LC 72-132388. Repr. 24.75 (ISBN 0-404-00198-X). AMS Pr.
Miller, Floyd J. The Search for a Black Nationality: Black Colonization & Immigration, 1787-1863. LC 75-4650. (Blacks in the New World Ser.). 320p. 1975. 17.50 (ISBN 0-252-00263-6). U of Ill Pr.
Read, Hollis. Negro Problem Solved: Or, Africa As She Was, As She Is, & As She Shall Be. LC 71-78774. (Illus.). Repr. of 1864 ed. 15.50x (ISBN 0-8371-1394-6, Pub. by Negro U Pr). Greenwood.

NEGROES–ECONOMIC CONDITIONS

This heading discontinued January 1976. See Afro-Americans–Economic Conditions and Blacks–Economic Conditions for later materials. see also Negro Businessmen; Negroes–Employment

Atlanta University. Atlanta University Publications. LC 68-28985. (The American Negro: History & Literature, Ser. No. 3). 1970. Repr. of 1898 ed. No. 3. 5. 6. 7. 10. 12. 19. 20. 37.00 (ISBN 0-405-01914-9). Arno.
Bates, Timothy M. Black Capitalism: A Quantitative Analysis. LC 73-9060. (Special Studies in U.S. Economic,Social & Political Issues). 1973. 29.50x (ISBN 0-89197-680-9). Irvington.
Billingsley, Andrew. Black Families & the Struggle for Survival. (Orig.). 1974. pap. 2.95 (ISBN 0-377-00001-9). Friend Pr.
Brown, T. I., ed. Economic Co-Operation Among the Negroes of Georgia. (Atlanta Univ. Publ. Ser.: No. 19). (Orig.). Repr. of 1917 ed. pap. 4.00 (ISBN 0-527-03120-8). Kraus Repr.
Cash, William L., Jr. & Oliver, Lucy R., eds. Black Economic Development: Analysis & Implications. 360p. 1975. pap. 10.00 (ISBN 0-87712-170-2). U Mich Busn Div Res.
Coles, Flournoy A., Jr. Black Economic Development. LC 74-30495. 232p. 1975. 17.95x (ISBN 0-88229-176-9). Nelson-Hall.
Conference for the Study of Problems Concerning Negro City Life. Social & Physical Condition of Negroes in Cities. (Atlanta Univ. Publ. Ser.: No. 2). (Orig.). Repr. of 1897 ed. 4.00 (ISBN 0-527-03109-7). Kraus Repr.
Cross, Theodore L. Black Capitalism: Strategy for Business in the Ghetto. LC 72-80268. 1971. pap. 3.95 (ISBN 0-689-70266-3, 174). Atheneum.
Du Bois, W. E. B. Economic Co-Operation Among Negro Americans. (Atlanta Univ. Publ. Ser.: No. 12). (Orig.). 1907. Repr. of 1907 ed. pap. 6.00 (ISBN 0-527-03113-5). Kraus Repr.
Edwards, Paul K. Southern Urban Negro As a Consumer. LC 73-89022. (Illus.). Repr. of 1932 ed. 16.50x (ISBN 0-8371-1891-3, Pub. by Negro U Pr). Greenwood.
Gagala, Kenneth. Economics of Minorities: A Guide to Information Sources. LC 73-17573. (Economics Information Guide Ser: Vol. 2). 339p. 1976. 36.00 (ISBN 0-8103-1294-8). Gale.
Harris, Abram L. Negro As Capitalist. LC 73-117597. (Studies in Negro History & Culture, No. 54). 1970. Repr. of 1936 ed. lib. bdg. 33.95 (ISBN 0-8383-1030-3). Haskell.
--Negro As Capitalist: Study of Banking and Business Among American Negroes. LC 77-97425. Repr. of 1936 ed. 10.00x (ISBN 0-8371-2731-9, Pub. by Negro U Pr). Greenwood.
Hudson, Hosea. Black Worker in the Deep South: A Personal Account. LC 72-82078. 1972. 6.95 (ISBN 0-7178-0373-2); pap. 1.95 (ISBN 0-7178-0362-7). Intl Pub Co.
Irons, Edward D. On Black Economic Development: Myths & Facts. (Richard J. Gonzales Lectures Ser.: No. 4). 18p. 1971. pap. 1.00 (ISBN 0-87755-160-X). U of Tex Busn Res.
Jackson, Luther P. Free Negro Labor & Property Holding in Virginia, 1830-1860. LC 69-15524. (Studies in American Negro Life Ser). 1969. pap. 3.45 (ISBN 0-689-70107-1, NL15). Atheneum.
Killens, John O. Black Man's Burden. 4.95 (ISBN 0-671-09450-5). Trident.
Lacy, Dan. The White Use of Blacks in America. LC 77-175286. 288p. 1973. pap. 3.95 (ISBN 0-07-035751-X, SP). McGraw.
--White Use of Blacks in America. LC 77-175286. 1972. 7.95 (ISBN 0-689-10476-6). Atheneum.
Lee, Roy F. Setting for Black Business Development: A Study in Sociology & Political Economy. LC 72-619630. 1973. pap. 7.00 (ISBN 0-87546-039-9); pap. 10.00 special hard bdg (ISBN 0-87546-275-8). NY Sch Indus Rel.
Ofari, Earl. Myth of Black Capitalism. LC 70-105313. 1970. pap. 3.25 (ISBN 0-85345-163-X, PB-163X). Monthly Rev.
Purcell, Theodore & Cavanagh, Gerald. Blacks in the Industrial World: Issues for the Manager. LC 74-184530. 1972. 15.95 (ISBN 0-02-925520-1); pap. text ed. 5.95 (ISBN 0-02-925480-9). Free Pr.
Rodman, Hyman. Lower-Class Families: The Culture of Poverty in Negro Trinidad. 256p. 1971. pap. 4.50x (ISBN 0-19-501378-6). Oxford U Pr.
Rowan, Carl. Just Between Us Blacks. LC 74-9068. 1974. 10.00 (ISBN 0-394-47090-7). Random.
Stuart, M. S. An Economic Detour: A History of Insurance in the Lives of American Negroes. Repr. of 1940 ed. 19.50 (ISBN 0-384-58660-0). Johnson Repr.
Swinton, David H. & Ellison, Julian. Aggregate Personal Income of the Black Population in the United States: 1947-1980. 75p. (Orig.). 1974. pap. text ed. 3.95x (ISBN 0-87855-600-1). Transaction Bks.
Tabb, William K. Political Economy of the Black Ghetto. LC 70-124347. 1971. 5.95x (ISBN 0-393-05426-8); pap. text ed. 3.95x (ISBN 0-393-09930-X). Norton.
Thurow, Lester C. Poverty & Discrimination. (Studies in Social Economics). 1969. 10.95 (ISBN 0-8157-8444-9). Brookings.
United States Office Of Adviser On Negro Affairs. Urban Negro Worker in the United States, 1925-1936, 2 Vols. in 1. LC 79-82095. (Illus.). 1938-39. Repr. 25.00x (ISBN 0-8371-3209-6). Greenwood.
Wolters, Raymond. Negroes & the Great Depression: The Problem of Economic Recovery. Kutler, Stanley E., ed. LC 78-95510. (Contributions in American History: No. 6). 1970. lib. bdg. 19.95 (ISBN 0-8371-2341-0, WON/). Greenwood.

NEGROES–EDUCATION

This heading discontinued January 1976. See Afro-Americans–Education and Blacks–Education for later materials. see also Negro Students; Negro Teachers; Negro Universities and Colleges

Alexander's Magazine, 7 Vols. LC 73-15076. 1905-1909. Repr. Set. 305.00x (ISBN 0-8371-9105-X, Pub. by Negro U Pr). Greenwood.
American Unitarian Association. From Servitude to Service. Cremin, Lawrence A. & Barnard, Frederick A., eds. LC 74-101402. (American Education: Its Men, Institutions & Ideas, Ser. 1). 1969. Repr. of 1905 ed. 14.00 (ISBN 0-405-01382-5). Arno.
Andrews, Charles C. History of the New York African Free-Schools, from Their Establishment in 1787, to the Present Time. LC 68-55868. (Illus.). Repr. of 1830 ed. 10.00x (ISBN 0-8371-1064-5). Greenwood.
Banks, James A. Teaching the Black Experience: Methods & Materials. LC 74-126641. (Orig.). 1970. pap. 4.50 (ISBN 0-8224-6885-9). Pitman Learning.
Blascoer, Frances. Colored School Children in New York. Johnson, Eleanor H., ed. LC 73-100279. Repr. of 1915 ed. 10.00x (ISBN 0-8371-2935-4, Pub. by Negro U Pr). Greenwood.
Bond, Horace M. Black American Scholars: A Study of Their Beginnings. LC 72-78234. 210p. 1972. 8.95 (ISBN 0-913642-01-0); pap. 3.95 (ISBN 0-913642-04-5). Balamp Pub.
--Education of the Negro in the American Social Order. rev. ed. 1965. lib. bdg. 30.00x (ISBN 0-374-90760-9). Octagon.
--Negro Education in Alabama. 1969. Repr. of 1939 ed. lib. bdg. 17.50x (ISBN 0-374-90780-3). Octagon.
--Negro Education in Alabama: A Study in Cotton & Steel. LC 39-18307. (Studies in American Negro Life Ser). 1969. pap. 3.45 (ISBN 0-689-70019-9, NL17). Atheneum.
Brawley, Benjamin. Doctor Dillard of the Jeanes Fund. facsimile ed. LC 73-168511. (Black Heritage Library Collection). Repr. of 1930 ed. 13.50 (ISBN 0-8369-8864-7). Arno.
Brazziel, William F. Quality Education for All Americans: An Assessment of Gains of Black Americans with Proposals for Program Development in American Schools & Colleges for the Next Quarter Century. LC 73-88966. 288p. 1974. 8.95x (ISBN 0-88258-007-8). Howard U Pr.

Bullock, Henry A. History of Negro Education in the South: From 1619 to the Present. LC 67-20873. 1967. 18.50x (ISBN 0-674-39950-1). Harvard U Pr.
Caliver, Ambrose. Secondary Education for Negroes. LC 74-82091. (Illus.). Repr. of 1933 ed. 10.00x (ISBN 0-8371-2046-2). Greenwood.
--Vocational Education & Guidance of Negroes. LC 78-82092. (Illus.). Repr. 10.50x (ISBN 0-8371-3208-8). Greenwood.
Campbell, Thomas M. Movable School Goes to the Negro Farmer. Cremin, Lawrence A. & Barnard, Frederick A., eds. LC 78-101403. (American Education: Its Men, Institutions & Ideas, Ser. 1). 1969. Repr. of 1936 ed. 12.00 (ISBN 0-405-01398-1). Arno.
Commissioner Of Education In The District Of Columbia. History of Schools for the Colored Population. LC 74-101516. (American Negro: His History & Literature, Ser. No. 3). 1970. Repr. of 1871 ed. 9.00 (ISBN 0-405-01918-1). Arno.
Cooke, Dennis H. White Superintendent & the Negro Schools in North Carolina. Repr. of 1930 ed. 11.00x (ISBN 0-8371-3474-9). Greenwood.
Culp, D. W., ed. Twentieth Century Negro Literature. LC 69-18586. (American Negro: His History & Literature Ser., No. 2). 1969. Repr. of 1902 ed. 23.00 (ISBN 0-405-01856-8). Arno.
Dabney, Charles W. Universal Education in the South, 2 Vols. LC 70-89170. (American Education: Its Men, Institutions & Ideas, Ser. 1). 1969. Repr. of 1936 ed. Set. 50.00 (ISBN 0-405-01408-2). Arno.
Daniel, William A. Education of Negro Ministers. LC 77-78581. Repr. of 1925 ed. 12.00 (ISBN 0-8371-1410-1, Pub. by Negro U Pr). Greenwood.
Davis, William R. Development & Present Status of Negro Education in East Texas. LC 75-178798. (Columbia University. Teachers College. Contributions to Education: No. 626). Repr. of 1934 ed. 17.50 (ISBN 0-404-55626-4). AMS Pr.
Derbigny, Irving A. General Education in the Negro College. LC 72-97448. Repr. of 1947 ed. 12.75x (ISBN 0-8371-2694-0, Pub. by Negro U Pr). Greenwood.
Du Bois, W. E. The Education of Black People: Ten Critiques, 1906-1960. Aptheker, Herbert, ed. LC 72-90495. (Modern Reader Paperbacks Ser.). 192p. 1975. pap. 4.50 (ISBN 0-85345-363-2, PB-3632). Monthly Rev.
Du Bois, W. E. B. The Education of Black People: Ten Critiques, 1906-1960. Aptheker, Herbert, ed. LC 72-90495. 184p. 1973. 10.00x (ISBN 0-87023-130-8). U of Mass Pr.
Du Bois, W. E. B., ed. The College-Bred Negro American. (Orig.). Repr. of 1910 ed. pap. 4.00 (ISBN 0-527-03116-X). Kraus Repr.
--The Common School & the Negro American. (Atlanta Univ. Publ. Ser.: No. 16). (Orig.). 1911. Repr. of 1911 ed. pap. 5.00 (ISBN 0-527-03117-8). Kraus Repr.
Fader, Daniel. Naked Children. 1971. 10.95 (ISBN 0-02-536900-8). Macmillan.
Foster, Herbert L. Ribbin', Jivin', & Playin' the Dozens: The Unrecognized Dilemma of Inner-City Schools. LC 74-7393. 304p. 1974. pap. 10.95 (ISBN 0-88410-163-0). Ballinger Pub.
From Servitude to Service: Being the Old South Lecturer on the History & Work of Southern Institutions for the Education of the Negro. LC 70-88410. Repr. of 1905 ed. 12.75x (ISBN 0-8371-1841-7, Pub. by Negro U Pr). Greenwood.
George Washington University American Studies Program-Rose Bibl. Analytical Guide & Indexes to the Colored American Magazine: 1900-1909, 2 vols. LC 73-15077. 1974. lib. bdg. 75.00x set (ISBN 0-8371-7176-8, RBCAM). Greenwood.
Ginzberg, Eli. The Negro Potential. LC 56-9606. 144p. 1956. pap. 5.00x (ISBN 0-231-08546-X). Columbia U Pr.
Ginzberg, Eli, et al. The Middle-Class Negro in the White Man's World. LC 67-26364. 1967. 15.00x (ISBN 0-231-03096-7); pap. 5.00x (ISBN 0-231-08596-6). Columbia U Pr.
Greene, Harry W. Holders of Doctorates Among American Negroes. 275p. 1974. Repr. 15.00x (ISBN 0-89020-010-6). Crofton Pub.
Greer, Colin. Cobweb Attitudes: Essays on Educational & Cultural Mythology. LC 76-94368. 1970. pap. text ed. 4.75x (ISBN 0-8077-1468-2). Tchrs Coll.
Gregory, Susan. Hey, White Girl- LC 79-90978. 1970. 8.95 (ISBN 0-393-07450-1). Norton.
Guggisberg, Frederick G. Future of the Negro: Some Chapters in the Development of a Race. LC 71-97366. Repr. of 1929 ed. 10.00x (ISBN 0-8371-2427-1, Pub. by Negro U Pr). Greenwood.
Harris, Ruth M. Teachers' Social Knowledge & Its Relation to Pupils' Responses: A Study of Four St. Louis Negro Elementary Schools. LC 77-176843. (Columbia University. Teachers College. Contributions to Education: No. 816). Repr. of 1941 ed. 17.50 (ISBN 0-404-55816-X). AMS Pr.
Harrison, Bennett. Education, Training, & the Urban Ghetto. LC 72-4023. (Illus.). 287p. 1973. 20.00x (ISBN 0-8018-1366-2). Johns Hopkins.
Haskins, Jim, ed. Black Manifesto for Education. 1973. 7.95 (ISBN 0-688-00029-0); pap. 2.95 (ISBN 0-688-05029-8). Morrow.
Hayes, R. B. Teach the Freeman: The Correspondence of Rutherford B. Hayes & the Slater Fund for Negro Education 1881-1887, 2 Vols. in 1. Repr. of 1959 ed. 26.00 (ISBN 0-527-38930-7). Kraus Repr.
Holmes, Dwight O. Evolution of the Negro College. LC 74-128993. (Columbia University. Teachers College. Contributions to Education: No. 609). Repr. of 1934 ed. 8.50 (ISBN 0-404-00172-6). AMS Pr.
--Evolution of the Negro College. LC 69-18570. (American Negro: His History & Literature Ser. No. 2). 1969. Repr. of 1934 ed. 9.50 (ISBN 0-405-01871-1). Arno.
Johnson, Charles S. Negro College Graduate. LC 79-78768. (Illus.). Repr. of 1938 ed. 18.25x (ISBN 0-8371-1392-X, Pub. by Negro U Pr). Greenwood.
Johnson, Charles S., ed. Education & the Cultural Process: Papers Presented at Symposium Commemorating the Seventy-Fifth Anniversary of the Founding of Fisk University, April 29-May 4, 1941. LC 75-109340. Repr. of 1943 ed. 11.75x (ISBN 0-8371-3596-6, Pub. by Negro U Pr). Greenwood.
Jones, C. C. Religious Instruction of the Negroes in the United States. 1842. 14.00 (ISBN 0-527-46700-6). Kraus Repr.
Jones, Charles C. Religious Instruction of the Negroes in the United States. facs. ed. LC 70-149869. (Black Heritage Library Collection Ser). 1842. 14.50 (ISBN 0-8369-8718-7). Arno.
--Religious Instruction of the Negroes in the United States. LC 73-82466. Repr. of 1842 ed. 12.25x (ISBN 0-8371-1645-7). Greenwood.
Jones, Thomas J., ed. Negro Education: A Study of the Private & Higher Schools for Colored People in the United States. LC 69-18572. (American Negro-His History & Literature Ser., No.2). 1226p. Repr. of 1917 ed. 39.00 (ISBN 0-405-01874-6). Arno.
Kozol, Jonathan. Death at an Early Age: The Destruction of the Hearts & Minds of Negro Children in the Boston Public Schools. 1967. 7.95 (ISBN 0-395-07868-7). HM.
Leavell, Ullin W. Philanthropy in Negro Education. LC 77-138011. Repr. of 1930 ed. 12.25x (ISBN 0-8371-5658-0). Greenwood.
Long, Hollis M. Public Secondary Education for Negroes in North Carolina. LC 71-177008. (Columbia University. Teachers College. Contributions to Education: No. 529). Repr. of 1932 ed. 17.50 (ISBN 0-404-55529-2). AMS Pr.
Lyons, Charles H. To Wash an Aethiop White: British Ideas About Black Educability, 1530-1960. LC 74-23396. 1975. text ed. 9.25x (ISBN 0-8077-2464-5). Tchrs Coll.
McKinney, Richard I. Religion in Higher Education Among Negroes. LC 75-38785. (Religion in America, Ser. 2). 186p. 1972. Repr. of 1945 ed. 11.00 (ISBN 0-405-04075-X). Arno.
--Religion in Higher Education Among Negroes. LC 75-38785. (Religion in America, Ser. 2). 186p. 1972. Repr. of 1945 ed. 11.00 (ISBN 0-405-04075-X). Arno.
Meece, Leonard E. Negro Education in Kentucky: A Comparative Study of White & Negro Education on the Elementary & Secondary School Levels. LC 76-155706. (Illus.). Repr. of 1938 ed. 10.75x (ISBN 0-8371-6097-9, Pub. by Negro U Pr). Greenwood.
Noble, Stuart G. Forty Years of Public Schools in Mississippi: With Special Reference to the Education of the Negro. LC 73-177109. (Columbia University. Teachers College. Contributions to Education: No. 94). Repr. of 1918 ed. 8.50 (ISBN 0-404-55094-0). AMS Pr.
--Forty Years of the Public Schools in Mississippi. LC 73-89049. Repr. of 1918 ed. 10.00x (ISBN 0-8371-1939-1, Pub. by Negro U Pr). Greenwood.
O'Connor, Ellen M. & Miner, Myrtilla. Myrtilla Miner: A Memoir. Bd. with The School for Colored Girls in Washington, D. C. Repr. of 1854 ed. LC 73-92235. (American Negro, Ser. 3). 1970. Repr. of 1885 ed. 8.75 (ISBN 0-405-01933-5). Arno.
Redcay, Edward E. County Training Schools & Public Secondary: Education for Negroes in the South. LC 72-106864. Repr. of 1935 ed. 12.50x (ISBN 0-8371-3486-2, Pub. by Negro U Pr). Greenwood.
Rosenfeld, G. Shut Those Thick Lips: A Cultural Study of a Slum School. LC 73-159723. 1971. pap. text ed. 4.95 (ISBN 0-03-085350-8, HoltC). HR&W.
Smith, Elsie J. Counseling the Culturally Different Black Youth. LC 72-833444. 1973. pap. text ed. 6.95x (ISBN 0-675-09069-5). Merrill.
Stearns, C. Black Man of the South & the Rebels. 1872. 24.00 (ISBN 0-527-85900-1). Kraus Repr.
Stearns, Charles. Black Man of the South, & the Rebels. LC 77-76861. (Illus.). Repr. of 1871 ed. 24.25x (ISBN 0-8371-1164-1, Pub. by Negro U Pr). Greenwood.
Swint, Henry L. Northern Teacher in the South, 1862-1870. 1967. lib. bdg. 15.00x (ISBN 0-374-97676-7). Octagon.
Tuskegee Normal And Industrial Institute - Extension Department. Negro Rural School & Its Relation to the Community. LC 79-155416. (Illus.). Repr. of 1915 ed. 10.75x (ISBN 0-8371-6112-6, Pub. by Negro U Pr). Greenwood.
United States Office Of Education. Negro Education: A Study of the Private & Higher Schools for Colored People in the United States, 2 Vols. LC 72-75558. (Illus.). Repr. of 1917 ed. 58.00x (ISBN 0-8371-2513-8, Pub. by Negro U Pr). Greenwood.
--Survey of Negro Colleges & Universities. LC 72-82096. (Illus.). Repr. of 1929 ed. 40.00x (ISBN 0-8371-1878-6, Pub. by Negro U Pr). Greenwood.
Vontress, Clemmont E. Counseling Negroes. (Guidance Monograph). 1971. pap. 2.40 (ISBN 0-395-12048-9, 9-78857). HM.
Washington, Booker T. Character Building. LC 75-38848. (Studies in Black History & Culture, No. 54). 291p. 1972. Repr. of 1902 ed. lib. bdg. 53.95 (ISBN 0-8383-1394-9). Haskell.
--Sowing & Reaping. facsimile ed. LC 70-161275. (Black Heritage Library Collection). Repr. of 1900 ed. 8.75 (ISBN 0-8369-8834-5). Arno.
Wilcox, Roger N., ed. Psychological Consequences of Being a Black American: A Source Book of Research by Black Psychologists. LC 74-142720. 1971. pap. 14.95 (ISBN 0-471-94383-5). Wiley.
Wilkerson, Doxey A. Special Problems of Negro Education. LC 76-82097. (Illus.). Repr. of 1939 ed. 10.75x (ISBN 0-8371-3210-X, Pub. by Negro U Pr). Greenwood.
Wilson, Charles H., Sr. Education for Negroes in Mississippi: Since 1910. (Illus.). 641p. 1974. Repr. 20.00x (ISBN 0-89020-011-4). Crofton Pub.
Woodson, Carter G. Education of the Negro Prior to 1861. LC 68-29024. (American Negro: His History & Literature Series No. 1). 1968. Repr. of 1919 ed. 22.00 (ISBN 0-405-01846-0). Arno.
--Mis-Education of the Negro. LC 77-24332. Repr. of 1933 ed. 10.00 (ISBN 0-404-16027-1). AMS Pr.
Wright, Marion M. Education of Negroes in New Jersey. LC 77-165746. (American Education Ser, No. 2). 1972. Repr. of 1941 ed. 18.00 (ISBN 0-405-03617-5). Arno.
--The Education of Negroes in New Jersey. LC 76-177620. (Columbia University. Teachers College. Contributions to Education: No. 815). Repr. of 1941 ed. 17.50 (ISBN 0-404-55815-1). AMS Pr.

NEGROES–EMPLOYMENT

This heading discontinued January 1976. See Afro-Americans–Employment and Blacks–Employment for later materials.
see also Negro Businessmen

Banner, Melvin. The Black Pioneer in Michigan. LC 73-91313. 1973. pap. 7.00 (ISBN 0-87812-053-X). Pendell Pub.
Blumrosen, Alfred W. Black Employment & the Law. 1971. 30.00 (ISBN 0-8135-0682-4). Rutgers U Pr.
Brown, Earl L. & Leighton, George R. Negro & the War. LC 75-172045. Repr. of 1942 ed. 11.50 (ISBN 0-404-00194-7). AMS Pr.
Cantor, Milton, ed. Black Labor in America. LC 74-111265. (Contributions in Afro-American & African Studies, No. 2). 1969. 19.95x (ISBN 0-8371-4667-4, Pub. by Negro U Pr). Greenwood.
Christian, Marcus B. Negro Ironworkers in Louisiana. LC 72-85953. (Illus.). 64p. (Orig.). 1972. pap. 7.95 (ISBN 0-911116-74-5). Pelican.
Cull, John G. & Hardy, Richard E., eds. Career Guidance for Black Adolescents: A Guide to Selected Professional Occupations. (American Lectures in Social & Rehabilitation Psychology Ser.). 176p. 1975. text ed. 17.50 (ISBN 0-398-03119-3). C C Thomas.
Dubinsky, Irwin. Reform in Trade Union Discrimination in the Construction Industry: Operation Dig & Its Legacy. LC 72-12974. (Special Studies in U.S. Economic, Social, & Political Issues). 1973. 28.50x (ISBN 0-275-07080-8). Irvington.
Du Bois, W. E. Black Reconstruction in America, 1860-1880. LC 68-1237. (Studies in American Negro Life). 1969. pap. text ed. 7.95x (ISBN 0-689-70063-6, NL20). Atheneum.
--Black Reconstruction in America, 1860-1880. LC 68-1237. 1956. Repr. of 1935 ed. 30.00 (ISBN 0-8462-0172-0). Russell.
Du Bois, W. E. B., ed. The Negro-American Artisan. (Atlanta Univ. Publ.: No. 17). (Orig.). 1912. Repr. of 1912 ed. pap. 5.00 (ISBN 0-527-03118-6). Kraus Repr.
Ebony Editors. Ebony Success Library, Vols. 1-3. Incl. Vol. 1. One Thousand Successful Black (ISBN 0-87485-060-6); Vol. 2. Famous Blacks Give Secrets of Success (ISBN 0-87485-061-4); Vol. 3. Career Guide: Opportunities and Resources for You (ISBN 0-87485-062-2). (Illus.). 960p. 1973. Set. 27.95 (ISBN 0-87485-058-4). Johnson Chi.
Franklin, Charles L. Negro Labor Unionist of New York. LC 68-58573. (Columbia University. Studies in the Social Sciences: No. 420). Repr. of 1936 ed. 27.50 (ISBN 0-404-51420-0). AMS Pr.
Garfinkel, Herbert. When Negroes March. LC 69-15522. (Studies in American Negro Life Ser). 1969. pap. 3.25x (ISBN 0-689-70078-4, NL13). Atheneum.
Ginzberg, Eli. The Negro Potential. LC 56-9606. 144p. 1956. pap. 5.00x (ISBN 0-231-08546-X). Columbia U Pr.
Greene, Lorenzo J. & Woodson, Carter G. Negro Wage Earner. LC 76-126671. Repr. of 1930 ed. 10.25 (ISBN 0-404-00163-7). AMS Pr.
--Negro Wage Earner. LC 69-17839. 1969. Repr. of 1930 ed. 11.50 (ISBN 0-8462-1321-4). Russell.
Harrison, Bennett. Education, Training, & the Urban Ghetto. LC 72-4023. (Illus.). 287p. 1973. 20.00x (ISBN 0-8018-1366-2). Johns Hopkins.
Haynes, George E. Negro at Work in New York City. LC 77-76709. (Columbia University, Studies in the Social Sciences Ser.: No. 124). Repr. of 1912 ed. 5.50 (ISBN 0-404-51124-4). AMS Pr.
Hiestand, Dale L. Economic Growth & Employment Opportunities for Minorities. LC 64-20359. 127p. 1964. 17.50x (ISBN 0-231-02729-X). Columbia U Pr.
Jackson, Luther P. Free Negro Labor & Property Holding in Virginia, 1830-1860. LC 69-15524. (Studies in American Negro Life Ser). 1969. pap. 3.45 (ISBN 0-689-70107-1, NL15). Atheneum.
Jones, Thomas B. A Franchising Guide for Blacks. LC 73-12907. 48p. (Orig.). 1973. pap. 2.00 (ISBN 0-87576-004-X). Pilot Bks.
--A Franchising Guide for Blacks. LC 73-12907. 48p. (Orig.). 1973. pap. 2.00 (ISBN 0-87576-004-X). Pilot Bks.
Kennedy, Louise V. Negro Peasant Turns Cityward. LC 68-58597. (Columbia University Studies in the Social Sciences: No. 329). Repr. of 1930 ed. 14.00 (ISBN 0-404-51329-8). AMS Pr.
Lewis, Edward E. The Mobility of the Negro. LC 68-58603. (Columbia University. Studies in the Social Sciences: No. 342). Repr. of 1931 ed. 12.50 (ISBN 0-404-51342-5). AMS Pr.
Marshall, F. Ray. & Briggs, Vernon M., Jr. The Negro & Apprenticeship. LC 67-18561. 288p. 1967. 18.50x (ISBN 0-8018-0458-2). Johns Hopkins.
Marshall, Ray. The Negro Worker. 1967. pap. text ed. 3.60x (ISBN 0-394-30735-6). Phila Bk Co.
Norgren, Paul H. & Hill, Samuel E. Toward Fair Employment. LC 64-17756. 296p. 1964. 20.00x (ISBN 0-231-02716-8). Columbia U Pr.
Northrup, H. R. Organized Labor & the Negro. Repr. of 1944 ed. 18.00 (ISBN 0-527-67640-3). Kraus Repr.
Purcell, Theodore & Cavanagh, Gerald. Blacks in the Industrial World: Issues for the Manager. LC 74-184530. 1972. 15.95 (ISBN 0-02-925520-1); pap. text ed. 5.95 (ISBN 0-02-925480-9). Free Pr.
Ross, Frank A. Bibliography of Negro Migration. LC 78-80745. (Bibliography & Reference Ser.: No. 370). 1969. Repr. of 1934 ed. 21.00 (ISBN 0-8337-3057-6). B Franklin.
Ross, Jack C. & Wheeler, Raymond H. Black Belonging: A Study of the Social Correlates of Work Relations Among Negroes. LC 77-105974. (Contributions in Sociology: No. 7). 1971. lib. bdg. 15.95 (ISBN 0-8371-3298-3, RBB/); pap. 4.95 (ISBN 0-8371-5962-8). Greenwood.
Ross, Malcolm H. All Manner of Men. Repr. of 1948 ed. lib. bdg. 15.00x (ISBN 0-8371-0992-2, ROMM). Greenwood.

Ruchames, Louis. Race, Jobs & Politics: The Story of the FEPC. LC 78-142922. 255p. 1972. Repr. of 1953 ed. 15.25x (ISBN 0-8371-5948-2). Greenwood.

Twentieth Century Fund. Task Force on Employment Problem of Black Youth. The Job Crisis & Black Youth. Repr. of 1971 ed. 6.00 (ISBN 0-527-02855-X); pap. cancelled (ISBN 0-527-02842-8). Kraus Repr.

U. S. Department Of Labor - Division Of Negro Economics. Negro at Work During the World War & During Reconstruction. LC 70-88453. (Illus.). Repr. of 1921 ed. 10.50x (ISBN 0-8371-1909-X, Pub. by Negro U Pr). Greenwood.

--Negro Migration in 1916-1917 - Reports. LC 78-78580. Repr. of 1919 ed. 9.75x (ISBN 0-8371-1417-9, Pub. by Negro U Pr). Greenwood.

United States Office Of Adviser On Negro Affairs. Urban Negro Worker in the United States, 1925-1936, 2 Vols. in 1. LC 79-82095. (Illus.). 1938-39. Repr. 25.00x (ISBN 0-8371-3209-6). Greenwood.

Washington, Booker T. The Negro in Business. Repr. of 1907 ed. 19.50 (ISBN 0-384-65980-2). Johnson Repr.

--Negro in Business. LC 72-99418. 1969. Repr. of 1907 ed. lib. bdg. 17.50 (ISBN 0-8411-0092-6). Metro Bks.

Washington, Booker T. & Dubois, W. E. Negro in Business. LC 71-144699. (Illus.). Repr. of 1907 ed. 12.50 (ISBN 0-404-00237-4). AMS Pr.

Wegner, Kenneth W. Jobs & the Color Barrier. new ed. Burnes, Alan J., ed. (Urban America Ser.). (Illus.). 62p. (Orig.). (gr. 6-10). 1969. pap. 0.95 (ISBN 0-88301-021-6). Pendulum Pr.

Wesley, Charles H. Negro Labor in the United States, 1850-1925: A Study in American Economic History. LC 67-16001. 1967. Repr. of 1927 ed. 11.00 (ISBN 0-8462-0884-9). Russell.

Woodson, Carter G. Negro Professional Man & the Community, with Special Emphasis on the Physician & the Lawyer. Repr. of 1934 ed. 18.50 (ISBN 0-384-69208-7). Johnson Repr.

--Rural Negro. LC 69-16771. (Illus.). 1969. Repr. of 1930 ed. 12.50 (ISBN 0-8462-1324-9). Russell.

NEGROES–HISTORIOGRAPHY

This heading discontinued January 1976.

Aptheker, Herbert C. Afro-American History: The Modern Era. 1971. 7.95 (ISBN 0-8065-0228-2); pap. 2.95 (ISBN 0-8065-0362-9). Citadel Pr.

NEGROES–HISTORY

This heading discontinued January 1976. See Afro-Americans–History for later materials.

Alimayo, Chikuyo, pseud. A Garden on Cement. (Essays on Black America Ser.). (Illus.). 224p. 1973. 5.95 (ISBN 0-686-05439-3); pap. 2.95 (ISBN 0-686-05440-7). Eko Pubns.

Allen, Robert L. Black Awakening in Capitalist America: An Analytic History. LC 69-20059. pap. 3.50 (ISBN 0-385-07718-1, Anch). Doubleday.

Andrews, Sidney. South Since the War. LC 69-18546. (American Negro: His History & Literature Ser., No. 2). 1969. Repr. of 1866 ed. 14.00 (ISBN 0-405-01847-9). Arno.

Aptheker, Herbert. A Documentary History of the Negro People in the United States from Colonial Times to 1910. 15.00 (ISBN 0-8065-0346-7). Citadel Pr.

--A Documentary History of the Negro People in the United States, Vol. 3: 1932-1945. 640p. 1974. 17.50 (ISBN 0-8065-0438-2). Citadel Pr.

--Essays in the History of the American Negro. 1964. pap. 2.25 (ISBN 0-7178-0061-X). Intl Pub Co.

--To Be Free: Studies in American Negro History. 1968. pap. 2.25 (ISBN 0-7178-0204-3). Intl Pub Co.

Aptheker, Herbert, ed. Documentary History of the Negro People in the United States: Vol. 1 - from Colonial Times Through the Civil War. 1962. pap. 4.95 (ISBN 0-8065-0168-5, 109). Citadel Pr.

--Documentary History of the Negro People in the United States: Vol. 2 - from the Reconstruction Years to the Founding of the National Association for the Advancement of Colored People, 1910. 1964. pap. 4.95 (ISBN 0-8065-0167-7, 160). Citadel Pr.

--A Documentary History of the Negro People in the United States: 1910-1932. 832p. 1973. 17.50 (ISBN 0-8065-0355-6). Citadel Pr.

Aptheker, Herbert C. Afro-American History: The Modern Era. 1971. 7.95 (ISBN 0-8065-0228-2); pap. 2.95 (ISBN 0-8065-0362-9). Citadel Pr.

Association for the Study of Afro-American Life & History. Journal of Negro History, 56, Vols. 1-56. LC 70-102634. 1969. Set. 475.00 (ISBN 0-87781-001-X); Set. lib. bdg. 400.00 (ISBN 0-685-70331-2). Pubs Agency.

Atlanta University. Atlanta University Publications. LC 68-28985. (The American Negro: History & Literature, Ser. No. 3). 1970. Repr. of 1898 ed. No. 3. 5. 6. 7. 10. 12. 19. 20. 37.00 (ISBN 0-405-01914-9). Arno.

--Atlanta University Publications. LC 68-28965. (American Negro: His History & Literature, Ser. No. 1). 1968. Repr. of 1897 ed. No. 1. 2. 4. 8. 9. 11. 13. 14. 15. 16. 17. 18. 34.00 (ISBN 0-405-01804-5). Arno.

Banks, James A. & Banks, Cherry A. March Toward Freedom: A History of Black Americans. 2nd rev ed. LC 77-95084. (Illus.). (gr. 7-12). 1978. pap. text ed. 7.00 (ISBN 0-8224-4406-2). Pitman Learning.

Bardolph, Richard. The Negro Vanguard. LC 77-135592. 388p. 1972. Repr. of 1959 ed. text ed. 21.25x (ISBN 0-8371-5183-X, Pub. by Negro U Pr). Greenwood.

Barr, Alwyn. Black Texans: A History of Negroes in Texas 1528-1971. LC 72-97935. (Negro Heritage Ser., No. 12). (Illus.). 259p. 1973. 12.50 (ISBN 0-8363-0016-5). Jenkins.

Bennett, Lerene, Jr. Shaping of Black America. LC 74-20659. 1975. 15.95 (ISBN 0-87485-071-1). Johnson Chi.

Bennett, Lerone, Jr. Before the Mayflower: A History of Black America. 1969. 8.95 (ISBN 0-87485-029-0). Johnson Chi.

--Black Power U. S. A. The Human Side of Reconstruction, 1867-1877. 1967. 6.95 (ISBN 0-87485-023-1). Johnson Chi.

Berlin, Ira. Slaves Without Masters: The Free Negro in the Antebellum South. LC 74-4761. 448p. 1975. 15.00 (ISBN 0-394-49041-X). Pantheon.

Berry, M. Black Resistance - White Law: A History of Institutional Racism in America. 1971. pap. text ed. 11.95 (ISBN 0-13-077735-8). P-H.

Blackwell, James E. & Janowitz, Morris, eds. Black Sociologists: Historical & Contemporary Perspectives. LC 73-84187. (Heritage of Sociology Ser). xxii, 416p. 1975. Repr. of 1974 ed. 6.50x (ISBN 0-226-05566-3, Phoen). U of Chicago Pr.

Brawley, Benjamin G. A Social History of the American Negro. LC 70-37233. Repr. of 1921 ed. 12.50 (ISBN 0-404-00138-6). AMS Pr.

Brown, William J. The Life of William J. Brown, of Providence, R. I. With Personal Recollections of Incidents in Rhode Island. facsimile ed. LC 78-164382. (Black Heritage Library Collection). Repr. of 1883 ed. 15.50 (ISBN 0-8369-8841-8). Arno.

Brown, William W. Rising Son, Or, the Antecedents & Advancement of the Colored Race. LC 75-100258. Repr. of 1874 ed. 18.25x (ISBN 0-8371-2856-0). Greenwood.

Bruce, Philip A. The Plantation Negro As a Freeman: Observations on His Character, Condition & Prospects in Virginia. LC 79-99354. ix, 262p. 1972. Repr. of 1889 ed. lib. bdg. 14.75 (ISBN 0-8411-0025-X). Metro Bks.

Bunche, Ralph J. The Political Status of the Negro in the Age of F.D.R. Grantham, Dewey W., ed. LC 72-96327. (Illus.). xxxiv, 682p. 1975. pap. 7.95x (ISBN 0-226-08029-3). U of Chicago Pr.

Cantor, Milton, ed. Black Labor in America. LC 74-111265. (Contributions in Afro-American & African Studies, No. 2). 1969. 19.95x (ISBN 0-8371-4667-4, Pub. by Negro U Pr). Greenwood.

Chittenden, L. E. Personal Reminiscences, Eighteen Forty - Eighteen Ninety. facsimile ed. LC 72-37302. (Black Heritage Library Collection). Repr. of 1893 ed. 23.75 (ISBN 0-8369-8939-2). Arno.

Comer, James P. Beyond Black & White. LC 76-162812. 1974. 7.95 (ISBN 0-8129-0220-3); pap. 2.95 (ISBN 0-8129-6231-1). Times Bks.

Conrad, Earl. Invention of the Negro. LC 66-26645. 1969. Repr. of 1967 ed. 5.95 (ISBN 0-8397-3700-9). Eriksson.

Coombs, Norman. The Black Experience in America. LC 73-186717. (The Immigrant Heritage of America Ser.). 1972. lib. bdg. 10.95 (ISBN 0-8057-3208-X). Twayne.

Cummings, John. Negro Population in the United States, 1790-1915. LC 68-28992. (American Negro: His History & Literature Ser., No. 1). 1968. Repr. of 1918 ed. 26.00 (ISBN 0-405-01811-8). Arno.

Davis, Daniel S. Struggle for Freedom: The History of Black Americans. LC 71-187857. (Illus.). 256p. (gr. 9 up). 1972. 6.50 (ISBN 0-15-281815-4, HJ). HarBraceJ.

Dennis, R. Ethel. Black People of America. (gr. 9-12). 1970. 13.72 (ISBN 0-07-016397-9, W); pap. 10.60 (ISBN 0-07-016398-7). McGraw.

Dick, Robert C. Black Protest: Issues & Tactics. LC 72-794. 320p. 1974. lib. bdg. 16.95 (ISBN 0-8371-6366-8, DNA/); pap. 5.95 (ISBN 0-8371-8922-5). Greenwood.

Dubois, William E. The Gift of Black Folk. LC 70-144598. Repr. of 1924 ed. 15.00 (ISBN 0-404-00152-1). AMS Pr.

--The Gift of Black Folk. LC 70-144598. Repr. of 1924 ed. 15.00 (ISBN 0-404-00152-1). AMS Pr.

Ebony Editors. Ebony Pictorial History of Black America, 4 vols. 1971 ed. Bennett, Lerone, Jr., ed. Incl. Vol. 1; Vol. 2; Vol. 3; Vol. 4. The 1973 Yearbook. 312p. 10.95 (ISBN 0-87485-059-2). boxed set of 3 vols. 27.95 (ISBN 0-87485-049-5); deluxe slip-case set of 4 vols. 38.90 (ISBN 0-87485-073-8). Johnson Chi.

--Ebony Success Library, Vols. 1-3. Incl. Vol. 1. One Thousand Successful Black (ISBN 0-87485-060-6); Vol. 2. Famous Blacks Give Secrets of Success (ISBN 0-87485-061-4); Vol. 3. Career Guide: Opportunities and Resources for You (ISBN 0-87485-062-2). (Illus.). 960p. 1973. Set. 27.95 (ISBN 0-87485-058-4). Johnson Chi.

Ferguson, Franklin. Negro American: A History. 173p. 1969. pap. 5.00x (ISBN 0-89039-151-3). Ann Arbor Pubs.

Fishel, Leslie H., Jr. & Quarles, Benjamin. The Black American: A Brief Documentary History. 2nd, brief ed. 1970. pap. 7.95x (ISBN 0-673-07576-1). Scott F.

Fogel, Robert W. & Engerman, Stanley L. Time on the Cross, 2 vols. Incl. Vol. 1. The Economics of American Negro Slavery. LC 73-18347. 8.95 (ISBN 0-316-28699-0); Vol. 2. Evidence & Methods-a Supplement. 12.50 (ISBN 0-316-28700-8). 1974. Little.

Foner, Eric, ed. America's Black Past: A Reader in Afro-American History. 1970. pap. text ed. 14.50 scp (ISBN 0-06-042115-0, HarpC). Harrow.

Foner, Philip S. History of Black Americans: From Africa to the Emergence of the Cotton Kingdom, 4 vols, Vol. 1. LC 74-5987. (Contributions in American History: Vol. 1, No. 40). 680p. 1975. lib. bdg. 27.00 (ISBN 0-8371-7529-1, FBA/1). Greenwood.

Foster, William Z. Negro People in American History. 1970. 8.50 (ISBN 0-7178-0275-2); pap. 3.45 (ISBN 0-7178-0276-0). Intl Pub Co.

Fowler, Charles H. Historical Romance of the American Negro. Repr. of 1902 ed. 23.00 (ISBN 0-384-16530-3). Johnson Repr.

Fox, Stephen R. Guardian of Boston: William Monroe Trotter. LC 78-108822. (Studies in American Negro Life). 1971. pap. text ed. 3.45x (ISBN 0-689-70256-6, NL26). Atheneum.

Franklin, John H. Free Negro in North Carolina, 1790-1860. (Illus.). 1971. pap. 2.25x (ISBN 0-393-00579-8, Norton Lib). Norton.

--Illustrated History of Black Americans. 1970. 7.95 (ISBN 0-8094-0803-1). Time-Life.

Gage, Frank W. Negro Problem in the United States, Its Rise, Development & Solution. LC 74-110111. Repr. of 1892 ed. 10.00x (ISBN 0-8371-4116-8, Pub. by Negro U Pr). Greenwood.

Garnet, Henry H. Past & Present Condition, & the Destiny of the Colored Race. facs. ed. LC 77-79010. (Black Heritage Library Collection Ser). 1848. 7.00 (ISBN 0-8369-8576-1). Arno.

Gatewood, Willard B., Jr. Black Americans & the White Man's Burden, 1898-1903. LC 75-9945. (Blacks in the New World Ser). 350p. 1975. 19.95 (ISBN 0-252-00475-2). U of Ill Pr.

Guzman, Jessie, ed. Negro Year Book, 1941-1946. 1947. 12.50 (ISBN 0-685-02663-9). Univ Place.

Halliburton, R. The Tulsa Race War of 1921. LC 74-31767. 1975. soft bdg. 9.00 (ISBN 0-88247-333-6). R & E Res Assoc.

Harris, Middleton, et al. The Black Book. 1973. pap. 9.95 (ISBN 0-394-70622-6). Random.

Haygood, Atticus G. Our Brother in Black: His Freedom and His Future. LC 77-107806. (Select Bibliographies Reprint Ser). 1881. 17.00 (ISBN 0-8369-5214-6). Arno.

Helm, Mary. From Darkness to Light: The Story of Negro Progress. LC 76-88433. Repr. of 1909 ed. 12.75x (ISBN 0-8371-1908-1, Pub. by Negro U Pr). Greenwood.

Henry, George. Life of George Henry. facsimile ed. LC 73-164389. (Black Heritage Library Collection). Repr. of 1894 ed. 13.25 (ISBN 0-8369-8848-5). Arno.

Herskovits, M. J. The Myth of the Negro Past. 7.75 (ISBN 0-8446-0695-2). Peter Smith.

Hill, Roy L., ed. Rhetoric of Racial Revolt. 2nd ed. 1963. 5.50 (ISBN 0-87315-033-3). Golden Bell.

Jackson, Giles B. & Davis, D. Webster. Industrial History of the Negro Race of the United States. facs. ed. LC 73-152923. (Black Heritage Library Collection Ser). 1908. 32.75 (ISBN 0-8369-8767-5). Arno.

James, C. L. History of the Negro Revolt. LC 75-101141. (Studies in Black History & Culture, No. 54). 1970. Repr. of 1938 ed. lib. bdg. 27.95 (ISBN 0-8383-1217-9). Haskell.

Johnson, Edward A. School History of the Negro Race in America, 2 Vols. in 1. LC 73-100532. Repr. of 1911 ed. 26.50 (ISBN 0-404-00176-9). AMS Pr.

Johnson, William H. Autobiography of William Henry Johnson. LC 72-129569. (Studies in Black History & Culture, No. 54). 1970. Repr. of 1900 ed. lib. bdg. 53.95 (ISBN 0-8383-1155-5). Haskell.

Jordan, Winthrop. White Man's Burden: Historical Origins of Racism in the United States. 224p. 1974. 13.95 (ISBN 0-19-501742-0). Oxford U Pr.

Jordan, Winthrop D. White Over Black: American Attitudes Toward the Negro, 1550-1812. LC 68-13295. (Institute of Early American History & Culture Ser.). (Illus.). 1968. 27.00x (ISBN 0-8078-1055-X). U of NC Pr.

Katz, William L., ed. American Negro: History & Literature, Ser. 1, 44 bks. 1968. Set. 736.50 (ISBN 0-405-01800-2). Arno.

--American Negro: History & Literature, Ser. 2, 66 bks. 1969. Set. 893.00 (ISBN 0-405-01801-0). Arno.

--American Negro: History & Literature, Ser. 3, 30 bks. 1970. Set. 406.00 (ISBN 0-405-01912-2). Arno.

Kletzing, Henry F. & Crogman, William H. Progress of a Race, Or, the Remarkable Advancement of the American Negro. LC 12-4245. (American Studies). 1970. Repr. of 1898 ed. 38.00 (ISBN 0-384-29805-2). Johnson Repr.

Kusmer, Kenneth L. A Ghetto Takes Shape: Black Cleveland, 1870-1930. (Blacks in the New World Ser.). (Illus.). 320p. 1976. 15.00 (ISBN 0-252-00289-X); pap. 5.95 (ISBN 0-252-00690-9). U of Ill Pr.

Lyons, T. T. Black Leadership in American History. 1971. pap. 5.64 (ISBN 0-201-04288-6). A-W.

McPherson, James M. Struggle for Equality: Abolitionists & the Negro in the Civil War & Reconstruction. (Illus.). 1964. 27.50 (ISBN 0-691-04566-6); pap. 8.95 (ISBN 0-691-00555-9). Princeton U Pr.

McQuilkin, Frank. Thinking Black: An Introduction to Black Political Power. 1970. pap. 2.95 (ISBN 0-685-03350-3, 80510). Macmillan.

Malcolm X. Malcolm X on Afro-American History. expanded ed. LC 72-103696. (Illus.). 1972. pap. 2.25 (ISBN 0-87348-085-6). Path Pr NY.

Meier, August. Negro Thought in America, 1880-1915: Racial Ideologies in the Age of Booker T. Washington. LC 63-14008. 1963. 8.95 (ISBN 0-472-64230-8). U of Mich Pr.

--Negro Thought in America, 1880-1915: Racial Ideologies in the Age of Booker T. Washington. 1963. pap. 4.95 (ISBN 0-472-06118-6, 118, AA). U of Mich Pr.

Meier, August & Rudwick, Elliott M., eds. Making of Black America. LC 67-25486. (Studies in American Negro Life). (Orig.). 1969. Vol. 1: The Origins Of Black Americans. pap. text ed. 4.95x (ISBN 0-689-70141-1, NL8A); Vol. 2: The Black Community In Modern America. pap. text ed. 5.95x (ISBN 0-689-70143-8, NL8B). Atheneum.

Mitchell, George W. Question Before Congress. LC 70-100270. Repr. of 1918 ed. 12.25x (ISBN 0-8371-2861-7). Greenwood.

Morris, Thomas D. Free Men All: The Personal Liberty Laws of the North, 1780-1861. LC 73-8126. 265p. 1974. 17.50x (ISBN 0-8018-1505-3). Johns Hopkins.

The Negro in American History, 3 vols. (Illus.). 1972. 43.00 (ISBN 0-87827-007-8). Ency Brit Ed.

Nichols, J. L. & Crogman, William H. Progress of a Race. LC 69-18552. (American Negro: His History & Literature Ser., No. 2). 1969. Repr. of 1920 ed. 19.00 (ISBN 0-405-01883-5). Arno.

Pease, Jane & Pease, William H. They Who Would Be Free: The Blacks' Search for Freedom. LC 74-77620. (Studies in American Negro Life). 1974. pap. text ed. 4.95x (ISBN 0-689-70517-4, NL33). Atheneum.

Pendleton, Leila A. A Narrative of the Negro. facsimile ed. LC 78-178481. (Black Heritage Library Collection). Repr. of 1912 ed. 18.25 (ISBN 0-8369-8930-9). Arno.

Pictorial History of Black Americans. rev. ed. 1973. pap. 5.95 (ISBN 0-517-50622-X); 7.95 (ISBN 0-517-50621-1). Crown.

Pierson, Hamilton W. A Letter to Hon. Charles Sumner. facsimile ed. LC 78-38018. (Black Heritage Library Collection). Repr. of 1866 ed. 10.50 (ISBN 0-8369-8985-6). Arno.

Pinkney, Alphonse. Black Americans. 2nd ed. (Ethnic Groups in American Life Ser.). (Illus.). 272p. 1975. pap. text ed. 8.95x (ISBN 0-13-077529-0). P-H.

Porter, Kenneth W. The Negro on the American Frontier. LC 77-135872. Repr. of 1971 ed. 15.00 (ISBN 0-405-01983-1). Arno.

Quarles, Benjamin. Negro in the Making of America. (Orig.). (gr. 9 up). 1964. pap. 2.95 (ISBN 0-02-036130-0, Collier). Macmillan.

Roucek, Joseph S. & Kiernan, Thomas. Negro Impact on Western Civilization. LC 72-86509. 1970. 15.00 (ISBN 0-8022-2329-X). Philos Lib.

Ruffin, E. Anticipations of the Future. facsimile ed. LC 70-38021. (Black Heritage Library Collection). Repr. of 1860 ed. 21.00 (ISBN 0-8369-8988-0). Arno.

Scheiner, Seth M. & Edelstein, Tilden G., eds. The Black Americans: Interpretive Readings. LC 75-4844. 512p. 1975. pap. 11.50 (ISBN 0-88275-287-1). Krieger.

Sernett, Milton C. Black Religion & American Evangelicalism: White Protestants, Plantation Missions, & the Flowering of Negro Christianity, 1787-1865. LC 75-4754. (ATLA Monograph: No. 7). (Illus.). 320p. 1975. 15.00 (ISBN 0-8108-0803-X). Scarecrow.

Sinclair, William A. Aftermath of Slavery - a Study of the Condition & Environment of the American Negro. LC 69-18548. (American Negro: His History & Literature, Ser. No. 2). 1969. Repr. of 1905 ed. 13.00 (ISBN 0-405-01894-0). Arno.

--Aftermath of Slavery: A Study of the Condition & Environment of the American Negro. LC 71-99490. 1969. Repr. of 1905 ed. lib. bdg. 11.50 (ISBN 0-8411-0079-9). Metro Bks.

Synnestvedt, Sig. The White Response to Black Emancipation: Second-Class Citizenship in the United States Since Reconstruction. 288p. 1972. pap. text ed. 6.50x (ISBN 0-02-418750-X). Macmillan.

Taylor, J. Troup. Prophetic Families, or, the Negro: His Origin, Destiny & Status. facs. ed. LC 70-89442. (Black Heritage Library Collection Ser). 1895. 8.00 (ISBN 0-8369-8664-4). Arno.

Thomas, William H. American Negro. LC 74-95449. (Studies in Black History & Culture, No. 54). 1970. Repr. of 1901 ed. lib. bdg. 59.95 (ISBN 0-8383-1206-3). Haskell.

Toppin, Edgar A. The Black American in United States History. new ed. (gr. 9-12). 1973. text ed. 12.20 (ISBN 0-205-03303-2, 7833032); tchrs.' guide 4.12 (ISBN 0-205-03304-0, 7833040). Allyn.

Tuskegee Institute, Alabama, Dept. of Records & Research. Pamphlets: 1949-1961, 1 vol, Nos. 1-10. 24.00 (ISBN 0-527-91250-6). Kraus Repr.

U.S. House of Representatives-Executive Document No. 30. Use of the Army in Certain of the Southern States: 44th Congress, Second Session. LC 75-90201. (Mass Violence in America Ser). Repr. of 1876 ed. 19.00 (ISBN 0-405-01314-0). Arno.

Washington, Booker T. New Negro for a New Century. pap. 3.95 (ISBN 0-685-16793-3, N185P). Mnemosyne.

--New Negro for a New Century: An Accurate & Up-To-Date Record of the Upward Struggles of the Negro Race. facs. ed. LC 79-81134. (Black Heritage Library Collection Ser). 1900. 16.50 (ISBN 0-8369-8679-2). Arno.

--The Story of the Negro: The Rise of the Race from Slavery, 2 vols. 16.00 (ISBN 0-8446-0955-2). Peter Smith.

Washington, Booker T., et al. New Negro for a New Century. LC 69-18559. (American Negro: His History & Literature, Ser., No. 2). 1969. Repr. of 1900 ed. 16.00 (ISBN 0-405-01904-1). Arno.

Weatherford, Willis D. Negro from Africa to America. LC 69-16565. Repr. of 1924 ed. 16.50x (ISBN 0-8371-2399-2, Pub. by Negro U Pr). Greenwood.

Williams, George W. History of the Negro Race in America from 1619 to 1880, 2 vols. LC 69-19636. (American Negro: His History & Literature Ser., No. 1). 1968. Repr. of 1883 ed. Set. 39.00 (ISBN 0-405-01844-4). Arno.

Williamson, Joel. After Slavery: The Negro in South Carolina During Reconstruction, 1861-1877. 464p. 1975. pap. 5.95 (ISBN 0-393-00759-6, Norton Lib). Norton.

Wolters, Raymond. Negroes & the Great Depression: The Problem of Economic Recovery. Kutler, Stanley E., ed. LC 78-95510. (Contributions in American History: No. 6). 1970. lib. bdg. 19.95 (ISBN 0-8371-2341-0, WON/). Greenwood.

Work, Monroe, ed. Negro Year Book: An Annual Encyclopedia of the Negro, 1918-1919. 523p. pap. 7.50 (ISBN 0-685-26800-4). Univ Place.

NEGROES–HISTORY–BIBLIOGRAPHY

This heading discontinued January 1976. See Afro-Americans–History for later materials.

George Washington University American Studies Program-Rose Bibl. Analytical Guide & Indexes to the Colored American Magazine: 1900-1909, 2 vols. LC 73-15077. 1974. lib. bdg. 75.00x set (ISBN 0-8371-7176-8, RBCAM). Greenwood.

--Analytical Guide & Indexes to The Crisis: 1910-1960, 3 vols. LC 73-15078. 1975. lib. bdg. 195.00x (ISBN 0-8371-7175-X, RBCRR). Greenwood.

Kumatz & Wolf. The Black Experience. 1971. 5.00 (ISBN 0-913252-05-0). LIU Univ.

Smith, Dwight L., ed. Afro-American History: A Bibliography. new ed. LC 73-87155. (Clio Bibliography Ser.: No. 2). 856p. 1974. text ed. 55.00 (ISBN 0-87436-123-0). ABC-Clio.

Williams, D. T., compiled by. Eight Negro Bibliographies. 1969. 30.00 (ISBN 0-527-96840-4). Kraus Repr.

NEGROES–HISTORY–SOURCES

This heading discontinued January 1976. See Afro-Americans–History for later materials.

Bell, Howard H., ed. Minutes of the Proceedings of the National Negro Conventions 1830-1864. LC 72-105552. (American Negro: His History & Literature, Ser. No. 3). 1970. Repr. of 1969 ed. 19.50 (ISBN 0-405-01916-5). Arno.

Frazier, Thomas R., ed. Afro-American History: Primary Sources. (Shorter ed.). 1971. pap. text ed. 2.50 (ISBN 0-15-502051-X, HC). HarBraceJ.

Meltzer, Milton. In Their Own Words: A History of the American Negro, 1619-1865, Vol. 1. LC 64-22541. (Illus.). (gr. 5 up). 1964. 8.95 (ISBN 0-690-44691-8, TYC-J). Har-Row.

--In Their Own Words: A History of the American Negro, 1916-1966, Vol. 3. LC 66-1439. (Illus.). (gr. 5 up). 1967. 8.95 (ISBN 0-690-44693-4, TYC-J). Har-Row.

Minutes of the Proceedings at a Court Martial, Assembled for the Trial of Capt. John Moutray of His Majesty's Ship the Ramillies. LC 77-81076. (Eyewitness Accounts of the American Revolution Ser., No. 2). Repr. of 1781 ed. 10.00 (ISBN 0-405-01163-6). Arno.

Storing, J. J., ed. Writings of Black Americans. 1970. pap. 6.95 (ISBN 0-312-86520-1, W21001). St Martin.

Wade, Richard C. & Anderson, Howard R., eds. Negro in American Life. (Life in America Ser). (gr. 9-12). 1970. pap. 4.56 (ISBN 0-395-03147-8, 2-33480). HM.

Westmoreland, Guy T., Jr. An Annotated Guide to Basic Reference Books on the Black American Experience. LC 74-79558. 1974. 14.00 (ISBN 0-8420-1738-0). Scholarly Res Inc.

NEGROES–HISTORY–STUDY AND TEACHING

This heading discontinued January 1976. See Afro-Americans–History for later materials.

Ward, Olivia. ABC's of Black History: Educational Multi-Media Program. LC 74-77593. 1974. complete pkg. 79.50 (ISBN 0-913024-04-X). Tandem Pr.

NEGROES–HISTORY–1960-

This heading discontinued January 1976. See Afro-Americans–History for later materials.

Brisbane, Robert H. Black Activism. LC 74-2892. 336p. 1974. 10.00 (ISBN 0-8170-0619-2); pap. 5.95 (ISBN 0-8170-0674-5). Judson.

Good, Paul. The Trouble I've Seen: White Journalist - Black Movement. LC 74-10923. 354p. 1975. 9.95 (ISBN 0-88258-020-5). Howard U Pr.

Hallie Q. Brown Memorial Library. Index to Periodical Articles by & About Negroes, 1960-1970, Cumulation. 1971. 55.00 (ISBN 0-8161-0847-1). G K Hall.

King, Martin L., Jr. Where Do We Go from Here? Chaos or Community. pap. 4.95 (ISBN 0-8070-0571-1, BP285). Beacon Pr.

--Where Do We Go from Here: Chaos or Community. 1967. 11.95 (ISBN 0-06-012394-X, HarpT). Har-Row.

Wolters, Raymond. Negroes & the Great Depression: The Problem of Economic Recovery. Kutler, Stanley E., ed. LC 78-95510. (Contributions in American History: No. 6). 1970. lib. bdg. 19.95 (ISBN 0-8371-2341-0, WON/). Greenwood.

NEGROES–HOUSING

This heading discontinued January 1976. See Afro-Americans–Housing for later materials.

Clark, Henry. The Church & Residential Desegregation. 1965. 6.00x (ISBN 0-8084-0076-2). Coll & U Pr.

Deutsch, Morton & Collins, Mary E. Interracial Housing: A Psychological Evaluation of a Social Experiment. LC 68-25056. (Illus.). 1968. Repr. of 1951 ed. 7.00 (ISBN 0-8462-1196-3). Russell.

Meyer, David R. Spatial Variation of Black Urban Households. LC 72-128466. (Research Papers Ser.: No. 129). 127p. 1970. pap. 8.00 (ISBN 0-89065-036-5). U Chicago Dept Geog.

Meyerson, Martin & Banfield, Edward C. Politics, Planning & the Public Interest. LC 55-7335. 1964. pap. text ed. 5.95 (ISBN 0-02-921230-8). Free Pr.

Openshaw, Howard. Race & Residence: An Analysis of Property Values in Transitional Areas, Atlanta, Georgia, 1960-1971. LC 74-620726. (Research Monograph: No. 53). 1973. spiral bdg. 10.00 (ISBN 0-88406-019-5). Ga St U Busn Pub.

President's Conference On Home Building And Home Ownership. Negro Housing. Gries, John M. & Ford, James, eds. LC 79-89053. Repr. of 1932 ed. 13.75x (ISBN 0-8371-1921-9, Pub. by Negro U Pr). Greenwood.

Stacey, William A. Black Home Ownership: A Sociological Case Study of Metropolitan Jacksonville. LC 73-186201. (Special Studies in U.S. Economic, Social & Political Issues). 1972. 29.50x (ISBN 0-275-04810-1). Irvington.

Vose, Clement E. Caucasians Only: The Supreme Court, the NAACP, & the Restrictive Covenant Cases. LC 59-8758. 1959. 22.75x (ISBN 0-520-01308-5); pap. 5.95x (ISBN 0-520-01309-3, CAMPUS1). U of Cal Pr.

NEGROES–INTELLECTUAL LIFE

This heading discontinued January 1976.

Cruse, Harold. The Crisis of the Negro Intellectual. 1967. pap. 7.95 (ISBN 0-688-25224-9). Morrow.

Pickens, William. New Negro, His Political, Civil & Mental Status & Related Essays. LC 72-95399. Repr. of 1916 ed. 10.00 (ISBN 0-404-00271-4). AMS Pr.

Thorpe, Earl E. Mind of the Negro: An Intellectual History of Afro-Americans. LC 76-100313. Repr. of 1961 ed. 28.00x (ISBN 0-8371-3863-9, Pub. by Negro U Pr). Greenwood.

Woodson, Carter G., ed. Mind of the Negro As Reflected in Letters Written During the Crisis 1800-1860. Repr. of 1926 ed. lib. bdg. 17.00x (ISBN 0-8371-1179-X, WOM&). Greenwood.

NEGROES–JUVENILE LITERATURE

This heading discontinued January 1976. Later juvenile materials on Afro-Americans or Blacks are classified with adult titles and identified by grade range.

see also Negroes–Biography–Juvenile Literature; Negroes–Civil Rights–Juvenile Literature

Bontemps, Arna. Story of the Negro. 5th ed. (Illus.). (gr. 7 up). 1958. PLB 5.99 (ISBN 0-394-91690-5). Knopf.

Goodman, M. C. Junior History of the American Negro, 2 vols. Incl. Vol. 1. Discovery to Civil War. 1969 (ISBN 0-8303-0072-4); Vol. 2. Civil War to Civil Rights War. LC 73-76026. 1970 (ISBN 0-8303-0073-2). (Illus.). (gr. 6-12). 6.50 ea.; text ed. avail. (ISBN 0-8303-0162-3); teaching manual 0.50 ea. Fleet.

Heard, J. Norman. Black Frontiersmen: Adventures of Negroes Among American Indians, 1528-1918. LC 79-89317. (Illus.). (gr. 6 up). 1969. 7.95 (ISBN 0-381-99799-5, A09050, JD-J). Har-Row.

Hunter, Kristin. Guests in the Promised Land. 144p. (gr. 5 up). 1973. 5.95 (ISBN 0-684-13227-3, ScribJ). Scribner.

Johnston, Johanna A. Special Bravery. LC 67-20777. (Illus.). (gr. 2-5). 1967. 5.95 (ISBN 0-396-06728-X). Dodd.

Lester, Julius. Long Journey Home: Stories from Black History. LC 75-181791. 176p. (gr. 7 up). 1972. 7.95 (ISBN 0-8037-4953-8). Dial.

Meltzer, Ida S. Black History: Events in February. Thomas, Nestina, ed. (Ethnic Reading Series). (Illus.). 32p. (Orig.). (gr. 4-9). 1972. pap. text ed. 6.75 set of ten (ISBN 0-87594-171-0, 4604). Book-Lab.

--Blacks in Early American History. Thomas, Nestina, ed. (Ethnic Reading Series). (Illus.). 32p. (Orig.). (gr. 4-9). 1972. pap. text ed. 6.75 set of ten (ISBN 0-87594-168-0, 4601). Book-Lab.

--A School at Midnight. Thomas, Nestina, ed. (Ethnic Reading Ser). (Illus.). 32p. (Orig.). (gr. 4-9). 1972. pap. text ed. 6.75 set of ten (ISBN 0-87594-170-2, 4603). Book-Lab.

Schraff, A. E. Black Courage. LC 76-87984. (Illus.). (gr. 3 up). 1969. PLB 5.97 (ISBN 0-8255-7801-9). Macrae.

NEGROES–LEGAL STATUS, LAWS, ETC.

This heading discontinued January 1976. See Afro-Americans–Legal Status, Laws, Etc. for later materials.

Berry, M. Black Resistance - White Law: A History of Institutional Racism in America. 1971. pap. text ed. 11.95 (ISBN 0-13-077735-8). P-H.

Catterall, Helen H., ed. Judicial Cases Concerning American Slavery & the Negro, 5 Vols. LC 68-55875. 1926-1937. Set. 139.50x (ISBN 0-8371-0343-6, Pub. by Negro U Pr). Greenwood.

Catterall, Helen T., ed. Judicial Cases Concerning American Slavery & the Negro, 5 Vols. 1968. Repr. of 1937 ed. Set. lib. bdg. 115.00 (ISBN 0-374-91330-7). Octagon.

Friedman, Leon, ed. Southern Justice. LC 75-33296. 306p. 1976. Repr. of 1965 ed. lib. bdg. 17.50x (ISBN 0-8371-8489-4, FRSJ). Greenwood.

Greenberg, Jack & Lambert, Richard D., eds. Blacks & the Law. new ed. LC 72-93252. (Annals of the American Academy of Political & Social Science: No. 407). 250p. 1973. 7.50 (ISBN 0-87761-163-7); pap. 6.00 (ISBN 0-87761-162-9). Am Acad Pol Soc Sci.

Guild, June. Black Laws of Virginia. LC 78-98721. Repr. of 1936 ed. 12.25x (ISBN 0-8371-2777-7, Pub. by Negro U Pr). Greenwood.

Mangum, Charles S. The Legal Status of the Negro. Repr. of 1940 ed. 21.00 (ISBN 0-384-35150-6). Johnson Repr.

Martin, Carl. To Hell with the Constitution: An Expose. Owens, Ethel E., ed. (Orig.). 1971. pap. 7.50 (ISBN 0-911734-11-2). Commonsense.

Yates, William. Rights of Colored Men to Suffrage, Citizenship, & Trial by Jury. facs. ed. LC 71-89437. (Black Heritage Library Collection Ser). 1838. 9.25 (ISBN 0-8369-8695-4). Arno.

NEGROES–MORAL AND SOCIAL CONDITIONS

This heading discontinued January 1976. See Afro-Americans–Social Conditions for later materials.

Billingsley, Andrew. Black Families in White America. LC 68-54602. 1968. pap. 2.95 (ISBN 0-13-077453-7, Spec). P-H.

Bond, Horace M. Education of the Negro in the American Social Order. rev. ed. 1965. lib. bdg. 30.00x (ISBN 0-374-90760-9). Octagon.

Caliver, Ambrose. Background Study of Negro College Students. LC 76-82089. (Illus.). Repr. of 1933 ed. 10.00x (ISBN 0-8371-3205-3, Pub. by Negro U Pr). Greenwood.

--Personnel Study of Negro College Students: A Study of the Relations Between Certain Background Factors of Negro College Studens & Their Subsequent Careers in College. LC 73-107470. Repr. of 1931 ed. 10.75x (ISBN 0-8371-3749-7). Greenwood.

Cohn, David. Where I Was Born & Raised. 1967. pap. 2.75x (ISBN 0-268-00299-1). U of Notre Dame Pr.

Conference for the Study of Problems Concerning Negro City Life. Social & Physical Condition of Negroes in Cities. (Atlanta Univ. Publ. Ser.: No. 2). (Orig.). Repr. of 1897 ed. 4.00 (ISBN 0-527-03109-7). Kraus Repr.

Doyle, Bertram W. Etiquette of Race Relations in the South. LC 68-25198. 1968. Repr. of 1937 ed. 12.00 (ISBN 0-8046-0115-1). Kennikat.

Du Bois, W. E. B. Efforts for Social Betterment Among Negro Americans. (Atlanta Univ. Publ. Ser.: No. 14). (Orig.). 1909. Repr. of 1909 ed. 5.00 (ISBN 0-527-03115-1). Kraus Repr.

Du Bois, W. E. B., ed. Morals & Manners Among Negro Americans. (Atlanta Univ. Publ. Ser.: No. 18). (Orig.). 1914. Repr. of 1914 ed. pap. 5.00 (ISBN 0-527-03119-4). Kraus Repr.

Frazier, E. Franklin. Negro Family in the United States. rev. & abr ed. LC 66-13868. 1966. pap. 2.95 (ISBN 0-226-26141-7, P205, Phoen). U of Chicago Pr.

Gillard, John T. The Catholic Church & the Negro. (Basic Afro-American Reprint Library). 1969. Repr. of 1929 ed. 15.50 (ISBN 0-384-18550-9). Johnson Repr.

Goldman, Peter. Report from Black America. LC 77-130194. 1970. 6.95 (ISBN 0-671-20609-5). S&S.

--Report from Black America. LC 77-130194. 1971. pap. 2.95 (ISBN 0-671-20899-3, Touchstone Bks). S&S.

Greene, Lorenzo J. & Woodson, Carter G. Negro Wage Earner. LC 76-126671. Repr. of 1930 ed. 10.25 (ISBN 0-404-00163-7). AMS Pr.

--Negro Wage Earner. LC 69-17839. 1969. Repr. of 1930 ed. 11.50 (ISBN 0-8462-1321-4). Russell.

Hendin, Herbert. Black Suicide. LC 72-92476. 1969. 15.00x (ISBN 0-465-00705-8). Basic.

Herbst, Alma. Negro in the Slaughtering & Meat-Packing Industry in Chicago. LC 73-156417. (American Labor Ser., No. 2). 1971. Repr. of 1932 ed. 12.00 (ISBN 0-405-02925-X). Arno.

Johnson, Charles S. Negro College Graduate. LC 79-78768. (Illus.). Repr. of 1938 ed. 18.25x (ISBN 0-8371-1392-X, Pub. by Negro U Pr). Greenwood.

Jones, William H. Recreation & Amusement Among Negroes in Washington, D. C. LC 72-88440. Repr. of 1927 ed. 15.25x (ISBN 0-8371-1847-6). Greenwood.

Kardiner, Abram & Ovesey, Lionel. Mark of Oppression: Explorations in the Personality of the American Negro. pap. 3.95 (ISBN 0-452-00141-2, FM141, Mer). NAL.

Kennedy, Louise V. Negro Peasant Turns Cityward. LC 68-58597. (Columbia University Studies in the Social Sciences: No. 329). Repr. of 1930 ed. 14.00 (ISBN 0-404-51329-8). AMS Pr.

McCord, Charles H. The American Negro As Dependent, Defective & Delinquent. 59.95 (ISBN 0-87968-609-X). Gordon Pr.

Morel, Edmund D. The Black Man's Burden. LC 75-99396. 241p. 1972. Repr. of 1920 ed. lib. bdg. 11.00 (ISBN 0-8411-0067-5). Metro Bks.

Negro Young People's Christian & Educational Congress Atlanta 1902. United Negro: His Problems & His Progress. Penny, Irvine G. & Bowen, John W., eds. LC 71-77210. (Illus.). Repr. of 1902 ed. 27.75x (ISBN 0-8371-1309-1). Greenwood.

Osofsky, Gilbert, ed. Puttin' on Ole Massa: The Slave Narratives of Henry Bibb, William W. Brown, & Solomon Northrup. 1969. pap. 7.50x (ISBN 0-06-131432-3, TB1432, Torch). Har-Row.

Patterson, William L., ed. We Charge Genocide: The Crime of Government Against the Negro People. LC 76-140208. 1970. 5.95 (ISBN 0-7178-0311-2); pap. 1.95 (ISBN 0-7178-0312-0). Intl Pub Co.

Powdermaker, Hortense. After Freedom: A Cultural Study in the Deep South. LC 68-16415. (Studies in American Negro Life). 1968. pap. 3.45 (ISBN 0-689-70160-8, NL3). Atheneum.

President's Conference On Home Building And Home Ownership. Negro Housing. Gries, John M. & Ford, James, eds. LC 79-89053. Repr. of 1932 ed. 13.75x (ISBN 0-8371-1921-9, Pub. by Negro U Pr). Greenwood.

Rainwater, Lee. Behind Ghetto Walls: Black Family Life in a Federal Slum. LC 77-113083. 1970. text ed. 24.95x (ISBN 0-202-30113-3); pap. text ed. 11.95x (ISBN 0-202-30114-1). Aldine Pub.

Ross, Frank A. Bibliography of Negro Migration. LC 78-80745. (Bibliography & Reference Ser.: No. 370). 1969. Repr. of 1934 ed. 21.00 (ISBN 0-8337-3057-6). B Franklin.

Sanders, Wiley B. Negro Child Welfare in North Carolina. LC 68-55782. (Criminology, Law Enforcement, & Social Problems Ser.: No. 18). (Illus.). 1968. Repr. of 1933 ed. 15.00 (ISBN 0-87585-018-9). Patterson Smith.

Staples, Robert. The Black Woman in America: Sex, Marriage & the Family. LC 72-95280. 287p. 1973. 17.95x (ISBN 0-911012-55-9); pap. 9.95x (ISBN 0-685-99065-6). Nelson-Hall.

Sterner, Richard E. Negro's Share: A Study of Income, Consumption, Housing & Public Assistance. LC 72-138018. (Illus.). 1971. Repr. of 1943 ed. text ed. 21.25x (ISBN 0-8371-5665-3, Pub. by Negro U Pr). Greenwood.

Warner, Robert A. New Haven Negroes, a Social History. LC 78-94138. (American Negro: His History & Literature, Ser. No. 3). 1970. Repr. of 1940 ed. 16.00 (ISBN 0-405-01940-8). Arno.

Warner, William L. Color & Human Nature: Negro Personality Development in a Northern City. LC 78-106844. Repr. of 1941 ed. 15.50x (ISBN 0-8371-3466-8, Pub. by Negro U Pr). Greenwood.

Weatherford, Willis D. Race Relations: Adjustment of Whites & Negroes in the United States. LC 73-97459. Repr. of 1934 ed. 24.75x (ISBN 0-8371-2691-6). Greenwood.

White House Conference on Child Health & Protection. The Young Child in the Home: A Survey of Three Thousand American Families. LC 71-169371. (Family in America Ser). 446p. 1972. Repr. of 1936 ed. 22.00 (ISBN 0-405-03847-X). Arno.

Woodson, Carter G. Rural Negro. LC 69-16771. (Illus.). 1969. Repr. of 1930 ed. 12.50 (ISBN 0-8462-1324-9). Russell.

Woofter, Thomas J. Negro Problems in Cities. LC 70-89064. Repr. of 1928 ed. 12.25x (ISBN 0-8371-1942-1, Pub. by Negro U Pr). Greenwood.

Wright, Richard. Twelve Million Black Voices: A Folk History of the Negro in the U.S. LC 69-18562. (American Negro: His History & Literature Ser., No. 2). 1969. Repr. of 1941 ed. 14.00 (ISBN 0-405-01909-2). Arno.

NEGROES–PERIODICALS

This heading discontinued January 1976. See Afro-American Press for later materials.

Anglo-African Magazine, Vol. 1. Eighteen Fifty-Nine. LC 68-28984. (American Negro - His History & Literature, Ser No. 1). 14.00 (ISBN 0-405-01803-7). Arno.

Brown American: National Association of Negroes in America in Industries, No. 8. 1936-1945. Repr. 250.00x (ISBN 0-8371-9374-5, Pub. by Negro U Pr). Greenwood.

Color Line: A Monthly Round up of the Facts of Negro American Progress & of Growth of American Democracy, Vols. 1-2. 1946-1947. Repr. 16.00x (ISBN 0-8371-3052-2, Pub. by Negro U Pr). Greenwood.

Colored American Magazine, Vols. 1-17 No. 5. 1900-1909. Repr. Set. 845.00x (ISBN 0-8371-9108-4, Pub. by Negro U Pr). Greenwood.

Competitor, Vols. 1-3 No. 4. 1920-1921. Repr. Set. 160.00x (ISBN 0-8371-9109-2, Pub. by Negro U Pr). Greenwood.

George Washington University American Studies Program-Rose Bibl. Analytical Guide & Indexes to the Voice of the Negro: 1904-1907. LC 73-15079. 1974. lib. bdg. 54.00x (ISBN 0-8371-7174-1, RBVON). Greenwood.

Hallie Q. Brown Memorial Library. Index to Periodical Articles by & About Negroes, Annual, 1972. 826p. 1974. lib. bdg. 49.00 (ISBN 0-8161-1106-5). G K Hall.

--Index to Periodicals Articles by & About Negroes, Annual, 1971. lib. bdg. 42.00 (ISBN 0-8161-0869-2). G K Hall.

Harlem Quarterly, No. 1-4. 1949-1950. Repr. 15.50x (ISBN 0-8371-3051-4, Pub. by Negro U Pr). Greenwood.

Messenger: World's Greatest Negro Monthly, Vols. 1-10, No. 5. 1917-1928. Repr. 545.00x (ISBN 0-8371-9112-2, Pub. by Negro U Pr). Greenwood.

National Association for the Advancement of Colored People. Crisis, A Record of the Darker Races, Vols. 1-47. 1910-1940. Repr. Set. 675.00x (ISBN 0-8371-9113-0, Pub. by Negro U Pr). Greenwood.

National Negro Health News, Vol. 1-18. 1933-1950. Repr. 270.00x (ISBN 0-8371-9115-7, Pub. by Negro U Pr). Greenwood.

Negro Quarterly Magazine: A Review of Negro Life & Culture, Vols. 1-4. 1942-1943. Repr. 21.50x (ISBN 0-8371-1223-0, Pub. by Negro U Pr). Greenwood.

New Challenge, Vol. 1-2. 1934-1937. Repr. 23.75x (ISBN 0-8371-3049-2, Pub. by Negro U Pr). Greenwood.

Quarterly Review of Higher Education Among Negroes, Vols. 1-28. 1933-1960. Repr. 395.00x (ISBN 0-8371-9120-3). Greenwood.

Race: Devoted to Social, Political, & Economic Equality No. 1-2. 1935-1936. Repr. 16.50x (ISBN 0-8371-3047-6). Greenwood.

Race Relations Magazine: A Monthly Summary & Events & Trends, Vol. 1-5. 1943-1948. Repr. 130.00x (ISBN 0-8371-9121-1). Greenwood.

Smith, Dwight L., ed. Afro-American History: A Bibliography. new ed. LC 73-87155. (Clio Bibliography Ser.: No. 2). 856p. 1974. text ed. 55.00 (ISBN 0-87436-123-0). ABC-Clio.

Southern Frontier, Vols. 1-6. 1940-1945. Repr. 39.00x (ISBN 0-8371-1260-5, Pub. by Negro U Pr). Greenwood.

NEGROES–POLITICS AND SUFFRAGE

This heading discontinued January 1976. See Afro-Americans-politics and Suffrage and Blacks-Politics and Government for later materials.

see also Negroes–Civil Rights

Altshuler, Alan. Community Control: The Black Demand for Participation in Large American Cities. LC 72-110439. 1970. pap. 5.50 (ISBN 0-672-63517-8). Pegasus.

Alvarez, Joseph A. From Reconstruction to Revolution: The Blacks' Struggle for Equality. LC 71-154747. (Illus.). 1971. 6.50 (ISBN 0-689-10485-5). Atheneum.

Bond, Julian. A Time to Speak, A Time to Act. 1972. pap. 1.95 (ISBN 0-671-21345-8, Touchstone Bks). S&S.

Braxton, Bernard. Women, Sex, & Race: A Realistic View of Sexism & Racism. LC 72-91049. 228p. 1973. 7.95 (ISBN 0-930876-01-6); pap. 3.95 (ISBN 0-930876-02-4). Verta Pr.

Brink, William & Harris, Louis. Negro Revolution in America. 1963. pap. 2.25 (ISBN 0-671-20419-X, Touchstone Bks). S&S.

Brisbane, Robert H. Black Activism. LC 74-2892. 336p. 1974. 10.00 (ISBN 0-8170-0619-2); pap. 5.95 (ISBN 0-8170-0674-5). Judson.

Bunche, Ralph J. The Political Status of the Negro in the Age of FDR. Grantham, Dewey W., ed. LC 72-96327. (Documents in American History Ser.). 704p. 1973. 27.50x (ISBN 0-226-08028-5). U of Chicago Pr.

Buni, Andrew. Negro in Virginia Politics, 1902-1965. LC 67-21659. 1967. 9.75 (ISBN 0-8139-0058-1). U Pr of Va.

Callcott, Margaret Law. The Negro in Maryland Politics, 1870-1912. LC 69-15395. (Historical & Political Science: Eighty-Seventh Series No. 1 (1969)). (Illus.). 358p. 1969. 22.50x (ISBN 0-8018-1023-X); pap. 5.95x (ISBN 0-8018-1556-8). Johns Hopkins.

Carmichael, Stokely S. & Hamilton, Charles V. Black Power: The Politics of Liberation in America. 1967. pap. 2.95 (ISBN 0-394-70033-3, V33, Vin). Random.

Champion, Jackson R. Blacks in the Republican Party? LC 75-29732. (Illus.). 1976. 5.95 (ISBN 0-917230-03-5). LenChamps Pubs.

Clayton, Edward T. Negro Politician. 1964. 4.95 (ISBN 0-87485-008-8). Johnson Chi.

Douglass, Frederick. Frederick Douglass: Selections. Foner, Philip S., ed. (Orig.). (YA) (gr. 7-12). 1945. pap. 1.00 (ISBN 0-7178-0071-7). Intl Pub Co.

Du Bois, W. E. Black Reconstruction in America, 1860-1880. LC 68-1237. (Studies in American Negro Life). 1969. pap. text ed. 7.95x (ISBN 0-689-70063-6, NL20). Atheneum.

--Black Reconstruction in America, 1860-1880. LC 68-1237. 1956. Repr. of 1935 ed. 30.00 (ISBN 0-8462-0172-0). Russell.

Garfinkel, H. When Negroes March. 1959. 5.95 (ISBN 0-02-911290-7). Free Pr.

Gilliam, Reginald E., Jr. Black Political Development: An Advocacy Analysis. LC 73-88999. 1974. 18.50 (ISBN 0-8046-7089-7). Kennikat.

Gosnell, Harold F. Negro Politicians: The Rise of Negro Politics in Chicago. LC 66-30216. 1935. 7.95x (ISBN 0-226-30493-0). U of Chicago Pr.

Greenberg, E. S., et al. The Inevitability of a Conflict-Readings. 383p. 1971. pap. 9.95 (ISBN 0-03-084739-7, Pub. by HR&W). Krieger.

Grossman, Lawrence. The Democratic Party & the Negro: Northern & National Politics, 1868-92. LC 75-30546. (Blacks in the New World Ser). 320p. 1976. 12.50 (ISBN 0-252-00575-9). U of Ill Pr.

Hamilton, Charles V. The Bench & the Ballot: Southern Federal Judges & Black Votes. 270p. 1974. pap. 5.95x (ISBN 0-19-501719-6). Oxford U Pr.

Hawley, Willis D. Blacks & Metropolitan Governance: The Stakes of Reform. LC 72-5145. 34p. (Orig.). 1972. pap. 1.50x (ISBN 0-87772-153-X). Inst Gov Stud Berk.

Hensel, William U. Christiana Riot & Treason Trials of 1851. facs. ed. LC 70-89415. (Black Heritage Library Collection Ser). 1911. 10.50 (ISBN 0-8369-8598-2). Arno.

Herring, Bryan W. Unprotected: Or, Mistakes of the Republican Party. facs. ed. LC 74-83892. (Black Heritage Library Collection Ser). 1890. 13.50 (ISBN 0-8369-8599-0). Arno.

Holloway, Harry. The Politics of the Southern Negro: From Exclusion to Big City Organization. 1969. text ed. 11.95x (ISBN 0-685-77213-6, 0-394-30283). Phila Bk Co.

Hunt, William H. Argument of William H. Hunt, Esq. facsimile ed. LC 71-168516. (Black Heritage Library Collection). Repr. of 1873 ed. 9.50 (ISBN 0-8369-8868-X). Arno.

Jordan, June. Dry Victories. (gr. 5 up). 1975. pap. 1.50 (ISBN 0-380-00476-3, 34835). Avon.

Ladd, Everett C., Jr. Negro Political Leadership in the South. LC 69-13435. (Studies in American Negro Life). 1969. pap. 3.95 (ISBN 0-689-70120-9, NL19). Atheneum.

--Negro Political Leadership in the South. 348p. 1966. 22.50x (ISBN 0-8014-0240-9). Cornell U Pr.

Langston, John M. Freedom & Citizenship. facs. ed. LC 74-79012. (Black Heritage Library Collection Ser). 1883. 13.75 (ISBN 0-8369-8618-0). Arno.

Lewinson, Paul. Race, Class, & Party: A History of Negro Suffrage & White Politics in the South. LC 63-15168. (Illus.). 1963. Repr. of 1932 ed. 21.00 (ISBN 0-8462-0366-9). Russell.

Mabry, William A. Negro in North Carolina Politics Since Reconstruction. LC 75-110130. (Duke University. Trinity College Historical Society. Historical Papers: No. 23). Repr. of 1940 ed. 17.50 (ISBN 0-404-51773-0). AMS Pr.

Matthews, Donald R. & Prothro, James W. Negro Political Participation Study, 1961-1962. 2nd ed. 1975. codebk. 18.00 (ISBN 0-89138-112-0). ICPSR.

--Negroes & the New Southern Politics. LC 66-28289. (Illus.). 551p. 12.50 (ISBN 0-15-165011-X). HarBraceJ.

Moon, H. L. Balance of Power: The Negro Vote. 1948. 13.00 (ISBN 0-527-64800-0). Kraus Repr.

Morris, Milton D. The Politics of Black America. 336p. 1975. pap. text ed. 11.50 scp (ISBN 0-06-044619-6, HarpC). Har-Row.

Nowlin, William F. Negro in American National Politics. LC 74-81461. 1970. Repr. of 1931 ed. 7.50 (ISBN 0-8462-1367-2). Russell.

--Negro in American National Politics. LC 71-173802. Repr. of 1931 ed. 7.50 (ISBN 0-404-00204-8). AMS Pr.

Olbrich, Emil. Development of Sentiment on Negro Suffrage to Eighteen Sixty. LC 77-88444. (Wisconsin University History Ser., Vol. 3, No. 1). Repr. of 1912 ed. 10.00x (ISBN 0-8371-1757-7, Pub. by Negro U Pr). Greenwood.

--Development of Sentiment on Negro Suffrage to 1860. facs. ed. Fish, Carl R., ed. LC 72-154085. (Black Heritage Library Collection Ser). 1912. 13.25 (ISBN 0-8369-8796-9). Arno.

Pickens, William. New Negro, His Political, Civil & Mental Status & Related Essays. LC 72-95399. Repr. of 1916 ed. 10.00 (ISBN 0-404-00271-4). AMS Pr.

Porter, Kirk H. History of Suffrage in the United States. LC 70-137272. Repr. of 1918 ed. 21.00 (ISBN 0-404-00207-2). AMS Pr.

--History of Suffrage in the United States. LC 18-22279. 1969. Repr. of 1918 ed. lib. bdg. 16.75x (ISBN 0-8371-0620-6, POHS). Greenwood.

Price, Hugh D. The Negro & Southern Politics: A Chapter of Florida History. LC 73-3027. (Illus.). 133p. 1973. Repr. of 1957 ed. lib. bdg. 15.00x (ISBN 0-8371-6824-4, PRNS). Greenwood.

Record, Wilson. Negro & the Communist Party. LC 76-162279. (Studies in American Negro Life). 1971. pap. text ed. 3.45x (ISBN 0-689-70279-5, NL29). Atheneum.

Roman, Charles V. American Civilization & the Negro: The Afro-American in Relation to National Progress. LC 70-140820. Repr. of 1916 ed. 23.75x (ISBN 0-8371-5851-6, Pub. by Negro U Pr). Greenwood.

Sherman, Richard B. The Republican Party & Black America: From McKinley to Hoover, 1896-1933. LC 72-96714. 1973. 12.95x (ISBN 0-8139-0467-6). U Pr of Va.

Stephenson, Gilbert T. Race Distinctions in American Law. LC 10-21327. (Basic Afro-American Reprint Library). 18.50 (ISBN 0-384-58030-0). Johnson Repr.

Storing, J. J., ed. Writings of Black Americans. 1970. pap. 6.95 (ISBN 0-312-86520-1, W21001). St Martin.

Strong, Donald S. Negroes, Ballots, & Judges. LC 68-23477. 100p. 1968. 8.00x (ISBN 0-8173-4715-1). U of Ala Pr.

Tatum, Elbert L. The Changed Political Thought of the Negro, 1915-1940. LC 73-16739. 205p. 1974. Repr. of 1951 ed. lib. bdg. 15.00x (ISBN 0-8371-7217-9, TACP). Greenwood.

Taylor, A. A. Negro in South Carolina During the Reconstruction. LC 69-14219. (Illus.). 1969. Repr. of 1924 ed. 10.00 (ISBN 0-8462-1312-5). Russell.

*Thomas, Tony & Oliver, Norman. What Road to Black Liberation: The Democratic Party or an Independent Black Party. 1974. pap. 0.50 (ISBN 0-87348-336-7). Path Pr NY.

Turner, Robert P. Up to the Front of the Line: The Black Man in the American Political System. 1975. 12.95 (ISBN 0-8046-9097-9, Natl U). Kennikat.

Walton, Hanes, Jr. Black Political Parties: An Historical & Political Analysis. LC 76-143514. 1972. 10.95 (ISBN 0-02-933870-0). Free Pr.

--Black Republicans: The Politics of the Black & Tans. LC 75-6718. 217p. 1975. 10.00 (ISBN 0-8108-0811-0). Scarecrow.

--The Study & Analysis of Black Politics: A Bibliography. LC 73-12985. 1973. 10.00 (ISBN 0-8108-0665-7). Scarecrow.

Watters, Pat & Cleghorn, Reese. Climbing Jacob's Ladder: The Arrival of Negroes in Southern Politics. LC 67-20324. 1970. pap. 2.95 (ISBN 0-15-618105-3, H080, Hbgr). HarBraceJ.

Williams, Joyce E. Black Community Control: A Study of Transition in a Texas Ghetto. LC 72-85984. (Special Studies in U.S. Economic, Social & Political Issues). 1973. 29.50x (ISBN 0-89197-681-7). Irvington.

Wilson, J. Q. Negro Politics. LC 60-10906. 1960. pap. 2.95 (ISBN 0-02-935390-4). Free Pr.

Wolfe, Tom. Radical Chic & Mau-Mauing the Flak Catchers. 153p. 1970. 5.95 (ISBN 0-374-24600-9). FS&G.

Wynn, Daniel W. The Black Protest Movement. LC 73-88710. 259p. 1974. 7.50 (ISBN 0-8022-2129-7). Philos Lib.

NEGROES–PSYCHOLOGY

This heading discontinued January 1976. See Afro-Americans–Psychology for later materials.

Atwood, Jesse H., et al. Thus Be Their Destiny: The Personality Development of Negro Youth in Three Communities. LC 71-155631. Repr. of 1941 ed. 12.50 (ISBN 0-404-00135-1). AMS Pr.

Baughman, E. Earl. Black Americans: A Psychological Analysis. LC 70-152748. 1971. pap. text ed. 7.50 (ISBN 0-12-083040-X). Acad Pr.

Comer, James P. Beyond Black & White. LC 76-162812. 1974. 7.95 (ISBN 0-8129-0220-3); pap. 2.95 (ISBN 0-8129-6231-1). Times Bks.

Crain, Robert L. & Weisman, Carlos S. Discrimination, Personality & Achievement: A Survey of Northern Negroes. LC 72-10104. (Quantitative Studies in Social Relations Er). 1972. 30.50 (ISBN 0-12-785142-9). Acad Pr.

DeCoy, Robert H. Cold Black Preach. 224p. 1971. pap. 1.95 (ISBN 0-87067-627-X, BH627). Holloway.

Ferguson, George O. Psychology of the Negro: An Experimental Study. LC 74-107481. Repr. of 1916 ed. 10.50x (ISBN 0-8371-3783-7). Greenwood.

Grier, William H. & Cobbs, Price M. Black Rage. LC 68-29925. 1968. 10.00 (ISBN 0-465-00702-3). Basic.

Hall, W. S. & Freedle, R. O. Culture & Language: The Black American Experience. LC 75-12534. 191p. 1975. 10.95 (ISBN 0-470-34156-4). Halsted Pr.

Hendin, Herbert. Black Suicide. LC 72-92476. 1969. 15.00x (ISBN 0-465-00705-8). Basic.

Hill, John L. Negro: National Asset or Liability. Repr. of 1930 ed. 11.50 (ISBN 0-384-23270-1). Johnson Repr.

Kardiner, Abram & Ovesey, Lionel. Mark of Oppression: Explorations in the Personality of the American Negro. pap. 3.95 (ISBN 0-452-00141-2, FM141, Mer). NAL.

Karon, Bertram P. Black Scars: A Rigorous Investigation of the Effects of Discrimination, New Edition of the Negro Personality. LC 74-79412. 220p. 1975. 10.95 (ISBN 0-8261-1540-3). Springer Pub.

McDonald, Marjorie. Not by the Color of Their Skin: The Impact of Racial Differences on the Child's Development. LC 73-134334. Orig. Title: Integration & Skin Color. 1971. text ed. 17.50 (ISBN 0-8236-3690-9); pap. text ed. 5.95 (ISBN 0-8236-8166-1, 023690). Intl Univs Pr.
Miller, Kent S. & Dreger, Ralph M., eds. Comparative Studies of Blacks & Whites in the United States. LC 72-82126. (Quantitative Studies in Social Relations Ser). 1973. 46.50 (ISBN 0-12-785526-2). Acad Pr.
Smith, Sidonie. Where I'm Bound. new ed. LC 73-20973. 194p. 1974. lib. bdg. 15.00 (ISBN 0-8371-7337-X, SPS/). Greenwood.
Sutherland, Robert L. Color, Class, & Personality. LC 78-155413. (Illus.). 135p. 1972. Repr. of 1942 ed. lib. bdg. 15.00x (ISBN 0-8371-3347-5, SUCC). Greenwood.
Thomas, Charles W. Boys No More: A Black Psychologist's View of Community. 1971. pap. text ed. 4.95x (ISBN 0-02-478890-2, 47889). Macmillan.
Thorpe, Earl E. Mind of the Negro: An Intellectual History of Afro-Americans. LC 76-100313. Repr. of 1961 ed. 28.00x (ISBN 0-8371-3863-9, Pub. by Negro U Pr). Greenwood.
Wilcox, Roger N., ed. Psychological Consequences of Being a Black American: A Source Book of Research by Black Psychologists. LC 74-142720. 1971. pap. 14.95 (ISBN 0-471-94383-5). Wiley.

NEGROES–RACE IDENTITY
This heading discontinued January 1976. See Afro-Americans–Race Identity and Blacks–Race Identity for later materials.
Angeles, Peter A. Possible Dream: Toward Understanding the Black Experience. (Orig.). 1971. pap. 1.95 (ISBN 0-377-01211-4). Friend Pr.
Ba, Sylvia W. The Concept of Negritude in the Poetry of Leopold Sedar Senghor. LC 72-7797. 250p. 1973. 20.00 (ISBN 0-691-06251-X). Princeton U Pr.
Carroll, Charles. Negro a Beast. facs. ed. LC 74-89419. (Black Heritage Library Collection Ser). 1900. 18.75 (ISBN 0-8369-8533-8). Arno.
Clark, Chris & Rush, Sheila. How to Get Along with Black People: A Handbook for White Folks & Some Black Folks Too. LC 73-162960. 156p. 1971. 8.95 (ISBN 0-89388-018-3). Okpaku Communications.
--How to Get Along with Black People: A Handbook for White Folks & Some Black Folks Too. LC 73-162960. 143p. 1973. pap. 5.95 (ISBN 0-89388-019-1). Okpaku Communications.
Congress On Africa. Africa & the American Negro. facs. ed. Bowen, J. W., ed. LC 74-79020. (Black Heritage Library Collection Ser). 1896. 13.50 (ISBN 0-8369-8547-8). Arno.
Ebony Editors. Black Revolution: An Ebony Special Issue. LC 72-128545. (Illus.). 1970. 5.95 (ISBN 0-87485-039-8). Johnson Chi.
Gurin, Patricia & Epps, Edgar G. Black Consciousness, Identity & Achievement: A Study of Students in Historically Black Colleges. LC 75-5847. 545p. 1975. text ed. 28.95 (ISBN 0-471-33670-X). Wiley.
Kletzing, Henry F. & Crogman, William H. Progress of a Race, Or, the Remarkable Advancement of the American Negro. LC 12-4245. (American Studies). 1970. Repr. of 1898 ed. 38.00 (ISBN 0-384-29805-2). Johnson Repr.
Petroni, Frank A. & Hirsch, Ernest A. Two, Four, Six, Eight, When You Gonna Integrate? 1971. pap. 2.75 (ISBN 0-87140-041-3). Liveright.
Poinsett, Alex. Black Power Gary Style: The Making of Mayor Richard Gordon Hatcher. LC 72-128545. 1970. 6.95 (ISBN 0-87485-042-8). Johnson Chi.
Preto-Rodas, Richard A. Negritude As a Theme in the Poetry of the Portuguese-Speaking World. LC 79-107879. (U of Fla. Humanities Monographs Ser.: No. 31). 1970. pap. 3.00 (ISBN 0-8130-0297-4). U Presses Fla.
Rogers, J. A. Nature Knows No Color Line. 242p. 1952. 7.95 (ISBN 0-9602294-5-0). H M Rogers.
Smith, Sidonie. Where I'm Bound. new ed. LC 73-20973. 194p. 1974. lib. bdg. 15.00 (ISBN 0-8371-7337-X, SPS/). Greenwood.
Weisbord, Robert G. Ebony Kinship: Africa, Africans & the Afro-American. LC 72-847. (Contributions in Afro-American & African Studies: No. 14). 256p. 1973. lib. bdg. 14.95 (ISBN 0-8371-6416-8, WEA&); pap. 4.95 (ISBN 0-8371-7340-X). Greenwood.
Woodson, Carter G., ed. Mind of the Negro As Reflected in Letters Written During the Crisis, 1800-1860. LC 69-14222. 1969. Repr. of 1926 ed. 17.50 (ISBN 0-8462-1314-1). Russell.

NEGROES–RELIGION
This heading discontinued January 1976. See Afro-Americans–Religion and Blacks–Religion for later materials.
Boatright, Mody C. & Day, Donald, eds. From Hell to Breakfast. LC 45-1540. (Texas Folklore Society Publications: No. 19). (Illus.). 1967. Repr. of 1944 ed. 6.95 (ISBN 0-87074-012-1). SMU Press.
Catto, William T. Semi-Centenary Discourse. facs. ed. LC 78-154073. (Black Heritage Library Collection Ser). 1857. 12.25 (ISBN 0-8369-8784-5). Arno.
Cleage, Albert B., Jr. Black Christian Nationalism: New Directions for the Black Church. 1972. pap. 5.95 (ISBN 0-688-06019-6). Morrow.
Cone, James H. Black Theology of Liberation. LC 74-120333. 1970. pap. 4.50 (ISBN 0-397-10098-1). Har-Row.
Essays & Pamphlets on Antislavery. LC 68-55924. 1833-1898. Repr. 14.25x (ISBN 0-8371-1795-X, Pub. by Negro U Pr). Greenwood.
Fauset, Arthur H. Black Gods of the Metropolis, Negro Religious Cults of the Urban North. LC 73-120251. 1970. Repr. lib. bdg. 12.00x (ISBN 0-374-92714-6). Octagon.
--Black Gods of the Metropolis: Negro Religious Cults of the Urban North. LC 75-133446. 1971. pap. 4.50x (ISBN 0-8122-1001-8, Pa Paperbks). U of Pa Pr.
Frazier, E. Franklin & Lincoln, C. Eric. The Negro Church in America. new ed. Bd. with The Black Church Since Frazier. LC 72-96201. (Sourcebooks in Negro History Ser.). 1973. 10.00x (ISBN 0-8052-3508-6); pap. 4.95 (ISBN 0-8052-0387-7). Schocken.
Gardiner, James J. & Roberts, J. Deotis, eds. Quest for a Black Theology. LC 76-151250. 128p. 1971. 6.95 (ISBN 0-8298-0196-0). Pilgrim NY.
Gillard, John T. The Catholic Church & the Negro. (Basic Afro-American Reprint Library). 1969. Repr. of 1929 ed. 15.50 (ISBN 0-384-18550-9). Johnson Repr.
Harrison, William P. Gospel Among the Slaves. LC 70-168249. Repr. of 1893 ed. 27.50 (ISBN 0-404-00263-3). AMS Pr.
Helm, Mary. From Darkness to Light: The Story of Negro Progress. LC 76-88433. Repr. of 1909 ed. 12.75x (ISBN 0-8371-1908-1, Pub. by Negro U Pr). Greenwood.
Hood, James W. Negro in the Christian Pulpit: Or the Two Characters & Two Destinies, As Delineated in 21 Practical Sermons. LC 79-109995. Repr. of 1884 ed. 18.00x (ISBN 0-8371-4119-2, Pub. by Negro U Pr). Greenwood.
Johnson, Clifton H., ed. God Struck Me Dead. LC 78-77839. 1969. pap. 3.95 (ISBN 0-8298-0050-6). Pilgrim NY.
Jones, J. Christian Ethics for Black Theology. LC 74-8680. 208p. (Orig.). 1974. pap. 4.50 (ISBN 0-687-07208-5). Abingdon.
McKinney, Richard I. Religion in Higher Education Among Negroes. LC 75-38785. (Religion in America, Ser. 2). 186p. 1972. Repr. of 1945 ed. 11.00 (ISBN 0-405-04075-X). Arno.
Massie, Priscilla, ed. Black Faith & Black Solidarity. (Illus.). 1974. pap. 2.50 (ISBN 0-377-00014-0). Friend Pr.
Mays, Benjamin E. Negro's God As Reflected in His Literature. LC 69-16578. (Illus.). Repr. of 1938 ed. 16.50x (ISBN 0-8371-1139-0, Pub. by Negro U Pr). Greenwood.
Mays, Benjamin E. & Nicholson, Joseph W. Negro's Church. LC 70-83430. (Religion in America, Ser. 1). 1969. Repr. of 1933 ed. 19.00 (ISBN 0-405-00255-6). Arno.
--Negro's Church. LC 68-15142. (Illus.). 1969. Repr. of 1933 ed. 13.00 (ISBN 0-8462-1311-7). Russell.
Miller, Harriet P. Pioneer Colored Christians. facsimile ed. LC 73-37313. (Black Heritage Library Collection). Repr. of 1911 ed. 13.50 (ISBN 0-8369-8950-3). Arno.
Negro Pew. facs. ed. LC 76-149873. (Black Heritage Library Collection Ser). 1837. 10.00 (ISBN 0-8369-8753-5). Arno.
Negro Young People's Christian & Educational Congress Atlanta 1902. United Negro: His Problems & His Progress. Penny, Irvine G. & Bowen, John W., eds. LC 71-77210. (Illus.). Repr. of 1902 ed. 27.75x (ISBN 0-8371-1309-1). Greenwood.
Nelsen, Hart M. & Nelsen, Anne K. Black Church in the Sixties. LC 74-18937. 184p. 1975. pap. 5.50x (ISBN 0-8131-0137-9). U Pr of Ky.
Nelsen, Hart M., et al, eds. Black Church in America. LC 79-147014. 1971. text ed. 10.75x (ISBN 0-465-00691-4). Basic.
Pipes, William H. Say Amen Brother, Old-Time Negro Preaching: A Study in American Frustration. LC 73-111585. Repr. of 1951 ed. 13.75x (ISBN 0-8371-4611-9). Greenwood.
Sernett, Milton C. Black Religion & American Evangelicalism: White Protestants, Plantation Missions, & the Flowering of Negro Christianity, 1787-1865. LC 75-4754. (ATLA Monograph: No. 7). (Illus.). 320p. 1975. 15.00 (ISBN 0-8108-0803-X). Scarecrow.
Thomas, George B. Young Black Adults: Liberation & Family Attitudes. 1974. pap. 1.95 (ISBN 0-377-00002-7). Friend Pr.
Thomas, Issac L. Methodism & the Negro. LC 75-155415. (Illus.). Repr. of 1910 ed. 16.75x (ISBN 0-8371-6111-8, Pub. by Negro U Pr). Greenwood.
Traynham, Warner R. Christian Faith in Black & White: A Primer in Theology from the Black Perspective. LC 73-85538. 128p. (Orig.). 1973. pap. 5.20 (ISBN 0-88203-003-5). Parameter Pr.
Williams, Melvin D. Community in a Black Pentecostal Church: An Anthropological Study. LC 74-5108. 1974. 11.95 (ISBN 0-8229-3290-3). U of Pittsburgh Pr.

NEGROES–SEGREGATION
This heading discontinued January 1976. See Afro-Americans–Segregation and Blacks–Segregation for later materials.
Bunche, Ralph J. The Political Status of the Negro in the Age of F.D.R. Grantham, Dewey W., ed. LC 72-96327. (Illus.). xxxiv, 682p. 1975. pap. 7.95x (ISBN 0-226-08029-3). U of Chicago Pr.
Carter, Hodding. South Strikes Back. Repr. of 1959 ed. 12.25x (ISBN 0-8371-5178-3). Greenwood.
Clark, Kenneth B. Dark Ghetto: Dilemmas of Social Power. pap. 3.50x (ISBN 0-06-131317-3, TB1317, Torch). Har-Row.
Coles, Robert. Children of Crisis. 1968. pap. 3.95 (ISBN 0-440-51235-2, Delta). Dell.
--Children of Crisis, Vol. 1: A Study of Courage & Fear. (Children of Crisis Ser.). (Illus.). 1967. 16.95 (ISBN 0-316-15159-9, Pub. by Atlantic Monthly Pr); pap. 6.95 (ISBN 0-316-15154-8). Little.
Crain, Robert L. & Weisman, Carlos S. Discrimination, Personality & Achievement: A Survey of Northern Negroes. LC 72-10104. (Quantitative Studies in Social Relations Er). 1972. 30.50 (ISBN 0-12-785142-9). Acad Pr.
Deutsch, Morton & Collins, Mary E. Interracial Housing: A Psychological Evaluation of a Social Experiment. LC 68-25056. (Illus.). 1968. Repr. of 1951 ed. 7.00 (ISBN 0-8462-1196-3). Russell.
Free People of Color: On the Condition of the Free People of Color in the United States(Present Condition of the Free Colored People in the United States. LC 75-92232. (American Negro: His History & Literature, Ser. No. 3). 1970. Repr. of 1853 ed. 7.50 (ISBN 0-405-01928-9). Arno.
Jacobstein, Helen L. The Segregation Factor in the Florida Democratic Gubernatorial Primary of 1956. LC 72-3302. (U of Fla. Social Sciences Monographs: No. 47). 1972. pap. 3.25 (ISBN 0-8130-0359-8). U Presses Fla.
King, Martin L. Stride Toward Freedom. LC 58-7099. 1958. 10.95 (ISBN 0-06-064690-X, HarpR). Har-Row.
Lee, Frank F. Negro & White in a Connecticut Town: A Study in Race Relations. 1961. 7.50x (ISBN 0-8084-0403-2); pap. 2.25 (ISBN 0-8084-0404-0, B3). Coll & U Pr.
Litwack, Leon F. North of Slavery: The Negro in the Free States, 1790-1860. LC 61-10869. 1961. 14.00x (ISBN 0-226-48585-4). U of Chicago Pr.
--North of Slavery: The Negro in the Free States, 1790-1860. LC 61-10869. 1965. pap. 4.95 (ISBN 0-226-48586-2, P179, Phoen). U of Chicago Pr.
Martin, John B. Deep South Says, Never. LC 77-135604. Repr. of 1957 ed. 10.75x (ISBN 0-8371-5179-1, Pub. by Negro U Pr). Greenwood.
Negro Pew. facs. ed. LC 76-149873. (Black Heritage Library Collection Ser). 1837. 10.00 (ISBN 0-8369-8753-5). Arno.
Newby, I. A. Challenge to the Court: Social Scientists & the Defense of Segregation, 1954-1966. rev ed. McGurk, Gregor, et al, eds. LC 69-17623. 1969. 25.00x (ISBN 0-8071-0628-3). La State U Pr.
Reimers, David M. White Protestantism & the Negro. 1965. 11.95 (ISBN 0-19-501195-3). Oxford U Pr.
Tumin, Melvin M. Desegregation: Resistance & Readiness. 1958. 20.00x (ISBN 0-691-09313-X). Princeton U Pr.
--Segregation & Desegregation, a Digest of Recent Research. LC 74-73. 112p. 1975. Repr. of 1957 ed. lib. bdg. 15.00x (ISBN 0-8371-7365-5, TUSD). Greenwood.
Warren, Robert P. Segregation: The Inner Conflict of the South. 1956. 10.95 (ISBN 0-394-44456-6). Random.
Yinger, John M. Minority Group in American Society. 1965. text ed. 10.95 (ISBN 0-07-072271-4, C); pap. text ed. 6.95 (ISBN 0-07-072270-6). McGraw.
Young, Whitney M., Jr. Beyond Racism: Building an Open Society. 1971. pap. 2.95 (ISBN 0-07-072373-7, SP). McGraw.

NEGROES–SOCIAL CONDITIONS
This heading discontinued January 1976. See Afro-Americans–Social Conditions and Blacks–Social Conditions for later materials.
Blackwell, James E. The Black Community: Diversity & Unity. LC 74-28532. (Illus.). 336p. (Orig.). 1975. pap. text ed. 14.50 scp (ISBN 0-06-040735-2, HarpC). Har-Row.
Chevigny, Paul. Cops & Rebels. LC 72-570. 1972. 24.00x (ISBN 0-394-47218-7). Irvington.
Greenberg, E. S., et al. The Inevitability of a Conflict-Readings. 383p. 1971. pap. 9.95 (ISBN 0-03-084739-7, Pub. by HR&W). Krieger.
Halpern, Florence. Survival: Black & White. 225p. 1973. text ed. 23.00 (ISBN 0-08-016994-5); pap. text ed. 10.00 (ISBN 0-08-017193-1). Pergamon.
Kornweibel, Theodore, Jr. No Crystal Stair: Black Life & the Messenger, 1917-1928. LC 75-16967. (Contributions in Afro-American & African Studies: No. 20). 306p. 1975. lib. bdg. 14.25x (ISBN 0-8371-8284-0, KCS/). Greenwood.
Ley, David. The Black Inner City As Frontier Outpost. LC 74-82116. (Monograph: No. 7). pap. 6.95 (ISBN 0-89291-086-0). Assn Am Geographers.
Miller, Kent S. & Dreger, Ralph M., eds. Comparative Studies of Blacks & Whites in the United States. LC 72-82126. (Quantitative Studies in Social Relations Ser). 1973. 46.50 (ISBN 0-12-785526-2). Acad Pr.
Muraskin, William A. Middle-Class Blacks in a White Society. 1975. 26.50x (ISBN 0-520-02705-1). U of Cal Pr.
Rowan, Carl. Just Between Us Blacks. LC 74-9068. 1974. 10.00 (ISBN 0-394-47090-7). Random.
Thompson, Daniel C. Sociology of the Black Experience. LC 73-20974. (Contributions in Sociology: No. 14). 261p. 1974. lib. bdg. 15.75 (ISBN 0-8371-7336-1, TBE/); pap. 4.95 (ISBN 0-8371-8928-4, TBE). Greenwood.
Wiley, Bell I. Southern Negroes, 1861-1865. LC 38-12709. 378p. 1974. pap. text ed. 7.95x (ISBN 0-8071-0090-0). La State U Pr.
Wolfe, Tom. Radical Chic & Mau-Mauing the Flak Catchers. 153p. 1970. 5.95 (ISBN 0-374-24600-9). FS&G.

NEGROES–SOCIAL LIFE AND CUSTOMS
This heading discontinued January 1976. See Afro-Americans–Social Life and Customs for later materials.
Angelou, Maya. I Know Why the Caged Bird Sings. (gr. 9-12). 1971. pap. 2.50 (ISBN 0-553-13904-5, 13904-5). Bantam.
Cohn, David. Where I Was Born & Raised. 1967. pap. 2.75x (ISBN 0-268-00299-1). U of Notre Dame Pr.
Goldstein, Rhoda L., ed. Black Life & Culture in the United States. LC 74-146281. (Apollo Eds.). 1971. pap. 3.95 (ISBN 0-8152-0294-6, A294). T Y Crowell.
Gordon, Asa H. Sketches of Negro Life & History in South Carolina. 2nd ed. LC 76-122358. 1971. pap. 2.25 (ISBN 0-87249-202-8). U of SC Pr.
Halpern, Florence. Survival: Black & White. 225p. 1973. text ed. 23.00 (ISBN 0-08-016994-5); pap. text ed. 10.00 (ISBN 0-08-017193-1). Pergamon.
Harrison, Paul C. The Drama of Nommo. LC 72-86051. 245p. 1972. 12.50 (ISBN 0-394-48275-1). Ultramarine Pub.
Heller, Murray, ed. Black Names in America: Origins & Usage. (Reference Bks.). 1975. lib. bdg. 29.50 (ISBN 0-8161-1140-5). G K Hall.
Hopkins, Pauline E. Contending Forces: Romances Illustrative of Negro Life, North & South. LC 72-83909. (Black Heritage Library Collection Ser.). 1900. 16.00 (ISBN 0-8369-8602-4). Arno.
Porter, Grace C. Negro Folk Singing Games & Folk Games of the Habitants. (Folklore Ser.). Repr. of 1914 ed. 6.50 (ISBN 0-88305-506-6). Norwood Edns.
Rainwater, Lee. Behind Ghetto Walls: Black Family Life in a Federal Slum. LC 77-113083. 1970. text ed. 24.95x (ISBN 0-202-30113-3); pap. text ed. 11.95x (ISBN 0-202-30114-1). Aldine Pub.

NEGROES–SOCIETIES
This heading discontinued January 1976. See Afro-Americans–Societies, Etc. for later materials.
Stuart, M. S. An Economic Detour: A History of Insurance in the Lives of American Negroes. Repr. of 1940 ed. 19.50 (ISBN 0-384-58660-0). Johnson Repr.

NEGROES–STATISTICS, VITAL
This heading discontinued January 1976. See Afro-Americans–Statistics, Vital for later materials.
U. S. Bureau of the Census & Hall, Charles E. Negroes in the United States, 1920-1932. Repr. of 1935 ed. lib. bdg. 46.00x (ISBN 0-8371-2076-4, NUS&). Greenwood.

NEGROES IN AFRICA
This heading discontinued January 1976. See Blacks for later materials.

Gollock, Georgina A. Lives of Eminent Africans. LC 70-91256. Repr. of 1928 ed. 13.00x (ISBN 0-8371-2062-4, Pub. by Negro U Pr). Greenwood.

--Sons of Africa. LC 75-89001. Repr. of 1928 ed. 12.75x (ISBN 0-8371-1746-1). Greenwood.

Guggisberg, Frederick G. Future of the Negro: Some Chapters in the Development of a Race. LC 71-97366. Repr. of 1929 ed. 10.00x (ISBN 0-8371-2427-1, Pub. by Negro U Pr). Greenwood.

Herskovits, Melville J. Background of African Art. lim. ed. LC 67-18433. (Cooke-Daniels Lecture Ser., Denver Art Museum). (Illus.). 1945. 10.50x (ISBN 0-8196-0201-9). Biblo.

Lynch, Hollis, ed. Black Africa. LC 73-8774. (Great Contemporary Issues Ser). 1973. 35.00 (ISBN 0-405-04165-9, Co-Pub by New York Times). Arno.

Mylius, N. Afrika Bibliographia, Nineteen Forty-Three to Nineteen Fifty-One. 1952. 20.00 (ISBN 0-527-66120-1). Kraus Repr.

Ojigbo, A. Okion, ed. Young & Black in Africa: Personal Accounts by Eight Africans. (Sundial Paperbks.). 1974. pap. 1.50 (ISBN 0-394-70802-4, Vin). Random.

Sachs, Wulf. Black Anger. LC 68-23323. 1968. Repr. of 1947 ed. lib. bdg. 16.75x (ISBN 0-8371-0244-8, SABA). Greenwood.

Sweeney, James J. African Negro Art. LC 66-26124. (Museum of Modern Art-Publications in Reprint Ser). Repr. of 1935 ed. 19.00 (ISBN 0-405-01517-8). Arno.

Tillinghast, Joseph A. Negro in Africa & America. facs. ed. LC 77-89441. (Black Heritage Library Collection Ser). 1902. 12.25 (ISBN 0-8369-8667-9). Arno.

--Negro in Africa & America. LC 68-58070. Repr. of 1902 ed. 10.75x (ISBN 0-8371-0686-9, Pub. by Negro U Pr). Greenwood.

Woodson, Carter G. African Background Outlined: Or, Handbook for the Study of the Negro. LC 68-55922. (Illus.). Repr. of 1936 ed. 16.50x (ISBN 0-8371-0760-1, Pub. by Negro U Pr). Greenwood.

NEGROES IN AFRICA-HISTORY
This heading discontinued January 1976.

Malcolm X. Malcolm X on Afro-American History. expanded ed. LC 72-103696. (Illus.). 1972. pap. 2.25 (ISBN 0-87348-085-6). Path Pr NY.

Sik, Endre. History of Black Africa, 4 vols. Simon, Sandor, tr. (Illus.). Vol. 1. 27.50 (ISBN 0-8044-1853-5); Vol. 2. 27.50 (ISBN 0-8044-1854-3); Vol.3. 32.50 (ISBN 0-8044-1855-1); Vol.4. 32.50 (ISBN 0-8044-1857-8); 105.00 set (ISBN 0-8044-1852-7). Ungar.

NEGROES IN AMERICA
This heading discontinued January 1976. For later works on Negroes in the United States see Afro-Americans and subdivisions under this heading. For works on Negroes during the discovery and exploration period of the Americas see Blacks-America-History. For works on Negroes in areas of the Americas other than the United States see Blacks or geographical subdivisions under this heading, e.g. Blacks-Latin America.

Abajian, James De T., compiled by. Blacks & Their Contributions to the American West: A Bibliography & Union List of Library Holdings Through 1970. (Seventy Ser). 483p. 1974. lib. bdg. 29.50 (ISBN 0-8161-1139-1). G K Hall.

Alexander, Rae P. & Lester, Julius, eds. Young & Black in America. (Sundial Paperbks.). 1972. pap. 1.95 (ISBN 0-394-70804-0, VS4, Vin). Random.

Aptheker, Herbert. The Negro People in America. LC 46-8650. 1946. pap. 4.50 (ISBN 0-527-02770-7). Kraus Repr.

Atkinson, J. Edward, ed. Black Dimensions in Contemporary American Art. 3.95 (ISBN 0-452-25041-2, Z5041, Plume). NAL.

Beecher, Henry W. American Rebellion. facsimile ed. LC 70-168510. (Black Heritage Library Collection). Repr. of 1864 ed. 13.50 (ISBN 0-8369-8863-9). Arno.

Blake, Clarence N. & Martin, Donald F. Quiz Book on Black America. (gr. 7 up). 1976. pap. 3.95 (ISBN 0-395-24974-0, Sandpiper). HM.

Coles, Robert. Children of Crisis, Vol. 3: The South Goes North. LC 70-162332. (Children of Crisis Ser.). (Illus.). 704p. 1972-73. 15.00 (ISBN 0-316-15172-6, Pub. by Atlantic Monthly Pr); pap. 7.95 (ISBN 0-316-15177-7). Little.

Coombs, Norman. The Black Experience in America. LC 73-186717. (The Immigrant Heritage of America Ser.). 1972. lib. bdg. 10.95 (ISBN 0-8057-3208-X). Twayne.

Cooper, Elizabeth K. Attitude of Children & Teachers Toward Mexican, Negro & Jewish Minorities. LC 72-86399. pap. 7.00 (ISBN 0-88247-184-8). R & E Res Assoc.

Davis, Frank M. I Am the American Negro. facsimile ed. LC 70-178471. (Black Heritage Library Collection). Repr. of 1937 ed. 10.00 (ISBN 0-8369-8920-1). Arno.

Davis, Lenwood G. The Black Woman in American Society: An Annotated Bibliography. (Series Seventy). 244p. 1975. lib. bdg. 17.00 (ISBN 0-8161-7858-5). G K Hall.

Du Bois, W. E. B. The Gift of Black Folk: The Negroes in the Making of America. LC 75-1447. 1975. Repr. of 1924 ed. 17.00 (ISBN 0-527-25310-3). Kraus Repr.

Dunn, Lynn P. Black Americans: A Study Guide & Source Book. LC 74-31621. 1975. soft bdg. 6.00 (ISBN 0-88247-306-9). R & E Res Assoc.

Ebony Editors. Ebony Pictorial History of Black America, 4 vols. 1971 ed. Bennett, Lerone, Jr., ed. Incl. Vol. 1; Vol. 2; Vol. 3; Vol. 4. The 1973 Yearbook. 312p. 10.95 (ISBN 0-87485-059-2). boxed set of 3 vols. 27.95 (ISBN 0-87485-049-5); deluxe slip-case set of 4 vols. 38.90 (ISBN 0-87485-073-8). Johnson Chi.

--Ebony Success Library, Vols. 1-3. Incl. Vol. 1. One Thousand Successful Black (ISBN 0-87485-060-6); Vol. 2. Famous Blacks Give Secrets of Success (ISBN 0-87485-061-4); Vol. 3. Career Guide: Opportunities and Resources for You (ISBN 0-87485-062-2). (Illus.). 960p. 1973. Set. 27.95 (ISBN 0-87485-058-4). Johnson Chi.

Ebony Editors & Saunders, Doris E., eds. The Ebony Handbook. LC 73-16179. 569p. 1974. 20.00 (ISBN 0-87485-064-9). Johnson Chi.

Elman, Richard M. Ill-at-Ease in Compton. LC 67-13322. 1967. 15.00 (ISBN 0-89366-095-7). Ultramarine Pub.

Farge, Emile J. La Vida Chicana: Health Care Attitudes & Behaviors of Houston Chicanos. LC 74-31766. 1975. soft bdg. 11.00 (ISBN 0-685-59169-7). R & E Res Assoc.

Frucht, Richard, ed. Black Society in the New World. 1971. pap. text ed. 3.95 (ISBN 0-685-55623-9, 30181). Phila Bk Co.

Grissom, Mary A. Negro Sings a New Heaven. 5.00 (ISBN 0-8446-0663-4). Peter Smith.

Haygood, Atticus G. Our Brother in Black: His Freedom & His Future. facs. ed. LC 72-78994. (Black Heritage Library Collection Ser). 1896. 14.50 (ISBN 0-8369-8697-0). Arno.

Helps, Arthur. Conquerors of the New World & Their Bondsmen, 2 Vols. facs. ed. LC 77-83945. (Black Heritage Library Collection Ser). 1852. 24.50 (ISBN 0-8369-8597-4). Arno.

History of Prince Lee Boo, to Which Is Added, the Life of Paul Cuffee, a Man of Colour: Also Some Account of John Sackhouse, the Esquimaux. facs. ed. LC 72-89405. (Black Heritage Library Collection Ser). 1820. 10.00 (ISBN 0-8369-8601-6). Arno.

Hosmer, William. Higher Law, in Its Relations to Civil Government: With Particular Reference to Slavery, & the Fugitive Slave Law. facs. ed. LC 70-83946. (Black Heritage Library Collection Ser). 1852. 12.25 (ISBN 0-8369-8604-0). Arno.

Howard, James H. Bond & Free: True Tale of Slave Times. facs. ed. LC 79-83908. (Black Heritage Library Collection Ser). 1886. 15.00 (ISBN 0-8369-8605-9). Arno.

Jenkins, Edward S., et al. American Black Scientists & Inventors. 1975. pap. 2.50 (ISBN 0-87355-003-X). Natl Sci Tchrs.

Johnston, Harry H. Negro in the New World, (Social & Economic History Ser). 1969. Repr. of 1910 ed. 27.00 (ISBN 0-384-27700-4). Johnson Repr.

Kronus, Sidney. Black Middle Class. LC 79-148247. 1971. pap. text ed. 3.95x (ISBN 0-675-09218-3). Merrill.

Meier, August & Rudwick, Elliott. From Plantation to Ghetto. 3rd ed. (Illus.). 1976. 12.95 (ISBN 0-8090-4792-6, AmCen); pap. 5.95 (ISBN 0-8090-0122-5). Hill & Wang.

Micheaux, Oscar. Conquest: The Story of a Negro Pioneer. facs. ed. LC 75-89391. (Black Heritage Library Collection Ser). 1913. 14.00 (ISBN 0-8369-8632-6). Arno.

Miller, Kelly. Appeal to Conscience: America's Code of Caste, a Disgrace to Democracy. facs. ed. LC 71-89390. (Black Heritage Library Collection Ser). 1918. 8.75 (ISBN 0-8369-8633-4). Arno.

Mitchell, George. I'm Somebody Important: Young Black Voices from Rural Georgia. LC 72-75489. (Illus.). 288p. 1973. 12.95 (ISBN 0-252-00268-7). U of Ill Pr.

Northrop, Henry D. College of Life or Practical Self Educator. facs. ed. LC 71-79014. (Black Heritage Library Collection Ser). (Illus.). 1895. 37.50 (ISBN 0-8369-8638-5). Arno.

Pease, William H. & Pease, Jane H. Black Utopia: Negro Communal Experiments in America. LC 63-64494. 1972. pap. 2.95 (ISBN 0-87020-066-6). State Hist Soc Wis.

Planter: Or, Thirteen Years in the South. facs. ed. LC 75-83958. (Black Heritage Library Collection Ser). 1853. 13.50 (ISBN 0-8369-8642-3). Arno.

Porter, A. Toomer. Led on! Step by Step: Scenes from Clerical, Military, Educational & Plantation Life in the South. facs. ed. LC 75-89383. (Black Heritage Library Collection Ser). 1898. 16.75 (ISBN 0-8369-8643-1). Arno.

Rogers, J. A. Africa's Gift to America. rev. ed. (Illus.). 272p. 1961. 9.95 (ISBN 0-9602294-6-9). H M Rogers.

Rudd, Daniel & Bond, Theophilus. From Slavery to Wealth: The Life of Scott Bond. facsimile ed. LC 73-173615. (Black Heritage Library Collection). Repr. of 1917 ed. 31.00 (ISBN 0-8369-8907-4). Arno.

Simmons, Charles W. & Morris, Harry W. Afro-American History. LC 71-184567. 344p. 1972. pap. text ed. 7.95x (ISBN 0-675-09131-4). Merrill.

Stanford, P. Thomas. The Tragedy of the Negro in America. facsimile 2nd ed. LC 75-178483. (Black Heritage Library Collection). Repr. of 1897 ed. 19.50 (ISBN 0-8369-8932-5). Arno.

Thompson, Daniel C. Sociology of the Black Experience. LC 73-20974. (Contributions in Sociology: No. 14). 261p. 1974. lib. bdg. 15.75 (ISBN 0-8371-7336-1, TBE/); pap. 4.95 (ISBN 0-8371-8928-4, TBE). Greenwood.

Thum, Marcella. Exploring Black America. LC 74-19428. (gr. 7 up). 1975. 10.95 (ISBN 0-689-30462-5). Atheneum.

Tillinghast, Joseph A. Negro in Africa & America. facs. ed. LC 77-89441. (Black Heritage Library Collection Ser). 1902. 12.25 (ISBN 0-8369-8667-9). Arno.

Trow, John F. Alton Trials: Of Winthrop S. Gilman. facs. ed. LC 73-89440. (Black Heritage Library Collection Ser). 1838. 9.50 (ISBN 0-8369-8671-7). Arno.

Tuskegee Institute, Alabama, Dept. of Records & Research. Pamphlets: 1949-1961, 1 vol, Nos. 1-10. 24.00 (ISBN 0-527-91250-6). Kraus Repr.

Washington, Booker T. Up from Slavery. 1971. Repr. of 1900 ed. 9.50 (ISBN 0-87928-021-2). Corner Hse.

Winslow, Eugene. Afro-American Seventy Six. LC 75-23936. (Illus.). 80p. 1975. 8.95 (ISBN 0-910030-20-0); pap. 5.95 (ISBN 0-910030-21-9). Afro-Am.

Writers Program, Illinois. Cavalcade of the American Negro. LC 73-3614. (American Guide Ser.). Repr. 11.50 (ISBN 0-404-57917-5). AMS Pr.

NEGROES IN ART
This heading discontinued January 1976. See Afro-Americans In Art for later materials. see also Negro Art; Negro Artists

Brawley, Benjamin G. Negro Genius. LC 66-17517. 1966. Repr. of 1937 ed. 10.50x (ISBN 0-8196-0184-5). Biblo.

Coen, Rena N. Black Man in Art. LC 78-84405. (Fine Art Books). (Illus.). (gr. 5-11). 1970. PLB 4.95 (ISBN 0-8225-0163-5). Lerner Pubns.

Locke, Alain. Negro & His Music. Bd. with Negro Art: Past & Present. LC 69-18592. (American Negro-His History & Literature Ser., No.2). 1969. Repr. of 1936 ed. 8.00 (ISBN 0-405-01879-7). Arno.

--Negro in Art: A Pictorial Record of the Negro Artist & the Negro Theme in Art. LC 79-99389. 1969. Repr. of 1940 ed. lib. bdg. 24.50 (ISBN 0-8411-0060-8). Metro Bks.

Locke, Alain, ed. Negro in Art: A Pictorial Record of the Negro Artist & of the Negro Theme in Art. LC 68-9006. (Illus.). 1971. Repr. of 1940 ed. lib. bdg. 25.00 buckram (ISBN 0-87817-013-8). Hacker.

Murray, Freeman H. Emancipation & the Freed in American Sculpture. facsimile ed. LC 70-38016. (Black Heritage Library Collection). Repr. of 1916 ed. 25.00 (ISBN 0-8369-8983-X). Arno.

NEGROES IN LITERATURE
This heading discontinued January 1976. See Afro-Americans In Literature for later materials. see also Negro Authors

Broderick, Dorothy. Image of the Black in Children's Fiction. LC 72-1741. 215p. 1973. 15.95 (ISBN 0-8352-0550-9). Bowker.

Brown, Sterling. Negro in American Fiction. 1969. Repr. of 1937 ed. 12.50 (ISBN 0-87266-002-8). Argosy.

--Negro in American Fiction. Bd. with Negro Poetry & Drama. LC 69-18582. (American Negro-His History & Literature Ser., No.2). 372p. Repr. of 1937 ed. 13.00 (ISBN 0-405-01851-7). Arno.

--Negro Poetry & Drama & the Negro in American Fiction. LC 69-15521. (Studies in American Negro Life Ser). 1969. pap. text ed. 3.45x (ISBN 0-689-70024-5, NL12). Atheneum.

Ford, Aaron N. & Turpin, Waters. Extending Horizons. 1969. pap. text ed. 3.95x (ISBN 0-685-55622-0, 30181). Phila Bk Co.

Gayle, Addison, Jr. The Way of the New World: The Black Novel in America. LC 74-9449. 440p. 1976. pap. 3.95 (ISBN 0-385-04135-7, Anch). Doubleday.

Gloster, Hugh M. Negro Voices in American Fiction. LC 65-17895. 1965. Repr. of 1948 ed. 17.00 (ISBN 0-8462-0577-7). Russell.

Gregoire, Abbe H. De la Litterature des Negres, ou Recherches sur Leurs Facultes Intellectuelles, Leurs Qualites Morals et Leur Litterature. (Slave Trade in France, 1744-1848, Ser.). 302p. (Fr.). 1974. Repr. of 1808 ed. lib. bdg. 80.00x (ISBN 0-8287-0399-X, TN121). Clearwater Pub.

Gross, Seymour L. & Hardy, John E., eds. Images of the Negro in American Literature. LC 66-23689. (Patterns of Literary Criticism Ser.). 1966. 8.75x (ISBN 0-226-30983-5); pap. 2.95 (ISBN 0-226-30984-3, PLC5). U of Chicago Pr.

Hallie Q. Brown Memorial Library. Index to Periodical Articles by & About Negroes, Annuals, 1960-1969. 1971. lib. bdg. 15.00 ea. G K Hall.

Harrison, Paul C. The Drama of Nommo. LC 72-86051. 245p. 1972. 12.50 (ISBN 0-394-48275-1). Ultramarine Pub.

Hughes, Langston, ed. The Best Short Stories by Negro Writers. 1967. 12.50 (ISBN 0-316-38032-6); pap. 6.95 (ISBN 0-316-38031-8). Little.

Johnson, Lemuel A. Devil, the Gargoyle, & the Buffoon: The Negro As Metaphor in Western Literature. LC 76-139355. 1971. 12.00 (ISBN 0-8046-9006-5, Natl U); pap. 7.95 (ISBN 0-8046-9047-2). Kennikat.

Locke, Alain, ed. Negro in Art: A Pictorial Record of the Negro Artist & of the Negro Theme in Art. LC 68-9006. (Illus.). 1971. Repr. of 1940 ed. lib. bdg. 25.00 buckram (ISBN 0-87817-013-8). Hacker.

Nelson, John H. Negro Character in American Literature. LC 73-128982. Repr. of 1926 ed. 11.50 (ISBN 0-404-00203-X). AMS Pr.

Shackelford, Otis M. Seeking the Best. LC 73-18606. Repr. of 1911 ed. 16.00 (ISBN 0-404-11416-4). AMS Pr.

Tischler, Nancy M. Black Masks: Negro Characters in Modern Southern Fiction. LC 68-8187. 1969. 12.95x (ISBN 0-271-00082-1). Pa St U Pr.

Wagner, Jean. Black Poets of the United States: From Paul Laurence Dunbar to Langston Hughes. Douglas, Kenneth, tr. from Fr. LC 72-75141. 580p. 1973. 20.00 (ISBN 0-252-00292-X); pap. 8.95 (ISBN 0-252-00341-1). U of Ill Pr.

Walker, Margaret. How I Wrote Jubilee. (Black Paper Ser). 1972. pap. 1.00 (ISBN 0-88378-023-2). Third World.

Wegelin, Oscar. Jupiter Hammon, American Negro Poet. facs. ed. LC 70-83900. (Black Heritage Library Collection Ser). 1915. 7.00 (ISBN 0-8369-8682-2). Arno.

Williams, John A., ed. Beyond the Angry Black. LC 66-28491. 198p. 1966. 11.00x (ISBN 0-8154-0260-0). Cooper Sq.

Yellin, Jean Fagan. The Intricate Knot: Black Figures in American Literature, 1776-1863. LC 72-76556. 1972. 12.00x (ISBN 0-8147-9650-8); pap. 4.95x (ISBN 0-8147-9651-6). NYU Pr.

NEGROES IN MEDICINE
This heading discontinued January 1976. See Afro-Americans In Medicine for later materials. see also Negro Physicians

Curtis, James L. Blacks, Medical Schools, & Society. LC 76-184249. 1971. 7.95 (ISBN 0-472-26900-3). U of Mich Pr.

NEGROES IN MOVING-PICTURES
This heading discontinued January 1976. See Afro-Americans In Motion Pictures for later materials. Here are entered works discussing the portrayal of Negroes in motion pictures. Works discussing all aspects of Negro involvement in motion pictures are entered under Negroes in the Moving-Picture Industry. Works dissusing specific aspects of Negro involvement are entered under the particular subject, e.g. Negro Moving-Picture Actors and Actresses.

Cripps, Thomas. Slow Fade to Black: The Negro in American Film, 1900-1942. (Illus.). 1977. pap. 7.95 (ISBN 0-19-502130-4, 484, GB). Oxford U Pr.

Noble, Peter. Negro in Films. LC 72-124022. (Literature of Cinema, Ser. 1). Repr. of 1949 ed. 15.00 (ISBN 0-405-01629-8). Arno.

Null, Gary. Black Hollywood: The Negro in Motion Pictures. (Illus.). 1975. 12.00 (ISBN 0-8065-0263-0). Citadel Pr.

Powers, Anne. Blacks in American Movies: A Selected Bibliography. LC 74-1925. 1974. 10.00 (ISBN 0-8108-0753-X). Scarecrow.

NEGROES IN SCIENCE
This heading discontinued January 1976.

Jay, James M. Negroes in Science: Natural Science Doctorates, 1876-1969. LC 74-28394. (Illus.). 87p. 1971. pap. 2.50 (ISBN 0-913642-00-2). Balamp Pub.

Jenkins, Edward S., et al. American Black Scientists & Inventors. 1975. pap. 2.50 (ISBN 0-87355-003-X). Natl Sci Tchrs.

NEGROES IN THE MOVING-PICTURE INDUSTRY
This heading discontinued January 1976. See Afro-Americans In The Motion Picture Industry for later materials. Here are entered works discussing all aspects of Negro involvement in motion pictures. Works discussing the portrayal of Negroes in motion pictures are entered under Negroes in Moving-Pictures. Works discussing specific aspects of Negro involvement are entered under the particular subject, e.g. Negro Moving-Picture Actors and Actresses.
see also Negro Moving-Picture Actors and Actresses; Negroes in Moving-Pictures

NEHASANE PARK
Pinchot, Gifford. Adirondack Spruce, a Study of the Forest in Ne-Ha-Sa-Ne Park. LC 77-125756. (American Environmental Studies). 1971. Repr. of 1907 ed. 10.00 (ISBN 0-405-02682-X). Arno.

NEHEMIAH
Barber, Cyril J. Nehemiah & the Dynamics of Effective Leadership. 1980. study guide 3.25 (ISBN 0-87213-022-3). Loizeaux.
--Nehemiah & the Dynamics of Effective Leadership. LC 76-22567. 1976. pap. 3.00 (ISBN 0-87213-021-5). Loizeaux.
Berg, Jean H. Nehemiah Builds the Wall. (Illus.). (ps-3). 1978. pap. 3.95 (ISBN 0-87510-114-3). Chr Science.
Campbell, Donald K. Nehemiah: Man in Charge. 1979. pap. 3.50 (ISBN 0-88207-781-3). Victor Bks.
Getz, Gene A. Nehemiah: A Man of Prayer & Persistence. LC 80-53102. 1981. pap. 4.95 (ISBN 0-8307-0778-6). Regal.
Lindsay, Gordon. Ezra & Nehemiah & the Return from Babylon. (Old Testament Ser.). 1.25 (ISBN 0-89985-154-1). Christ Nations.
Seume, Richard. Nehemiah: God's Builder. 1978. pap. 2.95 (ISBN 0-8024-5868-8). Moody.

NEHRU, JAWAHARLAL, 1889-1964
Alphonso-Karkala, John B. Jawaharlal Nehru. (World Authors Ser.: India: No. 345). 1975. lib. bdg. 10.95 (ISBN 0-8057-2649-7). Twayne.
Brecher, Michael. Nehru's Mantle: The Politics of Succession in India. LC 75-32653. 1976. Repr. of 1966 ed. lib. bdg. 17.75x (ISBN 0-8371-8553-X, BRNM). Greenwood.
Chakraborty, A. K. Jawaharlal Nehru's Writings. 1981. 15.00x (ISBN 0-685-59378-9). South Asia Bks.
Chhibber, V. N. Jawaharlal Nehru - Man of Letters. 1970. 7.50x (ISBN 0-8426-0011-6). Verry.
Copland, Ian. Jawaharlal Nehru of India Eighteen Eighty-Nine to Nineteen Sixty-Four. (Leaders of Asia Ser.). 53p. (Orig.). 1980. pap. 3.00x (ISBN 0-7022-1506-6). U of Queensland Pr.
Dutt, R. C. Socialism of Jaharwalal Nehru. 1981. 18.50x (ISBN 0-8364-0708-3, Pub. by Abhinav India). South Asia Bks.
Dutt, Subimal. With Nehru in the Foreign Office. 1977. 14.00x (ISBN 0-88386-905-5). South Asia Bks.
Dutt, Vishnu. Gandhi, Nehru & the Challenge. 1979. 14.00x (ISBN 0-8364-0322-3). South Asia Bks.
Gopal, Ram. Trials of Jawaharlal Nehru. 133p. 1964. 24.00x (ISBN 0-7146-1557-9, F Cass Co). Biblio Dist.
Gopal, Sarvepalli. Jawaharlal Nehru: A Biography, Vol. 2, 1947-1956. LC 75-33411. (Illus.). 1979. 20.00x (ISBN 0-674-47311-6). Harvard U Pr.
--Jawaharlal Nehru: A Biography, Vol. 1, 1889-1947. 416p. 1976. 18.50x (ISBN 0-674-47310-8). Harvard U Pr.
Gopal, Sarvepalli, ed. A Nehru Anthology. 648p. 1981. 27.00x (ISBN 0-19-561220-5). Oxford U Pr.
Kamath, H. V. Last Days of Jawaharial Nehru. 1977. 8.50x (ISBN 0-8002-0330-5). Intl Pubns Serv.
Nanda, B. R., ed. Indian Foreign Policy: The Nehru Years. 1976. 12.00x (ISBN 0-8248-0486-4, Eastwest Ctr). U Pr of Hawaii.
Nanda, B. R., et al. Gandhi & Nehru. 76p. 1979. pap. text ed. 4.50x (ISBN 0-19-561148-9). Oxford U Pr.
Nasenko, Yuri. Jawaharlal Nehru & India's Foreign Policy. 1977. text ed. 22.50x (ISBN 0-8426-1040-5). Verry.
Neeraj, Miss Nehru & Democracy in India. LC 73-928017. 301p. 1972. 15.00x (ISBN 0-8002-1746-2). Intl Pubns Serv.
Nehru, J. & Gopal, S. Selected Works of Jawaharlal Nehru, Vol.8. 1976. 15.00x (ISBN 0-88386-376-6); Vol. 9. 1977 15.00x (ISBN 0-685-66727-8); Vol. 10. 1977 15.00x (ISBN 0-8364-0344-4); Vol. 11. 1978 16.00 (ISBN 0-8364-0345-2). South Asia Bks.
Nehru, J. & Nanda, B. R., eds. Selected Writings of Jawaharlal Nehru. 1981. 26.00x (ISBN 0-8364-0672-9, Orient Longman). South Asia Bks.
Pandey, B. N. Nehru. LC 75-37858. (Illus.). 356p. 1976. 25.00 (ISBN 0-8128-1931-4). Stein & Day.
Pradhan, Benudhar. The Socialist Thought of Jawaharlal Nehru. LC 74-902421. 400p. 1974. 17.50x (ISBN 0-88386-387-1). South Asia Bks.
Prashad, G. Nehru: A Study in Colonial Liberalism. 1976. text ed. 15.00x (ISBN 0-8426-0925-3). Verry.
Rau, M. Nehru for Children. (Illus.). (gr. 4-12). 1979. 3.50 (ISBN 0-89744-159-1). Auromere.
Rau, M. C. Gandhi & Nehru. 1967. 4.50x (ISBN 0-8188-1116-1). Paragon.
Sharma, Jagdish S. Jawaharlal Nehru, a Descriptive Bibliography. (National Bibliography No. 2). 1955. 8.50x (ISBN 0-8426-1520-2). Verry.
Zaidi, Sabira K. Education & Humanism. 170p. 1971. 11.25x (ISBN 0-8002-0585-5). Intl Pubns Serv.
Zakaria, Rafiq, ed. A Study of Nehru. 2nd rev. ed. (Illus.). 478p. 1964. Repr. of 1959 ed. 22.50x (ISBN 0-7146-1574-9, F Cass Co). Biblio Dist.

NEHRU, KAMALA, 1899-1936
Kalhan, Promilla. Kamala Nehru: An Intimate Biography. (Illus.). 1973. 7.50x (ISBN 0-686-20265-1). Intl Bk Dist.

NEHRU FAMILY
Nanda, B. R. The Nehrus: Motilal & Jawaharlal. 358p. 1974. pap. 3.95 (ISBN 0-226-56806-7, P582, Phoen). U of Chicago Pr.

NEIDHART VON RUENTHAL, fl. 13TH CENTURY
Brill, Richard. Schule Neidharts. Repr. of 1908 ed. 29.00 (ISBN 0-384-05840-X); pap. 26.00 (ISBN 0-685-02227-7). Johnson Repr.
Simon, Eckehard. Neidhart Von Reuenthal. LC 75-2067. (World Authors Ser.: Germany: No. 364). 1975. lib. bdg. 12.50 (ISBN 0-8057-6215-9). Twayne.

NEIGHBORHOOD
Bayor, Ronald H. Neighborhoods in Urban America. (Interdisciplinary Urban Ser.). 1981. 19.50 (ISBN 0-8046-9284-X). Kennikat.
Clay, Phillip L. Neighborhood Renewal: Trends & Strategies. LC 78-14153. 1979. 14.95 (ISBN 0-669-02681-6). Lexington Bks.
Downs, Anthony. Neighborhoods & Urban Development. LC 81-66190. 250p. 1981. 22.95 (ISBN 0-8157-1920-5); pap. 8.95 (ISBN 0-8157-1919-1). Brookings.
Fisher, Robert & Romanofsky, Peter, eds. Community Organization for Urban Social Change: A Historical Perspective. LC 80-21498. (Illus.). 280p. 1981. lib. bdg. 29.95 (ISBN 0-313-21427-1, RCO/). Greenwood.
Greeley, Andrew. Neighborhood. LC 77-7119. (Illus.). 1977. 10.95 (ISBN 0-8164-9331-6). Continuum.
Hester, Randolph T., Jr., ed. Neighborhood Space: User Needs & Design Responsibility. LC 75-30669. (Community Development Ser.: Vol. 17). 1975. 40.00 (ISBN 0-87933-173-9). Hutchinson Ross.
Keller, Suzanne. Urban Neighborhood: A Sociological Perspective. (Orig.). 1968. pap. text ed. 4.95 (ISBN 0-394-30773-9, RanC). Random.
--The Urban Neighborhood: A Sociological Perspective. 5.50 (ISBN 0-8446-2360-1). Peter Smith.
McNutley, Robert & Kliment, Stephen A. Neighborhood Conservation: A Handbook of Methods & Techniques. (Illus.). 1979. pap. 9.95 (ISBN 0-8230-7381-5). Watson-Guptill.
Morris, David & Hess, Karl. Neighborhood Power: The New Localism. LC 74-16663. (Institute for Policy Studies Ser.). 192p. 1975. pap. 4.95 (ISBN 0-8070-0875-3, BP516). Beacon Pr.
Mueller, Virginia. Who Is Your Neighbor? Sparks, Judith, ed. (A Happy Day Book). (Illus.). 24p. (gr. k-2). 1980. 0.98 (ISBN 0-87239-412-3, 3644). Standard Pub.
Myers, Phyllis. Neighborhood Conservation & the Elderly. LC 78-70572. 1978. pap. text ed. 4.00 (ISBN 0-89164-050-9). Conservation Foun.
Myers, Phyllis & Binder, Gordon. Neighborhood Conservation: Lessons from Three Cities. LC 77-88157. (Illus.). 1977. pap. 4.00 (ISBN 0-89164-045-2). Conservation Foun.
Sesame Street. Who Are the People in Your Neighborhood? (Sesame Street Pop-up Ser.: No. 7). (ps). 1974. 4.95 (ISBN 0-394-82827-5, BYR). Random.
Spergel, Irving. Racketville, Slumtown, Haulburg: An Exploratory Study of Delinquent Subcultures. LC 64-17165. (Midway Reprint Ser). 1973. pap. 7.00x (ISBN 0-226-76934-8). U of Chicago Pr.
Tomasic, Roman & Feeley, Malcolm M., eds. Neighborhood Justice. (Illus.). 1981. text ed. 27.50x tent. (ISBN 0-582-28253-5). Longman.
Wolpert, J., et al. Metropolitan Neighborhoods: Participation & Conflict Over Change. LC 72-75260. (CCG Resource Papers Ser.: No. 16). (Illus.). 1972. pap. text ed. 4.00 (ISBN 0-89291-063-1). Assn Am Geographers.

NEIGHBORHOOD CENTERS
see Social Settlements

NEIGHBORHOOD GILDS
see Social Settlements

NEIGHBORHOOD NEWSPAPERS
see Community Newspapers

NEILL, ALEXANDER SUTHERLAND, 1883-1973
Hemmings, Ray. Children's Freedom: A. S. Neill & the Evolution of the Summerhill Idea. LC 72-94295. (Illus.). 240p. 1972. pap. 3.45 (ISBN 0-8052-0455-5). Schocken.
Perry, L., ed. Bertrand Russell, A. S. Neill, Homer Lane, W. H. Kilpatrick: Four Progressive Educators. 1968. pap. text ed. 1.95x (ISBN 0-02-975150-0). Macmillan.
Placzek, Beverley, ed. Record of a Friendship: The Correspondence of Wilhelm Reich and A.S. Neill. 1981. 20.00 (ISBN 0-374-24807-9). FS&G.

NEIZVESTNYI, ERNEST, 1926-
Berger, John. Art in Revolution. LC 68-26045. 1969. pap. 4.95 (ISBN 0-394-41562-0). Pantheon.
Obigenin, Boris. Ernst Neizvestny: Createur D'une Archaique Nouvelle. 15p. 1977. pap. text ed. 3.00x (ISBN 90-316-0022-9). Humanities.

NEKRASOV, NIKOLAY ALEKSEYEVICH, 1821-1877
Chukovsky, Kornei. The Poet & the Hangman: Nekrasov & Muravyov. Rotsel, R. W., tr. from Russian. (Ardis Essay Ser.: No. 5). 1977. 10.00 (ISBN 0-88233-217-1); pap. 2.95 (ISBN 0-88233-218-X). Ardis Pubs.

NELSON, HORATIA, 1801-1881
Gerin, Winifred. Horatia Nelson. 1970. 19.50x (ISBN 0-19-822331-5). Oxford U Pr.

NELSON, HORATIO NELSON, VISCOUNT, 1758-1805
Grenfell, Russell. Horatio Nelson: A Short Biography. LC 78-6150. (Illus.). 1978. Repr. of 1968 ed. lib. bdg. 24.25x (ISBN 0-313-20481-0, GRHN). Greenwood.
Jeaffreson, John C. Lady Hamilton & Lord Nelson. Repr. of 1897 ed. lib. bdg. 35.00 (ISBN 0-8495-2724-4). Arden Lib.
Lenanton, Carola M. Nelson. LC 77-100166. (Illus.). xiv, 748p. Repr. of 1946 ed. lib. bdg. 29.50x (ISBN 0-8371-3976-7, LENE). Greenwood.
Lloyd, Christopher. Nelson & Sea Power. (Men & Their Times Ser.). (Illus.). 1973. 5.50x (ISBN 0-340-12413-X). Verry.
Mahan, A. T. Life of Nelson: The Embodiment of the Sea Power of Great Britain, 2 Vols. LC 68-26361. (English Biography Ser., No. 31). 1969. Repr. of 1897 ed. lib. bdg. 69.95 (ISBN 0-8383-0182-7). Haskell.
Mahan, Alfred T. Life of Nelson: Embodiment of the Sea Power of Great Britain, 2 Vols. LC 68-23312. (Illus.). 1968. Repr. of 1897 ed. Set. lib. bdg. 28.75x (ISBN 0-8371-2667-3, MALN). Greenwood.
--Life of Nelson, the Embodiment of the Sea Power of Great Britain, 2 vols in one. 1899. 27.00 (ISBN 0-403-00076-9). Scholarly.
Oman, Carola. Lord Nelson. (Makers of History Ser). 1968. 14.50 (ISBN 0-208-00205-7, Archon). Shoe String.
Russell, William C. Horatio Nelson & the Naval Supremacy of England. LC 73-14467. (Heroes of the Nation Ser.). Repr. of 1890 ed. 30.00 (ISBN 0-404-58285-0). AMS Pr.
Sabatini, Rafael. Heroic Lives. facs. ed. LC 70-99648. (Essay Index Reprint Ser). 1934. 17.50 (ISBN 0-8369-2071-6). Arno.
Southey, Robert. Life of Horatio, Lord Nelson. 1962. 8.95x (ISBN 0-460-00052-7, Evman). Biblio Dist.
--Southey's Life of Nelson. Callender, G., ed. LC 71-153357. Repr. of 1922 ed. 24.50 (ISBN 0-404-07828-1). AMS Pr.
Warner, Oliver. A Portrait of Lord Nelson. (Illus.). 1979. 8.95 (ISBN 0-7011-1809-1, Pub. by Chatto Bodley Jonathan). Merrimack Bk Serv.

NELSON, HORATIO NELSON, VISCOUNT, 1758-1805–JUVENILE LITERATURE
Warner, Oliver & Nimitz, Chester W. Nelson & the Age of Fighting Sail. LC 63-10165. (Horizon Caravel Bks). (Illus.). 153p. (gr. 6 up). 1963. 9.95 (ISBN 0-8281-0397-6, J02414, Dist. by Har-Row); PLB 12.89 (ISBN 0-06-026380-6, Dist. by Har-Row). Am Heritage.

NELSON, WILLIAM ROCKHILL, 1841-1915
Members of the Staff of Kansas City Star. William Rockhill Nelson: Story of a Man, a Newspaper, & a City. (American Newspapermen Ser.: 1770-1933). Repr. of 1915 ed. 17.50 (ISBN 0-8464-0017-0). Beekman Pubs.

NEMATHELMINTHES
see also Nematoda

NEMATODA
Allen, M. W. & Noffsinger, Ella M. A Revision of the Marine Nematodes of the Superfamily Draconematoidea Filipjev. (Publications in Zoology Ser.: Vol. 109). 1978. 10.00x (ISBN 0-520-09583-9). U of Cal Pr.
Behme, R., et al. Biology of Nematodes: Current Studies. LC 72-8856. 218p. 1972. text ed. 28.50x (ISBN 0-8422-7043-4). Irvington.
Bird, Alan F. Structure of Nematodes. 1971. 50.00 (ISBN 0-12-099650-2). Acad Pr.
Chitwood, B. Introduction to Nematology. 1975. 29.50 (ISBN 0-8391-0697-1). Univ Park.
Croll, N. A., ed. The Organisation of Nematodes. 1977. 69.00 (ISBN 0-12-196850-2). Acad Pr.
Croll, Neil A. Behaviour of Nematodes: Their Activity, Senses & Responses. LC 75-124954. 1971. 17.95 (ISBN 0-312-07245-7). St Martin.
Croll, Neil A. & Matthews, B. E. Biology of Nematodes. LC 75-505520. (Tertiary Level Biology Ser.). 1977. 20.95 (ISBN 0-470-99028-7). Halsted Pr.
Diffusion & Absorption of the Nematicide 1,3-Dichloropropene in Soil. (Agricultural Research Reports Ser.: 769). 1972. pap. 13.75 (ISBN 90-220-0378-7, PUDOC). Unipub.
Dropkin, Victor H. Introduction to Plant Nematology. LC 80-13556. 293p. 1980. 27.50 (ISBN 0-471-05578-6, Pub. by Wiley Interscience). Wiley.
Hetherington, Duncan C. Comparative Studies on Certain Features of Nematodes & Their Significance. (Illinois Biological Monographs Ser: Vol. 3, No. 2). 1924. pap. 6.00 (ISBN 0-384-22760-0). Johnson Repr.
Ivashkin, V. M. Essentials of Nematodology: Camallanata of Animals & Man & Diseases Caused by Them, Vol. 22. 1977. 71.95 (ISBN 0-470-99321-9). Halsted Pr.
Lamberti, F. & Taylor, C. E., eds. Root-Knot Nematodes: Meloidogyne Species: Systematics, Biology & Control. 1979. 40.00 (ISBN 0-12-434850-5). Acad Pr.
Lamberti, F., et al, eds. Nematode Vectors of Plant Viruses. (Nato Advanced Study Institutes Ser. A Life Sciences: Vol. 2). 460p. 1975. 45.00 (ISBN 0-306-35602-3, Plenum Pr). Plenum Pub.
Lee, Donald Lewis & Atkinson, H. J. Physiology of Nematodes. 2d ed. LC 77-1232. (Illus.). 215p. 1977. 20.00x (ISBN 0-231-04358-9). Columbia U Pr.
Mai, W. F. & Lyon, H. H. Pictorial Key to Genera of Plant-Parasitic Nematodes. 4th ed. LC 74-14082. (Illus.). 224p. 1975. 17.50x (ISBN 0-8014-0920-9). Comstock.
Nicholas, Warwick L. The Biology of Free-Living Nematodes. (Illus.). 224p. 1975. 42.00x (ISBN 0-19-854379-4). Oxford U Pr.
Norton, Don C. Ecology of Plant-Parasitic Nematodes. LC 78-1052. 268p. 1978. 34.50 (ISBN 0-471-03188-7, Pub. by Wiley-Interscience). Wiley.
Plant Parasitic Nematodes of the Pacific. (Technical Report Ser.: No. 8). 192p. 1981. 50.00 (ISBN 0-686-71822-4, CAB 11, CAB). Unipub.
Poinar, George O. Nematodes for Biological Control of Insects. 304p. 1979. 74.95 (ISBN 0-8493-5333-5). CRC Pr.
Radewald, John D. Nematode Diseases of Food & Fiber Crops of the Southwestern United States. LC 77-81143. 1978. pap. 6.00x (ISBN 0-931876-16-8, 4083). Ag Sci Pubns.
Rysavy, B. & Ryzhikov, K. M., eds. Helminths of Fish Eating Birds of the Palaeartic Region: Volume 1, Nematoda. (Illus.). 1978. lib. bdg. 50.00 (ISBN 90-6193-551-2, Pub. by Junk Pubs Nethherlands). Kluwer Boston.
Skrjabin, K. I., et al, eds. Oxyurata of Animals & Man: Oxyuroidea, Pt. 1. Lavoott, R., tr. from Rus. (Essentials of Nematodology Ser.: Vol. 8, Pt. 1). Orig. Title: Oksiuraty Zhivothykh I Cheloveka. (Illus.). 526p. 1974. 47.50x (ISBN 0-7065-1361-4, Pub. by IPST). Intl Schol Bk Serv.
Skrjabin, K. U., et al. Oxyurata of Animals & Man, Pt. 2. Skrjabin, K. I. & Theodor, O., eds. Lavoott, R., tr. from Rus. (Essentials of Nematodology Ser.: Vol. 10). (Illus.). 462p. 1974. 47.50x (ISBN 0-7065-1449-1, Pub. by IPST). Intl Schol Bk Serv.
Smart, Grover C., Jr. & Perry, V. G., eds. Tropical Nematology. LC 68-28872. 1968. 9.50 (ISBN 0-8130-0275-3). U Presses Fla.
Tarjan, Armen C. Supplement to Check List of Plant & Soil Nematodes, 1961-1965: A Nomenclatorial Compilation. LC 60-10226. 1967. 6.75 (ISBN 0-8130-0224-9). U Presses Fla.
Wallace, H. R. Nematode Ecology & Plant Disease. LC 73-90720. 1973. 32.50x (ISBN 0-8448-0271-9). Crane Russak Co.
Yorke, Warrington & Maplestone, P. A. Nematode Parasites of Vertebrates. (Illus.). 1968. Repr. of 1926 ed. 17.50 (ISBN 0-02-855550-3). Hafner.
Zuckerman, B. M., et al, eds. Plant Parasitic Nematodes: Morphology, Anatomy, Taxonomy, & Ecology, Vols. 1 & 2. 1971. Vol. 1. 58.00 (ISBN 0-12-782201-1); Vol. 2. 54.50 (ISBN 0-12-782202-X); Set. 94.00 (ISBN 0-686-76834-5). Acad Pr.
Zuckerman, Bert M. Nematodes As Biological Models: Vol. 1 Behavioral & Developmental Models. LC 79-8849. 1980. 35.00 (ISBN 0-12-782401-4). Acad Pr.

Zuckerman, Bert M. & Rohde, Richard A. Plant Parasitic Nematodes, Vol. 3. 1981. price not set (ISBN 0-12-782403-0). Acad Pr.

Zuckerman, Bert M., ed. Nematodes As Biological Models: Vol. 2 Aging, & Other Model Systems. LC 79-8849. 1980. 35.00 (ISBN 0-12-782402-2). Acad Pr.

NEMATOSPORA

see Yeast

NEMBE, NIGERIA

Alagoa, Ebiegberi J. Small Brave City-State: A History of Nembe-Brass in the Niger Delta. (Illus.). 1964. 15.00x (ISBN 0-299-03110-1). U of Wis Pr.

NEMEA, GREECE

Hill, Bert H. Temple of Zeus at Nemea. rev., suppl. ed. Williams, Charles, ed. (Illus.). 1966. portfolio 22.00x (ISBN 0-87661-921-9). Am Sch Athens.

NEMEROV, HOWARD

Bartholomay, Julia A. The Shield of Perseus: The Vision & Imagination of Howard Nemerov. LC 70-137851. 172p. 1972. 6.75 (ISBN 0-8130-0317-2). U Presses Fla.

Duncan, Bowie. Critical Reception of Howard Nemerov: A Selection of Essays & a Bibliography. LC 70-154299. 1971. 10.00 (ISBN 0-8108-0400-X). Scarecrow.

--Critical Reception of Howard Nemerov: A Selection of Essays & a Bibliography. LC 70-154299. 1971. 10.00 (ISBN 0-8108-0400-X). Scarecrow.

Labrie, Ross. Howard Nemerov. (United States Authors Series: No. 356). 1980. lib. bdg. 9.50 (ISBN 0-8057-7298-7). Twayne.

Meinke, Peter. Howard Nemerov. LC 68-64753. (Pamphlets on American Writers Ser: No. 70). (Orig.). 1968. pap. 1.25x (ISBN 0-8166-0484-3, MPAW70). U of Minn Pr.

Mills, William. The Stillness in Moving Things: The World of Howard Nemerov. LC 75-31619. 160p. 1975. 9.95x (ISBN 0-87870-026-9). Memphis St Univ.

NEMERTINEA

Coe, Wesley R. Biology of the Nemerteans of the Atlantic Coast of North America. 1943. pap. 34.50x (ISBN 0-686-51347-9). Elliots Bks.

NENETS LANGUAGE

Decsy, Gyula. Yurak Chrestomathy. LC 65-63391. (Uralic & Altaic Ser: Vol. 50). (Orig., Yurak). 1966. pap. text ed. 4.00x (ISBN 0-87750-004-5). Res Ctr Lang Semiotic.

NEOCLASSICAL SCHOOL OF ECONOMICS

Collected Economic Papers of Joan Robinson, 5 vols. 1980. Set. text ed. 125.00x (ISBN 0-262-18099-5); text ed. 25.00x ea. Vol. 1 (ISBN 0-262-18093-6). Vol. 2 (ISBN 0-262-18094-4). Vol. 3 (ISBN 0-262-18095-2). Vol. 4 (ISBN 0-262-18096-0). Vol. 5 (ISBN 0-262-18097-9). Index. text ed. 12.50x (ISBN 0-262-18098-7). MIT Pr.

Ferguson, C. E. Neoclassical Theory of Production & Distribution. (Illus.). 1969. 27.50x (ISBN 0-521-07453-3). Cambridge U Pr.

Steinfels, Peter. The Neo-Conservatives. 1980. 5.95 (ISBN 0-671-41384-8, Touchstone). S&S.

NEOCLASSICISM (ARCHITECTURE)

Broadbent, Geoffrey, et al. Neo-Classicism. (Architectural Design Profiles Ser.). (Illus.). 72p. 1980. pap. 12.50 (ISBN 0-8478-5310-1). Rizzoli Intl.

Eitner, Lorenz. Neoclassicism & Romanticism: 1750-1850, 2 vols. Incl. Vol. 1. Enlightenment-Revolution. 1970 (ISBN 0-13-610907-1); Vol. 2. Restoration-the Twilight of Humanism. (Illus.). 1970 (ISBN 0-13-610915-2). pap. 11.95 ea. ref. ed. P-H.

Honour, Hugh. Neo-Classicism. (Illus.). 1978. pap. 5.95 (ISBN 0-14-020978-6, Pelican). Penguin.

Watkin, D. The Triumph of the Classical. LC 77-12164. (Illus.). 1977. 16.00 (ISBN 0-521-21854-3); pap. 8.95 (ISBN 0-521-29292-1). Cambridge U Pr.

NEO-CONFUCIANISM

Chan, Wing Tstit, tr. Reflections on Things at Hand: The Neo-Confucian Anthology. LC 65-22548. (Records of Civilization Sources Studies). 441p. 1967. 27.50x (ISBN 0-231-02819-9). Columbia U Pr.

Chang, Carsun. The Development of Neo-Confucian Thought. LC 77-8338. 1977. Repr. of 1957 ed. lib. bdg. 26.25x (ISBN 0-8371-9693-0, CHDN). Greenwood.

--The Development of Neo-Confucian Thought, Vol. 1. 1957. pap. 2.95x (ISBN 0-8084-0105-X, P6). Coll & U Pr.

De Bary, W. Theodore, ed. The Unfolding of Neo-Confucianism. LC 74-10929. (Neo-Confucian Ser. & Studies in Oriental Culture Ser.: No. 10). 593p. 1975. 25.00x (ISBN 0-231-03828-3); pap. 12.50x (ISBN 0-231-03829-1). Columbia U Pr.

De Bary, W. Theodore & Bloom, Irene, eds. Principle & Practicality: Essays in Neo-Confucianism & Practical Learning. LC 78-11530. (Neo-Confucian Ser. & Studies in Oriental Culture). 1979. 27.50x (ISBN 0-231-04612-X); pap. 12.00x (ISBN 0-231-04613-8). Columbia U Pr.

Huang, Hsiu-Chi. Lu Hsiang-Shan: A 12th Century Chinese Idealist Philosopher. LC 75-39028. (China Studies: from Confucius to Mao Ser.). (Illus.). 116p. 1976. Repr. of 1944 ed. 16.50 (ISBN 0-88355-384-8). Hyperion-Conn.

Liu, James T. Ou-yang Hsiu: An Eleventh-Century Neo-Confucianist. 1967. 10.00x (ISBN 0-8047-0262-4). Stanford U Pr.

Taylor, Rodney L. The Cultivation of Sagehood As a Religious Goal in Neo-Confucianism: A Study of Selected Writings of Kao P'an-Lung (1562-1626) LC 78-18685. 1978. pap. 7.50 (ISBN 0-89130-239-5). Scholars Pr Ca.

NEO-DADAISM

see Pop Art

NEO-EMPIRICISM

see Logical Positivism

NEO-FACISM

see Fascism

NEO-IMPRESSIONISM (ART)

see Impressionism (Art)

NEO-LATIN LANGUAGES

see Romance Languages

NEO-LITERATES, WRITING FOR

see New Literates, Writing for

NEOLITHIC PERIOD

Burkitt, M. C. Our Early Ancestors: An Introductory Study of Mesolithic, Neolithic, & Copper Age Cultures in Europe & Adjacent Regions. LC 72-80142. (Illus.). Repr. of 1926 ed. 15.00 (ISBN 0-405-08331-9, Blom Pubns). Arno.

Dumitrescu, Vladimir. The Neolithic Settlement of East (South-West Oltenia, Romania) 1980. 72.00x (ISBN 0-86054-076-6, Pub. by BAR). State Mutual Bk.

Knox, D. M. The Neolithic Revolution. Yapp, Malcolm, et al, eds. (World History Ser.). (Illus.). 32p. (gr. 10). 1980. lib. bdg. 5.95 (ISBN 0-89908-130-4); pap. text ed. 1.95 (ISBN 0-89908-105-3). Greenhaven.

Kosse, Krisztina. Settlement Ecology of the Early & Middle Neolithic Koros & Linear Pottery Cultures in Hungary. 1979. 40.00x (ISBN 0-86054-066-9, Pub. by BAR). State Mutual Bk.

Kruk, Janusz. The Neolithic Settlement of Southern Poland. Howell, J. M. & Starling, N. J., eds. Hejwoska, M., tr. from Polish. 129p. 1980. 36.00x (ISBN 0-86054-107-X, Pub. by BAR). State Mutual Bk.

Rowlett, Elsebet S., et al. Neolithic Levels on the Titelberg, Luxembourg. LC 76-623772. (Museum Brief: No. 18). iii, 61p. 1976. pap. write for info. (ISBN 0-913134-83-X). Mus Anthro Mo.

Tyler, Alan. Neolithic Flint Axes from the Cotswold Hills. 1976. 10.00x (ISBN 0-904531-28-7, Pub. by BAR). State Mutual Bk.

NEOLOGISMS

see Words, New

NEO-MELANESIAN LANGUAGE

see Pidgin English

NEON LAMPS

Miller, Samuel C. Neon Techniques & Handling: Handbook of Neon Sign & Cold Cathode Lighting. 1977. 21.00 (ISBN 0-911380-41-8). Signs of Times.

Stern, Rudi. Let There Be Neon. LC 77-25900. (Illus.). 1979. 19.95 (ISBN 0-8109-1255-4); pap. 8.95 o. p. (ISBN 0-8109-2164-2). Abrams.

NEONATAL DEATH

see Infants–Mortality

NEONATAL SURGERY

see Infants (Newborn)–Surgery

NEONATES

see Infants (Newborn)

NEONATOLOGY

Avery, Gordon B. Neonatology. 2nd ed. (Illus.). 129p. 1981. text ed. 79.50 (ISBN 0-397-50429-2, JBL-Med-Nursing). Har-Row.

Behrman, Richard E., ed. Neonatal-Perintal Medicine: Disease of the Fetus & Infant. 2nd ed. LC 77-1734. (Illus.). 1977. 58.50 (ISBN 0-8016-0579-2). Mosby.

Black, J. Neonatal Emergencies & Other Problems. 288p. 1972. 27.50 (ISBN 0-407-32780-0). Butterworth.

Brown, Edwin & Sweet, Avron Y., eds. Neonatal Necrotizing Enterocolitis. (Monographs in Neonatology Ser.). 224p. 1980. 21.50 (ISBN 0-8089-1244-5). Grune.

Dick, George. Immunisation. (Illus.). 1978. text ed. 12.50x (ISBN 0-906141-10-9, Pub. by Update Pubns England). Kluwer Boston.

Ferrara, Angelo & Harin, Anantham. Emergency Transfer of the High Risk Neonate: A Working Manual for Medical, Nursing & Administrative Personnel. LC 79-17689. (Illus.). 1979. pap. text ed. 25.00 (ISBN 0-8016-1565-8). Mosby.

Harper, Rita G. & Yoon, Jing J. Handbook of Neonatology. (Illus.). 305p. 1974. 16.50 (ISBN 0-8151-4149-1). Year Bk Med.

Hathaway, William E. & Bonnar, J. Perinatal Coagulation. (Monographs in Neonatology). 256p. 1978. 25.75 (ISBN 0-8089-1119-8). Grune.

Hirnle, Robert W. Clinical Simulations in Neonatal Respiratory Therapy. 300p. 1982. pap. 16.00 (ISBN 0-471-08266-X, Pub. by Wiley Medical). Wiley.

Jonsen, Albert R. & Garland, Michael J., eds. Ethics of Newborn Intensive Care. LC 76-47016. 1976. pap. 4.00x (ISBN 0-87772-216-1). Inst Gov Stud Berk.

Lassau, J. P., et al. Atlas of Neonatal Anatomy: Correlation of Gross Anatomy, Computed Tomography & Ultrasonography. (Illus.). 136p. 1981. write for info. (ISBN 0-89352-139-6). Masson Pub.

Lough, Marvin D., et al. Newborn Respiratory Care. (Illus.). 1979. 20.95 (ISBN 0-8151-5635-9). Year Bk Med.

Mansubi, Fereydun. Self-Assessment of Current Knowledge in Neonatology & Perinatal Medicine. 1976. spiral bdg. 14.50 (ISBN 0-87488-240-0). Med Exam.

Maragos, G. D., ed. Seminar on Neonatology. (Paediatrician: Vol. 5, No. 5). (Illus.). 1977. 18.00 (ISBN 3-8055-2702-0). S Karger.

Moragas, Augusto, et al. Atlas of Neonatal Histopathology. Valdes-Dapena, Antonio & Valdes-Dapena, Marie A., trs. LC 76-45960. (Illus.). 1978. text ed. 62.50 (ISBN 0-7216-6542-X). Saunders.

Odell, Gerard. Neonatal Hyperbilirubinemia. (Monographs in Neonatology Ser.). 176p. 1980. 19.00 (ISBN 0-8089-1247-X). Grune.

Oehler, Jerri M. Family-Centered Neonatal Nursing Care. (Illus.). 399p. 1981. pap. text ed. 17.50 (ISBN 0-397-54300-X, JBL-Med-Nursing). Har-Row.

Overbach, A. M. & Rodman, M. J. Drugs Used with Neonates & During Pregnancy. 1975. pap. 3.50 (ISBN 0-87489-061-6). Med Economics.

Philip, Alistair G. Neonatology - A Practical Guide. 2nd ed. LC 80-21108. 1980. pap. 18.50 (ISBN 0-87488-671-6). Med Exam.

Scanlon, John W. & Daze, Ann M. Code Pink: A Practical System for Neonatal-Perinatal Resuscitation. 192p. 1981. pap. text ed. 16.95 (ISBN 0-8391-1670-5). Univ Park.

Sheldon, Roger & Dominiak, Pati, eds. The Expanding Role of the Nurse in Neonatal Intensive Care. 1980. 17.50 (ISBN 0-8089-1270-4). Grune.

Sherwood, William & Cohen, Alan, eds. Transfusion Therapy in Infancy & Childhood: The Fetus, Infant, & Child. LC 80-80304. (Masson Monographs in Pediatrics - Pediatric Hematology Oncology: Vol. 1). (Illus.). 232p. 1980. text ed. 34.50x (ISBN 0-89352-074-8). Masson Pub.

Swinyard, Chester A. Decision Making & the Defective Newborn. (Illus.). 672p. 1978. 32.75 (ISBN 0-398-03662-4). C C Thomas.

Taylor, Paul M., ed. Parent-Infant Relationship. (Monographs in Neonatology). (Illus.). 371p. 1980. 24.50 (ISBN 0-8089-1289-5). Grune.

NEO-NAZISM

see Fascism–Germany

NEO-ORTHODOXY

see also Fundamentalism

NEOPLASMS

see Tumors

NEOPLATONISM

Armstrong, A. H. An Introduction to Ancient Philosophy. 3rd ed. (Littlefield, Adams Quality Paperbacks Ser.: No. 418). 250p. 1981. pap. 5.95 (ISBN 0-8226-0418-3). Littlefield.

Coulter, James. The Literary Microcosm: Theories of Interpretation of the Later Neoplatonists. (Columbia Studies in the Classical Tradition: No. II). 1976. text ed. 27.50x (ISBN 90-04-04489-2). Humanities.

Dodds, E. R. Select Passages Illustrating Neoplatonism. 128p. 1980. 12.50 (ISBN 0-89005-302-2). Ares.

Ellrodt, Robert. Neoplatonism in the Poetry of Spenser. LC 75-11942. 1960. lib. bdg. 25.00 (ISBN 0-8414-3991-5). Folcroft.

--Neoplatonism in the Poetry of Spenser. 1978. Repr. of 1960 ed. lib. bdg. 35.00 (ISBN 0-8495-1318-9). Arden Lib.

Elsas, Christoph. Neuplatonische und gnostische Weltablehnung in der Schule Plotins. (Religionsgeschichtliche Versuche und Vorarbeiten, Vol. 34). 1975. 57.25x (ISBN 3-11-003941-9). De Gruyter.

Goudard, Sr. M. Lucien. Etude Sur les Epistres Morales D'Honore D'Urfe. LC 70-94204. (Catholic University of America Studies in Romance Languages & Literatures Ser: No. 8). (Fr). Repr. of 1933 ed. 16.50 (ISBN 0-404-50308-X). AMS Pr.

Greive, Hermann. Studien zum juedischen Neuplatonismus: Die Religionsphilosophie des Abraham Ibn Ezra. (Studia Judaica Vol. 7). 225p. 1973. 45.00x (ISBN 3-11-004116-2). De Gruyter.

Harris, R. Baine, ed. Neoplatonism & Indian Thought. (Ancient & Modern Ser.). 353p. 1981. lib. bdg. 39.00x (ISBN 0-87395-545-5, HANI); pap. 12.95x (ISBN 0-87395-546-3, HANI-P). State U NY Pr.

--The Significance of Neoplatonism. LC 76-21254. 1976. 24.00 (ISBN 0-87395-800-4). State U NY Pr.

--The Structure of Being: A Neoplatonic Interpretation. LC 81-5627. (Neoplatonism: Ancient & Modern Ser.). 320p. 1981. 39.00x (ISBN 0-87395-532-3, HASB); pap. 12.95x (ISBN 0-87395-533-1, HASB-P). State U NY Pr.

Katz, Steven, ed. Jewish Neo-Platonism: Selected Essays. An Original Anthology. LC 79-7178. (Jewish Philosophy, Mysticism & History of Ideas Ser.). 1980. lib. bdg. 42.00x (ISBN 0-405-12236-5). Arno.

Koch, Hal. Pronoia und Paideusis: Studien Uber Origenes und Sein Verhaltnis Zum Platonismus. LC 78-66597. (Ancient Philosophy Ser.). 347p. 1979. lib. bdg. 34.00 (ISBN 0-8240-9592-8). Garland Pub.

Lowry, James. The Logical Principles of Proclus' As Systematic Ground of the Cosmos. (Elementa Ser.: No. 13). 118p. 1980. text ed. 17.25x (ISBN 90-6203-781-X). Humanities.

O'Meara, Dominic J. Neoplatonism & Christian Thought. LC 81-5272. (Neoplatonism: Ancient & Modern Ser.). 270p. 1981. 39.00x (ISBN 0-87395-492-0, OMNC); pap. 12.95x (ISBN 0-87395-493-9, OMNC-P). State U NY Pr.

Robb, Nesca A. Neoplatonism of the Italian Renaissance. 1968. lib. bdg. 17.00x (ISBN 0-374-96840-3). Octagon.

Stahl, W. H., tr. Commentary on the Dream of Scipio. LC 52-1644. 1952. 20.00x (ISBN 0-231-01737-5). Columbia U Pr.

Whittaker, Thomas. Neo-Platonists. facsimile ed. LC 76-114901. (Select Bibliographies Reprint Ser). 1918. 19.50 (ISBN 0-8369-5305-3). Arno.

Wilder, Alexander. New Platonism & Alchemy. (Secret Doctrine Reference Ser). 1975. pap. 2.50 (ISBN 0-913510-18-1). Wizards.

NEO-POSITIVISM

see Logical Positivism

NEOPRENE

see Rubber, Artificial

NEO-SCHOLASTICISM

Cantin, Stanislas. Precis De Psychologie Thomiste. 2nd ed. (Fr). 1960. pap. 2.70x (ISBN 2-7637-6128-3, Pub. by Laval). Intl Schol Bk Serv.

John, Sr. Helen. Thomist Spectrum. LC 66-23619. (Orestes Brownson Ser: No. 5). 1966. 20.00 (ISBN 0-8232-0715-3). Fordham.

Miethe, Terry L. & Bourke, Vernon J., eds. Thomistic Bibliography, 1940-1978. LC 80-1195. xxii, 318p. 1980. lib. bdg. 39.95 (ISBN 0-313-21991-5, MTH/). Greenwood.

Morreall, John S. Analogy & Talking About God: A Critique of the Thomistic Approach. LC 77-18494. 1978. pap. text ed. 7.75 (ISBN 0-8191-0423-X). U Pr of Amer.

NEO-THOMISM

see Neo-Scholasticism

NEPAL

Hedrick, Basil C., et al. A Bibliography of Nepal. LC 73-10075. 1973. 11.50 (ISBN 0-8108-0649-5). Scarecrow.

Hitchcock, John & Jones, Rex, eds. Spirit Possession in the Nepal Himalayas. 401p. 1976. text ed. 43.00x (ISBN 0-85668-029-X, Pub. by Aris & Phillips England). Humanities.

Kazami, Takehide. Himalayas: A Journey to Nepal. LC 68-17456. (This Beautiful World Ser.: Vol. 1). (Illus.). 1968. pap. 4.95 (ISBN 0-87011-052-7). Kodansha.

Pratapaditya Pal. Nepal: Where the Gods Are Young. LC 75-769. (Illus.). 136p. 1975. 19.95 (ISBN 0-87848-045-5). Asia Soc.

Rahul, Ram. The Himalaya As a Frontier. 154p. 1978. 10.00x (ISBN 0-7069-0564-4, Pub. by Croom Helm Ltd. England). Biblio Dist.

Regmi, Mahesh C. Landownership in Nepal. LC 74-77734. 1976. 27.50x (ISBN 0-520-02750-7). U of Cal Pr.

Shaha, Rishikesh. An Introduction to Nepal. (Illus.). 1976. 8.50x (ISBN 0-685-89510-6). Himalaya Hse.

Tuladhar, Jayanti M., et al. The Population of Nepal: Structure & Change. (Research Monograph: No. 17). (Illus.). 1977. 8.00 (ISBN 0-686-23610-6, Ctr South & Southeast Asia Studies). Cellar.

Von Furer-Haimendorf, Christoph. Himalayan Traders. LC 75-755. (Illus.). 325p. 1975. 21.50 (ISBN 0-312-37310-4). St Martin.

--The Sherpas of Nepal: Buddhist Highlanders. 1979. Repr. of 1964 ed. text ed. 21.00x (ISBN 0-391-01044-1). Humanities.

Von-Furer-Haimendorf, Christoph, ed. Contributions to the Anthropology of Nepal. 260p. 1974. text ed. 34.00 (ISBN 0-85668-021-4, Pub. by Aris & Phillips England); pap. text ed. 18.00 (ISBN 0-686-72789-4, Pub. by Aris & Phillips England). Humanities.

NEPAL–DESCRIPTION AND TRAVEL

Armington, Stan. Exploring Nepal. (Illus.). 1976. pap. text ed. 3.50 (ISBN 0-910856-62-1). La Siesta.

--Trekking in the Himalayas. (Illus.). 1979. pap. 5.95 (ISBN 0-908086-06-7). Hippocrene Bks.

Bendall, Cecil. A Journey in Nepal & Northern India. (Illus.). 1975. 5.95x (ISBN 0-685-89508-4). Himalaya Hse.

Bezruchka, Stephen. A Guide to Trekking in Nepal. 4th ed. LC 80-72091. (Illus.). 256p. 1981. pap. 8.95 (ISBN 0-89886-003-2). Mountaineers.

Casimaty, Nina, ed. India & Nepal: A Travel Handbook. 1979. pap. 4.00x (ISBN 0-686-19964-2). Intl Learn Syst.

--India & Nepal: A Travel Handbook 1979-1980. (Illus.). 56p. (Orig.). 1979. pap. 6.50x (ISBN 0-8002-2430-2). Intl Pubns Serv.

Engstrom, Barbie. India Nepal & Sri Lanka: A Guide to a Travel Experience. (Engstrom's Travel Exprience Guide Ser.). (Illus.). 228p. (Orig.). 1981. pap. 14.50 (ISBN 0-916588-06-8). Kurios Pr.

Fodor's India, 1981. 1980. 14.95 (ISBN 0-679-00696-6). McKay.

Hitchcock, John. A Mountain Village in Nepal. LC 79-20086. 143p. 1980. pap. text ed. 6.95 (ISBN 0-03-045386-0, HoltC). HR&W.

Monuments of the Katmandu Valley. 129p. 1980. pap. 7.00 (ISBN 92-3-101644-X, U 981, UNESCO). Unipub.

Murphy, Dervla. Waiting Land: A Spell in Nepal. (Illus.). 1969. 8.95 (ISBN 0-7195-1745-1). Transatlantic.

Nagel's Encyclopedia Guide: India & Nepal. (Illus.). 832p. 1980. 55.00 (ISBN 0-686-74058-0). Masson Pub.

Northey, William B. The Land of the Gurkhas. LC 78-179229. (Illus.). Repr. of 1937 ed. 27.50 (ISBN 0-404-54856-3). AMS Pr.

Thapa, N. B. & Thapa, D. P. Geography of Nepal: Physical, Economic, Cultural & Regional. 220p. 1981. 10.00x (ISBN 0-86125-657-3, Pub. by Orient Longman India). State Mutual Bk.

NEPAL–ECONOMIC CONDITIONS

Banskota, N. P. Indo-Nepal Trade & Economic Relations. 299p. 1981. text ed. 25.00x (ISBN 0-391-02337-3, Pub. by Concept India). Humanities.

Blaikie, M. P., et al. The Struggle for Basic Needs in Nepal. (Illus.). 100p. (Orig.). 1980. pap. 6.50x (ISBN 92-64-12101-3). OECD.

Blaikie, Pers, et al. Nepal in Crisis: Growth & Stagnation at the Periphery. (Illus.). 328p. 1980. 49.95x (ISBN 0-19-828414-4). Oxford U Pr.

Nepal Trade Directory. 2nd ed. 348p. 1979. pap. 25.00x (ISBN 0-8002-0983-4). Intl Pubns Serv.

Poffenberger, Mark. Patterns of Change in the Nepal Himalaya. 111p. 1981. lib. bdg. 15.50x (ISBN 0-86531-184-6). Westview.

Rawat, P. C. Indo-Nepal Economic Relations. 1974. text ed. 13.00x (ISBN 0-8426-0656-4). Verry.

Regmi, M. C. A Study in Nepali Economic History, 1768-1846. (Bibliotheca Himalayica Ser.: No. 1, Vol. 14). (Illus.). 235p. 1973. text ed. 12.00x (ISBN 0-8426-0485-5). Verry.

Regmi, Mahesh C. Land Tenure & Taxation in Nepal, Vol. 4, Religious & Charitable Land Endowments, Guthi Tenure. (Research Ser.: No. 12). 1968. pap. 2.75x (ISBN 0-87725-112-6). U of Cal Intl St.

--Thatched Huts & Stucco Places: Peasants & Landlords in Nineteenth Century Nepal. 173p. 1978. 14.00x (ISBN 0-7069-0672-1, Pub. by Croom Helm Ltd. England). Biblio Dist.

Seddon, D., et al, eds. Peasants & Workers in Nepal: The Condition of the Lower Classes. 214p. 1979. text ed. 34.00x (ISBN 0-85668-112-1, Pub. by Aris & Phillips England); pap. text ed. 24.00x (ISBN 0-85668-197-0, Pub. by Aris &Phillips England). Humanities.

NEPAL–FOREIGN RELATIONS

Mojumdar, Kanchanmoy. Anglo-Nepalese Relations in the Nineteenth Century. LC 73-906205. vi, 195p. 1973. 9.00x (ISBN 0-88386-214-X). South Asia Bks.

Muni, S. D. Foreign Policy of Nepal. (Illus.). 320p. 1973. 15.00x (ISBN 0-8002-1430-7). Intl Pubns Serv.

Ramakant. Indo-Nepalese Relations 1816-77. 1968. 10.00x (ISBN 0-8426-1482-6). Verry.

--Nepal-China & India. 1976. 12.00x (ISBN 0-88386-796-6). South Asia Bks.

Rawat, P. C. Indo-Nepal Economic Relations. LC 74-901654. 287p. 1974. 12.00x (ISBN 0-8002-0054-3). Intl Pubns Serv.

Rose, Leo E. Nepal: Strategy for Survival. LC 75-100022. (Center of South & Southeast Asia Studies, UC Berkeley). 1971. 27.50x (ISBN 0-520-01643-2). U of Cal Pr.

NEPAL–HISTORY

Bhooshan, B. S. The Development Experience of Nepal. 1980. text ed. 15.00x (ISBN 0-391-01819-1). Humanities.

Charak, Sukhder S. History & Culture of Himalayan States, Vol. 2. (Himachal Pradesh Ser.: Pt. 2). 1979. text ed. 35.00x (ISBN 0-391-01176-6). Humanities.

Messerschmidt, Donald A. The Gurungs of Nepal - Conflict & Change in Village Society. 155p. 1976. text ed. 18.00 (ISBN 0-85668-032-X, Pub. by Aris & Phillips England); pap. text ed. 10.00 (ISBN 0-85668-050-8, Pub. by Aris & Phillips England). Humanities.

Monuments of the Katmandu Valley. 129p. 1980. pap. 7.00 (ISBN 92-3-101644-X, U 981, UNESCO). Unipub.

Regmi, Mahesh C. Thatched Huts & Stucco Places: Peasants & Landlords in Nineteenth Century Nepal. 173p. 1978. 14.00x (ISBN 0-7069-0672-1, Pub. by Croom Helm Ltd. England). Biblio Dist.

Rose, Leo E. & Scholz, John T. Nepal: Profile of a Himalayan Kingdom. LC 79-17857. (Nations of Contemporary Asia Ser.). (Illus.). 150p. 1980. lib. bdg. 16.50x (ISBN 0-89158-651-2). Westview.

Wright, D., ed. History of Nepal. Singh, M. S., tr. 1972. Repr. of 1877 ed. 18.00 (ISBN 0-8426-0478-2). Verry.

Wright, Daniel, ed. History of Nepal. 1972. 9.50x (ISBN 0-685-89512-2). Himalaya Hse.

NEPAL–POLITICS AND GOVERNMENT

Agarwal, H. N. Administrative System of Nepal. 1976. 15.00 (ISBN 0-7069-0395-1). Intl Bk Dist.

Baral, Lok R. Opposition Politics in Nepal. 1977. 12.00x (ISBN 0-8364-0049-6). South Asia Bks.

Caplan, Lionel. Administration & Politics in a Nepalese Town. (Illus.). 304p. 1975. 16.95x (ISBN 0-19-713585-4). Oxford U Pr.

Chatterji, Bhola. Study of Recent Nepalese Politics. (Illus.). 1967. 6.50x (ISBN 0-8426-1195-9). Verry.

Gaige, Frederick H. Regionalism & National Unity in Nepal. LC 74-30520. 1975. 24.50x (ISBN 0-520-02728-0). U of Cal Pr.

Hamilton, Francis B. An Account of the Kingdom of Nepal & of the Territories Annexed to This Dominion by the House of Gorkla. (Bibliotheca Himalayica Ser.: No. 1, Vol. 10). (Illus.). 364p. 1973. Repr. of 1819 ed. text ed. 22.00x (ISBN 0-8426-0484-7). Verry.

Kumar, D. P. Nepal: Year of Decision. 208p. 1980. text ed. 18.00 (ISBN 0-7069-1031-1, Pub. by Vikas India). Advent NY.

Mojumdar, Kanchanmoy. Nepal & the Indian Nationalist Movement. LC 76-902010. 1975. 6.50x (ISBN 0-88386-703-6). South Asia Bks.

Rose, Leo E. & Fisher, Margaret W. Politics of Nepal: Persistence & Change in an Asian Monarchy. Park, Richard L., ed. LC 77-4792. (South Asian Political Systems Ser). (Illus.). 1970. 19.50x (ISBN 0-8014-0574-2). Cornell U Pr.

Shaha, Rishikesh. Nepali Politics: Retrospect & Prospect. 2nd ed. 1978. 11.50x (ISBN 0-19-560890-9). Oxford U Pr.

NEPAL–SOCIAL LIFE AND CUSTOMS

Bahadur, Kaisher. Judicial Customs of Nepal, Part 1. rev. 2nd ed. LC 78-919265. (Illus.). 432p. 1972. 37.50x (ISBN 0-8426-0432-4). Verry.

Borgstrom, Bengt-Erik. The Patron & the Panca. 184p. 1980. text ed. 15.00 (ISBN 0-7069-0997-6, Pub. by Vikas India). Advent NY.

Furer-Haimendorf, Christoph Von, ed. Caste & Kin in Nepal India & Ceylon: Anthropological Studies in Hindu-Buddhist Contact Zones. (Illus.). 1978. text ed. 22.50x (ISBN 0-391-01073-5). Humanities.

Hitchcock, John T. & Jones, Rex L., eds. Spirit Possession in the Nepal Himalayas. (Central Asian Studies). (Illus.). 1976. 43.00 (ISBN 0-85668-029-X, Pub. by Aris & Phillips); pap. 20.00x (ISBN 0-85668-049-4, Pub. by Aris & Phillips). Intl Schol Bk Serv.

Larsen, Peter. Boy of Nepal. LC 75-99179. (Illus.). (gr. 2 up). 1970. PLB 5.95 (ISBN 0-396-06063-3). Dodd.

Lorrance, Arleen. Hello, Goodbye, I Love You. (Illus., Orig.). 1981. pap. price not set (ISBN 0-916192-18-0). L P Pubns.

Messerschmidt, Donald A. The Gurungs of Nepal: Conflict & Change in a Village Society. (Central Asian Studies). (Illus.). 1976. 18.00x (ISBN 0-85668-032-X, Pub. by Aris & Phillips); pap. 10.00x (ISBN 0-85668-050-8, Pub. by Aris & Phillips). Intl Schol Bk Serv.

Pignede, Bernard. Les Gurungs: Une Population Himalayenne Du Nepal. (Le Monde D'outre-Mer Passe et Present, Etudes: No. 21). 1966. pap. 59.00x (ISBN 0-686-21823-X). Mouton.

Seddon, D., et al, eds. Peasants & Workers in Nepal: The Condition of the Lower Classes. 214p. 1979. text ed. 34.00x (ISBN 0-85668-112-1, Pub. by Aris & Phillips England); pap. text ed. 24.00x (ISBN 0-85668-197-0, Pub. by Aris &Phillips England). Humanities.

Seddon, David, et al. Peasants & Workers in Nepal: The Condition of the Lower Classes. 1979. 34.00x (ISBN 0-85668-112-1, Pub. by Aris & Phillips). Intl Schol Bk Serv.

Shadap-Sen, Namita C. Origin & Early History of the Khasi-Sunteng People. 1981. 28.50x (ISBN 0-8364-0767-9, Pub. by Mukhopadhyay). South Asia Bks.

Slusser, Mary S. Nepal Mandala: A Cultural Study of the Kathmandu Valley, 2 vols. LC 80-36662. (Illus., Vol.1, 580pp.; vol2, 350pp.). 1982. Set. 75.00x (ISBN 0-691-03128-2). Princeton U Pr.

Taylor, Daniel & Hamal, Hem B. Population Education for Nepal. 81p. 1974. pap. 4.00 (ISBN 0-89055-110-3). Carolina Pop Ctr.

NEPALESE TALES

see Tales, Nepalese

NEPALI LANGUAGE

Clark, N. Introduction to Nepali. 1977. 24.00x (ISBN 0-88386-385-5). South Asia Bks.

Dasgupta, B. Nepali Self Taught. 4.50x (ISBN 0-686-00877-4). Colton Bk.

Hale, Austin, ed. Clause, Sentence & Discourse Patterns in Selected Languages of Nepal, 4 pts. Pt. 1. pap. 10.50 (ISBN 0-88312-043-7); Pt. 2. pap. 7.50 (ISBN 0-88312-044-5); Pt. 3. pap. 10.00 (ISBN 0-88312-045-3); Pt. 4. pap. 8.50 (ISBN 0-88312-046-1); Set. pap. 35.00 (ISBN 0-88312-042-9); microfiche pt. 1 3.00, (0-88312-443-2), microfiche pt. 2 2.00, (0-88312-444-0), microfiche pt. 3 3.00, (0-88312-445-9), microfiche pt. 4 1.50. (0-88312-446-7), set 10.60, (0-88312-442-4) (ISBN 0-686-67020-5). Summer Inst Ling.

Hari, Anna M., ed. Conversational Nepali. 1971. Summer Inst Ling.

Rai, Krishna P., et al. Kulung-Nepali-English Glossary. 1975. pap. 2.00x (ISBN 0-88312-780-6). Summer Inst Ling.

Verma, M. K. & Sharma, T. N. Intermediate Nepali Reader, 2 vols. 1980. Vol.1. write for info. (ISBN 0-8364-0652-4, Pub. by Manohar India); Vol. 2. write for info. (ISBN 0-8364-0653-2); Set. 32.50 (ISBN 0-686-69016-8). South Asia Bks.

NEPHRITE

see Jade

NEPHRITIS

see Kidneys–Diseases

NEPHROLOGY

see also Kidneys

Asscher, et al. Nephrology Illustrated. Date not set. text ed. price not set (ISBN 0-7216-1447-7). Saunders.

Becker, E. Lovell, ed. Cornell Seminars in Nephrology. 272p. 1973. 29.50 (ISBN 0-471-06144-1). Krieger.

Brenner, Barry M. & Stein, Jay H., eds. Hormonal Function & the Kidney. (Contemporary Issues in Nephrology: Vol. 4). (Illus.). 1979. text ed. 29.00 (ISBN 0-443-08039-9). Churchill.

Brod, J., et al, eds. Proteinuria. (Contributions to Nephrology: Vol. 1). (Illus.). 250p. 1975. 35.50 (ISBN 3-8055-2183-9). S Karger.

Cameron, J. Stewart, et al. Nephrology for Nurses - A Modern Approach to the Kidney. 2nd ed. 1977. sprial bdg. 9.50 (ISBN 0-87488-869-7). Med Exam.

Cameron, Stewart, et al. Nephrology for Nurses: A Modern Approach to the Kidney. 2nd ed. (Illus.). 330p. 1976. pap. 16.95x (ISBN 0-433-05111-6). Intl Ideas.

Cheigh, Jhoong S., et al, eds. Manual of Clinical Nephrology of the Rogosin Kidney Center. (Developments in Nephrology: No. 1). (Illus.). 470p. 1981. PLB 65.00 (ISBN 90-247-2397-3, Pub. by Martinus Nijhoff Netherlands). Kluwer Boston.

Coe, Fredric L., et al, eds. Nephrolithiasis, Vol. 5. (Contemporary Issues in Nephrology Ser.). (Illus.). 280p. 1980. text ed. 35.00 (ISBN 0-443-08048-8). Churchill.

--Nephrolithiasis, Vol. 5. (Contemporary Issues in Nephrology Ser.). (Illus.). 280p. 1980. text ed. 35.00 (ISBN 0-443-08048-8). Churchill.

Congress on Toxic Nephropathies, 6th, Parma, June 1977. Toxic Nephropathies: Proceedings. Berlyne, G. M., et al, eds. (Contributions to Nephrology: Vol. 10). (Illus.). 1978. 29.50 (ISBN 3-8055-2832-9). S Karger.

Controversies in Nephrology Conference Sponsored by the American Kidney Fund. Controversies in Nephrology, Vol. 2: Proceedings. Schreiner, George E., ed. (Controversies in Nephrology, 2nd). 390p. 1981. text ed. 49.50 (ISBN 0-89352-144-2). Masson Pub.

David, David S. Calcium Metaboloism in Renal Failure & Nephrolithiasis. LC 76-30308. 418p. 1977. 54.50 (ISBN 0-471-19673-8). Krieger.

Diamond, L. H. Nephrology Reviews, Vol. 2. 320p. 1981. 25.00 (ISBN 0-471-07956-1, Pub. by Wiley Medical). Wiley.

European Dialysis & Transplant Assoc., 1974, Tel Aviv. Dialysis, Transplantation & Nephrology: Proceedings, Vol. 11. Moorhead, John, ed. (Illus.). 600p. 1975. 45.00x (ISBN 0-8464-0326-9). Beekman Pubs.

Flamenbaum, Walter. Basic Nephrology: An Approach to the Patient with Renal Disease. (Illus.). 640p. 1981. text ed. price not set (ISBN 0-397-50533-7, JBL-Med-Nursing). Har-Row.

Forland, Marvin. Nephrology-A Review of Clinical Nephrology. 1977. pap. 16.00 (ISBN 0-87488-622-8). Med Exam.

Friedman, E. A., ed. The John P. Merrill Festschrift: Nephrological Research Papers by Past & Present Members of the Merrill School of Nephrology. (Nephron: Vol. 22, Nos. 1-3). (Illus.). 1978. pap. 39.00 (ISBN 3-8055-2981-3). S Karger.

Gnnick, Harvey C., ed. Current Nephrology, Vol. 4. (Current Ser.). (Illus.). 500p. 1980. text ed. 48.00 (ISBN 0-471-09519-2, Pub. by Wiley Med). Wiley.

Hamburger, J., et al. Nephrology. 1193p. 1979. 110.00 (ISBN 0-471-01762-0, Pub. by Wiley Med). Wiley.

Hamburger, Jean, ed. Advances in Nephrology, Vol. 9. 1980. 49.95 (ISBN 0-8151-4118-1). Year Bk Med.

--Advances in Nephrology, Vol. 10. 1980. 48.95 (ISBN 0-8151-4119-X). Year Bk Med.

--Advances in Nephrology, Vol. 11. 1980. 48.95 (ISBN 0-8151-4134-3). Year Bk Med.

Heidelberg Seminars in Nephrology, Heidelberg, September 1978. Pathophysiological Problems in Clinical Nephrology. Ritz, E., et al, eds. (Contributions to Nephrology: Vol. 14). (Illus.). 1978. pap. 52.75 (ISBN 3-8055-2910-4). S Karger.

Hodson, C. J., ed. Radiology & the Kidney: Some Present Concepts. (Contributions to Nephrology: Vol. 5). (Illus.). 1977. 29.50 (ISBN 3-8055-2385-8). S Karger.

Hollerman, Charles E. Pediatric Nephrology. (Medical Outline Ser.). 1979. pap. 18.00 (ISBN 0-87488-590-6). Med Exam.

International Symposium on: HBsAg Containing Immune Complexes: Renal & Other Extra-Hepatic Manifestations: Italy, Sept. 1979, et al. Systematic Effects of HBsAg Immune Complexes: Proceedings. Chiandussi, L. & Sherlock, S., eds. 308p. 1981. text ed. 33.00 (ISBN 0-686-31134-5, Pub. by Piccin Italy). J K Burgess.

International Symposium on Parathyroid in Uremia, 1st, N.Y., May, 1979. Parathyroid Hormone in Kidney Failure: Proceedings. Avran, M. M. & Berlyne, G. M., eds. (Contributions to Nephrology: Vol. 20). 1980. soft cover 45.00 (ISBN 3-8055-0151-X). S Karger.

Klahr, Saulo & Massry, Shaul G., eds. Contemporary Nephrology, Vol. 1. 692p. 1981. 49.50 (ISBN 0-306-40664-0, Plenum Pr). Plenum Pub.

Massry, S. G., ed. Kidney in Systemic Diseases. (Contributions to Nephrology: Vol. 7). (Illus.). 1977. 58.75 (ISBN 3-8055-2445-5). S Karger.

Metaxas, P., ed. Eighth International Congress of Nephrology, Athens, June 1981. (Illus.). xiv, 786p. 1981. 143.75 (ISBN 3-8055-2532-X). S Karger.

Migone, L., ed. Urinary Proteins. (Contributions to Nephrology Ser.: Vol. 26). (Illus.). vi, 150p. 1981. pap. 54.00 (ISBN 3-8055-1848-X). S Karger.

Papper, Solomon. Clinical Nephrology. 2nd ed. 539p. 1978. 25.00 (ISBN 0-316-69045-7). Little.

Pascual, J. F. & Calcagno, P. L., eds. Nephrologic Problems of the Newborn. (Contributions to Nephrology: Vol. 15). (Illus.). 1979. pap. 19.75 (ISBN 3-8055-2947-3). S Karger.

--Recent Advances in Pediatric Nephrology. (Contributions to Nephrology Ser.: Vol. 27). (Illus.). vi, 150p. 1981. pap. 54.00 (ISBN 3-8055-1851-X). S Karger.

Registry of Nephrology Training Centers. 1972. pap. 4.00 (ISBN 0-87493-030-8, 73-307A). Am Heart.

Robinson, Brian. Dialysis, Transplantation, Nephrology: Proceedings, European Dialysis & Transplant Asso., Volume 14. (Illus.). 1978. 49.95x (ISBN 0-8464-0329-3). Beekman Pubs.

Robinson, Brian, ed. Dialysis, Transplantation, Nephrology: Proceedings European Dialysis & Transplant Assoc. Volume 13. (Illus.). 1977. 59.95x (ISBN 0-8464-0328-5). Beekman Pubs.

--Dialysis, Transplantation, Nephrology: Proceedings, European Dialysis & Transplant Association, Vol. 15. (Illus.). 662p. 1979. 69.95x (ISBN 0-8464-1087-7). Beekman Pubs.

Robinson, J. H., et al, eds. Dialysis, Transplantation, Nephrology: Proceedings, European Dialysis & Transplant Association, Vol. 16. (Illus.). 785p. 1979. 69.95x (ISBN 0-8464-1067-2). Beekman Pubs.

Rossi, E. & Oetliker, O., eds. Nephrologie im Kindesalter III. (Paediatrische Fortbildungskurse fuer die Praxis: Bd. 45). (Illus., Ger.). 1978. 38.50 (ISBN 3-8055-2825-6). S Karger.

Rossmann, P. & Jirka, I. Rejection Nephropathy. 1977. 66.00 (ISBN 0-444-80032-8, North-Holland). Elsevier.

Royer, Pierre, et al. Pediatric Nephrology. LC 74-4585. (Major Problem in Clinical Pediatrics Ser.: Vol. 11). (Illus.). 415p. 1974. text ed. 25.00 (ISBN 0-7216-7776-2). Saunders.
Schlotter, Lowanna, ed. Nursing & the Nephrology Patient: A Symposium on Current Trends & Issues. 1973. spiral bdg. 9.50 (ISBN 0-87488-376-8). Med Exam.
Schreiner, G. E. Controversies in Nephrology. (Illus.). 722p. 1979. 49.50x (ISBN 0-686-77785-9). Masson Pub.
Sophian, J. Pregnancy Nephropathy, 2 vols. (Illus.). 1972. Set. 65.00 (ISBN 0-407-36200-2). Butterworth.
Stolte, H. & Alt, Jeannette. Research Animals & Experimental Design in Nephrology. (Contributions to Nephrology: Vol. 19). (Illus.). x, 250p. 1980. soft cover 49.25 (ISBN 3-8055-3075-7). S Karger.
Strauss, Jose. Pediatric Nephrology, Vol. 4: Renal Failure. Current Concepts in Diagnosis & Management. new ed. 1978. text ed. 29.50x (ISBN 0-8240-7011-9, Garland STPM Pr). Garland Pub.
Strauss, Jose, ed. Pediatric Nephrology, Vol. 5. LC 78-26304. 1979. lib. bdg. 37.50 (ISBN 0-8240-7031-3). Garland Pub.
--Renal Failure. 1978. lib. bdg. 37.50 (ISBN 0-8240-7011-9). Garland Pub.
Symposium on Nephrology, 6th, Hannover, May 1978. Interstitial Nephropathies. Kuhn, K., ed. (Contributions to Nephrology: Vol. 16). (Illus.). 1979. pap. 48.00 (ISBN 3-8055-2979-1). S Karger.
Ueda, Y., ed. Current Research in Nephrology in Japan. (Contributions to Nephrology: Vol. 4). 1976. 29.50 (ISBN 3-8055-2383-1). S Karger.
Wardle, E. N. Renal Medicine, Vol. 2. (Guidelines in Medicine). 435p. text ed. 27.50 (ISBN 0-8391-1454-0). Univ Park.
Weise, M., ed. Experimental & Clinical Aspects of Proteinuria. (Contributions to Nephrology: Vol. 24). (Illus.). x, 166p. 1981. pap. 49.75 (ISBN 3-8055-1655-X). S Karger.

NEPTUNE (PLANET)
Grosser, Morton. The Discovery of Neptune. 7.50 (ISBN 0-8446-5766-2). Peter Smith.
--The Discovery of Neptune. LC 78-68017. 1979. pap. 3.00 (ISBN 0-486-23726-5). Dover.

NERELEOPARDS
see Leopard Men

NERNST, WALTHER HERMANN, 1864-1941
Mendelssohn, K. The World of Walther Nernst: The Rise & Fall of German Science, 1864-1941. LC 73-7605. 1973. 12.95 (ISBN 0-8229-1109-4). U of Pittsburgh Pr.

NERO, EMPEROR OF ROME, 37-68
Abbott, Jacob. The History of Nero. Repr. of 1854 ed. 15.00 (ISBN 0-686-20102-7). Quality Lib.
Claudius Tiberius Nero. LC 71-133646. (Tudor Facsimile Texts. Old English Plays: No. 117). Repr. of 1913 ed. 31.50 (ISBN 0-404-53417-1). AMS Pr.
Colony, Horatio. The Emperor & the Bee Boy. 1000p. 1976. 4.75 (ISBN 0-8283-1638-4). Branden.
Diderot, Denis. Essai sur les Regnes de Claude et de Neron, 2 vols. 1972. 7.95 ea. French & Eur.
Walter, Gerard. Nero. Craufurd, Emma, tr. from Fr. LC 76-45165. 1977. Repr. of 1957 ed. lib. bdg. 20.50x (ISBN 0-8371-9302-8, WANER). Greenwood.
Weigall, Arthur. Nero: The Singing Emperor of Rome. 1930. 20.00 (ISBN 0-686-20106-X). Quality Lib.

NERUDA, PABLO, 1904-
Belitt, Ben. Adam's Dream: A Preface to Translation. LC 78-51399. 1978. 12.50 (ISBN 0-394-50288-4, GP815). Grove.
Bizzarro, Salvatore. Pablo Neruda: All Poets the Poet. LC 78-24437. 1979. lib. bdg. 10.00 (ISBN 0-8108-1189-8). Scarecrow.
DeCosta, Rene. The Poetry of Pablo Neruda. LC 78-18008. 1979. 12.50x (ISBN 0-674-67980-6). Harvard U Pr.
Duran, Manuel & Safir, Margery. Earth Tones: The Poetry of Pablo Neruda. LC 80-8095. (Illus.). 288p. 1981. 22.50x (ISBN 0-253-16662-4). Ind U Pr.
Neruda, Pablo. Memoirs. St. Martin, Hardie, tr. from Span. 370p. 1977. 11.95 (ISBN 0-374-20660-0). FS&G.
--Memoirs. St. Martin, Hardie, tr. from Span. 1978. pap. 4.95 (ISBN 0-14-004661-5). Penguin.
Sola, Maria M. Poesia y Politica in Pablo Neruda: Analisis del "Canto General". (Coleccion Mente y Palabra Ser.). (Sp.). 1979. 12.00 (ISBN 0-8477-0560-9); pap. 2.00 (ISBN 0-8477-0561-7). U of PR Pr.

NERVAL, GERARD DE, PSEUD., I.E. GERARD LABRIENIE, 1808-1855
Beauchamp, William. The Style of Nerval's Aurelia. (De Proprietatibus Litterarum Series Practica: No. 109). 108p. 1976. pap. text ed. 23.75x (ISBN 90-2793-284-0). Mouton.
Knapp, Bettina L. Gerard De Nerval: The Mystic's Dilemma. LC 75-40296. 400p. 1980. 21.50x (ISBN 0-8173-7608-9). U of Ala Pr.

NERVE-CELLS
see Nerves; Neurons

NERVE ENDINGS
Halata, Z. The Mechanoreceptors of the Mammalian Skin: Ultrastructure & Morphological Classification. (Advances in Anatomy, Embryology & Cell Biology: Vol. 50, Pt. 5). (Illus.). 77p. 1975. pap. 31.90 (ISBN 0-387-07097-4). Springer-Verlag.
Winkelmann, R. K. Nerve Endings in Normal & Pathologic Skin: Contributions to the Anatomy of Sensation. (American Lectures Dermatology). (Illus.). 204p. 1960. photocopy ed. spiral 19.75 (ISBN 0-398-02088-4). C C Thomas.

NERVE TISSUE
see also Neuroglia; Neurons
Cowen, David. The Cells of Neural Tissue & Their Pathologic Reactions. LC 76-720307. (Neuropathology, an Illustrated Course Ser.). 1977. 100.00 (ISBN 0-8036-2911-7). Davis Co.
Davidson, A. N., et al. Functional & Structural Proteins of the Nervous System. LC 72-91937. (Advances in Experimental Medicine & Biology Ser.: Vol. 32). 286p. 1972. 32.50 (ISBN 0-306-39032-9, Plenum Pr). Plenum Pub.
Popp, A. John, et al, eds. Neural Trauma. LC 78-24627. (Seminars in Neurological Surgery). 408p. 1979. text ed. 38.00 (ISBN 0-89004-257-8). Raven.
Ratliff, Floyd. Mach Bands: Quantitative Studies on Neural Networks in the Retina. LC 65-10436. 1965. 25.95x (ISBN 0-8162-7045-7). Holden-Day.
Sandri, C., et al. Membrane Morphology of the Vertebrate Nervous System. (Progress in Brain Research: Vol. 46). 1977. 85.50 (ISBN 0-444-41479-7, North Holland). Elsevier.
Sato, Gordon, ed. Tissue Culture of the Nervous System. LC 73-79426. (Current Topics in Neurobiology Ser.: Vol. 1). (Illus.). 282p. 1973. 25.00 (ISBN 0-306-36701-7, Plenum Pr). Plenum Pub.
Sokoloff, Louis, ed. Regulatory Biochemistry in Neural Tissues. 1976. pap. text ed. 4.95x (ISBN 0-262-69052-7). MIT Pr.

NERVE TRANSMISSION
see Neural Transmission

NERVES
see also Myoneural Junction; Nervous System; Neuroglia; Neuromuscular Transmission; Synapses;
also particular nerves, e.g. Olfactory Nerve, Optic Nerve
Aguayo, A. G. & Karpati, G., eds. Current Topics in Nerve & Muscle Research. LC 79-13037. (International Congress Ser.: No. 455). 328p. 1979. 58.75 (ISBN 0-444-90057-8, North Holland). Elsevier.
Bourne, Geoffrey H., ed. The Structure & Function of Nervous Tissue. Incl. Vol. 1. 1968. 74.00, by subscription 59.50 (ISBN 0-12-119281-4); Vol. 2. 1969. 74.00, by subscription 59.50 (ISBN 0-12-119282-2); Vol. 3. 1969. 74.00, by subscription 59.50 (ISBN 0-12-119283-0); Vol. 4. 1972. 74.00, by subscription 59.50 (ISBN 0-12-119284-9); Vol. 5. 1972. 74.00, by subscription 59.50 (ISBN 0-12-119285-7); Vol. 6. 1972. 74.00, by subscription 59.50 (ISBN 0-12-119286-5). Acad Pr.
Brooks, Frank P. & Evers, Patricia W., eds. Nerves & the Gut. LC 77-72998. (Illus.). 1977. pap. 36.00 (ISBN 0-913590-48-7). C B Slack.
Conesa, Salvador H. & Argote, M. L. A Visual Aid to the Examination of Nerve Roots. (Illus.). 1976. text ed. 10.95 (ISBN 0-02-858080-X). Macmillan.
Coupland, R. E. & Forssmann, W. G., eds. Peripheral Neuroendocrine Interaction. (Illus.). 1978. pap. 45.10 (ISBN 0-387-08779-6). Springer-Verlag.
Das, G. D. & Kreutzberg, G. W. Evaluation of Interstitial Nerve Cells in the Central Nervous System: A Correlative Study Using Acetylcholinesterase & Golgi Techniques. LC 64-20582. (Advances in Anatomy, Embryology & Cell Biology: Vol. 41, Pt. 1). (Illus.). 1968. pap. 17.70 (ISBN 0-387-04091-9). Springer-Verlag.
Eccles, John C. The Physiology of Nerve Cells. LC 68-9181. 288p. 1957. pap. 4.95x (ISBN 0-8018-0182-6). Johns Hopkins.
Eranko, E. O., ed. Histochemistry of Nervous Transmission. LC 70-168912. (Progress in Brain Research Ser: No. 34). 541p. 1971. 109.75 (ISBN 0-444-40951-3). Elsevier.
Fraser, Harris D. The A B C of Nerves. Repr. of 1929 ed. 20.00 (ISBN 0-89987-052-X). Darby Bks.
Gutmann, Ernest, ed. Denervated Muscle. 486p. 1962. 50.00 (ISBN 0-306-10653-1, Consultants). Plenum Pub.
Hammer, Kathryne. Nerve Conduction Studies. (Illus.). 160p. 1981. spiral bdg. 18.75 (ISBN 0-398-04519-4). C C Thomas.
Holbrook, Martin L. Hygiene of the Brain & Nerves & the Cure of Nervousness. LC 78-72799. Repr. of 1878 ed. 27.50 (ISBN 0-404-60862-0). AMS Pr.
International Society for Cell Biology. Cellular Dynamics of the Neuron. Barondes, Samuel H., ed. (Proceedings: Vol. 8). 1970. 56.00 (ISBN 0-12-611908-2). Acad Pr.
Jenkner, F. L. Peripheral Nerve Block. LC 77-8317. (Illus.). 1977. 13.50 (ISBN 0-387-81426-4). Springer-Verlag.
Johnston, P. & Roots, B. Nerve Membranes: A Study of the Biological & Chemical Aspects of Neuron Glia Relationships. 279p. 1972. text ed. 55.00 (ISBN 0-08-013222-7). Pergamon.
Junge, Douglas. Nerve & Muscle Excitation. 2nd ed. LC 80-18158. (Illus.). 230p. 1981. pap. text ed. 12.95x (ISBN 0-87893-410-3). Sinauer Assoc.
Landon, D. H., ed. The Peripheral Nerve. LC 75-26738. 836p. 1976. text ed. 79.95x (ISBN 0-412-11740-1, Pub. by Chapman & Hall England). Methuen Inc.
Mannheimer, Jeffrey S. & Lampe, Gerald N. Clinical Transcutaneous Electrical Nerve Stimulation. 1982. 22.50 (ISBN 0-8036-5832-X). Davis Co.
Mei Liu, H. Biology & Pathology of Nerve Growth. 1981. 35.00 (ISBN 0-12-452960-7). Acad Pr.
Meisami, Esmail & Brazier, Mary A. Neural Growth & Differentiation. (International Brain Research Organization Monographs: Vol. 5). 546p. 1979. text ed. 52.00 (ISBN 0-89004-378-7). Raven.
Nachmanpohn, David. Chemical & Molecular Basis of Nerve Activity. 2nd & rev. ed. 1975. 36.00 (ISBN 0-12-512757-X). Acad Pr.
Omer, George E., Jr. & Spinner, Morton. Management of Peripheral Nerve Problems. LC 77-27753. (Illus.). 1034p. 1980. text ed. 65.00 (ISBN 0-7216-6975-1). Saunders.
Oosterveld, W. J., ed. Audio-Vestibular System & Facial Nerve in Honour of B. W. Jongkees. (Advances in Orl: Vol. 22). (Illus.). 160p. 1977. 38.50 (ISBN 3-8055-2354-8). S Karger.
Palo, Jarma, ed. Myelination & Demyelination. (Advances in Experimental Medicine & Biology Ser.: Vol. 100). 651p. 1978. 49.50 (ISBN 0-306-32700-7, Plenum Pr). Plenum Pub.
Pease, Daniel C., ed. Cellular Aspects of Neural Growth & Differentiation. LC 73-126760. (UCLA Forum in Medical Sciences: No. 14). (Illus.). 1971. 57.50x (ISBN 0-520-01793-5). U of Cal Pr.
Prasad, Keder N. Regulation of Differentiation in Mammalian Nerve Cells. (Illus.). 260p. 1980. 24.50 (ISBN 0-306-40365-X, Plenum Pr). Plenum Pub.
Proceedings of a Workshop, Palo Alto, California, July 1979, et al. Conduction Velocity Distributions: A Population Approach to Electrophysiology of Nerve. Dorfman, Leslie J. & Cummins, Kenneth L., eds. LC 80-29130. (Progress in Clinical & Biological Research Ser.: No. 52). 338p. 1981. 30.00x (ISBN 0-8451-0052-1). A R Liss.
Reuben, John P., et al, eds. Electrobiology of Nerve, Synapse & Muscle. LC 75-14587. 405p. 1976. 34.50 (ISBN 0-89004-030-3). Raven.
Rogers, M. How to Overcome Nervousness. 1973. lib. bdg. 59.95 (ISBN 0-87968-552-2). Krishna Pr.
Ruscak, M. & Ruscakova, D. Metabolism of the Nerve Tissue in Relation to Ion Movements in Vitro & in Situ. (Illus.). 1972. 24.50 (ISBN 0-8391-0031-0). Univ Park.
Shkolnik-Yarros, Ekaterina G. Neurons & Interneuronal Connections of the Central Visual System. LC 69-18115. 295p. 1971. 32.50 (ISBN 0-306-30429-5, Plenum Pr). Plenum Pub.
Tribe, M. A. & Eraut, M. R. Nerves & Muscle. LC 76-55511. (Basic Biology Course Ser.: Bk. 10). (Illus.). 1977. 32.50 (ISBN 0-521-21369-X); pap. 11.95x (ISBN 0-521-21368-1). Cambridge U Pr.
Weiss, Paul A. From Cell Research to Nerve Repair. LC 75-27230. 1976. 25.00 (ISBN 0-87993-070-5). Futura Pub.
Wolf, Steven L., ed. Transcutaneous Electrical Nerve Stimulation. 1978. pap. 2.25 (ISBN 0-912452-21-8). Am Phys Therapy Assn.
Zaimis, Eleanor, ed. Nerve Growth Factor & Its Antiserum. (Illus.). 384p. 1972. text ed. 25.00x (ISBN 0-485-11132-2, Athlone Pr). Humanities.

NERVES-ANATOMY
see Neuroanatomy

NERVES-DISEASES
see Nervous System-Diseases

NERVES-SECRETIONS
see Neurosecretion

NERVES-SURGERY
see Nervous System-Surgery

NERVES-WOUNDS AND INJURIES
see Nervous System-Wounds and Injuries

NERVES, CRANIAL
see also Acoustic Nerve
Bischoff, Ernst P. Microscopic Analysis of the Anastomoses between the Cranial Nerves. Sachs, Ernest, Jr. & Valtin, Eva W., eds. LC 77-72520. (Illus.). 148p. 1977. text ed. 13.50x (ISBN 0-87451-143-7). U Pr of New Eng.
Dubner, et al, eds. The Neural Basis of Oral & Facial Function. LC 78-4048. (Illus.). 495p. 1978. 37.50 (ISBN 0-306-31094-5, Plenum Pr). Plenum Pub.
Goltz, Ronald. Checking Cranial Nerves. 1978. wkbk. 20.00 (ISBN 0-916750-14-0, CX-17). Dayton Labs.
Samii, M. & Jannetta, P. J., eds. The Cranial Nerves: Anatomy-Pathology-Pathophysiology-Diagnosis-Treatment. (Illus.). 610p. 1981. 106.00 (ISBN 0-387-10620-0). Springer-Verlag.

NERVES, SPINAL
Hoppenfeld, Stanley. Orthopaedic Neurology: A Diagnostic Guide to Neurologic Levels. LC 77-9316. (Illus.). 1977. 21.50 (ISBN 0-397-50368-7, JBL-Med-Nursing). Har-Row.
Phillips, C. G., ed. Corticospinal Neurones: Their Role in Movement. (Monographs of the Physiological Society Ser.). 1978. 69.00 (ISBN 0-12-553950-9). Acad Pr.

NERVOUS SYSTEM
see also Biological Control Systems; Brain; Central Nervous System; Excitation (Physiology); Nerve Endings; Nerves; Neural Tube; Neuroanatomy; Neurologic Examination; Neurosecretion; Shock; Solar Plexus; Spinal Cord; Tremor
Adrian, Edgar D. Mechanism of Nervous Action. rev ed. LC 33-4029. 1959. 12.50x (ISBN 0-8122-7118-1). U of Pa Pr.
American Physiological Society & Kandell, Eric R. The Nervous System, Section 1: Celluar Biology of Neurons, 2 bks, Vol. 1. 1977. Set. 135.00 (ISBN 0-683-04505-9). Williams & Wilkins.
Asanuma, Hiroshi, ed. & pref. by. Intergration in the Nervous System. LC 79-84783. (Illus.). 1979. 52.50 (ISBN 0-89640-033-6). Igaku-Shoin.
Asratian, E. A. Compensatory Adaptations, Reflex Activity & the Brain. 1965. text ed. 37.00 (ISBN 0-08-010591-2). Pergamon.
Association for Research in Nervous Mental Disease. Patterns of Organization in the Central Nervous System. 1968. 30.25 (ISBN 0-02-846370-6). Hafner.
Bailey, Orville T., ed. Central Nervous System. (International Academy of Pathology Monographs Ser: No. 9). (Illus.). 377p. 1968. 21.50 (ISBN 0-683-00337-2, Pub. by Williams & Wilkins). Krieger.
Barnes, C. D & Kircher, Christopher, eds. Readings in Neurophysiology. 482p. 1968. text ed. 14.25 (ISBN 0-471-05060-1, Pub. by Wiley). Krieger.
Barr, Murray L. The Human Nervous System. 3rd ed. (Illus.). 1979. pap. text ed. 19.50 (ISBN 0-06-140312-1, Harper Medical). Har-Row.
--El Sistema Nervioso Humano. 2nd ed. 1975. text ed. 16.00 (ISBN 0-06-310057-6, IntlDept). Har-Row.
Bellairs, R. & Gray, E. G., eds. Essays on the Nervous System: A Festschrift for Professor J. Z. Young. (Illus.). 500p. 1974. text ed. 45.50x (ISBN 0-19-857364-2). Oxford U Pr.
Blumenthal, H. T., ed. The Regulatory Role of the Nervous System in Aging. (Interdisciplinary Topics in Gerontology: Vol. 7). 1970. 31.25 (ISBN 3-8055-0508-6). S Karger.
Bradshaw, Ralph & Schneider, Diana, eds. Proteins of the Nervous System. 2nd ed. 407p. 1980. 45.00 (ISBN 0-89004-327-2). Raven.
Brazier, Mary A. The Electrical Activity of the Nervous System. 4th ed. 260p. 1977. 17.50 (ISBN 0-272-79403-1). Krieger.
Breakefield, X. O., ed. Neurogenetics: Genetic Approaches to the Nervous System. 1979. 29.50 (ISBN 0-444-00295-2, North-Holland). Elsevier.
Breig, Alf. Adverse Mechanical Tension of the Central Nervous System: An Analysis of Cause & Effect. LC 77-88852. 1978. 84.50 (ISBN 0-471-04137-8, Pub. by Wiley Medical). Wiley.
Butter, Charles M. Neuropsychology: The Study of Brain & Behavior. LC 68-21883. (Basic Concepts in Psychology Ser). (Orig.). 1968. pap. text ed. 6.95 (ISBN 0-8185-0308-4). Brooks-Cole.
Campbell, H. J. Correlative Physiology of the Nervous System. 1966. 48.00 (ISBN 0-12-157650-7). Acad Pr.
Cort, Joseph. Electrolytes, Fluid Dynamics, & the Nervous System. 1966. 38.00 (ISBN 0-12-190150-5). Acad Pr.
Cotman, Carl W. & Jenson, Robert. Instructor's Manual for Behavioral Neuroscience: An Introduction. 1979. 3.00 (ISBN 0-12-191655-3). Acad Pr.

Cotman, Carl W., ed. Neuronal Plasticity. LC 77-72807. 349p. 1978. 31.50 (ISBN 0-89004-210-1). Raven.
Cowan, W. M., et al, eds. Annual Review of Neuroscience, Vol. 4. (Illus.). 1981. text ed. 20.00 (ISBN 0-8243-2404-8). Annual Reviews.
Curtis, D. R. & McIntyre, A. K., eds. Studies in Physiology Presented to John C. Eccles. (Illus.). 1965. 20.90 (ISBN 0-387-03411-0). Springer-Verlag.
Detwiler, S. R. Neuroembryology: An Experimental Study. 1964. Repr. of 1936 ed. 10.75 (ISBN 0-02-843900-7). Hafner.
Dunkerley, Gary B. A Basic Atlas of the Human Nervous System. LC 75-14044. (Illus.). 216p. 1975. pap. text ed. 9.95 (ISBN 0-8036-2940-0). Davis Co.
Essman, Walter B., ed. Neurotransmitters, Receptors, & Drug Action. LC 79-23862. (Illus.). 220p. 1980. text ed. 35.00 (ISBN 0-89335-108-3). Spectrum Pub.
Everett, N. B. Functional Neuroanatomy. 6th ed. LC 70-135680. (Illus.). 357p. 1971. text ed. 14.50 (ISBN 0-8121-0324-6). Lea & Febiger.
Eyzaguirre, Carlos & Fidone, Salvatore J. Physiology of the Nervous System. 2nd ed. (Illus.). 430p. 1975. 20.00 (ISBN 0-8151-3182-8); pap. 15.50 (ISBN 0-8151-3183-6). Year Bk Med.
Fessard, A., ed. Handbook of Sensory Physiology: Electrorecptors & Other Specialized Receptors in Lower Verterbrates. (Vol. 3, Pt. 1). (Illus.). viii, 333p. 1975. 72.70 (ISBN 0-387-06872-4). Springer-Verlag.
Freeman, Walter J. Mass Action in the Nervous System: Examination of the Neurophysiological Basis of Adaptive Behavior Through the EEG. 1975. 57.00 (ISBN 0-12-267150-3). Acad Pr.
Ganong, William F. The Nervous System. 2nd. ed. LC 79-89454. (Illus.). 243p. 1979. lexotone cover 11.00 (ISBN 0-87041-241-8). Lange.
Garrod, D. R. & Feldman, J. D., eds. Development in the Nervous System. LC 80-42151. (British Society for Developmental Biology Symposium Ser.). (Illus.). 350p. Date not set. price not set (ISBN 0-521-23493-X). Cambridge U Pr.
Gaze, R. M. Formation of Nerve Connections. 1970. 46.00 (ISBN 0-12-278550-9). Acad Pr.
Gibson, John. A Guide to the Nervous System. 3rd ed. 118p. 1974. pap. text ed. 4.95 (ISBN 0-571-04967-2, Pub. by Faber & Faber). Merrimack Bk Serv.
Glass, David C., ed. Neurophysiology & Emotion. LC 67-31389. (Illus.). 1967. 11.00 (ISBN 0-87470-006-X). Rockefeller.
Grenell, Robert. From Nerve to Mind. 244p. 1972. 52.25x (ISBN 0-677-12310-8). Gordon.
Guyton, Arthur C. Organ Physiology: Structure & Function of the Nervous System. 2nd ed. LC 75-40636. (Illus.). 312p. 1976. text ed. 14.50 (ISBN 0-7216-4366-3). Saunders.
Harnad, S., ed. Lateralization in the Nervous System. 1977. 36.50 (ISBN 0-12-325750-6). Acad Pr.
Hausman, Louis. Atlas of Consecutive Stages in the Reconstruction of the Nervous System: Atlas II. (Illus.). 100p. 1965. photocopy ed. spiral 9.50 (ISBN 0-398-00799-3). C C Thomas.
--Illustrations of the Nervous System: Atlas Three. (Illus.). 208p. 1971. 18.75 (ISBN 0-398-00800-0). C C Thomas.
Haymaker, Webb & Adams, Raymond D. Histology & Histopathology of the Nervous System, 2 vols. in slipcase. (Illus.). 3520p. 1981. Set. 295.00 (ISBN 0-398-03482-6). C C Thomas.
House, E. Lawrence, et al. A Systematic Approach to Neuroscience. 3rd ed. (Illus.). 1979. text ed. 27.00 (ISBN 0-07-030468-8, HP). McGraw.
Hubbard, John I., ed. The Peripheral Nervous System. LC 74-6258. (Illus.). 530p. 1974. 37.50 (ISBN 0-306-30764-2, Plenum Pr). Plenum Pub.
Hughes, Arthur F. Aspects of Neural Ontogeny. 1968. 38.00 (ISBN 0-12-360550-4). Acad Pr.
International Symposium on Neurophysiology. Recent Contributions to Neurophysiology: Proceedings. Cordeau, J., ed. & 1972. 44.00 (ISBN 0-444-40963-7, North Holland). Elsevier.
Jacobson, Edmund. You Must Relax. 5th, rev. ed. LC 75-33112. (Illus.). 256p. 1976. 8.95 (ISBN 0-07-032182-5, GB). McGraw.
Jensen, David. The Human Nervous System. (Illus.). 416p. 1980. pap. text ed. 14.95x (ISBN 0-8385-3944-0). ACC.
Kalter, Harold. Teratology of the Central Nervous System: Induced & Spontaneous Malformations of Laboratory, Agricultural, & Domestic Mammals. LC 68-14628. (Illus.). 1968. 20.00x (ISBN 0-226-42268-2). U of Chicago Pr.
Kempf, Edward J. Autonomic Functions & the Personality. (Nervous & Mental Disease Monographs: No. 28). 1918. 15.50 (ISBN 0-384-29175-9). Johnson Repr.
Kocen, K. S. The Neuromuscular System. (Penguin Library of Nursing). (Illus.). 1977. pap. text ed. 5.75 (ISBN 0-443-01496-5). Churchill.
Kuffler, Stephen W. & Nicholls, John G. From Neuron to Brain: A Cellular Approach to the Function of the Nervous System. LC 75-32228. 1976. text ed. 19.50x (ISBN 0-87893-442-1). Sinauer Assoc.
Leibovic, K. N. Nervous System Theory: An Introductory Study. 1973. 38.00 (ISBN 0-12-441250-5). Acad Pr.
Levi, Giulio, ed. Transport Phenomena in the Nervous System: Physiological & Pathological Aspects. LC 76-4839. (Advances in Experimental Medicine & Biology Ser.: Vol. 69). 541p. 1976. 45.00 (ISBN 0-306-39069-8, Plenum Pr). Plenum Pub.
Lierse, W. & Beck, F., eds. Studies of Normal & Abnormal Devlopment, of the Nervous System. (Bibliotheca Anatomica Ser.: No. 19). (Illus.). viii, 328p. 1980. softcover 112.00 (ISBN 3-8055-1039-X). S Karger.
McGraw, Myrtle B. Neuromuscular Maturation of the Human Infant. (Illus.). 1963. Repr. of 1945 ed. 10.75 (ISBN 0-02-849080-0). Hafner.
Maletta, Gabe J. & Pirozzolo, Francis J., eds. The Aging Nervous System. LC 79-21167. (Advances in Neurogerontology: Vol. 1). 344p. 1980. 28.95 (ISBN 0-03-052136-X). Praeger.
Mann, Michael D. The Nervous System & Behavior: An Introduction. 500p. 1981. pap. text ed. write for info. (ISBN 0-06-141576-6, Harper Medical). Har-Row.
Maser, Jack D., ed. Efferent Organization & the Integration of Behavior. 1973. 43.00 (ISBN 0-12-476950-0). Acad Pr.
Millar, R. P., ed. Neuropeptides: Biochemical & Physiological Studies. (Illus.). 368p. 1981. lib. bdg. 50.00 (ISBN 0-443-02265-8). Churchill.
Mitchell, Clifford L., ed. Nervous System Toxicology. (Target Organ Toxicology Ser.). 1982. text ed. price not set (ISBN 0-89004-473-2). Raven.
Monnier, M. Functions of the Nervous System: Sensory Functions, Pt. 3. 1975. 196.00 (ISBN 0-444-41231-X, North Holland). Elsevier.
Monnier, Marcel. Functions of the Nervous System: Motor Functions, Vol. 2. 1971. 174.75 (ISBN 0-444-40690-5, North Holland). Elsevier.
--Functions of the Nervous System: Psychic Functions, Vol. 4. Date not set. price not set (ISBN 0-685-05583-3). Elsevier.
Montgomery, Royce L., et al, eds. Nervous System Basic Sciences. 2nd ed. 1977. spiral bdg. 11.75 (ISBN 0-87488-210-9). Med Exam.
Nathan, Peter. The Nervous System. 2nd ed. (Illus.). 400p. 1981. text ed. 22.95x (ISBN 0-19-261344-8). Oxford U Pr.
Nebylitsyn, V. D. Fundamental Properties of the Human Nervous System. LC 76-75768. (Monographs in Psychology). 333p. 1972. 32.50 (ISBN 0-306-30512-7, Plenum Pr). Plenum Pub.
Nesmeyanova, T. S. Experimental Studies in Regeneration of Spinal Neurons. LC 77-22460. 1977. 27.50 (ISBN 0-470-99152-6). Halsted Pr.
Neumann, John Von. Computer & the Brain. LC 58-6542. (Silliman Lectures Ser.). 1958. 12.50x (ISBN 0-300-00793-0); pap. 3.45 (ISBN 0-300-02415-0). Yale U Pr.
Newman, P. P. Visceral Afferent Functions of the Nervous System. 273p. 1974. 28.50 (ISBN 0-683-06179-8, Pub. by W & W). Krieger.
Newth, D. R. & Usherwood, P. N., eds. Simple Nervous Systems. LC 75-7810. 1975. 47.50x (ISBN 0-8448-0713-3). Crane-Russak Co.
Noback, Charles & Demarest, Robert. The Human Nervous System: Basic Principles of Neurobiology. 3rd ed. (Illus.). 1980. text ed. 24.00 (ISBN 0-07-046851-6, HP). McGraw.
Ojai Symposium-1962. Neural Theory & Modeling: Proceedings. Reiss, Richard F., ed. (Illus.). 1964. 18.50x (ISBN 0-8047-0194-6). Stanford U Pr.
Olson, Willard C. The Measurement of Nervous Habits in Normal Children. LC 73-9228. 97p. 1973. Repr. of 1929 ed. lib. bdg. 15.00 (ISBN 0-8371-6991-7, CWOH). Greenwood.
Palmeri, Rosario. Sources of Instinctive Life. LC 65-27461. 1966. 3.00 (ISBN 0-8022-1260-3). Philos Lib.
Patton, Harry D., et al. Introduction to Basic Neurology. LC 75-31299. (Illus.). 1976. text ed. 19.00 (ISBN 0-7216-7113-6). Saunders.
Pease, Daniel C., ed. Cellular Aspects of Neural Growth & Differentiation. LC 73-126760. (UCLA Forum in Medical Sciences: No. 14). (Illus.). 1971. 57.50x (ISBN 0-520-01793-5). U of Cal Pr.
Pinsker, Harold & Willis, William D., Jr., eds. Information Processing in the Nervous System. 378p. 1980. text ed. 38.00 (ISBN 0-89004-422-8). Raven.
Pittendrigh, Colin S., ed. Circadian Oscillations & Organization in Nervous Systems. 120p. 1976. pap. text ed. 4.95x (ISBN 0-262-66024-5). MIT Pr.
Porcellati, Giuseppe, et al, eds. Function & Metabolism of Phospholipids in the Central & Peripheral Nervous Systems. LC 76-15617. (Advances in Experimental Medicine & Biology Ser.: Vol. 72). 412p. 1976. 45.00 (ISBN 0-306-39072-8, Plenum Pr). Plenum Pub.
--Ganglioside Function: Biochemical & Pharmacological Implications. LC 76-7403. (Advances in Experimental Medicine & Biology Ser.: Vol. 71). 306p. 1976. 35.00 (ISBN 0-306-39071-X, Plenum Pr). Plenum Pub.
Prochaska, Georg. Dissertation on the Functions of the Nervous System. Laycock, T., tr. Bd. with On the Study of Character. (Contributions to the History of Psychology Ser., Vol. XIV, Pt. A: Orientations). 1980. Repr. of 1851 ed. 30.00 (ISBN 0-89093-316-2). U Pubns Amer.
--A Dissertation on the Functions of the Nervous System. Laycock, T., tr. LC 78-72819. (Brainedness, Handedness, & Mental Abilities Ser.). Repr. of 1851 ed. 27.50 (ISBN 0-404-60888-4). AMS Pr.
Ranson, Stephen W. Anatomy of the Nervous System. 10th rev. ed. Clark, Sam L., ed. LC 59-5080. (Illus.). 1959. 18.00 (ISBN 0-7216-7455-0). Saunders.
Roberts, E., et al, eds. GABA in Nervous System Function. LC 74-21983. 576p. 1976. 36.50 (ISBN 0-89004-043-5). Raven.
Ross, R. T. How to Examine the Nervous System: Techniques & Methods. (Illus.). 136p. 1978. 8.25 (ISBN 0-398-03731-0). C C Thomas.
Sarnat, Harvey B. & Netsky, Martin G. Evolution of the Nervous System. 2nd ed. (Illus.). 520p. 1981. text ed. 23.95x (ISBN 0-19-502775-2); pap. text ed. 16.95x (ISBN 0-19-502776-0). Oxford U Pr.
Schade, J. P. Ythe Peripheral Nervous System. 2nd ed. 1973. 14.75 (ISBN 0-444-40509-7, North Holland). Elsevier.
Schlesinger, Benno. Higher Cerebral Functions & Their Clinical Disorders: The Organic Basis of Psychology & Psychiatry. LC 59-10265. (Illus.). 576p. 1961. 56.25 (ISBN 0-8089-0413-2). Grune.
Schmitt, F. O., ed. Neurosciences: Second Study Program. LC 78-136288. (Illus.). 1088p. (Charts, Photos, Micrographs, Tabs). 1971. ref. ed. 60.00 (ISBN 0-87470-014-0); prof. ed. 30.00 (ISBN 0-685-04785-7). Rockefeller.
Schoffeniels, E., et al, eds. Dynamic Properties of Glia Cells: An Interdisciplinary Approach to Their Study in the Central & Peripheral Nervous System. LC 78-40218. 1978. text ed. 69.00 (ISBN 0-08-021555-6). Pergamon.
Sherrington, Charles. The Integrative Activity of the Nervous System. 2nd ed. LC 73-2989. (Classics in Psychology Ser.). Repr. of 1947 ed. 20.00 (ISBN 0-405-05162-X). Arno.
Siegel, R. E. Galen on Psychology, Psychopathology & Function & Disease of the Nervous System: An Analysis of His Doctrines Observations & Experiments. 300p. 1973. 70.75 (ISBN 3-8055-1479-4). S Karger.
Sleight, Peter, ed. Arterial Baroreceptors & Hypertension. (Illus.). 380p. 1981. text ed. 69.50x (ISBN 0-19-261259-X). Oxford U Pr.
Sokolov, E. N. & Vinogradova, O. S., eds. Neuronal Mechanisms of the Orienting Reflex. LC 75-23135. 302p. 1975. 19.95 (ISBN 0-470-92562-0, Pub. by Wiley). Krieger.
Somjen, George. Sensory Coding in the Mammalian Nervous System. LC 75-31519. 286p. 1975. softcover 7.95 (ISBN 0-306-20020-1, Rosetta). Plenum Pub.
Sommerhoff, Gerd. Logic of the Living Brain. LC 73-8198. 440p. 1974. 42.00 (ISBN 0-471-81305-2, Pub. by Wiley-Interscience). Wiley.
Stein, Donald G., et al, eds. Plasticity & Recovery of Function in the Central Nervous System. 1974. 40.50 (ISBN 0-12-664350-4). Acad Pr.
Stent, Gunther S., ed. Function & Formation of Neural Systems, LSRR 6. (Dahlem Workshop Reports Ser.: L.S.R.R. No. 6). 1977. pap. 33.90 (ISBN 0-89573-090-1). Verlag Chemie.
Symposium of the Group of European Nutritionists, 9th, Chianciano, 1970. Nutrition & Nervous System: Proceedings. Somogyi, J. C. & Fidanza, F., eds. (Bibliotheca Nutritio et Dieta: No. 17). (Illus.). 202p. 1972. pap. 46.75 (ISBN 3-8055-1309-7). S Karger.
Symposium On Information Processing In The Nervous System - Buffalo - 1968. Proceedings. Leibovic, K. N., ed. 1970. 53.30 (ISBN 0-387-04885-5). Springer-Verlag.
Symposium on the Physiology & the Pharmacology of Vascular Neuroeffector Systems, Interlaken, 1969. Vascular Neuroeffector Systems, Physiology & Pharmacology: Proceedings. Bevan, J. A., et al, eds. (Illus.). viii, 350p. 1971. 43.25 (ISBN 3-8055-1184-1). S Karger.
Szentagothai, John & Arbib, Michael A. Conceptual Models of Neural Organization. LC 75-18837. 510p. 1975. text ed. 17.50x (ISBN 0-262-19144-X). MIT Pr.
Tower, D. B., ed. The Nervous System, 3 vols. Incl. Vol. 1. Basic Neurosciences. 20.00 (ISBN 0-89004-075-3); Vol. 2. Clinical Neurosciences. 20.00 (ISBN 0-89004-076-1); Vol. 3. Human Communication & Its Disorders. 20.00 (ISBN 0-89004-077-X). LC 75-33499. 1800p. 1975. Set. 59.50 (ISBN 0-685-61107-8). Raven.
Volk, Bruno W. & Schneck, Larry, eds. The Gangliosidoses. LC 75-11708. (Illus.). 270p. 1975. 29.50 (ISBN 0-306-30838-X, Plenum Pr). Plenum Pub.
Von Euler, U. S., et al, eds. Structure & Function of Inhibitory Neuronal Mechanisms. 1968. 79.00 (ISBN 0-08-012414-3). Pergamon.
Weizman Institute of Science, Rehovot, Israel, Feb. 1980 & Littauer, U. Z. Neurotransmitters & Their Receptors Organization: Proceedings. LC 80-41130. 570p. 1981. 42.00 (ISBN 0-471-27893-9, Pub. by Wiley-Interscience). Wiley.
Werner, Joan K. Neuroscience: A Clinical Perspective. LC 79-64779. (Illus.). 225p. 1980. text ed. 13.95 (ISBN 0-7216-9116-1). Saunders.
Williams, Peter L. & Warwick, Roger. Functional Neuroanatomy of Man. LC 74-10038. (Illus.). 460p. 1975. text ed. 23.50 (ISBN 0-7216-9450-0). Saunders.
Wilson, S. Kinnier. Neurology, 2 Vols. Bruce, A. Ninian, ed. (Illus.). 1969. Repr. of 1940 ed. Set. 79.00 (ISBN 0-02-854870-1). Hafner.
Young, J. Z. Evolution of Memory. Head, J. J., ed. LC 76-28270. (Carolina Biology Readers Ser.). (Illus.). (gr. 11-12). 1976. pap. 1.65 (ISBN 0-89278-233-1, 45-9633). Carolina Biological.
Young, John Z. Anatomy of the Nervous System of Octopus Vulgaris. (Illus.). 1971. 89.00x (ISBN 0-19-857340-5). Oxford U Pr.

NERVOUS SYSTEM–AMPHIBIANS

Horstadius, Sven. Neural Crest: Its Properties & Derivatives in the Light of Experimental Research. (Illus.). 1969. Repr. of 1950 ed. 12.50 (ISBN 0-02-846080-4). Hafner.

NERVOUS SYSTEM–ARTHROPODA

Treherne, J. E. Neurochemistry of Arthropods. (Cambridge Monographs in Experimental Biology). 1966. 28.95 (ISBN 0-521-06645-X). Cambridge U Pr.

NERVOUS SYSTEM–DEGENERATION AND REGENERATION

Birren, James E., et al. The Process of Aging in the Nervous System. (Illus.). 240p. 1959. ed. spiral bdg. 22.50photocopy (ISBN 0-398-00156-1). C C Thomas.
Buda, Francis B. The Neurology of Developmental Disabilities. (Illus.). 280p. 1981. 27.50 (ISBN 0-398-04373-6). C C Thomas.
Frolkis, V. V. & Bezrukov, V. V. Aging of the Central Nervous System. (Interdisciplinary Topics in Gerontology: Vol. 16). (Illus.). 1979. pap. 39.75 (ISBN 3-8055-2995-3). S Karger.
Fuxe, K., et al, eds. Dynamics of Degeneration & Growth in Neurons. 1974. text ed. 115.00 (ISBN 0-08-017917-7). Pergamon.
Rockstein, Morris & Sussman, Marvin L., eds. Development & Aging in the Nervous System. 1973. 21.50 (ISBN 0-12-591650-7). Acad Pr.
Sobur, Itsurd. Spinocerebellar Degenerations. 377p. text ed. 64.50 (ISBN 0-8391-4123-8). Univ Park.

NERVOUS SYSTEM–DISEASES

see also Demyelination; Fear; Nervous System–Radiography; Neurologic Manifestations of General Diseases; Neurological Nursing; Pediatric Neurology; Perception, Disorders of; Trance; Veterinary Neurology; Worry;
also specific diseases, e.g. Insanity, Neurasthenia, Neuritis

Asbury, Arthur K. & Johnson, Peter C. Pathology of Peripheral Nerve. LC 77-11328. (Major Problems in Pathology Ser.: No. 9). (Illus.). 1978. pap. text ed. 32.00 (ISBN 0-7216-1426-4). Saunders.
Association for Research in Nervous & Mental Disease. Effect of Pharmacologic Agents on the Nervous System: Proceedings, Vol. 37. (Illus.). 1969. Repr. of 1959 ed. 30.25 (ISBN 0-02-846400-1). Hafner.
Barbeau, Andre & Huxtable, Ryan, eds. Taurine & Neurological Disorders. LC 77-85076. 1978. 45.00 (ISBN 0-89004-202-0). Raven.
Blackwood, W. Greenfield's Neuropathology. 3rd ed. (Illus.). 1976. 89.50 (ISBN 0-8151-0840-0). Year Bk Med.
Boese, A., ed. Search for the Cause of Multiple Sclerosis & Other Chronic Diseases of the Central Nervous System. (Illus.). 516p. (Orig.). pap. text ed. 55.00 (ISBN 3-527-25875-2). Verlag Chemie.
Brain. Brain's Diseases of the Nervous System. 8th ed. Walton, John N., ed. (Illus.). 1977. text ed. 57.50x (ISBN 0-19-261309-X). Oxford U Pr.
Burrow, Trigant. The Biology of Human Conflict: An Anatomy of Behavior, Individual & Social. LC 73-14149. (Perspectives in Social Inquiry Ser.). 510p. 1974. Repr. 27.00x (ISBN 0-405-05495-5). Arno.

Canal, N. & Pozza, G., eds. Peripheral Neuropathies. (Developments in Neurology Ser.: Vol. 1). 1978. 70.75 (ISBN 0-444-80079-4, Biomedical Pr). Elsevier.
Cash, Joan, ed. Neurology for Physiotherapists. 2nd ed. LC 77-83951. (Illus.). 1978. soft cover 15.00 (ISBN 0-397-58230-7, JBL-Med-Nursing). Har-Row.
Cates, Paul W. Neurological Impairment. 30.00 (ISBN 0-686-22194-X). Freedom U Pr.
Charcot, Jean M. Clinique des maladies du Systeme nerveux, 2 vols. LC 71-169469. (Illus.). Repr. of 1893 ed. Set. 57.50 (ISBN 0-404-10017-1); 30.00 ea. Vol. 2 (ISBN 0-404-10018-X). Vol. 2 (ISBN 0-404-10019-8). AMS Pr.
Cohen, Maynard M., ed. Biochemistry of Neural Disease. (Illus.). 1975. text ed. 27.50x (ISBN 0-06-140646-5, Harper Medical). Har-Row.
Cooper, I. S. Living with Chronic Neurologic Disease: A Handbook for Patient & Family. 1976. 8.95 (ISBN 0-393-06409-3); pap. 4.95 (ISBN 0-393-06416-6). Norton.
Coping with Neurologic Problems, Proficiently. LC 78-27545. (Nursing Skillbook Ser.). (Illus.). 192p. 1979. text ed. 10.95 (ISBN 0-916730-12-3). InterMed Comm.
Coping with Neurological Disorders. (Nursing Photobook Ser.). (Illus.). 160p. 1981. text ed. 12.95 (ISBN 0-916730-42-5). Intermed Comm.
Cumings, J. N., ed. Biochemical Aspects of Nervous Diseases. LC 70-178775. 256p. 1972. 29.50 (ISBN 0-306-30564-X, Plenum Pr). Plenum Pub.
Darley, Frederick L., et al. Audio Seminars in Motor Speech Disorders. 1975. pap. 65.00 incl. cassettes (ISBN 0-7216-9892-1). Saunders.
--Motor Speech Disorders. LC 74-25475. (Illus.). 304p. 1975. text ed. 22.00 (ISBN 0-7216-2878-8). Saunders.
Detmar, Bernhard. Nervous Disorders & Hysteria. 1955. 1.50 (ISBN 0-685-06585-5). Assoc Bk.
Dunsker, Stewart, ed. Cervical Spondylosis. (Seminars in Neurological Surgery). 229p. 1980. text ed. 25.00 (ISBN 0-89004-421-X). Raven.
Dyck, Peter J., et al, eds. Peripheral Neuropathy. LC 73-81830. (Illus.). 1975. text ed. 150.00 set (ISBN 0-686-67128-7). Vol. 1 (ISBN 0-7216-3270-X). Vol. 2 (ISBN 0-7216-3271-8). Saunders.
Elwood, J. Mark & Elwood, J. Harold. Epidemiology of Anencephalus & Spina Bifida. (Illus.). 424p. 1980. text ed. 69.50x (ISBN 0-19-261220-4). Oxford U Pr.
Escourolle, Raymond & Poirier, Jacques. Manual of Basic Neuropathology. 2nd ed. Rubinstein, Lucien J., tr. LC 77-80748. (Illus.). 1978. pap. text ed. 13.50 (ISBN 0-7216-3406-0). Saunders.
Esslen, E. The Acute Facial Palsies. (Schrifterreihe Neurologie Ser.: No. 18). 1977. 27.00 (ISBN 0-387-08018-X). Springer-Verlag.
Fielding, Stuart, ed. Neuroleptics. LC 73-80698. (Industrial Pharmacology Ser: Vol. 1). (Illus.). 320p. 1974. 19.50 (ISBN 0-87993-026-8). Futura Pub.
Fishman, Robert A. Cerebrospinal Fluid in Diseases of the Nervous System. LC 79-67304. (Illus.). 384p. 1980. text ed. 32.00 (ISBN 0-7216-3686-1). Saunders.
Friede, R. L. Developmental Neuropathology. (Illus.). 550p. 1976. 65.80 (ISBN 0-387-81325-X). Springer-Verlag.
Friesen, Stanley R., ed. Surgical Endocrinology: Clinical Syndromes. LC 78-68. 1978. 34.50 (ISBN 0-397-50384-9, JBL-Med-Nursing). Har-Row.
Giles, Floyd H., et al. Developing Human Brain: Growth & Epidemiologic Neuropathology. Date not set. write for info. (ISBN 0-88416-254-0). Wright-PSG.
Goldblatt, David. Neuroscience & Clinical Nuerology Review. LC 78-8560. (Arco Medical Review Ser.). (Illus.). 1979. pap. text ed. 10.00 (ISBN 0-668-03370-3). Arco.
Goldensohn, Eli S. & Appel, Stanley H., eds. Scientific Approaches to Clinical Neurology, 2 vols. LC 75-135684. (Illus.). 2040p. 1977. text ed. 230.00 (ISBN 0-8121-0363-7). Lea & Febiger.
Gowers, William R. A Manual of Diseases of the Nervous System, 2 vols. Taylor, James, ed. Incl. Vol. 1. Diseases of the Nerves & Spinal Cord. (Illus.); Vol. 2. Diseases of the Brain & Crainal Nerves: General & Functional Diseases of the Nerves System. (Illus.). 1970. Repr. of 1899 ed. Set. 66.00 (ISBN 0-02-845390-5). Hafner.
Haley, Thomas J. & Snider, Ray S., eds. Response of the Nervous System to Ionizing Radiation: Proceedings. 1962. 64.50 (ISBN 0-12-318650-1). Acad Pr.
Herlin, Lennart. Sciatic & Pelvic Pain Due to Lumbosacral Nerve Root Compression. (Illus.). 264p. 1966. pap. 27.50 (ISBN 0-398-00829-9). C C Thomas.
Hirano, Asao. A Guide to Neuropathology. LC 80-83980. (Illus.). 1981. 41.00 (ISBN 0-89640-047-6). Igaku-Shoin.
Hirano, Asao, et al. Color Atlas of Pathology of the Nervous System. LC 80-81620. (Illus.). 222p. 1980. 74.00 (ISBN 0-89640-045-X). Igaku Shoin.
Hornabrook, R. W. Topics in Tropical Neurology. LC 74-11300. (Comtemporary Neurology Ser.: No. 12). (Illus.). 320p. 1975. 40.00 (ISBN 0-8036-4680-1). Davis Co.
Jane, John A. & Yashon, David. Cytology of Tumors Affecting the Nervous System. (Illus.). 232p. 1969. photocopy ed. spiral 23.50 (ISBN 0-398-00918-X). C C Thomas.
Jellinger, K., et al, eds. Experimental & Clinical Neuropathology: Proceedings. (Acta Neuropathologica Ser.: Supplementum 7). (Illus.). 409p. 1981. pap. 87.20 (ISBN 0-387-10449-6). Springer-Verlag.
Jelsma, Franklin. Primary Tumors of the Calvaria: With Special Consideration of the Clinical Problems. (Illus.). 128p. 1960. photocopy ed. spiral 12.75 (ISBN 0-398-00923-6). C C Thomas.
Johnson, Richard T. Viral Infections of the Nervous System. 1981. write for info. (ISBN 0-89004-426-0, 484). Raven.
Karcher, D., et al, eds. Humoral Immunity in Neurological Diseases. LC 79-15096. (Nato Advanced Study Institutes Ser. A: Life Sciences: Vol. 24). 684p. 1979. 59.50 (ISBN 0-306-40195-9, Plenum Pr). Plenum Pub.
Kim, Ronald C., ed. Metabolic & Degenerative Diseases of the Nervous System. LC 76-720135. (Neuropathology: An Illustrated Course). 1976. 100.00 (ISBN 0-8036-2914-1). Davis Co.
Kopell, Harvey P. & Thompson, Walter A. Peripheral Entrapment Neuropathies. rev. ed. LC 76-5448. 198p. 1976. Repr. of 1963 ed. 16.50 (ISBN 0-88275-214-6). Krieger.
Korney, S., et al, eds. Neuropathology, 2 vols. (International Congress Ser.: No. 362). 1700p. 1976. 186.50 set (ISBN 0-444-15177-X, Excerpta Medica). Elsevier.
Lees, F. Diagnosis & Treatment of Diseases of the Nervous System, 2 vols. 1970. 65.00 set (ISBN 0-444-19729-X). Elsevier.
Legg, N., ed. Neurotransmitter Systems & Their Clinical Disorders. 1979. 23.00 (ISBN 0-12-443050-3). Acad Pr.
Lewis, Anthony J. Mechanisms of Neurological Disease. 1976. 27.95 (ISBN 0-316-52336-4). Little.
Lierse, W. & Beck, F., eds. Studies of the Normal & Abnormal Development of the Nervous System. (Bibliotheca Anatomica Ser.: No. 19). (Illus.). 1980. soft cover 112.00 (ISBN 3-8055-1039-X). S Karger.
Lissak, K., ed. Results in Neurochemistry, Neuroendocrinology, Neurophysiology, & Behavior, Neuropharmacology, Neurpathology, Cybernetics. 1976. 20.00x (ISBN 963-05-0595-9). Intl Pubns Serv.
McDaniel, Lucy V., et al. Selected Neurological Disabilities. LC 74-78553. (Prog. Bk.). 1974. pap. text ed. 5.95x (ISBN 0-913590-19-3); wkbk 1.50x (ISBN 0-913590-20-7); plate 1.95 (ISBN 0-685-50191-4). C B Slack.
Malamud, Nathan & Hirano, Asao. Atlas of Neuropathology. (Illus.). 1975. 65.00x (ISBN 0-520-02221-1). U of Cal Pr.
Martin, Joseph, et al. Clinical Neuroendocrinology. LC 77-3601. (Contemporary Neurology Ser: Vol. 14). (Illus.). 410p. 1977. text ed. 33.00 (ISBN 0-8036-5885-0). Davis Co.
Meulen, V. Ter & Katz, M., eds. Slow Virus Infections of the Central Nervous System. LC 77-1570. 1977. 33.30 (ISBN 0-387-90188-4). Springer-Verlag.
Miller, Nancy & Cohen, Gene D., eds. Clinical Aspects of Alzheimer's Disease & Senile Dementia. (Aging Ser.: Vol. 15). 372p. 1981. text ed. 39.00 (ISBN 0-89004-326-4). Raven.
Mitchell, Clifford L., ed. Nervous System Toxicology. (Target Organ Toxicity Ser.). 1981. write for info. (ISBN 0-89004-473-2, 405). Raven.
Morariu, Mircea A. Major Neurological Syndromes. (Illus.). 368p. 1979. text ed. 25.75 (ISBN 0-398-03831-7). C C Thomas.
Neuwelt, Edward A. & Clark, W. Kemp. Clinical Aspects of Neuroimmunology. LC 78-2213. 292p. 1978. 29.50 (ISBN 0-683-06437-1). Krieger.
Olson, William H., et al. Practical Neurology for the Primary Care Physician. (Illus.). 456p. 1981. lexotone spiral bdg. 21.75 (ISBN 0-398-04135-0). C C Thomas.
Peele, Talmage L. The Neuroanatomic Basis for Clinical Neurology. 3rd ed. 1976. 33.50 (ISBN 0-07-049175-5, HP). McGraw.
Pellegrino, L. J., et al. A Sterotaxic Atlas of the Rat Brain. 2nd ed. LC 79-9438. 279p. 1979. 22.50 (ISBN 0-306-40269-6, Plenum Pr). Plenum Pub.
Pochedly, Carl. Leukemia & Lymphoma in the Nervous System. (Illus.). 248p. 1977. 30.00 (ISBN 0-685-73596-6). C C Thomas.
Prikhozhan, V. M. Affection of the Nervous System in Diabetes Mellitus. 309p. 1977. 5.70 (ISBN 0-8285-0750-3, Pub. by Mir Pubs Russia). Imported Pubns.
Prusiner, Stanley B. & Hadlow, William J., eds. Slow Transmissible Diseases of the Nervous System: Pathogenesis, Immunology, Virology & Molecular Biology of the Spongiform Encephalopathies, Vol. 2. LC 79-18087. 1979. 46.50 (ISBN 0-12-566302-1). Acad Pr.
--Slow Transmissible Diseases of the Nervous System: Vol. 1 Clinical, Epidemiological, Genetic & Pathological Aspects of the Spongiform Encephalopathie. LC 79-18087. 1980. 39.50 (ISBN 0-12-566301-3). Acad Pr.
Reeves. Disorders of the Nervous System. 1980. 22.95 (ISBN 0-8151-7136-6). Year Bk Med.
Riccardi, Vincent M. & Mulvihill, John J., eds. Neurofibromatosis (von Recklinghausen's Disease) (Advances in Neurology Ser.: Vol. 29). 293p. 1981. text ed. 29.50 (ISBN 0-686-64310-0). Raven.
Roizin, L. & Shiraki, H., eds. Neurotoxicology, Vol. 1. LC 77-4632. 686p. 1977. 68.50 (ISBN 0-89004-148-2). Raven.
Rottenberg, David A. & Hochberg, Fred H., eds. Neurological Classics in Modern Translation. LC 77-74853. (Illus.). 316p. 1977. 24.75 (ISBN 0-02-851180-8). Hafner.
Rowland, Lewis P., ed. Immunological Disorders of the Nervous System. LC 72-139827. (ARNMD Research Publications Ser: Vol. 49). 482p. 1971. 31.50 (ISBN 0-683-00243-0). Raven.
Schochet, Sydney S., Jr. & McCormick, William F. Essentials of Neuropathology. (Illus.). 191p. 1979. pap. 14.95 (ISBN 0-8385-2269-6). ACC.
--Neuropathology Case Studies. 2nd ed. 1979. pap. 16.50 (ISBN 0-87488-046-7). Med Exam.
Serratrice, G., ed. Peroneal Atrophy & Related Disorders. Roux, H. LC 78-62593. (Illus.). 376p. 1979. 45.50x (ISBN 0-89352-028-4). Masson Pub.
Slemmer, Robert E. An Atlas of Gross Neuropathology. (Illus.). 236p. (Orig.). 1981. 42.50 (ISBN 0-87527-239-8). Green.
Smith & Cavanagh, eds. Recent Advances in Neuropathology, No. 1. 1979. text ed. 52.00 (ISBN 0-443-01383-7). Churchill.
Smith, B. Neuropathology of the Alimentary Tract. 128p. 1972. 15.95 (ISBN 0-685-78092-9, Pub. by William & Wilkins). Krieger.
Spencer, Peter S. & Schaumburg, Herbert. Experimental & Clinical Neurotoxicology. (Illus.). 956p. 1980. lib. bdg. 110.00 (ISBN 0-683-07854-2). Williams & Wilkins.
Spillane, John D., ed. Tropical Neurology. (Illus.). 500p. 1973. text ed. 31.00x (ISBN 0-19-264154-9). Oxford U Pr.
Startsev, V. G. Primate Models of Human Neurogenic Disorders. Bowden, D. M., tr. LC 76-21626. 1976. 19.95 (ISBN 0-470-15193-5). Halsted Pr.
Teitelbaum, Harry A. Psychosomatic Neurology. LC 64-20775. 414p. 1964. 54.50 (ISBN 0-8089-0499-X). Grune.
Thompson, Richard A. & Green, John R., eds. Complications of Nervous System Trauma. LC 78-52425. (Advances in Neurology Ser.: Vol. 22). 345p. 1979. text ed. 34.50 (ISBN 0-89004-295-0). Raven.
Treip, C. S. Color Atlas of Neuropathology. (Illus.). 1978. 48.95 (ISBN 0-8151-8841-2). Year Bk Med.
Van Buchem, F. S., et al. Hyperostosis Corticalis Generalisata Familiaris (Van Buchem's Disease) 1976. 44.00 (ISBN 90-219-2070-0, North Holland). Elsevier.
Vinken, P. J. & Bruyn, G. W. Handbook of Clinical Neurology: Metabolic & Deficiency Diseases of the Nervous System, Part 1, Vol. 27. (Handbook of Clinical Neurology Ser.: Vol. 27). 1976. 109.75 (ISBN 0-7204-7227-X, North-Holland). Elsevier.
Vinken, P. J. & Bruyn, G. W., eds. Handbook of Clinical Neurology, Vols. 1-15. Incl. Vol. 1. Disturbances of Nervous Function. 1969. 136.75 (ISBN 0-444-10298-1); Vol. 2. Localization in Clinical Neurology. 1969. 158.75 (ISBN 0-444-10299-X); Vol. 3. Disorders of Higher Nervous Activity. 1969. 88.00 (ISBN 0-444-10300-7); Vol. 4. Disorders of Speech Perception & Symbolic Behavior. 1969. 95.25 (ISBN 0-444-10301-5); Vol. 5. Headaches & Cranial Neuralgias. 1969. 83.00 (ISBN 0-444-10302-3); Vol. 6. Diseases of the Basal Ganglia. 1968. 173.25 (ISBN 0-444-10303-1); Vol. 7. Diseases of the Nerves: Pt. 1. 1971. 134.25 (ISBN 0-444-10017-2); Vol. 8. Diseases of the Nerves: Pt. 2. 1970. 109.75 (ISBN 0-444-10018-0); Vol. 9. Multiple Sclerosis & Other Demyelinating Diseases. 1971. 139.00 (ISBN 0-444-10019-9); Vol. 10. Leucodystrophies & Lipidases. 1971. 139.00 (ISBN 0-444-10059-8); Vol. 11. Vascular Diseases of the Nervous System: Pt. 1. 1972. 141.50 (ISBN 0-444-10060-1); Vol. 12. Vascular Diseases of the Nervous System: Pt. 2. 136.75 (ISBN 0-444-10061-X); Vol. 13. Neuroretinal Degenerations & Phacomatoses. 1973. 97.75 (ISBN 0-444-10062-8); Vol. 14. The Phacomatoses. LC 68-8297. 1973. 161.00 (ISBN 0-444-10375-9); Vol. 15. The Epilepsies. 1974. 168.50 (ISBN 0-444-10457-7). (Illus., North-Holland). Elsevier.
--Handbook of Clinical Neurology, Vol. 29: Metabolic & Deficiency Diseases of the Nervous System, Pt. 3. 1977. 102.00 (ISBN 0-7204-7229-6, North-Holland). Elsevier.
Vital, Claude & Vallat, Jean M. Ultrastructural Study of the Human Diseased Peripheral Nerve. (Illus.). 200p. 1980. 35.00x (ISBN 0-89352-096-9). Masson Pub.
Warfel, John H. & Schlagenhauff, Reinhold E. Understanding Neurological Disease: A Textbook for Therapists. LC 79-28455. (Illus.). 128p. 1980. 11.95 (ISBN 0-8067-2131-6). Urban & S.
Weller, R. O. & Navarro, J. Cervos. Pathology of Peripheral Nerves: A Practical Approach. (Postgraduate Pathology Ser.). 1977. 39.95 (ISBN 0-407-00073-9). Butterworth.
Willson, Nicholas, ed. Infections of the Nervous System. LC 77-720159. (Neuropathology: An Illustrated Course). 1979. 100.00 (ISBN 0-8036-2913-3). Davis Co.
Wilson, S. Kinnier. Neurology, 2 Vols. Bruce, A. Ninian, ed. (Illus.). 1969. Repr. of 1940 ed. Set. 79.00 (ISBN 0-02-854870-1). Hafner.
Zimmerman, Harry, ed. Progress in Neuropathology, Vol. IV. (Vol 4). 424p. 1979. 41.00 (ISBN 0-89004-388-4). Raven.
Zimmerman, Harry M., ed. Progress in Neuropathology, Vol. I. LC 70-133553. (Illus.). 320p. 1971. 74.00 (ISBN 0-8089-0668-2). Grune.
--Progress in Neuropathology, Vol. II. LC 70-133553. (Illus.). 480p. 1973. 74.00 (ISBN 0-8089-0775-1). Grune.
--Progress in Neuropathology, Vol. III. LC 70-133553. (Illus.). 512p. 1976. 74.00 (ISBN 0-8089-0957-6). Grune.

NERVOUS SYSTEM–DISEASES–DIAGNOSIS

see also Clinical Psychology; Neuroses–Diagnosis

Balla. Pathways in Neurological Diagnosis. 1980. 23.95 (ISBN 0-8151-0414-6). Year Bk Med.
Bender, Morris B., ed. Approach to Diagnosis in Modern Neurology. LC 66-29189. (Illus.). 192p. 1967. 33.75 (ISBN 0-8089-0051-X). Grune.
Collins, R. Douglas. Illustrated Manual of Neurologic Diagnosis. (Illus.). 1962. 24.50 (ISBN 0-397-50078-5, JBL-Med-Nursing). Har-Row.
Diamond, E. Nervous System: Disease, Diagnosis, Treatment. (Clinical Monographs Ser.). (Illus.). 1976. pap. 7.95 (ISBN 0-87618-065-9). R J Brady.
Duus, Peter. Neurologic Diagnosis. 430p. 1980. pap. write for info. (ISBN 0-8151-2960-2). Year Bk Med.
Haymaker, Webb. Bing's Local Diagnosis in Neurological Diseases. 15th ed. LC 69-17488. (Illus.). 1969. 56.00 (ISBN 0-8016-2108-9). Mosby.
Hildebrand, J., ed. Lesions of the Nervous System in Cancer Patients. LC 78-3000. (European Organization for Research on Treatment of Cancer Monograph: Vol. 5). 162p. 1978. 20.00 (ISBN 0-89004-269-1). Raven.
Patten, J. P. Neurological Differential Diagnosis: An Illustrated Approach. (Illus.). 1977. 29.00 (ISBN 0-387-90264-3). Springer-Verlag.
Renfrew, Stewart. An Introduction to Diagnostic Neurology, Vol. 1. 2nd ed. (Illus.). 1967. pap. 6.25x (ISBN 0-443-00409-9). Churchill.
Schafer, Roy. Clinical Application of Psychological Tests. (Menninger Foundation Monograph Ser.: No. 6). 1967. text ed. 22.50 (ISBN 0-8236-0900-6). Intl Univs Pr.
Simpson, John F. & Magee, Kenneth R. Clinical Evaluation of the Nervous System. (Illus.). 1973. 9.95 (ISBN 0-316-79184-9). Little.

Slager, Ursula T. Basic Neuropathology. 330p. 1970. 17.50 (ISBN 0-683-07729-5, Pub. by W & W). Krieger.
Smorto, M. P. & Basmajian, John V. Clinical Electroneurography: An Introduction to Nerve Conduction Tests. 2nd ed. 1979. 27.95 (ISBN 0-683-07812-7). Williams & Wilkins.
Steefel, Jill S. Dysphagia Rehabilitation for Neurologically Impaired Adults. (Illus.). 152p. 1981. price not set (ISBN 0-398-04556-9). C C Thomas.
Steegmann, A. Theodore. Examination of the Nervous System. 3rd ed. (Illus.). 1970. 14.75 (ISBN 0-8151-8167-1). Year Bk Med.
Van Allen, Maurice W. Pictorial Manual of Neurological Tests. 1980. 17.95 (ISBN 0-8151-8960-5). Year Bk Med.

NERVOUS SYSTEM–INSECTS

Miller, T. A. Insect Neurophysiological Techniques. (Springer Ser. in Experimental Entomology). (Illus.). 1979. 27.10 (ISBN 0-387-90407-7). Springer-Verlag.
Roeder, Kenneth D. Nerve Cells and Insect Behavior. rev. ed. LC 67-27092. (Books in Biology Ser: No. 4). 1967. 10.00x (ISBN 0-674-60800-3). Harvard U Pr.
Strausfeld, N. J. & Miller, T. A., eds. Neuroanatomical Techniques: Insect Nervous System. LC 79-10145. (Springer Ser. in Experimental Entomology). (Illus.). 1979. 55.00 (ISBN 0-387-90392-5). Springer-Verlag.
Treherne, J. E. & Beament, J. W. Physiology of the Insect Central Nervous System. 1965. 42.50 (ISBN 0-12-698650-9). Acad Pr.

NERVOUS SYSTEM–INVERTEBRATES

Bullock, Theodore H. & Horridge, G. Adrian. Structure & Function in the Nervous Systems of Invertebrates, 2 Vols. (Biology Ser.). (Illus.). 1965. 160.00x (ISBN 0-7167-0626-1). W H Freeman.
Lentz, Thomas L. Primitive Nervous Systems. LC 68-27760. (Illus.). 1968. 13.50x (ISBN 0-300-00680-2). Yale U Pr.
Salanki, J., ed. Neurobiology of Invertebrates. LC 68-20453. 501p. 1969. 39.50 (ISBN 0-306-30341-8, Plenum Pr). Plenum Pub.
Wiersma, Cornelius G. Invertebrate Nervous Systems, Their Significance for Mammalian Neurophysiology. Conference on Invertebrate Nervous Systems-California Institute of Technology, ed. LC 66-23704. (Illus.). 370p. 1967. 17.50x (ISBN 0-226-89638-2). U of Chicago Pr.

NERVOUS SYSTEM–JUVENILE LITERATURE

The Brain & Nervous System. (The Human Body Ser.). (Illus.). 48p. (gr. 4up). 1981. PLB 7.90 (ISBN 0-531-04288-X). Watts.
Kalina, Sigmund. Your Nerves & Their Messages. LC 72-9360. (Illus.). (gr. 2-5). 1973. PLB 6.48 (ISBN 0-688-50045-5). Lothrop.
Weart, Edith L. The Story of Your Brain & Nerves. (Health Bks.). (Illus.). (gr. 4-7). 1961. PLB 6.59 (ISBN 0-698-30334-2). Coward.

NERVOUS SYSTEM–MATHEMATICAL MODELS

Deutsch, Sid. Models of the Nervous System. (Illus.). 266p. 1967. text ed. 12.75 (ISBN 0-471-21137-0, Pub. by Wiley). Krieger.
MacGregor, R. J. & Lewis, E. R., eds. Neural Modeling: Electrical Signal Processing in Nervous Systems. LC 77-8122. (Current Topics in Neurobiology Ser.). (Illus.). 414p. 1977. 25.00 (ISBN 0-306-30871-1, Plenum Pr). Plenum Pub.
Ojai Symposium-1962. Neural Theory & Modeling: Proceedings. Reiss, Richard F., ed. (Illus.). 1964. 18.50x (ISBN 0-8047-0194-6). Stanford U Pr.

NERVOUS SYSTEM–PROGRAMMED INSTRUCTION

McMillan, Donald E. Central Nervous System Pharmacology: A Self Instruction Text. 2nd ed. 1979. 12.95 (ISBN 0-316-56242-4). Little.

NERVOUS SYSTEM–RADIOGRAPHY

Burrows, E. H. & Leeds, Norman E. Neuroradiology, 2 vols. (Illus., Vol. 1, 800 p., vol. 2, 384 p.). 1981. text ed. 175.00x set (ISBN 0-443-08016-X). Churchill.
Davidoff, L. M., et al. Neuroradiology Workshop. Incl. Vol. 1. Scalp, Skull & Meninges. (Illus.). 264p. 1961. 68.00 (ISBN 0-8089-0112-5); Vol. 2. Intracranial Tumors Other Than Meningiomas. (Illus.). 410p. 1963. 83.75 (ISBN 0-8089-0113-3); Vol. 3. Non-Neoplastic Intracranial Lesions. (Illus.). 584p. 1968. 104.00 (ISBN 0-8089-0114-1). LC 60-16433. Grune.
Peterson, Harold O. & Kieffer, Stephen A. Introduction to Neuroradiology. (Illus.). 1972. 40.00x (ISBN 0-06-142150-2, Harper Medical). Har-Row.
Sano, Keiji, ed. Atlas of Stereoscopic Neuroradiology. 1976. 52.50x (ISBN 0-86008-163-X, Pub by U of Tokyo Pr). Intl Schol Bk Serv.
Taveras, Juan & Wood, Ernest H. Diagnostic Neuroradiology. 2nd ed. (Golden's Diagnostic Radiology Ser: Section 1). 1408p. 1976. 104.95 (ISBN 0-683-08111-X). Williams & Wilkins.

NERVOUS SYSTEM–SECRETIONS

see Neurosecretion

NERVOUS SYSTEM–SURGERY

see also Brain–Surgery

Allen, Marshall B. Manual of Neurosurgery. LC 77-25278. 1977. pap. 24.95 (ISBN 0-8391-1174-6). Univ Park.
Annual Meeting of the Japanese Society for Stereotactic & Functional Neurosurgery, 15th, Maebashi, October 1976. Recent Studies on the Human Thalamus: Proceedings. Gildenberg, Ph. L. & Ohye, C., eds. (Applied Neurophysiology: Vol. 39, No. 3-4). (Illus.). 1977. 34.75 (ISBN 3-8055-2847-7). S Karger.
Annual Meeting on Brain Edema, 24th, 1973. Brain Edema, Pathophysiology & Therapy, Cerebello Pontine Angle Tumors, Diagnosis & Surgery: Proceedings. Schuermann, et al, eds. LC 73-14237. (Advances in Neurosurgery Ser.: Vol. 1). (Illus.). 400p. 1974. pap. 36.40 (ISBN 0-387-06486-9). Springer-Verlag.
Asenjo, Alfonso. Neurosurgical Techniques. (Illus.). 360p. 1963. ed. spiral bdg. 30.75photocopy (ISBN 0-398-00058-1). C C Thomas.
Bonica, John J., ed. Pain. (Association for Research in Nervous & Mental Disease Publications Ser.: Vol. 58). 424p. 1979. text ed. 38.00 (ISBN 0-89004-376-0). Raven.
Bories, J., ed. The Diagnostic Limitations of Computerised Axial Tomography. (Illus.). 1978. pap. 31.20 (ISBN 0-387-08593-9). Springer-Verlag.
Brackman, Derald E., ed. Neurological Surgery of the Ear & Skull Base. 1982. text ed. price not set (ISBN 0-89004-691-3). Raven.
Brihaye, J., ed. Proceedings of the Sixth European Congress of Neurosurgery: Organized by the European Association of Neurosurgical Societies of Paris, July 15-20, 1979. (Act Neurochirurgica Supplements: Vol. 28). (Illus.). 1979. pap. 115.10 (ISBN 0-387-81534-1). Springer-Verlag.
Burger, Peter C. & Vogel, F. Stephen. Surgical Pathology of the Nervous System & Its Coverings. LC 76-6492. 1976. 75.00 (ISBN 0-471-12347-1, Pub. by Wiley Med). Wiley.
Campkin, T. V. & Turner, J. M. Neurosurgical Anesthesia & Intensive Care. LC 79-41659. (Illus.). 1980. text ed. 49.95 (ISBN 0-407-00185-9). Butterworth.
Cantu, Robert C., et al. Ventriculocis-Ternostomy: Long-Term Experiences. (Illus.). 152p. 1970. ed. spiral bdg. 14.75photocopy (ISBN 0-398-00282-7). C C Thomas.
Carmel, Peter W., ed. Clinical Neurosurgery, Vol. 28. (Congress of Neurological Surgeons Ser.). (Illus.). 534p. 1981. lib. bdg. 43.00 (ISBN 0-683-02023-4). Williams & Wilkins.
Cassinari, Valentino & Pagni, Carlo A. Central Pain: A Neurosurgical Survey. LC 68-54017. (Illus.). 1969. text ed. 8.50x (ISBN 0-674-10540-0). Harvard U Pr.
Congress of Neurological Surgeons. Clinical Neurosurgery, Vol. 23. Keener, Ellis B., ed. 1976. 30.00 (ISBN 0-683-02010-2). Williams & Wilkins.
Cottrell, James E. & Turndorf, Herman. Anesthesia & Neurosurgery. LC 79-24676. (Illus.). 1979. text ed. 54.50 (ISBN 0-8016-1036-2). Mosby.
Davis, Richard A., compiled by. Neurosurgical Contributions of Loyal Davis: Selected Papers & Retrospective Commentaries. LC 72-93113. (Illus.). 1973. text ed. 12.00 (ISBN 0-7216-2990-3). Saunders.
DeJong, Russell N. Yearbook of Neurology & Neurosurgery, 1979. 1979. 28.95 (ISBN 0-8151-2419-8). Year Bk Med.
DeJong, Russell N., ed. Yearbook of Neurology & Neurosurgery, 1981. 1981. 30.00 (ISBN 0-8151-2421-X). Year Bk Med.
DeJong, Russell N. & Sugar, Oscar, eds. Year Book of Neurology & Neurosurgery 1980. 1980. 30.00 (ISBN 0-8151-2420-1). Year Bk Med.
Dellon, A. Lee. Evaluation of Sensibility & Reeducation of Sensation in the Hand. (Illus.). 388p. 1981. 35.00 (ISBN 0-686-77746-8, 2427-2). Williams & Wilkins.
Fein, J. M. & Reichman, O. H., eds. Microvascular Anastomoses for Cerebral Ischemia. (Illus.). 1978. 49.10 (ISBN 0-387-90240-6). Springer-Verlag.
German Society for Neurosurgery, Dusseldorf, Nov. 1971. Modern Aspects of Neurosurgery, Vol. 3. Kuhlendahl, H. & Hensell, V., eds. LC 73-152681. (International Congress Ser.: No. 287). 320p. 1973. 55.75 (ISBN 0-444-15036-6, Excerpta Medica). Elsevier.
Gildenberg, P. L., ed. Symposium of the International Society for Research in Stereoencephalotomy, 7th, Sao Paulo, June 24, 1977. (Advances in Stereoencephalotomy Ser.: Vol. 8). (Illus.). 1978. pap. 58.75 (ISBN 3-8055-2946-5). S Karger.
Gillingham, F. J. Advances in Stereotactic & Functional Neurosurgery Four: Proceedings. (Acta Neurochirurgica Supplementum: Vol. 30). (Illus.). 444p. 1981. pap. 29.80 (ISBN 0-387-90501-4). Springer-Verlag.
Gurdjian, E. S., et al, eds. Glossary of Neurotraumatology. (Acta Neurochirurgica: Supplementum 25). 1978. pap. 11.70 (ISBN 0-387-81481-7). Springer-Verlag.
Gurdjian, E. Stephen & Thomas, L. Murray. Operative Neurosurgery. 3rd ed. LC 74-11097. 632p. 1975. Repr. of 1970 ed. 27.50 (ISBN 0-88275-191-3). Krieger.
Handa, H., ed. Microneurosurgery. (Illus.). 230p. 1975. 49.50 (ISBN 0-8391-0832-X). Univ Park.
Horrax, Gilbert. Neurosurgery: An Historical Sketch. (American Lecture Neurosurgery). (Illus.). 160p. 1952. photocopy ed. spiral 19.50 (ISBN 0-398-04287-X). C C Thomas.
Horwitz, Norman H. Post-Operative Complications in Neurosurgical Practice: Recognition, Prevention & Management. LC 66-28163. 440p. 1973. Repr. of 1967 ed. 22.00 (ISBN 0-88275-124-7). Krieger.
Howe, James R. Patient Care in Neurosurgery. 1977. spiral 12.95 (ISBN 0-316-37564-0). Little.
Irsigler, F. J. Neurosurgical Approach to Intracranial Infections: A Review of Personal Experiences 1940-1960. (Illus.). 1961. 52.00 (ISBN 0-387-02700-9). Springer-Verlag.
Jacobson, Sherwood A. The Post-Traumatic Syndrome Following Head Injury: Mechanisms & Treatment. (Illus.). 106p. 1963. photocopy ed. spiral 11.75 (ISBN 0-398-00913-9). C C Thomas.
Jennett, Bryan. A Introduction to Neurosurgery. 3rd ed. (Illus.). 1977. 28.95 (ISBN 0-8151-4868-2). Year Bk Med.
Jewett, Don L. & McCarroll, H. Relton, Jr. Nerve Repair & Regeneration: Its Clinical & Experimental Basis. LC 79-19276. 1979. pap. text ed. 52.50 (ISBN 0-8016-2507-6). Mosby.
Kempe, L. G. Operative Neurosurgery, 2 vols. Incl. Vol. 1. Cranial, Cerebral & Intracranial Vascular Disease. (Illus.). xiii, 269p. 1968. 94.70 (ISBN 0-387-04208-3); Vol. 2. Posterior Fossa, Spinal Cord & Peripheral Nerve Disease. (Illus.). viii, 281p. 1970. 94.70 (ISBN 0-387-04890-1). Springer-Verlag.
Kendall, Henry O., et al. Posture & Pain. 212p. 1971. Repr. of 1952 ed. 16.50 (ISBN 0-88275-031-3). Krieger.
Koos, W. Th., et al. Clinical Microneurosurgery. LC 75-16107. (Illus.). 334p. 1976. 39.50 (ISBN 0-88416-068-8). Wright-PSG.
Krayenbuehl, H., et al. Advances & Technical Standards in Neurosurgery, Vol. 6. LC 74-10499. (Illus.). 1979. 41.00 (ISBN 0-387-81518-X). Springer-Verlag.
Krayenbuehl, H., et al, eds. Advances & Technical Standards in Neurosurgery, Vol. 5. LC 74-10499. (Illus.). 1978. 50.60 (ISBN 0-387-81441-8). Springer-Verlag.
--Advances & Technical Standards in Neurosurgery, Vol. 7. (Illus.). 217p. 1980. 57.90 (ISBN 0-387-81592-9). Springer-Verlag.
--Progress in Neurological Surgery, Vol. 4. 1971. 105.00 (ISBN 3-8055-1166-3). S Karger.
--Craniocerebral Trauma. (Progress in Neurological Surgery Ser.: Vol. 10). (Illus.). xiv, 402p. 1981. 178.50 (ISBN 3-8055-0134-X). S Karger.
--Microsurgical Approach to Cerebro-Spinal Lesions. (Progress in Neurological Surgery: Vol. 9). (Illus.). 1978. 117.50 (ISBN 3-8055-2819-1). S Karger.
Krayenbuhl, H., ed. Advances & Technical Standards in Neurosurgery, Vol. 2. LC 74-10499. (Illus.). 217p. 1975. 48.60 (ISBN 0-387-81293-8). Springer-Verlag.
--Advances & Technical Standards in Neurosurgery, Vol. 3. LC 74-10499. (Illus.). 1976. 39.40 (ISBN 0-387-81381-0). Springer-Verlag.
Krayenbuhl, H., et al, eds. Advances & Technical Standards in Neurosurgery, Vol. 1. LC 74-10499. (Illus.). 220p. 1974. 55.20 (ISBN 0-387-81218-0). Springer-Verlag.
Kuntz, Albert. The Neuroanatomic Basis of Surgery of the Autonomic Nervous System. (Illus.). 96p. 1949. photocopy ed. spiral 10.50 (ISBN 0-398-04320-5). C C Thomas.
Lassan, N. A. Advances & Technical Standards in Neurosurgery, Vol. 4. LC 74-10499. 1977. 40.30 (ISBN 0-387-81423-X). Springer-Verlag.
Lee, J. Fletcher, ed. Pain Management: Symposium on the Neurosurgical Treatment of Pain. LC 77-1475. 210p. 1977. 12.50 (ISBN 0-683-04918-6). Krieger.
Litel, Gerald R. Neurosurgery & the Clinical Team: A Guide for Nurses, Technicians, & Students. LC 80-195. 1980. text ed. 23.95 (ISBN 0-8261-2970-6). Springer Pub.
Long, Donlin & Hopkins, Leo N., eds. Neurosurgery of Aneurisms: Seminars in Neurological Surgery. 1981. write for info. (ISBN 0-89004-481-3). Raven.
McMurtry, James G., 3rd. Neurological Surgery. 2nd ed. (Medical Examination Review Bk.: Vol. 19). 1975. spiral bdg. 16.50 (ISBN 0-87488-119-6). Med Exam.
Marguth, F., et al, eds. Neurovascular Surgery: Specialized Neurosurgical Techniques. (Advances in Neurosurgery: Vol. 7). (Illus.). 420p. 1980. pap. 51.80 (ISBN 0-387-09675-2). Springer-Verlag.
Marmo, Leonard. Peripheral Nerve Regeneration Using Nerve Grafts. (Illus.). 120p. 1967. photocopy ed. spiral 11.75 (ISBN 0-398-01217-2). C C Thomas.
Maroun, F. B. Diastematomyelia. LC 75-17393. (Illus.). 164p. 1976. 12.50 (ISBN 0-87527-143-X). Green.
Matson, Donald D. Neurosurgery of Infancy & Childhood. 2nd ed. (Illus.). 952p. 1969. photocopy ed. spiral 89.75 (ISBN 0-686-71888-7). C C Thomas.
Milhorat, Thomas H. Pediatric Neurosurgery. LC 77-22740. (Contemporary Neurology Ser.: Vol. 16). (Illus.). 398p. 1978. 38.00 (ISBN 0-8036-6180-0). Davis Co.
Morley, T. P., ed. Current Controversies in Neurosurgery. LC 75-21149. (Illus.). 1976. text ed. 42.00 (ISBN 0-7216-6557-8). Saunders.
Mullan, Sean. Essentials of Neurosurgery for Students & Practitioners. LC 61-12028. (Illus.). 1961. text ed. 14.95 (ISBN 0-8261-0479-7). Springer Pub.
O'Brien, Mark S., ed. Pediatric Neurological Surgery. LC 78-3005. (Seminars in Neurological Surgery Ser.). 216p. 1978. 26.00 (ISBN 0-89004-178-4). Raven.
October 1976. Pediatric Neurosurgery: Proceedings. Villani, R. & Giovanelli, M., eds. (Modern Problems in Peadiatrics: Vol. 18). (Illus.). 1977. 84.00 (ISBN 3-8055-2668-7). S Karger.
Orf, G. Critical Resection Length & Gap Distance in Peripheral Nerves: Experimental & Morphological Studies. LC 78-9048. (Acta Neurochirurgica Supplementum: No. 26). (Illus.). 1978. pap. 34.30 (ISBN 0-387-81482-5). Springer-Verlag.
Pasztor, E. Concise Neurosurgery. (Illus.). 292p. 1980. 56.50 (ISBN 3-8055-1431-X). S Karger.
Quintero, Jorge A. Laws, Theories & Values. 2nd ed. (Illus.). 144p. 1980. 10.50 (ISBN 0-87527-147-2). Green.
Ramamurthi, B. & Tandon, P. N., eds. Textbook of Neurosurgery, Vols. 1 & 2. 1286p. 1981. 75.00x set (ISBN 0-686-72504-2, Pub. by Orient Longman India). State Mutual Bk.
Rand, Carl W. The Neurosurgical Patient: His Problems of Diagnosis & Care. (Illus.). 591p. 1944. photocopy ed. spiral 58.75 (ISBN 0-398-04402-3). C C Thomas.
Rand, Robert W. Microneurosurgery. 2nd ed. LC 78-7230. 1978. text ed. 74.50 (ISBN 0-8016-4077-6). Mosby.
Rasmussen, Theodore & Marino, Raul, eds. Functional Neurosurgery. LC 77-85871. 288p. 1979. text ed. 34.50 (ISBN 0-89004-228-4). Raven.
Salmon, James H. & Pearson, Donald H. Self-Assessment of Current Knowledge in Neurological Surgery. 1976. spiral bdg. 14.50 (ISBN 0-87488-247-8). Med Exam.
Schiefer, W., et al. Brain Abscess & Meningitis Subarachnoid Hemorrhage: Timing Problems. (Advances in Neurosurgery Ser.: Vol. 9). (Illus.). 519p. 1981. pap. 76.70 (ISBN 0-387-10539-5). Springer-Verlag.
Schmidek, Henry H. & Sweet, William D., eds. Current Techniques in Operative Neurosurgery. 624p. 1978. 87.50 (ISBN 0-8089-1026-4). Grune.
Schneider, Richard C. Correlative Neurosurgery, 2 vols. 3rd ed. (Illus.). 1808p. 1982. Set. slipcase 225.00 (ISBN 0-398-04037-0). C C Thomas.
Seddon, Herbert. Surgical Disorders of Peripheral Nerves. 2nd ed. LC 75-9991. (Illus.). 352p. 1975. text ed. 46.25 (ISBN 0-443-01264-4). Churchill.
Shainberg, Lawrence. Brain Surgeon: An Intimate View of His World. 1979. 10.95 (ISBN 0-397-01310-8). Lippincott.
Smith, Robert R. Essentials of Neurosurgery. (Illus.). 295p. 1980. text ed. 27.50 (ISBN 0-397-50416-0). Lippincott.
Walker, Arthur E. History of Neurological Surgery. 1967. Repr. of 1951 ed. 35.75 (ISBN 0-02-854400-5). Hafner.
White, James C. & Sweet, William H. Pain & the Neurosurgeon: A Forty-Year Experience. (Illus.). 1032p. 1969. text ed. 52.75 (ISBN 0-398-02058-2). C C Thomas.

Wilkins, Robert H., ed. Neurosurgical Classics. 1965. 50.00 (ISBN 0-384-41180-0). Johnson Repr.
Wullenweber, R., et al, eds. Advances in Neurosurgery, Vol. 4. LC 76-57741. 1977. pap. 42.60 (ISBN 0-387-08100-3). Springer-Verlag.

NERVOUS SYSTEM–TUMORS

Bohoun, C., ed. Neuroblastomas: Biochemical Studies. (Recent Results in Cancer Research: Vol. 2). (Illus.). 1966. 15.40 (ISBN 0-387-03641-5). Springer-Verlag.
Chang. Tumors of the Central Nervous System. 1981. write for info (ISBN 0-89352-137-X). Masson Pub.
Duffy, Philip E., ed. Tumors of the Nervous System. LC 75-735757. (Neuropathology Ser). 1976. 195.00 (ISBN 0-8036-2917-6). Davis Co.
Pool, J. Lawrence, et al. Acoustic Nerve Tumors: Early Diagnosis & Treatment. 2nd ed. (Illus.). 252p. 1970. 18.75 (ISBN 0-398-01507-4). C C Thomas.
Rand, Robert W. & Rand, Carl W. Intraspinal Tumors of Childhood. (American Lecture Neurosurgery). (Illus.). 544p. 1960. photocopy ed. 53.75 (ISBN 0-398-01546-5). C C Thomas.
Russell, Dorothy S. & Rubinstein, Lucien J. Pathology of Tumors of the Nervous System. 4th ed. (Illus.). 460p. 1977. 55.00 (ISBN 0-683-07461-X). Williams & Wilkins.
Scharenberg, Konstantin & Liss, Leopold. The Neuroectodermal Tumors of the Central & Peripheral Nervous System. 248p. 1969. 25.00 (ISBN 0-683-07575-6, Pub. by Williams & Wilkins). Krieger.
Wagner, Franklin, ed. Neurosurgery of Tumors. (Seminars in Neurological Surgery Ser.). 1982. write for info. (ISBN 0-89004-448-1, 508). Raven.

NERVOUS SYSTEM–VERTEBRATES

Ariens, C. U., et al. The Comparative Anatomy of the Nervous System of Vertebrates Including Man, 3 vols. 2nd ed. (Illus.). 1845p. 1936. 97.50 (ISBN 0-02-840400-9). Hafner.
Coghill, G. E. Anatomy & the Problem of Behavior. 1929. 9.75 (ISBN 0-02-843050-6). Hafner.
Craigie, Edward H. Craigie's Neuroanatomy of the Rat. rev. ed. Zeman, Wolfgang & Innes, James R., eds. 1963. 37.50 (ISBN 0-12-195450-1). Acad Pr.
Kuhlenbeck, H. Central Nervous System of Vertebrates: A General Survey of Its Comparative Anatomy with an Introduction to Pertinent Fundamental Biologic & Logical Concepts, 5 vols. Incl. Vol. 1. Propaedeutics to Comparative Neurology. 1967. 54.00 (ISBN 3-8055-0897-2); Vol. 2. Invertebrates & Origin of Vertebrates. 1967. 54.00 (ISBN 3-8055-0896-4); Vol. 3, Pt. 1. Structural Elements: Biology of Nervous Tissue. 1970. 129.50 (ISBN 3-8055-0900-6); Vol. 3, Pt. 2. Overall Morphology Pattern. 1973. 203.75 (ISBN 3-8055-1393-3); Vol. 4. Spinal Cord & Deuterencephalon. 1975. 238.50 (ISBN 3-8055-1732-7); Vol. 5, Pt. 1. Derivatives of the Proencephalon: Diencephalon & Telencephalon. 1977. 238.50 (ISBN 3-8055-2638-5); Vol. 5, Pt. 2. Mammalian Telencephalon: Surface Morphology & Cerebral Cortex. The Vertebrate Neuraxis As a Whole. Subject & Authors Index to Vols. 1-5. 1978. 191.75 (ISBN 3-8055-2645-8). (Illus.). Set. 776.25 (ISBN 3-8055-1725-4). S Karger.
--Central Nervous System of Vertebrates, 3 vols. 1967-70. (ISBN 0-685-05124-2); Vol. 1. 46.00 (ISBN 0-12-427901-5); Vol. 2. 46.00 (ISBN 0-12-427902-3); Vol. 3, Pt. 1. 86.00 (ISBN 0-12-427903-1). Acad Pr.
Kuroda, Ryo. Experimental Researches Upon the Sense of Hearing in Lower Vertebrates, Including Reptiles, Amphibians, & Fishes. LC 26-12355. 1926. pap. 5.00 (ISBN 0-527-24851-7). Kraus Repr.
Manocha, S. L., et al. Macaca Mulatta Enzyme Histochemistry of the Nervous System. 1970. 50.00 (ISBN 0-12-469350-4). Acad Pr.
Masterton, R. B., et al, eds. Evolution, Brain & Behavior in Vertebrates, 2 vols. Incl. Vol. 1. Modern Concepts. 482p. 29.95 (ISBN 0-470-15045-9); Vol. 2. Persistent Problems. 276p. 14.95 (ISBN 0-470-15046-7). LC 76-6499. 1976. Halsted Pr.
NASA Symposium, Ames Research Center, Moffett Field, Calif., Nov 1973. Eighth Nerve Systems in Vertebrates Other Than Mammals: Proceedings. Mehler, W. R. & Riss, W., eds. (Brain, Behavior & Evolution: Vol. 10, Nos. 1-3). (Illus.). 264p. 1974. pap. 52.25 (ISBN 3-8055-2164-2). S Karger.
Ryall, R. W. & Kelly, J. S., eds. Iontophoresis & Transmitter Mechanisms in the Mammalian Central Nervous System: Proceedings of a Satellite Symposium. 1978. 70.75 (ISBN 0-444-80012-3, Biomedical Pr). Elsevier.
Sandri, C., et al. Membrane Morphology of the Vertebrate Nervous System. (Progress in Brain Research: Vol. 46). 1977. 85.50 (ISBN 0-444-41479-7, North Holland). Elsevier.
Santiago, Ramon & Santiago, Cajal. Studies on Vertebrate Neurogenesis. Guth, Lloyd, tr. (Illus.). 448p. 1960. pap. 43.75 (ISBN 0-398-04401-5). C C Thomas.

NERVOUS SYSTEM–WOUNDS AND INJURIES

Keith, Arthur. Menders of the Maimed: The Anatomical & Physiological Principles Underlying the Treatment of Injuries to Muscles, Nerves, Bones & Joints. LC 75-19489. 352p. 1975. Repr. of 1919 ed. 17.50 (ISBN 0-88275-341-X). Krieger.
Mitchell, Silas W. Injuries of Nerves & Their Consequences. 5.50 (ISBN 0-8446-2600-7). Peter Smith.
Oester, Y. T. & Mayer, John H., Jr. Motor Examination of Peripheral Nerve Injuries. (Illus.). 96p. 1960. photocopy ed. spiral 10.50 (ISBN 0-398-01413-2). C C Thomas.
Seddon, Herbert. Surgical Disorders of Peripheral Nerves. 2nd ed. LC 75-9991. (Illus.). 352p. 1975. text ed. 46.25 (ISBN 0-443-01264-4). Churchill.
Sunderland, Sydney. Nerves & Nerve Injuries. 2nd ed. (Illus.). 1979. text ed. 125.00 (ISBN 0-443-01653-4). Churchill.

NERVOUS SYSTEM, AUTONOMIC

see also Nervous System, Sympathetic

Appenzeller, O. The Autonomic Nervous System. 2nd ed. 1976. 73.25 (ISBN 0-7204-0670-6, North-Holland). Elsevier.
Barber, Theodore X., et al, eds. Biofeedback & Self-Control: An Aldine Reader on the Regulation of Bodily Processes & Consciousness. LC 71-167858. 1971. 39.95x (ISBN 0-202-25048-2). Aldine Pub.
Bhagat, Budh D., et al. Fundamentals of Visceral Innervation. (Illus.). 216p. 1977. 31.25- (ISBN 0-398-03388-9); pap. 21.50 (ISBN 0-398-03390-0). C C Thomas.
Brooks, C. M., et al, eds. Integrative Functions of the Autonomic Nervous System. 1979. 85.50 (ISBN 0-444-80140-5, North Holland). Elsevier.
DiCara, Leo V., ed. Limbic & Autonomic Nervous Systems Research. LC 74-17327. (Illus.). 428p. 1975. 27.50 (ISBN 0-306-30786-3, Plenum Pr). Plenum Pub.
Gabella, G. Structure of the Automatic Nervous System. LC 75-29233. 214p. 1976. text ed. 35.00x (ISBN 0-412-13620-1, Pub. by Chapman & Hall England). Methuen Inc.
Gellhorn, Ernst. Autonomic Imbalance & the Hypothalamus: Implications for Physiology, Medicine, Psychology & Neuropsychiatry. LC 57-8919. (Illus.). 1957. 15.00x (ISBN 0-8166-0141-0). U of Minn Pr.
--Principles of Autonomic-Somatic Integrations: Physiological Basis & Psychological & Clinical Implications. LC 66-24533. (Illus.). 1967. 15.00x (ISBN 0-8166-0414-2). U of Minn Pr.
Hockman, Charles H., ed. Limbic System Mechanisms & Autonomic Function. (Illus.). 312p. 1972. 36.25 (ISBN 0-398-02315-8). C C Thomas.
International Society for Neurovegatative Research-Tinany-1972. Neurovegetative Transmission Mechanisms: Proceedings. Csillik, B. & Kappers, J. A., eds. (Journal of Neural Transmission: Suppl. 11). (Illus.). 350p. 1974. 91.50 (ISBN 0-387-81173-7). Springer Verlag.
Johnson, R. H. & Spalding, J. M. Disorders of the Autonomic Nervous System. (Contemporary Neurology Ser.: No. 11). 300p. 1974. 25.00 (ISBN 0-8036-5030-2). Davis Co.
Kalsner, Stanley. Trends in Autonomic Pharmacology, Vol. 1. LC 79-17275. (Illus.). 508p. 1979. text ed. 35.00 (ISBN 0-8067-1001-2). Urban & S.
Lacey, John I. Psychophysiology of the Autonomic Nervous System: Some Conceptual & Methodological Considerations. (Master Lectures on Physiological Psychology: Manuscript No. 1327). 4.00x (ISBN 0-912704-29-2). Am Psychol.
Pickering, S. G. Exercises for the Autonomic Nervous System: You Need Them! (Illus.). 128p. 1981. 10.75 (ISBN 0-398-04454-6); pap. 7.50 (ISBN 0-398-04466-X). C C Thomas.
Shapiro, David, et al, eds. Biofeedback & Self-Control, 1972: An Aldine Annual on the Regulation of Bodily Processes & Consciousness. LC 73-75702. 513p. 1973. 39.95x (ISBN 0-202-25107-1). Aldine Pub.
Skok, Vladimir I. Physiology of Autonomic Ganglia. (Illus.). 1973. 26.00 (ISBN 0-89640-009-3). Igaku-Shoin.
Stoyva, Johann, et al, eds. Biofeedback & Self-Control, 1971: An Aldine Annual on the Regulation of Bodily Processes & Consciousness. LC 74-151109. 350p. 1972. 39.95x (ISBN 0-202-25085-7). Aldine Pub.
Triggle, D. J. Chemical Aspects of the Autonomic Nervous System. (Theoretical & Experimental Biology: Vol. 4). 1966. 52.00 (ISBN 0-12-700250-2). Acad Pr.
Van Toller, C. The Nervous Body: An Introduction to the Autonomic Nervous System & Behaviour. LC 78-16758. 1979. 38.50 (ISBN 0-471-99703-X); pap. 15.25 (ISBN 0-471-99729-3, Pub. by Wiley-Interscience). Wiley.

NERVOUS SYSTEM, EFFECT OF RADIATION ON

Gilbert, Harvey A. & Kagan, Robert A. Radiation Damage to the Nervous System: A Delayed Therapeutic Hazard. (Illus.). 225p. 1980. text ed. 27.00 (ISBN 0-89004-418-X). Raven.
Haley, Thomas J. & Snider, Ray S., eds. Response of the Nervous System to Ionizing Radiation: Proceedings. 1962. 64.50 (ISBN 0-12-318650-1). Acad Pr.

NERVOUS SYSTEM, SYMPATHETIC

see also Chromaffin Cells

Friedhoff, Arnold J., ed. Catecholamines & Behavior. Incl. Vol. 1, Basic Neurobiology. 235p (ISBN 0-306-38411-6); Vol. 2, Neuropsychopharmacology. 255p (ISBN 0-306-38412-4). LC 75-11697. (Illus.). 1975. 22.50 ea. (Plenum Pr). Plenum Pub.
Iversen, Leslie L. Uptake & Storage of Noradrenaline in Sympathic Nerves. 1967. 35.50 (ISBN 0-521-05390-0). Cambridge U Pr.

NERVOUS SYSTEM, VEGETATIVE

see Nervous System, Autonomic

NERVOUS TISSUE

see Nerve Tissue

NERVOUS TRANSMISSION

see Neural Transmission

NESS, LOCH

Baumann, Elwood. The Loch Ness Monster. LC 72-182896. (Illus.). 160p. (gr. 6 up). 1972. PLB 7.45 (ISBN 0-531-02031-2). Watts.
Berke, Sally. Monster at Loch Ness. LC 77-24715. (Great Unsolved Mysteries Ser.). (Illus.). (gr. 4-5). 1977. PLB 10.65 (ISBN 0-8172-1054-7). Raintree Pubs.
Cornell, James. The Monster of Loch Ness. (gr. 7 up). 1978. pap. 1.25 (ISBN 0-590-11872-2, Schol Pap). Schol Bk Serv.
Dinsdale, Tim. Loch Ness Monster. 3rd ed. (Illus.). 1976. pap. 7.95 (ISBN 0-7100-8394-7). Routledge & Kegan.
--Project Water Horse. (Illus.). 1975. 16.95 (ISBN 0-7100-8029-8); pap. 7.95 (ISBN 0-7100-8030-1). Routledge & Kegan.
Gould, Rupert T. The Loch Ness Monster. (Illus.). 1976. pap. 3.95 (ISBN 0-8065-0555-9). Citadel Pr.
Holiday, F. W. Great Orm of Loch Ness. LC 68-15754. (Illus.). 1969. 6.95 (ISBN 0-393-06345-3). Norton.
Mackal, Roy P. The Monsters of Loch Ness: The First Complete Scientific Study & Its Startling Conclusions. LC 76-3139. (Illus.). 401p. 1980. pap. 8.95 (ISBN 0-8040-0704-7). Swallow.
Meredith, Dennis L. Search at Loch Ness: A Report on the Expedition of the New York Times-Academy of Applied Science. LC 76-50826. 1977. 9.95 (ISBN 0-8129-0677-2). Times Bks.
Smith, Warren. Strange Secrets of the Loch Ness Monster. 256p. 1976. pap. 1.75 (ISBN 0-89083-175-0). Zebra.
Snyder, Gerald S. Is There a Loch Ness Monster? LC 78-26263. (Illus.). (gr. 4-8). 1979. pap. 3.95 (ISBN 0-671-33029-2). Wanderer Bks.
Thorne, Ian. The Loch Ness Monster. Schroeder, Howard, ed. LC 78-6193. (Search for the Unknown Ser.). (Illus.). (gr. 4). 1978. PLB 6.95 (ISBN 0-913940-83-6); pap. 3.25 (ISBN 0-89686-004-3). Crestwood Hse.
Witchell, Nicholas. The Loch Ness Story. (Illus.). 1979. 18.50 (ISBN 0-900963-68-9, Pub. by Terence Dalton England). State Mutual Bk.

NESSANA–ANTIQUITIES

Colt, H. Dunscombe, ed. Excavations at Nessana, Vol. I. (Colt Archaeological Institute). (Illus.). 311p. 1962. text ed. 72.00x (ISBN 0-85668-071-0, Pub. by Aris & Phillips England). Humanities.
--Excavations at Nessana, Vol. 1. (Illus.). 1976. 72.00x (ISBN 0-85668-071-0, Pub. by Aris & Phillips). Intl Schol Bk Serv.

NESTORIAN CHURCH

Isho-Yabah. Book of Consolations. Scott-Moncreiff, Phillip, ed. LC 77-87669. (Luzac's Semitic Text & Translation Ser.: No. 16). Repr. of 1904 ed. 21.50 (ISBN 0-404-11350-8). AMS Pr.
Stewart, John. Nestorian Missionary Enterprise. LC 78-63172. (Heresies of the Early Christian & Medieval Era: Second Ser.). Repr. of 1928 ed. 32.50 (ISBN 0-404-16187-1). AMS Pr.
Vine, Aubrey R. The Nestorian Churches. LC 78-63173. (Heresies of the Early Christian & Medieval Era: Second Ser.). Repr. of 1937 ed. 21.50 (ISBN 0-404-16188-X). AMS Pr.

NESTORIAN TABLET OF SIAN-FA

Legge, James. Nestorian Monument of Hsi-an Fu in Shen-Hsi, China. 1966. Repr. of 1888 ed. 5.50 (ISBN 0-8188-0062-3). Paragon.

NESTORIANS

see also Nestorian Church

Abramowski, Luise & Goodman, Allan E., eds. Nestorian Collection of Christological Texts, 2 vols. Incl. Vol. 1. Syriac Text. 58.00 (ISBN 0-521-07578-5); Vol. 2. Introduction, Translation & Indexes. 49.50 (ISBN 0-521-08126-2). LC 77-130904. (Oriental Publications Ser.: No. 18, 19). 1972. Cambridge U Pr.
Emhardt, William C. & Lamsa, G. M. Oldest Christian People. LC 71-126651. Repr. of 1926 ed. 14.50 (ISBN 0-404-02339-8). AMS Pr.
Montgomery, James A., ed. History of Yaballaha III. 1967. lib. bdg. 12.00x (ISBN 0-374-95814-9). Octagon.

NESTORIUS, PATRIARCH OF CONSTANTINOPLE, fl. 428

Bethune-Baker, J. F. Nestorius & His Teaching. 1908. 12.00 (ISBN 0-527-07500-0). Kraus Repr.
Loofs, Richard. Nestorius & His Place in the History of the Christian Doctrine. LC 75-1225. 1975. Repr. of 1914 ed. 18.50 (ISBN 0-8337-4903-X). B Franklin.

NESTROY, J. N., 1801-1862

Harding, Laurence V. The Dramatic Art of Ferdinand Raimund & Johann Nestroy: A Critical Study. (Studies in German Literature: No. 3). 1974. text ed. 40.00x (ISBN 90-2792-615-8). Mouton.

NESTS OF BIRDS

see Birds–Eggs and Nests

NET NATIONAL PRODUCT

see National Income

NETBALL

Dewhurst-Hands, Sally. Netball: A Tactical Approach. (Illus.). 80p. 1980. 12.95 (ISBN 0-571-11496-2, Pub. by Faber & Faber); pap. 6.95 (ISBN 0-571-11542-X). Merrimack Bk Serv.
Edwards, Phyl & Campbell, Sue. Netball Today. 1980. 20.00x (ISBN 0-86019-049-8, Pub. by Kimpton). State Mutual Bk.
Martin, Toy. Netball Fundamentals. LC 80-66418. (Illus.). 96p. 1980. 11.95 (ISBN 0-7153-7984-4). David & Charles.
Wheeler, Joyce. Better Netball. LC 74-22591. (Illus.). 96p. 1976. 8.50x (ISBN 0-7182-0151-5). Intl Pubns Serv.

NETHERLANDIC LANGUAGE

see Dutch Language

NETHERLANDS

see also names of cities, towns, geographic areas, etc. in the Netherlands

Coleman, John A. The Evolution of Dutch Catholicism, 1958-1974. LC 74-22958. 1979. 28.50x (ISBN 0-520-02885-6). U of Cal Pr.
Colijn, Helen. Of Dutch Ways. LC 79-24545. (Heritage Books). (Illus.). 1980. 8.95 (ISBN 0-87518-198-8). Dillon.
Edwards, George W. Holland of Today. 1909. 20.00 (ISBN 0-8495-1355-3). Arden Lib.
Fokkema, D. C. Introduction to Dutch Law. Lisser, E. C. & Hondius, E. H., eds. 1978. lib. bdg. 69.50 (ISBN 90-2680-897-6, Pub. by Kluwer Law Netherlands). Kluwer Boston.
Institute for Political Science & Baschwitz Institute for Public Opinion & Mass Psychology. Dutch Continuous Survey, 1972. University of Amsterdam, 1974. codebk. 8.00 (ISBN 0-89138-074-4). ICPSR.
Lambert, A. M. The Making of the Dutch Landscape: An Historical Geography of the Netherlands. LC 70-162378. 424p. 1971. 39.50 (ISBN 0-12-785450-9). Acad Pr.
Moors, H. G., et al, eds. Population & Family in the Low Countries, No. 1. 1976. pap. 21.00 (ISBN 90-247-1859-7, Pub. by Martinus Nijhoff Netherlands). Kluwer Boston.
Netherlands. (Panorama Bks.). (Illus., Fr.). 3.95 (ISBN 0-685-11418-X). French & Eur.
Netherlands Central Bureau of Statistics. Statistical Yearbook of the Netherlands 1976. (Illus.). 368p. 27.50x (ISBN 0-8002-2023-4). Intl Pubns Serv.
Werner, A. The Humour of Holland. Repr. of 1893 ed. lib. bdg. 30.00 (ISBN 0-8495-5901-4). Arden Lib.
Wohlrabe, Raymond A. The Land & People of Holland. LC 79-37249. 160p. (YA) (gr. 6-9). 1972. lib. bdg. 8.79 (ISBN 0-397-31254-7, JBL-J). Har-Row.

NETHERLANDS–BIBLIOGRAPHY

Bibliotheca Belgica: Bibliographie Generale des Pays-Bas, 7 vols. 5500p. (Fr.). 1975. Set, Vols. 1-6. 550.00x (ISBN 0-8002-2158-3); Vol. 7: General Index. 100.00x (ISBN 0-8002-2159-1). Intl Pubns Serv.

NETHERLANDS–BIOGRAPHY

Blok, Petrus J. The Life of Admiral De Ruyter. Renier, G. J., tr. LC 74-9393. (Illus.). 388p. 1975. Repr. of 1933 ed. lib. bdg. 21.75x (ISBN 0-8371-7666-2, BLAR). Greenwood.
Hoffman, William. Queen Juliana: The Richest Woman in the World. Hill, Carol, ed. LC 79-1827. 1979. 11.95 (ISBN 0-15-146531-2). HarBraceJ.
Rowen, Herbert H. John De Witt: Grand Pensionary of Holland, 1625-1672. LC 76-45909. 1978. text ed. 55.00 (ISBN 0-691-05247-6). Princeton U Pr.

Thrane, Carl. Friedrich Kuhlau. (Facsimilies of Early Biographies Ser.: Vol. 6). iv, 110p. 17.50 (ISBN 90-6027-356-7, Pub. by Frits Knuf Netherlands). Pendragon NY.

Tilstra, Albertine J. A Dutchman Bound for Paradise. Van Dolson, Bobbie J., ed. 128p. 1980. pap. write for info. (ISBN 0-8280-0021-2). Review & Herald.

--A Dutchman Bound for Paradise. Van Dolson, Bobbie J., ed. 128p. 1980. pap. write for info. (ISBN 0-8280-0021-2). Review & Herald.

NETHERLANDS–CIVILIZATION

Cochrane, Candace. Outport: A Newfoundland Fishing Village. Page, Roger, ed. (Illus.). 1981. 24.95 (ISBN 0-201-10090-8). A-W.

Hough, P. M. Dutch Life in Town & Country. LC 77-87698. Repr. of 1901 ed. 24.00 (ISBN 0-404-16494-3). AMS Pr.

Newton, Gerald. The Netherlands: An Historical & Cultural Survey 1795-1977. LC 77-16100. (Nations of the Modern World Ser.). 1978. lib. bdg. 29.75x (ISBN 0-89158-802-7). Westview.

Wilson, Charles. Dutch Republic. (Illus., Orig.). 1968. pap. 3.95 (ISBN 0-07-070653-0, SP). McGraw.

NETHERLANDS–COLONIES

Altmeyer, Jean J. Histoire des relations commerciales et diplomatiques des Pays-Bas avec le nord de l'Europe pendant le sixieme siecle. LC 66-20684. 1970. Repr. of 1840 ed. lib. bdg. 32.00 (ISBN 0-8337-0052-9). B Franklin.

Colquhoun, Archibald R. Mastery of the Pacific. LC 70-111750. (American Imperialism: Viewpoints of United States Foreign Policy, 1898-1941). 1970. Repr. of 1904 ed. 20.00 (ISBN 0-405-02009-0). Arno.

Goslinga, Cornelis C. Dutch in the Caribbean & on the Wild Coast, 1580-1680. LC 72-93193. (Illus.). 1971. 20.00 (ISBN 0-8130-0280-X). U Presses Fla.

Hiss, P. Netherlands America. 1976. lib. bdg. 59.95 (ISBN 0-8490-2336-X). Gordon Pr.

Masselman, George. Cradle of Colonialism. 1963. 47.50x (ISBN 0-685-69840-8). Elliots Bks.

Mitchell, Harold P. Europe in the Caribbean. LC 73-75777. (Illus.). xi, 211p. 1973. Repr. of 1963 ed. lib. bdg. 10.00x (ISBN 0-8154-0479-4). Cooper Sq.

Nijhoff, Martinus. The Hollanders in America. LC 74-167568. 94p. 1972. Repr. of 1925 ed. lib. bdg. 7.00 (ISBN 0-88247-168-6). R & E Res Assoc.

NETHERLANDS–COMMERCE

Coke, Roger. A Discourse of Trade. (History of English Economic Thought Ser). 1970. Repr. of 1670 ed. 12.50 (ISBN 0-384-09502-X). Johnson Repr.

Hyma, Albert. History of the Dutch in the Far East. 1953. 4.95x (ISBN 0-685-21788-4). Wahr.

Masselman, George. Cradle of Colonialism. 1963. 47.50x (ISBN 0-685-69840-8). Elliots Bks.

Newes Out of Holland, of the East India Trade There. LC 73-6145. (English Experience Ser.: No. 609). 14p. 1973. Repr. of 1622 ed. 3.50 (ISBN 90-221-0609-8). Walter J Johnson.

Van Winter, Pieter. American Finance & Dutch Investment, 1780-1805. Wilkins, Mira, ed. LC 76-46251. (European Business Ser.). (Illus.). 1977. Repr. of 1977 ed. lib. bdg. 68.00x (ISBN 0-405-09860-X). Arno.

Wilson, Charles Henry. Anglo-Dutch Commerce & Finance in the Eighteenth Century. Wilkins, Mira, ed. LC 76-29980. (European Business Ser.). (Illus.). 1977. Repr. of 1941 ed. lib. bdg. 16.00x (ISBN 0-405-09746-8). Arno.

NETHERLANDS–DESCRIPTION AND TRAVEL

Allen, Zachariah. The Practical Tourist; or, Sketches of the State of the Useful Arts, & of Society, Scenery in Great Britain, France & Holland, 2 vols. in 1. LC 73-38258. (The Evolution of Capitalism Ser.). 896p. 1972. Repr. of 1832 ed. 39.00 (ISBN 0-405-04111-X). Arno.

Benest, E. E. Inland Waterways of the Netherlands, 3 vols. (Illus.). 1966-71. 40.00 set (ISBN 0-685-36177-2). Heinman.

Brereton, William. Travels in Holland, the United Provinces, England, Scotland & Ireland. Repr. of 1844 ed. 17.00 (ISBN 0-384-05670-9). Johnson Repr.

Cochrane, Candace. Outport: A Newfoundland Fishing Village. Page, Roger, ed. (Illus.). 1981. 24.95 (ISBN 0-201-10090-8). A-W.

De Amicis, Edmondo. Holland & Its People. Tilton, Caroline, tr. from It. LC 72-3433. (Essay Index Reprint Ser.). Repr. of 1880 ed. 33.00 (ISBN 0-8369-2887-3). Arno.

De Bakker, H. Major Soils & Soil Regions in the Netherlands. (Illus.). 1979. lib. bdg. 53.00 (ISBN 9-06193-590-3, Pub. by Junk Pubs Netherlands). Kluwer Boston.

Edwards, G. W. Holland of Today. 59.95 (ISBN 0-8490-0367-9). Gordon Pr.

Edwards, George W. Holland of Today. 1978. Repr. lib. bdg. 45.00 (ISBN 0-8414-3986-9). Folcroft.

Gibbon, David. Holland: A Picture Book to Remember Her by. (Illus.). 3.98 (ISBN 0-517-28857-5). Bonanza.

Le Petit, Jean Francois. The Low Country Commonwealth. Grimeston, E., tr. LC 72-25634. (English Experience Ser.: No. 208). 1969. Repr. of 1609 ed. 30.00 (ISBN 90-221-0208-4). Walter J Johnson.

Magi, Giovanna. Holland. (Illus., Orig.). 1978. pap. 16.00x (ISBN 88-7009-046-9). Intl Pubns Serv.

Pilkington, Roger. Small Boat Through Holland. 1979. 15.00x (ISBN 0-86025-807-6, Pub. by Ian Henry Pubns England). State Mutual Bk.

Sitwell, Sacheverell. The Netherlands. 1974. 24.00 (ISBN 0-7134-2779-5, Pub. by Batsford England). David & Charles.

Southey, Robert. Journal of a Tour in the Netherlands in the Autumn of 1815. Repr. of 1903 ed. lib. bdg. 35.00 (ISBN 0-8495-5020-3). Arden Lib.

Vries, David P. De. Voyages from Holland to America, A. D. 1632 to 1644. Murphy, H. C., tr. from Dutch. LC 2-7761. Repr. of 1853 ed. 23.00 (ISBN 0-527-93460-7). Kraus Repr.

Weaver, Rex. Behold: New Holland! Date not set. 7.95 (ISBN 0-392-16428-0, ABC). Sportshelf.

NETHERLANDS–DESCRIPTION AND TRAVEL–GUIDEBOOKS

Arthur Frommer's Guide to Amsterdam - Holland, 1981-82. 224p. 1981. pap. 2.95 (ISBN 0-671-41427-5). Frommer-Pasmantier.

Bristow, Philip. Through the Dutch Canals. 250p. 1980. 15.00x (ISBN 0-686-69886-X, Pub. by Nautical England). State Mutual Bk.

Evans, Craig. On Foot Through Europe: A Trail Guide to France & the Benelux Nations. Whitney, Stephen, ed. (Illus.). 496p. 1980. lib. bdg. 13.95 (ISBN 0-933710-17-8); pap. 7.95 (ISBN 0-933710-16-X). Foot Trails.

Fodor's Holland, 1981. 1980. 11.95 (ISBN 0-679-00695-8). McKay.

Michelin. Michelin Green Guide to Hollande. 1979. pap. 7.95 (ISBN 2-06-005530-X). Michelin.

Michelin Guides & Maps. Michelin Red Guide to Benelux: Belgium, Luxembourg, Netherlands. (Red Guide Ser.). 1980. 12.95 (ISBN 2-06-006001-X). Michelin.

Michelin Red Guide to Benelux: Michelin Guides & Maps. (Red Guide Ser.). 1981. 12.95 (ISBN 2-06-006301-9). Michelin.

Nagel Travel Guide to Holland. 704p. 1974. 38.00 (ISBN 2-8263-0606-5). Hippocrene Bks.

NETHERLANDS–ECONOMIC CONDITIONS

Abert, James G. Economic Policy & Planning in the Netherlands, 1950-1965. (Illus.). 1969. 25.00x (ISBN 0-300-01108-3). Yale U Pr.

Dekker, H. C., et al. Planning in a Dutch & a Yugoslav Steelworks: A Comparative Study. (Illus.). 1976. pap. text ed. 23.00x (ISBN 90-6032-078-6). Humanities.

De La Court, Pieter. The True Interest & Political Maxims of the Republic of Holland. LC 78-38278. (The Evolution of Capitalism Ser.). 520p. 1972. Repr. of 1746 ed. 26.00 (ISBN 0-405-04117-9). Arno.

Ellis, M. J. & Juch, D. The Participation Exemption in the Netherlands. pap. 14.00 (ISBN 90-200-0501-4, Pub. by Kluwer Law Netherlands). Kluwer Boston.

Griffiths, Richard T. Industrial Retardation in the Netherlands: 1830-1850. (Illus.). xviii, 235p. 1980. lib. bdg. 34.00 (ISBN 90-247-2199-7, Martinus Nijhoff Pub). Kluwer Boston.

Hofstee, E. W. Rural Life & Rural Welfare in the Netherlands: Division of Documentation, Ministry of Agriculture, Fisheries & Food. LC 77-87697. (Illus.). Repr. of 1957 ed. 47.50 (ISBN 0-404-16493-5). AMS Pr.

Lawrence, G. R. Randstad, Holland. (Problem Areas of Europe Ser.). (Illus.). 1973. pap. 7.95x (ISBN 0-19-913101-5). Oxford U Pr.

Mokyr, Joel. Industrialization in the Low Countries, 1795-1850. LC 75-43326. (Economic in History Ser.). 1976. 25.00x (ISBN 0-300-01892-4). Yale U Pr.

Riley, R. C. & Ashworth, Gregory. Benelux: An Economic Geography of Belgium, the Netherlands, & Luxembourg. LC 74-84586. (Illus.). 256p. 1975. text ed. 25.00 (ISBN 0-8419-0174-0). Holmes & Meier.

Schiff, Eric. Industrialization Without National Patents: The Netherlands 1869-1912, Switzerland 1850-1907. LC 71-120761. 1971. 17.00x (ISBN 0-691-04197-0). Princeton U Pr.

Van Der Meer, S. W. Corporate Law of the Netherlands & of the Netherlands Antilles. 7th ed. viii, 128p. 1980. lib. bdg. 15.00 (ISBN 90-2711-632-6, Pub. by Kluwer Law Netherlands). Kluwer Boston.

Van Houtte, J. A. An Economic History of the Low Countries 800-1800. LC 77-81397. (Illus.). 1977. 19.95x (ISBN 0-312-23320-5). St Martin.

Vries, J. de. The Netherlands Economy in the Twentieth Century: An Examination of the Most Characteristic Feature in the Period 1900-1970. (Aspects of Economic History, the Low Countries Ser.: No. 3). 1978. pap. text ed. 13.50x (ISBN 90-232-1594-X). Humanities.

NETHERLANDS–EMIGRATION AND IMMIGRATION

Wabeke, Bertus H. Dutch Emigration to North America, 1624-1860. facs. ed. LC 78-119946. (Select Bibliographies Reprint Ser). 1944. 17.00 (ISBN 0-8369-5389-4). Arno.

NETHERLANDS–FOREIGN RELATIONS

Altmeyer, Jean J. Histoire des relations commerciales et diplomatiques des Pays-Bas avec le nord de l'Europe pendant le sixieme siecle. LC 66-20684. 1970. Repr. of 1840 ed. lib. bdg. 32.00 (ISBN 0-8337-0052-9). B Franklin.

An Answere to the Hollanders Declaration, Concerning the Occurrents of the East India. LC 72-168. (English Experience Ser.: No. 327). 1971. Repr. of 1622 ed. 7.00 (ISBN 90-221-0327-7). Walter J Johnson.

Carter, Alice C. Neutrality or Commitment: The Evolution of Dutch Foreign Policy, 1667-1795. (Foundations of Modern History). (Illus.). 120p. 1976. 10.00x (ISBN 0-393-05577-9). Norton.

De La Court, Pieter. The True Interest & Political Maxims of the Republic of Holland. LC 78-38278. (The Evolution of Capitalism Ser.). 520p. 1972. Repr. of 1746 ed. 26.00 (ISBN 0-405-04117-9). Arno.

De Ligt, Barthelemy. Conquest of Violence. LC 76-147627. (Library of War & Peace; Non-Resis. & Non-Vio.). lib. bdg. 38.00 (ISBN 0-8240-0402-7). Garland Pub.

Dorsten, J. A. Ten Studies in Anglo-Dutch Relations. (Publications of Sir Thomas Browne Institute Ser: No. 5). 1974. lib. bdg. 34.00 (ISBN 90-6021-217-7, Pub. by Leiden Univ. Holland). Kluwer Boston.

Dudley, Robert. Correspondence of Robert Dudley. 1844. 46.00 (ISBN 0-384-32130-5). Johnson Repr.

Edler, Friedrich. Dutch Republic & the American Revolution. LC 78-149686. Repr. of 1911 ed. 23.00 (ISBN 0-404-02246-4). AMS Pr.

The Hollanders Declaration of the Affaires of the East Indies. LC 72-187. (English Experience Ser.: No. 326). 12p. Repr. of 1622 ed. 7.00 (ISBN 90-221-0326-9). Walter J Johnson.

Pearson, Frederic S. The Weak State in International Crisis: The Case of the Netherlands in the German Invasion Crisis of 1939-1940. LC 80-69042. 182p. 1981. lib. bdg. 17.75 (ISBN 0-8191-1558-4); pap. text ed. 8.75 (ISBN 0-8191-1559-2). U Pr of Amer.

Scott, Thomas. Relation of Some Special Points Concerning the State of Holland...Shewing Why for the Security of the United Provinces Warre Is Better Than Peace. LC 73-6160. (English Experience Ser.: No. 623). 20p. 1973. Repr. of 1621 ed. 5.00 (ISBN 90-221-0623-3). Walter J Johnson.

Vandenbosch, Amry. Dutch Foreign Policy Since Eighteen Fifteen: A Study in Small Power Politics. LC 79-2292. 1981. Repr. of 1959 ed. 23.50 (ISBN 0-88355-968-4). Hyperion Conn.

Voorhoeve, J. Joris. Peace, Profits & Principles. 1979. lib. bdg. 23.00 (ISBN 90-247-2237-3); pap. 16.50 (ISBN 90-247-2203-9). Kluwer Boston.

Wilson, Charles. Queen Elizabeth & the Revolt of the Netherlands. LC 76-119009. 1970. 22.75x (ISBN 0-520-01744-7). U of Cal Pr.

NETHERLANDS–HISTORY

see also Dutch War, 1672-1678

Altmeyer, Jean J. Histoire des relations commerciales et diplomatiques des Pays-Bas avec le nord de l'Europe pendant le sixieme siecle. LC 66-20684. 1970. Repr. of 1840 ed. lib. bdg. 32.00 (ISBN 0-8337-0052-9). B Franklin.

Blok, Petrus J. History of the People of the Netherlands, 5 Vols. Bierstadt, O. A. & Putnam, Ruth, trs. LC 76-109911. (Illus.). Repr. of 1912 ed. Set. 75.00 (ISBN 0-404-00900-X); 16.50 ea. AMS Pr.

--The Life of Admiral De Ruyter. Renier, G. J., tr. LC 74-9393. (Illus.). 388p. 1975. Repr. of 1933 ed. lib. bdg. 21.75x (ISBN 0-8371-7666-2, BLAR). Greenwood.

Boxer, C. R. The Dutch Seaborne Empire, Sixteen Hundred to Eighteen Hundred. 1980. pap. text ed. 11.75x (ISBN 0-09-131051-2, Hutchinson U Lib). Humanities.

A Breefe Declaration of That Which Is Happened As Well Within As Without Oastend. LC 70-171781. (English Experience Ser.: No. 406). 8p. Repr. of 1602 ed. 11.50 (ISBN 90-221-0406-0). Walter J Johnson.

Certayne News of Christian Princes. LC 74-38155. (English Experience Ser.: No. 442). 16p. 1972. Repr. of 1547 ed. 7.00 (ISBN 90-221-0442-7). Walter J Johnson.

Clark, George N. Dutch Alliance & the War Against French Trade, 1688-1697. LC 71-139911. (Illus.). 1971. Repr. of 1923 ed. 10.50 (ISBN 0-8462-1576-4). Russell.

Crew, P. Mack. Calvinist Preaching & Iconoclasm in the Netherlands, 1544-1569. LC 77-77013. (Studies in Early Modern History). 1978. 32.95 (ISBN 0-521-21739-3). Cambridge U Pr.

Dudley, Robert. A Briefe Report of the Militaire Services Done in the Low Countries by the Erle of Leicester. LC 72-192. (English Experience Ser.: No. 201). 36p. 1969. Repr. of 1587 ed. 7.00 (ISBN 90-221-0201-7). Walter J Johnson.

--Correspondence of Robert Dudley. 1844. 46.00 (ISBN 0-384-32130-5). Johnson Repr.

Fredericq, Paul. The Study of History in Holland & Belgium. LC 78-63797. (Johns Hopkins University. Studies in the Social Sciences. Eighth Ser. 1890: 10). Repr. of 1890 ed. 11.50 (ISBN 0-404-61062-5). AMS Pr.

Gascoigne, George. The Spoyle of Antwerpe Faithfully Reported by a True Englishman. LC 74-25952. (English Experience Ser.: No. 180). 52p. 1969. Repr. of 1576 ed. 8.00 (ISBN 90-221-0180-0). Walter J Johnson.

Geyl, Pieter. The Revolt of the Netherlands Fifteen Fifty-Five to Sixteen Hundred & Nine. 2nd ed. LC 79-53235. (Illus.). 1980. text ed. 18.50x (ISBN 0-06-492382-7); pap. text ed. 6.95x (ISBN 0-06-492383-5). B&N.

Griffiths, Richard T. Industrial Retardation in the Netherlands: 1830-1850. (Illus.). xviii, 235p. 1980. lib. bdg. 34.00 (ISBN 90-247-2199-7, Martinus Nijhoff Pub). Kluwer Boston.

Guttman, Myron P. War & Rural Life in the Early Modern Low Countries. LC 79-3237. (Illus.). 1980. 22.50x (ISBN 0-691-05291-3). Princeton U Pr.

Kossman, E. H. Low Countries Seventeen Eighty to Ninteen Forty. (History of Modern Europe Ser.). 1978. 59.00x (ISBN 0-19-822108-8). Oxford U Pr.

Kossmann, E. H. & Mellink, A. F., eds. Texts Concerning the Revolt of the Netherlands. LC 73-83103. (Studies in the History & Theory of Politics). 320p. 1975. 33.95 (ISBN 0-521-20014-8). Cambridge U Pr.

Maximillian. Correspondance De l'Empereur Maximilien Premier et De Marguerite D'Autriche: Emperor of Germany, 2 Vols. Le Glay, M., ed. Set. 71.00 (ISBN 0-384-36006-8); Set. pap. 61.50 (ISBN 0-685-13400-8). Johnson Repr.

Meteren, Emanuel van. A True Discourse Historicall, of the Succeeding Gouernours in the Netherlands. Churchyard, T. & Robinson, R., trs. LC 68-54653. (English Experience Ser.: No. 57). 154p. 1968. Repr. of 1602 ed. 16.00 (ISBN 90-221-0057-X). Walter J Johnson.

Parker, Geoffrey. Army of Flanders & the Spanish Road: 1567-1659. LC 76-180021. (Cambridge Studies in Early Modern History). (Illus.). 288p. 1972. 43.95 (ISBN 0-521-08462-8); pap. 11.95x (ISBN 0-521-09907-2). Cambridge U Pr.

--The Dutch Revolt. 320p. 1977. 22.50x (ISBN 0-8014-1136-X). Cornell U Pr.

--Spain & the Netherlands, Fifteen Fifty Nine to Sixteen Fifty Nine. LC 79-12356. 1979. 16.95x (ISBN 0-89490-029-3). Enslow Pubs.

Pearson, Frederic S. The Weak State in International Crisis: The Case of the Netherlands in the German Invasion Crisis of 1939-1940. LC 80-69042. 182p. 1981. lib. bdg. 17.75 (ISBN 0-8191-1558-4); pap. text ed. 8.75 (ISBN 0-8191-1559-2). U Pr of Amer.

Regin, Deric. Traders, Artists, Burghers: A Cultural History of Amsterdam in the 17th Century. (Illus.). 1976. pap. text ed. 18.00x (ISBN 9-0232-1427-7). Humanities.

Rogers, James E. The Story of Holland. 1977. lib. bdg. 59.95 (ISBN 0-8490-2680-6). Gordon Pr.

Schama, Simon. Patriots & Liberators: Revolution in the Netherlands, 1780-1813. 1977. 20.00 (ISBN 0-394-48516-5). Knopf.

Schoffer, I., et al, eds. The Low Countries History Yearbook 1978. (Acta Historiae Neederlandicae: Vol. XI). 1979. lib. bdg. 38.00 (ISBN 90-247-2122-9, Pub. by Martinus Nijhoff Netherlands). Kluwer Boston.

--Acta Historiae Neerlandicae, Vol. 10. 1978. lib. bdg. 43.50 (ISBN 90-247-2021-4, Pub. by Martinus Nijhoff Netherlands). Kluwer Boston.

Scott, Thomas. Relation of Some Special Points Concerning the State of Holland...Shewing Why for the Security of the United Provinces Warre Is Better Than Peace. LC 73-6160. (English Experience Ser.: No. 623). 20p. 1973. Repr. of 1621 ed. 5.00 (ISBN 90-221-0623-3). Walter J Johnson.

Shetter, W. Z. The Pillars of Society: Six Centuries of Civilization in the Netherlands. 1971. pap. 15.00 (ISBN 9-0247-5080-6). Heinman.

Smit, P. & Smit, J. W. The Netherlands: A Chronology & Fact Book. LC 73-5599. (World Chronology Ser.). 160p. 1973. lib. bdg. 8.50 (ISBN 0-379-16301-2). Oceana.

Vere, Francis. Extremities Urging Sir F. Veare to the Anti-Parle with the Archduke Albertus. LC 68-54668. (English Experience Ser.: No. 28). 21p. 1968. Repr. of 1602 ed. 7.00 (ISBN 90-221-0028-6). Walter J Johnson.

--True Newes from One of Sir F. Veres Companie. LC 78-38227. (English Experience Ser.: No. 491). 24p. 1972. Repr. of 1591 ed. 5.00 (ISBN 90-221-0491-5). Walter J Johnson.

Wedgwood, Cicely V. William the Silent: William of Nassau, Prince of Orange, 1533-1584. 1960. text ed. 6.50x (ISBN 0-224-60761-8). Humanities.

--William the Silent: William of Nassau, Prince of Orange, 1533-1584. (Illus.). 1968. pap. 3.95x (ISBN 0-393-00185-7, Norton Lib). Norton.

Williams, Roger. The Actions of the Lowe Countries. LC 72-25705. (English Experience Ser.: No. 280). 134p. 1970. Repr. of 1618 ed. 16.00 (ISBN 90-221-0280-7). Walter J Johnson.

Wilson, Charles. Dutch Republic. (Illus., Orig.). 1968. pap. 3.95 (ISBN 0-07-070653-0, SP). McGraw.

--Queen Elizabeth & the Revolt of the Netherlands. 2nd ed. (Illus.). 168p. 1980. pap. 19.00 (ISBN 90-247-2273-X, Pub. by Martinus Nijhoff Netherlands). Kluwer Boston.

--Queen Elizabeth & the Revolt of the Netherlands. LC 76-119009. 1970. 22.75x (ISBN 0-520-01744-7). U of Cal Pr.

NETHERLANDS-HISTORY-FICTION

Dumas, Alexandre. Black Tulip. 1961. 10.95x (ISBN 0-460-00174-4, Evman). Biblio Dist.

NETHERLANDS-HISTORY-GERMAN OCCUPATION, 1940-1945

Frank, Anne. Anne Frank: The Diary of a Young Girl. rev. ed. (YA) 1967. 9.95a (ISBN 0-385-04019-9); PLB (ISBN 0-385-09190-7). Doubleday.

--Diary of Anne Frank. 1958. 3.95 (ISBN 0-394-60298-6, M298). Modern Lib.

German Institute of Archaeology Rome. Catalogs from the Library of the German Institute of Archaeology, 3 pts. Incl. Pt. 1. Author & Periodical Catalogs, 7 vols. Set. 600.00 (ISBN 0-8161-0824-2); Pt. 2. Classified Catalog, 3 vols. Set. 355.00 (ISBN 0-8161-0103-5); Pt. 3. Author Catalog of Periodicals, 3 vols. Set. 200.00 (ISBN 0-8161-0104-3). 1969. G K Hall.

Janssen, Pierre. Moment of Silence. Tyler, William R., tr. LC 76-115085. (Illus.). (gr. 5 up). 1970. PLB 4.25 (ISBN 0-689-20603-8). Atheneum.

Saillant, Las Teyrie Du. Bibliographie Generale des Travaux Historiques et Archeologiques Publies Par les Societes Savantes en France Depuis les Origines, 6 vols. LC 66-20686. 4529p. (Fr.). 1972. Repr. Set. lib. bdg. 30.50 (ISBN 0-8337-2015-5). B Franklin.

Schnabel, Ernst. Anne Frank: A Portrait in Courage. LC 53-12702. 1967. pap. 0.65 (ISBN 0-15-607530-X, HPL16, HPL). HarBraceJ.

Warmbrunn, Werner. The Dutch Under German Occupation, 1940-1945. 1963. 17.50x (ISBN 0-8047-0152-0). Stanford U Pr.

NETHERLANDS-HISTORY-GERMAN OCCUPATION, 1940-1945-DRAMA

Goodrich, Frances & Hackett, Albert. Diary of Anne Frank, Drama. (YA) 1956. 9.95 (ISBN 0-394-40564-1). Random.

NETHERLANDS-JUVENILE LITERATURE

Barnouw, Adriaan J. & Wohlrabe, Raymond A. Land & People of Holland. rev. ed. LC 79-37249. (Ports. of the Nations Ser.). (Illus.). (gr. 6 up). 1972. PLB 8.79 (ISBN 0-397-31254-7, JBL-J). Har-Row.

Carew, Dorothy. Netherlands. (Illus.). (gr. 7 up). 1965. 4.95g (ISBN 0-02-716500-0). Macmillan.

Loman, Anna. Looking at Holland. LC 66-10905. (Illus.). 64p. 1966. 8.95 (ISBN 0-397-30893-0, JBL-J). Har-Row.

Sterling Publishing Company Editors. Holland in Pictures. LC 62-18637. (Visual Geography Ser). (Illus., Orig.). (gr. 6 up). 1962. PLB 4.99 (ISBN 0-8069-1033-X); pap. 2.95 (ISBN 0-8069-1032-1). Sterling.

NETHERLANDS-POLITICS AND GOVERNMENT

Attitudes of the Dutch Population on Alternative Life Styles & Environmental Deterioration. 40p. pap. 5.00 (ISBN 92-808-0138-4, TUNU 065, UNU). Unipub.

Eldersveld, Samuel J., et al. Elite Images of Dutch Politics: Accommodation & Conflict. 296p. 1981. text ed. 16.50 (ISBN 0-472-10009-2). U of Mich Pr.

Heunks, Felix. Dutch Election Study, 1970-1973. LC 75-41583. 1976. codebk. 26.00 (ISBN 0-89138-124-4). ICPSR.

Lijphart, Arend. The Politics of Accommodation: Pluralism & Democracy in the Netherlands. new ed. 1976. 24.00x (ISBN 0-520-02918-6); pap. 7.95x (ISBN 0-520-02900-3). U of Cal Pr.

Mokken, Robert J. & Roschar, Frans M. Dutch Parliamentary Election Study, 1971. LC 75-32254. 650p. 1975. codebk. 24.00 (ISBN 0-89138-118-X). ICPSR.

Overbury, Thomas. Sir T. Overbury His Observations in His Travailes. LC 70-26399. (English Experience Ser.: No. 154). 28p. 1969. Repr. of 1626 ed. 7.00 (ISBN 90-221-0154-1). Walter J Johnson.

NETHERLANDS-RELATIONS (GENERAL) WITH FOREIGN COUNTRIES

Dickman, Ilka D. Appointment to Newfoundland. 1981. pap. 6.00 (ISBN 0-89745-018-3). Sunflower U Pr.

Duke, A. C. & Tamse, C. A., eds. Britain & the Netherlands: War and Society. (Britain & the Netherland Ser: Vol. VI.). 1977. lib. bdg. 26.00 (ISBN 90-247-2012-5, Pub. by Martinus Nijhoff Netherlands). Kluwer Boston.

NETHERLANDS-SOCIAL CONDITIONS

De Vries, Jan. The Dutch Rural Economy in the Golden Age: 1500-1700. LC 73-86889. (Economic History Ser). (Illus.). 326p. 1974. 25.00x (ISBN 0-300-01608-5). Yale U Pr.

Goudsblom, Johan. Dutch Society. 1966. pap. text ed. 2.95 (ISBN 0-394-30771-2). Phila Bk Co.

Hofstee, E. W. Rural Life & Rural Welfare in the Netherlands: Division of Documentation, Ministry of Agriculture, Fisheries & Food. LC 77-87697. (Illus.). Repr. of 1957 ed. 47.50 (ISBN 0-404-16493-5). AMS Pr.

Moors, H. G., et al, eds. Population & Family in the Low Countries, No. 2. (Publication of NIDI & CBGS: Vol. 6). 1978. pap. 17.00 (ISBN 90-207-0687-X, Pub. by Martinus Nijhoff Netherlands). Kluwer Boston.

--Population & Family in the Low Countries, No. 1. 1976. pap. 21.00 (ISBN 90-247-1859-7, Pub. by Martinus Nijhoff Netherlands). Kluwer Boston.

Moors, Hein G. Child Spacing & Family Size in the Netherlands. 1974. pap. 18.00 (ISBN 90-207-0491-5, Pub. by Martinus Nijhoff Netherlands). Kluwer Boston.

NETHERLANDS-SOCIAL LIFE AND CUSTOMS

Attitudes of the Dutch Population on Alternative Life Styles & Environmental Deterioration. 40p. pap. 5.00 (ISBN 92-808-0138-4, TUNU 065, UNU). Unipub.

Blanken, M. C. Force of Order & Methods... (1976) An American View into the Dutch Directed Society. (Studies in Social Life: Vol. 19). pap. 22.50 (ISBN 9-0247-1849-X). Heinman.

De Josselin De Jong, P. E., ed. Structural Anthropology in the Netherlands. (Translation Ser.: No. 17). (Illus.). 1977. pap. 31.00 (ISBN 90-247-1944-5, Pub. by Martinus Nijhoff Netherlands). Kluwer Boston.

Huizinga, J. Waning of the Middle Ages. LC 54-4529. pap. 3.95 (ISBN 0-385-09288-1, A42, Anch). Doubleday.

Huizinga, Johan. Waning of the Middle Ages: Study of the Forms of Life, Thought & Art in France & the Netherlands in the 14th & 15th Centuries. (Illus.). 1924. 25.00 (ISBN 0-312-85540-0). St Martin.

NETHERLANDS WEST INDIES

Boeke, Julius H. The Structure of the Netherlands Indian Economy. LC 75-30047. (Institute of Pacific Relations). Repr. of 1942 ed. 16.50 (ISBN 0-404-59509-X). AMS Pr.

Bousquet, Georges H. A French View of the Netherlands Indies. Lilienthal, Philip E., tr. from Fr. LC 75-30048. (Institute of Pacific Relations). Repr. of 1940 ed. 12.50 (ISBN 0-404-59510-3). AMS Pr.

Goslinga, Cornelis C. A Short History of the Netherlands Antilles & Surinam. 1978. pap. 20.00 (ISBN 90-247-2118-0, Pub. by Martinus Nijhoff Netherlands). Kluwer Boston.

Van De Poll, Willem. The Netherlands West Indies: A Pictorial Guide to Curacao, Aruba, St. Martin, Bonaire, Saba & St. Eustace. (Studies in the Caribbean). 1980. lib. bdg. 69.95 (ISBN 0-8490-3068-4). Gordon Pr.

Van Der Meer, S. W. Corporate Law of the Netherlands & of the Netherlands Antilles. 7th ed. viii, 128p. 1980. lib. bdg. 15.00 (ISBN 90-2711-632-6, Pub. by Kluwer Law Netherlands). Kluwer Boston.

NETHERLANDS WEST INDIES COMPANY

Bachman, Van Cleaf. Peltries or Plantations: The Economic Policies of the Dutch West India Company in New Netherland, 1623-1639. LC 74-91336. (Studies in Historical & Political Science: Eighty-Seventh Series No. 1 (1969)). 292p. 1970. 18.50x (ISBN 0-8018-1064-7). Johns Hopkins.

Furber, Holden. John Company at Work. LC 70-96181. 1969. Repr. lib. bdg. 24.00x (ISBN 0-374-92945-9). Octagon.

Murphy, Henry C. Henry Hudson in Holland: An Inquiry into the Origin & Objects of the Voyage Which Led to the Discovery of the Hudson River. LC 72-85105. xii, 150p. 1972. Repr. of 1909 ed. lib. bdg. 17.50 (ISBN 0-8337-2489-4). B Franklin.

NETS

Garner, John. How to Make & Set Nets. 1978. 15.00 (ISBN 0-685-63427-2). State Mutual Bk.

Graumont, Raoul & Wenstrom, Elmer. Fisherman's Knots & Nets. LC 48-423. (Illus.). 1948. pap. 6.50 (ISBN 0-87033-024-1). Cornell Maritime.

Klust, Gerhard. Netting Materials for Fishing Gear. 1978. 19.50 (ISBN 0-685-63444-2). State Mutual Bk.

Libert, L. & Maucoips, A. Mending of Fishing Nets. 1978. 12.95 (ISBN 0-685-63435-3). State Mutual Bk.

Mending of Fishing Nets. (FAO Fishing Manuals). (Illus.). 102p. (Orig.). 1974. pap. 10.00 (ISBN 0-85238-062-3, FAO). Unipub.

NETSUKES

Barker, Richard & Smith, Lawrence. Netsuke: The Miniature Sculpture of Japan. (British Museum Publications Ser.). (Illus.). 1977. o. p. 29.95 (ISBN 0-8120-5182-3). Barron.

Brockhous, Albert. Netsukes. LC 71-78364. (Illus.). 1969. Repr. of 1924 ed. 25.00 (ISBN 0-87817-025-1). Hacker.

Bushell, Raymond. Collectors' Netsuke: An in Depth Study of Japanese Miniature Sculptures. LC 70-139687. (Illus.). 200p. 1971. 45.00 (ISBN 0-8348-0056-X). Weatherhill.

--Introduction to Netsuke. LC 78-147176. (Illus.). 1971. 6.50 (ISBN 0-8048-0905-4). C E Tuttle.

--Netsuke Familiar & Unfamiliar. LC 75-22420. (Illus.). 256p. 1976. 75.00 (ISBN 0-8348-0115-9). Weatherhill.

--Wonderful World of Netsuke. LC 64-24948. (Illus.). 1964. 8.50 (ISBN 0-8048-0631-4). C E Tuttle.

Davey, Neil K. Netsuke: A Comprehensive Study Based on the M. T. Hindson Collection. (Illus.). 580p. 1974. 120.00 (ISBN 0-85667-013-8, Pub. by Sotheby Park Bernet England). Biblio Dist.

Hibbs, Michele & Altman, H. B. A Guide to Collecting & Selling Netsuke. LC 77-7060. 1977. 2.50 (ISBN 0-87576-061-9). Pilot Bks.

Hurtig, Bernard, ed. Masterpieces of Netsuke Art. LC 73-3202. (Illus.). 256p. 1973. 125.00 (ISBN 0-8348-0085-3). Weatherhill.

Jonas, F. M. Netsuke. LC 60-11840. (Illus.). 1960. 13.50 (ISBN 0-8048-0422-2). C E Tuttle.

Kinsey, Miriam. Contemporary Netsuke. LC 77-72596. (Illus.). 1978. 42.50 (ISBN 0-8048-1159-8). C E Tuttle.

Lazarnick, George. Netsuke & Lacquer Artists, & How to Read Their Signatures, 2. 1981. Set. write for info. (ISBN 0-917064-02-X, Pub by Reed Books Australia). Vol. 1 (ISBN 0-917064-03-8). Vol. 2 (ISBN 0-917064-04-6). C E Tuttle.

--The Signature Book of Netsuke, Inro & Ojime Artists in Photographs. LC 76-9504. 1976. 85.00 (ISBN 0-917064-01-1). Reed Pubs.

O'Brien, Mary L. Netsuke: A Guide for Collectors. LC 65-11837. (Illus.). 1965. 29.50 (ISBN 0-8048-0423-0). C E Tuttle.

Ueda, Reikichi. Netsuke Handbook of Ueda Reikichi. Bushell, Raymond, tr. LC 61-8139. (Illus.). 1961. 22.50 (ISBN 0-8048-0424-9). C E Tuttle.

NETTING

Garner, John. How to Make & Set Nets: The Technology of Netting. (Illus.). 96p. 15.00 (ISBN 0-85238-031-3, FN 53, FNB). Unipub.

Holdgate, Charles. Net Making. LC 72-84056. (Illus.). (gr. 7 up). 1972. 8.95 (ISBN 0-87523-180-2). Emerson.

Klust, Gerhard. Netting Materials for Fishing Gear. (Illus.). 184p. 13.25 (ISBN 0-85238-060-7, FN 26, FNB). Unipub.

Thomson, David. The Seine Net: Its Origin, Evolution & Use. 13.25 (ISBN 0-686-70988-8, FN 22, FNB). Unipub.

Waller, Irene. Knots & Netting. LC 76-55911. (Illus.). 1977. 8.95 (ISBN 0-8008-4484-X). Taplinger.

NETWORK ANALYSIS (PLANNING)

see also PERT (Network Analysis)

Ahuja, H. N. Construction Performance Control by Networks. LC 76-4774. (Construction Management & Engineering Ser.). 688p. 1976. 46.00 (ISBN 0-471-00960-1, Pub. by Wiley-Interscience). Wiley.

Barr, R. S., et al. Enhancements of Spanning Tree Labeling Procedures for Network Optimization. 1977. 2.50 (ISBN 0-686-64192-2). U CO Busn Res Div.

Bazaraa, Mokhtar S. & Jarvis, John J. Linear Programming & Network Flows. LC 76-42241. 565p. 1977. text ed. 32.95 (ISBN 0-471-06015-1). Wiley.

Boesch, Francis T., ed. Large-Scale Networks: Theory & Design. LC 75-25324. 1976. 28.95 (ISBN 0-87942-063-4). Inst Electrical.

Burman, P. J. Precedence Networks for Project Planning & Control. 20.00 (ISBN 0-9606344-0-1). Blitz Pub Co.

Elmaghraby, F. E. Activity Networks: Project Planning & Control by Network Models. LC 77-9501. 443p. 1977. 41.95 (ISBN 0-471-23869-4, Pub. by Wiley-Interscience). Wiley.

Elmaghraby, S. E. Some Network Models in Management Science. (Lecture Notes in Operations Research & Mathematical Systems: Vol. 29). 1970. pap. 10.90 (ISBN 0-387-04952-5). Springer-Verlag.

Faulkner, Edward E. Project Management with CPM. 3rd. ed. (Illus.). 150p. 1973. spiral bdg. 14.50 (ISBN 0-911950-21-4). Means.

Glover, Fred & Mulvey, John M. Network-Related Scheduling Models for Problems with Quasi-Adjacency & Block Adjacency Structures. 1976. 2.50 (ISBN 0-686-64194-9). U CO Busn Res Div.

Greenberger, Martin, et al, eds. Networks for Research & Education: Sharing of Computer & Information Resources Nationwide. 1974. 16.00x (ISBN 0-262-07057-X). MIT Pr.

Hoare, H. R. Project Management Using Network Analysis. 1973. 19.95 (ISBN 0-07-084436-4, P&RB). McGraw.

Iri, M. Network Flow, Transportation & Scheduling: Theory & Algorithms. (Mathematics in Science & Engineering Ser., Vol. 57). 1969. 54.00 (ISBN 0-12-373850-4). Acad Pr.

Kochhar, A. K. Development of Computer-Based Production Systems. LC 79-902. 274p. 1979. 42.95 (ISBN 0-470-26693-7). Halsted Pr.

Lawler, Eugene L. Combinatorial Optimization Networks & Matroids. LC 76-13516. 1976. text ed. 30.95 (ISBN 0-03-084866-0, HoltC). HR&W.

Mandl, Christoph. Applied Network Optimization. LC 79-40808. 1980. 31.00 (ISBN 0-686-75174-4). Acad Pr.

Moore, Laurence J. & Clayton, Edward R. Gert Modeling & Simulation. (Modern Decision Analysis Ser.). (Illus.). 230p. 1976. 17.95x (ISBN 0-442-80328-1). Van Nos Reinhold.

Newell, G. F. Traffic Flow on Transportation Networks. (MIT Press Series Intransportation Studies: No. 5). (Illus.). 288p. 1980. 30.00x (ISBN 0-262-14032-2). MIT Pr.

Nineteen Seventy Six 5th World Congress. Internet: Proceedings. (Illus.). 322p. 1976. pap. 110.00x (ISBN 0-85012-182-5). Intl Pubns Serv.

Offler, F. Networks Explained: A Course in Network Analysis. (Illus.). 1977. 35.00x (ISBN 0-85012-174-4). Intl Pubns Serv.

Phillips, Don T. & Garcia-Diaz, Alberto. Fundamentals of Network Analysis. (Illus.). 496p. 1981. text ed. 26.95 (ISBN 0-13-341552-X). P-H.

Reynaud, C. B. Critical Path: Network Analysis & Resource Scheduling. 2nd ed. 1970. text ed. 17.50x (ISBN 0-7121-3301-1). Intl Ideas.

Schnackenberg, J. Thermodynamic Network Analysis of Biological Systems. (Universitext Ser.). (Illus.). 150p. 1981. pap. 24.80 (ISBN 0-387-10612-X). Springer-Verlag.

Walton, H., ed. Programs for Network Analysis. LC 76-360389. 50p. 1974. pap. 22.50x (ISBN 0-85012-124-8). Intl Pubns Serv.

Whitehouse, Gary E. Systems Analysis & Design Using Network Techniques. (Industrial & Systems Engineering Ser). (Illus.). 464p. (Reference ed.). 1973. 27.95 (ISBN 0-13-881474-0). P-H.

Woodgate, H. S. Planning by Network. 330p. 1977. text ed. 24.50x (ISBN 0-220-66312-2, Pub. by Busn Bks England). Renouf.

NETWORK ANALYZERS

see Electric Network Analyzers

NETWORK THEORY

see Electric Networks; System Analysis

NETWORKS, ELECTRIC

see Electric Networks

NETWORKS OF LIBRARIES

see Library Information Networks

NEUMANN, JOHN NEPOMUCENE, BP. 1811-1860

Douglas, Philip. Sajnt of Philadelphia: The Life of Bishop John Neumann. 1977. 7.95 (ISBN 0-911218-07-6); pap. 3.50 (ISBN 0-911218-08-4). Ravengate Pr.

Hindman, Jane F. An Ordinary Saint, John Neumann. 1977. pap. 1.95 (ISBN 0-685-67952-7). Arena Lettres.

Ready, Dolores. A Traveler for God: A Story About John Neumann. (Stories About Christian Heroes Ser). (gr. 1-5). 1977. pap. 1.95 (ISBN 0-03-022111-0). Winston Pr.

Rush, Alfred C., ed. Autobiography of St. John Neumann. 1977. 3.50 (ISBN 0-8198-0384-7); pap. 2.50 (ISBN 0-8198-0385-5). Dghtrs St Paul.

NEUMANN, THERESA

Carty, Charles M. Who Is Teresa Neumann? 1974. pap. 1.00 (ISBN 0-89555-093-8, 156). TAN Bks Pubs.

Steiner, Johannes. Therese Neumann. LC 66-27536. (Illus.). 1967. pap. 4.50 (ISBN 0-8189-0144-6). Alba.

Vogl, Albert. Life & Death of Therese Neumann: Mystic & Stigmatist. 1978. 7.50 (ISBN 0-533-03379-9). Vantage.

NEUMANN ALGEBRAS

see Von Neumann Algebras

NEURAL TISSUE

see Nerve Tissue

NEURAL TRANSMISSION

Adrian, R. H. The Nerve Impulse. 2nd, rev. ed. Head, J. J., ed. LC 78-54975. (Carolina Biology Readers Ser.). 16p. 1981. pap. text ed. 1.65 (ISBN 0-89278-267-6, 45-9667). Carolina Biologial.

Ajmone-Marson, Cosimo, et al, eds. Neuropeptides & Neural Transmission. (International Brain Research Organization (IBRO) Monograph: Vol. 7). 412p. 1980. text ed. 45.50 (ISBN 0-89004-501-1). Raven.

Bacq, Z. M. Chemical Transmission of Nerve Impulses: A Historical Sketch. 1975. text ed. 27.00 (ISBN 0-08-020512-7). Pergamon.

Bennett, M. V., ed. Synaptic Transmission & Neuronal Interaction. LC 73-83886. (Society of General Physiologists Ser: Vol. 28). 401p. 1974. 34.50 (ISBN 0-911216-56-1). Raven.

Berl, Soll, et al, eds. Metabolic Compartmentation & Neurotransmission: Relation to Brain Structure & Function. (Illus.). 721p. 1975. 49.50 (ISBN 0-306-35606-6, Plenum Pr). Plenum Pub.

Bradley, P. B. & Dhawan, B. N., eds. Drugs & Central Synaptic Transmission. 1976. 49.50 (ISBN 0-8391-0942-3). Univ Park.

Ceccarelli, Bruno & Clementi, Francesco, eds. Neurotoxins: Tools in Neurobiology. LC 78-57244. (Advances in Cytopharmacology Ser.: Vol. 3). 1979. text ed. 49.00 (ISBN 0-89004-303-5). Raven.

Choux, M., ed. Shunts & Problems in Shunts. (Monographs in Neural Sciences: Vol. 8). (Illus.). 250p. 1981. pap. 90.00 (ISBN 3-8055-2465-X). S Karger.

Davidson, Neil. Neurotransmitter Amino Acids. 1976. 26.00 (ISBN 0-12-205950-6). Acad Pr.

Edelman, Gerald M. & Mountcastle, Vernon B. The Mindful Brain: Cortical Organization & the Group - Selective Theory of Higher Brain Function. 1978. text ed. 10.00x (ISBN 0-262-05020-X). MIT Pr.

Essman, Walter B., ed. Neurotransmitters, Receptors, & Drug Action. LC 79-23862. (Illus.). 220p. 1980. text ed. 35.00 (ISBN 0-89335-108-3). Spectrum Pub.

Feldman, J., et al, eds. Receptors & Recognition, Ser. B, Vol. 2: Intercellular Junctions & Synapses. 246p. 1976. text ed. 37.95x (ISBN 0-412-14820-X, Pub. by Chapman & Hall England). Methuen Inc.

Fonnum, Frade, ed. Amino Acids As Chemical Transmitters. LC 78-2362. (NATO Advanced Study Institutes Ser.: Series A, Life Sciences, Vol. 16). 759p. 1978. 49.50 (ISBN 0-306-35616-3, Plenum Pr). Plenum Pub.

Gispen, W. H. Molecular & Functional Neurobiology. 1976. 85.50 (ISBN 0-444-41365-0, North Holland). Elsevier.

Goldberg, Alan M. & Hanin, Israel, eds. Biology of Cholinergic Function. LC 74-14473. 730p. 1976. 48.00 (ISBN 0-911216-98-7). Raven.

Granit, Ragnar. Receptors and Sensory Perception. LC 75-14597. (Mrs. Hepsa Ely Silliman Memorial Lectures). (Illus.). 369p. 1975. Repr. of 1955 ed. lib. bdg. 21.75x (ISBN 0-8371-8213-1, GRRS). Greenwood.

Heimer, L. & Robards, M. J., eds. Neuroanatomical Tract-Tracing Methods. 540p. 1981. 49.50 (ISBN 0-306-40593-8, Plenum Pr). Plenum Pub.

Hockman, C. Chemical Transmission in the Mammalian Central Nervous System. (Illus.). 1976. 44.50 (ISBN 0-8391-0863-X). Univ Park.

Hungarian Pharmacological Society, 3rd Congress, Budapest, 1979. Modulation of Neurochemical Transmission: Proceedings. Knoll, J. & Vizi, E. S., eds. LC 80-41281. (Advances in Pharmacological Research & Practice Ser.: Vol. II). (Illus.). 450p. 1981. 84.00 (ISBN 0-08-026387-9). Pergamon.

Iggo, A. & Ilyinsky, B. Somatosensory & Visceral Receptor Mechanism. (Progress in Brain Research: Vol. 43). 1976. 68.50 (ISBN 0-444-41342-1, North Holland). Elsevier.

International Society for Neurovegatative Research-Tinany-1972. Neurovegetative Transmission Mechanisms: Proceedings. Csillik, B. & Kappers, J. A., eds. (Journal of Neural Transmission: Suppl. 11). (Illus.). 350p. 1974. 91.50 (ISBN 0-387-81173-7). Springer Verlag.

Kharkevich, D. A., ed. Pharmacology of Ganglionic Transmission. LC 79-9406. (Handbook of Experimental Pharmacology: Vol. 53). (Illus.). 1980. 141.50 (ISBN 0-387-09592-6). Springer-Verlag.

Kopin, Irwin J., ed. Neurotransmitters. LC 72-75942. (ARNMD Research Publications Ser: Vol. 50). 565p. 1972. 34.50 (ISBN 0-683-00244-9). Raven.

Kruk, Z. L. & Pycock, C. J. Neurotransmitters & Drug. 160p. 1980. 35.00x (ISBN 0-85664-865-5, Pub. by Croom Helm England). State Mutual Bk.

Legg, N., ed. Neurotransmitter Systems & Their Clinical Disorders. 1979. 23.00 (ISBN 0-12-443050-3). Acad Pr.

Moore, John W., ed. Membranes, Ions, & Impulses. LC 76-13841. (FASEB Monographs: Vol. 5). 195p. 1976. 25.00 (ISBN 0-306-34505-6, Plenum Pr). Plenum Pub.

Myers, R. D. & Drucker-Colin, R. R., eds. Neurohumoral Coding of Brain Function. LC 74-7408. (Advances in Behavioral Biology Ser.: Vol. 10). 480p. 1974. 39.50 (ISBN 0-306-37910-4, Plenum Pr). Plenum Pub.

Pycock, C. J. & Taberner, P. V., eds. Central Neurotransmitters Turnover. 197p. 1981. text ed. 39.50 (ISBN 0-8391-1644-6). Univ Park.

Satellite Symposium on Maturational Aspects of Neurotransmission Mechanisms, Saint-Vincent, August 1977. Maturation of Neurotransmission: Proceedings. Vernadakis, Antonia, et al, eds. (Illus.). 1978. 46.75 (ISBN 3-8055-2833-7). S Karger.

Shute, C. D. The McCollough Effect. LC 78-15609. (Illus.). 1979. 32.95 (ISBN 0-521-22395-4). Cambridge U Pr.

Smorto, M. P. & Basmajian, John V. Clinical Electroneurography: An Introduction to Nerve Conduction Tests. 2nd ed. 1979. 27.95 (ISBN 0-683-07812-7). Williams & Wilkins.

Szekely, Gy., et al, eds. Neural Communication & Control: Satellite Symposium of the 28th International Congress of Physiological Sciences, Debrechen, Hungary, 1980. (Advances in Physiological Sciences: Vol. 30). (Illus.). 350p. 1981. 35.00 (ISBN 0-08-027351-3). Pergamon.

Thompson, Richard F., et al, eds. Neural Mechanisms of Goal-Directed Behavior & Learning. LC 79-6775. 1980. 49.50 (ISBN 0-12-688980-5). Acad Pr.

Torda, Clara. A Depolarization-Repolarization Cycle: A Molecular Model. (Illus.). 100p. 1972. 5.50 (ISBN 0-686-14970-X, 430426). W Torda.

Triggle, D. J. & Triggle, C. R. Chemical Pharmacology of the Synapse. 1977. 92.50 (ISBN 0-12-700340-1). Acad Pr.

NEURAL TUBE

Crandall, B. F. & Brazier, A. B, eds. Prevention of Neural Tube Defects: the Role of Alpha-Feto-Protein. (UCLA Forum in Medicinal Sciences: Vol. 20). 1978. 21.50 (ISBN 0-12-195350-5). Acad Pr.

NEURALGIA

Hirsch, C. Cervical Pain. Zotterman, Y., ed. 232p. 1972. text ed. 50.00 (ISBN 0-08-016875-2). Pergamon.

White, James C. & Sweet, William H. Pain & the Neurosurgeon: A Forty-Year Experience. (Illus.). 1032p. 1969. text ed. 52.75 (ISBN 0-398-02058-2). C C Thomas.

NEURALGIA, SCIATIC

see Sciatica

NEURASTHENIA

see also Depression, Mental

Beard, G. M. Practical Treatise on Nervous Exhaustion (Neurasthenia) Its Symptoms, Nature, Sequences, Treatment. 5th enl. ed. Rockwell, A. D., ed. Repr. of 1905 ed. 18.00 (ISBN 0-527-06340-1). Kraus Repr.

Beard, George M. American Nervousness, Its Causes & Consequences: A Supplement to Nervous Exhaustion. LC 72-180552. (Medicine & Society in America Ser). 382p. 1972. Repr. of 1881 ed. 18.00 (ISBN 0-405-03932-8). Arno.

--Sexual Neurasthenia, Its Hygiene, Causes, Symptoms & Treatment with a Chapter on Diet for the Nervous. 5th ed. Rockwell, A. D., ed. LC 76-180553. (Medicine & Society in America Ser). 312p. 1972. Repr. of 1898 ed. 15.00 (ISBN 0-405-03933-6). Arno.

Myerson, Abraham. The Nervous Housewife. LC 72-2616. (American Women Ser: Images & Realities). 278p. 1972. Repr. of 1927 ed. 14.00 (ISBN 0-405-04470-4). Arno.

NEUROANATOMY

Angevine, Jay B., Jr. & Cotman, Carl W. Principles of Neuroanatomy. (Illus.). 300p. 1981. 29.95x (ISBN 0-19-502885-6); pap. 16.95 (ISBN 0-19-502886-4). Oxford U Pr.

Augustine, James R. Medical Neuroanatomy. (Illus.). 500p. Date not set. price not set (ISBN 0-8121-0801-9). Lea & Febiger.

Carpenter, Malcolm B. Core Text of Neuroanatomy. 2nd ed. (Illus.). 354p. 1978. pap. 17.50 (ISBN 0-683-01453-6). Williams & Wilkins.

--Human Neuroanatomy. 7th ed. 741p. 1976. 39.95 (ISBN 0-683-01460-9). Williams & Wilkins.

Chusid, Joseph G. Correlative Neuroanatomy & Functional Neurology. 17th ed. LC 78-71797. (Illus.). 464p. 1979. lexotone cover 12.00 (ISBN 0-87041-011-3). Lange.

Crosby, Elizabeth C., et al, eds. Comparative Correlative Neuroanatomy of the Vertebrate Telencephalon. Carey, Joshua. (Illus.). 1981. text ed. 65.00 (ISBN 0-02-325690-7). Macmillan.

DeLahunta, Alexander. Veterinary Neuroanatomy & Clinical Neurology. LC 76-4246. (Illus.). 1977. text ed. 24.50 (ISBN 0-7216-3024-3). Saunders.

DeLisa, Joel A. & Mackenzie, Keith. Manual of Nerve Conduction Velocity Techniques. 1981. text ed. 12.50 (ISBN 0-89004-656-5). Raven.

Dublin, William B. & Dublin, Arthur B. Atlas of Neuroanatomy for Radiologists: Surface & Sectional-with CT Scanning Correlation. (Illus.). 250p. 1981. 37.50 (ISBN 0-87527-204-5). Green.

Everett, N. B. Functional Neuroanatomy. 6th ed. LC 70-135680. (Illus.). 357p. 1971. text ed. 14.50 (ISBN 0-8121-0324-6). Lea & Febiger.

Folk, Dean. External Neuroanatomy of Old World Monkeys (Cercopithecoidea) Szalay, F. S., ed. (Contributions to Primatology: Vol. 15). (Illus.). 1978. 35.50 (ISBN 3-8055-2834-5). S Karger.

Frontera, Jose G. Neuroanatomy Laboratory Guide. pap. 6.25 (ISBN 0-8477-2310-0). U of PR Pr.

Garoutte, Bill. A Survey of Functional Neuroanatomy. LC 80-84809. (Illus.). 217p. 1981. pap. text ed. 9.75x (ISBN 0-930010-04-3). Jones Med.

Gilman, Sid & Winans, Sarah. Manter & Gatz's Essentials of Clinical Neuroanatomy & Neurophysiology. 6th ed. (Illus.). 225p. Date not set. pap. 10.95 (ISBN 0-8036-4155-9). Davis Co.

Gispen, W. H. & Van Wimersma, Greidanus, eds. Hormones Homeostasis & the Brain. Bohus, B., tr. (Progress in Brain Research Ser.: Vol. 42). 400p. 1975. 83.00 (ISBN 0-444-41300-6, North Holland). Elsevier.

Goldberg, Stephen. Clinical Neuroanatomy Made Ridiculously Simple. (Illus.). 89p. (Orig.). pap. text ed. 9.95 (ISBN 0-940780-00-3). MedMaster.

Greengard, Paul. Cyclic Nucleotides, Phosphorylated Proteins, & Neuronal Function. LC 78-66349. (Distinguished Lecture Series of the Society of General Physiologists). 302p. 1978. 15.00 (ISBN 0-89004-281-0). Raven.

Hausman, Louis. Clinical Neuroanatomy, Neurophysiology & Neurology: With a Method of Brain Reconstruction. rev. 3rd ed. (Illus.). 484p. 1971. text ed. 31.75 lexotone (ISBN 0-398-00803-5). C C Thomas.

--Clinical Neuroanatomy with a Method of Brain Reconstruction. 120p. 1963. photocopy ed. spiral 14.75 (ISBN 0-398-04273-X). C C Thomas.

Heimer, L. & Robards, M. J., eds. Neuroanatomical Tract-Tracing Methods. 540p. 1981. 49.50 (ISBN 0-306-40593-8, Plenum Pr). Plenum Pub.

House, E. Lawrence, et al. A Systematic Approach to Neuroscience. 3rd ed. (Illus.). 1979. text ed. 27.00 (ISBN 0-07-030468-8, HP). McGraw.

Ingram, W. A Review of Anatomical Neurology. (Illus.). 1976. 19.50 (ISBN 0-8391-0961-X). Univ Park.

Jenkins, Thomas W. Functional Mammalian Neuroanatomy: With Emphasis on the Dog and Cat, Including an Atlas of the Central Nervous System of the Dog. 2nd ed. LC 77-17308. (Illus.). 480p. 1978. text ed. 24.50 (ISBN 0-8121-0627-X). Lea & Febiger.

Krieger, Dorothy T., ed. Endocrine Rhythms: Comprehensive Endocrinology. LC 77-75655. 344p. 1979. 34.50 (ISBN 0-89004-234-9). Raven.

Lindsay, Robert, ed. Computer Analysis of Neuronal Structures. LC 76-50605. (Computers in Biology & Medicine Ser.). (Illus.). 210p. 1977. 27.50 (ISBN 0-306-30964-5, Plenum Pr). Plenum Pub.

Lissak, K., ed. Results in Neuroanatomy, Motor Organization, Cerebral Circulation & Modelling: Recent Developments in Neurobiology in Hungary, Vol. VIII. 1981. 60.00x (ISBN 0-569-08549-7, Pub. by Collet's). State Mutual Bk.

--Results in Neuroanatomy, Motor Organization, Cerebral Circulation & Modelling. (Recent Developments of Neurobiology in Hungary Ser.: Vol. 8). (Illus.). 243p. 1979. 25.00x (ISBN 963-05-1594-6). Intl Pubns Serv.

--Results in Neuroanatomy, Motor Organization, Cerebral Circulation and Modelling. (Recent Developments of Neurobiology in Hungary: Vol. 8). 1979. 24.00 (ISBN 0-9960011-1-5, Pub. by Kaido Hungary). Heyden.

Lockard, L. Desk Reference for Neuroanatomy: A Guide to Essential Terms. LC 77-21707. 1977. 16.40 (ISBN 0-387-90278-3). Springer Verlag.

Martinez & Martinez. Neuroanatomy. 1981. text ed. write for info. (ISBN 0-7216-6147-5). Saunders.

Matzke, Howard A. & Foltz, Floyd M. Synopsis of Neuroanatomy. 3rd ed. (Illus.). 1979. pap. text ed. 6.95x (ISBN 0-19-502551-2). Oxford U Pr.

Meisami, Esmail & Brazier, Mary A. Neural Growth & Differentiation. (International Brain Research Organization Monographs: Vol. 5). 546p. 1979. text ed. 52.00 (ISBN 0-89004-378-7). Raven.

Miller, Richard A. & Burack, Ethel. Atlas of the Central Nervous System in Man. 2nd ed. (Illus.). 150p. 1977. 21.00 (ISBN 0-683-06127-5). Williams & Wilkins.

Miller, Richard A. & Burack, Ethel M. Atlas of the Central Nervous System in Man. 3rd. ed. (Illus.). 208p. 1981. text ed. 22.95 (ISBN 0-683-05933-5). Williams & Wilkins.

Mitchell, George & Mayor, Donald. Essentials of Neuroanatomy. 3rd ed. LC 77-3105. (Illus.). 1977. pap. text ed. 8.75 (ISBN 0-443-01449-3). Churchill.

Moyer, K. E. Neuroanatomy: Text & Illustration. 1980. pap. text ed. 19.50 scp (ISBN 0-06-044639-0, HarpC). Har-Row.

Nieuwenhuys, R., et al. The Human Central Nervous System: A Pictorial Survey. (Illus.). 1978. pap. 26.40 (ISBN 0-387-08903-9). Springer-Verlag.

Pellegrino, L. J., et al. A Sterotaxic Atlas of the Rat Brain. 2nd ed. LC 79-9438. 279p. 1979. 22.50 (ISBN 0-306-40269-6, Plenum Pr). Plenum Pub.

Peters, Alan, et al. The Fine Structure of the Nervous System: The Neurons & Supporting Cells. LC 75-28797. (Illus.). 365p. 1976. text ed. 37.50 (ISBN 0-7216-7207-8). Saunders.

Reid, Cynthia. A Primer of Human Neuroanatomy. 1978. softcover 10.00 (ISBN 0-397-58237-4, JBL-Med-Nursing). Har-Row.

Robertson, Richard T., ed. Neuroanatomical Research Technique. (Methods in Physiological Psych. Ser.: Vol. 2). 1978. 43.00 (ISBN 0-12-590350-2). Acad Pr.

Smith, C. G. Basic Neuroanatomy. 2nd ed. 1971. 15.00x (ISBN 0-8020-2057-7). U of Toronto Pr.

Snell, Richard S. Clinical Neuroanatomy for Medical Students. 1980. text ed. 21.95 (ISBN 0-316-80213-1). Little.

Thalamocortical Organization of the Auditory System in the Cat: Studied by Retrograde Axonal Transport of Horseradish Peroxidase. (Advances in Anatomy, Embryology, & Cell Biology Ser.: Vol. 57). (Illus.). 1979. pap. 20.20 (ISBN 0-387-09449-0). Springer-Verlag.

Truex, R. C. & Carpenter, M. B. Human Neuroanatomy. 6th ed. 1981. 40.00x (ISBN 0-686-72952-8, Pub. by Oxford & IBH India). State Mutual Bk.

Verwoerd, C. D. A. & Van Oostrom, C. G. Cephalic Neural Crest & Placodes. (Advances in Anatomy, Embryology & Cell Biology: Vol. 58). (Illus.). 1980. 27.70 (ISBN 0-387-09608-6). Springer-Verlag.

Watson, Craig. Basic Human Neuroanatomy: An Introductory Atlas. 2nd ed. LC 74-128. (Illus.). 106p. 1977. pap. text ed. 9.95 (ISBN 0-316-92463-6). Little.

Wolf, John K. Classical Brain Stem Syndromes: Translations of the Original Papers with Notes on the Evolution of Clinical Neuroanatomy. (Illus.). 186p. 1971. text ed. 13.75 (ISBN 0-398-02170-8). C C Thomas.

Zilles, K. J. Ontogenesis of the Visual System. (Advances in Anatomy, Embryology & Cell Biology: Vol. 54, Pt. 3). (Illus.). 1978. pap. 27.50 (ISBN 0-387-08726-5). Springer-Verlag.

NEUROANATOMY-PROGRAMMED INSTRUCTION

Liebman, Michael. Neuroanatomy Made Easy & Understandable. 103p. pap. text ed. 9.95 (ISBN 0-8391-1513-X). Univ Park.

Sidman, Richard L. & Sidman, Murray. Neuroanatomy: A Programmed Text. 645p. spiral bdg. 18.95 (ISBN 0-316-78985-2). Little.

NEUROBIOLOGY

Aschoff, Jurgen, ed. Handbook of Behavioral Neurobiology: Biological Rythms, Vol. 4. 563p. 1981. 45.00 (ISBN 0-306-40585-7, Plenum Pr). Plenum Pub.

Bernstein, J. J. Neural Prostheses: Materials, Physiology & Histopathology of Electrical Stimulation of the Nervous System. (Brain, Behavior & Evolution: Vol. 14, No. 1-2). (Illus.). 1977. 44.50 (ISBN 3-8055-2640-7). S Karger.

Bradley, P. B., ed. Methods in Brain Research. LC 74-404. 557p. 1975. 93.00 (ISBN 0-471-09514-1, Pub. by Wiley-Interscience). Wiley.

Brodal, A. Neurological Anatomy in Relation to Clinical Medicine. 3rd ed. (Illus.). 1074p. 1981. text ed. 35.00x (ISBN 0-19-502694-2). Oxford U Pr.

Brown, Ian, ed. Molecular Approaches to Neurobiology. (Cell Biology Ser.). 1982. price not set (ISBN 0-12-137020-8). Acad Pr.
Brown, Paul B., ed. Computer Technology in Neuroscience. LC 76-6884. 1976. 28.95 (ISBN 0-470-15061-0). Halsted Pr.
Bullock, Theodore H., et al. Introduction to Nervous Systems. LC 76-3735. (Illus.). 1977. pap. text ed. 24.95x (ISBN 0-7167-0030-1). W H Freeman.
Caplan, David, ed. Biological Studies of Mental Processes. (Illus.). 1980. text ed. 24.95x (ISBN 0-262-03061-6). MIT Pr.
Chalmers, Neil, et al, eds. Biological Bases of Behavior. 1971. pap. text ed. 8.40 (ISBN 0-06-318007-3, IntlDept). Har-Row.
Chronister, R. B. & De France, J. F., eds. The Neurobiology of the Nuclear Accumbens. (Illus.). 380p. (Orig.). 1981. pap. 24.95 (ISBN 0-940090-00-7). Haer Inst.
Di Chiara, G. & Gessa, G. L., eds. Glutamate As a Neurotransmitter. (Advances in Biochemical Psychopharmacology Ser.: Vol. 27). 464p. 1981. text ed. 49.50 (ISBN 0-89004-420-1). Raven.
Ebadi, M. & Costa, E., eds. Role of Vitamin B-Six in Neurobiology. LC 73-84113. (Advances in Biochemical Psychopharmacology Ser.: Vol. 4). (Illus.). 248p. 1972. 24.50 (ISBN 0-911216-18-9). Raven.
Eccles, John C. The Understanding of the Brain. 2nd ed. (Illus.). 1976. pap. text ed. 8.50 (ISBN 0-07-018865-3, HP). McGraw.
Ehrenpreis, S. & Solnitsky, O., eds. Neurosciences Research. Incl. Vol. 1. 1968. 53.50 (ISBN 0-12-512501-1); Vol. 2. 1969. 53.50 (ISBN 0-12-512502-X); Vol. 3. 1970. 53.50 (ISBN 0-12-512503-8); Vol. 4. 1971. 53.50 (ISBN 0-12-512504-6); Vol. 5. 1973. 40.50 (ISBN 0-12-512505-4). 221.50 set (ISBN 0-685-30528-7). Acad Pr.
Eisenstein, Edward M., ed. Aneural Organisms. LC 74-28345. (Advances in Behavioral Biology Ser.: Vol. 13). 145p. 1975. 25.00 (ISBN 0-306-37913-9, Plenum Pr). Plenum Pub.
Faber, Donald & Korn, Henri, eds. Neurobiology of the Mauthner Cell. LC 78-66351. 302p. 1978. 31.50 (ISBN 0-89004-233-0). Raven.
Falkner, F. & Tanner, J. M., eds. Human Growth, Vol. 3: Neurobiology & Nutrition. 624p. 1979. 37.50 (ISBN 0-306-34463-7, Plenum Pr). Plenum Pub.
Federoff, S. & Hertz, L., eds. Advances in Cellular Neurobiology, Vol. 2. 1981. 49.00 (ISBN 0-12-008302-7). Acad Pr.
Fedoroff, S. & Hertz, Leif, eds. Cell, Tissue & Organ Cultures in Neurobiology. 1978. 40.50 (ISBN 0-12-250450-X). Acad Pr.
Gainer, Harold, ed. Peptides in Neurobiology. LC 76-54766. (Current Topics in Neurobiology: Vol. 2). (Illus.). 464p. 1977. 34.50 (ISBN 0-306-30978-5, Plenum Pr). Plenum Pub.
Garrod, D. R. & Feldman, J. D., eds. Development in the Nervous System. LC 80-42151. (British Society for Developmental Biology Symposium Ser.). (Illus.). 350p. Date not set. price not set (ISBN 0-521-23493-X). Cambridge U Pr.
Giacobini, Ezio, et al, eds. Tissue Culture in Neurobiology. 536p. 1980. text ed. 52.00 (ISBN 0-89004-461-9). Raven.
Gispen, W. H. Molecular & Functional Neurobiology. 1976. 85.50 (ISBN 0-444-41365-0, North Holland). Elsevier.
Griffith, J. S. Mathematical Neurobiology: An Introduction to the Mathematics of the Nervous System. 162p. 1971. 24.50 (ISBN 0-12-303050-1). Acad Pr.
Heiligenberg, W. Principles of Electrolocation & Jamming Avoidance in Electric Fish: A Neuroethological Approach. (Studies of Brain Functions: Vol. 1). (Illus.). 1977. pap. 13.30 (ISBN 0-387-08367-7). Springer-Verlag.
Heldman, E., et al, eds. Neurobiology of Cholinergic & Adrenergic Transmitters. (Monographs in Neural Sciences: Vol. 7). (Illus.). xvi, 200p. 1981. pap. 53.50 (ISBN 3-8055-0828-X). S Karger.
Himwich, Williamina A. Developmental Neurobiology. (Illus.). 788p. 1970. photocopy ed. spiral 68.75 (ISBN 0-398-00837-X). C C Thomas.
Horn, A. S., et al, eds. The Neurobiology of Dopamine. LC 78-72547. 1980. 136.00 (ISBN 0-12-354150-6). Acad Pr.
Icn-Ucla Symposium on Neurobiology, Squaw Valley, Cal., Mar. 1976. Cellular Neurobiology: Proceedings. Hall, Zach, et al, eds. LC 77-3386. (Progress in Clinical & Biological Research: Vol. 15). 340p. 1977. 44.00x (ISBN 0-8451-0015-7). A R Liss.
Jacobson, Marcus. Developmental Neurobiology. 2nd ed. LC 77-26068. (Illus.). 574p. 1978. 37.50 (ISBN 0-306-31075-9, Plenum Pr). Plenum Pub.
Kandel, Eric R. Cellular Basis of Behavior: An Introduction to Behavioral Neurobiology. LC 76-8277. (Psychology Ser.). (Illus.). 1976. text ed. 56.00x (ISBN 0-7167-0523-0); pap. text ed. 27.95x (ISBN 0-7167-0522-2). W H Freeman.
Kater, S. B. & Nicholson, C., eds. Intracellular Staining in Neurobiology. LC 73-77837. (Illus.). 332p. 1973. 32.90 (ISBN 0-387-06261-0). Springer-Verlag.
Kerkut, G. A. Progress in Neurobiology, Vol. 12. (Illus.). 312p. 1980. 103.00 (ISBN 0-08-024888-8). Pergamon.
Kerkut, G. A., ed. Progress in Neurobiology, Vol. 13, Complete. (Illus.). 440p. 1980. pap. 103.00 (ISBN 0-08-026039-X). Pergamon.
Kerkut, G. A. & Phillis, J. W., eds. Progress in Neurobiology, Vols. 1-9. Incl. Vol. 1. pap. 20.00 ea.; Vol. 1, Pt. 1. pap. (ISBN 0-08-017044-7); Pt. 2. pap. (ISBN 0-08-017187-7); Pt. 3. pap. (ISBN 0-08-017650-X); Pt. 4. pap. (ISBN 0-08-017661-5); Vol. 1. Complete (cloth) 62.50 (ISBN 0-686-57467-2); Vol. 2. pap. 20.00 ea.; Vol. 2, Pt. 1. pap. (ISBN 0-08-017688-7); Pt. 2. pap. (ISBN 0-08-017752-2); Pt. 3. pap. (ISBN 0-08-017812-X); Pt. 4. pap. (ISBN 0-08-017929-0); Vol. 2. Complete (cloth) 97.00 (ISBN 0-08-017882-0); Vol. 3. pap. 20.00 ea.; Vol. 3, Pt. 1. pap. (ISBN 0-08-017956-8); Pt. 2. pap. (ISBN 0-08-018009-4); Pt. 3. pap. (ISBN 0-08-018023-X); Pt. 4. pap. (ISBN 0-08-018092-2); Vol. 3 Complete. (cloth) 97.00 (ISBN 0-08-017963-0); Vol. 4. Pt. 1. pap. 16.25 (ISBN 0-08-018093-0); Pt. 2. pap. 24.00 (ISBN 0-08-018127-9); Pt. 3. pap. 20.00 (ISBN 0-08-018157-0); Pt. 4. pap. 20.00 (ISBN 0-08-018208-9); Vol. 4 Complete (cloth) 97.00 (ISBN 0-08-018094-9); Vol. 5. Vol. 5, Complete (cloth) 97.00 (ISBN 0-08-018973-3); Pt. 1. pap. 14.00 (ISBN 0-08-018969-5); Pt. 2. pap. 11.00 (ISBN 0-08-018970-9); Pt. 3. pap. 14.00 (ISBN 0-08-018971-7); Pt. 4. pap. 18.50 (ISBN 0-08-018972-5); Vol. 6. Vol. 6, Complete (cloth) 97.00 (ISBN 0-08-020319-1); Pt. 1. pap. 15.50 (ISBN 0-08-020615-8); Pt. 2. pap. 15.50 (ISBN 0-08-020966-1); Pts. 3-4. pap. 28.00 (ISBN 0-08-020976-9); Vol. 7. 97.00 (ISBN 0-686-66316-0); Pts. 1-4. pap. Pt. 2. pap. (ISBN 0-08-021116-X); Pt. 2. pap. (ISBN 0-08-021259-X); Pt. 3. pap. (ISBN 0-08-021261-1); Pt. 4. pap. (ISBN 0-08-021263-8); Vol. 7, Complete (cloth) 50.00 (ISBN 0-08-020321-3). LC 72-12616. Pergamon.
--Progress in Neurobiology, Vol. 11. 1979. 103.00 (ISBN 0-08-024857-8). Pergamon.
--Progress in Neurobiology, Vol. 14 Complete. 344p. 1980. 103.00 (ISBN 0-08-027114-6). Pergamon.
Korr, I. M., ed. The Neurobiologic Mechanisms in Manipulative Therapy. LC 78-4667. 488p. 1978. 25.00 (ISBN 0-306-31150-X, Plenum Pr). Plenum Pub.
Kravitz, E. A. & Treherne, J. E., eds. Neurotransmission, Neurotransmitters & Neuromodulators. (Special Issue of the Journal of Experimental Biology Ser.). (Illus.). 250p. 1981. 40.00 (ISBN 0-521-23651-7). Cambridge U Pr.
Lahue, Robert, ed. Methods in Neurobiology. 1981. 50.00 ea.; Set. 89.50 (ISBN 0-686-69459-7); Vol. 1, 640 Pp. for two vol. set 89.50 (ISBN 0-306-40517-2). Vol. Ii, 700 Pp (ISBN 0-306-40518-0). Plenum Pub.
--Methods in Neurobiology, Vol. 2. 726p. 1981. text ed. 50.00 (ISBN 0-306-40518-0, Plenum Pr). Plenum Pub.
Laughlin, Charles D. & D'Aquili, Eugene G. Biogenetic Stucturalism. LC 74-13245. (Illus.). 211p. 1974. text ed. 12.00x (ISBN 0-231-03817-8). Columbia U Pr.
Lissak, K., ed. Neural & Neurohumoral Organization of Motivated Behaviour. (Recent Developments of Neurobiology in Hungary Ser.). (Illus.). 1978. 16.00x (ISBN 963-05-1316-1). Intl Pubns Serv.
--Neural & Neurohumoral Organization of Motivated Behaviour: Neural & Neurohumoral Organization of Motivated Behaviour. 1978. casebound 18.50 (ISBN 0-9960012-9-8, Pub. by Kiado Hungary). Heyden.
--Results in Neuroanatomy, Motor Organization, Cerebral Circulation & Modelling. (Recent Developments of Neurobiology in Hungary Ser.: Vol. 8). (Illus.). 243p. 1979. 25.00x (ISBN 963-05-1594-6). Intl Pubns Serv.
McGeer, Edith G., et al, eds. Kainic Acid As a Tool in Neurobiology. LC 78-55812. 283p. 1978. 29.00 (ISBN 0-89004-279-9). Raven.
McGeer, P. L., et al. Molecular Neurobiology of the Mammalian Brain. (Illus.). 669p. 1978. 37.50 (ISBN 0-306-31095-3, Plenum Pr); pap. 14.95 (ISBN 0-306-40073-1). Plenum Pub.
Mandell, Arnold J., ed. Neurobiological Mechanisms of Adaptation & Behavior. LC 74-14475. (Advances in Biochemical Psychopharmacology Ser.: Vol. 13). 314p. 1975. 27.00 (ISBN 0-89004-001-X). Raven.
Marler, P. & Vandenberg, J. G., eds. Handbook of Behavioral Neurobiology-Vol. 3: Social Behavior & Communication. LC 79-308. 427p. 1979. 39.50 (ISBN 0-306-40218-1, Plenum Pr). Plenum Pub.
Masterton, R. Bruce, ed. Handbook of Behavioral Neurobiology, Vol. 1: Sensory Integration. new ed. LC 78-17238. 595p. 1978. 39.50 (ISBN 0-306-35191-9, Plenum Pr). Plenum Pub.
Mogenson, Gordon J. The Neurobiology of Behavior: An Introduction. LC 77-18283. 1977. 14.95 (ISBN 0-470-99341-3). Halsted Pr.
Myers, R. D., ed. Methods in Psychobiology. Incl. Vol. 1. Laboratory Techniques in Neuropsychology & Neurobiology. 1972. 56.50 (ISBN 0-12-512301-9); Vol. 2. Specialized Techniques in Neuropsychology & Neurobiology. 1973. 63.00 (ISBN 0-12-512302-7); Vol. 3. Advanced Laboratory Techniques in Neuropsychology & Neurobiology. 1977. 35.00 (ISBN 0-12-461003-X). Acad Pr.
Noback, Charles R. The Human Nervous System: Basic Principles of Neurobiology. 2nd ed. (Illus.). 1975. text ed. 24.00 (ISBN 0-07-046848-6, HP). McGraw.
Oakley, Bruce & Schafer, Rollie. Experimental Neurobiology: A Laboratory Manual. LC 76-49153. 14.95x (ISBN 0-472-08690-1). U of Mich Pr.
Otsuka, Masanori & Hall, Z. W., eds. Neurobiology of Chemical Transmission. LC 78-24602. 1979. 36.50 (ISBN 0-471-03974-8, Pub. by Wiley-Medical). Wiley.
Peele, Talmage L. The Neuroanatomic Basis for Clinical Neurology. 3rd ed. 1976. 33.50 (ISBN 0-07-049175-5, HP). McGraw.
Progress in Neurobiology, Vol. 15, No.4. pap. 26.00 (ISBN 0-08-027148-0). Pergamon.
Reichardt, Werner E. & Poggio, Tomaso, eds. Theoretical Approaches in Neurobiology. (Illus.). 208p. 1980. text ed. 20.00x (ISBN 0-262-18100-2). MIT Pr.
Salanki, J., ed. Neurobiology of Invertebrates Gastropoda Brain. 1976. 45.00x (ISBN 963-05-1080-4). Intl Pubns Serv.
Schmitt, Francis O. & Worden, Frederic G., eds. The Neurosciences: Third Study Program. 1250p. 1974. 50.00x (ISBN 0-262-19112-1). MIT Pr.
Siddiqui, O., et al, eds. Development & Neurobiology of Drosophila. (Basic Life Sciences Ser.: Vol. 16). 485p. 1980. 49.50 (ISBN 0-306-40559-8, Plenum Pr). Plenum Pub.
Smythies, John R. & Bradley, Ronald J. International Review of Neurobiology, Vol. 22. (Serial Publication). 1981. 39.50 (ISBN 0-12-366822-0). Acad Pr.
Towe, Arnold L. & Luschei, Erich S., eds. Handbook of Behavioral Neurobiology: Motor Coordination, Vol. 5. 610p. 1981. text ed. 45.00 (ISBN 0-306-40613-6, Plenum Pr). Plenum Pub.
Wasserman. Neurobiological Theory of Psychological Phenomena. 1978. 52.50 (ISBN 0-8391-1286-6). Univ Park.
Willis, William D. & Grossman, Robert G. Medical Neurobiology: Neuroanatomical & Neurophysiological Principles Basic to Clinical Neuroscience. 2nd ed. LC 76-41192. (Illus.). 1977. 29.50 (ISBN 0-8016-5583-8). Mosby.
Willis, William D., Jr. & Grossman, Robert G. Medical Neurobiology: Neuroanatomical & Neurophysiological Principles Basic to Clinical Neuroscience. 3rd ed. LC 81-1390. (Illus.). 593p. 1981. text ed. 35.00 (ISBN 0-8016-5584-6). Mosby.
Windle, William F. The Pioneering Role of Clarence Luther Herrick in American Neuroscience. 1979. 7.50 (ISBN 0-682-49340-6, University). Exposition.
Young, D., ed. Developmental Neurobiology of Arthropods. (Illus.). 200p. 1973. 47.50 (ISBN 0-521-20229-9). Cambridge U Pr.

NEUROCHEMISTRY

see also Brain Chemistry

Agranoff, B. W. & Aprison, M. H., eds. Advances in Neurochemistry, Vols. 1-3. Incl. Vol. 1. 309p. 1975. 29.50 (ISBN 0-306-39221-6); Vol. 2. 346p. 1977. 35.00 (ISBN 0-306-39222-4); Vol. 3. 318p. 1978. 32.50 (ISBN 0-306-39223-2). LC 75-8710. (Illus., Plenum Pr). Plenum Pub.
Agranoff, Bernard W. & Aprison, M. H. Advances in Neurochemistry, Vol. 4. 215p. 1981. text ed. price not set (ISBN 0-306-40678-0, Plenum Pr). Plenum Pub.
Bazan, N. G. & Lolley, R. N., eds. Neurochemistry of the Retina: Proceedings of the International Symposium on the Neurochemistry of the Retina, 28 August - 1 September 1979, Athens, Greece. (Illus.). 584p. 1980. 80.00 (ISBN 0-08-025485-3). Pergamon.
Bowman, Robert E. & Datta, Surinder P., eds. Biochemistry of Brain & Behavior. LC 76-133840. 364p. 1970. 34.50 (ISBN 0-306-30507-0, Plenum Pr). Plenum Pub.
Brunngraber, Eric G. Neurochemistry of Aminosugars: Neurochemistry & Neuropathology of the Complex Carbohydrates. (Illus.). 720p. 1979. text ed. 34.75 (ISBN 0-398-03843-0). C C Thomas.
Corning, W. C. & Ratner, S. C., eds. Chemistry of Learning: Invertebrate Research. LC 67-25103. 468p. 1967. 42.50 (ISBN 0-306-30305-1, Plenum Pr). Plenum Pub.
Daly, John. Cyclic Nucleotides in the Nervous System. LC 76-62999. (Illus.). 401p. 1977. 39.50 (ISBN 0-306-30971-8, Plenum Pr). Plenum Pub.
Davidson, A. N., et al. Functional & Structural Proteins of the Nervous System. LC 72-91937. (Advances in Experimental Medicine & Biology Ser.: Vol. 32). 286p. 1972. 32.50 (ISBN 0-306-39032-9, Plenum Pr). Plenum Pub.
Delgado, J. M., ed. Behavioral Neurochemistry. DeFeudis, F. V. LC 76-22627. 1977. 20.00 (ISBN 0-470-15179-X). Halsted Pr.
DeRobertis, Eduardo & Schacht, Jochen, eds. Neurochemistry of Cholinergic Receptors. LC 73-91105. 156p. 1974. 18.00 (ISBN 0-911216-66-9). Raven.
Eiduson, Samuel, et al. Biochemistry & Behavior. (Illus.). 1964. 19.50x (ISBN 0-442-02252-2). Van Nos Reinhold.
Erlich, Y. H., et al, eds. Modulators, Mediators, & Specifiers in Brain Function. (Advances in Experimental Medicine & Biology Ser.: Vol. 116). 343p. 1979. 35.00 (ISBN 0-306-40173-8, Plenum Pr). Plenum Pub.
Fried, Rainer, ed. Methods of Neurochemistry, Vol. 2. 1972. 49.75 (ISBN 0-8247-1216-1). Dekker.
--Methods of Neurochemistry, Vol. 4. 252p. 1973. 49.75 (ISBN 0-8247-6024-7). Dekker.
--Methods of Neurochemistry, Vol. 5. 296p. 1973. 49.75 (ISBN 0-8247-6073-5). Dekker.
Friede, Reinhard L. Topographic Brain Chemistry. 1966. 65.00 (ISBN 0-12-268350-1). Acad Pr.
Furst, Susanna & Knoll, J., eds. Opiate Receptors & the Neurochemical Correlates of Pain: Proceedings of the Third Congress of the Hungarian Pharmacological Society, Budapest, 1979. LC 80-41281. (Advances in Pharmacological Research & Practice Ser.: Vol. V). 240p. 1981. 45.00 (ISBN 0-08-026390-9). Pergamon.
Haber, Bernard & Aprison, M. H., eds. Neuropharmacology & Behavior. LC 77-14178. (Illus.). 225p. 1978. 24.50 (ISBN 0-306-31056-2, Plenum Pr). Plenum Pub.
Haber, Bernard, et al, eds. Serotonin: Current Aspects of Neurochemistry & Function. (Advances in Experimental Medicine & Biology Ser.: Vol. 133). 780p. 1981. 75.00 (ISBN 0-306-40579-2, Plenum Pr). Plenum Pub.
Himwich, Williamina & Himwich, Harold. Biogenic Amines. (Progress in Brain Research: Vol. 8). 1964. 53.75 (ISBN 0-444-40285-3). Elsevier.
Hungarian Pharmacological Society, 3rd Congress, Budapest, 1979. Modulation of Neurochemical Transmission: Proceedings. Knoll, J. & Vizi, E. S., eds. LC 80-41281. (Advances in Pharmacological Research & Practice Ser.: Vol. II). (Illus.). 450p. 1981. 84.00 (ISBN 0-08-026387-9). Pergamon.
Karczmar, A. G. & Eccles, John C., eds. Brain & Human Behavior. LC 78-160592. (Illus.). 1972. 42.00 (ISBN 0-387-05331-X). Springer-Verlag.
Lajtha, Abel, ed. Handbook of Neurochemistry, Vols. 1-7. Incl. Vol. 1. Chemical Architecture of the Nervous System. 484p. 1969 (ISBN 0-306-37701-2); Vol. 2. Structural Neurochemistry. 562p. 1969 (ISBN 0-306-37702-0); Vol. 3. Metabolic Reactions in the Nervous System. 590p. 1970 (ISBN 0-306-37703-9); Vol. 4. Control Mechanisms in the Nervous System. 516p. 1970 (ISBN 0-306-37704-7); Vol. 5A. Metabolic Turnover in the Nervous Systems. 438p. 1971 (ISBN 0-306-37705-5); Vol. 5B. Metabolic Turnover in the Nervous System. 399p. 1971 (ISBN 0-306-37715-2); Vol. 6. Alterations of Chemical Equilibrium in the Nervous System. 584p. 1971 (ISBN 0-306-37706-3); Vol. 7. Pathological Chemistry of the Nervous System. 675p. 1972 (ISBN 0-306-37707-1). LC 68-28097. 45.00 ea. (Plenum Pr). Plenum Pub.
--Protein Metabolism of the Nervous System. LC 74-85373. 732p. 1970. 55.00 (ISBN 0-306-30418-X, Plenum Pr). Plenum Pub.
Lissak. Results in Neurochemistry, Neuroendocrinology, Neurophysiology & Behavior, Neuropharmacology, Neuropathology, Cybernetics, Vol. 15. 1976. 19.50 (ISBN 0-9960007-2-0, Pub. by Kaido Hungary). Heyden.
Lissak, K., ed. Results in Neurochemistry, Neuroendocrinology, Neurophysiology, & Behavior, Neuropharmacology, Neurpathology, Cybernetics. 1976. 20.00x (ISBN 963-05-0595-9). Intl Pubns Serv.

--Results in Neuroendocrinology, Neurochemistry & Sleep Research. LC 76-379912. (Recent Developments of Neurobiology in Hungary: Vol. VII). (Illus.). 190p. 1978. 20.00x (ISBN 963-05-1587-3). Intl Pubns Serv.
--Results in Neuroendocrinology, Neurochemistry and Sleep Research. (Recent Developments of Neurobiology in Hungary Ser.: Vol. VII). 1978. 19.00 (ISBN 0-9960011-0-7, Pub. by Kaido Hungary). Heyden.
Loh, Horace H. & Ross, David H., eds. Neurochemical Mechanisms of Opiates & Endorphins. LC 78-24623. (Advances in Biochemical Pharmacology Ser.: Vol. 20). 475p. 1979. text ed. 44.50 (ISBN 0-89004-166-0). Raven.
Mandel, Paul & DeFeudis, F. V., eds. GABA: Biochemistry & CNS Function. LC 79-22019. (Advances in Experimental Medicine & Biology Ser.: Vol. 123). 517p. 1979. 42.50 (ISBN 0-306-40325-0, Plenum Pr). Plenum Pub.
Mandell, A. J. & Mandell, M. P., eds. Psychochemical Research in Man: Methods, Strategy & Theory. 1969. 55.00 (ISBN 0-12-468050-X). Acad Pr.
Margolis, R. U. & Margolis, R. K., eds. Complex Carbohydrates of Nervous Tissue. LC 78-26881. (Illus.). 419p. 1979. 39.50 (ISBN 0-306-40135-5, Plenum Pr). Plenum Pub.
Marks, Neville & Rodnight, Richard, eds. Research Methods in Neurochemistry, Vol. 5. 318p. 1981. 35.00 (ISBN 0-306-40583-0, Plenum Pr). Plenum Pub.
Neuhoff, V. Proceedings of the European Society for Neurochemistry, Vol. 1. (Illus.). 1978. pap. 51.80 (ISBN 0-89573-018-9). Verlag Chemie.
Osborne, Neville N., ed. Biochemistry of Characterized Neurons. LC 76-55379. 1978. text ed. 50.00 (ISBN 0-08-021503-3). Pergamon.
Pevzner, L. V. Functional Biochemistry of the Neuroglia. LC 78-26386. (Illus.). 320p. 1979. 35.00 (ISBN 0-306-10954-9, Consultants). Plenum Pub.
Polli, E., ed. Neurochemistry of Hepatic Coma. (Experimental Biology & Medicine: Vol. 4). 1971. 21.00 (ISBN 3-8055-1187-6). S Karger.
Richter, D., ed. Biochemical Factors Concerned in the Functional Activity of the Nervous System. 1969. pap. 27.00 (ISBN 0-08-013311-8). Pergamon.
Roberts, Peter J., et al, eds. Dopamine. LC 78-4355. (Advances in Biochemical Psychopharmacology Ser.: Vol. 19). 440p. 1978. 31.50 (ISBN 0-89004-239-X). Raven.
Siegel, George, et al. Basic Neurochemistry. 2nd ed. LC 75-36763. 1977. pap. text ed. 18.95 (ISBN 0-316-79002-8). Little.
Siegel, George J. & Albers, R. Wayne. Basic Neurochemistry. 3rd ed. 1981. pap. text ed. price not set (ISBN 0-316-79002-8). Little.
Svennerholm, Lars, et al, eds. Structure & Function of the Gangliosides. (Advances in Experimental Medicine & Biology Ser.: Vol. 125). 580p. 1980. 49.50 (ISBN 0-306-40332-3, Plenum Pr). Plenum Pub.
Treherne, J. E. Neurochemistry of Arthropods. (Cambridge Monographs in Experimental Biology). 1966. 28.95 (ISBN 0-521-06645-X). Cambridge U Pr.
Triggle, D. J. Chemical Aspects of the Autonomic Nervous System. (Theoretical & Experimental Biology: Vol. 4). 1966. 52.00 (ISBN 0-12-700250-2). Acad Pr.
Von Euler, U. S., et al, eds. Mechanisms of Release of Biogenic Amines. 1966. 60.00 (ISBN 0-08-011698-1). Pergamon.
Warburton, David M. Brain, Behavior & Drugs: Introduction to the Neurochemistry of Behaviour. LC 74-20789. 280p. 1975. 42.00 (ISBN 0-471-91991-8, Pub. by Wiley-Interseience). Wiley.
WHO Scientific Group. Geneva, 1968. Biochemistry of Mental Disorders: Report. (Technical Report Ser.: No. 427). (Also avail. in French). 1969. pap. 2.00 (ISBN 92-4-120427-3). World Health.
Youdim, M. B. & Lovenberg, W., eds. Essays in Neurochemistry & Neuropharmacology, Vol. 5. Sharman, D. F. & Lagnado, J. R., trs. LC 80-40964. 152p. 1981. 47.00 (ISBN 0-471-27879-3, Pub. by Wiley-Interscience). Wiley.
Zambotti, V., et al, eds. Glycolipids, Glycoproteins, & Mucopolysaccharides of the Nervous System. LC 72-78628. (Advances in Experimental Medicine & Biology Ser.: Vol. 25). 334p. 1972. 35.00 (ISBN 0-306-39025-6, Plenum Pr). Plenum Pub.

NEUROCYTE
see Neurons

NEUROENDOCRINOLOGY
Adler, Norman T., ed. Neuroendocrinology of Reproduction: Physiology & Behavior. 549p. 1981. 42.00 (ISBN 0-306-40600-4, Plenum Pr); pap. 18.95 (ISBN 0-306-40611-X). Plenum Pub.
Alcaraz, Manuel, et al. Sexual Hormones: Influence on the Electrophysiology of the Brain. LC 74-4137. 223p. 1974. text ed. 28.00x (ISBN 0-8422-7214-3). Irvington.
Ariens-Kappers, J. Topics in Neuroendocrinology. (Progress in Brain Research: Vol. 38). 1973. 73.25 (ISBN 0-444-41049-X, North Holland). Elsevier.
Bargmann, W., et al, eds. Neurosecretion & Neuroendocrine Activity: Evolution, Structure & Function. (Illus.). 1978. 56.70 (ISBN 0-387-08637-4). Springer-Verlag.
Carenza, L., et al, eds. Clinical Psychoneuroendocrinology in Reproduction. (Proceedings of the Serono Symposia). 1979. 49.00 (ISBN 0-12-159450-5). Acad Pr.
Clemens, James A., et al. Non-Sexual Hormonal Influences on the Electrophysiology of the Brain. LC 74-6074. (Biology of Sex Ser.). 188p. 1974. text ed. 24.50x (ISBN 0-8422-7223-2). Irvington.
Conference of the Int. Society for Psychoneuroendocrinology, Mieken, Sep, 1973. Psychoneuroendocrinology: Proceedings. Hatotani, N., ed. (Illus.). 450p. 1974. 80.25 (ISBN 3-8055-1711-4). S Karger.
Coupland, R. E. & Forssmann, W. G., eds. Peripheral Neuroendocrine Interaction. (Illus.). 1978. pap. 45.10 (ISBN 0-387-08779-6). Springer-Verlag.
Dorner, G. & Kawakami, M., eds. Hormones & Brain Development. LC 78-25863. (Developments in Endocrinology Ser.: Vol. 3). 1979. 70.25 (ISBN 0-444-80091-3, Biomedical Pr). Elsevier.
Endroczi. Cellular & Molecular Bases of Neuroendocrine Processes. 1976. 41.50 (ISBN 0-9960007-1-2, Pub. by Kaido Hungary). Heyden.
Ganong, W. F. & Martini, L., eds. Frontiers in Neuroendocrinology, Vol. 7. (Frontiers in Neuroendocrinology Ser.). 1982. text ed. price not set (ISBN 0-89004-694-8). Raven.
Ganong, William F. & Martini, Luciano, eds. Frontiers in Neuroendocrinology, Vol. 5. LC 77-82030. 409p. 1978. 31.00 (ISBN 0-89004-135-0). Raven.
--Frontiers in Neuroendocrinology, 1969. (Illus.). 1969. text ed. 29.50x (ISBN 0-19-501130-9). Oxford U Pr.
--Frontiers in Neuroendocrinology: 1973. (Illus.). 450p. 1973. text ed. 29.50x (ISBN 0-19-501672-6). Oxford U Pr.
International Conference on Neuroendocrinology, 0f Cns-Hormone-Interactions, Chapel Hill, 1974. Anatomical Neuroendocrinology: Proceedings. Stumpf, W. E. & Grant, L. D., eds. 300p. 1975. 77.25 (ISBN 3-8055-2154-5). S Karger.
International Seminar on Reproductive Physiology & Sexual Endocrinology, 6th, Brussels, May-June, 1976. Clinical Reproductive Neuroendocrinology: Proceedings. Hubinont, P. O., ed. (Progress in Reproductive Biology: Vol. 2). (Illus.). 1977. 69.50 (ISBN 3-8055-2382-3). S Karger.
International Symposium Held in Boston, 1975, et al. Subcellular Mechanisms in Reproductive Neuroendocrinology: Proceedings. Naftolin, F., ed. Ryan, K. J., ed. 1976. 99.50 (ISBN 0-444-41442-8, North Holland). Elsevier.
International Symposium, Kyoto, 1975. Endocrine Gut & Pancreas: Proceedings. Fujita, Tsunoo, ed. 1976. 86.00 (ISBN 0-444-41449-5, North Holland). Elsevier.
International Symposium on Brain-Endocrine Interaction, 2nd, Tokyo, October 1974. Brain Endocrine Interaction II: the Ventricular System in Neuroendocrine Mechanisms: Proceedings. Knigge, K. M. & Scott, D. E., eds. (Illus.). x, 406p. 1975. 85.25 (ISBN 3-8055-2176-6). S Karger.
International Symposium on Brain-Endocrine Interaction, 3rd, Wurzburg, July 1977. Neural Hormones & Reproduction: Proceedings. Scott, D. E., et al, eds. (Brain-Endocrine Interaction III). (Illus.). 1978. 118.75 (ISBN 3-8055-2798-5). S Karger.
International Symposium on Neurosecretion, 6th, London, 1973. Neurosecretion - the Final Neuroendocrine Pathway: Proceedings. Knowles, F. & Vollrath, L., eds. LC 74-13218. (Illus.). xii, 345p. 1975. 61.40 (ISBN 0-387-06821-X). Springer-Verlag.
Kawakami, Masazumi, intro. by. Biological Rhythms in Neuroendocrine Activity. (Illus.). 1974. 43.00 (ISBN 0-89640-017-4). Igaku-Shoin.
Krieger, Dorothy T. & Hughes, Joan, eds. Neuroendocrinology. LC 79-28123. (Illus.). 1980. 25.00x (ISBN 0-87893-425-1). Sinauer Assoc.
--Neuroendocrinology. 1979. text ed. write for info. HP Pub Co.
Lissak. Results in Neurochemistry, Neuroendocrinology, Neurophysiology & Behavior, Neuropharmacology, Neuropathology, Cybernetics, Vol. 15. 1976. 19.50 (ISBN 0-9960007-2-0, Pub. by Kaido Hungary). Heyden.
Lissak, K., ed. Hormones & Brain Function. LC 72-87943. 529p. 1974. 45.00 (ISBN 0-306-30712-X, Plenum Pr). Plenum Pub.
--Results in Neurochemistry, Neuroendocrinology, Neurophysiology, & Behavior, Neuropharmacology, Neurpathology, Cybernetics. 1976. 20.00x (ISBN 963-05-0595-9). Intl Pubns Serv.
--Results in Neuroendocrinology, Neurochemistry & Sleep Research. LC 76-379912. (Recent Developments of Neurobiology in Hungary: Vol. VII). (Illus.). 190p. 1978. 20.00x (ISBN 963-05-1587-3). Intl Pubns Serv.
--Results in Neuroendocrinology, Neurochemistry and Sleep Research. (Recent Developments of Neurobiology in Hungary Ser.: Vol. VII). 1978. 19.00 (ISBN 0-9960011-0-7, Pub. by Kaido Hungary). Heyden.
Martin, Joseph, et al. Clinical Neuroendocrinology. LC 77-3601. (Contemporary Neurology Ser: Vol. 14). (Illus.). 410p. 1977. text ed. 33.00 (ISBN 0-8036-5885-0). Davis Co.
Martini, L. & Ganong, W. F., eds. Frontiers in Neuroendocrinology, Vol. 4. LC 77-82030. 304p. 1976. 29.50 (ISBN 0-89004-033-8). Raven.
Martini, L. & Ganong, William F., eds. Neuroendocrinology, 2 Vols. 1966-67. 78.50 ea. Vol. 1 (ISBN 0-12-475351-5). Vol. 2 (ISBN 0-12-475352-3). Acad Pr.
Martini, Luciano & Ganong, William F. Frontiers in Neuroendocrinology, 1971. (Illus.). 1971. text ed. 29.50x (ISBN 0-19-501415-4). Oxford U Pr.
Martini, Luciano & Besser, G. M., eds. Clinical Neuroendocrinology. 1978. 49.50 (ISBN 0-12-475360-4). Acad Pr.
Martini, Luciano & Ganong, William F., eds. Frontiers in Neuroendocrinology, Vol. 6. 430p. 1979. text ed. 42.50 (ISBN 0-89004-404-X). Raven.
Meites, Joseph, et al, eds. Pioneers in Neuroendocrinology, No. 2: (Perspectives in Neuroendocrine Research Ser.: Vol. 2). (Illus.). 430p. 1978. 32.50 (ISBN 0-306-34902-7, Plenum Pr). Plenum Pub.
--Pioneers in Neuroendocrinology, No. 1. (Perspectives in Neuroendocrine Research Ser., Vol. 1). (Illus.). 327p. 1975. 27.50 (ISBN 0-306-34901-9, Plenum Pr). Plenum Pub.
Mendlewicz, J., ed. Psychoneuroendocrinology & Abnormal Behavior. (Advances in Biological Psychiatry: Vol. 5). (Illus.). vi, 130p. 1980. pap. 34.75 (ISBN 3-8055-0599-X). S Karger.
Muller, E. E. & Agnoli, A., eds. Neuroendocrine Correlates in Neurology & Psychiatry. (Developments in Neurology Ser.: Vol. 2). 1979. 46.50 (ISBN 0-444-80121-9, North Holland). Elsevier.
Nemeroff, C. B. & Dunn, A. J., eds. Behavioral Neuroendocrinology. (Illus.). 500p. Date not set. text ed. 45.00 (ISBN 0-89335-138-5). SP Med & Sci Bks.
Ruf, K. B. & Tolis, G., eds. Advances in Neuroendocrine Physiology. (Frontiers of Hormone Research Ser.: Vol. 10). (Illus.). 250p. 1981. 90.00 (ISBN 3-8055-2949-X). S Karger.
Stark, E., et al, eds. Endocrinology, Neuroendocrinology, Neuropeptides- Part 1: Proceedings of the 28th International Congress of Physiological Sciences, Budapest, 1980. LC 80-42047. (Advances in Physiological Sciences: Vol. 13). (Illus.). 350p. 1981. 40.00 (ISBN 0-08-026827-7). Pergamon.
--Endocrinology, Neuroendocrinology, Neuropeptides-Part II: Proceedings of the 28th International Congress of Physiological Sciences, Budapest, 1980. LC 80-42046. (Advances in Physiological Sciences Ser.: Vol. 14). (Illus.). 350p. 1981. 40.00 (ISBN 0-08-026871-4). Pergamon.
Symposium of the International Society of Psychoneuroendocrinology Visgrad, Hungary, Dec. 1975 & Endroczi, E. Cellular & Molecular Bases of Neuroendocrine Processes: Proceedings. 1977. 40.00x (ISBN 0-8002-0436-0). Intl Pubns Serv.
Symposium on the Physiology & Pathology of Human Reproduction, Fourth Annual. The Neuroendocrinology of Human Reproduction: Biological & Clinical Perspectives: Proceedings. Mack, Harold C. & Sherman, Alfred I., eds. (Illus.). 224p. 1972. photocopy ed. spiral 22.50 (ISBN 0-398-02348-4). C C Thomas.
Tolis, George, et al, eds. Clinical Neuroendocrinology: A Pathophysiological Approach. LC 78-64844. 492p. 1979. text ed. 50.00 (ISBN 0-89004-355-8). Raven.
Zimmerman, et al. Drug Effects on Neuroendocrine Regulation. LC 73-77069. (Progress in Brain Research Ser.: Vol. 39). 500p. 1973. 107.50 (ISBN 0-444-41129-1). Elsevier.

NEUROFIBROMATOSIS
Crowe, Frank W., et al. A Clinical, Pathological & Genetic Study of Multiple Neurofibromatosis. (American Lecture Dermatology). (Illus.). 192p. 1956. ed. spiral bdg. 18.75photocopy (ISBN 0-398-00370-X). C C Thomas.

NEUROGLIA
De Robertis, E. D. & Carrea, R. Biology of Neuroglia. (Progress in Brain Research: Vol. 15). 1965. 63.50 (ISBN 0-444-40165-2, North Holland). Elsevier.
Pevzner, L. V. Functional Biochemistry of the Neuroglia. LC 78-26386. (Illus.). 320p. 1979. 35.00 (ISBN 0-306-10954-9, Consultants). Plenum Pub.

NEUROKERATIN
see Keratin

NEUROLEPTANESTHESIA
Gordon, E., ed. A Basis & Practice of Neuroanaesthesia. LC 74-21859. (Monographs in Anesthesiology: Vol. 2). 288p. 1975. 53.75 (ISBN 0-444-15157-5, Excerpta Medica). Elsevier.

NEUROLOGIC EXAMINATION
Aminoff, Michael J. Electrodiagnosis in Clinical Neurology. 1980. text ed. 45.00 (ISBN 0-443-08021-6). Churchill.
DeMyer, William. Technique of the Neurologic Examination. 3rd, rev. ed. (Illus.). 1980. text ed. 19.00 (ISBN 0-07-016352-9). McGraw.
Denny-Brown, Derek E. Handbook of Neurological Examination & Case Recording. rev. ed. LC 58-2654. 1957. pap. 3.95x (ISBN 0-674-37100-3). Harvard U Pr.
Liveson, Jay A. & Spielholz, Neil I. Peripheral Neurology: Case Studies in Electrodiagnosis. LC 78-13583. (Illus.). 434p. 1979. 21.00 (ISBN 0-8036-5650-5). Davis Co.
Simpson, John F. & Magee, Kenneth R. Clinical Evaluation of the Nervous System. (Illus.). 1973. 9.95 (ISBN 0-316-79184-9). Little.
Smorto, Mario P. & Basmajian, John V. Neuromotor Examination of the Limbs: A Photographic Atlas. (Illus.). 120p. 1980. lib. bdg. 17.95 (ISBN 0-683-07790-2). Williams & Wilkins.
Strub, Richard L. & Black, F. William. The Mental Status Examination in Neurology. LC 76-30734. (Illus.). 180p. 1977. pap. text ed. 9.95 (ISBN 0-8036-8208-5). Davis Co.
Uemura, T., et al. Neuro-Otological Examination. (Illus.). 1977. 49.50 (ISBN 0-8391-0887-7). Univ Park.
Van Allen, Maurice W. Pictorial Manual of Neurological Tests. 1980. 17.95 (ISBN 0-8151-8960-5). Year Bk Med.

NEUROLOGIC MANIFESTATIONS OF GENERAL DISEASES
Aita, John A. Neurocutaneous Diseases. 96p. 1966. ed. spiral bdg. 12.75photocopy (ISBN 0-398-00020-4). C C Thomas.
--Neurologic Manifestations of General Diseases. 936p. 1975. 69.50 (ISBN 0-398-02675-0). C C Thomas.
Association for Research in Nervous & Mental Disease. Brain Dysfunction in Metabolic Disorders, Vol. 53. Plum, Fred, ed. LC 74-79190. 1974. 34.50 (ISBN 0-911216-81-2). Raven.
Bell, William E. & McCormick, William. Neurologic Infections in Children. 2nd ed. (Major Problems in Clinical Pediatrics Ser.: Vol. 12). (Illus.). 600p. 1981. text ed. write for info. (ISBN 0-7216-1676-3). Saunders.
Brain, R. L. & Norris, F. H., Jr., eds. Remote Effects of Cancer on the Nervous System. LC 65-21048. (Contemporary Neurology Symposia: Vol. 1). 240p. 1965. 55.75 (ISBN 0-8089-0070-6). Grune.
Broder, L. E. & Carter, S. K. Meningeal Leukemia. LC 74-190394. 132p. 1972. 25.00 (ISBN 0-306-30594-1, Plenum Pr). Plenum Pub.
Corkin, Suzanne, et al, eds. Alzheimer's Disease: A Review of Progress. 1981. text ed. price not set (ISBN 0-89004-685-9). Raven.
Karcher, D., et al, eds. Humoral Immunity in Neurological Diseases. LC 79-15096. (Nato Advanced Study Institutes Ser. A: Life Sciences: Vol. 24). 684p. 1979. 59.50 (ISBN 0-306-40195-9, Plenum Pr). Plenum Pub.
Locke, Simeon, et al. A Study in Neurolinguistics. (Illus.). 160p. 1973. text ed. 13.75 (ISBN 0-398-02738-2). C C Thomas.
Nakano, Kenneth K. Neurology of Musculoskeletal & Rheumatic Disorders. (Illus.). 1979. 50.00 (ISBN 0-471-09491-9, Pub. by Wiley Med). Wiley.
Rapport, Maurice M. & Gorio, Alfredo, eds. Gangliosides in Neurological & Neuromuscular Function, Development, & Repair. 300p. 1981. text ed. 33.00 (ISBN 0-89004-660-3). Raven.
Speer, Frederic. Allergy of the Nervous System. (Illus.). 280p. 1970. text ed. 27.50 (ISBN 0-398-01822-7). C C Thomas.

Vinken, P. J. & Bruyn, G. W., eds. Enurological Manifestations of Systemic Diseases, Part One. LC 68-8297. (Handbook of Clinical Neurology: Vol. 38). 704p. 1979. 146.50 (ISBN 0-686-63100-5, North Holland). Elsevier.

NEUROLOGICAL NURSING

Conway, Barbara L. Carini & Owens' Neurological & Neurosurgical Nursing. 7th ed. LC 78-609. 1978. text ed. 18.95 (ISBN 0-8016-0946-1). Mosby.

Coping with Neurologic Problems, Proficiently. LC 78-27545. (Nursing Skillbook Ser.). (Illus.). 192p. 1979. text ed. 10.95 (ISBN 0-916730-12-3). InterMed Comm.

Davis, Joan E. & Mason, Celestine B. Neurologic Critical Care. 1979. text ed. 16.95 (ISBN 0-442-22004-9). Van Nos Reinhold.

Hickey, Joanne V. X. The Clinical Practice of Neurological & Neurosurgical Nursing. 473p. 1981. text ed. 19.50 (ISBN 0-397-54244-5, JBL-Med-Nursing). Har-Row.

Hooper, Reginald. Neurosurgical Nursing. (Illus.). 248p. 1964. photocopy ed. spiral 22.50 (ISBN 0-398-00868-X). C C Thomas.

Jacobs, Erwin M. & DeNault, Phyllis M. Neurology for Nurses: Including Nursing Technics in Neurology. (Illus.). 208p. 1964. 13.75 (ISBN 0-398-00908-2). C C Thomas.

Klemme, Roland M. Nursing Care of Neurosurgical Patients. (Illus.). 134p. 1949. photocopy ed. spiral 13.75 (ISBN 0-398-04314-0). C C Thomas.

O'Connor, Andrea B., ed. Nursing in Neurological Disorders. LC 78-140949. (Contemporary Nursing Ser.). 258p. 1976. pap. text ed. 6.50 (ISBN 0-937126-15-2). Am Journal Nurse.

Smith, Barnard H. Differential Diagnosis in Neurology. LC 78-31117. (Illus.). 1979. pap. text ed. 14.00x (ISBN 0-668-04033-5). Arco.

Snyder, Mariah & Jackle, Mary. Neurologic Problems: A Critical Care Nursing Focus. (Critical Care Ser.). (Illus.). 352p. 1980. pap. text ed. 19.95 (ISBN 0-87619-713-6). R J Brady.

Swift, Nancy & Mabel, Robert M. Manual of Neurological Nursing. 1978. 8.95 (ISBN 0-316-82539-5). Little.

Taylor, Joyce & Ballenger, Sally. Neurological Dysfunction & Nursing Interventions. (Illus.). 1980. text ed. 15.95 (ISBN 0-07-063170-0). McGraw.

Van Zwanenberg, Dinah & Adams, C. B. Neurosurgical Nursing Care. 128p. 1979. 13.50 (ISBN 0-571-11295-1, Pub. by Faber & Faber); pap. 4.50 (ISBN 0-571-11296-X). Merrimack Bk Serv.

Wehrmaker, Suzanne & Wintermute, Joann. Case Studies in Neurological Nursing. 1978. pap. text ed. 8.95 (ISBN 0-316-92800-3). Little.

Wilson, Susan F. Neuronursing. LC 78-21635. 1979. text ed. 17.50 (ISBN 0-8261-2280-9). Springer Pub.

Wise, Burton L. Preoperative & Postoperative Care in Neurological Surgery. 2nd ed. (Illus.). 208p. 1978. 19.75 (ISBN 0-398-03825-2). C C Thomas.

NEUROLOGISTS

see also Psychiatrists

Austin, James H. Chase, Chance, & Creativity. LC 77-23011. 236p. 1978. 15.00x (ISBN 0-231-04294-9). Columbia U Pr.

Schiller, Francis. A Mobius Strip: Fin-de-Sicle Neuropsychiatry & Paul Mobius. LC 81-40317. (Illus.). 110p. 1981. 12.50x (ISBN 0-520-04467-3). U of Cal Pr.

Walter, Richard D. & Mitchell, S. Weir. Neurologist: A Medical Biography. (Illus.). 244p. 1970. photocopy ed. spiral 22.75 (ISBN 0-398-02014-0). C C Thomas.

NEUROLOGY

see also Electrophysiology; Inhibition; Nervous System; Neurobiology; Neurochemistry; Neuroendocrinology; Neuropsychiatry; Neuro-Psychopharmacology; Pediatric Neurology; Psychology, Pathological; Psychology, Physiological; Veterinary Neurology; Veterinary Neurology

Aarli, J. A. & Toender, O. Immunological Aspects of Neurological Diseases. (Monographs in Neural Sciences: Vol. 6). (Illus.). xiv, 190p. 1980. pap. 58.75 (ISBN 3-8055-0814-X). S Karger.

Abrams, R. & Essman, W. B., eds. Electroconvulsive Therapies: Biological Foundations & Clinical Applications. (Illus.). 320p. 1981. text ed. 45.00 (ISBN 0-89335-144-X). SP Med & Sci Bks.

Adams, R. D. & Victor, M. Principles of Neurology. 2nd ed. 1981. 42.00 (ISBN 0-07-000294-0). McGraw.

Adams, Raymond D. & Victor, Maurice. Principles of Neurology. 1st ed. (Illus.). 1977. text ed. 31.00 (ISBN 0-07-000293-2, C). McGraw.

Afifi, Adel & Bergman, Ronald. Basic Neuroscience. LC 79-17727. (Illus.). 523p. 1980. text ed. 24.50 (ISBN 0-8067-0101-3). Urban & S.

Aidley, D. J. The Physiology of Excitable Cells. 2nd ed. LC 77-87375. (Illus.). 1979. 65.50 (ISBN 0-521-21913-2); pap. 17.95x (ISBN 0-521-29308-1). Cambridge U Pr.

Ajmone-Marson, Cosimo, et al, eds. Neuropeptides & Neural Transmission. (International Brain Research Organization (IBRO) Monograph: Vol. 7). 412p. 1980. text ed. 45.50 (ISBN 0-89004-501-1). Raven.

Amaducci, L., et al, eds. Aging of the Brain & Dementia. (Aging Ser.). 1980. text ed. 35.00 (ISBN 0-89004-457-0). Raven.

American Neurological Assoc. Transactions: 1978, Vol. 103. Duvoisin, Roger, ed. LC 61-705. 1979. text ed. 34.50 (ISBN 0-8261-0478-9). Springer Pub.

Appel, Stanley H., ed. Current Neurology, Vol. 3. LC 78-68042. (Current Ser.). (Illus.). 545p. 1981. text ed. 50.00 (ISBN 0-471-09501-X, Pub by Wiley Med). Wiley.

Ashworth, Bryan & Saunders, Michael. Management of Neurological Disorders. 1978. 15.00 (ISBN 0-397-58238-2, JBL-Med-Nursing). Har-Row.

Association for Research in Nervous & Mental Disease. Neurology & Psychiatry in Childhood: Proceedings, Vol. 34. 1969. Repr. of 1954 ed. 30.25 (ISBN 0-02-846380-3). Hafner.

Ayres, A. Jean. Sensory Integration & Learning Disorders. LC 72-91446. 294p. 1973. 22.80x (ISBN 0-87424-303-3). Western Psych.

Baker, Elsworth. Man in the Trap. LC 79-26675. 384p. 1980. pap. 5.95 (ISBN 0-02-083650-3, Collier). Macmillan.

Baker, Mary, et al. Developing Strategies for Biofeedback Applications in Neurologically Handicapped Patients. 1977. pap. 1.00 (ISBN 0-912452-09-9). Am Phys Therapy Assn.

Bannister, Roger, ed. Brain's Clinical Neurology. 5th ed. (Illus.). 1978. 25.00x (ISBN 0-19-519957-X); pap. 17.95x (ISBN 0-19-261308-1). Oxford U Pr.

Barrows, Howard S. Guide to Neurological Assessment. (Illus.). 144p. 1980. text ed. 9.95 (ISBN 0-397-52093-X, JBL-Med-Nursing). Har-Row.

Baru, A. V. The Brain & Hearing: Hearing Disturbances Associated with Local Brain Lesions. LC 72-82624. (Neuropsychology Ser). 116p. 1972. 22.50 (ISBN 0-306-10876-3, Consultants). Plenum Pub.

Behan, P. O. & Currie, S. Clinical Neuroimmunology. (Major Problems in Neurology: Vol. 8). 1978. text ed. 20.00 (ISBN 0-7216-1672-0). Saunders.

Behan, Peter O. Progress in Neurological Research. 232p. text ed. 39.50 (ISBN 0-8391-1542-3). Univ Park.

Benson, D. Frank. Aphasia, Alexia, & Agraphia. (Clinical Neurology & Neurosurgery Monographs: Vol. 1). (Illus.). 1979. text ed. 25.00 (ISBN 0-443-08041-0). Churchill.

Benson, D. Frank & Blumer, Dietrich, eds. Psychiatric Aspects of Neurologic Disease. (Seminars in Psychiatry Ser). (Illus.). 336p. 1975. 35.00 (ISBN 0-8089-0860-X). Grune.

Berenberg, Samuel R. Brain: Fetal & Infant. 1977. lib. bdg. 53.00 (ISBN 90-247-2022-2, Pub. by Martinus Nijhoff Netherlands). Kluwer Boston.

Beresford, H. Richard. Legal Aspects of Neurologic Practice. LC 75-16362. (Contemporary Neurology Ser.: No. 13). 150p. 1975. text ed. 22.00 (ISBN 0-8036-0730-X). Davis Co.

Bernbeck, Rupprecht & Sinios, Alexander. Neuro-Orthopedic Screening in Infancy: Schedules, Examination & Findings. LC 78-2505. (Illus.). 120p. 1978. text ed. 16.50 (ISBN 0-8067-0231-1). Urban & S.

Bernhard, C. G. & Schade, J. Developmental Neurology. (Progress in Brain Research: Vol. 26). 1967. 53.75 (ISBN 0-444-40040-0, North Holland). Elsevier.

Bevan, John A., et al, eds. Vascular Neuroeffector Mechanisms. 1979. 42.50 (ISBN 0-89004-302-7). Raven.

Bishop, Beverly. Neurophysiology Study Guide. 2nd ed. (Illus.). 1973. spiral bdg. 8.50 (ISBN 0-87488-600-7). Med Exam.

Blunt, Michael J & Girgis, M. Multiple Choice Questions in Anatomy & Neurobiology for Undergraduates. (Illus.). 1979. pap. 8.50 (ISBN 0-407-00153-0). Butterworth.

Boller, Francois & Frank, Ellen. Sexual Dysfunctions in Neurological Disorders: Management & Rehabilitation. 1981. text ed. price not set (ISBN 0-89004-500-3). Raven.

Bondy, St. C. & Margolis, F. L. Sensory Deprivation & Brain Development: The Avian Visual System As a Model. (Illus.). 1971. wrappers 21.50 (ISBN 0-685-39788-2). Adler.

Bonica, John J., ed. Pain. (Association for Research in Nervous & Mental Disease Publications Ser.: Vol. 58). 424p. 1979. text ed. 38.00 (ISBN 0-89004-376-0). Raven.

Bories, J., ed. The Diagnostic Limitations of Computerised Axial Tomography. (Illus.). 1978. pap. 31.20 (ISBN 0-387-08593-9). Springer-Verlag.

Botez, M. I. & Reynolds, E. H., eds. Folic Acid in Neurology, Psychiatry, & Internal Medicine. LC 78-57243. 550p. 1979. text ed. 49.50 (ISBN 0-89004-338-8). Raven.

Bradford, Marsden, ed. Biochemistry & Neurology. 304p. 1976. pap. 47.50 (ISBN 0-12-123750-8). Acad Pr.

Brobeck, John R. Neural Control Systems. LC 72-85159. 108p. 1973. pap. 9.50 (ISBN 0-686-65351-3, Pub. by Williams & Wilkens). Krieger.

Brodie, Bernard B. & Bressler, R., eds. Minireviews of the Neurosciences from Life Sciences, Vols. 13-15. LC 75-8733. 493p. 1975. text ed. 32.00 combined ed. (ISBN 0-08-019724-8); pap. text ed. 16.00 combined ed. (ISBN 0-08-019723-X). Pergamon.

Brown, Donald R. Neurosciences for Allied Health Therapies. LC 79-19685. (Illus.). 1980. text ed. 18.95 (ISBN 0-8016-0827-9). Mosby.

Buchanan, Joseph R. Outlines of Lectures on the Neurological System of Anthropology. LC 74-29282. Repr. of 1854 ed. 30.00 (ISBN 0-404-13402-5). AMS Pr.

Burr, H. S. Classics in Neurology. 184p. 1963. pap. 14.50 photocopy ed. spiral (ISBN 0-398-00263-0). C C Thomas.

Calne, D. B., et al, eds. Dopaminergic Mechanisms. LC 74-13904. (Advances in Neurology Ser: Vol. 9). 445p. 1975. 41.50 (ISBN 0-911216-93-6). Raven.

Carpenter, David O. Cellular Pacemakers: Function in Normal & Diseased States, Vol. 2. 325p. 1982. 35.00 (ISBN 0-471-09608-3, Pub. by Wiley-Interscience). Wiley.

Cash, Joan, ed. Neurology for Physiotherapists. 2nd ed. LC 77-83951. (Illus.). 1978. soft cover 15.00 (ISBN 0-397-58230-7, JBL-Med-Nursing). Har-Row.

Cervos-Navarro, J. & Fritschka, E., eds. Cerebral Microcirculation & Metabolism. 1981. text ed. 49.50 (ISBN 0-89004-590-9). Raven.

Cervos-Navarro, J., et al, eds. Pathology of Cerebrospinal Microcirculation. LC 77-84125. (Advances in Neurology Ser.: Vol. 20). 1978. 56.00 (ISBN 0-89004-237-3). Raven.

Chaplin, James P. & Demers, Aline. Primer of Neurology & Neurophysiology. LC 78-6680. 1978. pap. text ed. 12.50 (ISBN 0-471-03027-9, Pub. by Wiley Med). Wiley.

Chusid, Joseph G. Correlative Neuroanatomy & Functional Neurology. 17th ed. LC 78-71797. (Illus.). 464p. 1979. lexotone cover 12.00 (ISBN 0-87041-011-3). Lange.

Clark, Ronald G. Manter & Gatz's Essentials of Clinical Neuroanatomy & Neurophysiology. 5th ed. LC 74-10887. (Illus.). 181p. 1975. pap. text ed. 7.95 (ISBN 0-8036-1850-6). Davis Co.

Claussen, Claus F. & Desa, Joe V. Clinical Study of Human Equilibrium by Electonystagmography & Allied Tests. (Illus.). xiii, 437p. 1980. text ed. 50.00x (ISBN 0-86590-002-7). Apt Bks.

Clemente, Carmine D. & Purpura, Dominick P., eds. Sleep & the Maturing Nervous System. (Illus.). 1972. 47.50 (ISBN 0-12-176250-5). Acad Pr.

Cohen, M. M., et al, eds. Biochemistry, Ultrastructure & Physiology of Cerebral Anoxia, Hypoxia & Ischaemia. (Monographs in Neural Science: Vol. 1). (Illus.). 1973. 29.50 (ISBN 3-8055-1420-4). S Karger.

Conesa, Salvador H. & Argote, M. L. A Visual Aid to the Examination of Nerve Roots. (Illus.). 1976. text ed. 10.95 (ISBN 0-02-858080-X). Macmillan.

Cooper, I. S., ed. Cerebellar Stimulation in Man. LC 77-76925. 232p. 1978. 28.00 (ISBN 0-89004-206-3). Raven.

Costa, E. & Trabucchi, Marco, eds. The Endorphins. LC 77-18301. (Advances in Biochemical Psychopharmacology Ser.: Vol. 18). 397p. 1978. 35.00 (ISBN 0-89004-226-8). Raven.

Costa, Erminio & Trabucchi, Marco, eds. Neural Peptides & Neural Communication. (Advances in Biochemical Psychopharmacology Ser.). 670p. 1980. text ed. 61.50 (ISBN 0-89004-375-2). Raven.

Cotman, Carl W. & McGaugh, James L. Behavioral Neuroscience: An Introduction. LC 79-50214. 1979. 21.95 (ISBN 0-12-191650-2). Acad Pr.

Courjon, Jean, et al, eds. Clinical Applications of Evoked Potentials in Neurology. 500p. 1981. text ed. 48.00 (ISBN 0-89004-619-0). Raven.

Cowan, W. Maxwell, et al, eds. Annual Review of Neuroscience, Vol. 1. (Illus.). 1978. text ed. 17.00 (ISBN 0-8243-2401-3). Annual Reviews.

--Annual Review of Neuroscience, Vol. 3. (Illus.). 1980. text ed. 17.00 (ISBN 0-8243-2403-X). Annual Reviews.

Cranefield, Paul F. The Way in & the Way Out. LC 73-86969. (History of Medicine Ser: No. 41). 686p. 1973. 25.00 (ISBN 0-87993-035-7). Futura Pub.

Curtis, Brian A., et al. An Introduction to the Neurosciences. LC 74-145556. (Illus.). 830p. 1972. 25.00 (ISBN 0-7216-2810-9); 15.00, filmstrip (ISBN 0-7216-9818-2). Saunders.

Daube, Jasper R., et al. Medical Neurosciences: An Approach to Anatomy, Pathology, & Physiology by Systems & Levels. 1978. text ed. 22.95 (ISBN 0-316-17361-4, Little Med Div); pap. text ed. 17.95 (ISBN 0-316-17362-2). Little.

Dejong, Russell N. A History of American Neurology. 1981. text ed. 16.50 (ISBN 0-89004-680-8). Raven.

--The Neurological Examination. 4th ed. (Illus.). 1979. text ed. 56.50 (ISBN 0-06-140692-9, Harper Medical). Har-Row.

--Yearbook of Neurology & Neurosurgery, 1979. 1979. 28.95 (ISBN 0-8151-2419-8). Year Bk Med.

DeJong, Russell N., ed. Yearbook of Neurology & Neurosurgery, 1981. 1981. 30.00 (ISBN 0-8151-2421-X). Year Bk Med.

DeJong, Russell N. & Sugar, Oscar, eds. Year Book of Neurology & Neurosurgery 1980. 1980. 30.00 (ISBN 0-8151-2420-1). Year Bk Med.

Dekaban, Anatole. Neurology of Early Childhood. 524p. 1970. 31.50 (ISBN 0-683-02419-1, Pub. by W & W). Krieger.

DeMyer, William, ed. Psychiatry-Neurology: PreTest Self-Assessment & Review. (Illus.). 250p. (Orig.). 1981. pap. 25.00 (ISBN 0-07-051660-X, HP). McGraw.

Desmedt, J. E., ed. New Developments in Electromyography & Clinical Neurophysiology. Incl. Vol. 1. New Concepts of the Motor Unit, Neuromuscular Disorders, Electromyographic Kinesiology. (Illus.). x, 700p. 143.75 (ISBN 3-8055-1451-4); Vol. 2. Pathological Conduction in Nerve Fibers, Electromyography of Sphincter Muscles, Automatic Analysis of Electrogram with Computers. (Illus.). x, 500p. 108.00 (ISBN 3-8055-1452-2); Vol. 3. Human Reflexes, Pathophysiology of Motor Systems, Methodology of Human Reflexes. (Illus.). x, 850p. 145.00 (ISBN 3-8055-1453-0). 1973. Set. 359.50 (ISBN 3-8055-1409-3). S Karger.

Deutsche Gesellschaft Fuer Neurochirurgie, 25th, Bochum, Germany, September 1974. Proceedings. Klug, W., et al, eds. LC 75-8941. (Advances in Neurosurgery Ser.: Vol. 2). (Illus.). 500p. 1975. pap. 44.20 (ISBN 0-387-07237-3). Springer-Verlag.

Diamond, Charles & Frew, Ivor. The Facial Nerve. (Illus.). 1979. text ed. 37.50x (ISBN 0-19-261128-3). Oxford U Pr.

Dilts, R., et al. Neuro-Linguistic Programming, Vol. 1. LC 80-50147. 1980. limited boxed ed. 24.00x (ISBN 0-916990-07-9). Meta Pubns.

Directory of Certified Psychiatrists & Neurologists. LC 78-72017. 1979. pap. 19.50 (ISBN 0-8379-5301-4). Marquis.

Divac, Ivan, et al, eds. The Neostriatum: Proceedings of a Workshop Sponsored by the European Brain & Behaviour Society, Denmark, 17-19 April 1978. (Illus.). 1979. 55.00 (ISBN 0-08-023174-8). Pergamon.

Domino, E. F. & Davis, J. M., eds. Neurotransmitter Balances Regulating Behavior. LC 75-21131. 240p. 1975. 25.00x (ISBN 0-916182-00-2). NPP Bks.

Donaldson, James O. Neurology of Pregnancy. LC 76-58600. (Major Problems in Neurology: Vol. 7). (Illus.). 1978. text ed. 27.00 (ISBN 0-7216-3139-8). Saunders.

Dyken, Paul D. & Miller, Max D. Facial Features in Neurologic Syndromes. LC 79-17012. (Illus.). 1979. text ed. 56.50 (ISBN 0-8016-1485-6). Mosby.

Ebbesson, Sven, ed. Comparative Neurology of the Telencephalon. (Illus.). 528p. 1980. 45.00 (ISBN 0-306-40237-8, Plenum Pr). Plenum Pub.

Ehrenpreis, Seymour & Kopin, Irwin J., eds. Reviews of Neuroscience, Vol. 1. LC 74-80538. 361p. 1974. 34.50 (ISBN 0-911216-84-7). Raven.

--Reviews of Neuroscience, Vol. 2. LC 74-80538. 280p. 1976. 27.00 (ISBN 0-89004-105-9). Raven.

--Reviews of Neuroscience, Vol. 3. LC 74-80538. 238p. 1978. 24.50 (ISBN 0-89004-168-7). Raven.

Eldridge, Roswell & Fahn, Stanley, eds. Dystonia. LC 75-25112. (Advances in Neurology Ser: Vol. 14). 510p. 1976. 48.00 (ISBN 0-89004-070-2). Raven.

Eliasson, Sven G., et al, eds. Neurological Pathophysiology. 2nd ed. (Pathophysiology Ser.). 1978. text ed. 18.95x (ISBN 0-19-502337-4); pap. text ed. 11.95x (ISBN 0-19-502338-2). Oxford U Pr.

Emmers, Raimond. Pain: A Spike-Interval Coded Message in the Brain. 200p. 1981. text ed. 20.00 (ISBN 0-89004-650-6). Raven.

Enna, S. J., et al, eds. Brain Neurotransmitters & Receptors in Aging & Age-Related Disorders. (Aging Ser.). 275p. 1981. text ed. 32.00 (ISBN 0-89004-643-3). Raven.

Eppinger, Hans & Hess, Leo. Vagotonia: A Clinical Study in Vegetative Neurology. Kraus, Walter G. & Jelliffe, Smith E., trs. (Nervous & Mental Disease Monographs: No. 20). 1915. 15.50 (ISBN 0-384-14525-6). Johnson Repr.

Ersek, Robert A. Pain Control with Transcutaneous Electrical Neuro Stimulation (Tens) LC 78-50175. 280p. 1981. 18.50 (ISBN 0-87527-168-5). Green.

Everett, N. B. Functional Neuroanatomy. 6th ed. LC 70-135680. (Illus.). 357p. 1971. text ed. 14.50 (ISBN 0-8121-0324-6). Lea & Febiger.

Ewert, J. P. Neuroethology. (Illus.). 1980. pap. 24.80 (ISBN 0-387-09790-2). Springer-Verlag.

Farquhar, Judith & Gajdusek, D. Carleton, eds. Kuru: Early Letters & Field Notes from the Collection of D. Carleton Gajdusek. 366p. 1980. text ed. 40.00 (ISBN 0-89004-359-0). Raven.

Fein, J. M. & Reichman, O. H., eds. Microvascular Anastomoses for Cerebral Ischemia. (Illus.). 1978. 49.10 (ISBN 0-387-90240-6). Springer-Verlag.

Fenichel, Gerald M. Neonatal Neurology. (Clinical Neurology & Neurosurgery Monographs: Vol. 2). (Illus.). 270p. 1980. text ed. 25.00 (ISBN 0-443-08052-6). Churchill.

Fields, William S., ed. Neural Organization & Its Relevance to Prosthetics. LC 73-82041. (Illus.). 1973. 25.00 (ISBN 0-8151-3221-2, Pub. by Symposia Special). Year Bk Med.

--Neurological & Sensory Disorders in the Elderly. LC 75-18335. (Symposia Ser.). (Illus.). 256p. 1975. text ed. 30.00 (ISBN 0-8151-3218-2, Pub. by Symposia Special). Year Bk Med.

Finelli, Pasqual F. Diagnostic Reference Index of Clinical Neurology: A Problem-Oriented Approach. 518p. 1980. lib. bdg. 33.00 (ISBN 0-683-03215-1). Williams & Wilkins.

Flohr, H. & Precht, W., eds. Lesion-Induced Neuronal Plasticity in Sensorimotor Systems. (Proceedings in Life Sciences Ser.). (Illus.). 400p. 1981. 46.70 (ISBN 0-387-10747-9). Springer-Verlag.

Forster, Francis M. Clinical Neurology. 4th ed. LC 78-7343. 1978. pap. text ed. 11.45 (ISBN 0-8016-1637-9). Mosby.

Fried, Rainer, ed. Methods of Neurochemistry, Vol. 1. 1971. 49.75 (ISBN 0-8247-1215-3). Dekker.

Friedlander, W., ed. Current Reviews. LC 75-14572. (Advances in Neurology Ser.: Vol. 13). 404p. 1975. 36.00 (ISBN 0-89004-000-1). Raven.

Garattini, S., et al, eds. Interactions Between Putative Neurotransmitters in the Brain. LC 77-83686. (Monographs of the Mario Negri Institute for Pharmacological Research). 431p. 1978. 34.50 (ISBN 0-89004-196-2). Raven.

Gazzaniga, Michael S., et al. Functional Neuroscience. LC 78-21508. 1979. text ed. 20.95 scp (ISBN 0-06-042291-2, HarpC); test items free (ISBN 0-06-362358-7). Har-Row.

Ghils, Paul. Language & Thought: A Survey of the Problem. 80p. 1980. 5.95 (ISBN 0-533-02649-0). Vantage.

Gilroy, John & Meyer, John S. Medical Neurology. 3rd ed. (Illus.). 1979. text ed. 29.95 (ISBN 0-02-343640-9). Macmillan.

Goldblatt, David. Neuroscience & Clinical Nuerology Review. LC 78-8560. (Arco Medical Review Ser.). (Illus.). 1979. pap. text ed. 10.00 (ISBN 0-668-03370-3). Arco.

Gross, Mortimer D. Neurology Primer for Non-Physicians: A Guide for Clinicians. (Postgraduate International Behavioral Science Ser). 1981. 18.95 (ISBN 0-918924-04-9). Postgrad Intl.

Haerer, Armin & Currier, Robert D. Neurology Notes. 1977. pap. text ed. 12.95 (ISBN 0-316-33780-3). Little.

Haerer, Armin F., ed. Self-Assessment of Current Knowledge in Neurology. 3rd ed. LC 80-81657. 1980. spiral bdg. 17.00 (ISBN 0-87488-254-0). Med Exam.

Harmony, Thalia. Neurometric Assessment of Brain Dysfunction in Neurological Patients. (Functional Neuroscience: Vol. 3). 500p. 1982. text ed. price not set (ISBN 0-89859-044-2). L Erlbaum Assocs.

Hassell, Thomas, et al, eds. Phenytoin-Induced Teratology & Gingival Pathology. 252p. 1980. text ed. 27.00 (ISBN 0-89004-412-0). Raven.

Hausman, Louis. Clinical Neuroanatomy, Neurophysiology & Neurology: With a Method of Brain Reconstruction. rev. 3rd ed. (Illus.). 484p. 1971. text ed. 31.75 lexotone (ISBN 0-398-00803-5). C C Thomas.

Haymaker, Webb & Schiller, Francis. The Founders of Neurology: One Hundred & Forty-Six Biographical Sketches by Eighty-Nine Authors. 2nd ed. (Illus.). 640p. 1970. 24.75 (ISBN 0-398-00809-4). C C Thomas.

Heiden, U. Analysis of Neural Networks. (Lecture Notes in Biomathematics: Vol. 35). 159p. 1980. pap. text ed. 13.00 (ISBN 0-387-09966-2). Springer-Verlag.

Heilman. A Handbook for Differential Diagnosis of Neurologic Signs & Symptoms. (Illus.). 1977. pap. text ed. 14.50 (ISBN 0-8385-3617-4). ACC.

Himwich, Williamina, ed. Biochemistry of the Developing Brain, Vol. 1. 408p. 1973. 49.75 (ISBN 0-8247-1316-8). Dekker.

Himwich, Williamina A., ed. Biochemistry of the Developing Brain, Vol. 2. 346p. 1974. 49.75 (ISBN 0-8247-6035-2). Dekker.

Hobson, J. Allan & Brazier, Mary A., eds. The Reticular Formation. (International Brain Research Organization Monograph: Vol. 6). 564p. 1979. text ed. 53.50 (ISBN 0-89004-379-5). Raven.

Hodson, C. J., et al. The Pathogenesis of Reflux Nephropathy. Maling, T. M. & McManamon, P. J., eds. 1980. 10.00x (ISBN 0-686-69953-X, Pub. by Brit Inst Radiology). State Mutual Bk.

Holmes, Gordon. Selected Letters of Gordon Holmes. Phillips, C. G., ed. (Illus.). 500p. 1979. text ed. 53.00 (ISBN 0-19-920105-6). Oxford U Pr.

Horn, G. & Hinde, R. A., eds. Short-Term Changes in Neural Activity & Behaviour. LC 71-121367. (Illus.). 1970. 92.00 (ISBN 0-521-07942-X). Cambridge U Pr.

International Conference on Parkinson's Disease, No. 6. The Extrapyramidal System & Its Disorders. Poirier, Louis J., et al, eds. LC 78-57817. (Advances in Neurology Ser.: Vol. 24). 551p. 1979. text ed. 53.00 (ISBN 0-89004-369-8). Raven.

International Congress of Primatology, 3rd, Zurich, 1970. Primatology: Proceedings, 3 vols. Incl. Vol. 1. Taxonomy, Anatomy, Reproduction. Biegert, J. & Leutenegger, W., eds. (Illus.). xvi, 278p. 57.75 (ISBN 3-8055-1244-9); Vol. 2. Neurobiology, Immunology, Cytology. Biegert, J. & Leutenegger, W., eds. (Illus.). x, 245p. 54.00 (ISBN 3-8055-1245-7); Vol. 3. Behavior. Kummer, H., ed. (Illus.). x, 191p. 35.00 (ISBN 3-8055-1246-5). 1971. Set. 152.75 (ISBN 3-8055-1247-3). S Karger.

International Symposium of the Austrian Society for Election Microscopy, Vienna, Nov. 30, 1973. Principles of Neurotransmission: Proceedings. Stockinger, L., ed. LC 75-2395. (Journal of Neural Transmission Ser: Suppl. 12). (Illus.). vii, 151p. 1975. 52.60 (ISBN 0-387-81277-6). Springer-Verlag.

International Symposium on Neurophysiology. Recent Contributions to Neurophysiology: Proceedings. Cordeau, J., ed. & 1972. 44.00 (ISBN 0-444-40963-7, North Holland). Elsevier.

Ito, Masao. The Cerebellum & Neural Control. 1982. write for info (ISBN 0-89004-106-7). Raven.

Jacobs, Erwin M. & DeNault, Phyllis M. Neurology for Nurses: Including Nursing Technics in Neurology. (Illus.). 208p. 1964. 13.75 (ISBN 0-398-00908-2). C C Thomas.

Jacobson, M., ed. Development of Sensory Systems. (Handbook of Sensory Physiology: Vol. 9). (Illus.). 1978. 120.80 (ISBN 0-387-08632-3). Springer-Verlag.

Jacoby, J. H. & Lytle, L. D., eds. Serotonin Neurotoxins. (Annals of the New York Academy of Sciences: Vol. 305). 702p. 1978. pap. 66.00x (ISBN 0-89072-061-4). NY Acad Sci.

Jennett, Bryan & Teasdale, Graham. Management of Head Injuries. LC 80-16785. (Contemporary Neurology Ser.: Vol. 20). (Illus.). 361p. 1981. text ed. 35.00 (ISBN 0-8036-5017-5). Davis Co.

Katsuki, Yasuji & Sato, Masayasu. Brain Mechanisms of Sensation. LC 81-2320. 320p. 1981. 32.50 (ISBN 0-471-08148-5, Pub. by Wiley Med). Wiley.

Katzman, Robert & Terry, Robert. Katzman & Terry: The Neurology of Aging. (Contemporary Neurology Ser.: No. 24). (Illus.). 300p. 1982. price not set (ISBN 0-8036-5231-3). Davis Co.

Katzman, Robert, ed. Congenital & Acquired Cognitive Disorders. LC 77-87458. (Association of Research in Nervous & Mental Disease Research Publication Ser.: Vol. 57). 326p. 1979. 29.00 (ISBN 0-89004-255-1). Raven.

Kaufman, David M. Clinical Neurology for Psychiatrists. (Illus.). 384p. 1981. 29.50 (ISBN 0-8089-1321-2). Grune.

Kaufmann, H. J., ed. Skull, Spine & Contents: Part 1: Proceedures & Indications. (Progress in Pediatric Radiology: Vol. 5). 300p. 1976. 77.25 (ISBN 3-8055-1382-8). S Karger.

Kelly, Emerson C., ed. Classics of Neurology. LC 78-158127. 384p. 1971. 19.50 (ISBN 0-88275-029-1). Krieger.

Kety, Seymour S., ed. Genetics of Neurological & Psychiatric Disorders. (Association for Research in Nervous & Mental Disease (ARNMD Research Publications). 1981. text ed. write for info. (ISBN 0-89004-626-3). Raven.

Kissel, P., et al. The Neurocristopathies. LC 79-89479. (Illus.). 1980. 57.50x (ISBN 0-89352-039-X). Masson Pub.

Kitamura, K. & Newton, T. H. Recent Advances in Diagnostic Neuroradiology. (Illus.). 1976. 55.00 (ISBN 0-685-83834-X). Year Bk Med.

Klawans, H. L., Jr., ed. The Pharmacology of Extrapyramidal Movement Disorders. (Monographs in Neural Sciences: Vol. 2). 1973. 29.50 (ISBN 3-8055-1421-2). S Karger.

Klawans, Harold L. Clinical Neuropharmacology, Vol. 4. 238p. 1979. 24.50 (ISBN 0-89004-350-7). Raven.

Klawans, Harold L., ed. Clinical Neuropharmacology, Vol. 3. LC 75-14581. 221p. 1978. 24.50 (ISBN 0-89004-266-7). Raven.

Kolb, Lawrence C. The Painful Phantom-Psychology, Physiology & Treatment. (American Lecture Neurology). (Illus.). 64p. 1954. pap. 6.75 (ISBN 0-398-04315-9). C C Thomas.

Krayenbuehl, H., et al. Progress in Neurological Surgery, Vol. 5. (Illus.). 500p. 1973. 103.00 (ISBN 3-8055-1499-9). S Karger.

Kreutzberg, G. W., ed. Physiology & Pathology of Dendrites. LC 74-14474. (Advances in Neurology Ser: Vol. 12). 523p. 1975. 43.50 (ISBN 0-911216-99-5). Raven.

Krogsgaard-Larsen, P., et al, eds. Gaba-Neurotransmitters. (Alfred Benson Symposium: No. 12). 1979. 66.50 (ISBN 0-12-426730-0). Acad Pr.

Kruk, Zygmunt L. Neurotransmitters & Drugs. 176p. pap. text ed. 6.95 (ISBN 0-8391-1483-4). Univ Park.

Kurland, Leonard T., et al. Epidemiology of Neurologic & Sense Organ Disorders. LC 72-90644. (Vital & Health Statistics Monographs, American Public Health Association). (Illus.). 801p. 1973. 22.50x (ISBN 0-674-25875-4). Harvard U Pr.

Lance, J. G. & McLeod, J. G. A Physiological Approach to Clinical Neurology. 2nd ed. LC 80-49872. 1975. 32.95 (ISBN 0-407-00022-4). Butterworth.

Lance, James W. & McLeod, James G. A Physiological Approach to Clinical Neurology. 3rd ed. (Illus.). 368p. 1981. text ed. 49.95 (ISBN 0-407-00196-4). Butterworth.

Langer, S. Z., et al. Presynadtic Receptors: Proceedings of the Satellite Symposium, Paris, July 22-23 1978, 7th International Congress of Pharmacology. (Illus.). 414p. 1979. 65.00 (ISBN 0-08-023190-X). Pergamon.

Leigh, R. John & Zee, David S. Leigh & Zee: The Neurology of Ocular Movement. (Contempory Neurology Ser., No.22: No. 22). 1982. price not set (ISBN 0-8036-5524-X). Davis Co.

Le Winn, Edward B. Human Neurological Organization. (Illus.). 244p. 1977. 14.75 (ISBN 0-398-01122-2). C C Thomas.

Loose Leaf Reference Services. Baker's Clinical Neurology, 3 vols. Baker, Abe B., et al, eds. loose leaf bdg. 250.00 (ISBN 0-06-148006-1, Harper Medical); revision pages 30.00 (ISBN 0-685-57884-4). Har-Row.

Lorente De No, Raphael, ed. The Primary Acoustic Nuclei. Orig. Title: The Cochlear Nuclei. (Illus.). 189p. 1981. text ed. 32.00 (ISBN 0-89004-318-3). Raven.

McComish, P. B. & Bodley, P. O. Anaesthesia for Neurological Surgery. (Illus.). 1971. 27.50 (ISBN 0-8151-5811-4). Year Bk Med.

McHenry, Lawrence C., Jr., ed. Garrison's History of Neurology. (Illus.). 568p. 1969. 22.75 (ISBN 0-398-01261-X). C C Thomas.

McKay, Ron, et al, eds. Monoclonal Antibodies to Neural Antigens. LC 81-10185. (Cold Spring Harbor Reports in the Neurosciences: Vol. 2). 250p. 1981. 35.00x (ISBN 0-87969-138-7). Cold Spring Harbor.

Magoun, Horace W. & Rhines, Ruth. Spasticity: The Stretch Reflex & Extrapyramidal Systems. (American Lecture Physiology). (Illus.). 70p. 1948. photocopy ed. spiral 9.75 (ISBN 0-398-04353-1). C C Thomas.

Magrab, Phyllis R., ed. Sensorineural Conditions & Social Concerns, Vol. II. (Psychological Management of Pediatric Problems Ser.). 321p. text ed. 22.50 (ISBN 0-8391-1245-9). Univ Park.

Mancall, Elliott L. Alpers & Mancall's Essentials of the Neurological Examination. 2nd ed. LC 81-919. (Illus.). 225p. 1981. pap. text ed. 10.95 (ISBN 0-8036-5805-2). Davis Co.

Mandell, A. J., ed. New Concepts in Neurotransmitter Regulation. LC 73-79222. 316p. 1973. 27.50 (ISBN 0-306-30737-5, Plenum Pr). Plenum Pub.

Mark, Vernon H. & Ervin, Frank R. Violence & the Brain. (Illus.). 1970. pap. 12.50x (ISBN 0-06-141698-3, Harper Medical). Har-Row.

Marks, Charles E. Commissurotomy, Consciousness & Unity of Mind. (Bradford Monograph Series in Cognitive & Neuro-Sciences). (Illus.). 64p. (Orig.). 1980. pap. 4.00x (ISBN 0-262-63076-1, Pub. by Bradford). MIT Pr.

Marler, P. & Vandenberg, J. G., eds. Handbook of Behavioral Neurobiology-Vol. 3: Social Behavior & Communication. LC 79-308. 427p. 1979. 39.50 (ISBN 0-306-40218-1, Plenum Pr). Plenum Pub.

Maroun, F. B. Diastematomyelia. LC 75-17393. (Illus.). 164p. 1976. 12.50 (ISBN 0-87527-143-X). Green.

Matthews, W. B. & Glaser, Gilbert H. Recent Advances in Clinical Neurology, No. 2. (Illus.). 1978. text ed. 32.50 (ISBN 0-443-01793-X). Churchill.

Meldrum, B. S. & Marsden, C. D., eds. Primate Models of Neurological Disorders. LC 74-21980. (Advances in Neurology: Vol. 10). 378p. 1975. 36.00 (ISBN 0-89004-002-8). Raven.

Menkes, John H. Textbook of Child Neurology. 2nd ed. LC 79-10975. (Illus.). 695p. 1980. text ed. 38.00 (ISBN 0-8121-0661-X). Lea & Febiger.

Merikangas, James R. Preventing Neurologic Syndromes. 250p. 1981. 22.50 (ISBN 0-87527-224-X). Green.

Merritt, H. Houston, ed. A Textbook of Neurology. 6th ed. LC 78-24403. (Illus.). 962p. 1979. text ed. 26.00 (ISBN 0-8121-0629-6). Lea & Febiger.

Meyer, John S., et al. Research on the Cerebral Circulation: Fifth International Salzburg Conference. (Illus.). 544p. 1972. photocopy ed. spiral 49.75 (ISBN 0-398-02524-X). C C Thomas.

Milner, Brenda, ed. Hemispheric Specialization & Interaction. 100p. 1975. pap. text ed. 4.95x (ISBN 0-262-63057-5). MIT Pr.

Mohedlishvili, G. I., et al, eds. Regulation of Cerebral Circulation. (Illus.). 267p. 1979. 27.50x (ISBN 963-05-2209-8). Intl Pubns Serv.

Morariu, Mircea A. Major Neurological Syndromes. (Illus.). 368p. 1979. text ed. 25.75 (ISBN 0-398-03831-7). C C Thomas.

Muller, E. E. & Agnoli, A., eds. Neuroendocrine Correlates in Neurology & Psychiatry. (Developments in Neurology Ser.: Vol. 2). 1979. 46.50 (ISBN 0-444-80121-9, North Holland). Elsevier.

Mumenthaler, Mark. Neurology. (Illus.). 1977. pap. 15.95 (ISBN 0-8151-6228-6). Year Bk Med.

Naumenko, E. V. Central Regulation of the Pituitary-Adrenal Complex. LC 73-17250. (Studies in Soviet Science - Life Sciences). (Illus.). 200p. 1973. 30.00 (ISBN 0-306-10902-6, Consultants). Plenum Pub.

Nelson, J. Craig, ed. Psychiatry: PreTest Self-Assessment & Review. 2nd ed. (Illus.). 225p. 1981. 9.95 (ISBN 0-07-050974-3, HP). McGraw.

Nikas, Diana L. Critical Neurological Surgical Assessment & Management: Contemporary Issues in Critical Care Nursing. (Illus.). 224p. Date not set. lib. bdg. 20.00 (ISBN 0-443-08158-1). Churchill.

Nomura, T. Atlas of Cerebral Angiography. (Illus.). 1970. 44.30 (ISBN 0-387-05222-4). Springer-Verlag.

O'Doherty, Desmond S. Handbook of Neurologic Emergencies. 1977. spiral bdg. 10.00 (ISBN 0-87488-643-0). Med Exam.

Oehman, R. L. & Axelsson, R. A. Prolactin Responses to Neuroleptics. (Journal of Neural Transmission Supplementum: Vol. 17). (Illus.). 75p. 1981. pap. 17.70 (ISBN 0-387-81605-4). Springer-Verlag.

Pansky, Ben & Allen, Delmas J. Review of Neuroscience. (Illus.). 1980. pap. text ed. 18.95 (ISBN 0-02-390610-3). Macmillan.

Parker, Harry L. Clinical Studies in Neurology. 384p. 1969. 12.75 (ISBN 0-398-01449-3). C C Thomas.

Paton, D. M., ed. The Transport of Neurotransmitters. (Journal: Pharmacology: Vol. 21, No. 2). (Illus.). 74p. 1980. pap. 14.50 (ISBN 3-8055-1316-X). S Karger.

Pearce, John & Miller, Edgar. Clinical Aspects of Dementia. (Illus.). 1973. text ed. 14.95 (ISBN 0-02-858870-3). Macmillan.

Pediatric Neurology for the House Officer. 2nd ed. (House Officer Ser.). (Illus.). 266p. 1981. pap. 9.95 (ISBN 0-683-08903-X). Williams & Wilkins.

Pellettieri, L. Surgical Versus Conservative Treatment of Intracranial Arteriovenous Malformations. (Acta Niurochirurgica Supplementum: Vol. 29). (Illus.). 86p. 1980. pap. 34.90 (ISBN 0-387-81561-9). Springer-Verlag.

Pepeu, Giancarlo, et al, eds. Receptors for Neurotransmitters & Peptide Hormones. (Advances in Biological Psychopharmacology Ser.: Vol. 21). 544p. 1980. text ed. 56.00 (ISBN 0-89004-408-2). Raven.

Peterson, Harold O. & Kieffer, Stephen A. Introduction to Neuroradiology. (Illus.). 1972. 40.00x (ISBN 0-06-142150-2, Harper Medical). Har-Row.

Pfeiffer, Carl C. & Smythies, John R., eds. International Review of Neurobiology, Vols. 1-19. Incl. Vol. 1. 1959. 57.00 (ISBN 0-12-366801-8); Vol. 2. 1960. 57.00 (ISBN 0-12-366802-6); Vol. 3. 1961. 57.00 (ISBN 0-12-366803-4); Vol. 4. 1962. 57.00 (ISBN 0-12-366804-2); Vol. 5. 1963. 57.00 (ISBN 0-12-366805-0); Vol. 6. 1964. 57.00 (ISBN 0-12-366806-9); Vol. 7. 1964. 57.00 (ISBN 0-12-366807-7); Vol. 8. 1965. 57.00 (ISBN 0-12-366808-5); Vol. 9. 1966. 57.00 (ISBN 0-12-366809-3); Vol. 10. 1967. 57.00 (ISBN 0-12-366810-7); Vol. 11. 1969. 57.00 (ISBN 0-12-366811-5); Vol. 12. 1970. 57.00 (ISBN 0-12-366812-3); Vol. 13. 1970. 57.00 (ISBN 0-12-366813-1); Vol. 14. 1971. 57.00 (ISBN 0-12-366814-X); Vol. 15. 1972. 57.00 (ISBN 0-12-366815-8); Suppl. 1. Neurobiology of the Trace Metals Zinc & Copper. 1972. 27.50 (ISBN 0-12-366851-4); Vol. 16. 1974. 57.00 (ISBN 0-12-366816-6); Vol. 17. 1975. 61.00 (ISBN 0-12-366817-4); Vol. 18. 1975. 53.50 (ISBN 0-12-366818-2); Vol. 19. 1976. 61.00 (ISBN 0-12-366819-0). Acad Pr.

Pincus, Jonathan H. & Tucker, Gary J. Behavioral Neurology. 2nd ed. (Illus.). 1978. text ed. 12.95x (ISBN 0-19-502306-4); pap. text ed. 7.95x (ISBN 0-19-502305-6). Oxford U Pr.

Pitcoff, Ramsey K. & Powell, Herb. Neuroradiology with Computed Tomography. 575p. 1981. text ed. write for info. (ISBN 0-7216-7444-5). Saunders.

Pool, J. Lawrence. Your Brain & Nerves. LC 79-143957. 1978. pap. 3.95 (ISBN 0-684-15894-9, ScribT). Scribner.

Pryse-Phillips, William & Murray, T. J. Essential Neurology. LC 77-91653. 1978. 25.00 (ISBN 0-87488-740-2). Med Exam.

Quintero, Jorge A. Laws, Theories & Values. 2nd ed. (Illus.). 144p. 1980. 10.50 (ISBN 0-87527-147-2). Green.

Renfrew, Stewart. An Introduction to Diagnostic Neurology, Vol. 1. 2nd ed. (Illus.). 1967. pap. 6.25x (ISBN 0-443-00409-9). Churchill.

--An Introduction to Diagnostic Neurology, Vol. 2. 2nd ed. Vol. 2. pap. 6.25x (ISBN 0-443-00410-2). Churchill.

Rockstein, Morris & Sussman, Marvin L., eds. Development & Aging in the Nervous System. 1973. 21.50 (ISBN 0-12-591650-7). Acad Pr.

Rose, Clifford F. & Bynum, W. F., eds. Historical Aspects of the Neurosciences: A Festschrift for Macdonald Critchley. 600p. 1981. text ed. 58.00 (ISBN 0-89004-661-1). Raven.

Rosenberg, Roger N., ed. Neurology. (The Science & Practice of Clinical Medecine Ser.). 740p. 1980. 39.50 (ISBN 0-8089-1196-1). Grune.

Round Table Conference, Rome, Oct. 30-31, 1974. Platelet Aggregation in the Pathogenesis of Cerebrovascular Disorders. Agnoli, A. & Fazio, C., eds. 1977. 27.00 (ISBN 0-387-08165-8). Springer-Verlag.

Salcman, Michael. Neurologic Emergencies: Recognition & Management. 266p. 1980. text ed. 27.00 (ISBN 0-89004-409-0). Raven.

Samuels, Martin A. Manual of Neurologic Therapeutics. 1978. spiral bound 13.95 (ISBN 0-316-76990-8). Little.

Schade & Ford. Basic Neurology: An Introduction to the Structure & Function of the Nervous System. 2nd, rev ed. (Illus.). 269p. 1973. text ed. 24.50 (ISBN 0-444-40940-8). Elsevier.

Schain, Richard J. Neurology of Childhood Learning Disorders. 2nd ed. (Illus.). 178p. 1977. 16.95 (ISBN 0-683-07566-7). Williams & Wilkins.

Schaumburg, Herbert H. & Scheinberg, Labe C., eds. Neurology Specialty Board Review. 2nd ed. 1972. spiral bdg. 16.50 (ISBN 0-87488-306-7). Med Exam.

Scheinberg, Labe C., et al. Neurology Handbook. 1972. spiral bdg. 11.00 (ISBN 0-87488-604-X). Med Exam.

Scheinberg, Peritz. Modern Practical Neurology. 2nd ed. 360p. 1981. 29.00 (ISBN 0-89004-521-6); pap. 16.50 (ISBN 0-686-69137-7). Raven.

Schmitt, Francis O. & Worden, Frederic G., eds. The Neurosciences: Fourth Study Program. 1979. 55.00x (ISBN 0-262-19162-8). MIT Pr.

Schmitt, Francis O., et al, eds. Neurosciences Research Symposium Summaries, Vols. 5-8. Incl. Vol. 5. 1971. 27.50x (ISBN 0-262-19100-8); Vol. 6. 1973. 27.50x (ISBN 0-262-19107-5); Vol. 7. 1975. 27.50x (ISBN 0-262-19117-2); Vol 8. 1977. 32.50x (ISBN 0-262-19141-5). LC 66-22645. MIT Pr.

Schneider, Diana S., ed. Reviews of Neuroscience, Vol. 4. 251p. 1979. text ed. 20.50 (ISBN 0-89004-282-9). Raven.

Schoenberg, Bruce S., ed. Neurological Epidemiology: Principles & Clinical Applications. LC 77-72796. (Advances in Neurology Ser.: Vol. 19). 678p. 1978. 63.50 (ISBN 0-89004-212-8). Raven.

Schoffeniels, E., et al, eds. Dynamic Properties of Glia Cells: An Interdisciplinary Approach to Their Study in the Central & Peripheral Nervous System. LC 78-40218. 1978. text ed. 69.00 (ISBN 0-08-021555-6). Pergamon.

Schulster, D. & Levitzki, A. Cellular Receptors for Hormones & Neurotransmitters. 412p. 1980. 77.00 (ISBN 0-471-27682-0, Pub. by Wiley-Interscience). Wiley.

Seiden, Margaret. Practical Management of Chronic Neurologic Problems. (Illus.). 405p. 1981. 26.50 (ISBN 0-8385-7871-3). ACC.

Serratrice, G., ed. Peroneal Atrophy & Related Disorders. Roux, H. LC 78-62593. (Illus.). 376p. 1979. 45.50x (ISBN 0-89352-028-4). Masson Pub.

Slade, Walter R., Jr., ed. Geriatric Neurology: Selected Topics. LC 81-66942. (Illus.). 350p. 1981. write for info. (ISBN 0-87993-164-7). Futura Pub.

Slosberg, Paul S. Neurology. 6th ed. (Medical Examination Review Book Ser.: Vol. 8). 1977. spiral bdg. 8.50 (ISBN 0-87488-108-0). Med Exam.

Smith, A. D., et al. Commentaries in the Neurosciences. (Illus.). 702p. 1980. 72.00 (ISBN 0-08-025501-9). Pergamon.

Smith, Barnard H. Differential Diagnosis in Neurology. LC 78-31117. (Illus.). 1979. pap. text ed. 14.00x (ISBN 0-668-04033-5). Arco.

Speckman, E. J. & Caspers, H. Origin of Cerebral Field Potentials. LC 78-24682. (Illus.). 230p. 1979. text ed. 28.00 (ISBN 0-88416-281-8). Wright-PSG.

Spicker, Stuart F. & Engelhardt, H. Tristram, Jr. Philosophical Dimensions of the Neuro-Medical Sciences. LC 76-1204. (Philosophy & Medicine Ser.: Vol. 2). 1976. lib. bdg. 34.00 (ISBN 90-277-0672-7, Pub. by Reidel Holland). Kluwer Boston.

Spiegel, E. A., ed. Progress in Neurology & Psychiatry, Vol. XXVII. 400p. 1972. 68.00 (ISBN 0-8089-0767-0). Grune.

--Progress in Neurology & Psychiatry, Vol. XXVIII. 464p. 1973. 64.50 (ISBN 0-8089-0829-4). Grune.

--Progress in Neurology & Psychiatry, Vols. 3-4, 11, 13-16, 20-26. Incl. Vol. III. 675p. 1948. 48.50 (ISBN 0-8089-0449-3); Vol. IV. 606p. 1949. 48.50 (ISBN 0-8089-0450-7); Vol. XI. 600p. 1956; Vol. XIII. 624p. 1958. 48.50 (ISBN 0-8089-0454-X); Vol. XIV. 670p. 1959. 48.50 (ISBN 0-8089-0455-8); Vol. XV. 632p. 1960. 48.50 (ISBN 0-8089-0456-6); Vol. XVI. 629p. 1961. 48.50 (ISBN 0-8089-0457-4); Vol. XX. 783p. 1965. 57.50 (ISBN 0-8089-0460-4); Vol. XXI. 672p. 1966. 57.50 (ISBN 0-8089-0461-2); Vol. XXII. 584p. 1967. 61.00 (ISBN 0-8089-0462-0); Vol. XXIII. 640p. 1969. 68.00 (ISBN 0-8089-0463-9); Vol. XXV. 495p. 1970. 69.00 (ISBN 0-8089-0667-4); Vol. XXIV. 552p. 1970. 62.50 (ISBN 0-8089-0464-7); Vol. XXVI. 597p. 1971. 71.75 (ISBN 0-8089-0708-5). Grune.

Spillane, John D. Atlas of Clinical Neurology. 2nd ed. (Illus.). 500p. 1975. text ed. 39.50x (ISBN 0-19-264172-7). Oxford U Pr.

--The Doctrine of the Nerves: Chapters in the History of Neurology. (Illus.). 500p. 1981. text ed. 50.00x (ISBN 0-19-261135-6). Oxford U Pr.

Stalberg & Young. Neurology: Clinical Neurophysiology, Vol. 1. (Butterworths International Medical Reviews Ser.). 1981. text ed. 29.95 (ISBN 0-407-02294-5). Butterworth.

Stark, Lawrence. Neurological Control Systems: Studies in Bioengineering. LC 68-14858. 428p. 1968. 29.50 (ISBN 0-306-30325-6, Plenum Pr). Plenum Pub.

Strub, Richard L. & Black, F. William. Organic Brain Syndromes: An Introduction to Neurobehavioral Disorders. LC 80-29400. (Illus.). 423p. 1981. text ed. 30.00 (ISBN 0-8036-8209-3). Davis Co.

Suchenwirth, Richard. Pocket Book of Clinical Neurology. 2nd ed. Burrows, E. H., tr. (Illus.). 1979. pap. 15.95 (ISBN 0-8151-8600-2). Year Bk Med.

Sutherland, John M. Fundamentals of Neurology. 272p. (Orig.). 1980. pap. 23.50x (ISBN 0-909337-29-2). ADIS Pr.

Symposium, New York, 1972. Neurobiological Aspects of Maturation & Ageing: Proceedings. Ford, ed. (Progress in Brain Research: Vol. 40). 535p. 1973. 109.75 (ISBN 0-444-41130-5, North Holland). Elsevier.

Taveras, Juan M. & Morello, Francesco. Normal Neuroradiology: And Atlas of the Skull, Sinuses & Facial Bones. (Illus.). 1979. 185.00 (ISBN 0-8151-8732-7). Year Bk Med.

Terry, R., et al, eds. Neural Aging & Its Implications in Human Neurological Pathology. 1981. text ed. 28.00 (ISBN 0-89004-677-8). Raven.

Torack, R. M. The Pathologic Physiology of Dementia: With Indications for Diagnosis & Treatment. (Psychiatry Ser.: Vol. 20). (Illus.). 1978. 36.90 (ISBN 0-387-08904-7). Springer-Verlag.

Triggle, D. J. Neurotransmitter-Receptor Interactions. 634p. 1971. 90.00 (ISBN 0-12-700350-9). Acad Pr.

Tyler, H. Richard & Dawson, David, eds. Current Neurology, Vol. 2. (Illus.). 1979. 40.00 (ISBN 0-471-09497-8, Pub. by Wiley Med). Wiley.

Tyler, Richard H., ed. Current Neurology. Dawson, David M. (Current Neurology Ser.: Vol. 1). 499p. 1978. 40.00 (ISBN 0-471-09521-4, Pub. by Wiley Med). Wiley.

Tyrer, J. Clinical & Experimental Neurology, Vol. 14. 1978. 37.50 (ISBN 0-8391-1267-X). Univ Park.

Tyrer, John & Sutherland, John. Exercises in Neurological Diagnosis. 2nd ed. LC 75-327559. (Illus.). 336p. 1975. pap. text ed. 17.50x (ISBN 0-443-01199-0). Churchill.

Van Meter, Marjie. Neurologic Care: A Guide for Patient Education. (Patient Education Series). (Illus.). 288p. pap. 11.50 (ISBN 0-8385-6706-1). ACC.

Vernadakis, Antonia & Weiner, Norman, eds. Drugs & the Developing Brain. LC 74-640. (Advances in Behavioral Biology Ser.: Vol. 8). 537p. 1974. 42.50 (ISBN 0-306-37908-2, Plenum Pr). Plenum Pub.

Vick, Nicholas A. Grinker's Neurology. 7th ed. (Illus.). 1104p. 1976. 49.75 (ISBN 0-398-03470-2). C C Thomas.

Vinken, P. J. & Bruyn, G. W. Handbook of Clinical Neurology, Vol. 20. 1976. 168.50 (ISBN 0-444-10929-3, North-Holland). Elsevier.

--Handbook of Clinical Neurology, Vol. 24. 1976. 168.50 (ISBN 0-444-10878-5, North-Holland). Elsevier.

--Handbook of Clinical Neurology Vol. 26: Injuries of the Spine & Spinal Cord & Column Pt. 2. LC 68-8297. 1976. 107.50 (ISBN 0-444-11016-X, North-Holland). Elsevier.

Vinken, P. J., ed. Handbook of Clinical Neurology, Vol. 23. LC 68-8297. 744p. 1975. 146.50 (ISBN 0-444-10877-7, North-Holland). Elsevier.

Vinken, P. J. & Bruyn, G. W., eds. Handbook of Clinical Neurology, Vols. 1-15. Incl. Vol. 1. Disturbances of Nervous Function. 1969. 136.75 (ISBN 0-444-10298-1); Vol. 2. Localization in Clinical Neurology. 1969. 158.75 (ISBN 0-444-10299-X); Vol. 3. Disorders of Higher Nervous Activity. 1969. 88.00 (ISBN 0-444-10300-7); Vol. 4. Disorders of Speech Perception & Symbolic Behavior. 1969. 95.25 (ISBN 0-444-10301-5); Vol. 5. Headaches & Cranial Neuralgias. 1969. 83.00 (ISBN 0-444-10302-3); Vol. 6. Diseases of the Basal Ganglia. 1968. 173.25 (ISBN 0-444-10303-1); Vol. 7. Diseases of the Nerves: Pt. 1. 1971. 134.25 (ISBN 0-444-10017-2); Vol. 8. Diseases of the Nerves: Pt. 2. 1970. 109.75 (ISBN 0-444-10018-0); Vol. 9. Multiple Sclerosis & Other Demyelinating Diseases. 1971. 139.00 (ISBN 0-444-10019-9); Vol. 10. Leucodystrophies & Lipidases. 1971. 139.00 (ISBN 0-444-10059-8); Vol. 11. Vascular Diseases of the Nervous System: Pt. 1. 1972. 141.50 (ISBN 0-444-10060-1); Vol. 12. Vascular Diseases of the Nervous System: Pt. 2. 136.75 (ISBN 0-444-10061-X); Vol. 13. Neuroretinal Degenerations & Phacomatoses. 1973. 97.75 (ISBN 0-444-10062-8); Vol. 14. The Phacomatoses. LC 68-8297. 1973. 161.00 (ISBN 0-444-10375-9); Vol. 15. The Epilepsies. 1974. 168.50 (ISBN 0-444-10457-7). (Illus., North-Holland). Elsevier.

--Handbook of Clinical Neurology: Congenital Malformations of the Brain & Skull, Pt. 1, Vol. 30. 1978. 136.75 (ISBN 0-7204-7230-X, North-Holland). Elsevier.

--Handbook of Clinical Neurology: Congenital Malformations of the Brain & Skull, Pt. 2, Vol. 31. 1977. 119.50 (ISBN 0-7204-7231-8, North-Holland). Elsevier.

--Handbook of Clinical Neurology: Infections of the Nervous System, Vol. 33, Pt. 1. 1978. 109.75 (ISBN 0-7204-7233-4, North-Holland). Elsevier.

--Handbook of Clinical Neurology, Vol. 28: Metabolic & Deficiency Diseases of the Nervous System, Pt. 2. 1976. 122.00 (ISBN 0-7204-7228-8, North-Holland). Elsevier.

Vinken, P. J., et al, eds. Handbook of Clinical Neurology: Intoxications of the Nervous System, Vol. 37, Pt. 2. LC 68-8297. (Pt. 2). 1979. 119.50 (ISBN 0-7204-7237-7, North Holland). Elsevier.

Volpe, Joseph J. Neonatal Neurologly. (Major Problems in Clinical Pediatrics Ser.). (Illus.). 300p. 1981. text ed. write for info. (ISBN 0-7216-9077-7). Saunders.

Walker, Arthur E. History of Neurological Surgery. 1967. Repr. of 1951 ed. 35.75 (ISBN 0-02-854400-5). Hafner.

Walton, John N. Essentials of Neurology. 4th ed. (Illus.). 1975. 18.00 (ISBN 0-397-58157-2). Lippincott.

Weiner, Howard L. Neurology for the House Officer. 2nd ed. (House Officer Ser.). 1978. pap. 9.95 (ISBN 0-683-08900-5). Williams & Wilkins.

Weinstein, Edwin A. & Friedland, Robert P., eds. Hemi-Inattention & Hemisphere Specialization. LC 77-5278. (Advances in Neurology Ser.: Vol. 18). 170p. 1977. 15.50 (ISBN 0-89004-115-6). Raven.

Wells, Charles E. & Duncan, Gary W. Neurology for Psychiatrists. LC 79-19972. (Illus.). 241p. 1980. text ed. 22.00 (ISBN 0-8036-9224-2). Davis Co.

Whitaker, Haiganoosh & Whitaker, Harry A., eds. Studies in Neurolinguistics, 2 vols. LC 75-13100. (Perspectives in Neurolinguistics & Psycholinguistics). 1976-79. Vol. 1. 37.50, subscription 33.50 (ISBN 0-12-746301-1); Vol. 2. 37.50, subscription 33.50 (ISBN 0-12-746302-X); Vol. 3. 28.00, subscription 27.00 (ISBN 0-12-746303-8); Vol. 4. 32.50, by subscription 28.00 (ISBN 0-12-746304-6). Acad Pr.

Wiederholt, Wigbert C. Nuerology Therapy. 448p. 1982. 50.00 (ISBN 0-471-09508-7, Pub. by Wiley Med). Wiley.

Wilder, B. Joseph & Bruni, Joseph. Seizure Disorders: A Pharmacological Approach to Treatment. 257p. 1981. text ed. 24.50 (ISBN 0-89004-539-9). Raven.

Wilkins, Robert H. & Brody, Irwin A. Neurological Classics. Repr. of 1973 ed. 35.00 (ISBN 0-384-68503-X). Johnson Repr.

Williams, D. Modern Trends in Neurology, Vol. 6. 1975. 19.95 (ISBN 0-407-00016-X). Butterworth.

Wilson, Charles B. & Hoff, Julian T. Current Surgical Management of Neurologic Disease. (Illus.). 355p. 1980. pap. 39.50 (ISBN 0-443-08042-9). Churchill.

Wolf, John K. Practical Clinical Neurology. LC 79-91846. 1980. pap. 13.75 (ISBN 0-87488-728-3). Med Exam.

Wolf, Sheldon M., et al. Neurology Case Studies. 2nd ed. 1975. spiral bdg. 13.75 (ISBN 0-87488-006-8). Med Exam.

Wolman, Benjamin B., ed. International Encyclopedia of Psychiatry, Psychology, Psychoanalysis, & Neurology, 12 vols. LC 76-54527. (Illus.). 1977. Set. 675.00 (ISBN 0-918228-01-8). Aesculapius Pubs.

Yahr, Melvin D. & Purpura, Dominick P., eds. Neurophysiological Basis of Normal & Abnormal Motor Activities. LC 67-28247. 512p. 1967. 37.50 (ISBN 0-911216-04-9). Raven.

Youmans, Julian R. Neurological Surgery, 6 vols. 2nd ed. LC 77-84693. (Illus.). 5152p. Vol. 1. text ed. write for info (ISBN 0-7216-9662-7); Vol. 2. text ed. write for info. (ISBN 0-7216-9663-5); Vol. 3. text ed. write for info. (ISBN 0-7216-9664-3); Vol. 4. text ed. write for info. (ISBN 0-7216-9665-1); Vol. 5. text ed. write for info. (ISBN 0-7216-9666-X); Vol. 6. text ed. write for info. (ISBN 0-7216-9667-8). Saunders.

NEUROLOGY–CONGRESSES

American Neurological Association. Transactions of the ANA, Vol. 105, 1980. 1981. PLB write for info. Springer Pub.

Carmel, Peter W. Congress of Neurological Surgeons: Clinical Neurosurgergy, Vol. 27. (CNS Ser.). (Illus.). 696p. 1981. lib. bdg. 44.00 (ISBN 0-683-02022-6). Williams & Wilkins.

Congress of Neurological Surgeons. Clinical Neurosurgery, Vol. 26. Carmel, Peter W., ed. 1979. 47.50 (ISBN 0-683-02021-8). Williams & Wilkins.

Scheinberg, Peritz, ed. Transactions of the American Neurological Association, Vol. 102 (1977) LC 61-705. 1978. text ed. 24.50 (ISBN 0-686-77343-8). Springer Pub.

Stent, Gunther S., ed. Function & Formation of Neural Systems: Report of the Dahlem Workshop on Function & Formation of Neural Systems, Berlin 1977. (Life Sciences Research Reports: Vol. 6). (Illus.). 1977. lib. bdg. 24.00 (ISBN 3-8200-1208-7). Dahlem.

NEUROLOGY–LABORATORY MANUALS

Halsey, James H., Jr., ed. Neurology Continuing Education Review. 3rd. ed. 1981. spiral bdg. 14.00 (ISBN 0-87488-345-8). Med Exam.

NEUROLOGY–PERIODICALS

Neurosciences Research Program Bulletin, Vol. 12. 1977. 27.50x (ISBN 0-262-19163-6). MIT Pr.

Neurosciences Research Program Bulletin, Vol. 13. 1977. 27.50x (ISBN 0-262-19164-4). MIT Pr.

Neurosciences Research Program Bulletin, Vol. 14. 1978. 27.50x (ISBN 0-262-19165-2). MIT Pr.

Neurosciences Research Program Bulletins, Vol. 15 & 16. (Neurosciences Research Program Ser. 1979 & 1980). 30.00x ea. Vol. 15 (ISBN 0-262-14030-6). Vol. 16 (ISBN 0-262-14033-0). MIT Pr.

NEUROMUSCULAR DISEASES

see also Amyotrophic Lateral Sclerosis; Muscular Dystrophy; Myasthenia Gravis

Brooke, Michael H. A Clinician's View of Neuromuscular Diseases. 1977. 25.00 (ISBN 0-683-01063-8). Williams & Wilkins.

Goldberg, Alan M. & Hanin, Israel, eds. Biology of Cholinergic Function. LC 74-14473. 730p. 1976. 48.00 (ISBN 0-911216-98-7). Raven.
Goodgold & Eberstein. Electrodiagnosis of Neuromuscular Diseases. 2nd ed. (Illus.). 230p. 1978. 28.00 (ISBN 0-683-03685-8). Williams & Wilkins.
Griggs, Robert C. & Moxley, R. T., eds. Treatment of Neuromuscular Diseases. LC 75-43197. (Advances in Neurology Ser: Vol. 17). 384p. 1977. 32.00 (ISBN 0-89004-113-X). Raven.
Hughes, J. Trevor. Pathology of Muscle. LC 73-89178. (Major Problems in Pathology Ser.: No. 4). (Illus.). 225p. 1974. text ed. 14.00 (ISBN 0-7216-4827-4). Saunders.
McComas, Alan. Neuromuscular Functions & Disorders. 1977. 59.95 (ISBN 0-407-00058-5). Butterworth.
Nakano, Kenneth K. Neurology of Musculoskeletal & Rheumatic Disorders. (Illus.). 1979. 50.00 (ISBN 0-471-09491-9, Pub. by Wiley Med). Wiley.
Rapport, Maurice M. & Gorio, Alfredo, eds. Gangliosides in Neurological & Neuromuscular Function, Development, & Repair. 300p. 1981. text ed. 33.00 (ISBN 0-89004-660-3). Raven.
Rose, Clifford F. Motor Neurone Disease. 160p. 1977. 27.00 (ISBN 0-8089-1047-7). Grune.
Smorto, Mario P. & Basmajian, J. V. Electrodiagnosis: A Handbook for Neurologists. (Illus.). 1977. text ed. 23.00 (ISBN 0-06-142410-2, Harper Medical). Har-Row.
Swaiman, Kenneth F. & Wright, Francis S. Pediatric Neuromuscular Diseases. LC 79-20238. 1979. text ed. 42.50 (ISBN 0-8016-4846-7). Mosby.
Swash, M. & Schwartz, M. S. Neuromuscular Diseases: A Practical Approach to Diagnosis & Management. (Illus.). 352p. 1981. 65.00 (ISBN 0-387-10548-4). Springer-Verlag.
Toole, James F., ed. Clinical Concepts of Neurological Disorders. LC 76-21328. 304p. 1977. 24.95 (ISBN 0-686-74099-8). Krieger.

NEUROMUSCULAR JUNCTION
see Myoneural Junction

NEUROMUSCULAR TRANSMISSION
see also Muscle; Nerves

Bennett, M. R. Automatic Neuromuscular Transmission. LC 76-182026. (Physiological Society Monographs: No. 30). (Illus.). 400p. 1973. 54.00 (ISBN 0-521-08463-6). Cambridge U Pr.
Betz, E., ed. Ionic Actions on Vascular Smooth Muscle. (Illus.). 1976. soft cover 15.30 (ISBN 0-387-07836-3). Springer-Verlag.
Cheymol, J. Neuromuscular Blocking & Stimulating Agents, Vols. 1 & 2. 654p. 1972. text ed. 145.00 (ISBN 0-08-016277-0). Pergamon.
Fields, William S., ed. Neurotransmitter Function: Basic & Clinical Aspects. LC 76-57012. (Illus.). 1977. text ed. 29.95 (ISBN 0-8151-3220-4, Pub. by Symposia Special). Year Bk Med.
Granit, Ragnar. Basis of Motor Control. 1970. 55.00 (ISBN 0-12-295350-9). Acad Pr.
Gydikov, Alexander A., et al, eds. Motor Control. LC 73-19722. 259p. 1973. 29.50 (ISBN 0-306-30771-5, Plenum Pr). Plenum Pub.
McComas, Alan. Neuromuscular Functions & Disorders. 1977. 59.95 (ISBN 0-407-00058-5). Butterworth.
Quantitative Methods of Investigations in the Clinics of Neuromuscular Diseases International Symposium, Giessen, April 1974. Studies on Neuromuscular Diseases: Proceedings. Kunze, K. & Desmedt, J. E., eds. 250p. 1975. 91.25 (ISBN 3-8055-1749-1). S Karger.
Shahani, M., ed. The Motor System: Neurophysiology & Muscle Mechanisms. 1976. 80.50 (ISBN 0-444-41374-X, North Holland). Elsevier.
Vrbova, G., et al. Nerve-Muscle Interaction. LC 78-13416. 233p. 1978. text ed. 43.00x (ISBN 0-412-15720-9, Pub. by Chapman & Hall England). Methuen Inc.

NEURONS

Barondes, Samuel H., ed. Neuronal Recognition. LC 75-45291. (Illus.). 367p. 1976. 32.50 (ISBN 0-306-30885-1, Plenum Pr). Plenum Pub.
Chalazonitis, N. & Boisson, M., eds. Abnormal Neuronal Discharges. LC 76-58750. 447p. 1978. 38.00 (ISBN 0-89004-238-1). Raven.
CINDA: Nineteen Thirty-Five to Nineteen Seventy-Six, 2 vols. 1929p. 1980. Set. pap. 86.75 (ISBN 0-686-60074-6, ICIN 35-76, IAEA); Vol. 1 Z-50. pap. (ISBN 92-0-039079-X); Vol. 2 Z-51. pap. (ISBN 92-0-039179-6). Unipub.
CINDA Seventy-Nine: An Index to the Literature on Microscopic Neutron Data. 1977-1979. 376p. 1980. pap. 30.00 (ISBN 92-0-039279-2, ICIN 77-79, IAEA); free supplement (ISBN 92-0-039379-9). Unipub.
Cold Spring Harbor Symposia on Quantitative Biology: The Neuron, Vol. 17. LC 34-8174. (Illus.). 317p. 1953. 30.00 (ISBN 0-87969-016-X). Cold Spring Harbor.
Costa, E. & Gessa, G. L., eds. Nonstriatal Dopaminergic Neurons. LC 76-5661. (Advances in Biochemical Psychopharmacology Ser.: Vol. 16). 728p. 1977. 59.50 (ISBN 0-89004-127-X). Raven.
Fuxe, K., et al, eds. Dynamics of Degeneration & Growth in Neurons. 1974. text ed. 115.00 (ISBN 0-08-017917-7). Pergamon.
International Symposium, Prilly-Lausanne, July 6-7, 1978. Transport Mechanisms of Tryptophan in Blood Cells, Nerve Cells, & at the Blood-Brain Barrier: Proceedings. Baumann, P., ed. (Journal of Neural Transmission: Suppl. 15). (Illus.). 1979. 64.40 (ISBN 0-387-81519-8). Springer-Verlag.
International Symposium, Switzerland, Sept. 1978. Development & Chemical Specificity Neurons: Proceedings. Cuenod, M., et al, eds. (Process in Brain Research Ser.: Vol. 51). 1980. 97.75 (ISBN 0-444-80128-6, North Holland). Elsevier.
Karlin, Arthur, et al, eds. Neuronal Information Transfer. (P & S Biomedical Sciences Symposia Ser.). 1978. 55.00 (ISBN 0-12-398450-5). Acad Pr.
Klopf, A. Harry. The Hedonistic Neuron: A Theory of Memory, Learning, & Intelligence. LC 80-16410. (Illus.). 112p. Date not set. pap. 19.95 (ISBN 0-89116-202-X). Hemisphere Pub.
Kojima, Tokuzo, et al. An Electron Microscopic Atlas of Neurons: A Complete Picture of the Neuron Soma & General Structures of the Neuron. (Illus.). 130p. 1975. 75.00x (ISBN 0-86008-127-3, Pub. by U of Tokyo Pr). Intl Schol Bk Serv.
Lindsay, Robert, ed. Computer Analysis of Neuronal Structures. LC 76-50605. (Computers in Biology & Medicine Ser.). (Illus.). 210p. 1977. 27.50 (ISBN 0-306-30964-5, Plenum Pr). Plenum Pub.
Mintz, Stephan L. & Widmayer, Susan M., eds. Progress in the Neurosciences & Related Fields. LC 74-10822. (Studies in the Natural Sciences: Vol. 6). 92p. 1974. 25.00 (ISBN 0-306-36906-0, Plenum Pr). Plenum Pub.
Nesmeyanova, T. S. Experimental Studies in Regeneration of Spinal Neurons. LC 77-22460. 1977. 27.50 (ISBN 0-470-99152-6). Halsted Pr.
Osborne, Neville N., ed. Biochemistry of Characterized Neurons. LC 76-55379. 1978. text ed. 50.00 (ISBN 0-08-021503-3). Pergamon.
Paton, David M., ed. The Mechanism of Neuronal & Extraneuronal Transport of Catecholamines. LC 74-14477. 384p. 1976. 37.50 (ISBN 0-89004-014-1). Raven.
Pinsker, Harold & Willis, William D., Jr., eds. Information Processing in the Nervous System. 378p. 1980. text ed. 38.00 (ISBN 0-89004-422-8). Raven.
Roberts, A. & Bush, B. M., eds. Neurones Without Impulses. LC 79-42572. (Society for Experimental Biology Seminar Ser.: No. 6). (Illus.). 250p. 1981. 59.50 (ISBN 0-521-23364-X); pap. 19.95 (ISBN 0-521-29935-7). Cambridge U Pr.
Rohkamm, R. Degeneration & Regeneration in Neurons of the Cerebellum. (Advances in Anatomy Embryology & Cell Biology: Vol. 53, Part 6). (Illus.). 1977. pap. 28.20 (ISBN 0-387-08519-X). Springer-Verlag.
Stevens, Leonard A. Neurons: Building Blocks of the Brain. LC 74-4399. (Illus.). 128p. (gr. 7 up). 1974. 7.95 (ISBN 0-690-00403-6, TYC-J). Har-Row.
Svendgaard, N. A., et al. Regenerative Properties of Central Monoamine Neurons: Studies in the Adult Rat Using Cerebral Iris Implants As Targets. (Advances in Anatomy, Embryology, & Cell Biology Ser.: Vol. 51, Pt. 4). (Illus.). 70p. (Orig.). 1975. pap. 34.30 (ISBN 0-387-07299-3). Springer-Verlag.
Szentagothai. Neuron Concept Today. 1977. 23.00 (ISBN 0-9960001-4-3, Pub. by Kaido Hungary). Heyden.
Waxman, Stephen G., ed. Physiology & Pathobiology of Axons. LC 77-17751. 462p. 1978. 41.00 (ISBN 0-89004-215-2). Raven.
Werner, Gerhard, ed. Feature Extraction by Neurons & Behavior. 100p. 1976. pap. text ed. 4.95x (ISBN 0-262-73044-8). MIT Pr.
Wiersma, C. A., ed. Invertebrate Neurons & Behavior. 100p. 1976. pap. text ed. 4.95x (ISBN 0-262-73045-6). MIT Pr.

NEURO-OPHTHALMOLOGY

Bajandas, Frank. Neuro-Ophthamology Board Review Manual. LC 80-50629. 1980. pap. 15.00 (ISBN 0-913590-71-1). C B Slack.
Cogan, David G. Neurology of the Visual System. (Illus.). 432p. 1977. 22.25 (ISBN 0-398-00322-X). C C Thomas.
Davidson, S. I., ed. Aspects of Neuro-Ophthalmology. 1974. 25.95 (ISBN 0-407-10980-3). Butterworth.
Deutman, A. F. & Cruysberg, J. R., eds. Neurogenetics & Neuro-Ophthalmology. (Documenta Ophthalmologica Proceedings Ser.: No. 17). 1978. lib. bdg. 87.00 (ISBN 90-6193-159-2, Pub. by Junk Pubs Netherlands). Kluwer Boston.
Glaser, Joel S. Neuro-Ophthalmology. (Illus.). 1978. text ed. 43.50x (ISBN 0-06-140941-3, Harper Medical). Har-Row.
--Neuro Ophthalmology, Vol. 10. LC 64-18729. (Illus.). 242p. 1980. text ed. 46.00 (ISBN 0-8016-1876-2). Mosby.
Hockwin, O. & Rathbun, W. B., eds. Progress in Anterior Eye Segment: Research & Practice. (Documenta Ophthalmologica Proceedings Ser.: No. 18). (Illus.). 1979. lib. bdg. 79.00 (ISBN 90-6193-158-4, Pub. by Junk Pubs Netherlands). Kluwer Boston.
Leisman, Gerald. Basic Visual Processes & Learning Disability. (Illus.). 456p. 1976. 35.75 (ISBN 0-398-03454-0). C C Thomas.
Lombardi, Guido. Radiology in Neuro-Ophthalmology. 252p. 1967. 14.50 (ISBN 0-683-05128-8, Pub. by Williams & Wilkins). Krieger.
Miller, Neil R. Sights & Sounds in Ophthalmology: Vol. 3, the Ocular Fundus in Neuroophtalmology. Fine, Stuart L., ed. (A slide-tape presentation). 1977. pap. 165.00 (ISBN 0-8016-3446-6). Mosby.
Neuro-Opthamology Symposia of the University of Miami & the Bascom Palmer Eye Institute. Proceedings, Vol. 8. Glaser, Joel S. & Smith, J. Lawton, eds. 1975. 37.50 (ISBN 0-8016-1846-0). Mosby.
Smith, J. Lawton. Neuro-Ophthalmology Update. LC 77-78562. (Illus.). 412p. 1977. 57.75x (ISBN 0-89352-005-5). Masson Pub.
Smith, J. Lawton, ed. Neuro-Ophthalmology Focus, 1980. LC 79-87484. (Illus.). 472p. 1979. text ed. 57.75x (ISBN 0-89352-071-3). Masson Pub.
--Neuro-Ophthalmology Nineteen Eighty-Two. Bascom Palmer Eye Institute, University of Miami School of Medicine. (Illus.). 320p. 1981. 49.00x (ISBN 0-89352-157-4). Masson Pub.
Thompson, H. Stanley. Topics in Neuro-Ophthalmology. (Handbook in Ophthalmology Ser.). (Illus.). 392p. 1979. 43.50 (ISBN 0-683-08178-0). Williams & Wilkins.
Walsh, Thomas J. Neuro-Ophthalmology: Clinical Signs & Symptoms. LC 78-2757. (Illus.). 294p. 1978. text ed. 22.50 (ISBN 0-8121-0631-8). Lea & Febiger.
Wolintz, Arthur H. Essentials of Clinical Neuro-Ophthalmology. 1976. pap. 13.50 (ISBN 0-316-95155-2). Little.
Zettler, F. & Weiler, R., eds. Neural Principles in Vision. LC 76-21804. (Proceedings in Life Sciences). (Illus.). 1976. 52.40 (ISBN 0-387-07839-8). Springer-Verlag.

NEUROPATHOLOGY
see Nervous System–Diseases

NEUROPHARMACOLOGY
see also Autonomic Drugs; Neuro-Psychopharmacology

Abel, Ernest L. Drugs & Behavior: A Primer in Neuropsychopharmacology. LC 80-11313. 240p. 1981. Repr. of 1974 ed. lib. bdg. write for info. (ISBN 0-89874-137-8). Krieger.
Bowman, W. C. Pharmacology of Neuromuscular Function. 186p. text ed. 19.75 (ISBN 0-8391-4144-0). Univ Park.
Essman, W. B. & Valzelli, L., eds. Clinical Applications of Neuropharmacology. (Illus.). 500p. 1981. text ed. price not set (ISBN 0-89335-154-7). SP Med & Sci Bks.
Giurgea, Corneliu E. Fundamentals to a Pharmacology of the Mind. (Illus.). 472p. 1981. text ed. 37.75 (ISBN 0-398-04130-X). C C Thomas.
Klawans, Harold L., ed. Clinical Neuropharmacology, Vol. 1. LC 75-14581. 238p. 1976. 26.00 (ISBN 0-89004-035-4). Raven.
--Clinical Neuropharmacology, Vol. 5. 225p. 1981. text ed. 26.00 (ISBN 0-89004-648-4). Raven.
Klawans, Harold L., et al. Textbook of Clinical Neuropharmacology. 325p. 1981. text ed. 30.00 (ISBN 0-89004-430-9). Raven.
Kruk, Z. L. & Pycock, C. J. Neurotransmitters & Drug. 160p. 1980. 35.00x (ISBN 0-85664-865-5, Pub. by Croom Helm England). State Mutual Bk.
Lissak. Results in Neurochemistry, Neuroendocrinology, Neurophysiology & Behavior, Neuropharmacology, Neuropathology, Cybernetics, Vol. 15. 1976. 19.50 (ISBN 0-9960007-2-0, Pub. by Kaido Hungary). Heyden.
Mandel, Paul & DeFeudis, F. V., eds. GABA: Biochemistry & CNS Function. LC 79-22019. (Advances in Experimental Medicine & Biology Ser.: Vol. 123). 517p. 1979. 42.50 (ISBN 0-306-40325-0, Plenum Pr). Plenum Pub.
Mitchell, Clifford L., ed. Nervous System Toxicology. (Target Organ Toxicology Ser.). 1982. text ed. price not set (ISBN 0-89004-473-2). Raven.
Youdim, M. B. & Lovenberg, W., eds. Essays in Neurochemistry & Neuropharmacology, Vol. 5. Sharman, D. F. & Lagnado, J. R., trs. LC 80-40964. 152p. 1981. 47.00 (ISBN 0-471-27879-3, Pub. by Wiley-Interscience). Wiley.
Youdim, M. B., et al, eds. Essays in Neurochemistry & Neuropharmacology, 4 vols. LC 76-21043. 1977-80. Vol. 1. 41.75 (ISBN 0-471-99424-3, Pub. by Wiley-Interscience); Vol. 2. 33.95 (ISBN 0-471-99516-9); Vol. 3. 36.95 (ISBN 0-471-99613-0, Pub. by Wiley-Interscience); Vol. 4. 74.25 (ISBN 0-471-27645-6). Wiley.

NEUROPHYSIOLOGY
see also Neural Transmission; Reflexes

Baloh, Robert W. & Honrubia, Vicente, eds. Clinical Neurophysiology of the Vestibular System. LC 78-15467. (Contemporary Neurology Ser.: No. 18). 1979. 33.00 (ISBN 0-8036-0580-3). Davis Co.
Barnes, Marylou R., et al. The Neurophysiological Basis of Patient Treatment: Reflexes in Motor Development, Vol. II. LC 72-87895. (Illus.). 1973. pap. 12.75x (ISBN 0-936030-01-1). Stokesville Pub.
Bechtereva, N. P. The Neurophysiological Aspects of Human Mental Activity. 2nd ed. (Illus.). 1978. text ed. 12.95 (ISBN 0-19-502131-2). Oxford U Pr.
Boudreau, James C. & Tsuchitani, Chiyeko. Sensory Neurophysiology: With Special Reference to the Cat. 1973. 27.50x (ISBN 0-442-20935-5). Van Nos Reinhold.
Buerger, A. A. & Tobis, Jerome S. Neurophysiologic Aspects of Rehabilitation Medicine. (Illus.). 352p. 1976. 35.00 (ISBN 0-398-03405-2). C C Thomas.
Byrne, John H. & Koester, John, eds. Molluscan Nerve Cells: From Biophysics to Behavior. LC 80-39967. (Cold Spring Harbor Reports in the Neurosciences Ser.: Vol. 1). 230p. 1980. 26.00x (ISBN 0-87969-135-2). Cold Spring Harbor.
Chaplin, James P. & Demers, Aline. Primer of Neurology & Neurophysiology. LC 78-6680. 1978. pap. text ed. 12.50 (ISBN 0-471-03027-9, Pub. by Wiley Med). Wiley.
Cobb, W. A. & Van Duyn, H. Contemporary Clinical Neurophysiology: Electroencephalography & Clinical Neurophysiology, Supplement. 1978. 95.25 (ISBN 0-444-80056-5, Biomedical Pr). Elsevier.
Conrad & Magar, eds. Physical Principles of Neuronal & Organismic Behavior. 1973. 46.25x (ISBN 0-677-12290-X). Gordon.
Cowan, W. Maxwell, et al, eds. Annual Review of Neuroscience, Vol. 2. (Illus.). 1979. text ed. 17.00 (ISBN 0-8243-2402-1). Annual Reviews.
Crain, Stanley M. Neurophysiologic Studies in Tissue Culture. LC 75-14567. 292p. 1976. 29.50 (ISBN 0-89004-048-6). Raven.
Crutchfield, Carolyn A. & Barnes, Marylou R. The Neurophysiological Basis of Patient Treatment: The Muscle Spindle, Vol. I. 2nd ed. LC 72-87895. (Illus.). 1978. pap. 9.75x (ISBN 0-936030-00-3). Stokesville Pub.
Desmedt, J. E., ed. Attention, Voluntary Contraction & Event-Related Cerebral Potentials. (Progress in Clinical Neurophysiology: Vol. 1). 1977. 58.75 (ISBN 3-8055-2438-2). S Karger.
--Auditory Evoked Potentials in Man: Psychopharmacology Correlates of EPS. (Progress in Clinical Neurophysiology: Vol. 2). 1977. 58.75 (ISBN 3-8055-2626-1). S Karger.
--Cognitive Components in Cerebral Event Related Potentials & Selective Attention. (Progress in Clinical Neurophysiology: Vol. 6). (Illus.). 1979. 70.75 (ISBN 3-8055-2760-8). S Karger.
--Language & Hemispheric Specialization in Man: Cerebral Event-Related Potentials. (Progress in Clinical Neurophysiology: Vol. 3). (Illus.). 1977. 58.75 (ISBN 3-8055-2629-6). S Karger.
--Motor Unit Types, Recruitment & Plasticity in Health & Disease. (Progress in Clinical Neurophysiology Ser.: Vol. 9). (Illus.). x, 418p. 1981. 88.75 (ISBN 3-8055-1929-X). S Karger.
--Physiological Tremor, Pathological Tremor & Clonus. (Progress in Clinical Neurophysiology: Vol. 5). (Illus.). 1977. 58.75 (ISBN 3-8055-2713-6). S Karger.
Desmedt, John E., ed. Clinical Uses of Cerebral, Brainstem & Spinal Somatosensory Evoked Potentials. (Progress in Clinical Neurophysiology: Vol. 7). (Illus.). 1979. 82.75 (ISBN 3-8055-2936-8). S Karger.
Freeman, Walter J. Mass Action in the Nervous System: Examination of the Neurophysiological Basis of Adaptive Behavior Through the EEG. 1975. 57.00 (ISBN 0-12-267150-3). Acad Pr.

Gildenberg, P. L., ed. Safety & Clinical Efficacy of Implanted Neuroaugmentive Devices. (Applied Neurophysiology: Vol. 40, Nos. 2-4). (Illus.). 1978. pap. 34.75 (ISBN 3-8055-2925-2). S Karger.
Granit, Ragnar. The Purposive Brain. 1977. text ed. 16.50x (ISBN 0-262-07069-3); pap. 5.95 (ISBN 0-262-57054-8). MIT Pr.
Hecaen, Henri & Albert, Martin L. Human Neuropsychology. LC 77-14158. 1978. 32.95 (ISBN 0-471-36735-4, Pub. by Wiley-Interscience). Wiley.
Heiniger, Margot C. Neurophysiological Concepts in Human Behavior: The Tree of Learning. LC 80-25454. (Illus.). 350p. 1981. text ed. 24.95 (ISBN 0-8016-2203-4). Mosby.
Hunt, C. Neurophysiology I. (International Review of Physiology Ser.: Vol. 3). 1975. 29.50 (ISBN 0-8391-1052-9). Univ Park.
Icn-Ucla Symposium on Neurobiology, Squaw Valley, Cal., Mar. 1976. Cellular Neurobiology: Proceedings. Hall, Zach, et al, eds. LC 77-3386. (Progress in Clinical & Biological Research: Vol. 15). 340p. 1977. 44.00x (ISBN 0-8451-0015-7). A R Liss.
Ingram, W. A Review of Anatomical Neurology. (Illus.). 1976. 19.50 (ISBN 0-8391-0961-X). Univ Park.
International Symposium on Neurophysiology. Recent Contributions to Neurophysiology: Proceedings. Cordeau, J., ed. & 1972. 44.00 (ISBN 0-444-40963-7, North Holland). Elsevier.
International Symposium on Radiofrequency Lesion Making Procedures, Chicago, Nov. 19, 1976. Proceedings. Gildenberg, ed. (Applied Neurophysiology: Vol. 39). (Illus.). 1977. 11.50 (ISBN 3-8055-2770-5). S Karger.
Karczmar, A. G. & Koella, W. P. Neurophysiological & Behavioral Aspects of Psychotropic Drugs. (Illus.). 224p. 1969. photocopy ed. spiral 19.75 (ISBN 0-398-00972-4). C C Thomas.
Kots, Ya. M. Organization of Voluntary Movement: Neurophysiological Mechanisms. LC 77-10938. (Illus.). 276p. 1977. 29.50 (ISBN 0-306-31038-4, Plenum Pr). Plenum Pub.
Lechner, H. & Aranibar, A., eds. EEG & Clinical Neurophysiology. (International Congress Ser.: No. 506). 128p. 1979. 24.50 (ISBN 0-444-90111-6, Excerpta Medica). Elsevier.
Leibovic, K. N. Nervous System Theory: An Introductory Study. 1973. 38.00 (ISBN 0-12-441250-5). Acad Pr.
Lissak. Results in Neurochemistry, Neuroendocrinology, Neurophysiology & Behavior, Neuropharmacology, Neuropathology, Cybernetics, Vol. 15. 1976. 19.50 (ISBN 0-9960007-2-0, Pub. by Kaido Hungary). Heyden.
Lissak, K., ed. Results in Neurochemistry, Neuroendocrinology, Neurophysiology, & Behavior, Neuropharmacology, Neurpathology, Cybernetics. 1976. 20.00x (ISBN 963-05-0595-9). Intl Pubns Serv.
Mandel, Paul & DeFeudis, F. V., eds. GABA: Biochemistry & CNS Function. LC 79-22019. (Advances in Experimental Medicine & Biology Ser.: Vol. 123). 517p. 1979. 42.50 (ISBN 0-306-40325-0, Plenum Pr). Plenum Pub.
Newman, P. P. Neurophysiology. (Illus.). 455p. 1980. text ed. 29.95 (ISBN 0-89335-107-5). Spectrum Pub.
Patton, Harry D., et al. Introduction to Basic Neurology. LC 75-31299. (Illus.). 1976. text ed. 19.00 (ISBN 0-7216-7113-6). Saunders.
Porter, R., ed. Neurophysiology II. (International Review of Physiology Ser: Vol. 10). (Illus.). 400p. 1976. 29.50 (ISBN 0-8391-1059-6). Univ Park.
--Neurophysiology III. (International Review of Physiology: Vol. 17). 1978. 24.50 (ISBN 0-8391-1067-7). Univ Park.
--Studies in Neurophysiology. LC 87-51674. (Illus.). 1978. 110.00 (ISBN 0-521-22019-X). Cambridge U Pr.
Remond, ed. EEG Informatics: A Didactic Review of Methods & Applications of EEG Data Processing. 1977. 44.00 (ISBN 0-444-80005-0, North Holland). Elsevier.
Roberts, T. D. M. Neurophysiology of Postural Mechanisms. 2nd ed. 1978. text ed. 99.95 (ISBN 0-408-70808-5). Butterworth.
Ryall, R. W. Mechanisms of Drug Action on the Nervous System. LC 78-5965. (Cambridge Texts in the Physiological Sciences Ser.: No. 1). (Illus.). 1979. 24.95 (ISBN 0-521-22125-0); pap. 7.95x (ISBN 0-521-29364-2). Cambridge U Pr.
Schmidt, R. F., et al, eds. Fundamentals of Neurophysiology: Springer Study Edition. 2nd ed. Jordan, D. & Jordan, I., trs. from Ger. 1978. pap. 15.50 (ISBN 0-387-08188-7). Springer-Verlag.
Serratrice, G., ed. Peroneal Atrophy & Related Disorders. Roux, H. LC 78-62593. (Illus.). 376p. 1979. 45.50x (ISBN 0-89352-028-4). Masson Pub.
Somjen, George. Sensory Coding in the Mammalian Nervous System. LC 72-78258. 386p. 1972. 32.50 (ISBN 0-306-50075-2, Plenum Pr). Plenum Pub.
Srinivasan, S. K. & Sampath, G. Stochastic Models for Spike Trains of Single Neurons. (Lecture Notes in Biomathematics: Vol. 16). 1977. 10.70 (ISBN 0-387-08257-3). Springer-Verlag.
Stalberg & Young. Neurology: Clinical Neurophysiology, Vol. 1. (Butterworths International Medical Reviews Ser.). 1981. text ed. 29.95 (ISBN 0-407-02294-5). Butterworth.
Stein, R. B. Nerve & Muscle: Membranes, Cells & Systems. (Illus.). 250p. 1980. 18.95 (ISBN 0-306-40512-1, Plenum Pr). Plenum Pub.
Stephenson, William K. Concepts in Neurophysiology. LC 79-19675. 175p. 1980. pap. text ed. 13.50x (ISBN 0-471-05585-9). Wiley.
Stevens, C. F. Neurophysiology: A Primer. 182p. 1966. 20.50 (ISBN 0-471-82436-4). Wiley.
Stratton, Donald B. Neurophysiology. 368p. Date not set. text ed. price not set (ISBN 0-07-062151-9). McGraw.
Thorp, John. Free Will: A Defence Against Neuro-Physiological Determinism. (International Library of Philosophy). 208p. 1980. 20.00 (ISBN 0-7100-0565-2). Routledge & Kegan.
Tighe, T. J. & Leaton, R. N. Habituation: Perspectives from Child Development, Animal Behavior & Neurophysiology. 1977. 19.95 (ISBN 0-470-99008-2). Halsted Pr.
Uttal, William R. Cellular Neurophysiology & Intergration: An Interpretive Introduction. LC 75-4673. 1975. 14.95 (ISBN 0-470-89655-8). Halsted Pr.
Willis, W. D. & Coggeshall, R. E., eds. Sensory Mechanisms of the Spinal Cord. LC 78-15764. 495p. 1978. 35.00 (ISBN 0-306-40083-9, Plenum Pr). Plenum Pub.
Wilson, V. J. & Melvill-Jones, G. Mammalian Vestibular Physiology. LC 78-26735. (Illus.). 377p. 1979. 32.50 (ISBN 0-306-40134-7, Plenum Pr). Plenum Pub.

NEUROPSYCHIATRY

see also Neurology; Psychiatry

Barbagallo-Sangiorgi, G. & Exton-Smith, A. N., eds. The Aging Brain: Neurological & Mental Disturbances. (Ettore Majorana International Science Series-Life Sciences: Vol. 5). 393p. 1981. 42.50 (ISBN 0-306-40625-X, Plenum Pr). Plenum Pub.
Baruk, Henri. Patients Are People Like Us: The Experiences of Half a Century in Neuropsychiatry. Finletter, Eileen & Ayer, Jean, trs. from Fr. LC 77-13692. 1978. 10.95 (ISBN 0-688-03271-0). Morrow.
Beckman, A. L., ed. The Neural Basis of Behavior. (Illus.). 447p. 1981. text ed. 35.00 (ISBN 0-89335-132-6). SP Med & Sci Bks.
Delgado, Jose M. Physical Control of the Mind: Toward a Psychocivilized Society. (Illus.). 1971. pap. 3.95x (ISBN 0-06-131914-7, TB1914, Torch). Har-Row.
Emrich, H. M., ed. The Role of Endorphins & Neuropsychiatry. (Modern Problems in Pharmacopsychiatry Ser.: Vol. 1). (Illus.). 250p. 1981. 90.00 (ISBN 3-8055-2918-X). S Karger.
Foster, F. Gordon & Goyette, Richert E., eds. Medical Psychiatry Journal Articles. 1974. spiral bdg. 15.50 (ISBN 0-87488-530-2). Med Exam.
Heilman, Kenneth M. & Valenstein, Edward, eds. Clinical Neuropsychology. (Illus.). 1979. 24.95x (ISBN 0-19-502477-X). Oxford U Pr.
Himwich, W. A. & Schade, J. P. Horizons in Neuropsychopharmacology. (Progress in Brain Research: Vol. 16). 1965. 73.25 (ISBN 0-444-40287-X, North Holland). Elsevier.
Marshall, Wallace. Immunologic Psychology & Psychiatry. LC 75-8713. 240p. 1977. 16.75x (ISBN 0-8173-2703-7). U of Ala Pr.
Riesen, Austin H. Developmental Neuropsychology of Sensory Deprivation. 1975. 32.00 (ISBN 0-12-588550-4). Acad Pr.
Schiller, Francis. A Mobius Strip: Fin-de-Sicle Neuropsychiatry & Paul Mobius. LC 81-40317. (Illus.). 110p. 1981. 12.50x (ISBN 0-520-04467-3). U of Cal Pr.
Shagass, Charles. Evoked Brain Potentials in Psychiatry. LC 76-157928. 244p. 1972. 29.50 (ISBN 0-306-30533-X, Plenum Pr). Plenum Pub.
Small, Leonard. Neuropsychodiagnosis in Psychotherapy. rev. ed. LC 80-19415. 480p. 1980. 25.00 (ISBN 0-87630-243-6). Brunner Mazel.
Smith, Selwyn M. & Koranyi, Erwin K. Self-Assessment of Current Knowledge in Forensic & Organic Psychiatry. 1978. spiral bdg. 15.00 (ISBN 0-87488-235-4). Med Exam.
Taylor, Michael A., ed. The Neuropsychiatric Mental Status Examination: A Phenomenologic Program Text. Date not set. text ed. price not set (ISBN 0-89335-130-X). Spectrum Pub.
Trimble, Michael R. Neuropsychiatry. LC 80-40766. 287p. 1981. 39.95 (ISBN 0-471-27827-0, Pub. by Wiley-Interscience). Wiley.
Usdin, Earl, et al, eds. Neuroregulators & Psychiatric Disorders. (Illus.). 1977. text ed. 35.00x (ISBN 0-19-502132-0). Oxford U Pr.
Weil, John L. A Neurophysiological Model of Emotional & Intentional Behavior. (Illus.). 204p. 1974. 22.75 (ISBN 0-398-02497-9). C C Thomas.

NEUROPSYCHOLOGY

Albert, Martin L. & Obler, Loraine K. The Bilingual Brain: Neuropsychological & Neurolinguistic Aspects of Bilingualism. LC 78-51243. (Perspectives in Neurolinguistics & Psycholinguistics Ser.). 1978. 24.50 (ISBN 0-12-048750-0). Acad Pr.
Alexander, P. E., ed. Electrolytes & Neuropsychiatric Disorders. (Illus.). 351p. 1981. text ed. 45.00 (ISBN 0-89335-122-9). Spectrum Pub.
Benedikt, Moriz. Anatomical Studies Upon Brains of Criminals. Fowler, E. P., tr. from Ger. (Historical Foundations of Forensic Psychiatry & Psychology Ser.). (Illus.). 185p. 1980. Repr. of 1881 ed. lib. bdg. 22.50 (ISBN 0-306-76071-1). Da Capo.
Blakemore, Colin. Mechanics of the Mind. LC 76-53515. (BBC Reith Lectures: 1976). 1977. 34.95 (ISBN 0-521-21559-5); pap. 8.95x (ISBN 0-521-29185-2). Cambridge U Pr.
Boddy, John. Brain Systems & Psychological Concepts. LC 77-21203. 1978. 43.75 (ISBN 0-471-99601-7); pap. 18.95 (ISBN 0-471-99600-9, Pub. by Wiley-Interscience). Wiley.
Brainedness, Handedness, & Mental Abilities: The Foundations of Neuropsychology, 40 titles in 44 vols. write for info. (ISBN 0-404-60850-7). AMS Pr.
Clark, Austen. Psychological Models & Neural Mechanisms: An Examination of Reductionism in Psychology. (CLLP Ser.). (Illus.). 216p. 1980. text ed. 34.50x (ISBN 0-19-824422-3). Oxford U Pr.
Dimond, S. J. Neuropsychology: A Textbook of Systems & Psychological Functions of the Human Brain. LC 79-40087. 1980. text ed. 72.95 (ISBN 0-407-00152-2). Butterworth.
Dimond, Stuart J. Introducing Neuropsychology: A Study of Brain & Mind. (Illus.). 236p. 1978. 15.25 (ISBN 0-398-03794-9). C C Thomas.
Ferguson, Norman B. Neuropsychology Laboratory Manual. (Psychology Ser.). 1977. 6.95x (ISBN 0-87843-630-8). Albion.
Filskov, Susan B. & Boll, Thomas J. Handbook of Clinical Neuropsychology. LC 80-15392. (Wiley Ser. on Personality Processes). 806p. 1981. 35.00 (ISBN 0-471-04802-X, Pub. by Wiley-Interscience). Wiley.
French, Gilbert M. Cortical Functioning in Behavior: Research & Commentary. 170p. 1973. pap. 5.95x (ISBN 0-673-05442-X). Scott F.
Gaddes, W. H. Learning Disabilities & Brain Function: A Neuropsychological Approach. (Illus.). 350p. 1980. 26.90 (ISBN 0-387-90486-7). Springer-Verlag.
Gazzaniga, Michael S., ed. Handbook of Behaviorial Neurobiology, Vol. 2: Neuropsychology. LC 78-21459. 586p. 1979. 35.00 (ISBN 0-306-35192-7, Plenum Pr). Plenum Pub.
Golden, C. J. Diagnosis & Rehabilitation in Clinical Neuropsychology. 2nd ed. 1981. 24.75 (ISBN 0-398-04438-4). C C Thomas.
Golden, Charles A., et al. Interpretation of the Halstead-Reitan Neuropsychological Test Battery: A Casebook Approach. (Illus.). 401p. 1980. 26.50 (ISBN 0-8089-1298-4). Grune.
Golden, Charles J. Diagnosis & Rehabilitation in Clinical Neuropsychology. (Illus.). 336p. 1981. 24.75 (ISBN 0-398-04438-4). C C Thomas.
Goldstein, Kurt. A Kurt Goldstein Reader: The Shaping of Neuropsychology. Rieber, R. W., ed. LC 78-22720. 32.50 (ISBN 0-404-60868-X). AMS Pr.
Guthrie, D. M. Neuroethology: An Introduction. 221p. 1981. pap. 27.95x (ISBN 0-470-26993-6). Halsted Pr.
Heilman, Kenneth M. & Valenstein, Edward, eds. Clinical Neuropsychology. (Illus.). 1979. 24.95x (ISBN 0-19-502477-X). Oxford U Pr.
Hirst, Donald V. Origins of Human Nature & Human Behavior. LC 74-30745. (Illus.). 106p. 1975. 10.00 (ISBN 0-8022-2162-9). Philos Lib.
Hynd, George & Obrzut, John E. Neuropsychological Assessment & the School-Age Child: Issues & Procedures. (Illus.). 1981. write for info. (ISBN 0-8089-1381-6). Grune.
Khomskaia. Brain & Activation. (National Library of Medicine Ser.). 380p. 1981. text ed. 18.50 (ISBN 0-08-025993-6). Pergamon.
Knights, Robert M. & Bakker, Dirk J., eds. The Neuropsychology of Learning Disorders: Theoretical Approaches. (Illus.). 1976. 24.50 (ISBN 0-8391-0951-2). Univ Park.
Kolb, Bryan & Whishaw, Ian Q. Fundamentals of Human Neuropsychology. LC 80-17987. (Psychology Ser.). (Illus.). 1980. text ed. 17.95x (ISBN 0-7167-1219-9). W H Freeman.
Laughlin, Charles D. & D'Aquili, Eugene G. Biogenetic Stucturalism. LC 74-13245. (Illus.). 211p. 1974. text ed. 12.00x (ISBN 0-231-03817-8). Columbia U Pr.
Lezak, Muriel D. Neuropsychological Assessment. (Illus.). 500p. 1976. text ed. 19.50x (ISBN 0-19-502037-5). Oxford U Pr.
Lohr, Thomas F. The Mechanics of the Mind. LC 75-175946. (Illus.). 515p. 1971. 11.95 (ISBN 0-9600432-1-7). Venture Bks.
Luria, A. R. The Neuropsychology of Memory. Haigh, B., tr. LC 76-10186. 1976. 22.95 (ISBN 0-470-15107-2). Halsted Pr.
McFadden, D., ed. Neural Mechanisms in Behavior: A Texas Symposium. (Illus.). 350p. 1980. 24.90 (ISBN 0-387-90468-9). Springer-Verlag.
Malmo, R. On Emotions, Needs, & Our Archaic Brain. LC 74-6356. (Persons in Psychology Ser). 1975. text ed. 7.95 (ISBN 0-03-078455-7, HoltC). HR&W.
Marler, P. & Vandenberg, J. G., eds. Handbook of Behavioral Neurobiology-Vol. 3: Social Behavior & Communication. LC 79-308. 427p. 1979. 39.50 (ISBN 0-306-40218-1, Plenum Pr). Plenum Pub.
Marshall, Wallace. Immunologic Psychology & Psychiatry. LC 75-8713. 240p. 1977. 16.75x (ISBN 0-8173-2703-7). U of Ala Pr.
Miller, Lyle H., et al. Neuropeptide Influences on the Brain & Behavior. LC 76-5663. (Advances in Biochemical Psychopharmacology: Vol. 17). 310p. 1977. 31.50 (ISBN 0-89004-130-X). Raven.
Phillips, M. Ian. Brain Unit Activity During Behavior. (Illus.). 376p. 1973. text ed. 22.50 (ISBN 0-398-02769-2). C C Thomas.
Pirozzolo, Francis J. & Wittrock, Merlin C. Neuropsychological & Cognitive Processes in Reading. (Perspectives in Neurolinguistics & Psycholinguistics Ser.). 1981. 29.50 (ISBN 0-12-557360-X). Acad Pr.
Pribram, Karl H. & Gill, Merton M. Freud's "Project" Reassessed: Preface to Contemporary Cognitive Theory & Neuropsychology. LC 74-25917. 1976. text ed. 14.50x (ISBN 0-465-02569-2). Basic.
Rieber, R. W., ed. Foundations of Neuropsychology: An Historical Reader. LC 78-72822. 1980. 32.50 (ISBN 0-404-60891-4, RC321). AMS Pr.
Robinson, Daniel N. Enlightened Machine: An Analytical Introduction to Neuropsychology. rev. ed. LC 79-29756. (Illus.). 1980. 17.50x (ISBN 0-231-04954-4); pap. 8.00x (ISBN 0-231-04955-2). Columbia U Pr.
Rose, Steven. The Conscious Brain. 1976. pap. 4.95 (ISBN 0-394-71146-7, Vin). Random.
Rosenthal, Joseph H. The Neuropsychopathology of Written Language. LC 77-2825. 1977. 18.95x (ISBN 0-88229-382-6). Nelson-Hall.
Shagass, Charles, et al, eds. Psychopathology & Brain Dysfunction. LC 76-55487. (American Psychopathological Association Ser). 399p. 1977. 28.00 (ISBN 0-89004-120-2). Raven.
Sinclair, John D. The Rest Principle: A Neurophysiological Theory of Behavior. LC 80-17396. 240p. 1981. text ed. 24.95x (ISBN 0-89859-065-5). L Erlbaum Assocs.
Smith, W. Lynn & Philippus, Marion J. Nueruropsychological Testing in Organic Brain Dysfunction. (Illus.). 356p. 1969. photocopy ed. spiral 34.75 (ISBN 0-398-01796-4). C C Thomas.
Stein, Donald & Rosen, Jeffrey J. Motivation & Emotion. (Illus.). 224p. 1974. pap. text ed. 6.50 (ISBN 0-02-416510-7). Macmillan.
Stein, Donald G. & Rosen, Jeffrey J. Learning & Memory. (Illus.). 224p. 1974. pap. text ed. 6.50 (ISBN 0-02-416520-4). Macmillan.
Sweet, William H. Neurosurgical Treatment in Psychiatry. (Illus.). 450p. 1977. 42.50 (ISBN 0-8391-0881-8). Univ Park.
Swiercinsky, Dennis. Manual for the Adult Neuropsychological Evaluation. (Illus.). 208p. 1978. spiral vinyl 19.75 (ISBN 0-398-03751-5). C C Thomas.
Usdih, Earl & Bunney, William E. Neuroreceptors Basic & Clinical Aspects. LC 80-40962. 279p. 1981. 60.50 (ISBN 0-471-27876-9, Pub. by Wiley-Interscience). Wiley.
Van Toller, C. The Nervous Body: An Introduction to the Autonomic Nervous System & Behaviour. LC 78-16758. 1979. 38.50 (ISBN 0-471-99703-X); pap. 15.25 (ISBN 0-471-99729-3, Pub. by Wiley-Interscience). Wiley.
Walsh, Kevin W. Neuropsychology: A Clinical Approach. LC 77-1451. (Illus.). 1977. pap. text ed. 22.00 (ISBN 0-443-01570-8). Churchill.
Weigl, Egon. Neuropsychology & Neurolinguistics. (Janua Linguarum, Ser. Maior: No. 78). 1980. text ed. 75.00x (ISBN 90-279-7956-1). Mouton.
Wilke, John T. A Neuropsychological Model of Knowing. LC 81-40175. 88p. (Orig.). 1981. lib. bdg. 16.50 (ISBN 0-8191-1768-4); pap. text ed. 6.75 (ISBN 0-8191-1769-2). U Pr of Amer.

NEURO-PSYCHOPHARMACOLOGY

Angrist, B., et al, eds. Recent Advances in Neuropsychopharmacology: Selected Papers from the 12th Congress of the Collegium Internationale Neuro-Psychopharmacologicum Goteborg, Sweden, 22-26 June, 1980. (Illus.). 422p. 1981. 80.00 (ISBN 0-08-026382-8). Pergamon.

Carpi, Amilcare, ed. The Pharmacology of Cerebral Circulation. LC 70-182263. 370p. 1972. text ed. 110.00 (ISBN 0-08-016209-6). Pergamon.

Cooper, Jack R., et al. The Biochemical Basis of Neuropharmacology. 3rd ed. (Illus.). 1978. text ed. 15.95x (ISBN 0-19-502346-3); pap. text ed. 8.95x (ISBN 0-19-502347-1). Oxford U Pr.

Costa, E. & Gessa, G. L., eds. Nonstriatal Dopaminergic Neurons. LC 76-5661. (Advances in Biochemical Psychopharmacology Ser.: Vol. 16). 728p. 1977. 59.50 (ISBN 0-89004-127-X). Raven.

Costa, E. & Giacobini, S., eds. Biochemistry of Simple Neuronal Models. (Advances in Biochemical Psychopharmacology Ser.: Vol. 2). 382p. 1970. text ed. 22.00 (ISBN 0-911216-10-3). Raven.

Deniker, P., ed. Collegium Internationale Neuro-Psychopharmacologicum, 10th Congress: Proceedings, 2 vols. 1977. Set. text ed. 255.00 (ISBN 0-08-021506-8). Pergamon.

Domino, Edward F. Neuropsychopharmacology Lecture Notes. (Illus.). 1979. pap. text ed. cancelled (ISBN 0-685-70075-5). NPP Bks.

Goldberg, Alan M. & Hanin, Israel, eds. Biology of Cholinergic Function. LC 74-14473. 730p. 1976. 48.00 (ISBN 0-911216-98-7). Raven.

Grof, P. & Saxena, B., eds. Recent Advances in Canadian Neuropsychopharmacology. x, 238p. 1981. pap. 58.75 (ISBN 3-8055-1459-X). S Karger.

Haber, Bernard & Aprison, M. H., eds. Neuropharmacology & Behavior. LC 77-14178. (Illus.). 225p. 1978. 24.50 (ISBN 0-306-31056-2, Plenum Pr). Plenum Pub.

International Congress, Paris, 1974. Neuropsychopharmacology: Proceedings. Boissier, J. R., et al, eds. (International Congress Ser: No. 359). 1080p. 1975. 170.75 (ISBN 0-444-15126-5, Excerpta Medica). Elsevier.

Jones, H. B. & Jones, Helen C. Sensual Drugs. LC 76-8154. (Illus.). 1977. 29.50 (ISBN 0-521-21247-2); pap. 7.95 (ISBN 0-521-29077-5). Cambridge U Pr.

Klawans, Harold L., ed. Clinical Neuropharmacology, Vol. 2. LC 75-14581. 218p. 1977. 24.00 (ISBN 0-89004-171-7). Raven.

--Clinical Neuropharmacology, Vol. 3. LC 75-14581. 221p. 1978. 24.50 (ISBN 0-89004-266-7). Raven.

Kornetsky, Conan. Pharmacology: Drugs Affecting Behavior. LC 76-6062. 275p. 1976. 28.95 (ISBN 0-471-50410-6, Pub. by Wiley-Interscience). Wiley.

Kutt & McDowell. Clinical Neuropharmacology. (Monographs in Clinical Pharmacology). 1979. text ed. 25.00 (ISBN 0-443-08009-7). Churchill.

Longo, V. G. Neuropharmacology & Behavior. LC 72-75588. (Illus.). 1972. text ed. 11.95x (ISBN 0-7167-0828-0); pap. text ed. 6.95x (ISBN 0-7167-0827-2). W H Freeman.

Palmer, Gene C., ed. Neuropharmacology of Central Nervous System & Behavioral Disorders. LC 80-1107. (Physiologic & Pharmacologic Bases of Drug Therapy Ser.). 1981. 59.00 (ISBN 0-12-544760-4). Acad Pr.

Radouco-Thomas, C. & Garcin, F., eds. Progress in Neuropsychopharmacology, Vol. 4, No. 6. (Illus.). 110p. 1981. pap. 25.00 (ISBN 0-08-027157-X). Pergamon.

Saletu, B., et al, eds. Neuro-Psychopharmacology: Proceedings of the Collegium Internationale Neuro-Psychopharmacologium 11th Congres S, Vienna, 1979. (Illus.). 1979. 140.00 (ISBN 0-08-023089-X). Pergamon.

Snyder, Solomon H. Perspectives in Neuropharmacology: A Tribute to Julius Axelrod. (Illus.). 400p. 1972. text ed. 22.95x (ISBN 0-19-501551-7). Oxford U Pr.

Symposia Held at the 7th Congress, Prague, 1970, et al. Advances in Neuro-Psychopharmacology: Proceedings. Vinar, ed. 1972. 46.50 (ISBN 0-444-10337-6, North-Holland). Elsevier.

Usdin, Earl, ed. Neuropsychopharmacology of Monoamines & Their Regulatory Enzymes. LC 74-77231. (Advances in Biochemical Psychopharmacology Ser: Vol. 12). 530p. 1974. 41.50 (ISBN 0-911216-77-4). Raven.

Valdman, A. V., ed. Pharmacology & Physiology of the Reticular Formation. (Progress in Brain Research: Vol. 20). 1967. 70.75 (ISBN 0-444-40589-5, North Holland). Elsevier.

Vernadakis, Antonia & Weiner, Norman, eds. Drugs & the Developing Brain. LC 74-640. (Advances in Behavioral Biology Ser.: Vol. 8). 537p. 1974. 42.50 (ISBN 0-306-37908-2, Plenum Pr). Plenum Pub.

Von Bruecke, Franz, et al. Pharmacology of Psychotherapeutic Drugs. Sigg, E. B., tr. (Heidelberg Science Library: Vol. 8). 1969. pap. 7.70 (ISBN 0-387-90009-8). Springer-Verlag.

Warburton, David M. Brain, Behavior & Drugs: Introduction to the Neurochemistry of Behaviour. LC 74-20789. 280p. 1975. 42.00 (ISBN 0-471-91991-8, Pub. by Wiley-Interscience). Wiley.

Yamamura, Henry I., et al, eds. Neurotransmitter Receptor Binding. LC 78-3010. 205p. 1978. 21.00 (ISBN 0-89004-231-4). Raven.

Youdim, M. B., et al, eds. Essays in Neurochemistry & Neuropharmacology, 4 vols. LC 76-21043. 1977-80. Vol. 1. 41.75 (ISBN 0-471-99424-3, Pub. by Wiley-Interscience); Vol. 2. 33.95 (ISBN 0-471-99516-9); Vol. 3. 36.95 (ISBN 0-471-99613-0, Pub. by Wiley-Interscience); Vol. 4. 74.25 (ISBN 0-471-27645-6). Wiley.

NEUROPTERA

see also Caddis-Flies; Stone-Flies; Termites

Elliott, J. M. A Key to the Larvae & Adults of British Freshwater Megaloptera & Neuroptera. 1977. 11.00x (ISBN 0-900386-27-4, Pub. by Freshwater Bio). State Mutual Bk.

NEUROSECRETION

see also Endocrinology

Bargmann, W., et al, eds. Neurosecretion & Neuroendocrine Activity: Evolution, Structure & Function. (Illus.). 1978. 56.70 (ISBN 0-387-08637-4). Springer-Verlag.

Brooks, Chandler M., et al. Humors, Hormones, & Neurosecretions: The Origins & Development of Man's Present Knowledge of the Humoral Control of Body Functions. LC 61-14336. 1962. 25.50 (ISBN 0-87395-006-2); microfiche 25.50 (ISBN 0-87395-106-9). State U NY Pr.

Farner, Donald S. & Lederis, Karl, eds. Neurosection: Molecules, Cells, Systems. 455p. 1981. text ed. 55.00 (ISBN 0-306-40760-4, Plenum Pr). Plenum Pub.

International Society For Neurovegetative Research - Amsterdam - 1967. Neurohormones & Neurohumors: Proceedings. (Illus.). 1969. 116.90 (ISBN 0-387-80914-7). Springer-Verlag.

International Symposium on Neurosecretion, 6th, London, 1973. Neurosecretion - the Final Neuroendocrine Pathway: Proceedings. Knowles, F. & Vollrath, L., eds. LC 74-13218. (Illus.). xii, 345p. 1975. 61.40 (ISBN 0-387-06821-X). Springer-Verlag.

Maddrell, Simon H. & Nordmann, Jean J. Neurosecretion. LC 79-63655. (Tertiary Level Biology Ser.). 173p. 1979. 27.95x (ISBN 0-470-26711-9). Halsted Pr.

Martin, Joseph B. & Reichlin, Seymour, eds. Neurosecretions & Brain Peptides: Implications for Brain Function & Neurological Disease, Vol. 14. (Advances in Biochemical Psychopharmacology Ser.). 727p. 1981. 65.00 (ISBN 0-89004-535-6). Raven.

Martin, Joseph B., et al, eds. Neurosecretion & Brain Peptides: Implications for Brain Function & Neurological Disease. (Advances in Biochemical Psychopharmacology Ser.: Vol. 28). 725p. 1981. 65.00 (ISBN 0-89004-535-6). Raven.

Snaith, Philip. Clinical Neurosis. 240p. 1981. pap. text ed. 17.95x (ISBN 0-19-261251-4). Oxford U Pr.

NEUROSES

see also Depression, Mental; Medicine, Psychosomatic; Mentally Ill; Obsessive-Compulsive Neuroses; Phobias; Psychological Manifestations of General Disease; Psychoses; also particular neuroses, e.g. Anxiety, Hysteria

Adler, Alfred. The Neurotic Constitution. LC 74-39684. (Select Bibliographies Ser). 1972. Repr. of 1926 ed. 28.00 (ISBN 0-8369-9925-8). Arno.

--Study of Organ Inferiority & Its Psychical Compensation: Contribution to Clinical Medicine. Jeliffe, Smith E., tr. (Nervous & Mental Disease Monographs: No. 24). 15.50 (ISBN 0-384-00340-0). Johnson Repr.

Andreev, B. V. Sleep Therapy in Neuroses. LC 60-13947. 114p. 1960. 30.00 (ISBN 0-306-10603-5, Consultants). Plenum Pub.

Baars, Conrad W. & Terruwe, Anna A. Healing the Unaffirmed: Recognizing the Deprivation Neurosis. LC 76-7897. 214p. 1979. pap. 4.95 (ISBN 0-8189-0329-5). Alba.

Beech, H. R. Obsessional States. 1976. pap. 16.95x (ISBN 0-416-70500-6). Methuen Inc.

Bellak, Leopold, et al. Ego Functions in Schizophrenics, Neurotics, & Normals: A Systematic Study of Conceptual, Diagnostic, & Therapeutic Aspects. LC 73-3199. (Personality Processes Ser.). 688p. 1973. 43.95 (ISBN 0-471-06413-0, Pub. by Wiley-Interscience). Wiley.

Bergler, Edmund. The Basic Neurosis: Oral Regression & Psychic Masochism. 371p. 1978. 13.75 (ISBN 0-8089-0054-4). Grune.

--Counterfeit Sex. 2nd rev. ed. LC 57-10688. 398p. 1958. 36.75 (ISBN 0-8089-0055-2). Grune.

--Curable & Incurable Neurotics. LC 61-10464. 8.95x (ISBN 0-87140-978-X, 1961); pap. 3.95 (ISBN 0-87140-066-9, 1972). Liveright.

--Parents Not Guilty of Their Children's Neuroses. LC 71-131274. 1964. 6.95x (ISBN 0-87140-977-1). Liveright.

Bisch, Louis E. Be Glad You're Neurotic. 2nd ed. 1956. pap. 3.95 (ISBN 0-07-005390-1, SP). McGraw.

Bosselman, Beulah C. Neurosis & Psychosis. 3rd ed. 216p. 1969. pap. 14.75 photocopy ed. spiral (ISBN 0-398-00195-2). C C Thomas.

Brill, A. A. Psychoanalysis, Its Theories & Practical Application. LC 78-180559. (Medicine & Society in America Ser). 346p. 1972. Repr. of 1913 ed. 16.00 (ISBN 0-405-03939-5). Arno.

Brooker, Andrew F. & Edwards, Charles. External Fixation: The Current State of the Art. (Illus.). 1979. pap. 23.50 (ISBN 0-683-01073-5). Williams & Wilkins.

Caine, Tom, et al. Personal Styles in Neurosis: Implications for Small Group Psychotherapy & Behavior Therapy. (International Library of Group Psychotherapy & Group Process). 224p. 22.50 (ISBN 0-7100-0617-9). Routledge & Kegan.

Castel, Emilio. Ideo-Symptomatic Origin of Neurosis & Phobias. 1981. 9.95 (ISBN 0-8062-1736-7). Carlton.

Dejerine, Joseph J. & Gauckler, E. Psychoneuroses & Their Treatment by Psychotherapy. Jelliffe, Smith E., tr. LC 75-16697. (Classics in Psychiatry Ser.). 1976. Repr. of 1913 ed. 23.00x (ISBN 0-405-07425-5). Arno.

Deutsch, Helene. Neuroses & Character Types: Clinical Psychoanalytic Studies. LC 65-15288. 1965. text ed. 22.50 (ISBN 0-8236-3560-0). Intl Univs Pr.

Ellis, Albert. How to Live with a Neurotic: At Work or at Home. rev. ed. 160p. 1974. 6.95 (ISBN 0-517-52035-4). Crown.

English, O. Spurgeon & Pearson, Gerald H. J. Emotional Problems of Living. 3rd ed. 640p. 1963. 10.95x (ISBN 0-393-01078-3, Norton Lib); pap. 7.95 (ISBN 0-393-00806-1). Norton.

English, Oliver S. & Pearson, G. H. Common Neuroses of Children & Adults. 1937. 6.95x (ISBN 0-393-01005-8, NortonC). Norton.

Eysenck, H. J. You & Neurosis. (Illus.). 224p. 1979. 16.95 (ISBN 0-8039-1287-0). Sage.

Eysenck, H. J. & Rachman, S. Causes & Cures of Neurosis. LC 64-21700. 1964. text ed. 11.95 (ISBN 0-912736-03-8). EDITS Pubs.

Fenichel, Otto. Psychoanalytic Theory of Neurosis. 1945. 24.95 (ISBN 0-393-01019-8). Norton.

Freud, Sigmund. Selected Papers on Hysteria & Other Psychoneuroses. Brill, A. A., tr. (Nervous & Mental Disease Monographs: No. 4). Repr. of 1912 ed. 15.50 (ISBN 0-384-16810-8). Johnson Repr.

Fromme, Allan. The Book for Normal Neurotics. 1981. 10.95 (ISBN 0-374-11544-3). FS&G.

Gardiner, Muriel, ed. The Wolf Man: With the Case of the Wolf Man by Sigmund Freud. LC 70-151227. 1971. pap. 5.95x (ISBN 0-465-09501-1, TB-5002). Basic.

Gossop, M. Theories of Neurosis. (Illus.). 161p. 1981. 35.00 (ISBN 0-387-10370-8). Springer-Verlag.

Gray, Melvin. Neuroses: A Comprehensive & Critical View. (Contemporary Psychology Ser.). 1979. pap. text ed. 8.95 (ISBN 0-442-22813-9). Van Nos Reinhold.

--Neuroses: A Comprehensive & Critical View. 1978. pap. 15.95x (ISBN 0-442-22814-7). Van Nos Reinhold.

Greenberg, Samuel. Neurosis Is a Painful Style of Living. rev. ed. 1978. pap. 1.50 (ISBN 0-451-07883-7, W7883, Sig). NAL.

Grotjahn, Martin. Psychoanalysis & the Family Neurosis. 1960. 5.95x (ISBN 0-393-01037-6, NortonC). Norton.

Guntrip, Harry. Your Mind & Your Health. (Unwin Bks.). 1970. pap. 2.95 (ISBN 0-04-132013-1). Allen Unwin.

Hine, Frederick R. Introduction to Psychodynamics: A Conflict-Adaptational Approach. LC 71-142292. 1971. 7.75 (ISBN 0-8223-0244-6). Duke.

Hitschmann, Edward. Freud's Theories of the Neuroses. Payne, C. R., tr. (Nervous & Mental Disease Monographs: No. 17). 1913. 15.50 (ISBN 0-384-23480-1). Johnson Repr.

Horney, Karen. Neurosis & Human Growth. 1950 7.95, (ISBN 0-393-01038-4). Norton.

--Neurosis & Human Growth. 1970. pap. 3.95 (ISBN 0-393-00135-0, Norton Lib). Norton.

--Neurotic Personality of Our Times. 1937. 6.75 (ISBN 0-393-01012-0, Norton Lib); pap. 3.95 (ISBN 0-393-00742-1). Norton.

--Our Inner Conflicts. 1945 6.45 (ISBN 0-393-01016-3, Norton Lib); pap. 2.95 1966 (ISBN 0-393-00133-4). Norton.

Hutchenecker, Arnold A. Will to Happiness. rev. ed. 1970. text ed. 4.95 (ISBN 0-671-27063-X). Trident.

Jacobson, Edmund. Modern Treatment of Tense Patients: Including the Neurotic & Depressed with Case Illustrations, Follow-Ups, & EMG Measurements. (Illus.). 484p. 1970. text ed. 45.50 photocopy ed. (ISBN 0-398-00910-4). C C Thomas.

Janov, Arthur. The Primal Scream. 448p. 1981. pap. 6.95 (ISBN 0-399-50537-7, Perigee). Putnam.

Jonas, A. D. Ictal & Subictal Neurosis: Diagnosis & Treatment. 144p. 1965. photocopy ed. spiral 14.75 (ISBN 0-398-00942-2). C C Thomas.

Kubie, Lawrence S. Neurotic Distortion of the Creative Process. 152p. 1961. pap. 4.95 (ISBN 0-374-50180-7, N213). FS&G.

Kuiper, Pieter C. The Neuroses. LC 74-180732. 256p. 1972. text ed. 17.50 (ISBN 0-8236-3555-4). Intl Univs Pr.

Lederman, E. K. Existential Neurosis. (Illus.). 150p. 1972. 10.60 (ISBN 0-407-17040-5). Butterworth.

Levin, Kenneth. Freud's Early Psychology of the Neuroses: A Historical Perspective. LC 77-15734. 1978. 15.95 (ISBN 0-8229-3366-7). U of Pittsburgh Pr.

McNeil, Elton B. Neurosis & Personality Disorders. (Lives in Disorder Ser). 1970. pap. 8.95 ref. ed. (ISBN 0-13-611491-1). P-H.

Mares, Wilson J. The Exhilarating Experience of an Incurable Neurotic or How to Be a Neurotic & Enjoy Every Single Moment of Your Life. (Illus.). 137p. 1980. deluxe ed. 39.45 (ISBN 0-89920-012-5). Am Inst Psych.

Marks, Isaac. Cure & Care of Neuroses: Theory & Practice of Behavioral Psychotherapy. LC 80-26600. 331p. 1981. 26.95 (ISBN 0-471-08808-0, Pub. by Wiley-Interscience). Wiley.

Martin, Barclay. Anxiety & Neurotic Disorders. LC 76-151033. (Approaches to Behavior Pathology Ser). 1971. pap. text ed. 11.95 (ISBN 0-471-57353-1). Wiley.

Masserman, Jules H. Behavior & Neurosis: An Experimental Psychoanalytic Approach to Psychobiologic Principles. 1964. Repr. of 1943 ed. 13.75 (ISBN 0-02-848840-7). Hafner.

Mathews, Arthur G. Take It Easy: The Art of Conquering Your Nerves. (Illus.). 1945. 7.95 (ISBN 0-911378-25-1). Sheridan.

Merin, Joseph H., ed. Etiology of the Neuroses. LC 66-18125. (Orig.). 1966. pap. 4.95x (ISBN 0-8314-0008-0). Sci & Behavior.

Meyer, Joachim E. Death & Neurosis. Nunberg, Margarete, tr. LC 73-19951. 1975. text ed. 13.50 (ISBN 0-8236-1130-2). Intl Univs Pr.

Mosak, Harold H. & Shulman, Bernard H. The Neuroses: A Syllabus. 1966. pap. text ed. 1.50x (ISBN 0-918560-03-9). A Adler Inst.

Moses, Paul J. Voice of Neurosis. LC 54-8213. (Illus.). 140p. 1971. 28.65 (ISBN 0-8089-0334-9). Grune.

Nunberg, Herman. Principles of Psychoanalysis: Their Application to the Neuroses. LC 55-11549. 1969. text ed. 25.00 (ISBN 0-8236-4300-X); pap. text ed. 5.95 (ISBN 0-8236-8198-X, 024300). Intl Univs Pr.

Pickering, George. Creative Malady. 336p. 1976. pap. 3.95 (ISBN 0-440-54995-7, Delta). Dell.

Putney, Snell & Putney, Gail. The Adjusted American: Normal Neuroses in the Individual & Society. pap. 2.75 (ISBN 0-06-090095-4, CN95, CN). Har-Row.

Putney, Snell & Putney, Gail J. The Adjusted American: Normal Neuroses in the Individual & Society. Orig. Title: Normal Neurosis. 256p. 1972. pap. 1.95 (ISBN 0-06-080270-7, P270, PL). Har-Row.

Reich, Wilhelm. Selected Writings: An Introduction to Orgonomy. 576p. 1973. 15.00 (ISBN 0-374-26084-2); pap. 8.95 (ISBN 0-374-50197-1). FS&G.

Saul, Leon J. The Childhood Emotional Pattern & Maturity. 1979. text ed. 18.95 (ISBN 0-442-27356-8). Van Nos Reinhold.

Schilder, Paul. On Neuroses. Bender, Lauretta, ed. LC 78-61181. 1979. text ed. 35.00 (ISBN 0-8236-3810-3). Intl Univs Pr.

Zapotoczky, H. G. Neurosen - Mythen, Modelle, Fakten: Ein Beitrag zur Genese neurotischer Stoehrungen. Berner, P., ed. (Bibliotheca Psychiatrica: No. 153). (Illus.). 180p. 1976. 26.50 (ISBN 3-8055-2310-6). S Karger.

NEUROSES–DIAGNOSIS

see also Personality Tests; Rorschach Test

Baars, Conrad W. & Terruwe, Anna A. Healing the Unaffirmed: Recognizing the Deprivation Neurosis. LC 76-7897. 214p. 1979. pap. 4.95 (ISBN 0-8189-0329-5). Alba.

Laughlin, H. P. The Neuroses. 1088p. 1967. 35.95 (ISBN 0-407-99992-2). Butterworth.

NEUROSPORA CRASSA

Bachmann, Barbara J & Strickland, Walter L. Neurospora Bibliography & Index. 1965. 25.00x (ISBN 0-300-00282-3). Yale U Pr.

NEUROSURGERY
see Nervous System–Surgery
NEUROSURGICAL NURSING
see Neurological Nursing
NEUROTROPIC DRUGS
see Neuropharmacology
NEUTRAL TRADE WITH BELLIGERENTS
see also Continuous Voyages (International Law)
NEUTRALITY
see also Asylum, Right Of; Intervention (International Law); Prize Law; Search, Right of; War (International Law); War, Maritime (International Law)

Bailey, Thomas A. The Policy of the United States Towards the Neutrals, 1917-1918. 8.50 (ISBN 0-8446-1036-4). Peter Smith.

Bernard, Mountague. Historical Account of the Neutrality of Great Britain During the American Civil War. LC 70-146237. 1971. Repr. of 1870 ed. lib. bdg. 32.00 (ISBN 0-8337-0246-7). B Franklin.

Black, Cyril E., et al. Neutralization & World Politics. LC 68-29388. (Center of International Studies, Princeton Univ.). 1968. 15.50 (ISBN 0-691-05639-0); pap. 8.95 (ISBN 0-691-01056-0). Princeton U Pr.

Borchard, Edwin M. & Lage, William P. Neutrality for the U. S. LC 78-153305. (BCL Ser.: Ii). Repr. of 1940 ed. 20.00 (ISBN 0-404-04644-4). AMS Pr.

Coogan, John W. The End of Neutrality: The United States, Britian & Maritime Rights, 1899-1915. LC 81-66645. 256p. 1981. 19.50x (ISBN 0-8014-1407-5). Cornell U Pr.

Deak, Francis & Jessup, Philip, eds. A Collection of Neutrality Laws, Regulations & Treaties of Various Countries, 2 vols. LC 70-138607. 1970. Repr. of 1939 ed. lib. bdg. 53.00x (ISBN 0-8371-5715-3, DENL). Greenwood.

Ford, Guy S. Hanover & Prussia, 1795-1803. LC 72-168054. (Columbia University. Studies in the Social Sciences: No. 48). 18.00 (ISBN 0-404-51048-5). AMS Pr.

Gordon, David R. The Hidden Weapon. Dangerfield, Royden, ed. LC 76-5473. (World War II Ser.). 1976. Repr. of 1947 ed. 22.50 (ISBN 0-306-70769-1). Da Capo.

Jessup, Philip, ed. Neutrality: Its History, Economics & Law, 4 Vols. LC 73-159198. 1973. Repr. of 1936 ed. lib. bdg. 60.00x (ISBN 0-374-94207-2). Octagon.

Montefiore, A., ed. Neutrality & Impartiality. 320p. 1975. 38.50 (ISBN 0-521-20664-2); pap. 9.95x (ISBN 0-521-09923-4). Cambridge U Pr.

Orvik, Nils. Decline of Neutrality, 1914-1941. 310p. 1971. 25.00x (ISBN 0-7146-2696-1, F Cass Co). Biblio Dist.

Sigham & Van Dihn, eds. From Bandung to Colombo: Conference of the Non-Aligned Countries. LC 76-162957. 1975. 7.95 (ISBN 0-89388-221-6). Okpaku Communications.

NEUTRINOS

Allen, J. S. Neutrino. (Investigations in Physics Ser.: No. 5). 1958. 15.00 (ISBN 0-691-08009-7). Princeton U Pr.

Asimov, Isaac. The Neutrino. 1975. pap. 1.75 (ISBN 0-380-00483-6, 38109). Avon.

Chiu Hone-Yee. Neutrino Astrophysics. (Documents on Modern Physics Ser). 1965. 24.75x (ISBN 0-677-01110-5). Gordon.

Faissner, Helmut, ed. Proceedings of the International Neutrino Conference: AACHEH 1976. 1977. 84.00 (ISBN 0-9940011-5-0, Pub. by Vieweg & Sohn Germany). Heyden.

Fiorini, Ettore, ed. Neutrino Physics & Astrophysics. (Ettore Majorana International Science (Physical Sciences) Series: Vol. 12). 410p. 1981. text ed. price not set (ISBN 0-306-40746-9, Plenum Pr). Plenum Pub.

Jacob, M. Gauge Theories & Neutrino Physics. (Physics Reports Reprint Book: Vol. 2). 1979. 49.00 (ISBN 0-444-85191-7, North Holland). Elsevier.

Kuchowicz, B. Bibliography of the Neutrino. 1967. 93.00x (ISBN 0-677-11490-7). Gordon.

Lee, T. D., ed. Weak Interactions & High Energy Neutrino Physics. (Italian Physical Society,: Course 32). 1966. 50.00 (ISBN 0-12-368832-9). Acad Pr.

Lewis, G. M. & Wheatley, G. A. Neutrinos. LC 73-135382. (Wykeham Science Ser.: No. 12). 1970. 9.95x (ISBN 0-8448-1114-9). Crane-Russak Co.

Saenz, A. W. & Uberall, H., eds. Long-Distance Neutrino Detection - Nineteen Seventy-Eight: C. L. Cowan Memorial Symposium, Catholic Univeristy. LC 79-52078. (AIP Conference Proceedings Ser.: No. 52). (Illus.). 1979. lib. bdg. 16.50 (ISBN 0-88318-151-7). Am Inst Physics.

NEUTRON ACTIVATION ANALYSIS
see Radioactivation Analysis
NEUTRON TRANSPORT THEORY

Mingle, J. O. The Invariant Imbedding Theory of Nuclear Transport. LC 73-187686. (Modern Analytic & Computational Methods in Science & Mathematics Ser.: No. 39). 144p. 1973. 24.95 (ISBN 0-444-00123-9, North Holland). Elsevier.

Osborn, Richard K. & Yip, S. Foundations of Neutron Transport Theory. (U. S. Atomic Energy Commission Monographs Ser). 1966. 29.25x (ISBN 0-677-01170-9). Gordon.

Roos, Bernard W. Analytic Functions & Distributions in Physics & Engineering. 521p. 1969. text ed. 26.00 (ISBN 0-471-73334-2, Pub. by Wiley). Krieger.

Spanier, Jerome & Gelbard, Ely M. Monte Carlo Principles & Neutron Transport Problems. 1969. text ed. 17.50 (ISBN 0-201-07089-8, Adv Bk Prog). A-W.

Springer, T. Quasielastic Neutron Scattering for the Investigation of Diffusive Motions in Solids & Liquids. (Springer Tracts in Modern Physics: Vol. 64). (Illus.). 102p. 1972. 24.80 (ISBN 0-387-05808-7). Springer-Verlag.

NEUTRONS
see also Atoms; Electrons; Neutrinos; Positrons; Protons; Thermal Neutrons

Anderson, W. K. & Theilacker, J. S. Neutron Absorber Materials for Reactor Control. 862p. 1962. pap. 95.00 (ISBN 0-686-75856-0); microfilm 47.50 (ISBN 0-686-75857-9). DOE.

Bacon, G. E. & Noakes, G. R. Neutron Physics. (Wykeham Science Ser.: No. 2). 1969. 9.95x (ISBN 0-8448-1104-1). Crane-Russak Co.

Basov, N. G., ed. Pulsed Neutron Research. (P. N. Lebedev Physics Institutes Ser.: Vol. 94). (Illus.). 1979. 35.00 (ISBN 0-306-10950-6, Consultants). Plenum Pub.

Beckurts, K. H. & Wirtz, K. Neutron Physics. rev. ed. (Illus.). 1964. 44.70 (ISBN 0-387-03096-4). Springer-Verlag.

Biological Effects of Neutron & Proton Irradiation, 2 vols. (Illus., Orig.). 1964. 22.00 ea. (IAEA). Vol. 1 (ISBN 92-0-010064-3, ISP80-1). Vol. 2 (ISBN 92-0-010164-X, ISP80-2). Unipub.

Biological Effects of Neutron Irradiation. (Illus.). 484p. (Orig.). 1974. pap. 37.50 (ISBN 92-0-010474-6, ISP352, IAEA). Unipub.

Boutin, Henri & Yip, Sidney. Molecular Spectroscopy with Neutrons. LC 68-22823. 1968. 20.00x (ISBN 0-262-02042-4). MIT Pr.

Case, K. M., et al. Introduction to the Theory of Neutron Diffusion, Vol. 1. 174p. 1953. pap. 22.00 (ISBN 0-686-75866-8); microfilm 11.00 (ISBN 0-686-75867-6). DOE.

CINDA Eighty: An Index to the Literature on Microscopic Neutron Data. 442p. 1980. pap. 39.00 (ISBN 92-0-039180-X, ICIN77/80, IAEA). Unipub.

CINDA: Nineteen Seventy-Eight, an Index to the Literature on Microscopic Neutron Data, Suppl. 4. 1979. pap. 24.25 (ISBN 92-0-039078-1, ICIN78-4, IAEA). Unipub.

CINDA: 1978 Index to the Literature on Microscopic Neutron Data, Suppl. 5. 1979. pap. 25.75 (ISBN 92-0-039178-8, ICIN78-5, IAEA). Unipub.

Compendium of Neutron Spectra in Critically Accident Dosimetry. (Technical Report Ser: No. 180). 1978. pap. 23.75 (ISBN 92-0-125178-5, IDC 180, IAEA). Unipub.

Delayed Fission Neutrons. (Illus., Orig.). 1968. pap. text ed. 14.75 (ISBN 92-0-031068-0, ISP176, IAEA). Unipub.

Dorschel, Birgit & Herforth, Lieselott. Neutronen - Personendosimetrie. (Physikalische Reihe: No. 7). (Illus.). 364p. (Ger.). 1980. 49.50 (ISBN 3-7643-1037-5). Birkhauser.

Egelstaff, P. A. & Poole, M. J. Experimental Neutron Thermalization. LC 79-86201. 1970. 60.00 (ISBN 0-08-006533-3). Pergamon.

Erdtmann, Gerhard. Neutron Activation Tables. (Topical Presentations in Nuclear Chemistry Ser.: Vol. 6). (Illus.). 1976. 45.90 (ISBN 3-527-25693-8). Verlag Chemie.

Ero, J. & Szucs, J., eds. Nuclear Structure Study with Neutrons. LC 73-17651. 496p. 1974. 45.00 (ISBN 0-306-30770-7, Plenum Pr). Plenum Pub.

Foderaro, Anthony. Elements of Neutron Interaction Theory. LC 79-103896. 1971. text ed. 32.50x (ISBN 0-262-06033-7). MIT Pr.

Goldstein, Herbert. Fundamental Aspects of Reactor Shielding. Repr. of 1959 ed. 22.50 (ISBN 0-384-19100-2). Johnson Repr.

Guldberg, Jens, ed. Neutron-Transmutation-Doped Silicon. 502p. 1981. text ed. 59.50 (ISBN 0-306-40738-8, Plenum Pr). Plenum Pub.

Hetrick, David L. & Weaver, Lynn E., eds. Neutron Dynamics & Control. LC 66-60098. (AEC Symposium Ser.). 612p. 1966. pap. 6.00 (ISBN 0-686-75895-1); microfiche 3.00 (ISBN 0-686-75896-X). DOE.

Irvine, J. M. Heavy Nuclei, Superheavy Nuclei, & Neutron Stars. (Oxford Studies in Nuclear Physics). (Illus.). 200p. 1975. 34.95x (ISBN 0-19-851510-3). Oxford U Pr.

Koester, L. & Steyerl, A. Neutron Physics. (Tracts in Modern Physics: Vol. 80). (Illus.). 1977. 36.00 (ISBN 3-540-08022-8). Springer-Verlag.

Marchuk, Gurji I. Numerical Methods for Nuclear Reactor Calculations. LC 59-9229. 295p. 1959. 65.00 (ISBN 0-306-10561-6, Consultants). Plenum Pub.

Mezei, F., ed. Neutron Spin Echo: Proceedings. (Lecture Notes in Physics Ser.: Vol. 128). 253p. 1980. pap. 19.00 (ISBN 0-387-10004-0). Springer-Verlag.

Mezhiborskaya, Kh. B. Photoneutron Method of Determining Beryllium. LC 61-18758. 30p. 1962. 17.50 (ISBN 0-306-10568-3, Consultants). Plenum Pub.

Neutron Capture Gamma-Ray Spectroscopy. (Illus., Orig.). 1969. pap. 47.25 (ISBN 92-0-130369-6, ISP235, IAEA). Unipub.

Neutron Moisture Gauges. (Technical Reports Ser.: No. 112). (Illus., Orig.). 1970. pap. 9.50 (ISBN 92-0-165070-1, IDC112, IAEA). Unipub.

Neutron Monitoring for Radiation Protection Purposes, 2 vols. (Illus.). 355p. (Orig.). 1974. Vol. 1. pap. 28.00 (ISBN 92-0-020173-3, ISP 318-1, IAEA); Vol. 2. pap. 40.25 (ISBN 92-0-020273-X, ISP 318-2). Unipub.

Neutron Noise, Waves & Pulse Propagation. LC 66-60048. (AES Symposium Ser.). 788p. 1967. pap. 6.00 (ISBN 0-686-75897-8); microfiche 3.00 (ISBN 0-686-75898-6). DOE.

Neutron Nuclear Data Evaluation. (Technical Reports Ser.: No. 146). 127p. (Orig.). 1973. pap. 11.75 (ISBN 92-0-135173-9, IDC146, IAEA). Unipub.

Neutron Standard Reference Data: Proceedings. (Illus.). 369p. 1975. pap. 26.75 (ISBN 92-0-031074-5, ISP371, IAEA). Unipub.

Neutron Thermalization & Reactor Spectra, 2 vols. (Illus., Eng. , Fr. & Rus.). 1968. Vol. 1. pap. 39.00 (ISBN 92-0-050068-4, ISP160-1-2, IAEA); Vol. 2. pap. 32.50 (ISBN 92-0-050168-0). Unipub.

Nuclear Data for Reactors - 1966, 2 vols. 1967. Vol. 1. pap. 34.25 (ISBN 92-0-030167-3, 140-1-2, IAEA); Vol. 2. pap. 26.00 (ISBN 92-0-030267-X). Unipub.

Phillips, Gerald C., et al, eds. Progress in Fast Neutron Physics. LC 63-18849. (Illus.). 1963. 9.75x (ISBN 0-226-66735-9). U of Chicago Pr.

Pile Neutron Research in Physics. 1962. 27.75 (ISBN 92-0-030062-6, IAEA). Unipub.

Pohl, H. A. Dielectrophoresis. LC 77-71421. (Cambridge Monographs on Physics). (Illus.). 1978. 99.50 (ISBN 0-521-21657-5). Cambridge U Pr.

Prompt Fission Neutron Spectra. (Illus.). 176p. (Orig.). 1973. pap. 13.00 (ISBN 92-0-131172-9, IAEA). Unipub.

Protection Against Neutron Radiation. (NCRP Reports Ser.: No. 38). 1971. 9.00 (ISBN 0-913392-20-0). NCRP Pubns.

Radiobiological Applications of Neutron Irradiation. (Illus.). 263p. (Orig.). 1972. pap. 21.25 (ISBN 92-0-011172-6, ISP325, IAEA). Unipub.

Rybakov, Boris V. & Sidorov, V. A. Fast-Neutron Spectroscopy. LC 60-8723. 121p. 1960. 27.50 (ISBN 0-306-10532-2, Consultants). Plenum Pub.

Smith, Alan B. Neutron Standards & Flux Normaization: Proceedings. LC 77-611328. (AEC Symposium Ser.). 525p. 1971. pap. 6.00 (ISBN 0-686-75873-0); microfiche 3.00 (ISBN 0-686-75874-9). DOE.

Tyror, J. G. & Vaughan, R. I. Introduction to Neutron Kinetics of Nuclear Power Reactors. LC 76-94936. 1970. 25.00 (ISBN 0-08-006667-4). Pergamon.

USA National Neutron Cross-Section Center & USSR Nuclear Data Centre. CINDA: 1976-1977 Index to the Literature on Microscopic Neutron Data, 2 vols. (Orig.). 1976. pap. 114.50 ea. (IAEA). Vol. 1 (ISBN 92-0-039076-5). Vol. 2 (ICIN76/7). Unipub.

Yeater, M. L., ed. Neutron Physics: Proceedings. (Nuclear Science & Technology: Vol. 2). 1962. 46.50 (ISBN 0-12-769050-6). Acad Pr.

NEUTRONS–DIFFRACTION

Bacon, G. E. Neutron Diffraction. 3rd ed. (Monographs on the Physics & Chemistry of Materials). (Illus.). 652p. 1975. 125.00x (ISBN 0-19-851353-4). Oxford U Pr.

--X-Ray & Neutron Diffraction. 1966. text ed. 44.00 (ISBN 0-08-011999-9); pap. text ed. 19.50 (ISBN 0-08-011998-0). Pergamon.

Dachs, H., ed. Neutron Diffraction. LC 78-2969. (Topics in Current Physics: Vol. 6). (Illus.). 1978. 34.50 (ISBN 0-387-08710-9). Springer-Verlag.

Izyumov, Yurii A. & Ozerov, Ruslan P. Magnetic Neutron Diffraction. LC 68-21475. 598p. 1970. 47.50 (ISBN 0-306-30371-X, Plenum Pr). Plenum Pub.

NEUTRONS–MEASUREMENT
see also Time-Of-Flight Mass Spectrometry

Broerse, J. J., ed. Ion Chambers for Neutron Dosimetry Workshop, Rijswijk, the Netherlands, Sept. 1979. (European Applied Research Reports Special Topics). 364p. 1980. 62.75 (ISBN 3-7186-0048-X). Harwood Academic.

Measurement of Absorbed Dose of Neutrons & Mixtures of Neutrons & Gamma - Rays. (NCRP Reports Ser.: No. 25). 1961. 6.00 (ISBN 0-913392-08-1). NCRP Pubns.

Measurements of Neutron Flux & Spectra for Physical & Biological Applications. (NCRP Reports Ser.: No. 23). 1960. 6.00 (ISBN 0-913392-07-3). NCRP Pubns.

Neutron Fluence Measurements. (Technical Reports Ser.: No. 107). (Illus., Orig.). 1970. pap. 15.25 (ISBN 92-0-135070-8, IDC107, IAEA). Unipub.

Neutron Monitoring. 1967. pap. 33.25 (ISBN 92-0-020067-2, ISP136, IAEA). Unipub.

USA National Neutron Cross-Section Center & USSR Nuclear Data Centre. CINDA: 1976-1977 Index to the Literature on Microscopic Neutron Data, 2 vols. (Orig.). 1976. pap. 114.50 ea. (IAEA). Vol. 1 (ISBN 92-0-039076-5). Vol. 2 (ICIN76/7). Unipub.

NEUTRONS–SCATTERING

Egelstaff, P. A., ed. Thermal Neutron Scattering. 1966. 83.00 (ISBN 0-12-232950-3). Acad Pr.

Ghatak, A. K. & Kothari, L. S. Introduction to Lattice Dynamics. 1972. 22.50 (ISBN 0-201-02363-6, Adv Bk Prog). A-W.

Inelastic Scattering of Neutrons in Solids & Liquids: 1962, 2 vols. (Illus., Eng. , Fr. & Rus.). 1963. Vol. 1. 22.75 (ISBN 92-0-030363-3, ISP62-1, IAEA); Vol. 2. 23.75 (ISBN 92-0-030463-X, ISP62-2). Unipub.

Inelastic Scattering of Neutrons: 1964, 2 vols. (Illus., Eng. , Fr & Rus.). 1965. Vol. 1. 24.50 (ISBN 92-0-030365-X, ISP92-1, IAEA); Vol. 2. 29.25 (ISBN 92-0-030465-6, ISP92-2). Unipub.

Instrumentation for Neutron Inelastic Scattering Research. (Illus., Orig.). 1971. pap. 21.25 (ISBN 92-0-131070-6, ISP275, IAEA). Unipub.

Krivoglaz, M. A. Theory of X-Ray & Thermal Neutron Scattering by Real Crystals. LC 68-26771. (Illus.). 405p. 1969. 45.00 (ISBN 0-306-30347-7, Plenum Pr). Plenum Pub.

Lovesey, S. & Springer, T., eds. Dynamics of Solids & Liquids by Neutron Scattering. LC 77-4740. (Topics in Current Physics Ser: Vol. 3). 1977. 40.30 (ISBN 0-387-08156-9). Springer-Verlag.

Mason, Ronald & Mitchell, E. W. Neutron Scattering in Biology, Chemistry & Physics. (Phil. Trans. of the Royal Soc., Ser. B.: Vol. 290). (Illus.). 201p. 1981. Repr. text ed. 60.00x (ISBN 0-85403-151-0, Pub. by Royal Soc London). Scholium Intl.

Neutron Inelastic Scattering - 1968, 2 vols. 1968. Vol. 1. pap. 40.75 (ISBN 92-0-030268-8, ISP187-1-2, IAEA); Vol. 2. pap. 29.25 (ISBN 92-0-030368-4). Unipub.

Neutron Inelastic Scattering - 1972. (Illus.). 888p. (Orig.). 1973. pap. 65.00 (ISBN 92-0-030172-X, ISP 308, IAEA). Unipub.

Neutron Inelastic Scattering Nineteen Seventy-Seven, Vol. 1. 1978. pap. 66.75 (ISBN 92-0-030078-2, ISP 468-1, IAEA). Unipub.

Neutron Inelastic Scattering Nineteen Seventy-Seven, Vol. 2. 1978. pap. 57.00 (ISBN 92-0-030178-9, ISP468-2, IAEA). Unipub.

NEVADA
see also names of cities, counties, etc. in Nevada

Ashbaugh, Don. Nevada's Turbulent Yesterday. LC 63-16925. (Illus.). 349p. 14.00 (ISBN 0-87026-024-3). Westernlore.

Bailey, Bernadine. Picture Book of Nevada. rev. ed. LC 73-89402. (Illus.). (gr. 3-5). 1974. 5.50g (ISBN 0-8075-9531-4). A Whitman.

Carlson, Helen S. Nevada Place Names: A Geographical Dictionary. LC 74-13877. xiv, 282p. 1974. 15.00 (ISBN 0-87417-041-9). U of Nev Pr.

Carpenter, Allan. Nevada. new ed. LC 79-4355. (New Enchantment of America State Bks.). (Illus.). (gr. 4 up). 1979. PLB 10.60 (ISBN 0-516-04128-2). Childrens.

Constitutional Convention of the State of Nevada. Debates & Proceedings. Marsh, Andrew J., ed. LC 76-39613. 1976. Repr. lib. bdg. 25.00 (ISBN 0-930342-32-1). W S Hein.

Federal Writers' Project. Nevada: A Guide to the Silver State. 1940. Repr. 45.00 (ISBN 0-403-02178-2). Somerset Pub.

Fletcher, F. N. Early Nevada: The Period of Exploraton Seventeen Seventy-Six to Eighteen Forty-Eight. LC 80-19035. (Vintage Nevada Ser). (Illus.). xi, 195p. 1980. pap. 5.25 (ISBN 0-87417-061-3). U of Nev Pr.

Fradin, Dennis. Nevada: In Words & Pictures. LC 80-24179. (Young People's Stories of Our States Ser.). (Illus.). 48p. (gr. 2-6). 1981. PLB 9.25 (ISBN 0-516-03928-8). Childrens.

Gamett, James. Nevada Post Offices: An Illustrated History. 1981. 30.00 (ISBN 0-913814-40-7). Nevada Pubns.

Glass, Mary E. Silver & Politics in Nevada: 1892-1902. LC 72-92547. (Lancehead Ser). (Illus.). xi, 242p. 1970. 5.50 (ISBN 0-87417-026-5). U of Nev Pr.

Johns, Albert C. Nevada Politics. 3rd ed. (Government Ser.). 1978. perfect bdg. 7.95 (ISBN 0-8403-8001-1). Kendall-Hunt.

Lewis, Marvin. Martha & the Doctor: A Frontier Family in Central Nevada. Lewis, B. Betty, ed. LC 77-24964. (Bristlecone Paperback Ser.). (Illus.). xii, 247p. (Orig.). 1977. pap. 5.00 (ISBN 0-87417-049-4). U of Nev Pr.
Lillard, Richard G. Desert Challenge: An Interpretation of Nevada. LC 78-26286. (Illus.). 1979. Repr. of 1942 ed. lib. bdg. 32.50x (ISBN 0-313-20866-2, LIDC). Greenwood.
Mack, Effie M., et al. Nevada Government. 384p. 1953. octavo 5.00 (ISBN 0-686-70671-4). Holmes.
Miluck, Nancy C. Nevada: This Is Our Land. (Illus.). 148p. (Orig.). 1978. pap. 6.50 (ISBN 0-9606382-0-2). Dragon Ent.
Moody, Eric N. Southern Gentleman of Nevada Politics: Vail M. Pittman. LC 73-84927. (History & Political Science Ser: No. 13). (Illus.). viii, 136p. 1974. pap. 3.50x (ISBN 0-87417-039-7). U of Nev Pr.
Morgan, Dale L. Humboldt, Highroad of the West. facs. ed. LC 70-146867. (Select Bibliographies Reprint Ser). 1943. 22.00 (ISBN 0-8369-5634-6). Arno.
Nevada. 23.00 (ISBN 0-89770-104-6). Curriculum Info Ctr.
Olds, Sarah E. Twenty Miles from a Match: Homesteading in Western Nevada. LC 78-13766. (Illus.). xiii, 182p. 1978. 5.50 (ISBN 0-87417-052-4). U of Nev Pr.
Paber, Stanley W., ed. Fort Churchill: Nevada Military Outpost of the 1860's. (Illus.). 1981. pap. 2.95 (ISBN 0-913814-38-5). Nevada Pubns.
--Nevada Towns & Tales, Vol. 1. (Illus.). 1981. 9.95 (ISBN 0-913814-41-5). Nevada Pubns.
Paher, Stanley W. Goldfield Boomtown of Nevada. (Illus.). 1977. 1.95 (ISBN 0-913814-14-8). Nevada Pubns.
--Nevada: An Annotated Bibliography. (Illus.). 1980. 95.00x (ISBN 0-913814-26-1). Nevada Pubns.
--Nevada Ghost Towns & Mining Camps. LC 70-116733. (Illus.). 1970. 25.00 (ISBN 0-8310-7075-7). Howell-North.
Saville, Anthony & Kavina, George. The Will of the People: Education in Nevada. 1977. pap. text ed. 10.00 (ISBN 0-8191-0162-1). U Pr of Amer.
Shepperson, Wilbur S. Restless Strangers: Nevada's Immigrants & Their Interpreters. LC 78-117219. (Lancehead Ser). (Illus.). xiv, 287p. 1970. 7.00 (ISBN 0-87417-028-1). U of Nev Pr.
Townley, John M. Conquered Provinces: Nevada Moves Southeast, 1864-1871. (Charles Redd Monographs in Western History: No. 2). (Illus.). 66p. 1973. pap. 2.50 (ISBN 0-8425-0417-6). Brigham.
Wheeler, Sessions S. The Black Rock Dessert. LC 76-6648. 1978. pap. 5.95 (ISBN 0-87004-258-0). Caxton.

NEVADA-ANTIQUITIES

Wheeler, Sessions S. The Black Rock Dessert. LC 76-6648. 1978. pap. 5.95 (ISBN 0-87004-258-0). Caxton.
Wilson, Helen. Gold Fever. (Illus.). 1979. pap. 7.25 (ISBN 0-913814-27-X). Nevada Pubns.

NEVADA-DESCRIPTION AND TRAVEL

Arnold, Emmett. Gold-Camp Drifter: 1906-1910. LC 72-94360. (Bristlecone Paperback Ser.). (Illus.). 186p. (Orig.). 1973. pap. 4.00 (ISBN 0-87417-037-0). U of Nev Pr.
Beck, Eric. Climber's Guide to Lake Tahoe & Donner Summit. (Illus.). 48p. 1978. pap. 3.95 (ISBN 0-89646-046-0). Outbooks.
Berssen, William. Pacific Boating Almanac 1982: Northern California & Nevada Edition. annual ed. 432p. 1982. pap. 7.95 (ISBN 0-930030-21-4). Western Marine Ent.
De Serio, Louis F. & Greenwell, Glen H., Jr. A Last Look. LC 79-67536. (Illus.). 1979. 19.50x (ISBN 0-9603568-0-0). De Serio.
Dollarwise Guide to California & Las Vegas: 1981-82. pap. 5.95 (ISBN 0-671-41426-7). Frommer-Pasmantier.
Evans, Douglas B. Auto Tour Guide to the Lake Mead National Recreation Area. LC 76-160215. (Illus.). 40p. (Orig.). 1971. pap. 0.50 (ISBN 0-911408-22-3). SW Pks Mnmts.
Federal Writers' Project. Nevada: A Guide to the Silver State. 1940. Repr. 45.00 (ISBN 0-403-02178-2). Somerset Pub.
Fiero, G. William. Nevada's Valley of Fire. DenDooven, Gweneth R., ed. LC 75-18136. (Illus.). 1975. 7.95 (ISBN 0-916122-42-5); pap. 2.50 (ISBN 0-916122-17-4). KC Pubns.
Fox, Theron L. Nevada Treasure Hunter's Ghost Town Guide. (Illus.). 1960. pap. 1.95 (ISBN 0-913814-16-4). Nevada Pubns.
Glass, Mary E. Nevada's Turbulent Fifties: Decade of Political & Economic Change. LC 80-25651. (Nevada Studies in History & Political Science: No. 15). (Illus.). ix, 137p. (Orig.). 1981. pap. 5.75 (ISBN 0-87417-062-1). U of Nev Pr.
Hall, Shawn. A Guide to the Ghost Towns & Mining Camps of Nye County, Nevada. LC 81-1570. (Illus.). 256p. 1981. pap. 12.95 (ISBN 0-396-07955-5). Dodd.
Holland, James S., et al. Flowering Plants of the Lake Mead Region. LC 77-90742. (Popular Ser.: No. 23). (Illus.). 1978. pap. 3.00 (ISBN 0-911408-49-5). SW Pks Mnmts.
Kosoy, Ted. A Budget Guide to California & the Pacific Coast States. LC 76-62778. 288p. 1977. 10.00x (ISBN 0-312-10692-0); pap. 4.95 (ISBN 0-312-10693-9). St Martin.
Lewis, Paul M. Beautiful North Nevada. Shangle, Robert D., ed. 1981. 14.95 (ISBN 0-89802-101-4); pap. 7.95 (ISBN 0-89802-100-6). Beautiful Am.
Lillard, Richard G. Desert Challenge: An Interpretation of Nevada. LC 78-26286. (Illus.). 1979. Repr. of 1942 ed. lib. bdg. 32.50x (ISBN 0-313-20866-2, LIDC). Greenwood.
McDonald, Douglas. Nevada Lost Mines & Buried Treasure. (Illus.). 1981. 5.95 (ISBN 0-913814-37-7). Nevada Pubns.
Mitchell, Roger. Western Nevada Jeep Trails. (Illus.). 1973. wrappers 1.25 (ISBN 0-910856-50-8). La Siesta.
Paher, Stanley W. Death Valley Ghost Towns. LC 82-97900. (Illus.). 1981. pap. 2.95 (ISBN 0-913814-35-0). Nevada Pubns.
Pearl, Ralph. Las Vegas Is My Beat. 200p. 1973. 6.00 (ISBN 0-8184-0149-4). Lyle Stuart.
Remy, Jules & Brenchley, Julius. A Journey to Great Salt-Lake City, 2 vols. LC 75-134399. (Illus.). Repr. of 1861 ed. Set. write for info. (ISBN 0-404-08441-9). Vol. 1 (ISBN 0-404-08442-7). Vol. 2 (ISBN 0-404-08443-5). AMS Pr.
Sadovich, Maryellen V. Your Guide to Southern Nevada. (Nevada Historical Society Guide Book Ser.). (Illus.). 1976. pap. 2.95 (ISBN 0-686-10439-0). Nevada Hist Soc.
Truitt, Velma S. On the Hoof in Nevada. (Illus.). 1950. 50.00 (ISBN 0-913814-06-7). Nevada Pubns.
Will, Robin. Beautiful Nevada. Shangle, Robert D., ed. (Illus.). 72p. 1981. 14.95 (ISBN 0-89802-101-4); pap. 7.95 (ISBN 0-89802-100-6). Beautiful Am.

NEVADA-HISTORY

Angel, Myron, ed. History of Nevada. LC 72-9424. (The Far Western Frontier Ser.). (Illus.). 948p. 1973. Repr. of 1881 ed. 50.00 (ISBN 0-405-04956-0). Arno.
Bancroft, Hubert H. History of Nevada Fifteen Forty to Eighteen Eighty-Eight. (Vintage Nevada Ser.). (Illus.). 350p. 1981. pap. price not set (ISBN 0-87417-068-0). U of Nev Pr.
Bushnell, Eleanore & Driggs, Don W. The Nevada Constitution: Origin & Growth. 5th ed. LC 80-23682. (History & Political Science Ser.: No. 8). x, 221p. 1980. pap. text ed. 5.25x (ISBN 0-87417-060-5). U of Nev Pr.
Chan, Loren B. Sagebrush Statesman: Tasker L. Oddie of Nevada. LC 73-77715. (Nevada Studies in History & Political Science Ser.: No.12). (Illus.). 189p. (Orig.). 1974. pap. 4.00x (ISBN 0-87417-038-9). U of Nev Pr.
De Quille, Dan, pseud. A History of the Comstock Silver Lode & Mines, Nevada & the Great Basin Region, Lake Tahoe & the High Sierras. LC 72-9439. (The Far Western Frontier Ser.). 162p. 1973. Repr. of 1889 ed. 12.00 (ISBN 0-405-04969-2). Arno.
Elliott, Russell R. History of Nevada. LC 72-187809. (Illus.). 1973. 13.95x (ISBN 0-8032-0781-6). U of Nebr Pr.
Glass, Alton E., Jr. & Glass, Mary E. Western Nevada. (Nevada Historical Society Guide Book Ser.). (Illus.). 1975. pap. 2.95 (ISBN 0-686-10438-2). Nevada Hist Soc.
Hulse, James W. The Nevada Adventure: A History. 5th ed. LC 81-51475. (Illus.). 324p. 1981. 9.00 (ISBN 0-87417-067-2). U of Nev Pr.
Laxalt, Robert. Nevada: A History. (States & the Nation Ser.). (Illus.). 1977. 12.95 (ISBN 0-393-05628-7, Co-Pub. by AASLH). Norton.
Rusco, Elmer R. Good Time Coming? Black Nevadans in the Nineteenth Century. LC 75-16969. (Contributions in Afro-American & African Studies: No. 15). (Illus.). 230p. 1975. lib. bdg. 14.75x (ISBN 0-8371-8286-7; RGT/). Greenwood.
Shepperson, W., et al. Questions from the Past. new ed. LC 72-94356. (Nevada Studies in History & Political Science Ser: No. 11). (Illus.). xii, 216p. 1973. pap. 3.50x (ISBN 0-87417-036-2). U of Nev Pr.
Thompson & West. History of Nevada State to 1881. LC 64-2476. (Illus.). 1958. 25.00 (ISBN 0-8310-7006-4). Howell-North.
Townley, John M. Conquered Provinces: Nevada Moves Southeast, 1864-1871. (Charles Redd Monographs in Western History: No. 2). (Illus.). 66p. 1973. pap. 2.50 (ISBN 0-8425-0417-6). Brigham.

NEVADA-IMPRINTS

Armstrong, Robert D. Nevada Printing History: A Bibliography of Imprints & Publications, 1858-1880. LC 81-7422. (Illus.). 540p. 1981. price not set (ISBN 0-87417-063-X). U of Nev Pr.
Historical Records Survey: Check List of Nevada Imprints, 1859-1890. 1939. pap. 12.00 (ISBN 0-527-01904-6). Kraus Repr.

NEVADA CITY, CALIFORNIA

Morley, Jim & Foley, Doris. Gold Cities: Grass Valley & Nevada City. LC 65-18741. (Illus.). 1965. 9.95 (ISBN 0-8310-7048-X); pap. 3.50 (ISBN 0-8310-6004-2). Howell-North.

NEVADA CITY, NEVADA

Morely, Jim & Foley, Doris, eds. Gold Cities: Grass Valley & Nevada City. 2nd ed. (Illus.). 96p. 1980. 9.95 (ISBN 0-8310-7136-2); pap. 3.50 (ISBN 0-8310-7135-4). Howell-North.
Shepperson, Wilbur S. Retreat to Nevada: A Socialist Colony of World War One. LC 66-63539. (Lancehead Ser). xiv, 204p. 1966. 5.25 (ISBN 0-87417-015-X). U of Nev Pr.

NEVADA COUNTY, CALIFORNIA-HISTORY

Bean, Edwin F. Bean's History & Directory of Nevada County, California: Containing a Complete History of the Country, with Sketches of the Various Towns & Mining Camps..Also, a Full Statistics of Mining & All Other Industrial Sources. 1976. Repr. of 1867 ed. 52.00 (ISBN 0-403-06470-8, Regency). Scholarly.

NEVADA COUNTY NARROW GAUGE RAILROAD

Best, G. M. Nevada County Narrow Gauge. LC 65-18740. (Illus.). 1965. 12.95 (ISBN 0-8310-7049-8). Howell-North.
Nevada County Narrow Gauge. 12.95 (ISBN 0-685-83362-3). Chatham Pub CA.

NEVELSON, LOUISE, 1900-

Albee, Edward, intro. by. Louise Nevelson: Atmospheres & Environments. (Illus.). 192p. 1980. 35.00 (ISBN 0-517-54054-1). Potter.

NEVIN, JOHN WILLIAMSON, 1803-1886

Appel, Theodore. Life & Work of John Williamson Nevin. LC 71-83409. (Religion in America, Ser. 1). 1969. Repr. of 1889 ed. 30.00 (ISBN 0-405-00230-0). Arno.
Nevin, John W. My Own Life: The Earlier Years. LC 64-57065. 1964. pap. 5.00 (ISBN 0-685-09356-5). Evang & Ref.

NEVINS, ALLAN, 1890-

Sheehan, Donald & Syrett, Harold C., eds. Essays in American Historiography. LC 72-9833. (Illus.). 320p. 1973. Repr. of 1960 ed. lib. bdg. 15.25x (ISBN 0-8371-6268-8, SMAH). Greenwood.

NEW AGE

Spangler, David, ed. Conversation with John. 32p. 1980. pap. 2.00 (ISBN 0-936878-03-7). Lorian Pr.

NEW BEDFORD, MASSACHUSETTS

Wolfbein, Seymour L. Decline of a Cotton Texile City. LC 74-76648. (Columbia University. Studies in the Social Sciences: No. 507). Repr. of 1944 ed. 17.50 (ISBN 0-404-51507-X). AMS Pr.

NEW BRITAIN (ISLAND)

Epstein, Scarlett. Capitalism, Primitive & Modern: Some Aspects of Tolai Economic Growth. x, 200p. 1969. 7.50 (ISBN 0-87013-133-8). Mich St U Pr.
Salisbury, Richard F. Vunamami: Economic Transformation in a Traditional Society. LC 70-79062. 1970. 27.50x (ISBN 0-520-01647-5). U of Cal Pr.

NEW BRUNSWICK (PROVINCE)

Aunger, Edmund A. In Search of Political Stability: A Comparative Study of New Brunswick & Northern Ireland. 238p. 1981. 21.95x (ISBN 0-7735-0366-8). McGill-Queens U Pr.
Cate, Margaret D. Our Todays & Yesterdays, a Story of Brunswick & the Coastal Islands. LC 77-187380. (Illus.). 302p. 1972. Repr. of 1930 ed. 18.75 (ISBN 0-87152-075-3). Reprint.
Ludman, Allan, ed. Guidebook for Field Trips in Southeastern Maine & South Western New Brunswick. (Geological Bulletins). pap. text ed. 2.50 (ISBN 0-930146-05-0). Queens Coll Pr.
Marsden, Joshua. The Narrative of a Mission to Nova Scotia, New Brunswick & the Somers Islands. Repr. of 1816 ed. 19.50 (ISBN 0-384-35430-0). Johnson Repr.
Vroom, Richard, ed. Old New Brunswick: A Victorian Portrait. (Illus.). 1979. 19.95 (ISBN 0-19-540293-6). Oxford U Pr.

NEW BUSINESS ENTERPRISES

Barlow, Ronald S. How to Be Successful in the Antique Business: A Survival Handbook. LC 79-63492. (Illus.). 1980. pap. 7.95 (ISBN 0-933846-00-2). Windmill Pub Co.
Baty, Gordon B. Entrepreneurship: Playing to Win. LC 74-13215. 320p. 1974. ref. ed 15.95 (ISBN 0-87909-253-X); pap. text ed. 9.95 (ISBN 0-87909-242-4). Reston.
Baumback, Clifford M. & Mancuso, Joseph R. Entrepreneurship & Venture Management: Text & Readings. (Illus.). 368p. 1975. pap. text ed. 13.95 (ISBN 0-13-283119-8). P-H.
Bennett, Vivo & Clagett, Cricket. One Thousand & One Ways to Be Your Own Boss: A Unique Guide to Money-Making Enterprises for Financial Independence. LC 75-38940. 1976. 10.00 (ISBN 0-13-636985-5); pap. 4.95 (ISBN 0-13-636977-4). P-H.
Buskirk, Richard H. & Vaughn, Percy J. Managing New Enterprises. LC 75-37999. (Illus.). 400p. 1976. text ed. 13.95 (ISBN 0-8299-0071-3). West Pub.
Chapman, E. N. Getting into Business. LC 75-20279. 1976. 19.95 (ISBN 0-471-14600-5). Wiley.
Diener, Royce. How to Finance a Growing Business. rev. ed. 378p. 1974. 11.95 (ISBN 0-8119-0223-4). Fell.
Feinman, Jeffrey. One Hundred Surefire Businesses You Can Start with Little or No Investment. 1977. pap. 1.95 (ISBN 0-87216-368-7). Playboy Pbks.
Friedman, Robert E. & Schweke, William, eds. Expanding the Opportunity to Produce: Revitalizing the American Economy Through New Enterprise Development. LC 81-66853. 570p. (Orig.). 1981. pap. 19.95 (ISBN 0-9605804-0-9). Corp Ent Dev.
Gupta, Shiv K. & Hamman, Ray T. Starting a Small Business: A Simulation Game. (Illus.). 64p. 1974. pap. text ed. 10.95 (ISBN 0-13-842963-4). P-H.
Hewitt, Geoff. The Working for Yourself. LC 77-22783. 1977. 9.95 (ISBN 0-87857-162-0). Rodale Pr Inc.
How to Get Started in Exporting. pap. 1.95x (ISBN 0-686-02553-9). Dun.
How to Start Your Own Small Business, Vol. 4. 140p. 1975. pap. 4.95 (ISBN 0-8069-8416-3). Sterling.
Kamoroff, Bernard. Small Time Operator: How to Start Your Own Small Business, Keep Your Books, Pay Your Taxes, & Stay Out of Trouble. rev. ed. LC 76-29817. (Illus.). 192p. 1981. pap. 7.95 (ISBN 0-917510-00-3). Bell Springs Pub.
Kryszak, Wayne D. The Small Business Index. LC 78-17540. 1978. 12.00 (ISBN 0-8108-1150-2). Scarecrow.
Liles, Patrick R. New Business Ventures & the Entrepreneur. 1974. 19.50x (ISBN 0-256-01560-0). Irwin.
New Product-New Business Digest. 66p. 1980. 50.00 (ISBN 0-686-62469-6). B Klein Pubns.
Rosefsky, Robert S. Getting Free: How to Profit Most Out of Working for Yourself. LC 76-9728. 1977. 9.95 (ISBN 0-8129-0663-2). Times Bks.
Sacks, Stephen R. Entry of New Competitors in Yugoslav Market Socialism. LC 73-620046. (Research Ser.: No. 19). (Illus.). 1973. pap. 2.50x (ISBN 0-87725-119-3). U of Cal Intl St.
Schollhammer, Hans & Kuriloff, Arthur. Entrepreneurship & Small Business Management. LC 78-9443. (Management & Administration Ser.). 1979. text ed. 25.95 (ISBN 0-471-76260-1). Wiley.
Stanford, Mel. New Enterprise Management. (Illus.). 400p. 1982. text ed. 17.95 (ISBN 0-8359-4886-2); instr's. manual free (ISBN 0-8359-4887-0). Reston.
Starmark Publishing. The No-Nonsense Guide to Starting Your Own Business. 64p. 1980. write for info. spiral bound hard pressboard cover 14.95 (ISBN 0-936572-01-9). Starmark.
Sterne, George & Von Hoelscher, Russ. How to Start Making Money in a Business of Your Own. 420p. 1981. 24.95 (ISBN 0-940398-05-2). Profit Ideas.
Tarrant, John J. Making It Big on Your Own: How to Start, Finance & Manage a New Business in the 80's. LC 80-84882. 1981. pap. 13.95 (ISBN 0-87223-676-5). Playboy Pbks.
Thompson, R. How to Start Your Own Business & Make Money. 1979. pap. 7.95 (ISBN 0-89484-025-8). Merchants Pub Co.
Townsend, Carl & Miller, Merl. How to Make Money with Your Micro-Computer. LC 79-53477. 1979. pap. 9.95 (ISBN 0-89661-001-2). Robotics Pr.
White, Richard M. The Entrepreneur's Manual: Business Start-Ups, Spin-Offs, & Innovative Management. LC 76-55520. 1976. 17.50 (ISBN 0-8019-6454-7). Chilton.

NEW CALEDONIA

Howe, K. R. The Loyalty Islands: History of Culture Contacts, 1840-1900. LC 76-50009. 1977. 12.00x (ISBN 0-8248-0451-1). U Pr of Hawaii.
Sterling Publishing Company Editors. Tahiti & the French Islands of the Pacific in Pictures. LC 66-25202. (Visual Geography Ser). (Orig.). (gr. 6 up). 1967. PLB 4.99 (ISBN 0-8069-1093-3); pap. 2.95 (ISBN 0-8069-1092-5). Sterling.

NEW CHURCH

see New Jerusalem Church

NEW ENGLAND

Bollan, William. The Importance & Advantage of Cape Breton. Repr. of 1698 ed. 11.00 (ISBN 0-384-04965-6). Johnson Repr.

Bongartz, Roy. The New England Records. LC 78-4647. 1978. pap. 5.95 (ISBN 0-8289-0330-1). Greene.
Brereton, John. A Briefe & True Relation of the Discoverie of the North Part of Virginia. LC 72-5967. (English Experience Ser.: No. 449). 24p. 1973. Repr. of 1602 ed. 6.00 (ISBN 90-221-0499-0). Walter J Johnson.
Butterworth, Hezekiah. In Old New England. LC 73-19716. 1974. Repr. of 1895 ed. 19.00 (ISBN 0-8103-3686-3). Gale.
Dow, George F. Arts & Crafts in New England. 1704-1775. LC 67-2035. (Architecture & Decorative Art Ser). (Illus.). 1967. Repr. of 1927 ed. 29.50 (ISBN 0-306-70955-4). Da Capo.
Jennison, Keith. New England in the Off-Color Season. LC 80-67659. (Illus., Orig.). 1980. pap. 5.95 (ISBN 0-911764-23-2). Durrell.
Johnson, Clifton. New England & Its Neighbors. 1902. 20.00 (ISBN 0-8495-2775-9). Arden Lib.
McCabe, Inger. Week in Amy's World: New England. (Face to Face Bks.). (Illus.). (gr. k-3). 1970. (CCPr); text ed. 1.36 (ISBN 0-685-04413-0, CCPr). Macmillan.
Mahnke, Susan, ed. Index to Yankee Magazine, 1935-1978. LC 79-66743. 1979. 24.95 (ISBN 0-911658-98-X). Yankee Bks.
New England on Land & Sea. (Illus.). 1970. 2.75 (ISBN 0-87577-039-8). Peabody Mus Salem.
Reidel, Carl H. New England Prospects: Essays on the Future of a Region. LC 81-51604. (Futures of New England Ser.: Vol. 1). (Illus.). 180p. 1982. 12.50 (ISBN 0-87451-213-1). U Pr of New Eng.
Robert Long Adams Associates. The New England Job Bank. 400p. 1981. pap. 9.95 (ISBN 0-686-30612-0). Adams Inc MA.
Wenkam, Robert. New England. LC 74-10221. (Illus.). 1974. pap. 7.95 (ISBN 0-528-88163-9). Rand.
Westbrook, Perry D. The New England Town in Fact & Fiction. LC 80-67077. 380p. 1981. 27.50 (ISBN 0-8386-3011-1). Fairleigh Dickinson.
Wheelwright, Thea. The Andovers: Portrait of Two New England Towns. (Illus.). 96p. (Orig.). 1980. pap. 9.95 (ISBN 0-931474-10-8). TBW Bks.
Willoughby, Charles C. Antiquities of the New England Indians. LC 72-5012. (Harvard University. Peabody Museum of Archaeology & Ethnology. Antiquities of the New World: No. 17). (Illus.). Repr. of 1935 ed. 25.00 (ISBN 0-404-57317-7). AMS Pr.

NEW ENGLAND–BIOGRAPHY

Beals, Carleton. Our Yankee Heritage. facsimile ed. LC 73-111814. (Essay Index Reprint Ser). 1955. 19.50 (ISBN 0-8369-1593-3). Arno.
Forbes, Harriette M., compiled by. New England Diaries, 1602-1800. LC 67-28478. 1967. Repr. of 1923 ed. 10.00 (ISBN 0-8462-0989-6). Russell.
Jantz, Harold S. The First Century of New England Verse. LC 74-6159. 1944. Repr. lib. bdg. 25.00 (ISBN 0-8414-5291-1). Folcroft.
Long, Peirce. The Journal of Zadoc Long: 1800-1873. LC 43-7563. (Illus.). 316p. 1943. 4.00 (ISBN 0-87004-090-1). Caxton.
Macy, Eliot E. The Captain's Daughters of Martha's Vineyard. LC 78-62650. (How We Lived Ser.: No. 1). 1978. 10.00 (ISBN 0-85699-141-4). Chatham Pr.
Mather, Cotton. Magnalia Christi Americana: Or the Ecclesiastical History of New England. Cunningham, Raymond J., ed. LC 75-12340. (Milestones of Thought Ser). 1971. 8.50 (ISBN 0-8044-5668-2); pap. 4.95 (ISBN 0-8044-6478-2). Ungar.
Myerson, Joel, ed. The American Renaissance in New England. LC 77-82803. (Dictionary of Literary Biography Ser.: Vol. 1). (Illus.). 1978. 58.00 (ISBN 0-8103-0913-0, Bruccoli Clark Bk). Gale.
Shipton, Clifford K. New England Life in the Eighteenth Century: Representative Biographies from Sibley's Harvard Graduates. LC 63-9562. (Illus.). 1963. 30.00x (ISBN 0-674-61250-7, Belknap Pr). Harvard U Pr.
Whitehill, Walter M. Analecta Biographica: A Handful of New England Portraits. Repr. of 1969 ed. 5.00 (ISBN 0-87577-048-7). Peabody Mus Salem.

NEW ENGLAND–CHURCH HISTORY

Backus, Isaac. History of New England. LC 76-83410. (Religion in America, Ser. 1). 1969. Repr. of 1871 ed. 45.00 (ISBN 0-405-00231-9). Arno.
Bacon, Leonard. The Genesis of the New England Churches. LC 74-38435. (Religion in America, Ser. 2). 510p. 1972. Repr. of 1874 ed. 25.00 (ISBN 0-405-04056-3). Arno.
Earle, Alice M. Sabbath in Puritan New England. 1969. Repr. of 1891 ed. 8.50 (ISBN 0-87928-005-0). Corner Hse.
Fleming, Sanford. Children & Puritanism: The Place of Children in the Life & Thought of the New England Churches, 1620-1847. LC 70-89178. (American Education: Its Men, Institutions & Ideas Ser). 1969. Repr. of 1933 ed. 13.00 (ISBN 0-405-01416-3). Arno.
Hall, David D. The Faithful Shepherd: A History of the New England Ministry in the Seventeenth Century. LC 72-81326. 328p. 1972. 22.00x (ISBN 0-8078-1193-9). U of NC Pr.
Lechford, Thomas. Plain Dealing: Or News from New England. 1969. Repr. of 1867 ed. 15.50 (ISBN 0-384-31985-8). Johnson Repr.
Levy, Babette M. Preaching in the First Half Century of New England History. LC 66-27116. 1967. Repr. of 1945 ed. 8.50 (ISBN 0-8462-0900-4). Russell.
Mansur, Ina. A New England Church: Its First Hundred Years. LC 74-76868. (Illus.). 256p. 1974. 10.95 (ISBN 0-87027-139-3); pap. 5.95 (ISBN 0-87027-140-7). Wheelwright.
Mather, Cotton. Magnalia Christi Americana, or the Ecclesiastical History of New-England from the Year 1620, Unto the Year 1698, 7 Bks. LC 74-141092. (Research Library of Colonial Americana). (Illus.). 1971. Repr. of 1702 ed. 48.00 (ISBN 0-405-03297-8). Arno.
--Magnalia Christi Americana: Or the Ecclesiastical History of New England. Cunningham, Raymond J., ed. LC 75-12340. (Milestones of Thought Ser). 1971. 8.50 (ISBN 0-8044-5668-2); pap. 4.95 (ISBN 0-8044-6478-2). Ungar.
Morse, James K. Jedidiah Morse: A Champion of New England Orthodoxy. LC 39-11247. Repr. of 1939 ed. 10.00 (ISBN 0-404-04504-9). AMS Pr.
Riegler, Gordon A. The Socialization of the New England Clergy 1800-1860. LC 79-13027. (Perspectives in American Hist. Ser.: No. 37). 187p. Repr. of 1945 ed. lib. bdg. 15.00x (ISBN 0-87991-361-4). Porcupine Pr.
Slafter, Edmund F. & Slafter, Edmund F., eds. John Checkley, or, Evolution of Religious Tolerance in Massachusetts, 2 vols. (Prince Soc. Pubns: Nos. 22 & 23). 1966. 39.00 (ISBN 0-8337-0553-9). B Franklin.
Stauffer, Vernon. New England & the Bavarian Illuminati. LC 66-27153. 1967. Repr. of 1918 ed. 8.50 (ISBN 0-8462-0953-5). Russell.
Tracy, Joseph. The Great Awakening. 1976. 11.95 (ISBN 0-85151-233-X). Banner of Truth.
Walker, Williston. Ten New England Leaders. LC 76-83445. (Religion in America Ser). 1969. Repr. of 1901 ed. 22.00 (ISBN 0-405-00278-5). Arno.
Winslow, Ola E. Meetinghouse Hill, 1630-1783. 1972. pap. 2.95x (ISBN 0-393-00632-8, Norton Lib). Norton.

NEW ENGLAND–CIVILIZATION

Adams, Herbert B. The Germanic Origin of New England Towns. LC 78-63731. (Johns Hopkins University. Studies in the Social Sciences. First Ser. 1882-1883: 2). Repr. of 1882 ed. 11.50 (ISBN 0-404-61002-1). AMS Pr.
Beals, Carleton. Our Yankee Heritage. facsimile ed. LC 73-111814. (Essay Index Reprint Ser). 1955. 19.50 (ISBN 0-8369-1593-3). Arno.
Lockridge, Kenneth A. Literacy in Colonial New England: An Inquiry into the Social Context of Literacy in the Early Modern West. (Illus.). 1974. 6.95x (ISBN 0-393-05522-1); pap. 3.95x (ISBN 0-393-09263-1). Norton.
Rogers, Barbara R. An Introduction to Twenty One Traditional Yankee Home Crafts. LC 78-66324. (Illus.). 1979. pap. 9.95 (ISBN 0-911658-85-8). Yankee Bks.
Vaughan, Alden T. & Bremer, Francis J. Puritan New England. LC 76-52589. 1977. pap. text ed. 7.95 (ISBN 0-312-65695-5). St Martin.
Weeden, William B. Indian Money As a Factor in New England Civilization. LC 78-63747. (Johns Hopkins University. Studies in the Social Sciences. Second Ser. 1884: 8-9). Repr. of 1884 ed. 11.50 (ISBN 0-404-61017-X). AMS Pr.

NEW ENGLAND–COMMERCE

Albion, Robert G., et al. New England & the Sea. LC 72-3694. (The American Maritime Library: Vol. 5). (Illus.). 303p. 1972. 15.95 (ISBN 0-8195-4052-8); pap. 9.00 (ISBN 0-913372-23-4); ltd. ed. 40.00 (ISBN 0-8195-4053-6). Mystic Seaport.
Carroll, Charles F. The Timber Economy of Puritan New England. LC 73-7122. (Illus.). xiv, 221p. 1973. pap. 15.00x (ISBN 0-87057-142-7, Pub. by Brown U Pr). U Pr of New Eng.
Dart, Margaret S. Yankee Traders at Sea & Ashore. 1965. 3.00 (ISBN 0-87164-011-2). William-F.
Smith, John. New England Trials. LC 70-171793. (English Experience Ser.: No. 416). 1971. Repr. of 1620 ed. 7.00 (ISBN 90-221-0416-8). Walter J Johnson.
Weedon, William B. Economic & Social History of New England 1620-1789, 2 Vols. 1963. Set. text ed. 25.00x (ISBN 0-391-00493-X). Humanities.

NEW ENGLAND–DESCRIPTION AND TRAVEL

Abbott, Katharine M. Old Paths & Legends of the New England Border: Connecticut, Deerfield, Berkshire. LC 72-75227. 1970. Repr. of 1907 ed. 22.00 (ISBN 0-8103-3562-X). Gale.
Abbott, Katherine M. Old Paths & Legends of New England: Saunterings Over Historic Roads with Glimpses of Picturesque Fields & Old Homesteads in Massachusetts, Rhode Island & New Hampshire. LC 76-75228. Repr. of 1903 ed. 22.00 (ISBN 0-8103-3564-6). Gale.
Andrews, Peter, et al. Lower New England. LC 79-22906. (Country Inns of America Ser.). (Illus.). 96p. (Orig.). 1980. pap. 6.95 (ISBN 0-03-043716-4). HR&W.
--Upper New England. LC 79-22906. (Country Inns of America Ser.). (Illus.). 96p. (Orig.). 1980. pap. 6.95 (ISBN 0-03-043711-3). HR&W.
Atkinson, Brooks & Olson, W. Kent. New England's White Mountains: At Home in the Wild. LC 78-55506. 1978. 35.00 (ISBN 0-913890-18-9, 936065). NYGS.
Beach, Stewart. New England in Color. (Profiles of America Ser). 1969. 7.95 (ISBN 0-8038-5013-1). Hastings.
Berrill, Michael & Berrill, Deborah. A Sierra Club Naturalist's Guide to the North Atlantic Coast. (Sierra Club Naturalist's Guides). (Illus.). 512p. 1981. 24.95 (ISBN 0-87156-242-1); pap. 10.95 (ISBN 0-87156-243-X). Sierra.
Brooks, Van Wyck. A Chilmark Miscellany: Essays Old & New. LC 73-3227. 315p. 1973. Repr. of 1948 ed. lib. bdg. 17.00x (ISBN 0-374-90999-7). Octagon.
Bryfonski, Dedria. The New England Beach Book. LC 73-93682. (Illus.). 192p. 1975. 6.95 (ISBN 0-8027-0453-0); pap. 3.95 (ISBN 0-8027-7093-2). Walker & Co.
Cameron, Barry, ed. Carboniferous Basins of Southeastern New England. LC 79-51602. 1979. pap. 10.00 (ISBN 0-913312-14-2). Am Geol.
Chase, Heman. More Than Land: Stories of New England Country Life & Surveying. LC 78-604. (Illus.). 1978. pap. 4.95 (ISBN 0-87233-045-1). Bauhan.
Clayton, Barbara & Whitley, Kathleen. Guide to New Bedford. LC 79-54908. (Illus.). 1979. pap. 4.95 (ISBN 0-87106-035-3). Globe Pequot.
Country New England Inns: 1981-1982. 1981. 4.95 (ISBN 0-89102-232-5). B Franklin.
Crain, Jim & Milne, Terry. Camping Around New England. (YA) 1975. pap. 3.95 (ISBN 0-394-70644-7). Random.
Drake, Samuel A. Nooks & Corners of the New England Coast. LC 69-19883. 1969. Repr. of 1875 ed. 24.00 (ISBN 0-8103-3827-0). Gale.
Dwight, Timothy. Travels in New England & New York, 4 Vols. Solomon, Barbara M., ed. LC 69-12735. (The John Harvard Library). (Illus.). 1969. Repr. of 1821 ed. Set. boxed 40.00x (ISBN 0-674-90670-5). Harvard U Pr.
Fellows, Henry P. Boat Trips on New England Rivers. 1977. lib. bdg. 59.95 (ISBN 0-8490-1518-9). Gordon Pr.
Griffin, Arthur. New England: The Four Seasons. 1980. 35.00 (ISBN 0-395-29164-X). HM.
Hall, Donald. String Too Short to Be Saved: Recollections of Summers on a New England Farm. LC 78-74249. 1979. pap. 6.95 (ISBN 0-87923-282-X, Nonpareil Books). Godine.
Hansen, Harry. Longfellow's New England. (Illus.). 192p. 1972. 8.75 (ISBN 0-8038-4279-1). Hastings.
Harris, John & Taylor, Robert. Treasures of New England. (Illus.). 1976. 5.95 (ISBN 0-87106-008-6). Globe Pequot.
Higginson, Francis. New England's Plantation. LC 78-154869. (Research & Source Works Ser: No. 719). 1971. Repr. of 1630 ed. lib. bdg. 12.00 (ISBN 0-8337-1700-6). B Franklin.
--New-Englands Plantation. LC 76-25635. (English Experience Ser.: No. 256). 24p. 1970. Repr. of 1630 ed. 7.00 (ISBN 90-221-0256-4). Walter J Johnson.
Hitchcock, Anthony & Lindgren, Jean. Country New England Antiques, Crafts, & Factory Outlets. rev. ed. 1979. pap. 3.95 (ISBN 0-89102-137-X). B Franklin.
Holbrook, Stewart H. Old Post Road. 1971. pap. 3.50 (ISBN 0-07-029536-0, SP). McGraw.
Jorgensen, Neil. A Guide to New England's Landscape. LC 77-75660. (Illus.). 1977. pap. 5.95 (ISBN 0-87106-088-4). Globe Pequot.
Josselyn, John. New-Englands Rarities Discovered. (Massachusetts Historical Society Picture Bks.). 1972. 10.00 (ISBN 0-686-21442-0). Mass Hist Soc.
Kingsbury, John M. Rocky Shore. LC 71-122758. (Illus.). 1970. 4.95 (ISBN 0-85699-015-9). Chatham Pr.
Knight. Journal of Madam Knight. Winship, ed. 7.00 (ISBN 0-8446-1268-5). Peter Smith.
Ludlum, David. The Country Journal New England Weather Book. 1976. 10.95 (ISBN 0-395-24299-1); pap. 7.95 (ISBN 0-395-24402-1). HM.
McManis, Douglas R. European Impressions of the New England Coast, 1497-1620. LC 70-187026. (Research Papers Ser: No. 139). (Illus.). 147p. 1972. pap. 8.00 (ISBN 0-89065-046-2, 139). U Chicago Dept Geog.
Miser, A. & Pennypincher, A. Factory Store Guide to All New England. 4th ed. LC 76-51130. (Illus.). 1979. pap. 4.95 (ISBN 0-686-77704-2). Globe Pequot.
Morton, Thomas. New English Canaan or New Canaan. Cantaining an Abstract of New England. LC 76-25966. (English Experience Ser.: No. 140). 192p. 1969. Repr. of 1637 ed. 28.00 (ISBN 90-221-0140-1). Walter J Johnson.
Newhall, Nancy, ed. Time in New England. LC 80-65763. (Illus.). 256p. 1980. 40.00 (ISBN 0-89381-060-6); ltd. ed. 175.00 (ISBN 0-686-76136-7). Aperture.
Parks, Roger, ed. The New England Galaxy. LC 80-66598. (Illus., Orig.). 1980. pap. 6.95 (ISBN 0-87106-040-X). Globe Pequot.
Pearson, Haydn S. Sea Flavor. facs. ed. LC 68-58809. (Essay Index Reprint Ser). 1948. 15.00 (ISBN 0-8369-0051-0). Arno.
Peirce, Neal R. The New England States: People, Politics & Power in the Six New England States. (Illus.). 1976. 15.95 (ISBN 0-393-05558-2). Norton.
A Place to Begin: The New England Experience. LC 76-21312. 1976. write for info. (ISBN 0-87156-182-4, Pub. by Sierra). Black Ice.
Pownall, Thomas. A Topographical Description of the Dominions of the United States of America. Mulkearn, Lois, ed. LC 75-22835. (America in Two Centuries Ser). 1975. Repr. of 1949 ed. 15.00x (ISBN 0-405-07706-8). Arno.
Putz & Spectre. The Down East Companion. 1979. pap. 10.95 (ISBN 0-89272-060-3). Down East.
Robinson, William F. Abandoned New England: Its Hidden Ruins & Where to Find Them. LC 75-24590. (Illus.). 1978. pap. 9.95 (ISBN 0-8212-0734-2). NYGS.
Ross, Corinne M. & Woodward, Ralph. New England: Off the Beaten Path. LC 80-27680. (Illus.). 128p. 1981. pap. 4.95 (ISBN 0-914788-40-X). East Woods.
Sandler, Martin. As New Englanders Played. LC 79-55211. (Illus.). 1979. pap. 5.95 (ISBN 0-87106-034-5). Globe Pequot.
Smith, Clyde H., photos by. New England. LC 74-33866. (Belding Imprint Ser.). (Illus.). 192p. (Text by Ann Glickman). 1975. 30.00 (ISBN 0-912856-17-3). Graphic Arts Ctr.
--New England Coast. LC 75-41843. (Belding Imprint Ser.). (Illus.). 128p. (Text by Cronan Minton). 1976. 27.50 (ISBN 0-912856-24-6). Graphic Arts Ctr.
Tanner, Ogden. The New England Wilds. (The American Wilderness Ser.). (Illus.). 184p. 1974. 12.95 (ISBN 0-8094-1229-2). Time-Life.
Thollander, Earl. Back Roads of New England. (Illus.). 224p. 1974. 10.95 (ISBN 0-517-51422-2). Potter.
Tobey, Eric & Wolkenberg, Richard. Northeast Bicycle Tours. (Illus.). 286p. 1973. pap. 3.95 (ISBN 0-686-10413-7, 440-6233-395). Tobey Pub.
Tolman, Newton F. North of Monadnock. LC 78-544. 1978. pap. 5.45 (ISBN 0-87233-044-3). Bauhan.
Trent, Sophie. My New England. 1973. 4.00 (ISBN 0-87164-105-4). William-F.
Ward, Edward. A Trip to New England: With a Character of the Country & People. LC 68-57126. (Research & Source Works Ser.: No. 312). Orig. Title: Club for Colonial Reprints, Vol. (2). 1969. Repr. of 1905 ed. 19.00 (ISBN 0-8337-3686-8). B Franklin.
Weber, Ken. Canoeing Massachusetts, Rhode Island & Connecticut. LC 79-90812. (Illus.). 1980. pap. 6.95 (ISBN 0-89725-009-5). NH Pub Co.
Winchester, Kenneth & Dunbar, David. Walking Tours of New England. LC 79-7884. (Illus., Orig.). 1980. pap. 8.95 (ISBN 0-385-15296-5, Dolp). Doubleday.
Winship, George P., ed. Sailors' Narratives of Voyages Along the New England Coast, 1524-1624. (Research & Source Works Ser.: No. 188). (Maps). 1968. Repr. of 1905 ed. 23.50 (ISBN 0-8337-3819-4). B Franklin.
Ziegler, Katey, ed. Ski Touring Guide to New England. 4th ed. (Illus.). 1979. pap. 7.95 (ISBN 0-910146-23-3). Eastern Mount.

NEW ENGLAND–DESCRIPTION AND TRAVEL–GUIDEBOOKS

Anderson, Jane. Inn Perspective: A Guide to New England Country Inns. LC 74-1785. (Illus.). 288p. 1976. pap. 4.95 (ISBN 0-06-010137-7, HarpT, TD-223, HarpT). Har-Row.

Clayton, Barbara & Whitley, Kathleen. Exploring Coastal New England: Gloucester to Kennebunkport. LC 79-624. (Illus.). 1979. 10.95 (ISBN 0-396-07572-X); pap. 6.95 (ISBN 0-396-07698-X). Dodd.
Country New England Historical & Sightseeing Guide. 1981. 4.95 (ISBN 0-89102-177-9). B Franklin.
Day Trips in New England: A Yankee Magazine Guidebook. (Illus.). 176p. 1982. pap. 7.95 (ISBN 0-911658-45-9). Yankee Bks.
Duncan, Roger F. & Ware, John P. A Cruising Guide to the New England Coast. rev. ed. LC 78-22734. (Illus.). 1979. 19.95 (ISBN 0-396-07629-7). Dodd.
Farny, Michael. New England Over the Handlebars: A Cyclist's Guide. (Illus., Orig.). 1975. pap. 5.95 (ISBN 0-316-27465-8). Little.
Federal Writers' Project. Here's New England: A Guide to Vacationland. 1939. Repr. 29.00 (ISBN 0-403-02207-X). Somerset Pub.
Fodor's New England, 1981. 1980. pap. 7.95 (ISBN 0-679-00608-7). McKay.
Gordon, Bernard L. A Guide to Historical Southern New England. (Illus.). 24p. 0.75 (ISBN 0-910258-06-6). Book & Tackle.
Hitchcock, Anthony & Lindgren, Jean. The Compleat Traveler's Guide to Antiques Shops, Craft Shops & Factory Outlets. pap. 4.95 (ISBN 0-89102-137-X). B Franklin.
--The Compleat Traveler's Guide to Inns & Guesthouses of Country New England. (Illus.). pap. 4.95 (ISBN 0-89102-135-3). B Franklin.
--Country New England Historical & Sightseeing Guide. rev. ed. 1979. pap. 4.95 (ISBN 0-89102-136-1). B Franklin.
--Country New England Recreation & Sports Guide. rev. ed. 1979. pap. 4.95 (ISBN 0-89102-138-8). B Franklin.
Kidstuff in New England: A Yankee Magazine Guidebook. (Illus.). 256p. 1982. pap. price not set (ISBN 0-911658-44-0). Yankee Bks.
Mallett, Sandy. A Year with New England's Birds: A Guide to Twenty-Five Field Trips. LC 77-26352. (Illus.). 1978. 10.00 (ISBN 0-912274-91-3); pap. 2.95 (ISBN 0-912274-87-5). NH Pub Co.
Robbins, Sarah F. & Yentsch, Clarice. Sea Is All About Us: A Guide to Marine Environments of Cape Ann & Other Northern New England Waters. 1973. pap. 6.25 (ISBN 0-87577-046-0, Cape Ann Soc. for Marine Research, Inc.). Peabody Mus Salem.
Schneider. Guide to New England Country Inns. 3.75 (ISBN 0-915248-36-0). Vermont Crossroads.
Smith, Sharon, ed. Yankee Magazine's Travel Guide to New England: Summer-Fall 1981. (Illus.). 200p. 1981. pap. 1.95 (ISBN 0-911658-31-9). Yankee Bks.
Squier, Elizabeth & Chapin, Suzy. Guide to the Recommended Country Inns of New England. 6th ed. Kennedy, Linda, ed. LC 73-83255. (Illus.). 360p. (Orig.). pap. 6.95 (ISBN 0-87106-045-0). Globe Pequot.
Stevens, Austin, ed. Yankee Magazine's Travel Maps of New England. 1979. pap. 3.95 (ISBN 0-911658-93-9, 3058). Yankee Bks.
Waters, John F. Exploring New England Shores: A Beachcomber's Handbook. LC 73-93310. (Illus.). 228p. 1974. 7.95 (ISBN 0-913276-09-X). Stone Wall Pr.
Yankee Magazine's Travel Guide to New England. (Illus.). 200p. 1982. pap. price not set (ISBN 0-911658-43-2). Yankee Bks.

NEW ENGLAND–ECONOMIC CONDITIONS

American Geographical Society. New England's Prospect: 1933. Adams, James T., et al, eds. LC 78-111763. Repr. of 1933 ed. 34.00 (ISBN 0-404-00354-0). AMS Pr.
Anderson, Terry L. The Economic Growth of Seventeenth Century New England: A Measurement of Regional Income. LC 75-2574. (Dissertations in American Economic History). (Illus.). 1975. 16.00x (ISBN 0-405-07255-4). Arno.
Bidwell, Percy W. Rural Economy in New England at the Beginning of the 19th Century. LC 68-55480. (Illus.). Repr. of 1916 ed. 12.50x (ISBN 0-678-00815-9). Kelley.
Burrows, Fredrika A. Cannonball & Cranberries. LC 76-3143. (Illus.). 1976. 4.95 (ISBN 0-88492-011-9); pap. 2.50 (ISBN 0-88492-012-7). W S Sullwold.
Eisenmenger, Robert W. The Dynamics of Growth in New England's Economy, 1870-1964. LC 66-23926. (New England Research Ser: No. 2). 1967. 15.00x (ISBN 0-8195-8013-9, Pub. by Wesleyan U Pr). Columbia U Pr.
Hoy, John C. & Bernstein, Melvin, eds. Higher Education & the New England Economy in the Nineteen-Eighties. 160p. 1981. 12.00 (ISBN 0-87451-197-6). U Pr of New Eng.
National Planning Association. The Economic State of New England: Report of the Committee of New England of the National Planning Association, 2 vols. LC 74-12446. (Illus.). Repr. of 1954 ed. 37.50x (ISBN 0-8046-1316-8). Kennikat.
New England Regional Commission. The New England Regional Plan: An Economic Development Strategy. LC 81-50584. (Illus.). 176p. 1981. 18.00x (ISBN 0-686-29652-4); pap. 12.00 (ISBN 0-87451-203-4). U Pr of New Eng.
Weeden, William B. Indian Money As a Factor in New England Civilization. LC 78-63747. (Johns Hopkins University. Studies in the Social Sciences. Second Ser. 1884: 8-9). Repr. of 1884 ed. 11.50 (ISBN 0-404-61017-X). AMS Pr.
Weedon, William B. Economic & Social History of New England 1620-1789, 2 Vols. 1963. Set. text ed. 25.00x (ISBN 0-391-00493-X). Humanities.
Wilson, Harold F. Hill Country of Northern New England: Its Social & Economic History 1790-1930. LC 79-182730. Repr. of 1936 ed. 21.50 (ISBN 0-404-06994-0). AMS Pr.
Zevin, Robert B. The Growth of Manufacturing in Early Nineteenth Century New England. LC 75-2603. (Dissertations in American Economic History). (Illus.). 1975. 11.00x (ISBN 0-405-07224-4). Arno.

NEW ENGLAND–EMIGRATION AND IMMIGRATION

Banks, Charles E. Topographical Dictionary of 2885 English Emigrants to New England, 1620-1650. LC 63-4154. 1976. Repr. of 1937 ed. 15.00 (ISBN 0-8063-0019-1). Genealog Pub.
Bolton, Ethel S. Immigrants to New England, 1700-1775. LC 66-28669. 1979. Repr. of 1931 ed. 12.50 (ISBN 0-8063-0047-7). Genealog Pub.

NEW ENGLAND–GENEALOGY

Adams, Herbert B. The Germanic Origin of New England Towns. LC 78-63731. (Johns Hopkins University. Studies in the Social Sciences. First Ser. 1882-1883: 2). Repr. of 1882 ed. 11.50 (ISBN 0-404-61002-1). AMS Pr.
Bolton, Ethel S. Immigrants to New England, 1700-1775. LC 66-28669. 1979. Repr. of 1931 ed. 12.50 (ISBN 0-8063-0047-7). Genealog Pub.
Clough, Wilson O. Dutch Uncles & New England Cousins. 1977. 15.00 (ISBN 0-686-22208-3). Polyanthos.
The Crouch Families of New England. 2.00 (ISBN 0-940748-07-X). Conn Hist Soc.
Drake, Samuel G. Result of Some Researches Among the British Archives for Information Relative to the Founders of New England. LC 63-3218. 1969. Repr. of 1860 ed. 10.00 (ISBN 0-8063-0096-5). Genealog Pub.
Farmer, John. A Genealogical Register of the First Settlers of New England. lib. bdg. 59.95 (ISBN 0-8490-0214-1). Gordon Pr.
--A Genealogical Register of the First Settlers of New England: 1620-1675. LC 64-19761. 1979. Repr. of 1829 ed. 15.00 (ISBN 0-8063-0108-2). Genealog Pub.
Flagg, Ernest. Genealogical Notes on the Founding of New England. LC 72-10465. (Illus.). 1973. Repr. of 1926 ed. 17.50 (ISBN 0-8063-0533-9). Genealog Pub.
Holmes, Frank R. Directory of the Ancestral Heads of New England Families, 1620-1700. LC 64-19755. 1974. Repr. of 1923 ed. 15.00 (ISBN 0-8063-0182-1). Genealog Pub.
New England Historic Genealogical Society. New England Historical & Genealogical Register, 4 vols. LC 72-1957. 1972. Repr. of 1911 ed. Set. 70.00 (ISBN 0-8063-0512-6). Genealog Pub.
New England Historical Genealogical Society. The Greenlaw Index of the New England Historic Genealogical Society. 1979. lib. bdg. 195.00 (ISBN 0-8161-0312-7). G K Hall.
Savage, James. A Genealogical Dictionary of the First Settlers of New England, 4 vols. 450.00 (ISBN 0-8490-0213-3). Gordon Pr.
Savage, James E. A Genealogical Dictionary of the First Settlers of New England, 4 vols. LC 65-18541. 1977. 75.00 (ISBN 0-8063-0309-3). Genealog Pub.
Talcott, Sebastian V. Genealogical Notes of New York & New England Families. LC 72-5682. 1973. Repr. of 1883 ed. 25.00 (ISBN 0-8063-0537-1). Genealog Pub.
Towle, Laird C., ed. New England Annals: History & Genealogy, Vol. 1. 500p. 1980. 20.00 (ISBN 0-917890-19-1). Heritage Bk.
Weis, Frederick L. Ancestral Roots of Sixty Colonists Who Came to New England Between 1623 & 1650. 5th ed. LC 76-7243. 1979. 12.50 (ISBN 0-8063-0373-5). Genealog Pub.

NEW ENGLAND–HISTORIC HOUSES, ETC.

Baker, Norman B. Early Houses of New England. LC 67-11935. (Illus.). 1980. 29.50 (ISBN 0-8048-0154-1). C E Tuttle.
Brown, Louise K. A Revolutionary Town. LC 74-30897. (Illus.). 336p. 1975. 15.00 (ISBN 0-914016-14-8). Phoenix Pub.
Chamberlain, Samuel. Small House in the Sun. 1936. 12.50 (ISBN 0-8038-6704-2). Hastings.
Chamberlain, Samuel & Chamberlain, Narcissa G. The Chamberlain Selection of New England Rooms, 1639-1863. 1973. 20.00 (ISBN 0-8038-1176-4). Hastings.
Country New England Antiques, Crafts & Factory Outlets. 1981. 4.95 (ISBN 0-89102-178-7). B Franklin.
Country New England Historical & Sightseeing Guide. 1981. 4.95 (ISBN 0-89102-177-9). B Franklin.
Gillon, Edmond V. A New England Town in Early Photographs: 149 Illus. of Southbridge, Massachusetts,1878-1930. 8.00 (ISBN 0-8446-5491-4). Peter Smith.
Jewett, Kenneth & Whitney, Stephen. Early New England Wall Stencils: A Workbook. 1979. pap. 8.95 (ISBN 0-517-53561-0, Harmony). Crown.
Kull, Andrew. New England Cemeteries: A Collector's Guide. LC 74-27456. (Illus.). 224p. 1975. 10.95 (ISBN 0-8289-0246-1); pap. 5.95 (ISBN 0-8289-0245-3). Greene.
Morton, Nathaniel. New England's Memoriall. LC 38-10717. Repr. of 1669 ed. 23.00x (ISBN 0-8201-1184-8). Schol Facsimiles.

NEW ENGLAND–HISTORY

Abbott, Katherine M. Old Paths & Legends of New England: Saunterings Over Historic Roads with Glimpses of Picturesque Fields & Old Homesteads in Massachusetts, Rhode Island & New Hampshire. LC 76-75228. Repr. of 1903 ed. 22.00 (ISBN 0-8103-3564-6). Gale.
Adams, Henry, ed. Documents Relating to New England Federalism, 1800-1815. 1964. Repr. of 1905 ed. 24.50 (ISBN 0-8337-0012-X). B Franklin.
Adams, Herbert B. The Germanic Origin of New England Towns. LC 78-63731. (Johns Hopkins University. Studies in the Social Sciences. First Ser. 1882-1883: 2). Repr. of 1882 ed. 11.50 (ISBN 0-404-61002-1). AMS Pr.
Adams, J. T. New England in the Republic. (Illus.). 1958. 9.00 (ISBN 0-8446-1010-0). Peter Smith.
Adams, James T. History of New England, 3 Vols. 1971. Repr. of 1923 ed. 16.50 ea. (ISBN 0-403-03602-X); Set. 95.00 (ISBN 0-403-00820-4). Scholarly.
--New England in the Republic 1776-1850. LC 70-144854. Repr. of 1926 ed. 54.00 (ISBN 0-403-00821-2). Scholarly.
Adams, Thomas B. A New Nation. (Illus.). 164p. (Orig.). 1981. pap. 9.95 (ISBN 0-87106-959-8). Globe Pequot.
All Sorts of Good Sufficient Cloth. LC 79-92225. (Illus.). 1979. 7.95 (ISBN 0-686-28439-9). Merrimack Vall Textile.
Allman, Ruth. Canaan Valley & the Black Bear. 3rd ed. 1976. 6.00 (ISBN 0-87012-220-7). McClain.
Baylies, Francis. An Historical Memoir of the Colony of New Plymouth... 1608 to 1692, 2 vols. LC 75-31110. Repr. of 1866 ed. 91.00 set (ISBN 0-404-13630-3). AMS Pr.
Bemis, Edward W. Cooperation in New England. LC 78-63779. (Johns Hopkins University. Studies in the Social Sciences. Sixth Ser. 1888: 1). Repr. of 1888 ed. 11.50 (ISBN 0-404-61045-5). AMS Pr.
Brooks, Van W. The Flowering of New England, Eighteen Fifteen to Eighteen Sixty-Five. LC 80-2898. Repr. of 1936 ed. 45.00 (ISBN 0-404-18007-8). AMS Pr.
Brooks, Van Wyck. The Flowering of New England, 1815-1865. 1981. pap. 7.95 (ISBN 0-395-30522-5). HM.
Burns, James J. The Colonial Agents of New England. LC 75-29253. (Perspectives in American History Ser., No. 26). 156p. Repr. of 1935 ed. lib. bdg. 13.50x (ISBN 0-87991-350-9). Porcupine Pr.
Carroll, Gladys H. Dunnybrook. (Illus.). 1978. 11.95 (ISBN 0-393-08822-7). Norton.
Chapman, Edward M. New England Village Life. LC 72-143643. 1971. Repr. of 1937 ed. 22.00 (ISBN 0-8103-3699-5). Gale.
Chase, Francis. Gathered Sketches from the Early History of New Hampshire & Vermont: Containing Vivid & Interesting Account of a Great Variety of the Adventures of Our Forefathers, & of Other Incidents of Olden Time. LC 75-7092. (Indian Captivities Ser.: Vol. 68). 1976. Repr. of 1856 ed. lib. bdg. 44.00 (ISBN 0-8240-1692-0). Garland Pub.
Committee for a New England Bibliography Inc. the Bibliographies of New England History & Haskell, John, eds. Massachusetts: A Bibliography of Its History, Vol. 1. (Ser. Seventy). 1976. lib. bdg. 30.00 (ISBN 0-8161-1212-6). G K Hall.
Drake, S. A. The Border Wars of New England. 305p. 1973. Repr. of 1897 ed. 10.00 (ISBN 0-87928-045-X). Corner Hse.
Egleston, Melville. The Land System of the New England Colonies. LC 78-63767. (Johns Hopkins University. Studies in the Social Sciences. Fourth Ser. 1886: 11-12). Repr. of 1886 ed. 11.50 (ISBN 0-404-61034-X). AMS Pr.
Hale, Clarence E. From a New England Town. LC 75-21355. (Illus.). 104p. 1975. pap. 3.95 (ISBN 0-914016-23-7). Phoenix Pub.
Hohmann, Elmo P. The American Whaleman. 1977. lib. bdg. 59.95 (ISBN 0-8490-1418-2). Gordon Pr.
Hoy, John C. & Bernstein, Melvin, eds. Higher Education & the New England Economy in the Nineteen-Eighties. 160p. 1981. 12.00 (ISBN 0-87451-197-6). U Pr of New Eng.
Hubbard, William. General History of New England, from the Discovery to 1680. LC 72-141089. (Research Library of Colonial Americana). 1972. Repr. of 1848 ed. 46.00 (ISBN 0-405-03288-9). Arno.
--A Narrative of Troubles with the Indians in New England. 59.95 (ISBN 0-8490-0710-0). Gordon Pr.
Kingsbury, John M. Rocky Shore. LC 71-122758. (Illus.). 1970. 4.95 (ISBN 0-85699-015-9). Chatham Pr.
Lader, Lawrence. The Bold Brahmins: New England's War Against Slavery, 1831-1863. LC 73-11624. (Illus.). 318p. 1973. Repr. of 1961 ed. lib. bdg. 15.50x (ISBN 0-8371-7081-8, LABB). Greenwood.
Lauer, Paul E. Church & State in New England. 1973. Repr. of 1892 ed. pap. 9.50 (ISBN 0-384-31585-2). Johnson Repr.
McBryde, Isabel. Aboriginal Prehistory in New England: An Archaeological Survey of Northeastern New South Wales. (Illus.). 400p. 1974. 45.00x (ISBN 0-424-06530-4, Pub. by Sydney U Pr). Intl Schol Bk Serv.
Mather, Increase. Relation of the Troubles Which Have Happened in New-England, by Reason of the Indians There from the Year 1614 to the Year 1675. LC 78-141093. (Research Library of Colonial Americana). 1971. Repr. of 1677 ed. 10.00 (ISBN 0-405-03298-6). Arno.
Mitchell, Edwin V. Horse & Buggy Age in New England. LC 74-7066. 1974. Repr. of 1937 ed. 19.00 (ISBN 0-8103-3657-X). Gale.
Morton, Nathaniel. New-Englands Memoriall. LC 75-31124. Repr. of 1937 ed. 16.50 (ISBN 0-404-13605-2). AMS Pr.
Newman, Alan B., ed. New England Reflections, Eighteen Eighty-Two to Nineteen Seven: Photographs by the Howes Brothers. (Illus.). Date not set. 25.00 (ISBN 0-394-51375-4); pap. 12.95 (ISBN 0-394-74912-X). Pantheon.
Powell, Sumner C. Puritan Village: The Formation of a New England Town. LC 63-8862. (Illus.). 1963. 27.50x (ISBN 0-8195-3034-4, Pub. by Wesleyan U Pr); pap. 6.95 (ISBN 0-8195-6014-6). Columbia U Pr.
Prince, Thomas. A Chronological History of New England in the Form of Annals. LC 75-31100. Repr. of 1826 ed. 35.00 (ISBN 0-404-13517-X). AMS Pr.
Putnam, George G. Salem Vessels & Their Voyages, 4 vols. Incl. A History of the Pepper Trade with the Island of Sumatra. Vol. 1 (ISBN 0-88389-105-0); A History of the "George", "Glide", "Taria Topan" & "St Paul", in Trade with Calcutta, East Coast of Africa, Madagascar, & the Philippine Islands. Vol. 2 (ISBN 0-88389-106-9); History of the 'Astrea', 'Mindoro', 'Sooloo', 'Panay', 'Dragon', 'Highlander', 'Shirley', & 'Formosa', with Some Account of Their Masters, & Other Reminiscences of Salem Shipmasters. Vol. 3 (ISBN 0-88389-107-7); A History of the European, African, Australian, & South Pacific Islands Trade As Carried on by Salem Merchants, Particularly the Firm of N. L. Rogers & Brothers. Vol. 4 (ISBN 0-88389-108-5). LC 30-1353. (Illus.). 680p. 1924-30. 55.00 set (ISBN 0-88389-017-8); 15.00 ea. Essex Inst.
Quinn, William P. Shipwrecks Around New England. LC 79-8876. (Illus.). 240p. 1979. 30.00 (ISBN 0-936972-00-9). Lower Cape.
Russell, Howard S. A Long, Deep Furrow: Three Centuries of Farming in New England. abr. ed. Lapping, Mark, ed. LC 81-51605. (Illus.). 400p. 1982. pap. 9.95 (ISBN 0-87451-214-X). U Pr of New Eng.
--A Long, Deep Furrow: Three Centuries of Farming in New England. LC 73-91314. (Illus.). 688p. 1976. text ed. 22.50x (ISBN 0-87451-093-7). U Pr of New Eng.
Sandler, Martin W. This Was New England: Images of a Vanished Past. LC 77-8604. (Illus.). 1978. 19.95 (ISBN 0-8212-0715-6, 839604). NYGS.
Scott, Donald M. From Office to Profession: The New England Ministry, 1750-1850. LC 77-20304. 1978. 16.00x (ISBN 0-8122-7737-6). U of Pa Pr.
Smith, John. Generall Historie of Virginia, New England & the Southern Isles. Repr. of 1624 ed. 12.00 (ISBN 0-930230-10-8). Johnson NC.
Tapley, Harriet S. Early Coastwise & Foreign Shipping of Salem: A Record of the Entrances & Clearances of the Port of Salem, 1750-1769. (Illus.). 217p. 1934. 10.00 (ISBN 0-88389-019-4). Essex Inst.

Taylor, William L., ed. Readings in New Hampshire & New England History. 282p. 1971. pap. text ed. 14.95x (ISBN 0-8422-0184-X). Irvington.

Thayer, Henry. The Sagadahoc Colony: Comprising the Relation of a Voyage into New England. LC 76-173865. (Illus.). Repr. of 1892 ed. 18.50 (ISBN 0-405-09026-9). Arno.

Towle, Laird C., ed. New England Annals: History & Genealogy, Vol. 1. 500p. 1980. 20.00 (ISBN 0-917890-19-1). Heritage Bk.

Tree, Christina. How New England Happened: The Modern Traveler's Guide to New England's Historical Past. 1976. pap. 6.95 (ISBN 0-316-85260-0). Little.

Vaughan, Alden T. & Richter, Daniel K. Crossing the Cultural Divide: Indians & New Englanders, 1605-1763. 76p. 1980. pap. 5.00 (ISBN 0-912296-48-8, Dist. by U Pr of Va). Am Antiquarian.

Wagenknecht, Edward. A Pictorial History of New England. (Illus.). 352p. 1975. 12.95 (ISBN 0-517-52346-9). Crown.

Webster, Clarence M. Town Meeting Country. Repr. of 1945 ed. lib. bdg. 15.00 (ISBN 0-8371-2979-6, WETM). Greenwood.

Weeden, W. B. Indian Money As a Factor in New England Civilization. 59.95 (ISBN 0-8490-0399-7). Gordon Pr.

Weedon, William B. Economic & Social History of New England 1620-1789, 2 Vols. 1963. Set. text ed. 25.00x (ISBN 0-391-00493-X). Humanities.

Weis, Frederick L. Ancestral Roots of Sixty Colonists Who Came to New England Between 1623 & 1650. 5th ed. LC 76-7243. 1979. 12.50 (ISBN 0-8063-0373-5). Genealog Pub.

Wilson, Harold F. Hill Country of Northern New England: Its Social & Economic History 1790-1930. LC 79-182730. Repr. of 1936 ed. 21.50 (ISBN 0-404-06994-0). AMS Pr.

Zuckerman, Michael. Peaceable Kingdoms: New England Towns in the Eighteenth Century. 1978. pap. 5.95x (ISBN 0-393-00895-9, N895, Norton Lib). Norton.

NEW ENGLAND–HISTORY–ANECDOTES

Snow, Edward R. Marine Mysteries & Dramatic Disasters of New England. LC 76-28985. 1976. 8.95 (ISBN 0-396-07378-6). Dodd.

NEW ENGLAND–HISTORY–COLONIAL PERIOD, ca. 1600-1775

Adams, James T. Revolutionary New England, Sixteen Ninety One to Seventeen Seventy Six. LC 68-19139. 1968. Repr. of 1923 ed. 17.50x (ISBN 0-8154-0002-0). Cooper Sq.

Akagi, R. H. Town Proprietors of the New England Colonies. 1963. 8.50 (ISBN 0-8446-1012-7). Peter Smith.

Bailyn, Bernard. The New England Merchants in the Seventeenth Century. 1979. pap. 4.95x (ISBN 0-674-61280-9). Harvard U Pr.

Baxter, James P. The Pioneers of New France in New England. 450p. 1980. Repr. of 1894 ed. 20.00 (ISBN 0-917890-20-5). Heritage Bk.

--Sir Ferdinando Gorges (1565-1647) & His Province of Maine, 3 vols. 1966. Set. 62.00 (ISBN 0-8337-0190-8). B Franklin.

Bodge, George M. Soldiers in King Philip's War. LC 67-30755. (Illus.). 1976. Repr. of 1906 ed. 20.00 (ISBN 0-8063-0043-4). Genealog Pub.

Bolton, Charles K. The Real Founders of New England: Stories of Their Life Along the Coast 1602-1628. LC 74-467. (Illus.). 192p. 1974. Repr. of 1929 ed. 15.00 (ISBN 0-8063-0614-9). Genealog Pub.

Bowen, Richard L. Early Rehoboth, Vol. 4. 1950. 10.00 (ISBN 0-685-67655-2). RI Hist Soc.

A Briefe Relation of the Discovery & Plantation of New England. LC 74-28876. (English Experience Ser.: No. 754). 1975. Repr. of 1622 ed. 3.50 (ISBN 90-221-0754-X). Walter J Johnson.

Brown, J. Pilgrim Fathers of New England & Their Puritan Successors. 4th ed. (Illus.). Repr. of 1920 ed. 24.00 (ISBN 0-527-12050-2). Kraus Repr.

Carroll, Gladys H. Dunnybrook. (Illus.). 1978. 11.95 (ISBN 0-393-08822-7). Norton.

Clap, Roger. Memoirs of Roger Clap: Collections of the Dorchester Antiquarian & Historical Society, No. 1. facsimile ed. LC 73-150176. (Select Bibliographies Reprint Ser.). 1972. Repr. of 1843 ed. 10.00 (ISBN 0-8369-5689-3). Arno.

Cobbett, Thomas. Civil Magistrate's Power in Matters of Religion Modestly Debated, London, 1653. LC 74-141104. (Research Library of Colonial Americana). 1972. Repr. of 1653 ed. 18.00 (ISBN 0-405-03318-4). Arno.

Company for the Propagation of the Gospel in New England & the Parts Adjacent in America, London. Some Correspondence Between the Governors & Treasurers of the New England Company in London & the Commissioners of the United Colonies in America the Missionaries of the Company & Others Between the Years 1657 & 1712. Ford, John W., ed. LC 73-126413. (Research & Source Works: No. 524). 1970. Repr. of 1896 ed. lib. bdg. 29.50 (ISBN 0-8337-1185-7). B Franklin.

Douglas, James. New England & New France: Contrasts & Parallels in Colonial History. LC 79-173516. (Illus.). iii, 560p. 1972. Repr. of 1913 ed. 24.00 (ISBN 0-8462-1653-1). Russell.

Dow, George F. & Edmonds, John H. Pirates of the New England Coast 1630-1730. (Illus.). 1968. Repr. of 1923 ed. 27.50 (ISBN 0-87266-008-7). Argosy.

Doyle, John A. The English in America, 5 vols. Incl. Vol. 1. Puritan Colonies, Pt. 1 (ISBN 0-404-02181-6); Vol. 2. Puritan Colonies, Pt. 2 (ISBN 0-404-02182-4); Vol. 3. The Middle Colonies (ISBN 0-404-02183-2); Vol. 4. Virginia, Maryland & the Carolinas (ISBN 0-404-02184-0); Vol. 5. The Colonies Under the House of Hanover (ISBN 0-404-02185-9). (Illus.). Repr. of 1907 ed. Set. 34.50 ea.; 172.50 (ISBN 0-404-02180-8). AMS Pr.

Drake, Samuel G. Result of Some Researches Among the British Archives for Information Relative to the Founders of New England. LC 63-3218. 1969. Repr. of 1860 ed. 10.00 (ISBN 0-8063-0096-5). Genealog Pub.

Dummer, Jeremiah. Defence of the New-England Charters. LC 71-141122. (Research Library of Colonial Americana). 1972. Repr. of 1721 ed. 13.00 (ISBN 0-405-03333-8). Arno.

Earle, Alice M. Customs & Fashions in Old New England. 1979. Repr. of 1894 ed. lib. bdg. 30.00 (ISBN 0-8495-1326-X). Arden Lib.

Egleston, Melville. The Land System of the New England Colonies. 1973. pap. 7.00 (ISBN 0-384-13963-9). Johnson Repr.

Fiske, John. The Beginnings of New England. 1978. lib. bdg. 25.00 (ISBN 0-8492-0899-8). R West.

Forbes, Harriette M., compiled by. New England Diaries, 1602-1800. LC 67-28478. 1967. Repr. of 1923 ed. 10.00 (ISBN 0-8462-0989-6). Russell.

Fox, Dixon R. Yankees & Yorkers. LC 79-15575. (Illus.). 1980. Repr. of 1940 ed. lib. bdg. 20.50x (ISBN 0-8371-5720-X, FOYY). Greenwood.

Geddes, Gordon E. Welcome Joy: Death in Puritan New England. Berkhofer, Robert, ed. (Studies in American History & Culture: No. 28). 1981. 39.95 (ISBN 0-8357-1181-1, Pub. by UMI Res Pr). Univ Microfilms.

Haffenden, Philip S. New England in the English Nation 1689-1713. 328p. 1974. text ed. 22.50x (ISBN 0-19-821124-4). Oxford U Pr.

Haller, William, Jr. Puritan Frontier: Town Planning in New England Colonial Development, 1630-60. (Columbia University. Studies in the Social Sciences: No. 568). Repr. of 1951 ed. 12.50 (ISBN 0-404-51568-1). AMS Pr.

Holmes, Frank R. Directory of the Ancestral Heads of New England Families, 1620-1700. LC 64-19755. 1974. Repr. of 1923 ed. 15.00 (ISBN 0-8063-0182-1). Genealog Pub.

Hoover, Gladys N. Elegant Royalls of Colonial New England. 10.00 (ISBN 0-533-01315-1). Vantage.

Howe, Henry F. Prologue to New England. LC 68-26231. (Illus.). 1968. Repr. of 1943 ed. 15.00 (ISBN 0-8046-0218-2). Kennikat.

Hubbard, W. History of the Indian Wars in New England, 2 Vols. in 1. 1865. 30.00 (ISBN 0-527-43000-5). Kraus Repr.

Hubbard, William. General History of New England, 1620-1680, Vols. 5-6. 1815. Vol. 5. 26.00 (ISBN 0-384-24800-4); Vol. 6. 32.00 (ISBN 0-384-24801-2). Johnson Repr.

Jennings, Francis. The Invasion of America: Indians, Colonialism, and the Cant of Conquest. (Illus.). 384p. 1976. pap. 4.95 (ISBN 0-393-00830-4, Norton Lib). Norton.

Lincoln, Charles H., ed. Narratives of the Indian Wars, Sixteen Seventy-Five to Sixteen Ninety-Nine. (Original Narratives). 1959. Repr. of 1913 ed. 18.50x (ISBN 0-06-480540-9). B&N.

Mather, Cotton. Magnalia Christi Americana: Or the Ecclesiastical History of New England. Cunningham, Raymond J., ed. LC 75-12340. (Milestones of Thought Ser). 1971. 8.50 (ISBN 0-8044-5668-2); pap. 4.95 (ISBN 0-8044-6478-2). Ungar.

Miller, Perry. Sources for The New England Mind: The Seventeenth Century. Hoopes, James, ed. 156p. (Orig.). 1981. pap. text ed. 5.95 (ISBN 0-910776-01-6). Inst Early Am.

Morison, Samuel E., et al, eds. Winthrop Papers, Prepared for the Massachusetts Historical Society, 2 vols. Incl. Vol. 1. 1498-1628. (Illus.). Repr. of 1929 ed. 15.00 (ISBN 0-8462-1089-4); Vol. 2. 1623-1630. Mitchell, Stewart, ed. (Illus.). Repr. of 1931 ed. 12.50 (ISBN 0-8462-1132-7). LC 68-10956. 1968. Russell.

Neal, Daniel. The History of New-England... to the Year of Our Lord, 1700, 2 vols. LC 75-31125. Repr. of 1747 ed. Set. 64.00 (ISBN 0-404-13760-1). AMS Pr.

Palfrey, John G. History of New England, 5 Vols. LC 1-7587. Repr. of 1890 ed. Set. 197.50 (ISBN 0-404-04910-9); 39.50 ea. Vol. 1 (ISBN 0-404-04911-7). Vol. 2 (ISBN 0-404-04912-5). Vol. 3 (ISBN 0-404-04913-3). Vol. 4 (ISBN 0-404-04914-1). Vol. 5 (ISBN 0-404-04915-X). AMS Pr.

Penhallow, S. History of the Wars of New England with the Eastern Indians. 1859. 12.00 (ISBN 0-527-70500-4). Kraus Repr.

Randolph, Edward. Edward Randolph Including His Letters & Official Papers, 7 Vols. Toppan, R. N., ed. 1966. 183.00 (ISBN 0-685-06751-3). B Franklin.

Reid, John G. Maine, Charles II & Massachusetts: Governmental Relationships in Early Northern New England. LC 77-18562. (Maine Historical Society Research Ser.: No. 1). 1977. 28.00 (ISBN 0-915592-28-2, IS-00041, Pub. by Maine Historical Soc.). Univ Microfilms.

Rosenblatt, F. F. The Chartist Movement in Its Social & Economic Aspects, 2 vols. LC 74-120203. (Columbia University Studies in the Social Sciences Ser.: No. 171-172). Repr. of 1916 ed. Set. 35.00 (ISBN 0-404-51696-3); 17.50 ea. AMS Pr.

Slosson, P. W. The Decline of the Chartist Movement. (Columbia University. Studies in the Social Sciences: No. 172). Repr. of 1916 ed. 17.50 (ISBN 0-404-51172-4). AMS Pr.

Smith, John. Advertisements for the Unexperienced Planters of New England. LC 77-171792. (English Experience Ser.: No. 356). 40p. 1971. Repr. of 1631 ed. 8.00 (ISBN 90-221-0356-0). Walter J Johnson.

--New England Trials. LC 70-171793. (English Experience Ser.: No. 416). 1971. Repr. of 1620 ed. 7.00 (ISBN 90-221-0416-8). Walter J Johnson.

--Travels & Works of Captain John Smith, President of Virginia, & Admiral of New England, 2 Vols. rev. ed. Arber, Edward & Bradley, A. G., eds. (Illus.). 1965. 75.50 (ISBN 0-8337-0080-4). B Franklin.

Weis, Frederick L. The Colonial Clergy & the Colonial Churches of New England. LC 77-82296. (Illus.). 1977. 15.00 (ISBN 0-8063-0779-X). Genealog Pub.

Winthrop, John. History of New England from 1630-1649, 2 Vols. in One. Savage, James, ed. LC 70-141103. (Research Library of Colonial Americana). (Illus.). 1972. Repr. of 1825 ed. Set. 50.00 (ISBN 0-405-03315-X). Arno.

--Winthrop's Journal, History of New England: Sixteen Thirty to Sixteen Forty-Nine, 2 Vols. Hosmer, James K., ed. (Original Narratives). 1959. Repr. of 1908 ed. Set. 37.00x (ISBN 0-06-480384-8). B&N.

Woodard, Florence M. Town Proprietors in Vermont. LC 68-58646. (Columbia University. Studies in the Social Sciences: No. 418). Repr. of 1936 ed. 16.50 (ISBN 0-404-51418-9). AMS Pr.

NEW ENGLAND–HISTORY–COLONIAL PERIOD, ca. 1600-1775–HISTORIOGRAPHY

Gay, Peter. A Loss of Mastery: Puritan Historians in Colonial America. LC 67-10969. (Jefferson Memorial Lectures). 1966. 16.75x (ISBN 0-520-00456-6). U of Cal Pr.

NEW ENGLAND–HISTORY–REVOLUTION, 1775-1783

Adams, J. T. New England in the Republic. (Illus.). 1958. 9.00 (ISBN 0-8446-1010-0). Peter Smith.

Adams, James T. Revolutionary New England, Sixteen Ninety One to Seventeen Seventy Six. LC 68-19139. 1968. Repr. of 1923 ed. 17.50x (ISBN 0-8154-0002-0). Cooper Sq.

Brown, Louise K. A Revolutionary Town. LC 74-30897. (Illus.). 336p. 1975. 15.00 (ISBN 0-914016-14-8). Phoenix Pub.

Forbes, Harriette M., compiled by. New England Diaries, 1602-1800. LC 67-28478. 1967. Repr. of 1923 ed. 10.00 (ISBN 0-8462-0989-6). Russell.

Hatch, Nathan O. The Sacred Cause of Liberty: Republican Thought & the Millenium in Revolutionary New England. LC 77-76299. 1977. 16.00x (ISBN 0-300-02092-9). Yale U Pr.

NEW ENGLAND–INTELLECTUAL LIFE

Bercovitch, Sacvan. The Puritan Origins of the American Self. LC 74-29713. 272p. 1975. 20.00x (ISBN 0-300-01754-5); pap. 5.95x (ISBN 0-300-02117-8). Yale U Pr.

Carroll, Peter N. Puritanism & the Wilderness: The Intellectual Significance of the New England Frontier, 1629-1700. LC 78-84673. 1969. 17.50x (ISBN 0-231-03253-6). Columbia U Pr.

Lowance, Mason I, Jr. The Language of Canaan: Metaphor & Symbol in New England from the Puritans to the Transcendentalists. LC 79-21179. 1980. 20.00x (ISBN 0-674-50949-8). Harvard U Pr.

Morison, Samuel E. The Intellectual Life of Colonial New England. LC 79-20246. 1980. Repr. of 1956 ed. lib. bdg. 22.50x (ISBN 0-313-22032-8, MOIL). Greenwood.

--Intellectual Life of Colonial New England. 288p. (YA) (gr. 9-12). 1960. pap. 7.95 (ISBN 0-8014-9011-1, CP11). Cornell U Pr.

Sullivan, Wilson. New England Men of Letters. LC 75-165574. (Illus.). 272p. (gr. 9 up). 1972. 9.95 (ISBN 0-02-788680-8). Macmillan.

NEW ENGLAND–JUVENILE LITERATURE

McCabe, Inger. Week in Amy's World: New England. (Face to Face Bks.). (Illus.). (gr. k-3). 1970. (CCPr); text ed. 1.36 (ISBN 0-685-04413-0, CCPr). Macmillan.

Mathieu, Joe. The Olden Days. (Pictureback Ser.). (Illus.). 32p. (ps-3). 1981. PLB 4.99 (ISBN 0-394-94085-7); pap. 1.25 (ISBN 0-394-84085-2). Random.

Pettengill, Samuel B. The Yankee Pioneers: A Saga of Courage. Bohannon, Laura, ed. (Bicentennial Historiettes). (Illus.). 86p. (gr. 7-9). 1977. pap. text ed. 0.95x (ISBN 0-915892-11-1). Regional Ctr Educ.

NEW ENGLAND–POLITICS

Hatch, Nathan O. The Sacred Cause of Liberty: Republican Thought & the Millenium in Revolutionary New England. LC 77-76299. 1977. 16.00x (ISBN 0-300-02092-9). Yale U Pr.

Koch, Stuart G. Water Resources Planning in New England. LC 79-66453. (Illus.). 200p. 1980. text ed. 15.00x (ISBN 0-87451-176-3). U Pr of New Eng.

Lauer, Paul E. Church & State in New England. LC 78-63809. (Johns Hopkins University. Studies in the Social Sciences. Tenth Ser. 1892: 2-3). Repr. of 1892 ed. 11.50 (ISBN 0-404-61072-2). AMS Pr.

Lechford, Thomas. Plain Dealing: Or News from New England. 1969. Repr. of 1867 ed. 15.50 (ISBN 0-384-31985-8). Johnson Repr.

McLaughlin, Andrew C. Foundations of American Constitutionalism. 6.50 (ISBN 0-8446-2565-5). Peter Smith.

Milburn, Josephine & Shuck, Victoria, eds. New England Politics. LC 80-14530. 320p. 1981. text ed. 27.00x (ISBN 0-87073-356-7); pap. text ed. 10.95x (ISBN 0-87073-357-5). Schenkman.

Peirce, Neal R. The New England States: People, Politics & Power in the Six New England States. (Illus.). 1976. 15.95 (ISBN 0-393-05558-2). Norton.

Stauffer, Vernon. New England & the Bavarian Illuminati. LC 66-27153. 1967. Repr. of 1918 ed. 8.50 (ISBN 0-8462-0953-5). Russell.

Trow, Martin A. Right-Wing Radicalism & Political Intolerance: A Study of Support for McCarthy in a New England Town. Zuckerman, Harriet & Merton, Robert K., eds. LC 79-9035. (Dissertations on Sociology Ser.). 1980. lib. bdg. 28.00x (ISBN 0-405-13002-3). Arno.

NEW ENGLAND–SOCIAL CONDITIONS

American Geographical Society. New England's Prospect: 1933. Adams, James T., et al, eds. LC 78-111763. Repr. of 1933 ed. 34.00 (ISBN 0-404-00354-0). AMS Pr.

Doherty, Robert. Society & Power: Five New England Towns, 1800-1860. LC 77-73477. 1977. 10.00x (ISBN 0-87023-242-8). U of Mass Pr.

Holmes, Richard. Communities in Transition: Bedford & Lincoln, Massachusetts, Seventeen Twenty-Nine to Eighteen Fifty. Berkhofer, Robert, ed. (Studies in American History & Culture: No. 16). 285p. 1980. 27.95 (ISBN 0-8357-1098-X, Pub by UMI Res Pr). Univ Microfilms.

NEW ENGLAND–SOCIAL LIFE AND CUSTOMS

Axtell, James, ed. The American People in Colonial New England. new ed. LC 72-95867. (American People Ser.). (Illus.). 175p. (Orig.). (gr. 9-12). 1973. PLB 7.95 (ISBN 0-88301-085-2); pap. 2.50 (ISBN 0-88301-069-0). Pendulum Pr.

Benton, Josiah H. Warning Out in New England. facs. ed. LC 70-137370. (Select Bibliographies Reprint Ser). 1911. 11.00 (ISBN 0-8369-5571-4). Arno.

Bowles, Ella S. About Antiques. LC 70-174011. (Tower Bks). (Illus.). 1971. Repr. of 1929 ed. 22.00 (ISBN 0-8103-3921-8). Gale.

Bremer, Francis J. The Puritan Experiment: New England Society from Bradford to Edwards. LC 75-38014. 256p. 1976. 15.95 (ISBN 0-312-65625-4); pap. text ed. 6.95 (ISBN 0-312-65660-2). St Martin.

Crawford, Mary C. Social Life in Old New England. LC 71-102645. (Tower Bks). (Illus.). 1971. Repr. of 1914 ed. 34.00 (ISBN 0-8103-3924-2). Gale.

Deetz, James. In Small Things Forgotten: The Archaeology of Early American Life. LC 76-50760. 1977. pap. 2.50 (ISBN 0-385-08031-X, Anch). Doubleday.

Dow, George F. Domestic Life in New England in the Seventeenth Century. LC 72-83087. (Illus.). Repr. of 1925 ed. 9.00 (ISBN 0-405-08462-5, Blom Pubns). Arno.

Earle, Alice M. Customs & Fashions in Old New England. 1969. Repr. of 1893 ed. 8.50 (ISBN 0-87928-007-7). Corner Hse.

--Customs & Fashions in Old New England. LC 71-142765. 1971. pap. 5.25 (ISBN 0-8048-0960-7). C E Tuttle.

--Customs & Fashions in Old New England. LC 68-17959. 1968. Repr. of 1893 ed. 19.00 (ISBN 0-8103-0155-5). Gale.

--Sabbath in Puritan New England. LC 68-17961. 1968. Repr. of 1891 ed. 19.00 (ISBN 0-8103-3430-5). Gale.

Felt, Joseph B. Customs of New England. 1967. Repr. of 1853 ed. 19.00 (ISBN 0-8337-1105-9). B Franklin.

Forbes, Harriette M., compiled by. New England Diaries, 1602-1800. LC 67-28478. 1967. Repr. of 1923 ed. 10.00 (ISBN 0-8462-0989-6). Russell.

Hale, Edward E. New England Boyhood. LC 72-131731. 1970. Repr. of 1927 ed. 10.00 (ISBN 0-403-00618-X). Scholarly.

Holmes, Richard. Communities in Transition: Bedford & Lincoln, Massachusetts, Seventeen Twenty-Nine to Eighteen Fifty. Berkhofer, Robert, ed. (Studies in American History & Culture: No. 16). 285p. 1980. 27.95 (ISBN 0-8357-1098-X, Pub by UMI Res Pr). Univ Microfilms.

Larcom, Lucy. New England Girlhood. 7.00 (ISBN 0-8446-2431-4). Peter Smith.

Loeb, Robert H., Jr. New England Village: Everyday Life in 1810. LC 76-2791. (gr. 4-5). 1976. 6.95a (ISBN 0-385-11488-5); PLB (ISBN 0-385-11489-3). Doubleday.

Lowell, James R. Among My Books. LC 75-126666. 1970. 11.50 (ISBN 0-404-04039-X). AMS Pr.

Morgan, E. S. Puritan Family. 8.00 (ISBN 0-8446-2609-0). Peter Smith.

Morgan, Edmund S., ed. Puritan Family: Religion & Domestic Relations in 17th Century New England. rev. ed. pap. 3.95x (ISBN 0-06-131227-4, TB1227, Torch). Har-Row.

Poggie, John J. & Gersuny, Carl. Fishermen of Galilee: The Human Ecology of a New England Coastal Community. LC 73-93703. (Marine Bulletin: No. 17). 1974. pap. 3.00 (ISBN 0-938412-09-4). URI MAS.

Ross, Corinne M. The New England Guest House Book. LC 79-4899. (Illus.). 192p. 1979. pap. 6.95 (ISBN 0-914788-15-9). East Woods.

Simpson, Ruth M. Hand-Hewn in Old Vermont. LC 78-78015. (Illus.). 240p. 1980. pap. 5.00 (ISBN 0-9604048-0-5). R M R Simpson.

--Out of the Saltbox: The Savour of Old Vermont. LC 74-27620. (Illus.). 273p. 1980. pap. 6.00 (ISBN 0-9604048-1-3). R M R Simpson.

Smith, Seba. Letters Written During the President's Tour 'Down East' facs. ed. LC 78-76929. (American Fiction Reprint Ser). 1833. 9.00 (ISBN 0-8369-7008-X). Arno.

Solomon, Barbara M. Ancestors & Immigrants: A Changing New England Tradition. LC 73-172102. 1972. pap. 2.95 (ISBN 0-226-76808-2, P446, Phoen). U of Chicago Pr.

Stiles, H. R. Bundling. 59.95 (ISBN 0-87968-804-1). Gordon Pr.

Stiles, Henry R. Bundling: Its Origin, Progress & Decline in America. LC 72-9681. Repr. of 1871 ed. 16.00 (ISBN 0-404-57499-8). AMS Pr.

Tolman, Newton F. & Gilbert, Kay. Nelson Music Collection. pap. 5.95x (ISBN 0-89190-952-4). Am Repr-Rivercity Pr.

Tyler, Royall. Algerine Captive. LC 67-10272. 1967. Repr. of 1797 ed. 48.00x (ISBN 0-8201-1046-9). Schol Facsimiles.

Weedon, William B. Economic & Social History of New England 1620-1789, 2 Vols. 1963. Set. text ed. 25.00x (ISBN 0-391-00493-X). Humanities.

Whittier, John G. The Supernaturalism of New England. Wagenknecht, Edward, ed. LC 69-10628. 1969. Repr. of 1847 ed. 7.95 (ISBN 0-8061-0824-X). U of Okla Pr.

NEW ENGLAND, AUSTRALIA (PROPOSED STATE)

Walker, R. B. Old New England. 1966. 7.50x (ISBN 0-424-05090-0, Pub by Sydney U Pr). Intl Schol Bk Serv.

NEW ENGLAND EMMIGRANT AID COMPANY

Johnson, Samuel A. The Battle Cry of Freedom: New England Emigration Aid Company in the Kansas Crusade. LC 77-11619. (Illus.). 1977. Repr. of 1954 ed. lib. bdg. 25.00x (ISBN 0-8371-9813-5, JOBC). Greenwood.

NEW ENGLAND FOOTBALL TEAM (AMERICAN CONFERENCE)

Fox, Larry. The New England Patriots: Triumph & Tragedy. LC 79-1992. (Illus.). 1979. 11.95 (ISBN 0-689-10992-X). Atheneum.

McGuane, George. New England Patriots: A Pictorial History. LC 80-84555. (Illus.). 176p. 1981. 16.95 (ISBN 0-938694-00-6). JCP Corp VA.

NEW ENGLAND IN LITERATURE

Westbrook, Perry D. The New England Town in Fact & Fiction. LC 80-67077. 380p. 1981. 27.50 (ISBN 0-8386-3011-1). Fairleigh Dickinson.

NEW ENGLAND MISSISSIPPI LAND COMPANY

Magrath, C. Peter. Yazoo: Law & Politics in the New Republic-The Case of Fletcher vs. Peck. LC 66-19584. (Illus.). 259p. 1966. text ed. 12.00x (ISBN 0-87057-100-1, Pub. by Brown U Pr). U Pr of New Eng.

NEW ENGLAND PRIMER

Ford, Paul L., ed. New England Primer. LC 62-20977. (Orig.). 1962. pap. text ed. 4.00x (ISBN 0-8077-1368-6). Tchrs Coll.

NEW ENGLAND SHIPBUILDING CORPORATION, SOUTH PORTLAND, MAINE

Jones, Herbert G. Portland Ships Are Good Ships. (Illus.). 101p. 1945. 7.50 (ISBN 0-686-00798-0); pap. 3.50 (ISBN 0-686-00799-9). O'Brien.

NEW ENGLAND THEOLOGY

Boardman, George N. A History of New England Theology. 1976. Repr. of 1899 ed. 29.00 (ISBN 0-403-06708-1, Regency). Scholarly.

Conforti, Joseph. Samuel Hopkins & the New Divinity Movement: Calvinism, the Congregational Ministry, & Reform in New England Between the Great Awakenings. 240p. (Orig.). 1981. pap. 16.95 (ISBN 0-8028-1871-4). Eerdmans.

Fleming, Sanford. Children & Puritanism: The Place of Children in the Life & Thought of the New England Churches, 1620-1847. LC 70-89178. (American Education: Its Men, Institutions & Ideas Ser). 1969. Repr. of 1933 ed. 13.00 (ISBN 0-405-01416-3). Arno.

Foster, Frank H. Modern Movement in American Theology. facs. ed. LC 76-86751. (Essay Index Reprint Ser). 1939. 12.50 (ISBN 0-8369-1131-8). Arno.

McKinsey, Elizabeth R. The Western Experiment: New England Transcendentalists in the Ohio Valley. LC 72-83467. (Essays in History & Literature Ser.). 80p. 1973. pap. 3.95x (ISBN 0-674-95040-2). Harvard U Pr.

NEW ENGLAND TRANSCENDENTALISM

see Transcendentalism (New England)

NEW ENGLAND WITCHCRAFT

see Witchcraft-New England

NEW ENGLANDERS

Burnett, Arthur C. Yankees in the Republic of Texas: Their Origin & Impact. 1952. wrappers 7.00 (ISBN 0-685-05007-6). A Jones.

Green, Fletcher. The Role of the Yankee in the Old South. LC 68-54086. (Mercer University Lamar Lecture Ser: No. 11). 156p. 1972. 9.95x (ISBN 0-8203-0233-3). U of Ga Pr.

Holbrook, Stewart H. Yankee Exodus: An Account of Migration from New England. LC 50-7972. (Illus.). 440p. 1968. Repr. of 1950 ed. 11.50 (ISBN 0-295-73726-3). U of Wash Pr.

Webster, Clarence M. Town Meeting Country. Repr. of 1945 ed. lib. bdg. 15.00 (ISBN 0-8371-2979-6, WETM). Greenwood.

NEW FOREST, ENGLAND

De Bairacli Levy, Juliette. Wanderers in the New Forest. 208p. 1977. pap. 4.95 (ISBN 0-571-11087-8, Pub. by Faber & Faber). Merrimack Bk Serv.

Vesey-Fitzgerald, Brian. Portrait of the New Forest. LC 67-70400. (Portrait Bks.). (Illus.). 1966. 10.50x (ISBN 0-7091-6400-9). Intl Pubns Serv.

NEW FRANCE

Biggar, H. P. & Litt, B. A. The Early Trading Companies of New France. LC 77-108460. 320p. 1972. Repr. of 1901 ed. 25.00 (ISBN 0-403-00452-7). Scholarly.

Cahall, Raymond D. Sovereign Council of New France: A Study in Canadian Constitutional History. LC 15-13350. (Columbia University Studies in the Social Sciences: No. 156). Repr. of 1915 ed. 21.00 (ISBN 0-404-51156-2). AMS Pr.

Faribault, George B., ed. Catalogue D'Ouvrages Sur l'Histoire De l'Amerique. 1966. Repr. of 1837 ed. 13.00 (ISBN 0-384-15145-0). Johnson Repr.

NEW FRANCE-BIBLIOGRAPHY

Dionne, Narcisse E. Inventaire Chronolgique des Ouvrages Publies a l'Etranger en Diverses Langues sur Quebec et la Nouvelle France, 5 vols. in 2. 1969. 45.50 (ISBN 0-8337-0866-X). B Franklin.

Faribault, G. B. Catalogue D'ourvages Sur L'histoire De L'amerique, et En Particulier Sur Celle Du Canada, Da la Louisiane, De L'acadie et Autres Lieux. (Canadiana Avant 1867: No. 13). 1966. 20.50x (ISBN 90-2796-330-4). Mouton.

Harrisse, Henry. Notes pour servir a L'histoire, a la bibliographie et a la cartographie De la Nouvelle-France et Des pays adjacents, 1545-1700. (French-Canadian Civilization Ser.). (Fr.). Repr. of 1872 ed. lib. bdg. 24.50x (ISBN 0-697-00006-0). Irvington.

NEW FRANCE-DISCOVERY AND EXPLORATION

Cartier, Jacques. A Shorte & Briefe Narration of the Two Navigations to Newe Fraunce. Florio, J., tr. LC 73-6110. (English Experience Ser.: No. 718). 1975. Repr. of 1580 ed. 8.00 (ISBN 90-221-0718-3). Walter J Johnson.

Champlain, Samuel. Voyages of Samuel De Champlain, 3 Vols. Slafter, Edmund F., ed. Otis, Charles P., tr. (Illus.). Set. 62.00 (ISBN 0-8337-3287-0). B Franklin.

Champlain, Samuel De. The Voyages & Explorations of Samuel De Champlain, Sixteen Four to Sixteen Sixteen, 2 vols. LC 72-2825. (Illus.). Repr. of 1922 ed. Set. 37.50 (ISBN 0-404-54905-5). AMS Pr.

Grant, W. L., ed. Voyages of Samuel De Champlain, Sixteen Four to Sixteen Eighteen. (Original Narratives). 1967. Repr. of 1907 ed. 18.50x (ISBN 0-06-480330-9). B&N.

Lavender, David. The Trans-Canada Canoe Trail. LC 77-4864. (American Trail Ser.). 1977. 11.50 (ISBN 0-07-036678-0, GB). McGraw.

La Verendrye, Pierre G. Journals & Letters of Pierre Gaultier De Varennes De la Verendrye & His Sons, with Correspondence Between the Governors of Canada & the French Court, Touching the Search for the Western Sea. Burpee, Lawrence J., ed. LC 68-28605. 1968. Repr. of 1927 ed. lib. bdg. 44.00x (ISBN 0-8371-5055-8, LAJL). Greenwood.

Lescarbot, Marc. History of New France, Vol. 1. LC 68-28596. 1968. Repr. of 1907 ed. Vol. 1. lib. bdg. 27.50x (ISBN 0-8371-5039-6, LHFA); Vol. 2. 37.75x (ISBN 0-8371-5040-X, LHFB); Vol. 3. 35.25x (ISBN 0-8371-5041-8, LHFC). Greenwood.

Morison, Samuel E. Samuel De Champlain: Father of New France. 1972. 10.00 (ISBN 0-316-58399-5, Pub. by Atlantic Monthly Pr). Little.

Nute, Grace Lee. Caesars of the Wilderness: Medard Chouart, Sieurdes Groseilliers & Pierre Espirt Radisson, 1618-1710. Wilkins, Mira, ed. LC 76-29750. (European Business Ser.). (Illus.). 1977. Repr. of 1943 ed. lib. bdg. 24.00x (ISBN 0-405-09766-2). Arno.

Parkman, Francis. Works, 20 vols. LC 69-19160. (Illus.). Repr. of 1902 ed. Set. 550.00 (ISBN 0-404-04920-6); 27.50 ea. AMS Pr.

Sagard-Theodat, Gabriel. Long Journey to the Country of the Hurons. Wrong, George M., ed. Langton, H. H., tr. LC 68-28613. 1968. Repr. of 1939 ed. lib. bdg. 29.25x (ISBN 0-8371-3861-2, SAJC). Greenwood.

Winsor, Justin. From Cartier to Frontenac: Geographical Discovery in the Interior of North America in Its Historical Relations 1534-1700. LC 79-114670. (Illus.). 1970. Repr. of 1894 ed. lib. bdg. 15.00x (ISBN 0-8154-0323-2). Cooper Sq.

NEW FRANCE-HISTORY

see Canada-History-To 1763 (New France); Mississippi Valley-History

NEW GRANADA

Graham, R. Cunninghame. The Conquest of New Grenada, Being the Life of Gonzalo Jimenez De Quesada. LC 77-88572. 1977. Repr. of 1922 ed. lib. bdg. 30.00 (ISBN 0-89341-279-1). Longwood Pr.

Kuethe, Allan J. Military Reform & Society in New Granada, 1773-1808. LC 77-21908. (Latin American Monographs: Ser. 2, No. 22). 1978. 11.00 (ISBN 0-8130-0570-1). U Presses Fla.

NEW GUARD

Campbell, Eric. Rallying Point. 1965. 12.50x (ISBN 0-522-83555-4, Pub. by Melbourne U Pr). Intl Schol Bk Serv.

NEW GUINEA

Bayliss-Smith, Timothy & Feachem, Richard, eds. Subsistence & Survival: Rural Ecology in the Pacific. 1978. 68.00 (ISBN 0-12-083250-X). Acad Pr.

Beier, Ulli, ed. Black Writing from New Guinea. (Asian & Pacific Writing Ser.). 1973. 14.95x (ISBN 0-7022-0835-3); pap. 8.50x (ISBN 0-7022-0846-9). U of Queensland Pr.

Burton-Bradley, B. G. Stone Age Crisis: A Psychiatric Appraisal. LC 75-4944. (Flexner Lectures in Medicine, 1973). 128p. 1975. 8.95x (ISBN 0-8265-1199-6). Vanderbilt U Pr.

Capell, A. A Survey of New Guinea Languages. LC 68-21925. (Illus.). 158p. 1971. 14.00x (ISBN 0-424-05420-5, Pub. by Sydney U Pr). Intl Schol Bk Serv.

Cilento, Raphael W. Causes of Depopulation in the Western Islands of the Territory of New Guinea. LC 75-32809. Repr. of 1928 ed. 14.50 (ISBN 0-404-14113-7). AMS Pr.

Ekman, Paul. The Face of Man: Expressions of Universal Emotions in a New Guinea Village. LC 79-12934. 154p. 1980. lib. bdg. 25.00 (ISBN 0-8240-7130-1). Garland Pub.

Groves, William. Native Education & Culture-Contact in New Guinea, a Scientific Approach. LC 75-32819. Repr. of 1936 ed. 17.50 (ISBN 0-404-14123-4). AMS Pr.

Hays, Terence E. Anthropology in the New Guinea Highlands: An Annotated Bibliography. LC 75-24102. (Reference Library of Social Science: Vol. 17). 200p. 1975. lib. bdg. 26.00 (ISBN 0-8240-9972-9). Garland Pub.

Keysser, Christian. A People Reborn. Allin, Alfred & Kuder, John, trs. from Ger. LC 79-23623. 306p. (Orig.). 1980. pap. 9.95x (ISBN 0-87808-174-7). William Carey Lib.

Koch, Klaus-Friedrich. War & Peace in Jalemo: The Management of Conflict in Highland New Guinea. LC 73-92579. 288p. 1974. text ed. 15.00x (ISBN 0-674-94590-5). Harvard U Pr.

Lagerberg, Kees. West Irian & Jakarat Imperialism. LC 79-11232. 1979. 18.95x (ISBN 0-312-86322-5). St Martin.

Longacre, Robert A. Hierarchy & Universality of Discourse Constituents in New Guinea Languages: Discussion. LC 72-81353. 176p. 1972. pap. 4.00 (ISBN 0-87840-154-7). Georgetown U Pr.

--Hierarchy & Universality of Discourse Constituents in New Guinea Languages: Texts. LC 72-81353. 268p. 1972. pap. 4.25 (ISBN 0-87840-155-5). Georgetown U Pr.

Mead, Margaret. Sex & Temperament in Three Primitive Societies. 10.00 (ISBN 0-8446-2568-X). Peter Smith.

Pataki-Schweizer, K. J. A New Guinea Landscape: Community, Space & Time in the Eastern Highlands. LC 78-21211. (Anthropological Studies in the Eastern Highlands of New Guinea: Vol. 4). (Illus.). 188p. 1980. 40.00 (ISBN 0-295-95656-9). U of Wash Pr.

Reed, Stephen W. The Making of Modern New Guinea. LC 75-30077. (Institute of Pacific Relations). Repr. of 1943 ed. 28.50 (ISBN 0-404-59554-5). AMS Pr.

Rowley, Charles D. The Australians in German New Guinea, 1914-1921. 1958. 16.50x (ISBN 0-522-83725-5, Pub. by Melbourne U Pr). Intl Schol Bk Serv.

Sack, Peter & Clark, Dymphna, eds. German New Guinea: The Annual Reports. LC 78-52786. (Illus.). 1979. text ed. 34.95 (ISBN 0-7081-1806-2, 0411, Pub. by ANUP Australia). Bks Australia.

Sillitoe, Paul. Give & Take: Exchange in Wola Society. LC 79-5084. 1979. 32.50x (ISBN 0-312-32735-8). St Martin.

Sinclair, James. Faces of New Guinea. (Illus.). 94p. 1973. 10.50x (ISBN 0-8002-1414-5). Intl Pubns Serv.

Smith, Henry. Voyage to New Guinea. 1744. 28.00 (ISBN 0-403-00290-7). Scholarly.

Willey, Keith. Assignment New Guinea. 1965. 10.00x (ISBN 0-8002-0668-1). Intl Pubns Serv.

Wurm, S. A., ed. New Guinea & Neighboring Areas: A Sociolinguistic Laboratory. (Contributions to the Sociology of Language Ser.: No. 24). 1979. text ed. 38.25x (ISBN 90-279-7848-4). Mouton.

NEW GUINEA-ART

see Art, New Guinea

NEW GUINEA-DESCRIPTION AND TRAVEL

Archbold, Richard & Rand, Austin L. New Guinea Expedition, Fly River Area, 1936-1937. LC 75-32797. (Illus.). Repr. of 1940 ed. 30.00 (ISBN 0-404-14100-5). AMS Pr.

Beaver, Wilfred N. Unexplored New Guinea. LC 75-32799. (Illus.). Repr. of 1920 ed. 32.50 (ISBN 0-404-14102-1). AMS Pr.

Bleeker, P. Explanatory Notes to the Land Limitation & Agricultural Land Use Potential Map of Papua New Guinea. (Land Research Ser.: No. 36). (Illus.). 1977. pap. 7.25x (ISBN 0-643-00164-6, Pub. by CSIRO). Intl Schol Bk Serv.

Brown, Paula. The Chimbu: A Study of Change in the New Guinea Highlands. (Illus.). 192p. 1972. 15.25x (ISBN 0-87073-756-2); pap. 8.95 (ISBN 0-87073-757-0). Schenkman.

Champion, Ivan F. Across New Guinea from the Fly to the Sepik. LC 75-32804. (Illus.). 1976. Repr. of 1932 ed. 27.50 (ISBN 0-404-14108-0). AMS Pr.

Holmes, John H. In Primitive New Guinea. LC 75-35120. Repr. of 1924 ed. 26.50 (ISBN 0-404-14137-4). AMS Pr.

Kirk, Malcolm. Man As Art: New Guinea. LC 81-835. (Illus.). 144p. 1981. 45.00 (ISBN 0-670-45223-8, Studio). Viking Pr.
Loffler, E. Explanatory Notes to the Geomorphological Map of Papua New Guinea. (Land Pesearch Ser.: No. 33). (Illus.). 19p. 1977. pap. 7.25x (ISBN 0-643-00092-5, Pub. by CSIRO). Intl Schol Bk Serv.
MacKay, Ray. New Guinea. (World's Wild Places Ser.). (Illus.). 1976. 12.95 (ISBN 0-8094-2056-2). Time-Life.
--New Guinea. (The World's Wild Places Ser.). (Illus.). 1978. lib. bdg. 11.97 (ISBN 0-686-51022-4). Silver.
Marshall, Alan J. The Men & Birds of Paradise: Journeys Through Equatorial New Guinea. LC 75-35141. Repr. of 1938 ed. 25.50 (ISBN 0-404-14157-9). AMS Pr.
Nolan, Riall, et al. Mountain Walking in Papua New Guinea. new ed. (Illus., Orig.). Date not set. pap. cancelled (ISBN 0-913140-32-5). Signpost Bk Pub.
O'Neill, Jack. Up from the South: A Prospector in New Guinea, Nineteen Thirty-One to Nineteen Thirty-Seven. Sinclair, James, ed. (Illus.). 224p. 1979. text ed. 23.50x (ISBN 0-19-550567-0). Oxford U Pr.
Paijmans, K. Explanatory Notes to the Vegetation Map of Papua New Guinea. (Land Research Ser.: No. 35). (Illus.). 46p. 1977. pap. 7.25x (ISBN 0-643-00138-7, Pub. by CSIRO). Intl Schol Bk Serv.
Robbins, R. G., ed. Lands of the Ramu - Madang Area, Papua New Guinea. (Land Research Ser.: No. 37). (Illus.). 1977. pap. 7.25x (ISBN 0-643-00175-1, Pub. by CSIRO). Intl Schol Bk Serv.
Wheeler, Tony. Papua, New Guinea. 2nd ed. (Travel Paperbacks Ser.). (Illus.). 224p. 1981. pap. 7.95 (ISBN 0-88254-612-0, Pub. by Lonely Australia). Hippocrene Bks.
--Papua New Guinea, a Travel Survival Kit. (Illus.). 1979. pap. 3.95 (ISBN 0-908086-05-9). Hippocrene Bks.

NEW GUINEA–HISTORY

Amarshu, Azeem, et al. Development & Dependency: The Political Economy of Papua New Guinea. (Illus.). 306p. 1979. text ed. 28.00x (ISBN 0-19-550582-4). Oxford U Pr.
Finney, Ben R. Big-Men & Business: Entrepreneurship & Economic Growth in the New Guinea Highlands. LC 72-93151. (Illus.). 250p. 1973. 12.00x (ISBN 0-8248-0262-4, Eastwest Ctr). U Pr of Hawaii.
Mayo, Lida. Bloody Buna. LC 79-88829. (World War II Ser.). 1979. pap. 2.25 (ISBN 0-87216-583-3). Playboy Pbks.
Monckton, Charles A. Last Days in New Guinea. LC 75-35142. Repr. of 1922 ed. 25.00 (ISBN 0-404-14158-7). AMS Pr.
--Taming New Guinea. LC 75-35143. (Illus.). Repr. of 1921 ed. 28.50 (ISBN 0-404-14159-5). AMS Pr.
Mouton, J. B. The New Guinea Memoirs of Jean Baptiste Octave Mouton. Biskup, Peter, ed. LC 74-76379. (Pacific History Ser.: No. 7). (Illus.). 164p. 1974. 15.00x (ISBN 0-8248-0328-0). U Pr of Hawaii.
Park, Edwards. Nanette. 1977. 9.95 (ISBN 0-393-05618-X). Norton.
Sack, Peter & Clark, Dymphna, eds. German New Guinea: The Draft Annual Report for 1913-14. 170p. (Orig.). 1980. pap. text ed. 13.95 (ISBN 0-909596-45-X, 0565). Bks Australia.
Sack, Peter G. & Clark, Dymphna, eds. Albert Hail: Governor in New Guinea. LC 79-51490. (Illus.). 164p. 1981. 27.95 (ISBN 0-7081-1820-8, 0028, Pub. by ANUP Australia). Bks Australia.
Watson, Virginia D. & Cole, J. David. Prehistory of the Eastern Highlands of New Guinea. LC 76-49166. (Anthropological Studies in the Eastern Highlands of New Guinea: No. 3). (Illus.). 243p. 1978. 35.00 (ISBN 0-295-95541-4). U of Wash Pr.

NEW GUINEA–SOCIAL LIFE AND CUSTOMS

Berndt, Ronald M. & Lawrence, Peter, eds. Politics in New Guinea: Traditional & in the Context of Change, Some Anthropological Perspectives. LC 73-172827. (Illus.). 448p. 1973. text ed. 18.50 (ISBN 0-295-95235-0). U of Wash Pr.
Bone, Robert C., Jr. Dynamics of the Western New Guinea (Irian Barat) Problem. (Interim Reports Ser). (Illus.). 1958. pap. 3.00 (ISBN 0-685-08663-1). Cornell Mod Indo.
Clarke, William C. Place & People: An Ecology of a New Guinean Community. LC 78-126764. (Illus.). 1971. 26.75x (ISBN 0-520-01791-9). U of Cal Pr.
Cook, Edwin A. & O'Brien, Denise, eds. Blood & Semen: Kinship Systems of Highland New Guinea. LC 80-21559. (Anthropology Ser.: Studies in Pacific Anthropology). (Illus.). 532p. (Orig.). 1980. pap. 38.50 (ISBN 0-472-02710-7, IS-00117, Pub. by U of Mich Pr). Univ Microfilms.
Firth, Raymond W. Art & Life in New Guinea. LC 75-32815. Repr. of 1936 ed. 24.50 (ISBN 0-404-14119-6). AMS Pr.
Gell, Alfred. Metamorphosis of the Cassowaries: Umeda Society, Language & Ritual. (London School of Economics Monographs on Social Anthropology Ser). (Illus.). 385p. 1975. text ed. 39.00x (ISBN 0-391-00388-7, Athlone Pr). Humanities.
Kirk, Malcolm. Man As Art: New Guinea. LC 81-835. (Illus.). 144p. 1981. 45.00 (ISBN 0-670-45223-8, Studio). Viking Pr.
Lewis, Gilbert. Knowledge of Illness in a Sepik Society: A Study of the Gnau, New Guinea. (Monographs on Social Anthropology). (Illus.). 372p. 1975. text ed. 42.00x (ISBN 0-391-00389-5, Athlone Pr). Humanities.
Newton, Henry. In Far New Guinea. LC 75-35145. (Illus.). Repr. of 1914 ed. 27.00 (ISBN 0-404-14161-7). AMS Pr.
Read, Kenneth E. The High Valley. 265p. 1980. pap. 7.50x (ISBN 0-231-05035-6). Columbia U Pr.
Riley, E. Baxter. Among Papuan Headhunters. LC 75-35155. (Illus.). Repr. of 1925 ed. 28.00 (ISBN 0-404-14170-6). AMS Pr.
Robbins, Sterling. Auyana: Those Who Held onto Home. LC 81-2707. (Anthropological Studies in the Eastern Highlands of New Guinea: No. 3). 304p. 1981. 35.00 (ISBN 0-686-73346-0). U of Wash Pr.
Serpenti, L. M. Cultivators in the Swamps. 2nd ed. (Studies of Developing Countries: No. 5). 1977. pap. text ed. 25.75x (ISBN 90-232-0078-0). Humanities.
Whiting, John W. Becoming a Kwoma: Teaching & Learning in a New Guinea Tribe. LC 75-35163. Repr. of 1941 ed. 20.50 (ISBN 0-404-14178-1). AMS Pr.

NEW HAMPSHIRE

see also names of cities, counties, towns etc. in New Hampshire

Belknap, Jeremy. The History of New Hampshire, 2 Vols. (Sources of Science Ser: No. 88). Repr. of 1812 ed. Set. 54.00 (ISBN 0-384-03803-4). Johnson Repr.
Carpenter, Allan. New Hampshire. LC 79-11454. (New Enchantment of America State Bks.). (Illus.). (gr. 4 up). 1979. PLB 10.60 (ISBN 0-516-04129-0). Childrens.
Federal Writers' Project. New Hampshire: A Guide to the Granite State. 559p. 1938. Repr. 45.00 (ISBN 0-403-02179-0). Somerset Pub.
Fradin, Dennis. New Hampshire: In Words & Pictures. LC 80-25421. (Young People's Stories of Our States Ser.). (Illus.). 48p. (gr. 2-5). 1981. PLB 9.25 (ISBN 0-516-03929-6). Childrens.
Holbrook, Jay M. New Hampshire Seventeen Thirty-Two Census. LC 81-80038. 75p. 1981. lib. bdg. 30.00 (ISBN 0-931248-10-8). Holbrook Res.
Jennison, Keith. New Hampshire. 1973. pap. 2.95 (ISBN 0-87233-828-2). Bauhan.
Mowrer, Paul S. On Going to Live in New Hampshire. 5.00 (ISBN 0-87482-101-0). Wake-Brook.
New Hampshire. 23.00 (ISBN 0-89770-105-4). Curriculum Info Ctr.
New Hampshire Register 1981-1982. 900p. 1981. 65.00 (ISBN 0-89442-026-7). Tower Pub Co.
New Hampshire Register: 1981-1982. 1981. 65.00 (ISBN 0-89442-018-6). Tower Pub Co.
State Industrial Directories Corp. New Hampshire State Industrial Directory 1978-79. (New Hampshire State Industrial Directory Ser.). 1977. soft cover 20.00 (ISBN 0-916112-60-8). State Indus Dir.
Tolman, Newton F. North of Monadnock. Repr. of 1957 ed. lib. bdg. 13.85x (ISBN 0-89190-953-2). Am Repr-Rivercity Pr.
--Our Loons Are Always Laughing. Repr. of 1963 ed. lib. bdg. 12.05x (ISBN 0-89190-951-6). Am Repr-Rivercity Pr.

NEW HAMPSHIRE–DESCRIPTION AND TRAVEL

Bailey, Bernadine. Picture Book of New Hampshire. rev. ed. LC 61-9971. (Illus.). (gr. 3-5). 1971. 5.50g (ISBN 0-8075-9532-2). A Whitman.
Blaisdell, Paul H. Twenty-Five Walks in the Lakes Region of New Hampshire. LC 76-53697. (Illus.). 1977. 10.00 (ISBN 0-912274-68-9); pap. 2.95 (ISBN 0-912274-80-8). NH Pub Co.
Doan, Daniel. Fifty More Hikes in New Hampshire. LC 77-94004. (Illus.). 1978. 12.50 (ISBN 0-912274-89-1); pap. 6.95 (ISBN 0-912274-85-9). NH Pub Co.
Federal Writers' Project. New Hampshire: A Guide to the Granite State. 559p. 1938. Repr. 45.00 (ISBN 0-403-02179-0). Somerset Pub.
Gambee, Robert. Exeter Impressions. new ed. (Illus.). 206p. 1980. 14.95 (ISBN 0-8038-1961-7). Hastings.
Goodwin, Del & Chaffee, Dorcas, eds. Perspectives Seventy Six, a Compendium of Useful Knowledge About Old-Time Vermont & New Hampshire. (Illus.). (gr. 6-12). 1975. pap. text ed. 4.95 (ISBN 0-915892-02-2); 6.95 (ISBN 0-686-64804-8). Regional Ctr Educ.
Heavey, Thomas & Heavey, Susan. Twenty Bicycle Tours in New Hampshire. LC 78-71716. (Illus.). 1979. pap. 5.95 (ISBN 0-89725-001-X). NH Pub Co.
Hill, Evan. The Primary State: An Historical Guide to New Hampshire. 144p. (Orig.). 1976. pap. 6.95 (ISBN 0-914378-16-3). Countryman.
Kibling, Mary L. Twenty-Five Walks in the Dartmouth-Lake Sunapee Region of New Hampshire. LC 78-74156. (Illus.). 1979. pap. 4.95 (ISBN 0-89725-003-6). NH Pub Co.
Lane, Paula, ed. The New Hampshire Atlas & Gazatteer. 2nd ed. 67p. 1979. pap. 7.95 (ISBN 0-89933-004-5). DeLorme Pub.
Lewis, Paul M. Beautiful New Hampshire. Shangle, Robert D., ed. (Illus.). 72p. 1981. 14.95 (ISBN 0-89802-289-4); pap. 7.95 (ISBN 0-89802-288-6). Beautiful Am.
Older, Julia & Sherman, Steve. The New Hampshire Dining Guide: A Compendium of Dining Places of Note & Flavorful Recipes Therefrom. LC 79-10289. (Illus.). 1979. pap. 5.95 (ISBN 0-914016-58-X). Phoenix Pub.
Preston, Philip. White Mountains - East. (Illus.). 270p. (Orig.). Date not set. pap. 8.50 (ISBN 0-9603106-1-4). Waumbek.
Preston, Philip & Kannair, Jonathan A. White Mountains-West. LC 79-66098. (Illus., Orig.). 1979. pap. 7.50 (ISBN 0-9603106-0-6). Waumbek.
Quinn, John R. The Winter Woods. LC 76-18486. (Illus.). 1976. 8.95 (ISBN 0-85699-138-4). Chatham Pr.
Randall, Peter. New Hampshire: Four Seasons. LC 79-67492. (Illus.). 104p. 1979. 14.95 (ISBN 0-89272-067-0, 447). Down East.
Randall, Peter E. All Creation & the Isles of Shoals. (Illus.). 72p. (Orig.). 1980. pap. 4.95 (ISBN 0-89272-089-1). Down East.
Schweiker, Roioli. Canoe Camping Vermont & New Hampshire Rivers. Baker, Catherine J., ed. LC 76-52884. (Illus.). 1977. pap. 4.95 (ISBN 0-912274-71-9). NH Pub Co.
Teg, William. Almuchicoitt. 1950. 4.00 (ISBN 0-8158-0196-3). Chris Mass.

NEW HAMPSHIRE–GENEALOGY

Child, William H. History of the Town of Cornish New Hampshire with Genealogical Record, 1763-1910, 2 vols in 1. LC 75-28084. (Illus.). 879p. 1975. Repr. of 1911 ed. 30.00 (ISBN 0-87152-213-6). Reprint.
Goss, Mrs. Charles C. Colonial Gravestone Inscriptions in the State of New Hampshire. LC 74-15654. 1974. Repr. of 1942 ed. 12.50 (ISBN 0-8063-0634-3). Genealog Pub.
Hadley, Alice M. Where the Winds Blow Free: The History of Dunbarton, N.H. LC 76-47005. (Illus.). 1977. 15.00x (ISBN 0-914016-33-4). Phoenix Pub.
Holbrook, Jay M. New Hampshire Seventeen Seventy-Six Census. LC 76-151110. 170p. 1976. pap. 20.00 (ISBN 0-931248-02-7). Holbrook Res.
Jackson, Ronald V. & Teeples, Gary R. New Hampshire Census Index 1810. (Illus.). lib. bdg. 24.00 (ISBN 0-685-59759-8). Accelerated Index.
--New Hampshire Cenus Index 1800. LC 77-85979. (Illus.). lib. bdg. 23.00 (ISBN 0-89593-083-8). Accelerated Index.
--New Hampshire Cenus Index 1820. LC 77-85981. (Illus.). lib. bdg. 29.00 (ISBN 0-89593-085-4). Accelerated Index.
--New Hampshire Cenus Index 1830. LC 77-85983. (Illus.). lib. bdg. 31.00 (ISBN 0-89593-086-2). Accelerated Index.
--New Hampshire Cenus Index 1840. LC 77-85984. (Illus.). lib. bdg. 34.00 (ISBN 0-89593-087-0). Accelerated Index.
--New Hampshire Cenus Index 1850. LC 77-86133. (Illus.). lib. bdg. 40.00 (ISBN 0-89593-088-9). Accelerated Index.
Noyes, Sybil, et al. Genealogical Dictionary of Maine & New Hampshire. LC 79-88099. 1979. Repr. of 1939 ed. 25.00 (ISBN 0-8063-0502-9). Genealog Pub.
Stiles, Henry R. History of Ancient Wethersfield Connecticut, Vol. 2. LC 74-83524. (Illus.). 946p. 1975. Repr. of 1904 ed. 45.00x (ISBN 0-912274-50-6). NH Pub Co.
Thompson, Alice Smith, compiled by. The Drake Family of New Hampshire: Robert, of Hampton, & Some of His Descendants, A Geneology. LC 63-62916. (Illus.). 354p. 1962. text ed. 15.00x (ISBN 0-915916-03-7). U Pr of New Eng.
U. S. Bureau of the Census. Heads of Families at the First Census of the United States Taken in the Year 1790: New Hampshire. LC 73-8202. 1973. Repr. of 1907 ed. 15.00 (ISBN 0-8063-0571-1). Genealog Pub.
--Heads of Families at the First Census of the United States Taken in the Year 1790: New Hampshire. LC 73-8202. 1973. Repr. of 1907 ed. 15.00 (ISBN 0-8063-0571-1). Genealog Pub.
--Heads of Families, First Census of the United States, 1790: New Hampshire. LC 64-61301. 1961-64. Repr. of 1908 ed. 15.00 (ISBN 0-87152-018-4). Reprint.
Wade, Hugh M. A Brief History of Cornish, N. H., 1763-1974. LC 75-22518. (Illus.). 208p. 1976. text ed. 15.00x (ISBN 0-87451-129-1). U Pr of New Eng.

NEW HAMPSHIRE–HISTORY

Addresses Delivered at the Observance of the Centennial of the New Hampshire Historical Society, September 27, 1923. 71p. 1923. text ed. 2.50x (ISBN 0-915916-11-8). U Pr of New Eng.
At the Edge of Megalopolis: A History of Salem, N. H. 1900-1974. LC 74-21031. (Illus.). 1974. 12.00x (ISBN 0-914016-11-3). Phoenix Pub.
Belknap, Jeremy. History of New Hampshire, 3 vols. LC 73-141081. (Research Library of Colonial Americana). (Illus.). 1971. Repr. of 1792 ed. 90.00 (ISBN 0-405-03272-2); 30.00 ea. Vol. 1 (ISBN 0-405-03273-0). Vol. 2 (ISBN 0-405-03274-9). Vol. 3 (ISBN 0-405-03275-7). Arno.
--The History of New Hampshire, 2 Vols. (Sources of Science Ser: No. 88). Repr. of 1812 ed. Set. 54.00 (ISBN 0-384-03803-4). Johnson Repr.
Bell, Charles H. The History of Exeter, N.H. rev., 2nd ed. LC 79-1226. (Illus.). 1979. Repr. of 1888 ed. 35.00 (ISBN 0-917890-14-0). Heritage Bk.
Bradford Town History Committee, ed. Two Hundred Plus: History of Bradford, New Hampshire. LC 76-26494. (Illus.). 1976. 20.00x (ISBN 0-914016-31-8). Phoenix Pub.
Bundy, David. One Hundred Acres-More or Less: History of Bow, New Hampshire. LC 75-38922. (Illus.). 576p. 1975. 20.00x (ISBN 0-914016-24-5). Phoenix Pub.
Child, William H. History of the Town of Cornish New Hampshire with Genealogical Record, 1763-1910, 2 vols in 1. LC 75-28084. (Illus.). 879p. 1975. Repr. of 1911 ed. 30.00 (ISBN 0-87152-213-6). Reprint.
Cleveland, Mather. New Hampshire Fights the Civil War. LC 69-19751. (Illus.). 230p. 1969. text ed. 20.00x (ISBN 0-87451-057-0). U Pr of New Eng.
Close, Virginia L., compiled by. Historical New Hampshire: Index to Volumes 1-25 (1944-1970) 203p. 1974. pap. text ed. 10.00x (ISBN 0-915916-05-3). U Pr of New Eng.
Cobb, David A. New Hampshire Maps to Nineteen Hundred: An Annotated Checklist. LC 78-63588. 126p. 1981. pap. 12.00x (ISBN 0-87451-166-6). U Pr of New Eng.
Cogswell, Elliot C. The History of Nottingham, Deerfield & Northwood, N.H. LC 72-80064. 1972. Repr. of 1878 ed. 45.00 (ISBN 0-912274-18-2). NH Pub Co.
Dean, John W., ed. Captain John Mason Fifteen Eighty-Six to Sixteen Thirty-Five. LC 3-24569. (Prince Society Pubns.: No. 17). 1966. Repr. of 1887 ed. 32.00 (ISBN 0-8337-0810-4). B Franklin.
Dedication of the Building of the New Hampshire Historical Society: The Gift of Edward Tuck. (Illus.). 132p. 1912. text ed. 12.50x (ISBN 0-915916-00-2). U Pr of New Eng.
Downey, Fairfax. It Happened in New Hampshire. 93p. (Orig.). 1981. pap. 4.95 (ISBN 0-686-75397-6). Shoe String.
--Tales of New Hampshire. (Illus.). 93p. 1981. pap. 4.95 (ISBN 0-936988-03-7). Tompson & Rutter.
Farmer, John. An Historical Sketch of the Town of Amherst. LC 72-91706. 64p. 1972. Repr. of 1837 ed. 10.00 (ISBN 0-912274-26-3). NH Pub Co.
Federal Writers' Project. New Hampshire Hands That Built New Hampshire. LC 73-3635. Repr. of 1940 ed. 27.50 (ISBN 0-404-57935-3). AMS Pr.
Giffen, Daniel H. New Hampshire Colony. LC 76-93178. (Forge of Freedom Ser). (Illus.). (gr. 5-8). 1970. 7.95 (ISBN 0-02-735890-9, CCPr). Macmillan.
Griffinn, S. G. & Whitcomb, M. A. A History of the Town of Keene (N.H.), Seventeen Thirty-Two to Nineteen Hundred & Four. (Illus.). 792p. (Orig.). 1980. Repr. of 1904 ed. 38.00 (ISBN 0-917890-21-3). Heritage Bk.
Hadley, Alice M. Where the Winds Blow Free: The History of Dunbarton, N.H. LC 76-47005. (Illus.). 1977. 15.00x (ISBN 0-914016-33-4). Phoenix Pub.
Hammond, Otis G. Hammond's Check List of New Hampshire Local History. rev. ed. Hanrahan, Jack, ed. LC 72-179458. (Bibliographies of New Hampshire History). Orig. Title: Check List of New Hampshire Local History. 1971. Repr. of 1925 ed. pap. 10.00 (ISBN 0-912274-10-7). NH Pub Co.

--Tories of New Hampshire in the War of the Revolution. LC 72-8758. (American Revolutionary Ser.). Repr. of 1917 ed. lib. bdg. 34.50x (ISBN 0-8398-0799-6). Irvington.
Hancock History Committee, ed. The Second Hundred Years of Hancock, New Hampshire. LC 79-14026. (Illus.). 1979. 15.00x (ISBN 0-914016-61-X). Phoenix Pub.
Hanlan, James P. The Working Population of Manchester, New Hampshire, 1840-1886. Berkhofer, Robert, ed. LC 81-3355. (Studies in American History & Culture: No. 29). 1981. 31.95 (ISBN 0-8357-1193-5, Pub. by UMI Res Pr). Univ Microfilms.
Hareven, Tamara K. & Langenbach, Randolph. Amoskeag: Life & Work in an American Factory-City. LC 78-52862. (Illus.). 1978. 15.00 (ISBN 0-394-49941-7). Pantheon.
Henniker History Committee. The Only Henniker on Earth. LC 79-28597. (Illus.). 376p. 1980. 18.50x (ISBN 0-914016-67-9). Phoenix Pub.
History of Temple, N. H. 1768-1976. LC 76-20435. 1976. 29.50x (ISBN 0-87233-040-0). Bauhan.
Holbrook, Jay M. New Hampshire Residents Sixteen Thirty-Three to Sixteen Ninety-Nine. LC 79-88038. 1979. lib. bdg. 35.00 (ISBN 0-931248-01-9). Holbrook Res.
Hollis History Committee. Where the Past Has Been Preserved: Hollis, New Hampshire Eighteen Seventy-Nine to Nineteen Seventy-Nine. LC 79-27118. (Illus.). 1980. 15.00 (ISBN 0-914016-65-2). Phoenix Pub.
Jager, Ronald & Jager, Grace. Portrait of a Hill Town: A History of Washington, N. H., 1876-1976. LC 76-62912. (Illus.). 1977. 22.00 (ISBN 0-686-22158-3). Wash Hist Comm.
Mitchell, et al. Exeter & Hampton, New Hampshire, Census & Business Directory 1908. LC 79-1145. 1979. Repr. of 1908 ed. 15.00 (ISBN 0-917890-15-9). Heritage Bk.
Morison, Elting E. & Morison, Elizabeth F. New Hampshire. (States & the Nation Ser). (Illus.). 1976. 12.95 (ISBN 0-393-05583-3, Co-Pub by AASLH). Norton.
Morrison, L. A. History of Windham in New Hampshire, 1719-1883, Vol. 1. Incl. Rural Oasis: History of Windham, New Hampshire, 1883-1975. Windham History Committee. (Illus.). 224p. 7.95x (ISBN 0-914016-29-6). LC 75-20931. (Illus.). 976p. 1975. Set. 30.00x (ISBN 0-914016-19-9). Phoenix Pub.
Musgrove, Richard W. History of the Town of Bristol, New Hampshire. LC 76-53696. (Illus.). 1976. Repr. of 1904 ed. 35.00 (ISBN 0-912274-67-0). NH Pub Co.
The Nashua Experience. LC 78-980. 1978. 15.95x (ISBN 0-914016-50-4); pap. 8.95x (ISBN 0-914016-51-2). Phoenix Pub.
New Hampshire State Legislature. Provincial & State Papers, 18 Vols. Bouton, Nathaniel & Hammond, I. W., eds. LC 70-173073. Repr. of 1867 ed. Set. 891.00 (ISBN 0-404-07450-2); 49.50 ea. AMS Pr.
Page, Elwin L. Judicial Beginnings in New Hampshire,1640-1700. LC 59-3040. (Illus.). 278p. 1959. text ed. 10.00x (ISBN 0-915916-02-9). U Pr of New Eng.
Parades and Promenades: History of Antrim, N. H. LC 76-30841. (Illus.). 1977. 15.00x (ISBN 0-914016-39-3). Phoenix Pub.
Pennacook-Sokoki Inter-Tribal Nation, compiled by. Historical Indian-Colonial Relations of New Hampshire. Williams, W. L., ed. (Illus., Orig.). 1977. pap. text ed. 8.50 (ISBN 0-9601834-1-8); pap. text ed. 5.00 five or more copies (ISBN 0-685-52520-1). Pennacook-Sokoki.
Poling, Evangeline K. Welcome Home to Deering, New Hampshire. LC 78-808. (Illus.). 1978. 12.00x (ISBN 0-914016-48-2). Phoenix Pub.
Pope, Charles H. Pioneers of Maine & New Hampshire, 1623 to 1660. LC 65-22477. 1973. Repr. of 1908 ed. 15.00 (ISBN 0-8063-0278-X). Genealog Pub.
Potter, Chandler E. The Military History of the State of New Hampshire. LC 72-4444. 1972. Repr. of 1866 ed. 30.00 (ISBN 0-8063-0514-2). Genealog Pub.
Sanborn, Franklin B. New Hampshire: An Epitome of Popular Government. LC 72-3768. (American Commonwealths: No. 16). Repr. of 1904 ed. 24.50 (ISBN 0-404-57216-2). AMS Pr.
Scales, John. Colonial Era History of Dover. LC 77-17541. (Illus.). 1977. Repr. of 1923 ed. 27.50 (ISBN 0-917890-03-5). Heritage Bk.
Smeal, Lee. New Hampshire Historical & Biographical Index. LC 78-53707. (Illus.). Date not set. lib. bdg. price not set (ISBN 0-685-59736-9). Accelerated Index.
Squires, James D. New Hampshire. LC 66-13065. (Orig.). 1966. pap. 2.95 (ISBN 0-8077-2194-8). Tchrs Coll.
Stiles, Henry R. History of Ancient Wethersfield Connecticut, Vol. 2. LC 74-83524. (Illus.). 946p. 1975. Repr. of 1904 ed. 45.00x (ISBN 0-912274-50-6). NH Pub Co.
Tardiff, Olive. They Paved the Way: A History of N. H. Women. vi, 98p. (gr. 9-12). 1980. pap. text ed. 3.95 (ISBN 0-917890-22-1). Heritage Bk.
Taylor, William L., ed. Readings in New Hampshire & New England History. 282p. 1971. pap. text ed. 14.95x (ISBN 0-8422-0184-X). Irvington.
Upton, Richard F. Revolutionary New Hampshire. LC 70-120896. (American Bicentennial Ser). 1970. Repr. of 1936 ed. 13.00 (ISBN 0-8046-1289-7). Kennikat.
--Revolutionary New Hampshire. LC 74-148460. 1970. Repr. lib. bdg. 16.50x (ISBN 0-374-98061-6). Octagon.
Van Deventer, David E. The Emergence of Provincial New Hampshire, 1623-1741. LC 75-33758. (Illus.). 320p. 1976. 19.50x (ISBN 0-8018-1730-7). Johns Hopkins.
Veblen, Eric P. The Manchester "Union Leader" in New Hampshire Elections. LC 74-15446. (Illus.). 218p. 1975. text ed. 12.50x (ISBN 0-87451-106-2). U Pr of New Eng.
Wade, Hugh M. A Brief History of Cornish, N. H., 1763-1974. LC 75-22518. (Illus.). 208p. 1976. text ed. 15.00x (ISBN 0-87451-129-1). U Pr of New Eng.
Washington History Committee. History of Washington: New Hampshire, 1768-1886. 1976. Repr. ltd. ed. 20.00 (ISBN 0-686-23110-4). Wash Hist Comm.
Webster, Kimball. History of Hudson, New Hampshire: 1673-1913, Vol. I. Incl. Vol. 2. Town in Transition: 1914-1977. Hudson Historical Committee. 15.00 (ISBN 0-914016-45-8). LC 77-21829. (Illus.). 1977. Set. 30.00x (ISBN 0-914016-44-X). Phoenix Pub.
Wheelwright, John. John Wheelwright: His Writings, Including His Fast-Day Sermon, 1637. 1966. 24.00 (ISBN 0-8337-3763-5). B Franklin.
--John Wheelwright's Writings, Including His Fast-Day Sermon, 1637, & His Mercurius Americanus, 1645. facs. ed. LC 70-128897. (Select Bibliographies Reprint Ser). 1876. 16.00 (ISBN 0-8369-5517-X). Arno.
Wood, James P. Colonial New Hampshire. LC 73-10270. (Colonial History Ser.). (Illus.). 160p. (gr. 5 up). 1973. 7.95 (ISBN 0-525-66316-9). Elsevier-Nelson.

NEW HAMPSHIRE–POLITICS AND GOVERNMENT

Anderson, Leon W. To This Day: The Three Hundred Years of the New Hampshire Legislature. LC 80-28564. (Illus.). 416p. 1981. 20.00x (ISBN 0-914016-75-X). Phoenix Pub.
Cole, Donald B. Jacksonian Democracy in New Hampshire, 1800-1851. LC 79-127878. 1970. 15.00x (ISBN 0-674-46990-9). Harvard U Pr.
Cushing, John D., compiled by. The First Laws of the State of New Hampshire. (Law Ser.). 1981. 35.00 (ISBN 0-89453-215-4). M Glazier.
Daniell, Jere R. Experiment in Republicanism: New Hampshire Politics & the American Revolution, 1741-1794. LC 75-122219. 1970. 15.00x (ISBN 0-674-27806-2). Harvard U Pr.
Fry, William H. New Hampshire As a Royal Province. LC 73-130938. (Columbia University. Studies in the Social Sciences: No. 79). Repr. of 1908 ed. 32.50 (ISBN 0-404-51079-5). AMS Pr.

NEW HAMPSHIRE GRANTS

Jones, Matt B. Vermont in the Making, 1750-1777. 1968. Repr. of 1939 ed. 25.00 (ISBN 0-208-00620-6, Archon). Shoe String.
New Hampshire State Legislature. Provincial & State Papers, 18 Vols. Bouton, Nathaniel & Hammond, I. W., eds. LC 70-173073. Repr. of 1867 ed. Set. 891.00 (ISBN 0-404-07450-2); 49.50 ea. AMS Pr.

NEW HARMONY, INDIANA

Brown, Paul. An Enquiry Concerning the Nature, End, & Practicability of a Course of Philosophical Education. LC 75-305. (The Radical Tradition in America Ser). 394p. 1975. Repr. of 1822 ed. 25.00 (ISBN 0-88355-210-8). Hyperion Conn.
--Twelve Months in New Harmony. LC 78-187439. (The American Utopian Adventure Ser.). 128p. Repr. of 1827 ed. lib. bdg. 13.50x (ISBN 0-87991-000-3). Porcupine Pr.
Lockwood, George B. The New Harmony Communities. LC 72-134410. Repr. of 1902 ed. 22.50 (ISBN 0-404-08456-7). AMS Pr.
--The New Harmony Movement. (Illus.). 8.75 (ISBN 0-8446-0187-X). Peter Smith.
--New Harmony Movement. LC 68-56245. (Illus.). Repr. of 1905 ed. 9.25x (ISBN 0-678-00667-9). Kelley.
Macdonald, Donald. Diaries of Donald Macdonald. Snedker, Caroline D., ed. LC 72-77060. Repr. of 1942 ed. lib. bdg. 15.00x (ISBN 0-678-00914-7). Kelley.
Maclure, William & Fretageot, Marie D. Education & Reform at New Harmony: Correspondence of Wm. Maclure & Marie Duclos Fretageot, 1820-1833. Bestor, Arthur E., Jr., ed. LC 72-77059. Repr. of 1948 ed. lib. bdg. 12.50x (ISBN 0-678-00722-5). Kelley.
Owen, Robert D. Threading My Way: Twenty-Seven Years of Autobiography. LC 67-18582. Repr. of 1874 ed. 15.00x (ISBN 0-678-00261-4). Kelley.
Pears, Thomas & Pears, Sarah. New Harmony, an Adventure in Happiness: Papers of Thomas & Henry Pears. Pears, Thomas C., Jr., ed. LC 72-77058. Repr. of 1933 ed. lib. bdg. 11.50x (ISBN 0-678-00908-2). Kelley.

NEW HAVEN

Brown, Elizabeth M. New Haven: A Guide to Architecture & Urban Design. LC 75-18166. (Illus.). 1976. pap. 5.95 (ISBN 0-300-01993-9). Yale U Pr.
Calder, Isabel M. New Haven Colony. 1970. Repr. of 1934 ed. 18.00 (ISBN 0-208-00836-5, Archon). Shoe String.
Dahl, Robert A. Who Governs: Democracy & Power in an American City. LC 61-16913. (Studies in Political Science: No. 4). (Illus.). 1961. 27.50x (ISBN 0-300-00395-1); pap. 5.95x (ISBN 0-300-00051-0, Y73). Yale U Pr.
Dahl, Robert A. & Flanigan, William. New Haven Community Study, 1959. 2nd ed. LC 75-38491. 1975. Repr. of 1971 ed. codebk. 10.00 (ISBN 0-89138-024-8). ICPSR.
Hegel, Richard. Nineteenth Century Historians of New Haven. (Illus.). 1972. 11.50 (ISBN 0-208-01262-1, Archon). Shoe String.
Levermore, Charles H. Republic of New Haven: A History of Municipal Evolution. LC 66-25926. 1886. 14.50 (ISBN 0-8046-0269-7). Kennikat.
--The Republic of New Haven: A History of Municipal Evolution. LC 78-64245. (Johns Hopkins University. Studies in the Social Sciences. Extra Volumes: 1). Repr. of 1886 ed. 12.00 (ISBN 0-404-61350-0). AMS Pr.
--Town & City Government of New Haven. 1973. Repr. of 1886 ed. pap. 9.50 (ISBN 0-384-32415-0). Johnson Repr.
--The Town & City Government of New Haven. LC 78-63766. (Johns Hopkins University. Studies in the Social Sciences. Fourth Ser. 1886: 10). Repr. of 1886 ed. 11.50 (ISBN 0-404-61033-1). AMS Pr.
McConnell, John W. Evolution of Social Classes. LC 72-86977. (Illus.). xii, 228p. 1973. Repr. of 1942 ed. 15.00 (ISBN 0-8462-1705-8). Russell.
Osterweis, Rollin G. The New Haven Green & the American Bicentennial. (Illus.). 129p. 1976. 13.50 (ISBN 0-208-01578-7, Archon). Shoe String.
--Three Centuries of New Haven, 1638-1938. (Illus.). 1953. 29.50 (ISBN 0-300-00812-0). Yale U Pr.
Polsby, Nelson W. Community Power & Political Theory: A Further Look at Problems of Evidence & Inference. 2nd rev. ed. LC 79-22966. 1980. text ed. 25.00 (ISBN 0-300-02445-2); pap. 6.95x (ISBN 0-300-02528-9). Yale U Pr.
Powledge, Fred. Model City. LC 75-130487. (Illus.). 1970. 7.95 (ISBN 0-671-20670-2). S&S.
Warner, Robert A. New Haven Negroes, a Social History. LC 78-94138. (American Negro: His History & Literature, Ser. No. 3). 1970. Repr. of 1940 ed. 16.00 (ISBN 0-405-01940-8). Arno.

NEW HAVEN RAILROAD

see New York, New Haven, and Hartford Railroad

NEW HEBRIDES

Deacon, Bernard. Malekula: A Vanishing People in the New Hebrides. Wedgwood, Camilla H., ed. 1970. Repr. of 1934 ed. text ed. 35.25x (ISBN 90-6234-006-7). Humanities.
--Malekula: A Vanishing People in the New Hebrides. Wedgwood, Camilla H., ed. 1970. Repr. of 1934 ed. text ed. 35.25x (ISBN 90-6234-006-7). Humanities.
McGee, T. G., et al. Food Distribution in the New Hebrides. (Development Studies Centre-Monographs: No. 25). 268p. 1981. pap. text ed. 13.95 (ISBN 0-909150-19-2, 0068, Pub. by ANUP Australia). Bks Australia.
Sterling Publishing Company Editors. Tahiti & the French Islands of the Pacific in Pictures. LC 66-25202. (Visual Geography Ser). (Orig.). (gr. 6 up). 1967. PLB 4.99 (ISBN 0-8069-1093-3); pap. 2.95 (ISBN 0-8069-1092-5). Sterling.

NEW JERSEY

see also names of individual cities, counties, towns, etc. in New Jersey

Beale, David T. Pollution Control on the Passaic River. 1972. 3.00 (ISBN 0-686-23339-5). Ctr Analysis Public Issues.
Burr, Nelson R. A Narrative & Descriptive Bibliography of New Jersey. 1970. 12.50 (ISBN 0-8135-0639-5). Rutgers U Pr.
Cavanaugh, Cam. Saving the Great Swamp: The People, the Power Brokers & an Urban Wilderness. LC 78-8132. (Illus.). 1978. 11.95 (ISBN 0-914366-11-4). Columbia Pub.
Dickey, Ronald W. & Klachko, Wolodymyr. Investing in New Jersey. LC 79-93331. 1980. 14.95 (ISBN 0-686-64291-0). W H Wise.
Gordon, Thomas F. Gazetteer of the State of New Jersey. 1975. 15.00 (ISBN 0-686-20869-2). Polyanthos.
Greenberg, Michael R. & Neuman, Nancy. New Jersey Toward the Year Two Thousand: Projections of Population. LC 77-87163. (Illus.). 1977. pap. 10.00 (ISBN 0-88285-044-X). Ctr Urban Pol Res.
Laccetti, Silvio R., ed. The Outlook on New Jersey. new ed. LC 79-64897. 488p. 1979. 14.95x (ISBN 0-8349-7540-8). W H Wise.
Michaelson, Connie & Greenberg, Michael. New Jersey Toward the Year Two Thousand: Employment Projections. LC 77-87163. 1978. pap. text ed. 10.00 (ISBN 0-88285-054-7). Ctr Urban Pol Res.
Nelson, William. New Jersey Marriage Records: 1665-1800. LC 67-18088. (Illus.). 1973. Repr. of 1900 ed. 30.00 (ISBN 0-8063-0254-2). Genealog Pub.
New Jersey. 28.00 (ISBN 0-89770-106-2). Curriculum Info Ctr.
New Jersey-Encyclopedia of the United States. 1981. lib. bdg. 45.00 (ISBN 0-403-04754-4). Scholarly.
New Jersey's Money. LC 76-3234. 1977. 17.50 (ISBN 0-932828-03-5). Newark Mus.
Pippines, Pamela & Ripmaster, Terence. The Arts Catalogue of New Jersey. LC 78-67411. 1978. 12.95 (ISBN 0-89529-123-1); pap. 9.95 (ISBN 0-685-60817-4). Avery Pub.
State Industrial Dirctories Corp. New Jersey State Industrial Directory, 1978. (State Industrial Directory Ser.). 1978. 87.50 (ISBN 0-916112-70-5). State Indus Dir.
State Industrial Directories Corp. New Jersey Industrial Directory 1980. 1980. pap. 90.00 (ISBN 0-89910-027-9). State Indus Dir.
Statistical Almanac: New Jersey. LC 79-55809. 1981. 15.95 (ISBN 0-8349-7541-6). W H Wise.
Sternlieb, George S. & Beaton, W. Patrick. The Zone of Emergence: A Case Study of an Older Suburb. LC 78-186710. 1972. 14.95x (ISBN 0-87855-035-6). Transaction Bks.
Weygandt, Cornelius. Down Jersey. LC 80-51866. 1980. 11.95 (ISBN 0-8349-7544-0). W H Wise.

NEW JERSEY–DESCRIPTION AND TRAVEL

Bailey, Rosalie F. Pre-Revolutionary Dutch Houses & Families in Northern New Jersey & Southern New York. (Illus.). 1968. pap. 6.00 (ISBN 0-486-21985-2). Dover.
Balleine, G. R. Bailiwick of Jersey. rev. ed. LC 72-505688. (The Queen's Channel Islands Ser.). 211p. 1970. 8.75x (ISBN 0-340-00267-0). Intl Pubns Serv.
Barber, John W. & Howe, Henry. Historical Collections of New Jersey. LC 66-63919. (Illus.). 1966. Repr. of 1868 ed. 25.00 (ISBN 0-87152-029-X). Reprint.
Beck, Henry C. The Roads of Home: Lanes & Legends of New Jersey. 1962. pap. 3.25 (ISBN 0-8135-0405-8). Rutgers U Pr.
--Tales & Towns of Northern New Jersey. (Illus., Orig.). 1967. pap. 2.95 (ISBN 0-8135-0534-8). Rutgers U Pr.
Beil, Preston J. & Brown, Florence, eds. What to Do in New Jersey. rev. ed. (What to Do Ser.). (Illus.). 160p. 1980. pap. 2.50x (ISBN 0-686-28502-6). What to Do.
Cawley, Margaret & Cawley, James. Exploring the Little Rivers of New Jersey. 3rd rev. ed. 1971. pap. 4.50 (ISBN 0-8135-0685-9). Rutgers U Pr.
Cazenove, Theophile. Cazenove Journal, 1794: A Journey Through New Jersey & Pennsylvania. Kelsey, Rayner W., ed. (Haverford Coll. Studies: No. 13). 1922. 15.00x (ISBN 0-686-17388-0). R S Barnes.
Cunningham, John. New Jersey, A Scenic Discovery. Patrick, James B., ed. (A Scenic Discovery Ser.). (Illus.). 120p. 1981. 25.00 (ISBN 0-940078-00-7). Foremost Pubs.
Cunningham, John T. This Is New Jersey. 3rd ed. 1978. 14.95 (ISBN 0-8135-0859-2); pap. 7.95 (ISBN 0-8135-0862-2). Rutgers U Pr.
Federal Writer's Project, Illinois. Princeton Guide. LC 73-3618. (American Guide Ser.). Repr. of 1939 ed. 14.00 (ISBN 0-404-57920-5). AMS Pr.
Federal Writers Project, New Jersey. Stories of New Jersey, Its Significant Places, People & Activities. LC 73-3639. (American Guide Ser.). Repr. of 1938 ed. 22.00 (ISBN 0-404-57939-6). AMS Pr.
Groff, Sibyl M. New Jersey's Historic Houses: A Guide to Homes Open to the Public. LC 75-139754. (Illus.). 1971. 8.95 (ISBN 0-498-07842-6); pap. 4.95 (ISBN 0-498-07878-7). A S Barnes.
Hagstrom Atlases, 8 bks. Incl. Bergen County. 8.95 (ISBN 0-686-67907-5); Mercer County; Middlesex County; Monmouth County; Morris-Somerset Counties; Ocean County; Passaic County; Union, Essex & Hudson County. 1977. Wehman.

Hudgins, Barbara. Trips & Treks: A Guide to Family Outings in the New Jersey Area. (Illus.). 121p. (Orig.). 1980. pap. text ed. 3.95 (ISBN 0-686-31589-8). Woodmont Pr.

Kelland, Frank & Kelland, Marilyn. New Jersey: Garden or Suburb? (Regional Georgraphy Ser.). (Illus.). 1978. pap. text ed. 12.95 (ISBN 0-8403-1839-1). Kendall-Hunt.

Lewis, Paul M. Beautiful New Jersey. Shangle, Robert D., ed. LC 80-23325. (Illus.). 72p. 1980. 14.95 (ISBN 0-89802-113-8); pap. 7.95 (ISBN 0-89802-112-X). Beautiful Am.

McPhee, John. The Pine Barrens. rev. ed. (Illus.). 1981. 22.50 (ISBN 0-374-17451-2). FS&G.

Meyer, Joan & Meyer, Bill. Canoe Trails of the Jersey Shore. (Illus.). 1974. pap. 2.95 (ISBN 0-913556-39-4). Spec Pr NJ.

Newberry, Lida. One-Day Adventures by Car: With Full Directions for Drivers Out of New York City. rev. ed. (Illus.). 288p. 1980. pap. 6.95 (ISBN 0-8038-5393-9). Hastings.

Newberry, Lida & Hansen, Harry, eds. New Jersey: A Guide to Its Present & Past. rev. ed. (American Guide Ser.). 1977. 14.95 (ISBN 0-8038-5048-4). Hastings.

Pepper, Adeline. Tours of Historic New Jersey. rev. ed. (Illus.). 280p. 1973. pap. 3.25 (ISBN 0-8135-0759-6). Rutgers U Pr.

Poor, Harold L. Bicycling in New Jersey: Thirty Tours. LC 78-1996. 1978. pap. 5.95 (ISBN 0-89490-013-7). Enslow Pubs.

Tice, George A. Paterson. LC 79-163964. 1972. pap. 9.00 (ISBN 0-8135-0719-7). Rutgers U Pr.

Wolfe, P. E. The Geology & Landscapes of New Jersey. LC 77-73871. (Illus.). 1977. 22.50x (ISBN 0-8448-1101-7). Crane-Russak Co.

Writers Program, New Jersey. Entertaining a Nation: The Career of Long Branch. LC 73-3637. (American Guide Ser.). (Illus.). 1940. Repr. 14.00 (ISBN 0-404-57937-X). AMS Pr.

NEW JERSEY–HISTORICAL GEOGRAPHY

Balleine, G. R. Bailiwick of Jersey. rev. ed. LC 72-505688. (The Queen's Channel Islands Ser.). 211p. 1970. 8.75x (ISBN 0-340-00267-0). Intl Pubns Serv.

Federal Writers' Project, New Jersey. The Swedes & Finns in New Jersey. LC 73-3640. (American Guide Ser.). (Illus.). Repr. of 1938 ed. 20.00 (ISBN 0-404-57940-X). AMS Pr.

Snyder, John P. The Mapping of New Jersey: The Men & the Art. (Illus.). 256p. 1973. 15.00 (ISBN 0-8135-0780-4). Rutgers U Pr.

Wacker, Peter O. The Musconetcong Valley of New Jersey: A Historical Geography. LC 68-18694. (Illus.). 1968. 15.00 (ISBN 0-8135-0575-5). Rutgers U Pr.

NEW JERSEY–GENEALOGY

Armstrong, William C. Pioneer Families of Northwestern New Jersey. 1979. lib. bdg. 25.00 (ISBN 0-912606-04-5). Hunterdon Hse.

Chambers, Theodore F. Early Germans of New Jersey: Their History, Churches & Genealogies. LC 78-85697. (Illus.). 1969. Repr. of 1895 ed. 25.00 (ISBN 0-8063-0070-1). Genealog Pub.

Cooley, Eli F. Genealogy of Early Settlers in Trenton & Ewing, "Old Hunterdon County," New Jersey. 1976. Repr. of 1883 ed. 15.00 (ISBN 0-912606-03-7). Hunterdon Hse.

Cooley, Eli F. & Cooley, William S. Genealogy of Early Settlers in Trenton & Ewing, "Old Hunterdon County," New Jersey. LC 76-45636. 1977. 15.00 (ISBN 0-8063-0744-7). Genealog Pub.

Gannett, Henry. A Geographic Dictionary of New Jersey. LC 78-59122. 1978. Repr. of 1894 ed. 8.50 (ISBN 0-8063-0819-2). Genealog Pub.

Howe, Paul S. Mayflower Pilgrim Descendants in Cape May County, New Jersey. LC 76-46706. (Illus.). 1977. 17.50 (ISBN 0-8063-0747-1). Genealog Pub.

Jackson, Ronald V. & Teeples, Gary R. Index to Military Men of New Jersey 1775-1815. LC 77-86053. lib. bdg. 24.00 (ISBN 0-89593-157-5). Accelerated Index.

--New Jersey Census Index 1800. LC 77-86134. (Illus.). lib. bdg. 16.00 (ISBN 0-89593-089-7). Accelerated Index.

--New Jersey Census Index 1830. LC 77-86130. (Illus.). lib. bdg. 34.00 (ISBN 0-89593-092-7). Accelerated Index.

--New Jersey Census Index 1840. LC 77-86131. (Illus.). lib. bdg. 44.00 (ISBN 0-89593-093-5). Accelerated Index.

--New Jersey Census Index 1850. LC 77-86122. (Illus.). lib. bdg. 50.00 (ISBN 0-89593-094-3). Accelerated Index.

Matlack, Edward R. Sense & Nonsense, History & Genealogy. 1978. 5.00 (ISBN 0-682-49085-7). Exposition.

Nelson, William. New Jersey Biographical & Genealogical Notes. LC 73-7838. (Collections of the New Jersey Historical Society Ser: Vol. 9). 1973. Repr. of 1916 ed. 15.00 (ISBN 0-8063-0562-2). Genealog Pub.

--Patents & Deeds & Other Early Records of New Jersey, 1664-1703. LC 76-252. 1976. Repr. of 1899 ed. 25.00 (ISBN 0-8063-0711-0). Genealog Pub.

New Jersey Adjutant-General's Office. Records of Officers & Men of New Jersey in Wars, 1791-1815. LC 78-117069. 1970. Repr. of 1909 ed. 25.00 (ISBN 0-8063-0417-0). Genealog Pub.

Scott, Kenneth, ed. Abstracts from Ben Franklin's Pennsylvania Gazette, 1728-1748. LC 74-29164. 720p. 1975. 25.00 (ISBN 0-8063-0661-0). Genealog Pub.

Stewart, Frank H. Notes on Old Gloucester County, New Jersey, 4 vols. in 2. LC 76-46705. (Illus.). 1977. 60.00 (ISBN 0-8063-0746-3). Genealog Pub.

Stillwell, John E. Historical & Genealogical Miscellany, 5 vols. LC 72-86805. 1970. Repr. of 1932 ed. Set. 100.00 (ISBN 0-8063-0392-1); 25.00 ea. Genealog Pub.

Stryker-Rodda, Kenn. Given-Name Index to the Genealogical Magazine of New Jersey, Vols. 1 & 2. 1975. 40.00 (ISBN 0-686-20877-3). Polyanthos.

--Given-Name Index to the Genealogical Magazine of New Jersey, Vol. 3. 1977. 25.00 (ISBN 0-686-20870-6). Polyanthos.

--Some Early Records of Morris Co., N. J. 1740-1799. 1976. 12.50 (ISBN 0-686-20894-3). Polyanthos.

NEW JERSEY–HISTORY

see also St. Clair'S Campaign, 1791

Barber, John W. & Howe, Henry. Historical Collections of New Jersey. LC 66-63919. (Illus.). 1966. Repr. of 1868 ed. 25.00 (ISBN 0-87152-029-X). Reprint.

Beck, Henry C. Forgotten Towns of Southern New Jersey. 1962. pap. 3.95 (ISBN 0-8135-0391-4). Rutgers U Pr.

--More Forgotten Towns of Southern New Jersey. 1963. pap. 5.95 (ISBN 0-8135-0432-5). Rutgers U Pr.

--The Roads of Home: Lanes & Legends of New Jersey. 1962. pap. 3.25 (ISBN 0-8135-0405-8). Rutgers U Pr.

--Tales & Towns of Northern New Jersey. (Illus., Orig.). 1967. pap. 2.95 (ISBN 0-8135-0534-8). Rutgers U Pr.

Bill, Alfred H. New Jersey & the Revolutionary War. (New Jersey Historical Ser). (Illus.). 117p. 1970. pap. 3.25 (ISBN 0-8135-0642-5). Rutgers U Pr.

Bischoff, Henry & Kahn, Mitchell. From Pioneer Settlement to Suburb: A History of Mahwah, New Jersey, 1700-1976. LC 78-55451. (Illus.). 1979. 15.00 (ISBN 0-498-02218-8). A S Barnes.

Budd, Thomas. Good Order Established in Pennsylvania & New Jersey. LC 68-56749. (Research & Source Works Ser.: No. 232). 1971. Repr. of 1685 ed. lib. bdg. 21.00 (ISBN 0-8337-0413-3). B Franklin.

Collins, Varnum L., ed. Brief Narrative of the Ravages of the British & Hessians at Princeton in 1776-1777. LC 67-29024. (Eyewitness Accounts of the American Revolution, Ser. No. 1). 1968. Repr. of 1906 ed. 9.50 (ISBN 0-405-01110-5). Arno.

Cooley, Henry S. A Study of Slavery in New Jersey. LC 78-63853. (Johns Hopkins University. Studies in the Social Sciences. Fourteenth Ser. 1896: 9-10). Repr. of 1896 ed. 11.50 (ISBN 0-404-61109-5). AMS Pr.

Cunningham, Barbara, ed. The New Jersey Ethnic Experience. LC 77-77851. (Illus.). 1977. 14.95 (ISBN 0-8349-7534-3). W H Wise.

Federal Writers' Project. New Jersey: A Guide to Its Present & Past. 735p. 1939. Repr. 49.00 (ISBN 0-403-02180-4). Somerset Pub.

Guthorn, Peter J. John Hills, Assistant Engineer: With a Collection of Plans of the Provinces of New Jersey. LC 76-1497. 1977. pap. text ed. 28.50 (ISBN 0-916762-01-7). Portolan.

Leiby, James. Charity & Correction in New Jersey: A History of State Welfare Institutions. 1967. 27.50 (ISBN 0-8135-0560-7). Rutgers U Pr.

Levine, Peter. The Behavior of State Legislative Parties in the Jacksonian Era New Jersey: 1829-1844. LC 75-18248. 285p. 1977. 18.00 (ISBN 0-8386-1800-6). Fairleigh Dickinson.

Lundin, Leonard. Cockpit of Revolution: The War for Independence in New Jersey. LC 74-159210. xiv, 463p. 1971. Repr. of 1940 ed. lib. bdg. 25.00x (ISBN 0-374-95143-8). Octagon.

McCormick, Richard P. Experiment in Independence: New Jersey in the Critical Period 1781-1789. 1950. 17.50 (ISBN 0-8135-0120-2). Rutgers U Pr.

--New Jersey. LC 65-15071. 1965. pap. 2.95 (ISBN 0-8077-1734-7). Tchrs Coll.

--New Jersey from Colony to State, 1609-1789. (New Jersey Historical Classics Ser.). (Illus.). 191p. pap. 5.95 (ISBN 0-911020-02-0). NJ Hist Soc.

McMahon, William. South Jersey Towns: History & Legend. LC 78-163961. (Illus.). 384p. 1973. pap. 4.95 (ISBN 0-8135-0718-9). Rutgers U Pr.

The Movies Begin: Making Movies in New Jersey 1887-1920. LC 77-73649. 1977. 13.95 (ISBN 0-87100-121-7). Newark Mus.

Nelson, William. Patents & Deeds & Other Early Records of New Jersey, 1664-1703. LC 76-252. 1976. Repr. of 1899 ed. 25.00 (ISBN 0-8063-0711-0). Genealog Pub.

New Jersey Archives - First Series: Documents Relating to the Colonial, Revolutionary, & Post-Revolutionary History of the State of New Jersey, 42 vols. LC 74-20233. Repr. of 1880 ed. 2022.50 set (ISBN 0-404-12700-2); 47.50 ea.; index 27.50 (ISBN 0-685-70881-0). AMS Pr.

Nissen, Mrs. Carl. Index to the New Jersey Genesis, 1953-1971. 172p. 1973. 16.00 (ISBN 0-913478-03-2). Hermosa.

O'Connor, John E. William Paterson: Lawyer & Statesman, 1745-1806. 1979. 25.00 (ISBN 0-8135-0880-0). Rutgers U Pr.

Pierce, Arthur D. Iron in the Pines: The Story of New Jersey's Ghost Towns & Bog Iron. (Illus.). 1966. pap. 3.95 (ISBN 0-8135-0514-3). Rutgers U Pr.

Pomfret, John E. The Province of West New Jersey, 1609-1702. 1973. lib. bdg. 18.50x (ISBN 0-374-96516-1). Octagon.

Sinclair, Donald A., compiled by. Index to the Cushing & Sheppard History of Gloucester, Salem, & Cumberland Counties, New Jersey. 1975. 17.50 (ISBN 0-686-20875-7). Polyanthos.

Smeal, Lee. New Jersey Historical & Biographical Index. LC 78-53708. (Illus.). Date not set. lib. bdg. price not set (ISBN 0-89593-191-5). Accelerated Index.

Steiner-Scott, Elizabeth & Wagle, Elizabeth P. New Jersey Women Seventeen Seventy to Nineteen Seventy: A Bibliography. 167p. 1978. 18.50 (ISBN 0-8386-1967-3). Fairleigh Dickinson.

Stockton, Frank R. Stories of New Jersey. (Illus.). 1961. pap. 4.50 (ISBN 0-8135-0369-8). Rutgers U Pr.

Stryker-Rodda, Kenn. Some Early Records of Morris Co., N. J. 1740-1799. 1976. 12.50 (ISBN 0-686-20894-3). Polyanthos.

Turp, Ralph K. West Jersey: Under Four Flags. (Illus.). 344p. 1975. 10.00 (ISBN 0-8059-2152-4). Dorrance.

Van Hoesen, Walter H. Early Taverns & Stagecoach Days in New Jersey. LC 74-198. (Illus.). 184p. 1976. 14.50 (ISBN 0-8386-1535-X). Fairleigh Dickinson.

Winston. Our Great State Papers. 1972. text ed. 2.72 (ISBN 0-03-085669-8); pap. text ed. 2.48 (ISBN 0-03-085670-1). HR&W.

Writers Program, New Jersey. Livingston: The Story of a Community. LC 73-3638. 1939. Repr. 10.00 (ISBN 0-404-57938-8). AMS Pr.

NEW JERSEY–HISTORY–COLONIAL PERIOD, ca. 1600-1775

Cook, Fred J. New Jersey Colony. LC 69-10893. (Forge of Freedom Ser). (Illus.). (gr. 4-7). 1969. 8.95 (ISBN 0-02-724360-5, CCPr). Macmillan.

Gerlach, Larry R. Prologue to Independence: New Jersey in the Coming of the American Revolution. 1976. 33.00 (ISBN 0-8135-0801-0). Rutgers U Pr.

Lundin, Leonard. Cockpit of Revolution: The War for Independence in New Jersey. LC 74-159210. xiv, 463p. 1971. Repr. of 1940 ed. lib. bdg. 25.00x (ISBN 0-374-95143-8). Octagon.

McLachlan, J. Princetonians, 1748-1768: A Biographical Dictionary. 1976. 45.00 (ISBN 0-691-04639-5). Princeton U Pr.

Myers, Albert C., ed. Narratives of Early Pennsylvania, West New Jersey & Delaware, 1630-1707. (Original Narratives). 1967. Repr. of 1912 ed. 18.50x (ISBN 0-06-480612-X). B&N.

Pomfret, John E. Province of East New Jersey, Sixteen Hundred & Nine to Seventeen Hundred & Two. 1980. Repr. of 1962 ed. lib. bdg. 24.00x (ISBN 0-374-96515-3). Octagon.

Promfret, John E. Colonial New Jersey: A History. LC 72-1228. (A History of the American Colonies Ser.). 1973. lib. bdg. 25.00 (ISBN 0-527-18716-X). Kraus Intl.

Proud, Robert. The History of Pennsylvania, 2 Vols. LC 66-25101. 1967. Repr. of 1797 ed. 20.00 ea. Vol. 1 (ISBN 0-87152-031-1). Vol. 2 (ISBN 0-87152-032-X). Set. 40.00 (ISBN 0-87152-305-1). Reprint.

Scott, Austin. The Influence of the Proprietors in Founding the State of New Jersey. LC 78-63755. (Johns Hopkins University. Studies in the Social Sciences. Third Ser. 1885: 8). Repr. of 1885 ed. 11.50 (ISBN 0-404-61023-4). AMS Pr.

Smith, Samuel. History of the Colony of Nova-Caesaria or New Jersey. LC 66-63920. (Illus.). 1966. Repr. of 1890 ed. 27.50 (ISBN 0-87152-028-1). Reprint.

--History of the Colony of Nova-Caesaria, or New Jersey to the Year 1721. LC 71-141094. (Research Library of Colonial Americana). 1971. Repr. of 1765 ed. 36.00 (ISBN 0-405-03299-4). Arno.

Wacker, Peter O. Land & People: A Cultural Geography of Preindustrial New Jersey--Origins & Settlement Patterns, Vol. 1. 520p. 1975. 35.00 (ISBN 0-8135-0742-1). Rutgers U Pr.

NEW JERSEY–HISTORY–REVOLUTION, 1775-1783

Jones, Edward A. The Loyalists of New Jersey; Their Memorials, Claims, Petitions, Etc., from English Records. LC 72-10759. (American Revolutionary Ser.). 1927. lib. bdg. 38.50x (ISBN 0-8398-0961-1). Irvington.

Leiby, Adrian C. The Revolutionary War in the Hackensack Valley: The Jersey Dutch & Neutral Ground, 1775 - 1783. 329p. 1980. pap. 5.95 (ISBN 0-8135-0898-3). Rutgers U Pr.

New Jersey Archives - Second Series: Documents Relating to the Revolutionary History of the State of New Jersey, 5 vols. LC 74-20234. Repr. of 1901 ed. 237.50 set (ISBN 0-404-12744-4); 47.50 ea. AMS Pr.

Stryker-Rodda, Kenn. Revolutionary Census of New Jersey: 1773-1784. 1976. 20.00 (ISBN 0-686-20892-7). Polyanthos.

White, Donald W. A Village at War: Chatham, New Jersey, & the American Revolution. LC 77-74400. (Illus.). 311p. 1978. 19.50 (ISBN 0-8386-2103-1). Fairleigh Dickinson.

NEW JERSEY–IMPRINTS

Humphrey, C. H. Checklist of New Jersey Imprints. Repr. of 1930 ed. pap. 6.00 (ISBN 0-527-43300-4). Kraus Repr.

Morsch, Lucille M. Historical Records Survey: Check List of New Jersey Imprints, 1784-1800. 1939. pap. 10.00 (ISBN 0-527-01906-2). Kraus Repr.

NEW JERSEY–JUVENILE LITERATURE

Carpenter, Allan. New Jersey. LC 78-14891. (New Enchantment of America State Bks). (Illus.). (gr. 4 up). 1979. PLB 10.60 (ISBN 0-516-04130-4). Childrens.

Cook, Fred J. New Jersey Colony. LC 69-10893. (Forge of Freedom Ser). (Illus.). (gr. 4-7). 1969. 8.95 (ISBN 0-02-724360-5, CCPr). Macmillan.

Fradin, Dennis. New Jersey: In Words & Pictures. LC 80-19688. (Young People's Stories of Our States Ser.). (Illus.). 48p. (gr. 2-5). 1980. PLB 9.25 (ISBN 0-516-03930-X). Childrens.

Murray, Thomas C. & Barnes, Valerie. The Seven Wonders of New Jersey--& Then Some. LC 80-16424. (Illus.). 128p. 1981. pap. 6.95 (ISBN 0-89490-017-X). Enslow Pubs.

NEW JERSEY–POLITICS AND GOVERNMENT

Cavanaugh, Cam. Saving the Great Swamp: The People, the Power Brokers & an Urban Wilderness. LC 78-8132. (Illus.). 1978. 11.95 (ISBN 0-914366-11-4). Columbia Pub.

Commerce Clearing House. Guidebook to New Jersey Taxes: 1982. 1982. 10.00 (ISBN 0-686-76129-4). Commerce.

Cushing, John D., compiled by. The First Laws of the State of New Jersey. (Earliest Laws of the Original Thirteen States Ser.). 1981. 49.00 (ISBN 0-89453-217-0). M Glazier.

Edge, Walter E. Jerseyman's Journal, Fifty Years of American Business & Politics. LC 48-10223. 1971. Repr. of 1948 ed. 25.00 (ISBN 0-384-13855-1, P514). Johnson Repr.

Fisher, Edgar J. New Jersey As a Royal Province, 1738-1776. LC 75-168028. (Columbia University. Studies in the Social Sciences: No. 107). Repr. of 1911 ed. 23.50 (ISBN 0-404-51107-4). AMS Pr.

Keodel, R. Craig. South Jersey Heritage: A Social, Economic & Cultural History. 190p. 1977. pap. text ed. 9.00 (ISBN 0-8191-0246-6). U Pr of Amer.

League of Women Voters of New Jersey. New Jersey: Spotlight on Government. 1978. 15.00 (ISBN 0-8135-0854-1); pap. 6.95 (ISBN 0-8135-0860-6). Rutgers U Pr.

MacCracken, Henry N. Prologue to Independence: The Trials of James Alexander 1715-1756. 1965. 4.95 (ISBN 0-685-11978-5). Heineman.

McKean, Dayton D. Pressures on the Legislature of New Jersey. LC 66-27121. 1967. Repr. of 1938 ed. 8.00 (ISBN 0-8462-0850-4). Russell.

The Nineteen Eighty N. J. Political Almanac. 1980. 4.00 (ISBN 0-686-26948-9). Ctr Analysis Public Issues.

Pasler, Rudolph J. & Pasler, Margaret C. The New Jersey Federalists. LC 73-22570. 256p. 1975. 16.50 (ISBN 0-8386-1525-2). Fairleigh Dickinson.

Prince, Carl E. New Jersey's Jeffersonian Republicans: The Genesis of an Early Party Machine 1789-1817. (Institute of Early American History & Culture Ser.). 1967. 18.00x (ISBN 0-8078-1027-4). U of NC Pr.

Scott, A. Influence of the Proprietors in Founding the State of New Jersey. Repr. of 1885 ed. pap. 7.00 (ISBN 0-384-54441-X). Johnson Repr.

Semel, Vicki G. At the Grass Roots in the Garden State: Reform & Regular Democrats in New Jersey. LC 75-5246. 287p. 1976. 20.00 (ISBN 0-8386-1737-9). Fairleigh Dickinson.

Shank, Alan. New Jersey Reapportionment Politics, Strategies & Tactics in the Legislative Process. LC 69-18908. (Illus.). 308p. 1968. 15.00 (ISBN 0-8386-6950-6). Fairleigh Dickinson.

Tanner, Edwin P. Province of New Jersey, 1664-1738. LC 8-33297. (Columbia University. Studies in the Social Sciences: No. 80). Repr. of 1908 ed. 42.50 (ISBN 0-404-51080-9). AMS Pr.

NEW JERSEY–SOCIAL LIFE AND CUSTOMS

Foresta, Ronald. Open Space Policy: New Jersey's Green Acres Program. 173p. (Orig.). 1981. 15.00 (ISBN 0-8135-0923-8). Rutgers U Pr.

Fradin, Dennis. New Jersey: In Words & Pictures. LC 80-19688. (Young People's Stories of Our States Ser.). (Illus.). 48p. (gr. 2-5). 1980. PLB 9.25 (ISBN 0-516-03930-X). Childrens.

Keodel, R. Craig. South Jersey Heritage: A Social, Economic & Cultural History. 190p. 1977. pap. text ed. 9.00 (ISBN 0-8191-0246-6). U Pr of Amer.

Turp, Ralph K. West Jersey: Under Four Flags. (Illus.). 344p. 1975. 10.00 (ISBN 0-8059-2152-4). Dorrance.

NEW JERUSALEM CHURCH

Field, G. Memoirs, Incidents, Reminiscences of the Early History of the New Church in Michigan, Indiana, Illinois, & Adjacent States, & Canada. LC 70-134423. 1972. Repr. of 1879 ed. 27.00 (ISBN 0-404-08463-X). AMS Pr.

Keller, Helen, tr. My Religion: Large Print Edition. LC 74-11645. 1979. 4.75 (ISBN 0-87785-158-1). Swedenborg.

Swedenborg, Emmanuel. Four Leading Doctrines of the New Church. LC 71-134426. Repr. of 1882 ed. 21.00 (ISBN 0-404-08466-4). AMS Pr.

NEW JERUSALEM CHURCH–DOCTRINAL AND CONTROVERSIAL WORKS

Barnitz, Harry W. Existentialism & the New Christianity. LC 69-14353. 1969. 10.00 (ISBN 0-8022-2279-X). Philos Lib.

James, Henry, Sr. Tracts for the New Times: No. 1 Letter to a Swedenborgian. LC 72-916. (The Selected Works of Henry James, Sr.: Vol. 9). Repr. of 1850 ed. 15.00 (ISBN 0-404-10089-9). AMS Pr.

Keller, Helen. My Religion. LC 74-11654. 1972. 2.50 (ISBN 0-87785-102-6); pap. 1.25 (ISBN 0-87785-103-4); Span. ed. 5.00 (ISBN 0-87785-114-X); pap. 2.00 (ISBN 0-87785-115-8). Swedenborg.

Kingslake, Brian. Aqueduct Papers. 1970. 4.95 (ISBN 0-8158-0239-0). Chris Mass.

Mayer, Fred S. Why Two Worlds: Relation of Physical to Spiritual Realities. LC 78-134425. Repr. of 1934 ed. 21.00 (ISBN 0-404-08465-6). AMS Pr.

Reed, Sampson. Observations on the Growth of the Mind Including GENIUS. 5th ed. LC 72-4971. (The Romantic Tradition in American Literature Ser.). 110p. 1972. Repr. of 1859 ed. 13.00 (ISBN 0-405-04641-3). Arno.

--Observations on the Growth of the Mind with Remarks on Other Subjects. LC 78-100126. 1970. Repr. of 1838 ed. 22.00x (ISBN 0-8201-1070-1). Schol Facsimiles.

Sechrist, Alice S., ed. Dictionary of Bible Imagery. LC 79-63409. 1972. 3.95 (ISBN 0-87785-118-2). Swedenborg.

Swedenborg, Emanuel. Divine Love & Wisdom. LC 75-37094. student ed. 6.50 (ISBN 0-87785-056-9); trade ed. 8.25 (ISBN 0-87785-057-7); pap. 1.25 (ISBN 0-87785-058-5). Swedenborg.

--Four Doctrines. LC 67-1465. 1971. trade ed. 8.25 (ISBN 0-87785-065-8); student ed. 6.50 (ISBN 0-87785-063-1); pap. 1.50 (ISBN 0-87785-064-X). Swedenborg.

--Miscellaneous Theological Works. LC 76-46143. 1970. trade ed. 8.25 (ISBN 0-87785-071-2); student ed. 6.50 (ISBN 0-87785-070-4). Swedenborg.

--Posthumous Theological Works, 2 vols. LC 38-24293. 634p. trade ed. 8.25 ea. Vol.1 (ISBN 0-87785-076-3). Vol.2 (ISBN 0-87785-077-1). Set. 14.00 (ISBN 0-87785-078-X); student ed. 6.50 ea. Vol.1 (ISBN 0-87785-073-9). Vol.2 (ISBN 0-87785-074-7). Set. 11.00 (ISBN 0-87785-075-5). Swedenborg.

--True Christian Religion, 2 vols. LC 63-1799. 1098p. trade ed. 8.25 ea. Vol. 1 (ISBN 0-87785-087-9). Vol. 2 (ISBN 0-87785-088-7). Set. 14.00 (ISBN 0-87785-089-5); student ed. 6.50 ea. Vol. 1 (ISBN 0-87785-084-4). Vol. 2 (ISBN 0-87785-085-2). Set. 11.00 (ISBN 0-87785-086-0). Swedenborg.

NEW LANARK ESTABLISHMENT

Cullen, Alex. Adventures in Socialism. LC 68-55519. Repr. of 1910 ed. 10.50x (ISBN 0-678-00804-3). Kelley.

--Adventures in Socialism New Lanark Establishment & Orbiston Community. LC 70-134404. Repr. of 1910 ed. 11.00 (ISBN 0-404-08448-6). AMS Pr.

Owen, Robert. Report of the County of Lanark of a Plan for Relieving Public Distress & Removing Discontent by Giving Permanent, Productive Employment to the Poor & Working Classes. LC 72-2942. Repr. of 1821 ed. 15.00 (ISBN 0-404-10708-7). AMS Pr.

Robert Owen at New Lanark: 1824-1838. LC 72-2543. (British Labour Struggles Before 1850 Ser). 1972. 10.00 (ISBN 0-405-04435-6). Arno.

NEW LEFT

see College Students–Political Activity; Radicalism; Right and Left (Political Science)

NEW LITERATES, WRITING FOR

Gerstner, Karl. Compendium for Literates: A System of Writing. Stephenson, Dennis Q., tr. from Ger. LC 73-21246. 180p. 1974. 20.00 (ISBN 0-262-07061-8); pap. 10.00 (ISBN 0-262-57055-6). MIT Pr.

Neijs, Karel. Literacy Primers: Construction, Evaluation & Use. 1965. pap. 2.25 (ISBN 92-3-100597-9, U361, UNESCO). Unipub.

Richards, Charles G., ed. The Provision of Popular Reading Materials. 298p. (Orig.). 1959. pap. 5.25 (ISBN 92-3-100438-7, U499, UNESCO). Unipub.

NEW LITERATES AND LIBRARIES

see Libraries and New Literates

NEW MADRID, MISSOURI–EARTHQUAKE, 1811-1812

Ben-Chieh Liu, et al. Earthquake Risk & Damage Functions: Applications to New Madrid. (Special Studies in Earth Sciences). 300p. 1981. lib. bdg. 32.00x (ISBN 0-86531-144-7). Westview.

Fuller, Myron. New Madrid Earthquake. 4.00 (ISBN 0-911208-11-9). Ramfre.

NEW MEXICO

see also names of cities, towns, counties, etc. in New Mexico

Bailey, Bernadine. Picture Book of New Mexico. rev. ed. LC 60-11568. (Illus.). (gr. 3-5). 1966. 5.50g (ISBN 0-8075-9534-9). A Whitman.

Calvin, Ross. Sky Determines: An Interpretation of the Southwest. rev ed. LC 48-6466. (Illus.). 1965. pap. 5.95 (ISBN 0-8263-0011-1). U of NM Pr.

Carpenter, Allan. New Mexico. new ed. LC 78-2695. (Enchantment of America State Books Ser.). (Illus.). (gr. 4 up). 1978. PLB 10.60 (ISBN 0-516-04131-2). Childrens.

Conron, John P. Socorro: A Historic Survey. LC 79-56821. (Illus.). 144p. 1980. 12.95 (ISBN 0-8263-0528-8). U of NM Pr.

Davis, William W. El Gringo. LC 72-9438. (The Far Western Frontier Ser.). (Illus.). 436p. 1973. Repr. of 1857 ed. 20.00 (ISBN 0-405-04968-4). Arno.

Espinosa, Carmen G. Shawls, Crinolines & Filigree: Dress & Adornment of the Women of New Mexico. LC 72-138042. (Illus.). 1971. 7.95 (ISBN 0-87404-026-4). Tex Western.

Fradin, Dennis. New Mexico: In Words & Pictures. LC 81-298. (Young People's Stories of Our States Ser.). (Illus.). 48p. (gr. 2-5). 1981. PLB 9.25 (ISBN 0-516-03931-8). Childrens.

Gregg, Josiah. Commerce of the Prairies. Quaife, Milo M., ed. & intro. by. 5.50 (ISBN 0-8446-2165-X). Peter Smith.

--Commerce of the Prairies. Moorhead, Max, ed. (American Exploration & Travel Ser.: No. 17). (Illus.). 1974. 19.95 (ISBN 0-8061-0299-3); pap. 7.95 (ISBN 0-8061-1059-7). U of Okla Pr.

Hillerman, Tony, ed. The Spell of New Mexico. LC 76-21523. (Illus.). 105p. 1976. 7.50 (ISBN 0-8263-0420-6). U of NM Pr.

Lummis, Charles F. Land of Poco Tiempo. LC 66-22698. (Illus.). 1981. pap. 5.95 (ISBN 0-8263-0071-5). U of NM Pr.

Mann, Edward B. & Harvey, Fred. New Mexico: Land of Enchantment. (Illus.). 312p. 1955. 5.00 (ISBN 0-87013-011-0). Mich St U Pr.

Nelson, Dick & Nelson, Sharon. Easy Field Guide to Common Mammals of New Mexico. (Illus.). 32p. (Orig.). (gr. 1-12). 1977. pap. 1.00 (ISBN 0-915030-12-8). Tecolote Pr.

--Easy Field Guide to Common Trees of New Mexico. (Illus.). 32p. (Orig.). (gr. 1-12). 1977. pap. 1.00 (ISBN 0-915030-14-4). Tecolote Pr.

Parish, William J. Charles Ilfeld Company: A Study in the Rise & Decline of Mercantile Capitalism in New Mexico. LC 61-9687. (Studies in Business History: No. 20). (Illus.). 1961. 20.00x (ISBN 0-674-11075-7). Harvard U Pr.

Perkins, Dixie L. Meaning of the New Mexico Mystery Stone. (Illus.). 1979. pap. 3.50 (ISBN 0-89540-039-1, SB-039). Sun Pub.

Reeve, Frank & Cleaveland, Alice A. New Mexico: Land of Many Cultures. rev. ed. (Illus.). (gr. 7-8). 1980. 7.25 (ISBN 0-87108-230-6); Creative Handbk. 12.50x (ISBN 0-87108-233-0). Pruett.

Ritch, William G., ed. New Mexico Blue Book, 1882. LC 68-56224. (Illus.). 1968. Repr. of 1882 ed. slipcased 10.00 (ISBN 0-8263-0086-3). U of NM Pr.

Robb, John D. Hispanic Folk Music of New Mexico & the Southwest: A Self-Portrait of the People. LC 78-21392. (Illus.). 1980. 35.00 (ISBN 0-8061-1492-4). U of Okla Pr.

State Industrial Directories Corp. New Mexico State Industrial Directory 1980. 1980. pap. write for info. (ISBN 0-89910-037-6). State Indus Dir.

Westphall, Victor. Public Domain in New Mexico, 1854-1891. LC 64-17807. (Illus.). 212p. 1965. 7.50x (ISBN 0-8263-0104-5). U of NM Pr.

Zubrow, Ezra B. Population, Contact, & Climate in the New Mexican Pueblos. LC 73-86447. (The Anthropological Papers: No. 24). 1974. pap. 4.95x (ISBN 0-8165-0344-3). U of Ariz Pr.

NEW MEXICO–ANTIQUITIES

Cosgrove, Cornelius B. Caves of the Upper Gila & Hueco Areas in New Mexico & Texas. 1947. pap. 25.00 (ISBN 0-527-01261-0). Kraus Repr.

De Luxan, Diego P. Expedition into New Mexico Made by Antonio De Espejo 1582-1583. Hammond, George P., ed. LC 67-24713. (Quivira Society Publications, Vol. 1). 1967. Repr. of 1929 ed. 12.00 (ISBN 0-405-00088-X). Arno.

Dickson, D. Bruce. Prehistoric Pueblo Settlement Patterns: The Arroyo Hondo, New Mexico, Site Survey. LC 79-21542. (Arroyo Hondo Archaeological Ser.: Vol. 2). (Illus.). 1979. pap. 6.25 (ISBN 0-933452-02-0). Schol Am Res.

Eddy, Frank W. Prehistory in the Navajo Reservoir District, 2 pts. (Illus.). 1966. pap. 7.95 ea. Pt. 1 (ISBN 0-89013-023-X). Pt. 2 (ISBN 0-89013-024-8). Museum NM Pr.

Fewkes, Jessie W. & Gilman, Benjamin I. A Few Summer Ceremonials at Zuni Pueblo: Zuni Melodies, Reconnaissance of Ruins in or Near the Zuni Reservation. LC 76-21216. (A Journal of American Ethnology & Archaeology: Vol. 1). Repr. of 1891 ed. 20.00 (ISBN 0-404-58041-6). AMS Pr.

Harris, et al. An Archaeological Survey of the Chuska Valley & the Chaco Plateau, New Mexico. (Illus.). 1967. pap. 4.50 (ISBN 0-89013-028-0). Museum NM Pr.

Hibben, Frank C. Kiva Art of the Anasazi at Pottery Mound, N.M. DenDooven, Gweneth R., ed. LC 75-19742. (Illus.). 1975. 35.00 (ISBN 0-916122-16-6); signed, limited ed. 100.00 (ISBN 0-685-60911-1). KC Pubns.

Hough, Walter. Antiquities of the Upper Gila & Salt River Valleys in Arizona & New Mexico. Repr. of 1907 ed. 19.00 (ISBN 0-403-03512-0). Scholarly.

Jelinek, Arthur. A Pre-Historic Sequence in the Middle Pecos Valley, New Mexico. (Anthropological Papers: No. 31). 1967. pap. 3.00x (ISBN 0-686-53049-7). U Mich Mus Anthro.

Kelley, N. Edmund. The Contemporary Ecology of Arroyo Hondo, New Mexico. LC 79-21351. (Arroyo Hondo Archaeological Ser.: Vol. 1). (Illus., Orig.). 1979. pap. 6.25 (ISBN 0-933452-01-2). Schol Am Res.

Kidder, A. Pecos, New Mexico: Archaeological Notes, Vol. 5. LC 58-4944. 1958. 12.50 (ISBN 0-939312-06-9). Peabody Found.

Kidder, Alfred V. Pottery of the Pajarito Plateau & of Some Adjacent Regions in New Mexico. LC 16-15195. 1915. pap. 7.00 (ISBN 0-527-00511-8). Kraus Repr.

Lister, Robert H. & Lister, Florence C. Chaco Canyon: Archaeology & Archaeologists. (Illus.). 312p. 1981. 29.95 (ISBN 0-8263-0574-1). U of NM Pr.

McGimsey, Charles R., 3rd. Mariana Mesa. (Peabody Museum Papers Ser.: Vol. 72). pap. 25.00 (ISBN 0-87365-198-7). Peabody Harvard.

Martin, Paul S. SU Site Excavations at a Mongollon Village, Western New Mexico, 1st, 2nd, & 3rd Seasons. (Illus.). 1940-1947. pap. 21.00 (ISBN 0-527-01892-9). Kraus Repr.

Mera, Harry P. Reconnaissance & Excavation in Southeastern New Mexico. LC 39-14217. (AAA Memoirs: No. 51). 1938. pap. 7.00 (ISBN 0-527-00550-9). Kraus Repr.

New Mexico. 23.00 (ISBN 0-89770-107-0). Curriculum Info Ctr.

Northrop, Stuart A. & Kues, Barry S. Bibliography of New Mexico Paleontology. 160p. (Orig.). 1981. pap. 9.95x (ISBN 0-8263-0600-4). U of NM Pr.

Reher, Charles A., ed. Settlement & Subsistence Along the Lower Chaco River: The CGP Survey. LC 77-71906. (Illus.). 614p. 1977. pap. 15.00x (ISBN 0-8263-0449-4). U of NM Pr.

Richert, Roland. Excavation of a Portion of East Ruin, Aztec Ruins National Monument, New Mexico. LC 64-22380. (Illus.). 1964. pap. 3.50x (ISBN 0-911408-13-4). Sw Pks Mnmts.

Smith, Watson. Excavation of Hawikuh by Frederick Webb Hodge: Report of the Hendricks-Hodge Expedition, 1917-1923, Vol. 20. LC 66-27358. (Contributions Ser.). 1966. soft cover 8.50 (ISBN 0-934490-29-5). Mus Am Ind.

--The Williams Site: A Frontier Mongollon Village in West-Central New Mexico. LC 73-86928. (Peabody Museum Papers: Vol. 39, No. 2). 1973. pap. text ed. 10.00 (ISBN 0-87365-190-1). Peabody Harvard.

Speth, John D. & Parry, William J. Late Prehistoric Bison Procurement in Southeastern New Mexico: The 1978 Season at the Garnsey Site (LA-18399) (Museum of Anthropology, The University of Michigan, Technical Reports: No. 12). 369p. 1980. pap. 9.00x (ISBN 0-686-66027-7). U Mich Mus Anth.

--Late Prehistoric Bison Procurement in Southeastern New Mexico: The 1977 Season at the Garnsey Site. (Technical Reports Ser.: No. 8). (Contribution 4 in research reports in archacology). 1978. pap. 4.00x (ISBN 0-932206-73-5). U Mich Mus Anthro.

Vivian, Gordon, et al. Kin Kletso, a Pueblo Three Community in Chaco Canyon, New Mexico, & Tree-Ring Dating of the Archeological Sites in the Chaco Canyon Region, New Mexico, Vol. 6, Pts. 1&2. LC 42-40993. (Illus.). 1973. pap. 4.00x (ISBN 0-911408-15-0). SW Pks Mnmts.

Vivian, R. Gwinn, et al. Wooden Ritual Artifacts from Chaco Canyon, New Mexico: The Chetro Ketl Collection. LC 78-10684. (Anthropological Papers: No. 32). 1978. pap. 5.95x (ISBN 0-8165-0576-4). U of Ariz Pr.

NEW MEXICO–BIBLIOGRAPHY

Myers, Dwight & Myers, Carol, eds. In Celebration of the Book: Literary New Mexico. 160p. 1982. deluxe ed. 49.95 (ISBN 0-89016-063-5). Lightning Tree.

Shelton, Wilma Loy. Checklist of New Mexico Publications, 1850-1953. LC 54-12989. 1954. pap. 3.50 (ISBN 0-8263-0092-8). U of NM Pr.

Swadesh, Frances L. Twenty Thousand Years of History: A New Mexico Bibliography. 1973. pap. 4.95 (ISBN 0-913270-14-8). Sunstone Pr.

Vexler, R. I. New Mexico Chronology & Factbook, Vol. 31. 1978. 8.50 (ISBN 0-379-16156-7). Oceana.

NEW MEXICO–DESCRIPTION AND TRAVEL

Adams, Eleanor B., ed. The Missions of New Mexico, 1776: A Description by Fray Francisco Atanasio Dominguez with Other Contemporary Documents. LC 55-12223. 1975. Repr. of 1956 ed. 35.00 (ISBN 0-8263-0373-0); deluxe ed. 100.00 (ISBN 0-8263-0418-4). U of NM Pr.

Adams, Emma H. To & Fro in Southern California: With Sketches in Arizona & New Mexico. Cortes, Carlos E., ed. LC 76-1220. (Chicano Heritage Ser.). 1976. Repr. of 1887 ed. 16.00x (ISBN 0-405-09481-7). Arno.

Armstrong, Ruth. New Mexico. 2nd ed. LC 74-30975. (Illus.). 192p. 1975. 9.50 (ISBN 0-498-01722-2). A S Barnes.

Armstrong, Ruth & New Mexico Magazine. Enchanted Trails. Tryk, Sheila & King, Scottie, eds. LC 80-82644. (Illus.). vi, 249p. (Orig.). 1980. pap. 7.95 (ISBN 0-937206-01-6, Pub. by NM Magazine). U of NM Pr.

Bartlett, John R. Personal Narrative of Explorations & Incidents in Texas, New Mexico, California, Sonora, & Chihuahua, Connected with the United States & Mexican Boundary Commission, During the Years 1850 51, 52 & 53. 1976. Repr. of 1854 ed. 145.00 (ISBN 0-403-06367-1, Regency). Scholarly.

Bullock, Alice. Mountain Villages. (Illus.). 1973. pap. 4.25 (ISBN 0-913270-13-X). Sunstone Pr.

Bunting, Bainbridge. Of Earth & Timbers Made: New Mexico Architecture. LC 73-91766. (Illus.). 85p. 1974. pap. 9.95 (ISBN 0-8263-0318-8). U of NM Pr.

Coles, Robert. The Old Ones of New Mexico. LC 73-82776. (Illus.). 74p. 1980. Repr. of 1973 ed. 7.95 (ISBN 0-8263-0301-3). U of NM Pr.

Conklin, Paul S. Cimarron Kid. LC 72-7917. (Illus.). 64p. (gr. 3 up). 1973. 5.95 (ISBN 0-396-06747-6). Dodd.

Cozzens, Samuel W. Marvelous Country. 1967. Repr. 12.50 (ISBN 0-87018-011-8). Ross.

De Luxan, Diego P. Expedition into New Mexico Made by Antonio De Espejo 1582-1583. Hammond, George P., ed. LC 67-24713. (Quivira Society Publications, Vol. 1). 1967. Repr. of 1929 ed. 12.00 (ISBN 0-405-00088-X). Arno.

Dillon, Richard H., ed. A Cannoneer in Navajo Country: Journal of Private Josiah M. Rice, 1851. (Illus.). 1970. limited ed. 14.50 (ISBN 0-912094-15-X). Old West.

Fowler, Jacob. Journal Narrating an Adventure from Arkansas Through Indian Territory Etc. Coues, Elliot, ed. Orig. Title: Narrating an Adventure from Arkansas Through Indian Territory Etc. 1965. Repr. 8.75 (ISBN 0-87018-019-3). Ross.

French, William. Some Recollections of a Western Ranchman, New Mexico 1883-1899, 2 Vols. 1965. Set. 35.00 (ISBN 0-87266-011-7). Argosy.
Hammond, George P. & Rey, Agapito. Rediscovery of New Mexico, 1580-1594. LC 66-14778. (Coronado Cuarto Centennial Ser: Vol. 3). 1966. 17.50x (ISBN 0-8263-0049-9). U of NM Pr.
Kluckhohn, Clyde M. To the Foot of the Rainbow. LC 80-12317. (Beautiful Rio Grande Classics Ser.). (Illus.). 412p. lib. bdg. 25.00 (ISBN 0-87380-136-9); pap. 15.00 (ISBN 0-87380-137-7). Rio Grande.
Lizar, Thomas. New Mexico Mountain Access. (Illus.). 95p. (Orig.). 1980. pap. 7.95 (ISBN 0-939866-02-1). Woodstone Bks.
McCall, George A. New Mexico in Eighteen Fifty: A Military View. Frazer, Robert W., ed. LC 68-15682. (Illus.). 1968. 12.95 (ISBN 0-8061-0800-2). U of Okla Pr.
McCliney, Eugene B. Clanton Draw & Box Canyon. (Illus.). 1962. pap. 2.50 (ISBN 0-89013-116-3). Museum NM Pr.
Muench, David, photos by. New Mexico. LC 74-75125. (Belding Imprint Ser.). (Illus.). 192p. (Text by Tony Hillerman). 1974. 29.50 (ISBN 0-912856-14-9). Graphic Arts Ctr.
Nichols, John Treadwell & Davis, William. If Mountains Die: A New Mexico Memoir. LC 78-20440. (Illus.). 1979. 20.00 (ISBN 0-394-42480-8); pap. 11.95 (ISBN 0-394-73614-1). Knopf.
Nymeyer, Robert. Carlsbad, Caves, & a Camera. (Speleologia Ser.). (Illus.). 224p. 1978. 17.00 (ISBN 0-914264-23-0); pap. 10.50 (ISBN 0-914264-24-9). Cave Bks TN.
Pike, Zebulon M. Account of Expeditions to the Source of the Mississippi, the Southwest, Etc, 2 vols. facsimile ed. 1965. Set. boxed 22.50 (ISBN 0-87018-049-5). Ross.
--The Journals of Zebulon Montgomery Pike, with Letters & Related Documents, 2 Vols. Jackson, Donald, ed. (American Exploration & Travel Ser.: No. 48). (Illus.). 1966. boxed 42.50 (ISBN 0-8061-0699-9). U of Okla Pr.
Sinclair, John L. New Mexico: The Shining Land. 224p. 1980. 14.95 (ISBN 0-8263-0548-2). U of NM Pr.
Territorial Bureau of Immigration. The Resources of New Mexico. LC 73-80703. 76p. 1973. Repr. of 1881 ed. lib. bdg. 9.50x (ISBN 0-88307-504-0); pap. 1.25 o. p. (ISBN 0-88307-503-2). Gannon.
Weigle, Marta. Hispanic Villages of Northern New Mexico. LC 73-89795. 1975. 18.00 (ISBN 0-89016-030-9); pap. 10.00 (ISBN 0-89016-031-7); pap. 3.00 bibliography (ISBN 0-89016-032-5). Lightning Tree.
Wislizenus, Frederick A. Tour to Northern Mexico with Col. Doniphan, 1846-1847. LC 74-85495. (Beautiful Rio Grande Classic Ser). (Illus.). 160p. 1969. Repr. of 1848 ed. lib. bdg. 10.00 (ISBN 0-87380-003-6). Rio Grande.

NEW MEXICO–DESCRIPTION AND TRAVEL–GUIDEBOOKS

Beard, Sam. Ski Touring in Northern New Mexico. (Illus., Orig.). 1979. pap. 3.95 (ISBN 0-933004-05-2). Adobe Pr.
Federal Writers' Project. New Mexico: A Guide to the Colorful State. 1940. Repr. 49.00 (ISBN 0-403-02181-2). Somerset Pub.
Hart, Herbert M. Tour Guide to Old Forts of New Mexico, Arizona, Nevada, Utah, Colorado, Vol. 2. (Illus.). 65p. (Orig.). 1981. pap. 3.95 (ISBN 0-87108-581-X). Pruett.
Hoard, Dorothy. A Hiker's Guide to Bandelier National Monument. (Illus.). 1979. pap. 3.50 (ISBN 0-933004-01-X). Adobe Pr.
Looney, Ralph. Haunted Highways: The Ghost Towns of New Mexico. (Illus.). 1979. pap. 8.95 (ISBN 0-8263-0506-7). U of NM Pr.
Ryan, Craig A. Beautiful New Mexico. Shangle, Robert D., ed. LC 79-16748. (Illus.). 80p. 1979. 14.95 (ISBN 0-89802-073-5); pap. 7.95 (ISBN 0-89802-072-7). Beautiful Am.
Ungnade, Herbert E. Guide to the New Mexico Mountains. enl. & rev. 2nd ed. LC 72-80752. (Illus.). 235p. 1972. 7.50 (ISBN 0-8263-0241-6); pap. 5.95 (ISBN 0-8263-0242-4). U of NM Pr.

NEW MEXICO–HISTORY

Alcala, Gaspar. History of New Mexico, 1610. Espinos, Gilberto & Hodge, F. W., eds. LC 67-24716. (Quivira Society Publications, Vol. 4). 1967. Repr. of 1933 ed. 12.00 (ISBN 0-405-00074-X). Arno.
Beck, Warren A. New Mexico: A History of Four Centuries. (Illus.). 1979. Repr. of 1962 ed. 12.95 (ISBN 0-8061-0533-X). U of Okla Pr.
Beck, Warren A. & Haase, Ynez D. Historical Atlas of New Mexico. LC 68-31366. (Illus.). 1969. pap. 6.95 (ISBN 0-8061-0817-7). U of Okla Pr.
Brown, Lorin W., et al. Hispano Folklife of New Mexico: The Lorin W. Brown Federal Writers' Project Manuscripts. LC 78-51578. (Illus.). 279p. 1978. 16.95 (ISBN 0-8263-0475-3). U of NM Pr.
Bullock, Alice. Mountain Villages. (Illus.). 1973. pap. 4.25 (ISBN 0-913270-13-X). Sunstone Pr.
Calvin, Ross, ed. Lieutenant Emory Reports: A Reprint of Lieutenant W. H. Emory's "Notes of a Military Reconnoissance". LC 51-10795. 1968. pap. 3.95 (ISBN 0-8263-0009-X). U of NM Pr.
Carroll, H. Bailey & Haggard, J. Villasana, eds. Three New Mexico Chronicles. Incl. Exposicion. Pino, Pedro B; Ojeada. Barreiro, Antonio; Addition. De Escudero, Jose A. LC 67-24722. (Quivira Society Publications Ser). 342p. 1967. Repr. of 1942 ed. 12.00 (ISBN 0-405-00085-5). Arno.
Chavez, Angelico. My Penitente Land. LC 79-63671. 1979. Repr. of 1974 ed. lib. bdg. 27.50x (ISBN 0-88307-568-7). Gannon.
--New Mexico Triptych. LC 75-31416. 84p. 1976. lib. bdg. 12.50x (ISBN 0-88307-520-2). Gannon.
Cleaveland, Agnes M. No Life for a Lady. LC 75-25302. 366p. 1976. Repr. of 1941 ed. 15.00 (ISBN 0-88307-519-9). Gannon.
Cohrs, Timothy. Fort Selden, New Mexico. (Illus.). 1974. pap. 1.50 (ISBN 0-89013-084-1). Museum NM Pr.
Cooke, Philip St. G. The Conquest of New Mexico & California: An Historical & Personal Narrative. 1977. Repr. 39.00 (ISBN 0-403-07682-X). Scholarly.
Cooke, Philip St George. The Conquest of New Mexico & California: An Historical & Personal Narrative. Cortes, Carlos E., ed. LC 76-1244. (Chicano Heritage Ser.). 1976. Repr. of 1878 ed. 18.00x (ISBN 0-405-09497-3). Arno.
Ellis, Richard N., ed. New Mexican Past & Present: A Historical Reader. LC 71-153941. 140p. 1971. 9.95x (ISBN 0-8263-0210-6); pap. 6.95 (ISBN 0-8263-0215-7). U of NM Pr.
--New Mexico Historic Documents. LC 75-14656. 140p. 1975. 7.50 (ISBN 0-8263-0385-4); pap. 3.95 (ISBN 0-8263-0386-2). U of NM Pr.
Fergusson, Erna. New Mexico: A Pageant of Three Peoples. 2nd ed. LC 72-94664. Orig. Title: New Mexico. (Illus.). 408p. 1973. pap. 8.95 (ISBN 0-8263-0271-8). U of NM Pr.
Forrest, James T. New Mexico. LC 70-118833. 1971. pap. text ed. 2.95 (ISBN 0-8077-1372-4). Tchrs Coll.
French, William. Further Recollections of a Western Ranchman: New Mexico 1883-1889, Vol. II. (Illus.). 1965. 20.00 (ISBN 0-87266-012-5). Argosy.
Ganaway, Loomis M. New Mexico & the Sectional Controversy 1846-1861. LC 76-8250. (Perspectives in American History Ser., No. 28). (Illus.). x, 140p. Repr. of 1944 ed. lib. bdg. 13.50x (ISBN 0-87991-352-5). Porcupine Pr.
Hackett, Charles W., ed. Revolt of the Pueblo Indians of New Mexico & Otermin's Attempted Reconquest, 1680-82, 2 Vols. LC 42-22191. (Coronado Cuarto Centennial Ser.: Vols. VIII & IX). 1942. Set. 30.00x (ISBN 0-8263-0161-4). U of NM Pr.
Hammond, George P. & Rey, Agapito, eds. New Mexico in Sixteen Two. LC 67-24719. (Quivira Society Publications, Vol. 8). 1967. Repr. of 1938 ed. 12.00 (ISBN 0-405-00082-0). Arno.
Hodge, F. W. The History of Hawikuh, New Mexico: One of the So-Called Cities of Cibola. (Illus.). 1937. 10.00 (ISBN 0-686-20671-1). Southwest Mus.
Huber, Leonard V. New Orleans: A Pictorial History. (Illus.). 352p. 1971. 19.95 (ISBN 0-517-50688-2). Crown.
Ingersoll, et al. New Mexico One Hundred Years Ago. (Sun Historical Ser.). (Illus.). pap. 3.50 (ISBN 0-89540-057-X). Sun Pub.
Inman, Henry. Old Santa Fe Trail. 1897. Repr. 12.50 (ISBN 0-87018-031-2). Ross.
Jackson, Ronald V. & Teeples, Gary R. New Mexico Census Index 1850. LC 77-86123. (Illus.). lib. bdg. 26.00 (ISBN 0-89593-095-1). Accelerated Index.
Jenkins, Myra E. & Schroeder, Albert H. A Brief History of New Mexico. LC 74-21917. (Illus.). 89p. (Orig.). 1974. pap. 3.95 (ISBN 0-8263-0370-6). U of NM Pr.
Keleher, William A. Memoirs: A New Mexico Item, 1892-1969. 1970. 7.50 (ISBN 0-911292-02-0). Adobe Pr.
Kenner, Charles L. History of New Mexican-Plains Indian Relations. LC 68-31375. (Illus.). 1969. 13.95 (ISBN 0-8061-0829-0). U of Okla Pr.
Kimball, Clark & Smith, Marcus J. The Hospital at the End of the Santa Fe Trail. (Illus.). 1977. pap. 6.95 (ISBN 0-686-00322-5). St Vincent Hosp.
Larson, Robert W. New Mexico Populism: A Study of Radical Protest in a Western Territory. LC 73-89256. 1974. 12.50x (ISBN 0-87081-054-5). Colo Assoc.
Lopez, Thomas R., Jr. Prospects for the Spanish American Culture of New Mexico. LC 73-82391. 1974. 12.00 (ISBN 0-88247-243-7). R & E Res Assoc.
Loyola, Mary. The American Occupation of New Mexico, 1821-1852. Cortes, Carlos E., ed. LC 76-1281. (Chicano Heritage Ser.). 1976. Repr. of 1939 ed. 10.00x (ISBN 0-405-09512-0). Arno.
McCall, George A. New Mexico in Eighteen Fifty: A Military View. Frazer, Robert W., ed. LC 68-15682. (Illus.). 1968. 12.95 (ISBN 0-8061-0800-2). U of Okla Pr.
Melzer, Richard. Madrid Revisited: Life & Labor in a New Mexican Mining Camp in the Years of the Great Depression. LC 76-18599. (Illus.). 1976. 9.95 (ISBN 0-89016-025-2); pap. 5.95 (ISBN 0-89016-024-4). Lightning Tree.
Motto, Sytha. More Than Conquerors Makers of History. LC 80-26706. (Illus.). 300p. 1981. 17.50 (ISBN 0-937268-05-4). Alpha Printing.
Murphy, Lawrence R. Philmont: A History of New Mexico's Cimarron Country. 2nd ed. LC 72-76828. (Illus.). 261p. 1976. pap. 6.95 (ISBN 0-8263-0244-0). U of NM Pr.
Nims, F. C. Health, Wealth & Pleasure in Colorado & New Mexico. (Illus.). 1980. pap. 4.95 (ISBN 0-89013-126-0). Museum NM Pr.
Otero, Miguel A. Otero, 3 vols. in 1. LC 73-14420. (The Mexican American Ser.). 1036p. 1974. Repr. 52.00x (ISBN 0-405-05685-0). Arno.
Parsons, Jack & Earney, Michael. Land & Cattle: Conversations with Joe Pankey, A New Mexico Rancher. LC 78-56950. (Illus.). 120p. 1978. 15.00 (ISBN 0-8263-0491-5). U of NM Pr.
Read, Benjamin M. Illustrated History of New Mexico. Cortes, Carlos E., ed. LC 76-1562. (Chicano Heritage Ser.). (Illus.). 1976. Repr. of 1912 ed. 48.00x (ISBN 0-405-09521-X). Arno.
Ream, Glen O. Out of New Mexico's Past. LC 80-166. (Illus.). 160p. (Orig.). 1980. pap. 6.95 (ISBN 0-913270-86-5, Sundial Bks). Sunstone Pr.
Robe, Stanley L., ed. Hispanic Legends from New Mexico: Narratives from the R. D. Jameson Collection. (U. C. Publications in Folkore & Mythology Studies: Vol. 31). pap. 27.50 (ISBN 0-520-09614-2). U of Cal Pr.
Scholes, France V. Troublous Times in New Mexico, 1659-1670. LC 75-41242. (New Mexico Hist. Society. Publications in History: Vol. 11). Repr. of 1942 ed. 21.50 (ISBN 0-404-14701-1). AMS Pr.
Sherman, James E. & Sherman, Barbara H. Ghost Towns & Mining Camps of New Mexico. LC 72-9525. (Illus.). 270p. 1975. 14.95 (ISBN 0-8061-1066-X); pap. 7.95x (ISBN 0-8061-1106-2). U of Okla Pr.
Simmons, Marc. New Mexico. (States & the Nation Ser.). (Illus.). 1977. 12.95 (ISBN 0-393-05631-7, Co-Pub by AASLH). Norton.
--Taos to Tome: True Tales of Hispanic New Mexico. (Illus., Orig.). 1978. pap. 4.95 (ISBN 0-933004-04-4). Adobe Pr.
--Turquoise & Six-Guns: The Story of Cerrillos, New Mexico. new rev. ed. (Illus.). 1975. pap. 3.95 (ISBN 0-913270-33-4). Sunstone Pr.
Smeal, Lee. New Mexico Historical & Biographical Index. LC 78-53709. (Illus.). Date not set. lib. bdg. price not set (ISBN 0-89593-192-3). Accelerated Index.
Stratton, Porter A. Territorial Press of New Mexico, 1834-1912. LC 78-78556. 1969. 15.00x (ISBN 0-8263-0141-X). U of NM Pr.
Sunseri, Alvin. Seeds of Discord: New Mexico in the Aftermath of the American Conquest, 1846-1861. LC 78-24315. 1979. 16.95x (ISBN 0-88229-141-6). Nelson-Hall.
Swadesh, Frances L. Los Primeros Pobladores: Hispanic Americans of the Ute Frontier. LC 73-11566. 288p. 1974. text ed. 3.95x (ISBN 0-268-00505-2). U of Notre Dame Pr.
Territorial Bureau of Immigration. The Resources of New Mexico. LC 73-80703. 76p. 1973. Repr. of 1881 ed. lib. bdg. 9.50x (ISBN 0-88307-504-0); pap. 1.25 o. p. (ISBN 0-88307-503-2). Gannon.
Twitchell, Ralph E. The History of the Military Occupation of the Territory of New Mexico from 1846-1851: With Biographical Sketches of Men Prominent in Government. Cortes, Carlos E., ed. LC 76-1601. (Chicano Heritage Ser.). (Illus.). 1976. Repr. of 1909 ed. 24.00x (ISBN 0-405-09528-7). Arno.
Ulibarri, Sabine R. Tierra Amarilla: Stories of New Mexico, Cuentos De Nuevo Mexico. LC 75-153942. (Illus.). 167p. (Eng. & Span.). 1978. pap. 5.95 (ISBN 0-8263-0212-2). U of NM Pr.
U. S. House of Representatives. California & New Mexico: Message from the President of the United States, January 21, 1850. Cortes, Carlos E., ed. LC 76-1618. (Chicano Heritage Ser.). (Illus.). 1976. Repr. of 1850 ed. 55.00x (ISBN 0-405-09530-9). Arno.
Vexler, R. I. New Mexico Chronology & Factbook, Vol. 31. 1978. 8.50 (ISBN 0-379-16156-7). Oceana.
Wiggins, Walt. Lincoln, New Mexico: As It Was One Day. LC 75-7275. Date not set. pap. 4.95 (ISBN 0-686-24292-0). Pintores Pr.
Wilson, John P. Fort Sumner, New Mexico. (Illus.). 1974. pap. 1.50 (ISBN 0-89013-083-3). Museum NM Pr.
Woods, Betty. Ghost Towns & How to Get Them. Smith, James C., ed. LC 77-78518. 1978. pap. 2.95 (ISBN 0-913270-30-X). Sunstone Pr.

NEW MEXICO–HISTORY–BIBLIOGRAPHY

Twitchell, Ralph E. The Spanish Archives of New Mexico, 2 vols. Cortes, Carlos E., ed. LC 76-1607. (Chicano Heritage Ser.). (Illus.). 1976. Repr. of 1914 ed. Set. 74.00x (ISBN 0-405-09529-5); Vol. 1. 34.00x (ISBN 0-405-09544-9); Vol. 2. 40.00x (ISBN 0-405-09549-X). Arno.

NEW MEXICO–HISTORY–FICTION

Bullock, Alice. Living Legends. LC 72-90383. (Illus.). 1978. pap. 4.25 (ISBN 0-913270-06-7). Sunstone Pr.
Cather, Willa. Death Comes for the Archbishop. 1971. pap. 2.95 (ISBN 0-394-71679-5, Vin). Random.

NEW MEXICO–HISTORY–SOURCES

De Luxan, Diego P. Expedition into New Mexico Made by Antonio De Espejo 1582-1583. Hammond, George P., ed. LC 67-24713. (Quivira Society Publications, Vol. 1). 1967. Repr. of 1929 ed. 12.00 (ISBN 0-405-00088-X). Arno.
Hammond, George P. & Rey, Agapito. Rediscovery of New Mexico, 1580-1594. LC 66-14778. (Coronado Cuarto Centennial Ser: Vol. 3). 1966. 17.50x (ISBN 0-8263-0049-9). U of NM Pr.
Thomas, Alfred B., ed. Forgotten Frontiers: A Study of the Spanish Indian Policy of Don Juan Bautista De Anza, Governor of New Mexico, 1777-1787. (Civilization of the American Indian Ser.: No. 1). 1969. Repr. of 1932 ed. 19.95 (ISBN 0-8061-0014-1). U of Okla Pr.
Twitchell, Ralph E. The Spanish Archives of New Mexico, 2 vols. LC 74-20571. Repr. of 1914 ed. Set. 75.00 (ISBN 0-404-12292-2). AMS Pr.
--The Spanish Archives of New Mexico, 2 vols. Cortes, Carlos E., ed. LC 76-1607. (Chicano Heritage Ser.). (Illus.). 1976. Repr. of 1914 ed. Set. 74.00x (ISBN 0-405-09529-5); Vol. 1. 34.00x (ISBN 0-405-09544-9); Vol. 2. 40.00x (ISBN 0-405-09549-X). Arno.

NEW MEXICO–IMPRINTS

Historical Records Survey: Check List of New Mexico Imprints & Publications, 1784-1876. Imprints, 1834-1876. Publications, 1784-1876. 1942. pap. 10.00 (ISBN 0-527-01920-8). Kraus Repr.

NEW MEXICO–POLITICS AND GOVERNMENT

Barker, Ruth L. Caballeros. Cortes, Carlos E., ed. Van Sweringen, Norma, tr. LC 76-1237. (Chicano Heritage Ser.). (Illus.). 1976. Repr. of 1932 ed. lib. bdg. 22.00x (ISBN 0-405-09484-1). Arno.
Fincher, E. B. Spanish-Americans As a Political Factor in New Mexico, 1912-1950. LC 73-14202. (The Mexican American Ser.). 332p. 1974. 19.00x (ISBN 0-405-05676-1). Arno.
Garcia, F. Chris & Hain, Paul. New Mexico Government. rev. ed. 280p. 1981. pap. 6.50 (ISBN 0-8263-0560-1). U of NM Pr.
Garcia, F. Chris, et al. State & Local Government in New Mexico. LC 79-2189. (Illus., Orig.). (gr. 9). 1979. pap. 6.95x (ISBN 0-8263-0511-3). U of NM Pr.
Holmes, Jack E. Politics in New Mexico. LC 67-22734. 1967. 7.95x (ISBN 0-8263-0055-3). U of NM Pr.
Kimzey, Bruce W. The Property Tax in New Mexico. 1977. pap. text ed. 7.50x (ISBN 0-8191-0131-1). U Pr of Amer.
Larson, Robert W. New Mexico's Quest for Statehood, 1846-1912. LC 68-23022. 1968. 12.00x (ISBN 0-8263-0062-6). U of NM Pr.
Meriwether, David. My Life in the Mountains & on the Plains: A Newly Discovered Autobiography. Griffen, Robert A., ed. (American Exploration & Travel Ser.: No. 46). 1966. Repr. of 1965 ed. 16.95 (ISBN 0-8061-0668-9). U of Okla Pr.
New Mexico Statutes Annotated, Nineteen Seventy-Eight Compilation. 1978. write for info. (ISBN 0-87215-224-3). Michie-Bobbs.
Ritch, William G., ed. New Mexico Blue Book, 1882. LC 68-56224. (Illus.). 1968. Repr. of 1882 ed. slipcased 10.00 (ISBN 0-8263-0086-3). U of NM Pr.
Roberts, Susan A., et al. Civics for New Mexicans. LC 80-52284. 375p. 1980. 25.00 (ISBN 0-8263-0547-4). U of NM Pr.
Vigil, Maurilio. Los Patrones: Profiles of Hispanic Political Leaders in New Mexico History. LC 79-6813. 179p. 1980. 17.75 (ISBN 0-8191-0962-2); pap. 8.75 (ISBN 0-8191-0963-0). U Pr of Amer.
WhisenHunt, Donald W. New Mexico Courthouses. (Southwest Studies Ser.: No. 57). 1979. pap. text ed. 3.00 (ISBN 0-87404-117-1). Tex Western.

NEW MEXICO–SOCIAL LIFE AND CUSTOMS

Brown, Lorin W., et al. Hispano Folklife of New Mexico: The Lorin W. Brown Federal Writers' Project Manuscripts. LC 78-51578. (Illus.). 279p. 1978. 16.95 (ISBN 0-8263-0475-3). U of NM Pr.

Bullock, Alice. The Squaw Tree: Ghost, Miracles & Mysteries of New Mexico. LC 77-86728. 1978. 9.95 (ISBN 0-89016-041-4); pap. 5.95 (ISBN 0-89016-040-6). Lightning Tree.

Buss, Fran L. La Partera: Story of a Midwife. 1980. 10.95x (ISBN 0-472-09322-3); pap. 6.95 (ISBN 0-472-06322-7). U of Mich Pr.

Cortes, Carlos E., ed. The New Mexican Hispano. LC 73-14210. (The Mexican American Ser.). (Illus.). 510p. 1974. Repr. 30.00x (ISBN 0-405-05684-2). Arno.

De Baca Gilbert, Fabiola C. The Good Life: New Mexico Traditions & Food. (Illus.). 96p. 1981. pap. 6.95 (ISBN 0-89013-137-6). Museum NM Pr.

Field, Matthew C. Matt Field on the Santa Fe Trail. Sunder, John E., et al, eds. (American Exploration & Travel Ser.: No. 29). (Illus.). 1960. 17.95 (ISBN 0-8061-0456-2). U of Okla Pr.

Kutsche, Paul & Van Ness, John R. Canones: Values, Crisis, & Survival in a Northern New Mexico Village. (Illus.). 280p. 1981. 17.50x (ISBN 0-8263-0570-9). U of NM Pr.

Museum of International Folk Art. Days of Plenty, Days of Want: Spanish Folklife & Art in New Mexico. Cuesta, Benedicto, tr. (Eng. & Span.). 1976. pap. 2.00 (ISBN 0-89013-109-0). Museum NM Pr.

NEW ORLEANS

Bruce, Curt. The Great Houses of New Orleans. 1977. 15.00 (ISBN 0-394-40716-4). Knopf.

Cable, Mary. Lost New Orleans. 256p. 1980. 21.95 (ISBN 0-395-27623-3). HM.

Davis, W. Hardy. Aiming for the Jugular in New Orleans. LC 75-16561. 1976. 8.95 (ISBN 0-87949-035-7). Ashley Bks.

Federal Writers' Project. New Orleans: A City Guide. 416p. 1938. Repr. 45.00 (ISBN 0-403-02203-7). Somerset Pub.

Jacobs, Howard. Charlie the Mole & Other Droll Souls. LC 73-12219. (Illus.). 288p. 1973. 5.95 (ISBN 0-88289-001-8). Pelican.

Lewis, Peirce F. New Orleans: The Making of an Urban Landscape. LC 76-4797. (Contemporary Metropolitan Analysis Ser.). (Illus.). 1976. pap. text ed. 7.95 (ISBN 0-88410-433-8). Ballinger Pub.

NEW ORLEANS–BIOGRAPHY

Coleman, James J., Jr. Gilbert Antoine de St. Maxent: The Spanish-Frenchman of New Orleans. LC 68-54600. 136p. 1980. 10.00 (ISBN 0-911116-06-0). Pelican.

Morazan, Ronald R. Biographical Sketches of the Veterans of the Battalion of Orleans, 1814 - 1815. LC 79-65180. 1980. 12.50 (ISBN 0-918784-51-4). Legacy Pub Co.

NEW ORLEANS–CARNIVAL

Hardy, Arthur. New Orleans Mardi Gras Guide, Nineteen Eighty One. rev. ed. (Illus.). 82p. 1981. pap. 2.95x (ISBN 0-930892-05-4). A Hardy & Assocs.

--New Orleans Mardi Gras Guide: 1977. 1977. pap. 2.95 (ISBN 0-930892-01-1). A Hardy & Assocs.

--New Orleans Mardi Gras Guide: 1978. 2nd annual ed. LC 77-93191. (Illus.). 64p. 1977. pap. 2.95 (ISBN 0-930892-02-X). A Hardy & Assocs.

--New Orleans Mardi Gras Guide: 1979. 3rd annual ed. LC 78-71117. (Illus.). 1979. pap. 2.95 (ISBN 0-930892-03-8). A Hardy & Assocs.

--New Orleans Mardi Gras Guide, 1980. 4th rev. ed. LC 79-92736. (Illus.). 1980. pap. 2.95 (ISBN 0-930892-04-6). A Hardy & Assocs.

Huber, Leonard. Mardi Gras: A Pictorial History of Carnival in New Orleans. LC 76-39911. (Illus.). 1977. pap. 5.95 (ISBN 0-88289-160-X). Pelican.

Laborde, Errol. Mardi Gras! Rogers, Mary A., ed. (Illus.). 200p. 1981. 29.95 (ISBN 0-937430-03-X); pap. 14.95 (ISBN 0-686-72682-0). Picayune Pr.

Tallant, Robert. Mardi Gras. LC 48-5068. 263p. 1976. 5.95 (ISBN 0-88289-108-1). Pelican.

Williams, Jonathan, ed. The Sleep of Reason. LC 74-76880. (Illus.). 120p. 1974. 12.50 (ISBN 0-912330-04-X, Dist. by Gnomon Pr); pap. 7.50 (ISBN 0-912330-23-6). Jargon Soc.

NEW ORLEANS–DESCRIPTION

Arthur Frommer's Guide to New Orleans, 1981-82. 224p. 1981. pap. 2.95 (ISBN 0-671-41437-2). Frommer-Pasmantier.

Berger, Brian. Beautiful New Orleans. Shangle, Robert D., ed. (Illus.). 72p. 1981. 14.95 (ISBN 0-89802-123-5); pap. 7.95 (ISBN 0-89802-122-7). Beautiful Am.

Castellanos, Henry C. New Orleans As It Was. Reinecke, George F., ed. LC 78-13014. 1979. (Louisiana Bicentennial Reprint Ser.). 1979. 14.95x (ISBN 0-8071-0457-4). La State U Pr.

Christovich, et al. New Orleans Architecture, Vol. 5: Esplanade Ridge. LC 72-172272. (New Orleans Architecture Ser.). (Illus.). 1977. 21.95 (ISBN 0-88289-151-0). Pelican.

Collin, Richard & Collin, Rima. The New Orleans Restaurant Guide. (Illus.). 1980. pap. 4.75 (ISBN 0-931522-02-1). Strether & Swann.

Costa, Louis, et al. Streetcar Guide to Uptown New Orleans. Swords, David, ed. (Illus.). 136p. (Orig.). 1980. pap. 5.00 (ISBN 0-939108-00-3). Transitour.

Dollarwise Guide to the Southeast & New Orleans, 1980-81. 300p. pap. 4.95 (ISBN 0-671-25175-9). Frommer-Pasmantier.

Dufour, Charles P. New Orleans. 1981. english ed. 19.95 (ISBN 0-8071-0799-9); french ed. 19.95 (ISBN 0-8071-0851-0). La State U Pr.

Faucheux, Kathryn E. Footnotes: French Quarter Walking Tour. 49p. 1977. pap. 2.95 (ISBN 0-88289-209-6). Pelican.

Faulkner, William. New Orleans Sketches. Collier, Carvel, ed. LC 68-14495. 1968. 10.00 (ISBN 0-394-43818-3). Random.

Federal Writers' Project. New Orleans: A City Guide. 416p. 1938. Repr. 45.00 (ISBN 0-403-02203-7). Somerset Pub.

Griffin, Thomas K. Pelican Guide to New Orleans. 4th, rev. ed. LC 74-182889. (Pelican Guide Ser.). (Illus.). 160p. 1980. pap. 3.95 (ISBN 0-88289-010-7). Pelican.

Hall, A. Oakey. The Manhattaner in New Orleans - Phases of Crescent City Life. Kmen, Henry A., ed. LC 75-21960. 240p. 1976. Repr. 10.00x (ISBN 0-8071-0167-2). La State U Pr.

Hennick, Louis & Charlton, E. Harper. Streetcars of New Orleans. rev. ed. LC 75-4489. (Illus.). 240p. 1975. 19.95 (ISBN 0-88289-066-2). Pelican.

Holland, Claude V. French Quarter, U. S. A. (Illus.). 1978. 5.00 (ISBN 0-932092-17-9); pap. 2.95 (ISBN 0-932092-16-0). Hol-Land Bks.

Huber, Leonard, et al. New Orleans Architecture, Vol. 3: The Cemeteries. Wilson, Samuel, Jr., ed. LC 72-172272. (New Orleans Architecture Ser.). (Illus.). 208p. 1974. 21.95 (ISBN 0-88289-020-4). Pelican.

Ingraham, Joseph H. South-West, 2 Vols. LC 68-55895. 1835. 29.00x (ISBN 0-8371-0493-9, Pub. by Negro U Pr). Greenwood.

Joynes, St. Leger M. & Du'Arte, Jack. Insiders' Guide to New Orleans. (Insiders' Guides Ser.). (Illus., Orig.). 1981. pap. 4.95 (ISBN 0-932338-03-8). Insiders Pub.

Kirk, Susan, et al. The Architecture of St. Charles Avenue. LC 77-23486. (Illus.). 1977. 15.00 (ISBN 0-88289-174-X). Pelican.

Kolb, Carolyn. New Orleans. LC 71-160873. 1972. pap. 3.95 (ISBN 0-385-02460-6, Dolp). Doubleday.

Lester, John. I'll Take New Orleans. 1971. pap. 2.50 (ISBN 0-88289-005-0). Pelican.

Matthews, E. C. Joseph Pennell's Sketches of Old New Orleans. 64p. 1966. pap. 2.00 (ISBN 0-911116-85-0). Pelican.

Moore, Fred W. Texas Short Stories & a Look at Puerto Rico. LC 78-64775. 57p. 1980. 4.95 (ISBN 0-533-04043-4). Vantage.

Norman, Benjamin M. Norman's New Orleans & Environs. Schott, Matthew J., ed. LC 75-21961. (Illus.). 256p. 1976. Repr. 10.00x (ISBN 0-8071-0168-0). La State U Pr.

Register, James. Shadows of Old New Orleans. 1967. 12.50 (ISBN 0-685-08206-7). Claitors.

Reinders, Robert C. End of an Era: New Orleans 1850-1860. 1964. 15.00 (ISBN 0-911116-18-4). Pelican.

Sims, Patsy. New Orleans: The Passing Parade. LC 80-82442. (Illus.). 132p. 1980. 26.50 (ISBN 0-937430-01-3); pap. 14.95 (ISBN 0-937430-00-5). Picayune Pr.

Swanson, Betsy. Historic Jefferson Parish. LC 74-23204. (Illus.). 176p. (Orig.). 1975. 20.95 (ISBN 0-88289-048-4). Pelican.

Toledano, Roulhac B. & Christovich, Mary Louise. New Orleans Architecture, Vol. 6: Faubourg Treme & the Bayou Road. (New Orleans Architecture Ser.). (Illus.). 224p. 1980. 34.95 (ISBN 0-88289-166-9). Pelican.

NEW ORLEANS–HISTORY

Barker, Jacob. Incidents in the Life of Jacob Barker of New Orleans, Louisiana. LC 74-121487. (Select Bibliographies Reprint Ser.). 1972. Repr. of 1855 ed. 18.00 (ISBN 0-8369-5455-6). Arno.

Bezou, Henry C. Metairie: A Tongue of Land to Pasture. new ed. LC 73-17038. (Illus.). 224p. 1973. 17.50 (ISBN 0-88289-012-3). Pelican.

Carter, Hodding, intro. by. Past As Prelude: New Orleans 1718-1968. LC 68-25161. (Illus.). 1968. 10.00 (ISBN 0-911116-02-8). Pelican.

Castellanos, Henry C. New Orleans As It Was. Reinecke, George F., ed. LC 78-13014. (Louisiana Bicentennial Reprint Ser.). 1979. 14.95x (ISBN 0-8071-0457-4). La State U Pr.

Chase, John. Frenchmen, Desire, Good Children & Other Streets of New Orleans. (Illus.). 1949. 9.95 (ISBN 0-685-08692-5). Crager.

Clapp, Theodore. Autobiographical Sketches & Recollections: During a Thirty-Five Years Residence in New Orleans. LC 77-38346. (Select Bibliographies Reprint Ser.). Repr. of 1857 ed. 21.00 (ISBN 0-8369-6763-1). Arno.

Clark, John G. New Orleans, 1718-1812: An Economic History. LC 77-119115. (Illus.). 1970. 27.50 (ISBN 0-8071-0346-2). La State U Pr.

DeGrummond, Jane L. & Morazan, Ronald R. The Baratarians & the Battle of New Orleans with Biographical Sketches of the Veterans of the Battalion of Orleans, 1814-1815. LC 79-65176. (Illus.). 1980. 15.00 (ISBN 0-918784-23-9). Legacy Pub Co.

Hair, William I. Carnival of Fury: Robert Charles & the New Orleans Race Riot of 1900. LC 75-34856. (Illus.). 224p. 1976. 15.00 (ISBN 0-8071-0178-8). La State U Pr.

Haskins, James. Creoles of Color of New Orleans. LC 74-12487. (Illus.). 164p. (gr. 5 up). 1975. 8.95 (ISBN 0-690-00224-6, TYC-J). Har-Row.

Howe, William W. Municipal History of New Orleans. LC 78-63788. (Johns Hopkins University. Studies in the Social Sciences. Seventh Ser. 1889: 4). Repr. of 1889 ed. 11.50 (ISBN 0-404-61053-6). AMS Pr.

King, Grace E. New Orleans: The Place & the People. LC 68-55897. (Illus.). Repr. of 1895 ed. 20.75x (ISBN 0-8371-0512-9, Pub. by Negro U Pr). Greenwood.

Madeull, Charles. New Orleans Marriage Contracts: 1804-1820. 1977. 17.50 (ISBN 0-686-20421-2). Polyanthos.

Maduell, Charles R., Jr. Federal Land Grants in the Territory of New Orleans: The Delta Parishes. 1975. 20.00 (ISBN 0-686-20865-X). Polyanthos.

Martinez, Raymond J. Rousseau: The Last Days of Spanish New Orleans. rev. 2nd ed. 148p. 1975. pap. 3.25 (ISBN 0-911116-87-7). Pelican.

Niehaus, Earl F. Irish in New Orleans, Eighteen Hundred to Eighteen Sixty. LC 76-6359. (Irish Americans Ser). 1976. Repr. of 1965 ed. 15.00 (ISBN 0-405-09352-7). Arno.

Reinders, Robert C. End of an Era: New Orleans 1850-1860. 1964. 15.00 (ISBN 0-911116-18-4). Pelican.

Rose, Al. Storyville, New Orleans: Being an Authentic Illustrated Account of the Notorious Redlight District. LC 74-491. (Illus.). 256p. 1974. pap. 11.95 (ISBN 0-8173-4404-7). U of Ala Pr.

Siegel, M. New Orleans: A Chronological & Documentary History. LC 75-4578. 1975. 8.50 (ISBN 0-379-00601-4). Oceana.

Tassin, Myron, ed. The Last Line: A Streetcar Named St. Charles. LC 79-21438. (Illus.). 97p. (Orig.). 1980. pap. 8.95 (ISBN 0-88289-250-9). Pelican.

Toledano, Roulhac, et al. New Orleans Architecture, Vol. 4: Creole Faubourgs. LC 74-16744. (New Orleans Architecture Ser.). (Illus.). 192p. 1974. 21.95 (ISBN 0-88289-037-9). Pelican.

United States House Of Representatives - 39th 2nd Session - Select Committee On New Orleans Riots. Report of Select Committee on New Orleans Riots. (Basic Afro-American Reprint Library). Repr. of 1867 ed. 31.00 (ISBN 0-384-62885-0). Johnson Repr.

United States 39th Congress, 2nd Session, 1866-1867, House. Report of the Select Committee on the New Orleans Riots: House Report No. 16. facsimile ed. LC 75-170706. (Black Heritage Library Collection). Repr. of 1867 ed. 30.75 (ISBN 0-8369-8896-5). Arno.

U.S. House of Representatives. New Orleans Riots of July Thirtieth, Eighteen Sixty-Six: 39th Congress, Second Session, House Report No. 16. LC 79-90200. (Mass Violence in America Ser). Repr. of 1867 ed. 21.00 (ISBN 0-405-01317-5). Arno.

NEW ORLEANS–HISTORY–POETRY

Boudreau, Amy. Mighty Mississippi. 1967. pap. 2.00 (ISBN 0-685-08193-1). Claitors.

NEW ORLEANS–POLITICS AND GOVERNMENT

Haas, Edward F. DeLesseps S. Morrison & the Image of Reform: New Orleans Politics, 1946-1961. LC 73-90867. (Illus.). 432p. 1974. 25.00x (ISBN 0-8071-0073-0). La State U Pr.

Howard, L. V. & Friedman, R. S. Government in Metropolitan New Orleans, Vol. 6. 1959. 5.00 (ISBN 0-930598-05-9). Tulane Stud Pol.

Howe, W. W. Municipal History of New Orleans. 1973. Repr. of 1889 ed. pap. 7.00 (ISBN 0-384-24440-8). Johnson Repr.

Howe, William W. Municipal History of New Orleans. LC 78-63788. (Johns Hopkins University. Studies in the Social Sciences. Seventh Ser. 1889: 4). Repr. of 1889 ed. 11.50 (ISBN 0-404-61053-6). AMS Pr.

Kemp, John R., ed. Martin Behrman of New Orleans: Memoirs of a City Boss. LC 77-6781. 1977. 20.00x (ISBN 0-8071-0275-X). La State U Pr.

Reisman, L., et al. The New Orleans Voter: A Handbook of Political Description, Vol. 2. Bd. with Republicanism in New Orleans. Vines, K. N. 1955. 5.00 (ISBN 0-930598-01-6). Tulane Stud Pol.

Reynolds, George M. Machine Politics in New Orleans, 1897-1926. LC 68-58617. (Columbia University. Studies in the Social Sciences: No. 421). Repr. of 1936 ed. 20.00 (ISBN 0-404-51421-9). AMS Pr.

NEW ORLEANS–SOCIAL CONDITIONS

Nau, John F. The German People of New Orleans: 1850-1900. 1975. pap. 4.95 (ISBN 0-88289-100-6). Pelican.

Ross, Elmer L. Factors in Residence Patterns Among Latin Americans in New Orleans, Louisiana. Cortes, Carlos E., ed. LC 79-6223. (Hispanics in the United States Ser.). (Illus.). 1981. lib. bdg. 23.00x (ISBN 0-405-13170-4). Arno.

NEW ORLEANS–SOCIAL LIFE AND CUSTOMS

Martinez, Raymond J. & Holmes, Jack D. L. New Orleans: Facts & Legends. pap. 3.50 (ISBN 0-911116-86-9). Pelican.

Ripley, Eliza. Social Life in Old New Orleans: Being Recollections of My Girlhood. facsimile ed. LC 75-1867. (Leisure Class in America Ser.). (Illus.). 1975. Repr. of 1912 ed. 22.00x (ISBN 0-405-06933-2). Arno.

Young, Perry. The Mistick Kreeve: Mardi Gras in N. Orl. 1969. 25.00 (ISBN 0-685-42979-2). Claitors.

NEW ORLEANS, BATTLE OF, 1815

Baumbach, Richard O., Jr. & Borah, William E. The Second Battle of New Orleans: A History of the Vieux Carre Riverfront Expressway Controversy. (Illus.). 1981. 27.50x (ISBN 0-8173-4840-9); pap. 12.95 (ISBN 0-8173-4841-7). U of Ala Pr.

Landry, Stuart O. Sidelights on the Battle of New Orleans. 1965. pap. 3.95 (ISBN 0-911116-14-1). Pelican.

Owsley, Frank L., Jr. The Struggle for the Gulf Borderlands: The Creek War & the Battle of New Orleans, Eighteen Twelve to Eighteen Fifteen. LC 80-11109. (Illus.). vii, 255p. 1981. 20.00 (ISBN 0-8130-0662-7). U Presses Fla.

Roosevelt, T. Naval War of Eighteen Twelve. LC 68-24994. (American History & Americana Ser., No. 47). 1969. Repr. of 1882 ed. lib. bdg. 43.95 (ISBN 0-8383-0235-1). Haskell.

Roosevelt, Theodore. Naval War of 1812 or the History of the United States Navy During the Last War with Great Britain to Which Is Appended an Account of the Battle of New Orleans. LC 74-108533. (Illus.). 1971. Repr. of 1882 ed. 32.00 (ISBN 0-403-00312-1). Scholarly.

NEW PRODUCTS

see also Design, Industrial

American Management Association. New Products - New Profits. Marting, Elizabeth, ed. LC 64-12772. (Illus.). 1964. 12.95 (ISBN 0-8144-5088-1). Am Mgmt.

Bacon, Frank R., Jr. & Butler, Thomas W., Jr. Planned Innovation: A Dynamic Approach for Selecting, Evaluating, & Guiding Successful Development of New Products. (Illus.). 89p. 1980. 12.00 (ISBN 0-686-72887-4, PLAN I). Indus Dev Inst Sci.

Balachandran, Sarojini, ed. New Product Planning. LC 79-24046. (Management Information Guide Ser.: No. 38). 1980. 36.00 (ISBN 0-8103-0838-X). Gale.

Berridge, A. E. Product Innovation & Development. 236p. 1977. text ed. 24.50x (ISBN 0-220-66325-4, Pub. by Busn Bks England). Renouf.

Biggadike, E. Ralph. Corporate Diversification: Entry, Strategy, & Performance. (Harvard Business School Publications, Division of Research Ser.). (Illus.). 1979. 16.00x (ISBN 0-87584-118-X). Harvard U Pr.

Borden, Neil H., Jr. Acceptance of New Food Products by Supermarkets. LC 68-15544. 248p. 1969. pap. 3.00 (ISBN 0-87005-000-1). Fairchild.

Buck, C. H. Problems of Product Design & Development. 1963. 13.75 (ISBN 0-08-009794-4); pap. 6.25 (ISBN 0-08-009793-6). Pergamon.

Buggie, Frederick D. New Product Development Strategies. 192p. 1981. 16.95 (ISBN 0-8144-5626-X). Am Mgmt.

Davis, Harry L. & Silk, Alvin J. Behavioral & Management Science in Marketing. LC 77-18878. 1978. 32.95 (ISBN 0-471-07179-X). Ronald Pr.

Desrosier, Norman W. & Desrosier, John N. Economics of New Food Product Development. (Illus.). 1971. 28.50 (ISBN 0-87055-102-7). AVI.

Douglas, A. G., et al. Systematic New Product Development. LC 78-2398. 1978. 27.95 (ISBN 0-470-26328-8). Halsted Pr.

Hanan, Mack. Life-Styled Marketing: How to Position New or Established Products for Premium Profits. rev. ed. (Illus.). 1980. 17.95 (ISBN 0-8144-5567-0). Am Mgmt.

Hise, Richard T. Product Service Strategy. (Priorities in Marketing Ser). 1977. text ed. 16.50x (ISBN 0-442-80348-6); pap. text ed. 9.00x (ISBN 0-442-80337-0). Van Nos Reinhold.
Holt, Knut. Product Innovation-Models & Methods: A Workbook for Management in Industry. new ed. 1978. 14.95 (ISBN 0-408-00288-3). Butterworth.
Hopkins, David S. Options in New-Product Organization. (Report Ser: No. 613). 55p. (Orig.). 1974. pap. 15.00 (ISBN 0-8237-0041-0). Conference Bd.
Ironmonger, D. S. New Commodities & Consumer Behaviour. new ed. LC 75-163056. (Department of Applied Economics Monographs: No. 20). (Illus.). 1972. 36.00 (ISBN 0-521-08337-0). Cambridge U Pr.
Karger, Delmar & Murdick, Robert. New Product Venture Management. 288p. 1972. 41.25x (ISBN 0-677-03960-3). Gordon.
Kracke, Don & Honkanen, Roger. How to Turn Your Idea into a Million Dollars. LC 76-23775. 1977. 7.95 (ISBN 0-385-11608-X). Doubleday.
Kraushar, P. New Products & Diversifications-New Edition. 1977. 21.00x (ISBN 0-8464-0672-1). Beekman Pubs.
Leduc, Robert. How to Launch a New Product. 130p. 1966. 14.95x (ISBN 0-8464-1107-5). Beekman Pubs.
Leontiades, Milton. Strategies for Diversification & Change. (Little, Brown Ser. in Strategy & Policy). (Illus.). 199p. 1980. pap. text ed. 7.95 (ISBN 0-316-52103-5). Little.
Lorsch, Jay W. Product Innovation & Organization. LC 65-28374. 200p. 1965. 7.50 (ISBN 0-913456-25-X). Interbk Inc.
McGuire, E. Patrick. Spin-off Products & Services: The Commercialization of Internally Supported Resources. (Report Ser.: No. 695). 1976. pap. 30.00 (ISBN 0-8237-0129-8). Conference Bd.
McGuire, Patrick E. Evaluating New-Product Proposals. (Report Ser: No. 604). 108p. (Orig.). 1973. pap. 22.50 (ISBN 0-8237-0017-8). Conference Bd.
--Evaluating New-Product Proposals. (Report Ser: No. 604). 108p. (Orig.). 1973. pap. 22.50 (ISBN 0-8237-0017-8). Conference Bd.
New Product-New Business Digest. 66p. 1980. 50.00 (ISBN 0-686-62469-6). B Klein Pubns.
Null, Gary & Simonson, Richard. How to Turn Your Ideas into Dollars. LC 71-85821. (Orig.). 1976. pap. 2.50 (ISBN 0-87576-023-6). Pilot Bks.
Nye, B. C. & Dorr, E. L. Product Planning. (Occupational Manuals & Projects in Marketing). 1970. text ed. 5.96 (ISBN 0-07-047561-X, G); tchr's manual o.p. 3.50 (ISBN 0-07-047593-8). McGraw.
Pessemier, Edgar A. New Product Decisions. 1966. pap. text ed. 7.95 (ISBN 0-07-049517-3, C). McGraw.
Peters, Michael P. & Hisrich, Robert D. Marketing a New Product: Its Planning, Development & Control. LC 77-84070. 1978. 17.95 (ISBN 0-8053-4102-1). Benjamin-Cummings.
Ramsey, Jackson E. Research & Development: Project Selection Criteria. LC 78-27294. (Research for Business Decisions: No. 1). 1978. 24.95 (ISBN 0-8357-0966-3). Univ Microfilms.
Rothberg, Robert R. & Mellott, Douglas W., Jr., eds. New Product Planning: Management of the Markting-R&D Interface-an Annotated Bibliography. LC 76-57928. (AMA Bibliography Ser.: No. 26). 1977. pap. text ed. 5.50 (ISBN 0-87757-091-4). Am Mktg.
Schoenfeld, Gerald. Schoenfeld's New Product Success Book. 150p. 1981. 50.00 (ISBN 0-932648-10-X). Boardroom.
Slocum, D. H. New Venture Methodology. 1972. 12.75 (ISBN 0-8144-5297-3, 49571). Am Mgmt.
Thorpe & Middendorf. Product Liability. (What Every Engineer Should Know About Ser.: Vol. 2). 1979. 12.75 (ISBN 0-8247-6876-0). Dekker.
Urban, Glen & Hauser, John R. Design & Marketing of New Products. (Illus.). 1980. 28.00 (ISBN 0-13-201269-3); text ed. 25.00 (ISBN 0-686-66020-X). P-H.

NEW SALEM, ILLINOIS

Horgan, Paul. Citizen of New Salem. LC 61-9893. (Illus.). 332p. (gr. 7 up). 1962. 3.75 (ISBN 0-374-31320-2). FS&G.

NEW SHAKESPEARE SOCIETY, LONDON

Swinburne, Algernon C. Study of Shakespeare. LC 9-30432. Repr. of 1880 ed. 10.00 (ISBN 0-404-06315-2). AMS Pr.

NEW SOUTH WALES

Caley, George. Reflections on the Colony of New South Wales. Currey, J. E., ed. 10.00x (ISBN 0-8426-1188-6). Verry.
Coley. Reflections of the Colony of New South Wales. 14.50x (ISBN 0-392-04392-0, ABC). Sportshelf.
Halliday, James. Wines & Wineries of New South Wales. 165p. 1981. text ed. 10.95x (ISBN 0-7022-1570-8). U of Queensland Pr.
Hayden, Albert A. New South Wales Immigration Policy, 1856-1900. LC 75-153382. (Transactions Ser.: Vol. 61, Pt. 5). 1971. pap. 2.25 (ISBN 0-87169-615-0). Am Philos.
Jeans, D. N. & Spearritt, Peter. The Open Air Museum: The Cultural Landscape of New South Wales. (Illus.). 154p. 1981. 25.00 (ISBN 0-86861-066-6). Allen Unwin.
Mitchell, Thomas L. Journal of an Expedition into the Interior of Tropical Australia, in Search of Route from Sydney to the Gulf of Carpentaria. LC 68-55204. (Illus.). 1968. Repr. of 1848 ed. lib. bdg. 18.75x (ISBN 0-8371-1319-9, MITA). Greenwood.
Thomas, Gilbert. Voyage from New South Wales to Canton in the Year Seventeen Eighty-Eight. (Illus.). 85p. 1968. Repr. of 1789 ed. 25.00 (ISBN 0-8398-0659-0). Parnassus Imprints.

NEW SOUTH WALES–HISTORY

Larcombe, F. A. The Advancement of Local Government in New South Wales, 1906 to the Present. (History of Local Government in New South Wales Ser., 1931 to the Present: Vol. 3). 1978. 35.00x (ISBN 0-424-00037-7, Pub. by Sydney U Pr). Intl Schol Bk Serv.
--Stabilization of Local Government in New South Wales, 1858-1906. (History of Local Government in New South Wales Ser.: Vol. 2). 352p. 1975. 25.00x (ISBN 0-424-00001-6, Pub. by Sydney U Pr). Intl Schol Bk Serv.
O'Kane, Frances. A Path Is Set. (Illus.). 200p. 1976. 20.50x (ISBN 0-522-84087-6, Pub. by Melbourne U Pr). Intl Schol Bk Serv.
Phillips, Marion. A Colonial Autocracy: New South Wales Under Governor Macquarie, 1810-1821. 336p. 1971. Repr. of 1909 ed. 15.00x (ISBN 0-424-06300-X, Pub. by Sydney U Pr). Intl Schol Bk Serv.
--Colonial Autocracy: New South Wales Under Governor Macquarie, 1810-1821. 336p. 1971. Repr. of 1906 ed. 25.00x (ISBN 0-7146-2658-9, F Cass Co). Biblio Dist.
Tapp, E. J. Early New Zealand. (Illus.). 1958. 14.00x (ISBN 0-522-83878-2, Pub. by Melbourne U Pr). Intl Schol Bk Serv.
Walker, R. B. The Newspaper Press in New South Wales 1803-1920. (Illus.). 1976. 15.00x (ISBN 0-424-00023-7, Pub. by Sydney U Pr). Intl Schol Bk Serv.
Wallace, Judith. Memories of a Country Childhood. (Illus.). 1978. 12.95x (ISBN 0-7022-1067-6); pap. 7.75 (ISBN 0-7022-1626-7). U of Queensland Pr.

NEW SOUTH WALES–POLITICS AND GOVERNMENT

Loveday, Peter. Parliament, Factions & Parties. 1966. 16.00x (ISBN 0-522-83659-3, Pub. by Melbourne U Pr). Intl Schol Bk Serv.
Parker, R. S. Government of New South Wales. (Governments of the Australian States & Territories Ser.). (Illus.). 1979. 30.00x (ISBN 0-7022-1139-7); pap. 19.95x (ISBN 0-7022-1145-1). U of Queensland Pr.
Parkes, Henry. Fifty Years in the Making of Australian History, 2 vols. facsimile ed. LC 74-150195. (Select Bibliographies Reprint Ser). Repr. of 1892 ed. Set. 45.00 (ISBN 0-8369-5708-3). Arno.
Power, J. Politics in a Suburban Community: Manly. 1968. 8.00x (ISBN 0-424-05710-7, Pub by Sydney U Pr). Intl Schol Bk Serv.

NEW SOUTH WALES–RELIGION

Macintosh, Neil K. Richard Johnson: Chaplain to the Colony of New South Wales. 150p. 1981. 15.95 (ISBN 0-908120-16-8, Pub by Lib Australian Hist). Bks Australia.
Phillips, Walter. Defending "A Christian Country". Churchmen & Society in New South Wales in the 1880's & After. (Illus.). 332p. 1981. text ed. 36.25 (ISBN 0-7022-1539-2). U of Queensland Pr.
Waldersee, James. Catholic Society in New South Wales 1788-1860. (Illus.). 348p. 1974. 22.50x (ISBN 0-424-06460-X, Pub. by Sydney U Pr). Intl Schol Bk Serv.

NEW STATES

see States, New

NEW STONE AGE

see Neolithic Period

NEW SUPER-REALISM

see Pop Art

NEW SWEDEN–HISTORY

Acrelius, Israel. History of New Sweden; or the Settlements on the River Delaware. LC 70-141080. (Research Library of Colonial Americana). (Illus.). 1971. Repr. of 1874 ed. 30.00 (ISBN 0-405-03271-4). Arno.
Du Ponceau, Peter S. Campanius Holm, Tomas: Description of the Province of New Sweden. LC 1-1320. Repr. of 1834 ed. 13.00 (ISBN 0-527-03241-7). Kraus Repr.
Johnson, Amandus. Instruction for Johan Printz: Governor of New Sweden. LC 79-83486. (Keystone State Historical Publications Ser: No. 5). (Illus.). 1969. Repr. of 1930 ed. 15.00 (ISBN 0-87198-505-5). Friedman.
--Swedish Settlements on the Delaware: Their History & Relation to the Indians, Dutch & English, 1638-1664, 2 vols. LC 69-17934. (Research & Source Works: No. 427). (Illus.). 1970. Repr. of 1911 ed. Set. text ed. 43.00 (ISBN 0-8337-1858-4). B Franklin.
--Swedish Settlements on the Delaware 1638-1664, 2 Vols. LC 76-80644. (Illus.). 1969. Repr. of 1911 ed. Set. 40.00 (ISBN 0-8063-0194-5). Genealog Pub.
Myers, Albert C., ed. Narratives of Early Pennsylvania, West New Jersey & Delaware, 1630-1707. (Original Narratives). 1967. Repr. of 1912 ed. 18.50x (ISBN 0-06-480612-X). B&N.
Proud, Robert. The History of Pennsylvania, 2 Vols. LC 66-25101. 1967. Repr. of 1797 ed. 20.00 ea. Vol. 1 (ISBN 0-87152-031-1). Vol. 2 (ISBN 0-87152-032-X). Set. 40.00 (ISBN 0-87152-305-1). Reprint.
Wuorinen, John H. Finns on the Delaware 1638-1655. LC 38-14748. Repr. of 1938 ed. 17.50 (ISBN 0-404-07057-4). AMS Pr.

NEW SWEDEN–HISTORY–FICTION

Paulding, James K. Koningsmarke: Or Old Times in, 2 Vols. Set. 16.00 (ISBN 0-403-00336-9). Scholarly.

NEW TESTAMENT GREEK

see Greek Language, Biblical

NEW THOUGHT

see also Jesus Christ–New Thought Interpretations; Psychology, Applied

Addington, Jack & Addington, Cornelia. The Perfect Power Within You. new ed. LC 73-87712. 167p. 1973. pap. 3.95 (ISBN 0-87516-179-0). De Vorss.
Addington, Jack E. Psychogenesis: Everything Begins in the Mind. LC 79-145391. 1971. 8.95 (ISBN 0-396-06334-9). Dodd.
Allen, James. As a Man Thinketh. pap. 0.50 (ISBN 0-87516-000-X). De Vorss.
--As a Man Thinketh. 1959. 2.95 (ISBN 0-448-01631-1). G&D.
--As a Man Thinketh. (Inspirational Classics Ser.). 4.95 (ISBN 0-8007-1142-4). Revell.
--As a Man Thinketh. blue leatheroid 1.95 (ISBN 0-529-05675-5, D6); leatheroid 2.95, slipcased (ISBN 0-529-05677-1, F12). Collins Pubs.
Andersen, Uell S. Magic in Your Mind. pap. 4.00 (ISBN 0-87980-089-5). Wilshire.
--Secret of Secrets. pap. 4.00 (ISBN 0-87980-134-4). Wilshire.
Barker, Raymond C. The Science of Successful Living. LC 57-11392. 1957. 4.95 (ISBN 0-396-03987-1). Dodd.
Behrend, Genevieve. Your Invisible Power. 1921. pap. 2.00 (ISBN 0-87516-004-2). De Vorss.
Berger, Hilbert J. Time to Negotiate. 1973. pap. 2.95 (ISBN 0-377-43001-3). Friend Pr.
Bristol, C. & Sherman, H. TNT: The Power Within You. 1954. 6.95 (ISBN 0-13-922682-6); pap. 2.95 (ISBN 0-13-922674-5). P-H.
Curtis, Donald. Live It Up. LC 76-47419. 1977. pap. 2.00 (ISBN 0-87707-187-X). CSA Pr.
--Your Thoughts Can Change Your Life. pap. 3.00 (ISBN 0-87980-179-4). Wilshire.
Fox, Emmet. Alter Your Life. 1950. 7.95 (ISBN 0-06-062850-2, HarpR). Har-Row.
--Around the Year with Emmet Fox. LC 58-13248. 1958. 8.95 (ISBN 0-06-062870-7, HarpR). Har-Row.
--Find & Use Your Inner Power. 1941. 7.95 (ISBN 0-06-062890-1, HarpR). Har-Row.
--Make Your Life Worthwhile. 1946. 7.95 (ISBN 0-06-062910-X, HarpR). Har-Row.
--Power Through Constructive Thinking. 1940. 7.95 (ISBN 0-06-062930-4, HarpR). Har-Row.
--Stake Your Claim. LC 52-11683. 1952. 7.95 (ISBN 0-06-062970-3, HarpR). Har-Row.
--Ten Commandments. LC 53-8369. 1953. 7.95 (ISBN 0-06-062990-8, HarpR). Har-Row.
Goldsmith, Joel. Beyond Words & Thoughts. 6.00 (ISBN 0-8216-0041-9). Univ Bks.
--Conscious Union with God. 6.00 (ISBN 0-8216-0050-8). Univ Bks.
--Master Speaks. 6.00 (ISBN 0-8216-0049-4). Univ Bks.
Goldsmith, Joel S. Art of Meditation. LC 56-13258. 1957. 7.95 (ISBN 0-06-063150-3, HarpR). Har-Row.
--Art of Spiritual Healing. LC 59-14532. 1959. 7.95 (ISBN 0-06-063170-8, HarpR). Har-Row.
--The Contemplative Life. 212p. 1976. pap. 4.95 (ISBN 0-8065-0523-0). Citadel Pr.
--Living the Infinite Way. rev. ed. LC 61-9646. 1961. 7.95 (ISBN 0-06-063190-2, HarpR). Har-Row.
--Mystical I. Sinkler, Lorraine, ed. LC 73-149745. 1971. 7.95 (ISBN 0-06-063195-3, HarpR). Har-Row.
--Parenthesis in Eternity. LC 64-10368. 1963. 9.95 (ISBN 0-06-063230-5, HarpR). Har-Row.
--Thunder of Silence. LC 61-7340. 1961. 7.95 (ISBN 0-06-063270-4, HarpR). Har-Row.
--The World Is New. LC 62-7953. 1978. 8.95 (ISBN 0-06-063291-7, HarpR). Har-Row.
Holmes, Ernest. The Basic Ideas of Science of Mind. 1957. pap. 3.50 (ISBN 0-911336-23-0). Sci of Mind.
--Creative Ideas. 1964. pap. 3.50 (ISBN 0-911336-00-1). Sci of Mind.
--Creative Mind & Success. 1947. 4.95 (ISBN 0-396-02070-4). Dodd.
--Discover a Richer Life. 1961. pap. 3.50 (ISBN 0-911336-27-3). Sci of Mind.
--Effective Prayer. 1966. pap. 2.50 (ISBN 0-911336-02-8). Sci of Mind.
--Freedom from Stress. 1964. pap. 3.50 (ISBN 0-911336-30-3). Sci of Mind.
--Freedom to Live. 1969. pap. 3.50 (ISBN 0-911336-35-4). Sci of Mind.
--How to Use the Science of Mind. 1950. 4.95 (ISBN 0-396-03212-5). Dodd.
--It Can Happen to You. Kinnear, Willis, ed. 1959. pap. 3.50 (ISBN 0-911336-25-7). Sci of Mind.
--Journey into Life. 1967. pap. 4.50 (ISBN 0-911336-05-2). Sci of Mind.
--Keys to Wisdom. 1965. pap. 4.50 (ISBN 0-911336-06-0). Sci of Mind.
--Living Without Fear. 1962. pap. 3.50 (ISBN 0-911336-28-1). Sci of Mind.
--Observations. 1968. pap. 4.50 (ISBN 0-911336-12-5). Sci of Mind.
--The Power of an Idea. 1965. pap. 3.50 (ISBN 0-911336-31-1). Sci of Mind.
--Science of Mind. rev. & enl. ed. 12.50 (ISBN 0-396-02069-0). Dodd.
--Ten Ideas That Make a Difference. 1966. pap. 3.50 (ISBN 0-911336-32-X). Sci of Mind.
--Think Your Troubles Away. 1963. pap. 3.50 (ISBN 0-911336-29-X). Sci of Mind.
--This Thing Called Life. 1947. 4.95 (ISBN 0-396-02851-9). Dodd.
--Words That Heal Today. 1948. 6.95 (ISBN 0-396-03093-9). Dodd.
Holmes, Ernest & Hornaday, William H. Help for Today. 1969. pap. 6.50 (ISBN 0-911336-04-4). Sci of Mind.
Holmes, Ernest & Kinnear, Willis. Know Yourself. (Orig.). 1970. pap. 3.50 (ISBN 0-911336-36-2). Sci of Mind.
--The Magic of the Mind. 1960. pap. 3.50 (ISBN 0-911336-26-5). Sci of Mind.
--A New Design for Living. 1959. pap. 5.95 (ISBN 0-911336-11-7). Sci of Mind.
--Practical Application of Science of Mind. 1958. pap. 3.50 (ISBN 0-911336-24-9). Sci of Mind.
--Thoughts Are Things. 1967. pap. 3.50 (ISBN 0-911336-33-8). Sci of Mind.
Holmes, Ernest & Kinnear, Willis H. The Larger Life. 1969. pap. 4.50 (ISBN 0-911336-07-9). Sci of Mind.
Hornaday, William H. & Ware, Harlan. Your Aladdin's Lamp. 1978. pap. 7.95 (ISBN 0-911336-75-3). Sci of Mind.
Kinnear, Willis. Thirty Day Mental Diet. 1965. pap. 4.95 (ISBN 0-911336-20-6). Sci of Mind.
Lighton, Merle. Addict to Yearning: Inspirational Philosophy & Religion. 1952. 5.00 (ISBN 0-910892-00-8, 910892). Lighton Pubns.
Mary. You Are God. 1955. pap. 3.50 (ISBN 0-87516-057-3). De Vorss.
Murphy, Joseph. Amazing Laws of Cosmic Mind Power. 1965. pap. 3.95 (ISBN 0-13-023804-X, Reward). P-H.
--Infinite Power for Richer Living. 1969. 8.95 (ISBN 0-13-464396-8, Reward); pap. 3.95 (ISBN 0-685-93566-3). P-H.
--Living Without Strain. 157p. 1973. pap. 3.50 (ISBN 0-87516-187-1). De Vorss.
--Pray Your Way Through It. 171p. 1973. pap. 3.00 (ISBN 0-87516-190-1). De Vorss.
--Prayer Is the Answer. 190p. 1973. pap. 3.00 (ISBN 0-87516-189-8). De Vorss.
Nimick, John A. Be Still & Know. LC 67-11989. 1967. 3.00 (ISBN 0-8022-1222-0). Philos Lib.
Parker, Gail T. Mind Cure in New England: From the Civil War to World War I. LC 72-92704. 209p. 1973. text ed. 12.50x (ISBN 0-87451-073-2). U Pr of New Eng.
Ross, Rainbow. Apples of Gold. 1978. pap. 1.75 (ISBN 0-911336-71-0). Sci of Mind.
Sewell, Dolly. My Life Blossoms Like a Flower. 1978. pap. 1.75 (ISBN 0-911336-73-7). Sci of Mind.
Skarin, Annalee. Secrets of Eternity. 1960. pap. 4.95 (ISBN 0-87516-092-1). De Vorss.
--Temple of God. pap. 4.95 (ISBN 0-87516-093-X). De Vorss.
--To God the Glory. pap. 4.95 (ISBN 0-87516-094-8). De Vorss.
--Ye Are Gods. 343p. 1973. pap. 3.00 (ISBN 0-87516-344-0). De Vorss.
Trine, Ralph W. In Tune with the Infinite. LC 72-125594. 1970. pap. 4.95 (ISBN 0-672-51349-8). Bobbs.
--In Tune with the Infinite. (Pivot Family Reader Ser). 176p. 1973. pap. 1.25 (ISBN 0-87983-052-2). Keats.
Troward, Thomas. Creative Process in the Individual. rev. ed. 5.95 (ISBN 0-396-02064-X). Dodd.
--Dore Lectures on Mental Science. 1909. 4.95 (ISBN 0-396-02063-1). Dodd.
--Edinburgh Lectures on Mental Science. 1909. 5.50 (ISBN 0-396-02062-3). Dodd.
Werber, Eva B. Journey with the Master. 1950. pap. 1.75 (ISBN 0-87516-103-0). De Vorss.

--Quiet Talks with the Master. 1936. pap. 1.75 (ISBN 0-87516-104-9). De Vorss.
Wolhorn, Herman. Emmet Fox's Golden Keys to Successful Living. LC 76-62930. 1977. 7.95 (ISBN 0-06-069670-2, HarpR). Har-Row.

NEW TRIBES MISSION, CHICAGO

Jank, Margaret. Culture Shock. 1977. pap. 3.95 (ISBN 0-8024-1679-9). Moody.

NEW ULM, MINNESOTA

Iverson, Noel. Germania, U.S.A. Social Change in New Ulm, Minnesota. LC 66-22152. 1966. 7.50x (ISBN 0-8166-0413-4). U of Minn Pr.

NEW WORDS

see Words, New

NEW YEAR

Aliki. New Year's Day. LC 67-10069. (Holiday Ser.). (Illus.). (gr. 1-3). 1967. 7.95 (ISBN 0-690-58182-3, TYC-J). Har-Row.
Banh Chung Banh Day: The New Year's Rice Cakes. (gr. 2-5). 1972. 1.50x (ISBN 0-686-10279-7). SE Asia Res Ctr.
Cheng, Hou-Tien. The Chinese New Year. LC 76-8229. (Illus.). (gr. k-3). 1976. reinforced bdg. 5.50 (ISBN 0-03-017511-9). HR&W.
Groh, Lynn. New Year's Day. LC 64-11363. (Holiday Books Ser). (Illus.). (gr. 2-5). 1964. PLB 6.87 (ISBN 0-8116-6554-2). Garrard.

NEW YEAR, JEWISH

see Rosh ha-Shanah

NEW YORK (CITY)

see also New York Metropolitan Area; also specific sections of New York City, e.g. Greenwich Village, Harlem

Abram, Jaffe, ed. Puerto Rican Population of New York City. LC 74-14328. (The Puerto Rican Experience Ser). 65p. 1975. Repr. of 1954 ed. 7.00x (ISBN 0-405-06226-5). Arno.
Auletta, Ken. The Streets Were Paved with Gold: The Decline of New York--An American Tragedy. LC 79-22305. 1980. pap. 4.95 (ISBN 0-394-74355-5, V-355, Vin). Random.
Berkowitz, Marvin. The Social Costs of Human Underdevelopment: Case Study of Seven New York City Neighborhoods. LC 73-19440. (Special Studies in U.S. Economic, Social & Political Issues). 1974. 28.50x (ISBN 0-275-28821-8). Irvington.
Bowser, Benjamin P., et al, eds. Census Data with Maps for Small Areas of New York City 1910-1960. 1981. write for info. (ISBN 0-89235-028-8). Res Pubns Conn.
Children's Aid Society. New York Street Kids. (Illus.). 9.00 (ISBN 0-8446-5743-3). Peter Smith.
Christian, Charles. Brief Treatise on the Police of the City of New York. LC 76-112548. (Rise of Urban America). 1970. Repr. of 1812 ed. 10.00 (ISBN 0-405-02442-8). Arno.
Clines, Francis X. About New York. LC 80-16080. 288p. 1980. 12.95 (ISBN 0-07-011384-X). McGraw.
Columbia University: Center for Advanced Research in Urban & Environmental Affairs. The New York Federal Archive Building: A Proposal for Mixed Re-Use. (Working Papers Ser.: 1). (Illus.). 1976. pap. 7.95 (ISBN 0-686-20829-3). Pr of Nova Scotia.
Dix, John A. Sketch of the Resources of the City of New York: With a View of Its Municipal Government, Population, Etc. LC 79-112538. (Rise of Urban America). 1970. Repr. of 1827 ed. 12.00 (ISBN 0-405-02447-9). Arno.
Fottler, Myron D. Manpower Substitution in the Hospital Industry: A Study of New York City Voluntary & Municipal Hospital Systems. LC 73-173280. (Special Studies in U.S. Economic, Social & Political Issues). 1972. 32.50x (ISBN 0-275-06150-7). Irvington.
Fried, William & Watson, Edward B. New York in Aerial Views: Eighty-Six Photographs. (Illus.). 176p. (Orig.). 1981. pap. 6.50 (ISBN 0-486-24018-5). Dover.
Gambee, Robert. Manhattan Seascape. (Illus.). 256p. 1975. 15.00 (ISBN 0-8038-5043-3). Hastings.
Gittell, Marilyn, et al. Local Control in Education: Three Demonstration School Districts in New York City. LC 73-185779. (Special Studies in U.S. Economic, Social & Political Issues). 1972. 22.50x (ISBN 0-89197-827-5); pap. text ed. 12.50x (ISBN 0-89197-828-3). Irvington.
Hagevik, George H. Decision-Making in Air Pollution Control. LC 72-112981. (Special Studies in U.S. Economic, Social, & Political Issues). 1970. 28.00x (ISBN 0-89197-723-6); pap. text ed. 12.50x (ISBN 0-89197-724-4). Irvington.
Harris, Arthur S. New York. LC 72-96127. (This Beautiful World Ser.: Vol. 42). (Illus.). 142p. 1973. pap. 4.95 (ISBN 0-87011-197-3). Kodansha.
Johnson, Gus. F.D.N.Y. The Fire Buff's Handbook of the New York Fire Department. (Illus.). 1977. 9.95 (ISBN 0-88279-233-4). Western Islands.
Klein, Alexander, ed. Empire City: A Treasury of New York. facsimile ed. LC 75-152184. (Essay Index Reprint Ser). Repr. of 1955 ed. 24.00 (ISBN 0-8369-2236-0). Arno.
Lopez, Manuel D. New York: A Guide to Information & Reference Sources. LC 80-18634. x, 307p. 1980. 17.50 (ISBN 0-8108-1326-2). Scarecrow.
Mabie, Hamilton W. The Writers of Knickerbocker, New York. LC 13-55. Repr. of 1912 ed. 18.00 (ISBN 0-527-59000-2). Kraus Repr.
Millstein, Gilbert. New York. LC 77-1860. (Illus.). 1977. 18.50 (ISBN 0-8109-1350-X); pap. 10.95 (ISBN 0-8109-2071-9). Abrams.
Morand, Paul. New York. Repr. of 1930 ed. 10.00 (ISBN 0-686-19848-4). Ridgeway Bks.
New York. (International Showcase Ser.). (Illus.). 1979. 24.95 (ISBN 0-8317-6363-9, Mayflower Bks). Smith Pubs.
New York. (Panorama Bks.). (Illus., Fr.). 3.95 (ISBN 0-685-11420-1). French & Eur.
Research Libraries of the New York Public Library. Dictionary Catalog of Materials on New York City. 1977. lib. bdg. 225.00 (ISBN 0-8161-0079-9). G K Hall.
Scher, Steven. Fire. LC 77-27270. (Illus.). 1978. pap. 7.95 (ISBN 0-8109-2151-0). Abrams.
Schwartz, Harry & Abeles, Peter. Planning for the Lower East Side. LC 72-88988. (Special Studies in U. S. Economics, Social & Political Issues). 1973. 24.00x (ISBN 0-275-28805-6). Irvington.
Scully, Sally & Scully, James. Avenue of the Americas. LC 74-164444. 1971. 6.00 (ISBN 0-686-30814-X); pap. 3.50 (ISBN 0-686-30815-8). Ziesing Bros.
Todd, Charles B. In Olde New York. LC 68-18359. (Empire State Historical Publications Ser: No. 49). (Illus.). 1968. Repr. of 1907 ed. 8.50 (ISBN 0-87198-049-5). Friedman.
Trager, Philip. Philip Trager: New York. (Illus.). 120p. 1980. 39.95 (ISBN 0-8195-5051-5). Wesleyan U Pr.
Wright, Carroll D. Slums of Baltimore, Chicago, New York, & Philadelphia: Seventh Special Report of the Commissioner of Labor. LC 71-112587. (Rise of Urban America). 1970. Repr. of 1894 ed. 35.00 (ISBN 0-405-02489-4). Arno.

NEW YORK (CITY)–BELLEVUE HOSPITAL

Karp, Laurence E. The View from the Vue. LC 77-2628. 1977. 8.95 (ISBN 0-8246-0215-3). Jonathan David.

NEW YORK (CITY)–BRIDGES

see also New York and Brooklyn Bridge

NEW YORK (CITY)–BIOGRAPHY

Cappelli, Louis H. Gigi Bread, Gamblers & Friends. LC 79-67322. 195p. 1980. 7.95 (ISBN 0-533-04449-9). Vantage.
Fisher, Jacob. On Vanishing Ground. 318p. (Orig.). 1980. pap. 3.95 (ISBN 0-686-30197-8). Piney Branch.
Fiske, Stephen. Off-Hand Portraits of Prominent New Yorkers. facsimile ed. LC 75-1847. (Leisure Class in America Ser.). 1975. Repr. of 1884 ed. 21.00x (ISBN 0-405-06914-6). Arno.
King, Moses. Notable New Yorkers of 1896-1899. 1976. lib. bdg. 59.95 (ISBN 0-8490-2354-8). Gordon Pr.
Klein, Carole. Aline. LC 76-26239. (Illus.). 1979. 12.95 (ISBN 0-06-012423-7, HarpT). Har-Row.
Letters from John Pintard to His Daughter Eliza Noel Pintard Davison, 1816-1833: Collections 1937-1940, 4 vols. LC 40-30954. 20.00x (ISBN 0-685-73910-4, New York Historical Society). U Pr of Va.
Peebles, Robert W. Leonard Covello: A Study of an Immigrants Contribution to New York City. Cordasco, Francesco, ed. LC 77-90551. (Bilingual-Bicultural Education in U. S. Ser.). 1978. lib. bdg. 28.00x (ISBN 0-405-11090-1). Arno.
Schor, Amy. Line by Line. 256p. 1981. 11.95 (ISBN 0-399-90083-7). Marek.
Scoville, Joseph A. Old Merchants of New York City, 5 Vols. LC 68-28645. 1968. Repr. of 1870 ed. Set. lib. bdg. 105.00x (ISBN 0-8371-0214-6, SCOM). Greenwood.
Stoddard, Lothrop. Master of Manhattan: The Life of Richard Croker. Repr. of 1931 ed. lib. bdg. 20.00 (ISBN 0-8495-5019-X). Arden Lib.
The Wealthy Citizens of New York. LC 73-1992. (Big Business; Economic Power in a Free Society Ser.). Repr. of 1973 ed. 8.00 (ISBN 0-405-05117-4). Arno.

NEW YORK (CITY)–CARNEGIE HALL

see Carnegie Hall, New York

NEW YORK (CITY)–CENTRAL PARK

Cook, Clarence C. A Description of the New York Central Park. LC 70-174831. (Illus.). Repr. of 1869 ed. 18.00 (ISBN 0-405-08377-7, Blom Pubns). Arno.
Kinkead, Eugene. A Concrete Look at Nature: Central Park (& Other) Glimpses. LC 74-77936. (Illus.). 256p. 1974. 7.95 (ISBN 0-8129-0471-0). Times Bks.
Laredo, Victor & Reed, Henry H. Central Park: A Photographic Guide. LC 78-70158. (Illus.). 1979. pap. 5.00 (ISBN 0-486-23750-8). Dover.
Reed, Henry H. Central Park: A History & a Guide. rev. ed. (Illus.). 184p. 1972. pap. 2.50 (ISBN 0-517-50082-5). Crown.
Whitson, Skip, compiled by. New York City One Hundred Years Ago: Central Park. (Sun Historical Ser). (Illus., Orig.). 1976. pap. 3.50 (ISBN 0-89540-019-7, SB019). Sun Pub.

NEW YORK (CITY)–CHARITIES

Directory of Social & Health Agencies of New York City. 1979. 24.00 (ISBN 0-231-04650-2, Pub. by Columbia U Pr). Comm Coun Great NY.
Hosay, Philip M. The Challenge of Urban Poverty: Charity Reformers in New York City, 1835 to 1890. Cordasco, Francesco, ed. LC 80-864. (American Ethnic Groupgs Ser.). 1981. lib. bdg. 28.00x (ISBN 0-405-13427-4). Arno.
Reed, Ruth. The Illegitimate Family in New York City. LC 72-152395. 385p. 1972. Repr. of 1934 ed. 16.25x (ISBN 0-8371-6056-1, Pub. by Negro U Pr). Greenwood.
--The Illegitimate Family in New York City: Its Treatment by Social & Health Agencies. LC 78-169397. (Family in America Ser). 408p. 1972. Repr. of 1934 ed. 17.00 (ISBN 0-405-03874-7). Arno.
Salaries & Related Personnel Practices in Voluntary Social & Health Agencies in New York City. 1974. pap. 5.00 - bulletin 1, 2 & 3 (ISBN 0-86671-018-3). Comm Coun Great NY.

NEW YORK (CITY)–CHURCHES

Bayley, James R. A Brief Sketch of the Early History of the Catholic Church on the Island of New York. LC 77-359171. (Monograph Ser.: No. 29). 1973. Repr. of 1870 ed. 6.50x (ISBN 0-930060-09-1). US Cath Hist.
Bennett, William H. Catholic Footsteps in Old New York: A Chronicle of Catholicity in the City of New York from 1524 to 1808. LC 77-359169. (Monograph Ser.: No. 28). 1973. Repr. of 1909 ed. 8.00x (ISBN 0-930060-08-3). US Cath Hist.
Campbell, Helen. Darkness & Daylight: Or, Lights & Shadows of New York Life: A Pictorial Record of Personal Experiences by Day & Night in the Great Metropolis with Hundreds of Thrilling Anecdotes & Incidents. LC 76-81511. 1969. Repr. of 1895 ed. 28.00 (ISBN 0-8103-3566-2). Gale.
Carthy, Mary P. Old St. Patrick's: New York's First Cathedral. (Monograph Ser.: No. 23). (Illus.). 1947. 6.50x (ISBN 0-930060-05-9). US Cath Hist.
Cook, Lee. St. Patrick's Cathedral. (Illus.). 1979. text ed. 24.95 (ISBN 0-8256-3169-6); pap. 9.95 (ISBN 0-8256-3170-X). Music Sales.
Messiter, Arthur. History of the Choir & Music of Trinity Church. LC 72-137317. Repr. of 1906 ed. 21.45 (ISBN 0-404-04313-5). AMS Pr.
Walking Tour of St. Patrick's Cathedral. (Illus.). 1980. pap. cancelled (ISBN 0-8256-3183-1, Quick Fox). Music Sales.

NEW YORK (CITY)–COMMERCE

De Voe, Thomas F. Market Book, Containing a Historical Account of the Public Markets in the Cities of New York, Boston, Philadelphia & Brooklyn Etc. 1969. Repr. of 1862 ed. 29.00 (ISBN 0-8337-0847-3). B Franklin.
Foner, Philip S. Business & Slavery: The New York Merchants & the Irrepressible Conflict. LC 68-15122. 1968. Repr. of 1941 ed. 13.50 (ISBN 0-8462-1145-9). Russell.
Harrington, Virginia D. The New York Merchant on the Eve of the Revolution. 1964. 7.50 (ISBN 0-8446-1224-3). Peter Smith.

NEW YORK (CITY)–DEPARTMENT OF LICENSES

Carrow, Milton M. Licensing Power in New York City. LC 68-58863. (Illus.). 230p. 1968. pap. 12.50x (ISBN 0-8377-0401-4). Rothman.

NEW YORK (CITY)–DESCRIPTION

Abbott, Berenice. New York in the Thirties. LC 73-77375. Orig. Title: Changing New York. (Illus.). 112p. 1973. Repr. of 1939 ed. 5.00 (ISBN 0-486-22967-X). Dover.
Anderson, Alexandra & Archer, B. J. Anderson & Archer's Soho: The Essential Guide to Art & Life in Lower Manhattan. 1979. pap. 6.95 (ISBN 0-671-24859-6). S&S.
Andrews, W. L. New York As Washington Knew It After the Revolution. 59.95 (ISBN 0-8490-0726-7). Gordon Pr.
Bailey, V. H. Magical City: Intimate Sketches of New York. 1977. lib. bdg. 59.95 (ISBN 0-8490-2196-0). Gordon Pr.
Baral, Robert. Turn West on Twenty-Third. LC 65-24028. (Illus.). 1966. 8.95 (ISBN 0-8303-0055-4). Fleet.
Bayles, W. H. Old Taverns of New York. 1977. lib. bdg. 59.95 (ISBN 0-8490-2373-4). Gordon Pr.
Bergman, Edward F. & Pohl, Thomas W. A Geography of the New York Metropolitan Region. LC 75-20816. (Illus.). 1975. perfect bdg. 5.95 (ISBN 0-8403-1263-6). Kendall Hunt.
Black, Mary. Old New York in Early Photographs: Eighteen Fifty-Three to Nineteen Hundred & One. (Illus.). 200p. (Orig.). 1973. pap. 7.95 (ISBN 0-486-22907-6). Dover.
Brown, Henry C. In the Golden Nineties. facs. ed. LC 71-133516. (Select Bibliographies Reprint Ser). 1927. 29.00 (ISBN 0-8369-5548-X). Arno.
Burgess, Anthony, ed. New York. (The Great Cities Ser.). 1977. 14.95 (ISBN 0-8094-2270-0). Time-Life.
Burnham, Alan, ed. New York Landmarks: A Study & Index of Architecturally Notable Structures in Greater New York. LC 63-17794. (Illus.). 1963. 30.00x (ISBN 0-8195-3040-9, Pub. by Wesleyan U Pr); pap. 12.95 (ISBN 0-8195-6045-6). Columbia U Pr.
Byron, Joseph. New York Interiors at the Turn of the Century. (Illus.). 192p. (Orig.). 1976. pap. 6.00 (ISBN 0-486-23359-6). Dover.
Chester, Carole. New York. 1977. 22.50 (ISBN 0-7134-0183-4, Pub. by Batsford England). David & Charles.
Child, Lydia M. Letters from New York. facs. 3rd ed. LC 79-137726. (American Fiction Reprint Ser). 1845. 17.00 (ISBN 0-8369-7025-X). Arno.
--Letters of Lydia Maria Child. LC 72-82183. (Anti-Slavery Crusade in America Ser). 1969. Repr. of 1883 ed. 12.00 (ISBN 0-405-00622-5). Arno.
Cooper, James F. New York: Being an Introduction to an Unpublished Manuscript by the Author, Entitled The Towns of Manhattan. LC 73-16206. 1930. lib. bdg. 12.50 (ISBN 0-8414-3500-6). Folcroft.
Crockett, Albert S. Peacocks on Parade: A Narrative of a Unique Period in American Social History & Its Most Colorful Figures. facsimile ed. LC 75-1836. (Leisure Class in America Ser.). (Illus.). 1975. Repr. of 1931 ed. 20.00x (ISBN 0-405-06905-7). Arno.
Dadie, Barnard B. Patron de New-York. pap. 6.50 (ISBN 0-685-35940-9). French & Eur.
Delaney, Edmund T., et al. Greenwich Village: A Photographic Guide. LC 74-78593. (Illus.). 128p. (Orig.). 1976. pap. 4.00 (ISBN 0-486-23114-3). Dover.
Feldstein, Mark. Unseen New York. LC 75-2617. (Illus.). 96p. 1975. pap. 4.50 (ISBN 0-486-20166-X). Dover.
--Unseen New York. (Illus.). 7.50 (ISBN 0-8446-5183-4). Peter Smith.
Fried, William & Watson, Edward B. New York in Aerial Views. (Illus.). 12.50 (ISBN 0-8446-5764-6). Peter Smith.
Gayle, Margot & Gillon, Edmund, Jr. Cast-Iron Architecture in New York: A Photographic Survey. (Illus.). 12.50 (ISBN 0-8446-5034-X). Peter Smith.
Gillon, Edmund V. New York Then & Now: 83 Manhattan Sites Photographed in the Past & Present. 8.75 (ISBN 0-8446-5524-4). Peter Smith.
Goldberger, Paul. The City Observed - New York: A Guide to the Architecture of Manhattan. LC 78-21795. (Illus.). 1979. 15.00 (ISBN 0-394-50450-X). Random.
--The City Observed-New York: A Guide to the Architecture of Manhattan. LC 78-21797. (Illus.). 1979. pap. 7.95 (ISBN 0-394-72916-1, Vin). Random.
Halpern, John. New York-New York. 1978. pap. 8.95 (ISBN 0-525-47471-4). Dutton.
Hemp, William H. New York Enclaves. (Illus.). 64p. 1975. 6.95 (ISBN 0-517-51999-2). Potter.
Hollister, Paul. Glass Paperweights of the New York Historical Society. (Illus.). 192p. 1974. 25.00 (ISBN 0-517-51667-5). Potter.
Howe, William F. & Hummel, Abraham H. In Danger, or Life in New York, a True History of a Great Cities Wiles & Temptations. 34.95 (ISBN 0-8490-0389-X). Gordon Pr.
Jenkins, S. The Greatest Street in the World: The Story of Broadway. 1977. lib. bdg. 69.95 (ISBN 0-8490-1905-2). Gordon Pr.
Johnson, Harry & Lightfoot, Frederick S. Maritime New York in Nineteenth-Century Photographs. 15.00 (ISBN 0-8446-5777-8). Peter Smith.
Kertesz, Andre. Of New York. 1976. 22.50 (ISBN 0-394-40511-0). Knopf.
King, Moses, ed. King's Handbook of New York City: 1893, 2 vols. LC 72-87651. (Illus.). 1973. Repr. of 1893 ed. Set. lib. bdg. 35.00 (ISBN 0-405-08704-7, Blom Pubns); lib. bdg. 17.50 ea. Vol. 1 (ISBN 0-405-08705-5). Vol. 2 (ISBN 0-405-08706-3). Arno.
--King's Views of New York 1896-1915. LC 73-76084. (Illus.). 1974. Repr. of 1896 ed. lib. bdg. 35.00 (ISBN 0-405-08710-1). Arno.
Kouwenhoven, John A. Columbia Historical Portrait of New York: An Essay in Graphic History. (Icon Editions). (Illus.). 1972. pap. 15.95 (ISBN 0-06-430030-7, IN-30, HarpT). Har-Row.
--The Columbia Historical Portrait of New York. 1978. Repr. of 1953 ed. lib. bdg. 50.00x (ISBN 0-374-94625-6). Octagon.
Laredo, Victor. New York City: A Photographic Portrait. (Illus.). 188p. 1972. pap. text ed. 5.00 (ISBN 0-486-22852-5). Dover.
--New York City: A Photographic Portrait. 7.50 (ISBN 0-8446-4771-3). Peter Smith.

Lehnartz, Kalus & Talbot, Allan R. New York in the Sixties. (Illus.). 10.00 (ISBN 0-8446-5787-5). Peter Smith.
Marcinik, Roger & Marcinik, Gerda. New York in Your Pocket. (Illus.). 128p. 1981. pap. 1.95 (ISBN 0-8120-2476-1). Barron.
Maurice, Arthur B. New York in Fiction. LC 68-28930. (Empire State Historical Publications Ser: No. 6). (Illus.). 1969. Repr. of 1889 ed. 8.50 (ISBN 0-87198-061-4). Friedman.
Mayer, Grace. Once Upon a City: New York from Eighteen Ninety to Nineteen Ten As Photographed by Byron & Described by Grace M. Mayer. xii, 511p. 1980. Repr. of 1958 ed. lib. bdg. 90.00x (ISBN 0-374-95418-6). Octagon.
Michelin Green Travel Guide: New York City. (Illus., Fr. & Eng.). 1968. 4.95 (ISBN 0-685-11385-X). French & Eur.
Morris, James. Great Port: A Passage Through New York. LC 70-84872. (Helen & Kurt Wolff Bk). (Illus.). 1969. 5.95 (ISBN 0-15-136945-3). HarBraceJ.
Orkin, Ruth. A World Through My Window. LC 78-2153. (Illus.). 1978. 19.95 (ISBN 0-06-013293-0, HarpT). Har-Row.
Ôrth, Rene. New York: The Largest City in the United States. (Q Book: Famous Cities). (Illus.). (gr. 2-6). 1978. 3.95 (ISBN 0-8467-0447-1, Pub. by Two Continents). Hippocrene Bks.
Peebles Press International & Zabronski, Ann. Cheap & Cheaper Restaurant Guide to Manhattan. 192p. 1980. 8.95 (ISBN 0-13-128421-5, Spec); pap. 3.95 (ISBN 0-13-128413-4). P-H.
Pennell, Joseph. Pennell's New York Etchings: Ninety Prints. (Illus.). 12.50 (ISBN 0-686-74164-1). Peter Smith.
Pennell, Joseph & Bryant, Edward. Pennell's New York City Etchings: Ninety-One Prints. (Illus.). 112p. (Orig.). 1981. pap. 6.00 (ISBN 0-486-23913-6). Dover.
Pound, Arthur. The Golden Earth: The Story of Manhattan's Landed Wealth. facsimile ed. LC 75-1865. (Leisure Class in America Ser.). (Illus.). 1975. Repr. of 1935 ed. 21.00x (ISBN 0-405-06931-6). Arno.
Sanders, Ronald & Gillon, Edmund V. The Lower East Side: A Guide to Its Jewish Past with Ninety-Nine New Photographs. (Illus.). 1980. pap. 4.50 (ISBN 0-486-23871-7). Dover.
Sasek, M. This Is New York. abr. ed. (Illus.). 48p. (gr. 3-6). 1973. pap. 0.95 (ISBN 0-02-045160-1, Collier). Macmillan.
Shackleton, R. The Book of New York. 1977. lib. bdg. 59.95 (ISBN 0-8490-1532-4). Gordon Pr.
Shangle, Robert D. & Shngle, Robert D., eds. Beautiful New York City. LC 79-27008. (Illus.). 72p. 1980. 14.95 (ISBN 0-89802-096-4); pap. 7.95 (ISBN 0-89802-095-6). Beautiful Am.
Shopsin, William C. & Broderick, Mosette G. The Villard Houses: Life Story of a Landmark. LC 80-5357. (Illus.). 144p. 1980. 18.95 (ISBN 0-670-74685-1). Viking Pr.
Silver, Nathan. Lost New York. LC 66-11220. (Illus.). 1971. pap. 7.95 (ISBN 0-8052-0328-1). Schocken.
Simpson, Charles R. SoHo: The Artist in the City. LC 80-27083. 352p. 1981. 20.00 (ISBN 0-226-75937-7). U of Chicago Pr.
Sloan, John. New York Etchings Nineteen Hundred & Five to Nineteen Forty-Nine. Sloan, Helen F., ed. (Illus.). 8.75 (ISBN 0-8446-5814-6). Peter Smith.
Spero, James & Gillon, Edmund V., Jr. The Great Sights of New York: A Photographic Guide. LC 79-87807. (Illus.). 1980. pap. 5.00 (ISBN 0-486-23870-9). Dover.
Still, Bayrd. Mirror for Gotham: New York As Seen by Contemporaries from Dutch Days to the Present. LC 80-16246. (Illus.). xix, 417p. 1980. Repr. of 1956 ed. lib. bdg. 35.00x (ISBN 0-313-22439-0, STMG). Greenwood.
Tauranac, John. Essential New York. LC 78-12413. (Illus.). 1979. 14.95 (ISBN 0-03-042621-9); pap. 8.95 (ISBN 0-03-042626-X). HR&W.
Timolat, Lou. November Three-Three Delta: Watch Over New York. LC 74-81422. (Illus.). 128p. 1974. pap. 3.95 (ISBN 0-85699-116-3). Chatham Pr.
Tucker, Kerry. Greetings from New York: A Visit to Manhattan in Postcards. (Illus.). 112p. (Orig.). 1981. pap. 8.95 (ISBN 0-933328-04-4). Delilah Comm.
Tweedy, Bonnie. Champagne Days. 1980. 6.95 (ISBN 0-533-04685-8). Vantage.
Wilson, Earl. Earl Wilson's New York. (Illus.). 1964. pap. 4.95 (ISBN 0-671-20032-1). S&S.
Wolf, Reinhart. New York. (Illus.). 80p. 1981. 50.00 (ISBN 0-86565-010-1). Vendome.

NEW YORK (CITY)–DESCRIPTION–GUIDEBOOKS

Amin & Mayor. Seeing the Real New York. 1981. pap. 7.95 (ISBN 0-8120-2242-4). Barron.
Appleberg, Marilyn, compiled by. The I Love New York Guide. LC 79-15990. (Illus.). 1979. pap. 2.95 (ISBN 0-02-097210-5). Macmillan.
--The I Love New York Guide, 1981. (Illus.). 208p. 1981. pap. 3.95 (ISBN 0-02-097220-2, Collier). Macmillan.
Baker, Stephen. Hammond's Get Around Guide to New York & Vicinity. (Illus.). 96p. 1981. pap. 5.95 (ISBN 0-8437-3376-4). Hammond Inc.
Britchky, Seymour. The Restaurants of New York, Nineteen Eighty to Nineteen Eighty-One. 4th ed. 352p. 1980. 7.95 (ISBN 0-394-73758-X). Random.
Campbell, H. S. Darkness & Daylight: Or, Lights & Shadows of New York Life. 59.95 (ISBN 0-87968-997-8). Gordon Pr.
Canady, John. The New York Times Guide to Dining Out in N.Y. rev. ed. LC 75-13626. 1975. pap. 3.95 (ISBN 0-689-70528-X, 61). Atheneum.
Carlinsky, Dan & Heim, David. Bicycle Tours in & Around New York. LC 75-4036. 1975. pap. 2.95 (ISBN 0-02-938850-3). Hagstrom Co.
Cohen, Marjorie A. The Shopper's Guide to New York for International & U. S. Visitors. Soule, Sandra, ed. (Illus.). 256p. (Orig.). 1981. 10.95 (ISBN 0-9606054-0-1); pap. 6.95 (ISBN 0-9606054-1-X). Two Zees.
--Shopper's Guide to New York: For International & U. S. Visitors. 288p. 1981. pap. 6.95 (ISBN 0-525-20330-3). Dutton.
Ditmas, C. A. Historic Homesteads of Kings County. 59.95 (ISBN 0-8490-0306-7). Gordon Pr.
Eighteen Sixty-Six Guide to New York City. LC 74-26914. (Illus.). 1975. pap. 2.50 (ISBN 0-8052-0474-1). Schocken.
Federal Writers' Project. New York: A City Guide. LC 39-27593. (Illus.). 708p. 1939. Repr. 59.00 (ISBN 0-403-02921-X). Somerset Pub.
--New York City Guide. LC 75-124406. (Illus.). 1970. Repr. lib. bdg. 35.00x (ISBN 0-374-96103-4). Octagon.
--New York Panorama: A Comprehensive View of the Metropolis Presented in a Series of Articles. LC 76-145121. (American Guidebook Ser.). 1981. Repr. of 1941 ed. lib. bdg. 45.00 (ISBN 0-403-02152-9). Somerset Pub.
Fodor's New York, 1981. 1980. pap. 7.95 (ISBN 0-679-00610-9). McKay.
Ford, Clebert & McPherson, Cynthia. A Guide to the Black Apple. (Illus.). 1977. pap. 2.95 (ISBN 0-916800-12-1). L J Martin.
Frank, Gerry. Gerry Frank's Where to Find It, Buy It, Eat It & Save Time & Money in New York. LC 80-7802. (Illus.). 1980. pap. 9.95 (ISBN 0-8323-0356-9). Binford.
Frommer. New York on Ten & Fifteen Dollars a Day. reev. ed. (Frommer Travel Guides). (Illus.). 1976. 3.95 (ISBN 0-671-10851-4). S&S.
Glaser, Milton & Snyder, Jerome. New York Underground Gourmet. rev. ed. LC 73-130473. 1970. pap. 2.95 (ISBN 0-671-20285-5, Fireside). S&S.
--The New York Underground Gourmet. rev. ed. 1977. pap. 3.95 (ISBN 0-671-22443-3, Fireside). S&S.
Gordon, Raoul. The One Hundred Best Restaurants of New York City: A Guide to Good Eating at Good Prices for the Budget-Minded. 1981. lib. bdg. 59.95 (ISBN 0-8490-3219-9). Gordon Pr.
Hunter, Linell P. Eating What Comes Naturally: A Guide to Vegetarian Restaurants in New York City. (Illus.). 130p. (Orig.). 1980. pap. 4.95 (ISBN 0-934700-00-1). Old Mill.
Kadish, Ferne, et al. New York on Five Hundred Dollars a Day. 1977. pap. 4.95 (ISBN 0-02-097740-9, Collier). Macmillan.
--New York on Nine Hundred Dollars a Day: Before Lunch. 288p. 1981. pap. 7.95 (ISBN 0-02-052350-5, Collier). Macmillan.
Michelin Guides & Maps. Michelin Green Guide to New York City. 5th ed. (Green Guide Ser.). (Avail. in fr.). 1979. pap. 7.95 (ISBN 2-06-015510-X). Michelin.
Miller, Stanley, et al. New York's Chinese Restaurants: A Guide. LC 76-53403. 1977. pap. 4.95 (ISBN 0-689-70550-6). Atheneum.
Moldvay, Albert & Fabian, Erika. Photographing New York. (Amphoto Travel Guide Ser.). Orig. Title: Photographer's Guide to New York. (Illus.). 1980. pap. 5.95 (ISBN 0-8174-2123-8). Amphoto.
Murray, Elizabeth M. Trips: New York City & Out-of Town. rev. ed. (Illus.). 112p. 1980. pap. 3.95 (ISBN 0-936426-10-1). Play Schs.
The Nagel Travel Guide to New York City. (Nagel Travel Guide Ser.). (Illus.). 184p. 1973. 23.00 (ISBN 2-8263-0518-2). Hippocrene Bks.
Nagel's Encyclopedia Guide: New York City. (Illus.). 184p. 1973. 23.00 (ISBN 2-8263-0518-2). Masson Pub.
New York Community Trust. Heritage of New York: A Walking Guide. LC 69-13762. 1970. pap. 2.50 (ISBN 0-8232-0826-5). Fordham.
New York in Your Pocket: A Compact Directory of the Big Apple. 128p. Date not set. pap. 1.95 (ISBN 0-686-75967-2). Barron.
New York on Twenty Dollars a Day: 1980-81 Edition. 304p. 1981. pap. 4.95 (ISBN 0-671-25427-8). Frommer-Pasmantier.
New York Panorama: A Comprehensive View of the Metropolis. LC 72-10165. 1938. 59.00 (ISBN 0-403-02152-9). Somerset Pub.
Postal, Bernard & Koppman, Lionel. Jewish Landmarks of New York: A Travel Guide & History. LC 76-27400. (Orig.). 1978. 13.95 (ISBN 0-8303-0153-4). Fleet.
Robert Nicholson Publications. Nicholson's Guide to Historic Britain. 272p. (Orig.). 1981. pap. 7.95 (ISBN 0-684-17280-1, ScribT). Scribner.
Rosebrock, Ellen F. South Street: A Photographic Guide to New York City's Historic Seaport. 8.50 (ISBN 0-8446-5578-3). Peter Smith.
--South Street: A Photographic Guide to New York City's Historic Seaport. 1977. pap. 4.00 (ISBN 0-486-23396-0). Dover.
Ross, Colin & Haight, James T. New York After Dark - San Francisco After Dark. 1977. pap. 1.50 (ISBN 0-532-15241-7). Woodhill.
Seeman, Helene Z. & Siegfried, Alanna. SoHo. LC 78-22225. (Illus.). 1979. pap. 6.95x (ISBN 0-918212-09-X). Neal-Schuman.
Seidman, Lloyd. New York City -- Retirement Village: A Handy Reference of Resources for the Retired & Those Who Will Be Retired. LC 77-3771. 1977. 10.00 (ISBN 0-06-013796-7, HarpT); pap. 4.95 (ISBN 0-06-013793-2, TD-290, HarpT). Har-Row.
Seymour, Tryntje V. Dylan Thomas' New York. LC 78-13286. (Illus.). 1978. pap. 5.95 (ISBN 0-916144-32-1). Stemmer Hse.
Shapiro, Mary J. The Dover New York Walking Guide: From the Battery to Wall Street. (New York Walking Guide Ser.). (Illus.). 64p. 1982. pap. price not set (ISBN 0-486-24225-0). Dover.
--The Dover New York Walking Guide: From Wall Street to Chambers Street. (New York Walking Guide Ser.). (Illus.). 64p. 1982. pap. price not set (ISBN 0-486-24226-9). Dover.
Shepard, Richard F. Going Out in New York: A Guide for the Curious. LC 73-79933. (Illus.). 320p. (Orig.). 1974. pap. 4.50 (ISBN 0-8129-0425-7). Times Bks.
Sheraton, Mimi. Mimi Sherston's the New York Times Restaurant Guide. 352p. 1981. pap. 7.95 (ISBN 0-8129-0930-5). Times Bks.
Simon, Kate. New York Places & Pleasures: An Uncommon Guidebook. rev. 4th ed. LC 70-138761. (Illus.). 1980. pap. 5.95 (ISBN 0-06-090818-1, CN-0818, HarpT). Har-Row.
Ski-Touring Committee of the New York-New Jersey Trail Conference. A Guide to Ski-Touring in New York-New Jersey, 29 Areas. (Illus.). 64p. (Orig.). 1979. pap. 4.95 (ISBN 0-9603966-0-8). NY-NJ Trail Confer.
Spero, James & Gillon, Edmund V., Jr. The Great Sights of New York: A Photographic Guide. 11.50 (ISBN 0-8446-5818-9). Peter Smith.
Stendahl. Best Restaurants of New York. LC 78-9420. (Best Restaurant Ser.). (Illus.). pap. 3.95 (ISBN 0-89286-137-1). One Hund One Prods.
Stern, Ellen. The Best of New York "Best Bets". LC 77-78528. (Illus.). 1977. pap. 3.95 (ISBN 0-8256-3074-6, 030074, Quick Fox). Music Sales.
Stern, Zelda. The Complete Guide to Ethnic New York. 1980. 12.95 (ISBN 0-312-15735-5); pap. 6.95 (ISBN 0-312-15736-3). St Martin.
Ulmann, Albert. Landmark History of New York. LC 70-101023. 1969. Repr. of 1901 ed. 9.00 (ISBN 0-87198-070-3). Friedman.
Visitor's Guide to New York City. 1977. pap. 2.00 (ISBN 0-517-52944-0, 529440). Crown.
Waldo, Myra. Myra Waldo's Restaurant Guide to New York & Vicinity. 4th rev. ed. 1980. 5.95 (ISBN 0-02-098880-X, Collier). Macmillan.
Weil, Susanne & Singer, Barry. Steppin' Out: A Guide to Live Music in Manhattan. LC 79-23812. (Illus.). 160p. 1980. pap. 6.95 (ISBN 0-914788-24-8). East Woods.
Welcome to New York. LC 76-4380. 1976. pap. 1.50 (ISBN 0-02-938880-5). Hagstrom Co.
White, Nancye. Nueva York Alive. (Span.). 1980. pap. 6.95 (ISBN 0-935572-05-8). Alive Pubns.
White, Norval & Willensky, Elliot. AIA Guide to New York City. rev. ed. (Illus.). 1978. 14.95 (ISBN 0-02-626580-X). Macmillan.
White, Norval & Willensky, Elliot, eds. AIA Guide to New York City. rev. ed. 1978. pap. 12.95 (ISBN 0-02-000980-1, Collier). Macmillan.
Wolfe, Gerard R. New York: A Guide to the Metropolis; Walking Tours of Architecture and History. LC 74-21706. 434p. 1975. 22.50x (ISBN 0-8147-9160-3); pap. 8.95 (ISBN 0-8147-9163-8). NYU Pr.
Yeadon, David. Nooks & Crannies: A Walking Tour Guide to New York City. (Illus.). 1979. pap. 8.95 (ISBN 0-684-16084-6, ScribT). Scribner.

NEW YORK (CITY)–DESCRIPTION–POETRY

Garcia Lorca, Federico. Poet in New York. Belitt, Ben, tr. (Span. & Eng., Bilingual ed.). 1955. pap. 4.95 (ISBN 0-394-17205-1, E54, Ever). Grove.
--Poet in New York. Belitt, Ben, tr. (Span., Eng., Span). 8.00 (ISBN 0-8446-2486-1). Peter Smith.

NEW YORK (CITY)–DIRECTORIES

Dahl, A. M. & Joseph, Joan E., eds. Directory of Directors in the City of New York & Surburbs, 1980. rev. ed. 680p. 1980. 115.00 (ISBN 0-936612-01-0). DODC.
Directory of Social & Health Agencies of New York City, 1981 to 1982. 32.50 (ISBN 0-231-05134-4); pap. 24.00 (ISBN 0-231-05135-2). Comm Coun Great NY.
Filsinger, Cheryl. Locus Seventy-Seven Seventy-Eight Update. (Locus Ser.). 1977. pap. 10.00 (ISBN 0-916754-01-4). Filsinger & Co.
Forstmann, Charlotte F., et al. Charlotte, Isabelle, Phyllis & Susan's N.Y., N.Y. A Woman's Guide to Shops, Services & Restaurants. 1977. pap. 6.95 (ISBN 0-394-73333-9). Random.
Germano, William P. & Lecyn, Nancy, eds. Directory of Social & Health Agencies of New York City: 1981-1982. 576p. 1981. 32.50x (ISBN 0-231-05134-4); pap. 24.00x (ISBN 0-231-05135-2). Columbia U Pr.
Jacobs, Jay. New York a la Carte. LC 78-6515. (Illus.). 1978. 14.95 (ISBN 0-07-032151-5, GB). McGraw.
Lain, J. Brooklyn City Directory, 1859. 59.95 (ISBN 0-87968-796-7). Gordon Pr.
WMCA. Call for Action: A Survival Kit for New Yorkers. rev. ed. LC 74-24296. 320p. 1975. pap. 2.95 (ISBN 0-8129-6250-8). Times Bks.

NEW YORK (CITY)–ECONOMIC CONDITIONS

Blumberg, Barbara. The New Deal & the Unemployed: The View from New York City. 332p. 1979. 19.50 (ISBN 0-685-19073-0). Bucknell U Pr.
The City in Transition: Prospects & Policies for New York, Final Report of the Temporary Commission on City Finances. 1978. lib. bdg. 15.00x (ISBN 0-405-10526-6); pap. 7.50x (ISBN 0-685-48606-0). Arno.
Dix, John A. Sketch of the Resources of the City of New York: With a View of Its Municipal Government, Population, Etc. LC 79-112538. (Rise of Urban America). 1970. Repr. of 1827 ed. 12.00 (ISBN 0-405-02447-9). Arno.
Eiberson, Harold. Sources for the Study of the New York Area. LC 60-15982. 128p. 1960. 7.95x (ISBN 0-8147-0135-3). NYU Pr.
Ferretti, Fred. The Year the Big Apple Went Bust. LC 75-44452. 1976. 10.00 (ISBN 0-399-11643-5). Putnam.
Grossman, David A. The Future of New York City's Capital Plant. (America's Urban Capital Stock Ser.: Vol. 1). 112p. (Orig.). 1979. pap. text ed. 6.00 (ISBN 0-87766-249-5, 25700). Urban Inst.
Klebaner, Benjamin J., ed. New York City's Changing Economic Base. LC 81-40498. (Illus.). 208p. 1981. text ed. 32.50x (ISBN 0-87663-731-4, Pica Spec Stud). Universe.
Mermelstein, David & Alcaly, Roger. The Fiscal Crisis of American Cities: Essays on the Political Economy of Urban America with Special Reference to New York. 1977. pap. 5.95 (ISBN 0-394-72193-4, V-193, Vin). Random.
Morris, Charles R. The Cost of Good Intentions: New York City & the Liberal Experiment. 1980. 14.95 (ISBN 0-393-01339-1). Norton.
Ott, Attiat F. & Yoo, Jang H. New York City's Financial Crisis: Can the Trend Be Reversed? LC 75-39814. 1975. pap. 3.25 (ISBN 0-8447-3195-1). Am Enterprise.
Pratt, Edward E. Industrial Causes of Congestion of Population in New York City. LC 68-56682. (Columbia University. Studies in the Social Sciences: No. 109). Repr. of 1911 ed. 21.00 (ISBN 0-404-51109-0). AMS Pr.
Riis, Jacob A. How the Other Half Lives. 304p. 1981. Repr. of 1892 ed. lib. bdg. 25.00 (ISBN 0-89987-718-4). Darby Bks.
Tabb, William K. The Long Default: New York City & the Urban Fiscal Crisis. LC 80-8933. 1981. 16.00 (ISBN 0-85345-571-6). Monthly Rev.
Twentieth Century Fund Task Force. New York-World City: Report of the Twentieth Century Task Fund on the Future of New York City. LC 79-25129. (Orig.). 1980. text ed. 20.00 (ISBN 0-89946-009-7); pap. text ed. 8.95 (ISBN 0-89946-008-9). Oelgeschlager.
Wilkenfeld, Bruce M. The Social & Economic Structure of the City of New York, 1695-1796. LC 77-14797. (Dissertations in American Economic History Ser.). 1978. 23.00 (ISBN 0-405-11062-6). Arno.

NEW YORK (CITY)–EMPIRE STATE BUILDING

Heller, Steven, et al. The Empire State Building Book. (Illus.). 96p. 1980. 14.95 (ISBN 0-312-24456-8); pap. 7.95 (ISBN 0-686-65894-9). St Martin.

Rose, Alan. Build Your Own Empire State Building. (The World at Your Feet Ser.). 40p. (gr. 10 up). 1980. pap. 6.95 (ISBN 0-399-50506-7, Perigee). Putnam.

NEW YORK (CITY)–FIVE POINTS MISSION

Ladies Of The Mission. Old Brewery & the New Mission House at the Five Points. LC 72-112563. (Rise of Urban America). (Illus.). 1970. Repr. of 1854 ed. 20.00 (ISBN 0-405-02461-4). Arno.

NEW YORK (CITY)–GALLERIES AND MUSEUMS

Barr, Alfred H. Painting and Sculpture in the Museum of Modern Art, 1929-1967. LC 68-54923. (Illus.). 1977. 40.00 (ISBN 0-87070-540-7). Museum Mod Art.

Filsinger, Cheryl. Locus. (Illus.). 192p. 1975. pap. 10.00 (ISBN 0-916754-00-6). Filsinger & Co.

--Locus Seventy-Seven Seventy-Eight Update. (Locus Ser.). 1977. pap. 10.00 (ISBN 0-916754-01-4). Filsinger & Co.

Franc, Helen M. An Invitation to See: 125 Paintings from the Museum of Modern Art. LC 72-82887. (Illus.). 1973. 14.95 (ISBN 0-87070-231-9); pap. 7.95 (ISBN 0-87070-230-0). Museum Mod Art.

Freeman, Margaret B. The Unicorn Tapestries. LC 76-2466. 246p. 1976. 45.00 (ISBN 0-87099-147-7, Dist. by E. P. Dutton). Metro Mus Art.

Glaeser, Ludwig. Work of Frei Otto. LC 75-150084. (Illus.). 1972. pap. 6.95 (ISBN 0-87070-333-1). Museum Mod Art.

Ivins, William M., Jr. Prints & Books. LC 76-75295. (Graphic Art Ser). 1969. Repr. of 1927 ed. lib. bdg. 32.50 (ISBN 0-306-71288-1). Da Capo.

McDarrah, Fred W. Museums in New York. 1978. pap. 5.95 (ISBN 0-8256-3112-2, Quick Fox). Music Sales.

Metropolitan Museum of Art, New York. Library Catalog of the Metropolitan Museum of Art, New York, 25 vols. 1960. Set. lib. bdg. 1970.00 (ISBN 0-8161-0496-4); Suppls. 1-5. 115.00 ea. First Suppl. 1962 (ISBN 0-8161-0579-0). Second Suppl. 1965 (ISBN 0-8161-0670-3). Third Suppl. 1968 (ISBN 0-8161-0748-3). Fourth Suppl. 1970 (ISBN 0-8161-0846-3). Fifth Suppl (ISBN 0-8161-0936-2). G K Hall.

Metropolitan Museum Studies: Vol. 5, Part 1. LC 29-1016. (Metropolitan Museum of Art Publications in Reprint). (Illus.). 148p. 1972. Repr. of 1934 ed. 26.00 (ISBN 0-405-02262-X). Arno.

Rorex, Robert A. & Wen Fong, trs. Eighteen Songs of a Nomad Flute: The Story of Lady Wen-Chi. LC 74-11140. (Illus.). 1974. 9.95 (ISBN 0-87099-095-0). Metro Mus Art.

Rubin, William S. Miro in the Collection of the Museum of Modern Art. LC 72-95708. (Illus.). 1973. 17.50 (ISBN 0-87070-463-X); pap. 8.95 (ISBN 0-87070-462-1). Museum Mod Art.

--Picasso in the Collection of the Museum of Modern Art. LC 70-164877. (Illus.). 1972. 18.95 (ISBN 0-87070-537-7); pap. 9.95 (ISBN 0-87070-538-5). Museum Mod Art.

Rudenstine, Angelica Z. The Guggenheim Museum Collection: Paintings 1880-1945, 2 vols. LC 75-37356. (Illus.). 1976. Set. 85.00x (ISBN 0-89207-002-1); pap. 40.00x (ISBN 0-685-70089-5). S R Guggenheim.

NEW YORK (CITY)–GRANGE, THE

Headley, Joel T. The Great Riots of New York Seventeen Twelve to Eighteen Seventy-Three. (Illus.). 8.75 (ISBN 0-8446-0136-5). Peter Smith.

NEW YORK (CITY)–HISTORY

Abbott, Berenice. New York in the Thirties. Orig. Title: Changing New York. 10.00 (ISBN 0-8446-5000-5). Peter Smith.

Archdeacon, Thomas J. New York City, 1664-1710: Conquest & Change. LC 75-22893. 224p. 1976. 17.50x (ISBN 0-8014-0944-6). Cornell U Pr.

Birmingham, Stephen. Life at the Dakota: New York's Most Unusual Address. LC 79-4800. (Illus.). 1979. 12.50 (ISBN 0-394-41079-3). Random.

Black, Mary, ed. Old New York in Early Photographs, 1853-1901. (Illus.). 10.00 (ISBN 0-8446-5005-6). Peter Smith.

Bliven, Bruce, Jr. & Bliven, Naomi. New York: The Story of the World's Most Exciting City. (Landmark Giant Ser.: No. 19). (gr. 5-9). 1969. PLB 5.99 (ISBN 0-394-90289-0, BYR). Random.

Bolton, Reginald P. New York City in Indian Possession, Vol. 2, No. 7. 2nd ed. (Indian Notes & Monographs). (Illus.). 1975. soft cover 6.00 (ISBN 0-934490-02-3). Mus Am Ind.

Brown, H. C. The Story of Old New York. 1977. lib. bdg. 59.95 (ISBN 0-8490-2683-0). Gordon Pr.

Brown, Henry C. In the Golden Nineties. facs. ed. LC 71-133516. (Select Bibliographies Reprint Ser). 1927. 29.00 (ISBN 0-8369-5548-X). Arno.

Burgess, Anthony, ed. New York. (The Great Cities Ser.). 1977. 14.95 (ISBN 0-8094-2270-0). Time-Life.

Byron, Joseph & Lancaster, Clay. New York Interiors at the Turn of the Century: 131 Photo Graphs from the Byron Collection of the Museum of the City of New York. 10.00 (ISBN 0-8446-5518-X). Peter Smith.

Conant, Melvin. Heralds of Their Age. (Illus.). 24p. pap. 1.00 (ISBN 0-913344-04-4). South St Sea Mus.

Condit, Carl W. The Port of New York: A History of the Rail & Terminal System from the Beginnings to Pennsylvania Station. LC 79-16850. (Illus.). 1980. lib. bdg. 29.95x (ISBN 0-226-11460-0). U of Chicago Pr.

Curvin, Robert & Porter, Bruce. Blackout Looting: New York City, July 13, 1977. LC 78-20817. 1979. 13.95 (ISBN 0-470-26669-4); pap. text ed. 6.95 (ISBN 0-470-26627-9). Halsted Pr.

Dawson, H. B. New York City During the American Revolution. 59.95 (ISBN 0-8490-0727-5). Gordon Pr.

Decker, Malcolm. Brink of Revolution: New York in Crisis, 1765-1776. (Illus.). 1964. 10.00 (ISBN 0-87266-005-2). Argosy.

Earle, Alice M. Colonial Days in Old New York. LC 68-21767. 1968. Repr. of 1896 ed. 19.00 (ISBN 0-8103-3428-3). Gale.

Edwards, George W. & Peterson, Arthur E. New York As an Eighteenth Century Municipality, 2 pts. LC 68-56681. (Columbia University Studies in the Social Sciences: Nos. 177-178). Repr. of 1917 ed. Set. 28.00 (ISBN 0-404-51697-1); 14.00 ea. Pt. 1 Prior To 1731 (ISBN 0-404-51177-5). Pt. 2 1731-1776 (ISBN 0-404-51178-3). AMS Pr.

Eighteen Sixty-Six Guide to New York City. LC 74-26914. (Illus.). 1975. pap. 2.50 (ISBN 0-8052-0474-1). Schocken.

Ellis, David M. New York: State & City. LC 78-15759. (Illus.). 1979. 12.95 (ISBN 0-8014-1180-7). Cornell U Pr.

Ernst, Robert. Immigrant Life in New York City, Eighteen Twenty-Five to Eighteen Sixty-Three. LC 79-11450. 1979. Repr. of 1949 ed. lib. bdg. 17.50x (ISBN 0-374-92624-7). Octagon.

Federal Writers' Project. A Maritime History of New York. LC 76-44939. (American Guidebook Ser.). 1980. Repr. of 1941 ed. lib. bdg. 45.00 (ISBN 0-403-03823-5). Somerset Pub.

Feininger, Andreas. New York in the Forties. LC 77-8734. (New York Ser.). (Illus.). 1978. pap. 6.00 (ISBN 0-486-23585-8). Dover.

Fine, Jo Renee & Wolfe, Gerard R. The Synagogues of New York's Lower East Side. LC 75-15126. (Illus.). 1978. 16.95 (ISBN 0-8147-2559-7). NYU Pr.

Foner, Philip S. Business & Slavery: The New York Merchants & the Irrepressible Conflict. LC 68-15122. 1968. Repr. of 1941 ed. 13.50 (ISBN 0-8462-1145-9). Russell.

Furer, Howard B., ed. New York: A Chronological & Documentary History. LC 74-3044. (American Cities Chronology Ser: No. 66). 160p. 1974. lib. bdg. 8.50 (ISBN 0-379-00610-3). Oceana.

Gillon, Edmund V. New York Then & Now: 83 Manhattan Sites Photographed in the Past & Present. 8.75 (ISBN 0-8446-5524-4). Peter Smith.

Goldstone, Harmon H. & Dalrymple, Martha. History Preserved: A Guide to New York City Landmarks & Historic Districts. LC 76-9142. (Illus.). 1976. pap. 8.95 (ISBN 0-8052-0544-6). Schocken.

Goodwin, Maud W., et al, eds. Historic New York, 4 Vols, Series One & Two. LC 74-83482. (Empire State Historical Publications Ser). (Illus.). 1969. Repr. of 1898 ed. Set. 35.00 (ISBN 0-87198-064-9). Friedman.

Goren, Arthur A. New York Jews & the Quest for Community. LC 76-129961. 1979. 22.50x (ISBN 0-231-03422-9); pap. 10.00x (ISBN 0-231-08368-8). Columbia U Pr.

Grafton, John. New York in the Nineteenth Century: Engravings from Harper's Weekly & Other Contemporary Sources. LC 77-73339. (Illus.). 1977. pap. 6.95 (ISBN 0-486-23516-5). Dover.

Grafton, John, ed. New York in the Nineteenth Century: 321 Engravings from Harper's Weekly & Other Contemporary Sources. 12.50 (ISBN 0-8446-5581-3). Peter Smith.

Hammack, David C. Power & Society: Greater New York at the Turn of the Century. LC 81-66977. (Illus.). 450p. 1982. 29.95x (ISBN 0-87154-348-6). Russell Sage.

Harrington, Virginia D. The New York Merchant on the Eve of the Revolution. 1964. 7.50 (ISBN 0-8446-1224-3). Peter Smith.

Harris, C. T. Memories of Manhattan: In the Sixties & the Seventies. 1977. lib. bdg. 59.95 (ISBN 0-8490-2226-6). Gordon Pr.

Headley, Joel T. Great Riots of New York, 1712-1873. pap. 3.25 (ISBN 0-685-16785-2, N180P). Mnemosyne.

Heckscher, August & Robinson, Phyllis. When LaGuardia Was Mayor: New York's Legendary Years. (Illus.). 1978. 17.50 (ISBN 0-393-07534-6). Norton.

Hone, Philip. Diary of Philip Hone, 1828-1851, 2 Vols. in 1. 1927. 48.00 (ISBN 0-527-42100-6). Kraus Repr.

Horsmanden, Daniel. New York Conspiracy, or a History of the Negro Plot. LC 69-16546. (Illus.). Repr. of 1810 ed. 18.75x (ISBN 0-8371-0484-X, Pub. by Negro U Pr). Greenwood.

Hosay, Philip M. The Challenge of Urban Poverty: Charity Reformers in New York City, 1835 to 1890. Cordasco, Francesco, ed. LC 80-864. (American Ethnic Grouggs Ser.). 1981. lib. bdg. 28.00x (ISBN 0-405-13427-4). Arno.

Innes, J. H. New Amsterdam & Its People: Studies Social & Topographical, of the Town Under Dutch & Early English Rule, 2 Vols. LC 68-58927. (Empire State Historical Publications Ser: No. 63). (Illus.). 1969. Repr. of 1902 ed. Set. 15.00 (ISBN 0-87198-063-0). Friedman.

The Italians of New York City. LC 72-166660. 1938. 32.00 (ISBN 0-403-02215-0). Somerset Pub.

Jackson, Ronald V. & Teeples, Gary R. New York City Census Index 1850. LC 77-86121. (Illus.). lib. bdg. 65.00 (ISBN 0-89593-102-8). Accelerated Index.

Janvier, T. A. In Old New York. 1977. lib. bdg. 59.95 (ISBN 0-8490-2045-X). Gordon Pr.

Johnson, Harry & Lightfoot, Frederick S. Maritime New York in Nineteenth-Century Photographs. 15.00 (ISBN 0-8446-5777-8). Peter Smith.

Johnston, H. P. Campaign of Seventeen Seventy-Six Around New York & Brooklyn. LC 74-157827. (Era of the American Revolution Ser). 1971. Repr. of 1878 ed. lib. bdg. 42.50 (ISBN 0-306-70169-3). Da Capo.

Kelly, Frank B. Historical Guide to the City of New York. 1977. lib. bdg. 59.95 (ISBN 0-8490-1959-1). Gordon Pr.

Klein, Milton M., ed. New York: The Centennial Years, 1676-1976. (Interdisciplinary Urban Ser.). (Illus.). 250p. 1976. 13.95 (ISBN 0-8046-9143-6, Natl U). Kennikat.

Koolhaas, Rem. Delirious New York: A Retroactive Manifesto for Manhattan. LC 77-17418. (Illus.). 1978. 39.95 (ISBN 0-19-520035-7). Oxford U Pr.

Kouwenhoven, John A. Columbia Historical Portrait of New York: An Essay in Graphic History. (Icon Editions). (Illus.). 1972. pap. 15.95 (ISBN 0-06-430030-7, IN-30, HarpT). Har-Row.

--The Columbia Historical Portrait of New York. 1978. Repr. of 1953 ed. lib. bdg. 50.00x (ISBN 0-374-94625-6). Octagon.

Kraus, Harry P. The Settlement House Movement in New York City, 1886-1914. Cordasco, Francesco, ed. LC 80-872. (American Ethnic Groups Ser.). 1981. lib. bdg. 29.00x (ISBN 0-405-13434-7). Arno.

Lehnartz, Klaus. New York in the Sixties. LC 78-53190. (Illus.). 1978. pap. 5.00 (ISBN 0-486-23674-9). Dover.

Lightfoot, Frederick. Nineteenth-Century New York in Rare Photographic Views. (New York Ser.). (Illus.). 96p. (Orig.). 1981. pap. 6.95 (ISBN 0-486-24137-8). Dover.

Lockwood, Charles. Manhattan Moves Uptown: An Illustrated History. 1976. 17.50 (ISBN 0-395-24674-1). HM.

Lowenhardt, Werner. Amsterdam, Twelve Seventy-Five - Nieuw Amsterdam, Sixteen Twenty-Five - New York, Nineteen Seventy-Five. (Illus., Dutch & Eng.). 1975. 20.00 (ISBN 0-685-80129-2). Heinman.

Manhattan Company. Manna-Hatin: Story of New York. LC 68-18364. (Empire Historical Publications Ser: No. 55). (Illus.). 1968. Repr. of 1929 ed. 7.50 (ISBN 0-87198-055-X). Friedman.

Mayer, Grace. Once Upon a City: New York from Eighteen Ninety to Nineteen Ten As Photographed by Byron & Described by Grace M. Mayer. xii, 511p. 1980. Repr. of 1958 ed. lib. bdg. 90.00x (ISBN 0-374-95418-6). Octagon.

Mohl, Raymond A. Poverty in New York, 1783-1825. (Urban Life in America Ser). 1971. 15.95 (ISBN 0-19-501367-0). Oxford U Pr.

Monaghan, Frank & Lowenthal, Marvin. This Was New York: The Nation's Capital in 1789. facsimile ed. LC 70-117884. (Select Bibliographies Reprint Ser). Repr. of 1943 ed. 24.00 (ISBN 0-8369-5337-1). Arno.

Morris, Lloyd. Incredible New York: High Life & Low Life of the Last Hundred Years. facsimile ed. LC 75-1862. (Leisure Class in America Ser.). (Illus.). 1975. Repr. of 1951 ed. 22.00x (ISBN 0-405-06928-6). Arno.

Nevins, Allan, ed. Diary of Philip Hone 1828-1851, 2 Vols. in 1. LC 77-112559. (Rise of Urban America). (Illus.). 1970. Repr. of 1927 ed. 39.00 (ISBN 0-405-02468-1). Arno.

Nevins, Allan & Krout, John A., eds. The Greater City: New York, 1898 to 1948. LC 81-4173. (Illus.). vii, 260p. 1981. Repr. of 1948 ed. lib. bdg. 35.00x (ISBN 0-313-23072-2, NEGC). Greenwood.

New York Writer's Program. A Maritime History of New York. LC 72-2083. (American History & Americana Ser., No. 47). 1972. Repr. of 1941 ed. lib. bdg. 45.95 (ISBN 0-8383-1460-0). Haskell.

New Yorker Unlimited: Memoirs of Edward Larocque Tinker. (Illus.). 1970. 12.50 (ISBN 0-88426-027-5). Encino Pr.

Patterson, Jerry E. The City of New York. (Illus.). 1978. 19.95 (ISBN 0-8109-1708-4). Abrams.

Peterson, Arthur E. & Edwards, George W. New York As an Eighteenth Century Municipality, 2 Vols. in 1. LC 67-16260. (Empire State Historical Publications Ser: No. 46). 1917. 12.50 (ISBN 0-87198-046-0). Friedman.

Pound, Arthur. The Golden Earth: The Story of Manhattan's Landed Wealth. facsimile ed. LC 75-1865. (Leisure Class in America Ser.). (Illus.). 1975. Repr. of 1935 ed. 21.00x (ISBN 0-405-06931-6). Arno.

Rock, Howard B. Artisans of the New Republic: Tradesmen of New York City in the Age of Jefferson. LC 78-55570. 1979. 22.50x (ISBN 0-8147-7378-8). NYU Pr.

Rosebrock, Ellen F. Farewell to Old England, New York in Revolution. LC 75-3941. (Illus.). 64p. (Orig.). 1976. pap. 1.95 (ISBN 0-913344-21-4). South St Sea Mus.

Rosenwaike, Ira. Population History of New York City. LC 75-39829. (New York State Studies). (Illus.). 274p. 1972. 14.95x (ISBN 0-8156-2155-8). Syracuse U Pr.

Sanders, Ronald & Gillon, Edmund V. The Lower East Side: A Guide to Its Jewish Past in Ninety-Nine New Photographs. 10.00 (ISBN 0-8446-5809-X). Peter Smith.

Schoener, Allon. Portal to America: The Lower East Side, 1870-1925. 1967. pap. 7.95 (ISBN 0-03-086712-6). HR&W.

Serle, Ambrose. The American Journal of Ambrose Serle, Secretary to Lord Howe 1776-1778. Tatum, Edward H., Jr., ed. LC 72-76240. (Eyewitness Accounts of the American Revolution Ser. 2). (Illus.). 1969. Repr. of 1940 ed. 16.00 (ISBN 0-405-01183-0). Arno.

Shepherd, William R. Story of New Amsterdam. LC 75-118790. (Empire State Historical Publications Ser: No. 88). 1970. Repr. of 1926 ed. 8.50 (ISBN 0-87198-088-6). Friedman.

Shopsin, William C. & Broderick, Mosette G. The Villard Houses: Life Story of a Landmark. LC 80-5357. (Illus.). 144p. 1980. 18.95 (ISBN 0-670-74685-1). Viking Pr.

--The Villard Houses: Life Story of a Landmark. LC 80-5357. (Illus.). 144p. 1980. 18.95 (ISBN 0-670-74685-1). Viking Pr.

Simon, Kate. Fifth Avenue: A Very Special History. LC 79-11996. (Illus.). 1979. pap. 4.95 (ISBN 0-15-630712-X, Harv). HarBraceJ.

Simpson, Charles R. SoHo: The Artist in the City. LC 80-27083. 352p. 1981. 20.00 (ISBN 0-226-75937-7). U of Chicago Pr.

Smith, Mortimer. My School the City. LC 80-51727. 190p. 1980. 9.95 (ISBN 0-89526-674-1). Regnery-Gateway.

Spann, Edward K. The New Metropolis: New York City, 1840-1857. LC 81-91. (The Columbia History of Urban Life Ser.). (Illus.). 512p. 1981. 19.95 (ISBN 0-231-05084-4). Columbia U Pr.

Stanford, Peter. South Street Around 1900. (Illus.). 33p. 1970. pap. 1.50 (ISBN 0-913344-12-5). South St Sea Mus.

Still, Bayrd. New York City. LC 65-15067. (Illus.). 1965. pap. 2.95 (ISBN 0-8077-2209-X). Tchrs Coll.

Stone, William L. The Centennial History of New York City from the Discovery to the Present Day. 1977. lib. bdg. 75.00 (ISBN 0-8490-1591-X). Gordon Pr.

Tax Lists of the City of New York, December, 1695-July 15, 1699 & Assessment of the Real & Personal Property of the East Ward, City of New York, June 24, 1791: Collections 1910, 1911, 2 vols. LC 1-16508. 4.00x ea. (New York Historical Society). U Pr of Va.

Tomasi, Silvano M. Piety & Power: The Role of Italian Parishes in the New York Metropolitan Area (1880-1930) LC 74-79913. 201p. 1975. 14.95x (ISBN 0-913256-16-1, Dist. by Ozer). Ctr Migration.

Ulmann, A. A Landmark History of New York. 1977. lib. bdg. 59.95 (ISBN 0-8490-2128-6). Gordon Pr.

Ulmann, Albert. Landmark History of New York. LC 70-101023. 1969. Repr. of 1901 ed. 9.00 (ISBN 0-87198-070-3). Friedman.

Van Rensselaer, Mrs. John K. The Goede Vrouw of Mana-Ha-Ta: At Home & in Society, 1609-1760. LC 72-2629. (American Women Ser: Images & Realities). 422p. 1972. Repr. of 1898 ed. 18.00 (ISBN 0-405-04484-4). Arno.

Van Rensselaer, Mariana. History of the City of New York in the Seventeenth Century, 2 vols. LC 74-19732. Repr. of 1909 ed. Set. 75.00 (ISBN 0-404-12265-5). AMS Pr.

Walsh, George. Public Enemies: The Mayor, the Mob, & the Crime That Was. 1980. 14.95 (ISBN 0-393-01306-5). Norton.

Wertenbaker, Thomas J. Father Knickerbocker Rebels: New York City During the Revolution. LC 68-57282. (Illus.). Repr. of 1948 ed. 17.50x (ISBN 0-8154-0286-4). Cooper Sq.

Wurts, Richard. The New York World's Fair 1939-1940 in 155 Photographs. Appelbaum, S., ed. 10.00 (ISBN 0-8446-5622-4). Peter Smith.

Yellowitz, Irwin, ed. Essays in the History of New York City: A Memorial to Sidney Pomerantz. (National University Pubns. Interdisciplinary Urban Ser.). 1978. 13.95 (ISBN 0-8046-9208-4). Kennikat.

Younger, William L. Old Brooklyn in Early Photographs Eighteen Sixty-Five to Nineteen Twenty-Nine. 15.00 (ISBN 0-8446-5665-8). Peter Smith.

NEW YORK (CITY)–HISTORY–ANECDOTES

Botkin, Benjamin A. New York City Folklore: Legends, Tall Tales, Anecdotes, Stories, Sagas, Heroes & Characters, Customs, Traditions & Sayings. LC 76-43977. (Illus.). 1976. Repr. of 1956 ed. lib. bdg. 28.75x (ISBN 0-8371-9310-9, BONC). Greenwood.

Letter Book of John Watts, Merchant & Councillor of New York: Collections 1928. LC 28-27799. 10.00x (ISBN 0-685-73907-4, New York Historical Society). U Pr of Va.

Still, Bayrd. Mirror for Gotham: New York As Seen by Contemporaries from Dutch Days to the Present. LC 80-16246. (Illus.). xix, 417p. 1980. Repr. of 1956 ed. lib. bdg. 35.00x (ISBN 0-313-22439-0, STMG). Greenwood.

NEW YORK (CITY)–HISTORY–FICTION

Erenberg, Lewis A. Steppin' Out: New York Nightlife & the Transformation of American Culture, 1890-1930. LC 80-930. (Contributions in American Studies Ser.: No. 50). (Illus.). xix, 291p. 1981. lib. bdg. 23.95 (ISBN 0-313-21342-9, EUN/). Greenwood.

Lippard, George. Empire City. facs. ed. LC 70-76927. (American Fiction Reprint Ser). 1850. 14.00 (ISBN 0-8369-7006-3). Arno.

Sanders, Ed. Fame & Love in New York. (New World Writing Ser.: No. 17). (Illus.). 320p. 1980. 17.95 (ISBN 0-913666-31-9); pap. 7.95 (ISBN 0-913666-32-7). Turtle Isl Foun.

NEW YORK (CITY)–HISTORY–SOURCES

The Burghers of New Amsterdam & the Freeman of New York, 1675-1866: New York Historical Society Collections 1885. LC 1-13394. 8.00x (ISBN 0-685-73876-0). U Pr of Va.

Fernow, Berthold, ed. Minutes of the Executive Boards of the Burgomasters of New Amsterdam. LC 71-112544. (Rise of Urban America). 1970. Repr. of 1907 ed. 9.00 (ISBN 0-405-02453-3). Arno.

Furer, Howard B., ed. New York: A Chronological & Documentary History. LC 74-3044. (American Cities Chronology Ser: No. 66). 160p. 1974. lib. bdg. 8.50 (ISBN 0-379-00610-3). Oceana.

Halsey, R. Haines. Pictures of Early New York on Dark Blue Staffordshire Pottery. (Illus.). 8.00 (ISBN 0-8446-5044-7). Peter Smith.

O'Callaghan, Edmund B., tr. The Minutes of the Orphanmasters of New Amsterdam 1663-1668. LC 76-2198. 1976. 3.00 (ISBN 0-8063-0717-X). Genealog Pub.

--New York Historical Manuscripts: Dutch, the Register of Salomon Lachaire, Notary Public of New Amsterdam, 1661-1662. Scott, Kenneth & Stryker-Rodda, Kenn, eds. LC 77-85298. 1978. 17.50 (ISBN 0-8063-0787-0). Genealog Pub.

Scott, Kenneth, compiled by. Rivington's New York Newspaper: Excerpts from a Loyalist Press, 1773-1783. LC 73-84656. (Illus.). 1973. 15.00x (ISBN 0-685-73924-4, New York Historical Society). U Pr of Va.

NEW YORK (CITY)–HOSPITALS

Arnstein, Helene S. Billy & Our New Baby. LC 73-7951. (Illus.). 32p. (ps-3). 1973. 9.95 (ISBN 0-87705-093-7). Human Sci Pr.

Jonas, Steven. Quality Control of Ambulatory Care: A Task for Health Departments. LC 77-24502. (Health Care & Society Ser.: Vol. 1). 1977. text ed. 12.50 (ISBN 0-8261-2240-X). Springer Pub.

Vignec, Elsie E. Children of Hope, Some Stories of the New York Foundling Hospital. LC 64-7500. 1964. 4.95 (ISBN 0-396-05040-9). Dodd.

NEW YORK (CITY)–INTELLECTUAL LIFE

Anderson, Alexandra & Archer, B. J. Anderson & Archer's Soho: The Essential Guide to Art & Life in Lower Manhattan. 1979. pap. 6.95 (ISBN 0-671-24859-6). S&S.

Cultural Assistance Center, ed. America's Stake in New York City Arts & Culture. LC 78-56952. (Illus.). 72p. 1978. pap. 4.50x (ISBN 0-89062-030-X, Pub. by Cultural Assistance Center). Pub Ctr Cult Res.

Howe, Irving. World of Our Fathers. LC 75-16342. (Illus.). 736p. 1976. 14.95 (ISBN 0-15-146353-0). HarBraceJ.

--World of Our Fathers. LC 76-53818. 1977. pap. 6.95 (ISBN 0-671-22755-6, Touchstone). S&S.

Kazin, Alfred. New York Jew. LC 78-23501. 1979. pap. 2.95 (ISBN 0-394-72867-X, Vin). Random.

NEW YORK (CITY)–JUVENILE LITERATURE

Burgess, Anthony. New York. (The Great Cities Ser.). (Illus.). (gr. 6 up). 1977. PLB 14.94 (ISBN 0-8094-2271-9, Pub. by Time-Life). Silver.

Hutchinson, Warner. New York! (Readers Ser.: Stage 2). 1979. pap. text ed. 1.95 (ISBN 0-88377-158-6). Newbury Hse.

Jagendorf, Moritz A. Ghost of Peg-Leg Peter & Other Stories of Old New York. LC 65-17371. (Illus.). (gr. 3 up). 1965. 7.95 (ISBN 0-8149-0327-4). Vanguard.

One Hundred Seventy Children's Writers & Artists Celebrate New York City. The New York Kid's Book. LC 77-15171. (Illus.). 416p. 1979. pap. 8.95 (ISBN 0-385-12918-1). Doubleday.

Reit, Seymour. Rice Cakes & Paper Dragons. LC 72-7749. (Illus.). 80p. (gr. 2-5). 1973. 4.95 (ISBN 0-396-06735-2). Dodd.

NEW YORK (CITY)–LIBRARIES

Collectors Club Library. New York. Philately: The/Catalog of the Collectors Club Library. 1974. lib. bdg. 115.00 (ISBN 0-8161-1047-6). G K Hall.

New York Public Library. New York Public Library in Fiction, Poetry & Children's Literature. 1956. pap. 3.00 (ISBN 0-87104-132-4). NY Pub Lib.

New York State Library Association. Public Libraries in New York State: A 1977 Salary Survey. 1978. pap. text ed. 3.00 (ISBN 0-931658-00-4). NY Lib Assn.

Research Libraries of the New York Public Library. Catalog of the Theatre & Drama Collections, Supplement 1974. 1976. lib. bdg. 60.00 (ISBN 0-8161-0058-6). G K Hall.

Siegel, Morris. Mackenzie Collection: A Study of West African Carved Gambling Chips. LC 41-25906. 1940. pap. 6.00 (ISBN 0-527-00554-1). Kraus Repr.

Williams, Sam P. Guide to the Research Collections of the New York Public Library. LC 75-15878. 368p. 1975. text ed. 35.00 (ISBN 0-8389-0125-5). ALA.

NEW YORK (CITY)–LINCOLN CENTER FOR THE PERFORMING ARTS

Sokol, Martin. The New York City Opera: An American Adventure. (Illus.). 480p. 1981. 34.95 (ISBN 0-02-612280-4). Macmillan.

Young, Edgar B. Lincoln Center: The Building of an Institution. 320p. 1980. 24.95 (ISBN 0-8147-9656-7). NYU Pr.

NEW YORK (CITY)–MAPS

Bowser, Benjamin P., et al, eds. Census Data with Maps for Small Areas of New York City 1910-1960. 1981. write for info. (ISBN 0-89235-028-8). Res Pubns Conn.

Hagstrom: New York City (5 Boros) 1977. 5.95 (ISBN 0-685-83175-2). Wehman.

NEW YORK (CITY)–METROPOLITAN OPERA

Eaton, Quaintance. The Miracle of the Met. LC 76-11746. 1976. Repr. of 1968 ed. lib. bdg. 31.50x (ISBN 0-8371-8934-9, EAMM). Greenwood.

--Opera Caravan. LC 78-9128. (Music Reprint 1978 Ser.). (Illus.). 1978. lib. bdg. 29.50 (ISBN 0-306-77596-4); pap. 6.95 (ISBN 0-306-80089-6). Da Capo.

Herbert-Caesari, Edgar F. Tradition & Gigli. 6.95 (ISBN 0-8008-7827-2, Crescendo). Taplinger.

Heylbut, Rose & Gerber, Aime. Backstage at the Metropolitan Opera. Farkas, Andrew, ed. LC 76-29941. (Opera Biographies). Orig. Title: Backstage at the Opera. (Illus.). 1977. Repr. of 1937 ed. lib. bdg. 22.00x (ISBN 0-405-09683-6). Arno.

Peltz, Mary E. & Fitzgerald, Gerald, eds. Metropolitan Opera Annals: Third Supplement: 1966-1976. LC 47-11435. (Illus.). 1978. 17.50 (ISBN 0-88371-022-6). J T White.

Robinson, Francis. Celebration: The Metropolitan Opera. LC 78-69666. (Illus.). 1979. 14.00 (ISBN 0-385-12975-0). Doubleday.

Wright, Helen L. Metropolitan Opera House. 1980. pap. 14.95 (ISBN 0-686-70335-9). Greylock Pubs.

--Metropolitan Opera House. (Illus.). 1979. pap. 14.95 (ISBN 0-686-30652-X). Immediate Pr.

NEW YORK (CITY)–MUSIC HALLS (VARIETY-THEATER, CABARETS, ETC.)

Aldrich, Richard. Concert Life in New York from Nineteen Hundred & Two to Nineteen Hundred & Twenty-Three. LC 74-181102. 795p. 1941. Repr. 96.00 (ISBN 0-403-01501-4). Scholarly.

Erenberg, Lewis A. Steppin' Out: New York Nightlife & the Transformation of American Culture, 1890-1930. LC 80-930. (Contributions in American Studies Ser.: No. 50). (Illus.). xix, 291p. 1981. lib. bdg. 23.95 (ISBN 0-313-21342-9, EUN/). Greenwood.

Lee, Ronald S. & Lee, Patricia, eds. Stubs: The Seating Plan Guide for New York Theaters, Music Halls & Sports Stadia, 1981 Edition. (Illus.). 1980. pap. 3.95 (ISBN 0-911458-02-6, MNYE7). Stubs.

NEW YORK (CITY)–NEIGHBORHOOD PLAYHOUSE

Henderson, Mary C. The City & the Theatre. LC 73-9970. (Illus.). 335p. 1973. 14.95 (ISBN 0-88371-003-X). J T White.

NEW YORK (CITY)–OFFICIALS AND EMPLOYEES

Dahl, A. M. & Knick, Allison, eds. Directory of Directors in the City of New York & Suburbs. rev. ed. 725p. 1981. 125.00 (ISBN 0-936612-02-9). DODC.

Gerson, Simon W. Pete: The Story of Peter V. Cacchione, New York's First Communist Councilman. LC 76-29039. 1976. 10.00 (ISBN 0-7178-0482-8); pap. 3.50 (ISBN 0-7178-0473-9). Intl Pub Co.

Lowi, Theodore J. At the Pleasure of the Mayor. LC 64-11216. 1964. 12.95 (ISBN 0-02-919420-2). Free Pr.

NEW YORK (CITY)–OFFICIALS AND EMPLOYEES–EXAMINATIONS

see also Civil Service Examinations–New York (City)

Arco Editorial Board. Attorney-Assistant Trainee. 3rd. ed. (Orig.). 1975. pap. 8.00 (ISBN 0-668-01084-3); PLB 7.50 (ISBN 0-668-01707-4). Arco.

--Battalion & Deputy Chief, F. D. 4th ed. (Orig.). 1969. lib. bdg. 8.50 (ISBN 0-668-02064-4); pap. 6.00 (ISBN 0-668-00515-7). Arco.

--College Office Assistant. 3rd ed. (Orig.). 1970. pap. 5.00 (ISBN 0-668-00181-X). Arco.

--Gardener--Assistant Gardener. 2nd ed. LC 75-27588. (Orig.). 1975. pap. 8.00 (ISBN 0-668-01340-0, 1340). Arco.

--Housing Caretaker. 3rd ed. LC 67-16544. (Orig.). 1967. pap. 4.00 (ISBN 0-668-00504-1). Arco.

--Housing Inspector. 2nd ed. LC 67-23003. (Orig.). 1968. lib. bdg. 7.50 (ISBN 0-668-01804-6); pap. 5.00 (ISBN 0-668-00055-4). Arco.

--Mechanical Apprentice (Maintainer's Helper B) 3rd ed. LC 66-28182. (Orig.). 1966. pap. 5.00 (ISBN 0-668-00176-3). Arco.

--Motorman: Subways. 2nd ed. LC 75-83162. (Test Tutor Ser). 1969. pap. 6.00 (ISBN 0-668-00061-9). Arco.

--Nurse. 4th ed. LC 73-94658. (Orig.). 1970. pap. 6.00 (ISBN 0-668-00143-7). Arco.

--Parking Enforcement Agent. LC 59-15581. (Orig.). 1960. pap. 4.00 (ISBN 0-668-00701-X). Arco.

--Sanitation Foreman: Foreman & Asst. Foreman. 2nd ed. LC 78-78990. (Orig.). 1975. pap. 6.00 (ISBN 0-668-01958-1). Arco.

--Structural Apprentice: Maintainer's Helper, Group D. 2nd ed. LC 61-18201. (Orig.). 1969. pap. 5.00 (ISBN 0-668-00177-1). Arco.

--Surface Line Dispatcher. 4th ed. LC 78-86828. 1974. pap. 6.00 (ISBN 0-668-00140-2). Arco.

--Towerman: Municipal Subway System. 4th ed. LC 57-14743. (Orig.). 1971. pap. 5.00 (ISBN 0-668-00157-7). Arco.

--Trackman: Municipal Subway System. 6th ed. LC 72-2782. 1973. pap. 5.00 (ISBN 0-668-00075-9). Arco.

Rudman, Jack. Housing Sergeant. (Career Examination Ser.: C-344). (Cloth bdg. avail. on request). pap. 10.00 (ISBN 0-8373-0344-3). Natl Learning.

--Maintainer's Helper - Group A. (Career Examination Ser.: C-465). (Cloth bdg. avail. on request). pap. 8.00 (ISBN 0-8373-0465-2). Natl Learning.

--Maintainer's Helper - Group B. (Career Examination Ser.: C-466). (Cloth bdg. avail. on request). pap. 8.00 (ISBN 0-8373-0466-0). Natl Learning.

--Maintainer's Helper - Group C. (Career Examination Ser.: C-467). (Cloth bdg. avail. on request). pap. 8.00 (ISBN 0-8373-0467-9). Natl Learning.

--Maintainer's Helper - Group D. (Career Examination Ser.: C-468). (Cloth bdg. avail. on request). pap. 8.00 (ISBN 0-8373-0468-7). Natl Learning.

--Maintainer's Helper - Group E. (Career Examination Ser.: C-469). 14.00 (ISBN 0-8373-0469-5). Natl Learning.

--Motor Vehicle Operator. (Career Examination Ser.: C-507). (Cloth bdg. avail. on request). pap. 8.00 (ISBN 0-8373-0507-1). Natl Learning.

--Railroad Porter. (Career Examination Ser.: C-662). (Cloth bdg. avail. on request). pap. 8.00 (ISBN 0-8373-0662-0). Natl Learning.

--Sanitation Man. (Career Examination Ser.: C-700). (Cloth bdg. avail. on request). pap. 8.00 (ISBN 0-8373-0700-7). Natl Learning.

--Sergeant - Police Department. (Career Examination Ser.: C-733). (Cloth bdg. avail. on request). pap. 10.00 (ISBN 0-8373-0733-3). Natl Learning.

--Transit Captain. (Career Examination Ser.: C-819). (Cloth bdg. avail. on request). pap. 12.00 (ISBN 0-8373-0819-4). Natl Learning.

--Transit Lieutenant. (Career Examination Ser.: C-820). (Cloth bdg. avail. on request). pap. 10.00 (ISBN 0-8373-0820-8). Natl Learning.

--Transit Patrolman. (Career Examination Ser.: C-821). (Cloth bdg. avail. on request). pap. 8.00 (ISBN 0-8373-0821-6). Natl Learning.

--Transit Sergeant. (Career Examination Ser.: C-822). (Cloth bdg. avail. on request). pap. 10.00 (ISBN 0-8373-0822-4). Natl Learning.

Turner, David R. Electrician. 4th ed. LC 60-53307. (Illus.). 304p. (Orig.). 1972. pap. 8.00 (ISBN 0-668-00084-8). Arco.

--Electronic Equipment Maintainer. LC 68-55431. 160p. (Orig.). 1975. pap. 8.00 (ISBN 0-668-01836-4). Arco.

--Road Car Inspector - Transit Authority. LC 74-24568. 160p. (Orig.). 1976. pap. 8.00 (ISBN 0-668-03743-1). Arco.

--Teacher in Vacation Playgrounds: Health Education in Playgrounds. LC 65-22181. (Orig.). 1966. pap. 3.00 (ISBN 0-668-01305-2). Arco.

--Telephone Maintainer: New York Transit Authority. LC 74-24559. 96p. (Orig.). 1975. pap. 5.00 (ISBN 0-668-03742-3). Arco.

--Track Foreman, New York City Transit Authority. LC 74-24567. 160p. (Orig.). 1975. pap. 6.00 (ISBN 0-668-03739-3). Arco.

NEW YORK (CITY)–PARKS

Laredo, Victor & Reed, Henry H. Central Park: A Photographic Guide. 8.50 (ISBN 0-686-74163-3). Peter Smith.

Lewis, Richard. The Park. LC 68-28917. (Illus.). (ps-3). 1968. 3.95 (ISBN 0-671-65028-9, Juveniles). S&S.

Olmsted, Frederick L. Public Parks & the Enlargement of Towns. LC 76-112564. (Rise of Urban America). 1970. Repr. of 1870 ed. 8.00 (ISBN 0-405-02469-X). Arno.

NEW YORK (CITY)–POLICE

Alex, Nicholas. New York Cops Talk Back: A Study of a Beleaguered Minority. LC 76-1852. 225p. 1976. 20.95 (ISBN 0-471-02055-9, Pub. by Wiley-Interscience). Wiley.

Arco Editorial Board. Captain, Police Department. 4th ed. (Orig.). 1967. pap. 10.00 (ISBN 0-668-00184-4). Arco.

Board Of Aldermen. Police in New York City: An Investigation. LC 79-154565. (Police in America Ser). 1971. Repr. of 1913 ed. 22.00 (ISBN 0-405-03382-6). Arno.

Chamber Of Commerce Of The State Of New York. Papers & Proceedings of the Committee on the Police Problem, City of New York. LC 79-154581. (Police in America Ser). 1971. Repr. of 1905 ed. 35.00 (ISBN 0-405-03364-8). Arno.

Chevigny, Paul. Cops & Rebels. LC 72-570. 1972. 24.00x (ISBN 0-394-47218-7). Irvington.

Christian, Charles. Brief Treatise on the Police of the City of New York. LC 76-112548. (Rise of Urban America). 1970. Repr. of 1812 ed. 10.00 (ISBN 0-405-02442-8). Arno.

Costello, Augustine. Our Police Protectors: History of the New York Police. 3rd ed. LC 79-129324. (Criminology, Law Enforcement, & Social Problems Ser.: No. 127). (Illus.). 653p. (With intro. added). 1972. Repr. of 1885 ed. lib. bdg. 25.00 (ISBN 0-87585-127-4). Patterson Smith.

Daley, Robert. Prince of the City: The True Story of the Cop Who Knew Too Much. 1979. 10.95 (ISBN 0-395-27096-0). HM.

Kornblum, Allan N. The Moral Hazards: Police Strategies for Honesty & Ethical Behavior. LC 75-34614. 224p. 1976. 22.95 (ISBN 0-669-00378-6). Lexington Bks.

Lavine, Emanuel H. The Third Degree: A Detailed Account of Police Brutality. LC 74-676. (Civil Liberties in American History Ser.). 248p. 1974. Repr. of 1930 ed. lib. bdg. 27.50 (ISBN 0-306-70601-6). Da Capo.

Maas, Peter. Serpico. (Illus.). 320p. 1973. 7.95 (ISBN 0-670-63498-0). Viking Pr.

--Serpico. 320p. 1974. pap. 2.95 (ISBN 0-553-20449-1, 13424-8). Bantam.

Miller, Wilbur. Cops & Bobbies: Police Authority in New York & London, 1830-70. LC 76-27847. 1977. 16.00x (ISBN 0-226-52595-3). U of Chicago Pr.

New York City Common Council. Report of the Special Committee of the New York City Board of Aldermen on the New York City Police Department: New York City Common Council Document, No. 53. LC 72-154582. (Police in America Ser). 1971. Repr. of 1844 ed. 20.00 (ISBN 0-405-03378-8). Arno.

Report & Proceedings of the Senate Committee Appointed to Investigate the Police Department of the City of New York: The Lexow Committee Report, 6 vols. LC 75-154600. 1971. Repr. of 1895 ed. 300.00 set (ISBN 0-405-03399-0). Arno.

Reynolds, Quentin. Headquarters. LC 72-136080. 339p. 1972. Repr. of 1955 ed. lib. bdg. 15.75x (ISBN 0-8371-5230-5, REHQ). Greenwood.

Rudman, Jack. Patrolman - Police Department. (Career Examination Ser.: C-576). (Cloth bdg. avail. on request). pap. 8.00 (ISBN 0-8373-0576-4). Natl Learning.

--Police Patrolman. (Career Examination Ser.: C-595). (Cloth bdg. avail. on request). pap. 8.00 (ISBN 0-8373-0595-0). Natl Learning.

--Transit Captain. (Career Examination Ser.: C-819). (Cloth bdg. avail. on request). pap. 12.00 (ISBN 0-8373-0819-4). Natl Learning.

--Transit Lieutenant. (Career Examination Ser.: C-820). (Cloth bdg. avail. on request). pap. 10.00 (ISBN 0-8373-0820-8). Natl Learning.

--Transit Patrolman. (Career Examination Ser.: C-821). (Cloth bdg. avail. on request). pap. 8.00 (ISBN 0-8373-0821-6). Natl Learning.

--Transit Sergeant. (Career Examination Ser.: C-822). (Cloth bdg. avail. on request). pap. 10.00 (ISBN 0-8373-0822-4). Natl Learning.

Stead, William T. Satan's Invisible World Displayed: A Study of Greater New York. LC 73-19180. (Politics & People Ser.). (Illus.). 222p. 1974. Repr. 13.00x (ISBN 0-405-05901-9). Arno.

Turner, David R. Transit Patrolman. 4th ed. LC 49-5910. (Orig.). 1969. pap. 5.00 (ISBN 0-668-00092-9). Arco.

Walker, Tom. Fort Apache: Life & Death in NYC's Most Violent Police Precinct. LC 75-35906. 224p. 1976. 7.95 (ISBN 0-690-01047-8). T Y Crowell.

NEW YORK (CITY)–POLITICS AND GOVERNMENT

Abbott, David W., et al. Police, Politics & Race: The New York City Referendum on Civilian Review. 1969. pap. 2.50x (ISBN 0-674-68321-8). Harvard U Pr.

Advocacy Conference: Proceedings. 1978. 4.00 (ISBN 0-86671-039-6). Comm Coun Great NY.

Auletta, Ken. The Streets Were Paved with Gold. LC 78-21838. 1979. 12.95 (ISBN 0-394-50019-9). Random.

Barton, Allen, et al. Decentralizing City Government. (Illus.). 1977. 22.95 (ISBN 0-669-01098-7). Lexington Bks.

Bayor, Ronald H. Neighbors in Conflict: The Irish, Germans, Jews & Italians of New York City, 1929-1941. 2nd ed. LC 77-14260. 256p. 1980. pap. 5.95 (ISBN 0-8018-2370-6). Johns Hopkins.

Berger, Mark L. The Revolution in the New York Party System: 1840-1860. LC 72-89990. 1973. 11.00 (ISBN 0-8046-9030-8, Natl U). Kennikat.

Breen, Matthew P. Thirty Years of New York Politics, up to Date. LC 73-19132. (Politics & People Ser.). (Illus.). 918p. 1974. Repr. 48.00x (ISBN 0-405-05857-8). Arno.

Buckley, William F., Jr. The Unmaking of a Mayor. (Illus.). 1977. Repr. of 1966 ed. 9.95 (ISBN 0-87000-391-7). Arlington Hse.

Citron, Casper. John V. Lindsay. LC 65-26494. (Illus.). 1965. 6.95 (ISBN 0-8303-0045-7). Fleet.

Costikyan, Edward N. Behind Closed Doors: Politics in the Public Interest. LC 66-123599. 1968. pap. 5.75 (ISBN 0-15-611681-2, HB143, Harv). HarBraceJ.

Costikyan, Edward N & Lehman, Maxwell. Re-Structuring the Government of New York City: Report of the Scott Commission Task Force on Jurisdiction & Structure. LC 72-86838. (Special Studies in U. S. Economic, Social & Political Issues). 1972. 19.50x (ISBN 0-275-06320-8). Irvington.

Directory of Community Services: Directorio de Servicios Para la Comunidad (In The Bronx, Mahattan & Staten Island) bilingual ed. (Orig., Eng. Sp.). 1980. pap. 40.00 Spanish & English (ISBN 0-87104-634-2). NY Pub Lib.

Dix, John A. Sketch of the Resources of the City of New York: With a View of Its Municipal Government, Population, Etc. LC 79-112538. (Rise of Urban America). 1970. Repr. of 1827 ed. 12.00 (ISBN 0-405-02447-9). Arno.

Duffy, John. A History of Public Health in New York City, 1866-1966. LC 68-25852. 712p. 1974. text ed. 20.00 (ISBN 0-87154-213-7). Russell Sage.

Edwards, George W. & Peterson, Arthur E. New York As an Eighteenth Century Municipality, 2 pts. LC 68-56681. (Columbia University Studies in the Social Sciences: Nos. 177-178). Repr. of 1917 ed. Set. 28.00 (ISBN 0-404-51697-1); 14.00 ea. Pt. 1 Prior To 1731 (ISBN 0-404-51177-5). Pt. 2 1731-1776 (ISBN 0-404-51178-3). AMS Pr.

Eiberson, Harold. Sources for the Study of the New York Area. LC 60-15982. 128p. 1960. 7.95x (ISBN 0-8147-0135-3). NYU Pr.

Estades, Rosa. Patrones De Participacion Politica De los Puertorriquenos En la Ciudad De Nueva York. Gardenas-Ruiz, Manuel, tr. LC 77-12112. 1978. pap. 5.00 (ISBN 0-8477-2446-8). U of PR Pr.

--Patterns of Political Participation of Puerto Ricans in New York. LC 77-11625. 1978. pap. 5.00 (ISBN 0-8477-2445-X). U of PR Pr.

Farr, Walter G., Jr., et al. Decentralizing City Government: A Practical Study of a Radical Proposal for New York City. LC 72-83567. (Special Studies in U.S. Economic, Social, & Political Issues). 1972. 22.00x (ISBN 0-275-06330-5). Irvington.

Fitch, Lyle C. & Walsh, Annmarie H., eds. Agenda for a City: Issues Confronting New York. LC 77-110511. 718p. 1970. 25.00 (ISBN 0-8039-0076-7). Sage.

Gibson, Florence E. Attitudes of the New York Irish Toward State & National Affairs, 1848-1892. (Columbia University. Studies in the Social Sciences: No. 563). Repr. of 1951 ed. 24.50 (ISBN 0-404-51563-0). AMS Pr.

Hugins, Walter. Jacksonian Democracy & the Working Class: A Study of the New York Workingmen's Movement, 1829-1837. 1960. 15.00x (ISBN 0-8047-0026-5). Stanford U Pr.

Kivelson, Adrienne. What Makes New York City Run? LC 79-88289. 1979. pap. 2.50 (ISBN 0-916130-02-9). LWV NYC.

Kuo, Chia-Ling. Social & Political Change in New York's Chinatown: The Role of Voluntary Associations. LC 77-5328. (Special Studies). 1977. text ed. 24.95 (ISBN 0-03-021951-5). Praeger.

McBain, Howard L. De Witt Clinton & the Origin of the Spoils System in New York. LC 7-36153. (Columbia University. Studies in the Social Sciences: No. 75). Repr. of 1907 ed. 12.50 (ISBN 0-404-51075-2). AMS Pr.

Makielski, Stanislaw J. The Politics of Zoning: New York, 1916-1960. LC 65-25662. (Metropolitan Politics Ser.: No. 4). 1966. 17.50x (ISBN 0-231-02789-3). Columbia U Pr.

Merritt, Fred. The Building Code of the City of New York. 1970. 17.95x (ISBN 0-442-24970-5). Van Nos Reinhold.

Morris, C. R. The Cost of Good Intention: New York City & the Liberal Experiment. (McGraw-Hill Paperback Ser.). 1981. pap. price not set (ISBN 0-07-043280-5). McGraw.

Myers, Gustavus. History of Tammany Hall. 1971. pap. 4.50 (ISBN 0-486-21554-7). Dover.

--History of Tammany Hall. 2nd, rev., enl. ed. LC 68-56582. (Research & Source Works Ser: No. 298). 1967. Repr. of 1917 ed. 26.50 (ISBN 0-8337-2498-3). B Franklin.

Nevins, Allan. Abram S. Hewitt: With Some Account of Peter Cooper. 1967. Repr. lib. bdg. 35.00x (ISBN 0-374-96099-2). Octagon.

Newfield, Jack & DuBrul, Paul. The Permanent Government: Who Really Runs New York? rev. ed. 352p. 1981. pap. 9.95 (ISBN 0-8298-0466-8). Pilgrim NY.

Parkhurst, Charles H. Our Fight with Tammany. LC 73-112566. (Rise of Urban America). 1970. Repr. of 1895 ed. 17.00 (ISBN 0-405-02470-3). Arno.

Peel, Roy V. Political Clubs of New York City. LC 68-18356. (Empire State Historical Publications Ser: No. 48). (Illus.). 1968. Repr. of 1935 ed. 9.00 (ISBN 0-87198-048-7). Friedman.

Peterson, Arthur E. & Edwards, George W. New York As an Eighteenth Century Municipality, 2 Vols. in 1. LC 67-16260. (Empire State Historical Publications Ser: No. 46). 1917. 12.50 (ISBN 0-87198-046-0). Friedman.

Rogers, David. Can Business Management Save the Cities? The Case of New York. LC 77-18594. 1978. 13.95 (ISBN 0-02-926730-7). Free Pr.

--Management of Big Cities: Interest Groups & Social Change Strategies. LC 77-151671. 191p. 1971. pap. 9.95 (ISBN 0-8039-0936-5). Sage.

Sayre, Wallace S. & Kaufman, Herbert. Governing New York City. 1965. pap. 11.95x (ISBN 0-393-09657-2, NortonC). Norton.

--Governing New York City. LC 60-8408. 1960. 15.00 (ISBN 0-87154-732-5). Russell Sage.

Shaw, Frederick. History of New York City Legislature. LC 75-76659. (Columbia University. Studies in the Social Sciences: No. 581). Repr. of 1954 ed. 17.50 (ISBN 0-404-51581-9). AMS Pr.

Smith, Thelma E. Guide to the Municipal Government of the City of New York. rev. ed. LC 73-4426. 308p. 1973. pap. 4.95 (ISBN 0-88238-001-X). Law-Arts.

Stead, William T. Satan's Invisible World Displayed: A Study of Greater New York. LC 73-19180. (Politics & People Ser.). (Illus.). 222p. 1974. Repr. 13.00x (ISBN 0-405-05901-9). Arno.

NEW YORK (CITY)–POOR

Bahr, Howard M. & Caplow, Theodore. Old Men Drunk & Sober. LC 72-96370. (Illus.). 407p. 1974. 25.50x (ISBN 0-8147-0965-6). NYU Pr.

Brace, Charles L. The Dangerous Classes of New York. LC 73-84256. (NASW Classics Ser). (Illus.). 448p. 1973. pap. text ed. 5.95x (ISBN 0-87101-061-5, CBC-061-C). Natl Assn Soc Wkrs.

Cordasco, Francesco, ed. Jacob Riis Revisited. LC 72-93134. Repr. of 1970 ed. lib. bdg. 15.00x (ISBN 0-678-00706-3). Kelley.

Hosay, Philip M. The Challenge of Urban Poverty: Charity Reformers in New York City, 1835 to 1890. Cordasco, Francesco, ed. LC 80-864. (American Ethnic Groupgs Ser.). 1981. lib. bdg. 28.00x (ISBN 0-405-13427-4). Arno.

Koos, Earl L. Families in Trouble. LC 72-86976. (Illus.). xvi, 134p. 1973. Repr. of 1946 ed. 13.00 (ISBN 0-8462-1714-7). Russell.

Ostow, Miriam & Dutka, Anna B. Work & Welfare in New York City. LC 75-11357. (Policy Studies in Employment & Welfare: No. 21). (Illus.). 112p. 1975. 7.95x (ISBN 0-8018-1735-8); pap. 3.95x (ISBN 0-8018-1736-6). Johns Hopkins.

Puerto Rican Forum. The Puerto Rican Community Development Project. LC 74-14243. (A Puerto Rican Experience Ser). (Illus.). 162p. 1975. Repr. 9.00x (ISBN 0-405-06230-3). Arno.

Siegal, Harvey A. Outposts of the Forgotten: Socially Terminal People in Slum Hotels & Single Room Occupancy Tenements. LC 76-1777. 220p. 1978. 16.95 (ISBN 0-87855-141-7). Transaction Bks.

NEW YORK (CITY)–PUBLIC SCHOOLS

Berrol, Selma C. Immigrants at School: New York City, Eighteen Ninety-Eight to Nineteen Fourteen. Cordasco, Francesco, ed. LC 77-90872. (Bilingual-Bicultural Education in the U. S. Ser.). 1978. lib. bdg. 30.00x (ISBN 0-405-11077-4). Arno.

Bourne, William O. History of the Public School Society of the City of New York. LC 79-165733. (American Education Ser, No. 2). 1971. Repr. of 1870 ed. 36.00 (ISBN 0-405-03601-9). Arno.

Cohen, Rose N. The Financial Control of Education in the Consolidated City of New York. LC 79-176700. (Columbia University. Teachers College. Contributions to Education: No. 943). Repr. of 1948 ed. 17.50 (ISBN 0-404-55943-3). AMS Pr.

Dunn, Joan. Retreat from Learning: Why Teachers Can't Teach, a Case History. LC 75-16609. 224p. 1975. Repr. of 1955 ed. lib. bdg. 14.00x (ISBN 0-8371-8252-2, DURL). Greenwood.

Fuentes, Luis. La Lucha Contra el Racismo en Nuestras Escuelas: Control Comunal de las Escuelas Por las Comunidades Puertorriquenas, Negras y Chinas en la Ciudad de Nueva York. (Sp.). pap. 0.25 (ISBN 0-87348-327-8). Path Pr NY.

Gittell, Marilyn, et al. School Boards & School Policy: An Evaluation of Decentralization in New York City. LC 72-92475. (Special Studies in U. S. Social, Political & Economic Issues Ser.). (Illus.). 1973. text ed. 24.00x (ISBN 0-89197-929-8); pap. text ed. 12.50x (ISBN 0-89197-930-1). Irvington.

Kaestle, Carl F. The Evolution of an Urban School System: New York, 1750-1850. LC 72-93950. 1973. 12.50x (ISBN 0-674-27175-0). Harvard U Pr.

Lobman, Ethel & Sojourner, Katherine. The Struggle for Community Control in N. Y. School District One: Peurto Rican, Black & Chinese Parents Fight Racism. pap. 0.35 (ISBN 0-87348-344-8). Path Pr NY.

New York City. Board of Aldermen. Committee on General Welfare. Preliminary Report of the Committee on General Welfare in the Matter of a Request of the Conference of Organized Labor Relative to Educational Facilities. Meeting of June 26, 1917. LC 73-11924. (Metropolitan America Ser.). 350p. 1974. Repr. 19.00x (ISBN 0-405-05407-6). Arno.

Quance, Frank M. Part-Time Types of Elementary Schools in New York City: A Comparative Study of Pupil Achievement. LC 72-177173. (Columbia University. Teachers College. Contributions to Education: No. 249). Repr. of 1926 ed. 17.50 (ISBN 0-404-55249-8). AMS Pr.

Ravitch, Diane. The Great School Wars. LC 73-81136. 1975. pap. 5.95x (ISBN 0-465-09709-X, CN-5009). Basic.

Rich, Wilbur C. The Politics of Urban Personnel Policy: Reformers, Politicans & Bureaucrats. (Interdisciplinary Urban Ser.). 1981. 18.50 (ISBN 0-8046-9290-4). Kennikat.

Salley, Ruth E. Some Factors Affecting the Supply of & Demand for Pre-School Teachers in New York City. LC 78-177224. (Columbia University. Teachers College. Contributions to Education: No. 870). Repr. of 1943 ed. 17.50 (ISBN 0-404-55870-4). AMS Pr.

Tractenberg, Paul, ed. Selection of Teachers & Supervisors in Urban School Systems: A Transcript of the New York City Commission on Human Rights Public Hearings on the Procedures of the N. Y. C. Board of Examiners, January 25-29, 1971. LC 72-81915. 1972. 25.00x (ISBN 0-87988-001-5). Agathon.

NEW YORK (CITY)–PUBLIC WORKS

Arco Editorial Board. Sanitation Man. 4th ed. LC 65-26085. (Orig.). 1965. pap. 4.00 (ISBN 0-668-00025-2). Arco.

Millett, J. D. The Works Progress Administration in New York City. LC 77-74950. (American Federalism-the Urban Dimension). 1978. Repr. of 1938 ed. lib. bdg. 15.00x (ISBN 0-405-10496-0). Arno.

Pratt Institute, ed. Pratt Guide to Planning & Renewal for New Yorkers. LC 72-94651. (Illus.). 1973. 15.00 (ISBN 0-8129-0345-5). Times Bks.

NEW YORK (CITY)–SOCIAL CONDITIONS

Atkins, Gordon. Health, Housing & Poverty in New York City: 1865-1898. (Perspectives in American History: No. 51). (Illus.). Repr. of 1947 ed. lib. bdg. 19.50x (ISBN 0-87991-374-6). Porcupine Pr.

Benjamin, Gerald. Race Relations & the New York City Commission on Human Rights. LC 73-20790. (Illus.). 304p. 1974. 22.50x (ISBN 0-8014-0826-1). Cornell U Pr.

Brace, Charles L. Dangerous Classes of New York & Twenty Years's Work Among Them. 3rd ed. LC 67-26666. (Criminology, Law Enforcement, & Social Problems Ser.: No. 3). 1967. Repr. of 1880 ed. 17.00 (ISBN 0-87585-003-0). Patterson Smith.

Brager, George A. & Purcell, Francis P., eds. Community Action Against Poverty: Readings from the Mobilization Experience. 1967. 7.00x (ISBN 0-8084-0087-8); pap. 3.45 (ISBN 0-8084-0088-6, B44). Coll & U Pr.

Browne, Junius H. The Great Metropolis: A Mirror of New York... facsimile ed. LC 75-1833. (Leisure Class in America Ser.). (Illus.). 1975. Repr. of 1869 ed. 42.00x (ISBN 0-405-06902-2). Arno.

Campbell, Helen. Darkness & Daylight: Or, Lights & Shadows of New York Life: A Pictorial Record of Personal Experiences by Day & Night in the Great Metropolis with Hundreds of Thrilling Anecdotes & Incidents. LC 76-81511. 1969. Repr. of 1895 ed. 28.00 (ISBN 0-8103-3566-2). Gale.

Carlson, Karin. New York Self Help Handbook: A Step by Step Guide to Neighborhood Improvement Projects. LC 77-90736. (Illus.). 1978. pap. 4.95 (ISBN 0-9601496-1-9). Citizens Comm NY.

Characteristics of the Population in New York City Health Areas. Incl. No. 1. Age with an Analysis of the Distribution of Children & Youth; No. 2. Family Income, with an Analysis of the Distribution of Low Income Groups; No. 3. Race & Ethnicity. 1970. pap. 4.00 ea.; pap. 12.00 set of 3 (ISBN 0-686-11739-5). Comm Coun Great NY.

Characteristics of the Population in New York City Health Areas: Family Composition, No. 3. 1973. 4.00 (ISBN 0-86671-014-0). Comm Coun Great NY.

Citizens' Association Of New York. Report of the Council of Hygiene & Public Health of the Citizens' Association of New York Upon the Sanitary Condition of the City. LC 77-112532. (Rise of Urban America). (Illus.). 1970. Repr. of 1866 ed. 35.00 (ISBN 0-405-02443-6). Arno.

Cole, Mary. Summer in the City. (Illus.). 1968. 4.95 (ISBN 0-02-832040-9, 83204). Kenedy.

Cordasco, Francesco, ed. Italians in the City: An Original Anthology. LC 74-17933. (Italian American Experience Ser). (Illus.). 1975. Repr. 13.00x (ISBN 0-405-06405-5). Arno.

Crapsey, Edward. Nether Side of New York. LC 69-14919. (Criminology, Law Enforcement, & Social Problems Ser.: No. 46). 1969. Repr. of 1872 ed. 12.00 (ISBN 0-87585-046-4). Patterson Smith.

DeForest, Robert W. & Veiller, Lawrence, eds. Tenement House Problem: Including the Report of the New York State Tenement House Commission of 1900, 2 Vols. in 1. LC 75-112537. (Rise of Urban America). (Illus.). 1970. Repr. of 1903 ed. 45.00 (ISBN 0-405-02446-0). Arno.

Dorman, Michael. The Making of a Slum. 1972. 6.95 (ISBN 0-440-05192-4). Delacorte.

Eichner, Alfred S. & Brecher, Charles. Controlling Social Expenditures: The Search for Output Measures. LC 78-59180. (Conservation of Human Resources Ser.: No. 8). 224p. 1979. text ed. 23.50 (ISBN 0-916672-83-2). Allanheld.

Fitch, Lyle C. & Walsh, Annmarie H., eds. Agenda for a City: Issues Confronting New York. LC 77-110511. 718p. 1970. 25.00 (ISBN 0-8039-0076-7). Sage.

Ford, James. Slums & Housing, with Special Reference to New York City. LC 76-142935. (Illus.). 1972. Repr. of 1936 ed. 64.00x (ISBN 0-8371-5936-9). Greenwood.

Horlick, Allan S. Country Boys & Merchant Princes: The Social Control of Young Men in New York. LC 73-2887. 278p. 1975. 18.00 (ISBN 0-8387-1361-0). Bucknell U Pr.

Howe, Irving. World of Our Fathers. LC 75-16342. (Illus.). 736p. 1976. 14.95 (ISBN 0-15-146353-0). HarBraceJ.

--World of Our Fathers. LC 76-53818. 1977. pap. 6.95 (ISBN 0-671-22755-6, Touchstone). S&S.

Jenkins, Shirley. Comparative Recreation Needs & Services in New York Neighborhoods. 1963. 4.00 (ISBN 0-86671-000-0). Comm Coun Great NY.

Jones, Thomas J. Sociology of a New York City Block. (Columbia University. Studies in the Social Sciences: No. 55). Repr. of 1904 ed. 11.50 (ISBN 0-404-51055-8). AMS Pr.

Kane, Geoffrey. Inner-City Alcoholism: An Ecological Analysis & Cross-Cultural Study. 264p. 1981. 19.95x (ISBN 0-89885-023-1). Human Sci Pr.

Kantrowitz, Nathan. Ethnic & Racial Segregation Patterns in the New York City Metropolis: Residential Patterns Among White Ethnic Groups, Blacks & Puerto Ricans. LC 72-86840. (Special Studies in U.S. Economic, Social & Political Issues). 1973. 29.50x (ISBN 0-275-06550-2). Irvington.

Kaufmen, Michael. Rooftops & Alleys: Adventures with a City Kid. (gr. 4-6). 1973. 4.95 (ISBN 0-394-82486-5). Knopf.

Kessner, Thomas. The Golden Door: Italian & Jewish Immigrant Mobility in New York City, 1880-1915. 1977. text ed. 14.95 (ISBN 0-19-502116-9); pap. 4.95 (ISBN 0-19-502161-4). Oxford U Pr.

Ladies Of The Mission. Old Brewery & the New Mission House at the Five Points. LC 72-112563. (Rise of Urban America). (Illus.). 1970. Repr. of 1854 ed. 20.00 (ISBN 0-405-02461-4). Arno.

Longchamp, Ferdinand. Asmodeus in New York. facsimile ed. LC 75-1854. (Leisure Class in America Ser.). 1975. Repr. of 1868 ed. 22.00x (ISBN 0-405-06920-0). Arno.

Mariano, John H. The Italian Contribution to American Democracy. LC 74-17938. (Italian American Experience Ser). (Illus.). 336p. 1975. Repr. 19.00x (ISBN 0-405-06409-8). Arno.

Mohl, Raymond A. Poverty in New York, 1783-1825. (Urban Life in America Ser). 1971. 15.95 (ISBN 0-19-501367-0). Oxford U Pr.

People Who Live Alone in New York City: An Analysis of 1970 Census Facts. 1974. pap. 2.00 (ISBN 0-86671-021-3). Comm Coun Great NY.

Pratt, Edward E. Industrial Causes of Congestion of Population in New York City. LC 68-56682. (Columbia University. Studies in the Social Sciences: No. 109). Repr. of 1911 ed. 21.00 (ISBN 0-404-51109-0). AMS Pr.

Research Utilization Inventory: A Survey of Current Research of Social & Health Agencies in New York City. 1976. pap. 6.00 (ISBN 0-86671-033-7). Comm Coun Great NY.

Riis, Jacob. How the Other Half Lives. 1959. 6.00 (ISBN 0-8446-2807-7). Peter Smith.

--How the Other Half Lives. 231p. 1957. pap. 4.95 (ISBN 0-8090-0012-1, AmCen). Hill & Wang.

Riis, Jacob A. Battle with the Slum. LC 69-16245. (Criminology, Law Enforcement, & Social Problems Ser.: No. 77). (Illus.). 1969. Repr. of 1902 ed. 15.00 (ISBN 0-87585-077-4). Patterson Smith.

--How the Other Half Lives. 304p. 1981. Repr. of 1892 ed. lib. bdg. 25.00 (ISBN 0-89987-718-4). Darby Bks.

--How the Other Half Lives: Studies Among the Tenements of New York. Warner, Sam B., Jr., ed. LC 70-120321. (The John Harvard Library). (Illus.). 1970. 14.00x (ISBN 0-674-41006-8). Harvard U Pr.

--How the Other Half Lives: Studies Among the Tenements of New York. (Illus.). 10.00 (ISBN 0-8446-0233-7). Peter Smith.

--Out of Mulberry Street. LC 74-104550. Repr. of 1898 ed. lib. bdg. 17.50x (ISBN 0-8398-1758-4). Irvington.

--Ten Years' War: An Account of the Battle with the Slum in New York. facsimile ed. LC 70-103655. (Select Bibliographies Reprint Ser). 1900. 24.00 (ISBN 0-8369-5155-7). Arno.

Spier, Peter. The Legend of New Amsterdam. LC 78-6032. (Illus.). 32p. 1979. 7.95a (ISBN 0-385-13179-8); PLB (ISBN 0-385-13180-1). Doubleday.

This Is New York City: Facts & Trends for Social Planning. 1980. 2.00 (ISBN 0-86671-066-3). Comm Coun Great NY.

U.S. Bureau of Labor. Slums of Baltimore, Chicago, New York & Philadelphia. LC 73-89065. Repr. of 1894 ed. 30.00x (ISBN 0-8371-1922-7). Greenwood.

Wakefield, Dan. Island in the City: The World of Spanish Harlem. LC 74-14257. (A Puerto Rican Experience Ser). 290p. 1975. Repr. 19.00x (ISBN 0-405-06242-7). Arno.

Ware, Caroline F. Greenwich Village, 1920-1930: A Comment on American Civilization in the Post-War Years. LC 76-51282. 1977. Repr. lib. bdg. 30.00x (ISBN 0-374-98230-9). Octagon.

Warren, John H., Jr. Thirty Years' Battle with Crime: Or, the Crying Shame of New York, As Seen Under the Broad Glare of an Old Detective's Lantern. LC 73-112582. (Rise of Urban America). (Illus.). 1970. Repr. of 1875 ed. 19.00 (ISBN 0-405-02484-3). Arno.

Welfare Council, New York City. Puerto Ricans in New York City. LC 74-14230. (The Puerto Rican Experience Ser). (Illus.). 64p. 1975. Repr. 7.00x (ISBN 0-405-06219-2). Arno.

NEW YORK (CITY)-SOCIAL LIFE AND CUSTOMS

Birmingham, Stephen. Life at the Dakota: New York's Most Unusual Address. LC 79-4800. (Illus.). 1979. 12.50 (ISBN 0-394-41079-3). Random.

Botkin, Benjamin A. New York City Folklore: Legends, Tall Tales, Anecdotes, Stories, Sagas, Heroes & Characters, Customs, Traditions & Sayings. LC 76-43977. (Illus.). 1976. Repr. of 1956 ed. lib. bdg. 28.75x (ISBN 0-8371-9310-9, BONC). Greenwood.

Brown, Henry C. In the Golden Nineties. facs. ed. LC 71-133516. (Select Bibliographies Reprint Ser). 1927. 29.00 (ISBN 0-8369-5548-X). Arno.

Browne, Junius H. The Great Metropolis: A Mirror of New York... facsimile ed. LC 75-1833. (Leisure Class in America Ser.). (Illus.). 1975. Repr. of 1869 ed. 42.00x (ISBN 0-405-06902-2). Arno.

Child, Lydia M. Letters from New York. facs. 3rd ed. LC 79-137726. (American Fiction Reprint Ser). 1845. 17.00 (ISBN 0-8369-7025-X). Arno.

--Letters of Lydia Maria Child. LC 72-82183. (Anti-Slavery Crusade in America Ser). 1969. Repr. of 1883 ed. 12.00 (ISBN 0-405-00622-5). Arno.

Colon, Jesus. A Puerto Rican in New York & Other Sketches. LC 74-14229. (The Puerto Rican Experience Ser). 206p. 1975. Repr. 13.00x (ISBN 0-405-06218-4). Arno.

Crockett, Albert S. Peacocks on Parade: A Narrative of a Unique Period in American Social History & Its Most Colorful Figures. facsimile ed. LC 75-1836. (Leisure Class in America Ser.). (Illus.). 1975. Repr. of 1931 ed. 20.00x (ISBN 0-405-06905-7). Arno.

Earle, Alice M. Colonial Days in Old New York. LC 68-21767. 1968. Repr. of 1896 ed. 19.00 (ISBN 0-8103-3428-3). Gale.

Ellington, George. The Women of New York: The Underworld of the Great City. LC 72-2600. (American Women Ser: Images & Realities). 770p. 1972. Repr. of 1869 ed. 33.00 (ISBN 0-405-04456-9). Arno.

Fairfield, Francis G. & Croly, Jane. The Clubs of New York: Sorosis, 2 vols. in 1. facsimile ed. LC 75-1845. (Leisure Class in America Ser.). 1975. Repr. of 1873 ed. 23.00x (ISBN 0-405-06944-8). Arno.

Hamburger, Robert & Fowler-Gallagher, Susan. A Stranger in the House. 14.95 (ISBN 0-02-547610-6). Macmillan.

Hone, Philip. Diary of Philip Hone, 1828-1851, 2 Vols. in 1. 1927. 48.00 (ISBN 0-527-42100-6). Kraus Repr.

Kaufmen, Michael. Rooftops & Alleys: Adventures with a City Kid. (gr. 4-6). 1973. 4.95 (ISBN 0-394-82486-5). Knopf.

Laredo, Victor. New York City: A Photographic Portrait. (Illus.). 188p. 1972. pap. text ed. 5.00 (ISBN 0-486-22852-5). Dover.

Lehnartz, Kalus & Talbot, Allan R. New York in the Sixties. (Illus.). 10.00 (ISBN 0-8446-5787-5). Peter Smith.

Longchamp, Ferdinand. Asmodeus in New York. facsimile ed. LC 75-1854. (Leisure Class in America Ser.). 1975. Repr. of 1868 ed. 22.00x (ISBN 0-405-06920-0). Arno.

Maurice, Arthur B. Fifth Avenue. facsimile ed. LC 75-1860. (Leisure Class in America Ser.). (Illus.). 1975. Repr. of 1918 ed. 22.00x (ISBN 0-405-06926-X). Arno.

Mayer, Grace. Once Upon a City: New York from Eighteen Ninety to Nineteen Ten As Photographed by Byron & Described by Grace M. Mayer. xii, 511p. 1980. Repr. of 1958 ed. lib. bdg. 90.00x (ISBN 0-374-95418-6). Octagon.

Morris, Lloyd. Incredible New York: High Life & Low Life of the Last Hundred Years. facsimile ed. LC 75-1862. (Leisure Class in America Ser.). (Illus.). 1975. Repr. of 1951 ed. 22.00x (ISBN 0-405-06928-6). Arno.

Nevins, Allan, ed. Diary of Philip Hone 1828-1851. 2 Vols. in 1. LC 77-112559. (Rise of Urban America). (Illus.). 1970. Repr. of 1927 ed. 39.00 (ISBN 0-405-02468-1). Arno.

The New York Cultural Consumer. 264p. 1976. pap. 7.50x (ISBN 0-89062-019-9, Pub. by NYSCA). Pub Ctr Cult Res.

Pulitzer, Ralph. New York Society on Parade. facsimile ed. LC 75-1866. (Leisure Class in America Ser.). (Illus.). 1975. Repr. of 1910 ed. 10.00x (ISBN 0-405-06932-4). Arno.

Report of the Mayor's Committee on Cultural Policy, October 15, 1974. LC 74-20048. 100p. 1974. pap. 2.00x (ISBN 0-89062-014-8, Pub. by Mayor's Comm Cultural). Pub Ctr Cult Res.

Segal, Ryna A. New York City Department of Cultural Affairs, 1976-1973: A Record of Government's Involvement in the Arts. LC 76-22386. 88p. 1976. pap. 1.75x (ISBN 0-89062-037-7, Pub. by NYC Cultural). Pub Ctr Cult Res.

Seventy-Six - Seventy-Seven Directory of Educational Resources of New York City's Museums, Zoos & Botanical Gardens. 188p. 1976. pap. 5.00 (ISBN 0-89062-038-5, Pub. by Museums Collaborative). Pub Ctr Cult Res.

Singleton, Esther. Dutch New York. LC 68-20248. (Illus.). 1968. Repr. of 1909 ed. 20.00 (ISBN 0-405-08972-4, Pub. by Blom). Arno.

--Social New York Under the Georges 1714-1776, 2 Vols. LC 68-58928. (Empire State Historical Publications Ser: No. 60). (Illus.). 1969. Repr. of 1902 ed. Set. 15.00 (ISBN 0-87198-060-6). Friedman.

--Social New York Under the Georges 1717-1776. LC 68-26018. (Illus.). 1968. Repr. of 1902 ed. 20.00 (ISBN 0-405-08973-2, Pub. by Blom). Arno.

This Is New York City: Facts & Trends for Social Planning. 1980. 2.00 (ISBN 0-86671-066-3). Comm Coun Great NY.

Van Rensselaer, Mrs. John K. The Goede Vrouw of Mana-Ha-Ta: At Home & in Society, 1609-1760. LC 72-2629. (American Women Ser: Images & Realities). 422p. 1972. Repr. of 1898 ed. 18.00 (ISBN 0-405-04484-4). Arno.

Van Rensselaer, May K. The Social Ladder. facsimile ed. LC 75-911. (Leisure Class in America Ser.). (Illus.). 1975. Repr. of 1924 ed. 21.00x (ISBN 0-405-06937-5). Arno.

WMCA. Call for Action: A Survival Kit for New Yorkers. rev. ed. LC 74-24296. 320p. 1975. pap. 2.95 (ISBN 0-8129-6250-8). Times Bks.

NEW YORK (CITY)-SUBURBS AND ENVIRONS

Jamaica Bay & Kennedy Airport: A Multidisciplinary Environmental Study, 2 vols. 1971. Set. 9.75 (ISBN 0-309-01871-4). Natl Acad Pr.

NEW YORK (CITY)-THEATERS

Brown, T. A. A History of the New York Stage. 59.95 (ISBN 0-8490-0358-X). Gordon Pr.

Hughes, Catharine R., ed. American Theatre Annual, 1978-1979. (Illus.). 1980. 38.00 (ISBN 0-8103-0418-X, Incorporates New York Theatre Annual). Gale.

Lawliss, Chuck. The New York Theatre Guide. (Illus.). 320p. 1981. pap. 8.95 (ISBN 0-686-30979-0, Rutledge Pr). Smith Pubs.

Lee, Ronald S. & Lee, Patricia, eds. Stubs: The Seating Plan Guide for New York Theaters, Music Halls & Sports Stadia, 1981 Edition. (Illus.). 1980. pap. 3.95 (ISBN 0-911458-02-6, MNYE7). Stubs.

Off off Broadway Alliance & Levine, Mindy N. New York's Other Theatre: A Guide to off off Broadway. 256p. 1981. pap. 4.50 (ISBN 0-380-77909-9, 77909, Discus). Avon.

NEW YORK (CITY)-TRANSIT SYSTEMS

Arco Editorial Board. Trackman: Municipal Subway System. 6th ed. LC 72-2782. 1973. pap. 5.00 (ISBN 0-668-00075-9). Arco.

Condit, Carl W. The Port of New York: A History of the Rail & Therminal System from the Grand Central Electrification to the Present, Vol. 2. LC 79-16850. 384p. 35.00 (ISBN 0-226-11461-9). U of Chicago Pr.

Cudahy, Brian J. Under the Sidewalks of New York: The Story of the Greatest Subway System in the World. LC 79-15221. (Illus.). 1979. 16.95 (ISBN 0-8289-0352-2). Greene.

Sontheimer, Stanley & Fink, Howard D. Taxi Passengers Sertem: New York City Edition. Scudder, Janet, ed. LC 78-55544. (Illus.). 1978. pap. 2.50 (ISBN 0-9601694-1-5). Bradley David Assocs.

Walker, James B. Fifty Years of Rapid Transit 1864-1917. LC 70-112581. (Rise of Urban America). (Illus.). 1970. Repr. of 1918 ed. 17.00 (ISBN 0-405-02480-0). Arno.

NEW YORK (CITY)-ZOOLOGICAL PARK

Bridges, William. Zoo Doctor. (Illus.). (gr. 3-6). 1957. 7.25 (ISBN 0-688-21499-1). Morrow.

Buchenholz, Bruce, photos by. Doctor in the Zoo. (Illus.). 192p. (gr. 8 up). 1974. 12.95 (ISBN 0-670-27527-1, Studio). Viking Pr.

Lyle, Sparky & Golenbock, Peter. The Bronx Zoo. 1979. 8.95 (ISBN 0-517-53726-5). Crown.

NEW YORK (CITY) IN LITERATURE

Craige, Betty Jean. Lorca's "Poet in New York". The Fall into Consciousness. LC 76-24339. (Studies in Romance Languages: No. 15). 112p. 1977. 10.50x (ISBN 0-8131-1349-0). U Pr of Ky.

Maurice, A. B. New York in Fiction. 59.95 (ISBN 0-8490-0728-3). Gordon Pr.

NEW YORK (STATE)

see also names of cities, counties, and geographic areas in New York (State), e.g. Rochester; Dutchess County; Mohawk River and Valley

Bliven, Bruce, Jr. New York. (States & the Nation Ser.). (Illus.). 1981. 12.95 (ISBN 0-393-05665-1). Norton.

Bronin, Andrew. New York State. (Jackdaw Ser: No. A7). (Illus.). 1973. 6.95 (ISBN 0-670-50915-9, Grossman). Viking Pr.

Brownell, Joseph W. Census Statistics in Geography: A Manual for New York State. (Illus.). 1975. pap. 3.50x (ISBN 0-910042-23-3). Allegheny.

Goldman, Lawrence S. New York Criminal Law Handbook. 500p. Date not set. 60.00x (ISBN 0-07-023669-0). Dist. by Shepard's Inc. McGraw.

Jensen, David E. Minerals of New York State. LC 78-66426. (Illus.). 1978. 12.95 (ISBN 0-932142-00-1); pap. 7.95 (ISBN 0-932142-01-X). Ward Pr.

Lopez, Manuel D. New York: A Guide to Information & Reference Sources. LC 80-18634. x, 307p. 1980. 17.50 (ISBN 0-8108-1326-2). Scarecrow.

Miller, John. New York Considered & Approved. LC 72-78784. 1903. Repr. 6.00 (ISBN 0-403-01944-3). Somerset Pub.

New York. 33.00 (ISBN 0-89770-108-9). Curriculum Info Ctr.

New York Public Library, Research Libraries. Dictionary Catalog of the Local History & Genealogy Division, 20 vols. 1974. Set. lib. bdg. 1540.00 (ISBN 0-8161-0784-X). G K Hall.

Thompson, H. W. New York State Folktales, Legends & Ballads. Orig. Title: Body,Boots &Britches. (Illus.). 7.00 (ISBN 0-8446-3066-7). Peter Smith.

NEW YORK (STATE)-ANTIQUITIES

Ferguson, Henry L. Archeological Exploration of Fishers Island, New York. (Indian Notes & Monographs: Vol. 11, No. 1). 1935. pap. 1.50 (ISBN 0-934490-13-9). Mus Am Ind.

Granger, Joseph E., Jr. Meadowood Phase Settlement Pattern in the Niagara Frontier Region of Western New York State. (Anthropological Papers Ser.: No. 65). (Illus., Orig.). 1978. pap. 8.00x (ISBN 0-932206-76-X). U Mich Mus Anthro.

Ritchie, William A. Archaeology of New York State. rev ed. LC 80-13378. (Illus.). 1980. Repr. of 1969 ed. write for info (ISBN 0-916346-41-2). Harbor Hill Bks.

NEW YORK (STATE)-BIOGRAPHY

Lape, Fred. A Farm & Village Boyhood. LC 80-17303. (Illus.). 200p. 9.95 (ISBN 0-8156-0162-X, York State Bks). Syracuse U Pr.

Penney, Sharon H. Patrician in Politics: Daniel Dewey Barnard of New York. new ed. LC 74-77652. 220p. 1974. 15.00 (ISBN 0-8046-9067-7, Natl U). Kennikat.

Zistel, Era. Good Companions. large print ed. LC 80-29117. 1981. Repr. of 1980 ed. 7.95 (ISBN 0-89621-265-3). Thorndike Pr.

NEW YORK (STATE)-CHURCH HISTORY

Kreider, Harry J. Lutheranism in Colonial New York. LC 78-38452. (Religion in America, Ser. 2). 184p. 1972. Repr. of 1942 ed. 11.00 (ISBN 0-405-04072-5). Arno.

Smith, George L. Religion & Trade in New Netherland: Dutch Origins & American Development. LC 73-8403. 272p. 1973. 22.50x (ISBN 0-8014-0790-7). Cornell U Pr.

Taylor, Mary C. A History of the Foundations of Catholicism in Northern New York. LC 77-359034. (Monograph Ser.: No. 32). (Illus.). 12.00x (ISBN 0-930060-12-1). US Cath Hist.

Zwierlein, Frederick K. Religion in the New Netherland, 1623-1664. LC 72-120851. (Civil Liberties in American History Ser). 1970. Repr. of 1910 ed. lib. bdg. 35.00 (ISBN 0-306-71960-6). Da Capo.

NEW YORK (STATE)-COMMERCE

Condon, Thomas J. New York Beginnings: The Commercial Origins of New Netherland. LC 68-28003. (Illus.). 1968. 10.00x (ISBN 0-8147-0099-3). NYU Pr.

Smith, George L. Religion & Trade in New Netherland: Dutch Origins & American Development. LC 73-8403. 272p. 1973. 22.50x (ISBN 0-8014-0790-7). Cornell U Pr.

NEW YORK (STATE)-CONSTITUTION

Root, Elihu. Addresses on Government & Citizenship. facs. ed. LC 70-86779. (Essay Index Reprint Ser). 1916. 24.00 (ISBN 0-8369-1190-3). Arno.

NEW YORK (STATE)–COURT OF APPEALS

Smith, Franklin A. Judicial Review of Legislation in N.Y. 1906-1938. LC 71-76658. (Columbia University. Studies in the Social Sciences: No. 574). Repr. of 1952 ed. 16.00 (ISBN 0-404-51574-6). AMS Pr.

NEW YORK (STATE)–DESCRIPTION AND TRAVEL

Bailey, Rosalie F. Pre-Revolutionary Dutch Houses & Families in Northern New Jersey & Southern New York. (Illus.). 1968. pap. 6.00 (ISBN 0-486-21985-2). Dover.

Bloomfield, J. A., ed. The Lakes of New York State, 2 vols. Incl. Vol. 1. Ecology of the Finger Lakes. 34.50, by subscription 34.50 (ISBN 0-12-107301-7); Vol. 2. The Lakes of Western New York. 31.00, by subscription 31.00 (ISBN 0-12-107302-5). 1978. Acad Pr.

Blumin, Stuart & Durlach, Hansi. The Short Season of Sharon Springs: Perspectives on Another New York. (Illus.). 128p. 1980. 19.95 (ISBN 0-8014-1303-6). Cornell U Pr.

Clardy, Andrea F., ed. Ithaca: A Book of Photographs. (Illus.). 96p. pap. 8.95 (ISBN 0-935526-03-X). Crossing Pr.

Clint, Florence & Fay, Loren V. New York State Area Key. 208p. 1979. pap. 12.00 (ISBN 0-686-27873-9). Keyline Pubs.

Conover, Jewel H. Nineteenth-Century Houses in Western New York. LC 66-63788. (Illus.). 1966. 17.00 (ISBN 0-87395-017-8); microfiche 17.00 (ISBN 0-87395-117-4). State U NY Pr.

Cooper, William. Guide in the Wilderness. facs. ed. LC 79-140352. (Select Bibliographies Reprint Ser). 1810. 10.00 (ISBN 0-8369-5595-1). Arno.

Covey, Frances A. The Earl Covey Story. (Illus.). 1979. 10.00 (ISBN 0-682-49443-7). Exposition.

Danckaerts, Jasper. Journal of Jasper Danckaerts, Sixteen Seventy-Nine to Sixteen Eighty. James, B. B. & Jameson, J. Franklin, eds. (Original Narratives). 1969. Repr. of 1913 ed. 18.50x (ISBN 0-06-480422-4). B&N.

Dwight, Timothy. Travels in New England & New York, 4 Vols. Solomon, Barbara M., ed. LC 69-12735. (The John Harvard Library). (Illus.). 1969. Repr. of 1821 ed. Set. boxed 40.00x (ISBN 0-674-90670-5). Harvard U Pr.

Federal Writers Project, New York. Rochester & Monroe County. LC 73-3646. (American Guide Ser.). Repr. of 1937 ed. 25.00 (ISBN 0-404-57945-0). AMS Pr.

Federal Writers Project, Pennsylvania. Erie: A Guide to the City & County. LC 73-3649. Repr. of 1938 ed. 17.00 (ISBN 0-404-57948-5). AMS Pr.

Fowler, Barney. Adirondack Album, Vol. 2. (Illus.). 200p. (Orig.). 1980. pap. 10.25 (ISBN 0-9605556-0-9). Outdoor Assocs.

Fowler, John. Journal of a Tour in the State of New York in the Year 1830. LC 70-122073. Repr. of 1831 ed. 19.50x (ISBN 0-678-00582-6). Kelley.

Giambarba, Paul. Blue Water Views of Old New York. (Illus.). pap. 3.95 (ISBN 0-87155-115-2). Scrimshaw.

Gould, Jay. Delaware County, New York. 1977. Repr. 20.00 (ISBN 0-686-22207-5). Polyanthos.

Holbrook, Stewart H. Old Post Road. 1971. pap. 3.50 (ISBN 0-07-029536-0, SP). McGraw.

Howison, John. Sketches of Upper Canada, Domestic, Local, & Characteristic. 1965. Repr. of 1821 ed. 17.00 (ISBN 0-384-24490-4). Johnson Repr.

Johnson, Harry & Lightfoot, Frederick. Maritime New York in Nineteenth Century Photographs. (Illus.). 160p. (Orig.). 1980. pap. 7.95 (ISBN 0-486-23963-2). Dover.

Johnson, Herbert A. Historic Courthouses of New York State: 18th. & 19th. Century Halls of Justice Across the Empire State. Andrist, Ralph K., ed. LC 77-23962. (Illus.). 175p. 1977. 20.00x (ISBN 0-231-04432-1). Columbia U Pr.

Macia, Rafael. The New York Bicycler. LC 75-185628. (Illus.). 1972. pap. 2.50 (ISBN 0-671-21176-5, Fireside). S&S.

Miller, John. New York Considered & Improved Sixteen Ninety-Five. LC 73-114816. (Illus.). 1970. Repr. of 1903 ed. 23.50 (ISBN 0-8337-2392-8). B Franklin.

O'Connor, Lois. A Finger Lakes Odyssey. 1975. soft cover 5.95 (ISBN 0-932052-04-5). North Country.

Reynolds, Helen W. Dutch Houses in the Hudson Valley Before 1776. (Illus.). 12.50 (ISBN 0-8446-2796-8). Peter Smith.

--Dutch Houses in the Hudson Valley Before 1776. (Illus.). 1965. pap. 6.95 (ISBN 0-486-21469-9). Dover.

Roseberry, C. R. From Niagra to Montauk: The Scenic Pleasures of New York State. LC 81-5640. (Illus.). 242p. 1981. 33.50x (ISBN 0-87395-496-3, ROFN); pap. 10.95 (ISBN 0-87395-497-1, ROFN-P). State U NY Pr.

Schwarz, Jeanne. Student Guide to Richards Atlas of New York State. 1976. pap. 6.95x ea. (ISBN 0-88323-108-5, 304). Richards Pub.

Spafford, Horatio G. Eighteen Twenty-Four Gazetteer of the State of New York. 1981. lib. bdg. 25.00 (ISBN 0-932334-39-3); pap. 20.00 (ISBN 0-932334-40-7). Heart of the Lakes.

Stewart, Donald H. Opposition Press of the Federalist Period. LC 69-11319. 1969. 59.00 (ISBN 0-87395-042-9); microfiche 59.00 (ISBN 0-87395-142-5). State U NY Pr.

Street, Alfred B. Woods & Waters: Or, the Saranacs & Racket. LC 75-45369. (Illus.). 1976. Repr. of 1860 ed. 14.50 (ISBN 0-916346-18-8). Harbor Hill Bks.

Sylvester, Nathaniel B. Historical Sketches of Northern New York & the Adirondack Wilderness: Including Traditions of the Indians, Early Explorers, Pioneer Settlers, Hermit Hunters. LC 73-5937. (Illus.). 324p. 1973. Repr. of 1877 ed. pap. 8.95 (ISBN 0-916346-00-5). Harbor Hill Bks.

Thompson, John H., ed. Geography of New York State. LC 66-14602. (Illus.). 1977. pap. 27.50x (ISBN 0-8156-2182-5); supplement & 3 color maps o.p. 6.95x (ISBN 0-8156-2185-X); supplement only o.p. 2.95 (ISBN 0-8156-2190-6). Syracuse U Pr.

Tobey, Eric & Wolkenberg, Richard. Northeast Bicycle Tours. (Illus.). 286p. 1973. pap. 3.95 (ISBN 0-686-10413-7, 440-6233-395). Tobey Pub.

Van Der Donck, Adriaen. Description of the New Netherlands. O'Donnell, Thomas F., ed. LC 68-29420. (New York State Studies). 1968. 10.00x (ISBN 0-8156-2127-2). Syracuse U Pr.

Van Diver, Bradford B. Rocks & Routes of the North Country, New York. LC 76-46243. (Illus.). 1976. pap. text ed. 6.95 (ISBN 0-685-83503-0). Van Diver.

Wade, Richard C., ed. Regional Survey of New York & Its Environs, 10 vols. (Metropolitan America Ser.). (Illus.). 1974. Set. 170.00x (ISBN 0-405-05439-4). Arno.

NEW YORK (STATE)–DESCRIPTION AND TRAVEL–GUIDEBOOKS

Andrews, Peter, et al. New York& Mid-Atlantic. LC 79-22906. (Country Inns of America Ser.). (Illus.). 96p. (Orig.). 1980. pap. 6.95 (ISBN 0-03-043721-0). HR&W.

Arthur Frommer's Guide to New York, 1981-82. 224p. 1981. pap. 2.95 (ISBN 0-671-41438-0). Frommer-Pasmantier.

Bolton, Robert. A Guide to New Rochelle & Its Vicinity: Pelham, West Chester, West Farms, Morrisania, Fordham, Yonkers, East Chester, White Plains, Mamaroneck & Rye. Weigold, Marilyn, ed. LC 76-6922. (Illus.). 1976. pap. 2.95 (ISBN 0-916346-22-6). Harbor Hill Bks.

Brush, John E. & Carey, George W., eds. Guidebook for Field Excursions, New York, 1976. (Illus.). 1976. pap. 2.00 (ISBN 0-89291-112-3). Assn Am Geographers.

Curran, William. Beautiful New York. LC 79-90287. 80p. 1979. 14.95 (ISBN 0-89802-004-2); pap. 7.95 (ISBN 0-89802-003-4). Beautiful Am.

Dumbleton, Susanne & Older, Anne. In & Around Albany: A Guide for Residents, Students & Visitors. (Illus.). 183p. (Orig.). 1980. pap. 4.50 (ISBN 0-9605460-0-6). Wash Park.

Ehling, Bill. Twenty-Five Ski Tours in Central New York. (Illus.). 128p. 1980. pap. 5.95 (ISBN 0-89725-019-2). NH Pub Co.

--Twenty-Five Walks in the Finger Lakes Region of New York. LC 78-71718. (Illus.). 1979. pap. 5.95 (ISBN 0-89725-004-4). NH Pub Co.

Federal Writers Project. New York: Guide to the Empire State. (American Guide Ser). 1940. 14.95 (ISBN 0-19-500038-2). Oxford U Pr.

Federal Writers' Project. New York State: A Guide to the Empire State. 782p. 1940. Repr. 59.00 (ISBN 0-403-02151-0). Somerset Pub.

New York World. The Conning Tower Book. 59.95 (ISBN 0-87968-931-5). Gordon Pr.

Newberry, Lida. One-Day Adventures by Car: With Full Directions for Drivers Out of New York City. rev. ed. (Illus.). 288p. 1980. pap. 6.95 (ISBN 0-8038-5393-9). Hastings.

Osler, Jack M. Fifty Great Mini-Trips for New York. (Jack Osler's Mini-Trips Ser.). (Illus.). Date not set. pap. cancelled (ISBN 0-89645-010-4). Media Ventures.

Philipsburg Manor: A Guidebook. LC 72-89495. (Illus.). 56p. 1969. pap. 0.85 (ISBN 0-912882-01-8). Sleepy Hollow.

Robert Nicholson Publications. Nicholson's New York Guide. 152p. (Orig.). 1981. pap. 4.95 (ISBN 0-684-17279-8, ScribT). Scribner.

Scheller, William G. AMC Guide to Country Walks Near New York City. (Illus.). 200p. (Orig.). 1980. pap. 6.95 (ISBN 0-910146-29-2). Appalach Mtn.

Titterton, Pat & Bassett, Sara. Capitol Cuisine. 1979. pap. 3.95 (ISBN 0-932052-21-5). North Country.

Tomlan, Mary R. A Walking Tour in Canadaigua, New York. (Illus.). 1977. pap. text ed. 3.00 (ISBN 0-89257-024-5). Am Life Foun.

NEW YORK (STATE)–ECONOMIC CONDITIONS

Blumin, Stuart M. The Urban Threshold: Growth & Change in a Nineteenth-Century American Community. LC 75-27891. 1976. lib. bdg. 15.00x (ISBN 0-226-06169-8). U of Chicago Pr.

Brenner, M. Harvey. Mental Illness & the Economy. LC 72-85144. 320p. 1973. 16.50x (ISBN 0-674-56875-3). Harvard U Pr.

Cochran, Thomas C. New York in the Confederation. LC 72-77054. (Illus.). Repr. of 1932 ed. 5.75x (ISBN 0-678-00911-2). Kelley.

Commerce Clearing House. Tax Law of the State of New York: 1980 Edition. 1980. 15.00 (ISBN 0-686-75932-X). Commerce.

Edwards, Richard, ed. New York's Great Industries. LC 73-2504. (Big Business; Economic Power in a Free Society Ser.). Repr. of 1884 ed. 23.00 (ISBN 0-405-05086-0). Arno.

McClelland, Peter D. & Magdovitz, Alan L. Crisis in the Making: The Political Economy of New York State Since 1945. LC 80-24167. (Studies in Economic History & Policy: the United States in the Twentieth Century). (Illus.). 512p. 1981. 24.95 (ISBN 0-521-23807-2). Cambridge U Pr.

Miller, Nathan. Enterprise of a Free People: Aspects of Economic Development in New York State During the Canal Period, 1792-1838. LC 62-8487. (Beveridge Award Books Ser.). 293p. 1962. 19.50x (ISBN 0-8014-0300-6). Cornell U Pr.

National Research Center of the Arts, Inc. A Second Look: The Nonprofit Arts & Cultural Industry of New York State 1975-76. 308p. 1978. pap. 8.50x (ISBN 0-89062-097-0, Pub. by NY Found Arts). Pub Ctr Cult Res.

Ringenbach, Paul T. Tramps & Reformers, 1873-1916: The Discovery of Unemployment in New York. LC 77-175610. (Contributions in American History: No. 27). (Illus.). 224p. 1973. lib. bdg. 15.00 (ISBN 0-8371-6266-1, RAT/). Greenwood.

Ritchie, Robert C. The Duke's Province: A Study of New York Politics & Society, 1664-1691. LC 77-681. 1977. 21.00x (ISBN 0-8078-1292-7). U of NC Pr.

Zinser, Charles I. The Economic Impact of the Adirondack Park Private Land Use & Development Plan. LC 79-15569. 1980. 29.00 (ISBN 0-87395-399-1). State U NY Pr.

NEW YORK (STATE)–EMIGRATION AND IMMIGRATION

Kapp, Friedrich. Immigration & the Commissioners of Emigration of the State of New York. LC 69-18782. (American Immigration Collection Ser., No. 1). 1969. Repr. of 1870 ed. 7.50 (ISBN 0-405-00530-X). Arno.

NEW YORK (STATE)–FAMILY COURT

Biskind, Elliott L., ed. Boardman's New York Family Law. rev. ed. LC 64-17549. 1972. looseleaf with 1980 suppl. 60.00 (ISBN 0-87632-058-2). Boardman.

Gould Editorial Staff. Family Court Act (N.Y.) 250p. (Supplemented annually). looseleaf 10.00 (ISBN 0-87526-143-4). Gould.

Samuels, Aaron. Family Court Law & Practice in New York. rev. ed. 1972. 35.00 (ISBN 0-685-05161-7). Acme Law.

NEW YORK (STATE)–GENEALOGY

Abstracts of Wills on File in the Surrogate's Office, City of New York, 1665-1801: Collections, New York Historical Society, 1892-1908, 17 vols. 8.00 ea.; Set. 100.00x (ISBN 0-685-73867-1). U Pr of Va.

Bull Family. Fifty Years of the Bull Family Picnic, 1922-1972. 4.95x (ISBN 0-686-14963-7). T E Henderson.

DeLong, Thomas A. The DeLongs of New York & Brooklyn: A Huguenot Family Portrait. LC 75-189091. (Illus.). 203p. 1972. 9.95 (ISBN 0-912980-01-X). Sasco.

Eager. Marriage of William Bull. 4.95x (ISBN 0-686-14960-2). T E Henderson.

Hamm, M. A. Famous Families of New York, 2 vols. in one. (Illus.). 1971. 12.50 (ISBN 0-685-22782-0). Heraldic Pub.

Joel Munsell's Sons. American Ancestry: Giving the Name & Descent, in the Male Line, of Americans, Whose Ancestors Settled in the U. S. Previous to the Declaration of Independence, Vols. 1-12. LC 67-30977. 1968. 15.00 ea. (ISBN 0-8063-0239-9); Set. 175.00 (ISBN 0-685-11727-8). Genealog Pub.

LeFevre, Ralph. History of New Paltz, New York & Its Old Families, from 1678 to 1820. LC 70-105530. (Illus.). 1973. Repr. of 1909 ed. 35.00 (ISBN 0-8063-0551-7). Genealog Pub.

Luther, Leslie L. A Complete Name Index to the History of Cayuga Co., NY of Eighteen Seventy-Nine. 1978. 15.50x (ISBN 0-932334-07-5); pap. 10.00x (ISBN 0-932334-08-3). Heart of the Lakes.

Luther, Leslie L. & Luther, Bertha K. A Complete Name Index of the Biographical Review of Cayuga County, NY (Edition of Eighteen Ninety-Four) 1977. 10.50x (ISBN 0-932334-00-8); pap. 5.00x (ISBN 0-932334-01-6). Heart of the Lakes.

MacWethy, Lou D. Book of Names Especially Relating to the Early Palatines & the First Settlers in the Mohawk Valley. LC 69-17132. (Illus.). 1969. Repr. of 1933 ed. 12.50 (ISBN 0-8063-0231-3). Genealog Pub.

McWhorter, Emma. History & Genealogy of the Bull Family. LC 73-89689. 1976. 35.00x (ISBN 0-686-14954-8). T E Henderson.

O'Callaghan, Edmund B. Lists of Inhabitants of Colonial New York. LC 79-52062. (Repr. of 1849-1851 ed.). 1979. 17.50 (ISBN 0-8063-0847-8). Genealog Pub.

Orange County Genealogical Society. Index to the Eighteen Eighty-One Ruttenber & Clark History of Orange County, New York. LC 79-84908. 1980. 20.00 (ISBN 0-9604116-1-5). Orange County Genealog.

Papers of the Lloyd Family of the Manor of Queens Village, Lloyd's Neck, Long Island, New York, 1654-1826, 2 vols. LC 28-6973. 10.00x (ISBN 0-685-73920-1, New York Historical Society). U Pr of Va.

Pearson, Jonathan. Contributions for the Genealogies of the Descendants of the First Settlers of the Patent & City of Schenectady N.Y. from 1662 to 1800. LC 76-20240. 1976. Repr. of 1873 ed. 15.00 (ISBN 0-8063-0730-7). Genealog Pub.

Predmore, Helen, et al, eds. Cemeteries of Chester, New York. LC 77-12179. (Orange County, New York Cemeteries Ser.: No. 1). 142p. (Orig.). 1977. pap. 6.95 (ISBN 0-912526-20-3). Orange County Genealog.

Presbyterian Church Historical Society of Campbell Hall, N.Y. Cemeteries of the Town of Hamptonburgh, Orange County, New York. LC 80-81240. (Orange County, New York Cemeteries Ser.: No. 2). 88p. (Orig.). 1980. pap. 3.95 (ISBN 0-9604116-2-3). Orange County Genealog.

Robison, Jeannie F. & Bartlett, Henrietta C. Genealogical Records: Manuscript Entries of Births, Deaths & Marriages, Taken from Family Bibles 1581-1917. LC 72-86813. (Illus.). xv, 331p. 1972. Repr. of 1917 ed. 15.00 (ISBN 0-8063-0487-1). Genealog Pub.

Scott, Kenneth. Genealogical Data from Colonial New York Newspapers. LC 77-79068. 1977. 15.00 (ISBN 0-8063-0777-3). Genealog Pub.

--Marriages & Deaths from the New Yorker: Double Quatro Edition 1836-1841. LC 80-80958. 308p. 22.75 (ISBN 0-915156-46-6, SP46). Natl Genealogical.

--New York State Census of Albany County Towns in 1790. LC 75-7592. 1975. wrappers 6.50 (ISBN 0-685-70661-3). Genealog Pub.

Scott, Kenneth & Conway, Rosanne. New York Alien Residents, 1825-1848. LC 78-57005. 1978. 10.00 (ISBN 0-8063-0814-1). Genealog Pub.

Scott, Kenneth & Gibbons, Kristin L. The New York Magazine: Marriages & Deaths, 1790-1797. 1976. 15.00 (ISBN 0-686-20885-4). Polyanthos.

Scott, Kenneth & Stryker-Rodda, Kenn. Denizations, Naturalizations & Oaths of Allegiance in Colonial New York. LC 75-10680. 1975. 12.00 (ISBN 0-8063-0679-3). Genealog Pub.

Talcott, Sebastian V. Genealogical Notes of New York & New England Families. LC 72-5682. 1973. Repr. of 1883 ed. 25.00 (ISBN 0-8063-0537-1). Genealog Pub.

Tyne, John J. Index of Names for the Eighteen Seventy-Eight History of Otsego Co., NY. 1978. 17.50x (ISBN 0-932334-09-1); pap. 12.00x (ISBN 0-932334-10-5). Heart of the Lakes.

--Index of Names in the Eighteen Eighty History of Chenango & Madison Counties, NY. 1978. 20.50x (ISBN 0-932334-03-2); pap. 15.00x (ISBN 0-932334-04-0). Heart of the Lakes.

--Index to Names in the History of the Century: Delaware Co., Ny. 1978. pap. 6.00x (ISBN 0-932334-11-3). Heart of the Lakes.

U. S. Bureau Of The Census. Heads of Families, First Census of the United States, 1790: New York. LC 64-62656. 1961-64. Repr. of 1908 ed. 15.00 (ISBN 0-87152-020-6). Reprint.

Wood, Ralph V., Jr., ed. Herkimer County New York State: Federal Population Census Schedules 1800, 1810, 1820 Transcripts & Index. LC 65-4818. viii, 186p. 1965. pap. 8.50 (ISBN 0-915184-05-2, Pub. by Oak Hill). R V Wood.

--Jefferson & St. Lawrence Counties, New York 1810 & 1820 Federal Population Census Schedules, Transcripts & Index. LC 63-42291. xi, 240p. 1963. pap. 9.75 (ISBN 0-915184-02-8, Pub. by Oak Hill). R V Wood.

--Oneida County New York 1800 Federal Population Census Schedule Transcript & Index. iv, 103p. 1962. pap. 4.75 (ISBN 0-915184-00-1, Pub. by Oak Hill). R V Wood.

--Ontario County New York State, 1800 Federal Population Census Schedule, Transcript & Index. LC 63-52558. (Illus.). vi, 59p. 1963. pap. 3.25 (ISBN 0-915184-01-X, Pub. by Oak Hill). R V Wood.

--Ontario County, New York State, 1810: Federal Population Census Schedule, Transcript & Index. LC 65-4110. (Illus.). vi, 162p. 1964. pap. 7.25 (ISBN 0-915184-03-6, Pub. by Oak Hill). R V Wood.

--Ostego County New York State, 1800: Federal Population Census Schedule, Transcript & Index. LC 65-4697. vii, 68p. 1965. pap. 4.50 (ISBN 0-915184-04-4, Pub. by Oak Hill). R V Wood.

NEW YORK (STATE)–HISTORY

Beauchamp, William M. Aboriginal Place Names of New York. LC 68-17915. 333p. 1972. Repr. of 1907 ed. 25.00 (ISBN 0-8103-3231-0). Gale.

--Moravian Journals Relating to Central New York. LC 72-8246. (Communal Societies in America Ser). Repr. of 1916 ed. 20.00 (ISBN 0-404-11000-2). AMS Pr.

Bernstein, Burton. The Sticks. LC 71-39651. 240p. 1972. 5.95 (ISBN 0-396-06528-7). Dodd.

Bolton, Reginald P. Indian Life of Long Ago in the City of New York. LC 71-151809. (Empire State Historical Publications Ser). (Illus.). 1971. Repr. of 1934 ed. 12.00 (ISBN 0-87198-094-0). Kennikat.

Briggs, Mary S., ed. The Ferguson-Jayne Papers, 2 vols. 1981. lib. bdg. price not set (ISBN 0-9606606-2-3). Davenport.

Calver, William L. & Bolton, Reginald P. History Written with Pick & Shovel. LC 50-10740. (New York Historical Society). (Illus.). 1970. 8.00x (ISBN 0-685-73900-7). U Pr of Va.

Chalmers, Harvey, 2nd. Tales of the Mohawk: Stories of Old New York State from Colonial Times to the Age of Homespun, 1st & 2nd Ser. LC 68-18354. (Empire State Historical Publications Ser). (Illus.). 1968. 8.50 ea.; 1st ser. (ISBN 0-8046-8057-4); 2nd ser. (ISBN 0-8046-8058-2). Friedman.

Collections of the New-York Historical Society, Vol. 1. LC 1-16509. (Second Ser.). (Illus.). 20.00x (ISBN 0-685-73881-7). U Pr of Va.

Collections of the New-York Historical Society, Vol. 2, Pt. 1. LC 1-16509. (Second Ser.). 1848. pap. 10.00x (ISBN 0-685-73882-5). U Pr of Va.

Collections of the New-York Historical Society, Vol. 3, Pt. 1. LC 1-16509. (Second Ser.). 1857. 20.00x (ISBN 0-685-73889-2). U Pr of Va.

Collections of the New-York Historical Society: 1882. LC 1-13394. (Illus.). 10.00x (ISBN 0-685-73883-3). U Pr of Va.

Collections of the New-York Historical Society: 1909. LC 1-16508. 5.00x (ISBN 0-685-73885-X). U Pr of Va.

Collections of the New-York Historical Society: 1913. LC 1-16508. 5.00x (ISBN 0-685-73886-8). U Pr of Va.

Collections of the New-York Historical Society: 1912. LC 1-16508. 5.00x (ISBN 0-685-73887-6). U Pr of Va.

Collections of the New-York Historical Society: 1875. LC 1-13394. 10.00x (ISBN 0-685-73888-4). U Pr of Va.

Collections of the New-York Historical Society: 1868. LC 1-16508. 10.00x (ISBN 0-685-73890-6). U Pr of Va.

Collections of the New-York Historical Society: 1869. LC 1-16508. 10.00x (ISBN 0-685-73891-4). U Pr of Va.

Collections of the New-York Historical Society: 1870. LC 1-16508. 5.00x (ISBN 0-685-73892-2). U Pr of Va.

Collections of the New-York Historical Society: 1878, 1879, 1880, 3 vols. LC 1-13394. 10.00x ea. U Pr of Va.

Conklin, Henry. Through Poverty's Vale: A Hardscrabble Boyhood in Upstate New York, 1832-1862. Tripp, Wendell, ed. LC 73-19980. (Illus.). 280p. 1974. 8.50 (ISBN 0-8156-0098-4); pap. 5.95 (ISBN 0-8156-0117-4). Syracuse U Pr.

Coolidge, Guy O. The French Occupation of the Champlain Valley: From 1609-1759. 1979. Repr. of 1938 ed. 9.75 (ISBN 0-916346-34-X). Harbor Hill Bks.

Countryman, Edward. A People in Revolution: The American Revolution & Political Society in New York, 1760-1790. LC 81-5993. (Studies in Historical & Political Science 99th Series: No. 2). 352p. 1981. text ed. 24.50x (ISBN 0-8018-2625-X). Johns Hopkins.

Davidson, Marshall B. New York: A Pictorial History. LC 77-3921. (Encore Edition). (Illus.). 356p. 1977. 9.95 (ISBN 0-684-16188-5, ScribT). Scribner.

Dunkelman, Mark H. & Winey, Michael J. The Hardtack Regiment: An Illustrated History of the 154th Regiment, New York State Infantry Volunteers. LC 79-64502. (Illus.). 216p. 1981. 19.50 (ISBN 0-8386-3007-3). Fairleigh Dickinson.

Dunlap, William. History of the New Netherlands, Province of New York, & State of New York, to the Adoption of the Federal Constitution, 2 Vols. LC 70-130594. 1970. Repr. of 1839 ed. Set. 48.00 (ISBN 0-8337-0963-1). B Franklin.

Ellis, David M. New York: State & City. LC 78-15759. (Illus.). 1979. 12.95 (ISBN 0-8014-1180-7). Cornell U Pr.

Ellis, David M., et al. History of New York State. rev. ed. (Illus.). 752p. 1967. 24.95 (ISBN 0-8014-0118-6); text ed. 19.50x (ISBN 0-8014-0119-4). Cornell U Pr.

Everest, Allan S. Rum Across the Border: The Prohibition Era in Northern New York. (York State Bks). (Illus.). 1978. 9.95 (ISBN 0-8156-0152-2). Syracuse U Pr.

Follett, Frederick. History of the Press in Western New York: From the Beginning to the Middle of the Nineteenth Century. LC 73-6520. (Illus.). 80p. 1973. Repr. of 1920 ed. 8.50 (ISBN 0-916346-03-X). Harbor Hill Bks.

French, J. H. Historical & Statistical Gazetteer of New York State. (Illus.). 782p. 1980. Repr. of 1860 ed. deluxe ed. 22.50 deluxe (ISBN 0-932334-31-8); pap. 17.50 (ISBN 0-932334-32-6). Heart of the Lakes.

French, Robert M. A Name Index for the Eighteen Seventy-Nine History of Allegany County, NY. 1978. 15.00x (ISBN 0-932334-05-9); pap. 10.00x (ISBN 0-932334-06-7). Heart of the Lakes.

Frese, Joseph R. & Judd, Jacob, eds. Business Enterprise in Early New York. LC 79-9346. 1979. 17.50 (ISBN 0-912882-38-7). Sleepy Hollow.

Friedman, Saul S. Incident at Massena: The Blood Libel in America. 1978. 9.95 (ISBN 0-8128-2526-8). Stein & Day.

Grinstein, Hyman B. The Rise of the Jewish Community of New York 1654-1860. LC 76-7555. (Perspectives in American History Ser., No. 27). (Illus.). xiii, 645p. Repr. of 1945 ed. lib. bdg. 27.50x (ISBN 0-87991-351-7). Porcupine Pr.

Hastings, Hugh & Noble, Henry H., eds. Military Minutes of the Council of Appointment of the State of New York, 1783-1821, 4 vols. LC 74-19724. Repr. of 1902 ed. Set. 348.50 (ISBN 0-404-12488-7). AMS Pr.

Hedrick, Ulysses P. A History of Agriculture in the State of New York. 6.95 (ISBN 0-686-16044-4); pap. 2.45 (ISBN 0-686-16045-2). Fenimore Bk.

Hershkowitz, Leo & Klein, Milton M., eds. Courts & Law in Early New York: Selected Essays. (National University Pubns., Multi-Disciplinary Series in the Law). 1978. 12.50 (ISBN 0-8046-9206-8). Kennikat.

Higgins, Ruth L. Expansion in New York: With Special Reference to the Eighteenth Century. LC 76-8251. (Perspectives in American History Ser., No. 30). (Illus.). xi, 209p. Repr. of 1931 ed. lib. bdg. 15.00x (ISBN 0-87991-354-1). Porcupine Pr.

Hulbert, Archer B. History of the Niagara River. LC 78-12656. (Illus.). 1978. Repr. of 1908 ed. 19.50 (ISBN 0-916346-29-3). Harbor Hill Bks.

Hutchinson, Lucille & Hutchinson, Theodore. The Centennial History of North Tarrytown. LC 74-18739. (Illus.). 1974. 11.95 (ISBN 0-9601366-1-4). T Hutchinson.

Irving, Washington. A History of New York from the Beginning of the World to the End of the Dutch Dynasty, 2 vols. LC 72-78760. 1809. Repr. 44.00 (ISBN 0-686-01681-5). Somerset Pub.

Jackson, Ronald V. & Teeples, Gary R. New York City Census Index 1800. LC 77-86124. (Illus.). lib. bdg. 40.00 (ISBN 0-89593-096-X). Accelerated Index.

--New York City Census Index 1810. LC 77-86125. (Illus.). lib. bdg. 44.00 (ISBN 0-89593-097-8). Accelerated Index.

--New York City Census Index 1820. LC 77-86116. (Illus.). lib. bdg. 61.00 (ISBN 0-89593-098-6). Accelerated Index.

--New York City Census Index 1840. LC 77-86118. (Illus.). lib. bdg. 110.00 (ISBN 0-89593-100-1). Accelerated Index.

--New York City Census 1830. LC 77-86117. (Illus.). lib. bdg. 90.00 (ISBN 0-89593-099-4). Accelerated Index.

--New York City Census 1850, 2 vols. LC 77-86120. (Illus.). Set. lib. bdg. 150.00 (ISBN 0-89593-101-X). Accelerated Index.

Judd, Jacob, ed. Correspondence of the Van Cortlandt Family of Cortlandt Manor, 1800-1814. LC 78-16849. (Van Cortlandt Family Papers: Vol. 3). 1978. 22.00 (ISBN 0-912882-34-4). Sleepy Hollow.

Lossing, Benson J. Empire State: A Compendious History of the Commonwealth of New York. LC 68-57492. (Illus.). 1968. Repr. of 1888 ed. 22.50 (ISBN 0-87152-050-8). Reprint.

Malo, Paul. Landmarks of Rochester & Monroe County: A Guide to Neighborhoods & Villages. LC 73-23095. (Illus.). 280p. 1974. 12.00 (ISBN 0-8156-0103-4); pap. 6.95 (ISBN 0-8156-0104-2). Syracuse U Pr.

Morton, Terry B., ed. Lyndhurst on the Hudson River, Tarrytown, N. Y. (National Trust Property Ser.). (Illus.). 48p. 1980. pap. 2.50 (ISBN 0-89133-078-X). Preservation Pr.

Myers, Andrew, ed. The Knickerbocker Tradition: Washington Irving's New York. LC 74-678. 160p. 1974. buckram bound 8.00 (ISBN 0-912882-08-5). Sleepy Hollow.

New York Constitutional Convention, 1821. Reports of the Proceedings & Debates. LC 72-133168. (Law, Politics & History Ser.). 1970. Repr. of 1821 ed. lib. bdg. 65.00 (ISBN 0-306-70069-7). Da Capo.

Nordstrom, Carl. Frontier Elements in a Hudson River Village. new ed. LC 72-91175. (National University Publications). 1973. 13.95 (ISBN 0-8046-9033-2). Kennikat.

Paltsits, Victor H., ed. Minutes of the Executive Council of the Province of New York, 2 vols. LC 74-19731. Repr. of 1910 ed. Set. 75.00 (ISBN 0-404-12262-0). AMS Pr.

Parker, Arthur C. The Archaeological History of New York, 2 vols. in 1. LC 76-43800. (New York State Museum. Bulletin: Nos. 235, 236, 237, 238). Repr. of 1922 ed. 53.50 (ISBN 0-404-15656-8). AMS Pr.

Proceedings & Addresses at the Freethinkers' Convention Held at Watkins, N. Y., 1878. LC 73-119051. (Civil Liberties in American History Ser). 1970. Repr. of 1878 ed. lib. bdg. 39.50 (ISBN 0-306-71937-1). Da Capo.

Rapp, Marvin A. New York. LC 68-9256. 1968. pap. 2.95 (ISBN 0-8077-2022-4). Tchrs Coll.

Roberts, Ellis H. New York: The Planting & the Growth of the Empire State, 2 vols. LC 72-3763. (American Commonwealths: Nos. 8-9). Repr. of 1904 ed. 54.00 (ISBN 0-404-57221-9). AMS Pr.

Robinton, Madeline R. Introduction to the Papers of the New York Prize Court, 1861-1865. 1971. lib. bdg. 13.00x (ISBN 0-374-96889-6). Octagon.

Schiro, George. Americans by Choice: Italians in Utica, New York. LC 74-17953. (Italian American Experience Ser). (Illus.). 192p. 1975. Repr. 11.00x (ISBN 0-405-06422-5). Arno.

Schull, Diantha D. Landmarks of Otsego County. (Illus.). 288p. 1980. 18.95 (ISBN 0-8156-0157-3); pap. 9.95 (ISBN 0-8156-0158-1). Syracuse U Pr.

Schwarz & Goldberg. New York State in Story, Pts. 1 & 2. 1962. comb. 7.95x (ISBN 0-88323-099-2, 280); wkbk. 2.50x (ISBN 0-88323-100-X, 283). Richards Pub.

--New York State in Story, Pt. 1. rev. ed. 1962. pap. 3.50x (ISBN 0-88323-096-8, 281). Richards Pub.

--The Story of New York State. 1962. pap. 3.50x (ISBN 0-88323-098-4, 282). Richards Pub.

Scott, Kenneth & Gibbons, Kristin L. The New York Magazine: Marriages & Deaths, 1790-1797. 1976. 15.00 (ISBN 0-686-20885-4). Polyanthos.

Seaver, James E. A Narrative of the Life of Mrs. Mary Jamison Who Was Taken by the Indians in the Year 1755 When Only About 12 Years of Age & Has Continued to Reside Amongst Them to the Present Time, Repr. Of 1824 Ed. Bd. with enl. ed. Morgan, Lewis H., ed. Repr. of 1856 ed. LC 75-7063. (Indian Captivities Ser.: Vol. 41). 1977. lib. bdg. 44.00 (ISBN 0-8240-1665-3). Garland Pub.

Smeal, Lee. New York Historical & Biographical Index. LC 78-53710. (Illus.). Date not set. lib. bdg. price not set (ISBN 0-89593-193-1). Accelerated Index.

The Smith & Telfer Photographic Collection of the New York State Historical Association. 18.75 (ISBN 0-686-16047-9); pap. 14.50 (ISBN 0-686-16048-7). Fenimore Bk.

Smith, Carlyle S. The Archaeology of Coastal New York. LC 76-43833. (AMNH. Anthropological Papers: Vol. 43, Pt. 2). Repr. of 1950 ed. 14.50 (ISBN 0-404-15687-8). AMS Pr.

Smith, James H. History of Dutchess County, New York: 1683-1882. 720p. 1980. Repr. of 1882 ed. 35.00 (ISBN 0-932334-35-0). Heart of the Lakes.

Smith, William, Jr. History of the Province of New York, 2 Vols. Kammen, Michael, ed. LC 78-160028. (The John Harvard Library). (Illus.). 1972. Set. 35.00x (ISBN 0-674-40321-5). Harvard U Pr.

Snyder, Charles M. Red & White on the New York Frontier: A Struggle for Survival, Insights from the Papers of Erastus Granger, Indian Agent, 1807-1819. LC 78-14239. (Illus.). 1978. 9.50 (ISBN 0-916346-28-5). Harbor Hill Bks.

Squier, Ephraim G. Antiquities of the State of New York. LC 76-43858. Repr. of 1851 ed. 24.50 (ISBN 0-404-15712-2). AMS Pr.

Street, Alfred B. Council of Revision in the State of New York. Repr. of 1859 ed. 35.00 (ISBN 0-89201-055-X). Zenger Pub.

U. S. Bureau of the Census. Heads of Families at the First Census of the United States Taken in the Year 1790: New York. LC 73-167707. 1976. Repr. of 1908 ed. 20.00 (ISBN 0-8063-0485-5). Genealog Pub.

Vanderhoof, Elisha W. Historical Sketches of Western New York. LC 71-134434. Repr. of 1907 ed. 14.00 (ISBN 0-404-08476-1). AMS Pr.

Van De Water, J. W. Chichee's Trunk: A Story of Roots & Branches. (Illus.). 130p. (Orig.). pap. 5.00x (ISBN 0-9606620-0-6). Jonsalvania.

Versteeg, Dingman, et al, trs. New York Historical Manuscripts: Dutch Kingston Papers, 2 vols. Scott, Kenneth & Stryker-Rodda, Kenn, eds. LC 75-5971. (Illus.). 1976. Set. 40.00 (ISBN 0-8063-0720-X). Genealog Pub.

Vinovskis, Maris A. Demographic History & the World Population Crisis. Billias, George A., ed. LC 76-50581. (Bland-Lee Lectures in History Ser.). (Illus.). 1976. pap. 2.00x (ISBN 0-914206-07-9). Clark U Pr.

Wolley, Charles. A Two Year's Journal in New York & Part of Its Territories in America. LC 73-5949. (Illus.). 96p. 1973. Repr. of 1902 ed. 7.50 (ISBN 0-916346-01-3). Harbor Hill Bks.

NEW YORK (STATE)–HISTORY–BIBLIOGRAPHY

Chronology & Documentary Handbook of the State of New York. 1974. 8.50 (ISBN 0-379-00610-3). Oceana.

Gocek, Matilda A. Orange County, New York: A Reader's Guide & Bibliography. LC 73-77313. 60p. 1973. pap. 2.45 (ISBN 0-912526-05-X). Lib Res.

Tyne, John J. Index to Names in the Eighteen Eighty-Five History of Broome County, New York. 131p. (Orig.). 1978. text ed. 15.50x (ISBN 0-932334-12-1); pap. 10.00x (ISBN 0-932334-13-X). Heart of the Lakes.

Vance, Mary. Historical Society Architectural Publications: New York, North Carolina, & North Dakota. (Architecture Ser.: Bibliography A-161). 72p. 1980. pap. 7.50 (ISBN 0-686-26908-X). Vance Biblios.

NEW YORK (STATE)–HISTORY–SOURCES

Barber, John W. & Howe, Henry. Historical Collections of the State of New York. LC 78-118780. (Empire State Historical Publications Ser). (Illus.). 1970. Repr. of 1841 ed. 27.50x (ISBN 0-87198-083-5). Friedman.

Christoph, Peter R., ed. New York Historical Manuscripts: English, Vol. 22. LC 79-92327. 261p. 1980. 18.50 (ISBN 0-8063-0880-X). Genealog Pub.

Corwin, E. T., ed. Ecclesiastical Records of the State of New York, 7 vols. LC 74-19602. Repr. of 1916 ed. Set. 440.00 (ISBN 0-404-12305-8); 63.00 ea.; Vol. 1. (ISBN 0-404-12306-6); Vol. 2. (ISBN 0-404-12307-4); Vol. 3. (ISBN 0-404-12308-2); Vol. 4. (ISBN 0-404-12309-0); Vol. 5. (ISBN 0-404-12310-4); Vol. 6. (ISBN 0-404-12311-2); Vol. 7. (ISBN 0-404-12312-0). AMS Pr.

Fowler, John. Journal of a Tour in the State of New York in the Year 1830. LC 70-122073. Repr. of 1831 ed. 19.50x (ISBN 0-678-00582-6). Kelley.

Gehring, Charles T., ed. New York Historical Manuscripts: Dutch Delaware Papers. LC 76-41652. (Illus.). 1977. 20.00 (ISBN 0-8063-0736-6). Genealog Pub.

--New York Historical Manuscripts: Dutch, Vols. GG, HH, & II. LC 73-14890. 141p. 1980. 16.50 (ISBN 0-8063-0876-1). Genealog Pub.

Judd, Jacob, ed. Correspondence of the Van Cortlandt Family of Cortlandt Manor, 1748-1800. LC 77-3281. (Van Cortlandt Family Papers: Vol. 2). (Illus.). 1977. 19.00 (ISBN 0-912882-29-8). Sleepy Hollow.

Loving, Jerome M., ed. Civil War Letters of George Washington Whitman. LC 74-83788. 1975. 12.75 (ISBN 0-8223-0331-0). Duke.

New York Historical Society. Collections of the New York Historical Society, First Series, 5 vols. in 4. Repr. of 1811 ed. Set. 130.00 (ISBN 0-404-11070-3); Vol. 1. 30.00 (ISBN 0-404-11071-1); Vol. 2. 30.00 (ISBN 0-404-11072-X); Vol. 3. 30.00 (ISBN 0-404-11073-8); Vols. 4 & 5. 40.00 (ISBN 0-404-11074-6). AMS Pr.

O'Callaghan, Edmund B., ed. Calandar of Historical Manuscripts in the Office of the Secretary of State, Albany, New York: Dutch Manuscripts 1630 - 1664, Pt. 1. 423p. 1968. Repr. of 1865 ed. 26.00 (ISBN 0-8398-1451-8). Parnassus Imprints.

--Calandar of Historical Manuscripts in the Office of the Secretary of State, Albany, New York: English Manuscripts 1664 - 1776, Pt. 2. 891p. 1968. Repr. of 1866 ed. 52.00 (ISBN 0-8398-1452-6). Parnassus Imprints.

Van Laer, Arnold J., tr. New York Historical Manuscripts: Dutch, 4 vols. LC 73-14890. 2032p. 1974. 75.00 set (ISBN 0-685-42613-0). Vol. 1 (ISBN 0-8063-0584-3). Vol. 2 (ISBN 0-8063-0585-1). Vol. 3 (ISBN 0-8063-0586-X). Vol. 4 (ISBN 0-8063-0587-8). Genealog Pub.

NEW YORK (STATE)–HISTORY–COLONIAL PERIOD, ca. 1600-1775

Bloch, Julius M., ed. An Account of Her Majesty's Revenue in the Province of New York, Seventeen Hundred & One to Seventeen Hundred & Nine. (Illus.). 1966. 25.00 (ISBN 0-8398-0059-2). Parnassus Imprints.

Bonomi, Patricia U. A Factious People: Politics & Society in Colonial New York. LC 74-156803. 342p. 1971. 20.00x (ISBN 0-231-03509-8); pap. 7.50x (ISBN 0-231-08329-7). Columbia U Pr.

Christensen, Gardell D. Colonial New York. LC 69-15223. (Colonial History Ser). (Illus.). (gr. 5 up). 1969. 7.95 (ISBN 0-525-67102-1). Elsevier-Nelson.

Colden, Cadwallader. History of the Five Indian Nations. 181p. (YA) (gr. 9-12). 1958. pap. 3.95 (ISBN 0-8014-9086-3, CP86). Cornell U Pr.

--The History of the Five Indian Nations of Canada Which Are Dependent on the Province of New York, & Are a Barrier Between the English & the French. LC 72-2827. (American Explorers Ser.). Repr. of 1922 ed. 37.50 (ISBN 0-404-54908-X). AMS Pr.

The Colonial Laws of New York from the Year 1664 to the Revolution, 5 vols. LC 74-19603. Repr. of 1896 ed. Set. 390.00 (ISBN 0-404-12313-9); 78.00 ea. AMS Pr.

Condon, Thomas J. New York Beginnings: The Commercial Origins of New Netherland. LC 68-28003. (Illus.). 1968. 10.00x (ISBN 0-8147-0099-3). NYU Pr.

Danckaerts, Jasper. Journal of Jasper Danckaerts, Sixteen Seventy-Nine to Sixteen Eighty. James, B. B. & Jameson, J. Franklin, eds. (Original Narratives). 1969. Repr. of 1913 ed. 18.50x (ISBN 0-06-480422-4). B&N.

Danckaerts, Jasper & Sluyter, Peter. Journal of a Voyage to New York & a Tour in Several of the American Colonies in Sixteen Seventy-Nine to Sixteen Eighty. Murphy, Henry C., ed. xv, 437p. 1967. Repr. of 1867 ed. 28.00 (ISBN 0-8398-0351-6). Parnassus Imprints.

Dawson, Henry B. Sons of Liberty in New York. LC 71-90172. (Mass Violence in America Ser). Repr. of 1859 ed. 11.00 (ISBN 0-405-01306-X). Arno.

Dunlap, William. History of the New Netherlands, Province of New York, & State of New York, to the Adoption of the Federal Constitution, 2 Vols. LC 70-130594. 1970. Repr. of 1839 ed. Set. 48.00 (ISBN 0-8337-0963-1). B Franklin.

Fox, Dixon R. Caleb Heathcote, Gentleman Colonist. LC 74-164523. (Illus.). viii, 301p. 1972. Repr. of 1926 ed. lib. bdg. 17.50x (ISBN 0-8154-0392-5). Cooper Sq.

--Yankees & Yorkers. LC 79-15575. (Illus.). 1980. Repr. of 1940 ed. lib. bdg. 20.50x (ISBN 0-8371-5720-X, FOYY). Greenwood.

Greenberg, Douglas. Crime & Law Enforcement in the Colony of New York, 1691-1776. LC 76-13658. (Illus.). 1976. 19.50x (ISBN 0-8014-1020-7). Cornell U Pr.

Hamlin, Paul L. Legal Education in Colonial New York. LC 70-129082. (American Constitutional and Legal History Ser.). (Illus.). 1970. Repr. of 1939 ed. lib. bdg. 25.00 (ISBN 0-306-70062-X). Da Capo.

Innes, J. H. New Amsterdam & Its People. 1902. Repr. 20.00 (ISBN 0-685-43210-6). Norwood Edns.

Irving, Washington. A History of New York. Bowden, Edwin T., ed. (Masterworks of Literature Ser). 1964. 7.50x (ISBN 0-8084-0158-0). Coll & U Pr.

--Knickerbocker's History of New York. Moore, Anne C., ed. LC 59-11666. (Illus.). 1959. 18.00 (ISBN 0-8044-1420-3). Ungar.

Janvier, Thomas A. Dutch Founding of New York. LC 67-16259. (Empire State Historical Publications Ser: No. 45). (Illus.). 1903. 8.95 (ISBN 0-87198-045-2). Friedman.

Jaray, Cornell, ed. Historic Chronicles of New Amsterdam, Colonial New York & Early Long Island, First & Second Series. LC 68-18355. (Empire State Historical Publications Ser: Nos. 35 & 36). ser. 1. 9.00 (ISBN 0-87198-035-5); ser. 2. 9.00 (ISBN 0-87198-036-3). Friedman.

Johnson, Herbert A. Essays on New York Colonial Legal History. LC 81-6204. (Contributions in Legal Studies: No. 21). (Illus.). 320p. 1981. lib. bdg. 29.95 (ISBN 0-313-20874-3, JNC/). Greenwood.

Kammen, Michael. Colonial New York: A History. LC 75-5693. (A History of the American Colonies Ser.). 1975. lib. bdg. 25.00 (ISBN 0-527-18717-8). Kraus Intl.

--Colonial New York: A History. (Illus.). 1978. pap. 6.95 (ISBN 0-527-18725-9, Pub. by Two Continents). Hippocrene Bks.

Kennedy, John H. Thomas Dongan, Governor of New York (1682-1688) LC 73-3564. (Catholic University of America. Studies in American Church History: No. 9). Repr. of 1930 ed. 15.45 (ISBN 0-404-57759-8). AMS Pr.

Ketchum, William. Authentic & Comprehensive History of Buffalo, 2 Vols. 1864-65. Set. 35.00 (ISBN 0-403-00372-5). Scholarly.

Launitz-Schurer, Leopold, Jr. Loyal Whigs & Revolutionaries: The Making of the Revolution in New York, 1765-1776. LC 79-53579. 1980. 20.00x (ISBN 0-8147-4994-1). NYU Pr.

Myers, Andrew B. & Myers, Andrew. Diedrich Knickerbocker's a History of New York. facsimile ed. (Illus.). 496p. 1981. Repr. of 1854 ed. 23.95 (ISBN 0-912882-46-8). Sleepy Hollow.

National Society Of The Colonial Dames Of America. Catalogue of the Genealogical & Historical Library of the Colonial Dames of the State of New York. LC 76-149778. 1971. Repr. of 1912 ed. 41.00 (ISBN 0-8103-3713-4). Gale.

Nissenson, S. G. The Patroon's Domain. LC 72-13740. x, 416p. 1971. Repr. lib. bdg. 20.00x (ISBN 0-374-96109-3). Octagon.

Nurenberg, Thelma. New York Colony. LC 77-77966. (Forge of Freedom Ser). (Illus.). (gr. 5-8). 1969. 7.95 (ISBN 0-02-768400-8, CCPr). Macmillan.

O'Callaghan, Edmund B. History of New Netherland: Or, New York Under the Dutch, 2 Vols. LC 66-25099. (Illus.). 1967. Repr. of 1846 ed. Vol. 1. 20.00 (ISBN 0-87152-033-8); Vol. 2. 25.00 (ISBN 0-87152-034-6); Set. 45.00 (ISBN 0-87152-332-9). Reprint.

Ritchie, Robert C. The Duke's Province: A Study of New York Politics & Society, 1664-1691. LC 77-681. 1977. 21.00x (ISBN 0-8078-1292-7). U of NC Pr.

Singleton, Esther. Dutch New York. LC 68-20248. (Illus.). 1968. Repr. of 1909 ed. 20.00 (ISBN 0-405-08972-4, Pub. by Blom). Arno.

Van Der Donck, Adriaen. Description of the New Netherlands. O'Donnell, Thomas F., ed. LC 68-29420. (New York State Studies). 1968. 10.00x (ISBN 0-8156-2127-2). Syracuse U Pr.

Van der Zee, Henri & Van der Zee, Barbara. A Sweet & Alien Land: The Story of the Dutch in New York. 1978. 19.95 (ISBN 0-670-68628-X). Viking Pr.

Zwierlein, Frederick K. Religion in the New Netherland, 1623-1664. LC 72-120851. (Civil Liberties in American History Ser). 1970. Repr. of 1910 ed. lib. bdg. 35.00 (ISBN 0-306-71960-6). Da Capo.

NEW YORK (STATE)–HISTORY–COLONIAL PERIOD, ca. 1600-1775–SOURCES

Brodhead, John R., et al, eds. Documents Relative to the Colonial History of the State of New York, 15 Vols. Repr. of 1887 ed. Set. 1275.00 (ISBN 0-404-01090-3); 85.00 ea. AMS Pr.

Jameson, J. Franklin, ed. Narratives of New Netherland, Sixteen Nine to Sixteen Sixty-Four. (Original Narratives). 1967. Repr. of 1909 ed. 18.50x (ISBN 0-06-480429-1). B&N.

Journal of the Legislative Council of the Colony of New York, 2 vols. LC 74-19723. Set. 125.00 (ISBN 0-404-12485-2). AMS Pr.

Journals of the Provincial Congress, Provincial Convention, Committee of Safety & Council of Safety of the State of New York, 2 vols. LC 74-19725. Repr. of 1842 ed. Set. 190.00 (ISBN 0-404-12493-3, J87). AMS Pr.

Scott, Kenneth & Stryker-Rodda, Kenn. Denizations, Naturalizations & Oaths of Allegiance in Colonial New York. LC 75-10680. 1975. 12.00 (ISBN 0-8063-0679-3). Genealog Pub.

Stevens, John A., Jr. Colonial Records with Historical & Biographical Sketches, 1768-1784, 2 vols. in 1. Incl. Colonial New York: Sketches, Biographical & Historical, 1768-1784. LC 78-153573. (New York State Chamber of Commerce Pubn.). Repr. of 1867 ed. 36.50 (ISBN 0-8337-3404-0). B Franklin.

NEW YORK (STATE)–HISTORY–REVOLUTION, 1775-1783

Abbott, W. C. New York in the American Revolution. LC 72-7428. (American History & Americana Ser., No. 47). 1973. Repr. of 1929 ed. lib. bdg. 37.95 (ISBN 0-8383-1668-9). Haskell.

Albany County Sessions. Minutes of the Commissioners for Detecting & Defeating Conspiracies in the State of New York, 2 vols. Paltsits, Victor H., ed. LC 72-1835. (Era of the American Revolution Ser.). (Illus.). 1972. Repr. of 1909 ed. Set. lib. bdg. 95.00 (ISBN 0-306-70504-4). Da Capo.

Boynton, Edward C. History of West Point. facs. ed. LC 71-126233. (Select Bibliographies Reprint Ser). 1863. 29.00 (ISBN 0-8369-5458-0). Arno.

Campbell, Patrick. Patrick Campbell's Travels. LC 78-50738. 1978. 12.50x (ISBN 0-8139-0858-2). U Pr of Va.

Cochran, Thomas C. New York in the Confederation. LC 71-118781. (Empire State Historical Publications Ser: No. 84). 1970. Repr. of 1932 ed. 7.50 (ISBN 0-87198-084-3). Friedman.

Countryman, Edward. A People in Revolution: The American Revolution & Political Society in New York, 1760-1790. LC 81-5993. (Studies in Historical & Political Science 99th Series: No. 2). 352p. 1981. text ed. 24.50x (ISBN 0-8018-2625-X). Johns Hopkins.

Fernow, Berthold. New York in the Revolution. 1976. 25.00 (ISBN 0-686-20884-6). Polyanthos.

Fish, Hamilton. New York State: The Battleground of the Revolutionary War. 1977. 7.95 (ISBN 0-533-02128-6). Vantage.

Flick, Alexander C. Loyalism in New York During the American Revolution. LC 75-120214. (Columbia University. Studies in the Social Sciences: No. 37). Repr. of 1901 ed. 10.00 (ISBN 0-404-51037-X). AMS Pr.

--Loyalism in New York During the American Revolution. LC 72-90175. (Mass Violence in America Ser). Repr. of 1901 ed. 13.00 (ISBN 0-405-01310-8). Arno.

Graymont, Barbara. Iroquois in the American Revolution. LC 73-170096. (New York State Studies). (Illus.). 1972. 14.95x (ISBN 0-8156-0083-6); pap. 6.95 (ISBN 0-8156-0116-6). Syracuse U Pr.

Gregory, James, compiled by. Narratives of The Revolution in New York. LC 75-2526. (Illus.). 1975. 12.95x (ISBN 0-685-73917-1, New York Historical Society). U Pr of Va.

Jones, Thomas. History of New York During the Revolutionary War, & of the Leading Events in the Other Colonies at That Period, 2 vols. De Lancey, Edward F., ed. LC 67-29030. (Eyewitness Accounts of the American Revolution Ser., No. 1). 1968. Repr. of 1879 ed. Set. 23.00 (ISBN 0-686-66373-X); Vol. 1. 13.00 (ISBN 0-405-01133-4); Vol. 2. 10.00 (ISBN 0-405-01128-8). Arno.

Launitz-Schurer, Leopold, Jr. Loyal Whigs & Revolutionaries: The Making of the Revolution in New York, 1765-1776. LC 79-53579. 1980. 20.00x (ISBN 0-8147-4994-1). NYU Pr.

Mather, Frederic G. The Refugees of Seventeen Seventy-Six from Long Island to Connecticut. LC 72-39173. (Illus.). 1204p. 1972. Repr. of 1913 ed. 37.50 (ISBN 0-8063-0495-2). Genealog Pub.

Minutes of the Committee & of the First Commission for Detecting & Defeating Conspiracies in the State of New York: Collections 1924, 1925, 2 vols. LC 25-1703. 20.00x (ISBN 0-685-73913-9, New York Historical Society). U Pr of Va.

Muster Rolls of New York Provincial Troops, 1755-1764: Collections 1891. LC 1-13394. 8.00x (ISBN 0-685-73916-3). U Pr of Va.

Onderdonk, Henry. Documents & Letters Intended to Illustrate the Revolutionary Incidents of Queens County. LC 73-118787. (Empire State Historical Publications No. 74: No. 74). 1970. Repr. of 1846 ed. 12.50 (ISBN 0-87198-074-6). Friedman.

Proceedings of a Board of General Officers of the British Army at New York, 1781: Collections 1916. LC 16-17940. 5.00x (ISBN 0-685-73922-8, New York Historical Society). U Pr of Va.

Roberts, Robert B. New York's Forts in the Revolution. LC 77-74395. 500p. 1979. 27.50 (ISBN 0-8386-2063-9). Fairleigh Dickinson.

Sabine, William H. Murder Seventeen Seventy-Six & Washington's Policy of Silence. LC 72-95279. (Illus.). 1973. 7.50 (ISBN 0-685-72747-5). Colburn & Tegg.

Willett, William M., ed. Narrative of the Military Actions of Colonel Marinus Willett, Taken Chiefly from His Own Manuscript. LC 74-71113. (Eyewitness Accounts of the American Revolution Ser., No. 2). (Illus.). 1969. Repr. of 1831 ed. 12.00 (ISBN 0-405-01186-5). Arno.

Yoshpe, Harry B. Disposition of Loyalist Estates in the Southern District of the State of New York. LC 39-31743. (Columbia University Studies in the Social Sciences: No. 458). Repr. of 1939 ed. 15.00 (ISBN 0-404-51458-8). AMS Pr.

NEW YORK (STATE)–HISTORY, LOCAL

Aber & King. Tales from an Adirondack County. 1961. 6.95 (ISBN 0-913710-07-5). Prospect.

Akers. Outposts of History. 4.95x (ISBN 0-686-14956-4). T E Henderson.

Barclay. History of Balmville. 3.98x (ISBN 0-686-14962-9). T E Henderson.

Blake. History of Putnam County. 15.75x (ISBN 0-686-14957-2). T E Henderson.

Briggs, John W. An Italian Passage: Immigrants to Three American Cities, 1890-1930. LC 77-22006. (Illus.). 1978. 25.00x (ISBN 0-300-02095-3). Yale U Pr.

Broderick, Warren F., ed. Brunswick, a Pictoral History. (Illus., Orig.). 1978. pap. 9.95 (ISBN 0-686-26173-9). Brunswick Hist Soc.

Butler, Joseph T. Van Cortlandt Manor. LC 77-17531. (A Sleepy Hollow Restorations Guidebook). (Illus.). 1978. pap. 1.95 (ISBN 0-912882-33-6). Sleepy Hollow.

Canning, Jeff & Buxton, Wally. History of the Tarrytowns. LC 75-22042. 340p. 1975. 12.95 (ISBN 0-916346-14-5). Harbor Hill Bks.

Chambers, Albert S. A Name Index to the Eighteen Seventy-Eight History of Montgomery & Fulton Counties, New York. 1979. 10.00x (ISBN 0-932334-30-X). Heart of the Lakes.

Cohen, David. The Ramapo Mountain People. (Illus.). 300p. 1974. 19.00 (ISBN 0-8135-0768-5). Rutgers U Pr.

DeCosta, Benjamin F. The Fight at Diamond Island, Lake George. 1977. Repr. 19.00 (ISBN 0-403-08069-X). Scholarly.

Durant, S. History of Oneida County, NY Nineteen Seventy-Four to Eighteen Seventy-Eight. 1982. Repr. of 1878 ed. 35.00 (ISBN 0-932334-41-5). Heart of the Lakes.

Dutchess County Genealogical Society. Name Index to the Eighteen Eighty-Two History of Duchess County, NY. 89p. 1981. 10.50x (ISBN 0-932334-38-5). Heart of the Lakes.

Freeland. Chronicles of Monroe, N.Y. 1977. 15.00x (ISBN 0-686-18935-3). T E Henderson.

Gardner, Emma B. Glimmerglass Country. 1980. 4.95 (ISBN 0-533-04258-5). Vantage.

Gardner, Virginia & Edwards, Myrtle S.pref. by. Cemeteries of Chester, New York. LC 77-12179. (Illus.). 142p. 1977. pap. 7.95 (ISBN 0-912526-20-3). Lib Res.

Gumaer. History of Deer Park. 10.30x (ISBN 0-686-14958-0). T E Henderson.

History of Montgomery & Fulton Countries, New York. 432p. 1979. Repr. of 1878 ed. 25.00 (ISBN 0-932334-14-8). Heart of the Lakes.

Johnson, Crisfield. History of Washington County, New York Seventeen Thirty-Seven to Eighteen Seventy-Eight. 1979. Repr. of 1878 ed. 30.00 (ISBN 0-932334-20-2). Heart of the Lakes.

McIntosh, W. H. History of Wayne County New York. LC 75-37578. (Illus.). 1975. Repr. of 1877 ed. 37.50 (ISBN 0-918426-01-4). Yankee Ped Bkshop.

Merrill, Robert, et al. New Rochelle: Portrait of a City. Greenberg, Mark D., ed. (Illus.). 224p. 1981. text ed. 25.00 (ISBN 0-89659-186-7). Abbeville Pr.

Oechsner, Carl. Ossining New York: An Informal Bicentennial History. LC 75-11853. (Illus.). 144p. 1975. 10.00 (ISBN 0-88427-016-5). North River.

Parrell, Mary Agnes, Sr. Profiles of Dobbs Ferry. LC 76-21031. (Illus.). 1976. lib. bdg. 7.50x (ISBN 0-379-01100-X). Oceana.

Pelletreau, William S. Early History of Putnam County, New York. LC 75-15223. (Illus.). 880p. 1975. Repr. of 1886 ed. 16.00 (ISBN 0-89062-006-7). Pub Ctr Cult Res.

Ritchie, Henry & Durkee, Cornelius. A Name Index to the Eighteen Seventy-Eight History of Saratoga Co., New York. 84p. 1979. 10.00x (ISBN 0-932334-24-5). Heart of the Lakes.

Roe, Alfred S. Rose Neighborhood Sketches. LC 76-11288. (Illus.). 1976. Repr. of 1893 ed. 18.75 (ISBN 0-918426-02-2). Yankee Ped Bkshop.

Roesch, John. Historic White Plains. LC 75-45366. (Illus.). 1976. Repr. of 1939 ed. 11.95 (ISBN 0-916346-16-1). Harbor Hill Bks.

Rosenblum, Beatrice. Handbook Guide to Orange County, N.Y., Bottles. LC 73-86871. 1974. 6.95x (ISBN 0-686-14955-6). T E Henderson.

Ruttenber, E. M. & Clark, L. H. History of Orange County, New York: 1683-1881, 2 vols. 1112p. 1980. Repr. of 1881 ed. 45.00 (ISBN 0-932334-33-4). Heart of the Lakes.

Ruttenber, E. M. & Clark, L. H., eds. Eighteen Eighty-One Ruttenber & Clark History of Orange County, New York. (Illus.). 820p. 1980. Repr. of 1881 ed. 45.00 (ISBN 0-9604116-0-7, Co-Pub. by Heart of the Lakes). Orange County Genealog.

Samson, Harold E. The Other Side of the Hill. 2nd ed. 1975. 7.95 (ISBN 0-932052-09-6). North Country.

--Tug Hill Country. 5th ed. 7.95 (ISBN 0-932052-13-4). North Country.

Savelle, Isabelle K. The Tonetti Years at Snedens Landing. (Illus.). pap. 8.95 (ISBN 0-89062-052-0). Rockland Count Hist.

Stickney. Woodburn Glen. 4.95x (ISBN 0-686-14959-9). T E Henderson.

Storke, Elliott G. History of Cayuga County, New York: Seventeen Eighty-Nine to Eighteen Seventy-Nine. 668p. 1979. Repr. of 1879 ed. 35.00 (ISBN 0-932334-27-X). Heart of the Lakes.

Sylvester, Nathaniel. History of Saratoga County, New York: Sixteen Hundred Nine to Eighteen Seventy-Eight. 732p. 1979. Repr. of 1878 ed. 35.00 (ISBN 0-932334-22-9). Heart of the Lakes.

Sylvester, Nathaniel B. History of Ulster County New York. LC 76-42094. (Illus.). 848p. 1977. 125.00 (ISBN 0-87951-053-6). Overlook Pr.

Talman, Wilfred B. How Things Began...in Rockland County & Places Nearby. (Illus.). 1977. 12.50 (ISBN 0-89062-052-0); pap. write for info. (ISBN 0-89062-052-0). Rockland County Hist.

Tholl, Claire K. Landmarks Map of Rockland County. 1975. 7.50 (ISBN 0-686-00573-2). Rockland County Hist.

Torres, Louis. Tuckahoe Marble: The Rise & Fall of an Industry in Eastchester, N. Y., 1822-1930. LC 76-26126. (Illus.). 1976. pap. 6.95 (ISBN 0-916346-21-8). Harbor Hill Bks.

Trager, Helen G. School House at Pine Tree Corner, North Salem, N. Y. 1784-1916: Teaching & Administrative Practices in a One-Room Rural School in Westchester County. LC 76-41367. (Illus.). 1976. pap. 7.95 (ISBN 0-916346-24-2). Harbor Hill Bks.

Van Loan, Schuyler & Smith, Mabel P. An Elegant Mistake: The Haight-Gantley-Van Loan Place at Athens, New York. 1973. pap. 2.95 (ISBN 0-685-40639-3). Hope Farm.

Webb, Franklin H. Claverack, Old & New. 1892. pap. 3.00 (ISBN 0-685-56523-8). Hope Farm.

Westmoreland Bicentennial Committee. Westmoreland: 200 Years. new ed. LC 76-19335. (Illus.). 256p. 1976. 6.95 (ISBN 0-914124-08-0). Arner Pubns.

NEW YORK (STATE)–IMPRINTS

Historical Records Survey: Check List of Utica, N. Y. Imprints, 1799-1830. 1942. pap. 17.00 (ISBN 0-527-01924-0). Kraus Repr.

NEW YORK (STATE)–JUVENILE LITERATURE

Bailey, Bernadine. Picture Book of New York. rev. ed. LC 66-1262. (Illus.). (gr. 3-5). 1968. 5.50g (ISBN 0-8075-9535-7). A Whitman.

Carpenter, Allan. New York. LC 78-3395. (New Enchantment of America State Bks.). (Illus.). (gr. 4 up). 1978. PLB 10.60 (ISBN 0-516-04132-0). Childrens.

Fradin, Dennis. New York: In Words & Pictures. LC 81-28366. (Young People's Stories of Our States Ser.). (Illus.). 48p. (gr. 2-5). 1981. PLB 9.25 (ISBN 0-516-03932-6). Childrens.

Yates, Raymond F. Under Three Flags. (Illus.). (gr. 7 up). 6.75 (ISBN 0-685-20416-2). Stewart.

NEW YORK (STATE)–POLITICS AND GOVERNMENT

Alexander, DeAlva S. Political History of the State of New York, 4 Vols. LC 72-87731. (Empire State Historical Publications Ser: No. 69). 1969. Repr. of 1906 ed. 52.50 (ISBN 0-87198-069-X). Friedman.

Becker, Carl L. History of Political Parties in the Province of New York, 1760-1776. 1960. pap. 7.95x (ISBN 0-299-02024-X). U of Wis Pr.

Bellush, Bernard. Franklin D. Roosevelt As Governor of New York. LC 68-54257. (Columbia University Studies in the Social Sciences: No. 585). Repr. of 1955 ed. 17.50 (ISBN 0-404-51585-1). AMS Pr.

Benson, Lee. Concept of Jacksonian Democracy: New York As a Test Case. 1961. 24.00x (ISBN 0-691-04513-5); pap. 6.95 (ISBN 0-691-00572-9). Princeton U Pr.

Berger, Mark L. The Revolution in the New York Party System: 1840-1860. LC 72-89990. 1973. 11.00 (ISBN 0-8046-9030-8, Natl U). Kennikat.

Berle, Peter A. Does the Citizen Stand a Chance? Politics of a State Legislature - New York. Dillon, Mary E., ed. LC 73-13013. (Politics of Government Ser). (gr. 11 up). 1974. pap. 2.50 (ISBN 0-8120-0480-9). Barron.

Breen, Matthew P. Thirty Years of New York Politics, up to Date. LC 73-19132. (Politics & People Ser.). (Illus.). 918p. 1974. Repr. 48.00x (ISBN 0-405-05857-8). Arno.

Brummer, Sidney D. Political History of New York State During the Period of the Civil War. LC 11-19977. (Columbia University Studies in the Social Sciences: No. 103). Repr. of 1911 ed. 23.50 (ISBN 0-404-51103-1). AMS Pr.

Canudo, Eugene R. Criminal Law of New York. 660p. (Supplemented annually). 1980. looseleaf 15.00 (ISBN 0-87526-201-5). Gould.

--Evidence (N.Y.) (Supplemented annually). looseleaf 9.50 (ISBN 0-87526-175-2). Gould.

Chamberlain, Lawrence H. Loyalty & Legislative Action: A Survey of Activity by the New York State Legislature 1919-1949. 1951. 15.50 (ISBN 0-384-08435-4). Johnson Repr.

Civil Practice Law & Rules of New York. (Supplemented annually). 1980. looseleaf 12.50 (ISBN 0-87526-155-8). Gould.

Cleveland, Grover. Writings & Speeches of Grover Cleveland. Parker, G. F., ed. 1892. 26.00 (ISBN 0-527-17900-0). Kraus Repr.

Clifford, Joseph A. Workmen's Compensation New York. 1982 ed. 75p. 1978. 5.00 (ISBN 0-87526-214-7). Gould.

Cochran, Thomas C. New York in the Confederation. LC 72-77054. (Illus.). Repr. of 1932 ed. 5.75x (ISBN 0-678-00911-2). Kelley.

The Colonial Laws of New York from the Year 1664 to the Revolution, 5 vols. LC 74-19603. Repr. of 1896 ed. Set. 390.00 (ISBN 0-404-12313-9); 78.00 ea. AMS Pr.

Correction Law of New York. (Supplemented annually). 1980. looseleaf 6.95 (ISBN 0-87526-198-1). Gould.

Criminal Law New York Questions & Answers. 1979 ed. 250p. 1981. 8.50 (ISBN 0-87526-203-1). Gould.

Criminal Procedure Law (N.Y.) (Supplemented annually). 1980. looseleaf 5.95 (ISBN 0-87526-138-8); pap. 5.50 (ISBN 0-87526-260-0). Gould.

Davis, M. L., ed. Memoirs of Aaron Burr, 2 Vols. LC 73-152836. (Era of the American Revolution Ser). 1971. Repr. of 1836 ed. Set. lib. bdg. 65.00 (ISBN 0-306-70139-1). Da Capo.

Davis, Matthew L. Memoirs of Aaron Burr, with Miscellaneous Selections from His Correspondence, 2 Vols. facsimile ed. (Select Bibliographies Reprint Ser). 1836. Set. 50.00 (ISBN 0-8369-5213-8). Arno.

De Pauw, Linda G. Eleventh Pillar: New York State & the Federal Constitution. 346p. 1966. 22.50x (ISBN 0-8014-0104-6). Cornell U Pr.

Dillon, Dorothy R. New York Triumvirate: A Study of the Legal & Political Careers of William Livingston, John Morin Scott, & William Smith Jr. LC 68-58567. (Columbia University Studies in the Social Sciences: No. 548). Repr. of 1949 ed. 18.50 (ISBN 0-404-51548-7). AMS Pr.

Dolbeare, Kenneth M. Trial Courts in Urban Politics: State Court Policy Impact & Functions in a Local Political System. LC 75-32506. 156p. 1976. Repr. of 1967 ed. 7.95 (ISBN 0-88275-360-6). Krieger.

Donovan, Herbert D. The Barnburners. LC 73-16337. (Perspectives in American History Ser.: No. 5). (Illus.). 140p. Repr. of 1925 ed. lib. bdg. 13.50x (ISBN 0-87991-337-1). Porcupine Pr.

Elting, Irving. Dutch Village Communities on the Hudson River. pap. 7.00 (ISBN 0-384-14288-5). Johnson Repr.

Fairlie, John A. Centralization of Administration in New York State. LC 77-77990. (Columbia University, Studies in the Social Sciences Ser.: Vol. 25). Repr. of 1898 ed. 18.00 (ISBN 0-404-51025-6). AMS Pr.

Fox, Dixon R. The Decline of Aristocracy in the Politics of New York. LC 70-161764. (Columbia University. Studies in the Social Sciences: No. 198). (Illus.). Repr. of 1919 ed. 24.50 (ISBN 0-404-51198-8). AMS Pr.

Gallet, Jeffrey H., et al. Rent Stabilization & Control Laws in N. Y. (Supplemented annually). 25.00 (ISBN 0-87526-082-9). Gould.

Gibson, Florence E. Attitudes of the New York Irish Toward State & National Affairs, 1848-1892. (Columbia University. Studies in the Social Sciences: No. 563). Repr. of 1951 ed. 24.50 (ISBN 0-404-51563-0). AMS Pr.

Gosnell, Harold F. Boss Platt & His New York Machine: A Study of the Political Leadership of Thomas C. Platt, Theodore Roosevelt, & Others. LC 75-95153. Repr. of 1924 ed. 27.00 (ISBN 0-404-02884-5). Ams Pr.

Gould Editorial Staff. Evidence Law of New York Quizzer 1981. 1981. text ed. 7.50x (ISBN 0-87526-220-1). Gould.

--Law Digest of New York. (Supplemented annually). looseleaf 7.50 (ISBN 0-87526-252-X). Gould.

--Multiple Dwelling Law of New York. 300p. 1979. 12.50x (ISBN 0-87526-246-5). Gould.

--Penal Law of New York Quizzer. 1981. looseleaf 5.50 (ISBN 0-87526-225-2). Gould.

--Vehicle & Traffic Law (N.Y.) 250p. (Supplemented annually). looseleaf 10.00 (ISBN 0-87526-130-2). Gould.

Graham, Frank, Jr. The Adirondack Park: A Political History. LC 78-54918. (Illus.). 1978. 15.00 (ISBN 0-394-42809-9). Knopf.

Hastings, Hugh & Noble, Henry H., eds. Military Minutes of the Council of Appointment of the State of New York, 1783-1821, 4 vols. LC 74-19724. Repr. of 1902 ed. Set. 348.50 (ISBN 0-404-12488-7). AMS Pr.

Henke, Jack. Lawyers & the Law in New York State: A Short History & Guide. (Illus.). 187p. 1979. 11.95 (ISBN 0-89062-066-0, Pub. by Hughes Press); pap. 6.95 (ISBN 0-89062-065-2). Pub Ctr Cult Res.

Herman, Harold. New York State & the Metropolitan Problem. LC 63-7856. 1963. 12.00x (ISBN 0-8122-7382-6). U of Pa Pr.

Hevesi, Alan G. Legislative Politics in New York State: A Comparative Analysis. LC 74-6864. (Special Studies). 265p. 1975. text ed. 24.95 (ISBN 0-275-05520-5). Praeger.

Ingalls, Robert P. Herbert H. Lehman & New York's Little New Deal. LC 75-13744. 287p. 1975. 16.00x (ISBN 0-8147-3750-1). NYU Pr.

Irwin, Ray W. Daniel D. Tompkins: Governor of New York & Vice President of the United States. LC 68-57031. (Illus.). 1968. 12.50x (ISBN 0-685-73895-7, New York Historical Society). U Pr of Va.

Johnson, Alexander B. Guide to the Right Understanding of Our American Union. Repr. of 1957 ed. lib. bdg. 20.00x (ISBN 0-8371-0500-5, JOGU). Greenwood.

Judd, Jacob & Polishook, Irwin H., eds. Aspects of Early New York Society & Politics. LC 73-6579. (Illus.). 160p. 1974. buckram bound 7.50 (ISBN 0-912882-06-9). Sleepy Hollow.

Kass, Alvin. Politics in New York State, 1800-1830. LC 65-11679. (New York State Studies). 1965. 10.00x (ISBN 0-8156-2074-8). Syracuse U Pr.

Katz, Stanley N. Newcastle's New York: Anglo-American Politics, 1732-1753. LC 68-14261. (Illus.). 1968. 15.00x (ISBN 0-674-62051-8, Belknap Pr). Harvard U Pr.

Klein, Milton M. Politics of Diversity: Essays in the History of Colonial New York. new ed. LC 74-77647. (National University Publications Ser.). 212p. 1974. 17.50 (ISBN 0-8046-9081-2). Kennikat.

League of Women Voters of New York State. The Judicial System in New York State. Anderson, Claire, ed. 48p. 1978. pap. 2.75 (ISBN 0-938588-01-X). LWV NYS.

--New York State: A Citizen's Handbook. Richman, Jeanne, ed. LC 79-24095. (Illus.). 119p. (Orig.). 1979. pap. 2.95 (ISBN 0-938588-03-6). LWV NYS.

--Toward an Evaluation of the Property Tax System in New York State. Amlung, Susan, ed. (Illus.). 125p. (Orig.). 1979. pap. 4.00 (ISBN 0-938588-02-8). LWV NYS.

Leder, Lawrence H. Robert Livingston 1654-1728, & the Politics of Colonial New York. (Institute of Early American History & Culture Ser.). 1961. 21.00x (ISBN 0-8078-0805-9). U of NC Pr.

Lichterman, Charlotte, ed. Women & the Law: A Look at Some of the Laws That Affect Women in New York State. LC 80-84197. 1980. 1.00 (ISBN 0-686-30852-2). LWV NYS.

Lincoln, Charles Z., ed. State of New York: Messages from the Governors, 11 vols. LC 74-19730. Repr. of 1909 ed. Set. 962.50 (ISBN 0-404-12280-9). AMS Pr.

McClelland, Peter D. & Magdovitz, Alan L. Crisis in the Making: The Political Economy of New York State Since 1945. LC 80-24167. (Studies in Economic History & Policy: the United States in the Twentieth Century). (Illus.). 512p. 1981. 24.95 (ISBN 0-521-23807-2). Cambridge U Pr.

McCormick, Richard L. From Realignment to Reform: Political Change in New York State 1893-1910. (Illus.). 1981. 25.00x (ISBN 0-8014-1326-5). Cornell U Pr.

MacCracken, Henry N. Prologue to Independence: The Trials of James Alexander 1715-1756. 1965. 4.95 (ISBN 0-685-11978-5). Heineman.

Milstein, Mike M. & Jennings, Robert E. Educational Policy-Making & the State Legislature: The New York Experience. LC 78-185780. (Special Studies in U.S. Economic, Social & Political Issues). 1973. 28.00x (ISBN 0-275-28719-X). Irvington.

Miner, Clarence E. Ratification of the Federal Constitution by the State of New York. LC 68-56671. (Columbia University. Studies in the Social Sciences: No. 214). Repr. of 1921 ed. 16.50 (ISBN 0-404-51214-3). AMS Pr.

Mitchell, Stewart. Horatio Seymour of New York. LC 69-19475. (American Scene Ser). 1970. Repr. of 1938 ed. lib. bdg. 59.50 (ISBN 0-306-71252-0). Da Capo.

Mohr, James C. The Radical Republicans & Reform in New York During Reconstruction. 300p. 1973. 24.50x (ISBN 0-8014-0757-5). Cornell U Pr.

Morgan, David. The Capitol Press Corps: Newsmen & the Governing of New York State. LC 77-84771. (Contributions in Political Science: No. 2). 1978. lib. bdg. 16.95 (ISBN 0-8371-9883-6, MCP/). Greenwood.

Moscow, Warren. Politics in the Empire State. LC 78-23664. 1979. Repr. of 1948 ed. lib. bdg. 18.50x (ISBN 0-313-20780-1, MOPE). Greenwood.

Munger, Frank J. & Straetz, Ralph A. New York Politics. LC 60-14315. (Illus., Orig.). 1960. pap. 1.95x (ISBN 0-8147-0404-2). NYU Pr.

Mushkat, Jerome. The Reconstruction of the New York Democracy, 1861-1874. LC 78-16826. 328p. 1981. 25.00 (ISBN 0-8386-3002-2, 3002). Fairleigh Dickinson.

O'Rourke, Vernon A. & Campbell, Douglas W. Constitution Making in a Democracy: Theory & Practice in New York State. LC 78-64298. (Johns Hopkins University. Studies in the Social Sciences. Extra Vols.: 29). Repr. of 1943 ed. 25.50 (ISBN 0-404-61398-5). AMS Pr.

Paltsits, Victor H., ed. Minutes of the Executive Council of the Province of New York, 2 vols. LC 74-19731. Repr. of 1910 ed. Set. 75.00 (ISBN 0-404-12262-0). AMS Pr.

Partnership New York. 1981 ed. 75p. 1978. 5.50 (ISBN 0-87526-187-6). Gould.

Penal Law of New York. (Supplemented annually). looseleaf 5.75 (ISBN 0-87526-145-0); pap. 4.50 (ISBN 0-87526-261-9). Gould.

Prescott, Frank W. & Zimmerman, Joseph F. The Politics of the Veto of Legislation in New York State, 2 vols. LC 79-9696. 649p. 1980. Vol. 1. pap. 17.50 (ISBN 0-8191-0985-1); softcover set 33.50 (ISBN 0-8191-0986-X); Vol. 2. 26.75 (ISBN 0-8191-0983-5); text ed. 51.50 hardback set (ISBN 0-8191-0984-3). U Pr of Amer.

Proceedings & Addresses at the Freethinkers' Convention Held at Watkins, N. Y., 1878. LC 73-119051. (Civil Liberties in American History Ser). 1970. Repr. of 1878 ed. lib. bdg. 39.50 (ISBN 0-306-71937-1). Da Capo.

Robinson, Frank S. Machine Politics: A Study of Albany's O'Connells. LC 76-3785. Orig. Title: Albany's O'Connell Machine. (Illus.). 260p. 1977. Repr. text ed. 12.95 (ISBN 0-87855-147-6). Transaction Bks.

Ruchelman, Leonard I. Political Careers: Recruitment Through the Legislature. LC 70-99325. 216p. 1970. 11.50 (ISBN 0-8386-7613-8). Fairleigh Dickinson.

Salisbury, Eugene W. Manual of Procedure for Town & Village Courts (N.Y., 2 vols. (Both volumes supplemented annually). 1978. Vol. 1. looseleaf 12.50 (ISBN 0-87526-180-9); Vol. 2. looseleaf 12.50 (ISBN 0-87526-181-7). Gould.

Scisco, Louis D. Political Nativism in New York State. LC 79-76668. (Columbia University. Studies in the Social Sciences: No. 35). 1968. Repr. of 1901 ed. 16.50 (ISBN 0-404-51035-3). AMS Pr.

Smith, Franklin A. Judicial Review of Legislation in N.Y. 1906-1938. LC 71-76658. (Columbia University. Studies in the Social Sciences: No. 574). Repr. of 1952 ed. 16.00 (ISBN 0-404-51574-6). AMS Pr.

Spann, Edward K. Ideals & Politics: New York Intellectuals & Liberal Democracy, 1820-1880. LC 72-7328. 1973. 21.00 (ISBN 0-87395-083-6); microfiche 21.00 (ISBN 0-87395-183-2). State U NY Pr.

Stebbins, Homer A. Political History of the State of New York, 1865-1869. LC 13-15791. (Columbia University. Studies in the Social Sciences: No. 135). Repr. of 1913 ed. 23.00 (ISBN 0-404-51135-X). AMS Pr.

Weeden, William B. War Government, Federal & State, 1861-65. LC 75-87685. (Law, Politics & History Ser.). 1972. Repr. of 1906 ed. lib. bdg. 39.50 (ISBN 0-306-71707-7). Da Capo.

Wesser, Robert F. Charles Evans Hughes: Politics & Reform in New York, 1905-1910. (Illus.). 366p. 25.00x (ISBN 0-8014-0446-0). Cornell U Pr.

White, Bouck. The Book of Daniel Drew. LC 73-2539. (Big Business; Economic Power in a Free Society Ser.). Repr. of 1910 ed. 20.00 (ISBN 0-405-05118-2). Arno.

Zeller, Belle. Pressure Politics in New York. LC 66-27184. 1967. Repr. of 1937 ed. 8.50 (ISBN 0-8462-0963-2). Russell.

Zimmerman, Joseph F. The Government & Politics of New York State. 376p. 1982. text ed. 30.00x (ISBN 0-8147-9657-5). NYU Pr.

NEW YORK (STATE)–SOCIAL CONDITIONS

D'Elia, Anthony N. The Adirondack Rebellion. (Illus.). 1979. text ed. 10.00 (ISBN 0-686-25749-9). Onchiota Bks.

Griffen, Clyde & Griffen, Sally. Natives & Newcomers: The Ordering of Opportunity in Mid-Nineteenth-Century Poughkeepsie. (Studies in Urban History). 1977. 18.50x (ISBN 0-674-60325-7). Harvard U Pr.

Ritchie, Robert C. The Duke's Province: A Study of New York Politics & Society, 1664-1691. LC 77-681. 1977. 21.00x (ISBN 0-8078-1292-7). U of NC Pr.

Rose, Peter I. Strangers in Their Midst: Small-Town Jews & Their Neighbors. 1977. lib. bdg. 12.95 (ISBN 0-915172-32-1). Richwood Pub.

Schneider, David M. History of Public Welfare in New York State: 1609-1866. LC 69-14944. (Criminology, Law Enforcement, & Social Problems Ser.: No. 44). (Illus.). 1969. Repr. of 1938 ed. 18.00 (ISBN 0-87585-044-8). Patterson Smith.

Schneider, David M. & Deutsch, Albert. History of Public Welfare in New York State: 1867-1940. LC 69-14944. (Criminology, Law Enforcement, & Social Problems Ser.: No. 45). (Illus.). 1969. Repr. of 1941 ed. 18.00 (ISBN 0-87585-045-6). Patterson Smith.

Williams, James M. Expansion of Rural Life. LC 72-1292. (Select Bibliographies Reprints Ser.). 1972. Repr. of 1926 ed. 20.00 (ISBN 0-8369-6841-7). Arno.

NEW YORK (STATE)-SOCIAL LIFE AND CUSTOMS

Erenberg, Lewis A. Steppin' Out: New York Nightlife & the Transformation of American Culture, 1890-1930. LC 80-930. (Contributions in American Studies Ser.: No. 50). (Illus.). xix, 291p. 1981. lib. bdg. 23.95 (ISBN 0-313-21342-9, EUN/). Greenwood.

Folwell, Betsy & Ingalls, Peggy A. Cultural Resources in New York's North Country. 188p. 1980. pap. 4.50 (ISBN 0-686-74845-X). Adirondack Mus.

Fradin, Dennis. New York: In Words & Pictures. LC 81-28366. (Young People's Stories of Our States Ser.). (Illus.). 48p. (gr. 2-5). 1981. PLB 9.25 (ISBN 0-516-03932-6). Childrens.

Humphreys, Mary G. Catherine Schuyler. LC 67-30160. 1968. Repr. of 1897 ed. 16.50 (ISBN 0-87152-040-0). Reprint.

Judd, Jacob & Polishook, Irwin H., eds. Aspects of Early New York Society & Politics. LC 73-6579. (Illus.). 160p. 1974. buckram bound 7.50 (ISBN 0-912882-06-9). Sleepy Hollow.

Kilpatrick, William H. Dutch Schools of New Netherland & Colonial New York. LC 76-89193. (American Education: Its Men, Institutions & Ideas Ser). 1969. Repr. of 1912 ed. 14.00 (ISBN 0-405-01431-7). Arno.

Spengler, Paul A. Yankee, Swedish & Italian Acculturation & Economic Mobility in Jamestown, New York from 1860 to 1920. Cordasco, Francesco, ed. LC 80-897. (American Ethnic Groups Ser.). 1981. lib. bdg. 35.00x (ISBN 0-405-13457-6). Arno.

NEW YORK (STATE)-STATE LABOR RELATIONS BOARD

Newhouse, Wade J. Public Sector Labor Relations Law in New York State. LC 78-50698. 1978. lib. bdg. 24.50 (ISBN 0-930342-57-7). W S Hein.

NEW YORK (STATE)-SUPREME COURT (1ST DISTRICT)

Hamlin, Paul M. & Baker, Charles E. Supreme Court of Judicature of the Province of New York, 1691-1704, 3 vols. LC 61-23396. 1959. 37.50x set (ISBN 0-685-73928-7, New York Historical Society). U Pr of Va.

NEW YORK AND BROOKLYN BRIDGE

Green, Samuel W. A Complete History of the New York & Brooklyn Bridge from Its Conception in 1866 to Its Completion 1883. 1979. lib. bdg. 59.95 (ISBN 0-8490-1655-X). Gordon Pr.

McCullough, David. The Great Bridge. (Illus.). 1976. pap. 8.95 (ISBN 0-380-00753-3, 49718). Avon.

Rose, Alan. Build Your Own Brooklyn Bridge. (The World at Your Feet Ser.). 40p. (gr. 10 up). 1980. pap. 6.95 (ISBN 0-399-50504-0, Perigee). Putnam.

NEW YORK BASEBALL CLUB (AMERICAN LEAGUE)

Anderson, Dave, et al. The Yankees: Nineteen Eighty-One Edition. 1981. 10.95 (ISBN 0-394-51902-7). Random.

--The Yankees: The Four Fabulous Eras of Baseball's Most Famous Team. rev. ed. (Illus.). 1980. 9.95 (ISBN 0-394-51133-6). Random.

Bove, Vincent. And on the Eighth Day God Created the Yankees. (Illus.). 176p. (Orig.). 1981. pap. write for info. (ISBN 0-88270-514-8, Pub. by Haven Bks). Logos.

Frommer, Harvey. New York City Baseball: The Last Golden Age, Nineteen Forty-Seven to Nineteen Fifty-Seven. (Illus.). 1980. 11.95 (ISBN 0-02-541700-2). Macmillan.

Golenbock, Peter. Dynasty: The New York Yankees 1949-1964. LC 75-4705. 1975. 9.95 (ISBN 0-13-222323-6, Reward); pap. 5.95 (ISBN 0-13-222208-6). P-H.

Honig, Donald. The New York Yankees: An Illustrated History. (Illus.). 1981. 19.95 (ISBN 0-517-54496-2). Crown.

--N.Y. Yankees: An Illustrated History. (Illus.). 320p. 1981. 19.95 (ISBN 0-517-54496-2). Crown.

Jacobsen, Steve. The Best Team Money Could Buy: The Turmoil & Triumph of the 1977 New York Yankees. (RL 7). 1978. pap. 1.95 (ISBN 0-451-08002-5, J8002, Sig). NAL.

Salant, Nathan. This Date in New York Yankees History. LC 78-24105. (Illus.). 1979. pap. 8.95 (ISBN 0-8128-6020-9). Stein & Day.

Schoor, Gene. Billy Martin. LC 79-7699. (Illus.). 1980. 11.95 (ISBN 0-385-15280-9). Doubleday.

Weil, Robert & Fitzgerald, James. The Yankee Quizbook. LC 80-1654. (Illus.). 144p. 1981. pap. 5.95 (ISBN 0-385-17178-1, Dolp). Doubleday.

NEW YORK BASEBALL CLUB (NATIONAL LEAGUE, GIANTS)

Frommer, Harvey. New York City Baseball: The Last Golden Age, Nineteen Forty-Seven to Nineteen Fifty-Seven. (Illus.). 1980. 11.95 (ISBN 0-02-541700-2). Macmillan.

NEW YORK BASEBALL CLUB (NATIONAL LEAGUE, METS)

D'Agostino, Dennis. This Date in New York Mets History. LC 80-6157. (This Date Ser.). 256p. 1981. pap. 9.95 (ISBN 0-8128-6068-3). Stein & Day.

Koppett, Leonard. The New York Mets. 1970. 9.95 (ISBN 0-02-578880-9). Macmillan.

--The New York Mets: The Whole Story. (Illus.). 448p. 1974. pap. 4.95 (ISBN 0-02-029180-9, Collier). Macmillan.

NEW YORK CENTRAL RAILROAD

Beebe, Lucius. Twentieth Century. LC 62-17074. (Illus.). 1962. 12.95 (ISBN 0-8310-7031-5). Howell-North.

Harwood, Herbert H., Jr. Fifty Best of New York Central Railroad, Bk. 1. (Illus.). 1977. 12.00 (ISBN 0-934118-09-4). Barnard Robert.

Hungerford, Edward. Men & Iron: The History of New York Central. LC 75-41763. (Companies & Men: Business Enterprises in America). (Illus.). 1976. Repr. of 1938 ed. 30.00x (ISBN 0-405-08078-6). Arno.

Taylor, Jeremy. Fifty Best of New York Central Railroad, Bk. 3. (Illus.). 1978. 12.00 (ISBN 0-934118-11-6). Barnard Robert.

NEW YORK CITY BALLET

Chujoy, Anatole. The New York City Ballet. (Da Capo Dance Ser.). (Illus.). xxviii, 382p. 1981. Repr. of 1953 ed. lib. bdg. 29.50 (ISBN 0-306-76035-5). Da Capo.

Kirstein, Lincoln. New York City Ballet. 1973. 30.00 (ISBN 0-394-46652-7). Knopf.

Mazo, Joseph H. Dance Is a Contact Sport. LC 76-6557. (Paperback Ser.). 1976. pap. 6.95 (ISBN 0-306-80044-6). Da Capo.

Reynolds, Nancy. Repertory in Review: 40 Years of the New York City Ballet. 1977. 22.50 (ISBN 0-8037-7368-4). Dial.

NEW YORK DAILY NEWS

Bessie, Simon M. Jazz Journalism: The Story of the Tabloid Newspapers. LC 68-27050. (Illus.). 1969. Repr. of 1938 ed. 10.00 (ISBN 0-8462-1246-3). Russell.

NEW YORK EMPLOYING PRINTERS' ASSOCIATION, INC.

Morgan, Charlotte E. Origin & History of the New York Employing Printers' Association. LC 68-58608. (Columbia University. Studies in the Social Sciences: No. 319). Repr. of 1930 ed. 15.00 (ISBN 0-404-51319-0). AMS Pr.

NEW YORK EVENING POST

Nevins, Allan. Evening Post: A Century of Journalism. LC 68-25047. (Illus., With a new preface). 1968. Repr. of 1922 ed. 16.00 (ISBN 0-8462-1174-2). Russell.

NEW YORK FOOTBALL CLUB (AMERICAN LEAGUE)

May, Julian. The New York Jets. (The NFL Today Ser.). (gr. 4-8). 1980. PLB 6.45 (ISBN 0-87191-726-2); pap. 2.95 (ISBN 0-89812-229-5). Creative Ed.

--New York Jets. LC 74-908. (Superbowl Champions Ser). 48p. 1974. PLB 6.45 (ISBN 0-87191-329-1); pap. 2.95 (ISBN 0-89812-089-6). Creative Ed.

--New York Jets. LC 74-908. (Superbowl Champions Ser). 48p. 1974. PLB 6.45 (ISBN 0-87191-329-1); pap. 2.95 (ISBN 0-89812-089-6). Creative Ed.

NEW YORK FOOTBALL CLUB (NATIONAL LEAGUE)

Stein, Fred. Under Coogan's Bluff. (Illus.). 160p. (Orig.). 1981. pap. 7.95 (ISBN 0-940056-00-3). Chapter & Cask.

NEW YORK HERALD TRIBUNE

Herzberg, Joseph G., et al. Late City Edition. 1969. Repr. of 1947 ed. 18.50 (ISBN 0-208-00739-3, Archon). Shoe String.

Laney, Al. Paris Herald, the Incredible Newspaper. LC 69-13963. 1969. Repr. of 1947 ed. lib. bdg. 15.00x (ISBN 0-8371-0524-2, LAPH). Greenwood.

NEW YORK HOSPITAL, CORNELL MEDICAL CENTER

Reader, George G. & Goss, Mary E., eds. Comprehensive Medical Care & Teaching: A Report on an Experimental Program of the New York Hospital-Cornell Medical Center. LC 67-23762. 391p. 1968. 27.50x (ISBN 0-8014-0352-9). Cornell U Pr.

NEW YORK HOUSE OF REFUGE, RANDALL'S ISLAND

Peirce, Bradford K. Half Century with Juvenile Delinquents, or the New York House of Refuge & Its Times. LC 69-16242. (Criminology, Law Enforcement, & Social Problems Ser.: No. 91). (Illus., With intro. added). 1969. Repr. of 1869 ed. 18.00 (ISBN 0-87585-091-X). Patterson Smith.

Pickett, Robert S. House of Refuge: Origins of Juvenile Reform in New York State, 1815-1857. LC 69-19745. (New York State Studies). (Illus.). 1969. 10.95x (ISBN 0-8156-2138-8). Syracuse U Pr.

NEW YORK MEDICAL COLLEGE, FLOWER AND FIFTH AVENUES HOSPITAL

Wershub, Leonard P. One Hundred Years of Medical Progress: A History of the New York Medical College Flower & Fifth Avenue Hospitals. (Illus.). 276p. 1967. pap. 27.75 (ISBN 0-398-04427-9). C C Thomas.

NEW YORK METROPOLITAN AREA

Carey, George W. A Vignette of the New York-New Jersey Metropolitan Region. LC 76-4796. (Contemporary Metropolitan Analysis Ser.). (Illus.). 1976. pap. text ed. 6.95 (ISBN 0-88410-436-2). Ballinger Pub.

Costikyan, Edward N. & Lehman, Maxwell. New Strategies for Regional Cooperation: A Model for the Tri-State New York-New Jersey-Connecticut Area. LC 73-9388. (Special Studies in U.S. Economic, Social & Political Issues). 1973. 27.50x (ISBN 0-275-28777-7). Irvington.

Doig, Jameson W. Metropolitan Transportation Politics & the New York Region. LC 66-16768. (Metropolitan Politics Ser.). (Illus.). 327p. 1966. 22.50x (ISBN 0-231-02791-5). Columbia U Pr.

Vernon, Raymond. Metropolis 1985: An Interpretation of the Findings of the New York Metropolitan Region Study. LC 60-15243. (New York Metropolitan Region Study). 1960. 12.50x (ISBN 0-674-57200-9). Harvard U Pr.

Wade, Richard C., ed. Regional Survey of New York & Its Environs, 10 vols. (Metropolitan America Ser.). (Illus.). 1974. Set. 170.00x (ISBN 0-405-05439-4). Arno.

NEW YORK, NEW HAVEN, AND HARTFORD RAILROAD

Weller, John L. New Haven Railroad: Its Rise & Fall. (Illus.). 1969. 9.95 (ISBN 0-8038-5017-4). Hastings.

NEW YORK, ONTARIO AND WESTERN RAILWAY

Helmer, William F. O. & W. LC 59-15621. (Illus.). 1959. 9.95 (ISBN 0-8310-7012-9). Howell-North.

NEW YORK PSYCHOANALYTIC INSTITUTE

Wangh, Martin, et al, eds. Fruition of an Idea: Fifty Years of Psychoanalysis in New York. LC 62-17380. 1962. text ed. 15.00 (ISBN 0-8236-2100-6). Intl Univs Pr.

NEW YORK PUBLIC LIBRARY

Brownrigg, Edwin B. Colonial Latin American Manuscripts & Transcripts in the Obadiah Rich Collection: An Inventory & Index. LC 77-20691. 1978. 20.00 (ISBN 0-87104-269-X). NY Pub Lib.

Catalog of Special & Private Presses in the Rare Book Division, the Research Libraries of the New York Public Library, 2 vols. (Printed Book Catalogs). 1978. Set. lib. bdg. 170.00 (ISBN 0-8161-0097-7). G K Hall.

Dain, Phyllis. The New York Public Library: A History of Its Founding & Early Years. LC 70-163359. (Illus.). 365p. (Orig.). 1972. 21.00 (ISBN 0-87104-131-6). NY Pub Lib.

New York Public Library, Research Libraries. The Dictionary Catalog of the Prints Division, 5 vols. 1975. Set. lib. bdg. 460.00 (ISBN 0-8161-1148-0). G K Hall.

--Dictionary Catalog of the Rare Book Division: First Supplement. 1973. 110.00 (ISBN 0-8161-1089-1). G K Hall.

Research Libraries of the New York Public Library. Catalog of Government Publications, Supplement 1974. 1976. lib. bdg. 200.00 (ISBN 0-8161-0060-8). G K Hall.

NEW YORK SOCIETY FOR PROMOTING THE MANUMISSION OF SLAVES

Andrews, Charles C. History of the New York African Free-Schools, from Their Establishment in 1787, to the Present Time. LC 68-55868. (Illus.). Repr. of 1830 ed. 10.00x (ISBN 0-8371-1064-5). Greenwood.

NEW YORK STATE PRISON, ATTICA

Wicker, Tom. A Time to Die. LC 74-77947. 256p. 1975. 10.00 (ISBN 0-8129-0487-7). Times Bks.

NEW YORK STATE PRISON, AUBURN

Osborne, Thomas M. Within Prison Walls, Being a Narrative of Personal Experience During a Week of Voluntary Confinement in the State Prison at Auburn, New York. LC 69-14940. (Criminology, Law Enforcement, & Social Problems Ser.: No. 72). 1969. Repr. of 1914 ed. 15.00 (ISBN 0-87585-072-3). Patterson Smith.

NEW YORK STATE REFORMATORY, ELMIRA

Brockway, Zebulon R. Fifty Years of Prison Service: An Autobiography. LC 69-14914. (Criminology, Law Enforcement, & Social Problems Ser.: No. 61). (Illus.). 1969. Repr. of 1912 ed. 17.00 (ISBN 0-87585-061-8). Patterson Smith.

Winter, Alexander. New York State Reformatory in Elmira. LC 74-172602. (Criminology, Law Enforcement, & Social Problems Ser.: No. 192). 1975. 12.00 (ISBN 0-87585-192-4). Patterson Smith.

NEW YORK STATE UNIVERSITY

Smith, Ruby G. People's Colleges: A History of the New York State Extension Service in Cornell University & the State, 1876-1948. (Illus.). 593p. 1949. 27.50x (ISBN 0-8014-0396-0). Cornell U Pr.

NEW YORK STATE UNIVERSITY COLLEGE OF EDUCATION, OSWEGO

Dearborn, Ned H. Oswego Movement in American Education. LC 74-89171. (American Education: Its Men, Institutions & Ideas, Ser. 1). 1969. Repr. of 1925 ed. 14.00 (ISBN 0-405-01409-0). Arno.

--Oswego Movement in American Education. LC 71-176709. (Columbia University. Teachers College. Contributions to Education: No. 183). Repr. of 1925 ed. 17.50 (ISBN 0-404-55183-1). AMS Pr.

NEW YORK STOCK EXCHANGE

see also Stock-Exchange

Black, Hillel. The Watchdogs of Wall Street. facsimile ed. LC 75-2621. (Wall Street & the Security Market Ser.). 1975. Repr. of 1962 ed. 15.00x (ISBN 0-405-06948-0). Arno.

Carosso, Vincent P., ed. Finance & Industry: The New York Stock Exchange: Banks, Bankers, Business Houses, and Moneyed Institutions of the Great Metropolis of the United States. facsimile ed. LC 75-2620. (Wall Street & the Security Markets Ser.). 1975. Repr. of 1886 ed. 17.00x (ISBN 0-405-06947-2). Arno.

--The New York Stock Market: An Original Anthology. LC 75-2656. (Wall Street & the Security Market Ser.). 1975. 36.00x (ISBN 0-405-06981-2). Arno.

--Wall Street & the Security Markets, 58 vols. facsimile ed. 1975. Repr. Vols. 1-29. 770.00x (ISBN 0-405-12493-7); Vols. 30-58. 771.00x (ISBN 0-405-19007-7). Arno.

Commerce Clearing House. New York Stock Exchange Inc. Directory Revised to August 1, 1980. 616p. 1980. 7.50 (ISBN 0-686-75922-2). Commerce.

Committee on Banking & Currency, U. S. Senate, 1934. Stock Exchange Practices. facsimile ed. LC 75-2678. (Wall Street & the Security Market Ser.). 1975. Repr. of 1934 ed. 23.00x (ISBN 0-405-07240-6). Arno.

Darvas, Nicolas. Wall Street, the Other Las Vegas. 1962. 4.95 (ISBN 0-8184-0092-7). Lyle Stuart.

Eames, Francis L. New York Stock Exchange. LC 68-28628. Repr. of 1968 ed. lib. bdg. 15.00x (ISBN 0-8371-0066-6, EANY). Greenwood.

Faber, Doris. Wall Street: A Story of Fortune & Finance. LC 78-19487. (gr. 8 up). 1979. 10.95 (ISBN 0-06-021868-1, HarpJ). Har-Row.

Hardy, Charles O. Odd-Lot Trading on the New York Stock Exchange. facsimile ed. LC 75-2639. (Wall Street & the Security Market Ser.). 1975. Repr. of 1939 ed. 15.00x (ISBN 0-405-06964-2). Arno.

Hodgson, James G., compiled by. Wall Street: Asset or Liability? facsimile ed. LC 75-2641. (Wall Street & the Security Market Ser.). 1975. Repr. of 1934 ed. 18.00x (ISBN 0-405-06966-9). Arno.

Lechner, Alan. Street Games: Inside Stories of the Wall Street Hustle. LC 79-2627. (Illus.). 1980. 8.95 (ISBN 0-06-012553-5, HarpT). Har-Row.

Manne, Henry G., et al. Wall Street in Transition: The Emerging System & Its Impact on the Economy. LC 74-15255. (Moskowitz Lectures). 206p. 1974. 13.50x (ISBN 0-8147-5369-8). NYU Pr.

Meeker, James E. The Work of the Stock Exchange (Revised Edition) facsimile ed. LC 75-2649. (Wall Street & the Security Market Ser.). (Illus.). 1975. Repr. of 1930 ed. 44.00x (ISBN 0-405-06974-X). Arno.

New York Stock Exchange, Constitution & Rules As of August 31, 1980. 1980. pap. 7.50 (ISBN 0-686-75921-4). Commerce.

Pecora, Ferdinand. Wall Street Under Oath. LC 68-20529. Repr. of 1939 ed. 15.00x (ISBN 0-678-00372-6). Kelley.

Sloane, Leonard. The Anatomy of the Floor: The Trillion Dollar Market at the New York Stock Exchange. LC 77-15173. 1980. 10.00 (ISBN 0-385-12249-7). Doubleday.

Sobel, Robert. Great Bull Market: Wall Street in the 1920's. LC 68-19795. (Essays in American History). 1968. pap. 5.95x (ISBN 0-393-09817-6, NortonC). Norton.

--Inside Wall Street: Continuity & Change in the Financial District. 1977. 12.95 (ISBN 0-393-05643-0). Norton.

Stedman, Edmund C. New York Stock Exchange. Repr. of 1905 ed. lib. bdg. 31.50x (ISBN 0-8371-0667-2, STSE). Greenwood.

NEW YORK TIMES

Berger, Meyer. Story of the New York Times: The First Hundred Years, 1851-1951. LC 75-122933. (American Journalists Ser). 1970. Repr. of 1951 ed. 12.00 (ISBN 0-405-01652-2). Arno.

Brown, Gene & Keylin, Arleen, eds. Sports: As Reported by the New York Times. new ed. LC 76-2450. (Illus.). 1976. 12.98 (ISBN 0-405-06689-9). Arno.

Claiborne, Craig. Craig Claiborne's Favorites from The New York Times. LC 75-10599. (Illus.). 1975. 12.50 (ISBN 0-8129-0584-9). Times Bks.

Davis, Elmer. History of the New York Times, 1851-1921. LC 70-144968. (Illus.). 1971. Repr. of 1921 ed. 35.00 (ISBN 0-403-00937-5). Scholarly.

Davis, Elmer H. History of the New York Times, 1851-1921. LC 72-95092. Repr. of 1921 ed. lib. bdg. 32.25x (ISBN 0-8371-2578-2, DAHT). Greenwood.

Dryfoos, Susan W., as told to. Iphigene: Memoirs of Iphigene Ochs Sulzberger of the New York Times Family. 304p. 1981. 12.95 (ISBN 0-396-08014-6). Dodd.

Falk, Bryon A. & Falk, Valerie. Personal Name Index to the New York Times Index: Eighteen Fifty One to Nineteen Seventy Four, Vol.15. 417p. 1980. lib. bdg. 38.25 (ISBN 0-89902-115-8). Roxbury Data.

Falk, Byron A. & Falk, Valerie R. Personal Name Index to the New York Times Index, Vols. 13 & 14: Eighteen Fifty-One to Nineteen Seventy-Four. LC 76-12217. 1980. lib. bdg. 52.50 ea. Vol. 13 (ISBN 0-89902-113-1). Vol. 14 (ISBN 0-89902-114-X). Roxbury Data.

--Personal Name Index to the New Youk Times Index: Eighteen Fifty One to Nineteen Seventy Four, Vol.16. 624p. 1980. lib. bdg. 50.50 (ISBN 0-89902-116-6). Roxbury Data.

Falk, Byron A., Jr. & Falk, Valerie R. Personal Name Index to the New York Times Index: Eighteen Fifty One to Nineteen Seventy Four, Vol. 17. 659p. 1981. lib. bdg. 62.00 (ISBN 0-89902-117-4). Roxbury Data.

New York Times. The Newspaper, Its Making & Its Meaning: Its Making & Its Meaning. LC 80-2891. (BCL Ser.: Vol. I & II). Repr. of 1945 ed. 26.00 (ISBN 0-404-18069-8). AMS Pr.

The New York Times Annual Review, 1981. 1981. write for info. Arno.

The New York Times Obituaries, Index 1858-1968. LC 72-113422. 1136p. 1970. pap. 95.00 (ISBN 0-667-00599-4). Microfilming Corp.

Rothman, John. Origin & Development of Dramatic Criticism in the New York Times 1851-1880. LC 78-126346. 1970. 8.00 (ISBN 0-405-02560-2). Arno.

Salisbury, Harrison. Without Fear or Favor: The New York Times & Our Times. 1980. 17.50 (ISBN 0-8129-0885-6). Times Bks.

Talese, Gay. The Kingdom & the Power. LC 78-7770. 1978. pap. 6.95 (ISBN 0-385-14404-0, Anch). Doubleday.

The Times in Review: New York Times Decade Books, 5 vols. Incl. Vol. 1. Nineteen Twenty-Nineteen Twenty Nine; Vol. 2. Nineteen Thirty-Nineteen Thirty Nine; Vol. 3. Nineteen Fourty-Nineteen Fourty Nine; Vol. J. Nineteen Fifty-Nineteen Fifty Nine; Vol. 5. Nineteen Sixty-Nineteen Sixty Nine. (Illus.). 50.00 ea. (Co-Pub by New York Times). Arno.

NEW YORK TRIBUNE

Baehr, Harry W., Jr. The New York Tribune Since the Civil War. LC 77-159164. xiii, 420p. 1972. Repr. of 1936 ed. lib. bdg. 22.00x (ISBN 0-374-90335-2). Octagon.

Isely, Jeter A. Horace Greeley & the Republican Party, 1853-1861. 1965. lib. bdg. 25.00x (ISBN 0-374-94123-8). Octagon.

NEW YORK UNIVERSITY

Brubacher, John S. The Judicial Power of the New York State Commissioner of Education. LC 78-176602. (Columbia University. Teachers College. Contributions to Education: No. 295). Repr. of 1927 ed. 17.50 (ISBN 0-404-55295-1). AMS Pr.

Frizzle, Arnold L. Study of Some of the Influences of Regents Requirements & Examinations in French. LC 70-176789. (Columbia University. Teachers College. Contributions to Education: No. 964). Repr. of 1950 ed. 17.50 (ISBN 0-404-55964-6). AMS Pr.

Jones, Theodore Francis, ed. New York University, 1832-1932. (Illus.). 1933. 12.00x (ISBN 0-8147-0221-X). NYU Pr.

Morello, Theodore, ed. The Hall of Fame for Great Americans at New York University: Official Handbook. rev. ed. LC 67-10691. (Illus.). 210p. 1967. 8.95x (ISBN 0-8147-0316-X). NYU Pr.

Sihler, Ernest. History of New York University. 1976. lib. bdg. 34.95 (ISBN 0-8490-0339-3). Gordon Pr.

Stoddard, George D., et al. The New York University Self-Study: Final Report. LC 56-12138. 436p. 1956. 10.00x (ISBN 0-8147-7807-0). Nyu Pr.

NEW YORK UNIVERSITY MEDICAL CENTER

De La Chapelle, Clarence E. & Jensen, Frode. A Mission in Action: The Story of The Regional Hospital Plan of New York University. LC 64-22262. 1964. 8.50x (ISBN 0-8147-0115-9). NYU Pr.

NEW YORK UNIVERSITY SCHOOL OF EDUCATION

Dossick, Jesse J. Doctoral Research at the School of Education, New York University, 1890-1970: A Classified List of 4,336 Dissertations with Some Critical & Statistical Analysis. LC 73-187304. 236p. 1972. 15.00x (ISBN 0-8147-1755-1). NYU Pr.

Hug, Elsie A. Seventy-Five Years in Education: The Role of the School of Education, New York University, 1890-1965. LC 65-13206. 1965. 8.95x (ISBN 0-8147-0211-2). NYU Pr.

NEW YORK WEEKLY JOURNAL

Alexander, James A. A Brief Narrative of the Case & Trial of John Peter Zenger, Printer of the New York Weekly. enl. ed. (Belknap Ser.). (Illus.). 953p. 1969. 25.00 (ISBN 0-674-37501-7). Harvard U Pr.

Rutherford, Livingston. John Peter Zenger, His Press, His Trial & a Bibliography of Zenger Imprints. LC 4-8588. (American Biography Ser). Repr. of 1904 ed. 14.50 (ISBN 0-384-52620-9). Johnson Repr.

Rutherfurd, L. John Peter Zenger: His Press, His Trial, & a Bibliography of Zenger Imprints. (With reprint of the first edition of his trial). 7.50 (ISBN 0-8446-1394-0). Peter Smith.

Rutherfurd, Livingston. John Peter Zenger, His Press, His Trial & a Bibliography of Zenger Imprints. LC 77-125713. (American Journalists). (Illus.). 1970. Repr. of 1904 ed. 20.00 (ISBN 0-405-01694-8). Arno.

NEW YORK YANKEES

see New York Baseball Club (American League)

NEW YORKER

Gill, Brendan. Here at the New Yorker. 1977. pap. 1.95 (ISBN 0-425-03043-1, Medallion). Berkley Pub.

Johnson, Robert O. An Index to Literature in the New Yorker, 1925-194, Vols. 1-15. LC 71-7740. 1969. 20.50 (ISBN 0-8108-0272-4). Scarecrow.

--An Index to Literature in the New Yorker, 1940-195, Vol. 16-30. 1970. 13.50 (ISBN 0-8108-0314-3). Scarecrow.

--An Index to Literature in the New Yorker, 1970-75, Vol. 46-50. LC 71-7740. 1976. 10.00 (ISBN 0-8108-0905-2). Scarecrow.

Kahn, E. J. About the New Yorker & Me: A Sentimental Journal. LC 78-11497. 1979. 12.95 (ISBN 0-399-12300-8). Putnam.

New Yorker. The New Yorker Twenty-Fifth Anniversary Album 1925-1950. 1977. pap. 8.95 (ISBN 0-06-090553-0, CN 553, CN). Har-Row.

NEW ZEALAND

Allison, K. W. & Child, John. The Mosses of New Zealand. 1971. 12.50x (ISBN 0-8002-0344-5). Intl Pubns Serv.

Bagnall, A. G., ed. New Zealand National Bibliography to the Year 1960, Vols. 2-4. Incl. Vol. 2. 1890-1960 (A-H) 620p. 1969. 22.50x (ISBN 0-8002-2190-7); Vol. 3. 1890-1960 (I-O) 583p. 1972. 30.00x (ISBN 0-8002-2191-5); Vol. 4. 1890-1960 (P-Z) 471p. 1975. 40.00x (ISBN 0-8002-2192-3). LC 71-18927. 1973. Intl Pubns Serv.

Begg, A. C. Dusky Bay: In the Steps of Captain Cook. 1975. 17.40x (ISBN 0-8002-1375-0). Intl Pubns Serv.

Begg, A. Charles. Port Preservation. 1973. 21.90x (ISBN 0-7233-0379-7). Intl Pubns Serv.

Blue Book Nineteen Seventy-Six: Leaders of the English-Speaking World, 2 vols. LC 73-13918. 1979. Set. 85.00 (ISBN 0-8103-0216-0). Gale.

Brunner, Edmund D. Rural Australia & New Zealand: Some Observations of Current Trends. LC 75-30123. (Institute of Pacific Relations). Repr. of 1938 ed. 11.50 (ISBN 0-404-59513-8). AMS Pr.

Buck, Peter H. Arts & Crafts of the Cook Islands. Repr. of 1941 ed. pap. 45.00 (ISBN 0-527-02287-X). Kraus Repr.

Concise Encyclopedia of Australia & New Zealand. (Illus.). 1977. 15.00x (ISBN 0-85835-198-6). Intl Pubns Serv.

Dixon, E. H. Red Deer Farming in New Zealand. (Illus.). 52p. 1975. pap. 6.25x (ISBN 0-8002-0479-4). Intl Pubns Serv.

Grayland, E. C. More Famous New Zealanders. LC 73-163033. 174p. 1972. 7.50x (ISBN 0-8002-0107-8). Intl Pubns Serv.

Grover, R. F. New Zealand. (World Biliographical Ser.: No. 13). 254p. 1981. 36.25 (ISBN 0-903450-31-3). ABC-Clio.

Hascombe, Jane. We Came to New Zealand. (Illus.). 1970. 7.50x (ISBN 0-09-457070-1). Intl Pubns Serv.

Hines, George H. The New Zealand Manager. LC 74-167425. 77p. 1973. pap. 7.00x (ISBN 0-8002-0094-2). Intl Pubns Serv.

Imber, Walter & Cumberland, K. B. New Zealand. LC 76-50908. (Illus.). 1976. 35.00 (ISBN 0-589-00773-4). J J Binns.

Jones, Tim. Hard-Won Freedom: Alternative Communities in New Zealand. (Illus.). 158p. 1975. 14.90x (ISBN 0-340-20406-0). Intl Pubns Serv.

Kingma, Jacobus. The Geological Structure of New Zealand. 407p. 1974. 73.50 (ISBN 0-471-47900-4, Pub. by Wiley). Krieger.

Knight, C. L. New Zealand Geography: A Systems Approach. 1973. 9.50x (ISBN 0-8002-0105-1). Intl Pubns Serv.

Marsh, Ngaio. New Zealand. 1976. Repr. of 1942 ed. lib. bdg. 13.30 (ISBN 0-88411-489-9). Amereon Ltd.

Morrell, W. P. Memoirs of W. P. Morrell. (Illus.). 1979. 17.50x (ISBN 0-908565-99-2). Intl Pubns Serv.

Morrell, William P. The Anglican Church in New Zealand: A History. LC 73-177145. (Illus.). 1973. 7.50x (ISBN 0-8002-0487-5). Intl Pubns Serv.

Morton, Harry. Why Not Together? Australia & New Zealand. 1978. 12.50x (ISBN 0-908565-84-4). Intl Pubns Serv.

Morton, John. Seacoast in the Seventies: The Future of the New Zealand Shoreline. LC 74-179330. (Illus.). 118p. 1974. pap. 9.90x (ISBN 0-340-15778-X). Intl Pubns Serv.

National Library of New Zealand. New Zealand National Bibliography, 1966 to 1978. Incl. Vol. 1. 1966. 1968. pap. 10.00x (ISBN 0-8002-2400-0); Vol. 2. 1967. 1968. pap. 10.00x (ISBN 0-8002-2401-9); Vol. 3. 1968. 1969. pap. 13.50x (ISBN 0-8002-2402-7); Vol. 4. 1969. 1970. pap. 13.50x (ISBN 0-8002-2403-5); Vol. 5. 1970. 1971. pap. 13.50x (ISBN 0-8002-2404-3); Vol. 6. 1971. 1972. pap. 13.50x (ISBN 0-8002-2405-1); Vol. 7. 1972. 1973. pap. 13.50x (ISBN 0-8002-2406-X); Vol. 8. 1973. 1974. pap. 13.50x (ISBN 0-8002-2407-8); Vol. 9. 1974. 1975. pap. 35.00x (ISBN 0-8002-0490-5); Vol. 10. 1975. 1976. pap. 13.50x (ISBN 0-8002-2408-6); Vol. 11. 1976. 1977. pap. 13.50x (ISBN 0-8002-2409-4); Vol. 12. 1977. 1978. pap. 13.50x (ISBN 0-8002-2410-8); Vol. 13. 1978. 1979. pap. 20.00x (ISBN 0-8002-2411-6). LC 73-640530. Intl Pubns Serv.

--New Zealand National Bibliography, 1979. 14th ed. LC 73-640530. 497p. 1980. 20.00x (ISBN 0-8002-2735-2). Intl Pubns Serv.

New Zealand Official Yearbook: 1978 Ed. 1979. lib. bdg. 17.00x (ISBN 0-8426-1107-X). Verry.

New Zealand Official Yearbook: 1976 Ed. 1976. lib. bdg. 10.50x (ISBN 0-8426-1036-7). Verry.

New Zealand Official Yearbook: 1977 Ed. (Illus.). 1977. lib. bdg. 16.00x (ISBN 0-8426-1073-1). Verry.

O'Regan, Rolland. Rating in New Zealand. 226p. 1973. pap. 4.00 (ISBN 0-685-46972-7). Schalkenbach.

Power, Elaine. Horse in New Zealand. 1976. 21.85x (ISBN 0-8002-0464-6). Intl Pubns Serv.

Pownall, Glen. Unique New Zealand. 156p. 1980. 3.95 (ISBN 0-85467-003-3, Pub. by Viking Sevenseas). Intl Schol Bk Serv.

Rijnhart, Hank, ed. Jobson's Yearbook of Public Companies of Australia & New Zealand: 1979. LC 72-200962. 847p. 1979. 90.00x (ISBN 0-8002-2223-7). Intl Pubns Serv.

Siers, James. New Zealanders. (Illus.). 252p. 1975. 26.50x (ISBN 0-8002-0474-3). Intl Pubns Serv.

Simmons, D. R. The Great New Zealand Myth. 1978. 27.75 (ISBN 0-589-00949-4, Pub. by Reed Books Australia). C E Tuttle.

Simpson, Colin J. Wake up to New Zealand. (Illus.). 1978. 21.95 (ISBN 0-589-07210-2, Pub. by Reed Books Australia). C E Tuttle.

Somerset, H. C. Littledene: Patterns of Change. 1974. text ed. 17.50x (ISBN 0-8426-0680-7). Verry.

Traue, J. E., ed. Who's Who in New Zealand. 11th ed. 1978. 24.75 (ISBN 0-589-01113-8, Pub. by Reed Books Australia). C E Tuttle.

--Who's Who in New Zealand. 11th ed. LC 27-18903. 1978. 30.00x (ISBN 0-589-01113-8). Intl Pubns Serv.

Wellington Dept. of Statistics, ed. New Zealand Official Yearbook 1978. 83rd ed. LC 7-21753. (Illus.). 991p. 1978. 17.50x (ISBN 0-8002-0450-6). Intl Pubns Serv.

Wood, Frederick L. Understanding New Zealand. facs. ed. LC 75-134163. (Essay Index Reprint Ser). 1944. 19.50 (ISBN 0-8369-2097-X). Arno.

NEW ZEALAND–CIVILIZATION

Challis, Aidan J. Motueka: An Archaeological Survey. (New Zealand Archaeological Assn. Monographs). (Illus.). 1978. text ed. 12.50x (ISBN 0-582-71758-2). Longman.

Downes, Peter. Shadows on the Stage: Theatre in New Zealand; the First Seventy Years. LC 76-352254. 166p. 1976. 16.50x (ISBN 0-8002-0481-6). Intl Pubns Serv.

Mitcalfe, Barry. Moana. 250p. 1975. 13.50x (ISBN 0-85467-030-0, Pub. by Viking New Zealand). Intl Schol Bk Serv.

Mol, Hans. The Fixed & the Fickle: Religion & Identity in New Zealand. 96p. 1981. text ed. 8.75x (ISBN 0-88920-113-7, Pub. by Laurier U Pr). Humanities.

Pearson, David. Johnsonville: Continuity & Change in a New Zealand Township. 200p. 1980. text ed. 21.00x (ISBN 0-86861-281-2); pap. text ed. 11.50x (ISBN 0-86861-289-8). Allen Unwin.

NEW ZEALAND–DESCRIPTION AND TRAVEL

Anderson, William. Milford Trails. (Illus.). 1971. 10.50 (ISBN 0-589-00472-7, Pub. by Reed Books Australia). C E Tuttle.

Angas, George F. Savage Life & Scenes in Australia & New Zealand: Being an Artist's Impressions of Countries & People at the Antipodes, 2 Vols. in 1. 2nd ed. (Illus.). 23.00 (ISBN 0-384-01465-8). Johnson Repr.

Badcock, Douglas. My Kind of Country: Paintings in Oil of Southern New Zealand. (Illus.). 87p. 1971. 29.00x (ISBN 0-7233-0304-5). Intl Pubns Serv.

Beckett, T. N. The Mountains of Erewhon. (Illus.). 1978. 19.50 (ISBN 0-589-01119-7, Pub. by Reed Books Australia). C E Tuttle.

Bigwood, Kenneth & Bigwood, Jean. New Zealand in Colour, Vol. 1. Baxter, James K., ed. (Illus.). 1962. 10.00 (ISBN 0-686-00956-8). Wellington.

Bolitho, Hector & Mulgan, John. Emigrants. facsimile ed. LC 70-108635. (Essay Index Reprint Ser). 1939. 16.00 (ISBN 0-8369-1547-X). Arno.

Bone, Robert W. Maverick Guide to New Zealand: 1981 Edition. LC 80-25250. (Illus.). 305p. (Orig.). 1981. pap. 9.95 (ISBN 0-88289-269-X). Pelican.

Burton, Robert E., ed. Travel in Oceania, Australia & New Zealand: A Guide to Information Sources. LC 80-15333. (Geography & Travel Information Guide Ser.: Vol. 2). 150p. 1980. 36.00 (ISBN 0-8103-1421-5). Gale.

Dykes, Merv. Time Out in New Zealand. (Tourist "Floppy" Ser.). (Illus.). 1979. pap. 8.95 (ISBN 0-589-01135-9, Pub. by Reed Books Australia). C E Tuttle.

Falla, Molly. Kea on My Bed. LC 75-327794. (Illus.). 40p. 1974. 7.00x (ISBN 0-8002-1626-1). Intl Pubns Serv.

Fodor's Australia, New Zealand & South Pacific, 1981. 1981. 13.95 (ISBN 0-679-00669-9); pap. 10.95 (ISBN 0-679-00670-2). McKay.

Forster, R. R. Small Land Animals of New Zealand. rev ed. (Illus.). 175p. 1975. pap. 13.55 (ISBN 0-8002-0482-4). Intl Pubns Serv.

Graham, Susan. This Land I Love: New Zealand. (Illus.). 1962. 6.00 (ISBN 0-686-00958-4). Wellington.

Henderson, Jim. New Zealand's South Island in Colour. LC 72-75989. (Illus.). 1966. 13.50 (ISBN 0-589-00275-9, Pub. by Reed Books Australia). C E Tuttle.

Hintz, O. S. Fisherman's Paradise. LC 75-322904. 192p. 1979. 9.95 (ISBN 0-370-10486-2, Pub. by Chatto Bodley Jonathan). Merrimack Bk Serv.

Hunter, Grant. The New Zealand Tramper's Handbook. (Illus.). 160p. (Orig.). 1981. pap. 10.50 (ISBN 0-589-01348-3, Pub. by Reed Books Australia). C E Tuttle.

King, Michael. New Zealand: Its Land & Its People. (Illus.). 152p. 1979. Repr. of 1977 ed. 22.50 (ISBN 0-589-01295-9, Pub. by Reed Bks Australia). C E Tuttle.

Linse, Linda & Cheledines, Gary. New Zealand on a Budget. (Illus.). 144p. (Orig.). 1979. pap. 4.95 (ISBN 0-934494-00-2). Odyssey Pub Co.

McFarlane, Shona. Dunedin: Portrait of a City. (Illus.). 95p. 1970. 12.50x (ISBN 0-7233-0171-9). Intl Pubns Serv.

McNeish, James. As for the Godwits... LC 78-670050. (Illus.). 1977. 12.50x (ISBN 0-340-22197-6). Intl Pubns Serv.

Miller, Michael. Reef & Beach Life of New Zealand. LC 74-180221. (Illus.). 141p. 1973. 21.20x (ISBN 0-8002-0084-5). Intl Pubns Serv.

Momatiuk, Yva & Eastcott, John. High Country. (Illus.). 128p. 1980. 37.50 (ISBN 0-589-01321-1, Pub. by Reed Bks Australia). C E Tuttle.

Morton, Harry. And Now New Zealand. 3rd ed. LC 77-353297. 1976. pap. 5.00x (ISBN 0-908565-07-0). Intl Pubns Serv.

Morton, John. The New Zealand Sea Shore. (Illus.). 638p. 1968. 25.00x (ISBN 0-8002-0070-5). Intl Pubns Serv.

Murray-Oliver, Anthony. Augustus Earle in New Zealand. (Illus.). 1968. text ed. 22.00x (ISBN 0-391-01948-1). Humanities.

Natusch, Sheila. Animals of New Zealand. (Illus.). 1967. 10.00x (ISBN 0-8426-1448-6). Verry.

Pask, Raymond & Bryant, Lee. Australia & New Zealand: A New Geography. 1976. pap. text ed. 9.00x (ISBN 0-435-34682-2); resources pack 47.00x (ISBN 0-435-34683-0). Heinemann Ed.

Pope, Diana, compiled by. Mobil New Zealand Travel Guide-North Island. (Illus.). 1973. pap. 11.95 (ISBN 0-589-00721-1, Pub. by Reed Books Australia). C E Tuttle.
--Mobil New Zealand Travel Guide: South Island. LC 74-76513. (Illus.). 1975. pap. 14.95 (ISBN 0-589-00861-7, Pub. by Reed Books Australia). C E Tuttle.
Radcliffe, Peter. Land of Mountains: Hiking & Climbing in New Zealand. (Illus.). 1979. 27.50 (ISBN 0-916890-69-4). Mountaineers.
Reed, Alfred H. From North Cape to Bluff. (Illus.). 6.00 (ISBN 0-686-00954-1). Wellington.
Ross, John. Lighthouses of New Zealand. (Illus.). 155p. 1975. 10.50x (ISBN 0-8002-0468-9). Intl Pubns Serv.
Shadbolt, Maurice, ed. The Shell Guide to New Zealand. 3rd rev. ed. 1976. 15.00x (ISBN 0-7181-0704-7). Intl Pubns Serv.
Siers, James. New Zealand. (Illus.). 84p. 1980. 12.50x (ISBN 0-908582-09-9). Intl Pubns Serv.
Silcock, Richard. New Zealand, Land of Scenic Contrasts. LC 76-364286. (Illus.). 1974. Repr. 10.00x (ISBN 0-600-07342-4). Intl Pubns Serv.
Skinner, Gwen. Simply Living: A Gather's Guide to New Zealand's Fields, Forests & Shores. (Illus.). 152p. (Orig.). 1981. pap. 20.95 (ISBN 0-589-01338-6, Pub. by Reed Books Australia). C E Tuttle.
Sunset Editors. New Zealand. 3rd ed. LC 77-90726. (Illus.). 128p. 1978. pap. 5.95 (ISBN 0-376-06534-6, Sunset Bks). Sunset-Lane.
Temple, Philip. Castles in the Air: Men & Mountains in New Zealand. LC 74-177859. (Illus.). 1973. pap. 8.50x (ISBN 0-8002-0342-9). Intl Pubns Serv.
--Patterns of Water: The Great Southern Lakes of New Zealand. LC 75-323384. (Illus.). 136p. 1974. 23.50x (ISBN 0-7233-0405-X). Intl Pubns Serv.
--South Island of New Zealand. 151p. 1975. 22.70x (ISBN 0-8002-1996-1). Intl Pubns Serv.
Turnbull, Michael. The Changing Land: A Short History of New Zealand. 2nd ed. LC 78-670072. (Illus.). 1975. pap. 10.00x (ISBN 0-582-68751-9). Intl Pubns Serv.
Turner, Gwenda. Akaroa: Banks Penisula, New Zealand. 1977. 20.00x (ISBN 0-908565-41-0). Intl Pubns Serv.
Warwick, Wayne. Surfriding in New Zealand. 84p. 1980. 10.00 (ISBN 0-85467-046-7, Pub. by Viking Sevenseas). Intl Schol Bk Serv.
Wheeler, Tony. New Zealand: A Travel Survival Kit. (Illus.). 112p. 1980. pap. 5.95 (ISBN 0-9598080-9-4, Pub by Lonely Planet Australia). Hippocrene Bks.

NEW ZEALAND–DISCOVERY AND EXPLORATION

Wakefield, Jerningham E. Adventure in New Zealand. 1977. 8.50 (ISBN 0-85558-440-8). Transatlantic.

NEW ZEALAND–ECONOMIC CONDITIONS

Blyth, Conrad. Inflation in New Zealand. 1978. pap. text ed. 4.95x (ISBN 0-86861-016-X). Allen Unwin.
Condliffe, J. B. Economic Outlook for New Zealand. 1969. 7.50x (ISBN 0-8426-1214-9). Verry.
Condliffe, John B. The Welfare State in New Zealand. LC 73-19123. (Illus.). 396p. 1975. Repr. of 1959 ed. lib. bdg. 21.25x (ISBN 0-8371-7298-5, CONZ). Greenwood.
Dale, D. A. The New Zealand Commercial Dictionary. 2nd ed. 338p. 1967. 11.00x (ISBN 0-8002-0077-2). Intl Pubns Serv.
Dean, Roderick S. Foreign Investment in New Zealand Manufacturing. LC 77-850163. 540p. 1970. 30.00x (ISBN 0-457-01010-X). Intl Pubns Serv.
Fogelberg, Graeme. New Zealand Case Studies in Marketing. 2nd ed. 240p. 1976. pap. 16.50x (ISBN 0-456-02090-X). Intl Pubns Serv.
Franklin, S. Harvey. Trade, Growth & Anxiety: New Zealand Beyond the Welfare State. (Illus.). 1979. 34.00x (ISBN 0-456-02320-8). Methuen Inc.
Hines, George H. Organizational Behaviour: Human Relations in New Zealand Industry. LC 72-194707. 250p. 1972. 16.00x (ISBN 0-457-01250-1). Intl Pubns Serv.
Holmes, Frank W. Money, Finance, & the Economy: An Introduction to the New Zealand Financial System. 210p. 1972. pap. 9.00x (ISBN 0-8002-0073-X). Intl Pubns Serv.
Rimmer, J. O., ed. Marketing in New Zealand. 308p. 1972. pap. text ed. 17.00x (ISBN 0-457-01140-8). Intl Pubns Serv.
Rogers, Frank & Sharp, Andrew. The Road to Maturity. (Studies in 20th Century History Ser.). 1977. pap. text ed. 4.50x (ISBN 0-686-71782-1, 00548). Heinemann Ed.

NEW ZEALAND–FOREIGN RELATIONS

Burnett, Robin & Burnett, Alan, eds. Australia-New Zealand Economic Relations: Issues for the 1980's. 183p. 1981. pap. text ed. 15.95 (ISBN 0-86784-011-0, 0102, Pub. by ANUP Australia). Bks Australia.
Dalziel, R. M. Origins of New Zealand Diplomacy. 1975. 6.00x (ISBN 0-7055-0550-2). Intl Pubns Serv.
Kay, Robin. The Australian New Zealand Agreement, 1944 (Canberra Pact) (Documents on New Zealand External Relations Ser: Vol. 1). 292p. 1973. text ed. 12.50x (ISBN 0-8426-0425-1). Verry.
Kennaway, Richard. New Zealand Foreign Policy 1951-1971. (Illus.). 174p. 1972. pap. 15.00x (ISBN 0-456-01460-8). Intl Pubns Serv.
Lissington, M. P. New Zealand & Japan, Nineteen Hundred to Nineteen Forty-One. (Illus.). 206p. 1972. 12.00x (ISBN 0-8426-0449-9). Verry.
--New Zealand & the United States, Eighteen Forty to Nineteen Forty-Four. (Illus.). 114p. 1972. 6.00x (ISBN 0-8426-0450-2). Verry.
New Zealand Institute of Intl. Affairs, ed. New Zealand in World Affairs, Vol. 1. (New Zealand in World Affairs Ser.). 1977. pap. 11.50x (ISBN 0-7055-0638-X). Intl Pubns Serv.
Sinclair, Keith. Towards Independence. (Studies in 20th Century History Ser.). 1976. pap. text ed. 4.50x (ISBN 0-686-71787-2, 00546). Heinemann Ed.
Stenson, M. R. New Zealand & the Global Ecological Crisis. LC 78-670045. (Illus.). 1975. pap. 7.50x (ISBN 0-7055-0551-0). Intl Pubns Serv.

NEW ZEALAND–HISTORY

Adams, Peter. Fatal Necessity: British Intervention in New Zealand 1830-1847. 1978. 23.00x (ISBN 0-19-647950-9). Oxford U Pr.
Buddle, Thomas. The Maori King Movement in New Zealand. LC 75-35241. Repr. of 1860 ed. 12.50 (ISBN 0-404-14416-0). AMS Pr.
Buick, Thomas L. The Moa-Hunters of New Zealand: Sportsmen of the Stone Age. LC 75-35242. Repr. of 1937 ed. 22.50 (ISBN 0-404-14417-9). AMS Pr.
Clark, Paul. Hauhau: The Pai Marire Search for Maori Identify. (Illus.). 1976. 13.95x (ISBN 0-19-647935-5). Oxford U Pr.
Cowan, James. New Zealand Wars, 2 Vols. LC 76-100514. (BCL Ser. II). Repr. of 1922 ed. 37.50 (ISBN 0-404-00600-0). AMS Pr.
Dalton, B. War & Politics in New Zealand, 1855-1870. 1967. 14.00x (ISBN 0-424-05250-4, Pub by Sydney U Pr). Intl Schol Bk Serv.
Enting, Brian. Neath the Mantle of Rangi. (Illus.). 148p. 1980. 20.50 (ISBN 0-85467-036-X, Pub. by Viking Sevenseas). Intl Schol Bk Serv.
Gibson, Tom. The Maori Wars: The British Army in New Zealand 1840-1872. (Nineteenth Century Military Campaigns Ser.). (Illus.). 266p. 1974. 19.50 (ISBN 0-85052-133-5). Shoe String.
Grey, George. Polynesian Mythology & Ancient Traditional History of the New Zealanders As Furnished by Their Priests & Chiefs. LC 75-35253. Repr. of 1906 ed. 20.50 (ISBN 0-404-14425-X). AMS Pr.
Hall-Jones, John. Bluff Harbour. 1976. 11.50x (ISBN 0-8002-0455-7). Intl Pubns Serv.
Hargreaves, R. P. & Hearn, T. J. New Zealand in the Mid-Victorian Era: An Album of Contemporary Engravings. (Illus.). 1977. 15.00x (ISBN 0-908565-39-9). Intl Pubns Serv.
Harrop, Angus J. England & the Maori Wars. facsimile ed. LC 74-169763. (Select Bibliographies Reprint Ser). Repr. of 1937 ed. 27.00 (ISBN 0-8369-5983-3). Arno.
Hillary, J. H. Westland: Journal of John Hillar, Emigrant to New Zealand, 1879. 111p. 1979. 20.00x (ISBN 0-906554-01-2, Pub. by Acorn England). State Mutual Bk.
Holcroft, M. H. Carapace. (Illus.). 1979. 13.50x (ISBN 0-908565-91-7). Intl Pubns Serv.
--The Line of the Road: A History of Manawatu County 1876-1976. LC 78-670039. (Illus.). 1977. 13.50x (ISBN 0-8002-0227-9). Intl Pubns Serv.
--Old Invercargill. LC 77-481152. (Illus.). 1976. 13.50x (ISBN 0-908565-08-9). Intl Pubns Serv.
--The Shaping of New Zealand. LC 78-670174. (Illus.). 1974. 12.50x (ISBN 0-600-07277-0). Intl Pubns Serv.
Holland, H. S. Tragic Story of the Waihi Strike. LC 76-353273. (Illus.). 202p. 1975. Repr. of 1913 ed. 12.00x (ISBN 0-8002-0484-0). Intl Pubns Serv.
Horsman, John. The Coming of the Pakeha to Auckland Province. 248p. 1971. 9.90x (ISBN 0-456-00590-0). Intl Pubns Serv.
Kenny, Robert W., ed. New Zealand Journal, 1842-1844. 3.00 (ISBN 0-87577-012-6). Peabody Mus Salem.
Knight, Hardwicke, ed. Dunedin Then. LC 75-312803. (Illus.). 1977. pap. 7.50x (ISBN 0-908565-38-0). Intl Pubns Serv.
Livingston, William S. & Louis, W. Roger, eds. Australia, New Zealand, & the Pacific Islands Since the First World War. 261p. 1979. text ed. 17.95x (ISBN 0-292-70344-9). U of Tex Pr.
Manson, Celia. Story of a New Zealand Family. LC 75-308156. 288p. 1975. 12.00x (ISBN 0-8002-0483-2). Intl Pubns Serv.
Marais, Johannes S. Colonization of New Zealand. LC 77-137258. Repr. of 1927 ed. 24.75 (ISBN 0-404-04184-1). AMS Pr.
Munz, P. Feel of Truth. 1969. 15.00x (ISBN 0-589-04070-7). Intl Pubns Serv.
Oliver, W. H., ed. The Oxford History of New Zealand. (Illus.). 550p. 1981. 39.95 (ISBN 0-19-558062-1). Oxford U Pr.
Reed, A. W. The Story of New Zealand. (Illus.). 1945. 5.95 (ISBN 0-589-00339-9, Pub. by Reed Books Australia). C E Tuttle.
Rogers, Frank & Sharp, Andrew. The Road to Maturity. (Studies in 20th Century History Ser.). 1977. pap. text ed. 4.50x (ISBN 0-686-71782-1, 00548). Heinemann Ed.
Scott, Dick. Ask That Mountain. LC 75-315794. (Illus.). 216p. 1975. 13.00x (ISBN 0-86863-375-5). Intl Pubns Serv.
Sewell, Henry. New Zealand Native Rebellion. 1974. 10.00x (ISBN 0-8002-1752-7). Intl Pubns Serv.
Shadbolt, Maurice. Love & Legend: Some 20th Century New Zealanders. (Illus.). 1976. 14.00x (ISBN 0-340-21455-4). Intl Pubns Serv.
Sinclair, Keith. Towards Independence. (Studies in 20th Century History Ser.). 1976. pap. text ed. 4.50x (ISBN 0-686-71787-2, 00546). Heinemann Ed.
Sinclair, Keith & Harrex, Wendy. Looking Back: A Photographic History of New Zealand. (Illus.). 240p. 1978. text ed. 34.00x (ISBN 0-19-558036-2). Oxford U Pr.
Smith, Stephenson P. Maori Wars of the Nineteenth Century. 2nd enl. ed. LC 75-35271. Repr. of 1910 ed. 41.50 (ISBN 0-404-14440-3). AMS Pr.
Tapp, E. J. Early New Zealand. (Illus.). 1958. 14.00x (ISBN 0-522-83878-2, Pub. by Melbourne U Pr). Intl Schol Bk Serv.
Turnbull, Michael. The Changing Land: A Short History of New Zealand. 2nd ed. LC 78-670072. (Illus.). 1975. pap. 10.00x (ISBN 0-582-68751-9). Intl Pubns Serv.
Williams, John B. The New Zealand Journal, Eighteen Forty-Two to Eighteen Forty-Four, of John B. Williams of Salem, Massachusetts. Kenny, Robert W., ed. LC 56-3911. (Illus.). xii, 120p. 1956. 12.00 (ISBN 0-87057-041-2). U Pr of New Eng.
--New Zealand Journal, 1842-1844, of John B. Williams of Salem, Massachusetts. Kenny, Robert W., ed. (Illus.). 132p. 1956. text ed. 12.00x (ISBN 0-87057-041-2, Pub. by Brown U Pr). U Pr of New Eng.
Wright, Harrison M. New Zealand, 1769-1840: Early Years of Western Contact. LC 59-12979. (Historical Monographs Ser: No. 42). 1959. 12.50x (ISBN 0-674-62000-3). Harvard U Pr.

NEW ZEALAND–HISTORY–FICTION

Hyde, Robin. Check to Your King. 1977. 8.50 (ISBN 0-85558-448-3). Transatlantic.

NEW ZEALAND–INTELLECTUAL LIFE

Fitzgerald, Thomas K. Education & Identity: A Study of the New Zealand Maori Graduate. (Illus.). 1977. text ed. 17.50x (ISBN 0-908567-01-4). Verry.
McLeod, Alan L., ed. Pattern of New Zealand Culture. LC 68-9751. 301p. 1968. 25.00x (ISBN 0-8014-0286-7). Cornell U Pr.
Smyth, Bernard W. The Role of Culture in Leisure-Time in New Zealand. LC 73-83403. (Studies & Documents on Cultural Policies Ser.). (Illus.). 88p. (Orig.). 1973. pap. 3.25 (ISBN 92-3-101041-7, U560, UNESCO). Unipub.

NEW ZEALAND–JUVENILE LITERATURE

Baldwin, Olive. Aotearoa: A Children's History of New Zealand. (Illus.). 52p. (gr. 3-8). 1975. 7.50x (ISBN 0-8002-0452-2). Intl Pubns Serv.
Klemm, Edward G., Jr. Precious Heritage. 228p. 1974. 5.00 (ISBN 0-912852-07-0). Echo Pubs.
Lawson, Pat. Kuma Is a Maori Girl. (Children Everywhere Ser). (Illus.). (gr. k-2). 1967. PLB 4.95 (ISBN 0-8038-3939-1); PLB 4.33 i.T.A. ed. (ISBN 0-8038-3940-5). Hastings.
Marsh, Ngaio. New Zealand. (Illus.). (gr. 7 up). 1964. 5.95g (ISBN 0-02-762380-7). Macmillan.
Sterling Publishing Company Editors. New Zealand in Pictures. LC 64-24690. (Visual Geography Ser.). (Orig.). (gr. 6 up). PLB 4.99 (ISBN 0-8069-1047-X); pap. 2.95 (ISBN 0-8069-1046-1). Sterling.

NEW ZEALAND–MAPS

Anderson, A. Grant, ed. New Zealand in Maps. LC 77-18023. (Illus.). 1978. text ed. 35.00x (ISBN 0-8419-0324-7). Holmes & Meier.
Automobile Associations of New Zealand. AA Road Atlas of New Zealand. LC 77-372880. (Illus.). 1975. 15.00x (ISBN 0-600-07347-5). Intl Pubns Serv.
Wards, Ian, ed. New Zealand Atlas. (Illus.). 1976. text ed. 60.00 (ISBN 0-477-01000-8). Verry.

NEW ZEALAND–NATIVE RACES

Raymond, Val. Taupo. (Illus.). 1976. 12.50x (ISBN 0-340-21453-8). Intl Pubns Serv.
Siers, James & Ngata, W. T. The Maori People of New Zealand. LC 78-670037. (Illus.). 1976. pap. 6.50 (ISBN 0-85467-037-8). Intl Pubns Serv.

NEW ZEALAND–POLITICS AND GOVERNMENT

Bedggood, David. Rich & Poor in New Zealand. 200p. 1980. text ed. 21.00x (ISBN 0-86861-377-0); pap. text ed. 11.50x (ISBN 0-86861-385-1). Allen Unwin.
Buick, T. Lindsay. Treaty of Waitangi. LC 72-1294. (Select Bibliographies Reprint Ser.). 1972. Repr. of 1936 ed. 29.00 (ISBN 0-8369-6822-0). Arno.
Bush, Graham. Local Government & Politics in New Zealand. 200p. 1980. text ed. 22.95x (ISBN 0-86861-074-7); pap. text ed. 14.95x (ISBN 0-86861-082-8). Allen Unwin.
Cleveland, Les. The Anatomy of Influence: Pressure Groups & Politics in New Zealand. LC 72-170757. 144p. 1972. pap. 11.70x (ISBN 0-457-01050-9). Intl Pubns Serv.
Davis, Richard P. Irish Issues in New Zealand Politics, 1868-1922. LC 75-332097. 248p. 1974. 19.25x (ISBN 0-8002-0466-2). Intl Pubns Serv.
Goldstein, Ray & Alley, Rod, eds. Labour in Power: Promise & Performance. LC 76-367719. 1975. pap. 7.50x (ISBN 0-7055-0611-8). Intl Pubns Serv.
Hill, Larry B. The Model Ombudsman: Institutionalizing New Zealand's Democratic Experiment. LC 76-3258. 1976. 30.00 (ISBN 0-691-07579-4). Princeton U Pr.
--Parliament & the Ombudsman in New Zealand. (Legislative Research Ser.: No. 8). 1973. pap. 3.50 (ISBN 0-686-18649-4). Univ OK Gov Res.
Levine, S. The New Zealand Political System: Politics in a Small Society. LC 78-74191. 1979. text ed. 18.95x (ISBN 0-86861-073-9); pap. text ed. 9.95x (ISBN 0-86861-081-X). Allen Unwin.
Levine, S., ed. New Zealand Politics: A Reader. 1975. 18.00 (ISBN 0-7015-1753-0). Verry.
Levine, Stephen & Robinson, Alan. The New Zealand Voter: A Survey of Public Opinion & Electoral Behaviour. (New Zealand Studies in Politics Ser.). 1976. pap. 12.50x (ISBN 0-7055-0652-5). Intl Pubns Serv.
Levine, Stephen, ed. Politics in New Zealand. 1978. text ed. 29.95x (ISBN 0-86861-056-9); pap. text ed. 14.95x (ISBN 0-86861-064-X). Allen Unwin.
McRobie, Alan & Roberts, Nigel S. Election Nineteen Hundred & Seventy Eight: 1977 Electoral Redistribution & the 1978 General Election in New Zealand. 1978. pap. 12.50x (ISBN 0-908565-49-6). Intl Pubns Serv.
Olssen, Erick. John A. Lee. LC 78-302192. (Illus.). 1977. 20.00x (ISBN 0-908569-04-1). Intl Pubns Serv.
Palmer, Geoffrey. Compensation for Incapacity: A Study of Law & Social Change in New Zealand & Australia. 460p. 1980. 49.50x (ISBN 0-19-558045-1). Oxford U Pr.
Penniman, Howard R., ed. New Zealand at the Polls: The General Election of 1978. 1980. pap. 7.95 (ISBN 0-8447-3376-8). Am Enterprise.
Scholefield, Guy H. Notable New Zealand Statesmen: Twelve Prime Ministers. LC 72-5588. (Biography Index Reprint Ser.). 1972. Repr. of 1947 ed. 19.00 (ISBN 0-8369-8139-1). Arno.
Scott, Claudia D. Local & Regional Government in New Zealand. LC 78-73729. 1979. text ed. 16.50x (ISBN 0-86861-041-0); pap. text ed. 9.95x (ISBN 0-86861-049-6). Allen Unwin.

NEW ZEALAND–ROYAL AIR FORCE

Francillon, Rene J. Royal Australian Air Force & Royal New Zealand Air Force in the Pacific. LC 76-114412. (Aero Pictorial Ser.: Vol. 3). (Illus., Orig.). 1970. pap. 4.95 (ISBN 0-8168-0308-0). Aero.

NEW ZEALAND–SOCIAL CONDITIONS

Condliffe, John B. The Welfare State in New Zealand. LC 73-19123. (Illus.). 396p. 1975. Repr. of 1959 ed. lib. bdg. 21.25x (ISBN 0-8371-7298-5, CONZ). Greenwood.
Easton, Brian. Social Policy & the Welfare State in New Zealand. 200p. 1980. text ed. 25.00x (ISBN 0-86861-393-2); pap. text ed. 12.50x (ISBN 0-86861-002-X). Allen Unwin.
King, Michael. New Zealand: Its Land & Its People. (Illus.). 152p. 1979. Repr. of 1977 ed. 22.50 (ISBN 0-589-01295-9, Pub. by Reed Bks Australia). C E Tuttle.
The Nature & Future of Development in New Zealand. 34p. 1980. pap. 5.00 (ISBN 92-808-0081-7, TUNU 042, UNU). Unipub.
Neville & O'Neill. Population New Zealand. 1979. pap. text ed. 17.50x (ISBN 0-582-71771-X). Longman.
Pool, D. Ian. The Maori Population of New Zealand 1769-1971. (Illus.). pap. 15.25x (ISBN 0-19-647947-9). Oxford U Pr.
Ritchie, Jane & Ritchie, James. Growing up in New Zealand. LC 78-52238. 1978. text ed. 13.50x (ISBN 0-86861-104-2). Allen Unwin.

Sutch, W. B. The Responsible Society in New Zealand. 141p. 1971. 5.00x (ISBN 0-8002-0111-6). Intl Pubns Serv.
Thomson, K. W., ed. Contemporary New Zealand: Essays on the Human Resource, Urban Growth, & Problems of Society. LC 74-176480. 218p. 1973. pap. 13.80x (ISBN 0-456-01440-3). Intl Pubns Serv.
Thorns, D. C. & Kilmartin, L. R. Cities Unlimited: Urbanization in Australia & New Zealand. LC 78-55230. (Studies in Society). 1978. text ed. 15.95x (ISBN 0-86861-288-X); pap. text ed. 8.95x (ISBN 0-86861-296-0). Allen Unwin.

NEW ZEALAND-SOCIAL LIFE AND CUSTOMS

Armstrong, Alan. Maori Customs & Crafts. 60p. 1973. pap. 2.50x (ISBN 0-85467-009-2, Pub. by Viking New Zealand). Intl Schol Bk Serv.
Ausubel, David P. The Fern & the Tiki. 1977. pap. 5.95 (ISBN 0-8158-0359-1). Chris Mass.
Colless, Brian & Donovan, Peter, eds. Religion in New Zealand Society. 215p. 1980. Repr. text ed. 17.50x (ISBN 0-567-09303-4). Attic Pr.
Forster, John, ed. Social Process in New Zealand. LC 76-460703. (Illus.). 1970. 10.00x (ISBN 0-8002-2331-4). Intl Pubns Serv.
Friedlander, M. & McNeish, J. Larks in a Paradise: New Zealand Portraits. LC 74-325408. (Illus.). 208p. 1974. 18.00x (ISBN 0-8002-0469-7). Intl Pubns Serv.
Johnston, R. J. The New Zealanders: How They Live & Work. LC 75-34976. 168p. 1976. text ed. 8.95 (ISBN 0-686-70219-0, HoltC). HR&W.
Main, William. Auckland Through a Victorian Lens. LC 78-670050. (Illus.). 1977. 22.50x (ISBN 0-908582-05-6). Intl Pubns Serv.
Morton, Harry. Which Way New Zealand? 244p. 1975. 11.50x (ISBN 0-908565-11-9). Intl Pubns Serv.
Pearson, David. Johnsonville: Continuity & Change in a New Zealand Township. 200p. 1980. text ed. 21.00x (ISBN 0-86861-281-2); pap. text ed. 11.50x (ISBN 0-86861-289-8). Allen Unwin.
Scholefield, Guy H., ed. Richmond-Atkinson Papers, 2 vols. (Illus.). 1960. 16.50x (ISBN 0-8426-1502-4). Verry.
Smyth, Bernard W. The Role of Culture in Leisure-Time in New Zealand. LC 73-83403. (Studies & Documents on Cultural Policies Ser.). (Illus.). 88p. (Orig.). 1973. pap. 3.25 (ISBN 92-3-101041-7, U560, UNESCO). Unipub.
Sorrenson, Keith. Integration or Identity? (Studies in 10th Century Hisory). (Orig.). 1977. pap. text ed. 4.50x (ISBN 0-686-71775-9, 00547). Heinemann Ed.

NEW ZEALAND AUTHORS

see Authors, New Zealand

NEW ZEALAND COMPANY, LONDON

Marais, Johannes S. Colonization of New Zealand. LC 77-137258. Repr. of 1927 ed. 24.75 (ISBN 0-404-04184-1). AMS Pr.
Wakefield, Edward J. The London Journal of Edward Jerningham Wakefield 1845-46. Stevens, Joan, ed. LC 75-316765. (Illus.). 1972. 6.00x (ISBN 0-8002-0244-9). Intl Pubns Serv.

NEW ZEALAND DRAWINGS

see Drawings, New Zealand

NEW ZEALAND FICTION-HISTORY AND CRITICISM

Burns, James. New Zealand Novels & Novelists Eighteen Sixty-One to Nineteen Seventy-Nine: A Bibliography. 1981. text ed. 20.00x (ISBN 0-686-73388-6, 00563). Heinemann Ed.

NEW ZEALAND LEGENDS

see Legends, New Zealand

NEW ZEALAND LITERATURE (COLLECTIONS)

Contemporary Maori Writing. 153p. 1970. 5.95 (ISBN 0-589-00447-6, Pub. by Reed Books Australia). C E Tuttle.

NEW ZEALAND LITERATURE-HISTORY AND CRITICISM

Curnon, Wystan. Essays on New Zealand Literature. LC 74-179530. 192p. 1973. pap. 11.50x (ISBN 0-435-18195-5). Intl Pubns Serv.
Curnow, Wystan, ed. Essays on New Zealand Literature. 1973. pap. text ed. 15.00x (ISBN 0-435-18195-5). Heinemann Ed.
McNaughton, Howard. New Zealand Drama. (World Authors Ser.: No. 626). 1981. lib. bdg. 14.95 (ISBN 0-8057-6468-2). Twayne.
Mulgan, Alan. Literature & Authorship in New Zealand. LC 72-18707. lib. bdg. 6.50 (ISBN 0-8414-0512-3). Folcroft.
Wilkes, G. A. & Reid, J. C. Literatures of Australia & New Zealand. McLeod, A. L., ed. LC 71-121856. 1971. 15.95x (ISBN 0-685-01602-1). Pa St U Pr.

NEW ZEALAND PAINTING

see Painting, New Zealand

NEW ZEALAND POETRY-HISTORY AND CRITICISM

Thompson, John, ed. New Zealand Literature to Nineteen Seventy-Seven: A Guide to Information Sources. LC 74-11537. (American Literature, English Literature, & World Literature in English Information Guide Ser.: Vol. 30). 250p. 1980. 36.00 (ISBN 0-8103-1246-8). Gale.

NEWARK, NEW JERSEY

Churchill, Charles W. The Italians of Newark. LC 74-17922. (Italian American Experience Ser). (Illus.). 220p. 1975. 18.00x (ISBN 0-405-06395-4). Arno.
Gwyn, William B. Barriers to Establishing Urban Ombudsmen: The Case of Newark. new ed. LC 74-11446. 93p. 1974. pap. 4.50x (ISBN 0-87772-200-5). Inst Gov Stud Berk.
Kolesar, John. The Newark Experiment: A New Direction for Urban Health Care. 1975. 2.00 (ISBN 0-686-23338-7). Ctr Analysis Public Issues.
Rice, Arnold S. Newark: A Chronological & Documentary History. LC 77-23412. (American Cities Chronology Ser.). 1977. 8.50 (ISBN 0-379-00608-1). Oceana.
Winters, Stanley B., ed. From Riot to Recovery: Newark After Ten Years. LC 79-66424. 1979. text ed. 22.25 (ISBN 0-8191-0822-7); pap. text ed. 14.75 (ISBN 0-8191-0823-5). U Pr of Amer.

NEWBERRY, TRUMAN HANDY, 1864-1945

Ervin, Spencer. Henry Ford Vs. Truman H. Newberry: The Famous Senate Election Contest. LC 73-19143. (Politics & People Ser.). 634p. 1974. Repr. 32.00x (ISBN 0-405-05867-5). Arno.

NEWBERY, JOHN, 1713-1761

Welsh, Charles. Bookseller of the Last Century. LC 79-179343. (English Book Trade). Repr. of 1885 ed. lib. bdg. 17.50x (ISBN 0-678-00883-3). Kelley.

NEWBERY, FIRM, PUBLISHERS, LONDON

Welsh, Charles. Bookseller of the Last Century. LC 79-179343. (English Book Trade). Repr. of 1885 ed. lib. bdg. 17.50x (ISBN 0-678-00883-3). Kelley.

NEWBERY MEDAL BOOKS

Kingman, Lee, ed. Newbery & Caldecott Medal Books: 1956-1965. LC 65-26759. (Illus.). 1965. 17.00 (ISBN 0-87675-002-1). Horn Bk.
--Newbery & Caldecott Medal Books: 1966-1975. LC 75-20167. (Illus.). 325p. 1975. 17.00 (ISBN 0-87675-003-X). Horn Bk.
Miller, Bertha M. & Field, Elinor W., eds. Newbery Medal Books, 1922-1955. LC 55-13968. (Illus.). 1955. 17.00 (ISBN 0-87675-000-5). Horn Bk.

NEWBOLD, DOUGLAS, SIR, 1894-1945

Newbold, Douglas. The Making of the Modern Sudan. LC 73-16800. (Illus.). 601p. 1974. Repr. of 1953 ed. lib. bdg. 29.50x (ISBN 0-8371-7233-0, NEMS). Greenwood.

NEWBORN INFANTS

see Infants (Newborn)

NEWBURYPORT, MASSACHUSETTS

Currier, John J. History of Newburyport, Massachusetts. LC 77-88166. (Illus.). 1977. Repr. of 1905 ed. Vol. 1. 22.50x (ISBN 0-912274-70-0). NH Pub Co.
--History of Newburyport, Massachusetts. LC 77-88166. (Illus.). 1978. Repr. Vol. 2. 22.50x (ISBN 0-912274-97-2). NH Pub Co.
Labaree, Benjamin W. Patriots & Partisans: The Merchants of Newburyport, 1764-1815. new ed. 272p. 1975. pap. 2.95 (ISBN 0-393-00786-3, Norton Lib). Norton.
Thernstrom, Stephan. Poverty & Progress: Social Mobility in a Nineteenth Century City. LC 64-21793. (Joint Center for Urban Studies Publications Ser). 1964. 16.00x (ISBN 0-674-69500-3); pap. 4.95x (ISBN 0-674-69501-1). Harvard U Pr.

NEWCASTLE, MARGARET (LUCAS) CAVENDISH, DUCHESS OF, 1624-1674

Perry, Henry T. E. First Duchess of Newcastle & Her Husband, As Figures in Literary History. (Harvard Studies in English). 1969. Repr. of 1918 ed. 19.50 (ISBN 0-384-45800-9). Johnson Repr.

NEWCASTLE, THOMAS PELHAM-HOLLES, 1ST DUKE OF, 1693-1768

Browning, Reed. The Duke of Newcastle. LC 74-77597. 416p. 1975. 29.50x (ISBN 0-300-01746-4). Yale U Pr.
Henretta, James A. Salutary Neglect: Colonial Administration Under the Duke of Newcastle. LC 70-166377. 388p. 1972. 26.00x (ISBN 0-691-05196-8). Princeton U Pr.
Kelch, Ray A. Newcastle: A Duke Without Money; Thomas Pelham-Holles, 1693-1768. LC 73-83064. 1974. 25.00x (ISBN 0-520-02537-7). U of Cal Pr.
Perry, Henry T. E. First Duchess of Newcastle & Her Husband, As Figures in Literary History. (Harvard Studies in English). 1969. Repr. of 1918 ed. 19.50 (ISBN 0-384-45800-9). Johnson Repr.
Williams, Basil. Carteret & Newcastle: A Contrast in Contemporaries. (Illus.). 240p. 1966. 25.00x (ISBN 0-7146-1524-2, F Cass Co). Biblio Dist.

NEWCASTLE, AUSTRALIA

Shaw, W. H. Newcastle Directory & Almanac, 1880. (Facsimile Ser. No.14). 165p. 1981. 12.95 (ISBN 0-908120-20-6, Pub. by Lib Australian Hist). Bks Australia.
Windross, John. Historical Records of Newcastle 1797-1897. (Facsimile Ser. No.13). 100p. 1981. 11.95 (ISBN 0-908120-19-2, Pub. by Lib Australian Hist). Bks Australia.

NEWCASTLE DISEASE

Hanson, Robert P., ed. Newcastle Disease Virus: An Evolving Pathogen. (Illus.). 366p. 1964. 30.00x (ISBN 0-299-03410-0). U of Wis Pr.
Newcastle Disease Vaccines: Their Production & Use. (Animal Production & Health Ser.: No. 10). 1979. pap. 14.25 (ISBN 92-5-100484-6, F1602, FAO). Unipub.

NEWCASTLE-UPON-TYNE, ENGLAND

Pickering, W. S. F. A Social History of the Diocese of Newcastle. (Illus.). 1981. 35.00 (ISBN 0-85362-189-6, Oriel). Routledge & Kegan.

NEWE METAMORPHOSIS

Lyon, John H. Study of the Newe Metamorphosis. LC 20-3786. Repr. of 1919 ed. 19.75 (ISBN 0-404-04087-X). AMS Pr.

NEWFOUNDLAND

Laird, M. Bibliography of the Natural History of Newfoundland & Labrador. 1980. 66.50 (ISBN 0-12-434050-4). Acad Pr.
Mackay, Robert A., ed. Newfoundland: Economic, Diplomatic & Strategic Studies. LC 76-46180. Repr. of 1946 ed. 39.50 (ISBN 0-404-15366-6). AMS Pr.
Noel, S. J. Politics in Newfoundland. LC 73-151382. (Canadian Government Ser.). 1971. pap. 5.50 (ISBN 0-8020-6187-7). U of Toronto Pr.
Peckham, Sir George. A True Reporte of the Late Discoueries of the Newfound Landes. LC 78-25630. (English Experience Ser.: No. 341). 1971. Repr. of 1583 ed. 11.50 (ISBN 90-221-0341-2). Walter J Johnson.

NEWFOUNDLAND-BIBLIOGRAPHY

Dean, John W., ed. Captain John Mason Fifteen Eighty-Six to Sixteen Thirty-Five. LC 3-24569. (Prince Society Pubns.: No. 17). 1966. Repr. of 1887 ed. 32.00 (ISBN 0-8337-0810-4). B Franklin.

NEWFOUNDLAND-DESCRIPTION AND TRAVEL

Hansen, Ben. Newfoundland Portfolio. (Illus.). 1979. 15.00 (ISBN 0-919948-40-5, Pub. by Co-Operative Union of Canada). Eastview.
Kerr, James L. Wilfred Grenfell, His Life & Work. LC 73-21177. 1977. lib. bdg. 19.50x (ISBN 0-8371-6068-5, KEWG). Greenwood.
Lysaght, A. M., ed. Joseph Banks in Newfoundland & Labrador, 1766: His Diary, Manuscripts & Collections. LC 70-81800. (Illus.). 1971. 65.00 (ISBN 0-520-01780-3). U of Cal Pr.
Whetbourne, Richard. A Discourse & Discovery of New-Found-Land. LC 78-38113. (English Experience Ser.: No. 419). 96p. 1971. Repr. of 1620 ed. 14.00 (ISBN 90-221-0419-2). Walter J Johnson.

NEWFOUNDLAND-HISTORY

Dean, John W., ed. Captain John Mason Fifteen Eighty-Six to Sixteen Thirty-Five. LC 3-24569. (Prince Society Pubns.: No. 17). 1966. Repr. of 1887 ed. 32.00 (ISBN 0-8337-0810-4). B Franklin.
Gunn, Gertrude E. Political History of Newfoundland, 1832-1864. LC 67-397. 1966. pap. 10.00 (ISBN 0-8020-6323-3). U of Toronto Pr.
Halpert, Herbert & Story, G. M., eds. Christmas Mumming in Newfoundland: Essays in Anthropology, Folklore & History. LC 71-391290. 1969. 27.50x (ISBN 0-8020-7065-5). U of Toronto Pr.
Hiller, James & Neary, Peter, eds. Newfoundland in the Nineteenth & Twentieth Centuries. 1980. 20.00x (ISBN 0-8020-5486-2); pap. 7.50 (ISBN 0-8020-6391-8). U of Toronto Pr.
Lounsbury, Ralph G. British Fishery at Newfoundland, 1634-1763. LC 69-19217. 1969. Repr. of 1934 ed. 25.00 (ISBN 0-208-00795-4, Archon). Shoe String.
Marshall, Ingeborg. The Red Ochre People: How Newfoundland's Beothuck Indians Lived. 8.50 (ISBN 0-88894-157-9, Pub. by Douglas & McIntyre). Intl Schol Bk Serv.
Prowse, D. W. History of Newfoundland from the English, Colonial & Foreign Records. 1971. Repr. of 1895 ed. pap. text ed. 51.50x (ISBN 90-6041-084-X). Humanities.
Reeves, John. History of the Government of the Island of Newfoundland. 1793. 14.00 (ISBN 0-384-50131-1). Johnson Repr.
Tuck, James A. Newfoundland & Labrador Prehistory. 1976. pap. 8.50x (ISBN 0-442-29889-7). Van Nos Reinhold.

NEWFOUNDLAND-SOCIAL LIFE AND CUSTOMS

Halpert, Herbert & Story, G. M., eds. Christmas Mumming in Newfoundland: Essays in Anthropology, Folklore & History. LC 71-391290. 1969. 27.50x (ISBN 0-8020-7065-5). U of Toronto Pr.

NEWFOUNDLAND DOG

see Dogs-Breeds-Newfoundland

NEWGATE PRISON, EAST GRANBY, CONNECTICUT

Phelps, Richard H. History of Nowgate of Connecticut, at Simsbury, New East Granby: It's Insurrections & Massacres. LC 74-90189. (Mass Violence in America). Repr. of 1860 ed. 7.50 (ISBN 0-405-01331-0). Arno.

NEWMAN, BARNETT

Richardson, Brenda. Barnett Newman: The Complete Drawings, 1944-1969. LC 79-63430. 1979. 17.50 (ISBN 0-912298-48-0). Baltimore Mus.
Rosenberg, Harold. Barnett Newman. LC 77-25433. (Contemporary Artist Ser.). (Illus.). 1978. 65.00 (ISBN 0-8109-1360-7). Abrams.

NEWMAN, ERNEST, 1868-1959

Van Thal, Herbert M., ed. Fanfare for Ernest Newman. LC 72-181288. 191p. 1955. Repr. write for info. (ISBN 0-403-01711-4). Scholarly.

NEWMAN, FRANCIS, 1805-1897

Robbins, William. Newman Brothers: An Essay in Comparative Intellectual Biography. LC 66-4976. (Illus.). 1966. 10.00x (ISBN 0-674-62200-6). Harvard U Pr.

NEWMAN, JOHN HENRY, CARDINAL, 1801-1890

Allen, Louis, ed. John Henry Newman & the Abbe Jager: A Controversy on Scripture & Tradition (1834-1836) 1976. 27.50x (ISBN 0-19-713138-7). Oxford U Pr.
Allenson, Robert D., compiled by. John Henry Newman, 1801-1890: A Preliminary Register of Editions from 1818 to 1890. 1976. pap. text ed. 2.00x (ISBN 0-8401-0050-7, Aleph Pr). Allenson-Breckinridge.
Barry, William. Cardinal Newman. 1973. Repr. of 1904 ed. 20.00 (ISBN 0-8274-1797-7). R West.
Blehl, Vincent & Connolly, Francis X., eds. Newman's Apologia: A Classic Reconsidered. LC 64-18283. 1964. 4.50 (ISBN 0-15-165204-X). HarBraceJ.
Blehl, Vincent F. John Henry Newman: A Bibliograhical Catalogue of His Writings. LC 77-12141. 1978. 17.50x (ISBN 0-8139-0738-1). U Pr of Va.
Coulson, John & Allchin, Arthur M., eds. The Rediscovery of Newman: An Oxford Symposium. 1967. text ed. 10.00x (ISBN 0-8401-0458-8). Allenson-Breckinridge.
Culler, Arthur D. The Imperial Intellect. LC 55-8700. Repr. of 1955 ed. lib. bdg. 15.50x (ISBN 0-8371-7683-2, CUII). Greenwood.
D'Arcy, Martin C. The Nature of Belief. facsimile ed. (Select Bibliographies Reprint Ser). Repr. of 1931 ed. 19.00 (ISBN 0-8369-5930-2). Arno.
Dessain, C. S. The Spirituality of John Henry Newman. 160p. 1980. pap. 4.95 (ISBN 0-03-057843-4). Winston Pr.
Dessain, Charles S. John Henry Newman. 2nd ed. 1971. 7.50x (ISBN 0-8047-0778-2). Stanford U Pr.
Donald, Gertrude. Men Who Left the Movement. facs. ed. LC 67-23207. (Essay Index Reprint Ser). 1933. 18.00 (ISBN 0-8369-0385-4). Arno.
Downes, David. The Temper of Victorian Belief: Studies in the Religious Novels of Pater, Kingsley & Newman. 8.95 (ISBN 0-685-60146-3, Pub by Twayne). Cyrco Pr.
Elwood, J. Murray. Kindly Light: The Spiritual Vision of John Henry Newman. LC 79-52444. 128p. (Orig.). 1979. pap. 2.95 (ISBN 0-87793-185-2). Ave Maria.
Garraghan, Gilbert J. Prose Studies in Newman. 1915. Repr. 25.00 (ISBN 0-8274-3216-X). R West.
Gates, Lewis E. Three Studies in Literature: Jeffrey, Newman, Arnold. LC 72-195408. 1899. lib. bdg. 15.00 (ISBN 0-8414-4640-7). Folcroft.
Gornall, Thomas. The Letters & Diaries of John Henry Newman: Liberalism in Oxford, January 1835 to December 1836, Vol. 5. 464p. 1981. 65.00x (ISBN 0-19-920117-X). Oxford U Pr.
Griffin, John R. Newman: A Bibliography of Secondary Studies. 150p. (Orig.). 1980. pap. text ed. 12.00 (ISBN 0-931888-04-2, Chr Coll Pr). Christendom Pubns.
Harrold, Charles F. John Henry Newman: An Expository & Critical Study of His Mind, Thought & Art. 1966. Repr. of 1945 ed. 22.50 (ISBN 0-208-00128-X, Archon). Shoe String.
Hicks, John. Critical Studies in Arnold, Emerson, & Newman. LC 75-35962. 1975. Repr. of 1942 ed. lib. bdg. 27.50 (ISBN 0-8414-4749-7). Folcroft.

Houghton, Walter E. Art of Newman's Apologia. 1970. Repr. of 1945 ed. 13.50 (ISBN 0-208-00954-X, Archon). Shoe String.

Hutton, Richard H. Cardinal Newman. 249p. 1980. Repr. of 1891 ed. lib. bdg. 20.00 (ISBN 0-89987-356-1). Darby Bks.

--Cardinal Newman. LC 75-30029. Repr. of 1891 ed. 21.00 (ISBN 0-404-14033-5). AMS Pr.

Kenny, Terence. The Political Thought of John Henry Newman. LC 73-16741. 208p. 1974. Repr. of 1957 ed. lib. bdg. 15.00x (ISBN 0-8371-7226-8, KEJU). Greenwood.

Leslie, Shane. Studies in Sublime Failure. LC 70-117817. (Essay Index Reprint Ser). 1932. 18.00 (ISBN 0-8369-1670-0). Arno.

Levine, George. Boundaries of Fiction: Carlyle, Macaulay, Newman. LC 68-11445. 1968. 20.00 (ISBN 0-691-06140-8). Princeton U Pr.

McGrath, Fergal. Consecration of Learning: Lectures on Newman's Idea of a University. LC 62-22015. 1963. 25.00 (ISBN 0-8232-0485-5). Fordham.

May, J. Lewis. Cardinal Newman. 1945. Repr. lib. bdg. 20.00 (ISBN 0-8414-6605-X). Folcroft.

Middleton, Robert D. Newman & Bloxam: An Oxford Friendship. LC 74-104246. (Illus.). 1971. Repr. of 1947 ed. lib. bdg. 15.00 (ISBN 0-8371-3986-4, MINB). Greenwood.

Moody, John. John Henry Newman. 1946. Repr. 20.00 (ISBN 0-685-43377-3). Norwood Edns.

Newman, J. H. Index. Rickaby, ed. 1977. 12.50 (ISBN 0-87061-042-2). Chr Classics.

Newman, John H. The Letters & Diaries of John Henry Cardinal Newman: Ealing, Trinity, Oriel, February 1801 to December 1826, Vol. I. Ker, Ian & Gornall, Thomas, eds. 364p. 1978. 48.00x (ISBN 0-19-920102-1). Oxford U Pr.

--The Letters & Diaries of John Henry Cardinal Newman: The Oxford Movement, July 1833 to December 1834, Vol. IV. Ker, Ian & Gornall, Thomas, eds. 428p. 1980. 55.00x (ISBN 0-19-920112-9). Oxford U Pr.

--The Letters & Diaries of John Henry Newman: A Cardinal's Apostolate, October 1881-December 1884, Vol. 30. Dessain, Charles S., ed. 496p. 1976. 44.00x (ISBN 0-19-920060-2). Oxford U Pr.

--The Letters & Diaries of John Henry Newman: New Bearings, January 1832 to June 1833, Vol. 3. Ker, Ian & Gornall, Thomas, eds. 1979. 49.95 (ISBN 0-19-920109-9). Oxford U Pr.

--The Letters & Diaries of John Henry Newman: The Cardinalate, January 1878-September 1881, Vol. 29. Dessain, Charles S. & Gornall, Thomas, eds. 480p. 1976. 44.00x (ISBN 0-19-920059-9). Oxford U Pr.

--The Letters & Diaries of John Henry Newman: The Last Years, January 1885 to August 1890, Vol.31. Dessain, Charles S. & Gornall, Thomas, eds. 1977. 48.00x (ISBN 0-19-920083-1). Oxford U Pr.

--The Letters & Diaries of John Henry Newman: Tutor of Oriel, January 1827 to December 1831, Vol. II. Ker, Ian & Gornall, Thomas, eds. 1979. 53.00x (ISBN 0-19-920108-0). Oxford U Pr.

--The Letters & Diaries of John Henry Newman, Vols. 27 & 28. Dessain, Stephen & Gornall, Thomas, eds. Incl. Vol. 27. Controversy with Gladstone, January 1874-December 1875. 480p (ISBN 0-19-920057-2); Vol. 28. Fellow of Trinity, January 1876-December 1878. 500p (ISBN 0-19-920058-0). 1975. 48.00x ea. Oxford U Pr.

--Loss & Gain: The Story of a Convert, 1848. Wolff, Robert L., ed. Bd. with Callista: A Sketch of the Third Century, 1856. (Victorian Fiction Ser.). 1975. lib. bdg. 66.00 (ISBN 0-8240-1530-4). Garland Pub.

Newman, Cardinal John H. Characteristics from the Writings of John Henry Newman. LC 76-45366. 1976. Repr. of 1875 ed. lib. bdg. 40.00 (ISBN 0-8414-5813-8). Folcroft.

O'Faolain, Sean. Newman's Way. 7.50 (ISBN 0-8159-6303-3). Devin.

Powell, Jouett L. Three Uses of Christian Discourse in John Henry Newman. LC 75-29423. (American Academy of Religion. Dissertation Ser.). 1975. pap. 7.50 (ISBN 0-89130-042-2, 010110). Scholars Pr Ca.

Robbins, William. Newman Brothers: An Essay in Comparative Intellectual Biography. LC 66-4976. (Illus.). 1966. 10.00x (ISBN 0-674-62200-6). Harvard U Pr.

Sarolea, Charles. Cardinal Newman. 174p. 1980. Repr. of 1908 ed. lib. bdg. 30.00 (ISBN 0-89987-759-1). Darby Bks.

--Cardinal Newman & His Influence on Religious Life & Thought. 182p. Repr. of 1908 ed. 4.95 (ISBN 0-567-04523-4). Attic Pr.

Selby, Robin. The Principle of Reserve in the Writings of John Henry, Cardinal Newman. (Oxford Theological Monographs). 120p. 1975. 21.95x (ISBN 0-19-826711-8). Oxford U Pr.

Sencourt, Robert. The Life of Newman. 1973. Repr. of 1948 ed. 30.00 (ISBN 0-8274-1085-9). R West.

Trevor, Mariol. Newman's Journey. (Fount Religious Paperbacks Ser.). 1977. pap. 2.95 (ISBN 0-00-643568-8, FA3568). Collins Pubs.

Ward, Wilfred. The Life of John Henry Newman Based on His Private Journals & Correspondence, 2 vols. 1912. Repr. 50.00 (ISBN 0-8274-2889-8). R West.

Ward, Wilfrid P. Last Lectures. facs. ed. LC 67-26793. (Essay Index Reprint Ser). 1918. 17.50 (ISBN 0-8369-0976-3). Arno.

Weatherby, Harold L. Cardinal Newman in His Age: His Place in English Theology & Literature. LC 72-1347. 320p. 1973. 11.50 (ISBN 0-8265-1182-1). Vanderbilt U Pr.

Whyte, Alexander. Newman: An Appreciation. 1973. Repr. of 1901 ed. 30.00 (ISBN 0-8274-0570-7). R West.

Yearley, Lee H. The Ideas of Newman: Christianity & Human Religiosity. LC 77-13894. 1978. 14.95x (ISBN 0-271-00526-2). Pa St U Pr.

NEWMAN, PAUL, 1925-

Godfrey, Lionel. Paul Newman Superstar. LC 78-66404. (Illus.). Date not set. 8.95 (ISBN 0-312-59819-X). St Martin.

Paige, David. Paul Newman. (Stars of Stage & Screen Ser.). (Illus.). (gr. 4-12). 1977. PLB 5.95 (ISBN 0-87191-553-7). Creative Ed.

Quirk, Lawrence J. Films of Paul Newman. (Illus.). 1971. 9.95 (ISBN 0-8065-0233-9); pap. 6.95 (ISBN 0-8065-0385-8). Citadel Pr.

Thompson, Kenneth. The Films of Paul Newman. Castell, David, ed. (The Films of...Ser.). (Illus.). (gr. 7-12). 1978. Repr. of 1974 ed. PLB 5.95 (ISBN 0-912616-87-3). Greenhaven.

NEWMAN FAMILY

Mozley, Dorothea, ed. Newman Family Letters. 1962. 12.00x (ISBN 0-8401-1686-1). Allenson Breckinridge.

NEWPORT, RHODE ISLAND

Boss, Judith A. Newport: A Pictorial History. Friedman, Donna R., ed. LC 80-22896. (Illus.). 208p. 1981. pap. 12.95 (ISBN 0-89865-097-6). Donning Co.

Dow, Richard A. & Mowbray, E. Andrew. Newport. LC 76-23489. (Illus.). 1976. pap. 4.00 (ISBN 0-917218-05-1). Mowbray Co.

Downing, A. F. & Scully, V. J., Jr. Architectural Heritage of Newport, Rhode Island: 1640-1915. 2nd ed. (Illus.). 1967. 25.00 (ISBN 0-517-09719-2). Potter.

Elliott, Maud H. This Was My Newport. facsimile ed. LC 75-1842. (Leisure Class in America Ser.). (Illus.). 1975. Repr. of 1944 ed. 18.00x (ISBN 0-405-06911-1). Arno.

Gannon, Tom. A Guide to Newport Rhode Island. LC 78-51228. (Illus.). 1978. pap. 4.95 (ISBN 0-87106-097-3). Globe Pequot.

Lincoln, Jonathan T. The City of the Dinner-Pail. Stein, Leon, ed. LC 77-70511. (Work Ser.). 1977. Repr. of 1909 ed. lib. bdg. 15.00x (ISBN 0-405-10181-3). Arno.

Van Rensselaer, May K. Newport: Our Social Capital. facsimile ed. LC 75-910. (Leisure Class in America Ser.). (Illus.). 1975. Repr. of 1905 ed. 30.00x (ISBN 0-405-06936-7). Arno.

NEWS, FOREIGN

see Foreign News

NEWS AGENCIES

see also Foreign News

Berger, Joel S., ed. Making Your News Service More Effective. 3rd ed. 200p. 1981. loose leaf bdg. 19.50 (ISBN 0-89964-177-6). CASE.

Boyd-Barrett, Oliver. The International News Agencies. LC 80-51779. (Constable Communication & Society Ser.: Vol. 13). (Illus.). 284p. 1980. 25.00 (ISBN 0-8039-1511-X); pap. 12.50 (ISBN 0-8039-1512-8). Sage.

Cooper, Kent. Barriers Down. LC 73-94560. 1969. Repr. of 1942 ed. 13.50 (ISBN 0-8046-0689-7). Kennikat.

Desmond, Robert W. The Information Process: World News Reporting to the Twentieth Century. LC 77-9491. 1978. text ed. 22.50x (ISBN 0-87745-070-6). U of Iowa Pr.

Metgler, K. Newsgathering. pap. 14.50 (ISBN 0-13-621037-6). P-H.

News Bureaus in the U.S. 1972p. 1979. 22.00 (ISBN 0-686-62470-X). B Klein Pubns.

News Dictionary. 1977. 14.95 (ISBN 0-87196-105-9). Facts on File.

News Dictionary. 1978. 14.95 (ISBN 0-87196-107-5); pap. 6.95 (ISBN 0-87196-108-3). Facts on File.

Righter, Rosemary. Whose News? Politics, the Press & the Third World. LC 78-14433. 1978. 12.50 (ISBN 0-8129-0797-3). Times Bks.

Rosewater, Victor. History of Cooperative News-Gathering in the United States. LC 30-10687. Repr. of 1930 ed. 23.00 (ISBN 0-384-52020-0). Johnson Repr.

UNESCO. News Agencies, Their Structure & Operation. Repr. of 1953 ed. lib. bdg. 21.25x (ISBN 0-8371-2501-4, UNNA). Greenwood.

Williams, Francis. Transmitting World News: A Study of Telecommunciations & the Press. LC 72-4686. (International Propaganda & Communications Ser.). (Illus.). 95p. 1972. Repr. of 1953 ed. 12.00 (ISBN 0-405-04770-3). Arno.

NEWS BROADCASTS

see Radio Journalism; Television Broadcasting of News

NEWS-LETTERS

Arth, Marvin & Ashmore, Helen. Newsletter Editor's Desk Book. 2nd rev. ed. LC 80-83042. (Illus.). 168p. (gr. 11-12). 1980. pap. 9.95 (ISBN 0-938270-00-1). Kindinger.

--The Newsletter Editor's Desk Book. 2nd, rev. ed. 168p. (Orig.). 14.95 (ISBN 0-938270-00-1); pap. 8.95 (ISBN 0-686-28910-2). Kindinger.

--The Newsletter Editor's Deskbook. 1981. 14.95 (ISBN 0-938270-01-X). Kindinger.

Davidson, John. Newsletter Publishing for the Entrepreneur. 1982. pap. write for info. (ISBN 0-940544-01-6). Briar Co.

Helmken, Charles M. Creative Newsletter Graphics. 1976. 40.00 (ISBN 0-89964-014-1). CASE.

Hoody, John, ed. Oxbridge Directory of Newsletters: 1981-1982. 2nd ed. 400p. 1981. pap. 45.00 (ISBN 0-917460-09-X). Oxbridge Comm.

Nanfria, Linda. How to Publish an Organization Newsletter. 1976. pap. 3.30 (ISBN 0-88409-040-X). Creative Bk Co.

Newsletter Yearbook Directory. 200p. 1979. 35.00 (ISBN 0-686-62471-8). B Klein Pubns.

Oaks, L. Robert. Newsletters As Promotional Media. 24p. 1978. pap. 1.50 (ISBN 0-916068-07-2). Groupwork Today.

Reid, Gerene. How to Write Company Newsletters. LC 79-66676. (Illus.). 80p. 1980. 7.95x (ISBN 0-931882-08-7). D W Carrey.

--How to Write Company Newsletters. LC 79-66676. (Illus., Orig.). 1980. pap. 7.95 (ISBN 0-931882-08-7). TIB Pubns.

Thomas, Robert C., et al, eds. National Directory of Newsletters & Reporting Services, 4 pts. 2nd ed. LC 77-99180. 669p. 1981. pap. 70.00 (ISBN 0-8103-0676-X). Gale.

Wales, La Rae H. A Practical Guide to Newsletter Editing & Design. (Illus.). 48p. 1976. pap. text ed. 4.50x (ISBN 0-8138-1145-7, 1145-7). Iowa St U Pr.

NEWS PHOTOGRAPHY

see Photography, Journalistic

NEWS SERVICES

see News Agencies

NEWSPAPER ADVERTISING

see Advertising, Newspaper

NEWSPAPER CLIPPING BUREAUS

see Clipping Bureaus

NEWSPAPER COURT REPORTING

see also Contempt of Court; Crime and the Press

Bennett, Robert E. Courtroom Procedures for Court Reporters: Syllabus. 1977. pap. text ed. 5.95 (ISBN 0-89420-031-3, 456010); cassette recordings 41.75 (ISBN 0-89420-137-9, 456000). Natl Book.

Fretz, Donald R. Courts & the News Media. (Ser. 810). 1977. 7.50 (ISBN 0-686-00408-6). Natl Judicial Coll.

Sullivan, Harold W. Contempts by Publication: The Law of Trial by Newspaper. 3rd ed. xiv, 230p. 1980. Repr. of 1941 ed. lib. bdg. 24.00x (ISBN 0-8377-1114-2). Rothman.

NEWSPAPER LAYOUT AND TYPOGRAPHY

see also Advertising Layout and Typography

Allen, John E. Newspaper Designing. 1977. Repr. of 1947 ed. lib. bdg. 15.00 (ISBN 0-686-19822-0). Havertown Bks.

Allen, Wallace W. A Design for News. LC 81-2022. (Illus.). 1981. spiral bdg. 10.95 (ISBN 0-932272-04-5). Minneapolis Star.

Arnold, Edmund C. Designing the Total Newspaper. LC 80-8788. (Illus.). 320p. 1981. 25.00x (ISBN 0-06-014836-5, HarpT). Har-Row.

Cushman, Kathleen, et al. How to Produce a Small Newspaper: Fundamentals of Typography, Layout, & Design. LC 76-46794. (Illus., Orig.). 1978. 9.95 (ISBN 0-916782-07-7); pap. 8.95 (ISBN 0-916782-04-2). Harvard Common Pr.

Garcia, Mario R. Contemporary Newspaper Design: A Structural Approach. (Illus.). 240p. 1981. text ed. 27.95 (ISBN 0-13-170381-1); pap. text ed. 13.95 (ISBN 0-13-170373-0). P-H.

Hutt, Allen. The Changing Newspaper. (Illus.). 224p. 1981. 29.50 (ISBN 0-913720-34-8). Sandstone.

Nelson, Roy P. Publication Design. 2nd ed. 288p. 1978. text ed. write for info. (ISBN 0-697-04324-X). Wm C. Brown.

Olson, Kenneth E. Typography & Mechanics of the Newspaper. 1977. Repr. of 1930 ed. lib. bdg. 15.00 (ISBN 0-686-19828-X). Havertown Bks.

Presson, Hazel. The Student Journalist-Layout. LC 72-163949. (Illus.). 160p. (gr. 7 up). 1972. PLB 7.97 (ISBN 0-8239-0253-6). Rosen Pr.

Radder, Norman. Newspaper Make-up & Headlines. 1977. Repr. of 1924 ed. lib. bdg. 15.00 (ISBN 0-686-19823-9). Havertown Bks.

Sherbow, Benjamin. Making Type Work. 1977. Repr. of 1916 ed. lib. bdg. 12.50 (ISBN 0-686-19817-4). Havertown Bks.

Smith, Anthony. Goodbye Gutenberg: The Newspaper Revolution of the 1980's. (Illus.). 382p. 1981. pap. 6.95 (ISBN 0-19-503006-0, GB 660, GB). Oxford U Pr.

Sutton, Albert A. Design & Makeup of the Newspaper. LC 71-110838. (Illus.). 1971. Repr. of 1948 ed. lib. bdg. 29.50x (ISBN 0-8371-2510-3, SUDM). Greenwood.

--Design & Makeup of the Newspaper. LC 71-110838. (Illus.). 1971. Repr. of 1948 ed. lib. bdg. 29.50x (ISBN 0-8371-2510-3, SUDM). Greenwood.

NEWSPAPER OFFICE LIBRARIES

Anderson, Elizabeth, ed. Directory of Newspaper Libraries in the U. S. & Canada. 2nd ed. LC 80-25188. 1980. 17.50 (ISBN 0-87111-265-5). SLA.

NEWSPAPER PUBLISHING

Argyris, Chris. Behind the Front Page: Organizational Self-Renewal in Metropolition News Papers. LC 73-22558. (Social & Behavioral Science Ser.). 320p. 1974. 16.95x (ISBN 0-87589-223-X). Jossey-Bass.

Belfrage, Cedric & Aronson, James. Something to Guard: The Stormy Life of the National Guardian. LC 78-3530. 362p. 1978. 25.00x (ISBN 0-231-04510-7). Columbia U Pr.

Cleverley, Graham. The Fleet Street Disaster: British National Newspapers As a Case Study in Mismanagement. LC 76-25733. (Communication & Society: Vol. 7). 175p. 1976. 21.00 (ISBN 0-8039-9989-5, Co-Pub with Constable). Sage.

Cline, C. L. The Fate of Cassandra: The Newspaper War of 1821-22 & Sir Walter Scott. LC 72-5780. (Quarterly Ser). 1971. 5.95 (ISBN 0-87959-069-6). U of Tex Hum Res.

Compaine, Benjamin. The Newspaper Industry in the Nineteen Eighties: An Assessment of Economics & Technology. (Communications Library). 1980. 29.95x (ISBN 0-914236-37-7). Knowledge Indus.

Diehl, Digby. Front Page Eighteen Eighty-One to Nineteen Eighty-One: One Hundred Years of the Los Angeles Times. (Illus.). 288p. 1981. 25.00 (ISBN 0-8109-0925-1). Abrams.

Educational Research Council of America. Managing Editor. Ferris, Theodore N. & Marchak, John P., eds. (Real People at Work: Series O). (Illus., Orig.). (gr. 5). 1976. pap. text ed. 2.25 (ISBN 0-89247-098-4). Changing Times.

Gormley, William T., Jr. Effects of Newspaper-Television Cross-Ownership on News Homogeneity. LC 76-21859. 1976. pap. text ed. 5.00 (ISBN 0-89143-065-2). U NC Inst Res Soc Sci.

Hale, Oron J. Captive Press in the Third Reich. LC 64-12182. (Illus.). 368p. 1964. 23.00x (ISBN 0-691-05109-7); pap. 7.95 (ISBN 0-691-00770-5). Princeton U Pr.

Kahn, E. J. Jock: The Life & Times of John Hay Whitney. LC 81-43052. (Illus.). 264p. 1981. 15.95 (ISBN 0-385-14932-8). Doubleday.

Lown, Edward. An Introduction to Technological Changes in Journalism. LC 77-2544. 1977. pap. 10.00 (ISBN 0-8357-0256-1, SS-00031). Univ Microfilms.

McKinney, John. How to Start Your Own Community Newspaper. LC 77-78181. 1977. pap. 19.95 (ISBN 0-931058-01-5). Meadow Pr.

Moghdam, Dineh. Computers in Newspaper Publishing: User Oriented Systems. (Books in Library & Information Science Ser.: Vol. 22). 1978. 31.50 (ISBN 0-8247-6620-2). Dekker.

Morse, R. C. An A,B,C of Publishing Literary Magazines. LC 78-54855. (Illus., Orig.). 1978. pap. text ed. 1.00 (ISBN 0-9601668-1-5). Upsala Coll.

Newsom, D. E. The Newspaper: Everything You Need to Know to Make It in the Newspaper Business. (Illus.). 256p. 1981. 19.95 (ISBN 0-13-616045-X, Spec); pap. 10.95 (ISBN 0-13-616037-9). P-H.

Notman, Larry. Community Newspaper: Front Office Worker. (Illus.). 1978. pap. 4.00x (ISBN 0-918488-07-9). Newspaper Serv.

--Community Newspaper Management: Starting Out. 48p. 1981. pap. 10.00x (ISBN 0-918488-10-9). Newspaper Serv.

Potter, Jeffrey. Men, Money & Magic: The Story of Dorothy Schiff. (Illus.). 1977. pap. 2.25 (ISBN 0-451-07691-5, E7691, Sig). NAL.

Rogers, Jason. Fundamentals of Newspaper Building. 1977. Repr. of 1919 ed. lib. bdg. 10.00 (ISBN 0-686-19806-9). Havertown Bks.

Smith, Anthony. Goodbye Gutenberg: The Newspaper Revolution of the 1980's. (Illus.). 382p. 1981. pap. 6.95 (ISBN 0-19-503006-0, GB 660, GB). Oxford U Pr.

Smith, C. R. Management of Newspaper Correspondents. 1977. Repr. of 1944 ed. lib. bdg. 12.50 (ISBN 0-686-19818-2). Havertown Bks.

Van Benthuysen, A. S. Newspaper Organization & Accounting. 1977. lib. bdg. 59.95 (ISBN 0-8490-2342-4). Gordon Pr.

Williams, Herbert L. Newspaper Organization & Management. 5th ed. 580p. 1978. text ed. 18.95x (ISBN 0-8138-1150-3, 1150-3). Iowa St U Pr.

NEWSPAPER STYLE

see Journalism–Handbooks, Manuals, Etc.

NEWSPAPERS

see also Advertising, Newspaper; Foreign News; Journalistic Ethics; Liberty of the Press; News Agencies; Newspaper Layout and Typography; Newspaper Publishing; Periodicals; Press; Press Law; Reporters and Reporting;

also names of individual newspapers, e.g. New York Times; Washington Post; American Newspapers, English, etc.

Acheson, Sam H. Thirty-Five Thousand Days in Texas: A History of the Dallas News & Its Forbears. LC 72-136510. (Illus.). xi, 337p. Repr. of 1938 ed. lib. bdg. 16.50x (ISBN 0-8371-5428-6, ACTD). Greenwood.

Adams, Anne H. & Woods, Elsa E. Reading the Newspaper. LC 76-28149. (Reading Ser.). 1976. 1-20 copies 3.00 ea.; 21-50 copies 2.75 ea.; 51-99 copies 2.50 ea.; 100 or more copies 2.00 ea. Perry-Neal Pubs.

Auchterlonie, Paul & Safadi, Yasin H., eds. Union Catalogue of Arabic Serials & Newspapers in British Libraries. 1977. 25.00 (ISBN 0-7201-0636-2, Pub. by Mansell England). Merrimack Bk Serv.

Azzi, Abderrahmane. News Cross Culturally. 1981. 6.95 (ISBN 0-8062-1840-1). Carlton.

Behind the Headlines: A Program Technique for Studying Intergroup Relations. 24p. 0.35 (ISBN 0-686-74909-X). ADL.

Bogart, Leo. The Press & Public: Who Reads What, Where, & Why in American Newspapers. LC 80-18357. 304p. 1981. text ed. 19.95 (ISBN 0-89859-077-9). L Erlbaum Assocs.

Bowen, Francis A. How to Produce a Church Newspaper... & Other Ways Churches Communicate. (Illus.). 1974. 5.00 (ISBN 0-9602830-1-3). F A Bowen.

Brinckmeyer, Edward, ed. Mitternachzeitung Fuer Gebildete Stand, Vol 11, Nos 1-212. 1973. Repr. of 1836 ed. 110.00 (ISBN 0-384-39224-5). Johnson Repr.

Cary, Melbert B., Jr. A Bibliography of the Village Press 1903-1938: Including an Account of the Genesis of the Press by Frederick W. Goudy & a Portion of the 1903 Diary of Will Ransom, Co-Founder. (Illus.). 224p. 1981. Repr. of 1938 ed. 22.50x (ISBN 0-935164-08-1). N T Smith.

Chamberlin, Vernon A. & Schulman, Ivan A. La Revista Ilustrada de Nueva York. LC 75-35891. 1976. 16.50x (ISBN 0-8262-0189-X). U of Mo Pr.

Chapman, John. Tell It to Sweeney: The Informal History of the New York Daily News. LC 77-8991. (Illus.). 1977. Repr. of 1961 ed. lib. bdg. 24.00x (ISBN 0-8371-9724-4, CHTS). Greenwood.

Crawford, Nelson A. The Ethics of Journalism. (American Studies). 1969. Repr. of 1924 ed. 19.50 (ISBN 0-384-10130-5). Johnson Repr.

Dann, F. Know Your Newspaper. (Orig.). 1977. pap. 2.95 (ISBN 0-671-18772-4). Monarch Pr.

Desmond, Robert W. The Information Process: World News Reporting to the Twentieth Century. LC 77-9491. 1978. text ed. 22.50x (ISBN 0-87745-070-6). U of Iowa Pr.

Duller, Edward & Gutzkow, Karl, eds. Phonix: Fruhlings-Zeitung Fur Deutschland, 2 vols. 1973. Repr. of 1835 ed. vol. 1 nos. 1-309 77.00 (ISBN 0-384-46413-0). Johnson Repr.

Engwall, Lars. Newspapers As Organisations. 1979. text ed. 34.00x (ISBN 0-566-00262-0, Pub. by Gower Pub Co England). Renouf.

Floherty, John J. Your Daily Paper. 1977. Repr. of 1938 ed. lib. bdg. 10.00 (ISBN 0-686-19833-6). Havertown Bks.

Furst, Arnold. How to Get Publicity in Newspapers. pap. 3.95 (ISBN 0-685-64526-6). Borden.

Gilmore, Gene & Root, Robert. Modern Newspaper Editing. 2nd ed. 1976. 14.95x (ISBN 0-87835-054-3). Boyd & Fraser.

Golder, Diane. The Newspaper & You. (Orig.). (gr. 9). 1980. wkbk. 5.83 (ISBN 0-87720-300-8). AMSCO Sch.

Gramling, Oliver. A P: Story of News. LC 77-94561. 1969. Repr. of 1940 ed. 22.50 (ISBN 0-8046-0690-0). Kennikat.

Greenberg, Cory. How to Start a High School Underground Newspaper. 5th ed. (Illus.). 1977. saddle-stitched 1.50 (ISBN 0-918946-09-3). Youth Lib.

Gregorich, Barbara & Zack, Carol. The Newspaper: Reading Skills. LC 78-730963. (Illus.). 1978. pap. text ed. 135.00 (ISBN 0-89290-114-4, A160). Soc for Visual.

Hammond, Otis G. Notices from the New Hampshire Gazette 1765-1800. 1970. lib. bdg. 10.00 (ISBN 0-912606-01-0). Hunterdon Hse.

History of Kansas Newspapers. (Illus.). pap. 1.00 (ISBN 0-87726-012-5). Kansas St Hist.

Hulteng, John L. Playing It Straight. LC 81-65984. (Orig.). 1981. pap. 4.95 (ISBN 0-87106-955-5). Globe Pequot.

Hurlburt, Allen. The Grid System. 1978. 18.95 (ISBN 0-442-23598-4). Van Nos Reinhold.

Hynds, Ernest C. American Newspapers in the Nineteen Eighties. rev. ed. (Studies in Media Management). 368p. 1980. 18.95 (ISBN 0-8038-0490-3, Communication Arts); pap. 9.95x (ISBN 0-8038-0491-1). Hastings.

Jackson, Mason. Pictorial Press: Its Origin & Progress. (Illus.). 1969. 13.00 (ISBN 0-8337-1815-0). B Franklin.

--Pictorial Press, Its Origin & Progress. LC 68-21776. (Illus.). 1968. Repr. of 1885 ed. 19.00 (ISBN 0-8103-3355-4). Gale.

Johnson, Walter C. & Robb, Arthur T. The South & Its Newspapers, Nineteen Hundred Three to Nineteen Fifty-Three. LC 78-136935. 386p. 1974. Repr. of 1954 ed. lib. bdg. 22.00x (ISBN 0-8371-5407-3, JOSN). Greenwood.

Kobre, Sidney. The Development of the Colonial Newspaper. 7.50 (ISBN 0-8446-1269-3). Peter Smith.

Laube, Heinrich, ed. Zeitung fuer Die elegante Welt, 3 vols. 1973. Repr. of 1833 ed. 70.00 ea. (ISBN 0-384-70845-5). Johnson Repr.

Lyons, Louis M. Newspaper Story: One Hundred Years of the Boston Globe. LC 74-152697. (Illus.). 1971. 22.50x (ISBN 0-674-62225-1, Belknap Pr). Harvard U Pr.

McAuliffe, Kevin. The Great American Newspaper: The Story of the Village Voice. (Encore Edition). (Illus.). 1978. 4.95 (ISBN 0-684-16588-0). Scribner.

Malmquist, O. N. The First Hundred Years: A History of the Salt Lake Tribune, 1871-1971. LC 74-158989. (Illus.). 496p. 1971. 8.00 (ISBN 0-913738-21-2). Utah St Hist Soc.

Mankekar, D. R. The Press Under Pressure. LC 73-907825. 167p. 1973. 7.75x (ISBN 0-8002-1832-9). Intl Pubns Serv.

Mansoor, Menahem. Hebrew Newspaper Reader. 1971. pap. 9.95x (ISBN 0-87068-579-1). Ktav.

Mavity, Nancy B. The Modern Newspaper. 1977. Repr. of 1930 ed. lib. bdg. 10.00 (ISBN 0-686-19819-0). Havertown Bks.

Merrill, John C. & Fisher, Hal. The World's Great Dailies: Profiles of Fifty Newspapers. (Illus.). 416p. 1980. 18.50 (ISBN 0-8038-8095-2, Communication Arts); pap. text ed. 10.50x (ISBN 0-8038-8096-0, Communication Arts). Hastings.

Mookini, Esther K. The Hawaiian Newspapers. 1974. 9.00 (ISBN 0-914916-34-3); pap. 3.00 (ISBN 0-914916-05-X). Topgallant.

Morton, Brian N. & Morton, Jacqueline. Presse Deux. 2nd ed. 1977. pap. text ed. 8.95x (ISBN 0-669-01636-5). Heath.

News Dictionary, Vol. 9: 1972. annual 1973. 14.95 (ISBN 0-87196-095-8). Facts on File.

Nord, David P. Newspapers & New Politics: Midwestern Municipal Reform. Berkhofer, Robert, ed. (Studies in American History & Culture: No. 27). 1981. 31.95 (ISBN 0-8357-1168-4, Pub. by UMI Res Pr). Univ Microfilms.

Popkin, Jeremy D. The Rightwing Press in France, Seventeen Ninety-Two to Eighteen Hundred. LC 79-14067. (Illus.). 1980. 22.00x (ISBN 0-8078-1393-1). U of NC Pr.

Pour une Histoire Du Quotidien Au XIXe Siecle En Nivernais. 1977. 45.50x (ISBN 90-279-7883-2). Mouton.

Press: A Handbook of Elementary Classroom Ideas to Motivate Teaching Through the Use of the Newspaper. (Spice Ser.). 1978. 6.50 (ISBN 0-89273-126-5). Educ Serv.

Reddick, De Witt C. The Mass Media & the School Newspaper. 1976. text ed. 13.95x (ISBN 0-534-00436-9). Wadsworth Pub.

Rhoades, Lynn & Rhoades, George. Teaching with Newspapers: The Living Curriculum. LC 80-82682. (Fastback Ser.: No. 149). 1980. pap. 0.75 (ISBN 0-87367-149-X). Phi Delta Kappa.

Salmon, Lucy M. The Newspaper & Authority. 1972. lib. bdg. 25.00x (ISBN 0-374-97018-1). Octagon.

--The Newspaper & the Historian. 1972. lib. bdg. 30.00x (ISBN 0-374-97020-3). Octagon.

Schudson, Michael. Discovering the News: A Social History of American Newspapers. LC 78-54997. 1978. 11.95x (ISBN 0-465-01669-3). Basic.

Shepard, Leslie. The Broadside Ballad: The Development of the Street Ballad from Traditional Song to Popular Newspaper. LC 78-50797. (Illus.). 9.95 (ISBN 0-913714-00-3); pap. 4.95 (ISBN 0-913714-01-1). Legacy Bks.

Short, J. Rodney & Dickerson, Beverly. The Newspaper: An Alternative Textbook. LC 79-54759. (gr. 6-11). 1980. pap. 5.95 (ISBN 0-8224-4661-8). Pitman Learning.

Smiley, Nixon. Knights of the Fourth Estate: The Story of the Miami Herald. LC 74-75298. (Illus.). 344p. 1974. 14.95 (ISBN 0-912458-42-9). E A Seemann.

Smith, Anthony. Goodbye Gutenberg: The Newspaper Revolution of the 1980's. LC 79-24263. (Illus.). 1980. 16.95 (ISBN 0-19-502709-4). Oxford U Pr.

--The Newspaper: An International History. 1979. 14.95 (ISBN 0-500-01204-0). Thames Hudson.

Smith, Anthony, ed. Newspapers & Democracy. 320p. 1980. text ed. 25.00x (ISBN 0-262-19184-9). MIT Pr.

Spurgeon, C. H. The Bible & the Newspaper. pap. 2.25 (ISBN 0-686-09104-3). Pilgrim Pubns.

Stone, Candace. Dana & the Sun. 1977. Repr. of 1938 ed. lib. bdg. 17.50 (ISBN 0-686-19802-6). Havertown Bks.

Udell, Jon G. The Economics of the American Newspaper. (Illus.). 1978. 12.95 (ISBN 0-8038-1932-3); pap. text ed. 5.95x (ISBN 0-8038-1933-1). Hastings.

Walker, R. B. The Newspaper Press in New South Wales 1803-1920. (Illus.). 1976. 15.00x (ISBN 0-424-00023-7, Pub. by Sydney U Pr). Intl Schol Bk Serv.

Weed, Katherine K. & Bond, Richmond P. Studies of British Newspapers & Periodicals from Their Beginning to 1800. Repr. of 1946 ed. pap. 7.00 (ISBN 0-384-66370-2). Johnson Repr.

Weigle, Clifford F. American Newspaper by William Irwin. (Illus.). 1969. pap. 3.95x (ISBN 0-8138-0095-1). Iowa St U Pr.

Wilds, John. Afternoon Story: History of the New Orleans Statesitem. LC 76-27188. (Illus.). 1976. 17.50x (ISBN 0-8071-0192-3). La State U Pr.

NEWSPAPERS–BIBLIOGRAPHY

Cary, Melbert B., Jr. A Bibliography of the Village Press 1903-1938: Including an Account of the Genesis of the Press by Frederick W. Goudy & a Portion of the 1903 Diary of Will Ransom, Co-Founder. (Illus.). 224p. 1981. Repr. of 1938 ed. 22.50x (ISBN 0-935164-08-1). N T Smith.

Contemporary China Institute, ed. A Bibliography of Chinese Newspapers & Periodicals in European Libraries. LC 75-12135. (Contemporary China Institute Publications). 1100p. 1975. 97.50 (ISBN 0-521-20950-1). Cambridge U Pr.

Fabisoff, Sylvia G. & Tripp, Wendell, eds. A Bibliography of Newspapers in Fourteen New York Counties. 14.00 (ISBN 0-686-26190-9). Fenimore Bk.

Hansen, James L. Wisconsin Newspapers, Eighteen Thirty-Three to Eighteen Fifty: An Analytical Bibliography. LC 79-10411. (Orig.). 1979. pap. 4.00 (ISBN 0-87020-179-4). State Hist Soc Wis.

Hewett, Daniel. Daniel Hewett's List of Newspapers & Periodicals in the United States in 1828. 32p. 1935. pap. 3.00x (ISBN 0-912296-22-4, Dist. by U Pr of Va). Am Antiquarian.

Kestercanek, Nada. Croatian Newspapers & Calendars in the U. S. LC 79-146896. 1951. softcover 8.00 (ISBN 0-88247-116-3). Ragusan Pr.

Thompson, Gary B., ed. Index to the Newspapers Published in Geneva, New York 1806-1819, Vol. I. 118p. 1981. lib. bdg. 18.00 (ISBN 0-939624-00-1). Smith Lib.

Webber, R. World List of National Newspapers. 1977. 19.95 (ISBN 0-408-70817-4). Butterworth.

Yale Univ. Library. List of Newspapers in Library of Yale. (Yale Historical Pubs., Miscellany Ser.: No. II). 1916. 42.50x (ISBN 0-685-69889-0). Elliots Bks.

NEWSPAPERS–DIRECTORIES

Baird, Donald, ed. Press Radio & TV Guide: Australia, New Zealand, & the Pacific Islands. 23rd ed. 1978. 27.50x (ISBN 0-8002-1831-0). Intl Pubns Serv.

Gebbie Press All-in-One Directory. 520p. 1980. 50.00 (ISBN 0-686-62458-0). B Klein Pubns.

Greenberg, Howard, ed. Oxbridge Directory of Newsletters - 1979. 1979. pap. 35.00 (ISBN 0-917460-04-9). Oxbridge Comm.

Grove, Pearce S., et al. New Mexico Newspapers: A Comprehensive Guide to Bibliographical Entries & Locations. LC 74-84232. Orig. Title: A Guide to New Mexico Newspapers. (Illus.). 680p. 1975. pap. 12.00x (ISBN 0-8263-0336-6). U of NM Pr.

King, Frank H. & Clarke, Prescott, eds. Research Guide to China-Coast Newspapers, 1822-1911. LC 65-5287. (East Asian Monographs Ser: No. 18). 1965. pap. 9.00x (ISBN 0-674-76400-5). Harvard U Pr.

Newspaper Press Directory. 1979. 2 vol. set 95.00 (ISBN 0-685-79498-9). State Mutual Bk.

Wynar, Lubomyr R. & Wynar, Anna T. Encyclopedic Directory of Ethnic Newspapers & Periodicals in the United States. 2nd rev. ed. LC 76-23317. 248p. 1976. PLB 20.00x (ISBN 0-87287-154-1). Libs Unl.

NEWSPAPERS–HEADLINES

Garst, Robert E. & Bernstein, Theodore M. Headlines & Deadlines: A Manual for Copy Editors. 3rd ed. LC 61-7716. 237p. 1961. 17.50x (ISBN 0-231-02450-9); pap. 5.00x (ISBN 0-231-08541-9, 41). Columbia U Pr.

Wimer, Arthur & Brix, Dale. Workbook for Head Writing & News Editing. 4th ed. 230p. 1978. write for info. wire coil (ISBN 0-697-04328-2). Wm C Brown.

NEWSPAPERS–INDEXES

Brooklyn Eagle. Brooklyn Eagle Index: July 1, 1891 to December 31, 1902, 3 vols. 1980. Set. lib. bdg. 79.95 (ISBN 0-8490-3102-8). Gordon Pr.

Falk, Byron A. & Falk, Valerie R. Personal Name Index to the New York Times Index, Vols. 13 & 14: Eighteen Fifty-One to Nineteen Seventy-Four. LC 76-12217. 1980. lib. bdg. 52.50 ea. Vol. 13 (ISBN 0-89902-113-1). Vol. 14 (ISBN 0-89902-114-X). Roxbury Data.

Jacobs, Donald M. Antebellum Black Newspapers: Indices to New York Freedom's Journal (1827-1829), Rights of All (1829) The Weekly Advocate (1837) & The Colored American (1837-1841) LC 76-2119. 600p. (Orig.). 1976. lib. bdg. 37.00 (ISBN 0-8371-8824-5, JWA/). Greenwood.

Johnson, Rubellite K., ed. Ka Nupepa Ku'oko'a: A Chronicle of Entries, 1861-1862. 1975. pap. 4.95 (ISBN 0-914916-04-1). Topgallant.

Lathrop, Norman M. & Lathrop, Mary Lou, eds. Lathrop Report on Newspaper Indexes. (Illus.). 1979. pap. 60.00 (ISBN 0-910868-10-7). Lathrop.

Milner, Anita C. Newspaper Indexes: A Location & Subject Guide for Researchers, Vol. II. LC 77-7130. 303p. 1979. 11.00 (ISBN 0-8108-1244-4). Scarecrow.

--Newspaper Indexes: A Location & Subject Guide for Researchers. LC 77-7130. 1977. 10.00 (ISBN 0-8108-1066-2). Scarecrow.

Paneth, Donald, ed. News Dictionary Nineteen Seventy-Eight. (Illus.). 1979. 14.95x (ISBN 0-87196-107-5); pap. 6.95 (ISBN 0-87196-108-3). Facts on File.

Perica, Esther. Newspaper Indexing for Historical Societies, Colleges & High Schools. LC 74-20822. 60p. 1975. pap. 2.45 (ISBN 0-912526-15-7). Lib Res.

NEWSPAPERS–JUVENILE LITERATURE

Debnam, Betty. The Best of "The Mini Page". 1977. pap. 6.95 (ISBN 0-8362-0760-2). Andrews & McMeel.

Fenton, Don & Fenton, Barb. Behind the Newspaper Scene. Schroeder, Howard, ed. LC 80-14593. (Behind the Scenes Ser.). (Illus.). (gr. 4). 1980. PLB 6.95 (ISBN 0-89686-058-2); pap. 3.25 (ISBN 0-89686-063-9). Crestwood Hse.

Fisher, Leonard E. The Newspapers. LC 80-8812. (A Nineteenth Century America Book). (Illus.). 64p. (gr. 5 up). 1981. PLB 7.95 (ISBN 0-8234-0387-4). Holiday.

Larned, Phyllis & Randall, Nick. Reading a Newspaper. (Survival Guides Ser.). (Illus.). 64p. (gr. 7-12). 1978. pap. text ed. 2.85 (ISBN 0-915510-26-X). Janus Bks.

Lerner, Mark. Careers with a Newspaper. LC 77-72422. (Early Career Bks.). (Illus.). (gr. 2-5). 1977. PLB 4.95 (ISBN 0-8225-0330-1). Lerner Pubns.

Touster, Irwin & Payne, C. Washington Post Book: Insiders Speak Out. LC 74-20725. (Illus.). (gr. 7 up). 1976. 7.95 (ISBN 0-13-944405-X). P-H.

NEWSPAPERS–SECTIONS, COLUMNS, ETC.

see also Book Reviewing

Barnes, Robert. Marriages & Deaths from the Maryland Gazette, 1727 to 1839. LC 73-12383. 234p. 1979. Repr. of 1973 ed. 15.00 (ISBN 0-8063-0580-0). Genealog Pub.

Bode, Carl. Highly Irregular: The Newspaper Columns of Carl Bode. LC 74-8704. 176p. 1974. 7.95x (ISBN 0-8093-0684-0). S Ill U Pr.

Crume, Marion, ed. The World of Paul Crume. 320p. 1980. 15.00 (ISBN 0-87074-176-4). SMU Press.

Folio Magazine. Nineteen Eighty Edition Folio: Annual. (Folio Annual Ser.). (Orig.). 1981. pap. 20.00 (ISBN 0-918110-05-X). Folio.

McKnight, Pete C., frwd. by. Kays Gary, Columnist. 256p. 1981. 10.95 (ISBN 0-914788-43-4). East Woods.

Neal, Lois S. Abstracts of Vital Records from Raleigh, North Carolina, Newspapers 1820-1829. LC 79-13328. (Abstracts of Vital Records from Raleigh, North Carolina, Newspapers 1799-1915 Ser.). (Illus.). 940p. 1980. 50.00 (ISBN 0-686-77631-3). Vol. 2 (ISBN 0-87152-316-7). Reprint.

Shore, Elliot, et al, eds. The Alternative Papers: Selections from the Alternative Press, 1979-1980. (Illus.). 448p. 1982. 30.00 (ISBN 0-87722-243-6); pap. 14.95 (ISBN 0-87722-244-4). Temple U Pr.

Smith, Jack. Jack Smith's L. A. 224p. 1981. pap. 4.95 (ISBN 0-523-41493-5). Pinnacle Bks.

Starr, Lloyd C. Could This Be the Way It Is? 1981. 6.00 (ISBN 0-8062-1780-4). Carlton.

Thomas, W. H. Road to Syndication. pap. 5.00 (ISBN 0-8303-0066-X). Fleet.
Van Buren, Abigail. The Best of Dear Abby. 250p. 1981. 9.95 (ISBN 0-8362-7907-7). Andrews & McMeel.
West Publications Editors, ed. Thirty-One Flavors: A Newsmagazine. 56p. (Orig.). pap. 0.95 (ISBN 0-935954-06-6). Beacon Presse IA.

NEWSPAPERS, COMMUNITY
see Community Newspapers

NEWSPAPERS, PUBLISHING OF
see Newspaper Publishing

NEWSPRINT
Pollock, Vera & Weiner, Jack. Newsprint. LC 76-28671. (Bibliographic Ser.: No. 272). 1976. pap. 25.00 (ISBN 0-87010-047-5). Inst Paper Chem.

NEWSREEL
see also Photography, Journalistic
Aldgate, Anthony. Cinema & History: British Newsreels & the Spanish Civil War. (Illus., Orig.). 1980. pap. 11.95 (ISBN 0-85967-486-X). NY Zoetrope.
Fielding, Raymond. The American Newsreel, 1911-1967. LC 73-177334. (Illus.). 392p. 1981. pap. 7.95 (ISBN 0-8061-1717-6). U of Okla Pr.
--The March of Time: 1935-1951. (Illus.). 1978. 18.95 (ISBN 0-19-502212-2). Oxford U Pr.
Nichols, Bill. Newsreel: Documentary Filmaking on the American Left. LC 79-6681. (Dissertations on Film Ser.). 313p. 1980. 25.00 (ISBN 0-405-12914-9). Arno.
Nichols, William J. Newsreel. Jowett, Garth S., ed. LC 79-6681. (Dissertations on Film, 1980). 1980. lib. bdg. 25.00x (ISBN 0-405-12914-9). Arno.
Stone, Vernon & Hinson, Bruce. Television Newsfilm Techniques. (Communication Arts Bks.). (Illus.). 1974. pap. text ed. 4.95x (ISBN 0-8038-7141-4). Hastings.

NEWTON, HUEY P.
Erikson, Erik H. & Newton, Huey P. In Search of Common Ground. Erikson, Kai T., ed. 160p. 1973. 12.95 (ISBN 0-393-05483-7). Norton.
Keating, Edward M. Free Huey: The True Story of the Trial of Huey P. Newton for Murder. LC 79-144055. 280p. 1971. lib. bdg. 7.95 (ISBN 0-87867-000-9). Ramparts.
Newton, Huey P. & Blake, Herman. Revolutionary Suicide. LC 72-93749. 1973. 8.95 (ISBN 0-15-177092-1). HarBraceJ.

NEWTON, ISAAC, SIR, 1642-1727
Andrade, E. N. Isaac Newton. 1979. Repr. of 1950 ed. lib. bdg. 12.50 (ISBN 0-8414-3014-4). Folcroft.
--Isaac Newton. 1950. 17.50 (ISBN 0-932062-04-0). Sharon Hill.
Andrade, Edward N. Sir Isaac Newton. LC 79-15162. 140p. 1979. Repr. of 1958 ed. lib. bdg. 14.50x (ISBN 0-313-22022-0). Greenwood.
Ball, Rouse W. An Essay on Newton's Principia. Repr. of 1893 ed. 23.00 (ISBN 0-384-03141-2, S155). Johnson Repr.
Brewster, David. Memoirs of the Life, Writings & Discoveries of Sir Isaac Newton, 2 Vols. Repr. of 1855 ed. Set. 54.00 (ISBN 0-384-05703-9). Johnson Repr.
Brodetsky, S. Sir Isaac Newton. 1927. Repr. 20.00 (ISBN 0-8274-3425-1). R West.
Brougham, Henry & Routh, E. J. Analytical View of Sir Isaac Newton's Principia. 1972. Repr. of 1855 ed. 34.50 (ISBN 0-384-05960-0). Johnson Repr.
Burtt, Edwin A. Metaphysical Foundations of Modern Physical Science. 2nd ed. (International Library of Psychology, Philosophy & Scientific Method). 1967. Repr. of 1932 ed. text ed. 27.50x (ISBN 0-7100-3032-0); pap. text ed. 5.95x (ISBN 0-391-01633-4). Humanities.
Castillejo'S, David. The Expanding Force in Newton's Cosmos. 128p. 1981. 35.00x (ISBN 84-85005-49-X). State Mutual Bk.
Clarke, John. Demonstration of Some of the Principal Sections of Sir Isaac Newton's Principles of Natural Philosophy. 1972. Repr. of 1730 ed. 23.00 (ISBN 0-384-09226-8). Johnson Repr.
Cohen, I. B. The Newtonian Revolution. LC 79-18637. 1981. 37.50 (ISBN 0-521-22964-2). Cambridge U Pr.
De Villamil, Richard. Newton, the Man. 112p. 1972. Repr. of 1931 ed. 19.50 (ISBN 0-685-27503-5). Johnson Repr.
Dobbs, Betty J. The Foundation of Newton's Alchemy; or, "the Hunting of the Greene Lyon". LC 74-31795. (Illus.). 320p. 1976. 47.50 (ISBN 0-521-20786-X). Cambridge U Pr.
Dow, T. W. Repeal Kepler's Laws. LC 60-13372. 1960. 5.00 (ISBN 0-910340-02-1). Celestial Pr.
--Reshape Newton's Laws. LC 64-19218. 1965. 5.00 (ISBN 0-910340-03-X). Celestial Pr.
Edelston, J., ed. Correspondence of Sir Issac Newton & Professor Cotes. 323p. 1969. 35.00x (ISBN 0-7146-1597-8, F Cass Co). Biblio Dist.
Hall, A. R. & Tilling, Laura, eds. The Correspondence of Isaac Newton, 1718-1727, Vol. VII. LC 59-65134. (Illus.). 1978. 95.00 (ISBN 0-521-08723-6). Cambridge U Pr.
Hall, R., ed. Unpublished Scientific Papers of Isaac Newton. Hall, Marie B. (Illus.). 1979. pap. 29.95 (ISBN 0-521-29436-3). Cambridge U Pr.
Harrison, J. The Library of Isaac Newton. LC 77-83994. (Illus.). 1978. 75.00 (ISBN 0-521-21868-3). Cambridge U Pr.
Hessen, B. The Social & Economic Roots of Newton's Principia. 12.50 (ISBN 0-86527-182-8). Fertig.
Koyre, Alexander. Newtonian Studies. 1965. pap. 7.50x (ISBN 0-226-45176-3). U of Chicago Pr.
Lerner, Aaron B. Einstein & Newton: A Comparison of the Two Greatest Scientists. LC 72-7653. (Adult & Young Adult Bks.). (Illus.). (gr. 9 up). 1973. PLB 8.95 (ISBN 0-8225-0752-8). Lerner Pubns.
Maclaurin, Colin. Account of Sir Isaac Newton's Philosophical Discoveries. 1968. Repr. of 1748 ed. 27.00 (ISBN 0-384-34900-5). Johnson Repr.
--An Account of Sir Isaac Newton's Philosophical Discoveries. 1970. Repr. of 1748 ed. 46.00 (ISBN 3-487-04002-6). Adler.
McMullin, Ernan. Newton on Matter & Activity. LC 77-82480. 1979. pap. text ed. 3.95x (ISBN 0-268-01343-8). U of Notre Dame Pr.
--Newton on Matter & Activity. LC 77-82480. 1978. text ed. 7.95x (ISBN 0-268-01342-X). U of Notre Dame Pr.
Manuel, Frank E. The Religion of Isaac Newton: The Fremantle Lectures 1973. 155p. 1974. 22.50x (ISBN 0-19-826640-5). Oxford U Pr.
More, Louis T. Isaac Newton: A Biography. 6.50 (ISBN 0-8446-2605-8). Peter Smith.
Newton, Isaac. The Correspondence, 1713-1718, Vols. 6 & 7. Hall, A. R. & Tilling, Laura, eds. (Correspondence of Isaac Newton Ser.). (Illus.). 500p. 1976. Vol. 6. 95.00 ea. (ISBN 0-521-08722-8). Vol. 7 (ISBN 0-521-08723-6). Cambridge U Pr.
--Mathematical Papers of Isaac Newton: 1691-1695, Vol. 7. Whiteside, D. T. & Hoskin, M. A., eds. LC 65-11203. 1977. 175.00 (ISBN 0-521-08720-1). Cambridge U Pr.
--Optique De Newton: Traduit Par Jean Paul Marat. Repr. of 1787 ed. 149.00 (ISBN 0-8287-0653-0). Clearwater Pub.
Nicholson, Marjorie H. Newton Demands the Muse: Newton's "Opticks" & the Eighteenth Century Poets. LC 78-13146. 1979. Repr. of 1966 ed. lib. bdg. 16.75x (ISBN 0-313-21044-6, NIND). Greenwood.
Pemberton, Henry. A View of Sir Isaac Newton's Philosophy. 1972. Repr. of 1728 ed. 31.00 (ISBN 0-384-45695-2). Johnson Repr.
Pullin, V. E. Sir Issac Newton: A Biographical Sketch. 1979. Repr. of 1927 ed. lib. bdg. 15.00 (ISBN 0-8495-4334-7). Arden Lib.
Rigaud, Stephen P. Historical Essay on the First Publication of Sir Isaac Newton's Principia. 1972. Repr. of 1838 ed. 19.50 (ISBN 0-384-50845-6). Johnson Repr.
Ronan, C. A. Isaac Newton. (Clarendon Biography Ser.). (Illus.). 1976. pap. 3.50 (ISBN 0-912728-05-1). Newbury Bks.
Snow, A. J. Matter & Gravity in Newton's Physical Philosophy. LC 74-26293. (History, Philosophy & Sociology of Science Ser). 1975. Repr. 19.00x (ISBN 0-405-06619-8). Arno.
Tiner, John H. Isaac Newton: The True Story of His Life. LC 75-32562. (Sower Series). (Illus.). (gr. 3-6). 1976. 6.95 (ISBN 0-915134-06-3). Mott Media.
Westfall, R. S. Never at Rest: A Biography of Isaac Newton. LC 77-84001. (Illus.). 850p. 1981. 49.50 (ISBN 0-521-23143-4). Cambridge U Pr.
Whiston, William. Sir Isaac Newton's Mathematick Philosophy More Easily Demonstrated. Repr. of 1716 ed. 31.00 (ISBN 0-384-67976-5). Johnson Repr.
Wright, J. M. A Commentary on Newton's Principia: With a Supplementary Volume, Designed for the Use of Students at the Universities, 2 Vols. 1972. Repr. of 1833 ed. Set. 54.00 (ISBN 0-384-69445-4). Johnson Repr.

NEWTON, JOHN, 1725-1807
Cecil, Richard. Life of John Newton. (Summit Bks). 1978. pap. 3.95 (ISBN 0-8010-2418-8). Baker Bk.
Deal, William S. John Newton, Author of Amazing Grace. 0.95 (ISBN 0-686-13719-1). Deal Pubns.
Guerlac, Henry. Newton on the Continent. LC 81-3187. (Illus.). 160p. 1981. 12.50x (ISBN 0-8014-1409-1). Cornell U Pr.
McLachlan, Herbert. The Religious Opinions of Milton, Locke & Newton. LC 74-20740. 1974. Repr. of 1941 ed. lib. bdg. 11.95 (ISBN 0-8414-5930-4). Folcroft.
Newton, John. Letters of John Newton. 1976. pap. 2.45 (ISBN 0-85151-120-1). Banner of Truth.
--Out of the Depths. LC 80-85340. (Shepherd Illustrated Classics Ser.). (Illus.). 1981. pap. 5.95 (ISBN 0-87983-243-6). Keats.
Pollock, John. Amazing Grace: John Newton's Story. LC 78-3142. 192p. 1981. 9.95 (ISBN 0-06-066653-6, HarpR). Har-Row.

NEWTON'S RINGS
see Interference (Light)

NEWTS
see also Salamanders

NEX, MARTIN ANDERSEN, b. 1869
Slochower, Harry. Three Ways of Modern Man. LC 37-17328. 1968. Repr. of 1937 ed. 12.00 (ISBN 0-527-83656-7). Kraus Repr.

NEY, MICHEL, MARSHAL OF FRANCE, 1769-1815
Foster, John. Napoleon's Marshal: The Life of Michel Ney. (Illus.). (gr. 7 up). 1968. 7.75 (ISBN 0-688-21606-4). Morrow.

NEZ PERCE INDIANS
see Indians of North America–The West

NEZ PERCE LANGUAGE
see also Shahaptian Languages
Phinney, Archie. Nez Perce Texts. LC 73-82344. (Columbia Univ. Contributions to Anthropology Ser.: Vol. 25). Repr. of 1934 ed. 34.50 (ISBN 0-404-50575-9). AMS Pr.

NGALA LANGUAGE
see Bangala Language

NGANASANI
Popov, A. A. Nganasan: The Material Culture of the Tavgi Samoyeds. Ristenen, Elaine K., tr. LC 66-63668. (Uralic & Altaic Ser: Vol. 56). (Orig.). 1966. pap. text ed. 7.00x (ISBN 0-87750-020-7). Res Ctr Lang Semiotic.

NG'ANGA LANGUAGE
see Nyanja Language

NGGERIKUDI LANGUAGE
see also Australian Languages

NGOMBE (BANTU TRIBE)
Thayer, James E. The Deep Structure of the Sentence in Sara-Ngambay Dialogues. (Linguistics & Related Fields Ser.: No. 57). 1978. 10.00x (ISBN 0-88312-071-2); microfiche 2.00 (ISBN 0-88312-470-X). Summer Inst Ling.

NGONDE (AFRICAN TRIBE)
see also Makonde (Bantu Tribe); Nyakyusa (African Tribe)
Mackenzie, D. R. Spirit-Ridden Konde, a Record of the Interesting. 1925. 25.00 (ISBN 0-403-00354-7). Scholarly.
Wilson, Monica. For Men & Elders: Change in the Relations of Generations & of Men & Women Among the Nyakyusa-Ngonde People, 1875-1971. LC 77-4203. 1978. 29.50x (ISBN 0-8419-0313-1, Africana). Holmes & Meier.

NGONI
see Angoni

NGUNA LANGUAGE
Schutz, Albert J. Nguna Texts: A Collection of Traditional & Modern Narratives from the Central New Hebrides. (Oceanic Linguistics Special Publication: No. 4). (Orig., Nguna & Eng). 1969. pap. text ed. 7.00x (ISBN 0-87022-745-9). U Pr of Hawaii.

NIAGARA FALLS
Donaldson, Gordon. Niagara: The Eternal Circus. LC 79-7328. (Illus.). 1979. 9.95 (ISBN 0-385-12309-4). Doubleday.
Loker. Guide to Niagara Falls. (Illus.). 1975. pap. 1.50 (ISBN 0-685-20409-X). Stewart.
Tesmer, Irving H., ed. Colossal Cataract: The Geological History of Niagara Falls. LC 80-26858. (Illus.). 210p. 1981. text ed. 34.00x (ISBN 0-87395-522-6, TECC); pap. text ed. 9.95x (ISBN 0-87395-523-4, TECC-P). State U NY Pr.
Yates, Raymond F. Niagara Story. (Illus.). 1980. pap. 2.00 (ISBN 0-685-20411-1). Stewart.

NIAGARA FALLS (CITY) NEW YORK–HISTORY
Gillard, William H. & Tooke, Thomas R. The Niagara Escarpment: From Tobermory to Niagara Falls. LC 73-84434. (Illus.). 1974. pap. 6.00 (ISBN 0-8020-6214-8). U of Toronto Pr.
Stokes, Peter J. Old Niagara on the Lake. LC 74-151393. 1971. pap. 10.95 (ISBN 0-8020-6318-7). U of Toronto Pr.

NIAGARA FORT, NEW YORK
Ford, Paul L. Short History & Description of Fort Niagara with an Account of Its Importance to Great Britain. LC 72-173994. (Research & Source Works Ser.: No. 847). 1971. pap. text ed. 10.00 (ISBN 0-8337-1199-7). B Franklin.

NIAGARA FRONTIER–HISTORY
Boning, Richard A. Blondin: Hero of Niagara. (Incredible Ser). (Illus.). (gr. 5-11). 1972. PLB 5.95 (ISBN 0-87966-101-1, Pub. by Dexter & Westbrook). B Loft.
Cruikshank, Ernest A., ed. Documentary History of the Campaign Upon the Niagara Frontier, 1812-1814, 4 Vols. LC 74-146387. (First American Frontier Ser). (Illus.). 1971. Repr. of 1909 ed. 128.00 (ISBN 0-405-02838-5). Arno.
Hulbert, Archer B. History of the Niagara River. LC 78-12656. (Illus.). 1978. Repr. of 1908 ed. 19.50 (ISBN 0-916346-29-3). Harbor Hill Bks.
Severance, Frank H. Old Frontier of France, the Niagara Region & Adjacent Lakes Under French Control, 2 Vols. in 1. LC 77-146421. (First American Frontier Ser). (Illus.). 1971. Repr. of 1917 ed. 42.00 (ISBN 0-405-02885-7). Arno.

NIAM-NIAM
see Azande

NIANTIC LANGUAGE
see Massachuset Language

NIBELUNGENLIED
Abeling, Theodor. Nibelungenlied und Seine Literatur: Eine Bibliographie und Vier Abhandlungen. LC 70-123508. (Bibliography & Reference Ser: No. 363). (Ger). 1970. Repr. of 1907 ed. lib. bdg. 23.50 (ISBN 0-8337-0003-0). B Franklin.
Cleather, Alice L. The Ring of the Nibelung. LC 77-18100. 1977. Repr. of 1924 ed. lib. bdg. 20.00 (ISBN 0-8414-1844-6). Folcroft.
Fischer, Rudolf. Zu Den Kunstformen Des Mittelalterlichen Epos. 1965. pap. 21.00 (ISBN 0-384-15765-3). Johnson Repr.
Gentry, Francis G. Triuwe & Vriunt in the Nibelungenlied. Minis, Cola, ed. (Amsterdamer Publikationen Zur Sprache und Literatur: Vol. 19). 94p. 1975. pap. text ed. 17.25x (ISBN 90-6203-368-7). Humanities.
Lachmann, Karl, ed. Nibelunge Noth und die Klage: Nach Den Aelesten Ueberlieferungen Mit Bezeichnung Des Unechten und Mit Den Abweichungen der Gemeinen Lesart. 6th ed. (Ger). 1960. 15.75x (ISBN 3-11-000177-2). De Gruyter.
Langosch, Karl, ed. Nibelunge Not in Auswahl: Mit Kurzem Woerterbuch. 11th ed. (Sammlung Goeschen, No. 1). (Ger). 1966. 3.25x (ISBN 3-11-002722-4). De Gruyter.
Mueller, Werner A. Nibelungenlied Today. LC 70-181961. (North Carolina. University. Studies in the Germanic Languages & Literatures: No. 34). Repr. of 1962 ed. 18.50 (ISBN 0-404-50934-7). AMS Pr.
Shumway, Daniel B. The Nibelungenlied. 1909. Repr. 15.00 (ISBN 0-8274-3034-5). R West.

NICAEA, COUNCIL OF, 325
Haase, Felix A. Die Koptischen Quellen Zum Konzil Von Nicaa. pap. 9.50 (ISBN 0-384-20630-1). Johnson Repr.

NICARAGUA
Adams, Richard N. Cultural Surveys of Panama, Nicaragua, Guatemala, El Salvador, Honduras. LC 76-41776. 1976. Repr. of 1957 ed. 35.00 (ISBN 0-87917-056-5). Blaine Ethridge.
Aldaraca, Bridget, et al, eds. Nicaragua in Revolution: The Poets Speak. LC 80-16304. (Studies in Marxism: Vol. 5). 310p. (Bilingual: spanish & english). 1980. 12.95 (ISBN 0-930656-10-5); pap. 6.95 (ISBN 0-930656-09-1). Marxist Educ.
Bell, Belden, ed. Nicaragua: An Ally Under Seige. 1978. pap. 10.00 (ISBN 0-685-59450-5). Coun Am Affair.
Belt, Thomas. The Naturalist in Nicaragua: A Narraitive of a Residence at the Gold Mines of Chontales; Journeys in the Savannahs & Forests; with Obervations on Animals & Plants in Reference to the Theory of Evolution of Living Forms. 1976. Repr. of 1888 ed. 54.00 (ISBN 0-403-06615-8, Regency). Scholarly.
Booth, John A. The End & the Beginning: The Nicaraguan Revolution. (Special Studies on Latin America & the Caribbean). (Illus.). 225p. (Orig.). Date not set. lib. bdg. 20.00x (ISBN 0-89158-939-2); pap. text ed. 10.00x (ISBN 0-86531-148-X). Westview.
Camejo, Pedro & Murphy, Fred, eds. The Nicaraguan Revolution. LC 79-55833. (Illus.). 1979. lib. bdg. 8.00 (ISBN 0-87348-573-4); pap. 2.25 (ISBN 0-87348-574-2). Path Pr NY.
Carpenter, Allan & Balow, Tom. Nicaragua. LC 76-160842. (Enchantment of Central America Ser). (Illus.). (gr. 5 up). 1971. PLB 9.25 (ISBN 0-516-04519-9). Childrens.
Cox, Isaac J. Nicaragua & the United States. 1976. lib. bdg. 59.95 (ISBN 0-8490-2344-0). Gordon Pr.
De Nogales, Rafael. The Looting of Nicaragua. 1976. lib. bdg. 59.95 (ISBN 0-8490-0555-8). Gordon Pr.
Healy, Paul F. Archaeology of the Rivas Region, Nicragua. 382p. 1980. text ed. 15.50x (ISBN 0-88920-094-7, Pub. by Laurier U Pr). Humanities.
International Bank for Reconstruction & Development. Economic Development of Nicaragua. LC 77-86381. Repr. of 1953 ed. 57.50 (ISBN 0-404-60307-6). AMS Pr.
Kamman, William. Search for Stability: United States Diplomacy Toward Nicaragua 1925-1933. (International Studies Ser). 1968. 9.95x (ISBN 0-268-00249-5). U of Notre Dame Pr.
Macaulay, Neill. Sandino Affair. 320p. (Orig.). 1971. 6.95 (ISBN 0-8129-0100-2); pap. 3.45 (ISBN 0-8129-6128-5). Times Bks.

Roberts, Orlando W. Narrative of Voyages & Excursions on the East Coast & in the Interior of Central America. Craggs, Hugh, ed. LC 65-28696. (Latin American Gateway Ser). 1965. Repr. of 1827 ed. 9.00 (ISBN 0-8130-0199-4). U Presses Fla.

Scroggs, William O. Filibusters & Financiers: The Story of William Walker & His Associates. LC 72-83846. (Illus.). 1969. Repr. of 1916 ed. 13.00 (ISBN 0-8462-1419-9). Russell.

Sims, Harold. Nicaragua's Revolutionary Economy: ISHI Occasional Papers in Social Change. (No. 7). 1981. pap. text ed. 2.95x (ISBN 0-89727-027-4). Inst Study Human.

Somoza, Anastasio. Nicaragua Traicionada. 1980. pap. 7.95 (ISBN 0-88279-128-1). Western Islands.

Squier, Ephraim G. Nicaragua. 1977. lib. bdg. 95.00 (ISBN 0-8490-2343-2). Gordon Pr.

--Nicaragua, Its People, Scenery, Monuments, Resources, Condition & Proposed Canal. LC 73-176006. (Illus.). Repr. of 1860 ed. 42.50 (ISBN 0-404-06220-2). AMS Pr.

Strachan, Harry W. Family & Other Business Groups in Economic Development: The Case of Nicaragua. LC 75-25025. (Special Studies). (Illus.). 160p. 1976. text ed. 21.95 (ISBN 0-275-56050-3). Praeger.

Walker, Thomas W. Nicaragua: A Profile. (Nations of Contemporary Latin America). 128p. 1981. lib. bdg. 18.00x (ISBN 0-89158-947-3). Westview.

Walker, William. War in Nicaragua. LC 72-165663. 1971. Repr. of 1860 ed. 20.00x (ISBN 0-87917-018-2). Blaine Ethridge.

Wilcox, John C. El Aliento de la Vida: Cuentos Nicaraguenses. LC 79-56364. (Coleccion Caniqui Ser.). 214p. (Orig., Span.). 1981. pap. 8.95 (ISBN 0-89729-244-8). Ediciones.

Wyckoff, Lydia L. A Suggested Nicaraguan Pottery Sequence Based on the Museum Collection. LC 75-139868. (Miscellaneous Ser.: No. 58). (Illus.). 1971. pap. 2.50 (ISBN 0-934490-35-X). Mus Am Ind.

NICARAGUA-HISTORY

Black, George. Triumph of the People: The Sandinista Revolution in Nicaragua. 320p. 1981. 18.95 (ISBN 0-686-74772-0, Pub. by Zed Pr England); pap. 7.95 (ISBN 0-86232-036-4). Lawrence Hill.

--Triumph of the People: The Sandinista Revolution in Nicaragua. 320p. 1981. 18.95 (ISBN 0-686-76757-8, Pub. by Zed Pr England); pap. 7.95 (ISBN 0-86232-036-4). Lawrence Hill.

Crawley, Eduardo. Dictators Never Die: Nicaragua & the Somoza Dynasty. LC 78-31151. 1979. 14.50x (ISBN 0-312-20007-2). St Martin.

Diederich, Bernard. Somoza: American Made Dictator. 1981. 19.75 (ISBN 0-525-20670-1). Dutton.

Dilling, Yvonne & Wheaton, Philip, eds. Nicaragua: A People's Revolution. (Illus.). 103p. 1980. pap. text ed. 4.25 (ISBN 0-918346-04-5). EPICA.

Elman, Richard. Cocktails at Somoza's: A Reporter's Sketchbook of Events in Revolutionary Nicaragua. 196p. 1981. 10.95 (ISBN 0-918222-28-1). Apple Wood.

Ignatiev, O. & Borovik, G. La Agonia De una Dictadura: Cronica Nicaraguense. 190p. (Span.). 1980. pap. 3.00 (ISBN 0-8285-1596-4, Pub. by Progress Pubs Russia). Imported Pubns.

Meiselas, Susan. Nicaragua-June Nineteen Seventy-Eight to July Nineteen Seventy-Nine. (Illus.). 1981. 22.95 (ISBN 0-394-51265-0); pap. 11.95 (ISBN 0-394-73931-0). Pantheon.

Millett, Richard. Guardians of the Dynasty: A History of the U.S. Created Guardia Nacional De Nicaragua and the Somoza Family. LC 76-49499. 1977. pap. 6.95 (ISBN 0-88344-171-3). Orbis Bks.

Selser, Gregorio. Sandino. Belfrage, Cedric, tr. LC 80-8086. 256p. 1981. 16.00 (ISBN 0-85345-558-9). Monthly Rev.

Somoza, Anastasio. Nicaragua Betrayed. 1980. 15.00 (ISBN 0-88279-235-0). Western Islands.

Stimson, Henry L. American Policy in Nicaragua. LC 76-111733. (American Imperialism: Viewpoints of United States Foreign Policy, 1898-1941). 1970. Repr. of 1927 ed. 8.00 (ISBN 0-405-02051-1). Arno.

NICARAGUA CANAL

Du Val, Miles P. Cadiz to Cathay: The Story of the Long Diplomatic Struggle for the Panama Canal. 2nd ed. LC 68-23284. Repr. of 1947 ed. lib. bdg. 30.00x (ISBN 0-8371-0065-8, DUCC). Greenwood.

Folkman, David I., Jr. The Nicaragua Route. LC 73-180827. (University of Utah Publications in the American West: Vol. 8). 1976. pap. 15.00 (ISBN 0-87480-117-6). U of Utah Pr.

Miller, Hugh G. Isthmian Highway: A Review of the Problems of the Caribbean. LC 76-111725. (American Imperialism: Viewpoints of United States Foreign Policy, 1898-1941). 1970. Repr. of 1929 ed. 18.00 (ISBN 0-405-02039-2). Arno.

NICCOLI, NICCOLO, 1364-1437?

Gordan, Phyllis G., ed. Two Renaissance Book Hunters: The Letters of Poggius Bracciolini to Nicolaus De Niccolis. LC 74-1401. (Records of Civilization, Sources & Studies). 393p. 1974. 25.00x (ISBN 0-231-03777-5). Columbia U Pr.

NICENE CREED

The Ante-Nicene Fathers, 10 vols. Repr. Set. 139.50 (ISBN 0-686-12358-1); 15.00 ea. Church History.

Bassett, Bernard. And Would You Believe It! Thoughts About the Creed. 1978. pap. 2.45 (ISBN 0-385-13367-7, Im). Doubleday.

Bull, George. Harmony on Justification, Defense of the Nicene Creed, Judgement of the Catholic Church, 5 vols. LC 71-39556. (Library of Anglo-Catholic Theology: No. 4). Repr. of 1855 ed. Set. 150.00 (ISBN 0-404-52070-7). AMS Pr.

MacGregor, Geddes. The Nicene Creed Illumined by Modern Thought. 1981. pap. 7.95 (ISBN 0-8028-1855-2). Eerdmans.

Nicene & Post Nicene Fathers. Repr. of 14 vols. 196.00 set (ISBN 0-686-12360-3); 15.00 ea. (ISBN 0-686-12362-X). Church History.

NICEPHORUS, SAINT, PATRIARCH OF CONSTANTINOPLE

Alexander, Paul J. The Patriarch Nicephorus of Constantinople: Ecclesiastical Policy & Image Worship in the Byzantine Empire. LC 78-63177. (Heresies Ser.: No. II). Repr. of 1958 ed. 31.00 (ISBN 0-404-16195-2). AMS Pr.

Jenkins, R. J., ed. & tr. Nicholas I, Patriarch of Constantinople: Letters. LC 74-28930. (Dumbarton Oaks Texts: Vol. 2). 668p. 1973. 45.00x (ISBN 0-88402-039-8, Ctr Byzantine). Dumbarton Oaks.

Westerink, L. G., ed. Nicholas I, Patriarch of Constantinople: Miscellaneous Writings. LC 80-70736. (Dumbarton Oaks Texts Ser.: Vol. 6). 160p. 1981. 18.00x (ISBN 0-88402-089-4, Ctr Byzantine). Dumbarton Oaks.

NICHIREN, 1222-1282

Anesaki, Masharu. Nichiren: The Buddhist Prophet. 1916. 7.75 (ISBN 0-8446-1029-1). Peter Smith.

Rodd, Laurel R. Nichiren: A Biography. (Occasional Paper; Arizona State Univ., Center for Asian Studies: No. 11). 86p. 1978. pap. text ed. 3.00x (ISBN 0-939252-07-4). ASU Ctr Asian.

--Nichiren: Selected Readings. LC 79-17054. (Asian Studies in Hawaii: No. 26). 224p. 1980. pap. text ed. 9.75x (ISBN 0-8248-0682-4). U Pr of Hawaii.

NICHOLAS 1ST, EMPEROR OF RUSSIA, 1796-1855

Gallet De Kulture, Achille. Le Tsar Nicolas et la Sainte Russie. (Nineteenth Century Russia Ser.). 306p. (Fr.). 1974. Repr. of 1855 ed. lib. bdg. 81.00x (ISBN 0-8287-0362-0, R8). Clearwater Pub.

Lincoln, W. Bruce. Nicholas I: Emperor & Autocrat of All the Russias. LC 77-15764. (Midland Bks.: No. 254). 424p. 1980. pap. 7.95x (ISBN 0-253-20254-X). Ind U Pr.

--Nicholas I: Emperor & Autocrat of All the Russias. LC 77-15764. 424p. 1978. 20.00x (ISBN 0-253-34059-4). Ind U Pr.

Presniakov, Alexander E. Emperor Nicholas the First of Russia: The Apogee of Autocracy, 1825-1855. Zacek, Judith C., tr. from Rus. Bd. with Nicholas the First & the Course of Russian History, Vol. 23. Riasanovsky, Nicholas V. LC 73-90779. (Russian Ser: No. 23). (Illus.). 1974. 11.00 (ISBN 0-87569-053-X). Academic Intl.

Riasanovsky, Nicholas V. Nicholas I & Official Nationality in Russia, 1825-1855. (Russian & East European Studies). 1959. 23.50x (ISBN 0-520-01064-7); pap. 6.95x (ISBN 0-520-01065-5, CAMPUS 120). U of Cal Pr.

Sazonov, Nicolas I. La Verite sur l'Empereur Nicholas. (Nineteenth Century Russia Ser.). 319p. (Fr.). 1974. Repr. of 1854 ed. lib. bdg. 84.00x (ISBN 0-8287-0764-2, R49). Clearwater Pub.

NICHOLAS 2ND, EMPEROR OF RUSSIA, 1868-1918

Bulygin, Paul & Kerensky, Alexander. The Murder of the Romanovs. LC 74-10075. (Russian Studies: Perspectives on the Revolution Ser). (Illus.). 286p. 1974. Repr. of 1935 ed. 27.50 (ISBN 0-88355-183-7). Hyperion Conn.

Gilliard, Pierre. Thirteen Years at the Russian Court a Personal Record of the Last Years & Death of the Czar Nicholas Second & His Family. LC 75-115539. (Russia Observed, Series I). 1970. Repr. of 1921 ed. 15.00 (ISBN 0-405-03029-0). Arno.

Massie, Robert K. Nicholas & Alexandra. LC 67-24627. (gr. 7 up). 1967. 24.50 (ISBN 0-689-10177-5). Atheneum.

--Nicholas & Alexandra. 1978. pap. 3.95 (ISBN 0-440-16358-7). Dell.

Nicholas, II. Letters of the Tsar to the Tsaritsa, 1914-1917. Vulliamy, C. E., ed. Hynes, A. L., tr. 1976. lib. bdg. 59.95 (ISBN 0-8490-2155-3). Gordon Pr.

Richards, Guy. Imperial Agent: The Goleniewski-Romanov Case. 1966. 7.95 (ISBN 0-8159-5804-8). Devin.

--The Rescue of the Romanovs. LC 74-27953. (Illus.). 1975. 8.95 (ISBN 0-8159-6717-9). Devin.

Sokolov, Nicolai. Sokolov Investigation into the Mysterious Disappearance of the Russian Imperial Family. O'Conor, John F., tr. 1968. 8.95 (ISBN 0-8315-0110-3). Speller.

Trewin, J. C. The House of Special Purpose: An Intimate Portrait of the Last Years of the Russian Imperial Family Compiled from the Papers of Their English Tutor Charles Sydney Gibbes. LC 74-30457. (Illus.). 200p. 1975. 10.00 (ISBN 0-8128-1796-6). Stein & Day.

NICHOLAS, SAINT, BP. OF MYRA

Jones, Charles W. Saint Nicholas of Myra, Bari & Manhattan: Biography of a Legend. LC 77-51487. 1978. lib. bdg. 32.50x (ISBN 0-226-40699-7). U of Chicago Pr.

McKnight, George H. Saint Nicholas: His Legend & His Role in the Christmas Celebration & Other Popular Customs. (Illus.). 153p. 1974. Repr. of 1917 ed. 8.50 (ISBN 0-87928-051-4). Corner Hse.

NICHOLAS OF CUSA

see Nicolaus Cusanus, Cardinal, 1401-1464

NICHOLS, JOHN, 1745-1826

Upcott, William. Bibliographical Account of the Principal Works Relating to English Topography, 3 vols. LC 68-57921. (Illus.). 1968. Repr. of 1818 ed. 102.00 set (ISBN 0-8337-3598-5). B Franklin.

NICHOLSON, BEN, 1894-

Ben Nicholson. LC 74-91553. (Tate Gallery Ser.). (Illus.). 1977. 5.75 (ISBN 0-8120-5174-2). Barron.

Harrison, Charles. Ben Nicholson. (Tate Gallery Publications). Repr. of 1969 ed. 7.00 (ISBN 0-405-00220-3). Arno.

Nash, Steven A. Ben Nicholson: Fifty Years of His Art. LC 78-62949. (Illus.). 1978. 14.00 (ISBN 0-914782-21-5). Buffalo Acad.

Spaulding, Karen L., ed. Ben Nicholson: Fifty Years of His Art. LC 78-6249. (Illus.). 1978. pap. 14.00 (ISBN 0-914782-21-5, Pub. by Albright-Knox Art Gallery). C E Tuttle.

NICHOLSON, JACK

Braithwaite, Bruce. The Films of Jack Nicholson. Castell, David, ed. (The Films of...Ser.). (Illus.). (gr. 7-12). 1978. Repr. PLB 5.95 (ISBN 0-912616-76-8). Greenhaven.

Fryer, Christopher & Crane, Robert D. Jack Nicholson, Face to Face. LC 74-31265. (Illus.). 192p. 1975. 9.95 (ISBN 0-87131-175-5); pap. 5.95 (ISBN 0-87131-176-3). M Evans.

NICHOLSON, JOHN, 1822-1857

Abdullah, Achmed & Pakenham, Thomas C. Dreamers of Empire. facs. ed. LC 68-57300. (Essay Index Reprint Ser). 1929. 16.00 (ISBN 0-8369-0099-5). Arno.

NICHOLSON, WILLIAM, SIR, 1872-1949

Steen, Marguerite. William Nicholson. Repr. of 1943 ed. 25.00 (ISBN 0-685-76624-1). Norwood Edns.

NICKEL

American Welding Society. Nickel & Nickel-Alloy Bare Welding Rods & Electrodes: A5.14-76. 5.00 (ISBN 0-685-65976-3). Am Welding.

--Nickel & Nickel-Alloy Covered Welding Electrodes: A5.11-76. 5.00 (ISBN 0-685-65973-9). Am Welding.

Betteridge, W. Nickel & Its Alloys. (Illus.). 160p. 1977. pap. 12.95x (ISBN 0-7121-0947-1, Pub. by Macdonald & Evans England). Intl Ideas.

Brown, Stanley S. & Sunderman, F. William, Jr., eds. Nickel Toxicology. 1981. 36.00 (ISBN 0-12-137680-X). Acad Pr.

Brugger, Robert. Nickel Plating. LC 70-523834. 1970. 32.50x (ISBN 0-85218-031-4). Intl Pubns Serv.

Cohen, Annette & Druley, Ray. Buffalo Nickel. 1980. softcover 7.00 (ISBN 0-686-64449-2). S J Durst.

Committee on Medical & Biological Effects of Environmental Pollutants. Nickel. 1975. pap. 15.00 (ISBN 0-309-02314-9). Natl Acad Pr.

Everhart, John L., ed. Engineering Properties of Nickel & Nickel Alloys. LC 74-141242. 229p. 1971. 29.50 (ISBN 0-306-30513-5, Plenum Pr). Plenum Pub.

Friend, Wayne Z. Corrosion of Nickel & Nickel-Base Alloys. LC 79-11524. (Corrosion Monographs). 1980. 46.00 (ISBN 0-471-28285-5, Pub. by Wiley-Interscience). Wiley.

Jolly, P. W. & Wilke, G. The Organic Chemistry of Nickel, 2 vols. (Organometallic Chemistry Ser.). Vol. 1, 1974. 92.00 (ISBN 0-12-388401-2); Vol. 2, 1975. 76.00 (ISBN 0-12-388402-0). Acad Pr.

Max Planck Society for the Advancement of Science, Gmelin Institute for Inorganic Chemistry. Organonickel Compounds. (Gmelin Handbuch der Anorganischen Chemie, 8th Ed., New Suppl.: Vol. 16, Pt. 1). (Illus.). 419p. 1975. 409.50 (ISBN 0-387-93294-1). Springer-Verlag.

Max Plank Society for the Advancement of Science, Gmelin Institute for Inorganic Chemistry. Nickel-Organische Verbibdunger Register-Organohickel Compounds Index for Pts. 1 & 2 of the Gmelin Handbuch. (Gmelin Handbuch der Anoranischew Chenill, 8th Ed, New Suppl.: Vol. 18). 129p. 1975. 116.90 (ISBN 0-387-93296-8). Springer-Verlag.

Nriagu, Jerome O. Nickel in the Environment. LC 80-16600. (Environmental Science & Technology: a Wiley Interscience Ser. of Texts & Monographs). 833p. 1980. 65.00 (ISBN 0-471-05885-8, Pub. by Wiley Interscience). Wiley.

Prokop, F. W. The Future Economic Significance of Large Lowgrade Copper & Nickel Deposits. Borchert, H., ed. (Illus.). 67p. (Orig.). 1975. pap. 32.50x (ISBN 3-443-12013-X). Intl Pubns Serv.

Such, Dennis T. Nickel & Chromium Plating. 1972. pap. text ed. 34.95 (ISBN 0-408-00086-4). Butterworth.

NICKEL-CHROMIUM ALLOYS

see also Nimonic Alloys

Friend, Wayne Z. Corrosion of Nickel & Nickel-Base Alloys. LC 79-11524. (Corrosion Monographs). 1980. 46.00 (ISBN 0-471-28285-5, Pub. by Wiley-Interscience). Wiley.

Gawrilov, G. G. Chemical (Electroless) Nickel Plating. (Illus.). 189p. 1979. 42.50x (ISBN 0-86108-023-8). Intl Pubns Serv.

NICKEL INDUSTRY

Gawrilov, G. G. Chemical (Electroless) Nickel Plating. (Illus.). 189p. 1979. 42.50x (ISBN 0-86108-023-8). Intl Pubns Serv.

The Nickel Industry & the Developing Countries. 100p. 1980. pap. 8.00 (ISBN 0-686-70505-X, UN80-2A2, UN). Unipub.

NICKERSON, EUGENE H.

Gonzalez, Arturo. Eugene H. Nickerson: Statesman of a New Society. (Future Maker Ser). (Illus.). 1964. 3.95 (ISBN 0-685-11955-6). Heineman.

NICKLAUS, JACK

Deegan, Paul J. Jack Nicklaus. LC 73-12190. (Creative Superstars Ser.). PLB 5.95 (ISBN 0-87191-259-7). Creative Ed.

Taylor, Paula. Golf's Great Winner: Jack Nicklaus. (The Allstars Ser.). (Illus.). 1977. PLB 5.95 (ISBN 0-87191-591-X). Creative Ed.

Van Riper, Guernsey, Jr. Golfing Greats: Two Top Pros. LC 74-16266. (Sports Library Ser). (Illus.). 96p. (gr. 3-6). 1975. PLB 6.48 (ISBN 0-8116-6669-7). Garrard.

NICKNAMES

Dawson, Lawrence H. Nicknames & Pseudonyms. LC 73-164216. viii, 312p. 1974. Repr. of 1908 ed. 28.00 (ISBN 0-8103-3177-2). Gale.

Frey, Albert R. Sobriquets & Nicknames. LC 66-22671. 1966. Repr. of 1888 ed. 22.00 (ISBN 0-8103-3003-2). Gale.

Kane, Joseph N. & Alexander, Gerard L. Nicknames & Sobriquets of U. S. Cities, States, & Counties. 3rd ed. LC 79-20193. 445p. 1979. 19.00 (ISBN 0-8108-1255-X). Scarecrow.

Latham, Edward. Dictionary of Names, Nicknames, & Surnames. LC 66-22674. 1966. Repr. of 1904 ed. 22.00 (ISBN 0-8103-0157-1). Gale.

Morgan, Jane, et al. Nicknames: Their Origins & Social Consequences. (Social Worlds of Childhood Ser.). 1979. 16.00x (ISBN 0-7100-0139-8). Routledge & Kegan.

Mossman, Jennifer. New Pseudonyms & Nicknames--Supplements: Supplements to Pseudonyms & Nicknames Dictionary, 2 vols. 1981. 50.00 set, softbound (ISBN 0-8103-0548-8). Gale.

Ruffner, Frederick G., Jr. & Thomas, Robert C., eds. Code Names Dictionary: A Guide to Code Names, Slang, Nicknames, Journalese, & Similar Terms. LC 63-21847. 1963. 24.00 (ISBN 0-8103-0685-9). Gale.

Shankle, George E. American Nicknames. 2nd ed. 1955. 15.00 (ISBN 0-8242-0004-7). Wilson.

Sharp, Harold S. Handbook of Geographical Nicknames. LC 79-26860. 153p. 1980. lib. bdg. 10.00 (ISBN 0-8108-1280-0). Scarecrow.

--Handbook of Pseudonyms & Personal Nicknames, 2 vols. LC 71-189886. 1972. Set. 35.00 (ISBN 0-8108-0460-3). Scarecrow.

Urdang, Laurence, ed. Twentieth-Century American Nicknames. 1979. 18.00 (ISBN 0-8242-0642-8). Wilson.

NICOBAR ISLANDS

Man, Edward H. The Nicobar Islands & Their People. LC 77-86996. (Royal Anthropological Institute of Great Britain & Ireland). Repr. of 1932 ed. 29.50 (ISBN 0-404-16767-5). AMS Pr.

Mathur, K. K. Nicobar Islands. (India - Land & People Ser). (Illus.). 1967. 4.25x (ISBN 0-8426-1380-3). Verry.
Singh, N. Iqbal. The Andaman Story. (Illus.). 321p. 1978. 20.00x (ISBN 0-7069-0632-2, Pub. by Croom Helm Ltd. England). Biblio Dist.
Whitehead, George. In the Nicobar Islands. LC 77-87005. Repr. of 1924 ed. 22.50 (ISBN 0-404-16786-1). AMS Pr.

NICOLAS DE LYRE, d. 1349

Gosselin, Edward A. Listing of the Printed Editions of Nicolaus of Lyra. 1970. pap. 3.00 (ISBN 0-8232-0040-X). Fordham.

NICOLAUS CUSANUS, CARDINAL, 1401-1464

Bett, Henry. Nicholas of Cusa. LC 76-1131. (Great Medieval Churchmen Ser). x, 210p. 1976. Repr. of 1932 ed. lib. bdg. 17.50 (ISBN 0-915172-05-4). Richwood Pub.
Biechler, James E. The Religious Language of Nicholas of Cusa. LC 75-23096. (American Academy of Religion. Dissertation Ser.). 1975. pap. 7.50 (ISBN 0-89130-021-X, 010108). Scholars Pr Ca.
Hopkins, Jasper. Nicholas of Cusa on Learned Ignorance: A Translation & an Appraisal of De Docta Ignorantia. LC 80-82907. (Illus.). 216p. 1981. text ed. 27.00x (ISBN 0-938060-23-6). Banning Pr.
Jaspers, Karl. Anselm & Nicholas of Cusa. Arendt, Hannah, ed. Manheim, Ralph, tr. from Ger. LC 74-4484. (From the Great Philosophers: Vol. No. 2). 208p. 1974. pap. 3.50 (ISBN 0-15-607600-4, HB289, Harv). HarBraceJ.

NICOLAUS DE AUTRICURIA, fl. 14TH CENTURY

Weinberg, Julius R. Nicolaus of Autrecourt. Repr. of 1948 ed. lib. bdg. 15.00 (ISBN 0-8371-2529-4, WENA). Greenwood.

NICOLAY, JOHN GEORGE, 1832-1901

Nicolay, Helen. Lincoln's Secretary: A Biography of John G. Nicolay. LC 70-138169. (Illus.). 363p. 1972. Repr. of 1949 ed. lib. bdg. 17.50x (ISBN 0-8371-5626-2, NILS). Greenwood.
--Lincoln's Secretary: A Biography of John G. Nicolay. LC 70-138169. (Illus.). 363p. 1972. Repr. of 1949 ed. lib. bdg. 17.50x (ISBN 0-8371-5626-2, NILS). Greenwood.

NICOLET, JEAN, d. 1642

Butterfield, C. W. History of the Discovery of the Northwest by John Nicolet in 1634. LC 68-26262. 1969. Repr. of 1881 ed. 12.00 (ISBN 0-8046-0059-7). Kennikat.

NICOLSON, HAROLD

Olson, Stanley. Harold Nicolson Diaries & Letters Nineteen Thirty - Nineteen Sixty-Four. LC 80-66005. 1980. 15.00 (ISBN 0-689-11097-9). Atheneum.

NICOMACHUS GERASENUS

Levin, Flora R. The Harmonics of Nicomachus & the Pythagorean Tradition. (American Philological Association, American Classical Studies). 1975. pap. 4.50 (ISBN 0-89130-241-7, 400401). Scholars Pr Ca.
Taran, Leonardo. Asclepius of Tralles: Commentary to Nicomachus' Introduction to Arithmetic. LC 69-18747. (Transactions Ser.: Vol. 59, Pt. 4). 1969. pap. 2.00 (ISBN 0-87169-594-4). Am Philos.

NICOTINE

see also Tobacco

Fazey, C. The Aetiology of Psychoactive Substance Use: A Report & Critically Annotated Bibliography on Research into the Aetiology of Alcohol, Nicotine, Opiate & Other Psychoactive Substance Use. 1978. pap. 18.00 (ISBN 92-3-101508-7, U776, UNESCO). Unipub.
International Workshop, Zurich, September 15-17, 1976. Behavioral Effects of Nicotine: Proceedings. Baettig, K., ed. (Illus.). 1977. 29.50 (ISBN 3-8055-2763-2). S Karger.
Remond, A. & Izard, C., eds. Electrophysiological Effects of Nicotine. 254p. 1979. 46.50 (ISBN 0-444-80183-9, North Holland). Elsevier.
Specifications for Plant Protection Products Nicotine Sulphate. (FAO Specifications for Plant Protection Products). 1979. pap. 7.50 (ISBN 92-5-100552-4, F1468, FAO). Unipub.

NIDOLOGY

see Birds-Eggs and Nests

NIEBUHR, HELMUT RICHARD, 1894-

Davies, D. R. Reinhold Niebuhr: Prophet from America. facs. ed. (Select Bibliographies Reprint Ser). 1945. 11.00 (ISBN 0-8369-5324-X). Arno.
Hoedemaker, Libertus. The Theology of H. Richard Niebuhr. LC 78-139271. 1979. pap. 6.95 (ISBN 0-8298-0186-3). Pilgrim NY.
Kliever, Lonnie. H. Richard Niebuhr. LC 77-92452. (Makers of the Modern Theogolical Mind Ser.). 1978. 7.95 (ISBN 0-8499-0078-6, 0078-6). Word Bks.
Ramsey, Paul, ed. Faith & Ethics: The Theology of H. Richard Neibuhr. 7.00 (ISBN 0-8446-2778-X). Peter Smith.

NIEBUHR, REINHOLD, 1892-1971

Bingham, June. Courage to Change: An Introduction to the Life & Thought of Reinhold Niebuhr. Repr. of 1961 ed. lib. bdg. 15.00x (ISBN 0-678-02766-8). Kelley.
Dibble, Ernest F. Young Prophet Niebuhr: Reinhold Niebuhr's Early Search for Social Justice. 1978. pap. text ed. 11.50 (ISBN 0-8191-0377-2). U Pr of Amer.
Fadner, Donald E. The Responsible God: A Study of the Christian Philosophy of H. Richard Niebuhr. LC 75-29373. (American Academy of Religion. Dissertation Ser.). 1975. pap. 7.50 (ISBN 0-89130-041-4, 010113). Scholars Pr Ca.
King, Rachel H. Omission of the Holy Spirit from Reinhold Niebuhr's Theology. LC 64-13324. 1964. 5.75 (ISBN 0-8022-0865-7). Philos Lib.
Landon, Harold R., ed. Reinhold Niebuhr: A Prophetic Voice in Our Time. (Essay Index Reprint Ser.). Repr. of 1962 ed. 11.00 (ISBN 0-518-10150-9). Arno.
Merkley, Paul. Reinhold Niebuhr: A Political Account. 304p. 1975. 13.95x (ISBN 0-7735-0216-5). McGill-Queens U Pr.
Meyer, Donald B. The Protestant Search for Political Realism, 1919-1941. LC 72-12314. 482p. 1973. Repr. of 1960 ed. lib. bdg. 25.00x (ISBN 0-8371-6698-5, MEPR). Greenwood.
Odegard, Holtan P. Sin & Science: Reinhold Niebuhr As Political Theologian. 245p. 1956. 13.00 (ISBN 0-9600524-1-0). Advance Planning.
Patterson, Bob E. Reinhold Niebuhr. LC 76-46783. (Makers of the Modern Theological Mind Series). 1977. 6.95 (ISBN 0-87680-508-X). Word Bks.
Plaskow, Judith. Sex, Sin & Grace: Women's Experience & the Theologies of Reinhold Niebuhr & Paul Tillich. LC 79-5434. 1980. pap. text ed. 9.25 (ISBN 0-8191-0882-0). U Pr of Amer.
Reinitz, Richard. Irony & Consciousness: American Historiography & Reinhold Niebuhr's Vision. LC 77-92574. 232p. Date not set. 19.50 (ISBN 0-8387-2062-5). Bucknell U Pr.
Robertson, D. B. Reinhold Niebuhr's Works: A Bibliography. (Reference Bks.). 1979. lib. bdg. 24.00 (ISBN 0-8161-8237-X). G K Hall.
Scott, Nathan A., Jr. Reinhold Niebuhr. (Pamphlets on American Writers Ser: No. 31). (Orig.). 1963. pap. 1.25 (ISBN 0-8166-0305-7, MPAW31). U of Minn Pr.
Scott, Nathan A., Jr., ed. Legacy of Reinhold Niebuhr. LC 74-30714. xxiv, 124p. 1975. 8.00x (ISBN 0-226-74297-0). U of Chicago Pr.
Stone, Ronald H. Reinhold Niebuhr: Prophet to Politicians. 270p. 1981. lib. bdg. 19.25 (ISBN 0-8191-1540-1); pap. text ed. 10.50 (ISBN 0-8191-1541-X). U Pr of Amer.
Wurth, G. Niebuhr. (Modern Thinkers Ser.). pap. 1.50 (ISBN 0-87552-586-5). Presby & Reformed.

NIELLO

Passavant, Johann D. Peintre-Graveur: Contenant l'histoire De la Gravare Sur Bois, Sur Metal et Au Burin Jusque Vers la Fix Du Seizieme Siecle, 6 Vols in 3. 1966. 99.50 (ISBN 0-8337-2682-X). B Franklin.

NIELSEN, CARL, 1865-1931

Simpson, Robert. Carl Nielsen: Symphonist. LC 79-63622. 1979. 14.95 (ISBN 0-8008-1260-3, Crescendo). Taplinger.
Simpson, Robert W. Carl Nielsen, Symphonist, 1865-1931. LC 78-59043. (Encore Music Editions). (Illus.). 1979. Repr. of 1952 ed. 21.50 (ISBN 0-88355-715-0). Hyperion Conn.

NIEMEYER SOARES, OSCAR, 1907

Papadaki, Stamo. Oscar Niemeyer. LC 60-13307. (Masters of World Architecture Ser). 1960. 7.95 (ISBN 0-8076-0131-4); pap. 3.95 (ISBN 0-8076-0231-0). Braziller.

NIEMOLLER, MARTIN, 1892-

Davidson, Clarissa S. God's Man: The Story of Pastor Niemoeller. LC 78-21065. 1979. Repr. of 1959 ed. lib. bdg. 19.75x (ISBN 0-313-21065-9, DAGM). Greenwood.

NIEN REBELLION, 1853-1868

Perry, Elizabeth J. Chinese Perspectives on the Nien Rebellion. 150p. 1981. 18.50 (ISBN 0-87332-191-X). M E Sharpe.

NIETZSCHE, FRIEDRICH WILHELM, 1844-1900

Abraham, G. Nietzsche. 59.95 (ISBN 0-8490-0731-3). Gordon Pr.
--Nietzsche. LC 73-20387. (Nietzsche Ser., No. 89). 1974. lib. bdg. 49.95 (ISBN 0-8383-1764-2). Haskell.
Alderman, Harold G. Nietzsche's Gift. LC 76-25612. xvi, 184p. 1977. 15.00x (ISBN 0-8214-0231-5); pap. 6.95x (ISBN 0-8214-0385-0). Ohio U Pr.
Allison, David, ed. The New Nietzsche: Contemporary Styles of Interpretation. 1977. pap. 3.95 (ISBN 0-440-55876-X, Delta). Dell.
Andreas-Salome, L. Frederic Nietzsche. 310p. 1971. 23.75x (ISBN 0-677-50405-5). Gordon.
Barth, Hans. Truth & Ideology. LC 74-81430. Orig. Title: Wahrheit und Ideologie. 1977. 21.75x (ISBN 0-520-02820-1). U of Cal Pr.
--Wahrheit und Ideologie: Truth & Ideology. LC 74-25738. (European Sociology Ser.). 352p. 1975. Repr. 19.00x (ISBN 0-405-06494-2). Arno.
Behler, Ernst, et al, eds. Nietzsche-Studien. (Internationales Jahrbuch Fur Die Nietzsche-Forschung: Vol. 9). 400p. 1980. text ed. 92.50x (ISBN 3-11-008241-1). De Gruyter.
Bohlmann, Otto. Yeats & Nietzsche: An Exploration of Major Nietzschean Echoes in the Writings of William Butler Yeats. 390p. 1981. 28.50x (ISBN 0-389-20065-4). B&N.
Brandes, George. Friedrich Nietzsche. LC 72-2133. (Studies in German Literature, No. 13). 1972. Repr. of 1914 ed. lib. bdg. 49.95 (ISBN 0-8383-1463-5). Haskell.
Carroll, John. Break-Out from the Crystal Palace: The Anarcho-Psychological Critique-Stirner, Nietzsche, Dostoevsky. (International Library of Sociology). 1974. 18.00x (ISBN 0-7100-7750-5). Routledge & Kegan.
Carus, Paul. Nietzsche. LC 72-2039. (Studies in German Literature, No. 13). 1972. Repr. of 1914 ed. lib. bdg. 33.95 (ISBN 0-8383-1464-3). Haskell.
Chatterton-Hill, Georges. Philosophy of Nietzsche: An Exposition & Appreciation. LC 70-152409. (Studies in German Literature, No. 13). 1971. Repr. of 1914 ed. lib. bdg. 53.95 (ISBN 0-8383-1232-2). Haskell.
Clive, Geoffrey. Philosophy of Nietzsche. pap. 3.50 (ISBN 0-451-61994-3, ME1994, Ment). NAL.
Colli, C. & Montinari, M. Nietzsche Briefwechsel: Briefe an Nietzsche 1869-1872, Vol. 2, Section 2. 1977. 79.75x (ISBN 3-11-006635-1). De Gruyter.
Colli, G. & Montinari, M. Nietzsche Briefwechsel: Briefe April 1869-1872, Vol. 1, Section 2. 1977. 48.75x (ISBN 3-11-006633-5). De Gruyter.
Colli, Giorgio & Montinari, Mazzino, eds. Nietzsche - Werke Kritische Gesamtausgabe. (Vol. 1, Sect. 7). 1976. 79.50x (ISBN 3-11-004979-1). De Gruyter.
Copleston, Frederick. Friedrich Nietzsche: Philosopher of Culture. 2nd ed. LC 74-15182. 273p. 1975. text ed. 16.50x (ISBN 0-06-491283-3). B&N.
Dannhauser, Werner J. Nietzsche's View of Socrates. LC 73-20797. 283p. 1974. 22.50x (ISBN 0-8014-0827-X). Cornell U Pr.
Danto, A. Nietzche As Philosopher. 1965. 9.95 (ISBN 0-02-529490-3); pap. 2.45 (ISBN 0-02-084570-7). Macmillan.
Danto, Arthur. Nietzsche As Philosopher. 250p. 1980. pap. 6.95x (ISBN 0-231-05053-4). Columbia U Pr.
Davis, Helen E. Tolstoy & Nietzsche. LC 72-119083. (Studies in Comparative Literature, No. 35). 1970. Repr. of 1929 ed. lib. bdg. 33.95 (ISBN 0-8383-1079-6). Haskell.
Derrida, Jacques. Spurs: Nietzsche's Styles: Eperons: les Styles De Nietzsche. Harlow, Barbara, tr. LC 79-31. 1979. 8.95 (ISBN 0-226-14330-9). U of Chicago Pr.
Dionne, James R. Pascal & Nietzche: Etude Historique & Comparee. LC 74-3300. (Fr.). 1976. lib. bdg. 18.00 (ISBN 0-89102-032-2). B Franklin.
Donadio, Stephen. Nietzsche, Henry James, & the Artistic Will. LC 77-15657. 1978. 16.95x (ISBN 0-19-502358-7). Oxford U Pr.
Faguet, E. On Reading Nietzsche. 75.00 (ISBN 0-87968-278-7). Gordon Pr.
Figgis, John N. Will to Freedom. LC 68-8236. 1969. Repr. of 1917 ed. 13.50 (ISBN 0-8046-0147-X). Kennikat.
Fischer-Dieskau, Dietrich. Wagner & Nietzsche. Neugroschel, Joachim, tr. from Ger. LC 75-45489. 1976. 12.95 (ISBN 0-8164-9280-8). Continuum.
Flaccus, Louis W. Artists & Thinkers. facs. ed. LC 67-23218. (Essay Index Reprint Ser). 1916. 15.00 (ISBN 0-8369-0444-3). Arno.
Foster, George B. & Reese, Curtis W. Friedrich Nietzsche. 250p. 1981. Repr. of 1931 ed. lib. bdg. 40.00 (ISBN 0-89760-226-9). Telegraph Bks.
Foster, John B., Jr. Heirs to Dionysus: A Nietzschean Current in Literary Modernism. LC 81-47127. 450p. 1981. 27.50x (ISBN 0-691-06480-6). Princeton U Pr.
Geffre, Claude & Jossua, Jean-Pierre, eds. Nietzche & Christianity, Vol. 145. (Concilium 1981). 128p. (Orig.). 1981. pap. 6.95 (ISBN 0-8164-2312-1). Seabury.
Grimm, Ruediger H. Nietzsche's Theory of Knowledge. (Monographien und Texte Zur Nietzsche-Forschung: Vol. 4). 1977. 48.75x (ISBN 3-11-006568-1). De Gruyter.
Halevy, D. Life of Friedrich Nietzsche. 59.95 (ISBN 0-8490-0529-9). Gordon Pr.
Harper, Ralph. The Seventh Solitude: Metaphysical Homelessness in Kierkegaard, Dostoevsky, & Nietzsche. LC 65-11662. 163p. 1965. 11.50x (ISBN 0-8018-0256-3); pap. 3.95 (ISBN 0-8018-0257-1). Johns Hopkins.
Hatab, Lawrence J. Nietzsche & Eternal Recurrence: The Redemption of Time & Becoming. LC 78-62266. 1978. pap. text ed. 7.75 (ISBN 0-8191-0564-3). U Pr of Amer.
Hayman, Ronald. Nietzsche. (Illus.). 1980. 19.95 (ISBN 0-19-520204-X). Oxford U Pr.
Heidegger, Martin. Nietzsche, 2 Vols. (Ger.). 1961. Set. 53.50 (ISBN 3-7885-0115-4). Adler.
--Nietzsche: The Will to Power As Art, Vol. 1. Krell, David F., tr. LC 78-19509. 1979. 12.95 (ISBN 0-06-063847-8, HarpR). Har-Row.
--Nietzsche: Vol. IV, Nihilism. Capuzzi, Frank, tr. from Ger. LC 78-19509. 352p. 1981. 16.95 (ISBN 0-06-063857-5, HarpR). Har-Row.
Heller, Erich. The Poet's Self & the Poem: Essays on Goethe, Nietzsche & Thomas Mann. 1976. text ed. 13.00x (ISBN 0-485-11164-0, Athlone Pr). Humanities.
Heller, Otto. Prophets of Dissent: Essays on Maeterlinck, Strindberg, Nietzsche & Tolstoy. LC 68-26246. 1968. Repr. of 1918 ed. 12.00 (ISBN 0-8046-0200-X). Kennikat.
Heller, Peter. Dialectics & Nihilism: Essays on Lessing, Nietzsche, Mann & Kafka. LC 65-26240. 1969. Repr. of 1966 ed. 15.00x (ISBN 0-87023-019-0). U of Mass Pr.
--Von Den ersten und letzten Dingen: Studien und Kommentar zu einer Aphorismenreihe von Friedrich Nietzsche. (Monographien und Texte zur Nietzsche-Forschung Vol. 1). 1972. 68.25x (ISBN 3-11-003943-5). De Gruyter.
Hollingdale, R. J. Nietzsche. (Author Guides Ser). 238p. 1973. 17.50x (ISBN 0-7100-7562-6); pap. 8.95 (ISBN 0-7100-7563-4). Routledge & Kegan.
Hubbard, Stanley. Nietzche und Emerson. LC 80-2538. Repr. of 1958 ed. 25.50 (ISBN 0-404-19264-5). AMS Pr.
Hubben, William. Dostoevsky, Kierkegaard, Nietzsche & Kafka. Orig. Title: Four Prophets of Our Destiny. 1962. pap. 1.95 (ISBN 0-02-065750-1, Collier). Macmillan.
Jaspers, Karl. Nietzsche: An Introduction to His Philosophical Activity. Wallraff, Charles F. & Schmitz, Frederick J., trs. LC 65-12660. (Orig.). 1969. pap. 6.95 (ISBN 0-89526-971-6). Regnery-Gateway.
--Nietzsche: Einfuehrung in das Verstaendnis seines Philosophierens. 4th ed. (Ger., Footnotes). 1974. 36.25x (ISBN 3-11-004892-2). De Gruyter.
--Reason & Existenz. Earle, William, tr. from Ger. pap. 3.95 (ISBN 0-374-50060-6, N117). FS&G.
Kashyap, Subhash C. The Unknown Nietzsche: His Socio-Political Thought & Legacy. 299p. 1970. 12.50x (ISBN 0-8002-2125-7). Intl Pubns Serv.
Kaufmann, W. Nietzsche: Philosopher, Psychologist, Antichrist. 4th ed. 1975. 30.00 (ISBN 0-691-07207-8); pap. 6.95 (ISBN 0-691-01983-5). Princeton U Pr.
Kennedy, J. M. Nietzsche. LC 73-21622. (Nietzsche Ser., No. 89). 1974. lib. bdg. 39.95 (ISBN 0-8383-1791-X). Haskell.
Knapp, Arthur. Friedrich Nietzsche. 59.95 (ISBN 0-8490-0200-1). Gordon Pr.
Knight, Arthur H. Some Aspects of the Life & Work of Nietzsche. LC 66-27192. 1967. Repr. of 1933 ed. 8.00 (ISBN 0-8462-1026-6). Russell.
Knight, G. Wilson. Christ & Nietzsche. 1948. lib. bdg. 15.00 (ISBN 0-8414-5590-2). Folcroft.
Krummel, Richard F. Nietzsche und der deutsche Geist: Ausbreitung und Wirkung des Nietzscheschen Werkes im Deutschen Sprachraum bis zum Todesjahr des Philosophen: ein Schrifttumsverzeichnis der Jahre 1867-1900. LC 72-81559. (Monographien und Texte Zur Nietzsche-Forschung, Vol. 3). 1974. 69.50x (ISBN 3-11-004019-0). De Gruyter.
Lavrin, Janko. Nietzsche: A Biographical Introduction. LC 79-174651. 1972. pap. 2.45 (ISBN 0-684-12672-9, SL320, ScribT). Scribner.
--Nietzsche & Modern Consciousness. LC 72-2094. (Studies in German Literature, No. 13). 1972. Repr. of 1922 ed. lib. bdg. 49.95 (ISBN 0-8383-1481-3). Haskell.
Love, Frederick R. Young Nietzsche & the Wagnerian Experience. LC 63-63585. (North Carolina. University. Studies in the Germanic Languages & Literatures: No. 39). Repr. of 1963 ed. 18.50 (ISBN 0-404-50939-8). AMS Pr.
Ludovici, A. M. Who Is to Be Master of the World? an Introduction to the Philosophy of Friedrich Nietzsche. 59.95 (ISBN 0-8490-1295-3). Gordon Pr.
Ludovici, Anthony M. Nietzsche & Art. LC 72-148824. (Studies in German Literature, No. 13). 1971. Repr. lib. bdg. 38.95 (ISBN 0-8383-1229-2). Haskell.

McDonough, B. T. Nietzsche & Kazantzakis. LC 78-61302. 1978. pap. text ed. 7.25 (ISBN 0-8191-0607-0). U Pr of Amer.

Magnus, Bernd. Nietzsche's Existential Imperative. LC 77-9864. (Studies in Phenomenology & Existential Philosophy Ser.). 256p. 1978. 17.50x (ISBN 0-253-34062-4). Ind U Pr.

Mann, Heinrich. The Living Thoughts of Nietzsche. Mendel, Alfred O., ed. 170p. 1981. Repr. of 1939 ed. lib. bdg. 20.00 (ISBN 0-89984-343-3). Century Bookbindery.

Manthey-Zorn, Otto. Dionysus: The Tragedy of Nietzsche. LC 75-14146. 210p. 1975. Repr. of 1956 ed. lib. bdg. 15.00x (ISBN 0-8371-8137-2, MADIO). Greenwood.

Mencken, Henry L. Gist of Nietzsche. LC 73-1156. 1910. lib. bdg. 10.00 (ISBN 0-8414-2306-7). Folcroft.

--The Philosophy of Frederich Nietzsche. 1978. Repr. of 1908 ed. lib. bdg. 30.00 (ISBN 0-8492-6719-6). R West.

Monarch Notes on Nietzsche's the Philosophy. 1965. pap. 2.75 (ISBN 0-671-00534-0). Monarch Pr.

Montinari, M., et al, eds. Nietzsche-Studien: Internationales Jahrbuch fur die Nietzsche-Forschung, Vol. 4. 466p. 1975. 82.75x (ISBN 3-11-005844-8). De Gruyter.

Morgan, George A., Jr. What Nietzsche Means. LC 74-2555. 408p. 1975. Repr. of 1943 ed. lib. bdg. 24.00x (ISBN 0-8371-7404-X, MOWN). Greenwood.

Mugge, M. Friedrich Nietzsche. 59.95 (ISBN 0-8490-0201-X). Gordon Pr.

Mugge, Maximilian A. Friedrich Nietzsche. LC 78-103207. 1970. Repr. of 1912 ed. 9.00 (ISBN 0-8046-0844-X). Kennikat.

Muhlenberg, William A. Plato, Nietzsche & the Insuperability of the Totalitarian State. (The Great Currents of History Library Book). (Illus.). 135p. 1981. 49.85 (ISBN 0-89266-307-3). Am Classical Coll Pr.

Neilson, Francis. The Nietzsche-Wagner Rift. 1979. lib. bdg. 39.95 (ISBN 0-685-96632-1). Revisionist Pr.

Nicholls, Roger A. Nietzsche in the Early Work of Thomas Mann. LC 73-89426. 119p. 1976. Repr. of 1955 ed. 12.00 (ISBN 0-8462-1770-8). Russell.

Nicolas, M. P. From Nietzsche Down to Hitler. LC 70-102579. 1970. Repr. of 1938 ed. 12.50 (ISBN 0-8046-0739-7). Kennikat.

Nietzche & Wagner. Nietzche-Wagner Correspondence. new ed. Foerster-Nietzche, Elizabeth, ed. Kerr, Caroline V., tr. from Ger. LC 72-131285. 1970. pap. 4.95 (ISBN 0-87140-030-8). Liveright.

Nietzsche, Briefwechsel, Kritische Gesamtausgabe: Section I. Incl. Vol. 3. Nietzsches Briefe Mai 1872-Dezember 1874. 48.00x (ISBN 3-11-007194-0); Vol. 4. Briefe an Nietzsche Mai 1872-Dezember 1874. 81.00x (ISBN 3-11-007196-7). 1978. De Gruyter.

Nietzsche, Friedrich. Briefwechsel: Kritische Gesamtausgabe, Section 1, Vols. 2 & 3. Incl. Vol. 2. September 1864 - April 1869. 48.75x (ISBN 3-11-006515-0); Vol. 3. October 1864 - March 1869. 45.00x (ISBN 3-11-006559-2). 1975. De Gruyter.

--Ecce Homo (Nietzsche's Autobiography) 1974. 100.00 (ISBN 0-87968-211-6). Gordon Pr.

--Index to Nietzsche. Guppy, Robert, ed. Cohn, Paul V., tr. 1974. lib. bdg. 100.00 (ISBN 0-87968-212-4). Gordon Pr.

--Nietzsche-Studien: Internationales Jahrbuch fuer Die Nietzsche - Forschung, Vol. 2. Montinari, Mazzino, et al, eds. vi, 368p. 1973. 53.50x (ISBN 3-11-004332-7). De Gruyter.

--Nietzsche-Studien: Internationales Jahrbuch fuer Die Nietzsche-Forschung, Vol. 3. Montinari, Mazzino, et al, eds. (Ger.). 1974. 48.75x (ISBN 3-11-004726-8). De Gruyter.

--Nietzsche Werke. Colli, Giorgio & Montinari, Mazzino, eds. Incl. Sect 4, Vol. 1. Richard Wagner in Bayreuth: Unzeitgemaesse Betrachtungen, Nummer 4; Nachgelassene Fragmente, Anfang 1875 bis Fruehjahr, 1876. iv, 366p. 1967. 24.00x (ISBN 3-11-005170-2); Sect 4, Vol. 2. Menschliches, Allzumenschliches: Band 1; Nachgelassene Fragmente, 1876 bis Winter, 1877-78. iv, 586p. 1967. 35.00x (ISBN 3-11-005171-0); Sect 4, Vol. 3. Menschliches, Allzumenschliches: Band 2; Nachgelassene Fragmente, Fruehling, 1878 Bis November, 1879. iv, 482p. 1967. 30.00x (ISBN 3-11-005172-9); Sect 4, Vol. 4. Nachbericht zur vierten Abteilung: Richard Wagner in Bayreuth; Menschliches, Allzumenschliches, Baende 1 & 2, Nachgelassene Fragmente, 1875-79. (Illus.). viii, 615p. 1969. 42.25x (ISBN 0-685-24224-2); Sect. 6, Vol 1. Also Sprach Zarathustra: Ein Buch fuer Alle und Keinen, 1883-85. iv, 410p. 1968. 25.75x (ISBN 3-11-005174-5); Sect. 6, Vol. 2. Jenseits von Gut und Boese; Zur Genealogie der Moral: 1886-87. iv, 436p. 1968. 27.00x (ISBN 3-11-005175-3); Sect. 6, Vol. 3. Der Fall Wagner; Goetzen-Daemmerung; Nachgelassene Schriften, August, 1888 bis Anfang Januar, 1889; der Antichrist; Ecce Homo; Dionysius-Dithyramben; Nietsche Contra Wagner. iv, 449p. 1969. 42.25x (ISBN 0-685-24225-0); Sect. 8, Vol. 2. Nachgelassene Fragmente: Herbst, 1887 bis Maerz, 1888. xii, 477p. 1970. 36.25x (ISBN 3-11-006393-X). (Ger.). De Gruyter.

--Nietzsche Werke, Kritische Gesamtausgabe, Sect. 3, Vol. 1: Die Geburt der Tragoedie. Unzeitgemaesse Betrachtungen I-III (1872-1874) Colli, Giorgio & Montinari, Mazzino, eds. iv, 427p. 1972. 42.25x (ISBN 3-11-004227-4). De Gruyter.

--Nietzsche Werke, Kritische Gesamtausgabe, Sect. 5, Vol. 1: Morgenroethe, Nachgelassene Fragmente Anfang 1880 bis Fruehjahr 1881. 1971. 48.75x (ISBN 3-11-001828-4). De Gruyter.

--Nietzsche Werke: Kritische Gesamtausgabe, Section 7, Vol. 3: Nachgelassene Fragmente Herbst 1884 bis Herbst 1885. iv, 476p. 1974. 57.25x (ISBN 3-11-004983-X). De Gruyter.

--Nietzsche Werke: Kritische Gesamtausgabe Sect. 8, Vol. 3: Nachgelasssene Fragmente Anfang 1888-Anfang Januar 1889. Colli, Giorgio & Montinari, Mazzino, eds. LC 68-84293. 484p. 1972. 46.25x (ISBN 3-11-004192-8). De Gruyter.

Nietzsche-Studien. (Internationale Jahrbuch Fur Die Nietzsche-Forschung: Vol. 5). 1976. 82.00x (ISBN 3-11-006656-4). De Gruyter.

Nietzsche-Studien, Vol. 6. 1977. 73.50x (ISBN 3-11-007166-5). De Gruyter.

Nietzsche Werke. Incl. Vol. 3, Section III. Nachgelassene Fragmente, 1869-1872. 55.00x (ISBN 3-11-007469-9); Vol. 4. Nachgelassene Fragmente, 1872-1873. 51.75x (ISBN 3-11-007471-0). 1978. De Gruyter.

O'Brien, E. J. Son of the Morning. 1973. Repr. of 1932 ed. 20.00 (ISBN 0-8274-1204-5). R West.

O'Flaherty, James C., et al, eds. Studies in Nietzsche & the Classical Tradition. (Germanic Languages & Literatures Ser: No. 85). 1976. 18.00x (ISBN 0-8078-8085-X). U of NC Pr.

Orage, A. R. Nietzsche in Outline & Aphorism. 59.95 (ISBN 0-8490-0733-X). Gordon Pr.

Pasley, Malcolm, ed. Nietzsche: Imagery & Thought. LC 77-85748. 1978. 26.50x (ISBN 0-520-03577-1). U of Cal Pr.

Pfeffer, Rose. Nietzsche: Disciple of Dionysus. LC 76-178041. 297p. 1972. 18.00 (ISBN 0-8387-1069-7). Bucknell U Pr.

Podach, E. The Madness of Nietzsche. 69.95 (ISBN 0-87968-179-9). Gordon Pr.

Reichert, Herbert W. Friedrich Nietzsche's Impact on Modern German Literature. (Studies in Comparative Literature Ser.: No. 84). 1975. 10.50x (ISBN 0-8078-8084-1). U of NC Pr.

Reichert, Herbert W. & Schlechta, Karl, eds. International Nietzsche Bibliography. (Studies in Comparative Literature Ser.: No. 45). 1969. 11.50x (ISBN 0-8078-7045-5). U of NC Pr.

Reyburn, H. A., et al. Nietzsche: The Story of a Human Philosopher. 499p. 1973. Repr. of 1948 ed. lib. bdg. 24.50x (ISBN 0-8371-6674-8, RENI). Greenwood.

Richardson, Larry N. The Philosophy of Nietzsche in Dramatic Representational Expressions. (Essence of the Great Philosophers Ser.). (Illus.). 134p. 1981. 31.45 (ISBN 0-89266-277-8). Am Classical Coll Pr.

Rivinak, Joseph D. Schopenhauer, Nietzsche, & the Individual, Social, Political & International Conditions of the Modern World. (The Essential Library of the Great Philosophers). (Illus.). 113p. 1981. 41.35 (ISBN 0-89266-305-7). Am Classical Coll Pr.

Roettges, Heinz. Nietzsche und die Dialektik der Aufklaerung. (Monographien und Texte zur Nietzsche-Forschung, Vol. 2). 1972. 61.00x (ISBN 3-11-004018-2). De Gruyter.

Rosenberg, Alfred. Nietzsche. 1975. lib. bdg. 59.95 (ISBN 0-8490-0732-1). Gordon Pr.

Shestov, Lev. Dostoevsky, Tolstoy & Nietzsche. Martin, Bernard & Roberts, Spencer E., trs. LC 74-78504. xxx, 322p. 1969. 16.00x (ISBN 0-8214-0053-3). Ohio U Pr.

Silk, M. S. & Stern, J. P. Nietzsche on Tragedy. LC 80-40433. 500p. 1981. 56.50 (ISBN 0-521-23262-7). Cambridge U Pr.

Solomon, Robert C., ed. Nietzsche: A Collection of Critical Essays. LC 80-10457. (Modern Studies in Philosophy). 400p. text ed. 20.00 (ISBN 0-268-01454-X); pap. text ed. 6.95 (ISBN 0-268-01455-8). U of Notre Dame Pr.

Stavrou, C. N. Whitman & Nietzsche: A Comparative Study of Their Thought. LC 64-65034. (North Carolina University. Studies in the Germanic Languages & Literatures: No. 48). Repr. of 1964 ed. 18.50 (ISBN 0-404-50948-7). AMS Pr.

Stern, J. P. Friedrich Nietzsche. (Penguin Modern Masters Ser.). 1979. pap. 3.95 (ISBN 0-14-005168-6). Penguin.

--A Study of Nietzsche. LC 78-54328. (Major European Authors Ser.). Date not set. pap. price not set (ISBN 0-521-28380-9). Cambridge U Pr.

--A Study of Nietzsche. LC 78-54328. (Major European Authors Ser.). 1979. 26.95 (ISBN 0-521-22126-9). Cambridge U Pr.

Strong, Tracy B. Friedrich Nietzche & the Politics of Transfiguration. LC 74-81442. 380p. 1976. 28.50x (ISBN 0-520-02810-4). U of Cal Pr.

Valery, Paul. Quatre Lettres au Sujet de Nietzsche. 6.95 (ISBN 0-685-36623-5). French & Eur.

Van Riessen, H. Nietzsche. (Modern Thinkers Ser.). pap. 1.25 (ISBN 0-87552-587-3). Presby & Reformed.

NIGER EXPEDITION, 1841

Allen, William & Thomson, T. R. Narrative of the Expedition Sent by Her Majesty's Government to the River Niger in 1841, 2 Vols. (Illus.). Repr. of 1848 ed. Set. 69.50 (ISBN 0-384-00803-8). Johnson Repr.

NIGER RIVER

Allen, William & Thomson, T. R. Narrative of the Expedition Sent by Her Majesty's Government to the River Niger in 1841, 2 Vols. (Illus.). Repr. of 1848 ed. Set. 69.50 (ISBN 0-384-00803-8). Johnson Repr.

Baikie, W. B. Narrative of an Exploring Voyage up to the Rivers Kuora & Binue Commonly Known As the Niger & Tsadda in 1854. new ed. 456p. 1966. 32.50x (ISBN 0-7146-1788-1, F Cass Co). Biblio Dist.

Basden, G. T. Niger Ibos. (Illus.). 456p. 1966. Repr. of 1938 ed. 27.50x (ISBN 0-7146-1632-X, F Cass Co). Biblio Dist.

De Gramont, Sanche. The Strong Brown God: The Story of the Niger River. LC 75-33298. 356p. 1976. 12.50 (ISBN 0-395-19782-1). HM.

Forde, D., ed. Peoples of the Niger-Benue Confluence. LC 78-23171. (International African Institute Ethnographic Survey of Africa Ser.). (Illus.). 1970. pap. 15.00x (ISBN 0-8002-0260-0). Intl Pubns Serv.

Jenness, Aylette. Along the Niger River: An African Way of Life. LC 73-20061. (Illus.). (gr. 5-12). 1974. 8.95 (ISBN 0-690-00514-8, TYC-J). Har-Row.

Nzewunwa, Nwanna. The Niger Delta: Aspects of Its Prehistoric Economy & Culture. (Cambridge Monographs in African Archaeology: No. 1). 60.00x (ISBN 0-86054-083-9, Pub. by BAR). State Mutual Bks.

Park, Mungo. Travels in the Interior Districts of Africa. LC 70-116312. 362p. 1973. Repr. of 1813 ed. 27.00 (ISBN 0-403-00338-5). Scholarly.

Thomson, Joseph. Mungo Park & the Niger. (Illus.). 1970. Repr. of 1890 ed. 15.00 (ISBN 0-87266-040-0). Argosy.

Watson, Jane W. The Niger: Africa's River of Mystery. LC 76-135581. (Rivers of the World Ser.). (Illus.). (gr. 4-7). 1971. PLB 3.68 (ISBN 0-8116-6374-4). Garrard.

NIGERIA

Akpabot, Samuel E. Ibibi Music in Nigerian Culture. (Illus.). 140p. 1975. 7.50x (ISBN 0-87013-193-1). Mich St U Pr.

Anamaleze, John, Jr. The Nigerian Press: The People's Conscience? 1978. 6.95 (ISBN 0-533-03788-3). Vantage.

Balewa, Alhaji A. Nigeria Speaks: Speeches Made Between 1957 & 1964. Epelle, Sam, compiled by. 1964. text ed. 6.00x (ISBN 0-582-64017-2). Humanities.

Coleman, James S. Nigeria: Background to Nationalism. LC 58-10286. (California Library Reprint Series: No. 28). 1971. 35.75x (ISBN 0-520-02070-7). U of Cal Pr.

Communication Policies in Nigeria. 67p. 1980. pap. 4.75 (ISBN 92-3-101743-8, U 1002, UNESCO). Unipub.

Crowder, Michael. The Story of Nigeria. 4th ed. 432p. 1978. 17.95 (ISBN 0-571-04946-X, Pub. by Faber & Faber); pap. 9.95 (ISBN 0-571-04947-8). Merrimack Bk Serv.

Damachi, Ukandi G. Nigerian Modernization. LC 75-183394. 160p. 1972. 7.95 (ISBN 0-89388-030-2). Okpaku Communications.

Hazzledine, George D. White Man in Nigeria. LC 74-78370. (Illus.). Repr. of 1904 ed. 14.50x (ISBN 0-8371-1338-5). Greenwood.

Ikime, Obaro. Nana of the Niger Delta. (African Historical Biographies Ser.). pap. text ed. 2.75x (ISBN 0-435-94465-7). Heinemann Ed.

Kirk-Greene, A. H. M., ed. Gazetteers of the Northern Provinces of Nigeria, 4 vols. rev. ed. Incl. Vol. 1. The Hausa Emirates. 232p. 40.00x (ISBN 0-7146-2933-2); Vol. 2. The Eastern Kingdoms. 264p. 40.00x (ISBN 0-7146-2934-0); Vol. 3. The Central Kingdoms. 264p. 40.00x (ISBN 0-7146-2539-6); Vol. 4. The Highland Chieftaincies. rev. ed. 368p. 40.00x (ISBN 0-7146-2936-7). (Illus.). 1972. 160.00x set (ISBN 0-7146-1665-6, F Cass Co). Biblio Dist.

Ogunsola, Albert F. Legislation & Education in Northern Nigeria. (Illus.). 124p. 1975. 9.95x (ISBN 0-19-575237-6). Oxford U Pr.

Orimoloya, S. A. Biographia Nigeriana: A Biographical Dictionary of Eminent Nigerians. (Reference Publications Ser.). 1977. lib. bdg. 40.00 (ISBN 0-8161-8049-0). G K Hall.

Smock, David R. & Smock, Audrey C. Cultural & Political Aspects of Rural Transformation: A Case Study of Eastern Nigeria. LC 71-165837. (Special Studies in International Economics & Development). 1972. 39.50x (ISBN 0-89197-716-3). Irvington.

NIGERIA–ANTIQUITIES

Connah, Graham. Three Thousand Years in Africa: Man & His Environment in the Lake Chad Region of Nigeria. LC 79-41508. (New Studies in Archaeology). (Illus.). 268p. 1981. 59.50 (ISBN 0-521-22848-4). Cambridge U Pr.

Shaw, Thurstan. Igbo-Ukwu, 2 vols. (Illus.). 888p. 1970. 68.00 set (ISBN 0-686-31721-1, Pub. by Faber & Faber). Vol. 1 (ISBN 0-571-09123-7). Vol. 2 (ISBN 0-571-09124-5). Merrimack Bk Serv.

--Nigeria. (Illus.). 1978. 16.95 (ISBN 0-500-02086-8). Thames Hudson.

Stevens, Phillips, Jr. The Stone Images of Esie, Nigeria. (Illus.). 398p. 1979. text ed. 65.00x (ISBN 0-8419-9850-7, Ibadan University Press & the Nigerian Federal Department of Antiquities). Holmes & Meier.

Willet, Frank & Eyo, Ekpo. Treasures of Ancient Nigeria. LC 79-3497. (Illus.). 1980. 18.95 (ISBN 0-394-50975-7); pap. 11.95 (ISBN 0-394-73858-6). Knopf.

NIGERIA–BIBLIOGRAPHY

Baum, Edward, compiled by. A Comprehensive Periodical Bibliography of Nigeria: 1960-1970. LC 75-620025. (Papers in International Studies: Africa: No. 24). 1975. pap. 13.00x (ISBN 0-89680-057-1). Ohio U Ctr Intl.

Ita, Nduntuei O., ed. Bibliography of Nigeria: Survey of Anthropological & Linguistic Writings from the Earliest Times to Nineteen Sixty-Six. 273p. 1971. 45.00x (ISBN 0-7146-2458-6, F Cass Co). Biblio Dist.

Tilman, Robert O. & Cole, Taylor, eds. Nigerian Political Scene. LC 62-18315. (Commonwealth Studies Center: No. 17). 1962. 17.75 (ISBN 0-8223-0178-4). Duke.

NIGERIA–CENSUS, 1921

Census of Nigeria, 1931, 7 vols. in 6. LC 74-15073. Repr. of 1934 ed. Set. 285.00 (ISBN 0-404-12117-9). AMS Pr.

Meek, Charles K. Northern Tribes of Nigeria, 2 vols. LC 78-97428. (Illus.). Repr. of 1925 ed. 39.00x (ISBN 0-8371-2737-8, Pub. by Negro U Pr). Greenwood.

NIGERIA–DESCRIPTION AND TRAVEL

Allen, William & Thomson, T. R. H. A Narrative of the Expedition Sent by Her Majesty's Government to the River Niger in 1841 Under the Command of Captain H.D. Trotter, 2 vols. 1968. Repr. of 1848 ed. Set. 85.00x (ISBN 0-7146-1784-9, F Cass Co). Biblio Dist.

Balagum, Olga. Nigeria. Magic of a Land. (Illus.). 1980. 60.00 (ISBN 2-85258-106-X). Hippocrene Bks.

Delany, M. R. & Campbell, Robert. Search for a Place: Black Separatism & Africa, 1860. Bell, Howard, ed. 1971. pap. 2.25 (ISBN 0-472-06179-8, AA). U of Mich Pr.

Faw, Chalmer, ed. Lardin Gabas: A Land, a People, a Church. new ed. (Illus.). 128p. 1973. 2.50 (ISBN 0-87178-511-0). Brethren.

Lanier, Alison R. Update -- Nigeria. LC 80-83925. (Country Orientation Ser.). 1980. pap. text ed. 25.00x (ISBN 0-933662-27-0). Intercult Pr.

Leith-Ross, Sylvia. Beyond the Niger. LC 79-142917. (Illus.). 1972. Repr. of 1951 ed. 10.50x (ISBN 0-8371-5943-1, Pub. by Negro U Pr). Greenwood.

Robinson, Charles H. Nigeria, Our Latest Protectorate. LC 69-16569. Repr. of 1900 ed. 18.00x (ISBN 0-8371-1542-6, Pub. by Negro U Pr). Greenwood.

Rosenberger, Homer T. Letters from Africa. LC 65-16638. 209p. 1965. pap. 3.50 (ISBN 0-917264-04-5). Rose Hill.

Talbot, Percy A. In the Shadow of the Bush. LC 73-79821. (Illus.). Repr. of 1912 ed. 35.00x (ISBN 0-8371-1468-3, Pub. by Negro U Pr). Greenwood.

--Tribes of the Niger Delta: Their Religions & Customs. (Illus.). 350p. 1967. Repr. of 1932 ed. 32.50x (ISBN 0-7146-1013-5, F Cass Co). Biblio Dist.

Tolman, Newton F. Our Loons Are Always Laughing. Repr. of 1963 ed. lib. bdg. 12.05x (ISBN 0-89190-951-6). Am Repr-Rivercity Pr.

Udo, Reuben K. Geographical Regions of Nigeria. LC 70-94980. (Illus.). 1970. 31.50x (ISBN 0-520-01588-6). U of Cal Pr.

Violi, Paul. Harmatan: A Poem. LC 77-3648. 1977. pap. 4.00 (ISBN 0-915342-24-3). Sun.

NIGERIA–COMMERCE

Belasco, Bernard. The Entrepreneur As Culture Hero: Preadaptations for Nigerian Economic Development. LC 79-10475. (Illus.). 256p. 1980. 23.95 (ISBN 0-03-052096-7). Praeger.

Lawn, M., ed. Major Companies of Nigeria 1980. 225p. 1980. 66.00x (ISBN 0-86010-230-0, Pub. by Graham & Trotman England); 55.00x (ISBN 0-86010-197-5). State Mutual Bk.

Major Companies of Nigeria 1979. 1979. 57.00x (ISBN 0-685-94073-X). Nichols Pub.

Major Companies of Nigeria 1980. 1980. 69.00 (ISBN 0-531-03943-9); pap. 58.00 (ISBN 0-531-03949-8). Watts.

Metra Consulting. Nigeria. (Business Opportunity Report Ser.). 300p. 1980. 275.00x (ISBN 0-686-64703-3, Pub. by Graham & Trotman England). State Mutual Bk.

Okigbo, P. N. Nigeria's Financial System. (Illus.). 320p. 1981. text ed. 25.00x (ISBN 0-582-59733-1). Longman.

Oxford University Press & Graham & Trotman Ltd. Business Map of Nigeria. 1979. 15.50x (ISBN 0-86010-194-0, Pub. by Graham & Trotman England). State Mutual Bk.

Rogers, M. Business Laws & Practices of Nigeria. 300p. 1980. 110.00x (ISBN 0-86010-216-5, Pub. by Graham & Trotman England). State Mutual Bk.

NIGERIA–ECONOMIC CONDITIONS

Ajayi, Simeon & Ojo, Oladeji O. Money & Banking Analysis & Policy in the Nigerian Context. (Illus.). 272p. 1981. pap. text ed. 13.50x (ISBN 0-04-330318-8). Allen Unwin.

Anaejionu, Paul. X-Ray Diffraction Study to Assess the Potential Economic-Pharmaceutical Uses for Nigerian Clays. (Science & Development in Africa Ser.). 1979. pap. 10.00x (ISBN 0-914970-22-4). Conch Mag.

Balbkins, Nicholas. Indigenization & Economic Development: The Nigerian Experience, Vol. 33. Altman, Edward I. & Walter, Ingo, eds. LC 81-81654. (Contemporary Studies in Economic & Financial Analysis). 300p. 1981. 32.50 (ISBN 0-89232-227-6). Jai Pr.

Berry, Sara S. Cocoa, Custom, & Socio-Economic Change in Rural Western Nigeria. (Oxford Studies in African Affairs Ser). (Illus.). 256p. 1975. 48.00x (ISBN 0-19-821697-1). Oxford U Pr.

Bienen, Henry & Diejomaoh, V. P., eds. The Political Economy of Income Distribution in Nigeria. LC 80-16860. (The Political Economy of Income Distribution in Developing Countries Ser.: No. 2). 500p. 1981. text ed. 49.50x (ISBN 0-8419-0618-1). Holmes & Meier.

Calvert, Albert F. Nigeria & Its Tin Fields. Wilkins, Mira, ed. LC 76-29763. (European Business Ser.). (Illus.). 1977. Repr. of 1910 ed. lib. bdg. 24.00x (ISBN 0-405-09778-6). Arno.

Directory of Incorporated (Registered) Companies in Nigeria 1912-1974. LC 74-647895. 351p. 1970. 12.50x (ISBN 0-8002-0620-7). Intl Pubns Serv.

Eicher, Carl K. & Liedholm, Carl, eds. Growth & Development of the Nigerian Economy. 445p. 1970. text ed. 12.50x (ISBN 0-87013-147-8). Mich St U Pr.

Ekundare, R. O. Economic History of Nigeria 1860-1960. LC 72-94209. 480p. 1973. text ed. 29.50x (ISBN 0-8419-0135-X, Africana). Holmes & Meier.

Freund, Bill. Capital & Labour in the Nigerian Tin Mines. (Ibadan History Ser.). 1980. text ed. write for info. (ISBN 0-391-02155-9). Humanities.

Hill, Polly. Population, Prosperity, & Poverty. LC 77-23167. (Illus.). 1977. 27.50 (ISBN 0-521-21511-0). Cambridge U Pr.

--Rural Hausa: A Village & a Setting. LC 75-161287. 1972. 34.50 (ISBN 0-521-08242-0). Cambridge U Pr.

Hogendorn, J. S. Nigerian Groundnut Exports: Origins & Early Developments. (Illus.). 1979. 29.95x (ISBN 0-19-575443-3). Oxford U Pr.

Igbozurike, Martin. Problem-Generating Structures in Nigeria's Rural Development. 1976. pap. text ed. 11.00x (ISBN 0-8419-9721-7). Holmes & Meier.

International Bank for Reconstruction & Development. Economic Development of Nigeria. LC 77-86382. Repr. of 1960 ed. 57.50 (ISBN 0-404-60308-4). AMS Pr.

International Labour Office with Jobs & Skills Programme for Africa. First Things First: Meeting the Basic Needs of the People of Nigeria. Report to the Government of Nigeria by a JASPA Basic Needs Mission. x, 256p. (Orig.). 1981. pap. 13.00 (ISBN 92-2-102682-5). Intl Labour Office.

Maclean, Ian & Arnold, Guy. Statistical Guide to the Nigerian Market. 1978. 62.50 (ISBN 0-85038-107-X, Pub by Kogan Pg). Nichols Pub.

Nafzinger, E. Wayne. African Capitalism: A Case Study in Nigerian Entrepreneurship. LC 76-48484. (Publication Ser: No. 169). (Illus.). 1977. 11.95 (ISBN 0-8179-6691-9). Hoover Inst Pr.

Nigeria: Options for Long Term Development. (IBRD Country Economic Reports). 1974. 19.00x (ISBN 0-8018-1602-5); pap. 6.00x (ISBN 0-8018-1603-3). Johns Hopkins.

Nigerian Cocoa Marketing Board, et al. Nigerian Cocoa Farmers. LC 70-142920. (Illus.). xxxix, 744p. Repr. of 1956 ed. lib. bdg. 28.00x (ISBN 0-8371-5946-6, NCF&). Greenwood.

Nnoli, Okwudiba, ed. Path to Nigerian Development. 360p. 1981. pap. 9.95 (ISBN 0-86232-021-6, Pub. by Zed Pr England). Lawrence Hill.

Nwanko, G. O. The Nigerian Financial System. 400p. 1980. text ed. 43.50x (ISBN 0-8419-5076-8). Holmes & Meier.

Odetola, Theophilus O. Military Politics in Nigeria: Economic Development & Political Stability. LC 76-58232. (Illus.). 1978. 14.95 (ISBN 0-87855-100-X). Transaction Bks.

Olaloku, F. Akin, et al. The Structure of the Nigerian Economy. LC 78-14765. 1979. 19.95x (ISBN 0-312-76777-3). St Martin.

Onoh, J. K., ed. The Foundations of Nigeria's Financial Infrastructure. 318p. 1980. 50.00x (ISBN 0-7099-0448-7, Pub. by Croom Helm Ltd England). Biblio Dist.

Peace, Adrian J. Choice, Class & Conflict: A Study of Southern Nigerian Factory Workers. LC 79-12658. (Harvester Studies in African Political Economy.). 1979. text ed. 38.75x (ISBN 0-391-01027-1). Humanities.

Pearson, Scott R. Petroleum & the Nigerian Economy. LC 76-130830. 1970. 12.50x (ISBN 0-8047-0749-9). Stanford U Pr.

Perham, M. F. The Economics of Tropical Dependency, 2 vols. 1976. lib. bdg. 200.00 (ISBN 0-8490-1748-3). Gordon Pr.

Schatz, Sayre P. Nigerian Capitalism. LC 74-16718. 1978. 33.75x (ISBN 0-520-02859-7). U of Cal Pr.

Tilman, Robert O. & Cole, Taylor, eds. Nigerian Political Scene. LC 62-18315. (Commonwealth Studies Center: No. 17). 1962. 17.75 (ISBN 0-8223-0178-4). Duke.

Uyanga, Joseph T. A Geography of Rural Development in Nigeria. LC 79-9601. 188p. 1980. pap. text ed. 9.00 (ISBN 0-8191-0956-8). U Pr of Amer.

Van Apeldoorn, G. Jan. Perspectives on Drought & Famine in Nigeria. write for info. Allen Unwin.

Williams, Gavin, ed. Nigeria: Economy & Society. 226p. 1976. 17.50x (ISBN 0-8476-1429-8). Rowman.

NIGERIA–FOREIGN RELATIONS

Akinyemi, A. Bolaji, ed. Nigeria & the World: Readings in the Nigerian Foreign Policy. 166p. 1979. text ed. 28.00 (ISBN 0-19-575444-1). Oxford U Pr.

Aluko, Olajide. Essays on Nigerian Foreign Policy. write for info. Allen Unwin.

Aluko, Olajide, ed. Ghana & Nigeria 1957-1970: A Study in Inter-African Discord. LC 75-1614. (Illus.). 275p. 1976. text ed. 18.50x (ISBN 0-06-490163-7). B&N.

Davis, Morris. Interpreters for Nigeria: The Third World & International Public Relations. LC 77-2345. 208p. 1977. 12.50 (ISBN 0-252-00552-X). U of Ill Pr.

Ohaegbulam, Festus U. Nigeria & the U. N. Mission to the Democratic Republic of the Congo: A Case Study of the Formative Stages of Nigeria's Foreign Policy. 1981. write for info. (ISBN 0-8130-0709-7). U Presses Fla.

NIGERIA–HISTORY

Adewoye, O. The Judicial System in Southern Nigeria, 1854-1954: Law & Justice in a Dependency. (Ibadan History Ser.). 1977. text ed. 17.00x (ISBN 0-391-00735-1). Humanities.

Afigbo, A. E. Some Thoughts on History Teaching in Nigeria & Other Essays. LC 79-88988. 1979. 20.50 (ISBN 0-686-52504-3). NOK Pubs.

Ajayi, J. F. Milestones in Nigerian History. new ed. (Illus.). 1980. pap. text ed. 2.95x (ISBN 0-582-60363-3). Longman.

Anene, J. C. Southern Nigeria in Transition, Eighteen Eighty-Five - Nineteen Six. 1966. 29.95 (ISBN 0-521-04033-7). Cambridge U Pr.

Asiwaju, A. I. Western Yorubaland Under European Rule 1889-1945. LC 76-10146. (Ibadan History Ser). 1976. text ed. 14.74x (ISBN 0-391-00605-3). Humanities.

Atanda, J. A. The New Oyo Empire: A Study of British Indirect Rule in Oyo Province 1894-1934. (Ibadan History Ser.). (Illus.). 332p. 1973. text ed. 12.50x (ISBN 0-391-00252-X). Humanities.

Ayandele, E. A. Nigerian Historical Studies. 305p. 1979. 27.50x (ISBN 0-7146-3113-2, F Cass Co). Biblio Dist.

Balagum, Olga. Nigeria, Magic of a Land. (Illus.). 1980. 60.00 (ISBN 2-85258-106-X). Hippocrene Bks.

Bradbury, R. E. Benin Studies. Morton-Williams, Peter, intro. by. (International African Institute Ser). (Illus.). 1973. pap. 17.50x (ISBN 0-19-724198-0). Oxford U Pr.

Burns, Alan. History of Nigeria. 1972. pap. text ed. 17.95x (ISBN 0-04-966014-4). Allen Unwin.

Burns, Alan C. History of Nigeria. 1976. lib. bdg. 59.95 (ISBN 0-8490-1981-8). Gordon Pr.

Cook, Arthur N. British Enterprise in Nigeria. 330p. 1964. Repr. of 1943 ed. 27.50x (ISBN 0-7146-1644-3, F Cass Co). Biblio Dist.

Crowder, Michael. Revolt in Bussa. (Illus.). 274p. 1973. 12.95 (ISBN 0-571-09395-7, Pub. by Faber & Faber). Merrimack Bk Serv.

Dudley, Billy J. Murtala Muhammed. 1981. 27.50x (ISBN 0-7146-3130-2, F Cass Co). Biblio Dist.

English, Maurice C. Outline of Nigerian History. (Illus., Orig.). 1959. pap. text ed. 2.25x (ISBN 0-582-60241-6). Humanities.

Geary, William M. Nigeria Under British Rule. 312p. 1965. 27.50x (ISBN 0-7146-1666-4, F Cass Co). Biblio Dist.

Ifemesia, C. C. Southeastern Nigeria in the Nineteenth Century. LC 78-55572. 1978. pap. 3.95 (ISBN 0-88357-066-1). NOK Pubs.

Ikime, Obaro. The Fall of Nigeria: The British Conquest. (Illus.). 1977. text ed. 15.00x (ISBN 0-8419-5318-X). Holmes & Meier.

Isichei, Elizabeth, ed. Studies in the History of Plateau State, Nigeria. (Illus.). 1979. text ed. 45.00x (ISBN 0-333-26931-4). Humanities.

Kirk-Greene, A H., ed. Lugard & the Amalgamation of Nigeria: A Documentary Record. 281p. 1968. 32.50x (ISBN 0-7146-1685-0, F Cass Co). Biblio Dist.

Kirk-Greene, Anthony & Rimmer, Douglas. Nigeria Since Nineteen Seventy: A Political & Economic Outline. LC 81-3609. 176p. 1981. text ed. 25.00x (ISBN 0-8419-0721-8, Africana); pap. text ed. 12.50x (ISBN 0-8419-0712-9). Holmes & Meier.

Luckham, Robin. Nigerian Military: A Sociological Analysis of Authority & Revolt, 1960-67. (African Studies: No. 4). (Illus.). 1971. 39.95 (ISBN 0-521-08129-7); pap. 11.95x (ISBN 0-521-09882-3). Cambridge U Pr.

Nair, Kannan K. The Origins & Development of Efik Settlements: Southeastern Nigeria. LC 75-620111. (Papers in International Studies: Southeast Asia: No. 26). (Illus.). 1976. pap. 4.00 (ISBN 0-89680-059-8). Ohio U Ctr Intl.

Nkemdirim, Bernard. Social Change & Political Violence in Colonial Nigeria. 1976. text ed. 6.25x (ISBN 0-7223-0693-8). Verry.

Northrup, David. Trade Without Rulers: Pre-Colonial Economic Development in South-Eastern Nigeria. (Studies in African Affairs). (Illus.). 1978. 47.50x (ISBN 0-19-822712-4). Oxford U Pr.

Nwabara. Iboland: A Century of Conflict with Britain 1860-1960. (Illus.). 1978. pap. text ed. 14.50x (ISBN 0-391-00552-9). Humanities.

Obichere, Boniface I., ed. Studies in Southern Nigerian History. 278p. 1981. 28.50x (ISBN 0-7146-3106-X, F Cass Co). Biblio Dist.

Okoli, Ekwueme F. Institutional Structure & Conflict in Nigeria. LC 79-3425. 1980. pap. text ed. 7.75 (ISBN 0-8191-0888-X). U Pr of Amer.

Orr, Sir C. Making of Northern Nigeria. 2nd ed. (Illus.). 306p. 1965. 27.50x (ISBN 0-7146-1707-5, F Cass Co). Biblio Dist.

Osuntokun, Akinjide. Nigeria in the First World War. (Ibadan History Ser.). 1979. text ed. 30.75x (ISBN 0-391-00916-8). Humanities.

Oyediran, Oyeleye. Survey of Nigerian Affairs, Nineteen Seventy-Five. (Illus.). 364p. 1979. text ed. 49.95x (ISBN 0-19-575450-6). Oxford U Pr.

Smith, Robert S. The Lagos Consulate, 1851-1861. 1979. 26.75x (ISBN 0-520-03746-4). U of Cal Pr.

Thom, Derrick J. The Niger-Nigerian Boundary: 1890-1906. LC 75-620024. (Papers in International Studies: Africa: No. 23). (Illus.). 1975. pap. 4.75 (ISBN 0-89680-056-3). Ohio U Ctr Intl.

Uwechue, Raph. Reflections on the Nigerian Civil War: Facing the Future. LC 71-105095. 1971. 17.50x (ISBN 0-8419-0037-X, Africana). Holmes & Meier.

Wellington, Dorothy Violet. Sir George Goldie, Founder of Nigeria: A Memoir. Wilkins, Mira, ed. LC 76-29765. (European Business Ser.). (Illus.). 1977. Repr. of 1934 ed. lib. bdg. 13.00x (ISBN 0-405-09779-4). Arno.

White, Jeremy J. Central Administration in Nigeria, Nineteen Fourteen to Nineteen Fifty-One: The Problem of Polarity. 250p. Date not set. 39.00x (ISBN 0-686-28430-5, Pub. by Irish Academic Pr Ireland). Biblio Dist.

NIGERIA–HISTORY–CIVIL WAR, 1967-1969

Aguolu, Christian. Nigerian Civil War, 1967-1970: An Annotated Bibliography. (Seventy Ser.). 197p. 1973. lib. bdg. 9.50 (ISBN 0-8161-1074-3). G K Hall.

Akpan, Ntieyong U. Struggle for Succession, 1966-1970: Personal Account of the Nigerian Civil War. 220p. 1972. 24.00x (ISBN 0-7146-2930-8, F Cass Co); pap. 9.95x (ISBN 0-7146-2949-9). Biblio Dist.

Cervenka, Zdenek. The Nigerian War: 1967-70. LC 73-885548. (Illus.). 459p. 1971. pap. 40.00x (ISBN 3-7637-0210-5). Intl Pubns Serv.

De St. Jorre, John. The Brothers' War: Biafra & Nigeria. 1972. 10.00 (ISBN 0-395-13934-1). HM.

Gold, Herbert. Biafra Goodbye. (Orig.). 1970. pap. 4.25 (ISBN 0-685-04864-0, Pub. by Twowindows Pr). SBD.

Obasanjo, Olusegun. My Command. 1981. text ed. 30.00x (ISBN 0-435-96533-6). Heinemann Ed.

Okpaku, Joseph, ed. Nigeria, Dilemma of Nationhood: An African Analysis of the Biafran Conflict. LC 78-111266. (Contributions in Afro-American & African Studies: No. 12). 1971. lib. bdg. 19.95 (ISBN 0-8371-4668-2, OKN/). Greenwood.

St. Jorre, John De. The Nigerian Civil War. (Illus.). 437p. 1972. 17.50x (ISBN 0-340-12640-X). Intl Pubns Serv.

--The Nigerian Civil War. (Illus.). 437p. 1972. 17.50x (ISBN 0-340-12640-X). Intl Pubns Serv.

Schabowska, Henryka & Himmelstrand, Ulf. Africa Reports on the Nigerian Crisis: News, Attitudes & Background Information. (Scandinavian Institute of African Studies, Uppsala). 1979. text ed. 23.50x (ISBN 0-8419-9733-0). Holmes & Meier.

Stremlau, John J. The International Politics of the Nigerian Civil War, 1967-1970. LC 76-24298. 1977. text ed. 32.50 (ISBN 0-691-07587-5); pap. 12.50 (ISBN 0-691-10051-9). Princeton U Pr.

NIGERIA–HISTORY–SOURCES

Hodgkin, Thomas, ed. Nigerian Perspectives: An Historical Anthology. 2nd ed. 450p. 1975. 15.95x (ISBN 0-19-215434-6). Oxford U Pr.

NIGERIA–JUVENILE LITERATURE

Carpenter, Allan. Nigeria. LC 77-2093. (Enchantment of Africa Ser.). (Illus.). (gr. 5 up). 1978. PLB 10.60 (ISBN 0-516-04579-2). Childrens.

Ikime, Obaro. Chief Dogho of Warri. (African Historical Biographics Ser.). (Illus.). 48p. 1977. pap. text ed. 2.75x (ISBN 0-435-94473-8). Heinemann Ed.

Johnston, Rhod O. Iyabo of Nigeria. (Illus.). (gr. 5-12). 1973. pap. 3.75 (ISBN 0-914522-01-9, 163808). Alpha Iota.

Latchem, Colin. Looking at Nigeria. LC 75-15967. (Looking at Other Countries Ser.). (gr. 4-7). 1976. 8.95 (ISBN 0-397-31652-6, JBL-J). Har-Row.

NIGERIA–LANGUAGES

Bendor-Samuel, John. Ten Nigerian Tone Languages. (Language Data, African Ser.: No. 4). 129p. 1974. pap. 3.00x (ISBN 0-88312-604-4); microfiche 1.60 (ISBN 0-88312-704-0). Summer Inst Ling.

Dunstan, Elizabeth. Twelve Nigerian Languages. LC 70-95611. (Orig.). 1969. pap. text ed. 8.95x (ISBN 0-8419-0031-0, Africana). Holmes & Meier.

Hansford, Kier, et al. Index of Nigerian Languages. (Studies in Nigerian Languages: No. 5). (Illus.). 204p. (Orig.). 1978. pap. 3.75 (ISBN 0-88312-613-3); microfiche 2.80 (ISBN 0-88312-713-X). Summer Inst Ling.

Newton, Sir Isaac. Mathematical Principles of Natural Philosophy and His System of the World. (Principia) Cajori, Florian, rev. by. Motte, Andrew, tr. Incl. Vol. I. The Motions of Bodies. pap. 5.95x (ISBN 0-520-00928-2, CAMPUS70); Vol. II. The System of the World. pap. 5.95 (ISBN 0-520-00929-0, CAMPUS71). 1962. U of Cal Pr.

Waddell, Hope M. A Vocabulary of the Efik or Old Calabar Language. 2nd ed. 94p. 1972. Repr. of 1849 ed. 7.00x (ISBN 0-8002-1353-X). Intl Pubns Serv.

NIGERIA–MAPS

Iloeje, N. P. New Geography of Nigeria. (Illus.). 1978. pap. text ed. 6.50x (ISBN 0-582-65510-2). Longman.

NIGERIA–NATIVE RACES

Boston, J. S. Ikenga: Figures Among the North West Igbo & Igala. 1977. text ed. 31.25x (ISBN 0-905788-01-X). Humanities.

Delano, Isaac O. The Soul of Nigeria. LC 74-15026. (Illus.). Repr. of 1937 ed. 26.00 (ISBN 0-404-12024-5). AMS Pr.

Leonard, Arthur G. Lower Niger & Its Tribes. 564p. 1968. Repr. of 1906 ed. 32.50x (ISBN 0-7146-1687-7, F Cass Co). Biblio Dist.

Meek, Charles Kingsley. Northern Tribes of Nigeria: Ethnographical Account of the Northern Provinces of Nigeria Together with a Report of the 1921 Decennial Census, 2 vols. (Illus.). 1971. Repr. of 1929 ed. 75.00x (ISBN 0-7146-2686-4, F Cass Co). Biblio Dist.

Perham, M. F. Tribes of the Niger Delta: Their Religion & Customs. 1976. lib. bdg. 59.95 (ISBN 0-8490-2768-3). Gordon Pr.

Perham, Margery F. Native Administration in Nigeria. LC 74-15078. Repr. of 1937 ed. 24.50 (ISBN 0-404-12127-6). AMS Pr.

Talbot, Percy. The Peoples of Southern Nigeria, 4 vols. 1976. lib. bdg. 400.00 (ISBN 0-8490-2420-X). Gordon Pr.

Talbot, Percy A. Peoples of Southern Nigeria, 4 vols. (Illus.). 1969. 195.00x set (ISBN 0-7146-1725-3, F Cass Co). Biblio Dist.

Temple, Charles L. Native Races & Their Rulers: Sketches & Studies of Official Life & Administrative Problems in Nigeria. (Illus.). 352p. 1968. Repr. of 1918 ed. 30.00x (ISBN 0-7146-1727-X, F Cass Co). Biblio Dist.

Temple, O. Notes on the Tribes, Provinces, Emirates & States of the Northern Province of Nigeria. 595p. 1965. 35.00x (ISBN 0-7146-1728-8, F Cass Co). Biblio Dist.

White, Stanhope. Dan Bana: The Memoirs of a Nigerian Official. (Illus.). 1967. 5.50 (ISBN 0-685-11953-X). Heineman.

Wilson-Haffenden, J. R. W. Red Men of Nigeria: Account of a Lengthy Residence Amoung the Fulani. (Illus.). 318p. 1967. Repr. 29.50x (ISBN 0-7146-1111-5, F Cass Co). Biblio Dist.

NIGERIA–POLITICS AND GOVERNMENT

Adebayo, Augustus. Principles & Practice of Public Administration in Nigeria. LC 80-41173. 192p. 1981. 27.00 (ISBN 0-471-27897-1, Pub. by Wiley-Interscience); pap. 13.50 (ISBN 0-471-27898-X). Wiley.

Adewoye, O. The Judicial System in Southern Nigeria, 1854-1954: Law & Justice in a Dependency. (Ibadan History Ser.). 1977. text ed. 17.00x (ISBN 0-391-00735-1). Humanities.

Aihe, D. O. & Oluyede, P. A. Cases & Materials on Constitutional Law in Nigeria. 1979. text ed. 27.50x (ISBN 0-19-575519-7). Oxford U Pr.

Akpan, Moses E. Nigerian Politics: A Search for National Unity & Stability. 170p. 1977. pap. text ed. 9.00 (ISBN 0-8191-0104-4). U Pr of Amer.

Aluko, Olajide, ed. Ghana & Nigeria 1957-1970: A Study in Inter-African Discord. LC 75-1614. (Illus.). 275p. 1976. text ed. 18.50x (ISBN 0-06-490163-7). B&N.

Anifowose, F. O. The Politics of Violence in Nigeria: A Case-Study of the Tiv & Yoruba. LC 79-88590. 1980. 21.50 (ISBN 0-686-52503-5). NOK Pubs.

Arnold, Guy. Modern Nigeria. 1977. pap. text ed. 9.95x (ISBN 0-582-64643-X). Longman.

Berger, Manfred. Industrialisation Policies in Nigeria. (Afrika Studien Ser.: No. 88). 333p. 1975. text ed. 19.00x (ISBN 3-8039-0111-1). Humanities.

Bienen, Henry & Diejomaoh, V. P., eds. Inequality & Social Change in Nigeria. LC 81-4145. (The Political Economy of Income Distribution in Developing Countries Ser.). 312p. (Orig.). 1981. pap. text ed. 14.50x (ISBN 0-8419-0710-2). Holmes & Meier.

Crocker, Walter. Nigeria: A Critique of British Colonial Administration. 1976. lib. bdg. 59.95 (ISBN 0-8490-2345-9). Gordon Pr.

Crocker, Walter R. Nigeria: A Critique of British Colonial Administration. facsimile ed. LC 76-160964. (Select Bibliographies Reprint Ser). Repr. of 1936 ed. 20.00 (ISBN 0-8369-5832-2). Arno.

Dudley, B. J. Parties & Politics in Northern Nigeria. 352p. 1968. 27.50x (ISBN 0-7146-1658-3, F Cass Co). Biblio Dist.

Fasuyi, T. A. Cultural Policy in Nigeria. LC 72-95232. (Studies & Documents on Cultural Policies). (Illus.). 63p. 1973. pap. 5.00 (ISBN 92-3-101029-8, U133, UNESCO). Unipub.

Gailey, Harry A., Jr. The Road to Aba: A Study of British Administrative Policy in Eastern Nigeria. LC 77-11519. 1970. 12.00x (ISBN 0-8147-0461-1). NYU Pr.

Kasunmu, A. B. The Supreme Court of Nigeria. LC 79-670156. 1977. text ed. 42.00 (ISBN 0-435-89057-3). Heinemann Ed.

Lagos Conference, 1964. Final Report. 1964. pap. 2.50 (ISBN 92-3-100565-0, U243, UNESCO). Unipub.

Murray, D. J. Studies in Nigerian Administration. 342p. 1978. pap. text ed. 13.75x (ISBN 0-8419-6602-8). Holmes & Meier.

Nadanugu, Edwin. Problems of Socialism: The Nigerian Challenge. 144p. 1981. pap. 9.95 (ISBN 0-686-76755-1, Pub. by Zed Pr England). Lawrence Hill.

Nair, K. K. Politics & Society in South Eastern Nigeria: A Study of Politics, Diplomacy and Commerce in a Southern Nigerian State. (Illus.). 328p. 1972. 27.50x (ISBN 0-7146-2296-6, F Cass Co). Biblio Dist.

Newbury, Colin W. West African Commonwealth. LC 64-22875. (Commonwealth Studies Center: No. 22). 1964. 7.75 (ISBN 0-8223-0121-0). Duke.

Nkemdirim, Bernard. Social Change & Political Violence in Colonial Nigeria. 1976. text ed. 6.25x (ISBN 0-7223-0693-8). Verry.

O'Connell, James & Beckett, Paul. Education & Power in Nigeria. LC 77-15452. 1978. text ed. 29.50x (ISBN 0-8419-0346-8, Africana). Holmes & Meier.

Odetola, Theophilus O. Military Politics in Nigeria: Economic Development & Political Stability. LC 76-58232. (Illus.). 1978. 14.95 (ISBN 0-87855-100-X). Transaction Bks.

Ofiaja, Nicholas D. Stability & Instability in Politics: The Case of Nigeria & Cameroon. 1979. 9.95 (ISBN 0-533-04210-0). Vantage.

Okoli, Ekwueme F. Institutional Structure & Conflict in Nigeria. LC 79-3425. 1980. pap. text ed. 7.75 (ISBN 0-8191-0888-X). U Pr of Amer.

Okonjo, I. M. British Administration in Nigeria, 1900-1950: A Nigerian View. LC 73-84372. (The NOK Library of African Affairs). 450p. 1974. text ed. 18.50x (ISBN 0-88357-002-5). NOK Pubs.

Olorunsola, Victor A. Soldiers & Power: The Development Performance of the Nigerian Military Regime. LC 76-48485. (Publication Ser: No. 168). 1977. pap. 10.95 (ISBN 0-8179-6681-1). Hoover Inst Pr.

Omu, Fred I. Press & Politics in Nigeria Eighteen Eighty-Nineteen Thirty Seven. (Ibadan History Ser.). 1978. text ed. 20.75x (ISBN 0-391-00561-8). Humanities.

Onyejekwe, Okey. The Role of the Military in Economic & Social Development: A Comparative Regime Performance in Nigeria, 1960-1979. LC 80-8181. 300p. 1981. lib. bdg. 20.75 (ISBN 0-8191-1608-4); pap. text ed. 10.75 (ISBN 0-8191-1609-2). U Pr of Amer.

Ostheimer, John M. Nigerian Politics. (Harper's Comparative Governmental Ser.). (Illus.). 1973. pap. text ed. 9.95 scp (ISBN 0-06-044958-6, HarpC). Har-Row.

Oyediran, Oyeleye, ed. Nigerian Government & Politics Under Military Rule 1966-1979. LC 79-15018. 1979. 25.00x (ISBN 0-312-57272-7). St Martin.

Paden, John N. Religion & Political Culture in Kano. LC 74-153548. 1973. 34.50x (ISBN 0-520-02020-0). U of Cal Pr.

Panter-Brick, Keith, ed. Soldiers & Oil: The Transformation of Nigeria. 375p. 1978. 28.00x (ISBN 0-7146-3098-5, F Cass Co). Biblio Dist.

Panter-Brick, S. K., ed. Nigerian Politics & Military Rule: Prelude to the Civil War. (Athlone Commonwealth Papers: No. 13). 1970. text ed. 9.75x (ISBN 0-485-17613-0, Athlone Pr). Humanities.

Perham, Margery F. Native Administration in Nigeria. LC 74-15078. Repr. of 1937 ed. 24.50 (ISBN 0-404-12127-6). AMS Pr.

Post, K. W. & Jenkins, G. D. The Price of Liberty: Personality & Politics in Colonial Nigeria. LC 70-186251. (African Studies, No. 7). (Illus.). 500p. 1973. 37.50 (ISBN 0-521-08503-9). Cambridge U Pr.

Post, Kenneth & Vickers, Michael. Structure & Conflict in Nigeria. 256p. 1973. 22.50 (ISBN 0-299-06470-0). U of Wis Pr.

Shegari, Shehu. Shehu Shegari: My Vision of Nigeria. Tijjani, Aminu & Williams, David, eds. (Illus.). 448p. 1981. 25.00x (ISBN 0-7146-3181-7, F Cass Co). Biblio Dist.

Sklar, R. Nigerian Political Parties: A Study of the Political Parties of the First Republic. 1980. pap. text ed. 9.95x (ISBN 0-686-52500-0). NOK Pubs.

Smith, John H. Colonial Cadet in Nigeria. LC 68-8589. (Commonwealth Studies Center: No. 34). 1968. 10.50 (ISBN 0-8223-0161-X). Duke.

Tamuno, T. N. The Evolution of the Nigerian State: The Southern Phase, 1898-1914. (Ibadan History Ser.). (Illus.). 250p. 1972. text ed. 14.00x (ISBN 0-391-00232-5). Humanities.

--Herbert Macaulay: Nigerian Patriot. (African Historical Biographics Ser.). (Illus.). 48p. 1977. pap. text ed. 2.75x (ISBN 0-435-94472-X). Heinemann Ed.

Tilman, Robert O. & Cole, Taylor, eds. Nigerian Political Scene. LC 62-18315. (Commonwealth Studies Center: No. 17). 1962. 17.75 (ISBN 0-8223-0178-4). Duke.

Uche, U. U. Contractual Obligations in Ghana & Nigeria. 300p. 1971. 29.50x (ISBN 0-7146-2611-2, F Cass Co). Biblio Dist.

Uku, Skyne R. The Pan-African Movement & the Nigerian Civil War: A Critical Analysis. 1978. 7.50 (ISBN 0-533-03271-7). Vantage.

Wayas, Joseph. Nigeria's Leadership Role in Africa. 1979. text ed. 26.00x (ISBN 0-333-26295-6). Humanities.

Wheare, Joan. The Nigerian Legislative Council. 1976. lib. bdg. 59.95 (ISBN 0-8490-2347-5). Gordon Pr.

Whitaker, C. S. Politics of Tradition: Continuity & Change in Northern Nigeria Nineteen Forty-Six to Nineteen Sixty-Six. 1980. pap. text ed. 9.95x (ISBN 0-686-52502-7). NOK Pubs.

Whitaker, C. S., Jr. Politics of Tradition: Continuity & Change in Northern Nigeria, 1946-1966. LC 68-56323. (Center of International Studies Ser). 1969. 28.50x (ISBN 0-691-03079-0). Princeton U Pr.

White, Jeremy J. Central Administration in Nigeria, Nineteen Fourteen to Nineteen Fifty-One: The Problem of Polarity. 250p. Date not set. 39.00x (ISBN 0-686-28430-5, Pub. by Irish Academic Pr Ireland). Biblio Dist.

Wolpe, Howard. Urban Politics in Nigeria: A Study of Port Harcourt. 1975. 34.50x (ISBN 0-520-02451-6). U of Cal Pr.

NIGERIA–RELIGION

Hambly, W. D. Serpent Worship in Africa - the Ovimbundu of Angola: Culture Areas of Nigeria. (Chicago Field Museum of Natural History Fieldiana Anthropology Ser). Repr. of 1935 ed. pap. 35.00 (ISBN 0-527-01881-3). Kraus Repr.

Isichei, Elizabeth. Varieties of Christian Experience in Nigeria. 256p. 1981. text ed. 45.00x (ISBN 0-333-31027-6, Pub. by Macmillan England). Humanities.

Johnston, G. Of God & Maxim Guns: Studies in the Presbytarian Church in Nigeria. 1980. 12.50x (ISBN 0-686-52501-9). NOK Pubs.

Kraft, Marguerite G. Worldview & Communication of the Gospel. LC 78-10196. (Illus.). 1978. pap. 7.95 (ISBN 0-87808-324-3). William Carey Lib.

Paden, John N. Religion & Political Culture in Kano. LC 74-153548. 1973. 34.50x (ISBN 0-520-02020-0). U of Cal Pr.

Rubingh, Eugene. Sons of Tiv: A Study of the Rise of the Church Among the Tiv of Central Nigeria. 1969. 5.95 (ISBN 0-8010-7643-9). Baker Bk.

NIGERIA–SOCIAL CONDITIONS

Bienen, Henry & Diejomaoh, V. P., eds. Inequality & Social Change in Nigeria. LC 81-4145. (The Political Economy of Income Distribution in Developing Countries Ser.). 312p. (Orig.). 1981. pap. text ed. 14.50x (ISBN 0-8419-0710-2). Holmes & Meier.

Buchanan, Keith & Pough, J. C. Land & People in Nigeria. 1976. lib. bdg. 60.00 (ISBN 0-8490-2122-7). Gordon Pr.

Cohen, Abner. Custom & Politics in Urban Africa: A Study of Hausa Migrants in Yoruba Towns. LC 68-55743. 1969. 20.00x (ISBN 0-520-01571-1); pap. 6.95x (ISBN 0-520-01836-2, CAMPUS43). U of Cal Pr.

Damachi, Ukandi G. Nigerian Modernization. LC 75-183394. 160p. 1972. 7.95 (ISBN 0-89388-030-2). Okpaku Communications.

Hill, Polly. Rural Hausa: A Village & a Setting. LC 75-161287. 1972. 34.50 (ISBN 0-521-08242-0). Cambridge U Pr.

LeVine, Robert A. Dreams & Deeds: Achievement Motivation in Nigeria. LC 66-20580. 123p. 1981. pap. price not set (ISBN 0-226-47572-7). U of Chicago Pr.

Lewis, L. J. Society, Schools & Progress in Nigeria. 1965. 22.00 (ISBN 0-08-011340-0); pap. 11.25 (ISBN 0-08-011339-7). Pergamon.

Lloyd, P. C. Power & Independence: Urban Africans' Perception of Social Inequality. (International Library of Anthropology Ser). (Illus.). 1974. 24.00x (ISBN 0-7100-7973-7). Routledge & Kegan.

Morel, E. D. Nigeria: Its Peoples & Its Problems. 3rd ed. (Illus.). 264p. 1968. 26.00x (ISBN 0-7146-1703-2, F Cass Co). Biblio Dist.

Nair, K. K. Politics & Society in South Eastern Nigeria: A Study of Politics, Diplomacy and Commerce in a Southern Nigerian State. (Illus.). 328p. 1972. 27.50x (ISBN 0-7146-2296-6, F Cass Co). Biblio Dist.

Nkemdirim, Bernard. Social Change & Political Violence in Colonial Nigeria. 1976. text ed. 6.25x (ISBN 0-7223-0693-8). Verry.

Obiechina, E. N. Onitsha Market Literature. LC 72-76469. 200p. 1972. text ed. 8.75x (ISBN 0-8419-0122-8, Africana). Holmes & Meier.

Okpaku, Joseph, ed. Nigeria-Dilemma of Nationhood: An African Analysis of the Biafran Conflict. LC 73-83162. 426p. 1974. pap. 5.95 (ISBN 0-89388-088-4). Okpaku Communications.

Oton, E. U., ed. Nigeria's Educator-Statesman: Selected Writings of Eyo Ita. 1981. 25.00x (ISBN 0-7146-2731-3, F Cass Co). Biblio Dist.

Peace, Adrian J. Choice, Class & Conflict: A Study of Southern Nigerian Factory Workers. LC 79-12658. (Harvester Studies in African Political Economy.). 1979. text ed. 38.75x (ISBN 0-391-01027-1). Humanities.

Smith, Victor E. Efficient Resource Use for Tropical Nutrition: Nigeria. LC 74-620058. 401p. 1975. pap. 9.50 (ISBN 0-87744-126-X). Mich St U Busn.

Smythe, Hugh H. & Smythe, Mabel M. The New Nigerian Elite. 1960. 10.00x (ISBN 0-8047-0521-6). Stanford U Pr.

Van Den Berghe, Pierre L. Power & Privilege at an African University. 288p. 1972. text ed. 14.95x (ISBN 0-87073-968-9). Schenkman.

Williams, Gavin, ed. Nigeria: Economy & Society. 226p. 1976. 17.50x (ISBN 0-8476-1429-8). Rowman.

NIGERIA–SOCIAL LIFE AND CUSTOMS

Balagum, Olga. Nigeria, Magic of a Land. (Illus.). 1980. 60.00 (ISBN 2-85258-106-X). Hippocrene Bks.

Meek, Charles K. Tribal Studies in Northern Nigeria, 2 vols. LC 32-2870. Repr. of 1931 ed. Set. 76.00 (ISBN 0-527-62650-3). Kraus Repr.

Nwosu, Joy, et al. Nigerian Hairstyles: A Photo Essay. (Illus.). 1980. 30.00 (ISBN 0-686-52499-3). NOK Pubs.

Talbot, Percy A. Life on Southern Nigeria: Magic, Beliefs & Customs of the Ibibio Tribe. (Illus.). 356p. (Orig.). 1967. 29.50x (ISBN 0-7146-1726-1, F Cass Co). Biblio Dist.

NIGERIAN ART

see Art, Nigerian

NIGERIAN COAL MINERS' UNION

Smock, David R. Conflict & Control in an African Trade Union: A Study of the Nigerian Coal Miner's Union. LC 75-76971. (Studies Ser.: No. 23). 170p. 1969. 11.95 (ISBN 0-8179-3231-3); pap. 5.95 (ISBN 0-8179-3232-1). Hoover Inst Pr.

NIGERIAN CULTUS

see Cultus, Nigerian

NIGERIAN FOLK-LORE

see Folk-Lore, Nigerian

NIGERIAN NATIONAL CHARACTERISTICS

see National Characteristics, Nigerian

NIGERIAN TALES

see Tales, Nigerian

NIGHT

Showers, Paul. In the Night. LC 61-6138. (A Let's-Read-&-Find-Out Science Bk). (Illus.). (gr. k-3). 1961. PLB 8.79 (ISBN 0-690-44621-7, TYC-J). Har-Row.

Wilson, Beth P. I Like Nighttime. (Illus.). 48p. (gr. k-6). 1976. 6.95 (ISBN 0-89185-047-3); pap. 2.95 (ISBN 0-89185-046-5). Anthelion Pr.

NIGHT CLUBS

see Music-Halls (Variety-Theaters, Cabarets, etc.)

NIGHT IN LITERATURE

Peake, Charles, ed. Poetry of the Landscape & the Night: Two Eighteenth-Century Traditions. LC 79-116474. (English Library). (Orig.). 1970. pap. 3.95x (ISBN 0-87249-161-7). U of SC Pr.

NIGHT PHOTOGRAPHY

see Photography, Night

NIGHT SCHOOLS

see Evening and Continuation Schools

NIGHT STICKS

see Truncheons

NIGHT WATCHMEN

see Watchmen

NIGHT WORK

see also Children–Employment; Shift Systems

Reinberg, A., et al, eds. Night & Shift Work-Biological & Social Aspects: Proceedings of the Vth International Symposium on Night and Shift Work-Scientific Committee on Shift Work of the Permanent Commission & International Association on Occupational Health (PCIAIH, Rouen, 12-16 May 1980. (Illus.). 516p. 1981. 80.00 (ISBN 0-08-025516-7). Pergamon.

NIGHTINGALE, FLORENCE, 1820-1910

Florence Nightingale. 1975. 2.95 (ISBN 0-442-82560-9). Peter Pauper.

Gordon, Richard. The Private Life of Florence Nightingale. LC 78-56342. 1979. 9.95 (ISBN 0-689-10929-6). Atheneum.

Hebert, Raymond G. Florence Nightingale: Saint, Reformer, or Rebel? 128p. 1980. 6.50 (ISBN 0-89874-127-0). Krieger.

Hume, Ruth F. Florence Nightingale. (World Landmark Ser.: No. 46). (Illus.). (gr. 6-10). 1960. PLB 5.99 (ISBN 0-394-90546-6, BYR). Random.

Keele, Mary, ed. Florence Nightingale in Rome: Letters Written 1847 to 1848. LC 80-68490. (Memoirs Ser.: Vol. 143). 1981. 12.00 (ISBN 0-87169-143-4). Am Philos.

Nightingale, Florence. Notes on Nursing. 80p. 1978. Repr. 16.00 (ISBN 0-7156-0528-3, Pub. by Duckworth England). Biblio Dist.

Pickering, George. Creative Malady. 1974. 13.95 (ISBN 0-19-519800-X). Oxford U Pr.

Sabatini, Rafael. Heroic Lives. facs. ed. LC 70-99648. (Essay Index Reprint Ser). 1934. 17.50 (ISBN 0-8369-2071-6). Arno.

Strachey, Lytton. Eminent Victorians. 7.50 (ISBN 0-8446-5836-7). Peter Smith.
--Eminent Victorians. 1969. pap. 4.50 (ISBN 0-15-628697-1, HPL40, HPL). HarBraceJ.

NIGHTINGALE, FLORENCE, 1820-1910–JUVENILE LITERATURE

Colver, Anne. Florence Nightingale. (Illus.). (gr. 1-7). 1966. pap. 1.25 (ISBN 0-440-42620-0, YB). Dell.
Koch, Charlotte. Florence Nightingale. LC 78-64424. (Illus.). (gr. 2-5). 1979. 3.50 (ISBN 0-89799-105-2); pap. 1.50 (ISBN 0-89799-038-2). Dandelion Pr.

NIGRILLOS

see Negrillos

NIHILISM

see also Anarchism and Anarchists; Russia–History–19th Century; Terrorism

Figner, Vera N. Memoirs of a Revolutionist. Daniels, Camilla-Chapin, et al, trs. LC 68-30820. (Illus.). 1968. Repr. of 1927 ed. lib. bdg. 15.25x (ISBN 0-8371-0418-1, FIRE). Greenwood.
Glicksberg, Charles. The Literature of Nihilism. 354p. 1975. 20.00 (ISBN 0-8387-1520-6). Bucknell U Pr.
Goudsblom, Johan. Nihilism & Culture. 213p. 1980. 27.50x (ISBN 0-8476-6766-9). Rowman.
Heidegger, Martin. Nietzsche: Vol. IV, Nihilism. Capuzzi, Frank, tr. from Ger. LC 78-19509. 352p. 1981. 16.95 (ISBN 0-06-063857-5, HarpR). Har-Row.
Heller, Peter. Dialectics & Nihilism: Essays on Lessing, Nietzsche, Mann & Kafka. LC 65-26240. 1969. Repr. of 1966 ed. 15.00x (ISBN 0-87023-019-0). U of Mass Pr.
Holbrook, David. Education, Nihilism & Survival. 1978. pap. 7.50 (ISBN 0-232-51384-8). Attic Pr.
Kravchinsky, Sergiei M. Underground Russia. LC 73-846. (Russian Studies: Perspectives on the Revolution Ser.). 272p. 1973. Repr. of 1883 ed. 22.50 (ISBN 0-88355-041-5). Hyperion Conn.
Murphy, Dennis D. Ethics, Nihilism, & the State. Date not set. pap. price not set (ISBN 0-918788-04-8). D D Murphy.
Novak, Michael. Experience of Nothingness. 1971. pap. 3.95x (ISBN 0-06-131938-4, TB 1938, Torch). Har-Row.
Paterson, R. W. Nihilist Egoist: Max Stirner. 1971. 24.95x (ISBN 0-19-713413-0). Oxford U Pr.
Rosen, Stanley. Nihilism: A Philosophical Essay. LC 70-81428. 1969. 20.00x (ISBN 0-300-01140-7). Yale U Pr.
Sogomonov, Y. & Landesman, P. Nihilism Today. 228p. 1977. 4.80 (ISBN 0-8285-0202-1, Pub. by Progress Pubs Russia). Imported Pubns.
Stack, George J. Kierkegaard's Existential Ethics. LC 75-16344. (Studies in Humanities: No. 16). 240p. 1977. 15.00x (ISBN 0-8173-6624-5); pap. 5.50 (ISBN 0-8173-6626-1). U of Ala Pr.
Thun, Alphons. Geschichte der Revolutionaren Bewegungen in Russland. 1964. Repr. of 1883 ed. 24.00 (ISBN 0-8337-3536-5). B Franklin.
Weber, Alfred. Farewell to European History: or, the Conquest of Nihilism. Hull, R. F., ed. LC 76-52396. 1977. Repr. of 1948 ed. lib. bdg. 15.25x (ISBN 0-8371-9447-4, WEFA). Greenwood.
Weischedel, Wilhelm, et al. Philosophische Theologie im Schatten des Nihilismus. Salaquarda, Joerg, ed. (Ger). 1971. pap. 15.25x (ISBN 3-11-001604-4). De Gruyter.

NIHON KYOSANTO

Langer, Paul F. Communism in Japan. LC 73-152426. (Studies: No. 30). 112p. 1972. 7.95 (ISBN 0-8179-3301-8). Hoover Inst Pr.

NIHON SHAKITO

Cole, Allan B., et al. Socialist Parties in Postwar Japan. (Illus.). 1966. 40.00x (ISBN 0-300-00371-4). Yale U Pr.
Stockwin, J. A. Japanese Socialist Party & Neutralism. 1968. 18.50x (ISBN 0-522-83838-3, Pub. by Melbourne U Pr). Intl Schol Bk Serv.

NIJINSKY, WASLAW, 1890-1950

Beaumont, C. W. Vaslav Nijinsky. LC 74-1080. (Studies in Music, No. 42). 1974. lib. bdg. 22.95 (ISBN 0-8383-1752-9). Haskell.
Bourman, Anatole. Tragedy of Nijinsky. LC 70-98822. Repr. of 1936 ed. lib. bdg. 16.50x (ISBN 0-8371-2965-6, BOTN). Greenwood.
Buckle, Richard. Nijinsky. (Illus.). 1975. pap. 5.95 (ISBN 0-380-00459-3, 40667). Avon.
Gelatt. Nijinsky: The Film. 29.95 (ISBN 0-345-28899-8). Ballantine.
Kirstein, Lincoln. Nijinsky Dancing. 1975. 40.00 (ISBN 0-394-48961-6). Knopf.
Krasovskaya, Vera. Nijinsky. Bowlt, John E., tr. from Rus. LC 79-7368. (Illus.). 1979. 15.00 (ISBN 0-02-871870-4). Schirmer Bks.
Magriel, Paul, ed. Nijinsky, Pavlova, Duncan: Three Lives in Dance. LC 76-30403. (Ser. in Dance). 1977. lib. bdg. 22.50 (ISBN 0-306-70845-0); pap. 6.95 (ISBN 0-306-80035-7). Da Capo.
Nijinska, Irina & Rawlinson, Jean, eds. Bronislava Nijinska: Early Memoirs. LC 80-21825. (Illus.). 576p. 1981. 22.50 (ISBN 0-03-020951-X). HR&W.
Nijinsky, Romola. Last Years of Nijinsky. LC 68-54284. Repr. of 1952 ed. 16.00 (ISBN 0-404-04775-0). AMS Pr.
--Nijinsky. LC 68-54285. Repr. of 1934 ed. 23.00 (ISBN 0-404-04776-9). AMS Pr.
--Nijinsky & the Last Days of Nijinsky. 1980. 16.95 (ISBN 0-671-41123-3). S&S.
Van Vechten, Carl. Interpreters. rev. ed. Farkas, Andrew, ed. LC 76-29975. (Opera Biographies). (Illus.). 1977. Repr. of 1920 ed. lib. bdg. 15.00 (ISBN 0-405-09713-1). Arno.
Whitworth, Geoffrey. Art of Nijinsky. LC 72-83753. (Illus.). Repr. of 1913 ed. 14.00 (ISBN 0-405-09073-0). Arno.

NIKON CAMERA

see Cameras–Types–Nikon

NIKONOS CAMERA

see Cameras–Types–Nikonos

NILE RIVER AND VALLEY

Burckhardt, John L. Travels in Nubia. LC 74-15014. Repr. of 1882 ed. 37.50 (ISBN 0-404-12009-1). AMS Pr.
Burton, Richard F. Nile Basin. 2nd ed. LC 65-23403. 1967. Repr. of 1864 ed. 19.50 (ISBN 0-306-70926-0). Da Capo.
Cheesman, R. E. Lake Tana & the Blue Nile: Abyssinian Quest. (Illus.). 400p. 1967. 35.00x (ISBN 0-7146-1641-9, F Cass Co). Biblio Dist.
Dunham, Dows. Second Cataract Forts, 2 vols. Incl. Vol. 1. Semna-Kumma. Janssen, Jozef M; Vol. 2. Uronarti, Shalfak, Mirgissa. 50.00 (ISBN 0-87846-107-8). Mus Fine Arts Boston.
Engstorm, Barbie. Egypt: Nile Cruise. (Engstrom's Travel Experience Guides Ser.). (Illus.). 228p. Date not set. 17.95 (ISBN 0-916588-07-6). Kurios Pr.
Engstrom, Barbie. Egypt: Nile Cruise. (Engstrom's Travel Experience Guides Ser.). (Illus.). 228p. (Orig.). Date not set. pap. 14.95 (ISBN 0-916588-05-X). Kurios Pr.
Geere, H. Valentine. By Nile & Euphrates: A Record of Discovery & Adventure. (Illus.). 367p. 1904. 6.50 (ISBN 0-567-02116-5). Attic Pr.
Gladstone, Penelope. Travels of Alexine. (Illus.). 1971. 12.50 (ISBN 0-7195-2044-4). Transatlantic.
Goddard, John. Kayaks Down the Nile. LC 78-14203. (Illus.). 1979. 15.95 (ISBN 0-8425-1575-5); pap. 7.95 (ISBN 0-8425-1365-5). Brigham.
Johnston, Harry. Nile Quest. 1903. 29.00 (ISBN 0-403-00378-4). Scholarly.
Kassas, M. & Ghabbour, I., eds. The Nile & Its Environment. 136p. 1980. pap. 20.15 (ISBN 0-08-026081-0). Pergamon.
Moorehead, Alan. The Blue Nile. LC 73-186776. 1980. pap. 4.95 (ISBN 0-06-090776-2, CN 776, CN). Har-Row.
Moret, Alexandre. The Nile & Egyptian Civilization. (History of Civilization Ser.). (Illus.). 1972. 26.50x (ISBN 0-7100-7241-4). Routledge & Kegan.
O'Clery, Helen. Nile. LC 76-512551. (Pegasus Books: No. 30). (Illus.). 1970. 10.50x (ISBN 0-234-77483-5). Intl Pubns Serv.
Peel, Sidney C. Binding of the Nile & the New Soudan. LC 74-94484. Repr. of 1904 ed. 14.50x (ISBN 0-8371-2369-0, Pub. by Negro U Pr). Greenwood.
Speke, John H. Journal of the Discovery of the Source of the Nile. 1969. 8.95x (ISBN 0-460-00050-0, Evman). Biblio Dist.
--Journal of the Discovery of the Source of the Nile. LC 68-55222. 1968. Repr. of 1863 ed. lib. bdg. 48.75x (ISBN 0-8371-1431-4, SPSN). Greenwood.
--What Led to the Discovery of the Nile, 1864. (Illus.). 372p. 1967. 24.00x (ISBN 0-7146-1854-3, F Cass Co). Biblio Dist.
Waterbury, John. Hydropolitics of the Nile Valley. (Illus.). 320p. 1979. 20.00x (ISBN 0-8156-2192-2). Syracuse U Pr.
Worthington, Barton. The Nile. LC 78-62991. (Rivers of the World Ser.). (Illus.). 1978. lib. bdg. 7.95 (ISBN 0-686-51136-0). Silver.

NILES, HEZEKIAH, 1777-1839

Stone, Richard G. Hezekiah Niles As an Economist. LC 78-64152. (Johns Hopkins University. Studies in the Social Sciences. Fifty-First Ser. 1933: 5). Repr. of 1933 ed. 16.50 (ISBN 0-404-61262-8). AMS Pr.

NILKANTA MOUNTAIN

Kumar, N. Nilakantha: Story of the Indian Expedition of 1961. 1965. 2.75x (ISBN 0-8426-1344-7). Verry.

NILO-HAMITIC TRIBES

see also Barabaig (African People); Jie (African Tribe); Kipsigis; Nandi (African Tribe); Turkana (African People)

Gulliver, Pamela & Gulliver, P. H. Central Nilo-Hamites. 1968. 10.50x (ISBN 0-8002-0278-3). Intl Pubns Serv.
Huntingford, G. W. Northern Nilo-Hamites. LC 77-408451. 1968. 10.00 (ISBN 0-85302-032-9). Intl Pubns Serv.
--Southern Nilo-Hamites. (Illus., Orig.). 1970. pap. 11.50x (ISBN 0-8002-2009-9). Intl Pubns Serv.

NILOTES

see Nilotic Tribes

NILOTIC LANGUAGES

see also Nuer Language

NILOTIC TRIBES

see also Dinka (Nilotic Tribe); Luo (Nilotic Tribe)

Ogot, Bethwell A. History of the Southern Luo, Vol. 1, Migration & Settlement 1500-1900. (Illus.). 1967. 7.50x (ISBN 0-8002-1512-5). Intl Pubns Serv.

NIMITZ, CHESTER WILLIAM, 1885-1966

Fleet Admiral Chester W. Nimitz of Fredericksburg, Texas. 1971. pap. 0.50 (ISBN 0-686-24072-3). Adm Nimitz Foun.
Nimitz: Reflections on Pearl Harbor. 1971. pap. 0.50 (ISBN 0-686-24071-5). Adm Nimitz Foun.
Potter, Elmer B. Nimitz. LC 76-1056. 608p. 1976. 18.95 (ISBN 0-87021-492-6). Naval Inst Pr.

NIMONIC ALLOYS

Betteridge, W. & Heslop, J., eds. The Nimonic Alloys. 2nd ed. LC 74-79862. (Illus.). 498p. 1974. 59.00x (ISBN 0-8448-0370-7). Crane-Russak Co.

NIMZOWITSCH, ARON, 1886-1935

Reinfeld, Fred. Hypermodern Chess. 1948. pap. 3.50 (ISBN 0-486-20448-0). Dover.

NIN, ANAIS, 1903-

Evans, Oliver. Anais Nin. LC 67-11703. (Crosscurrents-Modern Critiques Ser.). 239p. 1968. 7.95 (ISBN 0-8093-0285-3). S Ill U Pr.
Franklin, Benjamin & Schneider, Duane. Anais Nin: An Introduction. LC 79-10635. 309p. 1980. pap. 10.00x (ISBN 0-8214-0432-6). Ohio U Pr.
--Anais Nin: An Introduction. LC 79-10635. 1980. 17.50x (ISBN 0-8214-0395-8). Ohio U Pr.
Harms, Valerie. Stars in My Sky: Maria Montessori, Anais Nin, Frances Steloff. LC 74-82389. (Illus.). 160p. (Orig.). (YA) 1976. 8.00 (ISBN 0-8027-0536-7, Dist. by Walker & Co). Magic Circle Pr.
--Stars in My Sky: Maria Montessori, Anais Nin, Frances Steloff. (Illus.). 1976. 8.00 (ISBN 0-8027-0536-7). Walker & Co.
Hinz, Evelyn, ed. A Woman Speaks: The Lectures, Seminars, & Interviews of Anais Nin. LC 75-15111. 270p. 1975. 13.95x (ISBN 0-8040-0693-8); pap. 6.95x (ISBN 0-8040-0694-6). Swallow.
Hipskind, Judith. Palm Prints of Anais Nin. Date not set. price not set (ISBN 0-686-15714-1). Merging Media.
Jason, Philip K., ed. Anais Nin Reader. LC 72-91913. 316p. 1973. pap. 7.95 (ISBN 0-8040-0596-6). Swallow.
Knapp, Bettina L. Anais Nin. LC 78-57692. (Modern Literature Ser.). 1978. 10.95 (ISBN 0-8044-2481-0); pap. 4.95 (ISBN 0-8044-6371-9). Ungar.
Nin, Anais. Diary of Anais Nin, 7 vols. 1978. Set. pap. 22.50 (ISBN 0-15-626034-4, Harv). HarBraceJ.
--The Diary of Anais Nin: Vol. VII, 1966-1974. LC 66-12917. (Illus.). 432p. 1980. 14.95 (ISBN 0-15-125596-2). HarBraceJ.
--The Diary of Anais Nin: 1966-1974, Vol. VII. Stuhlmann, Gunther, ed. LC 66-12917. (Illus.). 368p. 1981. pap. 7.95 (ISBN 0-15-626028-X). HarBraceJ.
--Linotte; the Early Diary of Anais Dir: Nineteen Fourteen to Nineteen Twenty. Sherman, Jean, tr. LC 79-18962. (Illus.). 1980. pap. 7.50 (ISBN 0-15-652386-8, Harv). HarBraceJ.
Snyder, Robert. Anais Nin Observed: From a Film Portrait of a Woman As Artist. LC 76-3123. (Illus.). 116p. 1976. pap. 9.95 (ISBN 0-8040-0708-X). Swallow.
Spencer, Sharon. Collage of Dreams: The Writings of Anais Nin. LC 77-78781. 188p. 1977. 12.95 (ISBN 0-8040-0760-8). Swallow.

NINE (THE NUMBER)

Wallace, William, Jr. Rule of Nine. LC 59-12077. 1959. pap. 1.25 (ISBN 0-87021-555-8). Naval Inst Pr.

NINETEENTH CENTURY

Burchell, Samuel C. Age of Progress. (Great Ages of Man Ser). (Illus.). 1966. 12.95 (ISBN 0-8094-0351-X). Time-Life.
Chamberlain, Houston S. Foundations of the Nineteenth Century, 2 vols. LC 67-29735. 1968. Repr. Set. 85.00 (ISBN 0-86527-069-4). Fertig.
Clarke, Helen A. Browning & His Century. LC 73-18248. (Studies in Browning, No. 4). 1974. lib. bdg. 49.95 (ISBN 0-8383-1734-0). Haskell.
Cooper, F. T. & Maurice, A. B. History of the Nineteenth Century in Caricature. 59.95 (ISBN 0-8490-0359-8). Gordon Pr.
Ellis, H. Nineteenth Century. an Utopian Retrospect. LC 5-3952. Repr. of 1901 ed. 14.00 (ISBN 0-527-26930-1). Kraus Repr.
History of Mankind: Cultural & Scientific Development: The Nineteenth Century 1775-1905: Vol. 5, Pt. 3; Social, Cultural & Religious Aspects. (Illus.). 1970. text ed. 42.50x (ISBN 0-04-900027-6). Allen Unwin.
History of Mankind: Cultural & Scientific Development: The Nineteenth Century 1775-1905: Vol. 5, Pt. 4; European Empires, Technical & Scientific Progress, Cultural Conflicts. (Illus.). text ed. 42.50x (ISBN 0-04-900028-4). Allen Unwin.
Holman, Dennis & Millward, J. S., eds. Earlier Nineteenth Century, Seventeen Eighty Three-Eighteen Sixty Seven. (Portraits & Documents Ser.). 1968. pap. text ed. 2.25x (ISBN 0-09-075640-1). Humanities.
Jackson, Holbrook. Dreamers of Dreams: The Rise & Fall of 19th Century Idealism. LC 78-15808. 1978. Repr. of 1948 ed. lib. bdg. 35.00 (ISBN 0-8414-5410-8). Folcroft.
--The Ideas: A Review of the Art & Ideas at the Close of the 19th Century. LC 78-145104. 304p. 1972. Repr. of 1922 ed. 21.00 (ISBN 0-403-01041-1). Scholarly.
McCarthy, Mary. A Nineteenth-Century Childhood. (Educational Ser.). 1924. Repr. 25.00 (ISBN 0-685-43096-0). Norwood Edns.
Maurice, Arthur B. & Cooper, Frederic T. History of the Nineteenth Century in Caricature. LC 79-136560. (Tower Bks). (Illus.). 1971. Repr. of 1904 ed. 32.00 (ISBN 0-8103-3909-9). Gale.
Rickett, Arthur. Prophets of the Century: Wordsworth, Shelley, Carlyle, Emerson, Tennyson, Eliot, Ruskin, Whitman, Morris, Tolstoy, Ibsen. 1977. Repr. of 1898 ed. lib. bdg. 25.00 (ISBN 0-8495-4507-2). Arden Lib.
Roberts, John. Revolution & Improvement, 1775-1848. LC 75-17288. 1976. 32.50x (ISBN 0-520-03076-1). U of Cal Pr.
Roubiczek, Paul. Misinterpretation of Man: A Study of European Thought in the 19th Century. LC 67-27641. Repr. of 1947 ed. 12.50 (ISBN 0-8046-0394-4). Kennikat.
Somervell, David C. English Thought in the Nineteenth Century. LC 77-21468. 1977. Repr. of 1962 ed. lib. bdg. 18.50x (ISBN 0-8371-9793-7, SOET). Greenwood.
Sternberger, Dolf. Panorama of the Nineteenth Century. Neugroschel, Joachim, tr. from Ger. (Mole-Editions Ser.). Date not set. pap. cancelled (ISBN 0-916354-25-3). Urizen Bks.
--Panorama of the 19th Century. Neugroschel, Joachim, tr. from Ger. (Mole-Editions). 1977. 15.00 (ISBN 0-916354-24-5). Urizen Bks.
Twentieth Century. Nineteenth Century Opinion: An Anthology of Extracts from the First 50 Volumes of the Nineteenth Century, 1877-1901. Goodwin, Michael, ed. LC 79-9966. 1979. Repr. of 1951 ed. lib. bdg. 22.75x (ISBN 0-313-21276-7, TCNC). Greenwood.
Willey, Basil. More Nineteenth-Century Studies: A Group of Honest Doubters. LC 80-40635. 304p. 1981. pap. 9.95 (ISBN 0-521-28067-2). Cambridge U Pr.
--More Nineteenth Century Studies: A Group of Honest Doubters. LC 57-13564. 1956. 20.00x (ISBN 0-231-02187-9). Columbia U Pr.
--Nineteenth Century Studies: Coleridge to Mathew Arnold. LC 49-50265. 1949. 20.00x (ISBN 0-231-01789-8). Columbia U Pr.
Wrigley, E. A., ed. The Study of Nineteenth Century Society. LC 71-174258. (Illus.). 512p. 1972. 46.50 (ISBN 0-521-08412-1). Cambridge U Pr.

NINEVEH

Brackman, Arnold C. The Luck of Nineveh. 352p. 1981. pap. 8.95 (ISBN 0-442-28260-5). Van Nos Reinhold.
--The Luck of Nineveh. LC 78-1893. 1978. 14.95 (ISBN 0-07-007030-X, GB). McGraw.

NIOBIUM

Niobium: Physico-Chemical Properties of Its Compounds & Alloys. (Atomic Energy Review Ser.: Special Issue No. 2). 1968. pap. 13.00 (ISBN 92-0-149068-2, IAER2, IAEA). Unipub.
Sisco, F. T. & Epremian, E. Columbium & Tantalum. 635p. 1963. 36.00 (ISBN 0-471-79347-7, Pub. by Wiley). Krieger.

NIPPUR

Chiera, E. Lists of Personal Names from the Temple School of Nippur: A Syllabary of Personal Names. (Publications of the Babylonian Section: Vol. 11-1). (Illus.). 88p. 1916. soft bound 7.00 (ISBN 0-686-11923-1). Univ Mus of U PA.
--Lists of Personal Names from the Temple School of Nippur: Lists of Akkadian Personal Names. (Publications of the Babylonian Section: Vol. 11-2). (Illus.). 85p. 1916. soft bound 7.00 (ISBN 0-686-11924-X). Univ Mus of U PA.
Clay, A. T. Documents from the Temple Archives of Nippur Dated in the Reigns of Cassite Rulers with Incomplete Dates. (Publications of the Babylonian Section, Ser. A: Vol. 15). (Illus.). 68p. 1906. soft bound 8.00 (ISBN 0-686-11914-2). Univ Mus of U PA.

--Legal & Commercial Transactions Dated in the Assyrian, Neo-Babylonian & Persian Periods, Chiefly from Nippur. (Publications of the Babylonian Section, Ser. A: Vol 8). (Illus.). 85p. 1908. soft bound 8.00 (ISBN 0-686-11913-4). Univ Mus of U PA.
Gibson, McGuire. Excavations at Nippur. LC 75-9054. (Oriental Institute Communications Ser.: No. 22). 1976. pap. 15.00x (ISBN 0-226-62339-4). U of Chicago Pr.
Gibson, McGuire, et al. Excavations at Nippur: Twelfth Season. LC 78-59117. (Oriental Institute Communications Ser.: No. 23). (Illus.). 1978. pap. 22.00x (ISBN 0-918986-22-2). Oriental Inst.
Heimerdinger, J. Sumerian Literary Fragments from Nippur. (Occasional Pubns. of the Babylonian Fund Ser.: Vol. 4). 1980. 20.00 (ISBN 0-934718-31-8). Univ Mus of U PA.
Hilprecht, H. V. The Earliest Version of the Babylonian Deluge Story & the Temple Library of Nippur. (Publications of the Babylonian Section, Ser. D: Vol. 5-1). (Illus.). 65p. 1910. soft bound 1.50 (ISBN 0-686-11918-5). Univ Mus of U PA.
Hinke, W. J. A New Boundary Stone of Nebuchadrezzar I from Nippur. (Publications of the Babylonian Section, Ser. D: Vol. 4). (Illus.). 323p. 1907. soft bound 5.00 (ISBN 0-686-11917-7). Univ Mus of U PA.
Legrain, L. Terra-Cottas from Nippur. (Publications of the Babylonian Section: Vol. 16). (Illus.). 52p. 1930. bound with folio of plates 25.00 (ISBN 0-686-11926-6). Univ Mus of U PA.
McCown, Donald E. & Haines, Richard C. Nippur One: Temple of Enlil, Scribal Quarter & Soundings. LC 66-17104. (Illus.). 1967. 10.00 (ISBN 0-226-55688-3, OIP78). U of Chicago Pr.
Radau, Hugo. Letters to the Cassite Kings, from the Temple Archives of Nippur. (Publications of the Babylonian Section, Ser. A: Vol. 17). (Illus.). 174p. 1908. soft bound 8.00 (ISBN 0-686-11915-0). Univ Mus of U PA.
--Ninib, the Determiner of Fates from the Temple Library of Nippur. (Publications of the Babylonian Section, Ser. D: Vol. 5-2). (Illus.). 73p. 1910. soft bound 2.00 (ISBN 0-686-11919-3). Univ Mus of U PA.
Swindler, D. R. Study of Cranial & Skeletal Material Excavated at Nippur. (Museum Monographs). (Illus.). 40p. 1956. soft bound 1.50 (ISBN 0-934718-04-0). Univ Mus of U PA.

NIRVANA
Carus, Paul. Karma; Nirvana: Two Buddhist Tales. LC 73-82781. (Illus.). 160p. 1973. 12.95 (ISBN 0-87548-249-X); pap. 4.95 (ISBN 0-686-76973-2). Open Court.
Evans-Wentz, W. Y., ed. Tibetan Book of the Great Liberation. 1954. 15.95x (ISBN 0-19-501437-5). Oxford U Pr.
--Tibetan Book of the Great Liberation. (Illus.). 1968. pap. 6.95 (ISBN 0-19-500293-8, GB). Oxford U Pr.
Rajneesh, Bhagwan Sri. Nirvana: The Last Nightmare. Rajneesh Foundation, ed. (Illus.). 278p. (Orig.). 1981. pap. 8.95 (ISBN 0-914794-37-X). Wisdom Garden Bks.

NISEI
see Japanese in the United States

NISHI, AMANE, 1829-1897
Havens, Thomas R. Nishi Amane & Modern Japanese Thought. LC 75-90950. 1970. 17.50 (ISBN 0-691-03080-4). Princeton U Pr.

NISQUALLI LANGUAGE
Gibbs, George. Dictionary of the Nisqually Indian Language of Western Washington. Repr. of 1877 ed. pap. 12.50 (ISBN 0-8466-4022-8, SJI22). Shorey.

NITRATES
Committee on Environmental Pollutants, National Research Council. Nitrates: An Environmental Assessment. (Scientific & Technical Assessments of Environmental Pollutants Ser.). 1978. pap. text ed. 15.25 (ISBN 0-309-02785-3). Natl Acad Pr.
Committee on Nitrate Accumulation. Accumulation of Nitrate. vii, 106p. 1972. pap. text ed. 6.00 (ISBN 0-309-02038-7). Natl Acad Pr.
Effects of Agricultural Production on Nitrates in Food & Water with Particular Reference to Isotope Studies. (Illus.). 158p. (Orig.). 1974. pap. 13.00 (ISBN 92-0-111174-6, ISP361, IAEA). Unipub.
Needleman, P., ed. Organic Nitrates. (Handbook of Experimental Pharmacology Ser.: Vol. 40). (Illus.). xiii, 196p. 1975. 53.00 (ISBN 0-387-07048-6); by subscription 33.40 (ISBN 0-685-52192-3). Springer-Verlag.
Wilcox. Growth Mechanisms & Silicon Nitride. (Preparation & Properties of Solid State Materials Ser.: Vol. 7). price not set (ISBN 0-8247-1368-0). Dekker.

NITRATION
Albright, Lyle F. & Hanson, Carl, eds. Industrial & Laboratory Nitrations. LC 75-38712. (ACS Symposium Ser.: No. 22). 1976. 23.50 (ISBN 0-8412-0306-7). Am Chemical.
Hoggett, J. G., et al. Nitration & Aromatic Reactivity. LC 76-138374. (Illus.). 1971. 42.50 (ISBN 0-521-08029-0). Cambridge U Pr.
Schofield, K. Aromatic Nitration. (Illus.). 350p. 1981. 67.50 (ISBN 0-521-23362-3). Cambridge U Pr.

NITRENES
Gilchrist, T. L. & Rees, C. W. Carbenes, Nitrenes, & Arynes. 131p. 1969. pap. 12.50 (ISBN 0-306-50026-4, Plenum Pr). Plenum Pub.
Lwowski, Walter. Nitrenes. LC 76-97256. (Reactive Intermediates Ser). 1970. 48.50 (ISBN 0-471-55710-2, Pub. by Wiley-Interscience). Wiley.

NITRIC ACID
Chilton, Thomas. Strong Water: Nitric Acid, Its Sources, Methods of Manufacture, & Uses. 1968. 10.00x (ISBN 0-262-03023-3). MIT Pr.

NITRILES
Grundmann, C. & Gruenanger, P. Nitrile Oxides, Versatile Tools of Theoretical & Preparative Chemistry. (Organische Chemie in Einzeldarstellungen: Vol. 13). 1971. 52.90 (ISBN 0-387-05226-7). Springer-Verlag.
Taylor, E. C. & McKillop, A. Advances in Organic Chemistry: Methods & Results: the Chemistry of Cyclic Enaminonitriles & O-Aminonitriles, Vol. 7. 415p. 1970. 60.00 (ISBN 0-471-84661-9). Wiley.

NITRO COMPOUNDS
Eidus, J., et al. Atlas of Electronic Spectra of Five-Nitrofuran Compounds. 1972. 25.95 (ISBN 0-470-23430-X). Halsted Pr.
Feuer, Henry, ed. The Chemistry of the Nitro & Nitroso Groups: Part 1. LC 80-21491. 996p. 1981. Repr. of 1969 ed. text ed. write for info. (ISBN 0-89874-271-4). Krieger.
--The Chemistry of the Nitro & Nitroso Groups: Part 2. LC 80-21491. 450p. 1981. Repr. text ed. write for info. (ISBN 0-89874-272-2). Krieger.
Schmaehl, Dietrich. Risk Assessment of N-Nitroso Compounds for Human Health: Oncology. (Oncology Journal: Vol. 37). (Illus.). 120p. 1980. pap. 36.75 (ISBN 3-8055-1137-X). S Karger.

NITROCELLULOSE
see also Explosives

NITROGEN
see also Nitrogen Fertilizers
Bahn, Gilbert S., ed. Reaction Rate Compilation for the H-O-N System. LC 68-20396. 1968. Repr. of 1967 ed. 57.75x (ISBN 0-677-12750-2). Gordon.
Bartholomew, W. V. & Clark, Francis E., eds. Soil Nitrogen. (Illus.). 1965. 11.00 (ISBN 0-89118-011-7). Am Soc Agron.
Battino, R. Nitrogen: Gas Solubilities. (Solubility Data Ser.). Date not set. 100.01 (ISBN 0-08-023922-6). Pergamon.
Bothe, H. & Trebst, A., eds. Biology of Inorganic Nitrogen & Sulfur Metabolism. (Proceedings in Life Sciences Ser.). (Illus.). 370p. 1981. 49.80 (ISBN 0-387-10486-0). Springer-Verlag.
Colburn, C. B., ed. Developments in Inorganic Nitrogen Chemistry, Vol. 2. 1973. 49.00 (ISBN 0-444-40962-9). Elsevier.
Gorrod, J. W., ed. Biological Oxidation of Nitrogen: Proceedings of the 2nd International Symposium on the Biological Oxidation of Nitrogen in Organic Molecules, Chelsea College, London, Sept. 1977. 1978. 69.75 (ISBN 0-444-80039-5, North-Holland). Elsevier.
Grosjean, Daniel, ed. Nitrogenous Air Pollutants: Chemical & Biological Implications. LC 79-84379. 1979. 37.50 (ISBN 0-250-40294-7). Ann Arbor Science.
Heal, Henry. The Inorganic Heterocyclic Chemistry of Sulphur, Nitrogen & Phosphorus. 1981. 86.00 (ISBN 0-12-335680-6). Acad Pr.
Honti, G. D. The Nitrogen Industry. 1976. 85.00x (ISBN 963-05-0228-3). Intl Pubns Serv.
Hsu, Donald K., et al. Spectral Atlas of Nitrogen Dioxide: 5530a to 6480a. 1978. 49.50 (ISBN 0-12-357950-3). Acad Pr.
Interlaboratory Cooperative Study of the Precision & Accuracy of the Measurement of Nitrogen Dioxide Content in the Atmosphere Using ASTM D 1607. 1974. pap. 5.00 (ISBN 0-686-51980-9, 05-055000-17). ASTM.
Mosby, W. L., ed. Bridgehead Nitrogen Atoms, Vol. 15, Pt. 1. 758p. 1961. 75.00 (ISBN 0-470-38049-7). Krieger.
--Bridgehead Nitrogen Atoms, Vol. 15, Pt. 2. 730p. 1961. 85.50 (ISBN 0-470-38082-9). Krieger.
Nielsen, D. R. Nitrogen in the Environment, Vol. 1. 1978. 32.00 (ISBN 0-12-518401-8). Acad Pr.
Patai, Paul, ed. Chemistry of Carbon-Nitrogen Double Bond. LC 70-104166. (Chemistry of Functional Groups Ser.). 1970. 126.00 (ISBN 0-471-66942-3, Pub. by Wiley-Interscience). Wiley.
Schofield, K. Hetero-Aromatic Nitrogen Compounds. LC 67-26477. 434p. 1968. 42.50 (ISBN 0-306-30631-X, Plenum Pr). Plenum Pub.
Sittig, Marshall. Nitrogen in Industry. (Illus.). 1965. 11.50x (ISBN 0-442-07629-0). Van Nos Reinhold.
Stewart, W. D. & Sprent, Janet. Nitrogen Fixation in Plants. 1980. cancelled (ISBN 0-485-11155-1, Athlone Pr). Humanities.
Streuli, C. A. The Analytical Chemistry of Nitrogen & Its Compounds, 2 pts. Averell, P. R., ed. LC 68-8112. 428p. 1970. 65.00 (ISBN 0-686-74224-9). Krieger.
Wright, A. Nelson & Winkler, Carl A. Active Nitrogen. (Physical Chemistry Ser.: Vol. 14). 1968. 73.50 (ISBN 0-12-765150-0). Acad Pr.

NITROGEN-ASSIMILATION AND EXCRETION
see Nitrogen Metabolism

NITROGEN-FIXATION
Ayanaba, A. & Dart, P. J., eds. Biological Nitrogen Fixation in Farming Systems of the Tropics. LC 77-1304. 377p. 1978. 65.95 (ISBN 0-471-99499-5, Pub. by Wiley-Interscience). Wiley.
Bergersen, F. J., ed. Methods for Evaluating Biological Nitrogen Fixation. LC 79-41785. 702p. 1980. 114.00 (ISBN 0-471-27759-2, Pub. by Wiley-Interscience). Wiley.
Biological Nitrogen Fixation by Epiphytic Microorganisms in Rice Fields. (IRRI Research Paper Ser.: No. 47). 14p. 1981. pap. 5.00 (ISBN 0-686-69532-1, R 117, IRRI). Unipub.
Broughton, W. J. Nitrogen Fixation, Vol. 1: Ecology. (Illus.). 350p. 1981. 65.00x (ISBN 0-19-854540-1). Oxford U Pr.
Burns, R. C. & Hardy, R. W. Nitrogen Fixation in Bacteria & Higher Plants. LC 75-2164. (Molecular Biology, Biochemistry, & Biophysics Ser.: Vol. 21). (Illus.). 225p. 1975. 32.80 (ISBN 0-387-07192-X). Springer-Verlag.
Chatt, J., et al, eds. New Trends in the Chemistry of Nitrogen Fixation. 1980. 54.00 (ISBN 0-12-169450-X). Acad Pr.
Colowick, Sidney & Kaplan, Nathan, eds. Methods in Enzymology: Vol. 69 Photosynthesis & Nitrogen Fixation, Pt. C. LC 54-9110. 1980. 58.00 (ISBN 0-12-181969-8). Acad Pr.
Dobereiner, J., et al, eds. Limitations & Potentials for Biological Nitrogen Fixation in the Tropics. LC 77-28218. (Basic Life Sciences Ser.: Vol. 10). 412p. 1978. 39.50 (ISBN 0-306-36510-3, Plenum Pr). Plenum Pub.
Hardy, R. W. A Treatise on Dinitrogen Fixation: Agronomy & Ecology, Sect. 4. 527p. 1977. 53.00 (ISBN 0-471-02343-4, Pub. by Wiley-Interscience). Wiley.
--A Treatise on Dinitrogen Fixation: Biology, Sect. 3. 675p. 1977. 55.00 (ISBN 0-471-35138-5, Pub. by Wiley-Interscience). Wiley.
Isotopes in Biological Dinitrogen Fixation. 1979. pap. 31.75 (ISBN 92-0-011078-9, ISP478, IAEA). Unipub.
Lyons, J. M., et al, eds. Genetic Engineering of Symbiotic Nitrogen Fixation & Conservation of Fixed Nitrogen. LC 81-4683. (Basic Life Sciences Ser.: Vol. 17). 675p. 1981. text ed. 69.50 (ISBN 0-306-40730-2, Plenum Pr). Plenum Pub.
Mishustin, E. N. & Shil'nikova, V. K. Biological Fixation of Atmospheric Nitrogen. Crozy, Alan, tr. LC 78-177914. (Illus.). 420p. 1972. 22.50x (ISBN 0-271-01110-6). Pa St U Pr.
Newton, W. Recent Developments in Nitrogen Fixation. 1978. 74.00 (ISBN 0-12-517350-4). Acad Pr.
Newton, William E. Nitrogen Fixation, Vol. 1. Orme-Johnson, William H., ed. (Steenboek Symposia Ser.: No. 7). 414p. 1980. text ed. 39.50 (ISBN 0-8391-1560-1). Univ Park.
Newton, William E. & Orme-Johnson, William, eds. Nitrogen Fixation, Vol. 2. 352p. 1980. text ed. 39.50 (ISBN 0-8391-1561-X). Univ Park.
Postgate. Nitrogen Fixation. (Studies in Biology: No. 92). 1978. 5.95 (ISBN 0-7131-2688-4). Univ Park.
Postgate, J. R., ed. Chemistry & Biochemistry of Nitrogen Fixation. LC 70-161303. 326p. 1971. 35.00 (ISBN 0-306-30459-7, Plenum Pr). Plenum Pub.
Quispel, A. Biology of Nitrogen Fixation. (Frontiers of Biology Ser.: Vol. 33). 769p. 1974. 117.00 (ISBN 0-444-10630-8, North-Holland). Elsevier.
Sprent, Janet. The Biology of Nitrogen Fixing Organisms. (Illus.). 1979. text ed. 23.95 (ISBN 0-07-084087-3). McGraw.
Stewart, W. D., ed. Nitrogen Fixation by Free-Living Micro-Organisms. LC 75-2731. (International Biological Programme Ser.: Vol. 6). (Illus.). 448p. 1976. 72.00 (ISBN 0-521-20708-8). Cambridge U Pr.
Subba Rao, N. S., ed. Recent Advences in Biological Nitrogen Fixation. 500p. 1980. text ed. 45.00x (ISBN 0-8419-5825-4). Holmes & Meier.
Takahasi, H., ed. Nitrogen Fixation & Nitrogen Cycle. (Japan International Biological Program Synthetics Ser.: Vol. 12). 1975. pap. 20.00x (ISBN 0-86008-222-9, Pub. by U of Tokyo Pr). Intl Schol Bk Serv.

NITROGEN COMPOUNDS
see also Alkaloids; Organonitrogen Compounds
Allen, C. F. Six-Membered Heterocyclic Nitrogen Compounds with Three Condensed Rings, Vol. 12. 646p. 1958. 83.50 (ISBN 0-470-37851-4, Pub. by Wiley-Interscience). Wiley.
Anselme, Jean-Pierre, ed. N-Nitrosamines. LC 79-12461. (ACS Symposium Ser.: No. 101). 1979. 22.50 (ISBN 0-8412-0503-5). Am Chemical.
Immobilization & Mineralization of Nitrogen in Pasture Soil. (Agricultural Research Reports Ser.: 781). 1972. pap. 4.00 (ISBN 9-0220-0403-1, PUDOC). Unipub.
Jones, Gurnos. Quinoline & Its Derivatives. LC 76-26941. (The Chemistry of Heterocyclic Compounds Ser.: Vol. 32, Pt. 1). 898p. 1977. 174.75 (ISBN 0-471-99437-5, Pub. by Wiley-Interscience). Wiley.
Matasa, Claudius & Matasa, Eugenia. Basic Nitrogen Compounds. 1972. 56.50 (ISBN 0-8206-0009-1). Chem Pub.
Niedenzu, Kurt, ed. Boron-Nitrogen Chemistry. LC 63-23167. (Advances in Chemistry Ser: No. 42). 1964. 27.25 (ISBN 0-8412-0043-2). Am Chemical.
Schofield, K., et al. Heteroaromatic Nitrogen Compounds: The Azoles. LC 74-17504. (Illus.). 500p. 1976. 85.00 (ISBN 0-521-20519-0). Cambridge U Pr.
Streuli, C. A. The Analytical Chemistry of Nitrogen & Its Compounds, 2 pts. Averell, P. R., ed. LC 68-8112. 428p. 1970. 65.00 (ISBN 0-686-74224-9). Krieger.
Witanowski, M. & Webb, G. A., eds. Nitrogen NMR. LC 72-95065. 403p. 1973. 45.00 (ISBN 0-306-30734-0, Plenum Pr). Plenum Pub.

NITROGEN EXCRETION
see also Urea

NITROGEN FERTILIZERS
Denitrification Loss of Fertilizer Nitrogen in Paddy Soils - Its Recognition & Impact. (IRRI Research Paper Ser.: No. 37). 10p. 1979. pap. 5.00 (ISBN 0-686-70539-4, R077, IRRI). Unipub.
Gasser, J. K., ed. Modelling Nitrogen from Farm Wastes. (Illus.). 1979. 22.60x (ISBN 0-85334-869-3). Intl Ideas.
Nitrogen & Rice. 499p. 1979. pap. 32.50 (ISBN 0-686-70587-4, R026, IRRI). Unipub.
Recent Developements in Research on Nitrogen Fertilizers for Rice. (IRRI Research Paper Ser.: No. 49). 11p. 1981. pap. 5.00 (ISBN 0-686-69535-6, R 119, IRRI). Unipub.
The Role of Nitrogen in Intensive Grassland Production. 171p. 1981. pap. 30.00 (ISBN 90-220-0734-0, PDC 214, Pudoc). Unipub.
Simulation of Nitrogen Behaviour of Soil-Plant Systems. 277p. 1980. pap. 47.75 (ISBN 90-220-0735-9, PDC 223, Pudoc). Unipub.
Utilization of the Azolla-Anabaena Complex As a Nitrogen Fertilizer for Rice. (IRRI Research Paper Ser.: No. 11). 15p. 1977. pap. 5.00 (ISBN 0-686-70663-3, R051, IRRI). Unipub.

NITROGEN FIXATION
see Nitrogen-Fixation

NITROGEN INDUSTRIES
see also Fertilizer Industry; Munitions
Honti. The Nitrogen Industry I-II. 1976. 92.00 (ISBN 0-9960003-4-8, Pub. by Kaido Hungary). Heyden.

NITROGEN METABOLISM
American Physiological Society & American Society of Zoologists, Joint Symposium. Nitrogen Metabolism & the Environment. Campbell, J. W. & Goldstein, L., eds. 1972. 49.50 (ISBN 0-12-157850-X). Acad Pr.
Campbell, J. W., ed. Comparative Biochemistry of Nitrogen Metabolism, Vols. 1 & 2. 1970. Vol. 1. 71.00 (ISBN 0-12-157901-8); Vol. 2. 60.50 (ISBN 0-12-157902-6). Acad Pr.
Hewitt, E. J. & Cutting, C. V. Recent Aspects of Nitrogen Metabolism in Plants. 1968. 45.00 (ISBN 0-12-346250-9). Acad Pr.
Isotope Studies on the Nitrogen Chain. (Illus., Orig., Eng. , Fr. & Rus.). 1968. pap. 21.75 (ISBN 92-0-010068-6, ISP161, IAEA). Unipub.
Takahasi, H., ed. Nitrogen Fixation & Nitrogen Cycle. (Japan International Biological Program Synthetics Ser.: Vol. 12). 1975. pap. 20.00x (ISBN 0-86008-222-9, Pub. by U of Tokyo Pr). Intl Schol Bk Serv.
Tracer Studies on Non-Protein Nitrogen for Ruminants I. 1972. pap. 14.75 (ISBN 92-0-111072-3, ISP 302-1, IAEA). Unipub.

NITROGEN ORGANIC COMPOUNDS
see Organonitrogen Compounds

NITROGEN OXIDE
Bridges, J. W., et al. Biological Oxidation of Nitrogen in Organic Molecules. 269p. 1972. 30.95 (ISBN 0-470-10380-9). Halsted Pr.

Kimisch, Richard L. & Larson, John G., eds. The Catalytic Chemistry of Nitrogen Oxides. LC 75-22332. (General Motors Research Symposia Ser.). 340p. 1975. 32.50 (ISBN 0-306-30875-4, Plenum Pr). Plenum Pub.

Lee, S. D., ed. Nitrogen Oxides & Their Effects on Health. LC 79-53421. 1980. 39.95 (ISBN 0-250-40289-0). Ann Arbor Science.

Yaverbaum, L. H. Nitrogen Oxides Control & Removal. LC 79-16141. (Pollution Technology Review Ser., No. 60: Chemical Technology Review Ser., No. 136). (Illus.). 1980. 42.00 (ISBN 0-8155-0768-2). Noyes.

NITROSO COMPOUNDS

see also Chemical Reactions

Working Conference. International Agency for Research on Cancer. Lyon, France Oct. 17-20, 1973. N-Nitroso Compounds in the Environment: Proceedings. Bogovski, P., et al, eds. (IARC Scientific Pub.: No. 9). 1974. 20.00 (ISBN 0-686-16788-0). World Health.

Working Conference.Deutsches Krebsforschungszentrum, Heidelberg, Germany.Oct. 13-15, 1971. N-Nitroso Compounds-Analysis & Formation: Proceedings. Bogovski, P., et al, eds. (IARC Scientific Pub.: No. 3). 1972. 10.00 (ISBN 0-686-16787-2). World Health.

NITROUS OXIDE

Davy, H. Nitrous Oxide. (Illus.). 606p. 1972. 38.50 (ISBN 0-407-33150-6). Butterworth.

Delwiche, C. C. Denitrification, Nitrification, & Atmospheric Nitrous Oxide. LC 80-22698. 286p. 1981. 40.00 (ISBN 0-471-04896-8, Pub. by Wiley-Interscience). Wiley.

Sheldin, et al. Laughing Gas. 1973. pap. 6.95 (ISBN 0-915904-00-4). And-or Pr.

NITROXYL

Rozantsev, E. G. Free Nitroxyl Radicals. LC 69-12541. 249p. 1970. 34.50 (ISBN 0-306-30396-5, Plenum Pr). Plenum Pub.

NIVEDITA, SISTER

Atmaprana, Pravrajika. Story of Sister Nivedita. pap. 1.95 (ISBN 0-87481-109-0). Vedanta Pr.

NIVEN, DAVID, 1910-

Garrett, Gerard. The Films of David Niven. (Illus.). 256p. 1976. 14.00 (ISBN 0-8065-0557-5). Citadel Pr.

NIXON, PAT

David, Lester. The Lonely Lady of San Clemente. 1979. pap. 2.50 (ISBN 0-425-04253-7). Berkley Pub.

NIXON, RICHARD MILHOUS, PRES. U. S., 1913-

Allen, Gary. Richard Nixon: The Man Behind the Mask. 434p. Date not set. 8.00 (ISBN 0-686-31148-5); pap. 4.00 (ISBN 0-686-31149-3). Concord Pr.

--Richard Nixon: The Man Behind the Mask. LC 73-31048. 433p. 1971. 8.00 (ISBN 0-88279-222-9); pap. 2.00 (ISBN 0-88279-110-9). Western Islands.

Ball, Howard. No Pledge of Privacy: The Watergate Tapes Litigation, 1973-1974. (National University Pubns. Multi-Disciplinary Studies in the Law). 1977. 15.00 (ISBN 0-8046-9181-9). Kennikat.

Bramwell, Dana G. The Tragedy of King Richard: Shakespearean Watergate. new ed. 96p. 1974. pap. 3.35 (ISBN 0-685-52670-4). Survey Pub Co.

Bremer, H. F., ed. Richard M. Nixon: Chronology; Documents; Bibliographical Aids. LC 75-23324. (Presidential Chronology Ser.). 256p. 1975. 15.00 (ISBN 0-379-12083-6). Oceana.

Brodie, Fawn M. Richard Nixon: The Shaping of His Character. (Illus.). 1981. 18.95 (ISBN 0-393-01467-3). Norton.

Burke, Vincent & Burke, Vee. Nixon's Good Deed: Welfare Reform. LC 69-16955. 243p. 1974. 15.00x (ISBN 0-231-03850-X); pap. 6.00x (ISBN 0-231-08346-7). Columbia U Pr.

Cavan, Sherri. Twentieth Century Gothic: America's Nixon. LC 79-65722. (Illus.). 1979. 15.00 (ISBN 0-934594-00-7). Wigan Pier.

The Cumulated Indexes to the Public Papers of the Presidents of the United States: Richard M. Nixon, 1969-1974. 1977. lib. bdg. 45.00 (ISBN 0-527-20750-0). Kraus Intl.

Drew, Elizabeth. Washington Journal: A Diary of the Events of 1973-1974. 448p. 1975. 12.95 (ISBN 0-394-49575-6). Random.

Ehrlichman, John D. Privileged Communication: The Nixon Years. 1981. 14.95 (ISBN 0-671-24296-2). S&S.

Friedman, Leon, ed. United States vs. Nixon: The President Before the Supreme Court. LC 74-16403. 644p. 1974. 15.00 (ISBN 0-8352-0802-8, Dist. by R.R. Bowker). Chelsea Hse.

Frost, David. I Gave Them a Sword: Behind the Scenes of the Nixon Interview. 1978. 9.95 (ISBN 0-688-03279-6). Morrow.

Haldeman, H. R. The Ends of Power. LC 77-79031. 1978. 12.95 (ISBN 0-8129-0724-8). Times Bks.

Haldeman, H. R. & Dimona, Joseph. The Ends of Power. 1978. pap. 2.75 (ISBN 0-440-12239-2). Dell.

Hall, Gus. Lame Duck in Turbulent Waters: The Next Four Years of Nixon. 64p. 1972. pap. 0.50 (ISBN 0-87898-097-0). New Outlook.

Herschensohn, Bruce. The Gods of Antenna. 1976. 7.95 (ISBN 0-87000-346-1). Arlington Hse.

Johnson, George W., ed. Nixon Presidential Press Conferences. LC 77-15612. 1978. text ed. 35.00 (ISBN 0-930576-00-4). E M Coleman Ent.

Klein, Herbert G. Making It Perfectly Clear. (Illus.). 408p. 1980. 14.95 (ISBN 0-385-14047-9). Doubleday.

Lehman, John. The Executive, Congress, & Foreign Policy: Studies of the Nixon Administration. LC 76-13835. (Special Studies). 1976. text ed. 23.95 (ISBN 0-275-56490-8). Praeger.

Levitt, Morton & Levitt, Michael. A Tissue of Lies: Nixon Vs. Hiss. 1979. 14.95 (ISBN 0-07-037397-3, GB). McGraw.

Longford, Lord. Nixon: A Study in Extremes of Fortune. (Illus.). 216p. 1980. 22.50x (ISBN 0-297-77708-4, Pub. by Weidenfeld & Nicolson England). Biblio Dist.

McGinniss, Joe. Selling of the President, 1968. LC 77-92157. 1969. 5.95 (ISBN 0-671-27043-5). Trident.

Mankiewicz, Frank. Perfectly Clear: Nixon from Whittier to Watergate. LC 73-82532. 289p. 1973. 8.95 (ISBN 0-8129-0405-2). Times Bks.

--U. S. Vs. Richard M. Nixon: The Final Crisis. LC 74-81001. 1975. 8.95 (ISBN 0-8129-0505-9). Times Bks.

Marvell, Charles. In Defense of Nixon: A Study in Political Psychology & Political Pathology. LC 76-25960. 1977. 39.65 (ISBN 0-913314-74-9). Am Classical Coll Pr.

Mazlish, Bruce. In Search of Nixon: A Psychohistorical Inquiry. LC 71-189669. (Illus.). 208p. 1972. 12.95 (ISBN 0-465-03219-2). Basic.

Mollenhoff, Clark R. Game Plan for Disaster. 384p. 1976. 9.95 (ISBN 0-393-05543-4). Norton.

Nathan, Richard P. The Plot That Failed: Nixon & the Administrative Presidency. LC 74-30272. 176p. 1975. pap. text ed. 10.95 (ISBN 0-471-63065-9). Wiley.

Neruda, Pablo. Incitement to Nixonicide. Kowit, Steve, tr. 1979. pap. 5.00 (ISBN 0-686-60610-8). Quixote.

The Nixon-Ford Years. (Political Profile Ser.). 1980. lib. bdg. 55.00 (ISBN 0-87196-454-6). Facts on File.

Nixon, Richard. The Memoirs of Richard Nixon, Vol. 1. 736p. 1981. pap. 2.95 (ISBN 0-446-93259-0). Warner Bks.

--The Memoirs of Richard Nixon, Vol. 2. 728p. 1981. pap. 2.95 (ISBN 0-446-93260-4). Warner Bks.

Nixon, Richard M. Memoirs. LC 77-87793. (Illus.). 1978. 19.95 (ISBN 0-448-14374-7). G&D.

Osborne, John. The Third Year of the Nixon Watch. (Illus.). 1972. 6.95 (ISBN 0-87140-551-2). Liveright.

Pearl, Arthur. Landslide. 224p. 1973. 7.95 (ISBN 0-8065-0382-3). Citadel Pr.

Rathiesberger, James, ed. Nixon & the Environment: The Politics of Devestation. 1972. pap. 2.45 (ISBN 0-686-72089-X). Random.

Rothschild, Eric, ed. Richard Nixon & Detente, Nineteen Sixty-Nine to Nineteen Seventy Two. (The New York Times School Microfilm Collection: Guide No. 12). 214p. (gr. 7-12). 1979. pap. 5.50 wkbk (ISBN 0-667-00561-7). Microfilming Corp.

--Richard Nixon & Watergate, Nineteen Seventy-Three to Nineteen Seventy-Four. (The New York Times School Microfilm Collection: Guide No. 13). 114p. (gr. 7-12). 1979. pap. 5.50 wkbk (ISBN 0-667-00562-5). Microfilming Corp.

Rowse, Arthur E. Slanted News: A Case Study of the Nixon & Stevenson Fund Stories. LC 72-7823. (Illus.). 139p. 1973. Repr. of 1957 ed. lib. bdg. 15.00x (ISBN 0-8371-6528-8, ROSN). Greenwood.

Schulte, Renee K., ed. The Young Nixon: An Oral Inquiry. 1978. 13.95 (ISBN 0-930046-02-1); pap. 7.95 (ISBN 0-930046-01-3). CSUF Oral Hist.

Smith, Franklin B. Assassination of President Nixon. LC 76-15444. 128p. 1976. 6.95 (ISBN 0-914960-08-3). Academy Bks.

Spalding, Henry D. The Nixon Nobody Knows. LC 70-188240. (Illus.). 456p. 1972. 8.95 (ISBN 0-8246-0142-4). Jonathan David.

Tretick, Stanley & Shannon, William V. They Could Not Trust the King. (Illus.). 192p. 1974. pap. 4.95 (ISBN 0-02-074740-3, Collier). Macmillan.

Vidal, Gore. An Evening with Richard Nixon. pap. 1.65 (ISBN 0-394-71869-0, V-869, Vin). Random.

Voorhis, Jerry. The Strange Case of Richard Milhous Nixon. LC 72-83711. 352p. 1972. 8.95 (ISBN 0-8397-7917-8). Eriksson.

White, Theodore. Breach of Faith: Fall of Richard Nixon. LC 74-20350. 1975. 10.95 (ISBN 0-689-10658-0). Atheneum.

Wills, Garry. Nixon Agonistes. LC 72-80426. 1978. pap. 25.00 (ISBN 0-910220-88-3). Larlin Corp.

--Nixon Agonistes: The Crisis of the Self Made Man. rev. ed. 1979. pap. 2.50 (ISBN 0-451-61750-9, ME1750, Ment). NAL.

Woodward, Bob & Bernstein, Carl. The Final Days. 1976. 13.95 (ISBN 0-671-22298-8). S&S.

NIXON, RICHARD MILHOUS, PRES. U. S., 1913--CARTOONS, SATIRE, ETC.

Block, Herbert. Herblock Special Report. (Illus.). 1974. 7.95 (ISBN 0-393-08708-5, Norton Lib); pap. 3.95 (ISBN 0-393-00838-X). Norton.

Peters, Mike. The Nixon Chronicles. 1976. pap. 6.95 (ISBN 0-89328-001-1). Lorenz Pr.

Roth, Philip. Our Gang. 1971. 7.95 (ISBN 0-394-47886-X). Random.

Seelye, John. Dirty Tricks: Or Nick Noxin's Natural Nobility. 152p. 1974. 5.95 (ISBN 0-87140-577-6). Liveright.

NIXON, RICHARD MILHOUS, PRES. U. S., 1913--IMPEACHMENT

Barrer, Lester A. & Barrer, Myra E., eds. Documentation Index to the Richard M. Nixon Impeachment Proceedings - Including the Watergate & Related Investigations, Hearings, & Prosecutions, 2 vols. Incl. Vol. 1. 1972, 1973, 1974. 500p. 1982. lib. bdg. 60.00 (ISBN 0-87999-008-2); Vol. 2. 1976-1977. 400p. 1982. lib. bdg. 60.00 (ISBN 0-87999-009-0). LC 74-19332. (Illus.). lib. bdg. 150.00 set (ISBN 0-87999-010-4). Today News.

Barth, Alan. Presidential Impeachment. 1974. pap. 4.50 (ISBN 0-8183-0134-1). Pub Aff Pr.

Drew, Elizabeth. Washington Journal: A Diary of the Events of 1973-1974. 448p. 1975. 12.95 (ISBN 0-394-49575-6). Random.

--Washington Journal: The Events of 1973-1974. 1976. pap. 4.95 (ISBN 0-394-72091-1, Vin). Random.

Fields, Howard. High Crimes & Misdemeanors: The Untold & Dramatic Story of the Rodino Committee. 1978. 10.95 (ISBN 0-393-05681-3). Norton.

Friedman, Leon, ed. United States Vs. Nixon: The President Before the Supreme Court. LC 74-16403. 644p. 1980. pap. 11.95 (ISBN 0-87754-144-2). Chelsea Hse.

Labovitz, John R. Presidential Inpeachment. LC 77-76300. 1978. 20.00x (ISBN 0-300-02213-1). Yale U Pr.

Oglesby, Carl. The Yankee & the Cowboy War. 1977. pap. 1.95 (ISBN 0-425-03493-3, Medallion). Berkley Pub.

Woodward & Bernstein. Final Days. 1976. pap. 2.50 (ISBN 0-380-00844-0, 31104). Avon.

NKRUMAH, KWAME, PRES. GHANA, 1909-1972

Alexander, H. T. African Tightrope: My Two Years As Nkrumah's Chief of Staff. 1966. 7.50 (ISBN 0-685-56706-0). Univ Place.

Chicago Center for Afro-American Studies & Research. Kwane Nkrukmah: A Bibliography. (Bibliographies in Black Studies). 1981. lib. bdg. 10.00x (ISBN 0-937954-06-3). Chi Ctr Afro-Am Stud.

Jarmon, Charles. The Nkrumah Regime: An Evaluation of the Role of Charismatic Authority. Nyang, Sulayman S., ed. (Third World Monograph Ser.). 24p. (Orig.). 1981. pap. 1.50x (ISBN 0-931494-05-2). Brunswick Pub.

Kesse-Adu, K. The Politics of Political Detention. (Illus.). 236p. 1971. pap. 5.00x (ISBN 0-8002-1817-5). Intl Pubns Serv.

Killingray, David. Nyerere & Nkrumah. Yapp, Malcolm & Killingray, Margaret, eds. (World History Ser.). (Illus.). 32p. (gr. 10). 1980. Repr. of 1977 ed. lib. bdg. 5.95 (ISBN 0-89908-129-0); pap. text ed. 1.95 (ISBN 0-89908-104-5). Greenhaven.

Nkrumah, Kwame. Revolutionary Path. LC 73-78905. 1973. 12.50 (ISBN 0-7178-0400-3); pap. 4.95 (ISBN 0-7178-0401-1). Intl Pub Co.

Omari, T. Peter. Kwame Nkrumah: The Anatomy of an African Dictatorship. LC 74-103939. 1970. 23.50x (ISBN 0-8419-0036-1, Africana). Holmes & Meier.

NO KYOGEN PLAYS

see Kyogen Plays

NO MAN'S LAND OKLAHOMA-HISTORY

Chrisman, Harry E. Lost Trails of the Cimarron. LC 61-14370. (Illus.). 313p. 1964. pap. 7.95 (ISBN 0-8040-0615-6, SB). Swallow.

NO ME MEUVE MI DIOS, PARA QUERERTE (SONNET)

Huff, Sr. M. Cyria. Sonnet - Ne Me Mueve, Mi Dios - Its Theme in Spanish Tradition. LC 73-94177. (Catholic University of America Studies in Romance Languages & Literatures Ser: No. 33). Repr. of 1948 ed. 16.00 (ISBN 0-404-50333-0). AMS Pr.

NO PLAYS

Chiba, Reiko. Painted Fans of Japan: Fifteen Noh Drama Masterpieces. LC 62-20775. (Illus., Fr., Or Eng). 1962. 15.50 (ISBN 0-8048-0468-0). C E Tuttle.

Fenollosa, Ernest F. & Pound, Ezra. The Classic Noh Theatre of Japan. LC 77-4057. 1977. Repr. of 1959 ed. lib. bdg. 15.00x (ISBN 0-8371-9580-2, FECN). Greenwood.

Keene, Donald. No: The Classical Theatre of Japan. LC 66-25756. (Illus.). 311p. 1966. 85.00 (ISBN 0-87011-034-9). Kodansha.

Keene, Donald, ed. Twenty Plays of the No Theatre. Tyler, et al, trs. from Japanese. LC 74-121556. (Records of Civilization Sources & Studies & Translations of the Oriental Classics Ser.). 336p. 1970. 22.50x (ISBN 0-231-03454-7); pap. 12.00x (ISBN 0-231-03455-5). Columbia U Pr.

Noh Drama: Ten Plays from the Japanese. LC 60-11007. 1960. 7.95 (ISBN 0-8048-0428-1). C E Tuttle.

O'Neill, P. G. Early No Drama: Its Background, Character, & Development, 1300-1450. LC 73-21264. (Illus.). 223p. 1974. Repr. of 1959 ed. lib. bdg. 13.75x (ISBN 0-8371-6104-5, ONND). Greenwood.

Pound, Ezra. Translations. rev. ed. LC 53-11965. 1953. pap. 7.95 (ISBN 0-8112-0164-3, NDP145). New Directions.

Pound, Ezra, ed. Classic Noh Theatre of Japan. LC 59-9488. Orig. Title: Noh, or Accomplishment, a Study of the Classical Stage of Japan. 1959. pap. 4.95 (ISBN 0-8112-0152-X, NDP79). New Directions.

Waley, Arthur. The No Play of Japan. LC 75-28969. 1976. pap. 5.95 (ISBN 0-8048-1198-9). C E Tuttle.

NOAH

Allen, Don C. The Legend of Noah: Renaissance Rationalism in Art, Science & Letters. LC 49-49065. (Reprint of Studies in Language & Literature Ser.: Vol. 33, No. 3-4, 1949). (Illus.). 1963. pap. 3.95 (ISBN 0-252-72516-6). U of Ill Pr.

Bennett, Marian. The Story of Noah. (Mini Pop-Ups). (Illus.). 12p. (gr. k-2). 1979. 2.50 (ISBN 0-87239-366-6, 3614). Standard Pub.

Fant, Louie J., Jr. Noah. new ed. (Illus.). 14p. 1973. pap. text ed. 2.50 (ISBN 0-917002-70-9). Joyce Media.

Greenfeld, Josh. A Place for Noah. 1978. 10.00 (ISBN 0-03-089896-X). HR&W.

Hajj 'Abd al-Hayy al-Amin. The Story of Noah. (Stories of the Prophets Ser.). (Illus.). 1980. pap. 3.50 (ISBN 0-935290-02-8). Iqra.

Hutton, Warwick. Noah & the Great Flood. LC 77-3217. (Illus.). 32p. (ps up). 1977. 7.95 (ISBN 0-689-50098-X, McElderry Bk). Atheneum.

Lindsay, Gordon. Enoch & Noah, Patriarchs of the Deluge. (Old Testament Ser.). 1.25 (ISBN 0-89985-125-8). Christ Nations.

Mee, Charles L., Jr. Noah. LC 77-11839. (Illus.). 1978. 5.95 (ISBN 0-06-024183-7, HarpJ); PLB 5.79 (ISBN 0-06-024184-5). Har-Row.

Wengrov, Charles. Tales of Noah & the Ark. (Biblical Ser.). (Illus.). (gr. 5-10). 1969. 6.00 (ISBN 0-914080-23-7). Shulsinger Sales.

NOAH'S ARK

Bailey, Lloyd R. Where Is Noah's Ark? Mystery on Mount Ararat. (Festival Bks). 1978. pap. 1.95 (ISBN 0-687-45093-4). Abingdon.

Balsiger, David W. & Sellier, Charles E., Jr. In Search of Noah's Ark. (Illus.). 1976. pap. 1.95 (ISBN 0-917214-01-3). Schick Sunn.

Berg, Jean H. Noah & the Ark. (Illus.). (gr. 2-6). 1974. pap. 3.95 (ISBN 0-87510-095-3). Chr Science.

Bolliger, Max. Noah & the Rainbow: An Ancient Story. Bulla, Clyde R., tr. LC 72-76361. (Illus.). (gr. k-3). 1972. 8.79 (ISBN 0-690-58448-2, TYC-J); pap. 9.95 (ISBN 0-690-58448-2). Har-Row.

Burman, Ben L. Children of Noah. 5.00 (ISBN 0-685-02658-2). Taplinger.

Cummings, Violet. Noah's Ark: Fable of Fact. 1973. pap. 1.95 (ISBN 0-685-79096-7). Creation Sci.

Duvoisin, Roger. A for the Ark. LC 52-12846. (Illus.). (gr. k-3). 1952. PLB 8.16 (ISBN 0-688-50985-1). Lothrop.

Hartley, Allan. Noah's Ark. (Spire Comics Ser.). 1976. pap. 0.49 (ISBN 0-8007-8522-3). Revell.

Hutton, Warwick. Noah & the Great Flood. LC 77-3217. (Illus.). 32p. (ps up). 1977. 7.95 (ISBN 0-689-50098-X, McElderry Bk). Atheneum.

Krentel, Mildred. Two by Two. LC 61-14915. (Illus.). (ps-3). 1961. 1.95 (ISBN 0-87213-471-7). Loizeaux.

Latourette, Jane & Mathews. Story of Noah's Ark. LC 63-23144. (Arch Bks: Set 2). 1965. laminated bdg. 0.79 (ISBN 0-570-06009-5, 59-1110). Concordia.

Lorimer, Lawrence T., retold by. Noah's Ark. LC 77-92377. (Picturebacks Ser.). (Illus.). (ps-2). 1978. PLB 4.99 (ISBN 0-394-93861-5, BYR); pap. 1.25 (ISBN 0-394-83861-0). Random.

Meyer, Nathan M. Noah's Ark, Pitched & Parked. pap. 3.00 (ISBN 0-88469-039-3). BMH Bks.
Montgomery, John W. Quest for Noah's Ark. rev. ed. LC 74-21993. (Illus.). 1972. pap. 3.95 (ISBN 0-87123-477-7, 200477). Bethany Hse.
Noah & the Ark. (MacDonald Educational Ser.). (Illus., Arabic.). 3.50 (ISBN 0-86685-212-3). Intl Bk Ctr.
Noah Builds a Big Boat. (Tell-a-Bible Story Ser.). (Illus.). 28p. bds. 0.79 (ISBN 0-686-68637-3, 3681). Standard Pub.
Noah's Ark. LC 76-11269. (Sunshine Bks). (Illus.). 20p. 1976. pap. 1.00 (ISBN 0-8006-1576-X, 1-1576). Fortress.
Segraves, Kelly L. Search for Noah's Ark. 1976. pap. 1.45 (ISBN 0-89293-052-7). Beta Bk.
Spier, Peter. Noah's Ark. 48p. (ps). 1981. pap. 3.95 (ISBN 0-385-17302-4, Zephyr). Doubleday.
--Noah's Ark. LC 76-43630. (gr. 1-3). 1977. 8.95a (ISBN 0-385-09473-6); PLB (ISBN 0-385-12730-8). Doubleday.
Teeple, Howard M. The Noah's Ark Nonsense. LC 78-53529. (Truth in Religion Ser.: No. 1). 1978. 10.00 (ISBN 0-914384-01-5). REI.
Wengrov, Charles. Tales of Noah & the Ark. (Biblical Ser.). (Illus.). (gr. 5-10). 1969. 6.00 (ISBN 0-914080-23-7). Shulsinger Sales.

NOAILLES, ANTOINE DE, 1504-1562

Harbison, E. Harris. Rival Ambassadors at the Court of Queen Mary. LC 73-107805. (Select Bibliographies Reprint Ser). 1940. 26.00 (ISBN 0-8369-5182-4). Arno.

NOBEL, ALFRED BERNHARD, 1833-1896

Gray, Tony. Champions of Peace: The Story of Alfred Nobel, the Peace Prize, & the Laureates. LC 76-3812. (Illus.). (YA) 1976. 10.95 (ISBN 0-448-23316-9). Paddington.
Marble, Annie. Nobel Prize Winners in Literature, 1901-1931. facs. ed. LC 70-84324. (Essay Index Reprint Ser). 1932. 25.00 (ISBN 0-8369-1185-7). Arno.

NOBEL PRIZES

Falnes, Oscar J. Norway & the Nobel Peace Prize. LC 72-168003. Repr. of 1938 ed. 14.50 (ISBN 0-404-02365-7). AMS Pr.
Heathcote, Niels H. Nobel Prize Winners in Physics, 1901-1950. facsimile ed. LC 76-167354. (Essay Index Reprint Ser: Life of Science Library). Repr. of 1953 ed. 36.00 (ISBN 0-8369-2455-X). Arno.
Kidd, Walter E., ed. British Winners of the Nobel Literary Prize. LC 72-9270. 250p. 1973. 13.95x (ISBN 0-8061-1075-9). U of Okla Pr.
Ludovici, Lionel J., ed. Nobel Prize Winners. (Illus.). 1957. 3.75 (ISBN 0-685-06587-1). Assoc Bk.
Marble, Annie. Nobel Prize Winners in Literature, 1901-1931. facs. ed. LC 70-84324. (Essay Index Reprint Ser). 1932. 25.00 (ISBN 0-8369-1185-7). Arno.
Meyer, Edith P. In Search of Peace: The Winners of the Nobel Peace Prize, 1901-1975. LC 77-24599. (Illus.). (gr. 5 up). 1978. 7.95 (ISBN 0-687-18969-1). Abingdon.
Milosz, Czleslaw. Nobel Lecture. bi-lingual ed. (Polish & Eng.). 1981. 8.95 (ISBN 0-374-22299-1); pap. 5.95 (ISBN 0-374-51654-5). FS&G.
Nobel Foundation. Nobel Lectures in Physics, 1901-1970, 4 vols. Incl. Vol. 1. 1901-1921. 1967. 44.00 (ISBN 0-444-40416-3); Vol. 2. 1922-1941. 1965. 44.00 (ISBN 0-444-40417-1); Vol. 3. 1942-1962. 1964. 44.00 (ISBN 0-444-40418-X); Vol. 4. 1963-1970. 1973. 58.75 (ISBN 0-444-40993-9). Elsevier.
--Nobel, Prizes, Presentations, Biographies & Lectures. 1979. text ed. 41.25x (ISBN 91-97007-28-5). Humanities.
--Prix Nobel En 1967. 1970. 44.00 (ISBN 0-444-99921-3). Elsevier.
--Les Prix Nobel En 1970. 1972. 44.00 (ISBN 0-444-99909-4). Elsevier.
--Les Prix Nobel En 1971. 1973. 44.00 (ISBN 0-685-34694-3). Elsevier.
--Prix Nobel En 1972. 1974. 44.00 (ISBN 0-444-99882-9). Elsevier.
--Les Prix Nobel En 1973. 252p. 1975. 44.00 (ISBN 0-444-99859-4). Elsevier.
--Les Prix Nobel En 1974. 1976. 44.00 (ISBN 0-444-99834-9). Elsevier.
--Prix Nobel 1968. 1971. 44.00 (ISBN 0-444-99935-3). Elsevier.
Nobel Foundation & Odelberg, W. Nobel, the Man & His Prizes. 1972. 35.00 (ISBN 0-444-00117-4, North Holland). Elsevier.
Nobel Foundation, ed. Les Prix Nobel en 1975. 1980. 49.00 (ISBN 0-444-99815-2). Elsevier.
Opfell, Olga S. The Lady Laureates: Women Who Have Won the Nobel Prize. LC 78-15995. 1978. 14.00 (ISBN 0-8108-1161-8). Scarecrow.
Solzhenitsyn, Alexander. Nobel Lecture. bi-lingual ed. Reeve, F. D., tr. from Rus. 80p. 1973. 4.00 (ISBN 0-374-22300-9); pap. 1.95 (ISBN 0-374-51063-6). FS&G.
Solzhenitsyn, Alexandr I. The Nobel Lecture on Literature. Whitney, Thomas P., tr. from Rus. LC 72-9890. 48p. (YA) 1972. 5.95 (ISBN 0-06-013943-9, HarpT). Har-Row.
Wade, Nicholas. The Nobel Duel: The Scientist's Twenty-One Year Race to Win the World's Most Coveted Research Prize. LC 79-7512. (Illus.). 312p. 1981. 15.95 (ISBN 0-385-14981-6, Anchor Pr). Doubleday.
Zuckerman, Harriet. Scientific Elite: Nobel Laureates in the United States. LC 76-26444. (Illus.). 1977. 14.95 (ISBN 0-02-935760-8); pap. text ed. 7.95 (ISBN 0-02-935880-9). Free Pr.

NOBILITY

see also Aristocracy; Heraldry; Knights and Knighthood; Titles of Honor and Nobility; also subdivision Nobility under names of countries, e.g. France–Nobility

Cheyette, Frederic, ed. Lordship & Community in Medieval Europe. LC 75-12657. 448p. 1975. Repr. of 1968 ed. 14.50 (ISBN 0-88275-283-9). Krieger.
De Syrmia, Edmond. At the Head of Nations: The Rise of the Papal & Princely House of Odescalchi. LC 76-44029. (Illus.). 1978. 7.00 (ISBN 0-914226-05-3). Cyclopedia.
Duby, Georges. The Chivalrous Society. Postan, Cynthia, tr. from Fr. LC 74-81431. 1978. 32.50x (ISBN 0-520-02813-9); pap. 4.95 (ISBN 0-520-04271-9). U of Cal Pr.
Halifax, George S. Complete Works of George Savile, First Marquess of Halifax. Raleigh, Walter, ed. LC 76-105080. (Illus.). Repr. of 1912 ed. 10.00x (ISBN 0-678-00605-9). Kelley.
Humphrey, Laurence. The Nobles, or of Nobilitye. with a Small Treatise of Philo a Jewe. LC 72-6008. (English Experience Ser.: No. 534). 416p. 1973. Repr. of 1563 ed. 30.00 (ISBN 90-221-0534-2). Walter J Johnson.
Pettigrew, Joyce. Robber Noblemen. 1975. 24.00 (ISBN 0-7100-7999-0). Routledge & Kegan.
Reuter, T. The Medieval Nobility. (Europe in the Middle Ages Ser.: Vol 14). 1978. 40.00 (ISBN 0-444-85136-4, North Holland). Elsevier.
Robinson, John R. The Last Earls of Barrymore, 1769-1824. LC 72-80506. Repr. of 1894 ed. 15.00 (ISBN 0-405-08895-7, Pub. by Blom). Arno.
Rosenthal, Joel T. Nobles & Noble Life Twelve Ninety-Five to Fifteen Hundred: Historical Problems: Studies & Documents. (Illus.). 208p. 1976. text ed. 18.95x (ISBN 0-04-942139-5). Allen Unwin.

NOBLE GASES

see Gases, Rare

NOCK, ALBERT JAY

Wreszin, Michael. The Superfluous Anarchist: Albert Jay Nock. LC 75-154339. (Illus.). xii, 196p. 1971. 10.00 (ISBN 0-87057-130-3, Pub. by Brown U Pr). U Pr of New Eng.

NOCTUIDAE

Ripley, Lewis B. The External Morphology & Postembryology of Noctuid Larvae. (Illinois Biological Monographs: Vol. 8). Repr. of 1924 ed. pap. 6.00 (ISBN 0-384-50920-7). Johnson Repr.

NOCTURNAL ANIMALS

Berrill, Jacquelyn. Wonders of the Woods & Desert at Night. LC 63-7626. (Wonders Ser.). (Illus.). (gr. 4-6). 1963. PLB 5.95 (ISBN 0-396-06395-0). Dodd.
Charles-Dominique, P. & Martin, R. D. Behavior & Ecology of Nocturnal Prosimians: Field Studies in Gabon & Madagascar. (Advances in Ethology Ser.: Vol. 9). (Illus.). 91p. (Orig.). 1972. pap. text ed. 23.50 (ISBN 3-4896-4536-7). Parey Sci Pubs.
Charles-Dominique, Pierre. Ecology & Behavior of Nocturnal Primates. Martin, R. D., tr. LC 77-1227. (Illus.). 277p. 1977. 20.00x (ISBN 0-231-04362-7). Columbia U Pr.
Gilbreath, Alice. Creatures of the Night: North America's Nocturnal Animals. (Illus.). (gr. 6 up). 1979. 7.95 (ISBN 0-679-20552-7). McKay.
Hamerstrom, Frances. Walk When the Moon Is Full. LC 75-33878. (Illus.). 64p. (gr. 3-8). 1975. 6.95 (ISBN 0-912278-69-2); pap. 3.95 (ISBN 0-912278-84-6). Crossing Pr.
Ricciuti, Edward R. Sounds of Animals at Night. LC 76-3843. (Illus.). (gr. 3-7). 1977. 8.95 (ISBN 0-06-024980-3, HarpJ); PLB 8.79 (ISBN 0-06-024981-1). Har-Row.
Tunney, Christopher. Exploring the Midnight World. (Explorer Books). (Illus.). (gr. 3-5). 1979. 2.95 (ISBN 0-531-09131-7); PLB 6.90 s&l (ISBN 0-531-09116-3). Watts.
Wallace, David R. The Dark Range: A Naturalist's Night Notebook. LC 78-1452. (Illus.). 1978. 15.00 (ISBN 0-87156-212-X); pap. 8.95 (ISBN 0-87156-251-0). Sierra.

NODIER, CHARLES EMMANUEL, 1780-1844

Bell, Sarah F. Charles Nodier: His Life & Works: A Critical Bibliography. (Studies in the Romance Languages & Literatures: No. 95). 1971. pap. 8.50x (ISBN 0-8078-9095-2). U of NC Pr.
Bender, Edmund J., ed. Bibliographie: Charles Nodier. LC 69-11276. (Fr). 1969. 4.50 (ISBN 0-911198-21-0). Purdue.
Cortey, Teresa. Le Rave Dans les Contes De Charles Nodier. 309p. (Fr.). 1977. pap. text ed. 11.25 (ISBN 0-8191-0225-3). U Pr of Amer.
Nelson, Hilda. Charles Nodier. (World Authors Ser.: France: No. 242). lib. bdg. 10.95 (ISBN 0-8057-2654-3). Twayne.
Oliver, A. Richard. Charles Nodier, Pilot of Romanticism. LC 64-8670. (Illus.). 1964. 14.95x (ISBN 0-8156-2073-X). Syracuse U Pr.

NODUS LYMPHATICUS

see Lymph Nodes

NOEL, CONRAD, 1869-1942

Groves, Reginald. Conrad Noel & the Thaxted Movement. LC 68-3219. 1968. lib. bdg. 15.00x (ISBN 0-678-08010-0). Kelley.

NOGUCHI, HIDEYO, 1876-1928

Plesset, Isabel R. Noguchi & His Patrons. LC 78-66819. 320p. 1980. 25.00 (ISBN 0-8386-2347-6). Fairleigh Dickinson.

NOGUCHI, ISAMU

Grove, Nancy & Botnick, Diane. The Sculpture of Isamu Noguchi, 1924-1979: A Catalogue. LC 70-28698. (Garland Reference Library of the Humanities: Vol. 207). 625p. 1980. lib. bdg. 40.00 (ISBN 0-8240-9550-2). Garland Pub.
Hunter, Sam. Isamu Noguchi. LC 78-5288. (Illus.). 1978. 75.00 (ISBN 0-89659-003-8). Abbeville Pr.
Tobias, Tobi. Isamu Noguchi: The Life of a Sculptor. LC 72-7560. (Illus.). 48p. (gr. 2-5). 1974. 8.79 (ISBN 0-690-45014-1, TYC-J). Har-Row.

NOISE

see also Electric Noise; Industrial Noise; Noise Control; Silence; Sound Pressure; Soundproofing; Traffic Noise

Blachman, Nelson M. Noise & Its Effect on Communication. 224p. 1981. Repr. of 1966 ed. lib. bdg. write for info. (ISBN 0-89874-256-0). Krieger.
Bragdon, Clifford R. Noise Pollution: The Unquiet Crisis. LC 70-157049. (Illus.). 1972. 18.00 (ISBN 0-8122-7638-8). U of Pa Pr.
Community Noise. (Special Technical Publications Ser.). 653p. 1979. 34.75x (ISBN 0-686-76039-5, 692, 04-692000-41). ASTM.
Connor, F. R. Noise. (Introductory Topics in Electronics & Telecommunication Ser.). (Illus.). 1973. pap. text ed. 11.00x (ISBN 0-7131-3306-6). Intl Ideas.
Cremer, L. & Heckl, M. Structure-Borne Sound: Structural Vibrations & Sound Radiation at Audio Frequencies. rev. ed. Ungar, E. E., tr. from Ger. LC 72-95350. (Illus.). xvi, 528p. 1973. 62.10 (ISBN 0-387-06002-2). Springer-Verlag.
Floyd, Mary K. A Bibliography of Noise for 1971. LC 72-87107. 150p. 1973. 10.00x (ISBN 0-87875-031-2). Whitston Pub.
--A Bibliography of Noise for 1971. LC 72-87107. 150p. 1973. 10.00x (ISBN 0-87875-031-2). Whitston Pub.
--Bibliography of Noise for 1972. LC 72-87107. xvii, 126p. 1974. 10.00x (ISBN 0-87875-054-1). Whitston Pub.
--A Bibliography of Noise for 1973. LC 72-87107. 1975. 10.00x (ISBN 0-87875-055-X). Whitston Pub.
--A Bibliography of Noise, 1965-1970. LC 72-87107. xxx, 375p. 1973. 17.00x (ISBN 0-87875-029-0). Whitston Pub.
Holmes, Jack K. Coherent Communication with Applications to Pseudo-Noise Spread Spectrum Synchronization. LC 81-4296. 850p. 1981. 50.00 (ISBN 0-471-03301-4, Pub. by Wiley-Interscience). Wiley.
Kavaler, Lucy. The Dangers of Noise. LC 77-26588. (Illus.). (gr. 4-7). 1978. 9.95 (ISBN 0-690-03905-0, TYC-J); PLB 8.79 (ISBN 0-690-03906-9). Har-Row.
King, Richard L. Airport Noise Pollution: A Bibliography of Its Effects on People & Property. LC 73-3370. 1973. 13.50 (ISBN 0-8108-0610-X). Scarecrow.
Kramer-Greene, Judith. A Bibliography of Noise for 1974. LC 72-82107. 1976. 10.00x (ISBN 0-87875-078-9). Whitston Pub.
Kryter, Karl D. Effects of Noise on Man. (Environmental Science Ser). 1970. 56.00 (ISBN 0-12-427450-1). Acad Pr.
May, Daryl. Handbook of Noise Assessment. 1978. text ed. 24.50 (ISBN 0-442-25197-1). Van Nos Reinhold.
Miller, Richard K. Energy & Noise. 45.00 (ISBN 0-915586-40-1). Fairmont Pr.
Milne, Antony. Noise Pollution: Impact & Countermeasures. 1979. 17.95 (ISBN 0-7153-7701-9). David & Charles.
Molek, Mary, compiled by. Comprehensive Bibliography of the Literary Works of Ivan (John) Molek. LC 76-50170. (Illus.). 82p. 1976. 3.50 (ISBN 0-9603142-0-2). M Molek Inc.
Newman, Frederick R. Mouthsounds. (Illus.). 128p. (Orig.). 1980. pap. 5.95 (ISBN 0-89480-128-7). Workman Pub.
Scheibel, M. Barbara. Noise: The Unseen Enemy. new ed. Eblen, William, ed. LC 72-79109. (Ecology Ser.). (Illus.). 64p. (Orig.). (gr. 7-12). 1972. pap. 1.45 (ISBN 0-88301-041-0). Pendulum Pr.
Schultz, Theodore J. Community Noise Ratings. 1972. text ed. 21.60x (ISBN 0-85334-551-1). Intl Ideas.
Welch, Bruce L. & Welch, Annemarie S., eds. Physiological Effects of Noise. LC 70-130586. 365p. 1970. 32.50 (ISBN 0-306-30503-8, Plenum Pr). Plenum Pub.

NOISE, ELECTRONIC

see Electronic Noise

NOISE, RANDOM

see Random Noise Theory

NOISE CONTROL

see also Soundproofing

Archibald, Claudia J. Noise Control Directory. pap. 24.50 (ISBN 0-915586-14-2). Fairmont Pr.
--Noise Control Directory, 1978-79. 1978. pap. text ed. 35.00x (ISBN 0-89671-012-2). Southeast Acoustics.
Assembly of Behavioral & Social Sciences. Noise Abatement: Policy Alternatives for Transportation. 1977. pap. 8.00 (ISBN 0-309-02648-2). Natl Acad Pr.
Atkins Research & Development Group. The Control of Noise in Ventilation Systems: A Designer's Guide. Iqbal, M. A., et al, eds. 107p. 1977. text ed. 24.50x (ISBN 0-419-11050-X, Pub. by E & FN Spon England). Methuen Inc.
Beranek, Leo L. Noise & Vibration Control. 1971. 39.50 (ISBN 0-07-004841-X, P&RB). McGraw.
--Noise Reduction. LC 79-26956. 762p. 1980. Repr. of 1960 ed. lib. bdg. 38.50 (ISBN 0-89874-108-4). Krieger.
Bragdon, Clifford R. Coping with the Barking Dog Noise Problem. 40p. 1978. pap. text ed. 35.00x (ISBN 0-89671-013-0). Southeast Acoustics.
--Municipal Noise Legislation. 35.00 (ISBN 0-89671-018-1). Fairmont Pr.
Cheremisinoff, Paul N. & Cheremisinoff, Peter P. Industrial Noise Control Handbook. LC 76-46023. 1977. 37.50 (ISBN 0-250-40144-4). Ann Arbor Science.
Clark, William D. Rotary Power Lawn Mower Noise. (Illus.). 1978. pap. text ed. 45.00x (ISBN 0-89671-015-7). Southeast Acoustics.
Cremer, L. & Heckl, M. Structure-Borne Sound: Structural Vibrations & Sound Radiation at Audio Frequencies. rev. ed. Ungar, E. E., tr. from Ger. LC 72-95350. (Illus.). xvi, 528p. 1973. 62.10 (ISBN 0-387-06002-2). Springer-Verlag.
Crocker, Malcolm J. & Price, A. J. Noise & Noise Control. new ed. (Uniscience Ser.). 1975. 49.95 (ISBN 0-87819-064-3). CRC Pr.
Duerden, C. Noise Abatement. LC 77-164907. (Illus.). 1971. 25.00 (ISBN 0-8022-2061-4). Philos Lib.
Fader, Bruce. Industrial Noise Control. LC 81-2158. 352p. 1981. 29.95 (ISBN 0-471-06007-0, Pub. by Wiley Interscience). Wiley.
Ghering, W. L., ed. Reference Data for Acoustic Noise Control. LC 78-62291. (Illus.). 1978. 30.00 (ISBN 0-250-40257-2). Ann Arbor Science.
Harris, Cyril M. Handbook of Noise Control. 2nd ed. (Illus.). 1979. 39.50 (ISBN 0-07-026814-2, P&RB). McGraw.
Hutchins, Carleen M. Who Will Drown the Sound? (Science Is What & Why Ser.). (Illus.). (gr. 1-3). 1972. PLB 5.99 (ISBN 0-698-30478-0). Coward.
Institute for Power System. Handbook of Noise & Vibration Control. 4th ed. 850p. 1979. 99.00x (ISBN 0-85461-073-1). State Mutual Bks.
Institution of Chemical Engineers, London & South-Eastern Branch & Association of Noise Consultants. It Smells Rotten & It Sounds Awful. 111p. 1981. 60.00x (ISBN 0-686-75383-6, Pub. by Inst Chem Eng England). State Mutual Bk.
Inter-Noise 79: Proceedings, 2 vols. 944p. 1980. write for info. Noise Control.
International Conference on Noise Control Engineering, Miami, Florida, December 1980. Inter-Noise 80: Proceedings, 2 vols. Maling, George C., Jr., ed. 1296p. 1980. Set. 49.50 (ISBN 0-931784-03-4). Noise Control.
Irwin, J. David & Graf, Edward R. Industrial Noise & Vibration Control. LC 78-7786. (Illus.). 1979. ref. 31.50 (ISBN 0-13-461574-3). P-H.
Lhuede, E. P. & Davern, W. A. Noise Levels in Australian Sawmills. 1980. 10.00x (ISBN 0-643-00348-7, Pub. by CSJRO Australia). State Mutual Bk.
Lipscomb, David M. & Taylor, Arthur C., eds. Noise Control: Handbook of Principles & Practices. 1978. text ed. 26.50x (ISBN 0-442-24811-3). Van Nos Reinhold.

Lord, Harold W., et al. Noise Control for Engineers. (Illus.). 448p. 1979. text ed. 24.95x (ISBN 0-07-038738-9); solutions manual 4.95 (ISBN 0-07-038739-7). McGraw.
Magrab, Edward B. Environmental Noise Control. LC 75-20233. 299p. 1975. 27.50 (ISBN 0-471-56344-7, Pub. by Wiley-Interscience). Wiley.
Miller, Richard K. City Noise Index. new ed. (Illus.). 1978. pap. text ed. 35.00x (ISBN 0-89671-005-X). Southeast Acoustics.
--Guide to the Noise Control Literature. 24.95 (ISBN 0-915586-09-6). Fairmont Pr.
--Handbook of Industrial Noise Management. 24.95 (ISBN 0-915586-02-9). Fairmont Pr.
--Industrial Noise Control 1978. new ed. 1978. pap. text ed. 35.00x (ISBN 0-89671-011-4). Southeast Acoustics.
--Noise Control in Buffing & Polishing. new ed. (Illus.). 1979. pap. text ed. 35.00x (ISBN 0-89671-009-2). Southeast Acoustics.
--Noise Control Solutions for Monument Manufacturing. 1979. pap. text ed. 45.00x (ISBN 0-89671-008-4). Southeast Acoustics.
--Noise Control Solutions for the Chemical & Petroleum Industries. new ed. 1979. pap. text ed. 45.00x (ISBN 0-89671-010-6). Southeast Acoustics.
--Noise Control Solutions for the Construction Industry. 45.00 (ISBN 0-686-74623-6). Fairmont Pr.
--Noise Control Solutions for the Rubber & Plastics Industry. new ed. (Illus.). 1979. pap. text ed. 45.00x (ISBN 0-89671-007-6). Southeast Acoustics.
--Noise Control Solutions for the Wire Industry. new ed. (Illus.). 1979. pap. text ed. 35.00x (ISBN 0-89671-006-8). Southeast Acoustics.
Miller, Richard K., et al. Noise Control Solutions for the Paper Products Industry. 45.00 (ISBN 0-89671-001-7). Fairmont Pr.
--Noise Control Solutions for the Textile Industry. 45.00 (ISBN 0-89671-004-1). Fairmont Pr.
--Noise Control Solutions for the Wood Products Industry. 45.00 (ISBN 0-89671-002-5). Fairmont Pr.
--Noise Control Soultions for the Food Products Industry. 45.00 (ISBN 0-89671-003-3). Fairmont Pr.
--Noise Control Solutions for the Chemical & Petroleum Industries. 45.00 (ISBN 0-89671-010-6). Fairmont Pr.
--Noise Control Solutions for the Metal Products Industry. 45.00 (ISBN 0-89671-000-9). Fairmont Pr.
--Noise Control Solutions for the Rubber & Plastics Industry. 45.00 (ISBN 0-686-74624-4). Fairmont Pr.
Moore, J. E. Design for Good Acoustics & Noise Control. 1979. pap. 16.95x (ISBN 0-333-24293-9). Scholium Intl.
Nelson, Jon P. Economic Analysis of Transportation Noise Abatement. LC 77-25404. 1978. 19.00 (ISBN 0-88410-456-7). Ballinger Pub.
Noise Abatement Policies. 392p. 1980. 16.00x (ISBN 92-64-12084-X). OECD.
Oviatt, Mark D. & Miller, Richard K. Industrial Pneumatic Systems: Noise Control & Energy Conservation. 27.95 (ISBN 0-915586-19-3). Fairmont Pr.
Petrusewicz, S. A., ed. Industrial Noise & Vibration Control. 1974. 30.00 (ISBN 0-444-19543-2). Elsevier.
Pipkin, Lewis S., et al. Relation of Highway Noise to Residential Property Values in Urban Areas of Tennessee. (Illus.). 1978. pap. text ed. 35.00x (ISBN 0-89671-014-9). Southeast Acoustics.
Royster, Larry H., et al, eds. Noise-Control Eighty-One: Proceedings. (National Conference on Noise Control Engineering Ser.). 488p. 1981. 42.00 (ISBN 0-931784-04-2). Noise Control.
Sharland, Ian. Woods Practical Guide to Noise Control. 3rd ed. LC 74-181675. (Illus.). 1979. 10.00x (ISBN 0-8002-0030-6). Intl Pubns Serv.
Society of Automotive Engineers. Vehicle Noise Regulation & Reduction. 1980. 22.50 (ISBN 0-89883-227-6). SAE.
Thumann, Albert & Miller, Richard K. Secrets of Noise Control. 27.50 (ISBN 0-915586-00-2). Fairmont Pr.
Trade & Technical Press Editors. Handbook of Noise & Vibration Control. 4th ed. 850p. 1979. 110.00 (ISBN 0-85461-073-1, Pub by Trade & Tech England). Renouf.
--Noise & Vibration Control. 120p. 1976. 19.00x (ISBN 0-85461-058-8, Pub by Trade & Tech England). Renouf.
Webb, J. D., ed. Noise Control in Industry. 421p. 1976. text ed. 28.95x (ISBN 0-419-11220-0, Pub. by E & FN Spon England). Methuen Inc.
Williams, M. M., ed. Reactor Noise. an International Symposium: Special Multi Issue of Journal of Annals of Nuclear Energy. 400p. 1975. pap. text ed. 55.00 (ISBN 0-08-019895-3). Pergamon.
Yerges, Lyle F. Sound, Noise & Vibration Control. 2nd ed. (Environmental Engineering Ser.). 1978. text ed. 19.95x (ISBN 0-442-29604-5). Van Nos Reinhold.

NOISE POLLUTION

Amann, Dick. Airplanes, Airports & Noise Pollution. 1981. 49.95x (ISBN 0-917194-11-X). Prog Studies.
Archibald, Claudia J. Noise Control Directory, 1978-79. 1978. pap. text ed. 35.00x (ISBN 0-89671-012-2). Southeast Acoustics.
Barden, R. G. Sound Pollution. (Australian Environment Ser.: No.4). (Illus.). 66p. 1976. 19.75 (ISBN 0-7022-1012-9); pap. 9.95x (ISBN 0-7022-1013-7). U of Queensland Pr.
Bragdon, Clifford R. Coping with the Barking Dog Noise Problem. 40p. 1978. pap. text ed. 35.00x (ISBN 0-89671-013-0). Southeast Acoustics.
Bragdon, Clifford R., ed. Noise Pollution: A Guide to Information Sources. LC 73-17535. (Man & the Environment Information Guide Ser.: Vol. 5). 600p. 1979. 36.00 (ISBN 0-8103-1345-6). Gale.
Bugliarello, George, et al. The Impact of Noise Pollution: A Socio-Technological Introduction. 475p. 1976. text ed. 39.50 (ISBN 0-08-018166-X). Pergamon.
Clark, William D. Rotary Power Lawn Mower Noise. (Illus.). 1978. pap. text ed. 45.00x (ISBN 0-89671-015-7). Southeast Acoustics.
Cunniff, Patrick F. Environmental Noise Pollution. LC 76-48146. 1977. 27.95 (ISBN 0-471-18943-X). Wiley.
Floyd, Mary K. A Bibliography of Noise for 1971. LC 72-87107. 150p. 1973. 10.00x (ISBN 0-87875-031-2). Whitston Pub.
--Bibliography of Noise for 1972. LC 72-87107. xvii, 126p. 1974. 10.00x (ISBN 0-87875-054-1). Whitston Pub.
--A Bibliography of Noise for 1973. LC 72-87107. 1975. 10.00x (ISBN 0-87875-055-X). Whitston Pub.
--A Bibliography of Noise, 1965-1970. LC 72-87107. xxx, 375p. 1973. 17.00x (ISBN 0-87875-029-0). Whitston Pub.
Ganguli, H. C. Human Factor Aspects of Aircraft Noise. 1972. 9.00 (ISBN 0-686-20244-9). Intl Bk Dist.
Hutchins, Carleen M. Who Will Drown the Sound? (Science Is What & Why Ser.). (Illus.). (gr. 1-3). 1972. PLB 5.99 (ISBN 0-698-30478-0). Coward.
Kavaler, Lucy. The Dangers of Noise. LC 77-26588. (Illus.). (gr. 4-7). 1978. 9.95 (ISBN 0-690-03905-0, TYC-J); PLB 8.79 (ISBN 0-690-03906-9). Har-Row.
King, Richard L. Airport Noise Pollution: A Bibliography of Its Effects on People & Property. LC 73-3370. 1973. 13.50 (ISBN 0-8108-0610-X). Scarecrow.
Kramer-Greene, Judith, compiled by. A Bibliography of Noise for Nineteen Seventy-Five. LC 72-87107. 171p. 1977. 10.00x (ISBN 0-87875-099-1). Whitston Pub.
Magrab, Edward B. Environmental Noise Control. LC 75-20233. 299p. 1975. 27.50 (ISBN 0-471-56344-7, Pub. by Wiley-Interscience). Wiley.
May, Daryl. Handbook of Noise Assessment. 1978. text ed. 24.50 (ISBN 0-442-25197-1). Van Nos Reinhold.
Miller, Richard K. City Noise Index. new ed. (Illus.). 1978. pap. text ed. 35.00x (ISBN 0-89671-005-X). Southeast Acoustics.
--Industrial Noise Control 1978. new ed. 1978. pap. text ed. 35.00x (ISBN 0-89671-011-4). Southeast Acoustics.
--Noise Control in Buffing & Polishing. new ed. (Illus.). 1979. pap. text ed. 35.00x (ISBN 0-89671-009-2). Southeast Acoustics.
--Noise Control Solutions for Monument Manufacturing. 1979. pap. text ed. 45.00x (ISBN 0-89671-008-4). Southeast Acoustics.
--Noise Control Solutions for the Chemical & Petroleum Industries. new ed. 1979. pap. text ed. 45.00x (ISBN 0-89671-010-6). Southeast Acoustics.
--Noise Control Solutions for the Rubber & Plastics Industry. new ed. (Illus.). 1979. pap. text ed. 45.00x (ISBN 0-89671-007-6). Southeast Acoustics.
--Noise Control Solutions for the Wire Industry. new ed. (Illus.). 1979. pap. text ed. 35.00x (ISBN 0-89671-006-8). Southeast Acoustics.
Pipkin, Lewis S., et al. Relation of Highway Noise to Residential Property Values in Urban Areas of Tennessee. (Illus.). 1978. pap. text ed. 35.00x (ISBN 0-89671-014-9). Southeast Acoustics.
Reducing Noise in OECD Countries. 1978. 7.00x (ISBN 92-64-11800-4). OECD.
Scheibel, M. Barbara. Noise: The Unseen Enemy. new ed. Eblen, William, ed. LC 72-79109. (Ecology Ser.). (Illus.). 64p. (Orig.). (gr. 7-12). 1972. pap. 1.45 (ISBN 0-88301-041-0). Pendulum Pr.
Stephens, Irving E. & Barnes, Dorothy L., eds. A Bibliography of Noise for Nineteen Seventy-Six. LC 72-87107. 202p. 1978. 12.50x (ISBN 0-87875-128-9). Whitston Pub.
Turner, Stephen. Our Noisy World. LC 79-13210. (Illus.). 64p. (gr. 3-5). 1979. PLB 6.97 (ISBN 0-671-32987-1). Messner.
Walters, J. K. & Wint, A., eds. Industrial Effluent Treatment: Air & Noise, Vol. 2. (Illus.). ix, 305p. 1981. 52.75x (ISBN 0-85334-939-8). Intl Ideas.
--Industrial Effluent Treatment: Vol. 2: Air & Noise. (Illus.). 308p. 1981. text ed. 44.00 (ISBN 0-85334-939-8, Pub. by Applied Sci England). J. K. Burgess.

NOLAN, PAUL T.

Nolan, Paul T. John Wallace Crawford. (U. S. Authors Ser.: No. 378). 10.95 (ISBN 0-8057-7201-4). Twayne.

NOLAND, KENNETH

Moffett, Kenworth. Kenneth Noland. LC 76-50564. (Contemporary Artist Ser.). 240p. 1977. 65.00 (ISBN 0-8109-1351-8). Abrams.
Waldman, Diane. Kenneth Noland: A Retrospective. LC 77-70424. (Illus.). 1977. pap. 9.95 (ISBN 0-89207-009-9). S R Guggenheim.

NOLLEKENS, JOSEPH, 1737-1823

Colson, Percy. Their Ruling Passions. facs. ed. LC 70-136645. (Biography Index Reprint Ser.). 1949. 19.00 (ISBN 0-8369-8040-9). Arno.

NOMADS

Barfield, Thomas. The Central Asian Arabs of Afghanistan. (Illus.). 208p. 1981. text ed. 22.50x (ISBN 0-292-71066-6). U of Tex Pr.
Bates, Daniel G. Nomads & Farmers: A Study of the Yordk of Southeastern Turkey. (Anthropological Papers: No. 52). (Illus.). 1973. pap. 5.00x (ISBN 0-932206-50-6). U Mich Mus Anthro.
Carr, Claudia J. Pastoralism in Crisis: The Desanetch & Their Ethiopian Lands. LC 77-1252. (Research Papers Ser.: No. 180). (Illus.). 1977. pap. 8.00 (ISBN 0-89065-087-X). U Chicago Dept Geog.
Cole, Donald P. Nomads of the Nomads: The Al Murrah Bedouin of the Empty Quarter. LC 74-18211. (Worlds of Man Ser.). 192p. 1975. pap. 5.95x (ISBN 0-88295-605-1). Harlan Davidson.
Dippie, Brian W., ed. Nomad: George A. Custer in Turf, Field & Farm, Vol 3. (John Fielding & Lois Lasater Maher Ser: No. 3). (Illus.). 192p. 1980. 22.50 (ISBN 0-292-75519-8). U of Tex Pr.
Equipe Ecologie et Anthropologie Des Societes Postorales, ed. Pastoral Production & Society. LC 78-19139. (Illus.). 1979. 44.95 (ISBN 0-521-22253-2); pap. 14.95x (ISBN 0-521-29416-9). Cambridge U Pr.
Faegre, Torvald. Tents: Architecture of the Nomads. LC 77-25588. 1979. pap. 5.95 (ISBN 0-385-11656-X, Anch). Doubleday.
Heape, W. Emigration, Migration, & Nomadism. Marshall, F., ed. LC 32-7492. Repr. of 1931 ed. 19.00 (ISBN 0-527-39100-X). Kraus Repr.
Johnson, Douglas L. The Nature of Nomadism. LC 69-18022. (Research Papers Ser.: No. 118). 200p. 1969. pap. 8.00 (ISBN 0-89065-025-X). U Chicago Dept Geog.
Monod, Theodore, ed. Pastoralism in Tropical Africa: International African Seminar, Niamey, December 1972. (Illus.). 512p. 1975. 49.50x (ISBN 0-19-724196-4). Oxford U Pr.
National Geographic Society, ed. Nomads of the World. LC 78-151946. (Special Publications Ser.). (Illus.). 1971. avail. only from natl. geog. 6.95 (ISBN 0-87044-098-5). Natl Geog.
Nelson, Cynthia, ed. The Desert & the Sown: Nomads in the Wider Society. LC 73-620208. (Research Ser.: No. 21). 183p. 1973. pap. 3.50x (ISBN 0-87725-121-5). U of Cal Intl St.
Oberling, Pierre. The Quashqa'i Nomads of Fars. LC 72-94492. (Near & Middle East Monographs: No. 6). (Illus.). 277p. 1974. text ed. 66.00x (ISBN 90-2793-442-8). Mouton.
Oxby, Clare. Pastoral Nomads & Development. 36p. 1975. pap. 6.50x (ISBN 0-85302-043-4). Intl Pubns Serv.
Salzman, Philip C. When Nomads Settle. (Praeger Special Studies Ser.). 192p. 1980. 18.95 (ISBN 0-03-052501-2). Praeger.
Salzman, Philip C., ed. When Nomads Settle: Processes of Sedentorization As Adaptation & Response. 192p. 1980. 18.95x (ISBN 0-686-75102-7). J F Bergin.
Vucinich, Wayne S. A Study in Social Survival: The Katun in Bileca Rudine. (Monograph Ser. in World Affairs: Vol. 13, 1975-76 Ser., Pt. A). pap. 4.00 perfect bdg. (ISBN 0-87940-045-5). U of Denver Intl.
Wace, Alan J. & Thompson, M. S. The Nomads of the Balkans: An Account of Life & Customs Among the Vlachs of Northern Pindus. facsimile ed. LC 70-37358. (Select Bibliographies Reprint Ser.). Repr. of 1914 ed. 29.00 (ISBN 0-8369-6705-4). Arno.
Wace, Alan J. B. Nomads of the Balkans. 1973. Repr. 19.50x (ISBN 0-685-30613-5). Biblo.
Weissleder, Wolfgang, ed. The Nomadic Alternative: Modes & Models of Interaction in the African-Asian Deserts & Steppes. (World Anthropology Ser.). 1978. 34.00x (ISBN 0-202-90053-3). Beresford Bk Serv.

NOME, ALASKA

Nome Telephone Directory. facs. ed. 28p. Repr. of 1905 ed. pap. 4.50 (ISBN 0-8466-0014-5, SJS14). Shorey.

NOMENCLATURE

see Names

NOMINALISM

see also Realism; Reality

Armstrong, D. M. Universals & Scientific Realism: Nominalism & Realism, Vol. 1. LC 77-80824. 1978. 23.95 (ISBN 0-521-21741-5). Cambridge U Pr.
Eberle, R. A. Nominalistic Systems. LC 78-131265. (Synthese Library: No. 30). 217p. 1970. lib. bdg. 29.00 (ISBN 90-277-0161-X, Pub. by Reidel Holland). Kluwer Boston.
Peterson, John. Realism & Logical Atomism: A Critique of Neo-Atomism from the Viewpoint of Classical Realism. LC 75-12712. (Studies in the Humanities Ser.: No. 14). 128p. 1976. 8.95x (ISBN 0-8173-6622-9). U of Ala Pr.
Veatch, Henry. Realism & Nominalism Revisited. (Aquinas Lecture Ser.). 1954. 6.95 (ISBN 0-87462-119-4). Marquette.

NOMINATIONS FOR OFFICE

see also Political Conventions; Primaries

American Enterprise Institute, ed. Candidates, Nineteen Eighty. 1980. pap. 4.25 (ISBN 0-8447-1336-8). Am Enterprise.
Congressional Quarterly, ed. National Party Conventions: Seventeen Thirty-One to Nineteen Seventy-Eight. 2nd ed. LC 76-10122. 1979. pap. text ed. 7.95 (ISBN 0-87187-189-0). Congr Quarterly.
Dallinger, Frederick W. Nominations for Elective Office in the United States. LC 73-19140. (Politics & People Ser.). 304p. 1974. Repr. 16.00x (ISBN 0-405-05865-9). Arno.
David, Paul T. & Ceasar, James W. Proportional Representation in Presidential Nominating Politics. LC 79-4387. 1980. 15.95x (ISBN 0-8139-0787-X). U Pr of Va.
Marshall, Thomas R. Presidential Nominations in a Reform Age. 224p. 1981. 21.95 (ISBN 0-03-057678-4). Praeger.
Sanford, Terry. A Danger of Democracy: The Presidential Nominating Process. LC 80-29535. 184p. 1981. 12.95 (ISBN 0-86531-159-5). Westview.

NOMOGRAPHY (MATHEMATICS)

Adams, Douglas P. Nomography: Theory & Application. (Illus.). 1964. 17.50 (ISBN 0-208-00435-1, Archon). Shoe String.
Epstein, L. Ivan. Nomography. LC 58-9222. 134p. 1958. 7.75 (ISBN 0-686-74220-6). Krieger.
Fasal, John. Nomography. LC 67-13614. 1968. 18.50 (ISBN 0-8044-4227-4). Ungar.
Johnson, Lee H. Nomography & Empirical Equations. LC 77-16063. 160p. 1978. Repr. of 1952 ed. lib. bdg. 12.50 (ISBN 0-88275-551-X). Krieger.
Kuong, Javier F. Applied Nomography, Vol. 1. (Illus.). 142p. 1965. 12.95x (ISBN 0-87201-585-8). Gulf Pub.
--Applied Nomography, Vol. 2. (Illus.). 140p. 1968. 12.95x (ISBN 0-87201-586-6). Gulf Pub.
--Applied Nomography, Vol. 3. (Illus.). 135p. 1969. 14.95x (ISBN 0-87201-587-4). Gulf Pub.
Moffat, Donald W. Charts & Nomographs for Technicians & Engineers. LC 65-16436. 1965. spiral bdg. 7.95 (ISBN 0-8306-5121-7, 121). TAB Bks.

NOMOS (THE WORD)

Maultsby, Hubert D. Paul & the American Nomos. 290p. 1977. pap. text ed. 10.25 (ISBN 0-8191-0076-5). U Pr of Amer.

NOMS DE PLUME

see Anonyms and Pseudonyms

NON-ALIGNMENT

see Neutrality

NONANTUM LANGUAGE

see Massachuset Language

NONAQUEOUS SOLVENTS

Janz, George J. & Tompkins, R. P. T. Non-Aqueous Electrolytes Handbook, 2 vols. Vol. 1, 1972. 100.50 (ISBN 0-12-380401-9); Vol. 2, 1974. 100.50 (ISBN 0-12-380402-7); Set. 162.00 (ISBN 0-685-36102-0). Acad Pr.
Popovych, Orest & Tomkins, Reginald. Nonaqueous Solution Chemistry. LC 80-21693. 500p. 1981. 52.50 (ISBN 0-471-02673-5, Pub. by Wiley-Interscience). Wiley.

NON-ARISTOTELIAN PHILOSOPHY

see General Semantics

NONASSOCIATIVE ALGEBRAS

Beck, R. E. & Kolman, B. Computers in Nonassociative Rings & Algebras. 1977. 25.00 (ISBN 0-12-083850-8). Acad Pr.

NONCONFORMISTS

see Dissenters

NONCONFORMISTS, RELIGIOUS

see Dissenters, Religious

NONCONFORMITY

see Conformity

NON-CONTENTIOUS JURISDICTION

see also Notaries; Probate Law and Practice

NON-DESTRUCTIVE TESTING

see also Automatic Checkout Equipment; Ultrasonic Testing

Erf, Robert K., ed. Holographic Nondestructive Testing. 1974. 55.00 (ISBN 0-12-241350-4). Acad Pr.
Fitting, Dale & Adler, Laszlo. Ultrasonic Spectral Analysis for Nondestructive Evaluation. 354p. 1981. 39.50 (ISBN 0-306-40484-2, Plenum Pr). Plenum Pub.
Halmshaw, R. Industrial Radiology Techniques. (Wykeham Technology Ser.: No. 3). 1971. 14.00x (ISBN 0-8448-1174-2). Crane Russak Co.
McGonnagle, W., ed. International Advances in Nondestructive Testing, Vol. 7. 440p. 1981. 84.50 (ISBN 0-677-15700-2). Gordon.
McGonnagle, Warren J. International Advances in Nondestructive Testing, Vol. 5. 1977. 64.50 (ISBN 0-677-12000-1). Gordon.
--Nondestructive Testing. 2nd ed. (Illus.). 468p. 1971. 50.75x (ISBN 0-677-00500-8). Gordon.
McGonnagle, Warren J., ed. International Advances in Nondestructive Testing, Vol. 6. 376p. 1979. 64.50 (ISBN 0-677-12470-8). Gordon.
--Physics & Nondestructive Testing, Vol. 1. 1967. 89.25x (ISBN 0-677-10580-0). Gordon.
--Physics & Nondestructive Testing, Vol. 2. LC 65-27852. (Illus.). 302p. 1971. 54.00x (ISBN 0-677-15250-7). Gordon.
--Physics & Nondestructive Testing, Vol. 3. LC 65-27852. (Illus.). 338p. 1971. 54.00x (ISBN 0-677-15260-4). Gordon.
Malhotra, V. M. Testing Hardened Concrete: Nondestructive Methods. (Monograph: No. 9). 1976. 19.95 (ISBN 0-685-85144-3, M-9) (ISBN 0-685-85145-1). ACI.
Monitoring Structural Integrity by Acoustic Emission. 1975. 23.75 (ISBN 0-686-52062-9, 04-571000-22). ASTM.
Nondestructive Evaluation & Flaw Criticality for Composite Materials. (Special Technical Publications Ser.). 364p. 1979. 34.50x (ISBN 0-686-76024-7, 969, 04-696000-33). ASTM.
Nondestructive Rapid Identification of Metals & Alloys by Spot Tests. 1973. pap. 4.00 (ISBN 0-686-52063-7, 04-550000-24). ASTM.
Real-Time Radiologic Imaging: Medical & Industrial. (Special Technical Publications Ser.). 352p. 1980. 36.50x (ISBN 0-686-76060-3, 716, 04-716000-22). ASTM.
Sharpe, R. S. Research Techniques in Non-Destructive Testing, Vol. 4. LC 79-109038. 1980. 81.00 (ISBN 0-12-639054-1). Acad Pr.
Stanford, Edwin G., et al, eds. Progress in Applied Materials Research, Vols. 4-6. 1963-65. Vol. 4. 54.50x (ISBN 0-677-00920-8); Vol. 5. 54.50x (ISBN 0-677-00930-5); Vol. 6. 63.75x (ISBN 0-677-00940-2). Gordon.
Stinchcomb, W. W., et al, eds. Mechanics of Nondestructive Testing. 415p. 1980. 47.50 (ISBN 0-306-40567-9). Plenum Pub.

NON-EUCLIDEAN GEOMETRY
see Geometry, Non-Euclidean

NONFERROUS METAL INDUSTRIES
Gill, C. B. Non-Ferrous Extractive Metallurgy. LC 79-28696. 346p. 1980. 41.00x (ISBN 0-471-05980-3, Pub. by Wiley-Interscience). Wiley.
Jensen, Vernon H. Heritage of Conflict: Labor Relations in the Nonferrous Metals Industry up to 1930. LC 69-10109. (Industrial & Labor Relations Ser). (Illus.). 1968. Repr. of 1950 ed. lib. bdg. 28.50x (ISBN 0-8371-0117-4, JEHC). Greenwood.
Preston, Lee E. Exploration for Non-Ferrous Metals: An Economic Analysis. LC 77-86409. (Resources for the Future, Inc. Publications). Repr. of 1960 ed. 19.00 (ISBN 0-404-60342-4). AMS Pr.
Robbins, Peter & Edwards, John. Guide to Non-Ferrous Metals & Their Markets. 1979. 32.50 (ISBN 0-89397-050-6). Nichols Pub.
Schmitz, Christopher J. World Non-Ferrous Metal Production & Prices, 1700-1976. 432p. 1979. 30.00x (ISBN 0-7146-3109-4, F Cass Co). Biblio Dist.
Urquhart, Elizabeth. The Canadian Nonferrous Metals Industry: An Industrial Organization Study. 159p. (Orig.). 1978. pap. text ed. 8.00x (ISBN 0-88757-005-4, Pub. by Ctr Resource Stud Canada). Renouf.

NONFERROUS METALS
see also Nonferrous Metal Industries
American Bureau of Metal Statistics Staff, compiled by. ABMS Non-Ferrous Metal Data Publication: 1974 Yearbook. rev. ed. LC 21-15719. 1975. 25.00 (ISBN 0-910064-08-3). Am Bur Metal.
American Bureau of Metal Statistics Staff, ed. ABMS Non-Ferrous Metal Data Publication: 1975 Yearbook. rev. ed. LC 21-15719. 1976. 25.00 (ISBN 0-910064-09-1). Am Bur Metal.
--ABMS Non-Ferrous Metal Data Publication: 1976 Year Book. rev. ed. LC 21-15719. 1977. 25.00 (ISBN 0-910064-10-5). Am Bur Metal.
American Bureau of Metal Statistics Inc. Non-Ferrous Metal Data Yearbook, 1978. (Illus.). 1979. 25.00 (ISBN 0-686-51336-3). Am Bur Metal.
Burkin, A. R. Topics in Non-Ferrous Extractive Metallugy. 134p. 1980. 28.95 (ISBN 0-470-27016-0). Halsted Pr.
Din Standards for Non-Ferrous Metals: Aluminium, Magnesium, Titanium, & Their Alloys. 657.00 (ISBN 0-01-007042-7, 10070-4/27). Heyden.
Din Standards for Non-Ferrous Metals: Nickel, Lead, Zinc & Tin & Their Alloys. 186.00 (ISBN 0-686-28189-6, 10709-2/54). Heyden.
Din Standards: Non-Ferrous Metals: Standards on Copper & Wrought Copper Alloys. 548.00 (ISBN 0-686-28175-6, 10069-4/26). Heyden.
Edwards, John & Robbins, Peter, eds. Guide to Non-Ferrous Metals & Their Markets. 2nd ed. 250p. 1980. 43.50x (ISBN 0-89397-096-4). Nichols Pub.
Material Specifications: Nonferrous Materials, 3 pts, Pt. B. (Boiler & Pressure Vessel Code Ser.: Sec. II). 1980. 110.00 (ISBN 0-686-70436-3, P0002B); loose-leaf 150.00 (ISBN 0-686-70437-1, V0002B). ASME.
Metals Handbook, Properties & Selection: Nonferrous Alloys & Pure Metals. 1979. 62.00 (ISBN 0-87170-008-5). ASM.
Non-Ferrous Metal Data Book: 1977. LC 21-15719. 1978. write for info. (ISBN 0-685-89355-3). Am Bur Metal.
Plaksin, I. N., ed. Flotation Properties of Rare Metal Minerals. LC 67-16333. (Illus.). 1967. 8.75x (ISBN 0-685-19585-6). Primary.
Schmitz, Christopher J. World Non-Ferrous Metal Production & Prices, 1700-1976. 432p. 1979. 30.00x (ISBN 0-7146-3109-4, F Cass Co). Biblio Dist.
Touloukian, Y. S. & Ho, C. Y. Properties of Selected Ferrous Alloying Elements, Vol. III. (M-H-CINDAS Data Series on Material Properties). 288p. 1981. text ed. 33.50 (ISBN 0-07-065034-9). McGraw.

NON-FORMAL EDUCATION
Clark, Noreen & McCaffery, James. Demystifying Evaluation. LC 78-65627. (Illus., Orig.). 1979. pap. text ed. 5.00 (ISBN 0-914262-11-4). World Educ.
Dejene, Alemneh. Non-Formal Education As a Strategy in Development: Comparative Analysis of Rural Development Projects. LC 80-5882. 131p. 1980. lib. bdg. 16.25 (ISBN 0-8191-1346-8); pap. text ed. 7.75 (ISBN 0-8191-1347-6). U Pr of Amer.
Kindervatter, Susan. Nonformal Education As an Empowering Process. Center for International Education, ed. 1979. pap. 5.00 (ISBN 0-932288-54-5). Ctr Intl Ed U of MA.
Mitchell, Rita K. Please Take Your Dead Bird Home Today: Portrait of an Alternative School. LC 77-79578. 1978. 7.95 (ISBN 0-87212-094-5). Libra.
Pettit, John. Facilitator Skills Training Kit. 1978. pap. text ed. 4.00 (ISBN 0-914262-12-2). World Educ.
Srinivasan, Lyra. Perspectives on Nonformal Adult Learning. LC 76-52678. (Orig.). 1977. pap. text ed. 5.00 (ISBN 0-914262-04-1). World Educ.
Teer, Fredrica & Hunter, Carman. Challenge! A Process Training Manual on Learner -Centered Education. 1979. pap. 6.50 (ISBN 0-914262-10-6). World Educ.
Vella, Jane K. Visual Aids for Nonformal Education. 1979. pap. 2.00 (ISBN 0-932288-53-7). Ctr Intl Ed U of MA.
Von Hahmann, Gail. Collaborative Programming for Nonformal Education. 1979. pap. 2.50 (ISBN 0-932288-51-0). Ctr Intl Ed U of MA.

NONFOSSIL FUELS
see Synthetic Fuels

NONGRADED SCHOOLS
Marshall, Max S. Teaching Without Grades. LC 68-56417. 1968. pap. 4.95 (ISBN 0-87071-317-5). Oreg St U Pr.

NON-IMPORTATION AGREEMENTS, 1768-1769
Andrews, Charles M. Boston Merchants & the Non-Importation Movement. LC 67-18290. 1968. Repr. of 1918 ed. 6.50 (ISBN 0-8462-1058-4). Russell.

NONLINEAR DIFFERENTIAL EQUATIONS
see Differential Equations, Nonlinear

NONLINEAR MECHANICS
Dickey, R. W. Bifurcation Problems in Nonlinear Elasticity. (Research Notes in Mathematics Ser.: No. 3). 119p. 1976. pap. text ed. 15.95 (ISBN 0-273-00103-5). Pitman Pub MA.
Hedrick, J. K. & Paynter, H. M., eds. Nonlinear System Analysis & Synthesis, Vol. 1: Fundamental Principles, No. G00138. 146p. 1978. pap. 15.00 (ISBN 0-685-99209-8). ASME.
Hoppensteadt, F. C., ed. Nonlinear Oscillations in Biology. (Lectures in Applied Mathematics: Vol. 17). 1980. 36.00 (ISBN 0-8218-1117-7). Am Math.
International School Of Nonlinear Mathematics And Physics - Munich - 1966. Topics in Nonlinear Physics: Proceedings of the Physics Session. Zabusky, N. J. & Kruskal, M. D., eds. LC 67-20647. 1968. 23.30 (ISBN 0-387-04363-2). Springer-Verlag.
Knops, R. J., ed. Nonlinear Analysis & Mechanics: Heriot-Watt Symposium, Vol. III. (Research Notes in Mathematics Ser.: No. 30). 173p. (Orig.). 1979. pap. text ed. 17.95 (ISBN 0-273-08432-1). Pitman Pub MA.
--Nonlinear Analysis & Mechanics: Heriot-Watt Symposium, Vol. IV. (Research Notes in Mathematics Ser.: No. 39). 212p. (Orig.). 1979. pap. text ed. 18.95 (ISBN 0-273-08461-5). Pitman Pub MA.
Krylov, N. M. Introduction to Nonlinear Mechanics. Repr. of 1943 ed. pap. 7.00 (ISBN 0-527-02727-8). Kraus Repr.
Lefschetz, Solomon. Stability of Nonlinear Control Systems. (Mathematics in Science & Engineering Ser.,: Vol. 13). 1965. 25.50 (ISBN 0-12-440350-6). Acad Pr.
Leigh, D. C. Nonlinear Continuum Mechanics. (Mechanical Engineering Ser.). 1968. text ed. 22.50 (ISBN 0-07-037085-0, C). McGraw.
Noor, A. K. & McComb, H. G., eds. Computational Methods in Nonlinear Structural & Solid Mechanics: Papers Presented at the Symposium on Computational Methods in Nonlinear Structural & Solid Mechanics, 6-8 October 1980. LC 80-41608. 1980. 70.00 (ISBN 0-08-027299-1). Pergamon.
Oden, J. T., ed. Computational Mechanics: Lectures in Computational Methods in Nonlinear Mechanics. (Lecturenotes in Mathematics Ser.: Vol. 461). vii, 328p. (Orig.). 1975. 16.50 (ISBN 0-387-07169-5). Springer-Verlag.
Starzhinskii, V. M. Applied Methods in the Theory of Nonlinear Oscillations. 1980. 8.00 (ISBN 0-8285-1802-5, Pub. by Mir Pubs Russia). Imported Pubns.
Stoker, J. J. Nonlinear Elasticity. (Notes on Mathematics & Its Applications Ser). (Illus., Orig.). 1968. 29.25x (ISBN 0-677-00660-8); pap. 9.50 (ISBN 0-677-00665-9). Gordon.
--Nonlinear Vibrations in Mechanical & Electrical Systems Pure & Aplied Mechanics, Vol. 2. 294p. 1950. 35.50 (ISBN 0-470-82830-7). Wiley.
Willson, Alan N., Jr., ed. Nonlinear Networks: Theory & Analysis. LC 74-19558. 1975. 14.45 (ISBN 0-87942-046-4). Inst Electrical.
Wunderlich, W., et al, eds. Nonlinear Finite Element Analysis in Structural Mechanics: Proceedings. (Illus.). 777p. 1981. 44.50 (ISBN 0-387-10582-4). Springer-Verlag.

NONLINEAR OPERATORS
Arnold, L. & Lefever, R., eds. Stochastic Nonlinear Systems. (Springer Series in Synergetics: Vol. 8). (Illus.). 237p. 1981. 29.50 (ISBN 0-387-10713-4). Springer-Verlag.
Bachar, J. M. & Hadwin, D. W., eds. Hilbert Space Operators: Proceedings, University of California Long Beach, LB CA, June 20-24, 1977. (Lecture Notes in Mathematics: Vol. 693). 1979. pap. 11.30 (ISBN 0-387-09097-5). Springer-Verlag.
Fucik, S., et al. Spectral Analysis of Nonlinear Operators. (Lecture Notes in Mathematics: Vol. 346). 340p. 1973. pap. 15.70 (ISBN 0-387-06484-2). Springer-Verlag.
Gossez, J. P., et al, eds. Nonlinear Operators & the Calculus & Variations: Summer School Held in Bruxelles, 8-19 Sept. 1975. (Lecture Notes in Mathematics: Vol. 543). 1976. soft cover 13.80 (ISBN 0-387-07867-3). Springer-Verlag.
Pimbley, George H., Jr. Eigenfunction Branches of Nonlinear Operators & Their Bifurcations. LC 70-79958. (Lecture Notes in Mathematics: Vol. 104). 1969. pap. 10.70 (ISBN 0-387-04623-2). Springer-Verlag.
Rall, Louis B. Computational Solution of Nonlinear Operator Equations. LC 78-2378. 236p. (Orig.). 1979. pap. Repr. of 1969 ed. 13.50 (ISBN 0-88275-667-2). Krieger.
Summer School,Babylon,Czechoslovakia, Sept. 1971. Theory of Nonlinear Operators. Kucera, M., ed. 1973. 36.00 (ISBN 0-12-427650-4). Acad Pr.
Symposia in Pure Mathematics-Chicago, May, 1968. Nonlinear Operators & Nonlinear Equations of Evolution: Proceedings, Pt. 2. Browder, F., ed. LC 73-91392. 1976. 46.80 (ISBN 0-8218-0244-5, PSPUM 18-2). Am Math.

NONLINEAR OPTICS
see also Lasers
Akhmanov, S. A. & Khoklov, R. V. Nonlinear Optics. Sen, R., ed. Jacobi, N., tr. from Russian. LC 78-131021. Orig. Title: Problems of Non-Linear Optics. 208p. 1972. 48.00x (ISBN 0-677-30400-5). Gordon.
Baldwin, George C. An Introduction to Nonlinear Optics. LC 69-16517. 155p. 1969. 22.50 (ISBN 0-306-30388-4, Plenum Pr). Plenum Pub.
--An Introduction to Nonlinear Optics. LC 73-23074. 155p. 1974. pap. 5.95 (ISBN 0-306-20004-X, Rosetta). Plenum Pub.
Bloembergen, Nicolaas. Nonlinear Optics. (Frontiers in Physics Ser.: No. 21). 1965. 13.50 (ISBN 0-8053-0938-1, Adv Bk Prog). Benjamin-Cummings.
Bogoliubov, N. M. & Mitropolsky, Y. A. Asymptotic Methods in the Theory of Non-Linear Oscillations. 1961. 104.00 (ISBN 0-677-20050-1). Gordon.
Feld, M. S. & Letokhov, V. S., eds. Coherent Nonlinear Optics: Recent Advances. (Topics in Current Physics: Vol. 21). (Illus.). 377p. 1980. 44.50 (ISBN 0-387-10172-1). Springer-Verlag.
Hanna, D. C., et al. Nonlinear Optics of Free Atoms & Molecules. MacAdam, D. L., ed. (Springer Series in Optical Sciences: Vol. 17). (Illus.). 1979. 44.00 (ISBN 0-387-09628-0). Springer-Verlag.
Harper, P. G. & Wherrett, B. S., eds. Non-Linear Optics. 1978. 69.00 (ISBN 0-12-325950-9). Acad Pr.
Shen, Y. R., et al, eds. Nonlinear Infrared Generation. (Topics in Applied Physics Ser.: Vol. 16). 1977. 49.40 (ISBN 0-387-07945-9). Springer-Verlag.
Skobel'tsyn, D. V., ed. Investigations in Nonlinear Optics & Hyperacoustics. LC 73-79425. (P. N. Lebedev Physics Institute Ser.: Vol. 58). (Illus.). 163p. 1973. 30.00 (ISBN 0-306-10893-3, Consultants). Plenum Pub.
--Luminescence & Nonlinear Optics. LC 73-83897. (P. N. Lebedev Physics Institute Ser.: Vol. 59). (Illus.). 285p. 1973. 35.00 (ISBN 0-306-10896-8, Consultants). Plenum Pub.
--Nonlinear Optics. LC 72-107530. (P. N. Lebedev Physics Institute Ser.: Vol. 43). 203p. 1970. 29.50 (ISBN 0-306-10840-2, Consultants). Plenum Pub.
Zernike, Frits & Midwinter, John E. Applied Nonlinear Optics. LC 72-8369. (Pure & Applied Optics Ser). 336p. 1973. 31.00 (ISBN 0-471-98212-1, Pub. by Wiley-Interscience). Wiley.

NONLINEAR PROGRAMMING
Avriel, Mordecai. Non Linear Programming: Analysis & Methods. (Illus.). 1976. 29.95 (ISBN 0-13-623603-0). P-H.
Bathe, K. J., ed. Nonlinear Finite Element Analysis & Adina: Proceedings of the 3rd Adina Conference, Massachussetts, USA, 10-12 June 1981. 206p. 1981. 50.00 (ISBN 0-08-027594-X). Pergamon.
Bazaraa, M. S. & Shetty, C. M. Foundations of Optimization. (Lecture Notes in Economics & Mathematical Systems Ser.: Vol. 122). 1976. pap. 9.50 (ISBN 0-387-07680-8). Springer-Verlag.
Bazaraa, Mokhtar S. & Shetty, C. M. Nonlinear Programming: Theory & Algorithms. LC 78-986. 560p. 1979. text ed. 32.95 (ISBN 0-471-78610-1). Wiley.
Ben-Israel, Adi, et al. Optimality in Nonlinear Programming: A Feasible Directions Approach. LC 80-36746. (Wiley Pure & Applied Mathematics Ser.). 144p. 1981. 21.95 (ISBN 0-471-08057-8, Pub. by Wiley-Interscience). Wiley.
Bradley, Stephen P., et al. Applied Mathematical Programming. LC 76-10426. (Illus.). 1977. text ed. 23.95 (ISBN 0-201-00464-X). A-W.
Conference on Numerical Methods for Non-Linear Optimization, University of Dundee, Scotland, June-July, 1971. Numerical Methods in Non-Linear Optimization. Lootsma, F. A., ed. 1973. 70.50 (ISBN 0-12-455650-7). Acad Pr.
Dan, S. Nonlinear & Dynamic Programming: An Introduction. LC 75-6503. (Illus.). vii, 164p. (Orig.). 1975. pap. text ed. 15.90 (ISBN 0-387-81289-X). Springer-Verlag.
International Conference on Computational Methods in Nonlinear Mechanics, 2nd, Univ. of Texas at Austin. Computational Methods in Nonlinear Mechanics: Selected Papers. Oden, J. T., ed. 160p. pap. 41.25 (ISBN 0-08-025068-8). Pergamon.
Luenberger, David G. Introduction to Linear & Nonlinear Programming. LC 72-186209. 1973. text ed. 19.50 (ISBN 0-201-04347-5). A-W.
Mangasarian, O., et al, eds. Nonlinear Programming Four. LC 81-8007. 1981. 40.00 (ISBN 0-12-468662-1). Acad Pr.
Mangasarian, O. L., et al, eds. Nonlinear Programming 2: Proceedings. 1975. 36.50 (ISBN 0-12-468650-8). Acad Pr.
--Nonlinear Programming 3. 1978. 42.50 (ISBN 0-12-468660-5). Acad Pr.
Mangasarian, Olvi L. Nonlinear Programming. LC 79-4458. 236p. 1979. Repr. of 1969 ed. lib. bdg. 19.50 (ISBN 0-88275-919-1). Krieger.
Martos. Nonlinear Programming Theory & Methods. 280p. 1975. 29.50 (ISBN 0-444-10738-X, North-Holland). Elsevier.
Pierre, Donald A. & Lowe, Michael J. An Introduction with Computer Programs. (Applied Mathematics & Computation: No. 9). 464p. 1975. text ed. 24.50 (ISBN 0-201-05796-4); pap. text ed. 14.50 (ISBN 0-201-05797-2). A-W.
Rauch, H. E., ed. Control Programs of Nonlinear Programming: Proceedings of the IFAC Workshop, Denver, Colorado, USA, June 1979. (IFAC Proceedings). 130p. 1980. 35.00 (ISBN 0-08-024491-2). Pergamon.

Schittkowski, K. Nonlinear Programming Codes. (Lecture Notes in Economics & Mathematical Systems Ser.: Vol. 183). 242p. 1981. pap. 19.00 (ISBN 0-387-10247-7). Springer-Verlag.

Sposito, Vincent A. Linear & Nonlinear Programming. (Illus.). 264p. 1975. text ed. 13.95x (ISBN 0-8138-1015-9). Iowa St U Pr.

NONLINEAR THEORIES

see also Differential Equations, Nonlinear; System Analysis

Amann, H., et al, eds. Applications of Nonlinear Analysis in the Physical Sciences. (Surveys & References Ser.: No. 6). 352p. 1981. text ed. 65.00 (ISBN 0-273-08501-8). Pitman Pub MA.

Atteia, M., et al. Nonlinear Problems of Analysis in Geometry & Mechanics. (Research Notes in Mathematics: No. 46). 203p. (Orig.). 1981. pap. text ed. 21.95 (ISBN 0-273-08493-3). Pitman Pub MA.

Barbu, V. Nonlinear Semigroups & Differential Equations in Banach Spaces. 252p. 1976. 32.50x (ISBN 90-286-0205-4). Sijthoff & Noordhoff.

Bazaraa, Mokhtar S. & Shetty, C. M. Nonlinear Programming: Theory & Algorithms. LC 78-986. 560p. 1979. text ed. 32.95 (ISBN 0-471-78610-1). Wiley.

Bellman, Richard E. Methods of Nonlinear Analysis. (Mathematics in Science & Engineering Ser.: Vol. 61). Vol. 1 1970. 44.50 (ISBN 0-12-084901-1); Vol. 2. 1973. 37.50 (ISBN 0-12-084902-X). Acad Pr.

Bhatnagar, Prabhu L. Non-Linear Waves in One-Dimensional Dispersive Systems. (OXMM Ser.). (Illus.). 154p. 1981. text ed. 22.50x (ISBN 0-19-853531-7). Oxford U Pr.

Blaquiere, Austin. Nonlinear System Analysis. (Electrical Science Ser.). 1966. 51.00 (ISBN 0-12-104350-9). Acad Pr.

Byrne, George D. & Hall, Charles A., eds. Numerical Solution of Systems of Nonlinear Algebraic Equations. 1973. 40.50 (ISBN 0-12-148950-7). Acad Pr.

Cronin, Jane. Fixed Points & Topological Degree in Nonlinear Analysis. LC 63-21550. (Mathematical Surveys Ser.: Vol. 11). 1978. Repr. of 1964 ed. 26.00 (ISBN 0-8218-1511-3, SURV-11). Am Math.

Hermann, Robert. Cartanian Geometry, Nonlinear Waves, & Control Theory, Pt. A. (Interdisciplinary Mathematics Ser.: No. 20). 1979. pap. 50.00 (ISBN 0-915692-27-9). Math Sci Pr.

Hermann, Robert, ed. The Nineteen Seventy Six Ames Research Center (NASA) Conference on Geometric Nonlinear Wave Theory. (Lie Groups; History, Frontiers & Applications: Vol. 6). 1977. pap. 13.00x (ISBN 0-915692-19-8). Math Sci Pr.

Himmelblau, David M. Applied Nonlinear Programming. LC 76-148127. (Illus.). 512p. 1972. text ed. 24.00 (ISBN 0-07-028921-2, C). McGraw.

Householder. Numerical Treatment of a Single Nonlinear Equation. 1970. text ed. 25.00 (ISBN 0-07-030465-3, C). McGraw.

Kalman, G. & Feix, M. R., eds. Nonlinear Effects in Plasmas. 1969. 80.25x (ISBN 0-677-12970-X). Gordon.

Karpman, V. I. Non-Linear Waves in Dispersive Media. Cap, Ferdinand, tr. 1974. text ed. 30.00 (ISBN 0-08-017720-4). Pergamon.

Knops, R. J., ed. Nonlinear Analysis & Mechanics: Heriot-Watt Symposium, Vol. III. (Research Notes in Mathematics Ser.: No. 30). 173p. (Orig.). 1979. pap. text ed. 17.95 (ISBN 0-273-08432-1). Pitman Pub MA.

--Nonlinear Analysis & Mechanics: Heriot-Watt Symposium, Vol. IV. (Research Notes in Mathematics Ser.: No. 39). 212p. (Orig.). 1979. pap. text ed. 18.95 (ISBN 0-273-08461-5). Pitman Pub MA.

Lakshmikantham, V., ed. Nonlinear Systems & Applications: An International Conference. 1977. 42.00 (ISBN 0-12-434150-0). Acad Pr.

Lakshmikanthan, V., ed. Applied Nonlinear Analysis. LC 79-10237. 1979. 47.50 (ISBN 0-12-434180-2). Acad Pr.

Langer, Rudolph E., ed. Nonlinear Problems. (Mathematics Research Center Pubns., No. 8). (Illus.). 336p. 1963. 17.00x (ISBN 0-299-02810-0). U of Wis Pr.

Leibovich, Sidney & Seebass, A. Richard, eds. Nonlinear Waves. LC 72-12285. (Illus.). 331p. 1974. 27.50x (ISBN 0-8014-0766-4). Cornell U Pr.

Martin, Robert H., Jr. Nonlinear Operators & Differential Equations in Banach Spaces. LC 76-15279. (Pure & Applied Mathematics Ser.). 544p. 1976. 45.00 (ISBN 0-471-57363-9, Pub. by Wiley-Interscience). Wiley.

Mintz, Stephan & Perlmutter, Arnold, eds. Orbis Scientiae, Nineteen Seventy-Seven: The Significance of Nonlinearity in the Natural Sciences. (Studies in the Natural Sciences Ser.: Vol. 13). 1977. 42.50 (ISBN 0-306-36913-3, Plenum Pr). Plenum Pub.

--Orbis Scientiae, Nineteen Seventy-Seven: The Significance of Nonlinearity in the Natural Sciences. (Studies in the Natural Sciences Ser.: Vol. 13). 1977. 42.50 (ISBN 0-306-36913-3, Plenum Pr). Plenum Pub.

Pascali, D. & Sburlan, S. Nonlinear Mappings of Monotone Type. 351p. 1979. 43.00x (ISBN 90-286-0118-X). Sijthoff & Noordhoff.

Rudenko, O. V. & Soluyan, S. I., eds. Theoretical Foundations of Nonlinear Acoustics. (Studies in Soviet Sciences - Physical Sciences Ser). (Illus.). 274p. 1977. 39.50 (ISBN 0-306-10933-6, Consultants). Plenum Pub.

Rugh, Wilson J. Nonlinear System Theory: The Volterra-Wiener Approach. LC 80-8874. (Johns Hopkins Series in Information Sciences & Systems). 336p. 1981. text ed. 32.50x (ISBN 0-8018-2549-0). Johns Hopkins.

Schetzen, Martin. The Volterra & Weiner Theories of Nonlinear Systems. LC 79-13421. 1980. 34.50 (ISBN 0-471-04455-5, Pub. by Wiley-Interscience). Wiley.

Schwartz, Jacob T. Nonlinear Functional Analysis. (Notes on Mathematics & Its Applications Ser.). 1969. 33.00x (ISBN 0-677-01500-3). Gordon.

Stability of Nonlinear Systems. LC 80-40947. (Control Theory & Applications Studies Ser.). 208p. 1981. 41.00 (ISBN 0-471-27856-4, Pub. by Wiley-Interscience). Wiley.

Symposium on Nonlinear Elasticity, University of Wisconsin, April, 1973. Nonlinear Elasticity: Proceedings. Dickey, R. W., ed. 1973. 21.50 (ISBN 0-12-215150-X). Acad Pr.

Toda, M. Theory of Nonlinear Lattices. (Springer Series in Solid-State Sciences: Vol. 20). (Illus.). 220p. 1981. 35.00 (ISBN 0-387-10224-8). Springer-Verlag.

Tsytovich, V. N. Nonlinear Effects in Plasma. LC 69-12545. 332p. 1970. 35.00 (ISBN 0-306-30425-2, Plenum Pr). Plenum Pub.

Vidyasagar, M. Non Linear Systems Analysis. LC 77-24379. (Illus.). 1978. ref ed. 28.95x (ISBN 0-13-623280-9). P-H.

Vojtasek, S. & Janac, K. Solution of Non-Linear Systems. Smart, G. D., ed. Dolan, Pavel, tr. from Czech. (Illus.). 1970. 14.75 (ISBN 0-8088-3929-2). Davey.

Weiland, J. C. & Wilhelmsson, H. Coherent Non-Linear Interaction of Waves in Plasmas. 1977. text ed. 46.00 (ISBN 0-08-020964-5). Pergamon.

Willson, Alan N., Jr. Nonlinear Networks: Theory & Analysis. LC 74-19558. (IEEE Selected Reprint Ser.). 397p. 1975. 14.50 (ISBN 0-471-94953-1, Pub. by Wiley-Interscience). Wiley.

Wismer. Introduction to Nonlinear Optimization. (System Science & Engineering Ser.). 1977. 21.95 (ISBN 0-444-00234-0, North-Holland). Elsevier.

Zacks, S. Parametric Statistical Inference: Basic Theory & Modern Approaches. LC 80-41715. (I.S. in Nonlinear Mathematics Series; Theory & Applications: Vol. 4). 400p. 1981. 48.00 (ISBN 0-08-026468-9). Pergamon.

NON-MAILABLE MATTER

see Postal Service–Laws and Regulations

NON-NEWTONIAN FLUIDS

Coleman, B. D., et al. Viscometric Flows of Non-Newtonian Fluids: Theory & Experiment. (Springer Tracts in Natural Philosophy: Vol. 5). (Illus.). 1966. 15.40 (ISBN 0-387-03672-5). Springer-Verlag.

Harris, John. Rhealogy & Non-Newtonian Flow. LC 76-49635. 1978. text ed. 45.00x (ISBN 0-582-46331-9). Longman.

Schowalter, William R. Mechanics of Non-Newtonian Fluids. LC 76-51440. 1978. text ed. 52.00 (ISBN 0-08-021778-8). Pergamon.

NONNUTRITIVE SWEETNERS

see also Sugar Substitutes

Hough, C. A., et al, eds. Developments in Sweeteners, Vol. 1. (Illus.). 1979. 38.90x (ISBN 0-85334-820-0, Pub. by Applied Science). Burgess-Intl Ideas.

NON-OBJECTIVE ART

see Art, Abstract

NONOBJECTIVE PHOTOGRAPHY

see Photography, Abstract

NONPARAMETRIC STATISTICS

see also Order Statistics

Buringer, Helmut & Schriever, Karl-Heinz. Nonparametric Sequential Selection Procedures. 500p. 1981. pap. 24.50 (ISBN 3-7643-3021-X). Birkhauser.

Conover, W. J. Practical Nonparametric Statistics. 2nd ed. LC 80-301. (Probability & Mathematical Statistics Ser.). 493p. 1980. 28.95 (ISBN 0-471-02867-3). Wiley.

Daniel, Wayne W. Applied Nonparametric Statistics. LC 77-74515. (Illus.). 1978. text ed. 21.50 (ISBN 0-395-25795-6); sol. manual 1.15 (ISBN 0-395-25796-4). HM.

Ferguson, George A. Nonparametric Trend Analysis. 61p. 1965. pap. 2.95 (ISBN 0-7735-0161-4). McGill-Queens U Pr.

Hollander, Myles & Wolfe, Douglas A. Nonparametric Statistical Methods. LC 72-11960. (Ser. in Probability & Mathematical Statistics). (Illus.). 496p. 1973. 34.00 (ISBN 0-471-40635-X, Pub. by Wiley-Interscience). Wiley.

Lehmann, E. L. Nonparametrics: Statistical Methods Based on Ranks. LC 72-93538. 1975. text ed. 29.95x (ISBN 0-8162-4994-6). Holden-Day.

Mosteller, F. R. & Rourke, Robert E. Sturdy Statistics: Nonparametrics & Order Statistics. LC 70-184162. 1973. text ed. 18.95 (ISBN 0-201-04868-X). A-W.

Puri, M. L. & Sen, P. K. Nonparametric Methods in Multivariate Analysis. LC 79-129052. (Ser. in Probability & Mathematical Statistics). 1971. 46.00 (ISBN 0-471-70240-4, Pub. by Wiley-Interscience). Wiley.

Puri, M. L., ed. Nonparametric Techniques in Statistical Inference. LC 74-116750. (Illus.). 1970. 86.50 (ISBN 0-521-07817-2). Cambridge U Pr.

Randles, Ronald H. & Wolfe, Douglas A. Introduction to the Theory of Nonparametric Statistics. LC 79-411. (Ser. in Probability & Mathematical Statistics). 1979. 32.00 (ISBN 0-471-04245-5, Pub. by Wiley-Interscience). Wiley.

Rey, J. J. Robust Statistical Methods. (Lecture Notes in Mathematics: Vol. 690). 1979. pap. 10.50 (ISBN 0-387-09091-6). Springer-Verlag.

Runyon, Richard P. Nonparametric Statistics: A Contemporary Approach. LC 76-55635. 1977. pap. text ed. 9.95 (ISBN 0-201-06547-9); avail test book 2.75 (ISBN 0-201-06548-7). A-W.

Tapia, Richard A. & Thompson, James R. Nonparametric Probability Density Estimation. LC 77-17249. (Illus.). 1978. text ed. 17.95x (ISBN 0-8018-2031-6). Johns Hopkins.

Walsh, John E. Handbook of Nonparametric Statistics. Vol. 2 1965. 27.50x (ISBN 0-442-09193-1); Vol. 3 1968. 27.50x (ISBN 0-442-39194-3). Van Nos Reinhold.

NONPROFIT CORPORATIONS

see Corporations, Nonprofit

NONREALISTIC PHOTOGRAPHY

see Photography, Abstract

NONRECOGNITION OF GOVERNMENTS

see Recognition (International Law)

NON-RESISTANCE TO EVIL

see Evil, Non-Resistance to

NON-RESISTANCE TO GOVERNMENT

see Government, Resistance to

NONSELFGOVERNING TERRITORIES

see Colonies; International Trusteeships

NONSENSE-VERSES

Aiken, Conrad & Lord, John V. Who's Zoo. LC 77-77868. (Illus.). (gr. k-4). 1977. 7.95 (ISBN 0-689-30607-5). Atheneum.

Cole, William. Oh, Such Foolishness! LC 78-1622. (Illus.). (gr. 3-6). 1978. 8.95 (ISBN 0-397-31807-3, JBL-J). Har-Row.

--Oh, That's Ridiculous. LC 70-183934. (Illus.). 80p. (gr. 4-7). 1972. PLB 6.95 (ISBN 0-670-52107-8). Viking Pr.

Hample, Stoo. Yet Another Big Fat Funny Silly Book. LC 80-66202. (Illus.). 96p. (gr. 1-4). 1980. 4.95 (ISBN 0-440-09796-7); PLB 6.46 (ISBN 0-440-09797-5). Delacorte.

Hunt, Bernice K. Your Ant Is a Which: Fun with Homophones. LC 75-37582. (Let Me Read Ser). (Illus.). (gr. 1-5). 1976. pap. 1.65 (ISBN 0-15-299881-0, VoyB). HarBraceJ.

Hunter, Julius. Absurd Alphabedtime Stories. (Illus.). (gr. k-4). 1976. 1.50 (ISBN 0-8272-0012-9). Bethany Pr.

Kennedy, X. J. The Phantom Ice Cream Man. LC 78-23681. (Illus.). 64p. (gr. 3 up). 1979. 7.95 (ISBN 0-689-50132-3, Mcelderry Bk). Atheneum.

Lear, Edward. A Book of Nonsense. (Illus.). 56p. (gr. 4 up). 1980. 9.95 (ISBN 0-670-18011-4, Studio). Viking Pr.

Lewis, D. B. The Nonsensibus. 1977. Repr. of 1936 ed. lib. bdg. 10.00 (ISBN 0-8495-3203-5). Arden Lib.

Reed, Langford. Nonsense Verse: An Anthology. 1977. lib. bdg. 10.00 (ISBN 0-8495-4500-5). Arden Lib.

Van Rooten, Luis. Mots D'Heures: Gousses, Rames. LC 67-21230. 1967. 8.95 (ISBN 0-670-49064-4, Grossman). Viking Pr.

Wells, Carolyn, ed. Nonsense Anthology. facs. ed. LC 76-128160. (Granger Index Reprint Ser). 1902. 17.00 (ISBN 0-8369-6189-7). Arno.

NONSENSE-VERSES–HISTORY AND CRITICISM

Cammaerts, Emile. The Poetry Nonsense. 1978. Repr. of 1925 ed. lib. bdg. 15.00 (ISBN 0-8495-0769-3). Arden Lib.

--Poetry of Nonsense. lib. bdg. 12.50 (ISBN 0-8414-3548-0). Folcroft.

Stewart, Susan. Nonsense: Aspects of Intertextuality in Folklore & Literature. LC 79-4950. 1980. text ed. 12.95x (ISBN 0-8018-2258-0). Johns Hopkins.

NON-SUPPORT

see Support (Domestic Relations)

NON-VASCULAR PLANTS

see Cryptogams

NONVERBAL COMMUNICATION

see also Expression; Gesture; Personal Space

Argyle, M. & Cook, M. Gaze & Mutual Gaze. LC 75-12134. (Illus.). 160p. 1976. 27.50 (ISBN 0-521-20865-3). Cambridge U Pr.

Argyle, Michael. Bodily Communication. LC 75-18679. 1975. text ed. 25.00 (ISBN 0-8236-0550-7). Intl Univs Pr.

Ashley Montagu. Touching: The Human Significance of Skin. 2nd ed. 1978. pap. 5.95 (ISBN 0-06-090630-8, CN 630, CN). Har-Row.

--Touching: The Human Significance of the Skin. rev. ed. LC 77-3762. 1978. 10.95 (ISBN 0-06-012979-4, HarpT). Har-Row.

Aylesworth, Thomas G. Understanding Body Talk. LC 78-12446. (Impact Bks.). (Illus.). (gr. 7 up). 1979. PLB 7.45 s&l (ISBN 0-531-02200-5). Watts.

Bauml, Betty J. & Bauml, Franz H. A Dictionary of Gestures. LC 75-3144. 1975. 12.00 (ISBN 0-8108-0863-3). Scarecrow.

Beier, Ernst G. & Valens, E. G., Jr. People-Reading: How We Control Others, How They Control Us. LC 74-26977. 256p. 1975. 8.95 (ISBN 0-8128-1781-8). Stein & Day.

Beier, Ernst G. & Valens, Evans G. People-Reading: How We Control Others, How They Control Us. 320p. 1976. pap. 2.95 (ISBN 0-446-93642-1). Warner Bks.

Birdwhistell, Ray L. Kinesics & Context: Essays on Body Motion Communication. LC 77-122379. (Conduct & Communication Ser.: No. 2). 1970. pap. 9.95x (ISBN 0-8122-1012-3, Pa Paperbks). U of Pa Pr.

Blondis, Marion N. & Jackson, Barbara. Nonverbal Communication with Patients: Back to the Human Touch. LC 76-30732. 1977. 9.95 (ISBN 0-471-01753-1, Pub. by Wiley Med). Wiley.

Body Talk: A Handbook on Non-Verbal Behavior. 1975. 2.95 (ISBN 0-442-82562-5). Peter Pauper.

Bosmajian, Haig. The Rhetoric of Nonverbal Communication: Readings. 1971. pap. 4.95x (ISBN 0-673-07608-3). Scott F.

Brodey, Warren. Earthchild: Glories of the Asphyxiated Spectrum. new ed. (Social Change Ser). 184p. 1974. 29.25x (ISBN 0-677-04300-7); pap. 9.95 (ISBN 0-677-04305-8). Gordon.

Brown, Charles T. & Keller, Paul T. Monologue to Dialogue: An Exploration of Interpersonal Commuication. 2nd ed. LC 78-16541. (Special Communication Ser.). 1979. pap. 11.95 (ISBN 0-13-600825-9). P-H.

Bullowa, Margaret, ed. Before Speech. LC 78-51671. (Illus.). 1979. 42.50 (ISBN 0-521-22031-9); pap. 11.95 (ISBN 0-521-29522-X). Cambridge U Pr.

Burgoon, Judee K. & Saine, Thomas. The Unspoken Dialogue: An Introduction to Nonverbal Communication. (Illus., LC 77-078913). 1978. text ed. 13.95 (ISBN 0-395-25792-1); inst. manual 0.75 (ISBN 0-395-25793-X). HM.

Castle, Sue. Face Talk, Hand Talk, Body Talk. (gr. k-3). 1977. 7.95a (ISBN 0-385-11018-9); PLB (ISBN 0-385-11019-7). Doubleday.

Corson, S. A. & Corson, E. O'Leary. Ethology & Nonverbal Communication in Mental Health: An Interdisciplinary Biopsychosocial Exploration. LC 79-41689. (International Ser. in Biopsychosocial Sciences). (Illus.). 290p. 1980. 48.00 (ISBN 0-08-023728-2). Pergamon.

Deich, Ruth F. & Hodges, Patricia M. Language Without Speech. LC 77-27371. (Illus.). 1978. 15.00 (ISBN 0-87630-166-9). Brunner-Mazel.

Delph, Edward W. The Silent Community: Public Homosexual Encounters. LC 78-629. 1978. 18.95x (ISBN 0-8039-0990-X); pap. 8.95x (ISBN 0-8039-0991-8). Sage.

Eisenberg, Abne M. & Smith, Ralph R., Jr. Nonverbal Communication. 146p. pap. text ed. 4.95x (ISBN 0-8290-0326-6). Irvington.

Fant, Louie J., Jr. Intermediate Sign Language. LC 78-61003. (Illus.). 225p. (gr. 7 up). 1980. text ed. 17.95 (ISBN 0-917002-54-7). Joyce Media.

Fast, Julius. Body Language. 1981. pap. 2.75 (ISBN 0-671-43904-9). PB.

--The Body Language of Sex, Power, & Aggression. LC 76-47665. 192p. 1977. 7.95 (ISBN 0-87131-222-0). M Evans.

Fast, Julius & Fast, Barbara. Talking Between Lines. 1980. pap. 2.50 (ISBN 0-671-83244-1). PB.

Frandsen & Benson. An Orientation to Nonverbal Communication. new ed. Applbaum, Ronald & Hart, Roderick, eds. (MODCOM Modules in Speech Communication Ser.). 1976. pap. text ed. 2.50 (ISBN 0-574-22514-5, 13-5514). SRA.

Frye, Jerry K. FIND: Frye's Index to Nonverbal Data. LC 80-51053. 344p. 1980. 39.95 (ISBN 0-936992-01-8); pap. 29.95 (ISBN 0-936992-02-6). U of Minn Comp Ctr.

Gay, Kathlyn. Body Talk. LC 74-7811. (Illus.). (gr. 3-8). 1974. reinforced bdg. 8.95 (ISBN 0-684-14006-3, ScribJ). Scribner.
Guthrie, Russell D. Body Hot Spots: The Anatomy of Human Social Organs & Behavior. (Illus.). 225p. 1976. 8.95 (ISBN 0-442-22982-8). Van Nos Reinhold.
Hall, Edward T. The Silent Language. LC 79-25399. xviii, 217p. 1980. Repr. of 1973 ed. lib. bdg. 19.75x (ISBN 0-313-22277-0, HASN). Greenwood.
Hanna, Judith Lynn. To Dance Is Human: A Theory of Nonverbal Communication. LC 78-21612. (Illus.). 343p. 1979. text ed. 17.50x (ISBN 0-292-78032-X); pap. 7.95x (ISBN 0-292-78042-7). U of Tex Pr.
Harper, Robert G., et al. Nonverbal Communication: The State of the Art. LC 77-19185. (Personality Processes Ser.). 1978. 31.95x (ISBN 0-471-02672-7, Pub. by Wiley-Interscience). Wiley.
Harrison, Randall P. Beyond Words: An Introduction to Nonverbal Communication. LC 73-17202. (Speech Communication Ser). (Illus.). 208p. 1974. ref. ed. 15.95 (ISBN 0-13-076141-9); pap. 11.95 (ISBN 0-13-076133-8). P-H.
Heisel, D. The Kairos Dimension. 304p. 1974. 19.25 (ISBN 0-677-04910-2); pap. 8.95 (ISBN 0-685-42134-1). Gordon.
Henley, Nancy M. Body Politics: Power, Sex, & Nonverbal Communication. (Patterns of Social Behavior Ser.). (Illus.). 1977. 10.95 (ISBN 0-13-079640-9, Spec); pap. 3.95 (ISBN 0-13-079632-8). P-H.
Hinde, R. A., ed. Non-Verbal Communication. LC 75-171675. (Illus.). 464p. 1972. 47.50 (ISBN 0-521-08370-2); pap. 14.95x (ISBN 0-521-29012-0). Cambridge U Pr.
Hofter, Bates L. & St. Clair, Robert N., eds. Developmental Kinesics: The Emerging Paradigm. 288p. 1981. text ed. 29.95 (ISBN 0-8391-1651-9). Univ Park.
Key, Mary R. Nonverbal Communication: A Research Guide & Bibliography. LC 76-53024. 1977. lib. bdg. 21.00 (ISBN 0-8108-1014-X). Scarecrow.
--Paralanguage & Kinesics: Nonverbal Communication with a Bibliography. LC 74-30217. 1975. 10.00 (ISBN 0-8108-0789-0). Scarecrow.
Key, Mary R., ed. The Relationship of Verbal & Non-Verbal Communication. (Contributions to the Sociology of Language: No. 25). 1980. text ed. 41.25x (ISBN 90-279-7878-6); pap. text ed. 12.50x (ISBN 90-279-7637-6). Mouton.
Knapp, Mark L. Essentials of Nonverbal Communication. LC 79-17769. 264p. (Orig.). 1980. pap. text ed. 9.95 (ISBN 0-03-049861-9, HoltC). HR&W.
--Nonverbal Communication in Human Interaction. 2nd ed. LC 77-21262. 1978. pap. text ed. 12.95 (ISBN 0-03-089962-1, HoltC); instructor's manual avail. (ISBN 0-685-87575-X). HR&W.
Krames, Lester, ed. Nonverbal Communication. LC 74-6325. (Advances in the Study of Communication & Affect Ser.: Vol. 1). (Illus.). 212p. 1974. 32.50 (ISBN 0-306-35901-4, Plenum Pr). Plenum Pub.
LaFrance, Marianne & Mayo, Clara. Moving Bodies: Nonverbal Communication in Social Relationships. LC 77-13569. (Psychology Ser.). 1978. pap. 9.95 (ISBN 0-8185-0259-2). Brooks-Cole.
Lamb, Warren & Watson, Elizabeth. Body Code: The Meaning in Movement. (Illus.). 1979. 16.00 (ISBN 0-7100-0017-0). Routledge & Kegan.
Lowenfeld, Margaret. The World Technique. 1979. text ed. 27.50x (ISBN 0-04-150067-9). Allen Unwin.
McCardle, Ellen S. Nonverbal Communication. (Communication Science & Technology Ser.: Vol. 5). 112p. 1974. 18.75 (ISBN 0-8247-6126-X). Dekker.
McCormack, William C. & Wurm, Stephen A., eds. Language & Man: Anthropological Issues. (World Anthropology Ser). (Illus.). 1976. 33.50x (ISBN 0-202-90035-5). Beresford Bk Serv.
McGough, Elizabeth. Your Silent Language. LC 73-4253. (Illus.). 128p. (gr. 7 up). 1974. PLB 6.96 (ISBN 0-688-31820-7). Morrow.
Machotka, Pavel & Spiegel, John P. Articulate Body. (Illus.). 250p. 1980. 19.50x (ISBN 0-8290-0229-4). Irvington.
May, Marianne. Nonverbal Communication & the Congenitally Blind. 59p. 3.50 (ISBN 0-89128-959-3, PEP959). Am Foun Blind.
Mehrabian, Albert. Nonverbal Communication. LC 72-172859. 336p. 1972. 22.95x (ISBN 0-202-25091-1). Aldine Pub.
--Silent Messages. 1971. pap. 8.95x (ISBN 0-534-00059-2). Wadsworth Pub.
Millar, Dan & Millar, Frank. Messages & Myths: Understanding Interpersonal Communication. LC 75-33811. 250p. 1976. pap. text ed. 7.95x (ISBN 0-88284-022-3). Alfred Pub.
Moerk, E. Pragmatic & Semantic Aspects of Early Language Development. 1977. 18.50 (ISBN 0-8391-1118-5). Univ Park.
Montagu, Ashley & Matson, Floyd. The Human Connection. 228p. 1981. pap. 4.95 (ISBN 0-07-042842-5, GB). McGraw.
Morain, Genelle G. Kinesics & Cross-Cultural Understanding. (Language in Education Ser.: No. 7). 1978. pap. 3.25x (ISBN 0-87281-089-5). Ctr Appl Ling.
Obudho, Constance E., compiled by. Human Nonverbal Behavior: An Annotated Bibliography. LC 79-7586. 1979. lib. bdg. 18.95 (ISBN 0-313-21094-2, OBH/). Greenwood.
Peng, Fred C. & Von Raffler-Engel, Walburga, eds. Languauge Acquisition & Developmental Kinesics. 1979. pap. 9.50x (ISBN 0-89955-238-2, Pub. by Bunka Hyoron). Intl Schol Bk Serv.
Pizer, Vernon. You Don't Say: How People Communicate Without Speech. LC 77-12576. (Illus.). (gr. 6 up). 1978. 7.95 (ISBN 0-399-20625-6). Putnam.
Poyatos, Fernando. Man Beyond Words: Theory & Methodology of Nonverbal Communication. 1976. pap. text ed. 6.75 (ISBN 0-930348-07-9). NY St Eng Coun.
Reed, Scott. Miracle of Psycho Command Power: The New Way to Riches, Love & Happiness. 1972. 12.95 (ISBN 0-13-585679-5, Reward); pap. 3.95 (ISBN 0-13-585596-9). P-H.
Rosenthal, Robert, ed. Skill in Nonverbal Communication: Individual Differences. LC 79-19063. 288p. 1980. pap. text ed. 9.95 (ISBN 0-89946-033-X). Oelgeschlager.
--Skill in Nonverbal Communication: Individual Differences. LC 79-19063. 288p. 1979. text ed. 22.50 (ISBN 0-89946-000-3). Oelgeschlager.
Rosenthal, Robert, et al. Sensitivity to Nonverbal Communication: The Pons Test. LC 78-17322. 1979. text ed. 20.00x (ISBN 0-8018-2159-2). Johns Hopkins.
Ruesch, Jurgen & Kees, Weldon. Nonverbal Communication: Notes on the Visual Perception of Human Relations. 1956. 16.95 (ISBN 0-520-01100-7); pap. 6.95 (ISBN 0-520-02162-2, CAL243). U of Cal Pr.
Rybak, B., ed. Bio-Informatics & Bio-Process Studies in the Physiology of Communication. (Health Communications & Informatics Biosciences Communications Ser.: Vol. 4, No. 3). (Illus.). 1978. 11.50 (ISBN 3-8055-2856-6). S Karger.
Scheflen, A., ed. How Behavior Means. (Social Change Ser.). 1973. 23.75x (ISBN 0-677-04050-4); pap. 12.25 (ISBN 0-677-04055-5). Gordon.
Scheflen, Albert E. Body Language & the Social Order. (Illus.). 192p. 1973. 12.95 (ISBN 0-13-079590-9, Spec); pap. 4.95 (ISBN 0-13-079582-8, Spec). P-H.
Schiefelbusch, R. Nonspeech Language & Communication. 1979. 24.95 (ISBN 0-8391-1558-X). Univ Park.
Schrank, Jeffrey. Deception Detection: An Educator's Guide to the Art of Insight. LC 75-5293. (Illus.). 208p. 1975. 8.95 (ISBN 0-8070-3160-7); pap. 3.95 (ISBN 0-8070-3161-5, BP526). Beacon Pr.
Sesame Street. Sesame Street Sign Language Fun. LC 79-5570. (Illus.). 72p. (ps-3). 1980. PLB 6.99 (ISBN 0-394-94212-4); pap. 5.95 (ISBN 0-394-84212-X). Random.
Speer, David C., ed. Nonverbal Communication. LC 73-90714. (Sage Contemporary Social Science Issues: No. 10). 140p. 1974. 5.95x (ISBN 0-8039-0339-1). Sage.
Szasz, Suzanne. The Body Language of Children. (Illus.). 1978. 14.95 (ISBN 0-393-01171-2). Norton.
--The Unspoken Language of Children. (Illus.). 160p. 1980. pap. 6.95 (ISBN 0-393-00989-0). Norton.
Van Schaack, M. Without Words: An Introduction to Nonverbal Communication. 1977. 600.00 (ISBN 0-13-961417-6). P-H.
Von Raffler-Engel, Walburga, ed. Aspects of Nonverbal Communication. 380p. 1980. text ed. 45.00 (ISBN 90-265-0322-9, Pub. by Swets Pub Serv Holland). Swets North Am.
Wandor, Micheline, ed. Body Politic. 1978. pap. 6.95 (ISBN 0-85035-029-8, Pub. by Stage One). Carrier Pigeon.
Weitz, Shirley. Nonverbal Communication: Readings with Commentary. 2nd ed. (Illus.). 1978. text ed. 15.95x (ISBN 0-19-502447-8); pap. text ed. 9.95x (ISBN 0-19-502448-6). Oxford U Pr.
Whiteside, Robert L. Face Language. 1981. pap. 2.95 (ISBN 0-671-43905-7). PB.
--Face Language. 1977. pap. 2.50 (ISBN 0-671-80033-7). PB.
Wolfgang, Aaron, ed. Nonverbal Behavior: Applications & Cultural Implications. 1979. 15.00 (ISBN 0-12-761350-1). Acad Pr.
Wood, Barbara. Children & Communication: Verbal & Non-Verbal Language Development. LC 75-22452. (Speech Communication Ser.). (Illus.). 336p. 1976. text ed. 15.95x (ISBN 0-13-131896-9). P-H.
Wright, Sam. Crowds & Riots: A Study in Social Organization. LC 78-626. (Sociological Observations Ser.: No. 4). 207p. 1978. 20.00x (ISBN 0-8039-0995-0); pap. 9.95x (ISBN 0-8039-0996-9). Sage.
Ziajka, Alan. Prelinguistic Communication in Infancy. 192p. 1981. 21.95 (ISBN 0-03-058649-6). Praeger.
Zsilka, Janos. The Dialects of the Motion Forms of Language. (Janua Linguarum, Series Minor). 1979. text ed. 30.75 (ISBN 0-686-27020-7). Mouton.

NONVIOLENCE

see also Pacifism; Passive Resistance

Bass, Henry. The Power of the People: Active Nonviolence in the U.S. Cooney, Robert J. & Michalowski, Helen, eds. LC 76-19519. (Illus.). 240p. 1977. pap. 9.95 (ISBN 0-915238-06-3). Peace Pr.
Bell, Inge P. CORE & the Strategy of Nonviolence. 1968. pap. text ed. 3.95x (ISBN 0-394-30776-3). Phila Bk Co.
Bondurant, Joan V. & Fisher, Margaret W., eds. Conflict: Violence & Non-Violence. (Controversy Ser). 206p. 1971. text ed. 9.95x (ISBN 0-88311-011-3); pap. 3.95 (ISBN 0-88311-012-1). Lieber-Atherton.
Bruyn, Severyn T. & Rayman, Paula, eds. Non-Violent Action & Social Change. (Orig.). 1980. pap. text ed. 8.95x (ISBN 0-8290-0271-5). Irvington.
Case, Clarence M. Non-Violent Coercion: A Study in Methods of Social Pressure. LC 78-137530. (Peace Movement in America Ser). viii, 423p. 1972. Repr. of 1923 ed. lib. bdg. 20.95x (ISBN 0-89198-058-X). Ozer.
Committee for Nonviolent Revolution. Alternative, Vols. 1-3, No. 5. 1948-1951. Repr. lib. bdg. 15.00x (ISBN 0-8371-9124-6, A100). Greenwood.
Del Vasto, Lanza. Definitions of Nonviolence. Sidgwick, Jean, tr. Orig. Title: Fr. 27p. (Orig.). 1972. pap. 1.00 (ISBN 0-934676-06-2). Greenlf Bks.
Gandhi, Mohandas K. The Science of Satyagraha. Hingorani, A. T., ed. 137p. (Orig.). 1980. pap. 2.00 (ISBN 0-934676-19-4). Greenlf Bks.
Ghandi, Mohandas K. Nonviolence in Peace & War, 1942, 2 vols. Incl. Nonviolence in Peace & War, 1949. Ghandi, Mohandas K. LC 72-147618. (Library of War & Peace; Non-Resis. & Non-Vio.). Set. lib. bdg. 76.00 (ISBN 0-8240-0375-6); lib. bdg. 38.00 ea. Garland Pub.
Gregg, Richard B. Power of Non-Violence. rev. ed. 1960. pap. 3.50 (ISBN 0-227-67567-3). Attic Pr.
--Psychology & Strategy of Gandhi's Nonviolent Resistance. LC 76-147619. (Library of War & Peace; Non-Resis. & N3n-Vio.). lib. bdg. 38.00 (ISBN 0-8240-0376-4). Garland Pub.
Guinan, Edward, ed. Peace & Non-Violence: Basic Writings. LC 73-75741. 192p. (Orig.). 1973. pap. 4.95 (ISBN 0-8091-1770-3). Paulist Pr.
Hare, A. Paul & Blumberg, Herbert H., eds. Liberation Without Violence: A Third Party Approach. 368p. 1978. 21.50x (ISBN 0-87471-998-4). Rowman.
Hope, Marjorie & Young, James. The Struggle for Humanity: Agents of Nonviolent Change in a Violent World. LC 77-5573. 1977. 8.95 (ISBN 0-88344-468-2); pap. 6.95 (ISBN 0-88344-469-0). Orbis Bks.
Judson, Stephanie, ed. A Manual on Nonviolence & Children. (Illus.). 115p. (Orig.). 1977. pap. 5.00 (ISBN 0-9605062-1-7). Friends Peace Comm.
Mabee, Carleton. Black Freedom: The Nonviolent Abolitionists from 1830 to the Civil War. 1969. 12.95 (ISBN 0-02-577170-1). Macmillan.
Merton, Thomas. The Nonviolent Alternative. 1981. 12.95 (ISBN 0-374-22312-2); pap. 6.95 (ISBN 0-374-51575-1). FS&G.
Moulton, Phillips P. Violence, or Aggressive Nonviolent Resistance. LC 76-170019. (Orig.). 1971. pap. 0.70x (ISBN 0-87574-178-9). Pendle Hill.
Pelton, Leroy H. The Psychology of Nonviolence. LC 74-2156. 310p. 1975. text ed. 23.00 (ISBN 0-08-018099-X). Pergamon.
Sandhu, Swaran S. Nonviolence in Indian Religious Thought & Political Action. 1977. 6.95 (ISBN 0-8059-2444-2). Dorrance.
Sharp, Gene. The Politics of Nonviolent Action. Finkelstein, Marina, ed. LC 72-95483. (Extending Horizons Ser.). 928p. 1973. 24.95 (ISBN 0-87558-068-8). Porter Sargent.
Shiridharani, Krishnalal. War Without Violence. LC 79-147633. (Library of War & Peace; Non-Resis. & Non-Vio.). lib. bdg. 38.00 (ISBN 0-8240-0409-4). Garland Pub.
Sibley, Mulford Q. Political Theories of Modern Pacifism. Bd. with Introduction to Non-Violence. Paulin, Theodore; Pacifist Living-Today & Tomorrow. Peace Station, AFSC. LC 70-147612. (Library of War & Peace; Non-Resis. & Non-Vio.). lib. bdg. 38.00 (ISBN 0-8240-0371-3). Garland Pub.
Templin, Ralph T. Democracy & Nonviolence. LC 64-66235. (Extending Horizons Ser). 1965. 4.00 (ISBN 0-87558-035-1). Porter Sargent.
Trocme, Andre. Jesus & the Nonviolent Revolution. Shenk, Michel, tr. from Fr. LC 73-9934. 296p. 1974. 7.95 (ISBN 0-8361-1719-0). Herald Pr.
Unnithan, T. K. & Singh, Y. Sociology of Non-Violence & Peace: Behavioural & Attitudinal Dimensions. 1969. 8.25x (ISBN 0-8426-1575-X). Verry.
Unnithan, T. K. & Singh, Yogendra, eds. Traditions of Non Violence. LC 74-906983. 317p. 1973. 8.00x (ISBN 0-88386-433-9). South Asia Bks.

NON-VIOLENT NON-COOPERATION

see Passive Resistance

NON-WAGE PAYMENTS

see also Bonus System; Labor and Laboring Classes–Medical Care; Old Age Pensions; Profit-Sharing; Social Security; Welfare Funds (Trade-Union); Welfare Work in Industry

Allen, Donna. Fringe Benefits: Wages or Social Obligation? LC 75-627371. (Cornell Studies Ser.: No. 13). 1969. pap. 4.00 (ISBN 0-87546-006-2); pap. 7.00 special hard bdg. (ISBN 0-87546-265-0). NY Sch Indus Rel.
Annual Educational Conference of the International Foundation of Employee Benefit Plans. Textbook for Employee Benefit Plan Trustees, Administrators & Advisors, 1978: Proceedings, Vol. 20. Hieb, Elizabeth A., ed. 27.00 (ISBN 0-89154-093-8). Intl Found Employ.
Barth, Peter S. & Hunt, H. Allen. Workers' Compensation & Work-Related Illnesses & Diseases. 1980. text ed. 29.95x (ISBN 0-262-02141-2). MIT Pr.
Brennan, Mary, ed. Employee Contributions & Delinquencies Under Erisa Institute, las Vegas, Nov. 12-15, 1978. (Orig.). 1979. pap. 7.50 (ISBN 0-89154-097-0). Intl Found Employ.
Brennan, Mary E., ed. Canadian Conference, 12th Annual, October 27-31, 1979: Proceedings. 177p. 1980. pap. 10.00 (ISBN 0-89154-129-2). Intl Found Employ.
--Corporate Benefits Management Conferences, Spring 1979: Proceedings. 1979. pap. text ed. 8.50 (ISBN 0-89154-111-X). Intl Found Employ.
Candian Conference, 13th Annual, 1980. Proceedings. Brennan, Mary E., ed. 145p. (Orig.). 1981. pap. 11.00 (ISBN 0-89154-145-4). Intl Found Employ.
Chadwick, William J. Regulation of Employee Benefits: Erisa & Other Federal Laws. 1978. 25.00 (ISBN 0-89154-078-4). Intl Found Employ.
Contemporary Benefit Issues & Administration: Answers to the Questions on Subject Matter for Learning Guide, CEBS Course X. 139p. (Orig.). 1980. pap. 10.00 (ISBN 0-89154-122-5). Intl Found Employ.
Contemporary Benefit Issues & Administration: Learning Guide, CEBS Course X. (Orig.). 1979. spiral 13.00 (ISBN 0-89154-118-7). Intl Found Employ.
Contemporary Benefit Issues & Administration: Readings; CEBS Course X. 1979. pap. 20.00 (ISBN 0-89154-119-5). Intl Found Employ.
Contemporary Legal Environment of Employee Benefit Plans: Answers to the Questions on Subject Matter for the Learning Guide CEBS Course I. 128p. 1979. pap. text ed. 10.00 (ISBN 0-89154-108-X). Intl Found Employ.
Contemporary Legal Environment of Employee Benefit Plans: Learning Guide CEBS Course I. 1979. spiral bdg. 13.00 (ISBN 0-89154-102-0). Intl Found Employ.
Costa, Michael L. Master Trust: Simplifying Employee Benefits Trust Fund Administration. 288p. 1980. 19.95 (ISBN 0-8144-5622-7). Am Mgmt.
Di Palma, Vera. Your Fringe Benefits. 1978. 5.95 (ISBN 0-7153-7517-2). David & Charles.
Educational Conference, 20th, 1974. Textbook for Employee Benefit Plan Trustees, Administrators & Advisors: Proceedings, Vol. 16. Koby, Carol J., ed. (Non Wage Payment Pensions). 401p. 1975. 12.50 (ISBN 0-89154-001-6). Intl Found Employ.
Educational Conference, 21st, 1975. Textbook for Employee Benefit Plan Trustees, Adminstrators, & Advisors: Proceedings, Vol.17. Hatch, Jan, ed. 1976. 12.50 (ISBN 0-89154-045-8). Intl Found Employ.
Egdahl, Richard, et al. Designing Cost-Effective Employee Health Plans. (Studies in Productivity-Highlights of the Literature: Vol. 22). (Orig.). Date not set. pap. 25.00 (ISBN 0-89361-032-1). Work in Amer.

Egly. Fringe Benefits for Classified Employees in Cities of 100,000 Population or Greater. (Research Bulletin: No. 19). pap. 0.50 (ISBN 0-685-57189-0). Assn Sch Busn.

Employee Befefits. LC 54-2030. 700p. 1979. 7.00 (ISBN 0-89834-030-6). Chamber Comm US.

Employee Benefit Plans: A Glossary of Terms. 3rd ed. 1976. pap. 7.00 (ISBN 0-89154-050-4). Intl Found Employ.

Employee Benefit Plans & the Economy: Learning Guide, CEBS Course IX. 2nd ed. 1980. spiral 13.00 (ISBN 0-89154-132-2). Intl Found Employ.

Employee Benefit Research Institute. A Review of Research, Vol. I, II, & III. (Orig.). 1980. pap. 25.00 (ISBN 0-86643-002-4). Employee Benefit.

Employee Benefits & Plans & the Economy: Answers to the Questions on the Subject Matter for the Learning Guide, CEBS Course IX. 2nd ed. 62p. spiral bdg. 13.00 (ISBN 0-89154-132-2); pap. text ed. 10.00 (ISBN 0-89154-133-0). Intl Found Employ.

Employee Health & Welfare Benefit Funds. (Industry Audit Guides). 1972. pap. 4.50 (ISBN 0-685-58478-X). Am Inst CPA.

Fringe Benefits: A Proposal for the Future. 1979. pap. 9.50 (ISBN 0-686-70229-8). Am Inst CPA.

Funding & Termination of Defined Benefit Plans. 1978. pap. 5.00 (ISBN 0-918734-15-0). Reymont.

Gilbert, Geoffrey M., et al. Accounting & Auditing for Employee Benefit Plans. 1978. 46.00 (ISBN 0-88262-217-X, 78-56016). Warren.

Greenhill, Richard. Employee Remuneration & Profit Sharing. 224p. 1980. 45.00x (ISBN 0-85941-123-0, Pub. by Woodhead-Faulkner England). State Mutual Bk.

Grisham, Roy A., Jr., ed. Encyclopedia of U. S. Government Benefits. 1024p. 1981. 14.95 (ISBN 0-89696-127-3). Everest Hse.

Hatch, Janice, ed. Canadian Conference on Employee Benefit Plans, Sept.-Oct. 1975: Proceedings. (Pensions Canada). 144p. 1976. spiral bdg. 8.75 (ISBN 0-89154-041-5). Intl Found Employ.

Hieb, Elizabeth, ed. Institute for Fund Advisors, Lake Tahoe, June, 1977: Proceedings. 1977. spiral bdg. 10.50 (ISBN 0-89154-067-9). Intl Found Employ.

--Textbook for Employee Benefit Plan Trustees, Administrators & Advisors 1976: Proceedings, Vol. 18. 1977. 12.50 (ISBN 0-89154-056-3). Intl Found Employ.

Hieb, Elizabeth A., ed. Canadian Conference, 11th Annual, Nov. 22-25, 1978: Proceedings. (Orig.). 1979. pap. 12.00 (ISBN 0-89154-090-3). Intl Found Employ.

--Collection of Employer Contributions Institute, Las Vegas, Nevada, June 15 to 18, 1980: Proceedings. 77p. (Orig.). 1980. pap. 8.00 (ISBN 0-89154-138-1). Intl Found Employ.

--Employer Contributions: Collection & Control, Payroll Auditing Institute Proceedings. 1978. spiral 8.75 (ISBN 0-89154-075-X). Intl Found Employ.

--Textbook for Employee Benefit Plan Trustees, Administrators & Advisors 1980: Proceedings, Vol. 22. 589p. 1981. text ed. 30.00 (ISBN 0-89154-150-0). Intl Found Employ.

Hilton, Anthony. Employee Reports: How to Communicate Financial Information to Employees. (Illus.). 200p. 1980. 29.95 (ISBN 0-85941-057-9). Herman Pub.

Hoffman, Marvin & Luck, David J. Salesmen's Fringe Benefits. LC 59-63656. 1959. pap. 2.00 (ISBN 0-87744-089-1). Mich St U Busn.

Illustrations of Accounting for Employee Benefits. (Financial Report Survey: No. 14). 1977. pap. 8.00 (ISBN 0-685-92034-8). Am Inst CPA.

Industrial Relations: Answers to the Questions on Subject Matter for the Learning Guide, CEBS Course VIII. 82p. 1979. pap. 10.00 (ISBN 0-89154-114-4). Intl Found Employ.

Ingraham, Mark H. & King, Francis P. Outer Fringe: Faculty Benefits Other Than Annuities & Insurance. 1965. pap. 5.95 (ISBN 0-299-03433-X). U of Wis Pr.

Jobin, Guy A. Canadian Trustees Handbook. 1979. pap. 25.00 (ISBN 0-89154-094-6). Intl Found Employ.

Jost, Lee F. & Sutherland, C. Bruce. Guide to Professional Benefit Plan Management & Administration. 405p. (Orig.). 1980. pap. 35.00 (ISBN 0-89154-096-2). Intl Found Employ.

Kennedy, James B. Beneficiary Features of American Trade Unions. LC 78-63929. (Johns Hopkins University. Studies in the Social Sciences. Twenty-Sixth Ser. 1908: 11-12). Repr. of 1908 ed. 16.00 (ISBN 0-404-61179-6). AMS Pr.

Kordus, Claude L., ed. Trustees Handbook: A Basic Text on Labor-Management Employee Benefit Plans. 3rd ed. 545p. pap. text ed. 35.00 (ISBN 0-89154-113-6). Intl Found Employ.

Landry, Richard S., intro. by. Employee Benefits, 1978. LC 54-2030. (Illus., Orig.). 1979. pap. 6.00 (ISBN 0-89834-015-2, 6142). Chamber Comm US.

Latta, Geoffrey W. Profit Sharing, Employee Stock Ownership, Savings, & Asset Formation Plans in the Western World. (Multinational Industrial Relations Ser.: No. 5). 1979. pap. 15.00 (ISBN 0-89546-015-7). Indus Res Unit-Wharton.

Lawson, J. W. & Smith, Ballard. Managements Complete Guide to Employee Benefits. 259p. 1980. 76.50 (ISBN 0-85013-119-7). Dartnell Corp.

Leshin, Geraldine. EEO Law: Impact on Fringe Benefits. Hinman, Faye, ed. (Policy & Practice Publication). 1979. 6.00 (ISBN 0-89215-102-1). U Cal LA Indus Rel.

Life, Health & Other Group Benefit Programs, 2 vols. (Readings, (CEBS): Course V). 1978. Set. pap. 20.00 (ISBN 0-89154-082-2). Intl Found Employ.

Life, Health & Other Group Benefit Programs. (Learning Guide (CEBS): Course V). 1978. spiral bdg. 13.00 (ISBN 0-89154-080-6). Intl Found Employ.

Life, Health & Other Group Benefit Programs. (Answers to the Questions on Subject Matter for Learning Guide (CEBS): Course V). 1978. pap. text ed. 10.00 (ISBN 0-89154-087-3). Intl Found Employ.

Lindsey, Fred. Employee Benefits: Nineteen Seventy-Seven. LC 54-2030. 1978. pap. 5.00 (ISBN 0-89834-001-2). Chamber Comm US.

Livingston, David T. Fiduciary Liability Insurance for Taft-Hartley Funds; a Comparison of Coverages. (Insurance, Liability Pensions). 68p. 1976. pap. 7.50 (ISBN 0-89154-042-3). Intl Found Employ.

Macaulay, Hugh H. Fringe Benefits & Their Federal Tax Treatment. LC 79-18950. (Columbia University. Studies in the Social Sciences: No. 600). Repr. of 1959 ed. 12.50 (ISBN 0-404-51600-9). AMS Pr.

McCaffery, Robert M. Managing the Employee Benefits Program. LC 77-159775. 1972. 16.50 (ISBN 0-8144-5266-3). Am Mgmt.

Manin, Mark B. Isolating Distortions in a Company's Compensation Program. 61p. (Orig.). 1980. pap. 2.00 (ISBN 0-89154-124-1). Intl Found Employ.

Meyer, Mitchell. Women & Employee Benefits. (Report Ser.: No. 752). (Illus.). 1978. pap. 15.00 (ISBN 0-8237-0188-3). Conference Bd.

Meyer, Mitchell & Fox, Harland. Profile of Employee Benefits. (Report Ser.: No. 645). (Illus.). 103p. 1974. pap. text ed. 15.00 (ISBN 0-8237-0064-X). Conference Bd.

Miller, Ned A. The Complete Guide to Employee Benefit Plans. rev. ed. LC 79-88343. 1979. 29.95 (ISBN 0-87863-149-6). Farnswth Pub.

Neitzel, James J., ed. Canadian Conference of the International Foundation of Employee Benefit Plans, Oct. 31-Nov. 3, 1976: Proceedings. 1977. spiral bdg 8.75 (ISBN 0-89154-057-1). Intl Found Employ.

O'Brien, David W. California Employer-Employee Benefits Handbook. 5th ed. LC 78-71230. 1979. pap. text ed. 29.95 (ISBN 0-9602204-0-2). Winter Brook.

Pearson, Jack, ed. Employee Benefits Institutes & Seminars for Company Sponsored Plans, 1978: Proceedings. (Orig.). 1979. pap. 7.50 (ISBN 0-89154-095-4). Intl Found Employ.

Quinn, Robert P. & Staines, Graham L. The Nineteen Seventy-Seven Quality of Employment Survey: Descriptive Statistics, with Comparison Data from the 1969-70 & 1972-73 Surveys. LC 78-71659. (Illus.). 1979. pap. text ed. 10.00 (ISBN 0-87944-231-X). Inst Soc. Res.

Rosenbloom, Jerry & Hallman, G. Victor. Employee Benefit Planning. (P-H Ser. in Risk, Insurance & Security). (Illus.). 544p. 1981. 24.95 (ISBN 0-13-274811-8). P-H.

Snider, H. Wayne, ed. Employee Benefits Management. 228p. 1981. 24.95 (ISBN 0-937802-00-X). Risk & Ins.

Special Institute, Chicago, March 1976. Technical Compliance Under ERISA: Proceedings. Neitzel, James & Hatch, Janice, eds. (Employee Retirement Income Security Act, Pensions). 1976. pap. 5.50 (ISBN 0-89154-048-2). Intl Found Employ.

Srb, Jozetta H. Communicating with Employees About Pension & Welfare Benefits. (Key Issues Ser.: No. 8). 1971. pap. 2.00 (ISBN 0-87546-244-8). NY Sch Indus Rel.

Steinforth, Alex. Employee Benefits: A Guide for Hospitals. LC 80-12159. 124p. 1980. 22.50 (ISBN 0-89443-290-7). Aspen Systems.

Stoeber, Edward A. Tax & Fringe Benefit Planning for Professional Corporations. 4th ed. LC 78-78161. 1979. pap. 13.75 (ISBN 0-87218-400-5). Natl Underwriter.

Stone, Morris. Benefit Plan Disputes: Arbitration Case Stories. 1977. spiral bdg. 8.75 (ISBN 0-89154-065-2). Intl Found Employ.

Van Beck, Donald L. Company Policy Manual. LC 78-63059. 1978. looseleaf 125.00 (ISBN 0-87822-190-5). Res Press.

Voorheis, Frank L. Bank Administered Pooled Equity Funds for Employee Benefit Plans. LC 67-64604. 1967. 4.00 (ISBN 0-87744-090-5). Mich St U Busn.

We Can Do It Together: Employee Benefits Historical Data 1951-1979. write for info. (ISBN 0-89834-038-1); pap. price not set. Chamber Comm US.

Weeks, David A., ed. Rethinking Employee Benefits Assumptions. LC 78-53106. (Report Ser.: No. 739). (Illus.). 1978. pap. 15.00 (ISBN 0-8237-0173-5). Conference Bd.

NONWOVEN FABRICS

Bhatnagar, VіJay M. Nonwovens & Disposables: New Technical-Marketing Developments. 86p. 1978. pap. 25.00 (ISBN 0-87762-256-6). Technomic.

Bhatnagar, ViJay M., ed. Nonwovens & Disposables: Proceedings of the First Canadian Symposium of Nonwovens & Disposables. LC 78-68591. (Illus.). 1978. pap. 25.00 (ISBN 0-87762-268-X). Technomic.

Dembeck, Adeline A. Guidebook to Man-Made Textile Fibers & Textured Yarns of the World: Film-To-Yarn Non-Wovens. 3rd ed. LC 68-28677. 1969. leatherette 11.00 (ISBN 0-911546-01-4). United Piece.

Lennox-Kerr, Peter. Nonwovens, '71. 26.00 (ISBN 0-87245-515-7). Textile Bk.

Weiner, Jack, et al. Nonwoven Fabrics. Incl. Vol. 1. General & Testing, Properties & Finishing, Supplement No. 2; Vol. 2. Forming Methods, Supplement No. 2; Vol. 3. Chemical & Mechanical Bonding, Supplement No. 3; Vol. 4. Uses. LC 74-100622. 1974. 15.00 ea. (ISBN 0-87010-027-0). Inst Paper Chem.

NOOTKA LANGUAGE

Sapir, Edward & Swadesh, Morris, eds. Nootka Texts: Tales & Ethnological Narratives, with Grammatical Notes & Lexical Materials. LC 78-11226. Repr. of 1939 ed. 35.00 (ISBN 0-404-11893-3). AMS Pr.

NOOTKA SOUND

Colnett, James. Colnett's Journal Aboard the Argonaut from April 26, 1789 to November 3, 1791. Howay, F. W., ed. LC 68-28614. 1968. Repr. of 1940 ed. lib. bdg. 30.75x (ISBN 0-8371-5063-9, COJC). Greenwood.

Meany, Edmond S. Vancouver's Discovery of Puget Sound. (Illus.). 1957. 10.00 (ISBN 0-8323-0103-5). Binford.

Pethick, Derek. The Nootka Connection. LC 80-51074. (Illus.). 288p. 1980. 17.95 (ISBN 0-295-95754-9). U of Wash Pr.

NORADRENALIN METABOLISM

Iversen, Leslie L. Uptake & Storage of Noradrenaline in Sympathic Nerves. 1967. 35.50 (ISBN 0-521-05390-0). Cambridge U Pr.

NORDAU, MAX SIMON, 1849-1943

Shaw, George B. Major Critical Essays. LC 74-145292. 1971. Repr. of 1932 ed. 29.00 (ISBN 0-403-01205-8). Scholarly.

NORDHOFF, CHARLES BERNARD, 1887-1947

Monarch Notes on Nordhoff & Hall's Mutiny on the Bounty. (Orig.). pap. 1.50 (ISBN 0-671-00857-9). Monarch Pr.

NORDIC COUNCIL

Anderson, Stanley V. Nordic Council: A Study of Scandinavian Regionalism. LC 67-21202. (American-Scandinavian Foundation Studies). (Illus.). 212p. 1967. 15.00 (ISBN 0-295-97865-1). U of Wash Pr.

NORDIC RACE

see Teutonic Race

NORE MUTINY, 1797

Manwaring, G. E. & Dobree, Bonamy. Floating Republic: The Mutinies at Spithead & the Nore, 1797. (Illus.). 299p. 1966. 26.50x (ISBN 0-7146-1497-1, F Cass Co). Biblio Dist.

Manwaring, George E. & Dobree, Bonamy. Floating Republic. LC 67-72366. (Illus.). Repr. of 1935 ed. 23.00x (ISBN 0-678-05185-2). Kelley.

NORFOLK, ENGLAND

Davenport, Frances G. Economic Development of a Norfolk Manor, 1086-1565. (Illus.). 106p. 1967. Repr. 25.00x (ISBN 0-7146-1297-9, F Cass Co). Biblio Dist.

NORFOLK, ENGLAND (COUNTY)

Browne, Thomas. Hydriotaphia, Urne-Buriall, or, a Discourse of the Sepulchrall Urnes Lately Found in Norfolk. Together with the Garden of Cyrus, or the Quincunciall Lozenge, or Network Plantations of the Ancients, Artificially, Naturally Mystically Considered. Kastenbaum, Robert, ed. LC 76-19562. (Death & Dying Ser.). 1977. Repr. of 1927 ed. lib. bdg. 12.00x (ISBN 0-405-09558-9). Arno.

Drackett, Phil. Inns & Harbours of North Norfolk. 150p. 1980. 11.00x (ISBN 0-902628-88-7, Pub. by RAC). State Mutual Bk.

Jennett, Sean, ed. Norfolk. LC 74-353603. (Travellers Guides Ser). (Illus.). 1969. pap. 3.50x (ISBN 0-232-51001-6). Intl Pubns Serv.

Ketton-Cremer, R. W. Norfolk in the Civil War: A Portrait of a Society in Conflict. (Illus.). 1970. 22.50 (ISBN 0-208-00977-9, Archon). Shoe String.

White, William. History Gazetteer & Directory of Norfolk. LC 70-9028. Repr. of 1845 ed. 27.50x (ISBN 0-678-05502-5). Kelley.

Young, Arthur. General View of the Agriculture of Norfolk. LC 69-13757. (Illus.). Repr. of 1804 ed. 25.00x (ISBN 0-678-05648-X). Kelley.

NORFOLK, VIRGINIA

Campbell, Ernest Q. When a City Closes Its Schools. LC 75-16840. (Univ. of N. Carolina, Institute for Research in Social Science Monographs). 195p. 1975. Repr. of 1960 ed. lib. bdg. 15.00 (ISBN 0-8371-8193-3, CAWC). Greenwood.

Harrod, Wilhelmine & Linnell, C. L. Norfolk: A Shell Guide. (Shell Guide Ser.). (Illus.). 88p. 1969. 7.95 (ISBN 0-571-06748-4, Pub. by Faber & Faber). Merrimack Bk Serv.

Jackson, A. B. As I See Ghent, a Visual Essay. LC 76-43065. (Illus.). 1979. 29.95 (ISBN 0-915442-22-1); pap. 16.95 (ISBN 0-915442-72-8). Donning Co.

Tarter, Brent, ed. The Order Book & Related Papers of the Common Hall of the Borough of Norfolk, Virginia, 1736-1798. 1979. 12.50 (ISBN 0-88490-072-X). VA State Lib.

Walker, Carroll. Norfolk: A Pictorial History. 2nd ed. Friedman, Donna R., ed. LC 80-39668. (Illus.). 208p. 1981. pap. 12.95 (ISBN 0-89865-129-8). Donning Co.

NORFOLK ISLAND

Belcher, Diana. The Mutineers of the Bounty & Their Descendants in Pitcairn & Norfolk Islands. LC 75-3439. Repr. of 1870 ed. 34.50 (ISBN 0-404-14443-8). AMS Pr.

Hoare, Merval. Norfolk Island, an Outline of Its History: 1774-1977. 2nd ed. (Illus.). 1978. pap. 12.00x (ISBN 0-7022-1187-7). U of Queensland Pr.

Murray, Thomas. Pitcairn's Island. LC 72-281. (World History Ser., No. 48). 1972. Repr. of 1860 ed. lib. bdg. 43.95 (ISBN 0-8383-1410-4). Haskell.

NORFOLK AND WESTERN RAILWAY

Jeffries, Lewis I. Nofolk & Western: The Giant of Steam. (Illus.). 1980. 35.00 (ISBN 0-87108-547-X). Pruett.

NORMAL SCHOOLS

see Teachers Colleges

NORMAN, MONTAGU COLLET NORMAN, BARON, 1871-1950

Clay, Henry. Lord Norman. Wilkins, Mira, ed. LC 78-3906. (International Finance Ser.). (Illus.). 1978. Repr. of 1957 ed. lib. bdg. 32.00x (ISBN 0-405-11211-4). Arno.

NORMAN ARCHITECTURE

see Architecture, Norman

NORMAN HORSE

see Percheron Horse

NORMANDY

Frere, Edouard B. Manuel Du Bibliographe Normand, ou, Dictionnaire Bibliographique et Historique Contenant, 2 Vols. 1964. Repr. of 1860 ed. 73.00 (ISBN 0-8337-1245-4). B Franklin.

Gunn, Peter. Normandy: Landscape with Figures. (Illus.). 1976. text ed. 20.00x (ISBN 0-575-01962-X). Verry.

Haskins, Charles H. Norman Institutions. LC 80-2026. 1981. Repr. of 1918 ed. 39.50 (ISBN 0-404-18568-1). AMS Pr.

History, People & Places Series. Incl. History, People & Places in Normandy. Whelpton, Barbara. LC 75-314602. 144p. 1975. 11.50x (ISBN 0-902875-57-4); History, People & Places in Yorkshire. Gaunt, Arthur. LC 75-331730. 160p. 1975. 11.50x (ISBN 0-902875-77-9); History, People & Places in New Oxfordshire. Martin, Frank. 144p. 1975. 12.50x (ISBN 0-902875-53-1); History, People & Places in the Thames Valley. Martin, Frank. LC 73-167149. 142p. 1972. 9.00x (ISBN 0-902875-15-9); History, People & Places in Chiltern Villages. Burden, Vera. LC 73-174593. 136p. 1972. 9.00x (ISBN 0-902875-21-3); History, People & Places in the Cotwolds. Cash, J. Allan. LC 75-307571. 160p. 1975. 11.50x (ISBN 0-902875-59-0). (Illus.). 1975. Intl Pubns Serv.

Links, J. G. The Ruskins in Normandy: A Tour in 1848 with Murrays Handbook. LC 78-134669. (Illus.). Date not set. 6.95 (ISBN 0-8149-0689-3). Vanguard.

Loyd, Lewis C. The Origins of Some Anglo-Norman Families. Clay, Charles T. & Douglas, David C., eds. LC 74-18109. 140p. 1980. Repr. of 1951 ed. 12.50 (ISBN 0-8063-0649-1). Genealog Pub.

Speidel, Hans. Invasion Nineteen Forty Four: Rommel & the Normandy Campaign. Repr. of 1950 ed. cancelled (ISBN 0-89201-056-8). Zenger Pub.

NORMANDY-DESCRIPTION AND TRAVEL

Blue Guide - Normandy, Brittany, Loire Valley. 1977. 28.95 (ISBN 0-528-84597-7); pap. 19.95 (ISBN 0-528-84598-5). Rand.

Colyer, P. Voyage en Normandie. (Illus.). 1977. pap. text ed. 2.50x (ISBN 0-582-31340-6). Longman.
Delmar-Morgan, Edward. Normandy Harbors & Pilotage. 1979. 29.95x (ISBN 0-8464-0073-1). Beekman Pubs.
Michelin Green Travel Guide: Normandy. (Fr. & Eng.). 4.95 (ISBN 0-685-11381-7). French & Eur.
Normandy. (Panorama Books Collection). (Fr.). 3.95 (ISBN 0-685-35939-5). French & Eur.
One Hundred Hours in Normandy. (One Hundred Hours in Ser.). (gr. 7). 1976. pap. 5.95 (ISBN 0-88332-017-7, 4113). Larousse.

NORMANDY-HISTORY-SOURCES

Hunt, Robert & Mason, David. The Normandy Campaign. 1976. 14.95 (ISBN 0-85052-209-9). Hippocrene Bks.
Lanfranc. The Letters of Lanfranc, Archbishop of Canterbury. Clover, Helen & Gibson, Margaret, eds. (Oxford Medieval Texts Ser.). (Illus.). 218p. 1979. text ed. 59.00x (ISBN 0-19-822235-1). Oxford U Pr.

NORMANDY-HISTORY-MEDIEVAL PERIOD

Chibnall, Marjorie, ed. The Ecclesiastical History of Orderic Vitalis, Vol. 1. (Oxford Medieval Texts Ser.). (Illus.). 416p. 1981. 98.00 (ISBN 0-19-822243-2). Oxford U Pr.
Douglas, David C. William the Conqueror: The Norman Impact Upon England. (English Monarchs Ser.). 1964. 25.00x (ISBN 0-520-00348-9); pap. 5.95 (ISBN 0-520-00350-0, CAL131). U of Cal Pr.
Gaimar, Geoffroy. L' Estoire des Engleis. Bell, Alexander, ed. 37.00 (ISBN 0-384-17555-4); pap. 31.00 (ISBN 0-384-17556-2). Johnson Repr.
Histoire Des Ducs De Normandie et Des Rois D'Angleterre. 1840. 35.50 (ISBN 0-384-23431-3); pap. 31.00 (ISBN 0-384-23430-5). Johnson Repr.
Ordericus Vitalis. Ecclesiastical History of England & Normandy, 4 Vols. Forrester, T., tr. LC 68-57872. (Bohn's Antiquarian Library Ser). Repr. of 1856 ed. Set. 115.00 (ISBN 0-404-50040-4). AMS Pr.
Ordericus, Vitalis. Historiae Ecclesiasticae Libri Tredecim, 5 Vols. Le Prevost, A., ed. Repr. of 1838 ed. Set. 177.00 (ISBN 0-384-43511-4); Set. pap. 154.00 (ISBN 0-384-43512-2). Johnson Repr.
Palgrave, Francis. The History of Normandy & England, 4 vols. LC 80-2218. Repr. of 1919 ed. 345.00 (ISBN 0-404-18770-6). AMS Pr.
Prentout, Henri. Essai Sur les Origines et la Fondation Du Duche De Normandie. LC 80-2214. Repr. of 1911 ed. 39.00 (ISBN 0-404-18776-5). AMS Pr.
Rabasse, Maurice. Du Regime Des Fiefs En Normandie Au Moyen Age. LC 80-2006. Repr. of 1905 ed. 29.50 (ISBN 0-404-18588-6). AMS Pr.
Strayer, Joseph R. Administration of Normandy Under Saint Louis. LC 72-171362. Repr. of 1932 ed. 16.00 (ISBN 0-404-06297-0). AMS Pr.

NORMANDY-POLITICS AND GOVERNMENT

Strayer, J. R. Administration of Normandy Under Saint Louis. 1932. 20.00 (ISBN 0-527-01686-1). Kraus Repr.

NORMANS

Adams, Herbert B. Norman Constables in America. LC 78-63738. (Johns Hopkins University. Studies in the Social Sciences. First Ser. 1882-1883: 8). Repr. of 1883 ed. 11.50 (ISBN 0-404-61008-0). AMS Pr.
Amato. L' Ystoire De Li Normant: Et la Chronique De Robert Viscart Par Aime, Moine Du Mont-Cassin. 35.00 (ISBN 0-384-01030-X); pap. 31.00 (ISBN 0-384-01031-8). Johnson Repr.
Brook, Christopher. Saxon & Norman Kings. 1978. 28.00 (ISBN 0-7134-1534-7, Pub. by Batsford England). David & Charles.
Chalandon, Ferdinand. Histoire de la domination normande en Italie et en Sicilie, 2 Vols. 1969. Repr. of 1912 ed. Set. 55.50 (ISBN 0-8337-0514-8). B Franklin.
Davis, R. H. The Normans & Their Myth. (Illus.). 1977. 8.95 (ISBN 0-500-25047-2). Thames Hudson.
Douglas, David C. The Norman Achievement: 1050-1100. LC 74-88028. 1969. 23.75x (ISBN 0-520-01383-2). U of Cal Pr.
--The Norman Fate, 1100-1154. LC 75-13155. 350p. 1976. 32.75x (ISBN 0-520-03027-3). U of Cal Pr.
--William the Conqueror: The Norman Impact Upon England. (English Monarchs Ser.). 1964. 25.00x (ISBN 0-520-00348-9); pap. 5.95 (ISBN 0-520-00350-0, CAL131). U of Cal Pr.
Haskins, C. H. The Normans in European History. 258p. 1980. Repr. lib. bdg. 25.00 (ISBN 0-89984-278-X). Century Bookbindery.
Haskins, Charles H. The Normans in European History. 249p. 1980. Repr. lib. bdg. 25.00 (ISBN 0-8495-2270-6). Arden Lib.
--Normans in European History. 1966. pap. 4.95x (ISBN 0-393-00342-6, Norton Lib). Norton.
Jewett, S. The Story of the Normans. 59.95 (ISBN 0-8490-1140-X). Gordon Pr.
Johnson, A. H. Normans in Europe. Repr. 25.00 (ISBN 0-685-43053-7). Norwood Edns.
Le Patourel, John. The Norman Empire. (Illus.). 426p. 1977. 59.00x (ISBN 0-19-822525-3). Oxford U Pr.
Macgearailt, Gearoid. Celts & Normans. (History of Ireland Ser.: Vol. 1). (Illus.). 288p. 1969. pap. text ed. 6.95 (ISBN 0-7171-0255-6). Irish Bk Ctr.
The Norman People & Their Existing Descendants in the British Dominions & in the United States of America. LC 74-18414. 484p. 1975. Repr. of 1874 ed. 17.50 (ISBN 0-8063-0636-X). Genealog Pub.
Ordericus Vitalis. Ecclesiastical History of England & Normandy, 4 Vols. Forrester, T., tr. LC 68-57872. (Bohn's Antiquarian Library Ser). Repr. of 1856 ed. Set. 115.00 (ISBN 0-404-50040-4). AMS Pr.
Ordericus, Vitalis. Historiae Ecclesiasticae Libri Tredecim, 5 Vols. Le Prevost, A., ed. Repr. of 1838 ed. Set. 177.00 (ISBN 0-384-43511-4); Set. pap. 154.00 (ISBN 0-384-43512-2). Johnson Repr.
Rooke, Patrick, et al. The Normans. LC 78-56586. (Peoples of the Past Ser.). (Illus.). 1978. lib. bdg. 7.95 (ISBN 0-686-51159-X). Silver.
Wilson, David M. & Klindt-Jensen, Ole. Viking Art. 2nd ed. (Nordic Ser.: Vol. 6). (Illus.). 253p. 1980. 29.50x (ISBN 0-8166-0974-8); pap. 12.95 (ISBN 0-8166-0977-2). U of Minn Pr.

NORMANS IN ENGLAND

Crispin, M. Jackson & Macary, Leonce. Falaise Roll: Recording Prominent Companions of William Duke of Normandy at the Conquest of England. LC 76-86814. (Illus.). 1969. Repr. of 1938 ed. 15.00 (ISBN 0-8063-0080-9). Genealog Pub.
Freeman, Edward A. History of the Norman Conquest of England: Its Causes & Its Results, 5 Vols. Repr. of 1879 ed. Set. 265.00 (ISBN 0-404-07980-6). Vol. 1 (ISBN 0-404-07981-4). Vol. 2 (ISBN 0-404-07982-2). Vol. 3 (ISBN 0-404-07983-0). Vol. 4 (ISBN 0-404-07984-9). Vol. 5 (ISBN 0-404-07985-7). AMS Pr.
Jewett, Sarah O. The Story of the Normans. 1979. Repr. of 1899 ed. lib. bdg. 35.00 (ISBN 0-8482-1393-9). Norwood Edns.
Le Patourel, John. The Norman Empire. (Illus.). 426p. 1977. 59.00x (ISBN 0-19-822525-3). Oxford U Pr.
Loyn, H. R. Anglo-Saxon England & the Norman Conquest. (Social & Economic History of England). (Illus.). 1962. pap. text ed. 11.95x (ISBN 0-582-48232-1). Longman.
Ritchie, Robert L. The Normans in Scotland. LC 80-2216. Repr. of 1954 ed. 57.50 (ISBN 0-404-18783-8). AMS Pr.
Walker, David. The Norman Conquerors. (A New History of Wales). (Illus.). 1977. text ed. 10.50x (ISBN 0-7154-0302-8). Humanities.

NORMED LINEAR SPACES

Day, M. M. Normed Linear Spaces. 3rd ed. (Ergebnisse der Mathematik und Ihrer Grenzgebiete: Vol. 21). viii, 211p. 1973. 28.80 (ISBN 0-387-06148-7). Springer-Verlag.
The Geometry of Metric & Linear Spaces: Proceedings. (Lecture Notes in Mathematics: Vol. 490). x, 244p. 1976. pap. 13.10 (ISBN 0-387-07417-1). Springer-Verlag.
Jameson, G. J. Topology & Normed Spaces. LC 73-22137. (Mathematics Ser.). 408p. 1974. text ed. 20.50x (ISBN 0-412-12340-1, Pub. by Chapman & Hall England). Methuen Inc.
Singer, I. Best Approximation in Normed Linear Spaces by Elements of Linear Subspaces. LC 73-110407. (Grundlehren der Mathematischen Wissenschaften: Vol. 171). 1970. 40.20 (ISBN 0-387-05116-3). Springer-Verlag.

NORMED RINGS

see Banach Algebras

NORRIS, FRANK, 1870-1902

Ahnebrink, Lars. Beginnings of Naturalism in American Fiction, 1891-1903. LC 61-13093. 1961. Repr. of 1950 ed. 18.50 (ISBN 0-8462-0105-4). Russell.
--The Influence of Emile Zola on Frank Norris. 1978. Repr. of 1947 ed. lib. bdg. 16.00 (ISBN 0-8495-0041-9). Arden Lib.
--The Influence of Emile Zola on Frank Norris. LC 73-12457. Repr. of 1947 ed. lib. bdg. 15.00 (ISBN 0-8414-2873-5). Folcroft.
Crisler, Jesse E. & McElrath, Joseph R., Jr. Frank Norris: A Reference Guide. (Series Seventy, Reference Guide: No. 3). 145p. 1975. 12.50 (ISBN 0-8161-1097-2). G K Hall.
Davison, Richard A. Merrill Studies in the Octopus. LC 79-93996. 1969. pap. text ed. 2.50x (ISBN 0-675-09408-9). Merrill.
Dillingham, William B. Frank Norris: Instinct & Art. LC 69-15257. 1969. 13.50x (ISBN 0-8032-0039-0). U of Nebr Pr.
French, Warren. Frank Norris. (Twayne's United States Authors Ser). 1962. pap. 3.45 (ISBN 0-8084-0134-3, T25, Twayne). Coll & U Pr.
Frohock, W. M. Frank Norris. LC 68-64751. (Pamphlets on American Writers Ser: No. 68). (Orig.). 1968. pap. 1.25x (ISBN 0-8166-0482-7, MPAW68). U of Minn Pr.
Gaer, Joseph. Frank Norris (Benjamin Franklin Norris) Bibliography & Biographical Data. LC 71-131408. 1970. Repr. of 1934 ed. 15.00 (ISBN 0-8337-1257-8). B Franklin.
--Frank Norris Bibliography & Biographical Data. LC 74-16033. 1974. Repr. of 1934 ed. lib. bdg. 9.95 (ISBN 0-8414-4566-4). Folcroft.
Graham, Don. Critical Essays on Frank Norris. 1980. lib. bdg. 25.00 (ISBN 0-8161-8307-4). G K Hall.
--The Fiction of Frank Norris: The Aesthetic Context. LC 77-18298. (Illus.). 1978. text ed. 13.00x (ISBN 0-8262-0252-7). U of Mo Pr.
Lohf, Kenneth A. & Sheehy, Eugene P. Frank Norris: A Bibliography. 1959. 10.00 (ISBN 0-527-58050-3). Kraus Repr.
McElrath, Joseph P., ed. Frank Norris: The Critical Reception. (American Critical Tradition Ser.: No. 7). (Illus.). 1979. lib. bdg. 21.50 (ISBN 0-89102-150-7). B Franklin.
Marchand, Ernest. Frank Norris: A Study. 1964. lib. bdg. 17.50x (ISBN 0-374-95282-5). Octagon.
Norris, Charles G. Frank Norris. LC 73-9950. Repr. of 1914 ed. lib. bdg. 8.50 (ISBN 0-8414-2366-0). Folcroft.
Norris, Frank. The Literary Criticism of Frank Norris. Pizer, Donald, ed. LC 73-86725. xxiv, 247p. 1976. Repr. of 1964 ed. 19.00 (ISBN 0-8462-1758-9). Russell.
Pizer, Donald. The Novels of Frank Norris. LC 72-6785. (Studies in Fiction, No. 34). 1972. Repr. of 1966 ed. lib. bdg. 49.95 (ISBN 0-8383-1666-2). Haskell.
Solibakke, Eric. Monarch Notes on Norris' the Octopus. pap. 1.95 (ISBN 0-671-00891-9). Monarch Pr.
Taylor, Harvey. Frank Norris: Two Poems & Kim Reviewed with a Bibliography. LC 73-10180. 1974. Repr. of 1930 ed. lib. bdg. 10.00 (ISBN 0-8414-2687-2). Folcroft.
Walker, Franklin D. Frank Norris: A Biography. LC 63-15186. (Illus.). 1963. Repr. of 1932 ed. 14.50 (ISBN 0-8462-0378-2). Russell.

NORRIS, GEORGE WILLIAM, 1861-1944

Lief, Alfred. Democracy's Norris: The Biography of a Lonely Crusade. 1977. Repr. of 1939 ed. lib. bdg. 25.00x (ISBN 0-374-94998-0). Octagon.
Lowitt, Richard. George W. Norris: The Making of a Progressive, 1861 to 1912. LC 79-18826. (Illus.). 1980. Repr. of 1963 ed. lib. bdg. 29.00x (ISBN 0-313-22103-0, LOGN). Greenwood.
--George W. Norris: The Persistence of a Progressive, 1913-1933. LC 76-147923. (Illus.). 605p. 1971. 27.50 (ISBN 0-252-00176-1). U of Ill Pr.
--George W. Norris: The Triumph of a Progressive, 1933-1944. LC 78-2033. (Illus.). 1978. 24.50 (ISBN 0-252-00223-7). U of Ill Pr.

NORRIS FAMILY

Heywood, Thomas, ed. Norris Papers. 1847. 20.00 (ISBN 0-384-22880-1). Johnson Repr.

NORRISTOWN, PENNSYLVANIA

Goldstein, Sidney. Norristown Study. LC 60-10607. 1961. 12.50x (ISBN 0-8122-7312-5). U of Pa Pr.

NORSE LANGUAGES

see Icelandic and Old Norse Languages; Scandinavian Languages

NORSE LEGENDS

see Legends, Norse

NORSE LITERATURE

see Icelandic and Old Norse Literature

NORSE MYTHOLOGY

see Mythology, Norse

NORSEMEN

see Northmen

NORTH, FRANK MASON, 1850-1935

Lacy, Creighton. Frank Mason North: His Social & Ecumenical Mission. LC 67-14983. 1967. 6.50 (ISBN 0-687-13464-1). Abingdon.

NORTH, FREDERICK NORTH, BARON, 1732-1792

Cannon, J. Fox-North Coalition. LC 70-85715. 1970. 35.50 (ISBN 0-521-07606-4). Cambridge U Pr.
Smith, Charles D. The Early Career of Lord North the Prime Minister, 1754-1770. LC 76-14765. (Illus.). 381p. 1979. 18.50 (ISBN 0-8386-1899-5). Fairleigh Dickinson.
Thomas, Peter D. Lord North. LC 75-29819. (British Political Biography Ser.). 175p. 1975. 17.95 (ISBN 0-312-49840-3). St Martin.
Valentine, Alan. Lord North, 2 Vols. (Illus.). 1967. Set. 27.50c (ISBN 0-8061-0752-9); Set. pap. 15.00x (ISBN 0-8061-1344-8). U of Okla Pr.

NORTH AFRICA

see Africa, North

NORTH AFRICANS

see also Arabs; Bedouins; Berbers

NORTH AMERICA

Conant, Melvin. The Long Polar Watch: Canada & the Defense of North America. LC 74-9874. (Published for the Council on Foreign Relations Ser). (Illus.). 204p. 1974. Repr. of 1962 ed. lib. bdg. 15.00x (ISBN 0-8371-7613-1, COPW). Greenwood.
Fenning, D., et al. An Encyclopaedia of North & South America 1786. 1980. 75.00x (ISBN 0-905418-02-6); pap. 25.00x (ISBN 0-9502121-6-4). State Mutual Bk.
Garreau, Joel. The Nine Nations of North America. LC 80-28556. (Illus.). 423p. 1981. 14.95 (ISBN 0-395-29124-0). HM.
Grant, George. Technology & Empire: Perspectives on North America. 143p. 1969. 12.95 (ISBN 0-88784-705-6, Pub. by Hse Anansi Pr Canada); pap. 4.95 (ISBN 0-88784-605-X). U of Toronto Pr.
Hudson, Fred S. North America. (Advanced Level Geography Ser.). (Illus.). 462p. 1974. pap. 11.25x (ISBN 0-7121-1408-4). Intl Pubns Serv.
Kroeber, A. L. Cultural & Natural Areas of Native North America. Repr. of 1939 ed. 35.00 (ISBN 0-527-01394-3). Kraus Repr.
Lenin, Vladimir I. Carta a los Obreros Norteamericanos. 26p. (Span.). 1978. pap. 0.80 (ISBN 0-8285-1364-3, Pub. by Progress Pubs Russia). Imported Pubns.
Livingston, Richard A., ed. North American Yacht Register 1980. LC 78-646613. (Illus.). 1980. 45.00 (ISBN 0-931938-02-3). Livingston Marine.
Research Libraries of the New York Public & the Library of Congress. Bibliographic Guide to North American History: 1978. (Library Catalogs-Bib. Guides). 1979. lib. bdg. 75.00 (ISBN 0-8161-6855-5). G K Hall.
Research Libraries of the New York Public Library & the Library of Congress. Bibliography Guide to North American History: 1979. (Library Catalogs-Bib. Guides). 1980. lib. bdg. 75.00 (ISBN 0-8161-6871-7). G K Hall.
Smith, Joseph R. & Phillips, Merton O. North America, Its People & the Resources, Development, & Prospects of the Continent As the Home of Man. (Illus.). Repr. of 1942 ed. lib. bdg. 51.50x (ISBN 0-8371-2519-7, SMNA). Greenwood.
Trollope, Anthony. North America, 2 vols. new ed. LC 79-350542. Repr. of 1869 ed. Set. 37.50x (ISBN 0-678-00770-5). Kelley.
Who Owns Whom: North America, 1980-81. 12th ed. LC 74-646353. 1100p. 1980. 225.00x (ISBN 0-8002-2417-5). Intl Pubns Serv.

NORTH AMERICA-ANTIQUITIES

Cleland, Charles E., ed. For the Director: Research Essays in Honor of James B. Griffin. (Anthropological Papers Ser.: No. 61). (Illus., Orig.). 1977. pap. 6.50x (ISBN 0-932206-59-X). U Mich Mus Anthro.
De Laguna, Frederica. The Prehistory of Northern North America As Seen from the Yukon. LC 76-43687. (Society for American Archaeology Memoirs.: No. 3). Repr. of 1947 ed. 54.50 (ISBN 0-404-15520-0). AMS Pr.
Fitting, James E., ed. The Development of North American Archaeology. LC 73-5862. 312p. 1973. 14.75x (ISBN 0-271-01161-0). Pa St U Pr.
Gorenstein, Shirley, et al. North America. (Pre History Ser). (Illus.). 200p. (Orig.). 1975. 15.95 (ISBN 0-312-57820-2); pap. text ed. 6.95 (ISBN 0-312-57855-5). St Martin.
Harvard University. Peabody Museum of Archaeology & Ethnology. Antiquities of the New World: Early Explorations in Archaeology, 18 titles in 19 vols. Repr. of 1949 ed. 753.00 (ISBN 0-404-57300-2). AMS Pr.
Jennings, Jesse D. Prehistory of North America. 2nd ed. (Illus.). 320p. 1974. text ed. 21.00 (ISBN 0-07-032454-9, C). McGraw.
Jennings, Jesse D., ed. Ancient Native Americans. LC 78-7989. (Illus.). 1978. pap. text ed. 21.95x (ISBN 0-7167-0074-3). W H Freeman.
Jennings, Jesse D., et al. Sudden Shelter. (University of Utah Anthropological Papers: No. 103). (Illus., Orig.). 1980. pap. 25.00x (ISBN 0-87480-166-4). U of Utah Pr.
Martin, Paul S., et al. Indians Before Columbus: Twenty Thousand Years of North American History Revealed by Archaeology. LC 47-1434. (Illus.). xxiv, 582p. 1975. pap. 6.95 (ISBN 0-226-50782-3, P630, Phoen). U of Chicago Pr.
Martineau, LaVan. The Rocks Begin to Speak. DenDooven, Gweneth R., ed. LC 72-85137. (Illus.). 1973. 10.95 (ISBN 0-916122-30-1). KC Pubns.
Spencer, Robert F., et al. The Native Americans: Ethnology & Backgrounds of the North American Indians. 2nd ed. (Illus.). 1977. text ed. 23.50 scp (ISBN 0-06-046371-6, HarpC). Har-Row.

Spiess, A. E., ed. Conservation Archaeology in the Northeast: Toward a Research Orientation. LC 78-56049. (Peabody Museum Bulletins Ser.: No. 3). 1978. pap. 8.00x (ISBN 0-87365-953-8). Peabody Harvard.

Thomas, Cyrus. Introduction to the Study of North American Archaeology. LC 72-5009. (Harvard University. Peabody Museum of Archaeology & Ethnology. Antiquities of the New World: No. 14). Repr. of 1898 ed. 34.00 (ISBN 0-404-57314-2). AMS Pr.

NORTH AMERICA–CLIMATE–MAPS

Bryson, R. A. & Hare, F., eds. Climates of North America. LC 74-477739. (World Survey of Climatology Ser.: Vol. 11). 1974. 97.75 (ISBN 0-444-41062-7). Elsevier.

NORTH AMERICA–DESCRIPTION AND TRAVEL

Arrow Pub Staff, ed. Arrow Street Guide of the North Shore. 1976. pap. 2.50 (ISBN 0-913450-30-8). Arrow Pub.

Beddis, R. A. Asia & North America. (New Secondary Geographies Ser: Pt. 3). 192p. 1969. 4.50x (ISBN 0-340-07414-0). Intl Pubns Serv.

Burman, Ben L. It's a Big Continent. LC 61-11648. 1961. 4.95 (ISBN 0-685-20504-5). Taplinger.

Dobbs, Arthur. An Account of the Counties Adjoining to Hudson's Bay, in the Northwest Part of America. 1744. 13.00 (ISBN 0-384-12045-8). Johnson Repr.

Douglas, David. Journal Kept by David Douglas During His Travels in North America, 1823-27. Repr. of 1959 ed. text ed. 22.50 (ISBN 0-934454-54-X). Lubrecht & Cramer.

Farkas, Sandor B. Journey in North America, 1831. Kadarkay, Arpad, tr. from Hung. LC 77-19145. 230p. 1978. text ed. 24.75 (ISBN 0-87436-270-9). ABC-Clio.

Haraszthy, Agoston. Travels in North America. Schoenman, Theodore & Schoenman, Helen B., trs. from Hungarian. (Illus.). 1980. 15.00 (ISBN 0-8424-0157-1). Nellen Pub.

Hudson, F. S. North America. 4th ed. (Illus.). 464p. 1978. pap. 15.95x (ISBN 0-7121-1410-6, Pub. by Macdonald & Evans England). Intl Ideas.

Knowles, R. North America in Maps: Topographical Map Studies of Canada & the USA. (Illus.). 1976. pap. text ed. 12.95x (ISBN 0-582-31017-2). Longman.

M'Robert, P. Tour Through Part of the North Provinces of America. LC 67-29039. (Eyewitness Accounts of the American Revolution Ser.). 1971. Repr. of 1776 ed. 10.00 (ISBN 0-405-01136-9). Arno.

The Magnificent Continent. LC 75-1928. (Illus.). 320p. 1975. 14.95 (ISBN 0-528-81013-8); deluxe ed. 30.00 (ISBN 0-528-81011-1). Rand.

Mead, W. R. & Brown, E. H. United States & Canada: A Regional Geography. 1964. text ed. 7.25x (ISBN 0-09-103750-6, Hutchinson U Pr). Humanities.

Milbert, Jacques. Picturesque Itinerary of the Hudson River & Peripheral Parts of North America. LC 67-29606. (American Environmental Studies). 1968. Repr. of 1928 ed. 20.00 (ISBN 0-405-02678-1). Arno.

Mirsky, Jeannette. Westward Crossings: Balboa, Mackenzie, Lewis & Clark. LC 70-116434. 1970. 11.00x (ISBN 0-226-53180-5). U of Chicago Pr.

Niemeier, Jean. Wild Blue Water. LC 62-22127. (Illus.). 1962. 8.95 (ISBN 0-8323-0196-5). Binford.

Paterson, J. H. North America. 6th ed. (Illus.). 1979. text ed. 18.95 (ISBN 0-19-502484-2). Oxford U Pr.

Quinn, David B., ed. North American Discovery, Circa 1000-1612. LC 72-174707. (Documentary History Ser). (Illus.). 1971. 14.95x (ISBN 0-87249-245-1). U of SC Pr.

Rogers, Robert. A Concise Account of North America. Repr. of 1765 ed. 14.50 (ISBN 0-384-51700-5). Johnson Repr.

Simpson, Thomas. Narrative of the Discoveries on the North Coast of America, Effected by the Officers of the Hudson's Bay Company During the Years 1836-39. LC 74-5877. Repr. of 1843 ed. 26.50 (ISBN 0-404-11685-X). AMS Pr.

Thorne, James. The Adventurers Guide to North America, 4 vols. LC 73-11796. 1974. pap. 2.95 ea. Bobbs.

Wilhelm, Paul. Travels in North America, 1822-1824. Lottinville, Savoie, ed. Nitske, W. Robert, tr. (Illus.). 1974. pap. text ed. 10.95 (ISBN 0-8061-1501-7). U of Okla Pr.

Williams, Lawrence. North America from the Air. 1976. pap. text ed. 5.25x (ISBN 0-435-34918-X). Heinemann Ed.

NORTH AMERICA–DESCRIPTION AND TRAVEL–GUIDEBOOKS

Dickerman, Pat. Adventure Travel, North America. LC 77-25745. (Illus.). 1978. pap. 5.95 (ISBN 0-690-01751-0). T y Crowell.

Four-Wheel-Drive North American Travel Guide. LC 79-63747. 1980. pap. 7.95 (ISBN 0-528-84110-6). Rand.

Gousha North American Road Atlas. rev. ed. 1981. pap. 4.50 (ISBN 0-451-82064-9, XE2064, Sig). NAL.

Leen, Daniel. The Freighthopper's Manual for North America. (Illus.). 1979. pap. 4.95 (ISBN 0-88496-129-X). Capra Pr.

Moneywise Guide to North America: Canada - U S. A. -Mexico 1980-81. (Illus.). 328p. 1980-81. pap. 9.95 (ISBN 0-88254-545-0, Pub. by Travelaid England). Hippocrene Bks.

A Moneywise Guide to North America: Canada, U. S. A., Mexico. 13th ed. 1979. pap. 9.95 (ISBN 0-902743-15-5, Pub. by Two Continents). Hippocrene Bks.

Wallace, Harriet E., ed. Union List of Geologic Field Trip Guidebooks of North America. 3rd ed. LC 78-52012. 1978. pap. 20.00 (ISBN 0-913312-05-3). Am Geol.

NORTH AMERICA–DISCOVERY AND EXPLORATION

see America–Discovery and Exploration

NORTH AMERICA–HISTORY

The American Nations Past & Present. Incl. Barbados. 1976 (ISBN 0-8270-4630-8); Bolivia. 1973 (ISBN 0-8270-4635-9); Brazil. 1975 (ISBN 0-8270-4640-5); Canada. 1974 (ISBN 0-8270-4645-6); Chile. 1971 (ISBN 0-8270-4650-2); Colombia. 1977 (ISBN 0-8270-4655-3); Costa Rica. 1973 (ISBN 0-8270-4660-X); Dominican Republic. 1976 (ISBN 0-8270-4665-0); Ecuador. 1972 (ISBN 0-8270-4670-7); El Salvador. 1979 (ISBN 0-8270-4675-8); Guatemala. 1972 (ISBN 0-8270-4680-4); Haiti. 1979 (ISBN 0-8270-4685-5); Jamaica. 1974 (ISBN 0-8270-4690-1); Mexico. 1978 (ISBN 0-8270-4925-0); Nicaragua. 1978 (ISBN 0-8270-4695-2); Panama. 1971 (ISBN 0-8270-4700-2); Paraguay. 1974 (ISBN 0-8270-4705-3); Peru. 1971 (ISBN 0-8270-4710-X); Trinidad & Tobago. 1974 (ISBN 0-8270-4715-0); Venezuela. 1978 (ISBN 0-8270-4915-3). (Image Ser.). (Illus., Span. eds. avail. for each bk.). pap. 1.00 ea. OAS.

Axtell, James. The European & the Indian: Essays in the Ethnohistory of Colonial North America. (Illus.). 256p. 1981. 19.95 (ISBN 0-19-502903-8). Oxford U Pr.

Babcock, William H. Early Norse Visits to North America. 1976. lib. bdg. 59.95 (ISBN 0-8490-1742-4). Gordon Pr.

Bolton, Herbert E. & Marshall, Thomas M. The Colonization of North America, 1492-1783. (Illus.). 1971. Repr. of 1920 ed. 24.75 (ISBN 0-02-841590-6). Hafner.

Brown, R., et al. Settlement in North America. 1974. pap. text ed. 3.95x (ISBN 0-435-34066-2). Heinemann Ed.

Educational Research Council. Early Years: Twenty Thousand B.C. to Seventeen Sixty-Three A. D. (The American Adventure Concepts & Inquiry Ser.). (gr. 8). 1975. pap. text ed. 8.96 (ISBN 0-205-04628-2, 804628X). Allyn.

Force, Peter, ed. Tracts & Other Papers Relating Principally to the Origin, Settlement & Progress of the Colonies in North America, 4 vols. Set. 44.00 (ISBN 0-8446-1188-3). Peter Smith.

Gibson, James R. European Settlement & Development in North America: Essays on Geographical Change in Honour & Memory of Andrew Hill Clark. (Dept. of Geography Research Ser.). 1978. 15.00x (ISBN 0-8020-5415-3); pap. 8.50x (ISBN 0-8020-3357-1). U of Toronto Pr.

Godfrey, William G. Pursuit of Profit & Preferment in Colonial North America: John Bradstreet's Quest. 346p. 1981. text ed. 14.75x (ISBN 0-88920-108-0, Pub. by Laurier U Pr). Humanities.

Graham, Gerald S. Empire of the North Atlantic: The Maritime Struggle for North America. 2nd ed. LC 50-14296. 1958. 25.00x (ISBN 0-8020-7051-5). U of Toronto Pr.

Handy, Robert T. A History of the Churches in the United States & Canada. 1977. 25.00 (ISBN 0-19-826910-2). Oxford U Pr.

Harrisse, H. Discovery of North America: A Critical Documentary & Historic Investigation. (Illus.). 1969. Repr. of 1892 ed. 80.00 (ISBN 0-685-12007-4). Heinman.

Horsford, E. N. Defences of Norumbega. 1977. 59.95 (ISBN 0-8490-1705-X). Gordon Pr.

Hutchinson, Bruce. The Struggle for the Border. facsimile ed. LC 70-140358. (Select Bibliographies Reprint Ser). Repr. of 1955 ed. 25.00 (ISBN 0-8369-5601-X). Arno.

Millar, John F. American Ships of the Colonial & Revolutionary Periods. (Illus.). 1979. 24.95 (ISBN 0-393-03222-1). Norton.

Neidhardt, W. S. Fenianism in North America. LC 74-31392. 216p. 1975. 12.95 (ISBN 0-271-01188-2). Pa St U Pr.

Phillips, Paul C. & Smurr, J. W. The Fur Trade, 2 Vols. (Illus.). 1967. Repr. of 1961 ed. 50.00 (ISBN 0-8061-0497-X). U of Okla Pr.

Pre-Columbian America. Incl. Mesoamerica. (Eng. & Span.). 1979. Eng. ed. (ISBN 0-8270-4270-1); Span. ed. (ISBN 0-8270-4265-5); The Araucanians. 1971 (ISBN 0-8270-4895-5); The Aztecs. 1972 (ISBN 0-8270-4890-4); The Incas. 1975. pap. 1.00 ea. OAS.

Savelle, Max. Empires to Nations: Expansion in America, 1713-1824. Shafer, Boyd C., ed. LC 74-78995. (Europe & the World in the Age of Expansion Ser: Vol. 5). (Illus.). 384p. 1974. 12.50x (ISBN 0-8166-0709-5); pap. 3.45x (ISBN 0-8166-0781-8). U of Minn Pr.

Schoenman, Theodore, ed. Journey in North America by Alexander Boloni Farkas (Kolozsvar, 1834) Schoenman, Helen B., tr. LC 77-2116. (Memoirs Ser.: Vol.120). (Illus.). 1977. 7.00 (ISBN 0-87169-120-5). Am Philos.

Weise, Arthur J. The Discoveries of America to the Year 1525. LC 73-15546. (Illus.). 392p. 1974. Repr. of 1884 ed. 40.00 (ISBN 0-87821-234-5). Milford Hse.

NORTH AMERICA–HISTORY–BIBLIOGRAPHY

Research Libraries of New York Public Library. Bibliographic Guide to North American History, 1977. 1978. lib. bdg. 65.00 (ISBN 0-8161-6843-1). G K Hall.

Research Libraries of the New York Public Library & the Library of Congress. Bibliographic Guide to North American History: 1980. (Library Catalogs Bib.Guides Ser.). 1981. lib. bdg. 85.00 (ISBN 0-8161-6892-X). G K Hall.

NORTH AMERICA–JUVENILE LITERATURE

Jones, Evan & Morgan, Dale L. Trappers & Mountain Men. LC 61-6561. (American Heritage Junior Library). (Illus.). 153p. (gr. 5 up). 1961. PLB 12.89 (ISBN 0-06-023056-8, Dist. by Har-Row). Am Heritage.

Shippen, Katherine B. Leif Eriksson: First Voyager to America. LC 51-14135. (gr. 7-9). 1951. PLB 7.89 (ISBN 0-06-025596-X, HarpJ). Har-Row.

NORTH AMERICA–MAPS

Black, Jeannette D., ed. Blathwayt Atlas, Vol. 1, The Maps. LC 78-654217. (Illus.). 1970. Set. text ed. 500.00x unbound boxed (ISBN 0-87057-125-7, Pub. by Brown U Pr). U Pr of New Eng.

Gousha Chek-Chart: The North American Atlas. 1979. pap. 3.95 (ISBN 0-451-82056-8, XE2056, Sig). NAL.

Karpinski, L. C. Maps of Famous Cartographers Depicting North America: An Historical Atlas of the Great Lakes & Michigan, with Bibliography of the Printed Maps of Michigan to 1880. 2nd ed. (Illus.). 1977. text ed. 82.75x (ISBN 90-6041-109-9). Humanities.

Klinefelter, Walter. Lewis Evans & His Maps. LC 72-153384. (Transactions Ser.: Vol. 61, Pt. 7). (Illus.). 1971. pap. 2.00 (ISBN 0-87169-617-7). Am Philos.

Knowles, R. North America in Maps: Topographical Map Studies of Canada & the USA. (Illus.). 1976. pap. text ed. 12.95x (ISBN 0-582-31017-2). Longman.

NORTH AMERICAN INDIANS

see Indians of North America

NORTH ARYAN LANGUAGE

see Khotanese Language

NORTH ATLANTIC REGION

Andersen, Raoul, ed. North Atlantic Maritime Cultures. (World Anthropology Ser.). 1979. text ed. 48.25x (ISBN 90-279-7830-1). Mouton.

Bensor, N. R. North Atlantic Seaway, Vol. III. (Illus.). 1980. 29.95 (ISBN 0-905824-01-6, ADON 4864-6). Arco.

Cordier, Sherwood S. The Air & Sea Lanes of the North Atlantic: Their Security in the Nineteen Eighties. LC 81-40180. 90p. (Orig.). 1981. pap. text ed. 6.25 (ISBN 0-8191-1587-8). U Pr of Amer.

Deutsch, Karl W., et al. Political Community & the North Atlantic Area: International Organization in the Light of Historical Experience. LC 69-13882. Repr. of 1957 ed. lib. bdg. 15.00x (ISBN 0-8371-1054-8, DEPO). Greenwood.

Edey, Maitland A. The Northeast Coast. (The American Wilderness Ser.). (Illus.). 184p. 1972. 12.95 (ISBN 0-8094-1148-2). Time-Life.

Klitz, J. Kenneth. North Sea Oil: Resource Requirements for UK Development. (Illus.). 1981. 36.00 (ISBN 0-08-024442-4). Pergamon.

Marcus, G. J. The Conquest of the North Atlantic. (Illus.). 256p. 1981. 25.00 (ISBN 0-19-520252-X). Oxford U Pr.

Mueller, Bernard. A Statistical Handbook of the North Atlantic Area: Apercu Statisque De la Region Atlantique Nord. LC 65-26294. (Eng & Fr.). 1965. pap. 7.00 (ISBN 0-527-02830-4). Kraus Repr.

Munk, Frank. Atlantic Dilemma, Partnership or Community? LC 64-12945. 1964. 7.50 (ISBN 0-379-00214-0). Oceana.

Renwick, Malcolm & Tolley, Harry. The North Atlantic. (Jackdaw Ser: No. 108). 1971. 6.95 (ISBN 0-670-51527-2, Grossman). Viking Pr.

NORTH ATLANTIC REGION–ECONOMIC INTEGRATION

Franck, Thomas M. & Weisband, Edward, eds. A Free Trade Association. LC 68-29429. (Studies in Peaceful Change: Vol. 2). 1968. 10.00x (ISBN 0-8147-0153-1). NYU Pr.

NORTH ATLANTIC REGION–POLITICS AND GOVERNMENT

Myers, Kenneth A. North Atlantic Security: The Forgotten Flank? LC 78-66209. (The Washington Papers: No. 62). 72p. 1979. pap. 4.00 (ISBN 0-8039-1231-5). Sage.

Philip, Andre. Counsel from an Ally: Reflections on Changes Within the Atlantic Community. LC 66-14033. 1966. 2.50 (ISBN 0-8262-0045-1). U of Mo Pr.

Spaak, Paul-Henri. Crisis of the Atlantic Alliance. LC 67-63351. (Orig.). 1967. pap. 1.50 (ISBN 0-8142-0116-4). Ohio St U Pr.

Strausz-Hupe, Robert & Dougherty, J. Building the Atlantic World. LC 74-1517. 400p. 1974. Repr. of 1963 ed. lib. bdg. 19.50x (ISBN 0-8371-7386-8, STAW). Greenwood.

NORTH ATLANTIC TREATY ORGANIZATION

Amme, Carl H., Jr. NATO Without France: A Strategic Appraisal. LC 67-31025. (Publications Ser.: No. 67). (Illus.). 195p. 1967. 9.95 (ISBN 0-8179-1671-7). Hoover Inst Pr.

Amundsen, Kirsten. Norway, NATO & the Forgotten Soviet Challenge. LC 81-80337. (Policy Papers in International Affairs Ser.: No. 14). (Illus.). iv, 50p. 1981. pap. 2.95x (ISBN 0-87725-514-8). U of Cal Intl St.

Ball, M. Margaret. NATO & the European Union Movement. LC 74-9319. (Library of World Affairs, London, Institute of World Affairs Ser.: No. 45). (Illus.). 486p. 1974. Repr. of 1959 ed. lib. bdg. 22.25x (ISBN 0-8371-7642-5, BANA). Greenwood.

Beer, Francis A. Integration & Disintegration in NATO: Processes of Alliance Cohesion & Prospects for Atlantic Community. LC 69-12762. 1969. 10.00 (ISBN 0-8142-0005-2). Ohio St U Pr.

Bray, Frank T. & Moodie, Michael. Defense Technology & the Atlantic Alliance: Competition or Collaboration? LC 77-80297. (Foreign Policy Report Ser.). 5.00 (ISBN 0-89549-000-5). Inst Foreign Policy Anal.

Burgess, Philip M. Elite Images & Foreign Policy Outcomes: A Study of Norway. LC 67-24453. 1968. 6.25 (ISBN 0-8142-0030-3). Ohio St U Pr.

Calleo, David. The Atlantic Fantasy: The U. S., NATO, & Europe. (No. 13). 192p. 1970. 13.00x (ISBN 0-8018-1222-4); pap. 3.95x (ISBN 0-8018-1196-1). Johns Hopkins.

Challener, Richard D., ed. The Vandenberg Resolution & the North Atlantic Treaty (May, June, 1948; February, March, April & June, 1949) (Legislative Origins of American Foreign Policy Ser.: Vol. 6). 1979. lib. bdg. 42.00 (ISBN 0-8240-3035-4). Garland Pub.

Couloumbis, Theodore A. Greek Political Reaction to American & NATO Influences. 1966. 20.00x (ISBN 0-300-00385-4). Yale U Pr.

Dougherty, James E. & Pfaltzgraff, Diane K. Eurocommunism & the Atlantic Alliance. LC 76-53142. (Special Reports Ser.). 1977. 3.00 (ISBN 0-89549-003-X). Inst Foreign Policy Anal.

Eren, Nuri. Turkey, NATO & Europe, No. 34. (The Atlantic Papers). 54p. 1979. pap. 4.75 (ISBN 0-86598-061-6, Pub. by Atlantic Inst France). Allanheld.

Fox, William T. & Fox, Annette B. NATO & the Range of American Choice. LC 67-11560. (Institute for War & Peace Studies). 352p. 1967. 22.50x (ISBN 0-231-03001-0). Columbia U Pr.

Fox, William T. & Schilling, Warner R, eds. European Security & the Atlantic System. LC 72-4248. (Institute for War & Peace Studies). 276p. 1973. 17.00x (ISBN 0-231-03640-X). Columbia U Pr.

Furniss, Edgar S., Jr., ed. Western Alliance: Its Status & Prospects. LC 65-25644. 1965. 4.75 (ISBN 0-8142-0051-6). Ohio St U Pr.

Goldberg, Edward D., ed. North Sea Science: Papers Presented at the Nato Science Committee Conference, November 1971. (Illus.). 420p. 1973. 26.00x (ISBN 0-262-07056-1). MIT Pr.

Gordon, Colin, ed. The Atlantic Alliance: A Selective Bibliography. 1978. 22.50x (ISBN 0-89397-041-7). Nichols Pub.

Graham, Daniel O. A New Strategy for the West: NATO After Detente. LC 77-89607. 1977. 3.00 (ISBN 0-89195-020-6). Heritage Found.

Hahn, Walter F. & Pfaltzgraff, Robert L., Jr., eds. Atlantic Community in Crisis: A Redefinition of the Transatlantic Relationship. (Pergamon Policy Studies). 386p. 1979. 42.00 (ISBN 0-08-023003-2). Pergamon.

Holst, Johan & Nerlich, Uwe, eds. Beyond Nuclear Deterrence: New Aims, New Arms. LC 76-20283. 1977. 19.50x (ISBN 0-8448-0974-8). Crane-Russak Co.
Ireland, Timothy P. Creating the Entangling Alliance: The Origins of the North Atlantic Treaty Organization. LC 80-655. (Contributions in Political Science: No. 50). x, 245p. 1981. lib. bdg. 27.50 (ISBN 0-313-22094-8, IRC/). Greenwood.
Johnson, U. Alexis & Packard, George R., eds. The Common Security Interests of Japan, the United States, & NATO. 200p. 1981. professional reference 19.50 (ISBN 0-88410-698-5). Ballinger Pub.
Jordan, Robert S. Political Leadership in NATO: A Study in Multilateral Diplomacy. 1979. lib. bdg. 28.75 (ISBN 0-89158-355-6). Westview.
Kaplan, Lawrence S. & Clawson, Robert W. NATO After Thirty Years. LC 80-53885. 262p. 1981. lib. bdg. 19.95 (ISBN 0-8420-2172-8); pap. 8.95 (ISBN 0-8420-2184-1). Scholarly Res Inc.
Kaplan, Morton A. The Rationale for NATO: European Collective Security - Past & Future. (AEI-Hoover Policy Studies). 1973. pap. 4.25 (ISBN 0-8447-3107-2). Am Enterprise.
Kennedy, Gavin. Burden Sharing in NATO. LC 79-12140. 1979. text ed. 24.95x (ISBN 0-8419-0515-0). Holmes & Meier.
Knorr, Klaus. The Atlantic Alliance: A Reappraisal. LC 74-78164. (Headline Ser.: No. 221). (Illus., Orig.). 1974. pap. 2.00 (ISBN 0-87124-026-2). Foreign Policy.
Lawrence, Richard D. & Record, K. Jeffrey. U. S. Force Structure in NATO: An Alternative. (Studies in Defense Policy). 136p. 1974. pap. 3.95 (ISBN 0-8157-5171-0). Brookings.
Link, Werner & Feld, Werner J., eds. The New Nationalism: Implications for Transatlantic Relations. new ed. LC 78-17144. (Pergamon Policy Studies). 1979. text ed. 19.25 (ISBN 0-08-023370-8); pap. text ed. 7.95 (ISBN 0-08-023369-4). Pergamon.
Loewenstein, Prince H. & Von Zuhlsdorff, Volkmar. NATO & the Defense of the West. Fitzgerald, Edward, tr. from Ger. LC 74-20276. 383p. 1975. Repr. of 1963 ed. lib. bdg. 21.00x (ISBN 0-8371-7855-X, LONA). Greenwood.
Ludz, Peter C., et al. Dilemmas of the Atlantic Alliance: Two Germanys, Scandinavia, Canada, Nato & the EEC. LC 75-25737. (Atlantic Institute Studies: No. 1). 1975. text ed. 25.95 (ISBN 0-275-01490-8). Praeger.
Mets, David R. NATO: Alliance for Peace. LC 81-1841. (Illus.). 224p. (gr. 7 up). 1981. PLB 10.79 (ISBN 0-671-34065-4). Messner.
Myers, Kenneth A., ed. NATO-the Next Thirty Years: The Changing Political, Economic, & Military Setting. 440p. 1980. lib. bdg. 36.25x (ISBN 0-89158-965-1). Westview.
NATO: The Next Thirty Years. (Significant Issues Ser.: Vol. I, No. 6). 25p. 1979. pap. 5.00 (ISBN 0-89206-012-3, CSIS007, CSIS). Unipub.
Nato: the Next Thirty Years: A Report of the Conference, Vol. I. LC 79-57250. (Significant Issues Ser.: No. 6). 25p. 1979. 4.00 (ISBN 0-89206-012-3). CSI Studies.
Nitz, Paul H., et al. Securing the Seas: The Soviet Naval Challenge & Western Alliance Options. (Illus.). 1979. lib. bdg. 30.75 (ISBN 0-89158-359-9); pap. text ed. 14.50x (ISBN 0-89158-360-2). Westview.
Norton, Augustus R. & Greenberg, Martin H. NATO: A Bibliography & Resource Guide. 1981. lib. bdg. 45.00 (ISBN 0-8240-9331-3). Garland Pub.
Owen, J. I., ed. Infantry Weapons of the NATO Armies. 2nd ed. 192p. 1980. pap. 22.50 (ISBN 0-08-027015-8). Pergamon.
Planck, Charles R. The Changing Status of German Reunification in Western Diplomacy, 1955-1966. LC 67-22894. (Studies in International Affairs: No.4). 72p. (Orig.). 1967. pap. 1.45x (ISBN 0-8018-0534-1). Johns Hopkins.
Record, Jeffrey. U. S. Nuclear Weapons in Europe: Issues & Alternatives. (Studies in Defense Policy). 70p. 1974. pap. 3.95 (ISBN 0-8157-7365-X). Brookings.
Reid, Escott. Time of Fear & Hope: The Making of the North Atlantic Treaty 1947-1949. 315p. 1981. text ed. 15.00 (ISBN 0-86598-055-1). Allanheld.
Richardson, James L. Germany & the Atlantic Alliance: The Interaction of Strategy & Politics. LC 66-13184. (Center for International Affairs Ser). 1966. 20.00x (ISBN 0-674-35200-9). Harvard U Pr.
Roach, James R., ed. United States & the Atlantic Community: Issues & Prospects. 95p. 1967. 7.50x (ISBN 0-292-73673-8). U of Tex Pr.
Royal Institute of Internatinal Affairs & Chatham House Study Group. Atlantic Alliance: NATO's Role in the Free World. LC 78-12995. 1979. Repr. of 1952 ed. lib. bdg. 16.50x (ISBN 0-313-20643-0, RIAN). Greenwood.
Salvadori, Massimo. NATO: A Twentieth Century Community of Nations. 6.00 (ISBN 0-8446-2859-X). Peter Smith.
Saulle, Maria R. NATO & Its Activities: A Political & Juridical Approach on Consultation. 1979. lib. bdg. 16.00 (ISBN 0-379-20459-2). Oceana.
Sloss, Leon. NATO Reform: Prospects & Priorities. LC 75-38321. (The Washington Papers: No. 30). 66p. 1975. 4.00 (ISBN 0-8039-0620-X). Sage.
Steinbruner, John D. The Cybernetic Theory of Decision: New Dimensions of Political Analysis. LC 73-2479. 312p. 1974. 26.00x (ISBN 0-691-07559-X); pap. 6.95 (ISBN 0-691-02175-9). Princeton U Pr.
Stewart-Smith, Geoffrey, ed. Brandt & the Destruction of NATO. LC 74-157269. 101p. 1973. pap. 5.00x (ISBN 0-900380-12-8). Intl Pubns Serv.
Strausz-Hupe, Robert & Dougherty, J. Building the Atlantic World. LC 74-1517. 400p. 1974. Repr. of 1963 ed. lib. bdg. 19.50x (ISBN 0-8371-7386-8, STAW). Greenwood.
Trezise, Philip H. The Atlantic Connection. 200p. 1975. pap. 3.95 (ISBN 0-8157-8527-5). Brookings.
Vali, Ferenc. The Turkish Straits & NATO. LC 70-170205. (Studies Ser.: No. 32). (Illus.). 200p. 1972. pap. 6.95 (ISBN 0-8179-3322-0). Hoover Inst Pr.
Williams, Geoffrey L. & Williams, Alan L. Crisis in European Defense. LC 74-81480. 356p. 1974. 22.50 (ISBN 0-312-17325-3). St Martin.
Yost, David S., ed. NATO's Strategic Options: Arms Control & Defense. (Pergamon Policy Studies on International Politics). (Illus.). 275p. 1981. 30.00 (ISBN 0-08-027184-7). Pergamon.

NORTH BORNEO

Evans, Ivor H. The Religion of the Tempusak Dusuns of North Borneo. LC 77-86972. Repr. of 1953 ed. 40.00 (ISBN 0-404-16707-1). AMS Pr.
Rutter, Owen. The Pagans of North Borneo. LC 77-87003. (Illus.). Repr. of 1929 ed. 32.00 (ISBN 0-404-16776-4). AMS Pr.

NORTH BRITON

Nobbe, George. North Briton: A Study in Political Propaganda. LC 39-24192. Repr. of 1939 ed. 17.50 (ISBN 0-404-04779-3). AMS Pr.

NORTH CAROLINA

see also Carolina;
also names of cities, counties, and towns in North Carolina

Clay, James W., et al, eds. North Carolina Atlas: Portrait of a Changing Southern State. LC 75-6984. 1975. 8.95 (ISBN 0-8078-1244-7). U of NC Pr.
Federal Writers' Project. North Carolina: A Guide to the Old North State. 649p. 1939. Repr. 54.00 (ISBN 0-403-02182-0). Somerset Pub.
Hamilton, C. Horace. North Carolina Population Trends: A Demographic Sourcebook, Vols. 1-3. 95p. 1974-75. pap. 4.00 ea. (ISBN 0-89055-109-X). Carolina Pop Ctr.
Hewlett, Crockette. Two Centuries of Art in New Hanover County. LC 76-12221. 1976. 15.000 (ISBN 0-87716-065-1, Pub. by Moore Pub Co). F Apple.
Holcomb, Brent H. Anson County, North Carolina Deed Abstracts, 1749 to 1766: Abstracts of Wills & Estates, 1749 to 1795. LC 79-67870. 170p. 1980. Repr. of 1974 ed. 15.00 (ISBN 0-8063-0871-0). Genealog Pub.
McCain, Paul M. County Court in North Carolina Before Seventeen Fifty. LC 70-115996. (Duke University. Trinity College Historical Society, Historical Papers: No. 31). Repr. of 1954 ed. 17.50 (ISBN 0-404-51781-1). AMS Pr.
North Carolina. 28.00 (ISBN 0-89770-109-7). Curriculum Info Ctr.
North Carolina Craftsmen Exhibition: 1973. (Illus.). 20p. 1973. pap. 0.75x (ISBN 0-88259-070-7). NCMA.
North Carolina in Maps. 36p. 1966. of 15 maps with booklet 12.00 set (ISBN 0-86526-137-7). NC Archives.
Ray, Worth S. Colonial Granville County, North Carolina, & Its People. LC 65-21371. 312p. 1979. Repr. of 1945 ed. 10.00 (ISBN 0-8063-0285-2). Genealog Pub.
Roberts, Bruce & Roberts, Nancy. The Goodliest Land: North Carolina. LC 72-89345. (Illus.). 160p. 1973. 11.95 (ISBN 0-385-04302-3). Doubleday.
Rosenberg, Harry M. & Krasowski, Robert S. Trends in Industry Employment for North Carolina, 1940-70: The State & Multicounty Planning Regions. 1976. pap. 3.00 (ISBN 0-89055-127-8). Carolina Pop Ctr.
State Industrial Directories Corp. North Carolina State Industrial Directory, 1980. 1980. pap. 60.00 (ISBN 0-89910-033-3). State Indus Dir.
State Industrial Directory Corp. North Carolina State Industrial Directory, 1978. (State Industrial Directory Ser.). 1979. 30.00 (ISBN 0-916112-99-3). State Indus Dir.
Steahr, Thomas E. North Carolina's Changing Population. 106p. 1973. pap. 2.00 (ISBN 0-89055-105-7). Carolina Pop Ctr.
Steila, et al. North Carolina: A Reader. 1975. perfect bdg. 6.95 (ISBN 0-88252-033-4). Paladin Hse.
Thornton, Mary L., compiled by. Bibliography of North Carolina, Fifteen Eighty-Nine to Nineteen Fifty-Six. LC 73-441. 597p. 1973. Repr. of 1958 ed. lib. bdg. 28.25x (ISBN 0-8371-6765-5, THNC). Greenwood.
Valentine, James, photos by. North Carolina. LC 79-51767. (Belding Imprint Ser.). (Illus.). 160p. (Text by Marguerite Schumann). 1979. 29.50 (ISBN 0-912856-50-5). Graphic Arts Ctr.
Walser, Richard, ed. North Carolina Miscellany. 1962. 9.95 (ISBN 0-8078-0842-3). U of NC Pr.
Witte, Ann D. Work Release in North Carolina: An Evaluation of Its Post-Release Effects. LC 75-44339. 190p. 1975. pap. text ed. 5.00 (ISBN 0-89143-064-4). U NC Inst Res Soc Sci.
Zopf, Paul E., Jr. A Demographic & Occupational Profile of State Planning Region G. LC 74-20614. 325p. 1974. pap. text ed. 4.00 (ISBN 0-89055-111-1). Carolina Pop Ctr.

NORTH CAROLINA-DESCRIPTION AND TRAVEL

Bartram, W. Travels Through North & South Carolina. 59.95 (ISBN 0-8490-1229-5). Gordon Pr.
Brickell, John. Natural History of North Carolina. (Illus.). 1968. Repr. of 1737 ed. 12.00 (ISBN 0-930230-17-5). Johnson NC.
--Natural History of North Carolina. (Illus.). 1968. Repr. of 1737 ed. 12.00 (ISBN 0-930230-17-5). Johnson NC.
--The Natural History of North Carolina. (American Studies). (Illus.). Repr. of 1737 ed. lib. bdg. 31.00 (ISBN 0-384-05740-3). Johnson Repr.
Byrd, William. Writings of Colonel William Byrd. Bassett, J. S., ed. LC 76-125631. (Research & Source Ser.: No. 518). (Illus.). 1970. Repr. of 1901 ed. lib. bdg. 32.00 (ISBN 0-8337-0442-7). B Franklin.
Camblos, Ruth & Winger, Virginia. North Carolina Round the Mountains Guide Book. 4th, rev. ed. (Round the Mountains Ser.). (Illus., Orig.). 1981. pap. write for info. (ISBN 0-9602706-3-9). Camblos-Winger.
Camblos, Ruth & Wnger, Virginia. North Carolina Round the Mountains Guide Book. 3rd, rev. ed. (Round the Mountains Ser.). (Illus., Orig.). 1978. pap. 3.50x perfect bdg. (ISBN 0-9602706-0-4). Camblos-Winger.
Doane, Jim. North Carolina: From the Mountains to the Sea. LC 80-80955. 72p. 1980. 10.95 (ISBN 0-936672-01-3); pap. text ed. 7.50 (ISBN 0-936672-00-5). Aerial Photo.
Dula, Lucile N. The Pelican Guide to Hillsborough: Historic Orange County, North Carolina. LC 78-26081. (The Pelican Guide Ser). (Illus.). 1979. pap. 4.95 (ISBN 0-88289-208-8). Pelican.
Fagan, John M. Beautiful North Carolina. Shangle, Robert D., ed. LC 79-18081. (Illus.). 72p. 1980. 14.95 (ISBN 0-89802-075-1); pap. 7.95 (ISBN 0-89802-074-3). Beautiful Am.
Federal Writers' Project. North Carolina: A Guide to the Old North State. 649p. 1939. Repr. 54.00 (ISBN 0-403-02182-0). Somerset Pub.
Guide to North Carolina Historical Highway Markers. 7th ed. (Illus.). 1979. pap. 2.50 (ISBN 0-86526-079-6). NC Archives.
Harriot, Thomas. A Briefe & True Report of the New Found Land in Virginia. LC 71-171785. (English Experience Ser.: No. 384). 48p. 1971. Repr. of 1588 ed. 7.00 (ISBN 90-221-0384-6). Walter J Johnson.
--A Briefe & True Report of the New Found Land of Virginia. (Illus.). 91p. 1972. pap. 4.50 (ISBN 0-486-21092-8). Dover.
Joynes, Leger M., et al. The Insiders' Guide to the Outer Banks of North Carolina. rev. ed. (Insiders' Guides). (Illus.). 1981. pap. 3.95 (ISBN 0-932338-01-1). Insiders Pub.
Lawson, John. New Voyage to Carolina. Lefler, Hugh T., ed. 1967. 14.95 (ISBN 0-8078-1042-8); limited ed. 25.00 (ISBN 0-8078-1041-X). U of NC Pr.
Schoenbaum, Thomas J. Islands, Capes, & Sounds: The North Carolina Coast. (Illus.). 352p. 1981. 16.95x (ISBN 0-89587-021-5). Blair.
Schumann, Marguerite. The Living Land: An Outdoor Guide to North Carolina. (Illus.). 200p. Date not set. pap. 4.25 (ISBN 0-914788-29-9). East Woods.
Tucker, Patsy M. Carolina Treasures. LC 78-78073. (Illus.). 1979. 7.95 (ISBN 0-87716-099-6, Pub. by Moore Pub Co). F Apple.

NORTH CAROLINA-GENEALOGY

Arthur, John P. History of Watauga County, North Carolina. (Illus.). 1976. Repr. of 1915 ed. 30.00 (ISBN 0-89308-001-2). Southern Hist Pr.
Bentley, Elizabeth P. Index to the Eighteen Hundred & Ten Census of North Carolina. LC 77-88140. 1978. 17.50 (ISBN 0-8063-0788-9). Genealog Pub.
--Index to the Eighteen Hundred Census of North Carolina. LC 76-53969. 1977. 17.50 (ISBN 0-8063-0104-X). Genealog Pub.
Broughton, Carrie L. Marriage & Death Notices from the Raleigh Register & North Carolina State Gazette 1846-1867, 2 vols. in 1. LC 75-7876. 1975. Repr. of 1949 ed. 12.50 (ISBN 0-8063-0677-7). Genealog Pub.
--Marriages & Death Notices from the Raleigh Register & North Carolina State Gazette: 1799-1825. LC 66-26935. 178p. 1975. Repr. of 1945 ed. 12.50 (ISBN 0-8063-0052-3). Genealog Pub.
Clemens, William M. North & South Carolina Marriage Records. LC 73-1942. 295p. 1977. Repr. of 1927 ed. 12.50 (ISBN 0-8063-0555-X). Genealog Pub.
Gwynn, Zae H. Abstracts of the Records at Jones County, North Carolina 1779-1868, Vol. 1. 1074p. 1963. 30.00 (ISBN 0-685-25482-8). Genealog Pub.
--Abstracts of the Records of Onslow County, North Carolina, 1734-1850, 2 vols. 1961. 50.00 (ISBN 0-685-34328-6). Genealog Pub.
--The Eighteen Fifty Census of Craven County, North Carolina. 1961. 12.50 (ISBN 0-685-34329-4). Genealog Pub.
Hathaway, James R. North Carolina Historical & Genealogical Register, Vol. 1 - Vol. 3, No. 3. LC 70-132931. 1979. Set. pap. 75.00 (ISBN 0-8063-0441-3); 7.50 ea. Genealog Pub.
Jackson, Ronald V. & Teeples, Gary R. North Carolina Census Index 1800. LC 77-86111. (Illus.). lib. bdg. 36.00 (ISBN 0-89593-103-6). Accelerated Index.
--North Carolina Census Index 1810. LC 77-86112. (Illus.). lib. bdg. 40.00 (ISBN 0-89593-104-4). Accelerated Index.
--North Carolina Census Index 1820. LC 77-86113. (Illus.). lib. bdg. 42.00 (ISBN 0-89593-105-2). Accelerated Index.
--North Carolina Census Index 1830. LC 77-86114. (Illus.). lib. bdg. 46.00 (ISBN 0-89593-106-0). Accelerated Index.
--North Carolina Census Index 1840. LC 77-86115. (Illus.). lib. bdg. 52.00 (ISBN 0-89593-107-9). Accelerated Index.
--North Carolina Census 1850. LC 77-86109. (Illus.). lib. bdg. 62.00 (ISBN 0-89593-108-7). Accelerated Index.
Jones, Gordon C. Abstracts of Wills & Other Records, Currituck & Dare Counties, North Carolina. LC 77-72077. 1977. 15.00 (ISBN 0-8063-0766-8). Genealog Pub.
Lindsay, Elizabeth D. The Diary of Elizabeth Dick Lindsay Eighteen Hundred Thirty-One to Eighteen Hundred Sixty-One: Guilford County, N. C. facsimile ed. (Illus.). 110p. 1975. 18.50 (ISBN 0-918470-10-2). J W Linn.
Linn, Jo W. Abstracts of the Wills & Estates Records of Rowan County, N.C., 1753-1805 & Tax Lists of 1759-1778. 216p. 1980. 25.00 (ISBN 0-918470-03-X). J W Linn.
--Davie County, N. C. Will & Deed Abstracts. 266p. 1973. softcover 15.00 (ISBN 0-918470-08-0). J W Linn.
--People Named Hanes. LC 80-52426. (Illus.). 300p. 1980. 25.00 (ISBN 0-918470-12-9). J W Linn.
Linn, Jo W. & Gray, Gordon. The Gray Family & Allied Lines. LC 76-42358. (Illus.). 1976. 27.50 (ISBN 0-918470-01-3). J W Linn.
Lucas, Silas, Jr. & Holcomb, Brent. Marriage & Death Notices from Raleigh, N.C. Newspapers, 1796-1826. 1978. Repr. 17.50 (ISBN 0-89308-046-2). Southern Hist Pr.
Newman, Harry W. Charles County Gentry. LC 75-88098. (Illus.). 1971. Repr. of 1940 ed. 15.00 (ISBN 0-8063-0486-3). Genealog Pub.
Potter, Dorothy W. Index to the Eighteen Twenty North Carolina Census: Supplemented from Tax Lists & Other Sources. LC 78-58459. 1978. Repr. of 1974 ed. 25.00 (ISBN 0-8063-0815-X). Genealog Pub.
Powell, William S., ed. Dictionary of North Carolina Biography, Vol. I: A-C. LC 79-10106. 1979. 45.00x (ISBN 0-8078-1329-X). U of NC Pr.
Ray, Worth S. Ray's Index & Digest to Hathaway's North Carolina Historical & Genealogical Register: With Genealogical Notes & Annotations. LC 67-121942. 192p. 1979. Repr. of 1945 ed. 12.00 (ISBN 0-8063-0288-7). Genealog Pub.
Shields, Ruth H. Abstracts of Wills Recorded in Orange County, North Carolina, 1752 to 1800 & 1800 to 1850. LC 72-78. 438p. 1979. Repr. of 1957 ed. 18.50 (ISBN 0-8063-0504-5). Genealog Pub.
Simpson, Thelma P. & Taylor, David R. Eighteen Fifty Federal Census of Carteret County, North Carolina. LC 72-7955. 1972. 12.50 (ISBN 0-8063-0526-6). Genealog Pub.

Smith, Clifford N., compiled by. British Colonial Land Grants in North Carolina. (British-American Genealogical Research Monograph: No. 3). 80p. 1981. pap. 12.00 (ISBN 0-915162-27-X). Westland Pubns.
U. S. Bureau of the Census. Heads of Families at the First Census of the United States Taken in the Year 1790: North Carolina. LC 73-8204. 1978. Repr. of 1908 ed. 20.00 (ISBN 0-8063-0572-X). Genealog Pub.
--Heads of Families at the First Census of the United States Taken in the Year 1790: North Carolina. LC 73-8204. 1978. Repr. of 1908 ed. 20.00 (ISBN 0-8063-0572-X). Genealog Pub.
--Heads of Families, First Census of the United States, 1790: North Carolina. LC 61-60771. 1961-64. Repr. of 1908 ed. 15.00 (ISBN 0-87152-011-7). Reprint.
Weathers, Lee B. The Living Past of Cleveland County: A History. LC 80-14289. (Illus.). 314p. 1980. Repr. of 1956 ed. 16.50 (ISBN 0-87152-320-5). Reprint.
Wheeler, John H. Reminiscences & Memoirs of North Carolina & Eminent North Carolinians. LC 66-18837. 1966. Repr. of 1884 ed. 20.00 (ISBN 0-8063-0375-1). Genealog Pub.
Wooley, J. E. Marriage Bonds of Haywood & Jackson Counties N.C. 1978. 20.00 (ISBN 0-89308-107-8). Southern Hist Pr.
Yearns, Wilfred B., ed. Papers of Thomas Jordan Jarvis, Vol. 1, 1869-1882. (Illus.). 1969. 10.00 (ISBN 0-86526-045-1). NC Archives.

NORTH CAROLINA–HISTORY

see also Raleigh'S Roanoke Colonies, 1584-1590

Absher, W. O. Surry County, N. C., Deed Books A, B, & C. 120p. 1981. Repr. 20.00 (ISBN 0-89308-172-8). Southern Hist.
Allen, William C. The Annals of Haywood County, North Carolina: Historical, Sociological, & Genealogical. LC 77-24593. (Illus.). 1977. Repr. of 1935 ed. 33.00 (ISBN 0-87152-251-9). Reprint.
Andrews, Melvin B. Carolina Adventures: Brief Sketches of Growing Up in Eastern North Carolina at the Turn of the Century (1889-1915) Andrews, J. David, ed. (Illus.). 92p. (Orig.). 1979. pap. 5.00 (ISBN 0-686-29310-X). Planetary Pr.
Arthur, John P. Western North Carolina: A History from 1730 to 1913. LC 73-1945. (Illus.). 710p. 1973. Repr. of 1914 ed. 30.00 (ISBN 0-87152-126-1). Reprint.
Ashe, Samuel A. History of North Carolina, 2 Vols. LC 72-149340. (Illus.). 1971. Repr. of 1908 ed. Vol. 1. 30.00 (ISBN 0-87152-059-1); Vol. 2. 40.00 (ISBN 0-87152-060-5); Set. 70.00 (ISBN 0-87152-323-X). Reprint.
Badger, Anthony J. Prosperity Road: The New Deal, Tobacco & North Carolina. LC 79-310. (Illus.). xviii, 295p. 1980. 20.00x (ISBN 0-8078-1367-2). U of NC Pr.
Barrett, John G. Civil War in North Carolina. LC 63-22810. 1963. 14.95 (ISBN 0-8078-0874-1). U of NC Pr.
--North Carolina As a Civil War Battleground, 1861-1865. (Illus.). 1975. pap. 1.00 (ISBN 0-86526-088-5). NC Archives.
Barringer, Bugs, et al. Rocky Mount: A Pictorial History. LC 77-8620. (Illus.). 1977. 14.95 (ISBN 0-915442-31-0). Donning Co.
Bassett, John S. The Constitutional Beginnings of North Carolina (1653-1729) LC 78-63829. (Johns Hopkins University. Studies in the Social Sciences. Twelfth Ser. 1894: 3). Repr. of 1894 ed. 11.50 (ISBN 0-404-61089-7). AMS Pr.
Billings, Dwight B., Jr. Planters & the Making of a "New South". Class, Politics, & Development in North Carolina, 1865-1900. LC 78-25952. xiii, 284p. 1979. 19.00x (ISBN 0-8078-1315-X). U of NC Pr.
Blackmun, Ora. Western North Carolina: Its Mountains & Its People to 1880. 2nd ed. LC 76-53030. (Illus., Orig.). 1977. 12.95 (ISBN 0-686-27857-7); pap. 6.95 (ISBN 0-686-27858-5). Appalach Consortium.
Bode, Frederick A. Protestantism & the New South: North Carolina Baptists & Methodists in Political Crisis, 1894-1903. LC 75-1289. 300p. 1976. 10.95x (ISBN 0-8139-0597-4). U Pr of Va.
Boyd, William K. History of North Carolina, Vol. 2: The Federal Period, 1783-1860. LC 73-1946. (Illus.). 416p. 1973. Repr. of 1919 ed. 25.00 (ISBN 0-87152-134-2). Reprint.
--Some Eighteenth Century Tracts Concerning North Carolina. LC 73-2625. 516p. 1973. Repr. of 1927 ed. 27.50 (ISBN 0-87152-127-X). Reprint.
Brant & Fuller. Cyclopedia of Eminent & Representative Men of the Carolinas of the Nineteenth Century, Vol. 2, North Carolina. LC 75-187377. (Illus.). 661p. 1973. Repr. of 1892 ed. 24.00 (ISBN 0-87152-131-8). Reprint.
Brown, Norman D. Edward Stanly: Whiggery's Tarheel "Conqueror". LC 74-2818. (Southern Historical Publications: No. 18). 373p. 1974. 21.25x (ISBN 0-8173-5262-7). U of Ala Pr.
Burgner, Goldene F. North Carolina Land Grants in Greene County, Tennessee. 160p. Date not set. 20.00 (ISBN 0-89308-204-X). Southern Hist.
--North Carolina Land Grants in Tennessee, 1778 to 1791. 200p. Date not set. 20.00 (ISBN 0-89308-205-8). Southern Hist.
Burney, Eugenia. Colonial North Carolina. LC 75-20192. (Colonial History Ser.). (Illus.). 160p. (gr. 5 up). 1975. 7.95 (ISBN 0-525-67134-X). Elsevier-Nelson.
Byrd, William. Histories of the Dividing Line Betwixt Virginia & North Carolina. 6.00 (ISBN 0-8446-1790-3). Peter Smith.
Chafe, William H. Civilities & Civil Rights: Greensboro, North Carolina, & the Black Struggle for Freedom. (Illus.). 1980. 15.95 (ISBN 0-19-502625-X). Oxford U Pr.
Coe, Joffre L. The Formative Cultures of the Carolina Piedmont. LC 64-21423. (Transaction Ser.: Vol. 54, Pt. 5). 1980. Repr. of 1964 ed. 8.00 (ISBN 0-87169-545-6). Am Philos.
Connor, R. D. Ante-Bellum Builders of North Carolina. LC 70-149342. 123p. 1971. Repr. of 1930 ed. 13.50 (ISBN 0-87152-064-8). Reprint.
--History of North Carolina, Vol. 1: The Colonial & Revolutionary Periods, 1584-1783. LC 73-1946. (Illus.). 530p. 1973. Repr. of 1919 ed. 21.00 (ISBN 0-87152-133-4). Reprint.
--North Carolina: Rebuilding an Ancient Commonwealth, 1584-1925, 2 vols. LC 73-1944. (Illus.). 1375p. 1973. Repr. of 1929 ed. Vol. 1. 24.00 (ISBN 0-87152-129-6); Vol. 2. 27.50 (ISBN 0-87152-130-X). Set (ISBN 0-87152-328-0). Reprint.
--Revolutionary Leaders of North Carolina. Jackson, W. C., ed. LC 77-149344. 125p. 1971. Repr. of 1916 ed. 13.50 (ISBN 0-87152-063-X). Reprint.
Connor, Robert D. Cornelius Harnett: An Essay in North Carolina History. facsimile ed. LC 76-148876. (Select Bibliographies Reprint Ser). Repr. of 1909 ed. 16.00 (ISBN 0-8369-5647-8). Arno.
Corbett, David L. Formation of the North Carolina Counties, 1663-1943. 1976. pap. 8.00 (ISBN 0-86526-032-X). NC Archives.
Creecy, Richard B. Grandfather's Tales of North Carolina History. LC 65-2488. (Illus.). 1965. Repr. of 1901 ed. 15.00 (ISBN 0-87152-022-2). Reprint.
Crow, Jeffrey J. & Tise, Larry E., eds. Writing North Carolina History. LC 79-439. 1979. 17.50x (ISBN 0-8078-1369-9). U of NC Pr.
Davis, Edward G. Maryland & North Carolina in the Campaign of 1780-1781, with a Preliminary Notice of the Revolution, in Which the Troops of the Two States Won Distinction. LC 72-14418. (Maryland Historical Society. Fund-Publications: No. 33). Repr. of 1893 ed. 10.00 (ISBN 0-404-57633-8). AMS Pr.
Drayton, John. Memoirs of the American Revolution, 2 Vols. Decker, Peter, ed. LC 77-76244. (Eyewitness Accounts of the American Revolution Ser., No. 2). 1969. Repr. of 1821 ed. Set. 34.00 (ISBN 0-405-01149-0); 17.00 ea. Vol. 1 (ISBN 0-405-01150-4). Vol. 2 (ISBN 0-405-01151-2). Arno.
Duke University. Trinity College Historical Society Historical Papers, Ser. 1-32. LC 74-115989. Repr. of 1956 ed. Set. 525.00 (ISBN 0-404-51750-1); 17.50 ea. AMS Pr.
--Trinity College Historical Society Papers, Ser. 1: Reconstruction & State Biography. Repr. of 1897 ed. 17.50 (ISBN 0-404-51751-X). AMS Pr.
--Trinity College Historical Society Papers, Ser. 11: 1915. Repr. 17.50 (ISBN 0-404-51761-7). AMS Pr.
--Trinity College Historical Society Papers, Ser. 15: 1925. Repr. 17.50 (ISBN 0-404-51765-X). AMS Pr.
--Trinity College Historical Society Papers, Ser. 14: 1922. Repr. 17.50 (ISBN 0-404-51764-1). AMS Pr.
--Trinity College Historical Society Papers, Ser. 10: 1914. Repr. 17.50 (ISBN 0-404-51760-9). AMS Pr.
--Trinity College Historical Society Papers, Ser. 13: 1919. Repr. 17.50 (ISBN 0-404-51763-3). AMS Pr.
--Trinity College Historical Society Papers, Ser. 12: 1916. Repr. 17.50 (ISBN 0-404-51762-5). AMS Pr.
--Trinity College Historical Society Papers, Ser. 2: Legal & Biographical Studies. Repr. of 1898 ed. 17.50 (ISBN 0-404-51752-8). AMS Pr.
--Trinity College Historical Society Papers, Ser. 3: Gov. W. W. Holden & Revolutionary Documents. Repr. of 1899 ed. 17.50 (ISBN 0-404-51753-6). AMS Pr.
--Trinity College Historical Society Papers, Ser. 4: 1900. Repr. 17.50 (ISBN 0-404-51754-4). AMS Pr.
--Trinity College Historical Society Papers, Ser. 5: 1905. Repr. 17.50 (ISBN 0-404-51755-2). AMS Pr.
--Trinity College Historical Society Papers, Ser. 6: 1906. Repr. 17.50 (ISBN 0-404-51756-0). AMS Pr.
--Trinity College Historical Society Papers, Ser. 8: 1908-1909. Repr. 17.50 (ISBN 0-404-51758-7). AMS Pr.
Dykeman, Wilma. The French Broad. LC 54-9347. (Illus.). 1965. 8.50 (ISBN 0-87049-056-7). U of Tenn Pr.
Ekirch, A. Roger. Poor Carolina: Politics & Society in North Carolina, 1729-1776. LC 80-39889. (Illus.). 336p. 1981. 19.00 (ISBN 0-8078-1475-X). U of NC Pr.
Griffin, Clarence W. History of Old Tryon & Rutherford Counties, North Carolina,1730-1936. LC 77-24691. (Illus.). 1977. Repr. of 1937 ed. 30.00 (ISBN 0-87152-252-7). Reprint.
Hamilton, J. G. History of North Carolina, Vol. 3: North Carolina Since 1860. LC 73-1946. (Illus.). 442p. 1973. Repr. of 1919 ed. 25.00 (ISBN 0-87152-135-0). Reprint.
Harden, John. Devil's Tramping Ground & Other North Carolina Mystery Stories. 1949. 7.95 (ISBN 0-8078-0561-0); pap. 4.95 (ISBN 0-8078-4070-X). U of NC Pr.
Hawks, Francis L. History of North Carolina, 2 Vols. LC 61-3775. 1961. Repr. of 1858 ed. Vol. 1. 15.00 (ISBN 0-87152-006-0); Vol. 2. 20.00 (ISBN 0-87152-007-9); Set. 35.00 (ISBN 0-87152-329-9). Reprint.
Holcomb, Brent. Bladen County, N. C., Abstracts of Early Deeds, Seventeen Eighty-Three to Eighteen Hundred & Four. 73p. 1979. 10.00 (ISBN 0-89308-189-2). Southern Hist Pr.
--Mecklenburg County, North Carolina Deed Abstracts, Books 1-9, 1763-1779. 1978. 27.50 (ISBN 0-89308-108-6). Southern Hist Pr.
Hughson, S. C. Carolina Pirates & Colonial Commerce: 1670-1740. 1973. Repr. of 1894 ed. pap. 11.50 (ISBN 0-384-24865-9). Johnson Repr.
Hunter, C. L. Sketches of Western North Carolina: Illustrating Principally the Revolutionary Period of Mecklenburg, Rowan, Lincoln & Adjoining Counties. LC 79-110328. 1970. Repr. of 1877 ed. 17.50 (ISBN 0-8063-7977-4). Regional.
James, Hunter. The Quiet People of the Land: A Story of the North Carolina Moravians in Revolutionary Times. LC 75-44042. (Old Salem Ser). (Illus.). 1976. 8.50 (ISBN 0-8078-1282-X). U of NC Pr.
Konkle, Burton A. John Motley Morehead & the Development of North Carolina 1796-1866. LC 78-149347. (Illus.). 1971. Repr. of 1922 ed. 20.00 (ISBN 0-87152-067-2). Reprint.
Kostyu, Frank A. & Kostyu, Joel A. Durham: A Pictorial History. LC 78-7817. (Illus.). 1978. pap. 12.95 (ISBN 0-915442-57-4). Donning Co.
Landrum, John B. Colonial & Revolutionary History of Upper South Carolina. LC 61-1396. (Illus.). 1959. 16.50 (ISBN 0-87152-001-X). Reprint.
Lee, E. Lawrence. Indian Wars in North Carolina, 1663-1763. (Illus.). 1968. pap. 1.00 (ISBN 0-86526-084-2). NC Archives.
Lefler, Hugh T. & Newsome, Albert R. North Carolina: The History of a Southern State. 3rd rev. ed. LC 72-81330. (Illus.). 822p. 1973. 16.95 (ISBN 0-8078-1207-2); text ed. 13.00x student ed. (ISBN 0-8078-1202-1). U of NC Pr.
Lefler, Hugh T. & Powell, William S. Colonial North Carolina: A History. LC 73-5188. (A History of the American Colonies Ser.). 1973. lib. bdg. 25.00 (ISBN 0-527-18718-6). Kraus Intl.
Lefler, Hugh T., ed. North Carolina History Told by Contemporaries. 4th ed. 1965. text ed. 17.95 (ISBN 0-8078-0165-8). U of NC Pr.
Lemmon, Sarah M. Frustrated Patriots: North Carolina & the War of 1812. 248p. 1973. 15.00 (ISBN 0-8078-1209-9). U of NC Pr.
--North Carolina & the War of 1812. (Illus.). 1971. pap. 1.00 (ISBN 0-86526-087-7). NC Archives.
--North Carolina's Role in the First World War. (Illus.). 1975. pap. 1.00 (ISBN 0-86526-094-X). NC Archives.
--North Carolina's Role in World War Two. (Illus.). 1969. pap. 1.00 (ISBN 0-86526-095-8). NC Archives.
Lemmon, Sarah M., ed. Pettigrew Papers, Sixteen Eighty-Five to Eighteen Eighteen, Vol. 1. (Illus.). 1971. 15.00 (ISBN 0-86526-068-0). NC Archives.
Linn, Jo W. Abstracts of the Wills & Estates Records of Rowan County, N.C., 1753-1805 & Tax Lists of 1759-1778. 216p. 1980. 25.00 (ISBN 0-918470-03-X). J W Linn.
McBee, May W. Anson County, North Carolina: Abstracts of Early Records. LC 77-88217. 1980. Repr. of 1950 ed. 12.50 (ISBN 0-8063-0790-0). Genealog Pub.
Manarin, Louis H., compiled by. North Carolina Troops, 1861-1865: A Roster, 7 vols, Vols 2-6. Incl. Vol. 1. Artillery. xx, 619p. 1966. o.p (ISBN 0-86526-006-0); Vol. 2. Cavalry. xvix, 789p. 1968; Vol. 3. Infantry. 1971; Vol. 4. Infantry. 1973. 12.00 (ISBN 0-86526-009-5); Vol. 5. Infantry. Jordan, Weymouth T. 1977. 20.00 (ISBN 0-86526-010-9); Vol. 6. Infantry. 1977. 22.00 (ISBN 0-86526-011-7); Vol. 7. Infantry. 1979. 22.00 (ISBN 0-86526-012-5). Set (ISBN 0-86526-005-2). NC Archives.
Mathis, Harry R. Along the Border: A History of Virgilina, Virginia & the Surrounding Area in Halifax & Mecklenburg Counties in Virginia & Person & Granville Counties in North Carolina. LC 64-7237. (Illus.). 344p. 1964. 9.00x (ISBN 0-685-65080-4). Va Bk.
Mitchell, Memory F. Legal Aspects of Conscription & Exemption in North Carolina, 1861-1865. (James Sprunt Study in History & Political Science: Vol. 47). (Orig.). 1965. pap. text ed. 5.00x (ISBN 0-8078-5047-0). U of NC Pr.
Morgan, David T. & Schmidt, William J. North Carolinians in the Continental Congress. LC 76-40113. (Illus.). (YA) 1976. 7.95 (ISBN 0-910244-89-8). Blair.
Neal, Lois S. Abstracts of Vital Records from Raleigh, North Carolina, Newspapers 1799-1819, Vol. I. LC 79-13328. (Illus.). 1979. 35.00 (ISBN 0-87152-297-7). Reprint.
North Carolina General Assembly. Colonial Records of North Carolina, 1662-1776, 10 Vols. Saunders, William L., ed. LC 72-130612. Repr. of 1890 ed. Set. 675.00 (ISBN 0-404-05590-7); 67.50 ea. AMS Pr.
The Old North State Fact Book. (Illus.). 1976. pap. 1.00 (ISBN 0-86526-099-0). NC Archives.
Paludan, Phillip S. Victims, a True Story of the Civil War. LC 81-2578. 160p. 1981. 11.95 (ISBN 0-87049-316-7). U of Tenn Pr.
Parramore, Thomas C. Carolina Quest. (gr. 7-8). 1978. text ed. 15.00 (ISBN 0-13-114900-8). P-H.
Patton, Sadie. Sketches of Polk County History. LC 76-4897. (Illus.). 178p. 1976. Repr. of 1950 ed. 15.00 (ISBN 0-87152-234-9). Reprint.
--The Story of Henderson County. LC 76-4904. (Illus.). 310p. 1976. Repr. of 1947 ed. 17.50 (ISBN 0-87152-233-0). Reprint.
Powell, William S. Annals of Progress: The Story of Lenoir County & Kinston, North Carolina. 1963. pap. 2.00 (ISBN 0-86526-124-5). NC Archives.
--North Carolina. LC 65-15069. (Orig.). 1965. pap. 2.95 (ISBN 0-8077-2012-7). Tchrs Coll.
--Proprietors of North Carolina. (Illus.). 1968. pap. 1.00 (ISBN 0-86526-101-6). NC Archives.
Powell, William S., ed. The Correspondence of William Tryon & Other Selected Papers, Vol. I: 1758-1767. (Illus.). lvi, 664p. 1980. 25.00 (ISBN 0-86526-141-5). NC Archives.
Rankin, Hugh F. North Carolina Continentals. LC 79-135311. 1971. 14.95 (ISBN 0-8078-1154-8). U of NC Pr.
--North Carolina in the American Revolution. (Illus.). 1975. pap. 1.00 (ISBN 0-86526-091-5). NC Archives.
--Pirates of Colonial North Carolina. (Illus.). 1979. pap. 1.00 (ISBN 0-86526-100-8). NC Archives.
Register, Alvaretta K. State Census of North Carolina, 1784-1787. 2nd ed. LC 73-3664. 1978. Repr. of 1971 ed. 12.50 (ISBN 0-8063-0556-8). Genealog Pub.
Rumple, Jethro. A History of Rowan County, North Carolina. LC 74-9870. (Illus.). 410p. 1978. Repr. of 1929 ed. 17.50 (ISBN 0-8063-7998-7). Regional.
Salley, Alexander S., Jr., ed. Narratives of Early Carolina, Sixteen Fifty to Seventeen Eight. (Original Narratives). (Illus.). 1967. Repr. of 1911 ed. 18.50x (ISBN 0-06-480758-4). B&N.
Savage, Henry, Jr. River of the Carolinas: The Santee. LC 56-6469. (Rivers of America: No. 51). 1968. Repr. of 1956 ed. 12.95 (ISBN 0-8078-1059-2). U of NC Pr.
Schenck, David. North Carolina 1780-1781: Being a History of the Invasion of the Carolinas. LC 68-18503. 1968. Repr. of 1889 ed. 20.00 (ISBN 0-87152-045-1). Reprint.
Shanks, Henry T., ed. The Papers of Willie Person Mangum, 5 vols. Incl. Vol. 1. 1807-1832. xli, 613p. 1950 (ISBN 0-86526-050-8); Vol. 2. 1833-1838. xxi, 573p. 1952 (ISBN 0-86526-051-6); Vol. 3. 1839-1843. xxi, 521p. 1953 (ISBN 0-86526-052-4); Vol. 4. 1844-1846. xxviii, 812p. 1955 (ISBN 0-86526-053-2); Vol. 5. 1847-1894. xxxvii, 812p. 1956 (ISBN 0-86526-054-0). (Illus.). Set. 10.00 ea. (ISBN 0-86526-049-4). NC Archives.
Shoaf, Mary J. & Reeves, Henry. Davidson County, North Carolina Will Summaries 1823-1846. LC 79-63429. 1979. pap. 15.00 (ISBN 0-9602520-0-2). M J D Shoaf.

Sikes, Enoch W. The Transition of North Carolina from Colony to Commonwealth. LC 78-63866. (Johns Hopkins University. Studies in the Social Sciences. Sixteenth Ser. 1898: 10-11). Repr. of 1898 ed. 11.50 (ISBN 0-404-61122-2). AMS Pr.

Smeal, Lee. North Carolina Historical & Biographical Index. LC 78-53711. (Illus.). Date not set. lib. bdg. price not set (ISBN 0-89593-194-X). Accelerated Index.

Sondley, Foster A. A History of Buncombe County, North Carolina, 2 vols. in 1. LC 77-24692. (Illus.). 1977. Repr. of 1930 ed. 40.00 (ISBN 0-87152-253-5). Reprint.

Sprunt, James. Chronicles of the Cape Fear River, 1660-1916. LC 73-2562. (Illus.). 744p. 1973. Repr. of 1916 ed. 30.00 (ISBN 0-87152-139-3). Reprint.

--Tales & Traditions of the Lower Cape Fear: 1661-1896. LC 73-2561. (Illus.). 281p. 1973. Repr. of 1896 ed. 16.50 (ISBN 0-87152-140-7). Reprint.

Stokes, Durward T. Company Shops, North Carolina: The Town Built by a Railroad. 1981. 14.95 (ISBN 0-89587-016-9). Blair.

Todd, Vincent H. Christoph von Graffenried's Account of the Founding of New Bern. LC 73-2697. (Illus.). 434p. 1973. Repr. of 1920 ed. 21.50 (ISBN 0-87152-141-5). Reprint.

Van Noppen, Ina & Van Noppen, John. Western North Carolina Since the Civil War. LC 73-1241. 1973. 12.95 (ISBN 0-686-27859-3); pap. 4.95 (ISBN 0-686-27860-7). Appalach Consortium.

Vexler, R. I. North Carolina Chronology & Factbook, Vol. 33. 1978. 8.50 (ISBN 0-379-16158-3). Oceana.

Waddell, Alfred M. A Colonial Officer & His Times, 1754-1773: A Biographical Sketch of Gen. Hugh Waddell of North Carolina. LC 73-2617. 242p. 1973. Repr. of 1890 ed. 12.00 (ISBN 0-87152-142-3). Reprint.

Wagstaff, Henry M. State Rights & Political Parties in North Carolina, 1776-1861. LC 78-63916. (Johns Hopkins University. Studies in the Social Sciences. Twenty-Fourth Ser. 1906: 7-8). Repr. of 1906 ed. 17.50 (ISBN 0-404-61167-2). AMS Pr.

Wall, James W. Davie County: A Brief History. (Illus.). 1976. pap. 2.00 (ISBN 0-86526-126-1). NC Archives.

Walser, Richard. North Carolina Legends. (Illus.). viii, 86p. (Orig.). 1980. 6.00 (ISBN 0-86526-145-8); pap. 2.50 (ISBN 0-86526-139-3). NC Archives.

Walser, Richard & Street, Julia M., eds. North Carolina Parade: Stories of History & People. (Illus.). (gr. 5-9). 1966. 9.95 (ISBN 0-8078-0988-8). U of NC Pr.

Watson, Alan D. Burke County: A Brief History. (Illus., Orig.). 1979. pap. 2.00 (ISBN 0-86526-130-X). NC Archives.

--Edgecombe County: A Brief History. (Illus.). 1979. pap. 2.00 (ISBN 0-86526-127-X). NC Archives.

Weathers, Lee B. The Living Past of Cleveland County: A History. LC 80-14289. (Illus.). 314p. 1980. Repr. of 1956 ed. 16.50 (ISBN 0-87152-320-5). Reprint.

Weaver, Charles C. Internal Improvements in North Carolina Previous to 1860. LC 75-149349. 1971. Repr. of 1903 ed. 13.50 (ISBN 0-87152-069-9). Reprint.

--Internal Improvements in North Carolina Previous to 1860. LC 78-63895. (Johns Hopkins University. Studies in the Social Sciences. Twenty-First Ser. 1903). Repr. of 1903 ed. 11.50 (ISBN 0-404-61148-6). AMS Pr.

Weeks, S. B. The Religious Development in the Province of North Carolina. Repr. of 1892 ed. pap. 7.00 (ISBN 0-384-66390-7). Johnson Repr.

Weeks, Stephen B. The Religious Development in the Province of North Carolina. LC 78-63811. (Johns Hopkins University. Studies in the Social Sciences. Tenth Ser. 1892: 5-6). Repr. of 1892 ed. 11.50 (ISBN 0-404-61074-9). AMS Pr.

Wellman, Manly W. The Kingdom of Madison: A Southern Mountain Fastness & It's People. LC 72-87495. (Illus.). 232p. 1973. 8.95 (ISBN 0-8078-1206-4). U of NC Pr.

Wheeler, John H. Historical Sketches of North Carolina, from 1584 to 1851, 2 vols. in 1. LC 64-8758. (Illus.). 1974. Repr. of 1851 ed. 25.00 (ISBN 0-8063-7972-3). Regional.

--Reminiscences & Memoirs of North Carolina & Eminent North Carolinians. LC 66-18837. 1966. Repr. of 1884 ed. 20.00 (ISBN 0-8063-0375-1). Genealog Pub.

Williams, Robert L. Gastonia: A Pictorial History. LC 79-18386. (Illus.). 1980. 16.95 (ISBN 0-89865-005-4); ltd. ed. 24.95 (ISBN 0-89865-004-6). Donning Co.

Williamson, Hugh. The History of North Carolina, 2 vols. LC 73-2572. 618p. 1973. Repr. of 1812 ed. Vol. 1. 16.50 (ISBN 0-87152-143-1); Vol. 2. 16.50 (ISBN 0-87152-144-X); Set. 33.00 (ISBN 0-87152-335-3). Reprint.

Winborne, Benjamin B. The Colonial & State History of Hertford County, North Carolina. LC 76-24025. (Illus.). 1976. 17.50 (ISBN 0-8063-0733-1). Genealog Pub.

Yearns, W. Buck & Barrett, John G., eds. North Carolina Civil War Documentary. LC 79-17604. (Illus.). xvii, 365p. 1980. 17.95x (ISBN 0-8078-1407-5). U of NC Pr.

York, Courtney & York, Gerlene. Bladen County North Carolina Census 1810. (Orig.). 1970. pap. 5.00 (ISBN 0-916660-10-9). Hse of York.

--Colombus County North Carolina Census 1810. (Orig.). 1970. pap. 5.00 (ISBN 0-916660-11-7). Hse of York.

--Northampton County North Carolina Census 1790. 1972. pap. 5.00 (ISBN 0-916660-08-7). Hse of York.

--Rutherford County North Carolina Census 1790. (Orig.). 1970. pap. 5.00 (ISBN 0-916660-13-3). Hse of York.

--Warren County North Carolina Census 1790. (Orig.). 1972. pap. 5.00 (ISBN 0-916660-09-5). Hse of York.

--Warren County North Carolina Census 1810. (Orig.). 1970. pap. 5.00 (ISBN 0-916660-14-1). Hse of York.

York, Curtney & York, Gerlene. Northampton County North Carolina Census 1810. (Orig.). 1970. pap. 5.00 (ISBN 0-916660-12-5). Hse of York.

Young, Joanne & Lewis, Taylor, Jr. North Carolina: A Pictorial History of the First Two Hundred Years. LC 75-17098. (Illus.). 160p. 1975. 12.95 (ISBN 0-8487-0402-9). Oxmoor Hse.

Zuber, Richard L. North Carolina During Recontruction. (Illus.). 1975. pap. 1.00 (ISBN 0-86526-089-3). NC Archives.

NORTH CAROLINA–HISTORY–BIBLIOGRAPHY

Guide to Research Materials in the North Carolina State Archives, Section B: County Records. 1979. 5.00 (ISBN 0-86526-133-4). NC Archives.

Robinson, Blackwell. The North Carolina Adventure. (Illus.). (gr. 3-6). 1969. text ed. 9.95 (ISBN 0-87716-017-1, Pub. by Moore Pub Co). F Apple.

Vance, Mary. Historical Society Architectural Publications: New York, North Carolina, & North Dakota. (Architecture Ser.: Bibliography A-161). 72p. 1980. pap. 7.50 (ISBN 0-686-26908-X). Vance Biblios.

NORTH CAROLINA–HISTORY–FICTION

Fletcher, Inglis. Bennett's Welcome. (The Albemarle Ser). 451p. 1976. Repr. of 1950 ed. lib. bdg. 21.30x (ISBN 0-89244-001-5). Queens Hse.

--Cormorant's Brood. 324p. 1976. Repr. of 1959 ed. lib. bdg. 17.15x (ISBN 0-89244-002-3). Queens Hse.

Pierson, Edna C. The Witch of Turner's Bald. (Illus.). 1971. 5.00 (ISBN 0-686-05889-5). Puddingstone.

Wellman, Manly W. Settlement on Shocco: Adventures in Colonial Carolina. LC 63-22549. (gr. 4-8). 1963. PLB 5.95 (ISBN 0-910244-35-9). Blair.

NORTH CAROLINA–JUVENILE LITERATURE

Bailey, Bernadine. Picture Book of North Carolina. rev. ed. LC 74-134956. (Illus.). (gr. 3-5). 1970. 5.50g (ISBN 0-8075-9536-5). A Whitman.

Carpenter, Allan. North Carolina. new ed. LC 79-682. (New Enchantment of America State Bks.). (Illus.). (gr. 4 up). 1979. PLB 10.60 (ISBN 0-516-04133-9). Childrens.

Fradin, Dennis. North Carolina: In Words & Pictures. LC 79-25291. (Young People's Stories of Our States Ser.). (Illus.). 48p. (gr. 2-5). 1980. PLB 9.25 (ISBN 0-516-03933-4). Childrens.

Robinson, Blackwell. The North Carolina Adventure. (Illus.). (gr. 3-6). 1969. text ed. 9.95 (ISBN 0-87716-017-1, Pub. by Moore Pub Co). F Apple.

Walser, Richard & Street, Julia M., eds. North Carolina Parade: Stories of History & People. (Illus.). (gr. 5-9). 1966. 9.95 (ISBN 0-8078-0988-8). U of NC Pr.

NORTH CAROLINA–POETRY

Andrews, John W. First Flight. 2.25 (ISBN 0-8283-1228-1). Branden.

Ray, Worth S. The Mecklenburg Signers & Their Neighbors. LC 67-8260. (Lost Tribes of North Carolina Ser: Pt. 3). (Illus.). 246p. 1975. Repr. of 1946 ed. 12.00 (ISBN 0-8063-0286-0). Genealog Pub.

NORTH CAROLINA–POLITICS AND GOVERNMENT

Ball, Clyde L., et al. The General Assembly of North Carolina: A Handbook for Legislators. 3rd ed. (Law & Government Ser.). 1973. pap. 4.00 (ISBN 0-686-17571-9); 1979 suppl. 2.50 (ISBN 0-686-28571-9). U of NC Inst Gov.

Bassett, John S. The Constitutional Beginnings of North Carolina: 1662-1729. Repr. of 1894 ed. pap. 7.00 (ISBN 0-384-03523-X). Johnson Repr.

Beyle, Thad L. & Black, Merle, eds. Politics & Policy in North Carolina. 294p. 1975. pap. text ed. 8.95x (ISBN 0-8422-0496-2, 0496). Irvington.

Commerce Clearing House. Guidebook to North Carolina Taxes: 1982. 1982. pap. 10.00 (ISBN 0-686-76131-6). Commerce.

Crabtree, Beth G. North Carolina Governors,1585-1975: Brief Sketches. rev. ed. (Illus.). 1974. pap. 3.00 (ISBN 0-86526-033-8). NC Archives.

Crow, Jeffrey J. & Durden, Robert F. Maverick Republican in the Old North State: A Political Biography of Daniel L. Russell. LC 77-3657. (Southern Biography Ser.). 1977. 14.95x (ISBN 0-8071-0291-1). La State U Pr.

Durden, Robert F. Reconstruction Bonds & Twentieth-Century Politics: South Dakota Versus North Carolina, 1904. LC 62-10051. 1962. 12.75 (ISBN 0-8223-0050-8). Duke.

Edmonds, Helen G. The Negro & Fusion Politics in North Carolina, 1894-1901. LC 72-84986. (Illus.). xv, 260p. 1973. Repr. of 1951 ed. 18.00 (ISBN 0-8462-1692-2). Russell.

Hamilton, Joseph G. Reconstruction in North Carolina. 1964. 12.50 (ISBN 0-8446-1219-7). Peter Smith.

Lee, Robert E. North Carolina Family Law, 3 vols. 3rd ed. 1963. 1979-1980 100.00 (ISBN 0-87215-098-4). Michie-Bobbs.

Michie Editorial Staff. General Statutes of North Carolina, Annotated with 1979 Cum. Suppl, 17 vols. Set. write for info. (ISBN 0-87215-132-8); write for info. 1979 suppl. & index (ISBN 0-87215-308-8); 1980 interim suppl. avail. (ISBN 0-87215-347-9). Michie-Bobbs.

North Carolina General Assembly. Index to Colonial & State Records of North Carolina, 1662-1790, 4 Vols. Weeks, Stephen B., ed. LC 72-1797. Repr. of 1914 ed. Set. 270.00 (ISBN 0-404-07487-1); 67.50 ea. AMS Pr.

--State Records of North Carolina, 1777-1790, 16 Vols. Clark, Walter, ed. LC 72-1798. Repr. of 1895 ed. Set. 1160.00 (ISBN 0-404-07470-7); 72.50 ea. AMS Pr.

Potter, J. Reid. North Carolina Appellate Handbook. 1978. 28.50 (ISBN 0-87215-211-1, Bobbs-Merrill Law). Michie-Bobbs.

Puryear, Elmer L. Democratic Party Dissension in North Carolina, 1928-1936. (James Sprunt Studies in History & Political Science: Vol. 44). 249p. 1962. pap. 6.00x (ISBN 0-8078-5044-6). U of NC Pr.

Spence, James R. The Making of a Governor: The Moore -Preyer - Lake Primaries of 1964. LC 68-25854. (Orig.). 1968. pap. 1.95 (ISBN 0-910244-49-9). Blair.

Wagstaff, Henry M. State Rights & Political Parties in North Carolina, 1776-1861. LC 78-63916. (Johns Hopkins University. Studies in the Social Sciences. Twenty-Fourth Ser. 1906: 7-8). Repr. of 1906 ed. 17.50 (ISBN 0-404-61167-2). AMS Pr.

Weeks, Stephen B. Church & State in North Carolina. LC 78-63820. (Johns Hopkins University. Studies in the Social Sciences. Eleventh Ser. 1893: 6). Repr. of 1893 ed. 11.50 (ISBN 0-404-61082-X). AMS Pr.

NORTH CAROLINA–POLITICS AND GOVERNMENT–COLONIAL PERIOD, ca. 1600-1775

Bassett, John S. The Constitutional Beginnings of North Carolina: 1662-1729. Repr. of 1894 ed. pap. 7.00 (ISBN 0-384-03523-X). Johnson Repr.

Greene, Jack P. Quest for Power: The Lower Houses of Assembly in the Southern Royal Colonies, 1689-1776. 1972. pap. 3.95x (ISBN 0-393-00591-7, Norton Lib). Norton.

--The Quest for Power: The Lower Houses of Assembly in the Southern Royal Colonies 1689-1776. (Institute of Early American History & Culture Ser.). 1963. 24.50x (ISBN 0-8078-0900-4). U of NC Pr.

Higginbotham, Don, ed. The Papers of James Iredell. 1976. Vol. 1, 1767-1771. 16.00 (ISBN 0-86526-042-7); Vol. 2, 1778-1783. 16.00 (ISBN 0-86526-043-5). NC Archives.

Parker, Mattie E. & Price, William S., Jr., eds. Colonial Records of North Carolina: Second Series, 5 vols. Incl. Vol. 1. North Carolina Charters & Constitutions, 1578-1698. 247p. 1963. 10.00 (ISBN 0-86526-022-2); Vol. 2. North Carolina Higher-Court Records, 1670-1696. 533p. 1968. 11.00 (ISBN 0-86526-023-0); Vol. 3. North Carolina Higher Court Records, 1697-1701. 622p. 1971. 12.00 (ISBN 0-86526-024-9); Vol. 4. North Carolina Higher-Court Records, 1702-1708. 533p. 1974. 16.00 (ISBN 0-86526-025-7); Vol. 5. North Carolina Higher Court Minutes, 1709-1723. 1977. 21.00 (ISBN 0-86526-026-5). Set (ISBN 0-86526-020-6). NC Archives.

Raper, Charles L. North Carolina: A Study in English Colonial Government. LC 73-2564. 274p. 1973. Repr. of 1904 ed. 15.00 (ISBN 0-87152-138-5). Reprint.

Robinson, Blackwell P. Five Royal Governors of North Carolina, 1729-1775. (Illus.). 1968. pap. 1.00 (ISBN 0-86526-076-1). NC Archives.

NORTH CAROLINA–POLITICS AND GOVERNMENT–1775-1865

Bassett, John S. Anti-Slavery Leaders of North Carolina. LC 76-149341. 74p. 1971. Repr. of 1898 ed. 13.50 (ISBN 0-87152-061-3). Reprint.

Gilpatrick, Delbert H. Jeffersonian Democracy in North Carolina, 1789-1816. 1967. lib. bdg. 15.00x (ISBN 0-374-93098-8). Octagon.

Higginbotham, Don, ed. The Papers of James Iredell. 1976. Vol. 1, 1767-1771. 16.00 (ISBN 0-86526-042-7); Vol. 2, 1778-1783. 16.00 (ISBN 0-86526-043-5). NC Archives.

Sikes, E. W. Transition of North Carolina from Colony to Commonwealth. Repr. of 1898 ed. pap. 8.00 (ISBN 0-384-55370-2). Johnson Repr.

Trenholme, Louise. Ratification of the Federal Constitution in North Carolina. LC 32-19030. (Columbia University. Studies in the Social Sciences: No. 363). Repr. of 1932 ed. 22.50 (ISBN 0-404-51363-8). AMS Pr.

Watson, Harry L. Jacksonian Politics & Community Conflict: The Emergence of the Second American Party System in Cumberland County, North Carolina. LC 81-2414. (Illus.). 432p. 1981. text ed. 32.50 (ISBN 0-8071-0857-X). La State U Pr.

NORTH CAROLINA–SOCIAL CONDITIONS

Bassett, John S. Slavery in the State of North Carolina. 1976. Repr. of 1899 ed. 25.00 (ISBN 0-403-06401-5, Regency). Scholarly.

Bode, Frederick A. Protestantism & the New South: North Carolina Baptists & Methodists in Political Crisis, 1894-1903. LC 75-1289. 300p. 1976. 10.95x (ISBN 0-8139-0597-4). U Pr of Va.

Herring, Harriet L. Welfare Work in Mill Villages: The Story of Extra-Mill Activities in North Carolina. LC 68-55773. (Criminology, Law Enforcement, & Social Problems Ser.: No. 20). 1968. Repr. of 1929 ed. 17.00 (ISBN 0-87585-020-0). Patterson Smith.

Learning Institute of North Carolina. Who Cares for Children? A Survey of Child Care Services in North Carolina. 1974. pap. 3.00 (ISBN 0-686-10550-8). Learning Inst NC.

Pope, Liston. Millhands & Preachers: A Study of Gastonia. (Studies in Religious Education Ser.: No. 15). (Illus.). 1965. pap. 5.95x (ISBN 0-300-00182-7). Yale U Pr.

Rhyne, Jennings J. Some Southern Cotton Mill Workers & Their Villages. Stein, Leon, ed. LC 77-70527. (Work Ser.). (Illus.). 1977. Repr. of 1930 ed. lib. bdg. 15.00x (ISBN 0-405-10195-3). Arno.

Rosenberg, Harry M., et al, eds. Proceedings of the North Carolina Demographic Data Workshop. 2nd ed. LC 76-25003. 54p. 1976. pap. text ed. 3.00 (ISBN 0-89055-116-2). Carolina Pop Ctr.

Sheppard, Muriel E. Cabins in the Laurel. 1935. 12.95 (ISBN 0-8078-0184-4). U of NC Pr.

NORTH CAROLINA–SOCIAL LIFE AND CUSTOMS

Bledsoe, Jerry. Just Folks: Visitin' with Carolina People. LC 80-36880. (Illus.). 208p. 1980. 9.95 (ISBN 0-914788-31-0). East Woods.

Ginns, Patsy M. Rough Weather Makes Good Timber: Carolinians Recall. LC 76-20765. 189p. 1977. 11.50 (ISBN 0-8078-1288-9); pap. 6.50 (ISBN 0-8078-4071-8). U of NC Pr.

McCourry, Donald L. Us Poor Folks & the Things of Dog Flat Hollow. LC 75-29138. (Illus.). 1975. 7.95 (ISBN 0-910244-85-5). Blair.

Taylor, Rosser H. Carolina Crossroads: A Study of Rural Life at the End of the Horse-and Buggy Era. (Illus.). 1966. 7.50 (ISBN 0-930230-05-1). Johnson NC.

Watson, Alan D. Society in Colonial North Carolina. (Illus.). 1975. pap. 1.00 (ISBN 0-86526-103-2). NC Archives.

NORTH CAROLINA–SUPREME COURT
Holt, Bryce R. Supreme Court of North Carolina & Slavery. LC 73-109913. (Duke University. Trinity College Historical Socity. Historical Papers: No. 17). Repr. of 1927 ed. 17.50 (ISBN 0-404-53167-9). AMS Pr.
NORTH CAROLINA, UNIVERSITY OF
Battle, Kemp P. History of the University of North Carolina, 2 vols. LC 74-13351. (Illus.). 1974. Repr. of 1907 ed. Set. 65.00 (ISBN 0-87152-308-6); 32.50 ea.; Vol. 1. (ISBN 0-87152-187-3); Vol. 2. (ISBN 0-87152-188-1). Reprint.
Books from Chapel Hill, 1922-1972: A Complete Catalog of the University of North Carolina Press. 244p. 1972. pap. 4.00x (ISBN 0-8078-1198-X). U of NC Pr.
Connor, Robert D., ed. Documentary History of the University of North Carolina, 1776-1799, 2 Vols. 1965. Set. 35.00 (ISBN 0-8078-0640-4). U of NC Pr.
Henderson, Archibald. Campus of the First State University. 1949. 12.50 (ISBN 0-8078-0565-3). U of NC Pr.
Powell, William S., ed. The First State University: A Pictorial History of the University of North Carolina at Chapel Hill. LC 78-26419. (Illus.). 350p. 1979. 25.00 (ISBN 0-8078-1190-4). U of NC Pr.
Schumann, Marguerite. The First State University: A Walking Guide. (Illus.). 96p. 1972. pap. 2.50 (ISBN 0-8078-1195-5). U of NC Pr.
NORTH CAROLINA GAZETTEER
Powell, William S. North Carolina Gazetteer. (Maps). 1968. pap. 8.95 (ISBN 0-8078-1247-1). U of NC Pr.
NORTH CAROLINA STATE PORTS AUTHORITY
Landon, Charles E. North Carolina State Ports Authority. LC 63-9009. (Illus.). 1963. 9.75 (ISBN 0-8223-0104-0). Duke.
NORTH CASCADES NATIONAL PARK
Darvill, Fred T., Jr. Darvill's Guide to the North Cascades National Park Associated Areas. rev. ed. 1975. Vol. 1. pap. 1.75 (ISBN 0-915740-01-X). Darvill Outdoor.
--North Cascades Highway Guide. 1973. pap. 1.00 (ISBN 0-915740-03-6). Darvill Outdoor.
Spring, Bob, et al. The North Cascades National Park. (Illus.). 32p. 1973. pap. 2.95 (ISBN 0-87564-613-1). Superior Pub.
NORTH CENTRAL STATES
see Middle West
NORTH DAKOTA
see also names of cities, counties, towns etc. in North Dakota
Bailey, Bernadine. Picture Book of North Dakota. rev. ed. LC 58-12319. (Illus.). (gr. 3-5). 1971. 5.50g (ISBN 0-8075-9537-3). A Whitman.
Berg, Francie M. North Dakota: Land of Changing Seasons. LC 76-45874. (Old West Region Ser.: Vol. I). (Illus.). 1977. 12.95 (ISBN 0-918532-01-9); pap. 8.95 (ISBN 0-918532-02-7). Flying Diamond Bks.
Butler, Mike. Ninety-Two Days in the Saddle. (Illus.). 1975. 8.95 (ISBN 0-88342-042-2). Old Army.
Carpenter, Allan. North Dakota. new ed. LC 79-11470. (New Enchantment of America State Bks.). (Illus.). (gr. 4 up). 1979. PLB 10.60 (ISBN 0-516-04134-7). Childrens.
Dietrich, Irvine T. & Hove, John. Conservation of Natural Resources: North Dakota. (Illus.). (gr. 7 up). 1962. 3.00 (ISBN 0-911042-06-7). N Dak Inst.
Dresden, Donald. Marquis De Mores: Emperor of the Badlands. LC 69-16720. (Illus.). 1970. 13.95x (ISBN 0-8061-0869-X). U of Okla Pr.
Federal Writers Project. North Dakota: Guide to the Northern Prairie State. 2nd ed. (American Guide Ser). 1950. 14.95 (ISBN 0-19-500043-9). Oxford U Pr.
Fradin, Dennis. North Dakota: In Words & Pictures. LC 80-26480. (Young People's Stories of Our States Ser.). (Illus.). 48p. (gr. 2-5). 1981. PLB 9.25 (ISBN 0-516-03934-2). Childrens.
Hanson, Nancy E. Bismarck & Mangan: A Pictorial History. LC 80-27784. (Illus.). 205p. 1981. pap. 12.95 (ISBN 0-89865-094-1). Donning Co.
--Fargo: A Pictorial History. LC 80-29178. (Illus.). 205p. 1981. pap. 12.95 (ISBN 0-686-77771-9). Donning Co.
Hart, Herbert M. Tourguide to Old Forts of Montana, Wyoming North & South Dakota, Vol. 4. (Illus.). 150p. 1980. pap. 3.95 (ISBN 0-87108-570-4). Pruett.
Hickey, Leo J. Stratigraphy & Paleobotany of the Golden Valley Formation (Early Tertiary) of Western North Dakota. LC 76-50970. (Memoir: No. 150). (Illus.). 1977. 34.00x (ISBN 0-8137-1150-9). Geol Soc.
Howard, Thomas W., ed. The North Dakota Political Tradition. 192p. 1981. 12.50 (ISBN 0-8138-0520-1). Iowa St U Pr.
Kazeck, Melvin E. North Dakota: A Human & Economic Geography. LC 56-13250. (Illus.). 264p. 1956. 4.75 (ISBN 0-911042-02-4). N Dak Inst.
Liddle, Janice. Index to Mary Ann Barnes Williams' Origins of North Dakota Place Names. LC 77-622724. 1977. pap. 2.00 (ISBN 0-911042-21-0). N Dak Inst.
Morrow, Patrick D. Growing up in North Dakota. 1979. pap. text ed. 2.25 (ISBN 0-8191-0650-X). U Pr of Amer.
North Dakota. 23.00 (ISBN 0-89770-110-0). Curriculum Info Ctr.
North Dakota: Guide to the Northern Prairie State. LC 72-84498. 1938. 54.00 (ISBN 0-403-02183-9). Somerset Pub.
Robinson, Elwyn B. History of North Dakota. LC 66-10877. (Illus.). 1966. 11.95 (ISBN 0-8032-0155-9). U of Nebr Pr.
Roehrick, Kaye L., ed. Brevet's North Dakota Historical Markers & Sites LC 74-79978. (Historical Markers-Sites Ser). (Illus.). 176p. 1975. pap. 6.95 (ISBN 0-88498-025-1). Brevet Pr.
Schneider, Bill. The Dakota Image. LC 80-83707. (Illus.). 96p. 1980. 20.00 (ISBN 0-934318-02-6). Falcon Pr MT.
Sletten, Harvey. Growing up on Bald Hill Creek. (Illus.). 1977. 6.95 (ISBN 0-8138-0080-3, 0080-3). Iowa St U Pr.
State Industrial Directories Corp. North Dakota State Industrial Directory, 1980. 1980. pap. 15.00 (ISBN 0-89910-034-1). State Indus Dir.
Tweton, D. Jerome & Jelliff, Theodore B. North Dakota: The Heritage of a People. LC 76-27123. (Illus.). (gr. 7 up). 1976. 9.85 (ISBN 0-911042-19-9). N Dak Inst.
Vance, Mary. Historical Society Architectural Publications: New York, North Carolina, & North Dakota. (Architecture Ser.: Bibliography A-161). 72p. 1980. pap. 7.50 (ISBN 0-686-26908-X). Vance Biblios.
Vexler, R. I. North Dakota Chronology & Factbook, Vol. 34. 1978. 8.50 (ISBN 0-379-16159-1). Oceana.
Wilkins, Robert P. & Wilkins, Wynona H. North Dakota. (States & the Nation Ser.). (Illus.). 1977. 12.95 (ISBN 0-393-05655-4, Co-Pub by AASLH). Norton.
NORTH DAKOTA STATE UNIVERSITY OF AGRICULTURE AND APPLIED SCIENCE, FARGO
Hoag, Donald G. Trees & Shrubs for Northern Plains. LC 65-65446. 376p. 1965. pap. 12.50 (ISBN 0-911042-10-5). N Dak Inst.
Hunter, William C. Beacon Across the Prairie. LC 61-63838. (Illus.). 309p. 1961. 5.50 (ISBN 0-911042-05-9). N Dak Inst.
NORTH EASTERN RAILWAY COMPANY (GREAT BRITAIN)
Irving, R. J. The North Eastern Railway 1870-1914: An Economic History. 1976. text ed. 28.75x (ISBN 0-7185-1141-7, Leicester). Humanities.
Locomotive of the North Eastern Railway. 14.95x (ISBN 0-392-08071-0, SpS). Sportshelf.
Nock, O. S. British Steam Railway Locomotive: Volume 2, 1925-1965. 31.50x (ISBN 0-392-07700-0, SpS). Sportshelf.
NORTH PACIFIC COAST RAILROAD
Graves, Al, et al. Narrow-Gauge to the Redwoods: The Story of the North Pacific Coast Railroad & San Francisco Bay Paddle-Wheel Ferries. 2nd rev. ed. 15.00 (ISBN 0-87046-010-2). Trans-Anglo.
Narrow Gauge to the Redwoods. 15.00 (ISBN 0-685-83361-5). Chatham Pub CA.
NORTH POLE
see also Arctic Regions
Brontman, Lazar K. On the Top of the World: The Soviet Expedition to the North Pole, 1937. Schmidt, O. J., ed. LC 68-55180. 1968. Repr. of 1938 ed. lib. bdg. 16.75x (ISBN 0-8371-0326-6, BRTW). Greenwood.
Henson, Matthew A. Negro Explorer at the North Pole. LC 69-18565. (American Negro: His History & Literature Ser., No. 2). 1969. Repr. of 1912 ed. 12.00 (ISBN 0-405-01868-1). Arno.
Hunt, Harrison J. North to the Horizon. Thompson, Ruth H., ed. LC 80-69081. (Illus.). 135p. 1981. 11.95 (ISBN 0-89272-080-8). Down East.
Hunt, William R. To Stand at the Pole: The Dr. Cook-Admiral Peary North Pole Controversy. LC 80-6156. 272p. 1981. 14.95 (ISBN 0-8128-2773-2). Stein & Day.
Lisker, Tom. First to the Top of the World: Admiral Peary at the North Pole. LC 78-14924. (Famous Firsts Ser.). (Illus.). 1978. lib. bdg. 7.35 (ISBN 0-686-51107-7). Silver.
Mirsky, Jeannette. To the Arctic: The Story of Northern Exploration from Earliest Times to the Present. LC 72-121386. 1970. 10.00x (ISBN 0-226-53178-3). U of Chicago Pr.
Peary, Robert E. North Pole, Its Discovery in 1909 Under the Auspices of the Peary Arctic Club. LC 68-55210. 1968. Repr. of 1910 ed. lib. bdg. 31.00x (ISBN 0-8371-0613-3, PENP). Greenwood.
--The North Pole: Its Discovery in 1909 Under the Auspices of the Peary Arctic Club. Repr. of 1910 ed. lib. bdg. 45.00 (ISBN 0-8495-4330-4). Arden Lib.
White, John. Pole Shift: Predictions & Prophecies of the Ultimate Disaster. LC 79-7704. (Illus.). 432p. 1980. 14.00 (ISBN 0-385-15374-0). Doubleday.
NORTH SEA
Delmar-Morgan, Edward. North Sea Harbors & Pilotage. 1979. 29.95x (ISBN 0-8464-0070-7). Beekman Pubs.
Lebour, M. V. The Planktonic Diatoms of Northern Seas. (Ray Society Publication: No. 116). (Illus.). 244p. 1978. Repr. of 1930 ed. lib. bdg. 30.00x (ISBN 3-87429-147-2). Lubrecht & Cramer.
Maclean, Ian. North Sea Oil Information Sources. 80p. 1975. 35.00x (ISBN 0-85038-311-0). Intl Pubns Serv.
Mason, C. M., ed. Effective Management of Resources: The International Politics of the North Sea. 1979. 22.50x (ISBN 0-89397-043-3). Nichols Pub.
Sibthorp, M. M. The North Sea: Challenge & Opportunity. LC 76-363368. 340p. 1975. 21.00x (ISBN 0-900362-76-6). Intl Pubns Serv.
Watt, D. C., ed. Greenwich Forum V: Europe & the Sea: the Cause for & Against a New International Regime for the North Sea and Its Approaches. 1981. text ed. 49.95 (ISBN 0-86103-039-7). Butterworth.
NORTHAMPTON, MASSACHUSETTS
Hannay, Agnes. A Chronicle of Industry on the Mill River. Stein, Leon, ed. LC 77-70501. (Work Ser.). 1977. Repr. of 1936 ed. lib. bdg. 12.00x (ISBN 0-405-10172-4). Arno.
Rupp, Daniel. History of Northampton: Lehigh Monroe Carbon Schuykill Counties, Pa. 1978. 18.50x (ISBN 0-916838-16-1). Schiffer.
NORTHAMPTONSHIRE, ENGLAND
Greenall, R. L. A History of Northamptonshire. (The Darwen County History Ser.). (Illus.). 128p. 1979. 20.75x (ISBN 0-8476-3167-2). Rowman.
Smith, Juliet. Northamptonshire & the Soke of Peterborough: A Shell Guide. (Shell Guide Ser.). (Illus.). 128p. 1968. 12.95 (ISBN 0-571-08420-6, Pub. by Faber & Faber). Merrimack Bk Serv.
Thorn, Frank & Thorn, Caroline, eds. Northamptonshire. (Domesday Bk.: Vol. 21). (Illus.). 231p. 1979. 24.00x (ISBN 0-8476-3142-7). Rowman.
NORTHCLIFFE, ALFRED CHARLES WILLIAM HARMSWORTH, 1ST VISCOUNT, 1865-1922
Fyfe, Henry H. Northcliffe: An Intimate Biography. LC 74-100527. (BCL Ser.: I). Repr. of 1930 ed. 26.00 (ISBN 0-404-00592-6). AMS Pr.
NORTHEAST BOUNDARY OF THE UNITED STATES
Corey, Albert B. Crisis of Eighteen Thirty to Eighteen Forty-Two in Canadian - American Relations. LC 77-102483. (Relations of Canada & the U. S. Ser). (Illus.). 203p. 1970. Repr. of 1941 ed. 11.00 (ISBN 0-8462-1356-7). Russell.
Edey, Maitland. The Northeast Coast. LC 70-187925. (American Wilderness Ser). (Illus.). (gr. 6 up). 1972. lib. bdg. 11.97 (ISBN 0-8094-1149-0, Pub. by Time-Life). Silver.
Gallatin, Albert, ed. Right of the United States of America to the Northeastern Boundary Claimed by Them. facs. ed. LC 70-117876. (Select Bibliographies Reprint Ser). 1840. 29.00 (ISBN 0-8369-5329-0). Arno.
Greenleaf, Moses. Survey of the State of Maine in Reference to Its Geographical Features, Statistics & Political Economy. LC 71-128108. 1970. 14.00 (ISBN 0-913764-00-0). Maine St Mus.
Merk, Frederick & Merk, Lois B. Fruits of Propaganda in the Tyler Administration. LC 79-135547. 1971. 15.00x (ISBN 0-674-32676-8). Harvard U Pr.
NORTHEAST PASSAGE
Amundsen, Ronald. The North East Passage, 2 vols. 1908. Set. 65.00 (ISBN 0-685-43784-1). Norwood Edns.
Asher, George M., ed. Henry Hudson the Navigator. (Hakluyt Soc. First Ser.: No. 27). (Illus.). 1964. Repr. of 1613 ed. 32.00 (ISBN 0-8337-0098-7). B Franklin.
De Veer, Gerrit. Three Voyages of William Barents to the Arctic Regions, 1594, 1595, & 1596. 2nd ed. Beynen, K., ed. 1964. 32.00 (ISBN 0-8337-3622-1). B Franklin.
Kish, G. North-East Passage: Adolf Erik Nordenskiold, His Life & Times. (Illus.). 1973. 30.00 (ISBN 9-0607-2720-7). Heinman.
Krypton, Constantine. Northern Sea Route & the Economy of the Soviet North. LC 76-9087. (Studies of the Research Program on the U.S.S.R: No.14). (Illus.). 1976. Repr. of 1956 ed. lib. bdg. 15.50x (ISBN 0-8371-8886-5, KRNS). Greenwood.
NORTHEASTERN STATES
Alexander, Lewis M. The Northeastern United States. (New Searchlight Ser.). 1976. pap. 4.50x (ISBN 0-442-29749-1). Van Nos Reinhold.
Berman, Steve. The Northeastern Outdoors: A Field & Travel Guide. LC 76-52519. (Illus.). 1977. pap. 7.95 (ISBN 0-913276-21-9). Stone Wall Pr.
Chinitz, Benjamin. The Declining Northeast: Demographic & Economic Analyses. LC 78-6137. 1978. 22.95 (ISBN 0-03-043476-9). Praeger.
Christopher, Bob & Christopher, Ellen. Christopher's America on Fifteen to Twenty-Five Dollars a Night: Northeast States. 80p. (Orig.). Date not set. pap. 3.95 (ISBN 0-930570-02-2). Travel Discover.
Fisher, Robert, ed. Fodor's Mid-Atlantic 1980. (Fodor Travel Guide Ser.). (Illus.). 1980. 10.95 (ISBN 0-679-00453-X); pap. 7.95 (ISBN 0-679-00454-8). McKay.
Franklin, John H. A Southern Odyssey - Travelers in the Antebellum North. LC 74-27190. (Illus.). 320p. 1976. 22.50x (ISBN 0-8071-0161-3); pap. 6.95x (ISBN 0-8071-0351-9). La State U Pr.
Gottmann, J. Megalopolis: The Urbanized Northeastern Seaboard of the United States. Repr. of 1961 ed. 12.00 (ISBN 0-527-02819-3). Kraus Repr.
Jennings, Jerry, ed. The Northeast. rev. ed. LC 78-54254. (United States Ser.). (Illus.). 320p. (gr. 5 up). 1979. text ed. 9.93 ea. 1-4 copies (ISBN 0-88296-057-1); text ed. 7.94 ea. 5 or more copies; tchrs.' annotated ed. 13.68 (ISBN 0-88296-347-3). Fideler.
Lape, James, ed. America in Literature: The Northeast. LC 78-25617. 280p. (gr. 9-12). 1979. pap. text ed. 6.50 (ISBN 0-684-16063-3, SSP-40). Scribner.
Peirce, Neal R. & Barone, Michael. The Mid-Atlantic States of America: People, Politics, & Power in the Five Mid-Atlantic States & the Nation's Capital. (Illus.). 1977. 15.95 (ISBN 0-393-05541-8). Norton.
NORTHEASTERN UNIVERSITY
Morris, Rudolph M. Where? on Huntington Avenue. (Illus.). 1977. 9.75 (ISBN 0-8158-0357-5). Chris Mass.
NORTHERN BUDDHISM
see Mahayana Buddhism
NORTHERN IRELAND
Arthur, Paul. Government & Politics of Northern Ireland. 1981. text ed. 12.95x (ISBN 0-582-35300-9); pap. text ed. 6.95x (ISBN 0-582-35301-7). Longman.
Aunger, Edmund A. In Search of Political Stability: A Comparative Study of New Brunswick & Northern Ireland. 238p. 1981. 21.95x (ISBN 0-7735-0366-8). McGill-Queens U Pr.
Barritt, Denis & Carter, Charles F. The Northern Ireland Problem: A Study in Group Relations. rev. 2nd ed. (Oxford Paperbacks Ser). (Illus.). 180p. 1972. pap. 2.95x (ISBN 0-19-285058-X). Oxford U Pr.
Beyond Orange & Green: The Political Eonomy of the Northern Ireland Crisis. 176p. 1978. 12.95 (ISBN 0-905762-16-9, Pub. by Zed Pr); pap. 5.95 (ISBN 0-905762-17-7). Lawrence Hill.
Birrell, Derek & Murie, Alan. Policy & Government in Northern Ireland: Lessons of Devolution. 353p. 1980. 32.50x (ISBN 0-389-20019-0). B&N.
Bow, Paul, et al. The State in Northern Ireland: Political Forces & Social Classes. LC 79-13020. 1979. 18.95x (ISBN 0-312-75608-9). St Martin.
Buckland, Patrick. The Factory of Grievances: Devolved Government in Northern Ireland, 1921-1939. LC 79-52164. 1979. text ed. 27.50x (ISBN 0-06-490752-X). B&N.
--A History of Northern Ireland. LC 81-909. 200p. 1981. text ed. 25.00x (ISBN 0-8419-0700-5). Holmes & Meier.
Carlton, Charles. Bigotry & Blood: Documents on the Ulster Crisis. LC 76-17018. 160p. 1977. 15.95x (ISBN 0-88229-278-1); pap. 8.95x (ISBN 0-88229-469-5). Nelson-Hall.
Clark, Dennis J. Irish Blood: Northern Ireland and the American Conscience. LC 76-21808. (National University Publications Ser. in American Studies). 1977. 11.00 (ISBN 0-8046-9163-0). Kennikat.
Darby, John & Williamson, Arthur. Violence & the Social Services in Northern Ireland. (Studies in Social Policy & Welfare). 1978. text ed. 29.95x (ISBN 0-435-82261-6). Heinemann Ed.
De Breffny, Brian. Land of Ireland. LC 79-11461. (Illus.). 1979. 35.00 (ISBN 0-8109-1250-3). Abrams.
Deutsch, Richard R. Northern Ireland, Nineteen Twenty-One to Nineteen Seventy-Four: A Select Bibliography. LC 75-5516. (Reference Library of Social Science: No. 2). 160p. 1974. lib. bdg. 21.00 (ISBN 0-8240-1060-4). Garland Pub.

Donaldson, Alfred G. Some Comparative Aspects of Irish Law. LC 57-8815. (Commonwealth Studies Center: No. 3). 1957. 14.75 (ISBN 0-8223-0047-8). Duke.

Elliot, Sydney, ed. Northern Ireland Parliamentary Election Results 1921-1972. (Illus.). 152p. 1973. 15.00x (ISBN 0-900178-12-4). Intl Pubns Serv.

Farell, Michael. Northern Ireland: Orange State. 408p. 1980. text ed. 22.00 (ISBN 0-904383-14-8); pap. 11.95 (ISBN 0-86104-300-6). Pluto Pr.

Fedden, Robin & Joekes, Rosemary, eds. The National Trust Guide to England, Wales, & Northern Ireland. rev. ed. (Illus.). 1978. 24.95 (ISBN 0-393-08813-8). Norton.

Fields, Rona M. Northern Ireland: Society Under Siege. LC 80-80316. 267p. 1981. pap. 5.95 (ISBN 0-87855-806-3). Transaction Bks.

--Society Under Siege: A Psychology of Northern Ireland. LC 76-21895. 1977. 17.50x (ISBN 0-87722-074-3). Temple U Pr.

Fraser. Children in Conflict: Growing up in Northern Ireland. LC 73-92721. 1977. 10.00x (ISBN 0-465-01043-1). Basic.

Gamble, John. Views of Society & Manners in the North of Ireland: Letters Written in the Year 1818. LC 77-87688. 1977. Repr. of 1819 ed. 34.00 (ISBN 0-404-16487-0). AMS Pr.

Greaves, C. Desmond. The Irish Crisis. new ed. LC 70-188753. 1974. pap. 1.95 (ISBN 0-7178-0405-4). Intl Pub Co.

Hastings, Max. Barricades in Belfast: The Fight for Civil Rights in Northern Ireland. LC 70-109178. 1970. 5.95 (ISBN 0-8008-0665-4). Taplinger.

Heskin, Ken. Northern Ireland: A Psychological Analysis. LC 80-13407. 192p. 1980. 17.50x (ISBN 0-231-05138-7). Columbia U Pr.

Hill, D. A. Northern Ireland. (Geography of the British Isles Ser.). (Illus.). 68p. 1974. 4.95x (ISBN 0-521-20027-X). Cambridge U Pr.

Holland, Jack. Too Long a Sacrifice: Life & Death in Northern Ireland Since 1969. LC 80-27267. (Illus.). 240p. 1981. 10.95 (ISBN 0-396-07934-2). Dodd.

Hull, Roger H. The Irish Triangle: Conflict in Northern Ireland. LC 75-17424. 1976. 23.00 (ISBN 0-691-07576-X); pap. 6.95 (ISBN 0-691-02181-3). Princeton U Pr.

Isles, Keith S. & Cuthbert, Norman. An Economic Survey of Northern Ireland. LC 74-33505. (Illus.). 646p. 1975. Repr. of 1957 ed. lib. bdg. 35.50x (ISBN 0-8371-7970-X, ISES). Greenwood.

McAllister, Ian. The Northern Ireland Social Democratic & Labour Party: Political Opposition in a Divided Society. 1978. text ed. 31.50x (ISBN 0-8419-5035-0). Holmes & Meier.

McCreary, Alf. Survivors: Documentary Account of the Victims of Northern Ireland. 1977. 21.00x (ISBN 0-8464-0904-6). Beekman Pubs.

Magee, John. Northern Ireland: Crises & Conflict. (World Studies). (Illus.). 212p. 1974. 16.00x (ISBN 0-7100-7946-X); pap. 7.95 (ISBN 0-7100-7947-8). Routledge & Kegan.

Mansbach, Richard W., ed. Northern Ireland: Half a Century of Partition. LC 72-81732. 221p. (Orig.). 1974. lib. bdg. 17.50 (ISBN 0-87196-182-2). Facts on File.

Miller, David. Queen's Rebels: Ulster Loyalism in Historical Perspective. LC 78-16943. 1978. text ed. 23.50x (ISBN 0-06-494829-3). B&N.

Moody, T. W. The Ulster Question, 1603-1973. (Illus.). 1974. pap. 4.95 (ISBN 0-85342-399-7). Irish Bk Ctr.

Murphy, John. Ireland in the Twentieth Century. (Gill History of Ireland: Vol. 11). 192p. 1975. pap. 5.50 (ISBN 0-7171-0568-7). Irish Bk Ctr.

O'Dowd, L., et al. Northern Ireland: Between Civil Rights & Civil War. 1981. text ed. 26.00x (ISBN 0-906336-18-X, Pub. by CSE Bks England); pap. text ed. 9.25x (ISBN 0-906336-19-8, Pub. by CSE Bks England). Humanities.

Rose, Richard. Northern Ireland: A Time of Choice. (Foreign Affairs Studies). 1976. pap. 6.25 (ISBN 0-8447-3206-0). Am Enterprise.

--Northern Ireland Loyalty Study, 1968. LC 75-32210. 1975. codebk. 14.00 (ISBN 0-89138-116-3). ICPSR.

Schutz, Barry & Scott, Douglas. Natives & Settlers: A Comparative Analysis of the Politics of Opposition & Mobilization in Northern Ireland & Rhodesia. (Monograph Ser. in World Affairs, Vol. 12: 1974-75 Ser., Pt.B). 4.00 (ISBN 0-87940-042-0). U of Denver Intl.

Skoogfors, L., et al. The Most Natural Thing in the World. 1974. pap. 3.95 (ISBN 0-06-090385-6, CN385, CN). Har-Row.

Stevens, Patricia B. God Save Ireland! The Irish Conflict in the Twentieth Century. LC 73-19067. 224p. (gr. 7 up). 1974. 10.95 (ISBN 0-02-788180-6). Macmillan.

Wilson, Ron. A Flower Grows in Ireland. 112p. pap. 3.95 (ISBN 0-912692-78-2, 95539). Cook.

Winchester, Simon. Northern Ireland in Crisis: Reporting the Ulster Troubles. LC 74-84649. 250p. 1975. 19.50x (ISBN 0-8419-0180-5). Holmes & Meier.

NORTHERN LIGHTS

see Auroras

NORTHERN NECK, VIRGINIA

Morrison, Charles. The Fairfax Line: A Profile in History & Geography. (Illus.). 1970. pap. 1.75 (ISBN 0-87012-085-9). McClain.

NORTHERN PACIFIC RAILROAD

Cotroneo, Ross R. History of the Northern Pacific Land Grant, 1900-1952. Bruchey, Stuart, ed. LC 78-56728. (Management in Public Lands in the U. S. Ser.). (Illus.). 1979. lib. bdg. 31.00x (ISBN 0-405-11329-3). Arno.

Harnsberger, John L. Jay Cooke & Minnesota: The Formative Years of the Northern Pacific Railroad, 1868-1873. Bruchey, Stuart, ed. LC 80-1281. (Railroads Ser.). 1981. lib. bdg. 35.00x (ISBN 0-405-13756-7). Arno.

Hedges, James B. Henry Villard & the Railways of the Northwest. LC 66-24704. (Illus.). 1967. Repr. of 1930 ed. 7.50 (ISBN 0-8462-0870-9). Russell.

Irwin, Leonard B. Pacific Railways & Nationalism in the Canadian American Northwest, 1845-1873. LC 69-10107. 1969. Repr. of 1939 ed. lib. bdg. 15.75x (ISBN 0-8371-0495-5, IRPR). Greenwood.

Ledger Stem Book Co. Tacoma: The Western Terminus of the Northern Pacific Railroad. Repr. of 1885 ed. pap. 4.50 (ISBN 0-8466-0311-X, SJS311). Shorey.

Leverty, Maureen J., compiled by. Guide to Records of Northern Pacific Branch Lines, Subsidiaries, & Related Companies in the Minnesota Historical Society. LC 77-227041. 15p. 1977. pap. 2.00 (ISBN 0-87351-117-4). Minn Hist.

Nothern Pacific. 9.95 (ISBN 0-685-83363-1). Chatham Pub CA.

Ocosta: The Ocean Terminus of the Northern Pacific Railroad & Ocean City of Washington. facs. ed. 40p. Repr. pap. 5.00 (ISBN 0-8466-0142-7, SJS142). Shorey.

Smalley, Eugene V. History of the Northern Pacific Railroad. facsimile ed. LC 75-120. (Mid-America Frontier Ser.). 1975. Repr. of 1883 ed. 27.00x (ISBN 0-405-06886-7). Arno.

Wood, Charles R. Northern Pacific. encore ed. LC 68-26752. (Illus.). 1968. 9.95 (ISBN 0-87564-504-6). Superior Pub.

NORTHERN RHODESIA

see also Zambia

Rau, William E., ed. A Bibliography of Pre-Independence Zambia: The Social Sciences. (Area Studies). 1978. lib. bdg. 45.00 (ISBN 0-8161-7872-0). G K Hall.

NORTHERN SPORADES ISLANDS

Carroll, Michael. Gates of the Wind. 8.95 (ISBN 0-7195-0197-0). Transatlantic.

NORTHMEN

see also Normans; Vikings

Anderson, R. B. Norse Mythology or the Religion of Our Forefathers. LC 77-6879. 1977. Repr. of 1891 ed. lib. bdg. 25.00 (ISBN 0-89341-147-7). Longwood Pr.

Bray, Olive, ed. & tr. Elder or Poetic Edda. LC 76-43949. (Viking Society for Northern Research: Translation Ser.: Vol. 2). Repr. of 1908 ed. 34.50 (ISBN 0-404-60012-3). AMS Pr.

Brown, George M. An Orkney Tapestry. (Illus.). 192p. 1969. 15.00x (ISBN 0-575-00318-9). Intl Pubns Serv.

Collingwood, W. G. & Steffanson, Jon, trs. Life & Death of Cormac the Skald. LC 76-43948. (Viking Society for Northern Research: Translation Ser.: Vol. 1). Repr. of 1902 ed. 24.00 (ISBN -0404-60011-5). AMS Pr.

Ekwall, Eilert, et al. Saga Book, 19 vols. (Viking Society for Northern Research). Repr. of 1895 ed. Set. 760.00 (ISBN 0-404-60030-1); 40.00 ea. AMS Pr.

Erlingsson, Thorsteinn. Ruins of the Saga-Time in Iceland. LC 76-43951. (Viking Society for Northern Research: Extra Ser.: Vol. 2). Repr. of 1899 ed. 27.00 (ISBN 0-404-60022-0). AMS Pr.

Ferguson, Sheila. Growing up in Viking Times. (Growing up Ser.). (Illus.). 72p. (gr. 6 up). 1981. 14.95 (ISBN 0-7134-2730-2, Pub. by Batsford England). David & Charles.

Froncek, Thomas. The Northmen. (The Emergence of Man Ser). (Illus.). 1974. 9.95 (ISBN 0-8094-1324-8); lib. bdg. avail. (ISBN 0-685-49690-2). Time-Life.

Hall, R. A., ed. Viking Age York & the North. (CBA Research Report Ser.: No.27). 73p. 1978. pap. text ed. 17.95x (ISBN 0-900312-65-3, Pub. by Coun Brit Archaeology). Humanities.

Horsford, E. N. Problem of the Northmen. 1977. lib. bdg. 59.95 (ISBN 0-8490-2483-8). Gordon Pr.

Johnston, Alfred W. & Johnston, Amy, eds. Caithness & Sutherland Records. (Viking Society for Northern Research: Old Lore Ser.). Repr. of 1928 ed. 27.50 (ISBN 0-404-60238-X). AMS Pr.

--Old-Lore Miscellany, 10 vols. (Viking Society for Northern Research: Old-Lore Ser.). Repr. of 1946 ed. Set. 275.00 (ISBN 0-404-60220-7). AMS Pr.

--Orkney & Shetland Records, 3 vols. (Viking Society for Northern Research: Old-Lore Ser.). Repr. of 1942 ed. Set. 82.50 (ISBN 0-404-60221-5). AMS Pr.

Leirfall, Jon. West Over Sea. 160p. 1980. 14.95 (ISBN 0-906191-15-7, Pub. by Thule Pr England). Intl Schol Bk Serv.

Mallet, Paul H. Northern Antiquities; or, a Description of the Manners, Customs, Religion & Laws of the Ancient Danes, & Other Northern Nations, 2 vols. Feldman, Burton & Richardson, Robert, eds. LC 78-60889. (Myth & Romanticism Ser.: Vol. 16). 1980. Set. lib. bdg. 132.00 (ISBN 0-8240-3565-8); lib. bdg. 66.00 ea. Garland Pub.

Nerman, Birger. Poetic Edda in the Light of Archaeology. LC 76-43954. (Viking Society for Northern Research: Extra Ser.: Vol. 4). Repr. of 1931 ed. 19.50 (ISBN 0-404-60024-7). AMS Pr.

The Norsemen. (gr. 1). 1974. pap. text ed. 2.80 (ISBN 0-205-03878-6, 8038783); tchrs.' guide 12.00 (ISBN 0-205-03866-2, 803866X). Allyn.

Schiller, Barbara. Eric the Red & Leif the Lucky. LC 78-18055. (Illus.). 48p. (gr. 4-7). 1979. PLB 5.89 (ISBN 0-89375-174-X); pap. 1.75 (ISBN 0-89375-166-9). Troll Assocs.

Smyth, Alfred P. Scandinavian Kings in the British Isles, 850-880. (Oxford Historical Monographs). 1978. 42.00x (ISBN 0-19-821865-6). Oxford U Pr.

Snorri. Heimskringla: From the Sagas of the Norse Kings. Monsen, Erling, tr. (Illus.). 398p. 1980. 35.00 (ISBN 0-906191-39-4, Pub. by Thule Pr England). Intl Schol Bk Serv.

Sturlason, S. The Heimskringla: A History of the Norse Kings, 3 vols. 1977. Set. lib. bdg. 300.00 (ISBN 0-8490-1939-7). Gordon Pr.

Turville-Petre, G. & Olszewska, E. S., trs. Life of Gudmund the Good, Bishop of Holar. LC 77-90461. (Viking Society for Northern Research: Translation Ser.: Vol. 3). Repr. of 1942 ed. 18.00 (ISBN 0-404-60013-1). AMS Pr.

Turville-Petre, J. E., tr. Story of Raud & His Sons. LC 77-90463. (Viking Society for Northern Research: Translation Ser.: Vol. 4). Repr. of 1947 ed. 11.00 (ISBN 0-404-60014-X). AMS Pr.

Viking Society for Northern Research, 41 vols. Repr. of 1977 ed. Set. 1329.00 (ISBN 0-404-60200-2). AMS Pr.

Wilson, David M. & Klindt-Jensen, Ole. Viking Art. 2nd ed. (Nordic Ser.: Vol. 6). (Illus.). 253p. 1980. 29.50x (ISBN 0-8166-0974-8); pap. 12.95 (ISBN 0-8166-0977-2). U of Minn Pr.

NORTHMEN-BIBLIOGRAPHY

Hermannsson, Halldor. Northmen in America, Nine Eighty Two-Fifteen Hundred. LC 9-18976. (Islandica Ser.: Vol. 2). 1909. pap. 8.00 (ISBN 0-527-00332-8). Kraus Repr.

NORTHMEN IN AMERICA

see America-Discovery and Exploration

NORTHUMBERLAND, ENGLAND-DESCRIPTION AND TRAVEL

Allsopp, Bruce & Clark, Ursula. Historic Architecture of Northumberland & Newcastle Upon Tyne. (Illus.). 1977. 15.00 (ISBN 0-85362-170-5, Oriel). Routledge & Kegan.

Fraser, Maxwell & Elmsley, Kenneth. Northumbria. 1978. 27.00 (ISBN 0-7134-1140-6, Pub. by Batsford England). David & Charles.

Ridley, Nancy. Portrait of Northumberland. LC 66-5457. (Portrait Bks.). (Illus.). 1966. 10.50x (ISBN 0-7091-6070-4). Intl Pubns Serv.

Sharp, Thomas. Northumberland: A Shell Guide. (Shell Guide Ser.). (Illus.). 128p. 1970. 7.95 (ISBN 0-571-04677-0, Pub. by Faber & Faber). Merrimack Bk Serv.

NORTHWEST, CANADIAN

see also Great Plains

Bryce, George. Remarkable History of the Hudson's Bay Company: Induding That of the French Traders of Northwestern Canada, & of the Astor Fur Companies. (Research & Source Works Ser.: No. 171). (Illus.). 1968. 29.50 (ISBN 0-8337-0407-9). B Franklin.

Carroll, John A., ed. Reflections of Western Historians. LC 68-9335. 1969. 2.00 (ISBN 0-8165-0187-4). U of Ariz Pr.

Faraud, Henri J. Dix-Huit Ans Chez Les Sauvages: Voyages Et Missions De Monseigneur Henry Faraud. Repr. of 1866 ed. 23.00 (ISBN 0-384-15135-3). Johnson Repr.

Gates, Charles M., ed. Five Fur Traders of the Northwest: Narrative of Peter Pond & the Diaries of John Macdonell et Al. LC 65-63528. 296p. 1971. Repr. of 1933 ed. 7.25 (ISBN 0-87351-024-0). Minn Hist.

Gluek, Alvin C., Jr. Minnesota & the Manifest Destiny of the Canadian Northwest: A Study in Canadian-American Relations. LC 77-536946. 1965. 25.00x (ISBN 0-8020-5162-6). U of Toronto Pr.

Hargrave, James. Hargrave Correspondence, 1821-1843. Glazebrook, G. P., ed. LC 68-28612. 1968. Repr. of 1938 ed. lib. bdg. 32.50x (ISBN 0-8371-5062-0, HAHC). Greenwood.

Hargrave, Letitia M. Letters of Letitia Hargrave. Macleod, Margaret A., ed. LC 69-14502. 1968. Repr. of 1947 ed. lib. bdg. 24.50x (ISBN 0-8371-5065-5, HALE). Greenwood.

Hearne, Samuel. Journals of Samuel Hearne & Philip Turnor. Tyrrell, J. B., ed. LC 68-28609. 1968. Repr. of 1934 ed. lib. bdg. 44.25x (ISBN 0-8371-5059-0, HEJH). Greenwood.

Innis, Harold A. Fur Trade in Canada: An Introduction to Canadian Economic History. rev. ed. LC 57-2937. 1956. pap. 10.00 (ISBN 0-8020-6001-3). U of Toronto Pr.

Irwin, Leonard B. Pacific Railways & Nationalism in the Canadian American Northwest, 1845-1873. LC 69-10107. 1969. Repr. of 1939 ed. lib. bdg. 15.75x (ISBN 0-8371-0495-5, IRPR). Greenwood.

Knauth, Percy. The North Woods. LC 72-88525. (American Wilderness Ser). (Illus.). (gr. 6 up). 1972. lib. bdg. 11.97 (ISBN 0-8094-1165-2, Pub. by Time-Life). Silver.

Lingard, C. Cecil. Territorial Government in Canada: The Autonomy Question in the Old North-West Territories. (Scholarly Reprint Ser.). 1980. Repr. 30.00x (ISBN 0-8020-7095-7). U of Toronto Pr.

Morton, Arthur S. History of the Canadian West to 1870-71. 2nd ed. Thomas, Lewis G., ed. LC 72-97150. (Illus.). 1973. 35.00x (ISBN 0-8020-4033-0). U of Toronto Pr.

Owram, Doug. Promise of Eden: The Canadian Expansionist Movement & the Idea of the West, 1856-1900. 1980. 25.00x (ISBN 0-8020-5483-8); pap. 10.00 (ISBN 0-8020-6385-3). U of Toronto Pr.

Radisson, Pierre E. Voyages of Peter Esprit Radisson, Being an Account of His Travels & Experiences Among the North American Indians, from 1652 to 1684. Scull, Gideon D., ed. (Illus.). 1885. 26.50 (ISBN 0-8337-3285-4). B Franklin.

Robson, Joseph. An Account of Six Years Residence in Hudson's Bay: From 1733 to 1736, & 1744 to 1747. Repr. of 1757 ed. 13.00 (ISBN 0-384-51580-0). Johnson Repr.

Sandoz, Mari. Beaver Men. (American Procession Ser). (Illus.). 1975. Repr. of 1964 ed. 10.95 (ISBN 0-8038-0674-4). Hastings.

Stanley, George F. Birth of Western Canada: A History of the Riel Rebellions. LC 61-1393. (Illus.). 1960. pap. 10.95 (ISBN 0-8020-6010-2). U of Toronto Pr.

Wallace, William S., ed. Documents Relating to the North West Company. LC 68-28610. 1968. Repr. of 1934 ed. lib. bdg. 33.00x (ISBN 0-8371-5060-4, WADR). Greenwood.

NORTHWEST, CANADIAN-DESCRIPTION AND TRAVEL

Anderson, David. The Net in the Bay: Or, Journal of a Visit to Moose & Albany. 18.50 (ISBN 0-384-01401-1). Johnson Repr.

Butler, William F. The Wild Northland, Being the Story of a Winter Journey, with Dogs, Across Northern North America. LC 72-2824. (American Explorers Ser.). Repr. of 1922 ed. 26.00 (ISBN 0-404-54904-7). AMS Pr.

Dawson, Simon J. Report on the Exploration of the Country Between Lake Superior & the Red River Settlement, & Between the Latter Place & the Assiniboine & Saskatchewan. LC 68-55184. 1968. Repr. of 1859 ed. lib. bdg. 40.00x (ISBN 0-8371-5031-0, DALS). Greenwood.

De Smet, P. J. Life, Letters, & Travels, Eighteen Hundred One to Eighteen Seventy Three, 4 Vols. in 2. 1905. Set. 60.00 (ISBN 0-527-83900-0). Kraus Repr.

Franchere, Gabriel. Adventure at Astoria, Eighteen Ten to Eighteen Fourteen. Franchere, Hoyt C., tr. (American Exploration & Travel Ser.: No. 53). (Illus.). 1967. 9.95 (ISBN 0-8061-0747-2). U of Okla Pr.

Franklin, John. Narrative of a Journey to the Shores of the Polar Sea, in the Years 1819 - 1822. LC 68-55187. 1968. Repr. of 1823 ed. lib. bdg. 40.25x (ISBN 0-8371-1447-0, FRPS). Greenwood.

--Narrative of a Second Expedition to the Shores of the Polar Sea. LC 71-133871. (Illus.). 1971. Repr. 23.10 (ISBN 0-8048-1008-7). C E Tuttle.

--Narrative of a Second Expedition to the Shores of the Polar Sea, in the Years 1825, 1826, & 1827. LC 68-55188. 1968. Repr. of 1828 ed. lib. bdg. 26.50x (ISBN 0-8371-1750-X, FRSE). Greenwood.

Harmon, Daniel W. A Journal of Voyages & Travels in the Interior of North America. LC 72-2829. (American Explorers Ser.). (Illus.). Repr. of 1922 ed. 27.00 (ISBN 0-404-54911-X). AMS Pr.
Hearne, Samuel. Journey from Prince of Wale's Fort in Hudson's Bay to the Northern Ocean. LC 78-133870. (Illus.). 1971. 19.25 (ISBN 0-8048-1007-9). C E Tuttle.
--Journey from Prince of Wales's Fort in Hudson's Bay to the Northern Ocean in the Years 1769-1772. LC 68-28601. (Illus.). 1968. Repr. of 1911 ed. lib. bdg. 32.75x (ISBN 0-8371-5045-0, HEJP). Greenwood.
Hind, Henry Y. Narrative of the Canadian Red River Exploring Expedition of 1857, 2 vols. in 1. LC 70-133868. (Illus.). 1971. 23.10 (ISBN 0-8048-1009-5). C E Tuttle.
--Narrative of the Canadian Red River Exploring Expedition of 1857, & of the Assiniboine & Saskatchewan Exploring Expedition of 1858, 2 Vols. LC 68-55195. (Illus.). 1968. Repr. of 1860 ed. Set. lib. bdg. 35.00x (ISBN 0-8371-3896-5, HIRR). Greenwood.
--North-West Territory: Reports of Progress. Bd. with Report on the Exploration. LC 68-55184. 1968. Repr. of 1859 ed. lib. bdg. 40.00x (ISBN 0-8371-5031-0, DALS). Greenwood.
Laut, Agnes C. Pathfinders of the West. LC 74-90651. (Essay Index Reprint Ser). 1904. 25.00 (ISBN 0-8369-1220-9). Arno.
Lavender, David. The Trans-Canada Canoe Trail. LC 77-4864. (American Trail Ser.). 1977. 11.50 (ISBN 0-07-036678-0, GB). McGraw.
Mackenzie, Alexander. First Man West. Sheppe, Walter, ed. LC 76-3568. (Illus.). 366p. 1976. Repr. of 1962 ed. lib. bdg. 24.00x (ISBN 0-8371-8789-3, SHFM). Greenwood.
--Voyages from Montreal Through the Continent of North America to the Frozen & Pacific Oceans in 1789 & 1793, with an Account of the Rise & State of the Fur Trade, 2 vols. LC 72-2721. (American Explorers Ser.). Repr. of 1922 ed. 47.50 (ISBN 0-404-54912-8). AMS Pr.
McLean, John. Notes of a Twenty-Five Years' Service in the Hudson's Bay Territory. Wallace, W. S., ed. LC 68-28607. 1968. Repr. of 1932 ed. lib. bdg. 29.50x (ISBN 0-8371-5057-4, MCNS). Greenwood.
Nickerson, E. B. Kayaks to the Arctic. LC 67-27369. (Illus.). 1967. 4.95 (ISBN 0-8310-7065-X). Howell-North.
Olson, Sigurd F. Runes of the North. 1963. 10.95 (ISBN 0-394-44348-9). Knopf.
Palliser, John. Exploration - British North America: Papers, 2 Vols. LC 68-55211. (Illus.). 1968. Repr. of 1860 ed. lib. bdg. 18.75x (ISBN 0-8371-1430-6, PABN). Greenwood.
Richardson, John. Arctic Searching Expedition: A Journal of a Boat Voyage Through Rupert's Land & the Arctic Sea, in Search of the Discovery Ships Under Command of Sir John Franklin, 2 Vols. LC 68-55214. 1968. Repr. of 1851 ed. Set. lib. bdg. 31.75x (ISBN 0-8371-3858-2, RIAS). Greenwood.
Robson, Joseph. An Account of Six Years Residence in Hudson's Bay: From 1733 to 1736, & 1744 to 1747. Repr. of 1757 ed. 13.00 (ISBN 0-384-51580-0). Johnson Repr.
Ross, Eric. Beyond the River & the Bay: The Canadian Northwest in 1811. LC 71-486954. (Illus.). 1970. pap. 6.00 (ISBN 0-8020-6188-5). U of Toronto Pr.
Savishinsky, Joel S. The Trail of the Hare. new ed. (Library of Anthropology Ser.). (Illus.). 304p. 1975. 27.00x (ISBN 0-677-04140-3). Gordon.
Simpson, George. Fur Trade & Empire: George Simpson's Journal, 1824-1825. rev. ed. Merk, Frederick, ed. LC 68-15646. 1968. 20.00x (ISBN 0-674-33500-7, Belknap Pr). Harvard U Pr.
Thompson, David. David Thompson's Narrative of His Explorations in Western America, 1784-1812. Tyrrell, J. B., ed. LC 68-28603. Repr. of 1916 ed. lib. bdg. 50.00x (ISBN 0-8371-3879-5, THNE). Greenwood.
Vandiveer, Clarence A. Fur-Trade & Early Western Exploration. LC 73-145876. (Illus.). 1971. Repr. of 1929 ed. lib. bdg. 14.50x (ISBN 0-8154-0381-X). Cooper Sq.
Voyage of Alexander Mackenzie. facs. ed. Repr. pap. 5.75 (ISBN 0-8466-0182-6, SJS182). Shorey.

NORTHWEST, NEW
see Northwestern States

NORTHWEST, OLD
see also Middle West

Bond, Beverley W., Jr. Civilization of the Old Northwest. LC 71-88787. (BCL Ser.: Ii). Repr. of 1934 ed. 12.50 (ISBN 0-404-00935-2). AMS Pr.
Hoffman, Charles F. Winter in the West, 2 Vols. LC 70-108493. 1970. Repr. of 1835 ed. Set. 35.00 (ISBN 0-403-00215-X). Scholarly.
Keating, William H. Narrative of the Expedition to the Source of St. Peter's River. facsimile ed. (Illus.). 1825. 12.50 (ISBN 0-87018-036-3). Ross.
Mason, Philipp, ed. Schoolcraft's Expedition to Lake Itasca: The Discovery of the Source of the Mississippi. xxvi, 390p. 1958. 10.00 (ISBN 0-87013-040-4). Mich St U Pr.
Ossoli, Margaret F. Summer on the Lakes. LC 68-24991. (Concordance Ser., No. 37). 1969. Repr. of 1844 ed. lib. bdg. 24.95 (ISBN 0-8383-0225-4). Haskell.
The Territory Northwest of the River Ohio, 1787-1803. (The Territorial Papers of the United States: Vol. 3). Repr. of 1934 ed. 69.50 (ISBN 0-404-01453-4). AMS Pr.

NORTHWEST, OLD-DESCRIPTION AND TRAVEL

Beste, J. Richard. Wabash, or Adventures of an English Gentleman's Family in the Interior of America, 2 Vols. facs. ed. LC 75-121498. (Select Bibliographies Reprint Ser). 1855. 36.00 (ISBN 0-8369-5456-4). Arno.
Davenport, Marge. Best of the Old Northwest. LC 80-83780. (Illus., Orig.). 1981. pap. 6.95 (ISBN 0-938274-00-7). Paddlewheel.
Loam, Jayson. Hot Springs & Pools of the Northwest. (Illus.). 160p. 1980. pap. 7.95 (ISBN 0-88496-143-5). Capra Pr.
Peck, John M. A Guide for Emigrants: Containing Sketches of Illinois, Missouri, & the Adjacent Parts. facsimile ed. LC 75-115. (Mid-American Frontier Ser.). 1975. Repr. of 1831 ed. 19.00x (ISBN 0-405-06881-6). Arno.
Schoolcraft, Henry R. Personal Memoirs of a Residence of Thirty Years with the Indian Tribes on the American Frontiers: 1812-1842. facsimile ed. LC 75-119. (Mid-American Frontier Ser.). 1975. Repr. of 1851 ed. 41.00x (ISBN 0-405-06885-9). Arno.

NORTHWEST, OLD-ECONOMIC CONDITIONS

Bond, Beverley W., Jr. Civilization of the Old Northwest. facs. ed. LC 73-124226. (Select Bibliographies Reprint Ser). 1934. 20.00 (ISBN 0-8369-5415-7). Arno.

NORTHWEST, OLD-HISTORY

Adams, Herbert B. Maryland's Influence Upon Land Cessions to the U. S. LC 77-97563. Repr. of 1885 ed. 11.50 (ISBN 0-404-00286-2). AMS Pr.
Benton, Elbert J. The Wabash Trade Route in the Development of the Old Northwest. LC 78-63893. (Johns Hopkins University. Studies in the Social Sciences. Twenty-First Ser. 1903: 1-2). Repr. of 1903 ed. 11.50 (ISBN 0-404-61147-8). AMS Pr.
Brady, Cyrus T. Northwestern Fights & Fighters. 1974. Repr. of 1907 ed. 10.00 (ISBN 0-685-56786-9). Corner Hse.
Burnet, Jacob. Notes on the Early Settlement of the North-Western Territory. facsimile ed. LC 75-90. (Mid-American Frontier Ser.). 1975. Repr. of 1847 ed. 28.00x (ISBN 0-405-06857-3). Arno.
Butterfield, C. W. History of the Discovery of the Northwest by John Nicolet in 1634. LC 68-26262. 1969. Repr. of 1881 ed. 12.00 (ISBN 0-8046-0059-7). Kennikat.
Dillon, John B. History of Indiana from Its Earliest Exploration by Europeans to the Close of Territorial Government in 1816. LC 73-146392. (First American Frontier Ser). (Illus.). 1971. Repr. of 1859 ed. 30.00 (ISBN 0-405-02845-8). Arno.
Dyer, Albion M. First Ownership of Ohio Lands. LC 69-18897. 1978. Repr. of 1911 ed. 7.50 (ISBN 0-8063-0098-1). Genealog Pub.
Fernow, Berthold. Ohio Valley in Colonial Days. LC 70-149231. 1971. Repr. of 1890 ed. 21.50 (ISBN 0-8337-1116-4). B Franklin.
Gates, Charles M., ed. Five Fur Traders of the Northwest: Narrative of Peter Pond & the Diaries of John Macdonell et Al. LC 65-63528. 296p. 1971. Repr. of 1933 ed. 7.25 (ISBN 0-87351-024-0). Minn Hist.
Gilpin, Alec R. War of Eighteen-Twelve in the Old Northwest. (Illus.). vii, 286p. 1958. 6.50 (ISBN 0-87013-032-3). Mich St U Pr.
Havighurst, Walter H. Upper Mississippi Valley. LC 66-19220. 1966. pap. 2.95 (ISBN 0-8077-1506-9). Tchrs Coll.
Hinsdale, Burke A. The Old Northwest: The Beginnings of Our Colonial System (Revised Edition) facsimile ed. LC 75-104. (Mid-American Frontier Ser.). 1975. Repr. of 1899 ed. 25.00x (ISBN 0-405-06872-7). Arno.
Kellogg, Louise P. French Regime in Wisconsin & the Northwest. LC 68-31296. 1968. Repr. of 1925 ed. 18.50x (ISBN 0-8154-0127-2). Cooper Sq.
Kellogg, Louise T. British Regime in Wisconsin & the Northwest. LC 74-124927. (American Scene Ser). (Illus.). 1970. Repr. of 1935 ed. lib. bdg. 35.00 (ISBN 0-306-71047-1). Da Capo.
Kohlemeier, A. L. Old Northwest As the Keystone of the Arch of American Federal Union: A Study in Commerce & Politics. 1938. 3.70 (ISBN 0-911536-25-6). Trinity U Pr.
Kohlmeier, Albert L. The Old Northwest As the Keystone of the Arch of American Federal Union: A Study in Commerce & Politics. LC 38-2230. (History of American Economy Ser.). 1970. Repr. of 1938 ed. 14.00 (ISBN 0-384-30070-7). Johnson Repr.
M'Clung, John A. Sketches of Western Adventure. LC 76-90184. (Mass Violence in America Ser). Repr. of 1832 ed. 13.00 (ISBN 0-405-01326-4). Arno.
Nute, Grace L. Rainy River Country: A Brief History of the Region Bordering Minnesota & Ontario. LC 71-96385. (Illus.). 143p. 1950. pap. 3.75 (ISBN 0-87351-008-9). Minn Hist.
Rohrbough, Malcolm J. The Trans-Appalachian Frontier. (Illus.). 1978. 22.50x (ISBN 0-19-502209-2). Oxford U Pr.
Roosevelt, Theodore. Winning of the West. Wish, Harvey, ed. & intro. by. 8.00 (ISBN 0-8446-2827-1). Peter Smith.
Russell, Nelson V. The British Regime in Michigan & the Old North-West 1760-1796. LC 78-10896. (Perspectives in Americn History Ser.: No. 40). xi, 302p. Repr. of 1939 ed. lib. bdg. 17.50x (ISBN 0-87991-364-9). Porcupine Pr.
Schuyler, Robert L. Transition in Illinois from British to American Government. Repr. of 1909 ed. 16.00 (ISBN 0-404-05627-X). AMS Pr.
Skaggs, David C., ed. Old Northwest in the American Revolution: An Anthology. LC 77-1757. 1977. 10.00 (ISBN 0-87020-164-6). State Hist Soc Wisc.
Thwaites, Reuben G. How George Rogers Clark Won the Northwest, & Other Essays in Western History. facs. ed. LC 68-22949. (Essay Index Reprint Ser). 1903. 19.50 (ISBN 0-8369-0943-7). Arno.
Van Every, Dale. A Company of Heroes: The American Frontier, 1775-1783. LC 76-1391. (Frontier People of America Ser.). 1976. Repr. of 1962 ed. 15.00x (ISBN 0-405-05542-0). Arno.

NORTHWEST, OLD-HISTORY-FICTION

Boyd, Thomas. Shadow of Long Knives. 6.75 (ISBN 0-8446-1086-0). Peter Smith.

NORTHWEST, OLD-HISTORY-SOURCES

Beers, Henry P. The French & British in the Old Northwest: A Bibliographical Guide to the Archive & Manuscript Sources. LC 64-13305. 1964. 12.95x (ISBN 0-8143-1235-7). Wayne St U Pr.
Kellogg, Louise P., ed. Early Narratives of the Northwest, 1634-1699. (Original Narratives). 1967. Repr. of 1917 ed. 18.50x (ISBN 0-06-480455-0). B&N.
Smith, William H. St. Clair Papers: The Life & Public Services of Arthur St. Clair, 2 Vols. facs. ed. LC 77-117894. (Select Bibliographies Reprint Ser). 1881. Set. 56.00 (ISBN 0-8369-5347-9). Arno.
--Saint Clair Papers: The Life & Public Services of Arthur St. Clair, with His Correspondence & Other Papers, 2 Vols. LC 79-119058. (Illus.). 1970. Repr. of 1882 ed. lib. bdg. 95.00 (ISBN 0-686-76847-7). Da Capo.

NORTHWEST, OLD-POLITICS AND GOVERNMENT

Bemis, Edward W. Local Government in Michigan & the Northwest. LC 78-63735. (Johns Hopkins University. Studies in the Social Sciences. First Ser. 1882-1883: 5). Repr. of 1883 ed. 11.50 (ISBN 0-404-61005-6). AMS Pr.
Bond, Beverley W., Jr. Civilization of the Old Northwest. facs. ed. LC 73-124226. (Select Bibliographies Reprint Ser). 1934. 20.00 (ISBN 0-8369-5415-7). Arno.
Shade, William G. Banks or No Banks: The Money Issue in Western Politics, 1832-1865. LC 72-4229. 1973. 15.95x (ISBN 0-685-30224-5). Wayne St U Pr.

NORTHWEST, OLD-SOCIAL LIFE AND CUSTOMS

Bond, Beverley W., Jr. Civilization of the Old Northwest. facs. ed. LC 73-124226. (Select Bibliographies Reprint Ser). 1934. 20.00 (ISBN 0-8369-5415-7). Arno.

NORTHWEST, PACIFIC
Here are entered works on the old Oregon country, comprising the present states of Oregon, Washington and Idaho, parts of Montana and Wyoming and the province of British Columbia.

Bellas, Carl J. Industrial Democracy & the Worker-Owned Firm: A Study of Twenty-One Plywood Companies in the Pacific Northwest. LC 72-80459. (Special Studies in U. S. Economic, Social,& Political Issues). 1972. 21.00x (ISBN 0-275-28616-9). Irvington.
Cunningham, Imogen. Imogen! Imogen Cunningham Photographs 1910-1973. LC 74-2490. (Index of Art in the Pacific Northwest Ser.: No. 7). (Illus.). 112p. 1974. 20.00 (ISBN 0-295-95332-2); pap. 10.95 (ISBN 0-295-95333-0). U of Wash Pr.
Doig, Ivan. Winter Brothers: A Season at the Edge of America. LC 80-7933. (Illus.). 352p. 1980. 12.95 (ISBN 0-15-197186-2). HarBraceJ.
Drazan, Joseph G. The Pacific Northwest: An Index to People & Places in Books. LC 79-16683. 176p. 1979. 10.00 (ISBN 0-8108-1234-7). Scarecrow.
Gibbs, James A. Sentinels of the North Pacific. (Illus.). 274p. 1975. pap. 5.95 (ISBN 0-8323-0254-6). Binford.
Hines, Gustavus. Oregon: Its History, Condition & Prospects. LC 72-9450. (The Far Western Frontier Ser.). (Illus.). 444p. 1973. Repr. of 1851 ed. 20.00 (ISBN 0-405-04978-1). Arno.
Lambert, Dale. The Pacific Northwest: Past, Present & Future. Belina, Tom, ed. (Illus.). 414p. (gr. 8-12). 11.95 (ISBN 0-939688-00-X); tchr's ed. 5.00 (ISBN 0-939688-01-8); wkbk. 2.95 (ISBN 0-939688-03-4); lab manual 9.95 (ISBN 0-939688-02-6). Directed Media.
Lee, Kai N., et al. Electric Power & the Future of the Pacific Northwest. LC 79-6762. (Illus.). 340p. 1980. 16.95 (ISBN 0-295-95720-4). U of Wash Pr.
Le Roy, Bruce, notes by. Northwest Forts & Trading Posts. (Illus.). 35p. 1968. pap. 2.00 (ISBN 0-917048-20-2). Wash St Hist Soc.
Speck, Gordon. Northwest Explorations. 2nd ed. LC 70-92541. (Illus.). 1970. 8.95 (ISBN 0-8323-0216-3). Binford.
Teben'Kov, Mikhail N. Atlas of the North Pacific. Pierce, Richard A., ed. (Alaska History Ser.: No. 21). (Illus.). 1981. 17.50x (ISBN 0-919642-55-1). Limestone Pr.
Thomas, Lewis H. The Struggle for Responsible Government in the North-West Territories 1870-97. 2nd ed. LC 56-3490. 1978. 22.50x (ISBN 0-8020-2287-1); pap. 7.50 (ISBN 0-8020-6327-6). U of Toronto Pr.

NORTHWEST, PACIFIC-ANTIQUITIES

Seaman, N. G. Indian Relics of the Pacific Northwest. 2nd enl. ed. LC 66-28021. (Illus.). 1967. pap. 5.95 (ISBN 0-8323-0236-8). Binford.
Stewart, Hilary. Indian Artifacts of the Northwest Coast. LC 73-84986. (Illus.). 172p. 1976. 20.00 (ISBN 0-295-95419-1). U of Wash Pr.

NORTHWEST, PACIFIC-BIBLIOGRAPHY

Connette, Earle. Pacific Northwest Quarterly Index: Vol. 1. 1906 - Vol. 53. 1962. 1964. 27.50 (ISBN 0-208-00036-4, Archon). Shoe String.
University of Washington at Seattle. The Dictionary Catalog of the Pacific Northwest Collection of the University of Washington Libraries, 6 vols. 1972. Set. lib. bdg. 640.00 (ISBN 0-8161-0985-0). G K Hall.

NORTHWEST, PACIFIC-DESCRIPTION AND TRAVEL

Arno, Stephen F. Northwest Trees. LC 77-82369. (Illus.). 1977. 30.00 (ISBN 0-916890-55-4); pap. 6.95 (ISBN 0-916890-50-3). Mountaineers.
Brogan, Phil F., ed. East of the Cascades. LC 63-23702. (Illus.). 1976. 9.95 (ISBN 0-8323-0005-5); pap. 6.50 (ISBN 0-8323-0277-5). Binford.
Busk, Fred & Andrews, Peter. Country Inns of America: Pacific Northwest. LC 81-1617. (Illus.). 96p. 1981. pap. 8.95 (ISBN 0-03-059181-3, Owl Bk). HR&W.
Byways of the Northwest. LC 76-662. (Illus.). 120p. (Photos & Text by R. Moland Reynolds). 1976. pap. 8.95 (ISBN 0-912856-29-7). Graphic Arts Ctr.
Ekman, Leonard C. Scenic Geology of the Pacific Northwest. 2nd. ed. LC 61-13278. (Illus.). 1970. 8.95 (ISBN 0-8323-0130-2). Binford.
Exploration Northwest. (Illus.). 1969. pap. 2.00 (ISBN 0-917048-51-2). Wash St Hist Soc.
Fanning, Edmund. Voyages to the South Seas & to the Northwest Coast of America. enl. ed. 1970. Repr. of 1838 ed. 14.95 (ISBN 0-87770-012-5). Ye Galleon.
Green, Jonathan. Journal of a Tour on the Northwest Coast in 1829. Date not set. 7.50 (ISBN 0-87770-013-3). Ye Galleon.
Gulick, Bill. Snake River Country. LC 71-140117. (Illus.). 1971. 35.00 (ISBN 0-87004-215-7). Caxton.
Hayden, Mike. Exploring the North Coast. (Illus.). 1976. pap. 4.95 (ISBN 0-87701-085-4). Chronicle Bks.
Highsmith, Richard M. & Kimerling, A. Jon, eds. Atlas of the Pacific Northwest. 6th ed. (Illus.). 1979. 20.00 (ISBN 0-87071-408-2); pap. text ed. 8.00x (ISBN 0-87071-409-0). Oreg St U Pr.
Mercer, Asa S. Washington Territory, the Great North-West, Her Material Resources & Claims to Emigration. 40p. Repr. of 1865 ed. pap. 4.95 (ISBN 0-87770-106-7). Ye Galleon.
Parker, Samuel. Journal of Exploring Tour Etc. Repr. 10.00 (ISBN 0-87018-046-0). Ross.
Ramsay, Cynthia. America's Spectacular Northwest. LC 80-7829. (Illus.). 200p. 6.95 (ISBN 0-87044-363-1); lib. bdg. 8.50 (ISBN 0-87044-368-2). Natl Geog.
Render, Lorne E. The Mountains & the Sky. LC 75-27295. (Illus.). 224p. 1976. 27.50 (ISBN 0-295-95462-0). U of Wash Pr.

Settle, Dionyse, ed. A True Report on the Last Voyage into the West & Northwest Regions, & C. 1577: Worthily Atchieued by Capteine Frobisher of the Sayde Voyage the First Finder & Generall. 63p. Date not set. pap. price not set (ISBN 0-87770-073-7). Ye Galleon.

Smith, Lynwood S. Living Shores of the Pacific Northwest. LC 76-17153. (Illus.). 160p. (YA) 1976. pap. 10.95 (ISBN 0-914718-14-2). Pacific Search.

Sunset Editors. Beautiful Northwest. 2nd ed. LC 77-78147. (Illus.). 224p. 1977. pap. 8.95 (ISBN 0-376-05053-5, Sunset Bks). Sunset-Lane.

Swan, James Gilchrist. The Northwest Coast, or Three Years Residence in Washington Territory. Date not set. Repr. of 1857 ed. price not set (ISBN 0-685-56554-8). Ye Galleon.

Thompson, David. David Thompson's Narrative of His Explorations in Western America, 1784-1812. Tyrrell, J. B., ed. LC 68-28603. Repr. of 1916 ed. lib. bdg. 50.00x (ISBN 0-8371-3879-5, THNE). Greenwood.

Trzyna, Thomas N., ed. The Northwest Handbook: A Guide to Organizations & Information Resources in the Pacific Northwest. LC 81-67063. (Western America Ser.). (Illus.). 150p. 1981. pap. 20.00x (ISBN 0-912102-55-1). Cal Inst Public.

Victor, Frances F. The River of the West: Life & Adventure in the Rocky Mountains & Oregon. LC 74-83523. (Illus.). 602p. 1974. Repr. of 1870 ed. 15.00 (ISBN 0-914418-02-5). Brooks-Sterling.

NORTHWEST, PACIFIC–DESCRIPTION AND TRAVEL–GUIDEBOOKS

Berssen, William, ed. Pacific Boating Almanac: Oregon, Wash., B.C. & Alaska. (Illus.). 432p. 1982. pap. 7.95 (ISBN 0-930030-22-2). Western Marine Ent.

Clark, Lewis J. Wild Flowers of Marsh & Waterway. (Lewis Clark's Field Guides: E.T.T.A.). 1974. pap. 4.95 (ISBN 0-88826-052-0). Superior Pub.

Guide to California & the Northwest. 1981. 4.95 (ISBN 0-89102-163-9). B Franklin.

Hitchcock, Anthony & Lindgren, Jean. California & the Pacific Northwest Historical & Sightseeing Guide. LC 79-16770. (The Compleat Traveler's Guides Ser.). (Illus.). 1980. pap. 4.95 (ISBN 0-89102-163-9). B Franklin.

Pacific Search Press. The Northwest Adventure Guide. LC 80-24309. (Illus.). 1981. pap. 5.95 (ISBN 0-914718-54-1). Pacific Search.

Rankin, Marni & Rankin, Jake. The Getaway Guide: Short Vacations in the Pacific Northwest. LC 79-17626. (Illus.). 192p. 1979. pap. 8.95 (ISBN 0-914718-47-9). Pacific Search.

Wood, Amos L. Hiking Trails in the Pacific Northwest. (Illus.). 1977. 5.95 (ISBN 0-8092-7238-5). Contemp Bks.

NORTHWEST, PACIFIC–HISTORY

Appleton, Marion B., ed. Index of Pacific Northwest Portraits. LC 70-38982. (Pacific Northwest Library Association, Reference Division). 220p. 1972. 15.00 (ISBN 0-295-95179-6). U of Wash Pr.

Bell, James C., Jr. Opening a Highway to the Pacific, 1838-1846. LC 68-56648. (Columbia University Studies in the Social Sciences: No. 217). Repr. of 1921 ed. 18.50 (ISBN 0-404-51217-8). AMS Pr.

Berthold, Mary P. Including Two Captains: A Later Look. LC 75-13400. 1975. 6.00 (ISBN 0-8187-0023-8). Harlo Pr.

Bingham, Edwin R. & Love, Glen A., eds. Northwest Perspectives: Essays on the Culture of the Pacific Northwest. LC 77-15189. 264p. 1979. 14.95 (ISBN 0-295-95594-5); pap. 7.95 (ISBN 0-295-95805-7). U of Wash Pr.

Cook, Warren L. Flood Tide of Empire: Spain & the Pacific Northwest, 1543-1819. LC 72-75187. (Western Americana Ser.: No. 24). (Illus.). 672p. 1973. 37.50x (ISBN 0-300-01577-1). Yale U Pr.

Dillon, Richard. The Siskiyou Trail: The Hudson's Bay Company Route to California. LC 74-23553. 416p. 1975. 9.95 (ISBN 0-07-016980-2, GB). McGraw.

Evans, Elwood. Washington Territory. facs. ed. Repr. of 1877 ed. pap. 5.75 (ISBN 0-8466-0129-X, SJS129). Shorey.

Fogdall, Alberta B. Royal Family of the Columbia. (Illus.). 1978. 14.95 (ISBN 0-87770-168-7). Ye Galleon.

Fuller, George W. A History of the Pacific Northwest. LC 75-41106. Repr. of 1931 ed. 32.50 (ISBN 0-404-14664-3). AMS Pr.

Hadley, Douglas. Stories Told in Winter. (Illus.). 76p. 1979. 50.00 (ISBN 0-918400-02-3, Pub. by Champoeg Pr). Intl Schol Bk Serv.

Hazard, Joseph T. Companion of Adventure. (Illus.). 1952. 8.95 (ISBN 0-8323-0059-4). Binford.

Henry & Thompson. New Light on Early History of the Greater Northwest, 2 vols. Repr. 22.50, boxed set (ISBN 0-87018-025-8). Ross.

Hines, Donald M. An Index of Archived Resources for a Folklife & Cultural History of the Inland Pacific Northwest Frontier. LC 76-15898. 190p. (Sponsored by the Eastern Washington State Historical Society). 1976. 18.25 (ISBN 0-8357-0174-3, SS-00010, Pub by University Microfilms International). Univ Microfilms.

Johansen, Dorothy O. & Gates, C. M. Empire of the Columbia: A History of the Pacific Northwest. 2nd ed. 1967. text ed. 21.50 scp (ISBN 0-06-043321-3, HarpC). Har-Row.

Judson, Phoebe Goodell. A Pioneer's Search for an Ideal Home. McClelland, John M., Jr., ed. LC 66-27824. (Illus.). 207p. 1966. 5.00 (ISBN 0-917048-22-9). Wash St Hist Soc.

Kip, Lawrence. Army Life on the Pacific. Date not set. price not set (ISBN 0-87770-016-8). Ye Galleon.

Lavender, David. Land of Giants: The Drive to the Pacific Northwest, 1750-1950. LC 78-27240. xii, 468p. 1979. 22.50x (ISBN 0-8032-2854-6); pap. 7.50 (ISBN 0-8032-7905-1, BB 679, Bison). U of Nebr Pr.

Miller, Don C. & Cohen, Stan B. Military & Trading Posts of Montana. LC 78-70407. (Illus.). 116p. 1978. 12.95 (ISBN 0-933126-01-8); pap. 7.95 (ISBN 0-933126-00-X). Pictorial Hist.

Ranck, Glenn N. Pictures from Northwest History. 38p. Repr. of 1902 ed. pap. 4.25 (ISBN 0-8466-0115-X, SJS115). Shorey.

Ray, Verne F. Cultural Relations in the Plateau of Northwestern America. LC 76-43807. Repr. of 1939 ed. 18.50 (ISBN 0-404-15664-9). AMS Pr.

--Cultural Relations in the Plateau Region of Northwestern America. (Illus.). 1954. 5.00 (ISBN 0-686-20673-8). Southwest Mus.

Richard, David B. Puget Sounds: A Nostalgic Review of Radio & TV in the Great Northwest. LC 80-26557. (Illus.). 192p. 1981. 19.95 (ISBN 0-87564-636-0). Superior Pub.

Rundall, Thomas, ed. Narratives of Voyages Toward the North-West in Search of a Passage to Cathay & India, 1496 to 1631. LC 78-134705. (Hakluyt Society Ser.: No. 5). 1970. lib. bdg. 30.50 (ISBN 0-8337-3095-9). B Franklin.

Saunders, Mary. The Whitman Massacre. 1978. 5.50 (ISBN 0-87770-188-1); pap. 2.95 (ISBN 0-685-87578-4). Ye Galleon.

Serven, James E. Conquering the Frontiers. LC 74-75583. 1974. 19.95 (ISBN 0-910618-39-9). Foun Pubns.

Settle, Dionyse, ed. A True Report on the Last Voyage into the West & Northwest Regions, & C. 1577: Worthily Atchieued by Capteine Frobisher of the Sayde Voyage the First Finder & Generall. 63p. Date not set. pap. price not set (ISBN 0-87770-073-7). Ye Galleon.

Speck, Gordon. Northwest Explorations. 2nd ed. LC 70-92541. (Illus.). 1970. 8.95 (ISBN 0-8323-0216-3). Binford.

Warren, Sidney. Farthest Frontier: The Pacific Northwest. LC 79-110332. 1970. Repr. of 1949 ed. 14.50 (ISBN 0-8046-0876-8). Kennikat.

Winther, O. O. Old Oregon Country. 1950. pap. 18.00 (ISBN 0-527-97400-5). Kraus Repr.

Work, John. The Snake Country Expedition of 1830-1831: John Work's Field Journal. Haines, Francis D., Jr., ed. (American Exploration & Travel Ser.: No. 59). (Illus.). 224p. 1971. 11.95 (ISBN 0-8061-0947-5). U of Okla Pr.

Wright, Elizabeth. Miller Freeman, Man of Action. LC 76-29566. (Illus.). 1977. pap. 10.00 (ISBN 0-87930-060-4). Miller Freeman.

NORTHWEST, PACIFIC–HISTORY–BIBLIOGRAPHY

Crumb, Lawrence N. Historic Preservation in the Pacific Northwest: A Bibliography of Sources, 1947-1978. (CPL Bibliographies: No. 11). 63p. 1979. pap. 7.00 (ISBN 0-86602-011-X). CPL Biblios.

Smith, Charles W. Pacific Northwest Americana. 3rd ed. Mayhew, Isabel, ed. pap. 10.00 (ISBN 0-8323-0352-6). Binford.

NORTHWEST BOUNDARY OF THE UNITED STATES

see also Washington, Treaty of, 1871

Barrows, William. Oregon: The Struggle for Possession. LC 72-3766. (American Commonwealths: No. 2). Repr. of 1892 ed. 25.50 (ISBN 0-404-57202-2). AMS Pr.

Cushing, Caleb. Treaty of Washington: Its Negotiation, Execution, & the Discussions Relating Thereto. facsimile ed. LC 72-114872. (Select Bibliographies Reprint Ser). 1873. 17.00 (ISBN 0-8369-5277-4). Arno.

Merk, Frederick. Oregon Question: Essays in Anglo-American Diplomacy & Politics. LC 67-14345. 1967. 20.00x (ISBN 0-674-64200-7, Belknap Pr). Harvard U Pr.

Murray, Keith A. The Pig War. LC 68-7256. (Illus.). 1968. pap. 2.00 (ISBN 0-917048-23-7). Wash St Hist Soc.

NORTHWEST COAST OF NORTH AMERICA

see also Bering's Expeditions, 1725-1743

Colnett, James. Colnett's Journal Aboard the Argonaut from April 26, 1789 to November 3, 1791. Howay, F. W., ed. LC 68-28614. 1968. Repr. of 1940 ed. lib. bdg. 30.75x (ISBN 0-8371-5063-9, COJC). Greenwood.

D'Wolf, John. Voyage to the North Pacific. 1968. Repr. of 1861 ed. 9.95 (ISBN 0-87770-011-7). Ye Galleon.

Espinosa y Tello, Jose. Spanish Voyage to Vancouver & the North-West Coast of America. Jane, Cecil, tr. LC 70-136389. (Illus.). Repr. of 1930 ed. 10.00 (ISBN 0-404-02356-8). AMS Pr.

Meany, Edmond S. Vancouver's Discovery of Puget Sound. (Illus.). 1957. 10.00 (ISBN 0-8323-0103-5). Binford.

Teichmann, Emil. Journey to Alaska in 1868. (Illus.). 1963. Repr. of 1925 ed. 17.50 (ISBN 0-87266-032-X). Argosy.

Williams, Richard. The Northwest Coast. LC 73-87559. (American Wilderness Ser). (Illus.). (gr. 6 up). 1973. lib. bdg. 11.97 (ISBN 0-8094-1193-8, Pub. by Time-Life). Silver.

--The Northwest Coast. (The American Wilderness Ser.). (Illus.). 240p. 1974. 12.95 (ISBN 0-8094-1192-X). Time-Life.

NORTHWEST COMPANY OF CANADA

Bryce, George. Remarkable History of the Hudson's Bay Company: Induding That of the French Traders of Northwestern Canada, & of the Astor Fur Companies. (Research & Source Works Ser.: No. 171). (Illus.). 1968. 29.50 (ISBN 0-8337-0407-9). B Franklin.

Davidson, Gordon C. North West Company. LC 66-27059. (Illus.). 1967. Repr. of 1918 ed. 30.00 (ISBN 0-8462-0894-6). Russell.

Thompson, David. David Thompson's Narrative of His Explorations in Western America, 1784-1812. Tyrrell, J. B., ed. LC 68-28603. Repr. of 1916 ed. lib. bdg. 50.00x (ISBN 0-8371-3879-5, THNE). Greenwood.

Wallace, William S., ed. Documents Relating to the North West Company. LC 68-28610. 1968. Repr. of 1934 ed. lib. bdg. 33.00x (ISBN 0-8371-5060-4, WADR). Greenwood.

NORTHWEST PASSAGE

Amundsen, Roald E. The North West Passage: Being the Record of a Voyage of Exploration of the Ship Gjoa 1903-1907, 2 vols. LC 74-5824. Repr. of 1908 ed. Set. 50.00 (ISBN 0-404-11625-6); Vol. 1. (ISBN 0-404-11626-4); Vol. 2. (ISBN 0-404-11627-2). AMS Pr.

Best, George. The Three Voyages of Martin Frobisher: In Search of a Passage to Cathaia & India by the Northwest, A.D. 1576-78. Collinson, Richard, ed. (Hakluyt Society, First Ser.: No. 38). (Illus.). 1964. 32.00 (ISBN 0-8337-0271-8). B Franklin.

Christy, Miller, ed. The Voyage of Captain Luke Foxe of Hull & Captain Thomas James of Bristol, in Search of a Northwest Passage, in 1631-32. (Hakluyt Society. Publications: Nos. 88-89). (Illus.). 1966. Repr. of 1894 ed. 63.00 (ISBN 0-8337-0568-7). B Franklin.

Davis, John. Voyages & Works of John Davis the Navigator. Markham, Albert H., ed. & intro. by. LC 71-134714. (Hakluyt Society, First Ser.: No. 59). (Illus.). 1970. Repr. of 1880 ed. lib. bdg. 32.00 (ISBN 0-8337-2241-7). B Franklin.

Ellis, Henry. Voyage to Hudson's Bay, by the Dobbs Galley & California, in the Years 1746 & 1747, for Discovering a North West Passage. 1748. 23.00 (ISBN 0-384-14200-1). Johnson Repr.

Espinosa y Tello, Jose. Spanish Voyage to Vancouver & the North-West Coast of America. Jane, Cecil, tr. LC 70-136389. (Illus.). Repr. of 1930 ed. 10.00 (ISBN 0-404-02356-8). AMS Pr.

Fox, Luke. North-West Fox, Or, Fox from the North-West Passage. (Illus.). 1965. Repr. of 1635 ed. 17.00 (ISBN 0-384-16550-8). Johnson Repr.

Gilbert, Humphrey. A Discourse of a Discoverie for a New Passage to Cataia. Gascoigne, George, ed. LC 68-54645. (English Experience Ser.: No. 72). 88p. 1968. Repr. of 1576 ed. 11.50 (ISBN 90-221-0072-3). Walter J Johnson.

Hakluyt, Richard & Jones, John W., eds. Divers Voyages Touching the Discovery of America & the Islands Adjacent. 30.50 (ISBN 0-8337-1867-3). B Franklin.

Hearne, Samuel. Journey from Prince of Wale's Fort in Hudson's Bay to the Northern Ocean. LC 78-133870. (Illus.). 1971. 19.25 (ISBN 0-8048-1007-9). C E Tuttle.

--Journey from Prince of Wales's Fort in Hudson's Bay to the Northern Ocean in the Years 1769-1772. LC 68-28601. (Illus.). 1968. Repr. of 1911 ed. lib. bdg. 32.75x (ISBN 0-8371-5045-0, HEJP). Greenwood.

Howard, Richard. North-West Passage. (Canadian Jackdaw Ser: No. C15). 1968. 6.95 (ISBN 0-670-51574-4, Grossman). Viking Pr.

James, Thomas. The Strange & Dangerous Voyage of Captaine T. James. LC 68-54650. (English Experience Ser.: No. 58). 1968. Repr. of 1633 ed. 22.00 (ISBN 90-221-0058-8). Walter J Johnson.

Lancaster, James. Voyages of Sir James Lancaster, Kt., to the East Indies. Markham, Clements R., ed. LC 78-134713. (Hakluyt Society First Ser: No. 56). 1970. Repr. of 1877 ed. lib. bdg. 32.00 (ISBN 0-8337-1995-5). B Franklin.

Lehane, Brendan & Time-Life Books Editors. The Northwest Passage. (The Seafarers Ser.). (Illus.). 192p. 1981. 13.95 (ISBN 0-8094-2730-3). Time-Life.

McClure, Robert J. The Discovery of the North-West Passage by H.M.S. Investigator: 1850-54. Osborn, Sherard, ed. LC 74-5853. Repr. of 1856 ed. 26.50 (ISBN 0-404-11660-4). AMS Pr.

McDonald, Lucile. Search for the Northwest Passage. LC 58-11860. (Illus.). 1958. 6.50 (ISBN 0-8323-0029-2). Binford.

--Search for the Northwest Passage. LC 58-11860. (Illus.). 142p. 1975. pap. 4.95 (ISBN 0-8323-0253-8). Binford.

Markham, Clements R., ed. The Voyages of William Baffin, 1612-1622. LC 74-20893. (Illus.). 192p. 1881. Repr. 28.50 (ISBN 0-8337-2240-9). B Franklin.

Middleton, Christopher. Vindication of the Conduct of Captain Christopher Middleton, in a Late Voyage on Board His Majesty's Ship the Furnace. (Illus.). Repr. of 1743 ed. 12.50 (ISBN 0-384-38831-0). Johnson Repr.

Orlob, Helen. The Northeast Passage: Black Water, White Ice. LC 77-9064. (gr. 5 up). 1977. 6.95 (ISBN 0-525-66564-1). Elsevier-Nelson.

Parry, William E. Journal of a Second Voyage for the Discovery of a Northwest Passage from the Atlantic to the Pacific. Repr. of 1824 ed. lib. bdg. 34.00x (ISBN 0-8371-1448-9, PASV). Greenwood.

--Journal of a Voyage for the Discovery of a Northwest Passage from the Atlantic to the Pacific, Performed in the Years 1819-20. LC 68-55209. 1968. Repr. of 1821 ed. lib. bdg. 28.50x (ISBN 0-8371-0608-7, PANP). Greenwood.

Ross, John. Narrative of a Second Voyage in Search of a North-West Passage, & of a Residence in the Arctic Regions During the Years 1829, 1830,1831, 1833, 2 Vols. LC 68-55217. 1968. Repr. of 1835 ed. Set. lib. bdg. 56.25x (ISBN 0-8371-3860-4, RONP). Greenwood.

Rundall, Thomas, ed. Narratives of Voyages Toward the North-West in Search of a Passage to Cathay & India, 1496 to 1631. LC 78-134705. (Hakluyt Society Ser.: No. 5). 1970. lib. bdg. 30.50 (ISBN 0-8337-3095-9). B Franklin.

Settle, Dionyse. A True Reporte of the Laste Voyage by Capteine Frobisher. LC 79-6343. (English Experience Ser.: No. 88). 48p. 1969. Repr. of 1577 ed. 11.50 (ISBN 90-221-0088-X). Walter J Johnson.

Stefansson, Vilhjalmur. Northwest to Fortune. LC 73-20881. (Illus.). 356p. 1974. Repr. of 1958 ed. lib. bdg. 17.25x (ISBN 0-8371-5729-3, STNF). Greenwood.

Swaine, Charles. Account of a Voyage for the Discovery of a North-West Passage by Hudson's Streights, to the Western & Southern Ocean of America, 2 Vols. (Illus.). Repr. of 1748 ed. 38.50 (ISBN 0-384-58960-X). Johnson Repr.

Veer, Gerrit de. A True & Perfect Description of Three Voyages by the Ships of Holland & Zeland. Phillip, W., tr. LC 75-25746. (English Experience Ser.: No. 274). 164p. 1970. Repr. of 1609 ed. 21.00 (ISBN 90-221-0274-2). Walter J Johnson.

Wallace, Hugh N. The Navy, the Company, & Richard King: British Exploration in the Canadian Arctic, 1829-1860. (Illus.). 265p. 1980. 21.95x (ISBN 0-7735-0338-2). McGill-Queens U Pr.

NORTHWEST REBELLION, 1885

see Riel Rebellion, 1885

NORTHWESTERN PACIFIC RAILROAD COMPANY

Kneiss, Gilbert H. Redwood Railways. LC 57-671. (Illus.). 1956. 6.00 (ISBN 0-8310-7005-6). Howell-North.

NORTHWESTERN STATES

Haas, Pamela. Northwest Coast Photographs of Edward Dossetter. 1981. write for info. Arno.

Meacham, Mary, ed. Reading for Young People: The Southeast. 8.50 (ISBN 0-686-75136-1). ALA.

Morgan, Lane, ed. Northwest Experience One. (Northwest Experience Ser.). 192p. (gr. 12). 1980. PLB 10.00x (ISBN 0-914842-47-1); pap. 4.95 (ISBN 0-914842-46-3). Madrona Pubs.

Robert Long Adams Associates. The Northwest Job Bank. 400p. 1981. pap. 9.95 (ISBN 0-686-30614-7). Adams Inc MA.

NORTHWESTERN STATES–DESCRIPTION AND TRAVEL

Berssen, William. Pacific Boating Almanac: Oregon, Washington, British Columbia & Alaska Edition 1981. annual ed. 432p. 1982. pap. 7.95 (ISBN 0-930030-22-2). Western Marine Ent.

Calhoun, Bruce. Northwest Passages: A Cruising Guide for Northwest Boatowners, Vol. 1. (Illus.). 1978. pap. 8.95 (ISBN 0-930030-06-0). Western Marine Ent.

Christopher, Bob & Christopher, Ellen. Christopher's America on Fifteen to Twenty-Five Dollars a Night: Northwest States. 80p. (Orig.). pap. 3.95 (ISBN 0-930570-06-5). Travel Discover.

De Smet, P. J. Life, Letters, & Travels, Eighteen Hundred One to Eighteen Seventy Three, 4 Vols. in 2. 1905. Set. 60.00 (ISBN 0-527-83900-0). Kraus Repr.

Drawson, Maynard C. Treasures of the Oregon Country: No. V. (Historical Travel Ser.). (Illus., Orig.). 1979. pap. 9.95 (ISBN 0-934476-04-7). Dee Pub Co.

Hewitt, Randall H. Across the Plains & Over the Divide. (Illus.). 1964. Repr. of 1906 ed. 15.00 (ISBN 0-87266-015-X). Argosy.

Irving, Washington. Adventures of Captain Bonneville. (Illus.). 1954. 10.00 (ISBN 0-8323-0100-0). Binford.

--Astoria. LC 67-25439. (Illus.). 1967. 10.00 (ISBN 0-8323-0101-9). Binford.

Palliser, John. Solitary Rambles & Adventures of a Hunter in the Prairies. LC 69-13511. (Illus.). 1969. Repr. of 1853 ed. 5.00 (ISBN 0-8048-0534-2). C E Tuttle.

Russell, Osborne. Journal of a Trapper. Haines, Aubrey L., ed. LC 56-52. (Illus.). xxiv, 203p. 1965. 14.50x (ISBN 0-8032-0897-9); pap. 3.50 (ISBN 0-8032-5166-1, BB 316, Bison). U of Nebr Pr.

Schwartz, Susan. Cascade Companion. LC 76-40369. (Illus.). 160p. (YA) 1976. 6.95 (ISBN 0-914718-16-9). Pacific Search.

Spring & Manning. National Parks of the Northwest. LC 76-6935. (Illus.). 184p. 1976. 14.95 (ISBN 0-87564-015-X). Superior Pub.

Winthrop, Theodore. Canoe & Saddle. 2nd ed. (Illus.). 1981. pap. 6.50 (ISBN 0-8323-0380-1). Binford.

NORTHWESTERN STATES–HISTORY

Armstrong, Moses K. History & Resources of Dakota, Montana & Idaho. 1968. 4.95 (ISBN 0-87770-031-1); pap. 3.00 (ISBN 0-87770-104-0). Ye Galleon.

Bancroft, Hubert H. History of the Northwest Coast, 2 vols. LC 67-29422. (Works of Hubert Howe Bancroft Ser.). 1967. Repr. of 1888 ed. 50.00x (ISBN 0-914888-31-5). Bancroft Pr.

--Popular Tribunals, 2 vols. LC 67-29422. (Works of Hubert Howe Bancroft Ser.). 1967. Repr. of 1888 ed. 50.00x (ISBN 0-914888-39-0). Bancroft Pr.

Benton, Elbert J. The Movement for Peace Without a Victory During the Civil War. LC 70-176339. (The American Scene Ser.). 1972. Repr. of 1918 ed. lib. bdg. 12.50 (ISBN 0-306-70420-X). Da Capo.

Dorman, C. C. North Western Album. (Illus.). 16.50x (ISBN 0-392-04067-0, SpS). Sportshelf.

Drawson, Maynard C. Treasures of the Oregon Country: No. V. (Historical Travel Ser.). (Illus., Orig.). 1979. pap. 9.95 (ISBN 0-934476-04-7). Dee Pub Co.

Langford, Nathaniel P. Vigilante Days & Ways, 2 Vols. LC 76-156021. Repr. of 1890 ed. Set. 35.00 (ISBN 0-404-09121-0); 18.00 ea. Vol. 1 (ISBN 0-404-09163-6). Vol. 2 (ISBN 0-404-09164-4). AMS Pr.

Morgan, Lane, ed. The Northwest Experience Two. 192p. 1981. lib. bdg. 10.00x (ISBN 0-914842-61-7); pap. 4.95 (ISBN 0-914842-60-9). Madrona Pubs.

Nelson, Bruce. Land of the Dacotahs. LC 65-108129. (Illus.). 1964. pap. 3.95 (ISBN 0-8032-5145-9, BB 176, Bison). U of Nebr Pr.

Prucha, F. P. Broadax & Bayonet: The Role of the United States Army in the Development of the Northwest, 1815-1860. (Illus.). 6.50 (ISBN 0-8446-2760-7). Peter Smith.

University of Illinois at Urbana-Champaign - Library. Mereness Calendar: Federal Documents on the Upper Mississippi Valley, 1780-1890, 13 vols. 1971. Set. 1470.00 (ISBN 0-8161-0915-X). G K Hall.

NORTHWESTERN STATES–HISTORY–FICTION

Morrow, Honore. On to Oregon. (Illus.). (gr. 5-9). 1946. Repr. of 1926 ed. 8.95 (ISBN 0-688-21639-0). Morrow.

NORTHWESTERN UNIVERSITY

Rein, Lynn. Ladies & Gentlemen: A History of the School of Speech of North Western University. 1980. 23.95 (ISBN 0-8101-0538-1). Northwestern U Pr.

Rein, Lynn Miller. Northwestern University School of Speech: A History. (Illus.). 300p. 1981. 16.95x (ISBN 0-8101-0538-1). Northwestern U Pr.

Williamson, Harold F. & Wild, Payson S. Northwestern University: A History, 1850-1975. 1976. cloth 12.50x (ISBN 0-8101-0463-6); pap. 4.75x (ISBN 0-8101-0462-8). Northwestern U Pr.

NORTON, CHARLES ELIOT, 1827-1908

Emerson, Edward W. Charles Eliot Norton: Two Addresses. 1973. Repr. of 1912 ed. 15.00 (ISBN 0-8274-1441-2). R West.

Vanderbilt, Kermit. Charles Eliot Norton: Apostle of Culture in a Democracy. LC 59-10321. (Illus.). 1959. 15.00x (ISBN 0-674-11025-0, Belknap Pr). Harvard U Pr.

Whitehill, Jane. Letters to Mrs. Gaskell & Charles Eliot Norton. LC 73-14667. 1932. lib. bdg. 20.00 (ISBN 0-8414-9450-9). Folcroft.

NORWAY

see also names of cities, towns, regions, etc. in Norway

Aftenposten, A., ed. Norway: Facts About. 16th ed. 1979. 6.00x (ISBN 82-516-0659-4, N451). Vanous.

Gathorne Hardy, G. Norway. LC 75-18358. 324p. 1975. Repr. of 1925 ed. lib. bdg. 16.50x (ISBN 0-8371-8325-1, GANO). Greenwood.

Hassing, Arne. Religion & Power: The Case of Methodism in Norway. (Jesse Lee Prize Ser.). (Illus.). 300p. 1980. 15.00 (ISBN 0-915466-03-1). United Meth Archives.

Rolvaag, O. E. Giants in the Earth. 465p. 1980. Repr. lib. bdg. 20.00 (ISBN 0-89987-700-1). Darby Bks.

Wergeland, Agnes M. Leaders in Norway, & Other Essays. facs. ed. Merrill, K., ed. LC 67-22127. (Essay Index Reprint Ser). 1916. 15.00 (ISBN 0-8369-0981-X). Arno.

NORWAY–ANTIQUITIES

Herteig, Asbiorn, et al. Archaeological Contributions to the Early History of Urban Communities in Norway. 1976. 14.50x (ISBN 82-00-09366-2). Universitet.

Skard, Sigmund. Classical Tradition in Norway. 204p. 1980. pap. 21.00x (ISBN 8-20001-972-1). Universitet.

NORWAY–CHURCH HISTORY

Hauglid, R. Norwegian Stave Churches. (Illus.). 1970. 22.00x (ISBN 8-2090-0937-0, N497). Vanous.

Molland, Einar. Church Life in Norway: 1800-1950. Harris, Kaasa, tr. LC 78-2711. 1978. Repr. of 1957 ed. lib. bdg. 14.50x (ISBN 0-313-20342-3, MOCL). Greenwood.

Undset, Sigrid. Saga of Saints. facs. ed. Ramsden, E. C., tr. LC 68-22952. (Essay Index Reprint Ser). 1968. Repr. of 1934 ed. 18.00 (ISBN 0-8369-0959-3). Arno.

Willson, Thomas B. History of the Church & State in Norway: From the 10th to the 16th Century. LC 72-145376. (Illus.). 1971. Repr. of 1903 ed. 29.00 (ISBN 0-403-01280-5). Scholarly.

NORWAY–DEFENSES

Burgess, Philip M. Elite Images & Foreign Policy Outcomes: A Study of Norway. LC 67-24453. 1968. 6.25 (ISBN 0-8142-0030-3). Ohio St U Pr.

NORWAY–DESCRIPTION AND TRAVEL

Brueckner, Hannes. Geographic Survey of Norway, No. 332, Bulletin 41. 1977. pap. 12.00x (ISBN 82-00-31366-2). Universitet.

Derry, T. Oslo. (Tanum of Norway Tokens Ser). pap. 7.00x (ISBN 0-89918-484-7, N484). Vanous.

Dreyers. Traveller Discovering Norway. 1968. 25.00x (ISBN 0-686-31693-2, N499). Vanous.

Froude, James A. Spanish Story of the Armada & Other Essays. LC 71-144613. Repr. of 1892 ed. 24.50 (ISBN 0-404-02628-1). AMS Pr.

Helvig, Magne & Johannessen, Viggo. Norway - Land, People, Industries: A Brief Geography. 2nd ed. (Norwegian Guides Ser). (Illus., Orig.). 1968. pap. 13.50x (ISBN 0-8002-1759-4). Intl Pubns Serv.

Holt-Jensen, Arild. The Norwegian Wilderness: National Parks & Protected Areas. LC 79-321366. (Tokens of Norway Ser.). (Illus.). 78p. (Orig.). 1978. pap. 10.50x (ISBN 82-518-0719-0). Intl Pubns Serv.

Lees, James A. Peaks & Pines. (Tokens of Norway Ser). (Illus., Orig.). 1971. pap. 8.00x (ISBN 0-8002-1783-7). Intl Pubns Serv.

Mittet, M. Norge - Norway - Norvege. (Illus.). 1980. 21.00x (ISBN 0-89918-437-5, N437). Vanous.

Norway. (Panorama Books Collections). (Fr.). 3.95 (ISBN 0-685-35938-7). French & Eur.

Ronning, Olaf & Bjaerevoll, Olav. Flowers of Svalbard. (Illus.). 56p. 1981. pap. 14.00x (ISBN 82-00-05398-9). Universitet.

Senje, Sigurd. The North Cape & Its Hinterland. (Tokens of Norway Ser.). (Illus.). 53p. (Orig.). 1979. pap. 12.50x (ISBN 82-518-0822-7). Intl Pubns Serv.

Somme, A. Norway-a Geography of Norden. rev. 2nd ed. 1968. 60.00x (ISBN 0-89918-418-9, N-418). Vanous.

Sverdrup, E. Norway's Delights Cookbook. 10th ed. (Tanum of Norway Tokens Ser). 1980. pap. 11.00x (ISBN 8-2518-0089-7, N429). Vanous.

Sylte, T. Rivers of Norway. (Illus.). 1966. 15.00x (ISBN 82-09-00841-2, N447). Vanous.

Vinland the Good. (Norwegian Guide Ser). 1966. 8.50x (ISBN 0-8002-2138-9). Intl Pubns Serv.

Welle, Strand. Norway (Pictures & Facts) 1977. pap. 6.00x (ISBN 8-2516-0659-4, N451). Vanous.

Welle-Strand. Norway Tourist. 5th ed. Lundevall, E., ed. (Illus.). 1974. pap. 7.50x (ISBN 8-2516-0269-6, N410). Vanous.

--Two Thousand Five Hundred Miles of the Norwegian Coastal Steamer. 1980. pap. 6.00x (ISBN 8-2901-0307-7, N416). Vanous.

Welle-Strand, E. Mountain Touring Holidays in Norway. (Illus.). 96p. (Orig.). 1974. pap. 5.00x (ISBN 8-2901-0315-8, N-528). Vanous.

NORWAY–ECONOMIC CONDITIONS

Allen, Hilary. Norway & Europe in the Nineteen Seventies. 1979. 31.00x (ISBN 82-00-05230-3, Dist. by Columbia U Pr.). Universitet.

Bryde, Konrad & Gyllstoem, Walter, eds. Norwegian Directory of Commerce, 1979, 2 vols. 54th ed. LC 66-4838. Orig. Title: Norges Handels-Kalendar. 1979. Set. 80.00x (ISBN 82-7030-054-3). Intl Pubns Serv.

Isachsen, Arne. The Demand for Money in Norway. 1976. pap. text ed. 6.00x (ISBN 8-200-01569-6, Dist. by Columbia U Pr). Universitet.

Knudsen, Ole. Norway at Work: A Survey of the Principal Branches of the Economy. (Tokens of Norway Ser). (Illus.). 83p. (Orig.). 1972. pap. 10.00x (ISBN 0-8002-1760-8). Intl Pubns Serv.

Leiserson, Mark W. Wages & Economic Control in Norway, 1945-1957. LC 59-5565. (Wertheim Publications in Industrial Relations Ser). 1959. 10.00x (ISBN 0-674-94470-4). Harvard U Pr.

Moe, Thorvald. Demographic Developments & Economic Growth in Norway 1740-1940: An Econometric Study. Bruchey, Stuart, ed. LC 77-77190. (Dissertations in European Economic History Ser.). 1977. lib. bdg. 20.00x (ISBN 0-405-10802-8). Arno.

Norway's One Thousand Largest Companies 1976. (One Thousand Largest Companies Ser). 202p. 1976. 42.00x (ISBN 0-8002-1761-6). Intl Pubns Serv.

The Norwegian Price & Income Freeze. 1980. 50.00x (ISBN 0-686-69880-0, Pub. by Norwegian Info Norway). State Mutual Bk.

NORWAY–FOREIGN RELATIONS

Amundsen, Kirsten. Norway, NATO & the Forgotten Soviet Challenge. LC 81-80337. (Policy Papers in International Affairs Ser.: No. 14). (Illus.). iv, 50p. 1981. pap. 2.95x (ISBN 0-87725-514-8). U of Cal Intl St.

Burgess, Philip M. Elite Images & Foreign Policy Outcomes: A Study of Norway. LC 67-24453. 1968. 6.25 (ISBN 0-8142-0030-3). Ohio St U Pr.

Oervik, Nils. Europe's Northern Cap & the Soviet Union. LC 73-38763. (Harvard University. Center for International Affairs. Occasional Papers in International Affairs: No. 6). Repr. of 1963 ed. 10.00 (ISBN 0-404-54606-4). AMS Pr.

Riggs, Robert E. & Mykletun, I. Jostein. Beyond Functionalism: Attitudes Toward International Organization in Norway & the United States. LC 79-11306. (Illus.). 1979. 19.50x (ISBN 0-8166-0898-9). U of Minn Pr.

Skard, Sigmund. The U. S. in Norwegian History. LC 76-5263. (Contributions in American Studies: No. 26). (Orig.). 1976. lib. bdg. 15.00 (ISBN 0-8371-8909-8, SKU/). Greenwood.

NORWAY–HISTORY

Blegen, Theodore. Norwegian Migration to America, 1825-60, 2 Vols. LC 68-31271. (American History & Americana Ser., No. 47). 1969. Repr. of 1931 ed. lib. bdg. 69.95 (ISBN 0-8383-0330-7). Haskell.

Boyesen, Hjalmar H. The Story of Norway. 1886. 40.00 (ISBN 0-685-43758-2). Norwood Edns.

Derry, T. K. A History of Modern Norway, 1814-1972. (Illus.). 1973. 45.00x (ISBN 0-19-822503-2). Oxford U Pr.

Derry, Thomas K. A Short History of Norway. LC 79-10688. (Illus.). 1979. Repr. of 1968 ed. lib. bdg. 22.50x (ISBN 0-313-21467-0, DESH). Greenwood.

Gjelsvik, Tore. Norwegian Resistance, Nineteen Forty to Nineteen Forty-Five: Nineteen Forty to Nineteen Forty-Five. 1979. 21.95x (ISBN 0-7735-0507-5). McGill-Queens U Pr.

Gjerset, Knut. History of the Norwegian People. LC 79-101272. (Illus.). Repr. of 1932 ed. 57.50 (ISBN 0-404-02818-7). AMS Pr.

Hermannsson, Halldor. Bibliography of the Sagas of the Kings of Norway & Related Sagas & Tales. LC 10-10613. (Islandica Ser.: Vol. 3). 1910. pap. 6.00 (ISBN 0-527-00333-6). Kraus Repr.

Jorgenson, Theodore J. Norway's Relation to Scandinavian Unionism 1815-1871. (Perspectives in European History Ser.: No. 22). v, 530p. Repr. of 1935 ed. lib. bdg. 35.00x (ISBN 0-87991-116-6). Porcupine Pr.

Koht, Halvdan & Skard, Sigmund. Voice of Norway. LC 75-181941. Repr. of 1944 ed. 24.00 (ISBN 0-404-03769-0). AMS Pr.

Larsen, Karen. History of Norway. (American-Scandinavian Foundation). 1948. 35.00 (ISBN 0-691-05127-5). Princeton U Pr.

--History of Norway. LC 71-135387. 1948. 25.00 (ISBN 0-89067-029-3). Am Scandinavian.

Larson, Laurence M., ed. The Earliest Norwegian Laws. xii, 451p. 1976. Repr. of 1935 ed. lib. bdg. 30.00x (ISBN 0-374-94777-5). Octagon.

Lindgren, Raymond E. Norway-Sweden: Union, Disunion, & Scandinavian Integration. LC 78-13451. 1979. Repr. of 1959 ed. lib. bdg. 22.50x (ISBN 0-313-21043-8, LINS). Greenwood.

Midgaard, J., ed. Norway-Brief History. 7th ed. (Tanum of Norway Tokens Ser.). 1979. pap. 12.50x (ISBN 82-518-0053-6, N-441). Vanous.

Midgaard, John. Brief History of Norway. 7th ed. LC 67-7814. (Norwegian Guides Ser). (Illus., Orig.). 1979. pap. 9.50x (ISBN 82-518-0053-6). Intl Pubns Serv.

Petrow, Richard. The Bitter Years: The Invasion & Occupation of Denmark & Norway April 1940 - May 1945. LC 74-9576. (Illus.). 1979. pap. 5.95 (ISBN 0-688-05275-4, Quill). Morrow.

Riste & Nokleby. Norway Nineteen-Forty to Nineteen Forty-Five: The Resistance Movement. (Tanum of Norway Tokens Ser). pap. 9.50x (ISBN 82-518-0164-8, N488). Vanous.

Sjovold, Thorleif. The Iron Age Settlement of Arctic Norway, Vol. II. 1974. pap. text ed. 27.00x (ISBN 82-00-06157-4, Dist. by Columbia U Pr). Universitet.

Sonsteby, Gunnar. Report from No. 24. 1964. 4.95 (ISBN 0-8184-0068-4). Lyle Stuart.

Sturluson, Snorri. Heims Kringla, History of the Kings of Norway. Hollander, Lee M., tr. from Old Norse. LC 64-10460. (Illus.). 1977. Repr. of 1964 ed. 32.50x (ISBN 0-89067-040-4). Am Scandinavian.

Vigness, Paul G. The Neutrality of Norway in the World War. LC 70-155601. (Stanford University. Stanford Studies in History, Economics, & Political Science: No. 4, Pt. 1). Repr. of 1932 ed. 18.00 (ISBN 0-404-50967-3). AMS Pr.

NORWAY–JUVENILE LITERATURE

Hall, Elvajean. The Land & People of Norway. rev ed. LC 72-10777. (Portraits of the Nations Series). (Illus.). 1973. 8.95 (ISBN 0-397-31408-6, JBL-J). Har-Row.

Sheridan, Irene. We Go to Norway & Sweden. LC 66-9556. (We Go to Ser.). 1965. 4.00x (ISBN 0-245-57971-0). Intl Pubns Serv.

Sterling Publishing Company Editors. Norway in Pictures. LC 67-16017. (Visual Geography Ser). (Orig.). (gr. 6 up). PLB 4.99 (ISBN 0-8069-1089-5); pap. 2.95 (ISBN 0-8069-1088-7). Sterling.

NORWAY–POLITICS AND GOVERNMENT

Allen, Hilary. Norway & Europe in the Nineteen Seventies. 1979. 31.00x (ISBN 82-00-05230-3, Dist. by Columbia U Pr.). Universitet.

Arneson, Ben A. The Democratic Monarchies of Scandinavia. LC 74-4728. (Illus.). 294p. 1975. Repr. of 1949 ed. lib. bdg. 18.50x (ISBN 0-8371-7485-6, ARDM). Greenwood.

Cowart, Andrew T. & Brofoss, Karl E. Decisions, Politics & Change: A Study of Norwegian Urban Budgeting. 1979. pap. 15.00x (ISBN 82-00-01882-2, Dist. by Columbia U. Pr.). Universitet.

Eckstein, Harry. Division & Cohesion in Democracy: A Study of Norway. (Center of International Studies Ser). 1966. 21.00x (ISBN 0-691-05611-0); pap. 6.95 (ISBN 0-691-01070-6). Princeton U Pr.

Higley, John, et al. Elite Structure & Ideology: A Theory with Applications to Norway. LC 75-40145. 377p. 1976. 20.00x (ISBN 0-231-04068-7). Columbia U Pr.

Koht, Halvdan & Skard, Sigmund. Voice of Norway. LC 75-181941. Repr. of 1944 ed. 24.00 (ISBN 0-404-03769-0). AMS Pr.

Kvavik, Robert B. Interest Groups in Norwegian Politics. 1976. pap. 17.00x (ISBN 8-200-01477-0, Dist. by Columbia U Pr). Universitet.

Lafferty, William M. Participation & Democracy in Norway: The "Distant Democracy" Revisited. 188p. 1981. 16.00x (ISBN 82-00-05606-6). Universitet.

Larson, Laurence M., tr. from Old Norse. The King's Mirror. LC 72-1542. (Library of Scandinavian Literature: Vol. 15). 8.50x (ISBN 0-89067-008-0). Am Scandinavian.

Lindgren, Raymond E. Norway-Sweden: Union, Disunion, & Scandinavian Integration. LC 78-13451. 1979. Repr. of 1959 ed. lib. bdg. 22.50x (ISBN 0-313-21043-8, LINS). Greenwood.

Omrcanin, Margaret. Norway-Sweden-Croatia: A Comparative Study of State Secession & Formation. 1976. pap. 6.95 (ISBN 0-8059-2309-8). Dorrance.

Sosin, Jack M. Whitehall & the Wilderness: The Middle West in British Colonial Policy, 1760 to 1775. LC 80-21061. (Illus.). xi, 307p. 1981. Repr. of 1961 ed. lib. bdg. 35.00x (ISBN 0-313-22678-4, SOWW). Greenwood.

Urwin, Derek W. From Ploughshare to Ballotbox. 356p. 1981. pap. 30.00x (ISBN 82-00-05394-6). Universitet.

NORWAY-POPULATION

Drake, Michael. Population & Society in Norway, 1735-1865. LC 69-14393. (Cambridge Studies in Economic History). (Illus.). 1969. 35.50 (ISBN 0-521-07319-7). Cambridge U Pr.

Dyrvik, Stale. Demographic Crises in Norway in the 17th & 18th Centuries. 1977. pap. 8.00x (ISBN 82-00-01627-7, Dist. by Columbia U Pr). Universitet.

Moe, Thorvald. Demographic Developments & Economic Growth in Norway 1740-1940: An Econometric Study. Bruchey, Stuart, ed. LC 77-77190. (Dissertations in European Economic History Ser.). 1977. lib. bdg. 20.00x (ISBN 0-405-10802-8). Arno.

NORWAY-SOCIAL CONDITIONS

Drake, Michael. Population & Society in Norway, 1735-1865. LC 69-14393. (Cambridge Studies in Economic History). (Illus.). 1969. 35.50 (ISBN 0-521-07319-7). Cambridge U Pr.

Gustavson, Bjorn & Hunius, Gerry. Improving the Quality of Life: The Case of Norway. 112p. 1981. pap. 11.00x (ISBN 82-00-05525-6). Universitet.

Larson, Laurence M., tr. from Old Norse. The King's Mirror. LC 72-1542. (Library of Scandinavian Literature: Vol. 15). 8.50x (ISBN 0-89067-008-0). Am Scandinavian.

Nordskog, John E. Social Reform in Norway. LC 72-13001. 184p. 1973. Repr. of 1935 ed. lib. bdg. 15.00 (ISBN 0-8371-6736-1, NOSR). Greenwood.

NORWAY-SOCIAL LIFE AND CUSTOMS

Dahl, Gundel K. Family Diary: Everyday Life in Norway. (Tokens of Norway Ser). (Orig.). 1971. pap. 7.50x (ISBN 82-518-0031-5). Intl Pubns Serv.

Daniels, H. K. Home Life in Norway. LC 77-87709. (Illus.). Repr. of 1911 ed. 24.50 (ISBN 0-404-16499-4). AMS Pr.

Howell, Ruth A. A Norwegian Birthday Party. 1980. 4.50 (ISBN 0-533-03978-9). Vantage.

Negative & Positive Sides of Norweigian Life Styles: An Empirical Assessmant of Overdevelopment. 32p. 1980. pap. 5.00 (ISBN 92-808-0137-6, TUNU 069, UNU). Unipub.

Ramsay, Natalie R. Norwegian Society. 1974. text ed. 22.00x (ISBN 82-00-04834-9, Dist. by Columbia U Pr); pap. text ed. 11.00x (ISBN 82-00-04610-9). Universitet.

Vanberg, Bent. Of Norwegian Ways. LC 78-107746. (Heritage Bks.). (Illus.). 1970. 8.95 (ISBN 0-87518-014-0). Dillon.

NORWEGIAN-AMERICAN LITERATURE

Undset, S. Longest Years. Chater, A. G., tr. Repr. of 1935 ed. 18.00 (ISBN 0-527-91500-9). Kraus Repr.

NORWEGIAN ART

see Art, Norwegian

NORWEGIAN AUTHORS

see Authors, Norwegian

NORWEGIAN BALLADS AND SONGS

see also Folk-Songs, Norwegian

NORWEGIAN-BRITISH-SWEDISH ANTARCTIC EXPEDITION, 1949-1952

Giaever, John. White Desert: The Official Account of the Norwegian-British-Swedish Antarctic Expedition. Huggard, E. M., tr. LC 69-10097. (Illus.). 1969. Repr. of 1954 ed. lib. bdg. 14.50x (ISBN 0-8371-1318-0, GIWD). Greenwood.

NORWEGIAN ELKHOUND

see Dogs-Breeds-Norwegian Elkhound

NORWEGIAN FOLK-LORE

see Folk-Lore, Norwegian

NORWEGIAN FOLK SONGS

see Folk-Songs, Norwegian

NORWEGIAN LANGUAGE

see also Danish Language

Abrahamsen, Samuel. Say It in Norwegian. LC 57-36629. 1957. lib. bdg. 8.50 (ISBN 0-88307-635-7). Gannon.

--Say It in Norwegian. (Orig.). 1957. pap. 1.75 (ISBN 0-486-20814-1). Dover.

Berulfsen, B. Norwegian Grammar. 4th ed. 1977. pap. text ed. 10.00x (ISBN 8-2030-4312-7, N436). Vanous.

Chapman, Kenneth G. Basic Norwegian Reader. LC 65-13020. 1966. text ed. 9.95 (ISBN 0-03-050855-X, HoltC). HR&W.

Falnes, Oscar J. National Romanticism in Norway. LC 68-54263. (Columbia University. Studies in the Social Sciences: No. 386). Repr. of 1933 ed. 21.50 (ISBN 0-404-51386-7). AMS Pr.

Flom, George T. The Phonology of the Dialect of Aurland Norway, Vol. 1 Nos. 1-2. pap. 5.50 (ISBN 0-384-16080-8). Johnson Repr.

Haugen, E. Beginning Norwegian: A Grammar & Reader. 3rd ed. 1957. text ed. 12.95 (ISBN 0-13-073239-7). P-H.

Haugen, Einar. Reading Norwegian. LC 75-24258. 1977. pap. 8.00x (ISBN 0-87950-172-3). Spoken Lang Serv.

Haugen, Einar & Chapman, K. G. Spoken Norwegian. rev. ed. LC 64-15729. 1964. text ed. 19.95 (ISBN 0-03-019065-7, HoltC). HR&W.

Hovdhaugen, Even, ed. The Nordic Languages & Modern Linguistics. 392p. 1981. 40.00x (ISBN 82-00-05569-8). Universitet.

Janus, Louis. Norsk, Nordmenn og Norge: Workbook. LC 81-50827. 184p. 1981. pap. text ed. 7.50x (ISBN 0-299-08774-3). U of Wis Pr.

Learn Norwegian for English Speakers. pap. 8.50 (ISBN 0-87557-055-0, 055-0). Saphrograph.

Norwegian in Three Months. (Hugo's Language Courses Ser.: No. 527). 1958. pap. 3.50 (ISBN 0-8226-0527-9). Littlefield.

Popperwell, R. G. Pronunciation of Norwegian. 35.00 (ISBN 0-521-05973-9). Cambridge U Pr.

Sommerfelt, A. & Marm, I. Teach Yourself Norwegian. (Teach Yourself Ser.). pap. 4.95 (ISBN 0-679-10221-3). McKay.

Stokker, Kathleen & Haddal, Odd. Norsk, Nordmenn og Norge. LC 81-50827. 528p. 1981. text ed. 17.50x (ISBN 0-299-08690-9). U of Wis Pr.

--Norsk, Nordmenn og Norge: Teachers Manual. LC 81-50827. 264p. 1981. pap. 17.50x (ISBN 0-299-08804-9). U of Wis Pr.

NORWEGIAN LANGUAGE-DICTIONARIES

Ansteinsson, J. Norwegian Technical Dictionary: English-Norwegian, Vol. 1. 3rd ed. 1973. 30.00x (ISBN 8-2702-8007-0, N433). Vanous.

Ansteinsson, J. & Andreassen, A. T. Norwegian-English, English-Norwegian Technical Dictionary, 2 Vols. Set. 60.00 (ISBN 8-2702-8007-0). Heinman.

Ansteinsson, J., ed. Norwegian Technical Dictionary: Norwegian-English, Vol. 2. rev. ed. 1954. 25.00x (ISBN 8-2702-8006-2, N432). Vanous.

Berulfsen, B. English-Norsk Dictionary: Gyldendals. new ed. 1978. 18.50x (ISBN 8-2573-0007-1, N481); Norsk-English. 18.50x (ISBN 8-2573-0006-3, N-482). Vanous.

Berulfsen, B. & Berulfsen, T. Norwegian Dictionary: Engelsk-Norwegina. rev. ed. 433p. 1978. 18.50x (ISBN 82-573-0007-1, N481). Vanous.

Berulfsen, B. & Svenkerud, A. Norwegian Deluxe Dictionary: English-Norse. 1968. 90.00x (ISBN 82-02-06627-1, N461). Vanous.

Berulfsen, B. & Scavenius, H., eds. McKay's Modern Norwegian-English & English-Norwegian Dictionary. (Modern Dictionaries). 1953. 14.95 (ISBN 0-679-10076-8). McKay.

Bjerke, L. & Soraas, H., eds. Norwegian Dictionary: English-Norwegian. 1963. 26.00x (ISBN 0-686-31692-4, N434). Vanous.

Christophensen, Scavenius. Norwegian Dictionary: Norsk-English, Vol. 2. Kirkeby, Willie, ed. 1978. 18.50x (ISBN 8-2573-0006-3, N482). Vanous.

Diccionario Lexicon Noruego-Espanol, Espanol-Noruego. 400p. (Nor. -Espn.). leatherette 4.95 (ISBN 84-303-0165-8, S-50418). French & Eur.

Diccionario Lexicon Noruego-Espanol, Espanol-Noruego. 400p. (Nor. -Espn.). pap. 4.50 (ISBN 84-303-0164-X, S-50417). French & Eur.

English-Norwegian Norwegian-English Pocket Dictionary. 1981. 6.95 (ISBN 0-88254-584-1). Hippocrene Bks.

Falk, H. S. & Torp, Alf. Norwegisch-Daenisches Etymologisches Woerterbuch, Vol. 1. 2nd ed. (Nor. -Dan.). 1960. 55.00 (ISBN 3-533-00505-4, M-7570, Pub. by Carl Winter). French & Eur.

--Norwegisch-Daenisches Etymologisches Woerterbuch, Vol. 2. 2nd ed. (Nor. -Dan.). 1960. 55.00 (ISBN 3-533-00506-2, M-7571, Pub. by Carl Winter). French & Eur.

--Norwegisch Daenisches Etymologisches Woerterbuch: Mit Literatur-Nachweisen Strittiger Etymologien Sowie Deutschem und Altnordischen Woerterverzeichnis. 2nd ed. 1722p. 1960. 80.00x (ISBN 8-200-00085-0, Dist. by Columbia U Pr). Universitet.

Gybdendaus. Norwegian Pocket Dictionary: English-Norwegian, Norwegian-English. rev. 2nd ed. 1980. 8.00x (ISBN 8-2573-0054-3, N-407). Vanous.

Haugen, Einar, ed. Norwegian-English Dictionary. 504p. 1965. pap. 17.50 (ISBN 0-299-03874-2). U of Wis Pr.

Haugen, G. Norwegian Dictionary: Norwegian-English. 1976. pap. 18.00x (ISBN 0-299-03874-2, N533). Vanous.

Kirkely, Willie. Norsk-Engelsk Ordbok. 4th ed. 482p. 1978. 18.50x (ISBN 82-573-0006-3, N482). Vanous.

Myklestad, J. Meyer & Soras, H. English-Norwegian, Norwegian-English Dictionary, Norwegian-English Dictionary. 17.50 (ISBN 0-87557-054-2, 054-2). Saphrograph.

Norwegian Pocket Dictionary. 7.00 (ISBN 82-517-8010-1). Heinman.

Slette, T. Norwegian-English Dictionary. 1977. 80.00x (ISBN 82-521-0692-7, N-537). Vanous.

NORWEGIAN LITERATURE

see also Icelandic and Old Norse Literature; Norwegian-American Literature

Burchardt, Carl J. Norwegian Life & Literature. LC 73-136521. 230p. 1974. Repr. of 1920 ed. lib. bdg. 15.00x (ISBN 0-8371-5442-1, BUNL). Greenwood.

Dasent, George W. Popular Tales from the Norse: With an Introductory Essay on the Origin & Diffusion of Popular Tales. 3rd ed. LC 74-136733. clii, 443p. 1971. Repr. of 1888 ed. 24.00 (ISBN 0-8103-3796-7). Gale.

NORWEGIAN LITERATURE-BIBLIOGRAPHY

Grondahl, Illit & Raknes, Ola. Chapters in Norwegian Literature; Being the Substance of Public Lectures, Given at University College, London, During the Sessions 1918-1922. LC 74-102241. (Select Bibliographies Reprint Ser). 1923. 24.00 (ISBN 0-8369-5126-3). Arno.

NORWEGIAN LITERATURE-HISTORY AND CRITICISM

Bauys, Harald. A History of Norwegian Literature. Haugen, Einar, tr. LC 56-6801. 1956. pap. 12.50x (ISBN 0-8147-1023-9). NYU Pr.

Beyer, Harald. History of Norwegian Literature. Haugen, Einar, ed. LC 56-6801. 1979. Repr. of 1952 ed. pap. 6.95 (ISBN 0-89067-032-3). Am Scandinavian.

Downs, Brian W. Modern Norwegian Literature, Eighteen Eighty-Nineteen Eighteen. 1966. 47.50 (ISBN 0-521-04854-0). Cambridge U Pr.

Grondahl, Carl H., intro. by. The Literary Masters of Norway. LC 79-309381. (Tokens of Norway Ser.). (Illus.). 89p. (Orig.). 1978. pap. 12.50x (ISBN 82-518-0727-1). Intl Pubns Serv.

Grondahl, Illit & Raknes, Ola. Chapters in Norwegian Literature; Being the Substance of Public Lectures, Given at University College, London, During the Sessions 1918-1922. LC 74-102241. (Select Bibliographies Reprint Ser). 1923. 24.00 (ISBN 0-8369-5126-3). Arno.

Jorgenson, Theodore. History of Norwegian Literature. LC 71-129968. (Studies in European Literature, No. 56). 1970. Repr. of 1933 ed. lib. bdg. 48.95 (ISBN 0-8383-1167-9). Haskell.

--Norwegian Literature in Medieval & Early Modern Times. LC 77-27602. 1978. Repr. of 1952 ed. lib. bdg. 17.25x (ISBN 0-313-20073-4, JONL). Greenwood.

Koht, Halvdan & Skard, Sigmund. Voice of Norway. LC 75-181941. Repr. of 1944 ed. 24.00 (ISBN 0-404-03769-0). AMS Pr.

McFarlane, James W. Ibsen & the Temper of Norwegian Literature. 1979. Repr. of 1960 ed. lib. bdg. 15.00x (ISBN 0-374-95479-8). Octagon.

Reich, Wilhelm. Ibsen's Peer Gynt. 74p. 1975. 10.00 (ISBN 0-374-17416-4). FS&G.

NORWEGIAN MUSIC

see Music, Norwegian

NORWEGIAN POETRY-TRANSLATIONS INTO ENGLISH

Stork, Charles W., ed. Anthology of Norwegian Lyrics. facs. ed. LC 68-57066. (Granger Index Reprint Ser). 1942. 15.00 (ISBN 0-8369-6043-2). Arno.

Vesaas, Tarjei. Land of Hidden Fires. Konig, Fritz & Crisp, Jerry, trs. from Norwegian. LC 72-11951. 132p. 1973. 9.95x (ISBN 0-8143-1496-1). Wayne St U Pr.

NORWEGIAN PRISONERS

see Prisoners, Norwegian

NORWEGIAN SCULPTURE

see Sculpture-Norway

NORWEGIAN TALES

see also Tales, Norwegian

Anderson, Poul. The Last Viking: Book One, The Golden Horn. 272p. (Orig.). 1980. pap. text ed. 2.50 (ISBN 0-89083-597-7). Zebra.

NORWEGIANS

see also Northmen

Leif Sverdrup. (Illus.). 435p. 1980. 14.95 (ISBN 0-935284-12-5). Patrice Pr.

Semmingsen, Ingrid. Norway to America: A History of the Migration. Haugen, Einar, tr. LC 78-3201. (Illus.). 1978. 12.95 (ISBN 0-8166-0842-3); pap. 7.95 (ISBN 0-8166-1000-2). U of Minn Pr.

NORWEGIANS IN THE UNITED STATES

Andersen, Arlow W. The Immigrant Takes His Stand: The Norwegian-American Press & Public Affairs, 1847-1872. LC 70-138098. vii, 176p. Repr. of 1953 ed. lib. bdg. 15.00 (ISBN 0-8371-5674-2, ANIS). Greenwood.

--The Norwegian-Americans. (The Immigrant Heritage of American Ser). 1975. lib. bdg. 9.95 (ISBN 0-8057-3249-7). Twayne.

Bergmann, Leola N. Americans from Norway. LC 72-12625. 324p. 1973. Repr. of 1950 ed. lib. bdg. 15.00x (ISBN 0-8371-6677-2, BEAN). Greenwood.

Blegen, Theodore. Norwegian Migration to America, 1825-60, 2 Vols. LC 68-31271. (American History & Americana Ser., No. 47). 1969. Repr. of 1931 ed. lib. bdg. 69.95 (ISBN 0-8383-0330-7). Haskell.

Blegen, Theodore C. Grass Roots History. LC 75-85987. 1969. Repr. of 1947 ed. 13.50 (ISBN 0-8046-0602-1). Kennikat.

--Norwegian Migration to America, 1825-1860. LC 69-18759. (American Immigration Collection Ser., No. 1). 1969. Repr. of 1931 ed. 12.50 (ISBN 0-405-00507-5). Arno.

Chrislock, Carl. Ethnicity Challenged: The Upper Midwest Norwegian-American Experience. Lovoll, Odd S., ed. (Topical Studies). (Illus.). 160p. 1981. 10.00 (ISBN 0-87732-066-7). Norwegian-Am Hist Assn.

Enger, Ralph. The History of the Norwegian Club of San Francisco. 1970. pap. 7.00 (ISBN 0-685-40339-4). R & E Res Assoc.

Fapso, Richard J. Norwegians in Wisconsin. (Illus.). 1977. pap. 1.25 (ISBN 0-87020-171-9). State Hist Soc Wis.

Gjerset, Knut. Norwegian Sailors on the Great Lakes. Scott, Franklyn D., ed. LC 78-15207. (Scandinavians in America Ser.). (Illus.). 1979. Repr. of 1928 ed. lib. bdg. 16.00x (ISBN 0-405-11636-5). Arno.

Gjetset, Knut. Norwegian Sailors in American Waters. Scott, Franklyn D., ed. LC 78-15186. (Scandinavians in American Ser.). (Illus.). 1979. Repr. of 1933 ed. lib. bdg. 20.00x (ISBN 0-405-11637-3). Arno.

Hillbrand, Percie V. Norwegians in America. LC 67-15683. (In America Bks.). (Illus.). (gr. 5-11). 1967. PLB 6.95g (ISBN 0-8225-0212-7). Lerner Pubns.

Holand, Hjalmar R. Norwegians in America. LC 78-55075. (Illus.). 1978. pap. 8.95 (ISBN 0-931170-07-9). Ctr Western Studies.

Larson, Laurence M. Changing West, & Other Essays. facs. ed. LC 68-16946. (Essay Index Reprint Ser). (Illus.). 1968. Repr. of 1937 ed. 15.00 (ISBN 0-8369-0606-3). Arno.

Lindberg, Duane R. Men of the Cloth & the Social-Cultural Fabric of the Norwegian Ethnic Community in North Dakota. Cordasco, Francesco, ed. LC 80-877. (American Ethnic Groups Ser.). 1981. lib. bdg. 35.00x (ISBN 0-405-13438-X). Arno.

Munch, Caja & Munch, Johan S. Strange American Way: Letters from Wiota, 1855-1859. Munch, Peter A. & Munch, Helene, trs. LC 74-112392. 288p. 1970. 12.50x (ISBN 0-8093-0440-6). S Ill U Pr.

Nelson, Clifford & Fevold, Eugene L. Lutheran Church Among Norwegian Americans, 2 Vols. LC 60-6438. 1960. Set. boxed 15.00 (ISBN 0-8066-0019-5, 10-4150). Augsburg.

Norlie, Olaf M. History of the Norwegian People in America. LC 72-1251. (American History & Americana Ser., No. 47). 1972. Repr. of 1925 ed. lib. bdg. 48.95 (ISBN 0-8383-1436-8). Haskell.

Qualey, Carlton C. Norwegian Settlement in the United States. LC 70-129409. (American Immigration Collection, Ser. 2). 1970. Repr. of 1938 ed. 15.00 (ISBN 0-405-00563-6). Arno.

Roinestad, Soren C. A Hundred Years with the Norwegians in the East Bay. 1970. pap. 6.00 (ISBN 0-685-23364-2). R & E Res Assoc.

Skard, Sigmund. Trans-Atlantica: Memoirs of a Norwegian Americanist. 1978. 20.50x (ISBN 82-00-05224-9, Dist. by Columbia U Pr.). Universitet.

Ylvisaker, Erling. Eminent Pioneers. LC 70-111875. (Essay Index Reprint Ser). 1934. 16.00 (ISBN 0-8369-1639-5). Arno.

NORWICH, ENGLAND

Evans, John T. Seventeenth-Century Norwich: Politics, Religion, & Government 1620-1690. (Illus.). 1980. 34.95 (ISBN 0-19-822476-1). Oxford U Pr.

NOSE

see also Nasopharynx; Olfactory Nerve; Smell

Dodd, Gerald D. & Jing, Bao-Shan. Radiology of the Nose, Paranasal Sinuses & Nasopharynx. (Golden's Diagnostic Radiology Ser.: Section 2). 264p. 1977. 46.00 (ISBN 0-683-02602-X). Williams & Wilkins.

Holmes, Thomas H., et al. The Nose: An Experimental Study of Reactions Within the Nose in Human Subjects During Varying Life Experiences. (Illus.). 173p. 1950. photocopy ed. spiral 16.75 (ISBN 0-398-04283-7). C C Thomas.

International Otoneurological Symposium. Transtemporal Surgery of the Internal Auditory Canal: Proceedings. Pfaltz, C. R. & Fisch, U., eds. (Advances in Oto-Rhino-Laryngology: Vol. 17). 1970. 49.75 (ISBN 3-8055-0237-0). S Karger.

Messerklinger, W. Endoscopy of the Nose. LC 77-17072. (Illus.). 187p. 1978. text ed. 78.00 (ISBN 0-8067-1211-2). Urban & S.

Wright, Jonathan. A History of Laryngology & Rhinology. 2nd rev. enl. ed. LC 75-23771. Repr. of 1914 ed. 30.50 (ISBN 0-404-13397-5). AMS Pr.
Zappler, Lisbeth. The Natural History of the Nose. LC 73-9051. (gr. 3-5). 1976. 4.95 (ISBN 0-385-00708-6). Doubleday.

NOSE-DISEASES

Ballantyne, John & Groves, John, eds. Scott Brown's Diseases of the Ear, Nose, & Throat. 4th ed. Incl. Vol. 1. Ear, Nose & Throat Diseases. 115.00 (ISBN 0-407-00147-6); Vol. 2. The Ear. 145.00 (ISBN 0-407-00148-4); Vol. 3. The Nose. 69.95 (ISBN 0-407-00149-2); Vol. 4. The Throat. 99.95 (ISBN 0-407-00150-6). LC 79-41008. (Illus.). 1979. Set. text ed. 400.00 (ISBN 0-407-00143-3). Butterworth.
Birrell, J. F. Logan Turner's Diseases of the Nose, Throat & Ear. 8th ed. (Illus.). 1977. 26.00 (ISBN 0-8151-0815-X). Year Bk Med.
Bull, T. R. Color Atlas of Ear, Nose, & Throat Diagnosis. (Year Book Color Atlas Ser.). (Illus.). 240p. 1974. 28.50 (ISBN 0-8151-1316-1). Year Bk Med.
Cody. Diseases of the Ears, Nose & Throat. 1980. 36.95 (ISBN 0-8151-1798-1). Year Bk Med.
Hall, Ian S. & Colman, Bernard H. Diseases of the Nose, Throat & Ear. 11th ed. LC 75-13874. (Illus.). 352p. 1976. pap. text ed. 12.50x (ISBN 0-443-01313-6). Churchill.
Likhachev, A. Diseases of the Ear, Nose & Throat. 1978. 8.75 (ISBN 0-8285-1888-2, Pub. by Mir Pubs Russia). Imported Pubns.
McCurdy, John A., Jr. The Complete Guide to Your Sinuses, Allergies, & Nasal Problems. LC 81-383. (Illus.). 256p. 1982. text ed. 12.95 (ISBN 0-8119-0429-6). Fell.
Saunders, William, et al. Nursing Care in Eye, Ear, Nose & Throat Disorders, Nineteen Seventy-Nine. 4th ed. LC 79-499. (Illus.). 1979. text ed. 19.95 (ISBN 0-8016-2113-5). Mosby.
Tambascia, John J. & Ritota, Michael C. The Sick Sinus & Conduction System Syndrome. Mancini, L. Phillip, ed. (Illus.). 1979. pap. text ed. write for info. (ISBN 0-916420-04-3). MEDS Corp.
Unger, June D. & Shaffer, Katherine A. Ear, Nose & Throat Radiology. LC 74-113034. (Advanced Exercises in Diagnostic Radiology Ser.: Vol. 14). (Illus.). 174p. 1980. pap. text ed. 13.95 (ISBN 0-7216-8946-9). Saunders.

NOSE-SURGERY

Ballantyne, J. & Smith, Rodney, eds. Nose & Throat. 3rd ed. (Operative Surgery Ser.). 1976. 67.00 (ISBN 0-407-00627-3). Butterworth.
Denecke, H. J. & Meyer, R. Corrective & Reconstructive Rhinoplasty. Oxtoby, L., tr. (Plastic Surgery of Head & Neck: Vol. 1). (Illus.). 1967. 289.10 (ISBN 0-387-03757-8). Springer-Verlag.
Fomon, Samuel & Bell, Julius. Rhinoplasty: New Concepts, Evaluation & Application. (Illus.). 332p. 1970. 37.75 (ISBN 0-398-00592-3). C C Thomas.
Millard. Symposium on Corrective Rhinoplasty, Vol. 13. LC 76-16519. (Illus.). 432p. 1976. 45.00 (ISBN 0-8016-3413-X). Mosby.
Portmann, Michel, et al. The Ear & Temporal Bone. LC 78-61476. (Illus.). 464p. 1979. 71.50 (ISBN 0-89352-034-9). Masson Pub.
Sheen, Jack H. Aesthetic Rhinoplasty. LC 78-27554. (Illus.). 1978. text ed. 87.50 (ISBN 0-8016-4575-1). Mosby.

NOSE, ACCESSORY SINUSES OF

Bonke, Felix I. The Sinus Node: Structure, Function, & Clinical Relevance. 1978. lib. bdg. 55.00 (ISBN 90-247-2064-8, Pub. by Martinus Nijhoff Netherlands). Kluwer Boston.
McCurdy, John A., Jr. The Complete Guide to Your Sinuses, Allergies, & Nasal Problems. LC 81-383. (Illus.). 256p. 1982. text ed. 12.95 (ISBN 0-8119-0429-6). Fell.
Ritter, Frank N. The Paranasal Sinuses: Anatomy & Surgical Techniques. 2nd ed. LC 78-7354. (Illus.). 1978. text ed. 31.50 (ISBN 0-8016-4129-2). Mosby.

NOSOLOGY

American Medical Association. Standard Nomenclature of Diseases & Operations. 5th ed. 1961. 26.00 (ISBN 0-07-001483-3, HP). McGraw.
Application of the International Classification of Diseases to Dentistry & Stomatology (ICD-DA) (Also avail. in French & Spanish). 1973. pap. 6.40 (ISBN 92-4-154029-X). World Health.
Current Procedural Terminology. 4th ed. 1970. pap. 12.00 (ISBN 0-89970-029-2, OP-041). AMA.
Faber, Knud H. Nosography. 2nd rev ed. LC 75-23706. (Illus.). 1976. Repr. of 1930 ed. 22.00 (ISBN 0-404-13258-8). AMS Pr.
Medical Certification of Cause of Death: Instructions for Physicians on Use of International Form of Medical Certificate of Cause of Death. 3rd ed. (Also avail. in French & Spanish). 1968. 1.20 (ISBN 92-4-156009-6). World Health.
Thompson & Hayden. Textbook & Guide to the Standard Nomenclature of Diseases & Operations. 1967. 14.50 (ISBN 0-917036-07-7). Physicians Rec.

NOSTOCACEAE

Drouet, F. Revision of the Nostocaceae with Constricted Trichomes. (Beihefte zur Nova Hedwigia: No. 57). (Illus.). 1978. text ed. 50.00 (ISBN 3-7682-5457-7). Lubrecht & Cramer.
Drouet, Francis. Revision of Nostocaceae with Cylindrical Trichomes. new ed. (Illus.). 256p. 1973. 16.25 (ISBN 0-02-844060-9). Hafner.

NOSTRADAMUS (MICHEL DE NOTRE DAME), 1503-1566

Nostradamus. Prophecies on World Events by Nostradamus. 4th ed. Robb, Stewart, tr. (Illus., Orig.). 1970. pap. 3.95 (ISBN 0-87140-020-0). Liveright.
Nostradamus: His Prophecies. 1973. 2.95 (ISBN 0-442-82353-3). Peter Pauper.
Prieditis, Arthur. The Fate of the Nations. LC 73-20450. 450p. 1975. 12.95 (ISBN 0-87542-624-7). Llewellyn Pubns.
Ward, Charles. Oracles of Nostradamus. 1974. 75.00 (ISBN 0-87968-232-9). Gordon Pr.

NOTARIES

see also Justices of the Peace

Arco Editorial Board. Notary Public. 5th ed. LC 76-106952. 1976. pap. 6.00 (ISBN 0-668-00180-1). Arco.
Brown, James C. The Origin & Early History of the Office of Notary. 1976. lib. bdg. 59.95 (ISBN 0-8490-2383-1). Gordon Pr.
Editors of The National Notary Magazine of the National Notary Assn. Journal of Notarial Acts & Recordkeeping Practices. 2nd ed. LC 73-75903. 1979. 11.65 (ISBN 0-933134-01-0). Natl Notary.
Editors of The National Notary Magazine of the National Notary Assn. The California Notary Law Primer. 3rd ed. 1980. pap. 5.95 (ISBN 0-933134-00-2). Natl Notary.
Editors of The National Notary magazine of the National Notary Association, ed. The Florida Notary Law Primer. 1980. pap. 5.95 (ISBN 0-933134-05-3). Natl Notary.
Editors of The National Notary Magazine of the National Notary Assn. The Missouri Notary Law Primer. 1981. pap. 5.95 (ISBN 0-933134-04-5). Natl Notary.
--The Pennsylvania Notary Law Primer. 1981. pap. 5.95 (ISBN 0-933134-07-X). Natl Notary.
--The Texas Notary Law Primer. 1981. pap. 5.95 (ISBN 0-933134-06-1). Natl Notary.
Gilmer, Wesley, Jr. Anderson's Manual for Notaries Public: With 1979 Supplement. 5th ed. 1976. text ed. 12.50 (ISBN 0-87084-039-8). Anderson Pub Co.
Green, Edward H. Guide to Notaries Public in West Virginia. 1965. 10.00 (ISBN 0-87215-090-9). Michie-Bobbs.
Rothman, Raymond C. Notary Public Practices & Glossary. 3rd ed. LC 77-93911. 1980. text ed. 13.95 (ISBN 0-933134-03-7). Natl Notary.
Rudman, Jack. Notary Public. (Career Examination Ser.: C-531). (Cloth bdg. avail. on request). pap. 6.00 (ISBN 0-8373-0531-4). Natl Learning.
Woodward, M. Truman. Louisiana Notarial Manual. 2nd ed. 1962. text ed. 35.00 including 1973 suppl. (ISBN 0-87473-016-3). A Smith Co.

NOTATION (FOR BOOKS IN LIBRARIES)

see Alphabeting

NOTATION, MATHEMATICAL

see Mathematical Notation

NOTATION, MUSICAL

see Musical Notation

NOTE-TAKING

Baird, Don O. A Study of Biology Notebook Work in New York State. LC 71-176532. (Columbia University. Teachers College. Contributions to Education: No. 400). Repr. of 1929 ed. 17.50 (ISBN 0-404-55400-8). AMS Pr.
Barton, William A. Outlining As a Study Procedure. LC 77-176539. (Columbia University. Teachers College. Contributions to Education: No. 411). Repr. of 1930 ed. 17.50 (ISBN 0-404-55411-3). AMS Pr.
Brown, Diane. Notemaking. 245p. 1977. text ed. 10.56x (ISBN 0-7715-0858-1); tchr's. manual 15.85x (ISBN 0-7715-0859-X). Forkner.
Leslie, Louis A., et al. Gregg Notehand. 2nd ed. 1968. text ed. 11.04 (ISBN 0-07-037331-0, G); instructor's guide 4.30 (ISBN 0-07-037338-8); exercises 5.18 (ISBN 0-07-037343-4); inst. key to exercises 4.30 (ISBN 0-07-037344-2). McGraw.
Weber, Gloria H., et al. Notetaking & Study Skills. (gr. 10-12). 1977. 11.96x (ISBN 0-912036-27-3); wkbk. 5.96x (ISBN 0-912036-28-1); instrs'. manual 2.00x (ISBN 0-912036-29-X); profiles pkg. of 25 6.96x (ISBN 0-912036-30-3); tape library (6 cassettes) 117.00x (ISBN 0-912036-43-5). Forkner.
Yates, Virginia. Listening & Note Taking. (McGraw-Hill Basic Skills System). (Illus.). 1979. pap. text ed. 7.95 (ISBN 0-07-044413-7, C); cassettes & transcripts 100.00 (ISBN 0-07-044414-5). McGraw.
Ziggy's Class Notes. 1980. 2.95 (ISBN 0-8362-1916-3). Andrews & McMeel.

NOTHING (PHILOSOPHY)

see also Ontology

Dorman, Peter J. The Quotable Nothing Book: Being a Book of Quotes About Nothing & Nothingness. (Illus.). 96p. 1980. lib. bdg. 12.90 (ISBN 0-89471-096-6); pap. 3.95 (ISBN 0-89471-097-4). Running Pr.
Novak, Michael. Experience of Nothingness. 1971. pap. 3.95x (ISBN 0-06-131938-4, TB 1938, Torch). Har-Row.

NOTICE OF DISMISSAL

see Employees, Dismissal of

NOTKER LABEO, 950-1022

Hoffmann, Paul. Mischprosa Notkers Des Deutschen. 1910. 21.50 (ISBN 0-384-23941-2); pap. 18.50 (ISBN 0-685-13518-7). Johnson Repr.

NOTRE DAME, MICHEL DE, 1503-1566

see Nostradamus (Michel de Notre Dame), 1503-1566

NOTRE DAME, UNIVERSITY OF

Bonifer & Weaver. Out of Bounds: An Anecdotal History of Notre Dame Football. LC 78-60060. (Illus.). 1978. 15.00 (ISBN 0-87832-043-1). Piper.
Condon, Dave, et al. Notre Dame Football: The Golden Tradition. (Illus.). 208p. 1981. 21.95 (ISBN 0-89651-510-9). Icarus.
Hope, Arthur J. Notre Dame: One Hundred Years. LC 78-23391. 532p. 1979. 15.95 (ISBN 0-89651-500-1); pap. 9.95 (ISBN 0-89651-501-X). Icarus.
Jeffers, Jeff. Rally: The Twelve Greatest Notre Dame Football Comebacks. (Illus.). 250p. 1981. 12.95 (ISBN 0-89651-651-2). Icarus.
Pagna, Tom & Best, Bob. Notre Dame's Era of Ara. LC 76-24238. (Illus.). 1976. 9.95 (ISBN 0-87397-104-3). Strode.
Rappoport, Ken. Wake Up the Echoes: Notre Dame Football. LC 75-26072. (College Sports Ser.). 1981. 11.95 (ISBN 0-87397-053-5). Strode.
Schlereth, Thomas J. The University of Notre Dame: A Portrait of Its History & Campus. LC 74-27890. 1976. pap. text ed. 7.95x (ISBN 0-268-01905-3). U of Notre Dame Pr.

NOTTINGHAM, ENGLAND

Bryson, Emrys. Portrait of Nottingham. (Portrait Bk.). (Illus.). 208p. 1974. 10.50x (ISBN 0-7091-4338-9). Intl Pubns Serv.
Church, Roy A. Economic & Social Change in a Midland Town: Victorian Nottingham, 1815-1900. LC 66-5409. (Illus.). 1966. 22.50x (ISBN 0-678-05038-4). Kelley.
--Economic & Social Change in a Midland Town: Victorian Nottingham, 1815-1900. (Illus.). 409p. 1966. 27.50x (ISBN 0-7146-1290-1, F Cass Co). Biblio Dist.
Thomis, Malcolm I. Old Nottingham. LC 68-9402. (Illus.). 1968. 10.95x (ISBN 0-678-05565-3). Kelley.
--Politics & Society in Nottingham 1785-1835. LC 78-92499. 1969. 15.00x (ISBN 0-678-06250-1). Kelley.

NOTTINGHAMSHIRE, ENGLAND

Chambers, Jonathan D. Nottinghamshire in the Eighteenth Century. LC 65-5293. Repr. of 1932 ed. 22.50x (ISBN 0-678-05036-8). Kelley.
--Nottinghamshire in the Eighteenth Century. new ed. 377p. 1966. 27.50x (ISBN 0-7146-1285-5, F Cass Co). Biblio Dist.
Morris, John, ed. Nottinghamshire. (The Domesday Bk Ser.). (Illus.). 160p. 1977. 18.00x (ISBN 0-8476-1427-1). Rowman.

NOUVELLE COMPAGNIE DES INDIES

Furber, Holden. John Company at Work. LC 70-96181. 1969. Repr. lib. bdg. 24.00x (ISBN 0-374-92945-9). Octagon.

NOUTKA LANGUAGE

see Nootka Language

NOVA SCOTIA

see also Acadia

Brebner, John B. Neutral Yankees of Nova Scotia: A Marginal Colony During the Revolutionary Years. LC 72-102471. 1970. Repr. of 1937 ed. 15.00 (ISBN 0-8462-1488-1). Russell.
Clark, Andrew H. Acadia: The Georgraphy of Early Nova Scotia to 1760. (Illus.). 470p. 1968. 27.50x (ISBN 0-299-05080-7). U of Wis Pr.
Columbia University Center for Advanced Research in Urban & Enviornmental Affairs. Working Paper 2. (Working Papers Ser.: 2). (Illus.). 1977. pap. 15.00 (ISBN 0-686-19302-4). Pr of Nova Scotia.
Laing, David, ed. Royal Letters, Charters, & Tracts. LC 70-171639. (Bannatyne Club, Edinburgh. Publications: No. 114). Repr. of 1867 ed. 42.50 (ISBN 0-404-52869-4). AMS Pr.
Murdoch, Beamish. Epitome of the Laws of Nova Scotia, 4 vols. LC 73-26626. 1034p. Repr. of 1833 ed. Set. 95.00x (ISBN 0-912004-04-5). W W Gaunt.

NOVA SCOTIA-DESCRIPTION AND TRAVEL

Armstrong, Bruce. Sable Island. LC 80-2745. (Illus.). 256p. 1981. 19.95 (ISBN 0-385-13113-5). Doubleday.
Clarke, Wayne, et al. Cruising Nova Scotia: From Yarmouth to Casuo. LC 79-11352. 1979. 12.95 (ISBN 0-396-07671-8). Dodd.
De Diereville, Sieur. Relation of the Voyage to Port Royal in Acadia or New France. Webster, John C., ed. LC 68-28608. 1968. Repr. of 1933 ed. lib. bdg. 28.00x (ISBN 0-8371-5058-2, DIRV). Greenwood.
Denys, Nicolas. Description - Natural History of the Coasts of North America. Ganong, William F., ed. LC 68-28597. 1968. Repr. of 1908 ed. lib. bdg. 42.25x (ISBN 0-8371-3873-6, DEDH). Greenwood.
Feild, Lance. Exploring Nova Scotia. LC 79-4903. (Illus.). 192p. 1978. pap. 6.95 (ISBN 0-914788-16-7). East Woods.
Furneaux, Rupert. The Money Pit Mystery: The Costliest Treasure Hunt Ever. new ed. LC 73-6030. (Illus.). 160p. 1973. 5.95 (ISBN 0-396-06833-2). Dodd.
Hines, Sherman. Nova Scotia: The Lighthouse & the Annapolis Valley. (Illus.). 1980. 14.95 (ISBN 0-19-540319-3). Oxford U Pr.
Howe, Joseph. Western & Eastern Rambles: Travel Sketches of Nova Scotia. Parks, M. G., ed. LC 72-97424. (Illus.). 1973. pap. 5.50 (ISBN 0-8020-6183-4). U of Toronto Pr.
Marsden, Joshua. The Narrative of a Mission to Nova Scotia, New Brunswick & the Somers Islands. Repr. of 1816 ed. 19.50 (ISBN 0-384-35430-0). Johnson Repr.
--The Narrative of a Mission to Nova Scotia, New Brunswick & the Somers Islands. Repr. of 1816 ed. 19.50 (ISBN 0-384-35430-0). Johnson Repr.

NOVA SCOTIA-HISTORY

Denys, Nicolas. Description - Natural History of the Coasts of North America. Ganong, William F., ed. LC 68-28597. 1968. Repr. of 1908 ed. lib. bdg. 42.25x (ISBN 0-8371-3873-6, DEDH). Greenwood.
Livingstone, W. Ross. Responsible Government in Nova Scotia: A Study of the Constitutional Beginnings of the British Commonwealth. (Perspectives in Canadian History: No. 7). Repr. of 1930 ed. lib. bdg. 17.50x (ISBN 0-87991-127-1). Porcupine Pr.
Perkins, Simeon. Diary of Simeon Perkins, 1766-1780, Vol. 1. Innes, Harold A., ed. LC 69-14503. 1969. Repr. of 1948 ed. lib. bdg. 18.25x (ISBN 0-8371-5067-1, PEDI). Greenwood.
--Diary of Simeon Perkins, 1780-1789, Vol. 2. Harvey, D. C., ed. LC 69-14503. 1969. Repr. of 1958 ed. lib. bdg. 33.50x (ISBN 0-8371-5068-X, PEDJ). Greenwood.
Pryke, Kenneth G. Nova Scotia & Confederation Eighteen Sixty-Four to Seventy-Four. LC 79-94235. (Canadian Studies in History & Government Ser.). 1979. 20.00x (ISBN 0-8020-5389-0). U of Toronto Pr.
Rawlyk, George A. Nova Scotia's Massachusetts: A Study of Massachusetts - Nova Scotia Relations, 1630 to 1784. (Illus.). 256p. 1973. 14.00x (ISBN 0-7735-0142-8). McGill-Queen's U Pr.
Slafter, Edmund F., ed. Sir William Alexander & American Colonization. 1966. 21.00 (ISBN 0-8337-3292-7). B Franklin.
Smith, Leonard H., Jr. Cape Sable Nova Scotia: Vital Records Seventeen Ninety-Nine to Eighteen Forty-One. LC 79-66242. 1979. text ed. 20.00x (ISBN 0-932022-13-8). L H Smith.
Stewart, Gordon & Rawlyk, George. A People Highly Favoured of God: The Nova Scotia Yankees & the American Revolution. LC 78-38968. 256p. 1972. 17.50 (ISBN 0-208-01283-4, Archon). Shoe String.

NOVA SCOTIA-HISTORY-SOURCES

Smith, Leonard H., Jr., ed. Index of Persons: Isiah W. Wilson's County of Digby Nova Scotia. pap. 12.50 (ISBN 0-932022-00-6). L H Smith.
--Salmon River, Digby County, Nova Scotia: Vital Records 1849-1907. LC 77-79479. pap. 20.00 (ISBN 0-932022-10-3). L H Smith.
Uniacke, Richard J. Nova Scotia Statutes: Statutes at Large, Vols. 1-4. LC 76-612783. 1970. Repr. Set. lib. bdg. 195.00x (ISBN 0-912004-06-1). W W Gaunt.

NOVA SCOTIA-SOCIAL LIFE AND CUSTOMS

Columbia University Center for Advanced Research in Urban & Environmental Affairs. Fifteen Families in Akcalan. (Working Papers Ser.: 2). (Illus.). 1977. pap. 15.00 (ISBN 0-686-19303-2). Pr of Nova Scotia.

NOVA-SCOTIAN FOLK-LORE

see also Folk-Lore, Nova-Scotian

NOVAE

see Stars, New

NOVALIS
see Hardenberg, Friedrich Leopold, Freiherr Von, 1772-1801
NOVARA, SIEGE OF, 1495
Benedetti, Alessandro. Diary of the Caroline War. Schullian, Dorothy M., tr. LC 66-21028. (Renaissance Text Ser.: Vol. 1). Orig. Title: Diaria De Bello Carolina. 15.00 (ISBN 0-8044-1105-0). Ungar.
NOVELISTS
see Authors
NOVELS
see Fiction; Plots (Drama, Novel, etc.)
Kramer, John E., Jr. The American College Novel: An Annotated Bibliography. 1981. lib. bdg. 40.00 (ISBN 0-8240-9365-8). Garland Pub.
NOVENAS
Cassidy, Norma C. Favorite Novenas & Prayers. 1973. pap. 2.95 (ISBN 0-8091-1761-4, Deus). Paulist Pr.
Lacy, C. Rosary Novenas. 1974. pap. 1.00 (ISBN 0-02-645810-1). Macmillan.
Rosary Novenas. 0.65 (ISBN 0-02-645810-1). Benziger Pub Co.
NOVGOROD, RUSSIA (CITY)
Chronicle of Novgorod, 1016-1471. (Russian Ser.: Vol. 18). Repr. of 1914 ed. 21.50 (ISBN 0-87569-017-3). Academic Intl.
Karger, M. Novgorod the Great. 255p. 1973. 10.00 (ISBN 0-8285-0890-9, Pub. by Progress Pubs Russia). Imported Pubns.
NOVGOROD, RUSSIA (CITY)–ANTIQUITIES
Mitchell, R. & Forbes, Nevill, trs. Chronicle of Novgorod, 1016-1471. Repr. of 1914 ed. 16.75 (ISBN 0-404-04799-8). AMS Pr.
NOVITIATE
Lynch, Joseph H. Simoniacal Entry into Religious Life, 1000 to 1260: A Social, Economic, & Legal Study. LC 76-22670. (Illus.). 1976. 15.00x (ISBN 0-8142-0222-5). Ohio St U Pr.
Philippe, Paul. Novitiate. (Religious Life in the Modern World Ser.: Vol. 2). (Orig.). 1961. pap. 1.95x (ISBN 0-268-00196-0). U of Notre Dame Pr.
NOYES, ALFRED, 1880-
Jerrold, Walter. Alfred Noyes. 1978. Repr. of 1931 ed. lib. bdg. 20.00 (ISBN 0-8495-2736-8). Arden Lib.
Walter, Jerrold. Alfred Noyes. 1978. Repr. of 1930 ed. lib. bdg. 20.00 (ISBN 0-8274-0000-4). R West.
NOYES, JOHN HUMPHREY, 1811-1886
Jacoby, John E. Two Mystic Communities in America. LC 75-326. (The Radical Tradition in America Ser). 104p. 1975. Repr. of 1931 ed. 13.50 (ISBN 0-88355-230-2). Hyperion Conn.
Noyes, George W., ed. John Humphrey Noyes: The Putney Community. (Illus.). 1931. 30.00x (ISBN 0-8156-8059-7). Syracuse U Pr.
--Religious Experience of John Humphrey Noyes. 1923. 15.00x (ISBN 0-8156-8060-0). Syracuse U Pr.
Noyes, John H. Religious Experience of John Humphrey Noyes, Founder of the Oneida Community. facsimile ed. Noyes, George W., ed. (Select Bibliographies Reprint Ser). Repr. of 1923 ed. 24.00 (ISBN 0-8369-5750-4). Arno.
Parker, Robert A. A Yankee Saint: John Humphrey Noyes & the Oneida Community. LC 75-187456. (The American Utopian Adventure Ser.). 322p. Repr. of 1935 ed. lib. bdg. 16.50x (ISBN 0-87991-009-7). Porcupine Pr.
--A Yankee Saint: John Humphrey Noyes & the Oneida Community. (Illus.). 327p. 1973. Repr. of 1935 ed. 19.50 (ISBN 0-208-01319-9, Archon). Shoe String.
NOYON, FRANCE–NOTRE-DAME (CATHEDRAL)
Seymour, Charles, Jr. Notre-Dame of Noyon in the Twelfth Century: A Study in the Early Development of Gothic Architecture. 1968. pap. 3.95x (ISBN 0-393-00464-3, Norton Lib). Norton.
NU, U
Butwell, Richard. U Nu of Burma. rev. ed. (Illus.). 1969. 12.50x (ISBN 0-8047-0155-5). Stanford U Pr.
NUBIA
Belzoni, Giovanni. Adventures, in Egypt & Nubia. 1843. 25.00 (ISBN 0-403-00454-3). Scholarly.
Burckhardt, John L. Some Account of the Travels in Egypt & Nubia. 2nd ed. 1971. 35.00 (ISBN 0-403-03692-5). Scholarly.
--Travels in Nubia. LC 74-15014. Repr. of 1882 ed. 37.50 (ISBN 0-404-12009-1). AMS Pr.
Fernea, Robert A. & Gerster, Georg. Nubians in Egypt: Peaceful People. LC 73-3078. (Illus.). 160p. 1973. 25.00 (ISBN 0-292-75504-X). U of Tex Pr.
Kennedy, John G. Struggle for Change in a Nubian Community. Edgerton, Robert B. & Langness, L. L., eds. LC 76-28115. (Explorations in World Ethnology Ser.). (Illus.). 194p. 1977. 6.95 (ISBN 0-87484-321-9). Mayfield Pub.
Kennedy, John G., ed. Nubian Ceremonial Life: Studies in Islamic Syncretism & Cultural Change. 1979. 16.50x (ISBN 0-520-02748-5). U of Cal Pr.
Marks, Anthony E. Preceramic Sites. Save-Soderbergh, Torgny, ed. (Scandinavian Joint Expedition to Sudanese Nubia). (Illus.). 1970. text ed. 13.50x (ISBN 0-8419-8801-3). Holmes & Meier.
Nordstrom, Hans-Ake & Haland, Randi. Neolithic & A-Group Sites, 2 vols. LC 73-851683. (Scandinavian Joint Expedition to Sudanese Nubia Ser). (Illus.). 420p. 1973. Set. text ed. 65.00x (ISBN 0-8419-8802-1, Africana). Holmes & Meier.
Porter, Bertha & Moss, Rosalind. Nubia, the Deserts & Outside Egypt, Seven. (Topographical Bibliography of Ancient Egyptian Hieroglypic Texts, Reliefs & Paintings Ser.). 453p. 1952. text ed. 49.00 (ISBN 0-900416-04-1, Pub. by Aris & Phillips England). Humanities.
Prime, William C. Boat Life in Egypt & Nubia. LC 77-87655. Repr. of 1872 ed. 34.50 (ISBN 0-404-16409-9). AMS Pr.
Trigger, Bruce G. The Late Nubian Settlement at Arminna West. (Pubns of the Penn-Yale Expedition to Egypt: No. 2). 1967. 16.00 (ISBN 0-686-17768-1). Univ Mus of U PA.
NUBIA–ANTIQUITIES
Africa in Antiquity: The Arts of Ancient Nubia & the Sudan - the Essays, Vol. 1. LC 78-10925. (Illus.). 1978. text ed. 26.00 (ISBN 0-87273-063-8); pap. text ed. 12.00 (ISBN 0-87273-065-4). Bklyn Mus.
Bergman, Ingrid. Late Nubian Textiles. Save-Soderbergh, Torgny, ed. (Scandinavian Joint Expedition to Sudanese Nubia). (Illus.). 1975. text ed. 25.00x (ISBN 0-8419-8807-2). Holmes & Meier.
Brown, Claudine K. Something Old, Something Nubian. (Illus.). 20p. (gr. 3-7). pap. 1.25 (ISBN 0-686-74788-7). Bklyn Mus.
Eckley B Coxe, Jr. Expedition to Nubia, 5 vols. Incl. Vol. 1. Areika. Randall-MacIver, D., et al. (Illus.). 56p. 1909. 7.00 (ISBN 0-686-11897-9); Vol. 3-4. Karanog, the Romano-Nubian Cemetery. Woolley, C. Leonard & Randall-MacIver, D. (Illus.). 286p. 1910. 28.00 (ISBN 0-686-11898-7); Vol. 5. Karanog, the Town. Woolley, C. Leonard. (Illus.). 51p. 1911. 7.00 (ISBN 0-686-11899-5); Vol. 6. Karanog, the Meroitic Inscriptions of Shablul & Karanog. Griffith, F. L. (Illus.). 181p. 1911. 14.00 (ISBN 0-686-11900-2); Vol. 7-8. Buhen. Randall-MacIver, D. & Woolley, C. Leonard. (Illus.). 243p. 1911. 28.00 (ISBN 0-686-11901-0). Univ Mus of U PA.
Hellstrom, Pontus & Langballe, Hans. The Rock Drawings, 2 pts. Save-Soderbergh, Torgny, ed. (Scandinavian Joint Expedition to Sudanese Nubia). (Illus.). 1970. Set. text ed. 55.00x (ISBN 0-8419-8800-5). Holmes & Meier.
Lister, Florence C. Ceramic Studies of the Historic Periods in Ancient Nubia. (Nubian Ser.: No. 2). Repr. of 1967 ed. 30.00 (ISBN 0-404-60686-5). AMS Pr.
Nielsen, Ole V. Human Remains: Metrical & Non-Metrical Anatomical Variations. Save-Soderbergh, Torgny, ed. (Scandinavian Joint Expedition to Sudanese Nubia Ser.). (Illus.). 1970. text ed. 20.00x (ISBN 0-8419-8808-0). Holmes & Meier.
Plumley, J. Martin. The Scrolls of Bishop Timotheos: Two Documents from Medieval Nubia. James, T. G., ed. (Texts from Excavations Ser.: 1st Memoir). (Illus.). 1976. 22.00x (ISBN 0-85698-044-7, Pub. by Aris & Phillips). Intl Schol Bk Serv.
Reisner, G. A. Excavations at Kerma, Pts. I-V. Hooton, E. A. & Bates, Natica I., eds. (Harvard African Studies: Vol. 5). Pts. I-III. lib. bdg. 81.00 set (ISBN 0-527-01028-6); Pts. IV-V. lib. bdg. 69.00 set (ISBN 0-527-01029-4). Kraus Repr.
Ricke, Herbert, et al. Ausgrabungen Von Khor Dehmit Bis Bet el-Wali. LC 68-15933. (Oriental Institute Nubian Expedition Pubns. Ser: Vol. 2). (Illus.). 1968. 30.00x (ISBN 0-226-62366-1, OINE2). U of Chicago Pr.
Shinnie, P. L. & Shinnie, Margaret. A Mediaeval Nubian Town. (Illus.). 107p. 1978. text ed. 69.00x (ISBN 0-85668-094-X, Pub. by Aris & Phillips England). Humanities.
Wendorf, Fred, ed. Contributions to the Prehistory of Nubia. LC 65-5730. (Contributions in Anthropology Ser.: No. 1). 200p. 1965. pap. 4.00 (ISBN 0-87074-124-1). SMU Press.
--The Prehistory of Nubia, 2 Vols. LC 68-18382. (Contributions in Anthropology: No. 2). (Illus.). 1968. Set. 50.00, with separate atlas (ISBN 0-87074-125-X). SMU Press.
Wenig, Steffen. Africa in Antiquity: The Arts of Ancient Nubia & the Sudan - the Exhibition, Vol. 2. LC 78-10925. (Illus.). 1978. text ed. 40.00 (ISBN 0-87273-064-6); pap. 18.00 (ISBN 0-87273-066-2). Bklyn Mus.
NUBIAN LANGUAGE
Armbruster, C. H. Dongolese Nubian: A Grammar. 1965. text ed. 170.00 (ISBN 0-521-04050-7). Cambridge U Pr.
--Dongolese Nubian, a Lexicon. 1965. text ed. 145.00 (ISBN 0-521-04051-5). Cambridge U Pr.
NUCLEAR ASTROPHYSICS
Arnett, W. B., et al, eds. Nucleosynthesis. LC 67-28241. 1968. 63.75x (ISBN 0-677-11580-6). Gordon.
Audouze, Jean & Vauclair, Sylvie. An Introduction to Nuclear Astrophysics: The Formation & Evolution of Matter in the Universe. (Geophysics & Astrophysics Monographs: No. 18). 1980. lib. bdg. 39.50 (ISBN 90-277-1012-0, Pub. by Reidel Holland); pap. 21.00 (ISBN 90-277-1053-8, Pub. by Reidel Holland). Kluwer Boston.
Chretien, M. & Lipworth, E., eds. Brandeis University Summer Institute in Theoretical Physics: 1969 Lectures: Atomic Physics & Astrophysics, 2 vols. Vol. 1. 1971 ed. 54.50x (ISBN 0-677-14900-X); Vol. 2. 1973 ed. 73.25x (ISBN 0-677-14910-7). Gordon.
Clayton, Donald D. Principles of Stellar Evolution & Nucleosynthesis. LC 68-12263. 1968. text ed. 29.95 (ISBN 0-07-011295-9, C). McGraw.
Fichtel, Carl E. & McDonald, Frank B., eds. High Energy Particles & Quanta in Astrophysics. 1974. 25.00x (ISBN 0-262-06048-5). MIT Pr.
Greisen, Kenneth. The Physics of Cosmic X-Ray, Gamma-Ray & Particle Sources. 2nd ed. Cameron, A. G. W. & Field, G. B., eds. LC 78-135063. (Topics in Astrophysics & Space Physics Ser.). (Illus.). 124p. 1971. 22.50 (ISBN 0-677-03380-X). Gordon.
Hazard, C. & Mitton, S., eds. Active Galactic Nuclei. LC 78-67426. 1979. 38.50 (ISBN 0-521-22494-2). Cambridge U Pr.
Krueger, A. Physics of Solar Continuum Radio Bursts. 200p. 1973. 26.50 (ISBN 0-685-39164-7). Adler.
Schild, A. & Schucking, E. L., eds. Quasers & High Energy Astronomy. 1969. 103.00 (ISBN 0-677-11520-2). Gordon.
Shen, Benjamin S. & Merker, Milton, eds. Spallation Nuclear Reactions & Their Applications. new ed. (Astrophysics & Space Science Library: No. 59). 1976. lib. bdg. 39.50 (ISBN 90-277-0746-4, Pub. by Reidel Holland). Kluwer Boston.
NUCLEAR CHEMISTRY
Here are entered works on the application of chemical techniques to the study of the structure and properties of atomic nuclei, their transformations and reactions. Works on the chemical effects of high energy radiation on matter are entered under Radiation chemistry. Works on the chemical properties of radioactive substances and their use in chemical studies are entered under Radiochemistry.
see also Nuclear Physics; Radiation Chemistry; Radiochemistry
Arnikar, Hari J. Essentials of Nuclear Chemistry. LC 81-6818. 256p. 1982. 17.95 (ISBN 0-470-27176-0). Halsted Pr.
Benedict, M. & Pigford, T. Nuclear Chemical Engineering. (Nuclear Engineering Ser). 1957. 27.95 (ISBN 0-07-004530-5, C). McGraw.
Benedict, Manson, et al. Nuclear Chemical Engineering. 2nd ed. (Illus.). 1008p. 1981. text ed. 37.95 (ISBN 0-07-004531-3, C). McGraw.
Cindro, N., ed. Nuclear Molecular Phenomena. 1978. 58.75 (ISBN 0-444-85116-X, North-Holland). Elsevier.
Erdtmann, Gerhard. Neutron Activation Tables. (Topical Presentations in Nuclear Chemistry Ser.: Vol. 6). (Illus.). 1976. 45.90 (ISBN 3-527-25693-8). Verlag Chemie.
Friedlander, Gerhart. Nuclear & Radiochemistry. 3rd ed. LC 81-1000. 650p. 1981. 36.50 (ISBN 0-471-28021-6, Pub. by Wiley-Interscience). Wiley.
Friedlander, Gerhart, et al. Nuclear & Radiochemistry. 3rd ed. 688p. 1981. pap. 29.50 (ISBN 0-471-86255-X, Pub. by Wiley-Interscience). Wiley.
Haissinsky, M. Nuclear Chemistry & Its Applications. 1964. 25.00 (ISBN 0-201-02705-4, Adv Bk Prog). A-W.
Harvey, Bernard G. Introduction to Nuclear Physics & Chemistry. 2nd ed. 1969. ref. ed. 27.95 (ISBN 0-13-491159-8). P-H.
Hot Atom Chemistry Status Report: Proceedings, Vienna, 1974. (Illus.). 332p. 1976. pap. 31.00 (ISBN 92-0-141075-1, ISP393, IAEA). Unipub.
Keller, Cornelius. The Chemistry of Transuranium Elements. LC 79-173366. (Topical Presentations in Nuclear Chemistry Ser.: Vol. 3). (Illus.). 1971. 110.60 (ISBN 3-527-25389-0). Verlag Chemie.
Krugers, Jan, ed. Instrumentation in Applied Nuclear Chemistry. LC 79-183561. (Illus.). 383p. 1973. 37.50 (ISBN 0-306-30562-3, Plenum Pr). Plenum Pub.
National Research Council - Committee For The Survey Of Chemistry. Nuclear Chemistry: A Current Review. 1966. pap. 3.00 (ISBN 0-309-01292-9). Natl Acad Pr.
Richards, W. G., et al. Bibliography of Ab Initio Molecular Wave Functions: Supplement for 1974-1977. (Science Research Papers Ser). 1979. pap. 45.00 (ISBN 0-19-855360-9). Oxford U Pr.
Tominaga, T. & Tachikawa, E. Modern Hot-Atom Chemistry & Its Applications. (Inorganic Chemistry Concepts Ser.). (Illus.). 160p. 1981. 49.50 (ISBN 0-387-10715-0). Springer-Verlag.
Whitson, Gary, ed. Nuclear-Cytoplasmic Interactions in the Cell Cycle. (Cell Biology Ser.). 1980. 39.00 (ISBN 0-12-747750-0). Acad Pr.
Yaffe, L., ed. Nuclear Chemistry, Vols. 1-2. 1968. 63.00 (ISBN 0-686-76855-8). Vol. 1 (ISBN 0-12-767901-4). Vol. 2 (ISBN 0-12-767902-2). Acad Pr.
NUCLEAR COUNTERS
see also Cold Cathode Tubes; Radiation Dosimetry; Radioactive Prospecting; Scintillation Counters; Semiconductor Nuclear Counters
DiIorio, Gino J. Direct Physical Measurement of Mass Yields in Thermal Fission of Uranium. LC 78-75005. (Outstanding Disserations on Energy Ser.). 1979. lib. bdg. 11.00 (ISBN 0-8240-3985-8). Garland Pub.
Helman, Edith Z. Basic Principles of Nuclear Counting: A Programmed Text. 1975. 10.00 (ISBN 0-930914-01-5). Sci Newsletters.
Korff, Serge A. Electron & Nuclear Counters: Theory & Use. Repr. of 1955 ed. lib. bdg. 16.25x (ISBN 0-8371-2395-X, KONC). Greenwood.
Low-Background High-Efficiency Geiger-Muller Counter. (Technical Reports Ser.: No. 33). 1964. pap. 5.50 (ISBN 92-0-135064-3, IDC33, IAEA). Unipub.
Miller, Dudley G. Radioactivity & Radiation Detection. LC 70-146446. (Illus.). 122p. 1972. 29.25x (ISBN 0-677-01490-2). Gordon.
Neutron Monitoring. 1967. pap. 33.25 (ISBN 92-0-020067-2, ISP136, IAEA). Unipub.
Ouseph, P. J. Introduction to Nuclear Radiation Detectors. LC 74-22364. (Laboratory Instrumentation & Techniques Ser.: Vol. 2). (Illus.). 194p. 1975. 25.00 (ISBN 0-306-35302-4, Plenum Pr). Plenum Pub.
Price, W. J. Nuclear Radiation Detection. 2nd ed. (Nuclear Engineering Ser.). 1964. text ed. 29.50 (ISBN 0-07-050860-7, P&RB). McGraw.
NUCLEAR DAMAGES, LIABILITY FOR
see Liability for Nuclear Damages
NUCLEAR ENERGY
see Atomic Energy
NUCLEAR ENGINEERING
see also Atomic Power; Nuclear Fuels; Nuclear Reactors; Radioisotopes; Shielding (Radiation)
Aron, Raymond. The Great Debate: Theories of Nuclear Strategy. Pawel, Ernst, tr. from Fr. LC 81-495. ix, 265p. 1981. Repr. of 1965 ed. lib. bdg. 27.50x (ISBN 0-313-22851-5, ARGR). Greenwood.
Ash, Milton S. Nuclear Reactor Kinetics. nd ed. (Illus.). 1979. text ed. 49.50 (ISBN 0-07-002380-8). McGraw.
ASME-ANS International Conference on Advanced Nuclear Energy Systems, 1976. 638p. 1976. pap. 55.00 (ISBN 0-685-78340-5, H00099). ASME.
Benedict, M. & Pigford, T. Nuclear Chemical Engineering. (Nuclear Engineering Ser). 1957. 27.95 (ISBN 0-07-004530-5, C). McGraw.
Benedict, Manson, et al. Nuclear Chemical Engineering. 2nd ed. (Illus.). 1008p. 1981. text ed. 37.95 (ISBN 0-07-004531-3, C). McGraw.
Bracco, F. V. Stratified Charge Engines. 100p. 1974. 36.25x (ISBN 0-677-05165-4). Gordon.
Companies Holding Nuclear Certificates of Authorization. (Bk. No. E00061). 55p. 1978. 45.00 (ISBN 0-685-37566-8). ASME.
Connolly, Thomas J. Foundations of Nuclear Engineering. LC 77-26916. 1978. text ed. 30.95 (ISBN 0-471-16858-0). Wiley.
Davey, W. G. & Redman, W. C. Techniques in Fast Reactor Critical Experiments. LC 79-119375. 314p. 1970. 20.40 (ISBN 0-677-02680-3). Am Nuclear Soc.
DeFelice, Gerald T. Nuclear Engineering. 400p. (Orig.). pap. text ed. 29.95 (ISBN 0-686-30241-9). Une Pub.
Division 1 - Nuclear Power Plant Components: General Requirements. (Boiler & Pressure Vessel Code Ser.: Sec. 3). 1980. 55.00 (ISBN 0-686-70367-7, P0003R); pap. 80.00 loose-leaf (ISBN 0-686-70368-5, V0003R). ASME.
Duderstadt, James J. & Hamilton, Louis J. Nuclear Reactor Analysis. LC 75-20389. 650p. 1976. text ed. 38.95 (ISBN 0-471-22363-8). Wiley.
Egelstaff, P. A. & Poole, M. J. Experimental Neutron Thermalization. LC 79-86201. 1970. 60.00 (ISBN 0-08-006533-3). Pergamon.
El Wakil, M. M. Nuclear Heat Transport. LC 78-61691. 1978. 28.60 (ISBN 0-89448-014-6). Am Nuclear Soc.

El-Wakil, M. M. Nuclear Power Engineering. (Nuclear Engineering Ser). 1962. text ed. 26.50 (ISBN 0-07-019300-2, C). McGraw.
Etherington, H. Nuclear Engineering Handbook. 1958. 55.00 (ISBN 0-07-019720-2, P&RB). McGraw.
Foderaro, Anthony. Elements of Neutron Interaction Theory. LC 79-103896. 1971. text ed. 32.50x (ISBN 0-262-06033-7). MIT Pr.
Foster, Arthur R. & Wright, Robert L., Jr. Basic Nuclear Engineering. 3rd ed. 1977. text ed. 29.95x (ISBN 0-205-05697-0); sol. manual free (ISBN 0-205-05698-9). Allyn.
Foust, O. J., ed. Sodium-Nak Engineering Handbook, 5 vols. (U.S. Atomic Energy Commission Monograhs). (Illus.). Vol. 3. 73.75 (ISBN 0-677-03040-1); Vol. 4. 73.75 (ISBN 0-677-03050-9). Vol. 5. Gordon.
--Sodium-Nak Engineering Handbook, 5 vols, Vol. 2. LC 70-129473. (U.S. Atomic Energy Commission Monographs). (Illus.). 1976. 82.00 (ISBN 0-677-03030-4). Gordon.
Garg, J. B., ed. Statistical Properties of Nuclei. LC 75-182409. 665p. 1972. 55.00 (ISBN 0-306-30576-3, Plenum Pr). Plenum Pub.
Gruen, D. M., ed. Chemistry of Fusion Technology. LC 72-89488. 394p. 1972. 37.50 (ISBN 0-306-30714-6, Plenum Pr). Plenum Pub.
Henley, E. J., et al, eds. Advances in Nuclear Science & Technology. Incl. Vol. 1. 1962 (ISBN 0-12-029301-3); Vol. 2. 1964 (ISBN 0-12-029302-1); Vol. 4. 1968 (ISBN 0-12-029304-8); Vol. 5. Henley, E. J. & Lewins, J., eds. 1969 (ISBN 0-12-029305-6); Vol. 6. 1972 (ISBN 0-12-029306-4); Vol. 7. 1973 (ISBN 0-12-029307-2); Vol. 9. 1976 (ISBN 0-12-029309-5). 55.00 ea. Acad Pr.
--Advances in Nuclear Science & Technology, Vol. 10. 600p. 1977. 45.00 (ISBN 0-306-38230-X, Plenum Pr). Plenum Pub.
Koen, Susan & Swaim, Nina. A Handbook for Women on the Nuclear Mentality. 74p. pap. 3.50 (ISBN 0-686-74728-3). Crossing Pr.
Lacey, Robert & Loeb, Sidney, eds. Industrial Processing with Membranes. LC 78-21889. 360p. 1979. Repr. of 1972 ed. lib. bdg. 25.00 (ISBN 0-88275-788-1). Krieger.
Lamarsh, John R. Introduction to Nuclear Engineering. LC 74-4718. (Nuclear Science & Engineering Ser.). (Illus.). 600p. 1975. text ed. 26.95 (ISBN 0-201-04160-X). A-W.
Lau, L. Wang. Elements of Nuclear Reactor Engineering. new ed. LC 77-156083. 256p. 1975. 54.50x (ISBN 0-677-02270-0). Gordon.
Lewins, Jeffrey & Becker, Martin, eds. Advances in Nuclear Science & Technology, Vol. 13. 471p. 1981. 55.00 (ISBN 0-686-73237-5, Plenum Pr). Plenum Pub.
Mader, Charles L., ed. LASL Phermex Data, Vol. 2. (The Los Alamos Scientific Series on Dynamic Material Properties). 768p. 1980. 47.50x (ISBN 0-520-04010-4). U of Cal Pr.
Morse, G. Nuclear Methods in Mineral Exploration & Production. 1977. 53.75 (ISBN 0-444-41567-X). Elsevier.
Murphy, Glenn. Elements of Nuclear Engineering. LC 74-16147. (Illus.). 248p. 1974. Repr. of 1961 ed. 18.50 (ISBN 0-88275-155-7). Krieger.
Nea & the U. S. Dept. of Energy, Workshop, Columbus, Ohio, May 1980. Borehole & Shaft Plugging: Proceedings. OECD Staff, ed. (Illus.). 422p. (Orig.). Date not set. pap. 30.00x (ISBN 92-64-02114-0). OECD.
Nicholson, P. W. Nuclear Electronics. LC 73-8196. 388p. 1974. 50.00 (ISBN 0-471-63697-5, Pub. by Wiley-Interscience). Wiley.
Noggle, Joseph H. & Schirmer, Richard E. Nuclear Overhauser Effect: Chemical Applications. 1971. 46.50 (ISBN 0-12-520650-X). Acad Pr.
Nuclear Quality Assurance: A Bibliography. (DOE Technical Information Center Ser.). 80p. 1978. write for info. DOE.
Nuclear Technology & Mineral Resources 1977. (Proceedings Ser). (Illus.). 1978. pap. 68.25 (ISBN 92-0-060077-8, ISP464, IAEA). Unipub.
Operating Experience with Nuclear Power Stations in Member States: Performance Analysis Report 1977. 27p. 1980. pap. 5.25 (ISBN 92-0-159179-9, ISP 543, IAEA). Unipub.
Pedersen, Knud, et al. Applied Nuclear Power for Practicing Engineers. (Professional Engineering Career Development). 1972. 15.95x (ISBN 0-8464-0143-6). Beekman Pubs.
--Applied Nuclear Power for Practicing Engineers. LC 78-170128. 1972. 12.95 (ISBN 0-8436-0326-7). CBI Pub.
Petrosyants, A. M. From Scientific Search to Atomic Industry. LC 74-24684. 374p. 1975. text ed. 17.90x (ISBN 0-8134-1661-2, 1661). Interstate.
Petrosy'Ants, A. M. Problems of Nuclear Science & Technology: The Soviet Union As a World Nuclear Power. 4th rev. & enl. ed. LC 80-40818. (Illus.). 400p. 1981. 56.00 (ISBN 0-08-025462-4). Pergamon.
Ram, K. S. Basic Nuclear Engineering. LC 77-795. 1977. 14.95 (ISBN 0-470-99105-4). Halsted Pr.
Research Applications of Nuclear Pulsed Systems. 1967. pap. 14.75 (ISBN 92-0-151067-5, ISP144, IAEA). Unipub.
Richels, Richard G. R & D Under Uncertainty. LC 78-74997. (Outstanding Dissertations on Energy Ser.). 1979. lib. bdg. 18.00 (ISBN 0-8240-3978-5). Garland Pub.
Roberts, J. T., ed. Structural Materials in Nuclear Power Systems. (Modern Perspectives in Energy Ser.). 480p. 1981. 39.50 (ISBN 0-306-40669-1). Plenum Pub.
Sample Analysis of a Piping System: Class One Nuclear. 1972. pap. text ed. 4.50 (ISBN 0-685-30778-6, E00063). ASME.
Shieh, Paulinus S. & Inam-Ur-Rahman. Introduction to Nuclear Engineering. LC 80-13160. 1981. text ed. write for info. (ISBN 0-88275-972-8). Krieger.
Specialists Meeting, Paris, Nov. 26-8, 1979. Calculation of Three-Dimensional Rating Distributions in Operating Reactors: Proceedings. 450p. (Orig., Eng. & Fr.). 1980. pap. 21.50x (ISBN 92-64-02052-7, 66-80-04-3). OECD.
Steel, L. E. Neutron Irradiation Embrittlement of Reactor Pressure Vessel Steels. (Technical Report Ser.: No. 163). (Illus.). 235p. 1975. pap. 24.00 (ISBN 92-0-155075-8, IDC163, IAEA). Unipub.
Steps to Nuclear Power: A Guidebook. (Technical Report Ser.: No. 164). (Illus.). 106p. 1975. pap. 13.00 (ISBN 92-0-155175-4, IAEA). Unipub.
Stewart, Hugh B. Transitional Energy Policy 1980-2030: Alternative Nuclear Technologies. (Pergamon Policy Studies on Science & Technology). 266p. 1981. 30.00 (ISBN 0-08-027183-9); pap. 12.50 (ISBN 0-08-027182-0). Pergamon.
Technical Committee, Vienna Jan. 20-24, 1975. Peaceful Nuclear Explosions - Four: Proceedings. (Illus.). 479p. 1975. pap. 44.75 (ISBN 92-0-061075-7, IAEA). Unipub.
Thermodynamics, 2 Vols. 1966. Vol. 1. 29.25 (ISBN 92-0-040066-3, ISP109-1-2, IAEA); Vol. 2. 35.75 (ISBN 92-0-040166-X). Unipub.
United States Atomic Energy Commission. Reactor Handbook, 2 vols. 2nd ed. Incl. Vol. 1. Materials. 1223p. 1960. 75.95 (ISBN 0-470-71082-9); Vol. 3, Pt. A. Physics. 313p. 1962. 34.00 (ISBN 0-470-71148-5); Vol. 3, Pt. B. Shielding. 287p. 1962. 30.00 (ISBN 0-470-71150-7). (Pub. by Wiley-Interscience). Wiley.
Villani, S., ed. Uranium Enrichment. (Topics in Applied Physics Ser.: Vol. 35). (Illus.). 1979. 51.50 (ISBN 0-387-09385-0). Springer-Verlag.

NUCLEAR ENGINEERING–DICTIONARIES

Carpovich, Eugene A. Russian-English Atomic Dictionary: Physics, Mathematics, Nucleonics. rev. ed. 2nd ed. LC 57-8256. 1959. 15.00 (ISBN 0-911484-00-0). Tech Dict.
Clason, W. E. Elsevier's Dictionary of Nuclear Science & Technology. 2nd rev. ed. (Polyglot). 1970. 85.50 (ISBN 0-444-40810-X). Elsevier.
Freyberger, G. H. Abbreviations of Nuclear Power Plant Engineering. 280p. (Eng. -Ger.). 1979. 28.95 (ISBN 0-686-56591-6, M-7288, Pub. by Verlag Karl Thiemig). French & Eur.
Stattmann, F. Dictionary of Power Plant Engineering: Nuclear Power Plants, Pt. II. 316p. (Ger. & Fr.). 1973. 15.95 (ISBN 3-521-06081-0, M-7102). French & Eur.

NUCLEAR ENGINEERING–INSTRUMENTS

Boland, James F. Nuclear Reactor Instrumentation (In-Core) LC 76-101310. 230p. 1970. 12.50 (ISBN 0-677-02420-7). Am Nuclear Soc.

NUCLEAR ENGINEERING–SAFETY MEASURES

see also Radiation–Dosage; Radioactive Decontamination; Radioactive Waste Disposal

Criticality Control of Fissile Materials. (Illus., Orig.). 1966. pap. 40.75 (ISBN 92-0-020066-4, ISP114, IAEA). Unipub.
Current Nuclear Power Plant Safety Issues, Vol. 1. (Proceeding Ser.). 518p. 1981. pap. 65.00 (ISBN 92-0-020181-4, ISP566, IAEA). Unipub.
External Man-Induced Events in Relation to Nuclear Power Plant Siting. (Safety Series: No. 50-SG-S5). 62p. 1981. pap. 11.50 (ISBN 92-0-123081-8, ISP 585, IAEA). Unipub.
Fitzgerald, J. J. Applied Radiation Protection & Control, 2 vols. LC 65-27846. 1018p. 1969. 62.70 (ISBN 0-685-58267-1). Am Nuclear Soc.
Guidelines for the Layout & Contents of Safety Reports for Stationary Nuclear Power Plants. (Safety Ser.: No. 34). (Orig.). 1970. pap. 6.50 (ISBN 92-0-123170-9, ISP272, IAEA). Unipub.
Marguglio, B. W. Quality Systems in the Nuclear Industry: And in Other High Technology Industries. (ASTM Special Technical Publication Ser.: No. 616). 1977. 37.75 (ISBN 0-8031-0197-X). ASTM.
Melville, Mary H. The Temporary Worker in the Nuclear Power Industry: An Equity Analysis. LC 81-65590. (CENTED Monographs: No. 1). (Illus.). 60p. 1981. pap. text ed. 5.00 (ISBN 0-939436-00-0). Ctr Tech Environ.
Radiation Protection Monitoring. 1969. pap. 35.75 (ISBN 92-0-020069-9, ISP199, IAEA). Unipub.
Spinrad, Bernard I. Use of Computers in Analysis of Experimental Data & the Control of Nuclear Facilities. LC 67-60057. (AEC Symposium Ser.). 306p. 1967. pap. 6.00 (ISBN 0-686-75753-X); microfiche 3.00 (ISBN 0-686-75754-8). DOE.
Symposium, Vienna, 20-24 October, 1975. Safeguarding Nuclear Materials, Vol. II: Proceedings. (Illus., Orig.). 1976. pap. 68.25 (ISBN 92-0-070176-0, ISP408-2, IAEA). Unipub.

NUCLEAR ENGINEERING AS A PROFESSION

Educational Research Council of America. Nuclear Plant Designer. Ferris, Theodore N., et al, eds. (Real People at Work Er: J). (Illus.). 1976. pap. text ed. 2.25 (ISBN 0-89247-079-8). Changing Times.
Manpower Development for Nuclear Power: A Guidebook. (Technical Reports Ser.: No. 200). 492p. 1980. pap. 65.50 (ISBN 92-0-155080-4, IDC200, IAEA). Unipub.

NUCLEAR EXCITATION

Belyaev, S. T. Collective Excitations in Nuclei. (Documents on Modern Physics Ser.). 1968. 29.75x (ISBN 0-677-01870-3). Gordon.
De Mayo, Paul, ed. Rearrangements in Ground & Excited States, Vol. 1. LC 79-51675. (Organic Chemistry Ser.). 1980. 84.00 (ISBN 0-12-481301-1); Set. 65.00 (ISBN 0-686-66014-5). Acad Pr.
--Rearrangements in Ground & Excited States, Vol. 2. LC 79-51675. (Organic Chemistry Ser.). 1980. 77.00 (ISBN 0-12-481302-X); Set. 60.00 (ISBN 0-686-66015-3). Acad Pr.
Devreese, J. T., et al, eds. Elementary Excitations in Solids, Molecules, & Atoms, 2 pts. Incl. Pt. A. 375p. 39.50 (ISBN 0-306-35791-7); Pt. B. 385p. 39.50 (ISBN 0-306-35792-5). (NATO Advanced Study Institutes Ser. B - Physics: Vols. 2A & 2B). 1974 (Plenum Pr). Plenum Pub.
Lawley, K. P., ed. Molecular Scattering: Physical & Chemical Applications. LC 74-23667. (Advances in Chemical Physics Ser.). 541p. 1975. 96.00 (ISBN 0-471-51900-6, Pub. by Wiley-Interscience). Wiley.
Lim, Edward C., ed. Excited States, Vols. 1 & 2. Vol. 1, 1974. 52.50 (ISBN 0-12-227201-3); Vol. 2, 1975. 60.00 (ISBN 0-12-227202-1); Vol. 3, 1978. 40.00 (ISBN 0-12-227203-X). Acad Pr.
--Excited States, Vol. 4. (Serial Publication). 1980. 48.50 (ISBN 0-12-227204-8); lib. ed. 63.00 (ISBN 0-12-227278-1); microfiche 30.00 (ISBN 0-12-227279-X). Acad Pr.
Maradudin, A. A. & Nardelli, G. F. Elementary Excitations in Solids. LC 68-26772. 526p. 1969. 49.50 (ISBN 0-306-30356-6, Plenum Pr). Plenum Pub.
Sherf, Libi & Neufeld, Henry N. Pre-Excitation Syndrome: Facts & Theories. LC 78-56930. 1978. 33.00 (ISBN 0-914316-13-3). Yorke Med.
Shoppee, Charles W., ed. Excited States of Matter. (Graduate Studies: No. 2). (Illus., Orig.). 1973. pap. 8.00 (ISBN 0-89672-009-8). Tex Tech Pr.
Thomas, E. W. Excitation in Heavy Particle Collisions. 436p. 1972. 33.50 (ISBN 0-471-85890-0, Pub. by Wiley). Krieger.
Ware, William R., ed. Creation & Detection of the Excited State, Vol. 2. 240p. 1974. 44.00 (ISBN 0-8247-6113-8). Dekker.
--Creation & Detection of the Excited State, Vol. 4. 1976. 58.25 (ISBN 0-8247-6451-X). Dekker.

NUCLEAR FISSION

see also Fission Products; Neutron Transport Theory

BCC Staff, ed. Advanced Fission, E-031: Economic Impact. 1978. 675.00 (ISBN 0-89336-143-7). BCC.
DiIorio, Gino J. Direct Physical Measurement of Mass Yields in Thermal Fission of Uranium. LC 78-75005. (Outstanding Disserations on Energy Ser.). 1979. lib. bdg. 11.00 (ISBN 0-8240-3985-8). Garland Pub.
Duderstadt, James J. & Hamilton, Louis J. Nuclear Reactor Analysis. LC 75-20389. 650p. 1976. text ed. 38.95 (ISBN 0-471-22363-8). Wiley.
Fong, Peter. Statistical Theory of Nuclear Fission. (Documents on Modern Physics Ser.). (Orig.). 1969. 54.50x (ISBN 0-677-01850-9). Gordon.
Graetzerk, Hans G. & Anderson, David L. The Discovery of Nuclear Fission. Cohen, I. Bernard, ed. LC 80-2123. (Development of Science Ser.). (Illus.). 1981. lib. bdg. 12.00x (ISBN 0-405-13846-6). Arno.
Hyde, Earl K., et al. Nuclear Properties of Heavy Elements, 3 vols. rev. ed. LC 70-153894. (Orig.). 1971. Repr. text ed. 15.00 ea. Vol. I (ISBN 0-486-62805-1). Vol. II (ISBN 0-486-62806-X). Vol. III (ISBN 0-486-62807-8). Dover.
Natural Fission Reactors. 1979. pap. 64.25 (ISBN 92-0-051078-7, ISP 475, IAEA). Unipub.
Physics & Chemistry of Fission - 1969. (Illus., Orig.). 1969. pap. 61.75 (ISBN 92-0-030269-6, IAEA). Unipub.
Physics & Chemistry of Fission - 1973, 2 vols. (Illus.). 579p. (Orig.). 1974. Vol. 1. pap. 44.75 (ISBN 92-0-030074-X, IAEA); Vol. 2. pap. 41.50 (ISBN 92-0-030174-6). Unipub.
Physics & Chemistry of Fission, Nineteen Seventy-Nine, Vol. 11. 501p. 1980. pap. 64.25 (ISBN 92-0-030180-0, ISP526-2, IAEA). Unipub.
Prompt Fission Neutron Spectra. (Illus.). 176p. (Orig.). 1973. pap. 13.00 (ISBN 92-0-131172-9, IAEA). Unipub.
Vandenbosch, Robert & Huizenga, John R. Nuclear Fission. 1973. 55.50 (ISBN 0-12-710850-5). Acad Pr.

NUCLEAR FORCES (PHYSICS)

see also Coulomb Functions

Austin, S. M. & Crawley, G. M. The Two-Body Force in Nuclei. LC 72-76009. 390p. 1972. 42.50 (ISBN 0-306-30598-4, Plenum Pr). Plenum Pub.
Davies, P. C. The Forces of Nature. LC 78-72084. (Illus.). 1979. 35.50 (ISBN 0-521-22523-X); pap. 9.95 (ISBN 0-521-29535-1). Cambridge U Pr.
Zingl, H., et al, eds. Few Body Systems & Nuclear Forces: 8th International Conference Held in Graz, Austria, August 24-30, 1978. LC 78-13440. (Lecture Notes in Physics: Vol. 82). 1978. pap. 21.30 (ISBN 0-387-08917-9). Springer-Verlag.

NUCLEAR FUEL ELEMENTS

Babu, Suresh B., ed. Trace Elements in Fuel. LC 75-15522. (Advances in Chemistry Ser.: No. 141). 1975. 20.00 (ISBN 0-8412-0216-8). Am Chemical.
Detection & Location of Failed Fuel Elements. (Illus., Orig.). 1968. pap. 15.50 (ISBN 92-0-051168-6, ISP204, IAEA). Unipub.
Holden, A. N. Dispersion Fuel Elements. LC 67-29666. 255p. 1967. 11.00 (ISBN 0-685-58274-4). Am Nuclear Soc.
Holden, Robert B. Ceramic Fuel Elements. LC 66-28066. 244p. 1966. 12.50 (ISBN 0-685-58271-X). Am Nuclear Soc.
Linder, P. Air Filters for Use at Nuclear Facilities. (Technical Reports Ser.: No. 122). (Illus.). 76p. (Orig.). 1970. pap. 8.75 (ISBN 92-0-125670-1, IDC122, IAEA). Unipub.
OECD. Storage of Spent Fuel Elements. 348p. (Orig.). 1978. pap. 15.00x (ISBN 92-64-01840-9). OECD.
Olander, Donald R. Fundamental Aspects of Nuclear Reactor Fuel Elements. LC 76-6485. 624p. 1976. pap. 16.25 (ISBN 0-686-75845-5); microfiche 3.00 (ISBN 0-686-75846-3); pap. 13.50 solutions to problems (ISBN 0-686-75847-1); solutions microfiche 3.00 (ISBN 0-686-75848-X). DOE.
Simnad, Massoud. Fuel Element Experience in Nuclear Power Reactors. LC 78-131892. 620p. 1971. 37.50 (ISBN 0-677-03260-9). Am Nuclear Soc.
Weissert & Schileo. Fabrication of Thorium Fuel Elements. LC 68-25126. 1968. 11.10 (ISBN 0-89448-007-3). Am Nuclear Soc.

NUCLEAR FUELS

see also Nuclear Fuel Elements; Reactor Fuel Reprocessing; Thorium; Uranium

Ahmed, S. Basheer. Nuclear Fuel & Energy Policy. LC 78-19673. 1979. 18.95 (ISBN 0-669-02714-6). Lexington Bks.
Brown, J. Coggin & Key, A. K. The Mineral & Nuclear Fuels of the Indian Subcontinent & Burma. 1976. 38.00x (ISBN 0-19-560172-6). Oxford U Pr.
Christensen, R. Thermal Mechanical Behavior of VO2 Nuclear Fuel: Multi-Cycle Test Description, Vol. IV. xiv, 325p. Date not set. 49.50 (ISBN 0-686-29433-5). Entropy Ltd.
--Thermal Mechanical Behavior of VO2 Nuclear Fuel: Statistical Analysis of Acoustic Emission Axial Elagation, & Crack Characteristics. xii, 238p. 1981. 34.50 (ISBN 0-686-28976-5). Entropy Ltd.
--Thermal Mechanical Behavior of VO2 Nuclear Fuel: Statistical Analysis of Acoustic Emission, Diametral Expansion,Anrol Elongation & Crash Characteristics. x, 238p. pap. 34.50 (ISBN 0-686-29430-0). Entropy Ltd.
--Thermal Mechanical Behavior of VO2 Nuclear Fuel: Single Cycle Test Discription, Vol. III. x, 308p. Date not set. 46.50 (ISBN 0-686-29432-7). Entropy Ltd.
--Thermal Mechanical Behavior of V02 Nuclear Fuel: Electrothermal Analysis, Vol. II. x, 122p. Date not set. 19.50 (ISBN 0-686-29431-9). Entropy Ltd.

Economics of Nuclear Fuels. (Illus., Orig.). 1968. pap. 37.50 (ISBN 92-0-050668-2, ISP188, IAEA). Unipub.
Elliott, David M. & Weaver, Lynn E. Education & Research in the Nuclear Fuel Cycle. LC 76-160491. (Illus.). 450p. 1972. pap. 8.95x (ISBN 0-8061-1116-X). U of Okla Pr.
Experience from Operating & Fuelling Nuclear Power Plants. (Illus.). 721p. (Orig., Eng. , Fr. & Span.). 1974. pap. 45.00 (ISBN 92-0-050274-1, ISP351, IAEA). Unipub.
Flagg, John F., ed. Chemical Processing of Reactor Fuels. (Nuclear Science and Technology Ser.: Vol. 1). 1961. 55.00 (ISBN 0-12-258250-0). Acad Pr.
Fuel & Fuel Elements for Fast Reactors, 2 vols. (Illus.). 906p. (Orig., Eng. , Fr. , Rus. & Span.). 1974. Vol. 1. pap. 32.50 (ISBN 92-0-050074-9, ISP346-1, IAEA); Vol. 2. pap. 39.00 (ISBN 92-0-050174-5, ISP346-2). Unipub.
Graves, Harvey W. Nuclear Fuel Management. LC 78-19119. 1979. text ed. 28.95 (ISBN 0-471-03136-4). Wiley.
International Nuclear Fuel Cycle Evaluation. Incl. Report of INFCE Working Group 1 - Fuel & Heavy Water Availability. 314p. pap. 40.75 (ISBN 92-0-159180-2, ISP534-1); Report of INFCE Working Group 2 - Enrichment Availability. 157p. pap. 21.25 (ISBN 92-0-159280-9, ISP534-2); Report of INFCE Working Group 3 - Assurances of Long-Term Supply of Technology, Fuel, & Heavy Water & Services in the Interest of National Needs Consistent with Non-Proliferation. 104p. pap. 14.75 (ISBN 92-0-159380-5, ISP534-3); Report of INFCE Working Group 4 - Reprocessing, Plutonium Handling, Recycle. 300p. pap. 39.00 (ISBN 92-0-159480-1, ISP534-4); Report of INFCE Working Group 5 - Fast Breeders. 217p. pap. 29.25 (ISBN 92-0-159580-8, ISP534-5); Report of INFCE Working Group 6 - Spent Fuel Management. 113p. pap. 16.25 (ISBN 92-0-159680-4, ISP534-6); Report of INFCE Working Group 7 - Waste Management & Disposal. 287p. pap. 36.75 (ISBN 92-0-159780-0, ISP534-7); Report of INFCE Working Group 8 - Advanced Fuel Cycle & Reactor Concepts. 181p. pap. 24.50 (ISBN 92-0-159880-7, ISP534-8); INFCE Summary Volume. 285p. pap. 35.00 (ISBN 92-0-159980-3, ISP534-9). 1980. 252.75 set (ISBN 0-686-77641-0, ISP534, IAEA). Unipub.
Joint Research Centre, Workshop, Karlsruhe Establishment (European Inst. for Transuranium Elements), Germany, October 1978. Fission Gas Behaviour in Nuclear Fuels: Proceedings. Ronchi, C., et al, eds. (European Applied Research Reports Special Topics Ser.). 350p. 1979. pap. text ed. 90.25 (ISBN 3-7186-0010-2). Harwood Academic.
Kruger, Owen & Kaznoll, Alexis, eds. Ceramic Nuclear Fuels. LC 77-11082. 20.00 (ISBN 0-916094-16-2). Am Ceramic.
Long, Justin T. Engineering for Nuclear Fuel Reprocessing. LC 78-50886. 1023p. 1978. 68.00 (ISBN 0-89448-012-X). Am Nuclear Soc.
Meller, Eberhard, ed. Internationalization: An Alternative to Nuclear Proliferation? LC 80-17265. (Salzburg Seminar on American Studies 1978 Ser.). 192p. 1980. text ed. 22.50 (ISBN 0-89946-049-6). Oelgeschlager.
Mining Journal Books Ltd. Uranium & Nuclear Energy. 326p. 1980. 36.00x (ISBN 0-900117-20-6, Pub. by Mining Journal England). State Mutual Bk.
Monitoring of Airborne & Liquid Radioactive Releases from Nuclear Facilities to the Environment. (Safety Ser.: No. 46). 1978. pap. 14.00 (ISBN 92-0-123178-4, ISP482, IAEA). Unipub.
Nuclear Fuel Quality Assurance. (Illus.). 1977. pap. 48.75 (ISBN 92-0-050276-8, ISP435, IAEA). Unipub.
Nuclear Materials Management. 1966. 48.75 (ISBN 92-0-050066-8, ISP110, IAEA). Unipub.
Occupational Radiation Exposure in Nuclear Fuel Cycle Facilities. 640p. 1980. pap. 79.25 (ISBN 92-0-020080-X, ISP527, IAEA). Unipub.
Plutonium As a Reactor Fuel. (Illus., Eng. , Fr. & Rus.). 1967. pap. 48.75 (ISBN 92-0-050167-2, ISP153, IAEA). Unipub.
Quality Assurance & Control in the Manufacture of Metal-Clad U02 Reactor Fuels. (Technical Reports Ser.: No. 173). (Illus.). 1976. pap. 9.50 (ISBN 92-0-155076-6, IDC173, IAEA). Unipub.
Reactor Burn-up Physics. (Illus.). 296p. (Orig.). 1973. pap. 22.75 (ISBN 92-0-051073-6, ISP336, IAEA). Unipub.
Regional Nuclear Fuel Cycle Centres, 2 vols. Incl. Vol. 1. Summary 1977 Report of the IAEA Study Project. pap. 15.00 (ISBN 92-0-159177-2, ISP445-1); Vol. 2. Basic Studies 1977 Report of the IAEA Study Project. pap. 32.25 (ISBN 92-0-159277-9). (Illus.). 1977 (IAEA). Unipub.
Reprocessing of Spent Nuclear Fuels in OECD Countries: Report by an Expert Group of the OECD Nuclear Energy Agency,January,1977. 1977. 5.00x (ISBN 92-64-11615-X). OECD.
Robertson, J. A. Irradiation Effects in Nuclear Fuels. LC 67-26575. 309p. 1969. 16.25 (ISBN 0-685-58270-1). Am Nuclear Soc.
Rodden, Clement J., ed. Selected Measurement Methods for Plutonium & Uranium in the Nuclear Fuel Cycle. 2nd ed. LC 72-600015. 440p. 1972. pap. 6.00 (ISBN 0-686-75747-5); microfiche 3.00 (ISBN 0-686-75748-3). DOE.
Silvennoinen, P. Reactor Core Fuel Management. 250p. 1976. text ed. 42.00 (ISBN 0-08-019853-8); pap. text ed. 18.75 (ISBN 0-08-019852-X). Pergamon.
Simnad, M. T. & Zumwatt, L. R., eds. Materials & Fuels for High-Temperature Nuclear Applications. 1964. 23.00x (ISBN 0-262-19012-5). MIT Pr.
Sol-Gel Processes for Ceramic Fuels. 1968. pap. 11.50 (ISBN 92-0-141068-9, ISP207, IAEA). Unipub.
Sorantin, H. Determination of Uranium & Plutonium in Nuclear Fuels. (Topical Presentations in Nuclear Chemistry Ser.: Vol. 5). (Illus.). 1975. 81.20 (ISBN 3-527-25475-7). Verlag Chemie.
Thermal Conductivity of Uranium Dioxide. (Technical Reports: No. 59). 1966. pap. 6.25 (ISBN 92-0-145166-0, IDC59, IAEA). Unipub.
Thermodynamic & Transport Properties of Uranium Dioxide & Related Phases. (Technical Reports: No. 39). 1965. pap. 8.00 (ISBN 92-0-145065-6, IDC39, IAEA). Unipub.
Urban District Heating Using Nuclear Heat. (Panel Proceedings Ser). (Illus.). 1977. pap. text ed. 22.75 (ISBN 92-0-051077-9, IAEA). Unipub.
Utilization of Thorium in Power Reactors. (Technical Reports: No. 52). 1966. pap. 23.25 (ISBN 92-0-055066-5, IDC52, IAEA). Unipub.
Warnecke, Steven J. Uranium, Nonproliferation & Energy Security, No. 37. (The Atlantic Papers). 121p. 1980. pap. 4.75 (ISBN 0-916672-77-8, Pub. by Atlantic Inst France). Allanheld.
World Uraniam Potential: An International Evaluation. 1979. 16.00 (ISBN 92-64-11883-7). OECD.
Wymer, Raymond G. & Vondra, Benedict L., Jr., eds. Light Water Reactor Nuclear Fuel Cycle. 256p. 1981. 69.95 (ISBN 0-8493-5687-3). CRC Pr.
Yemel'yanov, V. S. & Yevstyukin, A. I. Metallurgy of Nuclear Fuels. 1969. 94.00 (ISBN 0-08-012073-3). Pergamon.
Zimmermann, Charles F. Uranium Resources on Federal Lands. LC 78-20738. (Illus.). 1979. 28.95 (ISBN 0-669-02847-9). Lexington Bks.

NUCLEAR FUELS–BIBLIOGRAPHY

Nuclear Raw Materials: A Selected Bibliography. 1976. write for info. DOE.

NUCLEAR FUSION

see also Controlled Fusion; Hydrogen Bomb; Neutron Transport Theory

Committee on Nuclear & Alternative Energy Systems, National Research Council. Controlled Nuclear Fusion: Current Research & Potential Progress. 1978. pap. text ed. 4.75x (ISBN 0-309-02863-9). Natl Acad Pr.
Hulme, H. R. & Collieu, A. Nuclear Fusion. (Wykeham Science Ser.: No. 4). 1969. 9.95x (ISBN 0-8448-1106-8). Crane-Russak Co.
Miley, George H. Fusion Energy Conversion. LC 75-44554. (Nuclear Science Technology Ser.). (Illus.). 1976. text ed. 39.80 (ISBN 0-89448-008-1). Am Nuclear Soc.
Plasma Physics & Controlled Nuclear Fusion Research, 3 vols. (Illus.). 1977. Vol. 1. pap. 66.00 (ISBN 92-0-130077-8, IAEA); Vol. 2. pap. 67.50 (ISBN 92-0-130177-4); Vol. 3. pap. 64.25 (ISBN 92-0-130277-0). Unipub.
Plasma Physics & Controlled Nuclear Fusion Research - 1971, 3 vols. (Illus.). 673p. (Orig.). 1972. pap. 48.75 ea. (IAEA); Vol. 1. pap. (ISBN 92-0-030071-5); Vol. 2. pap. (ISBN 92-0-030171-1); Vol. 3. pap. (ISBN 92-0-030271-8). Unipub.
Plasma Physics & Controlled Nuclear Fusion Research - 1972: Supplement. (Illus.). 357p. (Orig.). 1973. pap. 24.25 (ISBN 92-0-139072-6, 1WFS72, IAEA). Unipub.
Plasma Physics & Controlled Nuclear Fusion Research 1978, 2 vols. 1979. Vol. 1. pap. 101.50 (ISBN 92-0-130079-4, ISP 495-1, IAEA); Vol. 2. pap. 77.25 (ISBN 92-0-130179-0, ISP 495-2). Unipub.
Plasma Physics & Controlled Nuclear Fusion Research 1978, Vol. 3. 552p. 1980. pap. 70.00 (ISBN 92-0-130279-7, ISP 495-3, IAEA). Unipub.
Schramm, David N. & Arnett, W. David, eds. Explosive Nucleosynthesis: Proceedings of the Conference on Explosive Nucleosynthesis Held in Austin, Texas, on April 2-3, 1973. 313p. 1973. 15.00x (ISBN 0-292-72006-8); pap. 8.95x (ISBN 0-292-72007-6). U of Tex Pr.

NUCLEAR GEOPHYSICS

see also Radioactive Dating; Radioactive Substances

Nuclear Techniques in Geochemistry & Geophysics: Proceedings. (Illus.). 271p. 1976. pap. 27.75 (ISBN 92-0-041076-6, ISP425, IAEA). Unipub.
Shen, Benjamin S. & Merker, Milton, eds. Spallation Nuclear Reactions & Their Applications. new ed. (Astrophysics & Space Science Library: No. 59). 1976. lib. bdg. 39.50 (ISBN 90-277-0746-4, Pub. by Reidel Holland). Kluwer Boston.

NUCLEAR INDUCTION

Das, T. P. & Hahn, E. L. Nuclear Quadrupole Resonance Spectroscopy. (Solid State Physics: Suppl. 1). 1958. 40.50 (ISBN 0-12-607761-4). Acad Pr.

NUCLEAR MAGNETIC RESONANCE

see also Cyclotron; Nuclear Induction; Nuclear Magnetism; Paramagnetism

Abraham, R. J. Analysis of High Resolution NMR Spectra. 1971. 53.75 (ISBN 0-444-40846-0). Elsevier.
--Nuclear Magnetic Resonance, Vols. 1-8. Incl. Vol. 1. 1970-71 Literature. 1972. 38.50 (ISBN 0-85186-252-7); Vol. 2. 1971-72 Literature. 1973. 41.25 (ISBN 0-85186-262-4); Vol. 3. 1972-73 Literature. 1974. 46.75 (ISBN 0-85186-272-1); Vol. 4. 1973-74 Literature. 1975. 49.50 (ISBN 0-85186-282-9); Vol. 5. 1974-75 Literature. 1976. 55.00 (ISBN 0-85186-292-6); Vol. 6. 1975-76 Literature. 1977. 57.75 (ISBN 0-85186-302-7); Vol. 7. 1976-77 Literature. 1978. 68.75 (ISBN 0-85186-312-4); Vol. 8. 1979. 57.75 (ISBN 0-85186-322-1). LC 72-78527. Am Chemical.
Aleksandrov, I. V. Theory of Nuclear Magnetic Resonance. 1966. 34.00 (ISBN 0-12-049850-2). Acad Pr.
Andrew, Edwin R. Nuclear Magnetic Resonance. (Cambridge Monographs on Physics Ser). 1956. 49.95 (ISBN 0-521-04030-2). Cambridge U Pr.
Ault, Addison & Ault, Margaret R. A Handy & Systematic Catalog of NMR Spectra: Instruction Through Examples. LC 79-57227. 425p. 1980. 15.00 (ISBN 0-935702-00-8). Univ Sci Bks.
Ault, Addison & Dudek, Gerald. An Introduction to Proton NMR Spectroscopy. LC 75-26286. 150p. 1976. pap. text ed. 7.50x (ISBN 0-8162-0331-8). Holden-Day.
Becker, Edwin D. High Resolution NMR: Theory & Chemical Applications. 2nd. ed. LC 79-20540. 1980. 24.00 (ISBN 0-12-084660-8). Acad Pr.
Bible, Roy H., Jr. Guide to the NMR Empirical Method: A Workbook. LC 66-11695. 305p. 1967. 22.50 (ISBN 0-306-30233-0, Plenum Pr). Plenum Pub.
--Interpretation of NMR Spectra: An Empirical Approach. LC 64-20741. 150p. 1965. 24.50 (ISBN 0-306-30187-3, Plenum Pr). Plenum Pub.
Bovey, Frank A. High Resolution NMR of Macromolecules. 1972. 56.00 (ISBN 0-12-119740-9). Acad Pr.
Breitmaier, E. & Bauer, G. Thirteen-C NMR Spectroscopy: A Working Manual with Exercises. Cassels, B. K., tr. from Ger. (MMI Press Polymer Monographs: Vol. 2). 400p. 1981. 80.00 (ISBN 3-7186-0022-6). Harwood Academic.
Brugel, Werner. Nuclear Magnetic Resonance Spectra & Chemical Structure. 1968. 58.50 (ISBN 0-12-137450-5). Acad Pr.
Bulthuis, Jakob. NMR in Liquid Crystalline Solvents: Complications in Determining Molecular Geometries. (Illus.). 104p. (Orig.). 1974. pap. text ed. 12.00x (ISBN 90-6203-111-0). Humanities.
Chamberlain, Nugent F. The Practice of NMR Spectroscopy: With Spectra-Structure Correlations for Hydrogen-One. LC 74-11479. (Illus.). 430p. 1974. 39.50 (ISBN 0-306-30766-9, Plenum Pr). Plenum Pub.
Chapman, Dennis & Magnus, P. D. Introduction to Practical High Resolution Nuclear Magnetic Resonance Spectroscopy. 1966. pap. 26.00 (ISBN 0-12-168550-0). Acad Pr.
Colloque A.M.P.E.R.E. - 15th - Grenoble. Magnetic Resonance & Radiofrequency Spectroscopy: Proceedings. Averbuch, P., ed. 1968. text ed. 30.25x (ISBN 0-7204-1206-4, Pub. by North Holland). Humanities.
Coogan, C. K., et al. Magnetic Resonance. LC 70-119613. 386p. 1970. 37.50 (ISBN 0-306-30487-2, Plenum Pr). Plenum Pub.
Corio, P. L. Structure of High Resolution Nuclear Magnetic Resonance Spectra. 1966. 63.00 (ISBN 0-12-188750-2). Acad Pr.
Danadian, R., ed. NMR in Medicine. (NMR--Basic Principles & Progress Ser.: Vol. 19). (Illus.). 230p. 1981. 57.90 (ISBN 0-387-10460-7). Springer-Verlag.
Diehl, P. & Khetrapel, C. L. N M R Studies of Molecules Oriented in the Nematic Phase of Liquid Crystals. Bd. with The Use of Symmetry in Nuclear Magnetic Resonance. Jones, R. G. (NMR Basic Principles & Progress: Vol. 1). (Illus.). v, 174p. 1969. 26.30 (ISBN 0-387-04665-8). Springer-Verlag.
Dwek, Raymond A. Nuclear Magnetic Resonance (Nmr) in Biochemistry: Applications to Enzyme Systems. (Monographs on Physical Biochemistry Ser.). 387p. 1974. 59.00x (ISBN 0-19-854614-9). Oxford U Pr.
Emsley, J. W. Progress in NMR Spectroscopy, Vol. 12. 288p. 1980. 87.50 (ISBN 0-08-024874-8). Pergamon.
Emsley, J. W. & Lindon, J. C. NMR Spectroscopy Using Liquid Crystal Solvents. 367p. 1975. text ed. 55.00 (ISBN 0-08-019919-4). Pergamon.
Emsley, J. W. & Sutcliffe, L. H., eds. Progress in Nuclear Magnetic Resonance Spectroscopy, Vols. 1-10. Incl. Vol. 1. 1962. 76.00 (ISBN 0-08-011322-2); Vol. 2. 1963. 76.00 (ISBN 0-08-012208-6); Vol. 3. 1965. 76.00 (ISBN 0-08-012446-1); Vol. 4. 1966. 76.00 (ISBN 0-08-012717-7); Vol. 5. 1970. 76.00 (ISBN 0-08-012834-3); Vol. 6. 1971; Vol. 7. 1971. 76.00 (ISBN 0-08-016267-3); Vol. 8, 3 pts. 1972. Vol. 8, Complete. 76.00 (ISBN 0-08-017018-8); Pts. 1-3. pap. 15.50 ea.; Pt. 1. pap. -1971 (ISBN 0-08-016662-8); Pt. 2. pap. -1971 (ISBN 0-08-016757-8); Pt. 3. pap. -1972 (ISBN 0-08-016857-4); Vol. 9, 3 pts. Vol. 9, Complete. 76.00 (ISBN 0-08-017704-2); Pts. 1-3. pap. 13.75 ea.; Vol. 10. Pt. 1, 1975. pap. 8.00 (ISBN 0-08-017703-4); Pt. 2, 1976. pap. 14.00 (ISBN 0-08-019463-X); Pts. 3 & 4, 1977. 75.00 (ISBN 0-08-019464-8); One Vol. Ed. (cloth) 76.00 (ISBN 0-08-019466-4). Pergamon.
Emsley, J. W., et al. High Resolution Nuclear Magnetic Resonance Spectroscopy, 2 Vols. 1966. 46.00 (ISBN 0-08-011824-0). Pergamon.
Forsen, S., et al. Chlorine, Bromine & Iodine NMR Physico-Chemicall & Biological Applications. Diehl, P., et al, eds. (Basic Principles & Progress: Vol. 12). (Illus.). 1976. 52.40 (ISBN 0-387-07725-1). Springer-Verlag.
Fukushima, E. & Roeder, S. B. W. Experimental Pulse NMR: A Nuts & Bolts Approach. 1981. 34.50 (ISBN 0-201-10403-2). A-W.
Gerven, Lieven Van, ed. Nuclear Magnetic Resonance in Solids. LC 77-1230. (NATO Advanced Study Institutes Ser.: Series B, Physics, Vol. 22). 429p. 1977. 47.50 (ISBN 0-306-35722-4, Plenum Pr). Plenum Pub.
Haeberlen, Ulrich. High Resolution NMR in Solids. (Advances in Magnetic Resonance Ser.: Supplement 1). 1976. 37.50 (ISBN 0-12-025561-8); lib. ed. 51.00 (ISBN 0-12-025569-3); microfiche 29.50 (ISBN 0-12-025570-7). Acad Pr.
Harris, Robin & Mann, Brian, eds. NMR & the Periodic Table. 1979. 102.50 (ISBN 0-12-327650-0). Acad Pr.
Hershenson, Herbert M. Nuclear Magnetic Resonance & Electron Spin Resonance, Index for 1958-1963. 1965. 30.00 (ISBN 0-12-343260-X). Acad Pr.
Hoehler, G., ed. Nuclear Magnetic Double Resonance. Principles & Applications in Solid State Physics. Incl. Vibrational Absorption of Electron & Hydrogen Centers in Tonic Crystals. Bauerle, D; Factor Group Analysis. Remlinger, J. (Springer Tracts in Modern Physics: Vol. 68). (Illus.). 200p. 1973. 52.00 (ISBN 0-387-06341-2). Springer Verlag.
Hoffman, R. A., et al. Analysis of NMR Spectra. LC 70-156999. (NMR-Basic Principles & Progress: Vol. 5). (Illus.). 1971. 35.30 (ISBN 0-387-05427-8). Springer-Verlag.
Howell, M. G., et al. Formula Index to NMR Literature Data, Vol. 2. LC 64-7756. 206p. 1966. 47.50 (ISBN 0-306-67002-X). IFI Plenum.
Humpert, B., ed. Dynamical Concepts on Scaling Violation & the New Resonances in e Positive e Negative Annihilation. (Lecture Notes in Physics Ser: Vol. 45). 1975. pap. 13.80 (ISBN 0-387-07539-9). Springer-Verlag.
Ionin, B. I. & Ershov, B. A. NMR Spectroscopy in Organic Chemistry. LC 66-18972. (Physical Methods in Organic Chemistry Ser.). 382p. 1970. 39.50 (ISBN 0-306-30424-4, Plenum Pr). Plenum Pub.
Jackman, L. M. & Sternhell, S. Applications of Nuclear Magnetic Resonance Spectroscopy in Organic Chemistry. 2nd ed. 1969. 50.00 (ISBN 0-08-012542-5). Pergamon.
Jackman, Lloyd M. & Cotton, F. A., eds. Dynamic Nuclear Magnetic Resonance Spectroscopy. 1975. 72.00 (ISBN 0-12-378850-1). Acad Pr.
James, Thomas L. Nuclear Magnetic Resonance in Biochemistry: Principles & Applications. 1975. 48.50 (ISBN 0-12-380950-9). Acad Pr.
Jardetzky, Oleg. NMR in Molecular Biology. LC 80-2337. 1981. price not set (ISBN 0-12-380580-5). Acad Pr.

Kaplan, Jerome I. & Fraenkel, Gideon. NMR in Chemically Exchanging Systems. LC 79-50217. 1980. 22.50 (ISBN 0-12-397550-6). Acad Pr.
Kasler, F. Quantitative Analysis by NMR Spectroscopy. 1973. 32.00 (ISBN 0-12-400850-X). Acad Pr.
Kaufman, Leon, et al, eds. Nuclear Magnetic Resonance Imaging in Medicine. LC 81-82043. (Illus.). 240p. 1981. 29.50 (ISBN 0-89640-057-3). Igaku-Shoin.
Khetrapal, C. L. Lyotropic Liquid Crystals. (NMR (Nuclear Magnetic Resonance) Ser.). (Illus.). 180p. 1975. 20.90 (ISBN 0-387-07303-5). Springer-Verlag.
Knowles, Peter F., et al. Magnetic Resonance of Biomolecules: An Introduction to the Theory & Practice of NMR & ESR in Biological Systems. LC 75-4872. 343p. 1976. 41.25 (ISBN 0-471-49575-1, Pub. by Wiley-Interscience); pap. 18.95 (ISBN 0-471-01672-1). Wiley.
Lenk, R. Brownian Motion & Spin Relaxation. 1977. 53.75 (ISBN 0-444-41592-0). Elsevier.
Levy, George C. Topics in Carbon-13 NMR Spectroscopy, Vol. 1. LC 72-1262. 336p. 1974. 32.00 (ISBN 0-471-53154-5, Pub. by Wiley-Interscience). Wiley.
Leyden, D. E. & Cox, R. H. Analytical Applications of NMR. LC 77-1229. (Chemical Analysis Ser: Vol. 48). 1977. 46.00 (ISBN 0-471-53403-X, Pub. by Wiley-Interscience). Wiley.
Low, William, ed. Paramagnetic Resonance, 2 Vols. 1963. Set. 64.00 (ISBN 0-12-456266-3); Vol. 1. 56.00 (ISBN 0-12-456201-9); Vol. 2. 56.00 (ISBN 0-12-456202-7). Acad Pr.
Mathieson, David W., ed. Nuclear Magnetic Resonance for Organic Chemists. 1967. 45.50 (ISBN 0-12-479950-7). Acad Pr.
Mooney, E. F., ed. Annual Reports on NMR Spectroscopy. Incl. Vol. 1. 1968. 56.50 (ISBN 0-12-505350-9); Vol. 5B. 1974. 71.50 (ISBN 0-12-505345-2); Vol. 6, 2 pts. 1976-78. Pt. B. 39.00 (ISBN 0-12-505346-0); Pt. C. 103.50 (ISBN 0-12-505347-9); Vol. 7. 1978. 50.00 (ISBN 0-12-505307-X); Vol. 8. 1978. 82.00 (ISBN 0-12-505308-8); Vol. 9. 1978. 66.50 (ISBN 0-12-505309-6). Acad Pr.
--Annual Reports on NMR Spectroscopy, Vol. 6a. 1975. 72.00 (ISBN 0-686-75173-6). Acad Pr.
Mullen, K. & Pregosin, P. S. Fourier Transform Nuclear Magnetic Resonance Techniques: A Practical Approach. 1977. 28.00 (ISBN 0-686-75175-2). Acad Pr.
Muus, L. T., et al, eds. Chemically Induced Magnetic Polarization. (Nato Advanced Study Institutes Ser. C: No. 34). 1977. lib. bdg. 50.00 (ISBN 90-277-0845-2, Pub. by Reidel Holland). Kluwer Boston.
Opella, S. J. & Lu, P. NMR & Biochemistry. 1979. 49.75 (ISBN 0-8247-6882-5). Dekker.
Paudler, William W. Nuclear Magnetic Resonance. 1971. pap. text ed. 12.95 (ISBN 0-205-02888-8, 6828884). Allyn.
Pesce, Biagio, ed. Nuclear Magnetic Resonance in Chemistry: Proceedings. 1965. 58.00 (ISBN 0-12-552350-5). Acad Pr.
Pintar, M. M., ed. Introductory Essays. (NMR Ser.: Vol. 13). 1976. 39.40 (ISBN 0-387-07754-5). Springer-Verlag.
Pople, J. A., et al. High Resolution Nuclear Magnetic Resonance. (Advanced Chemistry Ser.). 1959. text ed. 27.00 (ISBN 0-07-050516-0, C). McGraw.
Resonancia Magnetica Nuclear De Hidrogeno. (Serie De Quimica: No. 9). (Span.). 1973. pap. 1.25 (ISBN 0-8270-6365-2). OAS.
Richards, Rex, ed. Nuclear Magnetic Resonance Spectroscopy in Solids. (The Royal Society of London: Vol. 299). (Illus.). 210p. 1981. Repr. text ed. 58.00 (ISBN 0-85403-160-X, Pub. by Royal Soc London). Scholium Intl.
Rushworth, Francis A. & Tunstall, David P. Nuclear Magnetic Resonance. LC 72-89713. (Documents on Modern Physics Ser.). 266p. 1973. 37.50 (ISBN 0-677-04820-3). Gordon.
Semin, G. K., et al. Nuclear Quadrupole Resonance in Chemistry. Shelnitz, P., tr. from Rus. 517p. 1975. 71.95 (ISBN 0-470-77580-7). Halsted Pr.
Simons, W. W. & Zanger, M. The Sadtler Guide to NMR Spectra. 1972. 86.50 (ISBN 0-85501-074-6). Heyden.
Slichter, C. P. Principles of Magnetic Resonance 1980: Second Corrected Printing of the Second Revised & Expanded Edition. (Springer Ser. in Solid-State Sciences: Vol. I). 397p. 1980. 24.80 (ISBN 0-387-08476-2). Springer-Verlag.
Slonim, I. Ya. & Lyubimov, A. N. The NMR of Polymers. LC 69-12543. 365p. 1970. 37.50 (ISBN 0-306-30415-5, Plenum Pr). Plenum Pub.
Smith, J. A., ed. Advances in Nuclear Quadrupole Resonance. Vol. 3. 1978 ed. 97.00 (ISBN 0-85501-146-7); Vol. 2. 1975 ed. 97.00 (ISBN 0-85501-145-9); Vol. 1. 1974 ed. 97.00 (ISBN 0-85501-091-6). Heyden.
Stepin, L. D. Quantum Radio Frequency Physics. 1965. 17.50x (ISBN 0-262-19016-8). MIT Pr.
Szymanski, Herman & Yelin, R. E. NMR Band Handbook. LC 66-20321. 432p. 1968. 75.00 (ISBN 0-306-65127-0). IFI Plenum.
Turov, E. A. & Petrov, M. P. Nuclear Magnetic Resonance in Ferro & Antiferromagnetics. 206p. 1972. 54.95 (ISBN 0-470-89323-0). Halsted Pr.
Waugh, John, et al. Advances in Magnetic Resonance: The Principles of Biological & Medical Imaging by NMR, Supplement 2. 1982. price not set (ISBN 0-12-025562-6). Acad Pr.
Wertheim, G. K., et al. The Electronic Structure of Point Defects As Determined by Mossbauer Spectroscopy & by Spin Resonance. (Defects in Crystalline Solids: Vol. 4). 1972. 34.25 (ISBN 0-444-10125-X, North-Holland). Elsevier.
Wuthrich, K. NMR in Biological Research: Peptides & Proteins. 1976. 73.25 (ISBN 0-444-11031-3, North-Holland); pap. 29.50 (ISBN 0-7204-0389-8). Elsevier.
Zhernovoi, Aleksandr I. & Latyshev, Georgy D. Nuclear Magnetic Resonance in a Flowing Liquid. LC 65-13580. 166p. 1965. 32.50 (ISBN 0-306-10722-8, Consultants). Plenum Pub.

NUCLEAR MAGNETISM
see also Hyperfine Interactions; Nuclear Magnetic Resonance

Abragam, A. Principles of Nuclear Magnetism. (International Series of Monographs on Physics). 1961. 98.00x (ISBN 0-19-851236-8). Oxford U Pr.
Deutch, B. I., et al, eds. Hyperfine Interactions. 1977. 68.50 (ISBN 0-7204-0452-5, North-Holland). Elsevier.
Fogedby, Hans C. Theoretical Aspects of Mainly Low Dimensional Magnetic Systems. (Lecture Notes in Physics Ser.: Vol. 131). 163p. 1981. pap. 12.00 (ISBN 0-387-10238-8). Springer Verlag.
Rado, George T. & Suhl, H., eds. Magnetism: A Treatise on Modern Theory & Materials, 5 vols. 1963-1973. Vol. 1. 63.00 (ISBN 0-12-575301-2); Vol. 2A. 55.50 (ISBN 0-12-575302-0); Vol. 2B. 55.50 (ISBN 0-12-575342-X); Vol. 3. 56.00 (ISBN 0-12-575303-9); Vol. 4. 52.00 (ISBN 0-12-575304-7); Vol. 5. 60.00 (ISBN 0-12-575305-5). Acad Pr.

NUCLEAR MASSES
see Atomic Mass

NUCLEAR MEDICINE
see also Radioactivity–Physiological Effect; Radioisotopes in Pharmacology

Alderson, Philip O. Atlas of Pediatric Nuclear Medicine, Nineteen Seventy-Eight. LC 78-24369. (Illus.). 1978. text ed. 47.50 (ISBN 0-8016-0107-X). Mosby.
Ashkar, F., et al, eds. Nuclear Medicine: A Modern up-to-Date Presentation, Study Guide. (Illus.). 488p. 1975. 29.00 (ISBN 0-398-03029-4); pap. 22.25 (ISBN 0-398-03060-X). C C Thomas.
Ashkar, F. S., ed. Thyroid & Endocrine System Investigations with Radionuclides & Radioassays. (Illus.). 544p. 1979. 40.50 (ISBN 0-89352-070-5). Masson Pub.
Ashkar, Fued, ed. Practical Nuclear Medicine. LC 73-13794. 217p. 1974. 25.00 (ISBN 0-8463-0126-1, Pub. by W & W). Krieger.
Barnes, Broda O. & Barnes, Charlotte W. Heart Attack Rareness in Thyroid-Treated Patients. 104p. 1972. pap. 11.75 photocopy ed. spiral (ISBN 0-398-02519-3). C C Thomas.
Baum, Sheldon, et al. Atlas of Nuclear Medicine Imaging. (Illus.). 400p. 1981. 68.50x (ISBN 0-8385-0447-7). ACC.
Behrens, C. E., et al. Atomic Medicine. 5th ed. 892p. 1969. 38.50 (ISBN 0-683-00509-X, Pub. by Williams & Wilkins). Krieger.
Belcher, E. H. & Vetter, H., eds. Radioisotopes in Medical Diagnosis. 2nd ed. (Illus.). 1971. 69.50 (ISBN 0-407-38400-6). Butterworth.
Bennington, J. Financial Operation & Management Concepts in Nuclear Medicine. (Illus.). 1976. 19.50 (ISBN 0-8391-0953-9). Univ Park.
Bernier, Donald R., et al. Nuclear Medicine, Technology & Techniques. LC 80-17455. (Illus.). 538p. 1981. pap. text ed. 34.50 (ISBN 0-8016-0662-4). Mosby.
Billinghurst. Chemistry for Nuclear Medicine. Date not set. price not set (ISBN 0-8151-3295-6). Year Bk Med.
Blahd, William. Nuclear Medicine. 2nd ed. 1971. 44.00 (ISBN 0-07-005542-4, HP). McGraw.
Blaufox, M. Donald & Funck-Brentano, Jean-Louis, eds. Radionuclides in Nephrology: An International Symposium. LC 76-182811. (Illus.). 448p. 1972. 58.25 (ISBN 0-8089-0745-X). Grune.
Brucer, et al, eds. The Heritage of Nuclear Medicine. LC 79-65338. (Illus.). 167p. 1979. soft cover 17.00 (ISBN 0-932004-02-4). Soc Nuclear Med.
Catsch, Alexander. Radioactive Metal Mobilization in Medicine. Kawin, Bergene, tr. (American Lecture Living Chemistry). (Illus.). 184p. 1964. ed. spiral bdg. 17.50photocopy (ISBN 0-398-00296-7). C C Thomas.
Chandra, Ramesh. Introductory Physics of Nuclear Medicine. 2nd ed. (Illus.). 200p. Date not set. price not set (ISBN 0-8121-0826-4). Lea & Febiger.
Choppin, G. & Ryberg, J., eds. Nuclear Chemistry: Theory & Applications. (Illus.). 1980. text ed. 87.00 (ISBN 0-08-023826-2); pap. text ed. 29.50 (ISBN 0-08-023823-8). Pergamon.
Clifton, Nancy A. & Simmons, Pamela J. Basic Imaging Procedures in Nuclear Medicine. 159p. 1981. pap. 13.95 (ISBN 0-8385-0578-3). ACC.
Cremin, B. J., et al. Radiological Diagnosis of Digestive Tract Disorders in the Newborn: A Guide to Radiologists, Surgeons, & Paediatricians. (Illus.). 1973. 21.95 (ISBN 0-407-38375-1). Butterworth.
Czerniak, Pinchas. Radionuclides in Medicine & Biology Diagnosis, Pt. A. (Illus.). 308p. 1970. 14.50 (ISBN 0-88275-013-5). Krieger.
Danadian, R., ed. NMR in Medicine. (NMR--Basic Principles & Progress Ser.: Vol. 19). (Illus.). 230p. 1981. 57.90 (ISBN 0-387-10460-7). Springer-Verlag.
DeLand, Frank H. & Wagner, Henry W. Atlas of Nuclear Medicine: Reticuloendothelial System, Liver, Spleen & Thyroid, Vol. 3. LC 74-81820. (Illus.). 1972. 30.00 (ISBN 0-7216-3017-0). Saunders.
Donath, A. & Righetti, A., eds. Cardiovascular Nuclear Medicine. (Progress in Nuclear Medicine: Vol. 6). (Illus.). viii, 228p. 1980. 88.75 (ISBN 3-8055-0618-X). S Karger.
Dubovsky, E. V., et al. Nuclear Medicine Technology Continuing Education Review. 1976. sprial bdg. 13.50 (ISBN 0-87488-331-8). Med Exam.
Dynamic Studies with Radioisotopes in Medicine. (Illus., Orig.). 1971. pap. 66.00 (ISBN 92-0-010071-6, ISP263, IAEA). Unipub.
Dynamic Studies with Radioisotopes in Medicine, Vol. 1. (Illus.). 489p. 1975. pap. 44.00 (ISBN 92-0-010075-9, ISP376-1, IAEA). Unipub.
Early, Paul J., et al. Textbook of Nuclear Medicine Technology. 3rd ed. LC 78-31659. (Illus.). 1979. text ed. 34.95 (ISBN 0-8016-1488-0). Mosby.
Enlander, Derek, ed. Computers in Laboratory Medicine. 1975. 23.00 (ISBN 0-12-239950-1). Acad Pr.
ERDA Technical Information Center. Nuclear Medicine. 503p. 1976. write for info. DOE.
Esser, Peter, et al. Functional Mapping of Organ Systems. (Illus.). 300p. 1981. write for info. (ISBN 0-932004-09-1). Soc Nuclear Med.
Etter, Lewis E. Glossary of Words & Phrases Used in Radiology, Nuclear Medicine & Ultrasound. 2nd ed. 384p. 1970. pap. 32.50 photocopy ed. spiral (ISBN 0-398-00526-5). C C Thomas.
Fajman, W. A. Effect of Image Size on Lesion Detectability in Nuclear Medicine. Date not set. price not set (ISBN 0-685-96884-7). Green.
Freedman, Gerald S., ed. Tomographic Imaging in Nuclear Medicine. LC 73-82572. (Illus.). 271p. 1973. 14.50 (ISBN 0-932004-07-5). Soc Nuclear Med.
Freeman, Leonard, ed. Nuclear Medicine Annual, 1980. Weissmann, Heidi. 440p. 1980. text ed. 42.50 (ISBN 0-89004-472-4). Raven.
Freeman, Leonard M. & Blaufox, Donald, eds. Cardiovascular Nuclear Medicine: Current Methodology & Practice. (Seminars in Nuclear Medicine Reprint). 304p. 1980. write for info. (ISBN 0-8089-1292-5). Grune.
Freeman, Leonard M. & Blaufox, M. Donald, eds. Pediatric Nuclear Medicine. 224p. 1975. 34.50 (ISBN 0-8089-0920-7). Grune.
--Radionuclide Studies of the Genitourinary System. 224p. 1975. 34.25 (ISBN 0-8089-0921-5). Grune.
Freeman, Leonard M. & Weissmann, Heidi S., eds. Nuclear Medicine Annual, 1981. 360p. 1981. text ed. 39.00 (ISBN 0-89004-581-X). Raven.
Frey, G. Donald & Klobukowski, Christopher J. Nuclear Medicine Technology Examination Review Book. 1980. pap. 14.50 (ISBN 0-87488-457-8). Med Exam.
Goodwin, Paul N. & Rao, Dandamudi V. An Introduction to the Physics of Nuclear Medicine. (Illus.). 164p. 1977. 23.75 (ISBN 0-398-03569-5). C C Thomas.
Gottschalk, Alexander, et al. Diagnostic Nuclear Medicine. Robbins, Laurence L., ed. (Golden's Diagnostic Radiology Ser: Section 20). 57.00 (ISBN 0-683-03669-6). Williams & Wilkins.
Greig, William & Gillespie, Frank C. Recent Advances in Clinical Nuclear Medicine, No. 1. LC 74-21553. (Illus.). 1975. text ed. 26.50x (ISBN 0-443-01026-9). Churchill.
Group for the Advancement of Psychiatry. Psychological & Medical Aspects of the Use of Nuclear Energy, Vol. 4. (Symposium No. 6). 1960. pap. 2.00 (ISBN 0-87318-059-3, Pub. by Adv Psychiatry). Mental Health.
Guter, Marvin & Serafini, Aldo. Chest Nuclear Medicine Case Studies. 1979. spiral bdg. 14.50 (ISBN 0-87488-083-1). Med Exam.
Hayes, Raymond L., et al, eds. Radioisotopes in Medicine: In Vitro Studies. LC 68-60071. (AEC Symposium Ser.). 753p. 1968. pap. 6.00 (ISBN 0-686-75732-7); microfiche 3.00 (ISBN 0-686-75733-5). DOE.
Heindel, Ned D., et al, eds. The Chemistry of Radiopharmaceuticals. LC 77-94827. (Cancer Management Ser.: Vol. 3). (Illus.). 304p. 1978. 37.75x (ISBN 0-89352-019-5). Masson Pub.
Hirsch, et al, eds. Nuclear Medicine in Clinical Pediatrics. LC 74-25383. (Illus.). 296p. 1975. 25.00 (ISBN 0-88416-036-X). Soc Nuclear Med.
Hoffer. Yearbook of Nuclear Medicine, 1981. 1981. 38.95 (ISBN 0-8151-4525-X). Year Bk Med.
Hoffer, Paul B., et al. Gallium-67 Imaging. LC 77-13125. (Diagnostic & Therapeutic Radiology Ser.). 1978. 37.50 (ISBN 0-471-02601-8, Pub. by Wiley Medical). Wiley.
Hoffer, Paul B., et al, eds. Semiconductor Detectors in the Future of Nuclear Medicine. LC 77-159479. (Illus.). 306p. 1971. 10.00 (ISBN 0-686-74002-5). Soc Nuclear Med.
Holman, B. L. & Lindeman, J. F., eds. Regional Pulmonary Function in Health & Disease. (Progress in Nuclear Medicine: Vol. 3). 196p. 1973. 42.00 (ISBN 3-8055-1425-5). S Karger.
Holman, B. L., et al. Cardiac Nuclear Medicine. (Illus.). 1980. pap. 19.00 (ISBN 0-387-09803-8). Springer-Verlag.
Holman, B. Leonard, et al, eds. Principles of Cardiovascular Nuclear Medicine. 256p. 1978. 30.50 (ISBN 0-8089-1082-5). Grune.
Horst, W., et al, eds. Frontiers in Nuclear Medicine. (Illus.). 350p. 1980. pap. 54.90 (ISBN 0-387-09895-X). Springer-Verlag.
Howard, Phillip L. & Trainer, Thomas D. Radionuclides in Clinical Chemistry. 1980. text ed. 22.50 (ISBN 0-316-37470-9). Little.
IAEA-WHO Expert Committee on the Use of Ionizing Radiation & Radioisotopes for Medical Purposes. Geneva, 1975. Nuclear Medicine: Report. (Technical Report Ser.: No. 591). (Also avail. in French, Russian & Spanish). 1976. pap. 2.80 (ISBN 92-4-120591-1). World Health.
Iio, M. Nuclear Medicine in Japan. 310p. 1975. 60.00x (ISBN 0-89955-341-9, Pub. by Japan Sci Soc Japan). Intl Schol Bk Serv.
In Vitro Procedures with Radioisotopes in Medicine. (Illus., Orig., Eng., Fr. & Span.). 1970. pap. 50.50 (ISBN 92-0-010070-8, ISP237, IAEA). Unipub.
James, A. Everette, et al. Pediatric Nuclear Medicine. LC 72-97912. (Illus.). 560p. 1974. text ed. 35.00 (ISBN 0-7216-5108-9). Saunders.
Janisch, H., et al. Radioisotop in Geburtshilfe und Gynakologie. Gitsch, E., ed. 1977. 146.75x (ISBN 3-11-004532-X). De Gruyter.
Juge, O. & Donath, A., eds. Neuronuclear Medicine. (Progress in Nuclear Medicine Ser.: Vol. 7). (Illus.). vii, 240p. 1981. 90.00 (ISBN 3-8055-2319-X). S Karger.
Kaufman, Leon, et al, eds. Nuclear Magnetic Resonance Imaging in Medicine. LC 81-82043. (Illus.). 240p. 1981. 29.50 (ISBN 0-89640-057-3). Igaku-Shoin.
Kenny, Peter J. & Smith, Edward M., eds. Quantitative Organ Visualization in Nuclear Medicine: A Symposium. LC 71-125662. (Illus.). 1971. 29.95x (ISBN 0-87024-180-X). U of Miami Pr.
Keyes, John W., Jr., ed. CRC Manual of Nuclear Medicine Procedures. 3rd ed. 224p. 1978. 29.95 (ISBN 0-8493-0707-4). CRC Pr.
Kirchner, Peter T., ed. Nuclear Medicine Review Syllabus. LC 79-92990. (Illus.). 619p. 1980. pap. text ed. 32.50 (ISBN 0-932004-04-0). Soc Nuclear Med.
Lange, Robert C. Nuclear Medicine for Technicians. (Illus.). 1973. 16.75 (ISBN 0-8151-5300-7). Year Bk Med.
Lawrence, John H., ed. Recent Advances in Nuclear Medicine. LC 65-12654. (Illus.). 256p. Vol. III. 49.25 (ISBN 0-8089-0697-6). Grune.
--Recent Advances in Nuclear Medicine, Vol. IV. LC 65-299263. (Illus.). 256p. 1974. 54.25 (ISBN 0-8089-0837-5). Grune.
Lawrence, Jon H. & Budinger, Thomas, eds. Recent Advances in Nuclear Medicine, Vol. V. 1978. 36.00 (ISBN 0-8089-1068-X). Grune.
Lieberman, David E., ed. Computer Methods: The Fundamentals of Digital Nuclear Medicine. LC 77-10999. (Illus.). 1977. pap. 20.00 (ISBN 0-8016-3009-6). Mosby.
McAlister, Joan. Radionuclide Techniques in Medicine. LC 78-68348. (Techniques of Measurement in Medicine: No. 3). 1980. 41.50 (ISBN 0-521-22402-0); pap. 12.50x (ISBN 0-521-29474-6). Cambridge U Pr.

Maisey, Michael. Nuclear Medicine: A Clinical Introduction. (Illus.). 136p. 1980. lib. bdg. 24.50 (ISBN 0-906141-42-7, Pub. by Update Pubns England). Kluwer Boston.
Matin, Philip. Handbook of Clinical Nuclear Medicine. 1977. cancelled (ISBN 0-87488-610-4). Med Exam.
Mayneord, W. V. Some Applications of Nuclear Physics to Medicine. 1980. 15.00x (ISBN 0-686-69957-2, Pub. by Brit Inst Radiology). State Mutual Bk.
Medical Radioisotope Scanning-1959. 1959. pap. 9.75 (ISBN 92-0-010059-7, IS63, IAEA). Unipub.
Medical Radioisotope Scanning-1964, 2 vols. 1964. Vol. 1. pap. 27.75 (ISBN 92-0-010264-6, ISP82-1-2, IAEA); Vol. 2. pap. 23.75 (ISBN 92-0-010364-2). Unipub.
Medical Radioisotope Scintigraphy, 2 Vols. 1968. Vol. 1. pap. 57.75 (ISBN 92-0-010069-4, IAEA); Vol. 2. pap. 61.75 (ISBN 92-0-010169-0). Unipub.
Medical Radionuclide Imaging: Vol. 1, Proceedings of a Symposium, los Angeles 25-29 Oct, 1976. (Illus.). 1977. pap. 64.25 (ISBN 92-0-110077-9, ISP 440-1, IAEA). Unipub.
Medical Uses of Ca-47. (Technical Reports Ser.: No. 10). 1962. pap. 7.00 (ISBN 92-0-115162-4, IDC 10, IAEA). Unipub.
Medical Uses of Ca-47: Second Panel Report. (Technical Reports Ser.: No. 32). 1964. pap. 11.75 (ISBN 92-0-115264-7, IDC32, IAEA). Unipub.
Membership Directory 1979-80. 232p. 1979. write for info. (ISBN 0-932004-03-2). Soc Nuclear Med.
Nuclear Activation Techniques in the Life Sciences - 1972. (Illus.). 664p. (Orig.). 1973. pap. 51.25 (ISBN 92-0-010272-7, ISP310, IAEA). Unipub.
Nudelman, Sol & Patton, Dennis D., eds. Imaging for Medicine: Volume 1, Nuclear Medicine, Ultrasonics & Thermography. (Illus.). 494p. 1980. 49.50 (ISBN 0-306-40384-6, Plenum Pr). Plenum Pub.
O'Reilly, P H & Shields. Nuclear Medicine in Urology & Nephrology. (Illus.). 1979. text ed. 44.95 (ISBN 0-407-00151-4). Butterworth.
O'Rourke, J. Nuclear Opthalmology: Dynamic Function Studies in Intraocular Disease. LC 76-1257. (Illus.). 1976. text ed. 27.00 (ISBN 0-7216-7009-1). Saunders.
Parker, R. P., et al. Basic Science of Nuclear Medicine. LC 77-30087. 1978. 30.00 (ISBN 0-443-01460-4). Churchill.
Powsner, Edward R. & Raeside, David E. Diagnostic Nuclear Medicine. LC 72-130001. (Illus.). 640p. 1971. 81.75 (ISBN 0-8089-0639-9). Grune.
Precautions in the Management of Patients Who Have Received Theraputic Amounts of Radionuclides. (NCRP Reports Ser.: No. 37). 1970. 8.00 (ISBN 0-913392-19-7). NCRP Pubns.
Prince, John R. & Schmidt, Lewis D. Statistics & Mathematics in the Nuclear Medicine Laboratory. LC 75-39797. (Illus.). 89p. 1976. pap. text ed. 18.00 perfect bdg. (ISBN 0-89189-020-3, 45-8-007-00). Am Soc Clinical.
Quimby, Edith H., et al. Radioactive Nuclides in Medicine & Biology: Basic Physics & Instrumentation. 3rd ed. LC 68-18868. (Illus.). 390p. 1970. text ed. 12.50 (ISBN 0-8121-0197-9). Lea & Febiger.
Quinn, James L., III & Spies, Stewart M. Year Book of Nuclear Medicine, 1979. (Illus.). 1979. 31.95 (ISBN 0-8151-6988-4). Year Bk Med.
Quinn, James L., III, ed. Year Book of Nuclear Medicine 1980. (Illus.). 400p. 1980. 37.95 (ISBN 0-8151-6989-2). Year Bk Med.
Radioisotope Sample Measurement Techniques in Medicine & Biology. 1965. pap. 39.00 (ISBN 92-0-010165-8, ISP106, IAEA). Unipub.
Radioisotopes in Tropical Medicine. 1962. 13.50 (ISBN 92-0-010062-7, ISP31, IAEA). Unipub.
Radiopharmaceuticals from Generator-Produced Radionuclides. 205p. 1971. pap. 14.75 (ISBN 92-0-111471-0, ISP294, IAEA). Unipub.
Recommendations: Manual on Early Medical Treatment of Possible Radiation Injury. (IAEA Safety Ser.: No. 47). 1979. pap. 14.00 (ISBN 92-0-123278-0, ISP506, IAEA). Unipub.
Rocha, Antonio F. & Harbert, John C., eds. Textbook of Nuclear Medicine: Basic Science. LC 78-17195. (Illus.). 412p. 1978. text ed. 27.50 (ISBN 0-8121-0630-X). Lea & Febiger.
--Textbook of Nuclear Medicine: Clinical Applications. LC 78-31734. (Illus.). 495p. 1979. text ed. 32.50 (ISBN 0-8121-0648-2). Lea & Febiger.
Rose, Joseph L., et al. Basic Physics in Diagnostic Ultrasound. LC 79-14932. 1979. 34.50 (ISBN 0-471-05735-5, Pub. by Wiley Medical). Wiley.
Rothfeld, Benjamin, ed. Nuclear Medicine: Endocrinology. LC 78-3773. (Illus.). 1978. 43.50 (ISBN 0-397-50392-X, JBL-Med-Nursing). Har-Row.
--Nuclear Medicine: Hepatolineal. (Illus.). 288p. 1980. text ed. 45.00 (ISBN 0-397-50412-8, JBL-Med Nursing). Har-Row.
Schneider, P. B. & Treves, S. Nuclear Medicine in Clinical Practice. 1978. 92.75 (ISBN 0-444-80052-2, Biomedical Pr). Elsevier.
Selby, John B. & Frey, Donald G. Self-Assessment of Current Knowledge in Nuclear Medicine. 1977. spiral bdg. 12.00 (ISBN 0-87488-239-7). Med Exam.
Selected Papers on Nuclear Pharmacy. 1976. 12.00 (ISBN 0-917330-07-2). Am Pharm Assn.
Serafini, Aldo. Nuclear Cardiology: Principles & Methods. LC 76-39783. (Topics in Cardiovascular Disease Ser.). (Illus.). 249p. 1977. 27.50 (ISBN 0-306-30952-1, Plenum Pr). Plenum Pub.
Shipley, Reginald A. & Clark, Richard E. Tracer Methods for in Vitro Kinetics: Theory & Applications. 1972. 37.50 (ISBN 0-12-640250-7). Acad Pr.
Shtasel, Philip. Speak to Me in Nuclear Medicine. (Illus.). 1976. 25.00x (ISBN 0-06-142383-1, Harper Medical). Har-Row.
Sodee, D. Bruce & Early, Paul J. Mosby's Manual of Nuclear Medicine Procedures. 3rd ed. LC 80-26675. (Illus.). 601p. 1981. pap. 35.95 (ISBN 0-8016-4729-0). Mosby.
--Technology & Interpretation of Nuclear Medicine Procedures. 2nd ed. LC 75-15607. (Illus.). 544p. 1975. text ed. 31.95 (ISBN 0-8016-4732-0). Mosby.
Solomon, Nathan A., ed. Nuclear Medicine. 2nd. ed. (Medical Examination Review Bk. Ser.: Vol. 25). 1977. spiral bdg. 16.50 (ISBN 0-87488-133-1). Med Exam.
Sorenson, James A. & Phelps, Michael E. Physics in Nuclear Medicine. 416p. 1980. 39.50 (ISBN 0-8089-1238-0). Grune.
Sorenson, James A., ed. Nuclear Cardiology: Selected Computers Aspects, 1978 Symposium Proceedings. LC 78-58477. 203p. pap. 15.00 (ISBN 0-932004-00-8). Soc Nuclear Med.
Spencer, Richard P. Nuclear Medicine - Focus on Clinical Diagnosis. 2nd ed. 1980. pap. 18.00 (ISBN 0-87488-825-5). Med Exam.
Spencer, Richard P., ed. Therapy in Nuclear Medicine. 416p. 1978. 46.75 (ISBN 0-8089-1070-1). Grune.
Sprawls, Perry, Jr. The Physics & Instrumentation of Nuclear Medicine. 198p. 1981. text ed. 22.95 (ISBN 0-8391-0544-4). Univ Park.
Strauss, H. William & Pitt, Bertram. Cardiovascular Nuclear Medicine. 2nd ed. LC 79-18410. (Illus.). 1979. text ed. 54.50 (ISBN 0-8016-2409-6). Mosby.
Strauss, H. William, et al. Atlas of Cardiovascular Nuclear Medicine: Selected Case Studies. LC 77-22947. (Illus.). 1977. 46.50 (ISBN 0-8016-4811-4). Mosby.
--Cardiovascular Nuclear Medicine. LC 74-20982. 1974. text ed. 45.00 (ISBN 0-8016-2408-8). Mosby.
Symposium, Knoxville, July 15-19, 1974. Dynamic Studies with Radioisotopes in Medicine 1974, Vol. II: Proceedings. (Illus.). 443p. 1975. pap. 40.75 (ISBN 92-0-010175-5, ISP376-2, IAEA). Unipub.
Trainer, Thomas D., et al. Radioisotopes in the Clinical Laboratory. (Atlas Ser.). (Illus.). 1976. text & slides 70.00 (ISBN 0-89189-093-9, 15-8-01-00); microfiche 22.00 (ISBN 0-89189-094-7, 17-8-001-00). Am Soc Clinical.
Verdon, Thomas A., Jr. Nuclear Medicine for the General Physician. LC 78-26954. (Illus.). 244p. 1980. 25.00 (ISBN 0-88416-206-0). Wright-PSG.
Wegst, Audrey V., et al, eds. Nuclear Medicine Science Syllabus. LC 78-68703. 1978. loose-leaf text 33.00 (ISBN 0-932004-01-6). Soc Nuclear Med.
Wells, L. David & Bernier, Donald R. Radionuclide Imaging Artifacts. (Illus.). 1980. pap. 15.95 (ISBN 0-8151-9217-7). Year Bk Med.

NUCLEAR MEDICINE–EQUIPMENT AND SUPPLIES

Bennington, J. Financial Operation & Management Concepts in Nuclear Medicine. (Illus.). 1976. 19.50 (ISBN 0-8391-0953-9). Univ Park.
Berton, Alberta D., compiled by. Nuclear Medicine: A Comprehensive Bibliography. (Biomedical Information Guides Ser.: Vol. 2). 355p. 1980. 85.00 (ISBN 0-306-65178-5, IFI). Plenum Pub.
Hine, Gerald J., ed. Instrumentation in Nuclear Medicine, 2 vols. Vol. 1, 1967. 72.00 (ISBN 0-12-349450-8); Vol. 2, 1974. 71.00 (ISBN 0-12-349452-4). Acad Pr.
Hudak, Julia S. Handbook for Technologists of Nuclear Medicine. (Illus.). 168p. 1971. 12.75 (ISBN 0-398-02178-3). C C Thomas.
Medical Cyclotron Users Conference, 4th, Miami, 1976. Medical Cyclotrons in Nuclear Medicine: Proceedings. Roesler, H., et al, eds. (Progress in Nuclear Medicine: Vol. 4). 1977. 59.50 (ISBN 3-8055-2670-9). S Karger.
Quimby, Edith H., et al. Radioactive Nuclides in Medicine & Biology: Basic Physics & Instrumentation. 3rd ed. LC 68-18868. (Illus.). 390p. 1970. text ed. 12.50 (ISBN 0-8121-0197-9). Lea & Febiger.
Sodee, D. Bruce & Early, Paul J. Technology & Interpretation of Nuclear Medicine Procedures. 2nd ed. LC 75-15607. (Illus.). 544p. 1975. text ed. 31.95 (ISBN 0-8016-4732-0). Mosby.

NUCLEAR MODELS

see also Nuclear Shell Theory

Bohr, A. & Mottelson, B. R. Nuclear Structure, Vol. 3: Nucleonic Correlations. 1980. write for info (ISBN 0-8053-1017-7, Adv Bk Prog). Benjamin-Cummings.
Brown, G. E. Unified Theory of Nuclear Models & Forces. 3rd rev ed. 1972. 29.50 (ISBN 0-444-10107-1, North-Holland). Elsevier.
Davidson, John P. Collective Models of the Nucleus. LC 68-18665. 1968. 38.00 (ISBN 0-12-205250-1). Acad Pr.
Eisenberg, J. M. & Greiner, W. Nuclear Theory Vol. 3: Microscopic Theory of the Nucleus. 2nd ed. 1976. 36.75 (ISBN 0-7204-0484-3, North-Holland). Elsevier.
Green, A. E., et al. Nuclear Independent Particle Model. 1968. 56.00 (ISBN 0-12-297450-6). Acad Pr.
Irvine, J. M. Nuclear Structure Theory. 492p. 1972. text ed. 55.00 (ISBN 0-08-016401-3); pap. text ed. 32.00 (ISBN 0-08-018991-1). Pergamon.
Nemirovskii, P. E. Contemporary Models of the Atomic Nucleus. 1963. 37.00 (ISBN 0-08-009840-1); pap. 22.00 (ISBN 0-08-013582-X). Pergamon.
Ulehla, Ivan, et al. Optical Model of the Atomic Nucleus. Alter, G., tr. 1965. 29.50 (ISBN 0-12-707450-3). Acad Pr.
Wildermuth, K. & McClure, W. Cluster Representations of Nuclei. (Springer Tracts in Modern Physics, Vol. 41). (Illus.). 1966. 37.80 (ISBN 0-387-03670-9). Springer-Verlag.

NUCLEAR MOMENTS

see also Angular Momentum (Nuclear Physics); Nuclear Induction; Nuclear Magnetic Resonance; Nuclear Magnetism; Nuclear Spin; Paramagnetism

Eder, Gernot. Nuclear Forces: Introduction to Theoretical Nuclear Physics. 1968. pap. 6.95x (ISBN 0-262-55004-0). MIT Pr.
Lucken, E. A. Nuclear Quadrupole Coupling Constants. 1969. 57.50 (ISBN 0-12-458450-0). Acad Pr.
Rescigno, et al, eds. Electron-Molecule & Photon-Molecule Collisions. 1979. 39.50 (ISBN 0-306-40193-2, Plenum Pr). Plenum Pub.

NUCLEAR PARTICLES

see Particles (Nuclear Physics)

Michaudon, A., et al, eds. Nuclear Fission & Neutron-Induced Fission Cross-Sections. (Neutron Physics & Nuclear Data in Science & Technology Ser.: Vol. 1). (Illus.). 270p. 1981. 60.00 (ISBN 0-08-026125-6). Pergamon.

NUCLEAR PHYSICS

see also Angular Correlations (Nuclear Physics); Angular Momentum (Nuclear Physics); Atomic Energy; Atomic Mass; Auger Effect; Causality (Physics); Chemistry, Physical and Theoretical; Collisions (Nuclear Physics); Cosmic Rays; Cyclotron; Electric Discharges; Internal Conversion (Nuclear Physics); Isobaric Spin; Moessbauer Effect; Nuclear Astrophysics; Nuclear Chemistry; Nuclear Counters; Nuclear Engineering; Nuclear Excitation; Nuclear Fission; Nuclear Forces (Physics); Nuclear Geophysics; Nuclear Magnetism; Nuclear Models; Nuclear Moments; Nuclear Reactions; Nuclear Reactors; Nuclear Shell Theory; Nuclear Spin; Particle Accelerators; Particles (Nuclear Physics); Quantum Electrodynamics; Radioactivity; Radiobiology; Scattering (Physics); Transmutation (Chemistry); Triplet State

Abrahams, K., et al, eds. Nuclear Structure. (NATO Advanced Study Institute Series B-Physics: Vol. 67). 418p. 1981. 49.50 (ISBN 0-306-40728-0, Plenum Pr). Plenum Pub.
Ajzenberg-Selove, Fay, ed. Nuclear Spectroscopy, 2 Pts. (Pure & Applied Physics Ser.: Vol. 9). 1960. 66.50 ea. Pt. A (ISBN 0-12-046850-6). Pt. B (ISBN 0-12-046851-4). Acad Pr.
Alexander, G., ed. High Energy Physics & Nuclear Structure. 1967. 83.00 (ISBN 0-444-10133-0, North-Holland). Elsevier.
Arenhoevel, H. & Saruis, A. M., eds. From Collective States to Quarks in Nuclei: Proceedings. (Lecture Notes in Physics Ser.: Vol. 137). 414p. 1981. pap. 27.70 (ISBN 0-387-10570-0). Springer-Verlag.
Arenhovel, H. & Drechsel, D., eds. Nuclear Physics with Electromagnetic Interactions: Proceedings, International Conference, Mainz, Germany, June 1979. (Lecture Notes in Physics: Vol. 108). 1979. pap. 24.20 (ISBN 0-387-09539-X). Springer-Verlag.
Bacher, Robert F. & Goudsmit, Samuel, eds. Atomic Energy States, As Derived from the Analyses of Optical Spectra. LC 69-10066. 1969. Repr. of 1932 ed. lib. bdg. 29.50x (ISBN 0-8371-0290-1, BAES). Greenwood.
Baker, Wilfred E. Explosions in Air. (Illus.). 282p. 1973. 18.50x (ISBN 0-292-72003-3). U of Tex Pr.
Baranger, Michel & Vogt, Erich, eds. Advances in Nuclear Physics. Incl. Vol. 1. 416p. 1968. 37.50 (ISBN 0-306-39101-5); Vol. 2. 430p. 1969. 37.50 (ISBN 0-306-39102-3); Vol. 3. 480p. 1969. 37.50 (ISBN 0-306-39103-1); Vol. 4. 448p. 1971. 37.50 (ISBN 0-306-39104-X); Vol. 5. 484p. 1972. 32.50 (ISBN 0-306-39105-8); Vol. 6. 462p. 1973. 37.50 (ISBN 0-306-39106-6); Vol. 7. 329p. 1973. 32.50 (ISBN 0-306-39107-4); Vol. 8. 383p. 1975. 35.00 (ISBN 0-306-39108-2); Vol. 9. 264p. 1977. 24.50 (ISBN 0-306-39109-0); Vol. 10. 320p. 1978. 34.50 (ISBN 0-306-39110-4). LC 67-29001 (Plenum Pr). Plenum Pub.
Barnes, Arthur H., et al. Problems of Physics in the Ion Source. (National Nuclear Energy Ser.: Div. I, Vol. 8). 294p. 1951. pap. 36.20 (ISBN 0-686-75879-X); microfilm(35mm) 18.20 (ISBN 0-686-75880-3); microfilm(16mm) 10.00 (ISBN 0-686-75881-1). DOE.
Barrett, Roger C. & Jackson, Daphne F. Nuclear Sizes & Structure. (International Series of Monographs on Physics). 1977. 89.00x (ISBN 0-19-851272-4). Oxford U Pr.
Bates, D. R., et al, eds. Advances in Atomic & Molecular Physics, Vols. 1-14. Incl. Vol. 1. 1965. 50.00 (ISBN 0-12-003801-3); Vol. 2. 1966. 50.00 (ISBN 0-12-003802-1); Vol. 3. 1968. 57.00 (ISBN 0-12-003803-X); Vol. 4. 1968. 57.00 (ISBN 0-12-003804-8); Vol. 5. 1969. 57.00 (ISBN 0-12-003805-6); Vol. 6. 1970. 57.00 (ISBN 0-12-003806-4); Vol. 7. 1971. 57.00 (ISBN 0-12-003807-2); Vol. 8. 1972. 57.00 (ISBN 0-12-003808-0); Vol. 9. 1974. 57.00 (ISBN 0-12-003809-9); Vol. 10. 1974. 57.00 (ISBN 0-12-003810-2); Vol. 11. 1976. 76.50 (ISBN 0-12-003311-9); lib ed. 98.50 (ISBN 0-12-003874-9); microfiche 54.50 (ISBN 0-12-003875-7); Vol. 12. 1976. 67.50 (ISBN 0-12-003812-9); lib ed. 87.00 (ISBN 0-12-003876-5); microfiche 48.50 (ISBN 0-12-003877-3); Vol. 13. 1978. 66.50 (ISBN 0-12-003813-7); lib ed. 85.00 (ISBN 0-12-003878-1); microfiche 41.50 (ISBN 0-12-003879-X); Vol. 14. 1979. 55.50 (ISBN 0-12-003814-5); lib ed. 71.50 (ISBN 0-12-003880-3); microfiche 40.00 (ISBN 0-12-003881-1). Acad Pr.
Bates, David R., ed. Atomic & Molecular Processes. (Pure & Applied Physics Ser.: Vol. 13). 1962. 60.00 (ISBN 0-12-081450-1). Acad Pr.
Bates, Sir David R. & Bederson, Benjamin, eds. Advances in Atomic & Molecular Physics, Vol. 16. LC 65-18423. 1980. 47.50 (ISBN 0-12-003816-1); lib. ed. 61.50 (ISBN 0-12-003884-6); microfiche ed. 33.50 (ISBN 0-12-003885-4). Acad Pr.
Becker, Martin, et al, eds. Advances in Nuclear Science & Technology, Vol. 12. 350p. 1980. 39.50 (ISBN 0-306-40315-3, Plenum Pr). Plenum Pub.
Bederson, B., et al, eds. Atomic Physics, No. 1. LC 69-14560. 620p. 1969. 39.50 (ISBN 0-306-30383-3, Plenum Pr). Plenum Pub.
Beiser, Arthur. Perspectives of Modern Physics. 1969. text ed. 19.95 (ISBN 0-07-004350-7, C). McGraw.
Bhiday, M. R. & Joshi, V. A. Introduction to Nuclear Physics. 388p. 1981. 15.00x (ISBN 0-86125-503-8, Pub. by Orient Longman India). State Mutual Bk.
Birks, J. B. & Birks, J. B., eds. Rutherford Jubilee International Conference - Manchester, 1962. 83.50 (ISBN 0-12-101162-3). Acad Pr.
Blanchard, C., et al. Introduction to Modern Physics. 2nd ed. LC 69-10054. 1969. text ed. 17.95 (ISBN 0-13-488502-3). P-H.
Blatt, J. & Weisskopf, V. F. Theoretical Nuclear Physics. LC 79-4268. 1979. pap. 32.00 (ISBN 0-387-90382-8). Springer-Verlag.
Boffi, S. & Passatore, G., eds. Nuclear Optical Model Potential. (Lecture Notes in Physics: Vol. 55). 1976. soft cover 13.70 (ISBN 0-387-07864-9). Springer-Verlag.
Bogolyubov, N. N., ed. Particles & Nuclei. Incl. Vol. 1, Pt. 1. 189p (ISBN 0-306-17191-0); Vol. 1, Pt. 2. 191p (ISBN 0-306-17192-9); Vol. 2, Pt. 1. 171p (ISBN 0-306-17193-7); Vol. 2, Pt. 2. 138p (ISBN 0-306-17194-5); Vol. 2, Pt. 3. 178p (ISBN 0-306-17195-3); Vol. 2, Pt. 4. 178p (ISBN 0-306-17196-1). LC 72-83510. 1972. 45.00 ea. (Consultants). Plenum Pub.
Bonse, U. & Rauch, H., eds. Neutron Interferometry. (Illus.). 1980. 69.00x (ISBN 0-19-851947-8). Oxford U Pr.
Boschke, F., et al, eds. Nuclear Quadrupole Resonance. Boschke, F. (Topics in Current Chemistry: Vol. 30). (Illus.). 180p. (Eng. & Ger.). 1972. pap. 29.50 (ISBN 0-387-05781-1). Springer-Verlag.
Boulder Conference On High Energy Physics. Proceedings. Mahanthappa, K. T., et al, eds. LC 71-115692. (Illus.). 1970. 15.00x (ISBN 0-87081-002-2). Colo Assoc.

Bowcock, J. E., ed. Methods & Problems of Theoretical Physics in Honor of R. E. Peierls. 1971. 53.75 (ISBN 0-444-10040-7, North-Holland). Elsevier.
Bowler, M. G. Nuclear Physics. 444p. 1973. text ed. 42.00 (ISBN 0-08-016983-X); pap. text ed. 26.00 (ISBN 0-08-018990-3). Pergamon.
Brink, D. M. Nuclear Forces. 1965. 19.50 (ISBN 0-08-011034-7); pap. 9.75 (ISBN 0-08-011033-9). Pergamon.
Brink, D. M. & Mulvey, J., eds. Progress in Nuclear Physics. Incl. Vol. 10. 1968. 70.00 (ISBN 0-08-012682-0); Vol. 11. 1970. 70.00 (ISBN 0-08-006360-8); Vol. 12, Pt. 1. pap. text ed. 15.50 (ISBN 0-08-015766-1); Vol. 12, Pt. 2. pap. text ed. 15.50 (ISBN 0-08-016394-7). Pergamon.
Brittin, Wesley E. & Barut, A. O., eds. Boulder Lecture Notes in Theoretical Physics, 1967: Vol. 10-B, High Energy Physics & Fundamental Particles. 1968. 133.75x (ISBN 0-677-12900-9). Gordon.
Brittin, Wesley E., et al, eds. Boulder Lecture Notes in Theoretical Physics, 1963, Vol. 6. 1964. 133.75x (ISBN 0-677-13030-9). Gordon.
--Boulder Lecture Notes in Theoretical Physics, 1968: Vol. 11-B, Quantum Fluids & Nuclear Matter. 1969. 93.00x (ISBN 0-677-13120-8). Gordon.
--Boulder Lecture Notes in Theoretical Physics, 1968: Vol. 11-a, Elementary Particle Physics, Pts. 1 & 2. 1969. Pt. 1. 111.75 (ISBN 0-677-13110-0); Pt. 2. 76.00 (ISBN 0-677-13400-2). Gordon.
--Boulder Lecture Notes in Theoretical Physics, 1964: Vol. 7-A, Lorentz Group. 1968. 83.75x (ISBN 0-677-13040-6). Gordon.
--Boulder Lecture Notes in Theoretical Physics, 1964: Vol. 7-C, Statistical Phases, Weak Interactions, Field Theory. 1968. 104.50 (ISBN 0-677-13060-0). Gordon.
--Boulder Lecture Notes in Theoretical Physics, 1965: Vol. 8-C, Nuclear Structure Physics. 1966. 133.75x (ISBN 0-677-13090-2). Gordon.
--Boulder Lecture Notes in Theoretical Physics, 1966: Vol. 9-a, Mathematical Methods of Theoretical Physics. 1967. 81.00x (ISBN 0-677-11600-4). Gordon.
--Boulder Lecture Notes in Theoretical Physics, 1966: Vol. 9-B, High Energy & Particle Physics. 1967. 93.00 (ISBN 0-677-11610-1). Gordon.
Burcham, W. E. Elements of Nuclear Physics. (Illus.). 1979. pap. text ed. 19.95x (ISBN 0-582-46027-1). Longman.
Burge, E. J. Atomic Nuclei & Their Particles. (Oxford Physics Ser.). (Illus.). 1977. pap. text ed. 14.95x (ISBN 0-19-851835-8). Oxford U Pr.
Cagnac, B. & Pebay-Peyroula, J. C. Modern Atomic Physics. Incl. Vol. 1. Fundamentals & Principles. LC 74-28161. text ed. 27.95 (ISBN 0-470-12920-4); Vol. 2. Quantum Theory & Its Application. LC 74-26875. 1975. Halsted Pr.
Calder, Nigel. The Key to the Universe. (Large Format Ser.). 1978. pap. 7.95 (ISBN 0-14-005065-5). Penguin.
Cantore, Enrico. Atomic Order: An Introduction to the Philosophy of Microphysics. 1970. pap. text ed. 6.95x (ISBN 0-262-53028-7). MIT Pr.
Chandra, Ramesh. Introductory Physics of Nuclear Medicine. 2nd ed. (Illus.). 200p. Date not set. price not set (ISBN 0-8121-0826-4). Lea & Febiger.
Cherdyntsev, V. V. Abundance of Chemical Elements. rev. ed. Nichiporuk, Walter, tr. LC 61-11892. (Illus.). 1961. 12.00x (ISBN 0-226-10339-0). U of Chicago Pr.
Chretien, M. & Lipworth, E., eds. Brandeis University Summer Institute in Theoretical Physics: 1969 Lectures: Atomic Physics & Astrophysics, 2 vols. Vol. 1. 1971 ed. 54.50x (ISBN 0-677-14900-X); Vol. 2. 1973 ed. 73.25x (ISBN 0-677-14910-7). Gordon.
Clustering Phenomena in Nuclei. (Illus., Orig.). 1969. pap. 24.50 (ISBN 92-0-130269-X, ISP232, IAEA). Unipub.
Cohen, Bernard L. Concepts of Nuclear Physics. LC 70-138856. (Fundamentals of Physics Ser). (Illus.). 1971. text ed. 22.95 (ISBN 0-07-011556-7, C). McGraw.
Costing Methods for Nuclear Desalination. (Technical Reports Ser.: No. 69). (Orig.). 1966. pap. 5.50 (ISBN 92-0-145466-X, IDC69, IAEA). Unipub.
Davidson, J. P. & Kern, Bernard D., eds. Fifth Symposium on the Structure of Low-Medium Mass Nuclei. LC 73-77254. (Illus.). 312p. 1973. 17.00x (ISBN 0-8131-1293-1). U Pr of Ky.
Davis, George E. Radiation & Life. (Illus.). 344p. 1967. text ed. 7.95x (ISBN 0-8138-1330-1). Iowa St U Pr.
Deconninck, G. Introduction to Radioanalytical Physics. (Nuclear Methods Monograph: No. 1). 1978. 55.75 (ISBN 0-444-99796-2). Elsevier.
De Shalit, Amos & Feshbach, Herman. Theoretical Nuclear Physics, Vol. 1: Nuclear Structure. LC 73-17165. 979p. 1974. text ed. 55.00 (ISBN 0-471-20385-8). Wiley.
Devons, S. High-Energy Physics & Nuclear Structure. LC 72-112272. 859p. 1970. 65.00 (ISBN 0-306-30473-2, Plenum Pr). Plenum Pub.
Devreese, J. T., et al, eds. Recent Developments in Condensed Matter Physics, Vol. 1: Invited Papers. 838p. 1981. 85.00 (ISBN 0-306-40646-2, Plenum Pr). Plenum Pub.
DeWitt, C. & Gillet, V., eds. Les Houches Lectures: 1968, Nuclear Physics. 1969. 120.50 (ISBN 0-677-13380-4). Gordon.
Diamond, Sheldon. Fundamental Concepts of Modern Physics. (gr. 11-12). 1970. pap. text ed. 6.58 (ISBN 0-87720-178-1). AMSCO Sch.
Duncan, Thomas. Electronics & Nuclear Physics. (gr. 9-12). text ed. 14.95 (ISBN 0-7195-2003-7). Transatlantic.
Dyson, Freeman J., ed. Symmetry Groups in Nuclear & Particle Physics: A Lecture Note & Reprint Volume. (Mathematical Physics Monographs: No. 4). 1966. 17.50 (ISBN 0-8053-2370-8, Adv Bk Prog). Benjamin-Cummings.
Egelstaff, P. A. & Poole, M. J. Experimental Neutron Thermalization. LC 79-86201. 1970. 60.00 (ISBN 0-08-006533-3). Pergamon.
Eisenberg, J. M. & Greiner, W. Nuclear Theory: Nuclear Models, Vol. 1. 2nd ed. 1976. text ed. 29.50 (ISBN 0-444-10790-8, North-Holland). Elsevier.
--Nuclear Theory Vol. 3: Microscopic Theory of the Nucleus. 2nd ed. 1976. 36.75 (ISBN 0-7204-0484-3, North-Holland). Elsevier.
Eisenberg, Judah & Greiner, Walter. Nuclear Theory: Excitation Mechanisms of the Nucleus, Vol. 2. 2nd ed. LC 78-97200. 1976. pap. text ed. 34.25 (ISBN 0-7204-0158-5, North-Holland). Elsevier.
Eisenbud, L. & Wigner, E. P. Nuclear Structure. (Investigations in Physics Ser.: Vol. 8). 1958. 15.00x (ISBN 0-691-08010-0). Princeton U Pr.
El-Wakil, M. M. Nuclear Power Engineering. (Nuclear Engineering Ser). 1962. text ed. 26.50 (ISBN 0-07-019300-2, C). McGraw.
Engdahl, Sylvia Louise & Roberson, Rick. The Subnuclear Zoo. LC 77-1686. (Illus.). (gr. 6-9). 1977. 6.95 (ISBN 0-689-30582-6). Atheneum.
Enge, Harald A. Introduction to Nuclear Physics. 1966. 24.95 (ISBN 0-201-01870-5). A-W.
England, J. B. Techniques in Nuclear Structure Physics, 2 vols. LC 74-8171. 697p. 1974. 60.95 (ISBN 0-470-24161-6). Halsted Pr.
Esch, Gerald W. & McFarlane, Robert W., eds. Thermal Ecology II: Proceedings. LC 76-28206. (ERDA Symposium Ser.). 414p. 1976. pap. 11.00 (ISBN 0-686-75817-X); microfiche 3.00 (ISBN 0-686-75818-8). DOE.
Europhysics Study Conference, Plitvice Lakes, Yugoslavia, 1972. Intermediate Processes in Nuclear Reactions: Proceedings. Cindro, N., et al, eds. (Lecture Notes in Physics: Vol. 22). (Illus.). 349p. 1973. pap. 18.30 (ISBN 0-387-06526-1). Springer-Verlag.
Fenech, Henri, ed. Heat Transfer & Fluid Flow in Nuclear Systems. 300p. 1981. 49.51 (ISBN 0-08-027181-2). Pergamon.
Fleischer, Robert L., et al. Nuclear Tracks in Solids. LC 73-90670. 1975. 46.50x (ISBN 0-520-02665-9); pap. 16.95x (ISBN 0-520-04096-1). U of Cal Pr.
Fourteen International Universitaetswochen Fuer Kernphysik 1975 der Karlfranzens-Universitaet at Schladming. Electromagnetic Interactions & Field Theory: Proceedings. Urban, P., ed. (Acta Physica Austriaca: No. 14). (Illus.). v, 681p. 1975. 87.40 (ISBN 0-387-81333-0). Springer-Verlag.
Frauenfelder, Hans & Henley, Ernest M. Subatomic Physics. (Illus.). 544p. 1974. 31.95 (ISBN 0-13-859082-6). P-H.
Friedlander, Gerhart, et al. Nuclear & Radiochemistry. 2nd ed. 1964. 33.95 (ISBN 0-471-28020-8). Wiley.
Frisch, O. R., ed. Progress in Nuclear Physics, Vols. 2 & 5-9. Vol. 2. 1952. 81.00 (ISBN 0-08-013329-0); Vol. 5. 1956. 81.00 (ISBN 0-08-009043-5); Vol. 6. 1957. 81.00 (ISBN 0-08-009066-4); Vol. 7. 1959. 81.00 (ISBN 0-08-009186-5); Vol. 8. 1960. 81.00 (ISBN 0-08-009479-1); Vol. 9. 1963. 81.00 (ISBN 0-08-010063-5). Pergamon.
Fundamentals in Nuclear Theory. (Illus., Orig.). 1967. pap. 40.75 (ISBN 92-0-130067-0, ISP145, IAEA). Unipub.
Future of Nuclear Structure Studies. (Illus., Orig.). 1969. pap. 11.50 (ISBN 92-0-031069-9, ISP220, IAEA). Unipub.
Garg, J. B., ed. Statistical Properties of Nuclei. LC 75-182409. 665p. 1972. 55.00 (ISBN 0-306-30576-3, Plenum Pr). Plenum Pub.
Geramb, H. von, ed. Microscopic Optical Potentials: Proceedings of the Hamburg Topical Workshop on Nuclear Physics, Univ. of Hamburg, Germany, Sept. 25-27, 1978. (Lecture Notes in Physics Ser.: Vol. 89). 1979. pap. 22.40 (ISBN 0-387-09106-8). Springer-Verlag.
Goodman, Charles D., et al, eds. The p,n Reaction & the Nucleon-Nucleon Force. 550p. 1980. 55.00 (ISBN 0-306-40351-X, Plenum Pr). Plenum Pub.
Grant, P. J. Nuclear Science. (Illus.). 1971. pap. text ed. 11.95x (ISBN 0-245-50419-2). Intl Ideas.
Green, Alex E. & Wyatt, P. J. Atomic & Space Physics. 1965. 21.50 (ISBN 0-201-02570-1, Adv Bk Prog). A-W.
Harnwell, G. P. & Livingood, J. J. Experimental Atomic Physics. LC 77-10147. 486p. 1979. Repr. of 1933 ed. lib. bdg. 22.50 (ISBN 0-88275-600-1). Krieger.
Harvey, Bernard G. Introduction to Nuclear Physics & Chemistry. 2nd ed. 1969. ref. ed. 27.95 (ISBN 0-13-491159-8). P-H.
Heavy-Ion, High-Spin States & Nuclear Structure, 2 vols. (Illus.). 872p. 1975. Set. pap. 78.00 (ISBN 0-685-61024-1, ISP386-1-2, IAEA). Unipub.
Heisenberg, Werner. Nuclear Physics. Repr. of 1953 ed. lib. bdg. 15.00 (ISBN 0-8371-2089-6, HENP). Greenwood.
Henley, E. J. & Kouts, H. H., eds. Advances in Nuclear Science & Technology, Vol. 8. (Serial Publication). 1975. 55.00 (ISBN 0-12-029308-0). Acad Pr.
Henley, E. J., et al, eds. Advances in Nuclear Science & Technology. Incl. Vol. 1. 1962 (ISBN 0-12-029301-3); Vol. 2. 1964 (ISBN 0-12-029302-1); Vol. 4. 1968 (ISBN 0-12-029304-8); Vol. 5. Henley, E. J. & Lewins, J., eds. 1969 (ISBN 0-12-029305-6); Vol. 6. 1972 (ISBN 0-12-029306-4); Vol. 7. 1973 (ISBN 0-12-029307-2); Vol. 9. 1976 (ISBN 0-12-029309-9). 55.00 ea. Acad Pr.
--Advances in Nuclear Science & Technology, Vol. 10. 600p. 1977. 45.00 (ISBN 0-306-38230-X, Plenum Pr). Plenum Pub.
Hering, H. Robert Leroy Platzman Memorial. 428p. 1976. pap. text ed. 71.00 (ISBN 0-08-019957-7). Pergamon.
High-Energy Physics & Elementary Particles. (Illus., Orig.). 1965. pap. 35.75 (ISBN 92-0-530265-1, ISP117, IAEA). Unipub.
Hodgson, P. E. Growth Points in Nuclear Physics, Vol. 1. (Illus.). 1980. 21.00 (ISBN 0-08-023080-6); pap. 9.50 (ISBN 0-08-023079-2). Pergamon.
--Growth Points in Nuclear Physics, Vol. 2. (Illus.). 1980. 21.00 (ISBN 0-08-023082-2); pap. text ed. 9.50 (ISBN 0-08-023081-4). Pergamon.
--Nuclear Heavy-Ion Reactions. (Oxford Studies in Nuclear Physics). (Illus.). 598p. 1978. text ed. 85.00x (ISBN 0-19-851514-6). Oxford U Pr.
Hoehler, G., ed. Low Energy Hadron Interactions: Compilation of Coupling Constants & Low Energy Parameters. LC 25-9130. (Springer Tracts in Modern Physics: Vol. 55). (Illus.). 1970. 58.50 (ISBN 0-387-05250-X). Springer-Verlag.
--Nuclear Physics. LC 25-9130. (Springer Tracts in Modern Physics: Vol. 71). (Illus.). 255p. 1974. 57.90 (ISBN 0-387-06641-1). Springer-Verlag.
--Springer Tracts in Modern Physics, Vol. 53. (Illus.). 1970. 29.00 (ISBN 0-387-05016-7). Springer-Verlag.
Hoffmann, Banesh. Strange Story of the Quantum. 1959. pap. text ed. 3.00 (ISBN 0-486-20518-5). Dover.
Hornyak, William F. Nuclear Structure. 1975. 78.00 (ISBN 0-12-356050-0). Acad Pr.
Hurst, G. S. & Turner, J. E. Elementary Radiation Physics. 202p. 1981. Repr. of 1970 ed. text ed. 15.50 (ISBN 0-89874-249-8). Krieger.
Iachello, ed. Interacting Bosons in Nuclear Physics. (Ettore Majorana International Science Ser.--Physical Sciences: Vol. 1). 1979. 29.50 (ISBN 0-306-40190-8, Plenum Pr). Plenum Pub.
IAEA Laboratory Activities: 1st Report. (Technical Reports Ser.: No. 25). (Illus., Orig.). 1964. pap. 5.50 (ISBN 92-0-175064-1, IAEA). Unipub.
IAEA Laboratory Activities: 2nd Report. (Technical Reports Ser.: No. 41). (Illus., Orig.). 1965. pap. 5.50 (ISBN 92-0-175065-X, IDC41, IAEA). Unipub.
IAEA Laboratory Activities: 3rd Report. (Technical Reports Ser.: No. 55). (Illus., Orig.). 1966. pap. 5.50 (ISBN 92-0-175166-4, IDC55, IAEA). Unipub.
IAEA Laboratory Activities: 4th Report. (Technical Reports Ser.: No. 77). (Illus., Orig.). 1967. pap. 5.50 (ISBN 92-0-175167-2, IDC77, IAEA). Unipub.
IAEA Laboratory Activities: 6th Report. (Technical Reports Ser.: No. 98). (Illus., Orig.). 1969. pap. 12.00 (ISBN 92-0-175169-9, IDC98, IAEA). Unipub.
IAEA Laboratory Activities: 7th Report. (Technical Reports Ser.: No. 103). (Illus., Orig.). 1970. pap. 9.50 (ISBN 92-0-175070-6, IDC103, IAEA). Unipub.
International Atomic Energy Agency. INIS Reference Series, 16 vols. (Orig.). 1969-1974. pap. 72.25 (ISBN 0-685-02939-5, IAEA). Unipub.
International Conference, Harwell, Sept. 1978. Neutron Physics & Nuclear Data: Proceedings. 1979. 55.00x (ISBN 92-64-01870-0). OECD.
International Conference Held at Laval University, Quebec City, Canada. Aug. 27-31, 1974. Few Body Problems in Nuclear & Particle Physics. Slobodrian, R. J., et al, eds. (Illus., Eng. & Fr.). 1977. pap. 35.00x (ISBN 2-7637-6752-4, Pub. by Laval). Intl Schol Bk Serv.
International Conference on High-Energy Physics & Nuclear Structure, 5th. High Energy Physics& Nuclear Structure: Proceedings. Tibell, G., ed. 1974. 78.00 (ISBN 0-444-10688-X, North-Holland). Elsevier.
International Conference on High-Energy Physics & Nuclear Structure, 7th, Zurich, Aug - Sept. 1977. Proceedings. Locher, Milan P., ed. 1978. text ed. 64.25x (ISBN 3-7643-0987-3). Renouf.
International School of Elementary Particle Physics, Herceg-Novi. Methods in Subnuclear Physics: Proceedings, 1965-1969, Vols. 1-4. Nikolic, M., ed. Incl. Vol. 1. 514p. 1968. 87.00 (ISBN 0-677-11950-X); Vol. 2. 858p. 1968. 128.50 (ISBN 0-677-11960-7); Vol. 3. 882p. 1969. 145.75 (ISBN 0-677-12790-1); Vol. 4. 1970. Part 1. 93.00 (ISBN 0-677-14340-0); Part 2. 74.75 (ISBN 0-677-14350-8); Part 3. 93.00 (ISBN 0-677-14360-5); Three Part Set. 235.00 (ISBN 0-677-13530-0); Vol. 5. 1977. Pt. 1. (ISBN 0-677-15910-2); Pt. 2. (ISBN 0-677-15920-X); Two Part Set. 163.50 (ISBN 0-677-15960-9). Gordon.
International Summer Institute in Theoretical Physics. Strong Interaction Physics. (Springer Tracts in Modern Physics: Vol. 57). 1971. 56.70 (ISBN 0-387-05252-6). Springer-Verlag.
International Summer School for Theoretical Physics-2nd - University of Karlsruhe-1969. Weak Interactions: Invited Papers. Hoehler, G., ed. (Springer Tracts in Modern Physics: Vol. 52). (Illus.). v, 214p. 1970. 44.90 (ISBN 0-387-05015-9). Springer-Verlag.
Irvine, J. M. Nuclear Structure Theory. 492p. 1972. text ed. 55.00 (ISBN 0-08-016401-3); pap. text ed. 32.00 (ISBN 0-08-018991-1). Pergamon.
Jackson. Concepts of Atomic Physics. 1972. pap. text ed. 7.50 (ISBN 0-07-094160-2, I). McGraw.
Jackson, Herbert L. Basic Nuclear Physics for Medical Personnel. (Illus.). 164p. 1973. 13.75 (ISBN 0-398-02663-7). C C Thomas.
Jackson, J. D., et al, eds. Annual Review of Nuclear & Particle Science, Vol. 30. LC 53-995. (Annual Review of Nuclear Science Ser.: 1950-1977). (Illus.). 1980. text ed. 22.50 (ISBN 0-8243-1530-8). Annual Reviews.
Jackson, J. David, et al, eds. Annual Review of Nuclear & Particle Science, Vol. 28. LC 53-995. (Annual Review of Nuclear Science Ser.: 1950-1977). (Illus.). 1978. text ed. 19.50 (ISBN 0-8243-1528-6). Annual Reviews.
Jacob, M. R. & Chew, G. F. Strong Interaction Physics. 1964. 17.50 (ISBN 0-8053-5000-4, Adv Bk Prog). Benjamin-Cummings.
Jaech, John L. Statistical Methods in Nuclear Material Control. LC 73-600241. 409p. 1973. pap. 10.60 (ISBN 0-686-75751-3); microfiche 3.00 (ISBN 0-686-75752-1). DOE.
Jones, G. A. The Properties of Nuclei. (Oxford Physics Ser.). (Illus.). 1976. 21.00x (ISBN 0-19-851828-5). Oxford U Pr.
Jungk, Robert. Brighter Than a Thousand Suns: A Personal History of the Atomic Scientists. Cleugh, James, tr. from Ger. LC 58-8581. Orig. Title: Heller Als Tausend Sonnen. 1970. pap. 3.95 (ISBN 0-15-614150-7, HB182, Harv). HarBraceJ.
Kaplan, Irving. Nuclear Physics. 2nd ed. 1962. 24.95 (ISBN 0-201-03602-9). A-W.
Kieffer, F., ed. Trapped Charges. 236p. 1976. pap. text ed. 42.00 (ISBN 0-08-019961-5). Pergamon.
Kleppner, Daniel & Pipkin, Francis M., eds. Atomic Physics Seven. 580p. 1981. 69.50 (ISBN 0-306-40650-0, Plenum Pr). Plenum Pub.
Kopferman, Hans. Nuclear Moments. (Pure & Applied Physics Ser.). microfiche 58.00 (ISBN 0-12-419951-8). Acad Pr.
Landau, L. D. & Smorodinsky, Ya. Lectures on Nuclear Theory. LC 59-8865. 108p. 1959. 15.00 (ISBN 0-306-30134-2, Plenum Pr). Plenum Pub.

Lapp, Ralph & Andrews, Howard. Nuclear Radiation Physics. 4th ed. (Illus.). 1972. 24.95 (ISBN 0-13-625988-X). P-H.
Leighton, Robert B. Principles of Modern Physics. (International Ser. in Pure & Applied Physics). 1959. text ed. 22.95 (ISBN 0-07-037130-X, C). McGraw.
Leprince-Ringuet, Louis. Atoms & Men. LC 61-11292. 1961. 5.50x (ISBN 0-226-47290-6). U of Chicago Pr.
Levine, Raphael D. & Tribus, Myron, eds. The Maximum Entropy Formalism. 1979. text ed. 27.50x (ISBN 0-262-12080-1). MIT Pr.
Locher, M. P., ed. Seventh International Conference on High Energy Physics & Nuclear Structure. (Experientia Supplementa: 31). 436p. 1978. 68.00 (ISBN 3-7643-0987-3). Birkhauser.
McCarthy, I. E. Introduction to Nuclear Theory. 555p. 1968. text ed. 18.50 (ISBN 0-471-58140-2, Pub. by Wiley). Krieger.
McDaniel, E. W. & McDowell, M. R., eds. Case Studies in Atomic Physics, Vol. 4. 1975. 68.50 (ISBN 0-444-10882-3, North-Holland). Elsevier.
McDowell, M. R. & Ferendeci, A. M., eds. Atomic & Molecular Processes in Controlled Thermonuclear Fusion. (NATO Advanced Study Institutes Ser., Ser. B: Vol. 53). 500p. 1980. 55.00 (ISBN 0-306-40424-9, Plenum Pr). Plenum Pub.
Makhon'Ko, K. P. & Malakhov, S. G., eds. Nuclear Meteorology. Baruch, A. & Olaru, H., trs. from Rus. Orig. Title: Yadernaya Meteorologiya. (Illus.). 380p. 1974. lib. bdg. 39.50x (ISBN 0-7065-1445-9, Pub. by IPST). Intl Schol Bk Serv.
Marmier, Pierre & Sheldon, Eric. Physics of Nuclei & Particles, Vols. 1-2. 1969-70. 25.95 ea. Vol. 1 (ISBN 0-12-473101-5). Vol. 2 (ISBN 0-12-473102-3). Acad Pr.
--Physics of Nuclei & Particles, Vol. 3. Date not set. price not set (ISBN 0-12-473103-1). Acad Pr.
Marrus, Richard, et al, eds. Atomic Physics, 5. 573p. 1977. 49.50 (ISBN 0-306-37195-2, Plenum Pr). Plenum Pub.
Massey, Harrie. New Age in Physics. 2nd ed. (Illus.). 1966. text ed. 19.50x (ISBN 0-8464-0670-5). Beekman Pubs.
Massimo, L. Physics of High Temperature Reactors. 1975. text ed. 37.00 (ISBN 0-08-019616-0). Pergamon.
Meeting on Polarization Nuclear Physics, Ebermannstadt, Germany, 1973. Proceedings. Fick, D., ed. (Lecture Notes in Physics Ser.: Vol. 30). (Illus.). ix, 292p. 1974. pap. 13.10 (ISBN 0-387-06978-X). Springer-Verlag.
Messel, H. & Crawford, D. F. Electron-Photon Shower Distribution Function: Tables for Lead, Copper & Air Absorbers. LC 69-16049. 1970. 180.00 (ISBN 0-08-013374-6). Pergamon.
Meyerhof, Walter E. Elements of Nuclear Physics. 1967. text ed. 21.95 (ISBN 0-07-041745-8, C); 4.50 (ISBN 0-07-041746-6). McGraw.
Migdal, A. B. Nuclear Theory: The Quasiparticle Method. Leggett, Anthony J., tr. 1968. 17.50 (ISBN 0-8053-7060-9, Adv Bk Prog). Benjamin-Cummings.
Minerva Symposium on Physics, Rehovot, Israel, 1973. Nuclear Structure Physics: Proceedings. Smilansky, V., et al, eds. (Lecture Notes in Physics: Vol. 23). 296p. 1973. pap. 18.30 (ISBN 0-387-06554-7). Springer-Verlag.
Mit Students' System Project. Project Icarus. rev. ed. Li, Yao T. & Sandorf, Paul, eds. 1979. pap. 4.95 (ISBN 0-262-63068-0). MIT Pr.
Mitra, A. N., et al. Few Body Dynamics. 1976. 97.75 (ISBN 0-7204-0481-9, North-Holland). Elsevier.
Morinaga, H. Developments & Borderlines of Nuclear Physics. (Italian Physical Society Course: No. 53). 1974. 40.00 (ISBN 0-12-368853-1). Acad Pr.
Myers, W. D. Droplet Model of Atomic Nuclei. 158p. 1978. 75.00 (ISBN 0-306-65170-X). IFI Plenum.
Nato Advanced Study Institute, C15, Ramsau, Germany, 1974. Computational Techniques in Quantum Chemistry & Molecular Physics: Proceedings. Diercksen, G. H., ed. LC 75-9913. 568p. 1975. lib. bdg. 68.50 (ISBN 90-277-0588-7, Pub. by Reidel Holland). Kluwer Boston.
Negele & Vogt, eds. Advances in Nuclear Physics, Vol. 11. (Illus.). 1979. 37.50 (ISBN 0-306-40111-8, Plenum Pr). Plenum Pub.
Negele, J. W. & Vogt, E., eds. Advances in Nuclear Physics, Vol. 12. 240p. 1981. 35.00 (ISBN 0-306-40708-6, Plenum Pr). Plenum Pub.
Nuclear Data in Science & Technology, 2 vols. (Illus.). 1214p. (Orig.). 1974. pap. 48.75 ea. (IAEA); Vol. 1. pap. (ISBN 92-0-030073-1, ISP 343-1); Vol. 2. pap. (ISBN 92-0-030173-8, ISP 343-2). Unipub.
Nuclear Electronics - 1961, 3 vols. 1962. Vol. 1. 24.50 (ISBN 92-0-030162-2, IAEA); Vol. 2. 19.50 (ISBN 92-0-030262-9); Vol. 3. 24.50 (ISBN 92-0-030362-5). Unipub.
Nuclear IEEE Standards, 2 vols. LC 78-70585. 1978. 32.50 ea. Vol. 1 (ISBN 0-471-05321-X). Vol. 2 (ISBN 0-471-05320-1, Pub. by Wiley-Interscience). Wiley.
Nuclear Structure: Dubna Symposium, 1968. 1968. pap. 35.75 (ISBN 92-0-530068-3, ISP189, IAEA). Unipub.
Nuclear Techniques & Mineral Resources. 1969. pap. 35.75 (ISBN 92-0-040069-8, ISP198, IAEA). Unipub.
Nuclear Track Detection Conference, Neuherberg Munich, Sept. 30 to Oct. 6, 1976. Solid State Nuclear Track Detectors: Proceedings, 2 vols. Granzer, F., et al, eds. 1978. Set. text ed. 240.00 (ISBN 0-08-021659-5). Pergamon.
Oldenberg, Otto & Holladay, Wendell G. Introduction to Atomic & Nuclear Physics. LC 77-5544. 424p. 1977. Repr. of 1949 ed. 19.50 (ISBN 0-88275-548-X). Krieger.
Paic, Guy & Slaus, Ivo, eds. Few Body Problems, Light Nuclei & Nuclear Interactions, 2 Vols. 1969. Set. 104.00x (ISBN 0-677-13440-1); Vol. 1. 93.00x (ISBN 0-677-12760-X); Vol. 2. 94.50x (ISBN 0-677-13020-1). Gordon.
Phillips, Gerald C., et al, eds. Progress in Fast Neutron Physics. LC 63-18849. (Illus.). 1963. 9.75x (ISBN 0-226-66735-9). U of Chicago Pr.
Physics & Material Problems of Reactor Control Rods. 1964. 39.00 (ISBN 92-0-050364-0, IAEA). Unipub.
Pietschmann, H. Formulae & Results in Weak Interactions. (Acta Physica Austriaca: Suppl. 12). x, 64p. 1974. pap. text ed. 26.00 (ISBN 0-387-81258-X). Springer-Verlag.
Plasma Physics & Controlled Nuclear Fusion Research, 3 vols. (Illus.). 1977. Vol. 1. pap. 66.00 (ISBN 92-0-130077-8, IAEA); Vol. 2. pap. 67.50 (ISBN 92-0-130177-4); Vol. 3. pap. 64.25 (ISBN 92-0-130277-0). Unipub.
Preston, M. A. & Bhaduri, R. K. Structure of the Nucleus. 475p. 1975. 37.50 (ISBN 0-201-05976-2, Adv Bk Prog); pap. text ed. 25.50 (ISBN 0-201-05977-0, Adv Bk Prog). A-W.
Racah, G., ed. Nuclear Spectroscopy. (Italian Physical Society: Course 15). 1962. 49.50 (ISBN 0-12-368815-9). Acad Pr.
Ram, K. S. Basic Nuclear Engineering. LC 77-795. 1977. 14.95 (ISBN 0-470-99105-4). Halsted Pr.
Renner, B. Current Algebras & Their Applications. 1968. 34.00 (ISBN 0-08-012504-2). Pergamon.
Rho, M. & Wilkinson, D., eds. Mesons in Nuclei, 3 vols. 1979. Set Of 3 Vols. 186.50 (ISBN 0-444-85052-X, North Holland); Vol. 1. 88.00 (ISBN 0-444-85255-7); Vol. 2. 73.25 (ISBN 0-444-85256-5); Vol. 3. 73.25 (ISBN 0-444-85257-3). Elsevier.
Roberts, Albert O. The Nucleon Simplified. 1980. 4.95 (ISBN 0-533-04319-0). Vantage.
Robson, B. A., ed. Nuclear Interactions: Conference Held in Canberra, Aug. 28-Sept. 1, 1978. (Lecture Notes in Physics: Vol. 92). 1979. pap. 24.20 (ISBN 0-387-09102-5). Springer-Verlag.
Robson, D. & Fox, J. D., eds. Nuclear Analogue States. LC 76-17849. (Benchmark Papers in Nuclear Physics Ser.: Vol. 1). 1976. 55.50 (ISBN 0-12-787356-2). Acad Pr.
Rodean, Howard C. Nuclear-Explosion Seismology. LC 73-170333. (AEC Critical Review Ser.). 164p. 1971. pap. 3.00 (ISBN 0-686-75875-7); microfiche 3.00 (ISBN 0-686-75876-5). DOE.
Rose, M. E., ed. Nuclear Orientation. (International Science Review Ser.). (Illus.). 1963. 67.25x (ISBN 0-677-00730-2). Gordon.
Sandars, P. G. & Woodgate, G. K. Atomic Physics Two. 396p. 1972. 42.50 (ISBN 0-306-37192-8, Plenum Pr). Plenum Pub.
Segre, E., et al, eds. Annual Review of Nuclear Science, Vol. 22. LC 53-995. (Illus.). 1972. text ed. 19.50 (ISBN 0-8243-1522-7). Annual Reviews.
--Annual Review of Nuclear Science, Vol. 26. LC 53-995. (Illus.). 1976. text ed. 19.50 (ISBN 0-8243-1526-X). Annual Reviews.
Segre, Emilio. Nuclei & Particles: An Introduction to Nuclear & Subnuclear Physics. 2nd rev. ed. 1977. 34.50 (ISBN 0-8053-8601-7, Adv Bk Prog). Benjamin-Cummings.
Segre, Emilio, et al, eds. Annual Review of Nuclear Science, Vol. 24. LC 53-995. (Illus.). 1974. text ed. 19.50 (ISBN 0-8243-1524-3). Annual Reviews.
--Annual Review of Nuclear Science, Vol. 25. LC 53-995. (Illus.). 1975. text ed. 19.50 (ISBN 0-8243-1525-1). Annual Reviews.
--Annual Review of Nuclear Science, Vol. 27. LC 53-995. (Illus.). 1977. text ed. 19.50 (ISBN 0-8243-1527-8). Annual Reviews.
Selected Topics in Nuclear Theory. 1963. 21.25 (ISBN 92-0-030563-6, ISP67, IAEA). Unipub.
Shen, Benjamin S. & Merker, Milton, eds. Spallation Nuclear Reactions & Their Applications. new ed. (Astrophysics & Space Science Library: No. 59). 1976. lib. bdg. 39.50 (ISBN 90-277-0746-4, Pub. by Reidel Holland). Kluwer Boston.
Sitenko, A. G. & Tartakovsky, V. K. Lectures on the Theory of the Nucleus. LC 74-10827. 312p. 1975. text ed. 37.00 (ISBN 0-08-017876-6). Pergamon.
Skobel'tsyn, D. V., ed. Studies in Nuclear Physics. LC 72-94830. (P. N. Lebedev Physics Institute Ser.: Vol. 53). (Illus.). 246p. 1973. 35.00 (ISBN 0-306-10882-8, Consultants). Plenum Pub.
--Studies of Nuclear Reactions. LC 66-14741. (P. N. Lebedev Physics Institute Ser.: Vol. 33). 222p. 1966. 35.00 (ISBN 0-306-10767-8, Consultants). Plenum Pub.
Smith, S. J. Atomic Physics 3. LC 72-176581. 670p. 1973. 49.50 (ISBN 0-306-37193-6, Plenum Pr). Plenum Pub.
Soloviev, V. G. Theory of Complex Nuclei. 1976. 67.00 (ISBN 0-08-018053-1). Pergamon.
Stoler, ed. Photopion Nuclear Physics. 1979. 42.50 (ISBN 0-306-40148-7, Plenum Pr). Plenum Pub.
Theory of Nuclear Structure: Trieste Lectures, 1969. (Illus., Orig.). 1970. pap. 57.00 (ISBN 92-0-130070-0, ISP 249, IAEA). Unipub.
Thermodynamics of Nuclear Materials 1974, 2 vols. (Illus.). 469p. 1975. Vol. 1. pap. 42.25 (ISBN 92-0-040175-9, IAEA); Vol. 2. pap. 48.75 (ISBN 0-685-54200-9). Unipub.
Touschek, B., ed. Physics with Intersecting Storage Rings. (Italian Physical Society: Course 46). 1971. 67.00 (ISBN 0-12-368846-9). Acad Pr.
Tucson International Topical Conference on Nuclear Physics Held at the University of Arizona, Tucson, Jun 2-6, 1975. Effective Interactions & Operators in Nuclei: Proceedings. Barrett, B. R., ed. (Lecture Notes Physics: Vol. 40). xii, 339p. 1975. pap. 16.50 (ISBN 0-387-07400-7). Springer-Verlag.
Uhrig, Robert E., ed. Noise Analysis in Nuclear Systems. (AEC Symposium Ser.). 518p. 1964. pap. 6.00 (ISBN 0-686-75899-4); microfiche 3.00 (ISBN 0-686-75900-1). DOE.
Warren, J. B., ed. Nuclear & Particle Physics at Intermediate Energies. LC 76-8270. (NATO Advanced Study Institutes Ser. B: Physics, Vol. 15). 608p. 1976. 55.00 (ISBN 0-306-35715-1, Plenum Pr). Plenum Pub.
Weisskopf, Victor F., ed. Nuclear Physics. (Italian Physical Society: Course 23). 1963. 49.50 (ISBN 0-12-368823-X). Acad Pr.
Weneser, J. & Lederman, L., eds. Nuclear & Particle Physics, Vol. 1. 1969. 57.75x (ISBN 0-677-12780-4). Gordon.
--Vienna Conference Fourteen: High Energy Physics, Nineteen Sixty-Eight Supplement to Comments on Nuclear & Particle Physics. 1969. 16.00 (ISBN 0-677-13860-1). Gordon.
Wilkinson, D., ed. Proceedings of the International School of Nuclear Physics, Erice, 2-14 Sept. 1976. (Progress in Particle & Nuclear Physics Ser.: Vol. 1). 1978. 81.00 (ISBN 0-08-020327-2). Pergamon.
Wilkinson, Denys, ed. Progress in Particle & Nuclear Physics, Vol. 3. 1980. 81.00 (ISBN 0-08-025020-3). Pergamon.
--Progress in Particle & Nuclear Physics, Vol. 4. (Illus.). 600p. 1980. 81.00 (ISBN 0-08-025039-4). Pergamon.
--Progress in Particle & Nuclear Physics, Vol. 7. (Illus.). 270p. 1981. 84.00 (ISBN 0-08-027152-9). Pergamon.
--Progress in Particles & Nuclear Physics, Vol. 5. (Illus.). 280p. 1981. 81.00 (ISBN 0-08-027109-X). Pergamon.
--Progress in Particles & Nuclear Physics, Vol. 6. 350p. 1981. 81.00 (ISBN 0-08-027117-0). Pergamon.
Zichichi, A., ed. Lepton & Hadron Structure. 1975. 111.00 (ISBN 0-12-780589-3). Acad Pr.
--The Whys of Sub-Nuclear Physics. (Subnuclear Ser.). 1979. 0.85.00 (ISBN 0-306-40151-7, Plenum Pr). Plenum Pub.
Zichichi, Antonio, ed. The New Aspects of Subnuclear Physics. (The Subnuclear Ser.: Vol. 16). 800p. 1981. 75.00 (ISBN 0-306-40459-1, Plenum Pr). Plenum Pub.
Zingl, H., et al, eds. Few Body Systems & Nuclear Forces 2: 8th International Conferencce Held in Graz, August 24-30, 1978. (Lecture Notes in Physics: Vol. 87). 1979. pap. 26.60 (ISBN 0-387-09099-1). Springer-Verlag.
Zu Putlitz, G., et al, eds. Atomic Physics, No. 4. LC 72-176581. 780p. 1975. 59.50 (ISBN 0-306-37194-4, Plenum Pr). Plenum Pub.

NUCLEAR PHYSICS–ADDRESSES, ESSAYS, LECTURES

Balian, R., et al, eds. Claude Bloch Scientific Works, 2 vols. LC 74-84212. 1975. Set. 219.50 (ISBN 0-444-10853-X, North-Holland). Elsevier.
Becker, R. L., ed. Nuclear Physics. 1967. 60.00 (ISBN 0-12-084550-4). Acad Pr.
Bederson, B., et al, eds. Atomic Physics, No. 1. LC 69-14560. 620p. 1969. 39.50 (ISBN 0-306-30383-3, Plenum Pr). Plenum Pub.
Bloch, F., et al, eds. Spectroscopic & Group Theoretical Methods in Physics. 1968. 58.75 (ISBN 0-444-10147-0, North-Holland). Elsevier.
Cujec, B., et al, eds. Compte Rendu Du Symposium Sur les Mecanismes De Reaction Nucleaire et les Phenomenes De Polarisation: Symposium on Nuclear Reaction Mechanisms & Polarization Phenomena 1969. (Illus.). 503p. 1970. 15.00x (ISBN 2-7637-6474-6, Pub. by Laval). Intl. Schol Bk Serv.
Design of Radiotracer Experiments in Marine Biology Studies. (Technical Report Ser.: No. 167). (Illus.). 289p. 1975. pap. 29.00 (ISBN 92-0-125175-0, IDC167, IAEA). Unipub.
DeWitt, C. & Gillet, V., eds. Les Houches Lectures: 1968. Nuclear Physics. 1969. 120.50 (ISBN 0-677-13380-4). Gordon.
Frampton, P., et al, eds. First Workshop on Grand Unification. (Lie Groups; History, Frontiers & Applications: Vol. XI). 250p. 1980. text ed. 30.00 (ISBN 0-915692-31-7). Math Sci Pr.
International School of Elementary Particle Physics, Herceg-Novi. Methods in Subnuclear Physics: Proceedings, 1965-1969. Vols. 1-4. Nikolic, M., ed. Incl. Vol. 1. 514p. 1968. 87.00 (ISBN 0-677-11950-X); Vol. 2. 858p. 1968. 128.50 (ISBN 0-677-11960-7); Vol. 3. 882p. 1969. 145.75 (ISBN 0-677-12790-1); Vol. 4. 1970. Part 1. 93.00 (ISBN 0-677-14340-0); Part 2. 74.75 (ISBN 0-677-14350-8); Part 3. 93.00 (ISBN 0-677-14360-5); Three Part Set. 235.00 (ISBN 0-677-13530-0); Vol. 5. 1977. Pt. 1. (ISBN 0-677-15910-2); Pt. 2. (ISBN 0-677-15920-X); Two Part Set. 163.50 (ISBN 0-677-15960-9). Gordon.
Jean, M., ed. Nuclear Structure & Nuclear Reactions. (Italian Physical Society: Course 40). 1969. 76.50 (ISBN 0-12-368840-X). Acad Pr.
Klauder, John R., ed. Magic Without Magic: John Archibald Wheeler, a Collection of Essays in Honor of His 60th Birthday. LC 75-183745. (Illus.). 1972. text ed. 28.95x (ISBN 0-7167-0337-8). W H Freeman.
Lane, Anthony M. Nuclear Theory: Pairing Force Correlations & Collection Motion. (Frontiers in Physics Ser.: No. 13). 1964. 17.50 (ISBN 0-8053-5700-9, Adv Bk Prog). Benjamin-Cummings.
Maria Sklodowska-Curie: Centenary Lectures. 1968. pap. 12.25 (ISBN 92-0-030168-1, ISP179, IAEA). Unipub.
Morse, Philip M., et al. Nuclear, Particle & Many Body Physics, 2 vols. 1972. Vol. 1. 61.00 (ISBN 0-12-508201-0); Vol. 2. 58.00 (ISBN 0-12-508202-9); Set. 93.50 (ISBN 0-685-27233-8). Acad Pr.
Nagle, D. E., et al, eds. High Energy Physics & Nuclear Structure-1975: Conference Held at Santa Fe & Los Alamos. LC 75-26411. (AIP Conference Proceedings Ser.: No. 26). 712p. 1975. 20.50 (ISBN 0-88318-125-8). Am Inst Physics.
Nielsen, J. R. Niels Bohr Collected Works: Periodic System 1920-23, Vol. 4. 1977. 144.00 (ISBN 0-7204-1804-6, North-Holland). Elsevier.
Porter, Charles E., ed. Statistical Theories of Spectra: Fluctuations. (Perspectives in Physics Ser.). (Illus., Orig.). 1965. pap. 27.50 (ISBN 0-12-562356-9). Acad Pr.
Reines, Frederick, ed. Cosmology, Fusion & Other Matters: A Memorial to George Gamow. LC 77-159018. (Illus.). 336p. 1972. 15.00x (ISBN 0-87081-025-1). Colo Assoc.
Skolbel'Tsyn, D. V., ed. Nuclear Physics & Interaction of Particles with Matter. LC 70-120025. (P. N. Lebedev Physics Institute Ser.: Vol. 44). 269p. 1971. 37.50 (ISBN 0-306-10851-8, Consultants). Plenum Pub.
Verhaar, B. J., ed. Selected Topics in Nuclear Spectroscopy. 1964. 36.75 (ISBN 0-444-10332-5, North-Holland). Elsevier.
Woolf, Harry. Albert Einstein Centennial Celebration. (Illus.). 400p. 1980. text ed. 43.50 (ISBN 0-201-09924-1). A-W.

NUCLEAR PHYSICS–DICTIONARIES

Clason, W. E. Elsevier's Dictionary of Nuclear Science & Technology. 2nd rev. ed. (Polyglot). 1970. 85.50 (ISBN 0-444-40810-X). Elsevier.
Commissariat a l'Energie Atomique. Dictionnaire des Sciences et Techniques Nucleaires. 3rd ed. 492p. (Fr.). 1975. 67.50 (ISBN 0-686-56958-X, M-6081). French & Eur.
Del Vecchio, Alfred, ed. Concise Dictionary of Atomics. LC 64-13328. 1964. 6.00 (ISBN 0-8022-1771-0). Philos Lib.
INIS: Thesaurus. (Inis: Ser. No. 13: Rev. 18). 748p. 1980. pap. 45.00 (ISBN 92-0-178080-X, IAEA). Unipub.
INIS: Thesaurus. (INIS Ser.: No. 13, Rev. 19). 748p. 1980. pap. 45.00 (ISBN 92-0-178480-5, IN13/R19, IAEA). Unipub.

Lexico De Terminos Nucleares: Diccionario Vocabulario Triligue. 848p. (Span., Eng. & Fr.). 1974. 44.95 (ISBN 84-500-6295-0, S-50124). French & Eur.

Markus, John. Vocabulario Ingles-Espan0l De Electronica y Tecnica Nuclear. 2nd ed. 196p. (Span.-Eng.). pap. 16.75 (ISBN 84-267-0247-3, S-30684). French & Eur.

Richard, Robert, ed. Concise Dictionary of American Literature. (Illus.). 1955. 5.00 (ISBN 0-8022-1336-7). Philos Lib.

NUCLEAR PHYSICS–EXPERIMENTS

Avignone, Frank T. A Modern Nuclear Laboratory Course. LC 75-20288. 200p. 1975. pap. 7.95x (ISBN 0-87249-335-0). U of SC Pr.

Exponential & Critical Experiments, 3 vols. (Illus., Eng. , Fr. , Rus. & Span.). 1964. Vol. 1. 24.50 (ISBN 92-0-050064-1, ISP79-1, IAEA); Vol. 2. 29.25 (ISBN 92-0-050164-8, ISP79-2); Vol. 3. 24.50 (ISBN 92-0-050264-4, ISP79-3). Unipub.

Friedrich, et al. Experiments in Atomic Physics. (gr. 12). text ed. 6.95 (ISBN 0-7195-0467-8). Transatlantic.

NUCLEAR PHYSICS–HISTORY

AIP & American Academy of Arts & Sciences Joint Conference, Brookline, Mass., 1967 & 1969. Exploring the History of Nuclear Physics: Proceedings, No. 7. Weiner, Charles, ed. LC 72-81883. (Illus.). 271p. 1972. 13.00 (ISBN 0-88318-106-1). Am Inst Physics.

Anderson, David L. & Cohen, I. Bernard, eds. The Discovery of the Electron. LC 80-2114. (Development of Science Ser.). (Illus.). 1981. lib. bdg. 15.00x (ISBN 0-405-13834-2). Arno.

Stuewer, Roger H., ed. Nuclear Physics in Retrospect: Proceedings of a Symposium on the 1930's. (Illus.). 1979. 25.00x (ISBN 0-8166-0869-5). U of Minn Pr.

NUCLEAR PHYSICS–INSTRUMENTS

Fenyves, E. & Haiman, O. Physical Principles of Nuclear Radiation Measurements. 1969. 63.00 (ISBN 0-12-253150-7). Acad Pr.

National Academy Of Sciences Division Of Physical Sciences. Semiconductor Nuclear-Particle Detectors & Circuits. 1969. 26.00 (ISBN 0-309-01593-6). Natl Acad Pr.

Nuclear Electronic Instruments in Tropical Countries. (Technical Reports Ser.: No. 13). 1963. pap. 5.50 (ISBN 92-0-135063-5, IDC13, IAEA). Unipub.

NUCLEAR PHYSICS–JUVENILE LITERATURE

Engdahl, Sylvia Louise & Roberson, Rick. The Subnuclear Zoo. LC 77-1686. (Illus.). (gr. 6-9). 1977. 6.95 (ISBN 0-689-30582-6). Atheneum.

NUCLEAR PHYSICS–PROBLEMS, EXERCISES, ETC.

Smith, W. Problems in Modern Physics. 1970. 32.00x (ISBN 0-677-02850-4). Gordon.

NUCLEAR PHYSICS–RESEARCH

see Nuclear Research

NUCLEAR PHYSICS–STUDY AND TEACHING

Nuclear Science Teaching. (Technical Reports: No. 94). 1968. pap. 5.50 (ISBN 92-0-175368-3, IDC94, IAEA). Unipub.

Nuclear Science Teaching III. (Technical Reports Ser. No. 162). (Illus.). 34p. 1975. pap. 7.00 (ISBN 92-0-175075-7, IDC162, IAEA). Unipub.

Tipler, Paul A. Modern Physics. 2nd ed. LC 77-58725. 1977. text ed. 21.95x (ISBN 0-87901-088-6). H S Worth.

NUCLEAR PHYSICS–TABLES

Adams, F. & Dams, R. Applied Gamma-Ray Spectrometry. 2nd rev. ed. LC 79-114847. 1970. text ed. 92.00 (ISBN 0-08-006888-X). Pergamon.

Herman, Robert C. & Hofstadter, Robert. High-Energy Electron Scattering Tables. 1960. 10.00x (ISBN 0-8047-0588-7). Stanford U Pr.

NUCLEAR PHYSICS AS A PROFESSION

Thompson, William E., Jr. Your Future in Nuclear Energy Fields. LC 61-10801. (Careers in Depth Ser.). (gr. 7 up). PLB 5.97 (ISBN 0-8239-0058-4). Rosen Pr.

NUCLEAR POLARIZATION

see Polarization (Nuclear Physics)

NUCLEAR POWER

see Atomic Power

NUCLEAR POWER PLANTS, MARINE

see Marine Nuclear Reactor Plants

NUCLEAR-POWERED SHIPS

see Atomic Ships

NUCLEAR-POWERED VEHICLES

see Nuclear Propulsion

NUCLEAR PRESSURE VESSELS

Rules for Inservice Inspection of Nuclear Power Plant Components: Division 1. (Boiler & Pressure Vessel Code Ser.: Sec. XI). 1980. 80.00 (ISBN 0-685-76832-5, P00111); pap. 105.00 loose-leaf (ISBN 0-685-76833-3, V00111). ASME.

NUCLEAR PROPULSION

see also Nuclear Reactors; also specific applications, e.g. Nuclear Rockets

Heaps, Leo. Operation Morning Light. 1979. pap. 2.95 (ISBN 0-345-28101-2). Ballantine.

Kramer, A. W., ed. Nuclear Propulsion for Merchant Ships. 600p. 1962. pap. 73.20 (ISBN 0-686-75757-2); microfilm 36.60 (ISBN 0-686-75758-0). DOE.

NUCLEAR REACTIONS

see also Bremsstrahlung; Nuclear Fission; Photonuclear Reactions; Radioactivity; Weak Interactions (Nuclear Physics)

AIP Conference. Particles & Fields-1973: Proceedings, No. 14. Bingham, H. H., et al, eds. LC 73-91923. 680p. 1973. 18.50 (ISBN 0-88318-113-4). Am Inst Physics.

AIP Conference, Rochester 1971. Particles & Fields 1971: Proceedings, No. 2. Melissinos, A. C. & Slattery, P. S., eds. LC 71-184662. 323p. 1971. 13.00x (ISBN 0-88318-101-0). Am Inst Physics.

Alvarez, L. W., ed. Strong Interactions. (Italian Physical Society: Course 33). 1966. 49.50 (ISBN 0-12-368833-7). Acad Pr.

Bailen, D. Weak Interactions. LC 75-34572. 480p. 1977. pap. 24.95x (ISBN 0-8448-0851-2). Crane-Russak Co.

Bass, R. Nuclear Reactions with Heavy Ions. (Texts & Monographs in Physics). (Illus.). 1980. 48.40 (ISBN 0-387-09611-6). Springer-Verlag.

Blin-Stoyle, Roger J. Fundamental Interactions & the Nucleus. 1973. 34.25 (ISBN 0-444-10461-5, North-Holland). Elsevier.

Boschke, F., et al, eds. Nuclear Quadrupole Resonance. Boschke, F. (Topics in Current Chemistry: Vol. 30). (Illus.). 180p. (Eng. & Ger.). 1972. pap. 29.50 (ISBN 0-387-05781-1). Springer-Verlag.

Brown, G. E. & Jackson, A. D. The Nucleon-Nucleon Interaction. LC 75-37972. 242p. 1976. 36.75 (ISBN 0-444-10894-7, North-Holland). Elsevier.

Cannata, F. & Ueberall, H. Giant Resonance Phenomena in Intermediate-Energy Nuclear Reactions. (Springer Tracts in Modern Physics: Vol. 89). (Illus.). 112p. 1980. 29.80 (ISBN 0-387-10105-5). Springer-Verlag.

Cannon, R. D. Electron Transfer Reactions. LC 79-41278. 1981. text ed. 84.95 (ISBN 0-408-10646-8). Butterworth.

Chemical Effects of Nuclear Transformations - 1964, 2 vols. (Illus.). 1965. Vol. 1. 22.75 (ISBN 92-0-040065-5, ISP91-1, IAEA); Vol. 2. 29.25 (ISBN 92-0-040165-1, ISP91-2). Unipub.

Clementel, E. & Villi, C. Direct Interactions & Nuclear Reaction Mechanisms. 1963. 208.00 (ISBN 0-677-10070-1). Gordon.

Commins, E. Weak Interactions. 1973. text ed. 25.95 (ISBN 0-07-012372-1, C). McGraw.

Conference on the Present Status of Weak Interaction Physics, Indiana Univ., Bloomington, May 16-17, 1977. Weak Interaction Physics: 1977-Proceedings. Lichtenberg, D. B., ed. LC 77-83344. (AIP Conference Proceedings: Vol. 37). (Illus.). 1977. lib. bdg. 13.00 (ISBN 0-88318-136-3). Am Inst Physics.

Dean, B. Introduction to Strong Interactions. 394p. 1976. 57.75x (ISBN 0-677-02750-8). Gordon.

DeBenedetti, Sergio. Nuclear Interactions. LC 73-92136. 660p. 1974. Repr. of 1964 ed. 31.00 (ISBN 0-88275-143-3). Krieger.

De Shalit, Amos & Feshbach, Herman. Theoretical Nuclear Physics, Vol. 1: Nuclear Structure. LC 73-17165. 979p. 1974. text ed. 55.00 (ISBN 0-471-20385-8). Wiley.

Devons, S. High-Energy Physics & Nuclear Structure. LC 72-112272. 859p. 1970. 65.00 (ISBN 0-306-30473-2, Plenum Pr). Plenum Pub.

Ericson, T. E., ed. Interaction of High-Energy Particles with Nuclei. (Italian Physical Society: Course 38). 1967. 55.00 (ISBN 0-12-368838-8). Acad Pr.

Exchange Reactions. (Illus., Orig., Eng. & Fr.). 1965. pap. 22.75 (ISBN 92-0-040265-8, ISP107, IAEA). Unipub.

Faraggi, H. & Ricci, R. A. Nuclear Spectroscopy & Nuclear Reactions with Heavy Ions. 1976. 102.50 (ISBN 0-7204-0450-9, North-Holland). Elsevier.

Feshbach, H. & Levin, F. S. Reaction Dynamics, 2 pts. Incl. Pt. 1. Recent Developments in the Theory of Direct Reactions; Pt. 2. Topics in the Theory of Nuclear Reactions. LC 70-183847. (Documents on Modern Physics Ser.). 224p. 1973. 41.00x (ISBN 0-677-04330-9). Gordon.

Gell-Mann, Murray & Ne'eman, Yuval. The Eightfold Way. LC 65-13009. (Frontiers in Physics Ser.: No. 17). 1964. 19.50 (ISBN 0-8053-3150-6, Adv Bk Prog). Benjamin-Cummings.

Gibson, W. Martin. The Physics of Nuclear Reactions. LC 79-40063. (Illus.). 288p. 1980. 45.00 (ISBN 0-08-023078-4); pap. 16.75 (ISBN 0-08-023077-6). Pergamon.

Gorbachev, V. M. & Zamyatnin, A. A. Nuclear Reactions in Heavy Elements: A Data Handbook. LC 79-40928. 460p. 1980. 115.00 (ISBN 0-08-023595-6). Pergamon.

Gudehus, Tim, et al, eds. Fundamental Interactions at High Energy One. 1969. 83.75x (ISBN 0-677-13660-9). Gordon.

Harbottle, G. & Maddock, A. G., eds. Chemical Effects of Nuclear Transformations in Inorganic Systems. LC 78-10479. 1979. 88.00 (ISBN 0-444-85054-6, North Holland). Elsevier.

Horn, David & Zachariasen, Fredrik. Hadron Physics at Very High Energies. LC 73-9616. (Frontiers in Physics Ser: No. 40). xvi, 378p. 1973. text ed. 17.50 (ISBN 0-8053-4402-0, Adv Bk Prog); pap. text ed. 9.50 (ISBN 0-8053-4403-9, Adv Bk Prog). Benjamin-Cummings.

International Conference on High Energy Collisions, 3rd, Stony Brook. Proceedings. Cole, J. A., et al, trs. 1969. 73.00x (ISBN 0-677-13950-0). Gordon.

International Conference On The Nuclear Optical Model. Proceedings. Green, A. E., ed. (Florida State U. Studies: No. 32). 1959. pap. 4.50 (ISBN 0-8130-0474-8). U Presses Fla.

International Symposium Oln Electron & Photoninteractions at High Energies - Hamburg - 1965. Electron & Photon Interactions at High Energies: Invited Papers. (Springer Tracts in Modern Physics: Vol. 39). (Illus.). 1965. 34.30 (ISBN 0-387-03406-4). Springer-Verlag.

Jean, M., ed. Nuclear Structure & Nuclear Reactions. (Italian Physical Society: Course 40). 1969. 76.50 (ISBN 0-12-368840-X). Acad Pr.

Kabir, P. K., ed. Development of Weak Interaction Theory. (International Science Review Ser.). (Illus.). 1963. 43.00x (ISBN 0-677-00320-X). Gordon.

Kennedy, Hugh P. & Schrils, Rudolph, eds. Intermediate Structure in Nuclear Reactions. LC 67-29341. (Illus.). 232p. 1968. pap. 9.50x (ISBN 0-8131-1155-2). U Pr of Ky.

Lee, T. D., ed. Weak Interactions & High Energy Neutrino Physics. (Italian Physical Society,: Course 32). 1966. 50.00 (ISBN 0-12-368832-9). Acad Pr.

McCarthy, I. E. Nuclear Reactions. 1970. text ed. 35.00 (ISBN 0-08-006630-5); pap. text ed. 10.75 (ISBN 0-08-006629-1). Pergamon.

Mahanthappa, K. T. & Brittin, Wesley E., eds. Boulder Lecture Notes in Theoretical Physics, 1969: Vol. 12-B High Energy Collisions of Elementary Particles. 386p. 1973. 57.75x (ISBN 0-677-14560-8). Gordon.

Mahaux, C. & Weidenmuller, H. A. Shell-Model Approach to Nuclear Reactions. 1969. 39.00 (ISBN 0-444-10240-X, North-Holland). Elsevier.

Marshak, M. L., ed. High Energy Physics with Polarized Beams & Targets (Argonne, 1976) Proceedings. LC 76-50181. (AIP Conference Proceedings, No. 35: Subseries on Particles & Fields, No. 12). 543p. 1977. 21.50 (ISBN 0-88318-134-7). Am Inst Physics.

Non-Destructive Testing in Nuclear Technology, 2 vols. 1965. Vol. 1. 24.25 (ISBN 92-0-530065-9, ISP105-1-2, IAEA); Vol. 2. 28.00 (ISBN 92-0-530165-5). Unipub.

Okun, L. B. Weak Interaction of Elementary Particles. 1965. text ed. 30.00 (ISBN 0-08-011122-X); pap. text ed. 19.50 (ISBN 0-08-013702-4). Pergamon.

Park, David. Introduction to Strong Interactions. (Lecture Notes & Supplements in Physics Ser.: No. 8). 1966. 17.50 (ISBN 0-8053-7750-6, Adv Bk Prog). Benjamin-Cummings.

Perl, Martin L. High Energy Hadron Physics. LC 74-6348. 584p. 1974. 41.00 (ISBN 0-471-68049-4, Pub. by Wiley-Interscience). Wiley.

Preist, T. W. & Vick, L. L., eds. Particle Interactions at High Energies. LC 67-26706. 406p. 1967. 42.50 (ISBN 0-306-30314-0, Plenum Pr). Plenum Pub.

Proceedings of the International Conference, Los Angeles, 1972, et al. Few Particle Problems in the Nuclear Interaction. Moszkowski, Steven A. & Haddock, Roy P., eds. 1973. 97.75 (ISBN 0-444-10439-9, North-Holland). Elsevier.

Reeves, Hubert. Nuclear Reactions in Stellar Surfaces & Their Relations with Stellar Evolution. (Topics in Astrophysics & Space Physics Ser). (Illus.). 100p. 1971. 23.75x (ISBN 0-677-02960-8). Gordon.

Robinson, R. L., et al, eds. Reactions Between Complex Nuclei: Proceedings, 2 vols. LC 74-81324. 680p. 1975. Set. 92.75 (ISBN 0-685-57108-4); Vol. 1. 27.00 (ISBN 0-444-10664-2); Vol. 2. 78.00 (ISBN 0-444-10746-0). Elsevier.

Satchler, G. R. Introduction to Nuclear Reactions. LC 79-26275. 1980. 64.95 (ISBN 0-470-26467-5). Halsted Pr.

Skobel'tsyn, D. V., ed. Cosmic Rays & Nuclear Interactions at High Energies. LC 75-157933. (P. N. Lebedev Physics Institute Ser.: Vol. 46). 229p. 1971. 35.00 (ISBN 0-306-10862-3, Consultants). Plenum Pub.

--Nuclear Reactions & Charged-Particle Accelerators. LC 76-161. (P. N. Lebedev Physics Institute Ser.: Vol. 69). 144p. 1976. 47.50 (ISBN 0-306-10924-7, Consultants). Plenum Pub.

Skolbel'tsyn, D. V., ed. Nuclear Reactions & Interaction of Neutrons & Matter. LC 74-32059. (P. N. Lebedev Physics Institute Ser.: Vol. 63). (Illus.). 161p. 1974. 39.50 (ISBN 0-306-10907-7, Consultants). Plenum Pub.

The Structure of Nuclei: Trieste Lectures 1971. (Illus.). 599p. (Orig.). 1973. pap. 40.75 (ISBN 92-0-130072-7, ISP305, IAEA). Unipub.

Symposium - 3rd - Madison - 1970. Polarization Phenomena in Nuclear Reactions: Proceedings. Barschall, Henry H. & Haeberli, Willy, eds. LC 71-143762. 960p. 1971. text ed. 60.00 (ISBN 0-299-05890-5). U of Wis Pr.

Van Oers, W. T., et al, eds. Clustering Aspects of Nuclear Structure & Nuclear Reactions, Winnipeg, 1978. LC 78-64942. (AIP Conference Proceedings: No. 47). (Illus.). 1978. lib. bdg. 26.75 (ISBN 0-88318-146-0). Am Inst Physics.

Way, Katherine, ed. Atomic & Nuclear Data Reprints, 2 vols. Incl. Vol. 1. Internal Conversion Coefficients. 1973. 30.00 (ISBN 0-12-738901-6); Vol. 2. Reaction List for Charged-Particle-Induced Nuclear Reactions. McGowan, F. K. & Milner, W. T. 1973. 35.50 (ISBN 0-12-738902-4). Acad Pr.

Werle, J. Relativistic Theory of Reactions. 1970. 49.00 (ISBN 0-444-10307-4, North-Holland). Elsevier.

Wildermuth, K. & McClure, W. Cluster Representations of Nuclei. (Springer Tracts in Modern Physics, Vol. 41). (Illus.). 1966. 37.80 (ISBN 0-387-03670-9). Springer-Verlag.

Zichichi, A., ed. Hadrons & Their Interactions: Current - Field Algebra, Soft Pions, Supermultiplets, & Related Topics. 1968. 71.00 (ISBN 0-12-780540-0). Acad Pr.

--Strong & Weak Interactions. 1967. 71.00 (ISBN 0-12-780545-1). Acad Pr.

NUCLEAR REACTORS

see also Boiling Water Reactors; Breeder Reactors; Gas Cooled Reactors; Heavy Water Reactors; Marine Nuclear Reactor Plants; Neutron Transport Theory; Nuclear Propulsion; Organic Cooled Reactors; Pressurized Water Reactors; Pulsed Reactors; Reactor Fuel Reprocessing; Thermal Neutrons

Akcasu, Ziya, et al. Mathematical Methods in Nuclear Reactor Dynamics. (Nuclear Science & Technology Ser: Vol. 7). 1971. 67.50 (ISBN 0-12-047150-7). Acad Pr.

American Society of Civil Engineers, compiled by. International Seminar on Probabilistic & Extreme Load Design of Nuclear Plant Facilities. 464p. 1979. pap. text ed. 27.00 (ISBN 0-87262-146-4). Am Soc Civil Eng.

--Structural Design of Nuclear Plant Facilities. 1975. pap. text ed. 73.00 (ISBN 0-87262-172-3). Am Soc Civil Eng.

--Structural Design of Nuclear Plant Facilities. 1973. pap. text ed. 52.00 (ISBN 0-87262-155-3). Am Soc Civil Eng.

Argonne National Laboratory. Reactor Physics Constants. 2nd ed. 276p. 1963. write for info. DOE.

Ash, Milton. Optimal Shutdown Control of Nuclear Reactors. (Mathematics in Science and Engineering Ser.: Vol. 26). 1966. 32.00 (ISBN 0-12-065150-5). Acad Pr.

Ash, Milton S. Nuclear Reactor Kinetics. nd ed. (Illus.). 1979. text ed. 49.50 (ISBN 0-07-002380-8). McGraw.

Bankoff, S. George, et al, eds. Heat Transfer in Nuclear Reactor Sáfety. (International Centre for Heat & Mass Transfer Ser.). (Illus.). 1981. text ed. 95.00 (ISBN 0-89116-223-2). Hemisphere Pub.

Bell, George I. & Glasstone, Samuel. Nuclear Reactor Theory. LC 78-22102. 638p. 1979. Repr. of 1970 ed. lib. bdg. 32.50 (ISBN 0-88275-790-3). Krieger.

Boland, James F. Nuclear Reactor Instrumentation (In-Core) LC 76-101310. 230p. 1970. 12.50 (ISBN 0-677-02420-7). Am Nuclear Soc.

Butt, J. Reaction Kinetic & Reactor Design. 1980. 26.95 (ISBN 0-13-753335-7). P-H.

Clark, Melville & Hansen, K. F. Numerical Methods of Reactor Analysis. (Nuclear Science & Technology: Vol. 3). 1964. 50.00 (ISBN 0-12-175350-6). Acad Pr.

Coastal Resources Center. An Environmental Study of a Nuclear Plant at Charlestown: Rhode Island. (Marine Technical Report Ser.: No. 33). 1974. pap. 5.00 (ISBN 0-938412-07-8). URI MAS.

Codes for Reactor Computations. (Illus., Orig.). 1961. 17.25 (ISBN 92-0-050061-7, ISP24, IAEA). Unipub.

DeLeon, Peter. Development & Diffusion of the Nuclear Power Reactor: A Comparative Analysis (A Rand Graduate Institute Book) LC 79-12988. 350p. 1979. reference 19.50 (ISBN 0-88410-682-9). Ballinger Pub.

Determination of Absorbed Dose in Reactors. (Technical Reports Ser.: No. 127). (Illus.). 251p. (Orig.). 1972. pap. 20.00 (ISBN 92-0-157071-6, IDC127, IAEA). Unipub.

Developments in the Physics of Nuclear Power Reactors. (Technical Reports Ser.: No. 143). (Illus.). 291p. (Orig.). 1973. pap. 25.00 (ISBN 92-0-135073-2, IDC143, IAEA). Unipub.

Directory of Nuclear Reactors. Incl. Vol. 2. Research, Text & Experimental Reactors: Power Reactors. 1959. pap. 11.25 (ISBN 92-0-152159-6, ISP397); Vol. 3. Research, Test & Experimental Reactors, Supplement. 378p. 1960. pap. 12.50 (ISBN 92-0-152060-3, ISP397-3); Vol. 4. Power Reactors, Supplement. 324p. 1962. pap. 15.75 (ISBN 92-0-152062-X, ISP-397-4). (Technical Directories Ser., IAEA). Unipub.

Directory of Nuclear Reactors. Incl. Vol. 5. Research, Test & Experimental Reactors, Supplement. 1964. 16.25 (ISBN 92-0-152064-6, ISP397-5); Vol. 6. Research, Test & Experimental Reactors, Supplement. 1966. 13.50 (ISBN 92-0-152066-2, ISP397-6); Vol. 7. Power Reactors, Supplement. 1967. 20.50 (ISBN 92-0-152067-0, ISP397-7); Vol. 8. Research, Test & Experimental Reactors, Supplement. 1970. 17.75 (ISBN 92-0-152170-7, ISP397-8); Vol. 9. Power Reactors, Supplement. 1971. 17.25 (ISBN 92-0-152171-5, ISP397-9). IAEA). Unipub.

Directory of Nuclear Reactors: Power & Research Reactors, Vol. 10. (Directories of Nuclear Reactors). (Illus.). 1976. 42.25 (ISBN 92-0-152076-X, ISP397-10, IAEA). Unipub.

Division 2-Code for Concrete Reactor Vessels & Containments. (Boiler & Pressure Vessel Code Ser.: Sec. 3). 1980. 90.00 (ISBN 0-686-70386-3, P00032); pap. 125.00 loose-leaf (ISBN 0-686-70387-1, V00032). ASME.

Duderstadt, James J. & Hamilton, Louis J. Nuclear Reactor Analysis. LC 75-20389. 650p. 1976. text ed. 38.95 (ISBN 0-471-22363-8). Wiley.

Dyer, A. Gas Chemistry in Nuclear Reactors & Large Industrial Plants. 1980. 38.50 (ISBN 0-85501-449-0). Heyden.

Educational Research Council of America. Nuclear Reactor Operator. Ferris, Theodore N. & Marchak, John P., eds. (Real People at Work Ser: G). (Illus.). 1974. pap. text ed. 2.25 (ISBN 0-89247-059-3). Changing Times.

El-Wakil, M. M. Nuclear Power Engineering. (Nuclear Engineering Ser). 1962. text ed. 26.50 (ISBN 0-07-019300-2, C). McGraw.

Factors Relevant to the Decommissioning of Land-Based Nuclear Reactor Plants. (Safety Ser.: No. 52). 28p. 1981. pap. 6.50 (ISBN 9-2062-3080-8, ISP 541, IAEA). Unipub.

Fast Reactor Physics, 2 vols. (Illus., Orig., Eng. , Fr. & Rus.). 1968. Vol. 1. pap. 34.25 (ISBN 0-685-12710-9, ISP165-1, IAEA); Vol. 2. pap. 37.50 (ISBN 92-0-050568-6, ISP165-2). Unipub.

Fast Reactor Physics Nineteen Seventy-Nine, Vol. 1. 2nd ed. 611p. 1980. pap. 77.25 (ISBN 92-0-050180-X, ISP529-1, IAEA). Unipub.

Fuel Burn-up Predictions in Thermal Reactors. (Illus., Orig., Eng. & Fr.). 1968. pap. 15.25 (ISBN 92-0-051068-X, ISP172, IAEA). Unipub.

Fusion Reactor Design Concepts. 1979. pap. 41.50 (ISBN 92-0-131178-8, ISP487, IAEA). Unipub.

Fusion Reactor Design Problems. (Illus.). 540p. (Orig.). 1974. pap. 41.50 (ISBN 92-0-139074-2, ISP23-74, IAEA). Unipub.

Glasstone, Samuel & Sesonske, Alexander. Nuclear Reactor Engineering. 2nd ed. 800p. 1980. text ed. 39.50 (ISBN 0-442-20057-9). Van Nos Reinhold.

Gol'denblat, I. & Nikolaenko, N. A. Calculations of Thermal Stresses in Nuclear Reactors. LC 64-13143. 78p. 1964. 25.00 (ISBN 0-306-10671-X, Consultants). Plenum Pub.

Goodjohn, Albert J. & Pomraning, Gerald C., eds. Reactor Physics in the Resonance & Thermal Regions, 2 vols. Incl. Vol. 1. Neutron Thermalization. 450p (ISBN 0-262-07023-5); Vol. 2. Resonance Absorbtion. 450p (ISBN 0-262-07024-3). 1966. text ed. 30.00x ea. MIT Pr.

Greenspan, H., et al, eds. Computing Methods in Reactor Physics. (Orig.). 1968. 89.75 (ISBN 0-677-11890-2). Gordon.

Harrer, Joseph M. & Beckerley, James G., eds. Nuclear Power Reactor Instrumentation Systems Handbook, Vol. 1. LC 72-600355. 313p. 1973. pap. 7.60 (ISBN 0-686-75765-3); microfiche 3.00 (ISBN 0-686-75766-1). DOE.

--Nuclear Power Reactor Instrumentation Systems Handbook, Vol. 2. LC 72-600355. 282p. 1974. pap. 7.60 (ISBN 0-686-75767-X); microfiche 3.00 (ISBN 0-686-75768-8). DOE.

Henry, Allan. Nuclear Reactor Analysis. LC 74-19477. 1975. 39.95x (ISBN 0-262-08081-8). MIT Pr.

Hetrick, David L. Dynamics of Nuclear Reactors. LC 76-130109. 1971. text ed. 27.50 (ISBN 0-226-33166-0). U of Chicago Pr.

Hetsroni, G., ed. Basic Two Phase Flow Modeling in Reactor Safety & Performance: EPRI Workshop Held at Tampa, Fla. 27 Feb.--2 March 1979. 170p. 1980. pap. 45.00 (ISBN 0-08-026160-4). Pergamon.

Hickey, Albert E., ed. Simulator Training of Nuclear Reactor Operators. 151p. 1980. 15.00 (ISBN 0-89785-974-X). Am Inst Res.

Howe, P. J., ed. Advanced Converters & Near Breeders: Proceedings of the Wingspread Conference, Racine, Wisconsin, 1975. 1976. text ed. 37.00 (ISBN 0-08-020523-2). Pergamon.

International Atomic Energy Agency. Programming & Utilization of Research Reactors: Proceedings, 3 vols. Eklund, Sigvard, ed. (International Atomic Energy Agency Symposia). 1962. Vol. 1. 19.50 (ISBN 0-12-572501-9); Vol. 2, 1963. 19.50 (ISBN 0-12-572502-7); Vol. 3. 19.50 (ISBN 0-12-572503-5). Acad Pr.

International Tokamak Reactor: Zero Phase. (Panel Proceedings Ser.). 650p. 1980. pap. 83.75 (ISBN 92-0-131080-3, ISP556, IAEA). Unipub.

Irradiation Facilities for Research Reactors. (Illus.). 478p. (Orig., Eng. & Fr.). 1973. pap. 37.50 (ISBN 92-0-050073-0, ISP316, IAEA). Unipub.

Jaeger, T. A., ed. Structural Mechanics in Reactor Technology, 5 vols. in 8 bks. 1975. Set. 292.75 set (ISBN 0-444-10974-9, North-Holland). Elsevier.

Jaeger, T. A. & Baley, B. A., eds. Structural Mechanics in Reactor Technology, 13 vols. 5821p. 1979. Set. pap. 292.75 (ISBN 0-444-85356-1, North Holland). Elsevier.

Jaeger, T. A. & Boley, B. A., eds. Structural Mechanics in Reactor Technology: Transactions of the 4th International Conference, San Francisco, California, August 1977, 13 vols. 1978. pap. 292.75 (ISBN 0-444-85093-7, North-Holland). Elsevier.

Jones, Owen C., Jr., ed. Nuclear Reactor Safety Heat Transfer. LC 81-2932. (Proceedings of the International Centre for Heat & Mass Transfer Ser.). (Illus.). 1981. text ed. 99.00 (ISBN 0-89116-224-0). Hemisphere Pub.

Kallfelz, J. M. & Karam, R. A., eds. Advanced Reactors: Physics, Design, & Economics: Proceedings, International Conference, Atlanta, Georgia, Sept. 1974. LC 75-4642. 864p. 1975. text ed. 46.00 (ISBN 0-08-019610-1). Pergamon.

Keck, Otto. Policy-Making in a Nuclear Program: The Case of the West German Fast-Breeder Reactor. LC 79-3831. 1981. 27.95x (ISBN 0-669-03519-X). Lexington Bks.

Keepin, G. Robert. Physics of Nuclear Kinetics. 1965. 15.00 (ISBN 0-201-03682-7, Adv Bk Prog). A-W.

Kerlin, T. W. Frequency Response Testing in Nuclear Reactors. (Nuclear Science & Technology Ser.). 1974. 36.50 (ISBN 0-12-404850-1). Acad Pr.

Kinetics & Noise Analysis of Zero-Power Reactors: An NPY-Project Report. (Technical Reports Ser.: No. 138). (Illus.). 110p. (Orig.). 1973. pap. 11.25 (ISBN 92-0-135072-4, IDC138, IAEA). Unipub.

Lamarsh, J. R. Introduction to Nuclear Reactor Theory. 1966. 26.95 (ISBN 0-201-04120-0). A-W.

Lau, L. Wang. Elements of Nuclear Reactor Engineering. new ed. LC 77-156083. 256p. 1975. 54.50x (ISBN 0-677-02270-0). Gordon.

Layman, D. C. & Thornton, G. Remote Handling of Mobile Nuclear Systems. LC 66-60017. 655p. 1966. write for info. DOE.

Lewins, J. Nuclear Reactor Kinetics & Control. LC 77-8107. 1978. text ed. 45.00 (ISBN 0-08-021682-X); pap. text ed. 18.00 (ISBN 0-08-021681-1). Pergamon.

Lewis, E. E. Nuclear Power Reactor Safety. LC 77-21360. 1977. 50.00 (ISBN 0-471-53335-1, Pub. by Wiley-Interscience). Wiley.

Link, Leonard E. Reactor Technology, Selected Reviews, 1965. LC 66-60019. 445p. 1966. write for info. DOE.

Link, Leonard E., ed. Reactor Technology, Selected Reviews, 1964. 636p. 1964. write for info. DOE.

Long, Robert L. & O'Brien, Paul, eds. Fast Burst Reactors. LC 73-603552. (AEC Symposium Ser.). 646p. 1969. pap. 6.00 (ISBN 0-686-75893-5); microfiche 3.00 (ISBN 0-686-75894-3). DOE.

Manual on the Operation of Research Reactors. (Technical Reports Ser.: No. 37). 1964. pap. 11.75 (ISBN 92-0-155364-1, IDC37, IAEA). Unipub.

Marchuk, Gurii I. Theory & Methods for Nuclear Reactor Calculations. LC 63-21215. 199p. 1964. 45.00 (ISBN 0-306-10670-1, Consultants). Plenum Pub.

Marchuk, Gurji I. Numerical Methods for Nuclear Reactor Calculations. LC 59-9229. 295p. 1959. 65.00 (ISBN 0-306-10561-6, Consultants). Plenum Pub.

Massimo, L. Physics of High Temperature Reactors. 1975. text ed. 37.00 (ISBN 0-08-019616-0). Pergamon.

Meem, J. L. Two Group Reactor Theory. 1964. 65.00 (ISBN 0-677-00520-2). Gordon.

Meredith, Dennis L., ed. Nuclear Power Plant Siting: A Handbook for the Layman. rev. ed. (Marine Bulletin Ser.: No. 6). 1972. pap. 1.00 (ISBN 0-938412-11-6). URI MAS.

Mohler, R. R. & Shen, C. N. Optimal Control of Nuclear Reactors. (Nuclear Science & Technology Ser.: Vol. 6). 1970. 55.00 (ISBN 0-12-504150-0). Acad Pr.

Nau, Henry R. National Politics & International Technology: Nuclear Reactor Development in Western Europe. LC 73-19344. 304p. 1974. 18.50x (ISBN 0-8018-1506-1). Johns Hopkins.

Nero, Anthony V., Jr. A Guidebook to Nuclear Reactors. LC 77-76183. (Cal. Ser.: No. 393). 1979. 32.50x (ISBN 0-520-03482-1); pap. 11.95 (ISBN 0-520-03661-1). U of Cal Pr.

Neutron Thermalization & Reactor Spectra, 2 vols. (Illus., Eng. , Fr. & Rus.). 1968. Vol. 1. pap. 39.00 (ISBN 92-0-050068-4, ISP160-1-2, IAEA); Vol. 2. pap. 32.50 (ISBN 92-0-050168-0). Unipub.

Nuclear Activation Cross-Section Data: Neutron, Proton, & Charged Particle Nuclear Reaction Cross-Section Data. (Technical Reports Ser., No. 156). (Illus.). 558p. (Orig.). 1974. pap. 44.00 (ISBN 92-0-135074-0, IDC156, IAEA). Unipub.

Nuclear Data for Reactors - 1966, 2 vols. 1967. Vol. 1. pap. 34.25 (ISBN 92-0-030167-3, 140-1-2, IAEA); Vol. 2. pap. 26.00 (ISBN 92-0-030267-X). Unipub.

Nuclear Data in Science & Technology, 2 vols. (Illus.). 1214p. (Orig.). 1974. pap. 48.75 ea. (IAEA); Vol. 1. pap. (ISBN 92-0-030073-1, ISP 343-1); Vol. 2. pap. (ISBN 92-0-030173-8, ISP 343-2). Unipub.

Nuclear Electronics - 1965. 1966. pap. 26.75 (ISBN 92-0-030266-1, IAEA). Unipub.

Nuclear Power Plant Control & Instrumentation - 1973. (Illus.). 886p. (Orig.). 1974. pap. 65.00 (ISBN 92-0-050173-7, ISP341, IAEA). Unipub.

Nuclear Power Plant Control & Instrumentation. (Illus.). 3110p. (Orig.). 1971. pap. 24.50 (ISBN 92-0-051072-8, ISP301, IAEA). Unipub.

Nuclear Reactor Energy Spectra. 1974. pap. 26.00 (ISBN 0-686-52082-3, 05-592000-41). ASTM.

OECD Nuclear Energy Agency. Nuclear Data & Benchmarks for Reactor Shielding. 421p. (Orig., Eng. & Fr.). 1981. pap. 24.00x (ISBN 92-64-02118-3). OECD.

Operating Experience with Power Reactors, 2 vols. 1963. Vol 1. 24.00 (ISBN 92-0-050163-X, IAEA); Vol 2. 19.50 (ISBN 92-0-050263-6). Unipub.

Organization of Regulatory Activities for Nuclear Reactors. (Technical Reports). 57p. (Orig.). 1974. pap. 7.50 (ISBN 92-0-125174-2, IDC-153, IAEA). Unipub.

Pacilio, Nicola. Reactor-Noise Analysis in the Time Domain. LC 79-600321. 102p. 1969. pap. 6.00 (ISBN 0-686-75906-0); microfiche 3.00 (ISBN 0-686-75907-9). DOE.

Physics & Heat Technology of Reactors. (Illus.). 1958. 37.50 (ISBN 0-306-10571-3, Consultants). Plenum Pub.

Physics of Fast & Intermediate Reactors, 3 vols. 1962. Vol. 1. 16.25 (ISBN 92-0-050062-5, IAEA); Vol. 2. 16.25 (ISBN 92-0-050162-1); Vol. 3. 21.50 (ISBN 92-0-050262-8). Unipub.

Potter, Philip J. Power Plant Theory & Design. 2nd ed. (Illus.). 1959. 28.95 (ISBN 0-8260-7205-4). Wiley.

Power Reactors in Member States. 1978. pap. 10.25 (ISBN 92-0-152078-6, ISP423-78, IAEA). Unipub.

Power Reactors in Member States. 1977. pap. 13.50 (ISBN 92-0-152077-8, ISP423-77, IAEA). Unipub.

Power Reactors in Member States Nineteen Seventy-Nine. 1979. pap. 16.75 (ISBN 92-0-152079-4, ISP 423-79, IAEA). Unipub.

Power Reactors in Member States, 1976. 1976. pap. 9.75 (ISBN 92-0-152176-6, IAEA). Unipub.

Power Reactors in Member States 1980. 147p. 1980. pap. 19.50 (ISBN 92-0-152080-8, ISP423-80, IAEA). Unipub.

Profio, A. Edward. Experimental Reactor Physics. LC 75-35735. 832p. 1976. 46.00 (ISBN 0-471-70095-9, Pub. by Wiley-Interscience). Wiley.

Reactor Burn-up Physics. (Illus.). 296p. (Orig.). 1973. pap. 22.75 (ISBN 92-0-051073-6, ISP336, IAEA). Unipub.

Reactor Physics Studies of H20 - D20 Moderated U02 Cores: A NORA Project Report. (Technical Reports: No. 67). 1966. pap. 7.00 (ISBN 92-0-155166-5, IAEA). Unipub.

Reliability Problems of Reactor Pressure Components, Vol. 1. 1978. pap. 50.50 (ISBN 92-0-050078-1, ISP 467-1, IAEA). Unipub.

Rockwell, Theodore, 3rd, ed. Reactor Shielding Design Manual. 478p. 1956. write for info. DOE.

Safe Operation of Critical Assemblies & Research Reactors, 1971. (Safety Ser.: No. 35). (Orig.). 1971. pap. 15.25 (ISBN 92-0-123071-0, ISP225, IAEA). Unipub.

Schaeffer, N. M. Reactor Shielding for Nuclear Engineers. LC 73-600001. 801p. 1973. pap. 13.60 (ISBN 0-686-75908-7); microfiche 3.00 (ISBN 0-686-75909-5). DOE.

Shaw, J. Reactor Operation. 1969. 25.00 (ISBN 0-08-013325-8); pap. 12.25 (ISBN 0-08-013324-X). Pergamon.

Shimizu, Akinao & Aoki, Katsutada. Application of Invariant Imbedding to Reactor Physics. (Nuclear Science & Technology Ser). 1972. 34.50 (ISBN 0-12-640150-0). Acad Pr.

Small & Medium Power Reactors - 1970. 1971. pap. 39.00 (ISBN 92-0-050171-0, ISP267, IAEA). Unipub.

Specialists Meeting Held at the Central Bureau for Nuclear Measurements, Geel, Belgium, 5-8 Dec. 1977. Neutron Data of Structural Materials for Fast Reactors: Proceedings. Bockhoff, K. H., ed. (Illus.). 1979. text ed. 120.00 (ISBN 0-08-023424-0). Pergamon.

Stacey, W. H., Jr. Space-Time Nuclear Reactor Kinetics. (Nuclear Science & Technology Ser: Vol. 5). 1969. 35.50 (ISBN 0-12-662050-4). Acad Pr.

Stacey, Weston M., Jr. Modal Approximations: Theory & an Application to Fast-Reactor Physics. (Press Research Monographs: No. 41). 1967. 15.00x (ISBN 0-262-19038-9). MIT Pr.

--Variational Methods in Nuclear Reactor Physics. (Nuclear Science & Technology Ser.). 1974. 35.50 (ISBN 0-12-662060-1). Acad Pr.

Study on the Potentialities of the Use of a Nuclear Reactor for the Industrialization of Southern Tunisia. (Technical Reports: No. 35). 1964. pap. 5.50 (ISBN 92-0-155164-9, IDC35, IAEA). Unipub.

Subcommittee on Nuclear Reactors. Reactors for University Research. 1959. pap. 0.75 (ISBN 0-309-00075-0). Natl Acad Pr.

Symposia in Applied Mathematics-New York-1959. Nuclear Reactor Theory: Proceedings, Vol. 11. Birkhoff, G. & Wigner, E. P., eds. LC 50-1183. 1961. 23.20 (ISBN 0-8218-1311-0, PSAPM-11). Am Math.

Technical Information Center, U. S. Department of Energy. Nuclear Reactors Built, Being Built, or Planned. 44p. pap. 6.50 (ISBN 0-686-75903-6). DOE.

Thermal Discharges at Nuclear Power Stations. (Technical Reports Ser., No. 155). (Illus.). 155p. (Orig.). 1974. pap. 15.00 (ISBN 92-0-125274-9, IDC155, IAEA). Unipub.

Tyror, J. G. & Vaughan, R. I. Introduction to Neutron Kinetics of Nuclear Power Reactors. LC 76-94936. 1970. 25.00 (ISBN 0-08-006667-4). Pergamon.

United States Atomic Energy Commission. Reactor Handbook, 2 vols. 2nd ed. Incl. Vol. 1. Materials. 1223p. 1960. 75.95 (ISBN 0-470-71082-9); Vol. 3, Pt. A. Physics. 313p. 1962. 34.00 (ISBN 0-470-71148-5); Vol. 3, Pt. B. Shielding. 287p. 1962. 30.00 (ISBN 0-470-71150-7). (Pub. by Wiley-Interscience). Wiley.

Walsh, Edward M. Energy Conversion: Electromechanical, Direct, Nuclear. (Illus.). 1967. 23.95 (ISBN 0-8260-9125-3). Wiley.

Weaver, Lynn E., ed. Reactor Kinetics & Control. (AEC Symposium Ser.). 593p. 1964. pap. 6.00 (ISBN 0-686-75904-4); microfiche 3.00 (ISBN 0-686-75905-2). DOE.

Weinberg, Alvin M. & Wigner, Eugene P. Physical Theory of Neutron Chain Reactors. LC 58-8507. (Illus.). 1958. 30.00x (ISBN 0-226-88517-8). U of Chicago Pr.

Weisman, Joel. Elements of Nuclear Reactor Design. LC 76-41680. 1977. 60.50 (ISBN 0-444-41509-2). Elsevier.

Williams, M. M. Random Processes in Nuclear Reactors. LC 74-4066. 1974. text ed. 42.00 (ISBN 0-08-017920-7). Pergamon.

Williams, M. M., ed. Reactor Noise - Smorn II: Proceedings of the 2nd Specialists' Meeting on Reactor Noise 1977. 1978. pap. text ed. 182.00 (ISBN 0-686-68044-8). Pergamon.

--Reactor Noise. an International Symposium: Special Multi Issue of Journal of Annals of Nuclear Energy. 400p. 1975. pap. text ed. 55.00 (ISBN 0-08-019895-3). Pergamon.

Winterton, R. H. Thermal Design of Nuclear Reactors. LC 80-41187. (Illus.). 200p. 1981. 32.00 (ISBN 0-08-024215-4); pap. 18.00 (ISBN 0-08-024214-6). Pergamon.

Yeater, M. L., ed. Neutron Physics: Proceedings. (Nuclear Science & Technology: Vol. 2). 1962. 46.50 (ISBN 0-12-769050-6). Acad Pr.

NUCLEAR REACTORS–ACCIDENTS

Del Tredici, Robert. The People of Three Mile Island. LC 80-13558. (Illus.). 124p. (Orig.). 1980. pap. 7.95 (ISBN 0-87156-237-5). Sierra.

Environmental Action Foundation. Accidents Will Happen: The Case Against Nuclear Power. 6.00 (ISBN 0-8446-5850-2). Peter Smith.

Kemeny, John G., ed. The Accident at Three Mile Island: The Need for Change, the Legacy of TMI. (Illus.). 201p. 1980. 33.00 (ISBN 0-08-025949-9); pap. 25.00 (ISBN 0-08-025946-4). Pergamon.

Leppzer, Robert. Voices from Three-Mile Island: The People Speak Out. LC 80-20933. (Illus.). 1980. 8.95 (ISBN 0-89594-041-8); pap. 3.95 (ISBN 0-89594-042-6). Crossing Pr.

Medvedev, Zhores A. Nuclear Disaster in the Urals. 1979. 14.95 (ISBN 0-393-01219-0). Norton.

Moss, Thomas H. & Sills, David L., eds. The Three Mile Island Nuclear Accident: Lessons & Implications. 343p. 1981. 66.00 (ISBN 0-89766-115-X); pap. write for info. NY Acad Sci.

Stephens, Mark. Three Mile Island. (Illus.). 1981. 11.95 (ISBN 0-394-51092-5). Random.

Stever, Donald W., Jr. Seabrook & the Nuclear Regulatory Commission: The Licensing of a Nuclear Power Plant. LC 79-56160. (Illus.). 264p. 1980. 15.00 (ISBN 0-87451-181-X). U Pr of New En.

Williams, M. M. & McCormick, N. J., eds. Progress in Nuclear Energy: Staff Reports to the President's Commission on the Accident at Three Mile Island, Vol. 6. LC 77-25743. (Illus.). 431p. 1981. 97.00 (ISBN 0-08-027124-3). Pergamon.

NUCLEAR REACTORS–COOLING

Cohen, Paul. Water Coolant Technology of Power Reactors. Wallin, Diane, ed. LC 79-57306. (Monograph). 250p. 1980. Repr. of 1969 ed. write for info. (ISBN 0-89448-020-0). Am Nuclear Soc.

Foust, O. J. Sodium-Nak Engineering Handbook, Vol. 1: Sodium Chemistry & Physical Properties. LC 70-129473. (U. S. Atomic Energy Commission Monographs Ser.). 350p. 1972. 73.25x (ISBN 0-677-03020-7). Gordon.

NUCLEAR REACTORS–FUEL

see Nuclear Fuels

NUCLEAR REACTORS–FUEL ELEMENTS

see Nuclear Fuel Elements

NUCLEAR REACTORS–MATERIALS

see also Nuclear Fuels

Analytical Chemistry of Nuclear Materials. (Technical Reports Ser.: No. 18). 88p. (Orig.). 1963. pap. 6.25 (ISBN 92-0-145163-6, IDC18, IAEA). Unipub.

Analytical Chemistry of Nuclear Materials: Second Panel Report. (Technical Reports Ser.: No. 62). (Orig.). 1966. pap. 10.25 (ISBN 92-0-145266-7, IDC62, IAEA). Unipub.

Foell, Wesley K. Small-Sample Reactivity Measurements in Nuclear Reactors. LC 74-144051. (ANS Monographs). 272p. 1972. 23.50 (ISBN 0-89448-003-0). Am Nuclear Soc.

Nuclear Data for Reactors - 1970, 2 Vols. (Illus., Orig.). 1970. Vol. 1. pap. 52.00 (ISBN 92-0-030070-7, ISP 259-1, IAEA); Vol. 2. pap. 61.75 (ISBN 92-0-030170-3, ISP 259-2). Unipub.

Nuclear Materials Management. 1966. 48.75 (ISBN 92-0-050066-8, ISP110, IAEA). Unipub.

Okrent, Hummel. Reactivity Coefficients in Large Fast Power Reactors. LC 73-119000. (ANS Monographs). 386p. 1970. 18.40 (ISBN 0-89448-006-5). Am Nuclear Soc.

Rodden, C. J., ed. Analysis of Essential Nuclear Reactor Materials. LC 64-60035. 1291p. 1964. write for info. microfiche. DOE.

Simnad, M. T. & Zumwatt, L. R., eds. Materials & Fuels for High-Temperature Nuclear Applications. 1964. 23.00x (ISBN 0-262-19012-5). MIT Pr.

Smith, Charles O. Materials in Nuclear Reactors. 1967. 22.50 (ISBN 0-201-07061-8, Adv Bk Prog). A-W.

Thermodynamics of Nuclear Materials - 1967. (Eng., Fr. & Rus.). 1968. pap. 52.00 (ISBN 92-0-040068-X, ISP162, IAEA). Unipub.

NUCLEAR REACTORS–SAFETY MEASURES

ACI Committee 349. Code Requirements for Nuclear Safety Related Concrete Structures: ACI 349-76. 1976. 43.95 (ISBN 0-685-85087-0, 349-76) (ISBN 0-685-85088-9). ACI.

Application of Meteorology to Safety at Nuclear Plants. (Safety Ser.: No. 29). (Orig.). 1968. pap. 5.50 (ISBN 92-0-123368-X, ISP211, IAEA). Unipub.

Ballinger, Ronald G. The Anisotropic Mechanical Behavior of Zircalor-2. LC 78-74995. (Outstanding Dissertations on Energy Ser.). 1979. lib. bdg. 27.50 (ISBN 0-8240-3986-6). Garland Pub.

Bressler, M. N., et al. Criteria for Nuclear Safety Related Piping & Component Support Snubbers. (PVP: No. 45). 40p. 1980. 6.00 (ISBN 0-686-69846-0, H00172). ASME.

Containment & Siting of Nuclear Power Plants. (Illus., Orig.). 1967. pap. 45.50 (ISBN 92-0-020167-9, ISP154, IAEA). Unipub.

Detection & Location of Failed Fuel Elements. (Illus., Orig.). 1968. pap. 15.50 (ISBN 92-0-051168-6, ISP204, IAEA). Unipub.

Earthquake Guidelines for Reactor Siting. (Technical Reports Ser.: No. 139). 53p. (Orig.). 1973. pap. 5.50 (ISBN 92-0-125272-2, IDC139, IAEA). Unipub.

ECO Two: Atomic Reactor Safety Hearings. (The Energy Papers Ser). 1974. pap. 4.95 (ISBN 0-913890-12-X). Friends Earth.

Environmental Surveillance Around Nuclear Installations, 2 vols. (Illus.). 927p. (Orig.). 1974. Set. pap. 73.00 (ISBN 92-0-020074-5, ISP353, IAEA). Unipub.

Fire Protection Practice for Nuclear Reactor. (Eight Hundred & Nine Hundred Ser). 1974. pap. 3.50 (ISBN 0-685-58215-9, 802). Natl Fire Prot.

Freeman, Leslie J. Nuclear Witnesses: Insiders Speak Out. (Illus.). 1981. 16.95 (ISBN 0-393-01456-8). Norton.

Fussell, J. B. & Burdick, G. R., eds. Nuclear Systems Reliability Engineering & Risk Assessment. LC 77-91478. (Illus.). 1977. text ed. 38.50 (ISBN 0-686-24250-5). Soc Indus-Appl Math.

Graham, John. Fast Reactor Safety. (Nuclear Science & Technology Ser.: Vol. 8). 1971. 55.00 (ISBN 0-12-294950-1). Acad Pr.

Hakkila, E. Arnold, ed. Nuclear Safeguards Analysis: Nondestructive & Analytical Chemical Techniques. LC 78-12706. (ACS Symposium Ser.: No. 79). 1978. 22.00 (ISBN 0-8412-0449-7). Am Chemical.

I Mech E Conference, Manchester, U. K., Sept. 1977. Heat & Fluid Flow in Water Reactor Safety: Proceedings. new ed. Mechanical Engineering Publicatons Limited, Books & Academic Journals Managing Editor, ed. (Illus.). 1977. text ed. 50.00 (ISBN 0-85298-379-4). Hemisphere Pub.

International Colloquium on Irradiation Tests for Reactor Safety Programmes, Petten, Holland, June 1979 & Joint Research Center, Petten Establishment of the Commission of the European Communities. Aspects of Nuclear Reactor Safety: Proceedings. (European Applied Research Reports Special Topics Ser.). 600p. 1980. lib. bdg. 47.50 (ISBN 3-7186-0016-1). Harwood Academic.

Jones, O. C., Jr. & Bankoff, S. G., eds. Symposium on the Thermal & Hydraulic Aspects of Nuclear Reactor Safety-Light Water Reactors, Vol. 1. 1977. pap. text ed. 25.00 (ISBN 0-685-86878-8, G00127). ASME.

--Symposium on the Thermal & Hydraulic Aspects of Nuclear Reactor Safety-Liquid Metal Fast Breeder Reactors, Vol. 2. 1977. pap. text ed. 25.00 (ISBN 0-685-86879-6, G00128). ASME.

Nuclear Aerosols in Reactor Safety: June, 1979. (Document Ser.). 266p. 1979. 18.75x (ISBN 92-64-11977-9). OECD.

Nuclear Energy Agency & Organization for Economic Cooperation & Development. Plate Inspection Programme, PISC: November, 1979. (Illus.). 78p. (Orig.). 1980. pap. text ed. 7.50x (ISBN 92-64-12028-9, 66 80 02 1). OECD.

Nuclear Safeguards Technology Nineteen Seventy-Eight, Vol. 1. 1979. pap. 95.25 (ISBN 92-0-070079-9, ISP 497, IAEA). Unipub.

OECD-NEA. Reference Seismic Ground Motions in Nuclear Safety Assessments. (Illus.). 171p. (Orig.). 1980. pap. text ed. 16.00x (ISBN 92-64-12100-5). OECD.

Okrent, David. Nuclear Reactor Safety: On the History of the Regulatory Process. LC 80-53958. 480p. 1981. 29.50x (ISBN 0-299-08350-0). U of Wis Pr.

Osterhout, Marilyn M., ed. Decontamination & Decommissioning of Nuclear Facilities. 820p. 1980. 75.00 (ISBN 0-306-40429-X, Plenum Pr). Plenum Pub.

Principles & Standards of Reactor Safety. (Illus.). 650p. (Orig.). 1974. pap. 52.00 (ISBN 92-0-020373-6, ISP342, IAEA). Unipub.

Quality Assurance in the Manufacture of Items for Nuclear Power Plants. (Safety Ser.: No. 50-SG-QA8). 40p. 1981. pap. 8.50 (ISBN 92-0-123181-4, ISP577, IAEA). Unipub.

Reactor Safety: A Bibliography, Supplement 12, June 1977 to June 1980. (DOE Technical Information Center Ser.). 1980. write for info. DOE.

Reactor Safety: A Literature Search. (DOE Technical Information Center Ser.). 94p. 1978. write for info. DOE.

Rolph, Elizabeth S. Nuclear Power & the Public Safety: A Study in Regulation. LC 78-24795. (Illus.). 1979. 17.95 (ISBN 0-669-02822-3). Lexington Bks.

Russell, C. R. Reactor Safeguards. 1962. 40.00 (ISBN 0-08-009706-5); pap. 15.00 (ISBN 0-08-013610-9). Pergamon.

Safe Operation of Nuclear Power Plants. (Safety Ser.: No. 31). (Orig.). 1969. pap. 11.25 (ISBN 92-0-123169-5, ISP222, IAEA). Unipub.

Safety Functions & Component Classification from BWR, PWR & PTR. (Safety Ser.: No. 50-SG-D1). 55p. 1980. pap. 10.50 (ISBN 92-0-123979-3, IDC 542, IAEA). Unipub.

Shimizu, Akinao & Aoki, Katsutada. Application of Invariant Imbedding to Reactor Physics. (Nuclear Science & Technology Ser). 1972. 34.50 (ISBN 0-12-640150-0). Acad Pr.

Symposium Sponsored by the Healh Physics Society & Reinig, William C. Environmental Surveillance in the Vicinity of Nuclear Facilities: Proceedings. (Illus.). 480p. 1970. pap. 47.50 (ISBN 0-398-01568-6). C C Thomas.

Webb, Richard E. The Accident Hazards of Nuclear Power Plants. LC 75-37173. (Illus.). 1976. pap. 5.95 (ISBN 0-87023-210-X). U of Mass Pr.

Williams, M. M. Nuclear Safety. (Illus.). 1979. pap. 18.50 (ISBN 0-08-024752-0). Pergamon.

NUCLEAR REACTOR FUEL REPROCESSING

see Reactor Fuel Reprocessing

NUCLEAR RESEARCH

Braunbek, Werner. Pursuit of the Atom. 1959. 7.95 (ISBN 0-87523-115-2). Emerson.

Brookhaven National Laboratory. Brookhaven Lectures: Vistas in Research. Incl. Vol. 1. 220p. 1967 (ISBN 0-677-11550-4); Vol. 2. 204p. 1968 (ISBN 0-677-12950-5); Vol. 3. 198p. 1968 (ISBN 0-677-12990-4); Vol. 4. 188p. 1969 (ISBN 0-677-13500-9). 45.25x ea. Gordon.

Chemistry Research & Chemical Techniques Based on Research Reactors. (Technical Reports Ser.: No. 17). (Illus., Orig.). 1963. pap. 15.25 (ISBN 92-0-045063-6, IDC17, IAEA). Unipub.

Crewe, Albert V. & Katz, Joseph J. Nuclear Research U. S. A. Knowledge for the Future. (Illus.). 6.50 (ISBN 0-8446-0564-6). Peter Smith.

Henley, E. J., et al, eds. Advances in Nuclear Science & Technology, Vol. 11. 550p. 1978. 45.00 (ISBN 0-306-40030-8, Plenum Pr). Plenum Pub.

Hodgson, P. E. Growth Points in Nuclear Physics, Vol. 3. (Illus.). 200p. 1981. 21.60 (ISBN 0-08-026485-9); pap. 10.70 (ISBN 0-08-026484-0). Pergamon.

IAEA Laboratory Activities: 5th Report. (Technical Reports Ser.: No. 90). (Illus., Orig.). 1968. pap. 5.50 (ISBN 92-0-175168-0, IDC90, IAEA). Unipub.

IAEA Research Contracts: 10th Annual Report. (Technical Reports Ser.: No. 105). (Orig.). 1970. pap. 16.75 (ISBN 92-0-175170-2, IDC105, IAEA). Unipub.

IAEA Research Contracts: 12th Annual Report. (Technical Reports Ser.: No. 134). 191p. (Orig.). 1972. pap. 16.75 (ISBN 92-0-175072-2, IDC134, IAEA). Unipub.

International School on Electro & Photonuclear Reactions, First Course, Erice, June 2-17, 1976. International School on Electro & Photonuclear Reactions I: Proceedings. Schaerf, C., ed. (Lecture Notes in Physics: Vol. 61). 1977. soft cover 27.50 (ISBN 3-540-08139-9). Springer-Verlag.

--International School on Electro & Photonuclear Reactions II: Proceedings. Schaerf, C., ed. (Lecture Notes in Physics: Vol. 62). 1977. 17.40 (ISBN 0-387-08140-2). Springer-Verlag.

International University Courses on Nuclear Physics, 10th, Schladming, Austria, 1971. Concepts in Hadron Physics: Proceedings. (Acta Physica Austriaca: Suppl. 8). (Illus.). xvi, 424p. 1971. 63.80 (ISBN 0-387-81032-3). Springer-Verlag.

Jackson, J. D., et al, eds. Annual Review of Nuclear & Particle Science, Vol. 31. LC 53-995. Orig. Title: Annual Review of Nuclear Science. (Illus.). 446p. 1981. text ed. 22.50 (ISBN 0-8243-1531-6). Annual Reviews.

MacAvoy, Paul W. Economic Strategy for Developing Nuclear Breeder Reactors. 1969. 22.50x (ISBN 0-262-13054-8). MIT Pr.

Manual on the Operation of Research Reactors. (Technical Reports Ser.: No. 37). 1964. pap. 11.75 (ISBN 92-0-155364-1, IDC37, IAEA). Unipub.

Nuclear Research Index. 5th ed. LC 76-643048. 1975. 185.00x (ISBN 0-8002-1762-4). Intl Pubns Serv.

Schmid, Loren C. Critical Assemblies & Reactor Research. 400p. 1971. 33.00 (ISBN 0-471-76190-7, Pub. by Wiley). Krieger.

Segre, E., et al, eds. Annual Review of Nuclear Science, Vol. 23. LC 53-995. (Illus.). 1973. text ed. 19.50 (ISBN 0-8243-1523-5). Annual Reviews.

Siting of Reactors & Nuclear Research Centres. 1963. 22.75 (ISBN 92-0-020263-2, ISP72, IAEA). Unipub.

NUCLEAR ROCKETS

AGARD-NATO. Nuclear Thermal & Electric Rocket Propulsion. (Agardographs Ser.: No. 101). 1967. 135.25x (ISBN 0-677-11040-5). Gordon.

Bussard, R. W. & De Lauer, R. D. Fundamentals of Nuclear Flight. 1965. text ed. 26.95 (ISBN 0-07-009300-8, C). McGraw.

Loeb, Horst. Nuclear Engineering for Satellites & Rockets. (Illus.). 1970. 13.50x (ISBN 3-521-06053-5). Intl Pubns Serv.

NUCLEAR SALINE WATER CONVERSION PLANTS

Guide to the Costing of Water from Nuclear Desalination Plants. (Technical Reports Ser.: No. 80). (Illus., Orig.). 1967. pap. 7.00 (ISBN 92-0-145267-5, IDC80, IAEA). Unipub.

Guide to the Costing of Water from Nuclear Desalination Plants. (Technical Reports Ser.: No. 151). (Illus.). 79p. (Orig.). 1974. pap. 9.00 (ISBN 92-0-145273-X, IDC151, IAEA). Unipub.

Nuclear Energy for Water Desalination. 1966. pap. 10.25 (ISBN 92-0-145066-4, IDC51, IAEA). Unipub.

NUCLEAR SCATTERING

see Scattering (Physics)

NUCLEAR SHELL THEORY

Bogolyubov, N. N., ed. Structure of Complex Nuclei. LC 69-12510. 217p. 1969. 35.00 (ISBN 0-306-10815-1, Consultants). Plenum Pub.

Brody, T. A. & Moshinsky, M. Tables of Transformation Brackets for Nuclear Shell-Model Calculations. 2nd ed. 1967. 54.50x (ISBN 0-677-01320-5). Gordon.

Brussaard, P. J. & Glaudemans, P. W. Shell Model Applications in Nuclear Spectroscopy. 1977. 78.00 (ISBN 0-444-10895-5, North-Holland). Elsevier.

Craseman, Bernard, ed. Atomic Inner-Shell Processes, 2 vols. Incl. Vol. 1. Production & Decay of Inner-Shell Vacancies. 1975. 78.00 (ISBN 0-12-196901-0); Vol. 2. Experimental Approaches & Applications. 1975. 55.00 (ISBN 0-12-196902-9). Set. 107.50 (ISBN 0-686-67156-2). Acad Pr.

Griffith, John S. Theory of Transition-Metal Ions. 1961. 83.50 (ISBN 0-521-05150-9). Cambridge U Pr.

International Conference on Nuclear Self-Consistent Fields. Proceedings. Ripka, G. & Porneuf, M., eds. LC 75-23198. 1975. 44.00 (ISBN 0-444-10962-5, North-Holland). Elsevier.

Irvine, J. M. Heavy Nuclei, Superheavy Nuclei, & Neutron Stars. (Oxford Studies in Nuclear Physics). (Illus.). 200p. 1975. 34.95x (ISBN 0-19-851510-3). Oxford U Pr.

Lawson, R. D. Theory of the Nuclear Shell Model. (OSNP). (Illus.). 546p. 1980. text ed. 129.00x (ISBN 0-19-851516-2). Oxford U Pr.

Mahaux, C. & Weidenmuller, H. A. Shell-Model Approach to Nuclear Reactions. 1969. 39.00 (ISBN 0-444-10240-X, North-Holland). Elsevier.

Olszak, W., ed. Thin Shell Theory: New Trends & Applications. (CISM Courses & Lectures Ser.: Vol. 240). (Illus.). 301p. 1981. pap. 24.80 (ISBN 0-387-81602-X). Springer-Verlag.

The Structure of Nuclei: Trieste Lectures 1971. (Illus.). 599p. (Orig.). 1973. pap. 40.75 (ISBN 92-0-130072-7, ISP305, IAEA). Unipub.

Towner, I. S. A Shell Model Description of Light Nuclei. (Oxford Studies in Nuclear Physics Ser.). (Illus.). 1977. 74.00x (ISBN 0-19-851508-1). Oxford U Pr.

NUCLEAR SHIELDING

see Shielding (Radiation)

NUCLEAR SHIPS

see Atomic Ships

NUCLEAR SPECTROSCOPY

see also Hyperfine Interactions

Ajzenberg-Selove, Fay, ed. Nuclear Spectroscopy, 2 Pts. (Pure & Applied Physics Ser.: Vol. 9). 1960. 66.50 ea. Pt. A (ISBN 0-12-046850-6). Pt. B (ISBN 0-12-046851-4). Acad Pr.

Axenrod, Theodore & Webb, Graham. Nuclear Magnetic Resonance Spectroscopy of Nuclei Other Than Protons. LC 80-27361. 424p. 1981. Repr. of 1974 ed. lib. bdg. write for info. (ISBN 0-89874-290-0). Krieger.

Bertsch, G. F., ed. Nuclear Spectroscopy: Proceedings. (Lecture Notes in Physics: Vol. 119). 250p. 1980. pap. 19.00 (ISBN 0-387-09970-0). Springer-Verlag.

Boumans, P. W., ed. Atomic Absorption Spectroscopy: Past, Present & Future, Pt. 2: To Commemorate the 25th Anniversary of Alan Walsh's Landmark Paper in Spectrochimica Acta. (Spectrochimica Acta B: Vol. 36, No. 5). iv, 92p. 1981. pap. 16.00 (ISBN 0-08-026287-2). Pergamon.

--Line Coincidence Tables for Inductively Coupled Plasma Atomic Emission Spectrometry, 2 vols. (Illus.). 941p. (Fr.). 1981. 250.00 (ISBN 0-08-026269-4). Pergamon.

--Line Coincidence Tables for Inductively Coupled Plasma Atomic Emission Spectrometry, 2 vols. (Illus.). 941p. (Span.). 1981. 250.00 (ISBN 0-08-026270-8). Pergamon.

Brugel, W., ed. Handbook of NMR Spectral Parameters, 3 vols. casebound set 336.00 (ISBN 0-85501-170-X). Heyden.

Brugel, Werner. Nuclear Magnetic Resonance Spectra & Chemical Structure. 1968. 58.50 (ISBN 0-12-137450-5). Acad Pr.
Brussaard, P. J. & Glaudemans, P. W. Shell Model Applications in Nuclear Spectroscopy. 1977. 78.00 (ISBN 0-444-10895-5, North-Holland). Elsevier.
Caudano, R. & Verbist, J., eds. Electron Spectroscopy. 1136p. 1975. 88.00 (ISBN 0-444-41291-3). Elsevier.
Cerney, Joseph, ed. Nuclear Spectroscopy & Reactions, 4 pts. Set. 229.00 (ISBN 0-685-48719-9); Pt. A 1974. 76.50 (ISBN 0-12-165201-7); Pt. B 1974. 78.00 (ISBN 0-12-165202-5); Pt. C 1974. 78.00 (ISBN 0-12-165203-3); Pt. D 1975. 50.00 (ISBN 0-12-165204-1). Acad Pr.
Christian, Gary D. & Feldman, Fredric J. Atomic Absorption Spectroscopy: Applications in Agriculture, Biology & Medicine. LC 78-23204. 512p. 1979. Repr. of 1970 ed. lib. bdg. 28.50 (ISBN 0-88275-797-0). Krieger.
Emsley, J. W. Progress in NMR Spectroscopy, Vol. 12. 288p. 1980. 87.50 (ISBN 0-08-024874-8). Pergamon.
Emsley, J. W. & Lindon, J. C. NMR Spectroscopy Using Liquid Crystal Solvents. 367p. 1975. text ed. 55.00 (ISBN 0-08-019919-4). Pergamon.
Emsley, J. W. & Sutcliffe, L. H., eds. Progress in NMR Spectroscopy: Vol. 11 Complete. LC 66-17931. 282p. 1978. 87.50 (ISBN 0-08-020325-6). Pergamon.
--Progress in Nuclear Magnetic Resonance Spectroscopy, Vols. 1-10. Incl. Vol. 1. 1962. 76.00 (ISBN 0-08-011322-2); Vol. 2. 1963. 76.00 (ISBN 0-08-012208-6); Vol. 3. 1965. 76.00 (ISBN 0-08-012446-1); Vol. 4. 1966. 76.00 (ISBN 0-08-012717-7); Vol. 5. 1970. 76.00 (ISBN 0-08-012834-3); Vol. 6. 1971; Vol. 7. 1971. 76.00 (ISBN 0-08-016267-3); Vol. 8, 3 pts. 1972. Vol. 8, Complete. 76.00 (ISBN 0-08-017018-8); Pts. 1-3. pap. 15.50 ea.; Pt. 1. pap. -1971 (ISBN 0-08-016662-8); Pt. 2. pap. -1971 (ISBN 0-08-016757-8); Pt. 3. pap. -1972 (ISBN 0-08-016857-4); Vol. 9, 3 pts. Vol. 9, Complete. 76.00 (ISBN 0-08-017704-2); Pts. 1-3. pap. 13.75 ea.; Vol. 10. Pt. 1, 1975. pap. 8.00 (ISBN 0-08-017703-4); Pt. 2, 1976. pap. 14.00 (ISBN 0-08-019463-X); Pts. 3 & 4, 1977. 75.00 (ISBN 0-08-019464-8); One Vol. Ed. (cloth) 76.00 (ISBN 0-08-019466-4). Pergamon.
Emsley, J. W., et al. High Resolution Nuclear Magnetic Resonance Spectroscopy, 2 Vols. 1966. 46.00 (ISBN 0-08-011824-0). Pergamon.
Faraggi, H. & Ricci, R. A. Nuclear Spectroscopy & Nuclear Reactions with Heavy Ions. 1976. 102.50 (ISBN 0-7204-0450-9, North-Holland). Elsevier.
Hamilton, Joseph H. & Manthuruthil, Jose, eds. Radioactivity in Nuclear Spectroscopy, 2 vols. 1972. Vol. 1. 105.75 (ISBN 0-677-12410-4); Vol. 2. 138.00 (ISBN 0-677-12420-1); Set. 214.00 (ISBN 0-677-14220-X). Gordon.
Hamilton, W. D. The Electromagnetic Interaction in Nuclear Spectroscopy. LC 73-75533. 941p. 1975. 127.00 (ISBN 0-444-10519-0, North-Holland). Elsevier.
Hanle, W. & Kleinpoppen, H., eds. Progress in Atomic Spectroscopy: Pts. A & B, 2 vols. (Physics of Atoms & Molecules Ser.). 1978. 49.50 ea. (Plenum Pr); Pt. A, 755p. (ISBN 0-306-31115-1); Pt. B. 855p. (ISBN 0-306-31116-X); 95.00 set (ISBN 0-685-92702-4). Plenum Pub.
International Conference, 10th, Lyon, July 2-6, 1979. Solid State Nuclear Track Detectors: Proceedings. Francois, H., et al, eds. (Illus.). 1082p. 1980. 120.00 (ISBN 0-08-025029-7). Pergamon.
Jackman, L. M. & Sternhell, S. Applications of Nuclear Magnetic Resonance Spectroscopy in Organic Chemistry. 2nd ed. 1969. 50.00 (ISBN 0-08-012542-5). Pergamon.
Kirkbright, G. F., ed. Eighth International Conference on Atomic Spectroscopy. 284p. 1980. 50.50 (ISBN 0-85501-487-3). Heyden.
Levy, George C. & Lichter, Robert L. Nitrogen-Fifteen Nuclear Magnetic Resonance Spectroscopy. LC 78-4016. 1979. 23.50 (ISBN 0-471-02954-8, Pub by Wiley-Interscience). Wiley.
Maeir, Clifford L. The Role of Spectroscopy in the Acceptance of the Internally Structured Atom. Cohen, I. Bernard, ed. LC 80-2093. (Development of Science Ser.). (Illus.). 1981. lib. bdg. 50.00x (ISBN 0-405-13858-X). Arno.
Matthias, E. & Shirley, D. A., eds. Hyperfine Structure & Nuclear Radiations. 1968. 68.50 (ISBN 0-444-10246-9, North-Holland). Elsevier.
Mooney. An Introduction to Nineteen-F Nuclear Magnetic Resonance Spectroscopy. 1970. 35.00 (ISBN 0-85501-008-8). Heyden.
Mooney, E. F., ed. Annual Reports on NMR Spectroscopy. Incl. Vol. 1. 1968. 56.50 (ISBN 0-12-505350-9); Vol. 5B. 1974. 71.50 (ISBN 0-12-505345-2); Vol. 6, 2 pts. 1976-78. Pt. B. 39.00 (ISBN 0-12-505346-0); Pt. C. 103.50 (ISBN 0-12-505347-9); Vol. 7. 1978. 50.00 (ISBN 0-12-505307-X); Vol. 8. 1978. 82.00 (ISBN 0-12-505308-8); Vol. 9. 1978. 66.50 (ISBN 0-12-505309-6). Acad Pr.
Mooney, E. F. & Webb, G. A., eds. Annual Reports on NMR Spectroscopy, Vol. IIA. 1981. 84.00 (ISBN 0-12-505311-8). Acad Pr.
Nuclear Spectroscopy of Fission Products 1979: Grenoble. (Institute of Physics Conference Ser.: No. 51). 1980. 75.00 (ISBN 0-9960033-1-2, Pub. by Inst Physics England). Heyden.
Pecker-Wimel, C. Introduction a la Spectroscopie Des Plamas. (Cours & Documents de Mathematiques & de Physique Ser.). (Orig.). 1967. 34.75x (ISBN 0-677-50130-7). Gordon.
Racah, G., ed. Nuclear Spectroscopy. (Italian Physical Society: Course 15). 1962. 49.50 (ISBN 0-12-368815-9). Acad Pr.
Rybakov, Boris V. & Sidorov, V. A. Fast-Neutron Spectroscopy. LC 60-8723. 121p. 1960. 27.50 (ISBN 0-306-10532-2, Consultants). Plenum Pub.
Schrenk, William G. Analytical Atomic Spectroscopy. (Modern Analytical Chemistry Ser.). (Illus.). 380p. 1975. 37.50 (ISBN 0-306-33902-1, Plenum Pr). Plenum Pub.
Simons, W. W. & Zanger, M. Sadtler Guide to NMR Spectra. 1972. 38.50 (ISBN 0-85501-074-6). Sadtler Res.
--Sadtler Guide to the NMR Spectra of Polymers. 1973. 26.00 (ISBN 0-85501-098-3). Sadtler Res.
Sukhodrev, N. K. Research on Spectroscopy & Luminescence, Part 3: On Excitation Spectra in Spark Discharges. LC 62-12860. (P. N. Lebedev Physics Institute Ser.: Vol. 15). 53p. 1962. 22.50 (ISBN 0-306-17043-4, Consultants). Plenum Pub.
Topical Conference on Problems of Vibrational Nuclei, Sept. 24-27, 1974. Proceedings. Alaga, G., et al, eds. 458p. 1975. 53.75 (ISBN 0-444-10886-6, North-Holland). Elsevier.
Von Goeler, Eberhard & Weinstein, Roy, eds. Experimental Meson Spectroscopy, 1977. LC 77-94049. 456p. 1977. 22.00x (ISBN 0-930350-00-6). NE U Pr.
Welz, Bernhard. Atomic Absorption Spectroscopy. (Illus.). 1976. 40.00 (ISBN 3-527-25680-6). Verlag Chemie.
Wheatley, P. J. Chemical Consequences of Nuclear Spin. 1970. 24.50 (ISBN 0-444-10027-X, North-Holland). Elsevier.

NUCLEAR SPIN

see also Magnetic Resonance; Polarization (Nuclear Physics); Spin-Lattice Relaxation

Carruthers, Peter A. Spin & Isospin in Particle Physics. LC 72-160021. (Illus.). 268p. 1971. 54.50x (ISBN 0-677-02580-7). Gordon.
Conference On Isobaric Spin In Nuclear Physics - Tallahassee - 1966. Isobaric Spin in Nuclear Physics: Proceedings. Fox, John D. & Robson, D., eds. 1966. 55.00 (ISBN 0-12-263850-6). Acad Pr.
Daniels, James M. Oriented Nuclei: Polarized Targets & Beams. (Pure & Applied Physics Ser.: Vol. 20). 1965. 42.50 (ISBN 0-12-202950-X). Acad Pr.
McWeeny, R. Spins in Chemistry. (Current Chemical Concepts Ser). 1970. 27.50 (ISBN 0-12-486750-2). Acad Pr.
Wheatley, P. J. Chemical Consequences of Nuclear Spin. 1970. 24.50 (ISBN 0-444-10027-X, North-Holland). Elsevier.
Wolf, Dieter. Spin Temperature & Nuclear Spin Relaxation in Matter: Basic Principles & Applications. (International Series of Monographs on Physics). (Illus.). 480p. 1979. text ed. 59.00x (ISBN 0-19-851295-3). Oxford U Pr.

NUCLEAR TEST BAN TREATY, 1963

Seaborg, Glenn T. & Loeb, Benjamin S. Kennedy, Krushchev, & the Test Ban. LC 81-3051. (Illus.). 320p. 1981. 16.95 (ISBN 0-520-04332-4). U of Cal Pr.
Stockholm International Peace Research Institute. The Near-Nuclear Countries & the Npt. 150p. 1972. pap. text ed. 4.75x (ISBN 91-85114-14-6). Humanities.
Willrich, Mason. Non-Proliferation Treaty: Framework for Nuclear Arms Control. 1969. 15.00 (ISBN 0-87215-060-7). Michie-Bobbs.

NUCLEAR TRANSFORMATIONS

see Nuclear Reactions

NUCLEAR UNDERGROUND EXPLOSIONS

see Underground Nuclear Explosions

NUCLEAR WARFARE

see Atomic Warfare

NUCLEAR WASTES

see Radioactive Wastes

NUCLEAR WEAPONS

see Atomic Weapons

NUCLEATION

Lewis, B. & Anderson, J. C. Nucleation & Growth of Thin Films. 1979. 81.00 (ISBN 0-12-446680-X). Acad Pr.
Michaels, Alan S., ed. Nucleation Phenomena. LC 66-26717. 1966. 19.50 (ISBN 0-8412-0100-5). Am Chemical.
Zettlemoyer, A. C., ed. Nucleation Phenomena. (Advances in Colloid & Interface Science: Vol. 7). 1977. Repr. 58.75 (ISBN 0-444-41586-6). Elsevier.

NUCLEI, VESTIBULAR

see Vestibular Nuclei

NUCLEIC ACID METABOLISM

Cohn, Waldo E., ed. Progress in Nucleic Acid Research & Molecular Biology, Vol. 23. LC 63-15847. 1980. 40.00 (ISBN 0-12-540023-3); lib ed. 40.00 (ISBN 0-12-540090-X); microfiche ed. 22.00 (ISBN 0-12-540091-8). Acad Pr.
Cowdry, E. V. & Seno, S. Nucleic Acid Metabolism, Cell Differentiation & Cancer Growth. 1968. 75.00 (ISBN 0-08-013252-9). Pergamon.
Hayashi, T., ed. Symposium on Nucleic Acid Metabolism of Placenta & Fetus. (Gynecologic Investigation: Vol. 8, No. 3). (Illus.). 1977. 18.00 (ISBN 3-8055-2771-3). S Karger.
Research Symposium on Complexes of Biologically Active Substances with Nucleic Acids & Their Modes of Action. Proceedings. Hahn, F. E., et al, eds. (Progress in Molecular & Subcellular Biology: Vol. 2). (Illus.). 1971. 39.80 (ISBN 0-387-05321-2). Springer-Verlag.

NUCLEIC ACIDS

see also Nucleoproteins; Nucleotides

Balis, M. E. Antagonists & Nucleic Acids. Neuberger, A. & Tatum, E. L., eds. (Frontiers of Biology Ser.: Vol. 10). 1968. 26.50 (ISBN 0-444-10135-7, North-Holland). Elsevier.
Bogorad, L. & Weil, J. H., eds. Nucleic Acids & Protein Synthesis in Plants. (NATO Advanced Study Institutes Ser., Series A: Life Sciences, Vol. 12). 429p. 1977. 42.50 (ISBN 0-306-35612-0, Plenum Pr). Plenum Pub.
Chargaff, Erwin & Davidson, J. N., eds. The Nucleic Acids: Chemistry & Biology, 3 vols. Vol. 1 1955. 62.00 (ISBN 0-12-169201-9); Vol. 2 1955. 62.00 (ISBN 0-12-169202-7); Vol. 3 1960. 62.00 (ISBN 0-12-169203-5); Set. 148.00 (ISBN 0-685-23118-6). Acad Pr.
Cleveland Symposium on Macromolecules, 1st, Case Western Reserve Univ., Oct. 1976. Proceedings. Walton, A. G., ed. 1977. 53.75 (ISBN 0-444-41561-0). Elsevier.
Cohn, Waldo E., ed. Progress in Nucleic Acid Research & Molecular Biology, Vol. 24. 1980. 32.50 (ISBN 0-12-540024-1); lib. ed. 42.50 (ISBN 0-12-540092-6); microfiche ed. 22.50 (ISBN 0-12-540093-4). Acad Pr.
--Progress in Nucleic Acid Research & Molecular Biology, Vol. 25. (Serial Publication). 1981. 29.50 (ISBN 0-12-540025-X); lib. ed. 38.50 (ISBN 0-12-540094-2); microfiche ed. 20.00 (ISBN 0-12-540095-0). Acad Pr.
--Progress in Nucleic Acid Research & Molecular Biology: DNA: Multiprotein Interactions, Vol. 26. (Serial Publication Ser.). 1981. write for info. (ISBN 0-12-540026-8); lib. ed. (ISBN 0-12-540096-9); microfiche ed. (ISBN 0-12-540097-7). Acad Pr.
Cold Spring Harbor Symposia On Quantitative Biology. Nucleic Acids & Nucleoproteins: Proceedings, Vol. 12. Repr. of 1947 ed. 19.50 (ISBN 0-384-42250-0). Johnson Repr.
Davidson, J. N., et al, eds. Progress in Nucleic Acid Research & Molecular Biology: An International Series. Incl. Vol. 3. 1964. 55.00 (ISBN 0-12-540003-9); Vol. 4. 1965. 55.00 (ISBN 0-12-540004-7); Vol. 5. 1966. 55.00 (ISBN 0-12-540005-5); Vol. 6. 1967. 55.00 (ISBN 0-12-540006-3); Vol. 7. 1967. 55.00 (ISBN 0-12-540007-1); Vol. 8. 1968. 55.00 (ISBN 0-12-540008-X); Vol. 9. 1969. 55.00 (ISBN 0-12-540009-8); Vol. 10. 1970. 47.00 (ISBN 0-12-540010-1); Vol. 11. 1970. 58.50 (ISBN 0-12-540011-X); Vol. 12. 1972. 46.00 (ISBN 0-12-540012-8); Vol. 13. 1973. 51.00 (ISBN 0-12-540013-6); Vol. 20. 1977. 44.50 (ISBN 0-12-540020-9); lib. ed. 63.50 (ISBN 0-12-540084-5); microfiche 31.50 (ISBN 0-12-540085-3); Vol. 21. 1978. 32.00 (ISBN 0-12-540021-7); lib. ed. 40.00 (ISBN 0-12-540086-1); microfiche 24.00 (ISBN 0-12-540087-X); Vol. 22. 1979. 40.00 (ISBN 0-12-540022-5); lib ed. o. s. i. 54.50 (ISBN 0-12-540088-8); microfiche 29.00 (ISBN 0-12-540089-6). Acad Pr.
Dubes, George R. Methods for Transfecting Cells with Nucleic Acids of Animal Viruses: A Review. 1971. 5.50x (ISBN 3-7643-0574-6). Intl Pubns Serv.
Duchesne, J., ed. Physico-Chemical Properties of Nucleic Acids, 3vols. Incl. Vol.1. Electrical,Optical & Magnetic Properties of Nucleic Acids & Components. 48.00 (ISBN 0-12-222901-0); Vol.2. Structural Studies on Nucleic Acids & Other Biopolymers. 63.00 (ISBN 0-12-222902-9); Vol.3. Intra - & Intermolecular Interactions, Radiation Effects in Dnacells & Repair Mechanisms. 35.00 (ISBN 0-12-222903-7). 1973. Acad Pr.
The Eighth Symposium on Nucleic Acids Chemistry: Proceedings. (Nucleic Acids Symposium Ser.: No. 8). 198p. 1980. 20.00 (ISBN 0-904147-28-2). Info Retrieval.
Fasman, Gerald D, ed. Handbook of Biochemistry & Molecular Biology, CRC: Nucleic Acids Section, 2 vols. 3rd ed. LC 75-29514. (Handbook Ser.). 1976. Vol. 1. 79.95 (ISBN 0-87819-506-8); Vol. 2, 923p. 74.95 (ISBN 0-87819-507-6). CRC Pr.
Fraenkel-Conrat, H. & Wagner, R. R., eds. Comprehensive Virology, Vol. 5: Structure & Assembly - Virions, Pseudoyirions, & Intnaviral Nucleic Acids. LC 74-5494. (Illus.). 230p. 1975. 22.50 (ISBN 0-306-35145-5, Plenum Pr). Plenum Pub.
--Comprehensive Virology, Vol. 6: Reproduction - Small RNA Viruses. LC 75-46506. (Illus.). 220p. 1976. 29.50 (ISBN 0-306-35146-3, Plenum Pr). Plenum Pub.
Gould, H. & Matthews, H. R. Separation Methods for Nucleic Acids & Oligonucleotides. (Laboratory Techniques in Biochemistry & Molecular Biology: Vol. 4-2). 1976. 22.00 (ISBN 0-444-10868-8, North-Holland). Elsevier.
Gould, Meredith, et al. Invertebrate Oogenesis, Vol. 2. 300p. 1972. 32.50x (ISBN 0-8422-7030-2). Irvington.
Guschlbauer, W. Nucleic Acid Structure: An Introduction. LC 75-11796. (Heidelberg Science Library: Vol. 21). (Illus.). 180p. 1976. pap. 9.80 (ISBN 0-387-90141-8). Springer-Verlag.
Hall, Ross H. Modified Nucleosides in Nucleic Acids. LC 73-122745. (Molecular Biology Ser). 1971. 27.50x (ISBN 0-231-03018-5). Columbia U Pr.
Hall, Timothy C. & Davies, Jeffrey W. Nucleic Acids in Plants, 2 vols. 1979. Vol. 1, 272p. 69.95 (ISBN 0-8493-5291-6); Vol. 2, 256p. 64.95 (ISBN 0-8493-5292-4). CRC Pr.
Harbers, Eberhard. Introduction to Nucleic Acids: Chemistry, Biochemistry & Functions. (Books in Biochemistry & Biophysics Ser). (Illus.). 1968. 25.50x (ISBN 0-442-15595-6). Van Nos Reinhold.
Holmes, K. C. & Blow, D. M. The Use of X-Ray Diffraction in the Study of Protein & Nucleic Acid Structure. Glick, D., ed. LC 79-20293. 1979. Repr. of 1965 ed. lib. bdg. 9.50 (ISBN 0-89874-046-0). Krieger.
International Symposium in Chemical Synthesis of Nucleic Acids, Egestorf, West Germany, May 1980. Nucleic Acid Synthesis: Applications to Molecular Biology & Genetic Engineering. (Nucleic Acids Symposium Ser.: No. 7). 396p. 1980. 40.00 (ISBN 0-904147-27-4). Info Retrieval.
International Symposium on Molecular Biology, 4th, 1970. Biological Effects of Polynucleotides: Proceedings. Beers, R. F. & Braun, W., eds. LC 74-143500. (Illus.). 1971. 44.30 (ISBN 0-387-05345-X). Springer-Verlag.
Kersten, H. & Kersten, W. Inhibitors of Nucleic Acid Synthesis: Biophysical & Biochemical Aspects. (Molecular Biology Biochemistry & Biophysics Ser.: Vol. 18). (Illus.). ix, 184p. 1974. 35.40 (ISBN 0-387-06825-2). Springer-Verlag.
King, Robert, et al. Invertebrate Oogenesis, Vol. 1: Interactions Between Oocytes & Their Accessory Cells. 277p. 1972. text ed. 32.50x (ISBN 0-8422-7015-9). Irvington.
Kochetkov, N. K. & Budovsky, E. I., eds. Organic Chemistry of Nucleic Acids, Pts. A & B. LC 77-178777. 1972. Pt. A. 240pp. 37.50 (ISBN 0-306-37531-1, Plenum Pr); Pt. B. 330pp. 37.50 (ISBN 0-306-37532-X). Plenum Pub.
Konev, Sergei V. Fluorescence & Phosphorescence of Proteins & Nucleic Acids. LC 67-10309. 204p. 1967. 32.50 (ISBN 0-306-30271-3, Plenum Pr). Plenum Pub.
Laskin, Allen I. & Last, Jerold A., eds. Nucleic Acid Biosynthesis. (Methods in Molecular Biology Ser.: Vol. 4). 288p. 1973. 32.50 (ISBN 0-8247-6008-5). Dekker.
Legogki, A. B., ed. Translation of Natural & Synthetic Polynucleotides: Proceedings of the Meeting Held in Blazejewko, Pozan, May, 1977. 1978. pap. 97.00 (ISBN 0-444-80045-X, Biomedical Pr). Elsevier.
McLaren, A. D. & Shugar, D. Photochemistry of Proteins & Nucleic Acids. 1964. 46.00 (ISBN 0-08-010139-9); pap. text ed. 22.00 (ISBN 0-08-013569-2). Pergamon.
Mandeles, Stanley. Nucleic Acid Sequence Analysis. LC 79-186389. (Molecular Biology Ser). 282p. 1972. 20.00x (ISBN 0-231-03130-0). Columbia U Pr.
Moyer, Mary Pat & Moyer, Rex C. Membrane-Associated Nucleic Acids. (Vol. 12). (Illus., LC 76-052699). 1978. lib. bdg. 22.50 (ISBN 0-8240-9863-3, Garland STPM Pr). Garland Pub.
Neidle, Stephen. Topics in Nucleic Acid Structure. LC 81-1316. 230p. 1981. 59.95 (ISBN 0-470-27161-2). Halsted Pr.

Research Symposium on Complexes of Biologically Active Substances with Nucleic Acids & Their Modes of Action. Proceedings. Hahn, F. E., et al, eds. (Progress in Molecular & Subcellular Biology: Vol. 2). (Illus.). 1971. 39.80 (ISBN 0-387-05321-2). Springer-Verlag.
Ribbons, D. W., et al. Nucleic Acid-Protein Interactions & Nucleic Acid Synthesis in Viral Infection. LC 79-161446. (Miami Winter Symposia: No. 2). 508p. 1971. 39.00 (ISBN 0-444-10084-9, North-Holland). Elsevier.
Sarma, Ramaswamy H. Nucleic Acid Geometry & Dynamics. LC 80-10620. (Illus.). 424p. 1980. 55.00 (ISBN 0-08-024631-1); pap. 24.50 (ISBN 0-08-024630-3). Pergamon.
Science Press, ed. Nucleic Acids & Proteins: The Proceedings of a Symposium on Nucleic Acids & Proteins. 1981. text ed. 42.00 (ISBN 0-442-20072-2). Van Nos Reinhold.
Smellie & Adams. Biochemistry of Nucleic Acids. 9th ed. 38.00x (ISBN 0-412-22680-4, Pub. by Chapman & Hall); pap. 19.95x (ISBN 0-412-22690-1). Methuen Inc.
Spencer, John H. The Physics & Chemistry of DNA & RNA. LC 79-183458. (Science Library Ser). (Illus.). 143p. 1972. 12.50 (ISBN 0-7216-8513-7). HR&W.
Spiro, Thomas G., ed. Nucleic Acid-Metal Ion Interactions. LC 79-13808. (Metals Ions in Biology Ser.: Vol. 1). 1980. 30.50 (ISBN 0-471-04399-0, Pub. by Wiley-Interscience). Wiley.
Steiner, Robert F. & Weinryb, Ira, eds. Excited States of Proteins & Nucleic Acids. LC 75-138521. 478p. 1971. 49.50 (ISBN 0-306-30509-7, Plenum Pr). Plenum Pub.
Sundaralingham, M. & Rao, S. R., eds. Structure & Conformation of Nucleic Acids & Protein-Nuclein Acid Interactions. (Illus.). 1975. 49.50 (ISBN 0-8391-0764-1). Univ Park.
Symposium on Nucleic Acids, Chemistry, 4th, Kyoto, 1976. Proceedings. (Nucleic Acids Symposium Ser.: No. 2). 156p. 16.00 (ISBN 0-686-70819-9). Info Retrieval.
Symposium on Nucleic Acids Chemistry, 5th, Mishima, Japan, 1977. Proceedings. (Nucleic Acids Symposium Ser.: No. 3). 190p. 12.00 (ISBN 0-686-70820-2). Info Retrieval.
Symposium on Nucleic Acids Chemistry, 6th, Nagoya, Japan, 1978. Proceedings. (No. 5). 227p. 15.00 (ISBN 0-686-70821-0). Info Retrieval.
Symposium on Nucleic Acids Chemistry, 7th, Okayama, Japan, 1979. Proceedings. (Nucleic Acids Symposium Ser.: No. 6). 250p. 16.00 (ISBN 0-686-70822-9). Info Retrieval.
Symposium on the Chemistry of Nucleic Acids Components, 3rd, Czechoslovakia, 1975. Proceedings. (Nucleic Acids Symposium Ser.: No. 1). 183p. 15.00 (ISBN 0-686-70817-2). Info Retrieval.
Townsend, Leroy B. & Tipson, R. Stuart, eds. Nucleic Acid Chemistry: Improved & New Synthetic Procedures, Methods & Techniques, 2 pts. LC 77-22816. 1978. Set. 112.00 (ISBN 0-471-04738-4, Pub. by Wiley-Interscience); Pt. I. 52.50 (ISBN 0-471-88090-6); Pt. II. 55.00 (ISBN 0-471-04680-9). Wiley.
Ts'o. Basic Principles of Nucleic Chemistry. 1974. Vol. 1. 63.50, subscription 51.50 (ISBN 0-12-701901-4); Vol. 2, 1974. 60.00, subscription 48.50 (ISBN 0-12-701902-2). Acad Pr.
Ursprung, H., ed. Nucleic Acid Hybridization in the Study of Cell Differentiation. LC 70-188705. (Results & Problems in Cell Differentiation: Vol. 3). (Illus.). 120p. 1972. 19.20 (ISBN 0-387-05742-0). Springer-Verlag.
Vogel, H. J., ed. Nucleic Acid-Protein Recognition. 1977. 50.00 (ISBN 0-12-722560-9). Acad Pr.
Wang, Shih Y., ed. Photochemistry & Photobiology of Nucleic Acids, 2 vols. 1976. Vol. 1. 83.00 (ISBN 0-12-734601-5); Vol. 2. 70.50 (ISBN 0-12-734602-3); Set. 122.00 (ISBN 0-686-77181-8). Acad Pr.
Zorback, W. Werner & Tipson, R. Stuart, eds. Synthetic Procedures in Nucleic Acid Chemistry: Vol. 1. 570p. (Orig.). 1968. 28.25 (ISBN 0-470-98415-5). Krieger.
--Synthetic Procedures in Nucleic Acid Chemistry: Vol. 2. 686p. (Orig.). 1973. 54.25 (ISBN 0-471-98418-3). Krieger.

NUCLEONS
see Particles (Nuclear Physics)

NUCLEOPROTEINS
Busch, Harris. Histones & Other Nuclear Proteins. 1965. 43.00 (ISBN 0-12-147656-1). Acad Pr.

NUCLEOSIDES
Bloch, Alexander, ed. Chemistry, Biology, & Clinical Uses of Nucleoside Analogs, Vol. 255. (Annals of the New York Academy of Sciences). 610p. 1975. 69.00x (ISBN 0-89072-009-6). NY Acad Sci.
Hall, Ross H. Modified Nucleosides in Nucleic Acids. LC 73-122745. (Molecular Biology Ser). 1971. 27.50x (ISBN 0-231-03018-5). Columbia U Pr.
Harmon, Robert E., ed. Chemistry & Biology of Nucleosides & Nucleotides. 1978. 32.50 (ISBN 0-12-326140-6). Acad Pr.
Huang, C. C., et al. Molecular Studies on Halogenated Deoxynucleosides. 256p. 1972. text ed. 34.50x (ISBN 0-8422-7013-2). Irvington.
Suhadolnik, R. J. Nucleosides As Biological Probes. 346p. 1979. 53.50 (ISBN 0-471-05317-1). Wiley.
Suhadolnk, Robert J. Nucleoside Antibiotics. 1970. 35.00 (ISBN 0-471-83543-9, Pub. by Wiley). Krieger.
Tattersall, M. H. & Fox, R. M., eds. Nucleosides in Cancer Treatment: Rational Approaches to Antimetabolite Selectivity & Modulatiob. (Ludwig Symposia Ser.: Vol. 1). 1981. 26.00 (ISBN 0-12-683820-8). Acad Pr.
Walker, R. T., et al, eds. Nucleoside Analogues: Chemistry, Biology, & Medical Applications. LC 79-19432. (NATO Advanced Study Institutes, Ser. A, Life Sciences: Vol. 26). 468p. 1979. 39.50 (ISBN 0-306-40302-1, Plenum Pr). Plenum Pub.

NUCLEOTIDES
see also Nucleosides
Alfred Benzon Symposium - 1st. Role of Nucleotides for the Function & Conformation of Enzymes. Kalckar, H. M., et al, eds. 1970. 43.00 (ISBN 0-12-394550-X). Acad Pr.
Brooker, et al, eds. Current Methodology. LC 78-55806. (Advances in Cyclic Nucleotide Research Ser.: Vol. 10). 271p. 1979. 28.00 (ISBN 0-89004-265-9). Raven.
Chasin, Mark, ed. Methods in Cyclic Nucleotide Research. (Methods in Molecular Biology Ser: Vol. 3). 336p. 1972. 39.50 (ISBN 0-8247-6004-2). Dekker.
Cramer, H. & Schultz, J., eds. Cyclic Nucleotides: Mechanisms of Action. LC 76-45361. 1977. 67.50 (ISBN 0-471-99456-1, Pub. by Wiley-Interscience). Wiley.
Daly, John. Cyclic Nucleotides in the Nervous System. LC 76-62999. (Illus.). 401p. 1977. 39.50 (ISBN 0-306-30971-8, Plenum Pr). Plenum Pub.
Dumont, Jacques E., et al, eds. Fourth International Conference on Cyclic Nucleotides, Brussels, Belgium: Proceedings. (Advances in Cyclic Nucleotide Research: Vol. 14). 760p. 1981. text ed. 79.00 (ISBN 0-89004-546-1). Raven.
Dumont, Jaques E. & Greengard, Paul, eds. Fourth International Conference on Cyclic Nucleotides, Vol. 14. (Advances in Cyclic Nucleotide Research Ser.). 683p. 1981. 75.00 (ISBN 0-89004-546-1). Raven.
Folco, G. & Paoletti, R., eds. Molecular Biology & Pharmacology of Cyclic Nucleotides: Proceedings of the NATO Advanced Study Institute on Cyclic Nucleotides Held in Tremezzo, Italy, September, 1977, Vol. 1. (Symposia of the Giovanni Lorenzini Foundation). 1978. 49.75 (ISBN 0-444-80041-7, Biomedical Pr). Elsevier.
--Molecular Biology & Pharmacology of Cyclic Nucleotides: Proceedings of the NATO Advanced Study Institute on Cyclic Nucleotides Held in Tremezzo, Italy, September, 1977, Vol. 1. (Symposia of the Giovanni Lorenzini Foundation). 1978. 49.75 (ISBN 0-444-80041-7, Biomedical Pr). Elsevier.
Frunder, H., ed. Effects & Metabolism of Insulin & Cyclic Nucleotides. (Illus.). 1978. stitched 22.00 (ISBN 0-685-87201-7). Adler.
Greengard, P. & Robison, G. A., eds. Advances in Cyclic Nucleotide Research, Vol. 6. LC 71-181305. 368p. 1975. 34.50 (ISBN 0-89004-042-7). Raven.
Greengard, Paul. Cyclic Nucleotides, Phosphorylated Proteins, & Neuronal Function. LC 78-66349. (Distinguished Lecture Series of the Society of General Physiologists). 302p. 1978. 15.00 (ISBN 0-89004-281-0). Raven.
Greengard, Paul & Robison, Alan, eds. Advances in Cyclic Nucleotide Research, Vol. 13. 352p. 1980. text ed. 38.00 (ISBN 0-89004-471-6). Raven.
Greengard, Paul & Robison, G. Alan, eds. Advances in Cyclic Nucleotide Research, Vol. 4. LC 71-181305. 498p. 1974. 39.00 (ISBN 0-911216-76-6). Raven.
--Advances in Cyclic Nucleotide Research, Vol. 7. LC 71-181305. 302p. 1976. 34.50 (ISBN 0-89004-107-5). Raven.
--Advances in Cyclic Nucleotide Research, Vol. 8. LC 71-181305. 302p. 1977. 43.50 (ISBN 0-89004-169-5). Raven.
--Advances in Cyclic Nucleotide Research, Vol. 11. LC 71-181305. 1979. text ed. 39.00 (ISBN 0-89004-363-9). Raven.
Hamet, Pavel & Sands, Howard, eds. Pathophysiological Aspects of Cyclic Nucleotides, Vol. 12. (Advances in Cyclic Nucleotide Research). 470p. 1980. text ed. 48.50 (ISBN 0-89004-454-6). Raven.
Harmon, Robert E., ed. Chemistry & Biology of Nucleosides & Nucleotides. 1978. 32.50 (ISBN 0-12-326140-6). Acad Pr.
Henderson, J. Frank & Paterson, A. R. Nucleotide Metabolism. 1973. 38.50 (ISBN 0-12-340550-5). Acad Pr.
International Conference on Cyclic Amp, 2nd, July, 1974. Advances in Cyclic Nucleotide Research: Proceedings. Drummond, G. I., et al, eds. LC 74-24679. (Advances in Cyclic Nucleotide Research Ser.: Vol. 5). 886p. 1975. 67.00 (ISBN 0-89004-021-4). Raven.
International Conference on Cyclic Nucleotide, 3rd, New Orleans, la., July 1977. Advances in Cyclic Nucleotide Research: Proceedings, Vol. 9. George, William J. & Ignarro, Louis, eds. LC 77-84555. 831p. 1978. 72.50 (ISBN 0-89004-240-3). Raven.
Janik, Borek. Physicochemical Characteristics of Oligonucleotides & Polynucleotides. LC 70-165692. 213p. 1971. 24.50 (ISBN 0-306-65155-6). IFI Plenum.
Krause, E. G., et al, eds. Cyclic Nucleotides & Protein Phosphorylation in Cell Regulation: Proceedings of the 12th FEBS Meeting, Dresden, 1978. (Federation of European Biochemical Society. Symposia: Vol. 54). (Illus.). 1979. text ed. 60.00 (ISBN 0-08-023178-0). Pergamon.
Legogki, A. B., ed. Translation of Natural & Synthetic Polynucleotides: Proceedings of the Meeting Held in Blazejewko, Pozan, May, 1977. 1978. pap. 97.00 (ISBN 0-444-80045-X, Biomedical Pr). Elsevier.
Metrology of Radionuclides. 1960. 16.25 (ISBN 92-0-030060-X, ISP6, IAEA). Unipub.
Palmer, Gene C., ed. Neuropharmacology of Cyclic Nucleotides: Role of Camp in Affective Disorders, Epilepsy & Modified Behavioral States. LC 78-23490. (Illus.). 316p. 1979. text ed. 19.50 (ISBN 0-8067-1521-9). Urban & S.
Pettit, George R. Synthetic Nucleotides, Vol. 1. 1971. 25.50x (ISBN 0-442-26532-8). Van Nos Reinhold.
Scheit, Karl H. Nucleotide Analogs: Synthesis & Biological Function. LC 79-25445. 1980. 35.50 (ISBN 0-471-04854-2, Pub. by Wiley-Interscience). Wiley.
Sund, Horst, ed. Pyridine Nucleotide - Dependent Dehydrogenases. 513p. 1977. text ed. 97.00x (ISBN 3-11007-091-X). De Gruyter.
Weiss, Benjamin, ed. Cyclic Nucleotides in Disease. (Illus.). 400p. 1975. 39.50 (ISBN 0-8391-0765-X). Univ Park.

NUCLEUS (CELLS)
see Cell Nuclei; Cells

NUCLEUS OF THE ATOM
see Nuclear Physics

NUDE IN ART
see also Anatomy, Artistic; Art and Morals; Figure Drawing; Figure Painting; Human Figure in Art; Photography of the Nude
Archer, John F. Diana. (Illus.). 1978. ltd. 100.00 (ISBN 0-915718-04-9). Atavistic Pr.
--Susohn: A Personal Journey. LC 75-40290. (Illus.). 1976. ltd. 175.00 (ISBN 0-915718-01-4). Atavistic Pr.
Clark, Kenneth. Nude: A Study of Ideal Form. (Illus.). pap. 3.50 (ISBN 0-385-09388-8, A168, Anch). Doubleday.
Clark, Kenneth M. The Nude: A Study in Ideal Form. (Bollingen Series, No. 35: A. W. Mellon Lectures in the Fine Arts, Vol. 2). (Illus.). 458p. 1972. 50.00 (ISBN 0-691-09792-5); pap. 14.95 (ISBN 0-691-01788-3). Princeton U Pr.
Dean, Roy. Roy Dean Nudes. (Illus.). 1977. 10.00 (ISBN 0-685-82030-0). Rho-Delta Pr.
--A World of Nudes. (Illus.). 1975. 7.95 (ISBN 0-685-53563-0). Rho-Delta Pr.
Jacobs, Michael. Nude Painting. LC 78-25561. (The Mayflower Gallery Ser.). (Illus.). 1979. 12.50 (ISBN 0-8317-6465-1, Mayflower Bks); pap. 6.95 (ISBN 0-8317-6466-X). Smith Pubs.
Lange, E., et al. Shameless Nude. (Illus.). 12.50 (ISBN 0-910550-14-X). Elysium.
Machotka, Pavel. The Nude: Perception & Personality. LC 78-8515. 322p. 1979. 24.50 (ISBN 0-470-26426-8). Halsted Pr.
Parramon, J. M., ed. Painting the Nude. LC 77-361625. (Illus., Orig.). 1976. pap. 10.50x (ISBN 0-85242-449-3). Intl Pubns Serv.
Reid, Charles. Figure Painting in Watercolor. (Illus.). 176p. 1972. 19.95 (ISBN 0-8230-1710-9). Watson-Guptill.
Ruth, Jan De. Painting the Nude. (Illus.). 198p. 1976. pap. text ed. 9.95 (ISBN 0-8230-3726-6). Watson-Guptill.
Sheppard, Joseph. Drawing the Female Figure. (Illus.). 160p. 1975. 16.50 (ISBN 0-8230-1370-7). Watson-Guptill.
--Drawing the Male Figure. (Illus., Orig.). 1976. 16.50 (ISBN 0-8230-1405-3). Watson-Guptill.
Sullivan, Jeanne. Photographing the Nude. LC 77-75. (Illus.). 1977. 6.98 (ISBN 0-916800-11-3). Harbor Hse Bk.
Walters, Margaret. The Nude Male: A New Perspective. LC 77-20967. (Illus.). 1978. 12.95 (ISBN 0-448-23168-9). Paddington.

NUDISM
Douglas, Jack D., et al. The Nude Beach. LC 77-22287. (Sociological Observations: Vol. 1). 244p. 1977. 20.00 (ISBN 0-8039-0813-X); pap. 9.95 (ISBN 0-8039-0814-8). Sage.
Ilfeld, Fred, Jr. & Lauer, Roger. Social Nudism in America. 1964. pap. 2.95 (ISBN 0-8084-0281-1, B28). Coll & U Pr.
Lange, June. Wonderful Webbers. (Illus.). 1967. 12.95 (ISBN 0-910550-19-0). Elysium.
Merrill, Frances & Merrill, Mason. Among the Nudists. LC 72-9664. Repr. of 1931 ed. 16.00 (ISBN 0-404-57475-0). AMS Pr.
--Nudism Comes to America. LC 72-9773. Repr. of 1932 ed. 24.50 (ISBN 0-404-57476-9). AMS Pr.
Minkkinen, Arno R., ed. New American Nudes: Recent Trends & Attitudes. LC 81-80057. (Illus.). 1981. 19.95 (ISBN 0-87100-178-0). Morgan.
Reese, Ray. How Many Things Can You Do in the Nude? 256p. Date not set. pap. 9.95 (ISBN 0-686-30964-2). Everest Hse.
Rudofsky, Bernard. The Unfashionable Human Body. LC 74-160871. 288p. 1974. pap. 5.95 (ISBN 0-385-07818-8, Anch). Doubleday.
Smith, Dennis C. The Naked Child: The Long Range Effects of Family & Social Nudity. LC 80-69234. (Illus.). 180p. 1981. perfect bdg. 7.95 (ISBN 0-86548-056-7). Century Twenty One.

NUER (AFRICAN TRIBE)
Crazzolara, J. P. Zur Gesellschaft & Religion Der Nueer. 1953. 38.50 (ISBN 0-384-10150-X). Johnson Repr.
Evans-Pritchard, Edward E. Kinship & Marriage Among the Nuer. (Illus.). 1951. 24.00x (ISBN 0-19-823104-0). Oxford U Pr.
--Nuer: A Description of the Modes of Livelihood & Political Institutions of a Nilotic People. (Illus.). 1968. 24.00x (ISBN 0-19-823105-9); pap. 4.95x (ISBN 0-19-500322-5). Oxford U Pr.
--Nuer Religion. 348p. 1956. pap. 5.95x (ISBN 0-19-874003-4). Oxford U Pr.
Howell, Paul P. Manual of Nuer Law: Being an Account of Customary Law, Its Evolution & Development in the Courts Established by the Sudan Government. LC 73-106840. (Illus.). Repr. of 1954 ed. 15.00x (ISBN 0-8371-3462-5, Pub. by Negro U Pr). Greenwood.
Huffman, Ray. Nuer Customs & Folklore. (Illus.). 108p. 1970. Repr. of 1931 ed. 24.00x (ISBN 0-7146-2689-9, F Cass Co). Biblio Dist.

NUER LANGUAGE
Huffman, Ray. Nuer English Dictionary. 16.00 (ISBN 0-87559-060-8). Shalom.

NUEVA VIZCAYA, MEXICO
Griffen, William B. Culture Change & Shifting Populations in Central Northern Mexico. LC 69-16327. (Anthropological Papers, No. 13). 1969. pap. 5.95x (ISBN 0-8165-0140-8). U of Ariz Pr.
Mecham, John L. Francisco De Ibarra & Nueva Vizcaya. LC 68-23315. (Illus.). 1968. Repr. of 1927 ed. lib. bdg. 17.50x (ISBN 0-8371-0168-9, MEFI). Greenwood.

NUISANCES
see also Odors
A Briefe Declaration for What Manner of Speciall Nusance Man May Have His Remedy by Assise. LC 76-38169. (English Experience Ser.: No. 446). 1972. Repr. of 1636 ed. 7.00 (ISBN 90-221-0446-X). Walter J Johnson.
Tyrell, R. Emmett, Jr. Public Nuisances. LC 78-19940. 1979. 11.95 (ISBN 0-465-06772-7). Basic.

NULLIFICATION
see also Kentucky and Virginia Resolutions of 1798; Secession; State Rights
Bancroft, Frederic. Calhoun & the South Carolina Nullification Movement. 1966. 7.00 (ISBN 0-8446-1052-6). Peter Smith.
Boucher, Chauncey S. Nullification Controversy in South Carolina. LC 68-15103. (Illus.). 1968. Repr. of 1916 ed. 10.00 (ISBN 0-8462-1226-9). Russell.
Freehling, William. Prelude to Civil War: The Nullification Controversy in South Carolina, 1816-1836. (Illus.). 1968. pap. 5.95x (ISBN 0-06-131359-9, TB1359, Torch). Har-Row.
Houston, David F. Critical Study of Nullification in South Carolina. LC 66-27104. 1967. Repr. of 1896 ed. 6.50 (ISBN 0-8462-0991-8). Russell.
--A Critical Study of Nullification in South Carolina. 8.50 (ISBN 0-8446-1244-8). Peter Smith.
State Papers on Nullification. LC 69-16649. (American Constitutional & Legal History Ser). 1970. Repr. of 1834 ed. lib. bdg. 39.50 (ISBN 0-306-71126-5). Da Capo.

NULLITY
see also Sanctions (Law)

NULLITY OF MARRIAGE
see Marriage–Annulment

NUMBER ABILITY
see Mathematical Ability

NUMBER CONCEPT
see also Numeration

Carle, Eric. My Very First Book of Numbers. LC 72-83777. (Illus.). 10p. (ps-2). 1974. 3.95 (ISBN 0-690-57366-9, TYC-J). Har-Row.
Charosh, Mannis. Number Ideas Through Pictures. LC 73-4370. (Young Math Ser.). (Illus.). 40p. (gr. 1-5). 1974. PLB 8.79 (ISBN 0-690-00156-8, TYC-J). Har-Row.
Concepto De Numero. (Serie De Matematica: No. 7). (Span.). 1968. pap. 1.25 (ISBN 0-8270-6250-8). OAS.
Coutourat, Louis. De L'infini Mathematique. LC 68-56776. (Research & Source Works Ser.: No. 262). (Fr). 1969. Repr. of 1896 ed. 35.50 (ISBN 0-8337-0706-X). B Franklin.
Dantzig, Tobias. Number: The Language of Science. 4th ed. (Illus.). 1967. pap. text ed. 8.95 (ISBN 0-02-906990-4). Free Pr.
Dawson, Dan T. & Mellott, M. Numbers for You & Me. (gr. k-1). pap. text ed. 4.80 (ISBN 0-13-625392-X); teachers' manual o.p. 1.95 (ISBN 0-685-04689-3, 62654-9). P-H.
Drob, Ralph E. Number Mastery. Smith, Donald E., ed. (Michigan Tracking Ser.). 1974. pap. text ed. 1.95x (ISBN 0-914004-46-8). Ulrich.
Frege, Gottlob. Foundations of Arithmetic: A Logico-Mathematical Enquiry into the Concept of Numbers. Austin, J. L., tr. LC 68-8996. (Eng. & Ger.). 1968. 16.95x (ISBN 0-8101-0023-1). Northwestern U Pr.
Kohnstamm, Geldolph A. Piaget's Analysis of Class Inclusion: Right or Wrong. (Psychological Studies, Ser. Minor: No. 1). (Orig.). 1967. pap. text ed. 14.00x (ISBN 0-686-22452-3). Mouton.
Luce, Marnie. One Is Unique. LC 68-56701. (Math Concept Bks). (gr. 3-6). 1969. PLB 3.95 (ISBN 0-8225-0572-X). Lerner Pubns.
Moos. Number Systems: One Plus One Equals Ten. 1970. 17.50 (ISBN 0-85501-240-4). Heyden.
Piaget, Jean. Child's Conception of Number. 1965. pap. 4.25 (ISBN 0-393-00324-8, Norton Lib). Norton.
Smeltzer, Donald. Man & Number. (Illus.). (gr. 9 up). 1958. 7.95 (ISBN 0-87523-107-1). Emerson.
Sondheimer, E. & Rogerson, A. Numbers & Infinity: An Historical Account of Mathematical Concepts. LC 81-7660. 150p. Date not set. price not set (ISBN 0-521-24091-3); pap. price not set (ISBN 0-521-28433-3). Cambridge U Pr.
Waismann, Friedrich. Introduction to Mathematical Thinking. Benac, T., tr. 1951. 12.00 (ISBN 0-8044-4984-8). Ungar.

NUMBER CONCEPT- JUVENILE LITERATURE

Adler, Irving. Magic House of Numbers. LC 73-19471. (Illus.). 144p. (gr. 5-9). 1974. PLB 8.79 (ISBN 0-381-99986-6, JD-J). Har-Row.
Allen, Robert. One- Two-Three a First Counting Book. (Illus.). 72p. (ps-1). 1981. 3.95 (ISBN 0-448-41055-9). G&D.
Cartwright, Mary. One Two Three. (Illus.). 40p. (ps-1). 1981. 5.95 (ISBN 0-528-82406-6). Rand.
Fujikawa, Gyo. One, Two, Three, A Counting Book. (Tiny Board Bks.). (Illus.). 14p. (ps). 1981. 1.95 (ISBN 0-448-15085-9). G&D.
Gelman, Rochel & Gallistel, C. R. The Child's Understanding of Number. LC 78-5124. (Illus.). 1978. 15.00x (ISBN 0-674-11636-4). Harvard U Pr.
Gray, Les. Happy Helper One-Two-Three. (Illus.). (ps-2). 1971. PLB 5.38 (ISBN 0-307-68926-3, Golden Pr). Western Pub.
Korr, David. The Day the Count Stopped Counting. (Kid's Paperback Ser.). (Illus.). (ps-3). 1977. PLB 7.62 (ISBN 0-307-62358-0, Golden Pr). Western Pub.
Kunhardt, Edith. Ned's Number Book. (First Little Golden Bks.). (Illus.). (ps). 1981. 0.69 (ISBN 0-307-10103-7, Golden Pr); PLB 4.77 (ISBN 0-307-68103-3). Western Pub.
Luce, Marnie. Zero Is Something. LC 68-28034. (Math Concept Bks). (Illus.). (gr. 3-6). 1969. PLB 3.95 (ISBN 0-8225-0571-1). Lerner Pubns.
Manley, Deborah. Animals One to Ten. LC 78-26648. (Ready, Set, Look Ser.). (Illus.). (gr. k-3). 1979. PLB 10.65 (ISBN 0-8172-1302-3). Raintree Pubs.
My First Book of Numbers. (Puppet Boards Books Ser.). (ps-2). bds. 1.75 (ISBN 0-448-02679-1). G&D.
Newman, Georgiana C. & Dawson, Mildred A. Baker's Dozen. rev. ed. (Cornerstone Ser.). (gr. 2-3). 1978. pap. text ed. 4.52 (ISBN 0-201-41024-9, Sch Div); tchr's ed. 5.56 (ISBN 0-201-41025-7). A-W.
Porter Productions, ed. One Nose, Ten Toes. (Stretch Bks.). (Illus.). 16p. (ps). 1981. 3.50 (ISBN 0-686-73576-5). G&D.
Robinson, Shari. A First Number Book. LC 80-83587. (Illus.). 96p. (gr. k-4). 1981. PLB 11.85 (ISBN 0-448-13922-7); pap. 3.95 (ISBN 0-448-47335-6). Platt.
Sentlowitz, Michael & Thelen, James. Baseball: A Game of Numbers. (gr. 5-9). 1977. pap. text ed. 6.64 (ISBN 0-201-06798-6, Sch Div); tchr's man. 2.60 (ISBN 0-201-06816-8). A-W.
Sitomer, Harry & Sitomer, Mindel. Zero Is Not Nothing. LC 77-11562. (A Young Math Book). (gr. 1-3). 1978. PLB 8.79 (ISBN 0-690-03829-1, TYC-J). Har-Row.
Stiles, Norman. The Count's Number Parade. (Illus.). 24p. (ps-4). 1977. PLB 5.38 (ISBN 0-307-68876-3, Golden Pr). Western Pub.
Tallarico, Tony. The Numbers Flip Book Game. (Flip Bks.). (Illus.). 9p. (ps). 3.50 (ISBN 0-448-11498-4). G&D.
University of Oregon. Number Sense & Arithmetic Skills. 1977. 36.95 (ISBN 0-88488-089-3). Creative Pubns.
Wehrli, Kitty. Numbers & Numerals. (Michigan Arithmetic Program). (ps-2). 1976. 1.00x (ISBN 0-89039-199-8); wkbk. 5.00 (ISBN 0-89039-102-5). Ann Arbor Pubs.
Winnie-the-Pooh Do-It-Yourself Counting Book. (Golden Play & Learn Bk.). 14p. (ps). Date not set. pap. 2.95 (ISBN 0-307-10727-2, Golden Pr). Western Pub.
Youldon, Gillian. Numbers. (Picture Play Ser.). (Illus.). (ps-2). 1979. 2.95 (ISBN 0-531-02388-5); PLB 5.90 s&l (ISBN 0-531-00440-6). Watts.

NUMBER GAMES
see Arithmetic-Study and Teaching; Mathematical Recreations

NUMBER RHYMES
see Counting-Out Rhymes

NUMBER STUDY
see Arithmetic-Study and Teaching

NUMBER SYMBOLISM
see Symbolism of Numbers

NUMBER THEORY
see Numbers, Theory of

NUMBERS, COMPLEX
see also Algebra, Universal; Ausdehnungslehre; Functions; Numbers, Real; Quaternions; Vector Analysis

Beardon, A. F. Complex Analysis: The Argument Principle in Analysis & Topology. LC 78-8540. 239p. 1979. 48.95 (ISBN 0-471-99671-8, Pub. by Wiley-Interscience). Wiley.
Carico, Charles. Complex Numbers: Polynomial Functions. 1974. 4.95x (ISBN 0-534-00329-X). Wadsworth Pub.
Chillingworth, H. R. Complex Variables. LC 72-86178. 280p. 1973. text ed. 32.00 (ISBN 0-08-016938-4); pap. text ed. 18.75 (ISBN 0-08-016939-2). Pergamon.
Conway, J. B. Functions of One Complex Variable. 2nd ed. (Graduate Texts in Mathematics: Vol. 11). (Illus.). 1979. 24.00 (ISBN 0-387-90328-3). Springer-Verlag.
Deaux, Roland. Introduction to the Geometry of Complex Numbers. Eves, Howard, tr. LC 56-13198. 1956. 8.00 (ISBN 0-8044-4176-6). Ungar.
Ferrier, J. P. Spectral Theory & Complex Analysis. (Mathematical Studies Ser: No. 4). 1973. pap. 17.00 (ISBN 0-444-10429-1, North-Holland). Elsevier.
Hawkins, F. M. & Hawkins, J. Q. Complex Numbers & Elementary Complex Functions. 1970. 32.50x (ISBN 0-677-61110-2). Gordon.
Kogbetliantz, E. G. Handbook of First Complex Prime Numbers, 2 vol. set. LC 78-142082. 1010p. 1971. 146.25x (ISBN 0-677-02920-9). Gordon.
Ledermann, Walter. Complex Numbers. (Library of Mathematics). 1971. pap. 5.00 (ISBN 0-7100-4345-7). Routledge & Kegan.
Levi, Judith N. The Syntax & Semantics of Complex Nominals. 1978. 29.50 (ISBN 0-12-445150-0). Acad Pr.
Markushevich, A. I. Complex Numbers & Conformal Mapping. (Russian Tracts on the Physical Sciences Ser). 1962. 15.00x (ISBN 0-677-20280-6). Gordon.
Seminar on Complex Multiplication, Institute for Advanced Study, Princeton. Proceedings. Borel, A., et al, eds. (Lecture Notes in Mathematics: Vol. 21). 1966. pap. 10.70 (ISBN 0-387-03604-0). Springer-Verlag.

NUMBERS, INDEX
see Index Numbers (Economics)

NUMBERS, IRRATIONAL
see also Numbers, Transcendental

Delone, B. N. & Faddeev, D. K. Theory of Irrationalities of the Third Degree. LC 63-21548. (Translations of Mathematical Monographs: Vol. 10). 1964. 22.40 (ISBN 0-8218-1560-1, MMONO-10). Am Math.
Niven, Ivan. Irrational Numbers. (Carus Monograph: No. 11). 164p. 1956. 12.50 (ISBN 0-88385-011-7). Math Assn.
Nivien, Ivan. Numbers: Rational & Irrational. LC 61-6226. (New Mathematical Library: No.1). 1975. pap. 5.50 (ISBN 0-88385-601-8). Math Assn.

NUMBERS, LARGE
see Law of Large Numbers

NUMBERS, NATURAL
see also Numbers, Prime; Numbers, Theory of

Adler, Irving. Integers: Positive & Negative. LC 78-162589. (Reason Why Ser.). (Illus.). 48p. (gr. 3-6). 1972. PLB 8.79 (ISBN 0-381-99988-2, A39160, JD-J). Har-Row.
Froman, Robert. Less Than Nothing Is Really Something. LC 72-7546. (Young Math Ser). (Illus.). (gr. 1-5). 1973. 8.95 (ISBN 0-690-48862-9, TYC-J). Har-Row.
Howett, J. Basic Skills with Whole Numbers. 128p. 1980. pap. text ed. 3.00 (ISBN 0-8428-2116-3). Cambridge Bk.
O'Brien, Thomas C. Odds & Evens. (Young Math Ser.). (Illus.). (gr. 1-4). 1971. pap. 1.45 (ISBN 0-690-00207-6, TYC-J); filmstrip with record 12.85 (ISBN 0-690-59071-7); filmstrip with cassette 15.85 (ISBN 0-690-59073-3). Har-Row.
Sloans, N. J. A Handbook of Integer Sequences. 1973. 24.00 (ISBN 0-12-648550-X). Acad Pr.

NUMBERS, PRIME

Apostol, Tom M. Introduction to Analytic Number Theory. (Undergraduate Texts in Mathematics Ser.). (Illus.). 370p. 1976. text ed. 20.80 (ISBN 0-387-90163-9). Springer-Verlag.
Brown, Stephen I. & National Council of Teachers of Mathematics. Some "Prime" Comparisons. 1979. pap. 6.00 (ISBN 0-87353-131-0). NCTM.
Hooley, C. Applications of Sieve Methods to the Theory of Numbers. LC 75-27796. (Cambridge Tracts in Mathematics Ser.: No. 70). 122p. 1976. 32.95 (ISBN 0-521-20915-3). Cambridge U Pr.
Hua, Lo-Keng. Additive Theory of Prime Numbers. Ng, N. H., tr. LC 62-23103. (Translations of Mathematical Monographs: Vol. 13). 1966. Repr. of 1965 ed. 25.60 (ISBN 0-8218-1563-6, MMONO-13). Am Math.
Huxley, M. N. The Distribution of Prime Numbers: Large Sieves & Zero-Density Theorems. (Oxford Mathematical Monographs). (Illus.). 145p. 1972. text ed. 37.50x (ISBN 0-19-853518-X). Oxford U Pr.
Kogbetliantz, E. G. Handbook of First Complex Prime Numbers, 2 vol. set. LC 78-142082. 1010p. 1971. 146.25x (ISBN 0-677-02920-9). Gordon.
Landau, Edmund. Handbuch der Lehre von der Verteilung der Primzahlen, 2 vols. in 1. 3rd ed. LC 73-21539. 1974. text ed. 39.50 (ISBN 0-8284-0096-2). Chelsea Pub.
Luce, Marnie. Primes Are Builders. LC 68-56702. (Math Concept Bks). (Illus.). (gr. 3-6). 1969. PLB 3.95 (ISBN 0-8225-0573-8). Lerner Pubns.
Osborn, Roger. Tables of All Primitive Roots of Odd Primes Less Than 1,000. 70p. 1961. 6.00x (ISBN 0-292-73394-1). U of Tex Pr.

NUMBERS, RANDOM

Dudewicz, Edward J. & Ralley, Thomas G. The Handbook of Random Number Generation & Testing with TESTRAND Computer Code. LC 80-68286. (The American Sciences Press Ser. in Mathematical & Management Sciences: Vol. 4). 1981. text ed. 95.00 (ISBN 0-935950-01-X). Am Sciences Pr.
Lewis, Theodore G. Distribution Sampling for Computer Simulation. LC 74-25058. 128p. 1975. 19.95 (ISBN 0-669-97139-1). Lexington Bks.
Meeker, William Q., Jr., et al. The Product of Two Normally Distributed Random Variables. LC 74-6283. (TABLES Ser.: Vol. 7). Date not set. 12.40 (ISBN 0-8218-1907-0). Am Math.
Moses, Lincoln E. & Oakford, Robert V. Tables of Random Permutations. LC 63-12041. 1963. 20.00x (ISBN 0-8047-0148-2). Stanford U Pr.
Snyder, Donald L. Random Point Processes. LC 75-11556. 485p. 1975. 40.00 (ISBN 0-471-81021-5, Pub. by Wiley-Interscience). Wiley.

NUMBERS, RATIONAL
see also Fractions

Lang, S. & Trotter, H. F. Frobenius Distributions in GL-Two Extensions. (Lecture Notes in Mathematics: Vol. 504). 274p. 1976. pap. 13.80 (ISBN 0-387-07550-X). Springer-Verlag.
Nivien, Ivan. Numbers: Rational & Irrational. LC 61-6226. (New Mathematical Library: No.1). 1975. pap. 5.50 (ISBN 0-88385-601-8). Math Assn.
Shoemaker, Richard W. Perfect Numbers. LC 73-18012. 32p. 1973. pap. 1.70 (ISBN 0-87353-081-0). NCTM.

NUMBERS, REAL
see also Arithmetic; Numbers, Rational

Allen, Layman E. Real Numbers: Arithmetic. 2.50 (ISBN 0-911624-04-X). Wffn Proof.
Cohen, Leon W. & Ehrich, Gertrude. The Structure of the Real Number System. rev. ed. LC 76-7512. 122p. 1977. 9.95 (ISBN 0-88275-396-7). Krieger.
Galambos, J. Representations of Real Numbers by Infinite Series. LC 75-44296. (Lecture Notes in Mathematics: Vol. 502). 1976. pap. 9.90 (ISBN 0-387-07547-X). Springer-Verlag.
Hackworth, Robert D. & Howland, Joseph. Introductory College Mathematics: History of Real Numbers. LC 75-23623. 62p. 1976. pap. text ed. 2.95 (ISBN 0-7216-4416-3). HR&W.
--Introductory College Mathematics: Real Number System. LC 75-23632. (Illus.). 67p. 1976. pap. text ed. 2.95 (ISBN 0-7216-4425-2). HR&W.
Sanin, Nikolai A. Constructive Real Numbers & Function Spaces. LC 68-19437. (Translations of Mathematical Monographs: Vol. 21). 1968. 36.00 (ISBN 0-8218-1571-7, MMONO-21). Am Math.

NUMBERS, THEORY OF
see also Algebraic Number Theory; Cyclotomy; Diophantine Analysis; Fibonacci Numbers; Fields, Algebraic; Forms, Quadratic; Functions, Modular; Galois Theory; Goedel's Theorem; Groups, Theory of; Magic Squares; Numbers, Transfinite; Numeration; Partitions (Mathematics); Recursive Functions

Adams, W. & Goldstein, L. Introduction to Number Theory. 1976. text ed. 19.95 (ISBN 0-13-491282-9). P-H.
Adjan, S., et al. Eleven Papers on Number Theory, Algebra & Functions of a Complex Variable. LC 51-5559. (Translations, Ser.: No. 2, Vol. 46). 1965. 22.00 (ISBN 0-8218-1746-9, TRANS 2-46). Am Math.
Agnew, Jeanne. Explorations in Number Theory. LC 72-189515. (Contemporary Undergrad Math Ser). 1972. text ed. 17.95 (ISBN 0-8185-0041-7). Brooks-Cole.
Algebra, Theory of Numbers & Their Applications. LC 80-28539. (STEKLO Ser.: No. 148). Date not set. 88.00 (ISBN 0-8218-3046-5). Am Math.
Analytic Number Theory, Mathematical Analysis & Their Applications. LC 80-14363. 220p. 1977. 62.40 (ISBN 0-8218-3044-9). Am Math.
Andrews, George E. Number Theory: The Theory of Partitions. LC 76-41770. (Encyclopedia of Mathematics & Its Applications: Vol. 2). (Illus.). 1976. text ed. 21.50 (ISBN 0-201-13501-9). A-W.
--On the General Rogers-Ramanujan Theorem. LC 74-18067. (Memoirs: No. 152). 1974. pap. 8.40 (ISBN 0-8218-1852-X, MEMO-152). Am Math.
Andrunakievic, V. A., et al. Twelve Papers on Topology, Algebra & Number Theory. LC 51-5559. (Translations Ser.: No. 2, Vol. 52). 1966. 30.80 (ISBN 0-8218-1752-3, TRANS 2-52). Am Math.
Apostol, T. M. Modular Functions & Dirichlet Series in Number Theory. Gehring, F. W. & Moore, C. C., eds. LC 76-10236. (Graduate Texts in Mathematics: Vol. 41). 1976. 20.80 (ISBN 0-387-90185-X). Springer-Verlag.
Apostol, Tom M. Introduction to Analytic Number Theory. (Undergraduate Texts in Mathematics Ser.). (Illus.). 370p. 1976. text ed. 20.80 (ISBN 0-387-90163-9). Springer-Verlag.
Archibald, Ralph. Introduction to the Theory of Numbers. LC 76-118978. 1970. text ed. 19.95 (ISBN 0-675-09351-1). Merrill.
Armendariz, Efraim P. & McAdam, Stephen J. Elementary Number Theory. (Illus.). 1980. text ed. 18.95 (ISBN 0-02-303850-0). Macmillan.
Asimov, Isaac. Asimov on Numbers. (gr. 11-12). 1978. pap. 2.50 (ISBN 0-671-41186-1). PB.
--Asimov on Numbers. LC 76-23747. 1977. 9.95 (ISBN 0-385-12074-5). Doubleday.
Ayoub, Raymond. Introduction to the Analytic Theory of Numbers. LC 63-11989. (Mathematical Surveys Ser.: No. 10). 1974. Repr. of 1963 ed. 28.80 (ISBN 0-8218-1510-5, SURV-10). Am Math.
Bachmann, Paul. Zahlentheorie, 5 vols. (Nos. 15-20). (Ger). Repr. Set. 131.00 (ISBN 0-384-02990-6). Johnson Repr.
Beiler, Albert H. Recreations in the Theory of Numbers. (Orig.). 1964. pap. 5.50 (ISBN 0-486-21096-0). Dover.
Bellman, R. Analytic Number Theory: An Introduction. 1980. 19.50 (ISBN 0-8053-0360-X). A-W.
Bertin, M. J., ed. Seminaire De Theorie Des Nombres, Paris 1979-1980. (Progress in Mathematics Ser.). 404p. (Fr. & Eng.). 1981. 22.00 (ISBN 3-7643-3035-X). Birkhauser.
Birjukov, A. P., et al. Sixteen Papers on Number Theory & Algebra. LC 51-5559. (Translations Ser.: No. 2, Vol. 82). 1969. 29.60 (ISBN 0-8218-1782-5, TRANS 2-82). Am Math.
Borevich, Z. I. & Shafarevich, I. R. Number Theory. (Pure and Applied Mathematics: Vol. 20). 1966. text ed. 22.95 (ISBN 0-12-117850-1). Acad Pr.
Brainerd, Charles J. The Origins of the Number Concept. LC 78-21223. 1979. 22.60 (ISBN 0-275-24310-9). Praeger.
Brandt Corstius, H., ed. Grammars for Number Names. (Foundations of Language Supplementary Ser: No. 7). 123p. 1968. lib. bdg. 21.00 (ISBN 90-277-0023-0, Pub. by Reidel Holland). Kluwer Boston.
Brodskii, M. S., et al. Nine Papers on Number Theory & Theory of Operators. LC 51-5559. (Translations Ser.: No. 2, Vol. 13). 1980. Repr. of 1964 ed. 40.40 (ISBN 0-8218-1713-2, TRANS 2-13). Am Math.

Bureloff, Morris, et al. Number Triangles. Laycock, Mary & Merrick, Paul, eds. (Illus., Orig.). (gr. 5-12). 1977. pap. 4.95 (ISBN 0-918932-36-X). Activity Resources.
Burton. Elementary Number Theory. rev. ed. 390p. 1980. text ed. 22.95 (ISBN 0-205-06965-7, 5669650). Allyn.
Calenko, M. S., et al. Twelve Papers on Algebra, Number Theory & Topology. LC 51-5559. (Translations Ser.: No. 2, Vol. 58). 1966. 28.80 (ISBN 0-8218-1758-2, TRANS 2-58). Am Math.
--Twenty-Two Papers on Algebra, Number Theory, & Differential Geometry. LC 51-5559. (Translations Ser.: No. 2, Vol. 37). 1964. 28.80 (ISBN 0-8218-1737-X, TRANS 2-37). Am Math.
Carico, Charles C. The Real Number System. 1974. pap. 4.95x (ISBN 0-534-00316-8). Wadsworth Pub.
Chandrasekharan, K. Introduction to Analytic Number Theory. LC 68-21990. (Die Grundlehren der Mathematischen Wissenschaften: Vol. 14). (Illus.). 1968. 19.10 (ISBN 0-387-04141-9). Springer-Verlag.
Cohn, Harvey. Advanced Number Theory. (Illus.). 1980. pap. 5.00 (ISBN 0-486-64023-X). Dover.
Conway, John. On Numbers & Games. (London Mathematical Society Monographs). 1976. 27.00 (ISBN 0-12-186350-6). Acad Pr.
Cudakov, N. G., et al. Number Theory & Analysis. (Translations Ser.: No. 1, Vol. 2). 1970. Repr. of 1962 ed. 26.80 (ISBN 0-8218-1602-0, TRANS-1-2). Am Math.
Dedekind, Richard. Essays on the Theory of Numbers. Beman, Wooster W., tr. 1901. pap. 3.00 (ISBN 0-486-21010-3). Dover.
Dickson, Leonard E. History of the Theory of Numbers, 3 Vols. LC 66-26932. 49.50 (ISBN 0-8284-0086-5). Chelsea Pub.
--On Varients & Theory of Numbers. 1967. pap. 2.00 (ISBN 0-486-61667-3). Dover.
--Studies in the Theory of Numbers. LC 61-13494. 9.95 (ISBN 0-8284-0151-9). Chelsea Pub.
Dudley, Underwood. Elementary Number Theory. 2nd ed. LC 78-5661. (Mathematical Sciences Ser.). (Illus.). 1978. text ed. 17.95x (ISBN 0-7167-0076-X); instrs.' guide avail. W H Freeman.
Eichler, M. Einfuhrung in Die Theorie der Algebraischen Zahlen und Funktionen. (Mathematische Reihe Ser.: No. 27). 338p. (Ger.). 1963. 58.50 (ISBN 3-7643-0097-3). Birkhauser.
Eichler, Martin. Introduction to the Theory of Algebraic Numbers & Functions. (Pure & Applied Mathematics: Vol. 23). 1966. 55.00 (ISBN 0-12-233650-X). Acad Pr.
Eliott, P. D. Probabilistic Number Theory Two: Central Limit Theorems. (Grundlehren der Mathematischen Wissenschaften: Vol. 240). 1980. 35.00 (ISBN 0-387-90438-7). Springer-Verlag.
Elliot, P. D. Probabilistic Number Theory One: Mean-Value Theorems. (Grundlehren der Mathematischen Wissenschaften: Vol. 239). 1980. 36.80 (ISBN 0-387-90437-9). Springer-Verlag.
Ellis, Keith. Number Power: In Nature, Art, & Everyday Life. LC 78-3124. (Illus.). 1978. 10.00 (ISBN 0-312-57988-8). St Martin.
Faddeev, D. K., et al. Five Papers on Logic, Algebra, & Number Theory. LC 51-5559. (Translations Ser.: No. 2, Vol. 3). 1956. 20.80 (ISBN 0-8218-1703-5, TRANS 2-3). Am Math.
Fomin, S. V. Number Systems. 2nd ed. Teller, Joan W. & Branson, Thomas P., trs. from Rus. LC 73-89787. (Popular Lectures in Mathematics Ser). 48p. 1975. pap. text ed. 3.50x (ISBN 0-226-25669-3). U of Chicago Pr.
Freiman, G. A. Foundations of a Structural Theory of Set Addition. LC 73-9804. (Translations of Mathematical Monographs Ser.: Vol. 37). 1973. 31.20 (ISBN 0-8218-1587-3, MMONO-37). Am Math.
Galambos, J. Representations of Real Numbers by Infinite Series. LC 75-44296. (Lecture Notes in Mathematics: Vol. 502). 1976. pap. 9.90 (ISBN 0-387-07547-X). Springer-Verlag.
Gelbart, S. S. Weil's Representation & the Spectrum of the Metaplectic Group. (Lecture Notes in Mathematics: Vol. 530). 1976. soft cover 9.90 (ISBN 0-387-07799-5). Springer-Verlag.
Gel'fond, A. O., et al. Twelve Papers on Number Theory & Function Theory. LC 51-5559. (Translations Ser.: No. 2, Vol. 19). 1962. 23.60 (ISBN 0-8218-1719-1, TRANS 2-19). Am Math.
Gupta, H. Selected Topics in Number Theory. 1980. 55.00x (ISBN 0-85626-177-7, Pub. by Abacus Pr). Intl Schol Bk Serv.
Halberstam, H. & Hooley, C., eds. Recent Progress in Analytic Number Theory, Vol. II. LC 81-66693. 1981. write for info. (ISBN 0-12-318202-6). Acad Pr.
--Recent Progress in Analytic Number Theory, Vol. I. 1981. write for info. (ISBN 0-12-318201-8). Acad Pr.
Hardy, Godfrey H. Ramanujan. 3rd ed. LC 59-10268. 1978. 9.95 (ISBN 0-8284-0136-5). Chelsea Pub.
Hardy, Godfrey H. & Wright, E. M. Introduction to the Theory of Numbers. 5th ed. 1980. 49.95x (ISBN 0-19-853170-2); pap. 16.95x (ISBN 0-19-853171-0). Oxford U Pr.
Hasse, H. Number Theory. (Grundlehren der Mathematischen Wissenschaften: Vol 229). 1978. 49.00 (ISBN 0-387-08275-1). Springer-Verlag.
Hecke, Erich. Algebraische Zahlen. 2nd ed. LC 50-3732. (Ger). 1970. 11.95 (ISBN 0-8284-0046-6). Chelsea Pub.
Henrici, Peter. Computational Analysis with the Hp 25 Pocket Calculator. LC 77-1182. 1977. 19.95 (ISBN 0-471-02938-6, Pub. by Wiley-Interscience). Wiley.
How Numbers Lie: A Consumer's Guide to Numerical Hocus-Pocus. 1981. 12.95 (ISBN 0-86616-000-0); pap. 7.95 (ISBN 0-86616-001-9). Greene.
Hua, L. K. & Wang, Y. Applications of Number Theory to Numerical Analysis. 241p. 1981. 39.00 (ISBN 0-387-10382-1). Springer-Verlag.
Husserl. Philosophie der Arithmetik. (Husserliana Ser: No. 12). 1970. lib. bdg. 50.00 (ISBN 90-247-0230-5, Pub. by Martinus Nijhoff Netherlands). Kluwer Boston.
Igusa, J. I. Lectures on Forms of Higher Degree. (Tata Institute Lecture Notes). 1979. pap. 10.40 (ISBN 0-387-08944-6). Springer-Verlag.
International Conference, Sonderforschungsbereich Theoretische Mathematik,University of Bonn, July 1976. Modular Functions of One Variable: Proceedings, No. 6. Serre, J. P. & Zagier, D. B., eds. (Lecture Note in Mathematics: Vol. 627). 1977. pap. 18.30 (ISBN 0-387-08530-0). Springer-Verlag.
International Summer School, University of Antwerp, 1972. Modular Functions of One Variable 2: Proceedings. Kuyk, W. & Deligne, P., eds. (Lecture Notes in Mathematics: Vol. 349). v, 598p. 1974. pap. 21.50 (ISBN 0-387-06558-X). Springer-Verlag.
Iyanaga, S. The Theory of Numbers. (North-Holland Mathematical Library: Vol. 8). 1976. 73.25 (ISBN 0-444-10678-2, North-Holland). Elsevier.
Jackson, T. H. Number Theory. (Library of Mathematics). 1975. pap. 5.00 (ISBN 0-7100-7998-2). Routledge & Kegan.
Kac, Mark. Statistical Independence in Probability Analysis & Number Theory. (Carus Monograph: No. 12). 93p. 1959. 12.50 (ISBN 0-88385-012-5). Math Assn.
Khinchin, Aleksander Y. Three Pearls of Number Theory. LC 52-2385. 1952. 9.00x (ISBN 0-910670-04-8). Graylock.
Knopfmacher, J. Abstract Analytic Number Theory. (North-Holland Mathematical Library: Vol. 12). 1976. 49.00 (ISBN 0-444-10779-7, North-Holland). Elsevier.
Koblitz, N. P-Adic Analysis. (London Mathematical Society Lecture Note Ser.: No. 46). 150p. 1980. pap. 14.95 (ISBN 0-521-28060-5). Cambridge U Pr.
Korobov, N. M., et al. Eight Papers on Algebra & Number Theory. LC 51-5559. (Translations, Ser.: No. 2, Vol. 4). 1956. 20.00 (ISBN 0-8128-1704-4, TRANS 2-4). Am Math.
Kubilius, Jonas. Probabilistic Methods in the Theory of Numbers. LC 63-21549. (Translations of Mathematical Monographs: Vol. 11). 1968. Repr. of 1964 ed. 26.00 (ISBN 0-8218-1561-X, MMONO-11). Am Math.
Landau, Edmund. Elementare Zahlentheorie. LC 49-235. (Ger). 10.95 (ISBN 0-8284-0026-1). Chelsea Pub.
--Elementary Number Theory. 2nd ed. LC 57-8494. 12.00 (ISBN 0-8284-0125-X). Chelsea Pub.
--Foundations of Analysis. 2nd ed. LC 60-15580. (gr. 9 up). 1960. text ed. 8.95 (ISBN 0-8284-0079-2). Chelsea Pub.
--Grundlagen der Analysis: With Complete German-English Vocabulary. 4th ed. LC 60-7485. (Ger). o. p. 6.95 (ISBN 0-8284-0024-5); pap. 2.95 (ISBN 0-8284-0141-1). Chelsea Pub.
--Vorlesungen Ueber Zahlentheorie, 3 Vols. in One. LC 49-235. (Ger). 29.95 (ISBN 0-8284-0032-6). Chelsea Pub.
Lang, S. Introduction to Modular Forms. (No. 222). (Illus.). 1976. 29.60 (ISBN 0-387-07833-9). Springer-Verlag.
Leblanc, John F., et al. Mathematics-Methods Program: Number Theory. (Mathematics Ser.). (Illus.). 128p. 1976. pap. text ed. 3.50 (ISBN 0-201-14624-X); instr's manual 1.50 (ISBN 0-201-14625-8). A-W.
Lejeune-Dirichlet, P. G. & Dedekind, R. Zahlentheorie. 4th ed. LC 68-54716. (Ger). 1969. text ed. 29.95 (ISBN 0-8284-0213-2). Chelsea Pub.
LeVeque, W. J., ed. Studies in Number Theory. LC 75-76868. (MAA Studies: No. 6). 212p. 1969. 12.50 (ISBN 0-88385-106-7). Math Assn.
LeVeque, William J. Fundamentals of Number Theory. LC 76-55645. 1978. text ed. 19.95 (ISBN 0-201-04287-8). A-W.
Le Veque, William J., ed. Reviews in Number Theory. LC 74-11335. 1974. Set. 245.00 (ISBN 0-685-26205-7, REVNUM); Vol. 1. 67.00 (ISBN 0-8218-0203-8, REVNUM-1); Vol. 2. 67.00 (ISBN 0-8218-0204-6, REVNUM-2); Vol. 3. 51.00 (ISBN 0-8218-0205-4, REVNUM-3); Vol. 4. 67.00 (ISBN 0-8218-0206-2, REVNUM-4); Vol. 5. 51.00 (ISBN 0-8218-0207-0, REVNUM-5); Vol. 6. 51.00 (ISBN 0-8218-0208-9, REVNUM-6). Am Math.
Levi, Howard. Elements of Algebra. 4th ed. LC 61-16955. (gr. 9-12). 1961. text ed. 6.95 (ISBN 0-8284-0103-9). Chelsea Pub.
Lion, Gerard & Vergne, Michele, eds. The Weil Representation, Maslov Index & Theta Series. (Progress in Mathematics Ser.: No. 6). 346p. 1980. pap. text ed. 18.00 (ISBN 3-7643-3007-4). Birkhauser.
Luneburg, H. Vorlesungen uber Zalentheorie. (Elemente der Mathematik Von Hoeheren Standpunkt Aus: Vol. 8). 108p. (Ger.). 1978. pap. 18.50 (ISBN 3-7643-0932-6). Birkhauser.
MacMahon, Percy A. Combinatory Analysis, 2 Vols. in 1. LC 59-10267. 19.95 (ISBN 0-8284-0137-3). Chelsea Pub.
Malm, Donald G. A Computer Laboratory Manual for Number Theory. 256p. 1980. pap. text ed. 9.95x (ISBN 0-933694-13-X). COMPress.
Malyshev, A. V., ed. Studies in Number Theory. LC 68-31238. (Seminars in Mathematics Ser.: Vol. 1). 66p. 1968. 18.50 (ISBN 0-306-18801-5, Consultants). Plenum Pub.
Mann, Henry B. Addition Theorems: The Addition Theorems of Group Theory & Number Theory. LC 76-16766. 124p. 1976. Repr. of 1965 ed. text ed. 12.50 (ISBN 0-88275-418-1). Krieger.
Masi, Michael. Boethian Number Theory: A Translation of the De Institutione Arithmetica. 1979. pap. text ed. write for info. (ISBN 0-85635-155-5). Humanities.
Mathews, George B. Theory of Numbers. 2nd ed. LC 61-17958. 9.95 (ISBN 0-8284-0156-X). Chelsea Pub.
Mendelson, Elliot. Number Systems & the Foundations of Analysis. 1973. text ed. 19.95 (ISBN 0-12-490850-0). Acad Pr.
Minkowski, Hermann. Diophantische Approximationen. LC 56-13056. (Ger). 11.95 (ISBN 0-8284-0118-7). Chelsea Pub.
--Geometrie der Zahlen. (Bibliotheca Mathematica Teubneriana: No. 40). (Ger). 1969. Repr. of 1910 ed. 23.00 (ISBN 0-384-39040-4). Johnson Repr.
Montgomery, H. L. Topics in Multiplicative Number Theory. (Lecture Notes in Mathematics: Vol. 227). ix, 178p. 1971. pap. 8.20 (ISBN 0-387-05641-6). Springer-Verlag.
Mordell, L. J. Two Papers on Number Theory. 80p. 1972. 4.95 (ISBN 0-685-27556-6). Adler.
Nagell, Trygve. Introduction to Number Theory. 309p. 1981. 14.95 (ISBN 0-8284-0163-2). Chelsea Pub.
Nathanson, M. B., ed. Number Theory: Carbondale Nineteen Seventy-Nine. (Lecture Notes in Mathematics: Vol. 751). 342p. 1980. pap. 16.80 (ISBN 0-387-09559-4). Springer-Verlag.
--Number Theory Day: Proceedings of the Conference Held at Rockefeller University, New York, 1976. LC 77-26055. (Lecture Notes in Mathematics Ser: Vol. 626). 1977. pap. 14.60 (ISBN 0-387-08529-7). Springer-Verlag.
Niven, Ivan & Zuckerman, Herbert S. An Introduction to the Theory of Numbers. 4th ed. LC 79-24869. 355p. 1980. text ed. 22.95 (ISBN 0-471-02851-7); solutions manual avail. (ISBN 0-471-06394-0). Wiley.
Ore, Oyestein. Invitation to Number Theory. LC 67-20607. (New Mathematical Library: No. 20). 1975. pap. 5.50 (ISBN 0-88385-620-4). Math Assn.
Ore, Oystein. Number Theory & Its History. (Illus.). 1948. text ed. 15.95 (ISBN 0-07-047675-6, C). McGraw.
Pieper, H. Variationen Uber ein Zahlenthroretisches Them von Carl Friedrich Gauss. (Science & Civilization Ser.: No. 33). 160p. (Ger.). 1978. 14.50 (ISBN 3-7643-0959-8). Birkhauser.
Polya, G. & Szego, G. Problems & Theorems in Analysis II: Theory of Functions, Zeros, Polynomials, Determinants, Numger Theory, Geometry. Billigheimer, C. E., tr. (Illus.). 1977. pap. text ed. 18.90 (ISBN 0-387-90291-0). Springer-Verlag.
Pringsheim, Alfred. Vorlesungen Uber Zahlen & Funktionenlehre, 2 Vols. (Bibliotheca Mathematica Teubneriana Ser: Nos. 28-29). (Ger). 1969. Repr. of 1916 ed. Set. 100.00 (ISBN 0-384-47885-9). Johnson Repr.
Rademacher, H. Topics in Analytic Number Theory. LC 72-79326. (Die Grundelehren der Mathematischen Wissenschaften: Vol. 169). (Illus.). 340p. 1973. 52.50 (ISBN 0-387-05447-2). Springer-Verlag.
Rademacher, Hans. Lectures on Elementary Number Theory. LC 76-30495. 156p. 1977. Repr. of 1964 ed. lib. bdg. 10.50 (ISBN 0-88275-499-8). Krieger.
Reid, Constance. From Zero to Infinity. enl. rev. ed. (Apollo Eds.). (Illus.). (YA) (gr. 9-12). pap. 1.95 (ISBN 0-8152-0119-2, A119). T Y Crowell.
Roberts, Joe. Elementary Number Theory: A Problem-Oriented Approach. LC 76-46738. 1977. pap. text ed. 12.50x (ISBN 0-262-68028-9). MIT Pr.
Robinson, Abraham. Numbers & Ideals. LC 65-16747. (Illus.). 1965. 10.95x (ISBN 0-8162-7234-4). Holden-Day.
Rota, Gian-Carlo, ed. Studies in Algebra & Number Theory. LC 79-4638. (Advances in Mathematics Supplementary Studies Ser.: Vol. 6). 1979. 47.00 (ISBN 0-12-599153-3). Acad Pr.
Safarewic, I. R. & Borewicz, S. J. Zahlentheorie. (Mathematische Reihe Ser.: No. 32). (Illus.). 468p. (Ger.). 1966. 50.00 (ISBN 3-7643-0039-6). Birkhauser.
Schweiger, F. Metrical Theory of Jacobi-Perron Algorithm. LC 73-9201. (Lecture Notes in Mathematics: Vol. 334). v, 111p. 1973. pap. 9.70 (ISBN 0-387-06388-9). Springer-Verlag.
Seere, J. P. Local Fields. Greenberg, M. J., tr. from Fr. LC 79-12643. (Graduate Texts in Mathematics: Vol. 67). (Illus.). 1979. 24.80 (ISBN 0-387-90424-7). Springer-Verlag.
Seminar on Complex Multiplication, Institute for Advanced Study, Princeton. Proceedings. Borel, A., et al, eds. (Lecture Notes in Mathematics: Vol. 21). 1966. pap. 10.70 (ISBN 0-387-03604-0). Springer-Verlag.
Serre, J. A Course in Arithmetic. Gehring, F. W. & Moore, C. C., eds. LC 70-190089. (Graduate Texts in Mathematics: Vol. 7). (Illus.). 1979. 18.50 (ISBN 0-387-90040-3). Springer-Verlag.
Shanks, Daniel. Solved & Unsolved Problems in Number Theory. 2nd ed. LC 77-13019. 1978. text ed. 11.95 (ISBN 0-8284-0297-3). Chelsea Pub.
Shimura, G. Automorphic Functions & Number Theory. LC 68-25132. (Lecture Notes in Mathematics: Vol. 54). (Orig.). 1968. pap. 10.70 (ISBN 0-387-04224-5). Springer-Verlag.
Siegel, C. L. Topics in Complex Function Theory, 3 vols. Incl. Vol. 1. Elliptical Functions & Uniformization Theory. 1969. 31.00 (ISBN 0-471-79070-2); Vol. 2. Automorphic Functions & Abelian Integrals. 1972. 31.00 (ISBN 0-471-79080-X); Vol. 3. Abelian Functions & Modular Functions of Several Variables. Tretkoff, M. & Gottschling, E., trs. 244p. 1973. 39.95 (ISBN 0-471-79090-7). LC 69-19931. (Pure & Applied Mathematics Ser., Pub. by Wiley-Interscience). Wiley.
Sierpinski, W. Two Hundred Fifty Problems in Elementary Number Theory. (Modern Analytic & Computational Methods in Science& Mathematics: No. 26). 1970. 21.50 (ISBN 0-444-00071-2, North Holland). Elsevier.
Smith, Henry J. Report on the Theory of Numbers. LC 64-8080. 1966. 14.95 (ISBN 0-8284-0186-1). Chelsea Pub.
Sneath, Peter H. & Sokal, Robert R. Numerical Taxonomy: The Principles & Practice of Numerical Classification. LC 72-1552. (Biology Ser.). (Illus.). 1973. 36.95x (ISBN 0-7167-0697-0). W H Freeman.
Stark, Harold M. An Introduction to Number Theory. 1978. pap. text ed. 9.95x (ISBN 0-262-69060-8). MIT Pr.
Steklov Institute of Mathematics, Academy of Sciences, U S S R, No. 82 & Postinikov, A. G. Ergodic Problems in the Theory of Congruences & of Diophantine Approximations: Proceedings. 1967. 28.40 (ISBN 0-8218-1882-1, STEKLO-82). Am Math.
Steklov Institute of Mathematics, Academy of Sciences, U S S R, Vol. 132. International Conference on Number Theory: Proceedings. Vinogradov, I. M., et al, eds. LC 75-14189. 1975. 53.60 (ISBN 0-8218-3032-5, STEKLO-132). Am Math.
Swierczkowski, S. Sets & Numbers. (Library of Mathematics). 1972. pap. 5.00 (ISBN 0-7100-7137-X). Routledge & Kegan.
Symposia in Pure Mathematics-Houston-January-1967. Number Theory, Vol. 12. LeVeque, W. J., ed. LC 70-78057. 1969. 20.00 (ISBN 0-8218-1412-5, PSPUM-12). Am Math.

Symposia in Pure Mathematics-Pasadena-1963. Theory of Numbers: Proceedings, Vol. 8. Whiteman, A. L., ed. LC 65-17382. 1979. Repr. of 1965 ed. with additions 23.60 (ISBN 0-8218-1408-7, PSPUM-8). Am Math.

Symposia in Pure Mathematics - St. Louis, 1972. Analytic Number Theory: Proceedings, Vol. 24. Diamond, H. G., ed. LC 72-10198. 1973. 42.40 (ISBN 0-8218-1424-9, PSPUM-24). Am Math.

Symposia in Pure Mathematics-Stony Brook, N.Y. 1969. Number Theory Institute, 1969: Proceedings, Vol. 20. Lewis, Donald J., ed. LC 76-125938. 1971. 38.40 (ISBN 0-8218-1420-6, PSPUM-20). Am Math.

Symposium at the Centre for Research in Mathematics, University of Montreal, Sept., 1971. Applications of Number Theory to Numerical Analysis: Proceedings. Zaremba, S. K., ed. 1972. 46.50 (ISBN 0-12-775950-6). Acad Pr.

Theory of Numbers, Mathematical Analysis & Their Applications. LC 79-20552. (Proceedings of the Steklov Institute). 1979. 73.20 (ISBN 0-8218-3042-2, STEKLO 142). Am Math.

Toledo, S. A. Tableau Systems for First Order Number Theory & Certain Higher Order Theories. LC 75-6738. (Lecture Notes in Mathematics Ser.: Vol. 447). iii, 339p. 1975. pap. 16.50 (ISBN 0-387-07149-0). Springer-Verlag.

Trost, E. Primzahlen. 2nd rev. ed. (Elemente der Mathematik Von Hoeheren Standpunkt Aus: Vol. 2). 100p. (Ger.). 1968. pap. 14.50 (ISBN 3-7643-0387-5). Birkhauser.

Turan, P. Topics in Number Theory. (Colloquia Mathematica Societatis Janos Bolyai: Vol. 13). 1976. 61.00 (ISBN 0-7204-0454-1, North-Holland). Elsevier.

Valenza, Samuel W., Jr. The Professor Googol Flying Time Machine & Atomic Space Capsule Math Primer. 3rd ed. (Illus.). 196p. (gr. 7-12). 1974. 9.50 (ISBN 0-936918-00-4). Intergalactic NJ.

Vaughan, R. C. The Hardy-Littlewood Method. (Cambridge Tracts in Mathematics: No. 80). 160p. Date not set. 34.50 (ISBN 0-521-23439-5). Cambridge U Pr.

Vinogradov, I. Fundamentos De la Teoria De los Numeros. 107p. (Span.). 1977. 5.20 (ISBN 0-8285-1686-3, Pub. by Mir Pubs Russia). Imported Pubns.

Weil, A. Basic Number Theory. 3rd ed. LC 74-13963. (Die Grundlehren der Mathematischen Wissenschaften Ser.: Vol. 144). xviii, 325p. 1975. 24.90 (ISBN 0-387-06935-6). Springer-Verlag.

Weiss, Edwin. First Course in Algebra & Number Theory. 1971. text ed. 21.95 (ISBN 0-12-743150-0). Acad Pr.

Weyl, Hermann. Algebraic Theory of Numbers. rev. ed. (Annals of Mathematics Studies: No. 1). (Orig.). 1954. pap. 16.50x (ISBN 0-691-07908-0). Princeton U Pr.

Wright, C. Frege's Conception of Numbers As Objects. 150p. pap. 13.50 (ISBN 0-08-025726-7). Pergamon.

Zassenhaus, Hans. Number Theory & Algebra: Collected Papers Dedicated to Henry B. Mann, Arnold E. Ross & Olga Taussky-Todd. 1977. 56.00 (ISBN 0-12-776350-3). Acad Pr.

NUMBERS, TRANSCENDENTAL

Baker, A. Transcendental Number Theory. LC 74-82591. 148p. 1975. 19.95x (ISBN 0-521-20461-5). Cambridge U Pr.

Lang, Serge A. Introduction to Transcendental Numbers. 1966. 7.50 (ISBN 0-201-04176-6, Adv Bk Prog). A-W.

Mahler, K. Lectures on Transcendental Numbers. Divis, B. & Le Veque, W. J., eds. 1976. soft cover 13.70 (ISBN 0-387-07986-6). Springer-Verlag.

Sprindzuk, V. G. Mahler's Problem in Metric Number Theory. LC 73-86327. (Translations of Mathematical Monographs: Vol. 25). 1969. 21.20 (ISBN 0-8218-1575-X, MMONO-25). Am Math.

NUMBERS, TRANSFINITE

Dauben, Joseph W. Georg Cantor: His Mathematics & Philosophy of the Infinite. 1979. 27.50x (ISBN 0-674-34871-0). Harvard U Pr.

Zuckerman, M. M. Sets & Transfinite Numbers. 1974. 16.95 (ISBN 0-02-432110-9). Macmillan.

NUMBERS IN THE BIBLE

Davis, John J. Biblical Numerology. (Orig.). 1968. pap. 3.95 (ISBN 0-8010-2813-2). Baker Bk.

--Biblical Numerology. pap. 3.95 (ISBN 0-88469-063-6). BMH Bks.

Grant, Frederick W. Witness the Witness of Arithmetic to Christ. 64p. 1980. pap. 1.95 (ISBN 0-87213-272-2). Loizeaux.

Lucas, Jerry & Washburn, Del. Theomatics: God's Best Kept Secret Revealed. LC 76-49958. (Illus.). 1977. 8.95 (ISBN 0-8128-2181-5); pap. 6.95 (ISBN 0-8128-6017-9). Stein & Day.

Wenham, Gordon J. Numbers. Wiseman, D. J., ed. (Tyndale Old Testament Commentaries Ser.). 240p. 1981. 10.95 (ISBN 0-87784-891-2). Inter-Varsity.

NUMERALS

see also Numeration; Symbolism of Numbers

Allington, Richard L. Numbers. LC 79-19200. (Beginning to Learn About Ser.). (Illus.). (gr. k-2). 1979. PLB 10.65 (ISBN 0-8172-1278-7). Raintree Pubs.

Bing, Ilse. Numbers in Images: Illuminations of Numerical Meanings. LC 76-5739. (Illus.). 176p. 1976. 9.95 (ISBN 0-916832-00-7). Ilkon Pr.

Carson, R. A. & Kraay, C. M. Scripta Numaria Romana. 1979. 60.00 (ISBN 0-686-63876-X, Pub. by Spink & Son England). S J Durst.

Crone, Rainer F. Numerals, Nineteen Twenty-Four to Nineteen Seventy-Seven. (Illus.). 84p. 1978. pap. 10.00 (ISBN 0-87451-983-7). U Pr of New Eng.

--Numerals, Nineteen Twenty-Four to Nineteen Seventy-Seven. (Illus.). 84p. 1978. pap. 10.00 (ISBN 0-87451-983-7). U Pr of Amer.

Friend, J. Newton. Numbers: Fun & Facts. 1972. 5.95 (ISBN 0-684-10186-6, ScribT); (ScribT). Scribner.

Reid, Constance. From Zero to Infinity. enl. rev. ed. (Apollo Eds.). (Illus.). (YA) (gr. 9-12). pap. 1.95 (ISBN 0-8152-0119-2, A119). T Y Crowell.

Skinner, Hubert M. The Story of the Letters & Figures. LC 71-175744. (Illus.). 1971. Repr. of 1905 ed. 22.00 (ISBN 0-8103-3035-0). Gale.

Smith, David E. Number Stories of Long Ago. LC 70-167181. (Illus.). 150p. (gr. 1 up). 1973. Repr. of 1951 ed. 22.00 (ISBN 0-8103-3273-6). Gale.

Smith, David E. & Ginsburg, Jekuthiel. Numbers & Numerals. 1937. pap. 2.40 (ISBN 0-87353-078-0). NCTM.

Wehrli, Kitty. Numbers & Numerals. (Michigan Arithmetic Program). (ps-2). 1976. 1.00x (ISBN 0-89039-199-8); wkbk. 5.00 (ISBN 0-89039-102-5). Ann Arbor Pubs.

NUMERATION

see also Binary System (Mathematics); Decimal System; Number Concept; Numerals

Fair, Jan. Electric Drill-Whole Numbers. (Electric Drill Set Ser.). (gr. 5-12). 1977. 24.95 (ISBN 0-88488-076-1). Creative Pubns.

Fomin, S. V. Sistemas De Numeracion. 46p. (Span.). 1975. pap. 1.15 (ISBN 0-8285-1692-8, Pub. by Mir Pubs Russia). Imported Pubns.

Hackworth, Robert D. & Howland, Joseph. Introductory College Mathematics: Numeration. LC 75-23626. 60p. 1976. pap. text ed. 2.95 (ISBN 0-7216-4419-8). HR&W.

LeBlanc, John F., et al. Mathematics-Methods Program: Numeration. (Mathematics Ser.). 128p. 1976. pap. 3.95 (ISBN 0-201-14606-1); instr's man. 1.50 (ISBN 0-201-14607-X). A-W.

McNamara, Terry S. Numeracy & Accounting. (Illus.). 370p. 1979. pap. text ed. 16.95x (ISBN 0-7121-1411-4, Pub. by Macdonald & Evans England). Intl Ideas.

Pai, Hang Y. The Complete Book of Chisanbop: Original Finger Calculation Method. 340p. 1981. 17.95 (ISBN 0-442-27569-2); pap. 12.95 (ISBN 0-442-27568-4). Van Nos Reinhold.

Pohl, A. Principles of Counting. (Finite Math Text Ser.). write for info. (ISBN 0-685-84479-X). J W Wills.

NUMERATION-JUVENILE LITERATURE

Activity Fun with Words & Numbers. (Golden Fun at Home Workbooks). 64p. (ps). 1981. 0.99 (ISBN 0-307-01462-2, Golden Pr). Western Pub.

Adler, David A. Roman Numerals. LC 77-2270. (Young Math Ser.). (Illus.). (gr. 1-4). 1977. PLB 8.79 (ISBN 0-690-01302-7, TYC-J). Har-Row.

--Three, Two, One Number Fun. (Activity Bks.). 128p. 1981. pap. 2.95 (ISBN 0-385-15558-1). Doubleday.

Allen, Robert. Numbers. LC 68-19579. (Illus.). (ps-2). 1968. 3.50 (ISBN 0-448-41053-2). Platt.

Allington. Beginning to Learn About Numbers. Date not set. lib. bdg. 7.99 (ISBN 0-8172-1278-7). Raintree Pubs.

Animal Counting Book. (Children's Library of Picture Books). (Illus.). 10p. (ps). 1966. 1.95 (ISBN 0-89346-127-X, TA4, Pub. by Froebel-Kan Japan). Heian Intl.

Anno, Mitsumasa. Anno's Counting Book. LC 76-28977. (Illus.). (ps-3). 1977. 8.95 (ISBN 0-690-01287-X, TYC-J); PLB 9.89 (ISBN 0-690-01288-8). Har-Row.

Asch, Frank. Little Devil's One Two Three. LC 79-11867. (Illus.). (ps-1). 1979. 6.95 (ISBN 0-684-16294-6). Scribner.

Bayley, Nicola, illus. One Old Oxford Ox. LC 77-77866. (ps-3). 1977. 6.95 (ISBN 0-689-30608-3). Atheneum.

Berenstain, Stan & Berenstain, Janice. The Berenstain Bears' Counting Book. LC 75-36461. (Illus.). 14p. (ps-1). 1976. 2.95 (ISBN 0-394-83246-9, BYR). Random.

Bruna, Dick. I Know More About Numbers. (Bruna Books). (Illus.). (ps-2). 1981. 3.50 (ISBN 0-416-20870-3). Methuen Inc.

--One-Two-Three Frieze. (Bruna Books). (Illus.). 24p. (Orig.). (ps-2). 1976. pap. 5.50 four foldout paper panels (ISBN 0-416-80350-4). Methuen Inc.

Cory's Counting Game. (Surprise Books). (Illus.). (ps). 1979. 3.50 (ISBN 0-8431-0629-8). Price Stern.

Count to Ten. (Block Bk.). (Illus.). (ps). 1981. 2.50 (ISBN 0-686-69367-1, Golden Pr). Western Pub.

Counting. 8p. 1981. pap. 1.50 (ISBN 0-8431-0709-X). Price Stern.

Counting Friends. (Children's Library of Picture Books). (Illus.). 10p. (ps). 1.95 (ISBN 0-89346-133-4, TA64, Pub. by Froebel-Kan Japan). Heian Intl.

Counting Thymes Book: The Ten Little Indians. (Three-D Puppet Story Bk.). (ps). 1968. 1.95 (ISBN 0-448-00756-8). G&D.

Dodd, Lynley. The Nickle Nackle Tree. LC 77-12493. (Illus.). (gr. k-3). 1978. 8.95 (ISBN 0-02-732610-1, 73261). Macmillan.

Editions les Belles Images Staff, tr. from Fr. In My Garden: Learning to Count. (Butterfly Bks). (Illus.). 16p. (Orig.). (ps-2). 1976. pap. 1.50 (ISBN 0-8467-0219-3, Pub. by Two Continents). Hippocrene Bks.

Fairy Tale Counting Book. (Children's Library of Picture Bks.). (Illus.). 10p. (ps). 1966. 1.95 (ISBN 0-89346-138-5, TA42, Pub. by Froebel-Kan Japan). Heian Intl.

Fisher, Margery M. One & One. LC 63-9776. (gr. k-3). 1963. 2.95 (ISBN 0-8037-6626-2). Dial.

Godfrey, Elsa, illus. Count to Ten in No Man's Valley. LC 81-50716. (Shape Bks.). (Illus.). 24p. (ps-1). 1981. bds. 2.50 (ISBN 0-394-84980-9). Random.

Kenyon, Raymond G. I Can Learn About Calculators & Computers. LC 61-5771. (Illus.). (gr. 5 up). 1961. PLB 7.89 (ISBN 0-06-023141-6, HarpJ). Har-Row.

Kraus, Robert. Good Night Little One. (Good Night Bks.). (Illus.). 32p. (ps-2). 1981. paper over board 1.95 (ISBN 0-671-41091-1, Pub. by Windmill). S&S.

Kraus, Robert & Kraus, Pam. You Can Count on Brownies. LC 80-50808. (Big Brownie Bks). (Illus.). 32p. (ps up). 1981. pap. 2.95 (ISBN 0-671-43393-8). Windmill Bks.

Kulas, Jim. Puppy's One-Two-Three Book. (Illus.). (gr. k-1). 1978. PLB 5.38 (ISBN 0-307-68990-5, Golden Pr). Western Pub.

Laptev, V. One Two Three. 16p. 1976. pap. 0.75 (ISBN 0-8285-1217-5, Pub. by Progress Pubs Russia). Imported Pubns.

Leighton, Ralph & Feynman, Carl. How to Count Sheep Without Falling Asleep. LC 76-10237. (Illus.). (gr. 1-4). 1976. PLB 5.95 (ISBN 0-13-404459-2). P-H.

Luce, Marnie. Counting Systems: The Familiar & the Unusual. LC 68-56708. (Math Concept Bks). (gr. 3-6). 1969. PLB 3.95 (ISBN 0-8225-0579-7). Lerner Pubns.

McLeod, Emilie Warren. One Snail & Me. (Illus.). 32p. (ps-1). 1981. 9.95 (ISBN 0-316-56198-3, Pub. by Atlantic Monthly Pr); pap. 3.95 (ISBN 0-316-56199-1). Little.

McNaughton, Colin. A B C & One Two Three. LC 77-71993. (gr. 1 up). 1977. 5.95a (ISBN 0-385-13273-5); PLB (ISBN 0-385-13614-5). Doubleday.

Madell, Robert & Stahl, Elizabeth L. Picturing Numeration. (gr. k-3). 1977. wkbk. 8.50 (ISBN 0-88488-071-0). Creative Pubns.

Magarian, Judith A. Numbers Ten to Twenty. (Illus.). 24p. (gr. k-3). 1980. pap. 4.25 (ISBN 0-933358-58-X). Enrich.

Mahoney, Susan. Basic Number Concepts Learning Module. Molly, Julia S., ed. 1977. pap. text ed. 181.50 (ISBN 0-89290-147-0, CM-91). Soc for Visual.

Makakabilang Ako Ng Sampu. (Illus.). (ps). 1970. 4.25 (ISBN 0-686-09533-2). Cellar.

Mann, Philip. Contando Para Divertirme. Kreps, Georgian, tr. from Eng. (Shape Board Play Books). Orig. Title: Counting for Fun. (Illus.). 14p. (Span.). (ps-3). 1981. bds. 3.50 plastic com bdg (ISBN 0-89828-203-9, 5003SP). Tuffy Bks.

Miller, Roberta. Counting Book. (Golden Play & Learn Bks). (gr. k-2). 1967. 2.95 (ISBN 0-307-10735-3, Golden Pr). Western Pub.

Nedobeck, Don. Nedobeck's Numbers Book. 32p. (gr. k-6). 1981. 3.25 (ISBN 0-8249-8015-8). Ideals.

Nolan, Dennis. Monster Bubbles: A Counting Book. LC 76-10167. 1976. PLB 5.95 (ISBN 0-13-600635-3); pap. 1.95 (ISBN 0-13-600643-4). P-H.

Number Fun. (Golden Fun at Home Workbooks). 64p. (ps). 1981. 0.99 (ISBN 0-307-01435-5, Golden Pr). Western Pub.

Peppe, Rodney. Humphrey the Number Horse: Fun with Counting & Multiplication. LC 77-18782. (Illus.). (gr. k-3). 1978. 7.95 (ISBN 0-670-38666-9). Viking Pr.

Pienkowski, Jan. Numbers. Klimo, Kate, ed. (Concept Bks). (Illus.). 32p. 1981. Repr. 3.95 (ISBN 0-671-44456-5, Little Simon). S&S.

Rabens, Neil. One Happy Little Songbird. (A Happy Day Book). (Illus.). 24p. (gr. k-3). 1979. 0.98 (ISBN 0-87239-361-5, 3631). Standard Pub.

Richards, Dorothy F. Wise Owl's Counting Book. (The Wise Owl Ser.). (Illus.). 32p. (ps-2). Date not set. PLB price not set (ISBN 0-516-06565-3). Childrens.

Robertson, Patricia & Bounds, Barbara. Sunshine Math Numeration. (gr. k-3). 1977. wkbk. 6.95 (ISBN 0-88488-066-4). Creative Pubns.

Rosenburg, Amye, illus. One, Two, Buckle My Shoe. (Illus.). 6p. (ps-k). 1981. 3.50 (ISBN 0-671-42532-3, Little Simon). S&S.

Ross, H. L. Not Counting Monsters. LC 77-87557. (A Cricket Book). (Illus.). (gr. k-2). 1978. 1.95 (ISBN 0-448-46524-8). Platt.

Sazer, Nina. What Do You Think I Saw? A Nonsense Number Book. LC 75-26643. (Illus.). 32p. (gr. k-1). 1976. 2.95 (ISBN 0-394-83182-9). Pantheon.

Scarry, Richard. Learn to Count. (Golden Look-Look Bks.). (Illus.). (ps-1). 1976. PLB 5.38 (ISBN 0-307-61829-3, Golden Pr); pap. 0.95 (ISBN 0-307-11829-0). Western Pub.

--Richard Scarry's Best Counting Book Ever. LC 74-2544. (Illus.). 48p. (ps-2). 1975. 4.95 (ISBN 0-394-82924-7, BYR); PLB 5.99 (ISBN 0-394-92924-1). Random.

Schulz, Charles M., illus. Tubby Book Featuring Snoopy. (Tubby Bks.). (Illus.). 10p. (ps). 1980. vinyl book 2.95 (ISBN 0-671-41335-X, Pub. by Windmill). S&S.

Sendak, Maurice. Ten Little Rabbits: A Counting Book for Children with Mino the Magician. (Illus.). (ps). 1981. pap. 2.50 (ISBN 0-686-76779-9). U Pr of Va.

Sesame Street. The Counting Book. (Sesame Street Pop-Up Ser.: No. 2). (ps-2). 1971. span. ed. 2.95 (ISBN 0-394-83037-7, BYR). Random.

Sitomer, Mindel & Sitomer, Harry. How Did Numbers Begin? LC 75-11756. (Young Math Ser.). (Illus.). 40p. (gr. k-3). 1976. 8.79 (ISBN 0-690-00794-9, TYC-J). Har-Row.

Smith, David E. Number Stories of Long Ago. LC 70-167181. (Illus.). 150p. (gr. 1 up). 1973. Repr. of 1951 ed. 22.00 (ISBN 0-8103-3273-6). Gale.

Spires, Elizabeth. Count with Me. (Poke & Look Bks). (ps-1). 1981. 5.95 (ISBN 0-686-76681-4). Merrill.

Srivastava, Jane J. Number Families. LC 78-19511. (Illus.). (gr. 2-5). 1979. PLB 8.79 (ISBN 0-690-03924-7, TYC-J). Har-Row.

Steiner, Charlotte. Ten in a Family. (Illus.). (ps). 1960. PLB 4.99 (ISBN 0-394-91734-0). Knopf.

Sustendal, Pat, illus. Strawberry Shortcake's One-Two-Three. LC 80-85420. (Chunky Bks.). (Illus.). 28p. (ps). 1981. bds. 2.50 (ISBN 0-394-84896-9). Random.

Tod, M. N. Ancient Greek Numerical Systems. 128p. 1979. 20.00 (ISBN 0-89005-290-5). Ares.

Youldos, Gillian. Counting. (All a-Board Bks. Ser.). (ps-2). 1980. 2.95 (ISBN 0-531-02142-4). Watts.

Zaslavsky, Claudia. Count on Your Fingers African Style. LC 77-26586. (Illus.). 32p. (gr. k-3). 1980. 8.95 (ISBN 0-690-03864-X, TYC-J); PLB 8.79 (ISBN 0-690-03865-8). Har-Row.

NUMERATION-PROBLEMS, EXERCISES, ETC.

Rylands, Ljiljana. Counting Balloons. (ps-2). 1979. pap. 1.45 avail. in 5 pk. (ISBN 0-686-28363-5, Pub. by Dinosaur Pubns). Merrimack Bk Serv.

NUMERATION OF BOOKS IN LIBRARIES

see Alphabeting

NUMERICAL ANALYSIS

see also Digital Filters (Mathematics); Finite Element Method; Interpolation; Iterative Methods (Mathematics); Monte Carlo Method; Nomography (Mathematics); Numerical Calculations; Numerical Integration; Random Walks (Mathematics)

Acton, Forman S. Numerical Methods That Work. (Illus.). 1970. text ed. 31.50 scp (ISBN 0-06-040161-3, HarpC). Har-Row.

Altman. Contractors & Contractor Direction Theory & Applications: A New Approach to Solving Equations, Vol. 32. (Lecture Notes in Pure & Applied Math). 1977. 29.75 (ISBN 0-8247-6672-5). Dekker.

Ansorge, Rainer, et al. Numerical Mathematics-Numerische Mathematik. (International Series of Numerical Mathematics: No. 49). 207p. (Eng. Ger.). 1979. 28.00 (ISBN 3-7643-1099-5). Birkhauser.

Atkinson, Kendall E. An Introduction to Numerical Analysis. LC 78-6706. 587p. 1978. text ed. 29.95 (ISBN 0-471-02985-8); solutions manual o.p. 5.00 (ISBN 0-471-03749-4). Wiley.

Avriel, Mordecai, ed. Advances in Geometric Programming. (Mathematical Concepts & Methods in Science & Engineering Ser.: Vol. 21). 470p. 1980. 39.50 (ISBN 0-306-40381-1, Plenum Pr). Plenum Pub.

Baker, Christopher. The Numerical Treatment of Integral Equations. (Monographs on Numerical Analysis). (Illus.). 1048p. 1977. text ed. 69.00x (ISBN 0-19-853406-X). Oxford U Pr.

Bakhualov, N. S. Numerical Methods. 663p. 1977. 9.00 (ISBN 0-8285-0731-7, Pub. by Mir Pubs Russia). Imported Pubns.

Bavel, Zamir. A Math Companion for Computer Science. 1981. pap. 13.00 (ISBN 0-8359-4299-6). Reston.

Beck, R. E. & Kolman, B. Computers in Nonassociative Rings & Algebras. 1977. 25.00 (ISBN 0-12-083850-8). Acad Pr.

Berztiss, A. T. Data Structures: Theory & Practice. 2nd ed. (Computer Science & Applied Mathematics Ser.). 586p. 1975. 21.95 (ISBN 0-12-093552-X). Acad Pr.

Biennial Conference, Dundee, Great Britain, June 28-July 1, 1977. Numerical Analysis: Proceedings. Watson, G. A., ed. (Lecture Notes in Mathematics Ser.: Vol. 630). 1978. pap. 14.30 (ISBN 0-387-08538-6). Springer-Verlag.

Blum, E. K. Numerical Analysis Computation: Theory & Practice. LC 79-150574. 1972. text ed. 20.95 (ISBN 0-201-00614-6). A-W.

Bock, R. Darrell & Kolakowski, Donald. Logog: Maximum Likelihood Item Analysis & Test Scoring-Logical Model for Multiple Item Responses. pap. 2.75 (ISBN 0-89498-005-X). Natl Ed Res.

Bock, R. Darrell & Yates, George R. Multiqual: Log-linear Analysis of Nominal or Ordinal Qualitative Data by the Method of Maximum Likelihood. pap. 2.75 (ISBN 0-89498-008-4). Natl Ed Res.

Brezinski, C. Pade-Typed Approximation & General Orthogonal Polynomials. (International Series of Numerical Mathematics: No. 50). 250p. 1979. pap. 34.00 (ISBN 3-7643-1100-2). Birkhauser.

Burden, Richard, et al. Numerical Analysis. 2nd ed. LC 80-29558. 598p. 1981. text ed. write for info. (ISBN 0-87150-314-X, 33L 2511). Prindle.

Cabannes, H., et al, eds. Sixth International Conference on Numerical Methods in Fluid Dynamics: Proceedings of the Conference, Held in Tbilisi (USSR) June 21-24, 1978. (Lecture Notes in Physics: Vol. 90). 1979. pap. 28.40 (ISBN 0-387-09115-7). Springer-Verlag.

Carnahan, Brice, et al. Applied Numerical Methods. LC 67-27555. 1969. 31.95 (ISBN 0-471-13507-0). Wiley.

Cheney, Ward & Kincaid, David. Numerical Analysis & Computing. LC 79-17230. 1980. text ed. 19.95 (ISBN 0-8185-0357-2). Brooks-Cole.

Clifford & Clifford. Computer Mathematics Handbook. 15.95x (ISBN 0-205-04311-9, 2043114). Allyn.

Collatz, Lothar. Functional Analysis & Numerical Mathematics. Oser, H., tr. 1966. 52.50 (ISBN 0-12-180450-X). Acad Pr.

Conference on Applications of Numerical Analysis, Dundee, Scotland, 1971. Proceedings. Morris, J. L., ed. (Lecture Notes in Mathematics: Vol. 228). 358p. 1971. pap. 14.10 (ISBN 0-387-05656-4). Springer-Verlag.

--Proceedings. Morris, J. L., ed. (Lecture Notes in Mathematics: Vol. 228). 358p. 1971. pap. 14.10 (ISBN 0-387-05656-4). Springer-Verlag.

Conference on Linear Spaces & Approximation, Mathematical Research Institute Oberwolfach, Aug. 1977. Proceedings. Butzer, Paul L. & Sz.-Nagy, Bela, eds. (International Series of Numerical Mathematics: Vol. 40). 1978. text ed. 54.25x (ISBN 3-7643-0979-2). Renouf.

Conley, William. Computer Optimization Techniques. (Illus.). 266p. 1980. 24.00 (ISBN 0-07-091059-6). McGraw.

Conway, J. B. Numerical Methods for Creep & Rupture Analysis. 1967. 45.25 (ISBN 0-677-01090-7). Gordon.

Crowell, W., ed. Portability of Numerical Software: Proceedings. LC 77-13623. (Lecture Notes in Computer Science: Vol. 57). 1977. pap. text ed. 24.10 (ISBN 0-387-08446-0). Springer-Verlag.

Davies, Alan J. The Finite Element Method: A First Approach. (Oxford Applied Mathematics & Computing Science Ser.). (Illus.). 300p. 1980. 49.50x (ISBN 0-19-859630-8); pap. 27.50x (ISBN 0-19-859631-6). Oxford U Pr.

De Boor, Carl & Golub, Gene H., eds. Recent Advances in Numerical Analysis. (Mathematics Research Center Symposia Ser.). 1978. 19.50 (ISBN 0-12-208360-1). Acad Pr.

De Bruijn, N. G. Asymptotic Methods in Analysis. 3rd ed. (Bibliotheca Mathematica Ser.: Vol. 4). 1958. 24.50 (ISBN 0-444-10330-9, North-Holland). Elsevier.

DeVore, R. A. & Scherer, K., eds. Quantitative Approximation. LC 80-17554. 1980. 22.00 (ISBN 0-12-213650-0). Acad Pr.

Dodes. Numerical Analysis for Computer Science. 1978. text ed. 19.95 (ISBN 0-444-00238-3, North-Holland). Elsevier.

European Conference on Computational Physics, 2nd, Garching, Apr. 1976. Computing in Plasma Physics: Proceedings. Biskamp, D., ed. 1977. 36.75 (ISBN 0-7204-0713-3, North-Holland). Elsevier.

Faddeeva, V. N., ed. Automatic Programming & Numerical Methods of Analysis. LC 76-37618. (Seminars in Mathematics Ser.: Vol. 18). 1972. 25.00 (ISBN 0-306-18818-X, Consultants). Plenum Pub.

Fichera, G. Numerical & Quantitative Analysis. (Surveys & References Ser.). 218p. 1978. text ed. 39.95 (ISBN 0-273-00284-8). Pitman Pub MA.

Flynn, M. J., et al. Operating Systems: An Advanced Course. (Springer Study Editions). 593p. 1980. pap. 20.80 (ISBN 0-387-09812-7). Springer-Verlag.

Fox, Leslie & Mayers, D. F. Computing Methods for Scientists & Engineers. (Monographs in Numerical Analysis). (Illus.). 1968. 59.00x (ISBN 0-19-853404-3). Oxford U Pr.

Garbow, B. S. Matrix Eigensystem Routines-Eispack Guide Extension. (Lecture Notes in Computer Science: Vol. 51). 1977. 18.30 (ISBN 0-387-08254-9). Springer-Verlag.

GARP Program on Numerical Experimentation. (GARP Publications Ser: No. 7). (Illus., Orig.). 1972. pap. 10.00 (ISBN 0-685-02932-8, WMO). Unipub.

Gastinel, Noel. Linear Numerical Analysis. LC 70-108619. 1971. 49.50 (ISBN 0-12-277150-8). Acad Pr.

Gerald, Curtis F. Applied Numerical Analysis. 2nd ed. LC 77-79469. (Illus.). 1978. text ed. 21.95 (ISBN 0-201-02696-1). A-W.

Goldstine, H. H. A History of Numerical Analysis from the 16th to the 19th Century. LC 77-5029. (Studies in the History of Mathematics & Physical Sciences: Vol. 2). (Illus.). 1977. pap. text ed. 31.60 (ISBN 0-387-90277-5). Springer-Verlag.

Golub, Gene H. & Oliger, Joseph, eds. Numerical Analysis. LC 78-11096. 135p. 1980. pap. 11.20 (ISBN 0-8218-0122-8). Am Math.

Greenspan, Donald. Computer-Oriented Mathematical Physics. (I.S. in Nonlinear Mathematics Ser.: Vol. 3). (Illus.). 179p. 1981. 25.00 (ISBN 0-08-026471-9); pap. 9.70 (ISBN 0-08-026470-0). Pergamon.

--Discrete Numerical Methods in Physics & Engineering. (Mathematics in Science & Engineering Ser.). 1974. 34.00 (ISBN 0-12-300350-4). Acad Pr.

Grove, Wendell E. Brief Numerical Methods. 1966. text ed. 17.95x (ISBN 0-13-082917-X). P-H.

Haberman, Shelby. C-Tab: Analysis of Multidimensional Contingency Tables by Log-linear Models. pap. 2.25 (ISBN 0-89498-006-8). Natl Ed Res.

Hamming, Richard W. Introduction to Applied Numerical Analysis. 1970. text ed. 22.50 (ISBN 0-07-025889-9, C). McGraw.

Hansen, Eldon R. The Numerical Analysis CumIndex, Vol. 9. 1979. 60.00 (ISBN 0-88274-008-3). R & D Pr.

Hemker, P. W. & Miller, J. J., eds. Numerical Analysis of Singular Perturbation Problems. 1979. 47.00 (ISBN 0-12-340250-6). Acad Pr.

Henrici, Peter K. Elements of Numerical Analysis. LC 64-23840. 1964. 26.95 (ISBN 0-471-37241-2). Wiley.

Hildebrand, Francis B. Introduction to Numerical Analysis. 2nd ed. 1973. text ed. 22.50 (ISBN 0-07-028761-9, C); instructor's manual 3.50 (ISBN 0-07-028763-5). McGraw.

Hornbeck, Robert W. Numerical Methods. (QPI Ser.). 1975. pap. 7.95 (ISBN 0-934644-02-0). Quantum Pubs.

Householder, Alston S. The Theory of Matrices in Numerical Analysis. LC 74-83763. 288p. 1975. pap. text ed. 4.00 (ISBN 0-486-61781-5). Dover.

Hua, L. K. & Wang, Y. Applications of Number Theory to Numerical Analysis. 241p. 1981. 39.00 (ISBN 0-387-10382-1). Springer-Verlag.

Huelsman, Lawrence P. Digital Computation in Basic Circuit Theory. (Illus.). 1968. text ed. 18.50 (ISBN 0-07-030843-8, C). McGraw.

International Conference on Numerical Methods in Fluid Dynamics, 4th, University of Colorado, June 24-28, 1974. Meningiomas Diagnostic & Therapeutic Problems: Proceeding. Richtmyer, R. D., ed. (Lecture Notes in Physics Ser.: Vol. 35). (Illus.). vi, 457p. 1975. pap. 20.30 (ISBN 0-387-07139-3). Springer-Verlag.

International Symposium, Karlsruhe, West Germany, May 20-24, 1975. Interval Mathematics: Proceedings. Nickel, K., ed. (Lecture Notes in Computer Science Ser.: Vol. 29). vi, 331p. 1975. pap. 16.50 (ISBN 0-387-07170-9). Springer-Verlag.

International Symposium on Control Theory, Numerical Methods & Computer Systems Modelling, June, 1974. Proceedings. Bensoussan, A. & Lions, J. L., eds. LC 74-28484. (Lecture Notes in Economics & Mathematical Systems Ser.: Vol. 107). viii, 757p. 1975. pap. 29.00 (ISBN 0-387-07020-6). Springer-Verlag.

Isaacson, Eugene & Keller, H. B. The Analysis of Numerical Methods. LC 66-17630. 1966. 34.95 (ISBN 0-471-42865-5). Wiley.

Jacobs, D. A., ed. The State of the Art in Numerical an Analysis. (Mathematics & Its Application Ser.). 1977. 107.00 (ISBN 0-12-378650-9). Acad Pr.

Jaffe, Arthur & Taubes, Clifford. Vortices & Monopoles: Structure of Static Gauge Theories. 275p. 1980. text ed. 16.00 (ISBN 3-7643-3025-2). Birkhauser.

Jameson, W. J., Jr., ed. Studies in Numerical Analysis, One. (Illus.). 1968. text ed. 9.75 (ISBN 0-89871-042-1). Soc Indus-Appl Math.

Jensen, Jens A. & Rowland, John H. Methods of Computation: The Linear Space Approach to Numerical Analysis. 303p. 1975. text ed. 15.95x (ISBN 0-673-05394-6). Scott F.

John, F. Lectures on Advanced Numerical Analysis. (Notes on Mathematics & Its Applications Ser). 1967. 22.00 (ISBN 0-685-88495-3). Gordon.

Johnson, Lee W. & Riess, R. Dean. Numerical Analysis. LC 76-14658. (Illus.). 1977. text ed. 18.95 (ISBN 0-201-03442-5). A-W.

Kellison, Stephen G. Fundamentals of Numerical Analysis. LC 74-78157. 1974. 17.50x (ISBN 0-256-01612-7). Irwin.

Khabaza, I. M. Numerical Analysis. 1965. text ed. 25.00 (ISBN 0-08-010776-1); pap. text ed. 12.75 (ISBN 0-08-010775-3). Pergamon.

Kovach, Ladis. Computer-Oriented Mathematics: An Introduction to Numerical Methods. LC 64-21711. 1964. 6.95x (ISBN 0-8162-4794-3). Holden-Day.

Kulisch, Ulrich W. & Miranker, Willard L. Computer Arithmetic in Theory & Practice. LC 80-765. (Computer Science & Applied Mathematics Ser.). 1980. 25.00 (ISBN 0-12-428650-X). Acad Pr.

Kurata, Mamoru. Numerical Analysis for Semiconductor Devices. LC 80-8374. 1981. write for info. (ISBN 0-669-04043-6). Lexington Bks.

Lambert, J. D. Computational Methods in Ordinary Differential Equations. LC 72-5718. (Introductory Mathematics for Scientists & Engineers Ser.). 278p. 1973. text ed. 35.75 (ISBN 0-471-51194-3, Pub. by Wiley-Interscience). Wiley.

Lee, John A. Numerical Analysis for Computers. 1966. 14.95x (ISBN 0-442-17003-3). Van Nos Reinhold.

Lewis, R. W. & Morgan, K. Numerical Methods in Heat Transfer. Zienkiewicz, O. C., ed. LC 80-49973. (Numerical Methods in Engineering Ser.). 536p. 1981. 78.75 (ISBN 0-471-27803-3, Pub. by Wiley-Interscience). Wiley.

Linz, Peter. Theoretical Numerical Analysis: An Introduction to Advanced Techniques. LC 78-15178. (Pure & Applied Mathematics: Texts, Monographs & Tracts). 1979. 26.95 (ISBN 0-471-04561-6, Pub. by Wiley-Interscience). Wiley.

Lipson, John D. Elements of Algebra & Algebraic Computing. 420p. 1980. text ed. 34.50 (ISBN 0-201-04115-4). A-W.

Lyon, A. J. Dealing with Data. LC 76-92111. 1970. text ed. 28.00 (ISBN 0-08-006398-5); pap. text ed. 17.00 (ISBN 0-08-006397-7). Pergamon.

McCalla, Thomas R. Introduction to Numerical Methods & FORTRAN Programming. LC 66-28745. 1967. 26.75 (ISBN 0-471-58125-9, Pub. by Wiley-Interscience). Wiley.

Marchuk, G. I. Methods of Numerical Mathematics. Ruzicka, J., tr. from Rus. LC 75-15566. (Applications of Mathematics: Vol. 2). viii, 352p. 1975. 41.80 (ISBN 0-387-90156-6). Springer-Verlag.

Maron, Melvinj. Applied Numerical Analysis. 1982. text ed. 22.95 (ISBN 0-686-75013-6). Macmillan.

Medgyessy, Pal. Decomposition of Superpositions of Density Functions & Discrete Distributions. LC 75-46231. 308p. 1977. 43.95x (ISBN 0-470-15017-3). Halsted Pr.

Meinardus, Guenter. Approximation of Functions: Theory & Numerical Methods. Schumaker, L. L., tr. LC 67-21464. (Springer Tracts in Natural Philosophy: Vol. 13). (Illus.). 1967. 41.30 (ISBN 0-387-03985-6). Springer-Verlag.

Miller, J. H., ed. Topics in Numerical Analysis III. 1978. 75.50 (ISBN 0-12-496953-4). Acad Pr.

Miller, J. J., ed. Topics in Numerical Analysis II. 1976. 42.00 (ISBN 0-12-496952-6). Acad Pr.

Mittelmann, H., ed. Brfurcation Prpblems & Their Numerical Solution. (ISNM Ser.: No. 54). 252p. 1980. pap. 24.50 (ISBN 3-7643-1204-1). Birkhauser.

Moorhead, Jack, ed. Numerical Control Applications. LC 80-52613. (Manufacturing Update Ser.). (Illus.). 260p. 1980. 29.00 (ISBN 0-87263-058-7). SME.

--Numerical Control Fundamentals. LC 80-52723. (Manufacturing Update Ser.). (Illus.). 242p. 1980. 29.00 (ISBN 0-87263-057-9). SME.

Morton, B. R. Numerical Approximation. (Library of Mathematics). 1969. pap. 5.00 (ISBN 0-7100-4354-6). Routledge & Kegan.

Moursund, David G. & Duris, C. S. Elementary Theory & Application of Numerical Analysis. 1967. text ed. 18.95 (ISBN 0-07-043560-X, C). McGraw.

Nash, J. C. Compact Numerical Methods for Computers: Linear Algebra & Functional Minimization. LC 78-10144. 1979. 32.95x (ISBN 0-470-26559-0). Halsted Pr.

Ortega, James M. & Rheinboldt, Werner C., eds. Studies in Numerical Analysis, Two: Numerical Solutions of Nonlinear Problems. (Illus.). 1970. text ed. 9.75 (ISBN 0-89871-043-X). Soc Indus-Appl Math.

Prather, Ronald E. Discrete Mathematical Structures for Computer Science. LC 75-25014. (Illus.). 680p. 1976. text ed. 20.95 (ISBN 0-395-20622-7); solutions manual 1.50 (ISBN 0-395-20623-5). HM.

Pressman, R. S. & Williams, J. E. Numerical Control & Computer-Aided Manufacturing. 310p. 1977. text ed. 28.95 (ISBN 0-471-01555-5). Wiley.

Price, Wilson T. & Miller, M. Elements of Data Processing Mathematics. 2nd ed. LC 71-140239. 1971. text ed. 18.95 (ISBN 0-03-084745-1, HoltC). HR&W.

Proceedings of the Colloquium on Numerical Analysis, Lausanne, Oct. 11-13, 1976. Numerical Analysis. Descloux, J. & Marti, J. T., eds. (International Series of Numerical Mathematics: No. 37). 248p. 1977. pap. 32.50 (ISBN 3-7643-0939-3). Birkhauser.

Ralston, A. & Rabinowitz, Philip. A First Course in Numerical Analysis. (McGraw Hill Intl. Ser. in Pure & Applied Mathematics). (Illus.). 1978. text ed. 22.00 (ISBN 0-07-051158-6, C). McGraw.

Remson, Irwin, et al. Numerical Methods in Subsurface Hydrology. LC 75-142139. 1971. 43.50 (ISBN 0-471-71650-2, Pub. by Wiley-Interscience). Wiley.

Royal Irish Academy, Conference, 1972. Topics in Numerical Analysis: Proceedings. Miller, John J., ed. 1974. 57.50 (ISBN 0-12-496950-X). Acad Pr.

Samoilenko, A. M. & Ronto, N. I. Numerical-Analytic Methods of Investigating Periodic Solutions. 183p. 1979. pap. 3.50 (ISBN 0-8285-1514-X, Pub. by Mir Pubs Russia). Imported Pubns.

Sawyer, W. W. A First Look at Numerical Functional Analysis. (Oxford Applied Mathematics & Computing Science Ser.). (Illus.). 1978. pap. 9.95x (ISBN 0-19-859629-4). Oxford U Pr.

Scaife, B. K. Studies in Numerical Analysis. 1974. 44.50 (ISBN 0-12-621150-7). Acad Pr.

Scalzo, Frank & Hughes, Rowland. A Computer Approach to Introductory College Mathematics. 1977. pap. text ed. 13.95x (ISBN 0-442-80434-2). Van Nos Reinhold.

Scarborough, James B. Numerical Mathematical Analysis. 6th ed. 608p. 1966. 25.00x (ISBN 0-8018-0575-9). Johns Hopkins.

Scheid, Francis. Numerical Analysis. (Schaum's Outline Ser). (Orig.). 1968. pap. 6.95 (ISBN 0-07-055197-9, SP). McGraw.

Schwartz, J. T., ed. Mathematical Aspects of Computer Science: Proceedings of a Symposium, New York City, Apr. 1966. LC 67-16554. 1978. Repr. of 1967 ed. 17.20 (ISBN 0-8218-1319-6, PSAPM-19). Am Math.

Schwefel, Hans-Paul. Numerical Optimization of Computer Models. 389p. 1981. 32.95 (ISBN 0-471-09988-0, Pub. by Wiley-Interscience). Wiley.

Shaw, R., et al, eds. Innovative Numerical Analysis for the Engineering Sciences. LC 80-14005. 1980. 40.00x (ISBN 0-8139-0867-1). U Pr of Va.

Singer, James. Elements of Numerical Analysis. (Illus.). 1964. text ed. 21.95 (ISBN 0-12-646450-2). Acad Pr.

Southworth, R. & De Leeuw, S. Digital Computation & Numerical Methods. 1965. text ed. 24.50 (ISBN 0-07-059799-5, C); solutions manual 2.50 (ISBN 0-07-059801-0). McGraw.

Spaniol, Otto. Computer Arithmetic: Logic & Design. LC 80-41867. (Computing Ser.). 280p. 1981. 39.50 (ISBN 0-471-27926-9, Pub. by Wiley-Interscience). Wiley.

Stark, Peter A. Introduction to Numerical Methods. (Illus.). 1970. text ed. 22.95 (ISBN 0-02-416110-1). Macmillan.

Steklov Institute of Mathematics, Academy of Sciences, U S S R, No. 96. Automatic Programming, Numerical Methods & Functional Analysis: Proceedings. Faddeeva, V. N., ed. 1970. 41.20 (ISBN 0-8218-1896-1, STEKLO-96). Am Math.

Stoer, J. & Bulirsch, R. Introduction to Numerical Analysis. Bartels, R., et al, trs. from Ger. (Illus.). 1979. pap. 24.00 (ISBN 0-387-90420-4). Springer-Verlag.

Symposia in Applied Mathematics - Santa Monica Calif - 1953. Numerical Analysis: Proceedings, Vol. 6. Curtiss, J. H., ed. LC 50-1183. 1956. 29.60 (ISBN 0-8218-1306-4, PSAPM-6). Am Math.

Symposium on the Theory of Numerical Analysis. Proceedings. Morris, J. L., ed. LC 70-155916. (Lecture Notes in Mathematics: Vol. 193). 1971. pap. 8.20 (ISBN 0-387-05422-7). Springer-Verlag.

Szidarovszky, F. & Yakowitz, S., eds. Principles & Procedures of Numerical Analysis. (Mathematical Concepts & Methods in Science & Engineering Ser.: Vol. 14). 365p. 1978. 24.50 (ISBN 0-306-40087-1, Plenum Pr). Plenum Pub.

Tikhonov, A. N. & Arsenin, V. Y. Solutions of Ill-Posed Problems. LC 77-3422. 1977. 19.75 (ISBN 0-470-99124-0). Halsted Pr.

Todd, John. Basic Numerical Mathematics, Vol. 1: Numerical Analysis. (International Series of Numerical Mathematics: No. 14). 1981. 24.00 (ISBN 0-12-692401-5). Acad Pr.

Vandergraft, James S. Introduction to Numerical Computations. (Computer Science & Applied Mathematics Ser.). 1978. 31.50 (ISBN 0-12-711350-9). Acad Pr.

Watson, G. A., ed. Numerical Analysis. LC 75-45241. (Lecture Notes in Mathematics: Vol. 506). 1976. pap. 12.70 (ISBN 0-387-07610-7). Springer-Verlag.

--Numerical Analysis: Proceedings. (Lecture Notes in Mathematics Ser.: Vol. 773). 184p. 1980. pap. 11.80 (ISBN 0-387-09740-6). Springer-Verlag.

Westlake, Joan R. Handbook of Numerical Matrix Inversion & Solution of Linear Equations. LC 74-26623. 182p. 1975. Repr. of 1968 ed. 13.50 (ISBN 0-88275-225-1). Krieger.

Wilkes, Maurice V. Short Introduction to Numerical Analysis. (Illus., Orig.). pap. 6.95 (ISBN 0-521-09412-7, 412). Cambridge U Pr.

Zadeh, L. A., et al, eds. Computing Methods in Optimization Problems Two. 1969. 47.00 (ISBN 0-12-775250-1). Acad Pr.

NUMERICAL ANALYSIS–DATA PROCESSING

Arden, Bruce W. & Astill, Kenneth N. Numerical Algorithms: Origins & Applications. LC 76-100853. 1970. 17.95 (ISBN 0-201-00336-8). A-W.

Bjorck, Ake & Dahlquist, Germund. Numerical Methods. Anderson, N., tr. (Illus.). 576p. 1974. ref. ed. 26.95 (ISBN 0-13-627315-7). P-H.

Conte, S. D. & De Boor, C. W. Elementary Numerical Analysis: An Algorithmic Approach. 2nd ed. (International Ser. in Pure & Applied Mathematics). (Illus.). 408p. 1972. text ed. 21.95 (ISBN 0-07-012446-9, C). McGraw.

Dorn, William S. & McCracken, Daniel D., eds. Numerical Methods with Fortran IV Case Studies. LC 77-37365. 477p. 1972. 29.95 (ISBN 0-471-21918-5). Wiley.

Evans, D. J., ed. Software for Numerical Mathematics. 1974. 73.00 (ISBN 0-12-243750-0). Acad Pr.

Forsythe, George E., et al. Computer Methods for Mathematical Computations. (Illus.). 1977. ref. ed. 23.50x (ISBN 0-13-165332-6). P-H.

Gastinel, Noel. Linear Numerical Analysis. LC 70-108619. 1971. 49.50 (ISBN 0-12-277150-8). Acad Pr.

Gear, C. W. Numerical Initial Value Problems in Ordinary Differential Equations. (Automatic Computation Ser). (Illus.). 1971. ref. ed. 22.95 (ISBN 0-13-626606-1). P-H.

Gregory, Robert & Karney, David L. A Collection of Matrices for Testing Computational Algorithms. LC 77-19262. 164p. 1978. Repr. of 1969 ed. lib. bdg. 15.00 (ISBN 0-88275-649-4). Krieger.

Henrici, Peter. Computational Analysis with the Hp 25 Pocket Calculator. LC 77-1182. 1977. 19.95 (ISBN 0-471-02938-6, Pub. by Wiley-Interscience). Wiley.

--Essentials of Numerical Analysis with Pocket Calculator Demonstrations. LC 81-10468. 352p. 1982. text ed. 22.95 (ISBN 0-471-05904-8); price not set solutions manual (ISBN 0-471-09704-7). Wiley.

Kuo, Shan S. Computer Applications of Numerical Methods. LC 78-164654. 1972. text ed. 18.95 (ISBN 0-201-03956-7). A-W.

LaFara, Robert L. Computer Methods for Science & Engineering. (Illus.). 1973. 16.10 (ISBN 0-8104-5766-0). Hayden.

Liffick, Blaise W., ed. Numbers in Theory & Practice. (Orig.). 1979. pap. 8.95 (ISBN 0-07-037827-4, BYTE Bks). McGraw.

Miller, R. E. & Thatcher, J. W., eds. Complexity of Computer Computations. LC 72-85736. (IBM Research Symposia Ser.). 225p. 1972. 27.50 (ISBN 0-306-30707-3, Plenum Pr). Plenum Pub.

Mittelmann, H., ed. Brfurcation Prpblems & Their Numerical Solution. (ISNM Ser.: No. 54). 252p. 1980. pap. 24.50 (ISBN 3-7643-1204-1). Birkhauser.

Pennington, Ralph H. Introductory Computer Methods & Numerical Analysis. 2nd ed. (Illus.). 1970. text ed. 20.95 (ISBN 0-02-393830-7). Macmillan.

Pizer, Stephen M. Numerical Computing & Mathematical Analysis. (Computer Science Ser). (Illus.). 544p. 1975. text ed. 23.95 (ISBN 0-574-19155-0, 13-4025). SRA.

Poirot, James, et al. Practice in Computers & Mathematics. 227p. (Orig.). (gr. 11-12). 1980. pap. text ed. 5.95 (ISBN 0-88408-126-5). Sterling Swift.

Shampine, Lawrence F. & Allen, Richard C. Numerical Computing: An Introduction. LC 72-93122. 258p. 1973. text ed. 12.95 (ISBN 0-7216-8150-6). HR&W.

Smith, Donald N., ed. Numerical Control for Tomorrow. Peelle, David M. (Illus.). 181p. 1969. 12.00 (ISBN 0-686-72884-X, NC TOM). Indus Dev Inst Sci.

Smith, J. M. Mathematical Modeling & Digital Simulation for Engineers & Scientists. LC 76-52419. 1977. 30.00 (ISBN 0-471-80344-8, Pub. by Wiley-Interscience). Wiley.

Society for Industrial & Applied Mathematics - American Mathematical Society Symposia - New York - March, 1971. Computers in Algebra & Number Theory: Proceedings, Vol. 4. Birkhoff, Garrett & Hall, Marshall, Jr., eds. LC 76-167685. 208p. 1980. Repr. of 1971 ed. 16.00 (ISBN 0-8218-1323-4, SIAMS-4). Am Math.

Stummel, F. & Hainer, K. Introduction to Numerical Analysis. 276p. 1980. 22.00x (ISBN 0-7073-0130-0, Pub. by Scottish Academic Pr). Columbia U Pr.

Young, David M. & Gregory, Robert T. A Survey of Numerical Mathematics, Vol. 1. LC 78-168767. 1972. text ed. 21.95 (ISBN 0-201-08773-1). A-W.

--A Survey of Numerical Mathematics, Vol. 2. LC 78-168767. 1973. text ed. 22.95 (ISBN 0-201-08774-X). A-W.

NUMERICAL ANALYSIS LABORATORIES

see Computation Laboratories

NUMERICAL CALCULATIONS

see also Computation Laboratories; Differential Equations–Numerical Solutions; Differential Equations, Linear–Numerical Solutions; Differential Equations, Partial–Numerical Solutions; Digital Filters (Mathematics); Monte Carlo Method

Alefeld, G. & Grigorieff, R. D., eds. Fundamentals of Numerical Computation: International Conference. (Computing Supplementum: No. 2). (Illus.). 250p. 1980. pap. 57.90 (ISBN 0-387-81566-X). Springer-Verlag.

Balakrishnan, A. V. & Neustadt, Lucien W., eds. Computing Methods in Optimization Problems: Proceedings. 1964. 36.00 (ISBN 0-12-076950-6). Acad Pr.

Conference on Numerical Methods for Non-Linear Optimization, University of Dundee, Scotland, June-July, 1971. Numerical Methods in Non-Linear Optimization. Lootsma, F. A., ed. 1973. 70.50 (ISBN 0-12-455650-7). Acad Pr.

Faddeeva, V. N. Computational Methods of Linear Algebra. 1959. pap. 4.50 (ISBN 0-486-60424-1). Dover.

Fosdick, L., ed. Performance Evaluation of Numerical Software. 1979. 24.50 (ISBN 0-444-85330-8, North Holland). Elsevier.

Fox, Leslie. Introduction to Numerical Linear Algebra. (Monographs on Numerical Analysis Ser.). 1965. 12.95x (ISBN 0-19-500325-X). Oxford U Pr.

Furman, T. T. Approximate Methods in Engineering Design. LC 80-40891. (Mathematics in Science & Engineering Ser.). 408p. 1981. 59.00 (ISBN 0-12-269960-2). Acad Pr.

Glowinski, R., et al, eds. Computing Methods in Applied Sciences & Engineering. (Lecture Notes in Economics & Mathematical Systems Ser.: Vol. 134). 1976. soft cover 17.60 (ISBN 0-387-07990-4). Springer-Verlag.

--Computing Methods in Applied Sciences. (Lecture Notes in Physics Ser.: Vol. 58). (Eng. & Fr.). 1976. soft cover 19.40 (ISBN 0-387-08003-1). Springer-Verlag.

Henrici, Peter. Error Propagation for Difference Methods. LC 76-18838. 82p. 1977. Repr. of 1963 ed. 7.50 (ISBN 0-88275-448-3). Krieger.

Marchuk, G. I. Differential Equations & Numerical Mathematics: Proceedings of a USSR Council of Ministers for Science & Technology, Moscow. (Illus.). 130p. 1982. 50.00 (ISBN 0-08-026491-3). Pergamon.

Milne, W. E. Numerical Calculus. 1949. 25.00x (ISBN 0-691-08011-9). Princeton U Pr.

Rice, John R. The Approximation of Linear Functions, 2 vols, Vols. 1 & 2. 1964-69. Vol. 1: Linear Theory. 14.50 (ISBN 0-201-06430-8, Adv Bk Prog); Vol. 2: Nonlinear & Multivariate Theory. 18.00 (ISBN 0-201-06432-4, Adv Bk Prog). A-W.

Richtmyer, Robert D. & Morton, K. W. Difference Methods for Initial-Value Problems. 2nd ed. LC 67-13959. (Pure & Applied Mathematics Ser.). (Illus.). 1967. 41.50 (ISBN 0-470-72040-9, Pub. by Wiley-Interscience). Wiley.

Society for Industrial & Applied Mathematics-American Mathematical Society Symposia-N.C.-April, 1968. Numerical Solution of Field Problems in Continuum Physics: Proceedings, Vol. 2. Birkhoff, G. & Varga, R. S., eds. LC 75-92659. 1970. 24.40 (ISBN 0-8218-1321-8, SIAMS-2). Am Math.

Steffensen, John F. Interpolation. 2nd ed. LC 50-12797. 14.95 (ISBN 0-8284-0071-7). Chelsea Pub.

Stiefel, E. L. Introduction to Numerical Mathematics. Rheinboldt, W. C., tr. 1963. text ed. 18.95 (ISBN 0-12-671150-X); problem bklt. free (ISBN 0-685-05133-1). Acad Pr.

Symposia in Applied Mathematics-Atlantic City & Chicago-1962. Experimental Arithmetic, High Speed Computing & Mathematics: Proceedings, Vol. 15. Metropolis, N. C., et al, eds. LC 63-17582. 1963. 23.60 (ISBN 0-8218-1315-3, PSAPM-15). Am Math.

Symposium at the Centre for Research in Mathematics, University of Montreal, Sept., 1971. Applications of Number Theory to Numerical Analysis: Proceedings. Zaremba, S. K., ed. 1972. 46.50 (ISBN 0-12-775950-6). Acad Pr.

Todd, John. Basic Numerical Mathematics: Numerical Algebra, Vol. 2. 1978. 23.50 (ISBN 0-12-692402-3). Acad Pr.

Zienkiewicz, O. C., et al, eds. Numerical Methods in Offshore Engineering. LC 77-12565. (Numerical Methods in Engineering Ser.). 1978. 82.25 (ISBN 0-471-99591-6, Pub. by Wiley-Interscience). Wiley.

NUMERICAL FILTERS

see Digital Filters (Mathematics)

NUMERICAL INTEGRATION

Anderson, Norman H. Foundations of Integration Theory, Vol. 1. LC 80-1769. (Information Integration Ser.). 1981. price not set (ISBN 0-12-058101-9). Acad Pr.

Antoine, Jaen-Pierre & Tirapegui, Enrique, eds. Functional Integration--Theory & Applications. 355p. 1980. 42.50 (ISBN 0-306-40573-3, Plenum Pr). Plenum Pub.

Arthurs, A. M. & Bhagavan, M. R., eds. Functional Integration & Its Applications. 300p. 1975. 45.00x (ISBN 0-19-853346-2). Oxford U Pr.

Davis, Phillip J. & Rabinowitz, Philip. Methods of Numerical Integration. 1975. 54.00 (ISBN 0-12-206350-3). Acad Pr.

DeBarra, G. Measure Theory & Integration. (Mathematics & Its Applications). 260p. 1981. 69.95 (ISBN 0-470-27232-5). Halsted Pr.

Engels, H. Quadrature & Cubature. LC 79-41235. (Computational Mathematics and Application Ser.). 1980. 74.00 (ISBN 0-12-238850-X). Acad Pr.

Fichtenholz, G. M. The Definite Integral. Silverman, R. A., tr. from Rus. LC 78-149513. (Pocket Mathematical Library Ser.). (Illus.). 97p. 1973. 23.25x (ISBN 0-677-21090-6). Gordon.

Ghizzetti, A. & Ossicini, A. Quadrature Formulae. 1970. 31.50 (ISBN 0-12-281750-8). Acad Pr.

Hammerlin, Gunther. Numerische Integration. (Internationale Schriftenreihe zur Numerischen Mathematik: No. 45). 320p. (Ger., Eng.). 1979. pap. 29.80 (ISBN 3-7643-1014-6). Birkhauser.

Keenan, Edward P. & Dressler, Isidore. Integrated Mathematics: Course II. (Orig.). (gr. 10). 1981. text ed. 19.17 (ISBN 0-87720-251-6); pap. text ed. 12.08 (ISBN 0-87720-250-8). AMSCO Sch.

McShane, E. J. Order-Preserving Maps & Integration Processes. (Annals of Mathematics Studies). Repr. of 1953 ed. pap. 7.00 (ISBN 0-527-02747-2). Kraus Repr.

Rao, M. M. Stochastic Processes & Integration. 467p. 1979. 55.00x (ISBN 90-286-0438-3). Sijthoff & Noordhoff.

Stroud, A. H. Numerical Quadrature & Solution of Ordinary Differential Equations: A Textbook for a Beginning Course in Numerical Analysis. (Applied Mathematical Sciences Ser.: Vol. 10). (Illus.). 350p. 1974. pap. 13.10 (ISBN 0-387-90100-0). Springer-Verlag.

NUMERICAL SEQUENCES

see Sequences (Mathematics)

NUMERICAL WEATHER FORECASTING

Haltiner, G. J. & Williams, R. T. Numerical Prediction & Dynamic Meteorology. 2nd ed. 477p. 1980. 29.50 (ISBN 0-471-05971-4). Wiley.

NUMEROLOGY

see Symbolism of Numbers

NUMIPU LANGUAGE

see Nez Perce Language

NUMISMATICS

see also Bible–Numismatics; Medals; Seals (Numismatics)

Adams, John W., ed. Monographs on the United States Large Cent of 1793 & 1794. LC 75-28712. (Illus.). 240p. 1977. 30.00x (ISBN 0-88000-071-6). Quarterman.

Adelson, Howard L. American Numismatic Society Eighteen Fifty-Eight to Nineteen Fifty-Eight. (Illus.). 390p. 1958. 35.00 (ISBN 0-89722-045-5). Am Numismatic.

Album, Stephen. Marsden's Numismata Orientalia Illustrata. LC 76-24245. (Illus.). 1977. 21.50 (ISBN 0-915018-16-0). Attic Bks.

Alfoldi, A. The Numbering of the Victories of the Emperor Gallienus & of the Loyalty of His Legions. (Numismatic Chronicle Reprint Ser.). (Illus.). 62p. 1977. pap. 4.50 (ISBN 0-915018-28-4). Attic Bks.

Allenbaugh, Carl. Coins Questions & Answers. 3rd ed. LC 78-51021. 1978. pap. 1.95 (ISBN 0-87341-019-X). Krause Pubns.

American Numismatic Association. Official A.N.A. Grading Guide. (Whitman Coin Hobby Books). (Illus.). 1977. 5.95 (ISBN 0-307-09097-3). Western Pub.

American Numismatic Society. Dictionary & Auction Catalogues of the Library of the American Numismatic Society, New York, 7 Vols. 1962. Set. lib. bdg. 0.00 (ISBN 0-685-11673-5); lib. bdg. 530.00 dictionary catalog, 6 vols. (ISBN 0-8161-0630-4); lib. bdg. 90.00 auction catalog, 1 vol. (ISBN 0-8161-0102-7). G K Hall.

--A Survey of Numismatic Research, 1966-71, 3 vols. 1973. 40.00 set (ISBN 0-89722-069-2). Am Numismatic.

American Numismatic Society Museum Notes: Index to Vols. 1-20. 1977. pap. 2.50 (ISBN 0-89722-035-8). Am Numismatic.

American Numismatic Society Museum Notes, Vols. 19-22. Vol. 19. pap. 30.00 1974 (ISBN 0-89722-032-3); Vol. 20. pap. 20.00 1975 (ISBN 0-89722-033-1); Vol. 22. pap. 30.00 1977 (ISBN 0-89722-172-9). Am Numismatic.

American Numismatic Society, New York. Dictionary & Auction Catalogues of the Library of the American Numismatic Society, Second Supplement. 1973. lib. bdg. 105.00 (ISBN 0-8161-1058-1). G K Hall.

Angus, Ian. Fell's Guide to Coins & Money Tokens of the World. LC 74-75383. Orig. Title: Coins & Money Tokens. (Illus.). 128p. 1974. 8.95 (ISBN 0-8119-0237-4). Fell.

Bagg, Richard & Jelinski, James J., eds. Grading Coins: A Collection of Readings. LC 77-82246. (Illus.). 1977. pap. text ed. 9.95 (ISBN 0-930332-01-6). Essex Pubns.

Baldwin, Agnes. Symbolism on Greek Coins. LC 76-62839. (Illus.). 1977. Repr. of 1915 ed. lib. bdg. 16.50 (ISBN 0-915262-10-X). S J Durst.

Basso, Aldo P. Coins, Medals & Tokens of the Philippines. (Illus.). 144p. 1968. 5.95 (ISBN 0-912496-10-X). Shirjieh Pubs.

Beginners Coin Collecting Kit: For U. S. Coins. (gr. 4 up). 1980. 5.95 (ISBN 0-307-09394-8). Western Pub.

Bellinger, A. R. Essays on the Coinage of Alexander the Great. (Alexander the Great Ser.). (Illus.). 132p. 1981. 30.00 (ISBN 0-916710-93-9). Obol Intl.

Beresford-Jones, R. D. A Manual of Anglo-Gallic Gold Coins. 1964. 9.00 (ISBN 0-685-51544-3, Pub by Spink & Son England). S J Durst.

Berry, G. Medieval English Jetons. 1974. 9.00 (ISBN 0-685-51549-4, Pub by Spink & Son England). S J Durst.

Blum, G. Numismatique D'Antinoos. 1979. 20.00 (ISBN 0-916710-60-2). Obol Intl.

Brilliant, Richard. Gesture & Rank in Roman Art. (Connecticut Academy of Arts & Sciences Memoirs: No. 14). 1963. pap. 30.00 (ISBN 0-208-00639-7). Shoe String.

Brooke, G. C. English Coins. 1977. 17.00 (ISBN 0-685-51518-4, Pub by Spink & Son England). S J Durst.

Browning, A. W. Early Quarter Dollars. LC 77-74032. (Illus.). 1977. Repr. of 1925 ed. lib. bdg. 12.50 (ISBN 0-915262-15-0). S J Durst.

Burns, Arthur R. Money & Monetary Policy in Early Times. LC 65-19645. Repr. of 1927 ed. 19.50x (ISBN 0-678-00100-6). Kelley.

Carson, et al. Late Roman Bronze Coinage. 1977. 15.00 (ISBN 0-685-51531-1, Pub by Spink & Son England). S J Durst.

Carson, R. A. The Geneva Forgeries. (Numismatic Chronicle Reprint Ser.). pap. 2.50 (ISBN 0-915018-27-6). Attic Bks.

Casson, Lionel & Price, Martin. Coins, Culture, & History in the Ancient World: Numismatic & Other Studies in Honor of Bluma L. Trell. (Illus.). 250p. 1981. 22.50 (ISBN 0-8143-1684-0). Wayne St U Pr.

Clain-Stefanelli, E. E. Russian Gold Coins. 1962. 4.00 (ISBN 0-685-51560-5, Pub by Spink & Son England). S J Durst.

Codrington, O. A Manual of Musulman Numismatics. (Illus.). 1980. pap. 15.00 (ISBN 0-89005-200-X). Ares.

Cohen, Annette R. & Druley, Ray M. The Buffalo Nickel. (Illus.). 130p. (Orig.). 1979. pap. 6.95 (ISBN 0-939836-00-9). Potomac Ent.

Coin Collection, Their Preservation, Classification & Presentation. 1979. pap. 7.00 (ISBN 92-3-101619-9, U917, UNESCO). Unipub.

A Colloquium in Memory of George Carpenter Miles, 1904-1975. (Illus.). 49p. 1976. pap. 1.50 (ISBN 0-89722-064-1). Am Numismatic.

Davenport, John S., et al. Standard Price Guide to World Crowns & Talers. Bruce, Colin R., II, ed. (Illus.). 576p. (Orig.). 1981. pap. 19.50 (ISBN 0-87341-062-9). Krause Pubns.

Davis, T. W. Rhys. On the Ancient Coins & Measures of Ceylon. (Illus.). 1975. pap. 8.00 (ISBN 0-916710-24-6). Obol Intl.

De Vos, Raymond. History of the Monies Medals & Tokens of Monaco. 1978. write for info. (ISBN 0-685-51123-5); lib. bdg. 80.00x (ISBN 0-685-51124-3). S J Durst.

Dictionary & Auction Catalogues of the Library of the American Numismatic Society: Third Supplement. (Reference Supplements Ser.). 1978. lib. bdg. 195.00 (ISBN 0-8161-0247-3). G K Hall.

Dolley, M. The Norman Conquest & the English Coinage. 1966. 3.00 (ISBN 0-685-51535-4, Pub by Spink & Son England). S J Durst.

Dowle, A. & Finn, P. The Guide Book to the Coinage of Ireland. 1969. 6.00 (ISBN 0-685-51508-7, Pub by Spink & Son England). S J Durst.

Durst, Sanford J. Comprehensive Guide to American Colonial Coinage. LC 75-32796. (Illus.). 1976. lib. bdg. 15.00 (ISBN 0-915262-02-9). S J Durst.

Durst, Sanford J., ed. Early American Coppers Anthology. LC 76-62837. (Miscellaneous Bks.). (Illus.). 1977. Repr. lib. bdg. 39.50 (ISBN 0-915262-08-8). S J Durst.

Fleetwood, William. Chronicon Precosium. LC 68-55711. (Illus.). Repr. of 1745 ed. 15.00x (ISBN 0-678-00492-7). Kelley.

Frey, A. R. Dictionary of Numismatic Names. 1973. 18.00 (ISBN 0-685-51559-1, Pub by Spink & Son England). S J Durst.

Frey, Albert R. A Dictionary of Numismatic Names. pap. 18.00 (ISBN 0-384-16830-2). Johnson Repr.

Fuld, George & Fuld, Melvin. Patriotic Civil War Tokens. LC 81-423. (Illus.). 80p. Date not set. pap. 7.50 (ISBN 0-88000-128-3). Quarterman.

Gardiakos, S. A Catalogue of the Coins of Dalmatia et Albania, 1410-1797. (Illus.). 32p. 1970. pap. 5.00 (ISBN 0-916710-67-X). Obol Intl.

Gardiakos, Soterios, ed. The Coinages of Alexander the Great. (Illus.). 1007p. 1981. 295.00 (ISBN 0-916710-82-3). Obol Intl.

Gardner, Percy. History of Ancient Coinage: B. C. 700-300. LC 74-77879. (Illus.). 492p. 1975. Repr. 15.00 (ISBN 0-89005-007-4). Ares.

Gray, John C. Tranquebar: A Guide to the Coins of Danish India Circa 1620 to 1845. new ed. LC 74-84564. (Illus.). 96p. 1975. 20.00x (ISBN 0-88000-054-6). Quarterman.

Grierson, Philip. Numismatics. (Illus.). 232p. 1975. pap. 5.95 (ISBN 0-19-888098-7, GB440, GB). Oxford U Pr.

Hawkins, Edward. Silver Coins of England. LC 76-12920. (Illus.). 1977. Repr. of 1875 ed. lib. bdg. 45.00 (ISBN 0-915262-05-3). S J Durst.

Hazlitt, W. C. The Coinage of the European Countinent. LC 74-77880. 774p. 1975. 30.00 (ISBN 0-89005-037-6). Ares.

Head, Barclay V. Historia Numorum. 1977. 45.00 (ISBN 0-685-51525-7, Pub by Spink & Son England). S J Durst.

Herbert, Kevin. The John Max Wulfing Collection in Washington University. (ANS Ancient Coins in North American Collections). (Illus.). 1980. 20.00 (ISBN 0-89722-180-X). Am Numismatic.

Higgins, Frank C. The Copper Coins of Europe Till 1892. 1970. 3.00 (ISBN 0-685-51545-1, Pub by Spink & Son England). S J Durst.

Hill, P. V. The Coinage of Septimius Severus of the Mint of Rome. 1977. 9.00 (ISBN 0-685-51524-9, Pub by Spink & Son England). S J Durst.

--The Dating & Arrangement of the Undated Coins of Rome A.D. 98-148. 1970. 19.00 (ISBN 0-685-51523-0, Pub by Spink & Son England). S J Durst.

Hobson, Burton. Coin Collecting As a Hobby. 1973. Cornerstone.

Ingholt, Harald, ed. Centennial Publication of the American Numismatic Society. (Illus.). 712p. 1958. 60.00 (ISBN 0-89722-046-3). Am Numismatic.

Internaional Numismatic Symposium, Warsaw & Budapest, 1976. Proceedings. Niro-Sey, K. & Gedai, I., eds. (Illus.). 221p. 1980. 27.50x (ISBN 963-05-2055-9). Intl Pubns Serv.

Jones, J. R. Analytical Index to the Journal international d'archeologie numismatique: Numismatic Literature Supplement, No. 1. 49p. 1967. pap. 2.50 (ISBN 0-89722-054-4). Am Numismatic.

Kelly, E. M. Spanish Dollars & Silver Tokens: Of England. 1977. 25.00 (ISBN 0-685-51517-6, Pub by Spink & Son England). S J Durst.

Kent, E. Jackson. Some Notes & Observations of the Silver Coinage of William III, 1695-1701. 1974. 1.50 (ISBN 0-685-51505-2, Pub by Spink & Son England). S J Durst.

Kent, J. P., et al. Handbook of the Coins of Great Britain & Ireland in the British Museum. 1970. 22.00 (ISBN 0-685-51501-X, Pub by Spink & Son England). S J Durst.

Kenyon, Robert L. Gold Coins of England. LC 77-74031. (Illus.). 1980. Repr. of 1884 ed. lib. bdg. 25.00 (ISBN 0-686-52393-8). S J Durst.

Kleiner, G. Alexanders Reichmunzen. (Alexander the Great Ser.). (Illus.). 56p. 1981. 30.00 (ISBN 0-916710-91-2). Obol Intl.

Kouymjian, Dickran K. & Bacharach, Jere L., eds. Near Eastern Numismatics, Iconography, Epigraphy & History: Studies in Honor of George C. Miles. 1974. 55.00x (ISBN 0-8156-6041-3, Am U Beirut). Syracuse U Pr.

Kraay, Colin. Archaic & Classical Greek Coins. LC 76-14303. (Library of Numismatics). 1977. 65.00x (ISBN 0-520-03254-3). U of Cal Pr.

Kraay, Colin M. The Coinage of Sybaris After Five Hundred Ten B. C. (Numismatic Chronicle Reprint Ser.). pap. 2.50 (ISBN 0-915018-26-8). Attic Bks.

--The Coinage of Vindex & Galba, A. D. 68 & the Continuity of the Augustan Principate. (Numismatic Chronicle Reprint Ser.). 1977. pap. 2.50 (ISBN 0-915018-20-9). Attic Bks.

Krause, Chester L., et al. Standard Catalog of Twentieth Century World Coins. (Illus.). 512p. (Orig.). 1981. pap. 9.95 (ISBN 0-87341-063-7). Krause Pubns.

Kroha, Tyll. Lexikon der Numismatik. (Ger.). 1977. 48.00 (ISBN 3-570-01588-2, M-7241). French & Eur.

Lambros, P. The Coins of the Genoese Rulers of Chios (1314-1429) Barozzi, A., tr. (Illus.). 27p. 1968. pap. 5.00 (ISBN 0-916710-00-9). Obol Intl.

--Unpublished Coins Struck at Glarentza in Imitation of Venetian by Robert of Taranto, Sovereign of the Peloponnese: 1346-1364. Gardiakos, B., tr. (Illus.). 30p. 1969. pap. 5.00 (ISBN 0-916710-01-7). Obol Intl.

Lambros, Paul. Gold Coins of Philippi. (Illus.). 1975. pap. 3.00 (ISBN 0-916710-20-3). Obol Intl.

Linecar, H. W. & Stone, A. G. English Proof & Pattern Crown Size Pieces. 1968. 15.00 (ISBN 0-685-51507-9, Pub by Spink & Son England). S J Durst.

Linecar, Howard, ed. The Milled Coinage of England. 1971. 10.00 (ISBN 0-685-51502-8, Pub by Spink & Son England). S J Durst.

Loring, Denis W., ed. Monographs on Varieties of United States Large Cents, 1795-1803. LC 75-39497. (Illus.). 248p. 1976. 30.00x (ISBN 0-88000-075-9). Quarterman.

MacDonald, G. Coin Types: Their Origin & Development. LC 77-94599. 1979. Repr. of 1905 ed. lib. bdg. 30.00 (ISBN 0-89341-246-5). Longwood Pr.

--The Silver Coinage of Crete: A Metrological Note. (Illus.). 29p. 1974. pap. 5.00 (ISBN 0-916710-13-0). Obol Intl.

Mack, R. P. Coinage of Ancient Britain. 1975. 16.00 (ISBN 0-685-51540-0, Pub by Spink & Son England). S J Durst.

MacKay, James A. Value in Coins & Medals. (Illus.). 1969. 8.75 (ISBN 0-85307-013-X). Transatlantic.

Manley, Stephen G. The Lincoln Cent. LC 81-80366. (Illus.). 121p. (Orig.). 1981. pap. 7.95 (ISBN 0-939272-00-8). Libty Pr IA.

Mattingly, H. The Coinage of the Civil War of Sixty-Eight to Sixty-Nine A. D. (Numismatic Chronicle Reprint Ser.). 1977. pap. 2.50 (ISBN 0-915018-21-7). Attic Bks.

--Fel, Temp, Reparatio. (Numismatic Chronicle Reprint Ser.). 1977. pap. 2.50 (ISBN 0-915018-22-5). Attic Bks.

--Roman Coins. 1977. 17.00 (ISBN 0-685-51532-X, Pub by Spink & Son England). S J Durst.

Mattingly, H. & Robinson, E. S. G. The Date of the Roman Denarius & Other Landmarks in Early Roman Coinage. (Illus.). 59p. 1974. pap. 8.00 (ISBN 0-916710-17-3). Obol Intl.

Mattingly, Harold. The Roman Serrati. (Illus.). 22p. 1974. pap. cancelled (ISBN 0-915018-07-1). Attic Bks.

Mayer, L. A. A Bibliography of Jewish Numismatics, 1966. 10.00x (ISBN 0-685-38402-0). Ktav.

Metcalf, William E. The Cistophori of Hadrian. (ANS Numismatic Studies: No. 15). (Illus.). 164p. 1980. 65.00 (ISBN 0-89722-181-8). Am Numismatic.

Migne, J. P., ed. Dictionnaire de Numismatique et de Sigillographie Religieuses. (Nouvelle Encyclopedie Theologique Ser.: Vol. 32). (Fr.). Date not set. Repr. of 1852 ed. lib. bdg. 91.00x (ISBN 0-89241-274-7). Caratzas Bros.

Morgan, Jacques. Ancient Persian Numismatics: Elymais. Churchill, Dominique Gillain, tr. from Fr. & illus. LC 76-21027. Orig. Title: La Principaute D'elymaide. (Eng.). 1976. pap. 8.50 (ISBN 0-915018-15-2). Attic Bks.

Muller, L. Numismatique d'Alexandre le Grand: Suive D'un Appendice Contenant les Monnaies De Philippe 2 et 3. (Alexander the Great Ser.). (Illus.). 401p. 1981. 60.00 (ISBN 0-916710-83-1). Obol Intl.

--Numismatique De L'ancienne Afrique, 4 vols. in 1. 1978. heavy-duty bndg. 60.00 (ISBN 0-89005-269-7). Ares.

Museum Notes, No. 24. (Illus.). 282p. (Orig.). 1980. pap. 30.00 (ISBN 0-89722-024-2). Am Numismatic.

Museum Notes, No. 25. (Illus.). 232p. (Orig.). 1981. pap. 30.00 (ISBN 0-89722-186-9). Am Numismatic.

Newell, E. T. Some Cypriote "Alexanders". (Illus.). iii, 29p. 1974. pap. 5.00 (ISBN 0-916710-14-9). Obol Intl.

Newell, Edward T. The Dated Coinage of Sidon & Ake. (Alexander the Great Ser.). (Illus.). 96p. 1981. 40.00 (ISBN 0-916710-85-8). Obol Intl.

--Re-Attribution of Certain Tetradrachms of Alexander the Great. (Alexander the Great Ser.). (Illus.). 160p. 1981. 50.00 (ISBN 0-916710-84-X). Obol Intl.

Noe, S. P. The Alexander Coinage of Sicyon. (Alexander the Great Ser.). (Illus.). 64p. 1981. 30.00 (ISBN 0-916710-92-0). Obol Intl.

North, J. J. The Coinages of Edward I & II. 1968. 3.00 (ISBN 0-685-51543-5, Pub by Spink & Son England). S J Durst.

--English Hammered Coinage, Vol. I. 1963. 25.00 (ISBN 0-685-51541-9, Pub by Spink & Son England). S J Durst.

--English Hammered Coinage, Vol. II. 1977. 25.00 (ISBN 0-685-51542-7, Pub by Spink & Son England). S J Durst.

Numismatic Fine Arts Auction Catalogues. (Ancient Greek, Roman, Byzantine & Judaean Coins, Related Literature Ser.). (Illus.). 1981. pap. 15.00 (ISBN 0-686-66080-3). Numismatic Fine Arts.

Numismatic Literature, No. 104. xii, 277p. (Orig.). 1980. pap. 4.00 (ISBN 0-89722-188-5). Am Numismatic.

Pegge, Samuel. An Assemblage of Coins Fabricated by the Authority of the Archbishops of Canterbury. (Illus.). 1975. pap. 15.00 (ISBN 0-916710-23-8). Obol Intl.

Pradeau, Alberto. Numismatic History of Mexico. LC 77-93447. (Illus.). 1978. Repr. of 1938 ed. lib. bdg. 22.50 (ISBN 0-915262-20-7). S J Durst.

Price, Martin J., ed. Coins: An Illustrated Survey, 650 B.C. to the Present Day. (Illus.). 320p. 1980. slipcased 50.00 (ISBN 0-416-00691-4). Methuen Inc.

Pridmore, F. Coins & Coinages of the Straits Settlements & British Malaya, 1786-1951. 1968. 12.00 (ISBN 0-685-51510-9, Pub by Spink & Son England). S J Durst.

Robertson, Anne S. Roman Imperial Coins in the Hunter Coin Cabinet: Valerian I to Allectus, Vol. IV. (Glasgow University Publications). (Illus.). 1978. 94.00 (ISBN 0-19-713307-X). Oxford U Pr.

Rogers, Edgar. A Handy Guide to Jewish Coins. LC 77-77252. (Illus.). 1977. Repr. of 1915 ed. lib. bdg. 13.50 (ISBN 0-915262-14-2). S J Durst.

Ronning, Bjorn & Skaare, Kolbjorn, eds. Scandinavian Numismatic Journal 1975-76. 1978. 18.00x (ISBN 82-00-01667-6, Dist. by Columbia U Pr). Universitet.

Rosenfeld, Sam. Story of Coins. LC 67-16903. (Story of Science Ser.). (Illus.). (gr. 5 up). 1968. PLB 7.29 (ISBN 0-8178-3922-4). Harvey.

Sadow, Joseph & Sarro, Thomas, Jr. Coins & Medals of the Vatican. LC 76-40814. (Illus.). 1977. lib. bdg. 13.00 (ISBN 0-915262-06-1). S J Durst.

Schembri, H. C. Coins & Medals of the Knights of Malta. 1966. 18.00 (ISBN 0-685-51537-0, Pub by Spink & Son England). S J Durst.

Schon, Gunter. Simon & Schuster World Coin Catalogue 1979-1980. (Illus.). 1979. pap. 11.95 (ISBN 0-671-24639-9). S&S.

Schroetter, Friedrich Von, ed. Woerterbuch der Muenzkunde. 2nd ed. (Ger). 1970. 75.00x (ISBN 3-11-001227-8). De Gruyter.

Schulz, Otto T. Die Rechtstitel und Regierungsprogramme Auf Romischen Kaisermunzen. Repr. of 1925 ed. pap. 9.50 (ISBN 0-384-54310-3). Johnson Repr.

Schwan, Fred. Military Payment Certificates. 122p. 1981. lib. bdg. 25.00 (ISBN 0-931960-08-8); pap. 15.95 (ISBN 0-931960-07-X). BNR Pr.

Schwarz, Ted. Coins As Living History. LC 75-2708. (Illus.). 256p. 1976. 8.95 (ISBN 0-668-03791-1); pap. 4.95 (ISBN 0-668-04499-3). Arco.

Scott, Gavin J. British Countermarks on Copper & Bronze Coins. 1977. 26.00 (ISBN 0-685-51515-X, Pub by Spink & Son England). S J Durst.

Seltman, C. Greek Coins. 1977. 17.00 (ISBN 0-685-51533-8, Pub by Spink & Son England). S J Durst.

Skaare, Kolbjorn. Coins & Coinage in Viking-Age Norway. 1976. 36.00x (ISBN 8-200-01542-4, Dist. by Columbia U Pr). Universitet.

Stewart, I. H. The Scottish Coinage. 1977. 10.00 (ISBN 0-685-51519-2, Pub by Spink & Son England). S J Durst.

Storer, Malcolm. Numismatics of Massachusetts. LC 80-52820. 317p. 1981. Repr. of 1923 ed. 35.00x (ISBN 0-88000-117-8). Quarterman.

Sutherland, C. H. The Emperor & the Coinage: Julio-Claudian Studies. 1977. 30.00 (ISBN 0-685-51534-6, Pub by Spink & Son England). S J Durst.

Sutherland, C. H. & Carson, R. A. Roman Imperial Coinage, 11 vols. 1977. 500.00 set (ISBN 0-685-51530-3, Pub by Spink & Son England). S J Durst.

Sutherland, C. H. & Kraay, C. M. Catalogue of Coins of the Roman Empire in the Ashmolean Museum: Augustus (c. 31 B.C. - A.D. 14, Pt. 1. (Illus.). 60p. 1975. 65.00x (ISBN 0-19-813189-5). Oxford U Pr.

Sydenham, E. A. Historical References on Coins of the Roman Empire. 1968. 12.00 (ISBN 0-685-51527-3, Pub by Spink & Son England). S J Durst.

Sydenham, Edward. The Coinage of the Roman Republic. LC 76-12921. (Illus.). 1976. Repr. of 1952 ed. lib. bdg. 27.50 (ISBN 0-915262-04-5). S J Durst.

Sylloge Nummorum Graecorum: The Collection of the American Numismatic Society, Pt. 3, Bruttium-Sicily I - Abacaenum-Eryx. (Illus.). 1975. pap. 75.00 (ISBN 0-89722-063-3). Am Numismatic.

Tudeer, L. O. Die Tetradrachmenpragung Von Syrakus, in der Periode der Signierenden Kunstler. (Illus.). 1979. 40.00 (ISBN 0-916710-53-X). Obol Intl.

Vermeule, Cornelius. Numismatic Art in America: Aesthetics & the United States Coinage. LC 76-135549. (Illus.). 1971. 20.00x (ISBN 0-674-62840-3, Belknap Pr). Harvard U Pr.

Weiser, F. Contributions to the Monetary History of Serbia, Montenegro & Yugoslavia. 1975. 3.00 (ISBN 0-685-51550-8, Pub by Spink & Son England). S J Durst.

Welter, G. & Schulman, H. Cleaning & Preservation of Coins & Medals. LC 76-3964. (Illus.). 1976. Repr. of 1970 ed. lib. bdg. 12.00 (ISBN 0-915262-03-7). S J Durst.

Wismer, David. The Obsolete Bank Notes of New England, 1922. LC 72-85119. (Illus.). 1972. 20.00x (ISBN 0-88000-006-6). Quarterman.

Zu Aichholz, V. Miller, et al. Osterreichische Munzpragungen 1519-1938, 2 vols. (Illus., Ger.). 1981. 195.00 (ISBN 0-686-73165-4). Obol Intl.

NUMISMATICS–BIBLIOGRAPHY

American Numismatic Society, New York. Dictionary & Auction Catalogues of the Library of the American Numismatic Society, Second Supplement. 1973. lib. bdg. 105.00 (ISBN 0-8161-1058-1). G K Hall.

Attinelli, E. J. A Bibliography of American Numismatic Auction Catalogues, 1828-1875. LC 75-32394. (Illus.). 1976. Repr. of 1875 ed. 25.00x (ISBN 0-88000-072-4). Quarterman.

Brown, I. D. & Dolley, M. Bibliography of Coin Hoards of Great Britain & Ireland, Fifteen Hundred to Nineteen Sixty-Seven. 1977. 12.00 (ISBN 0-685-51521-4, Pub by Spink & Son England). S J Durst.

Bruce, Colin R., 2nd. Standard Catalog of Mexican Coins, Paper Money, Bonds & Medals. rev. ed. LC 81-80932. (Illus.). 352p. (Eng. & Span.). 1981. pap. 14.50 (ISBN 0-87341-060-2). Krause Pubns.

Library Catalogue of the American Numismatic Association. 2nd ed. LC 77-93078. 1977. perfect bdg. 25.00 (ISBN 0-89637-000-3). American Numismatic.

Newell, Edward T. Myriandros Alexandria Kat'isson. (Alexander the Great Ser.). (Illus.). 48p. 1981. 25.00 (ISBN 0-916710-88-2). Obol Intl.

--Tarsos Under Alexander. (Alexander the Great Ser.). (Illus.). 68p. 1981. 25.00 (ISBN 0-916710-87-4). Obol Intl.

Numismatisc Literature, Nos. 1-99. Nos. 1-77. 1.00 ea.; Nos. 78-94. 2.00 ea.; No. 95-101. 4.00 (ISBN 0-685-88664-6); Biennial Indexes 1947-65. 2.00 ea. No. 1 (ISBN 0-89722-073-0). No. 99 (ISBN 0-89722-171-0). No. 100 (ISBN 0-89722-177-X). No. 101 (ISBN 0-89722-178-8). No. 102 (ISBN 0-89722-182-6). Am Numismatic.

Soetbeer, Adolf. Liraturnachweis Ueber Geld-und Muenzwesen Insbesondere Weber der Waehrungsstreit, 1871-1891. LC 72-85106. iv, 322p. 1972. Repr. of 1892 ed. lib. bdg. 32.50 (ISBN 0-8337-3304-4). B Franklin.

NUMISMATICS–COLLECTORS AND COLLECTING

Andersen, Paul. Let's Collect Type Coins. LC 81-90057. (Illus.). 57p. 1981. pap. 2.95 (ISBN 0-9604720-1-0). P Andersen.

Andrews, Charles J. Fell's United States Coin Book. 9th rev. ed. (Illus.). 160p. 1981. 9.95 (ISBN 0-8119-0349-4); pap. 5.95 (ISBN 0-8119-0421-0). Fell.

Baldwin, Agnes. The Electrum & Silver Coins of Chios, Issued During the Sixth, Fifth & Fourth Centuries B.C. A Chronological Study. (Illus.). 60p. 1979. Repr. of 1915 ed. 20.00 (ISBN 0-916710-61-0). Obol Intl.

Bale, Don, Jr. Fabulous Investment Potental of Singles. 4th, rev. ed. 1980. pap. 5.00 (ISBN 0-686-70347-2). Bale Bks.

--Fabulous Investment Potential of Uncirculated Singles. 4th, rev. ed. 1980. pap. 5.00 (ISBN 0-686-70348-0). Bale Bks.

--Gold Mine in Gold. 4th, rev. ed. 1980. pap. 5.00 (ISBN 0-686-70349-9). Bale Bks.

--Gold Mine in Your Pocket. 4th, rev. ed. 1980. pap. 5.00 (ISBN 0-686-70350-2). Bale Bks.

--How to Find Valuable Old & Scarce Coins. 4th, rev. ed. 1980. pap. 5.00 (ISBN 0-686-70351-0). Bale Bks.

--How to Invest in Singles. 4th, rev. ed. 1980. pap. 5.00 (ISBN 0-686-70352-9). Bale Bks.

--How to Invest in Uncirculated Singles. 4th, rev. ed. 1980. pap. 5.00 (ISBN 0-686-70353-7). Bale Bks.

--Out of Little Coins, Big Fortunes Grow. 4th, rev. ed. 1980. pap. 5.00 (ISBN 0-686-70354-5). Bale Bks.

Bale, Don, Jr., ed. Fabulous Investment Potential of Liberty Walking Half Dollars. 4th, rev. ed. 1980. pap. 5.00 (ISBN 0-686-70346-4). Bale Bks.

Boy Scouts of America. Coin Collecting. LC 19-600. (Illus.). 32p. (gr. 6-12). 1975. pap. 0.70x (ISBN 0-8395-3390-X, 3390). BSA.

Buying & Selling United States Coins. 1974. pap. 1.95 (ISBN 0-307-21981-X, Whitman). Western Pub.

Coffin, Joseph. Complete Book of Coin Collecting. 6th, rev. ed. LC 78-10529. (Illus.). 1979. 8.95 (ISBN 0-698-10954-6); pap. 5.95 (ISBN 0-698-10967-8). Coward.

Coin Digest. Date not set. price not set (ISBN 0-685-69141-1). Krause Pubns.

Coin Year Book, 1981. 14th ed. LC 74-644812. (Illus.). 386p. (Orig.). 1980. pap. 13.50x (ISBN 0-901265-16-0). Intl Pubns Serv.

Cope, G. M. & Rayner, P. A. The Standard Catalogue of English Milled Coinage, 1662-1972. 1978. 22.00 (ISBN 0-685-51072-7, Pub by Spink & Son England). S J Durst.

Crumbley, Larry & Crumbley, Tony L. The Financial Management of Your Coin-Stamp Estate. LC 77-13026. 1978. 16.50 (ISBN 0-668-04444-6). Arco.

Davis, Norman M. The Complete Book of United States Coin Collecting. rev. ed. 336p. 1976. 11.95 (ISBN 0-02-529880-1). Macmillan.

DeMorgan, J. Manuel de Numismatique Orientale de l'Antiquite et du Moyen Age. (Illus., Fr.). 1979. 30.00 (ISBN 0-916710-44-0); pap. 20.00 (ISBN 0-916710-45-9). Obol Intl.

DeRouge, J. & Feaurdent, F. The Coins of the Nomes & Prefecture of Roman Egypt. (Illus., Fr.). 1979. 20.00 (ISBN 0-916710-41-6); pap. 10.00 (ISBN 0-685-95531-1). Obol Intl.

Durst, Sanford J. Investor-Collector Guidebook. LC 76-40813. (Illus.). 1977. lib. bdg. 15.00 (ISBN 0-915262-07-X). S J Durst.

Eddy, Samuel K. The Minting of Antoniniani A. D. 238-249 & the Smyrna Hoard. (Numismatic Notes & Monographs: 156). (Illus.). 133p. 1967. pap. 12.50 (ISBN 0-89722-055-2). Am Numismatic.

Forrer, L., compiled by. The Weber Collection: Descriptive Catalogue of the Collection of Greek Coins Formed by Sir Hermann Weber, M.D., 1823-1918, 3 vols. Incl. Vol. 1. Italy-Sicily; Vol. 2. Greece; Vol. 3. Asia-Africa. O.S.I. (ISBN 0-685-56025-2). LC 75-6022. (Illus.). 1975. Repr. of 1922 ed. 150.00 (ISBN 0-915018-08-X). Attic Bks.

Frey, Albert R. The Dated European Coinage Prior to 1501. Carvin, David R., ed. LC 76-62838. 1978. Repr. of 1915 ed. lib. bdg. 25.00 (ISBN 0-915262-09-6). S J Durst.

Friedberg, Robert. The Green Coin Book: Appraising & Selling Your Coins, 1982. 11th ed. Friedberg, Arthur & Friedberg, Ira, eds. LC 81-67499. (Illus.). 176p. 1981. 4.95 (ISBN 0-87184-211-4). Coin & Curr.

Ganz, David L. The World of Coins & Coin Collecting. (Illus.). 356p. 1980. 19.95 (ISBN 0-684-16625-9, ScribT). Scribner.

Garrett, Charles L. Successful Coin Hunting. rev. ed. Nelson, Bettye, ed. LC 73-87120. (Illus.). 100p. (Orig.). 1978. pap. 6.95 (ISBN 0-915920-30-1). Ram Pub.

Gould, Jean & Gould, Maurice. Story of Israel in Coins. pap. 2.00 (ISBN 0-87980-150-6). Wilshire.

Gould, Maurice. Gould's Gold & Silver Guide to Coins. LC 70-76025. (Illus.). 1969. 9.95 (ISBN 0-8303-0077-5). Fleet.

Grierson, Philip. Later Medieval Numismatics (11th-16th Centuries) 1980. 60.00x (ISBN 0-86078-043-0, Pub. by Variorum England). State Mutual Bk.

Gunstone, Anthony, ed. Sylloge of Coins of the British Isles, Lincolnshire Collection: Coins in the Lincolnshire Collection. (Illus.). 200p. 1980. 79.00x (ISBN 0-686-74009-2). Oxford U Pr.

Hawkins, E. Medallic Illustrations of the History of Great Britain & Ireland, 2 vols. 1978. 54.00 (ISBN 0-685-51071-9, Pub. by Spink & Son England). S J Durst.

Head, B. V. On the Chronological Sequence of the Coins of Ephesus. (Illus.). 1979. 20.00 (ISBN 0-916710-40-8). Obol Intl.

Hendin, David. Collecting Coins. (Illus.). (RL 8). 1978. pap. 1.95 (ISBN 0-451-08405-5, J8405, Sig). NAL.

Hobson, Burton. Coins & Coin Collecting. LC 70-168904. (Illus.). 1971. pap. 2.50 (ISBN 0-486-22763-4). Dover.

Hobson, Burton & Reinfeld, Fred. Coin Collecting for Beginners. pap. 3.00 (ISBN 0-87980-022-4). Wilshire.

Hobson, Burton H. Coin Collecting As a Hobby. rev. ed. LC 67-27759. (Illus.). (gr. 3 up). 1977. 7.95 (ISBN 0-8069-6018-3); lib. bdg. 7.49 (ISBN 0-8069-6019-1). Sterling.

Hosch, Charles R. Official Guide to World Proof Coins. rev. 2nd ed. LC 73-94075. (Collector's Ser.). (Illus.). 1975. pap. 10.50 (ISBN 0-87637-259-0). Hse of Collectibles.

Knox, John J. United States Notes. LC 78-54681. 1978. Repr. of 1885 ed. lib. bdg. 22.50 (ISBN 0-915262-17-7). S J Durst.

Krause, Chester L. & Mishler, Clifford. Standard Catalog of World Coins. 8th ed. Bruce, Colin R., ed. LC 79-640940. (Illus.). 2048p. 1981. pap. 29.50 (ISBN 0-87341-061-0). Krause Pubns.

--Standard Catalog of World Coins: 1981. Bruce, Colin R., II, ed. LC 79-640940. (Illus.). 2000p. 1980. pap. 29.50 (ISBN 0-87341-054-8). Krause Pubns.

Laythorpe, Mark. The Penny Pincher's Profit Portfolio: How to Make Dollars into Cents. (Illus.). 80p. 1981. pap. 19.95 (ISBN 0-939230-00-3). SNOWCO.

Linecar, Howard. Beginner's Guide to Coin Collecting. 9.95 (ISBN 0-7207-0015-9). Transatlantic.

Linecar, Howard A. The Commemorative Medal: Its Appreciation & Collection. LC 72-12989. (Illus.). 250p. 1974. 16.00 (ISBN 0-8103-2012-6). Gale.

Love, Morris. Profitable Coin Collecting. pap. 1.00 (ISBN 0-686-00713-1). Key Bks.

McLure, Dudley. Tales of the Golden Beavers. 1978. pap. 3.50 (ISBN 0-87341-022-X). Krause Pubns.

Mulligan, Tom. Better Coin Collecting. LC 73-155440. (Illus.). 96p. 1972. 8.50x (ISBN 0-7182-0481-6). Intl Pubns Serv.

The Numismatist Index: Vols. 1-91, (1888-1978) 1980. 4.95 (ISBN 0-686-75364-X). American Numismatic.

Raho, Rodolfo, compiled by. Collection Claudius Cote, de Lyon: Monnaies de Tarente. 42p. (French.). 1975. pap. 7.50 (ISBN 0-915018-09-8). Attic Bks.

Reinfeld, Fred. How to Build a Coin Collection. (Illus.). 160p. 1973. pap. 4.95 (ISBN 0-02-081230-2, Collier). Macmillan.

Reinfeld, Fred & Hobson, Burton H. How to Build a Coin Collection. LC 58-12544. (Illus.). (gr. 3 up). 1977. 7.95 (ISBN 0-8069-6068-X); PLB 7.49 (ISBN 0-8069-6069-8). Sterling.

Reinfeld, Fred & Obojski, Robert. Coin Collector's Handbook. rev. ed. 160p. 1980. 7.95 (ISBN 0-385-17078-5). Doubleday.

Schmeider, Thomas K. Collecting & Investing in U. S. Small Cents. 1979. softcover 7.00 (ISBN 0-686-64450-6). S J Durst.

Schwarz, Ted. Beginner's Guide to Coin Collecting. LC 78-22353. (Illus.). 1980. pap. 5.95 (ISBN 0-385-14491-1, Dolp). Doubleday.

Sey, Katalin B. Coins & Medals. LC 75-308639. (Illus.). 46p. 1973. 7.50x (ISBN 0-8002-0137-X). Intl Pubns Serv.

Sylloge Nummorum Graecorum: The Collection of the American Numismatic Society-Part 1-Etruria Calabria. (Illus.). 39p. 1970. pap. 75.00 (ISBN 0-89722-060-9). Am Numismatic.

Sylloge Nummorum Graecorum: The Collection of the American Numismatic Society, Part 2-Lucania. (Illus.). 38p. 1972. pap. 75.00 (ISBN 0-89722-061-7). Am Numismatic.

Terry, Thomas P. Coin Investments for Profit. rev. ed. (Illus.). 40p. (Orig.). 1975. pap. 2.00 (ISBN 0-939850-09-5). Spec Pub.

--Doubloons & Other Buried Treasure. (Illus.). 139p. (Orig.). 1970. pap. 5.95 (ISBN 0-939850-02-8). Spec Pub.

Thompson, J., ed. The Coin Chart Manual. (Illus.). 48p. 1974. 3.00 (ISBN 0-916710-16-5). Obol Intl.

Troxell, Hyla A. The Norman Davis Collection. (Illus.). 53p. 1969. pap. 15.00 (ISBN 0-89722-058-7). Am Numismatic.

Zimmerman, Walter J. Coin Collectors Fact Book. LC 73-77839. (Illus.). 192p. 1973. lib. bdg. 5.95 o. p. (ISBN 0-668-02991-9); pap. 3.95 (ISBN 0-668-02992-7). Arco.

NUNAMIUT (ESKIMO TRIBE)

Binford, Lewis R. Nunamiut Ethnoarchaeology. (Studies in Archaeology Ser.). 1978. 50.00 (ISBN 0-12-100040-0). Acad Pr.

NUNATOGMUIT (ESKIMO TRIBE)

see Nunamiut (Eskimo Tribe)

NUNCIOS, PAPAL

see also Legates, Papal

NUNEZ CABEZA DE VACA, ALVAR, 16TH CENTURY

Bishop, Morris. The Odyssey of Cabeza De Vaca. LC 70-139123. (Illus.). 306p. 1972. Repr. of 1933 ed. lib. bdg. 18.00x (ISBN 0-8371-5739-0, BICV). Greenwood.

Long, Haniel. The Marvellous Adventure of Cabera de Vaca. 1972. Repr. of 1939 ed. 3.00 (ISBN 0-285-64709-1). SMU Press.

Nunez Cabeza de Vaca, Alvar. The Journey of Alvar Nunez Cabeza de Vaca & His Companions from Florida to the Pacific, 1528-1536. Bandelier, A. F., ed. Bandelier, Fanny, tr. LC 72-2822. (American Explorers Ser.). Repr. of 1922 ed. 20.00 (ISBN 0-404-54915-2). AMS Pr.

NUNIVAK ISLAND

Matthiessen, Peter. Oomingmak: The Expedition to the Musk Ox Island in the Bering Sea. (Illus.). (gr. 6-9). 1967. 6.95 (ISBN 0-8038-5351-3). Hastings.

NUNS

see also Ex-Nuns

Bryce, Lawrence. To Love a Nun. (Illus.). 1978. 29.75 (ISBN 0-89266-114-3). Am Classical Coll Pr.

Campbell-Jones, Suzanne. In Habit: A Study of Working Nuns. LC 78-20410. 1979. 10.00 (ISBN 0-394-50666-9). Pantheon.

Gustafson, Janie. Celibate Passion. LC 77-20439. 1978. 8.95 (ISBN 0-06-063536-3, HarpR). Har-Row.

Holloway, Marcella. Should You Become a Sister? 1978. pap. 1.50 (ISBN 0-89243-073-7, 29553). Liguori Pubns.

McDonnell, Thomas. Listening to the Lord in Literature: The Sister's Life Revisited. LC 77-88108. (Orig.). 1978. pap. 1.85 (ISBN 0-8189-1154-9, 154, Pub. by Alba Bks). Alba.

Monk, Maria & Grob, Gerald. Awful Disclosures by Marcia Monk of the Hotel Dieu Nunnery of Montrial. LC 76-46089. (Anti-Movements in America). 1977. lib. bdg. 21.00 (ISBN 0-405-09962-2). Arno.

Moore, Sr. Mary E. And I Married the Son of a King. 185p. 1979. pap. 6.95 (ISBN 0-8059-2688-7). Dorrance.

Pearlstein, Edward W. Three Intellectual Plays: Jack Ruby, Marina Alcoforado, Pocahontas. 146p. 1979. pap. 1.95 (ISBN 0-917636-02-3). Edit Consult.

Target, C. M. The Nun in the Concentration Camp. 1977. pap. 1.55 (ISBN 0-08-017611-9). Pergamon.

NUPE (AFRICAN PEOPLE)

Nadel, Siegfried. Black Byzantium: The Kingdom of Nupe in Nigeria. 1976. lib. bdg. 59.95 (ISBN 0-8490-1510-3). Gordon Pr.

Nadel, Siegfried F. Black Byzantium: Kingdom of Nupe in Nigeria. (International Institute of African Languages & Cultures Ser). (Illus.). 1942. 49.00x (ISBN 0-19-724123-9). Oxford U Pr.

NUREMBERG

Goethe, Meredyth. Why Nurnberg. (Illus.). 256p. 1981. text ed. 12.95 (ISBN 0-9606714-0-4). Goethe Pubs.

Greenfield, Kent R. Sumptuary Law in Nuernberg: A Study in Paternal Government. LC 78-63964. (Johns Hopkins University. Studies in the Social Sciences. Thirty-Sixth Ser. 1918: 2). Repr. of 1918 ed. 16.50 (ISBN 0-404-61211-3). AMS Pr.

Headlam, C. The Story of Nuremberg. 59.95 (ISBN 0-8490-2682-2). Gordon Pr.

Kusch, Eugen. Immortal Nuremburg. 5th ed. LC 60-2788. 1972. 12.50x (ISBN 3-418-00429-6). Intl Pubns Serv.

Strauss, Gerald. Nuremberg in the Sixteenth Century: City Politics & Life Between Middle Ages & Modern Times. LC 76-12379. (Illus.). 320p. 1976. 12.50x (ISBN 0-253-34149-3); pap. text ed. 5.95x (ISBN 0-253-34150-7). Ind U Pr.

Sumberg, Samuel L. Nuremberg Schembart Carnival. (Columbia University. Germanic Studies, New Ser.: No. 12). Repr. of 1941 ed. 22.50 (ISBN 0-404-50462-0). AMS Pr.

NUREMBERG TRIAL OF MAJOR GERMAN WAR CRIMINALS, 1945-1946

Bardeche, Maurice. Nuremberg, 2 vols. 650p. 1975. lib. bdg. 250.00 (ISBN 0-8490-0742-9). Gordon Pr.

Benton, Wilbourn E. & Grimm, Georg, eds. Nuremberg: German Views of the War Trials. LC 55-5739. 1955. 5.95 (ISBN 0-87074-006-7). SMU Press.

Harris, Whitney R. Tyranny on Trial: The Evidence at Nuremberg. LC 54-11298. (Illus.). 1954. 12.50 (ISBN 0-87074-073-3). SMU Press.

Harwood, Richard. Nuremberg & Other War Crimes Trials. (Illus.). 70p. Date not set. pap. 2.50 (ISBN 0-911038-34-5). Inst Hist Rev.

--Nuremberg & Other War Crimes Trials: A New Look. (Illus.). 1978. pap. 2.50 (ISBN 0-911038-34-5, Inst Hist Rev). Noontide.

Heydecker, Joe & Leeb, Johannes. The Nuremberg Trail. LC 75-9111. 398p. 1975. Repr. of 1962 ed. lib. bdg. 24.25x (ISBN 0-8371-8131-3, HENT). Greenwood.

International Conference on Military Trials, London, 1945. Report of Robert H. Jackson, U.S. Representative to the International Conference on Military Trials, London, 1945. LC 72-178907. Repr. of 1949 ed. 31.00 (ISBN 0-404-10023-6). AMS Pr.

Jackson, Robert H. Nurnberg Case. LC 73-166584. 1972. Repr. of 1947 ed. 13.50x (ISBN 0-8154-0403-4). Cooper Sq.

Maser, Werner. Nuremberg: A Nation on Trial. 1979. 16.95 (ISBN 0-684-16252-0, ScribT). Scribner.

Maugham, Frederic H. U.N.O. & War Crimes. LC 74-27728. 143p. 1975. Repr. of 1951 ed. lib. bdg. 15.00 (ISBN 0-8371-7911-4, MAUN). Greenwood.

Miale, Florence & Selzer, Michael. The Nuremberg Mind: The Psychology of the Nazi Leaders. LC 75-8300. (Illus.). 256p. 1976. 10.95 (ISBN 0-686-67204-6); pap. 3.95 (1977) (ISBN 0-8129-6280-X). Times Bks.

Neave, Airey. On Trial at Nuremberg. LC 78-25626. (Illus.). 1979. 12.95 (ISBN 0-316-59930-1). Little.

Nuremburg War Trials. Trial of the Major War Criminals Before the International Military Tribunal, 44 vols. LC 70-145536. Repr. of 1949 ed. 57.50 ea.; Set. 2530.00 (ISBN 0-404-53650-6). AMS Pr.

Poltorak, A. The Nuremberg Epilogue. 477p. 1971. 4.80 (ISBN 0-8285-0486-5, Pub. by Progress Pubs Russia). Imported Pubns.

Robinson, Jacob & Sachs, Henry. The Holocaust: The Nuremberg Evidence, Part I: Documents, Digest, Index & Chronological Tables. (Yad Vashem-Yivo. Joint Documentary Projects). 1976. 30.00 (ISBN 0-914512-37-4). Yivo Inst.

Smith, Bradley. The Road to Nuremberg. LC 80-68174. 336p. 1980. 14.95 (ISBN 0-465-07056-6). Basic.

Smith, Bradley F. The American Road to Nuremberg: The Documentary Record, 1944-1945. LC 80-83830. 234p. 1981. 24.95 (ISBN 0-8179-7481-4). Hoover Inst Pr.

--Reaching Judgment at Nuremberg: The Untold Story of How the Nazi War Criminals Were Judged. 1979. pap. 5.95 (ISBN 0-452-00503-5, F503, Mer). NAL.

--Reaching Judgment at Nuremburg. LC 76-9345. 1977. 15.00x (ISBN 0-465-06839-1). Basic.

Thompson, Harold K., Jr. & Strutz, Henry. Doenitz at Nuremberg - a Re-Appraisal: War Crimes & the Military Professional. LC 75-26202. (Illus.). 1977. 10.00 (ISBN 0-916788-01-6). Amber Pub.

NUREYEV, RUDOLF, 1939-

Bland, Alexander. Fonteyn & Nureyev: The Story of a Partnership. LC 79-64452. (Illus.). 1979. 22.50 (ISBN 0-8129-0860-0). Times Bks.

--The Nureyev Image. LC 76-17509. (Illus.). 1976. 20.00 (ISBN 0-8129-0664-0). Times Bks.

Percival, John. Nureyev. 1977. pap. 2.25 (ISBN 0-445-04015-7). Popular Lib.

Vollmer, Jurgen & Devere, John. Nureyev in Paris. (Illus.). 80p. 1975. pap. 5.95 slipcase (ISBN 0-89237-002-5). Modernismo.

NURI AL SA'ID 1888-1958

Gallman, Waldemar J. Iraq under General Nuri: My Recollections of Nuri al-Said 1954-1958. (Illus.). 255p. 1964. 16.50x (ISBN 0-8018-0210-5). Johns Hopkins.

NURSE AND PATIENT

Blondis, Marion N. & Jackson, Barbara. Nonverbal Communication with Patients: Back to the Human Touch. LC 76-30732. 1977. 9.95 (ISBN 0-471-01753-1, Pub. by Wiley Med). Wiley.

Broadwell, Lucile & Milutnovic, Barbara. Medical-Surgical Nursing Procedures. LC 76-4305. 1977. pap. text ed. 12.40 (ISBN 0-8273-0353-X); instructor's guide 1.60 (ISBN 0-8273-0354-8). Delmar.

Brooks, Lucy. The Nurse Assistant. LC 77-73939. 1978. pap. text ed. 7.40 (ISBN 0-8273-1620-8); instructor's guide 1.60 (ISBN 0-8273-1621-6). Delmar.

Burnside, Irene & Ebersole, Priscilla. Psychosocial Caring Throughout the Life Span. (Illus.). 1979. text ed. 15.50 (ISBN 0-07-009213-3, HP). McGraw.

Freedman, Carol R. Teaching Patients: A Practical Handbook for the Health Care Professional. LC 78-73147. 1978. 10.50 (ISBN 0-89805-000-6). Courseware.

Gillies, Dee A. & Alyn, Irene B. Patient Assessment & Management by the Nurse Practitioner. LC 75-28793. (Illus.). 320p. 1976. text ed. 12.95 (ISBN 0-7216-4133-4). Saunders.

Glass, Marion & Atchison, Evelyn. Integrated Studies in Patient Care. LC 76-46127. 1978. pap. text ed. 9.00 (ISBN 0-8273-1608-9); instructor's guide 1.60 (ISBN 0-8273-1609-7). Delmar.

--Integrated Studies in Patient Care. 1978. 10.95 (ISBN 0-442-22699-3). Van Nos Reinhold.

Gordon, Laura B. Behavioral Intervention in Health Care. (Behavioral Sciences for Health Care Professionals Ser.). 128p. 1981. lib. bdg. 15.00x (ISBN 0-86531-018-1); pap. text ed. 6.75x (ISBN 0-86531-019-X). Westview.

Gow, Kathleen W. Emotional Involvement in Nursing: The Affective Dimensions of Care-Giving. 1981. text ed. price not set (ISBN 0-8261-3430-0); pap. text ed. price not set (ISBN 0-8261-3431-9). Springer Pub.

Gruendemann, Barbara J., et al. The Surgical Patient: Behavioral Concepts for the Operating Room Nurse. 2nd ed. LC 76-51725. (Illus.). 1977. pap. text ed. 10.50 (ISBN 0-8016-1981-5). Mosby.

Kraegel, Janet M., et al. Patient Care Systems. LC 74-7210. 150p. 1974. text ed. 12.95 (ISBN 0-397-54154-6, JBL-Med-Nursing). Har-Row.

Lewis, Garland K. Nurse-Patient Communication. 3rd ed. 125p. 1978. pap. text ed. write for info. (ISBN 0-697-05543-4). Wm C Brown.

Maas, Meridean & Jacox, Ada. Guidelines for Nurse Autonomy Patient Welfare. (Illus.). 1977. pap. 14.50 (ISBN 0-8385-3526-7). ACC.

O'Connor, Andrea B., ed. Nursing: Patient Education. LC 79-140955. (Contemporary Nursing Ser.). 224p. 1979. pap. text ed. 7.95 (ISBN 0-937126-22-5). Am Journal Nurse.

Padilla, Geraldine V., et al. Interacting with Dying Patients: An Inter-Hospital Nursing Research & Nursing Education Project. LC 75-32950. 219p. 1975. pap. 7.00 (ISBN 0-686-16747-3). City Hope.

Peitchinis, Jacquelyn. Staff-Patient Communication in the Health Services. LC 76-15415. 1976. text ed. 11.50 (ISBN 0-8261-2040-7); pap. text ed. 6.95 (ISBN 0-8261-2041-5). Springer Pub.

Robinson, Lisa. Psychiatric Nursing As a Human Experience. LC 76-41542. (Illus.). 1977. text ed. 12.50 (ISBN 0-7216-7621-9). Saunders.

Simmons, Janet A. The Nurse-Client Relationship in Mental Health Nursing: Workbook Guides to Understanding & Management. LC 75-40639. 240p. 1978. pap. 8.95 (ISBN 0-7216-8286-3). Saunders.

Sundeen, Sandra, et al. Nurse-Client Interaction: Implementing the Nursing Process. 2nd ed. LC 80-27585. (Illus.). 252p. 1981. pap. text ed. 11.95 (ISBN 0-8016-4844-0). Mosby.

Werner-Beland, Jean A. Grief Response for the Critically Ill. (Illus.). 1980. text ed. 14.95 (ISBN 0-8359-2591-9); pap. text ed. 9.95 (ISBN 0-8359-2590-0). Reston.

NURSE-PATIENT RELATIONSHIP

see Nurse and Patient

NURSERIES

Bergstrom, Joan L. & Gold, Jane R. Sweden's Day Nurseries: Focus on Programs for Infants & Toddlers. (Illus.). 144p. pap. 5.25 (ISBN 0-936746-08-4, L56). Day Care Coun.

Cohan & Yoshikawa. Nursery Management. 1982. text ed. 16.95 (ISBN 0-8359-5051-4); instr's. manual free (ISBN 0-8359-5052-2). Reston.

Cunningham, P. J., ed. Nursery Nursing. 3rd ed. 224p. 1978. pap. 5.95 (ISBN 0-571-04940-0, Pub. by Faber & Faber). Merrimack Bk Serv.

Freeman, Larry. Nursery Americana. (Orig.). 1947. pap. 3.50 (ISBN 0-87282-052-1, 20). Century Hse.

Miall, Antony & Miall, Peter. The Victorian Nursery Book. (Illus.). 1981. 14.95 (ISBN 0-394-51597-8). Pantheon.

NURSERIES (HORTICULTURE)

see also Plant Propagation

Berninger, Louis M. Profitable Garden Center Management. (Illus.). 1978. 15.95 (ISBN 0-8359-5632-6); instrs's manual avail. Reston.

Davidson, Harold & Mechlenburg, Roy. Nursery Management: Administration & Culture. (Illus.). 464p. 1981. text ed. 20.95 (ISBN 0-13-627455-2). P-H.

Educational Research Council of America. Nursery Worker. Ferris, Theodore N. & Marchak, John P., eds. (Real People at Work: Series M). (Illus., Orig.). (gr. 5). 1976. pap. text ed. 2.25 (ISBN 0-89247-099-2). Changing Times.

Lamb, et al. Nursery Stock Manual. (Illus.). 1979. pap. 15.00 (ISBN 0-901361-17-8, Pub. by Grower Books England). Intl Schol Bk Serv.

Nursery Source Guide. 1.95 (ISBN 0-686-21114-6). Bklyn Botanic.

Pinney, John J. Your Future in the Nursery Industry. LC 67-10084. (Careers in Depth Ser). (Illus.). (gr. 7 up). 1978. PLB 5.97 (ISBN 0-8239-0331-1). Rosen Pr.

Toogood, Alan & Stanley, John. The Modern Nurseryman. (Illus.). 432p. 1981. 45.00 (ISBN 0-571-11544-6, Pub. by Faber & Faber); pap. 22.00 (ISBN 0-571-11547-0). Merrimack Bk Serv.

NURSERY RHYMES

see also Children's Poetry; Counting-Out Rhymes

Adams, Pam, illus. There Was an Old Lady. (Books with Holes). (Illus.). 16p. Date not set. 6.00 (ISBN 0-85953-021-3, Pub. by Child's Play England). Playspaces.

--This Old Man. (Books with Holes Ser.). (Illus.). 16p. (Orig.). pap. 4.00 (ISBN 0-85953-026-4, Pub. by Childs Play England). Playspaces.

--This Old Man. (Books with Holes). (Illus.). 16p. 6.00 (ISBN 0-85953-027-2, Pub. by Child's Play England). Playspaces.

Ahlberg, Janet & Ahlberg, Allan. Peek-a-Boo! LC 81-1925. (Illus.). (ps-1). 1981. 9.95 (ISBN 0-670-54598-8). Viking Pr.

Anglund, Joan W. In a Pumpkin Shell. LC 60-10243. (Illus.). (ps-2). 1977. pap. 1.95 (ISBN 0-15-238273-9, VoyB). HarBraceJ.

Baber, Frank, illus. Frank Baber's Mother Goose. (Illus.). (gr. k-2). 1976. 4.95 (ISBN 0-517-52819-3). Crown.

Baring-Gould, S. A Book of Nursery Songs & Rhymes. 59.95 (ISBN 0-87968-768-1). Gordon Pr.

Baring-Gould, Sabine. Book of Nursery Songs & Rhymes. LC 68-23135. 1969. Repr. of 1895 ed. 19.00 (ISBN 0-8103-3471-2). Gale.

Battaglia, Aurelius, ed. Mother Goose. (ps-1). 1973. pap. 1.25 (ISBN 0-394-82661-2, BYR). Random.

Benvenuti, illus. Rhymes from Mother Goose. LC 79-18772. (Goodnight Bks). (Illus.). 24p. (gr. 1). 1980. 1.75 (ISBN 0-394-84383-5). Knopf.

--The Three Little Pigs. LC 78-12526. (A Good Night Bk.). (Illus.). (ps-1). 1979. 1.75 (ISBN 0-394-84104-2). Knopf.

Bett, H. Nursery Rhymes & Tales: Their Origin & History. 59.95 (ISBN 0-8490-0743-7). Gordon Pr.

Bett, Henry. Nursery Rhymes & Tales: Their Origin & History. LC 73-14839. 1924. lib. bdg. 6.50 (ISBN 0-8414-3274-0). Folcroft.

--Nursery Rhymes & Tales, Their Origin & History. LC 68-21756. 1968. Repr. of 1924 ed. 22.00 (ISBN 0-8103-3474-7). Gale.

The Big Book of Mother Goose. (Illus.). (ps-5). 1981. pap. 7.95 (ISBN 0-686-31167-1, 4900). Playmore & Prestige.

Blegvad, Erik, illus. Burnie's Hill: A Traditional Rhyme. LC 76-28515. (ps-3). 1977. 6.95 (ISBN 0-689-50070-X, Mcelderry Bk). Atheneum.

Brown, Marc. Finger Rhymes. LC 80-10173. (Illus.). 32p. (ps-2). 1980. 8.95 (ISBN 0-525-29732-4, Unicorn Bks). Dutton.

Chambers, Robert. Popular Rhymes of Scotland. LC 68-58902. 1969. Repr. of 1870 ed. 22.00 (ISBN 0-8103-3828-9). Gale.

Chorao, Kay. The Baby's Lap Book. (Illus.). (ps-k). 1977. 8.95 (ISBN 0-525-26100-1). Dutton.

Cole, William. The Square Bear & Other Riddle Rhymers. (gr. k-3). 1977. pap. 1.25 (ISBN 0-590-10320-2, Schol Pap). Schol Bk Serv.

Cooper, Helen. Great Grandmother Goose. LC 79-1081. (Illus.). (gr. k up). 1979. 7.95 (ISBN 0-688-80218-4); PLB 7.63 (ISBN 0-688-84218-6). Greenwillow.

De Angeli, Marguerite. Book of Nursery & Mother Goose Rhymes. (Illus.). (gr. k-3). 1954. 10.95a (ISBN 0-385-07232-5); PLB (ISBN 0-385-06246-X). Doubleday.

--Marguerite De Angeli's Book of Nursery & Mother Goose Rhymes. (Illus.). (gr. 1-3). 1979. pap. 4.95 (ISBN 0-385-15291-4, Zephyr). Doubleday.

De Paola, Tomie. The Comic Adventures of Old Mother Hubbard & Her Dog. LC 80-19270. (Illus.). 32p. (ps-3). 1981. pap. 5.95 (ISBN 0-15-219542-4, VoyB). HarBraceJ.

Dodson, Fitzhugh. I Wish I Had a Computer That Makes Waffles: Teaching Your Child with Modern Nursery Rhymes. LC 78-13178. (Illus.). 1978. 7.95 (ISBN 0-916392-27-9). Oak Tree Pubns.

Duvoisin, Roger. A for the Ark. LC 52-12846. (Illus.). (gr. k-3). 1952. PLB 8.16 (ISBN 0-688-50985-1). Lothrop.

Eckenstein, Lina. Comparative Studies in Nursery Rhymes. LC 68-23469. 1968. Repr. of 1906 ed. 19.00 (ISBN 0-8103-3479-8). Gale.

--Comparative Studies in Nursery Rhymes. 59.95 (ISBN 0-87968-912-9). Gordon Pr.

Farjeon, Eleanor. Nursery Rhymes of London Town. 2nd ed. (Illus.). 1977. pap. 4.50 (ISBN 0-7156-0736-7, Pub. by Duckworth England). Biblio Dist.

Fletcher, Cynthia H. My Jesus Pocketbook of Nursery Rhymes. LC 80-52041. (Illus.). 32p. (Orig.). (ps). 1980. pap. 0.49 (ISBN 0-937420-00-X). Stirrup Assoc.

Ford, Robert. Children's Rhymes, Children's Games, Children's Songs, Children's Stories. LC 69-16067. 1968. Repr. of 1904 ed. 22.00 (ISBN 0-8103-3526-3). Gale.

Fujikawa, Gyo, illus. Mother Goose. abr. ed. (Pandaback Ser.). (Illus.). 24p. (ps-2). 1980. 7.65 (ISBN 0-448-13146-3); pap. 1.25 (ISBN 0-448-49618-6). Platt.

Goldsborough, June, illus. The Dandelion Mother Goose. LC 78-72131. (Illus.). (gr. k-3). 1979. 3.50 (ISBN 0-89799-097-8); pap. 1.50 (ISBN 0-89799-052-8). Dandelion Pr.

Green, Percy B. History of Nursery Rhymes. LC 72-191809. 1899. lib. bdg. 8.25 (ISBN 0-8414-4506-0). Folcroft.

--History of Nursery Rhymes. LC 68-31082. 1968. Repr. of 1899 ed. 22.00 (ISBN 0-8103-3481-X). Gale.

--A History of Nursery Rhymes. 59.95 (ISBN 0-8490-0340-7). Gordon Pr.

Greg, R. P. A Selection of Old Nursery Rhymes. LC 74-17263. 1975. Repr. of 1903 ed. lib. bdg. 6.00 (ISBN 0-88305-232-6). Norwood Edns.

Halliwell-Phillipps, James O. Nursery Rhymes of England. LC 67-23936. 1969. Repr. of 1843 ed. 22.00 (ISBN 0-8103-3482-8). Gale.

--Popular Rhymes & Nursery Tales. LC 78-67715. (The Folktale). Repr. of 1849 ed. 25.00 (ISBN 0-404-16092-1). AMS Pr.

--Popular Rhymes & Nursery Tales. LC 68-23470. 1968. Repr. of 1849 ed. 22.00 (ISBN 0-8103-3484-4). Gale.

Halliwell-Phillips, J. O. The Nursery Rhymes of England. 59.95 (ISBN 0-8490-0744-5). Gordon Pr.

--Popular Rhymes & Nursery Tales. 59.95 (ISBN 0-8490-0878-6). Gordon Pr.

Halsey, Rosalie V. Forgotten Books of the American Nursery. 59.95 (ISBN 0-8490-0182-X). Gordon Pr.

Hazen, Barbara S. World, World, What Can I Do? LC 74-34186. (Illus.). (gr. k-3). 1976. 5.95 (ISBN 0-687-46384-X). Abingdon.

Hillman, Priscilla. A Merry-Mouse Book of Nursery Rhymes. LC 80-2053. (Illus.). 32p. (gr. k-1). 1981. 4.95a (ISBN 0-385-17102-1); PLB (ISBN 0-385-17103-X). Doubleday.

Hobbie, Holly, illus. Holly Hobbie's Nursery Rhymes. LC 76-52815. (Illus.). (gr. k-2). 1977. 4.95 (ISBN 0-448-47215-5). Platt.

Howard, Nina. Barber, Barber, Shave a Pig. 16p. (ps-k). 1981. tchr's ed. 4.95 (ISBN 0-917206-13-4). Children Learn Ctr.

Jeffers, Susan. If Wishes Were Horses: Mother Goose Rhymes. LC 79-9986. (Illus.). (ps-3). 1979. 9.95 (ISBN 0-525-32531-X). Dutton.

Joyful Nursery Rhymes. (Children's Library of Picture Bks.). (Illus.). 10p. (ps). 1979. 1.95 (ISBN 0-89346-179-2, TA63, Froebel-Kan Japan). Heian Intl.

Kent, Jack. Jack Kent's Book of Nursery Tales. (Illus.). (ps-1). 1970. 4.95 (ISBN 0-394-80288-8); PLB 5.99 (ISBN 0-394-90288-2). Random.

Kramer, Caroline. Read-Aloud Nursery Tales. (Illus.). (gr. k-3). 1957. 1.95 (ISBN 0-394-80673-5). Random.

Levy, Sara G. Mother Goose Rhymes for Jewish Children. (Illus.). (ps-2). 1979. Repr. of 1945 ed. 6.95 (ISBN 0-8197-0254-4). Bloch.

Little Boy Blue. (Vocabulary Builders). (Illus.). pap. 0.59 (ISBN 0-685-74083-8). Guild Bks.

Little Jack Horner. (Vocabulary Builders). (Illus.). pap. 0.59 (ISBN 0-685-74086-2). Guild Bks.

Lobel, Arnold. Gregory Griggs & Other Nursery Rhyme People. LC 77-22209. (Illus.). (gr. k-3). 1978. 9.25 (ISBN 0-688-80128-5); PLB 8.88 (ISBN 0-688-84128-7). Greenwillow.

Mary Had a Little Lamb. (Vocabulary Builders). (Illus.). pap. 0.59 (ISBN 0-685-74085-4). Guild Bks.

Mary-Mary Quite Contrary. (Vocabulary Builders). (Illus.). pap. 0.59 (ISBN 0-685-74084-6). Guild Bks.

Mason, Marianne H. Nursery Rhymes & Country Songs. LC 77-19041. 1909. 10.00 (ISBN 0-8414-2302-4). Folcroft.

Montgomerie, Norah & Montgomerie, William, eds. Scottish Nursery Rhymes. 158p. 1978. 7.95 (ISBN 0-7012-0003-0, Pub. by Chatto Bodley Jonathan). Merrimack Bk Serv.

Moorat, Joseph. Nursery Songs. (Illus.). 1980. 10.95 (ISBN 0-500-01242-3). Thames Hudson.

--Thirty Old-Time Nursery Songs. LC 80-16025. (Illus.). 33p. (ps). 1980. 10.95 (ISBN 0-87099-242-2). Metro Mus Art.

Newbery, John, et al, eds. Original Mother Goose's Melody. LC 68-31093. 1969. Repr. of 1892 ed. 19.00 (ISBN 0-8103-3485-2). Gale.

Nursery Rhymes. (Sturdy Shape Bks.). (Illus.). 14p. (ps). 1980. 2.95 (ISBN 0-307-12253-0, Golden Pr). Western Pub.

Old King Cole. (Vocabulary Builders). (Illus.). pap. 0.59 (ISBN 0-685-74103-6). Guild Bks.

The Old Woman Who Lived in a Shoe. (Vocabulary Builders). (Illus.). pap. 0.59 (ISBN 0-685-74082-X). Guild Bks.

Opie, Iona & Opie, Peter, eds. Oxford Dictionary of Nursery Rhymes. (Illus.). (ps-3). 1951. 42.50 (ISBN 0-19-869111-4). Oxford U Pr.

--Oxford Nursery Rhyme Book. (Illus.). (ps-3). 1955. 24.95 (ISBN 0-19-869112-2). Oxford U Pr.

Opie, Peter & Opie, Iona. Puffin Book of Nursery Rhymes. (Illus.). (ps-2). 1964. pap. 1.95 (ISBN 0-14-030200-X, Puffin). Penguin.

Peake, Mervyn, illus. Ride a Cock-Horse: & Other Nursery Rhymes. LC 75-509235. (Illus.). 32p. (ps-2). 1979. 12.95 (ISBN 0-7011-5015-7, Pub. by Chatto Bodley Jonathan); pap. 4.95 (ISBN 0-7011-1945-4, Pub. by Chatto Bodley Jonathan). Merrimack Bk Serv.

Petersham, Maud & Petersham, Miska. Rooster Crows. (Illus.). (gr. k-1). 1945. 10.95g (ISBN 0-02-773100-6). Macmillan.

Piper, Watty, ed. Mother Goose, a Treasury of Best Loved Rhymes. LC 72-185969. (Illus.). 64p. (ps-1). 1971. 4.95 (ISBN 0-448-47230-9). Platt.

Potts, William. Banbury Cross & the Rhyme. LC 76-25535. 1976. Repr. of 1930 ed. lib. bdg. 10.00 (ISBN 0-8414-6737-4). Folcroft.

Rackham, Arthur. Mother Goose, the Old Nursery Rhymes. (Illus.). 1978. Repr. of 1912 ed. lib. bdg. 9.95 luxury ed. (ISBN 0-932106-02-1, Pub by Marathon Pr). S J Durst.

Rockwell, Anne. Gray Goose & Gander & Other Mother Goose Rhymes. LC 79-6839. (Illus.). 64p. (ps-1). 1980. 8.95 (ISBN 0-690-04048-2, TYC-J); PLB 8.79 (ISBN 0-690-04049-0). Har-Row.

Rosenberg, Amye, illus. My Little Mother Goose. (First Little Golden Bks.). (Illus.). (ps). 1981. 0.69 (ISBN 0-307-10110-X, Golden Pr); PLB 4.77 (ISBN 0-307-68110-6). Western Pub.

Rossetti, Christina G. Sing Song: A Nursery Rhyme Book. LC 68-55822. (Illus.). (gr. 3-7). 1969. pap. 2.00 (ISBN 0-486-22107-5). Dover.

Ruth, Rod, illus. Humpty Dumpty & Other Nursery Rhymes. (Tell-a-Tale Reader). 32p. (ps-3). 1980. PLB 4.77 (ISBN 0-307-68415-6, Golden Pr). Western Pub.

Sechrist, Elizabeth H., ed. Merry Meet Again: Poems for Small Children to Recite. facsimile ed. LC 77-160908. (Granger Index Reprint Ser.). Repr. of 1941 ed. 17.00 (ISBN 0-8369-6272-9). Arno.

Simon, Iris, illus. This Is the House That Jack Built. LC 78-72322. (Illus.). (ps). 1979. 3.50 (ISBN 0-89799-139-7); pap. 1.50 (ISBN 0-89799-006-4). Dandelion Pr.

Smith, Doris, illus. The Tortoise & the Hare. LC 78-12525. (A Goodnight Bk.). (Illus.). (ps-1). 1979. 1.75 (ISBN 0-394-84102-6). Knopf.

Snowdon, Lynda, compiled by. Baa, Baa, Black Sheep & Other Rhymes. (First Nursery Rhyme Bks.). (Illus.). 12p. (ps-1). 1981. 1.95 (ISBN 0-517-54532-2). Crown.

--Doctor Foster & Other Rhymes. (First Nursery Rhyme Bks.). (Illus.). 12p. (ps-1). 1981. 1.95 (ISBN 0-517-54533-0). Crown.

--Hey Diddle Diddle & Other Rhymes. (First Nursery Rhyme Bks.). (Illus.). 12p. (ps-1). 1981. 1.95 (ISBN 0-517-54530-6). Crown.

--Jack & Jill & Other Rhymes. (First Nursery Rhyme Bks.). (Illus.). 12p. (ps-1). 1981. 1.95 (ISBN 0-517-54534-9). Crown.

--Tom, Tom, the Piper's Son & Other Rhymes. (First Nursery Rhyme Bks.). (Illus.). 12p. (ps-1). 1981. 1.95 (ISBN 0-517-54531-4). Crown.

Southern, Edward M. Are Nursery Rhymes for Children? 1978. 4.95 (ISBN 0-533-03277-6). Vantage.

Stanley, Diane. Fiddle-I-Fee. LC 79-14117. (Illus.). (gr. k-3). 1979. 7.95g (ISBN 0-316-81040-1). Little.

Stevens, Albert M. The Nursery Rhyme: Remnant of Popular Protest. 146p. 1968. 5.00x (ISBN 0-87291-056-3). Coronado Pr.

Stone, Evelyn, ed. Bedtime Mother Goose. (Look-Look Ser.). (Illus.). 24p. (Orig.). (ps). 1980. pap. 0.95 (ISBN 0-686-77804-9, Golden Pr). Western Pub.

Sutherland, Zena, compiled by. Nursery Rhymes, Songs & Stories. (Illus.). (gr. k-4). 1980. 10.95 (ISBN 0-525-66707-5). Elsevier-Nelson.

Walt Disney Productions. Nursery Rhymes. (ps-1). 1979. PLB 6.08 s&l (ISBN 0-307-61077-2, Golden Pr). Western Pub.
Watson, Clyde. Catch Me & Kiss Me & Say It Again. LC 78-17644. (Illus.). (gr. 1-12). 1978. 7.95 (ISBN 0-529-05436-1); PLB 7.99 (ISBN 0-529-05438-8). Philomel.
Wells, Edmund. More Gospel from Mother Goose. 120p. (Orig.). Date not set. pap. 2.95 (ISBN 0-8341-0727-9). Beacon Hill.
Wilkin, Eloise, illus. Ladybug, Ladybug, & Other Nursery Rhymes. LC 79-63899. (Shape Bks.). (Illus.). (ps-1). 1979. 2.50 (ISBN 0-394-84282-0, BYR). Random.
--Nursery Rhymes. LC 78-64606. (Board Bks). (Illus.). (ps). 1979. bds. 2.95 (ISBN 0-394-84129-8, BYR). Random.
--Rock-a-Bye, Baby: Nursery Songs & Cradle Games. LC 80-54774. (Rocking Bks.). (Illus.). 24p. (ps). 1981. 2.95 (ISBN 0-394-84824-1). Random.

NURSERY RHYMES–BIBLIOGRAPHY

Eckenstein, Lina. Comparative Studies in Nursery Rhymes. LC 68-23469. 1968. Repr. of 1906 ed. 19.00 (ISBN 0-8103-3479-8). Gale.

NURSERY SCHOOLS

see also Day Care Centers; Education, Preschool; Kindergartens

Allen, Susan W. & Talbot, Karen H. Preparing Preschoolers. 150p. (Orig.). 1981. pap. 12.95 (ISBN 0-88290-160-5, 2047). Horizon Utah.
Anbar, Ada. How to Choose a Nursery School: A Parent's Guide to Preschool Education. (Illus.). 1981. 12.95 (ISBN 0-87015-233-5). Pacific Bks.
Bartholomew, Robert, et al. Child Care Centers: Indoor Lighting - Outdoor Playspace. LC 72-90516. (Illus.). 1973. pap. 2.90 (ISBN 0-87868-099-3). Child Welfare.
Beer, Ethel S. Working Mothers & the Day Nursery. 1970. 4.50x (ISBN 0-8426-0374-3). Verry.
Boegehold, Betty. Education Before Five. 1978. pap. 7.50x (ISBN 0-8077-2557-9). Tchrs Coll.
Cass, Joan E. The Role of the Teacher in the Nursery School. 97p. 1975. 12.75 (ISBN 0-08-018282-8); pap. text ed. 7.00 (ISBN 0-08-018281-X). Pergamon.
Chenoweth, Linda. God's People: Nursery Leader's Guide. 64p. 1981. 2.95 (ISBN 0-686-74751-8). Westminster.
Cherry, Clare. Nursery School Bulletin Boards. 1973. pap. 3.95 (ISBN 0-8224-4786-X). Pitman Learning.
Cherry, Clare, et al. Nursery School & Day Care Center Management Guide. rev ed. 1978. looseleaf bdg. 22.50 (ISBN 0-8224-4791-6); pap. 18.95 (ISBN 0-8224-4792-4). Pitman Learning.
Clift, Phillip, et al. The Aims, Role & Deployment of Staff in the Nursery. (Report of the National Foundation for Educational Research in England & Wales). 224p. 1980. pap. text ed. 18.75x (ISBN 0-85633-197-X). Humanities.
Collier, et al. Kids' Stuff: Kindergarten - Nursery School. (The Kids' Stuff Set). (ps-k). 1969. pap. 10.95 (ISBN 0-913916-00-5, IP005). Incentive Pubns.
Dowling, Marion. The Modern Nursery. (Longman Early Childhood Education Ser.). 1977. text ed. 11.50x (ISBN 0-582-25004-8); pap. text ed. 6.95x (ISBN 0-582-25005-6). Longman.
Eliason, Claudia & Jenkins, Loa T. A Practical Guide to Early Childhood Curriculum. 2nd ed. LC 80-39694. (Illus.). 389p. 1981. pap. text ed. 12.95 (ISBN 0-8016-1511-9). Mosby.
Feshback, Norma D., et al. Early Schooling in England & Israel. (IDEA Reports on Schooling). 224p. 1973. 9.95 (ISBN 0-07-020635-X, P&RB). McGraw.
Garland, Caroline & White, Stephanie. Children & Day Nurseries. LC 80-24264. (Oxford Preschool Research Project Ser.: Vol. 4). 128p. 1980. pap. 8.95 (ISBN 0-931114-12-8). High-Scope.
Goldworthy, G. M. Why Nursery Schools? 1978. text ed. cancelled (ISBN 0-900675-57-8). Humanities.
Hurd, Edith T. Come with Me to Nursery School. (Illus.). (ps-2). 1970. PLB 5.49 (ISBN 0-698-30050-5). Coward.
Joffe, Carole E. Friendly Intruders: Childcare Professionals & Family Life. LC 74-27281. 1977. 16.95x (ISBN 0-520-02925-9); pap. 3.95 (ISBN 0-520-03934-3). U of Cal Pr.
Johnson, Harriet M. School Begins at Two. Biber, Barbara, ed. LC 70-108765. 1970. Repr. of 1936 ed. 8.50x (ISBN 0-87586-022-2). Agathon.
Johnson, John E. My School Book. LC 79-63898. (Shape Bks.). (Illus.). (ps-1). 1979. 2.50 (ISBN 0-394-84293-6, BYR). Random.
Lucas, James & Neufeld, Evelyn. Think & Color: The Cognitive Coloring Book. (Illus.). 95p. 1971. tchrs. ed. 4.25 (ISBN 0-912990-01-5). Ed Sci.
Mental Hygiene in the Nursery School. 1953. pap. 2.50 (ISBN 92-3-100418-2, U381, UNESCO). Unipub.
Read, Katherine & Patterson, June. Nursery School & Kindergarten. 4th ed. LC 79-25455. 419p. 1980. text ed. 18.95 (ISBN 0-03-055221-4, HoltC). HR&W.
Read, Katherine H. The Nursery School: Human Relationships & Learning. 6th ed. LC 75-28801. (Illus.). 480p. 1976. text ed. 15.95 (ISBN 0-7216-7488-7). HR&W.
Salley, Ruth E. Some Factors Affecting the Supply of & Demand for Pre-School Teachers in New York City. LC 78-177224. (Columbia University. Teachers College. Contributions to Education: No. 870). Repr. of 1943 ed. 17.50 (ISBN 0-404-55870-4). AMS Pr.
Sauerman, Thomas H. & Schomaker, Linda, eds. Starting a Church-Sponsored Weekday Preschool Program: A Manual of Guidance. LC 80-14160. 128p. (Orig.). 1980. pap. 5.95 (ISBN 0-8006-1377-5, 1-1377). Fortress.
Slater, E. C. Types, Levels-Irregularities of Response to a Nursery School Situation of 40 Children Observed with Special Reference to the Home Environment. 1939. pap. 9.00 (ISBN 0-527-01509-1). Kraus Repr.
Taylor, Katharine W. Parents & Children Learn Together. 2nd ed. LC 67-21500. 1968. pap. text ed. 8.95x (ISBN 0-8077-2257-X). Tchrs Coll.
--Parents & Children Learn Together: Parent Cooperative Nursery Schools. 3rd ed. 1981. text ed. 17.95 (ISBN 0-8077-2689-3); pap. 10.95 (ISBN 0-8077-2638-9). Tchrs Coll.
Tucker, Clara. A Study of Mothers' Practices & Children's Activities in a Co-Operative Nursery School. LC 79-177696. (Columbia University. Studies in the Social Sciences: No. 810). Repr. of 1940 ed. 17.50 (ISBN 0-404-55810-0). AMS Pr.
Twinn, Michael, illus. I Go to Nursery School. (Nursery Ser.). 8p. 1977. text ed. 1.75 (ISBN 0-85953-070-1, Pub. by Child's Play England). Playspaces.
Washburn, Ruth W. Re-Education in a Nursery Group: A Study in Clinical Psychology. (SRCO Ser.). 1944. pap. 9.00 (ISBN 0-527-01531-8). Kraus Repr.
Whitbread, Nanette. The Evolution of the Nursery-Infant School. (Students Library of Education). 1972. 12.50x (ISBN 0-7100-7290-2); pap. 6.00 (ISBN 0-7100-7291-0). Routledge & Kegan.
Wolffheim, Nelly. Psychology in the Nursery School. Hannam, Charles L., tr. LC 77-162630. 143p. 1972. Repr. of 1953 ed. lib. bdg. 16.00x (ISBN 0-8371-6197-5, WONS). Greenwood.
Woodhead, Martin. Intervening in Disadvantage: A Challenge for Nursery Education. (General Ser.). (Orig.). 1976. pap. text ed. 8.25x (ISBN 0-85633-095-7, NFER). Humanities.
Woodhead, Martin, ed. An Experiment in Nursery Education. (Orig.). 1976. pap. text ed. 13.75x (ISBN 0-85633-122-8, NFER). Humanities.

NURSERY SCHOOLS–MUSIC

see also Games with Music; Singing Games

Beyer, Evelyn M. Teaching Young Children. LC 67-21042. 1969. 18.95x (ISBN 0-672-53600-5). Irvington.
Bley, Edgar S. Best Singing Games for Children of All Ages. rev. ed. LC 57-1014. (Illus.). (gr. k-6). 1959. 8.95 (ISBN 0-8069-4450-1); PLB 8.29 (ISBN 0-8069-4451-X). Sterling.
Zeitlin, Patty. A Song Is a Rainbow: Body Movement, Music, & Rythym Instruments in the Nursery School & Kindergarten. 336p. (Orig.). pap. 12.95 (ISBN 0-8302-8196-7). Goodyear.

NURSERY STOCK

see also Nurseries (Horticulture); Plants, Ornamental; Shrubs; Trees

Lamb, Kelly & Lamb, Bowbrick. Nursery Stock Manual. 300p. 1981. 30.00x (ISBN 0-686-75420-4, Pub. by Grower Bks). State Mutual Bk.
Stooling Nursery Stock. 1981. 12.00x (ISBN 0-686-75427-1, Pub. by Grower Bks). State Mutual Bk.

NURSES–CORRESPONDENCE, REMINISCENCES, ETC.

Breckinridge, Mary. Wide Neighborhoods: A Story of the Frontier Nursing Service. LC 81-50181. (Illus.). 400p. 1981. 19.50 (ISBN 0-8131-1453-5); pap. 8.00 (ISBN 0-8131-0149-2). U Pr of Ky.

NURSES, AFRO-AMERICAN

see Afro-American Nurses

NURSES' AIDES

Being a Nursing Aide. 2nd ed. (Illus.). 1978. student manual 11.95 (ISBN 0-87914-050-X, 9760). Hosp Res & Educ.
Caldwell & Hegner. Health Assistant. LC 79-50661. (Illus.). 1980. pap. 8.60 (ISBN 0-8273-1337-3); instr's. guide 1.60 (ISBN 0-8273-1338-1). Delmar.
Caldwell, Esther & Hegner, Barbara. Health Assistant. 288p. 1981. text ed. 13.95 (ISBN 0-442-21850-8). Van Nos Reinhold.
Cherescavich, Gertrude D. A Textbook for Nursing Assistants. 3rd ed. LC 72-12852. (Illus.). 1973. 15.95 (ISBN 0-8016-0957-7). Mosby.
Hanebuth, Lorna, et al. Nursing Assistants & the Long-Term Health Care Facility. (Illus.). 1977. pap. text ed. 11.95x (ISBN 0-06-141090-X, Harper Medical). Har-Row.
Hospital Research & Educational Trust of the AHA. Being a Nursing Aide. 2nd ed. (Illus.). 1978. pap. 11.95 (ISBN 0-87914-050-X). R J Brady.
Isler, Charlotte. The Nurses' Aide. 2nd ed. LC 73-77723. 1973. pap. text ed. 5.95 (ISBN 0-8261-0913-6). Springer Pub.
--Workbook for the Nurses' Aide. 1973. pap. 2.95 (ISBN 0-8261-0912-8). Springer Pub.
Mayes, Mary E. Nurse's Aid Study Manual. 3rd ed. LC 75-28796. (Illus.). 285p. 1976. text ed. 8.50 (ISBN 0-7216-6191-2). Saunders.
Reese, Dorothy E. How to Be a Nurse's Aid in a Nursing Home: Resource Manual. 360p. 1978. 44.95 (ISBN 0-686-60068-1). CBI Pub.
--How to Be a Nurse's Aide in a Nursing Home. 120p. 1978. 13.50 (ISBN 0-686-60067-3). CBI Pub.
Rudman, Jack. Nurse's Aide. (Career Examination Ser.: C-535). (Cloth bdg. avail. on request). pap. 6.00 (ISBN 0-8373-0535-7). Natl Learning.
--Nursing Assistant. (Career Examination Ser.: C-534). (Cloth bdg. avail. on request). pap. 8.00 (ISBN 0-8373-0534-9). Natl Learning.
Stolten, Jane H. The Health Aide. 373p. 1972. pap. 9.95 (ISBN 0-316-81740-6). Little.

NURSES AND NURSING

see also Cancer Nursing; Cardiovascular Disease Nursing; Care of the Sick; Children–Care and Hygiene; Convalescence; Cookery for the Sick; Deaconesses; Diet in Disease; Dieticians; Disaster Nursing; Emergency Nursing; First Aid in Illness and Injury; Geriatric Nursing; Gynecologic Nursing; Home Nursing; Hospitalers; Hospitals; Industrial Nursing; Infants–Care and Hygiene; Labor and Laboring Classes–Medical Care; Men Nurses; Neurological Nursing; Nurse and Patient; Nurses' Aides; Obstetrical Nursing; Ophthalmic Nursing; Orthopedic Nursing; Pediatric Nursing; Practical Nursing; Psychiatric Nursing; Public Health Nursing; Red Cross; School Nursing; Sick; Sisters of Charity; Surgical Nursing; Team Nursing; Urological Nursing

also subdivisions Hospitals, Charities, etc. and Medical and Sanitary Affairs under names of wars, e.g. United States–History–Civil War, 1861-1865–Hospitals, Charities, etc.; World War, 1939-1945–Medical and Sanitary Affairs

Abdella, Fay G. & Levine, Eugene. Better Patient Care Through Nursing Research. 2nd ed. 1978. 18.95 (ISBN 0-02-300110-0). Macmillan.
Abdellah, Faye G. & Beland, Irene L. New Directions in Patient Centered Nursing: Guidelines for Systems of Service, Education & Research. 576p. 1973. 19.95 (ISBN 0-02-300050-3). Macmillan.
Abu-Saad, Huda. Nursing: A World View. LC 78-25860. (Illus.). 1979. text ed. 12.50 (ISBN 0-8016-0065-0). Mosby.
Ackerman, Winona B. & Lohnes, Paul R. Research Methods for Nurses. (Illus.). 304p. 1981. text ed. 16.95x (ISBN 0-07-000182-0, HP). McGraw.
Adler, Diane & Shoemaker, Norma J., eds. Organization & Management of Critical Care Facilities. LC 78-31498. (Illus.). 1979. text ed. 16.95 (ISBN 0-8016-0130-4). Mosby.
Aiken, Linda, ed. Health Policy & Nursing Practice. (Illus.). 308p. 1980. pap. text ed. 6.95 (ISBN 0-07-000745-4, HP). McGraw.
AJN: Five Year Cumulative Index, 1951-55 (XAO2. 134p. 1956. pap. text ed. 3.90 (ISBN 0-937126-95-0). Am Journal Nurse.
AJN: Five Year Cumulative Index, 1956-60 (XAO3) 117p. 1961. pap. text ed. 4.50 (ISBN 0-937126-94-2). Am Journal Nurse.
AJN: Five Year Cumulative Index, 1966-70 (XAO5) 1971. pap. text ed. 6.00 (ISBN 0-937126-92-6). Am Journal Nurse.
AJN: Five Year Cumulative Index, 1971-75 (XAO6) 128p. 1976. pap. text ed. 8.00 (ISBN 0-937126-91-8). Am Journal Nurse.
Albanese, Joseph. Nurses' Drug Reference. 1979. 16.95 (ISBN 0-07-000765-9, HP); pap. text ed. 11.95 (ISBN 0-07-000766-7). McGraw.
Alfano, Genrose. All-RN Nursing Staff. LC 81-80201. (Nursing Dimensions Administration Ser.). 133p. 1980. pap. text ed. 11.95 (ISBN 0-913654-68-X). Nursing Res.
American Alliance for Health, Physical Education & Recreation. Introduction to School Nursing Curriculum. 1973. pap. 3.75x (ISBN 0-685-42008-6, 244-25470). AAHPERD.
American Assoc. of Critical-Care Nurses. Critical Care Nursing of Children & Adolescents. Oakes, Annalee, ed. (Illus.). 750p. 1981. pap. write for info. (ISBN 0-7216-1003-X). Saunders.
American Association of Critical Care Nurses. Core Curriculum for Critical Care Nurses. Borg, Nan, ed. 400p. Date not set. write for info. soft cover (ISBN 0-7216-1215-6). Saunders.
--Critical Care Nursing of the Multi-Injured Patient. Mann, James K. & Oakes, Annalee R, eds. LC 79-67787. (Illus.). 168p. 1980. pap. 10.95 (ISBN 0-7216-1002-1). Saunders.
--Standards of Nursing Care of the Critically Ill. (Illus.). 368p. 1980. pap. text ed. 12.95 (ISBN 0-8359-7061-2). Reston.
Anderson, Peggy. Nurse. LC 78-3994. 1978. 10.95 (ISBN 0-312-58021-5). St Martin.
Andreoli, Kathleen, et al. Comprehensive Cardiac Care: A Text for Nurses, Physicians & Other Health Practitioners. 4th ed. LC 78-9905. (Illus.). 1979. text ed. 14.95 (ISBN 0-8016-0256-4). Mosby.
Arkhangelsky, G. Manual for Nurses. 398p. 1978. 9.00 (ISBN 0-8285-0762-7, Pub. by Mir Pubs Russia). Imported Pubns.
Armstrong, M., et al. McGraw-Hill's Handbook of Clinical Nursing. (Illus.). 1979. 24.95 (ISBN 0-07-045020-X, HP). McGraw.
Aspinall, Mary Jo & Tanner, Christine. Decision-Making for Patient Care: Applying the Nursing Process. 480p. 1981. pap. 15.95 (ISBN 0-8385-1555-X). ACC.
Assessing Vital Functions Accurately. LC 78-24419. (Nursing Skillbooks Ser.). (Illus.). 1977. text ed. 10.95 (ISBN 0-916730-05-0). InterMed Comm.
Assessing Your Patients. LC 80-36819. (Nursing Photobook Ser.). (Illus.). 160p. 1980. text ed. 12.95 (ISBN 0-916730-24-7). InterMed Comm.
Atkinson, Leslie D. & Murray, Mary E. Nursing Process: What It Is & How It Is Used. (Illus.). 1980. pap. text ed. 5.95 (ISBN 0-02-304600-7). Macmillan.
Auld, Margaret & Ehlke, Graceann. Guide to Camp Nursing. rev. ed. 1978. pap. 2.50 (ISBN 0-87603-028-2). Am Camping.
Austin, Eileen K. Guidelines for the Development of Continuing Education Offerings for Nurses. (Illus.). 176p. 1981. pap. 9.95 (ISBN 0-8385-3524-0). ACC.
Ayers, Rachel. Nursing Service in Transition: A Description of Organization for Classification & Utilization of Nurse Practitioners. 124p. 1972. pap. 5.00 (ISBN 0-686-16746-5). City Hope.
Ayers, Rachel, et al. The Clinical Nurse Specialist: An Experiment in Role Effectiveness & Role Development. 75p. 1971. pap. 5.00 (ISBN 0-686-16745-7). City Hope.
Bailey, June T. & Claus, Karen E. Decision Making in Nursing: Tools for Change. LC 74-28268. 168p. 1975. pap. text ed. 10.50 (ISBN 0-8016-0422-2). Mosby.
Baldwin, Linda & Pierce, Ruth. Mobile Intensive Care: A Problem Oriented Approach. LC 78-18240. (Illus.). 1978. pap. 12.95 (ISBN 0-8016-0428-1). Mosby.
Baly, Monica E. Nursing & Social Change. (Illus.). 1973. pap. text ed. 13.95x (ISBN 0-433-01160-2). Intl Ideas.
Banks, Ian. Nurse Allocation in Britain. (Illus.). 1972. wire bound 16.95x (ISBN 0-433-01165-3). Intl Ideas.
Barber, Janet M., et al. Adult & Child Care: A Client Approach to Nursing. 2nd ed. LC 76-26637. (Illus.). 1977. 26.95 (ISBN 0-8016-0444-3). Mosby.
Basic Attending Skills. 1974. participant manual. write for info. 6.95 (ISBN 0-917276-01-9); leader manual. write for info 12.95 (ISBN 0-917276-00-0). Microtraining Assocs.
Basic Influencing Skills. 1976. participant manual. write for info. 7.95 (ISBN 0-917276-03-5); leader manual. write for info. 13.95 (ISBN 0-917276-02-7). Microtraining Assocs.
Becknell, Eileen & Smith, Dorothy M. System of Nursing Practice: A Clinical Nursing Assessment Tool. 1975. pap. text ed. 8.50 (ISBN 0-8036-0695-8). Davis Co.
Beland, Irene & Passos, Joyce. Clinical Nursing: Pathophysiological & Psychosocial Approaches. 4th ed. 1981. text ed. 31.95x (ISBN 0-02-307890-1). Macmillan.
Beland, Irene L. & Passos, Joyce Y. Clinical Nursing. 3rd ed. (Illus.). 1086p. 1975. text ed. 24.95 (ISBN 0-02-307900-2). Macmillan.
Benson, Evelyn P. & DeVitt, Joan Q. Community Health & Nursing Practices. 2nd ed. (Illus.). 1980. text ed. 17.95 (ISBN 0-13-153171-9). P-H.
Bergersen, Betty S. Pharmacology in Nursing. 14th ed. LC 66-10935. (Illus.). 1979. text ed. 22.95 (ISBN 0-8016-0632-2). Mosby.
Bergersen, Betty S. & Sakalys, Jurate A. Review of Pharmacology in Nursing. 2nd ed. LC 78-5717. 1978. pap. text ed. 11.00 (ISBN 0-8016-0624-1). Mosby.

Bermosk, Loretta S. & Mordan, Mary J. Interviewing in Nursing. (Illus.). 208p. 1973. pap. text ed. 6.95 (ISBN 0-02-308550-9, 30855). Macmillan.
Bernzweig, Eli. The Nurse's Liability for Malpractice: A Programed Course. 3rd ed. 368p. 1981. pap. text ed. 11.95 (ISBN 0-07-005058-9, HP); prepub. 2.95 test bank (ISBN 0-07-005059-7). McGraw.
Beth Israel Hospital, Boston. Respiratory Intensive Care Nursing. 2nd ed. 1979. spiral bdg. 13.95 (ISBN 0-316-09237-1). Little.
Beyers, Marjorie & Dudas, Susan. The Clinical Practice of Medical-Surgical Nursing. 1977. pap. text ed. 19.95 (ISBN 0-316-09263-0). Little.
Beyers, Marjorie & Phillips, Carole. Nursing Management for Patient Care. 2nd ed. 1979. text ed. 12.95 (ISBN 0-316-09264-9, Little Med Div); pap. text ed. 9.95 (ISBN 0-316-09265-7). Little.
Bleier, Inge J. Workbook in Bedside Maternity Nursing. 2nd ed. LC 71-151675. (Illus.). 175p. 1974. pap. text ed. 7.95 (ISBN 0-7216-1746-8). Saunders.
Blevins, Dorothy. The Diabetic & Nursing Care. (Illus.). 1979. text ed. 14.95 (ISBN 0-07-005902-0, HP). McGraw.
Bliss, Ann & Cohen, Eva. The New Health Professionals: Nurse Practitioners & Physician's Assistants. LC 76-46831. 472p. 1977. 29.95 (ISBN 0-912862-35-1). Aspen Systems.
Block, Gloria & Nolan, Joellen. Health Assessment for Professional Nursing: A Developmental Approach. (Illus.). 496p. 1981. 19.75 (ISBN 0-8385-3660-3). ACC.
Bloom, Arnold. Toohey's Medicine for Nurses. 13th ed. (Illus.). 1981. pap. text ed. 17.50 (ISBN 0-443-02201-1). Churchill.
Bower, F. L. Nursing & the Concept of Loss. (Nursing Concept Modules Ser.). 214p. 1980. 12.50 (ISBN 0-471-04790-2). Wiley.
Bower, Fay L. Health Maintenance. LC 79-25269. (Wiley Nursing Concept Module Ser.). 1980. pap. 12.95 (ISBN 0-471-03782-6, Pub. by Wiley Med). Wiley.
--Nutrition in Nursing. LC 79-10562. (Nursing Concept Modules Ser.). 1979. pap. 12.50 (ISBN 0-471-04124-6, Pub. by Wiley Med). Wiley.
--The Process of Planning Nursing Care: A Model for Practice. 2nd ed. LC 76-44886. (Illus.). 1977. pap. 9.45 (ISBN 0-8016-0728-0). Mosby.
Bower, Fay L. & Bevis, Em O. Fundamentals of Nursing Practice: Concepts, Roles & Functions. LC 77-26885. (Illus.). 1978. text ed. 17.95 (ISBN 0-8016-0732-9). Mosby.
Bower, Fay L. & Wheeler, Robinetta T., eds. The Nursing Assessment. LC 77-5160. (Wiley Nursing Concept Modules). 1977. pap. 12.50 (ISBN 0-471-02167-9, Pub. by Wiley Med). Wiley.
Branch, Marie F. & Paxton, Phyliss P., eds. Providing Safe Nursing Care for Ethnic People of Color. (Illus.). 1976. pap. 12.50 (ISBN 0-8385-7943-4). ACC.
Brink, P. J. Transcultural Nursing: A Book of Readings. (Illus.). 320p. 1976. pap. 11.95 (ISBN 0-13-928101-0). P-H.
Britten, Jessie D. Practical Notes on Nursing Procedures. 7th ed. (Churchill Livingstone Nursing Text Ser.). (Illus.). 228p. 1980. pap. text ed. 7.50 (ISBN 0-443-01758-1). Churchill.
Britton, Frances. Basic Nursing Skills. (Illus.). 272p. 1981. pap. text ed. 7.95 (ISBN 0-87619-921-X). R J Brady.
Broadwell, Lucile & Milutnovic, Barbara. Medical-Surgical Nursing Procedures. LC 76-4305. 1977. pap. text ed. 12.40 (ISBN 0-8273-0353-X); instructor's guide 1.60 (ISBN 0-8273-0354-8). Delmar.
Broadwell, Lucille & Milutinovic, Barbara. Medical-Surgical Nursing Procedures. 1977. 15.95 (ISBN 0-442-21062-0). Van Nos Reinhold.
Brooks, Lucy. The Nurse Assistant. 1978. 9.95 (ISBN 0-442-20943-6). Van Nos Reinhold.
--The Nurse Assistant. LC 77-73939. 1978. pap. text ed. 7.40 (ISBN 0-8273-1620-8); instructor's guide 1.60 (ISBN 0-8273-1621-6). Delmar.
Brooks, Stewart M. Review of Nursing: Essentials for the State Boards. 1978. text ed. 11.95 (ISBN 0-316-10974-6). Little.
Brooten, Dorothy A., et al. Leadership for Change: A Guide for the Frustrated Nurse. LC 78-8661. pap. 8.25 (ISBN 0-397-54218-6). Har-Row.
Brotton, Joan, rev. by. Ward Pocket-Book for the Nurse. 7th ed. (Illus.). 1978. pap. 2.95 (ISBN 0-571-04966-4, Pub. by Faber & Faber). Merrimack Bk Serv.
Brown, Barbara. Nurse Staffing: A Practical Guide. 200p. 1980. 23.95 (ISBN 0-89443-291-5). Aspen Systems.
Brown, Marie S., et al. Student Manual of Physical Examination. LC 77-13693. 1977. pap. text ed. 8.95 (ISBN 0-397-54211-9, JBL-Med-Nursing). Har-Row.
Brown, Mary L. Occupational Health Nursing. LC 80-21024. 368p. 1981. text ed. 21.95 (ISBN 0-8261-2250-7); pap. text ed. cancelled (ISBN 0-8261-2251-5). Springer Pub.
Brown, R. G. The Male Nurse. 139p. 1973. pap. text ed. 5.00x (ISBN 0-7135-1879-0, Pub. by Bedford England). Renouf.
Brundage, Dorothy J. Nursing Management of Renal Problems. 2nd ed. LC 80-11720. (Illus.). 1980. pap. text ed. 10.45 (ISBN 0-8016-0849-X). Mosby.
--Nursing Management of Renal Problems. LC 75-22149. (Illus.). 204p. 1976. pap. text ed. 8.95 (ISBN 0-8016-0850-3). Mosby.
Brunner, Lillian S. The Lippincott Manual of Nursing Practice. 2nd ed. LC 78-6987. 1978. text ed. 32.50 (ISBN 0-397-54212-7, JBL-Med-Nursing). Har-Row.
Brunner, Lillian S. & Suddarth, Doris S. Textbook of Medical-Surgical Nursing. 4th ed. LC 79-27506. 1500p. 1980. text ed. 36.50 (ISBN 0-397-54238-0, JBL-Med-Nursing). Har-Row.
Bullough, Bonnie & Bullough, Vern, eds. Expanding Horizons for Nurses. LC 76-47020. 1977. pap. text ed. 11.95 (ISBN 0-8261-2061-X). Springer Pub.
Bullough, Bonnie, et al, eds. The Management of Common Human Miseries: A Text for Primary Health Care Practitioners. LC 78-24072. 1979. text ed. 26.50 (ISBN 0-8261-2190-X). Springer Pub.
Burgess, Ann W., ed. Nursing: Levels of Health Intervention. (P-H General Nursing Ser.). (Illus.). 1978. ref. 20.95 (ISBN 0-13-627687-3). P-H.
Burgess, Audrey. The Nurse's Guide to Fluid & Electrolyte Balance. 2nd ed. (Illus.). 1979. pap. text ed. 12.95 (ISBN 0-07-008955-8, HP). McGraw.
Burkhalter, Pamela & Donley, Diana, eds. Dynamics of Oncology Nursing. (Illus.). 1977. text ed. 15.95 (ISBN 0-07-009052-1, HP). McGraw.
Burns, Kenneth R. & Johnson, Patricia J. Health Assessment in Clinical Practice. (Illus.). 1980. text ed. 26.95 (ISBN 0-13-385054-4). P-H.
Burrell, Zeb, Jr. & Burrell, Lennette O. Critical Care. 3rd ed. LC 76-53564. (Illus.). 1977. lib. bdg. 15.95 (ISBN 0-8016-0914-3). Mosby.
Burton, J. L. Aids to Medicine for Nurses. 168p. 1976. pap. text ed. 5.75 (ISBN 0-443-01387-X). Churchill.
Bussman, John W. & Davidson, Sharon V. P.S.R.O: The Promise, Perspective, & Potential. 1981. 29.95 (ISBN 0-201-00790-8). A-W.
Butnarescu, G. F., et al. Perinatal Nursing. 553p. 1980. 24.95 (ISBN 0-686-74418-7). Wiley.
Butnaurescu, Glenda F. Perinatal Nursing: Reproductive Health, Vol. 1. LC 77-25924. 1978. 24.95 (ISBN 0-471-04361-3, Pub. by Wiley Med). Wiley.
Byers, Virginia B. Nursing Observation. 3rd ed. (Foundations of Nursing Ser.). 226p. 1977. pap. text ed. write for info. (ISBN 0-697-05542-6). Wm C Brown.
Byrne, Majorie L. & Thompson, Lida F. Key Concepts for the Study & Practice of Nursing. 2nd ed. LC 77-26957. (Illus.). 1978. pap. text ed. 8.00 (ISBN 0-8016-0920-8). Mosby.
Caldwell, Eva W., et al. Mosby's Review of Practical Nursing. 7th ed. LC 77-16207. (Illus.). 375p. 1978. text ed. 10.95 (ISBN 0-8016-3536-5). Mosby.
Calnan, James & Monks, Brenda. How to Speak & Write: A Practical Guide for Nurses. 178p. 1975. pap. 9.95x (ISBN 0-433-05010-1). Intl Ideas.
Campbell, Claire. Nursing Diagnosis & Intervention in Nursing Practice. LC 77-17095. 1978. text ed. 32.50 (ISBN 0-471-13307-8, Pub. by Wiley Medical). Wiley.
Cancer Nursing Conference, ed. Proceedings. 171p. 1979. text ed. 26.00 (ISBN 0-686-74060-2). Masson Pub.
Cantor, Marjorie M. Achieving Nursing Care Standards: Internal, External. LC 78-53072. 180p. 1978. 17.50 (ISBN 0-913654-47-7). Nursing Res.
Carter, Frances M. Psychosocial Nursing. 3rd ed. 1981. text ed. 19.95x (ISBN 0-02-319660-2). Macmillan.
Carter, Joan H., et al. Standards of Nursing Care: A Guide for Evaluation. 2nd ed. LC 72-75096. 304p. 1976. text ed. 20.50 (ISBN 0-8261-1361-3); pap. text ed. 12.95 (ISBN 0-8261-1362-1). Springer Pub.
Ceccio, Joseph F. & Ceccio, Cathy M. Effective Communication in Nursing: Theory & Practice. 344p. 1982. pap. 12.95 (ISBN 0-471-07911-1, Pub. by Wiley Med). Wiley.
Chapman, A. H. & Almeida, Elza M. The Interpersonal Basis of Psychiatric Nursing. 1972. 12.50n (ISBN 0-399-40047-8). Putnam.
Chaska. The Nursing Profession. (Illus.). 1977. pap. text ed. 12.50 (ISBN 0-07-010695-9, HP). McGraw.
Cherescavich, Gertrude D. A Textbook for Nursing Assistants. 3rd ed. LC 72-12852. (Illus.). 1973. 15.95 (ISBN 0-8016-0957-7). Mosby.
Chrisman, Marilyn K. Respiratory Nursing Continuing Education Review. 1976. spiral bdg. 9.50 (ISBN 0-87488-396-2). Med Exam.
Ciske, Karen & Mayer, Gloria, eds. Primary Nursing. LC 79-90370. (Nursing Dimensions Ser.: Vol. VII, No. 4). 101p. 1980. pap. text ed. 6.95 (ISBN 0-913654-60-4). Nursing Res.
Clark, Carolyn & Shea, Carole A. Management in Nursing. (Illus.). 1979. text ed. 12.95 (ISBN 0-07-011135-9, HP). McGraw.
Clark, Carolyn C. Assertive Skills for Nurses. LC 78-53071. 236p. 1978. pap. text ed. 9.75 (ISBN 0-913654-46-9). Nursing Res.
--Mental Health Aspects of Community Health Nursing. (Illus.). 1978. pap. text ed. 8.95 (ISBN 0-07-011150-2, HP). McGraw.
--The Nurse As Continuing Educator. LC 79-18283. (Teaching of Nursing Ser.: Vol. 6). 1979. pap. text ed. 12.95 (ISBN 0-8261-2791-6). Springer Pub.
--The Nurse As Group Leader. LC 77-7778. (Teaching of Nursing Ser.: Vol. 3). 1977. 15.95 (ISBN 0-8261-2330-9); pap. text ed. 9.50 (ISBN 0-8261-2331-7). Springer Pub.
--Nursing Concepts & Processes. LC 76-14095. 1977. pap. text ed. 11.60 (ISBN 0-8273-1318-7); instructor's guide 2.75 (ISBN 0-8273-1319-5). Delmar.
Clarke, D. B. & Barnes, A. D., eds. Intensive Care for Nurses. 2nd ed. (Illus.). 208p. 1975. 7.50 (ISBN 0-632-00696-X, Blackwell). Mosby.
Claus, Karen E. & Bailey, June T. Living with Stress & Promoting Well Being: A Handbook for Nurses. LC 80-14605. (Illus.). 1980. pap. text ed. 10.45 (ISBN 0-8016-1148-2). Mosby.
Clinical Experiences in Collegiate Nursing Education. LC 80-23401. 125p. 1981. soft bd. 11.50 (ISBN 0-8261-3391-6). Springer Pub.
Code for Nurses with Interpretive Statements: G-56. 1976. pap. 0.25 (ISBN 0-686-21448-X). ANA.
Cohen, Helen A. The Nurse's Quest for a Professional Identity. 1981. 14.95 (ISBN 0-201-00956-0, Med-Nurse); pap. 9.95 (ISBN 0-201-01157-3). A-W.
Collage, Malcolm, ed. Readings in Nursing. Jong, Dan O. (Illus.). 260p. 1979. pap. text ed. 18.75 (ISBN 0-686-31226-0). Churchill.
Conley, Virginia C. Curriculum & Instruction in Nursing. 1973. 19.95 (ISBN 0-316-15307-9). Little.
Cooke, R. Gordon & Miller, Ann. A Summary of Medicine for Nurses & Medical Auxiliaries. 7th ed. 156p. 1978. pap. 4.95 (ISBN 0-571-04942-7, Pub. by Faber & Faber). Merrimack Bk Serv.
Corbett, Nancy Ann & Beveridge, Phyllis. Clinical Simulations in Nursing Practice. LC 78-52724. 332p. 1980. pap. text ed. 9.95 (ISBN 0-7216-2722-6). Saunders.
Cosmoss, Patricia M., et al. Cardiac Rehabilitation: A Comprehensive Nursing Approach. LC 79-13050. 1979. text ed. 21.50 (ISBN 0-397-54322-0). Har-Row.
Culver, Vivian M. Modern Bedside Nursing. 8th ed. LC 73-88258. (Illus.). 862p. 1974. text ed. 17.95 (ISBN 0-7216-2782-X). Saunders.
Curry, Judith B. & Peppe, Kathryn K., eds. Mental Retardation: Nursing Approaches to Care. LC 77-26307. 1978. pap. text ed. 11.50 (ISBN 0-8016-1196-2). Mosby.
Darwin, Joan, et al. Bedside Nursing: An Introduction. 3rd ed. (Illus.). 236p. 1976. pap. 12.95x (ISBN 0-433-07133-8). Intl Ideas.
Davidson, Sharon V., et al. Nursing Care Evaluation: Concurrent & Retrospective Review Criteria. LC 77-5069. 1977. 20.95 (ISBN 0-8016-1210-1). Mosby.
Davis, Anne J. & Aroskar, Mila A. Ethical Dilemmas in Nursing Practice. (Illus.). 240p. 1978. pap. 12.95 (ISBN 0-8385-2273-4). ACC.
Davitz, Joel R. & Davitz, Lois L. Inferences of Patients' Pain & Psychological Distress: Studies of Nursing Behaviors. (Illus.). 1980. text ed. 25.00 (ISBN 0-8261-3360-6). Springer Pub.
Davitz, Lois J. Interpersonal Processes in Nursing-Case Histories. LC 74-130685. 1970. pap. text ed. 4.50 (ISBN 0-8261-1151-3). Springer Pub.
Davitz, Lois J. & Davitz, Joel R. Nurses Response to Patients' Suffering. (Orig.). 1980. pap. text ed. 12.95 (ISBN 0-8261-2921-8). Springer Pub.
Department of Clinical Practice, University of California. Mosby's Manual of Clinical Nursing Procedures. LC 80-1379. (Illus.). 394p. 1981. pap. text ed. 19.95 (ISBN 0-8016-3592-6). Mosby.
Deutsch, Beatrice L. Ambulatory Care Nursing Procedure & Employee Health Service Manual. 1977. spiral bdg. 12.00 (ISBN 0-87488-968-5). Med Exam.
DeYoung, Lillian. Dynamics of Nursing. 4th ed. LC 80-29477. (Illus.). 235p. 1981. pap. text ed. 13.95 (ISBN 0-8016-1283-7). Mosby.
Diekelman, Nancy. Primary Health Care of the Well Adult. (Illus.). 1977. pap. text ed. 8.50 (ISBN 0-07-016879-2, HP). McGraw.
Diekelmann, Nancy, et al. Fundamentals of Nursing. (Illus.). 1979. text ed. 16.95 (ISBN 0-07-016885-7, HP). McGraw.
Dingwall, Robert & McIntosh, Jean. Readings in the Sociology of Nursing. LC 78-40429. 1979. text ed. 21.25 (ISBN 0-443-01675-5). Churchill.
Dison, Norma. Clinical Nursing Techniques. 4th ed. LC 78-31262. (Illus.). 1979. pap. text ed. 15.95 (ISBN 0-8016-1308-6). Mosby.
--Simplified Drugs & Solutions for Nurses, Including Arithmetic. 7th ed. LC 79-28198. (Illus.). 1980. pap. text ed. 8.50 (ISBN 0-8016-1311-6). Mosby.
Documenting Patient Care Responsibly. LC 78-14232. (Nursing Skillbooks Ser.). (Illus.). 1978. text ed. 10.95 (ISBN 0-916730-10-7). InterMed Comm.
Donnelly, G. F., et al. The Nursing System: Issues, Ethics & Politics. LC 80-12402. 224p. 1980. 11.95 (ISBN 0-471-04441-5). Wiley.
Donovan, Joan, et al. The Nurse Assistant. 2nd ed. (Illus.). 1977. pap. text ed. 12.95 (ISBN 0-07-017675-2, HP); instructor's manual 3.95 (ISBN 0-07-017676-0). McGraw.
Doughty, Dorothy B. & Mash, Norma J. Nursing Audit. LC 77-9502. 1977. pap. text ed. 13.50 (ISBN 0-8036-2740-8). Davis Co.
Douglass, Laura M. The Effective Nurse: Leader & Manager. LC 80-10860. (Illus.). 1980. pap. text ed. 10.50 (ISBN 0-8016-1448-1). Mosby.
Douglass, Laura M. & Bevis, Em O. Nursing Management & Leadership in Action: Principles & Applications to Staff Situations. 3rd ed. LC 78-31960. (Illus.). 1979. pap. text ed. 12.75 (ISBN 0-8016-1441-4). Mosby.
Douville, Leone. Patient Care Services Policy Manual for the Nursing Department. LC 73-88318. (Illus.). 1974. pap. 8.00 (ISBN 0-87125-011-X). Cath Health.
Downs, Florence S. & Newman, Margaret A. A Source Book of Nursing Research. 3rd ed. (Illus.). 250p. Date not set. pap. price not set (ISBN 0-8036-2792-0). Davis Co.
Dreyer, Sharon, et al. A Guide to Nursing Management of Psychiatric Patients. 2nd ed. LC 78-31432. 1979. pap. text ed. 10.95 (ISBN 0-8016-0832-5). Mosby.
Driscoll, Dorothy L., et al. The Nursing Process in Later Maturity. (Illus.). 1980. text ed. 20.95 (ISBN 0-13-627570-2). P-H.
Du Gas, Beverly W. Introduction to Patient Care. 3rd ed. LC 76-58601. (Illus.). 1977. text ed. 16.95 (ISBN 0-7216-3226-2). Saunders.
Dutcher, Isabel E. & Fielo, Sandra B. Water & Electrolytes: Implications for Nursing Practice. 1967. 8.95 (ISBN 0-02-331050-2, 33105). Macmillan.
Edwards, Barbara J. & Brilhart, John K. Communications in Nursing Practice. LC 81-1960. (Illus.). 245p. 1981. pap. text ed. 9.95 (ISBN 0-8016-0786-8). Mosby.
Elhart, Dorothy, et al. Scientific Principles in Nursing. 8th ed. LC 77-23961. (Illus.). 1978. pap. text ed. 15.95 (ISBN 0-8016-1953-X). Mosby.
Eliopoulos, Charlotte K. Gerontological Nursing. LC 78-25587. 1979. text ed. 15.75x (ISBN 0-06-043754-5, JBL-Med-Nursing). Har-Row.
Elliott, Margaret. Nursing Rheumatic Disease. (Illus.). 1980. pap. 11.25 (ISBN 0-443-02002-7). Churchill.
Ellis, Janice & Nowlis, Elizabeth. Nursing: A Human Needs Approach. LC 76-12023. (Illus.). 416p. 1977. text ed. 16.75 (ISBN 0-395-24067-0); instructor's manual 1.25 (ISBN 0-395-24068-9). HM.
Ellis, Janice R. & Nowlis, Elizabeth A. Nursing: A Human Needs Approach. 2nd ed. LC 80-82841. (Illus.). 528p. 1981. text ed. 19.95 (ISBN 0-395-29642-0); instr's manual 0.45 (ISBN 0-395-29643-9); test bank 2.00 (ISBN 0-395-29644-7). HM.
Ellis, Janice R., et al. Modules for Basic Nursing Skills, 2 vols. 2nd ed. LC 79-89521. (Illus.). 1980. Vol. 1. pap. text ed. 10.00 (ISBN 0-395-28654-9); Vol. 2. pap. text ed. 9.50 (ISBN 0-395-28655-7). HM.
Emanuelsen, Kathy L. & Densmore, Mary J. Acute Respiratory Care. LC 81-50072. (The Fleschner Series in Critical Care Nursing). (Illus.). 216p. (Orig.). 1981. pap. text ed. 9.95 (ISBN 0-937878-01-4). Fleschner.
Emerton, M. D. Principles & Practice of Nursing. 2nd ed. (Nursing Ser.). (Illus.). 411p. (Orig.). 1980. pap. text ed. 15.75x (ISBN 0-7022-1522-8). U of Queensland Pr.
Ensuring Intensive Care. (Nursing Photobook Ser.). (Illus.). 160p. 1981. 12.95 (ISBN 0-916730-37-9). InterMed Comm.

Epstein, Charlotte. Leadership in Nursing. 225p. 1981. text ed. 19.95 (ISBN 0-8359-3970-7); pap. text ed. 13.95 (ISBN 0-8359-3969-3). Reston.

--The Nurse Leader: Philosophy & Practice. 304p. 1982. text ed. 16.00 (ISBN 0-8359-5027-1); pap. text ed. 13.95 (ISBN 0-8359-5026-3). Reston.

--Nursing the Dying Patient. 224p. 1975. pap. text ed. 9.95 (ISBN 0-87909-558-X). Reston.

Epstein, Laura. Helping People: The Task-Centered Approach. LC 79-21084. (Illus.). 1980. pap. text ed. 9.50 (ISBN 0-8016-1509-7). Mosby.

Eriksen, Karin. Human Services Today. 2nd ed. 192p. 1981. text ed. 14.95 (ISBN 0-8359-3004-1). Reston.

Estes, Nada J., et al. Nursing Diagnosis of the Alcoholic Person. LC 80-11057. (Illus.). 1980. pap. text ed. 10.45 (ISBN 0-8016-1558-5). Mosby.

Evans, M. L. & Hansen, B. D. Guide to Pediatric Nursing: A Clinical Reference. (Illus.). 284p. 1980. pap. 14.95 (ISBN 0-8385-3533-X). ACC.

The Expanded Role of the Nurse. (Contemporary Nursing Ser.). 325p. 1973. 6.50 (ISBN 0-937126-10-1, C10). Am Journal Nurse.

Facts About Nursing. LC 80-70580. 336p. 1981. pap. text ed. 18.95 (ISBN 0-937126-85-3). Am Journal Nurse.

Falconer, Mary W., et al. The Drug, the Nurse, the Patient. 6th ed. LC 77-84669. (Illus.). 1978. text ed. 19.95 (ISBN 0-7216-3549-0). Saunders.

Farley, Venner. Second Level Nursing: Study Modules. LC 80-70482. (Associate Degree Nursing Ser.). (Illus.). 272p. (Orig.). 1981. pap. text ed. 10.00 (ISBN 0-8273-1876-6); 5.95 (ISBN 0-8273-1877-4). Delmar.

Farley, Venner M. First Level Nursing-Study Modules. (Nursing-Registered Ser.). 1981. pap. 10.00 (ISBN 0-8273-1873-1); 5.50 (ISBN 0-8273-1875-8). Delmar.

Feeley, Ellen M., et al. Fundamentals of Nursing Care. (Illus.). 552p. 1980. text ed. 20.95 (ISBN 0-442-25708-2); instr's. manual 2.00 (ISBN 0-442-25709-0). Van Nos Reinhold.

Feller, Irving & Archambeault-Jones, Claudella. Nursing the Burned Patient. LC 77-169193. 1973. 25.00 (ISBN 0-917478-24-X). Natl Inst Burn.

Ferris, Elvira & Skelley, Esther G. Body Structures & Functions. LC 77-83347. 160p. 1979. pap. 7.20 (ISBN 0-8273-1322-5); instructor's guide 1.60 (ISBN 0-8273-1323-3); slide pocket 29.50 (ISBN 0-8273-1821-9). Delmar.

Ferster, Marilyn G. Arithmetic for Nurses-Programmed. 2nd ed. LC 73-75647. (Illus.). 1973. pap. text ed. 5.50 (ISBN 0-8261-0482-7). Springer Pub.

Fielo, S. B. A Summary of Integrated Nursing Theory. 1975. 8.50 (ISBN 0-07-020715-1, HP). McGraw.

Fielo, Sandra B. & Edge, Sylviac. Technical Nursing of the Adult: Medical, Surgical & Psychiatric Approaches. 2nd ed. 1974. 17.50x (ISBN 0-02-337280-X, 33728). Macmillan.

Fish, Sharon & Shelly, Judith A. Spiritual Care: The Nurse's Role. LC 77-27688. (Illus.). 1978. 8.95 (ISBN 0-87784-509-3); pap. text ed. 4.95 (ISBN 0-87784-506-9). Inter-Varsity.

Fitzpatrick, M. Louise, ed. Present Realities: Future Imperatives in Nursing Education. LC 76-55404. 1977. pap. text ed. 5.25x (ISBN 0-8077-2513-7). Tchrs Coll.

Flitter, Hessel H. An Introduction to Physics in Nursing. 7th ed. (Illus.). 294p. 1976. pap. 13.95 (ISBN 0-8016-1597-6). Mosby.

Flynn, Beverly. Current Perspectives in Nursing: Social Issues & Trends, Vol. 2. LC 76-57746. (Current Perspectives Ser.). (Illus.). 1979. pap. text ed. 10.50 (ISBN 0-8016-3466-0). Mosby.

Flynn, Patricia A. The Healing Continuum: Journeys in the Philosophy of Holistic Health. (Illus.). 568p. 1980. 16.95 (ISBN 0-87619-670-9). R J Brady.

--Holistic Health: The Art & Science of Care. (Illus.). 259p. 1980. pap. text ed. 12.95 (ISBN 0-87619-626-1). R J Brady.

Ford, Jo Ann G., et al. Applied Decision Making for Nurses. LC 78-15713. (Illus.). 1979. pap. text ed. 9.50 (ISBN 0-8016-1624-7). Mosby.

Fream, William C. Notes on Medical Nursing. 2nd ed. LC 77-1480. (Illus.). 1977. pap. text ed. 8.25 (ISBN 0-443-01612-7). Churchill.

Freeman, Ruth B. & Heinrich, Janet. Community Health Nursing Practice. 2nd ed. (Illus.). 500p. 1981. text ed. write for info. (ISBN 0-7216-3877-5). Saunders.

Friedman, Marilyn M. Family Nursing: Theory & Assessment. 352p. 1980. pap. 16.50 (ISBN 0-8385-2532-6). ACC.

Froebe, Doris J. & Bain. Quality Assurance Programs & Controls in Nursing. LC 76-165. (Illus.). 192p. 1976. pap. 9.95 (ISBN 0-8016-1695-6). Mosby.

Fromer, Margot J. Community Health Care & the Nursing Process. LC 78-16645. (Illus.). 1979. 17.95 (ISBN 0-8016-1707-3). Mosby.

Ganong, Warren & Ganong, Joan. Nursing Management. 2nd ed. LC 80-10865. 350p. 1980. text ed. 19.95 (ISBN 0-89443-278-8). Aspen Systems.

Gebbie, Kristine M. & Lavin, Mary A., eds. Classification of Nursing Diagnoses. LC 74-14869. 1975. pap. text ed. 9.50 (ISBN 0-8016-1769-3). Mosby.

Gerald, Michael C. & O'Bannon, Freda V. Nursing Pharmacology. (Illus.). 544p. 1981. text ed. 19.95 (ISBN 0-13-627505-2). P-H.

Gibson, John. Common Symptoms Described for Nurses. 2nd ed. (Blackwell Scientific Pubns.). 1978. 6.75 (ISBN 0-632-00442-8). Mosby.

Gillies, Dee A. & Alyn, Irene B. Saunders Tests for Self-Evaluation of Nursing Competence. rev. ed. 1980. text ed. write for info. (ISBN 0-7216-4157-1). Saunders.

Gillies, Dee Ann & Alyn, Irene B. Saunders Tests for Self-Evaluation of Nursing Competence. 3rd ed. LC 77-77100. 1978. 11.95 (ISBN 0-7216-4132-6). Saunders.

Given, Barbara A. & Simmons, Sandra J. Gastroenterology in Clinical Nursing. 3rd ed. LC 79-13048. (Illus.). 1979. pap. text ed. 17.95 (ISBN 0-8016-1855-X). Mosby.

Glass, Marion & Atchison, Evelyn. Integrated Studies in Patient Care. 1978. 10.95 (ISBN 0-442-22699-3). Van Nos Reinhold.

Glenn, J. Si Units for Nursing. 1981. pap. text ed. 4.95 (ISBN 0-06-318180-0, Pub. by Har-Row Ltd England). Har-Row.

Goddard, H. A. Principles of Administration Applied to Nursing Service. (Monograph Ser.: No. 41). (Also avail. in French & Spanish). 1958. 4.80 (ISBN 92-4-140041-2). World Health.

Goldman, Ralph. Principles of Medical Science. (Illus.). 416p. 1973. text ed. 12.95 (ISBN 0-07-023667-4, HP). McGraw.

Gomez, June F., ed. Nursing Eighty-One: Career Directory, Vol. 3, No. 1. 3rd ed. (Illus., Orig.). 1981. pap. 10.00 (ISBN 0-916730-30-1). Intermed Comm.

Gorton, John V. Behavioral Components of Patient Care. 1970. text ed. 11.50 (ISBN 0-02-345380-X, 34538). Macmillan.

Gow, Kathleen W. Emotional Involvement in Nursing: The Affective Dimensions of Care-Giving. 1981. text ed. price not set (ISBN 0-8261-3430-0); pap. text ed. price not set (ISBN 0-8261-3431-9). Springer Pub.

Grant, Marcia L., et al. Case Studies in Clinical Pharmacology. LC 77-519. 169p. 1977. pap. text ed. 8.95 (ISBN 0-8036-4280-6). Davis Co.

Grant, Nancy. Time to Care. (Royal College of Nursing Research Ser.). 186p. 1980. pap. text ed. 10.00x (ISBN 0-443-02330-1). Churchill.

Green, Joan L. & Stone, James C. Curriculum Evaluation: Theory & Practice, with a Case Study from Nursing Education. LC 77-8802. (Teaching of Nursing Ser.: Vol. 1). 1977. 14.95 (ISBN 0-8261-2110-1). Springer Pub.

Green, Marilyn L. & Harry, Joann. Nutrition in Contemporary Nursing Practice. LC 80-22426. 864p. 1981. 24.95 (ISBN 0-471-03892-X, Pub. by Wiley Med). Wiley.

Grimes, Jorge & Ianopollo, Elizabeth. Health Assessment in Nursing Practice. (Nursing Ser.). 835p. 1982. text ed. 23.00 (ISBN 0-87872-277-7). Brooks-Cole.

Grippando, Gloria M. Nursing Perspectives & Issues. LC 76-14090. 1977. pap. text ed. 11.60 (ISBN 0-8273-1314-4); instructor's guide 2.75 (ISBN 0-8273-1315-2). Delmar.

Gross, Linda & Bailey, Zeila. Enterostomal Therapy: Developing Institutional & Community Programs. LC 78-70682. 226p. 1979. pap. text ed. 15.95 (ISBN 0-913654-49-3). Nursing Res.

Grubb, Reba D. & Ondov, Geraldine. Planning Ambulatory Surgery Facilities. LC 79-10123. (Illus.). 1979. 18.95 (ISBN 0-8016-1986-6). Mosby.

Guinee, Kathleen K. Professional Nurse: Orientation, Roles & Responsibilities. (Illus.). 1970. text ed. 12.50 (ISBN 0-02-348390-3, 34839). Macmillan.

Hagarty, Catherine. Revelations of an Army Nurse. 1981. 6.75 (ISBN 0-8062-1591-7). Carlton.

Hagen, Elizabeth & Wolff, Luverne. Nursing Leadership Behavior in General Hospitals. LC 61-18762. 1961. pap. text ed. 4.75x (ISBN 0-8077-1482-8). Tchrs Coll.

Hall, Joanne E. & Weaver, Barbara R. Distributive Nursing Practice: A Systems Approach to Community Health. LC 77-6260. 1977. text ed. 17.95 (ISBN 0-397-54201-1, JBL-Med-Nursing). Har-Row.

Hamessley, Mary Lou. Handbook for Camp Nurses & Other Camp Health Workers. 2nd ed. LC 76-46061. (Illus.). 1977. flexible bdg. 7.95 (ISBN 0-913292-08-7). Tiresias Pr.

Hamilton, Ardith J. Critical Care Nursing Skills. (Illus.). 256p. 1981. pap. 12.95 (ISBN 0-8385-1242-9). ACC.

Hand, Lee. Nursing Supervision. (Illus.). 368p. 1980. text ed. 16.95 (ISBN 0-8359-5044-1); pap. 13.95 (ISBN 0-8359-5043-3). Reston.

Hardie, Melissa & Hockey, Lisbeth, eds. Nursing Auxiliaries in Health Care. 217p. 1978. 25.00x (ISBN 0-85664-529-X, Pub by Croom Helm Ltd England). Biblio Dist.

Hardy, Margaret E., et al. Theoretical Foundations for Nursing. 490p. 1974. text ed. 29.50x (ISBN 0-8422-5150-2); pap. text ed. 16.50x (ISBN 0-8422-0340-0). Irvington.

Hare, Ronald & Cooke, Mary. Bacteriology & Immunity for Nurses. 5th ed. (Churchill Livingstone Nursing Texts). 1979. pap. text ed. 11.25 (ISBN 0-443-01757-3). Churchill.

Harris, Cecelia C. A Primer of Cardiac Arrhythmias: A Self Instructional Program. LC 78-27022. 1979. pap. text ed. 9.50 (ISBN 0-8016-2070-8). Mosby.

Hart, Laura K. The Arithmetic of Dosages & Solutions: A Programmed Presentation. 5th ed. LC 80-29474. (Illus.). 68p. 1981. spiral bdg. 7.95 (ISBN 0-8016-2076-7). Mosby.

Hart, Laura K., et al. Concepts Common to Acute Illness: Indentification & Management. LC 80-28706. (Illus.). 371p. 1981. text ed. 19.95 (ISBN 0-8016-2117-8). Mosby.

Hasler, Doris. Practical Nurse & Today's Family. 2nd ed. 1972. pap. text ed. 9.50 (ISBN 0-02-351700-X). Macmillan.

Hawkins, Joellen W. Clinical Experiences in Collegiate Nursing Education: Selection of Nursing Agencies. LC 80-23401. (Springer Series on the Teaching of Nursing: Vol. 7). 128p. 1980. text ed. cancelled (ISBN 0-8261-3390-8); pap. text ed. 11.50 (ISBN 0-8261-3391-6). Springer Pub.

Hawkins, Joellen W. & Higgins, Loretta P. The Nurse in the American Health Care Delivery System. LC 81-50580. (Illus.). 192p. (Orig.). 1981. 12.95 (ISBN 0-913292-34-6); pap. 7.95 (ISBN 0-913292-33-8). Tiresias Pr.

Hazlett, C. B. Primary Care Nursing: A Manual of Clinical Skills. LC 77-7105. 387p. 1977. pap. text ed. 12.00 (ISBN 0-8036-4610-0). Davis Co.

Hector, Winifred. Modern Nursing: Theory & Practice. 6th ed. (Illus.). 1976. 19.95x (ISBN 0-433-14212-X). Intl Ideas.

Hector, Winifred & Malpas, J. S. Textbook of Medicine for Nurses. 3rd ed. (Illus.). 1977. pap. text ed. 21.95x (ISBN 0-433-14214-6). Intl Ideas.

Hein, Eleanor C. Communication in Nursing Practice. 2nd ed. 280p. 1980. pap. text ed. 8.95 (ISBN 0-316-35453-8). Little.

Hekelman, Francine & Ostendarp, Carol. Nephrology Nursing. (Illus.). 1979. text ed. 14.95 (ISBN 0-07-027948-9, HP). McGraw.

Henderson, M. A. Essential Surgery for Nurses. (Illus.). 240p. 1980. pap. text ed. 12.00 (ISBN 0-443-01737-9). Churchill.

Henderson, Virginia & Nite, Gladys. The Principles & Practice of Nursing. 6th ed. (Illus.). 1978. text ed. 28.95 (ISBN 0-02-353580-6). Macmillan.

Henrickson, Charles & Byrd, Larry. Chemistry for the Health Professions. (Illus.). 798p. 1980. text ed. 21.95 (ISBN 0-442-23258-6); instr's. manual 3.50 (ISBN 0-442-26252-3); Student Self Study Guide by John R. Wilson 7.95 (ISBN 0-686-77564-3). D Van Nostrand.

Herman, Sonya J. Becoming Assertive: A Guide for Nurses. 189p. (Orig.). 1978. pap. text ed. 10.95 (ISBN 0-442-23259-4). Van Nos Reinhold.

Hockey, Lisbeth, ed. Current Issues in Nursing. (Recent Advances in Nursing Ser.). 200p. 1981. pap. text ed. 14.00 (ISBN 0-443-02186-4). Churchill.

Hoffman, Claire P. & Lipkin, Gladys B. Simplified Nursing. 9th ed. (Illus.). 500p. 1981. pap. text ed. 12.75 (ISBN 0-397-54237-2, JBL-Med-Nursing). Har-Row.

Hohman, Jo. Focus on Nurse Credentialing. LC 80-17049. 96p. (Orig.). 1980. 10.00 (ISBN 0-87258-303-1, 1460). Am Hospital.

Holloway, Nancy M. Nursing the Critically Ill Adult. LC 78-21153. 1978. 21.95 (ISBN 0-201-02948-0, 02948, Med-Nurse). A-W.

Honesty, Henrene. Essentials of Abdominal Ostomy Care. LC 70-189308. (Illus.). 1972. pap. text ed. 5.95 (ISBN 0-8261-1380-X). Springer Pub.

Hood, Gail H. & Dincher, Judy. Medical-Surgical Nursing: Workbook for Nurses. 5th ed. LC 79-24346. (Illus.). 1980. pap. text ed. 8.95 (ISBN 0-8016-2567-X). Mosby.

--Total Patient Care: Foundations & Practice. 5th. ed. LC 79-23834. (Illus.). 1980. text ed. 17.95 (ISBN 0-8016-2574-2). Mosby.

Hoole, Axalla J. & Greenberg, Robert A. Patient Care Guidelines for Nurse Practitioners. 2nd ed. (Little, Brown SPIRA&L Manual Ser.: Nursing). 1981. price not set spiral bdg. Little.

Hoole, Axalla J., et al. Patient Care Guidelines for Family Nurse Practitioners. 1976. pap. 11.95 (ISBN 0-316-37221-8). Little.

Hopkins, S. J. Drugs & Pharmacology for Nurses. 7th ed. (Illus.). 1979. 12.50 (ISBN 0-443-01763-8). Churchill.

Hornemann, Grace V. Basic Nursing Procedures. LC 77-94835. (Illus.). 272p. 1980. pap. 9.80 (ISBN 0-8273-1320-9); instructors's guide 1.50 (ISBN 0-8273-1321-7). Delmar.

Horsley, Jo Anne, ed. Distress Reduction Through a Sensory Preparation: Using Research to Improve Nursing Practice Ser. 1981. write for info. (ISBN 0-8089-1400-6). Grune.

Howard, Rosanne B. & Herbold, Nancie. Nutrition in Clinical Care. (Illus.). 1977. text ed. 15.95 (ISBN 0-07-030545-5, HP). McGraw.

Howe, Jeanne. Nursing Care of Adolescents. (Illus.). 1980. text ed. 12.95 (ISBN 0-07-030585-4). McGraw.

Huckabay, Loucine M. Conditions of Learning & Instruction in Nursing: Modularized. LC 79-17015. 1979. text ed. 18.95 (ISBN 0-8016-2304-9). Mosby.

Huckbody, Eileen. Nursing Procedures for Skin Diseases. LC 76-41736. 1977. pap. text ed. 10.00 (ISBN 0-443-01538-4). Churchill.

Hymovich, Debra & Barnard, Martha. Family Health Care, Vol. I. (Illus.). 1979. pap. text ed. 8.95 (ISBN 0-07-031675-9, HP). McGraw.

Hynes, V. Barbara. Orthopedic & Rehabilitation Nursing Continuing Education Review. 1976. sprial bdg. 9.50 (ISBN 0-87488-397-0). Med Exam.

Infante, Mary S. The Clinical Laboratory in Nursing Education. LC 74-12454. 112p. 1975. text ed. 15.50 (ISBN 0-471-42715-2, Pub. by Wiley Medical). Wiley.

Ingalls, A. Joy & Salerno, M. Constance. Maternal & Child Health Nursing. 4th ed. LC 78-32131. (Illus.). 1979. text ed. 17.95 (ISBN 0-8016-2326-X). Mosby.

Irons, Patricia. Psychotropic Drugs & Nursing Intervention. (Illus.). 1978. pap. text ed. 7.95 (ISBN 0-07-032052-7, HP). McGraw.

Jacox, Ada. Organizing for Independent Nursing Practice. (Illus.). 270p. 1977. pap. 13.50 (ISBN 0-8385-7522-6). ACC.

Jacox, Ada, et al. A Primary Care Process Measure: The Nurse Practitioner Rating Form. LC 81-80621. (Nursing Dimensions Administration Ser.). 144p. 1981. pap. 19.95 (ISBN 0-913654-75-2). Nursing Res.

Jarvis, Linda L. Community Health Nursing: Keeping the Public Healthy. LC 80-16953. (Illus.). 896p. 1981. 22.00 (ISBN 0-8036-4925-8). Davis Co.

Jasmin, Sylvia & Trygstad-Durland, Louise. Behavioral Concepts & the Nursing Process. LC 78-26960. (Illus.). 1979. pap. text ed. 8.50 (ISBN 0-8016-2435-5). Mosby.

Jessop, Ann L. Nurse-Patient Communication: A Skills Approach. (Illus.). 1979. pap. text ed. 6.95 (ISBN 0-917276-05-1). Microtraining Assocs.

Johanson, Brenda C., et al. Standards for Critical Care. LC 80-15476. (Illus.). 536p. 1980. pap. text ed. 15.95 (ISBN 0-8016-2527-0). Mosby.

Johns, Marjorie P. & Inashima, O. James. Drug Therapy & Nursing Care. 1979. text ed. 19.95 (ISBN 0-02-360800-5). Macmillan.

Johnson, Grace G. Mathematics for Nurses. 208p. 1981. pap. text ed. 7.95 (ISBN 0-8385-6174-8). ACC.

--Mathematics for Nursing. 208p. 1981. pap. text ed. 7.95 (ISBN 0-8385-6174-8). ACC.

Johnson, Mae M., et al. Problem Solving in Nursing Practice. 3rd ed. 130p. 1980. pap. text ed. write for info. (ISBN 0-697-05545-0). Wm C Brown.

Johnson, R. Winifred & Johnson, Douglass W. Introduction to Nursing Care. 1976. text ed. 8.95 (ISBN 0-07-032595-2, G). McGraw.

Johnston, Dorothy F. & Hood, Gail H. Total Patient Care: Foundations & Practice. 4th ed. LC 75-15563. 1976. pap. text ed. 14.95 (ISBN 0-8016-2573-4). Mosby.

Jones, Claudella A. & Feller, Irving. Procedures for Nursing the Burned Patient. LC 75-15372. (Illus.). 1975. plastic 3-ring binder 30.00 (ISBN 0-917478-25-8). Natl Inst Burn.

Jones, Dorothy, et al. Medical Surgical Nursing: A Conceptual Approach. (Illus.). 1978. text ed. 26.95 (ISBN 0-07-032785-8, HP); instructors manual 2.95 (ISBN 0-07-032786-6). McGraw.

Journal of Nursing Administration. Quality Control & Performance Appraisal, Vol. 2. LC 75-41590. 48p. 1976. pap. 4.95 (ISBN 0-913654-34-5). Nursing Res.

Journal of Nursing Administration, Editorial Staff, ed. Clinical Specialists & Nurse Clinicians. LC 75-41601. 46p. 1976. pap. text ed. 4.95 (ISBN 0-913654-22-1). Nursing Res.

Journal of Nursing Administration Staff, ed. Primary Nursing. LC 77-18356. 44p. 1977. pap. text ed. 5.95 (ISBN 0-913654-38-8). Nursing Res.

--Quality Control & Performance Appraisal, Vol. 3. LC 77-85307. (Illus.). 1977. pap. 5.95 (ISBN 0-913654-37-X). Nursing Res.

Judd, Eloise W. Judd: Nursing Care of Thhe Adult Patient. (Illus.). 500p. 1982. price not set (ISBN 0-8036-5136-8). Davis Co.
Juneau, Patricia S. Dimensions of Practical Nursing. 1979. pap. text ed. 7.95 (ISBN 0-02-361520-6). Macmillan.
--Fundamentals of Nursing Care. (Illus.). 1979. text ed. 16.95 (ISBN 0-02-361540-0); instrs'. manual avail. Macmillan.
--Medical-Surgical Nursing. (Illus.). 1980. text ed. 17.95 (ISBN 0-02-361570-2). Macmillan.
Kandzari, Judith H. & Howard, Joan R. The Well Family: A Developmental Approach to Assessment. pap. text ed. write for info. (ISBN 0-316-48269-2). Little.
Karch, Amy. Concurrent Nursing Audit: Quality Assurance in Action. 1979. pap. 15.00 (ISBN 0-685-91500-X). C B Slack.
Keane, Claire. Management Essentials in Nursing. 1980. text ed. 15.95 (ISBN 0-8359-4220-1); pap. text ed. 12.95 (ISBN 0-8359-4202-3). Reston.
Keane, Claire B. Essentials of Nursing: A Medical Surgical Text for Practical Nurses. 4th ed. (Illus.). 558p. 1979. text ed. 17.95 (ISBN 0-7216-5313-8). Saunders.
Keenan, Terrance, et al, eds. Nurses & Doctors: Their Education & Practice. 128p. 1981. text ed. 20.00 (ISBN 0-89946-092-5). Oelgeschlager.
Kekstadt, H. & Primrose, D. A. Mental Subnormality. (Modern Practical Nursing Ser: N0. 15). (Illus.). 1975. pap. text ed. 9.95x (ISBN 0-685-83644-4). Intl Ideas.
Kellogg, Carolyn J. & Sullivan, Barbara P., eds. Current Perspectives in Oncologic Nursing, Vol. II. LC 78-492. (Current Perspectives Ser.). (Illus.). 1978. 12.50 (ISBN 0-8016-3794-5); pap. 9.50 (ISBN 0-8016-3795-3). Mosby.
Kelly, John, et al. Nursing Eighty One Career Directory. 2nd, rev. ed. Gomez, June F., ed. (Illus.). 320p. 1980. pap. 10.00 (ISBN 0-916730-23-9). InterMed Comm.
Kelly, Lucie Y. Dimensions of Professional Nursing. 4th ed. (Illus.). 1981. text ed. 16.95 (ISBN 0-02-362270-9). Macmillan.
Kennedy, Maureen O. & Molnar, Gail. Current Practice in Nursing Care of the Adult: Issues & Concepts, Vol. 1. LC 79-12298. (Current Practice Ser.). (Illus.). 1979. text ed. 12.50 (ISBN 0-8016-2646-3); pap. text ed. 9.50 (ISBN 0-8016-2635-8). Mosby.
Kenner, Cornelia V., et al. Critical Care Nursing: Body - Mind - Spirit. 1981. text ed. 29.95 (ISBN 0-316-48910-7). Little.
Kernicki, Jeanette & Weiler, Kathi. Electocardiography for Nurses: Physiological Correlates. LC 80-28705. 262p. 1981. 17.95 (ISBN 0-471-05752-5, Pub. by Wiley Med). Wiley.
Kilgour, O. F. Introduction to the Biological Aspects of Nursing Science. (Illus.). 1978. pap. text ed. 15.95x (ISBN 0-433-18473-6). Intl Ideas.
--Introduction to the Physical Aspects of Nursing Science. 3rd ed. (Illus.). 1979. pap. text ed. 18.50x (ISBN 0-433-18469-8). Intl Ideas.
Kim, Mi J. & Moritz, Derry A., eds. Classification of Nursing Diagnoses: Proceedings of the Third & Fourth National Conferences. (Illus.). 448p. 1981. pap. text ed. 13.95 (ISBN 0-07-034547-3, HP). McGraw.
Kin, Carole, et al. Basic Science Nursing Review. LC 80-22950. 208p. (Orig.). 1981. pap. text ed. 8.00x (ISBN 0-668-05133-7, 5133). Arco.
King, Eunice M., et al. Illustrated Manual of Nursing Techniques. 2nd ed. (Illus.). 831p. 1981. pap. text ed. 19.75 (ISBN 0-397-54284-4, JBL-Med-Nursing). Har-Row.
King, Imogene M. Toward a Theory for Nursing: General Concepts of Human Behavior. LC 70-136716. (Nursing Ser). 132p. 1971. pap. 10.95 (ISBN 0-471-47800-8, Pub. by Wiley-Medical). Wiley.
King, Virginia & Gerwig, Norma. Humanizing Nursing Education. LC 80-83678. (Nursing Dimensions Education Ser.). 206p. 1981. text ed. 15.95 (ISBN 0-913654-69-8). Nursing Res.
Kinlein, M. Lucille. Independent Nursing Practice with Clients. LC 77-3545. 1977. 9.75 (ISBN 0-397-54204-6, JBL-Med-Nursing). Har-Row.
Kinney, Marguerite, et al. AACN's Reference for Critical Care Nursing. (Illus.). Date not set. text ed. 44.00 (ISBN 0-07-001133-8, HP). McGraw.
Klaus, Billie J. Protocols Handbook for Nurse Practitioners. LC 79-14389. 240p. 1979. 15.95 (ISBN 0-471-05219-1, Pub. by Wiley-Medical). Wiley.
Knapp, Rebecca G. Basic Statistics for Nurses. LC 77-26950. 308p. 1978. pap. 11.95 (ISBN 0-471-03545-9, Wiley Medical). Wiley.
Kneisl, Carol R. & Ames, Sue Ann. Mental Health Concepts in Medical-Surgical Nursing: A Workbook. 2nd ed. LC 78-16371. (Illus.). 1979. pap. 9.50 (ISBN 0-8016-0161-4). Mosby.
Kohnke, Mary F., et al. The Independent Nurse Practitioner. LC 73-19784. 180p. 1974. 13.95 (ISBN 0-8463-0606-9). Trainex Pr.
Kolin, Philip C. & Kolin. Professional Writing for Nurses in Education, Practice & Research. LC 79-28258. 1980. pap. text ed. 10.95 (ISBN 0-8016-2724-9). Mosby.
Koltz, Charles J. Private Practice in Nursing. LC 79-9311. 257p. 1979. text ed. 25.50 (ISBN 0-89443-158-7). Aspen Systems.
Kozier, Barbara & Glenora, Erb. Fundamentals of Nursing: Concepts & Procedures. 1979. transparency resource kit 40.00 (ISBN 0-201-03918-4, Med-Nurse). A-W.
Kozier, Barbara B. & Erb, Glenora L. Fundamentals of Nursing: Concepts & Procedures. LC 78-7776. 1979. 25.95 (ISBN 0-201-03904-4, 03904, Med-Nurse); instr's guide 3.95 (ISBN 0-201-03905-2, 03905). A-W.
Kraegel, Janet M., et al. Patient Care Systems. LC 74-7210. 150p. 1974. text ed. 12.95 (ISBN 0-397-54154-6, JBL-Med-Nursing). Har-Row.
Kramer, Marlene. Reality Shock: Why Nurses Leave Nursing. LC 73-22243. (Illus.). 1974. pap. text ed. 13.95 (ISBN 0-8016-2741-9). Mosby.
Kramer, Marlene & Schmalenberg, Claudia. Path to Biculturalism. LC 77-7202. 315p. 1977. pap. text ed. 12.95 (ISBN 0-913654-30-2). Nursing Res.
Kratz, Charlotte R. Care of the Long-Term Sick in the Community. (Illus.). 1978. pap. text ed. 13.25 (ISBN 0-443-01689-5). Churchill.
Krieger, Dolores. Foundations for Holistic Health Nursing Practices: The Renaissance Nurse. (Illus.). 278p. 1981. pap. text ed. 13.50 (ISBN 0-397-54341-7, JBL-Med-Nursing). Har-Row.
Kviz, Frederick J. & Knafl, Kathleen A. Statistics for Nurses: An Introductory Text. 330p. 1980. pap. text ed. 10.95 (ISBN 0-316-50750-4). Little.
Laird, Elizabeth. Adult Medicine. (Modern Practical Nursing Ser.: No. 9). 1972. pap. 9.95x (ISBN 0-433-19050-7). Intl Ideas.
La Monica, Elaine L. The Nursing Process: A Humanistic Approach. 1979. text ed. 14.95 (ISBN 0-201-04138-3, 04138, Med-Nurse). A-W.
Lancaster, Arnold. Nursery & Midwifery Sourcebook. 304p. 1980. 25.00x (ISBN 0-686-69979-3, Pub. by Beaconsfield England). State Mutual Bk.
--Nursing & Midwifery Sourcebook. (Illus., Orig.). 1979. pap. text ed. 12.50x (ISBN 0-04-610013-X). Allen Unwin.
Lancaster, Jeanette. Concepts for Advanced Nursing Practice: The Nurse As a Change Agent. 1st ed. (Illus.). 496p. 1981. pap. text ed. 14.95 (ISBN 0-8016-2832-6). Mosby.
Lancaster, Jeanette, ed. Community Mental Health Nursing: An Ecological Perspective. LC 79-26185. (Illus.). 1980. pap. text ed. 11.45 (ISBN 0-8016-2816-4). Mosby.
Land, Loretta C. Hiram Hitchcock's Legacy: A History of the Mary Hitchcock Memorial Hospital School of Nursing. LC 80-13044. (Illus.). 160p. 1980. 10.00 (ISBN 0-914016-66-0). Phoenix Pub.
Langford, Teddy. Managing & Being Managed: Preparation for Professional Nursing Practice. (Illus.). 304p. 1981. text ed. 18.95 (ISBN 0-13-550525-9); pap. text ed. 13.95 (ISBN 0-13-550517-8). P-H.
Lapp, Rhonda S. Devotionals for Nurses. (Ultra Bks.). 4.95 (ISBN 0-8010-5539-3). Baker Bk.
Larkin, Patricia & Backer, Barbara. Problem-Oriented Nursing Assessment. 1977. pap. text ed. 8.50 (ISBN 0-07-036450-8, HP). McGraw.
Lasor, B. & Elliot, M. Issues in Canadian Nursing. 1977 (ISBN 0-13-506238-1). pap. 9.25 (ISBN 0-13-506238-1). P-H.
Law, Barbara. Family Planning in Nursing. (Illus.). 84p. 1973. 8.95x (ISBN 0-8464-0400-1). Beekman Pubs.
Leahy, Irene M., et al. The Nurse & Radiotherapy: A Manual for Daily Care. LC 78-12296. 1978. pap. text ed. 11.95 (ISBN 0-8016-2896-2). Mosby.
Leake, Mary J. Manual of Simple Nursing Procedures. 5th ed. LC 71-139430. (Illus.). 1971. pap. 8.95 (ISBN 0-7216-5662-5). Saunders.
Lee, Eloise R. Concepts in Basic Nursing: A Modular Approach. LC 79-66038. (Illus.). 366p. 1980. pap. text ed. 10.95 (ISBN 0-7216-5697-8). Saunders.
Leininger, Madeleine. Transcultural Nursing: Concepts, Theories & Practices. LC 77-28250. 1977. text ed. 29.50 (ISBN 0-471-52608-8, Pub by Wiley Medical). Wiley.
Leitch, Cynthia J. & Tinker, Richard V. Primary Care. LC 77-19147. (Illus.). 1978. text ed. 17.00 (ISBN 0-8036-5535-5). Davis Co.
Lewis, Laverne W. Fundamental Skills in Patient Care. 2nd ed. LC 79-27050. 1980. pap. text ed. 15.95 (ISBN 0-397-54283-6, 408 PGS., JBL-Med-Nursing); 8.75 (ISBN 0-397-54335-2, 257 PGS. FOR WKBK.). Har-Row.
Lewis, Lucile. Planning Patient Care. 2nd ed. (Foundations of Nursing Ser.). 224p. 1976. pap. text ed. write for info. (ISBN 0-697-05540-X). Wm C Brown.
Little, Dolores E. & Carnevali, Doris L. Nursing Care Planning. 2nd ed. LC 76-6949. 250p. 1976. pap. text ed. 9.95x (ISBN 0-397-54184-8). Har-Row.
Lockhart, Carol & Werther, William, eds. Labor Relations in Nursing. LC 79-90382. (Nursing Management Anthologies). 176p. 1980. pap. text ed. 8.95 (ISBN 0-913654-63-9). Nursing Res.
Long, Rosemary. Systematic Nursing Care. (Illus.). 96p. 1981. 21.00 (ISBN 0-571-11616-7, Pub. by Faber & Faber); pap. 7.95 (ISBN 0-571-11616-7). Merrimack Bk Serv.
Loomis, Maxine E. Group Process for Nurses. LC 78-31261. (Illus.). 1979. pap. text ed. 10.50 (ISBN 0-8016-3037-1). Mosby.
Lore, Ann. Effective Therapeutic Communications. (Illus.). 128p. 1981. pap. 10.95 (ISBN 0-87619-842-6). R J Brady.
Lucas, Elizabeth, ed. Nurses & Health Care. 1976. 17.50x (ISBN 0-8464-0679-9). Beekman Pubs.
Luckmann, Joan & Sorensen, Karen C. Medical-Surgical Nursing: A Psychophysiologic Approach. 2nd ed. LC 77-16973. (Illus.). 2276p. 1980. text ed. 34.00 (ISBN 0-7216-5806-7). Saunders.
Lysaught, Jerome, ed. A Luther Christman Anthology. LC 78-53078. 90p. 1978. pap. 6.95 (ISBN 0-913654-45-0). Nursing Res.
Lysaught, Jerome P. Action in Affirmation: Towards an Unambiguous Profession of Nursing. (Illus.). 224p. 1981. pap. text ed. 13.95 (ISBN 0-07-039271-4, HP). McGraw.
McBryde, Brenda. A Nurse's War. LC 79-63956. (Illus.). 1979. text ed. 15.00x (ISBN 0-87663-233-9). Universe.
McCaffery, Margo. Nursing Management of the Patient with Pain. 2nd ed. LC 79-19966. 1979. text ed. 18.50x (ISBN 0-397-54324-7, JBL-Med-Nursing). Har-Row.
McCloskey, Joanne C., et al. Current Issues in Nursing. (Illus.). 816p. (Orig.). 1981. pap. text ed. 19.95 (ISBN 0-86542-005-X). Blackwell Sci.
McElroy, Norman L. & Carr, Joseph J. Simplified Mathematics for Nurses. LC 76-53017. (Arco Nursing Ser.). (Illus.). 1977. lib. bdg. 9.00 (ISBN 0-668-04464-0, 4464); pap. text ed. 5.00 (ISBN 0-668-04197-8, 4197). Arco.
McFarland, Dalton E. & Shiflett, Nola, eds. Power in Nursing. LC 79-84506. (Nursing Dimensions Ser.: Vol. VII, No. 2). 86p. 1979. pap. text ed. 6.95 (ISBN 0-913654-54-X). Nursing Res.
MacGuire, Jillian. Threshold to Nursing. 271p. 1969. pap. text ed. 5.00x (ISBN 0-7135-1522-8, Pub. by Bedford England). Renouf.
McInnes, Mary E., ed. Essentials of Communicable Disease. 2nd ed. LC 74-28353. 402p. 1975. 14.95 (ISBN 0-8016-2545-9). Mosby.
McIntyre, H. Mildred, ed. Heart Disease: New Dimensions of Nursing Care. LC 73-18483. 331p. 1974. soft cover 16.95 (ISBN 0-686-63968-5). Trainex Pr.
Maclean, Una. Nursing in Contemporary Society. 184p. 1974. 10.95x (ISBN 0-7100-7751-3); pap. 6.00 (ISBN 0-7100-7752-1). Routledge & Kegan.
McManus, Rachel L. The Effect of Experience on Nursing Achievement. LC 70-177037. (Columbia University. Teachers College. Contributions to Education: No. 938). Repr. of 1949 ed. 17.50 (ISBN 0-404-55938-7). AMS Pr.
Malasanos, Lois, et al. Health Assessment. LC 77-2179. (Illus.). 1977. text ed. 22.95 (ISBN 0-8016-0478-8). Mosby.
Managing I. V. Therapy. LC 79-28050. (Nursing Photobook Ser.). (Illus.). 1979. text ed. 12.95 (ISBN 0-916730-18-2). InterMed Comm.
Manthey, Marie. The Practice of Primary Nursing. LC 79-92975. (Illus.). 128p. 1980. text ed. 8.95 (ISBN 0-86542-000-9). Blackwell Sci.
Marram, Gwen D. The Group Approach in Nursing Practice. 2nd ed. LC 77-14584. (Illus.). 1978. pap. text ed. 11.00 (ISBN 0-8016-3126-2). Mosby.
Marriner, Ann. Current Perspectives in Nursing Management, Vol. I. LC 78-31446. (Illus.). 1979. text ed. 12.50 (ISBN 0-8016-3119-X); pap. text ed. 9.50 (ISBN 0-8016-3120-3). Mosby.
--The Nursing Process: A Scientific Approach to Nursing Care. 2nd ed. LC 78-21093. (Illus.). 1979. pap. 11.50 (ISBN 0-8016-3122-X). Mosby.
Martin, et al. Comprehensive Rehabilitation Nursing. (Illus.). 816p. 1980. text ed. 22.95 (ISBN 0-07-040611-1, HP). McGraw.
Martin, Leonide L. Health Care of Women. LC 78-15633. 1978. text ed. 16.50 (ISBN 0-397-54219-4, JBL-Med-Nursing). Har-Row.
Massachusetts General Hospital. Manual of Nursing Procedures. 1975. spiral bdg. 14.95 (ISBN 0-316-54954-1). Little.
Massachusetts General Hospital Department of Nursing, et al, eds. Manual of Nursing Procedures. 1980. text ed. write for info. (ISBN 0-316-54958-4); pap. text ed. write for info. (ISBN 0-316-54958-4). Little.
Massachusetts General Hospital Department of Nursing. Massachusetts General Hospital Manual of Nursing Procedures. Kukuk, Helen M. & Murphy, Eleanor R., eds. (Little, Brown Spiral Manual Ser.). 520p. 1980. pap. text ed. 14.95 (ISBN 0-316-54958-4). Little.
Masson, VeNeta. International Nursing. 1981. text ed. write for info. (ISBN 0-8261-3170-0); pap. text ed. write for info. (ISBN 0-8261-3171-9). Springer Pub.
Mauksch, Ingeborg, ed. Primary Care: A Contemporary Nursing Perspectives. 1981. 12.50 (ISBN 0-8089-1392-1). Grune.
Mauksch, Ingeborg G. & Miller, Michael H. Implementing Change in Nursing. LC 80-16576. (Illus.). 195p. 1980. pap. text ed. 11.45 (ISBN 0-8016-3476-8). Mosby.
Mauksch, Ingeborg G., ed. Primary Care: A Contemporary Nursing Perspective. 1981. pap. write for info. (ISBN 0-8089-1392-1, 792813). Grune.
Mayers, Marlene & El Camino Hospital. Standard Nursing Care Plans: Labor-Delivery, Maternity, Nursery, Pediatric, Growth-Development, Vol. 3. 1977. 3 ring binder 37.50x (ISBN 0-686-18831-4). KP Med.
Mayers, Marlene, et al. Quality Assurance for Patient Care: Nursing Perspectives. (Illus.). 300p. 1977. pap. 14.50 (ISBN 0-685-78466-5). ACC.
Mayers, Marlene G. A Systematic Approach to the Nursing Care Plan. 2nd ed. (Illus.). 384p. 1978. pap. 13.95 (ISBN 0-8385-8790-9). ACC.
Mayfield, Peggy, et al. Health Assessment: A Modular Approach. Browning, Martha, ed. (Illus.). 1980. pap. text ed. 10.95 (ISBN 0-07-041027-5); ans. bklt. 2.95 (ISBN 0-07-041028-3). McGraw.
Medications & Mathematics for the Nurse. 288p. 1981. text ed. 13.95 (ISBN 0-442-21882-6). Van Nos Reinhold.
Medicii, Geraldine A. Drug Dosage Calculations: A Guide for Current Clinical Practice. (Illus.). 1980. pap. text ed. 10.95 (ISBN 0-13-220764-8). P-H.
Meltzer, L. E., et al. Concepts & Practices of Intensive Care for Nurse Specialists. 2nd ed. LC 75-27692. 1976. 24.95 (ISBN 0-913486-48-5). Charles.
Mercer, G. The Employment of Nurses: Nursing Labour Turnover in the NHS. 185p. 1979. 37.00x (ISBN 0-7099-0015-5, Pub. by Croom Helm Ltd England). Biblio Dist.
Mercer, Ramona. Nursing Care of Parents at Risk. LC 77-89905. 1977. pap. 12.00 (ISBN 0-913590-47-9). C B Slack.
Miller, Marv. Suicide Intervention by Nurses. 1981. text ed. price not set (ISBN 0-8261-3030-5); pap. text ed. price not set (ISBN 0-8261-3031-3). Springer Pub.
Miller, Michael H. & Flynn, Beverly, eds. Current Perspectives in Nursing: Social Issues & Trends. LC 76-57746. (Current Perspectives Ser.). (Illus.). 1977. 12.50 (ISBN 0-8016-3461-X); pap. 9.50 (ISBN 0-8016-3464-4). Mosby.
Miller, Robin. Flying Nurse. LC 70-174244. 1972. 8.95 (ISBN 0-8008-2892-5). Taplinger.
Millman, Michael, ed. Nursing Personnel & the Changing Health Care System. LC 77-16161. 1978. 16.00 (ISBN 0-88410-525-3). Ballinger Pub.
Mirenda, Rose, et al. Nutrition & Diet Therapy. 2nd ed. (Nursing Examination Review Book: Vol. 8). 1972. spiral bdg. 6.00 (ISBN 0-87488-508-6). Med Exam.
Mirin, Susan K. The Nurses Guide to Writing for Publication. LC 80-84085. (Nursing Dimensions Education Ser & Nursing Dimensions Administration Ser.: Vol. II, No. 1). 209p. 1981. text ed. 14.50 (ISBN 0-913654-71-X). Nursing Res.
Missen, Janet. Principles of Intensive Care for Nurses. (Illus.). 1975. pap. text ed. 14.95x (ISBN 0-433-22080-5). Intl Ideas.
Mitchell, P. Concepts Basic to Nursing. 3rd ed. (Illus.). 720p. text ed. 18.95 (ISBN 0-07-042582-5). McGraw.
Moidel, Harriet C., et al. Nursing Care of the Patient with Medical-Surgical Disorders. 2nd ed. 1976. 26.95 (ISBN 0-07-042655-4, HP). McGraw.
Montag, Mildred L. & Rines, Alice R. Handbook of Fundamental Nursing Techniques. LC 76-5246. 200p. 1976. 15.95 (ISBN 0-471-01475-3, Pub. by Wiley Medical); Arabic Translation avail. (ISBN 0-471-04525-X). Wiley.
Moore, Mary L. The Newborn & the Nurse. 2nd ed. (Illus.). 450p. 1981. text ed. write for info. (ISBN 0-7216-6491-1). Saunders.
Morrin, Helen C. Communication for Nurses. (Quality Paperback: No. 302). (Orig.). 1965. pap. 2.95 (ISBN 0-8226-0302-0). Littlefield.
Munn, Harry E., Jr. The Nurse's Communication Handbook. LC 80-13066. 187p. 1980. text ed. 22.95 (ISBN 0-89443-284-2). Aspen Systems.

Murray, Malinda. Fundamentals of Nursing. 2nd ed. (Illus.). 1980. text ed. 21.95 (ISBN 0-13-341313-6); pap. text ed. 8.95 study guide (ISBN 0-13-341347-0). P-H.

Murray, Rosemary & Kijek, Jean C. Current Perspectives in Rehabilitation Nursing. (Illus.). 1979. text ed. 12.50 (ISBN 0-8016-3605-1); pap. text ed. 10.50 (ISBN 0-8016-3606-X). Mosby.

Murray, Ruth B. & Zentner, Judith P. Nursing Assessment & Health Promotion Through the Life Span. 2nd ed. (Illus.). 1979. ref. 17.95 (ISBN 0-13-627588-5); pap. 13.95 (ISBN 0-13-627596-6). P-H.

--Nursing Concepts for Health Promotion. 2nd ed. (Illus.). 1979. ref. 17.95 (ISBN 0-13-627638-5); pap. text ed. 13.95 (ISBN 0-13-627620-2). P-H.

Narrow, Barbara W. Patient Teaching in Nursing Practice: A Patient & Family Centered Approach. LC 78-10241. 1979. pap. 9.95 (ISBN 0-471-04035-5, Pub. by Wiley Medical). Wiley.

Nash, D. F., et al. The Principles & Practice of Surgery for Nurses & Allied Professions. 7th ed. (Illus.). 800p. 1981. pap. text ed. 52.00x (ISBN 0-7131-4366-5). Intl Ideas.

Neal, Margo C. & Cohen, Patricia F. Nursing Care Planning Guide, Set 1. 2nd ed. 1980. pap. 11.95 (ISBN 0-935236-09-0). Nurseco.

--Nursing Care Planning Guide, Set 3. 1977. pap. 11.95 (ISBN 0-935236-05-8). Nurseco.

--Nursing Care Planning Guide, Set 4. 1978. pap. 11.95 (ISBN 0-935236-08-2). Nurseco.

--Nursing Care Planning Guides, Set 2. 2nd ed. 1980. pap. 11.95 (ISBN 0-935236-16-3). Nurseco.

--Nursing Care Planning Guides for Long Term Care. 1980. pap. 19.95 (ISBN 0-935236-13-9). Nurseco.

Neal, Margo C. & Cooper, Signe S., eds. Perspectives on Continuing Education in Nursing. 1980. pap. text ed. 15.95 (ISBN 0-935236-12-0). Nurseco.

Neal, Margo C., et al. Nursing Care Planning Guides, Set 5. 1981. pap. 11.95 (ISBN 0-935236-14-7). Nurseco.

Nichols, Arlene O. Pearls for Nursing Practice. LC 79-15387. 1979. pap. text ed. 9.95x (ISBN 0-397-54251-8, JBL-Med-Nursing); 13.75x (ISBN 0-686-65979-1). Har-Row.

Nightingale, Florence. Notes on Nursing. 80p. 1978. Repr. 16.00 (ISBN 0-7156-0528-3, Pub. by Duckworth England). Biblio Dist.

--Notes on Nursing: What It Is, & What It Is Not. LC 79-79233. 1969. pap. 2.50 (ISBN 0-486-22340-X). Dover.

--Notes on Nursing: What It Is & What It Is Not. facsimile ed. 1957. 6.75 (ISBN 0-397-54000-0, JBL-Med-Nursing). Har-Row.

--Notes on Nursing: What It Is & What It Is Not. 6.75 (ISBN 0-8446-0823-8). Peter Smith.

Nordmark, Madelyn T. & Rohweder, Ann W. Scientific Foundations of Nursing. 3rd ed. 1975. pap. 10.50 (ISBN 0-397-54166-X, JBL-Med-Nursing). Har-Row.

Norris, Walter & Campbell, Donald. A Nurses' Guide to Anaesthetics, Resuscitation & Intensive Care. rev. 6th ed. (Livingstone Nursing Text Ser.). (Illus.). 176p. 1976. pap. text ed. 9.50x (ISBN 0-443-01345-4). Churchill.

Norton, D. Hospitals & the Long-Stay Patient. 1967. 21.00 (ISBN 0-08-011053-3); pap. 9.75 (ISBN 0-08-011052-5). Pergamon.

Notes on Nursing, 2 bks. Incl. Bk. 1. The Science & the Art. Nightingale, Florence. 50p; Bk. 2. What It Is & What It Is Not. Skeet, Muriel. 75p. 1980. Set. 20.00 (ISBN 0-443-02130-9). Churchill.

Nowak, Janie B. The Forty-Seven Hundred: The Story of the Mount Sinai Hospital School of Nursing. LC 81-5202. (Illus.). 160p. 1981. 15.00 (ISBN 0-914016-79-2). Phoenix Pub.

Nurses in Action: Public Relations Manual, Ec-138. 1977. pap. 1.50 (ISBN 0-686-11642-9). ANA.

Nursing. LC 79-18811. (Nursing PreTest Self-Assessment & Review Ser.). (Illus.). 1979. 11.95 (ISBN 0-07-051574-3). McGraw-Pretest.

Nursing Audit. (QRB Special Edition). 1978. 25.00 (ISBN 0-86688-038-0, QRB-201). Joint Comm Hosp.

Nursing Critically Ill Patients, Confidently. LC 79-17515. (Nursing Skillbook Ser.). (Illus.). 1979. text ed. 10.95 (ISBN 0-916730-13-1). InterMed Comm.

Nursing Development Conference Group. Concept Formalization in Nursing: Process & Product. 2nd ed. LC 79-88164. 313p. 1979. text ed. 12.95 (ISBN 0-316-61421-1). Little.

Nursing Digest, Staff, ed. Nursing Digest Focus on Professional Issues. LC 75-27344. 143p. 1975. pap. text ed. 7.25 (ISBN 0-913654-14-0). Nursing Res.

Nursing Outlook Five Year Cumulative Index (XNO1) 1953-57. 80p. 1958. pap. 4.00 (ISBN 0-937126-98-5). Am Journal Nurse.

Nursing Outlook Five Year Cumulative Index (XNO2) 1958-62. 88p. 1963. text ed. write for info. (ISBN 0-937126-97-7). Am Journal Nurse.

The Nursing Process in Practice. (Contemporary Nursing Ser.). 290p. 1974. 6.50 (ISBN 0-937126-12-8, C12). Am Journal Nurse.

Nursing Theories Conference Group. Nursing Theories: The Base for Professional Nursing Practice. (Illus.). 1980. pap. text ed. 11.95 (ISBN 0-13-627703-9). P-H.

Nussbaum, Janet. Care Planning for Nurses. 2nd ed. LC 81-50882. 1981. pap. write for info. (ISBN 0-913590-78-9). C B Slack.

O'Brien, Mary T. & Pallett, Phyllis J. Total Care of the Stroke Patient. 1978. pap. text ed. 13.95 (ISBN 0-316-62202-8). Little.

O'Brien, Maureen. Communications & Relationships in Nursing. 2nd ed. LC 77-26260. (Illus.). 1978. pap. text ed. 9.50 (ISBN 0-8016-3700-7). Mosby.

Obstetric, Gynecologic, & Neonatal Nursing Functions & Standards. 7.50 (ISBN 0-686-24129-0). Am Coll Obstetric.

O'Conner, Andrea. Writing for Nursing Publications. 2nd ed. LC 81-50881. 1981. pap. 12.00 (ISBN 0-913590-77-0). C B Slack.

O'Connor, Andrea B., ed. Nursing in Respiratory Disease. 2nd ed. LC 78-140938. (Contemporary Nursing Ser.). 310p. 1977. pap. text ed. 6.50 (ISBN 0-937126-05-5). Am Journal Nurse.

--Nursing of Children & Adolescents. LC 78-140948. (Contemporary Nursing Ser.). 1975. pap. text ed. 6.50 (ISBN 0-937126-14-4). Am Journal Nurse.

--Nursing: Patients in Pain. LC 79-140957. (Contemporary Nursing Ser.). 256p. 1979. pap. text ed. 7.95 (ISBN 0-937126-24-1). Am Journal Nurse.

Oehler, Jerri M. Family-Centered Neonatal Nursing Care. (Illus.). 399p. 1981. pap. text ed. 17.50 (ISBN 0-397-54300-X, JBL-Med-Nursing). Har-Row.

Ohio State University. Nursing Skills. 1077p. 1980. pap. text ed. 18.95 (ISBN 0-8359-5039-5). Reston.

Oommen, T. K. Doctors & Nurses. 1978. 14.00x (ISBN 0-8364-0258-8). South Asia Bks.

Orem, Dorothea E. Nursing Concepts of Practice. 2nd ed. (Illus.). 1980. pap. text ed. 9.95 (ISBN 0-07-047718-3). McGraw.

Padilla, Geraldine V. The Clinical Nurse Specialist & Improvement of Nursing Practice. LC 78-78148. 83p. 1979. pap. text ed. 6.95 (ISBN 0-913654-51-5). Nursing Res.

Parker, William & Dietz, Lois. Nursing at Home. 1979. 14.95 (ISBN 0-517-52836-3). Crown.

Parks, Lucille M. Review Mathematics for Nurses & Health Professionals: A Textbook on Solutions & Dosage Calculations. LC 76-46122. 1977. pap. text ed. 9.95 (ISBN 0-8465-4890-9); test bklt. 6.50 (ISBN 0-8465-4891-7). Benjamin-Cummings.

Parse. Man-Living-Health: A Theory of Nursing. 202p. 1981. pap. 11.95 (ISBN 0-471-04443-1, Pub. by Wiley Med). Wiley.

Paterson, Josephine G. & Zderad, Loretta T. Humanistic Nursing. LC 75-40431. 1976. 17.50 (ISBN 0-471-66946-6, Pub. by Wiley Medical). Wiley.

Pearce, Evelyn. A General Textbook of Nursing: A Compendium of Nursing Knowledge. 20th ed. (Illus.). 448p. 1980. pap. 19.95 (ISBN 0-571-18005-1, Pub. by Faber & Faber). Merrimack Bk Serv.

Pembrey, Sue. The Ward Sister. (RCN Research Monograph). 184p. 1981. pap. text ed. 10.00 (ISBN 0-443-02411-1). Churchill.

Performing G. I. Procedures. LC 81-965. (Nursing Photobook Ser.). (Illus.). 1981. 12.95 (ISBN 0-916730-31-X). Intermed Comm.

Phaneuf, Maria C. The Nursing Audit: Self-Regulation in Nursing Practice. 2nd ed. (Illus.). 215p. 1976. pap. 13.50 (ISBN 0-8385-7005-4). ACC.

Phipps, Wilma J., et al. Medical-Surgical Nursing: Concepts & Clinical Practice. LC 78-27863. (Illus.). 1979. text ed. 31.95 (ISBN 0-8016-3932-8). Mosby.

Pillitteri, Adele. Child Health Nursing: Care of the Growing Family. 2nd ed. 1981. text ed. write for info (ISBN 0-316-70793-7). Little.

Pluckhan, Margaret. Human Communication: The Matrix of Nursing. (Illus.). 1977. pap. text ed. 8.50 (ISBN 0-07-050352-4, HP). McGraw.

Polslusny, Mary, et al, eds. Nursing & Thanatology. (Thanatology Ser.). 1978. 15.50x (ISBN 0-8422-7299-2). Irvington.

Pomeranz, Ruth. The Lady Apprentices. 144p. 1973. pap. text ed. 7.50x (ISBN 0-7135-1868-5, Pub. by Bedford England). Renouf.

Popiel, Elda S. Nursing & the Process of Continuing Education. 2nd ed. LC 76-57997. (Illus.). 1977. pap. text ed. 10.95 (ISBN 0-8016-3969-7). Mosby.

Popiel, Elda S., ed. Social Issues & Trends in Nursing: Chautauqua 1977. LC 78-66789. 1979. pap. 14.00 (ISBN 0-685-66972-6). C B Slack.

Price, Elmina. Staffing for Patient Care: A Guide for Nursing Service. LC 76-111051. 1970. pap. text ed. 6.95 (ISBN 0-8261-1111-4). Springer Pub.

Price, James L. & Mueller, Charles W. Professional Turnover: The Case of Nurses. (Health Systems Management Ser.). 218p. 1980. 20.00 (ISBN 0-89335-124-5). Spectrum Pub.

Price, Sylvia & Wilson, Lorraine. Pathophysiology: Clinical Concepts of Disease Processes. (Illus.). 1978. text ed. 22.95 (ISBN 0-07-050857-7, HP); test bank by Lewis 8.95 (ISBN 0-07-050858-5). McGraw.

Primary Care by Nurses: Sphere of Responsibility & Accountability. 1977. pap. 3.00 (ISBN 0-686-21451-X, G-127). ANA.

Providing Respiratory Care. LC 79-21639. (Nursing Photobook Ser.). (Illus.). 1979. text ed. 12.95 (ISBN 0-916730-17-4). InterMed Comm.

Putt, Arlene M. General Systems Theory Applied to Nursing. 1978. text ed. 10.95 (ISBN 0-316-72300-2). Little.

Quinn, Frances M. The Principles & Practice of Nurse Education. 336p. 1981. 34.00x (ISBN 0-85664-891-4, Pub. by Croom Helm Ltd England). Biblio Dist.

Quinn, Sheila, ed. Nursing in the European Community. 192p. 1980. 25.00x (ISBN 0-7099-0080-5, Pub. by Croom Helm Ltd England). Biblio Dist.

Radcliff, Ruth K. & Ogden, Shelia J. Nursing & Medical Terminology: A Workbook. LC 76-17597. (Illus.). 1977. pap. text ed. 12.50 (ISBN 0-8016-3714-7). Mosby.

Ram, Lily P. Manual of Nursing Arts & Procedures. 1978. 7.50 (ISBN 0-7069-0686-1, Pub. by Vikas India). Advent NY.

Readey, Helen, et al. Introduction to Nursing Essentials: A Handbook. LC 76-41198. (Illus.). 1977. pap. text ed. 9.50 (ISBN 0-8016-4099-7). Mosby.

Redland, A. & Leonard, B. Process in Clinical Nursing. 1981. pap. 14.95 (ISBN 0-13-723205-5). P-H.

Redman, Barbara K. Issues & Concepts in Patient Education. (The Patient Education Series). (Illus.). 160p. 1981. pap. 8.95 (ISBN 0-8385-4405-3). ACC.

--The Process of Patient Teaching in Nursing. 4th ed. LC 80-15310. (Illus.). 294p. 1980. pap. text ed. 12.95 (ISBN 0-8016-4100-4). Mosby.

Redman, Barbara K., ed. Patterns for Distribution of Patient Education. (The Patient Education Series). (Illus.). 176p. 1981. pap. 10.50 (ISBN 0-8385-7776-8). ACC.

Reilly, Dorothy E., ed. Teaching & Evaluating the Affective Domain in Nursing Programs. LC 77-93571. 1978. 12.00 (ISBN 0-913590-53-3). C B Slack.

Reimbursement for Nursing Services: A Position Statement, Ec-139. 1977. pap. 1.50 (ISBN 0-686-11641-0). ANA.

Reinhardt, Adina M. & Quinn, Mildred D. Family-Centered Community Nursing: A Sociocultural Framework, Vol. II. LC 73-8681. (Current Practice Ser.). (Illus.). 1980. pap. text ed. 13.95 (ISBN 0-8016-4121-7). Mosby.

Resford, Eliza. Yet Softly Tread the Leaves. 1981. 10.95 (ISBN 0-533-04949-0). Vantage.

Rezler, Agnes & Stevens, Barbara. The Nurse Evaluator in Education & Service. 1978. text ed. 18.95 (ISBN 0-07-052060-7, HP). McGraw.

Riehl, Joan P. & Roy, Sr. C. Conceptual Models for Nursing Practice. 2nd ed. (Illus.). 432p. 1980. pap. 14.00 (ISBN 0-8385-1200-3). ACC.

Riffle, Kathryn L., ed. Rehabilitative Nursing Case Studies. 1979. pap. 9.50 (ISBN 0-87488-035-1). Med Exam.

Riley, Mary Ann K. Case Studies in Nursing Fundamentals. 1979. pap. text ed. 7.95 (ISBN 0-02-401400-1). Macmillan.

Roberts, Sharon L. Behavioral Concepts & Nursing Throughout the Lifespan. 1978. ref. 16.95x (ISBN 0-13-074559-6); pap. text ed. 12.95x (ISBN 0-13-074567-7). P-H.

Robinson, Lisa. Psychological Aspects of the Care of Hospitalized Patients. 3rd ed. LC 75-28105. 122p. 1976. pap. text ed. 4.95 (ISBN 0-8036-7472-4). Davis Co.

Rodman, Morton J. & Smith, Dorothy W. Clinical Pharmacology in Nursing. LC 73-18194. 1974. text ed. 19.50 (ISBN 0-397-54132-5). Har-Row.

Roe, Anne K. & Sherwood, Mary C. Nursing in the Seventies. LC 73-2874. 272p. 1973. pap. text ed. 14.50 (ISBN 0-471-72962-0). Wiley.

Rogers, Martha E. Introduction to the Theoretical Basis of Nursing. 144p. 1970. pap. 9.95 (ISBN 0-8036-7490-2). Davis Co.

Roper, Nancy. Principles of Nursing. 2nd ed. 1973. pap. text ed. 8.75 (ISBN 0-443-00994-5). Churchill.

Roper, Nancy, et al. The Elements of Nursing. (Illus.). 1980. text ed. 44.00 (ISBN 0-443-02198-8); pap. text ed. 27.50x (ISBN 0-443-01577-5). Churchill.

Rosdahl, Caroline B. Textbook of Basic Nursing. 3rd ed. (Illus.). 864p. 1981. text ed. 22.50 (ISBN 0-397-54254-2, JBL-Med-Nursing); wkbk. 7.95 (ISBN 0-397-54359-X, JBL-Med-Nursing). Har-Row.

Rotkovich, Rachel, ed. Quality Patient Care & the Role of the Clinical Nurse Specialist. LC 76-5393. 1976. 22.00 (ISBN 0-471-74015-2, Pub. by Wiley Medical). Wiley.

Rowland, Howard & Rowland, Beatrice. Nursing Administration Handbook. LC 80-11857. 600p. 1980. text ed. 42.50 (ISBN 0-89443-275-3). Aspen Systems.

Rowland, Howard S. & Rowland, Beatrice L. The Nurse's Almanac. LC 78-311. (Illus.). 860p. 1978. 32.95 (ISBN 0-89443-031-9); pap. 21.95 (ISBN 0-89443-040-8). Aspen Systems.

Roy, Callista & Roberts, Sharon. Theory Construction in Nursing: An Adaptation Model. (Illus.). 352p. 1981. text ed. 17.95 (ISBN 0-13-913657-6). P-H.

Roy, Sr. Callista. Introduction to Nursing: An Adaptation Model. LC 75-43612. (Illus.). 400p. 1976. ref. ed. 17.95 (ISBN 0-13-491290-X). P-H.

Rubin, Marilyn B. Nursing Care for Myocarial Infarction. LC 76-6218. 288p. 1977. 10.50 (ISBN 0-87527-151-0). Green.

Rudman, Jack. Adult Nursing. (College Proficiency Examination Ser.: CLEP-35). (Cloth bdg. avail. on request). pap. 9.95 (ISBN 0-8373-5435-8). Natl Learning.

--Fundamentals of Nursing. (ACT Proficiency Examination Program: PEP-36). (Cloth bdg. avail. on request). pap. 14.95 (ISBN 0-686-77096-X). Natl Learning.

Sackheim, George I., et al. Programmed Mathematics for Nursing. 4th ed. 1979. pap. text ed. 8.95 (ISBN 0-02-405190-X). Macmillan.

St. Joseph Hospital. Patient-Centered Care Manual for the Nursing Department. new ed. LC 77-71736. 1977. pap. 13.00 (ISBN 0-87125-041-1). Cath Health.

Sana, Josephine & Judge, Richard D., eds. Physical Appraisal Methods in Nursing Practice. (Illus.). 402p. 1975. 15.95 (ISBN 0-316-76995-9); pap. 10.95 (ISBN 0-316-76996-7). Little.

Sanderson, Richard G., ed. Cardiac Patient: A Comprehensive Approach. LC 73-176215. (Monographs in Clinical Nursing: Vol. 2). (Illus.). 545p. 1972. text ed. 14.50 (ISBN 0-7216-7905-6). Saunders.

Saperstein, Arlyne B. & Frazier, Margaret A. Introduction to Nursing Practice. LC 79-17422. (Illus.). 1980. text ed. 21.00 (ISBN 0-8036-7729-4); instructor's guide avail. Davis Co.

Sauve, Mary J. & Pecherer, Angela. Concepts & Skills in Physical Assessment. LC 76-20120. 1977. pap. text ed. 13.50 (ISBN 0-7216-7939-0). Saunders.

Saxton, D. F., et al. Handbook of Nursing: Prescriptions for Patient Care. 1982. price not set (ISBN 0-201-07145-2). A-W.

Saxton, Dolores F. & Haring, Phyllis W. Care of Patients with Emotional Problems. 3rd ed. LC 78-31641. (Illus.). 1979. pap. text ed. 8.50 (ISBN 0-8016-4341-4). Mosby.

Saxton, Dolores F. & Hyland, Patricia A. Planning & Implementing Nursing Intervention: Stress & Adaptation Applied to Patient Care. 2nd ed. LC 78-31818. (Illus.). 1979. pap. 10.50 (ISBN 0-8016-4337-6). Mosby.

Saxton, Dolores F., et al, eds. Mosby's Comprehensive Review of Nursing. 9th ed. Nugent, Patricia M. & Pelikan, Phyllis K. LC 76-26682. 1977. text ed. 13.95 (ISBN 0-8016-3529-2). Mosby.

--Mosby's Comprehensive Review of Nursing. 10th ed. LC 80-26510. (Illus.). 1981. text ed. 13.95 (ISBN 0-8016-3530-6). Mosby.

Scherer, Jeanne C. Introductory Medical-Surgical Nursing. 2nd ed. LC 76-57782. 1977. text ed. 19.00 (ISBN 0-397-54200-3, JBL-Med-Nursing). Har-Row.

Schickedanz, H. Ruth & Mayhall, Pamela D. Restorative Nursing in a General Hospital. (Illus.). 232p. 1975. 19.75 (ISBN 0-398-03312-9); pap. 14.75 (ISBN 0-398-03313-7). C C Thomas.

Schmalenberg, Claudia & Kramer, Marlene. Coping with Reality Shock: The Voices of Experience. LC 78-70683. 339p. 1979. pap. text ed. 18.75 (ISBN 0-913654-50-7). Nursing Res.

Schmied, Elsie, ed. Maintaining Cost Effectiveness. LC 79-84505. (Management Anthology Ser.). 259p. 1979. pap. text ed. 12.50 (ISBN 0-913654-53-1). Nursing Res.

Schulze, Victor E. Electrocardiography & Related Coronary Care: A Complete Manual for the Nurse. LC 73-17201. 248p. 1974. soft cover 15.95 (ISBN 0-8463-0602-6). Trainex Pr.

Schweiger, Joyce F. Nurse As Manager. LC 80-17456. 194p. 1980. 11.95 (ISBN 0-471-04343-5, Pub. by Wiley Med). Wiley.

Secor, Jane. Patient Care in Respiratory Problems. LC 70-81827. (Monographs in Clinical Nursing: Vol. 1). (Illus.). 1969. 9.95x (ISBN 0-7216-8045-3). Saunders.

Seedor, Marie M. Aids to Nursing Diagnosis. 3rd ed. (Nursing Education Monograph: No. 6). 1980. pap. 8.95 (ISBN 0-397-54120-1, Pub. by Columbia U Pr). Lippincott.

--Aids to Nursing Diagnosis: A Programmed Unit in Fundamentals of Nursing. 3rd ed. 378p. (Orig.). 1980. pap. text ed. 8.95x (ISBN 0-8077-2630-3). Tchrs Coll.

Seedor, Marie M., ed. The Nursing Process: Proceedings. LC 73-85353. 51p. 1973. pap. text ed. 3.50x (ISBN 0-8077-2405-X). Tchrs Coll.

Self, Timothy H., et al. Systematic Patient Medication Record Review: A Manual for Nurses. LC 80-12481. 1980. pap. text ed. 9.45 (ISBN 0-8016-4479-8). Mosby.

Shader, Richard I. & Kerble, Judith, eds. Psychopharmacology in Psychiatric Nursing. 1982. write for info. (ISBN 0-89004-428-7, 486). Raven.

Shortridge, Lillie M. & Lee, Juanita E. Introduction to Nursing Practice. new ed. (Illus.). 1980. text ed. 16.95 (ISBN 0-07-057056-6, HP); introductory skills 11.95 (ISBN 0-07-057057-4). McGraw.

Sierra-Franco, Miriam. Therapeutic Communication in Nursing. 1977. pap. text ed. 9.95 (ISBN 0-07-057280-1, HP). McGraw.

Skelley, Esther G. Medications & Mathematics for the Nurse. LC 76-5302. 1976. pap. 7.40 (ISBN 0-8273-1343-8); instructor's guide 1.60 (ISBN 0-8273-1344-6). Delmar.

Smith. Nursing Science Applied to the Art of Nursing. (Illus.). 300p. 1981. text ed. price not set (ISBN 0-407-00202-2). Butterworth.

Smith, Dorothy W., et al. Survival of Illness: Implications for Nursing. 1981. pap. text ed. 9.95 (ISBN 0-8261-2871-8). Springer Pub.

Smith, James P. Sociology & Nursing. (Livingstone Nursing Texts Ser.). (Illus.). 1976. pap. text ed. 11.25 (ISBN 0-443-01473-6). Churchill.

Sorensen, Karen C. & Luckmann, Joan. Basic Nursing: A Psychophysiologic Approach. LC 77-84691. (Illus.). 1979. text ed. 29.00 (ISBN 0-7216-8498-X). Saunders.

Spicker, Stuart F. & Gadow, Sally. Nursing-Images & Ideals: Opening Dialogue with the Humanities. LC 79-15057. 1980. text ed. 20.95 (ISBN 0-8261-2740-1); pap. text ed. 12.95 (ISBN 0-8261-2741-X). Springer Pub.

Spicker, Stuart F. & Gadow, Sally, eds. Nursing, Images & Ideals: Opening Dialogue with the Humanities. LC 79-15057. xxvii, 193p. 1980. 20.95 (ISBN 0-8261-2740-1); pap. 12.95 (ISBN 0-8261-2741-X). Springer Pub.

Spradley, Barbara W. Community Health Nursing: Concepts & Practice. 1981. text ed. write for info. (ISBN 0-316-80748-6). Little.

Standards for Nursing Services in Camp Settings. 1978. pap. 1.00 (ISBN 0-686-11182-6). ANA.

Stevens, Barbara J. The Nurse As Executive. 2nd ed. LC 79-90379. 365p. 1980. text ed. 19.50 (ISBN 0-913654-62-0). Nursing Res.

--Nursing Theory: Analysis, Application, Evaluation. 1979. text ed. 10.95 (ISBN 0-316-81322-2, Little Med Div). Little.

Stevens, Marion K. The Practical Nurse in Supervisory Roles. LC 73-80982. (Illus.). 160p. 1973. text ed. 7.50x (ISBN 0-7216-8591-9). Saunders.

Stewart Conference on Research in Nursing, Sixteenth. Perspectives on Nursing Leadership: Proceedings. Ketefian, Shake, ed. LC 80-27464. (Orig.). 1981. pap. text ed. 6.50x (ISBN 0-8077-2637-0). Tchrs Coll.

Stone, Sandra, et al, eds. Management for Nurses: A Multidisciplinary Approach. LC 75-15561. 1976. pap. 9.95 (ISBN 0-8016-4812-2). Mosby.

Story, Donna K. & Rosdahl, Caroline B. Principles & Practices of Nursing Care. 1976. text ed. 13.95 (ISBN 0-07-061770-8); instructor's manual & key 4.00 (ISBN 0-07-061772-4); activities & projects 6.95 (ISBN 0-07-061771-6). McGraw.

Stromberg, Marilyn F. & Stromberg, Paul. Primary Care Assessment & Management Skills for Nurses: A Self-Assessment Manual. LC 79-14379. 1979. pap. 16.25x (ISBN 0-686-59574-2, JBL-Med-Nursing). Har-Row.

Stryker, Ruth. Rehabilitative Aspects of Acute & Chronic Nursing Care. 2nd ed. LC 76-54042. (Illus.). 1977. text ed. 11.95 (ISBN 0-7216-8637-0). Saunders.

Sultz, Harry A., et al. Nurse Practitioners: USA. LC 78-19728. 1979. 25.95 (ISBN 0-669-02727-8). Lexington Bks.

Summers, Anthony. Conspiracy. (McGraw-Hill Paperbacks Ser.). (Illus.). 656p. 1981. pap. 7.95 (ISBN 0-07-062400-3). McGraw.

Sundeen, Sandra J., et al. Nurse-Client Interaction: Implementing the Nursing Process. LC 75-32540. (Illus.). 240p. 1976. pap. 9.95 (ISBN 0-8016-4840-8). Mosby.

Survey of Salaries of Nursing Faculty in Educational Programs: D-61. 1978. pap. 3.00 (ISBN 0-686-11184-2). ANA.

Sutterley, Doris C. & Donnelly, Gloria F. Stress Management for Nurses. 250p. 1981. text ed. price not set (ISBN 0-89443-650-3). Aspen Systems.

Sutton, Audrey L. Bedside Nursing Techniques in Medicine & Surgery. 2nd ed. LC 69-12891. 1969. pap. 11.95 (ISBN 0-7216-8666-4). Saunders.

Swonger, Alvin K. Nursing Pharmacology: A Systems Approach to Drug Therapy & Nursing Practice. 1978. text ed. 9.95 (ISBN 0-316-82553-0). Little.

Taylor, Clarence E. Mathematics for Nursing. 1978. pap. text ed. 7.95 (ISBN 0-316-83304-5). Little.

Thompson, Lida F., et al. Sociology: Nurses & Their Patients in a Modern Society. 9th ed. LC 74-34417. 1975. text ed. 10.95 (ISBN 0-8016-4942-0). Mosby.

Tiffany, Robert, ed. Oncology for Nurses & Health Care Professionals, Vol. 1. (Illus.). 1978. text ed. 35.00x (ISBN 0-04-610009-1); pap. text ed. 18.95x (ISBN 0-04-610010-5). Allen Unwin.

Tinker, Jack & Porter, Susan W. A Course in Intensive Therapy Nursing. 294p. 1980. 30.00x (ISBN 0-7131-4347-9, Pub. by Arnold Pubs England). State Mutual Bk.

Tinkham, Catherine W. & Voorhies, Eleanor F. Community Health Nursing: Evolution & Process. 2nd ed. (Illus.). 315p. 1977. text ed. 15.50 (ISBN 0-8385-1188-0). ACC.

Tonkin, R. D. Nurses Handbook of Current Drugs. 3rd ed. 1979. pap. text ed. 14.95x (ISBN 0-433-32601-8). Intl Ideas.

Travelbee, Joyce. Interpersonal Aspects of Nursing. 2nd ed. 1971. text ed. 10.50 (ISBN 0-8036-8601-3). Davis Co.

Traver, Gayle A. Respiratory Nursing: The Science & the Art. 520p. 1982. 19.95 (ISBN 0-471-04539-X, Pub. by Wiley Med). Wiley.

Trounce, J. R. Clinical Pharmacology for Nurses. 9th ed. (Illus.). 432p. 1981. pap. text ed. 11.00 (ISBN 0-443-02333-6). Churchill.

Ujhely, Gertrud B. Determinants of the Nurse - Patient Relationship. LC 68-23551. 1968. pap. text ed. 8.50 (ISBN 0-8261-0971-3). Springer Pub.

--The Nurse & Her Problem Patients. LC 63-11842. 1963. pap. text ed. 5.50 (ISBN 0-8261-0601-3). Springer Pub.

Using Crisis Intervention Wisely. LC 79-14825. (Nursing Skillbook Ser.). (Illus.). 1979. text ed. 10.95 (ISBN 0-916730-15-8). InterMed Comm.

Using Monitors. LC 80-20948. (Nursing Photobook Ser.). (Illus.). 160p. 1980. text ed. 12.95 (ISBN 0-916730-26-3). Intermed Comm.

Van Zwanenberg, Dinah & Adams, C. B. Neurosurgical Nursing Care. 128p. 1979. 13.50 (ISBN 0-571-11295-1, Pub. by Faber & Faber); pap. 4.50 (ISBN 0-571-11296-X). Merrimack Bk Serv.

Vaughan-Wrobel, Beth C. & Henderson, Betty S. The Problem-Oriented System in Nursing: A Workbook. 2nd ed. (Illus.). 208p. 1982. pap. text ed. 11.95 (ISBN 0-8016-5222-7). Mosby.

Verner, Lawrence. Mathematics for Health Practitioners: Basic Concepts & Clinical Applications. LC 78-12176. 1978. pap. 8.75 (ISBN 0-397-54223-2). Lippincott.

Vredevoe, Donna L., et al. Concepts of Oncology Nursing. (Illus.). 400p. 1981. text ed. 18.95 (ISBN 0-13-166587-1). P-H.

Wade, Jacqueline F. Comprehensive Respiratory Nursing Care: Physiology & Technique. 3rd ed. (Illus.). 288p. 1981. pap. text ed. 12.95 (ISBN 0-8016-5282-0). Mosby.

Walsh, Angela. Expanded Role of the Rehabilitation Nurse. LC 80-50696. 1980. pap. 14.00 (ISBN 0-913590-69-X). C B Slack.

Walston, Betty J. & Walston. The Nurse Assistant in Long Term Care: A New Era. LC 80-12308. (Illus.). 1980. pap. text ed. 9.45 (ISBN 0-8016-5355-X). Mosby.

Walter, Judith, et al. Dynamics of Problem Oriented Approaches: Patient Care & Documentation. LC 76-11775. 1976. pap. text ed. 10.50x (ISBN 0-397-54187-2). Lippincott.

Wandelt, M. & Stewart, D. Slater Nursing Competencies Rating Scale. 92p. 1975. pap. 7.95 (ISBN 0-685-78468-1). ACC.

Wandelt, Mabel A. & Ager, Joel W. Quality Patient Care Scale. (Illus.). 92p. 1974. pap. 7.95 (ISBN 0-685-78465-7). ACC.

Wardell, Sandra C. Acute Intervention: Nursing Process Throughout the Life Span. (Illus.). 1979. text ed. 14.95 (ISBN 0-8359-0133-5); pap. text ed. 13.95 (ISBN 0-8359-0132-7); instrs'. manual avail. (ISBN 0-8359-0134-3). Reston.

Warner, Anne R., ed. Innovations in Community Health Nursing: Health Care Delivery in Shortage Areas. LC 77-20114. 1978. pap. text ed. 9.50 (ISBN 0-8016-5350-9). Mosby.

Warner, Steven D. & Schweer, Kathryn D. Author's Guide to Journals in Nursing & Related Fields. (Author's Guide to Journals Ser.). 1981. 19.95 (ISBN 0-917724-11-9). Haworth Pr.

Watson, Annita B. & Mayers, Marlene G. Assessment & Documentation: Theories in Action. LC 79-65450. 1981. write for info. (ISBN 0-685-91498-4); pap. 16.00 (ISBN 0-685-91499-2). C B Slack.

Watson, Jean. Nursing: The Philosophy & Science of Caring. 1979. 9.95 (ISBN 0-316-92464-4). Little.

Watson, Jeannette E. Medical-Surgical Nursing & Related Physiology. 2nd ed. LC 78-64732. (Illus.). 1043p. 1979. text ed. 22.00 (ISBN 0-7216-9136-6). Saunders.

Welsh, Elizabeth M., et al. Outline of Basic Nursing Care. (Illus.). 1975. pap. text ed. 11.95x (ISBN 0-433-35220-5). Intl Ideas.

Werley, Harriet H. & Grier, Margaret R. Nursing Information Systems. 1980. text ed. 27.50 (ISBN 0-8261-2520-4). Springer Pub.

Wessells & Nicholls. Nursing Standards & Nursing Process. LC 76-56882. 164p. 1977. pap. text ed. 9.50 (ISBN 0-913654-31-0). Nursing Res.

Whaley, Lucille F. & Wong, Donna. Nursing Care of Infants & Children. LC 78-31225. (Illus.). 1979. text ed. 27.95 (ISBN 0-8016-5417-3). Mosby.

White, Dorothy, et al. Fundamentals: The Foundations of Nursing. 324p. 1972. 16.95 (ISBN 0-13-331991-1). P-H.

WHO Expert Committee. Geneva, 1974. Community Health Nursing: Report. (Technical Report Ser.: No. 558). (Also avail. in French & Spanish). 1974. pap. 2.40 (ISBN 92-4-120558-X). World Health.

Wiedenbach, Ernestine & Falls, Caroline E. Communication: Key to Effective Nursing. LC 78-50063. (Illus.). 1978. pap. text ed. 4.95 (ISBN 0-913292-23-0). Tiresias Pr.

Wiener, M., et al. Clinical Pharmacology & Therapeutics in Nursing. 1979. text ed. 19.95 (ISBN 0-07-070138-5, HP); instructor's manual 3.95 (ISBN 0-07-070139-3). McGraw.

Williamson, Janet A. Current Perspectives in Nursing Education, Vol. 2. LC 75-32544. (Current Perspectives Ser.). (Illus.). 1978. 12.50 (ISBN 0-8016-5578-1); pap. 9.50 (ISBN 0-8016-5579-X). Mosby.

Wolff, LuVerne. Students Self-Evaluation Manual in Fundamentals of Nursing. pap. text ed. 8.75x (ISBN 0-397-54235-6). Lippincott.

Wolff, LuVerne, et al. Fundamentals of Nursing. 6th ed. LC 78-31576. 1979. text ed. 19.95x (ISBN 0-397-54234-8). Lippincott.

Wood, Lucile A., ed. Nursing Skills for Allied Health Services, Vol. 3. 2nd ed. Rambo, Beverly J. LC 76-41544. (Illus.). 467p. 1980. soft cover 10.95 (ISBN 0-7216-9607-4). Saunders.

Wood, Lucile A. & Rambo, Beverly J., eds. Nursing Skills for Allied Health Services. 2nd ed. (Illus.). 1977. Vol. 1. pap. text ed. 9.50 (ISBN 0-7216-9603-1); Vol. 2. 9.50 (ISBN 0-7216-9604-X); single vol. 14.00 (ISBN 0-7216-9606-6). Saunders.

Woolley, F. R., et al. Problem-Oriented Nursing. LC 74-79417. 1974. text ed. 11.95 (ISBN 0-8261-1721-X); pap. text ed. 6.25 (ISBN 0-8261-1720-1). Springer Pub.

Wu, Ruth. Behavior & Illness. (Scientific Foundations of Nursing Practice Ser.). (Illus.). 224p. 1973. pap. 12.95 ref. ed. (ISBN 0-13-074138-8). P-H.

Yedidia, Michael. Delivering Primary Health Care: Nurse Practitioners at Work. LC 81-1946. 160p. 1981. 19.95 (ISBN 0-86569-075-8). Auburn Hse.

Young, Linda L. Basic Skills for Nursing Assistants. 128p. 1980. wire coil & shrink wrap 9.95 (ISBN 0-8403-2219-4). Kendall-Hunt.

Yura, Helen. Nursing Leadership: Theory & Process. 2nd ed. (Illus.). 208p. 1980. pap. 11.95 (ISBN 0-8385-7028-3). ACC.

Yura, Helen & Walsh, Mary B. The Nursing Process: Assessing, Planning, Implementing, Evaluating. 3rd ed. (Illus.). 266p. 1978. pap. 12.50 (ISBN 0-8385-7032-1). ACC.

Yura, Helen & Walsh, Mary B., eds. Human Needs & the Nursing Process. LC 78-16148. (Illus.). 330p. 1978. pap. 12.50 (ISBN 0-8385-3941-6). ACC.

Zander, Karen S. Primary Nursing: Development & Management. LC 79-28837. 384p. 1980. text ed. 25.95 (ISBN 0-89443-170-6). Aspen Systems.

Zander, Karen S. & Bower, Kathleen A., eds. Practical Manual for Patient-Teaching. LC 78-7039. 1978. pap. text ed. 15.95 (ISBN 0-8016-5678-8). Mosby.

Zielstorff, Rita. Computers in Nursing. LC 80-80813. (Nursing Dimensions Administration Ser.: Vol. I, No. 3). 236p. 1980. pap. text ed. 10.95 (ISBN 0-913654-66-3). Nursing Res.

Ziff, Dolores & Filoromo, Tina. Nurse Recruitment: Strategies for Success. LC 80-14829. 208p. 1980. text ed. 25.00 (ISBN 0-89443-164-1). Aspen Systems.

NURSES AND NURSING–ADMINISTRATION

see Nursing Service Administration

NURSES AND NURSING–BIBLIOGRAPHY

American Journal of Nursing: Five Year Cumulative Indexes. 1971. 1966-1970 6.00 (ISBN 0-937126-92-6); 1951-1955 3.90 (ISBN 0-937126-95-0). Am Journal Nurse.

Annotated Bibliography of Teaching-Learning Materials for Schools of Nursing & Midwifery. (Offset Pub.: No. 19). (Also avail. in French & Spanish). 1975. pap. 20.40 (ISBN 92-4-052005-8). World Health.

Bullough, Bonnie, et al. Nursing: A Historical Bibliography. LC 80-836. 500p. 1981. lib. bdg. 50.00 (ISBN 0-8240-9511-1). Garland Pub.

Fanin, Ferne, ed. Cumulative Index to Nursing & Allied Health Literature, Vol. 24. LC 78-643434. 1979. 50.00 (ISBN 0-910478-15-5). Glendale Advent Med.

Grandbois, Mildred, ed. Cumulative Index to Nursing & Allied Health Literature, Vol. 22. LC 78-643434. 1977. 50.00 (ISBN 0-910478-13-9). Glendale Advent Med.

--Cumulative Index to Nursing Literature, Vol. 20. 1975. 40.00 (ISBN 0-686-74115-3). Glendale Advent Med.

--Cumulative Index to Nursing Literature, Vol. 21. 1976. 40.00 (ISBN 0-910478-12-0). Glendale Advent Med.

Grandbois, Mildred, et al, eds. Cumulative Index to Nursing Literature. Incl. Vols. 1-5, 5 vols. in 1. 1956-1960; Vols. 6-8, 3 vols. in 1. 1961-1963. 35.00 (ISBN 0-910478-01-5); Vols. 9-11, 3 vols. in 1. 1964-1966. 35.00 (ISBN 0-910478-02-3); Vols. 12-13, 2 vols. in 1. 1967-1968. 35.00 (ISBN 0-910478-03-1); Vol. 14. 1969. 40.00 (ISBN 0-910478-04-X); Vol. 15. 1970. 40.00 (ISBN 0-910478-06-6); Vol. 16. 1971. 40.00 (ISBN 0-910478-07-4); Vol. 17. 1972. 40.00 (ISBN 0-910478-08-2); Vol. 18. 1973. 40.00 (ISBN 0-910478-09-0); Vol. 19. 1974. 40.00 (ISBN 0-910478-10-4). LC 62-147. Glendale Advent Med.

Inman, Virginia, ed. Cumulative Index to Nursing & Allied Health Literature, Vol. 23. LC 78-643434. 1978. 50.00 (ISBN 0-910478-14-7). Glendale Advent Med.

Lockwood, DeLauna, ed. Cumulative Index to Nursing & Allied Health Literature, Vol. 25. 1980. 60.00 (ISBN 0-910478-16-3). Glendale Advent Med.

Strauch, K. P. & Brundage, D. J. Guide to Library Resources for Nursing. 509p. 1980. pap. 13.75 (ISBN 0-8385-3528-3). ACC.

Thompson, A. M. Bibliography of Nursing Literature: Eighteen Fifty-Nine to Nineteen Sixty. 1969. 27.95x (ISBN 0-85365-470-0, Pub. by Lib Assn England). Oryx Pr.

Thompson, A. M., ed. Bibliography of Nursing Literature: Nineteen Sixty-One to Nineteen Seventy. 1974. lib. bdg. 43.50x (ISBN 0-85365-316-X, Pub. by Lib Assn England). Oryx Pr.

NURSES AND NURSING–DICTIONARIES

Albanese, Joseph. The Nurses' Drug Reference. 2nd ed. (Illus.). 1184p. 1981. text ed. 24.95 (ISBN 0-07-000767-5, HP); pap. text ed. 17.95 (ISBN 0-07-000768-3, HP). McGraw.

Armstrong, M., et al. McGraw-Hill Nursing Dictionary. 1979. thumb-indexed 15.95 (ISBN 0-07-045019-6, HP). McGraw.

Deutsche Schwestergemeinschaft. Sprachfuehrer Fuer die Krankenpflege. 253p. (Ger., Eng., Fr. & Span., Elementary Guide of Nursing). 1968. pap. 7.95 (ISBN 3-8047-0338-0, M-7627, Pub. by Wissenschaftliche Vlg.). French & Eur.

Duncan, Helen A. Duncan's Dictionary for Nurses. LC 74-121974. (Illus.). 1971. pap. text ed. 6.25 (ISBN 0-8261-1121-1). Springer Pub.

Fitch, Grace E. & Dubiny, Mary J., eds. Macmillan Dictionary for the Practical & Vocational Nurse. 1966. 8.95 (ISBN 0-02-338160-4, 33816). Macmillan.

Garb, Solomon, et al. Abbreviations & Acronyms in Medicine & Nursing. LC 75-29483. 1976. text ed. 9.95 (ISBN 0-8261-2001-6); pap. text ed. 4.95 (ISBN 0-8261-2000-8). Springer Pub.

Miller, Benjamin F. & Keane, Claire B. Encyclopedia & Dictionary of Medicine & Nursing. LC 73-103569. (Illus.). 1972. text ed. 18.95 (ISBN 0-7216-6357-5); student ed. 15.95 (ISBN 0-7216-6358-3). Saunders.

Pearce, Evelyn, et al. Medical & Nursing Dictionary & Encyclopaedia. new ed. 545p. 1975. text ed. 15.95 (ISBN 0-571-04843-9, Pub. by Faber & Faber). Merrimack Bk Serv.

NURSES AND NURSING–EXAMINATIONS, QUESTIONS, ETC.

Allen, Hattie L. & Curlin, Vashti. Barron's How to Prepare for the Practical Nurse Licensing Examination. LC 78-27122. 1979. pap. 6.95 (ISBN 0-8120-0603-8). Barron.

Arco Editorial Board. Nurse. 4th ed. LC 73-94658. (Orig.). 1970. pap. 6.00 (ISBN 0-668-00143-7). Arco.

Bakutis, Alice R. Self-Assessment of Current Knowledge for the Nurse Anesthetist. 2nd ed. 1976. spiral bdg. 9.50 (ISBN 0-87488-715-1). Med Exam.

Carter, L. B., et al. Arco's Comprehensive State Board Examination Review for Nurses. LC 79-28537. 320p. (Orig.). 1980. pap. 8.95 (ISBN 0-668-04925-1, 4925-1). Arco.

Carter, Linda B. Fundamentals of Nursing Review. LC 79-1088. (Arco Nursing Review Ser.). 1979. pap. text ed. 6.00 (ISBN 0-668-04512-4). Arco.

Catlin, Alberta P. & Bachand, Shirley. Practical Nursing: PreTest Self-Assessment & Review. LC 78-70622. (Nursing: Pretest Self-Assessment & Review Ser.). (Illus.). 1979. pap. 8.95 (ISBN 0-07-051571-9). McGraw-Pretest.

Chuan, Helen, ed. Medical-Surgical Nursing: Pretest Self-Assessment & Review. Allman, Margaret. LC 78-50598. (PreTest Self-Assessment & Review). (Illus.). 1978. pap. 7.50 (ISBN 0-07-051567-0). McGraw-Pretest.

Feinstein, Maurice B. & Levine, Harriet. Pharmacology. 3rd ed. (Nursing Examination Review Bk.: Vol. 6). 1974. spiral bdg. 6.00 (ISBN 0-87488-506-X). Med Exam.

Gibson, John. Mental Nursing Examination Questions & Answers. 4th ed. 224p. 1978. pap. 6.95 (ISBN 0-571-04967-2, Pub. by Faber & Faber). Merrimack Bk Serv.

Gillies, Dee Ann & Alyn, Irene B. Saunders Tests for Self-Evaluation of Nursing Competence. 3rd ed. LC 77-77100. 1978. 11.95 (ISBN 0-7216-4132-6). Saunders.

Glynn, Maryanne C. Student Guide to the Registered Nurse (R.N.) Examination. Tarlow, David M., ed. (Illus.). 1981. pap. 9.00 (ISBN 0-931572-03-7). Datar Pub.

Green, Judith. Review of Maternal Child Nursing. 1978. pap. text ed. 6.95 (ISBN 0-07-024302-6, HP). McGraw.

Grippando, Gloria M. Nursing Perspectives & Issues. LC 76-14090. 1977. pap. text ed. 11.60 (ISBN 0-8273-1314-4); instructor's guide 2.75 (ISBN 0-8273-1315-2). Delmar.

Hazzard, Mary E. Medical Surgical Nursing Review. 2nd ed. LC 79-1288. (Arco Nursing Review Ser.). 224p. 1980. pap. text ed. 6.00 (ISBN 0-668-04823-9). Arco.

Holmes, Marguerite C., et al, eds. Basic Sciences. 3rd ed. (Nursing Examination Review Book Ser.: Vol. 4). 1973. spiral bdg. 5.00 (ISBN 0-87488-504-3). Med Exam.

Horemis, George. Nursing Comprehensive Examination Review. 2nd ed. LC 76-14832. 1976. pap. 6.00 (ISBN 0-668-02499-2). Arco.

Horemis, George & Matamors, Clemencia. Medical-Surgical Nursing Examination Review. LC 79-165611. (Orig.). 1973. pap. 6.00 (ISBN 0-668-02511-5). Arco.

Horemis, George & Matomors, Clemencia. Nursing Exam Review in Basic Sciences. LC 72-96307. 200p. (Orig.). 1973. pap. 4.00 (ISBN 0-668-02946-3). Arco.

Kaminsky, Daniel, et al. Microbiology. 3rd ed. (Nursing Examination Review Book: Vol. 7). 1974. spiral bdg. 6.00 (ISBN 0-87488-507-8). Med Exam.

Koch, Harry W. Nursing & Other Hospital Work. 1975. 5.00 (ISBN 0-913164-55-0). Ken-Bks.

Kurtz, Rosemary B. & Miller, Nancy F. Clinical Workbook in Medical-Surgical Nursing. (Illus.). 1978. pap. text ed. 9.95 (ISBN 0-7216-5580-7). Saunders.

Laliberte, Elizabeth & Daisy, Carol A., eds. Nursing Care of Children: PreTest Self-Assessment & Review. LC 78-50595. (PreTest Self-Assessment & Review Ser.). (Illus.). 1978. pap. 7.50 (ISBN 0-07-051568-9). McGraw-Pretest.

Lewis, Luverne W. Lippincott's State Board Examination Review for Nurses. LC 77-27368. 1978. pap. text ed. 15.75 (ISBN 0-397-54214-3, JBL-Med-Nursing). Har-Row.

--Lippincott's State Board Examination Review for Practical-Vocational Nurses. (Illus.). 465p. 1981. pap. text ed. 10.75 (ISBN 0-397-54351-4, JBL-Med-Nursing). Har-Row.

McMorrow, Mary E. & Malarkey, Louise M. Prentice-Hall R. N. Review for State Board Examinations. (Illus.). 352p. 1980. pap. text ed. 13.95 (ISBN 0-13-696559-8). P-H.

Magnus, Margaret. Fundamentals of Nursing. (Nursing Examination Review Books: Vol. 11). 1972. pap. 6.00 (ISBN 0-87488-511-6). Med Exam.

National Council of State Boards of Nursing, et al. The State Board Test Pool Examination for Registered Nurse Licensure. LC 81-6107. 150p. (Orig.). 1981. pap. 8.95 (ISBN 0-914091-02-6). Chicago Review.

Practical Nursing School Admission Test. pap. 4.95 (ISBN 0-8092-9392-7). Contemp Bks.

Preparation for Registered & Graduate Nursing Schools Entrance Examinations. 5.95 (ISBN 0-8092-9391-9). Contemp Bks.

Pretest Series, ed. PreTest for Students Preparing for the State Board Examinations for Practical Nurse Licensure. 2nd ed. LC 78-56568. 1979. pap. 14.95 (ISBN 0-07-079132-5). McGraw-Pretest.

--PreTest for Students Preparing for the State Board Examinations for Registered Nurse Licensure. 4th ed. LC 78-51705. 1979. pap. 14.95 (ISBN 0-07-079130-9). McGraw-Pretest.

Readey, Helen & Readey, William. Mathematical Concepts for Nursing: A Workbook. LC 79-20751. 1980. 7.95 (ISBN 0-201-06166-X). A-W.

Riddle, Janet T. Objective Tests for Nurses, Book 1. (Objective Tests for Nurses Ser.). (Illus.). 1980. pap. text ed. 4.95 (ISBN 0-443-01738-7). Churchill.

Riddle, Janet T. & Dinner, Joan. Objective Tests for Nurses, Book 2. (Objective Tests for Nurses Ser.). (Illus.). 112p. 1981. pap. text ed. 6.95 (ISBN 0-443-01740-9). Churchill.

Rozendal, Nancy & Fallon, Patricia. Psychiatric Nursing: PreTest Self-Assessment & Review. LC 78-50596. (Nursing: Pretest Self-Assessment & Review Ser.). 1978. pap. 7.50 (ISBN 0-07-051569-7). McGraw-Pretest.

Rudman, Jack. Adult Nursing. (ACT Proficiency Examination Program: PEP-39). (Cloth bdg. avail. on request). pap. 9.95 (ISBN 0-8373-5539-7). Natl Learning.

--Assistant Director of Nursing Care. (Career Examination Ser.: C-2858). (Cloth bdg. avail. on request). 1980. pap. 14.00 (ISBN 0-8373-2858-6). Natl Learning.

--Clinical Nurse. (Career Examination Ser.: C-947). (Cloth bdg. avail. on request). pap. 8.00 (ISBN 0-8373-0947-6). Natl Learning.

--Commonalities in Nursing Care - Area 1. (Regents External Degree Ser.: REDP-17). (Cloth bdg. avail. on request). pap. 9.95 (ISBN 0-8373-5617-2). Natl Learning.

--Commonalities in Nursing Care - Area 2. (Regents External Degree Ser.: REDP-18). (Cloth bdg. avail. on request). pap. 9.95 (ISBN 0-8373-5618-0). Natl Learning.

--Commonalities in Nursing Care: Area 1. (ACT Proficiency Examination Program: PEP-41). (Cloth bdg. avail. on request). pap. 9.95 (ISBN 0-8373-5541-9). Natl Learning.

--Commonalities in Nursing Care: Area 2. (ACT Proficiency Examination Program: PEP-42). (Cloth bdg. avail. on request). pap. 9.95 (ISBN 0-8373-5542-7). Natl Learning.

--Coordinator of Nursing Education. (Career Examination Ser.: C-1843). (Cloth bdg. avail on request). pap. 10.00 (ISBN 0-8373-1843-2). Natl Learning.

--Differences in Nursing Care: Area 1. (Regents External Degree Ser.: REDP-21). (Cloth bdg. avail. on request). pap. 9.95 (ISBN 0-8373-5621-0). Natl Learning.

--Differences in Nursing Care: Area 1. (ACT Proficiency Examination Program: PEP-43). (Cloth bdg. avail. on request). pap. 9.95 (ISBN 0-8373-5543-5). Natl Learning.

--Differences in Nursing Care: Area 2. (Regents External Degree Ser.: REDP-22). (Cloth bdg. avail. on request). pap. 9.95 (ISBN 0-8373-5622-9). Natl Learning.

--Differences in Nursing Care: Area 2. (ACT Proficiency Examination Program: PEP-44). (Cloth bdg. avail. on request). pap. 9.95 (ISBN 0-8373-5544-3). Natl Learning.

--Differences in Nursing Care: Area 3. (Regents External Degree Ser.: REDP-23). (Cloth bdg. avail. on request). pap. 9.95 (ISBN 0-8373-5623-7). Natl Learning.

--Differences in Nursing Care: Area 3. (ACT Proficiency Examination Program: PEP-45). (Cloth bdg. avail. on request). 9.95 (ISBN 0-8373-5545-1). Natl Learning.

--Director of Nursing Care. (Career Examination Ser.: C-2859). (Cloth bdg. avail. on request). 1980. pap. 14.00 (ISBN 0-8373-2859-4). Natl Learning.

--Fundamentals of Nursing. (College Proficiency Examination Ser.: CPEP-12). (Cloth bdg. avail. on request). pap. 9.95 (ISBN 0-8373-5536-2) (ISBN 0-8373-5412-9). Natl Learning.

--Fundamentals of Nursing. (College Level Examination Ser.: CLEP-30). (Cloth bdg. avail. on request). pap. 9.95 (ISBN 0-8373-5330-0). Natl Learning.

--Head Nurse. (Career Examination Ser.: C-321). (Cloth bdg. avail. on request). pap. 10.00 (ISBN 0-8373-0321-4). Natl Learning.

--Health Service Nurse. (Career Examination Ser.: C-350). (Cloth bdg. avail. on request). pap. 8.00 (ISBN 0-8373-0350-8). Natl Learning.

--Maternal & Child Nursing: Associate Degree. (ACT Proficiency Examination Program: PEP-37). (Cloth bdg. avail. on request). pap. 9.95 (ISBN 0-8373-5537-0). Natl Learning.

--Maternal & Child Nursing: Baccalaureate Degree. (ACT Proficiency Examination Program: PEP-38). (Cloth bdg. avail. on request). pap. 9.95 (ISBN 0-8373-5538-9). Natl Learning.

--Medical Surgical Nursing. (College Proficiency Examination Ser.: CPEP-24). 14.95 (ISBN 0-8373-5474-9); pap. 9.95 (ISBN 0-8373-5424-2). Natl Learning.

--Nurse. (Career Examination Ser.: C-532). (Cloth bdg. avail. on request). pap. 8.00 (ISBN 0-8373-0532-2). Natl Learning.

--Nurse GS4-GS7. (Career Examination Ser.: C-533). (Cloth bdg. avail. on request). pap. 8.00 (ISBN 0-8373-0533-0). Natl Learning.

--Nurse Instructor. (Career Examination Ser.: C-2108). (Cloth bdg. avail. on request). 1977. pap. 10.00 (ISBN 0-8373-2108-5). Natl Learning.

--Nursing Chairman (Questions Only) (Teachers License Examination Ser.: CH-31). (Cloth bdg. avail. on request). pap. 12.00 (ISBN 0-8373-8181-9). Natl Learning.

--Nursing Health Care. (Regents External Degree Ser.: REDP-19). (Cloth bdg. avail. on request). pap. 9.95 (ISBN 0-8373-5619-9). Natl Learning.

--Nursing Health Care. (ACT Proficiency Examination Program: PEP-46). (Cloth bdg. avail. on request). pap. 9.95 (ISBN 0-8373-5546-X). Natl Learning.

--Nursing: Senior H.S. (Teachers License Examination Ser.: T-44). (Cloth bdg. avail. on request). pap. 10.00 (ISBN 0-8373-8044-8). Natl Learning.

--Occupational Strategy (Nursing) (Regents External Degree Ser.: REDP-20). (Cloth bdg. avail. on request). pap. 9.95 (ISBN 0-8373-5620-2). Natl Learning.

--Occupational Strategy, Nursing. (ACT Proficiency Examination Program: PEP-47). (Cloth bdg. avail. on request). pap. 9.95 (ISBN 0-8373-5597-4). Natl Learning.

--Practical Nurse. (Admission Test Ser.: ATS-20). 300p. (Cloth bdg. avail. on request). pap. 9.95 (ISBN 0-8373-5020-4). Natl Learning.

--Professional Nurse. (Career Examination Ser.: C-624). (Cloth bdg. avail. on request). 14.00 (ISBN 0-8373-0624-8). Natl Learning.

--Registered & Graduate Nurses. (Admission Test Ser.: ATS-19). 300p. (Cloth bdg. avail. on request). pap. 9.95 (ISBN 0-8373-5019-0). Natl Learning.

--Registered Professional Nurse. (Career Examination Ser.: C-671). (Cloth bdg. avail. on request). pap. 10.00 (ISBN 0-8373-0671-X). Natl Learning.

--Staff Nurse. (Career Examination Ser.: C-756). (Cloth bdg. avail. on request). pap. 8.00 (ISBN 0-8373-0756-2). Natl Learning.

--State Nursing Boards for Practical Nurse. (Admission Test Ser.: ATS-46). (Cloth bdg. avail. on request). pap. 9.95 (ISBN 0-8373-5046-8). Natl Learning.

--State Nursing Boards for Registered Nurse. (Admission Test Ser.: ATS-45). (Cloth bdg. avail. on request). pap. 9.95 (ISBN 0-8373-5045-X). Natl Learning.

--Supervising Nurse. (Career Examination Ser.: C-1883). (Cloth bdg. avail. on request). pap. 10.00 (ISBN 0-8373-1883-1). Natl Learning.

--Supervising Public Health Nurse. (Career Examination Ser.: C-1748). (Cloth bdg. avail. on request). 1977. pap. 10.00 (ISBN 0-8373-1748-7). Natl Learning.

Scott, Lou. Programmed Instruction & Review for Practical & Vocational Nurses, 2 vols. Incl. Vol. 1. Foundations & Fundamentals of Nursing. 352p (40827); Vol. 2. Clinical & Community Nursing. 320p (40828). (Refs., review questions, related readings). 1968. text ed. 7.95x ea. Macmillan.

Scott, Lou P. Self Instruction & Review in Nursing. 2nd ed. (Illus.). 1980. pap. text ed. 9.95 ea. Vol. III (ISBN 0-02-408320-8). Vol. IV (ISBN 0-02-408370-4). Macmillan.

Speelman, Arlene. Examination Review for Practical Nurses. 3rd rev. ed. LC 76-14540. 384p. 1976. pap. text ed. 7.95 (ISBN 0-399-40052-4). Putnam.

Steele, Bonnie G. Self-Assessment of Current Knowledge in General Surgical Nursing. 1978. spiral bdg. 9.50 (ISBN 0-87488-290-7). Med Exam.

Stoltzfus, Doris. Self-Assessment of Current Knowledge in Mental Health Nursing. 1979. spiral bdg. 9.50 (ISBN 0-87488-264-8). Med Exam.

Sutton, et al. Barron's How to Prepare for the Registered Nurse Licensing Examination. 1982. pap. 4.95 (ISBN 0-8120-2301-3). Barron.

Turner, Phyllis S. Self-Assessment of Current Knowledge in Intensive Care Nursing. 1980. pap. 9.75 (ISBN 0-87488-227-3). Med Exam.

Watson, Joellen & Gorvine, Beverly, eds. Maternal-Newborn Nursing: Pretest Self-Assessment & Review. LC 78-50597. (Nursing: Pretest Self-Assessment & Review Ser.). 1978. pap. 7.50 (ISBN 0-07-051570-0). McGraw-Pretest.

NURSES AND NURSING–HISTORY

Breckinridge, Mary. Wide Neighborhoods: A Story of the Frontier Nursing Service. LC 81-50181. (Illus.). 400p. 1981. 19.50 (ISBN 0-8131-1453-5); pap. 8.00 (ISBN 0-8131-0149-2). U Pr of Ky.

Bullough, Bonnie, et al. Nursing: A Historical Bibliography. LC 80-836. 500p. 1981. lib. bdg. 50.00 (ISBN 0-8240-9511-1). Garland Pub.

Bullough, Vern & Bullough, Bonnie. The Care of the Sick: The Emergence of Modern Nursing. LC 78-14238. 1978. 17.50 (ISBN 0-88202-183-4). N Watson.

Butterworth, Vida. The Girls in White. LC 78-10862. 1979. pap. 6.25 (ISBN 0-8309-0230-9). Herald Hse.

Davies, Celia, ed. Rewriting Nursing History. 226p. 1980. 23.50x (ISBN 0-389-20153-7). B&N.

Deloughery, Grace L. History & Trends of Professional Nursing. 8th ed. LC 77-386. (Illus.). 1977. pap. 14.95 (ISBN 0-8016-1974-2). Mosby.

Dolan, Josephine A. Nursing in Society: A Historical Perspective. 14th ed. LC 77-88313. (Illus.). 380p. 1978. 22.00 (ISBN 0-7216-3133-9). Saunders.

Fitzpatrick, M. Louise, ed. Historical Studies in Nursing. LC 78-12192. 1978. text ed. 9.25x (ISBN 0-8077-2527-7). Tchrs Coll.

Kalisch, Philip A. & Kalisch, Beatrice J. The Advance of American Nursing. 1978. 18.95 (ISBN 0-316-48227-7); text ed. 13.95 (ISBN 0-316-48226-9). Little.

Kyle, Mabel R. White Caps: Nurse's Training Fifty Years Ago. 1978. 8.50 (ISBN 0-682-48974-3). Exposition.

Levine, Harriet & Minno, Frances P., eds. History & Law of Nursing. (Nursing Examination Review Books: Vol. 10). 1971. spiral bdg. 6.00 (ISBN 0-87488-510-8). Med Exam.

Mottus, Jane E. New York Nightingales: The Emergence of the Nursing Profession at Bellevue & New York Hospital, 1850-1920. Berkhofer, Robert, ed. (Studies in American History & Culture: No. 26). 1981. 31.95 (ISBN 0-8357-1167-6, Pub. by UMI Res Pr). Univ Microfilms.

Nicholson, G. W. Canada's Nursing Sisters. 1975. 12.95 (ISBN 0-88866-567-9). Samuel Stevens.

NURSES AND NURSING–JUVENILE LITERATURE

see also names of nurses, e.g. Nightingale, Florence; Richards, Linda Ann Judson

Bermosk, Loretta S. & Mordan, Mary J. Interviewing in Nursing. (Illus.). 208p. 1973. pap. text ed. 6.95 (ISBN 0-02-308550-9, 30855). Macmillan.

Greene, Carla. Doctors & Nurses: What Do They Do. LC 62-13313. (I Can Read Books). (Illus.). (gr. k-3). 1963. PLB 7.89 (ISBN 0-06-022076-7, HarpJ). Har-Row.

Tengbom, Mildred. No Greater Love. (Greatness with Faith Ser.). (Illus.). (gr. 5-8). 1978. 4.95 (ISBN 0-570-07878-4, 39-1203); pap. 2.95 (ISBN 0-570-07883-0, 39-1213). Concordia.

Witty, Margot. A Day in the Life of an Emergency Room Nurse. LC 78-68842. (Illus.). 32p. (gr. 4-8). 1981. PLB 6.89 (ISBN 0-89375-226-6); pap. 2.50 (ISBN 0-89375-230-4). Troll Assocs.

NURSES AND NURSING–LEGAL STATUS, LAWS, ETC.

Annas, George J. The Rights of Doctors, Nurses, & Allied Health Professionals. 416p. 1981. pap. 3.95 (ISBN 0-380-77859-9, 77859, Discus). Avon.

Bullough, Bonnie. The Law & the Expanding Nursing Role. 2nd ed. (Illus.). 238p. 1980. pap. 13.50 (ISBN 0-8385-5623-X). ACC.

Cazalas, Mary W. Nursing & the Law. 3rd ed. LC 78-24253. 294p. 1978. text ed. 17.50 (ISBN 0-89443-075-0). Aspen Systems.

Cowart, Marie & Allen, Rodney, eds. Changing Conceptions of Health Care: Public Policy & Ethical Issues for Nurses. LC 81-51721. 1981. pap. write for info. (ISBN 0-913590-81-9). C B Slack.

Creighton, Helen. Law Every Nurse Should Know. 4th ed. 480p. 1981. text ed. 14.95 (ISBN 0-7216-2573-8). Saunders.

--Law Every Nurse Should Know. 3rd ed. LC 74-31835. 385p. 1975. text ed. 13.00 (ISBN 0-7216-2752-8). Saunders.

Fenner, Kathleen. Ethics & Law in Nursing. 300p. (Orig.). 1980. pap. text ed. 10.95 (ISBN 0-442-25643-4). Van Nos Reinhold.

Lagerquist, S. L., et al. Addison-Wesley's Nursing Examination Review. LC 76-62905. 1977. 14.95 (ISBN 0-201-04141-3, Med-Nurse). A-W.

Lesnik, Milton & Anderson, Bernice E. Nursing Practice & the Law. LC 75-45453. 400p. 1976. Repr. of 1962 ed. lib. bdg. 25.00x (ISBN 0-8371-8729-X, LENP). Greenwood.

Levine, Harriet & Minno, Frances P., eds. History & Law of Nursing. (Nursing Examination Review Books: Vol. 10). 1971. spiral bdg. 6.00 (ISBN 0-87488-510-8). Med Exam.

Murchison, Irene, et al. Legal Accountability in the Nursing Process. LC 77-18063. 1978. pap. text ed. 10.50 (ISBN 0-8016-3603-5). Mosby.
Murchison, Irene A. & Nichols, Thomas S. Legal Foundations of Nursing Practice. 1970. text ed. 18.95 (ISBN 0-02-385130-9). Macmillan.
Perspectives on the Code for Nurses. 1978. pap. 2.00 (ISBN 0-686-09599-5). ANA.
Rothman, Daniel A. & Rothman, Nancy L. The Professional Nurse & the Law. 1977. 8.95 (ISBN 0-316-75768-3). Little.
Willig, S. Nurse's Guide to the Law. 1970. 13.95 (ISBN 0-07-070580-1, HP). McGraw.
Young, A. Legal Problems in Nursing Practice. 1981. text ed. 23.50 (ISBN 0-06-318181-9, Pub. by Har-Row Ltd England); pap. text ed. 15.50 (ISBN 0-06-318182-7). Har-Row.

NURSES AND NURSING–PROGRAMMED INSTRUCTION

Birmingham, Jacqueline. The Problem-Oriented Record: A Self-Learning Module. (Illus.). 1978. pap. text ed. 8.50 (ISBN 0-07-005385-5, HP). McGraw.
Ferster, Marilyn G. Arithmetic for Nurses-Programmed. 2nd ed. LC 73-75647. (Illus.). 1973. pap. text ed. 5.50 (ISBN 0-8261-0482-7). Springer Pub.
Forrest, Jane & Watson, Margaret. Practical Nursing & Anatomy for Pupil Nurses. 4th ed. (Illus.). 264p. 1981. pap. text ed. 16.95x (ISBN 0-7131-4392-4). Intl Ideas.
Franck, Phyllis & Price, Marjorie. Nursing Management: A Programmed Text. 2nd ed. 1980. pap. text ed. 10.95 (ISBN 0-8261-1663-9). Springer Pub.
Lipsey, Sally I. Mathematics for Nursing Science: A Programmed Text. 2nd ed. LC 76-44843. 1977. text ed. 10.95 (ISBN 0-471-01798-1, Pub. by Wiley-Medical). Wiley.
McInnes, Betty. Controlling the Spread of Infection: A Programmed Presentation. 2nd ed. LC 76-48945. (Illus.). 1977. pap. text ed. 8.00 (ISBN 0-8016-3334-6). Mosby.
Massachussetts General Hospital. Dept. of Nursing Staff Education Manual. Stetler, Cheryl B., et al, eds. 1981. text ed. 34.95 (ISBN 0-8359-1281-7). Reston.
Mundinger, Mary O. Autonomy in Nursing. LC 79-25630. (Illus.). 222p. 1980. text ed. 22.00 (ISBN 0-89443-171-4). Aspen Systems.
Price, Marjorie, et al. Nursing Management: A Programmed Text. LC 74-13978. (Illus.). 169p. 1974. pap. text ed. 7.50 (ISBN 0-8261-1660-4). Springer Pub.
Scott, Lou. Programmed Instruction & Review for Practical & Vocational Nurses, 2 vols. Incl. Vol. 1. Foundations & Fundamentals of Nursing. 352p (40827); Vol. 2. Clinical & Community Nursing. 320p (40828). (Refs., review questions, related readings). 1968. text ed. 7.95x ea. Macmillan.
Seedor, Marie. A Nursing Guide to Oxygen Therapy. 3rd ed. LC 79-23846. 1980. pap. text ed. 8.50x (ISBN 0-8077-2578-1). Tchrs Coll.
Seedor, Marie M. Body Mechanics & Patient Positioning: A Programmed Unit of Study for Nurses. LC 73-85804. 1977. pap. 8.75x (ISBN 0-8077-2524-2). Tchrs Coll.
--Introduction to Asepsis. 3rd ed. LC 79-514. 1979. pap. text ed. 8.95x (ISBN 0-8077-2555-2). Tchrs Coll.
Tinker, Jack & Porter, Susan W. A Course in Intensive Therapy Nursing. (Illus.). 304p. 1981. pap. text ed. 27.50x (ISBN 0-7131-4347-9). Intl Ideas.
Vitale, Barbara A., et al. A Problem Solving Approach to Nursing Care Plans: A Program. 2nd ed. LC 77-14222. (Illus.). 1978. pap. text ed. 9.50 (ISBN 0-8016-5243-X). Mosby.

NURSES AND NURSING–PSYCHOLOGICAL ASPECTS

Auger, J. Behavioral Systems & Nursing. (Illus.). 224p. 1976. ref. ed. 13.95x (ISBN 0-13-074484-0). P-H.
Becker, Betty G. & Fendler, Dolores T. Vocational & Personal Adjustments in Practical Nursing. 4th ed. (Illus.). 192p. 1982. pap. text ed. 9.50 (ISBN 0-8016-0566-0). Mosby.
Berni, Rosemarian & Fordyce, Wilbert E. Behavior Modification & the Nursing Process. 2nd ed. LC 76-57775. (Illus.). 1977. pap. text ed. 9.00 (ISBN 0-8016-0656-X). Mosby.
Bower, Fay L., ed. Distortions in Body Image in Illness & Disability. LC 77-4429. (Nursing Concept Modules Ser.). 1977. pap. 12.50 (ISBN 0-471-02169-5, Pub. by Wiley Med). Wiley.
Carlson, Carolyn E. & Blackwell, Betty. Behavioral Concepts & Nursing Intervention. 2nd ed. LC 78-8761. 1978. pap. text ed. 10.50x (ISBN 0-397-54217-8, JBL-Med-Nursing). Har-Row.
Carroll, Mary A. & Humphrey, Richard A. Moral Problems in Nursing: Case Studies. 1979. pap. text ed. 9.50 (ISBN 0-8191-0705-0). U Pr of Amer.
Earle, Ann M., et al, eds. The Nurse As Caregiver for the Terminal Patient & His Family. LC 76-14441. 252p. 1976. 20.00x (ISBN 0-231-04020-2). Columbia U Pr.
Gillis, Lynn. Human Behavior in Illness: Psychology & Interpersonal Relationships. 3rd ed. 224p. 1980. pap. 9.95 (ISBN 0-571-18025-6, Pub. by Faber & Faber). Merrimack Bk Serv.
Glaser, Barney G. & Strauss, Anselm L. Time for Dying. LC 67-17601. 1968. 19.95x (ISBN 0-202-30027-7). Aldine Pub.
Helping Cancer Patients-Effectively. LC 78-26288. (Nursing Skillbooks Ser.). (Illus.). 1977. text ed. 10.95 (ISBN 0-916730-06-9). InterMed Comm.
Johnson, Margaret A. Developing the Art of Understanding. 2nd ed. LC 72-184350. 1972. pap. text ed. 7.95 (ISBN 0-8261-0862-8). Springer Pub.
Kjervik, Diane K. & Martinson, Ida M., eds. Women in Stress: The Nursing Perspective. (Illus.). 352p. 1979. 12.95 (ISBN 0-8385-9829-3). ACC.
Kneisl, Carol R. & Ames, Sue Ann. Mental Health Concepts in Medical-Surgical Nursing: A Workbook. 2nd ed. LC 78-16371. (Illus.). 1979. pap. 9.50 (ISBN 0-8016-0161-4). Mosby.
Kramer, Marlene & Schmalenberg, Claudia. Path to Biculturalism. LC 77-7202. 315p. 1977. pap. text ed. 12.95 (ISBN 0-913654-30-2). Nursing Res.
Leininger, Madeline, ed. Transcultural Nursing, 1979. (Illus.). 742p. 1979. text ed. 32.50x (ISBN 0-89352-079-9). Masson Pub.
Long, Lynette & Prophit, Penny. Understanding Responding: A Communication Manual for Nurses. 1980. pap. text ed. 6.95 (ISBN 0-8185-0339-4). Brooks-Cole.
Longo, Diane C. & Williams, Reg A. Clinical Practice in Psychosocial Nursing: Assessment & Intervention. 382p. 1978. pap. 12.50 (ISBN 0-8385-1167-8). ACC.
McGhie, Andrew. Psychology As Applied to Nursing. 7th ed. (Livingstone Nursing Test Ser.). (Illus.). 309p. 1979. pap. text ed. 10.75 (ISBN 0-443-01827-8). Churchill.
Miller, Sally & Winstead-Fry, Patricia. Family Systems Theory & Nursing Practice. 176p. 1982. text ed. 13.95 (ISBN 0-686-76719-5); pap. text ed. 10.95 (ISBN 0-8359-1849-1). Reston.
Parent-Child Nursing: Psychosocial Aspects. 2nd ed. LC 77-26631. (Illus.). 1978. pap. text ed. 10.50 (ISBN 0-8016-3021-5). Mosby.
Parsons, Virgil & Sanford, Nancy. Interpersonal Interaction in Nursing. 1978. 8.95 (ISBN 0-201-05551-1, 05551, Med-Nurse). A-W.
Pesznecker, Betty L. & Hewitt, Helon E. Psychiatric Content in the Nursing Curriculum: A Study of Integration Process. LC 63-20537. 144p. 1963. pap. 6.50 (ISBN 0-295-73896-0). U of Wash Pr.
Quint, J. C. Nurse & the Dying Patient. 1973. 8.50 (ISBN 0-02-397230-0). Macmillan.
Reilly, Dorothy E. Behavioral Objectives-Evaluation in Nursing. 2nd ed. (Illus.). 200p. 1980. pap. text ed. 12.95 (ISBN 0-8385-0634-8). ACC.
Rudman, Jack. Behavioral Sciences for Nurses. (College Level Examination Ser.: CLEP-39). (Cloth bdg. avail. on request). 1977. pap. 9.95 (ISBN 0-8373-5389-0). Natl Learning.
Sanchez Hidalgo, Efrain & Sanchez Hidalgo, Lydia. La Psicologia De la Crianza. 4th, rev. ed. 5.00 (ISBN 0-8477-2902-8); pap. 3.75 (ISBN 0-8477-2903-6). U of PR Pr.
Schoenberg, Bernard, et al, eds. Teaching Psychosocial Aspects of Patient Care. LC 68-19757. 1968. 22.50x (ISBN 0-231-03162-9). Columbia U Pr.
Simon, Nathan, ed. The Psychological Aspects of Intensive Care Nursing. 295p. 1980. text ed. 17.95 (ISBN 0-87619-663-6). R J Brady.
Sugden, John. Psychology in Nursing. (Modern Practical Nursing Ser.: No. 16). 127p. 1975. pap. 9.95x (ISBN 0-433-31900-3). Intl Ideas.
Taves, Marvin J., et al. Role Conception & Vocational Success & Satisfaction: A Study of Student & Professional Nurses. (Illus.). 125p. 1963. pap. 3.00x (ISBN 0-87776-112-4, R-112). Ohio St U Admin Sci.

NURSES AND NURSING–RESEARCH

see Nursing Research

NURSES AND NURSING–STUDY AND TEACHING

see also Nursing Schools

Abdellah, Faye G. & Beland, Irene L. New Directions in Patient Centered Nursing: Guidelines for Systems of Service, Education & Research. 576p. 1973. 19.95 (ISBN 0-02-300050-3). Macmillan.
Annotated Bibliography of Teaching-Learning Materials for Schools of Nursing & Midwifery. (Offset Pub.: No. 19). (Also avail. in French & Spanish). 1975. pap. 20.40 (ISBN 92-4-052005-8). World Health.
Benner, Patricia & Benner, Richard V. The New Nurse's Work Entry: A Troubled Sponsorship. LC 78-68494. (Illus.). 160p. 1979. flexible 7.95 (ISBN 0-913292-09-5). Tiresias Pr.
Bevis, Em Olivia. Curriculum Building in Nursing: A Process. 2nd ed. LC 77-13045. (Illus.). 1978. pap. text ed. 12.95 (ISBN 0-8016-0668-3). Mosby.
Blomquist, Kathleen B., et al. Community Health Nursing Continuing Education Review. 1979. pap. 9.50 (ISBN 0-87488-401-2). Med Exam.
Brill, E. L. & Kilts, D. F. Foundations for Nursing. (Illus.). 813p. 1980. text ed. 24.95 (ISBN 0-8385-2687-X). ACC.
Caldwell, Eva W., et al. Mosby's Review of Practical Nursing. 8th ed. (Illus.). 464p. 1982. pap. text ed. 9.50 (ISBN 0-8016-3538-1). Mosby.
Carpenito, Lynda J. & Duespohl, T. Audean. A Guide for Effective Clinical Instruction. LC 81-82515. (Nursing Dimension Education Ser.). 200p. 1981. text ed. price not set (ISBN 0-913654-78-7). Nursing Res.
Carroll, Walter J., ed. Hospital-Health Care Training Media Profiles: 1974-1978, Vols. 1-7. 1979. 456.00x set (ISBN 0-88367-200-6). Olympic Media.
Chenevert, Melodie. Special Techniques in Assertiveness Training for Women in the Health Profession. LC 78-11635. (Illus.). 1978. pap. 9.50 (ISBN 0-8016-0971-2). Mosby.
Clark, Carolyn C. Classroom Skills for Nurse Educators. LC 78-4486. (Teaching of Nursing Ser.: Vol. 4). 1978. pap. 12.95 (ISBN 0-8261-2431-3). Springer Pub.
Coffey, Lou. Modules for Learning in Nursing: Life Cycle & Maternity Care. LC 75-5772. 196p. 1975. pap. text ed. 9.00 (ISBN 0-8036-1950-2). Davis Co.
Cooper, Signe S. Self-Directed Learning in Nursing. LC 80-80088. (Nursing Dimensions Education Ser.). 60p. 1980. pap. text ed. 11.95 (ISBN 0-913654-64-7). Nursing Res.
C.U.R.N. Project, Michigan Nurses Association. Structured Preoperative Teaching. (Using Research to Improve Clinical Practice: Vol. I). (Illus.). 165p. 1980. pap. 9.50 (ISBN 0-8089-1311-5). Grune.
Dempsey, Sheryll. Nursing Crosswords & Other Word Games. LC 73-17491. (Illus.). 100p. 1974. 5.95 (ISBN 0-8463-0600-X). Trainex Pr.
DeTornyay, Rheba. Strategies of Teaching Nursing. LC 73-134038. (Paperback Nursing Ser.). 1971. pap. 10.95 (ISBN 0-471-20395-5, Pub. by Wiley Medical). Wiley.
Fuhr, Sr. Mary T. Clinical Experience Record & Nursing Care Planning: A Guide for Student Nurses. 2nd ed. LC 77-22532. 1978. pap. text ed. 9.50 (ISBN 0-8016-1711-1). Mosby.
Guinee, Kathleen K. Teaching & Learning in Nursing. (Illus.). 1978. pap. text ed. 8.95 (ISBN 0-02-348360-1). Macmillan.
Hanton, E. Michael. The New Nurse. LC 74-79614. 122p. 1974. 10.00 (ISBN 0-914698-01-X); soft bdg. 6.95 (ISBN 0-914698-02-8). New Nurse.
Hastings, Glen E. & Murray, Louisa. The Primary Nurse Practitioner: A Multiple Track Curriculum. LC 76-5871. 1976. 7.95 (ISBN 0-916224-04-X). Banyan Bks.
Hinchliff, Susan M., ed. Teaching Clinical Nursing. LC 78-40434. (Illus.). 1979. pap. 15.75 (ISBN 0-443-01638-0). Churchill.
Innis, Mary Q., ed. Nursing Education in a Changing Society. LC 70-498725. 1970. pap. 4.00 (ISBN 0-8020-6112-5). U of Toronto Pr.
Keane, Claire B. Medical-Surgical Nursing for Practical Nurse: Study Guide & Workbook. LC 74-4573. 1974. pap. 9.95 (ISBN 0-7216-5331-6). Saunders.
Keenan, Terrance, et al, eds. Nurses & Doctors: Their Education & Practice. 128p. 1981. text ed. 20.00 (ISBN 0-89946-092-5). Oelgeschlager.
Knopke, Harry J. & Diekelmann, Nancy L. Approaches to Teaching Primary Health Care. LC 81-1552. 322p. 1981. text ed. 18.95 (ISBN 0-8016-2732-X). Mosby.
Leake, Mary J. Manual of Simple Nursing Procedures. 5th ed. LC 71-139430. (Illus.). 1971. pap. 8.95 (ISBN 0-7216-5662-5). Saunders.
McHenry, Ruth W., ed. Ends & Means: The National Conference on Continuing Education in Nursing, 1970. LC 70-157408. (Notes & Essays Ser., No. 69). 1971. pap. 2.50 (ISBN 0-87060-041-9). Syracuse U Cont Ed.
Macmillan, Patricia. Case Studies for Nursing Management. 1975. pap. text ed. 12.00x (ISBN 0-685-83073-X). State Mutual Bk.
Magner, Monica M. Inservice Education Manual for the Nursing Department. 2nd ed. LC 77-85484. 1978. pap. 10.00 (ISBN 0-87125-042-X). Cath Health.
Mason, M. A. Basic Medical-Surgical Nursing. 4th ed. 1978. 18.95 (ISBN 0-02-376950-5, 37695). Macmillan.
Meeks, Dorothy R., et al. Practical Nursing: A Textbook for Students & Graduates. 5th ed. LC 73-20244. 1974. text ed. 15.95 (ISBN 0-8016-3390-7). Mosby.
Megenity, Jean & Megenity, Jack. The Teaching Function in Nursing. 192p. 1982. pap. text ed. 12.95 (ISBN 0-89303-052-X). R J Brady.
Meyer, Genevieve R. Tenderness & Technique: Nursing Values in Transition. (Monograph Ser.: No. 6). 1960. 5.00 (ISBN 0-89215-008-4). U Cal LA Indus Rel.
Mirin, Susan K., ed. Teaching Tomorrow's Nurse: A Nurse Educator Reader. LC 79-90378. 1980. pap. text ed. 10.95 (ISBN 0-913654-59-0). Nursing Res.
Montag, Mildred L. Evaluation of Graduates of Associate Degree Nursing Programs. LC 72-84012. 1972. pap. text ed. 4.50x (ISBN 0-8077-1828-9). Tchrs Coll.
Olesen, Virginia L. & Whittaker, Elvi W. The Silent Dialogue: A Study in the Social Psychology of Professional Socialization. LC 68-21320. (Social & Behavioral Science Ser.). 1968. 17.95x (ISBN 0-87589-017-2). Jossey-Bass.
Parse, Rosemarie R., ed. Nursing Fundamentals. (Nursing Outline Ser.). 1974. 8.00 (ISBN 0-87488-378-4). Med Exam.
Pesznecker, Betty L. & Hewitt, Helon E. Psychiatric Content in the Nursing Curriculum: A Study of Integration Process. LC 63-20537. 144p. 1963. pap. 6.50 (ISBN 0-295-73896-0). U of Wash Pr.
Pivar, William H. Survival Manual for Nursing Students. LC 78-65973. (Illus.). 1979. pap. text ed. 6.50 (ISBN 0-7216-7252-3). HR&W.
Pohl, Margaret. Teaching Function of the Nursing Practitioner. 4th ed. 160p. 1981. pap. text ed. write for info. (ISBN 0-697-05546-9). Wm C Brown.
Puetz, Belinda E. & Peters, Faye L. Continuing Education for Nurses: A Complete Guide to Effective Programs. 250p. 1981. text ed. write for info. (ISBN 0-89443-373-3). Aspen Systems.
Reference Resources for Research Continuing Education in Nursing: G-125. 1976. pap. 2.00 (ISBN 0-686-21450-1). ANA.
Roe, A. K. & Sherwood, M. C. Learning Experience Guides for Nursing Students, 4 vols. 3rd ed. LC 78-8301. 1978. pap. 16.95 ea. Vol. 1 (ISBN 0-471-04186-6). Vol. 2 (ISBN 0-471-04614-0). Vol. 3 (ISBN 0-471-04187-4). Vol. 4 (ISBN 0-471-04613-2). Wiley.
Schoenberg, Bernard, et al, eds. Teaching Psychosocial Aspects of Patient Care. LC 68-19757. 1968. 22.50x (ISBN 0-231-03162-9). Columbia U Pr.
Schweer, Jean E. Creative Teaching in Clinical Nursing. 3rd ed. LC 75-31627. (Illus.). 316p. 1976. pap. 10.95 (ISBN 0-8016-4377-5). Mosby.
Searight, Mary. The Second Step: Baccalaureate Education for Registered Nurses. LC 76-3499. (Illus.). 250p. 1976. text ed. 16.50 (ISBN 0-8036-7780-4). Davis Co.
Simpson, Ida. From Student to Nurse. LC 78-31933. (ASA Rose Monographs). 1979. 19.95 (ISBN 0-521-22683-X); pap. 6.95x (ISBN 0-521-29616-1). Cambridge U Pr.
Smith, Dorothy W. Perspectives on Clinical Teaching. 2nd ed. LC 77-24283. (Teaching of Nursing Ser.: Vol. 2). 1977. pap. text ed. 13.50 (ISBN 0-8261-0932-2). Springer Pub.
Smola, B. K. & Mason, M. A. Basic Medical-Surgical Nursing Workbook. 2nd ed. 1978. pap. 6.95 (ISBN 0-02-412960-7, 41296). Macmillan.
Spiers, A. L. Basic Paediatrics for Nurses. (Illus.). 1973. text ed. 11.00x (ISBN 0-685-83070-5); pap. text ed. 5.00x (ISBN 0-685-83071-3). State Mutual Bk.
Standards for Nursing Education. pap. 2.00 (ISBN 0-686-21452-8). ANA.
Steele, Shirley. Educational Evaluation in Nursing. LC 77-93573. 1978. 14.00 (ISBN 0-913590-54-1). C B Slack.
Torres, Gertrude & Stanton, Marjorie. Curriculum Process in Nursing: A Guide to Curriculum Development. (Illus.). 208p. 1982. 16.95 (ISBN 0-13-196261-2). P-H.
Turnbull, L. M. & Pizurki, H. Family Planning in the Education of Nurses & Midwives. (Public Health Paper: No. 53). (Also avail. in French & Spanish). 1973. pap. 2.00 (ISBN 92-4-130053-1). World Health.
Vaughan-Wrobel, Beth C. & Henderson, Betty. The Problem-Oriented System in Nursing: A Workbook. (Illus.). 184p. 1976. pap. 9.00 (ISBN 0-8016-5221-9). Mosby.

NURSES AND NURSING–VOCATIONAL GUIDANCE

Alperin, Stanley. Careers in Nursing. 188p. 1981. prof. ref. 9.50 (ISBN 0-88410-731-0). Ballinger Pub.
Ayers, Rachel. Nursing Service in Transition: A Description of Organization for Classification & Utilization of Nurse Practitioners. 124p. 1972. pap. 5.00 (ISBN 0-686-16746-5). City Hope.

Becker, Betty G. & Fendler, Dolores T. Vocational & Personal Adjustments in Practical Nursing. 4th ed. (Illus.). 192p. 1982. pap. text ed. 9.50 (ISBN 0-8016-0566-0). Mosby.

--Vocational & Personal Adjustments in Practical Nursing. 3rd ed. LC 77-10153. (Illus.). 1978. pap. text ed. 9.50 (ISBN 0-8016-0565-2). Mosby.

Bernhard, Linda A. & Walsh, Michelle. Leadership: The Key to Professionalization of Nursing. (Illus.). 256p. 1981. pap. text ed. 8.95 (ISBN 0-07-004936-X, HP). McGraw.

Bullough, Bonnie & Bullough, Vern, eds. Expanding Horizons for Nurses. LC 76-47020. 1977. pap. text ed. 11.95 (ISBN 0-8261-2061-X). Springer Pub.

Chandler, Caroline A. & Kempf, Sharon H. Nursing As a Career. LC 74-123501. (Illus.). (gr. 9 up). 1970. 5.95 (ISBN 0-396-06230-X). Dodd.

DeYoung, Lillian. The Foundation of Nursing: As Conceived, Learned & Practiced in Professional Nursing. 3rd ed. LC 75-31536. (Illus.). 336p. 1976. pap. 10.95 (ISBN 0-8016-1282-9). Mosby.

Frederickson, Keville. Opportunities in Nursing. LC 76-42886. (Illus.). (YA) (gr. 8 up). 1977. lib. bdg. 6.60 (ISBN 0-8442-6536-5); pap. 4.95 (ISBN 0-685-77771-5). Natl Textbk.

Hammer, Hy, ed. Nurse. LC 81-1992. 352p. (Orig.). 1981. pap. 6.00 (ISBN 0-668-05248-1, 5248). Arco.

Health Professions Educational Association. Committee of Presidents, ed. A Guide to Education for the Health Professions. LC 79-11155. 1979. pap. 4.95 (ISBN 0-87491-242-3). Acropolis.

Lebowitz, Gordon. Exploring Health Careers Ser., Bk. 2: Nursing & Allied Careers. (Illus.). 128p. (Prog. Bk.). (gr. 7 up). 1973. text ed. 3.00 (ISBN 0-87005-120-2); tchrs' guide 1.50 (ISBN 0-87005-129-6). Fairchild.

Lotit, Mary Sue & Kostenbauer, Joyce. Advance: The Nurse's Guide to Success in Today's Job Market. 1981. pap. text ed. price not set. Little.

Nursing Job Guide to Over Seven Thousand Hospitals. 1982. softcover 15.00 (ISBN 0-932834-03-5). Prime NATL Pub.

Nursing Seventy Nine Career Directory. (Illus.). 1979. pap. 10.00 (ISBN 0-916730-16-6). InterMed Comm.

Robinson, Alice & Reres, Mary. Your Future in Nursing Careers. LC 72-75218. (Careers in Depth Ser.). (Illus.). 160p. (gr. 7 up). 1978. PLB 5.97 (ISBN 0-8239-0263-3). Rosen Pr.

--Your Future in Nursing Careers. LC 72-75218. (Illus.). 128p. 1975. pap. 3.95 (ISBN 0-668-03429-7). Arco.

Rose, et al. Being a Nursing Assistant. 3rd ed. (Illus.). 448p. 1981. pap. text ed. 13.95 (ISBN 0-89303-027-9). R J Brady.

Ross, Carmen F. Personal & Vocational Relationships in Practical Nursing. 5th ed. (Illus.). 290p. 1981. pap. text ed. 9.75 (ISBN 0-397-54281-X, JBL-Med-Nursing). Har-Row.

Schweer, Jean. Defining Behavioral Objectives for Continuing Education Offerings in Nursing: A Four Level Taxonomy. LC 80-54454. 1981. pap. 9.50 (ISBN 0-913590-75-4). C B Slack.

Searight, Mary W. Your Career in Nursing. rev. ed. LC 77-6180. (Messner Career Books). (Illus.). 192p. (gr. 7 up). 1977. PLB 7.79 (ISBN 0-671-32922-7). Messner.

NURSING (INFANT FEEDING)

see Breast Feeding

NURSING ADMINISTRATION

see Nursing Service Administration

NURSING ETHICS

see also Medical Ethics

Benjamin, Martin & Curtis, Joy. Ethics in Nursing. 192p. 1981. text ed. 13.95x (ISBN 0-19-502836-8); pap. text ed. 7.95x (ISBN 0-19-502837-6). Oxford U Pr.

Curtin, Leah & Flaherty, M. Josephine. Nursing Ethics: Theories & Pragmatics. (Illus.). 320p. 1982. text ed. 17.95 (ISBN 0-89303-051-1); pap. text ed. 13.95 (ISBN 0-89303-053-8). R J Brady.

Davis, Anne J. & Krueger, Janelle C., eds. Patients, Nurses, Ethics. LC 80-57573. 245p. 1980. pap. text ed. 9.95 (ISBN 0-937126-84-5). Am Journal Nurse.

Fenner, Kathleen M. Ethics & Law in Nursing. 220p. 1980. text ed. 13.95 (ISBN 0-442-23204-7). Van Nos Reinhold.

Shelly, Judith A. Dilemma: A Nurse's Guide for Making Ethical Decisions. LC 80-7788. (Orig.). 1980. pap. text ed. 4.95 (ISBN 0-87784-666-9). Inter-Varsity.

Smitherman, Colleen. Nursing Actions for Health Promotion. LC 80-17464. (Illus.). 415p. 1980. pap. text ed. 13.95 (ISBN 0-8036-7941-6). Davis Co.

Steele, Shirley M. & Harmon, Vera M. Values Clarification in Nursing. (Illus.). 1979. 8.95 (ISBN 0-8385-9337-2). ACC.

Tate, Barbara L. The Nurse's Dilemma: Ethical Considerations in Nursing Practice. 114p. 1977. pap. text ed. 3.50 (ISBN 0-937126-79-9). Am Journal Nurse.

Thompson, Joyce B. & Thompson, Henry O. Ethics in Nursing. 1981. pap. text ed. 12.95x (ISBN 0-02-420690-3). Macmillan.

NURSING HOMES

see also Geriatric Nursing

Alperin, Sondra P., ed. Guide Book to Florida Nursing Homes. 1979. 19.95 (ISBN 0-916524-12-4). US Direct Serv.

Aranyi, Laszlo & Goldman, Larry L. Design of Long-Term Care Facilities. 240p. 1980. text ed. 32.50 (ISBN 0-442-26120-9). Van Nos Reinhold.

Bednarski, Mary W. & Florczyk, Sandra E. Nursing Home Care As a Public Policy Issue. (Learning Packages in Policy Issues: No. 4). 62p. (Orig.). 1978. pap. text ed. 1.75 (ISBN 0-936826-13-4). Pol Stud Assocs.

Bennett, Clifford. Nursing Home Life: What It Is & What It Could Be. LC 80-52650. (Illus.). 192p. 1980. pap. text ed. 6.95 (ISBN 0-913292-19-2). Tiresias Pr.

Bloom, Barbara. Utilization Patterns and Financial Characteristics of Nursing Homes in the United States: 1977 Nnhs. Shipp, Audrey, ed. (Series Thirteen: No. 53). 50p. 1981. pap. 1.75 (ISBN 0-8406-0215-4). Natl Ctr Health Stats.

Brickner, Phillip W. Care of the Nursing-Home Patient. 1971. text ed. 14.95 (ISBN 0-02-314500-5, 31450). Macmillan.

Burger, Sarah G. & D'Erasmo, Martha. Living in a Nursing Home: A Guide for Residents, Their Families & Friends. LC 76-17890. 1976. 8.95 (ISBN 0-8164-9294-8). Continuum.

Burstein. The Get Well Hotel. 113p. Date not set. lib. bdg. 4.95 (ISBN 0-07-009244-3). McGraw.

Conger, Shirley & Moore, Kay. Social Work in Long-Term Care Facilities. 160p. 1981. 16.95 (ISBN 0-8436-0850-1). CBI Pub.

Corbus, Howard & Swanson, L. L. Adopting the Problem Oriented Medical Record in Nursing Homes. LC 78-53068. 98p. 1978. pap. text ed. 5.95 (ISBN 0-913654-44-2). Nursing Res.

Davies, Bleddyn & Knapp, Martin. Old People's Homes & the Production of Welfare. (Library of Social Work Ser.). 240p. 1981. 32.50 (ISBN 0-7100-0700-0). Routledge & Kegan.

Dunlop, Burton D. The Growth of Nursing Home Care. LC 78-14715. 1979. 18.95 (ISBN 0-669-02704-9). Lexington Bks.

Falk, Ursula A. & Falk, Gerhard. The Nursing Home Dilemma. LC 75-36565. 1976. softbound 8.00 (ISBN 0-88247-399-9). R & E Res Assoc.

Foley, Daniel J. Nursing Home Estimates for California, Illinois, Massachusetts, New York & Texas from the 1977 National Nursing Home Survey. Olmsted, Mary, ed. (Ser. 13-48). 50p. 1980. pap. text ed. 1.75 (ISBN 0-8406-0190-5). Natl Ctr Health Stats.

Foundaton of the American College of Nursing Home Administrators. State Licensure Requirements for Nursing Home Administrators. 2nd ed. 1979. 15.00 (ISBN 0-686-64025-X). Panel Pubs.

Gubrium, Jaber F. Living & Dying at Murray Manor. LC 74-23279. 256p. (Orig.). 1975. 8.95 (ISBN 0-312-48930-7); pap. text ed. 5.95 (ISBN 0-312-48965-X). St Martin.

Hing, Ester. Characteristics of Nursing Home Residents Health Status, & Care Received: National Nursing Home Survey, May-December 1977. Cox, Klaudia, ed. 60p. 1981. pap. 1.95 (ISBN 0-8406-0212-X). Natl Ctr Health Stats.

Huffman, Edna K. Medical Records in Nursing Homes. 1961. 5.00 (ISBN 0-917036-10-7). Physicians Rec.

Ingram, Donald K. Measures of Chronic Illness Among Residents of Nursing & Personal Care Homes, U. S., June-August, 1969. LC 74-4190. (Data from the Institutional Population Survey Ser. 12: No. 24). 60p. 1974. pap. text ed. 0.70 (ISBN 0-8406-0012-7). Natl Ctr Health Stats.

Jacobs, H. Lee & Morris, Woodrow W., eds. Nursing & Retirement Home Administration. (Illus.). 1966. 7.95x (ISBN 0-8138-1175-9). Iowa St U Pr.

Koch, Kenneth. I Never Told Anybody: Teaching Poetry Writing in a Nursing Home. 1978. pap. 2.95 (ISBN 0-394-72499-2, Vin). Random.

Koetting, Michael. Nursing-Home Organization & Efficiency: Profit Versus Non Profit. LC 79-2796. 160p. 1980. 19.95 (ISBN 0-669-03290-5). Lexington Bks.

Koncelik, Joseph A. Designing the Open Nursing Home. LC 76-11010. (Community Development Ser: Vol. 27). (Illus.). 1976. 26.00 (ISBN 0-87933-236-0). Hiutchinson Ross.

Kramer, Charles H. & Kramer, Jeannette R. Basic Principles of Long-Term Patient Care: Developing a Therapeutic Community. (Illus.). 380p. 1976. 26.75 (ISBN 0-398-03453-2). C C Thomas.

Laker, Mark. Nursing Home Activities for the Handicapped. 98p. 1980. pap. 9.75 (ISBN 0-398-04074-5). C C Thomas.

McQuillan, Florence. Fundamentals of Nursing Home Administration. 2nd ed. LC 73-89186. (Illus.). 430p. 1974. text ed. 12.50x (ISBN 0-7216-5971-3). Saunders.

Meiners, Mark P. Nursing Home Costs - Nineteen Seventy-Two United States: August 1973-April 1974 National Nursing Home Survey. Stevenson, Taoria, ed. (Ser. 13: No.39). 1978. pap. text ed. 1.75 (ISBN 0-8406-0136-0). Natl Ctr Health Stats.

Meiners, Mark R. Selected Operating & Financial Characteristics of Nursing Homes, United States, 1973-74 National Nursing Homes Survey. Shipp, Audrey M., ed. (Ser. 13: No. 22). 53p. 1976. pap. text ed. 1.25 (ISBN 0-8406-0064-X). Natl Ctr Health Stats.

Mendelson, Mary A. Tender Loving Greed: How the Incredibly Lucrative Nursing Home "Industry" Is Exploiting America's Old People & Defrauding Us All. LC 74-16496. 1975. pap. 2.95 (ISBN 0-394-71427-X, Vin). Random.

Miller, Dulcy B. & Barry, Jane T. Nursing Home Organization & Operation. LC 79-183. (Illus.). 1979. text ed. 20.95 (ISBN 0-8436-0782-3). CBI Pub.

Miller, Michael B. Current Issues in Clinical Geriatrics. LC 77-95435. 1979. casebound 13.50 (ISBN 0-913292-22-2). Tiresias Pr.

Moss, Frank E. & Halamandaris, Val J. Too Old, Too Sick, Too Bad. 1979. pap. 4.95 (ISBN 0-89185-211-5). Anthelion Pr.

--Too Old, Too Sick, Too Bad: Nursing Homes in America. LC 77-72515. 326p. 1977. 22.00 (ISBN 0-912862-43-2). Aspen Systems.

Neal, Margo C. & Cohen, Patricia F. Nursing Care Planning Guides for Long Term Care. 1980. pap. 19.95 (ISBN 0-935236-13-9). Nurseco.

Nursing Home Fires & Their Cures. (Illus.). 40p. 1972. pap. 2.50 (ISBN 0-685-58180-2, SPP-17). Natl Fire Prot.

The Nursing Home Volunteer's Handbook. 1979. pap. text ed. 2.45x (ISBN 0-918452-18-X). Learning Pubns.

Nursing Homes. (BTA Studies). 1979. 235.00 (ISBN 0-686-31561-8). Busn Trend.

Nursing Homes & County & Metropolitan Area Data Bank. 1973. 1.75 (ISBN 0-8406-0103-4). Natl Ctr Health Stats.

Patterson, Dorothy B. Nursing Home Administration. Date not set. price not set (ISBN 0-398-04610-7). C C Thomas.

Posyniak, Henry. Guide to Accounting Principles, Practices & Systems for Nursing Homes. new ed. LC 77-80740. 1978. pap. 10.00 (ISBN 0-87125-040-3). Cath Health.

Rausch, Erwin & Perper, Menna. Resident Care Management System. 162p. 1980. 12.95 (ISBN 0-8436-0793-9). CBI Pub.

Rhoads, Jerry L. Basic Accounting & Budgeting for Nursing Homes. 460p. 1981. 24.95 (ISBN 0-8436-0795-5). CBI Pub.

Rogers, Wesley W. General Administration in the Nursing Home. 3rd ed. LC 80-19106. 456p. 1980. text ed. 18.95 (ISBN 0-8436-0788-2). CBI Pub.

Rothert, Eugene A., Jr. & Daubert, James R. Horticultural Therapy for Nursing Homes, Senior Centers, & Retirement Living. (Illus.). 140p. (Orig.). 1981. pap. 10.00 (ISBN 0-939914-01-8). Chi Horticult.

Routh, Thomas A. Choosing a Nursing Home: The Problems & Their Solutions. 172p. 1970. text ed. 11.75 (ISBN 0-398-01617-8). C C Thomas.

Schneeweiss, Stephen M. & Davis, Stanley W., eds. Nursing Home Administration. 1974. 16.50 (ISBN 0-8391-0658-0). Univ Park.

Shipp, Audrey, ed. The National Nursing Home Survey: 1977 Summary for the United States. (Ser. 13: No. 43). 1979. pap. text ed. 1.75 (ISBN 0-8406-0166-2). Natl Ctr Health Stats.

Sirrocco, Al. Employees in Nursing Homes in the U. S. National Nursing Home Survey 1973-74. Kemper, Margot, ed. (Ser. 14: No. 20). 1978. text ed. 1.75 (ISBN 0-8406-0130-1). Natl Ctr Health Stats.

--Employees in Nursing Homes: National Nursing Home Survey, 1977. Cox, Klaudia, ed. (Ser. Fourteen: No. 25). 50p. 1981. pap. text ed. 1.50 (ISBN 0-8406-0213-8). Natl Ctr Health Stats.

Sirrocco, Al & Koch, Hugo. Nursing Homes in Profile: National Nursing Home Survey, 1973-74. (Ser. 14). 1976. pap. 1.50 (ISBN 0-8406-0084-4). Natl Ctr Health Stats.

--Nursing Homes in the United States: 1973-74 National Nursing Home Survey. Rutherford, Margaret, ed. (Ser. 14: No. 17). 1977. pap. 1.50 (ISBN 0-8406-0097-6). Natl Ctr Health Stats.

Smith, David B. Long-Term Care in Transition: Nursing Homes on the Cutting Edge. (Illus.). 350p. 1981. text ed. 20.00 (ISBN 0-914904-65-5). Health Admin Pr.

Sollenberger, Opal H. I Chose to Live in a Nursing Home. LC 79-57521. 1980. pap. 4.95 (ISBN 0-89191-242-8). Cook.

--I Chose to Live in a Nursing Home. 1981. pap. 4.95 (ISBN 0-89191-242-8). Caroline Hse.

Stevenson, Taloria, ed. Charges for Care & Sources of Payment for Residents in Nursing Homes, United States: National Nursing Home Survey August 1973-April 1974. (Ser. 13, No.32). 1977. pap. text ed. 1.50 (ISBN 0-685-85759-X). Natl Ctr Health Stats.

--Utilization of Nursing Homes, Unites States: 1973-74 National Nursing Homes Survey. (Ser. 13: No. 28). 1977. pap. 1.95 (ISBN 0-8406-0090-9). Natl Ctr Health Stats.

Stryker, R. How to Reduce Employee Turnover in Nursing Homes. 1981. 21.75 (ISBN 0-398-04510-0). C C Thomas.

Thomas, William C., Jr. Nursing Homes & Public Policy: Drift & Decision in New York State. LC 69-18221. 287p. 1969. 27.50x (ISBN 0-8014-0518-1). Cornell U Pr.

Tobin, Sheldon S. & Lieberman, Morton A. Last Home for the Aged: Critical Implications of Institutionalization. LC 76-11941. (Social & Behavioral Science Ser.). (Illus.). 1976. 16.95x (ISBN 0-87589-280-9). Jossey-Bass.

Vladeck, Bruce C. Unloving Care: The Nursing Home Tragedy. LC 79-3076. 305p. 1980. 13.95 (ISBN 0-465-08880-5). Basic.

Welter, Paul R. The Nursing Home: A Caring Community-Staff Manual. 96p. 1981. pap. 2.95 (ISBN 0-8170-0935-3). Judson.

--The Nursing Home: A Caring Community-Trainers' Manual. 176p. 1981. pap. 9.95 (ISBN 0-8170-0934-5). Judson.

Zaccarelli, Bro. Herman E. & Maggiore, Josephine. Nursing Home Menu Planning, Food Purchasing & Management. LC 73-182087. 1972. 15.95 (ISBN 0-8436-0541-3). CBI Pub.

Zappolo, Aurora. Characteristics & Social Contacts & Activities of Nursing Home Residents, United States: August 1973-April 1974, No. 13. 1977. pap. 1.75 (ISBN 0-8406-0085-2). Natl Ctr Health Stats.

--Discharge from Nursing Homes: 1977 National Nursing Home Survey. Cox, Klaudia, ed. (Ser. 13: No. 54). 60p. 1981. pap. 1.75 (ISBN 0-8406-0216-2). Natl Ctr Health Stats.

NURSING LAW

see Nurses and Nursing–Legal Status, Laws, etc.

NURSING PSYCHOLOGY

see Nurses and Nursing–Psychological Aspects

NURSING RESEARCH

Alpert, Joseph S. & Francis, Gary S. Manual of Coronary Care. 2nd ed. (Little, Brown SPIRAL TM Manual Ser.). 1980. pap. 11.95 (ISBN 0-316-03503-3). Little.

Chater, S. Understanding Research in Nursing. (Offset Pub.: No. 14). (Also avail. in French). 1975. pap. 2.40 (ISBN 92-4-170014-9). World Health.

Clemen & Eigsti. Comprehensive Family & Community Health Nursing. (Illus.). 544p. 1981. text ed. 19.95 (ISBN 0-07-011324-6, HP). McGraw.

Davis, Anne J. & Krueger, Janelle C., eds. Patients, Nurses, Ethics. LC 80-57573. 245p. 1980. pap. text ed. 9.95 (ISBN 0-937126-84-5). Am Journal Nurse.

Dempsey, Particia & Dempsey, Arthur. The Research Process in Nursing. 1980. 13.95 (ISBN 0-442-20884-7). D Van Nostrand.

Diers, Donna. Research in Nursing Practice. LC 79-878. 1979. text ed. 17.50x (ISBN 0-397-54221-6, JBL-Med-Nursing). Har-Row.

Downs, Florence S. & Newman, Margaret A. A Source Book of Nursing Research. 2nd ed. 200p. 1977. pap. text ed. 9.95 (ISBN 0-8036-2791-2). Davis Co.

Downs, Florence S. & Fleming, Juanita W., eds. Issues in Nursing Research. LC 78-21914. 176p. 1979. pap. 10.95 (ISBN 0-8385-4436-3). ACC.

Fox, D. J., ed. Readings on the Research Process in Nursing. Leeser, I. 232p. 1981. pap. 16.50 (ISBN 0-8385-8266-4). ACC.

Fox, David J. Fundamentals of Research in Nursing. 3rd ed. (Illus.). 313p. 1976. 15.95 (ISBN 0-8385-2796-5). ACC.

Krampitz, Sydney D. & Pavlovich, Natalie. Readings for Nursing Research. LC 80-18125. (Illus.). 285p. 1980. pap. text ed. 10.45 (ISBN 0-8016-2747-8). Mosby.

Kruegar, Janelle C. & Nelson, Allen H. Nursing Research: Development, Collaboration & Utilization. LC 78-26215. (Illus.). 324p. 1978. text ed. 25.00 (ISBN 0-89443-082-3). Aspen Systems.

Newman, Margaret A. Theory Development in Nursing. LC 79-12404. 96p. 1979. pap. text ed. 6.50 (ISBN 0-8036-6520-2). Davis Co.

Notter, Lucille E. Essentials of Nursing Research. 2nd ed. LC 78-16108. 1978. text ed. 13.95 (ISBN 0-8261-1592-6); pap. text ed. 8.50 (ISBN 0-8261-1593-4). Springer Pub.

Pavlovich, Natalie. Nursing Research: A Learning Guide. LC 77-22518. 1978. pap. text ed. 9.50 (ISBN 0-8016-3763-5). Mosby.

Polit, Denise & Hungler, Bernadette P. Nursing Research: Principles & Methods. LC 78-18493. 1978. text ed. 18.95 (ISBN 0-397-54220-8, JBL-Med-Nursing). Har-Row.
Reference Resources for Research Continuing Education in Nursing: G-125. 1976. pap. 2.00 (ISBN 0-686-21450-1). ANA.
Treece, Eleanor W. & Treece, James W., Jr. Elements of Research in Nursing. 2nd ed. LC 76-7521. (Illus.). 1977. pap. text ed. 12.95 (ISBN 0-8016-5104-2). Mosby.
Trussell, Patricia, et al. Using Nursing Research: Discovery, Analysis & Interpretation. LC 80-84150. 240p. 1981. text ed. 10.95 (ISBN 0-913654-70-1). Nursing Res.
Verhonick, P. & Seaman. Research Methods for Undergraduate Students in Nursing. (Illus.). 1978. pap. 9.95 (ISBN 0-8385-8407-1). ACC.
Verhonick, Phyllis. Nursing Research II. 1977. 13.50 (ISBN 0-316-90011-7). Little.
Verhonick, Phyllis J., ed. Nursing Research I. 1975. 13.50 (ISBN 0-316-90010-9). Little.
Waltz, Carolyn & Bausell, Barker. Nursing Research: Design Statistics & Computer Analysis. LC 80-18669. (Illus.). 362p. 1981. pap. text ed. 13.95 (ISBN 0-8036-9040-1). Davis Co.
Wechsler, Henry. Explorations in Nursing Research. Kibrick, Anne, ed. LC 79-719. 1979. text ed. 29.95 (ISBN 0-87705-379-0); pap. text ed. 12.95 (ISBN 0-87705-399-5). Human Sci Pr.
Werley, Harriet, et al, eds. Health Research: The Systems Approach. LC 73-92207. (Illus.). 330p. 1976. text ed. 17.95 (ISBN 0-8261-1710-4). Springer Pub.
Williamson, Yvonne M. Research Methodology & Its Application to Nursing. LC 80-22919. 325p. 1981. 14.95 (ISBN 0-471-03313-8, Pub. by Wiley Med). Wiley.
Wolanin, Mary O. & Phillips, Linda R. Confusion: Prevention & Care. LC 80-18508. (Illus.). 415p. 1980. pap. text ed. 18.95 (ISBN 0-8016-5629-X). Mosby.

NURSING SCHOOLS

Blurton-Jones, N. G., ed. Ethological Studies of Child Behaviour. (Illus.). 416p. 1974. 53.50 (ISBN 0-521-08260-9); pap. 14.95x (ISBN 0-521-09855-6). Cambridge U Pr.
Directory of Schools of Nursing (United Kingdom) 3rd ed. 1977. text ed. 22.50x (ISBN 0-11-320658-5). Intl Pubns Serv.
Greenblatt, Bernard. Responsibility for Child Care: The Changing Role of Family & State in Child Development. LC 76-50699. (Social & Behavioral Science Ser.). (Illus.). 1977. text ed. 17.95x (ISBN 0-87589-315-5). Jossey-Bass.
Grubb, Reba D. & Mueller, Carolyn J. Designing Hospital Training Programs. (Illus.). 216p. 1975. 20.50 (ISBN 0-398-03316-1). C C Thomas.
Harris, Lucy. Harris College of Nursing: Five Decades of Struggle for a Cause. new ed. LC 73-78068. 1973. 6.00 (ISBN 0-912646-43-8). Tex Christian.
Nursing School Entrance Examinations. 8th ed. LC 77-14090. 1978. pap. text ed. 6.00 (ISBN 0-668-01202-1). Arco.
Practical Nursing School Admission Test. pap. 4.95 (ISBN 0-8092-9392-7). Contemp Bks.
Sandri-White, Alex & Pokress, E. New Directory of Medical Schools. 1981. 9.50 (ISBN 0-685-22749-9). Aurea.
Tunis, Barbara L. In Caps & Gowns: The Story of the McGill School for Graduate Nurses, 1920-1964. 154p. 1966. 6.00 (ISBN 0-7735-9067-6). McGill-Queens U Pr.
Wold, Susan J. School Nursing: A Framework for Practice. LC 80-27711. (Illus.). 571p. 1981. pap. text ed. 19.95 (ISBN 0-8016-5611-7). Mosby.
World Directory of Post-Basic & Post-Graduate Schools of Nursing. 223p. (Eng, Fr, & Rus.). 1965. 7.20 (ISBN 92-4-150000-X). World Health.

NURSING SERVICE ADMINISTRATION

see also Team Nursing

Alexander, Edythe L. Nursing Administration in the Hospital Health Care System. 2nd ed. LC 77-18114. (Illus.). 1978. text ed. 16.95 (ISBN 0-8016-0110-X). Mosby.
Althus, Joan M., et al. Nursing Decentralization: The El Camino Experience. LC 81-83018. (Nursing Dimensions Administration Ser.). 200p. 1981. text ed. price not set (ISBN 0-913654-76-0). Nursing Res.
Arndt, Clara & Huckabay, Loucine. Nursing Administration: Theory for Practice with a Systems Approach. 2nd ed. LC 80-14034. (Illus.). 1980. pap. 16.95 (ISBN 0-8016-0305-6). Mosby.
Barrett. The Head Nurse: Her Leadership Role. 3rd ed. 450p. 1975. 18.00 (ISBN 0-8385-3651-4). ACC.
Berger, et al. Management for Nurses: A Multidisciplinary Approach. 2nd ed. LC 79-19965. 1980. pap. 12.00 (ISBN 0-8016-4815-7). Mosby.
Beyers, Marjorie, ed. Leadership in Nursing. LC 79-88377. (Management Anthology Ser.). 178p. 1979. pap. text ed. 9.50 (ISBN 0-913654-56-6). Nursing Res.
Blake, Robert R. & Mouton, Jane S. Grid Approaches for Managerial Leadership in Nursing. Tapper, Mildred, ed. LC 80-21583. (Illus.). 158p. 1980. pap. text ed. 9.95 (ISBN 0-8016-0696-9). Mosby.
Checklist for Nursing Service Policy Manual. 1968. pap. 0.50 (ISBN 0-87125-049-7). Cath Health.
Clark, Carolyn & Shea, Carole A. Management in Nursing. (Illus.). 1979. text ed. 12.95 (ISBN 0-07-011135-9, HP). McGraw.
Claus, Karen E. & Bailey, June T. Power & Influence in Health Care: A New Approach to Leadership. LC 76-57769. (Illus.). 1977. pap. 10.95 (ISBN 0-8016-0417-6). Mosby.
DiVincenti, Marie. Administering Nursing Service. 2nd ed. 350p. 1977. 15.95 (ISBN 0-316-18651-1). Little.
Donovan, Helen M. Nursing Service Administration: Managing the Enterprise. LC 75-26845. (Illus.). 272p. 1975. pap. 13.95 (ISBN 0-8016-1423-6). Mosby.
Douglass, Laura M. Review of Leadership in Nursing. 2nd ed. LC 76-41258. 1977. pap. text ed. 9.95 (ISBN 0-8016-1442-2). Mosby.
Ganong, Warren & Ganong, Joan. Cases in Nursing Management. LC 79-2572. 360p. 1979. text ed. 23.95 (ISBN 0-89443-152-8). Aspen Systems.
--Nursing Management. 2nd ed. LC 80-10865. 350p. 1980. text ed. 19.95 (ISBN 0-89443-278-8). Aspen Systems.
Guide for the Nursing Service Audit. 1971. pap. 2.00 (ISBN 0-87125-052-7). Cath Health.
Journal of Nursing Administration, Editorial Staff, ed. Quality Control & Performance Appraisal, Vol. 1. LC 75-41590. 61p. 1976. pap. text ed. 6.25 (ISBN 0-913654-23-X). Nursing Res.
Journal of Nursing Administration Staff, ed. Planning & Evaluating Nursing Care. 2nd ed. LC 76-11328. 1976. pap. text ed. 6.25 (ISBN 0-913654-29-9). Nursing Res.
--Staff Development, Vol. 1. LC 75-3506. 91p. 1975. pap. text ed. 8.95 (ISBN 0-913654-08-6). Nursing Res.
--Staff Development, Vol. 2. LC 77-85308. 61p. 1977. pap. 6.95 (ISBN 0-913654-40-X). Nursing Res.
--Staffing Three. LC 75-43268. 43p. 1976. pap. text ed. 4.95 (ISBN 0-913654-21-3). Nursing Res.
--Staffing Two. LC 75-1675. 47p. 1975. pap. text ed. 4.95 (ISBN 0-913654-06-X). Nursing Res.
Kirk, Roey. Nursing Management Tools. 1981. price not set (ISBN 0-316-49470-4). Little.
Kraegel, Janet, ed. Organization-Environment Relationships. LC 79-90380. (The Management Anthology Ser.). 233p. 1980. pap. text ed. 12.95 (ISBN 0-913654-58-2). Nursing Res.
Kron, Thora. The Management of Patient Care: Putting Leadership Skill to Work. 4th ed. LC 75-38153. (Illus.). 1976. pap. text ed. 9.95 (ISBN 0-7216-5528-9). Saunders.
Lemin, Brian. First Line Nursing Management. (Illus.). 1977. 15.95x (ISBN 0-8464-0415-X). Beekman Pubs.
McQuillan, Florence. Realities of Nursing Management: How to Cope. LC 78-8298. 384p. 1978. text ed. 19.95 (ISBN 0-87618-991-5). R J Brady.
Magula, Mary. Understanding Organization: A Guide for the Nurse Executive. (Nursing Management Anthologies Ser.). 200p. 1981. pap. price not set (ISBN 0-913654-72-8). Nursing Res.
Marriner, Ann. Contemporary Nursing Management: Issues & Practice. (Illus.). 368p. 1982. pap. text ed. 10.95 (ISBN 0-8016-3168-8). Mosby.
--Guide to Nursing Management. LC 79-24241. (Illus.). 1980. pap. 10.00 (ISBN 0-8016-3121-1). Mosby.
Munson, Fred C., et al. Nursing Assignment Patterns: User's Manual. (Illus.). 223p. (Orig.). 1980. pap. text ed. 32.50 (ISBN 0-914904-40-X). Health Admin Pr.
Neal, Margo C., ed. Nurses in Business. 1981. pap. price not set (ISBN 0-935236-21-X). Nurseco.
O'Rourke, Karen & Barton, S. R. Nurse Power: Unions & the Law. (Illus.). 420p. 1980. pap. text ed. 16.95 (ISBN 0-87619-669-5). R J Brady.
Planning & Programming for Nursing Services. (Public Health Paper: No. 44). (Also avail. in French & Spanish). 1971. pap. 3.60 (ISBN 92-4-130044-2). World Health.
Rowland, Howard & Rowland, Beatrice. Nursing Administration Handbook. LC 80-11857. 600p. 1980. text ed. 42.50 (ISBN 0-89443-275-3). Aspen Systems.
Schmied, Elsie. Organizing for Care: Nursing Units & Groups. LC 81-82833. (Nursing Management Anthologies Ser.). 180p. 1981. pap. 12.95 (ISBN 0-913654-74-4). Nursing Res.
Schmied, Elsie, ed. Maintaining Cost Effectiveness. LC 79-84505. (Management Anthology Ser.). 259p. 1979. pap. text ed. 12.50 (ISBN 0-913654-53-1). Nursing Res.
Schneider, Harriet. Evaluation of Nursing Competence. 1979. 7.95 (ISBN 0-316-77400-6). Little.
Stevens, Warren F. Management & Leadership in Nursing. (Illus.). 1978. text ed. 14.95 (ISBN 0-07-061260-9, HP). McGraw.
Stone, Sandra, et al, eds. Management for Nurses: A Multidisciplinary Approach. LC 75-15561. 1976. pap. 9.95 (ISBN 0-8016-4812-2). Mosby.
Tobin, Helen M. & Yoder, Pat S. The Process of Staff Development: Components for Change. 2nd ed. LC 78-31459. (Illus.). 1979. text ed. 17.95 (ISBN 0-8016-4996-X). Mosby.
Tobin, Helen M., et al. The Process of Staff Development: Components for Change. LC 73-13998. 1974. 10.50 (ISBN 0-8016-4995-1). Mosby.
You Are Barbara Jordan: An In-Basket Exercise on Nursing Service Administration. 1970. participant's kit 3.00 (ISBN 0-87914-015-1, 9630); instructor's guide 1.50 (ISBN 0-87914-016-X, 9631). Hosp Res & Educ.
Yura. Nursing Leadership: Theory & Process. (Illus.). 1976. pap. 11.50 (ISBN 0-8385-7027-5). ACC.
Zander, Karen S. Primary Nursing: Development & Management. LC 79-28837. 384p. 1980. text ed. 25.95 (ISBN 0-89443-170-6). Aspen Systems.

NURSING TEAM

see Team Nursing

NUSHAGAK RIVER, ALASKA–HISTORY

VanStone, James W. Eskimos of the Nushagak River: An Ethnographic History. LC 67-21203. (Publications in Anthropology: No. 15). (Illus.). 216p. 1967. 11.50 (ISBN 0-295-97864-3). U of Wash Pr.

NUSSBAUM, JEAN

Nusbaum, Rosemary. Tierra Dulce: The Jesse Nusbaum Papers. (Illus.). 128p. 1980. pap. 7.95 (ISBN 0-913270-83-0). Sunstone Pr.

NUT CULTURE

see Nuts

NUTATION

I.A.U Symposium No. 78, Kiev, USSR, May 23-28, 1977, et al. Nutation & the Earth's Rotation: Proceedings. Smith, M. L. & Bender, P. L., eds. 284p. 1980. lib. bdg. 34.00 (ISBN 90-277-1113-5, Pub. by Reidel Holland); pap. 21.00 (ISBN 90-277-1114-3). Kluwer Boston.
Klein, Felix. Ueber Die Theorie Des Kreisels. 1965. 46.00 (ISBN 0-384-29720-X). Johnson Repr.

NUTHATCHES

Bent, Arthur C. Life Histories of North American Nuthatches, Wrens, Thrashers & Their Allies. (Illus.). 11.50 (ISBN 0-8446-1640-0). Peter Smith.
--Life Histories of North American Nuthatches, Wrens, Thrashers, & Their Allies. (Illus.). 1948. pap. 7.00 (ISBN 0-486-21088-X). Dover.

NUTKA LANGUAGE

see Nootka Language

NUTRITION

see also Absorption (Physiology); Animal Nutrition; Artificial Feeding; Deficiency Diseases; Diet; Digestion; Feeds; Food; Food Habits; Malnutrition; Metabolism; Minerals in the Body; Trace Elements in Nutrition; Vitamins; also subdivision Nutrition under subjects, e.g. Children–Nutrition

Abelson, Philip H., ed. Food: Politics, Economics, Nutrition & Research. LC 75-18785. (Science Compendium Ser.: Vol. 2). (Illus.). 1975. casebound 12.00 (ISBN 0-87168-215-X); pap. 4.50 (ISBN 0-87168-226-5). AAAS.
Abraham, Sidney, et al. Caloria & Selected Nutrient Values of Persons Age 1-74 Years, U. S., 1971-74. Stevenson, Taloria, ed. (Ser. 11: No. 209). 1978. pap. 1.50 (ISBN 0-8406-0147-6). Natl Ctr Health Stats.
--Preliminary Findings of the First Health & Nutrition Examination Survey, U.S., Nineteen Seventy-One to Nineteen Seventy-Two, Dietary Intake & Biochemical Findings. 70p. 1974. pap. 1.25 (ISBN 0-8406-0028-3). Natl Ctr Health Stats.
Abrahamson, E. M. & Pezet, A. W. Body, Mind & Sugar. 3.95 (ISBN 0-686-29842-X). Cancer Bk Hse.
Action Center. Food on Campus. LC 78-947. 1978. pap. 3.95 (ISBN 0-87857-213-9). Rodale Pr Inc.
Adams, Ruth. Eating in Eden. 196p. (Orig.). 1976. pap. 1.75 (ISBN 0-915962-16-0). Larchmont Bks.
Adams, Ruth & Murray, Frank. All You Should Know About Beverages for Your Health & Well Being. 286p. 1976. pap. 1.75 (ISBN 0-915962-17-9). Larchmont Bks.
--All You Should Know About Health Foods. 352p. pap. 2.50 (ISBN 0-915962-01-2). Larchmont Bks.
--The Good Seeds, the Rich Grains, the Hardy Nuts for a Healthier, Happier Life. rev. ed. 303p. 1973. pap. 1.75 (ISBN 0-915962-07-1). Larchmont Bks.
--Is Blood Sugar Making You a Nutritional Cripple? rev. ed. 174p. (Orig.). 1975. pap. 2.25 (ISBN 0-915962-11-X). Larchmont Bks.
--Megavitamin Therapy. 277p. (Orig.). 1973. pap. 1.95 (ISBN 0-915962-03-9). Larchmont Bks.
--Minerals: Kill or Cure. rev. ed. 366p. (Orig.). 1974. pap. 1.95 (ISBN 0-915962-16-0). Larchmont Bks.
--The New High Fiber Diet. 319p. (Orig.). 1977. pap. 2.25 (ISBN 0-915962-21-7). Larchmont Bks.
--Seeds, Grains, Nuts. 1.75 (ISBN 0-686-29844-6). Cancer Bk Hse.
Aebi & Whitehead, eds. Maternal Nutrition During Pregnancy & Lactation. (Nestle Foundation Publication Ser.: No. 1). (Illus.). 354p. 1980. text ed. 31.00 (ISBN 3-456-80945-X, Pub. by Hans Huber Switzerland). J K Burgess.
Aebi, H. & Berger, E. Nutrition & Enzyme Regulation. (Current Problems in Clinical Biochemistry Ser.: Vol. 10). (Illus.). 144p. (Orig.). 1980. pap. text ed. 19.00 (ISBN 3-456-80931-X, Pub. by Hans Huber Switzerland). J K Burgess.
Aebi, H., et al. Problems in Nutrition Research Today. LC 81-66375. 1981. price not set (ISBN 0-12-044420-8). Acad Pr.
Ahnefeld, F. W., et al, eds. Parenteral Nutrition. Babad, A., tr. from Ger. LC 75-34213. (Illus.). 200p. 1976. pap. 17.00 (ISBN 0-387-07518-6). Springer-Verlag.
Ahrens, Richard A. Nutrition for Health. 1970. pap. 5.95x (ISBN 0-534-00675-2). Wadsworth Pub.
Aihara, Herman. Acid & Alkaline. 2nd ed. (Orig.). 1980. pap. 4.95 (ISBN 0-918860-35-0). G Ohsawa.
Airola, Paavo. Are You Confused? 1971. 5.95 (ISBN 0-932090-04-4). Health Plus.
Alacer Corp. Nutrition Minded Doctors U. S. & Canada. 0.50 (ISBN 0-686-29854-3). Cancer Bk Hse.
Alfin-Slater, Roslyn & Kritchevsky, David, eds. Human Nutrition, A Comprehensive Treatise: Vol. 3A, Nutrition & the Adult: Macronutrients. (Illus.). 300p. 1980. 25.00 (ISBN 0-306-40287-4, Plenum Pr). Plenum Pub.
--Human Nutrition, a Comprehensive Treatise: Vol. 3B, Nutrition & the Adult-Micronutrients. (Illus.). 444p. 1980. 39.50 (ISBN 0-306-40288-2, Plenum Pr). Plenum Pub.
Alfin-Slater, Roslyn B. & Aftergood, Lilla. Nutrition for Today. (Contemporary Topics in Health Science Ser). 1973. pap. write for info. (ISBN 0-697-07340-8). Wm C Brown.
Alford, Betty B. & Bogle, Margaret L. Nutrition During the Life Cycle. 384p. 1982. 19.95 (ISBN 0-686-76601-6). P-H.
Altschule, Mark D. Nutritional Factors in General Medicine: Effects of Stress & Distorted Diets. 200p. 1978. 14.75 (ISBN 0-398-03736-1). C C Thomas.
Arlin, Marian T. The Science of Nutrition. 2nd ed. (Illus.). 352p. 1977. text ed. 17.95 (ISBN 0-02-303840-3, 30384). Macmillan.
Arnold O. Beckman Conference in Clin. Chem., 4th. Human Nutrition: Clinical & Biochemical Aspects: Proceedings. Garry, Philip J., ed. LC 81-65736. 400p. 1981. 33.95 (ISBN 0-915274-15-9). Am Assn Clinical Chem.
Arnow, E. Earle. Food Power: A Doctor's Guide to Commonsense Nutrition. LC 75-185419. (Illus.). 320p. 1972. 16.95x (ISBN 0-911012-37-0). Nelson-Hall.
Aronson, Virginia & Fitzgerald, Barbara. Guidebook for Nutrition Counselors. 448p. 1980. 19.50 (ISBN 0-8158-0387-7). Chris Mass.
Asher, Ross. Discovery Two Thousand One. LC 78-51727. Date not set. 9.95 (ISBN 0-931662-00-1). Photo-Go Pr.
Ashley, Richard & Duggal, Heidi. Dictionary of Nutrition. 1976. pap. 2.50 (ISBN 0-671-83406-1). PB.
Austin, James E. & Hitt, Christopher. Nutrition Intervention in the United States: Cases & Concepts. LC 79-14494. 416p. 1979. reference 25.00 (ISBN 0-88410-370-6). Ballinger Pub.
Austin, James E., ed. Nutrition Programs in the Third World: Cases & Readings. LC 80-21083. 480p. 1981. lib. bdg. 27.50 (ISBN 0-89946-024-0). Oelgeschlager.

Austin, James E. & Zeitlin, Marian F., eds. Nutrition Intervention in Developing Countries: An Overview. LC 80-29223. (Nutrition Intervention in Developing Countries Ser.). 256p. 1981. lib. bdg. 22.50 (ISBN 0-89946-077-1). Oelgeschlager.
Balaam, David N. & Carey, Michael, eds. Food Politics: The Regional Conflict. LC 79-48097. 280p. 1981. write for info. (ISBN 0-916672-52-2). Allanheld.
Barness, Lewis A., et al, eds. Nutrition & Medical Practice. (Illus.). 1981. text ed. 19.50 (ISBN 0-87055-365-8). AVI.
Bass, Mary Ann & Wakefield, Lucille. Community Nutrition & Individual Food Behavior. 1979. text ed. 14.95x (ISBN 0-8087-0299-8). Burgess.
Bateman, Michael, et al. The World's Best Food: For Health & Long Life. (Illus.). 256p. 1981. 19.95 (ISBN 0-395-30529-2). HM.
Bauer, Cathy & Andersen, Juel. The Tofu Cookbook. 1979. 9.95 (ISBN 0-87857-246-5). Rodale Pr Inc.
Bayer, Leona M. & Green, Edith. Kitchen Strategy: The Family Angle on Nutrition. 3rd ed. (Illus.). 112p. 1952. photocopy ed. spiral 9.95 (ISBN 0-398-04201-2). C C Thomas.
Beal, Virginia A. Nutrition in the Life Span. LC 79-24610. 467p. 1980. text ed. 22.50 (ISBN 0-471-03664-1). Wiley.
Beasley, Sonia. The Spirulina Cookbook: Recipes for Rejuvenating the Body. (Illus.). 192p. (Orig.). 1981. pap. 6.95 (ISBN 0-916438-39-2). Univ of Trees.
Beaton, G. H. & McHenry, E. W., eds. Nutrition: A Comprehensive Treatise, 3 vols. Incl. Vol. 1. Macronutrients & Nutrient Elements. 1964. 71.00 (ISBN 0-12-084101-0); Vol. 2. Vitamins, Nutrient Requirements & Food Selections. 1964. 71.00 (ISBN 0-12-084102-9); Vol. 3. Nutritional Status: Assessment & Application. 1966. 60.50 (ISBN 0-12-084103-7). 163.50 (ISBN 0-685-23127-5). Acad Pr.
Beck, Mary E. Nutrition & Dietectics for Nurses. 6th ed. (Churchill Livingstone Nursing Texts Ser.). (Illus.). 288p. 1980. pap. text ed. 9.75 (ISBN 0-443-02009-4). Churchill.
Bedford, Stewart. Stress & Tiger Juice: How to Manage Your Stress & Improve Your Life & Health. LC 79-92277. 128p. 1980. 9.95x (ISBN 0-935930-00-0); pap. 5.95x (ISBN 0-935930-01-9). Scott Pubns CA.
Beebe, Brooke, et al. Nutrition & Good Health. LC 78-731300. (Illus.). 1978. pap. text ed. 135.00 (ISBN 0-89290-099-7, A576-SATC). Soc for Visual.
Beers, Roland F. & Bassett, Edward G., eds. Nutritional Factors: Modulating Effects on Metabolic Processes. (Miles International Symposium Ser.: Vol. 13). 1981. text ed. 55.00 (ISBN 0-89004-592-5). Raven.
Beeson, Kenneth & Matrone, Gennard. The Soil Factor in Nutrition: Animal & Human. (Nutrition & Clinical Nutrition Ser.: Vol. 2). 1976. 25.75 (ISBN 0-8247-6484-6). Dekker.
Beiler, Henry. Food Is Your Best Medicine. pap. 2.45 (ISBN 0-686-29865-9). Cancer Bk Hse.
Bender, A. E. Dictionary of Nutrition & Food Technology. 1977. 28.50 (ISBN 0-8206-0214-0). Chem Pub.
--Nutrition & Dietetic Foods. (Illus.). 1973. 30.00 (ISBN 0-8206-0231-0). Chem Pub.
Bender, Arnold. Food Processing & Nutrition. (Food Science & Technology Ser.). 1978. 33.00 (ISBN 0-12-086450-9). Acad Pr.
Bender, Arnold E. Dictionary of Nutrition & Food Technology. 4th ed. 1975. text ed. 19.95 (ISBN 0-408-00143-7). Butterworth.
Bennion, Marion. Clinical Nutrition. 1978. text ed. 30.50 scp (ISBN 0-06-453526-6, HarpC). Har-Row.
Berg, Alan. The Nutrition Factor: Its Role in National Development. 1973. 14.95 (ISBN 0-8157-0914-5); pap. 5.95 (ISBN 0-8157-0913-7). Brookings.
Bernard, Raymond. Eat Your Way to Better Health, Vol. 1. 1974. pap. 4.95 (ISBN 0-685-47352-X). Saucerian.
--Eat Your Way to Better Health, Vol. 2. 1974. pap. 4.95 (ISBN 0-685-47353-8). Saucerian.
Bernarde, M. A. Chemicals We Eat. 1971. 7.95 (ISBN 0-07-004422-8, GB); pap. 3.50 (ISBN 0-07-004424-4). McGraw.
Bijlani, L. Eating Scientifically. 188p. 1979. 10.00x (ISBN 0-86125-049-4, Pub. by Orient Longman India). State Mutual Bk.
Birch, G. G. & Parker, K. J., eds. Food & Health: Science & Technology. (Illus.). xii, 521p. 1980. 80.00x (ISBN 0-85334-875-8, Pub. by Applied Science). Burgess-Intl Ideas.
Blaine, Tom R. Mental Health Through Nutrition. 210p. 1974. 5.95 (ISBN 0-8065-0091-3); pap. 3.45 (ISBN 0-8065-0424-2). Citadel Pr.
--Nutrition & Your Heart. LC 79-87833. 1979. pap. 2.25 (ISBN 0-87983-178-2). Keats.
Bland, Jeffrey. Your Health Under Siege: Using Nutrition to Fight Back. 224p. 1981. 12.95 (ISBN 0-8289-0415-4). Greene.
Blaxter, Kenneth. Food Chains & Human Nutrition. (Illus.). x, 459p. 1980. 65.00x (ISBN 0-85334-863-4, Pub. by Applied Science). Burgess-Intl Ideas.
Block, Zenas. It's All on the Label: Understanding Food, Additives & Nutrition. 1981. pap. 7.95 (ISBN 0-316-09971-6). Little.
Board on Agriculture & Renewable Resources. Nutrient Requirements of Non Human Primates. 1978. pap. 5.00 (ISBN 0-309-02786-1). Natl Acad Pr.
Bodwell, C. E. Evaluation of Proteins for Humans. (Illus.). 1977. lib. bdg. 37.50 (ISBN 0-87055-215-5). AVI.
Borsook, Henry. Vitamins: What They Are. (Orig.). pap. 2.50 (ISBN 0-515-05834-3). Jove Pubns.
Bourne, C. H., ed. World Review of Nutrition & Dietetics, Vol. 22. (Illus.). 1975. 118.75 (ISBN 3-8055-2135-9). S Karger.
Bourne, G. H., ed. Aspects of Human Nutrition & Food Contaminants. (World Review of Nutritional Dietetics Ser.: Vol. 34). (Illus.). 1979. 99.50 (ISBN 3-8055-3069-2). S Karger.
--Human & Animal Nutrition. (World Review of Nutrition & Dietetics: Vol. 32). (Illus.). 1978. 88.75 (ISBN 3-8055-2855-8). S Karger.
--Human & Veterinary Nutrition. (World Review of Nutrition & Dietetics: Vol. 26). (Illus.). 1977. 99.50 (ISBN 3-8055-2392-0). S Karger.
--Human & Veterinary Nutrition, Biochemical Aspects of Nutrients. (World Review of Nutrition & Dietetics: Vol. 30). (Illus.). 1978. 88.75 (ISBN 3-8055-2789-6). S Karger.
--Human Nutrition & Animal Feeding. (World Review of Nutrition & Dietetics Ser.: Vol. 37). (Illus.). xii, 292p. 1981. 148.00 (ISBN 3-8055-2143-X). S Karger.
--Human Nutrition & Diet. (World Review of Nutrition & Dietetics Ser.: Vol. 36). (Illus.). x, 226p. 1981. 115.00 (ISBN 3-8055-1347-X). S Karger.
--Human Nutrition & Nutrition & Pesticides in Cattle, Vol. 35. (World Review of Nutrition & Dietetics: Vol. 35). (Illus.). 238p. 1980. 115.00 (ISBN 3-8055-0442-X). S Karger.
--World Review of Nutrition & Dietetics, Vol. 12. 1970. 115.00 (ISBN 3-8055-0663-5). S Karger.
--World Review of Nutrition & Dietetics, Vol. 13. 1971. 58.75 (ISBN 3-8055-1180-9). S Karger.
--World Review of Nutrition & Dietetics, Vol. 14. 1972. 80.25 (ISBN 3-8055-1282-1). S Karger.
--World Review of Nutrition & Dietetics, Vol. 15. (Illus.). 300p. 1972. 68.50 (ISBN 3-8055-1397-6). S Karger.
--World Review of Nutrition & Dietetics, Vol. 17. (Illus.). 300p. 1973. 86.25 (ISBN 3-8055-1336-4). S Karger.
--World Review of Nutrition & Dietetics, Vol. 18. 1973. 99.00 (ISBN 3-8055-1458-1). S Karger.
--World Review of Nutrition & Dietetics, Vol. 19. (Illus.). 319p. 1974. 99.00 (ISBN 3-8055-1589-8). S Karger.
--World Review of Nutrition & Dietetics, Vol. 21. (Illus.). x, 327p. 1975. 114.00 (ISBN 3-8055-2133-2). S Karger.
--World Review of Nutrition & Dietetics, Vol. 23. (Illus.). xii, 315p. 1975. 106.75 (ISBN 3-8055-2243-6). S Karger.
--World Review of Nutrition & Dietetics, Vol. 24. (Illus.). 250p. 1976. 91.25 (ISBN 3-8055-2344-0). S Karger.
--World Review of Nutrition & Dietetics, Vol. 25. (Illus.). 300p. 1976. 103.00 (ISBN 3-8055-2363-7). S Karger.
--World Review of Nutrition & Dietetics, Vol. 25. (Illus.). 300p. 1976. 103.00 (ISBN 3-8055-2363-7). S Karger.
--World Review of Nutrition & Dietetics, Vol. 37. (Illus.). x, 240p. 1981. 115.00 (ISBN 3-8055-2143-X). S Karger.
--World Review of Nutrition & Dietetics, Vol. 38. (Illus.). x, 220p. 1981. 85.75 (ISBN 3-8055-3048-X). S Karger.
Bourne, G. H. & Cama, H. R., eds. Vitamin & Carrier Functions of Polyprenoids. (World Review of Nutrition & Dietetrics: Vol. 31). (Illus.). 1978. 82.75 (ISBN 3-8055-2801-9). S Karger.
Bourne, Geoffrey H., ed. Some Aspects of Human & Veterinary Nutrition. (World Review of Nutrition & Dietetics: Vol. 28). 1978. 96.50 (ISBN 3-8055-2672-5). S Karger.
--Some Special Aspects of Nutrition. (World Review of Nutrition & Dietetics: Vol. 33). (Illus.). 1979. 94.75 (ISBN 3-8055-2942-2). S Karger.
Bourne, H. C., ed. Some Aspects of Human Nutrition. (World Review of Nutrition & Dietetics: Vol. 27). 1977. 68.50 (ISBN 3-8055-2393-9). S Karger.
Bower, Fay L. Nutrition in Nursing. LC 79-10562. (Nursing Concept Modules Ser.). 1979. pap. 12.50 (ISBN 0-471-04124-6, Pub. by Wiley Med). Wiley.
Bradley, Richard. The Country Housewife & Lady's Director. 500p. 1980. Repr. of 1736 ed. 37.50x (ISBN 0-907325-01-7, Pub. by Prospect England). U Pr of Va.
Bradshaw, Lois E. & Mazlen, Roger G. Nutrition in Health Care. 1979. vinyl 6.95 (ISBN 0-686-59813-X). Interfacia Inc.
--Nutrition in Health Care. LC 79-89882. 1979. pap. 6.95 (ISBN 0-917634-06-3). Creative Infomatics.
Bragg, Paul. Health Food Cookbook. 3.95 (ISBN 0-686-29872-1). Cancer Bk Hse.
--Hi-Protein, Meat-Less Health Recipes. 3.95 (ISBN 0-686-29871-3). Cancer Bk Hse.
--Toxicless Diet - Purification. 1.25 (ISBN 0-686-29873-X). Cancer Bk Hse.
Bragg, Paul C. & Bragg, Patricia. Healthful Eating Without Confusion. 10th ed. LC 71-152392. pap. 2.95 (ISBN 0-87790-024-8). Health Sci.
--Shocking Truth About Water. 22nd ed. LC 77-101348. pap. 2.95 (ISBN 0-87790-000-0). Health Sci.
Brandt, Johanna. The Grape Cure. 1.25 (ISBN 0-686-29874-8). Cancer Bk Hse.
Brennen, R. O. Nutrigenetics: Relieving Hypoglycemia. 8.95 (ISBN 0-686-29875-6). Cancer Bk Hse.
Brody, Jane. Jane Brody's Nutrition Book: A Lifetime Guide to Good Eating for Better Health & Weight Control by the Personal Health Columnist for the New York Times. LC 80-25117. (Illus.). 576p. 1981. 17.95 (ISBN 0-393-01429-0). Norton.
Bronfen, Nan. Nutrition for a Better Life: A Sourcebook for the 80's. (Illus.). 240p. (Orig.). 1980. pap. 8.95 (ISBN 0-88496-152-4). Capra Pr.
Brown, Jo G. The Food Compendium. pap. 10.95 (ISBN 0-385-13523-8, Dolp). Doubleday.
--The Good Food Compendium. LC 78-22306. (Illus.). 416p. 1981. pap. 12.95 (ISBN 0-385-13523-8, Dolp). Doubleday.
Bunnelle, Hasse. Food for Knapsackers & Other Trail Travellers. LC 74-162395. (Totebooks Ser.). 144p. 1971. pap. 4.95 (ISBN 0-87156-049-6). Sierra.
Burk, Dean. Vitamin B17, B15, Brief Foods-Vitamins. 1.50 (ISBN 0-686-29881-0). Cancer Bk Hse.
Burton, B. T. Human Nutrition. 3rd ed. Orig. Title: Heinz Handbook of Nutrition. (Illus.). 1975. 17.50 (ISBN 0-07-009282-6, HP); pap. 12.95 (ISBN 0-07-009281-8). McGraw.
Cadwallader, Sharon. Whole Earth Cooking for the Eighties. (Illus.). 128p. 1981. 9.95 (ISBN 0-312-87050-7); pap. 5.95 (ISBN 0-312-87051-5). St Martin.
Calabrese, Edward J. Nutrition & Environmental Health: The Influence of Nutritional Status on Pollutant Toxicity & Carcinogenicity, 2 vols. Incl. Vol. 1. The Vitamins. 60.00 (ISBN 0-471-04833-X); Vol. 2. Minerals & Macronutrients. 544p. 35.00 (ISBN 0-471-08207-4). LC 79-21089. (Environmental Science & Technology Ser.). 1980 (Pub. by Wiley-Interscience). Wiley.
Caliendo, Mary A. Nutrition & Preventative Health Care. (Illus.). 1981. text ed. 19.95 (ISBN 0-02-318330-6). Macmillan.
--The Nutrition Crisis: Alternatives for Change. (Illus.). 1979. pap. text ed. 10.95 (ISBN 0-02-318340-3). Macmillan.
Campbell, Diane. Step-by-Step to Natural Food. 6.95 (ISBN 0-686-29883-7). Cancer Bk Hse.
Cannon, Helen L. & Davidson, David F., eds. Relation of Geology & Trace Elements to Nutrition. LC 67-22340. (Special Paper: No. 90). (Illus., Orig.). 1968. pap. 5.50x (ISBN 0-8137-2090-7). Geol Soc.
Cantor, Alfred U. Doctor Cantor's Longevity Diet: How to Slow Down Aging & Prolong Youth & Vigor. 1967. 12.95 (ISBN 0-13-216267-9, Parker). P-H.
Carbohydrates in Human Nutrition. (Food & Nutrition Paper Ser.: No. 15). 82p. 1980. pap. 7.50 (ISBN 92-5-100903-1, F2040, FAO). Unipub.
Carlin, Joseph M. A Food Service Guide to the Nutrition Program for the Elderly. rev. ed. 1975. pap. text ed. 5.00 (ISBN 0-89634-013-9, 023). New England Geron.
--Nutrition Education for the Elderly: The Technique. (Serving the Elderly Ser.: Pt. 4). 1978. pap. text ed. 3.00 (ISBN 0-89634-009-0, 046). New England Geron.
Carpenter, Kathy & Calloway, Doris H. Nutrition & Health. 1981. text ed. 19.95 (ISBN 0-03-057711-X, HoltC); instr's manual 9.95 (ISBN 0-03-058274-1). HR&W.
Carper, Jean. Brand Name Nutrition Counter. 256p. 1975. pap. 2.50 (ISBN 0-553-06417-7, 14221-6). Bantam.
Carque, Otto. Vital Facts About Foods. LC 75-18697. 240p. 1975. pap. 3.50 (ISBN 0-87983-113-8). Keats.
Cathcart, E. P. Nutrition & Dietetics. 1928. 12.50 (ISBN 0-8274-4191-6). R West.
Chandra, R. K. & Newberne, P. M. Nutrition, Immunity & Infection: Mechanisms of Interaction. (Illus.). 262p. 1977. 22.50 (ISBN 0-306-31058-9, Plenum Pr). Plenum Pub.
Chaney, Margaret S., et al. Nutrition. 9th ed. LC 78-69546. (Illus.). 1979. text ed. 18.95 (ISBN 0-395-25448-5); o.p. inst. manual (ISBN 0-395-25449-3). HM.
Charley, Helen. Food Science. 2nd ed. 525p. 1982. text ed. 20.95 (ISBN 0-471-06206-5). Wiley.
--Food Science. LC 80-17047. 530p. 1970. 21.95 (ISBN 0-8260-1925-0). Wiley.
Chemical Feast. 1.95 (ISBN 0-686-29944-2). Cancer Bk Hse.
Cheraskin, E. & Ringsdorf, W. Diet & Disease. 5.95 (ISBN 0-686-29886-1). Cancer Bk Hse.
Chicago Dietetic Association & South Suburban Dietetic Association. Manual of Clinical Dietetics. 1981. text ed. write for info. (ISBN 0-7216-2537-1). Saunders.
Chomicki, William P. Your Secret to Vibrant Good Health. 1981. 4.95 (ISBN 0-8062-1802-9). Carlton.
Chrispeels, Maarten J. & Sadava, David. Plants, Food, & People. LC 76-46498. (Illus.). 1977. text ed. 19.95x (ISBN 0-7167-0378-5); pap. text ed. 9.95x (ISBN 0-7167-0377-7). W H Freeman.
Church, D. C., ed. Digestive Physiology & Nutrition of Ruminants: Nutrition, Vol. 2. 2nd ed. 1979. text ed. 25.00 (ISBN 0-9601586-5-0). O & B Bks.
Cilento. You Don't Have to Live with: Vitamin & Mineral Deficiences. 1978. 7.50x (ISBN 0-7233-5299-2). Intl Pubns Serv.
Clark, Linda. The Best of Linda Clark. LC 77-352686. (Orig.). 1976. pap. 4.50 (ISBN 0-87983-062-X). Keats.
--How to Improve Your Health. LC 78-61329. 1979. 8.95 (ISBN 0-87983-181-2); pap. 4.95 (ISBN 0-87983-180-4). Keats.
--Know Your Nutrition. rev. ed. LC 80-84437. 275p. 1981. pap. 4.95 (ISBN 0-87983-247-9). Keats.
--Know Your Nutrition. (Spanish ed.). 1980. pap. 5.95 (ISBN 0-87983-174-X). Keats.
--Know Your Nutrition. LC 73-84556. 276p. 1973. 6.95 (ISBN 0-87983-047-6); pap. 3.50 (ISBN 0-87983-048-4). Keats.
--Light on Your Health Problems. LC 72-83522. (Pivot Original Health Book). 240p. 1972. pap. 1.50 (ISBN 0-87983-026-3). Keats.
--The New Way to Eat. LC 79-55271. 1980. pap. 5.95 (ISBN 0-89087-263-5). Celestial Arts.
--Sepa Como Alimentarse. Orig. Title: Know Your Nutrition. (Orig., Span.). 1980. pap. 5.95 (ISBN 0-87983-174-X). Keats.
Clarkson, Kenneth W. Food Stamps & Nutrition. LC 75-4377. 1975. pap. 4.25 (ISBN 0-8447-3155-2). Am Enterprise.
Clerc, Michel. Contribution a l'Etude des Relations Vitaminiques A et C. (Black Africa Ser.). 182p. (Fr.). 1974. Repr. of 1963 ed. lib. bdg. 53.50x (ISBN 0-8287-0205-5, 71-2013). Clearwater Pub.
Clinical Nutrition Update: Amino Acids. pap. 7.00 (ISBN 0-89970-026-8, OP-040). AMA.
Clinkard, C. E. The Uses of Juices. 1981. pap. 1.95 (ISBN 0-87904-039-4). Lust.
Clydesdale, Fergus. Food Science & Nutrition: Current Issues & Answers. (Illus.). 1979. ref. 16.95 (ISBN 0-13-323162-3). P-H.
Clydesdale, Fergus S. & Francis, F. J. Food, Nutrition & You. (Illus.). 1977. lib. bdg. 13.95 (ISBN 0-13-323048-1); pap. text ed. 9.95 (ISBN 0-13-323030-9). P-H.
Colorado Dietectic Association Conference - 1969. Dimensions of Nutrition: Proceedings. Dupont, Jacqueline, ed. LC 71-134852. (Illus.). 1974. pap. 8.95x (ISBN 0-87081-006-5). Colo Assoc.
Commission on International Relations. World Food & Nutrition Study: Supporting Papers, 5 vols. 1977. Vol. I. pap. 6.75 (ISBN 0-309-02647-4); Vol. II. pap. 6.75 (ISBN 0-309-02726-8); Vol. III. pap. 7.00 (ISBN 0-309-02730-6); Vol. IV. pap. 6.00 (ISBN 0-309-02727-6); Vol. V. pap. 6.00 (ISBN 0-309-02646-6). Natl Acad Pr.
Consumer Beware. 4.95 (ISBN 0-686-29751-2). Cancer Bk Hse.
Corbin, Cheryl. Nutrition. LC 80-11138. (Illus.). 208p. 1981. 13.95 (ISBN 0-03-048281-X, Owl Bks); pap. 7.95 (ISBN 0-03-048276-3). HR&W.
Creff, Albert & Wernick, Robert. Dr. Creff's 1-2-3 Sports Diet. 1979. 8.95 (ISBN 0-698-10890-6). Coward.
Crisp, Arthur H. & Stonehill, Edward. Sleep, Nutrition & Mood. LC 75-16121. 1976. 30.75 (ISBN 0-471-18688-0, Pub. by Wiley-Interscience). Wiley.
CSPI Staff. The Midget Encyclopedia of Food & Nutrition. 1978. pap. 1.00 (ISBN 0-89329-008-4). Ctr Sci Public.
Culinary Arts Institute, ed. Nutrition Cookbook. LC 77-73012. (Adventures in Cooking Ser.). (Illus.). 1978. pap. 3.95 (ISBN 0-8326-0572-7, 2514). Delair.

Cumming, Candy & Newman, Vicky. Eater's Guide: Nutrition Basics for Busy People. (Illus.). 192p. 1981. 11.95 (ISBN 0-13-223057-7); pap. 5.95 (ISBN 0-13-223040-2). P-H.
Cunningham, John J., ed. Controversies in Clinical Nutrition. LC 80-50827. (Illus.). 240p. 1980. pap. 15.95x (ISBN 0-89313-021-4). G F Stickley Co.
Cureton, Thomas K. The Physiological Effects of Wheat Germ Oil on Humans in Exercise: Forty-two Physical Training Programs Utilizing 894 Humans. (Illus.). 552p. 1972. 46.50 (ISBN 0-398-02270-4). C C Thomas.
Cureton, Thomas K., Jr. & Stull, Allen, eds. Physical Fitness, Training Environment & Nutrition Related to Performance, Vol. II. (Encyclopedia of Physical Education, Fitness & Sports). (Illus.). 800p. 1980. 38.00 (ISBN 0-89832-016-X). Brighton Pub Co.
Darby, W. J., et al, eds. Annual Review of Nutrition, Vol. 1. (Illus.). 1981. text ed. 20.00 (ISBN 0-8243-2801-9). Annual Reviews.
Darden, Ellington. The Nautilus Nutrition Book. (Illus.). 352p. 1981. 14.95 (ISBN 0-8092-5891-9); pap. 7.95 (ISBN 0-8092-5890-0). Contemp Bks.
--Nutrition for Athletes. LC 77-76070. (Physical Fitness & Sports Medicine Ser.). 1978. pap. 3.95 (ISBN 0-89305-014-8). Anna Pub.
--Nutrition for Athletics. LC 76-10811. 1975. pap. 7.95 (ISBN 0-87095-058-4). Athletic.
--Olympic Athletes Ask Questions About Exercise & Nutrition. (Physical Fitness & Sports Medicine Ser.). pap. 2.95 (ISBN 0-89305-007-5). Anna Pub.
D'Asaro, Barbara. Be Young & Vital: The Nutrition Exercise Plan. LC 78-24260. (Illus.). 1979. pap. 7.95 (ISBN 0-89490-022-6). Enslow Pubs.
Davidson, Stanley, et al. Human Nutrition & Dietetics. 7th ed. (Illus.). 1979. text ed. 37.00 (ISBN 0-443-01765-4); pap. text ed. 35.00 (ISBN 0-443-01764-6). Churchill.
Davis, Adelle. Eat Right to Keep Fit. 2.50 (ISBN 0-686-29902-7). Cancer Bk Hse.
--Let's Cook It Right. rev. ed. LC 62-9440. (Illus.). 1962. 6.95 (ISBN 0-15-150166-1). HarBraceJ.
--Let's Cook It Right. LC 62-9440. 1970. pap. 2.50 (ISBN 0-685-72756-4, Pub. by NAL). Formur Intl.
--Let's Eat Right to Keep Fit. rev. ed. LC 75-134581. 1970. 8.95 (ISBN 0-15-150304-4). HarBraceJ.
--Let's Eat Right to Keep Fit. 1970. pap. 3.95 (ISBN 0-451-09644-4, AE1161, Sig). NAL.
--Let's Eat Right to Keep Fit. LC 71-128463. 1970. pap. 2.50 (ISBN 0-685-72755-6, Pub. by NAL). Formur Intl.
--Let's Get Well. LC 65-19054. 1972. pap. 2.50 (ISBN 0-685-72757-2, Pub. by NAL). Formur Intl.
--Let's Stay Healthy: A Guide to Lifelong Nutrition. Gildroy, Ann, ed. LC 80-8744. 320p. 1981. 12.95 (ISBN 0-15-150443-1). HarBraceJ.
DeJose, Grace. The Hempstead Plan: Sensible Approach to Dieting & Nutrition. (Illus.). 1980. 7.50 (ISBN 0-682-49516-6). Exposition.
Dennison, Darwin. The Dine System: For Better Nutrition & Health. 128p. 1981. pap. text ed. 7.95 (ISBN 0-8403-2371-9). Kendall-Hunt.
Department of School Nurses. Nutrition in Today's Education - As a School Nurse Sees It. 24p. 1972. 2.50 (ISBN 0-686-02359-5). Natl Assn Sch Nurses.
Deskins, Barbara B. Everyone's Guide to Better Food & Nutrition. LC 74-6570. 180p. 1974. 8.95 (ISBN 0-685-50524-3). Jonathan David.
De Spain, June. Litttle Cyanide Cookbook: B-17 Recipes. 4.95 (ISBN 0-686-29906-X). Cancer Bk Hse.
Detoxification Diet. 0.35 (ISBN 0-686-29908-6). Cancer Bk Hse.
Deutsch, Ronald. Realities of Nutrition. LC 76-23508. (Berkeley Series in Nutrition). (Illus.). 1976. 13.95 (ISBN 0-915950-07-3); pap. 10.95 (ISBN 0-915950-19-7). Bull Pub.
Deutsch, Ronald M. The New Nuts Among the Berries. LC 77-70401. 1977. pap. 5.95 (ISBN 0-915950-09-X). Bull Pub.
Deutsch-Skandinavisches Symposium, Kopenhagen, 1978. Parenterale Ernaehrung (Forschung und praxis) Zoellner, N., ed. (Beitraege zu Infusionstherapie und Klinische Ernaehrung: Band 1). (Illus.). 1978. pap. 12.00 (ISBN 3-8055-2963-5). S Karger.
Devadas, R. P. Nutrition in Tamil Nadu. (Madras Institute of Development Studies Ser., No. 3). 164p. 1973. text ed. 4.50x (ISBN 0-8426-0428-6). Verry.
Dickerson, John W. & Lee, H. A. Nutrition in the Clinical Management of Disease. 1978. 37.50 (ISBN 0-8151-2451-1). Year Bk Med.
Dietary Department Newark Beth Israel Medical Center. Diet Manual. LC 80-82889. 92p. (Orig.). 1980. pap. 10.00 (ISBN 0-937714-00-3). Newark Beth.
Dietary Fats & Oils in Human Nutrition. (FAO Food & Nutrition Paper Ser.: No. 3). 1978. pap. 7.50 (ISBN 92-5-100467-6, F1422, FAO). Unipub.
Dinaburg & Akel. Nutrition Survival Kit. (Orig.). pap. 1.75 (ISBN 0-515-04654-X). Jove Pubns.
Dobbing, John, ed. Maternal Nutrition in Pregnancy: Eating for Two? LC 80-41611. 1980. 33.50 (ISBN 0-12-218850-0). Acad Pr.
Draper, Harold H., ed. Advances in Nutritional Research, Vols. 1-3. Incl. Vol. 1. 362p. 1977. 27.50 (ISBN 0-306-34321-5); Vol. 2. 264p. 1979. 27.50 (ISBN 0-306-40213-0); Vol. 3. 300p. 1980. 32.50 (ISBN 0-306-40415-X). Plenum Pub. (Illus., Plenum Pr). Plenum Pub.
Duquet, Richard. Actively Seeking Nutrition. 27p. 1978. pap. 2.00 (ISBN 0-934332-20-7, Pub. by L'Epervier Pr). SBD.
Eagles, Juanita & Randall, Mildred. Handbook of Normal & Therapeutic Nutrition. 336p. 1979. text ed. 25.00 (ISBN 0-89004-325-6). Raven.
Eagles, Juanita, et al. Mary Swartz Rose, Eighteen Seventy Four-Nineteen Forty One: Pioneer in Nutrition. LC 79-4342. 1979. text ed. 9.95 (ISBN 0-8077-2556-0). Tchrs Coll.
Easter, Jade. The Healing Handbook. (Illus.). 128p. (Orig.). 1981. pap. 6.95 (ISBN 0-913300-15-2). Unity Pr.
Eating for Health. 1978. pap. 1.50 (ISBN 0-8277-5627-5). British Bk Ctr.
Echols, Barbara E. & Arena, Jay M. The Common-Sense Guide to Good Eating. LC 77-862. 1978. pap. text ed. 4.50 (ISBN 0-8120-0791-3). Barron.
Eckstein, Eleanor F. Food, People & Nutrition. (Illus.). 1980. text ed. 19.50 (ISBN 0-87055-355-0). AVI.
Eisenman, Patricia & Johnson, Dennis. Coaches Guide to Nutrition & Weight Control. (Illus.). 1981. pap. text ed. 12.95x (ISBN 0-931250-25-0). Human Kinetics.
Ellenbogen, Leon. Controversies in Nutrition. (Contemporary Issues in Clinical Nutrition Ser.). (Illus.). 224p. 1981. lib. bdg. 20.00 (ISBN 0-443-08127-1). Churchill.
Encouraging the Use of Protein-Rich Foods. 103p. 1974. pap. 10.00 (ISBN 0-685-48620-6, F123, FAO). Unipub.
Energy & Protein Requirements: Report of a Joint FAO-WHO Ad Hoc Expert Committee. (FAO Nutrition Meetings Report Ser.: No. 52). (Illus.). 118p. pap. 4.25 (ISBN 92-5-100303-3, F124, FAO). Unipub.
Eppright s, E., et al. Teaching Nutrition. 2nd ed. 1963. 7.95 (ISBN 0-8138-1660-2). Iowa St U Pr.
European Nutrition Conference, 2nd, Munich, 1976. Abstracts. Zoellner, N., et al, eds. (Nutrition & Metabolism: Vol. 20, No. 3). 1976. 22.25 (ISBN 3-8055-2441-2). S Karger.
--Proceedings. Incl. Vol. 21, Nos. 1-3. Main Papers. 54.00 (ISBN 3-8055-2704-7); Vol. 21, No. 4. Round Table on Comparison of Dietary Recommendation in Different European Countries. 9.00 (ISBN 3-8055-2705-5); Vol. 21, Suppl. 1. Short Communications. 54.00 (ISBN 3-8055-2636-9). (Nutrition & Metabolism: Vol. 21, Nos. 1-4 & Suppl. 1). 1977. complete 76.75 (ISBN 3-8055-2681-4). S Karger.
Eversaul, George A. Clinical Nutrition. 1979. 85.00 (ISBN 0-685-93704-6, 0-9601-7826). G A Eversaul.
Fabroni, Al G. Miracle of Natural Self-Cure. 1981. 6.00 (ISBN 0-8062-1581-X). Carlton.
Fabun, Don. Food: An Energy Exchange System. 1971. pap. text ed. 2.50x (ISBN 0-02-475370-X, 47537). Macmillan.
Falkner, F. & Tanner, J. M., eds. Human Growth, Vol. 3: Neurobiology & Nutrition. 624p. 1979. 37.50 (ISBN 0-306-34463-7, Plenum Pr). Plenum Pub.
FAO-WHO Expert Committee on Nutrition, Rome, 1974, 9th. Food & Nutrition Strategies in National Development: Report. (Technical Report Ser.: No. 584). (Also avail. in French & Spanish). 1976. pap. 2.80 (ISBN 92-4-120584-9). World Health.
FAO-WHO Joint Committee Expert Committee on Nutrition, 8th. Proceedings. (Technical Report Ser: No. 477). 80p. 1971. pap. 2.00 (ISBN 92-4-120477-X, 413). World Health.
Fat Emulsions in Parenteral Nutrition. pap. 7.00 (ISBN 0-89970-042-X, OP-140). AMA.
Fathman, George & Fathman, Doris. Live Foods (192) Recipes. 2.75 (ISBN 0-686-29918-3). Cancer Bk Hse.
Ferguson, James M. & Taylor, C. Barr. A Change for Heart: Your Family & the Food You Eat. 1978. pap. 5.95 (ISBN 0-915950-22-7). Bull Pub.
Fiennes, R. N., ed. Biology of Nutrition, Pts. 1-2. Incl. Pt. 1. The Evolution & Nature of Living Systems; Pt. 2. The Organizations & Nutritional Methods of Life Forms. 688p. 1972. Set. text ed. 125.00 (ISBN 0-08-016470-6). Pergamon.
Fitzgerald, Thomas K., ed. Nutrition & Anthropology in Action. (Studies of Developing Countries: No. 21). (Orig.). 1976. pap. text ed. 14.25x (ISBN 90-232-1447-1). Humanities.
Fleck, Henrietta. Introduction to Nutrition. 4th ed. 1981. text ed. 17.95x (ISBN 0-02-338280-5). Macmillan.
--Introduction to Nutrition. 3rd ed. (Illus.). 528p. 1976. text ed. 18.95 (ISBN 0-02-338430-1, 33843). Macmillan.
Fonosch, Gail & Kvitka, Elaine. Meal Management Concepts. 1978. text ed. 16.95 scp (ISBN 0-06-453520-7, HarpC); instructor's manual avail. (ISBN 0-06-453523-1). Har-Row.
Food & Nutrition Board. Recommended Dietary Allowances: Ninth Edition. (Illus.). 1980. pap. 6.00 (ISBN 0-309-02941-4). Natl Acad Pr.
Food and Nutrition Board - Division of Biology and Agriculture. Maternal Nutrition & the Course of Pregnancy. LC 72-605179. (Illus., Orig.). 1970. pap. text ed. 8.25 (ISBN 0-309-01761-0). Natl Acad Pr.
Food & Nutrition Education in the Primary School. (FAO Nutritional Studies: No. 25). (Illus.). 107p. (Orig.). 1971. pap. 8.25 (ISBN 0-685-29063-8, FAO). Unipub.
Food & Nutrition Planning. (Nutrition Consultants Reports Ser: No. 35). 1977. pap. 11.75 (ISBN 92-5-100263-0, F906, FAO). Unipub.
Food & Nutrition Strategies in National Development: Ninth Report of the Joint FAO-WHV Expert Committee on Nutrition, Rome, 1974. (FAO Nutrition Meetings Report Ser: No.56). 64p. (FAO Food & Nutrition Ser., No. 5). 1976. pap. 7.25 (ISBN 92-5-100262-2, P80, FAO). Unipub.
Food Combining Made Easy. pap. 2.15 (ISBN 0-686-20580-4). Willow Pub.
Food Deprivation. (Landmark Ser.). 1979. 25.00x (ISBN 0-8422-4127-2). Irvington.
Food Price Policies & Nutrition in Latin America. (Food & Nutrition Bulletin Ser.: Suppl. 3). 170p. 1980. pap. 15.00 (ISBN 92-808-0128-7, TUNU087, UNU). Unipub.
Foresman, Ethel. Health & Happiness Are Twins. 1961. 3.95 (ISBN 0-8315-0034-4). Speller.
Forman, Robert. How to Control Your Allergies. 256p. (Orig.). 1979. pap. 2.50 (ISBN 0-915962-29-2). Larchmont Bks.
Frankle, Reva T. & Owen, Anita Y. Nutrition in the Community: The Art of Delivering Services. LC 78-9144. 1978. text ed. 17.95 (ISBN 0-8016-1666-2). Mosby.
Frederick. Psycho-Nutrition. (Health, Nutrition & Well Being Bks). 5.95 (ISBN 0-448-14479-4). G&D.
Fredericks, Carlton. The Carlton Fredericks No-Nonsense Nutrition Guide. 1980. 9.95 (ISBN 0-448-12258-8). G&D.
--Dr. Carlton Fredericks' New & Complete Nutrition Handbook. 272p. (Orig.). 1978. pap. 1.95 (ISBN 0-89041-206-5, 3206). Major Bks.
--Eat Well, Get Well, Stay Well. LC 79-91618. 1980. 9.95 (ISBN 0-448-12258-8); pap. 5.95 (ISBN 0-448-12023-2). G&D.
--New & Revised Carlton Fredericks Cook Book for Good Nutrition. LC 73-15132. 304p. 1974. 3.95 (ISBN 0-448-11665-0, MSP). G&D.
--Nutrition: Your Key to Good Health. 1.95 (ISBN 0-686-29924-8). Cancer Bk Hse.
--Psycho-Nutrition. 224p. 1976. pap. 5.95 (ISBN 0-448-14479-4). G&D.
Fredericks, Carlton & Bailey, Herbert. Food Facts & Fallacies. LC 65-27390. (Charts). 1968. pap. 2.50 (ISBN 0-668-01726-0). Arco.
Freedland, R. A. & Briggs, S. A Biochemical Approach to Nutrition. (Outline Studies in Biology). 63p. 1977. pap. text ed. 5.95x (ISBN 0-412-13040-8, Pub. by Chapman & Hall England). Methuen Inc.
Freidman, Mendel, ed. Nutritional Improvement of Food & Feed Proteins. LC 78-17278. (Advances in Experimental Medicine & Biology Ser.: Vol. 105). 894p. 1978. 69.50 (ISBN 0-306-40026-X, Plenum Pr). Plenum Pub.
Friedman, Mendel, ed. Protein Nutritional Quality of Foods & Feeds, Pt. 2: Quality Factors - Plant Breeding, Composition, Processing & Antinutrients. (Nutrition & Clinical Nutrition Ser.: Vol. 1). 1975. 69.75 (ISBN 0-8247-6282-7). Dekker.
Frompovich, Catherine J. Preventing Burnout: The Nutritional Approach. (Illus.). 145p. Date not set. pap. cancelled (ISBN 0-935322-14-0). C J Frompovich.
Gallender, Carolyn N. & Gallender, Demos. Dietary Problems & Diets for the Handicapped. 224p. 1979. 16.25 (ISBN 0-398-03838-4). C C Thomas.
Gammon, Margaret & Read, Carol I. Edgar Cayce on Diet & Health. 192p. (Orig.). 1969. pap. 2.25 (ISBN 0-446-92690-6). Warner Bks.
Gastineau, Clifford F., et al, eds. Fermented Food Beverages in Nutrition. (Nutrition Foundation Ser.). 1979. 48.00 (ISBN 0-12-277050-1). Acad Pr.
Gati, T., et al, eds. Nutrition-Digestion-Metabolism: Proceedings of the 28th International Congress of Physiological Sciences, Budapest, 1980. LC 80-42185. (Advances in Physiological Sciences Ser.: Vol. 12). (Illus.). 400p. 1981. 50.00 (ISBN 0-08-026825-0). Pergamon.
Gazella, Jacqueline G. Nutrition for the Childbearing Year. LC 79-64367. (Illus.). 1979. spiralbound 8.95 (ISBN 0-934104-01-8). Woodland.
Gerard, Ralph W., ed. Food for Life. LC 52-14880. 1965. pap. 3.25 (ISBN 0-226-28790-4, P527, Phoen). U of Chicago Pr.
Gifft, Helen, et al. Nutrition, Behavior & Change. LC 79-170033. 1972. ref. ed. 18.95 (ISBN 0-13-627836-1). P-H.
Goldstein, Richard L. Eating & Weight Disorders. Date not set. price not set (ISBN 0-8261-3830-6). Springer Pub.
Good Food & Fitness. 1981. 4.95 (ISBN 0-696-00635-9). BH&G.
Goodhart, Robert S. & Shils, Maurice E., eds. Modern Nutrition in Health & Disease. 6th ed. LC 79-16842. (Illus.). 1370p. 1980. text ed. 47.50 (ISBN 0-8121-0645-8). Lea & Febiger.
Goulart, Frances S. Eating to Win. LC 77-8756. 1978. 25.00x (ISBN 0-8128-2322-2); pap. 6.95 (ISBN 0-686-67964-4). Stein & Day.
Grant, Doris. Recipe for Survival: Your Daily Food. LC 73-93654. 224p. 1974. 6.95 (ISBN 0-87983-069-7); pap. 3.95 (ISBN 0-87983-078-6). Keats.
Green, Lawrence S. & Johnston, Francis S., eds. Social & Biological Predictors of Nutritional Status, Physical Growth & Neurological Development. 1980. 25.00 (ISBN 0-12-299750-6). Acad Pr.
Green, Marilyn L. & Harry, Joann. Nutrition in Contemporary Nursing Practice. LC 80-22426. 864p. 1981. 24.95 (ISBN 0-471-03892-X, Pub. by Wiley Med). Wiley.
Grills, Norma J. & Bosscher, Marcia V. Manual of Nutrition & Diet Therapy. 10th ed. 1981. pap. text ed. 15.95x (ISBN 0-02-347280-4). Macmillan.
Group of European Nutritionists, 10th Meeting, Saltsjoebaden, 1971. Complete Intravenous Nutrition. Wretlind, A., ed. (Nutrition & Metabolism: Vol. 14, Suppl.). (Illus.). 300p. 1972. pap. 23.50 (ISBN 3-8055-1450-6). S Karger.
Group of European Nutritionists, 12th Symposium, Cambridge, July 1973. Gut & Nutrition: Proceedings. Somogyi, J. C. & MacDonald, eds. (Bibliotheca Nutritio et Dieta: No. 22). 200p. 1975. pap. 43.25 (ISBN 3-8055-1738-6). S Karger.
Gussow, Joan. The Feeding Web: Issues in Nutritional Ecology. LC 78-8579. 1978. 14.95 (ISBN 0-915950-14-6); pap. 11.95 (ISBN 0-915950-15-4). Bull Pub.
Guthrie, Helen. Introductory Nutrition. 4th ed. LC 78-16649. (Illus.). 1979. text ed. 19.95 (ISBN 0-8016-2001-5). Mosby.
Guthrie, Helen A. & Braddock, Karen S. Programmed Nutrition. 2nd ed. LC 77-15942. (Illus.). 1978. pap. text ed. 12.95 (ISBN 0-8016-2003-1). Mosby.
Gwatkin, Davidson R. & Wilcox, Janet R. Can Health & Nutrition Interventions Make a Difference? LC 80-80500. 76p. 1980. pap. 5.00 (ISBN 0-686-28117-9). Overseas Dev Council.
Hafen, Brent Q. Nutrition, Food & Weight Control: Expanded Edition. 400p. 1980. text ed. 19.95 (ISBN 0-205-06825-1, 6268250). Allyn.
--Nutrition, Food & Weight Control: Standard Edition. 320p. 1980. pap. text ed. 10.95 (ISBN 0-205-06826-X, 6268269); tchr's ed. free (ISBN 0-205-06828-6, 6268285). Allyn.
Hall, Ross H. Food for Nought: The Decline in Nutrition. (Illus.). 1974. pap. text ed. 15.00x (ISBN 0-06-141078-0, Harper Medical). Har-Row.
--Food for Nought: The Decline in Nutrition. 1976. pap. 3.95 (ISBN 0-394-71753-8, Vin). Random.
Halpern, Reuben & Halpern, Joshua. Live Your Health: The Art & Practice of Holistic Healing. (Healing Arts Ser.). 220p. 1980. 10.95 (ISBN 0-89496-028-8); pap. 5.95 (ISBN 0-89496-020-2). Ross Bks.
Halpern, Seymour L., ed. Quick Reference to Clinical Nutrition. LC 78-12175. 1979. flexible cover 19.75 (ISBN 0-397-50404-7, JBL-Med-Nursing). Har-Row.
Hambraeus, Leif, ed. Nutrition in Europe. 150p. 1981. text ed. 35.00 (ISBN 0-86598-059-4, Pub. by Almquist & Wiksell Sweden). Allanheld.
Hamilton, Eva M. & Whitney, Eleanor N. Nutrition: Concepts & Controversy. (Illus.). 1979. pap. text ed. 16.95 (ISBN 0-8299-0281-3, Pub by Hartnell); study guide 6.95 (ISBN 0-686-67552-5); study guide o.p. 4.95 (ISBN 0-8299-0288-0); instrs.' manual avail. (ISBN 0-8299-0485-9). West Pub.

Handbook on Human Nutritional Requirements. 66p. 1974. pap. 7.00 (ISBN 92-5-100129-4, F2128, FAO). Unipub.
Handbook on Human Nutritional Requirements. (Nutritional Studies: No. 28). (Illus.). 66p. 1975. pap. 7.25 (ISBN 0-685-54199-1, F223, FAO). Unipub.
Hansen, R. Gaurth & Wyse, Bonita W. Nutritional Quality Index of Foods. (Illus.). 1979. text ed. 35.00 (ISBN 0-87055-320-8). AVI.
Haresign, Lewis. Recent Advances in Animal Nutrition, 1981 (SAFS) 1982. text ed. price not set (ISBN 0-408-71014-4). Butterworth.
--Recent Development in Ruminant Nutrition & Feeding. 1982. price not set (ISBN 0-408-10804-5). Butterworth.
Hartbarger, Janie C. & Hartbarger, Neil J. Eating for the Eighties: A Complete Guide to Vegetarian Nutrition. LC 80-53187. 320p. text ed. 14.95 (ISBN 0-7216-4550-X); pap. text ed. 6.95 (ISBN 0-7216-4549-6). Saunders.
Hatfield, Antoinette K. & Stanton, Peggy S. How to Help Your Child Eat Right: The "Fun to Eat" Cookbook & Good to Nutrition. LC 78-6300. (Illus.). 1978. pap. 4.95 (ISBN 0-87491-253-9). Acropolis.
Hathcock, John N. & Coon, Julius, eds. Nutrition & Drug Interrelations. 1978. 58.00 (ISBN 0-12-332550-1). Acad Pr.
Hawkins, Harold F. Applied Nutrition. 1977. Repr. of 1947 ed. lexatone 7.50 (ISBN 0-87881-069-2). Mojave Bks.
Hefferren, John J. & Moller, Mary L., eds. Patterns & Effects of Diet & Disease Today. (AAAS Selected Symposium: No. 59). 225p. 1981. lib. bdg. 18.75x (ISBN 0-89158-844-2). Westview.
Hegne, Barbara. Everywoman's Every Day Exercise & Nutrition Book. LC 78-57649. (Illus.). 1979. pap. 10.95 (ISBN 0-87983-152-9). Keats.
Heineman, John. Human Nutrition the Value of Herbs. Date not set. cancelled (ISBN 0-89557-018-1). Bi World Indus.
Hensley, E. S. Basic Concepts of World Nutrition. 1981. pap. write for info. (ISBN 0-398-04544-5). C C Thomas.
Herbert, Victor. Nutrition Cultism. LC 80-51835. (Illus.). 240p. 1980. text ed. 12.95 (ISBN 0-89313-020-6). G F Stickley.
Hetzel, B. S. & Frith, H. J., eds. The Nutrition of Aborigines in Relation to the Ecosystem of Central Australia. 1979. 5.95x (ISBN 0-643-00306-1, Pub. by CSIRO). Intl Schol Bk Serv.
Hodges, Robert E. Nutrition in Medical Practice. LC 77-11337. (Illus.). 363p. 1980. text ed. 19.50 (ISBN 0-7216-4706-5). Saunders.
Hoffer, Abram & Walker, Morton. Ortho-Molecular Nutrition. (Orig.). 1981. pap. 4.95x (ISBN 0-686-76746-2). Regent House.
Hofmann, Lieselotte. The Great American Nutrition Hassle. LC 78-51947. 422p. 1978. pap. text ed. 10.95 (ISBN 0-87484-446-0). Mayfield Pub.
Holbrook, Iola B. Eat Your Way to Health. 1972. pap. 2.25 (ISBN 0-87516-162-6). De Vorss.
Hood, Lamartine F. & Wardrip, E. K. Carbohydrates & Health. (Illus.). 1977. text ed. 23.50 (ISBN 0-87055-223-6). AVI.
Hoorweg, Jan & Dowell, Ian. Evaluation of Nutrition Education in Africa: Community Research in Uganda, 1971-1972. 1979. pap. text ed. 13.00x (ISBN 0-686-27022-3). Mouton.
Howard, Rosanne B. & Herbold, Nancie. Nutrition in Clinical Care. (Illus.). 1977. text ed. 15.95 (ISBN 0-07-030545-5, HP). McGraw.
Howe, Phyllis. Basic Nutrition in Health & Disease: Including Selection & Care of Food. 7th ed. 450p. 1981. pap. text ed. write for info. (ISBN 0-7216-4796-0). Saunders.
Human Nutrition in Tropical Africa. (Food & Nutrition Ser: No. 11). 286p. 1980. pap. 21.25 (ISBN 92-5-100412-9, F2049, FAO). Unipub.
Hunt, Sara M., et al. Nutrition: Principles & Clinical Practice. LC 79-25899. 1980. text ed. 23.50 (ISBN 0-471-03149-6). Wiley.
Hunter, Beatrice. The Natural Foods Cookbook. 3.95 (ISBN 0-686-29750-4). Cancer Bk Hse.
Hunter, Beatrice T. The Great Nutrition Robbery. LC 78-1460. 1978. 9.95 (ISBN 0-684-15345-9, SL773, ScribT); pap. 4.95 (ISBN 0-684-15560-5, ScribT). Scribner.
--Natural Foods Primer. 2.95 (ISBN 0-686-29753-9). Cancer Bk Hse.
Hunter, Beatrice T., ed. Food & Your Health. LC 73-93651. (Pivot Original Health Book). 160p. 1974. pap. 1.50 (ISBN 0-87983-074-3). Keats.
Hunter, Kathleen. Health Foods & Herbs. LC 63-15194. (Orig.). 1968. pap. 1.50 (ISBN 0-668-01083-5). Arco.
Hurley, Lucille. Developmental Nutrition. (Illus.). 1979. text ed. 17.95 (ISBN 0-13-207639-X). P-H.
Inglett, G. E. & Charalambous, George, eds. Tropical Foods: Chemistry & Nutrition, Vol. 1. 1979. 29.50 (ISBN 0-12-370901-6). Acad Pr.
International Col.-Applied Nutrition. Nitrition-Applied Naturally. 3.00 (ISBN 0-686-29754-7). Cancer Bk Hse.
International Congress of Nutrition, Mexico, Sept. 1972. Proceedings, 4 vols. 1975. Set. 251.50 (ISBN 3-8055-1394-1). S Karger.
International Symposium on Protein Metabolism & Nutrition, 2nd, the Netherlands, May 2-6, 1977. Proceedings. (European Association for Animal Production (EAAP) Ser.: No. 20). 1977. pap. 28.00 (ISBN 9-0220-0634-4, Pub. by PUDOC). Unipub.
Jacobson, Michael F. Nutrition Scoreboard. 1975. pap. 2.25 (ISBN 0-380-00534-4, 44537). Avon.
Jansky, Robert C. Astrology, Nutrition & Health. Anderson, Margaret, ed. 1977. pap. 6.95 (ISBN 0-914918-08-7). Para Res.
Jarrett, R. J. Nutrition & Disease. 218p. text ed. 19.95 (ISBN 0-8391-1366-8). Univ Park.
Jelliffe, D. B. Assessment of the Nutritional Status of the Community. (Monograph Ser: No. 53). (Illus.). 271p. (Eng, Fr, Rus, & Span.). 1966. 18.80 (ISBN 92-4-140053-6). World Health.
Jelliffe, Derrick B., ed. Human Nutrition-A Comprehensive Treatise: Vol. 2: Nutrition & Growth. (Illus.). 472p. 1979. 37.50 (ISBN 0-306-40128-2, Plenum Pr). Plenum Pub.
Jenks, Jorian. The Stuff We're Made of. 1959. 6.00 (ISBN 0-8159-6829-9). Devin.
Jensen, Bernard D. Vital Foods-Total Health. 4.95 (ISBN 0-686-29759-8). Cancer Bk Hse.
Jerome, Norge W., et al, eds. Nutritional Anthropology: Contemporary Approaches to Diet & Culture. 1980. pap. 12.80 (ISBN 0-913178-55-1). Redgrave Pub Co.
--Nutritional Anthropology. 1980. pap. 12.80 (ISBN 0-913178-55-1, Pub. by Redgrave Pub. Co.). Hippocrene Bks.
Johnson, Roberta, ed. Whole Foods for the Whole Family. LC 81-81988. (Illus.). 352p. 1981. pap. 10.95 (ISBN 0-912500-09-3). La Leche.
Johnston, Joseph A. Nutritional Studies in Adolescent Girls: And Their Relation to Tuberculosis. (Illus.). 330p. 1953. photocopy ed. spiral 29.75 (ISBN 0-398-04296-9). C C Thomas.
Jones, Kenneth L., et al, eds. Foods, Diet & Nutrition. 2nd ed. 141p. 1975. pap. text ed. 8.95 scp (ISBN 0-06-384341-2, HarpC). Har-Row.
Jordan, Henry, et al. Eating Is Okay: A Radical Approach to Weight Loss. Gelman, Steve, ed. 1978. pap. 1.75 (ISBN 0-451-09305-4, E9305, Sig). NAL.
Junkin, Brock & Junkin, Elizabeth. Eat Cheaper. 80p. 1981. 5.50 (ISBN 0-682-49787-8). Exposition.
Jurgens, Marshall H. Animal Feeding & Nutrition. 4th ed. 1978. wire coil bdg. 11.95 (ISBN 0-8403-0600-8). Kendall Hunt.
Jussawalla, J. M. Natural Dietetics: A Handbook on Food, Nutrition & Health. 1979. text ed. 10.50 (ISBN 0-7069-0806-6, Pub. by Vikas India). Advent NY.
Kadans, Joseph N. Encyclopedia of Fruits, Vegetables, Nuts & Seeds for Healthful Living. 1973. 9.95 (ISBN 0-13-275412-6, Reward); pap. 3.95 (ISBN 0-13-275420-7). P-H.
Kaibara, Ekiken. Yojokun: Japanese Secret of Good Health. 1974. 9.95 (ISBN 0-89346-101-6, Pub. by Tokuma Shoten); pap. 2.95 (ISBN 0-89346-047-8). Heian Intl.
Kare, Morley R. & Maller, Owen, eds. The Chemical Senses & Nutrition. (Nutrition Foundation Ser.). 1977. 34.50 (ISBN 0-12-397850-5). Acad Pr.
Karow, Juliette. The Necessary Diet. LC 80-22565. (Orig.). 1981. pap. 5.95 (ISBN 0-89865-085-2). Donning Co.
Karran, S. J. Practical Nutritional Support. LC 79-56645. 351p. 1980. 32.50 (ISBN 0-471-08024-1, Pub. by Wiley Medical). Wiley.
Katzen, Howard M. & Mahler, Richard J., eds. Advances in Modern Nutrition: Vol. 2, Diabetes, Obesity & Vascular Disease, 2 pts. LC 77-24993. (Advances in Modern Nutrition Ser.). 1978. 24.50 ea.; Pt. 1. (ISBN 0-470-99360-X); Pt. 2. (ISBN 0-470-26286-9). Halsted Pr.
Kaufman, Willaim I. Guide to Calories. (Baronet's Handy Pocket Guide to Nutrition). 1978. pap. 1.50 (ISBN 0-89437-004-9). Baronet.
Kaufman, William I. Guide to Carbohydrates. (Baronet's Handy Pocket Guide to Nutrition). 1978. pap. 1.50 (ISBN 0-89437-003-0). Baronet.
--Guide to Cholesterol. (Baronet's Handy Guide to Nutrition Ser). 1978. pap. 1.50 (ISBN 0-89437-005-7). Baronet.
--Guide to Protein. (Baronet's Handy Pocket Guide to Nutrition). 1978. pap. 1.50 (ISBN 0-89437-006-5). Baronet.
Kerschner, Velma. Nutrition & Diet Therapy for Practical Nurses. 2nd ed. LC 75-33986. 280p. 1976. pap. text ed. 9.50 (ISBN 0-8036-5301-8). Davis Co.
Keyes, Ken, Jr. Loving Your Body. LC 74-84411. Orig. Title: How to Live Longer, Stronger, Slimmer. 252p. 1974. pap. 3.95 (ISBN 0-9600688-4-8). Living Love.
King, Maurice H., et al. Nutrition for Developing Countries: With Special Reference to the Maize, Cassava & Millet Areas of Africa. (Illus.). 240p. 1973. pap. text ed. 15.95x (ISBN 0-19-572244-2). Oxford U Pr.
Kirban, Salem. How to Eat Your Way Back to Vibrant Health. (Illus.). 1977. pap. 3.95 (ISBN 0-912582-25-1). Kirban.
--How to Keep Healthy & Happy by Fasting. (Illus.). 1976. 6.95 (ISBN 0-912582-23-5); pap. 2.95 (ISBN 0-912582-23-5). Kirban.
Kirschmann, John D., ed. Nutrition Almanac. rev. ed. (Illus.). 1979. pap. 7.95 (ISBN 0-07-034849-9, SP); pap. 6.95 (ISBN 0-07-034848-0). McGraw.
Kirschner, H. E. Live Food Juices. 3.00 (ISBN 0-686-29769-5). Cancer Bk Hse.
Kline, Monte L. & Strube, W. P. Eat, Drink & Be Ready. (Illus., Orig.). 1977. pap. 2.50 (ISBN 0-930718-38-0). Harvest Pr Texas.
Kohniechner, Manfred. Healing Wines: Celebrating Their Curative Powers. Blocher, Heidi, tr. from Ger. LC 81-66775. (Illus.). 160p. 1981. text ed. 14.95 (ISBN 0-914398-43-1). Autumn Pr.
Kolisko, Eugen. Nutrition I. 2nd ed. 1977. pap. 4.25x (ISBN 0-906492-04-1, Pub. by Kolisko Archives). St George Bk Serv.
Kolisko, Eugen, ed. Nurition Tl. 2nd ed. 1979. pap. 4.25x (ISBN 0-906492-12-2, Pub. by Kolisko Archives). St George Bk Serv.
Koniecko, Edward S. Nutritional Encyclopedia for the Elderly. 1981. 12.95 (ISBN 0-8062-1676-X). Carlton.
Koppert, Joan. Nutrition Rehabilitation-Its Practical Application. 144p. 1981. 10.50x (ISBN 0-905402-01-4, Pub. by Tri-Med England). State Mutual Bk.
Kordel, Lelord. You're Younger Than You Think. 1979. pap. 2.50 (ISBN 0-445-04507-8). Popular Lib.
Kordell, Lelord, ed. Health Through Nutrition. 4th ed. 1975. pap. 1.75 (ISBN 0-532-17121-7). Woodhill.
Kowtaluk, Helen. Discovering Nutrition. 1980. text ed. 10.00 (ISBN 0-87002-310-1); tchr's guide 6.00 (ISBN 0-87002-318-7); student guide 2.96 (ISBN 0-87002-317-9). Bennett IL.
Kraus, Barbara. Barbara Kraus Guide to Calories: 1982 Edition. (Orig.). 1982. pap. 1.95 (ISBN 0-451-11287-3, AJ1287, Sig). NAL.
--Calories & Carbohydrates. 4th, rev. ed. 1981. pap. 5.95 (ISBN 0-686-77707-7, Z5267, Plume). NAL.
--Calories & Carbohydrates. 4th, rev. ed. (Orig.). 1981. pap. 3.50 (ISBN 0-451-09774-2, E9774, Sig). NAL.
Krehl, Willard & Moss, N. Henry, eds. Clinical Nutrition in Health Care Facilities. LC 79-66103. (Orig.). 1979. pap. text ed. 4.95x (ISBN 0-89313-019-2). G F Stickley Co.
Krehl, Willard A. The Role of Citrus in Health & Disease. LC 76-4502. 1976. 6.50 (ISBN 0-8130-0532-9). U Presses Fla.
Kretchmer, Norman, intro. by. Human Nutrition: Readings from Scientific American. LC 78-17367. (Illus.). 1978. pap. text ed. 10.95x (ISBN 0-7167-0182-0). W H Freeman.
Kreutler, Patricia. Nutrition in Perspective. (Illus.). 1980. text ed. 20.95 (ISBN 0-13-627752-7); wkbk. 7.95 (ISBN 0-13-627778-0). P-H.
Kunin, Richard A. Mega-Nutrition: The New Prescription for Maximum Health, Energy & Longevity. 1981. pap. 6.95 (ISBN 0-452-25271-7, Plume). NAL.
Kupsinel, Penelope E. & Harker, Charlotte S. Questions & Problems on Nutrition. LC 74-81202. 1974. pap. text ed. 4.95x (ISBN 0-8134-1663-9, 1663). Interstate.
Labuza, T. P. & Sloan, A. Elizabeth. Food for Thought. 2nd ed. (Illus.). 1977. pap. text ed. 9.50 (ISBN 0-87055-244-9). AVI.
Labuza, Theodore P. Food & Your Well-Being. (Illus.). 1977. pap. text ed. 12.95 (ISBN 0-8299-0129-9); instrs.' manual & study guide 5.95 (ISBN 0-8299-0162-0). West Pub.
Labuza, Theodore P. & Sloan, A. Elizabeth. Contemporary Nutrition Controversies. (Illus.). 1979. pap. text ed. 12.95 (ISBN 0-8299-0258-9). West Pub.
Lag, Jul, ed. Survey of Geomedical Problems. 272p. 1980. 24.00x (ISBN 82-00-12654-4). Universitet.
Lamb, Lawrence E. Metabolics: Putting Your Food Energy to Work. LC 74-1829. (Illus.). 256p. 1974. 12.95 (ISBN 0-06-012484-9, HarpT). Har-Row.
Lamb, M. W. & Harden, M. L. Meaning of Human Nutrition. 1973. text ed. 18.50 (ISBN 0-08-017078-1); pap. text ed. 9.50 (ISBN 0-08-017079-X). Pergamon.
Lappe, Frances M. Diet for a Small Planet. rev ed. 432p. 1975. spiral bdg. 7.95 (ISBN 0-345-28919-6); pap. 2.75 (ISBN 0-345-29515-3). Ballantine.
Largen, Velda L. Guide to Nutrition. LC 80-25186. (Illus.). 144p. 1981. text ed. 8.96 (ISBN 0-87006-312-X). Goodheart.
Larsen, Carl. Even the Dog Won't Eat My Meat Loaf. LC 79-19887. 1980. pap. 5.95 (ISBN 0-89645-011-2). Media Ventures.
Larson, Gena. Fact-Book on Better Food for Better Babies & Their Families. LC 72-83519. (Pivot Original Health Book). 128p. 1972. pap. 1.75 (ISBN 0-87983-023-9). Keats.
--Fundamentals in Foods. 1.50 (ISBN 0-686-29781-4). Cancer Bk Hse.
Lasota, Marcia. The Fast Food Calorie Guide. (Illus., Orig.). 1980. pap. 3.95 (ISBN 0-933474-09-1, Gabriel Bks). Minn Scholarly.
Latham, Michael. Planning & Evaluation of Applied Nutrition Programmes. (FAO Nutritional Studies: No. 26). 125p. (Orig.). 1972. pap. 10.00 (ISBN 92-5-100439-0, F319, FAO). Unipub.
Latour, John. The A B C's of Vitamins, Minerals & Natural Foods. LC 72-3503. 96p. (Orig.). 1972. pap. 1.50 (ISBN 0-668-02655-3). Arco.
Leathem, James. Protein Nutrition & Free Amino Acid Patterns. 1968. 15.00x (ISBN 0-8135-0572-0). Rutgers U Pr.
Lee, H. A., ed. Parenteral Nutrition in Acute Metabolic Illness. 1974. 73.00 (ISBN 0-12-441750-7). Acad Pr.
Lesser, Michael. Nutrition & Vitamin Therapy. 7.95 (ISBN 0-686-29784-9). Cancer Bk Hse.
--Nutrition & Vitamin Therapy. 224p. 1981. pap. 2.50 (ISBN 0-553-14437-5). Bantam.
--Nutrition & Vitamin Therapy. LC 79-52100. 1980. pap. 7.95 (ISBN 0-394-17600-6, E748, Ever). Grove.
Leverton, Ruth M. Food Becomes You. facsimile ed. (Illus.). 1965. 9.45x (ISBN 0-8138-2405-2). Iowa St U Pr.
Levitt, Eleanor. Wonderful World of Natural Foods. LC 77-151462. (Illus.). 1971. 7.95 (ISBN 0-8208-0227-1). Hearthside.
Levy, Robert I., et al, eds. Nutrition, Lipids & Coronary Heart Disease. LC 78-67020. (Nutrition in Health & Disease Ser.: Vol. 1). 576p. 1979. 52.00 (ISBN 0-89004-181-4). Raven.
Lewin, Brenda. Sensuous Nutrition. 1977. pap. 1.50 (ISBN 0-89041-129-8, 3129). Major Bks.
Lewis, Christine. The Food Choice Jungle. 192p. 1979. 18.95 (ISBN 0-571-11424-5, Pub. by Faber & Faber); pap. 8.50 (ISBN 0-571-11425-3). Merrimack Bk Serv.
Lewis, Clara M. Nutrition & Diet Therapy. 1982. price not set (ISBN 0-8036-5624-6). Davis Co.
--Nutrition & Therapy. (Illus.). 250p. 1982. write for info. (ISBN 0-8036-5627-0). Davis Co.
--Nutrition: The Basis of Nutrition--Family Nutrition. LC 75-43830. (Illus.). 1977. pap. text ed. 7.00 (ISBN 0-8036-5639-4). Davis Co.
Li, A. K. C., et al. Fluid Electroytes, Acid Base & Nutrition. 1980. 8.50 (ISBN 0-12-448150-7). Acad Pr.
Lief, Stanley. How to Eat for Health. 1979. pap. 1.50 (ISBN 0-89437-067-7). Baronet.
Lindlahr, Victor. You Are What You Eat. 1971. pap. 2.95 (ISBN 0-87877-004-6, H-4). Newcastle Pub.
Lindlahr, Victor H. You Are What You Eat. LC 80-19722. 128p. 1980. Repr. of 1971 ed. lib. bdg. 9.95x (ISBN 0-89370-604-3). Borgo Pr.
Lindvig, Elise. Nutrition & Mental Health. LC 79-65602. 170p. (Orig.). 1979. pap. 5.95 (ISBN 0-89301-064-2). U Pr of Idaho.
Litchfield, Harry R. Live & Be Well. LC 72-76583. 300p. 1972. 6.00 (ISBN 0-87212-022-8). Libra.
Llewelyn-Jones, Derek. Every Body: A Nutritional Guide to Life. (Illus.). 1980. 16.95 (ISBN 0-19-217691-9). Oxford U Pr.
Lloyd, L. E., et al. Fundamentals of Nutrition. 2nd ed. LC 77-16029. (Animal Science Ser.). (Illus.). 1978. text ed. 23.95x (ISBN 0-7167-0566-4). W H Freeman.
Loewenfeld, Claire. Everything You Should Know About Your Food. 288p. 1978. pap. 9.95 (ISBN 0-571-11256-0, Pub. by Faber & Faber). Merrimack Bk Serv.
Lowenberg, Miriam E., et al. Food & People. 3rd ed. LC 78-19172. 1979. text ed. 20.95x (ISBN 0-471-02690-5). Wiley.
Luke, Barbara. Case Studies in Therapeutic Nutrition. 1977. pap. text ed. 6.95 (ISBN 0-316-53609-1). Little.
--Maternal Nutrition. 1980. text ed. 9.95 (ISBN 0-316-53610-5). Little.
Lusk, Graham. The Elements of the Science of Nutrition. 4th ed. (Nutrition Foundations' Reprint Ser.). (Illus.). Repr. 38.50 (ISBN 0-384-34203-5). Johnson Repr.
--The Fundamental Basis of Nutrition. 1923. 14.50x (ISBN 0-686-51390-8). Elliots Bks.
--Nutrition. LC 75-23660. (Clio Medica: No. 10). (Illus.). Repr. of 1933 ed. 13.00 (ISBN 0-404-58910-3). AMS Pr.
Lyon, Ninette & Benton, Peggie. Eggs, Milk & Cheese. 288p. 1971. 12.50x (ISBN 0-571-08302-1). Intl Pubns Serv.

MacAdie, Diana. Healthy Eating. (Illus.). 1978. 11.95 (ISBN 0-09-131260-4, Pub. by Hutchinson); pap. 5.95 (ISBN 0-09-131261-2). Merrimack Bk Serv.
McAfee, James W. Power to Live Through Nutrition. LC 80-82331. (Illus.). 196p. (Orig.). 1980. pap. 6.95 (ISBN 0-9604592-0-0). Image Awareness.
McEntire, Patricia. Mommy I'm Hungry: How to Feed Your Child Nutritiously. LC 81-68292. 168p. 1981. pap. 5.95 (ISBN 0-917982-11-8). Cougar Bks.
McGill, Marion & Pye, Orrea. The No-Nonsense Guide to Food & Nutrition. Speiser, Willa, ed. LC 77-92606. (Illus.). 1978. pap. 5.95 (ISBN 0-88421-054-5). Butterick Pub.
McGrath, William R. Bio-Nutronics. 224p. (RL 10). 1974. pap. 1.50 (ISBN 0-451-06065-2, W6065, Sig). NAL.
McGraw-Hill Editors. McGraw-Hill Encyclopedia of Food, Agriculture, & Nutrition. (Illus.). 1977. 24.50 (ISBN 0-07-045263-6, P&RB). McGraw.
McLaren, Donald S. Nutrition in the Community: A Text for Public Health Workers. LC 75-32565. 1976. 49.00 (ISBN 0-471-58556-4, Pub. by Wiley-Interscience). Wiley.
McLauren, Donald S. Nutritional Ophthalmology. 1980. 77.00 (ISBN 0-12-484240-2). Acad Pr.
McMillen, S. I. None of These Diseases. (Orig.). pap. 1.50 (ISBN 0-515-04604-3). Jove Pubns.
MacNeil, Karen. The Book of Whole Foods: Nutrition & Cuisine. (Orig.). 1981. pap. 8.95 (ISBN 0-394-74012-2, V-012, Vin). Random.
McNutt, Kristen W. & McNutt, David R. Nutrition & Food Choices. LC 77-13636. 1978. text ed. 17.95 (ISBN 0-574-20500-4, 13-3500). SRA.
McQueen-Williams, Morvyth & Apisson, Barbara. A Diet for 100 Healthy Happy Years: Health Secrets from the Caucasus. Ober, Norman, ed. LC 76-30710. 1977. 9.95 (ISBN 0-13-211185-3). P-H.
McQueen-Williams, Morvyth & Appisson, Barbara. A Diet for One Hundred Healthy, Happy Years. 1978. pap. 1.95 (ISBN 0-515-04523-3). Jove Pubns.
McWilliams, Margaret. Nutrition for the Growing Years. 3rd ed. LC 80-453. 491p. 1980. text ed. 22.95 (ISBN 0-471-02692-1). Wiley.
Mae, Eydie. Eydie Mae's Natural Recipes. 2.95 (ISBN 0-686-29794-6). Cancer Bk Hse.
Malstrom, Stan. Own Your Own Body. LC 76-58968. 414p. 1980. pap. 2.95 (ISBN 0-87983-215-0). Keats.
Mannerberg, Donald & Roth, Jane. Aerobic Nutrition: The Long-Life Plan for Ageless Health & Vigor. 1981. 14.95 (ISBN 0-8015-0070-2, Hawthorn). Dutton.
Manocha, S. L. Nutrition & Our Overpopulated Planet. (Illus.). 488p. 1975. 31.75 (ISBN 0-398-03180-0); pap. 22.50 (ISBN 0-398-03181-9). C C Thomas.
Marbach, Ellen S., et al. Nutrition in a Changing World: A Curriculum for Preschool. LC 79-11147. (Illus.). 1979. pap. 10.95x tchr's ed. (ISBN 0-8425-1658-1). Brigham.
Margen, Sheldon, ed. Progress in Human Nutrition, Vol. 2. (Illus.). 1978. text ed. 24.50 (ISBN 0-87055-255-4). AVI.
Marsh, Edward. Be Healthy with Natural Foods. 1.50 (ISBN 0-686-29799-7). Cancer Bk Hse.
Marsh, Edward E. How to Be Healthy with Natural Foods. LC 67-14909. 1968. pap. 1.50 (ISBN 0-668-01620-5). Arco.
Martin, Alice A. & Tenenbaum, Frances. Diet Against Disease: A New Plan for Safe & Healthy Eating. 1980. 11.95 (ISBN 0-395-29451-7). HM.
Martin, Ethel Austin & Coolidge, Ardath Anders. Nutrition in Action. 4th ed. LC 77-24031. 1978. 19.95 (ISBN 0-03-020336-8, HoltC). HR&W.
Martin, W. Coda. A Matter of Life. 1965. 4.95 (ISBN 0-8159-6202-9). Devin.
Mayer, Jean. Human Nutrition: Its Physiological, Medical & Social Aspects,A Series of 82 Essays. (Illus.). 740p. 1979. 23.75 (ISBN 0-398-02359-X). C C Thomas.
Mayer, Jean, ed. U. S. Nutrition Policies in the Seventies. LC 72-6548. 1973. text ed. 17.95x (ISBN 0-7167-0599-0); pap. text ed. 9.95x (ISBN 0-7167-0596-6). W H Freeman.
Mayer, Jean & Dwyer, Johanna, eds. Food & Nutrition Policy in a Changing World. (Illus.). 1978. text ed. 18.95x (ISBN 0-19-502363-3); pap. text ed. 11.95x (ISBN 0-19-502364-1). Oxford U Pr.
Meredith Corp. Editors & Deutsch, Ron. The Family Guide to Better Food & Better Health. 512p. 1973. pap. 2.50 (ISBN 0-553-13259-8, 13259-8). Bantam.
Metress, Seamus P. & Kart, Cary S. Nutrition & Aging: A Bibliographic Survey. (Public Administration Ser.: Bibliography P-309). 1979. pap. 9.50 (ISBN 0-686-26364-2). Vance Biblios.
Mier, G. F. & Hoogewerff, H. Fundamentals of Nutrition in the Light of Spiritual Science. LC 78-63296. (Illus.). 1978. pap. 4.95 (ISBN 0-916786-34-X). St George Bk Serv.
Millen, James W. The Nutritional Basis of Reproduction. (Illus.). 140p. 1962. photocopy ed. spiral 13.75 (ISBN 0-398-01308-X). C C Thomas.
Miller, C. D. Food Values of Poi, Taro, & Limu. Repr. of 1927 ed. pap. 5.00 (ISBN 0-527-02140-7). Kraus Repr.
The Mirage of Safety (Additives) 9.95 (ISBN 0-686-29752-0). Cancer Bk Hse.
Mitchell, H. H. & Edman, Marjorie. Nutrition & Climatic Stress: With Particular Reference to Man. (Illus.). 256p. 1951. photocopy ed. spiral 24.75 (ISBN 0-398-04365-5). C C Thomas.
Mitchell, Harold H. Comparative Nutrition of Man & Domestic Animals, Vol. 2. 1964. 63.50 (ISBN 0-12-499602-7). Acad Pr.
Mitchell, Helen S., et al. Nutrition in Health & Disease. 16th ed. LC 63-20822. 750p. 1976. text ed. 19.95x (ISBN 0-397-54177-5, JBL-Med-Nursing). Har-Row.
Mosley, W. H., ed. Nutrition & Human Reproduction. LC 77-28738. 526p. 1978. 42.50 (ISBN 0-306-31122-4, Plenum Pr). Plenum Pub.
Moss, N. Henry & Mayer, Jean, eds. Food & Nutrition in Health & Disease. (Annals of the New York Academy of Sciences: Vol. 300). 474p. 1977. 40.00x (ISBN 0-89072-046-0). NY Acad Sci.
Mulhauser, Roland. More Vitamins & Minerals with Fewer Calories. LC 77-91210. 1978. pap. 3.95 (ISBN 0-8048-1265-9). C E Tuttle.
Muller, H. G. & Tobin, G. Nutrition & Food Processing. 240p. 1980. 35.00x (ISBN 0-85664-540-0, Pub. by Croom Helm England). State Mutual Bk.
--Nutrition & Food Processing. (american) ed. 1980. pap. 30.00 (ISBN 0-87055-363-1). AVI.
Mulliss, Christine. Goodness! Eating Healthily. 64p. 1977. pap. 4.00x (ISBN 0-8464-1014-1). Beekman Pubs.
Nagy, Steven & Attaway, John, eds. Citrus Nutrition & Quality. LC 80-22562. (ACS Symposium Ser.: No. 143). 1980. 36.25 (ISBN 0-8412-0595-7). Am Chemical.
Naito, H., ed. Nutrition & Heart Disease. (Monographs of the American College of Nutrition: Vol. 5). 1981. text ed. 25.00 (ISBN 0-89335-119-9). Spectrum Pub.
National Research Council. World Food & Nutrition Study: Potential Contributions of Research, Commission on International Relations. 1977. pap. 10.50 (ISBN 0-309-02628-8). Natl Acad Pr.
Nearing, Helen. Simple Food for the Good Life. 1980. 13.00 (ISBN 0-686-30489-6). Soc Sci Inst.
Netter, Frank. Fad Diets Can Be Deadly: The Safe Sure, Way to Weight Loss & Good Nutrition. LC 74-21446. 1975. 8.00 (ISBN 0-682-48144-0, Banner). Exposition.
Neve, Vicki. Pat Neve's Bodybuilding Diet Book. rev. 2nd ed. De Mente, Boye, ed. (Illus.). 100p. (Orig.). 1981. pap. 7.95 (ISBN 0-914778-33-1). Phoenix Bks.
New York Academy of Sciences, Feb 20-22, 1980. Micronutrient Interactions: Vitamins, Minerals, & Hazardous Elements, Vol. 355. Levander, O. A. & Cheng, Lorraine, eds. LC 80-25622. 372p. 1980. 72.00x (ISBN 0-89766-099-4); pap. 72.00x (ISBN 0-686-77401-9). NY Acad Sci.
Newbold, H. L. Mega-Nutrients for Your Nerves. 416p. 1981. pap. 2.95 (ISBN 0-425-05010-6). Berkley Pub.
--Mega-Nutrients for Your Nerves. 1978. pap. 2.95 (ISBN 0-425-04653-2, Dist. by Putnam). Berkley Pub.
Newell, Guy R. & Ellison, Neil M., eds. Nutrition & Cancer: Etiology & Treatment. (Progress in Cancer Research & Therapy Ser.). 464p. write for info. (ISBN 0-89004-631-X). Raven.
--Nutrition & Cancer: Etiology & Treatment. 464p. 1981. 49.50 (ISBN 0-89004-631-X). Raven.
Nizel, Abraham E. Nutrition in Preventive Dentistry: Science & Practice. LC 74-165283. (Illus.). 1972. 18.925 (ISBN 0-7216-6809-7). Saunders.
No-Flab Diet. 9.00 (ISBN 0-686-29822-5). Cancer Bk Hse.
Nolfi, Kristine. Raw Food Treatment of Cancer-Other. 2.00 (ISBN 0-686-29817-9). Cancer Bk Hse.
Norris, P. About Honey: Nature's Elixir for Health. 1980. pap. 1.95 (ISBN 0-87904-043-2). Lust.
Null, Gary & Null, Steve. The Complete Handbook of Nutrition. LC 78-187994. (The Health Library: Vol. 1). 340p. 1972. 7.95 (ISBN 0-8315-0124-3). Speller.
--The Complete Handbook of Nutrition. 1973. pap. 2.50 (ISBN 0-440-11613-9). Dell.
Null, Gary & Null, Steven. How to Get Rid of the Poisons in Your Body. LC 76-28699. 192p. 1977. pap. 2.50 (ISBN 0-668-04114-5). Arco.
Null, Gary, et al. The Complete Question & Answer Book of General Nutrition. LC 79-187997. (The Health Library: Vol. 5). 184p. 1972. 5.95 (ISBN 0-8315-0128-6). Speller.
--The Complete Question & Answer Book of Natural Therapy. LC 75-187996. (The Health Library: Vol. 3). 272p. 1972. 5.95 (ISBN 0-8315-0127-8). Speller.
Nutritient Search Inc. Nutrient Alamanac-Diet-Ailment Contribution. 5.95 (ISBN 0-686-29818-7). Cancer Bk Hse.
Nutrition: A Review of the WHO Programme 1965-1971. (WHO Chronicle Reprint: Vol. 26, No. 4-5). (Also avail. in French & Spanish). 1972. pap. 0.80 (ISBN 92-4-156020-7). World Health.
Nutrition Almanac. LC 75-4193. 1975. pap. 6.95 (ISBN 0-685-72753-X, Pub. by McGraw). Formur Intl.
Nutrition & Cancer: Etiology & Treatment. (Progress in Cancer Research & Therapy Ser.: Vol. 17). 464p. 1981. write for info. (ISBN 0-89004-631-X). Raven.
Nutrition & Food Preparation & Preventive Care & Maintenance. (Lifeworks Ser.). 1981. 4.96 (ISBN 0-07-037094-X). McGraw.
Nutrition & Health: The Promotion of Health & the Prevention of Disease. 1981. 75.00x (ISBN 0-686-72936-6, Pub. by A B Academic England). State Mutual Bk.
Nutrition & Its Disorders. 3rd ed. (Livingston Medical Text Ser.). (Illus.). 1981. pap. text ed. 15.00 (ISBN 0-443-02158-9). Churchill.
Nutrition & Working Efficiency. (Freedom from Hunger Campaign Basic Ser: No. 5). 1966. pap. 4.50 (ISBN 0-685-27885-9, F302, FAO). Unipub.
The Nutrition of Aborigines in Relation to the Ecosystems of Central Australia. 149p. 1976. pap. 7.25 (ISBN 0-686-71836-4, CO 31, CSIRO). Unipub.
Nutrition Problems in Latin America, 4th Conference, Guatemala City, 1957. Report. 1959. pap. 4.25 (ISBN 0-685-36327-9, F370, FAO). Unipub.
Nutrition Status of the Rural Population of the Sahel. 92p. 1981. pap. 9.00 (ISBN 0-88936-277-7, IDRC 160, IDRC). Unipub.
Nutritional Assessment in Health Programs. 1973. 6.00x (ISBN 0-685-41636-4, 070). Am Pub Health.
Nutritional Evaluation of Cereal Mutants. (Illus.). 1978. pap. 19.50 (ISBN 92-0-111077-4, ISP 444, IAEA). Unipub.
O'Bannon, Dan R. The Ecological & Nutritional Treatment of Health Disorders. (Illus.). 206p. 1981. 21.75 (ISBN 0-398-04455-4). C C Thomas.
Obert, Jessie C. Community Nutrition. LC 77-13992. 452p. 1978. text ed. 22.50x (ISBN 0-471-65236-9). Wiley.
O'Reilly, Elizabeth, ed. Measure for Measure: Calorie & Carbohydrate Recipes. (Illus.). 1974. wire bound 11.95x (ISBN 0-433-24220-5). Intl Ideas.
Osborne, D. R. & Voogt, P. The Analysis of Nutrients in Foods. (Food Science & Technology Ser.). 1978. 32.00 (ISBN 0-12-529150-7). Acad Pr.
Overton, Meredith H. & Lukert, Barbara P. Clinical Nutrition: A Physiologic Approach. (Illus.). 1977. pap. 14.75 (ISBN 0-8151-5648-0). Year Bk Med.
Pacey, Arnold, compiled by. Gardening for Better Nutrition. (Illus.). 64p. (Orig.). 1980. pap. 3.50 (ISBN 0-903031-50-7, Pub. by Intermediate Tech England). Intermediate Tech.
Palma, Laurie D. The Good Morning Nutritional Breakfast Cookbook. LC 77-73996. 1978. 5.00 (ISBN 0-89430-005-9). Morgan-Pacific.
Passmore, R., et al. Handbook on Human Nutritional Requirements. (Also avail. in french, & spanish). 1974. pap. 4.80 (ISBN 92-4-140061-7). World Health.
Passwater, Richard. Supernutrition for Healthy Hearts. 1978. pap. 2.95 (ISBN 0-515-05725-8). Jove Pubns.
Passwater, Richard A. Super-Nutrition. 1981. pap. 2.95 (ISBN 0-671-44167-1). PB.
Pearson, Paul P. & Greenwell, J. Richard, eds. Nutrition, Food & Man: An Interdisciplinary Perspective. 1980. text ed. 11.50x (ISBN 0-8165-0691-4); pap. 5.95 (ISBN 0-8165-0706-6). U of Ariz Pr.
Pelstring, Linda & Mauck, JoAnn. Foods to Improve Your Health: A Complete Guide to Over Three Hundred Foods for One Hundred One Common Ailments. LC 73-83298. 224p. 1974. 3.95 (ISBN 0-8027-7147-5). Walker & Co.
Pennington, Jean & Church, Helen N. Food Values of Portions Commonly Used. 13th ed. LC 80-7594. 200p. 1980. 12.95 (ISBN 0-06-010767-7, Harpt); pap. 5.95 (ISBN 0-686-77497-3, CN 819). Har-Row.
Pennington, Jean A. Dietary Nutrient Guide. (Illus.). 1976. pap. text ed. 22.50 (ISBN 0-87055-196-5). AVI.
Pennsylvania State University Nutrition Education Curriculum Study. Nutrition in a Changing World: Grade Four. LC 80-20736. (Illus.). 152p. (Orig.). (gr. 4). 1981. pap. text ed. 11.95x (ISBN 0-8425-1864-9). Brigham.
Perrin, Arnold. The Care & Feeding of the Prostate. 1.00 (ISBN 0-686-31643-6). Wings ME.
--You Were Designed to Live for One Hundred & Forty Years. 1.00 (ISBN 0-939736-06-3). Wings ME.
Peshek, Robert J. Balancing Body Chemistry with Nutrition. 1977. 20.00 (ISBN 0-686-22958-4). Color Coded Charting.
--Nutrition for a Healthy Heart. (Illus.). 1979. 20.00 (ISBN 0-686-28350-3). Color Coded Charting.
--Student's Manual for Balancing Body Chemistry with Nutrition. 1977. 20.00 (ISBN 0-686-22959-2). Color Coded Charting.
Peterson, Vicki. Eat Your Way to Health. (Illus.). 208p. 1981. 10.95 (ISBN 0-312-22511-3). St Martin.
Pfeiffer & Banks. Dr. Pfeiffer's Total Nutrition. 1980. 9.95 (ISBN 0-671-24059-5, 24059). S&S.
Phillips, David A. Guidebook to Nutritional Factors in Foods. LC 79-10010. 1979. pap. 3.95 (ISBN 0-912800-71-2). Woodbridge Pr.
Pike, Arnold. Viewpoint on Nutrition. LC 80-24024. 221p. 1980. Repr. of 1973 ed. lib. bdg. 9.95x (ISBN 0-89370-621-3). Borgo Pr.
--Viewpoint on Nutrition. 224p. (Orig.). 1973. pap. 2.95 (ISBN 0-87877-021-6, H-21). Newcastle Pub.
Pike, Ruth L. & Brown, Myrtle L. Nutrition: An Integrated Approach. 2nd ed. LC 75-1488. 1082p. 1975. text ed. 31.95 (ISBN 0-471-68977-7). Wiley.
Plummer, Mary A. Foods & Nutrition: Syllabus. 1976. pap. text ed. 5.25 (ISBN 0-89420-001-1, 167070); cassette recordings 58.10 (ISBN 0-89420-147-6, 167040). Natl Book.
Polak, Jeanne E. Food Service for Fitness. (The Plycon Home Economics Ser.). 96p. 1981. spiral 7.95x (ISBN 0-8087-3418-0). Burgess.
Porter, J. W. & Rolls, B. A., eds. Proteins in Human Nutrition. 1973. 89.00 (ISBN 0-12-562950-8). Acad Pr.
Posner, Barbara M. Nutrition & the Elderly. LC 77-17683. 1979. 19.95 (ISBN 0-669-02085-0). Lexington Bks.
Powell, Eric F. A Home Course in Nutrition. 1980. 17.00x (ISBN 0-85032-158-1, Pub. by Daniel Co England). State Mutual Bk.
--A Home Course in Nutrition. 104p. 1978. pap. 7.50x (ISBN 0-8464-1019-2). Beekman Pubs.
Price, Weston. Nutrition & Physical Degeneration. 20.50 (ISBN 0-686-29940-X). Cancer Bk Hse.
Price, Weston A. Nutrition & Physical Degeneration. 9th ed. (Illus.). 560p. 1977. 20.50x (ISBN 0-916764-00-1). Price-Pottenger.
Prince, Francine. Diet for Life. 1981. pap. 6.95 (ISBN 0-346-12496-4). Cornerstone.
Protein-Energy Requirements Under Conditions Prevailing in Developing Countries: Current Knowledge & Research Needs. 73p. 1980. pap. 5.00 (ISBN 92-808-0018-3, TUNU 018, UNU). Unipub.
Protein Supply-Demands: Changing Styles GA-049. 1981. 800.00 (ISBN 0-89336-287-5). BCC.
Pyke, Magnus. Man & Food. 1970. pap. 3.95 (ISBN 0-07-050990-5, SP). McGraw.
Rajalakshmi, R. Applied Nutrition. 3rd ed. 700p. 1981. 50.00x (ISBN 0-686-72940-4, Pub. by Oxford & IBH India). State Mutual Bk.
Rajki, Sandor, ed. Proceedings of a Workshop on Agricultural Potentiality Directed by Nutritional Needs. (Illus.). 238p. 1979. 25.00x (ISBN 963-05-1991-7). Intl Pubns Serv.
Rall, Karen. Beautifood: Looking Better Through Nutrition. LC 80-83615. (Illus.). 160p. (Orig.). 1981. pap. 6.95 (ISBN 0-89087-307-0). Celestial Arts.
Ralph Nader Review. 0.50 (ISBN 0-686-29943-4). Cancer Bk Hse.
Raman, Pattabi. Nutrition & Human Development. 1976. 9.95x (ISBN 0-89223-028-2). Greylock Pubs.
Rechcigl, M. Nutrient Elements & Toxicants. (Comparative Animal Nutrition: Vol. 2). (Illus.). 1977. 58.75 (ISBN 3-8055-2351-3). S Karger.
Rechcigl, M., ed. Food, Nutrition & Health. (World Review of Nutrition & Dietetics: Vol. 16). (Illus.). 350p. 1973. 108.00 (ISBN 3-8055-1398-4). S Karger.
--Handbook of Nutritive Value of Processed Food: Food for Human Use, Vol. I. 608p. 1981. 79.95 (ISBN 0-8493-3951-0). CRC Pr.
Rechcigl, M., Jr., ed. Nitrogen, Electrolytes Water & Metabolism. (Comparative Animal Nutrition: Vol. 3). (Illus.). 1979. 78.00 (ISBN 3-8055-2829-9). S Karger.

Rechcigl, Miloslav, Jr., ed. Culture Media for Micro-Organisms & Plants, Vol. 3. 644p. 1977. 74.95 (ISBN 0-8493-2738-5). CRC Pr.
--Man, Food & Nutrition. LC 73-81478. (Uniscience Ser). 344p. 1973. 44.95 (ISBN 0-87819-040-6). CRC Pr.
--Nutritional Requirements, Vol. 1. (Comparative & Qualitative Requirements). (Illus.). 576p. 1977. 69.95 (ISBN 0-8493-2721-0). CRC Pr.
Rechigl, M., Jr., ed. Nutrition & the World Food Problem. (Illus.). 1978. 48.00 (ISBN 3-8055-2779-9). S Karger.
Recommended International Standard for Dextrose Anhydrous. 1970. pap. 4.50 (ISBN 0-685-36291-4, F671, FAO). Unipub.
Recommended International Standard for Dextrose Monohydrate. 1970. pap. 4.50 (ISBN 0-685-36292-2, F672, FAO). Unipub.
Reed, Pat B. Nutrition: An Applied Science. (Illus.). 650p. 1980. text ed. 21.95 (ISBN 0-8299-0311-9); instrs.' manual avail. (ISBN 0-8299-0570-7). West Pub.
Renwick, Ethel. Let's Try Real Food. 1981. pap. 5.95 (ISBN 0-310-31861-0). Zondervan.
--The Real Food Cookbook. 1978. spiral-bound kivar 7.95 (ISBN 0-310-31871-8). Zondervan.
Report of the Thirteenth Session Codex Alimentarius Commission. 103p. 1981. pap. 7.50 (ISBN 92-5-100912-0, F2071, FAO). Unipub.
Requirements of Vitamin A, Thiamine, Riboflavine & Niacin: Report of a Joint FAO-WHO Expert Group. (FAO Food & Nutritional Ser: No. 8). 1978. pap. 4.25 (ISBN 92-5-100453-6, F 1467, FAO). Unipub.
Reuben, David. Everything You Always Wanted to Know About Nutrition. 1979. lib. bdg. 14.95 (ISBN 0-8161-6673-0, Large Print Bks). G K Hall.
--Everything You Always Wanted to Know About Nutrition. 1979. pap. 2.75 (ISBN 0-380-44370-8, 44370). Avon.
--Save Your Life Diet. pap. 1.95 (ISBN 0-686-29951-5). Cancer Bk Hse.
Reutlinger, Shlomo & Selowsky, Marcelo. Malnutrition & Poverty: Magnitude & Policy Options. LC 76-17240. (A World Bank Staff Occasional Paper Ser: No. 23). (Illus.). 106p. 1976. pap. 4.75x (ISBN 0-8018-1868-0). Johns Hopkins.
Roberts, Lydia J. Nutricion. Torres, Rosa M., tr. LC 77-23108. 1978. pap. 9.00 (ISBN 0-8477-2777-7). U of PR Pr.
Robinson, Corinee H. & Lawler, Marilyn R. Normal & Therapeutic Nutrition. 6th ed. 1982. text ed. 19.95 (ISBN 0-02-402370-1). Macmillan.
Robinson, Corinne, et al. Case Studies in Clinical Nutrition: A Workbook & Study Guide for Students of Nursing & Dietetics. 1977. 6.50 (ISBN 0-02-402430-9, 40243). Macmillan.
Robinson, Corinne H. & Lawler, Marilyn R. Normal & Therapeutic Nutrition. 15th ed. (Illus.). 832p. 1977. text ed. 20.95 (ISBN 0-02-402300-0). Macmillan.
Robinson, Corinne H. & Weigley, Emma S. Fundamentals of Normal Nutrition. 3rd ed. (Illus.). 1978. 17.95 (ISBN 0-02-402330-2). Macmillan.
Robinson, Corrine H. Basic Nutrition & Diet Therapy. 4th ed. (Illus.). 1980. pap. text ed. 8.95 (ISBN 0-02-402450-3). Macmillan.
Robson, John R., et al. Malnutrition, Its Causation & Control. Set. 63.75x (ISBN 0-677-03140-8). Gordon.
Roche, Alex F. & Falkner, Frank. Nutrition & Malnutrition: Identification & Measurement. LC 74-13950. (Advances in Experimental Medicine & Biology Ser.: Vol. 49). 365p. 1974. 37.50 (ISBN 0-306-39049-3, Plenum Pr). Plenum Pub.
Roe, Daphne A. Clinical Nutrition for the Health Scientist. 144p. 1980. 44.95 (ISBN 0-8493-5417-X). CRC Pr.
Rolander-Chilo, Brita, ed. Nutritional Research: An International Approach. (Illus.). 1979. text ed. 28.00 (ISBN 0-08-024399-1). Pergamon.
Rosenbaum, Ernest, et al. Nutrition for the Cancer Patient. (Orig.). 1980. pap. 5.95 (ISBN 0-915950-38-3). Bull Pub.
Ross, Shirley. The Complex Carbohydrate Handbook. 192p. 1981. 9.95 (ISBN 0-688-00726-0, Quill); pap. 5.95 (ISBN 0-688-00593-4, Quill). Morrow.
Rosselin, G., et al, eds. Hormone Receptors in Digestion & Nutrition: Proceedings of the 2nd Int'l Symposium, France 797. 520p. 1979. 66.00 (ISBN 0-444-80155-3, North Holland). Elsevier.
Rossi, E., ed. Ernaehrung und Stoffwechsel: Die Adipositas im Kindesalter. (Paediatrische Forbildungkurse fuer die Praxis: Band 42). (Illus.). 113p. 1975. 25.25 (ISBN 3-8055-2158-8). S Karger.
Rotondi, Pietro. Vegetarian Cookery. 5.00 (ISBN 0-686-29955-8). Cancer Bk Hse.
Rubin, C., et al. Junk Food. (Orig.). 1980. pap. 9.95 (ISBN 0-440-54276-6, Delta). Dell.
Rubinstein, Helena. Food for Beauty. rev. ed. 256p. 1977. pap. 1.95 (ISBN 0-915962-19-5). Larchmont Bks.
Rudman, Jack. Chief Public Health Nutritionist. (Career Examination Ser.). (Cloth bdg. avail. on request). pap. 10.00 (ISBN 0-8373-3156-0). Natl Learning.
--Nutrition Education Consultant. (Career Examination Ser.: C-2740). (Cloth bdg. avail. on request). 1980. pap. 12.00 (ISBN 0-8373-2740-7). Natl Learning.
--Nutrition Services Consultant. (Career Examination Ser.: C-2836). (Cloth bdg. avail. on request). 1980. pap. 12.00 (ISBN 0-8373-2836-5). Natl Learning.
--Nutritionist. (Career Examination Ser.: C-2326). (Cloth bdg. avail. on request). pap. 10.00 (ISBN 0-8373-2326-6). Natl Learning.
--Principal Public Health Nutritionist. (Career Examination Ser.: C-1566). (Cloth bdg. avail. on request). pap. 10.00 (ISBN 0-8373-1566-2). Natl Learning.
--Senior Public Health Nutritionist. (Career Examination Ser.: C-1592). (Cloth bdg. avail. on request). pap. 10.00 (ISBN 0-8373-1592-1). Natl Learning.
Runyan, Thora J. Nutrition for Today. (Illus.). 384p. 1976. text ed. 20.95 scp (ISBN 0-06-045682-5, HarpC). Har-Row.
Rush, David, et al, eds. Diet in Pregnancy: A Randomized Controlled Trail of Nutritional Supplements. LC 79-3846. (Alan R. Liss Ser.: Vol. 16, No. 3). 1980. 26.00 (ISBN 0-8451-1037-3). March of Dimes.
Russell, Betsy. Wheatgrass Juice. 1.50 (ISBN 0-686-29956-6). Cancer Bk Hse.
Rynders, Barbara B. Eat It, Its Good for You! 1978. pap. 2.98 (ISBN 0-9601872-0-0). B Rynders Pubns.
Sanjur, Diva. Social & Cultural Perspectives in Nutrition. (Illus.). 352p. 1982. text ed. 18.95 (ISBN 0-13-815647-6). P-H.
Santos, W. J., et al, eds. Nutrition & Food Science: Present Knowledge & Utilization, 3 vols. 1980. 195.00 set (ISBN 0-686-77478-7, Plenum Pr); Vol. 1, 850p. 75.00 (ISBN 0-306-40342-0); Vol. 2, 900p. 79.50 (ISBN 0-306-40343-9); Vol. 3, 760p. 69.50 (ISBN 0-306-40344-7). Plenum Pub.
Sauberlich, Howerde E., et al. Laboratory Tests for the Assessment of Nutritional Status. LC 74-77908. (Monotopic Reprint Ser.). 136p. 1974. Repr. 17.95 (ISBN 0-8493-0121-1). CRC Pr.
Scarpa, Ioannis S., et al, eds. Sourcebook on Food & Nutrition. 2nd ed. LC 79-91584. 500p. 1980. 39.50 (ISBN 0-8379-4502-X). Marquis.
Schauss, Alexander. Diet, Crime & Delinquency. 3.95 (ISBN 0-686-29957-4). Cancer Bk Hse.
Schemmel, Rachel. Nutrition, Physiology & Obesity. 240p. 1980. 64.95 (ISBN 0-8493-5471-4). CRC Pr.
Schmandt, Jurgen, et al, eds. Nutrition Policy in Transition. LC 79-9628. (Illus.). 320p. 1980. 22.95x (ISBN 0-669-03596-3). Lexington Bks.
Schneider, Howard A., et al. Nutritional Support of Medical Practice. (Illus.). 1977. text ed. 30.00 (ISBN 0-06-140259-1, Harper Medical). Har-Row.
Schofield, Sue. Development & the Problems of Village Nutrition. LC 78-73290. 192p. 1979. Repr. of 1978 ed. text ed. 22.95 (ISBN 0-916672-21-2). Allanheld.
--Development & the Problems of Village Nutrition. 174p. 1979. 25.00x (ISBN 0-85664-836-1, Pub by Croom Helm Ltd. England). Biblio Dist.
Schwartz, George. Food Power. 1979. 10.95 (ISBN 0-07-055673-3, GB). McGraw.
--Food Power: How Foods Can Change Your Mind, Your Personality & Your Life. LC 78-32115. (McGraw-Hill Paperbacks Ser.). 204p. 1981. pap. 4.95 (ISBN 0-07-055674-1). McGraw.
Schwartz, Janet, et al. Nutrition Care in Family Planning: A Guide for Administrators. 68p. (Orig.). 1981. pap. text ed. 7.00 (ISBN 0-940050-00-5). Black & White.
Scientific American Editors. Food & Agriculture: A Scientific American Book. (Illus.). 1976. text ed. 16.95x (ISBN 0-7167-0382-3); pap. 8.95x (ISBN 0-7167-0381-5). W H Freeman.
Scott, Cyril. Crude Black Molasses. 1980. pap. 1.95 (ISBN 0-87904-010-6). Lust.
Scrimshaw, Nevin B., et al. Interactions of Nutrition & Infection. (Monograph Ser: No. 57). 329p. 1968. 11.20 (ISBN 92-4-140057-9, 790). World Health.
Scrimshaw, Nevin S. & Altschul, Aaron M., eds. Amino Acid Fortification of Protein Foods. 1971. 30.00x (ISBN 0-262-19091-5). MIT Pr.
Scrimshaw, Nevin S. & B'Ehar, Moises, eds. Nutrition & Agricultural Development. (Basic Life Sciences Ser.: Vol. 7). (Illus.). 500p. 1976. 39.50 (ISBN 0-306-36507-3, Plenum Pr). Plenum Pub.
Scrutton, Robert. Nature's Way to Nutrition & Vibrant Health. 1977. pap. 3.00 (ISBN 0-87980-344-4). Wilshire.
Shackelton, Alberta D. Practical Nurse Nutrition Education. 3rd ed. LC 77-176216. (Illus.). 1972. pap. 6.50 (ISBN 0-7216-8112-3). Saunders.
Shalhoub, Judy & Murray, Carol. Clinical Spanish for Dietitians. (Illus.). 1977. text ed. 6.95x (ISBN 0-916434-30-3). Plycon Pr.
Shank, et al. Guide to Modern Meals. 3rd ed. O'Neill, Martha, ed. (Illus.). 640p. (gr. 10-12). 1980. 17.28 (ISBN 0-07-056416-7, W); tchr's. resource guide 7.76 (ISBN 0-07-047514-8). McGraw.
Shannon, Barbara. The Student Supplement for Realities of Nutrition. 1977. 2.50 (ISBN 0-915950-13-8). Bull Pub.
Sheinken, David, et al. The Food Connection: How the Things You Eat Affect the Way You Feel. LC 78-11208. 1979. 10.00 (ISBN 0-672-52518-6). Bobbs.
Sheinkin, David, et al. Food, Mind & Mood. 304p. 1980. pap. 2.75 (ISBN 0-446-95551-5). Warner Bks.
Shell-Garner, Adeline & Reynolds, Kay. Feel Better After Fifty Food Book. 1979. lib. bdg. 13.95 (ISBN 0-8161-6692-7, Large Print Bks). G K Hall.
Shoden, Rebecca & Griffin, Sue. Fundamentals of Clinical Nutrition. (Illus.). 1980. pap. text ed. 5.95 (ISBN 0-07-056991-6). McGraw.
Simonton, O. Carl & Simonton, Stephanie. Getting Well Again. 8.95 (ISBN 0-686-29964-7). Cancer Bk Hse.
Sinclair, H. M. Progress in Food & Nutrition Science, Vol. 2, No. 11-12. LC 75-7734. (Illus.). 70p. 1979. pap. 23.00 (ISBN 0-08-023758-4). Pergamon.
Sinclair, H. M., ed. Progress in Food & Nutrition Science. Incl. Vol. 1, Pt. 1. pap. text ed. 10.00 (ISBN 0-08-019697-7); Vol. 1, Pt. 2. pap. text ed. 12.50 (ISBN 0-08-019782-5); Vol. 1, Pt. 3. pap. text ed. 12.50 (ISBN 0-08-019786-8); Vol. 1, Pt. 4. pap. text ed. 10.00 (ISBN 0-08-019789-2); Vol. 1, Pt. 5. pap. text ed. 12.50 (ISBN 0-08-019876-7); Vol. 1, Pt. 6. pap. text ed. 10.00 (ISBN 0-08-019878-3); Vol. 1, Pts. 7-8. pap. text ed. 22.00 (ISBN 0-08-019880-5); Vol. 1, Pt. 9. pap. text ed. 13.00 (ISBN 0-08-019942-9); Vol. 1, Pt. 10. pap. text ed. 11.00 (ISBN 0-08-019944-5); Vol. 2, Pt. 1. pap. text ed. 10.00 (ISBN 0-08-021025-2); Vol. 2, Pts. 2-3. pap. text ed. 19.00 (ISBN 0-08-021287-5); Vol. 2, Pt. 4. pap. text ed. 8.50 (ISBN 0-08-021764-8); Vol. 2, Pt. 5. pap. text ed. 9.80 (ISBN 0-08-021777-X); Vol. 2, Pt. 6. pap. text ed. 10.00 (ISBN 0-08-021921-7); Vol. 2, Pt. 7. pap. text ed. 8.50 (ISBN 0-08-021519-X); Vol. 2, Pt. 8. pap. text ed. 8.50 (ISBN 0-08-021532-7); Vol. 2, Pt. 9. pap. text ed. 8.50 (ISBN 0-08-021537-8). LC 75-7734. 1975-77. Pergamon.
Sinclair, H. M. & Howat, G. R., eds. World Nutrition & Nutrition Education. (Illus.). 272p. 1980. text ed. 42.50x (ISBN 0-19-261176-3). Oxford U Pr.
Sipple, Horace & McNutt, Kristen W., eds. Sugars in Nutrition. 1974. 66.00 (ISBN 0-12-646750-1). Acad Pr.
Smith, Anne. Eat Your Way to Health. 1.50 (ISBN 0-9601262-1-X). FairMail Serv.
Smith, C. Earle, Jr., ed. Man & His Foods: Studies in the Ethnobotany of Nutrition-Contemporary, Primitive & Prehistoric Non-European Diets. LC 77-38705. 120p. 1973. 8.95x (ISBN 0-8173-2400-3). U of Ala Pr.
Smith, Esther L. Good Foods That Go Together. LC 75-817. (Pivot a Health Books). 433p. 1975. pap. 3.95 (ISBN 0-87983-089-1). Keats.
Smith, Mildred N. Word of Wisdom, Principle with Promise. LC 76-46311. 1977. pap. 9.50 (ISBN 0-8309-0175-2). Herald Hse.
Soffer, Alfred. Potassium Therapy: A Seminar. (Illus.). 124p. 1968. photocopy ed. spiral 12.75 (ISBN 0-398-01807-3). C C Thomas.
Somogyi, J. C., ed. Ernaehrung und Alkoholismus. (Bibliotheca Nutritio et Dieta: Vol. 24). (Illus., Ger.). 1976. 51.50 (ISBN 3-8055-2376-9). S Karger.
--Foreign Substances & Nutrition. Tarjan, R. (Bibliotheca Nutritio et Dieta: No. 29). (Illus.). 1980. pap. 49.75 (ISBN 3-8055-0621-X). S Karger.
--Nutritional Aspects of Physical Performance. (Bibliotheca Nutritio et Dieta: No. 27). (Illus.). 1979. pap. 49.75 (ISBN 3-8055-2913-9). S Karger.
Somogyi, J. C. & Varela, G., eds. Nutritional Deficiencies in Industrialized Countries. (Bibliotheca Nutritic et Dieta Ser.: Vol. 30). (Illus.). 1981. 76.75 (ISBN 3-8055-1994-X). S Karger.
Sonntag, Ida M. Don't Drink the Water. (Illus.). 128p. 1980. 7.50 (ISBN 0-8158-0393-1). Chris Mass.
Soup, Stone. The Kitchen Almanac. 1977. pap. 8.95 (ISBN 0-425-03562-X, Windhover). Berkley Pub.
Sperber. Sociology of Nutrition & Public Health. (Traditional Healing Ser.: No. 9). Date not set. price not set (ISBN 0-932426-15-8, Trado-Medic Bks). Conch Mag.
Spiegel, Janet. Stretching the Food Dollar: Practical Solutions to the Challenges of the 80's. LC 81-4719. (Urban Life Ser.). (Illus.). 128p. (Orig.). 1981. pap. 4.95 (ISBN 0-87701-172-9). Chronicle Bks.
Spiller, Gene A., ed. Nutritional Pharmacology. LC 81-3766. (Current Topics in Nutrition & Disease Ser.: Vol. 4). 266p. 1981. 40.00 (ISBN 0-8451-1603-7). A R Liss.
Spira, Michael. How to Lose Weight Without Really Dieting. (Handbooks Ser). 1979. pap. 2.50 (ISBN 0-14-046368-2). Penguin.
Sprug, Joseph. Index to Nutrition & Health. (Useful Reference Ser. of Library Books: Vol. 119). 1981. 20.00 (ISBN 0-87305-125-4). Faxon.
Standardization of Analytical Methodology for Feeds. 128p. 1980. pap. 10.00 (ISBN 0-88936-217-3, IDRC 134, IDRC). Unipub.
Stare, Frederick & McWilliams, Margaret. Nutrition for Good Health. (The Plycon Home Economics Ser.). 177p. 1974. text ed. 8.95x (ISBN 0-686-75963-X). Burgess.
Stare, Frederick J. & McWilliams, Margaret. Living Nutrition. 3rd ed. LC 80-20470. 580p. 1981. text ed. 21.95 (ISBN 0-471-04940-9). Wiley.
Stare, Fredrick J. & McWilliams, Margaret. Nutrition for Good Health. LC 74-81644. 1974. 8.95x (ISBN 0-916434-11-7). Plycon Pr.
The State of Food & Agriculture, 1975. (FAO Agriculture Ser: No. 1). (Illus.). 150p. 1976. pap. 29.00 (ISBN 0-685-76006-5, FAO). Unipub.
Stevens, Laura J. & Stoner, Rosemary B. How to Improve Your Child's Behavior Through Diet. 1981. pap. 3.50 (ISBN 0-451-09812-9, E9812, Sig). NAL.
Stevenson, Taloria, ed. Dietary Intake Findings United States, 1971-1974. (Series 11: No. 202). 1977. pap. text ed. 1.75 (ISBN 0-8406-0094-1). Natl Ctr Health Stats.
Still, Jean. Food Selection & Preparation. 1981. text ed. 16.95x (ISBN 0-02-417510-2). Macmillan.
Suitor, Carol W. & Hunter, Merrily F. Nutrition: Principles & Application in Health Promotion. LC 79-22569. 468p. 1980. text ed. 18.25 (ISBN 0-397-54256-9). Lippincott.
Sumner, Margaret. Thought for Food. (Illus.). 129p. 1981. pap. text ed. 7.95x (ISBN 0-19-217690-0); pap. text ed. 7.95 (ISBN 0-19-286003-8). Oxford U Pr.
Super-Nutrition-Healthy Hearts. 2.50 (ISBN 0-686-29823-3). Cancer Bk Hse.
Superior Nutrition. pap. 4.00 (ISBN 0-686-20584-7). Willow Pub.
Supernutrition. 2.50 (ISBN 0-686-29824-1). Cancer Bk Hse.
Symposium, Copenhagen, 21st, March 1975. Parenteral Nutrition: Proceedings. (Nutrition & Metabolism: Vol. 20, Suppl. 1). 1977. 22.25 (ISBN 3-8055-2628-8). S Karger.
Symposium, Muenchen, 1974. Zucker und Zuckeraustauschstoffe. Zoellner, N. & Heuckenkamp, P., eds. (Nutrition & Metabolism: Vol. 18, Suppl. 1). (Illus.). 200p. 1975. 28.25 (ISBN 3-8055-2173-1). S Karger.
Symposium of the Group of European Nutritionists, 11th, Warsaw, April, 1972. Assessment of Nutritional Status & Food Consumption Surveys: Proceedings. Somogyi, J. C., ed. (Bibliotheca Nutritio et Dieta: No. 20). (Illus.). 224p. 1974. pap. 56.50 (ISBN 3-8055-1685-1). S Karger.
Symposium of the Group of European Nutritionists, Saltsjoebaden, June 10, 1971. Clinical Nutrition. Somogyi, J. C., ed. (Bibliotheca 'nutritio et Dieta': No. 19). (Illus.). 165p. 1973. pap. 39.00 (ISBN 3-8055-1500-6). S Karger.
Symposium of the Group of European Nutritionists, Zurich, 1971. Nutrition & Technology of Foods for Growing Humans: Proceedings. Somogyi, J. C., ed. (Bibliotheca Nutrition et Dieta: No. 18). (Illus.). 200p. (Eng.). 1973. pap. 55.25 (ISBN 3-8055-1317-8). S Karger.
Symposium of the Institute of Nutrition Research, Zurich, 1969. Biological Interrelations & Nutrition-Biologische Wechselbeziehungen und Ernaehrung: Proceedings. Somogyi, J. C., ed. (Bibliotheca Nutritio et Dieta: No. 15). (Illus.). 1970. pap. 38.50 (ISBN 3-8055-1155-8). S Karger.
Symposium on Toxicology & Nutrition, Paris, November 1976. Toxicology & Nutrition: Proceedings. Ferrando, R. & Truhaut, R., eds. (World Review of Nutrition & Dietetics: Vol. 29). (Illus.). 1977. 71.25 (ISBN 3-8055-2697-0). S Karger.
Symposium, Zuerich, March 1973. Entwicklungstendenzen in Ernaehrung und Diaetetik - Future Trends in Nutrition & Dietetics: Proceedings. Kopp, P., ed. (Bibliotheca Nutritio et Dieta: No. 21). 200p. 1975. pap. 58.25 (ISBN 3-8055-1737-8). S Karger.

Taylor. The Principles of Human Nutrition. (Studies in Biology: No. 94). 1978. 5.95 (ISBN 0-7131-2649-3). Univ Park.

Thurston, Emory. Nutrition for Tots to Teens. 4.50 (ISBN 0-686-29975-2). Cancer Bk Hse.

Thypin, Marilyn & Glasner, Lynne. More Food for Our Money: Food Planning, Buying, Nutrition. LC 78-13591. (Consumer Education Ser.). 1979. pap. text ed. 3.50 (ISBN 0-88436-502-6). EMC.

Time-Life Books Editors. Wholesome Diet. (Library of Health). (Illus.). 1981. 12.95 (ISBN 0-8094-3766-X). Time-Life.

Tobe, John. Sprouts: Elixir of Life. 2.00 (ISBN 0-686-29979-5). Cancer Bk Hse.

Tobin, Richard B. & Mehlman, Myron A., eds. Advances in Modern Human Nutrition. LC 80-81745. 1980. 28.00 (ISBN 0-930376-07-2). Pathotox Pubs.

Townsend, Carolyn. Nutrition & Diet Modification. 3rd ed. 301p. 1980. 11.95 (ISBN 0-442-26192-6). Van Nos Reinhold.

--Nutrition & Diet Modifications. 3rd ed. LC 78-74166. (Health Occupations Ser.). (gr. 9). 1980. pap. text ed. 10.40 (ISBN 0-8273-1324-1); instructor's guide 1.50 (ISBN 0-686-59749-4). Delmar.

Tucker, Rich. Biblical Nutrition. 1974. 9.95 (ISBN 0-913808-07-5). Madison Co.

Turner, M. R. Nutrition & Lifestyles. (Illus.). xi, 207p. 1980. 32.00x (ISBN 0-85334-874-X). Intl Ideas.

Turner, M. R., ed. Preventive Nutrition & Society. 1981. price not set (ISBN 0-12-704450-7). Acad Pr.

Tver, David F. & Russell, Percy. The Nutrition & Health Encyclopedia. LC 80-19933. (Illus.). 544p. 1981. text ed. 26.50 (ISBN 0-442-24859-8). Van Nos Reinhold.

U. S. Senate Select Committee on Nutrition & Human Needs. Eating in America. LC 77-73812. 1977. pap. 1.95 (ISBN 0-262-71004-8). MIT Pr.

U.S. Department of Agriculture. Handbook of Nutritional Contents of Foods. 9.50 (ISBN 0-8446-5252-0). Peter Smith.

--Handbook of the Nutritional Contents of Foods. LC 75-2616. (Illus.). 192p. 1975. pap. text ed. 4.00 (ISBN 0-486-21342-0). Dover.

--Yearbook of Agriculture, 1939: Food & Life; Part 1: Human Nutrition. LC 75-26321. (World Food Supply Ser). (Illus.). 1976. Repr. of 1939 ed. 24.00x (ISBN 0-405-07797-1). Arno.

Vander, Arthur J. Nutrition, Stress & Toxic Chemicals: An Approach to Environment - Health Controversies. 384p. 1981. text ed. 18.00x (ISBN 0-472-09329-0); pap. 9.95x (ISBN 0-472-06329-4). U of Mich Pr.

Van Wazer, Betty B. & Van Wazer, John R. Beneficial Nutrition & Naturally Splendid Food: The Intelligent Persons' Guide to a World of Enjoyment & Well-Being. (Illus.). 320p. 1981. lib. bdg. 18.95 (ISBN 0-939454-01-7); pap. 12.95 (ISBN 0-939454-00-9). Folio Pubs.

Vitale, Joseph J., ed. Advances in Human Clinical Nutrition. (Illus.). 160p. 1981. text ed. 22.50 (ISBN 0-88416-219-2). Wright-PSG.

Vitamins & Nutrients. (BTA Studies). 1981. 395.00 (ISBN 0-686-31557-X). Busn Trend.

Wade, Carlson. Arthritis, Nutrition & Natural Therapy. 1.95 (ISBN 0-686-29837-3). Cancer Bk Hse.

--Fact-Book on Hypertension, High Blood Pressure & Your Diet. LC 74-31668. (Pivot Original Health Book Ser). (Illus.). 128p. (Orig.). 1975. pap. 1.95 (ISBN 0-87983-095-6). Keats.

--Helping Your Health with Enzymes. LC 66-22102. 1970. pap. 2.50 (ISBN 0-668-02131-4). Arco.

--Key to Nutrition. pap. 1.00 (ISBN 0-686-00706-9). Key Bks.

--Magic Minerals: Your Key to Better Health. LC 67-27851. 1970. pap. 2.50 (ISBN 0-668-02135-7). Arco.

--What's in It for You? The Shoppers' Complete Guide to Health Store Products. rev. ed. LC 80-84443. (Pivot Original Health Bk.). 144p. (Orig.). 1981. pap. 2.95 (ISBN 0-87983-244-4). Keats.

Walczak, Michael & Ehrich, Benjamin B. Nutrition & Well-Being. LC 76-18447. 1977. 8.95 (ISBN 0-87881-054-4); pap. 6.50 (ISBN 0-87881-055-2). Mojave Bks.

Waldbott, George. Fluoridation Dilemma. 7.50 (ISBN 0-686-29987-6). Cancer Bk Hse.

Walker, Morton. Ortho-Molecular Nutrition. 2.25 (ISBN 0-686-29989-2). Cancer Bk Hse.

Walker, N. W. Diet: Salad Suggestions. 4.50 (ISBN 0-686-29992-2). Cancer Bk Hse.

--Raw Vegetables Juices. 1.50 (ISBN 0-686-29993-0). Cancer Bk Hse.

Wallis, Celestina, et al. Anushk's Complete Body Makeover Book. (Illus.). 224p. 1981. 11.95 (ISBN 0-399-12579-5). Putnam.

Waterlow, J. C., ed. Nutrition of Man: British Medical Bulletin, Jan. 1981, Vol.37. (No. 1). (Illus.). 104p. 1981. pap. text ed. 24.00 (ISBN 0-443-02449-9). Churchill.

Watson, George. Nutrition & Your Mind. 224p. 1974. pap. 2.75 (ISBN 0-553-14561-4). Bantam.

--Personality Strength & Psychochemical Energy. LC 79-1690. 1979. 9.95 (ISBN 0-06-014587-0, HarpT). Har-Row.

Watt, Bernice K. & Merrill, Annabel L. Handbook of the Nutritional Contents of Foods. LC 75-2616. 1975. lib. bdg. 12.50x (ISBN 0-88307-540-7). Gannon.

Webb, Sydney J. Nutrition, Time & Motion in Metabolism & Genetics. (Illus.). 426p. 1976. 39.75 (ISBN 0-398-03158-4). C C Thomas.

Weg, Ruth B. Nutrition & Aging. (Technical Bibliographies on Aging Ser.). 1978. 2.50 (ISBN 0-88474-041-2). USC Andrus Geron.

--Nutrition & the Later Years. LC 77-91696. 1978. pap. 6.50 (ISBN 0-88474-042-0). USC Andrus Geron.

Weider, Joe. Muscle & Fitness: Bodybuilding Nutrition & Training Programs. 1981. 12.95 (ISBN 0-686-77408-6); pap. 5.95 (ISBN 0-8092-5916-8). Contemp Bks.

Weiner, Michael A. The Sceptical Nutritionist. 256p. 1981. 9.95 (ISBN 0-02-625620-7). Macmillan.

--The Skeptical Nutritionist. 256p. 1981. 9.95 (ISBN 0-02-625620-7). Macmillan.

--The Way of the Skeptical Nutritionist: A Strategy for Designing Your Own Nutritional Profile. 212p. 1981. 11.95 (ISBN 0-686-30593-0). Macmillan.

Weinsier, Roland L. Handbook of Clinical Nutrition: Clinician's Manual for the Diagnosis & Management of Nutritional Problems. LC 80-20161. (Illus.). 231p. 1980. pap. text ed. 10.95 (ISBN 0-8016-5406-8). Mosby.

Welsh, Philip. Freedom-Arthritis Thru Nutrition. 7.95 (ISBN 0-686-29838-1). Cancer Bk Hse.

Wenck, Dorothy. Supermarket Nutrition. (Illus.). 336p. 1981. text ed. 14.95 (ISBN 0-8359-7321-2); pap. 9.95 (ISBN 0-8359-7320-4). Reston.

Wencke, et al. Nutrition. (Illus.). 1980. text ed. 17.95 (ISBN 0-8359-5061-1); instrs' manual avail. Reston.

Westberg, Marita. Eat Well, Live Longer: A Manual for a Healthy Heart. 4.95 (ISBN 0-7043-3219-1, Pub. by Quartet England). Charles River Bks.

White, R. Food & Your Future. text ed. 16.80 (ISBN 0-13-322982-3). P-H.

Whitney, Eleanor N. & Hamilton, Eva M. Understanding Nutrition. 2nd ed. (Illus.). 793p. 1981. text ed. 20.95 (ISBN 0-8299-0419-0). West Pub.

--Understanding Nutrition. (Illus.). 1977. text ed. 18.50 (ISBN 0-8299-0052-7); instrs.' manual avail. (ISBN 0-8299-0583-9). West Pub.

WHO Activities in Nutrition, 1948-1964. (WHO Chronicle Reprint: Vol. 19, Nos. 10-12). (Also avail in French & Spanish). 1965. pap. 1.20 (ISBN 92-4-156019-3). World Health.

WHO Expert Committee. Geneva, 1973. Trace Elements in Human Nutrition: Report. (Technical Report Ser.: No. 532). (Also avail. in French & Spanish). 1973. pap. 2.80 (ISBN 92-4-120532-6). World Health.

Whyte, Robert O. Rural Nutrition in Monsoon Asia. (Oxford in Asia College Texts Ser). 321p. 1974. pap. 29.50x (ISBN 0-19-580250-0). Oxford U Pr.

Wickham, Sandy J. Human Nutrition: A Self Instructional Text. 416p. 1981. pap. text ed. 14.95 (ISBN 0-87619-857-4). R J Brady.

Wigmore, Ann. Why Suffer? Wheatgrass, God's Manna! 2.95 (ISBN 0-686-29999-X). Cancer Bk Hse.

Wilcke, Harold L., et al, eds. Soy Protein & Human Nutrition. LC 78-25585. 1979. 32.00 (ISBN 0-12-751450-3). Acad Pr.

Williams, Melvin H. Nutritional Aspects of Human Physical & Athletic Performance. (Illus.). 456p. 1976. 21.50 (ISBN 0-398-03548-2). C C Thomas.

Williams, Roger J. Nutrition Against Disease. 384p. 1973. pap. 2.95 (ISBN 0-553-20086-0). Bantam.

--Nutrition in a Nutshell. LC 62-15322. pap. 2.50 (ISBN 0-385-03031-2, C396, Dolp). Doubleday.

--Physicians' Handbook of Nutritional Science. (American Lectures in Living Chemistry Ser.). 128p. 1978. 12.75 (ISBN 0-398-03256-4). C C Thomas.

--The Prevention of Alcoholism Through Nutrition. 176p. (Orig.). 1981. pap. 2.50 (ISBN 0-553-14502-9). Bantam.

Williams, Sue R. Essentials of Nutrition & Diet Therapy. 2nd ed. LC 77-18733. (Illus.). 1978. pap. text ed. 14.95 (ISBN 0-8016-5571-4). Mosby.

--Mowry's Basic Nutrition & Diet Therapy. 6th ed. LC 79-26165. (Illus.). 1980. pap. text ed. 10.50 (ISBN 0-8016-5556-0). Mosby.

--Nutrition & Diet Therapy. 4th ed. LC 80-27219. (Illus.). 840p. 1981. text ed. 19.95 (ISBN 0-8016-5554-4). Mosby.

--Self-Study Guide for Nutrition & Diet Therapy. 2nd ed. LC 77-18113. 1978. pap. text ed. 8.50 (ISBN 0-8016-5573-0). Mosby.

Wilson, E. D., et al. Principles of Nutrition. 4th ed. LC 78-11710. 1979. text ed. 23.95 (ISBN 0-471-02695-6); o.p. tchrs. manual (ISBN 0-471-04786-4); wkbk. 7.95 (ISBN 0-471-05766-5). Wiley.

Winber, Gloria K. Better Eating Habits - A Step by Step Approach. (Illus.). 170p. (Orig.). pap. 5.95 (ISBN 0-686-29292-8). Winfoto.

Wing, Elizabeth S. & Brown, Antoinette B. Paleonutrition: Prehistoric Foodways. LC 79-21034. (Studies in Archeology). 1979. 19.50 (ISBN 0-12-759350-0). Acad Pr.

Winick, M. Nutrition & the Killer Diseases. LC 81-3317. (Current Concepts in Nutrition Ser.: Vol. 10). 191p. 1981. 32.50 (ISBN 0-471-09130-8, Pub. by Wiley-Interscience). Wiley.

Winick, Myron. Nutrition & Cancer. LC 77-22650. (Current Concepts in Nutrition: Vol. 6). 1977. 31.50 (ISBN 0-471-03394-4, Pub. by Wiley-Interscience). Wiley.

--Nutrition & Gastroenterology. LC 80-16169. (Current Concepts in Nutrition Ser.: Vol. 9). 221p. 1980. 37.00 (ISBN 0-471-08173-6, Pub. by Wiley Interscience). Wiley.

Winick, Myron, ed. Human Nutrition-A Comprehensive Treatise, Vol. 1: Nutrition - Pre & Postnatal Development. LC 78-26941. (Human Nutrition--Comprehensive Treatise Ser.: Vol. 1). (Illus.). 516p. 1979. 39.50 (ISBN 0-306-40132-0, Plenum Pr). Plenum Pub.

--Nutritional Management of Genetic Disorders, Vol. 8. LC 79-16192. (Current Concepts in Nutrition Ser.). 1979. 32.50 (ISBN 0-471-05781-9, Pub. by Wiley-Interscience). Wiley.

Winikoff, Beverly, ed. Nutrition & National Policy. (Illus.). 1978. text ed. 26.50x (ISBN 0-262-23087-9). MIT Pr.

Wolf, Ray. Managing Your Personal Food Supply. LC 76-50569. 1977. 11.95 (ISBN 0-87857-121-3). Rodale Pr Inc.

Workshop on the Interfaces Between Agriculture, Nutrition, & Food Science, 1977. Proceedings. 143p. 1979. pap. 7.25 (ISBN 0-686-70590-4, R087, IRRI). Unipub.

World Nutrition & Nutrition Education. 226p. 1981. 50.50 (ISBN 92-3-101736-5, U1057, UNESCO). Unipub.

Worthington, Bonnie & Taylor, Lynda. Nutrition During Pregnancy & Breast Feeding. (Illus.). 1981. pap. 2.50 (ISBN 0-686-70167-4). Budlong.

Worthington, Bonnie S. & Williams, Sue R. Nutrition in Pregnancy & Lactation. LC 76-57760. (Illus.). 1977. pap. text ed. 9.95 (ISBN 0-8016-5237-5). Mosby.

Worthington-Roberts, Bonnie S. Contemporary Developments in Nutrition. LC 80-21557. (Illus.). 603p. 1980. pap. text ed. 18.95 (ISBN 0-8016-5627-3). Mosby.

Worthington-Roberts, Bonnie S., et al. Nutrition in Pregnancy & Lactation. 2nd ed. LC 80-39509. (Illus.). 309p. 1981. pap. text ed. 11.95 (ISBN 0-8016-5626-5). Mosby.

Wright, Helen S. & Sims, Laura S., eds. Community Nutrition: People, Policies, & Programs. 583p. 1981. pap. 11.95 (ISBN 0-87872-272-6). Wadsworth Pub.

Wright, Jonathan V. Dr. Wright's Book of Nutritional Therapy. 1979. 16.95 (ISBN 0-87857-270-8). Rodale Pr Inc.

Wurtman, Richard J. & Wurtman, Judith J., eds. Determinants of the Availability of Nutrients to the Brain. LC 75-14593. (Nutrition & the Brain Ser: Vol. 1). 336p. 1977. 31.50 (ISBN 0-89004-045-1). Raven.

--Nutrition & the Brain: Disorders of Eating & Nutrients in Treatment of Brain Diseases. (Nutrition & the Brain Ser.: Vol. 3). 314p. 1979. text ed. 32.00 (ISBN 0-89004-245-4). Raven.

--Nutrition & the Brain: Toxic Effects of Food Constituents on the Brain. LC 79-2073. (Nutrition & the Brain Ser.: Vol. 4). 232p. 1979. text ed. 25.00 (ISBN 0-89004-246-2). Raven.

Yagi, Kunio, ed. Biochemical Aspects of Nutrition. 238p. text ed. 57.50 (ISBN 0-8391-1444-3). Univ Park.

Yudkin, John. Lose Weight, Feel Great. (Illus.). 219p. 1974. pap. 1.75 (ISBN 0-915962-02-0). Larchmont Bks.

--This Nutrition Business. LC 77-10150. 1978. 10.00 (ISBN 0-312-80055-X). St Martin.

Zaccarell, Herman E. Cookbook That Tells You How. LC 75-6894. 1972. 16.95 (ISBN 0-8436-2078-1). CBI Pub.

Zaccarelli, Bro. Herman E. & Maggiore, Josephine. Nursing Home Menu Planning, Food Purchasing & Management. LC 73-182087. 1972. 15.95 (ISBN 0-8436-0541-3). CBI Pub.

Zales, Michael R. Eating, Sleeping & Sexuality: Recent Advances in Basic Life Functions. 320p. 1981. 25.00 (ISBN 0-87630-288-6). Brunner-Mazel.

Zebroff, Kareen. Yoga & Nutrition. LC 78-13437. (Illus.). 1979. pap. 3.95 (ISBN 0-668-04711-9). Arco.

NUTRITION–BIBLIOGRAPHY

Bender, Arnold F. The Facts of Food. (Illus.). 1975. 9.95x (ISBN 0-19-217632-3). Oxford U Pr.

Canon-Boventre, Kristina, et al. Cancer & Nutrition: A Bibliography & Resource Guide. 700p. 1981. lib. bdg. 75.00 (ISBN 0-8240-7133-6). Garland Pub.

Elias, Joel & Robson, John R. The Nutritional Value of Indigenous Wild Plants: An Annotated Bibliography. LC 76-51040. 1978. 18.50 (ISBN 0-87875-112-2). Whitston Pub.

Food & Nutrition: Annotated Bibliography, Author & Subject Index (1945-1972) (Special Index: No. 26). (Orig.). 1974. pap. 8.00 (ISBN 0-685-41433-7, FAO). Unipub.

Food & Nutrition Bibliography. 11th ed. 1982. pap. 18.00 (ISBN 0-89774-009-2). Oryx Pr.

Food & Nutrition Bibliography. 9th ed. 1980. pap. text ed. 18.00x (ISBN 0-912700-77-7). Oryx Pr.

Food & Nutrition Bibliography. 10th ed. 1981. pap. text ed. 18.00x (ISBN 0-912700-78-5). Oryx Pr.

Taylor, Clara M. & Riddle, Katharine P., eds. Annotated International Bibliography of Nutrition Education. LC 71-132937. 1971. pap. text ed. 5.75x (ISBN 0-8077-2255-3). Tchrs Coll.

NUTRITION–DATA PROCESSING

Maloff, Chalda & Zears, Russell. Computers in Nutrition. LC 79-4339. 1979. 33.00 (ISBN 0-89006-077-0). Artech Hse.

NUTRITION–JUVENILE LITERATURE

Adams, Marylou. Brighten up at Breakfast: Helpful Tips for Heavenly Bodies. LC 81-51601. (Illus.). 111p. (gr. 4-6). 1981. plastic comb 6.95 (ISBN 0-9606248-0-5). Starbright.

Berger, Melvin & Berger, Gilda. The New Food Book: Nutrition, Diet, Consumer Tips & Foods of the Future. LC 77-7976. (gr. 4-6). 1978. 7.95 (ISBN 0-690-01295-0, TYC-J); PLB 8.79 (ISBN 0-690-03841-0). Har-Row.

Fodor, Ronald V. What to Eat & Why: The Science of Nutrition. LC 78-24086. (Illus.). (gr. 4-6). 1979. 6.50 (ISBN 0-688-22189-0); PLB 6.24 (ISBN 0-688-32189-5). Morrow.

Frompovich, Catherine J. Nutrition Workbook for Children. 32p. (gr. 1-5). 1978. pap. 1.60 (ISBN 0-935322-00-0). C J Frompovich.

Gilbert, Sara. You Are What You Eat: A Common-Sense Guide to the Modern American Diet. LC 76-39806. (gr. 5 up). 1977. 8.95 (ISBN 0-02-736020-2, 73602). Macmillan.

Jones, Hettie. How to Eat Your ABC's: A Book About Vitamins. LC 75-41442. (Illus.). 96p. (gr. 2-5). 1976. 7.95 (ISBN 0-686-67313-1, Four Winds). Schol Bk Serv.

Margen, Sheldon, ed. Symposium: Progress in Human Nutrition. (Illus.). 1971. text ed. 24.50 (ISBN 0-87055-101-9). AVI.

Neff, Fred. Fred Neff's Keeping Fit Handbook for Physical Conditioning & Better Health. LC 75-38478. (Fred Neff's Self-Defense Library). (Illus.). 56p. (gr. 5 up). 1977. PLB 5.95g (ISBN 0-8225-1157-6). Lerner Pubns.

O'Connell, Lily H., et al. Nutrition in a Changing World: Grade Five. (Illus.). 152p. (Orig.). 1981. pap. text ed. 11.95 (ISBN 0-8425-1916-5). Brigham.

Peck, Leilani B., et al. Focus on Food. (Illus.). 432p. (gr. 7-9). 1974. text ed. 12.40 (ISBN 0-07-049145-3, W). McGraw.

Riedman, Sarah R. Food for People. rev. ed. LC 75-33193. 1976. 9.95 (ISBN 0-200-00161-2, AbS-J). Har-Row.

Simon, Seymour. About the Food You Eat. Date not set. price not set. McGraw.

Stitt, Paul, et al. Fighting the Food Giants. rev. ed. 1980. pap. 5.00 (ISBN 0-939956-00-4). Natural Pr.

Thompson, Paul. Nutrition. (First Bks.). 72p. 1981. lib. bdg. 7.40 (ISBN 0-531-04328-2). Watts.

Voelckers, Ellen. Food for Fitness & Sports. (YA) 1977. PLB 7.97 (ISBN 0-8239-0393-1). Rosen Pr.

Wilson, Wendy, et al, eds. Food Scoreboard. 30p. 1980. 60.00 (ISBN 0-89329-030-0). Ctr Sci Public.

NUTRITION–LABORATORY MANUALS

Krishna, G. & Ranjhan, S. K. Advanced Laboratory Manual for Nutrition Research. 150p. 1980. text ed. 13.95 (ISBN 0-7069-1125-3, Pub by Vikas India). Advent NY.

Pearson, David. Laboratory Techniques in Food Analysis. LC 72-14169. 315p. 1973. 28.95 (ISBN 0-470-67539-X). Halsted Pr.

Ranjhan, S. K. & Krishna, G. Laboratory Manual for Nutrition Research. 1980. lab manual 13.95 (ISBN 0-7069-1123-7, Pub. by Vikas India). Advent NY.

--Nutrition Research: Laboratory Manual. 1980. 13.95 (ISBN 0-7069-1123-7, Pub. by Vikas India). Advent NY.
Schatz, Pauline. Manual in Clinical Dietetics. 2nd ed. 1978. spiral bdg. 6.95x (ISBN 0-8087-2406-1). Plycon Pr.
Thompson, Nelle E. Meal Management. 2nd ed. 130p. 1968. pap. text ed. 7.95x (ISBN 0-8138-0564-3). Iowa St U Pr.

NUTRITION–RESEARCH
Abraham, Sidney, et al. Dietary Intake Source Data: United States, 1971-74. 1979. pap. text ed. 1.50 (ISBN 0-8406-0162-X). Natl Ctr Health Stats.
ARC-MRC Committee, ed. Food & Nutrition Research Report. 210p. 1975. pap. text ed. 44.50 (ISBN 0-444-99871-3). Elsevier.
Asahina, K. & Shigiya, R., eds. Physiological Adaptability & Nutritional Status of the Japanese (B) (Japan International Biological Program Synthetics Ser.: Vol. 4). 1975. pap. 32.50x (ISBN 0-86008-214-8, Pub. by U of Tokyo Pr). Intl Schol Bk Serv.
Beecher, Gary R., ed. Human Nutrition Research. LC 79-91006. (Beltsville Symposia in Agricultural Research Ser.: No. 4). (Illus.). 400p. 1981. text ed. 35.00 (ISBN 0-916672-48-4). Allanheld.
Bourne, G. H., ed. World Review of Nutrition & Dietetics, Vol. 20. (Illus.). 350p. 1975. 113.25 (ISBN 3-8055-1841-2). S Karger.
Campbell, Ada M. & Penfield, Marjorie. Experimental Study of Food. 2nd ed. LC 78-69535. (Illus.). 1979. text ed. 19.95 (ISBN 0-395-26666-1). HM.
Commission on International Relations, National Research Council. World Food & Nutrition Study: Interim Report. LC 75-37120. xix, 82p. 1975. pap. 5.50 (ISBN 0-309-02436-6). Natl Acad Pr.
Darden, Ellington. Nutrition & Athletic Performance. 1976. pap. 5.95 (ISBN 0-685-57677-9). Borden.
Draper, H. H., ed. Advances in Nutritional Research, Vol. 4. 340p. 1981. text ed. price not set (ISBN 0-306-40786-8, Plenum Pr). Plenum Pub.
Food & Nutrition Board. Nutrition and Fertility Interrelationships. 1975. pap. 4.50 (ISBN 0-309-02341-6). Natl Acad Pr.
Krishna, G. & Ranjhan, S. K. Advanced Laboratory Manual for Nutrition Research. 150p. 1980. text ed. 13.95 (ISBN 0-7069-1125-3, Pub by Vikas India). Advent NY.
Leklem, James E. & Reynolds, Robert D., eds. Methods in Vitamin B-6 Nutrition: Analysis & Status Assessment. 401p. 1981. 49.50 (ISBN 0-306-40640-3, Plenum Pr). Plenum Pub.
Mellanby, Edward. Story of Nutritional Research: The Effect of Some Dietary Factors on Bones & the Nervous System. LC 50-5910. (Abraham Flexner Lectures in Medicine, No. 9). 1950. 5.00x (ISBN 0-8265-0996-7). Vanderbilt U Pr.
Mrak, E. M. & Stewart, G. F., eds. Advances in Food Research: Supplements. Incl. Suppl. 1. Phenolic Substances in Grapes & Wine & Their Significance. Singleton, V. L. & Esau, P. 1969. 43.00 (ISBN 0-12-016461-2); Suppl. 2. The Chemical Constituents of Citrus Fruits. Kefford, J. F. & Chandler, B. V. 1970. 36.00 (ISBN 0-12-016462-0); Suppl. 3. Advances in the Chemistry of Plant Pigments. Chichester, O., ed. 1972. 36.00 (ISBN 0-12-016463-9). Acad Pr.
Mrak, E. M., et al, eds. Advances in Food Research, Vols. 1-24. Incl. Vol. 1. 1948 (ISBN 0-12-016401-9); Vol. 2. 1949 (ISBN 0-12-016402-7); Vols. 3-5. 1951-54. Vol. 3 (ISBN 0-12-016403-5). Vol. 4 (ISBN 0-12-016404-3). Vol. 5 (ISBN 0-12-016405-1); Vol. 6. 1955 (ISBN 0-12-016406-X); Vols. 7-8. 1957-58. Vol. 7 (ISBN 0-12-016407-8). Vol. 8 (ISBN 0-12-016408-6); Vol. 9. Chichester, C. O., et al, eds. 1960 (ISBN 0-12-016409-4); Vols. 11-13. 1963-64. Vol. 10. o.s.i (ISBN 0-12-016410-8). Vol. 11 (ISBN 0-12-016411-6). Vol. 12 (ISBN 0-12-016412-4). Vol. 13 (ISBN 0-12-016413-2); Vol. 14. 1965 (ISBN 0-12-016414-0); Vol. 15. 1967 (ISBN 0-12-016415-9); Vol. 16. 1968. o.s.i (ISBN 0-12-016416-7); Vol. 17. 1969 (ISBN 0-12-016417-5); Vol. 18. 1970 (ISBN 0-12-016418-3); Vol. 19. 1971 (ISBN 0-12-016419-1); Vol. 20. 1973 (ISBN 0-12-016420-5); Vol. 21. 1975 (ISBN 0-12-016421-3). lib ed. 68.00 (ISBN 0-12-016484-1); microfiche 38.50 (ISBN 0-12-016485-X); Vol. 22. 1976 (ISBN 0-12-016422-1). lib ed. 68.00 (ISBN 0-12-016486-8); microfiche 38.00 (ISBN 0-12-016487-6); Vol. 23. 1977. 46.00 (ISBN 0-12-016423-X); lib ed. 53.50 (ISBN 0-12-016488-4); microfiche 31.00 (ISBN 0-12-016489-2); Vol. 24. 1978. 46.00 (ISBN 0-12-016424-8) (ISBN 0-12-016490-6). med. ed. 33.50 (ISBN 0-12-016491-4). Vols. 1-22. 53.50 ea. Acad Pr.
Oddy, Derek T. & Miller, Derek S., eds. The Making of the Modern British Diet. 235p. 1976. 17.50x (ISBN 0-87471-803-1). Rowman.
Ordy, Mark & Harman, Denham, eds. Nutrition & Aging. 1981. write for info. (ISBN 0-89004-477-5, 531). Raven.
Pearson, Paul P. & Greenwell, J. Richard, eds. Nutrition, Food & Man: An Interdisciplinary Perspective. 1980. text ed. 11.50x (ISBN 0-8165-0691-4); pap. 5.95 (ISBN 0-8165-0706-6). U of Ariz Pr.
Peshek, Robert J. Clinical Nutrition Using the Seven Lines of Defense Against Disease. 1980. 10.00 (ISBN 0-686-27606-X). Color Coded Charting.
Wurtman, Judith J. Eating Your Way Through Life. LC 77-84121. 231p. 1979. text ed. 14.50 (ISBN 0-89004-280-2); pap. text ed. 10.50 (ISBN 0-685-99040-0). Raven.
Yoshimura, H. & Kobayashi, S, eds. Physiological Adaptability & Nutritional Status of the Japanese (A) (Japan International Biological Program Synthetics Ser.: Vol. 3). 1975. pap. 32.50x (ISBN 0-86008-213-X, Pub. by U of Tokyo Pr). Intl Schol Bk Serv.

NUTRITION–STUDY AND TEACHING
Audiovisual Resources in Food & Nutrition: 1970-1978. 1979. pap. text ed. 18.00 (ISBN 0-912700-50-5). Oryx Pr.
Bavly, Sarah. Family Food Consumption in Palestine. LC 76-176544. (Columbia University. Teachers College. Contributions to Education: No. 946). Repr. of 1949 ed. 17.50 (ISBN 0-404-55946-8). AMS Pr.
Beachy, Marlene K. Creative Nutrition for Kids: A Complete Teaching Unit for the Primary Grades. (Illus.). 136p. 1981. 11.95 (ISBN 0-9606052-0-7). Tchr Tested Materials.
Bingham, Nelson E. Teaching Nutrition in Biology Classes: An Experimental Investigation of High School Biology Pupils in Their Study of the Relation of Food to Physical Well-Being. LC 74-176565. (Columbia University. Teachers College. Contributions to Education; No. 772). Repr. of 1939 ed. 17.50 (ISBN 0-404-55772-4). AMS Pr.
Clarke, Helen. The Professional Training of the Hospital Dietician. LC 70-176651. (Columbia University. Teachers College. Contributions to Education: No. 602). Repr. of 1934 ed. 17.50 (ISBN 0-404-55602-7). AMS Pr.
Food & Nutrition Education in the Primary School. (FAO Nutritional Studies: No. 25). (Illus.). 107p. (Orig.). 1971. pap. 8.25 (ISBN 0-685-29063-8, FAO). Unipub.
Fremes, Ruth & Sabri, Zak. Nutriscore: The Rate-Yourself Plan for Better Nutrition. 262p. 1981. pap. 8.95 (ISBN 0-8264-0056-6). Continuum.
Holmes, Alan C. Visual Aids in Nutrition Education: A Guide to Their Preparation & Use. (Orig.). 1968. pap. 10.00 (ISBN 92-5-100502-8, F463, FAO). Unipub.
Hoover, Loretta & Moore, Aimee. Dietetic Com Pak Student Guide. 1978. text ed. 6.50x (ISBN 0-87543-094-5). Lucas.
Knight, Margaret. Teaching Nutrition & Food Science. 1976. pap. 13.50 (ISBN 0-7134-3099-0, Pub. by Batsford England). David & Charles.
LaBuza, Theodore P. The Nutrition Crisis: A Reader. LC 75-20459. (Illus.). 512p. 1975. pap. text ed. 12.95 (ISBN 0-8299-0063-2). West Pub.
McAfee, Oralie, et al. Cooking & Eating with Children: A Way to Learn. Markun, Patricia M., ed. (Illus.). 48p. 1979. pap. 3.00 (ISBN 0-87173-006-5). ACEI.
Marbach, Ellen S., et al. Nutrition in a Changing World: A Curriculum for Primary Level, Grades 1-3. LC 79-11776. (Illus., Orig.). 1979. pap. 8.95 (ISBN 0-8425-1660-3). Brigham.
Nutrition Education Curricula: Relevance Design & the Problem of Change. (Educational Studies & Documents Ser.: No. 18). 53p. 1976. pap. 3.25 (ISBN 92-3-101287-8, U433, UNESCO). Unipub.
Ritchie, Jean A. Learning Better Nutrition: A Second Study of Approaches & Techniques. (FAO Nutritional Studies: No. 20). (Orig.). 1973. pap. 14.25 (ISBN 0-685-09392-1, F254, FAO). Unipub.
Rudman, Jack. Public Health Nutritionist. (Career Examination Ser.: C-632). (Cloth bdg. avail. on request). pap. 8.00 (ISBN 0-8373-0632-9). Natl Learning.
Sinclair, H. M. & Howat, G. R., eds. World Nutrition & Nutrition Education. (Illus.). 272p. 1980. text ed. 42.50x (ISBN 0-19-261176-3). Oxford U Pr.
Taylor, Clara M. & Riddle, Katharine P., eds. Annotated International Bibliography of Nutrition Education. LC 71-132937. 1971. pap. text ed. 5.75x (ISBN 0-8077-2255-3). Tchrs Coll.
World Nutrition & Nutrition Education. 226p. 1981. 50.50 (ISBN 92-3-101736-5, U1057, UNESCO). Unipub.

NUTRITION AND DENTAL HEALTH
see also Teeth
Char, John K. Holistic Dentistry. Date not set. cancelled (ISBN 0-9601978-3-4). G A Eversaul.
Nizel, Abraham E. Nutrition in Preventive Dentistry: Science & Practice. 2nd ed. (Illus.). 704p. 1980. text ed. write for info. (ISBN 0-7216-6806-2). Saunders.
Randolph, Patricia M. Diet, Nutrition & Dentistry. LC 80-24809. (Illus.). 358p. 1980. pap. text ed. 14.95 (ISBN 0-8016-4088-1). Mosby.

NUTRITION AND INTELLECT
see Intellect–Nutritional Aspects

NUTRITION DISORDERS
see also Deficiency Diseases
Ahrens, Richard A. Nutrition for Health. 1970. pap. 5.95x (ISBN 0-534-00675-2). Wadsworth Pub.
Brewster, Marge A. & Naito, Herbert K., eds. Nutritional Elements & Clinical Biochemistry. 450p. 1980. 45.00 (ISBN 0-306-40569-5, Plenum Pr). Plenum Pub.
Chandra. Immunology of Nutritional Diseases. (Current Topics Immunology Ser.: Vol. 12). 1980. 23.75 (ISBN 0-8151-1640-3). Year Bk Med.
Cleave, T. L. Saccharine Disease: The Master Disease of Our Time. LC 75-15456. 224p. 1975. 7.95 (ISBN 0-87983-116-2); pap. 4.95 (ISBN 0-87983-117-0). Keats.
Dufty, William. Sugar Blues. 256p. 1976. pap. 2.95 (ISBN 0-446-93786-X). Warner Bks.
Feingold, Helene & Feingold, Ben. The Feingold Cookbook for Hyperactive Children & Others with Problems Associated with Food Additives & Salicylates. 1979. 10.95 (ISBN 0-394-41232-X); pap. 5.95 (ISBN 0-394-73664-8). Random.
Follis, Richard H., Jr. The Pathology of Nutritional Disease: Physiological & Morphological Changes Which Result from Deficiencies of the Essential Elements, Amino Acids, Vitamins, & Fatty Acids. (Illus.). 306p. 1948. photocopy ed. spiral 24.50 (ISBN 0-398-04255-1). C C Thomas.
Hodges, Robert E., ed. Human Nutrition-A Comprehensive Treatise, Vol. 4: Nutrition-Metabolic & Clinical Applications. (Illus.). 500p. 1979. 37.50 (ISBN 0-306-40203-3, Plenum Pr). Plenum Pub.
MacKeith, Ronald & Wood, Christopher. Infant Feeding & Feeding Difficulties. 5th ed. 1977. 14.95x (ISBN 0-443-01474-4). Churchill.
McLaren. Color Atlas of Nutritional Disorders. 1981. 39.95 (ISBN 0-8151-5833-5). Year Bk Med.
Palmer, Sushma & Ekvall, Shirley. Pediatric Nutrition in Developmental Disorders. (Illus.). 640p. 1978. 54.50 (ISBN 0-398-03652-7). C C Thomas.
Peshek, Robert J. Clinical Nutrition Using the Seven Lines of Defense Against Disease. 1980. 10.00 (ISBN 0-686-27606-X). Color Coded Charting.
Phillips, Marshall & Baetz, Albert, eds. Diet & Resistance to Disease. (Advances in Experimental Medicine & Biology Ser.: Vol. 135). 230p. 1981. 32.50 (ISBN 0-306-40636-5, Plenum Pr). Plenum Pub.
Rechcigl, Miloslav, Jr. Nutritional Requirements: Vol. 1, Effect of Nutrient Excesses & Toxicities in Animals & Man. 520p. 1978. 69.95 (ISBN 0-8493-2796-2). CRC Pr.
Rechcigl, Miroslav, ed. Nutritional Disorders, Vols. 2-3. 1978. Vol. II, 548p. 69.95 (ISBN 0-8493-2797-0); Vol. III, 388p. 59.95 (ISBN 0-8493-2798-9). CRC Pr.
Reuben, David. Everything You Always Wanted to Know About Nutrition. 1979. pap. 2.75 (ISBN 0-380-44370-8, 44370). Avon.
Schneider, Howard A., et al. Nutritional Support of Medical Practice. (Illus.). 1977. text ed. 30.00 (ISBN 0-06-140259-1, Harper Medical). Har-Row.
Serban, George, ed. Nutrition & Mental Functions. LC 74-28371. (Advances in Behavioral Biology Ser.: Vol. 14). (Illus.). 278p. 1975. 27.50 (ISBN 0-306-37914-7, Plenum Pr). Plenum Pub.
Somogyi, J. C., ed. Solution of Nutritional Problems: The Contribution of Producers, Distributors & Nutritionists. (Bibliotheca Nutritio et Dieta: No. 28). (Illus.). 1979. pap. 87.00 (ISBN 3-8055-3025-0). S Karger.
Symposium of the Group of European Nutritionists, 9th, Chianciano, 1970. Nutrition & Nervous System: Proceedings. Somogyi, J. C. & Fidanza, F., eds. (Bibliotheca Nutritio et Dieta: No. 17). (Illus.). 202p. 1972. pap. 46.75 (ISBN 3-8055-1309-7). S Karger.
WHO Activities in Nutrition, 1948-1964. (WHO Chronicle Reprint: Vol. 19, Nos. 10-12). (Also avail in French & Spanish). 1965. pap. 1.20 (ISBN 92-4-156019-3). World Health.
WHO Group of Experts. Geneva, 1971. Nutritional Anaemias: Report. (Technicalreport Ser.: No. 503). (Also avail. in French, Russian & Spanish). 1972. pap. 1.60 (ISBN 92-4-120503-2). World Health.
WHO Scientific Group. Geneva, 1967. Nutritional Anaemias: Report. (Technicalreport Ser.: No. 405). (Also avail. in French, Russian & Spanish). 1968. pap. 2.00 (ISBN 92-4-120405-2). World Health.
Winick, Myron. Nutritional Disorders of American Women. LC 76-54393. (Current Concepts in Nutrition Ser.: Vol. 5). 1977. 26.95 (ISBN 0-471-02393-0, Pub. by Wiley-Interscience). Wiley.

NUTRITION OF CHILDREN
see Children–Nutrition; Infants–Nutrition

NUTRITION OF PLANTS
see Plants–Nutrition

NUTRITION RESEARCH
see Nutrition–Research

NUTS
see also Cookery (Nuts); also names of nuts, e.g. Walnut
Adams, Ruth & Murray, Frank. Seeds, Grains, Nuts. 1.75 (ISBN 0-686-29844-6). Cancer Bk Hse.
Boethal, D. J. & Eikenbary, R. D., eds. Pest Management Programs for Deciduous Tree Fruits & Nuts. 256p. 1979. 29.50 (ISBN 0-306-40178-9, Plenum Pr). Plenum Pub.
Brooks, Reid M. & Olmo, Harold P. Register of New Fruit & Nut Varieties. 2nd rev. & enl. ed. LC 76-100017. 512p. 1972. 25.75x (ISBN 0-520-01638-6). U of Cal Pr.
Cashew Nut Processing. (Agricultural Services Bulletin: No. 6). (Illus.). 86p. 1971. pap. 7.50 (ISBN 0-685-62845-0, F131, FAO). Unipub.
Earle, Olive L. & Kantor, Michael. Nuts. LC 74-26800. (Illus.). 64p. (gr. 3-7). 1975. 6.75 (ISBN 0-688-22025-8); PLB 6.48 (ISBN 0-688-32025-2). Morrow.
Kadans, Joseph N. Encyclopedia of Fruits, Vegetables, Nuts & Seeds for Healthful Living. 1973. 9.95 (ISBN 0-13-275412-6, Reward); pap. 3.95 (ISBN 0-13-275420-7). P-H.
Lee, Hollis. Nuts, Berries & Grapes. (Country Home & Small Farm Guides). 96p. 1981. 5.95 (ISBN 0-442-27229-4); pap. 2.95 (ISBN 0-442-27228-6). Van Nos Reinhold.
--Nuts, Berries & Grapes. (Country Home & Small Farm Guides Ser.). (Illus.). 1978. pap. 2.95 (ISBN 0-88453-009-4). Barrington.
Logsdon, Gene. Organic Orcharding: A Grove of Trees to Live in. Wallace, Dan, ed. (Illus.). 424p. (Orig.). 1981. 16.95 (ISBN 0-87857-356-9). Rodale Pr Inc.
Menninger, Edwin A. Edible Nuts of the World. 1977. 14.95 (ISBN 0-9600046-4-5). Horticultural.
Micke, Warren, et al. Almond Orchard Management. LC 78-66204. 1978. pap. 6.00x (ISBN 0-931876-27-3, 4092). Ag Sci Pubns.
Organic Gardening & Farming Staff & Editors. Nuts & Seeds, the Natural Snacks. LC 72-93742. 1973. pap. 3.95 (ISBN 0-87857-064-0). Rodale Pr Inc.
Poole, Gray J. Nuts from Forest, Orchard & Field. LC 74-7662. (Illus.). 80p. (gr. 5 up). 1974. 5.95 (ISBN 0-396-06993-2). Dodd.
Recommended International Code of Hygienic Practice for Tree Nuts. (Codex Alimentarius Commission Reports). 12p. (Orig.). 1974. pap. 4.50 (ISBN 0-685-41472-8, F668, FAO). Unipub.
Riotte, Louise. Nuts for the Food Gardener: Growing Quick Crops Anywhere. LC 74-83146. (Illus.). 144p. 1975. pap. 4.95 (ISBN 0-88266-043-8). Garden Way Pub.
Schuler, Stanley. Gardens Are for Eating. 1971. 9.95 (ISBN 0-02-607410-9). Macmillan.
Weschcke, Carl. Growing Nuts in the North. (Illus.). 1954. 5.00 (ISBN 0-87542-881-9). Llewellyn Pubns.
Wilson, Edward E. & Ogawa, Joseph M. Fungal, Bacterial, & Certain Nonparasitic Diseases of Fruit & Nut Crops in California. LC 79-63107. 1979. 18.00x (ISBN 0-931876-29-X, 4090). Ag Sci Pubns.
Woodroof, J. G. Tree Nuts Production, Processing Products. 2nd ed. (Illus.). 1979. lib. bdg. 54.00 (ISBN 0-87055-254-6). AVI.

NUTTING, MARY ADELAIDE
Marshall, Helen E. Mary Adelaide Nutting: Pioneer of Modern Nursing. LC 72-174557. (Illus.). 396p. 1972. 20.00x (ISBN 0-8018-1365-4). Johns Hopkins.

NUZI, IRAQ
Cross, Dorothy. Movable Property in the Nuzi Documents. 1937. pap. 6.00 (ISBN 0-527-02684-0). Kraus Repr.
Lacheman, Ernest R. Excavations at Nuzi, Vol. 6. Repr. of 1955 ed. 19.50 (ISBN 0-384-30850-3). Johnson Repr.
Morrison, M. A. & Owen, D. I., eds. Studies on the Civilization of Nuzi & the Hurrians in Honor of E. R. Lacheman. 1981. text ed. price not set (ISBN 0-931464-08-0). Eisenbrauns.

NYAKYUSA (AFRICAN TRIBE)
see also Makonde (Bantu Tribe)
Wilson, Monica. For Men & Elders: Change in the Relations of Generations & of Men & Women Among the Nyakyusa-Ngonde People, 1875-1971. LC 77-4203. 1978. 29.50x (ISBN 0-8419-0313-1, Africana). Holmes & Meier.

NYAM-NYAM
see Azande

NYAMWEZI

Abrahams, R. C. Political Organization of Unyamwezi. (Cambridge Studies in Social Authropology Ser: No. 1). (Illus.). 1967. 21.95 (ISBN 0-521-04001-9). Cambridge U Pr.

Abrahams, R. G. The Nyamwezi Today: A Tanzanian People in the Seventies. LC 80-41012. (Changing Cultures Ser.). (Illus.). 176p. 1981. 29.50 (ISBN 0-521-22694-5); pap. 9.95 (ISBN 0-521-29619-6). Cambridge U Pr.

NYANJA LANGUAGE

see also Chewa Dialect

FSI Chinyanja Basic Course. 1973. pap. text ed. 4.60x (ISBN 0-686-10708-X); 15 cassettes 90.00x (ISBN 0-686-10709-8). Intl Learn Syst.

NYANJAN TALES

see Tales, Nyanjan

NYASA, LAKE

Johnson, William P. Nyasa, the Great Water. LC 77-97370. Repr. of 1922 ed. 12.75x (ISBN 0-8371-2431-X, Pub. by Negro U Pr). Greenwood.

Ransford, Oliver. Livingston's Lake - the Drama of Nyasa. 1977. 18.00 (ISBN 0-7195-1141-0). Transatlantic.

NYASALAND

see also Malawi; Rhodesia and Nyasaland

Duff, Hector L. Nyasaland Under the Foreign Office. LC 70-78369. (Illus.). Repr. of 1903 ed. 21.75x (ISBN 0-8371-1341-5, Pub. by Negro U Pr). Greenwood.

Great Britain - Admiralty. Handbook of Portuguese Nyasaland. LC 79-90115. Repr. of 1920 ed. 13.75x (ISBN 0-8371-2033-0, Pub. by Negro U Pr). Greenwood.

Great Britain Colonial Office. Colonial Reports: Nyasaland 1955. LC 70-180017. (Illus.). 143p. 1956. Repr. lib. bdg. 15.00x (ISBN 0-8371-6318-8, NYP&). Greenwood.

Werner, Alice. Natives of British Central Africa. LC 79-88458. Repr. of 1906 ed. 18.50x (ISBN 0-8371-1767-4, Pub. by Negro U Pr). Greenwood.

Worsfold, William B. Portuguese Nyassaland. LC 72-82325. (Illus.). Repr. of 1899 ed. 17.75x (ISBN 0-8371-1660-0). Greenwood.

NYASSA LANGUAGE

see Nyanja Language

NYAYA

Gautama. Gautama: The Nyaya Philosophy. Junankar, N. S., tr. from Sanskrit. 1978. 25.50 (ISBN 0-89684-002-6, Pub. by Motilal Banarsidass India). Orient Bk Dist.

Keith, Arthur B. Indian Logic & Atomism: An Exposition of the Nyaya & Vaicesika Systems. LC 68-54422. 1968. Repr. of 1921 ed. lib. bdg. 14.00x (ISBN 0-8371-0509-9, KEIL). Greenwood.

Matilal, Bimal K. Navya-Nyaya Doctrine of Negation. LC 67-27088. (Oriental Ser: No. 46). 1968. 10.00x (ISBN 0-674-60650-7). Harvard U Pr.

NYBERG, DOROTHEA

Meissonnier, Juste A. Oeuvre De Juste Aurele Meissonnier: The Complete Suite of Engravings of His Designs. LC 69-16909. (Illus.). 1969. Repr. of 1750 ed. 35.00 (ISBN 0-405-08785-3, Pub. by Blom). Arno.

NYE, GERALD PRENTICE, 1892-

Cole, Wayne S. Senator Gerald P. Nye & American Foreign Relations. LC 80-17370. (Illus.). 293p. 1980. Repr. of 1962 ed. lib. bdg. 25.00x (ISBN 0-313-22660-1, COSN). Greenwood.

NYERERE, JULIUS KAMBARAGE, PRES. TANZANIA, 1922-

Killingray, David. Nyerere & Nkrumah. Yapp, Malcolm & Killingray, Margaret, eds. (World History Ser.). (Illus.). 32p. (gr. 10). 1980. Repr. of 1977 ed. lib. bdg. 5.95 (ISBN 0-89908-129-0); pap. text ed. 1.95 (ISBN 0-89908-104-5). Greenhaven.

Nyerere, Julius K. Crusade for Liberation. (Illus). 1979. pap. 2.95x (ISBN 0-19-572462-3). Oxford U Pr.

NYGREN, ANDERS, BP., 1890-

Hall, Thor. Anders Nygren. (Makers of the Modern Theological Mind Ser.). 1978. 7.95 (ISBN 0-8499-0098-0). Word Bks.

NYIKIUSA (AFRICAN TRIBE)

see Nyakyusa (African Tribe)

NYIREGYHAZI, ERWIN, 1903-

Revesz, Geza. Psychology of a Musical Prodigy. Repr. of 1925 ed. lib. bdg. 15.00x (ISBN 0-8371-4004-8, REMP). Greenwood.

NYLON

see also Rayon

Kohan, Melvin J. Nylon Plastics. LC 73-9606. (Society of Plastics Engineers Monographs). 683p. 1973. 65.50 (ISBN 0-471-49780-0, Pub. by Wiley-Interscience). Wiley.

Redfarn & Nelson. Nylon Plastics Technology. 1977. 19.95 (ISBN 0-408-00251-4). Butterworth.

NYORO (BANTU PEOPLE)

see Banyoro

NYSTAGMUS

Aschan, Gunnar, et al. Nystagmography, Recording of Nystagmus in Clinical Neuro-Otological Examinations. pap. 9.00 (ISBN 0-384-02165-4). Johnson Repr.

Barber, Hugh O. & Stockwell. Manual of Electronystagmography. 2nd ed. LC 80-17349. (Illus.). 232p. 1980. text ed. 33.50 (ISBN 0-8016-0449-4). Mosby.

Henriksson, N. G. Speed of Slow Component & Duration in Caloric Nystagmus. 1956. pap. 9.00 (ISBN 0-384-22370-2). Johnson Repr.

NYUNGU-YA-MAWE

Shorter, Aylward. Nyungu-Ya-Mawe: Leadership in Nineteenth Century Tanzania. (Tanzania Historical Association Papers: No. 7). 29p. 1969. 4.00x (ISBN 0-8002-0609-6). Intl Pubns Serv.

NZOMBO LANGUAGE

see Congo Language

O

O. HENRY

see Porter, William Sydney, 1862-1910

OAHE DAM-JUVENILE LITERATURE

Coon, Martha. Oahe Dam, Master of the Missouri. LC 69-10752. (gr. 6-9). 1969. PLB 5.39 (ISBN 0-8178-4382-5). Harvey.

OAK

Hogan, Paula Z. The Oak Tree. LC 78-21183. (Life Cycles Ser.). (Illus.). (gr. k-3). 1979. PLB 11.15 (ISBN 0-8172-1251-5). Raintree Pubs.

Kohl, Herbert & Kohl, Judith. The View from the Oak. LC 76-57680. 1977. 8.95 (ISBN 0-684-15016-6); pap. 4.95 (ISBN 0-684-15017-4). Scribner.

Trelease, W. The American Oaks. (Plant Monograph Ser.). (Illus.). 1969. 75.00 (ISBN 3-7682-0600-9). Lubrecht & Cramer.

OAK RIDGE, LOUISIANA

Zimmer, Maude F. Door Without a Lock. LC 74-149634. 1972. 4.95 (ISBN 0-8315-0004-2). Speller.

--Village So Small. 1965. 3.95 (ISBN 0-8315-0006-9). Speller.

OAKLAND, CALIFORNIA

Bay Area Employer Directory: Nineteen Eighty to Nineteen Eighty-One Edition. 1980. 35.95 (ISBN 0-916210-80-4). Albin.

Bernhardi, Robert. Buildings of Oakland with a Section on Piedmont. 116p. 1979. 14.95 (ISBN 0-9605472-0-7). Forest Hill.

McCorry, Jesse J. Marcus Foster & the Oakland Public Schools: Leadership in an Urban Bureaucracy. LC 76-55567. 1978. 14.95 (ISBN 0-520-03397-3). U of Cal Pr.

Meltsner, Arnold J. & Kast, Gregory W. Political Feasibility of Reform in School Financing: The Case of California. LC 72-92461. (Special Studies in U.S. Economic, Social & Political Issues). 1973. 27.50x (ISBN 0-685-70526-9). Irvington.

Muir, William K., Jr. Police: Streetcorner Politicians. LC 76-8085. (Illus.). 1977. 15.00 (ISBN 0-226-54632-2); pap. 6.95 (ISBN 0-226-54633-0, P825, Phoen). U of Chicago Pr.

Pressman, Jeffrey L. Federal Programs & City Politics: The Dynamics of the Aid Process in Oakland. (Oakland Project Ser). 1975. 22.50x (ISBN 0-520-02749-3); pap. 5.95x (ISBN 0-520-03508-9). U of Cal Pr.

Weber, David O. Oakland: Hub of the West. Blakey, Ellen S., ed. LC 81-65674. (American Portrait Ser.). (Illus.). 224p. (gr. 11 up). 1981. 24.95 (ISBN 0-932986-16-1). Continental Herit.

--Oakland: Hub of the West. Blakey, Ellen S., ed. LC 81-65674. (American Potrait Ser.). (Illus.). 224p. 1981. 24.95 (ISBN 0-932986-16-1). Continent Herit.

OAKLAND, CALIFORNIA BASEBALL CLUB (AMERICAN LEAGUE, A'S)

Darlington, Sandy. Celebration: The New Oakland A's. (Illus.). 100p. (Orig.). 1981. pap. 7.95 (ISBN 0-9604152-2-X). Arrowhead Bks.

--The New Oakland A's. (Illus.). 96p. (Orig.). 1981. pap. 5.95 (ISBN 0-9604152-2-X). Arrowhead Bks.

OAKLAND, CALIFORNIA FOOTBALL CLUB (AMERICAN LEAGUE, RAIDERS)

Shadi, Lou. Ken Stabler & the Oakland Raiders. (gr. 7 up). 1977. pap. 1.25 (ISBN 0-590-11866-8, Schol Pap). Schol Bk Serv.

OAKLEY, ANNIE, 1860-1926

Alderman, Clifford L. Annie Oakley & the World of Her Time. LC 78-31838. (Illus.). (gr. 5-9). 1979. 9.95 (ISBN 0-02-700270-5, 70027). Macmillan.

Harrison, et al. Annie Oakley. (Illus.). 35p. (gr. 1-9). 1981. 2.95 (ISBN 0-86575-185-4). Dormac.

Sayers, Isabelle S. Annie Oakley & Buffalo Bill's Wild West: One Hundred & Two Illustrations. (Illus.). 96p. (Orig.). 1981. pap. 5.00 (ISBN 0-486-24120-3). Dover.

Wayne, Bennett, ed. & commentaries by. Women Who Dared to Be Different. LC 72-6802. (Target Ser.). (Illus.). 168p. (gr. 5-12). 1973. PLB 7.29 (ISBN 0-8116-4902-4). Garrard.

OAS

see Organization of American States

OASTLER, RICHARD, 1789-1861

Driver, Cecil H. Tory Radical - the Life of Richard Oastler. LC 75-120249. 1970. Repr. of 1946 ed. lib. bdg. 30.00x (ISBN 0-374-92348-5). Octagon.

Fleet Papers: Being Letters - from Richard Oastler with Occasional Communications from Friends, Vols. 1-4. 1841-44. Repr. lib. bdg. 82.50x (ISBN 0-8371-9168-8, FP00). Greenwood.

OATES, JOYCE CAROL

Creighton, Joanne V. Joyce Carol Oates. (United States Authors Ser.: No. 321). 1979. lib. bdg. 10.95 (ISBN 0-8057-7212-X). Twayne.

Friedman, Ellen G. Joyce Carol Oates. LC 79-4828. (Modern Literature Ser.). 1980. 13.50 (ISBN 0-8044-2221-4). Ungar.

Wagner, Linda W. Critical Essays on Joyce Carol Oates. 1979. lib. bdg. 25.00 (ISBN 0-8161-8224-8). G K Hall.

OATHS

see also Loyalty Oaths; Vows

Giesey, Ralph. If Not, Not: The Oath of the Aragonese & the Legendary Laws of the Sobrarbe. LC 67-21023. 1968. 19.00 (ISBN 0-691-05128-3). Princeton U Pr.

Stewart, George R. Year of the Oath. LC 77-150422. (Civil Liberties in American History Ser). 1971. Repr. of 1950 ed. lib. bdg. 25.00 (ISBN 0-306-70103-0). Da Capo.

OATMAN FAMILY

Lampman, Evelyn S. White Captives. LC 74-18187. 192p. (gr. 4-7). 1975. 6.95 (ISBN 0-689-50023-8, McElderry Bk). Atheneum.

OATS

Coffman, F. A., ed. Oats & Oat Improvement. (Illus.). 1961. 4.50 (ISBN 0-89118-009-5). Am Soc Agron.

OAXACA, MEXICO (STATE)

Berry, Charles R. The Reform in Oaxaca, 1856-76: A Microhistory of the Liberal Revolution. LC 80-15378. (Illus.). xx, 282p. 1981. 20.00x (ISBN 0-8032-1158-9). U of Nebr Pr.

Chance, John K. Race & Class in Colonial Oaxaca. LC 76-48011. 1978. 14.00x (ISBN 0-8047-0937-8). Stanford U Pr.

Flannery, Kent V. & Blanton, Richard, eds. Prehistory & Human Ecology of the Valley of Oaxaca: Memoirs, 1 vol, No. 10. Incl. Part 1. The Vegetational History of the Oaxaca Valley. Smith, C. Earle; Part 2. Zapotec Plant Knowledge: Classification, Uses & Communication About Plants in Mitla, Oaxaca, Mexico. Messer, Ellen. (Illus.). 1978. pap. 8.00x (ISBN 0-932206-72-7). U Mich Mus Anthro.

Paddock, John, ed. Ancient Oaxaca: Discoveries in Mexican Archeology & History. (Illus.). 1966. 25.00 (ISBN 0-8047-0170-9). Stanford U Pr.

Pires-Ferreira, Jane W. Formative Mesoamerican Exchange Networks with Special Reference to the Valley of Oaxaca. Flannery, Kent V., ed. (Memoirs No. 7; Prehistory & Human Ecology of the Valley of Caxaca Ser.: Vol. 3). (Illus.). 1975. pap. 6.00x (ISBN 0-932206-69-7). U Mich Mus Anthro.

OB-UGRIAN LANGUAGES

see also Finno-Ugrian Languages

OBEDIENCE

Adams, Jay E. Trust & Obey. pap. 3.95 (ISBN 0-8010-0145-5). Baker Bk.

Buerger, Jane. Obedience. LC 80-14590. (What Does the Bible Say? Ser.). (Illus.). 32p. (ps-2). 1980. PLB 4.95 (ISBN 0-89565-164-5). Childs World.

--Obedience. rev. ed. LC 80-39520. (What Is It? Ser.). (Illus.). 32p. (gr. k-3). 1981. PLB 5.50 (ISBN 0-89565-206-4). Childs World.

--Obedience: Values to Live by. (Illus.). (ps-3). 1981. PLB 8.65 (ISBN 0-516-06526-2). Childrens.

Cary-Elwes, Columbia. Law, Liberty & Love. 1950. 5.00 (ISBN 0-8159-6104-9). Devin.

Chimnoy, Sri. Obedience or Oneness. 54p. (Orig.). 1977. pap. 2.00 (ISBN 0-88497-374-3). Aum Pubns.

Chinmoy, Sri. Obedience. (A Supreme Virtue). 61p. (Orig.). 1977. pap. 2.00 (ISBN 0-88497-368-9). Aum Pubns.

Culliton, Joseph T. Obedience - Gateway to Freedom. 1978. pap. 3.95 (ISBN 0-88270-352-8). Logos.

Daughters Of St. Paul. Obedience: The Greatest Freedom. 1966. 4.00 (ISBN 0-8198-0106-2). Dghtrs St Paul.

Elliot, Elisabeth. The Liberty of Obedience. (Festival Bks). 1981. pap. 1.50 (ISBN 0-687-21730-X). Abingdon.

Gardiner, Stephen. Obedience in Church & State: Three Political Tracts. Janelle, Pierre, ed. LC 68-19272. 1968. Repr. of 1930 ed. lib. bdg. 14.00x (ISBN 0-8371-0081-X, GABW). Greenwood.

Milgram, Stanley. Obedience to Authority: An Experimental View. LC 71-138748. (Illus.). 320p. 1974. 12.95 (ISBN 0-06-012938-7, HarpT). Har-Row.

Parkinson, Virginia. Obedience. (Pointers for Little Persons Ser). (gr. k-3). 1961. PLB 5.99 (ISBN 0-8178-5052-X). Harvey.

Schonfeld, William R. Obedience & Revolt: French Behavior Toward Authority. LC 75-23616. (Sage Library of Social Research: Vol. 22). 256p. 1976. 20.00x (ISBN 0-8039-0515-7); pap. 9.95 (ISBN 0-8039-0516-5). Sage.

Woozley, A. D. Law & Obedience: The Arguments of Plato's Crito. LC 79-456. 1979. 14.00x (ISBN 0-8078-1366-4). U of NC Pr.

OBEDIENCE (CANON LAW)

MacDonald, Hope. Discovering the Joy of Obedience. 128p. (Orig.). 1980. pap. 3.95 (ISBN 0-310-28521-6). Zondervan.

OBERAMMERGAU-DESCRIPTION-VIEWS

Siegner, O. & Obergethmann, H. Oberammergau: The Passion-Play Village & Its Surrounding Country. (Illus.). 1981. 17.50 (ISBN 0-911268-34-0). Rogers Bk.

OBERLIN COLLEGE

Barnard, John. From Evangelicalism to Progressivism at Oberlin College, 1866-1917. LC 68-25865. 1969. 7.50 (ISBN 0-8142-0022-2). Ohio St U Pr.

Fletcher, Robert S. History of Oberlin College: From Its Foundation Through the Civil War, 2 vols. in 1. LC 75-165716. (American Education Ser, No. 2). 1971. Repr. of 1943 ed. 55.00 (ISBN 0-405-03705-8). Arno.

OBERLIN-WELLINGTON RESCUE, 1858

Shipherd, Jacob R. History of the Oberlin-Wellington Rescue. LC 71-97437. Repr. of 1859 ed. 14.75x (ISBN 0-8371-2729-7, Pub. by Negro U Pr). Greenwood.

--History of the Oberlin-Wellington Rescue. LC 77-127261. (Civil Liberties in American History Ser). 280p. 1972. Repr. of 1859 ed. lib. bdg. 32.50 (ISBN 0-306-71241-5). Da Capo.

OBESITY

Allen, Jean & Mix, Emily S. Build a Better - & Slimmer - You. 1977. 8.95 (ISBN 0-87000-369-0). Arlington Hse.

Asher, W. L., ed. Treating the Obese. LC 74-3289. 265p. 1974. 25.50 (ISBN 0-8463-0113-X, Pub. by W & W). Krieger.

Beller, Anne S. Fat & Thin: A Natural History of Obesity. 1978. pap. 4.95 (ISBN 0-07-004413-9, SP). McGraw.

--Fat & Thin: A Natural History of Obesity. 1977. 10.00 (ISBN 0-374-21964-8). FS&G.

Blundell, J. E. & McArthur, R. A. Obesity and Its Treatment. Horrobin, D. F., ed. (Obesity: Vol. I). 126p. 1979. 19.95 (ISBN 0-87705-967-5). Human Sci Pr.

Bonnet, F. P. Adipose Tissue in Childhood. 192p. 1981. 59.95 (ISBN 0-8493-5771-3). CRC Pr.

Bragg, Paul C. & Bragg, Patricia. Natural Way to Reduce. 14th ed. LC 66-30395. pap. 2.95 (ISBN 0-87790-007-8). Health Sci.

Bray, George A. The Obese Patient. LC 75-20798. (Major Problems in Internal Medicine Ser.: Vol. 9). (Illus.). 480p. 1976. 25.00 (ISBN 0-7216-1931-2). Saunders.

Bray, George A. & Bethune, John E., eds. Treatment & Management of Obesity. 1974. pap. text ed. 9.50x (ISBN 0-06-140544-2, Harper Medical). Har-Row.

Brown, Burnell R., Jr., ed. Anesthesia & the Obese Patient. (Contemporary Anesthesia Practice Ser.: Vol. 5). Date not set. price not set (ISBN 0-8036-1271-0). Davis Co.

Bruch, Hilde. Eating Disorders: Obesity, Anorexia Nervosa, & the Person Within. LC 72-89189. 1979. 16.50x (ISBN 0-465-01782-7, CN-5043); pap. 5.95 (ISBN 0-686-52338-5). Basic.

Bruno, Frank J. Think Yourself Thin. 265p. 1973. pap. 3.50 (ISBN 0-06-463348-9, EH 348, EH). Har-Row.

Cacciari, E., et al, eds. Obesity in Childhood. 1978. 40.50 (ISBN 0-12-154150-9). Acad Pr.

Collipp, Platon J., ed. Childhood Obesity. 2nd ed. LC 79-16052. (Illus.). 448p. 1980. 25.00 (ISBN 0-88416-221-4). Wright-PSG.

Cook, Shirley. Diary of a Fat Housewife. LC 77-71003. (Illus.). 1977. pap. 2.95 (ISBN 0-916406-65-2). Accent Bks.

Cordell, Franklin D. & Giebler, Gale R. Psychological War on Fat. LC 77-86484. 1977. pap. 3.50 (ISBN 0-913592-90-0). Argus Comm.

Coyle, Neva. Living Free. 160p. 1981. pap. 3.95 (ISBN 0-87123-346-0, 210346). Bethany Hse.

Craddock, D. How to Live with Obesity. 1976. pap. 9.95x (ISBN 0-433-06663-6). Intl Ideas.

Craddock, Denis. Obesity & Its Management. 3rd ed. (Illus.). 1978. pap. text ed. 18.75 (ISBN 0-443-01652-6). Churchill.

Dally, Peter & Gomez, Joan. Obesity & Anorexia Nervosa: A Question of Shape. 128p. 1980. 17.95 (ISBN 0-571-10542-4, Pub. by Faber & Faber); pap. 6.95 (ISBN 0-571-11472-5). Merrimack Bk Serv.

Darden, Ellington. How to Lose Body Fat. LC 77-75768. (Physical Fitness & Sports Medicine Ser.). (Illus.). 1977. pap. 4.95 (ISBN 0-89305-012-1). Anna Pub.
Dolit, Alan. You Can Lose Weight. LC 78-24472. 1979. 8.95 (ISBN 0-8424-0123-7). Nellen Pub.
Ellis, C. Arthur, Jr. & Ellis, Leslie E. Lose Weight by Surgery. new ed. (Illus.). 1977. 9.95 (ISBN 0-917172-01-9). Heritage Hse Pubs.
Enzi, G., et al, eds. Obesity: Pathogenesis & Treatment. (Serono Symposia Ser.: Vol. 28). 1981. 49.50 (ISBN 0-12-240150-6). Acad Pr.
Festing, Michael F., ed. Animal Models of Obesity. 1979. 35.00x (ISBN 0-19-520171-X). Oxford U Pr.
Foreyt, John P., ed. Behavioral Treatments of Obesity: A Practical Handbook. 1977. text ed. 21.00 (ISBN 0-08-019902-X). Pergamon.
Giammatteo, Michael C. Insights About Your Outsides. (Illus.). 1974. pap. 5.00 (ISBN 0-918428-00-9). Sylvan Inst.
Gilbert, Sara. Fat Free: Common Sense for Young Weight Worriers. LC 77-16186. (gr. 5 up). 1978. pap. 1.95 (ISBN 0-02-043250-X, 04325, Collier). Macmillan.
God's Answer to Overeating. (Aglow Bible Study: Bk. 7). 64p. 1975. 1.95 (ISBN 0-930756-15-0, 4220-7). Women's Aglow.
Goldberg, Larry. Goldberg's Diet Catalog. (Illus.). 1977. 17.50 (ISBN 0-02-544480-8). Macmillan.
--Goldberg's Diet Catalog. (Illus.). 1977. pap. 7.95 (ISBN 0-02-059000-8, Collier). Macmillan.
Howard, Alan, ed. Recent Advances in Obesity Research, Vol. 1. LC 76-11950. (Illus.). 1976. 32.50x (ISBN 0-87762-201-9). Technomic.
Kevorkian, Jack. Slimmeriks & the Demi-Diet. LC 78-70801. (Illus.). 1978. 8.95 (ISBN 0-9602030-0-1). Penumbra Inc.
Kiell, Norman, ed. The Psychology of Obesity: Dynamics & Treatment. (Illus.). 480p. 1973. 19.75 (ISBN 0-398-02685-8). C C Thomas.
Kirsch, Catherine A. All About Obesity. 146p. 1980. 20.00 (ISBN 0-916750-01-9). Dayton Labs.
Kline, Milton V., et al. Obesity: Etiology, Treatment, & Management. (Illus.). 480p. 1976. 29.50 (ISBN 0-398-03369-2). C C Thomas.
Klingman, Mildred. The Secret Lives of Fat People. 156p. 1981. 8.95 (ISBN 0-395-31006-7). HM.
Kordel, Lelord. Secrets for Staying Slim. 208p. 1972. pap. 2.25 (ISBN 0-451-09220-1, E9220, Sig). NAL.
Kraus, Barbara. Calories & Carbohydrates: A Dictionary of 7500 Brand Names & Basic Foods with Their Caloric & Carbohydrate Count. rev. ed. 384p. 1975. pap. 2.50 (ISBN 0-451-08544-2, E8544, Sig). NAL.
Kremer, William F. & Kremer, Laura. The Doctors' Metabolic Diet. 1976. pap. 1.75 (ISBN 0-380-00726-6, 29991). Avon.
LeShan, Eda. Winning the Losing Battle: Why I Will Never Be Fat Again. LC 79-7093. 1979. 8.95 (ISBN 0-690-01845-2). T Y Crowell.
Levine, R. & Pfeiffer, E. F., eds. Lipid Metabolism, Obesity & Diabetes Mellitis. 1974. 28.50 (ISBN 0-12-445350-3). Acad Pr.
Lindner, Peter G. Mind Over Platter. pap. 3.00 (ISBN 0-87980-099-2). Wilshire.
Lindsey, Jan H. & Tear, Jim. Fed up With Fat. 1978. pap. 3.95 (ISBN 0-8007-5022-5, Power Bks). Revell.
Lipe, Dewey & Wolff, Jurgen. Help for the Over-Weight Child: A Parent's Guide to Helping Children Lose Weight. 1978. 8.95 (ISBN 0-8128-2507-1). Stein & Day.
--Slimmanship. LC 74-17808. (Illus.). 224p. 1974. pap. 15.95 (ISBN 0-88229-161-0). Nelson-Hall.
Livingston, Carole. I'll Never Be Fat Again. 224p. 1981. pap. 2.50 (ISBN 0-345-28659-6). Ballantine.
--I'll Never Be Fat Again. 192p. 1980. 10.00 (ISBN 0-8184-0298-9). Lyle Stuart.
McHale, Kathryn. Comparative Psychology & Hygiene of the Overweight Child. LC 72-177027. (Columbia University. Teachers College. Contributions to Education: No. 221). Repr. of 1926 ed. 17.50 (ISBN 0-404-55221-8). AMS Pr.
Mahoney, Michael J. & Mahoney, Kathryn. Permanent Weight Control: A Total Solution to the Dieter's Dilemma. 192p. 1976. 13.95 (ISBN 0-393-08736-0). Norton.
Mancini, M., et al. Medical Complications of Obesity. LC 79-41151. (Serono Symposia: No.26). 1980. 50.00 (ISBN 0-12-467150-0). Acad Pr.
Mason, Edward E. Surgical Treatment of Obesity. (Major Problems in Clinical Surgery Ser.: Vol. 26). (Illus.). 512p. 1981. text ed. 32.50 (ISBN 0-7216-6141-6). Saunders.
Maxwell, J. D., et al, eds. Surgical Management of Obesity. (Illus.). 355p. 1980. 36.00 (ISBN 0-8089-1294-1). Grune.
Maynard, Leslie-Jane. When Your Child Is Overweight. LC 79-55863. (When Books). (Illus.). 96p. (Orig.). 1980. pap. 2.45 (ISBN 0-87029-162-9, 20263). Abbey.
Miller, Claude. Fat & Fed Up: Challenge to Weight Control. 1970. 5.95 (ISBN 0-8184-0031-5). Lyle Stuart.
Miller, William R. The Addictive Behaviors: Treatment of Alcoholism, Drug Abuse, Smoking & Obesity. (Illus.). 275p. 1980. 36.00 (ISBN 0-08-025203-6). Pergamon.
Millman, Marcia. Such a Pretty Face: Being Fat in America. (Illus.). 1980. 12.95 (ISBN 0-393-01317-0). Norton.
--Such a Pretty Face: Being Fat in America. 1981. pap. 2.75 (ISBN 0-425-04849-7). Berkley Pub.
Mulhauser, Roland A. Your Ideal Weight: A Calorie Counter. (Orig.). pap. 1.95 (ISBN 0-8048-0642-X). C E Tuttle.
Munro, J. F. The Treatment of Obesity. 234p. text ed. 27.50 (ISBN 0-8391-1424-9). Univ Park.
Nathan, Ruth, ed. That First Bite: Journal of a Compulsive Overeater. 1978. pap. 5.95 (ISBN 0-918732-07-7). Pomerica Pr.
Powers, Pauline S. Obesity: The Regulation of Weight. (Illus.). 448p. 1980. pap. 26.00 (ISBN 0-683-06953-5). Williams & Wilkins.
Rubin, Theodore I. Alive & Fat & Thinning in America. LC 78-2006. (Illus.). 1978. 8.95 (ISBN 0-698-10915-5). Coward.
Schachter, S. & Rodin, J. Obese Humans & Rats. LC 74-7179. (Complex Human Behavior Ser). 1974. 12.95 (ISBN 0-470-75679-9). Halsted Pr.
Schachter, Stanley & Rodin, Judith. Obese Humans & Rats. LC 74-7179. 182p. 1974. 12.95 (ISBN 0-470-75679-9, Pub. by Wiley). Krieger.
Schacter, Stanley. Emotion, Obesity & Crime. 1971. 22.50 (ISBN 0-12-621350-X). Acad Pr.
Scheimann, Eugene & Neimark, Paul. Doctor's Sensible Approach to Dieting & Weight Control. (Illus.). 1976. pap. 2.50 (ISBN 0-910304-19-X). Budlong.
Schemmel, Rachel. Nutrition, Physiology & Obesity. 240p. 1980. 64.95 (ISBN 0-8493-5471-4). CRC Pr.
Schwerdtfeger, Don. The Secret Truth About Fat People. LC 80-82369. 204p. 1980. 11.95 (ISBN 0-8119-0409-1, Pegasus Rex). Fell.
Shedd, Charlie W. The Fat Is in Your Head. LC 72-76443. 144p. 1972. 5.95 (ISBN 0-87680-202-1). Word Bks.
--The Fat Is in Your Head. LC 72-76443. 1977. pap. 2.25 (ISBN 0-8499-4103-2, 4103-2). Word Bks.
Silverstone, Trevor. Obesity: Its Pathogenesis & Management. LC 75-18338. (Illus.). 250p. 1975. 20.00 (ISBN 0-88416-038-6). Wright-PSG.
Silvestone, T. & Whelan, H., eds. Obesity: A Bibliography. 253p. 25.00 (ISBN 0-904147-01-0). Info Retrieval.
Smith, Anne, ed. Obesity: A Bibliography 1974-1979. 340p. 1980. 55.00 (ISBN 0-904147-17-7). Info Retrieval.
Somogyi, J. C., ed. Nutritional, Psychological & Social Aspects of Obesity. (Bibliotheca Nutritio et Dieta: No. 26). (Illus.). 1977. 51.50 (ISBN 3-8055-2764-0). S Karger.
Steib, Siobhan. Fat's Not Fun. (Illus., Orig.). 1979. pap. 5.00x (ISBN 0-901446-27-0). Intl Pubns Serv.
Stone. Fat Chance. 1980. 69.50 (ISBN 0-8151-8417-4). Year Bk Med.
Stuart, Richard B. & Davis, Barbara. Slim Chance in a Fat World: Behavioral Control of Obesity. professional ed. (Illus., Orig.). 1972. pap. 11.95 incl. materials (ISBN 0-87822-060-7); (bk. alone) 9.95 (ISBN 0-87822-064-X); (materials alone) 2.95 (ISBN 0-87822-061-5). Res Press.
--Slim Chance in a Fat World: Behavioral Control of Obesity. condensed ed. LC 78-62902. (Illus., Orig.). 1978. pap. 5.95 (ISBN 0-87822-193-X). Res Press.
Stuelke, Richard G. Thin for Life. LC 77-2469. 1977. 8.95 (ISBN 0-89437-000-6). Baronet.
Stunkard, Albert J. Obesity. LC 79-92616. (Illus.). 470p. 1980. text ed. 0.28.00 (ISBN 0-7216-8635-4). Saunders.
--The Pain of Obesity. 236p. 1980. pap. 7.95 (ISBN 0-915950-46-4). Bull Pub.
Title, Stanley H. & Klein, Charles M. Sensibly Thin. LC 78-27039. 1979. 14.95x (ISBN 0-88229-446-6); pap. 7.95 (ISBN 0-88229-665-5). Nelson-Hall.
Tyson, Mary C. & Tyson, Robert. Psychology of Successful Weight Control. LC 73-84207. 192p. 1974. 13.95 (ISBN 0-88229-103-3). Nelson-Hall.
Vague, J., ed. Diabetes & Obesity. LC 79-16232. 399p. 1979. 78.00 (ISBN 0-444-90058-6, Excerpta Medica). Elsevier.
Van Koevering, John A. Completely Natural Weight Control Primer. 1976. pap. 8.00x (ISBN 0-9601346-1-1). Caballero Pr.
Williams, Ben J., et al, eds. Obesity: Behavioral Approaches to Dietary Management. LC 75-40105. 1976. 15.00 (ISBN 0-87630-115-4). Brunner-Mazel.
Wolff, Jurgen M. & Lipe, Dewey. Help for the Overweight Child: A Parent's Guide to Helping Children Lose Weight. 1980. pap. 2.95 (ISBN 0-14-005318-2). Penguin.
Wolman, Benjamin B. Psychological Aspects of Obesity: A Handbook. 336p. 1981. text ed. 24.50 (ISBN 0-442-22609-8). Van Nos Reinhold.
Wurtman, Richard J. & Wurtman, Judith J., eds. Nutrition & the Brain: Disorders of Eating & Nutrients in Treatment of Brain Diseases. (Nutrition & the Brain Ser.: Vol. 3). 314p. 1979. text ed. 32.00 (ISBN 0-89004-245-4). Raven.
Young, Donald R. Physical Performance, Fitness & Diet. (Amer. Lec. Environmental Studies). (Illus.). 128p. 1977. 13.50 (ISBN 0-398-03642-X). C C Thomas.

OBITUARIES

Baker, Russell P. Marriages & Obituaries from the Tennessee Baptist, Eighteen Forty-Four to Eighteen Sixty-Two. 137p. 1979. 18.50 (ISBN 0-89308-127-2). Southern Hist Pr.
Boston Athenaeum. Index of Obituaries in Boston Newspapers, 1704-1800, 3 Vols. 1968. Set. 150.00 (ISBN 0-8161-0761-0). G K Hall.
Delisle, Leopold V., ed. Rouleaux Des Morts Du IXe Au XVe Siecle. 1866. 35.50 (ISBN 0-384-11361-3); pap. 31.00 (ISBN 0-384-11360-5). Johnson Repr.
Foley, Helen S. Obituaries from Babour County Newspapers, Eighteen Ninety to Nineteen Hundred Five. 146p. 1976. pap. 15.00 (ISBN 0-89308-182-5). Southern Hist Pr.
Keylin, Arleen, ed. Great Lives of the Century. LC 76-55945. 1977. 17.95 (ISBN 0-8129-0732-9). Times Bks.
Levy, Felice. Obituaries on File, 2 vols. 1979. Set. 75.00x (ISBN 0-686-31662-2). Vol. 1 (ISBN 0-87196-372-8). Vol. 2 (ISBN 0-87196-382-5). Facts on File.
Nangle, Benjamin. The Gentleman's Magazine Biographical & Obituary Notices, 1781-1819: An Index. LC 80-907. (Garland Reference Library of Humanities). 450p. 1980. 55.00 (ISBN 0-8240-9510-3). Garland Pub.
The New York Times Obituaries Index Nineteen Sixty-Nine to Nineteen Seventy-Eight. 341p. 1980. 95.00 (ISBN 0-667-00598-6). Microfilming Corp.
The New York Times Obituaries, Index 1858-1968. LC 72-113422. 1136p. 1970. pap. 95.00 (ISBN 0-667-00599-4). Microfilming Corp.
Penrose, Maryly B., ed. & compiled by. Philadelphia Marriages & Obituaries, 1857-1860 Philadelphia Saturday Bulletin. LC 74-84453. 294p. 1974. 35.00 (ISBN 0-918940-03-6); softcover 30.00 (ISBN 0-918940-04-4). Libty Bell Assoc.
Perry, Jeb H. Variety Obits: An Index to Obituaries in Variety 1905-1978. LC 80-10424. 322p. 1980. 16.00 (ISBN 0-8108-1289-4). Scarecrow.
Roberts, Frank, ed. Obituaries from the London Times, 1961-1970. 1977. 85.00x (ISBN 0-930466-08-X). Meckler Bks.
Roberts, Frank C. Obituaries from the London Times, 1971-1975. LC 77-22500. 1978. 75.00x (ISBN 0-930466-05-5). Meckler Bks.
Roberts, Frank C., compiled by. Obituaries from the Times, Nineteen Fifty-One to Sixty. LC 79-12743. 1979. lib. bdg. 85.00x (ISBN 0-930466-16-0). Meckler Bks.
Turner, Roland, ed. The Annual Obituary 1980. (Illus.). 900p. 1981. 69.50x (ISBN 0-312-03875-5). St Martin.
Whitman, Alden. Come to Judgment. 370p. 1980. 14.95 (ISBN 0-670-23169-X). Viking Pr.
Who Was Who, Vol. VII. 1981. 74.95x (ISBN 0-312-87746-3). St Martin.
Who Was Who: Index to Vols. 1-7. 1981. 74.95x (ISBN 0-686-72592-1). St Martin.

OBJECT-TEACHING

see also Children's Sermons; Project Method in Teaching; Visual Education

Biller, Tom A. & Biller, Martie. Simple Object Lessons for Children. (Object Lesson Ser.). 160p. 1980. pap. 4.95 (ISBN 0-8010-0793-3). Baker Bk.
Connelly, H. W. Forty-Seven Object Lessons for Youth Programs. (Object Lesson Ser). (YA) 1964. pap. 2.95 (ISBN 0-8010-2314-9). Baker Bk.
Cross, Luther. Object Lessons for Children. (Object Lesson Ser). (Illus., Orig.). (gr. 2-5). 1967. pap. 2.50 (ISBN 0-8010-2315-7). Baker Bk.
Dean, Bessie. Let's Go to Church. LC 76-3995. (Books for Lds Children Ser.). (Illus.). 64p. (ps-3). pap. 4.95 (ISBN 0-88290-062-5). Horizon Utah.
Hendricks, William C. & Den Bleyker, Merle. Object Lessons from Sports & Games. (Object Lessons Ser). 126p. 1975. pap. 2.50 (ISBN 0-8010-4134-1). Baker Bk.
Moore, Harvey D. & Moore, Patsie A. The Irritated Oyster & Other Object Lessons for Children. LC 75-30886. 80p. 1976. 3.95 (ISBN 0-687-19690-6). Abingdon.
Runk, Wesley T. The Devil Is a Mosquito Bite. 104p. 1976. pap. 4.05 (ISBN 0-89536-053-5). CSS Pub.
--I Am the Door. 18p. 1976. pap. 2.55 (ISBN 0-89536-104-3). CSS Pub.
Ryrie, Charles C. Easy Object Lesson. 1970. pap. 1.50 (ISBN 0-8024-2290-X). Moody.
Sargent, John H. Popular Object Lessons. (Object Lesson Ser). (gr. 3-8). 1969. pap. 1.95 (ISBN 0-8010-8015-0). Baker Bk.
Trull, Joe E. Forty Object Sermons for Children. (Object Lesson Ser.). 96p. 1975. pap. 2.95 (ISBN 0-8010-8831-3). Baker Bk.
Whitehead, Robert J. The Early School Years Read Aloud Program (Fall) LC 74-14891. (Read Aloud Program Ser.: No. 3). 104p. (gr. k-2). 1975. 8.95 (ISBN 0-88280-028-0); pap. 5.95 (ISBN 0-88280-029-9). ETC Pubns.

OBJECTIVITY

Haworth, Lawrence. Decandence & Objectivity. LC 77-4972. 1977. 15.00x (ISBN 0-8020-5387-4); pap. 6.50 (ISBN 0-8020-6398-5). U of Toronto Pr.
Scheffler, Israel. Science & Subjectivity. LC 67-27839. (Orig.). 1967. pap. 4.95 (ISBN 0-672-60724-7). Bobbs.

OBJECTS, MINIATURE

see Miniature Objects

OBLIGATION

see Duty; Responsibility

OBLIGATIONS (LAW)

see also Contracts; Damages; Debtor and Creditor; Liability (Law); Torts

Dainow, Joseph. Essays on the Civil Law of Obligations. LC 75-96256. 1969. 22.50 (ISBN 0-8071-0912-6). La State U Pr.
Hunting, Warren B. The Obligation of Contracts Clause of the United States Constitution. LC 75-31433. (Johns Hopkins Univ Studies in Hist & Pol. Science, Ser.: No. 37, Pt.4). 1976. Repr. of 1919 ed. lib. bdg. 15.00x (ISBN 0-8371-8524-6, HUOC). Greenwood.
Pennock, J. Roland & Chapman, John W., eds. Political & Legal Obligation. LC 70-105609. (Nomos Ser.: No. 12). 455p. 1970. text ed. 15.00x (ISBN 0-202-24086-X). Lieber-Atherton.
Tancelin, Maurice A. Theorie du Droit des Obligations. (Fr.). 1976. pap. 18.00x (ISBN 2-7637-6764-8, Pub. by Laval). Intl Schol Bk Serv.

OBOE

Bechler, Leo & Rahm, B. Die Oboe und die Ihr Verwandten Istrumente, Nebst Biographischen Skizzen der Bedeutendsten Ihrer Meister: Ph. Losch, Musikliteratur fur Oboe. 1978. Repr. of 1914 ed. 35.00 (ISBN 90-6027-165-3, Pub. by Frits Knuf Netherlands); wrappers 22.50 (ISBN 90-6027-164-5, Pub. by Frits Knuf Netherlands). Pendragon NY.
Fitch, William D. Study of the Oboe. 1968. 6.00x (ISBN 0-685-21807-4). Wahr.
Goosens, Leon & Roxburgh, Edwin. Oboe. LC 77-15886. (The Yehudi Menuhin Music Guides Ser.). (Illus.). 1978. 12.95 (ISBN 0-02-871450-4); pap. 6.95 (ISBN 0-02-871460-1). Schirmer Bks.
Ledet, David A. Oboe Reed Styles: Theory & Practice. LC 80-8152. (Illus.). 224p. 1981. 27.50x (ISBN 0-253-37891-5). Ind U Pr.
Mayer, Robert & Rohner, Traugott. Oboe Reeds: How to Make & Adjust Them. (Illus.). pap. 7.00 (ISBN 0-686-15900-4). Instrumental Co.
Rothwell, Evelyn. Oboe Technique. rev. ed. (YA) (gr. 9 up). 1962. 7.75 (ISBN 0-19-318602-0). Oxford U Pr.
--The Oboist's Companion: Lessons, Exercises, Music. (Illus.). 104p. 1976. Bk. 1. pap. 20.00 (ISBN 0-19-322335-X); Bk. 2. pap. 20.00 (ISBN 0-19-322336-8); Bk. 3. pap. 20.00 (ISBN 0-19-322337-6). Oxford U Pr.
Sprenkle, Robert & Ledet, David. Art of Oboe Playing. (Illus.). 1961. pap. text ed. 10.25 (ISBN 0-87487-040-2). Summy.

O'BRIEN, EDNA, 1932-

Eckley, Grace. Edna O'Brien. (Irish Writers Ser.). 88p. 1974. 4.50 (ISBN 0-8387-7838-0); pap. 1.95 (ISBN 0-8387-7976-X). Bucknell U Pr.

OBSCENE LITERATURE

see Literature, Immoral

OBSCENE WORDS

see Words, Obscene

OBSCENITY (LAW)

see also Postal Service–Laws and Regulations

Arts Council Of Great Britain - Conference. Obscenity Laws: Proceedings. 1970. 6.95 (ISBN 0-233-96204-2). Transatlantic.
Clor, Harry M. Obscenity & Public Morality: Censorship in a Liberal Society. LC 69-16772. 1969. 12.00x (ISBN 0-226-11033-8). U of Chicago Pr.
Daily, Jay E. The Anatomy of Censorship. (Bks. in Library & Information Science: Vol. 6). 424p. 1973. 22.50 (ISBN 0-8247-6065-4). Dekker.

De Grazia, Edward. Censorship Landmarks. LC 71-79424. 657p. 1969. 29.50 (ISBN 0-8352-0207-0). Bowker.
Dhavan, Rajeev & Davies, Christie, eds. Censorship & Obscenity. 187p. 1978. 16.50x (ISBN 0-8476-6054-0). Rowman.
Ernst, M. L. & Lindey, A. The Censor Marches on. LC 73-164512. (Civil Liberties in American History Ser.). 346p. 1971. Repr. of 1940 ed. lib. bdg. 32.50 (ISBN 0-306-70295-9). Da Capo.
Ernst, Morris L. & Schwartz, Alan U. Censorship. 1964. 6.95 (ISBN 0-685-14842-4). Macmillan.
Friedman, Leon, ed. Obscenity. 2nd ed. (Oral Arguments Before the Supreme Court Ser.). 365p. 1981. pap. 8.95 (ISBN 0-87754-211-2). Chelsea Hse.
Gerber, Albert B. Sex, Pornography & Justice. (Illus.). 1965. 10.00 (ISBN 0-8184-0079-X). Lyle Stuart.
Haney, Robert W. Comstockery in America: Patterns of Censorship & Control. LC 74-1241. (Civil Liberties Ser.). 199p. 1974. Repr. of 1960 ed. lib. bdg. 22.50 (ISBN 0-306-70654-7). Da Capo.
Kilpatrick, James J. The Smut Peddlers. LC 72-7506. (Illus.). 323p. 1973. Repr. of 1960 ed. lib. bdg. 18.75x (ISBN 0-8371-6515-6, KISP). Greenwood.
Lewis, Felice F. Literature, Obscenity, & Law. LC 75-42094. 310p. 1978. pap. 8.95 (ISBN 0-8093-0870-3). S Ill U Pr.
Oboler, Eli. The Fear of the Word: Censorship & Sex. LC 74-6492. 1974. 12.00 (ISBN 0-8108-0724-6). Scarecrow.
Obscenity Report. LC 70-127235. 1970. pap. 2.95 (ISBN 0-8128-1346-4). Stein & Day.
Paul, James C. & Schwartz, Murray L. Federal Censorship: Obscenity in the Mail. LC 77-10978. 1977. Repr. of 1961 ed. lib. bdg. 29.50x (ISBN 0-8371-9818-6, PAFC). Greenwood.
Ralph, C. H. Books in the Dock. 1970. 7.50 (ISBN 0-233-95901-7). Transatlantic.
Ringel, William E. Obscenity Law Today. 1970 ed. 1969. pap. text ed. 6.00x (ISBN 0-87526-048-9). Gould.
Schauer, Frederick F. The Law of Obscenity. LC 76-20445. 476p. 1976. 19.50 (ISBN 0-87179-254-0). BNA.
Schroeder, Theodore. Obscene Literature & Constitutional Law. 59.95 (ISBN 0-8490-0745-3). Gordon Pr.
Schroeder, Theodore A. Obscene Literature & Constitutional Law. LC 72-116913. (Civil Lib. in Am. Hist. Ser.). 440p. 1972. Repr. of 1911 ed. lib. bdg. 25.00 (ISBN 0-306-70156-1). Da Capo.
Sobel, Lester A., ed. Pornography, Obscenity & the Law. 1978. lib. bdg. 17.50x (ISBN 0-87196-299-3). Facts on File.

OBSCENITY (LAW)–GREAT BRITAIN

Clor, Harry M. Obscenity & Public Morality: Censorship in a Liberal Society. LC 69-16772. 1971. pap. 3.95 (ISBN 0-226-11034-6, P397, Phoen). U of Chicago Pr.
Craig, Alec. Above All Liberties. facsimile ed. LC 70-37839. (Essay Index Reprint Ser). Repr. of 1942 ed. 16.00 (ISBN 0-8369-2587-4). Arno.
--The Banned Books of England & Other Countries: A Study of the Conception of Literary Obscenity. LC 77-9968. 1977. Repr. of 1962 ed. lib. bdg. 17.50x (ISBN 0-8371-9709-0, CRBB). Greenwood.
St. John-Stevas, Norman. Obscenity & the Law. LC 74-8011. (Civil Liberties in American History Ser.). 289p. 1974. Repr. of 1956 ed. lib. bdg. 27.50 (ISBN 0-306-70602-4). Da Capo.

OBSEQUIES

see Funeral Rites and Ceremonies

OBSERVATION (EDUCATIONAL METHOD)

Anderson, D. C., ed. Strategies for Professional Development Evaluation by Classroom Experience. 1979. 6.50x (ISBN 0-905484-20-7, Pub. by Nafferton England). State Mutual Bk.
Beegle, Charles W. & Brandt, Richard M., eds. Observational Methods in the Classroom. LC 73-80535. 94p. 1973. 3.50 (ISBN 0-87120-047-3, 611-17948). Assn Supervision.
Boehm, Ann E. & Weinberg, Richard A. The Classroom Observer: Guide to Developing Observation Skills. LC 77-4316. (Illus.). 1977. pap. text ed. 7.50x (ISBN 0-8077-2506-4). Tchrs Coll.
Chatterton, Roland H. Methods of Lesson Observing by Preservice Student-Teachers; a Comparative Study. LC 72-178801. (Columbia University. Teachers College. Contributions to Education: No. 834). Repr. of 1941 ed. 17.50 (ISBN 0-404-55834-8). AMS Pr.
Mills, Richard W. Classroom Observation of Primary School Children: All in a Day. (Unwin Education Bks). (Illus.). 248p. (Orig.). 1980. text ed. 22.50x (ISBN 0-04-372028-5); pap. text ed. 9.95x (ISBN 0-04-372029-3). Allen Unwin.
Stallings, Jane. Learning to Look: A Handbook on Classroom Observation. 1977. pap. 12.95x (ISBN 0-534-00522-5). Wadsworth Pub.
Stubbs, Michael & Delamont, Sara, eds. Explorations in Classroom Observation. LC 74-13166. 221p. 1975. 36.95 (ISBN 0-471-83481-5, Pub. by Wiley-Interscience). Wiley.
Walker, Robert & Adelman, Clem. A Guide to Classroom Observation. (Illus.). 1975. pap. 9.50x (ISBN 0-416-81210-4). Methuen Inc.
West, Joe Y. A Technique for Appraising Certain Observable Behavior of Children in Science in Elementary Schools. LC 71-177651. (Columbia University. Teachers College. Contributions to Education: No. 728). Repr. of 1937 ed. 17.50 (ISBN 0-404-55728-7). AMS Pr.

OBSERVATIONS, METEOROLOGICAL

see Meteorology–Observations

OBSERVATORIES, ASTRONOMICAL

see Astronomical Observatories

OBSERVATORIES, METEOROLOGICAL

see Meteorological Stations; Meteorology–Observations

OBSERVER (LONDON NEWSPAPER)

Observer. Observer Profiles. Brown, Ivor, ed. LC 78-117330. (Biography Index Reprint Ser). Repr. of 1948 ed. 18.00 (ISBN 0-8369-8022-0). Arno.

OBSESSIVE-COMPULSIVE NEUROSES

Beech, H. R. & Vaughan, M. Behavioural Treatment of Obsessional States. LC 78-4552. 200p. 1978. 26.50 (ISBN 0-471-99646-7, Pub. by Wiley-Interscience). Wiley.
Broughton, Diane. Confessions of a Compulsive Eater. 1978. 8.95 (ISBN 0-525-66581-1). Elsevier-Nelson.
Edwards, S. Too Much Is Not Enough: An Insider's Answer to Compulsive Eating. 1981. 10.95 (ISBN 0-07-019032-1). McGraw.
Mule, S. Joseph, ed. Behavior in Excess: An Examination of the Volitional Disorders. LC 81-65506. (Illus.). 480p. 1981. 25.00 (ISBN 0-02-922220-6). Free Pr.
Nagera, Humbera. Obsessional Neuroses. LC 76-22918. 1977. 22.50x (ISBN 0-87668-271-9). Aronson.
Salzman, Leon. Treatment of the Obsessive Personality. LC 79-91903. 528p. 1980. 25.00 (ISBN 0-87668-392-8). Aronson.
Shapiro, David. Autonomy & Rigid Character. LC 80-68953. 167p. 1981. 12.95x (ISBN 0-465-00567-5). Basic.
Straus, Erwin W. On Obsession: A Clinical & Methodological Study. Repr. of 1948 ed. 11.50 (ISBN 0-384-58630-9). Johnson Repr.

OBSIDIONAL COINS

Hester, Thomas R., ed. Archaeological Studies of Mesoamerican Obsidian. (Ballena Press Studies in Mesoamerican Art, Archaeological & Ethnohistory Ser.: No. 3). (Illus.). 1979. pap. 9.95 (ISBN 0-87919-082-5). Ballena Pr.

OBSOLESCENCE (ACCOUNTING)

see Depreciation

OBSTETRICAL NURSING

Anderson, Barbara & Shapiro, Pamela. Obstetrics for the Nurse. 272p. 1981. text ed. 13.95 (ISBN 0-442-21840-0). Van Nos Reinhold.
--Obstetrics for the Nurse. LC 77-83424. 1979. pap. text ed. 7.40 (ISBN 0-8273-1330-6); instructor's guide 1.60 (ISBN 0-8273-1331-4). Delmar.
Anderson, Betty A., et al. The Childbearing Family, Vol. 1: Pregnancy & Family Health. 2nd ed. (Illus.). 1979. pap. text ed. 10.95 (ISBN 0-07-001683-6, HP). Macgraw.
--The Childbearing Family, Vol. 2: Interruptions in Family Health During Pregnancy. 2nd ed. (Illus.). 1979. pap. text ed. 10.95 (ISBN 0-07-001684-4, HP). McGraw.
Bethea, Doris C. Introductory Maternity Nursing. 3rd ed. LC 78-27877. 1979. pap. text ed. 11.50x (ISBN 0-397-54225-9, JBL-Med-Nursing); wkbk. 7.95x (ISBN 0-685-97151-1). Har-Row.
Bishop, Barbara E. The Maternity Cycle: One Nurse's Reflections. LC 79-13380. (Illus.). 325p. 1980. pap. 15.00 (ISBN 0-8036-0868-3). Davis Co.
Bleier, Inge J. Bedside Maternity Nursing. 4th ed. LC 78-65374. (Illus.). 362p. 1979. pap. 9.95 (ISBN 0-7216-1743-3). Saunders.
Clark, Ann L., et al. Childbearing: A Nursing Perspective. 2nd ed. LC 78-24575. (Illus.). 1979. text ed. 23.00 (ISBN 0-8036-1831-X). Davis Co.
Clausen, Joy, et al. Maternity Nursing Today. 2nd ed. (Illus.). 1976. text ed. 19.95 (ISBN 0-07-011284-3, HP). McGraw.
Dickason, Jean & Schult, Martha. Maternal & Infant Care. 2nd ed. (Illus.). 1979. text ed. 17.95 (ISBN 0-07-016796-6, HP); instructor's manual 2.95 (ISBN 0-07-016797-4). McGraw.
Dickason, Jean, et al. Maternal & Infant Drugs & Nursing Intervention. (Illus.). 1978. pap. text ed. 8.95 (ISBN 0-07-016788-5, HP). McGraw.
Disbrow, Mildred A., et al. Maternity Nursing Case Studies. 1976. spiral bdg. 9.50 (ISBN 0-87488-036-X). Med Exam.
Fream, William C. Notes on Obstetrics. LC 76-19020. (Livingston Nursing Notes). 1977. pap. 8.25 (ISBN 0-443-01451-5). Churchill.
Friesner, Arlyne. Maternity Nursing. 2nd ed. Raff, Beverly, ed. LC 77-80106. (Nursing Outline Ser.). 1977. pap. 8.50 (ISBN 0-87488-377-6). Med Exam.
Green, Judith. Review of Maternal Child Nursing. 1978. pap. text ed. 6.95 (ISBN 0-07-024302-6, HP). McGraw.
Griffin, Joanne K., et al. Maternal & Child Health Nursing. 3rd ed. (Nursing Examination Review Books: Vol. 3). 1972. pap. 6.00 spiral bdg. (ISBN 0-87488-503-5). Med Exam.
Hamilton, Persis M. Basic Maternity Nursing. 4th ed. LC 78-26998. (Illus.). 1979. pap. 10.95 (ISBN 0-8016-2031-7). Mosby.
Ingalls, A. Joy. Maternal & Child Health Nursing: A Study Guide. 2nd ed. (Illus.). 1980. pap. 10.45 wrk. bk. (ISBN 0-8016-2325-1). Mosby.
Jensen, Margaret & Bobak, Irene. Handbook of Maternity Care: A Guide for Nursing Practice. LC 79-18163. 1980. pap. text ed. 10.95 (ISBN 0-8016-2490-8). Mosby.
Jensen, Margaret, et al. Maternity Care: The Nurse & the Family. LC 76-48641. (Illus.). 1977. text ed. 22.95 (ISBN 0-8016-2489-4). Mosby.
Jensen, Margaret D., et al. Maternity Care: The Nurse & the Family. 2nd ed. LC 80-270023. (Illus.). 1013p. 1981. text ed. 23.95 (ISBN 0-8016-2492-4). Mosby.
Juneau, Patricia S. Maternal & Child Nursing-Associate. 1979. text ed. 16.95 (ISBN 0-02-361530-3). Macmillan.
Kalafatich, Audrey J., et al. Maternal & Child Health: A Handbook for Nurses. rev. ed. LC 77-417. (Quality Paperback Ser.: No. 303). (Illus.). 1977. pap. 3.50 (ISBN 0-8226-0303-9). Littlefield.
Lerch, Constance & Bliss, Jane. Maternity Nursing: A Self Study Guide. 4th ed. (Illus.). 1978. pap. text ed. 9.50 (ISBN 0-8016-2959-4). Mosby.
Lerch, Constance & Bliss, Virginia. Maternity Nursing. 3rd ed. LC 77-13983. (Illus.). 1978. text ed. 18.95 (ISBN 0-8016-2961-6). Mosby.
Lytle, Nancy A. Nursing of Women in the Age of Liberation. 1977. pap. text ed. 6.95x (ISBN 0-697-05516-7). Wm C Brown.
McNall, Lee. Contemporary Obstetric & Gynecologic Nursing, Vol. 3. LC 79-27333. (Current Practice Ser.). 1980. pap. 13.95 (ISBN 0-8016-3325-7). Mosby.
McNall, Leota K., ed. Current Practice in Obstetric & Gynecologic Nursing, Vol. 2. Galeener, Janet. LC 75-29240. (Current Practice Ser.). (Illus.). 1978. 11.95 (ISBN 0-8016-3326-5); pap. 8.95 (ISBN 0-8016-3327-3). Mosby.
Malinowski, Janet S., et al. Nursing Care of the Labor Patient. (Illus.). 1978. pap. text ed. 8.95 (ISBN 0-8036-5801-X). Davis Co.
Malo-Juvera, Dolores, et al, eds. Obstetrical Nursing Continuing Education Review. 2nd ed. 1979. pap. 9.50 (ISBN 0-87488-350-4). Med Exam.
Neeson, Jean D. & Stockdale, Connie R. The Practitioners Handbook of Ambulatory OB-GYN. LC 80-26151. 394p. 1981. 18.95 (ISBN 0-471-05670-7, Pub. by Wiley Medical). Wiley.
Olds, Sally. Obstetric Nursing. 1980. 24.95 (ISBN 0-201-02718-6, 170H00). A-W.
--Obstetric Nursing: Instructor's Guide. 1980. 3.95 (ISBN 0-201-02718-6, 170HOO, Med-Nurse). A-W.
Phillips, Celeste R. Family-Centered Maternity Newborn Care: A Basic Text. (Illus.). 1980. pap. text ed. 12.45 (ISBN 0-8016-3920-4). Mosby.
Pillitteri, Adele. Maternal-Newborn Nursing: Care of the Growing Family. 2nd ed. 1981. text ed. write for info. (ISBN 0-316-70792-9). Little.
Reeder, Sharon, et al. Maternity Nursing. LC 79-22993. 775p. 1980. text ed. 24.95x (ISBN 0-397-54253-4, JBL-Med-Nursing). Har-Row.
Sagebeer, Josephine. Maternal Health Nursing Review. 2nd ed. LC 79-1161. (Arco Nursing Review Ser.). (Illus.). 1980. pap. text ed. 6.00 (ISBN 0-668-04822-0). Arco.
Simpson, Mary S. Sister Stella's Babies. LC 78-67312. 143p. 1978. pap. text ed. 9.95 (ISBN 0-937126-81-0). Am Journal Nurse.
Tucker, Susan M. & Bryant, Sandra. Fetal Monitoring & Fetal Assesment in High Risk Pregnancy. LC 77-19098. 1978. pap. text ed. 11.95 (ISBN 0-8016-5121-2). Mosby.
Varney, Helen. Nurse-Midwifery. (Illus.). 672p. 1980. text ed. 37.50 (ISBN 0-86542-001-7). Blackwell Sci.
Ziegel, Erna & Cranley, Mecca. Obstetric Nursing. 7th ed. (Illus.). 1979. text ed. 18.95 (ISBN 0-02-431560-5). Macmillan.

OBSTETRICS

see also Abortion; Anesthesia in Obstetrics; Cesarean Section; Childbirth; Forceps, Obstetric; Hypnotism in Obstetrics; Labor (Obstetrics); Midwives; Obstetrical Nursing; Pelvis; Pregnancy; Puerperal Septicemia; Puerperium; Women–Diseases

Aladjem, Silvio. Obstetrical Practice. LC 80-17356. (Illus.). 877p. 1980. text ed. 41.50 (ISBN 0-8016-0114-2). Mosby.
Annotated Bibliography of Teaching-Learning Materials for Schools of Nursing & Midwifery. (Offset Pub.: No. 19). (Also avail. in French & Spanish). 1975. pap. 20.40 (ISBN 92-4-052005-8). World Health.
Arms, Suzanne. Immaculate Deception. 416p. 1977. pap. 2.95 (ISBN 0-553-13711-5, J13711-5). Bantam.
--Immaculate Deception: A New Look at Childbirth in America. LC 74-28129. (A San Francisco Ser.). 336p. 1975. 11.95 (ISBN 0-395-19893-3); pap. 6.95 (ISBN 0-395-19973-5). HM.
Babson, S. Gorham, et al. Diagnosis & Management of the Fetus & Neonate at Risk: A Guide for Team Care. 4th ed. LC 79-16957. (Illus.). 1979. text ed. 27.50 (ISBN 0-8016-0415-X). Mosby.
Barber, Hugh R., et al. Quick Reference to OB-Gyn Procedures. 2nd ed. 1979. pap. text ed. 19.50 (ISBN 0-397-50423-3, JBL-Med-Nursing). Har-Row.
Barnes, Allan C., ed. The Social Responsibility of Gynecology & Obstetrics. 225p. 1965. 15.50x (ISBN 0-8018-0055-2). Johns Hopkins.
Barnes, Cyril G. Medical Disorders in Obstetric Practice. 4th ed. (Illus.). 1974. text ed. 42.50 (ISBN 0-632-09810-4, Blackwell). Mosby.
Bayer, R., et al. Ultrasonographic Representation of Pregnancy: An Atlas for the Practioner in Obstetrics. (Illus.). 1979. text ed. 10.00 (ISBN 0-397-58234-X, JBL-Med-Nursing). Har-Row.
Bechard, L. Obstetrique. 160p. (Fr.). 1964. 3.75x (ISBN 2-7637-0031-4, Pub by Laval). Intl Schol Bk Serv.
Bender, S. Obstetrics for Student Midwives. 3rd ed. 1976. pap. text ed. 17.95x (ISBN 0-433-02402-X). Intl Ideas.
Benson, Ralph C. Handbook of Obstetrics & Gynecology. 7th ed. LC 80-81205. (Illus.). 808p. 1980. lexotone cover 10.00 (ISBN 0-87041-144-6). Lange.
Benson, Ralph C., ed. Current Obstetric & Gynecologic Diagnosis & Treatment. 3rd ed. LC 80-82160. (Illus.). 1001p. 1980. lexotone cover 21.00 (ISBN 0-87041-212-4). Lange.
Black, J. Neonatal Emergencies & Other Problems. 288p. 1972. 27.50 (ISBN 0-407-32780-0). Butterworth.
Black, M. & English, M., eds. Physical Science Techniques in Obstetrics & Gynecology. (Illus.). 1977. 39.50 (ISBN 0-8391-1145-2). Univ Park.
Bowers, John Z. & Purcell, Elizabeth, eds. The Current Status & Future of Academic Obstetrics. LC 80-80306. (Illus.). 184p. 1980. pap. 4.00 (ISBN 0-914362-31-3). J Macy Foun.
Breen, James L. & Jaffurs, William. Atlas of Gynecologic-Obstetric Pathology. (Complete print edition available). 1973. Two Parts. 90.00 (ISBN 0-8036-1136-6). Davis Co.
Brown, D. Obstetrics, Contraception, & Gynecology. 1977. 29.50 (ISBN 0-8391-1171-1). Univ Park.
Browne, J. C., et al. Antenatal Care. 11th ed. LC 77-1557. (Illus.). 1978. 35.00 (ISBN 0-443-01476-0). Churchill.
Burnett, C. W. The Anatomy & Physiology of Obstetrics. 6th ed. Anderson, Mary, ed. (Illus.). 1979. 9.95 (ISBN 0-571-04682-7, Pub. by Faber & Faber); pap. 7.95 (ISBN 0-571-04992-3). Merrimack Bk Serv.
Cadkin, Alan V. & Motew, Martin N. Clinical Atlas of Gray Scale Ultrasonography in Obstetrics. (Illus.). 384p. 1979. 77.50 (ISBN 0-398-03842-2). C C Thomas.
Campbell, John A. Obstetrical Diagnosis by Radiographic, Ultrasonic & Nuclear Methods. LC 77-6448. 220p. 1977. 25.00 (ISBN 0-683-01416-1). Krieger.
Caplan & Sweeney. Advances in Obstetrics & Gynecology. 1978. lib. bdg. 53.00 (ISBN 0-683-01435-8). Williams & Wilkins.
Castelazo-Ayala, L., et al, eds. Gynecology & Obstetrics: Proceedings of the VII World Congress of Gynecology & Obstetrics, Mexico City, October, 1976. (International Congress Ser: No. 412). 1978. 103.50 (ISBN 0-444-15251-2, Excerpta Medica). Elsevier.
Cavanagh, Denis, et al. Obstetric Emergencies. 2nd ed. (Illus.). 1978. pap. text ed. 22.50x (ISBN 0-06-140626-0, Harper Medical). Har-Row.
Chamberlain, Geoffrey. Contemporary Obstetrics & Gynaecology, Vol. 1. 440p. 90.00x (ISBN 0-7198-2546-6, Pub. by Northwood Bks). State Mutual Bk.
Chamberlain, Geoffrey & Dewhurst, C. J. Practice of Obstetrics & Gynecology. (Illus.). 271p. 1977. 21.00x (ISBN 0-8464-1120-2). Beekman Pubs.
Chamberlain, Geoffrey & Dewhurst, G. J. A Practice of Obstetrics & Gynocology. 1976. 19.00 (ISBN 0-685-85058-7). State Mutual Bk.

Chamberlin, Geoffrey. Contemporary Obstetrics & Gynaecology. (Illus.). 1977. 46.50x (ISBN 0-7198-2546-6). Intl Ideas.
Charles, David. Infections in Obstetrics & Gynecology. LC 79-67789. (Major Problems in Obstetrics & Gynecology Ser.: Vol. 12). (Illus.). 440p. 1980. text ed. 32.50 (ISBN 0-7216-2492-8). Saunders.
--Self-Assessment of Current Knowledge in Obstetrics & Gynecology. 3rd ed. LC 79-91970. 1980. pap. 16.50 (ISBN 0-87488-260-5). Med Exam.
Chef, R., ed. Real Time Ultrasound in Perinatal Medicine. (Contributions to Gynecology & Obstetrics: Vol. 6). (Illus.). 1979. pap. 47.50 (ISBN 3-8055-2976-7). S Karger.
Cibils, Luis A. Electronic Fetal-Material Monitoring: Antepartum-Intrapartum. (Illus.). 416p. 1981. text ed. 56.00 (ISBN 0-88416-192-7). Wright-PSG.
Clayton, Stanley & Newton, John R. A Pocket Obstetrics. 9th ed. (Illus.). 1979. pap. text ed. 9.50 (ISBN 0-443-02008-6). Churchill.
Clayton, Stanley G., et al, eds. Obstetrics by Ten Teachers. 13th ed. (Illus.). 552p. 1981. text ed. 43.50 (ISBN 0-7131-4365-7). Intl Ideas.
Clyne, Douglas G. A Concise Textbook for Midwives. 5th ed. (Illus.). 528p. 1980. pap. 17.95 (ISBN 0-571-18018-3, Pub. by Faber & Faber). Merrimack Bk Serv.
Cohen, Arnold W. Emergencies in Obstetrics & Gynecology. (Clinics in Emergency Medicine Ser.). (Illus.). 224p. Date not set. lib. bdg. price not set (ISBN 0-443-08130-1). Churchill.
Cosmi, Ermelando V. Obstetric Anesthesia & Perinatology. (Illus.). 769p. 1981. 42.50 (ISBN 0-8385-7196-4). ACC.
Cox, Helen. Midwifery Manual: A Guide for Auxiliary Midwives. (McGraw-Hill International Health Services Ser.). (Illus.). 1976. pap. text ed. 6.95 (ISBN 0-07-099250-9, C). McGraw.
Cumulative Index to Obstetrics & Gynecology, Vols. 1-40 (1953-1972) new ed. LC 74-10594. iv, 427p. 1975. 40.00 (ISBN 0-88471-033-5). Numarc Bk Corp.
Danforth, David N., ed. Obstetrics & Gynecology. 3rd ed. (Illus.). 1977. text ed. 52.50x (ISBN 0-06-140684-8, Harper Medical). Har-Row.
Davis, Elizabeth. A Guide to Midwifery: Heart & Hands. (Illus., Orig.). 1981. pap. 9.00 (ISBN 0-912528-22-2). John Muir.
--Midwifery: A Guide for Midwives & Parents. (Illus.). 8.00 (ISBN 0-686-74653-8). John Muir.
Day, Beth & Liley, H. I. Modern Motherhood: Pregnancy, Childbirth, & the Newborn Baby. rev. ed. 1969. 7.95 (ISBN 0-394-43661-X). Random.
DeCherney, Alan. Patient Management Problems: Obstetrics & Gynecology. LC 79-24563. 128p. (Orig.). 1980. pap. text ed. 9.00 (ISBN 0-668-04364-4). Arco.
De Cherney, Alan, ed. Obstetrics & Gynecology: PreTest Self-Assessment & Review. LC 77-78446. (Clinical Sciences: PreTest Self-Assessment & Review Ser.). (Illus.). 1978. pap. 9.95 (ISBN 0-07-051602-2). McGraw-Pretest.
Dill, L. V. The Obstetrical Forceps. (American Lecture Gynecology & Obstetrics). (Illus.). 175p. 1953. ed. spiral bdg. 24.50photocopy (ISBN 0-398-00457-9). C C Thomas.
Dilts, P. V., Jr., et al. Core Studies in Obstetrics & Gynecology. 3rd ed. (Illus.). 272p. 1981. softcover 17.95 (ISBN 0-686-77755-7, 2572-4). Williams & Wilkins.
Directory of Fellows with by-Laws, Councils Commissions, Committees & Task Forces, 1977-1978. 7.00 (ISBN 0-686-24121-5). Am Coll Obstetric.
Dixon, G., ed. Undergraduate Obstetrics & Gynecology. (Illus.). 280p. 1980. pap. text ed. 17.50 (ISBN 0-7236-0564-5). Wright-PSG.
Donald, Ian. Practical Obstetric Problems. 5th ed. (Illus.). 1979. text ed. 49.00 (ISBN 0-397-58247-1). Har-Row.
Douglas, C. P. & Holt, K. S., eds. Mental Retardation: Prenatal Diagnosis & Infant Assessment. (Illus.). 72p. 1972. 6.95 (ISBN 0-407-26850-2). Butterworth.
Eastman, Nicholas J. & Russell, Keith P. Expectant Motherhood. 5th rev. ed. (Illus.). 1970. 2.75 (ISBN 0-316-20394-7). Little.
Elam, Daniel. Building Better Babies. LC 80-66070. (Illus.). 168p. (Orig.). 1980. pap. 6.95 (ISBN 0-89087-274-0). Celestial Arts.
Elazo-Ayala, Cast & MacGregor, C., eds. Eighth World Congress of Gynecology & Obstetrics: Abstracts. (International Congress Ser.: No. 396). 1976. pap. 33.75 (ISBN 0-444-15235-0, Excerpta Medica). Elsevier.
Elder, M. G. & Hendricks, C. H. Obstetrics & Gynecology: Preterm Labor, Vol. 1. (Butterworths International Medical Reviews Ser.). 1981. text ed. 29.95 (ISBN 0-407-02300-3). Butterworth.
Eskes, T. K., et al, eds. Aspects of Obstetrics Today. 448p. 1975. 127.00 (ISBN 0-444-15151-6, Excerpta Medica). Elsevier.
European Congress on Perinatal Medicine, Sixth, Vienna, 1978. Perinatal Medicine: Proceedings. Thalhammer, O., et al, eds. (Illus.). 324p. 1979. pap. text ed. 30.00 (ISBN 0-88416-289-3). Wright-PSG.
Falkner, Frank & Macy, Christopher. Pregnancy & Birth: Pleasure & Problems. (Life Cycle Ser.). 1980. pap. text ed. 4.95 scp (ISBN 0-06-384741-8, HarpC). Har-Row.
Flatto, Edwin. Manual for Midwives: Home Birth. pap. 8.95 (ISBN 0-935540-02-4). Plymouth Pr.
Fream, William C. Notes on Obstetrics. LC 76-19020. (Livingston Nursing Notes). 1977. pap. 8.25 (ISBN 0-443-01451-5). Churchill.
Garrett, William J. & Robinson, David E. Ultrasound in Clinical Obstetrics. (Illus.). 128p. 1970. 16.50 (ISBN 0-398-00652-0). C C Thomas.
Garrey, Matthew M., et al. Obstetrics Illustrated. 3rd ed. (Illus.). 550p. 1980. pap. text ed. 22.00 (ISBN 0-443-02223-2). Churchill.
Gibbs, R. S. & Gibbs, C. E. Ambulatory Obstetrics: A Clinical Guide. LC 79-18554. 1979. pap. text ed. 12.95x (ISBN 0-471-05227-2, Pub. by Wiley Medical). Wiley.
Goldsmith, Jay P. & Karotkin, Edward H. Assisted Ventilation of the Neonate. LC 80-53489. (Illus.). 390p. Date not set. text ed. price not set (ISBN 0-7216-4154-7). Saunders.
Goldstein, Arthur I., ed. Advances in Perinatal Medicine. LC 77-74873. 1977. text ed. 25.00 (ISBN 0-8151-3763-X, Pub. by Symposia Special). Year Bk Med.
Goodlin, Robert C. Care of the Fetus. LC 78-62542. (Illus.). 580p. 1979. 43.50x (ISBN 0-89352-021-7). Masson Pub.
Graeff, H. & Kuhn, W. Coagulation Disorders in Obstetrics: Pathobiochemistry-Pathophysiology-Diagnosis-Treatment. Davis, A., tr. from Ger. LC 79-48020. (Major Problems in Obstetrics & Gynecology Ser.: No. 13). 1980. write for info. (ISBN 0-7216-4192-X). Saunders.
Greenhill, J. P. & Friedman, Emanuel A. Biological Principles & Modern Practice of Obstetrics. LC 73-77938. (Illus.). 837p. 1974. text ed. 30.00 (ISBN 0-7216-4257-8). Saunders.
Guillemeau, Jacques. Child-Birth. LC 77-38196. (English Experience Ser.: No. 464). 396p. 1972. Repr. of 1612 ed. 55.00 (ISBN 90-221-0464-8). Walter J Johnson.
Guttmacher, Alan. Pregnancy, Birth & Family Planning. (Reference Ser.). 352p. 1973. pap. 2.95 (ISBN 0-451-11193-1, AE1193, Sig). NAL.
Hallum, Jean. Midwifery. LC 73-93514. (Medibooks Ser.). 1972. pap. 5.00 (ISBN 0-668-03460-2). Arco.
Hassani, N. Ultrasound in Gynecology & Obstetrics. 1977. 26.30 (ISBN 0-387-90260-0). Springer-Verlag.
Hawkins, D. F. Obstetric Therapeutics: Clinical Pharmacology & Therapeutics in Obstetric Practice. (Illus.). 1974. text ed. 38.50 (ISBN 0-02-858030-3). Macmillan.
Heller. Emergencies in Gynecology & Obstetrics. 1981. 13.95 (ISBN 0-8151-4225-0). Year Bk Med.
Herrmann, W. L. & Heinrichs, W. L., eds. Forum of Modern Obstetrical Practice. (Gynecologic Investigations: Vol. 1, Supplement, 1970). 1970. pap. 8.50 (ISBN 3-8055-1144-2). S Karger.
Hersey, Thomas. The Midwife's Practical Directory: Woman's Confidential Friend. LC 73-20627. (Sex, Marriage & Society Ser.). 362p. 1974. Repr. of 1836 ed. 22.00x (ISBN 0-405-05803-9). Arno.
Hibbard, Lester T. Infections in Obstetrics & Gynecology. LC 80-18670. (Discussions in Patient Management Ser.). 1980. pap. 8.00 (ISBN 0-87488-896-4). Med Exam.
History of ACOG 1950-1976. 5.00 (ISBN 0-686-24124-X). Am Coll Obstetric.
Hobbins, John C., ed. Diagnostic Ultrasound in Obstetrics. (Clinics in Diagnostic Ultrasound Ser.: Vol. 3). (Illus.). text ed. 20.50 (ISBN 0-443-08055-0). Churchill.
Holmes, Helen B., et al, eds. The Custom-Made Child? Women-Centered Perspectives. (Contemporary Issues in Biomedicine, Ethics, & Society Ser.). 384p. 1981. 14.95 (ISBN 0-89603-024-5); pap. 7.95 (ISBN 0-89603-025-3). Humana.
Howells, John G., ed. Modern Perspectives in Psycho-Obstetrics. LC 72-79142. 600p. 1972. 35.00 (ISBN 0-87630-056-5). Brunner-Mazel.
Huff, R. W. & Pauerstein, C. J. Human Reproduction: Physiology & Pathophysiology. 497p. 1979. pap. 18.00 (ISBN 0-471-03562-9). Wiley.
Iffy, Leslie & Kaminetzky, Harold. Progress in Perinatology. (Illus.). 1977. text ed. 24.50x (ISBN 0-89313-006-0). G F Stickley Co.
Iffy, Leslie & Langer, Alvin. Perinatology Case Studies. 1978. pap. 18.75 (ISBN 0-87488-043-2). Med Exam.
Indices for Outcome Audit. 8.00 (ISBN 0-686-24125-8). Am Coll Obstetric.
Insler, Vaclav & Homburg, Roy. Practical Obstetrics & Gynecology: Manual of Selected Procedures & Treatments. (Illus.). 1979. bookblock 49.25 (ISBN 3-8055-2945-7). S Karger.
International Congress of Psychosomatic Obsterics & Gynecology, 5th. Emotion & Reproduction: Proceedings, Vol. 20B, Pt. B. Carenza, L. & Zinchella, L., eds. LC 78-54528. 1980. 86.50 (ISBN 0-12-159402-5). Acad Pr.
International Congress of Psychosomatic Medicine in Obstetrics & Gynecology, 3rd, London, 1971. Psychosomatic Medicine in Obstetrics & Gynecology: Proceedings. Morris, Norman, ed. (Illus.). 1972. 90.00 (ISBN 3-8055-1314-3). S Karger.
International Congress on Obstetrics & Gynecology, 12th, Moscow, 1973. Recent Progress in Obstetrics & Gyna Ecology: Proceedings. Persianinov, L. S., et al, eds. (International Congress Ser.: No. 329). 575p. 1975. 111.75 (ISBN 0-444-15081-1, Excerpta Medica). Elsevier.
Kaminetzky, Harold A. & Iffy, Leslie, eds. New Techniques & Concepts in Maternal & Fetal Medicine. (Semmelweis Memorial Ser.). 1979. text ed. 32.50 (ISBN 0-442-26244-2). Van Nos Reinhold.
Karim, S. Obstetric & Gunecological Uses of Prostaglandins. (Illus.). 1976. 34.50 (ISBN 0-8391-0950-4). Univ Park.
Kobayashi, Mitsunao. Illustrated Manual of Ultrasonography in Obstetrics & Gynecology. 2nd ed. LC 79-92555. (Illus.). 1980. 37.50 (ISBN 0-89640-040-9). Igaku-Shoin.
Kreutner, A. Karen & Reycroft-Hollingsworth, Dorothy. Adolescent Obstetrics & Gynecology. (Illus.). 1978. 44.95 (ISBN 0-8151-5200-0). Year Bk Med.
Kroger, William S. Psychosomatic Obstetrics, Gynecology & Endocrinology: Including Diseases of Metabolism. (American Lecture Gynecology & Obstetrics). (Illus.). 848p. 1962. photocopy ed. spiral 79.50 (ISBN 0-398-01052-8). C C Thomas.
Lackritz, Richard M. Current Literature Reveiw in Obstetrics & Gynecology. 175p. 1981. 18.50 (ISBN 0-8385-1409-X). ACC.
Lancaster, Arnold. Nursery & Midwifery Sourcebook. 304p. 1980. 25.00x (ISBN 0-686-69979-3, Pub. by Beaconsfield England). State Mutual Bk.
Ledger, William J. Infection in the Female. LC 76-21705. (Illus.). 240p. 1977. text ed. 12.00 (ISBN 0-8121-0560-5). Lea & Febiger.
Llewellyn-Jones, Derek. Fundamental of Obstetrics & Gynaecology, Vol. I: Obstetrics. rev. 2nd ed. (Illus.). 472p. 1977. 32.00 (ISBN 0-571-04913-3, Pub. by Faber & Faber); pap. 25.00 (ISBN 0-571-04914-1). Merrimack Bk Serv.
Loch, E. G. Ultrasonic Tomography in Obstetrics & Gynaecology. (Advances in Obstetrics & Gynaecology: Vol. 51). (Illus.). 1973. 24.00 (ISBN 3-8055-1585-5). S Karger.
Loose Leaf Reference Services. Gynecology & Obstetrics, 6 vols. Sciarra, John J., ed. Set. loose leaf bdg. 300.00 (ISBN 0-06-148008-8, Harper Medical); yearly revision pages 50.00 (ISBN 0-685-88067-2). Har-Row.
Luke, Barbara. Maternal Nutrition. 1980. text ed. 9.95 (ISBN 0-316-53610-5). Little.
McClure-Browne, J. C. Postgraduate Obstetrics & Gynaecology. 4th ed. (Illus.). 1973. 39.50 (ISBN 0-407-36121-9). Butterworth.
Macdonald, Ronald R., ed. Scientific Basis of Obstetrics & Gynecology. 2nd ed. (Illus.). 1978. text ed. 49.00 (ISBN 0-443-01580-5). Churchill.
McKenna, Julie & Polden, Margaret. You -- After Childbirth. (Churchill Livingstone Patient Handbook Ser.). 1980. pap. text ed. 2.25x (ISBN 0-443-02128-7). Churchill.
Marcus, C. C. & Marcus, S. L. Advances in Obstetrics & Gynecology. 717p. 1966. 23.50 (ISBN 0-683-05551-8, Pub. by Williams & Wilkins). Krieger.
Martius. Operative Obstetrics. LC 80-52240. 1980. 16.00 (ISBN 0-913258-76-8). Thieme Stratton.
Menon, M. K., et al. Post Graduate Obstetrics & Gynaecology. 450p. 1979. cloth with jacket 50.00x (ISBN 0-86131-207-4, Pub. by Orient Longman India). State Mutual Bk.
Meudt, R. O. & Hinselmann, M. Ultrasonoscopic Differential Diagnosis in Obstetrics & Gynecology. (Illus.). x, 138p. 1975. 51.00 (ISBN 0-387-06991-7). Springer-Verlag.
Midgley, A. Rees & Sadler, William A., eds. Ovarian Follicular Development & Function. LC 77-17750. 310p. 1978. 30.00 (ISBN 0-89004-186-5). Raven.
Minkowski, A. & Monset-Couchard, M., eds. Physiological & Biochemical Basis for Perinatal Medicine. (Illus.). xiv, 370p. 1981. 93.50 (ISBN 3-8055-1283-X). S Karger.
Model Screening Criteria for Hospital Admissions in Obstetrics & Gynecology. 2.50 (ISBN 0-686-24126-6). Am Coll Obstetric.
Monif, Gilles R., ed. Infectious Diseases in Obstetrics & Gynecology. (Illus.). 1974. text ed. 37.00x (ISBN 0-06-141795-5, Harper Medical). Har-Row.
Morselli, P. L., et al, eds. Basic & Therapeutic Aspects of Perinatal Pharmacology. LC 74-21981. (Monograph of the Mario Negri Institute of Pharmacological Research). 456p. 1975. 37.50 (ISBN 0-89004-016-8). Raven.
Mudaliar, A. L. & Menon, M. K. Clinical Obstetrics. 8th ed. 613p. 1979. 25.00x (ISBN 0-86131-037-3, Pub. by Orient Longman India). State Mutual Bk.
Myerscough, P. R. Munro Kerr's Operative Obstetrics. 9th ed. (Illus.). 1977. text ed. 55.00 (ISBN 0-02-858690-5). Macmillan.
Naftolin, Frederick & Stubblefield, Phillip G., eds. Dilation of the Uterine Cervix: Connective Tissue Biology & Clinical Management. 406p. 1979. text ed. 38.50 (ISBN 0-89004-300-0). Raven.
National Institutes of Health, the Chicago Heart Association & the University of Chicago, et al. Uteroplacental Blood Flow: Proceedings. Moawad, Atef M. & Lindheimer, Marshall D., eds. (Illus.). 300p. 1981. text ed. write for info. (ISBN 0-89352-146-9). Masson Pub.
Neubert, Diether & Merker, Hans J., eds. New Approaches to the Evaluation of Abnormal Embryonic Development. LC 76-4619. (Illus.). 844p. 1975. 32.00 (ISBN 0-88416-140-4). Wright-PSG.
Niswander, Kenneth R. Manual of Obstetrics: Diagnosis & Management. 1979. 12.95 (ISBN 0-316-61146-8, Little Med Div). Little.
--Obstetric & Gynecologic Disorders: A Practitioner's Guide. 1975. spiral bdg. 12.00 (ISBN 0-87488-704-6). Med Exam.
--Obstetrics: Essentials of Clinical Practice. 2nd ed. 1981. pap. text ed. 13.95 (ISBN 0-686-77387-X). Little.
--Obstetrics: Essentials of Clinical Practice. LC 75-41568. 1976. text ed. 18.95 (ISBN 0-316-61143-3); pap. text ed. 13.95 (ISBN 0-316-61144-1). Little.
Page, Ernest W., et al. Human Reproduction: Essentials of Obstetrics, Gynecology, & Reproductive Medicine. 1981. text ed. write for info. (ISBN 0-7216-7053-9). Saunders.
Percival, Robert. Holland & Brew's Manual of Obstetrics. 14th ed. (Illus.). 1980. text ed. 55.00 (ISBN 0-443-01604-6). Churchill.
Philipp, Elliott E., et al, eds. Scientific Foundations of Obstetrics & Gynecology. 2nd ed. (Illus.). 1977. 79.50 (ISBN 0-8151-6669-9). Year Bk Med.
Pitkin, Roy M., ed. Yearbook of Obstetrics & Gynecology, 1981. 1981. 29.95 (ISBN 0-8151-6690-7). Year Bk Med.
Pitkin, Roy M. & Zlatnik, Frank J., eds. Year Book of Obstetrics & Gynecology 1980. (Illus.). 1980. 29.95 (ISBN 0-8151-6689-3). Year Bk Med.
--Year Book of Obstetrics & Gynecology 1979. (Illus.). 1979. 27.50 (ISBN 0-8151-6688-5). Year Bk Med.
Precis: An Update in Obstetrics & Gynecology. 35.00 (ISBN 0-686-24130-4). Am Coll Obstetric.
Precis II: An Update in Obstetrics & Gynecology. 1981. 35.00 (ISBN 0-686-31638-X). Am Coll Obstetric.
Pritchard, Jack A. & MacDonald, Paul C. Williams Obstetrics. 16th ed. (Illus.). 1179p. 1980. 49.50 (ISBN 0-8385-9731-9). ACC.
Probst, Raymond E., ed. Obstetrics & Gynecology Specialty Board Review. 5th ed. 1977. spiral bdg. 16.50 (ISBN 0-87488-304-0). Med Exam.
Pschyrembel, W. & Dudenhausen, J. W. Grundriss der Perinatalmedizin. (Illus.). 336p. 1972. 24.00x (ISBN 3-11-003694-0). De Gruyter.
Quality Assurance in Obstetrics & Gynecology. 152p. 1981. 10.00 (ISBN 0-686-31636-3). Am Coll Obstetric.
Quilligan, E. J. & Kretchmer, Norman, eds. Fetal & Maternal Medicine. LC 79-4345. 1979. 48.00 (ISBN 0-471-50737-7, Pub. by Wiley Medical). Wiley.
Rathi, Manohar & Kumar, Sudhir, eds. Perinatal Medicine, Vol. 2. 224p. 1982. text ed. 35.00 (ISBN 0-89116-181-3). Hemisphere Pub.
Reid, Duncan E. & Christian, C. Donald, eds. Controversy in Obstetrics & Gynecology Two. 2nd ed. LC 73-93432. (Illus.). 365p. 1974. text ed. 38.00 (ISBN 0-7216-7528-X). Saunders.
Roch, Sara E. Midwifery Revision. (Illus.). 352p. 1980. text ed. 10.00 (ISBN 0-443-01964-9). Churchill.
Romney, S., et al. Gynecology & Obstetrics: The Health Care of Women. 1975. 37.00 (ISBN 0-07-053581-7, HP). McGraw.
Romney, Seymour, et al, eds. Gynecology & Obstetrics: The Health Care of Women. 2nd ed. (Illus.). 1980. text ed. 48.50 (ISBN 0-07-053582-5, HP). McGraw.

Rosenberg, Charles E. & Rosenberg, Carroll-Smith. The Male-Midwife & the Female Doctor. LC 73-20642. (Sex, Marriage & Society Ser.). (Illus.). 224p. 1974. Repr. 19.00x (ISBN 0-405-05810-1). Arno.

Russell, J. G. Radiology in Obstetrics & Antenatal Paediatrics. Trapnell, David H., ed. (Radiology in Clinical Diagnosis Ser.: Vol. 8). (Illus.). 1973. 18.95 (ISBN 0-407-38410-3). Butterworth.

Russell, J. G. B. & Fisher, A. S. Radiography in Obstetrics. 1975. 7.95 (ISBN 0-407-00009-7). Butterworth.

Ryan, George M., Jr., ed. Ambulatory Care in Obstetrics & Gynecology. 544p. 1980. 43.50 (ISBN 0-8089-1253-4). Grune.

Rydberg, Erik. The Mechanism of Labour. (American Lecture Gynecology & Obstetrics). (Illus.). 192p. 1954. photocopy ed. spiral 19.50 (ISBN 0-398-01636-4). C C Thomas.

Sabbagha, Rudy E. Ultrasound in High-Risk Obstetrics. LC 79-15161. (Illus.). 108p. 1979. text ed. 11.00 (ISBN 0-8121-0676-8). Lea & Febiger.

Sabbagha, Rudy E., ed. Diagnostic Ultrasound Applied to Obstetrics & Gynecology. (Illus.). 514p. 1980. text ed. 50.00 (ISBN 0-06-142310-6, Harper Medical). Har-Row.

St. Joseph Medical Center. Obstetrical Procedure Manual: Delivery Suite, Nursery, Post Partum. LC 75-18054. (Illus.). 1975. pap. 5.00 (ISBN 0-87125-027-6). Cath Health.

Sanders, Roger C. & James, A. E., Jr., eds. Principles & Practice of Ultrasonography in Obstetrics & Gynecology. 2nd ed. (Illus.). 466p. 1980. 52.50 (ISBN 0-8385-7955-8). ACC.

Scarpelli, Emile M. & Cosmi, Ermelando V., eds. Reviews in Perinatal Medicine. 1976. 29.50 (ISBN 0-8391-0150-3). Univ Park.

--Reviews in Perinatal Medicine, Vol. 2. LC 77-74616. 405p. 1978. 34.50 (ISBN 0-89004-195-4). Raven.

Scarpelli, Emilie & Cosmi, Ermelando, eds. Reviews in Perinatal Medicine, Vol. 4. 550p. 1981. 55.00 (ISBN 0-89004-364-7). Raven.

Schams, H. & Bretscher, J. Ultrasonographic Diagnosis in Obstetrics & Gynecology. (Illus.). 230p. 1975. text ed. 42.60 (ISBN 0-387-07254-3). Springer-Verlag.

Schwarz, Richard H., ed. Handbook of Obstetric Emergencies. 2nd ed. 1977. 11.00 (ISBN 0-87488-634-1). Med Exam.

Serio, Mario & Martini, Luciano, eds. Animal Models in Human Reproduction. 499p. 1980. text ed. 45.00 (ISBN 0-89004-522-4). Raven.

Sever, John L., et al. Handbook of Perinatal Infections. 1979. pap. text ed. 17.95 (ISBN 0-316-78170-3). Little.

Smith, Elizabeth D. Maternity Care: A Guide to Patient Education. (Illus.). 288p. pap. 11.50 (ISBN 0-8385-6170-5). ACC.

So You're Going to Have a Baby. (Illus.). 1972. pap. 1.50 (ISBN 0-87067-914-7, BH914, Melrose Sq). Holloway.

Spencer, Herbert R. The History of British Midwifery from 1650 to 1800. LC 75-23761. Repr. of 1927 ed. 19.00 (ISBN 0-404-13367-3). AMS Pr.

Stallworthy, John & Bourne, Gordon, eds. Recent Advances in Obstetrics & Gynaecology, No. 13. 1980. text ed. 42.50 (ISBN 0-443-01887-1). Churchill.

Standards for Obstetric, Gynecologic & Neonatal Nursing. 64p. 1981. 10.00 (ISBN 0-686-31637-1). Am Coll Obstetric.

Standards for Obstetric-Gynecologic Services. 1974. 10.00 (ISBN 0-686-24132-0). Am Coll Obstetric.

Stembera, Z. K., et al, eds. Perinatal Medicine: Fourth European Congress. LC 75-46148. (Illus.). 556p. 1975. 28.00 (ISBN 0-88416-080-7). Wright-PSG.

Stern, Leo, et al. Intensive Care of the Newborn II. LC 78-63400. (Illus.). 418p. 1979. 45.50x (ISBN 0-89352-022-5). Masson Pub.

Taber, Ben-Zion. Manual of Gynecologic & Obstetric Emergencies. new ed. LC 77-84692. (Illus.). 1979. pap. text ed. 26.00 (ISBN 0-7216-8721-0). Saunders.

Taylor, E. Stewart. Obstetrics & Fetal Medicine. 2nd ed. 1977. pap. text ed. 17.95 student ed. (ISBN 0-683-08103-9). Williams & Wilkins.

Taylor, R. W. & Brush, M. G. Obstetrics & Gynaecology: Concise Medical Textbook. (Illus.). 1979. pap. text ed. 13.95 (ISBN 0-02-859450-9). Macmillan.

Taylor, Stewart, ed. Beck's Obstetrical Practice & Fetal Medicine. 10th ed. (Illus.). 650p. 1976. 38.50 (ISBN 0-683-08123-3). Williams & Wilkins.

Thoms, Herbert. Chapters in American Obstetrics. 2nd ed. (Illus.). 172p. 1961. photocopy ed. spiral 16.75 (ISBN 0-398-01923-1). C C Thomas.

--Classical Contributions to Obstetrics & Gynecology. (Illus.). 265p. 1935. photocopy ed. spiral 26.50 (ISBN 0-398-04421-X). C C Thomas.

Tindall, V. R. Self Assessment in Obstetrics & Gynecology, Part 1: Basic Sciences. 1978. pap. 12.95 (ISBN 0-8151-8806-4). Year Bk Med.

Tulchinsky, Dan & Ryan, Kenneth J. Maternal-Fetal Endocrinology. LC 79-66046. (Illus.). 418p. 1980. text ed. 42.00 (ISBN 0-7216-8911-6). Saunders.

Van Bergen, William S. Obstetric Ultrasound for the Practitioner: Applications & Principals. LC 80-14969. 1980. 19.95 (ISBN 0-201-08001-X). A-W.

Van Wagenen, Gertrude & Simpson, Miriam E. Postnatal Development of the Ovary in Homo Sapiens & Macaca Mulatta & Induction of Ovulation in the Macaque. LC 72-91309. (Illus.). 384p. 1973. 45.00x (ISBN 0-300-01557-7). Yale U Pr.

Verralls, Sylvia. Anatomy & Physiology Applied to Obstetrics. rev ed. (Illus.). 1977. 15.00x (ISBN 0-8464-0131-2). Beekman Pubs.

--Anatomy & Physiology Applied to Obstetrics. (Illus.). 1977. pap. text ed. 15.00x (ISBN 0-685-82798-4). State Mutual Bk.

Vietor, Diana & McCutcheon, Maureen. Care of the Maternity Patient. 448p. 1971. pap. text ed. 20.50 (ISBN 0-07-067445-0, C). McGraw.

Vokaer, Roger & De Maubeuge, M. Sexual Endocrinology. LC 77-86694. (Illus.). 280p. 1978. 37.50x (ISBN 0-89352-017-9). Masson Pub.

Vontver, Louis A. Obstetrics & Gynecology Review. 2nd ed. LC 78-6768. (Arco Medical Review Ser.). (Illus.). 1978. pap. text ed. 9.00 (ISBN 0-668-03450-5). Arco.

Wachstein, Alison E. Pregnant Moments. LC 79-88347. 1979. pap. 10.95 (ISBN 0-87100-153-5, 2153). Morgan.

Walker, J., et al. Combined Textbook of Obstetrics & Gynecology. 9th ed. LC 76-8406. (Illus.). 1976. 98.00 (ISBN 0-443-01072-2). Churchill.

Wallace, Helen M., et al, eds. Maternal & Child Health Practices: Problems, Resources & Methods of Delivery. (Illus.). 1400p. 1973. 52.75 (ISBN 0-398-02617-3). C C Thomas.

Williams, Preston P. & Joseph, Marilyn S. Differential Diagnosis: Obstetrics. LC 78-1662. (Arco Diagnosis Ser.). (Illus.). 1978. pap. text ed. 12.00x (ISBN 0-668-04161-7). Arco.

Willocks, James. Essential Obstetrics & Gynaecology: A Guide for Postgraduates. (Illus.). 1978. pap. text ed. 14.50 (ISBN 0-443-01390-X). Churchill.

Willson, J. Robert. Obstetrics & Gynecology. 5th ed. LC 74-28270. 698p. 1975. text ed. 25.50 (ISBN 0-8016-5592-7). Mosby.

Willson, J. Robert & Carrington, Elsie R. Obstetrics & Gynecology. 6th ed. LC 78-31642. (Illus.). 1979. text ed. 34.50 (ISBN 0-8016-5595-1). Mosby.

Willughby, Percival. Observations in Midwifery. 1976. Repr. 17.50x (ISBN 0-85409-738-4). Charles River Bks.

Wolman, B. B., ed. Psychological Aspects of Gynecology & Obstetrics. 1978. 22.50 (ISBN 0-87489-009-8). Med Economics.

Wood, C. Intrauterine Devices. (Illus.). 1971. 6.95 (ISBN 0-407-21700-2). Butterworth.

Wren, Barry G. Handbook of Obstetrics & Gynaecology. (Illus.). 454p. 1979. pap. text ed. 14.95 (ISBN 0-02-859810-5). Macmillan.

Wynn, ed. Obstetrics & Gynecology Annual: 1977, Vol. 6. (Illus.). 1977. 28.75 (ISBN 0-8385-7181-6). ACC.

Wynn, Ralph M. Obstetrics & Gynecology: The Clinical Core. 2nd ed. LC 78-12821. 296p. 1979. text ed. 15.00 (ISBN 0-8121-0658-X). Lea & Febiger.

Wynn, Ralph M., ed. Obstetrics & Gynecology Annual 1978, Vol. 7. (Illus.). 476p. 1978. 32.50 (ISBN 0-8385-7182-4). ACC.

--Obstetrics & Gynecology Annual 1979, Vol. 8. (Illus.). 481p. 1979. 32.50 (ISBN 0-8385-7183-2). ACC.

--Obstetrics & Gynecology Annual 1980. (Obstetrics & Gynecology Ser.). (Illus.). 390p. 1980. 32.50x (ISBN 0-8385-7186-7). ACC.

--Obstetrics & Gynecology Annual, 1981. (Obstetrics & Gynecology Annual Series). (Illus.). 448p. 1981. 32.50 (ISBN 0-8385-7188-3). ACC.

Youngs, David D. & Ehrhardt, Anke A. Psychosomatic Obstetrics & Gynecology. (Illus.). 306p. 1980. 19.50 (ISBN 0-8385-8041-6). ACC.

Zuspan, Frederick P. & Quilligan, Edward J. Practical Manual of Obstetric Care: A Pocket Reference for Those Who Threat the Pregnant Patient. (Illus.). 480p. 1981. pap. text ed. 11.95 (ISBN 0-8016-4064-4). Mosby.

OBSTETRICS–DICTIONARIES

Baden, Wayne F., et al. The Obstetrician-Gynecologist & Primary Care. (Illus.). 197p. 1980. lib. bdg. 22.00 (ISBN 0-683-00301-1). Williams & Wilkins.

Cumulative Index to Clinical Obstetrics & Genecology, Vols. 1-17 (1958-1974) new ed. LC 75-45525. 1976. lib. bdg. 25.00 (ISBN 0-88471-035-1). Numarc Bk Corp.

OBSTETRICS–EXAMINATIONS, QUESTIONS, ETC.

Da Cruz, Vera. C. M. B. Questions & How to Answer Them. 5th ed. (Illus.). 1977. pap. 3.95 (ISBN 0-571-04919-2, Pub. by Faber & Faber). Merrimack Bk Serv.

Educational Materials for Obstetrics & Gynecology. 5.00 (ISBN 0-686-24122-3). Am Coll Obstetric.

Niswander, Kenneth R. Obstetrics & Gynecology. 4th ed. (Medical Examination Review Book: Vol. 4). 1971. spiral bdg. 8.50 (ISBN 0-87488-104-8). Med Exam.

Swartz, William H., ed. Obstetrics & Gynecology: PreTest Self-Assessment & Review. 2nd ed. (Illus.). 225p. 1981. pap. 9.95 (ISBN 0-07-050975-1, HP). McGraw.

Williams, Preston P. Specialty Board Review: Obstetrics & Gynecology. 2nd ed. LC 78-8734. (Arco Medical Review Ser.). (Illus.). 1979. pap. 14.00 (ISBN 0-668-03477-7). Arco.

Williams, Preston P. & Joseph, Marilyn S. Differential Diagnosis: Obstetrics. LC 78-1662. (Arco Diagnosis Ser.). (Illus.). 1978. pap. text ed. 12.00x (ISBN 0-668-04161-7). Arco.

OBSTETRICS–HISTORY

Aveling, James H. The Chamberlens & the Midwifery Forceps. LC 75-23677. Repr. of 1882 ed. 19.00 (ISBN 0-404-13230-8). AMS Pr.

Cianfrani, Theodore. A Short History of Obstetrics & Gynecology. (Illus.). 466p. 1960. ed. spiral bdg. 44.00photocopy (ISBN 0-398-00308-4). C C Thomas.

Thoms, Herbert. Classic Contributions to Obstertrics & Gynecology. (Historia Medicinae Ser.). (Illus.). Repr. of 1935 ed. lib. bdg. 17.50 (ISBN 0-87991-715-6). Porcupine Pr.

Wertz, Richard W. & Wertz, Dorothy C. Lying-in: A History of Childbirth in America. LC 77-72040. 1977. 10.00 (ISBN 0-02-934510-3). Free Pr.

OBSTETRICS–OUTLINES, SYLLABI, ETC.

Educational Materials for Obstetrics & Gynecology. 5.00 (ISBN 0-686-24122-3). Am Coll Obstetric.

NAACOG Conference Manual. 1978. 5.00 (ISBN 0-686-24127-4). Am Coll Obstetric.

NAACOG Officers Manual. 1976. 5.00 (ISBN 0-686-24128-2). Am Coll Obstetric.

OBSTETRICS–POPULAR WORKS

Braun, Jamy, et al. NAPSAC Directory of Alternative Birth Services & Consumer Guide: 1980 Edition. LC 77-93424. 1979. pap. 5.25 (ISBN 0-934426-01-5). NAPSAC.

Eastman, Nicholas J. & Russell, Keith P. Expectant Motherhood. 5th rev. ed. (Illus.). 1970. 2.75 (ISBN 0-316-20394-7). Little.

Gaskin, Ina May. Spiritual Midwifery. rev ed. (Illus.). 1978. 14.00 (ISBN 0-913990-19-1); pap. 10.00 (ISBN 0-913990-10-8). Book Pub Co.

Gillespie, Clark. Your Pregnancy Month by Month. LC 76-26229. (Illus.). 1977. 11.95 (ISBN 0-06-011538-6, HarpT). Har-Row.

Hall, Robert E., M.D. Nine Month's Reading: Medical Guide for Pregnant Women. rev. ed. LC 72-77076. 192p. 1972. 8.95 (ISBN 0-385-03688-4). Doubleday.

Russell, Keith P. Eastman's Expectant Motherhood Seventh Edition Revised. 1977. 6.95 (ISBN 0-316-20395-5). Little.

Seidman, Theodore R. & Albert, Marvin H. Becoming a Mother. rev. ed. 1978. pap. 1.95 (ISBN 0-449-23702-8, Crest). Fawcett.

Stewart, David, et al. The Five Standards for Safe Childbearing. LC 79-88699. (Illus.). 1981. pap. 9.50 (ISBN 0-934426-00-7). NAPSAC.

OBSTETRICS–SURGERY

see also Cesarean Section

Douglas, R. Gordon & Stromme, William B. Operative Obstetrics. 3rd ed. (Illus.). 986p. 1976. 52.50 (ISBN 0-8385-7403-3). ACC.

Myerscough, P. R. Munro Kerr's Operative Obstetrics. 9th ed. (Illus.). 1977. text ed. 55.00 (ISBN 0-02-858690-5). Macmillan.

Roberts, D. W. Gynecology & Obstetrics. (Operative Surgery Ser.). 1977. 49.95 (ISBN 0-407-00615-X). Butterworth.

Schaefer, George & Graber, Edward A., eds. Complications in Obstetric & Gynecologic Surgery. (Illus.). 492p. 1981. text ed. 40.00 (ISBN 0-06-142330-0, Harper Medical). Har-Row.

OBSTETRICS, ANESTHETICS IN

see Anesthesia in Obstetrics

OBSTETRICS, OPERATIVE

see Obstetrics–Surgery

OBSTETRICS, VETERINARY

see Veterinary Obstetrics

OBSTRUCTIONS, INTESTINAL

see Intestines–Obstructions

O'CASEY, SEAN, 1884-1964

Atkinson, Brooks. Sean O'Casey: From Times Past by Brooks Atkinson. Lowery, Robert G., ed. Date not set. 26.50x (ISBN 0-389-20180-4). B&N.

Ayling, Ronald. Continuity & Innovation in Sean O'Casey's Drama. (Salzburg Studies in English Literature Poetic Drama & Poetic Theory: No. 23). 1976. pap. 25.00x (ISBN 0-391-01304-1). Humanities.

Ayling, Ronald & Durkan, Michael J. Sean O'Casey: A Bibliography. LC 77-83181. 436p. 1978. 35.00 (ISBN 0-295-95566-X). U of Wash Pr.

Ayling, Ronald, ed. Sean O'Casey. LC 79-127563. (Modern Judgement Ser). 1970. pap. text ed. 2.50 (ISBN 0-87695-097-7). Aurora Pubs.

Benstock, Bernard. Sean O'Casey. LC 72-124101. (Irish Writers Ser). 123p. 1971. 4.50 (ISBN 0-8387-7748-1); pap. 1.95 (ISBN 0-8387-7618-3). Bucknell U Pr.

DaRin, Doris. Sean O'Casey. LC 75-10107. (World Dramatists Ser.). 1977. 10.95 (ISBN 0-8044-2136-6). Ungar.

Davis, Katie B. Federico Garcia Lorca & Sean O'Casey: Powerful Voices in the Wilderness. (Salzburg Studies in English Literature: Poetic Drama & Poetic Theory: No. 43). 1978. text ed. 25.00x (ISBN 0-391-01357-2). Humanities.

Frayne, John P. Sean O'casey - Columbia Essays on Modern Writers, No.73. 1976. pap. 2.00 (ISBN 0-231-03655-8). Columbia U Pr.

Greaves, C. Desmond. Sean O'Casey: Politics & Art. 1980. text ed. 18.25x (ISBN 0-391-01023-9). Humanities.

Hunt, Hugh. Sean O'Casey. (Gillis Irish Lives Ser.). 153p. 1980. 20.00 (ISBN 0-7171-1080-X, Pub. by Gill & Macmillan Ireland); pap. 6.50 (ISBN 0-7171-1034-6). Irish Bk Ctr.

Kaslow, Jules. Sean O'Casey: The Man & His Plays. Orig. Title: Green & the Red. 1966. pap. 1.75 (ISBN 0-8065-0061-1, 227). Citadel Pr.

Kilroy, T., ed. Sean O'Casey: A Collection of Critical Essays. 7.95 (ISBN 0-13-628941-X). Brown Bk.

Krause, David. Sean O'Casey & His World. LC 76-7182. (Encore Edition). (Illus.). 128p. 1976. 4.95 (ISBN 0-684-16547-3, ScribT). Scribner.

--A Self Portrait of the Artist As a Man: Sean O'Casey's Letters. 40p. 1968. pap. text ed. 2.50x (ISBN 0-85105-127-8, Dolmen Pr). Humanities.

Krause, David, ed. The Letters of Sean O'Casey, Nineteen Forty-Two to Nineteen Fifty-Four, Vol. II. 1980. 60.00 (ISBN 0-02-566670-3). Macmillan.

--The Letters of Sean O'Casey: 1910-1941, Vol. 1. (Illus.). 800p. 1975. 60.00 (ISBN 0-02-566660-6). Macmillan.

Krause, David & Lowery, Robert, eds. Sean O'Casey Centenary Essays: Irish Literary Studies. (No. 7). 257p. 1981. text ed. 24.00x (ISBN 0-86140-008-9, Pub. by Smythe England). Humanities.

Krause, David & Lowery, Robert G., eds. Sean O'Casey: Centenary Essays. (Irish Literary Studies 7). 258p. 1981. 24.75x (ISBN 0-389-20096-4). B&N.

Mikhail, E. H. Sean O'Casey: A Bibliography of Criticism. LC 76-37007. 164p. 1972. text ed. 16.50 (ISBN 0-295-95167-2). U of Wash Pr.

Mitchell, Jack. The Essential O'Casey. 435p. (Orig.). 1981. pap. 2.95 (ISBN 0-7178-0557-3). Intl Pub Co.

O'Casey, Sean. Autobiographies I. combined ed. 666p. 1980. pap. 7.50 (ISBN 0-330-26076-6, Pub. by Pan Bks England). Irish Bk Ctr.

--Autobiographies II. combined ed. 665p. 1980. pap. 7.50 (ISBN 0-330-26077-4, Pub. by Pan Bks England). Irish Bk Ctr.

Scrimgeour, James R. Sean O'Casey. (English Authors Ser.: No. 245). 1978. 12.50 (ISBN 0-8057-6735-5). Twayne.

Smith, B. L. O'Casey's Satiric Vision. LC 78-10583. 1979. 12.50x (ISBN 0-87338-218-8). Kent St U Pr.

Watson, G. J. Irish Identity & the Literary Revival: Synge, Yeats, Joyce & O'Casey. LC 79-54168. 1979. text ed. 27.50x (ISBN 0-06-497495-2). B&N.

Wilson, Donald D. Sean O'Casey's Tragi-Comic Vision. 1975. lib. bdg. 69.95 (ISBN 0-87700-237-1). Revisionist Pr.

OCCASIONAL SERMONS

Here are entered works containing sermons preached on special days or for special occasions, e.g. Christmas, Easter, dedications, anniversaries, etc. Single sermons or works containing sermons of one kind only, are entered under the specific subject, e.g. Confirmation Sermons.

Hobbs, Hershel H. Welcome Speeches. pap. 1.95 (ISBN 0-310-26151-1). Zondervan.

Miller, Charles E. Living in Christ: Sacramental & Occasional Homilies. LC 73-22092. 125p. 1974. pap. 2.95 (ISBN 0-8189-0284-1). Alba.

Poovey, W. A. Celebrate with Drama: Dramas & Meditations for Six Special Days. LC 74-14172. 88p. (Orig.). 1975. pap. 3.50 (ISBN 0-8066-1456-0, 10-1010); drama bklet 1.50 (ISBN 0-8066-1457-9, 10-1011). Augsburg.

Winter, Ole. A Living Sermon for Thanksgiving Day. 1973. 2.05 (ISBN 0-89536-124-8). CSS Pub.

Wood, Charles R., ed. Sermon Outlines for Special Days & Occasions. (Easy-To-Use Sermon Outlines Ser). 1970. pap. 1.95 (ISBN 0-8254-4006-8). Kregel.

OCCASIONALISM

see also Dualism

OCCIDENTAL ART

see Art

OCCIDENTAL CIVILIZATION

see Civilization, Occidental

OCCIDENTAL LANGUAGES

see Languages, Modern

OCCIDENTAL STUDIES

see also Civilization, Occidental

OCCITANE LANGUAGE

see Provencal Language

OCCLUSION (DENTISTRY)

Arnold, Norman R. & Frumker, Sanford C. Occlusal Treatment: Preventive & Corrective Occlusal Adjustment. LC 75-1306. (Illus.). 163p. 1976. text ed. 13.50 (ISBN 0-8121-0526-5). Lea & Febiger.

Celenza, Frank V. Occlusal Morphology. 110p. 1980. pap. 18.00 (ISBN 0-931386-33-0). Quint Pub Co.

Celenza, Frank V. & Nasedkin, John N. Occlusion, the State of the Art. (Illus.). 165p. 1978. 32.00 (ISBN 0-931386-00-4). Quint Pub Co.

Dawson, Peter E. Evaluation, Diagnosis, & Treatment of Occlusal Problems. LC 74-12409. 1974. 52.50 (ISBN 0-8016-1216-0). Mosby.

Ehrlich, Ann B. Training Therapists for Tongue Thrust Correction. (Illus.). 148p. 1973. 9.75 (ISBN 0-398-00503-6). C C Thomas.

Kraus, Bertram S., et al. Dental Anatomy & Occlusion. (Illus.). 333p. 1969. 23.00 (ISBN 0-683-04781-7). Williams & Wilkins.

Lundeen, Harry C. & Gibbs, Charles H., eds. Advances in Occlusion: Diagnosis & Treatment. (Illus.). 364p. 1981. 35.00 (ISBN 0-88416-168-4). Wright-PSG.

NCHS. An Assessment of the Occlusion of the Teeth of Youths 12-17 Years United States. LC 76-16152. (Ser. 4: No. 11). 65p. 1976. pap. 1.75 (ISBN 0-8406-0073-9). Natl Ctr Health Stats.

Perryman, James H., ed. Oral Physiology & Occlusion: An International Symposium. LC 78-17812. 268p. 1979. 30.00 (ISBN 0-08-023183-7). Pergamon.

Ramfjord, Sigurd & Ash, McKinley, Jr. Occlusion. 2nd ed. LC 78-151682. (Illus.). 1971. 22.00 (ISBN 0-7216-7441-0). Saunders.

Silverman, Meyer M. Occlusion in Prosthodontics & in the Natural Dentition. (Illus.). 1962. 16.50x (ISBN 0-9600244-1-7). Mutual.

--Occlusion in Prosthodontics & in the Natural Dentition. (Illus.). 1962. 16.50x (ISBN 0-9600244-1-7). Mutual.

Thomson, Hamish. Occlusion in Clinical Practice. (Dental Practitioner Handbook Ser.: No. 30). 248p. 1981. pap. text ed. 25.00 (ISBN 0-7236-0579-3). Wright-PSG.

Wheeler, Russell C. Dental Anatomy, Physiology & Occlusion. 5th ed. LC 72-95834. (Illus.). 520p. 1974. text ed. 19.50 (ISBN 0-7216-9262-1). Saunders.

OCCOM, SAMSON, 1723-1792

Blodgett, Harold. Samson Occom. LC 36-8648. (Dartmouth College Manuscript Ser.: No. 3). 230p. 1935. text ed. 10.00x (ISBN 0-87451-005-8). U Pr of New Eng.

McDonald, J. The Magic Story: Message of a Master. pap. 1.50 (ISBN 0-910140-23-5). Anthony.

Spalding. Life & Teaching of the Masters of the Far East, 5 vols. 25.00 set (ISBN 0-87516-088-3); pap. 15.00 set (ISBN 0-686-67590-8). De Vorss.

Steiner, Rudolf. Christianity & Occult Mysteries of Antiquity. 2nd ed. Allen, Paul M., ed. Frommer, E. A., et al, trs. from Ger. LC 61-18165. (The Major Writings of Rudolf Steiner in English Translation Ser.: The Centennial Edition). 256p. 1981. 12.00x (ISBN 0-8334-0718-X, Steinerbooks); pap. 7.50 (ISBN 0-8334-1719-3). Multimedia.

OCCULT MEDICINE

see Medicine, Magic, Mystic, and Spagiric

OCCULT SCIENCES

see also Alchemy; Astrology; Cabala; Clairvoyance; Conjuring; Crystal-Gazing; Demonology; Divination; Fortune-Telling; Geomancy; Incantations; Initiations (In Religion, Folk-Lore, etc.); Magic; Occultism in Literature; Oracles; Palmistry; Prophecies (Occult Sciences); Psychometry (Occult Sciences); Satanism; Second Sight; Spiritualism; Superstition; Witchcraft

Adams, W. H. Witch, Warlock & Magician. 59.95 (ISBN 0-8490-1310-0). Gordon Pr.

Adler, Margot. Drawing Down the Moon: Witches, Druids, Goddess-Worshippers & Other Pagans in America Today. LC 80-68170. (Illus.). 470p. 1981. pap. 8.95 (ISBN 0-8070-3237-9, BP 616). Beacon Pr.

Agrippa, Henry C. The Philosophy of Natural Magic. 1974. 8.95 (ISBN 0-8216-0218-7). Univ Bks.

Agrippa, Nettesheim & Heinrich, Cornelius. Three Books of Occult Philosophy or Magic. LC 79-8222. (Illus.). Repr. of 1898 ed. 34.50 (ISBN 0-404-18401-4). AMS Pr.

Akiba Ben Joseph. Book of Formation - Sepher Yetzirah. Stenring, Kurt, tr. 5.95x (ISBN 0-87068-008-0). Ktav.

Albertson, Edward. Prophecy for the Millions. 1978. 2.50 (ISBN 0-8202-0043-3). Sherbourne.

Alder, Vera S. Fifth Dimension. LC 78-16459. 1980. pap. 4.95 (ISBN 0-87728-055-X). Weiser.

--Finding of the Third Eye. 1980. pap. 4.95 (ISBN 0-87728-056-8). Weiser.

Alexander, Thea. A Macro Philosophy for the Aquarian Age. rev. 2nd ed. 160p. 1971. pap. 4.00 (ISBN 0-913080-01-2). Macro Bks.

Angebert, Jean-Michel. The Occult & the Third Reich: The Mystical Origins of Nazism & the Search for the Holy Grail. (McGraw-Hill Paperbacks Ser.). 336p. 1975. pap. 3.95 (ISBN 0-07-001850-2, SP). McGraw.

A.R.E. New York Members. Economic Healing. rev. ed. 29p. 1974. pap. 1.25 (ISBN 0-87604-074-1). ARE Pr.

Ares, Jacques d' Encyclopedia De L'esoterisme. 217p. (Fr.). 1975. pap. 19.95 (ISBN 0-686-56900-8, M-6010). French & Eur.

Arroyo, Stephen. Astrology, Karma & Transformation: The Inner Dimensions of the Birthchart. LC 76-21588. (Illus.). 1978. 11.95 (ISBN 0-916360-04-0); pap. 8.95 (ISBN 0-916360-03-2). CRCS Pubns NV.

Atwood, Mary Anne. A Suggestive Inquiry into the Hermetic Mystery. 597p. 1976. Repr. of 1918 ed. 15.50 (ISBN 0-911662-64-2). Yoga.

Bailey, Alice A. Consciousness of the Atom. 1972. 6.75 (ISBN 0-85330-001-1); pap. 3.00 (ISBN 0-85330-101-8). Lucis.

--The Destiny of the Nations. 1968. 11.00 (ISBN 0-85330-002-X); pap. 2.75 (ISBN 0-85330-102-6). Lucis.

--Discipleship in the New Age, 2 Vols. Vol. 1, 1971. 22.00 (ISBN 0-85330-003-8); Vol. 2, 1968. 13.50 (ISBN 0-85330-004-6); Vol. 1. pap. 9.00 (ISBN 0-85330-103-4); Vol. 2. pap. 10.25 (ISBN 0-85330-104-2). Lucis.

--Externalisation of the Hierarchy. 1968. 13.50 (ISBN 0-85330-006-2); pap. 7.50 (ISBN 0-85330-106-9). Lucis.

--Glamour: A World Problem. 1973. 8.25 (ISBN 0-85330-009-7); pap. 5.00 (ISBN 0-85330-109-3). Lucis.

--Initiation, Human & Solar. 1977. 11.25 (ISBN 0-85330-010-0); pap. 4.75 (ISBN 0-85330-110-7). Lucis.

--Letters on Occult Meditation. 1973. 8.50 (ISBN 0-85330-011-9); pap. 5.50 (ISBN 0-85330-111-5). Lucis.

--Ponder on This: A Compilation. 432p. 1980. pap. 5.75 (ISBN 0-85330-131-X). Lucis.

--Treatise on Cosmic Fire. 1973. 18.00 (ISBN 0-85330-017-8); pap. 11.75 (ISBN 0-85330-117-4). Lucis.

--Treatise on White Magic. 1979. 22.00 (ISBN 0-85330-023-2); pap. 7.25 (ISBN 0-85330-123-9). Lucis.

Bailey, Foster. Changing Esoteric Values. 2nd. rev. ed. 1974. pap. 2.50 (ISBN 0-85330-125-5). Lucis.

Baines, John. The Secret Science: For the Physical & Spiritual Transformation of Man--Hermetic Philosophy. (Bk. 1). 1980. pap. 5.95 (ISBN 0-87542-025-7). Llewellyn Pubns.

Ballard, Juliet B. Treasures from Earth's Storehouse. 311p. (Orig.). 1980. pap. 7.95 (ISBN 0-87604-128-4). ARE Pr.

Barbanell, Maurice. Works of Spiritualism & Healing, 6 vols. 800.00 (ISBN 0-8490-1331-3). Gordon Pr.

Baring-Gould, S. Freaks of Fanaticism, & Other Strange Events. 59.95 (ISBN 0-8490-0193-5). Gordon Pr.

Barrett, Francis. The Magus: A Complete System of Occult Philosophy. 200p. 1975. pap. 9.95 (ISBN 0-8065-0462-5). Citadel Pr.

Bayless, Raymond. Experiences of a Physical Researcher. 1972. 7.95 (ISBN 0-8216-0076-1). Univ Bks.

--The Other Side of Death. 1972. 5.95 (ISBN 0-8216-0134-2). Univ Bks.

Bazett, L. Margery. Beyond the Five Senses. 59.95 (ISBN 0-87968-726-6). Gordon Pr.

Beck, Jane C. To Windward of the Land: The Occult World of Alexander Charles. LC 79-84257. (Illus.). 360p. 1979. 17.50x (ISBN 0-253-16065-0). Ind U Pr.

Becker, Siegbert. Wizards That Peep. Kujath, Mentor, ed. 1978. pap. 5.95 (ISBN 0-8100-0054-7, 15N0366). Northwest Pub.

Benavides, Rodolfo. Dramatic Prophecies of the Great Pyramid. 44th ed. (The Living Path Ser: No. 1). (Illus.). 479p. 1974. 7.50 (ISBN 0-914732-00-5). Bro Life Bks.

--Raising the Curtain. 12th ed. (The Living Path Ser: No. 2). Orig. Title: Levantando la Cortina. 447p. (Orig.). 1974. pap. 7.50 (ISBN 0-914732-01-3). Bro Life Bks.

--Then We Shall Be Gods. (The Living Path Ser: No. 3). 1975. pap. 7.50 (ISBN 0-914732-03-X). Bro Life Bks.

Bennett, C. Practical Time Travel. (Paths to Inner Power Ser.). pap. 1.25 (ISBN 0-87728-156-4). Weiser.

Bennett, J. G. A Spiritual Psychology. rev. ed. LC 73-81620. 1974. 4.95 (ISBN 0-87707-128-4). CSA Pr.

Berger, Melvin. The Supernatural: From ESP to UFO's. LC 77-2829. (gr. 6 up). 1977. 8.95 (ISBN 0-381-90054-1, JD-J). Har-Row.

Besant, Annie. Esoteric Christianity. abr ed. LC 71-113470. 1971. pap. 3.50 (ISBN 0-8356-0028-9, Quest). Theos Pub Hse.

Birdsong, Robert E. Cosmic Cooperation: Aid for the Asking. (Aquarian Academy Monograph: Ser. E, No. 7). 1977. pap. 1.50 (ISBN 0-917108-18-3). Sirius Bks.

--The Revelations of Hermes: An Exposition of Adamic Christianity. LC 74-84553. (Illus.). 1975. 10.00 (ISBN 0-917108-11-6); pap. 6.95 (ISBN 0-917108-04-3). Sirius Bks.

--Ritual & Reality. (Aquarian Academy Monograph, Series F: Lecture No. 1). 1975. pap. 1.25 (ISBN 0-917108-05-1). Sirius Bks.

Biteaux, Armand. The New Consciousness. new ed. LC 74-84301. (Finder's Guide Ser.: No. 5). 300p. (Orig.). 1974. pap. 3.95 (ISBN 0-914400-04-5). Oliver Pr.

Bjornstad, James. Twentieth Century Prophecy: Jean Dixon-Edgar Cayce. 1969. pap. 1.95 (ISBN 0-87123-546-3, 200546). Bethany Hse.

Blair, Lawrence. Rhythms of Vision: The Changing Patterns of Belief. LC 75-34508. (Illus.). 256p. 1976. 8.95 (ISBN 0-8052-3610-4). Schocken.

Blavatsky, Helena P. Practical Occultism. 3rd ed. 1967. 2.25 (ISBN 0-8356-7124-0). Theos Pub Hse.

--The Secret Doctrine, 2 vols. facsimile reprint of 1888 ed. LC 74-76603. 1977. Set. 17.00 (ISBN 0-911500-00-6); Set. pap. 12.50 (ISBN 0-911500-01-4). Theos U Pr.

--Studies in Occultism. LC 67-18822. 1973. 6.00 (ISBN 0-911500-08-1); pap. 3.50 (ISBN 0-911500-09-X). Theos U Pr.

Blavatsky, Helene. The Theophysical Glossary. lib. bdg. 69.95 (ISBN 0-87968-487-9). Krishna Pr.

Boetger, Gary. In Search of Balance. LC 75-42602. 1976. 5.00 (ISBN 0-87212-051-1). Libra.

Bonaventura, Saint The Mind's Road to God. Boas, George, tr. 1953. pap. 2.50 (ISBN 0-672-60195-8, LLA32). Bobbs.

Bord, Janet & Bord, Colin. The Secret Country. 1977. 9.95 (ISBN 0-8027-0559-6). Walker & Co.

Boss, Judy. In Silence They Return. 1972. 5.95 (ISBN 0-87542-079-6). Llewellyn Pubns.

Bowman, Frank. New Horizons Beyond the World. 5.95 (ISBN 0-87516-006-9). De Vorss.

Bowness, Charles. Romany Magic. 96p. 1973. 4.50 (ISBN 0-87728-201-3). Weiser.

Boyle, John P. The Psionic Generator Pattern Book. LC 74-34292. (Illus.). 96p. 1975. pap. 5.95 (ISBN 0-13-736975-1). P-H.

Brennan, J. H. Astral Doorways. 5.95 (ISBN 0-87728-175-0). Weiser.

Bromage, B. Occult Arts in Ancient Egypt. pap. 4.95 (ISBN 0-87728-041-X). Weiser.

Brown, C. C. A New Look at Psychic Power. (Illus.). 1975. 4.95 (ISBN 0-9600378-1-0). C C Brown Pub.

Brown, Eric. Knave of Clubs. (Illus.). 12.50x (ISBN 0-392-03582-0, SpS). Sportshelf.

Brown, Hugh A. Cataclysms of the Earth. (Illus.). 288p. Date not set. pap. cancelled (ISBN 0-8334-1778-9). Steinerbks.

Brown, Michael H. PK: A Report on the Power of Psychokinesis; Mental Energy That Moves Matter. LC 76-21121. (Rudolf Steiner Publications). (Illus.). 320p. 1976. 12.00x (ISBN 0-8334-0716-3). Multimedia.

Brunton, Paul. Search in Secret Egypt. LC 78-16641. 1980. pap. 5.95 (ISBN 0-87728-060-6). Weiser.

--Search in Secret India. (Illus.). 1981. pap. 5.95 (ISBN 0-87728-061-4). Weiser.

--Wisdom of the Overself. 1970. pap. 7.50 (ISBN 0-87728-062-2). Weiser.

Bucke, Richard M. Cosmic Consciousness. 1970. pap. 4.95 (ISBN 0-8065-0211-8). Citadel Pr.

Buckland, Raymond. Anatomy of the Occult. 1976. pap. 2.95 (ISBN 0-87728-304-4). Weiser.

--The Tree: The Complete Book of Saxon Witchcraft. LC 74-79397. (Illus.). 158p. (Orig.). 1974. pap. 4.95 (ISBN 0-87728-258-7). Weiser.

Buckland, Raymond B. Practical Candle Burning. 2nd ed. (Illus.). 165p. 1981. pap. 4.95 (ISBN 0-87542-048-6). Llewellyn Pubns.

Budge, E. A. Book of the Mysteries of the Heavens & the Earth. 75.00 (ISBN 0-87968-772-X). Gordon Pr.

Busick, Armando. Pages from a Tree. (Artist's Note Book Ser.: No. 1). (Illus.). 64p. (Orig.). 1972. pap. 2.25 (ISBN 0-913300-14-4). Unity Pr.

Butler, W. E. How to Read the Aura. (Paths to Inner Power Ser.). pap. 2.25 (ISBN 0-87728-090-8). Weiser.

Butler, William. How to Read the Aura, Practice Psychometry Telepathy & Clairvoyance. (Warner Destiny Book). (Orig.). 1978. pap. 2.95 (ISBN 0-446-33075-2). Warner Bks.

Butler, William & Destiny, Warner. How to Read the Aura, Practice Psychometry, Telepathy, & Clairvoyancy. 2.25 (ISBN 0-446-82751-7). Inner Tradit.

Cameron, Verne L. Aquavideo: Locating Underground Water, a Complete Dowsing Method by the World Renowned Master. Cox, Bill, ed. LC 7-139236. (Illus.). 116p. 1970. pap. 6.95 (ISBN 0-686-57600-4). Life Understanding.

--Map Dowsing. (Dowser's Hdbk. Ser., No. 1). 40p. 1971. pap. 2.75 (ISBN 0-88234-003-4). Life Understanding.

--Oil Locating. (Dowser's Hdbk. Ser., No. 2). 40p. 1971. pap. 2.75 (ISBN 0-88234-004-2). Life Understanding.

Carey & Perry. Zodiac & the Salts of Salvation. LC 77-166412. 15.00 (ISBN 0-87728-143-2). Weiser.

Carrington, Hereward & Whitehead, Willis F. Keys to the Occult: Two Guides to Hidden Wisdom. LC 80-23835. 182p. 1980. Repr. of 1977 ed. lib. bdg. 10.95x (ISBN 0-89370-641-8). Borgo Pr.

Case, Paul F. The Magical Language. 320p. pap. 9.95 (ISBN 0-87728-526-8). Weiser.

Castilhon, Jean-Louis. Essai sur les Erreurs et les Superstitions. (Holbach & His Friends Ser). 485p. (Fr.). 1974. Repr. of 1765 ed. lib. bdg. 121.00 (ISBN 0-8287-0168-7, 1520). Clearwater Pub.

Cavendish, Richard, ed. Encyclopedia of the Unexplained. LC 73-7991. (Illus.). 304p. 1974. 19.95 (ISBN 0-07-010295-3, GB). McGraw.

Cayce, Edgar. Auras: An Essay on the Meaning of Colors. 1973. pap. 1.25 (ISBN 0-87604-012-1). ARE Pr.

Cayce, Hugh L. Earth Changes Update. 134p. (Orig.). 1980. pap. 4.95 (ISBN 0-87604-121-7). ARE Pr.

Cayce, Hugh L., ed. The Edgar Cayce Reader. 192p. 1969. pap. 2.25 (ISBN 0-446-92698-1). Warner Bks.

Chadwick, Henry. Priscillian of Avila: The Occult & the Charismatic in the Early Church. 1976. 37.50x (ISBN 0-19-826643-X). Oxford U Pr.

Chalk, John A., et al. The Devil, You Say? LC 74-6758. 160p. 1974. pap. 1.50 (ISBN 0-8344-0083-9). Sweet.

Chambers, A. Our Life After Death. 59.95 (ISBN 0-8490-0784-4). Gordon Pr.

Change: A Working Study of Concepts Found in the Edgar Cayce Readings & the Ancient Chinese Oracle, I Ching. (Orig.). 1971. pap. 1.95 (ISBN 0-87604-053-9). ARE Pr.

Chaplin, J. P. The Dictionary of the Occult & Paranormal. 1976. pap. 1.95 (ISBN 0-440-31927-7, LE). Dell.

Cheiro, pseud. Mysteries & Romances of the World's Greatest Occultists. 1972. 7.95 (ISBN 0-8216-0121-0). Univ Bks.

Chicorel, Marietta, ed. Chicorel Index to Parapsychology & Occult: Books. (Index Ser.: Vol. 24). 1978. text ed. 85.00 (ISBN 0-934598-33-9). Am Lib Pub Co.

Chinmoy, Sri. Astrology, the Supernatural & the Beyond. LC 74-75131. 123p. (Orig.). 1974. pap. 3.00 (ISBN 0-88497-037-X). Aum Pubns.

--Secrets of the Inner World. (Illus.). 54p. (Orig.). 1980. pap. 2.00 (ISBN 0-88497-499-5). Aum Pubns.

Christopher, Milbourne. Mediums, Mystics & the Occult. LC 74-26812. (Illus.). 288p. 1975. 9.95 (ISBN 0-690-00476-1, TYC-T). T Y Crowell.

Church of Light Research & Reference Cyclopedia, 2 vols. 1976. Vol. 1. pap. 7.50 (ISBN 0-87887-330-9); Vol. 2. pap. 7.50 (ISBN 0-87887-331-7). Church of Light.

Clarie, Thomas C. Occult Bibliography: An Annotated List of Books Published in English, 1971 Through 1975. LC 78-17156. 1978. 24.00 (ISBN 0-8108-1152-9). Scarecrow.

Clarke, Arthur C. Report on Planet Three & Other Speculations. 1973. pap. 1.50 (ISBN 0-451-07864-0, W7864, Sig). NAL.

Clymer, R. Swinburne. Compendium of Occult Laws. 1966. 4.95 (ISBN 0-686-09387-9). Philos Pub.

--Philosophy of Fire: Spiritual Light. 1964. 4.95 (ISBN 0-686-00823-5). Philos Pub.

--Teachings of the Masters. 1952. 5.00 (ISBN 0-686-00831-6). Philos Pub.

Coddington, Mary & Destiny, Warner. In Search of the Healing Energy. 2.25 (ISBN 0-446-82575-1). Inner Tradit.

Cohen, Daniel. Famous Curses. (gr. 3-6). pap. 1.75 (ISBN 0-671-41867-X). Archway.

--Ghostly Terrors. (High Interest, Low Vocabulary Ser.). (Illus.). 112p. (gr. 4-9). 1981. PLB 6.95 (ISBN 0-396-07996-2). Dodd.
--Masters of the Occult. LC 74-165669. (Illus.). 1971. 5.95 (ISBN 0-396-06407-8). Dodd.
--Voodoo, Devils & the New Invisible World. LC 72-2346. (Illus.). 232p. 1972. 5.95 (ISBN 0-396-06638-0). Dodd.
Collin De Plancy, J. A. Dictionnaire des Sciences Occultes, 2 vols. Migne, J. P., ed. (Encyclopedie Theologique Ser.: Vols. 48-49). 1116p. (Fr.). Date not set. Repr. of 1848 ed. lib. bdg. 143.00x (ISBN 0-89241-252-6). Caratzas Bros.
Collyns, Robin. Laser Beams from Star Cities. 128p. 1975. 10.95 (ISBN 0-7207-0756-0, Pub. by Michael Joseph). Merrimack Bk Serv.
Conway, David. Ritual Magic: An Occult Primer. 1978. pap. 5.95 (ISBN 0-525-47542-7). Dutton.
Cornillier, Pierre. The Survival of the Soul & Its Evolution After Death. lib. bdg. 59.95 (ISBN 0-87968-498-4). Krishna Pr.
Coxe, Francis. A Short Treatise Declaringe the Detestable Wickednesse of Magicall Sciences. LC 72-5971. (English Experience Ser.: No. 501). 32p. 1972. Repr. of 1561 ed. 5.00 (ISBN 90-221-0501-6). Walter J Johnson.
Crenshaw, James. Telephone Between Worlds. 1977. Repr. of 1950 ed. 6.95 (ISBN 0-87516-017-4). De Vorss.
Crookall, R. Interpretation of Cosmic & Mystical Experiences. 1969. 10.00 (ISBN 0-227-67729-3). Attic Pr.
Crow, W. B. Occult Properties of Herbs. (Paths to Inner Power Ser). 1980. pap. 2.25 (ISBN 0-87728-097-5). Weiser.
--Precious Stones: Their Occult Power. (Paths to Inner Power Ser). 1980. pap. 2.25 (ISBN 0-87728-093-2). Weiser.
--Witchcraft, Magic & Occultism. pap. 5.00 (ISBN 0-87980-173-5). Wilshire.
Crowley, Aleister. The Argonauts. 1973. lib. bdg. 59.95 (ISBN 0-87968-222-1). Krishna Pr.
--The Banned Lecture. LC 79-91571. Date not set. pap. 3.50 (ISBN 0-935458-99-9). Thirteenth Hse.
--Book Four. 1973. lib. bdg. 69.95 (ISBN 0-87968-114-4). Krishna Pr.
--Book of Lies. LC 79-16636. (Illus.). 1980. pap. 6.95 (ISBN 0-87728-018-5). Weiser.
--The Book of Lies. 1973. lib. bdg. 69.95 (ISBN 0-87968-115-2). Krishna Pr.
--The Book of Thoth. LC 79-16399. (Illus.). 287p. 1981. pap. 8.95 (ISBN 0-87728-268-4). Weiser.
--Clouds Without Water. 1973. lib. bdg. 59.95 (ISBN 0-87968-111-X). Krishna Pr.
--Clouds Without Water. 139p. 1973. Repr. 3.50 (ISBN 0-911662-50-2). Yoga.
--The Collected Works of Aleister Crowley, 3 vols. 1974. lib. bdg. 300.00 (ISBN 0-87968-130-6). Krishna Pr.
--Collected Works of Aleister Crowley, 3 vols. 280p. 1974. Repr. 8.00 ea.; Vol. 1. (ISBN 0-911662-51-0); Vol. 2. (ISBN 0-911662-52-9); Vol. 3. (ISBN 0-911662-53-7). Yoga.
--Creed of the Thelemites. 1973. lib. bdg. 59.95 (ISBN 0-87968-500-X). Krishna Pr.
--Dream of Scipio. 1973. lib. bdg. 59.95 (ISBN 0-87968-501-8). Krishna Pr.
--Energized Enthusiasm. (Equinox Reprints: Vol. 1, No. 9). 1976. pap. 1.50 (ISBN 0-87728-340-0). Weiser.
--Equinox of the Gods. 1973. lib. bdg. 69.95 (ISBN 0-87968-157-8). Krishna Pr.
--The High History of Good Sir Palamedes. 1973. lib. bdg. 59.95 (ISBN 0-87968-503-4). Krishna Pr.
--Holy Books. pap. 2.95 (ISBN 0-685-01086-4). Weiser.
--In Residence. 1973. lib. bdg. 59.95 (ISBN 0-87968-504-2). Krishna Pr.
--Jepthah & Other Mysteries. 1973. lib. bdg. 59.95 (ISBN 0-87968-217-5). Krishna Pr.
--Konx Om Pax. 108p. 1973. Repr. 3.50 (ISBN 0-911662-49-9). Yoga.
--Liber E & Liber O. (Equinox Reprints: Vol. 1, Nos. 1-2). 1976. pap. 1.50 (ISBN 0-87728-341-9). Weiser.
--The Magical Record of the Beast 666. Symonds, John & Grant, Kenneth, eds. 326p. 1979. 40.50 (ISBN 0-7156-0636-0, Pub. by Duckworth England); pap. 17.00 (ISBN 0-7156-1208-5, 386, Pub. by Duckworth England); limited ed. slipcase 95.00 (ISBN 0-7156-0636-0). Biblio Dist.
--Magick in Theory & Practice. 1973. lib. bdg. 75.00 (ISBN 0-87968-128-4). Krishna Pr.
--Moonchild. LC 72-142496. 1981. pap. 6.95 (ISBN 0-87728-147-5). Weiser.
--Olla: An Anthology of Sixty Years Song. 1973. lib. bdg. 59.95 (ISBN 0-87968-505-0). Krishna Pr.
--One Star in Sight. 1973. lib. bdg. 59.95 (ISBN 0-87968-506-9). Krishna Pr.
--Orpheus. 1973. lib. bdg. 59.95 (ISBN 0-87968-176-4). Krishna Pr.
--Seven Hundred Seventy-Seven & Other Qabilistic Writings. new ed. LC 73-80056. 274p. 1981. 12.95 (ISBN 0-87728-222-6). Weiser.
--The Soul of Osiris. 1973. lib. bdg. 59.95 (ISBN 0-87968-177-2). Krishna Pr.
--The Star & the Garter. 1973. lib. bdg. 59.95 (ISBN 0-87968-175-6). Krishna Pr.
--The Stratagem & Other Stories. 1973. lib. bdg. 59.95 (ISBN 0-87968-117-9). Krishna Pr.
--Tannhauser: A Story of All Time. 1973. lib. bdg. 59.95 (ISBN 0-87968-215-9). Krishna Pr.
--The Whirlpool. 1973. lib. bdg. 59.95 (ISBN 0-87968-507-7). Krishna Pr.
Crowley, Aleister & Motta, Marcelo R. Equinox, Vol. 5, No. 2. LC 78-68846. 1979. 31.00 (ISBN 0-933454-00-7, Pub. by Troll Pub); deluxe ed. 93.00 limited (ISBN 0-933454-01-5). SOTOA.
Culling, Louis T. Occult Renaissance 1972-2008. 1972. pap. 1.00 (ISBN 0-87542-133-4). Llewellyn Pubns.
Curtiss, H. A. & Curtiss, F. H. The Message of Aquaria. 487p. 1981. pap. 17.50 (ISBN 0-89540-065-0). Sun Pub.
Daniels, Cora L. Encyclopedia of Superstitions, Folklore & the Occult Sciences, 3 vols. 300.00 (ISBN 0-8490-0106-4). Gordon Pr.
Daniels, Cora L. & Stevans, C. M., eds. Encyclopedia of Superstitions, Folklore & the Occult Sciences of the World, 3 Vols. LC 70-141151. 1971. Repr. of 1903 ed. 80.00 (ISBN 0-8103-3286-8). Gale.
Darby & Joan. Our Unseen Guest. pap. 5.95 (ISBN 0-685-27817-4). Borden.
Darrow, Frank M., et al. An Experiment. (Orig.). 1977. pap. 2.50 (ISBN 0-685-80844-0). Darrow.
David-Neel, Alexandra. Magic & Mystery in Tibet. 1971. pap. 4.25 (ISBN 0-486-22682-4). Dover.
Davies, Thomas W. Magic, Divination & Demonology Among the Hebrews & Their Neighbors. 1898. 10.00x (ISBN 0-87068-051-X). Ktav.
Dawes, Walter A. Light Shines on Mystery Babylon the Great. (Orig.). 1981. pap. 10.95 (ISBN 0-938792-10-5). New Capernaum.
Dawson, W. R. Bride of Pegasus: Studies in Magic, Mythology & Folklore. lib. bdg. 59.95 (ISBN 0-87968-514-X). Krishna Pr.
DeA'Morelli, Richard. ESP Party Games: Psychic Tests for Everyone. (Illus.). 176p. (Orig.). 1976. pap. 1.25 (ISBN 0-89041-071-2, 3071). Major Bks.
De Camp, L. Sprague & De Camp, Catherine. Spirits, Stars & Spells. LC 65-25470. 10.00 (ISBN 0-940724-14-6). Canaveral.
DeGivry, Grillot. Witchcraft, Magic & Alchemy. lib. bdg. 95.00 (ISBN 0-87968-515-8). Krishna Pr.
DeHaan, Richard. El Culto a Satanas. De la Cerda, Rodolfo, tr. from Eng. 136p. (Orig., Span.). 1975. pap. 2.25 (ISBN 0-89922-059-2). Edit Caribe.
Delaney, Walter. Ultra-Psychonics: How to Work Miracles with the Limitless Power of Psycho-Atomic Energy. 1976. pap. 2.95 (ISBN 0-13-935627-4, Reward). P-H.
De Lubicz, Isha S. Her-Bak: Egyptian Initiate, Vol. 2. 1978. pap. 8.95 (ISBN 0-685-62083-2). Weiser.
--Her-Bak: The Living Face of Ancient Egypt, Vol. 1. 1978. pap. 8.95 (ISBN 0-685-62082-4). Weiser.
Demonolatry, 2 vols. Incl. Vol. 1. Demonolatry. Remy, Nicolas; Vol. 2. Compendium Maleficarum. Guazzo, Francesco M. 1975. Set. 25.00 (ISBN 0-8216-0215-2). Univ Bks.
Denning & Phillips. Triumph of Light. LC 75-2428. (Magical Philosophy Ser.: Vol. 4). (Illus.). 250p. 1978. 10.00 (ISBN 0-87542-179-2). Llewellyn Pubns.
De Purucker, G. Fountain-Source of Occultism. Knoche, Grace F., ed. LC 72-92155. 1974. 15.00 (ISBN 0-911500-70-7); pap. 9.00 (ISBN 0-911500-71-5). Theos U Pr.
--Golden Precepts: A Guide to Enlightened Living. rev. 3rd ed. Todd, Helen & Small, W. Emmett, eds. 170p. 1971. 3.50 (ISBN 0-685-29056-5, 913004-11); pap. 2.50 (ISBN 0-685-29057-3, 913004-02). Point Loma Pub.
--Mahatmas & Genuine Occultism. rev. ed. Small, Emmett & Todd, Helen, eds. Orig. Title: The Masters & the Path of Occultism. 100p. 1972. pap. 1.50 (ISBN 0-685-28754-8, 913004-07). Point Loma Pub.
--Studies in Occult Philosophy. LC 73-81739. 1973. 10.00 (ISBN 0-911500-52-9); pap. 6.50 (ISBN 0-911500-53-7). Theos U Pr.
--Wind of the Spirit. abr. ed. Small, W. Emmett & Todd, Helen, eds. 282p. 1971. pap. 3.25 (ISBN 0-685-29055-7, 913004-00). Point Loma Pub.
Devereux, George, ed. Psychoanalysis & the Occult. 1970. text ed. 25.00 (ISBN 0-8236-5180-0); pap. text ed. 6.95 (ISBN 0-8236-8240-4, 025180). Intl Univs Pr.
Dickinson, Peter. Chance, Luck & Destiny. (Illus.). (gr. 7 up). 1976. 9.95 (ISBN 0-316-18428-4, Pub. by Atlantic Monthly Pr). Little.
Dictionnaire des Songes, dans Dicitonnaire des Sciences Occultes. 416p. (Fr.). 1976. pap. 18.95 (ISBN 0-686-56865-6, M-6643). French & Eur.
Dictionnaires Sciences Occultes. 416p. (Fr.). 1976. pap. 19.95 (ISBN 0-686-57104-5, M-6130). French & Eur.
Don, Frank. Earth Changes Ahead: The Coming Great Catastrophes. 320p. (Orig.). 1981. pap. 2.75 (ISBN 0-446-85577-4). Warner Bks.
Douglas, Nik & Slinger, Penny. The Secret Dakini Oracle. (Illus.). 1979. pap. 5.95 (ISBN 0-89281-005-X, Destiny Books). Inner Tradit.
Downs. Magic Coin Tricks Anyone Can Do. 1.00 (ISBN 0-685-02621-3, 00545314). Stein Pub.
Drury, Nevill & Tillett, Gregory. The Occult Sourcebook. (Illus.). 1978. pap. 9.95 (ISBN 0-7100-8875-2). Routledge & Kegan.
Dubin, Reese P. Telecult Power: The Amazing New Way to Psychic & Occult Wonders. (Illus.). 1970. 12.95 (ISBN 0-13-902437-9, Reward); pap. 3.95 (ISBN 0-13-902411-5). P-H.
Dunsany, Lord. Gods, Men, & Ghosts. (Illus.). 6.75 (ISBN 0-8446-0081-4). Peter Smith.
Durckheim, Karlfried G. Way of Transformation. (Unwin Paperback Ser.). 112p. 1980. pap. 4.50 (ISBN 0-04-291014-5). Allen Unwin.
Ebon, Martin, ed. Mysterious Pyramid Power. 1976. pap. 1.75 (ISBN 0-451-08110-2, E8110, Sig). NAL.
--World's Great Unsolved Mysteries. (Orig.). 1981. pap. 2.50 (ISBN 0-451-09684-3, E9684, Sig). NAL.
Edmonds, I. G. The Kings of Black Magic. LC 79-19534. 160p. (gr. 4-8). 1981. 12.95 (ISBN 0-03-051376-6). HR&W.
Edwardes, Michael. The Dark Side of History. LC 76-45265. 1977. 10.00 (ISBN 0-8128-2320-6). Stein & Day.
Eichner. Atlantean Chronicles. 1972. 9.50 (ISBN 0-686-02510-5). Fantasy Pub Co.
The Encyclopedia of Occult Sciences. LC 75-78148. 1975. Repr. of 1939 ed. 26.00 (ISBN 0-8103-3120-9). Gale.
Esterer, Arnulf & Esterer, Louise. The Occult World. LC 78-18267. 224p. (gr. 7 up). 1978. PLB 8.29 (ISBN 0-671-32876-X). Messner.
Everard, John, tr. from Arabic. The Divine Pymander of Hermes Mercurius Trismegistus. LC 73-84044. (Secret Doctrine Reference Ser.). 140p. 1973. Repr. of 1884 ed. 7.95 (ISBN 0-913510-07-6). Wizards.
Farthing, Geoffrey. Exploring the Great Beyond. LC 77-17692. (Orig.). 1978. pap. 4.25 (ISBN 0-8356-0508-6, Quest). Theos Pub Hse.
Ferguson, Robert A. The Universal Law of Cosmic Cycles. 1980. 10.95 (ISBN 0-13-938738-2, Parker). P-H.
--Universal Mind: New Way to Mystic Power & Prosperity. (Illus.). 1978. 9.95 (ISBN 0-13-938035-3, Parker). P-H.
Fernie, W. T. Precious Stones for Curative Wear & Other Remedial Uses. 69.95 (ISBN 0-8490-0886-7). Gordon Pr.
Fernie, William T. The Occult & Curative Powers of Precious Stones. LC 80-8894. (The Harper Library of Spiritual Wisdom Ser.). 496p. 1981. pap. 7.95 (ISBN 0-06-062360-8, CN4009, HarpR). Har-Row.
Finch, Elizabeth & Finch, W. J. Photo-Chromotherapy. 2.50 (ISBN 0-89861-001-X). Esoteric Pubns.
Fletcher, Ella A. Law of the Rhythmic Breath. 1979. pap. 4.95 (ISBN 0-87877-044-5). Newcastle Pub.
Flinn, Avril. Come into My Parlor. 1980. pap. 2.50 (ISBN 0-88270-396-X). Logos.
Fodor, Nandor. Freud, Jung & Occultism. 1971. 7.95 (ISBN 0-8216-0081-8). Univ Bks.
Foli, P. R. Fortune Telling by Cards. 1.00 (ISBN 0-685-02613-2, 00545223). Stein Pub.
Fort, Charles. The Complete Books of Charles Fort, 4 vols. in 1. Incl. The Book of the Damned. Repr. of 1919 ed; New Lands. Repr. of 1923 ed; Lo! Repr. of 1931 ed; Wild Talents. Repr. of 1932 ed. 1975. 15.00 (ISBN 0-486-23094-5). Dover.
Fortune, Dion. Esoteric Orders. 1962. pap. 3.95 (ISBN 0-87542-226-8). Llewellyn Pubns.
--Sane Occultism. 1967. 3.95 (ISBN 0-685-22093-1). Wehman.
--Secrets of Dr. Taverner. 3rd rev. ed. 1979. pap. 3.95 (ISBN 0-87542-227-6). Llewellyn Pubns.
--Training & Work of an Initiate. 3.95 (ISBN 0-87728-400-8). Weiser.
Franklyn, Julian, ed. A Dictionary of the Occult. Repr. of 1935 ed. 22.00 (ISBN 0-685-32596-2). Gale.
Freeman, Hobart. Angels of Light? Deliverance from Occult Oppression. pap. 1.95 small type ed. (ISBN 0-912106-63-8). Logos.
French, Michael. Rhythms. 1981. pap. 2.75 (ISBN 0-425-05023-8). Berkley Pub.
Frith, Henry. Palmistry Secrets Revealed. pap. 3.00 (ISBN 0-87980-116-6). Wilshire.
Frost, Gavin & Frost, Yvonne. Power Secrets from a Sorcerer's Private Magnum Arcanum. (Illus.). 1980. 10.95 (ISBN 0-13-687251-4, Parker). P-H.
Gardner, Richard. Evolution Through the Tarot. rev. ed. Orig. Title: Accelerate Your Evolution. (Illus.). 1981. pap. 5.95 (ISBN 0-87728-371-0). Weiser.
Garvin, Richard M. & Burger, Robert E. The World of the Twilight Believers. 1978. pap. 4.95 (ISBN 0-8202-5023-6). Sherbourne.
George, Karl. Three-Fold Fortune. 1978. 6.50 (ISBN 0-533-03557-0). Vantage.
Gettings, Fred. Dictionary of Occult, Hermetic & Alchemical Sigils. 1981. 40.00 (ISBN 0-7100-0095-2). Routledge & Kegan.
--Fate & Prediction: An Historical Compendium of Astrology, Palmistry & Tarot. (Illus.). 14.95 (ISBN 0-89673-043-3). Bookthrift.
--The Occult in Art. LC 78-57910. (Illus.). 1979. 19.95 (ISBN 0-8478-0190-X). Rizzoli Intl.
Gipsy-Witch Dream Book. pap. 1.50 (ISBN 0-685-02616-7, 00545259). Stein Pub.
Godwin, John. Occult America. LC 79-168289. 1972. 8.95 (ISBN 0-385-03662-0). Doubleday.
--Occult America. LC 79-168289. 1972. 8.95 (ISBN 0-385-03662-0). Doubleday.
Godwin, William. Lives of the Necromancers. lib. bdg. 69.95 (ISBN 0-87968-281-7). Gordon Pr.
Gooch, Stan. The Paranormal. LC 78-69621. 1980. pap. 4.95 (ISBN 0-06-090749-5, CN 749, CN). Har-Row.
Goran, Morris. Fact, Fraud, & Fantasy: The Occult & Pseudosciences. (Littlefield, Adams Quality Paperback Ser.: No. 356). 189p. 1980. pap. 3.95 (ISBN 0-8226-0356-X). Littlefield.
--Fact, Fraud, & Fantasy: The Occult & Pseudosciences. LC 77-84569. 1979. 8.95 (ISBN 0-498-02122-X). A S Barnes.
Gosselin, Edward A. & Lerner, Lawrence S., eds. Giordano Bruno: The Ash Wednesday Supper (la Cena De le Ceneri) (Illus.). 1977. 19.50 (ISBN 0-208-01610-4, Archon). Shoe String.
Grand Orient, pseud. Complete Manual of Occult Divination, 2 vols. 1972. 20.00 set (ISBN 0-8216-0063-X). Univ Bks.
Grandville, J. J. Bizarreries & Fantasies of Grandville. Appelbaum, Stanley, ed. 1974. pap. 5.50 (ISBN 0-486-22991-2). Dover.
Grant, Kenneth. Aleister Crowley & the Hidden God. LC 73-93228. (Illus.). 245p. 1974. Repr. of 1973 ed. 8.95 (ISBN 0-87728-250-1). Weiser.
--Cults of the Shadow. 1976. 12.50 (ISBN 0-87728-310-9). Weiser.
--The Images & Oracles of Austin Osmond Spare. 1976. 27.50 (ISBN 0-87728-300-1). Weiser.
--Magical Revival. LC 72-185895. 7.95 (ISBN 0-87728-217-X). Weiser.
Graves, Tom & Hoult, Janet, eds. The Essential T. C. Lethbridge. 1980. 15.00 (ISBN 0-7100-0396-X). Routledge & Kegan.
Gray-Cobb, Geof. The Miracle of New Avatar Power. 1974. 10.95 (ISBN 0-13-585364-8, Parker). P-H.
Gray-Cobb, Geoff. The Miracle of New Avatar Power. 1974. 9.95 (ISBN 0-13-585372-9, Reward); pap. 3.45 (ISBN 0-13-585364-8). P-H.
Greenhouse, Herbert B. The Book of Psychic Knowledge: All Your Questions Answered. LC 72-6613. 1973. 7.50 (ISBN 0-8008-0932-7). Taplinger.
Greenhouse, Herbert K. Book of Psychic Knowledge. 1975. pap. 1.75 (ISBN 0-451-08035-1, E8035, Sig). NAL.
Grillot De Givry. Witchcraft, Magic & Alchemy. Locke, J. Courtney, tr. from Fr. (Illus.). 395p. 1971. pap. 6.50 (ISBN 0-486-22493-7). Dover.
Grillot De Givry, Emile. Illustrated Anthology of Sorcery, Magic & Alchemy. 1973. Repr. 15.00 (ISBN 0-685-70658-3). Gale.
Gross, Jim, et al. April Fourth, Nineteen Eighty-One: Pivotal Day in a Critical Year. (Illus.). 1980. pap. 7.00 (ISBN 0-933646-12-7). Aries Pr.
Gruss, E. C. Cults & the Occult in the Age of Aquarius. (Direction Bks). pap. 2.95 (ISBN 0-8010-3682-8). Baker Bk.
Gruss, Edmund C. Cults & the Occult. rev. ed. pap. 2.95 (ISBN 0-87552-308-0). Presby & Reformed.
Gurdjieff, G. Herald of Coming Good. LC 73-147105. 1979. pap. 3.95 (ISBN 0-87728-049-5). Weiser.
Gurdjieff, G. I. Beelzebub's Tales to His Grandson, 3 vols. 1973. Set. pap. 13.95 (ISBN 0-525-47351-3). Dutton.
Hack, G. Modern Psychic Mysteries. 59.95 (ISBN 0-8490-0651-1). Gordon Pr.
Haich, Elisabeth. Initiation. Robertson, John, tr. from Ger. 380p. (Orig.). 1974. pap. 7.00 (ISBN 0-916108-04-X). Seed Center.
Haining, Peter. Warlock's Book. (Illus.). 1971. 6.00 (ISBN 0-8216-0161-X). Univ Bks.
Haining, Peter, ed. The Magicians: The Occult in Fact & Fiction. LC 72-9806. 224p. 1973. 7.95 (ISBN 0-8008-5045-9). Taplinger.

Haislip, Barbara. Stars, Spells, Secrets, & Sorcery. (YA) 1978. pap. 1.50 (ISBN 0-440-98454-8, LFL). Dell.
Halevi, Z'Ev ben Shimon. A Kabbalistic Universe. 1977. pap. 5.00 (ISBN 0-87728-349-4). Weiser.
Hall, Manly. Secret of the Untroubled Mind. pap. 1.75 (ISBN 0-89314-352-9). Philos Res.
Hall, Manly P. The Inner Lives of Minerals, Plants, & Animals. pap. 1.75 (ISBN 0-89314-322-7). Philos Res.
--Magic: A Treatise on Esoteric Ethics. pap. 1.75 (ISBN 0-89314-384-7). Philos Res.
--Medicine of the Sun & Moon. pap. 1.75 (ISBN 0-89314-332-4). Philos Res.
--Old Testament Wisdom. 9.95 (ISBN 0-89314-515-7). Philos Res.
--Past Lives & Present Problems. pap. 1.75 (ISBN 0-89314-339-1). Philos Res.
--Postive Uses of Psychic Energy. pap. 1.75 (ISBN 0-89314-343-X). Philos Res.
--Psychic Self-Reproach. pap. 1.75 (ISBN 0-89314-344-8). Philos Res.
--Psychic Symbolism of Headaches, Insomnia & Upset Stomach. pap. 1.75 (ISBN 0-89314-345-6). Philos Res.
--Questions & Answers on Problems of Life. 7.90 (ISBN 0-89314-518-1). Philos Res.
--The Secret Teachings of All Ages: An Encyclopedia Guide to Masonic, Hermetic, Quabbalistic & Rosicrucian Symbolic Philosophy. (Illus.). 1978. pap. cancelled (ISBN 0-685-54894-5). Bolder Bks.
--Self-Unfoldment. 8.00 (ISBN 0-89314-524-6). Philos Res.
--Shadow Forms. pap. 4.95 (ISBN 0-89314-392-8). Philos Res.
--Space-Born. pap. 3.95 (ISBN 0-89314-399-5). Philos Res.
--The Spiritual Centers in Man. Orig. Title: Operative Occutism. pap. 1.75 (ISBN 0-89314-383-9). Philos Res.
--Super Faculties & Their Culture. pap. 1.75 (ISBN 0-89314-358-8). Philos Res.
--Talks to Students on Occult Philosophy. pap. 1.75 (ISBN 0-89314-361-8). Philos Res.
--Words to the Wise. 7.50 (ISBN 0-89314-528-9). Philos Res.
Hamel, Frank. Human Animals, Werewolves & Other Transformations. 7.95 (ISBN 0-8216-0092-3). Univ Bks.
Harlow, S. Ralph. A Life After Death. 224p. 1973. pap. 0.95 (ISBN 0-532-95222-7). Woodhill.
Harper, Charles G. Haunted Houses: Tales of the Supernatural with Some Account of Hereditary Curses & Family Legends. LC 79-164326. (Illus.). xvi, 283p. 1971. Repr. of 1907 ed. 28.00 (ISBN 0-8103-3928-5). Gale.
Harris, Iverson L. Mme. Blavatsky Defended. 174p. (Orig.). 1971. pap. 3.00 (ISBN 0-685-29053-0, 913004-01). Point Loma Pub.
Hart, F. The Ageless Mysteries: Karma, Reincarnation, Spiritualism, Astrology. 59.95 (ISBN 0-87968-586-7). Gordon Pr.
Hartmann, Franz. Magic White & Black; or, the Science of Finite & Infinite Life. LC 80-19323. 298p. 1980. Repr. of 1971 ed. lib. bdg. 11.95x (ISBN 0-89370-603-5). Borgo Pr.
Harvey, James M. Later Than You Think, 1975-2000. 33p. 1973. 2.95 (ISBN 0-686-02582-2). Publishers.
Hatt, Carolyn. The Maya: Based on the Edgar Cayce Readings. 67p. 1972. pap. 2.95 (ISBN 0-87604-059-8). ARE Pr.
Heline, Corinne. Beethoven's Nine Symphonies, & the Nine Lesser Mysteries. 4.50 (ISBN 0-87613-000-7). New Age.
--Color & Music in the New Age. 8th ed. 139p. 1981. pap. 3.95 (ISBN 0-87516-432-3). De Vorss.
--Occult Anatomy & the Bible. 6.00 (ISBN 0-87613-025-2). New Age.
Hills, Christopher. Nuclear Evolution: Discovery of the Rainbow Body. Hills, Norah, ed. LC 76-53180. (Illus.). 1024p. (Orig.). 1977. text ed. 18.95 (ISBN 0-916438-12-0); pap. 12.95 (ISBN 0-916438-09-0). Univ of Trees.
Hills, Norah, ed. You Are a Rainbow: Discovering Your Personality with the Rainbow Aura Pendulum. LC 79-13393. (Illus.). 128p. (Orig.). 1979. pap. 2.95 (ISBN 0-916438-25-2). Univ of Trees.
Hisey, Lehmann. Keys to Inner Space. 1975. pap. 1.95 (ISBN 0-380-00411-9, 25098). Avon.
Hitchcock, Ethan A. Red Book of Appin. 15.00 (ISBN 0-89314-413-4). Philos Res.
Hitchcock, Helyn. The Magic of Psychograms: New Way to Power and Prosperity. 1976. 10.95 (ISBN 0-13-545343-7). P-H.
Hodson, Geoffrey. Call to the Heights. LC 75-30656. 224p. (Orig.). 1975. pap. 3.50 (ISBN 0-8356-0477-2, Quest). Theos Pub Hse.
--Meditations on the Occult Life. 3rd ed. 1968. 2.50 (ISBN 0-8356-7225-5). Theos Pub Hse.
Holzer, Hans. Inside Witchcraft. (Orig.). 1980. pap. 2.25 (ISBN 0-532-23220-8). Woodhill.
--More Than One Life. (Orig.). 1980. pap. 2.25 (ISBN 0-532-23127-9). Woodhill.
Hoover, David W. How to Respond to the Occult. (The Response Ser.). 1977. 1.25 (ISBN 0-570-07678-1, 12-2661). Concordia.
Hudson, Thomson J. Law of Psychic Phenomena. Holland, Jack, ed. 220p. (Orig.). 1970. pap. 3.95 (ISBN 0-87852-000-7). Hudson-Cohan.
Huffman, Robert & Specht, Irene. Many Wonderful Things. 3rd ed. 1977. pap. 5.95 (ISBN 0-87516-027-1). De Vorss.
Hughes, Irene F. ESPecially Irene: A Guide to Psychic Awareness. LC 70-189997. 160p. 1972. pap. 1.95 (ISBN 0-8334-1730-4). Steinerbks.
Humphries, Joan R. The Application of Scientific Behaviorism to Humanistic Phenomena. LC 77-18593. 1978. pap. text ed. 6.50 (ISBN 0-8191-0163-X). U Pr of Amer.
Hyatt, Victoria & Charles, Joseph W. The Book of Demons. (Illus.). 1974. pap. 3.95 (ISBN 0-671-21907-3). S&S.
I Am Ishcomar. 1.00 (ISBN 0-89861-011-7). Esoteric Pubns.
Ibn Ezra, Abraham. Astrological Works. lib. bdg. 75.00 (ISBN 0-87968-525-5). Krishna Pr.
Imponderable Forces: Course XVIII, Lessons 183-9. (Illus.). 1976. pap. 6.95 (ISBN 0-87887-352-X). Church of Light.
Index to Occult Sciences. LC 76-40569. (New Library of the Supernatural). 1977. 8.95 (ISBN 0-385-11326-9). Doubleday.
Ingalese, Isabella. Occult Philosophy. LC 80-23861. 321p. 1980. Repr. lib. bdg. 12.95x (ISBN 0-89370-649-3). Borgo Pr.
--Occult Philosophy. 1980. pap. 5.95 (ISBN 0-87877-049-6). Newcastle Pub.
Ingalese, Richard. The History & Power of Mind. LC 80-19897. 332p. 1980. Repr. of 1976 ed. lib. bdg. 11.95x (ISBN 0-89370-637-X). Borgo Pr.
Irion, J. Everett. Vibrations. 125p. (Orig.). 1979. pap. 3.95 (ISBN 0-87604-120-9). ARE Pr.
Jacolliot, Louis. Occult Science in India & Among the Ancients. 1970. 5.95 (ISBN 0-8216-0130-X). Univ Bks.
James, Henry. Henry James: Stories of the Supernatural. rev. ed. Edel, Leon, ed. LC 78-125479. 1970. 10.00 (ISBN 0-8008-3830-0). Taplinger.
Jinarajadasa, C. The Divine Vision. LC 72-10072. 109p. 1973. pap. 1.45 (ISBN 0-8356-0433-0, Quest). Theos Pub Hse.
Jocelyn, Beredene. Citizens of the Cosmos: Life's Unfolding Through Death & Rebirth. 224p. 1981. 14.95 (ISBN 0-8264-0052-3). Continuum.
Johnson, Josephine L. Mysteries of the Space Age. 1966. 4.00 (ISBN 0-87164-006-6). William-F.
Jones, David E. Visions of Time. LC 78-64909. (Illus.). 1979. 12.95 (ISBN 0-8356-0525-6, Quest); pap. 7.50 (ISBN 0-8356-0523-X, Quest). Theos Pub Hse.
Judge, William Q. Echoes of the Orient, Vol. II. (Illus.). 1980. 12.00 (ISBN 0-685-95904-X, 913004-34). Point Loma Pub.
--Practical Occultism: From the Private Letters of William Q. Judge. LC 78-63320. 1979. 10.00 (ISBN 0-911500-29-4); pap. 6.00 (ISBN 0-911500-30-8). Theos U Pr.
Jung, C. G. Psychology & the Occult. 1976. pap. 2.95 (ISBN 0-691-01791-3). Princeton U Pr.
Karalius, Vince. Lucky Thirteen. 12.50x (ISBN 0-392-03839-0, SpS). Sportshelf.
Kardec, Allan. Book of Mediums. Wood, Emma A., tr. from Fr. LC 77-16630. 1970. pap. 5.95 (ISBN 0-87728-009-6). Weiser.
Kaye, Marvin. The Handbook of Mental Magic. LC 75-9830. 1977. 5.95 (ISBN 0-8128-2253-6). Stein & Day.
Kerval, Alastorde, pseud. Amrita - Liber CCCXLIII. LC 77-8311. 1980. 45.00 (ISBN 0-913576-29-8); deluxe ed. (ISBN 0-913576-19-0). Thelema Pubns.
Kettelkamp, Larry. Mischievous Ghosts: The Poltergeist & PK. LC 80-17138. (Illus.). 128p. (gr. 4-6). 1980. 6.95 (ISBN 0-688-22243-9); PLB 6.67 (ISBN 0-688-32243-3). Morrow.
Kiesewetter, Karl. Geschichte Des Nueren Occultismus: Vols. 1 & 2, Die Geheimwissenschaften, 2 vols. LC 75-36847. (Occult Sev.). (Illus., Ger.). 1976. Repr. of 1895 ed. Set. 88.00x (ISBN 0-405-07936-2); 44.00x ea. Vol. 1 (ISBN 0-405-07962-1). Vol. 2 (ISBN 0-405-07963-X). Arno.
--Der Occultismus Des Altertums, 2 vols. in 1. LC 75-36846. (Occult Ser.). (Ger.). 1976. Repr. of 1895 ed. 53.00x (ISBN 0-405-07958-3). Arno.
King, Francis & Skinner, Stephen. Techniques of High Magic: A Manual of Self Initiation. 1980. 17.50x (ISBN 0-85207-115-9, Pub. by Daniel Co England). State Mutual Bk.
Klein, Aaron E. Science & the Supernatural: A Scientific Overview of the Occult. LC 76-42339. (gr. 7-9). 1979. 7.95a (ISBN 0-385-12036-2); PLB (ISBN 0-385-12037-0). Doubleday.
Knight, G. Occult Exercises & Practices. (Paths to Inner Power Ser.). 1.25 (ISBN 0-685-01082-1). Weiser.
Koch, Kurt E. Between Christ & Satan. LC 79-160690. 1972. pap. 2.95 (ISBN 0-8254-3003-8). Kregel.
--Christian Counseling & Occultism. LC 65-23118. 1972. pap. 5.95 (ISBN 0-8254-3010-0). Kregel.
--Demonology, Past & Present. LC 72-93353. 1973. pap. 2.95 (ISBN 0-8254-3013-5). Kregel.
--Devil's Alphabet. LC 76-160692. 1972. pap. 2.95 (ISBN 0-8254-3004-6). Kregel.
--Occult ABC. LC 78-5066. Orig. Title: Satan's Devices. 1980. 7.95 (ISBN 0-8254-3031-3). Kregel.
--Occult Bondage & Deliverance. LC 72-160691. 1972. pap. 3.50 (ISBN 0-8254-3006-2). Kregel.
Kozminsky, Isidore. Numbers, Their Meaning & Magic. 1977. pap. 3.95 (ISBN 0-87728-184-X). Weiser.
LaChapelle, Dolores & Bourque, Janet. Earth Festivals: Seasonal Celebrations for Everyone, Young & Old. LC 76-15321. (Illus.). 196p. (Orig.). 1976. pap. 12.50 (ISBN 0-917270-00-2). Finn Hill.
LaDage, Alta J. Occult Psychology. 1978. 10.00 (ISBN 0-87542-409-0). Llewellyn Pubns.
Lamb, Geoffrey. Magic, Witchcraft & the Occult. LC 76-21194. 1977. 10.95 (ISBN 0-88254-422-5). Hippocrene Bks.
Laurence, Theodor. The Parker Lifetime Treasury of Mystic & Occult Powers. (Illus.). 1978. 9.95 (ISBN 0-13-650754-9, Parker). P-H.
LaVey, Anton S. The Satanic Rituals. 7.95 (ISBN 0-8216-0171-7). Univ Bks.
Laws of Occultism: Course I, Lessons 39-45. (Illus.). 1976. pap. 7.25 (ISBN 0-87887-344-9). Church of Light.
Leadbeater, Charles W. The Inner Life. LC 77-17044. 1978. pap. 5.95 (ISBN 0-8356-0502-7, Quest). Theos Pub Hse.
Leo, Alan. Jupiter: The Preserver. LC 72-16452. 1970. pap. 2.50 (ISBN 0-87728-020-7). Weiser.
--Mars: The War Lord. LC 79-16451. 1970. pap. 2.50 (ISBN 0-87728-021-5). Weiser.
--Saturn: The Reaper. LC 75-16450. 1981. pap. 3.95 (ISBN 0-87728-019-3). Weiser.
Lethbridge, T. C. The Power of the Pendulum. 1976. 12.00 (ISBN 0-7100-8337-8). Routledge & Kegan.
Leventhal, Herbert. In the Shadow of the Enlightenment: Occultism & Renaissance Science in Eighteenth-Century America. LC 75-13762. 336p. 1976. 17.50x (ISBN 0-8147-4965-8). NYU Pr.
Levi, Eliphas. The Book of Splendours. 191p. (Eng.). 1973. 8.95 (ISBN 0-87728-198-X). Weiser.
--The Great Secret. 1976. 10.00 (ISBN 0-87728-295-1). Weiser.
--Transcendental Magic. Waite, A. E., tr. from Fr. LC 72-16629. (Illus.). 1980. pap. 7.95 (ISBN 0-87728-079-7). Weiser.
Liebstoeckl, Hans. Secret Sciences in the Light of Our Time: Genesis, Golgotha's Mystery, Occultism, Philosopher's Stone, Rudolf Steiner. 59.95 (ISBN 0-8490-1014-4). Gordon Pr.
Lillie, Arthur. Modern Mystics & Modern Magic. LC 72-5680. (Essay Index Reprint Ser.). 1972. Repr. of 1894 ed. 16.00 (ISBN 0-8369-2996-9). Arno.
Lindsay, Gordon. Demons & the Occult. (Sorcery & Spirit World Ser.: Vol. 6). 0.95 (ISBN 0-89985-089-8). Christ Nations.
--Spiritualism, Telepathy, ESP, Ouija Board. (Sorcery in America Ser.: Vol. 1). pap. 0.95 (ISBN 0-89985-950-X). Christ Nations.
Lloyd, John U. Etidorhpa. 386p. 1974. pap. 15.00 (ISBN 0-89540-004-9). Sun Pub.
Lodge, Oliver. Spiritual Works, 4 vols. 400.00 (ISBN 0-8490-1114-0). Gordon Pr.
Long, Max F. Huna Code in Religions. 1965. 8.95 (ISBN 0-87516-044-1). De Vorss.
--Mana, or Vital Force. 5th ed. 1976. pap. 4.00x (ISBN 0-910764-04-2). Huna Res Inc.
--Recovering the Ancient Magic. (Illus.). 1978. pap. 5.95 (ISBN 0-910764-01-8). Huna Res Inc.
--Short Talks on Huna. 2nd rev. ed. 1978. pap. 5.00x (ISBN 0-910764-02-6). Huna Res Inc.
--Tarot Card Symbology. 2nd ed. Wingo, E. Otha, ed. (Illus.). 1972. pap. 8.50x (ISBN 0-910764-03-4). Huna Res Inc.
Lopez, Javier. El Moderno Manual de Magia y Hechiceria. (Compadre Collection Ser). 160p. (Orig., Span.). 1974. pap. 0.75 (ISBN 0-88473-704-7). Fiesta Pub.
Lowell, Percival. Occult Japan. 59.95 (ISBN 0-8490-0750-X). Gordon Pr.
Luster, Helen. I(EE), Bk. 2, Yellow Christmas. 2nd ed. (Illus.). 1977. text ed. 7.00 (ISBN 0-912662-14-X); pap. 3.00 (ISBN 0-912662-13-1). Fur Line Pr.
McIntosh, C. Eliphas Levi & the French Occult Revival. 7.95 (ISBN 0-87728-252-8). Weiser.
MacIvor, Virginia & LaForest, Sandra. Vibrations: Healing Through Color, Homeopathy & Radionics. 1979. pap. 5.95 (ISBN 0-87728-393-1). Weiser.
McKeever, Jim. Close Encounters of the Highest Kind. LC 78-70089. 1978. 7.95 (ISBN 0-931608-04-X); pap. 3.95 (ISBN 0-931608-03-1). Omega Pubns OR.
Mackey, Samson A. Mythological Astronomy of the Ancients Demonstrated, Pt. 1. Bd. with Pt. 2. The Key to Urania. LC 73-84043. (Secret Doctrine Reference Ser.). 380p. 1973. Repr. of 1822 ed. 15.00 (ISBN 0-913510-06-8). Wizards.
MacRae, Norman. Highland Second Sight. LC 77-19117. 1908. 20.00 (ISBN 0-8414-2305-9). Folcroft.
Maeterlinck, Maurice. The Unknown Guest. 1975. 7.95 (ISBN 0-8216-0220-9). Univ Bks.
Magic Card Tricks Anyone Can Do. 1.00 (ISBN 0-685-02620-5, 00545302). Stein Pub.
Manning, Al G. Helping Yourself with Psycho-Cosmic Power. 1968. pap. 3.95 (ISBN 0-13-386474-X, Reward). P-H.
Manning, Al. G. Miracle of Universal Psychic Power: How to Build Your Way to Prosperity. 1976. pap. 10.95 (ISBN 0-13-585794-5, Parker). P-H.
Marshall, Brenda & Mayo, Terry. The Occult. 6th ed. 1977. pap. 2.95 (ISBN 0-89596-220-9, Success). Merit Pubns.
Mason, Herbert M., Jr. Secrets of the Supernatural. LC 75-9729. (Illus.). 224p. (gr. 7-12). 1975. 7.95 (ISBN 0-590-17304-9, Four Winds). Schol Bk Serv.
Massy, Robert. Alive to the Universe! Layman's Handbook of Scientific Radiesthesia. new ed. Hills, Christopher, ed. LC 75-45901. (Illus.). 303p. (Orig.). 1976. pap. 9.95 (ISBN 0-916438-21-X). Univ of Trees.
Masters, G. Mallary. Rabelaisian Dialectic & the Platonic-Hermetic Tradition. LC 69-11316. 1969. 11.00 (ISBN 0-87395-039-9); microfiche 11.00 (ISBN 0-87395-139-5). State U NY Pr.
Mather, Increase. An Essay for the Recording of Illustrious Providences. LC 75-7021. (Indian Captivities Ser.: Vol. 2). 1977. Repr. of 1684 ed. lib. bdg. 40.00 (ISBN 0-8240-1626-2). Garland Pub.
Mathers, MacGregor. Grimoire of Armadel. 1979. 15.00 (ISBN 0-87728-255-2). Weiser.
Mathers, S. L. The Key of Solomon the King. 10.00 (ISBN 0-87728-211-0). Weiser.
Maya, Asura. Surya Siddhanta. Burgess, Ebeneezer & Whitney, William D., trs. from Sanscrit. LC 74-78001. (Secret Doctrine Reference Ser.). 368p. 1977. Repr. of 1860 ed. 17.50 (ISBN 0-913510-13-0). Wizards.
Mayo, Alzina. Tapestry of a Soul: An Inspirational Journey Experiencing Emotions. (Illus.). 1980. pap. 4.00 (ISBN 0-933646-13-5). Aries Pr.
Meek, G. From Enigma to Science. 6.95 (ISBN 0-87728-242-0). Weiser.
Messent, Peter B., ed. Literature of the Occult: A Collection of Critical Essays. (Twentieth Century Views Ser.). 224p. 1981. text ed. 12.95 (ISBN 0-13-537712-9, Spec); pap. text ed. 4.95 (ISBN 0-13-537704-8, Spec). P-H.
Metzner, Ralph. Maps of Consciousness. (Illus.). 1971. pap. 4.95 (ISBN 0-02-077400-1, Collier). Macmillan.
Michael X. Release Your Cosmic Powers. 1969. pap. 5.95 (ISBN 0-685-20201-1). Saucerian.
Mickaharic, Draja. Spiritual Cleansing. 128p. 1981. pap. 6.95 (ISBN 0-87728-531-4). Weiser.
Miller, Edith S., pseud. Occult Theocracy. 741p. Date not set. 15.00 (ISBN 0-913022-37-3). Angriff Pr.
Mishlove, Jeffrey. The Roots of Consciousness. LC 75-10311. (Illus.). 1975. pap. 12.95 (ISBN 0-394-73115-8). Random.
Monroe, Robert A. Journeys Out of the Body. LC 72-157612. 288p. 1977. pap. 6.50 (ISBN 0-385-00861-9, Anch). Doubleday.
Montgomery, Ruth. Strangers Among Us: Enlightened Beings from a World to Come. LC 79-10574. 1979. 9.95 (ISBN 0-698-10992-9). Coward.
Moore, Clara B. Keely & His Discoveries. 1972. 10.00 (ISBN 0-8216-0104-0). Univ Bks.
Morrill, Sibley S. Ambrose Bierce, F. A. Mitchell-Hedges & the Crystal Skull. LC 72-79466. 88p. 1972. pap. 3.95 (ISBN 0-9600310-3-0). Cadleon Pr.
Morrill, Sibley S., ed. Ponape: Where American Colonialism Confronts Black Magic, Five Kingdoms & the Mysterious Ruins of Nan Madol. LC 71-131215. 252p. 1970. pap. 2.95 (ISBN 0-9600310-1-4). Cadleon Pr.
Moss, Thelma. The Probability of the Impossible: Scientific Discoveries & Exploration in the Psychic World. 1975. pap. 4.95 (ISBN 0-452-25140-0, Z5140, Plume). NAL.
Murphet, H. Sai Baba, Man of Miracles. pap. 4.95 (ISBN 0-87728-240-4). Weiser.
Murphy, Joseph. Cosmic Power Within You. 1973. pap. 3.95 (ISBN 0-13-179176-1, Reward). P-H.
--Miracle Power for Infinite Riches. 1972. 8.95 (ISBN 0-13-585638-8, Parker); pap. 3.45 (ISBN 0-686-76982-1). P-H.

Myers, Erica. Akhenaten & Nefertiti: The Royal Rebels. (Orig.). 1979. pap. 2.25 (ISBN 0-532-23252-6). Woodhill.
Navon, Robert. Patterns of the Universe. 1977. pap. 3.50 (ISBN 0-685-91981-1). Weiser.
Neugroschel, Joachim. Yenne Velt: The Great Works of Jewish Fantasy & Occult. 1978. pap. 6.95 (ISBN 0-671-79006-4, Wallaby). PB.
Neugroschel, Joachim, ed. Yenne Velt: The Great Works of Jewish Fantasy & Occult, 2 vols. 736p. 1976. 25.00 (ISBN 0-88373-025-1). Stonehill Pub Co.
Nevius, John L. Demon Possession. LC 68-27729. (Orig.). 1973. 8.95 (ISBN 0-8254-3302-9). Kregel.
Nigosian, Solomon A. Occultism in the Old Testament. 119p. 1978. 6.95 (ISBN 0-8059-2537-6). Dorrance.
Noorbergen, Rene. Elena G. De White: Profeta Del Destino. Peyrera-Suarez, Hector, tr. from English. (Pivot Paperback). (Illus.). 272p. (Span.). 1974. pap. 1.95 (ISBN 0-87983-076-X). Keats.
--Ellen G. White Prophet of Destiny. LC 70-190456. (Pivot Paperback). (Illus.). 256p. 1974. pap. 1.75 (ISBN 0-87983-077-8). Keats.
North, Gary K. None Dare Call It Witchcraft. 1976. 8.95 (ISBN 0-87000-301-1). Arlington Hse.
Norvell. Cosmic Magnetism. pap. 3.95 (ISBN 0-13-179119-2). P-H.
--Universal Secrets of Telecosmic Power. 1977. 8.95 (ISBN 0-13-938993-8, Reward); pap. 3.95 (ISBN 0-13-938928-8). P-H.
Norvell, Anthony. Mind Cosmology. 1971. 10.95 (ISBN 0-13-583260-8, Parker). P-H.
--Money Magnetism: How to Grow Rich Beyond Your Wildest Dreams. 1974. 10.95 (ISBN 0-13-600338-9, Parker). P-H.
Notestein, W. A History of Witchcraft in England. 75.00 (ISBN 0-87968-448-8). Gordon Pr.
Novell, Anthony. How to Control Your Destiny. 1971. pap. 3.00 (ISBN 0-87980-055-0). Wilshire.
The Occult Technology of Power. 3rd ed. (Ruling Class Expose Ser.). 1978. 8.95 (ISBN 0-686-01314-X). Alpine Ent.
Occultism Applied to Daily Life: Course XIV, Lessons 141-50. (Illus.). 1976. pap. 7.95 (ISBN 0-87887-354-6). Church of Light.
O'Connor, Del, ed. Aries Press Journal: The New Age Anthology. (Illus.). 1980. pap. 3.00 quarterly (ISBN 0-933646-14-3); annual subscription 10.00 (ISBN 0-686-77568-6). Aries Pr.
O'Donnell, Elliott. Strange Disappearances. 1972. 7.95 (ISBN 0-8216-0155-5). Univ Bks.
Oesterreich, T. K. Obsession & Possession. 1935. 11.00 (ISBN 0-685-00906-8). Wehman.
Ophiel. Art & Practice of Astral Projection. pap. 4.95 (ISBN 0-87728-246-3). Weiser.
--Art & Practice of Getting Material Things Through Creative Visualization. pap. 5.95 (ISBN 0-87728-279-X). Weiser.
--Art & Practice of the Occult. pap. 4.50 (ISBN 0-87728-328-1). Weiser.
Osborn, Arthur W. Meaning of Personal Existence, in the Light of Paranormal Phenomena, Reincarnation & Mystical Experience. LC 67-8034. 1967. 3.95 (ISBN 0-8356-0417-9, Quest). Theos Pub Hse.
Oshawa, George. You Are All Sanpaku. 4.95 (ISBN 0-8216-0164-4). Univ Bks.
Ouspensky, P. D. New Model of the Universe. 1934. 8.95 (ISBN 0-394-43819-1). Knopf.
Panchadasi, Swami. Clairvoyance & Occult Powers. 7.00 (ISBN 0-911662-35-9). Yoga.
Pandit, M. P. Occult Lines Behind Life. LC 79-63488. 1979. pap. 3.95 (ISBN 0-89744-001-3). Auromere.
Papus. What Is Occultism? 104p. 1981. pap. 4.00 (ISBN 0-89540-073-1, SB-073). Sun Pub.
Patterson, Doris T. & Shelley, Violet M. Be Your Own Psychic. 1975. pap. 2.95 (ISBN 0-87604-079-2). ARE Pr.
Pauwels, Louis & Bergier, Jacques. The Morning of the Magicians. LC 77-22874. 1977. pap. 4.95 (ISBN 0-8128-2260-9). Stein & Day.
Percival, Harold W. Democracy Is Self-Government. LC 52-30629. 1952. 3.95 (ISBN 0-911650-05-9). Word Foun.
--Thinking & Destiny. LC 47-1811. 1978. 15.95 (ISBN 0-911650-01-6); deluxe ed. 18.95 in 2 vols. (ISBN 0-911650-02-4); pap. 8.95 (ISBN 0-911650-06-7). Word Foun.
Pernety, Antoine-Joseph. An Alchemical Treatise on the Great Art. Blitz, Edouard, ed. 255p. 1973. Repr. of 1898 ed. 12.50 (ISBN 0-87728-237-4). Weiser.
Petrie, Sidney & Stone, Robert B. Hypno-Cybernetics: Helping Yourself to a Rich New Life. 224p. 1973. 12.95 (ISBN 0-13-448530-0, Parker). P-H.
Petty, George R. & Gibson, William M. Project Occult: The Ordered Computer Collation of Unprepared Literary Text. LC 75-114767. 124p. 1970. 10.00x (ISBN 0-8147-0477-8). NYU Pr.
Phillips, Jill. Occult Bibliography. 1975. lib. bdg. 69.95 (ISBN 0-8490-0748-8). Gordon Pr.
Phillips, McCandlish. The Bible, the Supernatural & the Jews. LC 77-92532. 1970. pap. 6.95 (ISBN 0-87123-036-4, 210036). Bethany Hse.
Phylos The Tibetan. A Dweller on Two Planets. (Illus.). 450p. Date not set. pap. cancelled (ISBN 0-8334-1753-3). Steinerbks.
Pike, Diane K. & Lorrance, Arleen. Channeling Love Energy. rev ed. LC 75-42074. 88p. 1976. pap. 3.00 (ISBN 0-916192-02-4). L P Pubns.
Playfair, Guy L. The Indefinite Boundary. LC 76-28051. 1977. 8.95 (ISBN 0-312-41195-2). St Martin.
Popoff, Irmis B. The Enneagrama of the Man of Unity. (Illus.). 1978. pap. 4.50 (ISBN 0-87728-399-0). Weiser.
Pritchard. Using the Magnetic Forces of Your Mind. pap. 3.00 (ISBN 0-685-27818-2). Borden.
Puryear, Herbert B. Sex & the Spiritual Path. 225p. (Orig.). 1980. pap. 5.95 (ISBN 0-87604-129-2). ARE Pr.
Queen Of The Romanies. Gipsy-Witch Fortune Teller: Tea Leaves, Coffee Grounds, Cards, Etc. 1.00 (ISBN 0-685-02614-0, 00545235). Stein Pub.
Queenborough, Lady. Occult Theocracy, 2 vols. 300.00 (ISBN 0-8490-0751-8). Gordon Pr.
Rajneesh, Bhagwan Sri. Dimensions Beyond the Known. (Orig.). 1979. pap. 6.95 (ISBN 0-914794-35-3). Wisdom Garden.
Ramacharaka, Yogi. Advanced Course in Yogi Philosophy. 7.00 (ISBN 0-911662-02-2). Yoga.
Rampa, T. Lobsang. Beyond the Tenth. pap. 2.95 (ISBN 0-685-22168-7). Weiser.
--Candlelight. 174p. (Orig.). 1974. pap. 2.95 (ISBN 0-685-50987-7). Weiser.
--The Thirteenth Candle. pap. 2.95 (ISBN 0-685-27227-3). Weiser.
Randall, Edith L. & Campbell, Florence. Sacred Symbols of the Ancients. (Illus.). 1970. pap. 11.95 (ISBN 0-912504-00-5). Sym & Sign.
Randi, James. Flim-Flam. (Illus.). 1980. 12.95 (ISBN 0-690-01877-0). Har-Row.
Redgrove, H. Stanley. Bygone Beliefs. (An Excursion into the Occult and Alchemical Nature of Man). 287p. 1981. pap. 10.00 (ISBN 0-89540-078-2, SB-078). Sun Pub.
Redgrove, Stanley. Magic & Mysticism. pap. 2.95 (ISBN 0-8065-0301-7). Citadel Pr.
Regardie, Israel. A Garden of Pomegranates. 1978. pap. 4.95x (ISBN 0-87542-690-5). Llewellyn Pubns.
Regush, Nicholas M. Human Aura. 1977. pap. 1.95 (ISBN 0-425-04321-5, Medallion). Berkley Pub.
Rene, E. Hands & How to Read Them. 1.00 (ISBN 0-685-02618-3, 00545272). Stein Pub.
Richford, F. G. Common Sense Occultism. 69.95 (ISBN 0-87968-911-0). Gordon Pr.
Riffaterre, Hermine & Plottel, Jeanine P., eds. The Occult in Language & Literature. LC 77-18630. (New York Literary Forum Ser.). (Illus., Orig.). 1979. pap. 12.50 (ISBN 0-931196-03-5). NY Lit Forum.
Rogo, D. Scott. Parapsychology: A Century of Inquiry. LC 74-22890. 320p. 1975. 12.50 (ISBN 0-8008-6236-8). Taplinger.
Rosellemar, Kenneth. How to Master the Art of Spiritual Intercourse. (The Society of Psychic Research Library). (Illus.). 1981. 45.75 (ISBN 0-89920-025-7). Am Inst Psych.
Rudhyar, Dane. The Astrological Houses: The Spectrum of Individual Experience. LC 74-180105. pap. 4.95 (ISBN 0-385-03827-5). Doubleday.
--Occult Preparations for a New Age. LC 74-19054. 266p. (Orig.). 1975. pap. 5.50 (ISBN 0-8356-0460-8, Quest). Theos Pub Hse.
Rush, John A. Witchcraft & Sorcery: An Anthropological Perspective of the Occult. (Illus.). 176p. 1974. 14.75 (ISBN 0-398-02981-4); pap. 11.25 (ISBN 0-398-03019-7). C C Thomas.
Sana'I, Hakim A. Enclosed Garden of the Truth. Stephenson, J., ed. & pref. by. LC 71-16555. 1968. Repr. 12.50 (ISBN 0-87728-084-3). Weiser.
Saraydarian, Haroutiun. Cosmos in Man. 1974. 12.00 (ISBN 0-911794-31-X); pap. 10.00 (ISBN 0-911794-32-8). Aqua Educ.
Savoy, Gene. Project X. The Search for the Secrets of Immortality. LC 76-44670. (Illus.). 279p. 1977. text ed. 35.00 (ISBN 0-672-52181-4). Intl Comm Christ.
Sawyer, Michael E., compiled by. A Bibliographical Index of Five English Mystics. LC 73-110788. (Bibliographia Tripotamopolitana: No. 10). 1978. 10.00 (ISBN 0-931222-09-5). C E Barbour.
Schmidt, K. O. Applied Cybernetics. Muller, Leone H., tr. from Ger. LC 73-77609. 1973. 5.95 (ISBN 0-87707-124-1); pap. 3.00, (new. ed.) (ISBN 0-685-32271-8). CSA Pr.
Schulman, Martin. Karmic Relationships. 1981. pap. 6.951311 (ISBN 0-686-69318-3). Weiser.
Schwaller De Lubicz, R. A. The Sacred Science: The King of Pharaonic Theocracy. Vandenbroeck, A. & Vandenbroeck, G., trs. (Illus.). 1981. cloth 12.95 (ISBN 0-89281-007-6). Inner Tradit.
Scott, Cyril. Music: Its Secret Influence Throughout the Ages. LC 79-16380. 208p. 1973. pap. 4.95 (ISBN 0-87728-336-2). Weiser.
Scott, Walter. Letters on Demonology & Witchcraft. 75.00 (ISBN 0-87968-180-2). Gordon Pr.
Segno, A. Victor. Thought Vibrations. LC 80-23853. 208p. 1980. Repr. of 1973 ed. lib. bdg. 10.95x (ISBN 0-89370-625-6). Borgo Pr.
Sepharial. A Manual of Occultism. LC 80-53345. 356p. 1980. Repr. of 1979 ed. lib. bdg. 11.95x (ISBN 0-89370-646-9). Borgo Pr.
--A Manual of Occultism. LC 79-15179. 1979. pap. 4.95 (ISBN 0-87877-046-1). Newcastle Pub.
Shearman, Hugh. Approach to the Occult. 1.75 (ISBN 0-8356-7026-0). Theos Pub Hse.
Shepard, Leslie. Encyclopedia of Occultism & Parapsychology: A Compedium of Information on the Occult Sciences, Magic, Demonology, Superstitions, Spiritism, Mysticism, Metaphysics, Psychical Science & Parapsychology. 2nd ed. (Illus.). 400p. 1981. 125.00 (ISBN 0-8103-0196-2). Gale.
Shepard, Leslie, ed. Encyclopedia of Occultism & Parapsychology: A Compendium of Information on the Occult Sciences, Magic, Demonology, Superstition, Spiritism, Mysticism, Metaphysics, Psychical Science & Parapsychology, 2 vols. LC 77-92. (Illus., Supplemented by Occultism update). 1978. Set. 90.00 (ISBN 0-8103-0185-7); pap. 45.00 occultism update: a periodical supplement (4 issues subscription) (ISBN 0-685-79636-1). Gale.
Shepard, Leslie A. Encyclopedia of Occultism & Parapsychlogy: Vols. 1 & 2. 1980. pap. 19.90 boxed set (ISBN 0-380-50112-0). Vol. 1 (ISBN 0-380-48835-3, 48835). Vol. 2 (ISBN 0-380-48975-9, 48975). Avon.
Shirley, Ralph. Occultists & Mystics of All Ages. new ed. 1972. 7.95 (ISBN 0-8216-0165-2). Univ Bks.
Siegler, Bobbie. The Psychic Cookbook. LC 79-54187. 1980. pap. cancelled (ISBN 0-89087-258-9). Celestial Arts.
Silberer, Herbert. The Hidden Symbolism of Alchemy & the Occult Arts. Jelliffe, Smith E., tr. Orig. Title: Problems of Mysticism & Its Symbolism. 1971. pap. 5.00 (ISBN 0-486-20972-5). Dover.
Simon. Necronomicon. 288p. 1979. pap. 2.75 (ISBN 0-380-75192-5, 75192). Avon.
Skinner, J. Ralston. The Source of Measures: Key to the Hebrew Egyptian Mystery. LC 72-84846. (Secret Doctrine Reference Ser). (Illus.). 412p. 1972. Repr. of 1894 ed. 18.50 (ISBN 0-913510-00-9). Wizards.
Slater, Herman, ed. The Magickal Formulary. LC 81-90068. 112p. 1981. 29.25 (ISBN 0-939708-00-0); pap. 10.95 (ISBN 0-939708-01-9). Magickal Childe.
Smith, Alson. The Psychic Source Book. 6.50 (ISBN 0-685-32918-6). Assoc Bk.
Smith, Susy. Do We Live After Death? 192p. (Orig.). 1974. pap. 1.50 (ISBN 0-532-15134-8). Woodhill.
Somerlott, Robert. Here, Mr. Splitfoot: An Informal Exploration into Modern Occultism. LC 75-132185. (Illus.). 1971. 7.50 (ISBN 0-670-36876-8). Viking Pr.
Spangler, David. Revelation: The Birth of a New Age. 256p. 1979. pap. 5.95 (ISBN 0-936878-00-2). Lorian Pr.
Speare, Grace & Byars, Robert. Everything Talks to Me. (Orig.). 1979. pap. 2.25 (ISBN 0-440-01925-7). Dell.
Spears, Stanley. Mysteries of Eternal Life. 3rd ed. 1970. pap. 2.95 (ISBN 0-87516-095-6). De Vorss.
Spence, Lewis. Encyclopaedia of Occultism. (Illus.). 440p. 1974. pap. 8.95 (ISBN 0-8065-0427-7). Citadel Pr.
--Occult Sciences in Atlantis. LC 70-16446. 1970. pap. 5.00 (ISBN 0-87728-136-X). Weiser.
Steadman, Alice. Who's the Matter with Me? (Illus.). 1975. Repr. 4.95 (ISBN 0-917200-00-4). ESPress.
Stearn, Jess. The Search for a Soul: Taylor Caldwell's Psychic Lives. LC 72-84945. 336p. 1973. 7.95 (ISBN 0-385-02563-7). Doubleday.
Stebbing, L. Dictionary of the Occult Sciences. 1973. lib. bdg. 69.95 (ISBN 0-87968-449-6). Krishna Pr.
Steiger, Brad. Encounters of the Angelic Kind. 112p. (Orig.). 1979. pap. 4.50 (ISBN 0-89861-021-4). Esoteric Pubns.
--In My Soul I Am Free. 1968. pap. 2.50 (ISBN 0-914766-11-2). IWP Pub.
--Revelation: The Divine Fire. 1981. pap. 2.50 (ISBN 0-425-04615-X). Berkley Pub.
--Unknown Powers. 1981. pap. 2.50 (ISBN 0-425-05005-X). Berkley Pub.
Steiger, Francie. Reflections from an Angel's Eye. LC 79-50367. 4.50 (ISBN 0-89861-017-6). Esoteric Pubns.
Steinbach, Marten. Medical Palmistry: Health & Character in the Hand. 1975. 8.95 (ISBN 0-8216-0222-5). Univ Bks.
Steiner, Rudolf. Initiation, Eternity & the Passing Moment. Church, Gilbert, ed. 157p. 1981. 10.95 (ISBN 0-910142-84-X). Anthroposophic.
--The Occult Movement in the 19th Century. 190p. 1973. 12.50 (ISBN 0-85440-280-2). Anthroposophic.
--Outline of Occult Science. 352p. 1972. 9.95 (ISBN 0-910142-26-2); pap. 6.95 (ISBN 0-910142-75-0). Anthroposophic.
Stewart, Louis. Life Forces: A Contemporary Guide to the Cult & Occult. 1980. 20.00 (ISBN 0-8362-7903-4); pap. 9.95 (ISBN 0-8362-7906-9). Andrews & McMeel.
Stoessel, Fredric. Metaphysical Magnetism: Magic Force for Automatic Riches. 1976. 8.95 (ISBN 0-13-578567-7, Parker). P-H.
Storms, Godfried. Anglo-Saxon Magic. 75.00 (ISBN 0-87968-074-1). Gordon Pr.
Sturzaker, James. The Twelve Rays. 1977. pap. 1.50 (ISBN 0-87728-319-2). Weiser.
Summers, Montague. Witchcraft & Black Magic. LC 70-174114. (Illus.). 1971. Repr. of 1916 ed. 26.00 (ISBN 0-685-02995-6). Gale.
Summers, Montague, ed. The Supernatural Omnibus. 622p. 1980. Repr. of 1934 ed. lib. bdg. 25.00 (ISBN 0-89760-818-6). Telegraph Bks.
Swift, Edgar J. Jungle of the Mind. facsimile ed. LC 70-134140. (Essay Index Reprint Ser). Repr. of 1931 ed. 19.50 (ISBN 0-8369-2334-0). Arno.
Tabori, Paul & Raphael, Phyllis. Beyond the Senses: A Report on Psychical Research in the Sixties. LC 70-185482. (The Frontiers of the Unknown Ser.). 226p. 1972. 6.50 (ISBN 0-8008-0735-9). Taplinger.
Talbott, David N. The Saturn Myth. LC 76-51986. (Illus.). 1980. 15.95 (ISBN 0-385-11376-5). Doubleday.
Taylor, Ruth Mattson. Witness from Beyond. LC 79-52116. 152p. (Orig.). 1980. pap. 5.95 (ISBN 0-9602884-0-6, Pub by Forward Bk). Chicago Review.
Tester, M. H. Healing Touch. LC 70-119621. (Illus.). 1970. 5.95 (ISBN 0-8008-3818-1). Taplinger.
Thomas, Eugene E. Brotherhood of Mt. Shasta. 307p. 1981. pap. 10.00 (ISBN 0-89540-067-7). Sun Pub.
Three Initiates. Kybalion: Hermetic Philosphy. 1908. 7.00 (ISBN 0-911662-25-1). Yoga.
Thurston, Howard. Thurston's Card Tricks. 1.00 (ISBN 0-685-02625-6, 00545351). Stein Pub.
Tiryakian, Edward A., ed. On the Margin of the Visible: Sociology, the Esoteric, & the Occult. 364p. 1974. 11.50 (ISBN 0-471-87435-3, Pub. by Wiley). Krieger.
Toben, Bob, et al. Space-Time & Beyond: Toward an Explanation of the Unexplainable. 192p. 1975. pap. 8.95 (ISBN 0-525-47399-8). Dutton.
Todd, Helen. Psychic Powers. (Theosophical Manual: No. 11). 1975. pap. 2.00 (ISBN 0-7229-5044-6, 913004-38). Point Loma Pub.
Townley, John. The New Age Career Cycles. (Illus.). 192p. 1980. pap. 7.95 (ISBN 0-89281-006-8, Destiny Books). Inner Tradit.
Tralins, Robert. Visitantes Del Mas Alla. new ed. Rios, Juan A., tr. from Eng. (Compadre Collection Ser). Orig. Title: Weird People of the Unknown. 160p. (Span.). 1974. pap. 0.75 (ISBN 0-88473-706-3). Fiesta Pub.
Turizziani. Manu Genesis Speaks. 12.50 (ISBN 0-685-02592-6). Borden.
Twigg, Ena & Brod, Ruth H. Ena Twigg: Medium. LC 72-1970. 320p. 1973. pap. 1.50 (ISBN 0-532-15107-0). Woodhill.
Twitchell, Paul. Eckankar Dictionary. 1973. 6.95 (ISBN 0-914766-05-8). IWP Pub.
--Eckankar: La Cle Des Mondes Secrets. 1969. pap. 4.00 (ISBN 0-914766-27-9). IWP Pub.
--Eckankar: The Key to Secret Worlds. 1969. pap. 2.00 (ISBN 0-914766-06-6). IWP Pub.
--La Flute De Dieu. 1971. pap. 4.00 (ISBN 0-914766-28-7). IWP Pub.
--La Griffe De Tigre. 1967. pap. 4.00 (ISBN 0-914766-29-5). IWP Pub.
--Herbs, the Magic Healers. 1971. pap. 2.95 (ISBN 0-914766-10-4). IWP Pub.
Unger. Beyond the Crystal Ball. 1973. pap. 2.95 (ISBN 0-8024-0508-8). Moody.
Van Der Leeuw, J. J. Fire of Creation. rev. ed. LC 75-26823. 168p. 1976. pap. 2.95 (ISBN 0-8356-0470-5, Quest). Theos Pub Hse.
Vasarely, Victor. Victor Vasarely: Planetary Folklore. LC 73-86480. (Illus.). 1973. 19.95 (ISBN 0-8212-0584-6, 900605). NYGS.
Vassara. The Handbook of Supernatural Powers. 1977. pap. 3.95 (ISBN 0-686-10934-1). Virdon Assoc.

Verner, Alexander & Brahma, Swami. Five Booklets by Verner & Brahma, 5 bks. Incl. Bk. 1. Medical Hypnotism & Suggestion (ISBN 0-911662-14-6); Bk. 2. Psychometry (Reading by Vibration (ISBN 0-911662-15-4); Bk. 3. How to Converse with Spirit Friends (ISBN 0-911662-16-2); Bk. 4. Table Rapping & Automatic Writing (ISBN 0-911662-28-6); Bk. 5. How to Know Your Future (ISBN 0-911662-29-4). Set. pap. 3.00 (ISBN 0-685-24372-9). Yoga.
Von Reichenbach, Karl. The Mysterious Odic Force. Korth, Leslie O., tr. from Ger. Orig. Title: Magnetic-Odic Letters. 1977. pap. 1.95 (ISBN 0-685-79906-9). Weiser.
Wagner, Henry & Wagner, Mrs. Henry. Treasure Chest of Wisdom, Jewels of Thought. 1967. 6.00 (ISBN 0-911584-02-1). Green Dolphin.
Waite, Arthur E. The Alchemical Writings of Edward Kelly. LC 73-76949. 153p. 1973. Repr. of 1893 ed. 9.50 (ISBN 0-87728-137-8). Weiser.
--Azoth; or, the Star in the East. 1973. 10.00 (ISBN 0-8216-0201-2). Univ Bks.
--The Book of Black Magic & of Pacts. LC 72-77557. 326p. 1972. pap. 5.95 (ISBN 0-87728-207-2). Weiser.
--Brotherhood of the Rosy Cross. 10.00 (ISBN 0-8216-0169-5). Univ Bks.
--The Hermetic Museum, Restored & Enlarged, 2 vols. LC 73-76951. 1973. Repr. of 1893 ed. Set. 35.00 (ISBN 0-87728-221-8). Weiser.
--Occult Sciences. 7.95 (ISBN 0-8216-0214-4). Univ Bks.
--The Turba Philosophorum. LC 73-76950. 211p. 1973. Repr. of 1896 ed. 9.50 (ISBN 0-87728-139-4). Weiser.
Waldo-Schwartz, Paul. Art & the Occult. LC 75-7915. (Illus.). 192p. 1975. 17.50 (ISBN 0-8076-0784-3); pap. 7.95 (ISBN 0-8076-0785-1). Braziller.
Walker, Benjamin. The Encyclopedia of the Occult, the Esoteric, & the Supernatural. LC 79-42238. 335p. 1980. pap. 7.95 (ISBN 0-8128-6051-9). Stein & Day.
--Man & the Beasts Within. LC 76-42238. 1977. 35.00x (ISBN 0-8128-1900-4). Stein & Day.
Walker, Lynn. Supernatural Power & the Occult. 1977. pap. 3.00 (ISBN 0-686-23231-3). Firm Foun Pub.
Watson, Jane W. & Chaneles, Sol. The Golden Book of the Mysterious. (Illus.). (gr. 7 up). 1976. PLB 12.23 (ISBN 0-307-67862-8, Golden Pr). Western Pub.
Webb, James. The Occult Underground. LC 73-22458. (Illus.). 325p. 1974. 19.95 (ISBN 0-912050-46-2, Library Pr). Open Court.
Wedeck, Harry E. Treasury of Witchcraft. 1966. pap. 3.95 (ISBN 0-8065-0038-7, 214). Citadel Pr.
Weed, Joseph J. Psychic Energy: How to Change Your Desires into Realities. Orig. Title: Psychic Energy: Your Key to Transmute Desires into Realities. 1970. 9.95 (ISBN 0-13-732214-3, Reward); pap. 3.95 (ISBN 0-13-732784-6). P-H.
Weiner, H. Nine & a Half Mystics: The Kabbala Today. 1971. pap. 2.95 (ISBN 0-02-068140-2, Collier). Macmillan.
Weisman, Alan. We, Immortals: The Dick Sutphen Past Life Seminars. LC 77-71545. 1977. 3.95 (ISBN 0-911842-17-9). Valley Sun.
Weldon, John & Wilson, Clifford. Occult Shock & Psychic Forces. LC 80-81458. 496p. 1980. pap. 7.95 (ISBN 0-89051-065-2). CLP Pubs.
White, John & Krippner, Stanley, eds. Future Science: Life Energies & the Physics of Paranormal Phenomena. LC 76-23808. 600p. 1977. pap. 4.50 (ISBN 0-385-11203-3, Anch). Doubleday.
White, Nelson H. Magick & the Law, or, How to Organize & Operate Your Own Occult Church, Coven or Lodge. rev. ed. LC 76-7197. (Magick & the Law Ser.: Vol. 1). 48p. 1976. pap. 9.00 (ISBN 0-939856-02-6, Magick Circle). Tech Group.
White, Stewart E. Betty Book: Excursions into the World of Other Consciousness. 1977. pap. 5.50 (ISBN 0-525-47447-1). Dutton.
--Unobstructed Universe. 1959. pap. 4.50 (ISBN 0-525-47042-5). Dutton.
Whitman, Roback C. The Mysteries of Astrology & the Wonders of Magic. (Library of the Occult Bk). (Illus.). 121p. 1981. 59.85 (ISBN 0-89920-028-1). Am Inst Psych.
Wickland, Carl A. Thirty Years Among the Dead. LC 80-19669. 390p. 1980. Repr. of 1974 ed. lib. bdg. 12.95x (ISBN 0-89370-625-6). Borgo Pr.
--Thirty Years Among the Dead. 390p. 1974. pap. 5.95 (ISBN 0-87877-025-9, P-25). Newcastle Pub.
Wilcock, John. An Occult Guide to South America. LC 76-15933. (Illus.). 1976. 10.00 (ISBN 0-685-70124-7); pap. 5.95 (ISBN 0-685-70125-5). Stein & Day.
Wilcox, Laird M. Directory of the Occult & Paranormal. 1980. 9.95 (ISBN 0-933592-10-8). Edit Res Serv.
Wilcox, Laird M., compiled by. Bibliography on Astrology, Mysticism, & the Occult. 1981. pap. text ed. 9.95 (ISBN 0-933592-25-6). Edit Res Serv.
--Directory of the Occult & Paranormal. (Orig.). 1981. pap. text ed. 12.95 (ISBN 0-933592-18-3). Edit Res Serv.
Williams, Joseph J. Psychic Phenomena of Jamaica. LC 78-32183. 1979. Repr. of 1934 ed. lib. bdg. 19.75x (ISBN 0-8371-5669-6, WPP&). Greenwood.
Willis, Charles D. End of Days: Nineteen Seventy-One to Two Thousand One: an Eschatological Study. (Illus.). 1972. 7.50 (ISBN 0-682-47385-5). Exposition.
Wilson, Clifford. The Chariots Still Crash. 1976. pap. 1.50 (ISBN 0-451-06836-X, W6836, Sig). NAL.
--Crash Go the Chariots. rev. ed. LC 76-20176. 1976. pap. 2.95 (ISBN 0-89051-022-9, Master Bks). CLP Pubs.
Wilson, Clifford & Weldon, John. Occult Shock & Psychic Forces. LC 80-81458. 496p. (Orig.). 1980. pap. text ed. 7.95 - (ISBN 0-89051-065-2). Master Bks.
Wilson, Colin. Mysteries. 1980. pap. 8.95 (ISBN 0-686-65859-0). Putnam.
--Mysteries. LC 78-20286. 1978. 15.00 (ISBN 0-399-12246-X). Putnam.
--The Occult. 608p. 1973. pap. 5.95 (ISBN 0-394-71813-5, Vin). Random.
Wilson, Colin, ed. Dark Dimensions: A Celebration of the Occult. LC 78-56249. 1978. 7.95 (ISBN 0-89696-001-3). Everest Hse.
Wilson, Robert A. Cosmic Trigger: Final Secret of the Illuminati. LC 77-89429. 1977. pap. 4.95 (ISBN 0-915904-29-2). And-or Pr.
--The Illuminati Papers. LC 80-16641. 160p. 1980. pap. 7.95 (ISBN 0-915904-52-7). And-Or Pr.
Wingo, E. Otha. Letters on Huna: The Fundamentals of Huna Psychology. 1980. pap. write for info. (ISBN 0-910764-00-X). Huna Res Inc.
Winn, Ralph. Hypnotism Made Easy. pap. 3.00 (ISBN 0-87980-078-X). Wilshire.
Winston, Shirley R. Music As the Bridge: Based on the Edgar Cayce Readings. 68p. (Orig.). 1972. pap. 2.95 (ISBN 0-87604-058-X). ARE Pr.
Witch Hunting, Magic & the New Philosophy: An Introduction to Debates of the Scientific Revolution, 1450-1750. (Harvester Studies in Philosophy: No. 14). (Illus.). 283p. 1981. 42.50 (ISBN 0-391-01806-X); pap. 16.50 (ISBN 0-391-01808-6). Humanities.
Wood, Ernest. Questions on Occultism. Adzei, Kwaku, ed. LC 78-8791. (Orig.). 1978. pap. 3.75 (ISBN 0-8356-0517-5, Quest). Theos Pub Hse.
Wright, J. Stafford. La Mente y lo Desconocido. Gilchrist, James S., tr. from Eng. LC 76-9906. 228p. (Orig., Span.). 1976. pap. 3.50 (ISBN 0-89922-070-3). Edit Caribe.
Wynkoop, Mildred B. The Occult & the Supernatural. 1976. pap. 1.50 (ISBN 0-8341-0420-2). Beacon Hill.
Zacharias, Gerhard. The Satanic Cult. Trollope, Christine, tr. (Illus.). 208p. (Ger.). 1980. 22.50x (ISBN 0-04-133008-0). Allen Unwin.
Zeylmans, F. W. Epos-the Secret World. 1979. pap. 2.25 (ISBN 0-916786-43-9). St George Bk Serv.
Zolar. Everything You Want to Know About Black Magic, Metaphysical Astrology, Mediumship, Crystal Gazing, Revelations by Zolar. LC 72-3136. (Zolar's Everything You Want to Know About Ser). 224p. 1972. pap. 1.50 (ISBN 0-668-02658-8). Arco.
--Everything You Want to Know About Dreams, Lucky Numbers, Omens, Oils & Incense. LC 70-188859. (Zolar's Everything You Want to Know Ser.). 226p. 1972. pap. 1.95 (ISBN 0-668-02600-6). Arco.
--Everything You Want to Know About Fortune Telling with Cards, Karma System, Gypsy System, Professional System, Palmistry. LC 72-3138. (Zolar's Everything You Want to Know Ser.). 224p. 1972. pap. 0.95 (ISBN 0-668-02659-6). Arco.
Zoller, Robert E. Predictive Techniques: The Astrological Methods of the Sages. (Illus.). 456p. 1981. pap. 8.95 (ISBN 0-89281-035-1). Inner Tradit.

OCCULT SCIENCES–BIOGRAPHY

Allison, Dorothy & Jacobson, Scott. Dorothy Allison: A Psychic Story. (Orig.). 1980. pap. 2.50 (ISBN 0-515-05304-X). Jove Pubns.
Gagliardo, Pat. Why Me? Tales of a Reluctant Psychic. 1981. 5.95 (ISBN 0-8062-1745-6). Carlton.
Webb, Richard. These Came Back. (Orig.). 1976. pap. 1.75 (ISBN 0-89129-039-7). Jove Pubns.
Wilson, Colin. Strange Powers. 1976. pap. 1.95 (ISBN 0-394-71947-6, Vin). Random.

OCCULT SCIENCES–HISTORY

Aurigemma, Luigi. Le Signe Zodiacal Du Scorpion Dans les Traditions Occidentales De L'antiquite Grego-Latine a la Renaissance. (Civilisations et Societes.: No. 54). (Illus.). 1976. text ed. 47.05x (ISBN 90-2797-573-6). Mouton.
Copenhaver, Brian. Symphorien Champier & the Reception of the Occultist Tradition in Renaissance France. 1978. text ed. 51.00x (ISBN 90-279-7647-3). Mouton.
Dingwall, E. J. Ghosts & Spirits in the Ancient World. 59.95 (ISBN 0-8490-0233-8). Gordon Pr.
Dodds, Eric R. The Greeks & the Irrational. (Sather Classical Lectures: No. 25). 1951. pap. 4.95 (ISBN 0-520-00327-6, CAL74). U of Cal Pr.
Garrison, Omar V., ed. Lost Gems of Secret Knowledge. 304p. 1973. 7.95 (ISBN 0-8216-0205-5). Univ Bks.
Hall, Manly P. First Principles of Philosophy. 7.50 (ISBN 0-89314-508-4). Philos Res.
--Lectures on Ancient Philosophy. 10.75 (ISBN 0-89314-512-2). Philos Res.
--Man, the Grand Symbol of the Mysteries. 12.50 (ISBN 0-89314-513-0); pap. 8.95 (ISBN 0-89314-389-8). Philos Res.
--Phoenix. 13.90 (ISBN 0-89314-517-3). Philos Res.
Howe, Ellic. The Magicians of the Golden Dawn. (Illus.). 1978. pap. 5.95 (ISBN 0-87728-369-9). Weiser.
Hoyt, Olga. Demons, Devils & Djinn. LC 73-6190. (Illus.). 160p. (gr. 7 up). 1973. 8.95 (ISBN 0-200-00110-8, AbS-J). Har-Row.
Meier, Gerhard. Die Assyrische Beschwoerungssamlung Maqlu. LC 78-72751. (Ancient Mesopotamian Texts & Studies). Repr. of 1937 ed. 22.50 (ISBN 0-404-18194-5). AMS Pr.
Schure, Edouard. From Sphinx to Christ: An Occult History. LC 70-130818. 288p. 1981. 13.00x (ISBN 0-8334-0705-8, Steinerbooks); pap. 7.50 (ISBN 0-8334-1705-3). Multimedia.
Shumaker, Wayne. The Occult Sciences in the Renaissance: A Study in Intellectual Patterns. LC 70-153552. (Illus.). 1972. 29.50x (ISBN 0-520-02021-9); pap. 6.95 (ISBN 0-520-03840-1). U of Cal Pr.
Yates, Frances A. Giordano Bruno & the Hermetic Tradition. LC 64-10094. 1969. pap. 2.45 (ISBN 0-394-70546-7, V546, Vin). Random.
Zeylmans, F. The Reality in Which We Live: Occult Movements Through the Ages. 1973. lib. bdg. 59.95 (ISBN 0-87968-569-7). Krishna Pr.

OCCULTISM

see Occult Sciences; Occultism in Literature

OCCULTISM IN LITERATURE

see also Mysticism in Literature; Supernatural in Literature

Friedman, Susan S. Psyche Reborn: The Emergence of H. D. LC 80-8373. (Illus.). 416p. 1981. 22.50x (ISBN 0-253-37826-5). Ind U Pr.
Garrison, Omar V., ed. Lost Gems of Secret Knowledge. 304p. 1973. 7.95 (ISBN 0-8216-0205-5). Univ Bks.
Reed, Robert R., Jr. Occult on the Tudor & Stuart Stage. 1965. 6.50 (ISBN 0-8158-0170-X). Chris Mass.
St. John Barclay, Glen. Anatomy of Horror: The Masters of Occult Fiction. LC 78-70899. 1979. 8.95 (ISBN 0-312-03408-3). St Martin.
Saurat, Denis. Literature & Occult Traditions. LC 68-759. (Studies in Comparative Literature, No. 35). 1969. Repr. of 1930 ed. lib. bdg. 33.95 (ISBN 0-8383-0617-9). Haskell.
--Literature & the Occult Tradition. Bolton, D., tr. LC 65-27133. 1930. Repr. 12.00 (ISBN 0-8046-0405-3). Kennikat.
Senior, John. Way Down & Out: The Occult in Symbolist Literature. LC 68-23326. (Illus.). 1968. Repr. of 1959 ed. lib. bdg. 15.00x (ISBN 0-8371-0218-9, SESL). Greenwood.
Sinnett, A. P. Tennyson an Occultist. LC 72-2102. (Studies in Tennyson, No. 27). 1972. Repr. of 1920 ed. lib. bdg. 46.95 (ISBN 0-8383-1485-6). Haskell.
Tuveson, Ernest L. The Avatars of Thrice Great Hermes: An Approach to Romanticism. LC 78-75206. 280p. 1981. 17.50 (ISBN 0-8387-2264-4). Bucknell U Pr.
Yates, Frances A. The Occult Philosophy in the Elizabethan Age. (Illus.). 1979. 20.00 (ISBN 0-7100-0320-X). Routledge & Kegan.

OCCUPANCY (INTERNATIONAL LAW)

Lindley, Mark F. Acquisition & Government of Backward Territory in International Law. LC 77-78770. Repr. of 1926 ed. 18.50x (ISBN 0-8371-1401-2, Pub. by Negro U Pr). Greenwood.

OCCUPATION, CHOICE OF

see Vocational Guidance

OCCUPATION, MILITARY

see Military Occupation

OCCUPATION CURRENCY

Petrov, Vladimir. Money & Conquest: Allied Occupation Currencies in World War II. LC 66-26685. (Studies in Historical & Political Science: Eighty-Fourth Series No. 2 (1967)). 1967. 18.00x (ISBN 0-8018-0530-9). Johns Hopkins.
Rundell, Walter, Jr. Black-Market Money: The Collapse of U. S. Military Currency Control in World War 2. LC 64-15879. 1964. 10.00 (ISBN 0-8071-0725-5). La State U Pr.

OCCUPATION TAX

see Business Tax

OCCUPATION THERAPY

see Occupational Therapy

OCCUPATIONAL ACCIDENTS

see Industrial Accidents

OCCUPATIONAL APTITUDE TESTS

see Employment Tests

OCCUPATIONAL ASPIRATIONS

see Vocational Interests

OCCUPATIONAL CRIMES

see White Collar Crimes

OCCUPATIONAL DISEASES

see also Arsenic Poisoning; Caisson-Disease; Fatigue; Industrial Toxicology; Lead-Poisoning; Lungs–Dust Diseases; Medicine, Industrial; Nystagmus; Skin–Diseases; Workmen's Compensation

Agran, Larry. Cancer Connection: And What We Can Do About It. 1977. 10.95 (ISBN 0-395-25178-8). HM.
Cooper, Cary L. & Payne, Roy. Current Concerns in Occupational Stress. LC 79-40641. (Wiley Ser. on Studies in Occupational Stress). 1980. 43.75 (ISBN 0-471-27624-3, Pub. by Wiley-Interscience). Wiley.
Daugaard, J. Symptoms & Signs in Occupational Diseases. 1979. 14.75 (ISBN 0-8151-2293-4). Year Bk Med.
Dollberg, Donald D. & Verstuyft, Allen W., eds. Analytical Techniques in Occupational Health Chemistry. LC 79-28460. (ACS Symposium Ser.: No. 120). 1980. 28.00 (ISBN 0-8412-0539-6). Am Chemical.
Frazier, Claude A. Occupational Asthma. 384p. 1980. text ed. 22.50 (ISBN 0-442-21687-4). Van Nos Reinhold.
Gellin, Gerald A. Occupational Dermatoses. 37p. 1972. pap. 1.00 (ISBN 0-89970-064-0, OP108). AMA.
Goldberg, Rosamond W. Occupational Diseases in Relation to Compensation & Health Insurance. LC 68-58581. (Columbia University. Studies in the Social Sciences: No. 345). Repr. of 1931 ed. 22.50 (ISBN 0-404-51345-X). AMS Pr.
Hueper, W. C. Occupational & Environmental Cancers of the Respiratory System. (Recent Results in Cancer Research: Vol. 3). (Illus.). 1966. 31.90 (ISBN 0-387-03642-3). Springer-Verlag.
Hunter, Donald. The Diseases of Occupations. 6th ed. 1978. pap. 90.00 (ISBN 0-316-38260-4). Little.
Iijima, Nobuku. Pollution Japan: Historical Chronology. 401p. 1980. 64.00 (ISBN 0-08-026242-2). Pergamon.
McCann, Michael. Artists Health Hazards Manual. rev ed. LC 78-70898. (Illus.). 1978. pap. 3.50 (ISBN 0-933032-00-5). FCA Bks.
McCready, Benjamin W. On the Influence of Trades, Professions & Occupations in the United States in the Production of Disease. LC 78-180583. (Medicine & Society in America). 144p. 1972. Repr. of 1943 ed. 12.00x (ISBN 0-405-03960-3). Arno.
Parkes, W. Raymond. Occupational Lung Disorders. 2nd ed. 1981. text ed. 159.95 (ISBN 0-407-33731-8). Butterworth.
Peterson, Jack E. Industrial Health. (Illus.). 1977. ref. ed. 26.95 (ISBN 0-13-459552-1). P-H.
Plunkett, E. R. Folk Name & Trade Diseases. LC 78-72537. (Illus.). 1978. text ed. 17.95 (ISBN 0-932684-00-9). Barrett Bk.
--Occupational Diseases: A Syllabus of Signs & Symptoms. 1977. text ed. 24.95 (ISBN 0-89185-128-3). Barrett Bk.
Proctor, Nick H. & Hughes, James P. Chemical Hazards of the Workplace. LC 78-57614. 1978. 34.75 (ISBN 0-397-50398-9, JBL-Med-Nursing). Har-Row.
Robinson, D. W., ed. Occupational Hearing Loss. (British Acoustical Society Special: Vol. 1). 1971. 44.00 (ISBN 0-12-590150-X). Acad Pr.
Schneiderman, Marvin & Peto, Richard, eds. Quantification of Occupational Cancer. LC 81-10218. (Banbury Reports: Vol. 9). 750p. 1981. 89.00x (ISBN 0-87969-208-1). Cold Spring Harbor.
Shaw, Charles R., ed. Prevention of Occupational Cancer. 256p. 1981. 72.95 (ISBN 0-8493-5625-3). CRC Pr.
Stellman, Jeanne M. & Daum, Susan M. Work Is Dangerous to Your Health: A Handbook of Health Hazards in the Workplace & What You Can Do About Them. LC 72-12386. 1973. pap. 4.95 (ISBN 0-394-71918-2). Pantheon.

Vainio, Harri, et al, eds. Occupational Cancer & Carcinogenesis. LC 80-21703. (Illus.). 422p. 1980. text ed. 49.50 (ISBN 0-89116-193-7). Hemisphere Pub.

Weill & Turner. Occupational Lung Diseases. (Lung Biology in Health & Diseases Ser.: Vol. 18). 608p. 1981. price not set (ISBN 0-8247-1362-1). Dekker.

OCCUPATIONAL HEALTH AND SAFETY

see Industrial Safety

OCCUPATIONAL MEDICINE

see Medicine, Industrial

OCCUPATIONAL MOBILITY

Arbeiter, Solomon, et al. Forty Million Americans in Career Transition: The Need for Information. 1978. pap. 4.50 (ISBN 0-87447-050-1, 237403). College Bd.

Balan, Jorge, et al. Men in a Developing Society: Geographic & Social Mobility in Monterrey, Mexico. LC 72-6282. (Latin American Monographs Ser.: No. 30). 404p. 1973. 15.00x (ISBN 0-292-75004-8). U of Tex Pr.

Berliner, Don. Want a Job? Get Some Experience: Want Experience? Get a Job. 1978. 12.95 (ISBN 0-8144-5474-7). Am Mgmt.

Blau, Peter M. & Duncan, Otis D. The American Occupational Structure. LC 78-50657. 1978. pap. text ed. 8.95 (ISBN 0-02-903670-4). Free Pr.

Broom, Leonard & Jones, F. Lancaster. Opportunity & Attainment in Australia. LC 76-14271. 1977. 12.50x (ISBN 0-8047-0927-0). Stanford U Pr.

Conk, Margo A. The United States Census & Labor Force Change: A History of Occupation Statistics, 1870-1940. Berkhofer, Edward, ed. (Studies in American History & Culture: No. 11). 1980. 28.95 (ISBN 0-8357-1078-5, Pub. by UMI Res Pr). Univ Microfilms.

DeJong, Peter. Patterns of Intergenerational Occupational Mobility of American Females. LC 76-24720. 1977. soft bdg. 9.00 (ISBN 0-88247-416-2). R & E Res Assoc.

Fabun, Don. Mobility: From There to Here. 1971. pap. text ed. 2.50x (ISBN 0-02-475380-7, 47538). Macmillan.

Griffen, Clyde & Griffen, Sally. Natives & Newcomers: The Ordering of Opportunity in Mid-Nineteenth-Century Poughkeepsie. (Studies in Urban History). 1977. 18.50x (ISBN 0-674-60325-7). Harvard U Pr.

Horlick, Allan S. Country Boys & Merchant Princes: The Social Control of Young Men in New York. LC 73-2887. 278p. 1975. 18.00 (ISBN 0-8387-1361-0). Bucknell U Pr.

Kaye, Beverly L. Up Is Not the Only Way: A Guide for Career Development Practitioners. (Illus.). 256p. 1982. text ed. 17.95 (ISBN 0-13-939173-8). P-H.

Krantz, David L. Radical Career Change: Life Beyond Work. LC 78-50720. 1978. 9.95 (ISBN 0-02-916760-4). Free Pr.

Leigh, D. An Analysis of the Determinants of Occupational Upgrading. LC 78-3343. (Inst. for Research on Poverty Monagraph Ser.). 1978. 16.00 (ISBN 0-12-442850-9). Acad Pr.

Liveseu, Herbert. Second Chance: How to Change Your Career in Mid-Life. 1979. pap. 2.25 (ISBN 0-451-08469-1, E8469, Sig). NAL.

Mannari, Hiroshi. The Japanese Business Leaders. LC 74-84827. (Illus.). xxiv, 291p. 1975. 18.50x (ISBN 0-86008-122-2, Pub. by Lotus Pr Japan). Intl Schol Bk Serv.

Osherson, Samuel D. Holding on or Letting Go: Men & Career Change at Midlife. LC 79-7849. 1980. 19.95 (ISBN 0-02-923480-8). Free Pr.

Pomer, Marshall. Intergenerational Occupational Mobility in the United States: A Segmentation Perspective. LC 79-94804. (Social Sciences Monographs: No. 66). 1981. pap. write for info. (ISBN 0-8130-0674-0). U Presses Fla.

--Intergenerational Occupational Mobility in the United States. LC 80-20626. (University of Florida Social Science Monograph: No. 66). write for info. (ISBN 0-8130-0674-0). U Presses Fla.

Pullum, Thomas W. Measuring Occupational Inheritance. LC 74-10262. (Progress in Mathematical Social Sciences Ser: Vol. 5). 176p. 1975. 15.95 (ISBN 0-444-41260-3). Elsevier.

Robbins, Paula I. Successful Midlife Career Change: Self-Understanding & Strategies for Action. (Illus.). 1979. 14.95 (ISBN 0-8144-5480-1). Am Mgmt.

Rogoff, Natalie. Recent Trends in Occupational Mobility. Coser, Lewis A. & Powell, Walter W., eds. LC 79-7016. (Perennial Works in Sociology Ser.). (Illus.). 1979. Repr. of 1953 ed. lib. bdg. 13.00x (ISBN 0-405-12115-6). Arno.

Schreiber, Carol T. Changing Places: Men & Women in Transitional Occupations. 1979. 17.50 (ISBN 0-262-19177-6); pap. 6.95 (ISBN 0-262-69075-6). MIT Pr.

Stewart, Phyllis L. & Cantor, Muriel, eds. Varieties of Work Experience: The Social Control of Occupational Groups & Roles. LC 74-6158. 1974. text ed. 13.95x (ISBN 0-470-82477-8). Halsted Pr.

The Transition from Public Service Employment to Unsubsidized Jobs. (Policy Research Project: No. 37). 1981. 4.95 (ISBN 0-89940-637-8). LBJ Sch Public Affairs.

Warner, W. Lloyd & Abegglen, James C. Occupational Mobility in American Business & Industry, 1928-1952. Coser, Lewis A. & Powell, Walter W., eds. LC 79-7029. (Perennial Works in Sociology Ser.). (Illus.). 1979. Repr. of 1955 ed. lib. bdg. 21.00x (ISBN 0-405-12127-X). Arno.

Weaver, Peter A. You, Inc. A Detailed Escape Route to Being Your Own Boss. LC 72-97094. 312p. 1975. pap. 4.95 (ISBN 0-385-09895-2, Dolp). Doubleday.

OCCUPATIONAL RETRAINING

Here are entered works on retraining persons with obsolete vocational skills. Works on vocational instruction within the standard educational system are entered under Vocational Education. Works on the vocationally oriented process of endowing people with a skill after either completion or termination of their formal education are entered under Occupational Training. Works on training of employees on the job are entered under Employees, Training Of.

Blackler, F. H. & Brown, C. A. Job Redesign & Management Control. LC 78-60430. 1978. 22.95 (ISBN 0-03-046210-X). Praeger.

Borus, Michael E. Measuring the Impact of Employment Related Social Programs: A Primer on the Evaluation of Employment & Training, Vocational Education, Vocational Rehabilitation, Other Job Oriented Programs. LC 79-13151. 1979. pap. text ed. 3.50 (ISBN 0-911558-63-2). Upjohn Inst.

Conference on the Aging, 4th, University of Michican, 1951. Rehabilitation of the Older Worker: Proceedings. Donahue, Wilma, et al, eds. LC 76-44290. 1976. Repr. of 1953 ed. lib. bdg. 15.25x (ISBN 0-8371-9042-8, DORO). Greenwood.

Kennedy, Marilyn M. Career Knockouts: How to Battle Back. 228p. 1980. 10.95 (ISBN 0-8329-1474-6). New Century.

Krannich, Ronald L. & Banis, William J. Re-Careering in Turbulent Times: The Guide to Career Management & Change for the 80's. 1981. write for info. (ISBN 0-940010-04-6). Prog Concepts.

Levitan, Sar A. Antipoverty Work & Training Efforts: Goals & Reality. 2nd ed. (Policy Papers in Human Resources & Industrial Relations Ser.: No. 3). (Orig.). 1970. pap. 2.95x (ISBN 0-87736-103-7). U of Mich Inst Labor.

Mangum, Garth L. MDTA: Foundation of Federal Manpower Policy. LC 68-23905. 184p. 1968. 11.50x (ISBN 0-8018-0452-3). Johns Hopkins.

Miller, Kentalle & Miller, Isobel. Retraining & Tradition: Skilled Worker in an Era of Change. 192p. 1975. 18.95x (ISBN 0-8464-1127-X). Beekman Pubs.

Reubens, Beatrice G. The Hard-to-Employ: European Programs. (Illus.). 1970. 20.00x (ISBN 0-231-03388-5). Columbia U Pr.

Somers, Gerald G., ed. Retraining the Unemployed. 360p. 1968. 29.50x (ISBN 0-299-04820-9). U of Wis Pr.

Wolfbein, Seymour. Education & Training for Full Employment. LC 67-23754. 1967. 20.00x (ISBN 0-231-02946-2). Columbia U Pr.

OCCUPATIONAL THERAPY

see also Art Therapy; Handicraft; Music Therapy; Recreational Therapy

Banus, B. S., et al. The Developmental Therapist. 2nd ed. LC 79-65452. 1979. pap. 29.95 (ISBN 0-685-91501-8). C B Slack.

Briggs, Anne K., et al. Case Simulations in Psychosocial Occupational Therapy. LC 79-4674. 235p. 1979. pap. 14.95 (ISBN 0-8036-1201-X). Davis Co.

Briggs, L. Vernon. Occupation As a Substitute for Restraint in the Treatment of the Mentally Il: A History of the Passage of Two Bills Through the Massachusetts Legislature. LC 72-2387. (Mental Illness & Social Policy; the American Experience Ser.). Repr. of 1923 ed. 14.00 (ISBN 0-405-05195-6). Arno.

Cedoline, Anthony J. Occupational Stress & Job Burnout in Public Education: Symptoms, Causes, & Survival Skills. 1982. text ed. price not set (ISBN 0-8077-2694-X); pap. text ed. price not set (ISBN 0-8077-2693-1). Tchrs Coll.

Congress on Occupational Therapy, 5th International, Zurich, 1970. Occupational Therapy Today, Tomorrow, Proceedings: Its Present Position & the Possibilities of Development. Binswanger, Rotraut & De Spindler, Irene, eds. 1971. pap. 30.00 (ISBN 3-8055-1223-6). S Karger.

Copeland, Mildred, et al. Occupational Therapy for Mentally Retarded Children: Guidelines for Occupational Therapy Aides & Certified Occupational Therapy Assistants. (Illus.). 1976. 15.95 (ISBN 0-8391-0930-X). Univ Park.

Cynkin, Simme. Occupational Therapy. 1979. 9.95 (ISBN 0-316-16610-3). Little.

Dunton, William R. Occupational Therapy: Principles & Practice. 2nd ed. (Illus.). 384p. 1957. ed. spiral bdg. 32.50photocopy (ISBN 0-398-04249-7). C C Thomas.

Dunton, William R., Jr. Prescribing Occupational Therapy. 2nd ed. 164p. 1947. ed. spiral bdg. 14.75photocopy (ISBN 0-398-04250-0). C C Thomas.

Fidler, Gail S. & Fidler, Jay W. Occupational Therapy. 1963. text ed. 9.95 (ISBN 0-02-337190-0). Macmillan.

Gold, Marc. Marc Gold: "Did I Say That?". Articles & Commentary on the Try Another Way System. LC 80-51793. (Illus.). 347p. 1980. pap. text ed. 15.95 (ISBN 0-87822-219-7, 2197). Res Press.

Hephill, BJ. Evaluative Process in Psychiatric Occupational Therapy. 1981. pap. 19.50 (ISBN 0-913590-80-0). C B Slack.

Hopkins, Helen L. & Smith, Helen D., eds. Willard & Spackman's Occupational Therapy. 5th ed. LC 78-4607. 1978. text ed. 29.50 (ISBN 0-397-54216-X, JBL-Med-Nursing). Har-Row.

Hughes, Patricia & Mullins, Linda. Acute Psychiatric Care: An Occupational Therapist's Guide to Exercises in Daily Living Skills. LC 80-54633. 1981. pap. 16.50 (ISBN 0-913590-76-2). C B Slack.

Jackson, Elinor & Dundon, H. Dwyer, eds. Occupational Therapy Examination Review Book, Vol. 1. 3rd ed. 1974. pap. 9.50 (ISBN 0-87488-475-6). Med Exam.

Jones, M. S., ed. An Approach to Occupational Therapy. 3rd ed. Jay, P. 1977. 44.95 (ISBN 0-407-00053-4). Butterworth.

Kohn, Kate H., et al. Physical Medicine & Rehabilitation. 3rd ed. (Medical Examination Review Bk.: Vol. 20). 1979. spiral bdg. 19.50 (ISBN 0-87488-128-5). Med Exam.

Llorens, Lela A. & Rubin, Eli Z. Developing Ego Functions in Disturbed Children: Occupational Therapy in Milieu. LC 66-24385. (Lafayette Clinic Handbooks in Psychiatry Ser). (Orig.), 1967. pap. 4.95x (ISBN 0-8143-1307-8). Wayne St U Pr.

Lucci, Jennie A. Occupational Therapy Case Studies. 2nd ed. 1980. pap. 14.00 (ISBN 0-87488-034-3). Med Exam.

MacDonald, E. M., ed. Occupational Therapy in Rehabilitation. 4th ed. (Illus.). 1976. text ed. 20.95 (ISBN 0-02-858420-1). Macmillan.

Meldman, Monte J., et al. Occupational Therapy Manual. 88p. 1969. pap. 9.75 photocopy ed. spiral (ISBN 0-398-01283-0). C C Thomas.

Mosey, Anne C. Occupational Therapy: The Configuration of a Profession. 200p. 1981. text ed. 18.50 (ISBN 0-89004-655-7); pap. text ed. 12.50 (ISBN 0-89004-699-9). Raven.

Moyer, Elizabeth A. Self-Assessment of Current Knowledge in Occupational Therapy. 1976. spiral bdg. 9.50 (ISBN 0-87488-249-4). Med Exam.

O'Morrow, Gerald S. Administration of Activity Therapy Service. (Illus.). 440p. 1976. 22.50 (ISBN 0-398-01425-6). C C Thomas.

Pedretti, Lorraine W. Occupational Therapy: Practice Skills for Physical Dysfunction. LC 81-11076. (Illus.). 328p. 1981. pap. text ed. 24.95 (ISBN 0-8016-3772-4). Mosby.

Productivity Improvements in Physical and Occupational Therapies: An Examination of Case Studies. 215p. (Orig.). 1981. collection of papers 15.00 (ISBN 0-87258-339-2, 6024). Am Hospital.

Reed, Kathlyn L. & Sanderson, Sharon T. Concepts of Occupational Therapy. (Illus.). 312p. 1980. pap. 19.95 (ISBN 0-683-07200-5). Williams & Wilkins.

Rudman, Jack. Occupational Therapist. (Career Examination Ser.: C-558). pap. 10.00 (ISBN 0-8373-0558-6). Natl Learning.

--Occupational Therapist Aide. (Career Examination Ser.: C-1380). (Cloth bdg. avail. on request). pap. 8.00 (ISBN 0-8373-1380-5). Natl Learning.

--Occupational Therapist Assistant. (Career Examination Ser.: C-1381). (Cloth bdg. avail. on request). pap. 8.00 (ISBN 0-8373-1381-3). Natl Learning.

--Senior Occupational Therapist. (Career Examination Ser.: C-2174). (Cloth bdg. avail. on request). pap. 10.00 (ISBN 0-8373-2174-3). Natl Learning.

Schilling, R. S., ed. Occupational Health Practice. (Illus.). 1973. 32.95 (ISBN 0-407-33700-8). Butterworth.

Shopland, A. J. Refer to Occupational Therapy. 2nd ed. 1979. pap. text ed. 9.50 (ISBN 0-443-01866-9). Churchill.

Trombly, Catherine A. & Scott, Anna D. Occupational Therapy for Physical Dysfunction. 1977. pap. 28.00 (ISBN 0-683-08386-4). Williams & Wilkins.

Vash, Carolyn L. The Psychology of Disability. (Springer Ser. on Rehabilitation: Vol. 1). 1981. text ed. write for info. (ISBN 0-8261-3340-1); pap. text ed. price not set (ISBN 0-8261-3341-X). Springer Pub.

OCCUPATIONAL THERAPY AS A PROFESSION

Franciscus, Marie L. & Abbott, Marguerite. Opportunities in Occupational Therapy. rev. ed. LC 78-60522. (gr. 8 up). 1979. PLB 6.60 (ISBN 0-685-92740-7); pap. 4.95 (ISBN 0-685-92741-5). Natl Textbk.

Greenberg, Naomi S. Occupational Therapy Assistant's Handbook. (Allied Health Professions Monograph). (Illus.). 186p. 1981. 11.50 (ISBN 0-87527-270-3). Green.

Rudman, Jack. Certification Examination for Occupational Therapy Assistant (OTA) (Admission Test Ser.: ATS-69). (Cloth bdg. avail. on request). pap. 13.95 (ISBN 0-8373-5069-7). Natl Learning.

Shuff, Frances. Your Future in an Occupational Therapy Career. (Careers in Depth Ser.). (Illus.). (gr. 7-12). 1978. PLB 5.97 (ISBN 0-8239-0300-1). Rosen Pr.

Wolf, Stewart, et al. Occupational Health As Human Ecology. (Illus.). 128p. 1978. 14.75 (ISBN 0-398-03793-0). C C Thomas.

OCCUPATIONAL TRAINING

Here are entered works on the vocationally oriented process of endowing people with a skill after either completion or termination of their formal education. Works on vocational instruction within the standard educational system are entered under Vocational Education. Works on retraining persons with obsolete vocational skills are entered under Occupational Retraining. Works on training of employees on the job are entered under Employees, Training Of.

see also Non-Formal Education; Occupational Retraining

Alsup, Rea T. The Vocational Development of Welfare-Supported Youth. LC 74-28606. 1975. soft bdg. 9.00 (ISBN 0-685-59171-9). R & E Res Assoc.

American Society for Training & Development. Training & Development Handbook: A Guide to Human Resource Development. 2nd ed. (Handbook Ser.). (Illus.). 1976. 34.50 (ISBN 0-07-013350-6, P&RB); assessment supplement 4.95 (ISBN 0-07-013352-2). McGraw.

Appley, Lawrence A. & Irons, Keith L. Manager Manpower Planning: A Professional Management System. 128p. 1981. 14.95 (ISBN 0-8144-5707-X). Am Mgmt.

Auten, James H. Training in the Small Department. 144p. 1973. 12.75 (ISBN 0-398-02719-6). C C Thomas.

Baer, Max F. & Roeber, Edward C. Occupational Information: The Dynamics of Its Nature & Use. 1977. text ed. 15.93 (ISBN 0-574-50069-3, 5-0069). SRA.

Bahme, Charles W. Fire Officer's Guide to Disaster Control. Lyons, Paul R., ed. LC 77-76486. (Fire Officer's Guide Ser.). 1978. text ed. 16.50 (ISBN 0-87765-099-3, FSP-48A). Natl Fire Prot.

Bass, Bernard M. & Vaughan, James A. Training in Industry: The Management of Learning. LC 66-24534. (Behavioral Science in Industry Ser). (Orig.). 1968. pap. text ed. 6.95 (ISBN 0-8185-0319-X). Brooks-Cole.

Borus, Michael E. Measuring the Impact of Employment Related Social Programs: A Primer on the Evaluation of Employment & Training, Vocational Education, Vocational Rehabilitation, Other Job Oriented Programs. LC 79-13151. 1979. pap. text ed. 3.50 (ISBN 0-911558-63-2). Upjohn Inst.

Borus, Michael E. & Tash, William R. Measuring the Impact of Manpower Programs: A Primer. LC 73-633548. (Policy Papers in Human Resources & Industrial Relations Ser.: No. 17). (Orig.). 1970. pap. 2.50x (ISBN 0-87736-117-7). U of Mich Inst Labor.

Broadwell, Martin M. Supervisor & on the Job Training. 2nd ed. LC 74-30695. (Illus.). 176p. 1975. text ed. 8.95 (ISBN 0-201-00754-1). A-W.

Committee for Economic Development in Cooperation with Work in America Institute, Inc. Training & Jobs Programs in Action: Case Studies in Private-Sector Initiatives for the Hard-To-Employ. 1978. pap. 5.00 (ISBN 0-87186-332-4). Comm Econ Dev.

Cosmetology Teacher - Training Manual. 1976. 16.95 (ISBN 0-87350-069-5); wkbk. 11.95 (ISBN 0-87350-060-1). Milady.

Davies, Ivor K. Instructional Technique. (Illus.). 352p. 1980. text ed. 14.95x (ISBN 0-07-015502-X, TD). McGraw.

Drolet, Robert P. & Dowling, John R. Developing & Administering an Industrial Training Program. LC 79-10713. (Illus.). 1979. pap. 12.95 (ISBN 0-8436-0777-7). CBI Pub.

Engineering Industry Training Board, ed. First Year Training for Craftsmen & Technicians: An Introduction to General & Special Skills, 16 vols. (Illus.). 1975-1976. Set. spiral bdg. 77.00x (ISBN 0-89563-006-0). Intl Ideas.
--Model Schemes for the Training of Adult Operators in Technical Trades, 40 vols. (Illus.). 1968-1972. Set. 132.50x (ISBN 0-89563-011-7). Intl Ideas.
--Training Recommendations for Training Officers, 14 vols. Incl. Vol. 1. The Training of Supervisors; Vol. 2. Adult Operators; Vol. 3. Juvenile Operators; Vol. 4. Professional Engineers; Vol. 5. Managers; Vol. 6. Systems Analysts; Vol. 7. Clerks; Vol. 8. Technicians; Vol. 9. Supervisors; Vol. 10. Computer Operators; Vol. 11. Computer Programmers; Vol. 12. Secretaries; Vol. 13. Typists; Vol. 14. Machine Operators. (Illus.). 1973. Set. pap. text ed. 72.50x (ISBN 0-89563-032-X). Intl Ideas.
Erfurt, John C. A Compendium of Information Relevant to Manpower Agencies. 1973. pap. 7.00x (ISBN 0-87736-330-7). U of Mich Inst Labor.
Evans, Rupert, et al. Education for Employment: The Background & Potential of the 1968 Vocational Education Amendments. LC 70-627280. (Policy Papers in Human Resources & Industrial Relations Ser.: No. 14). 120p. (Orig.). 1969. pap. 2.50x (ISBN 0-87736-114-2). U of Mich Inst Labor.
Everybody Trains. 1975. 4.00 (ISBN 0-686-15332-4). Inst Urban Studies.
Ferman, Louis A. Job Development for the Hard-To-Employ. LC 71-626164. (Policy Papers in Human Resources & Industrial Relations Ser.: No. 11). (Orig.). 1969. pap. 2.50 (ISBN 0-87736-111-8). U of Mich Inst Labor.
Ferman, Louis A. & Manela, Roger. Agency Company Relationships in Manpower Operations for the Hard to Employ. 1973. pap. 6.50x (ISBN 0-87736-329-3). U of Mich Inst Labor.
Ferrin, Richard I. & Arbeiter, Solomon. Bridging the Gap: A Study of Education-to-Work Linkages. 1975. pap. 6.00 (ISBN 0-87447-008-0, 221762). College Bd.
Friedland, Dion, et al. People Productivity in Retailing: A Manpower Development Plan. LC 80-23109. 1980. 18.95 (ISBN 0-912016-91-4). Lebhar Friedman.
Gretler, Armin. The Training of Adult Middle-Level Personnel. LC 72-89860. (Illus.). 164p. (Orig.). 1973. pap. 7.00 (ISBN 92-3-100935-4, U685, UNESCO). Unipub.
Groves, S. L. & Groves, D. L. Occupational Development: Job Satisfaction & Productivity. 49p. 1981. pap. text ed. 5.00 (ISBN 0-940414-03-1). Appalach Assoc.
Harris, Norman C. & Grede, John F. Career Education in Colleges: A Guide for Planning Two- & Four-Year Occupational Programs. LC 77-82071. (Higher Education Ser.). 1977. text ed. 16.95x (ISBN 0-87589-342-2). Jossey-Bass.
Havelock, Ronald G. & Havelock, Mary C. Training for Change Agents: A Guide to the Design of Training Programs in Education & Other Fields. LC 72-86337. 262p. 1973. cloth 10.00 (ISBN 0-87944-126-7). Inst Soc Res.
How to Improve Training Skills. 1975. pap. 11.00 (ISBN 0-686-10814-0). Preston.
Human Resource Development Press. The Trainers Resource. Nadler, Leonard, ed. 340p. (Orig.). 1981. book with periodic supplements 75.00x (ISBN 0-914234-55-2). Human Res Dev.
International Labour Office. Equipment Planning Guide for Vocational & Technical Training & Education Programmes: Tool & Die Making Occupations. (Equipment Planning Guides: No. 2). x, 214p. (Orig.). 1980. pap. 22.80 (ISBN 92-2-101891-1). Intl Labour Office.
--Multinationals Training Practices & Development. viii, 138p. (Orig.). 1981. pap. 8.55 (ISBN 92-2-102569-1). Intl Labour Office.
--The Use of Sound in Workers' Education: An Instructional Aid for Workers' Educators & Trade Unionists. (A Workers' Education Manual). 121p. (Orig.). 1980. pap. 2.85 (ISBN 92-2-102228-5). Intl Labour Office.
International Labour Office Staff. Equipment Planning Guide for Vocational & Technical Training & Education Programmes: Electronics, No. 10. (Equipment Planning Guides Ser.). v, 276p. (Orig.). 1981. pap. 22.80 (ISBN 92-2-102588-8). Intl Labour Office.
Jacobs, Angeline M., et al. Handbook for Job Placement of Mentally Retarded Workers: Training, Opportunities, & Career Areas. LC 78-20654. (Garland Mental Retardation Ser.). 352p. 1979. lib. bdg. 27.50 (ISBN 0-8240-7061-5). Garland Pub.
Jones, Warren. Education & Employment, No. 11. (ACER Research Monograph). 209p. 1981. pap. text ed. 26.00x (ISBN 0-85563-217-8). Verry.
Kiefer, Nicholas M. The Economic Benefits from Four Employment & Training Programs. LC 78-75061. (Outstanding Dissertations in Economics Ser.). 1979. lib. bdg. 15.00 (ISBN 0-8240-4138-0). Garland Pub.
Killingsworth, Charles C. Jobs & Income for Negroes. (Policy Papers in Human Resources & Industrial Relations Ser.: No. 6). (Orig.). 1968. pap. 2.50x (ISBN 0-87736-106-1). U of Mich Inst Labor.
King, Kenneth. The African Artisan: Education & the Informal Sector in Kenya. LC 76-58316. 1977. pap. text ed. 8.75x (ISBN 0-8077-8023-5). Tchrs Coll.
Kobrak, Peter. Private Assumption of Public Responsibilities: The Role of American Business in Urban Manpower Programs. LC 72-83571. (Special Studies in U.S. Economic, Social & Political Issues). 1973. 29.50x (ISBN 0-275-07030-1). Irvington.
Levitan, Sar A., et al. Human Resources & Labor Markets: Employment and Training in the American Economy. 3rd ed. 576p. 1981. text ed. 21.50 scp (ISBN 0-06-044074-0, HarpC). Har-Row.
Macmillan. College Blue Book of Occupational Education. 4th ed. LC 79-66191. 1979. 37.50 (ISBN 0-02-695150-9). Macmillan.
Main, Earl D. A Nationwide Evaluation of M.D.T.A. (Manpower Development & Training Act) Institutional Job Training Programs. (Report Ser: No. 118). 1966. 6.25 (ISBN 0-932132-10-3). NORC.
Meyers, Frederic. Training in European Enterprises. (Monograph Ser.: No. 14). 1969. 5.00 (ISBN 0-89215-015-7). U Cal LA Indus Rel.
Miller, Harry G. & Verduin, John R. The Adult Educator: A Handbook for Staff Development. new ed. (Building Blocks of Human Potential). 178p. 1979. 12.95 (ISBN 0-87201-233-6). Gulf Pub.
Miller, Vincent A. The Guidebook for International Trainers in Business & Industry: Co-Published with the American Society for Training & Development, Inc. 1979. text ed. 16.95 (ISBN 0-442-25392-3). Van Nos Reinhold.
Moro-Oka, Kazufusa. Recurrent Education: Policy & Development in OECD Member Countries: Japan. 1976. 3.00x (ISBN 92-64-11579-X). OECD.
Multinationals' Training Practices & Development. 138p. 1981. pap. 9.50 (ISBN 92-2-102569-1, ILO 170, ILO). Unipub.
Myers, Charles A. The Role of the Private Sector in Manpower Development. LC 72-152912. (Policy Studies in Employment & Welfare: No. 10). 101p. 1971. 8.50x (ISBN 0-8018-1275-5); pap. 2.95x (ISBN 0-8018-1324-7). Johns Hopkins.
National Guide to Educational Credit for Training Programs. 1980. pap. 20.00 (ISBN 0-8268-1398-4). ACE.
The New Private Sector Initiative Program: A Source of Funds for Training Workers. LC 79-57737. Date not set. pap. 7.00 (ISBN 0-89834-009-8, 6036). Chamber Comm US.
Niland, John R., ed. The Production of Manpower Specialists: A Volume of Selected Papers. 248p. 1971. pap. 6.50 special hard bdg. (ISBN 0-87546-279-0); pap. 3.50 (ISBN 0-87546-045-3). NY Sch Indus Rel.
Nolfi, George J., ed. Experiences of Recent High School Graduates. new ed. LC 78-2075. 1978. 19.95 (ISBN 0-669-02264-0). Lexington Bks.
Nystrom, Dennis C. & Bayne, Keith G. Instructional Methods in Occupational Education. LC 76-43204. 1977. 13.50 (ISBN 0-672-97111-9). Bobbs.
Orna, Elizabeth, ed. Relevance of School Learning Experience to Performance in Industry. 1977. 22.95x (ISBN 0-85083-339-6). Intl Ideas.
Orr, David B., ed. New Directions in Employability: Reducing Barriers to Full Employment. LC 73-6094. (Special Studies in U.S. Economic, Social & Political Issues). 1973. 28.50x (ISBN 0-275-28838-2). Irvington.
Patten, Thomas H., Jr. Manpower Planning & the Development of Human Resources. LC 76-137109. 1971. 49.50 (ISBN 0-471-66944-X, Pub. by Wiley-Interscience). Wiley.
Pena, Alberto & De Bliek, Ruth. Cost Effectiveness in Training & Instruction. LC 80-82294. (Guideline Ser.). 60p. Date not set. pap. 6.95x (ISBN 0-931816-01-7). Kumarian Pr.
Pletcher, Barbara T. Saleswoman: A Career Guide. LC 78-59222. 1978. 9.95 (ISBN 0-87094-166-6). Dow Jones-Irwin.
Readings in Vocational Training for the Mentally Retarded. (Special Education Ser.). 1978. pap. 10.95 (ISBN 0-89568-084-X). Spec Learn Corp.
Ribich, Thomas I. Education & Poverty. LC 67-30600. (Studies in Social Economics). 1968. 10.95 (ISBN 0-8157-7430-3). Brookings.
Roberts, Kenneth & White, Graham E. The Character Training Industry: Adventure Training Schemes in Britain. 5.95 (ISBN 0-7153-6394-8). David & Charles.
Rudman, Jack. Manpower Program Coordinator. (Career Examination Ser.: C-2316). (Cloth bdg. avail. on request). pap. 10.00 (ISBN 0-8373-2316-9). Natl Learning.
--Manpower Training Coordinator. (Career Examination Ser.: C-1554). (Cloth bdg. avail. on request). pap. 10.00 (ISBN 0-8373-1554-9). Natl Learning.
--Training Specialist 2. (Career Examination Ser.: C-1768). (Cloth bdg. avail. on request). 1977. pap. 10.00 (ISBN 0-8373-1768-1). Natl Learning.
Smith, Wil J., ed. Poor & the Hard-Core Unemployed: Recommendations for New Approaches. LC 77-632182. 1970. pap. text ed. 4.00x (ISBN 0-87736-311-0). U of Mich Inst Labor.
Snedeker, Bonnie & Snedeker, David. CETA: Decentralization on Trial. LC 77-17956. 1978. 9.95 (ISBN 0-913420-73-5). Olympus Pub Co.
Srebalus, David J., et al. Promoting Career Development: Concepts & Procedures. (Counseling Ser.). 570p. 1982. text ed. 18.95 (ISBN 0-8185-0471-4). Brooks-Cole.
Staff of Universal Training Systems. How to Develop & Conduct Successful in-Company Training Program. 1972. 65.50 (ISBN 0-85013-037-9). Dartnell Corp.
Stockard, James G. Career Development & Job Training: A Manager's Handbook. new ed. 1977. 24.95 (ISBN 0-8144-5449-6). Am Mgmt.
Storm, George. Managing the Occupational Education Laboratory. LC 79-83724. (Illus.). 1979. 9.95x (ISBN 0-911168-42-7). Prakken.
The Training of Functional Literacy Personnel: A Practical Guide. 104p. (Orig.). 1974. pap. 4.75 (ISBN 92-3-101043-3, U686, UNESCO). Unipub.
Trebous, Madeleine. Migration & Development, the Case of Algeria. 244p. 1970. 4.00x (ISBN 0-686-14668-9). OECD.
U. S. Senate, Committee on Labor & Public Welfare. Bilingual Education, Health, & Manpower Programs. Cordasco, Francesco, ed. LC 77-90563. (Bilingual-Bicultural Education in the U. S. Ser.). 1978. Repr. of 1973 ed. lib. bdg. 14.00x (ISBN 0-405-11101-0). Arno.
Varny, Glenn H. Manpower Planning & Development for Managers. 1974. pap. 6.00x (ISBN 0-686-11618-6). Mgmt Advisory.
Wall, James E., ed. Vocational Education for Special Groups. (AVA Yearbook Ser.: 6). 351p. 1976. 12.00 (ISBN 0-89514-023-3, 01976). Am Voc Assn.
Wasserman, Paul, ed. New Training Organizations: Supplement to Training & Development Organizations Directory, 2nd Edition, 2 vols. 1981. Set. pap. 85.00 (ISBN 0-686-69180-6). Gale.
Zymelman, Manuel. Economic Evaluation of Vocational Training Programs. LC 76-4868. (A World Bank Occasional Paper Ser: No. 21). 136p. 1976. pap. 6.00x (ISBN 0-8018-1855-9). Johns Hopkins.

OCCUPATIONS

see also Civil Service Positions; Handicraft; Job Descriptions; Job Evaluation; Occupational Mobility; Professions; Vocation; Vocational Guidance; Vocational Interests;
also individual occupations and industries; also subdivision Vocational Guidance under appropriate subjects, e.g. Agriculture–Vocational Guidance

Amman, Jost & Sachs, Hans. The Book of Trades (Standebuch) (Illus.). 6.75 (ISBN 0-8446-4618-0). Peter Smith.
Anema, Durlynn. Get Hired: Thirteen Ways to Get a Job. (Illus.). 64p. (gr. 7-12). 1979. pap. text ed. 2.95 (ISBN 0-915510-35-9). Janus Bks.
Angle, John. Language Maintenance, Language Shift, & Occupational Achievement in the United States. LC 77-91426. 1978. soft cover 8.00 (ISBN 0-88247-542-8). R & E Res Assoc.
Austin, Michael J. Professionals & Paraprofessionals. LC 77-26273. 295p. 1978. text ed. 24.95 (ISBN 0-87705-305-7). Human Sci Pr.
Barnes, James S., ed. College & Career Directory: 1979-1980, Pennsylvania Edition. 238p. (gr. 11-12). 1979. soft cover 4.95 (ISBN 0-8352-1209-2). Bowker.
--College & Career Directory: 1980-1981, Maryland - Baltimore Edition. 325p. (gr. 11-12). 1980. soft cover 4.95 (ISBN 0-8352-1279-3). Bowker.
--College & Career Directory: 1980-1981, New Jersey Edition. 250p. (gr. 11-12). 1980. soft cover 4.95 (ISBN 0-8352-1208-4). Bowker.
Bennett, Wilma. Occupations Filing Plan & Bibliography. LC 68-56288. 138p. 1968. pap. text ed. 3.95x (ISBN 0-8134-1055-X, 1055). Interstate.
Billhartz, Celeste. The Complete Book of Job Hunting, Finding, Changing. (Illus., Orig.). 1980. pap. 7.95 (ISBN 0-935448-01-2). Rainbow Collect.
Blau, Peter M. & Duncan, Otis D. The American Occupational Structure. LC 78-50657. 1978. pap. text ed. 8.95 (ISBN 0-02-903670-4). Free Pr.
Bolles, Richard. Quick Job-Hunting Map, Beginning Version. 1977. pap. 1.25x (ISBN 0-913668-59-1). Ten Speed Pr.
Brunetti, Cledo & Higgerson, Clifford. Your Future in a Changing World. LC 70-87820. (Illus.). (gr. 9 up). 1970. PLB 5.97 (ISBN 0-8239-0181-5). Rosen Pr.
Campbell, Robert. London Tradesman. LC 68-26162. Repr. of 1747 ed. 19.50x (ISBN 0-678-05546-7). Kelley.
Caplow, Theodore. The Sociology of Work. LC 77-18112. (Illus.). 1978. Repr. of 1954 ed. lib. bdg. 25.75 (ISBN 0-313-20111-0, CASOW). Greenwood.
Career Employment Opportunities Directory, 4 vols. 1st ed. Set. 139.50 (ISBN 0-916270-11-4). Ready Ref Pr.
Cattell, Nancy G. & Sharp, Shirley I. College & Career: Adjusting to College & Selecting an Occupation. LC 78-111101. (Orig.). 1970. pap. text ed. 12.95x (ISBN 0-89197-085-1). Irvington.
Chapman, Elwood N. Scrambling. LC 78-73744. 1979. 7.95 (ISBN 0-312-90853-9). St Martin.
Christopher, Rachelle G. & Christopher, Edward E. Job Enrichment: How Far Have We Come? LC 79-8992. 1979. pap. text ed. 7.50 (ISBN 0-8191-0857-X). U Pr of Amer.
Cianflone, Ralph. This Could Be Your Life. 128p. 1980. 7.95 (ISBN 0-89962-039-6). Todd & Honeywell.
Congressional Quarterly Staff. Taxes, Jobs, & Inflation. LC 78-13735. 1978. pap. 6.95 (ISBN 0-87187-139-4). Congr Quarterly.
Coxon, Anthony P. & Jones, Charles L. Class & Hierarchy: The Social Meaning of Occupations. (Illus.). 1979. 21.95 (ISBN 0-312-14256-0). St Martin.
--The Images of Occupational Prestige: A Study in Social Cognition. LC 77-90093. 1978. 22.50x (ISBN 0-312-40928-1). St Martin.
Cummings, Donald W. & Herum, John, eds. Tempo: Life, Work & Leisure. (Illus.). 336p. 1974. pap. text ed. 9.95 (ISBN 0-395-17839-8, 3-12925); instructors' guide 1.50 (ISBN 0-395-17867-3, 3-12926). HM.
Dauten, Dale A. Quitting: Knowing When to Leave. 216p. 1980. 12.95 (ISBN 0-8027-0660-6). Walker & Co.
Davis, George. Your Career in Energy-Related Occupations. LC 79-17471. (Arco's Career Guidance Ser.). (Illus.). 1980. pap. 3.95 (ISBN 0-668-04798-4, 4798-4); pap. 3.50 (ISBN 0-668-04803-4, 4803-4). Arco.
Dean, H. Manufacturing: Industry & Careers. 1975. 7.20 (ISBN 0-13-555615-5); pap. text ed. 5.80 (ISBN 0-685-73756-X). P-H.
Derr, C. Brooklyn, ed. Work, Family & the Career: New Frontiers in Theory & Research. LC 80-13598. 320p. 1980. 27.95 (ISBN 0-03-056717-3). Praeger.
Deutsch, Arnold R. The Complete Job Book. 228p. (Orig.). 1980. pap. 6.95 (ISBN 0-346-12481-6). Cornerstone.
Djeddah, Eli. Moving up. rev. ed. LC 75-16692. (Illus.). 1978. pap. 4.95 (ISBN 0-913668-83-4). Ten Speed Pr.
DuBrin, Andrew J. Human Relations: A Job Oriented Approach. (Illus.). 1978. text ed. 17.95 (ISBN 0-87909-371-4); instrs'. manual avail. Reston.
Dudley, Gordon A. & Tiedeman, David V. Career Development: Exploration & Commitment. LC 75-10492. 1977. 10.95x (ISBN 0-915202-07-7). Accel Devel.
Dunkerley, David. Occupations & Society. (Students Library of Sociology). 96p. 1975. 13.00x (ISBN 0-7100-8239-8); pap. 6.00 (ISBN 0-7100-8240-1). Routledge & Kegan.
Durham. One Hundred Careers: How to Pick the One That's Best for You. 1977. 10.95 (ISBN 0-13-634717-7, Spec); pap. 4.95 (ISBN 0-13-634709-6). P-H.
E. A. Occupations. Incl. Blacksmith. 1957. (ISBN 0-87282-027-0); Primitive Painter. (ISBN 0-87282-030-0); Country Store. 1955. (ISBN 0-87282-031-9); Apothecary. 1956. (ISBN 0-87282-032-7); Frugal Housewife. 1957. (ISBN 0-87282-033-5); Music. 1958. (ISBN 0-87282-034-3); Gunsmith. 1959. (ISBN 0-87282-035-1). 3.00 ea. Century Hse.
Fashion Group Inc. Your Future in the Beauty Business. Le Vathes, Christine, ed. LC 68-31559. (Careers in Depth Ser). (Illus.). (gr. 9 up). 1979. PLB 5.97 (ISBN 0-8239-0482-2). Rosen Pr.
Feingold, S. Norman & Fins, Alice. Your Future in More Exotic Occupations. (Careers in Depth Ser.). (YA) 1978. PLB 5.97 (ISBN 0-8239-0412-1). Rosen Pr.

Fiarotta, Phyllis & Fiarotta, Noel. Be What You Want to Be. LC 76-52860. (Parents & Children Together Ser.). (Illus.). (gr. k-7). 1977. 10.95 (ISBN 0-911104-94-1); pap. 5.95 (ISBN 0-911104-95-X). Workman Pub.

Forrester, Gertrude. Occupational Literature: An Annotated Bibliography. 1971. 15.00 (ISBN 0-8242-0437-9). Wilson.

Fredrickson, Ronald H. Career Information. (Illus.). 416p. 1982. reference 19.95 (ISBN 0-13-114744-7). P-H.

Freedland, Mark R. The Contract of Employment. 400p. 1975. 39.50x (ISBN 0-19-825306-0). Oxford U Pr.

Fryklund, Verne C. Occupational Analysis. rev. ed. 1970. 10.95 (ISBN 0-02-816950-6). Glencoe.

Funes, Marilyn & Lazarus, Alan. Popular Careers. Piltch, Benjamin, ed. 64p. (gr. 5-12). 1980. wkbk 3.50 (ISBN 0-934618-01-1). Skyview Pub.

Gallagher, Bernard J. & Palazzolo, Charles S. The Social World of Occupations. LC 76-41981. 1976. pap. text ed. 10.95 (ISBN 0-8403-1620-8). Kendall-Hunt.

Garrison, Clifford B., et al. Finding a Job You Feel Good About. 1977. pap. 2.50 (ISBN 0-913592-88-9). Argus Comm.

Gautier, T. F. Dictionniare des Confreries et Corporations d'Arts et Metiers. Migne, J. P., ed. (Nouvelle Encyclopedie Theologique Ser.: Vol. 50). 562p. (Fr.). Date not set. Repr. of 1854 ed. lib. bdg. 72.00x (ISBN 0-89241-288-7). Caratzas Bros.

Gersoni-Edelman, Diane. Work-Wise: Learning About the World of Work from Books--Critical Guide to Book Selection & Usage. LC 79-11920. (Selection Guide Ser.: No. 3). 258p. 1980. 16.50 (ISBN 0-87436-264-4, Co-Pub. by Neal-Schuman). ABC-Clio.

Ginzberg, Eli, ed. Jobs for Americans. (The American Assembly Ser.). 1976. pap. 4.50 (ISBN 0-13-510016-X, Spec) (ISBN 0-13-510016-X). P-H.

Glasser, Ellen. Looking into the Future: An Occupational Worktext. 1975. pap. 2.50x (ISBN 0-88323-118-2, 206). Richards Pub.

Greenwood, John. Workers Sit-Ins & Job Protection. 144p. text ed. 22.75x (ISBN 0-566-02015-7, Pub by Teakfield Ltd England). Renouf.

Halcomb, Ruth. Recession-Proof Jobs. LC 75-36084. 192p. (Orig.). 1976. pap. 1.25 (ISBN 0-89041-053-4, 3053). Major Bks.

Hall, Douglas T. & Schneider, Benjamin. Organizational Climates & Careers: The Work Lives of Priests. LC 78-187261. (Quantitative Studies in Social Relation). 280p. 1972. 37.50 (ISBN 0-12-785300-6). Acad Pr.

Hall, Richard H. Occupations & the Social Structure. 2nd ed. LC 74-23243. (Illus.). 384p. 1975. text ed. 19.95 (ISBN 0-13-629345-X). P-H.

Hawes, Gene R., et al. Careers Today: A Guide to Good Jobs Without a Degree. LC 77-76039. 1977. Repr. 9.95 (ISBN 0-8008-1252-2). Taplinger.

Hoppock, Robert. Occupational Information. 4th ed. 1975. text ed. 19.95 (ISBN 0-07-030330-4). McGraw.

Horn, Yvonne. Dozens of Ways to Make Money. LC 76-39930. (gr. 7 up). 1977. pap. 2.95 (ISBN 0-15-224186-8, VoyB). HarBraceJ.

Jackson, Tom. Guerilla Tactics in the Job Market. 1978. pap. 2.95 (ISBN 0-553-14456-1). Bantam.

Jackson, Tom & Mayleas, Davidyne. The Hidden Job Market for the Eighties. 1981. pap. 9.95 (ISBN 0-8129-0973-9). Times Bks.

Johansen, I. Norman. Write Your Ticket to Success: A Do-It-Yourself Guide to Effective Resume Writing & Job Hunting. 2nd ed. 1976. 7.95 (ISBN 0-918350-00-X). Job Hunters Forum.

Jones, Edward S. Occupations Unlimited. pap. 1.25 (ISBN 0-685-20412-X). Stewart.

Kahn, Charles H. & Hanna, J. Bradley. Working Makes Sense. 1973. pap. 4.40 (ISBN 0-8224-7490-5); tchrs. manual free (ISBN 0-8224-5212-X). Pitman Learning.

Komar, John J. The Great Escape from Your Dead-End Job. 160p. (Orig.). 1980. pap. 4.95 (ISBN 0-695-81307-2). New Century.

Kruger, Charles. Eye on Careers, 4 vols. (gr. 8-12). 1981. Vol. 1. pap. text ed. write for info. (ISBN 0-86649-039-6, 039-6); Vol. 2. write for info. duplicate bk. (ISBN 0-86649-040-X, 040X); Vol. 3. write for info. tchrs. guide (ISBN 0-86649-041-8, 041-8); Vol. 4. write for info. audio cassettes (ISBN 0-86649-042-6, 042-6). Twentieth Century.

Laumann, Edward O. Prestige & Association in an Urban Community: An Analysis of an Urban Stratification System. LC 66-29709. (Orig.). 1966. pap. 4.95 (ISBN 0-672-60620-8). Bobbs.

--Prestige & Association in an Urban Community: An Analysis of an Urban Stratification System. LC 66-29709. 1966. 20.00x (ISBN 0-672-51165-7). Irvington.

Lieberman, Leo. What Can I Be? A Guide to 525 Liberal Arts & Business Careers. LC 75-26001. 12.95 (ISBN 0-935198-03-2). M M Bruce.

Linneman, Robert E. Turn Yourself On: Goal Planning for Success. LC 77-93292. (Personal Guidance, Social Adjustment Ser). (Illus.). (gr. 9 up). 1970. PLB 5.97 (ISBN 0-8239-0219-6). Rosen Pr.

Lobb, Charlotte. Exploring Careers Through Part-Time & Summer Employment. (gr. 7-12). 1977. PLB 5.97 (ISBN 0-8239-0371-0). Rosen Pr.

McCarthy, Marianthy. Readings in English: Careers 3. (Readings in English Ser.). 105p. (gr. 9-12). 1981. pap. text ed. 2.95 (ISBN 0-88345-425-4, 18884). Regents Pub.

McGrew, John F. Navigating Career Change. LC 80-80788. (Illus.). 124p. 1980. pap. 5.00x (ISBN 0-936544-00-7). New Vista.

Miller, Alden D. Principal Components & Curvature in Occupational Stratification. (Working Papers in Methodology Ser.: No. 2). 152p. 1967. pap. text ed. 4.00 (ISBN 0-89143-026-1). U NC Inst Res Soc Sci.

Montagna, Paul D. Occupations & Society: Toward a Sociology of the Labor Market. LC 76-40121. 1977. text ed. 21.50x (ISBN 0-471-61383-5). Wiley.

Morgan, Marilyn A., ed. Managing Career Development. 304p. 1980. text ed. 14.95 (ISBN 0-442-21914-8). Van Nos Reinhold.

Morrison, Peter & Twing, J. W. Getting the Right Job. (Career in the Modern Office Ser: Bk. 4). 1970. text ed. 5.36 (ISBN 0-07-043193-0, G); tchr's manual 6.95 (ISBN 0-07-043194-9). McGraw.

Mungo, Raymond. Cosmic Profit: How to Make Money Without Doing Time. LC 79-26366. 1980. 9.95 (ISBN 0-316-58933-0, Pub. by Atlantic-Little Brown); pap. 5.95 (ISBN 0-316-58934-9). Little.

Norback, Craig T., ed. Careers Encyclopedia. LC 80-69487. 456p. 1980. 27.50 (ISBN 0-87094-203-4). Dow Jones-Irwin.

Paige, Barbara E. Your Future in a Dental Hygiene Career. rev ed. LC 69-14464. (Careers in Depth Ser). (Illus.). (gr. 9 up). 1979. PLB 5.97 (ISBN 0-8239-0495-4). Rosen Pr.

Parsons, Frank. Choosing a Vocation. LC 67-20718. 1967. Repr. of 1909 ed. 6.00x (ISBN 0-87586-001-X). Agathon.

Prentice, Barbara A. & Sandman, Peter. Five Hundred Back to Work Ideas for Housewives. (Career Ser). Orig. Title: Back to Work Handbook for Housewives. 1971. pap. 1.50 (ISBN 0-02-081140-3, Collier). Macmillan.

Reiss, Albert J., et al. Occupations & Social Status. Stein, Leon, ed. LC 77-70525. (Work Ser.). (Illus.). 1977. Repr. of 1961 ed. lib. bdg. 22.00x (ISBN 0-405-10193-7). Arno.

Rettig, Jack L. Careers: Exploration & Decision. LC 74-611. (gr. 7-12). 1974. pap. text ed. 5.20 (ISBN 0-8224-4678-2); tchrs' guide 1.60 (ISBN 0-8224-4694-4). Pitman Learning.

Ritzer, George. Working: Conflict & Change. 2nd ed. (Illus.). 1977. text ed. 19.95 (ISBN 0-13-967638-4). P-H.

Robinson, John P., et al. Measures of Occupational Attitudes & Occupational Characteristics. LC 75-627966. 480p. 1969. pap. 9.00 (ISBN 0-87944-051-1). Inst Soc Res.

Roe, Anne. The Psychology of Occupations. Stein, Leon, ed. LC 77-70529. (Work Ser.). (Illus.). 1977. Repr. of 1956 ed. lib. bdg. 24.00x (ISBN 0-405-10197-X). Arno.

Roesch, Roberta. Jobs for Weekends. 1978. pap. 3.95 (ISBN 0-425-03635-9, Windhover). Berkley Pub.

Rosenberg, Morris. Occupations & Values. Zuckerman, Harriet & Merton, Robert K., eds. LC 79-9020. (Dissertations on Sociology Ser.). 1980. Repr. of 1957 ed. lib. bdg. 14.00x (ISBN 0-405-12989-0). Arno.

Rottenberg, Simon, ed. Occupational Licensure & Regulation. 1981. 16.25 (ISBN 0-686-73719-9); pap. 8.25 (ISBN 0-8447-2193-X). Am Enterprise.

Rudman, Jack. Associate Occupational Analyst. (Career Examination Ser.: C-2550). (Cloth bdg. avail. on request). pap. 14.00 (ISBN 0-8373-2550-1). Natl Learning.

--Occupational Analyst. (Career Examination Ser.: C-2548). (Cloth bdg. avail. on request). pap. 10.00 (ISBN 0-686-53725-4). Natl Learning.

--Occupational Competency Examination Series. (Individual Titles Listed by Subject). (Cloth bdg. avail. on request). pap. write for info. (ISBN 0-8373-5700-4). Natl Learning.

--Principal Occupational Analyst. (Career Examination Ser.: C-2535). (Cloth bdg. avail. on request). pap. 14.00 (ISBN 0-8373-2535-8). Natl Learning.

--Senior Occupational Analyst. (Career Examination Ser.: C-2549). (Cloth bdg. avail. on request). pap. 12.00 (ISBN 0-8373-2549-8). Natl Learning.

Rutkevich, M. N., ed. The Career Plans of Youth. Yanowitch, Murray, tr. LC 69-18828. (Orig.). 1969. 17.50 (ISBN 0-87332-027-1). M E Sharpe.

Schein, Edgar H. Career Dynamics: Matching Individual & Organizational Needs. 1978. pap. text ed. 7.50 (ISBN 0-201-06834-6). A-W.

Schill, William J. Career Choice & Career Preparation. LC 79-106130. (gr. 9-12). 1979. pap. text ed. 7.95x (ISBN 0-8134-2088-1, 2088). Interstate.

Schreiber, Carol T. Changing Places: Men & Women in Transitional Occupations. 1979. 17.50 (ISBN 0-262-19177-6); pap. 6.95 (ISBN 0-262-69075-6). MIT Pr.

Sinick, Daniel. Occupational Information & Guidance. (Guidance Monograph). 1970. pap. 2.40 (ISBN 0-395-09938-2). HM.

Stanat & Reardon. Job Hunting Secrets. pap. 5.95 (ISBN 0-686-31271-6). New Century.

Stewart, Alexander, et al. Social Stratification & Occupations. Prandy, Ken & Blackburn, R. M., eds. LC 80-16282. 320p. 1980. text ed. 36.00x (ISBN 0-8419-0629-7); pap. text ed. 19.95x (ISBN 0-8419-0630-0). Holmes & Meier.

Stickney, John. Self-Made: Braving an Independent Career in a Corporate Age. 1980. 10.95 (ISBN 0-686-65992-9). Putnam.

Strong, Arline. Veterinarian, Doctor for Your Pet. LC 76-46948. (Illus.). (gr. 2-5). 1977. 7.95 (ISBN 0-689-30575-3). Atheneum.

Treiman, D. J., ed. Occupational Prestige in Comparative Perspective. (Quantitative Studies in Social Discontinuity Ser.). 1977. 28.00 (ISBN 0-12-698750-5). Acad Pr.

Underhill, Ralph. Occupational Values & Post-College Career Change. (Report Ser: No. 120). 1967. 4.00 (ISBN 0-932132-12-X). NORC.

Vocational Research Group. Concise Occupational Reference Handbook. 1979. pap. 4.95 (ISBN 0-910164-01-0). Assoc Bk.

Vogelsang, John. Find the Career That's Right for You. 144p. (Orig.). 1978. pap. 4.95 (ISBN 0-89104-232-6). A & W Pubs.

Wilson, Sandra R. & Wise, Lauress L. The American Citizen: Eleven Years After High School, Vol. I. 1975. pap. 7.75 Research Report-Paper (ISBN 0-89785-518-3). Am Inst Res.

Winn, Charles S. & Davis, L. M. Exploring Occupations in Science, Fine Arts & Humanities. (Careers in Focus Ser.). 1975. text ed. 5.32 (ISBN 0-07-071045-7, G); tchr's. manual & key 3.30 (ISBN 0-07-071046-5); worksheets 8.08 (ISBN 0-07-071065-1). McGraw.

Winn, Charles S. & Peterson, M. Exploring Business & Office Occupations. (Careers in Focus Ser.). 1976. text ed. 5.32 (ISBN 0-07-071037-6, G); tchr's. manual & key 3.30 (ISBN 0-07-071038-4); pkg. of 10 wksheet bklets 13.28 (ISBN 0-07-071061-9). McGraw.

Winn, Charles S. & Vorndran, B. J. Exploring Occupations in Personal Services, Hospitality & Recreation. (Careers in Focus Ser.). 1975. text ed. 5.32 (ISBN 0-07-071033-3, G); tchr's manual & key 3.30 (ISBN 0-07-071034-1); pkg. of 10 wksheet bklets 13.28 (ISBN 0-07-071059-7). McGraw.

Winn, Charles S., et al. Exploring Occupations in Communication & Graphic Arts. (Careers in Focus Ser.). 1976. text ed. 5.32 (ISBN 0-07-071031-7, G); tchr's manual & key 3.30 (ISBN 0-07-071032-5); wksheets 8.08 (ISBN 0-07-071058-9). McGraw.

Wise, Lauress L., et al. The American Citizen: Eleven Years After High School, Vol. II. 1977. pap. 8.50 Research Report-Paper (ISBN 0-89785-519-1). Am Inst Res.

Wolfbein, Seymour L. Occupational Information: A Career Guidance View. 1968. pap. text ed. 3.45x (ISBN 0-685-41967-3). Phila Bk Co.

Yeomans, William N. Jobs Eighty & Eighty-One. LC 77-357858. 1979. 10.95 (ISBN 0-399-12418-7); pap. 4.95 (ISBN 0-399-50389-7, Perigee). Putnam.

Zaccaria, Joseph. Theories of Occupational Choice & Vocational Development. (Guidance Monograph). 1970. pap. 2.40 (ISBN 0-395-09934-X, 9-78834). HM.

OCCUPATIONS–CLASSIFICATION

Davis, Edwin W. Functional Pattern Technique for Classification of Jobs. LC 73-176712. (Columbia University. Teachers College. Contributions to Education: No. 844). Repr. of 1942 ed. 17.50 (ISBN 0-404-55844-5). AMS Pr.

Slocum, Walter. Occupational Careers: A Sociological Perspective. 2nd ed. 1974. lib. bdg. 14.50x (ISBN 0-202-30268-7). Beresford Bk Serv.

OCCUPATIONS–DISEASES

see Occupational Diseases

OCCUPATIONS–GREAT BRITAIN

More, Charles, ed. Skill & the English Working Class 1870-1914. LC 80-51895. 1980. 20.00 (ISBN 0-312-72772-0). St Martin.

Pyne, W. H. Picturesque Views of Rural Occupations in Early Nineteenth Century England, from Ackerman's Edition of Microcosm. 10.00 (ISBN 0-8446-5653-4). Peter Smith.

Spackman, William F. Analysis of the Occupations of the People. LC 68-58020. Repr. of 1847 ed. 17.50x (ISBN 0-678-00573-7). Kelley.

OCCUPATIONS–HYGIENIC ASPECTS

see Industrial Health

OCCUPATIONS–JUVENILE LITERATURE

Ancona, George. And What Do You Do? A Book About People & Their Work. 48p. (gr. 6). 1976. 9.95 (ISBN 0-525-25605-9). Dutton.

Bank, Ira M. Community Careering Gamebook. new ed. 59p. (gr. 3-6). 1974. wkbk. 1.50 (ISBN 0-912578-15-7). Chron Guide.

--Community Careering Guidebook. new ed. 16p. 1974. pap. 3.00 (ISBN 0-912578-14-9). Chron Guide.

Brunetti, Cledo & Higgerson, Clifford. Your Future in a Changing World. LC 70-87820. (Illus.). (gr. 9 up). 1970. PLB 5.97 (ISBN 0-8239-0181-5). Rosen Pr.

Freeman, Dorothy R., et al. Very Important People Who Work with Recreation Vehicles. LC 72-10385. (Very Important People Ser). (Illus.). 64p. (gr. 4-8). 1973. PLB 8.65 (ISBN 0-516-07452-0, Elk Grove Bks). Childrens.

Fries & Clayton. Timed Writings About Careers. 2nd ed. (gr. 9-12). 1975. text ed. 3.96 (ISBN 0-538-20740-X). SW Pub.

Frost, Jack M. & Ratliff, Linda. My Book of Workers: Book 1. new ed. 85p. (gr. 1). 1973. wkbk. 2.50 (ISBN 0-912578-18-1). Chron Guide.

--My Book of Workers: Book 2. new ed. 80p. (gr. 1). 1973. wkbk. 2.50 (ISBN 0-912578-19-X). Chron Guide.

Frost, Jack M & Ratliff, Linda. Workers We Know: Teacher's Manual, Level B. new ed. 166p. 1973. tchrs' manual 6.50 (ISBN 0-912578-20-3). Chron Guide.

Harper, Anita. How We Work. LC 77-5218. (Illus.). (ps-3). 1977. 2.95 (ISBN 0-06-022224-7, HarpJ); PLB 5.11 (ISBN 0-06-022225-5). Har-Row.

Jew, Wing & Tong, Robert. Janus Job Planner. (Illus.). 88p. (gr. 7-12). 1976. pap. text ed. 2.95 (ISBN 0-915510-12-X). Janus Bks.

Jones, Ann. Career Color-Cut-Out Book for Girls & Boys. (Coloring Experience Ser). (Illus.). (gr. 3-12). 1978. pap. 1.95 (ISBN 0-8431-0239-X). Price Stern.

Moncure, Jane B. Jobs People Do. LC 76-5452. (Illus.). (ps-3). 1976. 6.45 (ISBN 0-913778-37-0). Childs World.

--People Who Help People. LC 75-29225. (Illus.). (ps-3). 1975. 6.45 (ISBN 0-913778-16-8). Childs World.

Neigoff, Anne. Now You Know About People at Work, 5 bks. Incl. Where People Work; When People Work; Why People Work; Work You Can Do; Who Works. (Spanish edition available). 1974. 86.00 (ISBN 0-87827-181-3); tchr's guide incl. (ISBN 0-685-57300-1); inl. records & cassettes (ISBN 0-685-57301-X). Ency Brit Ed.

Ott, John & Stroer, Rosemary. Work As You Like It: A Look at Unusual Jobs. LC 78-26694. (Career Bk.). (Illus.). 192p. (gr. 7 up). 1979. PLB 7.79 (ISBN 0-671-32904-9). Messner.

Rockwell, Anne. When We Grow Up. LC 80-21768. (Illus.). (ps-1). 1981. 10.25 (ISBN 0-525-42575-6). Dutton.

Scarry, Richard. Mein Allerschonstes Buch Vom Backen Bauen und Flugzeugfliegen. (Illus., Ger.). 1970. 11.95x (ISBN 3-7735-4927-X). Intl Learn Syst.

--Richard Scarry's What Do People Do All Day? (Illus.). (ps-3). 1968. 4.95 (ISBN 0-394-81823-7); PLB 5.99 (ISBN 0-394-91823-1). Random.

Seed, Suzanne. Saturday's Child. LC 72-12599. (Illus.). (gr. 6-12). 1973. PLB 7.98 (ISBN 0-87955-803-2); pap. 4.95 (ISBN 0-87955-203-4). O'Hara.

Splaver, Sarah. Paraprofessions: Careers of the Future & the Present. LC 72-1417. (Career Bks.). 192p. (gr. 9 up). 1972. PLB 7.29 (ISBN 0-671-32546-9). Messner.

OCCUPATIONS, DANGEROUS

see also Accident Law; Arsenic Poisoning; Employers' Liability; Industrial Accidents; Lead-Poisoning; Mine Inspection; Occupational Diseases

Glassman. Dangerous Lives. (gr. 7-12). 1980. pap. 1.25 (ISBN 0-590-30875-0, Schol Pap). Schol Bk Serv.

Shafai-Sahrai, Yaghoub. Determinants of Occupational Injury Experience: A Study of Matched Pairs of Companies. LC 73-620211. 120p. 1973. pap. 4.50 (ISBN 0-87744-084-0). Mich St U Busn.

OCCUPATIONS, DANGEROUS–SAFETY APPLIANCES

see also Clothing, Protective

OCCUPATIONS AND BUSY WORK

see Creative Activities and Seatwork

OCCUPIED TERRITORY
see Military Occupation
OCEAN
see also Diving, Submarine; Underwater Exploration; Oceanography; also names of oceans, e.g. Pacific Ocean
Armstrong, John M. & Ryner, Peter C. Ocean Management: Seeking a New Perspective. 180p. 1981. text ed. 22.50 (ISBN 0-250-40470-2). Ann Arbor Science.
Barton, Robert. The Oceans. 336p. 1980. 19.95x (ISBN 0-87196-414-7). Facts on File.
Beazley, Mitchell, ed. Atlas of the Oceans. LC 77-73772. (Illus.). 1977. 35.00 (ISBN 0-528-83082-1). Rand.
Bolin, Bert, ed. The Atmosphere & the Sea in Motion. LC 59-14858. (Illus.). 1959. 20.00 (ISBN 0-87470-000-0). Rockefeller.
Borgese, Elisabeth M. Drama of the Oceans. LC 74-16165. (Illus.). 300p. 1976. 25.00 (ISBN 0-8109-0337-7). Abrams.
Borgese, Elisabeth M. & Ginsburg, Norton, eds. Ocean Yearbook Two. LC 79-642855. 1981. 35.00x (ISBN 0-226-06603-7). U of Chicago Pr.
Borgese, Elizabeth M. & Ginsburg, Norton, eds. Ocean Yearbook Nineteen Seventy-Seven. 1979. 25.00x (ISBN 0-226-06602-9). U of Chicago Pr.
Bowen, F. The Sea: Its History & Romance, 4 vols. 1977. lib. bdg. 400.00 (ISBN 0-8490-2581-8). Gordon Pr.
Carr, Roland T. To Sea in Haste. LC 75-13944. 1975. 12.50 (ISBN 0-87491-204-0); pap. 5.95 (ISBN 0-87491-020-X). Acropolis.
Carson, Rachel. Sea Around Us. rev. ed. (gr. 10 up). 1961. 15.00x (ISBN 0-19-500500-7). Oxford U Pr.
Carson, Rachel L. Sea Around Us. 1954. pap. 2.25 (ISBN 0-451-61873-4, ME1873, Ment). NAL.
Center for Oceans Law & Policy. Oceans Policy Studies, 6 vols. (Ocean Policy Studies Ser.). 1979. pap. 50.00 (ISBN 0-87215-297-9). Michie-Bobbs.
Coker, Robert E. This Great & Wide Sea: An Introduction to Oceanography & Marine Biology. (Illus.). pap. 4.95x (ISBN 0-06-130551-0, TB551, Torch). Har-Row.
Douglas, John S. Story of the Oceans. LC 78-106686. Repr. of 1952 ed. lib. bdg. 26.00x (ISBN 0-8371-3357-2, DOSO). Greenwood.
Engel, Leonard. The Sea. (Young Readers Library). (Illus.). 1977. lib. bdg. 7.95 (ISBN 0-686-51094-1). Silver.
Evans, I. O. Observer's Book of Sea & Seashore. (Observer Bks.). (Illus.). 1977. 4.95 (ISBN 0-684-15218-5, ScribT). Scribner.
Fishing News Bks. Ltd. Staff, ed. Study of the Sea: The Development of Marine Research Under the Auspices of the International Council for the Exploration of the Sea. 272p. 1981. 75.00x (ISBN 0-85238-112-3, Pub. by Fishing News England). State Mutual Bk.
Freuchen, Peter & Loth, David. Peter Freuchen's Book of the Seven Seas. (Illus.). 1966. 9.95 (ISBN 0-671-56671-7); deluxe ed. 10.00 (ISBN 0-671-56672-5); pap. 3.95 (ISBN 0-671-56674-1). S&S.
Garrett, William & Smagin, V. M. Determination of the Atmospheric Contribution of Petroleum Hydrocarbons to the Oceans. (Special Environmental Report Ser: No. 6). (Illus.). 27p. 1977. pap. 16.00 (ISBN 92-63-10440-9, WMO). Unipub.
Gibbs, R. J. & Shaw, R. P., eds. Transport Processes in Lakes & Oceans. (Marine Science Ser.: Vol. 7). 296p. 1977. 27.50 (ISBN 0-306-35507-8, Plenum Pr). Plenum Pub.
Goldberg, Edward D., ed. The Sea: Ideas & Observations on Progress in the Study of the Seas, Vol. 5, Marine Chemistry. LC 62-18366. 895p. 1974. 74.00x (ISBN 0-471-31090-5, Pub. by Wiley-Interscience). Wiley.
Gran Diccionario Infantil Marin, 4 vols. 840p. (Espn.). 1979. Set. 128.00 (ISBN 84-7102-150-1, S-50032). French & Eur.
Great Britain Challenger Office. Report on the Scientific Results of the Voyage of H. M. S. Challenger During the Years 1873-1876, 50 Vols. (Illus.). 1880-1895. Set. 3500.00 (ISBN 0-384-19750-7). Johnson Repr.
Groves, Donald G. & Hunt, Lee M. The Ocean World Encyclopedia. LC 79-21093. (Illus.). 1980. 29.95 (ISBN 0-07-025010-3). McGraw.
Heezen, B. C. Influence of Abyssal Circulation on Sedimentary Accumulations in Space & Time. (Developments in Sedimentology: 23). 1977. 39.00 (ISBN 0-444-41569-6). Elsevier.
Hill, M. N. The Sea: The Earth Beneath the Sea: History, Vol. 3. LC 80-248. (Vol. 3). 980p. 1963. Repr. of 1981 ed. 55.00 (ISBN 0-89874-099-1). Krieger.
Howard, George. How We Find Out About the Sea. (Illus.). 64p. (gr. 7-9). 1974. 6.50 (ISBN 0-212-98417-9). Transatlantic.
Idyll, C. P. Abyss: The Deep Sea & the Creatures That Live in It. 3rd rev. ed. (Apollo Eds.). (Illus.). pap. 6.95 (ISBN 0-8152-0400-0, A400). T Y Crowell.
Ippen, A. T. Estuary & Coastline Hydrodynamics. (Engineering Societies Monographs). 1966. text ed. 38.00 (ISBN 0-07-032015-2, C). McGraw.
Jacques Cousteau: The Ocean World. (Illus.). 1979. 55.00 (ISBN 0-8109-0777-1). Abrams.
Jones, Lewis. The Ocean. (Newbury Hse Raders Ser.: Stage 4 - Intermediate). (Illus.). 80p. (Orig.). (gr. 7-12). 1981. pap. text ed. cancelled (ISBN 0-88377-197-7). Newbury Hse.
Keller, W. Phillip. Ocean Glory. (Illus.). 160p. 1980. 22.95 (ISBN 0-8007-1104-1). Revell.
Lane, Ferdinand. Mysterious Sea. LC 73-128268. (Essay Index Reprint Ser). 1947. 20.00 (ISBN 0-8369-1971-8). Arno.
El Mar, Gran Enciclopedia Salvat, 10 vols. 3000p. (Espn.). 1975. Set. 320.00 (ISBN 84-7137-428-5, S-50560). French & Eur.
Marine Board. Toward Fulfillment of a National Ocean Commitment. LC 70-183067. (Illus.). 572p. 1972. 5.25 (ISBN 0-309-01936-2). Natl Acad Pr.
Mjelde, Michael J. Glory of the Seas. LC 77-105505. (The American Maritime Library: Vol. 1). (Illus.). 303p. 1970. 14.95 (ISBN 0-8195-4015-3). Mystic Seaport.
Monin, A. S., et al. Variability of the Oceans. LC 77-826. 1977. 39.50 (ISBN 0-471-61328-2, Pub. by Wiley-Interscience). Wiley.
Navarro Dagnino, Juan. Vocabulario Maritimo Ingles-Espanol y Espanol-Ingles. 5th ed. 151p. (Span.-Eng.). 1976. pap. 8.50 (ISBN 84-252-0225-6, S-12239). French & Eur.
The Ocean Realm. LC 77-93399. (Special Publication Ser.: 13). (Illus.). 1978. 6.95 (ISBN 0-87044-251-1); lib. bdg. 8.50 (ISBN 0-87044-256-2). Natl Geog.
Perry, A. H. & Walker, J. M. The Ocean-Atmosphere System. (Illus.). 1977. text ed. 22.00x (ISBN 0-582-48559-2); pap. text ed. 14.95x (ISBN 0-582-48560-6). Longman.
The Saturday Evening Post Book of the Sea & Ships. LC 78-61519. (Illus.). 1978. 11.95 (ISBN 0-89387-023-4). Sat Eve Post.
Saturday Evening Post Editors. The Saturday Evening Post Book of the Sea & Ships. LC 78-61519. (Illus.). 160p. 1978. 13.95 (ISBN 0-89387-023-4). Curtis Pub Co.
Sluyter, E. H. & Raddon, Ethel. Ocean Waves & Progressive Oscillatory Waves: Syllabus. 1977. pap. text ed. 3.95 (ISBN 0-89420-015-1, 234011); cassette recordings 38.90 (ISBN 0-89420-165-4, 234000). Natl Book.
Smith, Sandra. Discovering the Sea. (Discovering Ser.). (Illus.). 96p. 1981. 9.95 (ISBN 0-86706-000-X). Time-Life.
Sverdrup, H., et al. Oceans: Their Physics, Chemistry & General Biology. 1942. ref. ed. 33.95 (ISBN 0-13-630350-1). P-H.
Third United Nations Conference on the Law of the Sea: Official Records, Vol. IX. 191p. 1979. pap. 14.00 (ISBN 0-686-68976-3, UN79/5/3, UN). Unipub.
Thorndike, Joseph J., Jr. Discovery of Lost Worlds. LC 79-15881. (Illus.). 352p. 1980. pap. 14.95 (ISBN 0-8281-0312-7, Dist by Scribner). Scribner.
Vinogradov, A. P. & Udintsev, G. B., eds. The Rift Zones of the World Oceans. Kaner, N., tr. from Rus. LC 75-16178. 503p. 1975. 76.95 (ISBN 0-470-90838-6). Halsted Pr.
Wegener, A. The Origins of Continents & Oceans. (Illus.). 7.00 (ISBN 0-8446-3143-4). Peter Smith.
Wegener, Alfred. Origin of Continents & Oceans. Biram, John, tr. (Illus.). 1966. pap. 4.50 (ISBN 0-486-61708-4). Dover.
Wilson, David A. Song of the Sea. 1970. pap. 1.50 (ISBN 0-934852-04-9, LH-4). Lorien Hse.
Wirsing, Robert G., ed. International Relations & the Future of Ocean Space. LC 73-14938. (Studies in International Affairs: No. 10). (Illus.). 146p. 1974. 5.95x (ISBN 0-87249-303-2). U of SC Pr.
World Book-Childcraft International Inc. Staff. Childcraft Annual: Story of the Sea. LC 65-25105. (Childcraft-the How & Why Library). (Illus.). (gr. k-6). 1979. write for info. (ISBN 0-7166-0679-8). World Bk-Childcraft.
OCEAN–ECONOMIC ASPECTS
see Marine Resources; Shipping
OCEAN–JUVENILE LITERATURE
Aksyonov, Andrei & Chernov, Alexander. Exploring the Deep. (gr. 7 up). 1980. PLB 7.60 (ISBN 0-531-02126-2, BO3). Watts.
Bergaust, Erik. Colonizing the Sea. LC 76-21355. (Illus.). (gr. 6 up). 1976. PLB 4.96 (ISBN 0-399-61035-9). Putnam.
Berres, et al. Deep Sea Adventure Ser, 12 bks. (gr. 3-8). 1967. pap. text ed. 6.52 ea. (Sch Div); tchr's manual 2.52 (ISBN 0-201-40217-3). A-W.
Blau, Melinda. First Over the Oceans. LC 78-12960. (Famous Firsts Ser.). (Illus.). 1978. lib. bdg. 7.35 (ISBN 0-686-51103-4). Silver.
Cook, Jan L. The Mysterious Undersea World. LC 79-1791. (Ser. One). (Illus.). 100p. (gr. 3-8). 1980. 6.95 (ISBN 0-87044-317-8); PLB 8.50 (ISBN 0-87044-322-4). Natl Geog.
Davies, Eryl. Ocean Frontiers. LC 79-14041. (How It Works Ser.). (gr. 4-6). 1980. 5.95 (ISBN 0-670-52026-8). Viking Pr.
Griggs, Tamar. There's a Sound in the Sea: A Child's-Eye View of the Whale. (Illus.). 96p. (gr. 5-9). 1975. 10.95 (ISBN 0-912020-47-4); pap. 5.95 (ISBN 0-912020-46-6). Scrimshaw Calif.
A Look at the Earth Around Us: Oceans. 1981. 23.50 (ISBN 0-686-73885-3, 04916). Natl Geog.
Noel, Spike. Fish & the Sea. (Junior Reference Ser.). (Illus.). 64p. (gr. 7 up). 1972. 7.95 (ISBN 0-7136-1239-8). Dufour.
Reed, W. Maxwell & Bronson, Wilfrid S. Sea for Sam. rev. ed. Brandwein, Paul F., ed. LC 59-12826. (gr. 7 up). 1960. 7.95 (ISBN 0-15-271380-8, HJ). HarBraceJ.
Sabin, Louis. Wonders of the Sea. (Illus.). 32p. (gr. 2-4). 1981. PLB 7.29 (ISBN 0-89375-578-8); pap. text ed. 1.95 (ISBN 0-89375-579-6). Troll Assocs.
Selsam, Millicent E. & Morrow, Betty. See Through the Sea. LC 54-8990. 48p. (gr. 3-6). 1955. PLB 8.79 (ISBN 0-06-025456-4, HarpJ). Har-Row.
Simons, Barbara B. A Visit to the Ocean. LC 78-4602. (Adventures in Nature Ser). (Illus.). (gr. 2-6). 1978. lib. bdg. 6.95 (ISBN 0-916392-24-4); pap. 3.95 (ISBN 0-916392-23-6). Oak Tree Pubns.
Thompson, Brenda & Overbeck, Cynthia. Under the Sea. LC 76-22470. (First Fact Books Ser). (Illus.). (gr. k-3). 1977. PLB 4.95g (ISBN 0-8225-1363-3). Lerner Pubns.
Tyler, Jenny & Watts, Lisa. Children's Book of the Seas. LC 77-15549. (Children's Guides Ser.). (Illus.). (gr. 3 up). 1978. PLB 6.95 (ISBN 0-88436-464-X). EMC.
Waters, John F. Maritime Careers. (Career Concise Guides Ser.). (Illus.). 1977. 6.90 (ISBN 0-531-01283-2). Watts.
OCEAN–RESEARCH
see Oceanographic Research
OCEAN (IN RELIGION, FOLK-LORE, ETC.)
see Folk-Lore of the Sea
OCEAN-ATMOSPHERE INTERACTION
see also Ocean Waves
Dobson, F., et al, eds. Air-Sea Interaction: Instruments & Methods. 815p. 1980. 39.50 (ISBN 0-306-40543-1, Plenum Pr). Plenum Pub.
Hastenrath, Stefan & Lamb, Peter J. Heat Budget Atlas of the Tropical Atlantic & Eastern Pacific Oceans. LC 77-91052. (Illus.). 1978. pap. text ed. 50.00x (ISBN 0-299-07584-2). U of Wis Pr.
The Influence of the Ocean on Climate. (Reports on Marine Science Affairs: No. 11). 44p. 1977. pap. 10.00 (ISBN 92-63-10472-7, WMO). Unipub.
Monin, A. S., et al. Variability of the Oceans. LC 77-826. 1977. 39.50 (ISBN 0-471-61328-2, Pub. by Wiley-Interscience). Wiley.
NATO Advanced Study Institute, Sorrento, Italy, June, 1973. Modern Topics in Micro Wave Propagation & Air-Sea Interaction: Proceedings. Zancla, A., ed. LC 73-91210. (NATO Advance Study Institutes: No. C-5). 1973. lib. bdg. 45.00 (ISBN 90-277-0419-8, Pub. by Reidel Holland). Kluwer Boston.
OCEAN BIRDS
see Sea Birds
OCEAN BOTTOM
see also Abyssal Zone; Manned Undersea Research Stations; Marine Sediments; Sedimentation and Deposition; Submarine Geology; Submarine Topography
Barkenbus, Jack N. Deep Seabed Resources: Politics & Technology. LC 78-73024. 1979. 17.95 (ISBN 0-02-901830-7). Free Pr.
Belderson, R. H., et al. Sonographs of the Sea Floor: A Picture Atlas. 1972. 68.50 (ISBN 0-444-40984-X). Elsevier.
Booth, Eugene. Under the Ocean. LC 77-7983. (A Raintree Spotlight Book). (Illus.). (gr. k-3). 1977. PLB 9.30 (ISBN 0-8393-0108-1). Raintree Child.
Cohen, Phillip M. Bathymetric Navigation & Charting. LC 79-6107. (Navies & Men Ser.). (Illus.). 1980. Repr. of 1970 ed. lib. bdg. 12.00x (ISBN 0-405-13036-8). Arno.
Coulomb, J. Sea Floor Spreading & Continental Drift. Tanner, R. W., tr. from Fr. LC 79-179891. (Geophysics & Astrophysics Monographs: No. 2). 184p. 1972. lib. bdg. 31.50 (ISBN 90-277-0232-2, Pub. by Reidel Holland); pap. 18.50 (ISBN 90-277-0238-1). Kluwer Boston.
Emiliani, Cesare. The Oceanic Lithosphere. LC 62-18366. (The Sea: Ideas & Observations on Progress in the Study of the Seas: Vol. 7). 1712p. 1981. 55.00 (ISBN 0-471-02870-3, Pub. by Wiley-Interscience). Wiley.
Fanning, Kent A. & Manheim, Frank T. The Dynamic Environment of the Ocean Floor. LC 78-24651. 512p. 1981. 39.95 (ISBN 0-669-02809-6). Lexington Bks.
Fedorov, K. N., ed. The Thermohaline Finestructure of the Ocean. Brown, D. A. & Turner, J. S., trs. 1978. text ed. 45.00 (ISBN 0-08-021673-0). Pergamon.
Goldin, Augusta. Bottom of the Sea. LC 66-10194. (A Let's-Read-&-Find-Out Science Bk). (Illus.). (ps-3). 1967. bds. 8.95 (ISBN 0-690-15863-7, TYC-J). Har-Row.
Heezen, Bruce C. & Hollister, Charles D. Face of the Deep. 1971. pap. 13.95x (ISBN 0-19-501277-1). Oxford U Pr.
Hill, M. N. The Sea: The Earth Beneath the Sea: History, Vol. 3. LC 80-248. (Vol. 3). 980p. 1963. Repr. of 1981 ed. 55.00 (ISBN 0-89874-099-1). Krieger.
International Liege Colloquium on Ocean Hydrodynamics, 8th. Bottom Turbulence: Proceedings. Nihoul, J. C., ed. (Elsevier Oceanography Ser.: Vol. 19). 1977. 48.00 (ISBN 0-444-41574-2). Elsevier.
Johnson, Douglas W. Origin of Submarine Canyons: A Critical Review of Hypotheses. 1967. Repr. of 1939 ed. 13.75 (ISBN 0-02-847260-8). Hafner.
Luard, Evan. The Control of the Sea-Bed: An Updated Report. LC 76-11050. 320p. 1976. 16.50 (ISBN 0-8008-1811-3). Taplinger.
Maxwell, Arthur E., et al. Sea, Vol. 4 Pts 1-3. LC 62-18366. 1971. Pt. 1. 69.00 (ISBN 0-471-57910-6, Pub. by Wiley-Interscience). Wiley.
Mogi, Akio. An Atlas of the Sea Floor Around Japan. 1979. 60.00x (ISBN 0-86008-255-5, Pub. by U of Tokyo Pr). Intl Schol Bk Serv.
Nairn, A. E. & Stehli, F. G., eds. Ocean Basins & Margins, 5 vols. Incl. Vol. 1: The South Atlantic. 583p. 1973. 49.50 (ISBN 0-306-37771-3); Vol. 2: The North Atlantic. LC 73-21580. 598p. 1974. 49.50 (ISBN 0-306-37772-1); Vol. 3: The Gulf of Mexico & The Caribbean. 706p. 1975. 49.50 (ISBN 0-306-37773-X); Vol. 4A: The Eastern Mediterranean. 519p. 1977. 49.50 (ISBN 0-306-37774-8); Vol. 4B: The Western Mediterranean. 462p. 1977. 49.50 (ISBN 0-306-37779-9). (Illus., Plenum Pr). Plenum Pub.
Nelson, Bryan. Seabirds: Their Biology and Ecology. (Illus.). 248p. 1980. 14.95 (ISBN 0-89479-042-0). A & W Pubs.
Paton, Angus, pref. by. Sea Floor Development: Moving into Deep Water. LC 79-670284. (Royal Society). (Illus.). 1978. text ed. 45.00x (ISBN 0-85403-100-6). Scholium Intl.
Pettersson, Hans. Ocean Floor. (Illus.). 1969. Repr. of 1954 ed. 13.00 (ISBN 0-02-850260-4). Hafner.
Talwani, Manik & Pitman, Walter C., III, eds. Island Arcs, Deep Sea Trenches & Back-Arc Basins, Vol. 1. LC 76-58102. (Maurice Ewing Ser.). 1977. 18.00 (ISBN 0-87590-400-9). Am Geophysical.
Wertenbaker, William. The Floor of the Sea: Maurice Ewing & the Search to Understand the Earth. 1974. 10.00 (ISBN 0-316-93121-7). Little.
Wright, L. D. Circulation, Effluent Diffusion & Sediment Transport, Mouth of South Pass, Mississippi River Delta. LC 72-185845. (University Studies: Coastal Studies Ser 26). (Illus.). x, 56p. 1970. pap. 4.00x (ISBN 0-8071-0515-5). La State U Pr.
OCEAN CABLES
see Cables, Submarine
OCEAN CURRENTS
see also Gulf Stream
Briscoe, Melbourne, ed. Oceanic Internal Waves. 1976. pap. 15.00 (ISBN 0-87590-222-7). Am Geophysical.
Duing, Walter. Monsoon Regime of the Currents in the Indian Ocean. LC 76-104320. (International Indian Ocean Expedition Oceanographic Monographs: No. 1). (Illus.). 1970. 12.00x (ISBN 0-8248-0092-3, Eastwest Ctr). U Pr of Hawaii.
Kendall, T. Robert. The Pacific Equatorial Countercurrent. LC 71-125496. (Illus.). 78p. 1970. 8.00 (ISBN 0-914704-01-X). Intl Ctr Environment.
Leblond, P. H. & Mysak, L. A. Waves in the Ocean. (Elsevier Oceanography Ser.: Vol. 20). 1978. 115.75 (ISBN 0-444-41602-1). Elsevier.
Worthington, L. V. On the North Atlantic Circulation. LC 76-17244. (Oceanographic Studies: No. 6). (Illus.). 112p. 1977. 16.50x (ISBN 0-8018-1742-0). Johns Hopkins.
OCEAN CURRENTS–JUVENILE LITERATURE
Clemons, Elizabeth. Waves, Tides & Currents. (gr. 5 up). 1967. PLB 5.99 (ISBN 0-394-91824-X). Knopf.
OCEAN ENGINEERING
see also Manned Undersea Research Stations; Marine Geotechnique; Oceanographic Instruments; Offshore Structures

American Society Civil Engineers, compiled By. Civil Engineering in the Oceans, No. IV. 1104p. 1979. pap. text ed. 78.00 (ISBN 0-87262-191-X). Am Soc Civil Eng.
American Society of Civil Engineers, compiled By. Civil Engineering in the Oceans III. 1560p. 1976. pap. text ed. 59.00 (ISBN 0-87262-162-6). Am Soc Civil Eng.
ASCE Technical Council on Ocean Engineering, Dec. 1969. Civil Engineering in the Oceans: Proceedings, No. II. American Society of Civil Engineers, compiled By. 1280p. 1970. 38.00 (ISBN 0-87262-018-2). Am Soc Civil Eng.
Brahtz, John F., ed. Ocean Engineering: Goals, Environment, Technology. 732p. 1968. 39.00 (ISBN 0-471-09580-X). Krieger.
Bretschneider, Charles L. Topics in Ocean Engineering, Vol. 3. 339p. 1976. 26.50 (ISBN 0-87201-600-5). Gulf Pub.
Bretschneider, Charles L., ed. Topics in Ocean Engineering. Incl. Vol. 1. (Illus.). 428p. 1969. (ISBN 0-87201-598-X); Vol. 2. (Illus.). 229p. 1970 (ISBN 0-87201-599-8). 26.50x ea. Gulf Pub.
Capurro, Luis R. Oceanography for Practicing Engineers. LC 71-126339. 1970. 13.95 (ISBN 0-389-00503-7); pap. 10.95 (ISBN 0-8436-0323-2). CBI Pub.
Carmichael, A. Douglas. Ocean Engineering Power Systems. LC 74-4343. (Illus.). 1974. 8.00x (ISBN 0-87033-192-2). Cornell Maritime.
Craven, John. Ocean Engineering Systems. 1971. pap. 16.00x (ISBN 0-262-03040-3). MIT Pr.
English, T. Saunders, ed. Ocean Resources & Public Policy. LC 77-103298. (Public Policy Issues in Resource Management Ser.: No. 5). (Illus.). 192p. 1973. text ed. 15.00 (ISBN 0-295-95260-1). U of Wash Pr.
Evans, J. Harvey & Adamchak, John C. Ocean Engineering Structures. 1969. pap. 16.00x (ISBN 0-262-55001-6). MIT Pr.
Gaythwaite, John W. The Marine Environment & Structural Design. 236p. 1981. text ed. 22.50 (ISBN 0-442-24834-2). Van Nos Reinhold.
Geyer, R. A. Submersibles & Their Use in Oceanography & Ocean Engineering. (Elsevier Oceanography Ser.: 17). 1977. 63.50 (ISBN 0-444-41545-9). Elsevier.
Gillie, Angelo & Pratt, Arden. Marine Technology Programs. 1971. pap. 3.00 (ISBN 0-87117-026-4). Am Assn Comm Jr Coll.
International Conference on Port & Ocean Engineering Under Arctic Conditions, Third. Proceedings, 2 vols. Burrell, D. C. & Hood, D. W., eds. 1382p. 1976. Set. pap. 50.00 (ISBN 0-685-83273-2). U of AK Inst Marine.
Knight, H. Gary, et al, eds. Ocean Thermal Energy Conversion: Legal, Political & Institutional Aspects. LC 77-2049. 1977. 22.95 (ISBN 0-669-01441-9). Lexington Bks.
Lavi, A. Ocean Thermal Energy Conversion. 80p. 1981. pap. 30.00 (ISBN 0-08-026705-X). Pergamon.
McCormick, Michael E. Ocean Engineering Wave Mechanics. LC 72-12756. (Ocean Engineering Ser.). 192p. 1973. 29.50 (ISBN 0-471-58177-1, Pub. by Wiley-Interscience). Wiley.
McCormick, Michael E., ed. Port & Ocean Engineering Under Arctic Conditions: Selected Papers from the 3rd International Conference. 1977. pap. text ed. 24.00 (ISBN 0-08-021421-5). Pergamon.
Muga, Bruce J. & Wilson, James F. Dynamic Analysis of Ocean Structures. LC 77-122021. (Ocean Technology Ser.). 377p. 1970. 35.00 (ISBN 0-306-30483-X, Plenum Pr). Plenum Pub.
Myers, John J., ed. Handbook of Ocean & Underwater Engineering. LC 67-27280. 1969. 46.50 (ISBN 0-07-044245-2, P&RB). McGraw.
National Academy Of Sciences. Energy Systems of Extended Endurance in the 1-100 Kilowatt Range for Undersea Applications. 1968. 5.75 (ISBN 0-309-01702-5). Natl Acad Pr.
Paton, Angus, pref. by. Sea Floor Development: Moving into Deep Water. LC 79-670284. (Royal Society). (Illus.). 1978. text ed. 45.00x (ISBN 0-85403-100-6). Scholium Intl.
Penzias, Walter & Goodman, M. W. Man Beneath the Sea: A Review of Underwater Ocean Engineering. LC 70-148506. 1973. 69.00 (ISBN 0-471-68018-4). Wiley.
Schenck, Hilbert. Introduction to Ocean Engineering. (Illus.). 384p. 1975. text ed. 25.50 (ISBN 0-07-055240-1, C); solutions manual 3.50 (ISBN 0-07-055241-X). McGraw.
Smith, F. Walton & Kalber, F. A., eds. Handbook in Marine Science, CRC: Section A, Oceanography. LC 73-88624. 640p. 1974. Vol. 1. 59.95 (ISBN 0-87819-389-8); Vol. 2, 390p. 53.95 (ISBN 0-87819-390-1). CRC Pr.
U.S. Dept. of Energy. Ocean Energy Systems Program Summary: Fiscal Year 1979. 285p. 1981. Repr. of 1978 ed. pap. 30.00 (ISBN 0-89934-100-4, G.036). Solar Energy Info.
Wiegel, Robert L. Oceanographical Engineering. 1964. ref. ed. 34.95 (ISBN 0-13-629600-9). P-H.
Zienkiewicz, O. C., et al, eds. Numerical Methods in Offshore Engineering. LC 77-12565. (Numerical Methods in Engineering Ser.). 1978. 82.25 (ISBN 0-471-99591-6, Pub. by Wiley-Interscience). Wiley.

OCEAN FISHING
see Salt-Water Fishing

OCEAN FLOOR
see Ocean Bottom

OCEAN FREIGHTERS
see Cargo Ships

OCEAN IN ART
see Sea in Art

OCEAN IN LITERATURE
see Sea in Literature

OCEAN LIFE
see Marine Biology

OCEAN LINERS

Brinnin, John M. Beau Voyage: Life Aboard the Last Great Ships. (Illus.). 280p. 1981. until jan. 1982 50.00 (ISBN 0-312-92045-8); thereafter 60.00 (ISBN 0-686-30571-X). Congdon & Lattes.
Coleman, Terry. The Liners: A History of the North Atlantic Crossing. LC 77-76. (Illus.). 1977. 14.95 (ISBN 0-399-11958-2). Putnam.
Maber, John M. Channel Packets & Oceanliners. (The Ship Series, National Maritime Museum). (Illus.). 1980. 9.95 (ISBN 0-11-290316-9). Sheridan.
Maddocks, Melvin. The Great Liners. (The Seafarers). 1978. 14.95 (ISBN 0-8094-2662-5). Time-Life.
--The Great Liners. LC 78-1366. (The Seafarers Ser.). (Illus.). 1978. lib. bdg. 11.97 (ISBN 0-686-50986-2). Silver.
Marsden, Peter. The Wreck of the Amsterdam. LC 74-24329. (Illus.). 300p. 1975. 35.00x (ISBN 0-8128-1760-5). Stein & Day.
Martin, Simon. The Other Titanic. LC 79-56252. (Illus.). 208p. 1980. 19.95 (ISBN 0-7153-7755-8). David & Charles.
Maxtone-Graham, John. The Only Way to Cross. (Illus.). 480p. 1972. 15.95 (ISBN 0-02-582350-7). Macmillan.
--The Only Way to Cross. (Illus.). 1978. pap. 7.95 (ISBN 0-02-096010-7, Collier). Macmillan.
Miller, Byron. Sail, Steam & Splendour: A Picture History of Life Aboard the Transatlantic Liners. LC 76-9732. (Illus.). 1977. 35.00 (ISBN 0-8129-0638-1). Times Bks.
Miller, William H. Transatlantic Liners Nineteen Forty Five to Nineteen Eighty. LC 81-1526. (Illus.). 224p. 1981. 21.95 (ISBN 0-668-05267-8). Arco.
Miller, Williams H., Jr. Guide to North American Passenger Ships 1978-79. LC 78-52326. 1978. 9.95 (ISBN 0-88825-004-5). Nichols Pub.
Morris, Charles F. Origins, Orient & Oriana. LC 79-28664. (Illus.). xx, 491p. 1980. 56.00 (ISBN 0-935786-00-7). McCartan & Root.
Potter, Neil & Frost, Jack. The Queen Mary: Her Inception & History. LC 70-131366. (Illus.). 1971. 10.00 (ISBN 0-911302-14-X). San Francisco Pr.
Ransome-Wallis, P. North Atlantic Panorama. LC 77-74564. 1977. 19.95 (ISBN 0-8195-5016-7, Pub. by Wesleyan U Pr). Columbia U Pr.

OCEAN-METEOROLOGICAL RELATIONS
see Ocean-Atmosphere Interaction

OCEAN MINING
see also Manganese Mines and Mining, Submarine

Baram, Michael & Rice, David. Marine Mining of the Continental Shelf: An Assessment of Legal, Technical & Environmental Factors. LC 77-23831. 1978. 25.00 (ISBN 0-88410-616-0). Ballinger Pub.
Bulkley, Ian G. Who Gains from Deep Ocean Mining? Simulating the Impact of Regimes for Regulating Nodule Exploitation. LC 79-87567. (Research Ser.: No. 40). (Illus.). 1979. pap. 3.50x (ISBN 0-87725-140-1). U of Cal Intl St.
Cronan, David S. Underwater Minerals. (Ocean Science Resources & Technology Ser.). 1980. 57.50 (ISBN 0-12-197480-4). Acad Pr.
Earney, Fillmore C. Petroleum & Hard Minerals from the Sea. LC 80-17653. (Scripta Series in Geography). 291p. 1980. 32.95 (ISBN 0-470-27009-8, Pub. by Halsted Pr). Wiley.

OCEAN RESOURCES
see Marine Resources

OCEAN ROUTES
see Trade Routes

OCEAN TEMPERATURE

Colborn, J. G. The Thermal Structure of the Indian Ocean. (International Indian Ocean Expedition Oceanographic Monographs: No. 2). 144p. 1975. text ed. 15.00x (ISBN 0-8248-0349-3, Eastwest Ctr). U Pr of Hawaii.
Mamayev, O. I. Temperature-Salinity Analysis of World Ocean Waters. (Oceanography Ser.). 374p. 1975. 73.25 (ISBN 0-444-41251-4). Elsevier.
Sea-Surface Temperature. (Technical Note Ser.: No. 103). (Illus., Orig.). 1969. pap. 16.00 (ISBN 0-685-22338-8, WMO). Unipub.

OCEAN TRANSPORTATION
see Shipping

OCEAN TRAVEL
see also Steamboats and Steamboat Lines; Yachts and Yachting

Allen, Jim & Corris, Peter, eds. The Journal of John Sweatman: A Nineteenth Century Surveying Voyage in North Australia & Torres Strait. 1978. 29.00x (ISBN 0-7022-1441-8). U of Queensland Pr.
Augustus, Charles. Passage for Twelve. 1978. 6.95 (ISBN 0-533-03526-0). Vantage.
Beebe, Robert P. Voyaging Under Power. 1978. 12.50 (ISBN 0-685-56451-7). Seven Seas.
Bensor, N. R. P. North Atlantic Seaway, Vol.2. 1978. 19.95 (ISBN 0-905824-01-6, 4345-8, Pub. by Brookside Publications). Arco.
Brinnin, John M. Beau Voyage. (Illus.). 280p. 1981. 50.00 (ISBN 0-312-92045-8). St Martin.
Brower, Kenneth. The Starship & the Canoe. LC 77-15200. 1978. 8.95 (ISBN 0-03-039196-2). HR&W.
The Cape Route: Imperiled Western Lifeline. 84p. 1981. pap. 6.50 (ISBN 0-89549-028-5, IFPA18, IFPA). Unipub.
Chapman, Roger. No Time on Our Side. (Illus.). 163p. Date not set. pap. 8.95 (ISBN 0-686-74122-6). Superior Pub.
Daniels, Else & Daniels, Bennet. Vacation at Sea: A Travel Guide for Cruises. (Illus.). 1979. 12.95 (ISBN 0-671-18438-5); pap. 5.95 (ISBN 0-346-12423-9). Cornerstone.
Fielding's Worldwide Guide to Cruises. 320p. 1981. Fieldingflex 11.95 (ISBN 0-688-00422-9). Morrow.
Garland, Joseph E. Lone Voyager. rev. ed. LC 63-13452. (Illus.). 1978. pap. 4.95 (ISBN 0-930352-05-X). Nelson B Robinson.
Guillet, Edwin C. The Great Migration: The Atlantic Crossing by Sailing-Ship Since 1770. LC 73-145482. (The American Immigration Library). xii, 316p. 1971. Repr. of 1937 ed. lib. bdg. 15.95x (ISBN 0-89198-013-X). Ozer.
Johnson, Irving. The Peking Battles Cape Horn. (Illus.). 256p. 1977. 11.95 (ISBN 0-89046-070-1); pap. 5.95 (ISBN 0-89046-071-X). Herman Pub.
Kennedy, Ludovic, compiled by. A Book of Sea Journeys. (Illus.). 1981. 13.95 (ISBN 0-89256-178-5). Rawson Wade.
Maddocks, Melvin. The Atlantic Crossing. Time-Life Books, ed. (The Seafarers Ser.). (Illus.). 176p. 1981. 13.95 (ISBN 0-8094-2726-5). Time Life.
Motte, R. Weather Routeing of Ships. 150p. 1972. 9.50x (ISBN 0-540-00382-4). Sheridan.
Parker, David M. Ocean Voyaging. LC 74-78837. 1975. 15.00 (ISBN 0-8286-0068-6). De Graff.
Roth, Hal. Two on a Big Ocean. (Illus.). 1978. 17.95 (ISBN 0-393-03216-7). Norton.
Saunders, Jeraldine. The Complete Guide to a Successful Cruise. LC 77-91178. 1978. cancelled (ISBN 0-8092-7626-7); pap. 5.95 (ISBN 0-8092-7540-6). Contemp Bks.
Schoff, Wilfred A. The Periplus of the Erythraean Sea: Travel Ocean by a Merchant of the First Century. 324p. 1974. Repr. 18.50x (ISBN 0-8364-0444-0). South Asia Bks.
Ship's Routing. 4th ed. 150p. 1978. 55.00 (ISBN 0-686-70774-5, IMCO). Unipub.
Smith, Michael M. The Real Expedicion Maritima De la Vacuna in New Spain & Guatemala. LC 73-92725. (Transactions Ser.: Vol. 64, Pt. 1). 1974. pap. 4.00 (ISBN 0-87169-641-X). Am Philos.
Supplement Relating to the Annex to the Convention on Facilitation of International Maritime Traffic, 1965. 62p. 1979. 9.75 (ISBN 0-686-70773-7, IMCO). Unipub.
The Total Traveler by Ship. 3rd ed. 1981. 8.95 (ISBN 0-89102-165-5). B Franklin.
Underhill, H. A. Deep-Water Sail (1976) 2nd ed. (Illus.). 45.00 (ISBN 0-85174-172-X). Heinman.

OCEAN WAVES

American Society of Civil Engineers, compiled by. Ocean Wave Measure & Analysis. 1240p. 1974. pap. text ed. 62.00 (ISBN 0-87262-116-2). Am Soc Civil Eng.
Clemons, Elizabeth. Waves, Tides & Currents. (gr. 5 up). 1967. PLB 5.99 (ISBN 0-394-91824-X). Knopf.
Kinsman, Blair. Wind Waves: Their Generation & Propagation on the Ocean Surface. 1965. 30.95 (ISBN 0-13-960344-1). P-H.
Komar, Paul D. Beach Processes & Sedimentation. (Illus.). 464p. 1976. 32.95 (ISBN 0-13-072595-1). P-H.
McCormick, Michael E. Ocean Wave Energy Conversion. LC 81-494. (Alternate Energy Ser.). 233p. 1981. 39.95 (ISBN 0-471-08543-X, Pub. by Wiley-Interscience). Wiley.
Meyer, R. E. & Meyer, R. E., eds. Waves on Beaches & Resulting Sediment Transport. 1972. 24.00 (ISBN 0-12-493250-9). Acad Pr.
Phillips, O. M. The Dynamics of the Upper Ocean. 2nd ed. LC 76-26371. (Monographs on Mechanics & Applied Mathematics). (Illus.). 1977. 59.95 (ISBN 0-521-21421-1). Cambridge U Pr.
Price, W. G. & Bishop, R. E. Probabilistic Theory of Ship Dynamics. LC 74-911. 311p. 1974. 35.00x (ISBN 0-412-12430-0, Pub. by Chapman & Hall England). Methuen Inc.
Provis, D. G., ed. Waves on Water of Variable Depth. (Lecture Notes in Physics: Vol. 64). 1977. 14.40 (ISBN 0-387-08253-0). Springer-Verlag.
Roth, Hal. Two Against Cap Horn. (Illus.). 1978. 18.95 (ISBN 0-393-03223-X). Norton.
Russell, Robert C. Waves & Tides. LC 73-135252. (Illus.). 348p. Repr. of 1953 ed. lib. bdg. 16.00x (ISBN 0-8371-5171-6, RUWT). Greenwood.
Zim, Herbert S. Waves. (Illus.). (gr. 3-7). 1967. PLB 6.48 (ISBN 0-688-31479-1). Morrow.

OCEANARIUMS
see Marine Aquariums

OCEANEERING
see Ocean Engineering

OCEANFRONT GARDENING
see Seaside Gardening

OCEANIC LANGUAGES

Vanoverbergh, Morice. Isneg - English Vocabulary. (Oceanic Linguistics Special Publications: No. 11). 600p. 1972. pap. 10.00x (ISBN 0-8248-0235-7). U Pr of Hawaii.

OCEANICA
see also Geographic Areas, and names of islands or groups of islands, e.g. Islands of the Pacific, Polynesia, Samoan Islands, Tahiti

Bellwood, Peter. Man's Conquest of the Pacific: The Prehistory of Southeast Asia & Oceania. 1979. 35.00x (ISBN 0-19-520103-5). Oxford U Pr.
Boyd, Gavin, ed. Region Building in the Pacific. (Pergamon Policy Studies). 400p. Date not set. price not set (ISBN 0-08-025985-5). Pergamon.
Fanning, Edmund. Voyages to the South Seas & to the Northwest Coast of America. enl. ed. 1970. Repr. of 1838 ed. 14.95 (ISBN 0-87770-012-5). Ye Galleon.
Howard, Alan. Learning to Be Rotuman: Enculturation in the South Pacific. LC 77-122746. (Illus.). 1970. text ed. 11.00x (ISBN 0-8077-1520-4). Tchrs Coll.
Michener, James A. Return to Paradise. 1951. 16.95 (ISBN 0-394-44291-1). Random.
Morrell, Benjamin, Jr. A Narrative of Four Voyages to the South Sea, Eighteen Twenty-Two to Eighteen Thirty-One. 492p. 1970. Repr. of 1832 ed. 35.00 (ISBN 0-8398-1268-X). Parnassus Imprints.
Oceanic Abstracts: Five-Year Cumulative Index to Vols. 9-13. 1977. Vols. 9-13. 225.00 (ISBN 0-685-84407-2). Data Courier.

OCEANICA–ANTIQUITIES

Shutler, Richard, Jr. & Shutler, M. E. Oceanic Prehistory. 1975. pap. text ed. 5.95 (ISBN 0-8465-1938-0). Benjamin-Cummings.

OCEANICA–BIBLIOGRAPHY

Anderson, I. G., ed. Current Asian & Australian Directories. 264p. 1978. 85.00x (ISBN 0-900246-25-1). Intl Pubns Serv.
Day, A. Grove. Pacific Islands Literature: One Hundred Basic Books. LC 70-151452. 1971. 9.00x (ISBN 0-87022-180-9). U Pr of Hawaii.
McLean, Mervyn. Oceanic Music & Dance: An Annotated Bibliography. 1977. pap. text ed. 11.00x (ISBN 0-8248-0589-5). U Pr of Hawaii.
Sources of the History of North Africa, Asia, & Oceania in Scandinavia, 2 pts. Incl. Pt. 1. Sources of the History North Africa, Asia, & Oceania in Denmark. lib. bdg. 162.00 (ISBN 3-598-21474-X); Pt. 2. Sources of the History of North Africa, Asia, & Oceania in Finland, Norway, Sweden. lib. bdg. 80.00 (ISBN 3-598-21475-8). (Guides to the Sources for the History of the Nations). 1980 (Dist. by Gale Research Co.). K G Saur.

OCEANICA–DESCRIPTION AND TRAVEL

Burton, Robert E., ed. Travel in Oceania, Australia & New Zealand: A Guide to Information Sources. LC 80-15333. (Geography & Travel Information Guide Ser.: Vol. 2). 150p. 1980. 36.00 (ISBN 0-8103-1421-5). Gale.
California University Committee on International Relations. The Southwest Pacific & the War. LC 74-3750. 168p. 1974. Repr. of 1944 ed. lib. bdg. 15.00 (ISBN 0-8371-7473-2, CUSP). Greenwood.
Jacobs, Charles & Jacobs, Babette. South Pacific Travel Digest. 6th ed. (Travel Digests Ser.). (Illus.). 176p. Date not set. pap. 8.95 (ISBN 0-912640-23-5). Travel Digest.
Johnson, Martin. Through the South Seas with Jack London. (Illus.). 1976. Repr. of 1913 ed. 12.95 (ISBN 0-915046-07-5). Wolf Hse.
Orlebar, John. A Midshipman's Journal on Board H.M.S. Seringapatam During the Year, 1830. LC 76-11241. 1976. pap. 3.95 (ISBN 0-914488-10-4). Rand-Tofua.
Paulding, Hiram. Journal of a Cruise of the U. S. Schooner Dolphin in Pursuit of the Mutineers of the Whale Ship Globe. LC 77-119793. (Illus.). 1970. Repr. of 1831 ed. 7.50x (ISBN 0-87022-616-9). U Pr of Hawaii.

Ruhen, Olaf & Shadbolt, Maurice. Isles of the South Pacific. Breeden, Robert L., et al, eds. LC 68-10413. (Special Publications Ser.). (Illus.). 1968. Repr. 6.95, avail. only from natl. geog. (ISBN 0-87044-049-7). Natl Geog.

Wawn, William T. The South Sea Islanders & the Queensland Labour Trade. new ed. Corris, Peter, ed. & intro. by. LC 73-78979. (Pacific History Ser.: No. 5). 529p. 1973. text ed. 17.50x (ISBN 0-8248-0282-9). U Pr of Hawaii.

OCEANICA–DISCOVERY AND EXPLORATION

Allen, Oliver. The Pacific Navigators. Time-Life Books Editors, ed. (The Seafarers Ser.). (Illus.). 176p. 1980. 13.95 (ISBN 0-8094-2685-4). Time-Life.

Beaglehole, John C. The Exploration of the Pacific. 3rd ed. (Illus.). 1966. 15.00x (ISBN 0-8047-0310-8); pap. 6.95x (ISBN 0-8047-0311-6). Stanford U Pr.

Cook, James. Explorations of Captain James Cook in the Pacific, As Told by Selections of His Own Journals, 1768-1779. Price, A. Grenfell, ed. (Illus.). pap. 5.00 (ISBN 0-486-22766-9). Dover.

Fernandes de Queiros, Pedro. Terre Australis Incognita, or, a New Southerne Discoverie, Lately Found by F. De Quir. LC 68-54659. (English Experience Ser.: No. 246). 28p. 1976. Repr. of 1617 ed. 7.00 (ISBN 90-221-0246-7). Walter J Johnson.

Wilkes, Charles. United States Exploring Expedition During the Years 1838-42 Under the Command of Charles Wilkes: Botanical Section, Vols. 15-17. Incl. Vol. 15. Phanoregamia. Gray, A. 240.00 (ISBN 3-7682-0714-5); Vol. 16. Cryptogamia, Filices, Lycopodiaceae & Hydropterides. Brackenridge, W. D. (Illus.). 90.00 (ISBN 3-7682-0715-3); Vol. 17. Cryptogamia Musci, Lichenes, Algae, Fungi Phanerogamia of Pacific North America. Sullivent, W. B., et al. (Illus.). 100.00 (ISBN 3-7682-0716-1). 1968. Repr. of 1854 ed. Set. 420.00 (ISBN 3-7682-0709-9). Lubrecht & Cramer.

OCEANICA–ECONOMIC CONDITIONS

Holland, William L. Commodity Control in the Pacific Area. LC 75-30124. Repr. of 1935 ed. 36.00 (ISBN 0-404-59530-8). AMS Pr.

King, Frank P., ed. Oceania & Beyond: Essays on the Pacific Since 1945. LC 76-5261. (Illus., Orig.). 1976. lib. bdg. 24.00 (ISBN 0-8371-8904-7, KOB/). Greenwood.

OCEANICA–HISTORY

Brookes, Jean I. International Rivalry in the Pacific Islands, 1800-1875. LC 77-173529. 1972. Repr. of 1941 ed. 26.00 (ISBN 0-8462-1630-2). Russell.

Craig, Robert D. & King, Frank P., eds. Historical Dictionary of Oceania. LC 80-24779. (Illus.). 416p. 1981. lib. bdg. 55.00 (ISBN 0-313-21060-8, KHD/). Greenwood.

Grattan, C. Hartley. The Southwest Pacific: A Modern History, 2 vols. Incl. Vol. 1. The Southwest Pacific to 1900. LC 60-5670. (Illus.). 590p. 1963. 7.50 (ISBN 0-472-07110-6); Vol. 2. The Southwest Pacific Since 1900. LC 63-14013. 798p. 1963. 10.00 (ISBN 0-472-07112-2). (History of the Modern World Ser). U of Mich Pr.

Gunson, Niel, ed. Changing Pacific: Essays in Honour of H. E. Maude. (Illus.). 1978. text ed. 39.50x (ISBN 0-19-550518-2). Oxford U Pr.

Hempenstall, Peter J. Pacific Islanders Under German Rule: A Study in the Meaning of Colonial Resistance. LC 78-58251. (Illus.). 1979. text ed. 24.95 (ISBN 0-7081-1350-8, 0531, Pub. by ANUP Australia). Bks Australia.

Lloyd, Christopher. Pacific Horizons, the Exploration of the Pacific Before Captain Cook. LC 75-41177. Repr. of 1946 ed. 18.00 (ISBN 0-404-14710-0). AMS Pr.

Michener, James A. & Day, A. Grove. Rascals in Paradise. 1957. 17.95 (ISBN 0-394-44220-2). Random.

Trumbull, Robert. Tin Roofs & Palm Trees: A Report on the New South Seas. LC 76-49164. (Illus.). 344p. 1977. 18.95 (ISBN 0-295-95544-9). U of Wash Pr.

Wiltgen, R. M. The Founding of the Roman Catholic Church in Oceania 1825-1850. LC 78-74665. (Illus.). 610p. 1980. text ed. 36.95 (ISBN 0-7081-0835-0, 0572). Bks Australia.

OCEANICA–JUVENILE LITERATURE

Warner, Oliver & Beaglehole, J. C. Captain Cook & the South Pacific. LC 63-19987. (Horizon Caravel Bks). (Illus.). 153p. (gr. 6 up). 1963. 9.95 (ISBN 0-06-026355-5, Dist. by Har-Row); PLB 12.89 (ISBN 0-06-026356-3, Dist. by Har-Row). Am Heritage.

OCEANICA–RELIGION

Boutilier, James, et al, eds. Mission, Church, & Sect in Oceania. LC 78-11072. (Association for Social Anthropology in Oceania Monograph: No. 6). 1978. 36.75 (ISBN 0-472-02701-8, IS-00061, University of Michigan Press). Univ Microfilms.

OCEANICA–SOCIAL CONDITIONS

Boutilier, James, et al, eds. Mission, Church, & Sect in Oceania. LC 78-11072. (Association for Social Anthropology in Oceania Monograph: No. 6). 1978. 36.75 (ISBN 0-472-02701-8, IS-00061, University of Michigan Press). Univ Microfilms.

Gunson, Niel, ed. Changing Pacific: Essays in Honour of H. E. Maude. (Illus.). 1978. text ed. 39.50x (ISBN 0-19-550518-2). Oxford U Pr.

Lieber, Michael D., ed. Exiles & Migrants in Oceania. LC 77-10756. (Association for Social Anthropology in Oceania, Monograph No. 5). (Illus.). 1978. text ed. 17.50x (ISBN 0-8248-0557-7). U Pr of Hawaii.

Mander, Linden. Some Dependent Peoples of the South Pacific. LC 75-30071. (Institute of Pacific Relations). Repr. of 1954 ed. 44.50 (ISBN 0-404-59544-8). AMS Pr.

Trumbull, Robert. Tin Roofs & Palm Trees: A Report on the New South Seas. LC 76-49164. (Illus.). 344p. 1977. 18.95 (ISBN 0-295-95544-9). U of Wash Pr.

OCEANICA IN ART

Smith, Bernard. European Vision & the South Pacific, 1768-1850: A Study in the History of Art & Ideas. (Oxford Paperbacks Ser). (Illus.). 1969. pap. 4.95x (ISBN 0-19-881162-4). Oxford U Pr.

OCEANOGRAPHERS

see also Oceanography As a Profession

Educational Research Council of America. Oceanographers. Ferris, Theodore N. & Marchak, John P., eds. (Real People at Work: Series M). (Illus., Orig.). (gr. 5). 1976. pap. text ed. 2.25 (ISBN 0-89247-105-0). Changing Times.

Lewis, Charles L. Matthew Fontaine Maury. LC 79-6116. (Navies & Men Ser.). (Illus.). 1980. Repr. of 1927 ed. lib. bdg. 25.00x (ISBN 0-405-13045-7). Arno.

Ocean Affairs Board, National Research Council. U. S. Directory of Marine Scientists 1975. vii, 325p. 1975. pap. 6.50 (ISBN 0-309-02408-0). Natl Acad Pr.

Rudman, Jack. Oceanographer. (Career Examination Ser.: C-550). (Cloth bdg. avail. on request). pap. 10.00 (ISBN 0-8373-0550-0). Natl Learning.

Varley, Allen, ed. Who's Who in Ocean Freshwater Science. 336p. 150.00 (ISBN 0-686-75643-6, Pub. by Longman). Gale.

OCEANOGRAPHIC INSTRUMENTS

Dexter, Stephen C. Handbook of Oceanographic Engineering Materials. LC 78-26196. (Ocean Engineering Ser.). 1979. 33.50 (ISBN 0-471-04950-6, Pub. by Wiley-Interscience). Wiley.

Jerlov, N. G. Optical Aspects of Oceanography. 1974. 84.00 (ISBN 0-12-384950-0). Acad Pr.

Williams, Jerome. Oceanographic Instrumentation. LC 72-92657. (Illus.). 160p. 1973. 15.00x (ISBN 0-87021-503-5). Naval Inst Pr.

OCEANOGRAPHIC RESEARCH

see also Mohole Project; Underwater Exploration

Beebe, William. The Arcturus Adventure: An Account of the New York Zoological Society's First Oceanographic Expedition. 1926. 20.00 (ISBN 0-8482-0138-8). Norwood Edns.

Colwell, R. Effect of the Ocean Environment on Microbial Activities. 1974. 39.50 (ISBN 0-8391-0702-1). Univ Park.

Committee On Oceanography. Oceanography Nineteen Sixty-Six: Achievements & Opportunites. 1967. pap. 6.25 (ISBN 0-309-01492-1). Natl Acad Pr.

Cousteau, Jacques. Challenge of the Sea. LC 74-23066. (Ocean World of Jacques Cousteau Ser.: Vol. 18). (Illus.). 144p. 1975. 9.95 (ISBN 0-8109-0592-2). Abrams.

Dexter, Stephen C. Handbook of Oceanographic Engineering Materials. LC 78-26196. (Ocean Engineering Ser.). 1979. 33.50 (ISBN 0-471-04950-6, Pub. by Wiley-Interscience). Wiley.

Drew, E. A., et al, eds. Underwater Research. 1976. 68.00 (ISBN 0-12-221950-3). Acad Pr.

A Focus for Ocean Research. (Intergovernmental Oceanographic Commission Technical Ser.: No. 20). 64p. 1980. pap. 4.00 (ISBN 92-3-101754-3, U 1015, UNESCO). Unipub.

Global Ocean Research. (Marine Science Affairs Ser.: No. 1). (Orig.). 1970. pap. 5.00 (ISBN 0-685-04911-6, WMO). Unipub.

Guide to the Measurement of Marine Primary Production Under Some Special Conditions. (Monographs on Oceanographic Methodology, No. 3). (Illus.). 73p. (Orig.). 1973. pap. 4.75 (ISBN 92-3-101099-9, U278, UNESCO). Unipub.

Heintze, Carl. The Bottom of the Sea & Beyond. LC 74-34393. (Illus.). 128p. 1975. 7.95 (ISBN 0-525-66432-7). Elsevier-Nelson.

Hood, Donald W. Impingement of Man on the Oceans. 738p. 1971. 39.50 (ISBN 0-471-40870-0, Pub. by Wiley). Krieger.

Jane's Ocean Technology 1974-1975. Date not set. 55.00x (ISBN 0-531-02744-9). Key Bk Serv.

Jane's Ocean Technology 1976-1977. Date not set. 72.50x (ISBN 0-531-03257-4). Key Bk Serv.

Jane's Ocean Technology 1978. Date not set. 72.50x (ISBN 0-686-73472-6). Key Bk Serv.

Jane's Ocean Technology 1979-1980. Date not set. 89.50x (ISBN 0-686-73473-4). Key Bk Serv.

Kuperman, William A. & Jensen, Finn B., eds. Bottom-Interacting Ocean Acoustics. (NATO Conference Series IV-Marine Sciences: Vol. 5). 717p. 1981. 75.00 (ISBN 0-306-40624-1, Plenum Pr). Plenum Pub.

Means of Acquisition & Communication of Ocean Data, 2 vols. Incl. Vol. 1. Ocean Data Requirements & Communication Facilities. (Marine Science Affairs Ser.: No. 6). 267p. pap. 40.00 (ISBN 0-685-34558-0, 346); Vol. 2. Surface, Sub-Surface & Upper-Air Observations. (Marine Science Affairs Ser.: No. 7). 600p. pap. 80.00 (ISBN 0-685-34559-9, 350). (Illus., Orig.). 1973 (WMO). Unipub.

Montgomery, R. B. & Stroup, E. D. Equatorial Waters & Currents at 150 Degrees W in July, August, 1952. (No. 1). 68p. 1952. 8.50x (ISBN 0-8018-0472-8). Johns Hopkins.

Muratov, M. Origin of Continents & Ocean Basins. 191p. 1977. 4.80 (ISBN 0-8285-0797-X, Pub. by Mir Pubs Russia). Imported Pubns.

Ocean Research Index: Guide to Ocean & Freshwater Research Including Fisheries Research. 2nd ed. 1976. 135.00x (ISBN 0-8002-1764-0). Intl Pubns Serv.

The R-V Pillsbury Deep-Sea Biological Expedition to the Gulf of Guinea, 1964-1965. Incl. Part 1. 1966. 5.50x (ISBN 0-87024-085-4); Part 2. 1970. 7.95x (ISBN 0-87024-190-7). (Studies in Tropical Oceanography Ser: No. 4). U Miami Marine.

Rodenhuis, David R., ed. The Final Plan for the GATE Sub-Programme Data Centres. 1976. pap. 25.00 (ISBN 0-685-74526-0, WMO). Unipub.

Schlee, Susan. On Almost Any Wind: The Saga of the Oceanographic Research Vessel "Atlantis". LC 78-58038. (Illus.). 1978. 17.50 (ISBN 0-8014-1160-2). Cornell U Pr.

Shenton, Edward H. Diving for Science: The Story of the Deep Submersible. LC 74-90990. (Illus.). 1972. 8.95 (ISBN 0-393-06380-1). Norton.

Van Andel, Tjeerd. Tales of an Old Ocean: Exploring the Deep Sea World of the Geologist & Oceanographer. (Illus.). 1978. 8.95 (ISBN 0-393-03213-2, Norton Lib); pap. 3.95 (ISBN 0-393-00883-5). Norton.

Wooster, Warren S. Freedom of Oceanic Research. LC 73-81050. 256p. 1973. 18.50x (ISBN 0-8448-0214-X). Crane-Russak Co.

Zooplankton Sampling. (Monographs on Oceanographic Methodology: No. 2). 1974. pap. 13.75 (ISBN 92-3-101194-4, U737, UNESCO). Unipub.

OCEANOGRAPHIC RESEARCH–JUVENILE LITERATURE

Brindze, Ruth. All About Undersea Exploration. (Allabout Ser.: No. 35). (Illus.). (gr. 5-9). 1960. PLB 5.39 (ISBN 0-394-90235-1, BYR). Random.

Fichter, George S. The Future Sea. LC 78-57790. (Illus.). 1978. 14.95 (ISBN 0-8069-3106-X); lib. bdg. 13.29 (ISBN 0-8069-3107-8). Sterling.

OCEANOGRAPHIC RESEARCH STATIONS

see also Manned Undersea Research Stations

OCEANOGRAPHY

see also Abyssal Zone; Astronautics in Oceanography; Chemical Oceanography; Coasts; Diving; Hydrography; Diving, Submarine; Marine Biology; Meteorology, Maritime; Navigation; Ocean; Ocean-Atmosphere Interaction; Ocean Bottom; Ocean Currents; Ocean Engineering; Ocean Temperature; Ocean Waves; Oceanographers; Oceanographic Instruments; Oceanographic Research; Sea-Water; Submarine Geology; Tides; Underwater Exploration

Adam, Robert E. Oceans of the World: Syllabus. 1978. pap. text ed. 5.35 (ISBN 0-89420-041-0, 233021); cassette recordings 70.85 (ISBN 0-89420-166-2, 233000). Natl Book.

Agence de Cooperation Culturelle et Technique, ed. Vocabulaire De L'oceanologie. 431p. (Fr.). 1976. pap. 42.50 (ISBN 0-686-57252-1, M-6560). French & Eur.

Anderson, Franz E. Introductory Oceanography Laboratory Manual. 1979. pap. text ed. 9.95x (ISBN 0-8087-0146-0). Burgess.

Angel, M. V. Progress in Oceanography, Vol. 8. (Illus.). 296p. 1980. 76.00 (ISBN 0-08-022963-8). Pergamon.

Angel, M. V. & O'Brien, J. Progress in Oceanography, Vol. 9, Nos. 1-4. (Illus.). 246p. Date not set. 87.50 (ISBN 0-08-027116-2). Pergamon.

Angel, Martin V., ed. A Voyage of Discovery: George Deacon 70th Anniversary Volume. new ed. LC 76-57958. 1977. 120.00 (ISBN 0-08-021380-4). Pergamon.

Anikouchine, W. & Sternberg, R. World Ocean: An Introduction to Oceanography. 1973. 18.95 (ISBN 0-13-967752-6). P-H.

Anikouchine, William & Sternberg, Richard. The World Ocean. 2nd ed. (Illus.). 512p. 1981. 19.95 (ISBN 0-13-967778-X). P-H.

Baker, Joseph T. & Murphy, Vreni, eds. Handbook of Marine Science: Section B, Compounds from Marine Organisms, Vol. 1. LC 74-30747. 1976. 49.95 (ISBN 0-87819-391-X). CRC Pr.

Barkley, Richard A. Oceanographic Atlas of the Pacific Ocean. (Illus.). 1969. text ed. 40.00x (ISBN 0-87022-050-0). U Pr of Hawaii.

Barnes, H., ed. Oceanography & Marine Biology. Incl. Vol. 8. 1970. 40.50 (ISBN 0-02-840940-X); Vol. 10. 1972. 40.50 (ISBN 0-02-840960-4); Vol. 11. 1973. 40.50 (ISBN 0-02-840970-1); Vol. 12. 1974. 40.50 (ISBN 0-02-841010-6); Vol. 13. 1975. 57.75 (ISBN 0-02-841020-3). Hafner.

Barnes, Harold, ed. Oceanography & Marine Biology: An Annual Review, Vol. 15. 1977. 70.00 (ISBN 0-900015-39-X). Taylor-Carlisle.

--Oceanography & Marine Biology: An Annual Review, Vol. 16. 1978. 75.00 (ISBN 0-900015-44-6). Taylor-Carlisle.

--Oceanography & Marine Biology: Annual Review, Vol. 14. 1976. 70.00 (ISBN 0-900015-37-3). Taylor-Carlisle.

Barnes, Margaret & Barnes, Harold, eds. Oceanography & Marine Biology: An Annual Review, Vol. 18. (Illus.). 528p. 1980. 84.00 (ISBN 0-08-025732-1). Pergamon.

Barton, Robert. Atlas of the Sea. LC 73-18541. (John Day Bk.). (Illus.). 128p. 1974. 10.95 (ISBN 0-381-98267-X). T Y Crowell.

Beebe, William. The Arcturus Adventure: An Account of the New York Zoological Society's First Oceanographic Expedition. 1926. 20.00 (ISBN 0-8482-0138-8). Norwood Edns.

Belderson, R. H., et al. Sonographs of the Sea Floor: A Picture Atlas. 1972. 68.50 (ISBN 0-444-40984-X). Elsevier.

Bhatt, Jagdish J. Applied Oceanography: Mining, Energy & Management. LC 79-19517. (Illus.). 262p. (Orig.). 1979. pap. 17.75 (ISBN 0-8357-0463-7, SS-000108). Univ Microfilms.

Bischoff & Piper, eds. Marine Geology & Oceanography of the Pacific Manganese Nodule Province. (Marine Science Ser.: Vol. 9). 1979. 49.50 (ISBN 0-306-40187-8, Plenum Pr). Plenum Pub.

Boje, R. & Tomczak, M., eds. Upwelling Ecosystems. (Illus.). 1978. pap. 29.80 (ISBN 0-387-08822-9). Springer-Verlag.

Borgese, Elizabeth M., ed. Pacem in Maribus. LC 72-3140. 1972. 10.00 (ISBN 0-396-06417-5). Dodd.

Bowditch, Nathaniel. Waves, Wind & Weather: Selected from American Practical Navigator. (Nautical Ser.). (Illus.). 1977. 7.95 (ISBN 0-679-50753-1). McKay.

Bowman, M. J. & Esaias, W. E., eds. Oceanic Fronts in Coastal Processes: Proceedings of a Workshop Held at the Marine Science Research Center, May 25-27, 1977. (Illus.). 1978. pap. 13.90 (ISBN 0-387-08823-7). Springer-Verlag.

Boy Scouts Of America. Oceanography. LC 19-600. (Illus.). 48p. (gr. 6-12). 1965. pap. 0.70x (ISBN 0-8395-3306-3, 3306). BSA.

Boyer, Robert E. Oceanography Fact Book. new ed. LC 74-1649. (Fact Books). (Illus.). 48p. (gr. 7-12). 1974. 5.95 (ISBN 0-8331-1707-6). Hubbard Sci.

Braynard, Frank O., frwd. by. A Descriptive Catalogue of the Marine Collection to Be Found at India House. 2nd ed. LC 73-7088. (Illus.). 280p. 1973. 100.00x (ISBN 0-8195-4065-X, Pub. by Wesleyan U Pr). Columbia U Pr.

Bretschneider, Charles L., ed. Topics in Ocean Engineering. Incl. Vol. 1. (Illus.). 428p. 1969. (ISBN 0-87201-598-X); Vol. 2. (Illus.). 229p. 1970 (ISBN 0-87201-599-8). 26.50x ea. Gulf Pub.

Brindze, Ruth. Charting the Oceans. LC 77-134674. (Illus.). 128p. (gr. 6-12). 1972. 6.95 (ISBN 0-8149-0002-X). Vanguard.

Briscoe, Melbourne, ed. Oceanic Internal Waves. 1976. pap. 15.00 (ISBN 0-87590-222-7). Am Geophysical.

Brown, Seyom, et al. Regimes for the Ocean, Outer Space, & Weather. 1977. 14.95 (ISBN 0-8157-1156-5); pap. 5.95 (ISBN 0-8157-1155-7). Brookings.

Bruun Memorial Lectures, 1973. (Intergovernmental Oceanographic Commission Technical Ser.: No. 11). (Illus.). 63p. 1976. pap. 4.50 (ISBN 92-3-101274-6, U62, UNESCO). Unipub.

Bruun Memorial Lectures 1975: Intergovernmental Oceanographic Commission. (Technical Ser: No. 15). 1978. pap. 4.50 (ISBN 92-3-101526-5, U794, UNESCO). Unipub.

Burke, William T. Ocean Sciences, Technology, & the Future International Law of the Sea. LC 66-63004. (Orig.). 1966. pap. 1.50 (ISBN 0-8142-0031-1). Ohio St U Pr.

Capurro, L. R. & Reid, Joseph L., eds. Contributions on the Physical Oceanography of the Gulf of Mexico. LC 71-135998. (Texas A&M University Oceanographic Studies: Vol. 2). (Illus.). 288p. 1972. 19.95x (ISBN 0-87201-347-2). Gulf Pub.
Center for Ocean Management Studies. Comparative Marine Policy. 288p. 1981. 25.95 (ISBN 0-686-77546-5). J F Bergin.
Chapman, Roger. No Time on Our Side. (Illus.). 168p. 1975. 7.95 (ISBN 0-393-03186-1). Norton.
Charlier, Roger H. & Gordon, Bernard L. Ocean Resources: An Introduction to Economic Oceanography. LC 78-61393. (Illus.). 1978. pap. text ed. 9.00 (ISBN 0-8191-0599-6). U Pr of Amer.
Charlier, Roger H., et al. Marine Science & Technology: An Introduction to Oceanography. LC 80-5234. (Illus.). 498p. 1980. pap. text ed. 15.25 (ISBN 0-8191-1065-5). U Pr of Amer.
Charnock, H. Advances in Oceanography. Deacon, G., ed. 358p. 1978. 39.50 (ISBN 0-306-40019-7, Plenum Pr). Plenum Pub.
Chesapeake Research Consortium. Effects of Tropical Storm Agnes on the Chesapeake Bay Estuarine System. LC 76-47392. 1977. text ed. 35.00x (ISBN 0-8018-1945-8). Johns Hopkins.
Clay, Clarence S. & Medwin, Herman. Acoustical Oceanography: Principles & Applications. LC 77-1133. (Ocean Engineering Ser.). 1977. text ed. 44.00 (ISBN 0-471-16041-5, Pub. by Wiley-Interscience). Wiley.
Coggins, Jack. Hydrospace: Frontier Beneath the Sea. LC 65-27969. (Illus.). (gr. 5 up). 1966. 5.95 (ISBN 0-396-06723-9). Dodd.
Collias, Eugene E. & Andreeva, Svetlana I. Puget Sound Marine Environment: An Annotated Bibliography. LC 77-24231. (Washington Sea Grant). 402p. 1978. pap. 12.00 (ISBN 0-295-95570-8). U of Wash Pr.
Committee On Oceanography. Oceanography Nineteen Sixty-Six: Achievements & Opportunites. 1967. pap. 6.25 (ISBN 0-309-01492-1). Natl Acad Pr.
--Scientific Exploration of the South Pacific. LC 72-603750. (Orig.). 1970. 11.50 (ISBN 0-309-01755-6). Natl Acad Pr.
Committee On Oceanography & Committee On Ocean Engineering. Oceanic Quest: The International Decade of Ocean Exploration. (Orig.). 1969. pap. 5.00 (ISBN 0-309-01709-2). Natl Acad Pr.
Compendium of Meteorology: Marine Meteorology, Vol. 3. 121p. 1979. pap. 11.00 (ISBN 0-686-60082-7, W441, WMO). Unipub.
Costlow, John D., ed. Fertility of the Sea, 2 vols. LC 74-132383. (Illus.). 646p. 1971. Set. 95.25x (ISBN 0-677-14730-9). Gordon.
Council on Education in the Geological Sciences & Wright, F. F. Estuarine Oceanography. (Illus.). 80p. 1974. pap. text ed. 6.95 (ISBN 0-07-012336-5, C). McGraw.
Cousteau, Jacques. The Art of Motion. (Ocean World of Jacques Cousteau: Vol. 5). 9.95 (ISBN 0-8109-0579-5, A4505B). Abrams.
--Attack & Defense. LC 74-23980. (Ocean World of Jacques Cousteau: Vol. 6). 9.95 (ISBN 0-8109-0580-9). Abrams.
--Guide to the Sea. LC 74-23072. (Ocean World of Jacques Cousteau Ser.: Vol. 20). (Illus.). 144p. 1975. 9.95 (ISBN 0-8109-0594-9). Abrams.
--Invisible Messages. LC 74-23979. (Ocean World of Jacques Cousteau Ser.: Vol. 7). (Illus.). 9.95 (ISBN 0-8109-0581-7). Abrams.
--Quest for Food. (Ocean World of Jacques Cousteau: Vol. 3). (Illus.). 1973. 9.95 (ISBN 0-8109-0577-9). Abrams.
--Window in the Sea. (Ocean World of Jacques Cousteau: Vol. 4). (Illus.). 1973. 9.95 (ISBN 0-8109-0578-7). Abrams.
Cousteau, Jacques, intro. by. Outer & Inner Space. LC 74-28363. (Ocean World of Jacques Cousteau Ser: Vol. 15). (Illus.). 144p. 1975. 9.95 (ISBN 0-8109-0589-2). Abrams.
Cousteau, Jacques Y. The Act of Life. new ed. (Ocean World of Jacques Cousteau Ser.: Vol. 2). (Illus.). 144p. 1972. 9.95 (ISBN 0-8109-0576-0). Abrams.
Cousteau, Jacques-Yves & Diole, Philippe. Life & Death in a Coral Sea. LC 69-13003. (The Undersea Discoveries of Jacques-Yves Cousteau). (Illus.). 1978. pap. 8.95 (ISBN 0-89104-089-7). A & W Pubs.
--Three Adventures: Galapagos, Titcaca, the Blue Holes. LC 72-93396. (The Undersea Discoveries of Jacques-Yves Cousteau). (Illus.). 1978. pap. 8.95 (ISBN 0-89104-090-0). A & W Pubs.
Davis, Richard A. Principles of Oceanography. 2nd ed. LC 76-10436. (Illus.). 1977. text ed. 18.95 (ISBN 0-201-01464-5). A-W.
Deacon, Margaret B., ed. Oceanography: Concepts & History. (Benchmark Papers in Geology: Vol. 35). 1978. 36.50 (ISBN 0-12-786340-0). Acad Pr.
Deep Frontier. (Illus.). 296p. 1980. 14.95 (ISBN 0-87044-343-7). Natl Geog.
De Sylva, Donald P. The Alfred C. Glassell, Jr. - University of Miami Argosy Expedition to Ecuador: Part 1: Introduction & Narrative. LC 72-125657. (Studies in Tropical Oceanography Ser: No. 11). 1972. 6.95x (ISBN 0-87024-171-0). U Miami Marine.
Diemer, Ferdinand, et al, eds. Advanced Concepts in Ocean Measurements for Marine Biology. LC 79-24801. (Belle Baruch Library Ser.: Vol. 10). (Illus.). 572p. 1980. text ed. 27.50x (ISBN 0-87249-388-1). U of SC Pr.
Dietrich, Gunther, et al. General Oceanography: An Introduction. 2nd ed. LC 80-12919. 626p. 1980. 50.00 (ISBN 0-471-02102-4, Pub. by Wiley-Interscience). Wiley.
Directions for Data Buoy Technology, 1978-1983. 112p. 1974. pap. 3.50 (ISBN 0-309-02230-4). Natl Acad Pr.
Doak, Wade. The Blue Frontier. (Illus.). 1975. 14.00x (ISBN 0-8002-0799-8). Intl Pubns Serv.
Drake, Charles, et al. Oceanography. LC 77-13571. (Illus.). 1978. 22.95 (ISBN 0-03-085644-2, HoltC). HR&W.
Duing, Walter. Monsoon Regime of the Currents in the Indian Ocean. LC 76-104320. (International Indian Ocean Expedition Oceanographic Monographs: No. 1). (Illus.). 1970. 12.00x (ISBN 0-8248-0092-3, Eastwest Ctr). U Pr of Hawaii.
Duxbury, A. The Earth & Its Oceans. LC 73-131202. (Earth Science Ser.). 1971. 19.95 (ISBN 0-201-01616-8). A-W.
Earle & Malahoff, eds. Ocean Waye Climate. (Marine Sciences Ser.: Vol. 8). 1979. 36.00 (ISBN 0-306-40079-0, Plenum Pr). Plenum Pub.
Earle, Sylvia & Giddings, Al. Exploring the Deep Frontier: The Adventure of Man in the Sea. LC 80-7567. (Illus.). 300p. 1980. 14.95 (ISBN 0-87044-343-7). Natl Geog.
Eskinazi, S. Fluid Mechanics & Thermodynamics of Our Environment. 1975. 48.50 (ISBN 0-12-242540-5); lib ed 54.00 (ISBN 0-12-242541-3); microfiche 40.50 (ISBN 0-12-242542-1). Acad Pr.
Fairbridge, R, ed. Encyclopedia of Oceanography. LC 66-26059. (Encyclopedia of Earth Sciences Ser: Vol. I). 1966. 90.00 (ISBN 0-12-786457-1). Acad Pr.
Flatte, S. M., ed. Sound Transmission Through a Fluctuating Ocean. LC 77-88676. (Cambridge Monographs on Mechanics & Applied Mathematics). (Illus.). 1979. 44.50 (ISBN 0-521-21940-X). Cambridge U Pr.
Flemming, N. C., ed. The Undersea. LC 76-56827. 1977. 12.98 (ISBN 0-02-538740-5). Macmillan.
Freidheim, Robert L., ed. Managing Ocean Resources: A Primer. LC 79-53772. (Westview Special Studies in Natural Resources & Energy Management). 1979. lib. bdg. 23.25x (ISBN 0-89158-572-9). Westview.
Friedmann, Wolfgang. The Future of the Oceans. 1971. 6.95 (ISBN 0-8076-0602-2); pap. 3.95 (ISBN 0-8076-0601-4). Braziller.
Gibb, Thomas R., Jr., ed. Analytical Methods in Oceanography. new ed. LC 75-41463. (Advances in Chemistry Ser.: No. 147). 1975. 30.50 (ISBN 0-8412-0245-1). Am Chemical.
Goldberg, Edward D., ed. The Sea: Ideas & Observations on Progress in the Study of the Seas, Vol. 5, Marine Chemistry. LC 62-18366. 895p. 1974. 74.00x (ISBN 0-471-31090-5, Pub. by Wiley-Interscience). Wiley.
Goldberg, Edward D., et al, eds. The Sea; Ideas & Observations on Progress in the Study on the Seas, Vol. 6: Marine Modeling. LC 62-18366. 992p. 1977. 69.95 (ISBN 0-471-31091-3, Pub. by Wiley-Interscience). Wiley.
Gordon, A. Studies in Physical Oceanography. 1972. Set. 89.25 (ISBN 0-677-12910-6); Vol. 1. 45.25x (ISBN 0-677-15160-8); Vol. 2. 54.50x (ISBN 0-677-15170-5). Gordon.
Gordon, Bernard L., ed. Man & the Sea. rev. ed. (Illus.). 1980. pap. text ed. 7.50 (ISBN 0-910258-10-4). Book & Tackle.
Greenberg, Jerry. Adventures of a Reefcomber. (Illus.). saddlestiched 2.50 (ISBN 0-913008-03-6). Seahawk Pr.
Greis, Noel P. Oceans. Reed, Suzanne W., ed. LC 74-80547. (Illus., Orig.). (gr. 6-9). 1975. pap. text ed. 3.25 (ISBN 0-88301-154-9). Pendulum Pr.
Gross, Grant M. Ocean World. new ed. (Physical Science Ser.). (Orig.). 1976. pap. text ed. 7.95 (ISBN 0-675-08576-4); cassettes & filmstrips 135.00 (ISBN 0-675-08575-6); 2-4 sets 80.00, 5 or more sets 60.00 (ISBN 0-685-62201-0). Merrill.
Gross, M. Grant. Oceanography. 4th ed. (Physics & Physical Science Ser.). 152p. 1980. pap. text ed. 7.95 (ISBN 0-675-08110-6). Merrill.
--Oceanography: A View of the Earth. 2nd ed. (Illus.). 1977. 21.95 (ISBN 0-13-629675-0). P-H.
Groves, Donald G. & Hunt, Lee M. The Ocean World Encyclopedia. LC 79-21093. (Illus.). 1980. 29.95 (ISBN 0-07-025010-3). McGraw.
Guide on the Global Observing System. (WMO Ser: No. 365). (Illus.). 1978. pap. 42.00 (ISBN 0-685-87430-3, WMO 488, WMO). Unipub.
Hartwig, G. The Sea & Its Living Wonders, with 300 Woodcuts & Plates. lib. bdg. 95.00 (ISBN 0-8490-3066-8). Gordon Pr.
Harvey, J. G. Atmosphere & Ocean: Our Fluid Environments. LC 77-377903. 1978. pap. 14.50x (ISBN 0-8448-1293-5). Crane-Russak Co.
Hayes, Dennis E., ed. Antarctic Oceanology Two: The Australian-New Zealand Sector. LC 78-151300. (Antarctic Research Ser.: Vol. 19). (Illus.). 364p. 1972. 32.00 (ISBN 0-87590-119-0). Am Geophysical.
Herman, Y., ed. Marine Geology & Oceanography of the Arctic Seas. LC 73-22236. (Illus.). 416p. 1974. 43.90 (ISBN 0-387-06628-4). Springer-Verlag.
Heyerdahl, Thor. Albatros, Enciclopedia del Mar, 4 vols. 1256p. (Espn.). 1978. Set. 180.00 (ISBN 84-85004-07-8, S-50577). French & Eur.
Hickling, C. F. & Brown, Peter Lancaster. The Seas & the Oceans in Color. LC 73-18511. (Color Ser). (Illus.). 192p. 1974. 9.95 (ISBN 0-02-551380-X). Macmillan.
Hill, M. N. The Sea: Vol. 1 Physical Oceanography. 2nd ed. 880p. 1982. Repr. of 1962 ed. lib. bdg. cancelled (ISBN 0-89874-097-5). Krieger.
Hill, M. N., ed. The Sea: Vol. 2, Composition of Sea Water. 570p. 1982. Repr. of 1963 ed. lib. bdg. cancelled (ISBN 0-89874-098-3). Krieger.
--The Sea: Vol. 3 the Earth Beneath the Sea; History. LC 80-248. 980p. 1981. Repr. of 1963 ed. lib. bdg. write for info. (ISBN 0-89874-099-1). Krieger.
Hiscock, K. & Baume, A., eds. Proceedings of the Underwater Association Symposium, 1976. LC 76-53091. 1977. 24.00x (ISBN 0-8448-1078-9). Crane-Russak Co.
Hollaender, Alexander, ed. The Biosaline Concept: An Approach to the Utilization of Underexploited Resources. LC 79-18804. (Environmental Science Research Ser.: Vol. 14). 1979. 39.50 (ISBN 0-306-40295-5, Plenum Pr). Plenum Pub.
Hood, D. W. & Kelley, E. J., eds. Oceanography of the Bering Sea: With Emphasis on Renewable Resources. (Occasional Pub. Ser. No. 2). 20.00 (ISBN 0-914500-04-X). U of AK Inst Marine.
Hunt, Lee M. & Groves, Donald G. Glossary of Ocean Science & Undersea Technology Terms. (Illus., Orig.). pap. 5.95 (ISBN 0-685-08544-9). Compass Va.
Hydrological Application of Atmospheric Vapour-Flux Analyses. (WMO Ser: No. 476). (Illus.). 1978. pap. 10.00 (ISBN 92-63-10476-X, WMO). Unipub.
ICITA Equalant I & Equalant II: Oceanographic Atlas & Chemical & Biological Oceanography, Vol. 2. (Illus.). 1977. 81.00 (ISBN 0-685-86033-7, M76, UNESCO). Unipub.
ICITA Oceanographic Atlas, Equalant One & Equalant Two, Vol. 1: Physical Oceanography. (Illus.). 1974. 59.00 (ISBN 92-3-099996-2, M75, UNESCO). Unipub.
Implementation Plan for the Determination of the Atmospheric Contribution on Petroleum Hydrocarbons to the Oceans. 1979. pap. 10.00 (ISBN 92-63-10504-9, W430, WMO). Unipub.
Ingmanson, Dale E. & Wallace, William J. Oceanography: An Introduction. 2nd ed. 1979. text ed. 21.95x (ISBN 0-534-00538-1); lab manual 8.95x (ISBN 0-534-00624-8). Wadsworth Pub.
Integrated Global Ocean Station System: General Plan & Implementation Programme 1977-1982. (Technical Ser: No. 16). (Illus.). 36p. 1977. pap. 10.00 (ISBN 92-63-10466-2, WMO). Unipub.
International Conference on Tropical Oceanography, November 17-24, 1965, Miami Beach, Florida. Proceedings. LC 67-29907. (Studies in Tropical Oceanography Ser: No. 5). 1967. 25.00x (ISBN 0-87024-086-2). U Miami Marine.
International Oceanographic Congress, 2nd, Moscow, 1966. Morning Review Lectures: Proceeding. 256p. 1969. 29.95 (ISBN 92-3-000756-0, U390, UNESCO). Unipub.
International Oceanographic Tables, Vol. 1. 1966. 12.25 (ISBN 92-3-000906-7, U336, UNESCO). Unipub.
International Oceanographic Tables, Vol. 2. 141p. (Orig.). 1974. 15.75 (ISBN 92-3-001044-8, U337, UNESCO). Unipub.
Jerlov, N. G. Marine Optics. 2nd rev. & enl. ed. (Elsevier's Oceanography Ser: No. 14). 1976. 49.00 (ISBN 0-444-41490-8). Elsevier.
--Optical Aspects of Oceanography. 1974. 84.00 (ISBN 0-12-384950-0). Acad Pr.
Johnson, G. David. The Limits & Relationships of the Lutjanidae & Associated Families, Vol. 24. (Bulletin of the Scripps Institute of Oceanography). 1981. pap. 8.00x (ISBN 0-520-09642-8). U of Cal Pr.
Kamenkovich, J. M. Fundamentals of Ocean Dynamics. (Elsevier Oceanography Ser.: 16). 1977. 63.50 (ISBN 0-444-41546-7). Elsevier.
Kent, Peter, et al. The Evolution of Passive Continental Margins in the Light of Recent Deep Drilling Results. (Royal Society Ser.). (Illus.). 208p. 1980. Repr. of 1980 ed. text ed. 58.00x (ISBN 0-85403-129-4, Pub. by Royal Society London). Scholium Intl.
King, Cuchlaine. Introduction to Physical & Biological Oceanography. LC 74-81339. 1974. pap. 19.50x (ISBN 0-8448-0400-2). Crane-Russak Co.
Kirkland, Douglas W., ed. Marine Evaporites: Origin, Diagenesis & Geochemistry. Evans, Robert. LC 73-11151. (Benchmark Papers in Geology Ser.). 448p. 1973. text ed. 47.00 (ISBN 0-12-786850-X). Acad Pr.
Knauss, John A. Introduction to Physical Oceanography. (Illus.). 1978. 32.95 (ISBN 0-13-493015-0). P-H.
Krauss, Wolfgang. Methods & Results of Theoretical Oceanography: Dynamics of the Homogeneous & the Quasihomogeneous Ocean, Vol. 1. (Illus.). 1973. text ed. 63.00 (ISBN 3-443-01001-6). Lubrecht & Cramer.
Laevastu, Taivo & Hayes, Murray L. Fisheries Oceanography & Ecology. 1981. 75.00x (ISBN 0-686-75649-5, Pub. by Fishing News England). State Mutual Bk.
Lebow, Ruth & Garrison, Tom. Oceanus: The Marine Environment. 204p. 1979. 8.95x (ISBN 0-534-00841-0). Wadsworth Pub.
Levine, S. N. Selected Papers on Desalination & Ocean Technology. (Illus.). 8.50 (ISBN 0-8446-2459-4). Peter Smith.
Limburg, Peter R. Oceanographic Institutions: Science Studies the Sea. LC 78-12214. (Illus.). 1979. 9.95 (ISBN 0-525-66506-4). Elsevier-Nelson.
Lisitzin, E. Sea Level Changes. (Oceanography Ser: Vol. 8). 1974. 51.25 (ISBN 0-444-41157-7). Elsevier.
McCormick, J. Michael & Thiruvathukal, John V. Elements of Oceanography. 2nd ed. (Illus.). 437p. 1981. text ed. 20.95 (ISBN 0-03-057806-X, HoltC). HR&W.
--Elements of Oceanography. LC 75-10388. (Illus.). 350p. 1976. text ed. 17.95 (ISBN 0-7216-5900-4). HR&W.
McGraw-Hill Encyclopedia of Science & Technology Staff. McGraw-Hill Encyclopedia of Ocean & Atmospheric Sciences. Parker, Sybil P., ed. (Illus.). 1979. write for info. (ISBN 0-07-045267-9). McGraw.
McLellan, H. J. Elements of Physical Oceanography. 1966. 18.00 (ISBN 0-08-011320-6). Pergamon.
McLeod, G. C. Georges Bank: Past, Present, & Future. (Special Studies on Natural Resources & Energy Management). 225p. 1981. lib. bdg. 23.25x (ISBN 0-86531-199-4). Westview.
Marr, John, ed. Kuroshio: A Symposium on the Japan Current. 1970. 25.00x (ISBN 0-8248-0090-7, Eastwest Ctr). U Pr of Hawaii.
Matthews, H. Surface Wave Filters: Design, Construction, & Use. LC 77-3913. 1977. 43.00 (ISBN 0-471-58030-9). Wiley.
Maury, Matthew F. Physical Geography of the Sea, & Its Meteorology. Leighly, John, ed. LC 63-10870. (The John Harvard Library). (Illus.). 1963. pap. 8.95x (ISBN 0-674-66652-6). Harvard U Pr.
Maxwell, Arthur E., et al. Sea, Vol. 4 Pts 1-3. LC 62-18366. 1971. Pt. 1. 69.00 (ISBN 0-471-57910-6, Pub. by Wiley-Interscience). Wiley.
Means of Acquisition & Communication of Ocean Data, 2 vols. Incl. Vol. 1. Ocean Data Requirements & Communication Facilities. (Marine Science Affairs Ser.: No. 6). 267p. pap. 40.00 (ISBN 0-685-34558-0, 346); Vol. 2. Surface, Sub-Surface & Upper-Air Observations. (Marine Science Affairs Ser.: No. 7). 600p. pap. 80.00 (ISBN 0-685-34559-9, 350). (Illus., Orig.). 1973 (WMO). Unipub.
Menard, H. W., intro. by. Ocean Science: Readings from Scientific American. LC 77-23465. (Illus.). 1977. text ed. 19.95x (ISBN 0-7167-0014-X); pap. text ed. 9.95x (ISBN 0-7167-0013-1). W H Freeman.
Meteorological Aspects of the Contributions Presented at the Joint Oceanographic Assembly. (Reports on Marine Science Affairs Ser.: No. 12). 1979. pap. 10.00 (ISBN 92-63-10499-9, W 420, WMO). Unipub.
Monin, A. S., et al. Variability of the Oceans. LC 77-826. 1977. 39.50 (ISBN 0-471-61328-2, Pub. by Wiley-Interscience). Wiley.
Moore, Hilary B. Ecological Guide to Bermuda Inshore Water. (Bermuda Biological Station Special Pubn.: No. 5). (Illus.). ii, 42p. pap. 3.00 (ISBN 0-917642-05-8). Bermuda Bio.
Muir-Wood, A. M. Coastal Hydraulics. 1970. 45.25x (ISBN 0-677-61680-5). Gordon.

Murray, John. Selections from the Report on the Scientific Results of the Voyage of H.M.S. Challenger During the Years 1872-76. Egerton, Frank N., 3rd, ed. LC 77-74242. (History of Ecology Ser.). (Illus.). 1978. Repr. of 1895 ed. lib. bdg. 14.00x (ISBN 0-405-10411-1). Arno.
Neatby, L. H. Discovery in Russian & Siberian Waters. LC 72-85535. (Illus.). 226p. 1973. 15.00x (ISBN 0-8214-0124-6). Ohio U Pr.
Neumann, Gerhard & Pierson, W. J. Principles of Physical Oceanography. (Illus.). 1966. 35.95 (ISBN 0-13-709741-7). P-H.
Nihoul, J. C., ed. Modelling of Marine Systems. LC 74-77585. (Elsevier Oceanography Ser.: Vol. 10). 272p. 1975. 53.75 (ISBN 0-444-41232-8). Elsevier.
Ocean Affairs Board. International Marine Science Affairs. LC 74-183584. 104p. (Orig.). 1972. pap. text ed. 5.00 (ISBN 0-309-01937-0). Natl Acad Pr.
Ocean Science Board. Tropospheric Transport of Pollutants & Natural Substances to the Ocean. 1978. pap. 11.75 (ISBN 0-309-02735-7). Natl Acad Pr.
Ocean Sciences Board, National Research Council. Continental Margins: Geological & Geophysical Research Needs. 1979. pap. 16.25x (ISBN 0-309-02793-4). Natl Acad Pr.
--The Continuing Quest: Large Scale Ocean Science for the Future. (Orig.). 1979. pap. text ed. 7.25x (ISBN 0-309-02798-5). Natl Acad Pr.
Oceanographic Components of the Global Atmospheric Research Programme (GARP) (Intergovernmental Oceanographic Commission Technical Ser.: No. 17). 35p. 1978. pap. 3.25 (ISBN 92-3-101535-4, U828, UNESCO). Unipub.
Oceanographic Products & Methods of Analysis & Prediction. (Illus.). 1977. pap. 9.25 (ISBN 92-3-101453-6, U555, UNESCO). Unipub.
Oceanographic Sub-Programme for the GATE Atlantic Tropical Experiment. (GATE Report Ser.: No. 8). (Illus.). 135p. (Orig.). 1974. pap. 25.00 (ISBN 0-685-50263-5, WMO). Unipub.
Oceanography & Marine Biology: An Annual Review, Vol. 17. 1979. 80.00 (ISBN 0-08-023849-1). Taylor-Carlisle.
Oceanography & Marine Biology: An Annual Review, Vol. 18. 1980. 95.00 (ISBN 0-686-29371-1). Taylor Carlisle.
Oceanography in China. 1980. 7.00 (ISBN 0-309-03046-3). Natl Acad Pr.
Ol'shevskii, V. V. Characteristics of Sea Reverberations. LC 67-25401. 1967. 35.00 (ISBN 0-306-10796-1, Consultants). Plenum Pub.
Parker. The Study of Benthic Communities. LC 73-20941. (Oceanography Ser: Vol. 9). 279p. 1975. 53.75 (ISBN 0-444-41203-4). Elsevier.
Perry, Richard. Life at the Sea's Frontiers. LC 73-3969. (The Many Worlds of Wildlife Ser.). (Illus.). 320p. 1974. 7.95 (ISBN 0-8008-4795-4). Taplinger.
Phillips, O. M. The Dynamics of the Upper Ocean. LC 76-26371. (Cambridge Monographs on Mechanics & Applied Mathematics). 344p. 1980. pap. 21.50x (ISBN 0-521-29801-6). Cambridge U Pr.
Physical Oceanography in Canada. (Fisheries Research Board of Canada Reports). 23p. 1978. pap. 5.50 (ISBN 0-660-00531-X, SSC99, SSC). Unipub.
Pickard, G. L. Descriptive Physical Oceanography. 3rd ed. (International Series in Geophysics). (Illus.). 1979. text ed. 35.00 (ISBN 0-08-023824-6); pap. text ed. 11.50 (ISBN 0-08-023825-4). Pergamon.
Pickard, G. L. & Pond, S. Introductory Dynamic Oceanography. LC 77-4427. 1978. text ed. 45.00 (ISBN 0-08-021614-5); pap. text ed. 12.50 (ISBN 0-08-021615-3). Pergamon.
Pipkin, Bernard W., et al. Laboratory Exercises in Oceanography. (Illus.). 1977. lab. manual 9.95x (ISBN 0-7167-0181-2); tchrs. manual avail. W H Freeman.
Pirie, R. Gordon, ed. Oceanography: Contemporary Readings in Ocean Sciences. 2nd ed. (Illus.). 1977. pap. text ed. 8.95x (ISBN 0-19-502119-3). Oxford U Pr.
PROBES: A Prospectus on Processes & Resources of the Bering Sea Shelf Nineteen Seventy-Five to Nineteen Eighty-Five. write for info. (ISBN 0-914500-05-8). U of AK Inst Marine.
Regional Association Four, North & Central: Abridged Final Report of the Seventh Session. (Illus.). 1978. pap. 25.00 (ISBN 92-63-10479-4, WMO). Unipub.
Reid, Joseph L., ed. Antarctic Oceanology One. LC 78-151300. (Antarctic Research Ser.: Vol. 15). (Illus.). 1971. 22.00 (ISBN 0-87590-115-8). Am Geophysical.
Reid, Joseph L., Jr. Northwest Pacific Ocean Waters in Winter. LC 72-12351. (Oceanographic Studies: No. 5). (Illus.). 96p. 1973. 12.00x (ISBN 0-8018-1466-9). Johns Hopkins.
Report of the Fifth Session of WMO Executive Committee Inter-Governmental Panel on the First GARP Global Experiment. (GARP Special Report Ser.). (Illus.). 45p. 1978. pap. 15.00 (ISBN 0-685-27460-8, W-383, WMO). Unipub.
Report of the First Session of the Wamex Scientific & Management Committee. (GARP Special Report Ser.: No. 31). 1979. pap. 15.00 (ISBN 0-686-52645-7, W426, WMO). Unipub.
Report of the Fourth Planning Meeting for the Monsoon Experiment (MONEX) (GARP Special Report Ser.: No. 28). 1978. pap. 40.00 (ISBN 0-685-65240-8, W402, WMO). Unipub.
Report of the Fourth Session of WMO Executive Committee Inter-Governmental Panel on the First Garp Global Experiment. (Garp Special Report: No. 24). 1977. pap. 25.00 (ISBN 0-685-86035-3, WMO). Unipub.
Reports on Meteorological Aspects of the Contributions Presented at the Joint Oceanographic Assembly. (Marine Science Affairs Report Ser.: No. 12). 1979. pap. 10.00 (ISBN 92-63-10499-9, W420, WMO). Unipub.
Resolutions & Other Decisions of the Assembly Eleventh Session 1979. 328p. 1981. pap. 48.50 (ISBN 92-801-1102-7, IMCO 66, IMCO). Unipub.
Rezak, Richard & Henry, Vernon J., eds. Contributions on the Geological & Geophysical Oceanography of the Gulf of Mexico. LC 73-149761. (Texas A&M University Oceanographic Studies: Vol. 3). (Illus.). 303p. 1972. 19.95x (ISBN 0-87201-348-0). Gulf Pub.
Riley, S. P. & Skirrow, G., eds. Chemical Oceangraphy, 6 vols. 2nd ed. Vol. 1. 1975. 95.50 (ISBN 0-12-588601-2); Vol. 2. 1975. 103.00 (ISBN 0-12-588602-0); Vol. 3. 1975. 90.00 (ISBN 0-12-588603-9); Vol. 4. 1975. 57.00 (ISBN 0-12-588604-7); Vol. 5. 1976. 66.00 (ISBN 0-12-588605-5); Vol. 6. 1976. 66.00 (ISBN 0-12-588606-3). Acad Pr.
Rona, Peter A., ed. Mid-Atlantic Ridge, Part 1 & 2. LC 76-47736. (Microform Publication: No. 5). (Illus.). 1976. 9.00x (ISBN 0-685-88399-X). Geol Soc.
Ross, D. A. Opportunities & Uses of the Ocean. LC 79-12694. (Illus.). 1979. 19.80 (ISBN 0-387-90448-4). Springer-Verlag.
Ross, David. Introduction to Oceanography. 2nd ed. LC 76-17838. (Illus.). 1977. text ed. 19.95 (ISBN 0-13-491332-9). P-H.
Sachs, Moshe Y., ed. Sea-Bed Nineteen Sixty-Nine, 8 vols. LC 73-171925. 1971. Set. 450.00 (ISBN 0-405-02588-2). Arno.
Schopf, Thomas J. Paleoceanography. LC 79-12546. (Illus.). 1980. 25.00x (ISBN 0-674-65215-0). Harvard U Pr.
Scientific American Editors. The Ocean: A Scientific American Book. LC 71-102897. (Illus.). 1969. pap. text ed. 7.95x (ISBN 0-7167-0997-X). W H Freeman.
Sears, M. & Merriman, D., eds. Oceanography: The Past. (Illus.). 812p. 1980. 37.50 (ISBN 0-387-90497-2). Springer-Verlag.
Sears, M. & Warren, Bruce, eds. Progress in Oceanography, Vols. 1 & 4-6. LC 63-15353. text ed. 76.00 ea. Vol. 1 1963 (ISBN 0-08-010199-2). Vol. 4 1963 (ISBN 0-08-012124-1). Vol. 5 1968. (ISBN 0-08-012631-6). Vol. 6, 1974 (ISBN 0-08-017707-7). Pergamon.
Shepard, Francis & Dill, Robert. Submarine Canyons & Other Sea Valleys. 381p. 1966. 24.00 (ISBN 0-471-78315-3, Pub. by Wiley). Krieger.
Shepard, Francis P. Geological Oceanography. LC 76-54533. 1977. 19.50x (ISBN 0-8448-1064-9). Crane-Russak Co.
Sluyter, E. H. & Raddon, Ethel. Ocean Waves & Progressive Oscillatory Waves: Syllabus. 1977. pap. text ed. 3.95 (ISBN 0-89420-015-1, 234011); cassette recordings 38.90 (ISBN 0-89420-165-4, 234000). Natl Book.
Smith, F. Walton & Kalber, F. A., eds. Handbook in Marine Science, CRC: Section A, Oceanography. LC 73-88624. 640p. 1974. Vol. 1. 59.95 (ISBN 0-87819-389-8); Vol. 2, 390p. 53.95 (ISBN 0-87819-390-1). CRC Pr.
Sorensen, Robert M. Basic Coastal Engineering. LC 77-29256. (Ocean Engineering Ser.). 1978. 31.00 (ISBN 0-471-81370-2, Pub. by Wiley-Interscience). Wiley.
Stern, Melvin E. Ocean Circulation Physics. (International Geophysics Ser.). 1975. 36.50 (ISBN 0-12-666750-0). Acad Pr.
Stevenson, Merritt R., et al. A Marine Atlas of the Pacific Coastal Waters of South America. LC 79-85448. (Illus.). 1970. 90.00x (ISBN 0-520-01616-5). U of Cal Pr.
Stockman, Robert H. The Intergovernmental Oceanographic Commission: An Uncertain Future. (Washington Sea Grant Ser.). 150p. 1974. pap. 4.50 (ISBN 0-295-95371-3). U of Wash Pr.
Stommel, Henry & Fieux, Michele. Oceanographic Atlases: A Guide to Their Geographic Coverage & Contents. LC 78-70786. 1978. 15.00 (ISBN 0-915176-22-X); pap. 7.50x (ISBN 0-915176-21-1). Woods Hole.
Stommel, Henry & Yoshida, Kozo, eds. Kuroshio: Physical Aspects of the Japan Current. LC 72-378. (Illus.). 527p. 1972. 42.50 (ISBN 0-295-95225-3). U of Wash Pr.
Storr, John F. Ecology & Oceanography of the Coral-Reef Tract, Abaco Island, Bahamas. LC 64-66221. (Special Paper: No. 79). (Illus., Orig.). 1964. pap. 5.50x (ISBN 0-8137-2079-6). Geol Soc.
Stowe, Keith S. Ocean Science. LC 78-11962. 610p. 1979. pap. text ed. 23.95x (ISBN 0-471-04261-7); tchrs' manual avail. (ISBN 0-471-08084-5). Wiley.
Swallow, Mary, ed. Progress in Oceanography, Vol. 7. Incl. Pt. 1. Midwater Fishes in the Eastern North Atlantic. 1976. pap. 8.50 (ISBN 0-08-020877-0); Pt. 2. The Mixing & Spreading of Medoc. 1976. pap. 7.50 (ISBN 0-08-020888-6); Pt. 3. 1977. pap. 6.50 (ISBN 0-08-020890-8); Pt. 4. Observations of Rossby Waves Near Site D. 1977. pap. 6.00 (ISBN 0-08-020892-4); Pts. 5 & 6. Date not set. 17.50 (ISBN 0-08-022069-X); Vol. 7 Complete. Date not set. 76.00 (ISBN 0-08-020329-9). LC 63-15353. Pergamon.
Symposium on Progress in Marine Research in the Caribbean & Adjacent Regions: Cicar II. (FAO Fisheries Report Ser.: Suppl. 200). 1979. pap. 27.50 (ISBN 92-5-000707-8, F1598, FAO). Unipub.
Symposium on the Oceanography & Fisheries Resources of the Tropical Atlantic, Abidjan, 1966. Proceedings. LC 55-4606. (Illus.). 1969. 18.75 (ISBN 92-3-000749-8, U490, UNESCO). Unipub.
Takenouti, Y. & Hood, D. W., eds. Bering Sea Oceanography: An Update Nineteen Seventy-Two to Nineteen Seventy-Four. 12.00 (ISBN 0-914500-06-6). U of AK Inst Marine.
Taylor, Geoffrey I. Scientific Papers, 4 vols. Batchelor, G. K., ed. Incl. Vol. 1. Mechanics of Solids. 90.00 (ISBN 0-521-06608-5); Vol. 2. Meteorology, Oceanography & Turbulent Flow. 1960. 90.00 (ISBN 0-521-06609-3); Vol. 3. Aerodynamics & the Mechanics of Projectiles & Explosions. 1963. 90.00 (ISBN 0-521-06610-7); Vol. 4. Mechanics of Fluids: Miscellaneous Topics. (Illus.). 1971. 90.00 (ISBN 0-521-07995-0). Cambridge U Pr.
Tchernia, P. Descriptive Regional Oceanography. Densmore, D., tr. (Pergamon Marine Ser.: Vol. 3). (Illus.). 256p. 1980. 52.00 (ISBN 0-08-020925-4); pap. 19.50 (ISBN 0-08-020919-X). Pergamon.
--Regional Oceanography. 1980. text ed. 52.00 (ISBN 0-08-020925-4); pap. text ed. 19.50 (ISBN 0-08-020919-X). Pergamon.
Thurber, Walter A., et al. Oceanography. (Exploring Earth Science Program Ser.). (gr. 7-12). 1976. pap. text ed. 4.60 (ISBN 0-205-04745-9, 694745X). Allyn.
Thurman, Harold V. Introductory Oceanography. 3rd ed. (Illus.). 596p. 1981. text ed. 21.95 (ISBN 0-675-08058-4); tchr's. ed. 3.95 (ISBN 0-686-69493-7). Merrill.
--Introductory Oceanography. 2nd ed. 1978. text ed. 21.95 (ISBN 0-675-08428-8); instructor's manual 3.95 (ISBN 0-686-67980-6). Merrill.
Tooley, M. J. Sea-Level Changes: North-West England During the Flandrian Stage. (Research Studies in Geography Ser.). (Illus.). 1979. 45.00x (ISBN 0-19-823228-4). Oxford U Pr.
Turekian, Karl K. Oceans. 2nd ed. (Illus.). 160p. 1976. pap. 8.95 (ISBN 0-13-630418-4); 11.95 (ISBN 0-13-630426-5). P-H.
Tyler, John E., ed. Light in the Sea. (Benchmark Paper in Optics Ser.: Vol. 3). 1977. 44.50 (ISBN 0-12-787595-6). Acad Pr.
The Use of Satellite Imagery in Tropical Cyclone Analysis. (WMO Ser: No. 473). (Illus.). 1978. pap. 25.00 (ISBN 92-63-10473-5, W-369, WMO). Unipub.
Van Andel, Tjeerd H. Science at Sea: Tales of an Old Ocean. 1981. price not set (ISBN 0-7167-1363-2); pap. price not set (ISBN 0-7167-1364-0). W H Freeman.
Van Dorn, William G. Oceanography & Seamanship: A Guide for Ocean Cruising. LC 73-15377. (Illus.). 550p. 1974. 22.50 (ISBN 0-396-06888-X). Dodd.
Vinogradov, M. E. & Mills, H., eds. Life Activity of Pelagic Communities in the Ocean Tropics. Kaner, N., tr. from Rus. (Israel Program for Scientific Translations Ser). (Illus.). iv, 300p. 1972. 25.00x (ISBN 0-7065-1274-X, Pub. by IPST). Intl Schol Bk Serv.
Von Arx, William S. An Introduction to Physical Oceanography. (Illus.). 1962. 26.50 (ISBN 0-201-08174-1, Adv Bk Prog). A-W.
Voss, Gilbert L. Oceanography. (Golden Guide Ser). (Illus.). 160p. 1972. PLB 10.38 (ISBN 0-307-64352-2, Golden Pr). Western Pub.
Wallace. Development of the Chlorinity-Salinity Concept in Oceanography. LC 72-97440. (Elsevier Oceanography Ser: No. 7). 240p. 1974. 53.75 (ISBN 0-444-41118-6). Elsevier.
Warren, Bruce A. & Wunsch, Carl, eds. Evolution of Physical Oceanography: Scientific Surveys in Honor of Henry Stommel. 664p. 1980. 37.50x (ISBN 0-262-23104-2). MIT Pr.
Weihaupt, John G. Exploration of the Oceans: An Introduction to Oceanography. 1979. text ed. 19.95 (ISBN 0-02-425040-6). Macmillan.
Weisberg, Joseph S. & Parish, Howard I. Introductory Oceanography. (Illus.). 288p. 1974. text ed. 16.95 (ISBN 0-07-069046-4, C); instructor's manual 2.95 (ISBN 0-07-069047-2). McGraw.
Wenk, Edward, Jr. The Politics of the Ocean. LC 72-5814. (Illus.). 608p. 1972. 15.95 (ISBN 0-295-95240-7). U of Wash Pr.
Weyl, Peter K. Oceanography: An Introduction to the Marine Environment. 1970. 25.95 (ISBN 0-471-93744-4). Wiley.
Williams, Jerome, et al. Sea & Air: The Marine Environment. 2nd ed. LC 72-93196. 1973. 13.50x (ISBN 0-87021-596-5). Naval Inst Pr.
Wooster, Warren S. Freedom of Oceanic Research. LC 73-81050. 256p. 1973. 18.50x (ISBN 0-8448-0214-X). Crane-Russak Co.

OCEANOGRAPHY–BIBLIOGRAPHY

Gordon, Robert & Spaulding, Malcolm. A Bibliography of Numerical Models for Tidal Rivers, Estuaries & Coastal Waters. (Marine Technical Report Ser.: No. 32). 1974. pap. 2.00 (ISBN 0-938412-03-5). URI MAS.
Grier, Mary C., ed. Oceanography of the North Pacific Ocean, Bering Sea & Bering Strait. Repr. of 1941 ed. lib. bdg. 15.00x (ISBN 0-8371-2139-6, GROC). Greenwood.
Sears, Mary, compiled by. Oceanographic Index, Woods Hole Oceanographic Institution Auther Cumulation, 1971-1974. 1976. lib. bdg. 115.00 (ISBN 0-8161-0029-2). G K Hall.
--Oceanographic Index, Woods Hole Oceanographic Institution, Regional Cumulation, 1971-74. 1976. lib. bdg. 75.00 (ISBN 0-8161-0943-5). G K Hall.
--Oceanographic Index, Woods Hole Oceanographic Institution, Subject Cumulation 1971-74, 2 vols. 1976. Set. lib. bdg. 230.00 (ISBN 0-8161-0030-6). G K Hall.
--Oceanographic Index: Auther Cumulation, 1946-1970: Woods Hole Oceanographic Institution, Mass, 3 vols. 1972. Set. 265.00 (ISBN 0-8161-0931-1). G K Hall.
--Oceanographic Index: Organismal Cumulation, 1946-1973, Marine Organisms, Chiefly Planktonic: Woods Hole Oceanographic Institution, Mass, 3 vols. 1454p. 1974. Set. lib. bdg. 210.00 (ISBN 0-8161-0933-8). G K Hall.
--Oceanographic Index: Regional Cumulation, 1946-1970: Woods Hole Oceanographic Institution, Mass. 1972. 95.00 (ISBN 0-8161-0117-5). G K Hall.
--Oceanographic Index: Subject Cumulation, 1946-1970: Woods Hole Oceanographic Institution, Mass, 4 vols. 1972. Set. 365.00 (ISBN 0-8161-0932-X). G K Hall.
University of California - San Diego. Catalogs of the Scripps Institution of Oceanography Library, 4 pts. Incl. Pt. 1. Author-Title Catalog, 7 vols. 1970. Set. 640.00 (ISBN 0-8161-0860-9); Pt. 2. Subject Catalog, 2 vols. 1970. Set. 190.00 (ISBN 0-8161-0112-4); Pt. 3. Shelf List, 2 vols. 1970. Set. 175.00 (ISBN 0-8161-0113-2); Pt. 4. Shelf List of Documents, Reports & Translations Collection. 1970. 90.00 (ISBN 0-8161-0114-0). G K Hall.
--Catalogs of the Scripps Institution of Oceanography Library, First Supplement to Pt. 1, Author-Title Catalog, 3 vols. 1973. 315.00 (ISBN 0-8161-0897-8). G K Hall.
--Catalogs of the Scripps Institution of Oceanography Library, First Supplement to Pts. 2-4, Subject Catalog, Shelf List, Shelf List of Documents & Reports. 1974. 100.00 (ISBN 0-8161-1144-8). G K Hall.

OCEANOGRAPHY–JUVENILE LITERATURE

Boyer, Robert. Story of Oceanography. LC 74-25425. (Story of Science Ser). (Illus.). 128p. (gr. 5-12). 1975. PLB 7.29 (ISBN 0-8178-5162-3). Harvey.
Brown, Joseph E. Wonders of the Kelp Forest. LC 74-2601. (Wonders Ser.). (Illus.). 80p. (gr. 3-7). 1974. 5.95 (ISBN 0-396-06967-3). Dodd.
Colby, C. B. Underseas Frontiers: An Introduction to Oceanography. LC 77-7561. (Illus.). (gr. 4-7). 1977. PLB 5.29 (ISBN 0-698-30676-7). Coward.
Coombs, Charles. Deep-Sea World: The Story of Oceanography. (Illus.). (gr. 7 up). 1966. PLB 8.40 (ISBN 0-688-31226-8). Morrow.
Johnson, Robert L. Men Who Work & Explore Under the Sea. (Nature & Science Bk.). (Illus.). (gr. k-6). PLB 5.95 (ISBN 0-513-00438-6). Denison.
Pick, Christopher. The Young Scientist Book of the Undersea. LC 78-17796. (Young Scientist Ser.). (Illus.). (gr. 4-5). 1978. text ed. 6.95 (ISBN 0-88436-529-8). EMC.

Scharff, Robert. Oceanography. (How & Why Wonder Books Ser.). (Illus.). (gr. 4-6). pap. 1.00 (ISBN 0-685-56717-6). Wonder.
Spilhaus, Athelstan. Ocean Laboratory. LC 66-246868. (Illus., Orig.). (gr. 6 up). 1967. PLB 7.95 (ISBN 0-87191-009-8). Creative Ed.
Williams, Brian. Exploring Under the Sea. (Explorer Books). (Illus.). (gr. 3-5). 1979. 2.95 (ISBN 0-531-09133-3); PLB 6.45 s&l (ISBN 0-531-09118-X). Watts.

OCEANOGRAPHY–RESEARCH
see Oceanographic Research

OCEANOGRAPHY, PHYSICAL
see Oceanography

OCEANOGRAPHY AS A PROFESSION
Gordon, Bernard L., ed. Marine Careers: Selected Papers. 42p. 1974. 2.00 (ISBN 0-910258-02-3). Book & Tackle.
Ocean Sciences Board, National Research Council. Doctoral Scientists in Oceanography. 1981. pap. text ed. 9.25 (ISBN 0-309-03133-8). Natl Acad Pr.
Ross, Frank, Jr. Jobs in Marine Science. LC 73-17719. (Exploring Careers Ser.). (Illus.). 96p. (gr. 5 up). 1974. 7.25 (ISBN 0-688-75013-3). Lothrop.
Wood, Jonathan S. Your Future in the Science of Oceanography. (Careers in Depth Ser.). (Illus.). (gr. 7-12). 1979. PLB 5.97 (ISBN 0-8239-0438-5). Rosen Pr.

OCEANOLOGY
see Oceanography

OCELOTS
Travers, Jeanette. Starting from Scratch: Our Island for Ocelots. LC 75-37390. (Illus.). (YA) (gr. 9 up). 1976. 8.95 (ISBN 0-8008-7369-6). Taplinger.

OCHROLECHIA
Verseghy, K. Gattung Ochrolechia. 1962. pap. 20.00 (ISBN 3-7682-5401-1). Lubrecht & Cramer.

OCHS, ADOLPH SIMON, 1858-1935
Dryfoos, Susan W., as told to. Iphigene: Memoirs of Iphigene Ochs Sulzberger of the New York Times Family. 304p. 1981. 12.95 (ISBN 0-396-08014-6). Dodd.
Johnson, Gerald W. Honorable Titan, a Biographical Study of Adolph S. Ochs. Repr. of 1946 ed. lib. bdg. 14.25x (ISBN 0-8371-3836-1, JOHT). Greenwood.

OCHSNER MEDICAL CENTER, NEW ORLEANS, LOUISIANA
Caldwell, Guy A. Early History of the Ochsner Medical Center: The First Twenty-Two Years. (Illus.). 128p. 1965. ed. spiral bdg. 14.75photocopy (ISBN 0-398-00272-X). C C Thomas.

OCKHAM, WILLIAM, d. ca. 1349
Boehner, Philotheus & Buytaert, Eligius M. Collected Articles on Ockham. (Philosophy Ser). 1958. 20.00 (ISBN 0-686-11542-2). Franciscan Inst.
Boehner, Philotheus, ed. The Tractatus De Successivis Attributed to William Ockham. (Philosophy Ser). 1944. 7.00 (ISBN 0-686-11531-7). Franciscan Inst.
Boehner, Philotheus, et al, eds. Guillelmi De Ockham: Opera Philosophica, Vol. 1, Summa Philosophica. 1974. 45.00 (ISBN 0-686-11530-9). Franciscan Inst.
Brown, Stephen F., ed. Guillelmi De Ockham: Scriptum in Librum Primum Sententiarum, Ordinatio, Opera Theologica, Vol. 2, Distinction4es Secunda et Tertia. 1970. 32.00 (ISBN 0-686-11529-5). Franciscan Inst.
Buescher, Gabriel. The Eucharistic Teaching of William Ockham. (Theology Ser). 1974. Repr. of 1950 ed. 9.00 (ISBN 0-686-11585-6). Franciscan Inst.
Fuchs, Oswald. The Psychology of Habit According & William Ockham. (Philosophy Ser). 1952. 7.00 (ISBN 0-686-11538-4). Franciscan Inst.
Gal, Gedeon, ed. Guillelmi De Ockham: Scriptum in Librum Primum Sententiarum, Ordinatio, Vol. 1, Prologues et Distinctio Prima. 1967. 32.00 (ISBN 0-686-11528-7). Franciscan Inst.
Leff, Gordon. William of Ockham: The Metamorphosis of Scholastic Discourse. 666p. 1975. 45.00x (ISBN 0-87471-679-9). Rowman.
McGrade, A. S. The Political Thought of William of Ockham. LC 73-86044. (Studies in Medieval Life & Thought). 264p. 1974. 35.50 (ISBN 0-521-20284-1). Cambridge U Pr.
Menges, Matthew C. The Concept of Univocity Regarding the Predication of God & Creature According to William Ockham. (Philosophy Ser). 1952. 7.00 (ISBN 0-686-11539-2). Franciscan Inst.
Moody, Ernest A. Logic of William of Ockham. LC 65-17914. 1965. Repr. of 1935 ed. 20.00 (ISBN 0-8462-0666-8). Russell.
Ockham, William. Ockham's Theory of Terms. Loux, Michael J., tr. 234p. 1975. 14.95x (ISBN 0-268-00550-8); pap. 4.95x (ISBN 0-268-00551-6). U of Notre Dame Pr.
Ryan, John J. The Nature, Structure, & Function of the Church in William of Ockham. LC 78-2891. (American Academy of Religion: Studies in Religion, 16). 1979. o.s.i 12.00 (ISBN 0-89130-366-9, 010016); pap. 7.50 (ISBN 0-89130-230-1). Scholars Pr Ca.
Tierney, Brian. Ockham,The Conciliar Theory, & the Canonists. Oberman, Heiko A., ed. LC 74-157547. (Facet Bks). (Orig.). 1971. pap. 1.00 (ISBN 0-8006-3064-5, 1-3064). Fortress.
Webering, Damascene. Theory of Demonstration According to William Ockham. (Philosophy Ser). 1953. 7.00 (ISBN 0-686-11540-6). Franciscan Inst.
Weinberg, Julius R. Ockham, Descartes, & Hume: Self Knowledge, Substance, & Causality. Courtenay, William J., ed. 1977. 22.50 (ISBN 0-299-07120-0). U of Wis Pr.
Wey, Joseph C., ed. Guillelmi De Ockham: Quodlibeta Septem, Opera Theologica, Vol. 9. 1980. 50.00 (ISBN 0-686-28122-5). Franciscan Inst.

OCLC, INC.
Davis, Jinnie Y. & Abrera, Joseta B. Monographic Searching on the OCLC Terminal: A Programmed Text with Teacher's Guide. (Illus.). 136p. 1981. pap. 14.50x (ISBN 0-208-01843-3, Linnet). Shoe String.
Manheimen, Martha L. OCLC: An Introduction to Searching & Input. rev ed. 1981. write for info. (ISBN 0-918212-48-0). Neal-Schuman.
Maruskin. OCLC, Inc. Its Governance Function, Finance & Technology. (Books in Library & Information Science Ser.: Vol. 32). 160p. 1980. 22.75 (ISBN 0-8247-1179-3). Dekker.

O'CONNELL, DANIEL, 1775-1847
Dunlop, Robert. Daniel O'Connell & the Revival of National Life in Ireland. LC 73-14439. (Heroes of the Nations Ser.). Repr. of 1900 ed. 30.00 (ISBN 0-404-58258-3). AMS Pr.
Life & Speeches of Daniel O'Connell, M.P. 264p. 1980. Repr. of 1878 ed. lib. bdg. 65.00 (ISBN 0-89984-365-4). Century Bookbindery.
McCaffrey, Lawrence J. Daniel O'Connell & the Repeal Year. LC 65-27011. 272p. 1966. 10.00x (ISBN 0-8131-1115-3). U Pr of Ky.
Moley, Raymond. Daniel O'Connell: Nationalism Without Violence. LC 73-93142. 1974. 20.00 (ISBN 0-8232-0977-6). Fordham.
--Daniel O'connell: Nationalism Without Violence. 1975. pap. 8.00 (ISBN 0-8232-0978-4). Fordham.
Nowlan, Kevin B. The Politics of Repeal. LC 75-35339. 248p. 1976. Repr. of 1965 ed. lib. bdg. 15.25x (ISBN 0-8371-8562-9, NOPR). Greenwood.
O'Faolain, Sean. King of the Beggars. LC 75-7242. (Illus.). 338p. 1975. Repr. of 1938 ed. lib. bdg. 16.25x (ISBN 0-8371-8104-6, OFKB). Greenwood.

O'CONNOR, FLANNERY
Coles, Robert. Flannery O'Connor's South. LC 79-23057. (Walter Lynwood Fleming Lectures in Southern History). 1980. 14.95 (ISBN 0-8071-0655-0). La State U Pr.
Eggenschwiler, David. The Christian Humanism of Flannery O'Connor. LC 79-179560. 156p. 1972. 9.95x (ISBN 0-8143-1463-5). Wayne St U Pr.
Farmer, David. Flannery O'Connor: A Descriptive Bibliography. LC 80-8480. 1981. lib. bdg. 20.00 (ISBN 0-8240-9493-X). Garland Pub.
Fitzgerald, Sally, ed. The Habit of Being: Letters of Flannery O'Connor. LC 79-23319. 1980. pap. 6.95 (ISBN 0-394-74259-1, Vin). Random.
Friedman, Melvin J. The Added Dimension: The Art of Mind of Flannery O'Connor. 2nd ed. LC 66-11070. 1977. pap. 8.00 (ISBN 0-8232-0711-0). Fordham.
Getz, Lorine M. Flannery O'Connor: Her Life, Library & Book Reviews. (Studies in Women & Religion: Vol. 5). 1980. soft cover 24.95x (ISBN 0-88946-997-0). E Mellen.
Golden, Robert & Sullivan, Mary. Flannery O'Connor & Caroline Gordon: A Reference Guide. (Reference Publications Ser.). 1977. lib. bdg. 22.00 (ISBN 0-8161-7845-3). G K Hall.
Grimshaw, James A., Jr. The Flannery O'Connor Companion. LC 80-26828. (Illus.). 160p. 1981. lib. bdg. 22.50 (ISBN 0-313-21086-1, GRO/). Greenwood.
Hendin, Josephine. The World of Flannery O'connor. LC 76-108208. (Midland Bks.: No. 150). 192p. 1970. pap. 2.50x (ISBN 0-253-20150-0). Ind U Pr.
McFarland, Dorothy T. Flannery O'Connor. LC 74-78443. (Modern Literature Ser.). 140p. 1976. 10.95 (ISBN 0-8044-2609-0). Ungar.
McKenzie, Barbara. Flannery O'Connor's Georgia. LC 80-10936. (Illus.). 132p. 1980. 24.95 (ISBN 0-8203-0517-0); pap. 12.50 (ISBN 0-8203-0518-9). U of Ga Pr.
Muller, Gilbert H. Nightmares & Visions: Flannery O'Connor & the Catholic Grotesque. LC 75-184777. 134p. 1972. 9.95x (ISBN 0-8203-0284-8). U of Ga Pr.
O'Connor, Flannery. The Habit of Being: Letters. Fitzgerald, Sally, ed. & intro. by. 617p. 1979. 15.00 (ISBN 0-374-16769-9). FS&G.
Orvell, Miles. Invisible Parade: The Fiction of Flannery O'Connor. LC 72-91132. 250p. 1972. 19.50x (ISBN 0-87722-023-9). Temple U Pr.

O'CONNOR, FRANK
see O'Donovan, Michael, 1903-

O'CONNOR, WILLIAM DOUGLAS, 1832-1889
Loving, Jerome. Walt Whitman's Champion: William Douglas O'Connor. LC 77-89511. 284p. 1978. 13.50x (ISBN 0-89096-039-9). Tex A&M Univ Pr.
Resnick, Nathan D. Walt Whitman & the Authorship of The Good Gray Poet. pap. 9.00 (ISBN 0-8337-2947-0). B Franklin.

OCTAL SYSTEM
see also Arithmetic; Numeration

OCTOBER MIDDLE EAST WAR, 1973
see Israel-Arab War, 1973

OCTOPUS
see also Cephalopoda
Carrick, Carol. Octopus. LC 77-12769. (Illus.). 32p. (gr. 1-4). 1978. 7.95 (ISBN 0-395-28777-4, Clarion). HM.
Conklin, Gladys. The Octopus & Other Cephalopods. LC 77-3818. (Illus.). (gr. 4-6). 1977. 7.95 (ISBN 0-8234-0306-8). Holiday.
Cook, Joseph J. & Wisner, William L. Phantom World of the Octopus & Squid. LC 65-13029. (Illus.). (gr. 3-7). 1965. PLB 5.95 (ISBN 0-396-06792-1). Dodd.
Cousteau, Jacques-Yves & Diole, Philippe. Octopus & Squid: The Soft Intelligence. LC 72-76141. 304p. 1973. 12.95 (ISBN 0-385-06896-4). Doubleday.
--Octopus & Squid: The Soft Intelligence. (The Undersea Discoveries of Jacques-Yves Cousteau). (Illus.). 1978. pap. 8.95 (ISBN 0-89104-111-7). A & W Pubs.
Schultz, Ellen. I Can Read About the Octopus. new ed. LC 78-73715. (gr. 2-4). 1979. pap. 1.25 (ISBN 0-89375-213-4). Troll Assocs.
Shaw, Evelyn. Octopus. LC 74-135779. (Science I Can Read Books). (Illus.). (gr. k-3). 1971. PLB 7.89 (ISBN 0-06-025559-5, HarpJ). Har-Row.
Vevers, Gwynne. Octopus, Cuttlefish & Squid. LC 77-25083. (New Biology Ser.). (Illus.). 1978. 6.95 (ISBN 0-07-067405-1, GB). McGraw.
Wells, M. J. Octopus: Physiology & Behaviour of an Advanced Invertebrate. LC 77-2795. 471p. 1978. text ed. 55.00x (ISBN 0-412-13260-5, Pub. by Chapman & Hall England). Methuen Inc.
Young, John Z. Anatomy of the Nervous System of Octopus Vulgaris. (Illus.). 1971. 89.00x (ISBN 0-19-857340-5). Oxford U Pr.
--Model of the Brain. 1964. 39.50x (ISBN 0-19-857333-2). Oxford U Pr.

OCTOROONS
see Mulattoes

OCULAR BIOMICROSCOPY
L'Esperance, Francis A., Jr. Ocular Photocoagulation: A Stereoscopic Atlas. LC 75-33111. (Illus.). 338p. 1975. text ed. 77.50 (ISBN 0-8016-2824-5). Mosby.

OCULAR FUNDUS
see Fundus Oculi

OCULAR MANIFESTATIONS OF GENERAL DISEASES
Chester, Edward M. The Ocular Fundus in Systemic Disease: A Clinical Pathological Correlation. (Illus.). 245p. 1973. 52.50 (ISBN 0-8151-1657-8). Year Bk Med.
Goldberg, Morton F., ed. Genetic & Metabolic Eye Disease. 1974. 60.00 (ISBN 0-316-31923-6). Little.
Lee, W. R., ed. Current Research in Ophthalmic Electron Microscopy, 3. (Illus.). 160p. 1980. 28.40 (ISBN 0-686-62616-8). Springer-Verlag.
Nicholson. Pediatric Ocular Tumors. LC 81-2346. 320p. 1981. 66.50x (ISBN 0-89352-125-6). Masson Pub.
Ryan, Stephen J., Jr. & Smith, Ronald E., eds. Selected Topics on the Eye in Systemic Disease. LC 74-4471. (Illus.). 408p. 1974. 62.00 (ISBN 0-8089-0835-9). Grune.
Smolin, Gilbert & O'Connor, G. Richard. Ocular Immunology. LC 81-8218. (Illus.). 250p. 1981. text ed. price not set (ISBN 0-8121-0688-1). Lea & Febiger.
Sorsby, A. Diseases of the Fundus Oculi. 1976. 54.95 (ISBN 0-407-00023-2). Butterworth.
Watson, Peter G. & Hazleman, Brian L. The Sclera & Systemic Disorders. LC 76-26776. (Major Problems in Ophthalmology Ser.: Vol. 2). (Illus.). 1976. text ed. 24.00 (ISBN 0-7216-9134-X). Saunders.

OCULAR THERAPEUTICS
see Therapeutics, Ophthalmological

OCULISTS
see Optometrists

OCULOMOTOR SYSTEM
see Eye–Movements

ODEGAARD, CHARLES EDWIN, 1911-
Odegaard, Charles E., et al. Man & Learning in Modern Society. LC 59-15076. (Illus.). 203p. 1959. 10.50 (ISBN 0-295-73835-9). U of Wash Pr.
O'Neil, Robert M. Discriminating Against Discrimination: Preferential Admissions & the DeFunis Case. LC 75-3888. 288p. 1976. 10.95x (ISBN 0-253-31800-9). Ind U Pr.

ODER-NEISSE AREA
Here are entered works which discuss those former German areas of Poland that lie east of the Oder-Neisse line.
Czarnecki, Jan. The Goths in Ancient Poland. LC 74-20750. 1975. 12.50x (ISBN 0-87024-264-4). U of Miami Pr.
Jordan, Z. Oder-Neisse Line. 139p. 1952. 2.50 (ISBN 0-686-30934-0). Polish Inst Arts.
Kruszewski, Z. Anthony. The Oder-Neisse Boundary & Poland's Modernization: The Socioeconomic & Political Impact. LC 74-159411. (Special Studies in International Politics & Government). 1972. 28.00x (ISBN 0-275-28292-9). Irvington.

ODES
Fry, Paul H. The Poet's Calling in the English Ode. LC 79-20554. 1980. 21.00x (ISBN 0-300-02400-2). Yale U Pr.
Gosse, Edmund W. English Odes. 259p. 1980. Repr. of 1881 ed. lib. bdg. 25.00 (ISBN 0-8414-4625-3). Folcroft.
Hills, Elijah. The Odes of Bello, Olmedo & Heredia. 1920. 4.00 (ISBN 0-87535-003-8). Hispanic Soc.
Jump, John D. The Ode. (Critical Idiom Ser.). 1974. pap. text ed. 5.50x (ISBN 0-416-78820-3). Methuen Inc.
Lefkowitz, Mary. The Victory Ode: An Introduction. LC 76-11650. 1977. 18.00 (ISBN 0-8155-5045-6, NP). Noyes.
Niles, Nathaniel. The American Hero: A Sapphick Ode. 1975. 3.00 (ISBN 0-89073-039-3). Boston Public Lib.
Shafer, Robert. English Ode to Sixteen Sixty. LC 65-21090. (Studies in Poetry, No. 38). 1969. Repr. of 1918 ed. lib. bdg. 49.95 (ISBN 0-8383-0620-9). Haskell.
--English Ode to Sixteen Sixty: An Essay in Literary History. LC 66-29469. 1966. Repr. of 1918 ed. 6.50 (ISBN 0-87752-100-X). Gordian.
Sharp, William. Great Odes. 1977. Repr. of 1890 ed. 20.00 (ISBN 0-89984-114-7). Century Bookbindery.
--Great Odes: English & American. 1979. Repr. lib. bdg. 22.50 (ISBN 0-8495-4928-0). Arden Lib.
Shuster, George N. The English Ode from Milton to Keats. 1964. 7.50 (ISBN 0-8446-1405-X). Peter Smith.
Vega, Garcilaso De La. Odes & Sonnets. Cleugh, James, tr. from Span. LC 76-48423. (Library of World Literature Ser.). 1978. Repr. of 1930 ed. 12.50 (ISBN 0-88355-542-5). Hyperion Conn.

ODETS, CLIFFORD, 1906-
Brenman-Gibson, Margaret. Clifford Odets: American Playwright. LC 80-7927. 1981. 25.00 (ISBN 0-689-11160-6). Atheneum.
Cantor, Harold. Clifford Odets: Playwright-Poet. LC 77-27284. 1978. 12.00 (ISBN 0-8108-1107-3). Scarecrow.
Murray, Edward. Clifford Odets: The Thirties & After. LC 68-9397. 1968. 11.00 (ISBN 0-8044-2644-9). Ungar.
Shuman, R. Baird. Clifford Odets. (Twayne's United States Authors Ser). 1962. pap. 3.45 (ISBN 0-8084-0081-9, T30, Twayne). Coll & U Pr.

ODONATA
see Dragon Flies

O'DONNELL, PEADAR
Freyer, Grattan. Peadar O'Donnell. (Irish Writers Ser.). 128p. 1973. 4.50 (ISBN 0-8387-1362-9); pap. 1.95 (ISBN 0-8387-1369-6). Bucknell U Pr.

O'DONOVAN, MICHAEL, 1903-
Matthews, James. Frank O'Connor. LC 75-125470. (Irish Writers Ser.). 94p. 1975. 4.50 (ISBN 0-8387-7756-2); pap. 1.95 (ISBN 0-8387-7609-4). Bucknell U Pr.
O'Connor, Frank, pseud. My Father's Son. (Illus.). 188p. 1971. pap. 2.95 (ISBN 0-330-02637-2, Pub. by Pan Bks England). Irish Bk Ctr.
--An Only Child. 219p. 1970. Repr. of 1961 ed. pap. 2.95 (ISBN 0-686-30884-0, Pub. by Pan Bks England). Irish Bk Ctr.
Tomory, William M. Frank O'Connor. (English Authors Ser.: No. 297). 1980. 11.95 (ISBN 0-8057-6789-4). Twayne.

ODONTOGLOSSAE
see Flamingos

ODONTOLOGY
see Teeth

ODORS
see also Perfumes

Amoore, John E. Molecular Basis of Odor. (American Lecture in Living Chemistry Ser). (Illus.). 216p. 1970. 21.00 (ISBN 0-398-00039-5). C C Thomas.
Board on Toxicology & Environmental Health Hazards. Odors from Stationary & Mobile Sources. 1979. pap. 20.50 (ISBN 0-309-02877-9). Natl Acad Pr.
Compilation of Odor & Taste Threshold Values Data. 1973. 27.50 (ISBN 0-8031-0087-6, DS48). ASTM.
Hornstein, Irwin, ed. Flavor Chemistry. LC 66-27216. (Advances in Chemistry Ser: No. 56). 1966. 24.00 (ISBN 0-8412-0057-2). Am Chemical.
Jellinek, J. Stephan. The Use of Fragrance in Consumer Products. LC 75-2106. 219p. 1975. 31.50 (ISBN 0-471-44151-1, Pub. by Wiley-Interscience). Wiley.
Jennings, Walter & Shibamoto, Takayuki. Qualitative Analysis of Flavor & Fragrance Volatiles by Glass Capillary Gas Chromtography. LC 79-26034. 1980. 39.00 (ISBN 0-12-384250-6). Acad Pr.
Louden, Louise & Weiner, Jack. Odors & Odor Control. (Bibliographic Ser.: No. 267). 1976. pap. 25.00 (ISBN 0-87010-040-8). Inst Paper Chem.
Summer, W. Odour Pollution of Air: Causes & Control. 1972. 32.50x (ISBN 0-249-44022-9). Intl Ideas.
Turk, Amos & Johnston, James Jr., eds. Human Responses to Enviromental Odors. 1974. 46.00 (ISBN 0-12-703860-4). Acad Pr.
Water Pollution Control Federation. Odor Control for Wastewater Facilities ('79) (Manual of Practice No. 22). (Illus.). 70p. Date not set. pap. 8.00 (ISBN 0-686-30417-9). Water Pollution.

ODSCHI LANGUAGE
see Twi Language

O'DUFFY, EIMAR
Hogan, Robert. Eimar O'Duffy. LC 70-125469. (Irish Writers Ser.). 84p. 1972. 4.50 (ISBN 0-8387-7755-4). Bucknell U Pr.

ODYSSEUS
see Ulysses

OECANTHINAE
see Crickets

OEDIPUS
Kallich, Martin, et al, eds. Oedipus: Myth & Drama. LC 67-18744. 1968. pap. 7.95 (ISBN 0-672-63076-1). Odyssey Pr.
Money-Kyrle, Roger E. Meaning of Sacrifice. Repr. of 1930 ed. 13.00 (ISBN 0-384-39690-9). Johnson Repr.
Velikovsky, Immanuel. Oedipus & Akhnaton: Myth & History. LC 60-7886. 1960. 8.95 (ISBN 0-385-00529-6). Doubleday.

OEDIPUS COMPLEX
Green, Andre. The Tragic Effect. Sheridan, Alan, tr. LC 76-12629. 1979. 28.50 (ISBN 0-521-21377-0). Cambridge U Pr.
Hay, John. Oedipus Tyrannus: Lame Knowledge & the Homosporic Womb. LC 78-57075. 1978. pap. text ed. 8.00 (ISBN 0-8191-0518-X). U Pr of Amer.
Nagera, Humberto. Female Sexuality & the Oedipus Complex. LC 75-13505. 150p. 1975. 17.50x (ISBN 0-87668-206-9). Aronson.
Neilson, Francis. The Freudians & the Oedipus Complex. 69.95 (ISBN 0-87700-013-1). Revisionist Pr.
Rue, James & Shanahan, Louise. Daddy's Girl, Mama's Boy. 1979. pap. 2.25 (ISBN 0-451-08822-0, E8822, Sig). NAL.
Spotnitz, Hyman. Psychotherapy of Pre-Oedipal Conditions. LC 75-37489. 1976. 30.00x (ISBN 0-87668-242-5, 24257). Aronson.

OEDOGONIACEAE
Gauthier-Lievre, L. Oedogoniacees Africaines. (Illus.). 1964. 40.00 (ISBN 3-7682-0216-X). Lubrecht & Cramer.
Hirn, K. E. Monographie & Iconographie der Oedogoniaceen. (Illus.). 1960. pap. 100.00 (ISBN 3-7682-7056-4). Lubrecht & Cramer.

OEKUMENISCHE MARIENSCHWESTERNSCHAFT
Schlink, M. Basilea. Realities. 128p. 1972. pap. 2.50 (ISBN 0-310-32602-8). Zondervan.

OENOTHERA
Cleland, Ralph E. Oenothera: Cytogenetics & Evolution. (Experimental Botany Ser.: Vol. 5). 1973. 59.50 (ISBN 0-12-176450-8). Acad Pr.

OFF-BROADWAY THEATER
Farber, Donald C. From Option to Opening. rev. ed. LC 76-58845. 1977. text ed. 10.00x (ISBN 0-910482-80-2). Drama Bk.
Wetzsteon, Ross. The Obie Winners: The Best of off-Broadway. LC 79-6096. (Illus.). 816p. 1980. 15.95 (ISBN 0-385-17005-X). Doubleday.

OFF-TRACK BETTING
see Horse Race Betting

OFFENBACH, JACQUES, 1819-1880
Bekker, Paul. Jacques Offenbach. LC 74-24039. Repr. of 1909 ed. 14.50 (ISBN 0-404-12862-9). AMS Pr.
Faris, Alexander. Jacques Offenbach. 1981. 25.00 (ISBN 0-684-16797-2, ScribT). Scribner.
Hammond, Peter. Offenbach: His Life & Times. (Composers-Their Life & Times Ser.). (Illus.). 168p. 1981. 16.95 (ISBN 0-88254-526-4, Pub. by Midas England); pap. 9.95 (ISBN 0-686-71865-8, Pub. by Midas England). Hippocrene Bks.
--Offenbach: His Life & Times. (Life & Times Ser.). (Illus.). 192p. (YA) Date not set. Repr. of 1980 ed. 19.95 (ISBN 0-87666-583-0, Z-52). Paganiniana Pubns.
Kracauer, Siegfried. Jacques Offenbach und das Paris Seiner Zeit. (Illus.). 412p. 1980. text ed. 18.20 (ISBN 3-458-04927-4, Pub. by Insel Verlag Germany). Suhrkamp.
Kracaver, Siegfried. Orpheus in Paris: Offenbach & the Paris of His Time. David, Gwenda & Mosbacher, Eric, trs. LC 72-93827. 425p. 1972. Repr. of 1938 ed. 40.00 (ISBN 0-8443-0093-4). Vienna Hse.
Moss, Arthur & Marvel, Evalyn. Cancan & Barcarolle: The Life & Times of Jacques Offenbach. LC 75-2629. (Illus.). 280p. 1975. Repr. of 1954 ed. lib. bdg. 19.75x (ISBN 0-8371-8045-7, MOCB). Greenwood.
Offenbach, Jacques. Jacques Offenbach. 1981. 29.95 (ISBN 0-7145-3512-5); pap. 11.95 (ISBN 0-7145-3841-8). Riverrun NY.
--Offenbach in America: Notes of a Travelling Musician. LC 74-24172. Repr. of 1877 ed. 12.50 (ISBN 0-404-13076-3). AMS Pr.
--Offenbach's Songs from the Great Operettas: Complete Music for 38 Songs from 14 Operettas. (Illus., Orig.). 1976. pap. 7.00 (ISBN 0-486-23341-3). Dover.

OFFENDERS, FEMALE
see Female Offenders

OFFENSES, MILITARY
see Military Offenses

OFFENSES AFFECTING THE PUBLIC TRADE
see Commercial Crimes

OFFENSES AGAINST PROPERTY
see also Arson; Embezzlement; Extortion; Forgery; Fraud; Larceny; Poaching; Robbery; White Collar Crimes

OFFENSES AGAINST PUBLIC MORALITY
see Crimes without Victims

OFFENSES AGAINST PUBLIC PROPERTY
see also Sabotage

OFFENSES AGAINST PUBLIC SAFETY
see also Riots
Gurr, Ted R. Conflict. LC 76-17370. (A Sagemark Edition Ser.). (Illus.). 92p. 1976. 20.00x (ISBN 0-8039-0681-1); pap. 9.95x (ISBN 0-8039-0827-X). Sage.

OFFENSES AGAINST RELIGION
see also Apostasy; Blasphemy; Heresy

OFFENSES AGAINST THE PERSON
see also Abortion; Abduction; Assassination; Assault and Battery; Homicide; Infanticide; Murder; Sex Crimes; Suicide; Violent Deaths
Bailey, F. Lee & Rothblatt, Henry B. Crimes of Violence: Homicide & Assault. LC 72-97625. (Criminal Law Library). 543p. 1973. 47.50 (ISBN 0-686-05455-5). Lawyers Co-Op.
--Crimes of Violence: Rape & Other Sex Crimes. LC 72-97625. (Criminal Law Library). 1973. 47.50 (ISBN 0-686-14500-3). Lawyers Co-Op.
Block, Richard. Violent Crime. LC 76-40818. (Illus.). 1977. 15.95 (ISBN 0-669-01044-8). Lexington Bks.
Fanon, Frantz. Wretched of the Earth. Farrington, Constance, tr. 1965. pap. 2.95 (ISBN 0-394-17327-9, B342, BC). Grove.
National Commission on the Causes & Prevention of Violence & Moynihan, Daniel P. Violent Crime. LC 76-111638. 1970. pap. 2.50 (ISBN 0-8076-0531-X). Braziller.
Schur, Edwin M. Crimes Without Victims - Deviant Behavior & Public Policy: Abortion, Homosexuality, Drug Addiction. (Orig.). 1965. pap. 3.95 (ISBN 0-13-192930-5, S111, Spec). P-H.

OFFENSIVE FOOTBALL
see Football-Offense

OFFERINGS, VOTIVE
see Votive Offerings

OFFERTORIES
Gotwald, Frederick G. Offertory Prayers. 31p. 1976. pap. 2.25 (ISBN 0-89536-171-X). CSS Pub.
Ironside, H. A. Levitical Offerings. pap. 1.25 (ISBN 0-87213-375-3). Loizeaux.

OFFICE, ECCLESIASTICAL
see Clergy-Office

OFFICE, NOMINATIONS FOR
see Nominations for Office

OFFICE, TENURE OF
see Civil Service

OFFICE ADMINISTRATION
see Office Management

OFFICE BUILDINGS
see also Offices; Real Estate Management; Skyscrapers
Baron, Stephen L. Manual of Energy Saving in Existing Buildings & Plants, Vol. 1. (Illus.). 1978. 29.95 (ISBN 0-13-553578-6, Busn). P-H.
DeChiars, Joseph. Handbook of Architectural Details for Commercial Buildings. 512p. 1980. 32.50 (ISBN 0-07-016215-8, P&RB). McGraw.
Duffy, Francis, et al. Planning Office Space. (Illus.). 1976. 50.00 (ISBN 0-85139-505-8, Pub. by Architectural Pr). Nichols Pub.
Goddard, John B. Office Location in Urban & Regional Development. (Theory & Practice in Geography Ser.). (Illus.). 1975. pap. text ed. 5.95x (ISBN 0-19-874033-6). Oxford U Pr.
Institute of Real Estate Management. Income-Expense Analysis: Suburban Office Buildings. Anderson, Kenneth A., ed. (Orig.). 1980. pap. 35.00 (ISBN 0-912104-52-X). Inst Real Estate.
Joedicke, Jurgen. Office & Administration Building. 1975. 24.95x (ISBN 0-442-80005-3). Van Nos Reinhold.
Kirk, Nancye J., ed. Managing the Office Building. LC 80-82343. (Illus.). 414p. 1981. text ed. 21.95 (ISBN 0-912104-45-7). Inst Real Estate.
Ripnen, Kenneth H. Office Space Administration. (Illus.). 224p. 1974. 23.50 (ISBN 0-07-052936-1, P&RB). McGraw.
San Luis, Edward. Office & Office Building Security. LC 73-85627. (Illus.). 320p. 1973. 16.95 (ISBN 0-913708-12-7). Butterworth.
Scanzoni, L. & Scanzoni, J. Planning the New Office. (Illus.). 1978. 21.50 (ISBN 0-07-054721-1, P&RB). McGraw.

OFFICE EMPLOYEES
see Clerks

OFFICE EQUIPMENT AND SUPPLIES
see also Accounting Machines; Calculating-Machines; Electronic Office Machines; Typewriters; Writing-Materials and Instruments
Arco Editorial Board. Office Machines Operator. 3rd ed. LC 67-16547. (Orig.). 1967. pap. 4.00 (ISBN 0-668-00728-1). Arco.
Barr, Jene. Busy Office, Busy People. LC 67-26513. (Career Awareness-Community Helpers Ser.). (Illus.). (gr. k-2). 1968. 5.25g (ISBN 0-8075-0978-7). A Whitman.
BCC Staff. Office of the Future. 1980. cancelled (ISBN 0-89336-242-5, G-056). BCC.
Briggs, J. Robert & Kosy, Eugene J. Office Machines - a Collegiate Course. 2nd ed. 1973. pap. text ed. 6.48 (ISBN 0-538-13480-1, M48). SW Pub.
Bueromaschinen Lexikon. 18th ed. (Ger.). 1975. pap. 21.50 (ISBN 3-87264-001-1, M-7316, Pub. by Goeller Verlag). French & Eur.
The Business & Technology Videolog. LC 78-74186. 1981. pap. 39.50 (ISBN 0-88432-070-7, Pub. by Mord Media). Video-Forum.
Business Communications Staff. Markets for Office Products in the Home: G-007r. 1981. 850.00 (ISBN 0-89336-298-0). BCC.
Consumer Guide Editors. Decorating Your Office for Success. LC 78-20157. (Illus.). 1979. 12.95 (ISBN 0-06-010854-1, HarpT). Har-Row.
Davis, F. T. Business Acquisitions Desk Book. 2nd ed. 415p. 1981. 39.50 (ISBN 0-87624-049-X). Inst Busn Plan.
Encyclopedie des Equipements de Bureau et Materiels d'Informatique, 49 vols. (Fr.). Set. pap. 600.00 (ISBN 0-686-56734-X, M-6196). French & Eur.
Fasnacht, H. D., et al. How to Use Business Machines. 3rd ed. 1969. text ed. 5.96 (ISBN 0-07-019972-8, G); tchr's manual & key 3.25 (ISBN 0-07-019973-6). McGraw.
Galitz, Wilbur O. Human Factors in Office Automation. 237p. 1980. pap. 9.95 (ISBN 0-89435-089-7). QED Info Sci.
Gardiner, A. W. Typewriting & Office Duplicating Processes. 6.95 (ISBN 0-8038-7084-1). Hastings.
Gensler, M. Arthur & Brandt, Peter B. A Rational Approach to Office Planning. LC 77-28072. 1978. 7.50 (ISBN 0-8144-2217-9). Am Mgmt.
Giordano, Albert. Business Machine Calculation: Vol. I, Adding Machines & Printing Calculators. (Orig.). 1964. Vol. 1. pap. text ed. 9.95 (ISBN 0-13-104943-7). P-H.
Heyel, Carl & Business Equipment Manufacturers Association. Computers, Office Machines, & the New Information Technology. (Orig.). 1969. pap. 6.95x (ISBN 0-02-353980-1). Macmillan.
International Labour Office, Geneva. Audiovisual, Draughting, Office, Reproduction & Other Ancillary Equipment & Supplies: Equipment Planning Guide for Vocational & Technical Trading & Education Programmes. (No. 15). (Illus.). 279p. (Orig.). 1979. pap. 22.80 (ISBN 9-2210-2112-2). Intl Labour Office.
Kinzey, Vera G. Mastering Business Machines: A Text-Workbook. (Illus., Orig.). 1976. spiral bdg. 10.95 (ISBN 0-15-555124-8, HC); instructor's manual with tests avail. (ISBN 0-15-555125-6). HarBraceJ.
Logan, D. W. Setting up an Office. (Illus.). 232p. 1968. 14.95x (ISBN 0-8464-1135-0). Beekman Pubs.
McKenzie, Jimmy C. & Hughes, Robert J. Office Machines: A Practical Approach. 1978. write for info. wire coil (ISBN 0-697-08022-6); instr's manual avail. (ISBN 0-697-08024-2). Wm C Brown.
National Center for State Courts. Business Equipment & the Courts: Manual. (Illus.). 1977. pap. 35.00 (ISBN 0-89656-018-X, R0030R). Natl Ctr St Courts.
--Business Equipment & the Courts: Reference Guide. (Courts' Equipment Analysis Project Ser.). (Illus.). 1977. 4.50 (ISBN 0-89656-019-8, R0030G). Natl Ctr St Courts.
Office Furniture. (Home & Office Furnishings). 1981. 350.00 (ISBN 0-686-31550-2). Busn Trend.
Price, Judith. Executive Style. 1980. 19.95 (ISBN 0-671-25354-9, Linden). S&S.
Quinones De Perez, Josefina, et al. Maquinas De Oficina. rev., 2nd, enl. ed. LC 76-1024. (Illus.). 189p. (Span.). 1976. pap. text ed. 6.25 (ISBN 0-8477-2626-6). U of PR Pr.
Rudman, Jack. Addressograph Machine Operator. (Career Examination Ser.: C-1076). (Cloth bdg. avail on request). pap. 6.00 (ISBN 0-8373-1076-8). Natl Learning.
--Bookkeeping Machine Supervisor. (Career Examination Ser.: C-1140). (Cloth bdg. avail. on request). pap. 8.00 (ISBN 0-8373-1140-3). Natl Learning.
--Business Machine Maintainer & Repairer. (Career Examination Ser.: C-1155). (Cloth bdg. avail. on request). pap. 6.00 (ISBN 0-8373-1155-1). Natl Learning.
--Dictating Machine Transcriber. (Career Examination Ser.: C-1248). (Cloth bdg. avail. on request). pap. 8.00 (ISBN 0-8373-1248-5). Natl Learning.
--Duplicating Machine Operator. (Career Examination Ser.: C-1407). (Cloth bdg. avail. on request). pap. 8.00 (ISBN 0-8373-1407-0). Natl Learning.
--Duplicating Machine Supervisor. (Career Examination Ser.: C-1408). (Cloth bdg. avail. on request). pap. 8.00 (ISBN 0-8373-1408-9). Natl Learning.
--Office Appliance Operator. (Career Examination Ser.: C-551). (Cloth bdg. avail. on request). pap. 8.00 (ISBN 0-8373-0551-9). Natl Learning.
--Office Machine Aide. (Career Examination Ser.: C-1579). (Cloth bgd. avail. on request). pap. 8.00 (ISBN 0-8373-1579-4). Natl Learning.
--Office Machine Operating - Sr. H.S. (Teachers License Examination Ser.: T-45). (Cloth bdg. avail. on request). pap. 10.00 (ISBN 0-8373-8045-6). Natl Learning.
--Office Machine Operator. (Career Examination Ser.: C-559). (Cloth bdg. avail. on request). pap. 8.00 (ISBN 0-8373-0559-4). Natl Learning.
--Senior Office Machine Operator. (Career Examination Ser.: C-1480). (Cloth bdg. avail. on request). pap. 8.00 (ISBN 0-8373-1480-1). Natl Learning.
--Varitype Operator. (Career Examination Ser.: C-872). (Cloth bdg. avail. on request). pap. 8.00 (ISBN 0-8373-0872-0). Natl Learning.
Walsh, Jack, et al. Office Automation: A Manager's Guide for Improved Productivity. 250p. 1981. 21.95 (ISBN 0-471-07983-9, Pub. by Wiley-Interscience). Wiley.

OFFICE ETIQUETTE
see Business Etiquette

OFFICE MACHINES
see Electronic Office Machines; Office Equipment and Supplies

OFFICE MANAGEMENT
see also Business Etiquette; Business Records; Church Secretaries; Medical Office Management; Office Equipment and Supplies; Office Practice; Office Procedures; Personnel Management; Public Records; Receptionists; School Secretaries; Secretaries
Akers, Herbert. Modern Mailroom Management. (Illus.). 1979. 18.50 (ISBN 0-07-000760-8, P&RB). McGraw.
Arora, S. P. Office Organisation & Management. 1980. text ed. 18.95x (ISBN 0-7069-0795-7, Pub. by Vikas India). Advent NY.
Batty, J., ed. Developments in Office Management. (Illus.). 314p. 1972. 15.00x (ISBN 0-434-90109-1). Intl Pubns Serv.
Bayhylle, James E. Productivity Improvements in the Office. LC 79-523003. 1968. 7.50x (ISBN 0-85038-080-4). Intl Pubns Serv.
Betts, P. W. Office Management. (Teach Yourself Ser.). 1975. pap. 4.95 (ISBN 0-679-10383-X). McKay.
Bonamer, Charles. A Policy Manual for Real Estate Brokerage. 1981. pap. 25.00 (ISBN 0-915260-05-0). Atcom.
Capek, Leslie. The Ex-Urban Office. (Illus.). 150p. (Orig.). 1981. pap. price not set (ISBN 0-89708-080-7). And Bks.
Caruth, Donald L., et al. Office & Administrative Management. 3rd ed. 1970. text ed. 19.95 (ISBN 0-13-630996-8). P-H.
Cecil, Paula B. Management of Word Processing Operations. 1980. 18.95 (ISBN 0-8053-1759-7). Benjamin-Cummings.

Church, Olive. Office Dynamics Company: An Office Services & Temporary Help Practice Set. 250p. 1981. pap. text ed. 6.95 (ISBN 0-205-07136-8); free (ISBN 0-205-07361-1). Allyn.

Cutting Office Costs Through Work Simplification. pap. 12.00 (ISBN 0-686-02540-7). Preston.

Davison, D. J. The Environmental Factor: An Approach for Managers. LC 77-20123. 1978. 30.95 (ISBN 0-470-99351-0). Halsted Pr.

Didactic Systems Staff. Office Management. (Simulation Game Ser.). 1970. pap. 24.90 (ISBN 0-89401-070-0); pap. 21.50 two or more (ISBN 0-685-78139-9). Didactic Syst.

Earl, Ethel M. Professionalism, Legal Considerations, & Office Management. 3rd ed. (Dental Assisting Manuals: No. 1). 110p. 1980. 6.00 (ISBN 0-8078-1375-3). U of NC Pr.

Fetridge, Clark & Minor, Robert. Office Administration Handbook. 1981. 52.50 (ISBN 0-85013-123-5). Dartnell Corp.

Forsyth, Patrick. Running an Effective Sales Office. 142p. 1980. text ed. 37.25x (ISBN 0-566-02185-4, Pub. by Gower Pub Co England). Renouf.

Galloway, Lee. Organization & Management. LC 73-8517. (Management History Ser.: No. 40). (Illus.). 525p. 1973. Repr. of 1916 ed. 22.50 (ISBN 0-87960-045-4). Hive Pub.

Haszonics, Joseph J. Front Office Operation. LC 77-146929. 1971. text ed. 13.50 (ISBN 0-672-96074-5); tchr's manual 6.67 (ISBN 0-672-96076-1); wkbk. 6.95 (ISBN 0-672-96075-3). Bobbs.

Heyel, Carl, ed. Handbook of Modern Office Management & Administrative Services. LC 79-26821. 1214p. 1980. Repr. of 1972 ed. lib. bdg. 59.00 (ISBN 0-89874-088-6). Krieger.

Holmes, Ralph M. The Reference Guide: A Handbook for Office Personnel. (Illus.). 240p. 1979. spiral bound 3.30 (ISBN 0-395-27252-1). HM.

Institute of Real Estate Management. Income - Expense Analysis: Suburban Office Buildings - 1981 Edition. Anderson, Kenneth R., ed. 175p. 1981. pap. text ed. 35.00 (ISBN 0-912104-56-2). Inst Real Estate.

Johnson, H. Webster & Savage, William G. Administrative Office Management. 1968. 16.95 (ISBN 0-201-03325-9). A-W.

Kasavana, Michael L. Effective Front Office Operations. 352p. text ed. 16.95 (ISBN 0-8436-2200-8). CBI Pub.

Kennedy. Office Politics. 10.95 (ISBN 0-686-31280-5). New Century.

Kennedy, Marilyn M. Office Politics: Seizing Power, Wielding Clout. 1981. 2.95 (ISBN 0-686-73335-5). Warner Bks.

Kozoll, Charles E. Making It Work: The Secretary - Boss Team. LC 74-76071. 55p. 1974. pap. 2.50x (ISBN 0-914790-52-8). Avatar Pr.

Lazzaro, Victor. Systems & Procedures: A Handbook for Business & Industry. 2nd ed. 1968. text ed. 27.95 (ISBN 0-13-881425-2). P-H.

Leaming, Majorie P. & Motley, Robert J. Administrative Office Management: A Practical Approach. 570p. 1979. text ed. write for info. (ISBN 0-697-08030-7); instr's manual avail. (ISBN 0-685-91852-1). Wm C Brown.

Littlefield, C. L., et al. Management of Office Operations. (Illus.). 1978. ref. ed. 19.95 (ISBN 0-13-548834-6). P-H.

Longman, Harold H. How to Cut Office Costs. (Illus.). 304p. 1967. 15.00x (ISBN 0-900060-90-5). Intl Pubns Serv.

Motley, Robert J. & Leaming, Marjorie P. Cases in Administrative Office Management: A Problem-Solving Approach. 1979. pap. text ed. write for info. (ISBN 0-697-08031-5); pap. instr. man. 2.00 (ISBN 0-686-67715-3). Wm C Brown.

Neuner, John J., et al. Administrative Office Management. 6th ed. 1972. text ed. 13.50 (ISBN 0-538-07510-4). SW Pub.

Nolan, Robert E., et al. Improving Productivity Through Advanced Office Controls. 706p. 1981. 29.95 (ISBN 0-8144-5617-0). Am Mgmt.

Place, Irene, et al. Office Management. 3rd ed. LC 78-116569. 650p. 1974. pap. text ed. 16.95 scp (ISBN 0-06-453001-9, HarpC); scp study guide 8.50 (ISBN 0-06-453006-X) (ISBN 0-06-453002-7). Har-Row.

Quible, Zane K. Introduction to Administrative Office Management. (Illus.). 1980. text ed. 18.95 (ISBN 0-87626-418-6); pap. 6.95 student guide (ISBN 0-87626-420-8). Winthrop.

Robichaud, Beryl. Selecting, Planning & Managing Office Space. 1958. 13.95 (ISBN 0-07-053174-9, P&RB). McGraw.

Rudman, Jack. Business Environment & Strategy. (ACT Proficiency Examination Program: PEP-27). (Cloth bdg. avail. on request). pap. 9.95 (ISBN 0-8373-5527-3). Natl Learning.

--Chief Office Manager. (Career Examination Ser.: C-2400). (Cloth bdg. avail. on request). pap. 10.00 (ISBN 0-8373-2400-9). Natl Learning.

--Office Machine Associate. (Career Examination Ser.: C-2451). (Cloth bdg. avail. on request). pap. 8.00 (ISBN 0-8373-2451-3). Natl Learning.

--Office Manager. (Career Examination Ser.: C-2398). (Cloth bdg. avail. on request). pap. 10.00 (ISBN 0-8373-2398-3). Natl Learning.

--Principal Clerk. (Career Examination Ser.: C-611). (Cloth bdg. avail. on request). pap. 10.00 (ISBN 0-8373-0611-6). Natl Learning.

--Senior Office Manager. (Career Examination Ser.: C-2399). (Cloth bdg. avail. on request). pap. 10.00 (ISBN 0-8373-2399-1). Natl Learning.

--Supervisor Cf Office Services. (Career Examination Ser.: C-2533). (Cloth bdg. avail. on request). pap. 12.00 (ISBN 0-8373-2533-1). Natl Learning.

Saphier, M. Office Planning & Design. LC 68-11237. (Illus.). 1968. 27.50 (ISBN 0-07-054720-3, P&RB). McGraw.

Smith, Harold & Baker, William. The Administrative Manager. LC 78-6085. 1978. text ed. 17.95 (ISBN 0-574-20030-4, 13-3030); instr's guide avail. (ISBN 0-574-20031-2, 13-3031); study guide 6.95 (ISBN 0-574-20032-0, 13-3032). SRA.

Terry, George R. & Stallard, John J. Office Management & Control. 8th ed. 1980. 18.95x (ISBN 0-256-02271-2). Irwin.

Uhlig, R. P., et al. The Office of the Future. 415p. 1979. 41.50 (ISBN 0-686-63094-7, North Holland). Elsevier.

Walley, B. H. Office Administration Handbook. 470p. 1975. text ed. 25.75x (ISBN 0-220-66281-9, Pub. by Busn Bks England). Renouf.

--Office Administration Handbook. 1975. 34.95x (ISBN 0-8464-0680-2). Beekman Pubs.

Wylie, Harry L. & Harty, James Q., eds. Office Management Handbook. 2nd ed. (Illus.). 1958. 41.50 (ISBN 0-471-06604-4). Ronald Pr.

OFFICE PRACTICE

see also Calculating-Machines; Clerks; Commercial Correspondence; Electronic Data Processing; Electronic Office Machines; Files and Filing (Documents); Office Equipment and Supplies; Secretaries; Shorthand; Typewriting

Agnew, Peter L. & Cornelia. Machine Office Practice. 2nd ed. (gr. 9-12). 1971. pap. text ed. 3.84 (ISBN 0-538-13550-6). SW Pub.

Agnew, Peter L., et al. Clerical Office Practice. 4th ed. (gr. 9-12). 1967. text ed. 2.28 (ISBN 0-538-11360-X, K36); exercises 2.08 (ISBN 0-538-11361-8); tests 0.36 (ISBN 0-538-11362-6). SW Pub.

Albertson, Dorothy. RPM Unlimited: A Business Machines Practice Set. 2nd ed. (Illus.). (gr. 9-12). 1980. 6.48 (ISBN 0-07-000955-4, G); tchrs. manual & key 4.00 (ISBN 0-07-000956-2). McGraw.

Anderson, Thomas J. & Trotter, W. Word Processing. LC 73-94097. (Illus.). 192p. 1974. 21.95 (ISBN 0-8144-5356-2). Am Mgmt.

Andrews, M. E. Gregg Office Job Training Program, Classroom Installation. Incl. Mail Clerk. training manual 3.56 (ISBN 0-07-001811-1); resource material 4.80 (ISBN 0-07-001812-X); File Clerk. training manual 3.56 (ISBN 0-07-001813-8); resource material 4.80 (ISBN 0-07-001814-6); Payroll Clerk. training manual 3.56 (ISBN 0-07-001815-4); resource material 4.80 (ISBN 0-07-001816-2); Typist. training manual 3.56 (ISBN 0-07-001817-0); resource material 4.80 (ISBN 0-07-001818-9); Clerk Typist. training manual 3.56 (ISBN 0-07-001819-7); resource material 4.80 (ISBN 0-07-001820-0); Accounts Payable Clerk. training manual 3.56 (ISBN 0-07-001821-9); resource material 4.80 (ISBN 0-07-001822-7); Accounts Receivable Clerk. training manual 3.56 (ISBN 0-07-001823-5); resource material 4.80 (ISBN 0-07-001824-3); Order Clerk. training manual 3.56 (ISBN 0-07-001825-1); resource material 4.80 (ISBN 0-07-001826-X); Credit Clerk. training manual 3.56 (ISBN 0-07-001827-8); resource material 4.80 (ISBN 0-07-001828-6); Stock Control Clerk. training manual 3.56 (ISBN 0-07-001829-4); resource material 4.80 (ISBN 0-07-001830-8); Office Cashier. Andrews, M. E. training manual 3.56 (ISBN 0-07-001831-6); resource material 4.80 (ISBN 0-07-001832-4); Purchasing Clerk. training manual 3.56 (ISBN 0-07-001833-2); resource material 4.80 (ISBN 0-07-001834-0); Traffic Clerk. training manual 3.56 (ISBN 0-07-001835-9); resource material 4.80 (ISBN 0-07-001836-7); Personnel Clerk. training manual 3.56 (ISBN 0-07-001837-5); resource material 4.80 (ISBN 0-07-001838-3); Billing Clerk. Andrews, M. E. & Hodges. training manual 3.56 (ISBN 0-07-001839-1); resource material 4.80 (ISBN 0-07-001840-5). 1973. presentation pkg 290.00 (ISBN 0-07-079665-3, G); job selection guides 3.28 (ISBN 0-07-001841-3); supervisor's handbk. 10.35 (ISBN 0-07-001843-X); filing supplies 7.92 (ISBN 0-07-086301-6); display unit 53.50 (ISBN 0-07-086303-2); display unit replacement panels 5.35 (ISBN 0-07-086302-4). McGraw.

Archer, F. C. & Stewart, J. R. Model Office Practice Set. 2nd ed. 1975. text ed. 5.56 (ISBN 0-07-002306-9, G); tchr's manual & key 4.05 (ISBN 0-07-002307-7). McGraw.

Archer, F. C., et al. General Office Practice. 3rd ed. 1968. text ed. 12.04 (ISBN 0-07-002173-2, G); tchr's manual & key 6.90 (ISBN 0-07-002175-9); wkbk. 5.52 (ISBN 0-07-002174-0); tests 1.40 (ISBN 0-07-002169-4). McGraw.

--Office Cashiering Practice Set. 1969. text ed. 5.48 (ISBN 0-07-002167-8, G); tchr's manual & key 4.05 (ISBN 0-07-002166-X). McGraw.

Atkins, Hazel. Simple Office Practice. 112p. 1981. pap. 9.95x (ISBN 0-7131-0443-0). Intl Ideas.

Balsley, Irol W. & Robinson, Jerry W. Integrated Secretarial Studies. (gr. 9-12). 1964. text ed. 6.56 (ISBN 0-538-11240-9, K24); wkbk. 2.72 (ISBN 0-538-11241-7). SW Pub.

Barr, Jene. Busy Office, Busy People. LC 67-26513. (Career Awareness-Community Helpers Ser.). (Illus.). (gr. k-2). 1968. 5.25g (ISBN 0-8075-0978-7). A Whitman.

Bergerud, Marly & Gonzalez, Jean. Word Processing: Concepts & Careers. LC 77-15794. (Word Processing Ser.). 1978. pap. text ed. 13.95 (ISBN 0-471-02748-0); tchrs. manual o.p. 2.95 (ISBN 0-471-03778-8). Wiley.

Briggaman, Joan. Practical Problems in Mathematics for Office Workers. LC 76-54051. 1977. pap. text ed. 5.60 (ISBN 0-8273-1612-7); instructor's guide 1.60 (ISBN 0-8273-1613-5). Delmar.

Cecil, Paula B. Word Processing in the Modern Office: Instructor's Guide. 2nd ed. 1979. 3.95 (ISBN 0-8053-1760-0). Benjamin-Cummings.

Christie, Bruce. Face to File Communication: A Psychological Approach to Information Systems. 1981. price not set (ISBN 0-471-27939-0, Pub. by Wiley-Interscience). Wiley.

Church & Schatz. Office Systems & Careers: A Resource for the Administrative Assistants. 780p. 1981. text ed. 19.95 (ISBN 0-205-07134-1, 087134-6); tchrs' ed. avail. (ISBN 0-205-07135-X). Allyn.

Clark, Freda. Secretary's Desk Book of Shortcuts & Timesavers. 1978. 10.95 (ISBN 0-13-797720-4, Parker). P-H.

Clark, James L. & Clark, Lyn R. How Two: Handbook for Office Workers. 2nd ed. (Business Ser.). 280p. 1979. pap. text ed. 8.95x (ISBN 0-534-00635-3). Kent Pub Co.

Collins Publishers Staff, ed. Webster's New World Secretarial Handbook. 1980. 8.95 (ISBN 0-529-05751-4). Collins Pubs.

Connor, Donald. Filing Practice Workbook. 3rd ed. (gr. 9-12). 1975. pap. 2.40 (ISBN 0-8224-2002-3); key 1.20 (ISBN 0-8224-2006-6). Pitman Learning.

Crockford's Clerical Directory, 1977-1979. 1550p. 1980. 98.00x (ISBN 0-19-200009-8). Oxford U Pr.

Dallas, Richard J. & Thompson, James M. Clerical & Secretarial Systems for the Office. (Office Occupations Ser.). (Illus.). 448p. 1975. ref. ed. 16.95 (ISBN 0-13-136390-5). P-H.

De Vries, Mary. Follett Vest-Pocket Secretary's Handbook. 352p. 1980. pap. 2.95 (ISBN 0-695-81342-0). New Century.

DeVries, Mary A. Secretary's Standard Reference Manual & Guide. (Illus.). 1977. 12.95 (ISBN 0-13-797712-3, Parker). P-H.

Doris, Lillian & Miller, Besse M. Complete Secretary's Handbook. 4th ed. 1977. 12.95 (ISBN 0-13-163402-X, Busn). P-H.

Ettinger, Blanche & Popham, Estelle. Opportunities in Office Occupations. LC 76-1406. (Illus.). (gr. 8 up). 1976. PLB 6.60 (ISBN 0-8442-6401-6); pap. 4.95 (ISBN 0-8442-6400-8). Natl Textbk.

Finnegan, Edward G., ed. New Webster's Secretary's-Student's Guide: Vest Pocket Edition. 1978. pap. 1.75 (ISBN 0-8326-2220-6, 6451). Delair.

Fries, Albert C., et al. Applied Secretarial Procedures. 7th ed. (Illus.). 544p. (gr. 12). 1973. text ed. 2.36 (ISBN 0-07-022450-1, G); tchr's. manual & key 5.95 (ISBN 0-07-022452-8); wkbk. 5.52 (ISBN 0-07-022451-X). McGraw.

Goozner, Calman. Clerical Practice Skills. (gr. 10 up). 1978. pap. text ed. 7.08 (ISBN 0-87720-403-9). AMSCO Sch.

Gregg, John R., et al. Applied Secretarial Practice. 6th ed. 1967. text ed. 11.24 (ISBN 0-07-024380-8, G); tchr's. manual & key 5.95 (ISBN 0-07-024382-4); tests 1.56 (ISBN 0-07-024379-4). McGraw.

Hall, L. Secretarial & Administrative Practice. 4th ed. (Illus.). 288p. 1981. pap. 14.95 (ISBN 0-7121-1958-2, Pub. by Macdonald & Evans England). Intl Ideas.

Hanna, J. Marshall, et al. Secretarial Procedures & Administration. 6th ed. LC 68-12693. 1973. text ed. 11.70 (ISBN 0-538-11720-6). SW Pub.

Harrison, John. Secretarial Duties. 5th ed. (Pitman Secretarial Science Ser.). (Illus.). 328p. (Orig.). 1975. pap. text ed. 10.95x (ISBN 0-8464-0829-5). Beekman Pubs.

Hutchinson, Lois. Standard Handbook for Secretaries. 8th ed. 1969. 9.95 (ISBN 0-07-031537-X, GB). McGraw.

Jennings, Lucy M. Secretarial & Administrative Procedures. LC 77-5743. (Illus.). 1978. 16.95 (ISBN 0-13-797654-2). P-H.

Kennedy, Marilyn M. Office Politics. 262p. 1980. 10.95 (ISBN 0-695-81306-4). New Century.

Kestenbaum, Jack. Clerical Techniques for a Business Career. (Orig.). (gr. 9-12). 1975. text ed. 13.20 (ISBN 0-205-04507-3, 1745077); tchrs'. guide 3.80 (ISBN 0-205-04508-1, 1745085); workbook 5.92 (ISBN 0-205-04509-X, 1745093). Allyn.

Klein, A. E., ed. New World Secretarial Handbook: Compact Desk Ed. LC 68-12255. (Illus.). 1973. 7.95 (ISBN 0-529-05089-7, 2360N). Collins Pubs.

Konkel, Gilbert J. & Peck, Phyllis J. The Word Processing Explosion. LC 76-21172. (Illus.). 1976. pap. 8.50 (ISBN 0-911054-03-0). Office Pubns.

Lee, Dorothy E., et al. Secretarial Practices for Colleges. 2nd ed. 1965. text ed. 11.25 (ISBN 0-07-036987-9, G); tchr's manual & key 6.40 (ISBN 0-07-036985-2). McGraw.

McCabe, Helen M. & Popham, Estelle L. Word Processing: A Systems Approach to the Office. (Illus., Orig.). 1977. pap. text ed. 8.95 (ISBN 0-15-596666-9, HC); instructor's manual avail. (ISBN 0-15-596667-7). HarBraceJ.

McCauley, Rosemarie. Mini Sims Temporaries: Modern Office Simulations 1. 1979. pap. 9.95 (ISBN 0-672-97167-4); tchr's. resource 6.67 (ISBN 0-672-97168-2). Bobbs.

Mager, N. H. & Mager, S. K. The Office Encyclopedia. rev. ed. 1981. pap. price not set (ISBN 0-671-43530-2). PB.

Mason, Jennie. Word Processing Skills & Simulations. LC 78-15761. 1979. pap. 10.95 (ISBN 0-672-97197-6); tchr's manual 6.67 (ISBN 0-672-97135-6). Bobbs.

Meehan, et al. Clerical Office Procedures. 5th ed. 1973. text ed. 8.60 (ISBN 0-538-11370-7, K37). SW Pub.

Merriam-Webster Editorial Staff. Webster's Secretarial Handbook. 1976. 9.95 (ISBN 0-87779-036-1). Merriam.

Meyer, Lois & Moyer, Ruth. Machine Transcription in Modern Business. LC 77-25874. 1978. pap. text ed. 14.95 (ISBN 0-471-02735-9); scripts 3.75 (ISBN 0-471-03800-8). Wiley.

Monroe, K. M., et al. Secretary's Handbook. 9th rev. ed. 1969. 14.95 (ISBN 0-02-616230-X). Macmillan.

Morrison, Peter & Twing, J. W. Making the Most of Your Skills. 1969. text ed. 5.36 (ISBN 0-07-043192-2, G). McGraw.

Morrison, Peter, et al. Making the Most of Yourself. 1969. text ed. 5.36 (ISBN 0-07-043191-4, G). McGraw.

--Opportunities in Today's Office. (Career in the Modern Office Ser: Bk. 1). 1969. text ed. 5.36 (ISBN 0-07-043190-6, G). McGraw.
Mulkerne, D. D. & Andrews, M. E. Civil Service, Business & Industry Tests: Clerical & Stenographic. 2nd ed. 1982. price not set (ISBN 0-07-043987-7); price not set instr's guide & key (ISBN 0-07-043988-5). McGraw.
Nanassy, Louis C., et al. Reference Manual for Office Workers. 1977. text ed. 9.95 (ISBN 0-685-76202-5). Macmillan.
Parker Pub. Editorial Staff. One Hundred Fifty Five Office Shortcuts & Time Savers for the Secretary. 1964. pap. 1.95 (ISBN 0-13-635433-5, Reward). P-H.
Place, Irene & Strony, Madeline S. Road to Secretarial Success. (Illus.). 1954. 5.75 (ISBN 0-07-050279-X, GB); text-films avail. (ISBN 0-685-14475-5). McGraw.
Place, Irene, et al. College Secretarial Procedures. 4th ed. 1972. text ed. 15.80 (ISBN 0-07-050250-1, G); instructor's manual & key 6.50 (ISBN 0-07-050254-4); study guide 6.90 (ISBN 0-07-050251-X). McGraw.
Prentice-Hall Editorial Staff. Common Secretarial Mistakes & How to Avoid Them. (Illus.). 1963. pap. 2.95 (ISBN 0-13-152744-4, Reward). P-H.
Rosen, Arnold & Tunison, Eileen F. Administrative Procedures for the Electronic Office. 560p. 1982. text ed. 16.95 (ISBN 0-471-08700-9). Wiley.
Rudman, Jack. Senior Office Worker. (Career Examination Ser.: C-2519). (Cloth bdg. avail. on request). pap. 8.00 (ISBN 0-8373-2519-6). Natl Learning.
Slebert, J. & Schrag, A. Office Procedures Update: A Gregg Text Kit. 1982. price not set (ISBN 0-07-057291-7, G); price not set tchr's manual & key (ISBN 0-07-057292-5). McGraw.
Stankard, Martin F., Jr. Successful Management of Large Clerical Operations: A Guide to Improving Service Transaction Systems. LC 80-11991. (Illus.). 288p. 1980. 17.95 (ISBN 0-07-060831-8, P&RB). McGraw.
Stewart, et al. General Office Projects for Office Procedures. (Illus.). 160p. 1980. 5.20 (ISBN 0-07-061441-5, G). McGraw.
Strony, Madeline S., et al. Secretary at Work. 3rd ed. 1966. text ed. 11.20 (ISBN 0-07-062245-0, G); instructor's manual 3.75 (ISBN 0-07-062250-7). McGraw.
Turner, David R. Beginning Office Worker. 9th ed. LC 79-18112. (Arco Civil Service Test Tutor Ser.). 224p. (Orig.). 1980. pap. 8.00 (ISBN 0-668-04849-2, 4849-2). Arco.
--Office Aide. LC 78-16053. 1978. pap. 8.00 (ISBN 0-668-04704-6). Arco.
Wood, Merle & Sanders, Margaret M. General Office Procedures. (Office Procedures Ser.). (Illus.). 352p. 1981. pap. text ed. 13.95 (ISBN 0-07-071593-9, G); instr's. manual & key 6.50 (ISBN 0-07-071594-7). McGraw.
Woodward, Theodore, et al. Secretarial Office Procedures for Colleges. 6th ed. 1972. text ed. 5.96 (ISBN 0-538-11650-1). SW Pub.
--General Office Procedures for Colleges. 6th ed. 1972. 6.96 (ISBN 0-538-11640-4). SW Pub.
World Secretarial Handbook. new, rev ed. 1980. 8.95 (ISBN 0-529-05751-4, 2361). Collins Pubs.

OFFICE PRACTICE-AUTOMATION

Day, L. Automation in the Office. 1981. text ed. cancelled (ISBN 0-86103-044-3, Westbury Hse). Butterworth.
Galitz, Wilbur O. Human Factors in Office Automation. 237p. 1980. pap. 9.95 (ISBN 0-89435-089-7). QED Info Sci.
Rosen, Arnold & Tunison, Eileen F. Administrative Procedures for the Electronic Office. 560p. 1982. text ed. 16.95 (ISBN 0-471-08700-9). Wiley.

OFFICE PROCEDURES

Clark, James L. & Clark, Lyn. How Two: A Handbook for Office Workers. 2nd ed. 1979. pap. text ed. 8.95x (ISBN 0-534-00635-3). Wadsworth Pub.
Dukas, Peter. Hotel Front Office Management & Operation. 3rd ed. 186p. 1970. text ed. write for info. (ISBN 0-697-08400-0); solutions manual avail. (ISBN 0-686-66349-7). Wm C Brown.
Friedman, Sherwood & Grossman, Jack. Modern Clerical Practice. 4th ed. LC 74-26824. (gr. 9-12). 1975. text ed. 13.20 (ISBN 0-8224-2086-4); wkbk 6.00 (ISBN 0-8224-2087-2); key 2.60 (ISBN 0-8224-2088-0). Pitman Learning.
Hanna, J. Marshall, et al. Secretarial Procedures & Administration. 6th ed. LC 68-12693. 1973. text ed. 11.70 (ISBN 0-538-11720-6). SW Pub.
Holmes, Ralph M. The Reference Guide: A Handbook for Office Personnel. (Illus.). 240p. 1979. spiral bound 3.30 (ISBN 0-395-27252-1). HM.
House & Koebele. Reference Manual for Office Personnel. 5th ed. (gr. 9-12). 1970. pap. text ed. 2.80 (ISBN 0-538-11440-1). SW Pub.
Jennings, Lucy M. Secretarial & General Office Procedures. (Illus.). 400p. 1981. pap. text ed. 15.95 (ISBN 0-13-797803-0). P-H.
Lee, D. E. & Brower, W. A. Secretarial Office Procedures. 3rd ed. 1976. text ed. 13.50 (ISBN 0-07-037035-4, G); instructor's manual 6.40 (ISBN 0-07-037036-2). McGraw.
Lee, Dorothy E. & Brower, Walter A. Secretarial Office Procedures. 2nd, rev. ed. (Illus.). 416p. 1981. pap. text ed. 14.80 (ISBN 0-07-037037-0, G). McGraw.
McCook, Barbara. The Office: Procedures with Simulated Practice. 1972. pap. text ed. 5.95x (ISBN 0-685-02784-8, 47633). Glencoe.
Nanassy, Louis C. & Selden, William. Reference Manual for Office Workers. LC 74-6627. 1977. text ed. 11.20 (ISBN 0-02-476460-4); pap. text ed. 5.96 (ISBN 0-02-476470-1); 2.50 (ISBN 0-02-476560-0). Glencoe.
Piper, et al. Personal Shorthand for the Executive Secretary: Syllabus. 211p. 1977. pap. text ed. 9.95 (ISBN 0-89420-030-5, 217150); cassette recordings 243.95 (ISBN 0-89420-171-9, 217100). Natl Book.
Ross, H. John. Technique of Systems & Procedures. (Illus.). 17.50x (ISBN 0-911056-01-7). Office Res.
Sandry, Esther. Clerical Office Practice Set. 2nd ed. (gr. 9-12). 1973. pap. 3.32 (ISBN 0-8224-1741-3); supplies 6.60 (ISBN 0-8224-2082-1); tchrs'. manual 2.00 (ISBN 0-8224-2081-3). Pitman Learning.
Stewart, et al. General Office Projects for Office Procedures. (Illus.). 160p. 1980. 5.20 (ISBN 0-07-061441-5, G). McGraw.
Stewart, Jeffrey R., Jr. & Blockhus, Wanda A. Office Procedures. LC 79-9095. (Illus.). 1980. text ed. 12.95 (ISBN 0-07-061440-7); General Office Projects 5.20 (ISBN 0-07-061441-5); Administrative Projects 5.20 (ISBN 0-07-061442-3); tchrs. manual & key 5.50 (ISBN 0-07-061443-1). McGraw.
Westgate, Douglas G. Office Procedures 2000. 512p. 1977. text ed. 17.64x (ISBN 0-7715-0897-2); tchr's. manual 39.84x (ISBN 0-7715-0898-0). Forkner.
Yerian, et al. Personal Shorthand Student Dictionary. 1969. pap. text ed. 5.55 (ISBN 0-89420-025-9, 216711). Natl Book.

OFFICE RECORDS

see Business Records

OFFICE SUPPLIES

see Office Equipment and Supplies

OFFICES

see also Law Offices

Alexander, Ian. Office Location & Public Policy. (Topics in Applied Geography). (Illus.). 1979. pap. text ed. 11.50x (ISBN 0-582-48943-1). Longman.
Ballard, F. R. Directory of Manhattan Office Space. (Illus.). 1978. 79.50 (ISBN 0-07-003485-0). McGraw.
Daniels, P. W. Spatial Patterns of Office Growth & Location. LC 78-8386. 1979. 47.25 (ISBN 0-471-99675-0). Wiley.
DuBrin, Andrew J. Winning at Office Politics. Date not set. pap. 2.95 (ISBN 0-345-29532-3). Ballantine.
--Winning at Office Politics. 1978. 14.95 (ISBN 0-442-22187-8). Van Nos Reinhold.
Improving Office Environment. 1969. 7.00 (ISBN 0-686-00501-5). Busn Pr.
Klevins, Gil. Your Career in Office Occupations. LC 77-17377. (Arco Career Guidance Ser.). (Illus.). 1978. pap. 3.95 (ISBN 0-668-04449-7); pap. 3.50 (ISBN 0-668-04434-9). Arco.
Makower, Joel. Office Hazards: How Your Job Can Make You Sick. LC 81-51116. 244p. (Orig.). 1981. pap. 6.95 (ISBN 0-9605750-0-6). Tilden Pr.
Morris, Norma A. How to Set up a Business Office: The Complete Guide to Locating, Outfitting & Staffing. (Illus.). 210p. 1981. 14.95 (ISBN 0-913864-62-5). Enterprise Del.
Palmer, A. Planning the Office Landscape. (Architectural Ser.). 1977. 21.50 (ISBN 0-07-048415-5, P&RB). McGraw.
Pile, John. Interiors Third Book of Offices. (Illus., Orig.). 1976. 24.95 (ISBN 0-8230-7305-X, Whitney). Watson-Guptill.
--Open Office Planning: A Handbook for Interior Designers & Architects. (Illus.). 1978. 16.95 (ISBN 0-8230-7401-3, Whitney Lib). Watson-Guptill.
Price, Judith. Executive Style. 1980. 19.95 (ISBN 0-671-25354-9, Linden). S&S.
Regional Plan Association. Office Industry: Patterns of Growth & Location. Armstrong, R. B., ed. 1972. 22.50x (ISBN 0-262-18052-9). MIT Pr.
Roberts, Duane F. Marketing & Leasing of Office Space. Schleker, Peggy J., ed. LC 79-89774. 1979. 18.95 (ISBN 0-912104-42-2). Inst Real Estate.
Rudman, Jack. Office Services Supervisor. (Career Examination Ser.: C-2196). (Cloth bdg. avail. on request). pap. 10.00 (ISBN 0-8373-2196-4). Natl Learning.
San Luis, Edward. Office & Office Building Security. LC 73-85627. (Illus.). 320p. 1973. 16.95 (ISBN 0-913708-12-7). Butterworth.
Saphier, M. Office Planning & Design. LC 68-11237. (Illus.). 1968. 27.50 (ISBN 0-07-054720-3, P&RB). McGraw.
Scanzoni, L. & Scanzoni, J. Planning the New Office. (Illus.). 1978. 21.50 (ISBN 0-07-054721-1, P&RB). McGraw.
Schulak, Bernard. Executive's Guide to Office Leasing. 1978. pap. text ed. 17.50 (ISBN 0-685-65256-4). Schulak & Assoc.
Schwartz, Murray. Designing & Building Your Own Professional Office. (A Medical Economics Book). 1981. 22.50 (ISBN 0-686-71525-X). Van Nos Reinhold.
Shoshkes, Lila. Space Planning. LC 76-41305. (Illus.). 1977. 20.95 (ISBN 0-07-057060-4, Architectural Res Bks). McGraw.
Thomas, Diane C. How to Save Money on Your Business Rent: A Tenant's Guide to Office & Retail Leasing. LC 79-84224. 1979. 14.95 (ISBN 0-933690-00-2). Peachtree Park.

OFFICIAL LIBRARIES

see Libraries, Governmental, Administrative, etc.

OFFICIAL PUBLICATIONS

see Government Publications

OFFICIAL SECRETS

see also Defense Information, Classified

Dynamite Book of Top Secret Information. (gr. 3-5). pap. 1.50 (ISBN 0-590-11804-8, Schol Pap). Schol Bk Serv.
O'Brien, David M. The Public's Right to Know. 218p. 1981. 21.95 (ISBN 0-03-058029-3). Praeger.
Tefft, Stanton K., ed. Secrecy: A Cross-Cultural Perspective. LC 79-25454. 400p. 1980. text ed. 26.95 (ISBN 0-87705-442-8); pap. text ed. 12.95 (ISBN 0-87705-443-6). Human Sci Pr.

OFFICIALS AND EMPLOYEES, INTERNATIONAL

see International Officials and Employees

OFFSET PRINTING

Chambers, Harry T. The Management of Small Offset Print Departments. 2nd ed. 217p. 1979. text ed. 22.00x (ISBN 0-220-67007-2, Pub. by Busn Bks England). Renouf.
Clifton, Merritt. The Samisdat Method: A Guide to Do-It-Yourself Offset Printing. 1978. pap. 2.00 (ISBN 0-686-12106-6). Samisdat.
Eastman Kodak Company, ed. Lithographic Offset Presses: An Illustrated Guide. LC 78-58634. (Illus.). 1978. pap. 5.25 (ISBN 0-87985-219-4, Q-215). Eastman Kodak.
Lathrop, I. & Kunst, R. Photo-Offset. (Illus.). 1979. 12.33 (ISBN 0-8269-2750-5). Am Technical.
Latimer, Henry. Production Planning & Repro Mechanicals for Offset Printing. (Illus.). 1980. 21.95 (ISBN 0-07-036621-7). McGraw.
Rudman, Jack. Offset Photographer. (Career Examination Ser.: C-560). pap. 8.00 (ISBN 0-8373-0560-8). Natl Learning.
--Offset Pressman. (Career Examination Ser.: C-561). (Cloth bdg. avail. on request). pap. 8.00 (ISBN 0-8373-0561-6). Natl Learning.
--Offset Printing Machine Operator. (Career Examination Ser.: C-562). (Cloth bdg. avail. on request). pap. 8.00 (ISBN 0-8373-0562-4). Natl Learning.

OFFSHORE INSTALLATIONS

see Offshore Structures

OFFSHORE STRUCTURES

Armen, H. & Stiansen, S. Computational Methods for Offshore Structures. (AMD: Vol. 37). 154p. 1980. 24.00 (ISBN 0-686-69845-2, G00170). ASME.
Armer, G. S. & Garas, F. K., eds. Offshore Structures: The Use of Physical Models in Their Design. (Illus.). 420p. 1981. 55.00x (ISBN 0-86095-874-4). Longman.
Behavior of Offshore Structures, 2nd International Conference. Boss Seventy-Nine: Proceedings, 3 vols. 1500p. Set. pap. 169.00 (ISBN 0-906085-34-9, Dist. by Air Science Co). BHRA Fluid.
Beudel, Martin & De Keyser, Ethel, eds. Offshore Oil & Gas Yearbook Nineteen Seventy-Eight to Seventy-Nine: U. K. & Continental Europe. 1978. 62.50x (ISBN 0-85038-128-2, Pub by Kogan Pg). Nichols Pub.
Beudell, Martin, ed. Offshore Oil & Gas Yearbook 1980-81. 500p. 1980. 115.00x (ISBN 0-85038-336-6). Nichols Pub.
Block, Richard A. & Collins, Charles B., eds. Standard Operations Manual for the Marine Transportation Sector of the Offshore Mineral & Oil Industry. 61p. (Orig.). 1979. pap. text ed. 7.50 (ISBN 0-934114-09-9). Marine Educ.
Brebbia, C. A. Dynamic Analysis of Offshore Structures. (Illus.). 1979. 74.95 (ISBN 0-408-00393-6). Butterworth.
Carneiro, F. L., et al. Offshore Structures Engineering, Vol. 1. 424p. 1979. 39.95x (ISBN 0-87201-608-0). Gulf Pub.
Chryssostomidis, Marjorie, ed. Offshore Petroleum Engineering: A Bibliographic Guide to Publications & Information Sources. 1978. 50.00x (ISBN 0-89397-045-X). Nichols Pub.
Crawford. Marine & Offshore Pumping & Piping Systems. 1981. text ed. 48.95 (ISBN 0-408-00548-3). Butterworth.
Gowar, R. G., ed. Developments in Fire Protection of Offshore Platforms, Vol. 1. (Illus.). 1978. text ed. 42.80 (ISBN 0-85334-792-1, Pub. by Applied Science). Burgess-Intl Ideas.
Graff, William J. Introduction to Offshore Structures: Design, Fabrication, Installation. 300p. 1981. 24.95 (ISBN 0-87201-694-3). Gulf Pub.
Harris, L. M. An Introduction to Deepwater Floating Drilling Operations. LC 72-76603. 272p. 1972. 21.00 (ISBN 0-87814-011-5). Pennwell Pub.
Herbich. Offshore Pipeline Design Elements. (Ocean Engineering Ser.: Vol. 3). 240p. 1981. price not set (ISBN 0-8247-1388-5). Dekker.
Le Tirant, P. Seabed Reconnaissance & Offshore Soil Mechanics for the Installation of Petroleum Structures. 512p. 1980. 87.00x (ISBN 0-86010-196-7, Pub. by Graham & Trotman England). State Mutual Bk.
Mousseli, A. H. Offshore Pipeline Design, Analysis & Methods. 208p. 1981. 35.00 (ISBN 0-87814-156-1). Pennwell Pub.
Norwegian Petroleum Society. Corrosion Problems Related to Electrical, Instrumentation & Automation Components Offshore. 152p. 1980. 75.00x (ISBN 82-7270-007-7, Pub. by Norwegian Info Norway). State Mutual Bk.
--Engineering & Construction of an Oil Production Platform. 1980. 70.00x (ISBN 82-7270-015-8, Pub. by Norwegian Info Norway). State Mutual Bk.
--Marginal Fields-Criteria for Development. 197p. 1980. 60.00x (ISBN 82-7270-006-9, Pub. by Norwegian Info Norway). State Mutual Bk.
--Offshore North Sea 1978, 2 vols. 1980. 165.00x (ISBN 0-686-69882-7, Pub. by Norwegian Info Norway). State Mutual Bk.
--Quality Assurance Related to Offshore Activities. 336p. 1980. 95.00x (ISBN 82-7270-009-3, Pub. by Norwegian Info Norway). State Mutual Bk.
The Offshore Drilling Register: A Directory of Self-Contained Mobile Seal-Going Rigs 1980. 6th ed. (Illus.). 123p. 1980. 100.00 (ISBN 0-8002-2462-0). Intl Pubns Serv.
Ranney, M. W. Offshore Oil Technology: Recent Developments. LC 79-83771. (Energy Technology Review Ser. 38, Ocean Technology Review Ser. 8). (Illus.). 1979. 42.00 (ISBN 0-8155-0741-0). Noyes.
Sarpkaya, Turgut & Isaacson, Michael. Mechanics of Wave Forces on Offshore Structures. 624p. 1981. text ed. 37.50 (ISBN 0-442-25402-4). Van Nos Reinhold.
Thomas Telford Editorial Staff, Ltd. Design & Construction of Offshore Structures. 184p. 1980. 60.00x (ISBN 0-7277-0041-3, Pub. by Telford England). State Mutual Bk.
Thomas Telford Ltd, Editorial Staff. Maintenance of Maritime Structures. 252p. 1980. 40.00x (ISBN 0-7277-0050-2, Pub. by Telford England). State Mutual Bk.
Thomas Telford Ltd. Editorial Staff. The Marine Environment & Oil Facilities. 168p. 1980. 69.00x (ISBN 0-7277-0075-8, Pub. by Telford England). State Mutual Bk.
--Offshore Structures. 208p. 1980. 75.00x (ISBN 0-7277-0008-1, Pub. by Thomas Telford England). State Mutual Bk.
Zinkowski, Nicholas B. Commercial Oilfield Diving. nd ed. LC 78-7214. (Illus.). 1978. 19.00x (ISBN 0-87033-235-X). Cornell Maritime.
--Commercial Oilfield Diving. nd ed. LC 78-7214. (Illus.). 1978. 19.00x (ISBN 0-87033-235-X). Cornell Maritime.

O'FLAHERTY, LIAM, 1897-

Doyle, Paul A. Liam O'Flaherty. (English Authors Ser.: No. 108). lib. bdg. 10.95 (ISBN 0-8057-1424-3). Twayne.
--Liam O'Flaherty: An Annotated Bibliography. LC 71-161085. 1972. 7.50x (ISBN 0-87875-017-7). Whitston Pub.
O'Brien, James. Liam O'Flaherty. LC 78-126291. (Irish Writers Ser.). 124p. 1973. 4.50 (ISBN 0-8387-7772-4); pap. 1.95 (ISBN 0-8387-7773-2). Bucknell U Pr.
Sheeran, Patrick F. Novels of Liam O'Flaherty: A Study in Romantic Realism. 300p. 1976. text ed. 17.50x (ISBN 0-391-00643-6). Humanities.
Zneimer, John N. Literary Vision of Liam O'Flaherty. LC 74-130981. 1970. 10.00x (ISBN 0-8156-0073-9). Syracuse U Pr.

OGAREV, NIKOLAI PLATONOVICH, 1813-1877

Carr, Edward H. The Romantic Exiles. 391p. 1975. Repr. of 1933 ed. lib. bdg. 20.00x (ISBN 0-374-91297-1). Octagon.

OGATA, KENZAN, 1663-1743

Smith, Homer. Black Man in Red Russia. 1964. 4.95 (ISBN 0-87485-004-5). Johnson Chi.

OGATA, KORIN, 1658-1716

Mizuo, Hiroshi. Edo Painting - Sotatsu & Korin. LC 72-79122. (Heibonsha Survey of Japanese Art Ser). (Illus.). 1973. 17.50 (ISBN 0-8348-1011-5). Weatherhill.

OGDEN, PETER SKENE, 1790-1854

Binns, Archie. Peter Skene Ogden, Fur Trader. LC 67-23627. (Illus.). 1967. 8.95 (ISBN 0-8323-0054-3). Binford.

Cline, Gloria G. Peter Skene Ogden & the Hudson's Bay Company. (Illus.). 1979. pap. 7.95 (ISBN 0-8061-1595-5). U of Okla Pr.

OGLALA INDIANS

see Indians of North America–The West

OGLETHORPE, JAMES EDWARD, 1696-1785

Blackburn, Joyce. James Edward Oglethorpe. LC 75-117245. (Illus.). (gr. 6-9). 1970. 8.95 (ISBN 0-397-31127-3, JBL-J). Har-Row.

Church, Leslie F. Oglethorpe: A Study of Philanthropy in England & Georgia. 1932. 15.00x (ISBN 0-8401-0391-3). Allenson-Breckinridge.

Ettinger, Amos A. James Edward Oglethorpe, Imperial Idealist. (Illus.). 1968. Repr. of 1936 ed. 19.50 (ISBN 0-208-00664-8, Archon). Shoe String.

Parks, Aileen W. James Oglethorpe: Young Defender. LC 60-7711. (Childhood of Famous Americans Ser.). (Illus.). (gr. 3-7). 1957. 3.95 (ISBN 0-672-50085-X). Bobbs.

Spalding, Phinizy. Oglethorpe in America. LC 76-8092. 1977. lib. bdg. 12.50 (ISBN 0-226-76846-5). U of Chicago Pr.

OGLETHORPE COUNTY, GEORGIA

Rodgers, Ava D. The Housing of Oglethorpe County, Georgia, 1790-1860. LC 72-137857. (Illus.). xii, 79p. 1971. 12.00 (ISBN 0-8130-0434-9). U Presses Fla.

O'GRADY, STANDISH HAYES, 1832-1915

Marcus, Phillip L. Standish O'Grady. LC 74-124647. (Irish Writers Ser.). 92p. 1971. 4.50 (ISBN 0-8387-7751-1); pap. 1.95 (ISBN 0-8387-7660-4). Bucknell U Pr.

O'HARA, FRANK

Feldman, Alan. Frank O'Hara. (United States Authors Ser.: No. 347). 1979. 10.95 (ISBN 0-8057-7277-4). Twayne.

Smith, Alexander, Jr. Frank O'Hara: A Comprehensive Bibliography. LC 77-83403. (Garland Reference Library of the Humanities: No. 107). 1980. lib. bdg. 35.00 (ISBN 0-8240-9833-1). Garland Pub.

O'HARA, JAMES, 1752-1819–FICTION

Turnbull, Agnes S. King's Orchard. 1963. 8.95 (ISBN 0-395-08273-0). HM.

O'HARA, JOHN, 1905-1970

Bruccoli, Matthew J. John O'Hara: A Descriptive Bibliography. LC 77-15737. (Pittsburgh Ser. in Bibliography). (Illus.). 1978. 28.50x (ISBN 0-8229-3349-7). U of Pittsburgh Pr.

--The O'Hara Concern: A Biography of John O'Hara. LC 75-9736. (Illus.). 416p. 1975. 15.00 (ISBN 0-394-48446-0). Random.

Grebstein, Sheldon N. John O'Hara. (Twayne's United States Authors Ser.). 1966. pap. 3.45 (ISBN 0-8084-0187-4, T103, Twayne). Coll & U Pr.

Hawthorne, Mark D. John & Michael (the O'hara Brothers) A Study of the Early Development of the Anglo-Irish Novel. (Salzburg Studies in English Literature: Romantic Reassessment Ser.: No. 50). 1976. pap. text ed. 25.00x (ISBN 0-391-01401-3). Humanities.

MacShane, Frank. The Life of John O'Hara. (Illus.). 300p. 1981. 15.95 (ISBN 0-525-13720-3). Dutton.

--The Life of John O'Hara. (Illus.). 300p. 1981. 15.95 (ISBN 0-525-13720-3). Dutton.

O'Hara, John. An Artist Is His Own Fault: John O'Hara on Writers & Writing. Bruccoli, Matthew J., intro. by. LC 76-43279. 242p. 1977. 8.95 (ISBN 0-8093-0796-0). S Ill U Pr.

--Selected Letters of John O'Hara. Bruccoli, Matthew J., ed. 1978. 17.95 (ISBN 0-394-42133-7). Random.

Walcutt, Charles C. John O'Hara. (Pamphlets on American Writers Ser: No. 80). (Orig.). 1969. pap. 1.25x (ISBN 0-8166-0530-0, MPAW80). U of Minn Pr.

O'HARA, JOHN FRANCIS, 1888-1960

McAvoy, Thomas T. Father O'Hara of Notre Dame: The Cardinal-Archbishop of Philadelphia. 1967. 7.50x (ISBN 0-268-00097-2). U of Notre Dame Pr.

O'HIGGINS, AMBROSIO, MARQUES DE OSORNO, 1720-1801

Mehegan, J. J. O'Higgins of Chile. 1976. lib. bdg. 59.95 (ISBN 0-8490-2366-1). Gordon Pr.

OHIO

see also names of cities, counties, towns, etc. in Ohio

Bailey, Bernadine. Picture Book of Ohio. rev. ed. (Illus.). (gr. 3-5). 1967. 5.50g (ISBN 0-8075-9538-1). A Whitman.

Bogart, Ernest L. Internal Improvements & State Debt in Ohio. LC 68-55484. Repr. of 1924 ed. 15.00x (ISBN 0-678-01000-5). Kelley.

Carpenter, Allan. Ohio. LC 78-16162. (New Enchantment of America State Bks). (Illus.). (gr. 4 up). 1979. PLB 10.60 (ISBN 0-516-04135-5). Childrens.

Collins, William R. Ohio: The Buckeye State. 5th ed. (gr. 10-12). 1974. text ed. 13.76 (ISBN 0-13-633594-2). P-H.

Federal Writers' Project. The Ohio Guide. 634p. 1940. Repr. 49.00 (ISBN 0-403-02184-7). Somerset Pub.

Knepper, William E. & Frye, Richard. Ohio Eminent Domain Practice. 1977. text ed. 37.50 including 1979 suppl. (ISBN 0-87473-119-4). A Smith Co.

Lafferty, Michael B., ed. Ohio's Natural Heritage. LC 78-60505. 1979. 23.95 (ISBN 0-933128-01-0). Ohio Acad Sci.

Murphy, James L. A Bibliography of Ohio Archeology. LC 77-18486. 1977. pap. 29.50 (ISBN 0-8357-0293-6, SS-00058). Univ Microfilms.

Ohio. 33.00 (ISBN 0-89770-059-7). Curriculum Info Ctr.

OHIO–ANTIQUITIES

Atwater, Caleb. Description of the Antiquities Discovered in the State of Ohio & Other Western States. LC 72-4997. (Harvard University. Peabody Museum of Archaeology & Ethnology. Antiquities of the New World: No. 1). (Illus.). Repr. of 1820 ed. 21.50 (ISBN 0-404-57301-0). AMS Pr.

Brown, Jeffery D. The Tower Site & Late Prehistoric Cultures in Southeastern Ohio. 96p. 1981. 6.00 (ISBN 0-87338-263-3). Kent St U Pr.

Moorehead, Warren K. Fort Ancient, the Great Prehistoric Earthwork of Warren County, Ohio. LC 76-43781. (Illus.). Repr. of 1890 ed. 27.50 (ISBN 0-404-15637-1). AMS Pr.

Oplinger, Jon. Wise Cave: A Woodland Rockshelter in Jackson County, Ohio. 64p. 1981. 4.50 (ISBN 0-87338-262-5). Kent St U Pr.

Prufer, Olaf & Shane, Orrin C., 3rd. Blain Village & the Fort Ancient Tradition in Ohio. LC 79-99082. (Kent Studies in Archaeology & Anthropology Ser.: No. 1). (Illus.). 1970. 14.00x (ISBN 0-87338-090-8). Kent St U Pr.

Prufer, Olaf H. & McKenzie, Douglas H., eds. Studies in Ohio Archaeology. rev. ed. LC 66-28144. (Illus.). 400p. 1976. text ed. 14.00x (ISBN 0-87338-180-7). Kent St U Pr.

Thomas, Cyrus. The Problem of the Ohio Mounds. Repr. of 1889 ed. 17.00 (ISBN 0-403-03692-5). Scholarly.

OHIO–DESCRIPTION AND TRAVEL

Beatty, Charles. Journal of a Two-Months Tour, with a View to Promoting Religion. LC 72-108459. 1768. 17.00 (ISBN 0-403-00456-X). Scholarly.

Cutler, Jervis. Topographical Description of the State of Ohio, Indiana Territory, & Louisiana. LC 78-146388. (First American Frontier Ser). (Illus.). 1971. Repr. of 1812 ed. 12.00 (ISBN 0-405-02839-3). Arno.

--A Topographical Description of the State of Ohio, Indiana Territory, & Louisiana. Washburn, Wilcomb E., ed. LC 75-7056. (Narratives of North American Indian Captivities: Vol. 34). 1975. lib. bdg. 44.00 (ISBN 0-8240-1658-0). Garland Pub.

Durr, Eleanor. Lakeside Lore: Ohio's Chautauqua Vacationland. 1979. 9.00 (ISBN 0-682-49445-3). Exposition.

Federal Writers' Project. The Ohio Guide. 634p. 1940. Repr. 49.00 (ISBN 0-403-02184-7). Somerset Pub.

Fradin, Dennis. Ohio in Words & Pictures. LC 76-46941. (Young People's Stories of Our States). (Illus.). (gr. 2-5). 1977. PLB 9.25 (ISBN 0-516-03935-0). Childrens.

Frary, L. T. Early Homes of Ohio. (Illus.). 7.50 (ISBN 0-8446-0631-6). Peter Smith.

Gerrick, David J. Back Roads of Ohio: A Travel Guide to Back Road & Wilderness Areas in Ohio. 1974. pap. 4.95 (ISBN 0-916750-08-6). Dayton Labs.

Osler, Jack M. Fifty Great New Mini-Trips for Ohio. (Jack Osler's Mini-Trips Ser.). (Illus., Orig.). 1980. pap. 3.50 (ISBN 0-89645-013-9). Media Ventures.

Rucker, Marion E. & LaPidus, Anne. Ohio Magazine's Offical Guide to Columbus & Central Ohio. rev. ed. LC 80-53248. (Illus.). 272p. (Orig.). 1980. pap. 5.95 (ISBN 0-938040-00-6). Ohio Mag.

Van Voorhis, Eugene. Marine Directory of Ottawa County, Ohio. (Orig.). 1979. pap. 5.00 (ISBN 0-9603006-2-7). Freshwater Logistics.

Will, Robin. Beautiful Ohio. LC 78-9935. 72p. 1980. 14.95 (ISBN 0-915796-77-5); pap. 7.95 (ISBN 0-915796-76-7). Beautiful Am.

OHIO–ECONOMIC CONDITIONS

Craig, Paul G. & Yocum, James C. Trends in the Ohio Economy. 1955. pap. text ed. 1.00x (ISBN 0-87776-079-9, R79). Ohio St U Admin Sci.

Harwood, Bruce & Synek, Elmer. Ohio Real Estate. (Illus.). 640p. 1980. ref. ed 21.95 (ISBN 0-686-77509-0); pap. 18.95 (ISBN 0-8359-5189-8). Reston.

Humphrey, N., et al. The Future of Cincinnati's Capital Plant. (America's Urban Capital Stock Ser.: Vol. 3). 66p. (Orig.). 1980. pap. 6.00 (ISBN 0-87766-264-9, 27400). Urban Inst.

--The Future of Cleveland's Capital Plant. (America's Urban Capital Stock Ser.: Vol. 2). 77p. (Orig.). 1979. pap. text ed. 6.00 (ISBN 0-87766-264-9, 26900). Urban Inst.

Hunker, Henry L. Industrial Evolution of Columbus, Ohio. 1958. 4.00x (ISBN 0-87776-093-4, R93). Ohio St U Admin Sci.

McDermott, Thomas J. Ohio Real Estate Handbook. 2nd ed. 1980. text ed. 15.00 (ISBN 0-87473-130-5). A Smith Co.

--Ohio Real Property Law & Practice: 1980 Supplements. 1980. 26.50 (ISBN 0-685-31237-2). A Smith Co.

Minneman, Paul G. Large Land Holdings in Ohio & Their Operation. Bruchey, Stuart, ed. LC 78-56664. (Management of Public Lands in the U. S. Ser.). 1979. lib. bdg. 13.00x (ISBN 0-405-11344-7). Arno.

OHIO–GENEALOGY

Hanna, Charles A. Historical Collections of Harrison County, in the State of Ohio. LC 74-24735. 636p. 1975. Repr. of 1900 ed. 22.50 (ISBN 0-8063-0658-0). Genealog Pub.

Jackson, Ronald V. & Teeples, Gary R. Early Ohio Census Index. LC 77-86110. (Illus.). lib. bdg. 16.00 (ISBN 0-89593-109-5). Accelerated Index.

--Ohio Census Index 1820. LC 77-87432. (Illus.). lib. bdg. 59.00 (ISBN 0-89593-110-9). Accelerated Index.

--Ohio Census Index 1830. LC 77-86101. (Illus.). lib. bdg. 72.00 (ISBN 0-89593-111-7). Accelerated Index.

--Ohio Census Index 1840. LC 77-86102. (Illus.). lib. bdg. 80.00 (ISBN 0-89593-112-5). Accelerated Index.

--Ohio Census Index 1850. LC 77-86103. (Illus.). lib. bdg. 95.00 (ISBN 0-89593-113-3). Accelerated Index.

Rife, John M. & Rife, W. R. John & Mary J. Rife of Greene County Ohio: Their Ancestors & Descendants. LC 80-83318. 1980. 5.00 (ISBN 0-686-70943-8). Reiff Pr.

OHIO–HISTORY

Baskin, John. New Burlington: The Life & Death of an American Village. (Illus.). 1977. pap. 2.95 (ISBN 0-452-25156-7, Z5156, Plume). NAL.

Becker, Carl M. The Village: A History of Germantown, Ohio, 1804-1976. LC 80-16683. (Historical Society of Germantown, Ohio Ser.). (Illus.). xvi, 209p. 1980. 15.00 (ISBN 0-8214-0550-0). Ohio U Pr.

Bush, Fred W., ed. The Centennial Atlas of Athens County, Ohio 1905. LC 75-23393. (Illus.). 168p. (Facsimile Ed., reduced). 1975. 20.00 (ISBN 0-8214-0203-X). Ohio U Pr.

Caldwell, Nancy L. A History of Brooke County. 1975. 4.00 (ISBN 0-87012-235-5). McClain.

Carr, Carolyn K., ed. Ohio: A Photographic Portrait 1935-1941 - Farm Security Administration Photographs. LC 80-65227. (Illus.). 96p. 1980. pap. 8.75 (ISBN 0-87338-244-7). Kent St U Pr.

Cashdollar, Pat & Fabian, Miriam, eds. Ohio Almanac 1980. 9th ed. LC 68-3162. (Illus.). 544p. 1980. lib. bdg. 8.95 (ISBN 0-686-29709-1, B-14); pap. 4.95 (ISBN 0-686-29710-5). Kids Special.

Chaddock, Robert E. Ohio Before 1850. LC 8-18567. (Columbia University Studies in the Social Sciences: No. 82). Repr. of 1908 ed. 16.50 (ISBN 0-404-51082-5). AMS Pr.

Collins, William R. Ohio: The Buckeye State. 5th ed. (gr. 10-12). 1974. text ed. 13.76 (ISBN 0-13-633594-2). P-H.

Cradle of Greatness: National & World Achievements of Ohio's Western Reserve. 1977. pap. 3.75 (ISBN 0-686-22736-0). Shaker Savings.

Cutler, Julia P. Life & Times of Ephraim Cutler Prepared from His Journals & Correspondence by His Daughter Julia Perkins Cutler with Biographical Sketches of Jervis Cutler & William Parker Cutler. LC 71-146389. (First American Frontier). (Illus.). 1971. Repr. of 1890 ed. 18.00 (ISBN 0-405-02840-7). Arno.

Daily Nonpareil Office. Sketches of Springfield in 1856. (Annual Monograph Ser.). 96p. 1973. pap. 3.00 facsimile reprint (ISBN 0-686-29090-9). Clark County Hist Soc.

Dodge, Robert J. Isolated Splendor: Put-in-Bay & South Bass Island. 1975. 10.00 (ISBN 0-682-48233-1, Lochinvar). Exposition.

Eggleston, George C. The First of the Hoosiers. LC 72-78694. 1903. Repr. 14.50 (ISBN 0-403-02076-X). Somerset Pub.

Evans, Walter B., Jr. & Skardon, Mary A. Cedar Bog. (Annual Monograph Ser.). Orig. Title: Journal-Walter B. Evans. (Illus.). 54p. 1974. pap. 3.00 (ISBN 0-686-28231-0). Clark County Hist Soc.

Fradin, Dennis. Ohio in Words & Pictures. LC 76-46941. (Young People's Stories of Our States). (Illus.). (gr. 2-5). 1977. PLB 9.25 (ISBN 0-516-03935-0). Childrens.

Hanna, Charles A. Historical Collections of Harrison County, in the State of Ohio. LC 74-24735. 636p. 1975. Repr. of 1900 ed. 22.50 (ISBN 0-8063-0658-0). Genealog Pub.

Havighurst, Walter. Ohio: A Bicentennial History. (States & the Nation Ser.). (Illus.). 1976. 12.95 (ISBN 0-393-05613-9, Co-Pub by AASLH). Norton.

Holt, Edgar A. Party Politics in Ohio Eighteen Forty-Eighteen Fifty. (Perspectives in America Hist. Ser.: No. 38). (Illus.). 449p. Repr. of 1931 ed. lib. bdg. 25.00x (ISBN 0-87991-362-2). Porcupine Pr.

Howells, William C. Recollections of Life in Ohio from 1813 to 1840. LC 63-7082. 1977. Repr. of 1895 ed. 24.00x (ISBN 0-8201-1260-7). Schol Facsimiles.

Hull, Robert C. The Search for Adele Parker. LC 74-82751. (Illus.). 1975. 6.95 (ISBN 0-87212-046-5). Libra.

Hutchinson, William T. The Bounty Lands of the American Revolution in Ohio. Bruchey, Stuart, ed. LC 78-56675. (Management of Public Lands in the U. S. Ser.). (Illus.). 1979. lib. bdg. 25.00x (ISBN 0-405-11336-6). Arno.

Jackson, Ronald V. & Teeples, Gary R. Index to Ohio Tax Lists 1800-1810. LC 77-86051. lib. bdg. 32.00 (ISBN 0-89593-155-9). Accelerated Index.

Johnson, Tom L. My Story. Hauser, Elizabeth J., ed. LC 77-127899. Repr. of 1911 ed. 18.95 (ISBN 0-404-03593-0). AMS Pr.

Joiner, William A., compiled by. A Half Century of Freedom of the Negro in Ohio. LC 72-3347. (Black Heritage Library Collection Ser.). Repr. of 1915 ed. 20.50 (ISBN 0-8369-9083-8). Arno.

King, Rufus. Ohio: First Fruits of the Ordinance of 1787. new ed. LC 72-3755. (American Commonwealths: No. 13). Repr. of 1903 ed. 28.75 (ISBN 0-404-57213-8). AMS Pr.

Kinnison, William A. Wittenberg in Clark County. (Annual Monograph Ser.). 80p. (Orig.). 1970. pap. 3.00 (ISBN 0-686-28234-5). Clark County Hist Soc.

Kirke, et al. Ohio One Hundred Years Ago. (Sun Historical Ser.). (Illus.). pap. 3.50 (ISBN 0-89540-050-2). Sun Pub.

Miller, Betty. Amish Pioneers of the Walnut Creek Valley. 1978. pap. 2.50 (ISBN 0-685-87375-7). O R Miller.

Miller, Zane L. Suburb: Neighborhood & Community in Forest Park, Ohio, 1935-1976. LC 80-21828. (Twentieth-Century America Ser.). 296p. 1981. 18.50x (ISBN 0-87049-289-6). U of Tenn Pr.

Moorehead, Warren K. Primitive Man in Ohio. LC 76-43787. Repr. of 1892 ed. 19.00 (ISBN 0-404-15642-8). AMS Pr.

Ohio Family Historians. Eighteen Thirty Federal Population Census Index of Ohio, 2 vols. 1976. Repr. of 1964 ed. 42.50 set (ISBN 0-911060-06-5). Vol. 1 (ISBN 0-911060-04-9). Vol. 2 (ISBN 0-911060-05-7). Ohio Lib Foun.

--Eighteen Twenty Federal Population Census Index of Ohio. 1976. Repr. of 1964 ed. 29.75 (ISBN 0-685-70950-7). Ohio Lib Foun.

Old Ohio, 2 vols. Incl. Vol. I. Logan & Matthews.; Vol. II. Welch & Matthews.. (Sun Historical Ser.). pap. 3.50 ea. Sun Pub.

Parkinson, Cornelia M. Historical Tales of Old Reynoldsburg: Selections from the First Five Years of the Courier. (Illus.). 152p. (Orig.). 1980. pap. 7.50 (ISBN 0-938404-00-8). Hist Tales.

--History of Reynoldsburg & Truro Township, Ohio. (Illus.). 200p. 1981. 30.00 (ISBN 0-938404-02-4). Hist Tales.

Peters, William E. Ohio Lands & Their History. 3rd. ed. Bruchey, Stuart, ed. LC 78-53541. (Development of Public Land Law in the U. S. Ser.). (Illus.). 1979. Repr. of 1930 ed. lib. bdg. 23.00x (ISBN 0-405-11383-8). Arno.

Pieper, Thomas & Gidney, James B. Fort Laurens, 1778-1779: The Revolutionary War in Ohio. LC 75-44712. (Illus.). 128p. 1976. 7.95x (ISBN 0-87338-184-X). Kent St U Pr.

Pieper, Thomas I. & Gidney, James. Fort Laurens, Seventeen Seventy-Eight to Seventy-Nine: The Revolutionary War in Ohio. LC 75-44712. (Illus.). 1980. pap. 3.95 (ISBN 0-87338-240-4). Kent St U Pr.

Richardson, Robert H. Tilton Territory: A Historical Narrative--Warren Township, Jefferson County, Ohio. 1977. 10.00 (ISBN 0-8059-2362-4). Dorrance.

Skardon, Mary A., ed. Yester Year in Clark County, Ohio, 2 vols. in one. (Annual Monograph Ser.). 76p. (Repr. of 1947 & 1948 eds.). 1978. pap. 3.00 (ISBN 0-686-29091-7). Clark County Hist Soc.

Smeal, Lee. Ohio Historical & Biographical Index. LC 78-53712. (Illus.). Date not set. lib. bdg. price not set (ISBN 0-89593-195-8). Accelerated Index.

Smith, Thomas H. The Mapping of Ohio. LC 75-99081. (Illus.). 275p. 1977. 32.00x (ISBN 0-87338-054-1). Kent St U Pr.
Trautman, Milton B. The Ohio Country from 1750-1977--a Naturalist's View. 1977. 2.50 (ISBN 0-686-30341-5). Ohio Bio Survey.
Trent, William. Journal of Captain William Trent from Logstown to Pickawillany, A.D. 1752. LC 79-106114. (First American Frontier Ser). 1971. Repr. of 1871 ed. 9.00 (ISBN 0-405-02894-6). Arno.
Vexler, R. I. Ohio Chronology & Factbook, Vol. 35. 1978. 8.50 (ISBN 0-379-16160-5). Oceana.
Weisenburger, Francis P. Ohio. LC 64-8167. 1965. pap. 2.95 (ISBN 0-8077-2320-7). Tchrs Coll.
Wheeler, Kenneth W., ed. For the Union: Ohio Leaders in the Civil War. LC 67-25693. 1968. 10.00 (ISBN 0-8142-0129-6). Ohio St U Pr.
Woodward, R. C. & Thomas, I. Directory of the City of Springfield. (Annual Monograph Ser.). 219p. 1969. pap. 3.00 (ISBN 0-686-28233-7). Clark County Hist Soc.

OHIO-HISTORY-BIBLIOGRAPHY

Thomson, Peter G. Bibliography of the State of Ohio, 2 vols. LC 63-21499. 548p. Repr. of 1890 ed. Set. 25.00 (ISBN 0-686-66598-8); 12.50 ea. Vol. 1 (ISBN 0-405-03683-3). Vol. 2 (ISBN 0-405-03684-1). Arno.
Vance, Mary. Historical Society Architectural Publications: Ohio, Oklahoma, Oregon, & Pennsylvania. (Architecture Ser.: Bibliography A-162). 55p. 1980. pap. 6.00 (ISBN 0-686-26909-8). Vance Biblios.

OHIO-IMPRINTS

Historical Records Survey: Check List of Ohio Imprints, 1796-1820. 1941. pap. 17.00 (ISBN 0-527-01914-3). Kraus Repr.

OHIO-POLITICS AND GOVERNMENT

Allen Smith Co. Editorial Staff. Ohio Police Officers' Manual. 5th ed. 1979. text ed. 9.00 (ISBN 0-87473-123-2). A Smith Co.
Baldwin, William E., ed. Baldwin's Ohio Revised Code, with Rules of Practice, Annotated, 8 vols. 4th ed. 1971. Set. 475.00 (ISBN 0-8322-0006-9). Banks-Baldwin.
Baldwin's Ohio Bank Law & Regulation Manual. 3rd ed. 1978. 46.50 (ISBN 0-685-92084-4). Banks-Baldwin.
Baldwin's Ohio Legal Forms: An Encyclopedia of Legal & Business Forms, 6 vols. (Baldwin's Ohio Practice Ser.). 1962. Set. 275.00 (ISBN 0-8322-0003-4). Banks-Baldwin.
Baldwin's Ohio Tax Law & Rules, 2 vols. 3rd ed. (Baldwin's Ohio Practice Ser.). 1976. Set. 90.00 (ISBN 0-8322-0017-4). Banks-Baldwin.
Blackford, Jason C. Ohio Corporation Law & Practice: Including Ohio & Federal Securities Law & Regulation, 2 vols. (Baldwin's Ohio Practice Ser.). 1972. Set. 100.00 (ISBN 0-685-92082-8). Banks-Baldwin.
Brown, Wilmore. Ohio Domestic Authorities. 1978. 40.00 (ISBN 0-672-83380-8, Bobbs-Merrill Law). Michie-Bobbs.
Carlin, Angela G. & Schwartz, Richard W., eds. Merrick-Rippner Ohio Probate Law: Practice & Forms, Including Juvenile Law Practice & Forms. 3rd rev. ed. (Baldwin's Ohio Practice Ser.). 1978. 95.00 (ISBN 0-8322-0021-2). Banks-Baldwin.
Cornell, Meriss & Yocum, James C. Nineteen Sixty-Six Census Tract Street Directory: Columbus & Franklin County. 1966. pap. 4.00x (ISBN 0-87776-130-2, R130). Ohio St U Admin Sci.
Faske, Steve. Ohio Criminal Law Handbook. 1981. rev. ed. 1981. write for info. (ISBN 0-87084-641-8). Anderson Pub Co.
Gargan, John J. & Coke, James G. Political Behavior & Public Issues in Ohio. LC 72-78408. 1972. 12.00x (ISBN 0-87338-124-6). Kent St U Pr.
Gotherman, John E. Ohio Municipal Law: Procedure & Forms, 3 vols. 2nd rev. ed. (Baldwin's Ohio Practice Ser.). 1975. Set. 150.00 (ISBN 0-685-92079-8). Banks-Baldwin.
Gould Editorial Staff. Criminal Laws of Ohio. (Annual). 1981. looseleaf 10.50x (ISBN 0-87526-202-3). Gould.
Jacoby, Sidney B. Ohio Civil Practice: A Guide to Civil Practice in Ohio Under the Rules of Civil Procedure, 2 vols. (Baldwin's Ohio Practice Ser.). 1970. Set. 110.00 (ISBN 0-685-92074-7). Banks-Baldwin.
McDermott, Thomas J. Ohio Real Property Law & Practice, 3 vols. 3rd ed. 1966. Set. text ed. 97.50 including 1980 suppls. (ISBN 0-87473-026-0). A Smith Co.
Ohio Administrative Code: Rules of the Administrative Agencies of Ohio, 7 vols. 1977. Set. 395.00 (ISBN 0-8322-0018-2). Banks-Baldwin.
Ohio Basic Building Code: And Related Codes. 1979. 65.00 (ISBN 0-8322-0023-9). Banks-Baldwin.
Ohio Corporation Laws Annotated, 1977. 1977. 15.00 (ISBN 0-685-92086-0). Banks-Baldwin.
Orth, Samuel P. Centralization of Administration in Ohio. LC 68-56679. (Columbia University Studies in the Social Sciences Ser.: No. 43). Repr. of 1903 ed. 16.50 (ISBN 0-404-51043-4). AMS Pr.
Porter, George H. Ohio Politics During the Civil War Period. LC 76-76694. (Columbia University, Studies in the Social Sciences Ser.: No. 105). Repr. of 1911 ed. 21.00 (ISBN 0-404-51105-8). AMS Pr.
Sawyer, Charles. Concerns of a Conservative Democrat. LC 68-25553. (Illus.). 415p. 1968. 10.00x (ISBN 0-8093-0310-8). S Ill U Pr.
Schroeder, Oliver C. & Katz, Lewis R. Schroeder-Katz Ohio Criminal Law & Practice: A Guide to Ohio's New Criminal Law & Criminal Procedure Under the Rules, 2 vols. (Baldwin's Ohio Practice Ser.). 1974. Set. 110.00 (ISBN 0-8322-0011-5). Banks-Baldwin.
Shrimp, William G. & Pines, Denniss, eds. Baldwin's Ohio Township Law, with Text & Forms. 4th rev. ed. (Baldwin's Ohio Practice Ser.). 1977. 90.00 (ISBN 0-8322-0019-0). Banks-Baldwin.
Spayde, Paul E. Baldwin's Ohio School Law: A Complete Guide to Law & Fiscal Procedures. 8th ed. (Baldwin's Ohio Practice Ser.). 1973. 95.00 (ISBN 0-8322-0009-3). Banks-Baldwin.
Wheatley, Dennis. The KA of Gifford Hillary. 6.95 (ISBN 0-686-24101-0, Pub. by Hutchinson). Merrimack Bk Serv.
Whiteside, Alba L. Whiteside Ohio Appellate Practice: A Guide to Appellate Practice in Ohio Under the New Appellate Rules. (Baldwin's Ohio Practice Ser.). 1972. 60.00 (ISBN 0-8322-0008-5). Banks-Baldwin.
Whitlock, Brand. The Buckeyes: Politics & Abolitionism in an Ohio Town, 1836-1845. Miller, Paul W., ed. LC 76-8306. (Illus.). 273p. 1977. 12.95 (ISBN 0-8214-0222-6). Ohio U Pr.

OHIO COMPANY (1747-1779)

Bacon-Foster, Corra. Early Chapters in the Development of the Patomac Route to the West. LC 70-146134. (Research & Source Works Ser: No. 718). 1971. Repr. of 1912 ed. lib. bdg. 22.50 (ISBN 0-8337-0144-4). B Franklin.

OHIO RIVER AND VALLEY

Ambler, Charles H. History of Transportation in the Ohio Valley. LC 72-98804. Repr. of 1932 ed. lib. bdg. 18.25x (ISBN 0-8371-2905-2, AMTO). Greenwood.
Butler, Mann. Valley of the Ohio. Clift, G. Glenn & Tapp, Hambleton, eds. 1971. 5.00 (ISBN 0-916968-01-4). Kentucky Hist.
Ellet, Charles. Mississippi & Ohio Rivers, Containing Plans for the Protection of the Delta from Inundation & Investigations. LC 70-125738. (American Environmental Studies). 1970. Repr. of 1853 ed. 17.00 (ISBN 0-405-02663-3). Arno.
Pope, John. Tour Through the Southern & Western Territories of the United States of North America, the Spanish Dominions on the River Mississippi & the Floridas, the Countries of the Creek Nations, & Many Uninhabited Parts. LC 70-146411. (First American Frontier Ser). 1971. Repr. of 1792 ed. 9.00 (ISBN 0-405-02875-X). Arno.

OHIO RIVER AND VALLEY-DESCRIPTION AND TRAVEL

Baily, Francis. Journal of a Tour in Unsettled Parts of North America in 1796 & 1797. Holmes, Jack D., ed. LC 68-21414. (Travels on the Western Waters Ser.). (Illus.). 307p. 1969. Repr. of 1856 ed. 15.00x (ISBN 0-8093-0389-2). S Ill U Pr.
Bishop, Nathaniel Holmes. Four Months in a Sneak Box: A Boat Voyage of Twenty Six Hundred Miles Down the Ohio & Mississippi Rivers. LC 71-142572. (Illus.). xii, 322p. 1976. Repr. of 1879 ed. 30.00 (ISBN 0-8103-4170-0). Gale.
Blane, William N. Excursion Through the United States & Canada During the Years 1822-1823. LC 68-58049. (Illus.). Repr. of 1824 ed. 24.75x (ISBN 0-8371-4978-9, Pub. by Negro U Pr). Greenwood.
Brigham, Albert P. From Trail to Railway. LC 78-113279. 1970. Repr. of 1907 ed. 13.50 (ISBN 0-8046-1317-6). Kennikat.
Burmeister, Walter F. Appalachian Waters 5: The Upper Ohio & Its Tributaries. Mallinoff, Estelle, ed. 600p. 1978. pap. 12.50 (ISBN 0-912660-23-6). Appalachian Bks.
Flint, James. Letters from America: Containing Observations on the Climate & Agriculture of the Western States, the Manners of the People & the Prospects of Emigrants. 1971. Repr. of 1822 ed. 17.00 (ISBN 0-384-16028-X). Johnson Repr.
Forman, Samuel S. Narrative of a Journey Down the Ohio & Mississippi in 1789-90 with a Memoir & Illustrative Notes by Lyman C. Draper. LC 78-146396. (First American Frontier Ser). 1971. Repr. of 1888 ed. 9.00 (ISBN 0-405-02850-4). Arno.
Gerstacker, Friedrich. Wild Sports in the Far West. Steeves, Edna L. & Steeves, Harrison R., eds. LC 68-16624. 1968. 14.75 (ISBN 0-686-67566-5). Duke.
Imlay, Gilbert. Topographical Description of the Western Territory of North America. 3rd ed. 1797. 15.50 (ISBN 0-384-25685-6). Johnson Repr.
--Topographical Description of the Western Territory of North America. 3rd ed. LC 68-55739. (Illus.). Repr. of 1797 ed. 15.00x (ISBN 0-678-00541-9). Kelley.
Immunology of the Gut. (Ciba Foundation Symposium Ser: No. 46). 1977. 34.25 (ISBN 90-219-4052-3, Excerpta Medica). Elsevier.
Jakle, John A. Images of the Ohio Valley: A Historical Geography of Travel. (Illus.). 1977. text ed. 14.95 (ISBN 0-19-502240-8); pap. text ed. 6.95x (ISBN 0-19-502241-6). Oxford U Pr.
James, Edwin, compiled by. Account of An Expedition from Pittsburgh to the Rocky Mountains, Performed in the Years 1819 & 1820, 2 Vols. LC 68-55198. 1968. Repr. of 1823 ed. Set. lib. bdg. 21.75x (ISBN 0-8371-8599-8, JAPI). Greenwood.
Pownall, Thomas. A Topographical Description of the Dominions of the United States of America. Mulkearn, Lois, ed. LC 75-22835. (America in Two Centuries Ser). 1975. Repr. of 1949 ed. 15.00x (ISBN 0-405-07706-8). Arno.
Thwaites, Reuben G. On the Storied Ohio. facsimile ed. LC 75-127. (Mid-American Frontier Ser.). (Illus.). 1975. Repr. of 1903 ed. 20.00x (ISBN 0-405-06892-1). Arno.

OHIO RIVER AND VALLEY-ECONOMIC CONDITIONS

Barnhart, J. D. Valley of Democracy: The Frontier Versus the Plantation in the Ohio Valley, 1775-1818. Repr. of 1953 ed. 18.00 (ISBN 0-527-05350-3). Kraus Repr.
Hunter, Louis C. Studies in the Economic History of the Ohio Valley. LC 36-6753. (History of American Economy Ser). Repr. of 1934 ed. 9.50 (ISBN 0-384-24945-0). Johnson Repr.
--Studies in the Economic History of the Ohio Valley. LC 72-98689. (American Scene Ser.). 1969. Repr. of 1933 ed. lib. bdg. 19.50 (ISBN 0-306-71837-5). Da Capo.
Lippincott, Isaac. A History of Manufactures in the Ohio Valley to the Year 1860. LC 73-2518. (Big Business; Economic Power in a Free Society Ser.). Repr. of 1914 ed. 12.00 (ISBN 0-405-05098-4). Arno.
--A History of Manufactures in the Ohio Valley to the Year 1860. LC 73-19608. (Perspectives in American History: No. 14). Repr. of 1914 ed. lib. bdg. 11.95x (ISBN 0-87991-340-1). Porcupine Pr.

OHIO RIVER AND VALLEY-HISTORY

Adams, Herbert B. Maryland's Influence Upon Land Cessions to the U. S. LC 77-97563. Repr. of 1885 ed. 11.50 (ISBN 0-404-00286-2). AMS Pr.
--Maryland's Influence Upon Land Cessions to the United States. LC 4-8520. 1885. 1.00 (ISBN 0-403-00136-6). Scholarly.
Baldwin, Leland D. The Keelboat Age on Western Waters. LC 41-10342. 1941. 7.95 (ISBN 0-8229-1027-6). U of Pittsburgh Pr.
Banta, R. E. Ohio Valley. LC 66-19221. (gr. 7 up). 1967. pap. 2.95x (ISBN 0-8077-1044-X). Tchrs Coll.
Bolin, Daniel L. Ohio Valley History. 1976. 17.50 (ISBN 0-686-20887-0). Polyanthos.
Cist, Charles. Cincinnati Miscellany, or Antiquities of the West: Pioneer History & General & Local Statistics Compiled from the Western General Advertiser, 2 Vols. in 1. LC 72-146381. (First American Frontier Ser). 1971. Repr. of 1845 ed. 30.00 (ISBN 0-405-02832-6). Arno.
De Hass, Wills. History of the Early Settlement & Indian Wars of Western Virginia. 1980. Repr. of 1851 ed. 15.00 (ISBN 0-87012-002-6). McClain.
Doddridge, Joseph. Notes on the Settlement & Indian Wars. 1976. Repr. of 1824 ed. 15.00 (ISBN 0-87012-001-8). McClain.
Filson, John. Discovery, Settlement & Present State of Kentucke. 7.00 (ISBN 0-8446-2058-0). Peter Smith.
Hanna, Charles A. The Wilderness Trail, 2 vols. LC 77-149659. (Illus.). Repr. of 1911 ed. 67.50 set (ISBN 0-404-03097-1). AMS Pr.
Jacobs, Wilbur R. Wilderness Politics & Indian Gifts: The Northern Colonial Frontier, 1748-1763. LC 51-2149. Orig. Title: Anglo-French Rivalry Along the Ohio & Northwest Frontier-1748-1763. (Illus.). 1966. pap. 3.95x (ISBN 0-8032-5100-9, BB 351, Bison). U of Nebr Pr.
M'Clung, John A. Sketches of Western Adventure. LC 76-90184. (Mass Violence in America Ser). Repr. of 1832 ed. 13.00 (ISBN 0-405-01326-4). Arno.
McKnight, Charles. Our Western Border, Its Life, Combats, Adventures, Forays, Massacres, Captivities, Scouts, Red Chiefs, Pioneers, Women, One Hundred Years Ago, Carefully Written & Compiled. (Rediscovering America Ser). (Illus.). Repr. of 1876 ed. 42.50 (ISBN 0-384-34890-4, R174). Johnson Repr.
McMurtry, Richard K. John McMurtry & the American Indian: A Frontiersman in the Struggle for the Ohio Valley. LC 80-7469. (Illus., Orig.). 1980. pap. 9.95 (ISBN 0-936012-05-6). Current Issues.
Miller, James M. Genesis of Western Culture: The Upper Ohio Valley, 1800-1825. LC 77-87420. (American Scene Ser.). 1969. Repr. of 1938 ed. lib. bdg. 25.00 (ISBN 0-306-71566-X). Da Capo.
Roosevelt, Theodore. Winning of the West. Wish, Harvey, ed. & intro. by. 8.00 (ISBN 0-8446-2827-1). Peter Smith.
Thwaites, R. G. & Kellogg, L. P. Frontier Defense on the Upper Ohio: 1777-1778. LC 12-11742. Repr. of 1912 ed. 30.00 (ISBN 0-527-89980-1). Kraus Repr.
Thwaites, Reuben G. & Kellogg, Louise P., eds. Revolution on the Upper Ohio, 1775-1777. LC 76-120895. (American Bicentennial Ser). 1970. Repr. of 1908 ed. 13.50 (ISBN 0-8046-1288-9). Kennikat.
Trent, William. Journal of Captain William Trent from Logstown to Pickawillany, A.D. 1752. LC 79-106114. (First American Frontier Ser). 1971. Repr. of 1871 ed. 9.00 (ISBN 0-405-02894-6). Arno.

OHIO RIVER AND VALLEY-POLITICS

Barnhart, J. D. Valley of Democracy: The Frontier Versus the Plantation in the Ohio Valley, 1775-1818. Repr. of 1953 ed. 18.00 (ISBN 0-527-05350-3). Kraus Repr.
Barnhart, John D. Valley of Democracy: The Frontier Versus the Plantation in the Ohio Valley, 1775-1818. LC 53-10020. (Illus.). 1970. pap. 3.95x (ISBN 0-8032-5701-5, 330, Bison). U of Nebr Pr.

OHIO RIVER VALLEY WATER SANITATION COMMISSION

Cleary, Edward J. The ORSANCO Story: Water Quality Management in the Ohio Valley Under an Interstate Compact. LC 66-16036. (Resources for the Future Ser). 384p. (Orig.). 1967. 22.50x (ISBN 0-8018-0127-3); pap. 5.95x (ISBN 0-8018-0128-1). Johns Hopkins.

OHIO STATE UNIVERSITY, COLUMBUS

Eszterhas, Joe & Roberts, Michael D. Thirteen Seconds: Confrontation at Kent State. LC 74-135543. 1970. 7.50 (ISBN 0-396-06272-5). Dodd.
First Hundred Years: A Family Album of the Ohio State University, 1870-1970. LC 73-110667. (Orig.). 1970. pap. 7.00 (ISBN 0-8142-0138-5). Ohio St U Pr.
Kinnison, William A. Building Sullivant's Pyramid: An Administrative History of the Ohio State University, 1870-1907. LC 77-105722. 1970. 8.00 (ISBN 0-8142-0141-5). Ohio St U Pr.

OHMMETER

see also Voltohmmeter

OHM'S LAW

see also Electric Measurements

OIDIOMYCOSIS

see Candidiasis

OIL

see Mineral Oils; Oils and Fats; Petroleum

OIL AND GAS LAW

see Gas, Natural-Law and Legislation; Petroleum Law and Legislation

OIL AND GAS LEASES

Ballem, John B. Oil & Gas Lease in Canada. LC 72-75734. 352p. 1973. 30.00x (ISBN 0-8020-1879-3). U of Toronto Pr.
Brown, Keith C. Bidding for Offshore Oil: Toward an Optimal Strategy. LC 74-97802. 1969. pap. 3.00 (ISBN 0-87074-026-1). SMU Press.
California-Alaska Oil & Gas Review 1976. 1977. 30.00 (ISBN 0-686-28274-4). Munger Oil.
Cattan, H. The Law of Oil Concessions in the Middle East & North Africa. LC 67-1440. 1967. 15.00 (ISBN 0-379-00319-8). Oceana.
Hankinson, R. L. Landman's Encyclopedia. 2nd ed. 400p. 1981. 59.95 (ISBN 0-87201-420-7). Gulf Pub.
Kuntz, Eugene. The Law of Oil & Gas, Vols. 1-5, Vol. 6 Parts 1-4, 7 Part 1, 7 Part 2 With Supplements. Date not set. text ed. 550.00 (ISBN 0-87084-507-1). Anderson Pub Co.
Mosburg, Lewis G., Jr., ed. Contracts Used in Oil & Gas Operations. 1978. 45.00 (ISBN -089419-019-9). Inst Energy.
--Gas Contracts. 1978. 38.00 (ISBN 0-89419-020-2). Inst Energy.
--Practical Problems in Curing Land Titles. 1978. 39.00 (ISBN 0-89419-022-9). Inst Energy.
--Problems Arising Under the Oil & Gas Lease. 1977. 35.00 (ISBN 0-89419-007-5). Inst Energy.

Ramsey, James B., ed. Bidding & Oil Leases, Vol. 25. Walter, Ingo I. LC 79-3169. (Contemporary Studies in Economic & Financial Analysis Monographs). 320p. (Orig.). 1980. lib. bdg. 30.00 (ISBN 0-89232-148-2). Jai Pr.

OIL BURNERS

Burkhardt, Charles H. Domestic & Commercial Oil Burners. 3rd ed. LC 68-31659. (Illus.). 1969. text ed. 17.50 (ISBN 0-07-009039-4, G). McGraw.

Field, Edwin M. Oil Burners. 3rd ed. LC 76-45884. (Illus.). 1977. 9.95 (ISBN 0-672-23277-4, 23277). Audel.

Installation of Oil Burning Equipment. (Thirty Ser). 88p. 1973. pap. 3.50 (ISBN 0-685-44166-0, 31). Natl Fire Prot.

Mitchell, Frank V. & Mitchell, Robert W. Installation & Servicing of Domestic Oil Burners. LC 74-77492. 1974. pap. 10.00 (ISBN 0-668-00437-1). Arco.

Prevention of Furnace Explosions in Fuel Oil-Fired Multiple Burner Boiler-Furnace. (Eighty-Ninety Ser.). 84p. 1974. pap. 3.50 (ISBN 0-685-44131-8, 85D). Natl Fire Prot.

Rudman, Jack. Install Oil Burner Equipment (License) (Career Examination Ser.: C-1317). (Cloth bdg. avail. on request). pap. 10.00 (ISBN 0-8373-1317-1). Natl Learning.

OIL CONSERVATION

see Petroleum Conservation

OIL ENGINES

see Gas and Oil Engines

OIL FIELD WORKERS

see Petroleum Workers

OIL FIELDS

see also Oil Well Drilling; Petroleum; Petroleum-Pipe Lines

Allain, Louis J. Capital Investment Models of the Oil & Gas Industry: A Systems Approach. Bruchey, Stuart, ed. LC 78-22654. (Energy in the American Economy Ser.). (Illus.). 1979. lib. bdg. 36.00x (ISBN 0-405-11959-3). Arno.

Amyx, James W., et al. Petroleum Reservoir Engineering Physical Properties. 1960. 25.50 (ISBN 0-07-001600-3, C). McGraw.

Case, L. C. Water Problems in Oil Production: An Operator's Manual. 2nd ed. LC 75-118940. 168p. 1977. 28.00 (ISBN 0-87814-001-8). Pennwell Pub.

Conybeare, C. E. Geomorphology of Oil & Gas Fields in Sandstone Bodies. (Developments in Petroleum Science: Vol. 4). 1976. 44.00 (ISBN 0-444-41398-7). Elsevier.

Hughes, Richard V. Oil Property Valuation. 2rev. ed. LC 77-2945. (Illus.). 324p. 1978. Repr. of 1967 ed. lib. bdg. 19.50 (ISBN 0-88275-402-5). Krieger.

Impressions of the Taching Oil Field. 1978. pap. 0.75 (ISBN 0-8351-0494-X). China Bks.

Levorsen, Arville I. Stratigraphic Type Oil Fields, 2 vols. 1976. lib. bdg. 250.00 (ISBN 0-8490-2694-6). Gordon Pr.

Moltzer, J. Oelfeld-Fachwoerterbuch. (Eng., Fr., Span., Dutch & Ger., Dictionary of Oilfields). 1965. leatherette 37.50 (ISBN 3-486-31001-1, M-7576, Pub. by Oldenbourgy Verlag). French & Eur.

Noreng, Oystein. Economics & Politics of North Sea Oil. LC 80-81590. 1980. 27.50x (ISBN 0-918714-02-8). Intl Res Ctr Energy.

Shah, D. O. & Schechter, R. S., eds. Improved Oil Recovery by Surfactant & Polymer Flooding. 1977. 36.50 (ISBN 0-12-641750-4). Acad Pr.

Tiratsoo, E. N. Oilfields of the World. 2nd ed. (Illus.). 400p. 1976. 37.50x (ISBN 0-87201-630-7). Gulf Pub.

OIL HYDRAULIC MACHINERY

see also Hydraulic Servomechanisms

Pick, Christopher C. Oil Machines. LC 78-26333. (Machine World Ser.). (Illus.). (gr. 2-4). 1979. PLB 11.15 (ISBN 0-8172-1327-9). Raintree Pubs.

Thoma, Jean U. Modern Oil-Hydraulic Engineering. (Illus.). 1970. 52.00x (ISBN 0-85461-043-X). Intl Ideas.

OIL INDUSTRIES

see also Mineral Oils; Oils and Fats; Petroleum Industry and Trade

Adie, Ian W. Oil, Politics, & Seapower: The Indian Ocean Vortex. LC 74-29073. (Strategy Paper Ser: No. 24). 1975. 6.95x (ISBN 0-8448-0617-X); pap. 2.25x o. p. (ISBN 0-8448-0618-8). Crane-Russak Co.

Arab Petroleum Research Center. Arab Oil and Gas Directory: 1979-80. 450p. 1980. 143.00x (ISBN 0-686-64697-5, Pub. by Graham & Trotman England). State Mutual Bk.

Barton, Richard F. The Imaginit Oil Industry Game. 1980. pap. 11.98 (ISBN 0-933836-12-0). Simtek.

Commission of the European Communities. New Technologies for Exploration & Exploitation of Oil & Gas Resources, Vol. 1. 800p. 1979. 55.00x (ISBN 0-86010-158-4, Pub. by Graham & Trotman England). State Mutual Bk.

Commisssion of the European Communities. Oil & Gas Multilingual Glossary. 500p. 1979. 44.00x (ISBN 0-86010-170-3, Pub. by Graham & Trotman England). State Mutual Bk.

Dixon, Mim. What Happened to Fairbanks? The Effects of the Trans-Alaska Oil Pipeline on the Community of Fairbanks, Alaska. (Social Impact Assessment Ser.: No. 1). (Illus.). 337p. 1980. pap. text ed. 9.50x (ISBN 0-89158-961-9). Westview.

Eurocean. Petroleum & the Marine Environment. 750p. 1980. 55.00x (ISBN 0-86010-215-7, Pub. by Graham & Trotman England). State Mutual Bk.

Gagnacci-Schwicker, A. & Schwicker. International Dictionary of Metallurgy, Mineralogy, Geology and the Mining and Oil Industries. 1530p. (Eng., Fr., Ger. & It.). 1970. 88.00 (ISBN 3-7625-0751-1, M-7482, Pub. by Bauverlag). French & Eur.

Galvin, Michael E. Oilseed World Handbook. 450p. 1981. 50.00 (ISBN 0-937358-52-5). G D L Inc.

George, P. S. Oilseeds Economy of India. 1978. 11.00x (ISBN 0-8364-0243-X). South Asia Bks.

Giebelhaus, August W. Business & Government in the Oil Industry: A Case Study of Sun Oil, 1876 to 1945, Vol. 5. Porter, Glenn, ed. LC 77-7795. (Industrial Development & the Social Fabric Monographs). 425p. (Orig.). 1980. lib. bdg. 32.00 (ISBN 0-89232-089-3). Jai Pr.

Hall, Gus. The Energy Rip-off: Cause & Cure. LC 74-8897. (Orig.). 1974. pap. 1.75 (ISBN 0-7178-0421-6). Intl Pub Co.

Holden, David & Johns, Richard. The House of Saud: The Rise & Rule of the Most Powerful Dynasty in the Arab World. LC 81-47474. (Illus.). 464p. 1981. 17.95 (ISBN 0-03-043731-8). HR&W.

Jones, Charles S. From the Rio Grande to the Arctic: Story of the Richfield Oil Corporation. LC 70-160504. (Illus.). 1972. 19.95x (ISBN 0-8061-0976-9); pap. 8.95x (ISBN 0-8061-1155-0). U of Okla Pr.

Jones, G. G. The State & the Emergence of the British Oil Industry. 264p. 1981. text ed. 45.00x (ISBN 0-333-27595-0, Pub. by Macmillan England). Humanities.

Kaufman, Burton I. The Oil Cartel Case: A Documentary Study of Antitrust Activity in the Cold War Era. LC 77-87963. (Contributions in American History: No. 72). (Illus.). 1978. lib. bdg. 17.95x (ISBN 0-313-20043-2, KOC/). Greenwood.

Koury, Enver M. Oil & Geopolitics in the Persian Gulf Area: A Center of Power. LC 73-85565. 96p. 1973. pap. 5.00 (ISBN 0-934484-03-1). Inst Mid East & North Africa.

Kramer, K. Erdoel-Lexikon (Crude Oil Dictionary) 5th rev. ed. LC 72-313250. 1972. 20.00x (ISBN 3-7785-0233-6). Intl Pubns Serv.

LBJ School of Public Affairs & Eaton, David. Shale Oil Technology: Status of the Industry. (Working Paper Ser.: No. 7). 1977. 3.00 (ISBN 0-686-10611-3). LBJ Sch Public Affairs.

Lovegrove, Martin. Our Islands Oil. 1978. 30.00 (ISBN 0-900886-14-5, Pub. by Witherby & Co. Ltd.). State Mutual Bk.

Massie, Joseph L. Blazer & Ashland Oil: A Study in Management. LC 60-8519. (Illus.). 272p. 1960. 17.00x (ISBN 0-8131-1051-3). U Pr of Ky.

Megateli, Abderrahmane. Investment Policies of National Oil Companies: A Comparative Study of Sonatrach, Nioc & Pemex. LC 80-12841. 344p. 1980. 31.95 (ISBN 0-03-052736-8). Praeger.

Moureau, Magdeleine & Rouge, Janine. Dictionnaire Technique des Termes Utilises Dans l'Industrie du Petrole, Anglais-Francais, Francais-Anglais. 914p. (Eng. -Fr., Dictionary of Technical Terms Used in the Oil Industry, English-French, French-English). 1977. 95.00 (ISBN 0-686-56757-9, M-6419). French & Eur.

Odell, Peter R. Oil & World Power: Background to the Oil Crisis. 3rd rev. ed. LC 75-148830. (Illus.). 256p. 1975. 9.95 (ISBN 0-685-51711-X). Taplinger.

Oil & Gas International Yearbook 1981. 71st ed. LC 12-1196. (Illus.). 639p. 1981. 100.00x (ISBN 0-582-90307-6). Intl Pubns Serv.

Okura, Nagatsune. Seiyu Roku: On Oil Manufacturing. Ariga, Eiko, tr. LC 74-6761. (Illus.). 1974. 20.00 (ISBN 0-917526-01-5). Olearius Edns.

Salant, Stephen W. Imperfect Competition in the World Oil Market: A Computerized Nash-Cournot Model. LC 80-8737. 244p. 1981. 23.95x (ISBN 0-669-04344-3). Lexington Bks.

Shell UK Exploration & Production Ltd. Winning Supply & Service Business in Offshore Oil & Gas Markets. 112p. 1976. 77.00x (ISBN 0-86010-025-1, Pub. by Graham & Trotman England). State Mutual Bk.

Siksek, Simon G. The Legal Framework for Oil Concessions in the Arab World. LC 79-2882. 140p. 1981. Repr. of 1960 ed. 15.00 (ISBN 0-8305-0050-2). Hyperion Conn.

Stockholm International Peace Research Institute. Oil & Security. (SIPRI Monographs Ser.). (Illus.). 190p. 1974. pap. text ed. 14.25x (ISBN 0-391-00370-4). Humanities.

Weinberg, I. & Kalitenko, K. Instrumentation & Controls in the Oil & Petrochemical Industries. Mkrtchyan, G., tr. from Rus. (Illus.). 429p. 1971. 16.00x (ISBN 0-8464-0518-0). Beekman Pubs.

The Whole World Oil Directory, 2 vols. 920p. 1979. 60.00 set (ISBN 0-686-62484-X). B Klein Pubns.

Wilcox, Elliott. The Failure of the Twentieth Century Conspiracy for the Domination of the Third World. (Illus.). 111p. 1981. 51.75 (ISBN 0-930008-91-X). Inst Econ Pol.

Woerterbuch Fuer Metallurgie, Mineralogie, Geologie, Bergbau und die Oelindustrie. (Eng. , Fr. , Ger. & It., Dictionary of Metallurgy, Mineralogy, Geology, Mining and Oil Industry). 1970. 88.00 (ISBN 3-7625-0751-1, M-6912). French & Eur.

OIL LANDS

see Oil Fields

OIL LEASES

see Oil and Gas Leases

OIL-PAINTING

see Painting

OIL-PALM

Corley, R. H., et al. Oil Palm Research. (Developments in Crop Science Ser.: No. 1). 1976. 80.50 (ISBN 0-444-41471-1). Elsevier.

Hartley, C. W. The Oil Palm. 2nd ed. LC 76-23180. (Tropical Agriculture Ser.). 1977. text ed. 60.00x (ISBN 0-582-46809-4). Longman.

Van Der Vossen, H. A. Towards More Efficient Selection for Oil Yield in the Oil Palm. (Agricultural Research Reports: No. 823). (Illus.). iv, 107p. (Eng. & Dutch.). 1975. pap. 14.00 (ISBN 90-220-0522-4, Pub. by PUDOC). Unipub.

OIL POLLUTION OF RIVERS, HARBORS, ETC.

Becker, Mary K. & Coburn, Patricia. Superspill: An Account of the 1978 Grounding at Bird Rocks. LC 74-76954. 1974. pap. 3.95 (ISBN 0-914842-02-1). Madrona Pubs.

Boesch, Donald F., et al. Oil Spills & the Marine Environment. LC 74-7128. (Ford Foundation Energy Policy Project Ser.). 112p. 1974. text ed. 18.50 (ISBN 0-88410-310-2); pap. text ed. 8.95 (ISBN 0-88410-326-9). Ballinger Pub.

Environmental Factors in Operations to Combat Oil Spills. (Marine Science Affairs Ser.: No. 9). (Illus.). 25p. 1973. pap. 5.00 (ISBN 0-685-39017-9, WMO 359, WMO). Unipub.

Hoult, D. P. Oil on the Sea. LC 76-98411. (Ocean Technology Ser). 112p. 1969. 22.50 (ISBN 0-306-30443-0, Plenum Pr). Plenum Pub.

Impact of Oil on the Marine Environment. (GESAMP Reports & Studies Ser: No. 6, 1977). 1977. pap. 17.00 (ISBN 92-5-100219-3, F934, FAO). Unipub.

International Convention for the Prevention of Pollution of the Sea by Oil, 1954. 25p. 1978. 7.00 (ISBN 0-686-70802-4, IMCO). Unipub.

International Convention on Civil Liability for Oil Pollution Damage. 20p. 1977. 7.00 (ISBN 0-686-70807-5, IMCO). Unipub.

M'Gonigle, R. Michael & Zacher, Mark W. Pollution, Politics, & International Law: Tankers at Sea. 1979. 17.95 (ISBN 0-520-03690-5). U of Cal Pr.

Nash, A. E., et al. Oil Pollution & the Public Interest: A Study of the Santa Barbara Oil Spill. LC 72-5116. (Illus.). 157p. (Orig.). 1972. pap. 3.75x (ISBN 0-87772-085-1). Inst Gov Stud Berk.

Official Records of the Conference on the Establishment of an International Compensation Fund for Oil Pollution Damage, 1971. 742p. 1978. 33.60 (ISBN 0-686-70790-7, IMCO). Unipub.

Ross, William M. Oil Pollution as an International Problem: A Study of Puget Sound & the Strait of Georgia. LC 73-5610. (Illus.). 296p. 1973. 15.00 (ISBN 0-295-95275-X). U of Wash Pr.

Smith, James E., ed. Torrey Canyon-Pollution & Marine Life. (Illus.). 1968. 42.50 (ISBN 0-521-07144-5). Cambridge U Pr.

Vagners, Juris & Mar, Paul, eds. Oil on Puget Sound: An Interdisciplinary Study in Systems Engineering. LC 72-738. (Washington Sea Grant Ser.). (Illus.). 647p. 1972. 12.50 (ISBN 0-295-95239-3). U of Wash Pr.

Wardley-Smith, J. The Prevention of Oil Pollution. LC 79-63534. 1979. 54.95x (ISBN 0-470-26718-6). Halsted Pr.

Wardley-Smith, J., ed. Control of Oil Pollution on the Sea & Inland Waters. 251p. 1976. 26.00x (ISBN 0-686-64023-3, Pub. by Graham & Trotman England). State Mutual Bk.

--Control of Oil Pollution on the Sea & Inland Waters. 1976. 37.50x (ISBN 0-86010-021-9). Intl Pubns Serv.

Winslow, Ron. Hard Aground: The Story of the Argo Merchant Oil Spill. 1978. 10.95 (ISBN 0-393-05687-2). Norton.

OIL POLLUTION OF WATER

see also Oil Pollution of Rivers, Harbors, Etc.

Anderson, Madelyn K. The Black Tide: The Menace of Oil Spills. (Illus.). (gr. 4 up). 1980. cancelled (ISBN 0-8038-0796-1). Hastings.

--Oil on the Waters: Cleaning up Oil Spills. LC 80-21139. (Illus.). 128p. 1981. 8.95 (ISBN 0-8149-0842-X). Vanguard.

--Oil on Troubled Waters. Date not set. 8.95 (ISBN 0-8149-0842-X). Vanguard.

The Bravo Blow-Out. 287p. 1980. 100.00x (ISBN 8-272-70011-5, Pub. by Norwegian Info Norway). State Mutual Bk.

Breuel, A., ed. Oil Spill Cleanup & Protection Techniques for Shorelines & Marshlands. LC 81-2461. (Pollution Technology Review: No. 78). (Illus.). 404p. 1981. 42.00 (ISBN 0-8155-0848-4). Noyes.

Brown, Joseph E. Oil Spills: Danger in the Sea. LC 78-7743. (Illus.). (gr. 5 up). 1978. 5.95 (ISBN 0-396-07607-6). Dodd.

Chemical Dispersants for the Control of Oil Spills. 1978. 30.00 (ISBN 0-686-52111-0, 04-659000-24). ASTM.

Cole, H. A., ed. Petroleum & the Continental Shelf of North-West Europe, Volume 2: Environmental Protection. LC 75-14329. 126p. 1975. 32.95 (ISBN 0-470-16483-2). Halsted Pr.

Conference on the Establishment of an International Compensation Fund for Oil Pollution Damage, 1971. 94p. 1972. 11.00 (ISBN 0-686-70808-3, IMCO). Unipub.

Cox, Geraldine V., ed. Oil Spill Studies: Strategies & Techniques. LC 79-93237. (Vol. 3, No. 1-2). (Illus.). 148p. 1979. pap. 9.80 (ISBN 0-930376-12-9). Pathotox Pubs.

Fairhall, David & Jordan, Philip. The Wreck of the Amoco Cadiz. LC 80-17512. (Illus.). 256p. 1980. 12.95 (ISBN 0-8128-2743-0). Stein & Day.

Institute of Petroleum. Mechanical Systems for the Recovery of Oil Spilled on Water. (Illus.). 1975. 29.90x (ISBN 0-85334-451-5). Intl Ideas.

Institute of Petroleum Oil Pollution Analysis Committee, London. Marine Pollution by Oil. (Illus.). 1974. 30.40x (ISBN 0-85334-452-3). Intl Ideas.

International Convention Relating to Intervention on the High Seas in Cases of Oil Pollution Casualties (1969) 25p. 1977. 7.00 (ISBN 0-686-70804-0, IMCO). Unipub.

Johnston, C. S. & Morris, R. J., eds. Oily Water Discharges: Regulatory, Technical & Scientific Considerations. (Illus.). xv, 225p. 1980. 32.00x (ISBN 0-85334-876-6). Intl Ideas.

Jordan, Randolph E. & Payne, James R. Fate & Weathering of Petroleum Spills in the Marine Enviroment: A Literature Review & Synopsis. LC 80-66473. 170p. 1980. 20.00 (ISBN 0-250-40381-1). Ann Arbor Science.

Manual on Oil Pollution, 3 pts. Incl. Pt. 1. Prevention. 1976. pap. 8.25 (ISBN 0-686-64934-6, IMCO 23); Pt. II. Contingency Planning. 1978. pap. 11.00 (ISBN 0-686-64935-4, IMCO 24); Pt. IV. Practical Information on Means of Dealing with Oil Spillages. 1977. Repr. of 1972 ed. pap. 12.00 (ISBN 0-686-64936-2, IMCO-25). IMCO). Unipub.

Manual on Oil Pollution Section IV Practical Information on Means of Dealing with Oil Spillages. 143p. 1981. pap. 18.25 (ISBN 92-801-1096-9, IMCO 69, IMCO). Unipub.

Moghissi, A. A., ed. Oil Spills. 80p. 1980. pap. 12.80 (ISBN 0-08-026237-6). Pergamon.

Norwegian Petroleum Society. Contingency Planning. 223p. 1980. 75.00x (ISBN 8-27270-010-7, Pub. by Norwegian Info Norway). State Mutual Bk.

Recommendations on International Performance & Test Specifications for Oily-Water Separating Equipment & Oil Content Meters. 36p. 1978. 8.25 (ISBN 0-686-70801-6, IMCO). Unipub.

Spooner, M. F., ed. The Amoco Cadiz Oil Spill. (Illus.). 1979. pap. text ed. 7.75 (ISBN 0-08-023830-0). Pergamon.

Winslow, Ron. Hard Aground: The Story of the Argo Merchant Oil Spill. 1978. 10.95 (ISBN 0-393-05687-2). Norton.

OIL RESERVOIR ENGINEERING

Amyx, James W., et al. Petroleum Reservoir Engineering Physical Properties. 1960. 25.50 (ISBN 0-07-001600-3, C). McGraw.

Cole, Frank W. Reservoir Engineering Manual. 2nd ed. (Illus.). 393p. 1969. 22.95x (ISBN 0-87201-779-6). Gulf Pub.

Craft, Benjamin C. & Hawkins, M. F. Applied Petroleum Reservoir Engineering. 1959. 32.95 (ISBN 0-13-041285-6). P-H.

Dake, L. P. Fundamentals of Reservoir Engineering. (Developments in Petroleum Science Ser.: Vol. 8). 444p. 1979. pap. 29.50 (ISBN 0-444-41830-X). Elsevier.

Facilities in Ports for the Reception of Oil Residues: Results of an Enquiry Made in 1972. 145p. 1973. 16.50 (ISBN 0-686-70797-4, IMCO). Unipub.

Hurst, William. Advances in Petroleum Engineering. 400p. 1981. 35.00 (ISBN 0-87814-147-2). Pennwell Pub.
Langes, G. Secondary Recovery & Carbonate Reservoirs. 1972. 25.00 (ISBN 0-444-00116-6, North Holland). Elsevier.
Peaceman, D. W. Fundamentals of Numerical Reservoir Simulation. 1977. 48.00 (ISBN 0-444-41578-5). Elsevier.
Rebinder, P. A. Use of Surfactants in the Petroleum Industry. LC 64-23247. 346p. 1965. 49.50 (ISBN 0-306-10717-1, Consultants). Plenum Pub.
Slider, H. C. Practical Petroleum Reservoir Engineering Methods. LC 74-33712. 600p. 1976. 43.00 (ISBN 0-87814-061-1). Pennwell Pub.
Smith, Charles R. Mechanics of Secondary Oil Recovery. LC 74-32220. 512p. 1975. Repr. of 1966 ed. 25.50 (ISBN 0-88275-270-7). Krieger.

OIL ROYALITIES
see Oil and Gas Leases

OIL SEEDS
see Oilseeds

OIL-SHALES
see also Petroleum
Allred, V. Dean, ed. Oil Shale Processing Technology. 208p. Date not set. cancelled (ISBN 0-86563-001-1). Ctr Prof Adv.
Ellis, Theodore J. The Potential Role of Oil Shale in the U. S. Energy Mix: Questions of Development & Policy Formulation in an Environment Age. Bruchey, Stuart, ed. LC 78-22677. (Energy in the American Economy Ser.). (Illus.). 1979. lib. bdg. 20.00x (ISBN 0-405-11980-1). Arno.
Gary, Joseph H., ed. Thirteenth Oil Shale Symposium: Proceedings. (Oil Shale Ser.). (Illus.). 400p. (Orig.). 1980. pap. 16.00x (ISBN 0-918062-39-X). Colo Sch Mines.
Griest, W. H., et al, eds. Health Effects Investigation of Oil Shale Development. 1981. text ed. 29.50 (ISBN 0-250-40169-X). Ann Arbor Science.
Jensen, Howard, et al, eds. Analytical Chemistry of Liquid Fuel Sources: Tar Sands, Oil Shale, Coal & Petroleum. LC 78-10399. (Advances in Chemistry Ser.: No. 170). 1978. 32.00 (ISBN 0-8412-0395-4). Am Chemical.
Nowacki, Perry, ed. Oil Shale Technical Data Handbook. LC 80-27547. (Energy Tech. Rev. 63 Ser.: Chemical Tech. Rev. 182). (Illus.). 309p. 1981. 48.00 (ISBN 0-8155-0835-2). Noyes.
Oil Shale Symposium, 10th. Proceedings. Gary, J. H., ed. LC 75-17946. (Illus.). 256p. 1977. pap. 7.50 (ISBN 0-918062-01-2). Colo Sch Mines.
Oil Shale Symposium, 11th. Proceedings. Gary, James H., ed. (Illus.). 389p. 1978. pap. 12.00 (ISBN 0-918062-03-9). Colo Sch Mines.
Oil Shales & Tar Sands: A Bibliography. 1977. write for info. DOE.
Oil Shales: Selected Bibliography of DOE Sponsored Esearch. 1980. write for info. DOE.
Peterson, Kathy, ed. Oil Shale: The Environmental Challenges. (Proceedings of International Symposium Aug. 11-14, 1980, Vail, Colorado). (Illus.). 350p. 1981. text ed. 19.00 (ISBN 0-918062-43-8). Colo Sch Mines.
Ranney, M. W. Oil Shale & Tar Sands Technology. LC 79-16122. (Energy Technology Review No. 49; Chemical Technology Review No. 137). (Illus.). 1980. 48.00 (ISBN 0-8155-0769-0). Noyes.
Russell, Paul L. History of Western Oil Shale. LC 80-66410. (Illus.). 176p. 1980. 49.50 (ISBN 0-86563-000-3). Ctr Prof Adv.
Stauffer, H. C., ed. Oil Shale, Tar Sands, & Related Materials. (ACS Symposium Ser.: No. 163). 1981. write for info. (ISBN 0-8412-0640-6). Am Chemical.
Steele, Henry B. Economic Potentialities of Synthetic Liquid Fuels from Oil Shale. Bruchey, Stuart, ed. LC 78-22751. (Energy in the American Economy Ser.). (Illus.). 1979. lib. bdg. 35.00x (ISBN 0-405-12015-X). Arno.
Strausz, Otto P. & Lown, Elizabeth M., eds. Oil Sand & Oil Shale Chemistry. 1978. pap. text ed. 33.80 (ISBN 0-89573-102-9). Verlag Chemie.
Tissot, B., pref. by. Kerogen-Insoluble Organic Matter from Sedimentary Rocks. 560p. 1980. 95.00x (ISBN 0-86010-220-3, Pub. by Graham & Trotman England). State Mutual Bk.
Yen, T. F. & Chilingarian, G. V. Oil Shale. (Developments in Petroleum Science: Vol. 5). 1976. 53.75 (ISBN 0-444-41408-8). Elsevier.
Yen, T. F., ed. Science & Technology of Oil Shale. LC 75-10415. (Illus.). 1976. 32.50 (ISBN 0-250-40092-8); pap. 14.95 (ISBN 0-250-40242-4). Ann Arbor Science.

OIL TANKERS
see Tankers

OIL WELL BLOWOUTS
Adams, Neal. Workover Well Control. 320p. 1981. 45.00 (ISBN 0-87814-142-1). Pennwell Pub.

OIL WELL DRILLING
see also Drilling Muds; Oil Well Blowouts
Aguilera, Robert. Naturally Fractured Reservoirs. 703p. 1980. 49.00 (ISBN 0-87814-122-7). Pennwell Pub.
Angel, R. R. Volume Requirements for Air & Gas Drilling. 94p. 1958. 6.95x (ISBN 0-87201-890-3). Gulf Pub.
Baldwin, Pamela L. & Baldwin, Malcolm F. Onshore Planning for Offshore Oil: Lessons from Scotland. LC 75-606. (Illus.). 1975. pap. 5.00 (ISBN 0-89164-001-0). Conservation Foun.
Beudel, Martin & De Keyser, Ethel, eds. Offshore Oil & Gas Yearbook Nineteen Seventy-Eight to Seventy-Nine: U. K. & Continental Europe. 1978. 62.50x (ISBN 0-85038-128-2, Pub by Kogan Pg). Nichols Pub.
Brantly, J. E. History of Oil Well Drilling. (Illus.). 1578p. 1971. 59.95 (ISBN 0-87201-634-X). Gulf Pub.
Brown, Kermit. Technology of Artificial Lift Methods, Vols. 2a & 2b. 1980. 55.00 ea. Vol. 2a, 736 P (ISBN 0-87814-119-7). Vol. 2b, 607 P (ISBN 0-87814-133-2). Pennwell Pub.
Business Communications Staff. Oil Field Drilling Chemicals: C-034. 1982. 950.00 (ISBN 0-89336-297-2). BCC.
Carneiro, F. L., et al, eds. Offshore Structures Engineering, Vol. 2. (Illus.). 600p. 1980. 49.95x (ISBN 0-87201-609-9). Gulf Pub.
Chemicals for Enhanced Oil Recovery: C-014. 1980. 750.00 (ISBN 0-89336-210-7). BCC.
Chryssostomidis, Marjorie, ed. Offshore Petroleum Engineering: A Bibliographic Guide to Publications & Information Sources. 1978. 50.00x (ISBN 0-89397-045-X). Nichols Pub.
Commission of the European Communities. New Technologies for Exploration & Exploitation of Oil & Gas Resources, Vol. 11. 600p. 1979. 44.00x (ISBN 0-86010-159-2, Pub. by Graham & Trotman England). State Mutual Bk.
Cozzolino, John M. Management of Oil & Gas Exploration Risk. LC 77-84169. (Business Risk Analysis Ser.). 1977. 47.50 (ISBN 0-9601408-1-6). Cozzolino Assocs.
Craft, Benjamin C., et al. Well Design: Drilling & Production. 1962. ref. ed. 31.95x (ISBN 0-13-950022-7). P-H.
Educational Research Council of America. Oil Driller. Ferris, Theodore N. & Marchak, John P., eds. (Real People at Work Ser: C). (Illus.). 1974. pap. text ed. 2.25 (ISBN 0-89247-024-0). Changing Times.
Galtung, F. L., et al, eds. Automation in Offshore Oil Field Operation: Proceedings of the IFAC-IFIP Symposium, Bergen Norway, June 14-17, 1976. (Computer Applications in Shipping & Shipbuilding: Vol. 3). 1976. 66.00 (ISBN 0-7204-0516-5, North-Holland). Elsevier.
Geophysics Research Board. Continental Scientific Drilling. 1979. pap. 5.50 (ISBN 0-309-02872-8). Natl Acad Pr.
Gowar, R. G., ed. Developments in Fire Protection of Offshore Platforms, Vol. 1. (Illus.). 1978. text ed. 42.80 (ISBN 0-85334-792-1, Pub. by Applied Science). Burgess-Intl Ideas.
Grayson, C. Jackson, Jr. Decisions Under Uncertainty: Drilling Decisions by Oil & Gas Operators. Bruchey, Stuart, ed. LC 78-22686. (Energy in the American Economy Ser.). (Illus.). 1979. Repr. of 1960 ed. lib. bdg. 28.00x (ISBN 0-405-11989-5). Arno.
Harris, L. M. Design for Reliability in Deepwater Floating Drilling Operations. 266p. 1980. 39.00 (ISBN 0-87814-082-4). Pennwell Pub.
--An Introduction to Deepwater Floating Drilling Operations. LC 72-76603. 272p. 1972. 21.00 (ISBN 0-87814-011-5). Pennwell Pub.
Institut du Petrole Francaise, ed. Drilling Data Handbook. (Illus.). 420p. 1980. 39.95x (ISBN 0-87201-204-2). Gulf Pub.
Keto, David B. Law & Offshore Oil Development: The North Sea Experience. LC 78-19745. 1978. 20.95 (ISBN 0-03-046646-6). Praeger.
Knowles, Ruth S. The Greatest Gamblers. Orig. Title: The Epic of American Oil Exploration. 376p. 1980. pap. 7.95 (ISBN 0-8061-1654-4). U of Okla Pr.
Le Tirant, Pierre. Seabed Reconnaissance & Offshore Soil Mechanics for the Installation of Petroleum Structures. (Illus.). 508p. 1980. 75.00 (ISBN 0-87201-794-X). Gulf Pub.
Lynch, Philip F. Rig Equipment. (A Primer in Drilling & Production Equipment Ser.: Vol. 2). (Illus.). 134p. 1980. pap. 15.95x (ISBN 0-87201-199-2). Gulf Pub.
McCray, Arthur W. & Cole, Frank W. Oil Well Drilling Technology. (Illus.). 1979. Repr. of 1959 ed. 16.95x (ISBN 0-8061-0423-6). U of Okla Pr.
McNair, Will. Electric Drilling Rig Handbook. 222p. 1980. 37.50 (ISBN 0-87814-120-0). Pennwell Pub.
Maurer, William. Advanced Drilling Techniques. 698p. 1980. 49.00 (ISBN 0-87814-117-0). Pennwell Pub.
Moore, Preston L. Drilling Practices Manual. LC 74-80812. 448p. 1974. 39.50 (ISBN 0-87814-057-3). Pennwell Pub.
Neal, Harry E. The Story of Offshore Oil. LC 77-11175. (Illus.). 64p. (gr. 3 up). 1977. PLB 6.97 (ISBN 0-671-32888-3). Messner.
Nind, T. E. Principles of Oil Well Production. 2nd ed. (Illus.). 384p. 1981. 28.50 (ISBN 0-07-046576-2, P&RB). McGraw.
Oilfield Machinery & Equipment. (Industrial Equipment & Supplies Ser.). 1981. 495.00 (ISBN 0-686-31536-7). Busn Trend.
Olney, Ross R. Offshore! LC 80-10908. (Illus.). 96p. (gr. 5-9). 1981. 10.95 (ISBN 0-525-36305-X, 01117-330). Dutton.
Ostrovskii, A. P. Deep Hole Drilling with Explosives. LC 61-17718. 133p. 1962. 30.00 (ISBN 0-306-10524-1, Consultants). Plenum Pub.
Peterson, Kathy, ed. Oil Shale: The Environmental Challenges. (Proceedings of International Symposium Aug. 11-14, 1980, Vail, Colorado). (Illus.). 350p. 1981. text ed. 19.00 (ISBN 0-918062-43-8). Colo Sch Mines.
Ranney, M. Crude Oil Drilling Fluids. LC 78-70741. (Illus.). 1979. 39.00 (ISBN 0-8155-0732-1). Noyes.
Rogers, Walter F., et al. Composition & Properties of Oil Well Drilling Fluids. 4th rev. ed. Gray, George & Darley, H. C., eds. 42.50x (ISBN 0-87201-129-1). Gulf Pub.
Shah, D. O. Surface Phenomena in Enhanced Oil Recovery. 874p. 1981. write for info. (ISBN 0-306-40757-4, Plenum Pr). Plenum Pub.
Sheffield, Riley, Jr. Floating Drilling: Equipment & Its Use. (Illus.). 258p. 1980. 21.95 (ISBN 0-87201-289-1). Gulf Pub.

OIL WELL LOGGING
Norwegian Petroleum Society. Measuring Accuracy of Parameters Used in Formation Evaluation in the North Sea. 193p. 1980. 75.00x (ISBN 82-7270-002-6, Pub. by Norwegian Info Norway). State Mutual Bk.
Pirson, Sylvain J. Handbook of Well Log Analysis: For Oil & Gas Formation Evaluation. 1963. ref. ed. 33.95 (ISBN 0-13-382804-2). P-H.

OIL WELL LOGGING, ELECTRIC
Allaud, Louis & Martin, Maurice H. Schlumberger, The History of a Technique. LC 77-23566. 333p. 1977. 39.50 (ISBN 0-471-01667-5, Pub. by Wiley-Interscience). Wiley.
Wyllie, M. R. Fundamentals of Well Log Interpretation. 3rd ed. 1963. 38.00 (ISBN 0-12-767253-2). Acad Pr.

OIL WELL LOGGING, RADIATION
Alekseev, F. A., ed. Soviet Advances in Nuclear Geophysics. LC 64-18194. 189p. 1965. 39.50 (ISBN 0-306-10708-2, Consultants). Plenum Pub.

OIL WORKERS
see Petroleum Workers

OILS AND FATS
see also Essences and Essential Oils; Lubrication and Lubricants; Mineral Oils; Oil Industries; Oilseeds; Petroleum
also names of fats and oils
Applied Science Publishers Ltd London, ed. Metabolism of Hydrocarbons, Oils, Fuels & Lubricants. (Illus.). 1976. 50.40x (ISBN 0-85334-703-4). Intl Ideas.
Approaches to International Action on World Trade in Oilseeds, Oils & Fats. (FAO Commodity Policy Studies: No. 22). 129p. (Orig.). 1973. pap. 10.00 (ISBN 0-685-30139-7, F193, FAO). Unipub.
Fat & Oil Chemistry Composition Oxidation Processing. 1966. 63.75x (ISBN 0-677-11700-0). Gordon.
Hamilton, R. J. & Bhati, A., eds. Fats & Oils: Chemistry & Technology. (Illus.). 255p. 1980. text ed. 48.00 (ISBN 0-85334-915-0, Pub. by Applied Sci England). J K Burgess.
Intergovernmental Group Oilseeds, Oils, & Fats, 10th Session. Report. 19p. 1976. 7.50 (ISBN 0-685-68966-2, F1117, FAO). Unipub.
Intergovernmental Group on Oilseeds, Oil & Fats, 11th Session. Report. (Illus.). 29p. 1978. pap. 7.50 (ISBN 0-685-20384-0, F1143, FAO). Unipub.
Levitt, Benjamin. Oils, Detergents & Maintenance Specialties, 2 Vols. 1967. 25.00 ea. Vol. 1 (ISBN 0-8206-0232-9). Vol. 2 (ISBN 0-8206-0258-2). Chem Pub.
Somogyi, J. C., ed. Nutritional Aspects of Fats. (Bibliotheca Nutritio et Dieta: No. 25). (Illus.). 230p. 1977. 66.00 (ISBN 3-8055-2655-5). S Karger.
Swanson, Glen. Oil & Water. (Illus.). (gr. 3-7). 1981. 7.95 (ISBN 0-13-633677-9). P-H.
Swern, Daniel. Bailey's Industrial Oil & Fat Products, Vol. II. 4th ed. 675p. 1981. 50.00 (ISBN 0-471-83958-2, Pub. by Wiley-Interscience). Wiley.
--Bailey's Industrial Oil & Fat Products, Vol. 1. 4th ed. LC 78-31275. 841p. 1979. 62.50 (ISBN 0-471-83957-4, Pub. by Wiley-Interscience). Wiley.
Wade, Harlan. El Aceite. Contreras, Mamie M., tr. from Eng. LC 78-26613. (A Book About Ser.). (Illus., Sp.). (gr. k-3). 1979. PLB 7.95 (ISBN 0-8172-1485-2). Raintree Pubs.
--L' Huile. Potvin, Claude & Potvin, Rose-Ella, trs. from Eng. (A Book About Ser.). Orig. Title: Oil. (Illus., Fr.). (gr. k-3). 1979. PLB 7.95 (ISBN 0-8172-1460-7). Raintree Pubs.

OILS AND FATS–ANALYSIS
Bellanato, J. & Hidalgo, A. Infrared Analysis Ofessential Oils. 1971. 97.00 (ISBN 0-85501-022-3). Heyden.
Cocks, Leslie V. & Van Rede, C. Laboratory Handbook for Oil & Fat Analysts. 1966. 66.00 (ISBN 0-12-178550-5). Acad Pr.
Hamilton, R. J. & Bhati, A., eds. Fats & Oils: Chemistry & Technology. (Illus.). xii, 263p. 1981. 48.00x (ISBN 0-85334-915-0). Intl Ideas.
Masada, Yoshiro. Analysis of Essential Oils by Gas Chromatography & Mass Spectrometry. LC 75-46590. 334p. 1976. 65.95 (ISBN 0-470-15019-X). Halsted Pr.
Paquot, C., ed. Standard Methods for the Analysis of Oils, Fats & Derivatives. 6th ed. LC 78-40305. 1978. text ed. 25.00 (ISBN 0-08-022379-6). Pergamon.

OILS AND FATS, EDIBLE
see also Essences and Essential Oils;
also names of fats and oils
Gutcho, M. Edible Oils & Fats: Recent Developments. LC 78-70744. (Food Technology Review Ser.: No. 49). (Illus.). 1979. 39.00 (ISBN 0-8155-0735-6). Noyes.
Intergovernmental Group on Oilseeds, Oils & Fats. Report on the Fourteenth Session of the Intergovernmental Group on Oilseeds, Oils & Fats. 14p. 1980. pap. 7.50 (ISBN 92-5-100937-6, F2044, FAO). Unipub.
Recommended International Standard for Edible Arachia Oil. 1970. pap. 4.50 (ISBN 0-685-36341-4, F621, FAO). Unipub.
Recommended International Standard for Edible Cottonseed Oil. 1970. pap. 4.50 (ISBN 0-685-36342-2, F622, FAO). Unipub.
Recommended International Standard for Edible Fats & Oils Not Covered by Individual Codex Standards. 1970. pap. 1.50 (ISBN 0-685-36300-7, FAO). Unipub.
Recommended International Standard for Edible Fats & Oils. 1970. pap. 3.00 (ISBN 0-685-36343-0, FAO). Unipub.
Recommended International Standard for Edible Maize Oil. 1970. pap. 4.50 (ISBN 0-685-36345-7, F627, FAO). Unipub.
Recommended International Standard for Edible Mustardseed Oil. 1970. pap. 4.50 (ISBN 0-685-36346-5, F638, FAO). Unipub.
Recommended International Standard for Edible Rapeseed Oil. 1970. pap. 4.50 (ISBN 0-685-36347-3, F624, FAO). Unipub.
Recommended International Standard for Edible Soya Bean Oil. 1970. pap. 4.50 (ISBN 0-685-36350-3, F620, FAO). Unipub.
Recommended International Standard for Edible Safflower Oil. 1970. pap. 4.50 (ISBN 0-685-36348-1, F629, FAO). Unipub.
Recommended International Standard for Edible Sesameseed Oil. 1970. pap. 4.50 (ISBN 0-685-36349-X, F628, FAO). Unipub.
Recommended International Standard for Edible Tallow. 1970. pap. 4.50 (ISBN 0-685-36351-1, F633, FAO). Unipub.
Recommended International Standard for Olive Oil, Virgin & Refined, & for Refined Olive Residue Oil. 1970. pap. 4.50 (ISBN 0-685-36311-2, F636, FAO). Unipub.
Recommended International Standard for Lard. 1970. pap. 4.50 (ISBN 0-685-36306-6, F630, FAO). Unipub.
Recommended International Standard for Margarine. 1970. pap. 4.50 (ISBN 0-685-36307-4, F635, FAO). Unipub.
Recommended International Standard for Rendered Pork Fat. 1970. pap. 4.50 (ISBN 0-685-36326-0, F631, FAO). Unipub.
Weiss, Theodore J. Food Oils & Their Uses. (Illus.). 1970. lib. bdg. 27.50 (ISBN 0-87055-093-4). AVI.

OILSEED INDUSTRY
see Oil Industries

OILSEED PLANTS
see also Coconut-Palm; Cotton; Oil-Palm; Soy-Bean
Report of the Fifteenth Session of the Intergovernmental Group on Oilseeds, Oils & Fats to the Committee on Commodity Problems. 10p. 1981. pap. 7.50 (ISBN 92-5-101065-X, F2128, FAO). Unipub.

OILSEEDS
see also Oils and Fats; Seeds
Approaches to International Action on World Trade in Oilseeds, Oils & Fats. (FAO Commodity Policy Studies: No. 22). 129p. (Orig.). 1973. pap. 10.00 (ISBN 0-685-30139-7, F193, FAO). Unipub.
Intergovernmental Group Oilseeds, Oils, & Fats, 10th Session. Report. 19p. 1976. 7.50 (ISBN 0-685-68966-2, F1117, FAO). Unipub.

Intergovernmental Group on Oilseeds, Oil & Fats, 11th Session. Report. (Illus.). 29p. 1978. pap. 7.50 (ISBN 0-685-20384-0, F1143, FAO). Unipub.

Intergovernmental Group on Oilseeds, Oils & Fats. Report on the Fourteenth Session of the Intergovernmental Group on Oilseeds, Oils & Fats. 14p. 1980. pap. 7.50 (ISBN 92-5-100937-6, F2044, FAO). Unipub.

OJI LANGUAGE

see Twi Language

O'KEEFFE, GEORGIA

Georgia O'Keeffe: A Portrait by Alfred Stieglitz. (Illus.). 1978. museum edition 35.00 (ISBN 0-87099-182-5). Metro Mus Art.

Lisle, Laurie. Portrait of an Artist: A Biography of Georgia O'Keefe. 496p. 1981. 4.95 (ISBN 0-671-42182-4). WSP.

--Portrait of an Artist: A Biography of Georgia O'Keeffe. LC 79-66083. (Illus.). 1980. 14.95 (ISBN 0-87223-565-3, Dist. by Har-Row). Seaview Bks.

O'Keeffe, Georgia. Georgia O'Keeffe. (Illus.). 1978. 45.00 (ISBN 0-670-33710-2, Studio). Viking Pr.

--Georgia O'Keeffe: A Portrait by Alfred Stieglitz. LC 78-13467. (Illus., Co-pub. by Metropolitan Museum of Art). 1979. 45.00 (ISBN 0-670-51989-8, Studio). Viking Pr.

--Some Memories of Drawings. LC 74-14986. 1974. 250.00 (ISBN 0-686-17542-5). Atlantis.

Wilder, Mitchell A., ed. Georgia O'Keeffe. LC 66-20333. (Illus.). 30p. 1966. pap. 3.00 (ISBN 0-88360-009-9). Amon Carter.

O'KELLY, SEAMUS G.

Saul, George B. Seumas O'Kelly. LC 74-126030. (Irish Writers Ser.). 101p. 1971. 4.50 (ISBN 0-8387-7765-1); pap. 1.95 (ISBN 0-8387-7661-2). Bucknell U Pr.

OKIGBO, CHRISTOPHER, 1932-1967

Anozie, S. O. Christopher Okigbo: Creative Rhetoric. LC 77-182593. (Modern African Writers Ser). 225p. 1972. text ed. 18.50x (ISBN 0-8419-0086-8, Africana); pap. 7.95x (ISBN 0-8419-0117-1, Africana). Holmes & Meier.

OKINAWA, BATTLE OF, 1945

see World War, 1939-1945-Campaigns-Okinawa Island

OKINAWA ISLAND

Glacken, Clarence J. The Great Loochoo: A Study of Okinawan Village Life. LC 73-6394. (Illus.). 324p. 1973. Repr. of 1955 ed. lib. bdg. 17.25x (ISBN 0-8371-6897-X, GLGL). Greenwood.

Hogg, Clayton. Okinawa. LC 72-93532. (This Beautiful World Ser: Vol. 41). (Illus.). 114p. 1973. pap. 4.95 (ISBN 0-87011-189-2). Kodansha.

Kerr, George H. Okinawa: The History of an Island People. LC 58-12283. (Illus.). 542p. 1958. 22.50 (ISBN 0-8048-0437-0). C E Tuttle.

Lebra, William P. Okinawan Religion: Belief, Ritual, & Social Structure. LC 66-16506. (Illus., Orig.). 1966. pap. text ed. 6.00x (ISBN 0-87022-450-6). U Pr of Hawaii.

Watanabe, A. Okinawa Problem. 1970. 22.50x (ISBN 0-522-84000-0, Pub. by Melbourne U Pr). Intl Schol Bk Serv.

OKLAHOMA

see also names of cities, towns, etc. in Oklahoma

Broce, Thomas E. Directory of Oklahoma Foundations. LC 73-7430. 200p. 1974. 14.95x (ISBN 0-8061-1123-2); pap. 7.95 (ISBN 0-8061-1174-7). U of Okla Pr.

Chapman, Samuel G. & Peck, Gail. Dogs in Police Work in Oklahoma. 1978. 4.00 (ISBN 0-686-00896-0). Univ OK Gov Res.

Franks, Kenny A. The Oklahoma Petroleum Industry. LC 80-5242. (Oklahoma Horizons Ser.: Vol. 4). (Illus.). 320p. 1980. 17.50 (ISBN 0-8061-1625-0). U of Okla Pr.

Goins, Charles R. & Morris, John W. Oklahoma Homes: Past & Present. LC 80-5239. (Illus.). 288p. 1981. 25.00 (ISBN 0-8061-1668-4). U of Okla Pr.

Hebert, F. Ted. Oklahoma Legislative Voting: A Roll Call Analysis for 1970-1974. (Legislative Research Ser.: No. 12). 29p. 1978. 2.00 (ISBN 0-686-04909-8). Univ OK Gov Res.

Keegan, Marcia. Oklahoma. LC 79-5087. (Illus.). 112p. 1979. pap. 14.95 (ISBN 0-89659-063-1). Abbeville Pr.

Kirkpatrick, Samual A. The Legislative Process in Oklahoma: Policy Making, People & Politics. LC 77-26641. 1978. 14.95 (ISBN 0-8061-1421-5). U of Okla Pr.

McDonald, Jean G. Legislators & Patronage in Oklahoma. (Legislative Research Ser: No. 10). 1975. 2.50 (ISBN 0-686-18648-6). Univ OK Gov Res.

McLemore, Lelan E. Task-Related Norms in a State Legislature: The Case of Oklahoma. (Legislative Research Ser.: No. 5). 1973. pap. 2.00 (ISBN 0-686-18647-8). Univ OK Gov Res.

Moore, Lucille. Jake. 1978. 6.95 (ISBN 0-533-03052-8). Vantage.

Morgan, David R. & O'Brien, Joan. Oklahoma State Finance: A Longitudinal & Comparative Overview. 1977. 2.50 (ISBN 0-686-05891-7). Univ OK Gov Res.

Morgan, David R. & Petersen, Emily M. Oklahoma State Debt: A Longitudinal & Comparative Analysis. 1977. pap. 3.50 (ISBN 0-686-19374-1). Univ OK Gov Res.

Oklahoma. 28.00 (ISBN 0-89770-112-7). Curriculum Info Ctr.

Pelissero, John. Recruitment & Selection Practices in Oklahoma Police Departments. (Criminal Justice Policy & Administration Research Ser.). 47p. 1978. 3.00 (ISBN 0-686-00897-9). Univ OK Gov Res.

Shirk, George H. Oklahoma Place Names. 2nd ed. LC 73-7424. 248p. 1974. 10.95 (ISBN 0-8061-1140-2). U of Okla Pr.

State Industrial Directories Corp. Oklahoma State Industrial Directory 1981. 1980. pap. 35.00 (ISBN 0-89910-036-8). State Indus Dir.

Statistical Abstract of Oklahoma. 1980 ed. 511p. 1980. pap. 15.00 (ISBN 0-931880-01-7). U OK Ctr Econ.

OKLAHOMA-ANTIQUITIES

Bell, Robert E. Oklahoma Archaeology: An Annotated Bibliography. 2nd ed. LC 78-58141. 1978. pap. 8.95x (ISBN 0-8061-1497-5). U of Okla Pr.

Ferring, C. Reid, et al. An Archaelogical Reconnaissance of the Salt Plains Areas of Northwestern Oklahoma. (Contributions of the Museum of the Great Plains Ser.: No. 4). (Illus.). 1976. pap. 3.65 (ISBN 0-685-85503-1). Mus Great Plains.

Leonhardy, Frank C. Test Excavations in the Mangum Reservoir Area of Southwestern Oklahoma. (Contributions of the Museum of the Great Plains Ser.: No. 2). 1.50 (ISBN 0-685-85507-4). Mus Great Plains.

Northcutt, John D. An Archeological Survey in the Gypsum Breaks on the Elm Fork of the Red River. (Contributions of the Museum of the Great Plains Ser.: No. 8). (Illus.). 1979. pap. write for info. (ISBN 0-685-96445-0). Mus Great Plains.

Phillips, Philip & Brown, James A. Pre-Columbian Shell Engravings from the Craig Mound at Spiro, Oklahoma, 5 vols. Flnt, Emily & Condon, Lorna, eds. LC 74-77557. (Illus.). 1978. Limited Ed. Vols. 1-3. lib. bdg. 300.00 (ISBN 0-87365-777-2) (ISBN 0-87365-783-7). Limited Edition Vol. 5 (ISBN 0-87365-784-5). Peabody Harvard.

--Pre-Columbian Shell Engravings from the Craig Mound at Spiro, Oklahoma, Pt. 1. (Illus.). 1978. pap. 35.00 (ISBN 0-87365-795-0). Peabody Harvard.

Spivey, Towana, et al. Archaeological Investigations Along the Waurika Pipeline. (Contributions of the Museum of the Great Plains Ser.: No. 5). (Illus.). 1977. pap. 10.45 (ISBN 0-685-88670-0). Mus Great Plains.

OKLAHOMA-DESCRIPTION AND TRAVEL

Berger, Brian. Beautiful Oklahoma. LC 80-10968. (Illus.). 72p. 1980. 14.95 (ISBN 0-89802-008-5); pap. 7.95 (ISBN 0-89802-007-7). Beautiful Am.

Federal Writers' Project. Oklahoma: A Guide to the Sooner State. 532p. Repr. 49.00 (ISBN 0-403-02185-5). Somerset Pub.

Fitzgerald, David, photos by. Oklahoma. LC 79-92730. (Belding Imprint Ser.). (Illus.). 128p. (Text by Bill Burchardt). 1980. 27.50 (ISBN 0-912856-57-2). Graphic Arts Ctr.

Hart, Herbert M. Tour Guide to Old Forts of Texas, Kansas, Nebraska, Oklahoma, Vol. 4. (Illus.). 65p. (Orig.). 1981. pap. 3.95 (ISBN 0-87108-583-6). Pruett.

Hunt, David C. Guide to Oklahoma Museums. LC 80-5939. (Illus.). 256p. 1981. 17.50 (ISBN 0-8061-1567-X); pap. 9.95 (ISBN 0-8061-1752-4). U of Okla Pr.

Irving, Washington. Tour on the Prairies. McDermott, John F., ed. (Western Frontier Library: No. 7). 1971. Repr. of 1956 ed. 6.95 (ISBN 0-8061-0351-5). U of Okla Pr.

McCoy, Doyle. Roadside Trees & Shrubs of Oklahoma. LC 80-5944. (Illus.). 180p. (Orig.). 1981. pap. 9.95 (ISBN 0-8061-1556-4). U of Okla Pr.

Ruth, Kent. Oklahoma Travel Handbook. (Illus.). 1979. pap. 5.95 (ISBN 0-8061-1539-4). U of Okla Pr.

--Oklahoma Travel Handbook. LC 76-62517. (Illus.). 1977. 10.95 (ISBN 0-8061-1405-3). U of Okla Pr.

Silvey, Larry P. & Drown, Douglas S., eds. The Tulsa Spirit. new ed. LC 79-53563. (The American Portrait Ser.). (Illus.). 1979. 22.95 (ISBN 0-932986-07-2). Continent Herit.

Wilson, Steve. Oklahoma Treasures & Treasure Tales. 1976. 19.50 (ISBN 0-8061-1240-9). U of Okla Pr.

Wright, Muriel H., et al. Mark of Heritage. LC 75-40255. 1976. pap. 7.95 (ISBN 0-8061-1356-1). U of Okla Pr.

OKLAHOMA-HISTORY

Bernard, Richard M. The Poles in Oklahoma. LC 79-6714. (Newcomers to a New Land Ser.: Vol. 1). (Illus.). 96p. (Orig.). 1980. pap. 3.95 (ISBN 0-8061-1630-7). U of Okla Pr.

Bicha, Karel D. The Czechs in Oklahoma. LC 79-19734. (Newcomers to a New Land Ser.: Vol. 2). (Illus.). 96p. (Orig.). 1980. pap. 3.95 (ISBN 0-8061-1618-8). U of Okla Pr.

Bingham, Richard D. Reapportionment of the Oklahoma House of Representatives: Politics & Process. (Legislative Research Ser: No. 2). 33p. 1972. pap. 1.50 (ISBN 0-686-20792-0). Univ OK Gov Res.

Blessing, Patrick. The British & Irish in Oklahoma. LC 79-6722. (Newcomers to a New Land Ser.: Vol. 3). (Illus.). 96p. (Orig.). 1980. pap. 2.95 (ISBN 0-8061-1672-2). U of Okla Pr.

Bonnifield, Mathew P. Oklahoma Innovator: The Life of Virgil Browne. LC 75-41452. (Oklahoma Trackmaker Ser: Vol. 2). (Illus.). 190p. 1976. 9.75 (ISBN 0-8061-1326-X). U of Okla Pr.

Brown, Kenny L. The Italians in Oklahoma. LC 79-23342. (Newcomers to a New Land Ser.: Vol. 4). (Illus.). 96p. (Orig.). 1980. pap. 2.95 (ISBN 0-8061-1624-2). U of Okla Pr.

Burbank, Garin. When Farmers Voted Red: The Gospel of Socialism in the Oklahoma Countryside, 1910-1924. LC 76-5259. (Contributions in American History Ser.: No. 53). (Illus.). 1976. lib. bdg. 15.00 (ISBN 0-8371-8903-9, BSO/). Greenwood.

Burright, Orrin U. The Sun Rides High: Pioneering Days in Oklahoma, Kansas & Missouri. 1974. 8.95 (ISBN 0-89015-022-2). Eakin Pubns.

Chapman, Berlin B. Federal Management & Disposition of the Lands of Oklahoma Territory, 1866-1907. Bruchey, Stuart, ed. LC 78-56717. (Management of Public Lands in the U. S. Ser.). (Illus.). 1979. lib. bdg. 25.00x (ISBN 0-405-11325-0). Arno.

Cunningham, Robert E. Stillwater Through the Years. LC 79-89768. (Illus.). 1980. Repr. of 1974 ed. text ed. 14.95x (ISBN 0-934188-05-X). Evans Pubns.

--Stillwater Where Oklahoma Began. LC 79-89767. (Illus.). 1979. Repr. of 1969 ed. text ed. 14.95x (ISBN 0-934188-04-1). Evans Pubns.

Debo, Angie. Prairie City: The Story of an American Community. LC 77-93241. (Illus.). 1969. Repr. of 1944 ed. text ed. 8.50 (ISBN 0-87752-027-5). Gordian.

Erickson, John R. Panhandle Cowboy. LC 79-24929. (Illus.). xiv, 213p. 1980. 12.50 (ISBN 0-8032-1803-6); pap. 4.95 (ISBN 0-8032-6702-9, BB 777, Bison). U of Nebr Pr.

Fischer, John. From the High Plains: An Account of the Hard Men, High-Spirited Women -- & a Few Rascals -- Who Settled the Last Frontier of the Old West. LC 78-437. (Illus.). 1978. 10.00 (ISBN 0-06-011269-7, HarpT). Har-Row.

Franks, Kenny, et al. Early Oklahoma Oil: A Photographic History, 1859-1936. LC 76-51653. (The Montague History of Oil Ser.: No. 2). (Illus.). 260p. 1981. 27.95 (ISBN 0-89096-110-7). Tex A&M Univ Pr.

Gibson, Arrell. The Oklahoma Story. LC 77-18608. (Illus.). 1978. 10.95 (ISBN 0-8061-1461-4). U of Okla Pr.

Gibson, Arrell M. Oklahoma. LC 65-13131. (gr. 7 up). 1965. pap. 2.95 (ISBN 0-8077-1425-9). Tchrs Coll.

--Oklahoma: A History of Five Centuries. 2nd ed. LC 81-40284. (Illus.). 320p. 1981. Repr. 17.50 (ISBN 0-8061-1758-3). U of Okla Pr.

Goble, Danney. Progressive Oklahoma: The Making of a New Kind of State. LC 79-4734. (Illus.). 1980. 14.95 (ISBN 0-8061-1510-6). U of Okla Pr.

Hale, Douglas. The Germans from Russia in Oklahoma. LC 79-20152. (Newcomers to a New Land Ser.). (Illus.). 96p. (Orig.). 1980. pap. 3.95 (ISBN 0-8061-1620-X). U of Okla Pr.

Hawkins, B. Sketch of the Creek Country, in Seventeen Ninety-Eight to Ninety-Nine. Repr. of 1848 ed. 11.00 (ISBN 0-527-38850-5). Kraus Repr.

Kirkpatrick, Samuel A. & Morgan, David R. The Oklahoma Voter: Politics, Elections, & Political Parties in the Sooner State. (Illus.). 1978. pap. 8.95 (ISBN 0-8061-1498-3). U of Okla Pr.

McCoy, Doyle. Roadside Wild Fruits of Oklahoma. LC 79-6705. (Illus.). 96p. (Orig.). 1980. pap. 8.95 (ISBN 0-8061-1626-9). U of Okla Pr.

McReynolds, Edwin C. Oklahoma: History of the Sooner State. rev. ed. (Illus.). 1977. Repr. of 1954 ed. 14.95x (ISBN 0-8061-0302-7). U of Okla Pr.

McReynolds, Edwin C., et al. Oklahoma: The Story of Its Past & Present. rev. ed. (Illus.). 1980. Repr. of 1961 ed. 12.50x (ISBN 0-8061-0509-7). U of Okla Pr.

Miller, Benjamin S. Ranch Life in Southern Kansas & the Indian Territory, As Told by a Novice: How a Fortune Was Made in Cattle. facsimile ed. LC 75-111. (Mid-American Frontier Ser.). 1975. Repr. of 1896 ed. 12.00x (ISBN 0-405-06878-6). Arno.

Morgan, Anne H. & Strickland, Rennard. Oklahoma Memories. LC 81-2777. 336p. 1981. 16.95 (ISBN 0-8061-1689-7); pap. 8.95 (ISBN 0-8061-1767-2). U of Okla Pr.

Morgan, David R. Legislative Attitudes Toward State Constitutional Revision: The Oklahoma Case. (Legislative Research Ser: No. 1). 1971. pap. 1.00 (ISBN 0-686-20785-8). Univ OK Gov Res.

Morgan, H. Morgan & Morgan, Anne H. Oklahoma: A History. (The States & the Nation Ser.). (Illus.). 1977. 12.95 (ISBN 0-393-05642-2). Norton.

Morris, Cheryl H. The Cutting Edge: The Life of John Rogers. LC 75-37736. (Oklahoma Trackmaker: Vol. 3). (Illus.). 235p. 1976. 12.50 (ISBN 0-8061-1329-4). U of Okla Pr.

Morris, John W. Ghost Towns of Oklahoma. (Illus.). 1978. 15.95 (ISBN 0-8061-1358-8); pap. 8.95 (ISBN 0-8061-1420-7). U of Okla Pr.

Morris, John W., et al. Historical Atlas of Oklahoma. 2nd ed. LC 75-33129. 1976. 13.50 (ISBN 0-8061-1322-7); pap. 7.95 (ISBN 0-8061-1359-6). U of Okla Pr.

Okies: Mini-Play. (U.S. History Ser.). (gr. 7 up). 1974. 3.00 (ISBN 0-89550-351-4). RIM.

Rister, Carl C. Land Hunger: David L Payne & the Oklahoma Boomers. facsimile ed. LC 75-118. (Mid-American Frontier Ser.). (Illus.). 1975. Repr. of 1942 ed. 15.00x (ISBN 0-405-06884-0). Arno.

Rohrs, Richard C. The Germans in Oklahoma. LC 79-6715. (Newcomers to a New Land Ser.: Vol. 7). (Illus.). 96p. (Orig.). 1980. pap. 3.95 (ISBN 0-8061-1673-0). U of Okla Pr.

Sears, Roscoe H. Caddo Tribe-Wichita Reservation in Indian Territory, Oklahoma, As of March 2, 1895: Appraisal. (Library of American Indian Affairs). 112p. 1974. lib. bdg. 39.00 (ISBN 0-8287-0965-3). Clearwater Pub.

Shirley, Glenn. West of Hell's Fringe: Crime, Criminals, & the Federal Peace Officer in Oklahoma Territory, 1889-1907. LC 77-9112. (Illus.). 1978. 15.95 (ISBN 0-8061-1444-4). U of Okla Pr.

Silvey, Larry P. & Drown, Douglas S., eds. The Tulsa Spirit. new ed. LC 79-53563. (The American Portrait Ser.). (Illus.). 1979. 22.95 (ISBN 0-932986-07-2). Continent Herit.

Smallwood, James M., ed. And Gladly Teach: Reminiscences of Teachers from Frontier Dugout to Modern Module. LC 75-40961. (Illus.). 256p. 1976. 11.95 (ISBN 0-8061-1340-5). U of Okla Pr.

Smith, Michael M. The Mexicans in Oklahoma. LC 79-6716. (Newcomers to a New Land Ser.: Vol. 8). (Illus.). 96p. (Orig.). 1980. pap. 3.95 (ISBN 0-8061-1631-5). U of Okla Pr.

Strickland, Rennard. The Indians in Oklahoma. LC 79-6717. (Newcomers to a New Land Ser.: Vol. 9). (Illus.). 1980. 9.95 (ISBN 0-8061-1674-9); pap. 4.95 (ISBN 0-8061-1675-7). U of Okla Pr.

Thiel, Sidney. The Oklahoma Land Rush. (Jackdaw Ser: No. A12). (Illus.). 1973. 6.95 (ISBN 0-670-52192-2, Grossman). Viking Pr.

Tobias, Henry J. The Jews in Oklahoma. LC 79-6723. (Newcomers to a New Land Ser.: Vol. 10). (Illus.). 96p. (Orig.). 1980. pap. 3.95 (ISBN 0-8061-1676-5). U of Okla Pr.

Tyson, Carl N., et al. The McMan: The Lives of Robert M. McFarlin & James A. Chapman. LC 77-9113. (OT Ser.: Vol. 4). (Illus.). 1978. 12.50 (ISBN 0-8061-1446-0). U of Okla Pr.

Vance, Mary. Historical Society Architectural Publications: Ohio, Oklahoma, Oregon, & Pennsylvania. (Architecture Ser.: Bibliography A-162). 55p. 1980. pap. 6.00 (ISBN 0-686-26909-8). Vance Biblios.

Vexler, R. I. Oklahoma Chronology & Factbook, Vol. 36. 1978. 8.50 (ISBN 0-379-16161-3). Oceana.

Walker, Lloyd C. Catalog of Oklahoma Tokens. (Illus.). 1978. pap. 25.00 (ISBN 0-931960-03-7). BNR Pr.

OKLAHOMA-JUVENILE LITERATURE

Bailey, Bernadine. Picture Book of Oklahoma. rev. ed. (Illus.). (gr. 3-5). 1967. 5.50g (ISBN 0-8075-9540-3). A Whitman.

Carpenter, Allan. Oklahoma. new ed. LC 79-10592. (New Enchantment of America State Bks.). (Illus.). (gr. 4 up). 1979. PLB 10.60 (ISBN 0-516-04136-3). Childrens.

Fradin, Dennis. Oklahoma: In Words & Pictures. LC 80-26961. (Young People's Stories of Our States Ser.). (Illus.). 48p. (gr. 2-5). 1981. PLB 9.25 (ISBN 0-516-03936-9). Childrens.

OKLAHOMA, UNIVERSITY OF

Cross, George L. Blacks in White Colleges: Oklahoma's Landmark Cases. 1975. pap. 3.95x (ISBN 0-8061-1267-0). U of Okla Pr.

--Presidents Can't Punt: The OU Football Tradition. (Illus.). 1977. 11.95 (ISBN 0-8061-1419-3). U of Okla Pr.

--The University of Oklahoma & World War II: A Personal Account, 1941-1946. LC 80-16934. (Illus.). 320p. 1980. 15.95 (ISBN 0-8061-1662-5). U of Okla Pr.

Everett, Mark R. Medical Education in Oklahoma: The University of Oklahoma School of Medicine & Medical Center, 1900-1931. LC 70-177333. (Illus.). 300p. 1972. 17.50x (ISBN 0-8061-0988-2); pap. 8.95 (ISBN 0-8061-1237-9). U of Okla Pr.

Keith, Harold. Oklahoma Kickoff: An Informal History of the First Twenty-Five Years at the University of Oklahoma, & of the Amusing Hardships That Attended Its Pioneering. LC 78-58114. (Illus.). 1978. pap. 9.95 (ISBN 0-8061-1485-1). U of Okla Pr.

Roller, D. & Goodman, M. Catalogue of the History of Science, 2 vols. LC 76-381954. 1976. Set. 189.00x (ISBN 0-7201-0452-1, Pub. by Mansell England). Merrimack Bk Serv.

University Of Oklahoma Executive Planning Committee. Future of the University: A Report to the People. Christenson, Gordon A., ed. 1969. 12.50x (ISBN 0-8061-0820-7); pap. 4.95 (ISBN 0-8061-0821-5). U of Okla Pr.

OKRACOKE, NORTH CAROLINA

Goerch, Carl. Ocracoke. (Illus.). 1976. 7.95 (ISBN 0-910244-12-X). Blair.

OLAFFSON, EGGERT

Hermannsson, Halldor. Eggert Olafsson: A Biographical Sketch. LC 26-30. (Islandica Ser.: Vol. 16). 1925. pap. 6.00 (ISBN 0-527-00346-8). Kraus Repr.

OLCOTT, HENRY STEEL, 1832-1907

Murphet, Howard. Hammer on the Mountain: Life Story of Henry Steel Olcott (1832-1907) LC 72-76427. (Illus.). 352p. 1972. 7.95 (ISBN 0-8356-0210-9). Theos Pub Hse.

OLD AGE

see also Aged; Aging; Geriatrics; Longevity; Middle Age; Old Age Assistance; Old Age Pensions; Retirement

Achenbaum, W. Andrew. Old Age in the New Land: The American Experience Since 1790. LC 77-28666. 1979. 15.00x (ISBN 0-8018-2107-X); pap. 4.95 (ISBN 0-8018-2355-2). Johns Hopkins.

Anders, Rebecca. A Look at Aging. LC 75-38467. (Lerner Awareness Bks.). (Illus.). 36p. (gr. 3-6). 1976. PLB 4.95 (ISBN 0-8225-1304-8). Lerner Pubns.

Andrews, Elsie M. Facing & Fulfilling the Later Years. LC 68-16318. (Orig.). 1968. pap. 0.70x (ISBN 0-87574-157-6). Pendle Hill.

Baird, Janet H., ed. These Harvest Years. facsimile ed. LC 74-167308. (Essay Index Reprint Ser). Repr. of 1951 ed. 18.00 (ISBN 0-8369-2581-5). Arno.

Blythe, Ronald. The View in Winter. 288p. 1980. pap. 4.95 (ISBN 0-14-005663-7). Penguin.

Cicero, Marcus T. Cato Major. Kastenbaum, Robert, ed. LC 78-22193. (Aging & Old Age Ser.). 1979. Repr. of 1744 ed. lib. bdg. 12.00x (ISBN 0-405-11810-4). Arno.

Cowley, Malcolm. The View from Eighty. 96p. 1980. 6.95 (ISBN 0-670-74614-2). Viking Pr.

Department for the Aging, City of New York. Older Women in the City. Kastenbaum, Robert, ed. LC 78-73649. (Aging & Old Age Ser.). 1979. lib. bdg. 15.00x (ISBN 0-405-11839-2). Arno.

Derbers, Milton & Stein, Leon, eds. The Aged & Society. LC 79-8665. (Growing Old Ser.). (Illus.). 1980. Repr. of 1950 ed. lib. bdg. 19.00 (ISBN 0-405-12783-9). Arno.

Dyroff, Adolf. Der Peripatos Uber das Greisenalter. 1939. pap. 9.50 (ISBN 0-384-13655-9). Johnson Repr.

Farber, Norma. How Does It Feel to Be Old? LC 79-11516. (Illus.). (ps-3). 1979. 9.95 (ISBN 0-525-32414-3, Unicorn Bk.). Dutton.

Goodman, Jane G. Aging Parents: Whose Responsibility? LC 80-14945. (Workshop Models for Family Life Education Ser.). 168p. 1980. plastic bdg. 10.95 (ISBN 0-87304-175-5). Family Serv.

Greene, Eva & Greene, Barbara. Chance of a Lifetime: An Anthology for the Ageless. LC 67-16829. (Illus.). 1968. 6.95 (ISBN 0-87027-095-8). Wheelwright.

Gubrium, Jaber F. The Myth of the Golden Years: A Socio-Environmental Theory of Aging. (Illus.). 244p. 1973. 14.75 (ISBN 0-398-02703-X); pap. 9.75 (ISBN 0-398-02757-9). C C Thomas.

Gubrium, Jaber F., ed. Time, Roles & Self in Old Age. LC 74-12131. 1976. text ed. 29.95 (ISBN 0-87705-230-1); pap. text ed. 14.95 (ISBN 0-87705-350-2). Human Sci Pr.

Harbert, Anita S. & Ginsberg, Leon H. Human Services for Older Adults. 1979. pap. text ed. 15.95x (ISBN 0-534-00607-8). Wadsworth Pub.

Hess, Clinton W. & Kerschner, Paul A. The Silver Lobby: A Guide to Advocacy for Older Persons. LC 78-61804. 1978. pap. 2.50 (ISBN 0-88474-075-7). USC Andrus Geron.

International Association of Gerontology. Old Age in the Modern World: Report of the Third Congress of the International Association of Gerontology, London. Stein, Leon, ed. LC 79-8671. (Growing Old Ser.). 1980. Repr. of 1955 ed. lib. bdg. 50.00x (ISBN 0-405-12786-3). Arno.

Kastenbaum, Robert. Old Age on the New Scene. (Springer Series on Adulthood & Aging: No. 9). 1981. pap. text ed. 19.95 (ISBN 0-8261-2361-9). Springer Pub.

Kayser-Jones, Jeanie S. Old, Alone, & Neglected: Care of the Aged in Scotland & in the United States. LC 80-19711. 160p. 1981. 14.95 (ISBN 0-520-04153-4). U of Cal Pr.

Kessler, Julia. Getting Even with Getting Old. LC 80-11045. 228p. 1980. 16.95x (ISBN 0-88229-663-9); pap. 8.95 (ISBN 0-88229-754-6). Nelson-Hall.

Lawton, George, ed. New Goals for Old Age. LC 76-169390. (Family in America Ser). 230p. 1972. Repr. of 1943 ed. 14.00 (ISBN 0-405-03868-2). Arno.

Maclay, Elise. Green Winter: Celebrations of Old Age. 1977. 7.95 (ISBN 0-88349-122-2). Readers Digest Pr.

Miller, Mary. Suicide After Sixty: The Final Alternative. LC 79-4246. (Death & Suicide Ser.: Vol. 2). (Orig.). 1979. text ed. 12.95 (ISBN 0-8261-2780-0); pap. text ed. 6.95 (ISBN 0-8261-2781-9). Springer Pub.

Monk, Abraham, ed. The Age of Aging: A Reader in Social Gerontology. LC 79-2727. (Impact Ser.). 367p. 1979. 16.95 (ISBN 0-87975-111-8); pap. 8.95 (ISBN 0-87975-114-2). Prometheus Bks.

Morgan, John C. Becoming Old: An Introduction to Social Gerontology. LC 79-558. (Adulthood & Aging Ser.: Vol. 3). 1979. text ed. 6.50 (ISBN 0-8261-2621-9). Springer Pub.

Munnichs, Joep M., et al. Dependency or Interdependency in Old Age. 1976. lib. bdg. 26.00 (ISBN 9-0247-1895-3, Pub. by Martinus Nijhoff Netherlands). Kluwer Boston.

Neugarten, Bernice L., ed. Middle Age & Aging: A Reader in Social Psychology. LC 68-55150. 1968. 25.00x (ISBN 0-226-57381-8); pap. 10.00x (ISBN 0-226-57382-6). U of Chicago Pr.

O'Flaherty, Vincent M. The Grace of Old Age. LC 76-43314. 1977. pap. 1.95 (ISBN 0-8199-0611-5). Franciscan Herald.

Osterbind, Carter C., ed. Areawide Planning for Independent Living for Older People. LC 73-8869. (Center for Gerontological Studies & Programs Ser.: Vol. 22). 1973. pap. 5.00 (ISBN 0-8130-0396-2). U Presses Fla.

Parker, Pamela L., ed. Understanding Aging. LC 74-8795. (Shalom Resource Ser.). (Illus.). 48p. 1974. pap. 2.95 (ISBN 0-8298-0291-6). Pilgrim NY.

Petty, David L. An Analysis of Attitudes & Behaviors of Young Adults Toward the Aged. LC 78-68446. 1979. perfect bdg. 9.00 (ISBN 0-88247-573-8). R & E Res Assoc.

Pollak, Otto & Kelly, Nancy L. The Challenges of Aging. 1981. 9.95 (ISBN 0-88427-045-9). Caroline Hse.

Richardson, Bessie E. Old Age Among the Ancient Greeks. LC 74-93775. (Illus.). Repr. of 1933 ed. 21.50 (ISBN 0-404-05289-4). AMS Pr.

--Old Age Among the Ancient Greeks: The Greek Portrayal of Old Age in Literature, Art & Inscriptions. Repr. of 1933 ed. lib. bdg. 23.50x (ISBN 0-8371-0637-0, RIOA). Greenwood.

Russell, Cherry. The Aging Experience: Old Age in Australia Society. write for info. Allen Unwin.

Sanchez Hidalgo, Efrain & Sanchez Hidalgo, Lydia. La Psicologia De la Vejez. pap. 4.80 (ISBN 0-8477-2905-2). U of PR Pr.

Schmidt, K. O. The Beauty of Modern Maturity. Muller, Leone, tr. from German. LC 76-47421. 1977. pap. 4.25 (ISBN 0-87707-183-7). CSA Pr.

Scott-Maxwell, Florida. Measure of My Days. LC 68-13643. (YA) 1968. 7.95 (ISBN 0-394-43565-6). Knopf.

Simmons, Leo W. Role of the Aged in Primitive Society. (Illus.). 1970. Repr. of 1945 ed. 19.50 (ISBN 0-208-00824-1, Archon). Shoe String.

Smith, Bert K. Aging in America. LC 72-6232. 256p. 1973. pap. 4.95 (ISBN 0-8070-2769-3, BP502). Beacon Pr.

Smith, T. Lynn, ed. Living in the Later Years. (Center for Gerontological Studies & Programs Ser.: Vol. 2). (Illus.). 1952. pap. 3.75 (ISBN 0-8130-0212-5). U Presses Fla.

Stout, Ruth. Don't Forget to Smile or How to Stay Sane & Fit Over Ninety. 1981. 10.00 (ISBN 0-912846-21-6). Bookstore Pr.

Strehler, B., ed. Advances in Gerontological Research. Incl. Vol. 1. 1964. 52.50 (ISBN 0-12-019401-5); Vol. 2. 1967. 52.50 (ISBN 0-12-019402-3); Vol. 3. 1971. 52.50 (ISBN 0-12-019403-1); Vol. 4. 1972. 52.50 (ISBN 0-12-019404-X). Acad Pr.

Tibbitts, Clark & Stein, Leon, eds. Social Contribution by the Aging. LC 79-8690. (Growing Old Ser.). (Illus.). 1980. Repr. of 1952 ed. lib. bdg. 15.00x (ISBN 0-405-12806-1). Arno.

Turk, Ruth. You're Getting Older, So What? LC 76-39989. (Illus.). 8.00 (ISBN 0-8309-0166-3). Herald Hse.

Vining, Elizabeth G. Being Seventy: The Measure of a Year. 1978. 10.00 (ISBN 0-670-15539-X). Viking Pr.

Vischer, A. L. Old Age: Its Compensations & Rewards. LC 79-8698. (Growing Old Ser.). (Illus.). 1980. Repr. of 1947 ed. lib. bdg. 16.00x (ISBN 0-405-12809-6). Arno.

Warthin, Aldred S. Old Age: The Major Involution. Kastenbaum, Robert, ed. LC 78-22224. (Aging & Old Age Ser.). (Illus.). 1979. Repr. of 1929 ed. lib. bdg. 15.00x (ISBN 0-405-11837-6). Arno.

Webber, Irving L., ed. Society & the Health of Older People. LC 53-12339. (Center for Gerontological Studies & Programs Ser.: Vol. 9). 1959. pap. 3.75 (ISBN 0-8130-0239-7). U Presses Fla.

Withers, William. Crisis in Old Age Finance. 1979. 12.95 (ISBN 0-8120-5386-9). Barron.

OLD AGE-BIBLIOGRAPHY

Shock, Nathan W. Classified Bibliography of Gerontology & Geriatrics. LC 51-2115. Repr. of 1951 ed. 90.00 (ISBN 0-527-82450-X). Kraus Repr.

--Classified Bibliography of Gerontology & Geriatrics: Supplement Two, 1956-1961. 1963. 25.00x (ISBN 0-8047-0412-0). Stanford U Pr.

OLD AGE-DISEASES

see Geriatrics

OLD AGE, SURVIVORS AND DISABILITY INSURANCE

see Insurance, Disability; Old Age Pensions; Social Security

OLD AGE AND EMPLOYMENT

see Age and Employment

OLD AGE ASSISTANCE

see also Aged-Medical Care; Old Age Homes; Old Age Pensions

Alleger, Daniel E., ed. Social Change & Aging in the Twentieth Century. LC 53-12339. (Center for Gerontological Studies & Programs Ser.: Vol. 13). 1964. pap. 3.75 (ISBN 0-8130-0008-4). U Presses Fla.

Bowe, Frank. Rehabilitating America: Toward Independence for Disabled & Elderly People. LC 79-1654. 1980. 11.95 (ISBN 0-06-010436-8, HarpT). Har-Row.

Butler, Robert N. Why Survive? Being Old in America. LC 73-4066. 1977. pap. 5.95 (ISBN 0-06-090872-6, CN-872, HarpT). Har-Row.

Davis, Lenwood G. The Black Aged in the United States: An Annotated Bibliography. LC 80-1193. xviii, 200p. 1980. lib. bdg. 22.50 (ISBN 0-313-22560-5, DAB/). Greenwood.

Estes, Carroll L. The Aging Enterprise: A Critical Examination of Social Policies & Services for the Aged. LC 79-83571. (Social & Behavioral Science Ser.). 1979. 15.95x (ISBN 0-87589-410-0). Jossey-Bass.

Herzog, Barbara R., ed. Aging & Income: Programs & Prospects for the Elderly. LC 78-2510. 1978. 29.95 (ISBN 0-87705-369-3). Human Sci Pr.

International Association Of Gerontology - 5th Congress. Social Welfare of the Aging, Proceedings, Vol. 2. Kaplan, Jerome & Aldridge, G. J., eds. (Aging Around the World Ser.). 1962. 20.00x (ISBN 0-231-08950-3). Columbia U Pr.

Lawton, M. Powell, et al. Community Planning for an Aging Society: Designing Services & Facilities. LC 75-45302. (Community Development Ser.: Vol. 20). 1978. 25.00 (ISBN 0-87933-195-X). Hutchinson Ross.

Meltzer, Judith, et al, eds. Policy Options in Long-Term Care. LC 81-10445. 1981. lib. bdg. price not set (ISBN 0-226-51973-2); pap. price not set (ISBN 0-226-51974-0). U of Chicago Pr.

Parker, Florence E. & Stewart, Estelle M. Care of the Aged Persons in the United States. LC 75-17235. (Social Problems & Social Policy Ser.). 1976. Repr. of 1929 ed. 19.00x (ISBN 0-405-07504-9). Arno.

Pinner, Frank A., et al. Old Age & Political Behavior: A Case Study. Stein, Leon, ed. LC 79-8678. (Growing Old Ser.). (Illus.). 1980. Repr. of 1959 ed. lib. bdg. 28.00x (ISBN 0-405-12796-0). Arno.

Putnam, Jackson K. Old-Age Politics in California: From Richardson to Reagan. LC 70-107649. (Illus.). 1970. 10.00x (ISBN 0-8047-0734-0). Stanford U Pr.

Rudman, Jack. Senior Citizen Aide. (Career Examination Ser.: C-1473). (Cloth bdg. avail. on request). pap. 8.00 (ISBN 0-8373-1473-9). Natl Learning.

Smith, Bert K. The Pursuit of Dignity: New Living Alternatives for the Elderly. LC 76-48536. 1977. 9.95 (ISBN 0-8070-2736-7); pap. 4.95 (ISBN 0-8070-2737-5, BP587). Beacon Pr.

Starr, Bernard, et al. Projective Assessment of Aging Method. LC 79-13358. manual 31 cards 26.50 (ISBN 0-8261-2440-2). Springer Pub.

Stearns, Peter N. Old Age in European Society: The Case of France. LC 76-25603. 1976. text ed. 22.50 (ISBN 0-8419-0285-2). Holmes & Meier.

Tinker, Anthea. The Elderly in Modern Society. (Social Policy in Modern Britain Ser.). (Illus.). 320p. 1981. pap. text ed. 13.95x (ISBN 0-582-29513-0). Longman.

Viscusi, W. Kip. Welfare of the Elderly: An Economic Analysis & Policy Prescription. LC 78-31223. (Urban Research Ser.). 1979. 24.50 (ISBN 0-471-01506-7, Pub. by Wiley-Interscience). Wiley.

Webber, Irving L., ed. Services for the Aging. LC 53-12339. (Center for Gerontological Studies & Programs Ser.: Vol. 7). 1957. pap. 3.75 (ISBN 0-8130-0238-9). U Presses Fla.

OLD AGE HOMES

see also Almshouses; Nursing Homes

Aranyi, Laszlo & Goldman, Larry L. Design of Long-Term Care Facilities. 240p. 1980. text ed. 32.50 (ISBN 0-442-26120-9). Van Nos Reinhold.

Brearley, C. Residential Work with the Elderly. (Library of Social Work Ser.). 1977. 13.50x (ISBN 0-7100-8587-7); pap. 7.95 (ISBN 0-7100-8588-5). Routledge & Kegan.

Brody, Elaine. Long-Term Care of Older People: A Practical Guide. LC 77-5944. 402p. 1977. text ed. 24.95 (ISBN 0-87705-274-3). Human Sci Pr.

Clough, Roger. Old Age Homes. (National Institute Social Services Library Ser.: No. 42). 224p. 1981. text ed. 28.50 (ISBN 0-04-362043-4); pap. text ed. 12.50 (ISBN 0-04-362044-2). Allen Unwin.

Davis, Richard H., ed. Non-Profit Homes for the Aging: Planning, Development & Programming. 94p. 1973. pap. 3.00 (ISBN 0-88474-002-1). U of S Cal Pr.

Frush, James, Jr. The Retirement Residence: An Analysis of the Architecture & Management of Life-Care Housing. 116p. 1968. ed. spiral bdg. 11.75photocopy (ISBN 0-398-00626-1). C C Thomas.

Huttman, Elizabeth D. Housing & Social Services for the Elderly: Social Policy Trends. LC 75-44932. (Special Studies). 1977. text ed. 29.95 (ISBN 0-275-23830-X). Praeger.

McClure, Ethel. More Than a Roof: The Development of Minnesota Poor Farms & Homes for the Aged. LC 68-65534. (Illus.). 292p. 1968. 6.00 (ISBN 0-87351-043-7). Minn Hist.

Parker, Florence E. & Stewart, Estelle M. Care of the Aged Persons in the United States. LC 75-17235. (Social Problems & Social Policy Ser.). 1976. Repr. of 1929 ed. 19.00x (ISBN 0-405-07504-9). Arno.

Profiles of Two Adult Homes & Their Communities: The Need to Bridge the Gap. 1980. 4.00 (ISBN 0-86671-064-7). Comm Coun Great NY.

Regnier, Victor A. & Arch, M., eds. Environmental Planning. (Technical Bibliographies on Aging). 1975. 2.75 (ISBN 0-88474-080-3). USC Andrus Geron.

Smith, Viola B. Dear Ophelia. Michel, Sandra S., ed. 1978. pap. 3.95 (ISBN 0-917178-10-6). Lenape Pub.

Stephens, Joyce. Loners, Losers, & Lovers: Elderly Tenants in a Slum Hotel. LC 75-40874. 138p. 1976. pap. 6.95 (ISBN 0-295-95762-X). U of Wash Pr.

Teski, Marea. Living Together: An Ethnography of a Retirement Hotel. LC 79-88268. 1979. pap. text ed. 8.75 (ISBN 0-8191-0769-7). U Pr of Amer.

OLD AGE PENSIONS

see also Civil Service Pensions; Disability Evaluation; Pension Trusts; Welfare Funds (Trade-Union);

also subdivisions Pensions, and Salaries, Pensions, etc. under names of industries, professions, etc. e.g. Teachers-Salaries, Pensions, etc.

Bers, Melvin K. Union Policy & the Older Worker. LC 76-14986. 1976. Repr. of 1957 ed. lib. bdg. 15.00x (ISBN 0-8371-8655-2, BEUP). Greenwood.

Bronson, Dorrance C. Concepts of Actuarial Soundness in Pension Plans. 1957. 7.75x (ISBN 0-256-00641-5). Irwin.

Conference on Income Support Policies for the Aging-University of Chicago. Income Support Policies for the Aged. Tolley, George S. & Burkhauser, Richard V., eds. LC 77-4155. 1977. 16.50 (ISBN 0-88410-359-5). Ballinger Pub.

Davies, Bleddyn & Knapp, Martin. Old People's Homes & the Production of Welfare. (Library of Social Work Ser.). 240p. 1981. 32.50 (ISBN 0-7100-0700-0). Routledge & Kegan.

Douglas, Paul H. Social Security in the United States: An Analysis & Appraisal of the Federal Social Security Act. LC 71-137164. (Poverty U.S.A. Historical Record Ser). 1971. Repr. of 1936 ed. 16.00 (ISBN 0-405-03102-5). Arno.

Epstein, Abraham. Facing Old Age: A Study of Old Age Dependency in the United States & Old Age Pensions. LC 79-169381. (Family in America Ser). 374p. 1972. Repr. of 1922 ed. 16.00 (ISBN 0-405-03858-5). Arno.
Greenough, William C. & King, Francis P. Pension Plans & Public Policy. LC 76-13608. 311p. 1976. 17.50x (ISBN 0-231-04070-9). Columbia U Pr.
Katona, George. Private Pensions & Individual Saving. LC 65-64300. 114p. 1965. pap. 5.00 (ISBN 0-87944-043-0). Inst Soc Res.
Keeling, B. Lewis. Payroll Records & Accounting. 1975. text ed. 6.84 (ISBN 0-538-01460-1). SW Pub.
Kutza, Elizabeth A. The Benefits of Old Age: Social Welfare Policy for the Elderly. LC 80-24241. 176p. 1981. lib. bdg. 18.00x (ISBN 0-226-46565-9); pap. 5.95 (ISBN 0-226-46566-7). U of Chicago Pr.
McGill, Dan M. Fulfilling Pension Expectations. 1962. 9.25x (ISBN 0-256-00660-1). Irwin.
--Fundamentals of Private Pensions. 4th ed. 1979. 17.95x (ISBN 0-256-02252-6). Irwin.
McGill, Dan M., ed. Pensions: Problems & Trends. 1955. 6.95x (ISBN 0-256-00663-6). Irwin.
--Social Security & Private Pension Plans: Competitive or Complementary? 1977. 10.50x (ISBN 0-256-01968-1). Irwin.
McNulty, James E. Decision & Influence Processes in Private Pension Plans. 1961. 7.00x (ISBN 0-256-00667-9). Irwin.
Massachusetts Commission on Old Age Pensions, Annuities & Insurance. Report of the Commission on Old Age Pensions, Annuities & Insurance. LC 75-17233. (Social Problems & Social Policy Ser.). (Illus.). 1975. Repr. of 1910 ed. 23.00x (ISBN 0-405-07502-2). Arno.
Melone, Joseph J. Collectively Bargained Multi-Employer Pension Plans. 1963. 8.50x (ISBN 0-256-00654-7). Irwin.
Murray, Roger F. Economic Aspects of Pensions: A Summary Report. (General Ser.: No. 85). 1968. 10.00x (ISBN 0-87014-473-1, Dist. by Columbia U Pr). Natl Bur Econ Res.
Neuberger, Richard L. & Loe, Kelley. An Army of the Aged. LC 72-2379. (FDR & the New Deal Ser). 332p. 1973. Repr. of 1936 ed. lib. bdg. 32.50 (ISBN 0-306-70518-4). Da Capo.
Old Age Pension Schemes. 1977. 9.00x (ISBN 92-64-11599-4). OECD.
Patterson, Edwin W. Legal Protection of Private Pension Expectations. 1960. 9.25x (ISBN 0-256-00670-9). Irwin.
Pinner, Frank A., et al. Old Age & Political Behavior: A Case Study. Stein, Leon, ed. LC 79-8678. (Growing Old Ser.). (Illus.). 1980. Repr. of 1959 ed. lib. bdg. 28.00x (ISBN 0-405-12796-0). Arno.
Putnam, Jackson K. Old-Age Politics in California: From Richardson to Reagan. LC 70-107649. (Illus.). 1970. 10.00x (ISBN 0-8047-0734-0). Stanford U Pr.
Schulz, James H. The Economics of Aging. 3rd ed. 208p. 1979. pap. text ed. 8.95x (ISBN 0-534-00772-4). Wadsworth Pub.
Young, Fay & Young, Leo. Everything You Should Know About Pension Plans. LC 76-17381. 1976. pap. 5.95 (ISBN 0-9601308-1-0). Bethesda.

OLD AGE PENSIONS–GREAT BRITAIN
Booth, Charles. Pauperism: A Picture. Bd. with Endowment of Old Ages: An Argument. 188p. Repr. of 1892 ed. 12.50x (ISBN 0-678-01003-X). Kelley.

OLD AGE, SURVIVORS AND DISABILITY INSURANCE
see Social Security
OLD BACTRIAN LANGUAGE
see Avesta Language
OLD BULGARIAN LANGUAGE
see Church Slavic Language
OLD CATHOLIC CHURCH
Mathew, Arnold H., tr. Old Catholic Missal & Ritual. LC 73-84708. Repr. of 1909 ed. 27.45 (ISBN 0-404-01949-8). AMS Pr.
OLD CHURCH SLAVIC LANGUAGE
see Church Slavic Language
OLD ENGLISH LANGUAGE
see Anglo-Saxon Language; English Language–Middle English, 1100-1500
OLD ENGLISH LITERATURE
see Anglo-Saxon Literature (Collections); English Literature (Collections)–Middle English (1100-1500)
OLD ENGLISH SHEEPDOGS
see Dogs–Breeds–Old English Sheepdog
OLD FRENCH LANGUAGE
see French Language–To 1500
OLD FRENCH LITERATURE
see French Literature (Collections)–To 1500
OLD FRENCH POETRY
see French Poetry–To 1500
OLD HIGH GERMAN LANGUAGE
see German Language–Old High German, 750-1050
OLD ICELANDIC LANGUAGE
see Icelandic and Old Norse Languages
OLD ICELANDIC LITERATURE
see Icelandic and Old Norse Literature
OLD INDIC LANGUAGE
see Vedic Language
OLD IRONSIDES (SHIP)
see Constitution (Frigate)
OLD MILLS
see Flour Mills; Mills and Mill-Work
OLD MINE ROAD
Hine, Charles G. The Old Mine Road. (Illus.). 1963. pap. 2.75 (ISBN 0-8135-0427-9). Rutgers U Pr.
OLD NORSE LANGUAGE
see Icelandic and Old Norse Languages
OLD NORSE LITERATURE
see Icelandic and Old Norse Literature
OLD ORDER AMISH
see Amish
OLD PERSIAN INSCRIPTIONS
see also Cuneiform Inscriptions
OLD PERSIAN LANGUAGE
see also Avesta Language; Indo-Aryan Languages
Kent, Roland G. Old Persian Grammar Texts Lexicon. 2nd rev. ed. (American Oriental Ser.: Vol. 33). 1953. 13.00x (ISBN 0-940490-33-1). Am Orient Soc.
Utas, Bo. A Persian Sufi Poem: Vocabulary & Terminology. Concordance, Frequency Word-List, Statistical Survey, Arabic Loan-Words & Sufi-Religious Terminology in Tariq Ut-Tajqiq. (Scandinavian Institute of Asian Studies Monographs: No. 36). 1978. pap. text ed. 13.75x (ISBN 0-7007-0116-8). Humanities.
OLD RED SANDSTONE (GEOLOGY)
see Geology, Stratigraphic–Devonian
OLD SAXON LANGUAGE
see also Anglo-Saxon Language
Hinderschiedt, Ingeborg. Zur Heliandmetrik: Das Verhaltnis Von Rhythmus und Satzewicht Im Altachsischen. vi, 143p. 1979. 16.00 (ISBN 90-272-4001-9, GLLM 8). Benjamins North Am.
Sievers, Paul. Die Accente in Althochdeutschen und Altsachsischen Handschriften. Repr. of 1909 ed. 14.00 (ISBN 0-384-55360-5); pap. 11.00 (ISBN 0-685-13334-6). Johnson Repr.
Voyles, Joseph B. West Germanic Inflection, Derivation & Compounding. LC 72-94456. (Janua Linguarum, Ser. Practica: No. 145). 204p. (Orig.). 1974. pap. text ed. 35.00x (ISBN 90-2792-711-1). Mouton.
OLD SLOVENIAN LANGUAGE
see Church Slavic Language
OLD STONE AGE
see Paleolithic Period
OLD STONE FORT, MANCHESTER, TENNESSEE
Faulkner, Charles H. Old Stone Fort: Exploring an Archaeological Mystery. LC 68-17145. (Illus.). 1968. pap. 3.95 (ISBN 0-87049-086-9). U of Tenn Pr.
OLD STURBRIDGE VILLAGE, STURBRIDGE, MASSACHUSETTS
Bernheim, Marc & Bernheim, Evelyne. Growing Up in Old New England. LC 75-151160. (Illus.). (gr. 5-9). 1971. 9.95 (ISBN 0-02-709060-4, CCPr). Macmillan.
Old Sturbridge Village. Old Sturbridge Village Living History Calender for 1982. (Wall Calenders Ser.). 1981. pap. 6.95 (ISBN 0-8289-0437-5). Greene.
OLD TURKISH INSCRIPTIONS
see Inscriptions, Turkish (Old)
OLDCASTLE, SIR JOHN, called LORD COBHAM, d. 1417
Bale, John. Select Works of John Bale, Bishop of Ossory. 42.50 (ISBN 0-384-03135-8). Johnson Repr.
Drayton, Michael, et al. Sir John Oldcastle. LC 72-133657. (Tudor Facsimile Texts. Old English Plays: No. 89). Repr. of 1911 ed. 31.50 (ISBN 0-404-53389-2). AMS Pr.
OLDENBURG, CLAES
Baro, Gene, intro. By. Claes Oldenburg: Drawings & Prints. LC 68-8894. (Illus.). 274p. 1981. pap. 19.95 (ISBN 0-87754-202-3). Chelsea Hse.
Oldenburg, Claes. Raw Notes: Documents & Scripts of the Performances: Stars, Moveyhouse, Massage, the Typewriter with annotations by the author. LC 73-83224. (The Nova Scotia Ser). (Illus.). 544p. 1973. pap. 12.95, c (ISBN 0-919616-01-1). NYU Pr.
Oldenburg, Claes & Oldenburg, Coosje V. Claes Oldenburg: Large-Scale Projects, 1977 to 1980. LC 80-66728. (Illus.). 104p. (Orig.). 1980. pap. 20.00 (ISBN 0-8478-0351-1). Rizzoli Intl.
Rose, Barbara. Claes Oldenburg. 224p. 1979. 12.50 (ISBN 0-87070-509-1, Pub. by Museum Mod Art). NYGS.
OLDER, FREMONT, 1856-1935
Wells, Evelyn. Fremond Older. LC 70-125722. (American Journalists). 1970. Repr. of 1936 ed. 18.00 (ISBN 0-405-01705-7). Arno.
OLDER WORKERS
see Age and Employment
OLDHEIM, SAINT, BP. OF SHERBORNE, 640-709
Duckett, Eleanor S. Anglo-Saxon Saints & Scholars. 1967. Repr. of 1947 ed. 21.50 (ISBN 0-208-00200-6, Archon). Shoe String.
OLDKNOW, SAMUEL, 1756-1828
Unwin, George. Samuel Oldknow & the Arkwrights. LC 68-5554. (Illus.). Repr. of 1924 ed. 15.00x (ISBN 0-678-06767-8). Kelley.
OLDS, RANSOM ELI, 1864-1950
Niemeyer, Glenn A. Automotive Career of Ransom E. Olds. LC 63-63708. 1963. 7.50 (ISBN 0-87744-008-5). Mich St U Busn.
Yarnell, Duane. Auto Pioneering. 1949. 4.50 (ISBN 0-685-57228-5). Natl Heritage.
OLDSMOBILE AUTOMOBILE
see Automobiles–Types–Oldsmobile
OLDUVAI GORGE
see Paleontology–Africa
OLEFINS
Akhtar, M. Manipulation & Exploitation of Olefinic Linkages in Biological Systems. cancelled (ISBN 0-08-020462-7). Pergamon.
Albright, Lyle F. Processes for Major Addition-Type Plastics & Their Monomers. (Illus.). 388p. 1974. 34.50 (ISBN 0-07-000965-1, P&RB). McGraw.
Asinger, H. Mono-Olefins: Chemistry & Technology. 1969. text ed. 150.00 (ISBN 0-08-011547-0). Pergamon.
Fray, G. I. & Saxton, R. G. The Chemistry of Cyclo-Octatetraene & Its Derivatives. LC 76-57096. 1978. 95.00 (ISBN 0-521-21580-3). Cambridge U Pr.
Hudec, John. An Empirical Analysis of the Circular Dichroism of Chiral Olefins. 1977. pap. text ed. 12.75 (ISBN 0-08-021584-X). Pergamon.
Kennedy, J. P. Catonic Polymerization of Olefins: A Critical Inventory. 337p. 1975. 27.50 (ISBN 0-471-46909-2, Pub. by Wiley). Krieger.
Kresser, T. O. Polyolefin Plastics. 1969. 18.95x (ISBN 0-442-15632-4). Van Nos Reinhold.
Sittig, Marshall. Polyolefin Production Processes-Latest Developments. LC 76-9491. (Chemical Technology Review: No. 70). (Illus.). 1976. 39.00 (ISBN 0-8155-0622-8). Noyes.
OLEOMARGARINE
Committee on Agriculture, U.S. House of Representatives. Oleomargarine. LC 75-26318. (World Food Supply Ser). (Illus.). 1976. Repr. of 1949 ed. 23.00x (ISBN 0-405-07794-7). Arno.
Pabst, W. R., Jr. Butter & Oleomargarine. LC 70-76644. (Columbia University. Studies in the Social Sciences: No. 427). Repr. of 1937 ed. 15.00 (ISBN 0-404-51427-8). AMS Pr.
Wiest, Edward. Butter Industry in the United States: An Economic Study of Butter & Oleomargarine. LC 68-56696. (Columbia University. Studies in the Social Sciences: No. 165). Repr. of 1916 ed. 21.00 (ISBN 0-404-51165-1). AMS Pr.
OLEUM
see Sulphuric Acid
OLESH, JOHN AND ANNA–FICTION
Kauffman, Christmas-Carol. Hidden Rainbow. 1963. pap. 3.50 (ISBN 0-8024-3807-5). Moody.
OLESHA, YURY KARLOVICH, 1899-
Beaujour, Elizabeth K. The Invisible Land: A Study of the Artistic Imagination of Iurii Olesha. LC 71-130959. 222p. 1970. 20.00x (ISBN 0-231-03428-8). Columbia U Pr.
OLFACTORY BRAIN
see Rhinencephalon
OLFACTORY NERVE
see also Septum (Brain)
Cagan, Robert H. & Kare, Morley R., eds. Biochemistry of Taste & Olfaction. (Nutrition Foundation Ser.). 1981. 38.50 (ISBN 0-12-154450-8). Acad Pr.
International Symposium on Olfaction & Taste, 6th, Gif Sur Yvette, France, 1977. Olfaction & Taste VI: Proceedings. LeMagnen, J. & Macleod, P., eds. 500p. 25.00 (ISBN 0-904147-08-8). Info Retrieval.
Pfaffmann, Carl, ed. Olfaction & Taste. LC 67-2852. (Illus.). 1969. 23.00 (ISBN 0-87470-013-2). Rockefeller.
Valnet, Jean. The Practice of Aromatherapy. (Illus.). 1981. pap. 8.95 (ISBN 0-89281-026-2). Inner Tradit.
OLIGOCHAETA
Brinkhurst, Ralph O. & Cook, David G., eds. Aquatic Oligochaete Biology. 530p. 1980. 55.00 (ISBN 0-306-40338-2). Plenum Pub.
Gates, G. E. Burmese Earthworms: An Introduction to the Systematics & Biology of Megadrile Oligochaetes with Special Reference to Southeast Asia. LC 72-83461. (Transactions Ser.: Vol. 62, Pt. 7). (Illus.). 1972. pap. 5.00 (ISBN 0-87169-627-4). Am Philos.
Jamieson, B. G. Ultrastructure of the Oligochaeta. LC 81-66699. 1981. price not set (ISBN 0-12-380180-X). Acad Pr.
Kuhne, Walter G. The Liassic Therapsid Oligokyphus. (Illus.). iii, 150p. 1956. 17.50x (ISBN 0-565-00115-9, Pub. by British Mus Nat Hist England). Sabbot-Natural Hist Bks.
Stephenson, J. The Oligochaeta. (Illus.). 1930. 100.00 (ISBN 3-7682-0750-1). Lubrecht & Cramer.
OLIGOPHRENIA
see Mental Deficiency
OLIGOPOLIES
Blair, John M. Economic Concentration: Structure, Behavior, & Public Policy. LC 79-187702. (Harbrace Ser. in Business & Economics). (Illus.). 832p. 1972. 16.95 (ISBN 0-15-127425-8). HarBraceJ.
Eichner, A. S. The Megacorp & Oligopoly. LC 75-17115. (Illus.). 450p. 1976. 35.50 (ISBN 0-521-20885-8). Cambridge U Pr.
Fouraker, Lawrence E. & Seigel, Sidney. Bargaining Behavior. LC 77-23058. 1977. Repr. of 1963 ed. lib. bdg. 24.00x (ISBN 0-8371-9738-4, FOBB). Greenwood.
Friedman, James W. Oligopoly & the Theory of Games. (Advanced Textbooks in Economics Ser.: Vol. 8). 1977. 29.00 (ISBN 0-7204-0505-X, North-Holland). Elsevier.
Friedman, James W. & Hoggatt, Austin C., eds. An Experiment in Non-Cooperative Oligopoly. (Research in Experimental Economics Supplement Ser.: No. 1). 216p. 1980. 32.50 (ISBN 0-89232-121-0). Jai Pr.
Greenhut, Melvin L. A Theory of the Firm in Economic Space. LC 71-112946. (Illus.). 389p. 1974. Repr. of 1970 ed. text ed. 15.00x (ISBN 0-914872-00-1). Austin Pr.
Knickerbocker, Frederick T. Oligopolistic Reaction & Multinational Enterprise. LC 72-94361. 230p. 1973. 10.00x (ISBN 0-87584-102-3). Harvard Busn.
Lambin, J. J. Advertising, Competition & Market Conduct in Oligopoly Over Time. (Contributions to Economic Analysis: Vol. 94). 1976. 27.00 (ISBN 0-444-10905-6, North-Holland). Elsevier.
Long, Stewart L. The Development of the Television Network Oligopoly. new ed. Sterling, Christopher H., ed. LC 78-21725. (Dissertations in Broadcasting Ser.). (Illus.). 1979. lib. bdg. 12.00x (ISBN 0-405-11764-7). Arno.
Okuguchi, J. Expectations & Stability in Oligopoly Models. (Lecture Notes in Economics & Mathematical Systems Ser.: Vol. 138). 1977. soft cover 10.10 (ISBN 0-387-08056-2). Springer-Verlag.
Reid, Gavin. The Kinked Demand Curve Analysis of Oligopoly. 155p. 1981. 12.50x (ISBN 0-85224-390-1, Pub. by Edinburgh U Pr Scotland). Columbia U Pr.
Shubik, Martin & Levitan, Richard. Market Structure & Behavior. LC 79-27108. (Illus.). 267p. 1980. text ed. 18.50x (ISBN 0-674-55026-9). Harvard U Pr.
Tun Thin. Theory of Markets. LC 60-5398. (Economic Studies: No. 114). (Illus.). 1960. 6.95x (ISBN 0-674-88080-3). Harvard U Pr.
Vatter, Harold G. Small Enterprise & Oligopoly. Bruchey, Stuart & Carosso, Vincent P., eds. LC 78-18152. (Small Business Enterprise in America Ser.). 1979. Repr. of 1955 ed. lib. bdg. 10.00x (ISBN 0-405-11508-3). Arno.
Worcester, Dean A., Jr. Monopoly, Big Business, & Welfare in Postwar United States. LC 66-19564. 256p. 1967. 14.00 (ISBN 0-295-74059-0). U of Wash Pr.
OLIGOSACCHARIDES
Stanek, Jaroslav, et al. Oligosaccharides. Mayer, Karel, tr. 1965. 62.00 (ISBN 0-12-663756-3). Acad Pr.
OLIPHANT, LAURENCE, 1829-1888
Henderson, Philip. The Life of Laurence Oliphant: Traveller, Diplomat & Mystic. 281p. 1981. Repr. of 1956 ed. lib. bdg. 30.00 (ISBN 0-8495-2364-8). Arden Lib.
Oliphant, Margaret. Memoir of the Life of Laurence Oliphant & of Alice Oliphant, His Wife. LC 75-36915. (Occult Ser.). 1976. Repr. of 1892 ed. 24.00x (ISBN 0-405-07970-2). Arno.
Schneider, Herbert & Lawton, George. Prophet & a Pilgrim. LC 78-134433. (Illus.). Repr. of 1942 ed. 36.50 (ISBN 0-404-05610-5). AMS Pr.
OLIPHANT, MARGARET OLIPHANT (WILSON) 1828-1897
Clarke, Isabel C. Six Portraits. facs. ed. LC 67-26725. (Essay Index Reprint Ser). 1935. 18.00 (ISBN 0-8369-0309-9). Arno.
OLITSKI, JULES
Moffett, Kenworth. Jules Olitski. (Illus.). 240p. 1981. 65.00 (ISBN 0-8109-1403-4). Abrams.
OLIVE
Meeting, Cordoba, Spain, 19-20 September 1974. Establishment of Olive Research Networks: Report. (Illus.). 1975. pap. 7.50 (ISBN 0-685-62393-9, F1093, FAO). Unipub.
Report of the Third Session of the FAO Olive Production Committee. (Illus.). 1977. pap. 15.00 (ISBN 92-5-100223-1, F1098, FAO). Unipub.

Steffanides, George F. Olives & Olive Oil for the Gourmet. LC 38-9182. (Illus.). iv, 49p. 1980. pap. 2.50 (ISBN 0-686-61076-8). Steffanides.

OLIVE INDUSTRY AND TRADE

China: Development of Olive Production. 163p. 1981. pap. 10.50 (ISBN 92-5-100995-3, F2097, FAO). Unipub.

Manual of Olive Oil Technology. (Illus.). 164p. 1976. pap. 17.75 (ISBN 0-685-66348-5, F1038, FAO). Unipub.

Modern Olive-Growing. (Illus.). 1978. pap. 17.00 (ISBN 92-5-100249-5, F1351, FAO). Unipub.

OLIVER, MARIA ROSA, 1904-

Frank, Waldo D. City Block. LC 75-112789. Repr. of 1922 ed. 21.50 (ISBN 0-404-02546-3). AMS Pr.

OLIVER, ROBERT, 1757?-1834

Bruchey, Stuart W. Robert Oliver & Mercantile Bookkeeping in the Early Nineteenth Century. LC 75-18460. (History of Accounting Ser.). 1976. 12.00x (ISBN 0-405-07544-8). Arno.

--Robert Oliver: Merchant of Baltimore, 1783-1819. LC 78-64225. (Johns Hopkins University. Studies in the Social Sciences. Seventy-Fourth Ser. 1956: 1). Repr. of 1956 ed. 31.00 (ISBN 0-404-61327-6). AMS Pr.

--Robert Oliver, Merchant of Baltimore, 1783-1819. Carosso, Vincent P., ed. LC 78-18954. (Small Business Enterprise in America Ser.). 1979. Repr. of 1956 ed. lib. bdg. 28.00x (ISBN 0-405-11458-3). Arno.

OLIVIER, LAWRENCE KERR, SIR, 1907-

Daniels, Robert L. Lawrence Olivier: Theater & Cinema. LC 78-75346. (Illus.). 1980. 19.95 (ISBN 0-498-02287-0). A S Barnes.

Gourlay, Logan, ed. Olivier. LC 73-88745. 1975. pap. 4.95 (ISBN 0-8128-1859-8). Stein & Day.

Hirsch, Foster. Laurence Olivier. (Theatrical Arts Ser.). 1979. lib. bdg. 12.50 (ISBN 0-8057-9260-0). Twayne.

Kiernan, Thomas. Sir Larry. Chase, Edward T., ed. LC 81-50085. (Illus.). 384p. 1981. 15.00 (ISBN 0-8129-0989-5). Times Bks.

Morley, Margaret. The Films of Laurence Olivier. (Illus.). 1978. text ed. 14.95 (ISBN 0-8065-0613-X). Citadel Pr.

OLMECS

see also Indians of Mexico

Benson, Elizabeth P. An Olmec Figure at Dumbarton Oaks. LC 70-184640. (Studies in Pre-Columbian Art & Archaeology: No. 8). (Illus.). 95p. 1971. pap. 4.00x (ISBN 0-88402-035-5, Ctr Pre-Columbian). Dumbarton Oaks.

Benson, Elizabeth P., ed. The Olmec & Their Neighbors: Essays in Memory of Matthew W. Stirling. LC 79-49262. (Illus.). 346p. 1981. 30.00x (ISBN 0-88402-098-3, Ctr Pre-Columbian). Dumbarton Oaks.

Coe, Michael D. & Diehl, Richard A. In the Land of the Olmec, 2 vols. (Dancinger Ser.). (Illus.). 1980. Set. 100.00x (ISBN 0-292-77549-0); Vol. 1, The/archaeology Of San Lorenzo Techochtitan, 436pp. Vol. 2, The/people Of The River, 204pp. U of Tex Pr.

Gay, Carlo T. E. Xochipala: The Beginnings of Olmec Art. LC 70-187566. (Publications of the Princeton Univ. Art Museum). (Illus.). 64p. 1972. 16.00x (ISBN 0-691-03880-5). Princeton U Pr.

Luckert, Karl W. Olmec Religion: A Key to Middle America & Beyond. LC 75-12869. (The Civilization of the American Indian: Vol. 137). (Illus.). 250p. 1976. 11.95 (ISBN 0-8061-1298-0). U of Okla Pr.

OLMSTED, FREDERICK LAW, 1822-1903

Beveridge, Charles E. & McLaughlin, Charles C., eds. The Papers of Frederick Law Olmsted: Vol. II: Slavery & the South, 1852-1857. LC 80-8881. (The Papers of Frederick Law Olmsted). (Illus.). 528p. 1981. text ed. 27.50x (ISBN 0-8018-2242-4). Johns Hopkins.

Fabos, Julius G., et al. Frederick Law Olmsted Sr: Founder of Landscape Architecture in America. LC 68-19670. (Illus.). 1968. pap. 6.00x (ISBN 0-87023-052-2). U of Mass Pr.

McLaughlin, Charles Capen, ed. The Papers of Frederick Law Olmsted, Vol. 1: The Formative Years, 1822-1852. LC 76-47378. (The Papers of Frederick Law Olmsted Ser). (Illus.). 448p. 1977. 22.50x (ISBN 0-8018-1798-6). Johns Hopkins.

Mitchell, Broadus. Frederick Law Olmsted: A Critic of the Old South. LC 68-25677. 1968. Repr. of 1924 ed. 7.50 (ISBN 0-8462-1170-X). Russell.

--Frederick Law Olmsted, a Critic of the Old South. LC 78-64114. (Johns Hopkins University. Studies in the Social Sciences. Forty-Second Ser. 1924: 2). Repr. of 1924 ed. 11.50 (ISBN 0-404-61229-6). AMS Pr.

Olmsted, Frederick. The Papers of Frederick Law Olmsted: Slavery & the South 1852-1857, Vol. II. Beveridge, Charles E. & McLaughlin, Charles C., eds. 528p. 1981. 27.50 (ISBN 0-8018-2242-4). Johns Hopkins.

Olmsted, Frederick L. A Journey Through Texas; or, a Saddle-Trip on the Southwestern Frontier. LC 78-7028. (Barker Texas History Center Ser: No. 2). (Illus.). 564p. 1978. pap. 6.95 (ISBN 0-292-74008-5). U of Tex Pr.

Stevenson, Elizabeth. Park-Maker: A Life of Frederick Law Olmsted. (Illus.). 1977. 19.95 (ISBN 0-02-614440-9, 61444). Macmillan.

White, Dana F. & Kramer, Victor A., eds. Olmsted South: Old South Critic-New South Planner. LC 78-20019. (Contributions in American Studies: No. 43). 1979. lib. bdg. 27.50 (ISBN 0-313-20724-0, WOS/). Greenwood.

Wurman, Richard S., et al. The Nature of Recreation: A Handbook in Honor of Frederick Law Olmsted. 100p. 1972. pap. 5.95 (ISBN 0-262-73034-0). MIT Pr.

OLNEY, RICHARD, 1835-1917

Eggert, Gerald G. Richard Olney: Evolution of a Statesman. LC 73-6878. (Illus.). 432p. 1974. 17.50x (ISBN 0-271-01162-9). Pa St U Pr.

James, Henry. Richard Olney & His Public Service. LC 70-87445. (American Scene Ser). (Illus.). 1971. Repr. of 1923 ed. lib. bdg. 32.50 (ISBN 0-306-71516-3). Da Capo.

OLSON, BRUCE

Olson. Bruchko. LC 73-81494. 1977. pap. 2.45 (ISBN 0-88419-133-8). Creation Hse.

OLSON, CHARLES, 1910-1970

Byrd, Don. Charles Olson's Maximus. LC 79-21788. 225p. 1980. 15.00 (ISBN 0-252-00779-4). U of Ill Pr.

Christensen, Paul. Charles Olson: Call Him Ishmael. (Illus.). 261p. 1979. text ed. 12.95x (ISBN 0-292-71046-1). U of Tex Pr.

Merrill, Thomas F. The Poetry of Charles Olson: A Primer. LC 81-50341. 240p. 1982. 19.50 (ISBN 0-87413-196-0). U Delaware Pr.

Olson, Charles & Creeley, Robert. Charles Olson & Robert Creeley: The Complete Correspondence, Vol. 1. Butterick, George, ed. (Illus.). 200p. 1980. 20.00 (ISBN 0-87685-400-5); ltd. ed. 30.00 (ISBN 0-87685-401-3); pap. 7.50 (ISBN 0-87685-399-8). Black Sparrow.

--Charles Olson & Robert Creeley: The Complete Correspondence, Vol. 2. Butterick, George, ed. (Illus.). 200p. (Orig.). 1980. 20.00 (ISBN 0-87685-441-2); ltd. ed. 30.00 (ISBN 0-87685-442-0); pap. 7.50 (ISBN 0-87685-440-4). Black Sparrow.

--Charles Olson & Robert Creeley: The Complete Correspondence, Vol. 3. Butterick, George F., ed. (Illus.). 200p. (Orig.). 1981. 20.00 (ISBN 0-87685-483-8); deluxe ed. 30.00 (ISBN 0-87685-484-6); pap. 7.50 (ISBN 0-87685-482-X). Black Sparrow.

--Charles Olson & Robert Creeley: The Complete Correspondence, Vol. 4. Butterick, George F., ed. (Illus.). 200p. (Orig.). 1981. deluxe ed. 30.00 signed (ISBN 0-87685-486-2); pap. 7.50 (ISBN 0-87685-485-4); deluxe ed. 30.00 (ISBN 0-87685-487-0). Black Sparrow.

Olson, Charles F. Muthologos: The Collected Lectures & Interviews, Vol. I. Butterick, George F., ed. LC 77-1955. (Writing Ser.: No. 35). 1979. 12.00 (ISBN 0-87704-032-X); pap. 5.00 (ISBN 0-87704-031-1). Four Seasons Foun.

Paul, Sherman. Olson's Push: Origin, Black Mountain, & Recent American Poetry. LC 78-6694. 1978. 20.00x (ISBN 0-8071-0461-2). La State U Pr.

Von Hallberg, Robert. Charles Olson: The Scholar's Art. LC 78-4464. 1979. 15.00x (ISBN 0-674-11130-3). Harvard U Pr.

OLSON, FLOYD BJORNSTJERNE, 1891-1936

Mayer, George. Political Career of Floyd B. Olson. (Illus.). 1951. 10.00x (ISBN 0-8166-0071-6). U of Minn Pr.

OLYMPIA

Holmberg, E. J. Delphi & Olympia. (Studies in Mediterranean Archaeology Pocket Bk.). 1980. text ed. 14.00x (ISBN 91-85058-92-0). Humanities.

OLYMPIC GAMES

Africanus, Sextus J. List of Olympian Victors. Rutgers, I., ed. 196p. 1980. 20.00 (ISBN 0-89005-351-Q). Ares.

All About Discus. (Illus.). 7.95 (ISBN 0-87666-761-2, PS669). TFH Pubns.

American Alliance for Health, Physical Education & Recreation. Special Olympics Instructional Manual: From Beginners to Champions. 1972. pap. 2.75x (ISBN 0-685-42441-3, 245-25322). AAHPERD.

Associated Press & Grolier, eds. The Olympic Story Nineteen Eighty. (Illus.). 256p. 1981. 14.95 (ISBN 0-531-09942-3). Watts.

Basunov, B. A. Olympic Moscow. 172p. 1979. 13.00 (ISBN 0-8285-1585-9, Pub. by Progress Pubs Russia). Imported Pubns.

Booker, Christopher. The Games War: A Moscow Journal. 208p. 1981. 18.50 (ISBN 0-571-11755-4, Pub. by Faber & Faber); pap. 8.95 (ISBN 0-571-11763-5). Merrimack Bk Serv.

Brant, Marshall. The Games. (Illus.). 281p. 1980. pap. 7.95 (ISBN 0-906071-19-4). Proteus Pub NY.

Carroll, Walter J., ed. Olympic's Film Finder: Nineteen Eighty-One Business Edition. 1981. 24.00x (ISBN 0-88367-601-X). Olympic Media.

Christesen, Barbara. The First Olympic Games. LC 78-15976. (Famous Firsts Ser.). (Illus.). 1978. lib. bdg. 7.35 (ISBN 0-686-51102-6). Silver.

Daws, Ron. Self-Made Olympian. LC 75-20960. (Illus.). 158p. 1977. pap. 3.95 (ISBN 0-89037-103-2); handbk. 5.95 (ISBN 0-89037-104-0). Anderson World.

Dias, Susan. The Official NBC Olympic Activity Book for Kids. (gr. 2-5). 1980. pap. cancelled (ISBN 0-671-95641-8). Wanderer Bks.

Durant, John. Highlights of the Olympics. 5th ed. (Illus.). (gr. 6 up). 1977. 9.95 (ISBN 0-8038-3038-6); pap. 5.95 (ISBN 0-8038-3038-6). Hastings.

Espy, Richard. The Politics of the Olympic Games. LC 78-62861. 1979. 12.95 (ISBN 0-520-03777-4); pap. 6.95 (ISBN 0-520-04395-2, CAL 493). U of Cal Pr.

The Eternal Olympics. LC 79-51381. (Illus.). 308p. 1979. 50.00 (ISBN 0-89241-092-2). Caratzas Bros.

Gauer, Werner. Die Tongefaesse aus Dem Brunnen Unterm Stadion-Nordwall und Im Suedost-Gebiet. (Olympische Forschungen: Vol. 8). (Illus.). 254p. 1975. pap. 75.50x (ISBN 3-11-004602-4). De Gruyter.

Gault, Frank & Gault, Clare. Stories from the Olympics. LC 75-42823. (Illus.). 96p. 1976. 6.95 (ISBN 0-8027-6255-7). Walker & Co.

Gilbert, Doug. The Miracle Machine. LC 79-13603. (Illus.). 1980. 10.95 (ISBN 0-698-10952-X). Coward.

Giller, Norman. The Nineteen Eighty Olympics Handbook. LC 79-23124. (Illus.). 192p. (Orig.). 12.95 (ISBN 0-03-056054-3); pap. 6.95 (ISBN 0-03-056053-5). HR&W.

Glubok, Shirley & Tamarin, Alfred. Olympic Games in Ancient Greece. LC 74-25408. (Illus.). 120p. (gr. 5-9). 1976. PLB 9.89 (ISBN 0-06-022048-1, HarpJ). Har-Row.

Graham, Peter J. & Ueberhorst, Horst. The Modern Olympics. new ed. LC 76-27945. 1976. pap. text ed. 8.95 (ISBN 0-918438-05-5). Leisure Pr.

Grombach, John V. The Official Olympic Guide, 1980. 368p. 1980. pap. 5.95 (ISBN 0-8129-0869-4). Times Bks.

Guiney, David. The Dunlop Book of the Olympics. 1979. 12.00 (ISBN 0-903214-12-1, Pub. by Terence Dalton England). State Mutual Bk.

Hacker, Jeffrey H., ed. Spectator's Guide to the 1980 Olympics. LC 79-66059. (Illus.). 1979. write for info (ISBN 0-7172-8152-3). Grolier Ed Corp.

Harris, Harold A. Greek Athletes & Athletics. LC 78-10139. (Illus.). 1979. Repr. of 1966 ed. lib. bdg. 22.25x (ISBN 0-313-20754-2, HAGR). Greenwood.

Harrison, J. E. Themis: A Study of the Social Origins of Greek Religion. 10.00 (ISBN 0-8446-2212-5). Peter Smith.

Harrison, Jane. Themis. (Illus.). 1963. pap. 17.95 (ISBN 0-686-23502-9, Merlin Pr). Carrier Pigeon.

Harrison, Jane E. Themis: A Study of the Social Origins of Greek Religion. 1979. Repr. of 1912 ed. lib. bdg. 25.00 (ISBN 0-8482-4480-X). Norwood Edns.

Hazan, Baruch A. Olympic Sports & Propaganda Games: Moscow 1980. 250p. 1982. text ed. 19.95 (ISBN 0-87855-436-X); pap. text ed. 8.95 (ISBN 0-87855-881-0). Transaction Bks.

Hemery, David. Another Hurdle: The Making of an Olympic Champion. LC 76-364. (Illus.). (YA) (gr. 9 up). 1976. 9.95 (ISBN 0-8008-0233-0). Taplinger.

Hoberman, John M. The Olympic Crisis: To Moscow & Beyond. 220p. 1981. lib. bdg. 17.50 (ISBN 0-89241-224-0); pap. 8.95 (ISBN 0-89241-225-9). Caratzas Bros.

Holum, Dianne. World of Speed Skating. (Illus.). 320p. 1982. 17.50x (ISBN 0-89490-051-X). Enslow Pubs.

Kaneko, Akitomo. Olympic Gymnastics. LC 76-1171. (Illus.). 256p. 1980. pap. 7.95 (ISBN 0-8069-8926-2). Sterling.

Kanin, David B. A Political History of the Olympic Games. (Replica Edition Ser.). 160p. 1981. lib. bdg. 17.00x (ISBN 0-86531-109-9). Westview.

Killanin & Rodda, John. The Olympic Games 1980: Moscow & Lake Placid. LC 79-13769. (Illus.). 1979. 15.95 (ISBN 0-02-563060-1); pap. 9.95 (ISBN 0-02-029260-0). Macmillan.

Killanin, Lord. The Olympic Games. 272p. 1976. 22.95 (ISBN 0-02-563050-4). Macmillan.

Killanin, Lord & Rodda, John, eds. The Olympic Games: 80 Years of People, Events & Records. (Illus.). 1976. pap. 7.95 (ISBN 0-02-029220-1, Collier). Macmillan.

Kuse, James A., ed. The Thirteenth Summer Olympics Moscow, 1980. 1979. pap. 5.95 (ISBN 0-89542-014-7). Ideals.

--The Twenty Second Winter Olympic Games. (Illus.). 1979. pap. 5.95 (ISBN 0-89542-013-9). Ideals.

Litsky, Frank. The Summer Olympics. 4th rev. ed. (First Bks.). (Illus.). (gr. 4-6). 1979. PLB 6.90 s&l (ISBN 0-531-02935-2). Watts.

Lucas, John. The Modern Olympic Games. LC 79-52025. (Illus.). 240p. 1980. 12.95 (ISBN 0-498-02447-4). A S Barnes.

Lundberg, Knud. The Olympic Hope. Date not set. 9.95 (ISBN 0-392-15344-0, SpS). Sportshelf.

MacAloon, John J. This Great Symbol: Pierre De Courbertin & the Origins of the Modern Olympic Games. LC 80-21898. 1981. lib. bdg. 25.00x (ISBN 0-226-50000-4). U of Chicago Pr.

Mandell, Richard D. The First Modern Olympics. LC 75-3773. (Illus.). 256p. 1976. 12.95 (ISBN 0-520-02983-6). U of Cal Pr.

Olympic Story: Pursuit of Excellence. LC 80-67767. (Illus.). 1980. write for info. (ISBN 0-7172-8158-2). Grolier Ed Corp.

Ortloff, George C. & Ortloff, Stephen C. Lake Placid: The Olympic Years, 1932-1980. LC 76-45314. 1976. 19.95 (ISBN 0-9601170-1-6). Macromedia Inc.

Parandowski, Jan. Olympic Discus. Malecka, A. M. & Walewski, S. A., trs. LC 64-20050. (Illus.). 1964. pap. 4.95 (ISBN 0-8044-6620-3). Ungar.

Poole, Lynn & Poole, Gray. History of the Ancient Olympic Games. (Illus.). 1963. 6.95 (ISBN 0-8392-1049-3). Astor-Honor.

Schaap, Richard. The Illustrated History of the Olympics. 3rd enl. ed. 1975. 20.00 (ISBN 0-394-48757-5). Knopf.

Segrave, Jeffrey & Chu, Donald. Olympism. LC 80-85204. 393p. 1981. cancelled (ISBN 0-931250-20-X). Human Kinetics.

Thompson, Brett R. Olympiad. LC 79-5494. (Illus.). 128p. 1980. 30.00 (ISBN 0-498-02514-4). A S Barnes.

U. S. Olympic Committee. Olympic Sports. Date not set. pap. 2.00x (ISBN 0-392-08183-0, SpS). Sportshelf.

Walt Disney Productions. Goofy Presents the Olympics: A Fun & Exciting History of the Olympics from the Ancient Games to Today. LC 79-18177. (Illus.). 128p. (gr. 2-6). 1980. 6.95 (ISBN 0-394-84224-3, BYR); PLB 6.99 (ISBN 0-394-94224-8). Random.

Wimmer, Martin. Olympic Buildings. 225p. 1977. 32.85 (ISBN 0-8417-1060-0). Adler.

Yalouris, Nikolas, ed. The Olympic Games Through the Ages. (Illus.). 1977. 60.00 (ISBN 0-89241-021-3). Caratzas Bros.

OLYMPIC MOUNTAINS

Olympic Mountain Rescue. Climber's Guide to the Olympic Mountains. 2nd ed. LC 70-163356. (Illus.). 240p. (Orig.). 1979. pap. 7.95 (ISBN 0-916890-83-X). Mountaineers.

Wood, Robert L. Men, Mules & Mountains: Lt. O'Neil's Olympic Expeditions. LC 76-15458. (Illus.). 460p. 1976. 17.50 (ISBN 0-916890-43-0). Mountaineers.

OLYMPIC NATIONAL PARK

Leissler, Frederick. Roads & Trails of Olympic National Park. 4th rev. ed. (Illus.). 114p. 1981. pap. 7.95 (ISBN 0-295-95819-7). U of Wash Pr.

Radlauer, Ruth. Olympic National Park. LC 77-5836. (Parks for People Ser.). (Illus.). (gr. 3 up). 1978. 3.95 (ISBN 0-516-17494-0, Elk Grove Bks); PLB 10.00 (ISBN 0-516-07494-6). Childrens.

Spring, Bob & Spring, Ira. The Olympic National Park. LC 74-75655. 1974. pap. 2.95 (ISBN 0-87564-615-8). Superior Pub.

Tabor, Rowland W. Guide to the Geology of Olympic National Park. LC 74-32254. (Illus.). 160p. 1975. pap. 5.95 (ISBN 0-295-95395-0). U of Wash Pr.

OLYMPIC PENINSULA

Kirk, Ruth. Exploring the Olympic Pennisula. 3rd rev. ed. LC 80-51073. (Illus.). 128p. 1980. 7.95 (ISBN 0-295-95750-6). U of Wash Pr.

OLYMPUS CAMERA

see Cameras-Types-Olympus

OMAHA INDIANS

see Indians of North America-The West

OMAI, SOUTH SEA ISLANDER

Clark, Thomas B. Omai: First Polynesian Ambassador to England. 1969. Repr. of 1940 ed. 7.95 (ISBN 0-87022-140-X). U Pr of Hawaii.

OMAN

Anthony, John D. Historical & Cultural Dictionary of the Sultanate of Oman & the Emirates of Eastern Arabia. LC 76-42216. (Historical & Cultural Dictionaries of Asia Ser.: No. 9). 1976. 10.00 (ISBN 0-8108-0975-3). Scarecrow.

Clements, F. A. Oman: The Reborn Land. 181p. 1980. text ed. 25.00x (ISBN 0-582-78300-3). Longman.

Coupland, Reginald. East Africa & Its Invaders from the Earliest Times to the Death of Seyyid Said in 1856. LC 65-17886. (Illus.). 1965. Repr. of 1938 ed. 15.00 (ISBN 0-8462-0592-0). Russell.

Gallagher, Michael & Woodcock, Martin. The Birds of Oman. (Illus.). 138p. 1981. 75.00 (ISBN 0-7043-2216-1, Pub. by Quartet England). Charles River Bks.
Hill, Ann & Hill, Daryl. The Sultanate of Oman: A Heritage. LC 76-49444. (Illus.). 1977. text ed. 42.00x (ISBN 0-582-78050-0). Longman.
The Laws of the Sultanate of Oman: The Banking Law of 1974, Vol. 1. LC 75-15148. 800p. 1975. looseleaf bdg 25.00x (ISBN 0-379-00349-X). Oceana.
Narayan, B. K. Oman & Gulf Security. (Illus.). 192p. 1979. 17.50x (ISBN 0-8002-2244-X). Intl Pubns Serv.
Peterson, John. Oman in the Twentieth Century: Political Foundations of an Emerging State. LC 78-761. (Illus.). 1978. text ed. 25.00x (ISBN 0-06-495522-2). B&N.
Phillips, Wendell. Oman a History. 15.00x (ISBN 0-86685-024-4). Intl Bk Ctr.
--Unknown Oman. (Arab Background Ser.). 1972. 15.00x (ISBN 0-86685-025-2). Intl Bk Ctr.
Saleh, Nabh. The General Principals of Saudi Arabian & Omani Company Laws. 336p. 1981. 50.00 (ISBN 0-7043-2278-1, Pub. by Quartet England). Charles River Bks.
Searle, Pauline. Dawn Over Oman. (Illus.). 1979. 15.95 (ISBN 0-04-915023-5). Allen Unwin.
Shair Management Services, ed. Business Laws & Practices of Oman. 136p. 1979. 275.00x (ISBN 0-86010-907-0, Pub. by Graham & Trotman England). State Mutual Bk.
Tinson, A. R. Orders, Decorations & Medals of the Sultanate of Oman. 1979. 42.00 (ISBN 0-686-51597-8, Pub. by Spink & Son England). S J Durst.
Townsend, John. Oman: The Making of a Modern State. LC 76-62532. 1977. 17.95x (ISBN 0-312-58432-6). St Martin.

OMAR KHAYYAM

Bowen, J. C. A New Selection from the Rubaiyat of Omar Khayyam. (Middle East Studies). (Illus.). 1978. 12.75x (ISBN 0-85668-048-6, Pub. by Aris & Phillips). Intl Schol Bk Serv.
Draper, John W. Orientalia & Shakespeareana. LC 77-20542. 1978. 6.95 (ISBN 0-533-00608-2). Vantage.
Esfandiary, Hossein-Ali N., ed. The Rubaiyat of Omar Khayyam. (Illus.). 1977. 39.95 (ISBN 0-89955-247-1, Pub. by Esfandiary). Intl Schol Bk Serv.
Jackson, Abraham V. From Constantinople to the Home of Omar Khayyam. LC 74-149389. (Illus.). Repr. of 1911 ed. 33.75 (ISBN 0-404-09012-5). AMS Pr.
Jackson, Holbrook. Edward Fitzgerald & Omar Kayyam: An Essay & a Bibliography. LC 74-30069. 1972. Repr. of 1899 ed. lib. bdg. 8.50 (ISBN 0-8414-5339-X). Folcroft.
--Edward Fitzgerald & Omar Khayyam. 1980. Repr. lib. bdg. 8.50 (ISBN 0-8492-1274-X). R West.
Le Gallienne, Richard. Rubaiyat of Omar Khayyam. LC 78-11468. Repr. of 1902 ed. lib. bdg. 10.00 (ISBN 0-8414-5756-5). Folcroft.
Pattinson, J. S. The Symbolism of the Rubaiyat of Omar Khayyam. LC 74-9970. 1921. 8.50 (ISBN 0-8414-6779-X). Folcroft.
Rothfield, Otto. Omar Khayyam & His Age. LC 74-1126. 1974. Repr. of 1922 ed. lib. bdg. 12.50 (ISBN 0-8414-7309-9). Folcroft.
Saklatwalla, Jamshedji E. Omar Khayyam As a Mystic. LC 74-9971. 1928. 8.50 (ISBN 0-8414-7503-2). Folcroft.
Tutin, John R. Concordance to FitzGerald's Translation of the Rubaiyat of Omar Khayyam. LC 68-58471. (Bibliography & Reference Ser.: No. 256). 1969. Repr. of 1900 ed. 12.50 (ISBN 0-8337-3581-0). B Franklin.
--Concordance to Fitzgerald's Translation of the Rubaiyat of Omar Khayyam. Repr. of 1891 ed. 12.50 (ISBN 0-384-62040-X). Johnson Repr.

OMBUDSMAN

Anderson, Stanley V. & Moore, John E., eds. Transcript of Ombudsman Workshop: Recent Experience in the United States. LC 72-5772. 294p. (Orig., Obudsman workshop, honolulu, may 5-7, 1971). 1972. pap. 3.00x (ISBN 0-87772-154-8). Inst Gov Stud Berk.
Fitzharris, Timothy L. The Desirability of a Correctional Ombudsman. LC 72-13057. 114p. (Orig.). 1973. pap. 4.00x (ISBN 0-87772-155-6). Inst Gov Stud Berk.
Gellhorn, Walter. Ombudsmen & Others: Citizen's Protectors in Nine Countries. LC 66-23465. 1966. 22.50x (ISBN 0-674-63400-4). Harvard U Pr.
Gregory, Roy & Hutchesson, Peter. The Parliamentary Ombudsman. (Royal Institute of Public Administration). 1975. text ed. 50.00x (ISBN 0-04-328009-9). Allen Unwin.
Gwyn, William B. Barriers to Establishing Urban Ombudsmen: The Case of Newark. new ed. LC 74-11446. 93p. 1974. pap. 4.50x (ISBN 0-87772-200-5). Inst Gov Stud Berk.
--Ombudsman Policy Innovation in the English-Speaking World. LC 80-15829. (IGS Research Report: No. 80-2). 51p. 1981. pap. 5.75 (ISBN 0-87772-274-9). Inst Gov Stud Berk.
Hiden, Mikael. The Ombudsman in Finland: The First Fifty Years. Rowat, Donald C., ed. Bell, Aaron, tr. from Finnish. LC 73-14864. (Illus.). 198p. (Orig.). 1973. 8.00x (ISBN 0-87772-191-2). Inst Gov Stud Berk.
Hill, Larry B. The Model Ombudsman: Institutionalizing New Zealand's Democratic Experiment. LC 76-3258. 1976. 30.00 (ISBN 0-691-07579-4). Princeton U Pr.
--Parliament & the Ombudsman in New Zealand. (Legislative Research Ser.: No. 8). 1973. pap. 3.50 (ISBN 0-686-18649-4). Univ OK Gov Res.
Peel, Roy V. & Sellin, Thorsten, eds. Ombudsman or Citizen's Defender: A Modern Institution. LC 68-21996. (Annals of the American Academy of Political & Social Science: No. 377). (Orig.). 1968. 7.50 (ISBN 0-87761-107-6); pap. 6.00 (ISBN 0-87761-106-8). Am Acad Pol Soc Sci.
Rowat, Donald C., ed. Ombudsman: Citizen's Defender. 2nd ed. LC 69-138157. 1968. pap. 6.00 (ISBN 0-8020-6089-7). U of Toronto Pr.
Sawer, G. Ombudsmen. 2nd ed. 1968. pap. 3.00x (ISBN 0-522-83900-2, Pub. by Melbourne U Pr). Intl Schol Bk Serv.
Weeks, Kent M. Ombudsmen Around the World: A Comparative Chart. new ed. LC 73-13631. 101p. 1973. 3.00x (ISBN 0-87772-190-4). Inst Gov Stud Berk.
--Ombudsmen Around the World: A Comparative Chart. 2nd ed. LC 78-17224. 1978. pap. 7.00x (ISBN 0-87772-258-7). Inst Gov Stud Berk.
Wyner, Alan J. The Nebraska Ombudsman: Innovation in State Government. new ed. LC 74-8958. (Illus.). 160p. 1974. pap. 6.75x (ISBN 0-87772-199-8). Inst Gov Stud Berk.
Wyner, Alan J., ed. Executive Ombudsmen in the United States. LC 73-8971. (Illus.). 315p. 1973. 5.50x (ISBN 0-87772-156-4). Inst Gov Stud Berk.

OMELETS

see Cookery (Eggs)

OMENS

see also Divination; Dreams; Oracles; Signs and Symbols

Clay, Albert T. Epics, Hymns, Omens & Other Texts. LC 78-63519. (Babylonian Records in the Library of J. Pierpont Morgan: 4). Repr. of 1923 ed. 30.00 (ISBN 0-404-60124-3). AMS Pr.
Leichty, E. V. The Series Summa Izbu. LC 66-25697. 24.00 (ISBN 0-685-71732-1). J J Augustin.
Lewis, Naphtali. The Interpretation of Dreams & Portents. (Aspects of Antiquity Ser.). 1976. text ed. 9.00 (ISBN 0-88866-571-7); pap. text ed. 3.95 (ISBN 0-88866-572-5). Samuel Stevens.
Wasserzug, Dr. G. Signs & Wonders. 0.95 (ISBN 0-686-12836-2). Midnight Call.

OMNIBUS BILL, 1850

see Compromise of 1850

OMNIBUS SERVICE

see Motor Bus Lines

OMNIBUSES

see also Motor Buses

ON-LINE DATA PROCESSING

see also Real-Time Data Processing; Time-Sharing Computer Systems

Abbott, Joe. On-Line Programming: A Management Guide. 110p. (Orig.). 1981. pap. 17.50x (ISBN 0-85012-295-3). Intl Pubns Serv.
Atherton, Pauline & Christian, Roger W. Librarians & Online Services. LC 77-25275. (Professional Librarian Ser.). 1977. 24.50x (ISBN 0-914236-13-X). Knowledge Indus.
Automated Education Center. Management of On Line Systems. 1969. 19.00 (ISBN 0-686-01997-0). Mgmt Info Serv.
--On Line Computing Systems. LC 65-21221. 19.00 (ISBN 0-686-01993-8). Mgmt Info Serv.
Black, W. Wayne. An Introduction to On-Line Computers. LC 70-141580. (Illus.). 462p. 1971. 67.25x (ISBN 0-677-02930-6). Gordon.
Down, P. J. Fault Diagnosis in Data Communications Systems. LC 78-30112. (Illus.). 1977. pap. 30.00x (ISBN 0-85012-186-8). Intl Pubns Serv.
Hall, J. L. & Brown, M. J., eds. On-Line Bibliographic Data Bases: An International Directory. 2nd ed. 213p. 1981. 70.00 (ISBN 0-8103-0528-3, Pub. by Aslib England). Gale.
Henry, et al. Online Searching: An Introduction. LC 80-40242. 1980. 31.95 (ISBN 0-408-10696-4). Butterworth.
Hoadley, I. B. & Thorson, A. R., eds. Automated On-Line Circulation System. LC 73-620070. 1973. pap. 4.50 (ISBN 0-88215-031-6). Ohio St U Lib.
Houghton, Bernard & Convey, John. On-Line Information Retrieval Systems: A User's Manual. 1978. 15.00 (ISBN 0-208-01660-0, Linnet). Shoe String.
How to Go on-Line: Guidelines for the Establishment of on-Line Services in Public Libraries. 1981. 15.00x (ISBN 0-905984-57-9, Pub. by Brit Lib England). State Mutual Bk.
Juergens, Bonnie. Self Instruction to the OCLC Models 100 & 105 Terminals, No. 1. rev., 2nd ed. Duffy, Michelle, ed. (AMIGOS Training Series: No. 1). 40p. 3 hole punch, stapled 10.00 (ISBN 0-938288-00-8). AMIGOS Biblio.
Karplus, Walter J., ed. On-Line Computing: Time-Shared Man-Computer Systems. LC 79-13377. 348p. 1979. Repr. of 1967 ed. lib. bdg. 28.50 (ISBN 0-88275-989-2). Krieger.
Klerer, Melvin & Reinfelds, Juris, eds. Interactive Systems for Experimental Applied Mathematics. 1968. 50.00 (ISBN 0-12-414650-3). Acad Pr.
Lancaster, F. W. & Fayen, E. G. Information Retrieval on-Line. LC 73-9697. (Information Sciences Ser.). 597p. 1973. 32.95 (ISBN 0-471-51235-4, Pub. by Wiley-Interscience). Wiley.
Lefkovitz, David. File Structures for on-Line Systems. (Illus.). 1969. 14.85x (ISBN 0-8104-5943-4). Hayden.
Meadow, Charles T. & Cochrane. Basics of Online Searching. LC 80-23050. (Information Science Ser.). 245p. 1981. 15.95 (ISBN 0-471-05283-3, Pub. by Wiley-Interscience). Wiley.
On-Line Experiments in Public Libraries. 1981. 15.00x (ISBN 0-905984-56-0, Pub. by Brit Lib England). State Mutual Bk.
Orr, W. D. Conversational Computers. 227p. 1968. 16.00 (ISBN 0-471-65708-5, Pub. by Wiley). Krieger.
Pritchard, J. A. Selection & Use of Terminals in On-Line Systems. LC 74-76261. 120p. 1974. 21.00x (ISBN 0-85012-117-5). Intl Pubns Serv.
Rubin, Martin L. Documentation Standards & Procedures for Online Systems. 1979. text ed. 23.50 (ISBN 0-442-80042-8). Van Nos Reinhold.
Williams, Martha E. & Hogan, Thomas H., eds. National Online Meeting Proceedings, 1981. (Illus.). 554p. 1981. pap. text ed. 40.00 (ISBN 0-938734-02-4). Learned Info.
Yourdon, Edward. Design of on-Line Computer Systems. (Illus.). 576p. 1972. ref. ed. 25.95 (ISBN 0-13-201301-0). P-H.

ONANISM

see Masturbation

ONASSIS, JACQUELINE KENNEDY, 1929-

Birmingham, Stephen. Jacqueline Bouvier Kennedy Onassis. (Illus.). 1979. pap. 2.50 (ISBN 0-671-82862-2). PB.
Frischauer, Willi. Jackie. 256p. 1976. 13.95 (ISBN 0-7181-1545-7, Pub. by Michael Joseph). Merrimack Bk Serv.
Kelley, Kitty. Jackie Oh! 1978. 12.00 (ISBN 0-8184-0265-2). Lyle Stuart.
--Jackie Oh! 1979. pap. 2.50 (ISBN 0-345-28327-9). Ballantine.
Shulman, Irving. Jackie: The Exploitation of a First Lady. Orig. Title: Jackie Factories. 1970. 6.50 (ISBN 0-671-27052-4). Trident.
Watney, Hedda L. Jackie O. (Illus.). 1979. pap. 2.25 (ISBN 0-8439-0662-6, Leisure Bks). Nordon Pubns.

ONCHI, KOSHIRO, 1891-1945

Onchi, Koshiro, et al. Onchi: Prints of Onchi (Koshiro) (Illus.). 327p. 1975. 210.00x (ISBN 0-8150-0776-0). Wittenborn.

ONCHOCERIASIS

Buck, A. A., ed. Onchocerciasis: Symptomatology, Pathology, Diagnosis. (Also avail. in French). 1974. 4.80 (ISBN 92-4-156041-X). World Health.
Onchocerciasis & Filariasis. (Bulletin of WHO: Vol. 27, Nos. 4-5). 224p. (Eng. & Fr.). 1962. pap. 7.20 (ISBN 0-686-09187-6). World Health.
Rodger, Frederick C., ed. Onchocerciasis in Zaire. 1977. text ed. 50.00 (ISBN 0-08-020619-0). Pergamon.
WHO Expert Committee. Athens, 1973, 3rd. WHO Expert Committee on Filariasis: Report. (Technical Report Ser.: No. 542). (Also avail. in French & Spanish). 1974. pap. 2.00 (ISBN 92-4-120542-3). World Health.
WHO Expert Committee on Onchocerciasis, 2nd, Geneva, 1965. Report. (Technical Report Ser: No. 335). 96p. (Eng, Fr, Rus, & Span.). 1966. pap. 2.00 (ISBN 92-4-120335-8). World Health.

ONCOGENIC VIRUSES

Biology Colloquium, 34th, Oregon State University, 1973. The Biology of Tumor Viruses: Proceedings. Beaudreau, George S., ed. LC 52-19235. (Illus.). 144p. 1976. pap. text ed. 8.95 (ISBN 0-87071-173-3). Oreg St U Pr.
Cold Spring Harbor Symposia on Quantitative Biology: Tumor Viruses, Vol. 39. LC 34-8174. (Illus.). 1258p. 1975. 95.00 (ISBN 0-87969-038-0). Cold Spring Harbor.
Crowell, R., et al, eds. Tumor Virus Infections & Immunity. (Eastern Pennsylvania Branch of the American Society for Microbiology Symposia Ser). (Illus.). 250p. 1976. 29.50 (ISBN 0-8391-0891-5). Univ Park.
Gallo, Robert G., ed. Recent Advances in Cancer Research: Cell Biology, Molecular Biology & Tumor Virology. (Uniscience Ser.). 1977. Vol. 1, 280p. 64.95 (ISBN 0-8493-5138-3); Vol. 2, 240 Pgs. 59.95 (ISBN 0-8493-5139-1). CRC Pr.
Gross, Ludwik. Oncogenic Viruses. 3rd ed. 1200p. 1981. 150.00 (ISBN 0-08-026830-7); pap. 125.00 (ISBN 0-08-028003-X). Pergamon.
Hanna, Michael G., Jr. & Rapp, Fred, eds. Contemporary Tonics in Immunology: Immunology of Oncogenic Viruses. (Illus.). 289p. 1977. 27.50 (ISBN 0-306-37806-X, Plenum Pr). Plenum Pub.
Ikawa, Yoji & Odaka, Tadeshi, eds. Oncogenic Viruses & Host Cell Genes. LC 78-31253. 1979. 32.00 (ISBN 0-12-370650-5). Acad Pr.
Johnson, Richard T. Viral Infections of the Nervous System. 1981. write for info. (ISBN 0-89004-426-0, 484). Raven.
Kaplan, Albert S., ed. Viral Transformation & Endogenour Viruses. 1974. 25.50 (ISBN 0-12-397060-1). Acad Pr.
Klein, George, ed. Advances in Viral Oncology, Vol. 1. (Advances in Viral Oncology Ser.). 1982. text ed. price not set (ISBN 0-89004-692-1). Raven.
Koprowski, Hilary, ed. Neoplastic Transformation: Mechanisms & Consequences. (Dahlem Workshop Reports Ser.: L.S.R.R. No. 7). 1977. pap. 28.60 (ISBN 0-89573-091-X). Verlag Chemie.
--Neoplastic Transformation: Mechanisms & Consequences. (Dahlem Workshop Reports Ser.: L.S.R.R. No. 7). 1977. pap. 28.60 (ISBN 0-89573-091-X). Verlag Chemie.
Kurstak, Edouard & Maramorosch, Karl, eds. Viruses, Evolution & Cancer. 1974. 78.00 (ISBN 0-12-429760-9). Acad Pr.
Strayer, D. R. & Gillespie, D. H. The Nature & Organization of Retroviral Genes in Animal Cells. (Virology Monographs: Vol. 17). (Illus.). 117p. 1980. 39.80 (ISBN 0-387-81563-5). Springer-Verlag.
Symposium. Nuremberg, Germany, Oct. 14-16, 1974. Oncogenesis & Herpesviruses II: Proceedings, 2 pts. De The, G., et al, eds. Incl. Pt. 1. Biochemistry of Viral Replication & in Vitro Transformation. 40.00 (ISBN 0-686-16808-9); Pt. 2. Epidemiology, Host Response & Control. 32.00 (ISBN 0-686-16809-7). (IARC Scientific Pub.: No. 11). 1975. World Health.
Tooze, J. & Sambrook, J., eds. Selected Papers in Tumour Virology. LC 74-81418. (Illus.). 1040p. 1974. pap. text ed. 22.00x (ISBN 0-87969-112-3). Cold Spring Harbor.
Tooze, John, ed. DNA Tumor Viruses: Molecular Biology of Tumor Viruses. 2nd ed. LC 79-19882. (Cold Spring Harbor Monograph Series: Vol. 10b). 945p. 1980. 65.00 (ISBN 0-87969-126-3). Cold Spring Harbor.

ONCOLOGY

see also Cancer; Oncogenic Viruses; Tumors

American Society of Hospital Pharmacists Institute on Oncology Pharmacy Practice. Proceedings. Caro, J. P., ed. 128p. 1979. 23.00 (ISBN 0-444-00369-X); pap. 15.00 (ISBN 0-444-00373-8). Elsevier.
Anfinsen, C. B., et al, eds. Current Research in Oncology. 1973. pap. 20.00 (ISBN 0-12-058752-1). Acad Pr.
Auspices of the International Union Against Cancer, ed. Clinical Oncology: A Manual for Students & Doctors. 2nd ed. (Illus.). 1978. pap. 18.50 (ISBN 0-387-08868-7). Springer-Verlag.
Barber, Hugh R. Manual of Gynecologic Oncology. 356p. 1980. pap. text ed. 19.50 (ISBN 0-397-50474-8, JBL-Med-Nursing). Har-Row.
Bergevin, Patrick R., et al. Guide to Therapeutic Oncology. 624p. 1979. lib. bdg. 55.00 (ISBN 0-683-00599-5). Williams & Wilkins.
Block, Jerome B. Oncology. 320p. 1982. 35.00 (ISBN 0-471-09511-7, Pub. by Wiley Med). Wiley.
--Oncology: UCLA Postgraduate Medicine for the Internist. (Illus.). 1981. write for info. (ISBN 0-89289-376-1). HM.
Boclima, E. & Rumke, Ph, eds. Tumour Markers: Impact& Prospects. (Applied Methocs in Oncologyy Ser.: Vol. 2). 346p. 1979. 53.75 (ISBN 0-686-63097-1, North Holland). Elsevier.
Burkhalter, Pamela & Donley, Diana, eds. Dynamics of Oncology Nursing. (Illus.). 1977. text ed. 15.95 (ISBN 0-07-009052-1, HP). McGraw.
Carter, S. K., et al, eds. Antitumor Antibiotics. (Recent Results in Cancer Research Ser.: Vol. 63). (Illus.). 1978. 49.10 (ISBN 0-387-08624-2). Springer-Verlag.
Ceglowski, W. S. & Friedman, Herman, eds. Virus Tumorigenesis & Immunogenesis. 1973. 38.00 (ISBN 0-12-165050-2). Acad Pr.

Chandra, P., ed. Antiviral Mechanisms in the Control of Neoplasia. LC 78-10779. (NATO Advanced Study Institutes Ser.: Ser. A, Life Sciences, Vol. 20). 771p. 1979. 57.50 (ISBN 0-306-40063-4, Plenum Pr). Plenum Pub.
Clouse, Melvin E., ed. Lymphography. (Golden's Diagnostic Radiology Ser.: Section 7). (Illus.). 1977. 44.00 (ISBN 0-683-01883-3). Williams & Wilkins.
Cooper, Jay S. & Pizzarello, Donald J. Concepts in Cancer Care: A Practical Explanation of Radiotherapy & Chemotherapy for Primary Care Physicians. LC 80-10334. (Illus.). 273p. 1980. text ed. 16.50 (ISBN 0-8121-0716-0). Lea & Febiger.
Day, Stacey B., et al. Readings in Oncology. LC 80-80708. (Foundation Publication Ser.). (Illus.). 227p. (Orig.). 1980. pap. 15.00x (ISBN 0-934314-01-2). Intl Found Biosocial Dev.
Deeley, T. J. Monographs on Oncology-the Chest. Incl. The Chest. 1973. 13.20 (ISBN 0-407-32300-7). Butterworth.
Deeley, T. J., et al. Guide to Oncological Nursing. 1974. 7.50 (ISBN 0-443-01089-7). Churchill.
Delgado, Gregorio & Smith, Julian P. Management of Complications in Gynecologic Oncology. 344p. 1982. 35.00 (ISBN 0-471-05993-5, Pub. by Wiley Med). Wiley.
Dietz, J. Rehabiltation Oncology. LC 80-22911. 180p. 1981. 24.50 (ISBN 0-471-08414-X). Wiley.
DiSaia, Philip J. & Creasman, William T. Clinical Gynecologic Oncology. LC 80-18687. (Illus.). 478p. 1980. text ed. 30.50 (ISBN 0-8016-1314-0). Mosby.
Dodd, Marylin J. Oncology Nursing Case Studies. 1978. spiral bdg. 10.50 (ISBN 0-87488-044-0). Med Exam.
Ekert, H., ed. Seminar on Haematology & Oncology. (Journal: Paediatrician: Vol. 9, No. 2). (Illus.). 88p. 1980. softcover 19.75 (ISBN 3-8055-1302-X). S Karger.
Emanuel, N. M. & Evseenko, D. S. Clinical Oncology: A Quantitative Approach. Abramson, J. H., ed. Kaner, N., tr. from Rus. LC 73-16436. 272p. 1974. 50.95 (ISBN 0-470-23891-7). Halsted Pr.
Foley, John F. Self-Assessment of Current Knowledge in Oncology. 1975. spiral bdg. 14.00 (ISBN 0-87488-284-2). Med Exam.
Foulds, L. Neoplastic Development. Vol. 1. 1969. 58.50 (ISBN 0-12-262801-2); Vol. 2. 1975. 110.00 (ISBN 0-12-262802-0). Acad Pr.
Fuellenbach, D., ed. Adriamycin-Symposium. (Beitraege Zur Onkologie Ser. (Contributions to Oncology): Vol. 9). viii, 200p. 1981. pap. 28.75 (ISBN 3-8055-2966-X). S Karger.
Gerschenson, L. E. & Thompson, Brad E., eds. Gene Expression & Carcinogenesis in Cultured Liver. 1975. 42.50 (ISBN 0-12-281150-X). Acad Pr.
Gilbert, Harvey A. & Kagan, A. Robert, eds. Modern Radiation Oncology: Classic Literature & Current Management. (Illus.). 1978. text ed. 52.50x (ISBN 0-06-140910-3, Harper Medical). Har-Row.
Grundmann, E., ed. Carcinogenesis. LC 79-10558. (Current Topics in Pathology Ser.: Vol. 67). 1979. 57.80 (ISBN 0-387-09344-3). Springer-Verlag.
Halpern, Bernard, ed. Corynebacterium Parvum: Applications in Experimental & Clinical Oncology. LC 75-16310. (Illus.). 450p. 1975. 42.50 (ISBN 0-306-30837-1, Plenum Pr). Plenum Pub.
Hamperl, H. & Ackermann, L. V. Illustrated Tumor Nomenclature. 2nd ed. (Illus., Eng. Span, Fr, Ger. & Rus.). 1969. 39.00 (ISBN 0-387-04567-8). Springer-Verlag.
Hazra, Tapan A. & Beachley, Michael C., eds. Recent Advances in Clinical Oncology: Proceedings of a Conference Held in Williamsburg, Va., Feb.-March 1977. LC 78-14907. (Progress in Clinical & Biological Research: Vol. 25). (Illus.). 1978. 19.00x (ISBN 0-8451-0025-4). A R Liss.
Heuson, John C., et al, eds. Breast Cancer: Trends in Research & Treatment. LC 76-22910. (European Organization for Research on Treatment of Cancer Monograph: Vol. 2). 343p. 1976. 32.00 (ISBN 0-89004-096-6). Raven.
Hirsch, Martin S., et al. Investigation of Oncogenic Viruses, Vol. 2. 272p. 1974. text ed. 29.50x (ISBN 0-8422-7235-6). Irvington.
Hoerni, B., et al. Opportunistic Infections in Cancer Patients. Armstrong, Donald, tr. from Fr. LC 77-94828. (Illus.). 207p. 1978. text ed. 24.75 (ISBN 0-89352-014-4). Masson Pub.
Homburger, F., ed. Cancer Chemotherapy. (Karger Highlights, Oncology One). (Illus.). 1979. pap. 9.00 (ISBN 3-8055-3026-9). S Karger.
--Cancer Chemotherapy: Reprinted Selected Top Articles Published 1976 - 1978. (Karger Highlights, Oncology Two). (Illus.). 1979. pap. 9.00 (ISBN 3-8055-3029-3). S Karger.
Husband, Janet E. & Holiday, Pauline A. Computerized Axial Tomography in Oncology. 1981. text ed. 50.00 (ISBN 0-443-02196-1). Churchill.
Illiger, H. J., et al, eds. Hodentumoren. (Beitrage Zur Onkologie. Contributions to Oncology: Vol. 8). viii, 120p. 1981. pap. 18.00 (ISBN 3-8055-3065-X). S Karger.
International Vinca Alkaloid Symposium, Vindesine. Contributions to Oncology: Proceedings, Vol. 6. Brade, W., et al, eds. (Illus.). 1981. 57.00 (ISBN 3-8055-2501-X). S Karger.
Kaplan, Albert S., ed. The Herpesviruses. 1974. 58.50 (ISBN 0-12-397050-4). Acad Pr.
Kirsten, W. H., ed. Malignant Transformation by Viruses. (Recent Results in Cancer Research: Vol. 6). (Illus.). 1966. 23.60 (ISBN 0-387-03645-8). Springer-Verlag.
Klein, George, ed. Viral Oncology. 860p. 1980. text ed. 92.00 (ISBN 0-89004-390-6). Raven.
Konrad, Patricia & Ertl, John. Pediatric Oncology. (Medical Outline Ser.). 1978. spiral 14.50 (ISBN 0-87488-673-2). Med Exam.
Lagarde, Claude & Renaud-Salis, Jean-Louis. Clinical Judgement & Descision-Making in Oncology. (Illus.). 164p. 1981. pap. 22.50 (ISBN 0-89352-151-5). Mason Pub.
Lapis, K., ed. Developments of Cancer Chemotherapy. (Journal: Oncology: Suppl. 1, Vol. 37). (Illus.). iv, 120p. 1980. pap. 19.75 (ISBN 3-8055-1588-X). S Karger.
Lichtman, Marshall A., ed. Hematology & Oncology. (The Science & Practice of Clinical Medicine). 368p. 1980. 24.50 (ISBN 0-8089-1231-3). Grune.
McKerns, K. W. Hormones & Cancer. 1974. 56.00 (ISBN 0-12-485350-1). Acad Pr.
Marchesi, Vincent T., ed. Membranes & Neoplasia - New Approaches & Strategies: Proceedings of a Conference Held March 4-6, 1976 in Keystone, Co. LC 76-10605. (Progress in Clinical & Biological Research: Vol. 9). 292p. 1976. 41.00 (ISBN 0-8451-0009-2). A R Liss.
Morift, H. Mason & Ratzer, Erick R. Surgical Oncology Case Studies. 1977. 18.50 (ISBN 0-87488-063-7). Med Exam.
Morris, Harold P. & Criss, Wayne E., eds. Morris Hepatomas. LC 77-13136. (Advances in Experimental Medicine & Biology Ser.: Vol. 92). 785p. 1977. 49.50 (ISBN 0-306-32692-2, Plenum Pr). Plenum Pub.
Moss, William T., et al. Radiation Oncology: Rationale, Technique, Results. 5th ed. LC 79-14367. (Illus.). 1979. text ed. 49.50 (ISBN 0-8016-3556-X). Mosby.
Mulkerin, Larry E. Practical Points in Radiation Oncology. 1979. spiral bdg. 17.00 (ISBN 0-87488-726-7). Med Exam.
Murphy, Gerald P., ed. International Advances in Surgical Oncology, Vol. 1. LC 78-51119. 300p. 1978. 42.00 (ISBN 0-8451-0500-0). A R Liss.
--International Advances in Surgical Oncology, Vol. 2. LC 78-51119. 302p. 1979. 36.00x (ISBN 0-8451-0501-9). A R Liss.
--International Advances in Surgical Oncology, Vol. 3. LC 78-51119. 386p. 1980. 44.00x (ISBN 0-8451-0502-7). A R Liss.
--International Advances in Surgical Oncology, Vol. 4. LC 78-51119. 365p. 1981. 46.00x (ISBN 0-8451-0503-5). A R Liss.
Noltenius, Harald W., ed. Manual of Oncology, 2 vols. LC 80-18972. (Illus.). 1981. Set. text ed. 320.00 (ISBN 0-8067-1331-3). Urban & S.
O'Connor, Andrea B., ed. Nursing: The Oncology Patient. LC 80-140958. (Contemporary Nursing Ser.). 1980. pap. text ed. 7.95 (ISBN 0-937126-25-X). Am Journal Nurse.
Pinedo, H. M., ed. Clinical Pharmacology of Anti-Neoplastic Drugs. (Applied Methods in Oncology Ser.: Vol. 1). 1978. 52.75 (ISBN 0-444-80086-7, Biomedical Pr). Elsevier.
Portlock, Carol S. & Goffinet, Donald R. Manual of Clinical Problems in Oncology. (Little, Brown SPIRAI TM Manual Ser.). 1980. pap. text ed. 12.95 (ISBN 0-316-71424-0). Little.
Raven, Ronald W., ed. Principles of Surgical Oncology. LC 77-1804. (Illus.). 509p. 1977. 37.50 (ISBN 0-306-30979-3, Plenum Pr). Plenum Pub.
Rutledge, Felix, et al. Gynecologic Oncology. LC 75-30951. 272p. 1976. 37.50 (ISBN 0-471-74720-3, Pub. by Wiley Medical). Wiley.
Sarna, Gregory P., ed. Practical Oncology. (UCLA Postgraduate Medicine Ser.). 1980. text ed. 24.00 (ISBN 0-471-09494-3, Pub. by Wiley Med). Wiley.
See-Lasley, Kay & Ignoffo, Robert. Manual of Oncology Therapeutics. LC 81-1998. 457p. 1981. pap. text ed. 21.50 (ISBN 0-8016-4448-8). Mosby.
Silber, R., et al, eds. Contemporary Hematology-Oncology, Vol. 2. 536p. 1981. 49.50 (ISBN 0-306-40683-7, Plenum Pr). Plenum Pub.
Sinkovics, J. Medical Oncology: An Advanced Course. 1979. 49.50 (ISBN 0-8247-6863-9). Dekker.
Sutnick, Alton I. & Engstrom, Paul F., eds. Oncologic Medicine: Clinical Topics & Practical Management. (Illus.). 1976. 29.50 (ISBN 0-8391-0883-4). Univ Park.
Symington, T. Scientific Foundations of Oncology. (Illus.). 1976. 79.95 (ISBN 0-8151-8696-7). Year Bk Med.
Taylor, Samuel G., 3rd, ed. Oncology. (Medical Examination Review Bk. Ser.: Vol. 29). 1973. spiral bdg. 16.50 (ISBN 0-87488-146-3). Med Exam.
Temin, Howard M. The Biology of RNA-Tumor Viruses. (Perspectives of Current Research Ser.). 318p. 1974. text ed. 21.50x (ISBN 0-8422-7237-2). Irvington.
Theilen, Gordon H. & Madewell, Bruce R., eds. Veterinary Cancer Medicine. LC 79-905. (Illus.). 436p. 1979. text ed. 39.50 (ISBN 0-8121-0651-2). Lea & Febiger.
Tiffany, Robert, ed. Oncology for Nurses & Health Care Professionals, Vol. 1. (Illus.). 1978. text ed. 35.00x (ISBN 0-04-610009-1); pap. text ed. 18.95x (ISBN 0-04-610010-5). Allen Unwin.
--Oncology for Nurses & Health Care Professionals, Vol. 2. (Illus.). 1978. text ed. 25.00x (ISBN 0-04-610006-7); pap. text ed. 13.95x (ISBN 0-04-610007-5). Allen Unwin.
Todaro, George J., et al. Investigation of Oncogenic Viruses, Vol. 1. 234p. 1974. text ed. 29.50x (ISBN 0-8422-7234-8). Irvington.
Vicente, Jesus, et al, eds. Clinical Oncology: The Foundations of Current Patient Management. LC 80-80729. (Cancer Management Series: Vol. 4). (Illus.). 224p. 1980. 43.50 (ISBN 0-89352-083-7). Masson Pub.
Vredevoe, Donna L., et al. Concepts of Oncology Nursing. (Illus.). 400p. 1981. text ed. 18.95 (ISBN 0-13-166587-1). P-H.
Wang, Rosemary Y. & Kelley, Ann M. Self-Assessment of Current Knowledge in Oncology Nursing. 1979. spiral bdg. 10.50 (ISBN 0-87488-236-2). Med Exam.
West Coast Cancer Symposium, 9th Annual, San Francisco, 1973. Relationship of Histology to Cancer Treatment: Proceedings. Vaeth, J. M., ed. (Frontiers of Radiation Therapy & Oncology: Vol. 9). 200p. 1974. 85.25 (ISBN 3-8055-1748-3). S Karger.
Wiernik, Peter H. Controversies in Oncology. 448p. 1982. 38.75 (ISBN 0-686-76715-2, Pub. by Wiley Med). Wiley.
Williams, Thomas E. Self-Assessment of Current Knowledge in Pediatric Hematology & Oncology. 1974. 15.00 (ISBN 0-87488-277-X). Med Exam.
Willoughby, M. L. & Siegal, Stuart. B.I.M.R. Pediatrics: Volume I Hemotology & Oncology. (Butterworth International Medical Review, Pediatrics). 1981. text ed. price not set (ISBN 0-407-02308-9). Butterworth.
Wollard, Joy J. Nutritional Management of the Cancer Patient. LC 78-68523. 216p. 1979. text ed. 17.50 (ISBN 0-89004-357-4); pap. text ed. 12.00 (ISBN 0-685-94934-6). Raven.
Yarbro, John & Bornstein, Richard, eds. Oncologic Emergencies. (Clinical Oncology Monographs). (Illus.). 430p. 1980. 29.50 (ISBN 0-8089-1317-4). Grune.

ONE-ACT PLAYS

Cartmell, Van H. & Cerf, Bennett, eds. Twenty-Four Favorite One-Act Plays. LC 58-13274. pap. 3.95 (ISBN 0-385-06617-1, C423, Dolp). Doubleday.
Cerf, Bennett, ed. Thirty Famous One-Act Plays. 1949. 5.95 (ISBN 0-394-60722-8, G22). Modern Lib.
Cohen, Helen L., ed. One-Act Plays by Modern Authors. LC 34-8319. 1968. 8.95 (ISBN 0-15-169347-1). HarBraceJ.
France, Rachel, ed. A Century of Plays by American Women. (Theatre Student Ser.). (YA) 1979. PLB 12.50 (ISBN 0-8239-0472-5). Rosen Pr.
Gassner, John & Gassner, Mollie, eds. Fifteen International One-Act Plays. (Orig.). 1969. pap. 2.50 (ISBN 0-671-49110-5). WSP.
Kozlenko, William, ed. One-Act Play Today. LC 70-105022. (Essay Index Reprint Ser). 1938. 17.00 (ISBN 0-8369-1473-2). Arno.
The Provincetown Plays: Second Series. LC 76-40392. (One-Act Plays in Reprint Ser.). 1976. Repr. of 1916 ed. 12.50x (ISBN 0-8486-2007-0). Core Collection.
Selling, Gunter. Die Einakter und Einakterzyklen Arthur Schnitzlers. (Amsterdame Publikationen Zur Sprache und Literatur: No. 21). 254p. (Ger.). 1976. pap. text ed. 20.00x (ISBN 90-6203-358-X). Humanities.

ONE-ACT PLAYS–BIBLIOGRAPHY

Logasa, Hannah. Index to One-Act Plays for Stage, Radio, & Television, Suppl. 4, 1948-57. (The Useful Reference Ser. of Library Bks: Vol. 87). 1958. lib. bdg. 12.00x (ISBN 0-87305-087-8). Faxon.
--Index to One-Act Plays for Stage, Radio, & Television, Suppl. 5, 1956-64. LC 24-21477. (The Useful Reference Ser. of Library Bks: Vol. 94). 1966. lib. bdg. 11.00x (ISBN 0-87305-094-0). Faxon.
Logasa, Hannah & Ver Nooy, Winifred. Index to One-Act Plays, 1900-24. (The Useful Reference Ser. of Library Bks: Vol. 30). 1924. lib. bdg. 11.00x (ISBN 0-87305-030-4). Faxon.

ONE-ARMED BANDITS

see Slot Machines

ONE-PARENT FAMILY

see Single-Parent Family

ONE-ROOM SCHOOLS

see Rural Schools

ONEIDA COMMUNITY

see also Perfection

Carden, Maren L. Oneida: Utopian Community to Modern Corporation. 1977. pap. text ed. 4.95x (ISBN 0-06-131634-2, TB1634, Torch). Har-Row.
Daily Journal of Oneida Community, 5 vols. in 1. LC 74-32539. (American Utopian Adventure Ser.). (Illus., Vols. 1-3, bd. with the O.C. daily, vols. 4-5). Repr. lib. bdg. 67.50x (ISBN 0-87991-032-1). Porcupine Pr.
De Maria, Richard. Communal Love at Oneida: A Perfectionist Vision of Authority, Property & Sexual Order. LC 78-60958. (Texts & Studies in Religion: Vol. 2). xiii, 233p. 1978. soft cover 19.95x (ISBN 0-88946-986-5). E Mellen.
Eastlake, A. The Oneida Community. 69.95 (ISBN 0-8490-0769-0). Gordon Pr.
Eastman, Hubbard. Noyesism Unveiled. LC 72-134402. Repr. of 1849 ed. 30.00 (ISBN 0-404-08446-X). AMS Pr.
Ellis, John B. Free Love & Its Votaries. LC 77-134430. Repr. of 1870 ed. 35.00 (ISBN 0-404-08474-5). AMS Pr.
Estlake, Allan. The Oneida Community: A Record of an Attempt to Carry Out the Principles of Christian Unselfishnes & Scientific Race-Improvement. LC 72-4179. Repr. of 1900 ed. 11.50 (ISBN 0-404-10758-3). AMS Pr.
Foster, Lawrence. Religion & Sexuality: Three American Communal Experiments of the Nineteenth Century. 400p. 1981. 19.95 (ISBN 0-19-502794-9). Oxford U Pr.
Hostetler, John A. Communitarian Societies. LC 73-19897. (Basic Anthropology Units Ser). 1974. pap. text ed. 5.95 (ISBN 0-03-091291-1, HoltC). HR&W.
Jacoby, John E. Two Mystic Communities in America. LC 75-326. (The Radical Tradition in America Ser). 104p. 1975. Repr. of 1931 ed. 13.50 (ISBN 0-88355-230-2). Hyperion Conn.
Noyes, John H. Mutual Criticism. 128p. 1975. 8.50x (ISBN 0-8156-2169-8); pap. 4.75x (ISBN 0-8156-2170-1). Syracuse U Pr.
Oneida Community. Annual Report: 1848-1851, 3 vols. in 1. LC 78-72358. (Free Love in America). Repr. 18.50 (ISBN 0-404-60982-1). AMS Pr.
--Bible Communism. LC 76-187475. (The American Utopian Adventure Ser.). 128p. Repr. of 1853 ed. lib. bdg. 12.50x (ISBN 0-87991-015-1). Porcupine Pr.
--Bible Communism: A Compilation from the Annual Reports & Other Publications of the Oneida Association & Its Branches. LC 72-2978. Repr. of 1853 ed. 8.50 (ISBN 0-404-10742-7). AMS Pr.
--Hand-Book of the Oneida Community, with a Sketch of Its Founder, & an Outline of Its Constitution & Doctrines, 3 vols in 1. Incl. Hand-Book of the Oneida Community, Containing a Brief Sketch of Its Present Condition, Internal Economy & Leading Principles; Mutual Criticism. LC 72-2977. Repr. of 1876 ed. 23.50 (ISBN 0-404-10741-9). AMS Pr.
Parker, Robert A. A Yankee Saint: John Humphrey Noyes & the Oneida Community. LC 75-187456. (The American Utopian Adventure Ser.). 322p. Repr. of 1935 ed. lib. bdg. 16.50x (ISBN 0-87991-009-7). Porcupine Pr.
--A Yankee Saint: John Humphrey Noyes & the Oneida Community. (Illus.). 327p. 1973. Repr. of 1935 ed. 19.50 (ISBN 0-208-01319-9, Archon). Shoe String.
Robertson, C. N. Oneida Community Profiles. (Illus.). 1977. 10.00x (ISBN 0-8156-0140-9). Syracuse U Pr.
Robertson, Constance N. Oneida Community: The Breakup, 1876 - 1881. LC 72-38405. (New York State Studies). (Illus.). 330p. 1972. 9.95x (ISBN 0-8156-0086-0). Syracuse U Pr.
Robertson, Constance N., ed. Oneida Community: An Autobiography 1851-1876. LC 75-115417. (York State Bks.). (Illus.). 1981. pap. 9.95 (ISBN 0-8156-0166-2). Syracuse U Pr.

ONEIDA INDIANS

see Indians of North America–Eastern States

ONEIDA LANGUAGE

see also Iroquoian Languages

O'NEIL, KITTY

Ireland, Karen. Kitty O'Neil: Daredevil Woman. LC 80-80604. (Starpeople Ser.). (Illus.). 78p. (gr. 4 up). 1980. PLB 5.99 (ISBN 0-8178-0004-2). Harvey.

O'NEILL, EUGENE GLADSTONE, 1888-1953

Atkinson, Jennifer M. Eugene O'Neill: A Descriptive Bibliography. LC 73-13312. (Bibliography Ser.). (Illus.). 1974. 30.00x (ISBN 0-8229-3279-2). U of Pittsburgh Pr.

Bogard, Travis. Contour in Time: The Plays of Eugene O'Neill. 1972. 22.50x (ISBN 0-19-501573-8). Oxford U Pr.

Callahan, John. Barron's Simplified Approach to O'Neill's Mourning Becomes Electra. LC 77-89618. 1970. pap. text ed. 1.50 (ISBN 0-8120-0290-3). Barron.

Cargill, Oscar, et al, eds. O'Neill & His Plays: Four Decades of Criticism. LC 61-17631. (Gotham Library). 1961. pap. 6.95 (ISBN 0-8147-0076-4). NYU Pr.

Carpenter, Frederic I. Eugene O'neill. rev. ed. (United States Authors Ser.: No. 66). 1979. lib. bdg. 9.95 (ISBN 0-8057-7267-7). Twayne.

--Eugene O'Neill. rev. ed. (Twayne United States Authors Ser.). 1979. lib. bdg. 9.50 (ISBN 0-8057-7267-7). G K Hall.

--Eugene O'Neill. (Twayne's United States Authors Ser). 1964. pap. 3.45 (ISBN 0-8084-0126-2, T66, Twayne). Coll & U Pr.

Chabrowe, Leonard. Ritual & Pathos: The Theater of O'Neill. 226p. 1976. 14.50 (ISBN 0-8387-1575-3). Bucknell U Pr.

Chothia, J. Forging a Language. LC 78-73239. (Illus.). 1980. 29.50 (ISBN 0-521-22569-8). Cambridge U Pr.

Clark, Peter. O'Neill's Plays Notes. pap. 1.95 (ISBN 0-8220-0910-2). Cliffs.

Cronin, Harry C. Eugene O'Neill, Irish & American: A Study in Cultural Context. LC 76-6331. (Irish Americans Ser). 1976. 12.00 (ISBN 0-405-09327-6). Arno.

Falk, Doris V. Eugene O'Neill & the Tragic Tension: An Interpretive Study of the Plays. 1974. pap. 3.50 (ISBN 0-8135-0791-X). Rutgers U Pr.

--Eugene O'Neill & the Tragic Tention. 232p. 1981. Repr. of 1958 ed. 10.00 (ISBN 0-87752-222-7). Gordian.

Floyd, Virginia. Eugene O'Neill at Work: Newly Released Ideas for Plays. LC 81-40460. (Illus.). 416p. 1981. 19.95 (ISBN 0-686-73110-7). Ungar.

Floyd, Virginia, ed. Eugene O'Neill: A World View. LC 79-4826. 1980. 15.50 (ISBN 0-8044-2204-4). Ungar.

Frazer, Winifred D. Love As Death in "The Iceman Cometh: A Modern Treatment of an Ancient Theme. LC 67-65495. (U of Fla. Humanities Monographs: No. 27). 1967. pap. 3.00 (ISBN 0-8130-0081-5). U Presses Fla.

Frazer, Winifred L. E.G. & E.G.O. Emma Goldman & "The Iceman Cometh". LC 74-7361. (U of Fla. Humanities Monographs: No. 43). 106p. 1974. pap. 4.00 (ISBN 0-8130-0504-3). U Presses Fla.

Frenz, Horst. Eugene O'Neill. Sebba, Helen, tr. LC 79-143188. (Modern Literature Ser.). 1971. 10.95 (ISBN 0-8044-2211-7); pap. 4.95 (ISBN 0-8044-6159-7). Ungar.

Gannon, Paul. Monarch Notes on O'Neill's Long Day's Journey into Night. (Orig.). pap. 1.95 (ISBN 0-671-00752-1). Monarch Pr.

Gannon, Paul, ed. Monarch Notes on O'Neill's Desire Under the Elms. (Orig.). pap. 1.50 (ISBN 0-671-00750-5). Monarch Pr.

Gassner, J. O'Neill: A Collection of Critical Essays. 1964. 10.95 (ISBN 0-13-634279-5, Spec). P-H.

Geddes, Virgil. Melodramadness of Eugene O'Neill. LC 73-7589. 1934. lib. bdg. 7.50 (ISBN 0-8414-2032-7). Folcroft.

Greene, James. Monarch Notes on O'Neill's Strange Interlude. (Orig.). pap. 1.95 (ISBN 0-671-00754-8). Monarch Pr.

Griffin, E. Eugene O'Neill: A Collection of Criticism. 1976. 2.45 (ISBN 0-07-022769-1, SP). McGraw.

Harmon, Robert, compiled by. First Editions of Eugene O'Neill. (First Edition Pocket Guides Ser.). 15p. softcover 3.95 (ISBN 0-910720-16-9). Hermes.

Haywood, I. Strindbergs Influence on Eugene O'Neill. 59.95 (ISBN 0-8490-1145-0). Gordon Pr.

Josephson, Lennart. Role: O'neill's Cornelius Melody. Blair, Alan, tr. from Swedish. 1978. pap. text ed. 24.50x (ISBN 0-391-00811-0). Humanities.

Long, Chester C. Role of Nemesis in the Structure of Selected Plays by Eugene O'Neill. LC 68-15526. (Studies in American Literature: Vol. 8). 1968. text ed. 37.00x (ISBN 90-2790-240-2). Mouton.

Miller, Jordan Y. Eugene O'Neill & the American Critic: A Bibliographical Checklist. 2nd ed. 544p. 1973. 27.50 (ISBN 0-208-00939-6, Archon). Shoe String.

Nugent, Elizabeth. Monarch Notes on O'Neill's Iceman Cometh. (Orig.). pap. 1.50 (ISBN 0-671-00751-3). Monarch Pr.

--Monarch Notes on O'Neill's Mourning Becomes Electra. (Orig.). pap. 1.50 (ISBN 0-671-00753-X). Monarch Pr.

Raleigh, John H. Plays of Eugene O'Neill. LC 72-5503. (Arcturus Books Paperbacks). 320p. 1972. pap. 2.85 (ISBN 0-8093-0601-8). S Ill U Pr.

Reaver, J. Russell. O'Neill Concordance, 3 Vols. LC 73-75960. 1969. 130.00 (ISBN 0-8103-1001-5). Gale.

Rogers, David. Monarch Notes on O'Neill's Plays. (Orig.). pap. 1.95 (ISBN 0-671-00627-4). Monarch Pr.

Sanborn, Ralph & Clark, Barrett H., eds. Bibliography of the Works of Eugene O'Neill with Collected Poems by O'Neill. LC 65-16249. (Illus.). Repr. of 1931 ed. 12.50 (ISBN 0-405-08911-2). Arno.

Sheaffer, Louis. O'Neill, Son & Artist. LC 73-8610. (Illus.). 1973. 17.50 (ISBN 0-316-78336-6); pap. 8.95 (ISBN 0-316-78337-4). Little.

--O'Neill, Son & Playwright. LC 68-17278. (Illus.). 1968. 17.50 (ISBN 0-316-78335-8); pap. 8.95 (ISBN 0-316-78338-2). Little.

Shipley, Joseph T. Art of Eugene O'Neill. LC 74-11023. 1928. lib. bdg. 10.00 (ISBN 0-8414-7776-0). Folcroft.

Sinha, C. P. Eugene O'Neill's Tragic Vision. 1981. text ed. 16.50 (ISBN 0-391-02203-2). Humanities.

Skinner, Richard D. Eugene O'Neill: A Poet's Quest. LC 64-12398. 1964. Repr. of 1935 ed. 15.00 (ISBN 0-8462-0421-5). Russell.

Winther, Sophus K. Eugene O'Neill: A Critical Study. rev & enl ed. LC 61-13092. 1961. Repr. of 1934 ed. 17.00 (ISBN 0-8462-0305-7). Russell.

O'NEILL, MATILDA–JUVENILE LITERATURE

Hall, Marjory. The Gold-Lined Box. LC 68-17150. (gr. 7 up). 1968. 4.25 (ISBN 0-664-32420-7). Westminster.

O'NEILL, TIP

Clancy, Paul & Elder, Shirley. Tip: A Biography of Thomas P. O'Neill, Speaker of the House. 1981. 8.95 (ISBN 0-02-525700-5). Macmillan.

Clancy, Paul R. Untitled Biography of Tip N'Neill. 1980. 10.95 (ISBN 0-02-525700-5). Macmillan.

ONEIROMANCY

see Dreams

ONIN WAR, 1467-1477

Varley, H. Paul. Onin War: History of Its Origins & Background with a Selective Translation of the Chronicle of Onin. LC 66-14595. (Studies in Oriental Culture Ser.: No. 1). (Illus.). 1966. 17.50x (ISBN 0-231-02943-8). Columbia U Pr.

ONIONS

Bothwell, Jean. The Onion Cookbook. LC 75-35403. (Illus.). 180p. 1976. pap. 2.50 (ISBN 0-486-23312-X). Dover.

--The Onion Cookbook. 5.00 (ISBN 0-8446-5482-5). Peter Smith.

Kerch, Inez N. Onions: Secrets of Vegetable Cooking. 64p. 1981. pap. 3.95 (ISBN 0-517-54444-X). Crown.

Onion Storage. 1981. 12.00x (ISBN 0-686-75421-2, Pub. by Grower Bks). State Mutual Bk.

Voss, Ronald E. Onion Production in California. LC 79-55403. (Illus.). 1979. pap. 5.00x (ISBN 0-931876-35-4, 4086). Ag Sci Pubns.

ONOMATOPOEIA

Kayser, Wolfgang J. Klangmalerei Bei Harsdoerffer. 1932. 21.50 (ISBN 0-384-28831-6); pap. 18.50 (ISBN 0-384-28830-8). Johnson Repr.

Kloe, Donald R. A Dictionary of Onomatopoeic Sounds, Tones, & Noises in English & Spanish. LC 77-2627. 1977. 24.50 (ISBN 0-87917-059-X). Blaine Ethridge.

Swanson, Donald. Characterization of the Roman Poetic Onomasticon. LC 71-127397. 1970. pap. 5.00x (ISBN 0-271-00125-9). Pa St U Pr.

ONONDAGA COUNTY, NEW YORK

Sneller, Anne G. Vanished World. LC 64-16923. (Illus.). 1964. 6.00 (ISBN 0-8156-0037-2). Syracuse U Pr.

ONONDAGA LANGUAGE

see also Iroquoian Languages

Hale, Horatio E., ed. Iroquois Book of Rites. LC 74-83458. (Library of Aboriginal American Literature: No. 2). Repr. of 1883 ed. 20.00 (ISBN 0-404-52182-7). AMS Pr.

Shea, John D. French-Onondaga Dictionary, from a Manuscript of the Seventeenth Century. LC 10-30203. (Library of American Linguistics: No. 1). (Fr.). Repr. of 1860 ed. 12.50 (ISBN 0-404-50981-9). AMS Pr.

ONTARIO

Gourlay, Robert F. Statistical Account of Upper Canada, 2 Vols. 1967. Repr. of 1822 ed. 46.00 (ISBN 0-384-19475-3). Johnson Repr.

Krashinsky, M. Day Care & Public Policy in Ontario. (Ontario Economic Council Research Studies). 1977. pap. 7.50 (ISBN 0-8020-3349-0). U of Toronto Pr.

Landon, Fred. Western Ontario & the American Frontier. LC 78-102514. (Relations of Canada & the U. S. Ser). (Illus.). 1970. Repr. of 1967 ed. 20.00 (ISBN 0-8462-1375-3). Russell.

Smith, William. Political Leaders of Upper Canada. facs. ed. LC 68-26475. (Essay Index Reprint Ser.). 1931. 18.00 (ISBN 0-8369-0886-4). Arno.

ONTARIO–BIBLIOGRAPHY

Kingsford, William. Early Bibliography of the Province of Ontario, Dominion of Canada. LC 78-171543. Repr. of 1892 ed. 15.00 (ISBN 0-404-03704-6). AMS Pr.

ONTARIO–DESCRIPTION AND TRAVEL

Boyle, Terry. Under This Roof: Family Homes of Southern Ontario. LC 79-8925. (Illus.). 160p. 1980. 19.95 (ISBN 0-385-15636-7). Doubleday.

Dawson, Simon J. Report on the Exploration of the Country Between Lake Superior & the Red River Settlement, & Between the Latter Place & the Assiniboine & Saskatchewan. LC 68-55184. 1968. Repr. of 1859 ed. lib. bdg. 40.00x (ISBN 0-8371-5031-0, DALS). Greenwood.

Hayes, John, ed. Corpus Vasorum Antiquorum Canada: Royal Ontario Museum, Ontario. (Corpus Vasorum Antiquorum Ser.). (Illus.). 64p. 1981. 115.00x (ISBN 0-19-726000-4). Oxford U Pr.

Howison, John. Sketches of Upper Canada, Domestic, Local, & Characteristic. 1965. Repr. of 1821 ed. 17.00 (ISBN 0-384-24490-4). Johnson Repr.

Moodie, Susanna. Roughing It in the Bush. LC 70-104530. Repr. of 1852 ed. lib. bdg. 16.50x (ISBN 0-8398-1266-3). Irvington.

Smith, David W. Short Topographical Description of His Majesty's Province of Upper Canada in North America. (Canadiana Before 1867 Ser). 1969. Repr. of 1799 ed. 11.50 (ISBN 0-384-56150-0). Johnson Repr.

ONTARIO–ECONOMIC CONDITIONS

Bonsor, N. C. Transportation Rates & Economic Development in Northern Ontario. 1977. pap. 6.00 (ISBN 0-8020-3343-1). U of Toronto Pr.

Dean, W. G., ed. Economic Atlas of Ontario: Atlas Economique de L'ontario. LC 73-653512. 1969. 100.00x (ISBN 0-8020-3235-4). U of Toronto Pr.

Foot, D. K. Provincial Public Finance in Ontario: An Empirical Analysis of the Last Twenty-Five Years. (Ontario Economic Council Research Studies). 1977. 8.50 (ISBN 0-8020-3350-4). U of Toronto Pr.

Gentilcore, R. Louis, ed. Ontario. (Studies in Canadian Geography). (Illus.). 1972. 12.50x (ISBN 0-8020-1919-6); pap. 6.00x (ISBN 0-8020-6160-5). U of Toronto Pr.

Gilmour, James M. Spatial Evolution of Manufacturing: Southern Ontario 1851-1891. (Illus.). 1972. pap. 6.00x (ISBN 0-8020-3295-8). U of Toronto Pr.

Gourlay, Robert F. Statistical Account of Upper Canada, 2 Vols. 1967. Repr. of 1822 ed. 46.00 (ISBN 0-384-19475-3). Johnson Repr.

Williams, J. R. Resources, Tariffs, & Trade: Ontario's Stake. LC 76-26043. 1976. pap. 8.50 (ISBN 0-8020-3340-7). U of Toronto Pr.

ONTARIO–HISTORY

Byers, Mary, et al. Rural Roots: Pre-Confederation Buildings of the York Region of Ontario. LC 76-26867. (Illus.). 1976. 20.00 (ISBN 0-8020-2230-8); pap. 7.50 (ISBN 0-8020-6287-3). U of Toronto Pr.

Greenman, Emerson F. Old Birch Island Cemetery & the Early Historic Trade Route: Georgian Bay, Ontario. (Occasional Papers Ser.: No. 11). (Illus.). 1951. pap. 2.00x (ISBN 0-932206-03-4). U Mich Mus Anthro.

Mathews, Zena P. The Relation of Seneca False Face Masks to Seneca & Ontario Archeology. LC 77-94707. (Outstanding Dissertations in the Fine Arts Ser.). 1978. lib. bdg. 36.00x (ISBN 0-8240-3239-X). Garland Pub.

Miller, Orlo. A Century of Western Ontario: The Story of London, the Free Press, & Western Ontario, 1849-1949. LC 71-165443. (Illus.). 289p. 1972. Repr. of 1949 ed. lib. bdg. 15.75x (ISBN 0-8371-6226-2, MIWO). Greenwood.

--A Century of Western Ontario: The Story of London, the Free Press, & Western Ontario, 1849-1949. LC 71-165443. (Illus.). 289p. 1972. Repr. of 1949 ed. lib. bdg. 15.75x (ISBN 0-8371-6226-2, MIWO). Greenwood.

Morley, William F. Ontario & the Canadian North: A Bibliography. LC 78-4976. (Canadian Local Histories Ser). 1978. 27.50x (ISBN 0-8020-2281-2). U of Toronto Pr.

Nute, Grace L. Voyageur's Highway: Minnesota's Border Lake Land. LC 65-63529. (Illus.). 113p. 1976. pap. 3.75 (ISBN 0-87351-006-2). Minn Hist.

Palmer, Bryan D. A Culture in Conflict: Skilled Workers & Industrial Capitalism in Hamilton, Ontario 1860-1914. 1979. 23.50x (ISBN 0-7735-0346-3); pap. 10.95 (ISBN 0-7735-0347-1). McGill-Queens U Pr.

Prang, Margaret. N. W. Rowell: Ontario Nationalist. LC 73-89843. 1975. 27.50x (ISBN 0-8020-5300-9). U of Toronto Pr.

Talman, James J., ed. Loyalist Narratives from Upper Canada. LC 69-14505. 1969. Repr. of 1946 ed. lib. bdg. 27.50x (ISBN 0-8371-5064-7, TALN). Greenwood.

Wheeler, Robert C., et al. Voices from the Rapids: An Underwater Search for Fur Trade Artifacts, 1960-73. LC 75-1194. (Minnesota Historical Archaeology Ser., No. 3). (Illus.). 115p. 1975. pap. 6.50 (ISBN 0-87351-086-0). Minn Hist.

Wilson, Barbara. Ontario & the First World War, 1914-1918. (Ontario Series of the Champlain Society). 1977. 17.50 (ISBN 0-8020-2255-3). U of Toronto Pr.

ONTARIO–HISTORY–BIBLIOGRAPHY

Bishop, Olga B. Bibliography of Ontario History, 1867-1976: Cultural, Economic, Political, Social, 2 vols. 1980. 75.00 (ISBN 0-8020-2359-2). U of Toronto Pr.

ONTARIO–HISTORY–SOURCES

Edgar, Matilda R. Ten Years of Upper Canada in Peace & War, 1805-1815, Being the Ridout Letters with Annotations by Matilda Edgar: Also an Appendix of the Narrative of the Captivity Among the Shawanese Indians in 1788 of Thos. Ridout. LC 75-7125. (Indian Captivities Ser.: Vol. 98). 1977. Repr. of 1890 ed. lib. bdg. 44.00 (ISBN 0-8240-1722-6). Garland Pub.

ONTARIO–POLITICS AND GOVERNMENT

Armstrong, Christopher. The Politics of Federalism: Ontario's Relations with the Federal Government 1867-1942. (Ontario Historical Studies). 316p. 1981. 25.00 (ISBN 0-8020-2434-3). U of Toronto Pr.

Biggar, Charles R. Sir Oliver Mowat: A Biographical Sketch, 2 vols. (BCL Ser. I). Repr. of 1905 ed. Set. 24.00 (ISBN 0-404-00858-5); 12.50 ea. Vol. 1 (ISBN 0-404-08021-9). Vol. 2 (ISBN 0-404-08022-7). AMS Pr.

Bird, R. M. & Slack, N. E. Residential Property Tax Relief in Ontario. (Ontario Economic Council). 1978. 12.00 (ISBN 0-8020-3355-5). U of Toronto Pr.

Careless, J. M., ed. The Pre-Confederation Premiers: Ontario Government Leaders 1841 to 1867. (Ontario Historical Studies). 416p. 1980. 15.00 (ISBN 0-8020-3363-6). U of Toronto Pr.

Foot, D. K. Provincial Public Finance in Ontario: An Empirical Analysis of the Last Twenty-Five Years. (Ontario Economic Council Research Studies). 1977. 8.50 (ISBN 0-8020-3350-4). U of Toronto Pr.

Schindeler, Fred F. Responsible Government in Ontario. LC 70-390334. 1969. pap. 7.50 (ISBN 0-8020-6189-3). U of Toronto Pr.

Smith, William. Political Leaders of Upper Canada. facs. ed. LC 68-26475. (Essay Index Reprint Ser.). 1931. 18.00 (ISBN 0-8369-0886-4). Arno.

ONTARIO, LAKE

Cochrane, Hugh F. Gateway to Oblivion: The Great Lakes Vortex. 1981. pap. 2.50 (ISBN 0-380-54817-8, 54817). Avon.

Pound, Arthur. Lake Ontario. LC 70-118789. (Empire Historical Publications Ser: No. 87). 1970. Repr. of 1945 ed. 12.00 (ISBN 0-87198-087-8). Friedman.

ONTOGENY

see also Evolution

Ciba Foundation. Ontogeny of Acquired Immunity. (CIBA Foundation Symposium Ser.: No. 5). 1972. 20.50 (ISBN 0-444-10381-3, Excerpta Medica). Elsevier.

Davidson, Percy E. Recapitulation Theory & Human Infancy. LC 70-176714. (Columbia University. Teachers College. Contributions to Education: No. 65). Repr. of 1914 ed. 17.50 (ISBN 0-404-55065-7). AMS Pr.

Gould, Stephen J. Ontogeny & Phylogeny. 1977. 25.00x (ISBN 0-674-63940-5, Belknap Pr). Harvard U Pr.

Hamilton, T. H., et al, eds. Ontogeny of Receptors & Reproductive Hormone Action. LC 77-92523. 446p. 1979. text ed. 42.50 (ISBN 0-89004-254-3). Raven.

Medvedev, Zhores A. Molecular-Genetic Mechanisms of Development. LC 71-80754. 418p. 1970. 34.50 (ISBN 0-306-30403-1, Plenum Pr). Plenum Pub.

Moltz, Howard. Ontogeny of Vertebrate Behavior. 1971. 56.50 (ISBN 0-12-504350-3). Acad Pr.

ONTOLOGY

see also Absolute, the; Change; Demythologization; Existentialism; Identity; Metaphysics; Necessity (Philosophy); Nothing (Philosophy); Philosophical Anthropology; Philosophy; Situation (Philosophy); Substance (Philosophy)

Ahumada, Rodolfo. A History of Western Ontology from Thales to Heidegger. LC 78-60794. 1978. pap. text ed. 9.50 (ISBN 0-8191-0507-4). U Pr of Amer.

Barnes, Jonathan. The Ontological Argument. 1972. text ed. 12.95 (ISBN 0-312-58590-X). St Martin.

Bergmann, Gustav. Realism: A Critique of Brentano & Meinong. 468p. (Orig.). 1967. 25.00x (ISBN 0-299-04330-4); pap. 9.95x (ISBN 0-299-04334-7). U. of Wis Pr.
Bobik, Joseph, tr. Aquinas on Being & Essence: A Translation & Interpretation. 1965. 6.95x (ISBN 0-268-00009-3). U of Notre Dame Pr.
Bonevac, Daniel A. Reduction in the Abstract Sciences. 200p. 1981. lib. bdg. 18.50 (ISBN 0-915145-14-6); pap. text ed. 12.00 (ISBN 0-915145-15-4). Hackett Pub.
Buber, Martin. I & Thou. Kaufman, Walter, tr. LC 72-123845. 1970. 12.50 (ISBN 0-684-15575-3, ScribT); pap. 2.95 (ISBN 0-684-71725-5, SL243, ScribT). Scribner.
Coffey, Peter. Ontology. 9.00 (ISBN 0-8446-1119-0). Peter Smith.
Crist, Joseph F. The Divine Being: An Ontological Discourse. 1979. 6.95 (ISBN 0-533-03764-6). Vantage.
Deutsch, Eliot. On Truth: An Ontological Theory. LC 79-12754. 1979. text ed. 10.00x (ISBN 0-8248-0615-8). U Pr of Hawaii.
Earle, William. The Autobiographical Consciousness. 1972. 10.00 (ISBN 0-8129-0191-6); pap. 2.95 (ISBN 0-8129-6164-1). Times Bks.
Feibleman, James K. Ontology. LC 68-8333. (Illus.). 1968. Repr. of 1951 ed. lib. bdg. 29.75x (ISBN 0-8371-0072-0, FEON). Greenwood.
Feldstein, Leonard C. The Dance of Being: Man's Labyrinthe Rhythms, the Natural Ground of the Human. LC 77-75799. 1979. 25.00 (ISBN 0-8232-1032-4). Fordham.
--Homo Quaerens: The Seeker & the Sought Method Become Ontology. LC 76-18464. 1978. 20.00 (ISBN 0-8232-1019-7). Fordham.
Frank, S. L. Reality & Man: An Essay in the Metaphysics of Human Nature. LC 66-12950. 1966. 6.00 (ISBN 0-8008-6650-9). Taplinger.
Galvan, Enrique T. La Realidad Como Resultado. pap. 1.85 (ISBN 0-8477-2802-1). U of PR Pr.
Giles Of Rome. Giles of Rome: Theorems on Existence & Essence. Murray, Michael V., tr. (Medieval Philosophical Texts in Translation: No. 7). 1953. pap. 5.95 (ISBN 0-87462-207-7). Marquette.
Gottlieb, Dale. Ontological Economy: Substitutional Quantification & Mathematics. (Clarendon Library of Logic & Philosophy Ser.). 172p. 1980. 28.00 (ISBN 0-19-824420-7). Oxford U Pr.
Hartmann, Nicolai. New Ways of Ontology. Kuhn, Reinhard C., tr. from Ger. LC 75-1112. 145p. 1975. Repr. of 1953 ed. lib. bdg. 15.00 (ISBN 0-8371-7989-0, HANW). Greenwood.
Heidegger, Martin. Being & Time. LC 72-78334. 1962. 19.95x (ISBN 0-06-063850-8, HarpR). Har-Row.
--Discourse on Thinking. Anderson, J. M. & Freund, E. Hans, trs. from Ger. 1969. pap. 2.95x (ISBN 0-06-131459-5, TB 1459, Torch). Har-Row.
--Essence of Reasons. bilingual ed. Malick, Terrence, tr. (Studies in Phenomenology & Existential Philosophy Ser). (Ger. & Eng.). 1969. 9.95x (ISBN 0-8101-0004-5). Northwestern U Pr.
--On Time & Being. 1977. pap. 3.50x (ISBN 0-06-131941-4, TB 1941, Torch). Har-Row.
--The Question of Being. 1958. pap. 2.95x (ISBN 0-8084-0258-7, P9). Coll & U Pr.
--Sein und Zeit. (Ger.). 19.00 (ISBN 3-4847-0109-9). Adler.
Henke, Peter. Vor Dem Nichts. (Theologischo Bibliothe Toepelmann: Vol. 34). (Illus.). 1978. 35.75x (ISBN 3-11-007254-8). De Gruyter.
Henry, D. P. Medieval Logic & Metaphysics: A Modern Introduction. (Orig.). 1972. text ed. 7.50x (ISBN 0-09-110830-6, Hutchinson U Lib); pap. text ed. 6.75x (ISBN 0-09-110831-4, Hutchinson U Lib). Humanities.
Kaminsky, Jack. Language & Ontology. LC 69-11516. 330p. 1969. 12.50x (ISBN 0-8093-0367-1). S Ill U Pr.
Klubertanz, George P. & Holloway, Maurice R. Being & God: Introduction to the Philosophy of Being & to Natural Theology. LC 63-15359. 1963. 29.00x (ISBN 0-89197-045-2); pap. text ed. 16.50x (ISBN 0-89197-674-4). Irvington.
Lango, John. Whitehead's Ontology. LC 78-171184. 1972. 11.00 (ISBN 0-87395-093-3); microfiche 11.00 (ISBN 0-87395-193-X). State U NY Pr.
McCormick, John F. Scholastic Metaphysics. 1928. text ed. 2.90 (ISBN 0-8294-0092-3). Loyola.
McTaggart, John M. Nature of Existence, 2 Vols. 1968. 49.00x (ISBN 0-403-00129-3). Scholarly.
Marcel, Gabriel. Being & Having: An Existentialist Diary. 7.00 (ISBN 0-8446-2528-0). Peter Smith.
--The Mystery of Being, 2 vols. in 1. Hague, Rene, tr. from Fr. LC 77-27179. (Gifford Lectures: 1949-50). Repr. of 1951 ed. 44.50 (ISBN 0-404-60504-4). AMS Pr.
--The Mystery of Being, 2 vols. Incl. Vol. 1. Reflections & Mystery. 288p. pap. 4.25 (ISBN 0-89526-929-5); Vol. 2. Faith & Reality. 222p. pap. 3.95x (ISBN 0-89526-930-9). 1960. Repr. Regnery-Gateway.
Margolis, Joseph. Knowledge & Existence: An Introduction to Philosophical Problems. 304p. 1973. text ed. 8.95x (ISBN 0-19-501589-4). Oxford U Pr.
Merleau-Ponty, Maurice. Visible & the Invisible. Lingis, Alphonso, tr. LC 68-30125. (Studies in Phenomenology & Existential Philosophy Ser). 1969. 17.95x (ISBN 0-8101-0026-6); pap. 7.95x (ISBN 0-8101-0457-1). Northwestern U Pr.
Mohanty, J. N. Phenomenologie & Ontology. (Phaenomenologica Ser: No. 37). 1970. lib. bdg. 24.00 (ISBN 90-247-5053-9, Pub. by Martinus Nijhoff Netherlands). Kluwer Boston.
Moore, Jared S. Rifts in the Universe: A Study of the Historic Dichotomies & Modalities of Being. 1927. 22.50x (ISBN 0-686-51303-7). Elliots Bks.
Munitz, Milton K. Existence & Logic. LC 74-10417. 220p. 1974. 18.50x (ISBN 0-8147-5365-5). NYU Pr.
Nedoncelle, Maurice. Intersubjectivity & Ontology: The Personalist Challenge. Gerard, Francois C., tr. (Pittsburgh Theological Monographs: No. 27). 1982. pap. write for info (ISBN 0-915138-29-8). Pickwick.
Neville, Robert C. God the Creator: On the Transcendence & Presence of God. LC 68-13128. (Illus.). 1968. 12.50x (ISBN 0-226-57641-8). U of Chicago Pr.
Nunk, Arthur W. A Synoptic Approach to the Riddle of Existence. LC 77-818. 336p. 1977. 15.00 (ISBN 0-87527-165-0). Fireside Bks.
Owens, Joseph. Interpretation of Existence. (Horizons in Philosophy Ser). 1968. pap. 2.95x (ISBN 0-02-824320-X). Glencoe.
Pico Della Mirandola, Giovanni. On the Dignity of Man. Wallis, Charles G., et al, trs. Bd. with On Being & Unity; Heptaplus. LC 65-26540. 1965. pap. 5.50 (ISBN 0-672-60483-3, LLA227). Bobbs.
--Pico Della Mirandola: Of Being & Unity. Hamm, Victor M., tr. (Medieval Philosophical Texts in Translation: No. 3). 1943. pap. 5.95 (ISBN 0-87462-203-4). Marquette.
Pols, Edward. Recognition of Reason. LC 63-14296. (Philosophical Exploration Ser.). 269p. 1963. 9.95x (ISBN 0-8093-0111-3). S Ill U Pr.
Quine, Willard V. Ontological Relativity & Other Essays. LC 72-91121. (John Dewey Lectures Ser.: No. 1). 1969. 15.00x (ISBN 0-231-03307-9); pap. 5.00x (ISBN 0-231-08357-2). Columbia U Pr.
Reilly, John P. Cajetan's Notion of Existence. (Studies in Philosophy: No. 4). (Orig.). 1971. pap. text ed. 22.50x (ISBN 90-2791-559-8). Mouton.
Rescher, Nicholas, ed. Studies in Ontology. (American Philosophical Quarterly Monograph: No. 12). 67p. 1978. pap. 19.00x (ISBN 0-631-11560-9, Pub. by Basil Blackwell England). Biblio Dist.
Ross, Stephen D. Philosophical Mysteries. LC 80-26837. (Ser. in Philosophy). 160p. 1981. text ed. 34.00x (ISBN 0-87395-524-2, ROPM); pap. text ed. 9.95x (ISBN 0-87395-525-0, ROPM-P). State U NY Pr.
Royce, Josiah. World & the Individual, 2 Vols. (Series 1 & series 2). Set. 17.00 (ISBN 0-8446-2842-5). Peter Smith.
Russell, Bertrand. Essays in Analysis. Lackey, Douglas, ed. LC 73-79346. 340p. 1973. 8.95 (ISBN 0-8076-0698-7); pap. 3.95 (ISBN 0-8076-0699-5). Braziller.
Russell, E. S. Interpretation of Development & Heredity: A Study in Biological Method. LC 70-39699. (Select Bibliographies Reprint Ser.). 312p. 1972. Repr. of 1930 ed. 15.25 (ISBN 0-8369-9943-6). Arno.
Salmon, Elizabeth G. Good in Existential Metaphysics. (Aquinas Lecture). 1952. 6.95 (ISBN 0-87462-117-8). Marquette.
Salvan, Jacques. To Be & Not to Be: An Analysis of Jean-Paul Sartre's Ontology. (Waynebooks Ser: No. 5). (Orig.). 1962. pap. 4.95x (ISBN 0-8143-1166-0). Wayne St U Pr.
Samuel, Otto. Foundation of Onthology. 1954. 3.75 (ISBN 0-8022-1477-0). Philos Lib.
Santayana, George. The Realm of Essence: Book First of "Realms of Being". LC 72-11745. 183p. 1974. Repr. of 1928 ed. lib. bdg. 15.00x (ISBN 0-8371-6700-0, SARE). Greenwood.
--Realms of Being. LC 72-79638. xxxvi, 862p. 1972. Repr. of 1942 ed. lib. bdg. 24.00x (ISBN 0-8154-0425-5). Cooper Sq.
Schneider, Herbert W. Ways of Being. LC 72-9832. 116p. 1974. Repr. of 1962 ed. lib. bdg. 15.00x (ISBN 0-8371-6149-5, SCWB). Greenwood.
Sellars, Wilfrid. Naturalism & Ontology. viii, 182p. (Orig.). 1980. lib. bdg. 22.00 (ISBN 0-917930-36-3); pap. text ed. 7.50x (ISBN 0-917930-16-9). Ridgeview.
Sikora, Joseph J. Inquiry into Being. LC 65-26034. (Orig.). 1965. pap. 3.25 (ISBN 0-8294-0069-9). Loyola.
Simon, Y. Introduction a L 'ontologie du Connaitre. (Reprints in Philosophy Ser.). Repr. of 1934 ed. lib. bdg. 28.00x (ISBN 0-697-00049-4). Irvington.
Smith, Gerard. The Philosophy of Being. 1964. 9.95 (ISBN 0-87462-530-0). Marquette.
Sokolowski, Robert. Presence & Absence: A Philosophical Investigation of Language & Being. LC 77-23628. (Studies in Phenomenology & Existential Philosophy Ser.). 192p. 1978. 15.00x (ISBN 0-253-34600-2). Ind U Pr.
Sprung, Mervyn, ed. The Question of Being: East-West Perspectives. 1978. text ed. 12.95x (ISBN 0-271-01242-0). Pa St U Pr.
Starr, David E. Entity & Existence: An Ontological Investigation of Aristotle & Heidegger. LC 74-1463. 332p. 1976. lib. bdg. 20.00 (ISBN 0-89102-045-4). B Franklin.
Stoops, John A. Religious Values in Education. LC 67-25689. 1967. text ed. 4.95x (ISBN 0-8134-0950-0, 950). Interstate.
Tchurmin, Avrhum Y. Meditations from an Exploration of the Ultimate Mysteries. LC 72-85932. 110p. 1972. 3.95 (ISBN 0-8158-0295-1). Chris Mass.
Thatcher, Adrian. The Ontology of Paul Tillich. (Oxford Theological Monographs). 204p. 1978. text ed. 34.50x (ISBN 0-19-826715-0). Oxford U Pr.
Tillich, Paul. Courage to Be. (Terry Lectures Ser.). 1952. 15.00x (ISBN 0-300-00990-9); pap. 3.95 (ISBN 0-300-00241-6, Y11). Yale U Pr.
Vivante, Leone. Essays on Art & Ontology. Vivante, Arturo, tr. from It. 1980. 20.00x (ISBN 0-87480-100-1). U of Utah Pr.
Vollert, Cyril, tr. Francis Suarez: On the Various Kinds of Distinctions. (Medieval Philosophical Texts in Translation: No. 4). 1947. pap. 5.95 (ISBN 0-87462-204-2). Marquette.
Von Schelling, Friedrich. Ages of the World. Bolman, Frederick D., Jr., tr. LC 42-15925. Repr. of 1942 ed. 21.00 (ISBN 0-404-05586-9). AMS Pr.
Weinstein, Michael A. Structure of Human Life: A Vitalist Ontology. LC 79-2304. 1979. 16.50x (ISBN 0-8147-9189-1). NYU Pr.
Wells, Norman. Metaphysical Disputation, Xxxi, De Ento Finito, on Finite Being. Date not set. price not set. Marquette.
Wilkes, James. The Gift of Courage. 1981. pap. price not set. Westminster.
Wolterstorff, Nicholas. On Universals: An Essay in Ontology. LC 73-121819. 1970. 14.00x (ISBN 0-226-90565-9). U of Chicago Pr.

OOGENESIS
see also Ovum
Biggers, J. D. & Schuetz, A. W. Oogenesis. (Illus.). 1972. 35.00 (ISBN 0-8391-0676-9). Univ Park.
Gould, Meredith, et al. Invertebrate Oogenesis, Vol. 2. 300p. 1972. 32.50x (ISBN 0-8422-7030-2). Irvington.
King, Robert, et al. Invertebrate Oogenesis, Vol. 1: Interactions Between Oocytes & Their Accessory Cells. 277p. 1972. text ed. 32.50x (ISBN 0-8422-7015-9). Irvington.
King, Robert C. Ovarian Development in Drosophila Melanogaster. 1970. 42.00 (ISBN 0-12-408150-9). Acad Pr.
Peters, Hannah, et al. Mammalian Oogenesis. 169p. 1972. text ed. 32.50x (ISBN 0-8422-7042-6). Irvington.

OOLITE
see also Geology, Stratigraphic–Jurassic

OOLOGY
see Birds–Eggs and Nests

OOTACAMUND
Panter-Downes, Mollie. Ooty Preserved: A Victorian Hill Station in India. 134p. 1967. 4.95 (ISBN 0-374-22660-1). FS&G.

OPALS
Colahan, John. Australian Opal Safari. LC 72-83020. (Illus.). 128p. 1973. 15.00x (ISBN 0-85179-613-3). Intl Pubns Serv.
Eyles, Wilfred C. Book of Opals. LC 64-14193. (Illus.). 1964. 11.50 (ISBN 0-8048-0068-5). C E Tuttle.
Kalokerinos, Archie. Australian Precious Opal. LC 72-3320. (Illus.). 77p. 1972. 8.95 (ISBN 0-668-02684-7). Arco.
O'Leary, Barrie. A Field Guide to Australian Opals. (Illus.). 1977. 19.00x (ISBN 0-7270-0387-9). Intl Pubns Serv.

OPEL (AUTOMOBILE)
see Automobiles, Foreign–Types–Opel

OPELOUSAS, LOUISIANA–HISTORY
Gahn, Robert. The Opelousas Country. 1973. 6.95 (ISBN 0-685-37716-4). Claitors.

OPEN-AIR SCHOOLS
Wood, David E. & Gillis, James C. Adventure Education. 56p. 1979. pap. 2.50 (ISBN 0-686-63672-4, 1677-7-06). NEA.

OPEN AND CLOSED SHOP
Colberg, Marshall R. The Consumer Impact of Repeal of 14(B) LC 77-17061. 1978. 3.00 (ISBN 0-89195-021-4). Heritage Found.
Hoagland, H. E. Collective Bargaining in the Lithographic Industry. LC 73-76708. (Columbia University. Studies in the Social Sciences: No. 176). Repr. of 1917 ed. 16.50 (ISBN 0-404-51176-7). AMS Pr.
McCarthy, William E. The Closed Shop in Britain. 1964. 24.00x (ISBN 0-520-00837-5). U of Cal Pr.

OPEN CLASSROOM APPROACH TO TEACHING
see Open Plan Schools

OPEN-CUT MINING
see Strip Mining

OPEN DOOR POLICY (FAR EAST)
see Eastern Question (Far East)

OPEN EDUCATION
see Open Plan Schools

OPEN FORUM
see Forums (Discussion and Debate)

OPEN HOUSING
see Discrimination in Housing

OPEN-PIT MINING
see Strip Mining

OPEN PLAN SCHOOLS
see also Free Schools; Individualized Instruction
Alberty, Beth & Weber, Lillian. Continuity & Connection in Curriculum. 1979. pap. 3.50 (ISBN 0-918374-03-0). Workshop Ctr.
Alberty, Beth & Dropkin, Ruth, eds. The Open Education Advisor: Training, Role & Function of Advisors to the Open Corridor Program. Descriptions of Specific Help to Teachers. 92p. 1975. pap. 3.50 (ISBN 0-918374-10-3). Workshop Ctr.
Anderson, Iona L. The Effectiveness of an Open Classroom Approach on Second Language Acquisition. LC 78-62238. 1978. soft cover 10.00 (ISBN 0-88247-541-X). R & E Res Assoc.
Barth, Roland S. Open Education & the American School. LC 72-80265. 1972. 8.95x (ISBN 0-87586-036-2). Agathon.
Beach, Don M. Reaching Teenagers: Learning Centers for the Secondary Classroom. Hipple, Theodore W., ed. LC 76-40778. (Illus.). 1977. 12.95 (ISBN 0-87620-806-5); pap. text ed. 10.95 (ISBN 0-87620-805-7). Goodyear.
Bennett, Neville, et al. Open Plan Schools. 303p. 1981. pap. 27.00x (ISBN 0-85633-188-0, NFER). Humanities.
Bennie, Frances. Learning Centers: Development & Operation. LC 76-58528. 340p. 1977. 19.95 (ISBN 0-87778-097-8). Educ Tech Pubns.
Berger, Evelyn & Winters, Bonnie. Social Studies in the Open Classroom: A Practical Guide. LC 72-97667. 108p. 1973. pap. text ed. 5.00x (ISBN 0-8077-2398-3). Tchrs Coll.
Bogojavlensky, Ann, et al. The Great Learning Book. new ed. 1977. pap. text ed. 10.50 (ISBN 0-201-00844-0, Sch Div). A-W.
Borba, Craig & Borba, Michele. The Good Apple Guide to Learning Centers. (gr. k-6). 1978. 11.95 (ISBN 0-916456-33-1, GA86). Good Apple.
Breyfogle, Ethel, et al. Creating a Learning Environment: A Learning Center Handbook. LC 75-41859. (Illus.). 1976. case ed. 11.95 (ISBN 0-87620-204-0); pap. text ed. 10.95 (ISBN 0-87620-202-4). Goodyear.
Burba, Linda. Everybody Ought to Go to Learning Centers. (Illus.). 80p. (Orig.). 1980. pap. 2.95 (ISBN 0-8341-0634-5). Beacon Hill.
Charles, C. M., ed. Learning Centers That Teach. 1978. pap. 10.75 (ISBN 0-8191-0367-5). U Pr of Amer.
Davidson, Tom, et al. The Learning Center Book: An Integrated Approach. LC 74-33858. (Illus.). 176p. 1976. case ed. 12.95 (ISBN 0-87620-530-9); pap. text ed. 10.95 (ISBN 0-87620-528-7). Goodyear.
Day, Barbara. Open Learning in Early Childhood. 2nd ed. (Illus.). 224p. 1975. pap. text ed. 9.95 (ISBN 0-02-327950-8, 32795). Macmillan.
Devaney, Kathleen. Developing Open Education in America. new ed. LC 74-78803. (Illus.). 203p. 1974. pap. text ed. 2.00 (ISBN 0-912674-12-1). Natl Assn Child Ed.
Dropkin, Ruth, ed. Cumulative Index to Notes from Workshop Center for Open Education. 1979. pap. 1.00 (ISBN 0-918374-04-9). Workshop Ctr.
--Science in the Open Classroom: Approaches to & Samples of Science Teaching in the Elementary School. (Illus.). 50p. 1973. pap. 1.50 (ISBN 0-918374-14-6). Workshop Ctr.
--Teachers with Children: Curriculum in Open Classrooms. (Illus.). 68p. 1976. pap. 3.50 (ISBN 0-918374-16-2). Workshop Ctr.
Dropkin, Ruth & Tobier, Arthur, eds. Roots of Open Education in America: Reminiscences & Reflections on the Ways Americans Have Educated Themselves, in & Out of Schools. LC 76-53146. (Illus.). 1976. pap. 5.00x (ISBN 0-918374-01-4). Workshop Ctr.

Easthope, Gary. Community, Heirarchy & Open Education. 128p. 1975. 10.00x (ISBN 0-7100-8210-X); pap. 5.00 (ISBN 0-7100-8211-8). Routledge & Kegan.

Edelfelt, Roy A. & Orvell, Tamar. Teacher Centers: Where, What, Why? LC 78-61321. (Fastback Ser.: No. 117). 1978. pap. 0.75 (ISBN 0-87367-117-1). Phi Delta Kappa.

Forte, Imogene & Pangle, Mary A. Mini-Center Stuff. LC 76-29532. (The Learning Center Set). (Illus.). 1976. pap. 7.95 (ISBN 0-913916-25-0, IP 25-0). Incentive Pubns.

Gingell, Lesley. The ABCs of the Open Classroom. new ed. LC 72-12723. (Illus.). 288p. 1973. 12.95 (ISBN 0-88280-004-3). ETC Pubns.

Haynes, Carrie A. Good News on Grape Street: The Transformation of a Ghetto School. LC 75-25935. (Illus.). 176p. 1975. pap. text ed. 4.95 (ISBN 0-590-09606-0, Citation). Schol Bk Serv.

Hertzberg, Alvin & Stone, Edward F. Schools Are for Children: An American Approach to the Open Classroom. LC 77-163331. (Illus.). 1974. 6.95x (ISBN 0-8052-3418-7); pap. 3.75 (ISBN 0-8052-0440-7). Schocken.

Hoffman, Marvin. Vermont Diary: Language Arts in the Open Classroom. LC 78-16429. 1978. pap. 4.00 (ISBN 0-915924-07-2). Tchrs & Writers Coll.

Kelly, Lou. From Dialogue to Discourse: An Open Approach to Competence & Creativity. 371p. 1972. pap. 5.95x (ISBN 0-673-07821-3). Scott F.

Learning Centers. (Developments in Classroom Instruction Ser.). 1976. pap. text ed. 3.50 (ISBN 0-8106-1802-8). NEA.

Malehorn, Hal. Open to Change: Options for Teaching Self-Directed Learners. LC 77-28653. 1978. text ed. 12.95 (ISBN 0-87620-626-7); pap. text ed. 10.95 (ISBN 0-87620-625-9). Goodyear.

Meier. Facilitating Children's Development: A Systematic Guide to Open Learning, 2 vols. Incl. Vol. I. Infant & Toddler Learning Episodes. 22.95 (ISBN 0-686-77145-1); Vol. II. Learning Episodes for Older Preschoolers. 24.50 (ISBN 0-686-77146-X). 1979. Univ Park.

Moore, Elaine & Greenlee, Jerri. Ideas for Learning Centers: Discovery Learning for Children. 1974. pap. 7.95 spiral bdg (ISBN 0-8224-3840-2). Pitman Learning.

Morland, John, et al. Classroom Learning Centers. LC 73-77592. 1973. pap. 7.50 (ISBN 0-8224-1410-4). Pitman Learning.

Nyberg, David, intro. by. The Philosophy of Open Education. (International Library of the Philosophy of Education). 220p. 1975. 17.50x (ISBN 0-7100-8285-1). Routledge & Kegan.

The Open Corridor Program: Handbook for Parents. (Illus.). 12p. (Also avail. in Span. as El Programa Del Corredor Abierto). 1971. 0.50 (ISBN 0-918374-11-1). Workshop Ctr.

Open Space Schools. (ERIC Abstracts Ser.: No. 24). 14p. 1973. 2.00 (ISBN 0-686-12100-7, 021-00376). Am Assn Sch Admin.

Peterson, Gary T. The Learning Center: A Sphere for Non-Traditional Approaches to Education. (Illus.). 146p. (Orig.). 1975. 13.50 (ISBN 0-208-01421-7, Linnet). Shoe String.

Petreshene, Susan S. A Complete Guide to Learning Centers. LC 76-49794. (Educational Ser.). (Illus.). 1977. pap. 9.50 (ISBN 0-916988-08-2). Pendragon Hse.

--Supplement to the Complete Guide to Learning Centers. LC 77-71176. (Educational Ser.). (Illus.). 1977. pap. 5.00 (ISBN 0-916988-13-9). Pendragon Hse.

Rogers, Vincent R., et al. Open Education: Critique & Assessment. new ed. LC 75-18578. 106p. 1975. pap. 4.75 (ISBN 0-87120-074-0, 611-75054). Assn Supervision.

Rounds, Susan. Teaching the Young Child: A Handbook of Open Classroom Practice. LC 74-9315. (Illus.). 224p. 1975. 7.95x (ISBN 0-87586-048-6). Agathon.

Sabaroff, Rose & Hanna, Mary A. The Open Classroom: A Practical Guide for the Teacher of the Elementary Grades. LC 74-6442. (Illus.). 1974. 10.00 (ISBN 0-8108-0726-2). Scarecrow.

Seif, Elliott. Success with Open Education: A Manual for Educators & Parents. LC 75-27081. 1975. pap. 3.95 (ISBN 0-8224-6610-4). Pitman Learning.

Silberman, Charles E., ed. The Open Classroom Reader. LC 72-11430. 1973. 12.50 (ISBN 0-394-48221-2). Random.

Spodek, Bernard & Walberg, Herbert, eds. Studies in Open Education. LC 73-19109. 1975. 12.00x (ISBN 0-87586-045-1). Agathon.

Stoltz, Berdine & Saloom, Pamela. Why, What & How of Interest Development Centers. 1978. pap. text ed. 4.95 (ISBN 0-936386-02-9). Creative Learning.

Sullivan, LeRoy L. Sullivan's Guide to Learning Centers in Higher Education. 1978. pap. text ed. 49.50 (ISBN 0-87567-074-1). Entelek.

Terri, Jack D. The Administration of Learning Resource Centers. 1977. pap. text ed. 7.50 (ISBN 0-8191-0274-1). U Pr of Amer.

Tunstall, Jeremy, ed. The Open University Opens. LC 74-78983. 111p. 1974. 10.00x (ISBN 0-87023-167-7); pap. 4.00 (ISBN 0-87023-168-5). U of Mass Pr.

Waterman, Anita & Pflum, John. The New Open Education: A Program for Combining the Basics with Alternative Methods or Creative Teaching of the Basics, 2 vols. rev. ed. 1975. Set. 16.95 (ISBN 0-87491-025-0); Vol. 1. pap. 7.95 (ISBN 0-87491-021-8); Vol. 2. tchr's kit 5.95 (ISBN 0-87491-022-6). Acropolis.

OPEN SHOP

see Open and Closed Shop

OPEN-SPACE PLAN SCHOOLS

see Open Plan Schools

OPEN SPACES

see also Greenbelts; Recreation Areas

Foresta, Ronald. Open Space Policy: New Jersey's Green Acres Program. 173p. (Orig.). 1981. 15.00 (ISBN 0-8135-0923-8). Rutgers U Pr.

Hester, Randolph T., Jr., ed. Neighborhood Space: User Needs & Design Responsibility. LC 75-30669. (Community Development Ser.: Vol. 17). 1975. 40.00 (ISBN 0-87933-173-9). Hutchinson Ross.

Platt, Rutherford H. The Open Space Decision Process: Spatial Allocation of Costs & Benefits. LC 72-85930. (Research Papers Ser.: No. 184). (Illus.). 1972. pap. 8.00 (ISBN 0-89065-049-7, 142). U Chicago Dept Geog.

OPERA

see also Ballad Opera; Ballet; Liturgical Drama; Melodrama;

also names of specific opera companies, e.g. New York (City)-Metropolitan Opera

Abraham, Gerald E. Studies in Russian Music. facs. ed. LC 68-20285. (Essay Index Reprint Ser). 1936. 15.25 (ISBN 0-8369-0133-9). Arno.

Alda, Frances. Men, Women & Tenors. LC 75-149653. Repr. of 1937 ed. 18.00 (ISBN 0-404-00306-0). AMS Pr.

--Men, Women & Tenors. facsimile ed. LC 72-107790. (Select Bibliographies Reprint Ser). 1937. 24.00 (ISBN 0-8369-5174-3). Arno.

Aldrich, Richard. Concert Life in New York, Nineteen Hundred to Nineteen Twenty-Three. facsimile ed. Johnson, Harold, ed. LC 78-156603. (Essay Index Reprint Ser). Repr. of 1941 ed. 36.00 (ISBN 0-8369-2263-8). Arno.

Alexander, Alfred. Operanatomy. 1974. 7.50 (ISBN 0-8008-5838-7, Crescendo). Taplinger.

Armstrong, W. G. A Record of the Opera in Philadelphia. LC 74-27327. Repr. of 1884 ed. 22.50 (ISBN 0-404-12853-X). AMS Pr.

Arnold, Denis & Sadler, Graham, eds. The Baroque Operatic Arias: Andre Campra, Vol. 2. 104p. 1973. pap. 17.85x (ISBN 0-19-713417-3). Oxford U Pr.

Avery, Emmett L. London Stage, Seventeen Hundred to Seventeen Twenty-Nine: A Critical Introduction, Pt. 2. LC 60-6539. (Arcturus Books Paperbacks). (Illus.). 199p. 1968. pap. 5.95 (ISBN 0-8093-0337-X). S Ill U Pr.

Avery, Emmett L. & Scouten, Arthur H. London Stage, Sixteen Sixty to Seventeen-Hundred: A Critical Introduction, Pt. 1. LC 60-6539. (Arcturus Books Paperbacks Ser.). (Illus.). 203p. 1968. pap. 5.95 (ISBN 0-8093-0336-1). S Ill U Pr.

Biancolli, Louis, ed. The Opera Reader. 1977. Repr. of 1953 ed. lib. bdg. 43.00x (ISBN 0-8371-9722-8, BIOR). Greenwood.

Blaze, Francois H. De l'Opera En France, 2 vols. LC 80-2259. Repr. of 1820 ed. Set. 82.50 (ISBN 0-404-18810-9). AMS Pr.

--L' Opera-Italien de 1548 a 1856. LC 80-2260. Repr. of 1856 ed. 52.00 (ISBN 0-686-69547-X). Ams Pr.

Brown, Hubert. Success in Amateur Opera. 1976. lib. bdg. 19.00 (ISBN 0-403-03701-8). Scholarly.

Bulgarian Academy of Sciences, ed. Opera: Nikola D. Obrechkoff, Vol. I. (Illus.). 431p. 1978. 68.00 (ISBN 3-7643-0988-1). Birkhauser.

Camner, James. The Great Opera Stars in Historic Photographs: Three Hundred Thirty-Three Portraits from the 1850s to the 1940s. 12.50 (ISBN 0-8446-5672-0). Peter Smith.

--How to Enjoy Opera. LC 80-2325. (Illus.). 224p. 1981. 12.95 (ISBN 0-385-15850-5). Doubleday.

Camner, James, ed. The Great Opera Stars in Historic Photographs: Three Hundred & Forty Three Portraits from the 1850's to the 1940's. LC 77-86260. (Illus.). 1978. pap. 6.50 (ISBN 0-486-23575-0). Dover.

Capell, Richard. Opera. 1979. Repr. of 1930 ed. lib. bdg. 12.50 (ISBN 0-8495-0925-4). Arden Lib.

Cooper, Martin. Opera Comique. LC 70-181128. 70p. 1949. Repr. 20.00 (ISBN 0-403-01527-8). Scholarly.

Dean, Winton. Handel & the Opera Seria. LC 79-78567. (Ernest Bloch Lectures). 1969. 31.75x (ISBN 0-520-01438-3). U of Cal Pr.

Dent, Edward J. Foundations of English Opera. 2nd ed. LC 65-18501. (Music Ser). 1965. Repr. of 1928 ed. lib. bdg. 22.50 (ISBN 0-306-70905-8). Da Capo.

Donington, Robert. The Opera. (Harbrace History of Musical Forms Ser). (Illus.). 1978. pap. text ed. 9.95 (ISBN 0-15-567536-2, HC). HarBraceJ.

--The Rise of Opera. (Illus.). 362p. 1981. 45.00 (ISBN 0-684-17165-1). Scribner.

Drummond, Andrew H. American Opera Librettos. LC 72-8111. 1973. 10.00 (ISBN 0-8108-0553-7). Scarecrow.

Eaton, Quaintance. Opera Production 2: A Handbook. LC 61-16843. (Illus.). 328p. 1974. 18.95 (ISBN 0-8166-0689-7). U of Minn Pr.

Ebers, John. Seven Years of the King's Theatre. LC 79-88490. Repr. of 1828 ed. 17.50 (ISBN 0-405-08481-1, Blom Pubns). Arno.

Edwards, Henry S. The Lyrical Drama, 2 vols. LC 80-2274. Repr. of 1881 ed. 67.50 (ISBN 0-404-18840-0). AMS Pr.

Faner, Robert D. Walt Whitman & Opera. 260p. 1972. Repr. of 1951 ed. lib. bdg. 7.00x (ISBN 0-8093-0592-5). S Ill U Pr.

Farkas, Andrew, ed. Opera Biographies, 42 vols. (Opera Biographies). 1977. Repr. lib. bdg. 873.00 (ISBN 0-405-09666-6). Arno.

Frost, David, intro. by. The Bluffer's Guides, 6 bks. Incl. Bluff Your Way in Art. Lampitt, L; Bluff Your Way in Cinema. Wlaschin, Ken; Bluff Your Way in Literature. Seymoursmith, Martin; Bluff Your Way in Music. Gammond, Peter; Bluff Your Way in Opera. Coleman, Francis; Bluff Your Way in Wine. Clark, Wick. 64p. 1971. pap. 1.00 ea. Crown.

Genest, Emile. L' Opera-Comique Connu et Inconnu: Son Histoire Depuis l'origine Jusqu'a Nos Jours. LC 80-2277. Repr. of 1925 ed. 39.50 (ISBN 0-404-18845-1). AMS Pr.

Gilman, Lawrence. Aspects of Modern Opera: Estimates & Inquiries. LC 68-25288. (Studies in Music, No. 42). 1969. Repr. of 1909 ed. lib. bdg. 46.95 (ISBN 0-8383-0302-1). Haskell.

--Nature in Music, & Other Studies in the Tone Poetry of Today. facs. ed. LC 67-22096. (Essay Index Reprint Ser). 1914. 13.00 (ISBN 0-8369-0475-3). Arno.

Goldovsky, B. Bringing Opera to Life: Operatic Acting & Stage Direction. 1968. 20.95 (ISBN 0-13-083105-0). P-H.

Graf, Herbert. The Opera & Its Future in America. LC 78-154712. (Illus.). 305p. 1973. Repr. of 1941 ed. 19.50 (ISBN 0-8046-1744-9). Kennikat.

Grout, Donald J. A Short History of Opera. 2nd ed. LC 64-11043. 852p. (gr. 9 up). 1965. text ed. 20.00x (ISBN 0-231-02422-3). Columbia U Pr.

Hamm, Charles. Opera. (Music Reprint Ser: 1980). (Illus.). 1980. Repr. lib. bdg. 22.50 (ISBN 0-306-76013-4). Da Capo.

Harris, Kenn. Opera Quiz Book. 1982. pap. 6.95 (ISBN 0-14-005884-2). Penguin.

Hartmann, Rudolph, ed. Opera. LC 77-2896. (Illus.). 1977. 60.00 (ISBN 0-688-03212-5). Morrow.

Heriot, Angus. The Castrati in Opera. LC 74-1332. (Music Ser.). 243p. 1974. Repr. of 1956 ed. lib. bdg. 22.50 (ISBN 0-306-70650-4). Da Capo.

Heylbut, Rose & Gerber, Aime. Backstage at the Metropolitan Opera. Farkas, Andrew, ed. LC 76-29941. (Opera Biographies). Orig. Title: Backstage at the Opera. (Illus.). 1977. Repr. of 1937 ed. lib. bdg. 22.00x (ISBN 0-405-09683-6). Arno.

Higgins, John. The Making of an Opera. LC 78-55609. (Illus.). 1978. 12.95 (ISBN 0-689-10906-7). Atheneum.

Hogan, Charles B. London Stage, 1776-1800: A Critical Introduction. LC 60-6539. (Arcturus Books Paperbacks). (Illus.). 230p. 1968. pap. 6.95 (ISBN 0-8093-0340-X). S Ill U Pr.

Hogan, Charles B., ed. London Stage, 1660-1800, 3 vols, Pt. 5; 1776-1800. LC 60-6539. (London Stage Ser.). (Illus.). 2838p. 1968. Set. 100.00x (ISBN 0-8093-0437-6). S Ill U Pr.

Hogarth, G. Memoirs of the Opera, 2 vols. LC 71-166101. (Music Ser.). 1972. Repr. of 1851 ed. Set. lib. bdg. 49.50 (ISBN 0-306-70256-8). Da Capo.

Holbach, Paul T. Lettre a une Dame d'un Certain Age, sur l'Etat Present de l'Opera. (Holbach & His Friends Ser). (Fr.). 1974. Repr. of 1752 ed. lib. bdg. 20.00x (ISBN 0-8287-1383-9, 1522). Clearwater Pub.

Howard, Patricia. Gluck & the Birth of Modern Opera. (Illus.). 1963. 8.95 (ISBN 0-312-32970-9). St Martin.

--The Operas of Benjamin Britten: An Introduction. LC 76-7367. 1976. Repr. of 1969 ed. lib. bdg. 15.25x (ISBN 0-8371-8867-9, HOOB). Greenwood.

Hughes, Spike. Famous Mozart Operas. rev. ed. 256p. 1972. pap. 3.00 (ISBN 0-486-22858-4). Dover.

--Famous Mozart Operas: An Analytical Guide for the Opera-Goer & Armchair Listener. 2nd rev. ed. (Illus.). 6.00 (ISBN 0-8446-4559-1). Peter Smith.

--Famous Puccini Operas: An Analytic Guide for the Opera-Goer & Armchair Listener. 2nd rev. ed. (Illus.). 5.00 (ISBN 0-8446-4560-5). Peter Smith.

Kidson, Frank. Beggar's Opera: It's Predecessors & Successors. (Music - Practice & Theory Ser). 1969. Repr. of 1922 ed. 11.00 (ISBN 0-384-29395-6). Johnson Repr.

Krehbiel, Henry E. A Second Book of Operas, Their Histories, Their Plots & Their Music. LC 80-2280. Repr. of 1917 ed. 36.50 (ISBN 0-404-18852-4). AMS Pr.

Kupferberg, Herbert. Opera. LC 74-83891. (World of Culture Ser.). (Illus.). 192p. 1975. 12.95 (ISBN 0-88225-117-1). Newsweek.

Lahee, Henry C. Grand Opera in America. LC 72-2050. Repr. of 1902 ed. 16.45 (ISBN 0-404-09909-2). AMS Pr.

--Grand Opera in America. facsimile ed. LC 76-154157. (Select Bibliographies Reprint Ser). Repr. of 1901 ed. 21.00 (ISBN 0-8369-5773-3). Arno.

Lang, Paul H. The Experience of Opera. Orig. Title: Critic at the Opera. 336p. 1973. pap. 6.95 (ISBN 0-393-00706-5, Norton Lib). Norton.

Lapido, Duro. Eda: An Opera. Olayemi, Val, tr. 1970. 7.50x (ISBN 0-8002-1384-X). Intl Pubns Serv.

Lawrence, Robert. The World of Opera. LC 77-2268. (Illus.). 1977. Repr. of 1956 ed. lib. bdg. 17.75x (ISBN 0-8371-9551-9, LAWO). Greenwood.

Lee, E. M. The Story of Opera. 59.95 (ISBN 0-8490-1136-1). Gordon Pr.

Lee, Ernest M. Story of Opera. LC 69-16803. (Music Story Ser). 1968. Repr. of 1909 ed. 19.00 (ISBN 0-8103-3359-7). Gale.

Marek, George R. A Front Seat at the Opera. LC 71-138161. 307p. 1972. Repr. of 1948 ed. lib. bdg. 15.75x (ISBN 0-8371-5618-1, MAFS). Greenwood.

Maretzek, Max. Crochets & Quavers: Or Revelations of an Opera Manager in America. 2nd ed. LC 65-23397. (Music Ser). 1966. Repr. of 1855 ed. lib. bdg. 27.50 (ISBN 0-306-70915-5). Da Capo.

Mates, Julian. The American Musical Stage Before 1800. 1962. 20.00 (ISBN 0-8135-0393-0). Rutgers U Pr.

May, Robin. A Companion to the Opera. LC 76-52790. 1977. 12.95 (ISBN 0-88254-439-X). Hippocrene Bks.

Melitz, Leo L. The Opera Goers' Complete Guide. Hackney, Louise W., rev. by. Salinger, Richard, tr. LC 80-2293. Repr. of 1936 ed. 54.50 (ISBN 0-404-18859-1). AMS Pr.

Mondadori, Editore. Simon & Schuster's Book of the Opera. 1979. 32.50 (ISBN 0-671-24886-3). S&S.

Moore, Edward C. Forty Years of Opera in Chicago. Farkas, Andrew, ed. LC 76-29956. (Opera Biographies). (Illus.). 1977. Repr. of 1930 ed. lib. bdg. 30.00x (ISBN 0-405-09697-6). Arno.

Morley, Alexander F. Harrap Opera Guide. LC 79-558464. 320p. 1970. 17.50x (ISBN 0-245-50509-1). Intl Pubns Serv.

Moses, Montrose J. The Life of Heinrich Conried. Farkas, Andrew, ed. LC 76-29959. (Opera Biographies). (Illus.). 1977. Repr. of 1916 ed. lib. bdg. 25.00x (ISBN 0-405-09699-2). Arno.

Nuitter, C. & Thoinan, E. Les Origines De L'opera Francais. LC 77-4106. (Music Reprint Ser., 1977). 1977. Repr. of 1886 ed. lib. bdg. 32.50 (ISBN 0-306-70895-7). Da Capo.

Oliver, Alfred R. Encyclopedists As Critics of Music. LC 47-31483. Repr. of 1947 ed. 14.50 (ISBN 0-404-04817-X). AMS Pr.

Orrey, Leslie. A Concise History of Opera. LC 75-5192. (Illus.). 252p. 1973. pap. 5.95 (ISBN 0-684-13576-0, SL489, ScribT). Scribner.

Polfen, M. N. A Practical Guide to Grand Opera. 200p. (Orig.). 1981. pap. 7.95 (ISBN 0-934036-08-X). PMF Research.

Pougin, Arthur. Les Vrais Createurs De l'Opera Francais: Perrin et Cambert. LC 80-2296. Repr. of 1881 ed. 33.50 (ISBN 0-404-18862-1). AMS Pr.

Prunieres, Henry. L'Opera Italien En France Avant Lulli. Repr. of 1913 ed. 31.00 (ISBN 0-384-48061-6). Johnson Repr.

Remond De Saint-Mard, Toussaint. Reflexions Sur l'Opera. LC 80-2294. Repr. of 1741 ed. 18.50 (ISBN 0-404-18863-X). AMS Pr.

Rich, Allan. Listeners Guide to Opera. 1980. 9.95 (ISBN 0-671-25442-1). S&S.

Riemann, Hugo. Opern-Handbuch. LC 80-2295. 1981. 75.00 (ISBN 0-404-18864-8). AMS Pr.

Rolland, Romain. Some Musicians of Former Days. facs. ed. LC 68-8490. (Essay Index Reprint Ser). 1915. 19.00 (ISBN 0-8369-0831-7). Arno.

Der Rosenkavalier Kalsch. pap. write for info. (ISBN 0-8277-5226-1). British Bk Ctr.

Rosenthal, Harold D., ed. Opera, 5 vols. (Music Reprint Ser.: 1980). (Illus.). 1980. Repr. of 1955 ed. Set. lib. bdg. 250.00 (ISBN 0-306-79583-3); lib. bdg. 55.00 ea. Da Capo.
Schmidgall, Gary. Literature As Opera. (Illus.). 1980. pap. 7.95 (ISBN 0-19-502706-X, GB 598, GB). Oxford U Pr.
--Literature As Opera. LC 76-57264. (Illus.). 1977. 19.95 (ISBN 0-19-502213-0). Oxford U Pr.
Scott, R. H. Jean-Baptiste Lully, the Founder of French Opera. 1977. 6.95 (ISBN 0-8008-4320-7, Crescendo). Taplinger.
Scouten, Arthur H. London Stage, 1729-1747: A Critical Introduction. LC 60-6539. (Arcturus Books Paperbacks). (Illus.). 206p. 1968. pap. 6.95 (ISBN 0-8093-0338-8). S Ill U Pr.
Simon, Henry W. New Victor Book of the Opera. 1968. 19.95 (ISBN 0-671-20054-2). S&S.
Solerti, Angelo. Musica, Ballo E Drammatica Alla Corte Medicea Dal 1600 Al 1637. LC 67-12470. (It). 1968. Repr. of 1905 ed. 30.00 (ISBN 0-405-08987-2). Arno.
Sonneck, Oscar G. Early Opera in America. LC 63-23189. (Illus.). 1915. 18.00 (ISBN 0-405-08988-0). Arno.
Stone, George W., Jr. London Stage, 1747-1776: A Critical Introduction. LC 60-6539. (Arcturus Books Paperbacks). (Illus.). 224p. 1968. pap. 6.95 (ISBN 0-8093-0339-6). S Ill U Pr.
Swanston, Hamish. In Defence of Opera. 1978. pap. 3.95 (ISBN 0-14-022005-4, Pelican). Penguin.
Taubman, Hyman H. Opera: Front & Back. LC 80-2306. Repr. of 1938 ed. 51.50 (ISBN 0-404-18872-9). AMS Pr.
Thompson, Oscar. The American Singer: A Hundred Years of Success in Opera. Repr. of 1937 ed. 27.00 (ISBN 0-384-60280-0). Johnson Repr.
Thomson, Virgil. Art of Judging Music. LC 69-14114. 1969. Repr. of 1948 ed. lib. bdg. 20.50x (ISBN 0-8371-0683-4, THJM). Greenwood.
--Music, Right & Left. LC 68-55327. (Illus.). 1968. Repr. of 1951 ed. lib. bdg. 15.00x (ISBN 0-8371-0685-0, THMU). Greenwood.
--Musical Scene. Repr. of 1945 ed. lib. bdg. 15.75x (ISBN 0-8371-0684-2, THMS). Greenwood.
Wagner, Richard. Opera & Drama. (Richard Wagner's Prose Work Ser.: Vol. 2). 1967. Repr. of 1893 ed. only as part of set avail. (ISBN 0-8450-2102-8). Broude.
Who's Who in Opera. LC 75-7963. 1976. 65.00 (ISBN 0-405-06652-X). Arno.
Woodhouse, Frederick. Opera for Amateurs. 1951. 6.95 (ISBN 0-234-77225-5). Dufour.
Worsthorne, Simon T. Venetian Opera in the Seventeenth Century. 1954. 36.00x (ISBN 0-19-816116-6). Oxford U Pr.
Yaffee, Robert A. Subcultural Orientations Toward Opera: A Model of Marketing Research Concerning Opera Education & Potential Audience Development. 143p. (Orig.). 1980. pap. text ed. 11.95x (ISBN 0-536-03235-1). Ginn Custom.

OPERA–ADDRESSES, ESSAYS, LECTURES

Austin, William W., ed. New Looks at Italian Opera: Essays in Honor of Donald J. Grout. LC 76-1010. (Illus.). 290p. 1976. Repr. of 1968 ed. lib. bdg. 21.75 (ISBN 0-8371-8761-3, AUNL). Greenwood.
Clayton, Ellen C. Queens of Song: Being Memoirs of Some of the Most Celebrated Female Vocalists. facsimile ed. LC 77-38713. (Essay Index Reprint Ser). Repr. of 1865 ed. 30.00 (ISBN 0-8369-2640-4). Arno.
Dent, E. J. The Rise of Romantic Opera. Dean, W., ed. LC 76-14029. (Illus.). 1976. 32.95 (ISBN 0-521-21337-1). Cambridge U Pr.
Gilman, Lawrence. Aspects of Modern Opera: Estimates & Inquiries. LC 68-25288. (Studies in Music, No. 42). 1969. Repr. of 1909 ed. lib. bdg. 46.95 (ISBN 0-8383-0302-1). Haskell.
Goldovsky, Boris & Peltz, Mary E. Accents on Opera: A Series of Brief Essays Stressing Known & Little Known Facts & Facets of a Familiar Art. facsimile ed. LC 77-156651. (Essay Index Reprint Ser). Repr. of 1953 ed. 25.00 (ISBN 0-8369-2398-7). Arno.
Hussey, Dyneley. Some Composers of Opera. facsimile ed. LC 79-167360. (Essay Index Reprint Ser). Repr. of 1952 ed. 12.00 (ISBN 0-8369-2654-4). Arno.
Lang, Paul H. The Experience of Opera. Orig. Title: Critic at the Opera. 336p. 1973. pap. 6.95 (ISBN 0-393-00706-5, Norton Lib). Norton.
Wellesz, Egon. Essays on Opera. LC 71-181293. 158p. 1950. Repr. 17.00 (ISBN 0-403-01717-3). Scholarly.

OPERA–BIBLIOGRAPHY

Blyth, Alan. Opera on Record. LC 81-47801. 688p. 1982. pap. price not set (ISBN 0-06-090910-2, CN 910, CN). Har-Row.
Chusid, Martin. A Catalogue of Verdi's Operas. (Music Indexes & Bibliographies: No. 5). 1974. pap. 15.00 (ISBN 0-913574-05-8). Eur-Am Music.
Drone, Jeanette M. Index to Opera, Operetta & Musical Comedy Synopses in Collections & Periodicals. LC 77-25822. 1978. 10.00 (ISBN 0-8108-1100-6). Scarecrow.
Langbaine, Gerard. Account of the English Dramatick Poets. 2nd ed. 1965. Repr. of 1691 ed. 23.50 (ISBN 0-8337-2003-1). B Franklin.
Mattfeld, Julius. A Handbook of American Operatic Premieres, 1731-1962. (Detroit Studies in Music Bibliography Ser.: No. 5). 1963. pap. 2.00 (ISBN 0-911772-25-1). Info Coord.
Monterde Garcia Icazbalceta, Francisco. Bibliografia Del Teatro En Mexico. LC 72-132684. (Monografias Bibliograficas Mexicanas: No. 28). (Illus., Span). 1970. Repr. of 1934 ed. 43.00 (ISBN 0-8337-2440-1). B Franklin.
Sonneck, Oscar G. Dramatic Music: Catalogue of Full Scores. LC 69-12619. (Music Ser). 1969. Repr. of 1908 ed. lib. bdg. 25.00 (ISBN 0-306-71229-6). Da Capo.
U. S. Library of Congress. Catalogue of Opera Librettos Printed Before 1800, 2 vols. 1965. Repr. of 1914 ed. Set. 92.50 (ISBN 0-8337-3322-2). B Franklin.

OPERA–DICTIONARIES

see also Operas–Stories, Plots, etc.

Clement, Felix & Larousse, Pierre. Dictionnaire Des Operas, 2 Vols. LC 69-15617. (Music Reprint Ser). 1969. Repr. of 1905 ed. 95.00 (ISBN 0-306-71197-4). Da Capo.
Gammond, Peter. The Illustrated Encyclopedia of Recorded Opera. (Illus.). 1979. 17.95 (ISBN 0-517-53840-7). Crown.
Loewenberg, Alfred. Annals of Opera, Fifteen Ninety-Seven to Nineteen Forty, 2 vols. LC 72-166242. 879p. 1972. Repr. of 1943 ed. Set. 42.00 (ISBN 0-403-01376-3). Scholarly.
Moore, Frank L. Crowell's Handbook of World Opera. LC 73-3025. (Illus.). 683p. 1974. Repr. of 1961 ed. lib. bdg. 43.00x (ISBN 0-8371-6822-8, MOCH). Greenwood.
Orrey, Leslie & Chase, Gilbert, eds. The Encyclopedia of Opera. (Illus.). 376p. 1976. 22.50 (ISBN 0-684-13630-9, ScribT). Scribner.
Rosenthal, Harold & Warrack, John. Dictionnaire de L'opera. 420p. (Fr.). 1974. pap. 36.00 (ISBN 0-686-56799-4, M-416). French & Eur.
Rosenthal, Harold & Warrack, John, eds. The Concise Oxford Dictionary of Opera. 2nd ed. (Out-of-Ser. Paperback). 576p. 1979. pap. 11.95 (ISBN 0-19-311321-X). Oxford U Pr.
--The Concise Oxford Dictionary of Opera. 2nd ed. 1979. 25.00 (ISBN 0-19-311318-X). Oxford U Pr.
Ross, Anne. The Opera Dictionary. LC 71-166258. 566p. 1961. Repr. 35.00 (ISBN 0-403-01385-2). Scholarly.
Towers, John. Dictionary-Catalogue of Operas & Operettas, 2 Vols. LC 67-25996. (Music Ser). 1967. Repr. of 1910 ed. lib. bdg. 59.50 (ISBN 0-306-70962-7). Da Capo.

OPERA–DRAMATURGY

Kerman, Joseph. Opera As Drama. 1956. pap. 2.95 (ISBN 0-394-70088-0, Vin). Random.
Krehbiel, Henry E. Studies in the Wagnerian Drama. LC 74-24133. Repr. of 1891 ed. 12.50 (ISBN 0-404-12993-5). AMS Pr.
Mitchell, Ronald. Opera-Dead or Alive: Production, Performance, & Enjoyment of Musical Theatre. LC 73-121772. (Illus.). 334p. 1970. 25.00 (ISBN 0-299-05811-5); pap. 7.95 (ISBN 0-299-05814-X). U of Wis Pr.
Shea, George E. Acting in Opera. (Music Reprint Ser.: 1980). (Illus.). 1980. Repr. of 1915 ed. lib. bdg. 14.50 (ISBN 0-306-76004-5). Da Capo.

OPERA–HISTORY AND CRITICISM

Apthorp, W. F. The Opera, Past & Present. 59.95 (ISBN 0-8490-0770-4). Gordon Pr.
Apthorp, William F. The Opera Past & Present. LC 78-58193. 1978. Repr. of 1930 ed. lib. bdg. 25.00 (ISBN 0-89341-432-8). Longwood Pr.
Arundell, Dennis. The Critic at the Opera: Contemporary Comments on Opera in London Over Three Centuries. (Music Reprint Ser.: 1980). (Illus.). 1980. Repr. of 1957 ed. lib. bdg. 29.50 (ISBN 0-306-76026-6). Da Capo.
Bekker, Paul. The Changing Opera. Mendel, Arthur, tr. LC 80-2256. Repr. of 1935 ed. 35.50 (ISBN 0-404-18803-6). AMS Pr.
Bloomfield, Arthur. The San Francisco Opera: 1922-1978. 3rd, rev ed. (Illus.). 1978. pap. 11.95 (ISBN 0-89174-032-5). Comstock Edns.
Bordman, Gerald. American Operetta: From H.M.S. Pinafore to Sweeney Todd. (Illus.). 240p. 1981. 15.95 (ISBN 0-19-502869-4). Oxford U Pr.
Capell, Richard. Opera. LC 78-66894. (Encore Music Editions Ser.). 1981. Repr. of 1948 ed. 14.50 (ISBN 0-88355-730-4). Hyperion Conn.
A Checklist of Writings on Eighteenth Century French & Italian Opera (Excluding Mozart) (Music Indexes & Bibliographies: No. 3). pap. 8.00 (ISBN 0-913574-03-1). Eur-Am Music.
Colombani, Alfredo. L Opera Italiana Nel Secolo Xix: Dono Agli Abbonati Del Corriere Della Sera. LC 80-2266. Repr. of 1900 ed. 61.00 (ISBN 0-404-18819-2). AMS Pr.
Conrad, Peter. Romantic Opera & Literary Form. (Quantum Ser.). 1977. 14.00 (ISBN 0-520-03258-6). U of Cal Pr.
Cooper, Martin. Russian Opera. LC 77-181127. 65p. 1951. Repr. 25.00 (ISBN 0-403-01528-6). Scholarly.
Corte, Andrea Della. L' Opera Comica Italiana nel Settecento, Studi ed Appunti, 2 vols. LC 80-2269. Repr. of 1923 ed. Set. 62.50 (ISBN 0-404-18830-3). Vol. 1 (ISBN 0-404-18831-1). Vol. 2 (ISBN 0-404-18832-X). AMS Pr.
Cucuel, Georges. Les Createurs de l'Opera-Comique Francais. LC 80-2271. Repr. of 1914 ed. 29.50 (ISBN 0-404-18834-6). AMS Pr.
Davis, Ronald L. Opera in Chicago. (Illus.). 393p. 1981. Repr. of 1966 ed. text ed. 26.50x (ISBN 0-8290-0225-1). Irvington.
De Mably, Gabriel B. Lettres a Madame la marquise de Pompadour sur l'opera. LC 76-43925. (Music & Theatre in France in the 17th & 18th Centuries). Repr. of 1741 ed. 17.50 (ISBN 0-404-60169-3). AMS Pr.
Demuth, Norman. French Opera: Its Development to the Revolution. (Music Reprint, 1978 Ser.). (Illus.). 1978. Repr. of 1963 ed. lib. bdg. 27.50 (ISBN 0-306-77576-X). Da Capo.
Dent, Edward J. Opera. rev. ed. LC 78-14482. (Illus.). 1978. Repr. of 1968 ed. lib. bdg. 19.25x (ISBN 0-313-20563-9, DEOP). Greenwood.
--The Rise of Romantic Opera. Dean, Winton, ed. LC 78-62111. 1979. pap. 7.50 (ISBN 0-521-29659-5). Cambridge U Pr.
Desboulmiers, Jean A. Histoire du theatre de l'Opera comique, 2 vols. 2nd ed. LC 76-43914. (Music & Theatre in France in the 17th & 18th Centuries). Repr. of 1770 ed. 85.00 (ISBN 0-404-60160-X). AMS Pr.
Drummond, Andrew H. American Opera Librettos. LC 72-8111. 1973. 10.00 (ISBN 0-8108-0553-7). Scarecrow.
Drummond, John D. Opera in Perspective. (Illus.). 369p. 1980. 25.00 (ISBN 0-8166-0848-2). U of Minn Pr.
Edwards, Sutherland. History of the Opera: From Monteverdi to Donizetti, 2 vols. in one. LC 77-5587. 1977. Repr. of 1862 ed. lib. bdg. 49.50 (ISBN 0-306-77416-X). Da Capo.
Fernandez, Doreen G. The Iloilo Zarzuela: Nineteen Hundred & Three to Nineteen Thirty. (Illus.). 1979. 22.25x (ISBN 0-686-24651-9, Pub. by Ateneo Univ Pr). Cellar.
Flaherty, Gloria. Opera in the Development of German Critical Thought. LC 78-51163. 1978. 25.00 (ISBN 0-691-06370-2). Princeton U Pr.
Fortune, Nigel & Lewis, Anthony, eds. New Oxford History of Music, Vol. 5: Opera & Church Music 1630-1750. (Illus.). 800p. 1975. 49.95x (ISBN 0-19-316305-5). Oxford U Pr.
Freeman, Robert. Opera Without Drama: Currents of Change in Italian Opera, 1675-1725. Buelow, George, ed. LC 80-29133. (Studies in Musicology: No. 35). 358p. 1981. 81.95 (ISBN 0-8357-1152-8, Pub. by UMI Res Pr). Univ Microfilms.
Gammond, Peter, ed. An Illustrated Guide to Composers of Opera. LC 81-66319. (Illus.). 240p. 1981. 9.95 (ISBN 0-668-05317-8, 5317). Arco.
Gatti-Casazza, Guilio. Memories of the Opera. 1980. 19.95 (ISBN 0-7145-3518-4); pap. 9.95 (ISBN 0-7145-3665-2). Riverrun NY.
Gay, John. Polly - an Opera: Being the Second Part of the Beggar's Opera. 1922. 20.00 (ISBN 0-8274-3183-X). R West.
Goldovsky, Boris & Cate, Curtis. My Road to Opera: The Recollections of Boris Goldsovsky As Told to Curtis Cate. 1979. 15.00 (ISBN 0-395-27760-4). HM.
Graf, Herbert. The Opera & Its Future in America. LC 78-154712. (Illus.). 305p. 1973. Repr. of 1941 ed. 19.50 (ISBN 0-8046-1744-9). Kennikat.
--Opera for the People. LC 68-23811. (Music Reprint Ser.). 1973. Repr. of 1951 ed. lib. bdg. 27.50 (ISBN 0-306-70984-8). Da Capo.
Gregoir, Edouard-George-Jacques. Gretry (Andre-Ernest-Modeste) celebre compositeur belge. LC 76-43919. (Music & Theatre in France in the 17th & 18th Centuries). Repr. of 1883 ed. 42.50 (ISBN 0-404-60163-4). AMS Pr.
Grout, Donald J. Alessandro Scarlatti: An Introduction to His Operas. LC 78-54796. 1979. 16.50x (ISBN 0-520-03682-4). U of Cal Pr.
Hanning, Barbara R. Of Poetry & Music's Power: Humanism & the Creation of the Opera. Buelow, George, ed. (Studies in Musicology: No. 13). 1980. 34.95x (ISBN 0-8357-1071-8, Pub. by UMI Res Pr). Univ Microfilms.
Hewlett-Davies, Barry. A Night at the Opera. (Illus.). 160p. 1981. 10.95 (ISBN 0-312-57276-X). St Martin.
Hipsher, Edward E. American Opera & Its Composers. LC 77-25413. (Music Reprint Ser., 1978). (Illus.). 1978. Repr. of 1927 ed. lib. bdg. 35.00 (ISBN 0-306-77516-6). Da Capo.
Hogarth, G. Memoirs of the Opera, 2 vols. LC 71-166101. (Music Ser.). 1972. Repr. of 1851 ed. Set. lib. bdg. 49.50 (ISBN 0-306-70256-8). Da Capo.
Hughes, Spike. Famous Mozart Operas. rev. ed. 256p. 1972. pap. 3.00 (ISBN 0-486-22858-4). Dover.
Hussey, Dyneley. Eurydice: Or, the Nature of Opera. LC 80-2283. Repr. of 1929 ed. 17.50 (ISBN 0-404-18849-4). AMS Pr.
Iacuzzi, Alfred. The European Vogue of Favart: The Diffusion of the Opera-comique. LC 76-43946. (Music & Theatre in France in the 17th & 18th Centuries). Repr. of 1932 ed. 27.50 (ISBN 0-404-60165-0). AMS Pr.
Jell, George C. Master Builders of Opera. LC 78-134102. (Essay Index Reprint Ser). 1933. 17.00 (ISBN 0-8369-1964-5). Arno.
Jullien, Adolphe. La Cour et l'opera sous Louis XVI: Marie-Antoinette et Sacchini; Salieri; Favart et Gluck. LC 76-43947. (Music & Theatre in France in the 17th & 18th Centuries). Repr. of 1878 ed. 27.50 (ISBN 0-404-60166-9). AMS Pr.
Krehbiel, Henry. Chapters of Opera. (Music Reprint Ser.). (Illus.). xvii, 435p. 1980. Repr. of 1909 ed. lib. bdg. 39.50 (ISBN 0-306-76036-3). Da Capo.
Krehbiel, Henry E. More Chapters of Opera: Being Historical & Critical Observations & Records Concerning the Lyric Drama in New York from 1908-1918. LC 78-66910. (Encore Music Editions Ser.). 1981. Repr. of 1919 ed. 45.00 (ISBN 0-686-66139-7). Hyperion Conn.
Lahee, Henry C. Grand Opera in America. LC 72-2050. Repr. of 1902 ed. 16.45 (ISBN 0-404-09909-2). AMS Pr.
--Grand Opera in America. LC 72-2050. Repr. of 1902 ed. 16.45 (ISBN 0-404-09909-2). AMS Pr.
La Laurencie, Lionel de. Les Createurs De l'Opera Francais. LC 80-2287. Repr. of 1921 ed. 26.00 (ISBN 0-404-18854-0). AMS Pr.
Loewenberg, Alfred. Annals of Opera, Fifteen Ninety-Seven to Nineteen Forty, 2 vols. LC 72-166242. 879p. 1972. Repr. of 1943 ed. Set. 42.00 (ISBN 0-403-01376-3). Scholarly.
Loewenberg, Alfred, compiled by. Annals of Opera, Fifteen Ninety-Seven to Nineteen Forty, 2 vols. in 1. 3rd rev. ed. 878p. 1978. 49.50x (ISBN 0-87471-851-1). Rowman.
Lotti, Antonio. Alessandro Severo. LC 76-21046. (Italian Opera, 1640-1770 Ser.: Vol. 20). 1977. lib. bdg. 70.00 (ISBN 0-8240-2619-5). Garland Pub.
Lulu. (Opera Guides Ser.). (Illus.). 1981. pap. 4.95 (ISBN 0-7145-3847-7). Riverrun NY.
Mackinlay, Sterling. Origin & Development of Light Opera. 59.95 (ISBN 0-8490-0772-0). Gordon Pr.
Marek, George R., ed. World Treasury of Grand Opera: Its Triumphs, Trials & Great Personalities. LC 74-167383. (Essay Index Reprint Ser.). Repr. of 1957 ed. 32.00 (ISBN 0-8369-2463-0). Arno.
The Marriage of Figaro. (Opera Guides Ser.). (Illus.). 1981. pap. 4.95 (ISBN 0-686-71352-4). Riverrun NY.
Martens, Frederick H. The Book of the Opera & the Ballet & the History of the Opera. LC 80-2289. Repr. of 1925 ed. 22.50 (ISBN 0-404-18857-5). AMS Pr.
Martorella, Roseanne. The Sociology of the Opera. 256p. 1982. 24.95 (ISBN 0-686-76471-4). J F Bergin.
Mattfeld, Julius. A Hundred Years of Grand Opera in New York: 1825-1925. Repr. of 1927 ed. 12.00 (ISBN 0-404-13038-0). AMS Pr.
Merrill, Robert & Saffron, Robert. Between Acts: An Irreverent Look at Opera & Other Madness. LC 76-20467. 1976. 9.95 (ISBN 0-07-041501-3, GB). McGraw.
Mordden, Ethan. Opera in the Twentieth Century: Sacred, Profane, Godot. 1978. 13.95 (ISBN 0-19-502288-2). Oxford U Pr.
Newman, Ernest. Gluck & the Opera: A Study in Musical History. 1976. Repr. of 1967 ed. lib. bdg. 23.00x (ISBN 0-8371-8849-0, NEGO). Greenwood.
Newman, Joyce. Jean-Baptiste Lully & His Tragedies Lyriques. Buelow, George, ed. LC 79-12289. (Studies in Musicology: No. 1). 1979. 31.95 (ISBN 0-8357-1002-5, Pub. by UMI Res Pr). Univ Microfilms.
L Opera Buffa Napoletana Durante Il Settecento: Storia Letteraria. 2nd ed. LC 80-2298. Repr. of 1917 ed. 53.50 (ISBN 0-404-18867-2). AMS Pr.
Orrey, Lesley. Opera in the High Baroque. 1981. 27.50 (ISBN 0-7145-3658-X). Riverrun NY.
Pe-Chin Chang. Chinese Opera & Painted Face. 268p. 1980. 85.00x (ISBN 0-89955-142-4, Pub. by Mei Ya China). Intl Schol Bk Serv.

Petty, Fred C. Italian Opera in London, Seventeen Sixty to Eighteen Hundred. (Studies in Musicology: No. 16). 1980. 29.95x (ISBN 0-8357-1073-4). Univ Microfilms.
Planelli, Antonio. Dell'Opera in Musica. LC 80-2292. Repr. of 1772 ed. 31.50 (ISBN 0-404-18861-3). AMS Pr.
Rolland, Romain. Les Origines du Theatre Lyrique Moderne. facsimile ed. 332p. 1971. 55.00 (ISBN 0-686-55261-X). French & Eur.
Rubsamen, Walter H., ed. Scottish Ballad Operas, One: Pastoral Comedies. (The Ballad Opera Ser.). 1974. lib. bdg. 50.00 (ISBN 0-8240-0923-1). Garland Pub.
--Scottish Ballad Operas, Three: Farce & Satire. (The Ballad Opera Ser.). 1974. lib. bdg. 50.00 (ISBN 0-8240-0925-8). Garland Pub.
Salvatore, Paul J. Favart's Unpublished Plays: The Rise of the Popular Comic Opera. LC 76-43939. (Music & Theatre in France in the 17th & 18th Centuries). Repr. of 1935 ed. 29.50 (ISBN 0-404-60189-8). AMS Pr.
Scott, Michael. The Record of Singing. LC 79-28332. (Illus.). 1980. text ed. 49.50x (ISBN 0-8419-0599-1). Holmes & Meier.
Sokol, Martin. The New York City Opera: An American Adventure. (Illus.). 480p. 1981. 34.95 (ISBN 0-02-612280-4). Macmillan.
Sonneck, Oscar G. Early Opera in America. 59.95 (ISBN 0-8490-0073-4). Gordon Pr.
Stanislavski, Constantin & Rumyantsev, P. I. Stanislavski on Opera. LC 72-87119. (Illus.). 1975. pap. 11.95 (ISBN 0-87830-552-1). Theatre Arts.
Streatfeild, Richard A. The Opera: A Sketch of the Development of Opera. rev. ed. LC 79-109857. 402p. 1972. Repr. of 1932 ed. lib. bdg. 16.75x (ISBN 0-8371-4348-9, STOP). Greenwood.
Teasdale, May S. Handbook of 20th Century Opera. LC 76-4920. (Music Reprint Ser.). 1976. Repr. of 1938 ed. lib. bdg. 22.50 (ISBN 0-306-70783-7). Da Capo.
Troy, Charles E. The Comic Intermezzo: A Study in the History of Eighteenth-Century Italian Opera. LC 79-12295. (Studies in Musicology: No. 9). 1979. 31.95 (ISBN 0-8357-0992-2, Pub. by UMI Res Pr). Univ Microfilms.
Wagner, Richard. Opera & Drama. lib. bdg. 30.00 (ISBN 0-685-95458-7). Scholarly.
Walsh, T. J. Opera in Dublin Seventeen Five-Seventeen Ninety Seven: The Social Scene. (Illus.). 386p. 1973. 19.50x (ISBN 0-87471-704-3). Rowman.
--Second Empire Opera. 1981. 35.00 (ISBN 0-7145-3659-8). Riverrun NY.
Weinstock, Herbert. Donizetti & the World of Opera in Italy, Paris & Vienna in the First Half of the Nineteenth Century. 1979. Repr. of 1963 ed. lib. bdg. 24.00x (ISBN 0-374-98337-2). Octagon.
White, Eric W. Tippett & His Operas. (Music Reprint Ser.). 158p. 1981. Repr. of 1979 ed. 19.50 (ISBN 0-306-76111-4). Da Capo.
Yorke-Long, Alan. Music at Court: Four Eighteenth Century Studies. LC 78-66928. (Encore Music Editions Ser.). (Illus.). 1979. Repr. of 1954 ed. 18.50 (ISBN 0-88355-770-3). Hyperion Conn.

OPERA–JUVENILE LITERATURE

Brubaker, David. The Theatre Student-Court & Commedia. (Theatre Student Ser.). (Illus.). (gr. 7-12). 1975. PLB 12.50 (ISBN 0-8239-0317-6). Rosen Pr.
Kline, Peter. Enjoying the Arts: Opera. (YA) 1977. PLB 7.97 (ISBN 0-8239-0392-3). Rosen Pr.
Mozart. The Magic Flute. LC 72-90696. (Illus.). 32p. (gr. k-4). 1973. 5.50 (ISBN 0-87592-032-2). Scroll Pr.

OPERA–LIBRETTISTS

see Librettists

OPERA–LIBRETTOS

see Operas–Librettos

OPERA–PRODUCTION AND DIRECTION

Eaton, Quaintance. Opera Production One: A Handbook. LC 73-20232. (Music Ser.). 266p. 1974. Repr. of 1961 ed. lib. bdg. 22.50 (ISBN 0-306-70635-0). Da Capo.
Goldovsky, B. Bringing Opera to Life: Operatic Acting & Stage Direction. 1968. 20.95 (ISBN 0-13-083105-0). P-H.
Marek, George R. Cosima Wagner. LC 80-7591. (Illus.). 256p. 1981. 16.95 (ISBN 0-06-012704-X, HarpT). Har-Row.
Nagler, A. M. Misdirection: Opera Production in the Twentieth Century. 134p. 1981. 15.00 (ISBN 0-208-01899-9, Archon). Shoe String.
Robinson, Douglas. Act Two Beginners Please. Incl. Melody. 72p; Piano. 112p. 8.95 (ISBN 0-521-07416-9). LC 69-16285. 1970. Cambridge U Pr.
Volbach, Walther R. Problems of Opera Production. 2nd ed. 1967. pap. 7.50 (ISBN 0-208-00166-2, Archon). Shoe String.
Wallace, Mary E. & Wallace, Robert. Opera Scenes for Class & Stage. LC 78-11095. 314p. 1979. 18.95x (ISBN 0-8093-0903-3). S Ill U Pr.

OPERA–STORIES, PLOTS, ETC.

see Operas–Stories, Plots, etc.

OPERA–ENGLAND

Arundell, Dennis. The Critic at the Opera: Contemporary Comments on Opera in London Over Three Centuries. (Music Reprint Ser.: 1980). (Illus.). 1980. Repr. of 1957 ed. lib. bdg. 29.50 (ISBN 0-306-76026-6). Da Capo.
Chorley, Henry F. Thirty Years' Musical Recollections. LC 77-183330. 436p. 1972. Repr. of 1926 ed. 40.00x (ISBN 0-8443-0026-8). Vienna Hse.
Edgcumbe, Richard. Musical Reminiscences of the Earl of Mount Edgcumbe. LC 76-125071. 294p. 1973. Repr. of 1834 ed. lib. bdg. 27.50 (ISBN 0-306-70008-5). Da Capo.
Fitzgerald, S. J. The Story of the Savoy Opera in Gilbert & Sullivan Days. (Music Reprint Ser.). 1979. Repr. of 1925 ed. lib. bdg. 25.00 (ISBN 0-306-79543-4). Da Capo.
Forsyth, Cecil. Music & Nationalism: A Study of English Opera. LC 80-2276. Repr. of 1911 ed. 37.00 (ISBN 0-404-18844-3). AMS Pr.
--Music & Nationalism: A Study of the English Opera. (Perspectives in European History Ser.: No. 20). 359p. Repr. of 1911 ed. lib. bdg. 22.50x (ISBN 0-87991-950-7). Porcupine Pr.
Hughes, Spike. Glyndebourne: A History of the Festival Opera. LC 80-70705. (Illus.). 400p. 1981. 35.00 (ISBN 0-7153-7891-0). David & Charles.
John, Nicholas, ed. English National Opera Guides: Caida, Generentola, Fidelio, Magic Flute, Vol. I. 1981. 25.00 (ISBN 0-686-77656-9). Riverrun NY.
Lumley, Benjamin. Reminiscences of the Opera. LC 76-15185. (Music Reprint Ser.). 448p. 1976. Repr. of 1864 ed. 35.00 (ISBN 0-306-70842-6). Da Capo.

OPERA–ITALY

Adkins, Cecil. Orazio Vecchi's L'Amfiparnaso: A New Edition of the Music with Historical & Analytical Essays. LC 76-15183. (Early Musical Masterworks--Critical Editions & Commentaries). (Illus.). 1977. 19.50x (ISBN 0-8078-1287-0). U of NC Pr.
Ashbrook, William. Donizetti & His Operas. (Illus.). 650p. write for info. (ISBN 0-521-23526-X). Cambridge U Pr.
Austin, William W., ed. New Looks at Italian Opera: Essays in Honor of Donald J. Grout. LC 76-1010. (Illus.). 290p. 1976. Repr. of 1968 ed. lib. bdg. 21.75 (ISBN 0-8371-8761-3, AUNL). Greenwood.
Brown, John. Letters Upon the Poetry & Music of the Italian Opera: Addressed to a Friend. LC 80-2261. 1981. Repr. of 1789 ed. 22.50 (ISBN 0-404-18814-1). AMS Pr.
A Checklist of Writings on Eighteenth Century French & Italian Opera (Excluding Mozart) (Music Indexes & Bibliographies: No. 3). pap. 8.00 (ISBN 0-913574-03-1). Eur-Am Music.
Colombani, Alfredo. L Opera Italiana Nel Secolo Xix: Dono Agli Abbonati Del Corriere Della Sera. LC 80-2266. Repr. of 1900 ed. 61.00 (ISBN 0-404-18819-2). AMS Pr.
Cross, Eric. The Late Operas of Antonio Vivaldi, Seventeen Twenty-Seven to Seventeen Thirty-Eight, 2 vols. Fortune, Nigel, ed. LC 81-77. (British Studies in Musicology). 1981. Set. 59.95 (ISBN 0-8357-1158-7, Pub. by UMI Res Pr). Vol. 1 (ISBN 0-8357-1185-4). Vol. 2 (ISBN 0-8357-1186-2). Univ Microfilms.
Freeman, Robert. Opera Without Drama: Currents of Change in Italian Opera, 1675-1725. Buelow, George, ed. LC 80-29133. (Studies in Musicology: No. 35). 358p. 1981. 81.95 (ISBN 0-8357-1152-8, Pub. by UMI Res Pr). Univ Microfilms.
Henderson, William J. Some Forerunners of Italian Opera. facsimile ed. LC 70-160976. (Select Bibliographies Reprint Ser). Repr. of 1911 ed. 17.00 (ISBN 0-8369-5843-8). Arno.
Nagler, A. M. Theatre Festivals of the Medici, 1539-1637. LC 76-8447. 1976. Repr. of 1964 ed. lib. bdg. 25.00 (ISBN 0-306-70779-9). Da Capo.
Nicolaisen, Jay. Italian Opera in Transition, Eighteen Seventy-One to Eighteen Ninety-Three. Buelow, George, ed. (Studies in Musicology: No. 31). 273p. 1980. 34.95 (ISBN 0-8357-1121-8, Pub. by UMI Res Pr). Univ Microfilms.
L Opera Buffa Napoletana Durante Il Settecento: Storia Letteraria. 2nd ed. LC 80-2298. Repr. of 1917 ed. 53.50 (ISBN 0-404-18867-2). AMS Pr.
Porpora, Nicola A. Semiramide Riconosciuta. LC 76-20969. (Italian Opera, 1640-1770 Ser.: Vol. 30). 1977. lib. bdg. 70.00 (ISBN 0-8240-2629-2). Garland Pub.
Robinson, Michael F. Naples & Neapolitan Opera. (Oxford Monographs on Music). 200p. 1972. 36.00x (ISBN 0-19-816124-7). Oxford U Pr.
Schulze, Walter. Die Quellen der Hamburger Oper Sixteen Seventy Eight to Seventeen Thirty Eight. LC 80-2300. 1981. Repr. of 1938 ed. 25.50 (ISBN 0-404-18869-9). AMS Pr.
Smith, William C. The Italian Opera & Contemporary Ballet in London, 1789 to 1820. LC 73-166261. 191p. 1955. Repr. 19.00 (ISBN 0-403-01387-9). Scholarly.
Toye, Francis. Italian Opera. LC 70-181282. 65p. 1952. Repr. 17.00 (ISBN 0-403-01705-X). Scholarly.
Troy, Charles E. The Comic Intermezzo: A Study in the History of Eighteenth-Century Italian Opera. LC 79-12295. (Studies in Musicology: No. 9). 1979. 31.95 (ISBN 0-8357-0992-2, Pub. by UMI Res Pr). Univ Microfilms.
Vinci, Leonardo. Didone Abbandonata. LC 76-20964. (Italian Opera, 1640-1770 Ser.: Vol. 29). 1977. lib. bdg. 75.00 (ISBN 0-8240-2628-4). Garland Pub.
Weaver, William. The Golden Century of Italian Opera: From Rossini to Puccini. (Illus.). 256p. 1980. 27.50 (ISBN 0-500-01240-7). Thames Hudson.

OPERA, COMIC

see Opera

OPERA, CHINESE

Chang Pe-Chin. Chinese Opera & Painted Face. (Illus.). 1978. 85.00x (ISBN 0-89676-029-4). Drama Bk.
Peking Opera. 1981. 2.50 (ISBN 0-8351-0812-0). China Bks.
Peking Opera & Mei Lanfang. 1981. 5.95 (ISBN 0-8351-0837-6). China Bks.

OPERA-HOUSES

see Theaters

OPERANT BEHAVIOR

Bermant, Gordon, et al, eds. The Ethics of Social Intervention. LC 78-57507. (Series in Clinical & Community Psychology). 1978. 18.50 (ISBN 0-470-26362-8). Halsted Pr.
Blackman, Derek. Operant Conditioning: An Experimental Analysis of Behaviour. LC 74-18545. 247p. 1974. text ed. 13.95x (ISBN 0-416-13660-5); pap. text ed. 7.50x (ISBN 0-416-81480-8). Methuen Inc.
Blackwood, Ralph O. Operant Control of Behavior: Elimination of Misbehavior, Motivation of Children. 249p. 1971. pap. 4.95 (ISBN 0-912784-01-6). Exordium Pr.
Catania, Charles A. Contemporary Research in Operant Behavior. 1968. pap. 11.95x (ISBN 0-673-05496-9). Scott F.
Ferster, Charles B., et al. Behavior Principles. 2nd ed. LC 74-19287. (Illus.). 674p. 1975. Repr. text ed. 20.95 (ISBN 0-13-072611-7). P-H.
Flory, Randall K. & Sherman, J. Gilmour. Student Laboratory Experiments in Operant Conditioning. (Illus.). 100p. (Orig.). 1974. pap. text ed. 4.00 (ISBN 0-914044-02-8). Scholars Pr Ltd.
Friedlander, B. Z., et al, eds. Exceptional Infant: Assesment & Intervention, Vol. 3. LC 68-517. 700p. 1975. 22.50 (ISBN 0-87630-103-0). Brunner-Mazel.
Hall, Elizabeth. From Pigeons to People. (Illus.). 144p. (gr. 5 up). 1975. 6.95 (ISBN 0-395-21894-2). HM.
Harzem, P. & Miles, T. R. Conceptual Issues in Operant Psychology. LC 77-21280. 1978. 30.75 (ISBN 0-471-99603-3, Pub. by Wiley-Interscience). Wiley.
Henton, W. W. & Iverson, I. Classical Conditioning & Operant Conditioning: A Response Pattern Analysis. LC 78-16542. 1978. 28.30 (ISBN 0-387-90326-7). Springer-Verlag.
Honig, Werner K., ed. Operant Behavior: Areas of Research & Application. (Illus.). 1966. text ed. 32.95 (ISBN 0-13-637884-6). P-H.
Honig, Werner K. & Staddor, J., eds. Handbook of Operant Behavior. LC 76-26034. (Century Psychology Ser.). 1977. 46.95 (ISBN 0-13-380535-2). P-H.
Kazdin, Alan E., ed. The Token Economy: A Review & Evaluation. LC 76-44285. (Plenum Behavior Therapy Ser.). (Illus.). 342p. 1977. 16.95 (ISBN 0-306-30962-9, Plenum Pr). Plenum Pub.
Moore, T. W., et al. Conditioning & Instrumental Learning. 2nd ed. (Illus.). 1977. pap. text ed. 6.95 (ISBN 0-07-042902-2, C). McGraw.
Reynolds, George S. A Primer of Operant Conditioning. 2nd ed. 155p. 1975. text ed. 9.95x (ISBN 0-673-07964-3). Scott F.
Strain, James J. Psychological Interventions in Medical Practice. (Illus.). 224p. 1978. 16.00 (ISBN 0-8385-8014-9). ACC.
Walker, Edward L. Conditioning & Instrumental Learning. LC 67-17555. (Basic Concepts in Psychology Ser). (Orig.). 1967. pap. text ed. 6.95 (ISBN 0-8185-0299-1). Brooks-Cole.
Wheeler, Harvey, ed. Beyond the Punitive Society: Operant Conditioning, Social & Political Aspects. LC 73-1269. (Illus.). 1973. pap. text ed. 9.95x (ISBN 0-7167-0775-6). W H Freeman.

OPERAS

see also Musical Revues, Comedies, etc.

Abert, Hermann J. Grundprobleme der Operngeschichte. LC 80-2253. Repr. of 1926 ed. 14.00 (ISBN 0-404-18800-1). AMS Pr.
Abraham, Gerald E. On Russian Music. facs. ed. LC 73-134046. (Essay Index Reprint Ser). 1939. 16.00 (ISBN 0-8369-1900-9). Arno.
--On Russian Music: Critical & Historical Studies of Glinka's Operas. LC 39-32448. (Music Ser.: Practice & Theory). Repr. of 1939 ed. 17.00 (ISBN 0-384-00150-5). Johnson Repr.
Apthorp, William F. Opera, Past & Present. LC 72-4148. (Select Bibliographies Reprint Ser.). 1972. Repr. of 1901 ed. 19.00 (ISBN 0-8369-6870-0). Arno.
Auber, Daniel F. Gustave ou le Bal Masque, 2 vols. LC 76-49212. (Early Romantic Opera Ser.: Vol. 31). 1980. lib. bdg. 82.00 (ISBN 0-8240-2930-5). Garland Pub.
--La Muette De Portici, 2 vols. Grossett, Philip & Rosen, Charles, eds. LC 76-49211. (Early Romantic Opera Ser.: Vol. 30). 1980. lib. bdg. 82.00 (ISBN 0-8240-2929-1). Garland Pub.
Baily, Leslie. The Gilbert & Sullivan Book. 4th rev. ed. LC 75-181105. 475p. 1956. Repr. 59.00 (ISBN 0-403-01504-9). Scholarly.
Bellini, Vincenzo. Norma, 2 vols. Rosen, Charles & Gossett, Philip, eds. LC 76-49177. (Early Romantic Opera Ser.: Vol. 4). Date not set. lib. bdg. 82.00 (ISBN 0-8240-2903-8). Garland Pub.
Bizet, Georges. Carmen. Bleiler, Ellen, tr. 4.75 (ISBN 0-8446-0496-8). Peter Smith.
Broido, Lucy. French Opera Posters, 1868 - 1930. LC 75-32586. (Illus.). 80p. (Orig.). 1976. pap. 5.00 (ISBN 0-486-23306-5). Dover.
Budden, Julian. The Operas of Verdi: From Oberto to Rigoletto, Vol. 1. (Illus.). 1978. 35.00 (ISBN 0-19-520030-6). Oxford U Pr.
--The Operas of Verdi, Vol. 3: From Don Carlos to Falstaff. 1981. 39.95 (ISBN 0-19-520254-6). Oxford U Pr.
Chapin, Anna Alice. The Story of the Rhinegold: Der Ring Des Nibelungen. 138p. 1980. Repr. of 1897 ed. lib. bdg. 25.00 (ISBN 0-89760-119-X). Telegraph Bks.
Corsaro, Frank. Maverick: A Director's Personal Experience in Opera & Theatre. LC 77-77036. (Illus.). 1978. 12.95 (ISBN 0-8149-0790-3). Vanguard.
Crosten, William L. French Grand Opera: An Art & a Business. LC 73-171381. 132p. 1972. Repr. of 1948 ed. lib. bdg. 22.50 (ISBN 0-306-70405-6). Da Capo.
Donizetti, Gaetano. Dom Sebastien, 2 vols. Rosen, Charles & Gossett, Philip, eds. LC 76-49210. (Early Romantic Opera Ser.: Vol. 29). 1980. lib. bdg. 82.00 (ISBN 0-8240-2928-3). Garland Pub.
England, Paul. Favorite Operas by German & Russian Composers. 5.50 (ISBN 0-8446-4733-0). Peter Smith.
Goddard, Joseph. Rise & Development of Opera. 1976. lib. bdg. 19.00 (ISBN 0-403-03790-5). Scholarly.
Goslich, Siegfried. Beitrage Zur Geschicte der Deutschen Romantischen Oper Zwischen Spohrs "Faust" und Wagner's "Lohengrin". LC 80-2281. Repr. of 1937 ed. 31.50 (ISBN 0-404-18846-X). AMS Pr.
Green, Marlyn. Martyn Green's Treasury of Gilbert & Sullivan. 1976. pap. 8.95 (ISBN 0-671-22419-0, Fireside). S&S.
Green, Martyn, ed. Martyn Green's Treasury of Gilbert & Sullivan. 1961. 19.95 (ISBN 0-671-45250-9). S&S.
Gregor, Joseph. Kulturgeschichte der Oper. 2nd, rev. & enl. ed. LC 80-2282. Repr. of 1950 ed. 57.50 (ISBN 0-404-18847-8). AMS Pr.
Halevy, Jacques-Francois. La Juive, 2 vols. Gossett, Philip & Rosen, Charles, eds. LC 76-49218. (Early Romantic Opera Ser.). 1980. 82.00 (ISBN 0-8240-2935-6). Garland Pub.
Howard, John T. The World's Great Operas. LC 80-2278. Repr. of 1948 ed. 49.50 (ISBN 0-404-18848-6). AMS Pr.
Hughes, Spike. Famous Puccini Operas. rev. ed. 260p. 1972. pap. 3.00 (ISBN 0-486-22857-6). Dover.
Jacob, Naomi & Robertson, James C. Opera in Italy. facsimile ed. LC 74-140359. (Select Bibliographies Reprint Ser). Repr. of 1948 ed. 18.00 (ISBN 0-8369-5602-8). Arno.
Krehbiel, Henry E. Chapters of Opera: Being Historical & Critical Observations & Records Concerning the Lyric Drama in New York from Its Earliest Days Down to the Present Time. LC 78-66909. (Encore Music Editions Ser.). 1980. Repr. of 1911 ed. 45.00 (ISBN 0-88355-748-7). Hyperion Conn.
Kretzschmar, Hermann. Geschicte der Oper. LC 80-2285. Repr. of 1919 ed. 33.50 (ISBN 0-404-18853-2). AMS Pr.
Martens, Frederick H. The Book of the Opera & the Ballet & the History of the Opera. LC 80-2289. Repr. of 1925 ed. 22.50 (ISBN 0-404-18857-5). AMS Pr.
Mattfield, Julius. A Handbook of American Operatic Premieres, 1731-1962. LC 76-166243. 142p. 1963. Repr. 19.00 (ISBN 0-403-01377-1). Scholarly.

Meyerbeer, Giacomo. L' Etoile du Nord. Rosen, Charles & Gossett, Philip, eds. LC 76-49198. (Early Romantic Opera Ser.: Vol. 22). 1980. lib. bdg. 82.00 (ISBN 0-8240-2921-6). Garland Pub.
--Les Huguenots, 2 vols. Rosen, Charles & Gossett, Philip, eds. LC 76-49196. (Early Romantic Opera Ser.: Vol. 20). 1980. lib. bdg. 82.00 (ISBN 0-8240-2919-4). Garland Pub.
--L'Africaine, 2 vols. Grossett, Philip & Rosen, Charles, eds. LC 76-49200. (Early Romantic Opera Ser.: Vol. 24). 944p. 1980. lib. bdg. 82.00 (ISBN 0-8240-2923-2). Garland Pub.
Newmarch, Rosa. The Russian Opera. LC 72-109807. (Illus.). 403p. 1972. Repr. of 1914 ed. lib. bdg. 21.00x (ISBN 0-8371-4298-9, NERO). Greenwood.
Northouse, Cameron. Twentieth Century Operas in England & the United States: A Reference Guide. (Ser. Seventy). 1976. lib. bdg. 25.00 (ISBN 0-8161-7896-8). G K Hall.
Passano, Giambattista. Dizionario Di Opere Anonime & Pseudonime in Supplemento a Quello Di Gaetano Melzi. Incl. Anonimi & Pseudonimi Italiani. Rocco, Emmanuele. LC 61-3096. 1887-88. Repr. 39.00 (ISBN 0-8337-2351-0). B Franklin.
Rossini, Gioachino. Moise. Rosen, Charles & Gossett, Philip, eds. LC 76-49190. (Early Romantic Opera Ser.: Vol. 15). 1980. lib. bdg. 82.00 (ISBN 0-8240-2914-3). Garland Pub.
Rushton, Julian. W. A. Mozart: Don Giovanni. (Cambridge Opera Handbooks Ser.). (Illus.). Date not set. 22.50 (ISBN 0-521-22826-3); pap. 7.95 (ISBN 0-521-29663-3). Cambridge U Pr.
Schiedermair, Ludwig. Die Deutche Oper: Grundzuge Ihres Werdens & Wesens. LC 80-2299. Repr. of 1930 ed. 38.50 (ISBN 0-404-18868-0). AMS Pr.
Scrici. Physiology of the Opera (Philadelphia: Willis P. Hazard, 1852) LC 81-81546. (Special Publications: No. 2). 1981. pap. 6.00 (ISBN 0-914678-16-7). Inst Am Music.
Spontini, Gasparo. Olympie. Grossett, Philip & Rosen, Charles, eds. LC 76-49227. (Early Romantic Opera Ser.: Vol. 44). 1980. lib. bdg. 82.00 (ISBN 0-8240-2943-7). Garland Pub.
Taylor, Ian. How to Produce Concert Versions of Gilbert & Sullivan. 1972. 12.95x (ISBN 0-8464-0494-X). Beekman Pubs.
Upton, George P. The Standard Operas: Their Plots, Their Music, Their Composers, a Handbook. 1980. lib. bdg. 72.95 (ISBN 0-8490-3173-7). Gordon Pr.
Vickers, Hugh. Great Operatic Disasters. 1980. 7.95 (ISBN 0-312-34633-6). St Martin.
Weaver, William, tr. Seven Verdi Librettos. 1975 20.00x (ISBN 0-393-02181-5, N852, Norton Lib); pap. 5.95 1977 (ISBN 0-393-00852-5). Norton.
Webber, Andrew L. & Rice, Tim. Evita. LC 79-53888. (Illus.). 1979. 8.95 (ISBN 0-89676-030-8). Drama Bk.
White, Eric W. The Rise of English Opera. LC 78-87683. (Music Ser.). (Illus.). 374p. 1972. Repr. of 1951 ed. lib. bdg. 27.50 (ISBN 0-306-71709-3). Da Capo.

OPERAS-BIBLIOGRAPHY

White, Eric W. The Rise of English Opera. LC 78-87683. (Music Ser.). (Illus.). 374p. 1972. Repr. of 1951 ed. lib. bdg. 27.50 (ISBN 0-306-71709-3). Da Capo.

OPERAS-DISCOGRAPHY

Blyth, Alan. Opera on Record. LC 81-47801. 688p. 1982. pap. price not set (ISBN 0-06-090910-2, CN 910, CN). Har-Row.
Bontinck-Kueffel, Irmgard. Opern Auf Schallplatten Nineteen Hundred to Nineteen Sixty-Two. Blaukopf, Kurt & Wagner, Manfred, eds. (Ger.). 1974. pap. 15.50 (ISBN 3-7024-0014-1, 51-26205). Eur-Am Music.

OPERAS-LIBRETTOS

see also Ballad Operas-Librettos; Musical Revues, Comedies, etc.-Librettos; Operas-Stories, Plots, etc.

Bellini, Vincenzo. Beatrice Di Tenda, 2 vols. Rosen, Charles & Gosset, Philip, eds. LC 76-49178. (Early Romantic Opera Ser.: Vol. 5). 567p. 1980. lib. bdg. 82.00 (ISBN 0-8240-2904-6). Garland Pub.
Berlioz, Hector. Trojans. Dent, E. J., tr. 1957. 3.00 (ISBN 0-19-313303-2). Oxford U Pr.
Bizet, Georges. Carmen. Bleiler, Ellen, ed. & tr. LC 68-10868. (Opera Guide & Libretto Ser). (Illus., Orig.). 1970. pap. 4.00 (ISBN 0-486-22111-3). Dover.
--Doctor Miracle. Harris, David, tr. 1964. 2.00 (ISBN 0-19-335300-8). Oxford U Pr.
Bouilly, J. N. Fidelio, or Wedded Love. Dent, Edward J., tr. (Musical Score by Ludwig Van Beethoven). 1938. 2.50 (ISBN 0-19-313302-4). Oxford U Pr.
Brecht, Bertolt. Threepenny Opera. Bentley, Eric & Vesey, Desmond, trs. from German. (Orig.). 1964. pap. 1.95 (ISBN 0-394-17472-0, B333, BC). Grove.
Brown, Howard M. Italian Opera Librettos: 1640-1770. LC 76-20993. 1979. lib. bdg. 75.00 (ISBN 0-8240-2655-1). Garland Pub.
Brown, Howard M., ed. Italian Opera Librettos. LC 76-20993. (Italian Opera 1640-1770 Ser.: Vol. 52). 1979. lib. bdg. 75.00 (ISBN 0-8240-2651-9). Garland Pub.
--Italian Opera Librettos. LC 76-20993. (Italian Opera Ser. 1640 to 1770: Vol. 60). 1979. lib. bdg. 75.00 (ISBN 0-8240-2659-4); lib. bdg. 3700.00 set of 60 vols. (ISBN 0-686-60104-1). Garland Pub.
--Italian Opera Librettos: 1640-1770. Incl. Arsace (Sarri) Salvi, Antonio; Artaserse (Graun) Metastasio, Pietro; Il Bajazet (Gasparini) Piovene, Agostino; Catone in Utica (Piccinni) Metastasio, Pietro. LC 76-20993. (Italian Opera 1640-1770 Ser.: Vol. 53). 1978. lib. bdg. 75.00 (ISBN 0-8240-2652-7). Garland Pub.
--Italian Opera Librettos: 1640-1770. Incl. Demofoonte (Jommelli) Metastasio, Pietro; La Diavolessa (Galuppi) Goldoni, Carlo; Didone Abbandonata (Vinci) Metastasio, Pietro. LC 76-20993. (Italian Opera 1640-1770 Ser: Vol. 54). 1978. lib. bdg. 75.00 (ISBN 0-8240-2653-5). Garland Pub.
--Italian Opera Librettos: 1640-1770. Incl. L'Adelaide (Sartario) Dolfino, Pietro; Adriano in Siria (Maio) Metastasio, Pietro; Alessandro Severo (Lotti) Zeno, Apostolo; Gli Amanti Generosi (Mancini) Candi, Giovanni P; L' Amazore Corsara Overo L'alvilda Regina De Goti (Pallavicino) Corradi, Giulio C. LC 76-20993. (Italian Opera 1640-1770 Ser.: Vol. 51). 1978. lib. bdg. 75.00 (ISBN 0-8240-2650-0). Garland Pub.
Cammarano, Salvadore. Trovatore: Opera in Four Acts. Dent, E. J., ed. 1939. 1.50 (ISBN 0-19-313316-4). Oxford U Pr.
Cherubini, Maria L. Eliza Ou le Voyage Aux Glaciers Du Mont S. Bernard. Gossett, Philip & Rosen, Charles, eds. LC 76-49216. (Early Romantic Opera Ser.). 1979. lib. bdg. 82.00 (ISBN 0-8240-2933-X). Garland Pub.
De Wailly, Leon & Barbier, Auguste. Benvenuto Cellini: An Opera in Three Acts. Jacobs, Arthur, ed. 1963. pap. 1.80 (ISBN 0-19-313319-9). Oxford U Pr.
Donizetti, Gaetano. Don Pasquale: A Comic Opera in Three Acts. Dent, E. J., tr. 1946. 4.00 (ISBN 0-19-313304-0). Oxford U Pr.
--Elisir D'Amore. Jacobs, Arthur, tr. 1964. pap. 1.50 (ISBN 0-19-313320-2). Oxford U Pr.
--Lucia Di Lammermoor: Opera Guide & Libretto. Bleiler, Ellen, ed. & tr. (Ital-Eng, Fr-Eng). 1970. pap. 3.50 (ISBN 0-486-22110-5). Dover.
Herbert, David, ed. The Operas of Benjamin Britten. LC 79-2052. (Illus.). 1979. 65.00 (ISBN 0-231-04868-8). Columbia U Pr.
Leo, Leonardo. L' Andromaca. Brown, Howard M., ed. LC 76-21013. (Italian Opera Ser.). 1979. lib. bdg. 75.00 (ISBN 0-8240-2637-3). Garland Pub.
Le Seur, Jean F. Ossian Ou les Bardes. Geosset, Philip & Rosen, Charles, eds. LC 76-49219. (Early Romantic Opera Ser.). 1979. lib. bdg. 82.00 (ISBN 0-8240-2936-4). Garland Pub.
Lewis, Janet. Birthday of the Infanta. 22p. 1981. s & l, wrappers 25.00 (ISBN 0-936576-03-0). Symposium Pr.
Meyerbeer, Giacomo. Il Crociato in Egitto, 2 vols. Gossett, Philip & Rosen, Charles, eds. LC 76-49193. (Early Romantic Opera Ser.: Vol. 18). 1980. Set. lib. bdg. 164.00 (ISBN 0-8240-2917-8). Garland Pub.
Mozart, Wolfgang A. Don Giovanni. Bleiler, Ellen H., tr. & (Dover Opera Guide & Libretto Ser). 6.00 (ISBN 0-8446-2625-2). Peter Smith.
--Don Giovanni. Bleiler, Ellen, tr. (Illus., Orig.). 1964. pap. 3.00 (ISBN 0-486-21134-7). Dover.
Osborne, Charles. The Complete Operas of Verdi: An Interpretive Study of the Librettos & Music & Their Relation to the Composer's Life. LC 77-23409. 1977. pap. 7.95 (ISBN 0-306-80072-1). Da Capo.
Ponte, Lorenzo Da. Don Giovanni. Dent, Edward J., tr. 1938. 1.50 (ISBN 0-19-313307-5). Oxford U Pr.
--Marriage of Figaro. Dent, Edward J., tr. 1937. 2.25 (ISBN 0-19-313308-3). Oxford U Pr.
Provenzale, Francesco. Lo Schiavo Di Sua Moglie. Brown, Howard M., ed. LC 76-20973. (Italian Opera 1640-1770 Ser.). 1979. lib. bdg. 75.00 (ISBN 0-8240-2606-3). Garland Pub.
Puccini, Giacomo. La Boheme: Opera Guide & Libretto. Bleiler, Ellen, tr. (Illus., Orig.). 1962. pap. 1.75 (ISBN 0-486-20404-9). Dover.
Pushkin, Alexander. Eugene Onegin: An Opera in Three Acts. Dent, E. J., tr. 1946. 3.25 (ISBN 0-19-313312-1). Oxford U Pr.
Smith, Patrick J. The Tenth Muse: A Historical Study of the Opera Libretto. LC 73-111254. 1975. pap. 4.95 (ISBN 0-02-872450-X). Schirmer Bks.
Somma, Antonio. Ballo in Maschera. Dent, E. J., ed. 1952. 3.00 (ISBN 0-19-313313-X). Oxford U Pr.
Stephanie, Gottlieb. Abduction from the Seraglio. Dent, E. J., ed. 1952. 2.50 (ISBN 0-19-313309-1). Oxford U Pr.
Sterbini, Cesare. Barber of Seville. Dent, E. J., tr. 1940. 5.00 (ISBN 0-19-313311-3). Oxford U Pr.
Tchaikovsky, Modest & Pushkin, Alexander. Queen of Spades. Jacobs, Arthur, tr. 1961. 1.80 (ISBN 0-19-313318-0). Oxford U Pr.
Thane, Adele. Gilbert & Sullivan Operettas Adapted for Half-Hour Performance. (gr. 5-12). 1977. 15.00 (ISBN 0-8238-0188-8). Plays.
U. S. Library of Congress. Catalogue of Opera Librettos Printed Before 1800, 2 vols. 1965. Repr. of 1914 ed. Set. 92.50 (ISBN 0-8337-3322-2). B Franklin.
U. S. Library Of Congress Music Division. Catalogue of Opera Libretto Printed Before 1800, 2 Vols. Sonneck, George T., ed. Repr. of 1914 ed. Set. 115.50 (ISBN 0-384-63050-2). Johnson Repr.
Verdi, Giuseppe. Aida: Opera Guide & Libretto. Bleiler, Ellen, tr. (Illus., Orig.). 1962. pap. 2.25 (ISBN 0-486-20405-7). Dover.
Wagner, Richard. The Flying Dutchman: The Complete Text in German & English. Large, Brian & Butler, Peter, eds. (Illus.). 1975. text ed. 13.95x (ISBN 0-7156-0938-6). Intl Ideas.
--Ring of the Nibelung. Robb, Stewart, tr. (Illus.). 1960. pap. 5.95 (ISBN 0-525-47051-4). Dutton.
--The Ring of the Niblung, 2 vols. Armour, Margaret, tr. from Ger. Incl. Vol. 1. The Rheingold; The Valkyrie. Repr. of 1910 ed; Vol. 2. Siegfried; The Twilight of the Gods. Repr. of 1911 ed. LC 76-22301. 1976. 37.50 set (ISBN 0-913870-17-X). Abaris Bks.
--Tristan & Isolde. Robb, Stewart, tr. 1965. pap. 4.50 (ISBN 0-525-47173-1). Dutton.
Webber, Andrew L. & Rice, Tim. Evita. LC 79-53888. (Illus.). 1979. 8.95 (ISBN 0-89676-030-8). Drama Bk.

OPERAS-SCORES

Albinoni, Tomaso. Zenobia Regina Di Palmireni. Brown, Howard M., ed. LC 76-21018. (Italian Opera 1640-1770 Ser.: Vol. 15). 1979. lib. bdg. 75.00 (ISBN 0-8240-2614-4). Garland Pub.
DiCapua, Rinaldo. Vologeso Re De Parti. Brown, Howard M., ed. LC 76-20970. (Italian Opera, 1640-1770 Ser.: Vol. 38). (Libretto by G. E. Luccarelli). 1978. lib. bdg. 60.00 (ISBN 0-8240-2641-1). Garland Pub.
Grout, Donald J., ed. The Operas of Alessandro Scarlatti, Vol. 3: Griselda. (Publications in Music Ser.). 256p. 1976. pap. 25.00x (ISBN 0-674-64029-2). Harvard U Pr.
Handel, George F. & Brown, Howard M. Tamerlano. LC 76-21083. (Italian Opera 1640-1770 Ser.). 1979. lib. bdg. 75.00 (ISBN 0-8240-2626-8). Garland Pub.
Mozart, Wolfgang A. Bastien et Bastienne. Swift, Basil, tr. LC 68-8184. (Penn State Music Series, No. 23). 96p. 1969. 5.95x (ISBN 0-271-09130-4). Pa St U Pr.
--Don Giovanni. 15.00 (ISBN 0-8446-5069-2). Peter Smith.
Mussorgsky, Modeste. Boris Godunov. Lloyd-Jones, David, tr. 1968. 2.75 (ISBN 0-19-337704-7). Oxford U Pr.
Mussorgsky, Modesto. Boris Godunov: Full Score in Three Languages. Lloyd-Jones, David, ed. & tr. (Rus., Ger., & Engl., With cloth bound, a companion volume of notes, commentary & supplementary or alternative scenes in full score). 1975. boxed 175.00 (ISBN 0-19-337699-7); pap. 85.00 (ISBN 0-19-337700-4). Oxford U Pr.
Porsile, Giuseppe. Spartaco. Brown, Howard M., ed. LC 76-21089. (Italian Opera 1640-1770 Ser.). 1979. lib. bdg. 75.00 (ISBN 0-8240-2627-6). Garland Pub.
Rossini, Gioachino. Otello, 2 vols. Gossett, Philip & Rosen, Charles, eds. LC 76-49182. (Early Romantic Opera Ser.: Vol. 8). 1979. Set. lib. bdg. 164.00 (ISBN 0-8240-2907-0); lib. bdg. 82.00 ea. Garland Pub.
Scarlatti, Alessandro. The Operas of Alessandro Scarlatti: La Caduta de Decemviri, Vol. 6. Williams, Hermine W., ed. (Harvard Publications in Music: No. 11). 224p. 1980. pap. 28.00x (ISBN 0-674-64032-2). Harvard U Pr.
Stradella, Alessandro. Corispero. Brown, Howard M., ed. LC 76-20990. (Italian Opera 1640-1770 Ser.: Vol. 10). 1979. lib. bdg. 75.00 (ISBN 0-8240-2609-8). Garland Pub.
Vinci, Leonardo. Li Zite 'ngalera. Brown, Howard M., ed. LC 76-21072. (Italian Opera Ser.: Vol. 25). 1979. lib. bdg. 75.00 (ISBN 0-8240-2624-1). Garland Pub.
Wagner, Richard. The Ring of the Nibelung. Porter, Andrew, tr. from Ger. (Illus., Eng.). 1976. 26.95 (ISBN 0-393-02192-0); study guide 17.50 (ISBN 0-393-02200-5). Norton.
Weber, Carl M. Der Freischutz: Complete Vocal & Orchestral Score. 203p. 1977. pap. 6.00 (ISBN 0-486-23449-5). Dover.

OPERAS-STAGE GUIDES

see Opera-Dramaturgy

OPERAS-STORIES, PLOTS, ETC.

Biancolli, Louis, ed. The Opera Reader. 1977. Repr. of 1953 ed. lib. bdg. 43.00x (ISBN 0-8371-9722-8, BIOR). Greenwood.
Cross, Milton. New Milton Cross' Complete Stories of the Great Operas. 1955. 9.95 (ISBN 0-385-04324-4). Doubleday.
Cross, Milton & Kohrs, Karl. The New Milton Cross More Stories of the Great Operas. LC 79-8023. 816p. 1980. 17.95 (ISBN 0-385-14776-7). Doubleday.
Duncan, Edmonstoune. Opera Stories of Today & Yesterday. LC 77-75231. 1977. Repr. of 1923 ed. lib. bdg. 15.00 (ISBN 0-89341-083-7). Longwood Pr.
Earl Of Harewood, ed. The New Kobbe's Complete Opera Book. new rev. ed. LC 76-12106. 663p. 1976. 25.00 (ISBN 0-399-11633-8). Putnam.
Eaton, Quaintance. The Abaris Companion to Opera. (Illus.). 1980. 35.00 (ISBN 0-913870-71-4). Abaris Bks.
--Opera Production One: A Handbook. LC 73-20232. (Music Ser.). 266p. 1974. Repr. of 1961 ed. lib. bdg. 22.50 (ISBN 0-306-70635-0). Da Capo.
Elliott, Donald & Arrowood, Clinton. Lamb's Tales from the Great Operas. LC 80-84719. (Illus.). 80p. 1981. 10.95 (ISBN 0-87645-110-5). Gambit.
England, Paul. Favorite Operas by German & Russian Composers. LC 79-96409. Orig. Title: Fifty Favorite Operas. 269p. 1973. pap. 2.50 (ISBN 0-486-22933-5). Dover.
Ewen, David. The Book of European Light Opera. LC 77-1795. 1977. Repr. of 1962 ed. lib. bdg. 24.25x (ISBN 0-8371-9520-9, EWBE). Greenwood.
Fellner, Rudolph. Opera Themes & Plots. 1961. pap. 4.95 (ISBN 0-671-21215-X, Fireside). S&S.
Gatliff, Evelyn. Savoy Stories. 1950. 7.50x (ISBN 0-522-83611-9, Pub. by Melbourne U Pr); pap. 3.00 (ISBN 0-522-83795-6, Pub. by Melbourne U Pr). Intl Schol Bk Serv.
Guerber, H. A. Stories of the Wagner Operas. 1977. lib. bdg. 59.95 (ISBN 0-8490-2674-1). Gordon Pr.
Heath, Charles. Beauties of the Opera & Ballet. LC 76-58926. (Ser. in Dance). 1977. Repr. of 1845 ed. lib. bdg. 25.00 (ISBN 0-306-70844-2). Da Capo.
McSpadden, J. Walker. Opera Synopses: A Guide to the Plots & Characters of the Standard Operas. 1978. Repr. of 1915 ed. lib. bdg. 20.00 (ISBN 0-8414-6244-5). Folcroft.
Martens, Frederick K. A Thousand & One Nights of Opera. LC 77-25416. (Music Reprint Ser., 1978). 1978. Repr. of 1926 ed. lib. bdg. 32.50 (ISBN 0-306-77565-4). Da Capo.
Martin, George W. The Opera Companion to Twentieth-Century Opera. 1979. 19.95 (ISBN 0-396-07594-0). Dodd.
Mitchell, Jerome. The Walter Scott Operas. LC 76-7406. 384p. 1977. 21.95x (ISBN 0-8173-6401-3). U of Ala Pr.
Moore, Frank L. Crowell's Handbook of World Opera. LC 73-3025. (Illus.). 683p. 1974. Repr. of 1961 ed. lib. bdg. 43.00x (ISBN 0-8371-6822-8, MOCH). Greenwood.
Morley, Alexander F. The Harrap Opera Guide. 320p. 1971. 15.00 (ISBN 0-245-50509-1). Dufour.
Newman, Ernest. Stories of the Great Operas & Their Composers, 3 vols. in 1. Repr. of 1930 ed. 69.00 (ISBN 0-403-01632-0). Scholarly.
--Wagner Operas. (Illus.). 1949. 20.00 (ISBN 0-394-40880-2). Knopf.
Orrey, Leslie & Chase, Gilbert, eds. The Encyclopedia of Opera. (Illus.). 376p. 1976. 22.50 (ISBN 0-684-13630-9, ScribT). Scribner.
Simon, Henry W. One Hundred Great Operas & Their Stories. rev. ed. LC 68-27816. (Reference Bk.). 1968. pap. 4.50 (ISBN 0-385-05448-3, C100, Dolp). Doubleday.
Singleton, Esther. A Guide to the Opera. 350p. 1981. Repr. of 1912 ed. lib. bdg. 30.00 (ISBN 0-89987-769-9). Darby Bks.
Weaver, William, tr. Seven Puccini Librettos: In the Original Italian. (Eng. & It.). 1981. 25.00 (ISBN 0-393-01221-2); pap. 9.95 (ISBN 0-393-00930-0). Norton.
Weston, Jessie L. The Legends of the Wagner Drama. LC 74-24255. Repr. of 1896 ed. 24.00 (ISBN 0-404-13132-8). AMS Pr.

OPERATIC MOVING PICTURES

see Moving-Pictures, Musical

OPERATING ROOMS

Boba, Antonio. Death in the Operating Room. (American Lecture Anesthesiology). (Illus.). 120p. 1965. ed. spiral bdg. 12.75photocopy (ISBN 0-398-00181-2). C C Thomas.
Brooks, Shirley M. Fundamentals of Operating Room Nursing. 2nd ed. LC 79-500. (Illus.). 1979. pap. 11.50 (ISBN 0-8016-0814-7). Mosby.
Burns, Margaret A. & Morrissy, Lois E. Self-Assessment of Current Knowledge for the Operating Room Technician. 2nd ed. 1976. pap. 9.50 (ISBN 0-87488-474-8). Med Exam.
Productivity Improvements in Operating Rooms: An Examination of Case Studies. LC 80-22838. 236p. (Orig.). 1981. pap. 25.00 (ISBN 0-87258-335-X, 6021). Am Hospital.

OPERATING STATEMENTS
see Financial Statements

OPERATION PLUTO
see Cuba–History–Invasion, 1961

OPERATION SEA LION

Fleming, Peter. Operation Sea Lion: The Projected Invasion of England in 1940: An Account of the German Preparations & the British Countermeasures. LC 76-56777. (Illus.). 1977. Repr. of 1957 ed. lib. bdg. 24.25x (ISBN 0-8371-9429-6, FLOS). Greenwood.

Wheatley, Ronald. Operation Sea Lion: German Plans for the Invasion of England, 1939-1942. LC 78-16522. 1978. Repr. of 1958 ed. lib. bdg. 30.00 (ISBN 0-313-20605-8, WHOS). Greenwood.

OPERATIONAL AMPLIFIERS

Berlin, Howard M. The Design of Operational Amplifier Circuits, with Experiments. Titus, Christopher A., et al, eds. LC 77-10987. (Bugbook Reference Ser.). 1977. pap. text ed. 8.50 (ISBN 0-89704-014-7). E & L Instru.

Carr, Joseph. Op Amp Circuit Design & Applications. LC 75-41721. (Illus.). 1976. 9.95 (ISBN 0-8306-6787-3); pap. 6.95 (ISBN 0-8306-5787-8, 787). TAB Bks.

Clayton, G. Operational Amplifiers. 2nd ed. 1979. text ed. 26.95 (ISBN 0-408-00370-7). Butterworth.

Clayton, G. B. Eighty-Eight Practical OP AMP Circuits You Can Build. (Illus.). 1977. 7.95x (ISBN 0-8306-7912-X); pap. 4.95x (ISBN 0-8306-6912-4, 912). TAB Bks.

Coughlin, R. & Driscoll, F. Operational Amplifiers & Linear Integrated Circuits. 312p. 1977. text ed. 19.95 (ISBN 0-13-637850-1). P-H.

Coughlin, Robert F. & Driscoll, Frederick F., Jr. Operational Amplifiers & Linear Integrated Circuits. 2nd ed. (Illus.). 400p. 1982. 19.95 (ISBN 0-13-637785-8). P-H.

Faulkenberry, Luces M. An Introduction to Operational Amplifiers. LC 76-53778. (Electronic Technology Ser.). 1977. text ed. 22.95 (ISBN 0-471-01548-2); solutions manual avail. (ISBN 0-471-02531-3). Wiley.

Graeme, Jerald G. Designing with Operational Amplifiers: Applications, Alternatives. (Illus.). 1977. 24.50 (ISBN 0-07-023891-X, P&RB). McGraw.

Jung, Walter G. IC Op-Amp Cookbook. 2nd ed. LC 80-50052. (Illus.). 1980. pap. 14.95 (ISBN 0-672-21695-7). Sams.

Kalvoda, Robert. Operational Amplifiers in Chemical Instrumentation. LC 75-8866. (Ser. in Analytical Chemistry). 1975. 32.95 (ISBN 0-470-45566-7). Halsted Pr.

Lenk, J. Manual for Operational Amplifier Users. 1976. 19.95 (ISBN 0-87909-477-X). Reston.

Marston, R. M. One Hundred & Ten OP-AMP Projects. (Illus.). 128p. 1975. pap. 7.95 (ISBN 0-8104-0701-9). Hayden.

Melen, Roger & Garland, Harry. Understanding IC Operational Amplifiers. 2nd ed. LC 77-99109. 1978. pap. 4.95 (ISBN 0-672-21511-X). Sams.

Rutkowski, George B. Handbook of Integrated-Circuit Operational Amplifiers. (Illus.). 304p. 1975. ref. ed. 18.95 (ISBN 0-13-378703-6). P-H.

Towers, T. D. & Towers, N. S. Towers' International OpAmp Linear-IC Selector. (Illus.). 1979. vinyl 12.95 (ISBN 0-8306-9771-3); pap. 7.95 (ISBN 0-8306-1216-5, 1216). TAB Bks.

Wait, John V., et al. Introduction to Operational & Amplifier Theory Applications. (Illus.). 480p. 1975. text ed. 27.95 (ISBN 0-07-067765-4, C); solutions manual 3.00 (ISBN 0-07-067766-2). McGraw.

OPERATIONAL ANALYSIS
see Operations Research

OPERATIONAL AUDITING
see Management Audit

OPERATIONAL CALCULUS
see Calculus, Operational

OPERATIONAL RESEARCH
see Operations Research

OPERATIONS, CALCULUS OF
see Calculus of Operations

OPERATIONS, SURGICAL
see also Postoperative Care; Shock; Surgery–Cases, Clinical Reports, Statistics; Surgical Nursing

American College of Surgeons Committee on Pre & Postoperative Care. Manual of Preoperative & Postoperative Care. 2nd ed. Kinney, John M., et al, eds. LC 75-158397. (Illus.). 1971. 19.95 (ISBN 0-7216-5440-1). Saunders.

American Medical Association. Standard Nomenclature of Diseases & Operations. 5th ed. 1961. 26.00 (ISBN 0-07-001483-3, HP). McGraw.

Atkinson, L. J. & Kohn, M. J. Berry & Kohn's Introduction to Operating Room Technique. 1978. pap. text ed. 14.95 (ISBN 0-07-002540-1, HP). McGraw.

Bell, Sir Charles. Illustrations of the Great Operations of Surgery. 134p. 1975. 75.00 (ISBN 0-471-09474-9, Pub. by Wiley Med). Wiley.

Blanken, Gary E. Surgical Operations in Short-Stay Hospitals, U. S. 1971. LC 74-6259. (Data from the Hospital Discharge Survey Ser. 13: No. 18). 62p. 1974. pap. text ed. 1.10 (ISBN 0-8406-0017-8). Natl Ctr Health Stats.

Brigden, Raymond J. Operating Theatre Technique. 4th ed. (Illus.). 840p. 1980. text ed. 87.50x (ISBN 0-443-01999-1). Churchill.

Grubb, Reba D. & Ondov, Geraldine. Operating Room Guidelines: An Illustrated Manual. LC 78-31422. (Illus.). 1979. pap. text ed. 17.95 (ISBN 0-8016-1985-8). Mosby.

Horwitz, Norman H. Post-Operative Complications in Neurosurgical Practice: Recognition, Prevention & Management. LC 66-28163. 440p. 1973. Repr. of 1967 ed. 22.00 (ISBN 0-88275-124-7). Krieger.

Keen, Gerald, ed. Operative Surgery & Management. (Illus.). 880p. 1981. text ed. 89.50 (ISBN 0-7236-0548-3). Wright-PSG.

Lees, David H. & Singer, Albert. A Color Atlas of Gynecological Surgery Vol. 1: Vaginal Operations. (Illus.). 1978. 55.00 (ISBN 0-8151-5351-1). Year Bk Med.

Paget, G. E. & Thomson, R., eds. Standard Operating Procedures in Pathology. 520p. 1979. text ed. 84.50 (ISBN 0-8391-1311-0). Univ Park.

Ranofsky, Abraham L. Surgical Operations in Short-Stay Hospitals, U.S. 1973. Shipp, Audrey M., ed. (Ser. 13: No. 24). 61p. 1976. pap. text ed. 1.25 (ISBN 0-8406-0069-0). Natl Ctr Health Stats.

Sword, J. P. & Thompson, R., eds. Standard Operating Procedures in Vitro Toxicology. (Standard Operating Procedures Ser.). 268p. 1980. write for info. Univ Park.

Sword, J. P. & Waddell, A. W., eds. Standard Operating Procedures in Metabolism & Analytic Medicine. (Standard Operating Procedures Ser.: Vol. 4). 300p. 1981. 84.50 (ISBN 0-8391-1641-1). Univ Park.

OPERATIONS, SURGICAL–PSYCHOLOGICAL ASPECTS
see Surgery–Psychological Aspects

OPERATIONS AUDITING
see Management Audit

OPERATIONS RESEARCH
see also Maintainability (Engineering); Mathematical Optimization; Network Analysis (Planning); Queuing Theory; Research, Industrial; Scheduling (Management); Simulation Methods; Statistical Decision; Systems Engineering

Ackoff, R. L. Scientific Method: Optimizing Applied Research Decisions. LC 62-10914. 464p. 1962. 29.95 (ISBN 0-471-00297-6). Wiley.

Ackoff, R. L. & Rivett, Patrick. Manager's Guide to Operations Research. LC 63-14115. (Managers Guide Ser.). 107p. 1963. 17.95 (ISBN 0-471-00335-2, Pub. by Wiley-Interscience). Wiley.

Agrawal, R. C. & Heady, Earl O. Operations Research Methods for Agricultural Decisions. (Illus.). 1972. 10.95x (ISBN 0-8138-1200-3). Iowa St U Pr.

Albach, H. & Bergendahl, G., eds. Production Theory & Its Applications: Proceedings of a Workshop. (Lecture Notes in Economics & Mathematical Systems Ser.: Vol. 139). 1977. soft cover 10.10 (ISBN 0-387-08062-7). Springer-Verlag.

Annual Meeting in Operations Research, 1971. Proceedings. Henke, M., ed. (Illus.). 800p. (Eng. & Ger.). 1972. 32.50x (ISBN 3-7908-0119-4). Intl Pubns Serv.

Applied Operational Research. 27p. 1978. pap. 2.00 (ISBN 0-88936-144-4, IDRC 81, IDRC). Unipub.

Aronofsky, J. S., ed. Progress in Operations Research, Vol. 3. LC 61-10415. 570p. 1969. 29.50 (ISBN 0-471-03355-3, Pub. by Wiley). Krieger.

Au, Tung & Stelson, Thomas E. Introduction to Systems Engineering: Deterministic Models. (Civil Engineering Ser). (Illus.). 1969. text ed. 22.95 (ISBN 0-201-00363-5); instructor's manual 3.00 (ISBN 0-201-00364-3). A-W.

Avi-Itzhak, Benjamin. Developments in Operations Research, 2 vols. LC 78-141897. (Illus.). 642p. 1971. Set. 123.25 (ISBN 0-677-30510-9); Vol. 1. 63.75x (ISBN 0-677-30830-2); Vol 2. 73.25x (ISBN 0-677-30840-X). Gordon.

--Developments in Operations Research, 2 vols. LC 78-141897. (Illus.). 642p. 1971. Set. 123.25 (ISBN 0-677-30510-9); Vol. 1. 63.75x (ISBN 0-677-30830-2); Vol 2. 73.25x (ISBN 0-677-30840-X). Gordon.

Bailey, Norman T. Mathematics, Statistics & Systems for Health. LC 77-1307. (Wiley Ser. in Probability & Mathematical Statistics: Applied Probability & Statistics). 222p. 1977. 33.25 (ISBN 0-471-99500-2, Pub. by Wiley-Interscience). Wiley.

Bandyopadhyay, R. & Padwal, S. M. Introduction to Operational Research & Data Management. 400p. 1981. text ed. 25.00x (ISBN 0-7069-1234-9, Pub. by Vikas India). Advent NY.

Baumol, W. Economic Theory & Operations Analysis. 4th ed. 1977. 21.95 (ISBN 0-13-227132-X). P-H.

Beer, Stafford. Decision & Control: The Meaning of Operational Research & Management Cybernetics. LC 66-25668. 556p. 1966. 37.95 (ISBN 0-471-06210-3, Pub. by Wiley-Interscience). Wiley.

--Platform for Change. LC 73-10741. 460p. 1975. 36.25 (ISBN 0-471-06189-1, Pub. by Wiley-Interscience). Wiley.

Beilby, M. H. Economics & Operational Research. 1976. 27.00 (ISBN 0-12-085750-2). Acad Pr.

Bohigian, Haig E. The Foundations & Mathematical Models of Operations Research with Extensions to the Criminal Justice System. LC 75-186274. (Illus.). xxiii, 282p. (Orig.). 1972. 12.95 (ISBN 0-933390-01-7). Gazette Pr.

Boldy, Duncan, ed. Operational Research Applied to Health Services. 1981. 30.00x (ISBN 0-312-58682-5). St Martin.

Bonczek, Robert H., et al. Foundations of Decision Support Systems. LC 80-1779. (Operations Research & Industrial Engineering Ser.). 1981. 29.50 (ISBN 0-12-113050-9). Acad Pr.

Box, George E. & Draper, Norman R. Evolutionary Operation: A Statistical Method for Process Improvement. LC 68-56159. (Applied Probability & Mathematical Statistics Ser). 1969. 28.95 (ISBN 0-471-09305-X, Pub. by Wiley-Interscience). Wiley.

Bradley, Hugh E. The Operations Research & Management Science CumIndex, Vol. 10. 1979. 60.00 (ISBN 0-88274-009-1). R & D Pr.

Brennan, J., ed. Operational Research in Industrial Systems. (NATO Ser). 1972. 25.00 (ISBN 0-444-19642-0). Elsevier.

Bronson, R. Schaum's Outline of Operations Research. (Schaum Paperback Ser.). 1982. pap. price not set (ISBN 0-07-007977-3, SP). McGraw.

Brounstein, Sidney H. & Kamrass, Murray, eds. Operations Research in Law Enforcement & Societal Security. (Illus.). 1976. 21.95 (ISBN 0-669-00732-3). Lexington Bks.

Brown, A. R. Optimum Packing & Depletion. (Computer Monograph Ser: No. 14). 1972. 12.50 (ISBN 0-444-19588-2). Elsevier.

Budnick, Frank S., et al. Principles of Operations Research for Management. 1977. 22.95x (ISBN 0-256-01796-4). Irwin.

Buffa, Elwood S. & Dyer, James S. Essentials of Management Science-Operations Research. LC 77-23799. (Manangement & Administration Ser.). 1978. text ed. 25.95 (ISBN 0-471-02003-6). Wiley.

Burton, Ellison S., ed. Computers & Operations Research: Environmental Applications. 1977. pap. text ed. 34.50 (ISBN 0-08-021348-0). Pergamon.

Cabell, Randolph W. & Phillips, Almarin. Problems in Basic Operations Research Methods for Management. LC 75-11958. 122p. 1975. Repr. of 1961 ed. 11.50 (ISBN 0-88275-317-7). Krieger.

Cabot, A. Victor & Hartnett, Donald L. Introduction to Management Science. LC 76-20024. (Illus.). 1977. text ed. 18.95 (ISBN 0-201-02746-1). A-W.

Casti, John. Connectivity, Complexity, & Catastrophe in Large-Scale Systems. LC 79-40818. (Wiley IIASA International Ser. on Applied Systems Analysis). 1979. 40.75 (ISBN 0-471-27661-8, Pub. by Wiley-Interscience). Wiley.

Chacko, G. K. Applied Operations Research-Systems Analysis in Hierarchical Decision-Making, 2 vol. set. Incl. Vol. 1. Systems Approach to Public & Private Sector Problems; Vol. 2. Operations Research to Problem Formulation & Solution. (Studies in Management Science & Solution: Vol. 3). 1976. Set. 97.75 (ISBN 0-444-10768-1, North-Holland). Elsevier.

Clementson, Alan & Clewett, A. J., eds. Management, Operational Research & the Micro. 96p. 1981. pap. 14.00 (ISBN 0-08-025842-5). Pergamon.

Colin, A. Introduction to Operating Systems. 1972. text ed. 16.95 (ISBN 0-444-19589-0). Elsevier.

Colley, John L., Jr., et al. Operations Planning & Control. LC 77-4804. 1978. text ed. 18.95x (ISBN 0-8162-1736-X). Holden-Day.

Connolly, B. Techniques in Operational Research: Models, Search & Randomization, Vol. 2. 340p. 1981. 77.95 (ISBN 0-470-27130-2). Halsted Pr.

Converse, A. O. Optimization. LC 74-22103. 308p. 1975. Repr. of 1970 ed. 14.50 (ISBN 0-88275-236-7). Krieger.

Cook, Thomas M. & Russell, Robert A. Introduction to Management Science. 1977. text ed. 19.95 (ISBN 0-13-486084-5). P-H.

Cooper. Introd. Operations Research Models. 1977. 18.95 (ISBN 0-7216-2688-2). Dryden Pr.

Croucher, John S. Operations Research: A First Course. (Illus.). 320p. 1980. 27.00 (ISBN 0-08-024798-9); pap. 13.50 (ISBN 0-08-024797-0). Pergamon.

Daellenbach, Hans G. & George, John A. Introduction to Operations Research Techniques. 1978. text ed. 26.95 (ISBN 0-205-05755-1); answer book (ISBN 0-205-05756-X). Allyn.

Davar, Rustom S. Executive Decision Making: Modern Concepts & Techniques. (Progressive Management Ser). (Illus.). 1968. 12.50x (ISBN 0-8002-0598-7). Intl Pubns Serv.

Dean, Burton V., ed. Operations Research in Research & Development. LC 77-18041. 302p. 1978. Repr. of 1963 ed. lib. bdg. 13.50 (ISBN 0-88275-647-8). Krieger.

Doty, James. Journal of Operations. 5.50 (ISBN 0-87770-204-7). Ye Galleon.

Drake, Alvin W., et al, eds. Analysis of Public Systems. 480p. 1972. 26.50x (ISBN 0-262-04038-7). MIT Pr.

Duckworth, Walter E., et al. A Guide to Operational Research. 3d ed. LC 77-4247. 205p. 1977. text ed. 15.95x (ISBN 0-412-12370-3, Pub. by Chapman & Hall England). Methuen Inc.

Eck, Roger D. Operations Research for Business. 1976. text ed. 26.95x (ISBN 0-534-00424-5). Wadsworth Pub.

Eiselt, Horst A. & Von Frajer, Helmut. Operations Research Handbook: Standard Algorithms & Methods with Examples. 1977. 46.50x (ISBN 3-11-007055-3). De Gruyter.

Emshoff, James R. & Sisson, Roger L. Design & Use of Computer Simulation Models. (Illus.). 1970. 18.95 (ISBN 0-02-333720-6, 33372). Macmillan.

Gaither, Norman. Production & Operations Management. 784p. 1980. text ed. 23.95 (ISBN 0-03-042701-0). Dryden Pr.

Gal, Tomas. Postoptimal Analyses, Parametric Programming, & Related Topics. 1979. text ed. 54.50 (ISBN 0-07-022679-2, C). McGraw.

Gaver, Donald P. & Thompson, Gerald L. Programming & Probability Models in Operations Research. LC 72-90938. 1973. text ed. 29.95 (ISBN 0-8185-0057-3). Brooks-Cole.

Ghosal & Ghosal, A. Applied Cybernetics: It's Relevance to Operations Research. 1978. 29.75 (ISBN 0-677-05410-6). Gordon.

Ghosal, A., et al. Examples & Exercises in Operations Research. (Studies in Operations Research Ser.). 272p. 1975. 44.50x (ISBN 0-677-03910-7). Gordon.

Gillett, Billy E. Methods of Operations Research. (Illus.). 1976. text ed. 24.00 (ISBN 0-07-023245-8, C); solutions manual 7.95 (ISBN 0-07-023246-6). McGraw.

Gowan, J. C. Operations of Increasing Order. 408p. (Orig.). 1980. pap. 5.00x (ISBN 0-686-28154-3). Gowan.

Grouchko, Daniel, ed. Operations Research & Reliability. LC 72-172824. (Illus.). 642p. 1971. 104.00x (ISBN 0-677-14610-8). Gordon.

Gue, Ronald L. & Thomas, Michael E. Mathematical Methods in Operations Research. LC 68-18474. 1968. 16.50 (ISBN 0-02-348310-5, 34831). Macmillan.

Gupta, J. N. D. Postal Applications of Operations Research. 1978. text ed. 34.50 (ISBN 0-08-023011-3). Pergamon.

Gupta, Shiv K. & Cozzolino, John M. Fundamentals of Operations Research for Management. LC 73-94384. (Illus.). 1975. text ed. 22.95x (ISBN 0-8162-3476-0); solutions manual 6.50x (ISBN 0-8162-3486-8). Holden-Day.

Haehling von Lanzenauer, Christoph. Cases in Operations Research. 1975. 12.95x (ISBN 0-8162-3546-5); instr's manual 4.50x (ISBN 0-8162-3556-2). Holden-Day.

Hammer, L. Ivanescu & Rudeanu, S. Boolean Methods in Operations Research & Related Areas. LC 67-21932. (Econometrics & Operations Research Ser.: Vol. 7). (Illus.). 1968. 33.50 (ISBN 0-387-04291-1). Springer-Verlag.

Hanssmann, Fred. Operations Research Techniques for Capital Investment. LC 74-10988. 280p. 1974. Repr. of 1968 ed. 14.50 (ISBN 0-88275-181-6). Krieger.

Hanssmann, Fred, ed. Operational Research in the Design of Electronic Data Processing Systems. LC 72-95948. 1973. 27.50x (ISBN 0-8448-0161-5). Crane-Russak Co.

Hartley, Ronald V. Operations Research: A Managerial Emphasis. LC 75-23890. 1976. text ed. 23.95 (ISBN 0-87620-641-0). Goodyear.

Hax, A. Studies in Operations Management. (Studies in Management Science & Systems Ser.: Vol. 6). 1979. 78.00 (ISBN 0-444-85161-5, North Holland). Elsevier.

Henn, R., et al, eds. Optimization & Operations Research: Proceedings of a Workshop Held at the University of Bonn, October 2-8, 1977. (Lecture Notes in Econometrics & Operations Research Ser.: Vol. 157). 1978. pap. 13.90 (ISBN 0-387-08842-3). Springer-Verlag.
Hesse, Rick & Woolsey, Gene. Applied Management Science. 384p. 1980. pap. text ed. 15.95 (ISBN 0-574-19345-6, 13-2345); instr's. guide avail. (ISBN 0-574-19346-4, 13-2346). SRA.
Hettich, R., ed. Semi-Infinite Programming: Proceedings. (Lecture Notes in Control & Information Science: Vol. 15). (Illus.). 1979. pap. 10.30 (ISBN 0-387-09479-2). Springer-Verlag.
Hillier, Frederick S. & Lieberman, Gerald J. Introduction to Operations Research. 3rd ed. 848p. 1980. text ed. 28.95x (ISBN 0-8162-3867-7); solutions manual 7.50 (ISBN 0-8162-3868-5). Holden-Day.
--Operations Research. 2nd ed. LC 73-94383. 816p. 1974. text ed. 27.95x (ISBN 0-8162-3856-1); solutions manual o.p. 7.50 (ISBN 0-8162-3866-9). Holden-Day.
Holzman. Mathematical Programming for Operations Researchers. (Industrial Engineering Ser.: Vol. 6). 392p. 1981. 45.00 (ISBN 0-8247-1499-7). Dekker.
--Operations Research Support Methodology. (Industrial Engineering--a Ser. of Reference Books & Textbooks: Vol. 2). 1979. 39.75 (ISBN 0-8247-6771-3). Dekker.
Hopeman, Richard A. Production & Operations Management. 4th ed. (Marketing & Management Ser.). 608p. 1980. text ed. 21.95 (ISBN 0-675-08140-8); instructor's manual 3.95 (ISBN 0-686-63346-6). Merrill.
IFORS International Conference on Operational Research, 7th, Japan, 1975 & Haley, K. B. Operational Research '75: Proceedings. 1976. 68.50 (ISBN 0-444-11025-9, North-Holland). Elsevier.
Ignizio, James P., et al. Operations Research in Decision Making. LC 74-12829. 343p. 1975. 22.50x (ISBN 0-8448-0670-6); pap. 9.50x (ISBN 0-8448-0671-4). Crane-Russak Co.
Jaiswal, N. K. Priority Queues. (Mathematics in Science & Engineering Ser.: Vol. 50). 1968. 42.00 (ISBN 0-12-380050-1). Acad Pr.
Jardine, A. K. Operational Research in Maintenance. 242p. 1970. 45.00x (ISBN 0-7190-0389-X, Pub. by Manchester U Pr England). State Mutual Bk.
Johnson, Richard A., et al. Theory & Management of Systems. 3rd ed. (Management Ser). (Illus.). 544p. 1973. text ed. 17.95 (ISBN 0-07-032634-7, C); instructor's manual 4.95 (ISBN 0-07-032635-5). McGraw.
Johnson, Rodney D. & Siskin, Bernard R. Quantitative Techniques for Business Decisions. (Illus.). 544p. 1976. 22.95 (ISBN 0-13-746990-X). P-H.
Kaufmann, Arnold & Faure, R. Introduction to Operations Research. Sneyd, Henry C., tr. LC 67-23162. (Mathematics in Science & Engineering Ser.: Vol. 47). (Illus.). 1968. 43.50 (ISBN 0-12-402360-6). Acad Pr.
Kolbin, Vyacheslav V. Stochastic Programming. Grigoryev, Igor P., tr. (Theory & Decision Library: No. 14). 1977. lib. bdg. 34.00 (ISBN 90-277-0750-2, Pub. by Reidel Holland). Kluwer Boston.
Kovacs, Laszlo B. Combinatorial Methods of Discrete Programming. (Mathematical Methods of Operations Research: Vol. 2). 283p. 1980. 30.00x (ISBN 963-05-2004-4). Intl Pubns Serv.
Lange, Oskar. Optimal Decisions. 304p. 1972. text ed. 32.00 (ISBN 0-08-016053-0). Pergamon.
Levin, Richard I. & Kirkpatrick, Charles A. Quantitative Approaches to Management. 4th ed. (Illus.). 1978. text ed. 20.95 (ISBN 0-07-037423-6, C); instructor's manual 4.95 (ISBN 0-07-037424-4); student wkbk. 6.95 (ISBN 0-07-037434-1). McGraw.
Lewis, C. D. Operations Management in Practice. 304p. 1980. 36.00x (ISBN 0-86003-511-5, Pub. by Allan Pubs England); pap. 18.00x (ISBN 0-86003-611-1). State Mutual Bk.
Littlechild, S. C. Operational Research for Managers. 256p. 1977. 33.00x (ISBN 0-86003-504-2, Pub. by Allan Pubs England); pap. 16.50 (ISBN 0-86003-604-9). State Mutual Bk.
McCloskey, Joseph F., et al, eds. Operations Research for Management, Vol. 1. (Operations Research Ser). 410p. 1954. Vol. 1. 25.00x (ISBN 0-8018-0404-3). Johns Hopkins.
Makower, M. S. & Williamson, E. Operational Research. (Teach Yourself Ser.). 1973. pap. 4.95 (ISBN 0-679-10384-8). McKay.
Mansfield, Edwin, ed. Managerial Economics & Operations Research. 4th ed. 1980. 24.95 (ISBN 0-393-01271-9); pap. text ed. 7.95x (ISBN 0-393-95060-3). Norton.
--Managerial Economics & Operations Research. rev. ed. LC 70-95540. 1970. pap. text ed. 4.50x (ISBN 0-393-09919-9). Norton.
--Managerial Economics & Operations Research. 3rd ed. 1975. pap. 6.95x (ISBN 0-393-09297-6). Norton.
Markland, Robert E. Topics in Management Science. LC 78-17932. (Management & Administration Ser.). 1979. text ed. 28.95 (ISBN 0-471-01745-0). Wiley.
Marlow, W. H. Mathematics for Operations Research. LC 78-534. 1978. 33.95 (ISBN 0-471-57233-0, Pub. by Wiley-Interscience). Wiley.
Martin, M. J. & Denison, R. A., eds. Case Exercises in Operations Research. LC 75-146548. 1971. 23.25 (ISBN 0-471-57355-8, Pub. by Wiley-Interscience). Wiley.
Maslov, V. P. Operational Methods. 559p. 1976. 10.00 (ISBN 0-8285-0733-3, Pub. by Mir Pubs Russia). Imported Pubns.
Mercer, A., et al. Operational Distribution Research: Innovative Case Studies. (ORASA Text Ser.: No. 2). 1978. pap. 21.95x (ISBN 0-470-26537-X). Halsted Pr.
Miller, David W. & Starr, Martin K. Executive Decisions & Operations Research. 2nd ed. 1969. ref. ed. 21.00 (ISBN 0-13-294538-X). P-H.
Moder, Joseph J. & Elmaghraby, Salah E., eds. Handbook of Operations Research, 2 vols. 1978. Vols. 1 & 2, 32.50 ea. Vol. 1 (ISBN 0-442-24595-5). Vol. 2 (ISBN 0-442-24596-3). Vol. 3. 59.50 (ISBN 0-442-24597-1). Van Nos Reinhold.
Morse, Philip M. & Bacon, L. W. Operations Research for Public Systems. LC 67-27347. 1967. pap. text ed. 9.95x (ISBN 0-262-13010-6). MIT Pr.
Morse, Philip M. & Kimball, George E. Methods of Operations Research. (Illus.). 179p. 1980. pap. 14.95 (ISBN 0-932146-03-1). Peninsula.
Muth, Eginhard J. Transform Methods with Applications to Engineering & Operations Research. (Illus.). 1977. ref. ed. 25.95 (ISBN 0-13-928861-9). P-H.
Nagel, Stuart S. & Neef, Marian. Operations Research Methods. LC 76-25693. (Sage University Papers Ser.: Quantitative Applications in the Social Sciences, No. 2). 76p. 1976. pap. 4.00x (ISBN 0-8039-0651-X). Sage.
Nijkamp, Peter & Spronk, Jaap, eds. Multiple Criteria Analysis: Operational Methods. 288p. 1981. 18.95x (ISBN 0-566-00412-7, 04707-4, Pub. by Gower Pub Co England). Lexington Bks.
Oettli, W. K. & Ritter, K. G., eds. Optimization & Operations Research. (Lecture Notes in Economies & Math Systems: Vol. 117). 316p. 1976. pap. 15.30 (ISBN 0-387-07616-6). Springer-Verlag.
Operational Research 1972: Proceedings. Ross, M., ed. 690p. 1974. 63.50 (ISBN 0-444-10512-3, North-Holland). Elsevier.
Optner, Stanford L. Systems Analysis for Business Management. 3rd ed. (Illus.). 400p. 1974. ref. ed. 18.95 (ISBN 0-13-881276-4). P-H.
Palmer, Colin. Quantitative Aids for Management Decision Making. 1979. text ed. 21.50x (ISBN 0-566-00284-1, Pub. by Gower Pub Co England). Renouf.
Pearcy, Carl M. Some Recent Developments in Operator Theory. LC 78-8754. (Conference Board of the Mathematical Sciences Ser.: No. 36). 1980. Repr. of 1978 ed. 9.00 (ISBN 0-8218-1686-1, CBMS 36). Am Math.
Perraton, J. & Baxter, R., eds. Models, Evaluations & Information Systems for Planners. 1975. 33.00 (ISBN 0-85200-102-9). Elsevier.
Phillips, Don T., et al. Operations Research: Principles & Practices. LC 75-44395. 585p. 1976. text ed. 26.95 (ISBN 0-471-68707-3). Wiley.
Plane, Donald R. & Kochenberger, Gary A. Operations Research for Managerial Decisions. 1972. 14.95x (ISBN 0-256-00451-X). Irwin.
Poage, Scott. Quantitative Management Methods for Practicing Engineers. LC 77-133267. 1970. 13.95 (ISBN 0-389-00531-2); pap. 10.95 (ISBN 0-8436-0334-8). CBI Pub.
Prekopa, A., ed. Progress in Operations Research. (Colloquia Mathematica Societatis Janos Bolyai: No. 12). 1976. 92.75 (ISBN 0-7204-2836-X, North-Holland). Elsevier.
Reed, John H. The Application of Operations Research to Court Delay. LC 72-89647. (Special Studies in U.S. Economic, Social & Political Issues). 1973. 26.00x (ISBN 0-275-06690-8). Irvington.
Results of the 1975 National Operations & Automation Survey. 1975. 100.00 (ISBN 0-89982-171-5, 067100). Am Bankers.
Richmond, Samuel B. Operations Research for Management Decisions. LC 68-20552. (Illus.). 600p. 1968. 26.95 (ISBN 0-8260-7460-X). Wiley.
Rochat, Jean-Claude. Mathematiques pour la Question de l'Environment. (Interdisciplinary Systems Research Ser.: No. 74). (Illus.). 413p. (Fr.). 1980. pap. 39.50 (ISBN 3-7643-1126-6). Birkhauser.
Roubens, M. & European Congress on Operation Reserch, Second, Stockholm, Sweden, November 29, 1977. Advances in Operations Research: Proceedings. 1977. 70.75 (ISBN 0-7204-0718-4, North-Holland). Elsevier.
Rudman, Jack. Operations Research Analyst. (Career Examination Ser.: C-556). (Cloth bdg. avail. on request). pap. 12.00 (ISBN 0-8373-0556-X). Natl Learning.
Sargeaunt, M. J. Operational Research for Management. 1965. 16.95x (ISBN 0-89563-013-3). Intl Ideas.
Schaefer. What Is Operations? (Research Bulletin: No. 6). pap. 1.00 (ISBN 0-685-57183-1). Assn Sch Busn.
Schmidt, J. William & Davis, Robert P. Foundation of Analysis in Operations Research. LC 80-987. (Operations Research & Industrial Engineering Ser.). 1981. 27.00 (ISBN 0-12-626850-9). Acad Pr.
Schonberger, Richard J. Operations Management: Planning & Control of Operations & Operating Resources. 1981. text ed. 22.50x (ISBN 0-256-02442-1). Business Pubns.
Schultz, Randall L. & Slevin, Dennis P., eds. Implementing Operations Research - Management Science. LC 74-14467. (Illus.). 334p. 1975. 25.00 (ISBN 0-444-00150-6, North Holland). Elsevier.
Sengupta, J. K. & Fox, K. A. Economic Analysis & Operations Research: Optimization Techniques in Quantitative Economic Models, Vol. 10. Theil, Henri, ed. (Studies in Mathematical & Managerial Economics Ser.: Vol. 10). 1968. 44.00 (ISBN 0-444-10269-8, North-Holland). Elsevier.
Sengupta, S. Sankar. Operations Research in Sellers' Competition: A Stochastic Microtheory. 228p. 1967. 11.75 (ISBN 0-471-77625-4, Pub. by Wiley). Krieger.
Shamblin, James E. & Stevens, G. T. Operations Research. (Illus.). 416p. 1974. text ed. 21.00 (ISBN 0-07-056378-0, C); instructor's manual 5.50 (ISBN 0-07-056379-9). McGraw.
Shore, Barry. Operations Management. (Management Ser.). (Illus.). 544p. 1973. text ed. 21.00 (ISBN 0-07-057045-0, C); instructor's manual 7.95 (ISBN 0-07-057046-9). McGraw.
Siemens, Nicolai, et al. Operations Research: Planning, Operating & Information Systems. LC 70-184529. 1973. text ed. 19.95 (ISBN 0-02-928740-5). Free Pr.
Singh, Jagjit. Great Ideas of Operations Research. (Illus., Orig.). 1968. pap. text ed. 3.50 (ISBN 0-486-21886-4). Dover.
--Great Ideas of Operations Research. 5.50 (ISBN 0-8446-2947-2). Peter Smith.
Sivazlian, B. D. & Stanfel, Larry E. Optimization Techniques in Operations Research. (Industrial Engineering Ser). (Illus.). 448p. 1974. ref. ed. 26.95 (ISBN 0-13-638163-4). P-H.
Stoller, David S. Operations Research: Process & Strategy. 1964. 22.75x (ISBN 0-520-01222-4). U of Cal Pr.
Taha, Hamdy. Operations Research: An Introduction. 2nd ed. (Illus.). 1976. text ed. 22.95 (ISBN 0-02-418820-4). Macmillan.
Taha, Hamdy A. Operations Research. 3rd ed. 1982. text ed. 29.95 (ISBN 0-686-75042-X). Macmillan.
Thesen, Arne, ed. Computer Methods in Operations Research. (Operations Research & Industrial Engineering Ser). 1978. 21.00 (ISBN 0-12-686150-1). Acad Pr.
Thierauf, Robert J. An Introductory Approach to Operations Research. LC 77-23031. (Ser. on Management & Administration). 412p. 1978. text ed. 27.95 (ISBN 0-471-03125-9). Wiley.
Thierauf, Robert J. & Klekamp, Robert C. Decision Making Through Operations Research. 2nd ed. LC 74-19473. (Management & Administration Ser). 650p. 1975. 27.95 (ISBN 0-471-85861-7); instructors manual avail. (ISBN 0-471-85856-0); Wiley.
Thorelli, Hans B., et al. Player's Manual for International Operations Simulation. LC 63-13249. 1963. pap. text ed. 7.95 (ISBN 0-02-932530-7). Free Pr.
Thornton, Billy M. & Preston, Paul. An Introduction to Management Science: Quantitative Approach to Managerial Decisions. (Business Ser.). 1977. text ed. 19.95 (ISBN 0-675-08518-7); instructor's manual 3.95 (ISBN 0-686-67524-X); card deck o. p. 3.95 (ISBN 0-686-67525-8); transparencies 3.95 (ISBN 0-686-67526-6). Merrill.
Verma, Harish L. & Gross, Charles W. Introduction to Quantitative Methods: A Managerial Emphasis. LC 77-21089. 1978. text ed. 26.95 (ISBN 0-471-02610-7); tchrs. manual o.p. avail. (ISBN 0-471-02495-3, Pub. by Wiley-Hamilton). Wiley.
Wagner, Harvey M. Principles of Operations Research with Applications to Managerial Decisions. 2nd ed. (Illus.). 1088p. 1975. 31.00 (ISBN 0-13-709592-9). P-H.
Whisler, William D., ed. Applications on Management Science & Operations Research Methods. 249p. 1974. pap. text ed. 14.95x (ISBN 0-8422-0376-1). Irvington.
White, Douglas, et al. Operational Research Techniques, Vol. 2. 328p. 1974. 31.00x (ISBN 0-8464-0687-X). Beekman Pubs.
Whitehouse, Gary E. & Wechsler, Ben L. Applied Operations Research: A Survey. LC 76-16545. 1976. 25.95x (ISBN 0-471-02552-6); solutions manual 5.00 (ISBN 0-685-66900-9). Wiley.
Wilson, C. Operational Research for Students of Management. 1970. text ed. 16.95x (ISBN 0-7002-0159-9). Intl Ideas.
Woolsey, Robert E. & Swanson, Huntington S. Operations Research for Immediate Application: A Quick and Dirty Manual. Orig. Title: Quick & Dirty Manual: Operations Research for Immediate Application. 1975. pap. text ed. 11.50 scp (ISBN 0-06-047233-2, HarpC). Har-Row.
Worms, G. Modern Methods of Applied Economics. 1970. 43.00x (ISBN 0-677-01990-4). Gordon.

OPERATIVE DENTISTRY
see Dentistry, Operative
OPERATIVE OBSTETRICS
see Obstetrics-Surgery
OPERATIVE SURGERY
see Surgery, Operative
OPERATIVE UROLOGY
see Genito-Urinary Organs-Surgery
OPERATORS, DIFFERENTIAL
see Differential Operators
OPERATORS, LINEAR
see Linear Operators
OPERATORS, NONLINEAR
see Nonlinear Operators
OPERCULATES
see Discomycetes
OPERETTA
see also Melodrama; Musical Revue, Comedy, etc.
Kline, Peter. The Theatre Student: Gilbert & Sullivan Production. LC 74-170281. (Theatre Student Ser). (gr. 7 up). 1972. PLB 12.50 (ISBN 0-8239-0252-8). Rosen Pr.
Strang, Lewis C. Celebrated Comedians of Light Opera & Musical Comedy. LC 72-91574. (Illus.). 1901. 17.00 (ISBN 0-405-09005-6, Pub. by Blom). Arno.

OPERETTA-HISTORY AND CRITICISM
Allen, Reginald. Gilbert & Sullivan in America. LC 79-54098. (Illus.). 26p. 1979. pap. 3.00 (ISBN 0-686-70604-8). Pierpont Morgan.

OPERETTA-STORIES, PLOTS, ETC.
see Operas-Stories, Plots, etc.
OPERETTAS
see Musical Revues, Comedies, etc.; Operas
OPHIDIA
see Snakes
OPHIOLOGY
see Snakes
OPHIR
Peters, Karl. Eladorado of the Ancients. LC 70-88445. (Illus.). Repr. of 1902 ed. 31.00x (ISBN 0-8371-1905-7, Pub. by Negro U Pr). Greenwood.
--King Solomon's Golden Ophir: A Research into the Most Ancient Gold Production in History. LC 74-88446. Repr. of 1899 ed. 11.00x (ISBN 0-8371-1835-2, Pub. by Negro U Pr). Greenwood.
Price, Harry. The Royal Tour 1901: The Cruise of H.M.S. Ophir. LC 79-49267. (Illus.). 200p. 1980. 20.95 (ISBN 0-688-03667-8). Morrow.

OPHITES
see also Gnosticism
OPHTHALMIC NURSING
Rooke, F. E., et al. Ophthalmic Nursing: Its Practice & Management. (Illus.). 256p. 1980. pap. text ed. 13.50x (ISBN 0-443-01494-9). Churchill.

OPHTHALMIC OPTICIANS
see Optometrists
OPHTHALMOLOGICAL MANIFESTATIONS OF GENERAL DISEASES
see Ocular Manifestations of General Diseases
OPHTHALMOLOGY
see also Eye; Neuro-Ophthalmology; Pediatric Ophthalmology; Therapeutics, Ophthalmological; Ultrasonics in Ophthalmology
Abstracts of the Twenty-Third International Congress of Ophthalmology, Kyoto, Japan, May 1978. (International Congress Ser.: No. 442). 1978. 34.25 (ISBN 0-444-90027-6, Excerpta Medica). Elsevier.
Albert, Daniel M. & Scheie, Harold G. A History of Ophthalmology at the University of Pennsylvania. (Illus.). 420p. 1965. ed. spiral bdg. 36.50photocopy (ISBN 0-398-00024-7). C C Thomas.
Albert, Daniel M. & Puliafito, Carmen A., eds. Foundations of Ophthalmic Pathology. LC 78-9871. (Illus.). 664p. 1979. 52.00 (ISBN 0-8385-2690-X). ACC.
Allen, E. W. Essentials of Ophthalmic Optics. (Illus.). 1979. pap. text ed. 7.95x (ISBN 0-19-261173-9). Oxford U Pr.

Auerbach, E., ed. Experimental & Clinical Amblyopia. (Documenta Ophthalmologica Proceedings: Vol. 11). 1975. lib. bdg. 31.50 (ISBN 90-6193-151-7, Pub. by Junk Pubs. Netherlands). Kluwer Boston.

Bedford, M. A. Color Atlas of Ophthalmological Diagnosis. (Year Book Color Atlas Ser.). (Illus.). 1971. 25.00 (ISBN 0-8151-0623-8). Year Bk Med.

Bellows, John B., ed. Contemporary Ophthalomology. 554p. 1972. 34.75 (ISBN 0-685-90276-5, Pub. by W & W). Krieger.

Benson, William E. Retinal Detachment Diagnosis & Treatment. (Illus.). 208p. 1980. text ed. 28.75 (ISBN 0-06-140410-1, Harper Medical). Har-Row.

Bernard Becker, M.D. Collection in Ophthalmology. 1979. pap. 12.50x (ISBN 0-912260-09-2). Wash U Med Lib.

Blankenship, G., et al, eds. Current Concepts in Diagnosis & Treatment of Vitreoretinal Diseases. (Developments in Ophthalmology Ser.: Vol. 2). (Illus.). xxviii, 408p. 1981. 176.75 (ISBN 3-8055-1672-X). S Karger.

Bleeker, G. M., et al, eds. Orbital Disorders. (Illus.). 1978. lib. bdg. 34.00 (ISBN 90-6193-570-9, Pub. by Junk Pubs Netherlands). Kluwer Boston.

Brockhurst, Robert J., et al, eds. Controversy in Ophthalmology. LC 75-40634. (Illus.). 1977. text ed. 50.00 (ISBN 0-7216-1989-4). Saunders.

Brooks, Clifford F. & Borish, Irving. System for Ophthalmic Dispensing. 1979. 48.00 (ISBN 0-87873-025-7). Prof Press.

Campbell, Charles J., et al. Physiological Optics. (Illus.). 1974. text ed. 23.00x (ISBN 0-06-140616-3, Harper Medical). Har-Row.

Chance, Burton. Ophthalmology. LC 75-23693. (Clio Medica: No. 21). (Illus.). Repr. of 1939 ed. 21.00 (ISBN 0-404-58921-9). AMS Pr.

Char, Devron H. Immunology of Uveitis & Ocular Tumors. (Current Ophthalmology Monographs). 144p. 1978. 24.25 (ISBN 0-8089-1147-3). Grune.

Chignell, A. H. Retinal Detachment Surgery. (Illus.). 1979. 35.80 (ISBN 0-387-09475-X). Springer-Verlag.

Chumbley, Lee C. Ophthalmology in Internal Medicine. (Illus.). 288p. 1980. write for info. (ISBN 0-7216-2578-9). Saunders.

Colloque du Club Jules Gonin, 7th & Assemblee de la Societe Suisse d'ophtalmologie, 63rd, Lausanne, 1970. Secondary Detachment of the Retina: Proceedings. Dufour, R., ed. (Modern Problems in Ophthalmology: Vol. 10). (Illus.). 1972. 96.00 (ISBN 3-8055-1300-3). S Karger.

Corboy, J. M. The Retinoscopy Book: A Manual for Beginners. LC 79-65451. 1979. pap. text ed. 9.50 (ISBN 0-685-91503-4). C B Slack.

Cunha-Vaz, Jose G., ed. The Blood-Retinal Barriers. (NATO Advanced Study Institutes Ser., Ser. A: Life Sciences: Vol. 32). 405p. 1980. 39.50 (ISBN 0-306-40430-3, Plenum Pr). Plenum Pub.

Dausch, D. & Honegger, H. Timolol Ophthalmic Solution in the Treatment of Glaucoma. LC 78-72505. 1978. 3.00 (ISBN 0-911910-95-6). Merck-Sharp-Dohme.

Duke-Elder, Stewart, ed. System of Ophthalmology Series. Incl. Vol. 1. The Eye in Evolution. (Illus.). 843p. 1958. 61.50 (ISBN 0-8016-8282-7); Vol. 2. The Anatomy of the Visual System. (Illus.). 901p. 1961. 63.50 (ISBN 0-8016-8283-5); Vol. 3, Pt. 1. Normal & Abnormal Development: Embryology. (Illus.). 330p. 1963. 49.00 (ISBN 0-8016-8285-1); Vol. 3, Pt. 2. Normal & Abnormal Development: Congenital Deformities. (Illus.). 1190p. 1964. 69.00 (ISBN 0-8016-8286-X); Vol. 4. The Physiology of the Eye & of Vision. (Illus.). xx, 734p. 1968; Vol. 5. Ophthalmic Optics & Refraction. (Illus.). xix, 879p. 1970; Vol. 7. The Foundations of Ophthalmology: Heredity, Pathology, Diagnosis & Therapeutics. (Illus.). 829p. 1962. 65.50 (ISBN 0-8016-8284-3); Vol. 8. Diseases of the Outer Eye: Conjunctiva, Cornea & Sclera, 2 vols. (Illus.). 1339p. 1965. 100.00 (ISBN 0-8016-8287-8); Vol. 9. Diseases of Uveal Tract. (Illus.). xvi, 978p. 1966. 80.00 (ISBN 0-8016-8290-8); Vol. 10. Diseases of the Retina. (Illus.). xv, 878p. 1967. 80.00 (ISBN 0-8016-8295-9); Vol. 11. Diseases of the Lens & Vitreous: Glaucoma & Hypotony. (Illus.). xx, 779p. 1969. 80.00 (ISBN 0-8016-8297-5); Vol. 12. Neuro-Ophthalmology. (Illus.). xxi, 994p. 1971. 83.50 (ISBN 0-8016-8299-1); Vol. 14. Injuries, 2 vols. 1357p. 1972. Set. 117.00 (ISBN 0-8016-8300-9). Mosby.

Enoch, Jay M., et al. Quantitative Layer-by-Layer Perimetry: An Extented Analysis. (Current Ophthalmology Monographs). (Illus.). 256p. 1980. 29.50 (ISBN 0-8089-1282-8). Grune.

Francois, J. & De Rouck, A., eds. Electrodiagnosis, Toxic Agents & Vision. 1978. lib. bdg. 58.00 (ISBN 90-6193-155-X, Pub. by Junk Pubs. Netherlands). Kluwer Boston.

Frayer, William C., ed. Lancaster Course in Ophthalmic Histopathology. (Illus.). 325p. 1980. Text, Slides & Fourteen Units With Lectures. 936.00 (ISBN 0-8036-3827-2). Davis Co.

Gailloud, C., ed. Developments in Ophthalmology, Vol. 2. (Illus.). viii, 492p. 1981. 180.00 (ISBN 3-8055-1672-X). S Karger.

Gailloud, C., et al, eds. New Aspects of Vitreoretinopathology. (Modern Problems in Ophthalmology Ser.: Vol. 20). (Illus.). 1979. 155.75 (ISBN 3-8055-3038-2). S Karger.

Gardner & Klintworth. Pathobiology of Oscular Disease, Pt. A. 886p. 1981. price not set (ISBN 0-8247-1295-1). Dekker.

Gass, J. Donald. Stereoscopic Atlas of Macular Diseases: Diagnosis & Treatment. 2nd ed. LC 76-57176. (Illus.). 1977. 77.50 (ISBN 0-8016-1754-5). Mosby.

Gelatt, Kirk N., ed. Textbook of Veterinary Opthalmology. LC 80-17291. (Illus.). 788p. 1981. text ed. 85.00 (ISBN 0-8121-0686-5). Lea & Febiger.

Goldberg, Stephen. Ophthalmology Made Ridiculously Simple. (Illus.). 96p. (Orig.). 1982. pap. text ed. 9.50 (ISBN 0-940780-01-1). MedMaster.

Greve, E. L., ed. International Visual Field Symposium, 3rd. (Documenta Ophthalmologica Proceedings Ser.: Vol. 19). 1979. lib. bdg. 87.00 (ISBN 90-6193-160-6, Pub. by Junk Pubs Netherlands). Kluwer Boston.

--Symposium on Medical Therapy in Gloucoma. (Documenta Ophthalmologica Proceedings: Vol. 12). 1976. lib. bdg. 26.00 (ISBN 90-6193-152-5, Pub. by Junk Pubs Netherlands). Kluwer Boston.

Greve, Erik L., ed. Second International Visual Field Symposium. (Documenta Ophalmologica Proceedings Ser.: No. 14). (Illus.). 1977. lib. bdg. 79.00 (ISBN 90-6193-154-1). Kluwer Boston.

Guibor, Pierre, ed. Oculoplastic Surgery & Trauma. LC 75-27779. (Illus.). 1976. 25.00 (ISBN 0-8151-4033-9, Pub. by Symposia Special). Year Bk Med.

Hassani, N. Real Time Ophthalmic Ultrasonography. LC 78-17197. (Illus.). 1978. 39.80 (ISBN 0-387-90318-6). Springer-Verlag.

Havener, William H. Synopsis of Opthalmology. 5th ed. LC 79-12076. (Illus.). 1979. pap. text ed. 28.50 (ISBN 0-8016-2111-9). Mosby.

Henkind, Paul, ed. Classics in Opnthalmology Series, 5 vols. 1979. leather 295.00 (ISBN 0-88275-934-5); 169.00 (ISBN 0-88275-933-7). Krieger.

Hiles, David, ed. Intraocular Lens Implants in Children. (Current Ophthalmology Monographs). 304p. 1980. 23.50 (ISBN 0-8089-1234-8). Grune.

Hollwich, F. Ophthalmology. 9th ed. (Illus.). 380p. 1980. pap. 18.50 (ISBN 0-8151-4642-6). Year Bk Med.

Hughes, Carl W. & Bowers, Warner F. Traumatic Lesions of Peripheral Vessels. (Illus.). 208p. 1961. photocopy ed. spiral 19.75 (ISBN 0-398-00882-5). C C Thomas.

Hughes, William F., ed. Year Book of Ophthalmology 1979. (Illus.). 385p. 1979. 27.95 (ISBN 0-8151-4777-5). Year Bk Med.

--Yearbook of Ophthalmology, 1980. 1980. 31.50 (ISBN 0-8151-4778-3). Year Bk Med.

--Yearbook of Opthalmology, 1981. Date not set. price not set (ISBN 0-8151-4779-1). Year Bk Med.

Iliff, Charles E. & Ossofsky, Helen. Tumors of the Eye & Adnexa in Infancy & Childhood. (Pediatric Surgical Monograph). (Illus.). 168p. 1962. photocopy ed. spiral 16.75 (ISBN 0-398-00895-7). C C Thomas.

International Congress on Cataract Surgery, 1st Florence, 1978. Proceedings of the First International Congress on Cataract Surgery, Florence, 1978. Francois, J. & Maumenee, E., eds. (Documenta Opthalmologica Proceedings Ser.: No. 21). (Illus.). 1980. lib. bdg. 121.00 (ISBN 90-6193-162-2, Dr W Junk Pub). Kluwer Boston.

International Council of Opthalmology, ed. Perimetric Standards & Perimetric Glossary. 1979. lib. bdg. 29.00 (ISBN 90-6193-600-4, Pub. by Junk Pubs Netherlands). Kluwer Boston.

International Society for Ultrasonic Diagnosis in Ophthalmology, Ghent, May 1973. Ultrasonography on Ophthalmology, Siduo 5: Proceedings. Francois, J. & Goes, F., eds. (Bibliotheca Ophthalmologica: Vol. 83). (Illus.). 450p. 1975. 105.50 (ISBN 3-8055-1777-7). S Karger.

International Symposium on Acquired Colour Vision Deficiencies, Ghent, Belgium, 1971. Acquired Colour Vision Deficiencies: Proceedings. Verriest, G., ed. (Modern Problems in Ophthalmology.: Vol. 11). (Illus.). 1972. 44.50 (ISBN 3-8055-1303-8). S Karger.

International Symposium on Orbital Disorders, 2nd, Amsterdam, May 1973. Orbital Disorders: Proceedings. Bleeker, G. M., et al, eds. (Modern Problems in Ophthalmology: Vol. 14). 300p. 1975. 146.75 (ISBN 3-8055-2051-4). S Karger.

Jaffe, Norman S., et al. Pseudophakos. new ed. LC 77-27307. (Illus.). 1978. text ed. 45.50 (ISBN 0-8016-2401-0). Mosby.

Jayle, Gaetan E., et al. Night Vision. (Illus.). 432p. 1959. 43.50 (ISBN 0-398-00921-X). C C Thomas.

Jules Gonin Club, 9th Meeting, la Baule, May 1974. New Research on the Aetiology & Surgery of Retinal Detachment: Proceedings. Streiff, E. B., ed. (Modern Problems in Ophthalmology: Vol. 15). (Illus.). xiv, 338p. 1975. 91.25 (ISBN 3-8055-2141-3). S Karger.

Kaufman, Herbert E. & Zimmerman. Current Concepts in Ophthalmology, Vol. 6. (Illus.). 1979. text ed. 46.00 (ISBN 0-8016-2628-5). Mosby.

Keith, C. Gregory. Genetics & Ophthalmology. (Genetics in Medicine & Surgery Ser). (Illus.). 1978. text ed. 30.00 (ISBN 0-443-01323-3). Churchill.

King, John H. & Wadsworth, Joseph A. An Atlas of Ophthalmic Surgery. 3rd ed. 1980. text ed. 75.00 (ISBN 0-397-50481-0, JBL-Med-Nursing). Har-Row.

Kooi, Kenneth A. & Marshall, Robert E. Visual Evoked Potentials in Central Disorders of the Visual System. (Illus.). 1979. text ed. 30.00 (ISBN 0-06-141477-8, Harper Medical). Har-Row.

Kronfeld, Peter C. Introduction to Ophthalmology. (Illus.). 325p. 1938. photocopy ed. spiral 29.50 (ISBN 0-398-04318-3). C C Thomas.

Kwitko, Marvin L. & Praeger, Donald L. Pseudophakia: Current Trends & Concepts. (Illus.). 456p. 1980. lib. bdg. 50.00 (ISBN 0-683-04800-7). Williams & Wilkins.

Lawwill, T. ERG, VER & Psychophysics. (Documenta Ophthalmologica Proceedings: Vol. 13). 1976. lib. bdg. 63.00 (ISBN 90-6193-153-3, Pub. by Junk Pubs. Netherlands). Kluwer Boston.

Lebensohn, J. E., ed. An Anthology of Ophthamolic Classes. LC 76-94010. 424p. 1969. 17.50 (ISBN 0-683-04905-4, Pub. by Williams & Wilkins). Krieger.

Lerman, Sidney, ed. Radiant Energy & the Eye. (Illus.). 1979. text ed. 45.00 (ISBN 0-02-369970-1). Macmillan.

Lim Siew Ming, A. Practical Ophthalmic Microsurgery. (Illus.). 1980. 23.50 (ISBN 3-8055-3036-6). S Karger.

Loose Leaf Reference Service. Clinical Ophthalmology, 5 vols. & index. Duane, Thomas, ed. (Illus.). Set. looseleaf bdg. 325.00 (ISBN 0-06-148007-X, Harper Medical); annual revision pages 50.00 (ISBN 0-685-71848-4). Har-Row.

McLauren, Donald S. Nutritional Ophthalmology. 1980. 77.00 (ISBN 0-12-484240-2). Acad Pr.

Mann, Ida. Culture, Race, Climate & Eye Disease: An Introduction to the Study of Geographical Opthalmology. (Illus.). 592p. 1966. photocopy ed. spiral 59.50 (ISBN 0-398-01212-1). C C Thomas.

Martin-Doyle, J. L. Synopsis of Ophthalmology. 5th ed. 1976. 26.95 (ISBN 0-8151-5776-2). Year Bk Med.

Meeting of Jules Gonin Club, Lausanne, June 1976. Turning Points in Retinal Surgery: Proceedings. Norton, E. W., et al, eds. (Modern Problems in Ophthalmology: Vol. 18). (Illus.). 1977. 146.75 (ISBN 3-8055-2425-0). S Karger.

Merigan, William & Weiss, Bernard, eds. Neurotoxicity of the Visual System. 288p. 1980. text ed. 34.50 (ISBN 0-89004-400-7). Raven.

Milder, Benjamin & Rubin, Melvin L. The Fine Art of Prescribing Glasses Without Making a Spectacle of Yourself. LC 78-2812. (Illus.). 1978. 36.00x (ISBN 0-9600472-2-0). Triad Pub FL.

Miller, David. Ophthalmology: The Essentials. (Illus.). 1979. 16.00x (ISBN 0-471-09489-7, Pub. by Wiley Med). Wiley.

Morgan, Meredith. Optics of Ophthalmic Lenses. 1978. 42.00 (ISBN 0-87873-022-2). Prof Press.

Netherlands Opthalmological Society, 168th Meeting, Rotterdam, December 1973. Proceedings. (Ophthalmologica: Vol. 173, No. 3-4). 1976. 36.00 (ISBN 3-8055-2218-5). S Karger.

Newell, Frank W. Ophthalmology: Principles & Concepts. 4th ed. LC 78-6733. 1978. 34.50 (ISBN 0-8016-3640-X). Mosby.

Ophthalmic Microsurgery Study Group, 4th Lund, Sweden, July 4-7, 1972. Surgery of the Iris & the Ciliary Body: Proceedings. Palm, E. & Mackensen, G., eds. (Advances in Ophthalmology: Vol. 30). 300p. 1975. 118.75 (ISBN 3-8055-1844-7). S Karger.

O'Rourke, J. Nuclear Opthalmology: Dynamic Function Studies in Intraocular Disease. LC 76-1257. (Illus.). 1976. text ed. 27.00 (ISBN 0-7216-7009-1). Saunders.

Parr, John. Introduction to Ophthalmology. (Illus.). 1979. pap. text ed. 13.95x (ISBN 0-19-261162-3). Oxford U Pr.

--Introduction to Ophthalmology. 1976. pap. 24.50x (ISBN 0-908569-00-9). Intl Pubns Serv.

Patz, et al. Sights & Sounds in Ophthalmology: Diseases of the Macula, Vol. 1. (Illus.). 1976. pap. 165.00 incl. 2 one-hr. cassettes & 100 35mm slides (ISBN 0-8016-3761-9). Mosby.

Pavan-Langston, Deborah. Manual of Occular Diagnosis & Therapy. (Little, Brown SPIRAL TM Manual Ser.). 1980. 12.95 (ISBN 0-316-69537-8). Little.

Perkins, Edwards. & Hill, David W., eds. Scientific Foundations of Ophthalmogy. (Illus.). 1978. 70.00 (ISBN 0-8151-6666-4). Year Bk Med.

Peyman, Gholam A., et al, eds. Principles & Practice of Ophthalmology, 3 vols. (Illus.). 2000p. Date not set. Set. text ed. 250.00 (ISBN 0-7216-7228-0); Vol. 1. text ed. 82.50 (ISBN 0-7216-7211-6); Vol. 2. text ed. 82.50 (ISBN 0-7216-7212-4); Vol. 3. text ed. 85.00 (ISBN 0-7216-7213-2). Saunders.

Pritikin, Roland I. & Grace, Eugene V. Essentials of Ophthalmology. 3rd ed. LC 71-99301. (Illus.). 1979. 25.00 (ISBN 0-87716-028-7, Pub. by Moore Pub Co). F Apple.

Richards, Richard D. Ophthalmologic Disorders: A Practitioner's Guide. 1973. spiral bdg. 12.00 (ISBN 0-87488-703-8). Med Exam.

Robb, Richard M. Ophthalmic Considerations in the Pediatric Patient. (Clinical Pediatrics Ser.). 1981. text ed. write for info. Little.

Roper-Hall, M. J., et al, eds. Advances in Ophthalmology, Vol. 26. 1972. 80.25 (ISBN 3-8055-1354-2). S Karger.

--Commemorative Volume in Honour of Prof. Streiff. (Advances in Ophthalmology: Vol. 36). (Illus., Ger. & Fr.). 1978. 112.75 (ISBN 3-8055-2828-0). S Karger.

--Advances in Ophthalmology, Vol. 35. (Illus., Ger.). 1978. 79.25 (ISBN 3-8055-2657-1). S Karger.

--Advances in Ophthalmology, Vol. 39. (Illus.). 1979. 112.75 (ISBN 3-8055-3030-7). S Karger.

--Advances in Opthalmology, Vol. 40. (Illus.). 1979. 94.00 (ISBN 3-8055-3031-5). S Karger.

Rosen, George. The Specialization of Medicine with Particular Reference to Opthalmology. LC 79-180586. (Medicine & Society in America Ser). 106p. 1972. Repr. of 1944 ed. 9.00 (ISBN 0-405-03966-2). Arno.

Rycroft, P. V., ed. Corneo-plastic Surgery. LC 68-58885. 1969. 97.00 (ISBN 0-08-013013-5). Pergamon.

Scheie, Harold G. & Alert, Daniel M. Textbook of Ophthalmology. 9th ed. LC 75-19856. (Illus.). 1977. text ed. 32.50 (ISBN 0-7216-7951-X). Saunders.

Schlaegel, T. F., Jr. Ocular Histoplasmosis. (Current Ophthalmology Monographs). (Illus.). 320p. 1977. 49.00 (ISBN 0-8089-0994-0). Grune.

--Ocular Toxoplasmosis & Pars Planitis. (Current Ophthalmology Monographs Ser.). 400p. 1978. 49.00 (ISBN 0-8089-1078-7). Grune.

Schmoger, E. & Kelsey, J. H., eds. Visual Electrodiagnosis in Systematic Diseases. (Documenta Opthalmologica Ser.: No. 23). 290p. 1980. lib. bdg. 68.50 (ISBN 90-6193-163-0, Pub. by Junk Pubs Netherlands). Kluwer Boston.

Sears, Marvin L., ed. New Directions in Ophthalmic Research. LC 81-3368. (Illus.). 344p. 1981. text ed. 30.00x (ISBN 0-300-02749-4). Yale U Pr.

Shimigu, K. & Oasterhuis, J. A., eds. Ophthalmology, 2 vols. LC 79-724. (International Congress Ser.: No. 450). 2000p. 1979. Set. 214.75 (ISBN 0-444-90060-8, Excerpta Medica). Elsevier.

Shimizu, Koichi & Ujiie, Kasuyoshi. Structure of Ocular Vessels. LC 78-54736. 1978. 42.50 (ISBN 0-89640-029-8). Igaku-Shoin.

Sloan, Louise L. Reading Aids for the Partially Sighted: A Systematic Procedure for Prescribing Reading Aids. 1977. 14.95 (ISBN 0-683-07743-0). Williams & Wilkins.

Smelser, G. K., et al. La Morfologia del Ojo: Histologia y Estructura Microscopica, Cornea, y Esclera. Boschetti, Norma, tr. LC 78-15614. (Illus.). 1979. 25.00 (ISBN 0-8477-2322-4). U of PR Pr.

Smith, Joan F. & Nachazel, Delbert P. Ophthalmologic Nursing. 1980. text ed. 14.95 (ISBN 0-316-80158-5). Little.

Smith, Marvin B. Handbook of Ocular Pharmacology. 2nd ed. LC 77-94882. (Illus.). 258p. 1978. pap. 16.50 (ISBN 0-88416-246-X). Wright-PSG.

--Handbook of Ocular Toxicity. LC 75-12027. 526p. 1976. 25.00 (ISBN 0-88416-114-5). Wright-PSG.

Society of Photo-Optical Instrumentation Engineers, Seminar. Photo-Optical Data Reduction: Proceedings, Vol. 2. 28.00 (ISBN 0-89252-003-5). Photo-Optical.
Sommer, Alfred. Epidemiology & Statistics for the Ophthalmologist. (Illus.). 1980. pap. text ed. 11.95x (ISBN 0-19-502656-X). Oxford U Pr.
Sorsby, A. & Miller, S., eds. Modern Trends in Ophthalmology, Vol. 5. (Illus.). 256p. 1973. 29.95 (ISBN 0-407-30603-X). Butterworth.
Stein, Harold A. & Slatt, Bernard J. Ophthalmic Assistant: Fundamentals & Clinical Practice. 3rd ed. LC 75-43808. (Illus.). 1976. text ed. 30.50 (ISBN 0-8016-4772-X). Mosby.
Stein, Harold A., et al. Manual of Opthalmic Terminology. (Illus.). 218p. 1982. pap. text ed. 15.00 (ISBN 0-8016-4769-X). Mosby.
Straub, W., ed. Current Genetic, Clinical & Morphological Problems. (Developments in Ophthalmology: Vol. 3). (Illus.). vi, 218p. 1981. pap. 94.00 (ISBN 3-8055-2000-X). S Karger.
Streiff, E. B., ed. Advances in Ophthalmology, Vol. 41. (Illus.). xvii, 216p. 1980. 96.00 (ISBN 3-8055-0375-X). S Karger.
--Advances in Ophthalmology, Vol. 42. (Illus.). 164p. 1981. 58.75 (ISBN 3-8055-1025-X). S Karger.
Streiff, E. B., et al, eds. Advances in Ophthalmology, Vol. 32. (Illus.). 250p. 1976. 76.75 (ISBN 3-8055-2222-3). S Karger.
--Advances in Ophthalmology, Vol. 34. 1977. 77.25 (ISBN 3-8055-2406-4). S Karger.
--Advances in Ophthalmology, Vol. 29. 200p. 1975. 64.75 (ISBN 3-8055-1709-2). S Karger.
Symposium, 2nd, Edinburgh, June, 1973. Colour Vision Deficiencies, II: Proceedings. Verriest, G., ed. (Modern Problems in Ophthalmology: Vol. 13). 300p. 1974. 95.25 (ISBN 3-8055-1698-3). S Karger.
Taeumer, R., ed. Electro-Oculography-Its Clinical Importance: Proceedings. (Bibliotheca Ophthalmologica: No. 85). 130p. 1976. 38.50 (ISBN 3-8055-2301-7). S Karger.
Thomas, Charles I. Ophthalmology. 4th ed. (Medical Examination Review Book: Vol. 15). 1980. pap. 16.50 (ISBN 0-87488-115-3). Med Exam.
Trevor-Roper, P. D., ed. Sixth Congress of the European Society of Ophthalmology: The Cornea in Health & Disease. (Royal Society of Medicine International Congress & Symposium Ser.: No. 40). 1192p. 1981. 98.50 (ISBN 0-8089-1341-7). Grune.
Trier, H. G. Gewebsdifferenzierung mit Ultraschall. (Bibliotheca Ophthalmologica: No. 86). 1977. 29.50 (ISBN 3-8055-2404-8). S Karger.
Troutman, R. C., ed. Microsurgery of Ocular Injuries. (Advances in Ophthalmology: Vol. 27). 1972. 58.75 (ISBN 3-8055-1355-0). S Karger.
Twelfth I. S. C. E. R. G. Symposium. (Documenta Ophthalmologica Proceedings: Vol. 10). 1974. lib. bdg. 74.00 (ISBN 90-6193-150-9, Pub. by Junk Pubs Netherlands). Kluwer Boston.
Twenty Second Concilium Ophthalmologicum, Vols. 1 & 2. (Illus.). 1976. 241.50 set (ISBN 2-225-43164-7). Masson Pub.
Van Buren, J. M. The Retinal Ganglion Cell Layer: A Physiological Anatomical Correlation in Man & Primates of the Normal Topographical Anatomy of the Retinal Ganglion Cell Layer & Its Alterations with Lesions of the Visual Pathways. (Illus.). 160p. 1963. photocopy ed. spiral 16.00 (ISBN 0-398-04422-8). C C Thomas.
Van Scott, Timothy & Weiss, Sidney J. Self-Assessment of Current Knowledge in Ophthalmology. 1977. spiral bdg. 16.50 (ISBN 0-87488-255-9). Med Exam.
Vaughan, Daniel & Asbury, Taylor. General Ophthalmology. 9th, rev. ed. LC 79-92919. (Illus.). 410p. 1980. lexotone cover 15.00 (ISBN 0-87041-104-7). Lange.
Waltman, Stephen R. & Krupin, Theodore. Complications in Opthalmic Surgery. (Illus.). 333p. 1980. text ed. 37.00 (ISBN 0-397-50441-1). Lippincott.
Weinstein, E. S. Fundamentals of X-Ray Diagnosis in Opthalmology. 231p. 1975. 7.50 (ISBN 0-8285-0754-6, Pub. by Mir Pubs Russia). Imported Pubns.
Wilensky. Intraocular Lenses. (Illus.). 1822p. 1976. 21.00 (ISBN 0-8385-4304-9). ACC.
Workshop on Microsurgery, Singapore, May 1977. Ophthalmic Microsurgery: Proceedings. Ratnam, S. S., et al, eds. (Advances in Ophthalmology: Vol. 36). (Illus.). 1977. 70.75 (ISBN 3-8055-2782-9). S Karger.
Wybar, Kenneth. Ophthalmology: (Concise Medical Textbook) 2nd ed. (Illus.). 1974. text ed. 14.50 (ISBN 0-02-859840-7). Macmillan.

OPHTHALMOLOGY-ATLASES

Albert, Daniel M. Jaeger's Atlas of Diseases of the Ocular Fundus. LC 75-180175. (Illus.). 165p. 1972. 50.00 (ISBN 0-7216-1085-4). Saunders.
Helveston, Eugene M. Atlas of Strabismus Surgery. 2nd ed. LC 77-3542. (Illus.). 1977. text ed. 42.50 (ISBN 0-8016-2138-0). Mosby.
Hogan, Michael J., et al. Histology of the Human Eye. LC 78-135327. (Illus.). 1971. 45.00 (ISBN 0-7216-4720-0); slides 125.00 (ISBN 0-7216-9809-3). Saunders.
Lim, Arthur & Constable, Ian J. Colour Atlas of Ophthalmology. (Illus.). 1979. 14.00x (ISBN 0-471-09487-0, Pub. by Wiley Med). Wiley.
Thiel, Rudolf. Atlas of Diseases of the Eye, 2 vols. 1963. Set. 268.50 (ISBN 0-444-40566-6, North-Holland). Elsevier.
Twenty Second Concilium Ophthalmologicum, Vols. 1 & 2. (Illus.). 1976. 241.50 set (ISBN 2-225-43164-7). Masson Pub.

OPHTHALMOLOGY-EXAMINATIONS, QUESTIONS, ETC.

Thomas, Charles I., ed. Ophthalmology Review Book. 1972. spiral bdg. 13.00 (ISBN 0-87488-347-4). Med Exam.

OPHTHALMOLOGY-PRACTICE

Kupfer, Carl & Kupfer-Kaiser, Muriel. Differential Diagnosis: Disorders of the Eye & Visual Systems. LC 78-18208. (Arco Diagnosis Ser.). (Illus.). 1979. pap. text ed. 10.00x (ISBN 0-668-04315-6). Arco.

OPHTHALMOLOGY, INDUSTRIAL

see Industrial Ophthalmology

OPHTHALMOLOGY, VETERINARY

see Veterinary Ophthalmology

OPHTHALMOMETRY

see Eye-Examination

OPHTHALMOSCOPE AND OPHTHALMOSCOPY

see also Fundus Oculi; Ophthalmology-Atlases

International Symposium on Fluorescin Angiography, Miami, 1970. Photography in Ophthalmology: Proceedings. Ferrer, O., ed. (Modern Problems in Ophthalmology: Vol. 9). 1971. 41.24 (ISBN 3-8055-1165-5). S Karger.
Lee, W. R., ed. Current Research in Ophthalmic Electron Microscopy, Vol. 4. (Illus.). 140p. 1981. pap. 22.90 (ISBN 0-387-10651-0). Springer-Verlag.
Sorsby, A. Diseases of the Fundus Oculi. 1976. 54.95 (ISBN 0-407-00023-2). Butterworth.

OPIATES

see Narcotics

OPIE, AMELIA ALDERSON, 1769-1853

Opie, Amelia A. Memorials of the Life of Amelia Opie. LC 79-37711. Repr. of 1854 ed. 30.00 (ISBN 0-404-56774-6). AMS Pr.

OPINION, PUBLIC

see Public Opinion

OPINION EVIDENCE

see Evidence, Expert

OPINION POLLS

see Public Opinion Polls

OPINIONS, JUDICIAL

see Judicial Opinions

OPISTHOBRANCHIATA

Behrens, David W. Pacific Coast Nudibranchs: A Guide to the Opisthobranchs of the Northeastern Pacific. LC 80-51439. (Illus.). 112p. 1980. 24.95 (ISBN 0-930118-04-9, Dist. by Western Marine Enterprises); pap. 14.95 (ISBN 0-930118-05-7). Sea Chall.
Graham, Alistair. British Prosobranch & Other Operculate Gastropod Molluscs. (Synopses of the British Fauna: No. 2). 1972. 8.00 (ISBN 0-12-294850-5). Acad Pr.
MacFarland, Frank. Memoir IV: Studies of Opisthobranchiate Mollusks of the Pacific Coast of North America. Kessell, Howard L., ed. (Memoirs of the California Academy of Sciences Ser.). (Illus.). 546p. 1966. 25.00 (ISBN 0-940228-10-6). Calif Acad Sci.
Marcus, Eveline & Marcus, Ernst. American Opisthobranch Mollusks. LC 67-31694. (Studies in Tropical Oceanography Ser: No. 6). 1967. 10.00x (ISBN 0-87024-087-0). U Miami Marine.
Thompson, T. E. Biology of Opisthobranch Molluscs, Vol. 1. (Illus.). 1976. 37.50x (ISBN 0-903874-04-0, Pub. by Brit Mus Nat Hist). Sabbot-Natural Hist Bks.

OPIUM

see also Morphine

Abrams, M. H. Milk of Paradise: The Effects of Opium Visions on the Works of DeQuincey, Crabbe, Frances Thompson, & Coleridge. LC 79-120223. 1970. Repr. lib. bdg. 12.50 (ISBN 0-374-90028-0). Octagon.
Baudelaire, Charles P. Les Paradis Artificiels: Opium et haschisch. LC 77-10248. Repr. of 1860 ed. 23.50 (ISBN 0-404-16304-1). AMS Pr.
Bazilevskaya, N. A. On the Races of the Opium Poppy Growing in Semirech'e & the Origin of Their Culture. 1981. 25.00x (ISBN 0-686-76652-0, Pub. by Oxford & IBH India). State Mutual Bk.
Center for Opium Research. IROS: The International Review of Opium Studies, 1976, Vol. 1. Feingold, David A., ed. (Illus.). Date not set. 35.00x (ISBN 0-915980-75-4). Inst Study Human.
Drake, William D., Jr. International Cultivators Handbook. LC 74-80865. 100p. 1974. pap. 5.00 (ISBN 0-914728-02-4). Wingbow Pr.
Latimer, Dean & Goldberg, Jeff. Flowers in the Blood: The Story of Opium. (Illus.). 352p. 1981. 16.95 (ISBN 0-531-09853-2). Watts.
Prasad, Rajeshwari. Some Aspects of British Revenue Policy in India 1773-1833. 1970. 8.25x (ISBN 0-8426-0090-6). Verry.
Sala, Angelo. Opiologia, or, a Treatise Concerning the Nature & Safe Use of Opium. LC 77-7431. (English Experience Ser.: No. 892). 1977. Repr. of 1618 ed. lib. bdg. 11.50 (ISBN 90-221-0892-9). Walter J Johnson.
Schneider, Elisabeth. Coleridge, Opium & Kubla Khan. 1966. lib. bdg. 22.50x (ISBN 0-374-97144-7). Octagon.
Terry, Charles E. & Pellens, Mildred. Opium Problem. LC 76-108232. (Criminology, Law Enforcement, & Social Problems Ser.: No. 115). (Illus., With a new preface by Charles Winick & a new intro. by John C. Ball). 1970. Repr. of 1928 ed. 40.00 (ISBN 0-87585-115-0). Patterson Smith.
Willoughby, Westel W. Opium As an International Problem: The Geneva Conferences. LC 75-17252. (Social Problems & Social Policy Ser.). 1976. Repr. of 1925 ed. 33.00x (ISBN 0-405-07526-X). Arno.

OPIUM HABIT

Berridge, Virginia & Edwards, Griffith. Opium & the People: Opiate Use in Nineteenth Century England. 1981. 25.00 (ISBN 0-312-58684-1). St Martin.
Calkins, Alonzo. Opium & the Opium-Appetite. Grob, Gerald N., ed. LC 80-1215. (Addiction in America Ser.). 1981. Repr. of 1871 ed. lib. bdg. 35.00x (ISBN 0-405-13571-8). Arno.
Cobbe, William R. Doctor Judas: A Portrayal of the Opium Habit. Grob, Gerald N., ed. LC 80-1218. (Addiction in America Ser.). 1981. Repr. of 1895 ed. lib. bdg. 29.00x (ISBN 0-405-13574-2). Arno.
Cocteau, Jean. Opium. 1972. 3.95 (ISBN 0-686-54544-3). French & Eur.
--Opium: Journal D'une Desintoxication. 1930. pap. 15.75 (ISBN 0-685-11469-4). French & Eur.
Dai, Bingham. Opium Addiction in Chicago. LC 72-124503. (Criminology, Law Enforcement, & Social Problems Ser.: No. 126). (Intro. index added). 1970. 17.00 (ISBN 0-87585-126-6). Patterson Smith.
Day, Horace & Grob, Gerald N., eds. The Opium Habit, with Suggestions As to the Remedy. LC 80-1224. (Addiction in America Ser.). 1981. Repr. of 1868 ed. lib. bdg. 29.00x (ISBN 0-405-13580-7). Arno.
De Quincy, Thomas. Confessions of an English Opium Eater. Hayter, Alethea, ed. (English Library Ser.). 1971. pap. 1.95 (ISBN 0-14-043061-X, EL61). Penguin.
Gavit, John P. Opium. Grob, Gerald N., ed. LC 80-1228. (Addiction in America Ser.). 1981. Repr. of 1925 ed. lib. bdg. 28.00x (ISBN 0-405-13586-6). Arno.
Graham-Mulhall, Sara. Opium the Demon Flower. Grob, Gerald N., ed. LC 80-1229. (Addiction in America Ser.). 1981. Repr. of 1926 ed. lib. bdg. 28.00x (ISBN 0-405-13587-4). Arno.
Grob, Gerald N. The Medical Professions & Drug Addiction: Six Studies, 1882 to 1932, An Original Anthology. LC 80-1206. (Addiction in America Ser.). 1981. lib. bdg. 32.00x (ISBN 0-405-13560-2). Arno.
Grob, Gerald N., ed. American Perceptions of Drug Addiction: Five Studies, 1872 to 1912. an original anthology ed. LC 80-1209. (Addiction in America Ser.). 1981. lib. bdg. 30.00x (ISBN 0-405-13558-0). Arno.
--Opium Eating. LC 80-1241. (Addiction in America Ser.). 1981. Repr. of 1876 ed. lib. bdg. 15.00x (ISBN 0-405-13611-0). Arno.
Hawkins, John A. Opium Addicts & Addiction. Grob, Gerald N., ed. LC 80-1262. (Addiction in America Ser.). 1981. Repr. of 1937 ed. lib. bdg. 15.00x (ISBN 0-405-13588-2). Arno.
Hayter, Alethea. Opium & the Romantic Imagination. LC 68-29700. 1968. pap. 3.45 (ISBN 0-520-01746-3, CAL194). U of Cal Pr.
Hubbard, Fred H. The Opium Habit & Alcoholism. Grob, Gerald N., ed. LC 80-1232. (Addiction in America Ser.). 1981. Repr. of 1881 ed. lib. bdg. 25.00x (ISBN 0-405-13591-2). Arno.
Kane, Harry H. Opium Smoking in America & China: A Study of Its Prevalence, & Effects, Immediate & Remote, on the Individual & the Nation. LC 75-17227. (Social Problems & Social Policy Ser.). 1976. Repr. of 1882 ed. 10.00x (ISBN 0-405-07497-2). Arno.
Keeley, Leslie E. Opium: Its Use, Abuse, & Cure; or, from Bondage to Freedom. Grob, Gerald N., ed. LC 80-1270. (Addiction in America Ser.). (Illus.). 1981. Repr. of 1897 ed. lib. bdg. 12.00x (ISBN 0-405-13597-1). Arno.
Kroll, Larry J. & Silverman, Manuel S. Opiate Addiction: Theory & Process. LC 80-8283. 199p. 1980. lib. bdg. 17.50 (ISBN 0-8191-1324-7); pap. text ed. 9.00 (ISBN 0-8191-1325-5). U Pr of Amer.
Kurland, Albert A. Psychiatric Aspects of Opiate Dependence. (Uniscience Ser.). 1978. 59.95 (ISBN 0-8493-5056-5). CRC Pr.
LaMotte, Ellen N. The Ethics of Opium. Grob, Gerald N., ed. LC 80-1260. (Addiction in America Ser.). 1981. Repr. of 1924 ed. lib. bdg. 18.00x (ISBN 0-405-13601-3). Arno.
Mickel, Emanuel J., Jr. The Artificial Paradises: The Influence of Opium & Hashish on the Literature of French Romanticism & "les Fleurs du Mal". (Studies in the Romance Languages & Literatures: No. 84). 1969. pap. 10.50x (ISBN 0-8078-9084-7). U of NC Pr.
Snyder, Solomon H. & Matthysse, Steven. Opiate Receptor Mechanisms: Neurochemical & Neurophysiological Processes in Opiate Drug Action & Addiction. LC 75-7828. 172p. 1975. text ed. 17.50x (ISBN 0-262-19132-6). MIT Pr.
Terry, Charles E. & Pellens, Mildred. Opium Problem. LC 76-108232. (Criminology, Law Enforcement, & Social Problems Ser.: No. 115). (Illus., With a new preface by Charles Winick & a new intro. by John C. Ball). 1970. Repr. of 1928 ed. 40.00 (ISBN 0-87585-115-0). Patterson Smith.
Williams, Edward H. Opiate Addiction: Its Handling & Treatment. LC 75-17250. (Social Problems & Social Policy Ser.). 1975. Repr. of 1922 ed. 12.00x (ISBN 0-405-07524-3). Arno.

OPIUM TRADE

Allen, Nathan. The Opium Trade As Carried on in India & China. LC 77-91524. 1977. Repr. of 1853 ed. lib. bdg. 12.50 (ISBN 0-89341-504-9). Longwood Pr.
Beeching, Jack. The Chinese Opium Wars. LC 76-40223. (Illus.). 1977. pap. 4.95 (ISBN 0-15-617094-9, Harv). HarBraceJ.
Dai, Bingham. Opium Addiction in Chicago. LC 72-124503. (Criminology, Law Enforcement, & Social Problems Ser.: No. 126). (Intro. index added). 1970. 17.00 (ISBN 0-87585-126-6). Patterson Smith.
Gavit, John P. Opium. Grob, Gerald N., ed. LC 80-1228. (Addiction in America Ser.). 1981. Repr. of 1925 ed. lib. bdg. 28.00x (ISBN 0-405-13586-6). Arno.
Grob, Gerald N., ed. Narcotic Addiction & American Foreign Policy: Seven Studies, 1924 to 1938, An Original Anthology. LC 80-1207. (Addiction in America Ser.). (Illus.). 1981. lib. bdg. 32.00x (ISBN 0-405-13561-0). Arno.
Kalimtgis, Konstandinos, et al. DOPE, Inc. Britain's Opium War Against the U. S. Spannaus, N. & Frommer, L., eds. LC 78-26712. (Illus.). 400p. 1979. pap. 5.00 (ISBN 0-933488-00-9). New Benjamin.
--Dope, Inc.Ll. Britain's Opiun War Against the U. S. 2nd ed. 1981. pap. 6.00 (ISBN 0-686-30565-5). New Benjamin.
Lubbock, Alfred B. The Opium Clippers. LC 75-36235. Repr. of 1933 ed. 47.50 (ISBN 0-404-14483-7). AMS Pr.
Merrill, Frederick T. Japan & the Opium Menace. Grob, Gerald N., ed. LC 80-1264. (Addiction in America Ser.). 1981. Repr. of 1942 ed. lib. bdg. 15.00x (ISBN 0-405-13607-2). Arno.
The Opium Trade: 1910-1941, 6 vols. LC 74-19745. 1975. Set. 260.00 (ISBN 0-8420-1795-X). Scholarly Res Inc.
Owen, David E. British Opium Policy in China & India. 1968. Repr. of 1934 ed. 19.50 (ISBN 0-208-00676-1, Archon). Shoe String.
Stelle, Charles C. Americans & the China Opium Trade in the Nineteenth Century. Grob, Gerald N., ed. LC 80-1248. (Addiction in America Ser.). 1981. lib. bdg. 15.00x (ISBN 0-405-13557-2). Arno.
Terry, Charles E. & Pellens, Mildred. Opium Problem. LC 76-108232. (Criminology, Law Enforcement, & Social Problems Ser.: No. 115). (Illus., With a new preface by Charles Winick & a new intro. by John C. Ball). 1970. Repr. of 1928 ed. 40.00 (ISBN 0-87585-115-0). Patterson Smith.

OPIUM WAR, 1840-1842

see China-History-19th Century

OPOSSUMS

Lippincott, Joseph W. Persimmon Jim, the Possum. rev. ed. (Illus.). (gr. 4-6). 1955. 5.95 (ISBN 0-397-30306-8, JBL-J). Har-Row.
McClung, Robert M. Possum. (gr. 1-5). 1963. PLB 7.44 (ISBN 0-688-31508-9). Morrow.
Russell, Rupert. Spotlight on Possums. (Illus.). 91p. 1980. 18.00x (ISBN 0-7022-1478-7). U of Queensland Pr.

OPOSSUMS-JUVENILE LITERATURE

Freschet, Berniece. Possum Baby. LC 77-21000. (See & Read Nature Bks.). (Illus.). (gr. k-3). 1978. PLB 5.29 (ISBN 0-399-61105-3). Putnam.

OPPANOL

see Rubber, Artificial

OPPENHEIMER, ERNEST, SIR 1880-1957

Gregory, Theodore. Ernest Oppenheimer & the Economic Development of Southern Africa. Wilkins, Mira, ed. LC 76-29778. (European Business Ser.). (Illus.). 1977. Repr. of 1962 ed. lib. bdg. 42.00x (ISBN 0-405-09790-5). Arno.

OPPENHEIMER, J. ROBERT, 1904-1967

Goodchild, Peter J. Robert Oppenheimer: Shatterer of Worlds. 1981. 15.00 (ISBN 0-395-30530-6). HM.

Kunetka, James W. Oppenheimer: The Years of Risk. 256p. 1981. 14.95 (ISBN 0-13-638007-7). P-H.

Oppenheimer, Robert. Robert Oppenheimer: Letters & Recollections. Smith, Alice K. & Weiner, Charles, eds. LC 80-10106. (Harvard Paperbacks Ser.). 408p. 1981. pap. 8.95 (ISBN 0-674-77606-2). Harvard U Pr.

Smith, Alice K. & Weiner, Charles, eds. Robert Oppenheimer: Letters & Recollections. LC 80-10106. 1980. 20.00x (ISBN 0-674-52833-6). Harvard U Pr.

United States Atomic Energy Commission, ed. In the Matter of J. Robert Oppenheimer. 1971. 23.00x (ISBN 0-262-21003-7); pap. 5.95x (ISBN 0-262-71002-1). MIT Pr.

OPPENHEIMER, J. ROBERT, 1904-1967–DRAMA

Boskin, Joseph & Krinsky, Fred. Oppenheimer Affair: A Political Play in Three Acts. (Insight Series: Studies in Contemporary Issues). 1968. pap. text ed. 4.95x (ISBN 0-02-473760-7). Macmillan.

Kipphardt, Heinar. In the Matter of J. Robert Oppenheimer. Speirs, Ruth, tr. LC 68-18845. 1968. pap. 4.25 (ISBN 0-8090-1215-4, Mermaid). Hill & Wang.

OPPOSITES (IN RELIGION, FOLK-LORE, ETC.)

see Polarity (In Religion, Folk-Lore, etc.)

OPPOSITION (POLITICAL SCIENCE)

Botts, Hank. Encounter Time: Metro-Act & the Sores of Discontent. LC 81-66545. 220p. (Orig.). 1981. pap. 5.00 (ISBN 0-9606020-0-3). Edward Pr.

Dobrin, Arthur, et al. Convictions. LC 80-2787. 128p. (Orig.). 1981. pap. 5.95 (ISBN 0-88344-089-X). Orbis Bks.

Naik, J. A. An Alternative Polity for India. 1976. text ed. 9.00x (ISBN 0-8426-0895-8). Verry.

Pierce, John C. & Sullivan, John L., eds. The Electorate Reconsidered. LC 79-28415. (Sage Focus Editions Ser.: No. 20). (Illus.). 293p. 1980. 20.00 (ISBN 0-8039-1342-7); pap. 9.95 (ISBN 0-8039-1343-5). Sage.

Schutz, Barry & Scott, Douglas. Natives & Settlers: A Comparative Analysis of the Politics of Opposition & Mobilization in Northern Ireland & Rhodesia. (Monograph Ser. in World Affairs, Vol. 12: 1974-75 Ser., Pt.B). 4.00 (ISBN 0-87940-042-0). U of Denver Intl.

Stern, Robert W. Process of Opposition in India: Two Case Studies of How Policy Shapes Politics. LC 78-116029. 1970. 10.00x (ISBN 0-226-77314-0). U of Chicago Pr.

Turner, D. R. Shadow Cabinet in British Politics. 1969. text ed. 6.00x (ISBN 0-7100-6489-6). Humanities.

OPPRESSION (PSYCHOLOGY)

Dick, James C. Violence & Oppression. LC 78-2235. 224p. 1979. 12.00x (ISBN 0-8203-0446-8). U of Ga Pr.

Goldenberg, I. Ira. Oppression & Social Intervention: The Human Condition & the Problems of Change. LC 78-6869. (Illus.). 1978. 15.95x (ISBN 0-88229-349-4); pap. 8.95x (ISBN 0-88229-601-9). Nelson-Hall.

Grygier, Tadeusz. Oppression. LC 73-14194. (International Library of Sociology & Social Reconstruction: A Study in Social & Criminal Psychology). 362p. 1974. Repr. of 1954 ed. lib. bdg. 27.50x (ISBN 0-8371-7145-8, GROP). Greenwood.

Whitaker, Ben, ed. The Fourth World: Victims of Group Oppression. LC 72-93008. 1973. 10.00x (ISBN 0-8052-3482-9). Schocken.

OPTIC THALAMUS

see Thalamus

OPTICAL ART

Compton, Michael. Optical & Kinetic Art. (Tate Gallery: Little Art Book Ser.). 1977. pap. 1.95 (ISBN 0-8120-0859-6). Barron.

Lancaster, John. Introducing Op Art. 1973. 19.95 (ISBN 0-7134-2438-9, Pub. by Batsford England). David & Charles.

Ouchi, Hajime. Japanese Optical & Geometrical Art. LC 77-82360. (Orig.). 1977. pap. 5.00 (ISBN 0-486-23553-X). Dover.

Thurston, Jacqueline B. Optical Illusions & the Visual Arts. (Illus.). 1966. pap. 7.95 (ISBN 0-442-28511-6). Van Nos Reinhold.

OPTICAL COMPUTING

see Optical Data Processing

OPTICAL CRYSTALLOGRAPHY

see Crystal Optics

OPTICAL DATA PROCESSING

see also Computers–Optical Equipment; Information Display Systems; Optical Pattern Recognition

Andrews, Harry C. Computer Techniques in Image Processing. 1970. 32.00 (ISBN 0-12-058550-2). Acad Pr.

Barrekette, E. S., et al, eds. Optical Information Processing, Vol. 2. 1978. 37.50 (ISBN 0-306-34472-6, Plenum Pr). Plenum Pub.

Casasent, D., ed. Optical Data Processing: Applications. (Topics in Applied Physics: Vol. 23). (Illus.). 1978. 49.70 (ISBN 0-387-08453-3). Springer-Verlag.

Cathey, W. Thomas. Optical Information Processing & Holography. LC 73-14604. (Pure & Applied Optics Ser). 398p. 1974. 32.50 (ISBN 0-471-14078-3, Pub. by Wiley-Interscience). Wiley.

Fedida, Sam & Malik, Rex. The Viewdata Revolution. LC 79-23869. 186p. 1980. 38.95 (ISBN 0-470-26879-4). Wiley.

Frieden, B. R., ed. The Computer in Optical Research: Methods & Applications. (Topics in Applied Physics: Vol. 41). (Illus.). 400p. 1980. 58.00 (ISBN 0-387-10119-5). Springer-Verlag.

Harger, Robert O. Optical Communication Theory. (Benchmark Papers in Electrical Engineering & Computer Science: Vol. 18). 1977. 39.50 (ISBN 0-12-786630-2). Acad Pr.

Huang, T. S. & Tretiak, O. J. Picture Bandwidth Compression. LC 74-135062. 740p. 1972. 148.00x (ISBN 0-677-14680-9, 1468). Gordon.

International Workshop on Ergonomic Aspects of Visual Display Terminals, Milan, March 1980. Proceedings. Grandjean, Etienne & Vigliani, E., eds. (Illus.). 300p. 1980. 47.50x (ISBN 0-85066-211-7). Intl Pubns Serv.

Lee, S. H., ed. Optical Information Processing: Fundamentals. (Topics in Applied Physics Ser.: Vol. 48). (Illus.). 330p. 1981. 49.50 (ISBN 0-387-10522-0). Springer-Verlag.

Lipkin, Bernice S. & Rosenfeld, Azriel, eds. Picture Processing & Psychopictorics. 1970. 44.00 (ISBN 0-12-451550-9). Acad Pr.

Nesterikhin, Yu E., et al, eds. Optical Information Processing. 401p. 1976. 37.50 (ISBN 0-306-30899-1, Plenum Pr). Plenum Pub.

Preston, Kendall, Jr. Coherent Optical Computers. LC 73-152008. (Illus.). 336p. 1972. 36.50 (ISBN 0-07-050785-6, P&RB). McGraw.

Rogers, G. L. Noncoherent Optical Processing. LC 77-5453. (Pure & Applied Optics Ser.). 1977. 28.50 (ISBN 0-471-73055-6, Pub. by Wiley-Interscience). Wiley.

Rosenthal, David A. An Inquiry Driven Computer Vision System Based on Visual & Conceptual Hierarchies. Stone, Harold, ed. LC 81-7616. (Computer Science Ser.: Artificial Intelligence, No. 7). 1981. price not set (ISBN 0-8357-1214-1, Pub. by UMI Res Pr). Univ Microfilms.

Sandler, Sheldon S. Picture Processing & Reconstruction: Dimensional & Structural Analysis. LC 74-25087. (Illus.). 128p. 1975. 22.95 (ISBN 0-669-97683-0). Lexington Bks.

Society of Photo-Optical Instrumentation Engineers, Seminar. Acquisition & Analysis of Pictorial Data: Proceedings, Vol. 48. 1975. 28.00 (ISBN 0-89252-060-4). Photo-Optical.

--Image Information Recovery: Proceedings, Vol. 16. 28.00 (ISBN 0-89252-019-1). Photo-Optical.

Yu, Francis T. Optics & Information Theory. LC 76-23135. 1976. 24.00 (ISBN 0-471-01682-9, Pub. by Wiley-Interscience). Wiley.

OPTICAL ILLUSIONS

Beeler, Nelson F. & Branley, Franklyn M. Experiments in Optical Illusion. LC 51-5642. (Illus.). (gr. 5-9). 1951. 8.95 (ISBN 0-690-27507-2, TYC-J). Har-Row.

Brandreth, Gyles. Seeing Is Not Believing. LC 79-91401. (Illus.). 96p. (gr. 3-12). 1980. 5.95 (ISBN 0-8069-4615-6); PLB 6.69 (ISBN 0-8069-4615-6). Sterling.

Carini, E. Take Another Look. (ps-3). 1969. PLB 5.95 (ISBN 0-13-882530-0); pap. 1.50 (ISBN 0-13-882548-3). P-H.

Coren, Stanley & Girgus, Joan S. Seeing Is Deceiving: The Psychology of Visual Illusions. LC 78-13509. (Complex Human Behavior Ser.). 1978. 18.00 (ISBN 0-470-26522-1). Halsted Pr.

Gregory, R. L. & Gombrich, E. H. Illusion in Nature & Art. (Illus.). 1974. pap. 22.50 (ISBN 0-684-14185-X, SL618, ScribT). Scribner.

Held, Richard, intro. by. Image, Object, & Illusion: Readings from Scientific American. LC 74-11012. (Illus.). 1974. pap. text ed. 7.95x (ISBN 0-7167-0504-4). W H Freeman.

Ittleson, William H. Ames Demonstrations in Perception. (Illus., Together with an Interpretive Manual). 1968. Repr. of 1952 ed. 21.75 (ISBN 0-02-846990-9). Hafner.

Kettelkamp, Larry. Tricks of Eye & Mind, the Story of Optical Illusion: The Story of Optical Illusion. LC 74-5935. (Illus.). 128p. (gr. 5-9). 1974. PLB 6.96 (ISBN 0-688-31829-0). Morrow.

Kim, Scott. Inversions. 200p. 1980. pap. 8.95 (ISBN 0-07-034546-5). McGraw.

Koziakin, Vladimir. Color Designs 3: Optical Illusions. (Illus.). 64p. pap. 2.75 (ISBN 0-686-72255-8). Wanderer Bks.

Luckiesh, M. Visual Illusions: Their Causes, Characteristics & Applications. (Illus.). 8.50 (ISBN 0-8446-0780-0). Peter Smith.

Luckiesh, Matthew. Visual Illusions: Their Causes, Characteristics & Applications. (Illus.). 1965. pap. 3.50 (ISBN 0-486-21530-X). Dover.

Mastail, Marie-Louise D. Illusion in Art: A History of Pictorial Illusionism. LC 74-6501. (Illus.). 39.50 (ISBN 0-913870-03-X). Abaris Bks.

Paraquin, Charles H. Eye Teasers: Optical Illusion Puzzles. Kuttner, Paul, tr. LC 76-21844. (Illus.). (gr. 3 up). 1976. 5.95 (ISBN 0-8069-4538-9); PLB 6.69 (ISBN 0-8069-4539-7). Sterling.

Rainey, Patricia A. Illusions: A Journey into Perception. (Illus.). 112p. (Orig.). 1973. pap. 9.50 (ISBN 0-208-01212-5, Linnet). Shoe String.

Robinson, J. O. The Psychology of Visual Illusion. (Illus.). 288p. 1974. text ed. 10.75x (ISBN 0-09-112280-5, Hutchinson U Lib); pap. text ed. 5.50x (ISBN 0-09-112281-3). Humanities.

Simon, Seymour. The Optical Illusion Book. LC 75-33873. (Illus.). 80p. (gr. 2-6). 1976. 8.95 (ISBN 0-685-62042-5, Four Winds). Schol Bk Serv.

OPTICAL INSTRUMENTS

see also Astronomical Instruments; Computers–Optical Equipment; Glass; Lenses; Microscope and Microscopy; Mirrors; Petrographic Microscope; Telescope

also names of specific instruments, e.g. Spectroscope

Bindmann, W. Fachwoerterbuch Optik und Optischer Geraetebau. 408p. (Eng. & Ger., Dictionary of Optics and Optical Devices). 1974. 36.00 (ISBN 3-7684-6411-3, M-7402, Pub. by Dausien). French & Eur.

Bureau of Naval Personnel, compiled by. Basic Optics & Optical Instruments. (Illus.). 8.50 (ISBN 0-8446-0479-8). Peter Smith.

CISM (International Center for Mechanical Sciences), Dept. for General Mechanics, 1971. Optical Filtering. Parkus, H., ed. (CISM Pubns. Ser.: No. 94). (Illus.). 59p. 1973. pap. 10.70 (ISBN 0-387-81130-3). Springer-Verlag.

Horne, Douglas F. Optical Instruments & Their Applications. (Illus.). xiv, 270p. 1980. 90.00 (ISBN 0-9960019-6-4, Pub. by A Hilger England). Heyden.

Jurek, B. Optical Surfaces. 1976. 46.50 (ISBN 0-444-99868-3). Elsevier.

Kingslake, R., ed. Applied Optics & Optical Engineering: A Comprehensive Treatise, 5 vols. Incl. Vol. 1. Light: Its Generation & Modification. 1965 (ISBN 0-12-408601-2); Vol. 2. The Detection of Light & Infrared Radiation. 1965 (ISBN 0-12-408602-0); Vol. 3. Optical Components. 1965 (ISBN 0-12-408603-9); Vol. 4. Optical Instruments, Part I. 1967 (ISBN 0-12-408604-7); Vol. 5. Optical Instruments, Part 2. 1969 (ISBN 0-12-408605-5). 55.50 ea.; Set. 227.50 (ISBN 0-686-76926-0). Acad Pr.

Kingston, R. H. Detection of Optical & Infrared Radiation. (Springer Ser. in Optical Sciences: Vol. 10). (Illus.). 1978. 23.70 (ISBN 0-387-08617-X). Springer-Verlag.

Kressel, H., ed. Semiconductor Devices for Optical Communication. (Topics in Applied Physics: Vol. 39). (Illus.). 1980. 52.30 (ISBN 0-387-09636-1). Springer-Verlag.

Ross, Douglas A. Optoelectronic Devices & Optical Imaging Techniques. (Electrical & Electronic Engineering Ser.). (Illus.). 137p. 1979. text ed. 26.50 (ISBN 0-333-24292-0, Pub. by MacMillan London); pap. text ed. 15.95 (ISBN 0-333-25335-3, Pub. by MacMillan London). Scholium Intl.

Sixth European Conference on Optical Communication. (IEE Conference Publication Ser.: No. 190). (Illus.). 466p. (Orig.). 1980. soft cover 73.00 (ISBN 0-85296-223-1). Inst Elect Eng.

Smith, W. J. Modern Optical Engineering. 1966. 37.50 (ISBN 0-07-058690-X, P&RB). McGraw.

Society of Photo-Optical Instrumentation Engineers, Seminar. Application of Optical Instrumentation: Proceedings, Vol. 47. 1975. 15.00 (ISBN 0-89252-059-0). Photo-Optical.

--Effective Systems Integration & Optical Design: Proceedings, Vol. 54. 1975. 11.00 (ISBN 0-89252-066-3). Photo-Optical.

--Optical Instrumentation: A Problem-Solving Tool in Automotive Safety Engineering & Bio-Mechanics, Proceedings, Vol. 34. 28.00 (ISBN 0-89252-045-0). Photo Optical.

--Optical Instrumentation: A Tool for Solving Problems in Security, Surveillance & Law Enforcement, Proceedings, Vol. 33. 28.00 (ISBN 0-89252-044-2). Photo Optical.

Society of Photo-Optical Instrumentation Engineers, Annual Technical Symposium, 13th, Wash. D. C. Proceedings. 1968. 8.00 (ISBN 0-89252-086-8). Photo-Optical.

Society of Photo-Optical Instrumentation Engineers, Annual Technical Symposium, 14th San Francisco. Proceedings. 1969. 8.00 (ISBN 0-89252-087-6). Photo-Optical.

Society of Photo-Optical Instrumentation Engineers, Seminar. Remote Sensing of Earth Resources & the Environment: Proceedings, Vol. 27. 28.00 (ISBN 0-89252-037-X). Photo-Optical.

U. S. Navy (Bureau of Naval Personnel) Basic Optics & Optical Instruments. (Illus.). 1969. pap. 3.50 (ISBN 0-486-22291-8). Dover.

Whittaker, E. T. The Theory of Optical Instruments. 2nd ed. (Cambridge Tracts in Mathematics & Mathematical Physics Ser: No. 7). 1971. Repr. of 1915 ed. 7.50 (ISBN 0-02-854740-3). Hafner.

Zimmer, H. G. Geometrical Optics. Wilson, R. N., tr. LC 72-94095. (Applied Physics & Engineering Ser.: Vol. 9). (Illus.). 1970. 22.20 (ISBN 0-387-04771-9). Springer-Verlag.

OPTICAL MASERS

see Lasers

OPTICAL MEASUREMENTS

Barnes, K. R. Optical Transfer Function. (Applied Optics Monographs: No. 3). 1971. 20.00 (ISBN 0-444-19592-0). Elsevier.

Clarke, D. & Grainger, J. F. Polarized Light & Optical Measurements. 1971. text ed. 28.00 (ISBN 0-08-016320-3). Pergamon.

Levi, Leo, ed. Handbook of Tables of Functions for Applied Optics, CRC. LC 73-88627. (Handbook Ser). 640p. 1974. 69.95 (ISBN 0-87819-371-5). CRC Pr.

Lloyd, Peter H. Optical Methods in Ultracentrifugation, Electrophoresis, & Diffusion. (Monographs on Physical Biochemistry). (Illus.). 108p. 1974. 24.00x (ISBN 0-19-854605-X). Oxford U Pr.

Marcuse, D. Principles of Optical Fiber Measurements. LC 80-2339. 1981. 39.50 (ISBN 0-12-470980-X). Acad Pr.

Weissberger, Arnold, ed. Techniques of Chemistry: Physical Methods of Chemistry: Polarimetry, Vol. 1, Pt. 3c. LC 49-48584. 528p. 1972. 47.95 (ISBN 0-471-92732-5). Krieger.

OPTICAL MINERALOGY

Bambauer, H. U., et al. Optical Determination of Rock-Forming Minerals, Pt. 1. 1979. 35.00x (ISBN 3-510-65311-4). Intl Pubns Serv.

Jones, Norris W. & Bloss, Donald. Laboratory Manual for Optical Mineralogy. (Orig.). 1979. pap. text ed. 10.95x (ISBN 0-8087-1058-3). Burgess.

Kerr, Paul E. Optical Mineralogy. 4th ed. (Illus.). 1977. text ed. 25.00 (ISBN 0-07-034218-0, C). McGraw.

Marfunin, A. S. Spectroscopy, Luminescence & Radiation Centers in Minerals. Schiffer, W. W., tr. from Russ. (Illus.). 1979. 52.30 (ISBN 0-387-09070-3). Springer-Verlag.

Phillips, William R. Mineral Optics: Principles & Techniques. LC 78-134208. (Geology Ser.). (Illus.). 1971. text ed. 28.95x (ISBN 0-7167-0251-7). W H Freeman.

Phillips, Wm. Revell & Griffen, Dana T. Optical Mineralogy: The Nonopaque Minerals. LC 80-12435. (Illus.). 1981. text ed. 39.95x (ISBN 0-7167-1129-X). W H Freeman.

Shelley, D. Manual of Optical Mineralogy. 239p. 1975. 46.50 (ISBN 0-444-41303-0, North Holland); pap. 17.95 (ISBN 0-444-41387-1). Elsevier.

Uytenbogaaedt, W. & Burke, E. A. Tables for Microscopic Identification of Ore Minerals. 2nd ed. 1971. Repr. of 1973 ed. 46.50 (ISBN 0-444-40876-2). Elsevier.

OPTICAL OCEANOGRAPHY

see also Oceanography

OPTICAL PATTERN RECOGNITION

Biberman, L. M., ed. Perception of Displayed Information. LC 72-97695. (Optical Physics & Engineering Ser.). (Illus.). 345p. 1973. 35.00 (ISBN 0-306-30724-3, Plenum Pr). Plenum Pub.

Cathey, W. Thomas. Optical Information Processing & Holography. LC 73-14604. (Pure & Applied Optics Ser). 398p. 1974. 32.50 (ISBN 0-471-14078-3, Pub. by Wiley-Interscience). Wiley.

Chen, Chi-Hau. Statistical Pattern Recognition. (Illus.). 1973. 17.25x (ISBN 0-8104-9210-5, Spartan). Hayden.

DiBartolo, Baldassare. Optical Interactions in Solids. LC 67-31206. 260p. 1968. 32.50 (ISBN 0-471-21276-8). Krieger.

Grasselli, A., ed. Automatic Interpretation & Classification of Images. (NATO Advanced Study Institute). 1969. 50.00 (ISBN 0-12-295850-0). Acad Pr.

Kaufmann, A. Introduction to the Theory of Fuzzy Subsets, Vol. 1: Fundamental Theoretical Elements. 1975. 46.50 (ISBN 0-12-402301-0). Acad Pr.

Young, T. Y., ed. Classification, Estimation & Pattern Recognition. Calvert, T. 1974. 22.50 (ISBN 0-444-00135-2, North Holland). Elsevier.

Zadeh & Fu, King-Sun, eds. Fuzzy Sets & Their Applications to Cognitive & Decision Processes. 1975. 35.00 (ISBN 0-12-775260-9). Acad Pr.

OPTICAL ROTATION

see also Polarization (Light)

Crabbe, Pierre. ORD & CD in Chemistry & Biochemistry: An Introduction. 1972. 27.00 (ISBN 0-12-194650-9). Acad Pr.

Kirkwood, John G. Dielectrics-Intermolecular Forces-Optical Rotation. Cole, Robert H., ed. (Documents on Modern Physics Ser.). (Illus., Orig.). 1965. 34.75x (ISBN 0-677-00405-2). Gordon.

Lowry, T. Martin. Optical Rotatory Power. (Illus.). 8.75 (ISBN 0-8446-2493-4). Peter Smith.

Mason, Stephen F., ed. Optical Activity & Chiral Discrimination. (NATO Advanced Study Institutes Ser., Math & Physical Sciences: No. 48). 1979. lib. bdg. 45.00 (ISBN 90-277-0982-3). Kluwer Boston.

Mizushima, San-Ichiro. Structure of Molecules & Internal Rotation. (Physical Chemistry Ser.: Vol. 2). 1954. 38.00 (ISBN 0-12-501750-2). Acad Pr.

Snatzke, G., ed. Optical Rotatory Dispersion and Circular Dichroism in Organic Chemistry. 1976. 83.50 (ISBN 0-85501-000-2). Heyden.

OPTICAL SCANNERS

see also Perceptrons

Society of Photo-Optical Instrumentation Engineers, Seminar. Scanners & Imagery Systems for Earth Observation: Proceedings, Vol. 51. 1975. 28.00 (ISBN 0-89252-063-9). Photo-Optical.

OPTICAL WAVE GUIDES

Adams, M. J. An Introduction to Optical Waveguides. LC 80-42059. 384p. 1981. 67.50 (ISBN 0-471-27969-2, Pub. by Wiley Interscience). Wiley.

Barnoski, Michael K., ed. An Introduction to Integrated Optics. LC 74-5444. 515p. 1974. 39.50 (ISBN 0-306-30784-7, Plenum Pr). Plenum Pub.

Kapany, N. S. & Burke, J. J. Optical Waveguides. (Quantum Electronics Ser). 1972. 55.00 (ISBN 0-12-396760-0). Acad Pr.

Marcuse, Dietrich. Theory of Dielectric Optical Waveguides. (Quantum Electronics Ser.). 1974. 43.00 (ISBN 0-12-470950-8). Acad Pr.

Sodha, M. S. & Ghatak, A. K. Inhomogeneous Optical Waveguides. (Optical Physics & Engineering Ser.). (Illus.). 281p. 1977. 35.00 (ISBN 0-306-30916-5, Plenum Pr). Plenum Pub.

OPTICIANS

see also Eye-Glasses; Optometrists

Educational Research Council of America. Manufacturing Optician. Ferris, Theodore N. & Marchak, John P., eds. (Real People at Work Ser: B). (Illus.). 1974. pap. text ed. 2.25 (ISBN 0-89247-019-4). Changing Times.

Hirschhorn, Hans S. Your Future As an Optician. LC 70-89466. (Careers in Depth Ser). (Illus.). (gr. 9 up). 1970. PLB 5.97 (ISBN 0-8239-0065-7). Rosen Pr.

Stimson, Russel L. Ophthalmic Dispensing. 3rd ed. (Illus.). 720p. 1979. text ed. 33.75 (ISBN 0-398-03823-6). C C Thomas.

Stimson, Russell. Opportunities in Opticianry Today. LC 75-32613. (Illus.). (gr. 8 up). 1976. PLB 6.60 (ISBN 0-8442-6424-5); pap. text ed. 4.95 (ISBN 0-685-61136-1). Natl Textbk.

OPTICS

see also Color; Dispersion; Electron Optics; Electrooptics; Interference (Light); Light; Light Filters; Light, Wave Theory Of; Optical Measurements; Perspective; Photochemistry; Photometry; Polarization (Light); Quantum Optics; Radiation; Reflection (Optics); Refraction; Spectrum Analysis;
also headings beginning with the word Optical; also Optics, Geometrical; Optics, Physiological; and similar headings

Agarbiceanu, I. I. & Popescu, I. M. Optical Methods of Radio-Frequency Spectroscopy. 310p. Date not set. Repr. of 1975 ed. 53.00 (ISBN 0-470-00935-7). Krieger.

Alembert, Jean Le Rond. Opuscules Mathematiques. Repr. of 1761 ed. 906.00 (ISBN 0-8287-0012-5). Clearwater Pub.

Alhazen. Opticae Thesaurus: Alhazeni Arabis Libri Septem, Nunc Primum Editi, Eiusdem Liber De Crepusculis et Nubium Ascensionibus. (Lat). Repr. of 1572 ed. 61.50 (ISBN 0-384-00730-9). Johnson Repr.

Allen, E. W. Essentials of Ophthalmic Optics. (Illus.). 1979. pap. text ed. 7.95x (ISBN 0-19-261173-9). Oxford U Pr.

Arecchi, F. T. & Degiorgio, V., eds. Coherent Optical Engineering: A Series of Lectures Given at the International School of Quantum Electronics, Tuscany, Italy, September, 1976. 1978. 39.00 (ISBN 0-444-85080-5, North-Holland). Elsevier.

Baker, Daniel, et al. Projects in Optical Properties of the Atmosphere, Upper Atmospheric Turbulence & Structure, Ionospheric Reflection Properties, Plasma Physics, Data Reduction & Perspective Drawing. LC 72-135075. 152p. 1970. 14.00 (ISBN 0-686-01912-1). Mgmt Info Serv.

Baltes, H. P., ed. Inverse Scattering Problems in Optics. (Topics in Current Physics: Vol. 20). (Illus.). 313p. 1980. 42.00 (ISBN 0-387-10104-7). Springer-Verlag.

Barnoski, Michael K., ed. An Introduction to Integrated Optics. LC 74-5444. 515p. 1974. 39.50 (ISBN 0-306-30784-7, Plenum Pr). Plenum Pub.

Bindmann, W. Fachwoerterbuch Optik und Optischer Geraetebau. 408p. (Eng. & Ger., Dictionary of Optics and Optical Devices). 1974. 36.00 (ISBN 3-7684-6411-3, M-7402, Pub. by Dausien). French & Eur.

Bindmann, W., ed. Optics & Optical Instrumentation: Dictionary. 450p. (Eng. - Ger.). 1974. 30.60 (ISBN 0-685-42257-7); german-english ed. 30.60 (ISBN 0-686-66956-8). Adler.

Born, M. & Wolf, E. Principles of Optics: Electromagnetic Theory of Propagation, Interference & Diffraction of Light. 6th ed. (Illus.). 808p. 1980. 50.00 (ISBN 0-08-026482-4); pap. 27.50 (ISBN 0-08-026481-6). Pergamon.

Boutry, G. A. Instrumental Optics. (Illus.). 1962. 49.50 (ISBN 0-9960017-6-X, Pub. by A Hilger England). Heyden.

Brown, Earle B. Modern Optics. LC 73-92134. 656p. 1974. Repr. of 1965 ed. 32.50 (ISBN 0-88275-149-2). Krieger.

Bureau of Naval Personnel, compiled by. Basic Optics & Optical Instruments. (Illus.). 8.50 (ISBN 0-8446-0479-8). Peter Smith.

Carlson, Paul F., ed. Introduction to Applied Optics for Engineers. 1977. 29.50 (ISBN 0-12-160050-5). Acad Pr.

Charney, Elliott. Molecular Basis of Optical Activity: Optical Rotary Dispersion & Circular Dichroism. LC 79-9705. 1979. 35.00 (ISBN 0-471-14900-4, Pub. by Wiley-Interscience). Wiley.

Ciardelli, F. & Salvadori, P., eds. Fundamental Aspects & Recent Developments in Optical Rotatory Dispersion & Cincular Dichroism. 1973. 83.50 (ISBN 0-85501-060-6). Heyden.

Cornbleet, Sidney. Microwave Optics: The Optics of Microwave Antenna Design. (Pure & Applied Physics Ser.). 1977. 66.00 (ISBN 0-12-189650-1). Acad Pr.

Crew, Henry, tr. from Latin. The Photismi De Lumine of Maurolycus: A Chapter in Late Medieval Optics. Date not set. Repr. of 1940 ed. 12.50 (ISBN 0-686-30225-7). R S Barnes.

Dahl, Paul. Introduction to Electron & Ion Optics. 1973. 28.00 (ISBN 0-12-200650-X). Acad Pr.

Desirant, M., ed. Solid State Physics in Electronics & Telecommunications: Magnetic & Optical Properties. 1960. 87.50 (ISBN 0-12-211503-1); Vol. 4. Part 2. 64.50 (ISBN 0-12-211504-X). Acad Pr.

DeVany, A. S. Master Optical Techniques. LC 80-24442. (Pure & Applied Optics Ser.). 625p. 1981. 55.00 (ISBN 0-471-07720-8, Pub. by Wiley-Interscience). Wiley.

Divari, Nikolai B., ed. Atmospheric Optics, Vol. 2. LC 67-10534. 164p. 1972. 35.00 (ISBN 0-306-17172-4, Consultants). Plenum Pub.

Dowaliby, Margaret. Practical Aspects of Ophthalmic Optics. 222p. 1980. 27.00, leatherette (ISBN 0-87873-010-9). Prof Press.

Drouillard, T. F. Acoustic Emission: A Bibliography with Abstracts. 1979. 95.00 (ISBN 0-306-65179-3). IFI Plenum.

Enoch, J. M. & Tobey, F. L., eds. Vertebrate Photoreceptor Optics. (Springer Series in Optical Sciences: Vol. 23). (Illus.). 520p. 1981. 45.50 (ISBN 0-387-10515-8). Springer-Verlag.

Fincham, W. H. & Freeman, M. H. Optics. 9th rev. ed. LC 80-40274. (Illus.). 1980. 34.95 (ISBN 0-407-93422-7). Butterworth.

--Optics. 8th ed. 29.95 (ISBN 0-407-93421-9). Butterworth.

Fox, R W. Optoelectronics Guidebook - with Tested Projects. LC 76-45067. (Illus.). 1976. 8.95 (ISBN 0-8306-6836-5); pap. 5.95 (ISBN 0-8306-5836-X, 836). TAB Bks.

Francon, M. Optical Image Formation & Processing. 1979. 22.50 (ISBN 0-12-264850-1). Acad Pr.

Francon, M., et al. Experiences d'Optique Physique. (Fr). 1969. 81.00x (ISBN 0-677-50040-8). Gordon.

--Experiments in Physical Optics. 284p. 1970. 45.25x (ISBN 0-677-30040-9). Gordon.

Franke, G. Physical Optics in Photography. (Focal Library Ser.). (Illus.). 1966. 29.95 (ISBN 0-240-50643-X). Focal Pr.

Fresnel, Augustin J. Oeuvres Completes, 3 vols. (Lat.). Repr. of 1866 ed. 131.00 (ISBN 0-384-16770-5). Johnson Repr.

Frish, S. Problems of Wave Optics. 69p. 1976. pap. 1.50 (ISBN 0-8285-0831-3, Pub. by Mir Pubs Russia). Imported Pubns.

Gagliardi, Robert M. & Karp, Sherman. Optical Communications. LC 75-26509. 432p. 1976. 44.00x (ISBN 0-471-28915-9, Pub. by Wiley-Interscience). Wiley.

Garmire, E., et al. Integrated Optics. LC 75-14482. (Topics in Applied Physics Ser.: Vol. 7). (Illus.). 330p. 1975. 41.60 (ISBN 0-387-07297-7). Springer-Verlag.

Gaskill, Jack D. Linear Systems, Fourier Transforms & Optics. LC 78-1118. (Pure & Applied Optics Ser.). 1978. 35.00x (ISBN 0-471-29288-5, Pub. by Wiley-Interscience). Wiley.

Gerrard, A. & Burch, J. Introduction to Matrix Methods in Optics. LC 72-21192. (Pure & Applied Optics Ser.). 1975. 62.75x (ISBN 0-471-29685-6, Pub. by Wiley-Interscience). Wiley.

Ghatak, A. K. & Thyagarajan, eds. Contemporary Optics. (Optical Physics & Engineering Ser). (Illus.). 380p. 1978. 32.50 (ISBN 0-306-31029-5, Plenum Pr). Plenum Pub.

Goodman, Joseph W. Introduction to Fourier Optics. (Physical & Quantum Electronics Ser). 1968. text ed. 26.95 (ISBN 0-07-023776-X, C). McGraw.

Hansen, R. C., ed. Geometric Theory of Diffraction. LC 81-6198. 1981. 40.95 (ISBN 0-87942-149-5). Inst Electrical.

Harvey, A. F., ed. Bibliography of Microwave Optical Technology. (Solid State Physics Literature Guides Series: Vol. 8). 717p. 1976. 75.00 (ISBN 0-306-68328-8). IFI Plenum.

Hecht, E. & Zajac, A. Optics. 1974. 24.95 (ISBN 0-201-02835-2). A-W.

Hecht, Eugene. Optics. 256p. 1975. pap. text ed. 6.95 (ISBN 0-07-027730-3, SP). McGraw.

Hoehler, G., ed. Quantum Statistics in Optics & Solid-State Physics. (Springer Tracts in Modern Physics: Vol. 66). (Illus.). 173p. 1973. 46.10 (ISBN 0-387-06189-4). Springer-Verlag.

Horne. Optical Production Technology. 1972. 95.00 (ISBN 0-9960020-3-0, Pub. by A Hilger England). Heyden.

Horne, D. F. Optical Production Technology. 599p. 1980. Repr. 87.50x (ISBN 0-8448-1398-2). Crane-Russak Co.

International Commission on Optics International Congress, 9th. Space Optics: Proceedings. Thompson, B. J. & Shannon, R. R., eds. (Illus.). 849p. 1974. 37.50 (ISBN 0-309-02144-8). Natl Acad Pr.

Jaffe, Bernard. Michelson & the Speed of Light. LC 78-25969. (Illus.). 1979. Repr. of 1960 ed. lib. bdg. 16.75x (ISBN 0-313-20777-1, JAMI). Greenwood.

Jenkins, Francis A. Fundamentals of Optics. 4th ed. (Illus.). 672p. 1976. 23.95 (ISBN 0-07-032330-5, C); solutions manual 4.95 (ISBN 0-07-032334-8). McGraw.

Johnson, B. K. Optics & Optical Instruments. 3rd ed. Orig. Title: Practical Optics. 1947. pap. 4.00 (ISBN 0-486-60642-2). Dover.

Kingslake, R., ed. Applied Optics & Optical Engineering: A Comprehensive Treatise, 5 vols. Incl. Vol. 1. Light: Its Generation & Modification. 1965 (ISBN 0-12-408601-2); Vol. 2. The Detection of Light & Infrared Radiation. 1965 (ISBN 0-12-408602-0); Vol. 3. Optical Components. 1965 (ISBN 0-12-408603-9); Vol. 4. Optical Instruments, Part I. 1967 (ISBN 0-12-408604-7); Vol. 5. Optical Instruments, Part 2. 1969 (ISBN 0-12-408605-5). 55.50 ea.; Set. 227.50 (ISBN 0-686-76926-0). Acad Pr.

Kingslake, R. & Shannon, Robert R., eds. Applied Optics & Optical Engineering, Vol. 7. 1979. pap. text ed. 41.50 sub. 36.00 (ISBN 0-12-408607-1). Acad Pr.

Kingslake, Rudolf & Thompson, Brian J., eds. Applied Optics & Optical Engineering, Vol. 6. LC 65-17761. 1980. 49.50 (ISBN 0-12-408606-3); subscription 42.00 (ISBN 0-686-66188-5). Acad Pr.

Klein, Miles V. Optics. LC 73-107584. 647p. 1970. 36.50 (ISBN 0-471-49080-6). Wiley.

Kmetz, A. R. & Willisen, F. K. Von, eds. Nonemissive Electro-Optic Displays. LC 76-17060. (Brown Boveri Symposia Ser.). 360p. 1976. 42.50 (ISBN 0-306-30957-2, Plenum Pr). Plenum Pub.

Laser Induced Damage in Optical Materials: Nineteen Seventy-Seven. 1978. pap. 6.75 (ISBN 0-686-52051-3, 04-655000-46). ASTM.

Laser Induced Damage in Optical Materials: 1979. (Special Technical Publications Ser.). 538p. 1980. softcover 9.50 (ISBN 0-686-76054-9, 726, 04-726000-46). ASTM.

Laser Induced Damage in Optical Materials: 1978. (Special Technical Publications Ser.). 329p. 1978. softcover 5.50 (ISBN 0-686-76056-5, 689, 04-689000-46). ASTM.

Levi, L. Applied Optics: A Guide to Optical Systems Design, 2 vols. LC 67-29942. (Pure & Applied Optics Ser.). Vol. 1, 1968. 44.00 (ISBN 0-471-53110-3, Pub. by Wiley-Interscience); Vol. 2, 1980. 84.00 (ISBN 0-471-05054-7). Wiley.

Levi, Leo, ed. Handbook of Tables of Functions for Applied Optics, CRC. LC 73-88627. (Handbook Ser). 640p. 1974. 69.95 (ISBN 0-87819-371-5). CRC Pr.

Lindberg, David C. Theories of Vision from Al-Kindi to Kepler. LC 75-19504. (Chicago History of Science & Medicine Ser). 448p. 1976. lib. bdg. 22.50x (ISBN 0-226-48234-0). U of Chicago Pr.

Lothian, G. F. Optics & Its Uses. 1975. 22.50 (ISBN 0-442-30098-0); pap. 7.95x (ISBN 0-442-30099-9). Van Nos Reinhold.

MacAdam, D. L. Color Measurement: Theme & Variation. (Springer Ser. in Optical Sciences: Vol. 27). (Illus.). 250p. 1981. 39.50 (ISBN 0-387-10773-8). Springer-Verlag.

Mandel, L. & Wolf, E., eds. Coherence & Quantum Optics. LC 73-76700. 913p. 1973. 65.00 (ISBN 0-306-30731-6, Plenum Pr). Plenum Pub.

Marchand, Erich W. Gradient Index Optics. 1978. 25.50 (ISBN 0-12-470750-5). Acad Pr.

Marcuse, D. Integrated Optics. (IEEE Press Selected Reprint Ser.). 1973. text ed. 20.95 (ISBN 0-686-66849-9); pap. 13.50x (ISBN 0-471-56860-0, Pub. by Wiley-Interscience). Wiley.

Marcuse, Dietrich, ed. Integrated Optics. LC 72-92691. (Illus.). 304p. 1973. 20.95 (ISBN 0-87942-021-9). Inst Electrical.

Marechal, A. & Courtes, G., eds. Space Optics. new ed. 400p. 1974. 76.00x (ISBN 0-677-50680-5). Gordon.

Masten, Larry B. Understanding Optronics. (Understanding Ser.). (Illus.). 256p. (Orig.). 1981. pap. 6.95 (ISBN 0-89512-049-6, LCB5472). Tex Instr Inc.

Mathieu, Jean P. Optics, 2 pts. Incl. Pt. 1. Electromagnetic Optics; Pt. 2. Quantum Optics. LC 73-10408. 1974. text ed. 33.00 (ISBN 0-08-017157-5). Pergamon.

Meyer-Arendt, Jurgen. Introduction to Classical & Modern Optics. LC 71-157723. (Illus.). 1972. ref. ed. 25.95 (ISBN 0-13-479436-2). P-H.

Michelson, Albert A. Studies in Optics. 1962. pap. 2.45 (ISBN 0-226-52388-8, P514, Phoen). U of Chicago Pr.

Midwinter, John E. Optical Fibers for Transmission. LC 78-15797. (Pure & Applied Optics Ser.). 1979. 33.00 (ISBN 0-471-60240-X, Pub. by Wiley-Interscience). Wiley.

Morgan, Joseph. Introduction to Geometrical & Physical Optics. LC 77-13033. 462p. 1978. Repr. of 1953 ed. lib. bdg. 21.50 (ISBN 0-88275-620-6). Krieger.

Muetze. ABC der Optik. 960p. (Ger.). Repr. of 1961 ed. 38.95 (ISBN 0-686-56593-2, M-7290, Pub. by W. Dausien). French & Eur.

Mugler, Charles. Dictionnaire Historique de la Terminologie Optique des Grecs. 460p. (Fr.). 1964. pap. 110.00 (ISBN 0-686-57055-3, M-6421). French & Eur.

Nelson, Donald F. Electric, Optic, & Acoustic Interactions in Dielectrics. LC 78-25964. 1979. 41.00 (ISBN 0-471-05199-3, Pub. by Wiley-Interscience). Wiley.

Newman, Paul. Optical Resolution Procedures for Chemical Compounds, Vol. 1: Amines & Related Compounds. 1981. 31.50 (ISBN 0-686-76225-8). Optical Resolution.

--Optical Resolution Procedures for Chemical Compounds, Vol. 2: Carboxylic & Other Acids. 1981. write for info. Optical Resolution.

Newton, Isaac. Opticks. LC 52-12165. 1952. lib. bdg. 12.50 (ISBN 0-88307-624-1). Gannon.

--Opticks, or a Treatise of the Reflections, Refractions, Inflections & Colours of Light. 11.00 (ISBN 0-8446-5799-9). Peter Smith.

--Optics. 1952. pap. text ed. 5.50 (ISBN 0-486-60205-2). Dover.

Nicholson, Marjorie H. Newton Demands the Muse: Newton's "Opticks" & the Eighteenth Century Poets. LC 78-13146. 1979. Repr. of 1966 ed. lib. bdg. 16.75x (ISBN 0-313-21044-6, NIND). Greenwood.

Nussbaum, A. & Phillips, R. Contemporary Optics for Scientists & Engineers. 1976. 28.95 (ISBN 0-13-170183-5). P-H.

Omar, Saleh Beshara. Ibn Al-Haytham's Optics: A Study of the Origins of Experimental Science. LC 76-42611. (Studies in Islamic Philosophy & Science). (Illus.). 1977. 25.00x (ISBN 0-88297-015-1). Bibliotheca.

Optical Society of America. Optics Index. write for info. (ISBN 0-9600380-2-7). Optical Soc.

Overington, Ian. Vision & Acquisition. LC 75-45872. 1976. 44.50x (ISBN 0-8448-0917-9). Crane-Russak Co.

Palmer, C. Harvey. Optics: Experiments and Demonstrations. 340p. 1962. 20.00x (ISBN 0-8018-0518-X). Johns Hopkins.

Papoulis, Athanasios. Systems & Transforms with Applications in Optics. 484p. 1981. Repr. of 1968 ed. lib. bdg. price not set (ISBN 0-89874-358-3). Krieger.

Pecham, John. John Pecham & the Science of Optics: Perspectiva Communis. Lindberg, David C., ed. LC 72-98122. (Publication in Medieval Science No. 14). 1970. 22.00x (ISBN 0-299-05730-5). U of Wis Pr.

Pressley, Robert J. Handbook of Lasers, CRC: With Selected Data on Optical Technology. LC 72-163066. (Handbook Ser.). (Illus.). 631p. 1971. 49.95 (ISBN 0-87819-381-2). CRC Pr.

REA Staff. Optics: Problem Solver. 960p. 1980. 22.85 (ISBN 0-87891-526-5). Res & Educ.

Research & Education Ass. Optics: A Supplement to Any Class Text. LC 81-50899. 864p. (Orig.). 1981. pap. text ed. 22.85x (ISBN 0-87891-526-5). Res & Educ.

Robertson, E. R., ed. The Engineering Uses of Coherent Optics. LC 75-22978. 560p. 1976. 145.00 (ISBN 0-521-20879-3). Cambridge U Pr.

Robson, B. A. The Theory of Polarization Phenomena. (Oxford Studies in Physics). (Illus.). 200p. 1975. 35.00x (ISBN 0-19-851453-0). Oxford U Pr.

Rubin, Melvin L. Optics for Clinicians. 2nd ed. LC 72-97862. (Illus.). 1974. 25.00x (ISBN 0-9600472-1-2). Triad Pub FL.

Ruth, W. Lexikon der Schulphysik: Optik und Relativitaet, Vol. 4. (Ger.). 42.00 (ISBN 3-7614-0109-4, M-7226). French & Eur.

Safir, Aran. Refraction & Clinical Optics. (Illus.). 565p. 1980. text ed. 37.50 (ISBN 0-06-142318-1, Harper Medical). Har-Row.

Saleh, B. Photoelectronic Statistics: With Applications to Spectroscopy & Optical Communication. LC 77-9936. (Springer Ser. in Optical Sciences: Vol. 6). (Illus.). 1977. 39.30 (ISBN 0-387-08295-6). Springer-Verlag.

Schulz, Ernst. Woerterbuch der Optik und Feinmechanik, Vol. 1. (Fr., Ger. & Eng., Dictionary of Optics & Mechanical Engineering). 1961. pap. 12.00 (ISBN 3-87097-036-7, M-6978). French & Eur.

--Woerterbuch der Optik und Feinmechanik, Vol. 2. (Fr., Ger. & Eng., Dictionary of Optics & Mechanical Engineering). 1961. pap. 12.00 (ISBN 3-87097-037-5, M-6977). French & Eur.

Sears, Francis W. Optics. 3rd ed. 1949. 17.95 (ISBN 0-201-06915-6). A-W.

Skobel'tsyn, D. V., ed. Optical Studies in Liquids & Solids. LC 69-12523. (P. N. Lebedev Physics Institute Ser.: Vol. 39). 266p. 1969. 35.00 (ISBN 0-306-10821-6, Consultants). Plenum Pub.

Smith, F. Graham & Thomson, J. H. Optics. LC 71-146547. (Manchester Physics Ser). 1971. 17.50 (ISBN 0-471-80360-X, Pub. by Wiley-Interscience). Wiley.

Snyder, A. W. & Menzel, R., eds. Photoreceptor Optics. LC 75-6700. (Illus.). 550p. 1975. 53.00 (ISBN 0-387-07216-0). Springer-Verlag.

Soroko, L. M. Holography & Coherent Optics. (Illus.). 650p. 1978. 59.50 (ISBN 0-306-40101-0, Plenum Pr). Plenum Pub.

Steffens, Henry J. The Development of Newtonian Optics in England. (Illus.). 1977. 20.00 (ISBN 0-88202-048-X, Sci Hist). N Watson.

Stroke, George W. Introduction to Coherent Optics & Halography. (Illus.). 1969. 34.00 (ISBN 0-12-673956-0). Acad Pr.

Swenson, Loyd S., Jr. The Ethereal Aether: A History of the Michelson-Morley-Miller Aether-Drift Experiments, 1880-1930. (Illus.). 382p. 1972. 20.00x (ISBN 0-292-72000-9). U of Tex Pr.

Tamir, T., ed. Integrated Optics. (Topics in Applied Physics: Vol. 7). (Illus.). 1979. pap. 20.80 (ISBN 0-387-09673-6). Springer-Verlag.

Tenquist, D. W., et al. University Optics, 2 vols. 1970. Set. 103.50x (ISBN 0-677-62090-X); Vol. 1. 59.00x (ISBN 0-677-62070-5); Vol. 2. 59.00x (ISBN 0-677-62080-2). Gordon.

Topliss, W. S. The Optical Dispensing & Workshop Practice. 1975. 39.95 (ISBN 0-407-00025-9). Butterworth.

Van Heel, A. C., ed. Advanced Optical Techniques. 1967. 73.25 (ISBN 0-444-10291-4, North-Holland). Elsevier.

Walker, D. C., ed. Origins of Optical Activity in Nature. (Studies in Physical & Theoretical Chemistry: Vol. 7). 261p. 1979. 53.75 (ISBN 0-444-41841-5). Elsevier.

Ward, Gray, ed. Integrated Optics & Optical Communications. 1974. pap. 12.95x (ISBN 0-8422-0402-4). Irvington.

Weik, Martin H. Fiber Optics & Lightwave Communications Standard Dictionary. 320p. 1980. text ed. 18.50 (ISBN 0-442-25658-2). Van Nos Reinhold.

Weissberger, A. & Rossiter, B. W., eds. Techniques of Chemistry: Optical, Spectroscopic, & Radioactivity Methods: Iternferometry, Light Scattering, Microscopy, Microwave, & Magnetic Resonance Spectroscopy, Vol. 1, Pt. 3A. 791p. 1972. 49.50 (ISBN 0-471-92729-5). Kreiger.

Welford, W. T. & Winston, Roland. The Optics of Nonimaging Concentrators: Light & Solar Energy. 1978. 33.50 (ISBN 0-12-745350-4). Acad Pr.

Wheelock, Arthur K., Jr. Perspecture, Optics, & Delft Artists Around 1650. LC 76-23661. (Outstanding Dissertations in the Fine Arts - 17th Century). (Illus.). 1977. Repr. of 1973 ed. lib. bdg. 56.00 (ISBN 0-8240-2740-X). Garland Pub.

Williams, Charles S. & Becklund, Orville A. Optics: A Short Course for Engineers & Scientists. LC 73-39046. (Pure & Applied Optics Ser). 440p. 1972. 37.50 (ISBN 0-471-94830-6). Wiley.

Wolf. Progress in Optics, Vol 15. 1978. 61.00 (ISBN 0-7204-1515-2, North-Holland). Elsevier.

Wolf, E., ed. Progress in Optics, Vols. 1-2 & 6-15. LC 61-19297. 1961-74. Vol. 1. 39.00 (ISBN 0-444-10318-X, North-Holland); Vol. 2. 34.25 (ISBN 0-444-10319-8); Vol. 6. 41.50 (ISBN 0-444-10323-6); Vol. 7. 46.50 (ISBN 0-444-10324-4); Vol. 8. 49.00 (ISBN 0-444-10020-2); Vol. 9. 46.50 (ISBN 0-444-10111-X); Vol. 10. 53.75 (ISBN 0-444-10394-5); Vol. 11. 53.75 (ISBN 0-444-10497-6); Vol. 12. 58.75 (ISBN 0-7204-1512-8). Elsevier.

--Progress in Optics, Vol. 13. 46.50 (ISBN 0-444-10806-8, North-Holland). Elsevier.

--Progress in Optics, Vol. 14. 1976. 68.50 (ISBN 0-444-10914-5, North-Holland). Elsevier.

Young, Hugh D. Fundamentals of Waves, Optics & Modern Physics. 2nd ed. 1975. 19.95 (ISBN 0-07-072521-7, C). McGraw.

Young, M. Applied Optics. (Series in Optical Sciences: Vol. 5). 1977. 30.50 (ISBN 0-387-08126-7). Springer-Verlag.

Yu, Francis T. Optics & Information Theory. LC 76-23135. 1976. 24.00 (ISBN 0-471-01682-9, Pub. by Wiley-Interscience). Wiley.

OPTICS–ATLASES

Harburn, G., et al. Atlas of Optical Transforms. LC 75-14718. 104p. 1975. 27.50x (ISBN 0-8014-0986-1). Cornell U Pr.

OPTICS–TABLES, ETC.

Heller, Wilfried, et al. Tables of Angular Scattering Functions for Heterodisperse Systems of Spheres. LC 68-57471. 1969. 50.00x (ISBN 0-8143-1364-7). Wayne St U Pr.

Pangonis, William J. & Heller, Wilfried. Angular Scattering Functions for Spherical Particles. LC 60-8930. (Illus.). 1960. pap. 9.50x (ISBN 0-8143-1117-2). Wayne St U Pr.

Rousseau, M. & Mathieu, Jean P. Problems in Optics. 376p. 1973. text ed. 32.00 (ISBN 0-08-016980-5). Pergamon.

OPTICS, ELECTRONIC

see Electron Optics

OPTICS, FIBER

see Fiber Optics

OPTICS, GEOMETRICAL

Blaker, J. W. Geometric Optics: The Matrix Theory. 1971. 19.50 (ISBN 0-8247-1046-0). Dekker.

Buchdahl, H. A. Optical Aberration Coefficients. 2nd ed. LC 68-19165. 1969. pap. 5.00 (ISBN 0-486-62010-7). Dover.

--Optical Aberration Coefficients. 7.50 (ISBN 0-8446-1760-1). Peter Smith.

Buchdahl, Hans A. Introduction to Hamiltonian Optics. LC 69-19372. (Cambridge Monographs on Physics). (Illus.). 1970. 44.50 (ISBN 0-521-07516-5). Cambridge U Pr.

Herzberger, Max. Modern Geometrical Optics. LC 77-9030. 516p. 1978. Repr. 25.50 (ISBN 0-88275-585-4). Krieger.

Horemis, Spyros. Optical & Geometric Patterns & Designs. 1970. pap. 5.00 (ISBN 0-486-22214-4). Dover.

Kline, Morris & Kay, Irvin W. Electromagnetic Theory & Geometrical Optics. LC 78-14351. (Pure & Applied Mathemetics Ser.: Vol. 12). 340p. 1979. Repr. of 1965 ed. lib. bdg. 26.50 (ISBN 0-88275-739-3). Krieger.

Longhurst, R. S. Geometrical & Physical Optics. 3rd ed. LC 74-169158. (Illus.). 704p. 1974. pap. text ed. 19.95x (ISBN 0-582-44099-8). Longman.

Ogle, Kenneth N. Optics: An Introduction for Ophthalmologists. 2nd ed. (Illus.). 288p. 1979. 13.75 (ISBN 0-398-01417-5). C C Thomas.

Zimmer, H. G. Geometrical Optics. Wilson, R. N., tr. LC 72-94095. (Applied Physics & Engineering Ser.: Vol. 9). (Illus.). 1970. 22.20 (ISBN 0-387-04771-9). Springer-Verlag.

OPTICS, LINEAR

see Nonlinear Optics

OPTICS, METEOROLOGICAL

see Meteorological Optics

OPTICS, NONLINEAR

see Nonlinear Optics

OPTICS, PHOTOGRAPHIC

see Photographic Optics

OPTICS, PHYSICAL

see also Crystal Optics; Electromagnetic Theory; Photoelasticity

Egan, Walter G. & Hilgeman, Theodore W. Optical Properties of Inhomogeneous Materials: Applications to Geology, Astronomy, Chemistry & Engineering. LC 78-20043. 1979. 35.00 (ISBN 0-12-232650-4). Acad Pr.

Fowles, Grant R. Introduction to Modern Optics. 2nd ed. LC 74-23437. 1975. text ed. 25.95 (ISBN 0-03-089404-2, HoltC). HR&W.

Garbuny, Max. Optical Physics. 1965. text ed. 22.95 (ISBN 0-12-275350-X). Acad Pr.

Longhurst, R. S. Geometrical & Physical Optics. 3rd ed. LC 74-169158. (Illus.). 704p. 1974. pap. text ed. 19.95x (ISBN 0-582-44099-8). Longman.

Lorenz, Ludwig V. Oeuvres Scientifiques De L. Lorenz, 2 Vols. 1898-1904. Set. 38.50 (ISBN 0-384-33740-6). Johnson Repr.

Pockels, Friedrich C. Lehrbuch der Kristalloptik. (Bibliotheca Mathematica Teubneriana Ser: No. 39). (Ger). 1969. Repr. of 1906 ed. 46.00 (ISBN 0-384-47000-9). Johnson Repr.

Skolbel'Tsyn, D. V., ed. Optical Methods of Investigating Solid Bodies. LC 65-10524. (P. N. Lebedev Physics Institute Ser.: Vol. 25). 188p. 1965. 35.00 (ISBN 0-306-10713-9, Consultants). Plenum Pub.

Stokes, George G. Mathematical & Physical Papers, 5 Vols. 2nd ed. Repr. of 1905 ed. Set. 115.50 (ISBN 0-384-58370-9). Johnson Repr.

Strong, John. Concepts of Classical Optics. LC 57-6918. (Physics Ser.). (Illus.). 1958. 28.95x (ISBN 0-7167-0301-7). W H Freeman.

OPTICS, PHYSIOLOGICAL

see also Color Vision; Eye; Optical Illusions; Vision

Arden, G. B., ed. The Visual System: Neurophysiology, Biophysics, & Their Clinical Applications. LC 72-77461. (Advances in Experimental Medicine & Biology Ser.: Vol. 24). 340p. 1972. 35.00 (ISBN 0-306-39024-8, Plenum Pr). Plenum Pub.

Emsley. Visual Optics, 2 vols. 5th ed. (Illus.). 1976. Vol. 1. 34.95 (ISBN 0-407-93415-4); Vol. 2. 34.95 (ISBN 0-407-93414-6). Butterworth.

Helmholtz, H. Treatise on Physiological Optics, 3 vols. in 2. 30.00 (ISBN 0-8446-1231-6). Peter Smith.

Hering, Ewald. Outlines of a Theory of the Light Sense. LC 64-11130. (Illus.). 1964. 16.50x (ISBN 0-674-64900-1). Harvard U Pr.

Julesz, Bela. Foundations of Cyclopean Perception. LC 70-149594. (Illus.). 1971. text ed. 35.00x (ISBN 0-226-41527-9). U of Chicago Pr.

Kohler, Ivo. Formation & Transformation of the Perceptual World. LC 64-18328. (Psychological Issues Monograph: No. 12, Vol. 3, No. 4). (Orig.). 1964. text ed. 11.00 (ISBN 0-8236-2000-X). Intl Univs Pr.

LeGrand, Y. & El Hage, S. G. Physiological Optics. (Springer Ser. in Optical Sciences: Vol. 13). (Illus.). 350p. 1980. pap. 46.00 (ISBN 0-387-09919-0). Springer-Verlag.

Levene. Clinical Refraction & Visual Science. 375p. 1977. 39.95x (ISBN 0-407-00043-7). Butterworth.

Lindberg, David C. Theories of Vision from Al-Kindi to Kepler. LC 75-19504. (Chicago History of Science & Medicine Ser). 448p. 1976. lib. bdg. 22.50x (ISBN 0-226-48234-0). U of Chicago Pr.

Linksz, Arthur. Physiology of the Eye: Vol. I Optics. LC 50-5797. (Illus.). 366p. 1950. 43.00 (ISBN 0-8089-0267-9). Grune.

MacAdam, David L., ed. Sources of Color Science. LC 77-110231. 1970. pap. 5.95 (ISBN 0-262-63064-8). MIT Pr.

Miller, David & Benedek, George. Intraocular Light Scattering: Theory & Clinical Application. (Illus.). 132p. 1973. text ed. 11.75 (ISBN 0-398-02665-3). C C Thomas.

Murch, Gerald M. Visual & Auditory Perception. LC 74-172349. (Illus.). 1973. pap. 14.95 (ISBN 0-672-60779-4). Bobbs.

Reichardt, W., ed. Processing of Optical Data by Organisms & by Machines. (Italian Physical Society: Course No. 43). 1970. 76.50 (ISBN 0-12-368843-4). Acad Pr.

Rubin, Melvin L. & Walls, Gordon L. Studies in Physiological Optics. (Illus.). 144p. 1965. 10.50 (ISBN 0-398-01624-0). C C Thomas.

Wehner, R., ed. Information Processing in the Visual Systems of Arthropods. LC 72-91887. 340p. 1973. pap. 26.40 (ISBN 0-387-06020-0). Springer-Verlag.

Welford, W. T. Abberations of the Symmetrical Optical System. 1975. 40.50 (ISBN 0-12-742050-9). Acad Pr.

Zinchenko, V. P. & Vergiles, N. Yu. Formation of Visual Images: Studies of Stabilized Retinal Images. LC 70-185458. 58p. 1972. 20.00 (ISBN 0-306-10871-2, Consultants). Plenum Pub.

OPTICS, QUANTUM

see Quantum Optics

OPTIMISM

see also Pessimism

Bobrov, L. Grounds for Optimism. 278p. 1974. pap. 2.00 (ISBN 0-8285-0821-6, Pub. by Mir Pubs Russia). Imported Pubns.

Dana, William F. The Optimism of Ralph Waldo Emerson. LC 76-46925. 1976. Repr. of 1886 ed. lib. bdg. 10.00 (ISBN 0-8414-3806-4). Folcroft.

Kuznetsov, B. A. Philosophy of Optimism. 343p. 1977. 6.25 (ISBN 0-8285-1002-4, Pub. by Progress Pubs Russia). Imported Pubns.

Kuznetsov, Boris. The Philosophy of Optimism. 1977. 6.25 (ISBN 0-8285-1002-4, Pub. by Progress Pubs Russia). Imported Pubns.

Leland, Charles G. Sunshine in Thought. LC 59-6526. 1959. 21.00x (ISBN 0-8201-1055-8). Schol Facsimiles.

Matlin, Margaret & Stang, David. The Pollyanna Principle: Selectivity in Language, Memory, & Thought. LC 78-25548. 1979. text ed. 15.50 (ISBN 0-87073-815-1); pap. text ed. 7.95 (ISBN 0-87073-817-8). Schenkman.

Tiger, Lionel. Optimism. 1980. 4.95 (ISBN 0-671-25395-6, Touchstone). S&S.

OPTIMIZATION (MATHEMATICS)

see Mathematical Optimization

OPTIMIZATION THEORY

see Mathematical Optimization

OPTION (CONTRACT)

see also Put and Call Transactions

Cleeton, Claud E. Strategies for the Options Trader. LC 78-11230. 1979. 24.95 (ISBN 0-471-04973-5, Pub. by Wiley-Interscience). Wiley.

Henin, Claude G. & Ryan, Peter J. Options: Theory & Practice. LC 77-2687. 1977. 21.95 (ISBN 0-669-01623-3). Lexington Bks.

Little, Jeffrey B. & Rhodes, Lucien. Stock Options. 32p. 1977. pap. 2.95 (ISBN 0-89709-009-8). Liberty Pub.

Miller, Jarrott T. Options Trading Maximizing Profits, Minimizing Risks. new ed. 128p. 1975. 10.95 (ISBN 0-8092-8385-9). Contemp Bks.

Rogalski, Richard J. Dynamic Call Option Models: Theory & Evidence. (Michigan Business Studies, New Ser: Vol. 1, No. 4). 1978. text ed. 12.50 casebound (ISBN 0-87712-184-2). U Mich Busn Div Res.

OPTOMETRISTS

see also Eye-Accomodation and Refraction; Eye-Examination; Opticians; Optometry-Vocational Guidance

Elmstrom, George. Advanced Management for Optometrists. LC 73-75804. 1973. 42.00 (ISBN 0-87873-013-3). Prof Press.

Rudman, Jack. Optometrist. (Career Examination Ser.). (Cloth bdg. avail. on request). pap. 12.00 (ISBN 0-8373-0557-8). Natl Learning.

OPTOMETRY

see also Eye-Accomodation and Refraction

Cool, J. & Smith, E. L., eds. Frontiers in Visual Science: Proceedings of the University of Houston College of Optometry Dedication Symposium, Houston Texas, March, 1977. LC 78-24191. (Springer Ser. in Optical Sciences: Vol. 8). (Illus.). 1979. 43.30 (ISBN 0-387-09185-8). Springer-Verlag.

Gerstman, Daniel R. & Levene, John R. Optometry Examination Review Book: Clinical Optometry. 1975. spiral bdg. 12.00 (ISBN 0-87488-470-5). Med Exam.

Havener, William H. Ocular Pharmacology. 4th ed. LC 78-7208. 1978. text ed. 54.50 (ISBN 0-8016-2105-4). Mosby.

Hirsch, Monroe J. Dr. Thomson's 1895 Correspondence Course in Optics. LC 74-31552. 1975. 50.00 (ISBN 0-87873-017-6). Prof Press.

Kelley, Alberta. Lenses, Spectacles, & Contacts: The Story of Vision Aids. LC 78-14827. (Illus.). (gr. 6 up). 1979. 6.95 (ISBN 0-525-66617-6). Elsevier-Nelson.

Newcomb, Robert D. & Jolley, Jerry L. Public Health & Community Optometry. (Illus.). 534p. 1980. text ed. 24.75 (ISBN 0-398-03918-6). C C Thomas.

Rubin, L. Optometry Handbook. 1975. 17.95 (ISBN 0-407-98500-X). Butterworth.

Rubin, Leroy. Optometry Handbook. rev. 2nd ed. (Illus.). 1981. text ed. 34.95 (ISBN 0-409-95180-3). Butterworth.

Sloan, Louise L. Reading Aids for the Partially Sighted: A Systematic Procedure for Prescribing Reading Aids. 1977. 14.95 (ISBN 0-683-07743-0). Williams & Wilkins.

Tarlow, David M. Student Guide to the Optometry College Admission Test. (Illus.). 1981. pap. 9.50 (ISBN 0-931572-04-5). Datar Pub.

Victoreen, John A. Basic Principles of Otometry. (Illus.). 232p. 1973. 16.75 (ISBN 0-398-02616-5). C C Thomas.

OPTOMETRY-VOCATIONAL GUIDANCE

Gregg, James R. Your Future in New Optometric Careers. (Careers in Depth Ser). (gr. 7 up). 1978. PLB 5.97 (ISBN 0-8239-0449-0). Rosen Pr.

--Your Future in Optometry. LC 72-114107. (Career Guidance Ser). 1971. pap. 3.95 (ISBN 0-668-02259-0). Arco.
Kitchell, Frank M. Opportunities in Optometry. LC 74-82638. (Illus.). 128p. (gr. 8-12). 1974. PLB 6.60 (ISBN 0-685-50036-5); pap. 4.95 (ISBN 0-685-50037-3). Natl Textbk.
Koch, Hugo. Optometric Manpower: Characteristics of Optometric Practice, U. S. 1968. LC 74-2154. (Data on Health Resources: Manpower & Facilities Ser. 14: No. 13). 60p. 1974. pap. text ed. 1.25 (ISBN 0-8406-0004-6). Natl Ctr Health Stats.
Rudman, Jack. Optometry College Admission Test (OCAT) (Admission Test Ser.: ATS-27). (Cloth bdg. avail. on request). 1975. pap. 9.95 (ISBN 0-8373-5027-1). Natl Learning.

ORACLE, ARIZONA

Wood, Elizabeth L. Arizona Hoof Trails. 1956. 3.95 (ISBN 0-8323-0073-X). Binford.

ORACLES

see also Delphian Oracle; Divination; Sibyls

Abbott, Evelyn, ed. Hellenica: A Collection of Essays on Greek Poetry, Philosophy, History & Religion. LC 76-86577. (Classics Ser). 1971. Repr. of 1880 ed. 16.00 (ISBN 0-8046-1196-3). Kennikat.
Alexander, Paul J. The Oracle of Baalbek: The Tiburtine Sibyl in Greek Dress. LC 75-27113. (Dumbarton Oaks Studies: Vol. 10). (Illus.). 151p. 1967. 12.00x (ISBN 0-88402-020-7, Ctr Byzantine). Dumbarton Oaks.
Booker, John. The Dutch Oracle. (Illus.). 224p. 1981. pap. price not set (ISBN 0-931116-01-5). Ralston-Pilot.
Campbell, Alexander, tr. from Gk. Living Oracles. 1975. Repr. 12.00 (ISBN 0-89225-166-2); kivar 9.50 (ISBN 0-89225-117-4). Gospel Advocate.
Evans-Pritchard, Edward E. Witchcraft, Oracles & Magic Among the Azande. 1937. 52.50x (ISBN 0-19-823103-2). Oxford U Pr.
Flaceliere, Robert. Greek Oracles. Garman, Douglas, tr. (Illus.). 1977. 7.95 (ISBN 0-236-31145-X, Pub. by Paul Elek). Merrimack Bk Serv.
Loewe, Michael & Blacker, Carmen, eds. Oracles & Divination. LC 81-50968. (Illus.). 256p. (Orig.). 1981. pap. 7.95 (ISBN 0-394-74880-8). Shambhala Pubns.
Ophiel. Oracle of Fortuna. pap. 6.95 (ISBN 0-685-47280-9). Weiser.
Parke, Herbert W. Greek Oracles. 1967. pap. text ed. 6.25x (ISBN 0-09-084111-5, Hutchinson U Lib). Humanities.
Terry, Milton S., tr. from Gr. The Sibylline Oracles. new ed. LC 72-176141. Repr. of 1899 ed. 21.45 (ISBN 0-404-06362-4). AMS Pr.
Ward, Charles A. Oracles of Nostradamus. 400p. 1981. pap. 15.00 (ISBN 0-89540-084-7, SB-084). Sun Pub.

ORAGE, ALFRED RICHARD, 1873-1934

Carswell, John. Lives & Letters: A. R. Orage-Beatrice Hastings-Katherine Mansfield-John Middleton Murray-S. S. Koteliansky. LC 77-15986. (Illus.). 1978. 15.00 (ISBN 0-8112-0681-5). New Directions.
Mairet, P. A. R. Orage. 35.00 (ISBN 0-87968-572-7). Gordon Pr.

ORAIBI, ARIZONA

Titiev, Mischa. Old Oraibi. (Harvard Univ. PMP Ser.: Vol. 22, No. 1). (Illus.). 1944. pap. 30.00 (ISBN 0-527-01253-X). Kraus Repr.

ORAL COMMUNICATION

Here are entered works on speaking as a means of communication. Works on the oral production of meaningful sounds in language are entered under Speech.

see also Conversation; Oral Interpretation; Oral Tradition; Speech; Speech Processing Systems

Abernathy, Elton. Fundamentals of Speech Communication. 4th ed. 352p. 1976. pap. text ed. 7.95x (ISBN 0-697-04145-X); instr's man. 0.50 (ISBN 0-686-67110-4). Wm C Brown.
Adler, Ronald B. Confidence in Communication: A Guide to Assertive & Social Skills. LC 76-58530. 334p. 1979. pap. text ed. 12.95x (ISBN 0-03-016696-9, HoltC). HR&W.
Alexander, L. G. Question & Answer: Graded Oral Comprehension. new ed. (English As a Second Language Bk.). 1977. pap. text ed. 3.75x (ISBN 0-582-55206-0). Longman.
Allen, Roach V. Language Experiences in Communication. LC 75-31011. (Illus.). 512p. 1976. text ed. 17.95 (ISBN 0-395-18624-2); inst. manual 1.25 (ISBN 0-395-18798-2). HM.
Anastasiow, Nicholas. Oral Language: Expression of Thought. 1971. 2.00 (ISBN 0-87207-840-X). Intl Reading.
Auer, John J. An Introduction to Research in Speech. LC 77-5311. 1977. Repr. of 1959 ed. lib. bdg. 22.25 (ISBN 0-8371-9581-0, AUIR). Greenwood.
Baird. Orientations to Organizational Communication. Applbaum, Ronald & Hart, Roderick, eds. LC 77-21002. (MODCOM - Modules in Speech Communication). 1978. pap. text ed. 2.50 (ISBN 0-574-22533-1, 13-5533). SRA.
Baird, John E., Jr. Speaking for Results: Communication by Objectives. (Illus.). 301p. 1981. pap. text ed. 11.95 scp (ISBN 0-06-040457-4, HarpC); inst. manual available. Har-Row.
Beck, M. S. Baby Talk: How Your Child Learns to Speak. (Orig.). 1979. pap. 4.95 (ISBN 0-452-25253-9, Z5253, Plume). NAL.
Bellack, Arno A., et al. Language of the Classroom. LC 66-22926. 1966. pap. 7.50 (ISBN 0-8077-1063-6). Tchrs Coll.
Bending, C. W. Communication & the Schools. LC 71-103930. 1970. 22.00 (ISBN 0-08-015663-0); pap. 10.75 (ISBN 0-08-015662-2). Pergamon.
Bianchi, Doris B., et al. Easily Understood: A Basic Speech Text. 160p. (Orig.). 1981. pap. text ed. 7.95 (ISBN 0-89529-138-X). Avery Pub.
Bolenius, Emma M. The Teaching of Oral English. (Educational Ser.). 1914. Repr. 10.00 (ISBN 0-685-43089-8). Norwood Edns.
Bormann, Ernest & Bormann, Nancy C. Speech Communication: A Basic Approach. 3rd ed. 278p. 1981. pap. text ed. 11.50 scp (ISBN 0-06-040865-0, HarpC). Har-Row.
Bourke, S. F., et al. Oracy in Australian Schools. (Australian Council for Educational Research Ser.: No. 9). 258p. 1980. pap. text ed. 21.00x (ISBN 0-85563-212-7). Verry.
Bradley, Bert E., et al. Workbook for Fundamentals of Speech Communication. 144p. 1981. spiral bdg. 6.95 (ISBN 0-8403-2056-6). Kendall-Hunt.
Bradley, Patricia H. & Baird, John E., Jr. Communication for Business & the Professions. 300p. 1980. pap. text ed. write for info. (ISBN 0-697-04166-2); instrs' manual 3.00 (ISBN 0-697-04169-7). Wm C Brown.
Brooks, William D. & Friedrich, Gustav W. Teaching Speech Communication in the Secondary School. 368p. 1973. text ed. 19.50 (ISBN 0-395-12629-0, 3-06400). HM.
Bryant, Donald C. & Wallace, Karl R. Oral Communication: A Short Course in Speaking. 4th ed. (Illus.). 336p. 1976. pap. text ed. 11.95 (ISBN 0-13-638429-3). P-H.
Bryant, Donald C., et al. Oral Communication: A Short Course in Speaking. 5th ed. (Illus.). 288p. 1982. 12.95 (ISBN 0-13-638437-4). P-H.
Burby, Raymond J. Communicating with People: The Supervisor's Introduction to Verbal Communication & Decision-Making. LC 78-109507. (Supervision Ser). (Prog. Bk.). 1970. pap. text ed. 8.95 (ISBN 0-201-00735-5). A-W.
Bushman, John H. & Jones, Sandra K. Effective Communication: A Handbook of Discussion Skills. (Illus.). 1977. 2.50 (ISBN 0-914634-51-8, 7726). DOK Pubs.
Capp, Glenn R., et al. Basic Oral Communication. 3rd ed. (Illus.). 416p. 1981. pap. text ed. 13.95 (ISBN 0-13-065979-7). P-H.
Capps, Randall & O'Conner, J. Regis. Fundamentals of Effective Speech Communications. 1978. pap. text ed. 8.50 (ISBN 0-87626-318-X). Winthrop.
Carlson, Karen & Meyers, Alan. Speaking with Confidence. 1977. pap. 9.95x (ISBN 0-673-15022-4). Scott F.
Carlson, Ruth K. Speaking Aids Through the Grades. LC 74-14719. 1975. pap. text ed. 4.50x (ISBN 0-8077-2421-1). Tchrs Coll.
Carnegie. Quick & Easy Way Speaking. 8.95 (ISBN 0-686-31282-1). New Century.
Clevenger, Theodore, Jr. & Matthews, Jack. The Speech Communication Process. 1971. pap. 5.95x (ISBN 0-673-05734-8). Scott F.
Cole, Ronald A., ed. Perception & Production of Fluent Speech. LC 79-25481. (Illus.). 576p. 1980. text ed. 29.95x (ISBN 0-89859-019-1). L Erlbaum Assocs.
Cragan, John F. & Wright, David W. Introduction to Speech Communication. LC 80-52302. 400p. 1980. pap. text ed. 10.95x (ISBN 0-917974-45-X). Waveland Pr.
Day, Peter R. Methods of Learning Communication Skills. 324p. 1977. text ed. 35.00 (ISBN 0-08-018954-7); pap. text ed. 19.50 (ISBN 0-08-018953-9). Pergamon.
Dickens, Milton. Speech: Dynamic Communication. 3rd ed. 448p. 1974. text ed. 15.95 (ISBN 0-15-583193-3, HC); instructor's manual avail. (ISBN 0-15-583194-1). HarBraceJ.
Dickson, W. Patrick, ed. Children's Oral Communication Skills. (Developmental Psychology Ser.). 1981. 29.50 (ISBN 0-12-215450-9). Acad Pr.
Easley, Wayne & Creech, Kenneth. Communication: A Configurative Approach. 1979. pap. text ed. 6.95 (ISBN 0-8403-2059-0). Kendall-Hunt.
Eisenberg, Abne M. Speech Communication in Business & Professions. (Illus.). 1978. pap. text ed. 10.95 (ISBN 0-686-67728-5); pap. text ed. 6.95 (ISBN 0-686-67729-3). Macmillan.
Ervin-Tripp, S. & Mitchell-Kernan, C., eds. Child Discourse. 1977. 12.00 (ISBN 0-12-241950-2). Acad Pr.
Evans, W. Bryce. Improving Your Speech: "Here's How". 1976. perfect bdg. 9.50 (ISBN 0-8403-1404-3). Kendall Hunt.
Fellows, Hugh P. Art & Skill of Talking with People: A New Guide to Personal & Business Success. (Illus.). 1964. 10.95 (ISBN 0-13-046862-2). P-H.
Forrest, Mary & Olson, Margot. Exploring Speech Communication: An Introduction. 433p. 1981. pap. text ed. 13.50 (ISBN 0-8299-0381-X). West Pub.
Frank, Ted & Ray, David. Basic Business & Professional Speech Communication. (Speech Communication Ser.). (Illus.). 1979. pap. text ed. 14.95 (ISBN 0-13-057273-X). P-H.
Gabbard-Alley, Anne & Porter, M. Erin. An Interpersonal Approach to Business & Professional Speech Communication. 1977. pap. text ed. 7.95x (ISBN 0-89641-001-3). American Pr.
Gardner, Joyce & La Fleur, Ida. Oral Language Continuum Book. (gr. k-3). 1975. 9.00x (ISBN 0-933892-08-X). Child Focus Co.
Gilbert, John H., ed. Speech & Cortical Functioning. (Based upon a symposium). 1972. 28.00 (ISBN 0-12-282850-X). Acad Pr.
Gronbeck, Bruce E., et al. Principles & Types of Speech Communication. 9th ed. 1981. 11.95 (ISBN 0-673-15538-2). Scott F.
Gruner, Charles R., et al. Speech Communication in Society. 2nd ed. 1977. text ed. 14.95 (ISBN 0-205-05732-2, 4857321); instr's manual o.p. free (ISBN 0-205-05733-0). Allyn.
Heintz, Ann C. Persuasion. LC 71-123207. (Communication Education Ser). (Orig.). (gr. 9-12). 1974. pap. text ed. 3.20 (ISBN 0-8294-0193-8); tchrs guide 1.50 (ISBN 0-8294-0194-6); audio input tape 6.25 (ISBN 0-685-04189-1). Loyola.
Hughey, J. D. & Johnson, Arlee W. Speech Communication: Foundation & Challenges. 1975. pap. 13.95 (ISBN 0-02-358230-8). Macmillan.
Hunsinger, Carlos L. The Art of Argument. LC 79-15660. 1981. 10.95 (ISBN 0-87949-154-X). Ashley Bks.
Hyatt, Ada. The Place of Oral Reading in the School Program: Its History & Development from 1880-1941. LC 76-176891. (Columbia University. Teachers College. Contributions to Education: No. 872). Repr. of 1943 ed. 17.50 (ISBN 0-404-55872-0). AMS Pr.
Jabusch, David M. & Littlejohn, Stephen. Elements of Speech Communication: Achieving Competency. LC 80-82760. (Illus.). 464p. 1981. pap. text ed. 11.50 (ISBN 0-395-29730-3); instrs' manual 0.75 (ISBN 0-395-29731-1). HM.
Kelley, Joseph J., Jr. Speechwriting: A Handbook for All Occasions. 1981. pap. 6.95 (ISBN 0-452-25299-7, Z5299, Plume). NAL.
Lieberson, Stanley, ed. Explorations in Sociolinguistics. 3rd ed. LC 67-65323. (General Publications Ser: Vol. 44). (Orig.). 1971. pap. text ed. 8.00x (ISBN 0-87750-132-7). Res Ctr Lang Semiotic.
McCroskey, James. Introduction to Rhetorical Communication. 3rd ed. 1977. pap. 14.95 (ISBN 0-13-495432-7). P-H.
McGann, Mary. Coping with Language: Talk Your Way to Success. (Coping with Ser.). 1980. lib. bdg. 7.97 (ISBN 0-8239-0518-7). Rosen Pr.
Marcus, Marie. Diagnostic Teaching of the Language Arts. LC 76-52400. 1977. text ed. 24.95x (ISBN 0-471-56854-6). Wiley.
Mattes, Larry. Classroom Oral Language Development: An Elementary School Oral Language Curriculum. 126p. Date not set. price not set (ISBN 0-398-04584-4). C C Thomas.
Measell. An Overview of Speaking Situations. Applbaum, Ronald & Hart, Roderick, eds. LC 77-11907. (MODCOM - Modules in Speech Communication). 1978. pap. text ed. 2.50 (ISBN 0-574-22530-7, 13-5530). SRA.
Merenda, Merilyn & Polichak, C. W. Speech Communication & Theatre Arts: A Classified Bibliography of Theses & Dissertations, 1937-1978. LC 79-9373. 340p. 1979. 75.00 (ISBN 0-306-65182-3). IFI Plenum.
Minchew, Michael & Minchew, Norma. Oral Communication: The Essential Skill. 102p. (Orig.). 1980. pap. 5.95 (ISBN 0-89459-083-9). Hunter NC.
Monroe, Alan H., et al. Principles & Types of Speech Communication. 8th ed. 1978. text ed. 12.95x (ISBN 0-673-15118-2). Scott F.
Morlan, Don M. & Tuttle, George E., Jr. Specific Situations in Effective Oral Communication. (gr. 12). 1977. pap. 9.50 (ISBN 0-672-61410-3); tchr's manual 3.33 (ISBN 0-672-61411-1). Bobbs.
Murray, Edwood. The Speech Personality. 565p. 1981. Repr. of 1944 ed. lib. bdg. 30.00 (ISBN 0-89984-340-9). Century Bookbindery.
Murray, Elwood, et al. Speech: Science-Art. LC 79-77823. 1969. text ed. 11.50 (ISBN 0-672-60863-4). Bobbs.
Nadeau, Ray E. Speech-Communication: A Modern Approach. (gr. 9-12). 1973. text ed. 10.08 (ISBN 0-201-05001-3, Sch Div); text ed. 7.24 softbound (ISBN 0-201-05002-1). A-W.
Nadeau, Ray E. & Muchmore, John M. Speech Communication: A Career Education Approach. 2nd ed. LC 78-18640. (Speech Ser.). 1979. text ed. 12.50 (ISBN 0-201-05007-2). A-W.
Nadeau, Raymond E. A Modern Rhetoric of Speech-Communication. 2nd ed. LC 74-167994. (Speech Ser). 1972. text ed. 11.95 (ISBN 0-201-04999-6). A-W.
Nierenberg, Gerard & Calero, Henry. Meta-Talk. 1975. pap. 1.50 (ISBN 0-671-78879-5). PB.
Pelsma, John R. Essentials of Speech. 326p. 1981. Repr. of 1924 ed. lib. bdg. 25.00 (ISBN 0-89760-712-0). Telegraph Bks.
Pendergast, Kathleen, et al. Photo Articulation Test. text ed. 15.95x (ISBN 0-8134-1064-9, 1064). Interstate.
Possien, Wilma M. They All Need to Talk: Oral Communication in the Language Arts Program. (Orig.). 1969. pap. 9.95 (ISBN 0-13-917088-X). P-H.
Ross, Raymond S. Speech Communication: Fundamentals & Practice. 5th ed. (Communication Ser.). (Illus.). 1980. text ed. 12.95 (ISBN 0-13-827493-2). P-H.
St. Louis, Kenneth O. & Ruscello, Dennis M. Oral Speech Mechanism Screening Examination. 48p. 1981. pap. 13.95 (ISBN 0-8391-1665-9). Univ Park.
Samovar, Larry & Mills, Jack. Oral Communication: Message & Response. 4th ed. 310p. 1980. pap. text ed. write for info. (ISBN 0-697-04165-4); instr's. manual avail. (ISBN 0-697-04175-1). Wm C Brown.
Samovar, Larry A., et al. Speech Communication in Business & the Professions. 256p. 1981. pap. text ed. 10.95x (ISBN 0-534-00974-3). Wadsworth Pub.
Sarbaugh, Larry E. Teaching Speech Communication. (General Education Ser.). 1979. text ed. 15.95 (ISBN 0-675-08300-1). Merrill.
Schanker, Harry H. The Spoken Word. Rothermich, John A., ed. LC 80-24143. (Illus.). 384p. 1981. text ed. 11.96 (ISBN 0-07-055135-9); tchrs. manual 2.00 (ISBN 0-07-055136-7). McGraw.
Scheidel, Thomas M. Speech Communication & Human Interaction. 2nd ed. 1976. text ed. 10.95x (ISBN 0-673-15005-4). Scott F.
Sered, Joan B. Oral Communication. 1978. pap. text ed. 7.95x (ISBN 0-02-471260-4). Macmillan.
Snell, Frank. How to Stand up & Speak Well in Business. 1968. 3.95 (ISBN 0-346-12307-0). Cornerstone.
Speier, Matthew. How to Observe Face to Face Communication: A Sociological Introduction. LC 72-88567. 208p. 1973. pap. text ed. 11.95 (ISBN 0-87620-390-X). Goodyear.
Stewart, C. On Speech Communication. LC 75-187109. 1972. text ed. 7.95 (ISBN 0-03-086734-7, HoltC). HR&W.
Stolz, Benjamin A. & Shannon, Richard S., eds. Oral Literature & the Formula. LC 76-29202. 290p. (Orig.). 1976. pap. 10.00 (ISBN 0-915932-03-2). Trillium Pr.
Sudnow, D. Studies in Social Interaction. LC 79-168542. 1972. 14.95 (ISBN 0-02-932360-6). Free Pr.
Tacey, William S. Business & Professional Speaking. 3rd ed. 260p. 1980. pap. text ed. write for info. (ISBN 0-697-04163-8). Wm C Brown.
Thomlinson, T. Dean. Dialogic Communication. 1982. text ed. 14.95x (ISBN 0-582-28297-7); pap. text ed. 8.95x (ISBN 0-582-28296-9). Longman.
Tubbs, Stewart L. Systems Approach to Small Group Interaction. (Speech Communication Ser.). (Illus.). text ed. 13.95 (ISBN 0-201-07608-X); 2.00 (ISBN 0-201-07607-1). A-W.
Weaver, Richard, 2nd. Speech Communication: A Reader. 1975. text ed. 6.50 (ISBN 0-88429-014-X). Collegiate Pub.
Weiss, Harold & McGrath, J. B. Technically Speaking: Oral Communication for Engineers, Scientists & Technical Personnel. 1963. 16.75x (ISBN 0-07-069085-5, C). McGraw.
Welden, Terry A. & Ellingsworth, Huber W. Effective Speech-Communication: Theory in Action. 1970. pap. 6.95x (ISBN 0-673-05026-2). Scott F.
Werner, Heinz, ed. On Expressive Language. LC 55-4041. (Monographs in Psychology & Related Disciplines: No. 1). 81p. 1955. pap. 1.00x (ISBN 0-914206-02-8). Clark U Pr.
White, Eugene E., ed. Rhetoric in Transition: Studies in the Nature & Uses of Rhetoric. LC 79-15061. 1980. text ed. 15.95x (ISBN 0-271-00223-9). Pa St U Pr.
Wood, Barbara. Children & Communication: Verbal & Non-Verbal Language Development. LC 75-22452. (Speech Communication Ser.). (Illus.). 336p. 1976. text ed. 15.95x (ISBN 0-13-131896-9). P-H.

Young, Robert D. Be Brief About It. LC 80-16436. 1980. pap. 7.95 (ISBN 0-664-24321-5). Westminster.

Zannes, Estelle & Goldhaber, Gerald. Stand up & Speak Out. LC 77-76121. (Speech Communication Ser.). (Illus.). 1978. pap. text ed. 10.95 (ISBN 0-201-08987-4); instr's guide 2.50 (ISBN 0-201-08988-2). A-W.

Zelko, Harold P. & Dance, Frank E. Business & Professional Speech Communication. 2nd ed. LC 77-19074. 1978. 16.95 (ISBN 0-03-018891-1, HoltC). HR&W.

Zimmerman, Gordon, et al. Speech Communication: A Contemporary Introduction. 2nd ed. (Illus.). 1980. pap. 14.95 (ISBN 0-8299-0326-7). West Pub.

Zimmerman, Gordon I., et al. Speech Communication: A Contemporary Introduction. (Illus.). 1977. pap. text ed. 11.50 (ISBN 0-8299-0055-1); instrs.' manual avail. (ISBN 0-8299-0587-1). West Pub.

ORAL COMMUNICATION–RESEARCH

see Speech–Research

ORAL CONTRACEPTIVES

Bickerstaff, Edwin R. Neurological Complications of Oral Contraceptives. (Oxford Neurological Monographs). (Illus.). 120p. 1975. pap. text ed. 19.50x (ISBN 0-19-857207-7). Oxford U Pr.

Boffa, P. S., et al. Pathological Effects of Oral Contraceptives. LC 72-13565. (Illus.). 220p. 1973. text ed. 26.00x (ISBN 0-8422-7081-7). Irvington.

Briggs, Michael & Briggs, Maxine. Oral Contraceptives, Vol. 1. LC 77-670169. (Annual Research Reviews Ser.). 1977. 14.40 (ISBN 0-88831-005-6). Eden Med Res.

--Oral Contraceptives, Vol. 2. LC 77-670169. (Annual Research Reviews Ser.). 1978. 19.20 (ISBN 0-88831-020-X). Eden Med Res.

--Oral Contraceptives, Vol. 3. LC 77-670169. (Annual Research Reviews). 1979. 26.00 (ISBN 0-88831-053-6). Eden Med Res.

--Oral Contraceptives, Vol. 4. Horrobin, D. F., ed. (Annual Research Reviews Ser.). 232p. 1980. 30.00 (ISBN 0-88831-078-1). Eden Med Res.

Briggs, Michael, et al. Oral Contraceptives. (Annual Research Reviews: Vol. 5). 331p. 1981. 36.00 (ISBN 0-88831-096-X). Eden Med Res.

Dickey, Richard P. Managing Contraceptive Pill Patients. 2nd rev. ed. LC 76-29294. (Illus.). 116p. 1980. vinyl 7.95 (ISBN 0-917634-08-X). Creative Infomatics.

Guillebaud, John. The Pill. (Illus.). 196p. 1980. 16.95 (ISBN 0-19-217675-7); pap. 6.95 (ISBN 0-19-286002-X). Oxford U Pr.

Hepatic Tumors & Oral Contraceptives. (Landmark Ser.). 1979. 22.50x (ISBN 0-8422-4128-0). Irvington.

Kay, C. R. Oral Contraceptives & Health. 1974. pap. text ed. 11.00x (ISBN 0-272-79342-6). State Mutual Bk.

Kolbe, H. K. Oral Contraceptives Abstracts: A Guide to the Literature, 1977-1979. 1980. 75.00 (ISBN 0-306-65192-0). Plenum Pub.

Kolbe, Helen K. Oral Contraceptives Abstracts--a Guide to the Literature: 1977-1979. (Population Information Library Ser.: Vol. 2). 565p. 1980. 75.00 (ISBN 0-306-65192-0). IFI Plenum.

The Male Birth Control Pill. (Landmark Ser.). 1979. 22.50x (ISBN 0-8422-4110-8). Irvington.

Moghissi, Kamran S., ed. Controversies in Contraception. LC 78-15812. 250p. 1979. 15.00 (ISBN 0-686-74095-5). Krieger.

Oral Contraceptives. (Landmark Ser.). 1979. 22.50x (ISBN 0-8422-4129-9). Irvington.

Rose, David P., et al. Oral Contraceptives: Psychological & Physiological Effects. new ed. (Illus.). 220p. 1973. text ed. 29.00x (ISBN 0-8422-7101-5). Irvington.

Salhanick, Hilton A., et al. Metabolic Effects of Gonadal Hormones & Contraceptive Steroids. LC 71-89792. 762p. 1969. 49.50 (ISBN 0-306-30422-8, Plenum Pr). Plenum Pub.

Seaman, Barbara. The Doctors' Case Against the Pill. 264p. 1980. pap. 6.50 (ISBN 0-385-14575-6, Dolp). Doubleday.

Silverberg, Steven G. & Major, Francis J. Estrogens & Cancer. LC 78-17275. 1978. 37.95 (ISBN 0-471-04172-6, Pub. by Wiley Medical). Wiley.

ORAL HISTORY

see also History–Methodology

Baum, Willa K. Transcribing & Editing Oral History. (Illus.). 1977. pap. 6.75 (ISBN 0-910050-26-0). AASLH.

Cash, Joseph H., et al. The Practice of Oral History: A Handbook. Hoover, Herbert T., ed. LC 73-93526. 98p. 1975. 8.50 (ISBN 0-88455-001-X). Microfilming Corp.

Cook, Patsy A., ed. New York Times Oral History Guide, No. 2. 134p. 1979. pap. 17.50 (ISBN 0-667-00620-6). Microfilming Corp.

Curtiss, Richard D., et al, eds. A Guide for Oral History Programs. 10.00 (ISBN 0-930046-03-X). CSUF Oral Hist.

Davis, Cullom, et al. Oral History: From Tape to Type. LC 77-4403. pap. 10.00 (ISBN 0-8389-0230-8). ALA.

Epstein, Ellen R. & Mendelsohn, Rona. Record & Remember. LC 78-1411. 1978. pap. 2.95 (ISBN 0-671-18356-7). Monarch Pr.

Grele, Ronald J., ed. Envelopes of Sound: Six Practitioners Discuss the Method, Theory & Practice of Oral History & Oral Testimony. LC 74-18910. iii, 154p. 1975. 8.95 (ISBN 0-913750-07-7); 2 cassettes of panel discussion 17.95 (ISBN 0-685-51815-9). Precedent Pub.

Key, Betty M. Maryland Manual of Oral History. 1979. 4.00 (ISBN 0-938420-11-9). Md Hist.

Koster, Jeanne, ed. Oral History: Memoirs from Columbia University's Oral History Collection. (MicroSources: Social Science Skills Development Programs). 68p. (gr. 7-12). 1978. 7.95 (ISBN 0-667-00654-0). Microfilming Corp.

Moss, William W. Oral History Program Manual. LC 73-19446. (Special Studies). 122p. 1974. text ed. 24.95 (ISBN 0-275-08370-5). Praeger.

Neunschwander, John. Oral History. new ed. (Developments in Classroom Instruction Ser.). 1976. pap. 2.50 (ISBN 0-8106-1801-X). NEA.

New York Times Oral History Guide, No. 1. LC 76-5389. 244p. 1976. 17.50 (ISBN 0-88455-996-3). Microfilming Corp.

Oblinger, Carl. Interviewing the People of Pennsylvania: A Conceptual Guide to Oral History. 1978. pap. 3.00 (ISBN 0-911124-94-2). Pa Hist & Mus.

Perdue, Theda. Nations Remembered: An Oral History of the Five Civilized Tribes, 1865-1907. LC 79-6828. (Contributions in Ethnic Studies: No. 1). xxiv, 221p. 1980. lib. bdg. 23.95 (ISBN 0-313-22097-2, PFN/). Greenwood.

Thompson, Paul. The Voice of the Past: Oral History. 1978. text ed. 12.95x (ISBN 0-19-215833-3); pap. text ed. 5.95x (ISBN 0-19-289102-2, OPB). Oxford U Pr.

Thompson, Paul & Borrat, Joanna, eds. The Past in the Present: Essays in Oral History. 1980. 30.00x (ISBN 0-7129-0983-4, Pub. by Dawson). State Mutual Bk.

Zimmerman, William. How to Tape Instant Oral Biographies: Instant Oral Biographies. LC 79-56828. (Illus.). 96p. (Orig.). 1981. pap. 4.50 (ISBN 0-935966-00-5, 100). Guarionex Pr.

ORAL INTERPRETATION

see also Reading (Oral); Story-Telling

Aggertt, Otis J. & Bowen, Elbert R. Communicative Reading. 3rd ed. (Illus.). 512p. 1972. text ed. 13.95 (ISBN 0-02-301070-3, 30107). Macmillan.

Applbaum, Ronald & Hart, Roderick, eds. MODCOM Modules in Speech Communication, 22 modules. 1976. Individual Modules. pap. text ed. 2.50 (ISBN 0-686-68014-6); Set. pap. 55.00 (ISBN 0-574-22529-3, 13-5529). SRA.

Bacon, Wallace A. The Art of Interpretation. 3rd ed. LC 78-22101. 1979. pap. text ed. 16.95 (ISBN 0-03-089958-3, HoltC). HR&W.

Bowen, Elbert R., et al. Communicative Reading. 4th ed. (Illus.). 1978. 17.95 (ISBN 0-02-313000-8). Macmillan.

Cohen, Edwin. Oral Interpretation: The Communication of Literature. LC 77-8655. 1977. text ed. 12.95 (ISBN 0-574-22555-2, 13-5555). SRA.

Daniels, Earl, ed. Art of Reading Poetry. facsimile ed. LC 70-103087. (Granger Index Reprint Ser). 1941. 24.00 (ISBN 0-8369-6102-1). Arno.

Ecroyd, Donald & Wagner, Hilda S. Communicate Through Oral Reading. 1979. pap. text ed. 10.50x (ISBN 0-07-018970-6). McGraw.

Fernandez, T. L., ed. Oral Interpretation & the Teaching of English: A Collection of Readings. LC 75-91828. 1969. pap. 3.85 (ISBN 0-8141-3475-0). NCTE.

Geiger, Don. Dramatic Impulse in Modern Poetics. LC 67-26972. 1967. 12.50x (ISBN 0-8071-0506-6). La State U Pr.

Gilbert, Carolyn A. Communicative Performance of Literature. (Illus.). 1977. pap. 10.95 (ISBN 0-02-342900-3). Macmillan.

Gottlieb, Marvin. Oral Interpretation. (Illus.). 1980. text ed. 12.95x (ISBN 0-07-023838-3). McGraw.

Haas, Richard & Williams, David A. The Study of Oral Interpretation: Theory & Comment. LC 74-13539. 252p. 1975. pap. text ed. 5.95 (ISBN 0-672-61226-7). Bobbs.

Hartley, Helene. Tests of the Interpretive Reading of Poetry for Teachers of English. LC 78-176846. (Columbia University. Teachers College. Contributions to Education: No. 433). Repr. of 1930 ed. 17.50 (ISBN 0-404-55433-4). AMS Pr.

Henry, Mabel W., ed. Creative Experiences in Oral Language. 1967. pap. 5.00 (ISBN 0-8141-0902-0). NCTE.

Honko, Lauri & Voigt, Vilmos, eds. Genre, Structure & Reproduction in Oral Literature. (Bibliotheca Uralica: Vol. 5). 188p. 1980. 19.50x (ISBN 963-05-2215-2). Intl Pubns Serv.

Lee, Charlotte. Oral Interpretations. 5th ed. LC 76-13095. (Illus.). 1976. text ed. 16.50 (ISBN 0-395-24547-8). HM.

Lee, Charlotte E. Oral Reading of the Scriptures. 1974. text ed. 14.75 (ISBN 0-395-18940-3). HM.

Long, B., et al. Group Performance of Literature. (Illus.). 1977. pap. text ed. 15.95 (ISBN 0-13-365346-3). P-H.

Maclay, Joanna Hawkins. Readers Theatre: Toward a Grammar of Practise. 1970. pap. text ed. 3.50x (ISBN 0-394-30371-7). Phila Bk Co.

Maclay, Joanna M. & Sloan, Thomas O., eds. Interpretation: An Approach to the Study of Literature. 1972. pap. text ed. 3.95x (ISBN 0-685-69594-8). Phila Bk Co.

Robb, Mary M. Oral Interpretation of Literature in American Colleges & Universities. rev. ed. 1968. Repr. of 1941 ed. 15.50 (ISBN 0-384-51365-4). Johnson Repr.

Smith. Fundamentals of Oral Interpretation. Applbaum, Ronald & Hart, Roderick, eds. LC 77-12697. (MODCOM - Modules in Speech Communication Ser.). 1978. pap. text ed. 2.50 (ISBN 0-574-22532-3, 13-5532). SRA.

Trotter, Judy. Beyond Borrowed Bathrobes: Guide to Readers Theater Including Two Scripts for Youth & Adults. LC 75-32385. (Illus.). 64p. 1976. pap. 2.25 (ISBN 0-87239-082-9, 2721). Standard Pub.

ORAL LAW (JUDAISM)

see Tradition (Judaism)

ORAL MANIFESTATIONS OF GENERAL DISEASES

Bodak-Gyovai, L. Z. & Manzione, J. V., Jr. Oral Medicine: Patient Evaluation & Management. (Illus.). 202p. 1980. soft cover 17.95 (ISBN 0-683-00901-X). Williams & Wilkins.

Budnick. Handbook of Pediatric Oral Pathology. Date not set. price not set (ISBN 0-8151-1303-X). Year Bk Med.

Chisholm, Derrick M., et al. Introduction to Oral Medicine. (Illus.). 1979. text ed. 18.00 (ISBN 0-7216-2593-2). Saunders.

Frazier, Claude A., ed. Dentistry & the Allergic Patient. (Illus.). 456p. 1973. text ed. 28.75 (ISBN 0-398-02585-1). C C Thomas.

Gardner, A. F. Differential Oral Diagnosis in Systemic Disease. (Illus.). 1976. 22.50 (ISBN 0-8151-3312-X). Year Bk Med.

Gardner, Alvin F. Pathology of Oral Manifestations of Systematic Diseases. 1972. 30.25 (ISBN 0-02-845120-1). Hafner.

Leach, S. A., ed. Dental Plaque & Surface Interactions in the Oral Cavity: Proceedings. (Illus.). 340p. 1980. 40.00 (ISBN 0-904147-15-0); pap. 23.00 (ISBN 0-904147-16-9). Info Retrieval.

Lynch, Malcolm, ed. Burket's Oral Medicine. 7th ed. LC 77-2752. 1977. text ed. 45.00 (ISBN 0-397-52083-2, JBL-Med-Nursing). Har-Row.

McCarthy, Philip L. & Shklar, Gerald. Diseases of the Oral Mucosa. 2nd ed. LC 80-10335. (Illus.). 579p. 1980. text ed. 47.50 (ISBN 0-8121-0641-5). Lea & Febiger.

Mackenzie, Ian C., et al, eds. Oral Premalignancy: Proceedings of the First Dows Symposium. LC 80-17988. (Illus.). 336p. 1980. text ed. 32.50x (ISBN 0-87745-103-6). U of Iowa Pr.

Nally, F. F. & Eggleston, D. J. A Manual of Oral Medicine. 64p. 1973. 7.00x (ISBN 0-7190-0519-1, Pub. by Manchester U Pr England). State Mutual Bk.

Pierce, Roberta B. Tongue Thrust: A Look at Oral Myofunctional Disorders. LC 77-82567. (Cliffs Speech and Hearing Ser.). (Illus.). 1978. pap. text ed. 3.95 (ISBN 0-8220-1822-5). Cliffs.

Sedano, H. O., et al. Oral Manifestations of Inherited Disorders. 1977. 22.95 (ISBN 0-409-95050-5). Butterworth.

Shklar, G. & McCarthy, P. Oral Manifestations of Systemic Disease. 1976. 22.95 (ISBN 0-409-95002-5). Butterworth.

Smith, Roy M., et al. Atlas of Oral Pathology. LC 81-2388. (Illus.). 263p. 1981. text ed. 28.50 (ISBN 0-8016-4684-7). Mosby.

Strassburg, M. & Knolie, G. Disease of the Oral Mucosa: A Color Atlas. (Illus.). 270p. 1972. 58.00 (ISBN 0-686-29192-1). Quint Pub Co.

Wahl, Norman. Oral Signs & Symptoms: A Diagnostic Handbook, a Guide to the Identification of Lesions of the Mouth. (Illus.). 332p. 1969. photocopy ed. spiral 32.75 (ISBN 0-398-01999-1). C C Thomas.

Wood, Norman K. & Goaz, Paul W. Differential Diagnosis of Oral Lesions. 2nd ed. LC 80-18691. (Illus.). text ed. 39.50 (ISBN 0-8016-5617-6). Mosby.

Young, William G. & Sedano, Heddie O. Atlas of Oral Pathology. LC 80-29439. (Illus.). 256p. 1981. 25.00x (ISBN 0-8166-1040-1). U of Minn Pr.

ORAL MEDICATION

Anderson, J. A., ed. Self-Medication. 1979. text ed. 16.50 (ISBN 0-85200-282-3). Univ Park.

Bloomfield, Dennis A. & Simon, Hansjorg. Cardio Active Drugs: A Pharmacological Basis for Practice. 1982. price not set (ISBN 0-8067-1851-X). Urban & S.

Davis, Neil M. & Cohen, Michael R. Medication Errors: Causes & Prevention. (Illus.). 160p. 1981. text ed. 15.95 (ISBN 0-89313-051-6). G F Stickley.

Giving Medications. LC 80-14474. (Nursing Photobook). (Illus.). 160p. 1980. text ed. 12.95 (ISBN 0-916730-22-0). InterMed Comm.

Jones, Judith K. Good Housekeeping Family Guide to Medications. rev. ed. 320p. 1980. 16.95 (ISBN 0-87851-041-9). Hearst Bks.

Kisban, George. The Getting Well Timetable. 220p. (YA) 1981. pap. 7.00 (ISBN 0-939308-00-2, 81-83324). Med Info Pubns.

McEntyre, Robert L. Key Medications: A Practical Guide. LC 79-67794. 282p. 1980. pap. text ed. 9.95 (ISBN 0-7216-5904-7). Saunders.

Medications & Mathematics for the Nurse. 288p. 1981. text ed. 13.95 (ISBN 0-442-21882-6). Van Nos Reinhold.

Smith, Dorothy L. Medication Guide for Patient Counseling. 2nd ed. LC 81-6053. (Illus.). 445p. 1981. pap. write for info. (ISBN 0-8121-0791-8). Lea & Febiger.

Tyldesley, W. R. Color Atlas of Oral Medicine. (Illus.). 1978. 37.50 (ISBN 0-8151-8897-8). Year Bk Med.

ORAL MICROBIOLOGY

see Mouth–Microbiology

ORAL PLEADING

see also Forensic Orations

Re, Edward D. Brief Writing & Oral Argument. 4th rev ed. LC 73-11059. 400p. 1977. 15.00 (ISBN 0-686-57657-8). Oceana.

ORAL RADIOLOGY

see Teeth–Radiography

ORAL READING

see Reading (Oral)

ORAL SURGERY

see Mouth–Surgery

ORAL TRADITION

Finnegan, Ruth. Oral Poetry: Its Nature, Significance Social Context. LC 76-11077. (Illus.). 1977. 32.00 (ISBN 0-521-21316-9). Cambridge U Pr.

Honti, Janos. Studies in Oral Epic Tradition. 206p. 1976. 12.00x (ISBN 963-05-0418-9). Intl Pubns Serv.

Hymes, Dell. In Vain I Tried to Tell You: Essays in Native American Ethnopoetics. LC 81-51138. (Conduct & Communication Ser.). 416p. (Orig.). 1981. 35.00x (ISBN 0-8122-7806-2); pap. 12.95x (ISBN 0-8122-1117-0). U of Pa Pr.

Irwin, Paul. Liptako Speaks: History from Oral Tradition in Africa. LC 80-7531. (Illus.). 250p. 1981. 18.50 (ISBN 0-691-05309-X). Princeton U Pr.

Jason, Heda & Segal, Dimitri, eds. Patterns in Oral Literature. (World Anthropology Ser.). 1977. text ed. 33.00x (ISBN 90-279-7969-3). Mouton.

--Patterns in Oral Literature. (World Anthropology Ser.: Vol. 48). 1978. 28.00 (ISBN 0-202-90048-7). Beresford Bk Serv.

Kirk, G. S. Homer & the Oral Tradition. LC 76-7806. 1977. 28.50 (ISBN 0-521-21309-6). Cambridge U Pr.

Miller, Joseph C. The African Past Speaks: Essays on Oral Tradition & History. (Illus.). 248p. 1980. 27.50 (ISBN 0-208-01784-4, Archon). Shoe String.

Shils, Edward. Tradition. LC 80-21643. 320p. 1981. lib. bdg. 20.00x (ISBN 0-226-75325-5). U of Chicago Pr.

Wilson, Jane B. The Story Experience. LC 79-13888. 177p. 1979. 10.00 (ISBN 0-8108-1224-X). Scarecrow.

Wright, H. Curtis. The Oral Antecedents of Greek Librarianship. LC 77-73645. 1977. 19.95x (ISBN 0-8425-0623-3). Brigham.

ORAL TRADITION (JUDAISM)

see Tradition (Judaism)

ORANGE

McPhee, John. Oranges. 1967. 7.50 (ISBN 0-374-22688-1); pap. 3.95 (ISBN 0-374-51297-3). FS&G.

Opland, Jeff. Anglo-Saxon Oral Poetry: A Study of the Traditions. LC 79-24202. 304p. 1980. text ed. 25.00x (ISBN 0-300-02426-6). Yale U Pr.

ORANGE–MARKETING

Goldberg, Ray A. Agribusiness Coordination: A Systems Approach to the Wheat, Soybean & Florida Orange Economies. LC 68-118718. (Concepts in Agribusinesss Management Ser.). 256p. 1965. 25.00 (ISBN 0-88410-270-X). Ballinger Pub.

ORANGE COUNTY, CALIFORNIA

Lamb, Karl A. As Orange Goes: Twelve California Families & the Future of American Politics. 1974. 8.95x (ISBN 0-393-05520-5); pap. 6.95x (ISBN 0-393-09235-6). Norton.

Lewis, Paul M. Beautiful Orange County. Shangle, Robert D., ed. LC 80-25846. (Illus.). 72p. 1980. 14.95 (ISBN 0-89802-174-X); pap. 7.95 (ISBN 0-89802-173-1). Beautiful Am.

Meadows, Don. Historic Place Names of Orange County. (Illus.). 1966. 9.50 (ISBN 0-685-59751-2). Acoma Bks.

ORANGE COUNTY, VIRGINIA

Scott, William W. A History of Orange County, Virginia. (Illus.). 292p. Repr. of 1907 ed. 16.00x (ISBN 0-685-65084-7). Va Bk.

ORANGE FREE STATE

Bleloch, William E. New South Africa: Its Value & Development. LC 69-18973. (Illus.). Repr. of 1901 ed. 26.00x (ISBN 0-8371-0923-X, Pub. by Negro U Pr). Greenwood.

Botha, Colin G. Public Archives of South Africa, Sixteen Fifty-Two to Nineteen Hundred & Ten. LC 70-82015. 1969. Repr. of 1928 ed. lib. bdg. 19.50 (ISBN 0-8337-0340-4). B Franklin.

Braby's Orange Free State Directory 1979-80: Oranje Vrystaat Adresboek 1979-80. 64th ed. LC 53-32833. (Illus.). 168p. (Orig., Eng. & Afrikaans.). 1979. pap. 12.50x (ISBN 0-8002-2316-0). Intl Pubns Serv.

Collins, W. Free Statia, or Reminiscences of a Lifetime in the Orange Free State, South Africa, 1852-1875. (Africana Collectanea Ser: No. 12). 1965. Repr. of 1907 ed. 18.00x (ISBN 0-8426-1212-2). Verry.

The Orange Free State: Annotated Guide to the Pre-Union Government Publications,1854-1910. 1976. lib. bdg. 18.00 (ISBN 0-8161-7959-X). G K Hall.

ORANGE-NASSAU, HOUSE OF

Ryskamp, Charles & Vliegenthart, A. W. William & Mary & Their House. (Illus.). 266p. 1980. 59.00x (ISBN 0-19-520185-X). Oxford U Pr.

ORANGEBURG COUNTY, SOUTH CAROLINA

Salley, Alexander S., Jr. History of Orangeburg County, South Carolina: From Its First Settlement to the Close of the Revolutionary War. LC 70-88165. (Illus.). 1978. Repr. of 1898 ed. 20.00 (ISBN 0-8063-7964-2). Regional.

ORANGUTANS

Amon, Aline. Orangutan: Endangered Ape. LC 76-41354. (Illus.). (gr. 4-6). 1977. 7.95 (ISBN 0-689-30563-X). Atheneum.

Laidler, Kieth. The Talking Ape. LC 80-5388. (Illus.). 160p. 1980. 11.95 (ISBN 0-8128-2731-7). Stein & Day.

Maple, Terry L. Orang-Utan Behavior. (Van Nostrand Reinhold Primate Behavior & Development Ser.). 272p. 1980. text ed. 25.00 (ISBN 0-442-25154-8). Van Nos Reinhold.

Wildlife Education, Ltd. Orangutans. (Zoobooks). (Illus.). 20p. (Orig.). 1980. pap. 1.50 (ISBN 0-937934-02-X). Wildlife Educ.

ORATIONS

Here are entered collections of orations. Works on famous orations are entered under subdivision History and criticism.

see also Forensic Orations; Oratory; Public Speaking

also American Orations, English Orations and similar headings

Bechtel, John H., ed. Select Speeches for Declamation. facsimile ed. LC 75-103083. (Granger Index Reprint Ser). 1898. 15.00 (ISBN 0-8369-6098-X). Arno.

Brewer, David J., ed. World's Best Orations, 2 Vols. LC 75-15323. 1970. Repr. of 1901 ed. Set. 99.50 (ISBN 0-8108-0341-0). Scarecrow.

Brown, George, ed. The Voices of History. LC 79-65122. 1980. 12.95 (ISBN 0-8128-2691-4). Stein & Day.

Chandler, Raymond. Raymond Chandler Speaking. fascimile ed. Gardiner, Dorothy & Sorley, Kathrine, eds. LC 76-146855. (Select Bibliographies Reprint Ser.). 1972. Repr. of 1962 ed. 20.00 (ISBN 0-8369-5622-2). Arno.

Cicero. Cicero's Selected Orations. annotated ed. 232p. 1961. 2.00 (ISBN 0-685-27927-8). Landau.

--De Oratore, Bks 1 & 2, Vol. 3. (Loeb Classical Library: No. 348). 11.00x (ISBN 0-674-99383-7). Harvard U Pr.

Copeland, Lewis & Lamm, Lawrence, eds. World's Great Speeches. 3rd rev. ed. 1958. pap. 8.95 (ISBN 0-486-20468-5). Dover.

Demosthenes. Orations of Demosthenes, 2 vols. Kennedy, C. R., ed. 1977. Set. lib. bdg. 250.00 (ISBN 0-8490-2378-5). Gordon Pr.

Fobes, Walter K., ed. Five-Minute Declamations, First Pt. facs. ed. LC 71-139761. (Granger Index Reprint Ser). 1885. 15.00 (ISBN 0-8369-6215-X). Arno.

--Five-Minute Declamations, Second Pt. facs. ed. LC 71-139761. (Granger Index Reprint Ser). 1890. 16.00 (ISBN 0-8369-6216-8). Arno.

Godwin, Parke. Commemorative Addresses: G. W. Curtis, E. Booth, L. Kossuth, J. J. Audubon, W.C. Bryant. 1977. Repr. of 1895 ed. lib. bdg. 25.00 (ISBN 0-8414-4602-4). Folcroft.

Grimes, Joseph E. Papers on Discourse. (Publications in Linguistics & Related Fields Ser: No. 51). 1976. pap. 10.50 (ISBN 0-88312-061-5); microfiche 3.40 (ISBN 0-88312-461-0). Summer Inst Ling.

Hays, Edward M. Oraciones de la Familia hispan para todas ocasiones. Velasco, Amparo & Velasco, Asterio, trs. 56p. 1981. pap. 1.95 (ISBN 0-89570-202-9). Claretian Pubns.

Levens, R. G. Cicero: Verrine Orations V. 1946. 6.95 (ISBN 0-312-13825-3). St Martin.

Maurois, Andre. Discours de Reception a l'Academie Francaise. pap. 4.95 (ISBN 0-685-36933-1). French & Eur.

Terry, J. & Upton, D. Cicero: Speeches Against Antony, Philippics 4, 5, 6. (Modern School Classics Ser.). 1970. 5.95 (ISBN 0-312-13650-1). St Martin.

ORATIONS-INDEXS

Sutton, Roberta B. Speech Index. 4th ed. LC 66-13749. 1966. 29.50 (ISBN 0-8108-0138-8). Scarecrow.

ORATORIO

Baker, David E., et al. Biographia Dramatica, or Companion to the Playhouse, 4 pts. in 3 vols. LC 70-159990. (BCL Ser. I). Repr. of 1812 ed. Set. 110.00 (ISBN 0-404-00530-6); 39.50 ea. Vol. 1 (ISBN 0-404-00531-4). Vol. 2 (ISBN 0-404-00532-2). Vol. 3 (ISBN 0-404-00533-0). AMS Pr.

ORATORIO SOCIETY OF NEW YORK

Krehbiel, Henry E. Notes on the Cultivation of Choral Music & the Oratorio Society of New York. LC 75-137315. Repr. of 1884 ed. 11.00 (ISBN 0-404-03782-8). AMS Pr.

ORATORS

Auden, Wystan H. The Orators: An English Study. LC 77-131613. 116p. 1932. Repr. 19.00 (ISBN 0-403-00500-0). Scholarly.

Baskerville, Barnet. The People's Voice: The Orator in American Society. LC 79-4001. 272p. 1979. 17.00 (ISBN 0-8131-1385-7). U Pr of Ky.

Blyton, Gifford & Capps, Randall. Speaking Out: Two Centuries of Kentucky Orators. LC 77-88242. (Illus.). 1977. text ed. 10.00 (ISBN 0-89459-022-7). Hunter NC.

Boulware, Marcus H. Oratory of Negro Leaders: Nineteen Hunderd - Nineteen Sixty-Eight. LC 72-90794. 1969. lib. bdg. 16.95x (ISBN 0-8371-1849-2); pap. 4.95 (ISBN 0-8371-7353-1). Greenwood.

Dobson, John F. Greek Orators. facs. ed. LC 67-23205. (Essay Index Reprint Ser). 1919. 19.00 (ISBN 0-8369-0381-1). Arno.

Drerup, Engelbert. Aus Einer Alten Advokatenrepublik. 1916. pap. 12.50 (ISBN 0-384-12800-9). Johnson Repr.

Goodrich, Chauncey A. Essays from Select British Eloquence. Baird, A. Craig, ed. LC 63-7978. (Landmarks in Rhetoric & Public Address Ser.). 407p. 1963. 9.95x (ISBN 0-8093-0095-8). S Ill U Pr.

Hawthorne, Julian. Orations of American Orators, Including Biographical & Critical Sketches, 2 vols. 1900. Set. 45.00 (ISBN 0-686-17684-7). Quaker City.

--Orations of British Orators, 2 vols. 1900. Repr. 50.00 set (ISBN 0-8274-3076-0). R West.

Humes, James C. Roles Speakers Play. LC 75-25042. 256p. 1976. 10.95 (ISBN 0-06-012003-7, HarpT). Har-Row.

Jebb, Richard C. Attic Orators from Antiphon to Isaeos, 2 Vols. LC 62-8230. 1962. Repr. of 1875 ed. Set. 20.00 (ISBN 0-8462-0208-5). Russell.

Jones, Edgar D. Lords of Speech. facs. ed. LC 68-58799. (Essay Index Reprint Ser). 1937. 15.50 (ISBN 0-8369-1040-0). Arno.

Jones, Edgar DeWitt. Masters of Speech: Portraits of Fifteen American Orators. (Speakers' & Toastmasters' Library). Orig. Title: Lords of Speech. 362p. 1975. pap. 3.95 (ISBN 0-8010-5063-4). Baker Bk.

Kettle, T. M. Irish Orators & Oratory. Repr. lib. bdg. 50.00 (ISBN 0-8414-5570-8). Folcroft.

Langer, Howard J., ed. Directory of Speakers. 1981. pap. 37.50 (ISBN 0-912700-26-2). Oryx Pr.

Mark, Michael Z. The Struggle to Construct & Disseminate a Philosophy of Life: An Autobiography. 1978. 14.95 (ISBN 0-533-03055-2). Vantage.

Oliver, Robert T. Four Who Spoke Out. LC 75-101831. (Biography Index Reprint Ser). 1946. 17.00 (ISBN 0-8369-8005-0). Arno.

ORATORS, AFRO-AMERICAN

see Afro-American Orators

ORATORY

see also Debates and Debating; Gesture; Lectures and Lecturing; Orations; Persuasion (Rhetoric); Public Speaking

Adams, John Q. Lectures on Rhetoric & Oratory, 2 Vols. LC 62-18161. (With a new intro. by J. J. Auer & J. L. Banninga). 1962. Repr. of 1810 ed. Set. 30.00 (ISBN 0-8462-0104-6). Russell.

Austin, Gilbert. Chironomia: Or, a Treatise on Rhetorical Delivery. Robb, Mary M. & Thonssen, Lester, eds. LC 66-17967. (Landmarks in Rhetoric & Public Address Ser). (Illus.). 658p. 1966. 12.50x (ISBN 0-8093-0229-2). S Ill U Pr.

Barrett, Harold, ed. Rhetoric of the People: Is There Any Better or Equal Hope in the World? 335p. (Orig.). 1974. pap. text ed. 16.75x (ISBN 90-6203-001-7). Humanities.

Baskerville, Barnet. The People's Voice: The Orator in American Society. LC 79-4001. 272p. 1979. 17.00 (ISBN 0-8131-1385-7). U Pr of Ky.

Bloch, Maurice, ed. Political Language & Oratory in Traditional Society. 1975. 36.00 (ISBN 0-12-106850-1). Acad Pr.

Braden, Waldo W., ed. Oratory in the New South. LC 78-25909. 1979. 20.00x (ISBN 0-8071-0472-8). La State U Pr.

Bryant, Donald C. Rhetorical Dimensions in Criticism. LC 72-94149. 146p. 1973. 12.50x (ISBN 0-8071-0214-8). La State U Pr.

Buehler, Ezra C. & Johannesen, Richard L. Building the Contest Oration. 1965. 6.50 (ISBN 0-8242-0008-X). Wilson.

Bulwer, John. Chirologia; or the Natural Language of the Hand. Chironomia; or the Art of Manual Rhetoric. Cleary, James W., ed. LC 76-132492. (Landmarks in Rhetoric & Public Address Ser.). 380p. 1974. 19.50x (ISBN 0-8093-0497-X). S Ill U Pr.

Bury. Modern Oratory. 1929. Repr. 7.50 (ISBN 0-8274-2753-0). R West.

Chavez, Moises. Modelo de Oratoria. 144p. (Orig., Span.). 1979. pap. 3.50 (ISBN 0-89922-141-6). Edit Caribe.

Kettle, T. M. Irish Orators & Oratory. Repr. lib. bdg. 50.00 (ISBN 0-8414-5570-8). Folcroft.

Lawson, John. Lectures Concerning Oratory. facsimile ed. Claussen, E. Neal & Wallace, Karl R., eds. LC 78-156792. (Landmarks in Rhetoric & Public Address Ser.). 530p. 1972. 15.00x (ISBN 0-8093-0519-4). S Ill U Pr.

Logue, Cal M., ed. Oratory of Southern Demagogues. xxii, 234p. 1981. 22.50 (ISBN 0-8071-0792-1). La State U Pr.

McCurdy, Frances L. Stump, Bar & Pulpit: Speechmaking on the Missouri Frontier. LC 74-93050. 1969. 9.00x (ISBN 0-8262-0081-8). U of Mo Pr.

Nadeau, Raymond E. A Modern Rhetoric of Speech-Communication. 2nd ed. LC 74-167994. (Speech Ser). 1972. text ed. 11.95 (ISBN 0-201-04999-6). A-W.

Nichols, Marie H. Rhetoric & Criticism. LC 63-7958. 1967. pap. text ed. 4.95x (ISBN 0-8071-0122-2). La State U Pr.

Nilsen, Thomas R. Essays on Rhetorical Criticism. LC 68-13156. 1968. text ed. 8.50x (ISBN 0-685-19690-9). Phila Bk Co.

Oliver, Robert T. History of Public Speaking in America. LC 78-13428. 1978. Repr. of 1965 ed. lib. bdg. 43.00 (ISBN 0-313-21152-3, OLPS). Greenwood.

Quintilian. On the Early Education of the Citizen-Orator. rev. ed. Watson, John S., tr. 1965. pap. 5.50 (ISBN 0-672-60474-4). Bobbs.

Sears, Lorenzo. The History of Oratory from the Age of Pericles to the Present Time. 69.95 (ISBN 0-8490-0341-5). Gordon Pr.

--The History of Oratory from the Age of Pericles to the Present Time. Repr. 35.00 (ISBN 0-8274-2515-5). R West.

Shaw, Warren C. History of American Oratory, 2 vols. 1979. Repr. of 1928 ed. Set. lib. bdg. 65.00 (ISBN 0-8414-8023-0). Folcroft.

--History of American Oratory, 2 vols. 1928. Repr. 75.00 (ISBN 0-8274-2501-5). R West.

Sheridan, Thomas. Course of Lectures on Elocution. LC 67-23853. 1968. Repr. of 1798 ed. 15.00 (ISBN 0-405-08964-3). Arno.

Shurter, Edwin D. The Rhetoric of Oratory. 1978. Repr. of 1909 ed. lib. bdg. 35.00 (ISBN 0-8495-4860-8). Arden Lib.

Southwick, F. Townsend. Steps to Oratory: A School Speaker. facsimile ed. LC 72-167483. (Granger Index Reprint Ser.). Repr. of 1900 ed. 22.00 (ISBN 0-8369-6288-5). Arno.

Stolz, Benjamin A. & Shannon, Richard S., eds. Oral Literature & the Formula. LC 76-29202. 290p. (Orig.). 1976. pap. 10.00 (ISBN 0-915932-03-2). Trillium Pr.

Wallace, Karl R. Understanding Discourse: The Speech Act & Rhetorical Action. LC 76-103130. (Illus.). 1970. 12.50x (ISBN 0-8071-0925-8). La State U Pr.

ORATORY-BIBLIOGRAPHY

Cleary, James W. & Haberman, Frederick W., eds. Rhetoric & Public Address: A Bibliography, 1947-1961. 506p. 1964. 27.50 (ISBN 0-299-03350-3). U of Wis Pr.

ORATORY-COMPETITIONS

Schrier, William. Contest Oratory: A Handbook for High School & College Contestants & Coaches. LC 71-171595. 1971. 10.00 (ISBN 0-8108-0416-6). Scarecrow.

ORATORY-RESEARCH

see Speech-Research

ORATORY, ANCIENT

see also Greek Orations; Latin Orations

Caplan, Harry. Of Eloquence: Studies in Ancient & Medieval Rhetoric. King, Anne & North, Helen, eds. LC 66-24262. 289p. 1970. 22.50x (ISBN 0-8014-0486-X). Cornell U Pr.

Cicero, Marcus. Cicero's Brutus: Or, History of Famous Orators. Jones, Ernest, tr. LC 72-158313. Repr. of 1776 ed. 34.50 (ISBN 0-404-54106-2). AMS Pr.

Saunders, A. N. Greek Political Oratory. (Penguin Classic Ser.). 1978. pap. 1.95 (ISBN 0-14-044223-5). Penguin.

ORBISTON COMMUNITY

Cullen, Alex. Adventures in Socialism. LC 68-55519. Repr. of 1910 ed. 10.50x (ISBN 0-678-00804-3). Kelley.

Motherwell & Orbiston: The First Owenite Attempts at Cooperative Communities, 1822-1825. LC 72-2534. (British Labour Struggles Before 1850 Ser). 1972. 11.00 (ISBN 0-405-04427-5). Arno.

ORBITAL RENDEZVOUS (SPACE FLIGHT)

see also Project Apollo

ORBITALS, ATOMIC

see Atomic Orbitals

ORBITALS, MOLECULAR

see Molecular Orbitals

ORBITING VEHICLES

see Artificial Satellites; Space Stations

ORBITS

see also Artificial Satellites-Orbits; Mechanics, Celestial

Dow, T. W. Repeal Kepler's Laws. LC 60-13372. 1960. 5.00 (ISBN 0-910340-02-1). Celestial Pr.

Dubyago, A. D. Determination of Orbits. 1961. 16.95 (ISBN 0-02-330330-1, 33033). Macmillan.

Escobal, Pedro R. Methods of Orbit Determination. LC 75-11889. 500p. 1976. Repr. of 1965 ed. 28.50 (ISBN 0-88275-319-3). Krieger.

Moser, Jurgen & Kyner, Walter T. Lectures on Hamiltonian Systems, & Rigorous & Formal Stability of Orbits About an Oblate Planet. LC 52-42839. (Memoirs: No. 81). 1979. pap. 10.40 (ISBN 0-8218-1281-5, MEMO-81). Am Math.

Moulton, Forest R. Periodic Orbits. 1920. 31.00 (ISBN 0-384-40235-6). Johnson Repr.

Roy. Orbital Motion. 1978. 49.50 (ISBN 0-9960019-9-9, Pub. by A Hilger England). Heyden.

Symposia in Applied Mathematics - New York - 1957. Orbit Theory: Proceedings, Vol. 9. Birkhoff, G. & Langer, R. E., eds. LC 50-1183. 1959. 21.20 (ISBN 0-8218-1309-9, PSAPM-9). Am Math.

Symposium, University of Sao Paulo, Sao Paulo, 1969. Periodic Orbits, Stability & Resonances: Proceedings. Giacaglia, G. E., ed. LC 74-124848. 530p. 1970. lib. bdg. 50.00 (ISBN 90-277-0170-9, Pub. by Reidel Holland). Kluwer Boston.

Szebehely, Victor G. Theory of Orbits in the Restricted Problem of Three Bodies. 1967. 51.50 (ISBN 0-12-680650-0). Acad Pr.

ORCHARDS

see Fruit-Culture

ORCHESTRA

see also Bands (Music); Conducting; Conductors (Music); Instrumentation and Orchestration; Orchestral Music; Symphony Orchestras

Bekker, Paul. Orchestra. (Illus.). 1963. pap. 4.95 (ISBN 0-393-00219-5, Norton Lib). Norton.

Carse, Adam Von Ahn. The Orchestra from Beethoven to Berlioz. LC 79-181122. 514p. 1948. Repr. 49.00 (ISBN 0-403-01521-9). Scholarly.

--Orchestral Conducting, a Textbook for Students and Amateurs. LC 78-109716. (Illus.). iv, 100p. Repr. of 1929 ed. lib. bdg. 15.00x (ISBN 0-8371-4206-7, CAOC). Greenwood.

Duck, Leonard. Amateur Orchestra. (Student's Music Library Ser). 1949. 6.95 (ISBN 0-234-77312-X). Dufour.

Ewen, David. Man with the Baton. facs. ed. LC 68-57316. (Essay Index Reprint Ser). 1936. 19.50 (ISBN 0-8369-0433-8). Arno.

Hurd, Michael. The Orchestra. 224p. 1980. 24.95 (ISBN 0-87196-469-4). Facts on File.

Jefferson, Alan. Inside the Orchestra. 1976. 11.50x (ISBN 0-8448-1017-7). Crane-Russak Co.

Mueller, John H. The American Symphony Orchestra: A Social History of Musical Taste. LC 76-8875. (Illus.). 1976. Repr. of 1951 ed. lib. bdg. 27.25x (ISBN 0-8371-8915-2, MUAS). Greenwood.

Neel, Boyd. The Story of an Orchestra. LC 71-181218. 133p. 1950. Repr. 19.00 (ISBN 0-403-01629-0). Scholarly.

Previn, Andre. Orchestra. LC 79-7944. 192p. 1980. 16.95 (ISBN 0-385-15808-4). Doubleday.

Raynor, Henry. The Orchestra: A History. (Illus.). 1978. 12.50 (ISBN 0-684-15535-4; ScribT). Scribner.

Shore, Bernard. Orchestra Speaks. facsimile ed. LC 71-177966. (Essay Index Reprint Ser). Repr. of 1938 ed. 16.00 (ISBN 0-8369-2570-X). Arno.

Singleton, Esther. The Orchestra & Its Instruments. LC 76-22351. (Illus.). 1976. Repr. of 1917 ed. lib. bdg. 40.00 (ISBN 0-89341-004-7). Longwood Pr.

--Orchestra & Its Instruments. 1977. lib. bdg. 69.95 (ISBN 0-8490-2379-3). Gordon Pr.

Stewart, Madeau. The Music Lover's Guide to the Instruments of the Orchestra. 176p. 1980. 18.95 (ISBN 0-442-23358-2). Van Nos Reinhold.

Van Horn, James. The Community Orchestra: A Handbook for Conductors, Managers, & Boards. LC 78-60531. (Illus.). 1979. lib. bdg. 17.50 (ISBN 0-313-20562-0, VCO/). Greenwood.

ORCHESTRA–JUVENILE LITERATURE

Craig, Jean. Heart of the Orchestra: The Story of the Violin & Other Strings. LC 62-20802. (Musical Books for Young People Ser). (Illus.). (gr. 5-11). 1962. PLB 3.95 (ISBN 0-8225-0053-1). Lerner Pubns.

ORCHESTRAL MUSIC

see also Band Music; Concertos; Symphonies

Anthony, James R. Michel-Richard Delalande's "De Profundis:". Grand Motet for Soloists, Chorus, Woodwinds, Strings, & Continuo. LC 79-29740. (Early Musical Masterworks Ser.). viii, 173p. 1981. 21.00 (ISBN 0-8078-1439-3). U of NC Pr.

Biancolli, Louis L., ed. Analytical Concert Guide. LC 77-92295. lib. bdg. 33.75x (ISBN 0-8371-3074-3, BICG). Greenwood.

Churgin, Bathia. Giovanni Batista Sammartini's "Sonate a Tre Stromenti:". Six Notturnos for String Trio, Op. 7. LC 80-12339. (Early Musical Masterworks Ser.). 81p. 1981. 20.00x (ISBN 0-8078-1446-6). U of NC Pr.

Ferguson, Donald N. Masterworks of the Orchestral Repertoire: A Guide for Listeners. LC 54-12315. (Illus.). 1968. 15.00x (ISBN 0-8166-0461-4); pap. 5.95 (ISBN 0-8166-0467-3, MP14). U of Minn Pr.

Hale, Philip. Great Concert Music: Philip Hale's Boston Symphont Programme Notes. Burk, John N., ed. LC 75-109742. xix, 400p. Repr. of 1939 ed. lib. bdg. 17.25x (ISBN 0-8371-4232-6, HACM). Greenwood.

Hinson, Maurice. Music for Piano & Orchestra: An Annotated Guide. LC 80-8380. 352p. 1981. 25.00x (ISBN 0-253-12435-2). Ind U Pr.

Mordden, Ethan. A Guide to Orchestral Music: The Handbook for Non-Musicians. (Illus.). 1980. 19.95 (ISBN 0-19-502686-1). Oxford U Pr.

Newmarch, Rosa. The Concert-Goer's Library of Descriptive Notes, 2 vols. in 1. facsimile ed. LC 70-160984. (Select Bibliographies Reprint Ser). Repr. of 1929 ed. 17.00 (ISBN 0-8369-5852-7). Arno.

Prokofiev, Sergei. Four Orchestral Works: Complete Scores of Peter & the Wolf, Lieutenant Kije Suite, Classical Symphony, & Alexander Nevsky Cantata. Roth, Lewis, ed. 12.50 (ISBN 0-8446-5076-5). Peter Smith.

Smalle, P. W. Instruments & Art of the Orchestra. 1976. lib. bdg. 19.00 (ISBN 0-403-03782-4). Scholarly.

ORCHESTRAL MUSIC–BIBLIOGRAPHY

American Society of Composers, Authors & Publishers, ed. ASCAP Symphonic Catalog 1977. 3rd ed. LC 77-133. 1977. pap. 25.00 (ISBN 0-8352-0910-5). Bowker.

Daniels, David. Orchestral Music: A Source Book. LC 72-6274. 1972. 10.00 (ISBN 0-8108-0537-5). Scarecrow.

Farish, Margaret K., ed. Orchestral Music in Print. LC 79-24460. (Music in Print Ser.: Vol. 5). 1016p. 1979. lib. bdg. 100.00 (ISBN 0-88478-010-4). Musicdata.

--Orchestral Music in Print: Educational Section. LC 78-11929. (Music in Print Ser.). 78p. 1978. pap. 10.00 (ISBN 0-88478-009-0). Musicdata.

Mueller, Kate H. Twenty-Seven Major American Symphony Orchestras: A History & Analysis of Their Repertoires, Seasons 1842-43 Through 1969-1970. LC 72-96549. 464p. 1973. 15.00x (ISBN 0-253-36110-9). Ind U Pr.

Saltonstall, Cecilia D. & Saltonstall, Henry. A New Catalog of Music for Small Orchestra. (Music Indexes & Bibliographies Ser.: No. 14). 1978. 40.00 (ISBN 0-913574-14-7). Eur-Am Music.

Sonneck, Oscar G. Orchestral Music Catalog: Scores. LC 69-12692. (Music Reprint Ser). 1969. Repr. of 1912 ed. lib. bdg. 55.00 (ISBN 0-306-71228-8). Da Capo.

ORCHESTRAL MUSIC–HISTORY AND CRITICISM

Carse, Adam. The Orchestra from Beethoven to Berlioz. new ed. (Illus.). 528p. 1949. 15.00x (ISBN 0-8450-2550-3). Broude.

--The Orchestra in the XVIIIth Century. (Illus.). 184p. 1969. 10.00x (ISBN 0-8450-2551-1). Broude.

Ecorcheville, Jules, ed. Vingt suites d'orchestre du XVIIe siecle francais, 2 vols. (Illus.). 384p. (Fr.). 1971. Repr. of 1906 ed. 185.00x (ISBN 0-8450-1005-0). Broude.

Gal, Hans. Schumann Orchestral Music. LC 79-52145. (BBC Music Guides Ser.: No. 40). (Illus.). 64p. (Orig.). 1980. pap. 2.95 (ISBN 0-295-95696-8). U of Wash Pr.

Ulrich, Homer. Symphonic Music: Its Evolution Since the Renaissance. LC 52-12033. 1952. 20.00x (ISBN 0-231-01908-4). Columbia U Pr.

ORCHESTRATION

see Instrumentation and Orchestration

ORCHID CULTURE

Arditti, Joseph, ed. Orchid Biology: Reviews & Perspectives, I. LC 76-25648. (Illus.). 328p. 1977. 38.50x (ISBN 0-8014-1040-1). Comstock.

Bechtel, Helmut, et al. The Manual of Cultivated Orchid Species. (Illus.). 512p. 1981. 75.00 (ISBN 0-686-73529-3); deluxe ed. 200.00x (ISBN 0-262-02166-8). MIT Pr.

Bowen, Leslie. The Art & Craft of Growing Orchids. LC 75-39781. (Illus.). 1976. 10.95 (ISBN 0-399-11736-9). Putnam.

Correll, Donovan S. Native Orchids of North America North of Mexico. LC 78-62270. (Illus.). 1950. 28.50x (ISBN 0-8047-0999-8). Stanford U Pr.

Dressler, Robert L. The Orchids: Natural History & Classification. LC 80-24561. (Illus.). 352p. 1981. text ed. 27.50x (ISBN 0-674-87525-7). Harvard U Pr.

Hawkes, Alex D. Encyclopedia of Cultivated Orchids. (Illus.). 602p. 1965. 75.00 (ISBN 0-571-06502-3, Pub. by Faber & Faber). Merrimack Bk Serv.

Kramer, Jack. Growing Orchids at Your Window. 1979. pap. 4.50 (ISBN 0-8015-3175-6, Hawthorn). Dutton.

--Orchids for Your Home. 144p. 1974. pap. 1.95 (ISBN 0-346-12143-4). Cornerstone.

Northen, Rebecca T. Home Orchid Growing. rev. ed. & enl. 3rd ed. LC 74-90339. (Illus.). 1970. 25.95 (ISBN 0-442-06064-5). Van Nos Reinhold.

--Orchids As House Plants. rev. ed. (Illus.). 160p. 1976. pap. 2.50 (ISBN 0-486-23261-1). Dover.

Reinikka, Merle A. History of the Orchid. LC 74-125660. (Illus.). 1972. 17.50 (ISBN 0-87024-177-X). U of Miami Pr.

Rentoul, J. N. Growing Orchids: Cymbidiums & Slippers. LC 81-3023. (Illus.). 178p. 1981. 29.95 (ISBN 0-295-95839-1). U of Wash Pr.

Richter, Walter. Orchid Care: A Guide to Cultivation & Breeding. 1972. 13.50 (ISBN 0-442-26944-7). Van Nos Reinhold.

Sander, David. Orchids & Their Cultivation. (Illus.). 1979. 19.95 (ISBN 0-7137-0979-0, Pub. by Blandford Pr England). Sterling.

Sunset Editors. Orchids: How to Grow. 2nd ed. LC 76-46652. (Illus.). 64p. 1977. pap. 3.95 (ISBN 0-376-03554-4, Sunset Bks.). Sunset-Lane.

Watson, W. Orchids: Their Culture & Management. LC 79-52705. (Illus.). 1979. 24.95 (ISBN 0-87850-031-6). Darwin Pr.

Williams, B. S. & Williams, H. Orchid Growers Manual. 7th ed. 1973. Repr. of 1894 ed. 75.00 (ISBN 3-7682-0043-4). Lubrecht & Cramer.

Withner, Carl L., ed. The Orchids: Scientific Studies. LC 73-20496. (Illus.). 624p. 1974. 42.50 (ISBN 0-471-95715-1, Pub. by Wiley-Interscience). Wiley.

ORCHIDS

see also Orchid Culture

Ames, Blanche. Drawings of Florida Orchids. (Orchid Ser.). (Illus.). 1980. Repr. of 1959 ed. text ed. 15.00 (ISBN 0-930576-22-5). E M Coleman Ent.

Ames, Oakes. Orchidaceae: Illustrations & Studies of the Family Orchidaceae Volume IV: the Genus Habenaria in North America. (Orchid Ser.). (Illus.). 1980. Repr. of 1910 ed. text ed. 25.00 (ISBN 0-930576-23-3). E M Coleman Ent.

--Orchids in Retrospect: A Collection of Essays on the Orchidaceae. (Orchid Ser.). (Illus.). 1980. Repr. of 1948 ed. text ed. 15.00 (ISBN 0-930576-21-7). E M Coleman Ent.

Anderson, Frank. Orchids. (Abbeville Library of Art Ser.). (Illus.). 112p. 1981. pap. 4.95 (ISBN 0-89659-122-0). Abbeville Pr.

Black, Peter M. The Complete Handbook of Orchid Growing. 160p. 1980. 16.95 (ISBN 0-8129-0951-8). Times Bks.

Cady, Leo & Rotherham, E. R. Australian Native Orchids in Colour. (Reed Colourbook Ser.). (Illus.). 112p. 1970. 11.75 (ISBN 0-589-07011-8, Pub. by Reed Bks Australia). C E Tuttle.

Cameron, Jean W. The Orchids of Maine. 1976. pap. 3.50 (ISBN 0-89101-001-7). U Maine Orono.

Chew Kang, Lee. Orchids. (Illus.). 1979. 15.00 (ISBN 0-89860-032-4). Eastview.

Cogniaux, Alfredus. Orchidaceae, 4 vols. (Flora Brasiliensis Ser.: Vol. 3, Pts. 4-6). (Illus.). 970p. (Lat.). 1975. Repr. Set. lib. bdg. 225.00x (ISBN 3-87429-080-8). Lubrecht & Cramer.

Crockett, James U. & Skelsy, Alice F. Orchids. (The Time-Life Encyclopedia of Gardening Ser.). (Illus.). 1978. lib. bdg. 11.97 (ISBN 0-686-51061-5). Silver.

Darnell, A. W. Orchids for the Outdoor Garden: A Descriptive List of the World's Orchids for the Use of Amateur Gardeners. LC 76-23979. (Illus.). 512p. 1976. pap. 7.00 (ISBN 0-486-23406-1). Dover.

--Orchids for the Outdoor Garden: A Descriptive List of the World's Orchids for the Use of Amateur Gardeners. 10.00 (ISBN 0-8446-5497-3). Peter Smith.

Darwin, Charles. Fertilization of Orchids by Insects. (Orchid Ser.). 1980. Repr. of 1862 ed. text ed. 27.50 (ISBN 0-930576-20-9). E M Coleman Ent.

Dunsterville, G. C. & Garay, L. A. Orchids of Venezuela, 3 vols. 1980. pap. 40.00 (ISBN 0-686-74290-7). Museum Bks.

--Venezuelan Orchids Illustrated, 5 vols. Incl. Vol. 1. 448p. 1959; Vol. 2. 360p. 1961; Vol. 3. 350p. 1965; Vol. 4. 344p. 1966; Vol. 5. 1972. (Illus.). Vols. 1-5. 25.00 ea. Museum Bks.

--Venezuelan Orchids Illustrated, 6 vols, Vol. 6. 1975. 30.00 (ISBN 0-685-55087-7). Museum Bks.

Du Petit-Thouars, Aubert-Aubert. Histoire Particuliere Des Plantes Orchidees Recueillies sur les Trois Iles Australes d'Afrique. (Orchid Ser.). (Illus.). 1980. Repr. of 1822 ed. text ed. 15.00 (ISBN 0-930576-24-1). E M Coleman Ent.

Duthie, J. F. The Orchids of the Western Himalaya. (Illus.). 1967. Repr. of 1906 ed. 150.00 (ISBN 3-7682-0465-0). Lubrecht & Cramer.

Ettlinger, D. M. British & Irish Orchids, a Field Guide. (Illus.). 1976. text ed. 15.00x (ISBN 0-333-18262-6). Verry.

Fitch, Charles M. All About Orchids. LC 80-1806. (Illus.). 256p. 1981. 13.95 (ISBN 0-686-72827-0). Doubleday.

Fitch, W. H., illus. Refugium Botanicum or Figurs & Descriptions from Living Specimens of Little Known or New Plants of Botanical Interest, Vol. II. (Orchid Ser.). (Illus.). 1980. Repr. text ed. 27.50 (ISBN 0-930576-19-5). E M Coleman Ent.

Hooker, J. D. A Century of Indian Orchids. (Calutta Royal Bot. Gard. Ser.). (Illus.). 1967. 100.00 (ISBN 3-7682-0464-2). Lubrecht & Cramer.

Hooker, W. J. Icones Plantarum: On Orchids, Vols. 21 & 22. (Ser. 4). 1967. Vol. 21. 30.00 ea. Vol. 22 (ISBN 3-7682-0853-2) (ISBN 3-7682-0854-0). Lubrecht & Cramer.

Hunt, P. Francis. The Orchid. (Octopus Bk.). (Illus.). 1979. 40.00 (ISBN 0-7064-0808-X, Mayflower Bks). Smith Pubs.

Koester, Arthur R. The Cymbidium List: Species, Hybirds & Awards 1799-1976, Vol. 1. LC 79-84474. (Orig.). 1979. pap. 11.00x (ISBN 0-9602558-0-X). A R Koester Bks.

Kraenzlin, F. W. Orchidacearum Genera et Species. (Plant Monograph Reprint Ser.: No. 6). (Illus.). 1969. Repr. of 1904 ed. 100.00 (ISBN 3-7682-0649-1). Lubrecht & Cramer.

Kraenzlin, R. Monographie von Masdevallia Ruiz et Pavon Lothiana Kraenz: Scaphosepalum Pfitzer, Cryptophorantus Bearb, Rodr., Pseudostomeria Kraenzl. (Feddes Repertorium: Beiheft 34). 240p. (Ger.). 1980. Repr. of 1925 ed. lib. bdg. 47.85x (ISBN 3-87429-184-7). Lubrecht & Cramer.

Kramer, Jack. Orchids: Flowers of Romance & Mystery. (Illus.). 156p. 1980. 20.00 (ISBN 0-686-62708-3, 1401-8); pap. 9.95 (ISBN 0-686-62709-1, 2171-5). Abrams.

Lang, David C. Orchids of Britain: A Field Guide. (Illus.). 256p. 1980. 26.50x (ISBN 0-19-217692-7). Oxford U Pr.

Lindley, John. The Genera & Species of Orchidaceous Plants, 7vols. in 1. 1964. 45.00 (ISBN 90-6123-091-8). Lubrecht & Cramer.

Luer, Carlyle A. A Guide to Field Identification of Native Orchids of the U.S. & Canada. condensed ed. Date not set. 15.95 (ISBN 0-8120-5191-2); pap. 10.95 (ISBN 0-8120-0933-9). Barron.

--Native Orchids of Florida. (Illus.). 1972. 40.00 (ISBN 0-89327-014-8). NY Botanical.

--The Native Orchids of Florida. 1977. 39.95 (ISBN 0-8120-5183-1). Barron.

--Native Orchids of the United States & Canada. (Illus.). 1975. 45.00 (ISBN 0-89327-015-6). NY Botanical.

--Orchids of the United States & Canada Excluding Florida. (Illus.). 1977. 44.95 (ISBN 0-8120-5184-X). Barron.

Millar, Andree. Orchids of Papua New Guinea: An Introduction. LC 78-54152. (Illus.). 112p. 1978. 25.00 (ISBN 0-295-95605-4). U of Wash Pr.

Moir, W. W., et al. Breeding Variegata Oncidiums. LC 80-15946. (Illus.). 136p. 1980. pap. text ed. 12.00x (ISBN 0-8248-0712-X). U Pr of Hawaii.

Noble, Mary. You Can Grow Cattleya Orchids. rev. ed. (Illus.). 1980. pap. 6.50 (ISBN 0-913928-02-X). McQuerry-Orchid.

Northen, Rebecca T. Miniature Orchids. 264p. 1980. 26.95 (ISBN 0-442-25776-7). Van Nos Reinhold.

--Orchids As House Plants. 6.75 (ISBN 0-8446-5471-X). Peter Smith.

Orchids. 1.95 (ISBN 0-686-21148-0). Bklyn Botanic.

Petrie, W. & Campbell, M. Guide to Orchids of North America: Excluding the Tropicals of Florida & Hawaii & the Asiatics of Alaska. (Illus.). 220p. 1981. pap. 12.95 (ISBN 0-87663-635-0, Pub. by Hancock Hse). Universe.

Piers, Frank. Orchids of East Africa. 2nd rev. ed. (Illus.). 1968. pap. 50.00 (ISBN 3-7682-0569-X). Lubrecht & Cramer.

Reinikka, Merle A. History of the Orchid. LC 74-125660. (Illus.). 1972. 17.50 (ISBN 0-87024-177-X). U of Miami Pr.

Ritterhausen, Brian & Ritterhausen, Wilma. Orchids in Color. (Illus.). 1979. 12.50 (ISBN 0-7137-0859-X, Pub. by Blandford Pr England). Sterling.

Rittershausen, B. & Rittershausen, W. Popular Orchids. 1978. text ed. 15.00x (ISBN 0-7223-0940-6). Verry.

Rittershausen, Brian & Rittershausen, Wilma. Orchids As Indoor Plants. (Illus.). 90p. 1980. 12.50 (ISBN 0-7137-0998-7, Pub. by Blandford Pr England). Sterling.

Sander, David. Orchids & Their Cultivation. (Illus.). 1979. 19.95 (ISBN 0-7137-0979-0, Pub. by Blandford Pr England). Sterling.

Schlechter, R. Beitraege zur Orchideenkunde von Colombia. (Feddes Repertorium: Beiheft 27). 183p. (Ger.). 1980. Repr. of 1924 ed. lib. bdg. 40.55x (ISBN 3-87429-182-0). Lubrecht & Cramer.

--Beitraege zur Orchideenkunde von Zentralamerika, 2 vols. in one. (Feddes Repertorium: Beiheft 17 & 18). 402p. (Ger.). 1980. Repr. of 1922 ed. lib. bdg. 70.20x (ISBN 3-87429-181-2). Lubrecht & Cramer.

--Orchidaceae Perrierianae: Zur Orchideenkunde der Insel Madagascar. (Feddes Repertorium: Beiheft 33). 391p. (Ger.). 1980. Repr. of 1925 ed. lib. bdg. 59.80x (ISBN 3-87429-183-9). Lubrecht & Cramer.

--Orchideenflora von Rio Grande do Sul. (Feddes Repertorium: Beiheft 35). 108p. (Ger.). 1980. Repr. of 1925 ed. lib. bdg. 30.70x (ISBN 3-87429-185-5). Lubrecht & Cramer.

Sessler, Gloria J. Orchids & How to Grow Them. LC 78-9684. (Home Gardening Handbooks Ser.). (Illus.). 1978. 16.95 (ISBN 0-13-639617-8, Spec). P-H.

Sheehan, Tom & Sheehan, Marion. Orchid Genera Illustrated. 1979. 29.95 (ISBN 0-442-27529-3). Van Nos Reinhold.

Skelsey, Alice. Orchids. new ed. Time-Life Books, ed. (The Encyclopedia of Gardening). (Illus.). 1978. 12.95 (ISBN 0-8094-2591-2). Time-Life.

Taylor, George. Slipper Orchids: The Art of Digby Graham. (Illus.). 1981. price not set (Pub. by Reed Books Australia). C E Tuttle.

Van Der Pijl, L. & Dodson, Calaway H. Orchid Flowers: Their Pollination & Evolution. LC 66-28521. (Illus.). 1966. 14.95 (ISBN 0-87024-069-2). U of Miami Pr.

Van Royen, P. The Orchids of the High Mountains of New Guinea. (Illus.). 784p. 1980. 100.00x (ISBN 3-7682-1261-0). Lubrecht & Cramer.

Veitch, James. Manual of Orchidaceous Plants: 1887-1894, 2 vols. (Illus.). 1981. Set. 90.00 (ISBN 90-6123-180-9). Lubrecht & Cramer.

Watson, W. Orchids: Their Culture & Management. LC 79-52705. (Illus.). 1979. 24.95 (ISBN 0-87850-031-6). Darwin Pr.

Webber, G. Anyone for Orchids. 1979. 15.00 (ISBN 0-916838-12-9). Schiffer.

Williams, Brian & Dumbleton, Peter. Orchids for Everyone: A Practical Guide to the Home Cultivation of Over 200 of the World's Most Beautiful Varieties. (Illus.). 208p. 1980. 15.95 (ISBN 0-517-53989-6, Michelman Books). Crown.

Withner, C. L. The Orchids: Scientific Survey. (Illus.). 1959. 29.00 (ISBN 0-8260-9485-6, Pub. by Wiley-Interscience). Wiley.

You Can Grow Orchids. 4th, rev. ed. (Illus.). 136p. 1980. pap. 6.50 (ISBN 0-913928-04-6). McQuerry-Orchid.

ORDER

Beloff, Max. Public Order & Popular Disturbances: 1660-1714. 168p. 1963. 24.00x (ISBN 0-7146-1270-7, F Cass Co). Biblio Dist.

Loemker, Leroy E. Struggle for Synthesis: The Seventeenth Century Background of Leibniz's Synthesis of Order & Freedom. LC 72-79308. 529p. 1972. 16.50x (ISBN 0-674-84545-5). Harvard U Pr.

Olson, Marjorie E. Roxy the Robin: Sequence Relationships for Children. (Illus.). 48p. (gr. k-1). 1974. pap. text ed. 2.50x (ISBN 0-89039-126-2). Ann Arbor Pubs.

Order & Counter Order: Dualism in Western Culture. LC 65-20330. 1966. 4.57 (ISBN 0-8022-1815-6). Philos Lib.
Thompson, William I. Evil & World Order. (World Perspectives Ser.). 1977. pap. 4.95x (ISBN 0-06-131951-1, TB1951, Torch). Har-Row.

ORDER OF RUNNEMEDE

Browning, Charles H. Magna Charta Barons & Their American Descendants: Lineal Descents from Them of the Members of the Baronial Order of Runnemede. LC 69-17125. (Illus.). 1969. Repr. of 1915 ed. 17.50 (ISBN 0-8063-0056-6). Genealog Pub.
--Magna Charta Barons & Their American Descendants, Together with the Pedigrees of the Founders of the Order of Runnemede. LC 73-77634. (Illus.). 1969. Repr. of 1898 ed. 18.50 (ISBN 0-8063-0055-8). Genealog Pub.

ORDER OF ST. CLARE

see Poor Clares

ORDER OF THE EASTERN STAR

Bell. Eastern Star. 2.95 (ISBN 0-685-21937-2). Wehman.
Brunke, Ottillie. O.E.S. Floor Work. 18p. 1977. Repr. of 1960 ed. pap. 1.00 (ISBN 0-685-87985-2, S-241). Macoy Pub.
Hilburn, May S. Golden Tributes: Fraternal Ceremonies. 1977. Repr. text ed. 6.50 (ISBN 0-685-88789-8, S-113). Macoy Pub.
Lowe, Thomas. Adoptive Masonry. 1.50 (ISBN 0-685-19462-0). Powner.
Riegel, E. B., compiled by. Gems of Thoughts for Fraternal Speakers in Poetry & Prose. 1977. Repr. text ed. 5.00 (ISBN 0-685-88788-X, S-71). Macoy Pub.
Terry, Sarah H. The Second Mile. pap. 2.50 (ISBN 0-685-74614-3). Macoy Pub.
Voorhis, Harold V. The Eastern Star: The Evolution from a Rite to an Order. 1976. Repr. of 1954 ed. 5.95 (ISBN 0-685-74611-9, S-300). Macoy Pub.

ORDER OF THE EASTERN STAR–RITUAL

Adams, Ruth. One Little Candle. 1981. Repr. of 1966 ed. text ed. 6.50 (ISBN 0-685-88803-7, S-251). Macoy Pub.
Adams, Ruth, et al. Gathered Memories. 1978. Repr. of 1961 ed. text ed. 4.50 (ISBN 0-685-88787-1, S-76). Macoy Pub.
Alexander, J. L. Along the Starry Trail: Poems & Ceremonies. 1968. Repr. of 1954 ed. text ed. 3.00 (ISBN 0-685-88775-8, S-109). Macoy Pub.
Bell, F. A. Eastern Star Ritual. 2.00 (ISBN 0-685-19473-6). Powner.
Cooley, Doris H., ed. Ritual of Music. 12p. 1968. pap. text ed. 1.25 (ISBN 0-685-88807-X, S-79). Macoy Pub.
Daughter of Isis Ritual. pap. 1.00 (ISBN 0-685-19470-1). Powner.
Daughters of the Sphinx Ritual. 1.75 (ISBN 0-685-19471-X). Powner.
Gibbany, Etta M. Star Beams. 24p. 1958. pap. 1.50 (ISBN 0-685-88815-0, S-304). Macoy Pub.
Hansen, Vee & Shaw, Opal. Macoy's Short Addresses for Matron: Forty-Five Sentiments. 28p. 1975. Repr. pap. 1.00 (ISBN 0-685-88812-6, S-83). Macoy Pub.
Hansen, Vee, et al. Macoy's Short Addresses & Ceremonies for Matron's Use. 24p. 1975. Repr. pap. 1.00 (ISBN 0-685-88811-8, S-84). Macoy Pub.
Macoy, Robert. Adoptive Rite. 2.00 (ISBN 0-685-19463-9). Powner.
Meekins, Inez P. Old Dominion Addresses & Ceremonies. 1975. Repr. of 1972 ed. 2.50 (ISBN 0-685-88802-9, S-417). Macoy Pub.
Star Point Series. Incl. No. 1. Adah (S-181); No. 2. Ruth (S-182); No. 3. Esther (S-183); No. 4. Martha (S - 184); No. 5. Electa (S -185). 12p. 1981. Repr. of 1957 ed. pap. 1.60 ea. Macoy Pub.
Voorhis, Harold V. The Eastern Star: The Evolution from a Rite to an Order. 1976. Repr. of 1954 ed. 5.95 (ISBN 0-685-74611-9, S-300). Macoy Pub.

ORDER OF THE RAINBOW FOR GIRLS

Hilburn, May S. Rainbow in the Sky. 48p. 1966. pap. 1.00 (ISBN 0-685-88805-3, S-260). Macoy Pub.

ORDER STATISTICS

see also Nonparametric Statistics

Barlow, R. E., et al. Statistical Inference Under Order Restrictions: The Theory & Application of Isotonic Regression. LC 74-39231. (Probability & Statistics Ser.). (Illus.). 400p. 1972. 64.50 (ISBN 0-471-04970-0, Pub. by Wiley-Interscience). Wiley.
Gibbons, Jean D., et al. Selecting & Ordering Populations: A New Statistical Methodology. LC 77-3700. (Probability & Mathematical Statistics). 1977. 41.00x (ISBN 0-471-02670-0, Pub. by Wiley-Interscience). Wiley.
Harter, H. Leon. The Chronological Annotated Bibliography of Order Statistics: Vol. 1: Pre-1950. rev. ed. (The American Sciences Press Ser. in Mathematical & Management Sciences: Vol. 7). 1981. price not set. Am Sciences Pr.
Mosteller, F. R. & Rourke, Robert E. Sturdy Statistics: Nonparametrics & Order Statistics. LC 70-184162. 1973. text ed. 18.95 (ISBN 0-201-04868-X). A-W.

ORDERS, ANGLICAN

see Anglican Orders

ORDERS, ARCHITECTURAL

see Architecture–Orders

ORDERS, MAJOR

see Bishops; Clergy

ORDERS, MONASTIC

see Monasticism and Religious Orders

ORDERS IN COUNCIL

see also Continental System of Napoleon

ORDERS OF KNIGHTHOOD AND CHIVALRY

see also Chivalry; Knights and Knighthood

Joslin, E. C. The Standard Catalogue of British Orders, Decorations & Medals, 2 vols. 1979. 30.00 (ISBN 0-685-51506-0, Pub by Spink & Son England). S J Durst.
Risk, J. C. The History of the Order of the Bath & Its Insignia. 1972. 18.00 (ISBN 0-685-51511-7, Pub by Spink & Son England). S J Durst.
Rosignoli, Guido. Ribbons of Orders, Decorations, and Medals. LC 76-28307. (Arco Color Books). 1977. 7.95 (ISBN 0-668-04104-8, 4104); pap. 5.95 (ISBN 0-668-04253-2, 4253). Arco.
Shaw, William A. Knights of England: A Complete Record from the Earliest Time to the Present Day of the Knights of All the Orders of Chivalry in England, Scotland & Ireland, & of Knights Bachelor, 2 Vols. LC 74-129966. 1971. Repr. of 1906 ed. Set. 42.50 (ISBN 0-8063-0443-X). Genealog Pub.

ORDINAL POSITION OF CHILDREN

see Birth Order

ORDINALIA

Longsworth, Robert M. Cornish Ordinalia: Religion & Dramaturgy. LC 67-22869. 1967. 10.00x (ISBN 0-674-17200-0). Harvard U Pr.

ORDINARY'S COURTS

see Probate Law and Practice

ORDINATION

see also Priesthood

Ellard, G. Ordination Anointings in the Western Church Before 1000 A. D. 1932. 12.00 (ISBN 0-527-01688-8). Kraus Repr.
Hersey, Herman. Preparation for Ordination. 1981. pap. 1.25 (ISBN 0-89265-069-9). Randall Hse.
McEachern, Alton H. Set Apart for Service. LC 79-5114. 1980. 5.95 (ISBN 0-8054-2537-3). Broadman.
Reynolds, Roger E. The Ordinals of Christ from Their Origins to the Twelfth Century. 1978. 55.00x (ISBN 3-11-007058-8). De Gruyter.
Stendahl, Krister. The Bible & the Role of Women: A Case Study in Hermeneutics. Reumann, John, ed. Sander, Emilie T., tr. LC 66-25262. (Facet Bks). 64p. 1966. pap. 1.35 (ISBN 0-8006-3030-0, 1-3030). Fortress.
Watts, J. Wash. Ordination of Baptist Ministers. pap. 0.75 (ISBN 0-8054-9404-9). Broadman.

ORDINATION OF WOMEN

Heyer, Robert, ed. Women & Orders. LC 74-80262. 120p. (Orig.). 1974. pap. 2.45 (ISBN 0-8091-1841-6). Paulist Pr.
Malone, David M. The Church Cannot Ordain Women to the Priesthood. 1978. 0.75 (ISBN 0-8199-0724-3). Franciscan Herald.
Micks, Marianne & Price, Charles P., eds. Toward a New Theology of Ordination: Essays on the Ordination of Women. LC 76-634. 1976. pap. 3.95 (ISBN 0-913550-09-4). Greeno Hadden.
Stendahl, Krister. The Bible & the Role of Women: A Case Study in Hermeneutics. Reumann, John, ed. Sander, Emilie T., tr. LC 66-25262. (Facet Bks). 64p. 1966. pap. 1.35 (ISBN 0-8006-3030-0, 1-3030). Fortress.
Tiemeyer, Raymond. Ordination of Women. 1970. 1.00 (ISBN 0-8066-1013-1, 10-4815). Augsburg.

ORDNANCE

see also Antitank Guns; Artillery; Atomic Weapons; Ballistics; Bombs; Firearms Industry and Trade; Machine Guns; Naval Gunnery; Polaris (Missile); Weapons Systems; also heading Ordnance and Ordnance Stores under Armies and Navies, e.g. United States–Army–Ordnance and Ordnance Stores

Bruce, Robert V. Lincoln & the Tools of War. LC 73-15241. (Illus.). 368p. 1974. Repr. of 1956 ed. lib. bdg. 17.25x (ISBN 0-8371-7167-9, BRLS). Greenwood.
Chamberlain, Peter & Gander, Terry. Infantry, Mountain, & Airborne Guns. LC 75-10160. (World War II Fact Files Ser.). 1975. 5.95 (ISBN 0-668-03815-2); pap. 3.95 (ISBN 0-668-03819-5). Arco.
--Light & Medium Artillery. LC 75-10161. (World War II Fact Files Ser.). (Illus.). 1975. pap. 3.95 (ISBN 0-668-03820-9). Arco.
--Mortars & Rockets. LC 75-101158. (World War II Fact Files Ser.). 1975. 5.95 (ISBN 0-668-03813-6); pap. 3.95 (ISBN 0-668-03817-9). Arco.
Colby, C. B. Civil War Weapons: Small Arms, & Artillery of the Blue & Gray. (Illus.). (gr. 4-7). 1962. PLB 5.29 (ISBN 0-698-30046-7). Coward.
Foss, Christopher. Infantry Weapons of the World. rev. ed. LC 76-42911. (Illus.). 1979. 12.50 (ISBN 0-684-16246-6, ScribT); encore ed. 4.95 (ISBN 0-684-17183-X). Scribner.
Marchant-Smith, D. J. & Haslem, P. R. Small Arms & Cannons. (Brassey's Battlefield Weapons System & Technology: Vol. 5). 160p. 1982. 40.00 (ISBN 0-08-028330-6); pap. 16.00 (ISBN 0-08-028331-4). Pergamon.
Norton, Robert. The Gunner, Shewing the Whole Practise of Artillerie. LC 73-6155. (No. 617). 1973. Repr. of 1628 ed. 40.00 (ISBN 90-221-0617-9). Walter J Johnson.
Office Strategic Services. OSS Sabotage & Demolition Manual. (Illus.). 139p. 1973. pap. 12.95 (ISBN 0-87364-005-5). Paladin Ent.
Simon, Leslie E. Secret Weapons of the Third Reich: German Research in World War II. (Illus.). 258p. 1970. pap. 8.95 (ISBN 0-87364-227-9, Sycamore Island). Paladin Ent.

ORDNANCE, NAVAL

see also Naval Gunnery; Polaris (Missile)

Corse, Carl D., Jr. Introduction to Shipboard Weapons. LC 74-25032. (Fundamentals of Naval Science Ser.: No. 6). 1975. text ed. 16.95x (ISBN 0-87021-750-X). Naval Inst Pr.

ORDNANCE RESEARCH

William Roy, Seventeen Twenty-Six - Seventeen Ninety: Pioneer of the Ordnance Survey. 1981. pap. 6.00x (ISBN 0-7141-0387-X, Pub. by Brit Lib England). State Mutual Bk.

ORDOS LANGUAGE

Mostaert, Antoine. Dictionnaire Ordos, 3 Vols in 1. 2nd ed. 1968. Repr. of 1944 ed. 146.50 (ISBN 0-384-40225-9). Johnson Repr.

ORDOVICIAN PERIOD

see Geology, Stratigraphic–Ordovician

ORE-DEPOSITS

see also Ores

Barnes, H. L., ed. Geochemistry of Hydrothermal Ore Deposits. 2nd ed. LC 79-354. 798p. 1979. 36.50 (ISBN 0-471-05056-3, Pub. by Wiley-Interscience). Wiley.
Bauman, Ludwig. Introduction to Ore Deposits. 1976. 12.50x (ISBN 0-7073-0207-2, Pub. by Scottish Academic Pr Scotland). Columbia U Pr.
Baumann, Ludwig. Introduction to Ore Deposits. LC 74-26527. 163p. 1976. 21.95 (ISBN 0-470-05937-0). Halsted Pr.
Klemm, D. D. & Schneider, H. J., eds. Time- & Strata- Bound Ore Deposits. (Illus.). 1978. 49.70 (ISBN 0-387-08502-5). Springer-Verlag.
Lamey, C. A. Metallic & Industrial Mineral Deposits. 1966. text ed. 28.00 (ISBN 0-07-036091-X, C). McGraw.
Lebedev, L. M. Metacolloids in Endogenic Deposits. LC 65-25241. (Monographs in Geoscience Ser.). 1967. 42.50 (ISBN 0-306-30295-0, Plenum Pr). Plenum Pub.
Netschert, Bruce C. & Landsberg, Hans H. The Future Supply of the Major Metals: A Reconnaissance Survey. LC 76-58923. (Resources for the Future Ser.). (Illus.). 1978. Repr. of 1961 ed. lib. bdg. 15.00 (ISBN 0-8371-9472-5, NEMM). Greenwood.
Ore Deposits of the United States. LC 68-24170. 1968. 31.50x (ISBN 0-89520-008-2). Soc Mining Eng.
Park, Charles F., Jr. & MacDiarmid, Roy A. Ore Deposits. 3rd ed. LC 75-14157. (Geology Ser.). (Illus.). 1975. text ed. 28.95x (ISBN 0-7167-0272-X). W H Freeman.
Recent Advances in Mining & Processing of Low-Grade Submarginal Mineral Deposits. LC 76-11771. 1977. text ed. 25.00 (ISBN 0-08-021051-1). Pergamon.
Ridge, John D. Annotated Bibliographies of Mineral Deposits in the Western Hemisphere. LC 72-178773. (Memoir: No. 131). 1972. 14.00x (ISBN 0-8137-1131-2). Geol Soc.
Shand, S. James. Eruptive Rocks: Their Genesis, Composition, Classification, & Their Relation to Ore Deposits. 3rd ed. (Illus.). 1969. Repr. of 1949 ed. 17.50 (ISBN 0-02-852120-X). Hafner.
Wolf, K. H., ed. Handbook of Strata-Bound & Stratiform Ore Deposits. (Regional Studies: Vol. 5). 1976. 73.25 (ISBN 0-444-41405-3). Elsevier.
--Handbook of Strata-Bound & Stratiform Ore Deposits, Vols. 1-4. Incl. Vol. 1. Classifications & Historical Studies (ISBN 0-444-41401-0); Vol. 2. Geochemical Studies (ISBN 0-444-41402-9); Vol. 3. Supergene & Surficial Ore Deposits: Textures & Fabrics (ISBN 0-444-41403-7); Vol. 4. Tectonics & Metamorphism (ISBN 0-444-41404-5). 1976. 444.00 (ISBN 0-686-57861-9); Vols. 1-4. 241.50 (ISBN 0-685-74759-X); 66.00 ea. Elsevier.
--Handbook of Strata-Bound & Stratiform Ore Deposits, Vol. 5-7: Pt. 2. 1976. 241.50 (ISBN 0-685-74698-4). Elsevier.
--Handbook of Strata-Bound & Stratiform Ore Deposits, Vol. 6: Cu, Zn, Pb, Ag & Deposits. 1976. 117.00 (ISBN 0-444-41406-1). Elsevier.
--Handbook of Strata-Bound & Stratiform Ore Deposits, Vol. 7: Au, U, Fe, Mn, Hg, Sb, W, & P Deposits. 1976. 117.00 (ISBN 0-444-41407-X). Elsevier.

ORE-DRESSING

see also Flotation

Arbiter, N. Nathaniel, ed. Milling Methods in the Americas. 1964. 104.00x (ISBN 0-677-00950-X). Gordon.
Gaudin, Antoine M. Principles of Mineral Dressing. 1939. text ed. 27.95 (ISBN 0-07-023030-7, C). McGraw.
International Mineral Processing Congress - 7th - 1964. Proceedings. Arbiter, Nathaniel, ed. 1965. 113.00x (ISBN 0-677-10690-4). Gordon.
Lynch, A. J. Mineral Crushing & Grinding Circuits: Their Simulation, Design & Control. (Developments in Mineral Processing). 1977. 63.50 (ISBN 0-444-41528-9). Elsevier.
Milling & Lathe Cutting Tools. (Machinee Tool Ser.: Vol. 5). 1974. pap. text ed. 3.95 (ISBN 0-88462-246-0). Ed Methods.
• Milling Machine Work. 1953. pap. text ed. 7.40 (ISBN 0-8273-0185-5). Delmar.
Processing of Low-Grade Uranium Ores. 1967. pap. 14.75 (ISBN 92-0-041067-7, ISP146, IAEA). Unipub.
Taggart, Arthur F. Handbook of Mineral Dressing. 1905p. 1945. 64.00 (ISBN 0-471-84348-2, Pub. by Wiley-Interscience). Wiley.

OREGON

see also names of cities, counties and towns in Oregon

Bingham, Edwin. Oregon! LC 79-2296. (Illus.). (gr. 4). 1979. text ed. 14.00x (ISBN 0-87905-103-5). Peregrine Smith.
Brandt, Patricia & Guilford, Nancy, eds. Oregon Biography Index. (Bibliographic Ser.: No. 11). 1976. pap. 5.00 (ISBN 0-87071-131-8). Oreg St U Pr.
Carpenter, Allan. Oregon. LC 78-13955. (New Enchantment of America State Bks). (Illus.). (gr. 4 up). 1979. PLB 10.60 (ISBN 0-516-04137-1). Childrens.
Drake, Albert. Returning to Oregon. LC 74-28453. 1975. pap. 1.00 (ISBN 0-914994-07-7). Cider Pr.
Hall, Don Alan. On Top of Oregon. (Illus.). 1977. pap. 6.50 (ISBN 0-8323-0308-9). Binford.
Hines, Gustavus. Oregon: Its History, Condition & Prospects. LC 72-9450. (The Far Western Frontier Ser.). (Illus.). 444p. 1973. Repr. of 1851 ed. 20.00 (ISBN 0-405-04978-1). Arno.
Howison, Neil M. Oregon, a Report. 1976. pap. 4.00 (ISBN 0-87770-053-2). Ye Galleon.
Laidlaw, John R. These Things I Remembered & Poured Out My Soul in Me. 1977. 5.00 (ISBN 0-682-48767-8). Exposition.
Lockley, Fred. To Oregon by Ox Team in '47. facs. ed. 16p. Repr. pap. 3.75 (ISBN 0-8466-0145-1, SJS145). Shorey.
McArthur, Lewis A. Oregon Geographic Names. 4th ed. McArthur, Lewis L., ed. LC 72-86812. 1974. 19.95 (ISBN 0-87595-038-8). Oreg Hist Soc.
Oregon. 28.00 (ISBN 0-89770-113-5). Curriculum Info Ctr.
Preston, Ralph N. Early Oregon Atlas. (Illus.). 1978. pap. 6.50 (ISBN 0-8323-0304-6). Binford.

OREGON–ANTIQUITIES

Bedwell, Stephen. Fort Rock Basin: Prehistory & Environment. LC 74-169230. 1973. 10.00 (ISBN 0-87114-058-6). U of Oreg Bks.
Harpham, Josephine E. Doorways into History: The Early Houses & Public Buildings of Oregon. (Illus.). Repr. of 1966 ed. pap. 7.50 (ISBN 0-8466-0292-X, SJS292). Shorey.

OREGON–DESCRIPTION AND TRAVEL

Alt, David & Hyndman, Donald. Roadside Geology of Oregon. LC 77-2581. (Roadside Geology Ser.). (Illus.). 268p. 1978. pap. 7.95 (ISBN 0-87842-063-0). Mountain Pr.
Atkeson, Ray. Washington & Oregon in Color. (Illus.). 1954. pap. 1.00 (ISBN 0-8323-0077-2). Binford.
Atkeson, Ray, photos by. The Oregon Coast. LC 75-188295. (Belding Imprint Ser.). (Illus.). 128p. (Text by Archie Satterfield). 1972. 27.50 (ISBN 0-912856-06-8). Graphic Arts Ctr.
--Oregon II. LC 74-75124. (Belding Imprint Ser.). (Illus.). 192p. (Text by Archie Satterfield). 1974. 29.50 (ISBN 0-912856-15-7). Graphic Arts Ctr.
Barr, Tom. Portrait of Oregon. LC 79-91507. (Portrait of America Ser.). (Illus.). 80p. (Orig., Photos by ray atkeson). 1980. pap. 5.95 (ISBN 0-912856-52-1). Graphic Arts Ctr.
Bedrick, Ed & Bedrick, Christina. One Hundred Seventy Seven Free Oregon Campgrounds. new ed. LC 79-66696. (Illus., Orig.). 1980. pap. 6.95 (ISBN 0-913140-33-3). Signpost Bk Pub.
Berger, Brian. Beautiful Oregon Country. Shangle, Robert D., ed. LC 79-1107. (Illus.). 72p. 1979. 14.95 (ISBN 0-89802-092-1); pap. 7.95 (ISBN 0-89802-091-3). Beautiful Am.
--Beauty of Oregon. Shangle, Robert D., ed. (Illus.). 160p. 1980. 27.50 (ISBN 0-89802-128-6). Beautiful Am.

Bleything, Dennis & Hawkins, Susan. Getting off on 96 & Other Less Traveled Roads. LC 75-9248. (Illus.). 1975. pap. 3.95 (ISBN 0-911518-32-0). Touchstone Pr Ore.

Blood, Marje. Exploring the Oregon Coast by Car. LC 80-25484. (Illus.). 224p. (Orig.). 1980. pap. 6.95 (ISBN 0-916076-41-5). Writing.

Chase, Don & Helms, Marjory. Pack Saddles & Rolling Wheels: A Century of Travel & Transportation in N. W. California & South Oregon. (Illus.). 1959. pap. 3.00 (ISBN 0-918634-28-8). D M Chase.

Cloutier, James. The Alpine Tavern: Photographs of a Social Gathering Place. LC 77-77899. (Illus.). 1977. pap. 9.95x (ISBN 0-918966-00-0). Image West.

--Orygone IV; or, If This Is July & It's Raining, This Must Be Oregon. LC 78-71301. (Illus., Orig.). 1978. pap. 4.95 (ISBN 0-918966-03-5). Image West.

Cockrell, Nick & Cockrell, Bill. Roofs Over Rivers. Worcester, T. K., ed. 1978. pap. 6.95 (ISBN 0-911518-50-9). Touchstone Pr Ore.

Corning, Howard M. Willamette Landings: Ghost Towns of the River. 2nd ed. LC 73-81023. 272p. 1973. 8.95 (ISBN 0-87595-093-0); pap. 6.95 (ISBN 0-87595-042-6). Oreg Hist Soc.

Crawford, Meodrem. Journal of Meodrem Crawford. facs. ed. 26p. Repr. of 1897 ed. pap. 3.95 (ISBN 0-8466-0141-9, SJS141). Shorey.

Dart, John O. & Johnson, Daniel M. Oregon: Wet, High, & Dry. 500p. (Orig.). 1981. pap. 15.95x (ISBN 0-913244-53-8). Hapi Pr.

Dodge, Nicholas A. A Climbing Guide to Oregon. LC 75-16654. (Illus.). 1975. pap. 8.95 (ISBN 0-911518-33-9). Touchstone Pr Ore.

Drawson, Maynard C. Treasures of the Oregon Country: No. IV. (Illus.). 1977. pap. 9.95 (ISBN 0-934476-03-9). Dee Pub Co.

Farnham, Thomas J. Travels in the Great Western Prairies, 2 vols. in 1. LC 68-16231. (The American Scene Ser.). 612p. 1973. Repr. of 1843 ed. lib. bdg. 35.00 (ISBN 0-306-71012-9). Da Capo.

Federal Writers' Project. Oregon: End of the Trail. 548p. 1941. Repr. 49.00 (ISBN 0-403-02186-3). Somerset Pub.

Freemesser, Bernard. An Oregon Experience. Beltran, George, ed. LC 78-73426. (Illus.). 1979. 19.95 (ISBN 0-918966-04-3). Image West.

Friedman, Ralph. Oregon for the Curious. LC 75-151057. (Illus.). 1972. pap. 4.95 (ISBN 0-87004-222-X). Caxton.

--Tales Out of Oregon. 1976. pap. 1.95 (ISBN 0-89174-004-X). Comstock Edns.

--A Touch of Oregon. 1976. pap. 1.95 (ISBN 0-89174-005-8). Comstock Edns.

--Tracking Down Oregon. LC 76-6647. (Illus.). 1978. pap. 6.95 (ISBN 0-87004-257-2). Caxton.

Garren, John. Oregon River Tours. 1979. pap. 6.95 (ISBN 0-911518-57-6). Touchstone Pr Ore.

Hart, Herbert M. Tour Guide to Old Forts of Oregon, Idaho, Washington, California, Vol. 3. (Illus.). 65p. (Orig.). 1981. pap. 3.95 (ISBN 0-87108-582-8). Pruett.

Hastings, Lansford W. Emigrant's Guide to Oregon & California. 2nd ed. LC 68-8691. (American Scene Ser). 1969. Repr. of 1845 ed. lib. bdg. 19.50 (ISBN 0-306-71172-9). Da Capo.

Hatton, Raymond R. High Country of Central Oregon. LC 80-7801. (Illus.). 1980. 9.50 (ISBN 0-8323-0357-7); pap. 6.50 (ISBN 0-8323-0358-5). Binford.

--High Desert of Central Oregon. LC 77-85393. (Illus.). 1978. pap. 6.50 (ISBN 0-8323-0299-6). Binford.

Helm, Mike. Eugene, Oregon: A Guide. LC 79-63656. 1979. 5.95 (ISBN 0-931742-01-3). Rainy Day Oreg.

--A Guide to Eating Out in Eugene. new ed. Helm, Christine, ed. LC 79-65123. (Illus.). 1979. 3.25 (ISBN 0-931742-02-1). Rainy Day Oreg.

Jackman, E. R. & Long, R. A. The Oregon Desert. LC 64-15389. (Illus.). 1964. 9.95 (ISBN 0-87004-074-X). Caxton.

Jackman, E. R. & Scharff, John. Steen's Mountain in Oregon's High Desert Country. LC 67-24205. (Illus.). 1967. 35.00 (ISBN 0-87004-028-6). Caxton.

Lampman, Linda, et al. Oregon for All Seasons. 2nd ed. LC 79-67595. (Illus.). 160p. 1979. pap. 6.95 (ISBN 0-916076-39-3). Writing.

Lee, Daniel & Frost, Joseph H. Ten Years in Oregon. LC 72-9457. (The Far Western Frontier Ser.). (Illus.). 348p. 1973. Repr. of 1844 ed. 18.00 (ISBN 0-405-04985-4). Arno.

Lewis, Paul M. Beautiful Oregon. Shangle, Robert D., ed. LC 75-314222. (Illus.). 72p. 1974. 14.95 (ISBN 0-915796-04-X); pap. 7.95 (ISBN 0-915796-00-7). Beautiful Am.

--Beautiful Oregon, Vol. II. Shangle, Robert D., ed. LC 78-13762. (Illus.). 72p. 1978. 14.95 (ISBN 0-915796-79-1); pap. 7.95 (ISBN 0-915796-78-3). Beautiful Am.

--Beautiful Oregon Coast. Shangle, Robert D., ed. LC 78-102344. (Illus.). 72p. 1977. 14.95 (ISBN 0-915796-21-X); pap. 7.95 (ISBN 0-915796-20-1). Beautiful Am.

--Beautiful Oregon Mountains. (Illus.). Date not set. 14.95 (ISBN 0-915796-99-6); pap. 7.95 (ISBN 0-915796-98-8). Beautiful Am.

--Images of Oregon. new ed. Shangle, Robert D., ed. Orig. Title: Beautiful Oregon. (Illus.). 72p. Date not set. 11.95 (ISBN 0-89802-172-3); pap. 5.95 (ISBN 0-89802-171-5). Beautiful Am.

Love, Ken & Love, Ruth. A Guide to the Trails of Badger Creek. rev. ed. (Illus., Orig.). 1980. pap. 4.95 (ISBN 0-913140-38-4). Signpost Bk Pub.

Lowe, Don & Lowe, Roberta. Sixty Hiking Trails Central Oregon Cascades. (Trail Guide). (Illus.). 1978. pap. 6.95 (ISBN 0-911518-51-7). Touchstone Pr Ore.

Loy, William G. Atlas of Oregon. LC 76-13964. (Illus.). 1976. 29.95 (ISBN 0-87114-076-4). U of Oreg Bks.

McMullen, D. E. Oregon Underfoot. LC 75-9247. (Illus.). 1975. pap. cancelled (ISBN 0-911518-31-2). Touchstone Pr Ore.

Mainwaring, William L. Exploring the Oregon Coast. rev. ed. LC 77-77250. (Illus.). 1981. pap. 6.95 (ISBN 0-918832-01-2). Westridge.

Morse, Randy & McDougall, Keith. Oregon: The Coast. LC 81-50170. (Illus.). 128p. 1981. 27.50 (ISBN 0-939284-00-6). Reidmore Bks.

Museums & Sites of Historical Interest in Oregon. LC 74-647323. 206p. 1980. pap. 5.95 (ISBN 0-87595-075-2). Oreg Hist Soc.

Nash, Wallis. Oregon; There & Back in 1877. LC 76-9770. (Studies in History Ser.: No. 7). (Illus.). 1976. Repr. of 1878 ed. 10.00 (ISBN 0-87071-077-X). Oreg St U Pr.

Powell, Fred W., ed. Hall J. Kelley on Oregon. LC 79-87635. (The American Scene Ser). (Illus.). 412p. 1972. Repr. of 1932 ed. lib. bdg. 39.50 (ISBN 0-306-71796-4). Da Capo.

Puustinen, Toivo. Hello Kid. 1980. pap. 4.95 (ISBN 0-89260-144-2). Hwong Pub.

Reed, Ione. Twenty-Five Oregon Weekend Adventures, Vol. II. LC 75-27462. (Illus.). 1979. pap. 4.95 (ISBN 0-89802-064-6). Beautiful Am.

Shangle, Robert D., ed. Portland Dining Guide. LC 79-24804. (Illus.). 80p. 1980. pap. 4.95 (ISBN 0-89802-084-0). Beautiful Am.

Smith, Earl R. The Days of My Years. LC 68-64777. (Illus.). 322p. 1968. pap. 7.95 (ISBN 0-87595-001-9). Oreg Hist Soc.

Snively, Gloria. Exploring the Seashore: In British Columbia, Washington & Oregon. (Illus.). 1979. pap. 9.95 (ISBN 0-919574-25-4). Western Marine Ent.

Sunset Editors. Oregon: Travel Guide to. 4th ed. LC 80-53486. (Illus.). 128p. 1981. pap. 5.95 (ISBN 0-376-06615-6, Sunset Bks.). Sunset-Lane.

Thollander, Earl. Back Roads of Oregon. (Illus.). 1979. 14.95 (ISBN 0-517-53069-4, Dist. by Crown); pap. 9.95 (ISBN 0-517-53781-8). Potter.

Thornton, J. Quinn. Oregon & California in 1848, 2 vols. in 1. LC 72-9471. (The Far Western Frontier Ser.). (Illus.). 802p. 1973. Repr. of 1849 ed. 37.00 (ISBN 0-405-04998-6). Arno.

Ven Der Ree, Frieda. Exploring the Coast by Boat: British Columbia & Oregon. (Illus.). 1979. pap. 8.95 (ISBN 0-919574-24-6). Western Marine Ent.

Walsh, Frank K. & Halliday, William R. Oregon Caves: Discovery & Exploration. 2nd ed. (Illus.). 1976. pap. 1.95 (ISBN 0-913508-01-2). Te Cum Tom.

Will, Robin. Adventures in Oregon Country. Shangle, Robert D., ed. LC 79-28595. 64p. Date not set. pap. 4.95 (ISBN 0-89802-064-6). Beautiful Am.

--Beautiful Portland. Shangle, Robert D., ed. LC 79-778. 72p. 1979. 14.95 (ISBN 0-915796-91-0); pap. 7.95 (ISBN 0-915796-90-2). Beautiful Am.

Williams, Jerold. McKenzie Trails. LC 79-124290. (Illus.). 1979. pap. 5.00 (ISBN 0-935004-01-7). Calapooya Bks.

OREGON–HISTORY

Armstrong, A. N. History of Oregon. enl. ed. 1969. Repr. of 1857 ed. 9.95 (ISBN 0-87770-002-8). Ye Galleon.

Bancroft, Hubert H. History of Oregon, 2 vols. LC 67-29422. (Works of Hubert Howe Bancroft Ser.). 1967. Repr. of 1888 ed. 50.00x (ISBN 0-914888-34-X). Bancroft Pr.

Barlow, Jeffrey & Richardson, Christine. China Doctor of John Day, Oregon. (Illus.). 1979. pap. 5.95 (ISBN 0-8323-0327-5). Binford.

Barrows, William. Oregon: The Struggle for Possession. LC 72-3766. (American Commonwealths: No. 2). Repr. of 1892 ed. 25.50 (ISBN 0-404-57202-2). AMS Pr.

Bedingfield, Nancy. Oregon's One Hundred Years in Pictures. LC 56-12270. (Illus.). 1958. 3.95 (ISBN 0-8323-0364-X); pap. 1.00 (ISBN 0-8323-0001-2). Binford.

Bell, James C., Jr. Opening a Highway to the Pacific, 1838-1846. LC 68-56648. (Columbia University Studies in the Social Sciences: No. 217). Repr. of 1921 ed. 18.50 (ISBN 0-404-51217-8). AMS Pr.

Bensell, Royal A. All Quiet on the Yamhill: The Civil War in Oregon. Barth, Gunter, ed. LC 60-63172. 1959. 5.00 (ISBN 0-87114-005-5). U of Oreg Bks.

Bettis, Stan & Doornink, Jon. Place Called Oregon. (Illus.). Date not set. price not set (ISBN 0-685-52885-5). Pacific Bks.

Bowen, William A. Willamette Valley: Migration & Settlement on the Oregon Frontier. LC 77-15183. (Illus.). 134p. 1979. 17.50 (ISBN 0-295-95590-2). U of Wash Pr.

Browne, Aaron V. Oregon Territory. 24p. 1968. Repr. pap. 2.50 (ISBN 0-87770-034-6, A825). Ye Galleon.

Carey, Charles H. General History of Oregon. 3rd ed. LC 70-140122. (Illus.). 1971. 25.00 (ISBN 0-8323-0221-X). Binford.

Chinese Pheasants: Oregon Pioneers. (Illus.). 38p. 1964. pap. 0.50 (ISBN 0-686-75147-7). Oreg Hist Soc.

Cogswell, Philip, Jr. Capitol Names: Individuals Woven into Oregon's History. LC 76-56657. (Illus.). 133p. 1977. 4.95 (ISBN 0-87595-076-0); pap. 2.95 (ISBN 0-87595-054-X). Oreg Hist Soc.

Corning, Howard M., ed. Dictionary of Oregon History. 18.95 (ISBN 0-8323-0099-3). Binford.

Cross, Osborne. Report in the Form of a Journal, the March of the Regiment of Mounted Riflemen to Oregon in 1849. 1967. Repr. of 1851 ed. 14.95 (ISBN 0-87770-008-7). Ye Galleon.

Culp, Edwin D. Oregon, the Way It Was. LC 81-1266. (Illus.). 235p. 1981. pap. 12.95 (ISBN 0-87004-285-8). Caxton.

Dicken, Samuel N. & Dicken, Emily F. Making of Oregon: A Study in Historical Geography. LC 79-89087. (Two Centuries of Ocean Geography: Vol. 1). (Illus.). 222p. 19.95 (ISBN 0-87595-081-7); pap. 12.95 (ISBN 0-87595-061-2). Oreg Hist Soc.

Dodds, Gordon B. Oregon: A History. (States & the Nation Ser.). (Illus.). 1977. 12.95 (ISBN 0-393-05632-5, Co-Pub. by AASLH). Norton.

Drew, Charles S. Origin and Early Prosecution of the Indian War in Oregon. 48p. 1973. Repr. of 1860 ed. 4.95 (ISBN 0-87770-046-X). Ye Galleon.

Dryden, Cecil P. Give All to Oregon. (Illus.). 1968. 9.95 (ISBN 0-8038-2606-0). Hastings.

Due, John F. & French, Giles. Rails to the Mid Columbia Wheatlands: The Columbia Southern & Great Southern Railroads & the Development of Sherman & Wasco Counties, Oregon. LC 79-89206. (Illus.). 1979. pap. text ed. 13.50 (ISBN 0-8191-0798-0). U Pr of Amer.

Duniway, David C. & Riggs, Neil R., eds. Oregon Archives: 1841-1843. (Illus.). 72p. 1971. pap. 3.95 (ISBN 0-87595-055-8). Oreg Hist Soc.

Edson, Christopher H. Chinese in Eastern Oregon, Eighteen Sixty to Eighteen Ninety. LC 74-83262. (Illus.). 1974. soft bdg. 8.00 (ISBN 0-88247-238-0). R & E Res Assoc.

Edwards, Philip L. Sketch of the Oregon Territory: Or Emigrants Guide. enl. & facsimile ed. 20p. 1979. Repr. of 1842 ed. pap. 3.00 (ISBN 0-87770-047-8). Ye Galleon.

Fiske, John. Unpublished Orations: The Discovery of the Columbia River & the Whitman Controversy, the Crispus Attucks Memorial & Columbus Memorial. LC 77-168031. Repr. of 1909 ed. 14.00 (ISBN 0-404-02403-3). AMS Pr.

Fogdall, Alberta B. Royal Family of the Columbia. (Illus.). 1978. 14.95 (ISBN 0-87770-168-7). Ye Galleon.

Franchere, Gabriel. Adventure at Astoria, Eighteen Ten to Eighteen Fourteen. Franchere, Hoyt C., tr. (American Exploration & Travel Ser.: No. 53). (Illus.). 1967. 9.95 (ISBN 0-8061-0747-2). U of Okla Pr.

French, Giles. Homesteads & Heritages: A History of Morrow County, Oregon. (Illus.). 128p. 1971. 12.50 (ISBN 0-8323-0204-X). Binford.

Friedman, Ralph. This Side of Oregon. 1982. write for info. Caxton.

--Tracking Down Oregon. LC 76-6647. (Illus.). 1978. pap. 6.95 (ISBN 0-87004-257-2). Caxton.

Fussner, F. Smith, ed. Glimpses of Wheeler County's Past: An Early History of North Central Oregon. LC 75-11035. (Illus.). 1975. pap. 4.95 (ISBN 0-8323-0249-X). Binford.

Ghent, William J. Road to Oregon. LC 77-111787. (BCL Ser.: I). (Illus.). Repr. of 1929 ed. 22.00 (ISBN 0-404-02717-2). AMS Pr.

Gossett, Gretta P. Beyond the Bend. (Illus.). 1980. 18.95 (ISBN 0-87770-213-6). Ye Galleon.

Gray, William H. A History of Oregon, Seventeen Ninety-Two to Eighteen Forty-Nine. LC 72-9446. (The Far Western Frontier Ser.). (Illus.). 630p. 1973. Repr. of 1870 ed. 28.00 (ISBN 0-405-04974-9). Arno.

Hanft, Marshall. The Cape Forts: Guardians of the Columbia. rev. ed. (Illus.). 62p. 1973. pap. 3.95 (ISBN 0-87595-044-2). Oreg Hist Soc.

Hastings, Lansford W. Emigrant's Guide to Oregon & California. 2nd ed. LC 68-8691. (American Scene Ser). 1969. Repr. of 1845 ed. lib. bdg. 19.50 (ISBN 0-306-71172-9). Da Capo.

Hidden, Maria L. Oregon Pioneers. 19p. Repr. of 1910 ed. pap. 3.50 (ISBN 0-8466-0073-0, SJS73). Shorey.

Jackson, Ronald V. & Teeples, Gary R. Oregon Census Index 1850. LC 77-86104. (Illus.). lib. bdg. 22.00 (ISBN 0-89593-114-1). Accelerated Index.

Jacobs, Melvin C. Winning Oregon: A Study of an Expansionist Movement. (Perspectives in American History Ser.: No. 43). 261p. Repr. of 1938 ed. lib. bdg. 17.50x (ISBN 0-87991-367-3). Porcupine Pr.

Jensen-Worth, Veryl M. Early Days on the Upper Willamette. 2nd, rev. ed. (Illus.). 142p. 1981. 17.50 (ISBN 0-939248-03-4); pap. 9.95 (ISBN 0-686-29017-8). Worth Co.

Keller, Paul & Pement, Jack. Oregon Historical Vignettes. (Illus.). 104p. 1975. 10.00 (ISBN 0-8323-0247-3). Binford.

Kilkenny, John F. Shamrocks & Shepherds: The Irish of Morrow County. 2nd ed. (Illus.). 164p. 1981. pap. 3.95 (ISBN 0-87595-101-5). Oreg Hist Soc.

Klosky, Beth A. Pendleton Legacy: An Illustrated History of the District. LC 73-143043. 1971. 7.50 (ISBN 0-87844-005-4). Sandlapper Store.

Lee, Daniel & Frost, Joseph. Ten Years in Oregon. 1968. Repr. of 1844 ed. 14.95 (ISBN 0-87770-017-6). Ye Galleon.

Lockley, Fred. The Lockley Files, Vol. 1: Conversations with Pioneer Women. Helm, Mike, ed. LC 81-50485. (Illus.). 310p. (Orig.). 1981. pap. 8.95 (ISBN 0-931742-08-0). Rainy Day Oreg.

--To Oregon by Ox-Team in 1847. 1971. pap. 2.50 (ISBN 0-87770-061-3). Ye Galleon.

Loewenberg, Robert J. Equality on the Oregon Frontier: Jason Lee & the Methodist Mission, 1834-43. LC 75-40876. 300p. 1976. 18.50 (ISBN 0-295-95491-4). U of Wash Pr.

Lomax, Alfred L. Later Woolen Mills in Oregon. LC 73-89241. (Illus.). 1973. 12.50 (ISBN 0-8323-0238-4). Binford.

Longsworth, Basil N. Overland Journey from Washington Tp., Guernsey County Ohio, to Oregon in the Summer of 1853. 44p. 1971. Repr. 5.50 (ISBN 0-87770-120-2); pap. 3.00 (ISBN 0-87770-062-1). Ye Galleon.

McCornack, Ellen C., ed. Thomas Condon: Pioneer Geologist of Oregon. (Illus.). 1928. 10.00 (ISBN 0-87071-331-0). Oreg St U Pr.

M'Duffee, John. Oregon Crisis. 25p. 1970. Repr. of 1848 ed. pap. 3.00 (ISBN 0-87770-063-X). Ye Galleon.

McKay, Harvey J. St. Paul, Oregon, Eighteen Thirty to Eighteen Ninety. LC 80-69228. (Illus.). 1980. 15.00 (ISBN 0-8323-0384-4). Binford.

Marlitt, Richard. Nineteenth Street. rev. ed. LC 78-73291. (Illus.). 218p. 1978. 19.95 (ISBN 0-686-75145-0); pap. 12.95 (ISBN 0-686-75146-9). Oreg Hist Soc.

Memorial of the Legislative Assembly of Oregon Territory. (House Misc Doc: No. 98). 1972. pap. 2.50 (ISBN 0-87770-065-6). Ye Galleon.

Merk, Frederick. Oregon Question: Essays in Anglo-American Diplomacy & Politics. LC 67-14345. 1967. 20.00x (ISBN 0-674-64200-7, Belknap Pr). Harvard U Pr.

Miller, Donald C. Ghost Towns of Washington & Oregon. (Western Ghost Town Ser: Bk. 3). (Illus.). 1977. 12.50 (ISBN 0-87108-500-3). Pruett.

Miller, Emma G. Clatsop County, Oregon: Its History, Legends & Industries. LC 57-13209. (Illus.). 1958. 8.95 (ISBN 0-8323-0034-9). Binford.

Minto, John. Rhymes of Early Life in Oregon. 84p. pap. 8.95 (ISBN 0-8466-2185-1, SJS185). Shorey.

Mitchell, S. Augustus. Texas, Oregon & California. (California Heritage Ser.). 1948. lib. bdg. 10.00 (ISBN 0-685-86964-4). Sullivan Bks Intl.

Munnick, Harriet D. Catholic Church Records of the Pacific Northwest: St. Paul, Oregon 1839-1898. LC 79-3575. (Illus.). 1980. 25.00 (ISBN 0-8323-0348-8). Binford.

Museums & Sites of Historical Interest in Oregon. LC 74-647323. 206p. 1980. pap. 5.95 (ISBN 0-87595-075-2). Oreg Hist Soc.

Nelson, Ray. Memoirs of an Oregon Moonshiner. LC 75-21134. (Illus.). 110p. 1980. pap. 4.95 (ISBN 0-87004-255-6). Caxton.

Nesmith, James W. Two Addresses. 1978. 7.95 (ISBN 0-87770-200-4); pap. 4.95 (ISBN 0-87770-202-0). Ye Galleon.

Newsom, David. David Newsom: The Western Observer, 1805-1882. LC 72-92062. (Illus.). 330p. 1972. pap. 7.95 (ISBN 0-87595-040-X). Oreg Hist Soc.
Nicolay, Charles G. Oregon Territory. 1976. Repr. of 1846 ed. 8.50 (ISBN 0-87770-020-6). Ye Galleon.
Oakley, Obadiah. Expedition to Oregon. 17p. 1967. Repr. pap. 2.50 (ISBN 0-87770-067-2). Ye Galleon.
O'Callaghan, Jerry A. The Disposition of the Public Domain in Oregon. Bruchey, Stuart, ed. LC 78-53563. (Development of Public Lands in the U. S. Ser.). 1979. Repr. of 1960 ed. lib. bdg. 10.00x (ISBN 0-405-11382-X). Arno.
Ohrt, Wallace L. The Rogue I Remember. LC 79-17166. (Illus.). 128p. 1979. pap. 6.95 (ISBN 0-916890-94-5). Mountaineers.
Olson, Joan & Olson, Gene. Oregon Times & Trails. LC 65-23503. (Illus.). (gr. 7-12). 1965. pap. 6.47x (ISBN 0-913366-00-5). Windyridge.
Olson, John A. The Danish Settlement of Junction City, Oregon. LC 75-18125. 1975. soft bdg. 8.00 (ISBN 0-88247-364-6). R & E Res Assoc.
Pacific Northwest Letters of Geo Gibbs, 1850-53. 54p. 2.95 (ISBN 0-87595-018-3); pap. 1.95 (ISBN 0-686-75144-2). Oreg Hist Soc.
Potter, Miles. Oregon's Golden Years. LC 75-12292. 185p. 1976. pap. 9.95 (ISBN 0-87004-254-8). Caxton.
Powell, Fred W., ed. Hall J. Kelley on Oregon. LC 79-87635. (The American Scene Ser). (Illus.). 412p. 1972. Repr. of 1932 ed. lib. bdg. 39.50 (ISBN 0-306-71796-4). Da Capo.
Sampson, William R., ed. John McLoughlin's Business Correspondence, 1847-48. LC 73-8747. (Illus.). 232p. 1973. 16.50 (ISBN 0-295-95299-7). U of Wash Pr.
Smeal, Lee. Oregon Historical & Biographical Index. LC 78-53713. (Illus.). Date not set. lib. bdg. price not set (ISBN 0-89593-196-6). Accelerated Index.
Stein, Harry. Salem: A Pictorial History. LC 80-27805. (Illus.). 205p. 1981. pap. 12.95 (ISBN 0-89865-125-5). Donning Co.
Talbot, Theodore. Soldier in the West: Letters of Theodore Talbot During His Services in California, Mexico, & Oregon, 1845-53. Hine, Robert V. & Lottinville, Savoie, eds. LC 74-177337. (The American Exploration & Travel Ser.: Vol. 61). (Illus.). 200p. 1972. 11.95 (ISBN 0-8061-1002-3). U of Okla Pr.
Thompson, Erwin N. Shallow Grave at Waiilatpu: The Sagers' West. 2nd ed. LC 77-110668. (Illus.). 192p. 1973. pap. 6.95 (ISBN 0-87595-024-8). Oreg Hist Soc.
Throckmorton, Arthur L. Oregon Argonauts: Merchant Adventurers on the Western Frontier. LC 61-64035. (Illus.). 372p. 1961. 14.95 (ISBN 0-87595-009-4). Oreg Hist Soc.
Tucker, Ephraim W. History of Oregon. enl. ed. 1970. Repr. of 1844 ed. 9.00 (ISBN 0-87770-026-5). Ye Galleon.
Vance, Mary. Historical Society Architectural Publications: Ohio, Oklahoma, Oregon, & Pennsylvania. (Architecture Ser.: Bibliography A-162). 55p. 1980. pap. 6.00 (ISBN 0-686-26909-8). Vance Biblios.
Vexler, R. I. Oregon Chronology & Factbook, Vol. 37. 1978. 8.50 (ISBN 0-379-16162-1). Oceana.
Wallis, George A. J. P. Housman in Oregon's Wild West. (Western Biography). (Illus.). 1977. pap. 2.95 (ISBN 0-89288-016-3). Maverick.
Weatherford, Marion T. Arlington: Child of the Columbia. LC 77-80362. (Illus.). 280p. 1977. pap. 6.95 (ISBN 0-87595-056-6). Oreg Hist Soc.
Williams, Elsie H. Seaways, Trailways, Byways: Oregon. 1979. pap. 3.95 (ISBN 0-89185-183-6). Anthelion Pr.
Wilson, Fred W. & Stewart, Earle K. Steamboat Days on the Rivers. (Illus.). 118p. 1969. pap. 4.95 (ISBN 0-87595-022-1). Oreg Hist Soc.
Winther, Oscar O. Old Oregon Country: A History of Frontier Trade, Transportation, & Travel. LC 50-63368. (Illus.). 1969. pap. 7.95 (ISBN 0-8032-5218-8, BB 388, Bison). U of Nebr Pr.
Young, Frank G., ed. The Correspondence & Journals of Captain Nathaniel J. Wyeth, 1831-6. LC 72-9474. (The Far Western Frontier Ser.). (Illus.). 288p. 1973. Repr. of 1899 ed. 17.00 (ISBN 0-405-05001-1). Arno.

OREGON–HISTORY–FICTION

Slade, Ruth. Sarah-Christina: A Girl of Old Portland. Hunting, Constance, ed. (gr. 4-8). 1981. pap. text ed. 5.95 (ISBN 0-913006-19-X). Puckerbrush.

OREGON–IMPRINTS

Belknap, George N. Oregon Imprints 1845-1870. LC 78-1013. (Illus.). 1968. 10.00 (ISBN 0-87114-019-5). U of Oreg Bks.

OREGON–JUVENILE LITERATURE

Bailey, Bernadine. Picture Book of Oregon. rev. ed. LC 54-9942. (Illus.). (gr. 3-6). 1967. 5.50g (ISBN 0-8075-9541-1). A Whitman.
Cloutier, James. This Day in Oregon. LC 80-83719. (Illus.). 128p. 1981. pap. 6.95 (ISBN 0-918966-06-X). Image West.
Cooke, Clarence M. Our Daily Life: An Oregon Civics. (Illus.). 1946. text ed. 4.50 (ISBN 0-8323-0166-3). Binford.
Fradin, Dennis. Oregon: In Words & Pictures. LC 80-15183. (Young People's Stories of Our States Ser.). (Illus.). 48p. (gr. 2-5). 1980. PLB 9.25 (ISBN 0-516-03937-7). Childrens.

OREGON–POLITICS AND GOVERNMENT

Burton, Robert E. Democrats of Oregon: The Pattern of Minority Politics, 1900-1956. LC 70-20919. 1970. 7.50 (ISBN 0-87114-051-9). U of Oreg Bks.
Gugdger, Charles M. & Bailes, Jack C. The Economic Impact of Oregon's Bottle Bill. 1974. pap. 3.95 (ISBN 0-87071-037-0). Oreg St U Pr.
Hendrickson, James E. Joe Lane of Oregon: Machine Politics & the Sectional Crisis, 1849-1861. (Western Americana Ser: No. 16). (Illus.). 1967. 22.50x (ISBN 0-300-00547-4). Yale U Pr.
Neuberger, Richard L. Adventures in Politics. LC 74-153233. (American Government & Politics Ser). 1971. Repr. of 1954 ed. 12.50 (ISBN 0-8046-1543-8). Kennikat.
Onstine, Burton W. Oregon Votes: 1858-1972. LC 73-88980. 395p. 1973. pap. 9.95 (ISBN 0-87595-043-4). Oreg Hist Soc.

OREGON–SOCIAL CONDITIONS

Moline, Norman T. Mobility & the Small Town. LC 79-133029. (Research Papers Ser.: No. 132). (Illus.). 1971. pap. 8.00 (ISBN 0-89065-039-X, 132). U Chicago Dept Geog.

OREGON (BATTLESHIP)

Sternlicht, Stanford. McKinley's Bulldog: The Battleship Oregon. LC 77-8603. 1977. text ed. 15.95x (ISBN 0-88229-263-3); pap. 7.95 (ISBN 0-88229-516-0). Nelson-Hall.

OREGON HISTORICAL SOCIETY, PORTLAND

Guide to the Manuscript Collections of the Oregon Historical Society. LC 78-182344. (Research & Bibliography Ser: No. 1). 20.00 (ISBN 0-87595-031-0). Oreg Hist Soc.
Oregon Historical Quarterly Index: 1940-1960, Vol. 2. LC 6-13601. 712p. 25.00 (ISBN 0-87595-078-7); pap. 20.00 (ISBN 0-87595-079-5). Oreg Hist Soc.
Oregon Historical Society Microfilm Guide. LC 73-79868. (Research & Bibliography Ser: No. 4). 162p. pap. 7.50 (ISBN 0-87595-041-8). Oreg Hist Soc.

OREGON PINE

see Douglas Fir

OREGON QUESTION

see also Northwest Boundary of the United States

OREGON TRAIL

Blanchet, A. M. Journal of a Catholic Bishop on the Oregon Trail. Kowrach, Edward J., tr. 1979. 18.95 (ISBN 0-87770-166-0). Ye Galleon.
Denny, Arthur A. Pioneer Days on Puget Sound. rev. ed. 1980. 14.95 (ISBN 0-87770-226-8). Ye Galleon.
Dicken, Samuel N. Pioneer Trails of the Oregon Coast. 2nd ed. LC 70-176249. (Illus.). 78p. 1978. pap. 4.95 (ISBN 0-87595-030-2). Oreg Hist Soc.
Elliot, Thomas C. The Earliest Travelers on the Oregon Trail. 1975. pap. 3.00 (ISBN 0-87770-154-7). Ye Galleon.
Federal Writers Project. Oregon Trail: The Missouri River to the Pacific Ocean. LC 70-145012. (Illus.). 1971. Repr. of 1939 ed. 35.00 (ISBN 0-403-01290-2). Somerset Pub.
Franzwa, Gregory M. The Oregon Trail Revisited. 2nd ed. (Illus.). 1978. 12.95 (ISBN 0-935284-07-9); pap. 5.95 (ISBN 0-935284-06-0). Patrice Pr.
Ghent, William J. Road to Oregon. LC 77-111787. (BCL Ser.: I). (Illus.). Repr. of 1929 ed. 22.00 (ISBN 0-404-02717-2). AMS Pr.
--Road to Oregon: A Chronicle of the Great Emigrant Trail. (Illus.). 1971. Repr. of 1929 ed. 39.00 (ISBN 0-403-00987-1). Scholarly.
McIlwraith, W. F. Oregon Trail Wall Map. (Illus.). pap. 3.50 (ISBN 0-8323-0052-7). Binford.
Parkman, Frances. Oregon Trail. Feltskog, E. N., ed. (Illus.). 854p. 1969. 27.50 (ISBN 0-299-05070-X). U of Wis Pr.
Parkman, Francis. Oregon Trail. (Classics Ser). (gr. 6 up). 1964. pap. 1.50 (ISBN 0-8049-0037-X, CL-37). Airmont.
--Oregon Trail. (RL 8). pap. 1.75 (ISBN 0-451-51377-0, CE1377, Sig Classics). NAL.
Purcell, Polly Jane. Autobiography & Reminiscences of a Pioneer. 20p. 1974. 5.50 (ISBN 0-87770-138-5). Ye Galleon.
Sengstacken, Agnes. Destination, West! 2nd ed. LC 72-87307. 222p. 8.95 (ISBN 0-8323-0207-4). Binford.

OREGON TRAIL–JUVENILE LITERATURE

Place, Marian T. Westward on the Oregon Trail. LC 62-17442. (American Heritage Junior Library). 154p. (YA) (gr. 7 up). 1962. PLB 12.89 (ISBN 0-06-020321-8, HarpJ). Har-Row.

O'REILLY, JOHN BOYLE, 1870-1890

McManamin, Francis G. The American Years of John Boyle O'Reilly. LC 76-6356. (Irish American Ser). 1976. 20.00 (ISBN 0-405-09349-7). Arno.

ORELLANA, FRANCISCO DE, d. 1546

De Carvajal, Gaspar. Discovery of the Amazon According to the Accounts of Friar Gaspar De Carvajal & Other Documents. Heaton, H. C. & Lee, Bertram T., eds. LC 77-120567. Repr. of 1934 ed. 31.50 (ISBN 0-404-01404-6). AMS Pr.
Markham, Clements R., ed. & tr. Expeditions into the Valley of the Amazons, 1539-1540, 1639. (Hakluyt Society First Ser.: No. 24). (Illus.). 1964. Repr. of 1859 ed. 26.50 (ISBN 0-8337-2238-7). B Franklin.

ORES

see also Metallurgy; Metals; Mineralogy; Mines and Mineral Resources; Ore-Deposits; also names of specific ores, e.g. Iron Ores

Craig, James R. & Vaughan, David J. Ore Microscopy & Ore Petiography. LC 80-39786. 406p. 1981. 29.95 (ISBN 0-471-08596-0, Pub. by Wiley-Interscience). Wiley.
Freund, Hugo. Applied Ore Microscopy. 1966. 39.95 (ISBN 0-02-339710-1, 33971). Macmillan.
Muns, George F. Chemical Analysis of Ores & Minerals for Copper, Silver, Gold, & the Platinum Metals. (Illus.). 53p. (Orig.). 1980. pap. 6.50 (ISBN 0-9604924-0-2). Muns.
Ramdohr, P. The Opaque Minerals in Stony Meteorites. 1973. 68.50 (ISBN 0-444-41067-8). Elsevier.
Ramdohr, Paul. The Ore Minerals & Their Intergrowths, 2 vols. 2nd ed. LC 79-40745. (International Series in Earth Sciences: Vol. 35). (Illus.). 1269p. 1981. Set. 200.00 (ISBN 0-08-023801-7). Pergamon.
Wills, B. A. Mineral Processing Technology: An Introduction to the Practical Aspects of Ore Treatment & Mineral Recovery. 2nd ed. LC 80-41698. (International Series on Materials Science & Technology: Vol. 29). (Illus.). 450p. 1981. 60.00 (ISBN 0-08-027322-X); pap. 20.00 (ISBN 0-08-027323-8). Pergamon.

ORES–ANALYSIS

see Assaying

ORESME, NICOLE, 1323-1382

Grant, Edward, ed. Nicole Oresme & the Kinematics of Circular Motion: Tractatus De Commensurabilitate Vel Incommensurabilitate Motuum Celi. LC 79-133238. (Medieval Science Ser). 1971. 50.00 (ISBN 0-299-05830-1). U of Wis Pr.
Menut, Albert D., tr. Nicole Oresme: Highlights from His French Commentary on Aristotle's Politics. 237p. 1979. 15.00 (ISBN 0-87291-132-2). Coronado Pr.

ORFF, CARL

Keetman, Gunild. Elementaria, First Acquaintance with Orff-Schulwerk. LC 75-1152. (Illus.). 1974. 12.00 (ISBN 0-901938-04-1). Eur-Am Music.

ORGAN

see also Electronic Organ

Antony, Joseph. Geschichtliche Darstellung der Entstehung und Vervollkommnung der Orgel. (Bibliotheca Organologica: Vol. 26). 1971. Repr. of 1832 ed. wrappers 22.50 (ISBN 90-6027-239-0, Pub. by Frits Knuf Netherlands). Pendragon NY.
Audsley, G. A. Organ-Stops & Their Artistic Registration. LC 77-94542. 1978. Repr. of 1921 ed. lib. bdg. 30.00 (ISBN 0-89341-400-X). Longwood Pr.
Audsley, George A. Art of Organ Building, 2 vols. (Illus.). Set. 25.00 (ISBN 0-8446-1034-8). Peter Smith.
--The Organ of the Twentieth Century. (Illus.). 12.50 (ISBN 0-8446-0011-3). Peter Smith.
--Temple of Tone. LC 79-108119. (BCL Ser.: No. 1). (Illus.). 1970. Repr. of 1925 ed. lib. bdg. 19.50 (ISBN 0-404-00417-2). AMS Pr.
Azevedo, Carlos de. Baroque Organ-Cases of Portugal. (Bibliotheca Organologica Ser.: Vol. 50). (Illus.). 160p. 1972. 32.50 (ISBN 90-6027-238-2, Pub. by Frits Knuf Netherlands). Pendragon NY.
Banchieri, Adriano. L' Organo Suonarino: Venezia 1605, 1611, & 1638. (Bibliotheca Organologica Ser.: Vol. 27). 1969. 32.50 (ISBN 90-6027-076-2, Pub. by Frits Knuf Netherlands). Pendragon NY.
Bendeler, Johann P. Organopoeia, oder Unterweisung wie eine Orgel nach ihren Hauptstucken als Mensuriren, Abtheilung derer Laden, Zufall des Windes, Stimmung oder Temperatur etc., aus wahren Mathematischen Grunden zu erbauen. (Bibliotheca Organologica Ser.: Vol. 28). 1972. Repr. of 1690 ed. wrappers 22.50 (ISBN 90-6027-152-1, Pub. by Frits Knuf Netherlands). Pendragon NY.
Biermann, J. H. Organographia Hildesiensis Specialis Hildesheim. (Bibliotheca Organologica Ser.: Vol. 29). 1980. Repr. of 1930 ed. 37.50 (ISBN 90-6027-167-X, Pub. by Frits Knuf Netherlands); wrappers 25.00 (ISBN 90-6027-166-1, Pub. by Frit Knuf Netherlands). Pendragon NY.
Blanchard, Homer D., ed. Organs of Our Time II. (Illus.). 176p. (Orig.). 1981. pap. 21.00 (ISBN 0-930112-05-9). Praestant.
Bonavia-Hunt, Noel A. Modern Organ Stops. (Illus.). 1976. pap. 7.50x (ISBN 0-913746-05-3). Organ Lit.
Buck, Dudley. Influence of the Organ in History. 1976. lib. bdg. 19.00 (ISBN 0-403-03751-4). Scholarly.
Casson, Thomas. Lecture on the Pedal Organ. 1976. lib. bdg. 19.00 (ISBN 0-403-03627-5). Scholarly.
Cavaille-Coll, A. Complete Theoretical Works. Huybens, G., ed. (Bibliotheca Organologica Ser.: Vol. 45). (Illus.). xiii, 218p. (Fr.). 1980. 50.00 (ISBN 90-6027-192-0, Pub. by Frits Knuf Netherlands). Pendragon NY.
Clarke, William H. An Outline of the Structure of the Pipe Organ. (Illus.). 1977. pap. text ed. 8.00x (ISBN 0-913746-09-6). Organ Lit.
Dähnert, Ulrich. Die Orgeln Gottfried Silbermanns in Mitteldeutschland. (Bibliotheca Organologica Ser.: Vol. 34). 1971. Repr. of 1953 ed. 50.00 (ISBN 0-686-30876-X, Pub. by Frits Knuf Netherlands); wrappers 37.50 (ISBN 0-686-30877-8, Pub. by Frits Knuf Netherlands). Pendragon NY.
De Pontecoulant, Adolphe. Organographie, 2 vols. (Bibliotheca Organologica Ser.: Vol. 9). 1972. Repr. of 1861 ed. 137.50 (ISBN 90-6027-138-6, Pub. by Frits Knuf Netherlands). Pendragon NY.
Diruta, G. Il Transilvano, 1593-1609. facsimile ed. (Bibliotheca Organologica: Vol. 44). (Illus.). 154p. 1980. 75.00 (ISBN 90-6027-212-9, Pub. by Frits Knuf Netherlands). Pendragon NY.
Douglass, Fenner. Language of the Classical French Organ: A Musical Tradition Before 1800. LC 72-81415. (Studies in the History of Music Ser.: No. 5). (Illus.). 1969. 20.00x (ISBN 0-300-01117-2). Yale U Pr.
Earl, S. G. Repairing the Reed Organ & Harmonium. (Illus.). 1976. pap. 2.50x (ISBN 0-913746-06-1). Organ Lit.
Ellerhorst, Winfred. Handbuch der Orgelkunde: Die mathematischen und akustischen, technischen und kunstlerischen Grundlagen sowie die Geschichte und Pflege der Modernen Orgel, 2 vols. (Bibliotheca Organologica Ser.: Vol. 7). 1976. Repr. of 1936 ed. 102.50 (ISBN 90-6027-024-X, Pub. by Frits Knuf Netherlands); wrappers 77.50 (ISBN 90-6027-219-6, Pub. by Frits Knuf Netherlands). Pendragon NY.
Evans, Edwin. Technics of the Organ. 1976. lib. bdg. 25.00 (ISBN 0-403-03812-X). Scholarly.
Ferguson, John A. Walter Holtkamp: American Organ Builder. LC 78-26500. (Illus.). 1979. 11.00x (ISBN 0-87338-217-X). Kent St U Pr.
Fesperman, John. Two Essays on Organ Design. LC 75-10153. (Illus.). 104p. 1975. 9.25 (ISBN 0-915548-01-1). Sunbury Pr.
Gellerman, Robert F. The American Reed Organ. LC 73-81768. (Illus.). 13.95 (ISBN 0-911572-09-0). Vestal.
Goode, Jack C. Pipe Organ Registration. LC 64-16149. 1964. 8.95 (ISBN 0-687-31486-0). Abingdon.
Goodrich, Wallace. The Organ in France. LC 76-42038. 1977. Repr. of 1917 ed. lib. bdg. 20.00 (ISBN 0-89341-058-6). Longwood Pr.
Graaf, G. A. de. Literatuur over het orgel -- Literature on the Organ - Literatur uber die Orgel. (Bibliotheca Organolociga Ser.: Vol. 51). (Dutch, Eng., Ger.). 1957. wrappers 15.00 (ISBN 90-6027-229-3, Pub. by Frits Knuf Netherlands). Pendragon NY.
Havingha, Gerhardus. Oorspronk en Voortgang der Orgelen met de Voortreffelijkheit van Alkmaars groote Orgel. (Bibliotheca Organologica Ser.: Vol. 13). 1981. Repr. of 1727 ed. wrappers 35.00 (ISBN 90-6027-253-6, Pub. by Frits Knuf Netherlands). Pendragon NY.
Hill, Arthur G. The Organ-Cases & Organs of the Middle Ages & Renaissance. (Bibliotheca Organologica Ser.: Vol. 6). (Illus.). 1975. Repr. of 1891 ed. 42.50 (ISBN 90-6027-026-6, Pub. by Frits Knuf Netherlands); wrappers 30.00 (ISBN 90-6027-262-5, Pub. Frits Knuf Netherlands). Pendragon NY.
Hopkins, Edward J. & Rimbault, Edward F. The Organ: Its History and Construction. (Bibliotheca Organologica Ser.: Vol. 4). 1981. Repr. of 1877 ed. 55.00 (ISBN 90-6027-145-9, Pub. by Frits Knuf Netherlands). Pendragon NY.

Hulphers, A. Historisk Afhandling om Musik och Instrumenter sardeles om Orgwerks... An Historical Treatise on Music & Instruments Including the Arrangement of Organs in General, Together with a Brief Description of Organs in Sweden. (Bibliotheca Organologica Ser.: Vol. 35). 1972. Repr. of 1773 ed. 25.00 (ISBN 90-6027-146-7, Pub. by Frits Knuf Netherlands). Pendragon NY.

Klais, Hans G. & Steinhaus, Hans. The Bamboo Organ in the Catholic Parish Church of St. Joseph at las Pinas, Province of Rizal, on the Island of Luzon, Philippines. Blanchard, Homer, tr. from Ger. (Illus.). 30.00 (ISBN 0-930112-02-4). Praestant.

Kruys, M. H. Verzameling Van Disposities der Verschillende Orgels in Nederland. 2nd. ed. (Bibliotheca Organologica: Vol. 1). 1972. 35.00 (ISBN 90-6027-285-4, Pub. by Frits Knuf Netherlands); wrappers 22.50 (ISBN 90-6027-148-3). Pendragon NY.

Lahee, Henry C. The Organ & Its Masters. LC 76-22340. (Illus.). 1976. Repr. of 1903 ed. lib. bdg. 35.00 (ISBN 0-89341-002-0). Longwood Pr.

Lindow, Ch. W. Historic Organs in France. Blanchard, Homer D., tr. (The Little Organ Books Ser.: No. 1). (Illus.). 1980. pap. 21.00 (ISBN 0-930112-03-2). Praestant.

Locher, Carl & Dobler, J. Die Orgel-Register und Ihre Klangfarben: Ein Nachschlagewerk Fur Organisten, Physiker und Physiologen. (Bibliotheca Organologica: Vol. 12). 1971. 37.50 (ISBN 90-6027-290-0, Pub. by Frits Knuf Netherlands); wrappers 22.50 (ISBN 90-6027-151-3). Pendragon NY.

Matthews, E. N. Colonial Organs & Organ Builders. 1969. 32.00x (ISBN 0-522-83906-1, Pub by Melbourne U Pr). Intl Schol Bk Serv.

Miller, George L. Recent Revolution in Organ Building. (Illus.). 7.50 (ISBN 0-911572-02-3). Vestal.

Norman, Herbert & Norman, H. John. The Organ Today. (Illus.). 224p. 1981. 25.00 (ISBN 0-7153-8053-2). David & Charles.

Ochse, Orpha. The History of the Organ in the United States. LC 73-22644. (Illus.). 512p. 1975. 27.50x (ISBN 0-253-32830-6). Ind U Pr.

Ord-Hume, Arthur. The Barrel Organ. LC 73-22604. (Illus.). 1978. 25.00 (ISBN 0-498-01482-7). A S Barnes.

Owen, Barbara. The Organ in New England. (Illus.). 629p. 1980. 72.00 (ISBN 0-915548-08-9). Sunbury Pr.

Palmer, Susann & Palmer, Samuel. The Hurdy-Gurdy. LC 79-56052. (Illus.). 192p. 1980. 45.00 (ISBN 0-7153-7888-0). David & Charles.

Perrot, Jean. The Organ from Its Invention in the Hellenistic Period to the End of the Thirteenth Century. Deane, Norma, tr. 346p. 1971. 37.50 (ISBN 0-19-318418-4). Oxford U Pr.

Praetorius, Michael. The Syntagma Musicum, Vol. 2: De Organographica. Blumenfeld, Harold, tr. LC 72-14061. (Music Reprint Ser.). (Illus.). 1975. 16.50 (ISBN 0-306-70563-X). Da Capo.

Presley, Horton. Restoring & Collecting Antique Reed Organs. (Illus.). 1977. 12.95x (ISBN 0-8306-7911-1); pap. 8.95x (ISBN 0-8306-6911-6, 911). TAB Bks.

Rimbault, Edward. The Early English Organ Builders & Their Work. 1977. lib. bdg. 75.00 (ISBN 0-8490-1740-8). Gordon Pr.

Rimbault, Edward F. The Early English Organ Builders & Their Works: Fifteenth Century to the Great Rebellion. LC 74-24201. Repr. of 1865 ed. 14.00 (ISBN 0-404-12819-X). AMS Pr.

Roosevelt, Hilborne. Manufacturer of Church, Chapel, Concert & Chamber Organs. (Bibliotheca Organologica: Vol. 37). 117p. 22.50 (ISBN 90-6027-332-X, Pub. by Frits Knuf Netherlands). Pendragon NY.

Roosevelt, Hilborne L. Hilborne L. Roosevelt Organs. (Illus.). 1978. Repr. of 1888 ed. 20.00x (ISBN 0-913746-12-6). Organ Lit.

Schering, Arnold. Die Niederlandische Orgelmesse Im Zeitalter Des Josquin: Eine Stilkritische Untersuchung. (Bibliotheca Oeganologica: Vol. 16). 1971. Repr. of 1912 ed. wrappers 22.50 (ISBN 90-6027-154-8, Pub. by Frits Knuf Netherlands). Pendragon NY.

Schlick, Arnolt. Spiegel der Orgelmacher un(D) Organisten. (Bibliotheca Organologica: Vol. 63). 1981. 60.00 (ISBN 90-6027-395-8, Pub. by Frits Knuf Netherlands); wrappers 47.50 (ISBN 90-6027-338-9). Pendragon NY.

Schlimbach, Georg C. Ueber Die Structur, Erhaltung Stimmung, Prufung der Orgel: Leipzig 1801. (Bibliotheca Organologica: Vol. 8). Repr. of 1966 ed. wrappers 27.50 (ISBN 90-6027-025-8, Pub. by Frits Knuf Netherlands). Pendragon NY.

Seidel, J. J. The Organ & Its Construction. (Music Reprint Ser.). 218p. 1981. Repr. of 1855 ed. 22.50 (ISBN 0-306-76106-8). Da Capo.

Skinner, E. M. The Modern Organ. (Bibliotheca Organologica: Vol. 62). Repr. of 1974 ed. wrappers 15.00 (ISBN 90-6027-342-7, Pub. by Frits Knuf Netherlands). Pendragon NY.

Skinner, Ernest M. The Modern Organ: Including Ernest M. Skinner: Organ Builder. by T. Scott Buhrman. 1978. pap. text ed. 12.00x (ISBN 0-913746-11-8). Organ Lit.

Sorge, G. A. Die Geheim Gehaltene Kunst Von Mensuration Von Orgel-Pfeiffen: The Secretly Kept Art of the Scaling of Organ Pipes. (Bibliotheca Organologica: Vol. 33). 1979. 57.50 (ISBN 0-686-30869-7, Pub by Frits Knuf Netherlands); wrappers 45.00 (ISBN 90-6027-346-X). Pendragon NY.

Sponsel, Johann U. Orgelhistorie: Nurnberg 1771. (Bibliotheca Organologica: Vol. 18). Date not set. Repr. of 1968 ed. wrappers 20.00 (ISBN 90-6027-049-5, Pub. by Frits Knuf Netherlands). Pendragon NY.

A Study of Theater Organ Style. 1968. pap. 15.00 (ISBN 0-686-09506-5). Peer-Southern.

Sutton, F. H. A Short Account of Organs Built in England Eighteen Hundred & Forty - Seven. (Bibliotheca Organologica: Vol. 55). 113p. 1979. wrappers 20.00 (ISBN 90-6027-354-0, Pub. by Frits Knuf Netherlands). Pendragon NY.

Thornsby, Frederick W. Dictionary of Organs & Organists. 1978. Repr. of 1912 ed. lib. bdg. 29.95 (ISBN 0-89761-005-9). Dunn & Webster.

Truett, Everett E. Organ Registration: A Comprehensive Treatise on the Distinctive Quality of Tone & Organ Stops. LC 78-181284. 264p. 1919. Repr. 18.00 (ISBN 0-403-01707-6). Scholarly.

Truette, Everett E. Organ Registration: A Comprehensive Treatise on the Distinctive Quality of Tone of Organ Stops. LC 78-58192. 1978. Repr. of 1919 ed. lib. bdg. 25.00 (ISBN 0-89341-431-X). Longwood Pr.

Turk, Daniel G. Von Den Wichtigsten Pflichten Eines Organisten. (Bibliotheca Organologica: Vol. 5). Date not set. Repr. of 1966 ed. wrappers 27.50 (ISBN 90-6027-027-4, Pub. by Frits Knuf Netherlands). Pendragon NY.

Twinning, Walter L. The Art of Organ Accompaniment in the Church Services. 1976. lib. bdg. 17.00 (ISBN 0-403-03786-7). Scholarly.

Vente, Maarten A. Vijf Eeuwen Zwolse Orgels Fourteen Forty-Seven to Nineteen Seventy-One. (Bibliotheca Organologica: Vol. 49). 22.50 (ISBN 90-6027-240-4, Pub. by Frits Knuf Netherlands). Pendragon NY.

West, John E. Cathedral Organists Past & Present. 1978. Repr. of 1899 ed. lib. bdg. 12.95 (ISBN 0-89761-006-7). Dunn & Webster.

Whiting, Robert B. Estey Reed Organs on Parade:...a Pictorial Review of the Many Parlour, Boudoir, Philharmonic, & Other Types of Reed Organs Made Over a 100-Year Period by the Famous Estey Organ Company, Together with a Brief Corporate History. LC 81-7545. (Illus.). 1981. pap. 15.00 (ISBN 0-911572-21-X). Vestal.

Williams, C. F. The Story of the Organ. LC 78-90250. (Illus.). 328p. 1972. Repr. of 1903 ed. 22.00 (ISBN 0-8103-3067-9). Gale.

Williams, Charles F. The Story of Organ Music. LC 71-39643. (Select Bibliographies Reprint Ser). 1972. Repr. of 1905 ed. 18.25 (ISBN 0-8369-9948-7). Arno.

Williams, Peter. A New History of the Organ: From the Greeks to the Present Day. LC 79-2176. (Illus.). 234p. 1980. 27.50x (ISBN 0-253-15704-8). Ind U Pr.

Wilson, Michael. The English Chamber Organ: History & Development 1650-1850. LC 68-27600. 168p. 1968. 14.95x (ISBN 0-87249-119-6). U of SC Pr.

Wilson, Michael I. Organ Cases of Western Europe. (Illus.). 1979. 65.00 (ISBN 0-8390-0242-4). Allanheld & Schram.

Wolfram, J. C. Anleitung Zur Kenntnisz, Beurtheilung und Erhaltung der Orgeln. (Bibliotheca Organologica Ser.: Vol. 3). Repr. of 1972 ed. wrappers 25.00 (ISBN 90-6027-159-9, Pub. by Frits Knuf Netherlands). Pendragon NY.

ORGAN–CONSTRUCTION

Andersen, Poul-Gerhard. Organ Building & Design. Curnutt, Joanne, tr. (Illus.). 359p. 1969. 35.00 (ISBN 0-04-786003-0). Allen Unwin.

Audsley, George A. The Art of Organ Building, 2 vols. Incl. Vol. 1. Proem. (Illus.). x, 600p. 12.50 (ISBN 0-486-21314-5); Vol. 2. Specifications of Organs. (Illus.). iv, 750p. 12.50 (ISBN 0-486-21315-3). Dover.

Bonavia-Hunt, Noel A. Modern Organ Stops: A Practical Guide to Their Nomenclature, Construction, Voicing & Artistic Use. (Bibliotheca Organologica Ser.: Vol. 52). 1974. Repr. of 1923 ed. wrappers 15.00 (ISBN 90-6027-172-6, Pub. by Frits Knuf Netherlands). Pendragon NY.

Clarke, W. H. An Outline of the Structure of the Pipe Organ. (Bibliotheca Organologica: Vol. 59). 130p. 1978. wrappers 20.00 (ISBN 90-6027-374-5, Pub. by Frits Knuf Netherlands). Pendragon NY.

De Celles, Francois B. The Organ-Builder, 2 vols. Ferguson, Charles, tr. from Fr. LC 77-1443. Orig. Title: L'art Du Facteur D'orgues. (Illus.). 600p. 1977. Set. 320.00 (ISBN 0-915548-02-X). Sunbury Pr.

Earl, S. G. Repairing the Reed Organ & Harmonium. (Illus.). 1976. pap. 2.50x (ISBN 0-913746-06-1). Organ Lit.

Ferguson, John A. Walter Holtkamp: American Organ Builder. LC 78-26500. (Illus.). 1979. 11.00x (ISBN 0-87338-217-X). Kent St U Pr.

Fesperman, John. Organs in Mexico. (Illus.). 160p. 1981. 18.50 (ISBN 0-915548-07-0). Sunbury Pr.

Foort, Reginald. The Cinema Organ. LC 75-117943. (Illus.). 7.95 (ISBN 0-911572-05-8). Vestal.

Goodrich, Wallace. The Organ in France. 1978. Repr. of 1917 ed. lib. bdg. 18.95 (ISBN 0-89761-001-6). Dunn & Webster.

Heurn, J. van. De Orgelmaaker behelzende eene uitvoerige beschrijving van alle de uit en inwendige deelen des Orgels en handleiding tot het maaken, zamenbrengen en herstellen derzelven, benevens de beschrijving en afbeelding der werktuigen welke tot deze kunst gebezigd worden, 3 vols. (Bibliotheca Organologica Ser.: Vol. 56). 1976. Repr. of 1805 ed. Set. 137.50 (ISBN 90-6027-257-9, Pub. by Frits Knuf Netherlands). Pendragon NY.

Hill, Arthur G. The Organ Cases & Organs of the Middle Ages & Renaissance. 1978. lib. bdg. 11.95 (ISBN 0-89761-002-4). Dunn & Webster.

Klais, Hans G. & Steinhaus, Hans. The Bamboo Organ in the Catholic Parish Church of St. Joseph at las Pinas, Province of Rizal, on the Island of Luzon, Philippines. Blanchard, Homer, tr. from Ger. (Illus.). 30.00 (ISBN 0-930112-02-4). Praestant.

Klotz, Hans. Organ Handbook. LC 69-11068. 1969. 9.75 (ISBN 0-570-01306-2, 99-1187). Concordia.

Lewis, Walter & Lewis, Thomas. Modern Organ Building. LC 77-8738. 1977. Repr. of 1911 ed. lib. bdg. 30.00 (ISBN 0-89341-074-8). Longwood Pr.

Milne, H. F. How to Build a Small Two-Manual Chamber Pipe Organ. (Illus.). pap. 10.00x (ISBN 0-913746-03-7). Organ Lit.

--The Reed Organ: It's Design & Construction. (Bibliotheca Organologica: Vol. 58). 1930. wrappers 15.00 (ISBN 90-6027-303-6, Pub. by Frits Knuf Netherlands). Pendragon NY.

--The Reed Organ: Its Design & Construction. (Illus.). pap. 5.00x (ISBN 0-913746-02-9). Organ Lit.

Ogasapian, J. Organ Building in New York City Seventeen Hundred to Nineteen Hundred. (Bibliotheca Organologica: Vol. 61). 1977. wrappers 30.00 (ISBN 90-6027-309-5, Pub. by Frits Knuf Netherlands). Pendragon NY.

Ogasapian, John. Henry Erben: Portrait of a Nineteenth Century Organ Builder. (Illus.). 72p. 1980. pap. 10.00x (ISBN 0-913746-13-4). Organ Lit.

--Organ Building in New York City,1700 to 1900. LC 78-300889. (Illus.). 1977. pap. text ed. 20.75x (ISBN 0-913746-10-X). Organ Lit.

Rimbault, Edward F. The Early English Organ Builders & Their Works. LC 77-75182. 1977. Repr. of 1864 ed. lib. bdg. 15.00 (ISBN 0-89341-062-4). Longwood Pr.

Robertson, F. E. A Practical Treatise on Organ - Building. (Illus.). 370p. Set. pap. 35.00x (ISBN 0-913746-04-5). Organ Lit.

--A Practical Treatise on Organ Building, 2 vols. (Bibliotheca Organologica: Vol. 46). Repr. of 1972 ed. wrappers 22.50 (ISBN 90-6027-331-1, Pub. by Frits Knuf Netherlands); Vol. 1, Text. Vol. 2, Plates. Pendragon NY.

Seidel, J. J. The Organ & Its Construction. (Music Reprint Ser.). 218p. 1981. Repr. of 1855 ed. 22.50 (ISBN 0-306-76106-8). Da Capo.

--Die Orgel und Ihr Bau: Ein Systematisches Handbuch. (Bibliotheca Organologica: Vol. 2). Repr. of 1966 ed. wrappers 22.50 (ISBN 90-6027-001-0, Pub. by Frits Knuf Netherlands). Pendragon NY.

Sumner, William. The Organ: Its Evolution, Principles of Construction & Use. 3rd ed. LC 73-181272. 544p. 1962. Repr. 34.00 (ISBN 0-403-01695-9). Scholarly.

Die Theorie und Praxis Des Orgelbaues, 2 vols. (Bibliotheca Organologica: Vol. 20). Repr. of 1972 ed. Set. 145.00 (ISBN 90-6027-156-4, Pub. by Frits Knuf Netherlands). Pendragon NY.

Werckmeister, Andreas. Werckmeister in English. Krapf, Gerhard, tr. from Ger. LC 76-21064. Orig. Title: Erweiterte und Verbesserte Orgel-Probe. 1976. 9.00 (ISBN 0-915548-03-8). Sunbury Pr.

Whitworth, Reginald. The Cinema & Theatre Organ: A Comprehensive Description of This Instrument, Its Constituent Parts, & Its Use. (Illus.). 144p. 1981. pap. 15.00x (ISBN 0-913746-14-2). Organ Lit.

Wicks, Mark. Organ Building for Amateurs. (Illus.). pap. 15.00x (ISBN 0-913746-01-0). Organ Lit.

Williams, Peter. The European Organ, 1450-1850. LC 78-57080. (Illus.). 336p. 1978. Repr. of 1966 ed. 27.50x (ISBN 0-253-32083-6). Ind U Pr.

ORGAN–INSTRUCTION AND STUDY

Andrews, Mildred & Riddle, Pauline. Church Organ Method. 123p. 1973. pap. 12.00 (ISBN 0-686-64090-X, 04904). Fischer Inc NY.

Buck, Dudley. Illustrations in Choir Accompaniment. LC 79-137316. Repr. of 1892 ed. 18.00 (ISBN 0-404-01145-4). AMS Pr.

Conely, James. A Guide to Improvisation: An Introductory Handbook for Church Organists. LC 74-26945. 64p. 1975. pap. 2.95 (ISBN 0-687-16287-4). Abingdon.

DeVito, Albert. Chord Charts. 1980. 3.95 (ISBN 0-934286-00-0). Kenyon.

--Chord Dictionary. LC 75-40685. 1980. 3.95 (ISBN 0-934286-01-9). Kenyon.

--Chord Encyclopedia. LC 75-43441. 1980. 5.95 (ISBN 0-934286-02-7). Kenyon.

De Vito, Albert. Playing the Chord Organ & Learning to Read Music. 1974. 3.95 (ISBN 0-934286-08-6). Kenyon.

Evans, Edwin. Technics of the Organ. LC 78-13905. 1978. Repr. of 1938 ed. lib. bdg. 15.00 (ISBN 0-89341-437-9). Longwood Pr.

Gleason, Harole. Methods of Organ Playing. 6th ed. 1979. 19.95 (ISBN 0-13-579466-8). P-H.

Hull, A. Eaglefield. Organ Playing: Its Technique & Expression. (Music Ser.). (Illus.). viii, 256p. 1981. Repr. of 1911 ed. lib. bdg. 22.50 (ISBN 0-306-76134-3). Da Capo.

Hunt, Reginald. Extemporization for Music Students. (YA) (gr. 9 up). 1968. pap. 10.00 (ISBN 0-19-321380-X). Oxford U Pr.

Johnson, David N. Instruction Book for Beginning Organists. rev. ed. 1964. spiral bdg. 6.95 (ISBN 0-8066-0423-9, 11-9220). Augsburg.

--Organ Teacher's Guide. 48p. 1971. pap. 2.75 (ISBN 0-8066-1119-7, 11-9326). Augsburg.

Kittel, Johann C. Der Angehende Praktische Organist, Oder Anweisung Zum Zweckmassigen Gebrauch der Orgel Bei Gottesverehrungen in Beispielen: Erfurt 1801-1831. (Bibliotheca Organologica: Vol. 72). 75.00 (ISBN 90-6027-278-1, Pub. by Frits Knuf Netherlands). Pendragon NY.

Krapf, Gerhard. Organ Improvisation. 1967. pap. 5.25 (ISBN 0-8066-0727-0, 11-9310). Augsburg.

Phillips, Charles H. Modern Organ Pedalling. Blake, Leonard, ed. 1951. 10.00x (ISBN 0-19-322330-9). Oxford U Pr.

Ragatz, Oswald G. Organ Technique: A Basic Course of Study. LC 78-3244. (Illus.). 320p. 1980. soft cover, spiral bdg. 15.00x (ISBN 0-253-17146-6). Ind U Pr.

ORGAN, ELECTRONIC

see Electronic Organ

ORGAN CULTURE

see Organs, Culture of

ORGAN MUSIC

Bach, J. S. Organ Music. 357p. 1970. pap. 7.95 (ISBN 0-486-22359-0). Dover.

Bach, Johann. Organ Music. (The BachGesellschaft edition). 8.75 (ISBN 0-8446-0468-2). Peter Smith.

Belnap, Parley L. Hymn Studies for Organists. pap. 4.95 (ISBN 0-87747-418-4). Deseret Bk.

Bender, Jan. Organ Improvisation for Beginners. LC 75-2934. (Illus.). 71p. 1975. bds. 7.50 (ISBN 0-570-01312-7, 99-1229). Concordia.

Blanchard, Homer D. The Bach Organ Book. (The Little Organ Books Ser.: No. 3). (Illus.). Date not set. pap. price not set. Praestant.

Broadhouse, Joan. Compositions for the Organ. 1976. Repr. of 1880 ed. lib. bdg. 19.00 (ISBN 0-403-03764-6). Scholarly.

Cavaille-Coll, A. Devis d'un grand orgue a trois claviers et un pedalier complets projete pour la vieille Eglise Lutherienne Evangelique a Amsterdam. (Bibliotheca Organologica Ser.: Vol. 45). 52p. 1980. Repr. of 1881 ed. wrappers 17.50 (ISBN 90-6027-193-9, Pub. by Frits Knuf Netherlands). Pendragon NY.

Coleman, Henry. Church Organist. 2nd ed. 1968. 9.75 (ISBN 0-19-322100-4). Oxford U Pr.

Edson, Jean S. Organ Preludes: Supplement. 1974. 12.00 (ISBN 0-8108-0663-0). Scarecrow.

Gay, Harry W. Four French Organist-Composers: 1549-1720. LC 74-34396. 120p. 1975. incl. cassette 22.50x (ISBN 0-87870-022-6). Memphis St Univ.

Guilmant, Alexandre & Pirro, A., eds. Archives Des Maitres De L'orgue Des XVIe, XVIIe, et XVIIIe, 10 vols. 1898-1910. Set. 350.00 (ISBN 0-384-01893-9); 37.50 ea. Johnson Repr.

Harmon, Thomas. The Registration of J. S. Bach's Organ Works. (Bibliotheca Organologica Ser.: Vol. 70). 65.00 (ISBN 90-6027-245-5, Pub. by Frits Knuf Netherlands); wrappers 50.00 (ISBN 90-6027-243-9, Pub. by Frits Knuf Netherlands). Pendragon NY.
Irwin, Stevens. Dictionary of Hammond Organ Stops. 4th rev. ed. 1970. pap. 8.95 (ISBN 0-02-871110-6). Schirmer Bks.
--Dictionary of Pipe Organ Stops. rev. ed. 1965. pap. 10.95 (ISBN 0-02-871130-0). Schirmer Bks.
Keeler, J. J. & Blackham, E. Donnell. Basic Organ Technique & Repertoire. 4.95 (ISBN 0-87747-396-X). Deseret Bk.
Knock, N. A. Dispositien der Merkwaadigste Kerk-Orgelen, Welken in De Provincie Friesland, Groningen En Elders Aangetroffen Worden. (Bibliotheca Organologica: Vol. 24). 1972. Repr. of 1788 ed. 20.00 (ISBN 90-6027-147-5, Pub. by Frits Knuf Netherlands). Pendragon NY.
Kratzenstein, Marilou. Survey of Organ Literature & Editions. 1980. text ed. 14.75 (ISBN 0-8138-1050-7). Iowa St U Pr.
Lindow, Ch. W. & Blanchard, Homer D. A Little Organ Lexicon. (The Little Organ Book Ser.: No. 2). 44p. 1981. pap. 7.00 (ISBN 0-930112-04-0). Praestant.
Loewenfeld, Hans. Leonhard Kleber und Sein Orgeltabulaturbuch Als Beitrag Zur Geschicte der Orgelmusik Im Beginnenden XVI. (Bibliotheca Organologica: Vol. 19). 1968. Repr. of 1897 ed. 20.00 (ISBN 90-6027-050-9, Pub. by Frits Knuf Netherlands). Pendragon NY.
Lovelace, Austin C. The Organist & Hymn Playing. rev. ed. LC 81-80265. (Illus.). 61p. 1981. pap. 4.95 (ISBN 0-916642-16-X). Hope Pub.
Lully, Jean B. Nine Seventeenth Century Organ Transcriptions from the Operas of Lully. Howell, Almonte C., Jr., ed. LC 62-19378. 1963. pap. 3.50x (ISBN 0-8131-1078-5). U Pr of Ky.
Organ Chord Dictionary. 1981. 2.95 (ISBN 0-88284-156-4). Alfred Pub.
Pachelbel, Carl T. Magnificat for Double Chorus & Organ. David, Hans T., ed. pap. write to C. F. Peters Corps for prices (ISBN 0-685-18957-0). NY Pub Lib.
Radeker, Johannes. Korte Beschrijving Van Het Beroemde En Prachtige Orgel in De Groote of St. Bavooskerk Te Haerlem. (Bibliotheca Organologica: Vol. 14). 1974. Repr. of 1775 ed. wrappers 17.50 (ISBN 90-6027-323-0, Pub. by Frits/Netherlands). Pendragon NY.
Rietschel, Georg. Die Aufgabe der Orgel Im Gottesdienst Bis in das 18. (Bibliotheca Organologica: Vol. 53). iv, 72p. 1979. Repr. of 1893 ed. 36.50 (ISBN 90-6027-329-X, Pub. by Frits Knuf Netherlands); wrappers 24.00 (ISBN 90-6027-328-1). Pendragon NY.
Roseingrave, Thomas. Compositions for Organ & Harpsichord. Stevens, Denis, ed. LC 63-21370. (Penn State Music Series, No. 2). 44p. 1964. pap. 3.75x (ISBN 0-271-73054-4). Pa St U Pr.
Rowell, Lois. American Organ Music on Records. LC 76-360159. 122p. 1976. pap. 6.00x (ISBN 0-913746-08-8). Organ Lit.
Smits Van Waesberghe, J. Organicae Voces: Festschrift Joseph Smits Van Waesberghe Angeboten Anlasslich Seienes 60. 180p. 1963. 30.00 (ISBN 90-6027-344-3, Pub. by Frits Knuf Netherlands). Pendragon NY.
Tusler, Robert L. Style of J. S. Bach's Chorale Preludes. 2nd ed. LC 68-13275. (Music Ser). 1968. Repr. of 1956 ed. lib. bdg. 12.50 (ISBN 0-306-70942-2). Da Capo.

ORGAN MUSIC-BIBLIOGRAPHY

Edson, Jean S. Organ Preludes: An Index to Compositions on Hymn Tunes, Chorales, Plainsong Melodies, Gregorian Tunes & Carols, 2 Vols. LC 73-8960. 1970. Set. 45.00 (ISBN 0-8108-0287-2). Scarecrow.
Nardone, Thomas R., ed. Organ Music in Print. LC 75-16504. (Music in Print Ser.: Vol. 3). 262p. 1975. lib. bdg. 48.00 (ISBN 0-88478-006-6). Musicdata.
Rowell, Lois. American Organ Music on Records. (Bibliotheca Organologica: Vol. 71). 17.50 (ISBN 90-6027-333-8, Pub. by Frits Knuf Netherlands). Pendragon NY.

ORGAN MUSIC-HISTORY AND CRITICISM

Arnold, Corliss R. Organ Literature: A Comprehensive Survey. LC 72-8824. 1973. 18.50 (ISBN 0-8108-0559-6). Scarecrow.
Arnold, Denis. Giovanni Gabrieli. (Oxford Studies of Composers). (Illus.). 72p. 1974. pap. 7.95x (ISBN 0-19-315231-2). Oxford U Pr.
Banchieri, Adriano. Conclusioni Nel Suono Dell'Organo. (Monuments of Music & Music Literature in Facsimile: Series II, Vol. 101). 78p. (It.). 1975. Repr. of 1609 ed. 30.00x (ISBN 0-8450-2301-2). Broude.
Blanchard, Homer D. The Bach Organ Book. (The Little Organ Books Ser.: No. 3). (Illus.). Date not set. pap. price not set. Praestant.
Fellerer, K. G. Beitrage zur Choralbegleitung und Choralverarbeitung in der Orgelmusik des ausgehenden Eighteen und beginnenden Nineteen Jahrhunderts. (Sammlung Mw. Abh. 6-1932 Bibliotheca Organologica Ser.: Vol. 40). viii, 132p. 35.00 (ISBN 90-6027-225-0, Pub. by Frits Knuf Netherlands). Pendragon NY.
--Studien zur Orgelmusik des ausgehenden Eighteen und fruhen Nineteen Jahrhunderts. (Bibliotheca Organologica Ser.: Vol. 48). 1980. Repr. of 1932 ed. 47.50 (ISBN 90-6027-224-2, Pub. by Frits Knuf Netherlands); wrappers 32.50 (ISBN 90-6027-223-4, Pub. by Frits Knuf Netherlands). Pendragon NY.
Grace, Harvey. French Organ Music, Past & Present. LC 77-94581. 1979. Repr. of 1919 ed. lib. bdg. 25.00 (ISBN 0-89341-409-3). Longwood Pr.
Hathaway, Joseph W. An Analysis of Mendelssohn's Organ Works. LC 74-24107. Repr. of 1898 ed. 14.50 (ISBN 0-404-12956-0). AMS Pr.
Hess, Joachim. Dispositien der merkwaardigste Kerk-orgelen, welken in de zeven Vereenigde Provincien alsmede in Duytsland en Elders aangetroffen worden Gouda Seventeen Seventy-Four. (Bibliotheca Organologica Ser.: Vol. 11). 280p. 1981. Repr. of 1782 ed. 47.50 (ISBN 90-6027-385-0, Pub. by Frits Knuf Netherlands); wrappers 35.00 (ISBN 90-6027-256-0, Pub. by Frits Knuf Netherlands). Pendragon NY.
--Luister van het orgel, of nauwkeurige aanwijzinge Gouda Seventeen Seventy-Two. (Bibliotheca Organologica Ser.: Vol. 10). 1976. Repr. wrappers 22.50 (ISBN 90-6027-255-2, Pub. by Frits Knuf Netherlands). Pendragon NY.
Merian, Wilhelm. Die Tabulaturen Des Organisten Hans Kotter: Ein Beitrag Zur Musikgeschicte Des Beginnenden 16. (Bibliotheca Oranologica: Vol. 69). 1973. Repr. of 1916 ed. 40.00 (ISBN 90-6027-302-8, Pub. by Frits Knuf Netherlands). Pendragon NY.
Shannon, John R. A Treatise on Seventeenth-Century Organ Literature. (Illus.). 300p. 1978. 22.00 (ISBN 0-915548-06-2). Sunbury Pr.
Statham, Henry H. The Organ & Its Position in Musical Art. LC 77-75223. 1977. Repr. of 1910 ed. lib. bdg. 30.00 (ISBN 0-89341-122-1). Longwood Pr.
Stauffer, George B. The Organ Preludes of Johann Sebastian Bach. Buelow, George, ed. (Studies in Musicology: No. 27). 274p. 1980. 34.95 (ISBN 0-8357-1117-X, Pub. by UMI Res Pr). Univ Microfilms.
A Study of Theater Organ Style. 1968. pap. 15.00 (ISBN 0-686-09506-5). Peer-Southern.
Williams, C. Abdy. Story of Organ Music. LC 69-16789. 1968. Repr. of 1905 ed. 19.00 (ISBN 0-8103-3558-1). Gale.
Williams, Charles F. The Story of Organ Music. LC 71-39643. (Select Bibliographies Reprint Ser). 1972. Repr. of 1905 ed. 18.25 (ISBN 0-8369-9948-7). Arno.

ORGAN OF CORTI

see Corti's Organ

ORGAN TRADE

see Music Trade

ORGAN TRANSPLANTATION

see Transplantation of Organs, Tissues, Etc.

ORGANIC CHEMISTRY

see Chemistry, Organic

ORGANIC COOLED REACTORS

Organic Liquids As Reactor Coolants & Moderators. (Technical Reports: No. 70). 1967. pap. 11.25 (ISBN 92-0-055067-3, IAEA). Unipub.

ORGANIC FARMING

see also Organic Gardening

Bioconversion of Organic Residues for Rural Communities. (Food & Nutrition Bulletin Supplement Ser.: No. 2). 176p. 1980. pap. 15.00 (ISBN 92-808-0043-4, TUNU 039, UNU). Unipub.
Cocannouer, Joseph A. Organic Vegetable Gardening: The Better Way. LC 76-28226. 1977. pap. 1.75 (ISBN 0-668-04087-4). Arco.
Corley, Hugh. Organic Small Farming. Bargyla & Rateaver, Gylver, eds. LC 74-33122. (Conservation Gardening & Farming Ser: Ser. C). 1975. pap. 10.00 (ISBN 0-9600698-4-4). Rateavers.
Editors of Organic Gardening Magazine. Organic Farming Yesterday's & Tomorrow's Agriculture. (Illus.). 352p. 1977. pap. 5.95 (ISBN 0-87857-175-2). Rodale Pr Inc.
Foster, Catharine O. The Organic Gardener. 1972. 10.95 (ISBN 0-394-47210-1); pap. 4.95 (ISBN 0-394-71785-6). Knopf.
Globus, Diane. Digging It: How to Grow Things Naturally. (Illus.). 256p. 1973. 5.75 (ISBN 0-8037-2002-5). Dial.
Hainsworth, P. H. Agriculture, a New Approach. Bargyla & Rateaver, Gylver, eds. LC 74-33125. (Conservation Gardening & Farming Ser: Ser. C). 1976. pap. 13.00 (ISBN 0-9600698-5-2). Rateavers.
Howard, Sir Albert. The Soil & Health: A Study of Organic Agriculture. LC 70-179077. (Illus.). 335p. 1972. pap. 4.95 (ISBN 0-8052-0334-6). Schocken.
Jenks, Jorian. The Stuff We're Made of. 1959. 6.00 (ISBN 0-8159-6829-9). Devin.
Kohn, Bernice. The Organic Living Book. (Illus.). (gr. 7 up). 1972. PLB 7.95 (ISBN 0-670-52833-1). Viking Pr.
Leatherbarrow, Margaret. Gold in the Grass. Bargyla & Rateaver, Gylver, eds. LC 75-23179. (Conservation Gardening & Farming Ser: Ser. C). 1975. pap. 10.00 (ISBN 0-9600698-8-7). Rateavers.
Logsdon, Gene. Small Scale Grain Raising. LC 76-56102. 1977. 9.95 (ISBN 0-87857-134-5); pap. 7.95 (ISBN 0-87857-147-7). Rodale Pr Inc.
Null, Gary, et al. Grow Your Own Food Organically. LC 74-187993. (The Health Library: Vol. 6). 200p. 1972. 4.95 (ISBN 0-8315-0126-X). Speller.
Oelhaf, Robert C. Organic Agriculture: Economic & Ecological Comparisons with Conventional Methods. LC 78-7347. 300p. 1978. text ed. 18.00x (ISBN 0-916672-16-6). Allanheld.
--Organic Agriculture: Economic & Ecological Comparisons with Conventional Methods. 1979. 22.95 (ISBN 0-470-26427-6). Halsted Pr.
Ogden, Samuel. Step by Step to Organic Vegetable Growing. LC 74-149930. (Illus.). 182p. 1971. 5.95 (ISBN 0-87857-001-2). Rodale Pr Inc.
Organic Gardening & Farming Editors. Best Ideas for Organic Vegetable Growing. LC 77-90877. (Illus.). 1969. 7.95 (ISBN 0-87857-042-X). Rodale Pr Inc.
Organic Gardening & Farming Magazine Editors. Organic Way to Mulching. LC 70-170280. 208p. 1972. 8.95 (ISBN 0-87857-009-8). Rodale Pr Inc.
--Three Hundred of the Most Asked Questions About Organic Gardening. LC 72-84796. 1972. 7.95 (ISBN 0-87857-045-4). Rodale Pr Inc.
Organic Gardening & Farming Staff & Editors. The Calendar of Organic Gardening: A Guidebook to Successful Gardening Through the Year. LC 73-2280. (Illus.). 1973. 7.95 (ISBN 0-87857-067-5). Rodale Pr Inc.
Rateaver, Bargyla & Rateaver, Gylver. The Organic Method Primer: A Practical Explanation, the Why & How for the Beginner & the Experienced. LC 73-85165. (Conservation Gardening & Farming Ser). 1975. pap. 10.00 (ISBN 0-9600698-1-X). Rateavers.
Rodale, J. I. How to Grow Vegetables & Fruits by the Organic Method. 1961. 16.95 (ISBN 0-87596-066-9). Rodale Pr Inc.
Stephenson, W. A. Seaweed in Agriculture & Horticulture. 3rd ed. Bargyla & Rateaver, Gylver, eds. LC 74-12812. (Conservation Gardening & Farming Ser: Ser. C). 1974. pap. 7.00 (ISBN 0-9600698-3-6). Rateavers.
Stevens, Richard L. Organic Gardening in Hawaii. (Illus.). 72p. 1981. pap. 4.95 (ISBN 0-912180-40-4). Petroglyph.
Sykes, Friend. Humus Farming. Bargyla & Rateaver, Gylver, eds. (Conservation Gardening & Farming Ser). pap. write for info. (ISBN 0-9600698-7-9). Rateavers.
Terrell, Robert W. Soil 'neath My Feet. 1979. 5.50 (ISBN 0-533-03950-9). Vantage.
Turner, F. Newman. Fertility Farming. Rateaver, Bargyla & Rateaver, Gylver, eds. (Conservation Gardening & Farming Ser). pap. write for info (ISBN 0-685-61014-4). Rateavers.
--Fertility Pastures, & Cover Crops. Bargyla & Rateaver, Gylver, eds. LC 74-33123. (Conservation Gardening & Farming Ser: Ser. C). pap. 9.50 (ISBN 0-9600698-6-0). Rateavers.

ORGANIC GARDENING

see also Organic Farming

Abraham, George & Abraham, Katy. Organic Gardening Under Glass. LC 75-19310. 1975. 10.95 (ISBN 0-87857-104-3). Rodale Pr Inc.
Alth, Max. How to Farm Your Backyard the Mulch Organic Way. (Illus.). 1977. 9.95 (ISBN 0-07-001128-1, P&RB). McGraw.
Balfour, E. B. The Living Soil & the Haughley Experiment. LC 75-27030. 384p. 1976. 15.00x (ISBN 0-87663-269-X). Universe.
Cocannouer, Joseph A. Organic Vegetable Gardening: The Better Way. LC 76-28226. 1977. pap. 1.75 (ISBN 0-668-04087-4). Arco.
Davis, Burke. Newer & Better Organic Gardening. LC 75-42028. (Illus.). 96p. (gr. 5 up). 1976. 5.95 (ISBN 0-399-20510-1). Putnam.
Easey, Ben. Practical Organic Gardening. 152p. 1976. pap. 3.95 (ISBN 0-571-10314-6, Pub. by Faber & Faber). Merrimack Bk Serv.
Fatigati, Evelyn. Garden on Greenway Street. LC 77-2609. (Illus.). (gr. 5 up). 1977. 6.95 (ISBN 0-87857-166-3). Rodale Pr Inc.
Foster, Catharine O. The Ecological Garden. Ingraham, Erick, tr. (Illus.). 188p. (Orig.). 1981. cancelled (ISBN 0-8159-5407-7); pap. 6.95 (ISBN 0-8159-5408-5). Devin.
Foster, Catherine O. The Organic Gardener. pap. 2.95 (ISBN 0-394-71785-6, V-785, Vin). Random.
Hills, Lawrence D. Fertility Without Fertilizers: A Basic Approach to Organic Gardening. LC 76-41661. (Illus.). 1977. 12.50x (ISBN 0-87663-279-7); pap. 4.95 (ISBN 0-87663-944-9). Universe.
Kolisko, E. & Kolisko, L. Agriculture of Tomorrow. 2nd ed. (Illus.). 1978. Repr. of 1946 ed. 29.50x (ISBN 0-906492-00-9, Pub. by Kolisko Archive Publications). St George Bk Serv.
Logsdon, Gene. Gardener's Guide to Better Soil. LC 75-33191. 1976. 7.95 (ISBN 0-87857-106-X); pap. 4.95 (ISBN 0-87857-117-5). Rodale Pr Inc.
--Organic Orcharding: A Grove of Trees to Live in. Wallace, Dan, ed. (Illus.). 424p. (Orig.). 1981. 16.95 (ISBN 0-87857-356-9). Rodale Pr Inc.
MacLatchie, Sharon. Gardening with Kids. LC 77-24215. 1977. 8.95 (ISBN 0-87857-171-X); pap. 6.95 (ISBN 0-686-67633-5). Rodale Pr Inc.
Mintz, Lorelie M. Vegetables in Patches & Pots: A Child's Guide to Organic Vegetable Gardening. LC 76-46998. (Illus.). 128p. (gr. 4 up). 1976. 6.95 (ISBN 0-374-38091-0). FS&G.
Ogden, Samuel. Step-by-Step to Organic Vegetable Growing. 1976. pap. 3.95 (ISBN 0-87857-112-4). Rodale Pr Inc.
Organic Gardening & Minnich, Jerry. The Rodale Guide to Composting. (Illus.). 1979. 14.95 (ISBN 0-87857-212-0). Rodale Pr Inc.
Organic Gardening & Farming Editors. Organic Plant Protection. Yepsen, Roger, ed. LC 75-43829. 1976. 16.95 (ISBN 0-87857-110-8). Rodale Pr Inc.
Organic Gardening & Farming Magazine, ed. Encyclopedia of Organic Gardening. LC 77-25915. 1978. 21.95 (ISBN 0-87857-225-2). Rodale Pr Inc.
Perrin, Sandra. Organic Gardening in Montana & the Northwest. rev. ed. Vaughn, Bill & O'Loughlin, Jennifer, eds. (Illus.). 92p. (Orig.). pap. 3.95 (ISBN 0-939872-00-5). MRP.
Portugal, Nancy & Main, Jody. Potted Plant Organic Care. 3rd ed. LC 79-22173. (Living on This Planet Ser.). (Illus.). 1980. pap. 4.50 (ISBN 0-9601088-7-4). Wide World-Tetra.
Riotte, Louise. Planetary Planting. 1977. pap. 4.95 (ISBN 0-671-22772-6, Fireside). S&S.
--Planetary Planting: A Guide to Organic Gardening by the Signs of the Zodiac. LC 74-32481. 1976. 9.95 (ISBN 0-671-21953-7). S&S.
Scher, Cary. The Ten Week Garden. LC 73-76848. (Illus.). 1973. 17.50 (ISBN 0-87110-103-3); pap. 6.00 (ISBN 0-87110-101-7). Ultramarine Pub.
Shewell-Cooper, W. E. Compost Gardening. LC 74-18416. (Illus.). 1975. 10.75 (ISBN 0-02-852110-2). Hafner.
Smith, Marny. Gardening with Conscience: The Organic-Intensive Method. 96p. (Orig.). 1981. pap. 3.95 (ISBN 0-8164-2325-3). Seabury.
Smith, Robert F., Jr. Organic Gardening in the West: Raising Vegetables in a Short, Dry Growing Season. (Illus.). 1976. pap. 4.95 (ISBN 0-913270-60-1). Sunstone Pr.
Stevens, Richard L. Organic Gardening in Hawaii. (Illus.). 72p. 1981. pap. 4.95 (ISBN 0-912180-40-4). Petroglyph.
Wolf, Ray. Managing Your Personal Food Supply. LC 76-50569. 1977. 11.95 (ISBN 0-87857-121-3). Rodale Pr Inc.
Wordon, Diane, compiled by. Workshop on the Role of Earthworms in the Stabilization of Organic Residues, Vol. 2. (Orig.). 1981. pap. 70.00 (ISBN 0-939294-09-5). Beech Leaf.

ORGANIC MATTER IN SOIL

see Humus

ORGANICALLY GROWN FOOD

see Food, Natural

ORGANICULTURE

see Organic Farming; Organic Gardening

ORGANIZATION

see also Industrial Management; Industrial Organization; Management; Planning

Abrahamsson, Bengt. Bureaucracy or Participation: The Logic of Organization. LC 77-10023. (Sage Library of Social Research: Vol. 51). (Illus.). 1977. 20.00x (ISBN 0-8039-0836-9); pap. 9.95x (ISBN 0-8039-0837-7). Sage.
Albers, Henry H. Principles of Management: A Modern Approach. 4th ed. LC 73-12217. (Management & Administration Ser.). 560p. 1974. text ed. 22.50 (ISBN 0-471-01916-X); tchrs'. manual 3.95 (ISBN 0-471-01915-1). Wiley.
Alderfer, Clayton P. Existence, Relatedness & Growth: Human Needs in Organizational Settings. LC 78-156839. 1972. 15.95 (ISBN 0-02-900390-3). Free Pr.

Alderfer, Clayton P. & Cooper, Cary L. Advances in Experimental Social Processes, Vol. 2. 329p. 1980. 45.95 (ISBN 0-471-27623-5, Pub. by Wiley-Interscience). Wiley.

Allen, Louis A. Management & Organization. LC 57-13329. 353p. 1958. 17.50 (ISBN 0-686-65356-4). McGraw.

Argyris, C. Management & Organizational Development: The Paths from XA to YB. 1971. 18.50 (ISBN 0-07-002219-4, P&RB). McGraw.

Argyris, Chris & Schon, Donald A. Organizational Learning: A Theory of Action Perspective. LC 77-81195. 1978. text ed. 10.95 (ISBN 0-201-00174-8). A-W.

Armandi, Barry R. Organizational Structure & Efficiency. LC 80-69049. 276p. 1981. lib. bdg. 19.25 (ISBN 0-8191-1610-6); pap. text ed. 10.50 (ISBN 0-8191-1611-4). U Pr of Amer.

Arrow, Kenneth J. The Limits of Organization. (Fels Center of Government Ser.). 86p. 1974. pap. 3.95x (ISBN 0-393-09323-9). Norton.

Bacharach, Samuel B. & Lawler, Edward J. Power & Politics in Organizations: The Social Psychology of Conflict, Coalitions, & Bargaining. LC 79-92460. (Social & Behavioral Science Ser.). 1980. text ed. 15.95x (ISBN 0-87589-458-5). Jossey-Bass.

Baker, Frank, ed. Organizational Systems: General Systems Approaches to Complex Organizations. 1973. 17.50x (ISBN 0-256-00236-3). Irwin.

Becker, Selwyn W. & Neuhauser, Duncan. The Efficient Organization. LC 75-8269. 256p. 1975. 14.95 (ISBN 0-444-99004-6). Elsevier.

Bennis, Warren G. Beyond Bureaucracy: Essays on the Development & Evolution of Human Organization. 204p. 1973. pap. 3.50 (ISBN 0-07-004760-X, SP). McGraw.

Berkman, Harold W. The Human Relations of Management. 1974. text ed. 14.95x (ISBN 0-685-70780-6). Dickenson.

Blau, Peter M. On the Nature of Organizations. LC 74-7392. 358p. 1974. 31.95 (ISBN 0-471-08037-3, Pub. by Wiley-Interscience). Wiley.

Borman, Ernest, et al. Interpersonal Communication in the Modern Organization. 2nd ed. (Illus.). 304p. 1982. text ed. 18.95 (ISBN 0-13-475061-6). P-H.

Bramlette, Carl A., Jr. & Mescon, Michael H., eds. Individual & the Future of Organizations, Vol. 2. LC 72-619550. (Franklin Foundation Lecture Ser.). Orig. Title: Man & the Future of Organizations. 57p. (Orig.). 1973. pap. 3.75 (ISBN 0-88406-004-7). Ga St U Busn Pub.

Bramlette, Carl A., Jr., et al, eds. Individual & the Future of Organizations, Vol. 5. LC 72-619550. (Franklin Foundation Lecture Series). Orig. Title: Man & the Future of Organizations. 46p. 1976. pap. 3.75 (ISBN 0-88406-109-4). Ga St U Busn Pub.

Breadmore, R. G. Organization & Methods. (Teach Yourself Ser.). 1973. pap. 4.95 (ISBN 0-679-10509-3). McKay.

Brown, J. Douglas. The Human Nature of Organizations. LC 73-85862. 168p. 1973. 9.95 (ISBN 0-8144-5350-3). Am Mgmt.

Brown, Warrren B. & Moberg, Dennis G. Organization Management: A Macro Approach. LC 79-18709. (Wiley Ser. in Management). 1980. text ed. 23.95 (ISBN 0-471-02023-0). Wiley.

Buitenhuis, Cornelius. Organization in Innovation, Innovation in Organization: The Matrix As a Stimulus to Renewal. (Mensen En Organisaties in Beweging: No. 2). 1978. pap. text ed. 15.00x (ISBN 90-232-1660-1). Humanities.

Burack, Elmer H. & Negandhi, Anant, eds. Organization Design: Theoretical Perspectives & Empirical Findings. LC 77-24228. 1977. 17.50x (ISBN 0-87338-206-4, Pub. by Comparative Adm. Research Institute). Kent St U Pr.

Burke, W. Warner & Hornstein, Harvey A., eds. The Social Technology of Organization Development. LC 72-89997. 340p. 1972. pap. 10.00 (ISBN 0-88390-126-9). Univ Assocs.

Burrell, G. & Morgan, G. Sociological Paradigms & Organisational Analysis. 1979. text ed. 38.95x (ISBN 0-435-82130-X); pap. text ed. 14.95x (ISBN 0-435-82131-8). Heinemann Ed.

Cachenmeyer, Charles. Organizational Politica. (Analysis Ser.). 74p. (Orig.). 1979. pap. text ed. 18.00 (ISBN 0-938526-00-6). Inst Analysis.

Caplow, Theodore. How to Run Any Organization: A Manual of Practical Sociology. 1977. pap. text ed. 8.95 (ISBN 0-03-014886-3). HR&W.

Champion, Dean J. The Sociology of Organizations. LC 74-12245. (Illus.). 450p. 1975. 17.50 (ISBN 0-07-010492-1, C). McGraw.

Clark, Peter A. Action Research & Organizational Change. 1973. text ed. 9.80 (ISBN 0-06-318001-4, IntlDept); pap. text ed. 4.20 (ISBN 0-06-318004-9, IntlDept). Har-Row.

Clegg & Dunkerley. Critical Issues in Organizations. (Direct Edition Ser.). (Orig.). 1977. pap. 9.75 (ISBN 0-7100-8506-0). Routledge & Kegan.

Clegg, Stewart. The Theory of Power & Organization. 1979. 20.00x (ISBN 0-7100-0143-6). Routledge & Kegan.

Connor, Patrick E. Organizations: Theory & Design. 1979. text ed. 23.95 (ISBN 0-574-19380-4, 13-2380); instr's guide avail. (ISBN 0-574-19381-2, 13-2381). SRA.

Crozier, Michel & Friedberg, Erhard. Actors & Systems: The Politics of Collective Action. Goldhammer, Arthur, tr. LC 80-13803. 272p. 1980. lib. bdg. 25.00x (ISBN 0-226-12183-6). U of Chicago Pr.

Culbert, Samuel. The Organization Trap: & How to Get Out of It. LC 74-79281. 1974. 10.95x (ISBN 0-465-05320-3). Basic.

Dalton, Gene W. & Lawrence, Paul R., eds. Motivation & Control in Organizations. 1971. pap. 11.95x (ISBN 0-256-00609-1). Irwin.

Dalton, Gene W., et al, eds. Organizational Structure & Design. 1970. pap. 11.95x (ISBN 0-256-00607-5). Irwin.

DeGreene, K. B. The Adaptive Organization: Anticipation & Management of Crisis. 550p. 1982. 29.95 (ISBN 0-471-08296-1, Pub. by Wiley-Interscience). Wiley.

DeMare, George. Communicating at the Top: What You Need to Know About Communicating to Run an Organization. LC 78-31951. 1979. 15.95 (ISBN 0-471-05681-2, Pub. by Wiley-Interscience). Wiley.

Denhardt, Robert B. In the Shadow of Organization. LC 80-23775. 168p. 1981. 17.50x (ISBN 0-7006-0210-0). Regents Pr KS.

Dessler, G. Organization Theory: Integrating Structure & Behavior. 1980. 21.95 (ISBN 0-13-641886-4). P-H.

Dessler, Gary. Organization & Management: A Contingency Approach. ref. ed. (Illus.). 1976. 21.00 (ISBN 0-13-641225-4). P-H.

Dews, Jule N. Decision Structure of Organization. LC 78-53774. (Illus.). 120p. 1978. pap. 11.00 (ISBN 0-937300-00-4). Stoneridge Inst.

Diesing, Paul. Reason in Society: Five Types of Decisions & Their Social Conditions. LC 72-11328. 262p. 1973. Repr. of 1962 ed. lib. bdg. 18.50x (ISBN 0-8371-6660-8, DIRS); pap. 4.95 (ISBN 0-8371-8941-1, DIR). Greenwood.

Dowd, Ben, ed. Some Dimensions of the Formal Organization. 121p. 1972. pap. text ed. 7.95x (ISBN 0-8422-0205-6). Irvington.

Du Brin, Andrew J. Fundamentals of Organizational Behavior: An Applied Perspective. 2nd ed. LC 77-12720. 1978. text ed. 44.00 (ISBN 0-08-022252-8); pap. text ed. 15.00 (ISBN 0-08-022251-X). Pergamon.

Dunkerley, David. The Study of Organizations. (Students Library of Sociology). 1972. 8.95x (ISBN 0-7100-7231-7); pap. 3.00 (ISBN 0-7100-7232-5). Routledge & Kegan.

Dunkerley, David & Salaman, Graeme, eds. The International Yearbook of Organization Studies, 1980. 1981. 37.50 (ISBN 0-686-71902-6). Routledge & Kegan.

Dutton, Henry P. Principles of Organization As Applied to Business. (Management History Ser.: No. 33). 325p. Repr. of 1931 ed. 20.00 (ISBN 0-87960-067-5). Hive Pub.

Dyer, William G. Team Building: Issues & Alternatives. LC 77-76115. 1977. pap. text ed. 6.50 (ISBN 0-201-01191-3). A-W.

Eldridge, J. E. & Crombie, A. D. A Sociology of Organizations. LC 75-11335. (Studies in Sociology Ser.: No. 8). 218p. 1975. 12.50x (ISBN 0-8002-0156-6). Intl Pubns Serv.

Ends, E. & Page, C. Organizational Team Building. (Winthrop Mgt. Ser.). 1977. 5.95 (ISBN 0-87626-627-8). Winthrop.

England, George, et al, eds. Functioning of Complex Organizations. Negandhi, Anant & Wilpert, Bernard. LC 80-21966. 368p. 1981. lib. bdg. 27.50 (ISBN 0-89946-067-4). Oelgeschlager.

Etzioni, A. Modern Organizations. 1964. pap. 7.95 (ISBN 0-13-596049-5). P-H.

Etzioni, Amitai. Comparative Analysis of Complex Organizations. rev. ed. LC 74-21488. 1975. 19.95 (ISBN 0-02-909650-2); pap. text ed. 10.95 (ISBN 0-02-909620-0). Free Pr.

Evan, William M. Frontiers in Organization & Management. LC 79-20512. (Praeger Special Studies). 192p. 1980. 19.95 (ISBN 0-03-048441-3). Praeger.

Evatt, Crislynne. How to Organize Your Closet... & Your Life! 1981. pap. 2.95 (ISBN 0-345-29800-4). Ballantine.

Fordyce, Jack K. & Weil, Raymond. Managing with People: A Manager's Handbook of Organization Development. 2nd ed. 1979. pap. text ed. 8.95 (ISBN 0-201-02031-9). A-W.

Franklin, Jerome L., ed. Human Resource Development in the Organization: A Guide to Information Sources. LC 76-28289. (Management Information Guide Ser.: No. 35). 1978. 36.00 (ISBN 0-8103-0835-5). Gale.

French, Wendell L. & Bell, Cecil H., Jr. Organization Development: Behavioral Science Interventions for Organization Improvement. 2nd ed. 1978. ref. 16.95 (ISBN 0-13-641688-8); pap. 11.95 (ISBN 0-13-641670-5). P-H.

Fromkin, Howard L. & Sherwood, John J., eds. Integrating the Organization: A Social Psychological Analysis. LC 73-21306. (Illus.). 1974. 19.95 (ISBN 0-02-910920-5). Free Pr.

Frost, et al. Organizational Reality: Reports from the Firing Line. LC 77-20503. 1978. pap. text ed. 12.50 (ISBN 0-87620-654-2); instructor's manual free (ISBN 0-87620-656-9). Goodyear.

Fulmer, Robert M. Management & Organization. LC 78-15830. 1980. pap. 4.95 (ISBN 0-06-460176-5, CO 176, COS). Har-Row.

Galbraith, Jay. Designing Complex Organizations. LC 72-11887. 1973. pap. text ed. 6.50 (ISBN 0-201-02559-0). A-W.

--Organization Design. LC 76-10421. (Illus.). 1977. text ed. 18.95 (ISBN 0-201-02558-2). A-W.

Gannon, Martin J. Management: Organizational Perspective. 1977. text ed. 18.95 (ISBN 0-316-30326-7); tchr's manual free (ISBN 0-316-30328-3). Little.

Gibson, James L., et al. Organizations: Behavior, Structure, Processes. 3rd ed. 1979. 18.50x (ISBN 0-256-02210-0). Business Pubns.

--Readings in Organizations: Behavior, Structure, Processes. 3rd ed. 1979. pap. 9.95x (ISBN 0-256-02247-X). Business Pubns.

Gillespie, David F. & Mileti, Dennis S. Technostructures & Inter-Organizational Relations. LC 78-19543. (Illus.). 1978. 17.95 (ISBN 0-669-02542-9). Lexington Bks.

Goodman, Paul S., et al. New Perspectives on Organizational Effectiveness. LC 77-82916. (Social & Behavioral Science Ser). 1977. text ed. 16.95x (ISBN 0-87589-349-X). Jossey-Bass.

Gray, Jerry & Starke, Frederick. Readings in Organizational Behavior: Concepts and Applications. (Business Ser.). 1976. pap. text ed. 12.95 (ISBN 0-675-08522-5). Merrill.

--Readings in Organizational Behavior: Concepts and Applications. (Business Ser.). 1976. pap. text ed. 12.95 (ISBN 0-675-08522-5). Merrill.

Grusky, O. & Miller, G. A. Sociology of Organizations. LC 69-20286. 1970. text ed. 16.95 (ISBN 0-02-913180-4). Free Pr.

Haas, J. Eugene & Drabek, Thomas E. Complex Organizations: A Sociological Perspective. (Illus.). 416p. 1973. text ed. 19.95 (ISBN 0-02-348550-7, 34855). Macmillan.

Hage, Jerald. Theories of Organizations: Form, Process, & Transformation. LC 79-26715. 1980. 26.00x (ISBN 0-471-33859-1, Pub. by Wiley-Interscience). Wiley.

Hall, Douglas T. Careers in Organizations. Porter, Lyman W., ed. LC 75-13446. (Goodyear Series in Management & Organizations). 230p. 1976. pap. text ed. 9.95x (ISBN 0-87620-157-5); tchr's manual free (ISBN 0-685-63964-9). Goodyear.

Hall, Richard H. The Formal Organization. LC 72-76921. pap. 5.95x (ISBN 0-465-02492-0). Basic.

Hall, Richard S. Organizations: Structure & Process. 2nd ed. LC 76-45743. (Illus.). 384p. 1977. text ed. 18.95 (ISBN 0-13-642025-7). P-H.

Halsall, E., ed. Becoming Comprehensive: Case Histories. 1970. 18.00 (ISBN 0-08-015820-X); pap. 12.75 (ISBN 0-08-015819-6). Pergamon.

Handy, Charles. Understanding Organizations. (Education Ser.). 448p. 1976. pap. 5.95 (ISBN 0-14-080960-0). Penguin.

Harris, O. Jeff. How to Manage People at Work: A Short Course for Professionals. LC 76-45821. (Wiley Professional Development Programs Ser.). 300p. 1977. 45.95 (ISBN 0-471-01930-5). Wiley.

Heaton, Herbert. Productivity in Service Organizations: Organizing for People. (Illus.). 1977. 16.95 (ISBN 0-07-027705-2, P&RB). McGraw.

Heydebrand, Wolf. Comparative Organizations. (General Sociology Ser.). (Illus.). 608p. 1973. text ed. 24.95 (ISBN 0-13-153932-9). P-H.

Hicks, Herbert G. & Gullett, C. Ray. The Management of Organizations. 3rd ed. (Management Ser.). (Illus.). 1976. text ed. 16.95 (ISBN 0-07-028721-X, C); instructor's manual 4.95 (ISBN 0-07-028722-8). McGraw.

--Organizations: Theory & Behavior. (Management Ser.). (Illus.). 448p. 1975. text ed. 16.95 (ISBN 0-07-028730-9, C); instructors' manual by Slaughter 2.95 (ISBN 0-07-058160-6). McGraw.

Hicks, Herbert G. & Powell, James D. Management, Organizations & Human Resources: Selected Readings. 2nd ed. 1975. text ed. 9.95 (ISBN 0-07-028733-3, C). McGraw.

Hirschman, Albert O. Exit, Voice, & Loyalty: Responses to Decline in Firms, Organizations, & States. LC 77-99517. 1970. 8.95x (ISBN 0-674-27650-7); pap. 4.95x (ISBN 0-674-27660-4). Harvard U Pr.

Hodge, B. J. & Anthony, William P. Organizational Theory: An Environmental Approach. 1979. text ed. 18.95 (ISBN 0-205-06523-6, 0865230); instr's man. avail. (ISBN 0-205-06551-1, 086551-6). Allyn.

Hodgkinson, Christopher. Towards a Philosophy of Administration. LC 78-676. 1978. 18.50x (ISBN 0-312-81036-9). St Martin.

Hrebiniak, Lawrence G. Complex Organizations. (Management Ser.). 1978. text ed. 17.95 (ISBN 0-8299-0169-8). West Pub.

Hughes, Everett C. The Chicago Real Estate Board: The Growth of an Institution. Coser, Lewis A. & Powell, Walter W., eds. LC 79-6999. (Perennial Works in Sociology Ser.). 1979. Repr. of 1931 ed. lib. bdg. 13.00x (ISBN 0-405-12098-2). Arno.

Huse, Edgar F. Organization Development & Change. LC 75-631. 448p. 1975. text ed. 18.95 (ISBN 0-8299-0046-2). West Pub.

Hutton, Geoffrey. Thinking About Organization. 1979. 8.50x (ISBN 0-422-74100-0, Pub. by Tavistock England). Methuen Inc.

Indik, Bernard P. People, Groups & Organizations. LC 68-23785. 1968. text ed. 12.55x (ISBN 0-8077-1546-8). Tchrs Coll.

Industrial Relations Counselors Symposium, 1970. New Dimensions in Organization. 160p. pap. 4.50 (ISBN 0-87330-021-1). Indus Rel.

Jackson, J. & Morgan, C. Organization Theory: A Macro-Perspective for Management. 1978. 21.95 (ISBN 0-13-641407-9). P-H.

Janger, Allen R. Matrix Organization of Complex Businesses, Report No. 763. LC 79-66357. (Illus., Orig.). 1979. pap. 37.50 (ISBN 0-8237-0199-9). Conference Bd.

Jarett, Irwin M. & Brady, Patricia A., eds. A Conference on Key Factor Analysis: A Logic Leading to Social Accountability. LC 76-20624. 450p. 1976. 10.00x (ISBN 0-8093-0793-6); pap. 4.95x (ISBN 0-8093-0795-2). S Ill U Pr.

Jorge, Antonio. Competition, Cooperation, Efficiency & Social Organization. LC 76-20272. 89p. 1978. 12.00 (ISBN 0-8386-2026-4). Fairleigh Dickinson.

Jun, Jong S. & Storm, William B. Tomorrow's Organizations: Challenges & Strategies. 400p. 1973. pap. 8.95x (ISBN 0-673-07796-9). Scott F.

Kast, Fremont & Rosenzweig, James. Organization & Management: A Systems & Contingency Approach. 3rd rev. ed. (Management Ser.). (Illus.). 1979. text ed. 22.50x (ISBN 0-07-033346-7, C); instructor's manual 7.50 (ISBN 0-07-033347-5). McGraw.

Kast, Fremont E. & Rosenzweig, James. Organization & Management: Experiential Exercises. 1976. text ed. 12.95x (ISBN 0-07-033346-7, C); instructor's manual 4.95 (ISBN 0-07-033347-5). McGraw.

Kast, Fremont E. & Rosenzweig, James E. Contingency Views of Organization & Management. LC 73-75421. (Illus.). 355p. 1973. pap. text ed. 10.95 (ISBN 0-574-17135-5, 13-0135). SRA.

Katz, Fred E. Autonomy & Organization: The Limits of Social Control. 1968. text ed. 6.95x (ISBN 0-685-19686-0). Phila Bk Co.

Khandwalla, Pradip N. The Design of Organizations. 1977. text ed. 23.95 (ISBN 0-15-517366-9, HC). HarBraceJ.

Kiesler, Sara B. Interpersonal Processes in Groups & Organizations. Mackenzie, Kenneth D., ed. LC 77-86018. (Organizational Behavior Ser.). 1978. pap. text ed. 9.95x (ISBN 0-88295-451-2). Harlan Davidson.

Kilmann, Ralph H, et al. The Management of Organization Design, 2 vols. LC 76-23404. 1976. 22.95 ea. (North Holland). Vol. 1 (ISBN 0-444-00188-3). Vol. 2 (ISBN 0-444-00189-1). Elsevier.

Kimberly, John R., et al. The Organizational Life Cycle: Issues in the Creation, Transformation, & Decline of Organizations. LC 79-92446. (Social & Behavioral Science Ser.). 1980. text ed. 19.95x (ISBN 0-87589-459-3). Jossey-Bass.

Knight, Kenneth & McDaniel, Reuben. Organizations: An Information Systems Perspective. 1979. pap. 9.95x (ISBN 0-534-00583-7). Wadsworth Pub.

Knoeppel, C. E. Organization & Administration. LC 72-9516. (Management History Ser.: No. 48). 464p. Repr. of 1917 ed. 23.50 (ISBN 0-686-76978-3). Hive Pub.

Knowles, Michael. Organizational Functioning: A Behavioural Analysis. 1979. text ed. 34.25x (ISBN 0-566-00329-5, Pub. by Gower Pub Co England). Renouf.

Kossen, Stan. Human Side of Organizations. 2nd ed. 1978. text ed. 20.95 scp (ISBN 0-06-384719-1, HarpC); tchr's ed. free (ISBN 0-06-373618-7); scp wkbk. 6.50 (ISBN 0-06-384724-8). Har-Row.

Kotter, John P. Organizational Dynamics: Diagnosis & Intervention. 1978. pap. text ed. 6.50 (ISBN 0-201-03890-0). A-W.

Kotter, John P., et al. Organization. 1979. 19.95x (ISBN 0-256-02226-7). Irwin.

Kovach, Kenneth A. Organization Size, Job Satisfaction, Absenteeism & Turnover. 148p. 1977. pap. text ed. 7.75 (ISBN 0-8191-0242-3). U Pr of Amer.

Leavitt, Harold, et al, eds. Organizations of the Future: Interaction with the External Environment. LC 74-1733. (Special Studies). (Illus.). 220p. 1974. text ed. 25.95 (ISBN 0-275-28864-1). Praeger.

Leavitt, Harold J., et al. The Organizational World. 1973. pap. text ed. 10.95 (ISBN 0-15-567562-1, HC). HarBraceJ.

Lee, James A. The Gold & the Garbage in Management Theories & Prescriptions. LC 80-12758. (Illus.). x, 480p. 1980. 22.95x (ISBN 0-8214-0436-9); pap. 10.95x (ISBN 0-8214-0578-0). Ohio U Pr.

Lenin, V. I. On Organization. 235p. 1975. pap. text ed. 2.95 (ISBN 0-89380-007-4). Proletarian Pubs.

Levy, Marion J. Modernization & the Structure of Societies: A Setting for International Affairs, 2 vols. 1966. boxed 47.50 (ISBN 0-691-09320-2). Princeton U Pr.

Lewis, Phillip & Williams, John W. Readings for Organizational Communications. LC 79-19091. (Grid Ser. in Management). 1980. pap. text ed. 14.95 (ISBN 0-88244-200-7). Grid Pub.

Likert, Rensis & Likert, Jane G. New Ways of Managing Conflict. 1976. 19.95 (ISBN 0-07-037842-8, P&RB). McGraw.

Longenecker, Justin G. Essentials of Management: A Behavioral Approach. 1977. text ed. 15.95 (ISBN 0-675-08552-7); instructor's manual 3.95 (ISBN 0-686-67520-7). Merrill.

Lorsch, Jay W. & Lawrence, Paul R. Organizational Planning: Cases & Concepts. LC 72-79316. 1972. pap. 11.95x (ISBN 0-256-00456-0). Irwin.

Louis, Karen S. & Sieber, Sam D., eds. Bureaucracy & the Dispersed Organization: The Educational Extension Agent Experiment. LC 78-31623. (Modern Sociology Ser.). 1979. 19.95 (ISBN 0-89391-018-X). Ablex Pub.

McCarthy, Daniel J., et al. Business Policy & Strategy: Concepts & Readings. rev ed. 1979. pap. 13.95x (ISBN 0-256-02168-6). Irwin.

Mackenzie, Kenneth D. Organizational Structures. LC 77-86209. (Organizational Behavior Ser.). 1978. pap. text ed. 9.95x (ISBN 0-88295-452-0). Harlan Davidson.

McLennan, Roy. Cases in Organisational Behaviour. (Illus.). 282p. 1975. 29.50x (ISBN 0-8448-0761-3). Crane-Russak Co.

Magnusen, Karl O. Organizational Design, Development, & Behavior. 1977. pap. 8.95x (ISBN 0-673-15042-9). Scott F.

Managing & Developing New Forms of Work Organization. 158p. 1981. pap. 12.75 (ISBN 92-2-102145-9, ILO 166, ILO). Unipub.

March, James G. & Simon, Herbert A. Organizations. LC 58-13464. 1958. 22.50 (ISBN 0-471-56793-0). Wiley.

Marschak, J. Economic Information, Decision, & Prediction: Selected Papers, 3 vols. LC 74-81940. (Theory & Decision Library: No. 7). 1044p. 1974. lib. bdg. 189.50 (ISBN 90-277-0524-0, Pub. by Reidel Holland); lib. bdg. 63.00 ea. Kluwer Boston.

Masi, Dale A. Organizing for Women: Issues, Strategies, & Services. LC 78-19577. (Illus.). 240p. 1981. 22.95 (ISBN 0-669-02577-1). Lexington Bks.

Melcher, Arlyn J. Structure & Process of Organization: A Systems Approach. (Illus.). 480p. 1976. 21.00 (ISBN 0-13-855254-1). P-H.

Melcher, Arlyn J., ed. General Systems & Organization: Methodological Aspects. LC 74-11584. 120p. 1975. 9.50x (ISBN 0-87338-165-3, Pub. by Comp. Adm. Research Inst.). Kent St U Pr.

Mescon, Michael & Bramlette, Carl A., Jr., eds. The Individual & the Future of Organizations, Vol. 6. LC 72-619550. (Franklin Foundation Lecture Ser.). 1977. pap. 3.75 (ISBN 0-88406-116-7). Ga St U Busn Pub.

Mescon, Michael H., et al. The Management of Enterprise. Khedouri, Frank, ed. 242p. 1973. pap. text ed. 7.95 (ISBN 0-02-380600-1). Macmillan.

Meyer, Marshall W. Theory of Organizational Structure. LC 76-56415. (Studies in Sociology Ser.). 1977. pap. text ed. 3.95 (ISBN 0-672-61193-7). Bobbs.

Miles, Raymond E. & Snow, Charles C. Organizational Strategy: Structure & Process. (Management Ser.). (Illus.). 1978. text ed. 14.95 (ISBN 0-07-041932-9, C). McGraw.

Miller, Eric J., ed. Task & Organization. LC 75-12606. (Wiley Series Individuals, Groups & Organizations). 480p. 1976. 45.50 (ISBN 0-471-60605-7, Pub. by Wiley-Interscience). Wiley.

Mintzberg, Henry. Structuring of Organizations. (Theory of Management Policy Ser.). (Illus.). 1979. ref. ed. 22.95 (ISBN 0-13-855270-3). P-H.

Mohan, Raj P., ed. Management & Complex Organizations in Comparative Perspective. LC 78-22133. (Contributions in Sociology: No. 36). (Illus.). 1979. lib. bdg. 22.95 (ISBN 0-313-20752-6, MMA/). Greenwood.

Moore, Franklin G. Management of Organizations. LC 81-4665. 550p. 1982. text ed. 24.95 (ISBN 0-88244-234-1). Grid Pub.

Morowitz, Harold J. Ego Niches: An Ecological View of Organizational Behavior. LC 76-48588. (Illus.). 1977. pap. 4.95 (ISBN 0-918024-01-3). Ox Bow.

Mouzelis, Nicos P. Organisation & Bureaucracy: An Analysis of Modern Theories. LC 68-11361. 1968. 18.95x (ISBN 0-202-30072-2); pap. 7.95x (ISBN 0-202-30078-1). Aldine Pub.

Mulder, Mauk. The Daily Power Game. (Quality of Working Life Ser: No. 6). 1977. lib. bdg. 16.00 (ISBN 90-207-0707-8, Pub. by Martinus Nijhoff Netherlands). Kluwer Boston.

Naumes, William & Paine, Frank T. Cases for Organizational Strategy & Policy. LC 77-77104. (Illus.). 1978. pap. text ed. 12.95 (ISBN 0-7216-6662-0). HR&W.

Negandhi, Anant R., ed. Interorganization Theory. LC 74-21887. 1980. pap. text ed. 8.50x (ISBN 0-87338-239-0). Kent St U Pr.

--Modern Organizational Theory: Contextual, Environment & Socio-Cultural Variables. LC 72-619605. 350p. 1973. 14.00x (ISBN 0-87338-133-5). Kent St U Pr.

New Forms of Work Organization, No. 2. 145p. 1980. pap. 16.00 (ISBN 92-2-102110-6, ILO 135, ILO). Unipub.

Newman, Derek. Organization Design. 1973. 16.50x (ISBN 0-7131-3292-2). Intl Ideas.

Niewerth, Hans. Lexikon der Planun und Organisation. (Ger.). 1968. 37.00 (ISBN 3-87715-051-9, M-7235). French & Eur.

Nord, Walter R., ed. Concepts & Controversy in Organizational Behavior. 2nd ed. LC 75-10424. 700p. 1976. pap. text ed. 14.95 (ISBN 0-87620-164-8). Goodyear.

Olm, et al. Management Decisions & Organizational Policy. 3rd ed. 560p. 1981. text ed. 21.95 (ISBN 0-205-07215-1, 0872156); free tchr's ed. (ISBN 0-205-07216-X). Allyn.

Organizational Development: Theory & Practice. 1977. 10.50 (ISBN 0-8144-6513-7). Am Mgmt.

Osborn, Richard N., et al. Organization Theory: An Integrated Contingency Approach. (Wiley Ser. in Management). 1980. text ed. 23.95 (ISBN 0-471-02173-3). Wiley.

O'Shaughnessy, J. Business Organization. (Studies in Management). 1966. pap. text ed. 12.95x (ISBN 0-04-658043-3). Allen Unwin.

Paine, Frank T. & Naumes, William. Organizational Strategy & Policy. 2nd ed. LC 77-77106. (Illus.). 1978. pap. text ed. 10.95 (ISBN 0-7216-7048-2). HR&W.

Parsons, Talcott. Structure & Process in Modern Societies. 1960. 15.95 (ISBN 0-02-924340-8). Free Pr.

Perrow, Charles. Complex Organizations: A Critical Essay. 2nd ed. 1979. pap. text ed. 9.95x (ISBN 0-673-15205-7). Scott F.

--Organizational Analysis: A Sociological View. LC 70-98404. (Behavioral Science in Industry Ser). (Orig.). 1970. pap. text ed. 6.95 (ISBN 0-8185-0287-8). Brooks-Cole.

Perry, William E. How to Manage Management. LC 78-57259. 1979. 12.50 (ISBN 0-8149-0804-7). Vanguard.

Pfeffer, Jeffrey. Organizational Design. Mackenzie, Kenneth D., ed. LC 77-86024. (Organizational Behavior Ser.). (Illus.). 1978. pap. text ed. 9.95x (ISBN 0-88295-453-9). Harlan Davidson.

Pfiffner, John M. & Sherwood, F. Administrative Organization. 1960. 21.95x (ISBN 0-13-008615-0). P-H.

Pugh, D. S. & Hickson, D. J. Organizational Structure in Its Context: The Aston Programme One. LC 75-26469. 248p. 1976. 21.95 (ISBN 0-347-01114-4, 00206-2, Pub. by Saxon Hse). Lexington Bks.

Pugh, D. S., ed. Organization Theory. (Education Ser). 1972. pap. 3.95 (ISBN 0-14-080601-6). Penguin.

Ritchie, J. B. & Thompson, Paul H. Organization & People: Readings, Cases & Exercises in Organizational Behavior. LC 76-3566. (Management Ser.). (Illus.). 400p. 1976. pap. text ed. 12.50 (ISBN 0-8299-0103-5). West Pub.

Rosengren, William & Lefton, Mark. Organization & Clients: Essays in the Sociology of Service. LC 72-122308. 1970. text ed. 10.95x (ISBN 0-675-09313-9). Merrill.

Roy, Robert H. The Cultures of Management. LC 76-47385. (Illus.). 512p. 1977. 21.50x (ISBN 0-8018-1875-3); pap. text ed. 9.95 (ISBN 0-8018-2524-5). Johns Hopkins.

Salaman, G. & Thompson, K. People & Organizations. 384p. 1974. text ed. 10.95x (ISBN 0-582-48669-6). Longman.

Salaman, Graeme & Thompson, Kenneth, eds. Control & Ideology in Organizations. 350p. (Orig.). 1980. pap. 12.50x (ISBN 0-262-69069-1). MIT Pr.

Scanlan, B. K. Management Eighteen: Short Course for Managers. LC 74-9816. (Professional Development Programs, Business Administration Ser). 1974. 45.95 (ISBN 0-471-75633-4). Wiley.

Scott, William G. & Hart, David K. Organizational America. 1980. pap. 5.95 (ISBN 0-395-29698-6). HM.

Scott, William G., et al. Organization Theory: A Structural & Behavioral Analysis. 4th ed. 1981. 18.50 (ISBN 0-256-02515-0). Irwin.

Senger, John. Individuals, Groups, & the Organization. 328p. 1980. text ed. 13.95 (ISBN 0-87626-377-5). Winthrop.

Shepard, Jon M. Organizational Issues in Industrial Society: A Book of Readings. (General Sociology Ser.). 496p. 1972. ref. ed. 10.95 (ISBN 0-13-641001-4). P-H.

Silber, Mark B. & Sherman, V. Clayton. Managerial Performance & Promotability: The Making of an Executive. LC 73-75675. 192p. 1974. 12.95 (ISBN 0-8144-5325-2). Am Mgmt.

Silverman, David. Theory of Organizations. LC 72-150812. 1971. text ed. 8.95x (ISBN 0-465-08438-9). Basic.

Simmons, Robert H. Achieving Humane Organization. 300p. 1981. text ed. 15.00x (ISBN 0-936496-01-0). Spencer Pubs.

Sofer, Cyril. Organizations in Theory & Practice. LC 73-174821. 1972. text ed. 15.00x (ISBN 0-465-05324-6). Basic.

Steele, F. I. Open Organization: The Impact of Secrecy & Disclosure on People & Organizations. LC 74-12805. 240p. 1975. 10.95 (ISBN 0-201-07212-2). A-W.

Steele, Fritz & Jenks, Stephen. The Feel of the Work Place: Understanding & Improving Organization Climate. LC 76-12802. (Illus.). 1977. pap. text ed. 8.95 (ISBN 0-201-07213-0). A-W.

Steinberg, Rafael. Man & the Organization. (Human Behavior Ser). 176p. 1975. 9.95 (ISBN 0-8094-1912-2); lib. bdg. avail. (ISBN 0-685-52490-6). Time-Life.

Stout, Russell, Jr. Organizations, Management, & Control: An Annotated Bibliography. LC 79-3639. 208p. 1980. 15.00x (ISBN 0-253-14448-5). Ind U Pr.

Tannenbaum, Arnold S., et al. Hierarchy in Organizations: An International Comparison. LC 73-20963. (Social & Behavioral Science Ser.). 240p. 1974. 15.95x (ISBN 0-87589-219-1). Jossey-Bass.

Tannenbaum, R., et al. Leadership & Organization: A Behavioral Science Approach. (Management Ser.). 1961. text ed. 15.95 (ISBN 0-07-062845-9, C). McGraw.

Tausky, Curt. Work Organizations. 2nd ed. LC 77-83435. 1978. pap. text ed. 7.50 (ISBN 0-87581-226-0). Peacock Pubs.

Thayer, Frederick C. An End to Hierarchy, an End to Competition. 2nd ed. 224p. 1981. pap. 7.95 (ISBN 0-531-05631-7). Watts.

Thompson, Victor A. Modern Organization. 2d ed. LC 77-6664. 1977. pap. text ed. 3.50 (ISBN 0-8173-4838-7). U of Ala Pr.

Tosi, Henry L. Theories of Organization. LC 75-17063. (Illus.). 160p. 1975. pap. text ed. 9.95 (ISBN 0-914292-02-1). Wiley.

Tuggle, Francis D. Organizational Processes. Mackenzie, Kenneth D., ed. LC 77-86001. (Organizational Behavior Ser.). (Illus.). 1978. pap. text ed. 9.95x (ISBN 0-88295-455-5). Harlan Davidson.

Turk, Herman. Organizations in Modern Life: Cities & Other Large Networks. LC 76-50710. (Social & Behavioral Science Ser.). (Illus.). 1977. text ed. 17.95x (ISBN 0-87589-321-X). Jossey-Bass.

Ullrich, Robert A. & Wieland, George F. Organization Theory & Design. rev. ed. 1980. 20.95x (ISBN 0-256-02285-2). Irwin.

Van Maanen, J. Organizational Careers: Some New Perspectives. LC 76-13537. (Individuals, Groups & Organizations Ser). 1977. 23.95 (ISBN 0-471-99409-X, Pub. by Wiley-Interscience). Wiley.

Viola, Richard H. Organizations in a Changing Society: Administration & Human Values. 1977. text ed. 6.50 (ISBN 0-7216-9055-6). HR&W.

Vroom, Victor H. & Yetton, Philip W. Leadership & Decision-Making. LC 72-94068. 1976. pap. 5.95x (ISBN 0-8229-5265-3). U of Pittsburgh Pr.

Weber, Max. Max Weber on Charisma & Institution Building. Eisenstadt, S. N., ed. LC 68-54202. (Heritage of Sociology Ser). (Orig.). 1968. 15.00x (ISBN 0-226-87727-2); pap. text ed. 7.00x (ISBN 0-226-87724-8). U of Chicago Pr.

Westerlund, Gunnar & Sjostrand, Sven-Erik. Organizational Myths. 1979. text ed. 11.95 (ISBN 0-06-318074-X, IntlDept). Har-Row.

Wexley, Kenneth A. & Yukl, Gary A. Organizational Behavior & Personal Psychology. 1977. pap. 12.50x (ISBN 0-256-01884-7). Irwin.

White, Harrison C. Chains of Opportunity: System Models of Mobility in Organizations. LC 78-105374. 1970. 22.50x (ISBN 0-674-10674-1). Harvard U Pr.

Wickesberg, Albert K. Management Organization. (Illus., Orig.). 1966. pap. text ed. 6.95x (ISBN 0-89197-290-0). Irvington.

Wilm, Harold G. Organizations Are People. (Illus.). 1979. 7.95 (ISBN 0-8158-0377-X). Chris Mass.

Wright, Robert. The Nature of Organizations. 1977. pap. text ed. 10.95x (ISBN 0-8221-0188-2). Dickenson.

Wright, Robert G. Exploring Vital Elements of Organization & Management. 1978. pap. text ed. 6.50 (ISBN 0-8403-1384-5). Kendall-Hunt.

Zald, Mayer N., ed. Power in Organizations. LC 71-91949. 1970. 11.95 (ISBN 0-8265-1147-3). Vanderbilt U Pr.

Zaltman, Gerald, et al. Innovations & Organizations. LC 73-5873. 224p. 1973. 20.95 (ISBN 0-471-98129-X, Pub. by Wiley-Interscience). Wiley.

Zander, Alvin. Groups at Work: Unresolved Issues in the Study of Organizations. LC 77-82918. (Social & Behavioral Science Ser). 1977. text ed. 12.95x (ISBN 0-87589-347-3). Jossey-Bass.

ORGANIZATION–RESEARCH

see Organizational Research

ORGANIZATION, INDUSTRIAL

see Industrial Organization

ORGANIZATION, INTERNATIONAL

see International Organization

ORGANIZATION CHARTS

Famularo, Joseph J. Organization Planning Manual. rev. ed. (Illus.). 1979. 29.95 (ISBN 0-8144-5538-7). Am Mgmt.

ORGANIZATION DEVELOPMENT

see Organizational Change

ORGANIZATION FOR ECONOMIC COOPERATION AND DEVELOPMENT

Annual Reports on Competition Policy in OECD Member Countries, 1979, Vol. 2. (Document Ser.). 134p. 1979. 9.50x (ISBN 92-64-12009-2). OECD.

Bellagio Conference. Regional Economic Planning: Proceedings. Isard, Walter & Cumberland, John H., eds. 452p. 1961. 6.00x (ISBN 0-686-14693-X). OECD.

Brunner, Karl & Meltzer, A. H., eds. Institutions, Policies & Economic Performance. (Carnegie-Rochester Conference Series on Public Policy: Vol. 1V). 1976. pap. text ed. 19.50 (ISBN 0-7204-0564-5, North-Holland). Elsevier.

Economic Prospects Division. The Measurement of Domestic Cyclical Fluctuations. (Occasional Economic Studies Ser.). 1973. 2.50x (ISBN 92-64-11099-2). OECD.

Esman, Milton J. & Cheever, Daniel S. Common Aid Effort: The Development Assistance Activities of the Organization for Economic Cooperation & Development. LC 67-14403. 1967. 7.50 (ISBN 0-8142-0047-8). Ohio St U Pr.

Griffin, James M. Energy Conservation in the OECD: 1980 to 2000. LC 78-24109. 1979. reference 25.00 (ISBN 0-88410-087-1). Ballinger Pub.

Marsh, John S. European Economic Issues: Agriculture, Economic Security, Industrial Democracy, the OECD. LC 76-30359. (Special Studies). 1977. text ed. 28.95 (ISBN 0-275-24410-5). Praeger.

New Forms of Work Organization, No. 2. 145p. 1980. pap. 16.00 (ISBN 92-2-102110-6, ILO 135, ILO). Unipub.

OECD. Activities of OECD in 1980: Report by the Secretary-General. 130p. (Orig.). 1981. pap. 9.00x (ISBN 92-64-12206-0). OECD.

OECD Staff. Animal Feeding & Production: New Technical & Economic Development. (Agricultural Products & Markets Ser.). 214p. (Orig.). 1981. pap. 12.50x (ISBN 92-64-12167-6). OECD.

--Educational Statistics in OECD Countries. (Illus.). 231p. (Orig.). 1981. pap. text ed. 12.00x (ISBN 92-64-02119-1, 91-81-04-3). OECD.

--The Future of University Research. 78p. (Orig.). 1981. pap. 7.50 (ISBN 92-64-12160-9). OECD.

--National Accounts of OECD Countries 1950-1979, Vol. 1. 89p. (Orig.). 1981. pap. text ed. 7.50x (ISBN 92-64-02117-5, 30-81-01-3). OECD.

OECD Staff & IEA Staff. Energy Balances of OECD Countries 1975 - 1979. 162p. (Orig.). 1981. pap. 15.00x (ISBN 92-64-02178-7). OECD.

--Energy Statistics Nineteen Seventy-Five to Nineteen Seventy-Nine. 292p. (Orig.). 1981. pap. 20.00x (ISBN 92-64-02177-9). OECD.

Organization for Economic Cooperation & Development. Programme Budgets for Graduate Training. 247p. 1975. 10.00x (ISBN 92-64-11294-4). OECD.
--Promotion of Small & Medium-Sized Firms in Developing Countries Through Collective Actions. 374p. 1969. 6.50x (ISBN 0-686-14688-3). OECD.
--Re-Appraisal of Regional Policies in OECD Countries. 172p. 1974. 7.00x (ISBN 92-64-11286-3). OECD.
Regional Problems & Policies in OECD Countries: United Kingdom, Belgium, Netherlands, Norway, Finland, Spain, Austria, Germany, Canada, Switzerland. 1977. 10.00x (ISBN 92-64-11572-2). OECD.
The State of the Environment in OECD Member Countries. 177p. 1979. 10.00x (ISBN 92-64-11946-9). OECD.

ORGANIZATION FOR EUROPEAN ECONOMIC COOPERATION

Kravis, Irving B. Domestic Interests & International Obligations. LC 74-25537. 448p. 1975. Repr. of 1963 ed. lib. bdg. 27.75x (ISBN 0-8371-7870-3, KRDI). Greenwood.
New Forms of Work Organization, No. 2. 145p. 1980. pap. 16.00 (ISBN 92-2-102110-6, ILO 135, ILO). Unipub.

ORGANIZATION OF AFRICAN UNITY

Andemicael, Berhanykun. The OAU & the UN: Relations Between the Organization of African Unity & the United Nations. LC 74-84658. 350p. 1976. text ed. 32.50x (ISBN 0-8419-0186-4, Africana). Holmes & Meier.
Cervenka, Zdenek. The Unfinished Quest for Unity: Africa & the OAU. LC 77-16103. 1978. text ed. 26.00x (ISBN 0-8419-0353-0, Africana). Holmes & Meier.
Mbuyinga, Elenga. Pan Africanism or Neo-Colonialism: The Bankruptcy of the OAU. 224p. 1981. 25.00x (ISBN 0-86232-076-3, Pub. by Zed Pr). Lawrence Hill.

ORGANIZATION OF AMERICAN STATES

Actas y Documentos, Vol. II, Primera Parte: Quinto Periodo Ordinario de Sesiones. Wash. D.C., del 8 al 19 de Mayo de 1975. Actas de las Sesiones Plenarias. (General Assembly Ser.). 1976. 5.00 (ISBN 0-8270-0980-1). OAS.
Actas y Documentos, Vol. II, Segunda Parte: Actas De la Comision General y Actas Resumidas De las Comisiones I, II, III, y IV, y Anexos. (General Assembly Ser). 1976. 10.00 (ISBN 0-8270-0985-2). OAS.
Actas y Documentos Vol. 1, Sexto Periodo: Ordinario De Sesiones. Santiago, Chile, del 4 al 18 de Junio de 1976. Textos certificados de las resoluciones en espanol. (General Assembly Ser.). 1976. 3.00 (ISBN 0-8270-0995-X). OAS.
Ball, M. M. OAS in Transition. LC 70-86475. 1969. 27.75 (ISBN 0-8223-0207-1). Duke.
Barrett, John. The Pan American Union. 1977. lib. bdg. 59.95 (ISBN 0-8490-2401-3). Gordon Pr.
Bibliography of Books & Articles on the Organization of American States. 22p. (Eng. & Sp.). 1977. pap. text ed. 1.00 (ISBN 0-8270-3040-1). OAS.
Bosquejos de las Naciones Americanas. (Span.). 1977. pap. 1.00 (ISBN 0-8270-5135-2). OAS.
Catalogue of Technical Reports & Documents of the Oas, 1974-1976. (Eng. & Span.). 1977. 4.00 (ISBN 0-8270-0200-9). OAS.
Chiefs of State & Cabinet Ministers of the American Republics. 44p. (Semi-annual). pap. 1.00 (ISBN 0-8270-5685-0). OAS.
Convencion Sobre Asilo Diplomatico. (Treaty Ser.: No. 18). (Span. , Eng. , Fr. & Port.). 1954. pap. 1.00 (ISBN 0-8270-0360-9). OAS.
De Vries, H. P. & Rodriguez-Novas, J. The Law of the Americas. LC 66-27792. 1965. 20.00 (ISBN 0-379-00268-X). Oceana.
Documents & Notes on Privileges & Immunities with Special Reference to the Organization of American States. 1968. pap. 2.50 Eng. ed. (ISBN 0-8270-5220-0); pap. 2.50 Span. ed. (ISBN 0-8270-5215-4). OAS.
Extraordinario De Sesiones, Primer Periodo, Washington, D. C., 1970. Proceedings: Textos Certificados De las Resoluciones y Otros Documentos, Vol. 1. (General Assembly Ser.). (Fr., Span., Port.). pap. 2.00 (ISBN 0-8270-0880-5). OAS.
Extraordinario De Sesiones, Segundo Periodo, Washington, D. C., Del 24 Al 25 De Agosto De 1970. Actas y Documentos, Vol. 1. (General Assembly Ser.). (Span.). pap. 2.00 (ISBN 0-8270-0895-3). OAS.
Extraordinario De Sesiones, Tercer Periodo, Washington, D. C., Del 25 De Enero Al 2 De Febrero De 1971. Actas y Documentos, Vol. 2. (General Assembly Ser.). (Span.). pap. 2.00 (ISBN 0-8270-0905-4). OAS.
Informe Anual Del Secretario-General. (Span.). 1975. 7.00 (ISBN 0-8270-5040-2). OAS.
Informe De la XII Sesion De la Comision De Mejoramiento De las Estadisticas Nacionales (Coins) 1975. 4.00 (ISBN 0-8270-6720-8). OAS.
Inter-American Commission on Human Rights. Organization of American States & Human Rights 1960-1967. (Eng. & Span.). 1972. 15.00 (ISBN 0-8270-2520-3). OAS.
Inter-American Institute Of International Legal Studies. Inter-American System: Its Development & Strengthening. Garcia-Amador, F. V., ed. LC 66-17245. 1966. 20.00 (ISBN 0-379-00261-2). Oceana.
Inter-American Juridical Committee. Charter of the OAS & Inter-American Treaty of Reciprocal Assistance. (Treaty Ser.: No. 25). (Eng. & Span.). 1972. pap. 1.00 ea. (ISBN 0-8270-0395-1). OAS.
Inter-American Treaties & Conventions on Asylum & Extradition. (Treaty Ser.: No. 34). (Eng. & Span.). 1970. pap. 1.00 Eng. ed. (ISBN 0-8270-0440-0); pap. 1.00 Span ed. (ISBN 0-8270-0445-1). OAS.
Leblanc. The OAS & the Promotion & Protection of Human Rights. 1977. pap. 31.50 (ISBN 90-247-1943-7, Pub. by Martinus Nijhoff Netherlands). Kluwer Boston.
Lista General Vol. 11: No. 1 Enero-Julio, 1970. (Documentos Oficiales Ser). (Span.). pap. 1.50 (ISBN 0-8270-0090-1). OAS.
Lista General Vol. 11: No. 2 Julio-Diciembre, 1970. (Documentos Oficales Ser). 69p. (Span.). 1970. pap. 2.00 (ISBN 0-8270-0095-2). OAS.
Lista General Vol. 12: Enero-Diciembre, 1971. (Documentos Oficiales Ser). 190p. (Span.). 1971. pap. 2.00 (ISBN 0-8270-0100-2). OAS.
Martz, Mary Reid Jeanne. The Central American Soccer War: Historical Patterns & Internal Dynamics of Oas Settlement Procedures. LC 78-11595. (Papers in International Studies: Latin American: No. 4). 1978. pap. 7.00 (ISBN 0-89680-077-6). Ohio U Ctr Intl.
Metodologia Utilizada por las Naciones Americanas: (IASI) 1976. pap. text ed. 2.00 (ISBN 0-8270-6595-7). OAS.
O A S General Secretariat. Organization of American States Directory. 46p. 1981. pap. text ed. 1.00 (ISBN 0-686-73901-9). OAS.
OAS Department of Publication, ed. Actas y Documentos: Resoluciones Aprobadas. Septimo Periodo Extraordinario de Sesiones. Washington, D.C. 22 de Mayo de 1979. 266p. 1980. pap. text ed. 15.00 (ISBN 0-8270-1171-7). OAS.
OAS General Secretariat. Actas y Documentos Segunda Conferencia Especializada Interamericana Sobre Derecho Internacional Privado, 3 vols. (CIDIP-II Ser.: Vols. 1-3). 1980. Vol. 1, 455p. pap. text ed. 25.00 (ISBN 0-8270-1113-X); Vol. 2, 547p. pap. text ed. 25.00 (ISBN 0-8270-1114-8); Vol. 3, 469p. pap. text ed. 25.00 (ISBN 0-8270-1115-6). OAS.
--Aplicacoes Da Teoria De Grupos Na Espectroscopia De Raman E Do Infravermelho. (Fisica Monografia: No. 14). 102p. 1980. pap. text ed. 2.00 (ISBN 0-8270-1126-1). OAS.
--Decima Primeira Reunino Do Conselho Interamericano De Educacao, Ciencia E Cultura: Relatorio Final. 206p. (Port., 27 de julho a 2 de agosto de 1980, Bogota, Colombia). 1980. pap. text ed. 19.00 (ISBN 0-8270-1199-7). OAS.
--Guia De las Fuentes En Hispanoamerica Para el Estudio De la Administracion Virreinal Espanola En Mexico y En el Peru 1535-1700. 523p. 1980. pap. 15.00 (ISBN 0-8270-1091-5). OAS.
--Manual De Normas Vigentes En Materia De Direitos Humanos: Actualizado Em Julho De 1980. (Human Rights Ser.). 149p. (Port.). 1980. pap. text ed. 4.00 (ISBN 0-8270-1203-9). OAS.
--Onzieme Reunion Du Conseil Interamericain Pour L'education, la Science et la Culture: Rapport Final. 236p. (Fr.). 1980. pap. text ed. 19.00 (ISBN 0-8270-1198-9). OAS.
--Revista Interamericana De Bibliografia: (Inter-American Review of Bibliography) (Vol. XXX, No. 3). 116p. (Engl. & Span.). 1980. pap. text ed. 2.00 (ISBN 0-686-69868-1). OAS.
--Short-Term Economic Reports: Colombia, Vol. 1. 2nd ed. (Short Term Economic Reports Ser.). 77p. 1980. pap. text ed. 5.00 (ISBN 0-8270-1261-6). OAS.
--Sintesis De las Decisiones Tomadas En las Sesiones y Textos De las Resoluciones Aprobadas. (Vol. XXXI Enero-Diciembre De 1978). 174p. 1980. pap. text ed. 3.00 (ISBN 0-8270-6300-8). OAS.
--Trabajos Realizados Por el Comite Juridico Interamericano Durante el Periodo Ordinario De Sesiones. (International Law Ser.). 147p. 1980. text ed. 10.00 (ISBN 0-8270-1156-3). OAS.
--Trabajos Realizados Por el Comite Juridico Interamericano Durante el Periodo Ordinario De Sesiones: Celebrado Del 4 Al 29 De Agosto De 1980. (Comite Juridico Interamericano). 155p. (Span.). 1980. pap. text ed. 10.00 (ISBN 0-8270-1267-5). OAS.
--Trabalhos Realizados Pela Comissao Juridica Interamericana Durante Seu Periodo Ordinario De Sessoes: 30 de Julho a 16 de Agosto de 1979. 165p. (Port.). 1980. pap. text ed. 7.00 (ISBN 0-8270-1146-6). OAS.
--Tratados y Convenciones Interamerianos. (Serie Sobre Tratados: No. 9). 303p. 1980. pap. text ed. 15.00 (ISBN 0-8270-1159-8). OAS.
--Los Virus. (Serie De Biologia: No. 8). 72p. (Orig.). 1980. pap. text ed. 2.00 (ISBN 0-8270-1169-5). OAS.
--Work Accomplished by the Inter-American Juridical Committee During Its Regular Meeting: Held from January 14 to February 9, 1980. 127p. 1980. pap. text ed. 11.00 (ISBN 0-8270-1223-3). OAS.
OAS General Secretariat, ed. Boletin Estadistico de la OEA: Enero-Junio 1980, Vol. 2, Nos. 1-2. 221p. 1980. pap. text ed. 4.00 (ISBN 0-686-69867-3). OAS.
OAS General Secretariat for Legal Affairs. Relacion de Acuerdos Bilaterales: OEA Ser. B/II 1, 1949-1980. (Ser. Sobre Tratados: No. 59). 74p. (Span., Eng., Fr. & Port.). 1980. 4.00 (ISBN 0-8270-1283-7). OAS.
OAS General Secretariat for Management. Documentos Oficiales de la Organizacion de los Estados Americanos Lista General de Documentos, Volumen XX: OeA/Ser.Z/I. 1. Enero-Diciembre de 1979. 144p. (Span.). 1980. lib. bdg. 9.00 (ISBN 0-8270-1289-6). OAS.
OAS General Secretariat Inter-American Commission on Human Rights. Annual Report of the Inter-American Commission on Human Rights 1979-1980. OAS Staff, tr. (Inter-American Commission on Human Rights Ser.). 153p. 1980. lib. bdg. 6.00 (ISBN 0-8270-1285-3). OAS.
OAS General Secretariat Programa de Comercio Internacional y Desarrollo de las Exportaciones. Sistema Generalizado de Preferencias de Estados Unidos: Cobertura y Procedimientos Administrativos Vigentes En 1981. 59p. (Span.). Date not set. pap. 5.00 (ISBN 0-8270-1325-6). OAS.
OAS Opening Doors to Opportunity. (Eng & Span.). 1975. pap. 1.00 Eng. ed. (ISBN 0-8270-6500-0); pap. 1.00 Span. ed. (ISBN 0-8270-6495-0). OAS.
Octavia Reunion del Consejo Interamericano para la Educacion , la Ciencia & la Cultura: Informe Final. (Orig.). 1977. pap. text ed. 4.00 (ISBN 0-8270-1815-0). OAS.
Ondas, No.11. (Serie De Fisica). (Span.). 1975. pap. 1.25 (ISBN 0-8270-6195-1). OAS.
Ordinario De Sesiones, Tercer Periodo, Washington, D. C., Del 4 Al 15 De Abril De 1973. Actas y Documentos, Vol. 2. (General Assembly Ser.). (Span.). pap. 2.00 (ISBN 0-8270-0930-5). OAS.
Ordinariode Sesiones, Cuarto Periodo, Atlanta, Georgia, Del 19 De Abril Al 1 De Mayo De 1974. Actas y Documentos: Actas De las Sesiones Plenarias, Vol. 2, Pt. 1. (General Assembly Ser.). (Span.). pap. 2.00 (ISBN 0-8270-0970-4). OAS.
Organization of American States. Annual Report of the Secretary General. 104p. (Eng. & Span.). 1971 3.50 (ISBN 0-8270-5000-3); 1972 3.50 (ISBN 0-8270-5010-0); 1973 3.50 (ISBN 0-8270-5020-8); 1974 5.00 (ISBN 0-8270-5035-6); 1975 7.00 (ISBN 0-685-26562-5); 1976 5.00 (ISBN 0-685-26563-3); 1977 5.00 (ISBN 0-8270-5155-7). OAS.
--Charter of the Organization of American States, Bogota, 1948. (Treaty Ser.: No. 1). (Eng., Span., Port. & Fr.). 1948. pap. 1.00 (ISBN 0-8270-0245-9). OAS.
Organization of American States: A Handbook. rev. ed. (Span. & Eng.). 1977. pap. 1.00 Eng. ed. (ISBN 0-8270-0205-X); pap. 1.00 Span. ed. (ISBN 0-8270-0210-6). OAS.
The Pan American Highway System. (Travel Ser). 80p. 1969. pap. 1.00 (ISBN 0-8270-4825-4). OAS.
Sistema Generalizado De Preferencias De Estados Unidos: Material Informativo. (Programa Sector Externo). (Span. & Eng.). 1977. Span. pap. 6.00 (ISBN 0-8270-3335-4); Eng. pap. 3.00 (ISBN 0-8270-3325-7). OAS.
Slater, Jerome. OAS & United States Foreign Policy. LC 67-10162. 1967. 6.00 (ISBN 0-8142-0111-3). Ohio St U Pr.
Statements of the Laws of the OAS Member States in Matters Affecting Business. Incl. Brazil. 308p (ISBN 0-8270-5470-X); Colombia. 303p (ISBN 0-8270-5480-7); Dominica; Grenada; St. Lucia; Suriname. 1980. write for info. OAS.
Statements of the Laws of the OAS Member States in Matters Affecting Business. Incl. Argentina. 317p. 1975 (ISBN 0-8270-5635-4); Bolivia. 366p. 1974 (ISBN 0-8270-5465-3); Chile. 350p. 1977 (ISBN 0-8270-5560-9); Costa Rica. 332p. 1978 (ISBN 0-8270-5590-0); Dominican Republic. 300p. 1964 (ISBN 0-8270-5490-4); Ecuador. 296p. 1975 (ISBN 0-8270-5495-5); El Salvador. 230p. 1979 (ISBN 0-8270-5500-5); Guatemala. 367p. 1975 (ISBN 0-8270-5505-6); Haiti. 116p. 1974 (ISBN 0-8270-5510-2); Honduras. 275p. 1965 (ISBN 0-8270-5515-3). Suppl. No. 1, 1979, 54p (ISBN 0-8270-5651-6); Mexico. 300p. 1970 (ISBN 0-8270-5520-X); Nicaragua. 325p. 1978 (ISBN 0-8270-5570-6); Panama. 306p. 1974 (ISBN 0-8270-5530-7); Paraguay. 300p. 1973 (ISBN 0-8270-5595-1). Suppl. No. 1, 1979, 42p (ISBN 0-8270-5650-8); Peru. 290p. 1973 (ISBN 0-8270-5640-0); Uruguay. 275p. 1971 (ISBN 0-8270-5630-3); Venezuela. 350p. 1977 (ISBN 0-8270-5555-2). 10.00 ea.; suppl. where indicated 2.00 ea. OAS.
Tercer Curso de Derecho Internacional Organizado por el Comite Juridico Interamericano: (Julio-Agosto De 1976) 1977. 10.00 (ISBN 0-8270-5250-2). OAS.
Thomas, Ann V. & Thomas, A. J., Jr. Organization of American States. LC 63-9754. 1963. 12.50 (ISBN 0-87074-113-6). SMU Press.

ORGANIZATION OF PETROLEUM EXPORTING COUNTRIES

Allen, Loring. OPEC Oil. LC 79-19284. 288p. 1979. text ed. 25.00 (ISBN 0-89946-002-X). Oelgeschlager.
Ghadar, Fariborz. The Evolution of OPEC Strategy. LC 76-48377. 1977. 20.50 (ISBN 0-669-01147-9). Lexington Bks.
Jawdat, Nameer A., ed. Selected Documents of the International Petroleum Industry: 1967. 1968. 32.50x (ISBN 0-8002-0003-9). Intl Pubns Serv.
Johany, Ali D. The Myth of the OPEC Cartel: The Role of Saudi Arabia. LC 80-40959. 107p. 1980. 36.00 (ISBN 0-471-27864-5, Pub. by Wiley-Interscience). Wiley.
Landis, Robin C. OPEC: Policy Implications for the United States. Klass, Michael W., ed. LC 78-19457. (Praeger Special Studies). (Illus.). 304p. 1980. 29.95 (ISBN 0-03-044361-X). Praeger.
OPEC Official Resolutions & Press Releases 1960-1980. LC 80-41924. 224p. 1980. pap. 40.00 (ISBN 0-08-027335-1). Pergamon.
OPEC (Organization of Petroleum Exporting Companies) Annual Statistical Bulletin, 1978. LC 74-640556. (Illus.). 179p. 1979. pap. 22.50x (ISBN 0-8002-2211-3). Intl Pubns Serv.
OPEC Seminar Held in Vienna, Austria in Oct. 1979. OPEC & Future Energy Markets: Proceedings. OPEC Public Information Dept., ed. 300p. 1981. 35.00x (ISBN 0-312-58611-6). St Martin.
Selected Documents of the International Petroleum Industry: Saudi Arabia, pre-1966. 1976. 23.50x (ISBN 0-8002-0005-5). Intl Pubns Serv.
Selected Documents of the International Petroleum Industry: Socialist Peoples, Libyan Arab Jamahiriya & Quatar, Pre-1966. LC 79-311061. 1977. 23.50x (ISBN 0-8002-0006-3). Intl Pubns Serv.
Selected Documents of the International Petroleum Industry: 1974. 1976. 23.50x (ISBN 0-8002-0004-7). Intl Pubns Serv.
Servan-Schreiber, Jean-Jacques. The World Challenge: OPEC & the New World Order. 1981. 14.95 (ISBN 0-671-42524-2). S&S.
Seymour, Ian. OPEC: An Instrument of Change. 256p. 1981. 25.00x (ISBN 0-312-58605-1). St Martin.
Yuter, Seymour C. Cheap Oil: How to Break OPEC with a Comprehensive Mideast Peace Plan. LC 79-53854. (Illus., Orig.). 1979. pap. 9.95 (ISBN 0-9603122-1-8). Expedited.

ORGANIZATIONAL BEHAVIOR

Aldag, Ramon & Brief, Arthur. Managing Organizational Behavior. (Illus.). 510p. 1980. text ed. 19.95 (ISBN 0-8299-0306-2). West Pub.
Allen, Bud & Bosta, Diana. Library of Lesson Plans: Team Building & Listening Workshop. 75p. 1981. vinyl 49.95x (ISBN 0-939438-16-X). Rae John.
Altman. Readings: Organizational Behavior. 1979. pap. text ed. 11.95 (ISBN 0-7216-1140-0). Dryden Pr.
American Psychological Association. School Life & Organizational Psychology. (Human Behavior Curriculum Project Ser.). 64p. (Orig.). 1981. pap. text ed. 3.95x (ISBN 0-8077-2617-6); 9.95 (ISBN 0-8077-2618-4). Tchrs Coll.
Bass & Barrett. People, Work & Organizations: An Introduction to Industrial & Organizational Psychology. 2nd ed. 1980. text ed. 19.95 (ISBN 0-205-06809-X, 7968094). Allyn.

Bonoma, Thomas V. & Zaltman, Gerald. Psychology for Management. (Business Ser.). 337p. 1981. text ed. 11.95x (ISBN 0-686-73726-1). Kent Pub Co.
Boone, Louis E. & Bowen, Donald. Great Writings in Management & Organizational Behavior. 475p. 1980. pap. text ed. 13.90 (ISBN 0-87814-097-2). Pennwell Pub.
Bowers, Raymond V., ed. Studies on Behavior in Organizations: A Research Symposium. LC 65-28462. 364p. 1966. 20.00x (ISBN 0-8203-0171-X). U of Ga Pr.
Carroll, Stephen J. & Tosi, Henry L. Organizational Behavior. (Illus.). 1977. 23.95 (ISBN 0-914292-08-0). Wiley.
Carver, Fred D. & Sergiovanni, Thomas J. Organizations & Human Behavior: Focus on Schools. LC 69-13215. (Illus.). 1969. pap. text ed. 12.95 (ISBN 0-07-010191-4, C). McGraw.
Chapman, James E. & Bridges, F. J. Critical Incidents in Organizational Behavior & Administration: With Selected Readings. (Illus.). 1977. pap. text ed. 12.95 (ISBN 0-13-193896-7). P-H.
Chung, Kae H. & Megginson, Leon C. Organizational Behavior: Developing Managerial Skills. 560p. 1981. text ed. 18.95 (ISBN 0-06-041299-2, HarpC); instructor's manual avail. (ISBN 0-06-361217-8). Har-Row.
Coffey, Robert E., et al. Behavior in Organizations: A Multi-Dimensional View. 2nd ed. LC 74-12372. (Illus.). 608p. 1975. 22.95 (ISBN 0-13-073148-X). P-H.
Cohen, Allan R., et al. Effective Behavior in Organizations. rev. ed. 1980. 19.95x (ISBN 0-256-02283-6). Irwin.
Cooper, C. Behavioral Problems in Organizations. 1979. 16.95 (ISBN 0-13-073080-7). P-H.
Crozier, Michel & Friedberg, Erhard. Actors & Systems: The Politics of Collective Action. Goldhammer, Arthur, tr. LC 80-13803. 272p. 1980. lib. bdg. 25.00x (ISBN 0-226-12183-6). U of Chicago Pr.
Cummings, L. L. & Dunham, Randall B. Introduction to Organizational Behavior: Text & Readings. 1980. pap. 15.95x (ISBN 0-256-02043-4). Irwin.
Cummings, L. L. & Staw, Barry, eds. Research in Organizational Behavior, Vol. 3. 356p. 1981. 37.50 (ISBN 0-89232-151-2). Jai Pr.
Dauw, Dean C. Creativity & Innovation in Organizations. 380p. 1980. pap. text ed. 12.95x (ISBN 0-917974-42-5). Waveland Pr.
Davis, Keith. Organizational Behavior: A Book of Readings. 5th ed. 1977. pap. text ed. 9.95 (ISBN 0-07-015499-6, C). McGraw.
Davis, Keith & Newstrom, John. Organizational Behavior: Readings & Exercises. 6th ed. (Management Ser.). (Illus.). 468p. 1981. text ed. 11.95 (ISBN 0-07-015500-3, C). McGraw.
Day, Janis K. A Working Approach to Human Relations in Organizations. LC 79-24589. 1980. pap. text ed. 15.95 (ISBN 0-8185-0347-5). Brooks-Cole.
De Board, Robert. The Psychoanalysis of Organizations: A Psychoanalytic Approach to Behaviour in Groups & Organizations. 158p. 1978. 16.50x (ISBN 0-422-76520-1, Pub. by Tavistock England); pap. 6.95x (ISBN 0-422-76530-9). Methuen Inc.
Downey, H. Kirk, et al. Organizational Behavior: A Reader. (Illus.). 1977. pap. text ed. 13.95 (ISBN 0-8299-0137-X). West Pub.
Duncan, W. Jack. Organizational Behavior. 2nd ed. LC 80-82460. (Illus.). 464p. 1981. text ed. 20.95 (ISBN 0-395-29640-4); instr's manual 1.00 (ISBN 0-395-29641-2). HM.
Dutrich, John E. & Zawacki, Robert A. People & Organizations: Cases in Management & Organizational Behavior. 1981. pap. 9.95x (ISBN 0-256-02423-5). Business Pubns.
Falcione, Raymond L. & Greenbaum, Howard H. Organizational Communication: Abstracts, Analysis, & Overview, Vol. 5. (Illus.). 288p. 1980. 32.50x (ISBN 0-8039-1384-2); pap. 17.50 (ISBN 0-8039-1385-0). Sage.
Foy, Nancy. The Yin & Yang of Organizations. LC 80-18558. 1980. 11.95 (ISBN 0-688-03769-0). Morrow.
Gannon, Martin J. Organizational Behavior: A Managerial & Organizational Perspective. 1979. text ed. 19.95 (ISBN 0-316-30331-3); tchrs' manual free (ISBN 0-685-91891-2). Little.
Gibson, Cyrus F. Managing Organizational Behavior. 1980. 20.50x (ISBN 0-256-02237-2). Irwin.
Glen, Frederick. The Social Psychology of Organizations. (Essential Psychology Ser.). 1976. pap. 4.50x (ISBN 0-416-84050-7). Methuen Inc.
Gray, Jerry & Starke, Frederick. Readings in Organizational Behavior: Concepts and Applications. (Business Ser.). 1976. pap. text ed. 12.95 (ISBN 0-675-08522-5). Merrill.
Gray, Jerry L. & Starke, Frederick A. Organizational Behavior. 2nd ed. (Marketing & Management Ser.). 464p. 1980. text ed. 20.95 (ISBN 0-675-08141-6); instructor's manual 3.95 (ISBN 0-686-63343-1). Merrill.
Greenblatt, Sidney L., et al, eds. Organizational Behavior in Chinese Society. 300p. 1981. 27.95 (ISBN 0-03-053206-X). Praeger.
Hackman, Porter L., et al. Perspectives on Behavior in Organizations. 1977. pap. text ed. 11.95 (ISBN 0-07-025413-3, C). McGraw.
Hall, Douglas T., et al. Experiences in Management & Organizational Behavior. LC 75-1991. (Illus.). 1975. pap. text ed. 9.95 (ISBN 0-914292-03-X). Wiley.
Hamner, W. Clay & Organ, Dennis W. Organizational Behavior: An Applied Psychological Approach. 1978. 16.00x (ISBN 0-256-01811-1). Business Pubns.
Harlow, Dorothy N. & Hanke, Jean J. Situational Administration. LC 81-40339. Orig. Title: Behavior in Organizations. (Illus.). 674p. 1981. lib. bdg. 34.00 (ISBN 0-8191-1837-0); pap. text ed. 23.00 (ISBN 0-8191-1838-9). U Pr of Amer.
Hellriegel, Don & Slocum, John. Organizational Behavior. 2nd ed. (Management Ser.). (Illus.). 1979. text ed. 20.95 (ISBN 0-8299-0195-7); instrs.' manual avail. (ISBN 0-8299-0487-5). West Pub.
Herbert, Theodore T. Dimensions of Organizational Behavior. (Illus.). 640p. 1976. text ed. 17.50x (ISBN 0-02-353720-5). Macmillan.
Hersey, Paul & Blanchard, Kenneth H. Management of Organizational Behavior: Utilizing Human Resources. 4th ed. (Illus.). 368p. 1982. 16.95 (ISBN 0-13-549618-7); pap. text ed. 11.95 (ISBN 0-13-549600-4). P-H.
Higgins. Organizational Policy: Strat Mgmt. 1979. 22.95 (ISBN 0-03-022186-2). Dryden Pr.
Ho, Y. C. & Mitter, S., eds. Directions in Large-Scale Systems: Many-Person Optimization & Decentralized Control. 434p. 1976. 45.00 (ISBN 0-306-30937-8, Plenum Pr). Plenum Pub.
Hodge, Billy J. & Johnson, Herbert J. Management & Organizational Behavior: A Multidimensional Approach. (Management & Administration Ser.). 552p. 1981. Repr. of 1970 ed. lib. bdg. 21.50 (ISBN 0-89874-086-X). Krieger.
Hodgetts. Organizational Behavior. 1979. 21.95 (ISBN 0-7216-4713-8). Dryden Pr.
Howe, Roger J. Building Profits Through Organizational Change. 272p. 1981. 17.95 (ISBN 0-8144-5681-2). Am Mgmt.
Huse, Edgar F. & Bowditch, James L. Behavior in Organizations: A Systems Approach to Managing. 2nd ed. LC 76-9329. (Illus.). 1977. text ed. 18.95 (ISBN 0-201-02965-0). A-W.
Ingalls, John D. Human Energy: The Critical Factor for Individuals & Organizations. 285p. 1979. Repr. of 1976 ed. text ed. 18.95 (ISBN 0-89384-055-6). Learning Concepts.
Ivancevich, John M & Szilagyi, Andrew D. Organizational Behavior & Performance. LC 76-43427. (Illus.). 1977. 18.95 (ISBN 0-87620-635-6); instructors manual free (ISBN 0-87620-636-4). Goodyear.
Ivancevich, John M., et al, eds. Readings in Organizational Behavior & Performance. LC 77-1433. 1977. pap. 11.50 (ISBN 0-87620-634-8). Goodyear.
Jabes, Jak. Individual Processes in Organizational Behavior. MacKenzie, Kenneth D., ed. LC 77-86012. (Organizational Behavior Ser.). 1978. pap. text ed. 9.95x (ISBN 0-88295-450-4). Harlan Davidson.
Kanter, Rosabeth M. Men & Women of the Corporation. LC 76-43464. 1979. 15.00 (ISBN 0-465-04452-2, CN-5036); pap. 5.95x (ISBN 0-465-04453-0). Basic.
Karmel, Barbara. Point & Counterpoint in Organizational Behavior. 168p. 1980. pap. 8.95 (ISBN 0-03-054686-9). Dryden Pr.
Katz, Daniel, et al, eds. The Study of Organizations: Findings from Field & Laboratory. LC 80-15488. (Social & Behavioral Science Ser.). 1980. text ed. 28.95x (ISBN 0-87589-464-X). Jossey-Bass.
Kelly, Joe. Organizational Behavior. 3rd ed. 1980. 20.95x (ISBN 0-256-02284-4). Irwin.
Kerr, Steven, ed. Organizational Behavior. LC 78-26718. (Grid Series in Management). 1979. text ed. 22.00 (ISBN 0-88244-182-5). Grid Pub.
Klein, Stuart M. & Ritti, Richard R. Understanding Organizational Behavior. 592p. 1980. text ed. 20.95x (ISBN 0-534-00755-4, Kent Pub.). Kent Pub Co.
Kraus, William A. Collaboration in Organizations: Alternatives to Hierarchy. LC 80-11291. 274p. 1980. text ed. 22.95 (ISBN 0-87705-491-6). Human Sci Pr.
Lauderdale, Michael. Burnout: Strategies for Personal & Organizational Life: Speculations on Evolving Paradigms. 250p. 1981. text ed. price not set (ISBN 0-89384-063-7). Learning Concepts.
Lawler, Edward E., et al. Organizational Assessment: Perspectives on the Measurement of Organizational Behavior & the Quality of Working Life. (Wiley Series on Organizational Assessment & Change). 669p. 1980. 38.50 (ISBN 0-471-04836-4, Pub. by Wiley-Interscience). Wiley.
Lawrence, Paul R., et al, eds. Organizational Behavior & Administration: Cases & Readings. 3rd ed. 1976. 20.50x (ISBN 0-256-01760-3). Irwin.
Litterer, J. Organizations: Structure & Behavior. 3rd ed. LC 80-15645. (Wiley Series in Management). 625p. 1980. pap. 15.95 (ISBN 0-471-07786-0). Wiley.
Luthans, Fred. Contemporary Readings in Organizational Behavior. 2nd ed. (Illus.). 1976. pap. text ed. 9.95 (ISBN 0-07-039132-7, C). McGraw.
--Organizational Behavior. 3rd ed. (Illus.). text ed. 18.95 (ISBN 0-07-039144-0, C); instructor's manual 9.95 (ISBN 0-07-039145-9); test file 6.96 (ISBN 0-07-039146-7). McGraw.
--Organizational Behavior. 2nd ed. Davis, Keith, ed. (Management Ser.). (Illus.). 1976. text ed. 16.95 (ISBN 0-07-039130-0, C); instrs manual 4.95 (ISBN 0-07-039133-5); study guide 6.95 (ISBN 0-07-039131-9). McGraw.
Luthans, Fred & Martinko, Mark J. The Power of Positive Reinforcement. (Illus.). 1978. leader's guide 10.00 (ISBN 0-07-039138-6, T&D); wkbk. 6.95 (ISBN 0-07-039137-8). McGraw.
Luthans, Fred & Thompson, Kenneth R. Contemporary Readings in Organizational Behavior. 3rd ed. (Management Ser.). (Illus.). 528p. 1981. text ed. 12.95 (ISBN 0-07-039148-3). McGraw.
McGill, Michael. Organization Development for Operating Managers. 1980. pap. 5.95 (ISBN 0-8144-7529-9). Am Mgmt.
McLennan, Roy. Cases in Organisational Behaviour. (Illus.). 282p. 1975. 29.50x (ISBN 0-8448-0761-3). Crane-Russak Co.
March, James G. & Olsen, Johan P. Ambiguity & Choice in Organizations. 2nd ed. 420p. 1980. pap. 29.00x (ISBN 8-2000-1960-8). Universitet.
Martinez, Raul C. Organizational Behavior Management: A Manual for Supervisors. (Illus.). 148p. (Orig.). 1980. pap. 8.50 (ISBN 0-937230-00-6). NPD Corp.
Meister, David. Government Supported Behavioral Science Research: Civilian & Military R&D. (Pergamon Policy Studies on Science Policy). (Illus.). 300p. 1981. 27.51 (ISBN 0-08-024659-1). Pergamon.
Meltzer, H. & Nord, Walter R. Making Organizations Humane & Productive: A Handbook for Practitioners. 512p. 1981. 27.95 (ISBN 0-471-07813-1, Pub. by Wiley-Interscience). Wiley.
Meltzer, H. & Wickert, Frederic R. Humanizing Organizational Behavior. (Illus.). 456p. 1976. 37.75 (ISBN 0-398-03500-8). C C Thomas.
Merrell, V. Dallas. Huddling: The Informal Way to Management Success. LC 78-31941. 1979. 11.95 (ISBN 0-8144-5506-9). Am Mgmt.
Middlemist, R. Dennis & Hitt, Michael A. Organizational Behavior. 512p. 1981. text ed. 19.95 (ISBN 0-574-19390-1, 13-2390); instr's. guide avail. (ISBN 0-574-19391-X, 13-2391). SRA.
Miner, John B. Theories of Organizational Behavior. 416p. 1980. text ed. 21.95 (ISBN 0-03-054721-0). Dryden Pr.
Mink, Oscar G., et al. Developing & Managing Open Organizations. LC 79-10195. 1979. text ed. 17.95 (ISBN 0-89384-045-9). Learning Concepts.
Mitchell, T. R. People in Organizations: An Introduction to Organizational Behavior. 2nd ed. (Management Ser.). 1982. 20.95 (ISBN 0-07-042532-9, C); instr's manual 6.95 (ISBN 0-07-042533-7). McGraw.
Nadler, David A., et al. Managing Organizational Behavior. 1979. pap. text ed. 9.95 (ISBN 0-316-59679-5); tchrs' manual free (ISBN 0-316-59680-9). Little.
Naumes. Case Organizational Strategy Policy. 1978. pap. 12.95 (ISBN 0-7216-6662-0). Dryden Pr.
Naylor, James C., et al. A Theory of Behavior in Organizations. LC 79-6798. 1980. 24.00 (ISBN 0-12-514450-4). Acad Pr.
Owens, Robert G. Organizational Behavior in Education. 2nd ed. (Illus.). 368p. 1981. text ed. 19.95 (ISBN 0-13-641050-2). P-H.
Paine. Organizational Strategy & Policy. 2nd ed. 1978. pap. 16.95 (ISBN 0-7216-7048-2). Dryden Pr.
Parrino, John J. From Panic to Power: The Positive Use of Stress. LC 79-12027. 1979. 14.50 (ISBN 0-471-05303-1, Pub. by Wiley-Interscience). Wiley.
Pennings, Johannes M. Interlocking Directorates: Origins & Consequences of Connections Among Organizations' Boards of Directors. LC 80-8001. (Social & Behavioral Science Ser.). 1980. text ed. 16.95x (ISBN 0-87589-469-0). Jossey-Bass.
Pinder, Craig C. & Moore, Larry F., eds. Middle Range Theory & the Study of Organizatons. 1980. lib. bdg. 30.00 (ISBN 0-89838-021-9, Pub. by Martinus Nijhoff Netherlands). Kluwer Boston.
Porter, Lyman W., et al. Behavior in Organizations. (Psychology & Management Ser.). (Illus.). 561p. 1974. text ed. 17.95 (ISBN 0-07-050527-6, C); exam questions 2.95 (ISBN 0-07-050528-4). McGraw.
Preston, Lee E., ed. Research in Corporate Social Performance & Policy, Vol. 2. (Orig.). 1980. lib. bdg. 34.50 (ISBN 0-89232-133-4). Jai Pr.
Pruitt, Dean G. Negotiation Behavior. (Organizational & Occupational Psychology Ser.). 1981. price not set (ISBN 0-12-566250-5). Acad Pr.
Pugh, D. S., et al. Research in Organizational Behaviour. pap. text ed. 6.00x (ISBN 0-435-82692-1). Heinemann Ed.
Rashid, S. Anwar & Archer, Maurice. Case Problems in Organizational Behavior. 96p. 1980. pap. text ed. 5.95 (ISBN 0-8403-2222-4). Kendall-Hunt.
--Organizational Behavior. 336p. 1980. pap. text ed. 17.95 (ISBN 0-8403-2221-6). Kendall-Hunt.
Reber, Ralph W. & Terry, Gloria. Behavioral Insights for Supervision. 2nd ed. (Illus.). 240p. 1982. pap. 13.95 (ISBN 0-13-073114-5). P-H.
Reitz, H. Joseph. Behavior in Organizations. rev. ed. 1981. 19.95 (ISBN 0-256-02512-6). Irwin.
--Behavior in Organizations. rev. ed. 1980. 20.95x (ISBN 0-256-01792-1). Irwin.
Ritchie, J. B. & Thompson, Paul H. Organization & People: Readings, Cases & Exercises in Organizational Behavior. 2nd ed. (Ser. in Management). 1980. pap. 13.95 (ISBN 0-8299-0274-0); instrs.' manual avail. (ISBN 0-8299-0571-5). West Pub.
Schieve, William C. & Allen, Peter M., eds. Self-Organization & Dissipative Structures: Applications in the Physical & Social Sciences. (Illus.). 472p. 1981. text ed. 50.00x (ISBN 0-292-70354-6). U of Tex Pr.
Staw, Barry & Cummings, L. L., eds. Research in Organizational Behavior, Vol. 4. 425p. 1981. 37.50 (ISBN 0-89232-147-4). Jai Pr.
Staw, Barry M. & Cummings, Larry L., eds. Research in Organizational Behavior, Vol. 2. (Orig.). 1980. lib. bdg. 37.50 (ISBN 0-89232-099-0). Jai Pr.
Steers, Richard M. Introduction to Organizational Behavior. 1981. text ed. 19.95 (ISBN 0-8302-4459-X). Goodyear.
Stuart-Kotze, Robin. Introduction to Organizational Behavior: A Situational Approach. (Illus.). 1980. text ed. 17.95 (ISBN 0-8359-3259-1). Reston.
Swanda, John R., Jr. Organizational Behavior: Systems & Applications. LC 78-22719. (Illus.). 539p. 1979. text ed. 14.95 (ISBN 0-88284-054-1). Alfred Pub.
Tagliere, Daniel A. The Participative Prince: Techniques for Developing Your Organization & Improving Its Performance. LC 79-83886. (Illus.). 1979. 14.95 (ISBN 0-9602516-0-X). ODS Pubns.
Van de Ven, Andrew H., pseud. Perspectives on Organization Design & Behavior. (Organizational Assessment an Change Ser.). 448p. 1981. 28.95 (ISBN 0-471-09358-0, Pub. by Wiley-Interscience). Wiley.
Van de Ven, Andrew H. & Ferry, Diane L. Measuring & Assessing Organizations. LC 79-20003. (Organizational Assessment & Change Ser.). 1980. 38.95 (ISBN 0-471-04832-1, Pub. by Wiley-Interscience). Wiley.
Wallace, Melvin. Retreat: The Dynamic New Answer for Your Firm's Successful Future. LC 79-83673. 1979. 29.95 (ISBN 0-933460-00-7). Wintergreen.
Warmington, C., et al. Organizational Behavior & Performance. 1978. 14.95 (ISBN 0-87909-594-6). Reston.
Warner, Malcolm. Organizational Choice & Constraint. (Illus.). 1978. 24.95 (ISBN 0-566-00180-2, 01619-5, Pub. by Saxon Hse England). Lexington Bks.
White, Donald D. Contemporary Perspectives in Organizational Behavior. 500p. 1981. 9.96 (ISBN 0-205-07350-6, 0873500); free (ISBN 0-205-07351-4). Allyn.
White, Donald D. & Vroman, H. William. Action in Organizations. 2nd ed. 500p. 1981. write for info. (ISBN 0-205-07353-0); instructor manual free (ISBN 0-205-07354-9). Allyn.
Wilder, Claudyne & Rogers, William I. Taking Charge: Personal Effectiveness in Organizations. LC 79-9513. 1980. pap. text ed. 9.95 (ISBN 0-201-08624-7). A-W.

ORGANIZATIONAL CHANGE

Abramson, Robert. An Integrated Approach to Organization Development & Performance Improvement Training. (Library of Management for Development). 92p. (Orig.). 1978. pap. 4.95x (ISBN 0-931816-26-2). Kumarian Pr.

Adams, John D., ed. New Technologies in Organization Development: 2. LC 75-35017. 392p. 1974. pap. 9.95 (ISBN 0-88390-112-9). Univ Assocs.

Aiken, Michael & Hage, Jerald. Social Change in Complex Organization. 1970. pap. text ed. 5.95 (ISBN 0-394-30784-4). Random.

Alderfer, Clayton P. & Brown, L. Dave. Learning from Changing: Organizational Diagnosis & Development. LC 75-34081. (Sage Library of Social Research: Vol. 19). 256p. 1975. 20.00x (ISBN 0-8039-0554-8); pap. 9.95x (ISBN 0-8039-0555-6). Sage.

Anderson, Bijorn & Hedberg, Neils B. The Impact of Systems Change in Organizations, No. 2. (Information System Ser.). 356p. 1979. 47.50x (ISBN 90-286-0549-5). Sijthoff & Noordhoff.

Appley, Lawrence A. & Irons, Keith L. Manager Manpower Planning: A Professional Management System. 128p. 1981. 14.95 (ISBN 0-8144-5707-X). Am Mgmt.

Argyris, Chris. Intervention Theory & Method: A Behavioral Science View. LC 79-114331. (Business Ser). 1970. text ed. 18.95 (ISBN 0-201-00342-2). A-W.

Basil, Douglas & Cook, Curtis W. The Management of Change. 1974. 21.50 (ISBN 0-07-084440-2, P&RB). McGraw.

Beckhard, Richard. Organization Development: Strategies & Models. Schein, Edgar, et al, eds. (Ser. in Organization Development). 1969. pap. text ed. 6.50 (ISBN 0-201-00448-8). A-W.

Bell, Chip R. The Marketing of Change. 1982. text ed. price not set (ISBN 0-89384-051-3). Learning Concepts.

Bennis, Warren G. Organization Development: Its Nature, Origins & Prospects. Schein, Edgar, et al, eds. (Ser. in Organization Development). 1969. pap. text ed. 6.50 (ISBN 0-201-00523-9). A-W.

Bibeault, Donald. Corporate Turnaround: How Managers Turn Losers into Winners. 416p. 1981. 24.95 (ISBN 0-07-005190-9, P&RB). McGraw.

Blake, Robert R. & Mouton, Jane S. Building a Dynamic Corporation Through Grid Organization Development. Schein, Edgar, et al, eds. (Organization Development Ser). 1969. pap. text ed. 6.50 (ISBN 0-201-00612-X). A-W.

--The New Managerial Grid. 342p. 1978. 12.95 (ISBN 0-87201-473-8). Gulf Pub.

Burgher, Peter H. Changement: Understanding & Managing Business. 1979. 16.95 (ISBN 0-669-02569-0). Lexington Bks.

Burke, W. Warner. Current Issues & Strategies in Organization Development. LC 76-28755. 448p. 1977. 29.95 (ISBN 0-87705-270-0). Human Sci Pr.

Burke, W. Warner, ed. The Cutting Edge: Current Theory & Practice in Organization Development. LC 78-60935. 302p. 1978. pap. 16.50 (ISBN 0-88390-147-1). Univ Assocs.

--New Technologies in Organization Development: 1. LC 75-35017. 276p. 1972. pap. 8.95 (ISBN 0-88390-113-7). Univ Assocs.

Cizankas, Victor I. & Hanna, Donald G. Modern Police Management Organization. (Illus.). 256p. 1977. text ed. 15.95 (ISBN 0-13-597104-7). P-H.

Cooper, Cary L., ed. Organizational Development in the U.K. U.S.A. A Joint Evaluation. LC 77-15084. 1978. text ed. 10.00 (ISBN 0-89433-069-1). Petrocelli.

Cummings, Thomas G. & Molloy, Edmond S. Improving Productivity & the Quality of Work Life. LC 76-24348. (Praeger Special Studies). 1977. text ed. 29.95 (ISBN 0-275-56870-9); pap. 10.95 (ISBN 0-03-022601-5). Praeger.

Cummings, Thomas G., ed. Systems Theory for Organization Development. LC 79-42906. (Individuals, Groups & Organizations Ser.). 362p. 1980. 49.00 (ISBN 0-471-27691-X, Pub. by Wiley-Interscience). Wiley.

Dalton, Gene W., et al. The Distribution of Authority in Formal Organizations. (Paperback Ser). 240p. 1973. pap. 3.95 (ISBN 0-262-54021-5). MIT Pr.

Dalton, Gene W., et al, eds. Organizational Change & Development. 1970. pap. 11.95x (ISBN 0-256-00606-7). Irwin.

Fairweather, George W., et al. Creating Change in Mental Health Organizations. 200p. 1974. text ed. 19.75 (ISBN 0-08-017833-2); pap. text ed. 10.75 (ISBN 0-08-017832-4). Pergamon.

Filley, Alan C. The Compleat Manager: What Works When. LC 78-62907. (Illus., Orig.). 1978. pap. text ed. 9.95 (ISBN 0-87822-184-0). Res Press.

Francis, G. James. Organization Development: A Practical Approach. 200p. 1982. text ed. 17.95 (ISBN 0-8359-5301-7). Reston.

French, Wendell L., Jr., et al. Organization Development: Theory, Practice, & Research. 1978. pap. 16.50 (ISBN 0-256-02089-2). Business Pubns.

Gawthrop, Louis C. Bureaucratic Behavior in the Executive Branch. LC 69-10568. 1969. pap. text ed. 6.95 (ISBN 0-02-911400-4). Free Pr.

Gillespie, David, et al. Organizational Response to Changing Community Systems. LC 76-25890. (Illus.). 1976. pap. 4.50x (ISBN 0-87338-196-3, Pub. by Comp. Adm. Research Inst.). Kent St U Pr.

Goodman, Paul S. Assessing Organizational Change: Rushton Quality of Work Experiment. LC 78-31857. (Organizational Behavior Assessment & Change Ser.). 1979. 30.95x (ISBN 0-471-04782-1, Pub. by Wiley-Interscience). Wiley.

Goodstein, Leonard D., et al, eds. Organizational Change Sourcebook II: Cases in Conflict Management. LC 79-63006. 236p. 1979. pap. 12.95 (ISBN 0-88390-151-X). Univ Assocs.

Grossman, Lee. The Change Agent. LC 74-4744. 180p. 1974. 10.95 (ISBN 0-8144-5364-3). Am Mgmt.

Guest, R., et al. Organizational Change Through Effective Leadership. 1977. pap. text ed. 10.95 (ISBN 0-13-641308-0). P-H.

Hackman, J. Richard & Suttle, J. Lloyd, eds. Improving Life at Work: Behavorial Science Approaches to Organizational Change. LC 76-7667. 600p. 1977. pap. 13.95 (ISBN 0-87620-411-6). Goodyear.

Hall, Richard S. Organizations: Structure & Process. 2nd ed. LC 76-45743. (Illus.). 384p. 1977. text ed. 18.95 (ISBN 0-13-642025-7). P-H.

Harvey, D. & Brown, Donald R. An Experiential Approach to Organization Development. (Illus.). 336p. 1976. pap. text ed. 12.95 (ISBN 0-13-294983-0). P-H.

Harvey, D. & Brown, H. Experiemntal Approach to Organizational Developement. 2nd ed. 1981. pap. 18.95 (ISBN 0-13-295360-9). P-H.

Harvey, Donald F. & Brown, Donald R. An Experimental Approach to Organization Development. x2nd ed. (Illus.). 592p. 1982. pap. text ed. 18.95 (ISBN 0-13-295360-9). P-H.

Herman, Stanley & Korenich, Michael. Authentic Management: A Gestaelt Orientation to Organizations & Their Development. 1977. 10.95 (ISBN 0-201-02886-7). A-W.

Hofer, Charles W. & Schendel, Dan E. Strategy Formulation: Analytical Concepts. (West Ser. in Business Policy & Planning). (Illus.). 1978. pap. text ed. 10.50 (ISBN 0-8299-0213-9). West Pub.

Huse, Edgar F. Organization Development & Change. 2nd ed. (West Series in Management Ser.). (Illus.). 500p. 1980. text ed. 20.95 (ISBN 0-8299-0300-3). West Pub.

Ivancevich, John M & Szilagyi, Andrew D. Organizational Behavior & Performance. LC 76-43427. (Illus.). 1977. 18.95 (ISBN 0-87620-635-6); instructors manual free (ISBN 0-87620-636-4). Goodyear.

Jacobs, Bruce. The Political Economy of Organizational Change: Urban Institutional Response to War on Poverty. (Quantitative Studies in Social Relations). 1981. write for info. (ISBN 0-12-379660-1). Acad Pr.

Johns, E. A. The Sociology of Organizational Change. LC 73-8972. 182p. 1974. text ed. 25.00 (ISBN 0-08-017601-1); pap. text ed. 12.75 (ISBN 0-08-017602-X). Pergamon.

Jones, Andrew N. & Cooper, Cary L. Combating Managerial Obsolescence. LC 80-16307. xii, 176p. 1980. lib. bdg. 19.95 (ISBN 0-86003-509-3, JCO/). Greenwood.

Jones, Garth N., et al, eds. Planning, Development, & Change: A Bibliography on Development Administration. 1970. pap. text ed. 10.00x (ISBN 0-8248-0099-0, Eastwest Ctr). U Pr of Hawaii.

Jun, Jong S. & Storm, William B. Tomorrow's Organizations: Challenges & Strategies. 400p. 1973. pap. 8.95x (ISBN 0-673-07796-9). Scott F.

Kanh, Robert L. Work & Health. (Series in Organizational Assessment & Change). 160p. 1981. 15.95 (ISBN 0-471-05749-5, Pub. by Wiley-Interscience). Wiley.

Lawlor, Edward E., III. Pay & Organization Development. 230p. 1981. pap. text ed. 6.95 (ISBN 0-201-03990-7). A-W.

Lawrence, Paul R. & Lorsch, Jay W. Developing Organizations: Diagnosis & Action. LC 78-93985. (Organization Development Ser). (Orig.). 1969. pap. text ed. 6.50 (ISBN 0-201-04204-5). A-W.

Lievegoed, B. C. The Developing Organization. LC 80-66227. 228p. 1980. 12.95 (ISBN 0-89087-281-3). Celestial Arts.

Lippitt, Gordon L. Organizational Renewal: A Holistic Approach to Organization Development. 2nd ed. (Illus.). 464p. 1982. text ed. 19.95 (ISBN 0-13-641845-7). P-H.

--Visualizing Change: Model Building & the Change Process. LC 73-81361. (Illus.). 370p. 1973. pap. 14.50 (ISBN 0-88390-125-0). Univ Assocs.

Lubin, Bernard, et al, eds. Organizational Change Sourcebook I: Cases in Organization Development. LC 79-63006. 228p. 1979. pap. 12.95 (ISBN 0-88390-150-1). Univ Assocs.

Luthans, Fred & Martinko, Mark J. The Power of Positive Reinforcement. (Illus.). 1978. leader's guide 10.00 (ISBN 0-07-039138-6, T&D); wkbk. 6.95 (ISBN 0-07-039137-8). McGraw.

Lynton, Rolt P. & Pareek, Udai. Training for Development. LC 78-57232. 1978. pap. 7.95 (ISBN 0-931816-25-4). Kumarian Pr.

McGill, Michael E. Organization Development for Operating Managers. new ed. LC 76-50051. 240p. 1977. 14.95 (ISBN 0-8144-5381-3). Am Mgmt.

Mangham, Iain. The Politics of Organizational Change. LC 79-23. (Contributions in Economics & Economic History: No. 26). 1979. lib. bdg. 23.95 (ISBN 0-313-20981-2, MPC/). Greenwood.

Mangham, Iain, ed. Interactions & Interventions in Organizations. LC 78-2602. (Wiley Series on Individuals, Groups & Organizations). 1978. 29.75 (ISBN 0-471-99622-X, Pub. by Wiley-Interscience). Wiley.

Margulies, N. & Raia, A. Organizational Development: Values Process & Technology. 1971. 19.95 (ISBN 0-07-040357-0, C). McGraw.

Margulies, Newton & Raia, Anthony P. Conceptual Foundations of Organizational Development. (Management Ser.). (Illus.). 1978. text ed. 17.95 (ISBN 0-07-040360-0, C). McGraw.

Margulies, Newton & Wallace, John. Organizational Change: Techniques & Applications. 200p. 1973. pap. 8.95x (ISBN 0-673-07761-6). Scott F.

Marlow, Hugh. Managing Change. 1975. 20.00x (ISBN 0-85292-122-5). Intl Pubns Serv.

Meyer, M. W. Change in Public Bureaucracies. LC 76-47193. (Illus.). 1979. 22.50 (ISBN 0-521-22670-8). Cambridge U Pr.

Michael, Stephan, et al. Techniques of Organizational Change. LC 80-16243. (Illus.). 368p. 1981. write for info. (ISBN 0-07-041775-X, P&RB). McGraw.

Michael, Stephen R., et al. Techniques of Organizational Change. (Illus.). 363p. 1981. 16.95 (ISBN 0-07-041775-X). McGraw.

Miles, Raymond E. Theories of Management: Implications for Organizational Behavior & Development. Davis, Keith, ed. (Management Ser.). (Illus.). 256p. 1975. text ed. 14.95 (ISBN 0-07-041927-2, C). McGraw.

Mirvis, Philip H. & Berg, David N. Failures in Organization Development & Change: Cases & Essays for Learning. LC 77-21625. 1977. 31.50 (ISBN 0-471-02405-8). Ronald Pr.

Moore, Harvey A. Drug Users & Emergent Organizations. LC 77-9901. (University of Florida Social Sciences Monograph: No. 60). 1977. pap. 4.50 (ISBN 0-8130-0577-9). U Presses Fla.

Murray, Ruth B. & Zentner, Judith P. Nursing Assessment & Health Promotion Through the Life Span. 2nd ed. (Illus.). 1979. ref. 17.95 (ISBN 0-13-627588-5); pap. 13.95 (ISBN 0-13-627596-6). P-H.

National Retail Merchants Assn. Organization Survival & Growth Including Management by Objectives. 1976. 16.25 (ISBN 0-685-68875-5, P52776). Natl Ret Merch.

Ottaway, Richard N. Change Agents at Work. LC 79-24. (Contributions in Economics & Economic History: No. 27). 1979. lib. bdg. 23.95 (ISBN 0-313-21252-X, OCA/). Greenwood.

Owen, Trevor. Making Organisations Work. (International Ser. on the Quality of Working Life: Vol. 7). 1978. lib. bdg. 23.00 (ISBN 90-207-0778-7, Pub. by Martinus Nijhoff Netherlands); pap. 12.50 (ISBN 90-207-0779-5). Kluwer Boston.

Patten, Thomas H., Jr. Organizational Development Through Teambuilding. LC 80-20726. 295p. 1981. 22.95 (ISBN 0-471-66945-8, Pub. by Wiley-Interscience). Wiley.

Roeber, Richard J. The Organization in a Changing Environment. LC 72-11603. 1973. pap. text ed. 6.50 (ISBN 0-201-06501-0). A-W.

Rothman, Jack, et al. Changing Organizations & Community Programs. LC 81-4284. (Sage Human Services Guides Ser.: Vol. 20). 160p. 1981. 8.00 (ISBN 0-8039-1618-3). Sage.

Rush, Harold M. Organization Development: A Reconnaissance. (Report Ser: No. 605). 74p. (Orig.). 1973. pap. 15.00 (ISBN 0-8237-0043-7). Conference Bd.

Siu, Ralph G. The Craft of Power. LC 78-23393. 1979. 15.95 (ISBN 0-471-04628-0, Pub. by Wiley-Interscience). Wiley.

Sperry, Len, et al. You Can Make It Happen: A Guide to Self-Actualization & Organizational Change. LC 76-45156. (Illus.). 1977. pap. text ed. 8.95 (ISBN 0-201-07129-0). A-W.

Taylor, Bernard & Lippitt, Gordon. Management Development & Training Handbook. 1975. 34.95 (ISBN 0-07-084446-1, P&RB). McGraw.

Thayer, Frederick C. An End to Hierarchy, an End to Competition. 2nd ed. 224p. 1981. pap. 7.95 (ISBN 0-531-05631-7). Watts.

Van de Ven, Andrew H. & Ferry, Diane L. Measuring & Assessing Organizations. LC 79-20003. (Organizational Assessment & Change Ser.). 1980. 38.95 (ISBN 0-471-04832-1, Pub. by Wiley-Interscience). Wiley.

Woodcock, Mike & Francis, Dave. Organisation Development Through Teambuilding. LC 81-7399. 200p. 1981. 24.95 (ISBN 0-470-27205-8). Halsted Pr.

Yorks, Lyle. Job Enrichment Revisited. LC 78-21141. 1979. pap. 7.50 (ISBN 0-8144-2226-8). Am Mgmt.

Zaltman, Gerald & Duncan, Robert. Strategies for Planned Change. LC 76-39946. 1977. 28.95 (ISBN 0-471-98131-1, Pub. by Wiley-Interscience). Wiley.

ORGANIZATIONAL RESEARCH

Baer, George W. International Organizations, Nineteen Eighteen to Nineteen Forty-Five: A Guide to Research & Research Materials. Kimmich, Christoph M., ed. LC 80-53893. 261p. 1981. lib. bdg. 17.50 (ISBN 0-8420-2179-5). Scholarly Res.

Benson, J. Kenneth, ed. Organizational Analysis: Critique & Innovation. LC 77-80075. (Sage Conte,Mporary Socialscience Issues: Vol. 37). 160p. 1977. pap. 5.95x (ISBN 0-8039-0859-8). Sage.

Blake, Robert R. & Mouton, Jane S. Corporate Excellence Through Grid Organization Development. (Illus.). 392p. 1968. 11.95 (ISBN 0-87201-331-6). Gulf Pub.

Blau, Peter M. On the Nature of Organizations. LC 74-7392. 358p. 1974. 31.95 (ISBN 0-471-08037-3, Pub. by Wiley-Interscience). Wiley.

Bramlette, Carl A., Jr., ed. Individual & the Future of Organizations, Vol. 3. Mescon, Michael H. LC 72-619550. (Franklin Foundation Lecture Ser.). Orig. Title: Man & the Future of Organizations. 60p. (Orig.). 1974. pap. 3.75 (ISBN 0-88406-017-9). Ga St U Busn Pub.

Bryant, D. & Niehaus, R., eds. Manpower Planning & Organization Design. LC 78-4623. (NATO Conference Ser.: Series II,Systems Science, Vol. 7). 803p. 1978. 65.00 (ISBN 0-306-40006-5, Plenum Pr). Plenum Pub.

Clark, Alfred W., ed. Experimenting with Organizational Life: The Action Research Approach. LC 75-45035. (Illus.). 259p. 1976. 29.50 (ISBN 0-306-30879-7, Plenum Pr). Plenum Pub.

Cooper, C. L., ed. Group Training for Individual & Organizational Development. (Interpersonal Development: Vol. 3, Nos. 1-4). (Illus.). 1973. 36.00 (ISBN 3-8055-1481-6). S Karger.

Corwin, Ronald G. Reform & Organizational Survival. 496p. 1973. 19.50 (ISBN 0-471-17519-6, Pub. by Wiley). Krieger.

Domhoff, G. William, ed. Power Structure Research. (Sage Focus Editons: No. 17). (Illus.). 270p. 1980. 20.00 (ISBN 0-8039-1431-8); pap. 9.95 (ISBN 0-8039-1432-6). Sage.

Drucker, Peter. Age of Discontinuity. 1978. pap. 4.95 (ISBN 0-06-090591-3, CN591, CN). Har-Row.

Dubin, Robert. Human Relations in Administration. 4th ed. (Illus.). 640p. 1974. ref. ed. 21.00 (ISBN 0-13-446435-4). P-H.

Duncan, W. Jack. Organizational Behavior. LC 77-76344. (Illus.). 1978. text ed. 17.95 (ISBN 0-395-25744-1); inst. manual 0.50 (ISBN 0-395-25745-X). HM.

Evan, W. M. Organization Theory: Structures, Systems, & Environments. LC 76-22742. 1976. 27.50 (ISBN 0-471-01512-1). Wiley.

Frost, Carl, et al. The Scanlon Plan for Organization Development: Identity, Participation & Equity. 197p. 1974. 10.00x (ISBN 0-87013-184-2). Mich St U Pr.

Funk, David A. Group Dynamic Law. LC 80-84733. 650p. 1981. 29.50 (ISBN 0-8022-2378-8). Philos Lib.

Glaser, Barney G. Organizational Scientist: Their Professional Careers. LC 63-12180. 1964. pap. 2.50 (ISBN 0-672-60835-9). Bobbs.

Gorden, William I. & Howe, Roger J. Team Dynamics in Developing Organizations. 1977. pap. text ed. 10.95 (ISBN 0-8403-1718-2). Kendall-Hunt.

Kilmann, Ralph H. Social Systems Design: Normative Theory & the MAPS Design Technology. LC 76-46466. 1977. 22.95 (ISBN 0-444-00198-0, North Holland). Elsevier.

Margulies, N. & Raia, A. Organizational Development: Values Process & Technology. 1971. 19.95 (ISBN 0-07-040357-0, C). McGraw.

Meyer, Marshall W. Theory of Organizational Structure. LC 76-56415. (Studies in Sociology Ser.). 1977. pap. text ed. 3.95 (ISBN 0-672-61193-7). Bobbs.
Mowday, Richard & Steers, Richard. Research in Organizations: Issues & Controversy. LC 78-25809. 1979. pap. text ed. 14.95 (ISBN 0-87620-760-3). Goodyear.
Price, James L. Handbook of Organizational Measurement. 1972. text ed. 14.95x (ISBN 0-669-75200-2). Heath.
Roberts, Karlene H., et al. Developing an Interdisciplinary Science of Organizations. LC 78-62568. (Social & Behavioral Science Ser.). (Illus.). 1978. text ed. 14.95x (ISBN 0-87589-393-7). Jossey-Bass.
Rogers, Everett M. & Agarwala-Rogers, Rekha. Communication in Organizations. LC 75-32368. (Illus.). 1976. pap. text ed. 7.95 (ISBN 0-02-926710-2). Free Pr.
Rome, B. K. & Rome, S. C. Organizational Growth Through Decision-Making. 1971. 23.95 (ISBN 0-444-00095-X, North Holland). Elsevier.
Rothman, Jack. Using Research in Organizations: A Guide to Successful Application. LC 79-27947. (Sage Library of Social Research: Vol. 101). (Illus.). 229p. 1980. 20.00x (ISBN 0-8039-1442-3); pap. 9.95x (ISBN 0-8039-1443-1). Sage.
Scanlan, Burt & Keys, J. Bernard. Management & Organizational Behavior. LC 78-15477. (Management Ser.). 1979. text ed. 23.95 (ISBN 0-471-02484-8); study guide (ISBN 0-471-04773-2). Wiley.
Scott, William E. & Cummings, L. L. Readings in Organizational Behavior & Human Performance. rev ed. 1973. pap. 14.95x (ISBN 0-256-01398-5). Irwin.
Staw, Barry H., ed. Research in Organizational Behavior, Vol. 1. 1979. lib. bdg. 37.50 (ISBN 0-89232-045-1). Jai Pr.
Stone, Eugene. Research Methods in Organizational Behavior. 5th ed. LC 77-18755. (Goodyear Series in Management & Organizations). 1978. 13.95 (ISBN 0-87620-802-2); pap. 9.95 (ISBN 0-87620-801-4). Goodyear.
Taylor, James C. & Bowers, David G. Survey of Organizations. LC 72-619571. 172p. 1972. 12.00 (ISBN 0-87944-124-0). Inst Soc Res.
Thompson, James D. & Vroom, Victor H., eds. Organizational Design & Research: Approaches to Organizational Design & Methods of Organizational Research. LC 70-137859. 1971. pap. text ed. 4.95x (ISBN 0-8229-5222-X). U of Pittsburgh Pr.
Trela, James E. & O'Toole, Richard. Roles for Sociologists in Service Organizations. LC 74-81674. 100p. 1974. pap. 3.00x (ISBN 0-87338-142-4). Kent St U Pr.
Zwerman, William L. New Perspectives on Organization Theory: An Empirical Reconsideration of the Marxian & Classical Analyses. LC 71-90791. (Contributions in Sociology Ser.: No. 1). (Illus.). 1971. lib. bdg. 15.00x (ISBN 0-8371-1851-4, ZWN/); pap. 4.95 (ISBN 0-8371-5973-3). Greenwood.

ORGANIZATIONS
see Associations, Institutions, etc.

ORGANIZATIONS, INTERNATIONAL
see International Agencies

ORGANIZED CAMPS
see Camps

ORGANIZED CRIME
see also Gambling; Liquor Traffic; Mafia; Narcotics, Control of; Prostitution; Racketeering; Vice

Abadinsky, Howard. Organized Crime. 400p. 1980. text ed. 15.50 (ISBN 0-205-07098-1, 827097X); instrs' manual (ISBN 0-205-07098-1, 827097-X). Allyn.
Allen, Edward J. Merchants of Menace - the Mafia: A Study of Organized Crime. (Illus.). 344p. 1962. ed. spiral bdg. 24.50photocopy (ISBN 0-398-04187-3). C C Thomas.
Bequai, August. Organized Crime. LC 77-18574. 1979. 17.95 (ISBN 0-669-02104-0). Lexington Bks.
Bresler, Fenton. The Chinese Mafia. LC 80-5797. (Illus.). 256p. 1981. 12.95 (ISBN 0-8128-2752-X). Stein & Day.
Chambliss, William J. On the Take: From Petty Crooks to Presidents. LC 77-15213. 256p. 1978. 10.95 (ISBN 0-253-34244-9). Ind U Pr.
Cressey, Donald R. Theft of the Nation: Structure & Operation of Organized Crime in America. 9.00 (ISBN 0-8446-5848-0). Peter Smith.
Hanna, David. The Mafia: Two Hundred Years of Terror. (Orig.). 1980. pap. 2.25 (ISBN 0-532-23131-7). Woodhill.
Homer, Frederic D. Guns & Garlic: Myths & Realities of Organized Crime. LC 73-88132. 240p. 1974. lib. bdg. 7.95 (ISBN 0-911198-37-7); pap. 3.50 (ISBN 0-911198-38-5). Purdue.
Ianni, Francis A. & Ianni, Elizabeth R. A Family Business: Kinship & Social Control in Organized Crime. LC 72-75320. 1972. 10.00 (ISBN 0-87154-396-6). Russell Sage.
Iorizzo, Luciano J., ed. An Inquiry into Organized Crime. 1970. 2.50 (ISBN 0-686-21887-6). Am Italian.
Kwitny, Jonathan. Vicious Circles: The Mafia in the Marketplace. 432p. 1981. pap. 6.95 (ISBN 0-393-00029-X). Norton.
Landesco, John. Organized Crime in Chicago. 2nd ed. LC 68-24353. (Illinois Crime Survey 1929 Ser.: Pt. III). 1979. pap. text ed. 11.00x (ISBN 0-226-46824-0, Midway Reprint). U of Chicago Pr.
Nelli, Humbert S. The Business of Crime: Italians & Syndicate Crime in the United States. LC 75-32350. (Illus.). 304p. 1976. 17.95 (ISBN 0-19-502010-3). Oxford U Pr.
Opolot. Organised Crime in Africa. 1979. cancelled (ISBN 0-914970-39-9); pap. cancelled (ISBN 0-914970-41-0). Conch Mag.
Pace, Denny F. & Styles, Jimmie C. Organized Crime: Concepts & Control. (Law Enforcement Ser.). (Illus.). 352p. 1974. ref. ed. 16.95 (ISBN 0-13-640961-X). P-H.
Philcox, Norman W. An Introduction to Organized Crime. 108p. 1978. 8.75 (ISBN 0-398-03739-6). C C Thomas.
Pitkin, Thomas M. & Cordasco, Francesco. The Black Hand: A Chapter in Ethnic Crime. (Quality Paperback Ser: No. 333). (Illus.). 1977. pap. 4.95 (ISBN 0-8226-0333-0). Littlefield.
--The Black Hand: A Chapter in Ethnic Crime. (Illus.). 274p. 1977. 12.50x (ISBN 0-87471-886-4). Rowman.
Turkus, Burton. Murder, Inc. 448p. 1975. pap. 2.25 (ISBN 0-532-22101-X). Woodhill.

ORGANOALUMINUM COMPOUNDS

Crompton, T. R. The Analysis of Organoaluminium & Organozinc Compounds. 1968. text ed. 56.00 (ISBN 0-08-012578-6). Pergamon.
Mole, T. & Jeffery, E. A. Organoaluminum Compounds. LC 76-180005. 1973. 85.50 (ISBN 0-444-40911-4). Elsevier.

ORGANOBORON COMPOUNDS

Brown, Herbert C. Organic Syntheses Via Boranes. LC 74-20520. 320p. 1975. 31.50 (ISBN 0-471-11280-1, Pub. by Wiley-Interscience). Wiley.
Cragg, Gordon. Organoboranes in Organic Synthesis. (Studies in Organic Chemistry: Vol. 1). 440p. 1973. 46.50 (ISBN 0-8247-6018-2). Dekker.
Noeth, H. & Wrackmeyer, H. Nuclear Magnetic Resonance Spectroscopy of Boron Compounds. LC 77-14148. (NMR: Vol 14). 1978. 93.60 (ISBN 0-387-08456-8). Springer-Verlag.
Onak, Thomas. Organoborane Chemistry. (Organoborane Chemistry Ser.). 1975. 63.00 (ISBN 0-12-526550-6). Acad Pr.

ORGANOCHLORINE COMPOUNDS

Blair, Ectyl H., ed. Chlorodioxins - Origin & Fate. LC 73-84139. (Advances in Chemistry Ser: No. 120). 1973. 15.25 (ISBN 0-8412-0181-1). Am Chemical.
Committee on Impacts of Stratospheric Change, National Research Council. Halocarbons: Environmental Effects of Chlorofluoromethane Release. 1976. pap. 6.25 (ISBN 0-309-02529-X). Natl Acad Pr.
Moriarty, F., ed. Organochlorine Insecticides: Persistent Organic Pollutants. 1975. 49.50 (ISBN 0-12-506750-X). Acad Pr.

ORGANOFLUORINE COMPOUNDS
see also Fluorocarbons

Hudlicky, M. Chemistry of Organic Fluorine Compounds. 1962. 11.95 (ISBN 0-02-357750-9). Macmillan.
Hudlicky, Milos. Chemistry of Organic Fluorine Compounds. LC 73-14377. 903p. 1976. text ed. 160.95 (ISBN 0-470-41835-4). Halsted Pr.

ORGANOIRON COMPOUNDS

Lovenberg, Walter, ed. Iron-Sulfur Proteins, 3 vols. Incl. Biological Properties. Vol. 1, 1973. 60.50 (ISBN 0-12-456001-6); Molecular Properties. Vol. 2, 1974. 56.00 (ISBN 0-12-456002-4); Vol. 3. 1977. 63.00 (ISBN 0-12-456003-2). 1973. 147.00 set (ISBN 0-685-40605-9). Acad Pr.
Rosenblum, Myron. Chemistry of the Iron Group Metallocenes: Ferrocene, Ruthenocene, Osmocene, Pt. 1. 241p. 1965. text ed. 15.00 (ISBN 0-470-73671-2, Pub. by Wiley). Krieger.

ORGANOLEAD COMPOUNDS

Ratcliffe, J. M. Lead in Man & the Environment. 260p. 1981. 75.95 (ISBN 0-470-27184-1). Halsted Pr.
Seyferth, D., ed. Organometallic Chemistry Reviews: Annual Surveys - Silicon, Tin, Lead. (Journal of Organometallic Chemistry Library: Vol. 4). 1977. 73.25 (ISBN 0-444-41591-2). Elsevier.

ORGANOMAGNESIUM COMPOUNDS
see also Grignard Reagents

ORGANOMETALLIC COMPOUNDS
see also particular organometallic compounds, e.g. Organomagnesium Compounds

Abel, E. W. & Stone, F. G. Organometallic Chemistry, Vols. 1-7. Incl. Vol. 1. 1971 Literature. 1972. 44.00 (ISBN 0-85186-501-1); Vol. 2. 1972 Literature. 1973. 52.25 (ISBN 0-85186-511-9); Vol. 3. 1973 Literature. 1974. 57.75 (ISBN 0-85186-521-6); Vol. 4. 1974 Literature. 1975. 74.25 (ISBN 0-85186-531-3); Vol. 5. 1975 Literature. 1976. 79.75 (ISBN 0-85186-541-0); Vol. 6. 1976 Literature. 1977. 93.50 (ISBN 0-85186-551-8); Vol. 7. 1978. 101.75 (ISBN 0-85186-561-5). LC 72-83459. Am Chemical.
Alper, Howard. Transition Metal Organometallics in Organic Synthesis, 2 vols. (Organic Chemistry Ser.). Vol. 1, 1976. 47.00 (ISBN 0-12-053101-1); Vol. 2, 1978. 28.00 (ISBN 0-12-053102-X). Acad Pr.
Andrianov, K. A. Metalorganic Polymers. (Polymer Review Ser.: No. 8). 371p. 1965. 18.50 (ISBN 0-470-03185-9, Pub. by Wiley). Krieger.
Aylett, B. J. Organometallic Compounds, Vol. 1, Pt. 2, Groups IV & V. 4th ed. LC 79-42877. 550p. 1979. 76.00x (ISBN 0-412-13020-3, Pub. by Chapman & Hall England). Methuen Inc.
--Organometallic Derivatives of the Main Group Elements. (Mtp International Review of Science - Inorganic Chemistry Ser. 1: Vol. 4). (Illus.). 1972. 24.50 (ISBN 0-8391-1007-3). Univ Park.
--Organometallic Derivatives of the Main Group Elements. (MTP International Review of Science: Inorganic Chemistry Ser. 2: Vol. 4). (Illus.). 380p. 1975. 37.50 (ISBN 0-8391-0203-8). Univ Park.
Bauer, K. & Haller, G. Organometallic Compounds - Models of Synthesis, Physical Constants & Chemical Reactions, Vol. 1: Compounds of Transition Metals. 2nd ed. Dub, M., ed. LC 66-28249. xxvi, 1171p. 1975. 63.20 (ISBN 0-387-07196-2). Springer-Verlag.
Becker, Ernest I. & Tsutsui, Minoru, eds. Organometallic Reactions, 2 vols. LC 74-92108. 1971. Vol. 1, 389pp. 26.50 (ISBN 0-471-06135-2); Vol. 2, 450pp. 32.50 (ISBN 0-471-06130-1). Krieger.
Bird, C. W. Transition Metal Intermediates in Organic Synthesis. 1967. 48.50 (ISBN 0-12-099750-9). Acad Pr.
Blackborow, J. R. & Young, D. Metal Vapour Synthesis in Organometallic Chemistry. LC 79-9844. (Reactivity & Structure Ser.: Vol. 9). (Illus.). 1979. 56.50 (ISBN 0-387-09330-3). Springer-Verlag.
Brewster, ed. Aspects of Mechanism & Organometallic Chemistry. 1979. 39.50 (ISBN 0-306-40071-5, Plenum Pr). Plenum Pub.
Brinckman, F. E. & Bellama, J. M., eds. Organometals & Organometalloids: Occurrence & Fate in the Environment. LC 78-24316. (ACS Symposium Ser.: No. 82). 1978. 34.00 (ISBN 0-8412-0461-6). Am Chemical.
Carraher, Charles E. & Sheats, John, eds. Organometallic Polymers. 1978. 28.50 (ISBN 0-12-160850-6). Acad Pr.
Coates, G. E. & Wade, K. Organometallic Compounds, Vol. 1, Pt. 1, Groups I-III. 4th ed. 1981. 66.00x (ISBN 0-412-23120-4, Pub. by Chapman & Hall). Methuen Inc.
Collman, James P. & Hegedus, Louis S. Principles & Applications or Organotransition Metal Chemistry. LC 79-57228. 715p. 1980. 24.00 (ISBN 0-935702-03-2). Univ Sci Bks.
Crompton, T. R. Chemical Analysis of Organometallic Compounds, 5 vols. (Analysis of Organic Materials Ser). 1974-78. Vol. 1. 41.00 (ISBN 0-12-197301-8); Vol. 2. 28.50 (ISBN 0-12-197302-6); Vol.3. 31.50 (ISBN 0-12-197303-4); Vol. 4. 41.50 (ISBN 0-12-197304-2); Vol. 5. 70.50 (ISBN 0-12-197305-0). Acad Pr.
Deganello, G. Transition Metal Complexes of Cyclic Polyolefins. (Organometallic Chemistry Ser.). 1979. 91.50 (ISBN 0-686-74268-0). Acad Pr.
Dub, M., ed. Organometallic Compounds: Methods of Synthesis, Physical Constants & Chemical Reactions, 3 vols. Incl. Vol. 1. Compounds of Transition Metals. 2nd ed. xviii, 828p. 1966. 64.30 (ISBN 0-387-03632-6); Vol. 2. Compounds of Germanium, Tin & Lead, Including Biological Activity & Commercial Application. 2nd ed. Weiss, R. W., ed. xx, 627p. 1967. 64.30 (ISBN 0-387-03948-1); 1st suppl. 1973 70.10 (ISBN 0-387-06304-8); Vol. 3. Compounds of Arsenic, Antimony & Bismuth. 2nd ed. xx, 925p. 1968. 63.30 (ISBN 0-387-04296-2); Formula Index to Volumes 1-3. 2nd ed. vii, 343p. 1970. 43.50 (ISBN 0-387-04985-1). LC 66-28249. Springer-Verlag.
Eisch, J. J., ed. Organometallic Syntheses: Non-Transitional Compounds, Vol. 2. 1981. 29.50 (ISBN 0-12-234950-4). Acad Pr.
Geoffroy, Gregory L. & Wrighton, Mark S. Organometallic Photochemistry. LC 79-6933. 1979. 43.50 (ISBN 0-12-280050-8). Acad Pr.
Green, M. L. Organometallic Compounds, Vol. 2: The Transitions Elements. 3rd ed. 1968. 37.00x (ISBN 0-412-11580-8, Pub. by Chapman & Hall). Methuen Inc.
Hagihara, Nobue, et al, eds. Handbook of Organometallic Compounds. 1968. 45.00 (ISBN 0-8053-3780-6, Adv Bk Prog). A-W.
Heck, Richard F. Organotransition Metal Chemistry: A Mechanistic Approach. 1974. 55.50 (ISBN 0-12-336150-8). Acad Pr.
Houghton, R. P. Metal Complexes in Organic Chemistry. LC 78-51685. (Cambridge Texts in Chemistry & Biochemistry). 1979. 59.50 (ISBN 0-521-21992-2); pap. 18.50x (ISBN 0-521-29331-6). Cambridge U Pr.
Ishii, Yoshio & Tsutsui, Minori, eds. Organotransition-Metal Chemistry. LC 74-28165. 398p. 1975. 42.50 (ISBN 0-306-30832-0, Plenum Pr). Plenum Pub.
Johnson, B. L. & Goodman, Murray, eds. Elastomer Stereospecific Polymerization. LC 66-15861. (Advances in Chemistry Ser: No. 52). 1966. 15.50 (ISBN 0-8412-0053-X). Am Chemical.
King, R. B. Transition-Metal Organometallic Chemistry: An Introduction. 1969. 38.00 (ISBN 0-12-408040-5). Acad Pr.
Kochi, Jay. Organometallic Mechanism & Catalysis: The Role of Reactive Intermediates Organic Processes. 1979. 61.50 (ISBN 0-12-418250-X). Acad Pr.
Lukevits, E. Ya. & Voronkov, M. G. Organic Insertion Reactions of Group IV Elements. LC 65-22184. 413p. 1966. 45.00 (ISBN 0-306-10745-7, Consultants). Plenum Pub.
Marks, Tobin J. & Fischer, Dieter, eds. Organometallics of the F-Elements. (NATO Advanced Study Institutes Ser.: C-44). 1979. lib. bdg. 57.50 (ISBN 90-277-0990-4, Pub. by Reidel Holland). Kluwer Boston.
Morton, Avery A. Solid Organoalkali Metal Reagents. 1964. 54.50x (ISBN 0-677-00560-1). Gordon.
Negishi, Ei-Ichi. Organometallics in Organic Synthesis: General Discussions & Organometallics of Main Group Metals in Organic Synthesis, Vol. 1. LC 79-16818. 1980. 29.00 (ISBN 0-471-03193-3, Pub. by Wiley-Interscience). Wiley.
Pauson, P. L. Organometallic Chemistry. (Illus.). 1967. 19.95 (ISBN 0-312-58800-3). St Martin.
Seyferth, D. Organometallic Chemistry Reviews; Annual Surveys: Silicon-Germanium-Tin-Lead. (Journal of Organometallic Chemistry: Library 8). 1979. 105.00 (ISBN 0-444-41789-3). Elsevier.
Seyferth, D., et al, eds. Organometallic Chemistry Reviews. (Journal of Organometallic Chemistry Library: Vol. 5). 1977. 73.25 (ISBN 0-444-41633-1). Elsevier.
--Organometallic Chemistry Reviews. (Journal of Organometallic Chemistry, Library: No. 7). 1979. 105.00 (ISBN 0-444-41788-5). Elsevier.
Sittig, Marshall, ed. Metal-Organic Compounds. LC 60-3180. (Advances in Chemistry Ser: No. 23). 1959. 29.50 (ISBN 0-8412-0024-6). Am Chemical.
Stone, F. G. & West, Robert. Advances in Organometallic Chemistry, Vol. 19. 1980. 42.00 (ISBN 0-12-031119-4); 54.50 (ISBN 0-12-031183-6); 29.50 (ISBN 0-12-031184-4). Acad Pr.
Stone, F. G. & West, Robert, eds. Advances in Organometallic Chemistry. Incl. Vol. 1. 1964. 54.00 (ISBN 0-12-031101-1); Vol. 2. 1965. 54.00 (ISBN 0-12-031102-X); Vol. 3. 1966. 47.00 (ISBN 0-12-031103-8); Vol. 4. 1966. 54.00 (ISBN 0-12-031104-6); Vol. 5. 1967. 54.00 (ISBN 0-12-031105-4); Vol. 6. 1968. 54.00 (ISBN 0-12-031106-2); Vol. 7. 1969. 54.00 (ISBN 0-12-031107-0); Vol. 8. 1970. 54.00 (ISBN 0-12-031108-9); Vol. 9. 1971. 60.00 (ISBN 0-12-031109-7); Vol. 10. 1972. 60.00 (ISBN 0-12-031110-0); Vol. 11. 1973. 54.00 (ISBN 0-12-031111-9); Vol. 12. 1974. 60.00 (ISBN 0-12-031112-7); Vol. 13. 1975. 72.00 (ISBN 0-12-031113-5); lib ed. 92.50 (ISBN 0-12-031171-2); 51.50 (ISBN 0-12-031172-0); Vol. 14. 1976. 63.00 (ISBN 0-12-031114-3); lib ed. 81.00 (ISBN 0-12-031173-9); microfiche 45.50 (ISBN 0-12-031174-7); Vol. 15. 1977. 56.00 (ISBN 0-12-031115-1); lib ed. 72.00 (ISBN 0-12-031175-5); microfiche 40.50 (ISBN 0-12-031176-3); Vol. 16. 1977. 58.00 (ISBN 0-12-031116-X); lib ed. 74.50 (ISBN 0-12-031177-1); microfiche 40.00 (ISBN 0-12-031178-X); Vol. 17. 1979. 60.00 (ISBN 0-12-031117-8); lib ed. 77.00 (ISBN 0-12-031179-8); microfiche 43.00 (ISBN 0-12-031180-1). Acad Pr.
--Advances in Organometallic Chemistry, Vol. 18. LC 64-16030. 1980. 42.50 (ISBN 0-12-031118-6); lib ed. 55.50 (ISBN 0-12-031181-X); microfiche 29.50 (ISBN 0-12-031182-8). Acad Pr.

Swan, J. M. & Black, D. St. Clair. Organometallics in Organic Synthesis. LC 73-21334. 158p. (Orig.). 1974. pap. text ed. 11.95x (ISBN 0-412-10870-4, Pub. by Chapman & Hall England). Methuen Inc.

Tsutsui, M., et al. Introduction to Metal Pi-Complex Chemistry. LC 70-81164. (Monographs in Inorganic Chemistry Ser.). 210p. 1970. 29.50 (ISBN 0-306-30410-4, Plenum Pr). Plenum Pub.

Wailes, P. C., et al. Organmetallic Chemistry of Titanium, Zirconium, & Hafnium. 1974. 55.00 (ISBN 0-12-730350-2). Acad Pr.

Wakefield, B. J. The Chemistry of Organolithium Compounds. LC 73-10091. 336p. 1974. text ed. 49.00 (ISBN 0-08-017640-2). Pergamon.

ORGANOMETALLIC COMPOUNDS–SPECTRA

Becker, Ernest I. & Tsutsui, Minoru, eds. Organometallic Reactions, 2 vols. LC 74-92108. 1971. Vol. 1, 389pp. 26.50 (ISBN 0-471-06135-2); Vol. 2, 450pp. 32.50 (ISBN 0-471-06130-1). Krieger.

Ebsworth, E. A., ed. Spectroscopic Properties of Inorganic & Organometallic Compounds, Vols. 1-11. Incl. Vol. 1. 1967 Literature. 1968. 35.75 (ISBN 0-85186-003-6); Vol. 2. 1968 Literature. 1969. 38.50 (ISBN 0-85186-013-3); Vol. 3. 1969 Literature. 1970. 41.25 (ISBN 0-85186-023-0); Vol. 4. 1970 Literature. 1971. 44.00 (ISBN 0-85186-033-8); Vol. 5. 1971 Literature. 1972. 46.75 (ISBN 0-85186-043-5); Vol. 6. 1972 Literature. 1973. 49.50 (ISBN 0-85186-053-2); Vol. 7. 1973 Literature. 1974. 66.00 (ISBN 0-85186-063-X); Vol. 8. 1974 Literature. 1975. 68.75 (ISBN 0-85186-073-7); Vol. 9. 1975 Literature. 1976. 78.50 (ISBN 0-85186-083-4); Vol. 10. 1976 Literature. 1977. 88.00 (ISBN 0-685-55715-4); Vol. 11. 1977 Literature. 1978. 88.00 (ISBN 0-85186-103-2). LC 76-6662. Am Chemical.

Ramsey, Brian G. Electronic Transitions in Organometalloids. (Organometallic Chemistry Ser). 1969. 44.50 (ISBN 0-12-576950-4). Acad Pr.

ORGANONITROGEN COMPOUNDS

Dryhurst, Glenn, ed. Electrochemistry of Biological Molecules: Purines, Pyrimidines, Pteridines, Flavins, Pyrroles, Porphyrins and Pyridines. 1977. 71.50 (ISBN 0-12-222650-X). Acad Pr.

Krannich, Larry K., ed. Compounds Containing AS-N Bonds. LC 76-11783. (Benchmark Papers in Inorganic Chemistry: Vol. 5). 1976. 56.00 (ISBN 0-12-786869-0). Acad Pr.

ORGANOPHOSPHORUS COMPOUNDS

Bestmann, H. & Zimmermann, R. Chemistry of Organophosphorous Compounds, 2. (Topics in Current Chemistry: Vol. 20). 1971. 48.40 (ISBN 0-387-05459-6). Springer-Verlag.

Borisov, S. N., et al. Organosilicon Derivatives of Phosporus & Sulphur. LC 74-159028. (Monographs in Inorganic Chemistry Ser.). 338p. 1971. 45.00 (ISBN 0-306-30511-9, Plenum Pr). Plenum Pub.

Cadogan, J. I., ed. Organophosphorus Reagents in Organic Synthesis. LC 79-50307. (Organic Chemistry Ser.). 1980. 103.00 (ISBN 0-12-154350-1). Acad Pr.

Commission of the European Communities. Organophosphorus Pesticides Criteria (Dose-Effect Relationships) for Organophosphorus Compounds. Derache, R., ed. 1977. pap. text ed. 37.00 (ISBN 0-08-021993-4). Pergamon.

Critser, James R., Jr. Organophosphorus Compounds: Preparations & Applications, 1973. (Ser. 8-73). 1974. 145.00 (ISBN 0-914428-28-4). Lexington Data.

--Organophosphorus Compounds: Preparations & Applications, 1974. (Ser. 8-74). 1975. 150.00 (ISBN 0-914428-29-2). Lexington Data.

--Organophosphorus Compounds: Preparations & Applications, 1975. (Ser. 8-75). 1976. 150.00 (ISBN 0-914428-38-1). Lexington Data.

--Organophosphorus Compounds: Preparations & Applications (1976) (Ser. 8-76). 1977. 150.00 (ISBN 0-914428-52-7). Lexington Data.

Eto, Morifusa. Organophosphorus Pesticides: Organic & Biological Chemistry. LC 73-90239. (Uniscience Ser.). 375p. 1974. 67.95 (ISBN 0-8493-5021-2). CRC Pr.

Fest, C. & Schmidt, K. J. The Chemistry of Organophosphorus Pesticides: Reactivity-Synthesis-Mode of Action-Toxicology. LC 72-80294. (Illus.). 366p. 1973. 55.30 (ISBN 0-387-05858-3). Springer-Verlag.

Gefter, Y. Organophosphorus Monomers & Polymers. 1962. 32.00 (ISBN 0-08-009655-7). Pergamon.

Halmann, M., ed. Analytical Chemistry of Phosphorus Compounds. LC 70-37170. (Chemical Analysis Ser.: Vol. 37). 862p. 1972. 59.00 (ISBN 0-471-34558-X). Krieger.

Hudson, R. F. Structure & Mechanism in Organo-Phosphorus Chemistry. (Organic Chemistry Ser.: Vol. 6). 1966. 54.50 (ISBN 0-12-360250-5). Acad Pr.

Kirby, Anthony J. & Warren. The Organic Chemistry of Phosphorus. (Reaction Mechanisms in Organic Chemistry Ser.: Vol. 5). 1967. 66.00 (ISBN 0-444-40333-7). Elsevier.

Kosolapoff, G. M. & Maier, L. Organic Phosphorus Compounds, Vol. 6. 1980. Repr. of 1973 ed. lib. bdg. write for info. (ISBN 0-88275-802-0). Krieger.

Kosolapoff, G. M. & Maier, L., eds. Organic Phosphorus Compounds, Vols. 1-3, 5-6. LC 72-1359. 508p. 1972. Vol. 2. 58.00 (ISBN 0-471-50441-6); Vol. 5. 58.00 (ISBN 0-471-50444-0); (Pub. by Wiley-Interscience). Wiley.

McEwen, W. E. & Berlin, K. D., eds. Organophosphorous Stereochemistry, 2 pts. Incl. Pt. 1. Origins of P(3&4) Compounds. 387p. 55.50 (ISBN 0-12-787031-8); Pt. 2. P(5) Compounds. 48.50 (ISBN 0-12-787032-6). (Benchmark Papers on Organic Chemistry: Vols. 3 & 4). 1975. Acad Pr.

Maier, L. & Mislow, V. Chemistry of Organophosphorous Compounds, 1. LC 51-5497. (Topics in Current Chemistry: Vol. 19). (Illus.). 1971. pap. 32.50 (ISBN 0-387-05458-8). Springer-Verlag.

--Chemistry of Organophosphorous Compounds, 1. LC 51-5497. (Topics in Current Chemistry: Vol. 19). (Illus.). 1971. pap. 32.50 (ISBN 0-387-05458-8). Springer-Verlag.

Marcus, Y., et al, eds. Critical Evaluation of Some Equilibrium Constants Involving Organophosphorus Extractants, Vol. 1. 100p. 1976. pap. 22.00 (ISBN 0-08-020824-X). Pergamon.

Thomas, L. C. The Identification of Functional Groups in Organophosphorus Compounds. 1975. 28.50 (ISBN 0-12-688550-8). Acad Pr.

--Interpretation of the Infrared Spectra of Organophosphorus Compounds. 1974. 55.50 (ISBN 0-85501-034-7). Heyden.

Trippett, S. Organophosphorus Chemistry, Vols. 1-10. Incl. Vol. 1. 1968-69 Literature. 1970. 38.50 (ISBN 0-85186-006-0); Vol. 2. 1969-70 Literature. 1971. 41.25 (ISBN 0-85186-016-8); Vol. 3. 1970-71 Literature. 1972. 41.25 (ISBN 0-85186-026-5); Vol. 4. 1971-72 Literature. 1973. 41.25 (ISBN 0-85186-036-2); Vol. 5. 1972-73 Literature. 1974. 44.00 (ISBN 0-85186-046-X); Vol. 6. 1973-74 Literature. 1975. 44.00 (ISBN 0-85186-056-7); Vol. 7. 1974-75 Literature. 1976. 55.00 (ISBN 0-85186-066-4); Vol.8. 1975-76 Literature. 1977. 60.50 (ISBN 0-85186-076-1); Vol. 9. 1976-77 Literature. 1978. 66.00 (ISBN 0-85186-086-9); Vol. 10. 1979. 77.00 (ISBN 0-85186-096-6). LC 73-268317. Am Chemical.

ORGANOSILICON COMPOUNDS

Andrianov, K. A. Metalorganic Polymers. (Polymer Review Ser.: No. 8). 371p. 1965. 18.50 (ISBN 0-470-03185-9, Pub. by Wiley). Krieger.

Bazant, Vladimir, et al. Organosilicon Compounds, 3 vols. Incl. Vol. 1. Chemistry of Organosilicon Compounds. 75.00 (ISBN 0-12-083451-0); Vol. 2. Register of Organosilicon Compounds. Pt. 1. 75.00 (ISBN 0-12-083461-8); Pt. 2. 75.00 (ISBN 0-12-083462-6). 1965. Set. 168.00 (ISBN 0-12-083466-9). Acad Pr.

Bazant, Vladimir, et al, eds. Handbook of Organosilicon Compounds: Advances Since 1961, Vol. 2. 624p. 1975. 99.75 (ISBN 0-8247-6267-3). Dekker.

--Handbook of Organosilicon Compounds: Advances Since 1961, Vol. 3. 736p. 1975. 99.75 (ISBN 0-8247-6268-1). Dekker.

--Handbook of Organosilicon Compounds: Advances Since 1961, Vol. 4. 1008p. 1975. 99.75 (ISBN 0-8247-6269-X). Dekker.

--Handbook of Organosilicon Compounds: Advances Since 1961, Vol.1. 762p. 1975. 99.75 (ISBN 0-8247-6259-2). Dekker.

Borisov, S. N., et al. Organosilicon Derivatives of Phosporus & Sulphur. LC 74-159028. (Monographs in Inorganic Chemistry Ser.). 338p. 1971. 45.00 (ISBN 0-306-30511-9, Plenum Pr). Plenum Pub.

--Organosilicon Heteropolymers & Heterocompounds. LC 69-13393. (Monographs in Inorganic Chemistry Ser.). 633p. 1970. 55.00 (ISBN 0-306-30379-5, Plenum Pr). Plenum Pub.

Boschke, F. L., ed. Bioactive Organo-Silicon Compounds. LC 79-12799. (Topics in Current Chemistry Ser.: Vol. 84). (Illus.). 1979. 50.80 (ISBN 0-387-09347-8). Springer-Verlag.

International Union of Pure & Applied Chemistry. Organosilicon Chemistry-1: Proceedings of an International Symposium, Prague, 1965. 336p. 1976. 28.00 (ISBN 0-08-020807-X). Pergamon.

Kwart, H. & King, K. Delta-Orbital Involvement in the Organo-Chemistry of Silicon, Phosphorus & Sulfur. LC 77-1555. (Reactivity & Structure: Vol. 3). 1977. 50.40 (ISBN 0-387-07953-X). Springer-Verlag.

Seyferth, D., ed. Organometallic Chemistry Reviews: Annual Surveys - Silicon, Tin, Lead. (Journal of Organometallic Chemistry Library: Vol. 4). 1977. 73.25 (ISBN 0-444-41591-2). Elsevier.

Seyferth, D., et al, eds. Organometallic Chemistry Reviews: Organosilicon Reviews. (Journal of Organometallic Chemistry Library: Vol. 2). 1976. 73.25 (ISBN 0-444-41488-6). Elsevier.

Smith, A. L., ed. Analysis of Silicones. LC 74-13522. (Chemical Analysis Ser: Vol. 41). 512p. 1975. 43.00 (ISBN 0-471-80010-4, Pub. by Wiley-Interscience). Wiley.

ORGANOSULPHUR COMPOUNDS

Ando, W. Oxidation of Organo-Sulfur Compounds. (Sulfur Reports Ser.). 56p. 1980. flexicover 12.50 (ISBN 3-7186-0039-1). Harwood Academic.

Ashworth, M. R. The Determination of Sulphur-Containing Groups. (The Analysis of Organic Materials & International Series of Monographs, No. 2). Vol. 1 1973. 36.00 (ISBN 0-12-065001-0); Vol. 2 1976. 44.50 (ISBN 0-12-065002-9); Vol. 3 1977. 45.50 (ISBN 0-12-065003-7). Acad Pr.

Block, Eric, ed. Reactions of Organosulfur Compounds. 1978. 37.50 (ISBN 0-12-107050-6). Acad Pr.

Board on Toxicology & Environmental Health, National Research Council. Sulfur Oxides. 1979. pap. text ed. 9.00x (ISBN 0-309-02862-0). Natl Acad Pr.

Borisov, S. N., et al. Organosilicon Derivatives of Phosporus & Sulphur. LC 74-159028. (Monographs in Inorganic Chemistry Ser.). 338p. 1971. 45.00 (ISBN 0-306-30511-9, Plenum Pr). Plenum Pub.

Cavallini, D., et al, eds. Natural Sulfur Compounds: Novel Biochemical & Structural Aspects. 565p. 1980. 49.50 (ISBN 0-306-40335-8, Plenum Pr). Plenum Pub.

Freidlina, R. Kh., ed. Organic Sulfur Chemistry: Ninth International Symposium on Organic Sulfur Chemistry, Riga, USSR, 9-14 June 1980. (IUPAC Symposium Ser.). (Illus.). 270p. 1981. 65.00 (ISBN 0-08-026180-9). Pergamon.

Kwart, H. & King, K. Delta-Orbital Involvement in the Organo-Chemistry of Silicon, Phosphorus & Sulfur. LC 77-1555. (Reactivity & Structure: Vol. 3). 1977. 50.40 (ISBN 0-387-07953-X). Springer-Verlag.

Lovenberg, Walter, ed. Iron-Sulfur Proteins, 3 vols. Incl. Biological Properties. Vol. 1, 1973. 60.50 (ISBN 0-12-456001-6); Molecular Properties. Vol. 2, 1974. 56.00 (ISBN 0-12-456002-4); Vol. 3. 1977. 63.00 (ISBN 0-12-456003-2). 1973. 147.00 set (ISBN 0-685-40605-9). Acad Pr.

Preston, S. T. & Pankratz, Ronald. A Guide to the Analysis of Thioalcohols & Thioethers: (Mercaptans & Alkyl Sulfides) rev. ed. 1981. spiral plastic bdg. 25.00 (ISBN 0-913106-16-X). PolyScience.

Stirling, C. J. M., ed. Organic Sulpher Chemistry. 352p. 1975. 34.50 (ISBN 0-408-70711-9). Butterworth.

Suter, C. M. Organic Chemistry of Sulfur. 863p. 1971. 104.00x (ISBN 0-677-65130-9). Gordon.

Torchinskii, Yu M. Sulfhydyl & Disulfide Groups of Proteins. LC 73-83903. (Studies in Soviet Sciences - Life Sciences). (Illus.). 275p. 1974. 35.00 (ISBN 0-306-10888-7, Consultants). Plenum Pub.

Trost, Barry M. & Melvin, Lawrence S., Jr. Sulfer Ylides: Emerging Synthetic Intermediates. (Organic Chemistry Ser.). 1975. 55.00 (ISBN 0-12-701060-2). Acad Pr.

ORGANOTHERAPY

see also Cellular Therapy; Endocrinology; Rejuvenation; Serumtherapy

ORGANOTIN COMPOUNDS

Max Planck Society for the Advancement of Science, Gmelin Institute for Inorganic Chemistry. Organotin Compounds. (Gmelin Handbuch der Anorganischen Chemie, 8th Ed., New Suppl.: Vol. 26, Pt. 1). 182p. 1975. 177.60 (ISBN 0-387-93291-7). Springer-Verlag.

Poller, R. C. Chemistry of Organotin Compounds. (Organometallic Chemistry Ser). 1970. 56.00 (ISBN 0-12-560750-4). Acad Pr.

Seyferth, D., ed. Organometallic Chemistry Reviews: Annual Surveys - Silicon, Tin, Lead. (Journal of Organometallic Chemistry Library: Vol. 4). 1977. 73.25 (ISBN 0-444-41591-2). Elsevier.

Zuckerman, Jerold J., ed. Organotin Compounds: New Chemistry & Applications. LC 76-54338. (Advances in Chemistry Ser: 157). 1976. 37.50 (ISBN 0-8412-0343-1). Am Chemical.

ORGANOTITANIUM COMPOUNDS

Feld, Raoul & Cowe, Peter L. Organic Chemistry of Titanium. 213p. 1965. 29.50 (ISBN 0-306-30629-8, Plenum Pr). Plenum Pub.

ORGANS

see Organ

ORGANS (ANATOMY)

Banks, William J. Histology & Comparative Organology: A Text-Atlas. LC 79-24569. 296p. 1980. Repr. of 1974 ed. lib. bdg. 25.50 (ISBN 0-89874-084-3). Krieger.

Calne, R. Y. Organ Grafts. (Current Topics in Immunology: Vol. 4). (Illus.). 1978. pap. 12.95 (ISBN 0-8151-1415-X). Year Bk Med.

Kessel, Richard G. & Kardon, Randy H. Tissues & Organs: A Text-Atlas of Scanning Electron Microscopy. LC 78-23886. (Illus.). 1979. text ed. 34.95x (ISBN 0-7167-0091-3); pap. text ed. 16.95x (ISBN 0-7167-0090-5); slides avail. (ISBN 0-7167-1231-8). W H Freeman.

Pegg, D. E. & Jacobsen, I. A. Organ Preservation, Vol. II. (Symposium). (Illus.). 1979. text ed. 55.00 (ISBN 0-443-01781-6). Churchill.

ORGANS (ANATOMY)–PERFUSION

see Isolation Perfusion (Physiology)

ORGANS, ARTIFICIAL

see Artificial Organs

ORGANS, CULTURE OF

Balls, M. & Monnickendam, Marjorie, eds. Organ Culture in Biomedical Research. LC 75-21034. (British Society for Cell Biology Symposium Ser.: No. 1). (Illus.). 600p. 1976. 99.00 (ISBN 0-521-21001-1). Cambridge U Pr.

Cau, P., et al. Morphogenesis of Thyroid Follicles in Vitro. (Advances in Anatomy Embryology & Cell Biology: Vol. 52, Pt. 2). 1976. pap. 34.30 (ISBN 0-387-07654-9). Springer-Verlag.

Lutz, H., ed. Invertebrate Organ Cultures. (Documents in Biology Ser.: Vol. 2). 1970. 54.50x (ISBN 0-677-30100-6). Gordon.

Thomas, J. Andre, ed. Organ Culture. (Fr). 1970. 71.50 (ISBN 0-12-688150-2). Acad Pr.

ORGANUM

Ravina, Menasha. Organum & the Samaritans. LC 64-254. 1963. pap. 10.00 (ISBN 0-913932-35-3). Boosey & Hawkes.

Waite, William G. The Rhythm of Twelfth-Century Polyphony. LC 73-2648. (Illus.). 141p. 1973. Repr. of 1954 ed. lib. bdg. 47.50 (ISBN 0-8371-6815-5, WART). Greenwood.

ORGASM

Baker, Oleda. Twenty-Nine Forever. 1978. pap. 2.25 (ISBN 0-425-03813-0, Medallion). Berkley Pub.

Barbach, Lonnie G. For Yourself: Fulfillment of Female Sexuality - a Guide to Orgasmic Response. 1976. pap. 1.95 (ISBN 0-451-08969-3, J8969, Sig). NAL.

--For Yourself: The Fulfillment of Female Sexuality. 240p. 1976. pap. 3.95 (ISBN 0-385-11245-9, Anchor Pr). Doubleday.

The Female Orgasm Report. (Orig.). 1977. pap. 1.50 (ISBN 0-685-82434-9). Ideal World.

Hite, Shere. The Hite Report. (Illus.). 1976. 12.50 (ISBN 0-02-551850-X). Macmillan.

Kline-Graber, Georgia & Graber, Benjamin. Woman's Orgasm. 1976. pap. 2.50 (ISBN 0-445-08537-1). Popular Lib.

Linden, Millicent. Living in a State of Orgasm. LC 62-22285. (Illus., Orig.). 1967. pap. 5.00 (ISBN 0-912628-01-4). M Linden NY.

Lowen, Alexander. Love & Orgasm: A Revolutionary Guide to Sexual Fulfillment. (Illus.). 303p. 1975. pap. 2.95 (ISBN 0-02-077320-X, Collier). Macmillan.

Reich, Wilhelm. The Function of the Orgasm. Carfagno, V., tr. 416p. 1973. 10.95 (ISBN 0-374-15965-3). FS&G.

--Genitality: On the Theory & Therapy of Neurosis. rev., 2nd ed. Schmitz, Philip, tr. from Ger. 1981. 12.95 (ISBN 0-374-16112-7); pap. 7.95 (ISBN 0-374-51641-3). FS&G.

Rosenberg, Jack. Total Orgasm. 1976. 10.00 (ISBN 0-394-48501-7); pap. 4.95 (ISBN 0-394-73167-0). Random.

ORGONOMY

Baker, Elsworth F. Man in the Trap. 1967. 7.95 (ISBN 0-02-506300-6). Macmillan.

Eden, Jerome. View from Eden: Talks to Students of Orgonomy. 1976. 8.00 (ISBN 0-682-48570-5). Exposition.

Reich, Wilhelm. Ether, God & Devil & Cosmic Superimposition. Pol, Therese, tr. (Illus.). 260p. 1972. 10.00 (ISBN 0-374-14907-0); pap. 5.95 (ISBN 0-374-50991-3). FS&G.

--People in Trouble. Schmitz, Philip, tr. from Ger. 283p. 1976. 10.00 (ISBN 0-374-23068-4); pap. 5.95 (ISBN 0-374-51035-0). FS&G.

--Selected Writings: An Introduction to Orgonomy. 576p. 1973. 15.00 (ISBN 0-374-26084-2); pap. 8.95 (ISBN 0-374-50197-1). FS&G.

Wilson, Colin. The Quest for Wilhelm Reich. LC 78-22774. 12.95 (ISBN 0-385-01845-2). Doubleday.

ORIENT

see East

ORIENT, LATIN

see Latin Orient

ORIENT AND OCCIDENT

see East and West

ORIENT EXPRESS

see Compagnie Internationale Des Wagon-Lits et des Grands Express Europeens

ORIENTAL ANTIQUITIES
see also subdivision Antiquities under names of countries, cities, etc.
Andancht, Sandra, et al. Wallace-Homestead Price Guide to Oriental Antiques. (Illus.). 308p. 1980. pap. 17.95 (ISBN 0-87069-295-X). Wallace-Homestead.
Childe, V. Gordon. New Light on the Most Ancient East. 4th ed. (Library Ser). (Illus.). 1969. pap. 4.95x (ISBN 0-393-00469-4, Norton Lib). Norton.
Epigraphic Survey. The Temple of Khonsu, Vol. 1: Scenes of King Herihor in the Court. LC 78-59119. (Oriental Institute Publications: No. 100). (Illus.). 1979. 90.00x (ISBN 0-918986-20-6). Oriental Inst.
Riddell, Sheila. Dated Chinese Antiquities: Six Hundred to Sixteen Fifty. (Illus.). 256p. 1979. 50.00 (ISBN 0-571-09753-7, Pub. by Faber & Faber). Merrimack Bk Serv.
ORIENTAL ARCHITECTURE
see Architecture, Oriental
ORIENTAL ART
see Art, Oriental
ORIENTAL CHILDREN
Simon, Rita J. & Altstein, Howard. Transracial Adoption. LC 76-44817. 1977. 21.95 (ISBN 0-471-79208-X, Pub. by Wiley-Interscience). Wiley.
ORIENTAL CIVILIZATION
see Civilization, Oriental
ORIENTAL COINS
see Coins, Oriental
ORIENTAL LANGUAGES
see also particular languages or groups of languages, e.g. Afghan language; Indo-Aryan languages; Iranian Languages
Cerny, V., et al. Asian & African Languages in Social Context. (Oriental Institute Czechoslovakia Dissertationes Orientales Ser.: Vol. 34). 1974. pap. 6.00x (ISBN 0-685-88112-1). Paragon.
Dykstra, Andrew. The Kanji ABC. LC 76-58964. (Illus.). 195p. 1977. pap. 7.95 (ISBN 0-913232-37-8). W Kaufmann.
Egerod, Soren. Atayal-English Dictionary, 2 vols. (Scandinavian Institute of Asian Studies Monograph: No. 35). 830p. 1981. Set. pap. text ed. 41.25x (ISBN 0-7007-0117-6, Pub. by Curzon Pr England); Vol. 1. pap. text ed. (ISBN 0-7007-0118-4); Vol. 2. pap. text ed. (ISBN 0-7007-0119-2). Humanities.
Lyman, Thomas A. Dictionary of Mong Njua: A Miao (Meo) Language of Southeast Asia. LC 72-94484. (Janua Linguarum, Ser. Practica: No. 123). (Illus.). 403p. (Orig.). 1974. pap. text ed. 94.00x (ISBN 90-2792-696-4). Mouton.
Olson, Michael L. Barai Sentence Structure & Embedding. (Language Data, Asian-Pacific Ser.: No. 3). 1973. pap. 3.00x (ISBN 0-88312-303-7); microfiche 1.00x (ISBN 0-685-48708-3). Summer Inst Ling.
Svelmoe, Gordon & Svelmoe, Thelma. Notes on Mansaka Grammar. (Language Data Asian-Pacific Ser.: No. 6). 1974. pap. 3.75 (ISBN 0-88312-206-5); microfiche 1.50 (ISBN 0-88312-306-1). Summer Inst Ling.
Whitney, William D. Oriental & Linguistic Studies. 1980. Repr. of 1873 ed. lib. bdg. 45.00 (ISBN 0-89341-483-2). Longwood Pr.
--Oriental & Linguistic Studies, Vol. 1. LC 72-8581. (Essay Index Reprint Ser.). 1972. Repr. of 1872 ed. 23.00 (ISBN 0-8369-7342-9). Arno.
ORIENTAL LAW
see also Hindu Law
ORIENTAL LEGENDS
see Legends, Oriental
ORIENTAL LITERATURE
see also particular literatures, e.g. Chinese Literature
Befu, Ben. Ihara Saikaku: Worldy Mental Calculations. (Publications in Occasional Papers: No. 5). 1976. pap. 15.00x (ISBN 0-520-09406-9). U of Cal Pr.
Hearn, Lafcadio. Essays in European & Oriental Literature. Mordell, Alberrt, ed. 1977. Repr. of 1923 ed. 30.00 (ISBN 0-8495-2210-2). Arden Lib.
Johnston, Charles & Giles, Lionel, trs. Selections from the Upanishads & The Tao Te King. 142p. 1951. Repr. of 1897 ed. 3.00 (ISBN 0-938998-15-3). Cunningham Pr.
Miller, Barbara S., tr. Phantasies of a Love-Thief: The Caurapancasika Attributed to Bilhana. LC 77-122947. (Studies in Oriental Culture: No. 6). 233p. 1971. 17.50x (ISBN 0-231-03451-2). Columbia U Pr.
Nieh, Hualing, ed. Literature of the Hundred Flowers, 2 vols. (Modern Asian Literature Ser.). 1981. Set. 65.00x (ISBN 0-231-05264-2); Vol. I, Criticism & Polemics, 337pp. 27.50x (ISBN 0-231-05074-7); Vol. II, Poetry & Fiction, 618pp. 42.50x (ISBN 0-231-05076-3). Columbia U Pr.
Ortova, J. Etude Sur le Roman Au Cameroun. (Oriental Institute Czechoslovakia Dissertationes Orientales, Vol. 30). 1971. 6.00x (ISBN 0-685-25254-X). Paragon.
Prusek, Jaroslav, ed. Dictionary of Oriental Literatures, 3 vols. LC 73-82742. 1975. boxed set 48.50 (ISBN 0-465-01649-9). Basic.
Quackenbos, J. D. Ancient Literature: Oriental & Classical. 30.00 (ISBN 0-8274-3974-1). R West.
Shimer, Dorothy B., ed. Mentor Book of Modern Asian Literature. (Orig.). 1969. pap. 3.50 (ISBN 0-451-61914-5, ME1914, Ment). NAL.
Wilson, Epiphanius, ed. Oriental Literature. fasc. rev. ed. Incl. The Literature of Arabia. LC 71-174763. 14.50 (ISBN 0-8369-8229-0); The Literature of China. LC 78-174762. 18.00 (ISBN 0-8369-8228-2); The Literature of India. LC 79-174765. 25.00 (ISBN 0-8369-8226-6); The Literature of Japan. LC 75-174764. 19.25 (ISBN 0-8369-8227-4); Pts. 1 & 2. The Literature of Persia. Gottheil, Richard J., intro. by. LC 74-174766. 26.00 (ISBN 0-8369-8225-8). (Play Anthology Reprint Ser). 1900. Arno.
ORIENTAL LITERATURE–BIBLIOGRAPHY
De Bary, William T. Guide to Oriental Classics. 2nd ed. Embree, T., ed. LC 63-20463. (Companions to Asian Studies). 1974. 12.50x (ISBN 0-231-03891-7); pap. 7.50x (ISBN 0-231-03892-5). Columbia U Pr.
Halen, Harry. Handbook of Oriental Collections in Finland: Manuscripts, Xylographs, Inscriptions & Russian Minority Literature. (Scandinavian Institute of Asian Studies Monograph: No. 31). 1978. pap. 15.25x (ISBN 0-7007-0105-2). Humanities.
International Congress of Orientalists, Ann Arbor, 1967. Papers on Oriental Library Collections. Pearson, James D., ed. 1971. 27.50x (ISBN 0-8002-1330-0). Intl Pubns Serv.
McDowell, Robert E., et al. Asian - Pacific Literatures in English: Bibliographies. LC 78-62030. (Illus., Orig.). 1978. 22.00x (ISBN 0-89410-072-6); pap. 14.00x (ISBN 0-89410-073-4). Three Continents.
New York Public Library, Research Libraries. Dictionary Catalog of the Oriental Collection: First Supplement, 8 vols. 1976. Set. lib. bdg. 955.00 (ISBN 0-8161-0775-0). G K Hall.
--Dictionary Catalog of the Oriental Collection, 16 Vols. 1960. Set. lib. bdg. 1150.00 (ISBN 0-8161-0410-7). G K Hall.
Pearson, James D. Oriental Manuscripts in Europe & North America: A Survey. 1971. 57.50x (ISBN 0-8002-1326-2). Intl Pubns Serv.
Ross, Marion W. Bibliography of Vietnamese Literature in the Wason Collection at Cornell University. 179p. 1973. 4.50 (ISBN 0-87727-090-2, DP 90). Cornell SE Asia.
ORIENTAL LITERATURE–HISTORY AND CRITICISM
Bischoff, Friedrich, et al. K'uei Hsing: A Repository of Asian Literature in Translation. LC 74-149779. (East Asian Ser). 192p. 1974. 10.00x (ISBN 0-253-39101-6). Ind U Pr.
De Queljoe, David. Marginal Man in a Colonial Society: Abdoel Moeis' Salah Asuahan. LC 74-620028. (Papers in International Studies: Southeast Asia: No. 32). 1974. pap. 4.00x (ISBN 0-89680-019-9). Ohio U Ctr Intl.
Grinstead, Eric. Analysis of the Tangut Script. (Scandinavian Inst. of Asian Studies: No. 10). 376p. 1975. pap. text ed. 21.00x (ISBN 0-7007-0059-5). Humanities.
Jumsai, M. L. History of Thai Literature. 1973. pap. 6.50x (ISBN 0-685-42177-5). Paragon.
Nudas, Alfeo G. Telic Contemplation: A Study of Grace in Seven Filipino Writers. 1980. text ed. 12.00x (ISBN 0-8248-0659-X, Pub. by U of Philippines Pr); pap. text ed. 8.00x (ISBN 0-8248-0660-3). U Pr of Hawaii.
Sarkar, Himansu B. Indian Influence on the Literature of Java & Bali. LC 77-86977. Repr. of 1934 ed. 36.00 (ISBN 0-404-16777-2). AMS Pr.
ORIENTAL LITERATURE–TRANSLATIONS INTO ENGLISH
Anderson, G. L., ed. Asian Literature in English: A Guide to Information Sources. (American, English Literature & World Literatures in English Information Guide Ser.: Vol. 31). 300p. 1981. 36.00 (ISBN 0-8103-1362-6). Gale.
Anderson, G. L, ed. Masterpieces of the Orient. pap. 8.95x (ISBN 0-393-09542-8, NortonC); expanded pap. 1976 15.95x (ISBN 0-393-09196-1). Norton.
De Silva, D. M. Pemato Jayati Soko (Love Is the Bringer of Sorrow) De Silva, D. M., tr. from Singhalese. (Salzburg Studies in English Literature: Poetic Drama & Poetic Theory: No. 25). 55p. 1976. pap. text ed. 25.00x (ISBN 0-391-01524-9). Humanities.
Jose, F. Sionil, ed. Asian P. E. N. Anthology. LC 67-10849. 1967. 7.50 (ISBN 0-8008-0425-2). Taplinger.
Mueller, F. Max, ed. Sacred Books of the East, 50 Vols. Set. 700.00x (ISBN 0-8426-1420-6); 12.00x ea. Verry.
Pritchard, James B., ed. Ancient Near East in Pictures with Supplement. 2nd ed. Incl. Ancient Near Eastern Texts Relating to the Old Testament with Supplement. 3rd ed. Set. 50.00 ea. (ISBN 0-691-03503-2); 90.00 (ISBN 0-686-76919-8). 1969. deluxe ed. 46.50x ea. (ISBN 0-691-03502-4); Set. 82.50x (ISBN 0-686-66606-2). Princeton U Pr.
Yampolsky, Philip B., tr. from Jap. Zen Master Hakuin: Selected Writings. LC 75-145390. (Records of Civilization, Studies & Sources: No. 86). 1971. 17.50x (ISBN 0-231-03463-6). Columbia U Pr.
Yohannan, John D., ed. Treasury of Asian Literature. 1959. pap. 2.95 (ISBN 0-451-61936-6, ME1936, Ment). NAL.
ORIENTAL MUSIC
see Music, Oriental
ORIENTAL MYTHOLOGY
see Mythology, Oriental
ORIENTAL NATIONAL CHARACTERISTICS
see National Characteristics, Oriental
ORIENTAL PAINTING
see Painting, Oriental
ORIENTAL PHILOLOGY
The term oriental philology comprises ancient and modern oriental languages and literatures. Particular groups are entered under their specific names, e.g. Assyriology, Chinese Studies (Sinology), Indo-Iranian Philology, Semitic Philology.
Benfey, Theodore. Geschichte der Sprachwissenschaft und Orientalischen Philologie in Deutschland Seit Dem Anfange Des Neunzehnten Jahrhunderts. Repr. of 1869 ed. 41.50 (ISBN 0-384-03890-5). Johnson Repr.
Columbia University. Columbia University Contributions to Oriental History & Philology, 13 Vols. Repr. of 1927 ed. Set. 175.00 (ISBN 0-404-50530-9). AMS Pr.
East India Company Library. Catalogue of the Library of the Honorable East India Company, 2 Vols. 1969. Set. 43.50 (ISBN 0-8337-0494-X). B Franklin.
MacDonald Presentation Volume: A Tribute to Duncan Black Macdonald, Consisting of Articles by Former Students, Presented to Him on His Seventieth Birthday, April 9, 1933. facs. ed. LC 68-22109. (Essay Index Reprint Ser). 1933. 18.75 (ISBN 0-8369-0645-4). Arno.
ORIENTAL PHILOSOPHERS
see Philosophers, Oriental
ORIENTAL PHILOSOPHY
see Philosophy, Oriental
ORIENTAL POETRY–TRANSLATIONS INTO ENGLISH
Abdullah, Achmed, tr. Lute & Scimitar: Poems & Ballads of Central Asia. 1977. lib. bdg. 59.95 (ISBN 0-8490-2188-X). Gordon Pr.
Gooneratne, Yasmine, ed. Poems from India, Sri Lanka, Malaysia & Singapore. (Writing in Asia Ser.). 1980. 3.95x (ISBN 0-686-66066-8, 00219). Heinemann Ed.
Levy, Howard S. Lesser Known Japanese Poetry Classics, Vol.7. (East Asian Poetry in Translation Ser.). 1976. 4.00 (ISBN 0-89986-302-7). E Langstaff.
--One Hundred Haiku, Vol. 5. (East Asian Poetry in Translation Ser.). 1976. pap. 4.00 (ISBN 0-89986-300-0). E Langstaff.
--One Hundred Senryu, Vol. 6. (East Asian Poetry in Translation Ser.). 1976. pap. 4.00 (ISBN 0-89986-301-9). E Langstaff.
--One Hundred Shinkokinshu, Vol. 4. (East Asian Poetry in Translation Ser.). 1976. pap. 4.00 (ISBN 0-89986-299-3). E Langstaff.
Wells, Henry W., tr. Ancient Poetry from China, Japan, & India. LC 68-9365. 1968. 14.95x (ISBN 0-87249-132-3). U of SC Pr.
ORIENTAL POTTERY
see Pottery, Oriental
ORIENTAL RUGS
see Rugs, Oriental
ORIENTAL STUDIES
see also Assyriology; Civilization, Oriental; Egyptology; Oriental Antiquities; Oriental Philology; Orientalists; Philosophy, Comparative
American Geographical Society of New York. Oriental Explorations & Studies, 6 vols. & map vol. Repr. of 1928 ed. 300.00 set (ISBN 0-404-60230-4). AMS Pr.
Association for Asian Studies. Cumulative Bibliography of Asian Studies, 1941-1965, Author Bibliography, 4 Vols. 1969. Set. 390.00 (ISBN 0-8161-0805-6). G K Hall.
--Cumulative Bibliography of Asian Studies, 1941-1965, Subject Bibliography, 4 Vols. 1970. Set. 395.00 (ISBN 0-8161-0127-2). G K Hall.
Association for Asian Studies, Inc. Committee on East Asian Libraries. Library Resources on East Asia. LC 73-506629. 100p. 1967. 12.50x (ISBN 0-8002-1293-2). Intl Pubns Serv.
Bruce, David. Inquiry into Asia. (Orig.). 1981. pap. text ed. 8.00x (ISBN 0-686-73513-7, 00562). Heinemann Ed.
Cassuto, U. Biblical & Oriental Studies: Bible, Vol. 1. Abrahams, Israel, tr. from Hebrew. (Illus.). 298p. 1973. text ed. 23.00x (ISBN 0-686-74306-7, Pub. by Magnes Israel). Humanities.
--Biblical & Oriental Studies: Bible & Ancient Oriental Texts, Vol. 2. Abrahams, Israel, tr. from Hebrew. 286p. 1975. text ed. 23.00x (ISBN 0-686-74307-5, Pub. by Magnes Israel). Humanities.
Columbia University. Columbia University Oriental Studies, 26 Vols. Repr. of 1928 ed. Set. 495.00 (ISBN 0-404-50490-6). AMS Pr.
Deissman, Adolf. Light from the Ancient East. (Twin Brooks Ser). 1978. pap. 10.95 (ISBN 0-8010-2886-8). Baker Bk.
Dolezal, Ivan. Asian & African Studies, Vol. 11. 350p. 1975. text ed. 13.75x (ISBN 0-7007-0086-2). Humanities.
--Asian & African Studies, Vol. 12. 1977. text ed. 13.75x (ISBN 0-7007-0101-X). Humanities.
Dolezal, Ivan, ed. Asian & African Studies, Vol. 16. 360p. 1980. text ed. 13.75x (ISBN 0-7007-0137-0). Humanities.
--Asian & African Studies, Vol. 14, No. 14. 1978. text ed. 13.75x (ISBN 0-7007-0121-4). Humanities.
--Asian & African Studies: 1972, Vol. 8. 360p. 1972. text ed. 13.75x (ISBN 0-7007-0040-4). Humanities.
--Asian & African Studies: 1973, Vol. 9. 266p. 1974. text ed. 13.75x (ISBN 0-7007-0044-7). Humanities.
--Asian & African Studies: 1974, Vol. 10. 320p. 1975. text ed. 13.75x (ISBN 0-7007-0072-2). Humanities.
Endogenous Intellectual Creativity & the Emerging New International Order, with Special Reference to East Asia: Institutional Research Report. 33p. 1981. pap. 5.00 (ISBN 92-808-0307-7, TUNU161, UNU). Unipub.
Fersh, Seymour. Asia: Teaching About, Learning From. LC 77-16458. (Illus.). 1978. pap. text ed. 8.25x (ISBN 0-8077-2539-0). Tchrs Coll.
Iriye, Adira, et al. The World of Asia. new ed. (Orig.). pap. text ed. 12.95x (ISBN 0-88273-500-4). Forum Pr MO.
Kim, Hong N. Scholars' Guide to Washington, D.C. for East Asian Studies. LC 79-17344. (Scholars' Guide to Washington, D.C. Ser.: No. 3). 413p. 1979. text ed. 19.95x (ISBN 0-87474-582-9); pap. text ed. 8.95x (ISBN 0-87474-581-0). Smithsonian.
Kister, M. J., ed. Israel Oriental Studies, 8 vols. Incl. Vol. 1. 315p. 1971 (ISBN 0-87855-212-X); Vol. 2. 473p. 1972 (ISBN 0-87855-213-8); Vol. 3. 293p. 1973 (ISBN 0-87855-214-6); Vol. 4. 286p. 1974 (ISBN 0-87855-215-4); Vol. 5. 298p. 1975 (ISBN 0-87855-216-2); Vol. 6. 307p. 1976 (ISBN 0-87855-243-X); Vol. 7. 300p. 1977 (ISBN 0-87855-334-7); Vol. 8. 332p. 1981 (ISBN 0-87855-395-9). 39.95 ea.; Set. casebound 235.00 (ISBN 0-87855-220-0). Transaction Bks.
Klima, Otakar. Beitrage zur Geschichte des Mazdakismus. (Dissertationes Orientales: Vol. 37). (Ger.). 1978. pap. text ed. 6.00x (ISBN 0-685-24619-1). Paragon.
Lamley, Harry J., ed. East Asian Occasional Papers, 2 vols. Incl. Vol. 1. (Asian Studies at Hawaii: No. 3). 180p. 1969 (ISBN 0-87022-443-3); Vol. 2. (Asian Studies at Hawaii: No. 4). 176p. 1970 (ISBN 0-87022-444-1). pap. 4.50x ea. U Pr of Hawaii.
Morehouse, Ward, ed. The Comparative Approach in Area Studies & the Disciplines. (Occasional Publication). 68p. 1966. pap. 2.00 (ISBN 0-89192-135-4). Interbk Inc.
Orlin, Louis L., ed. Michigan Oriental Studies in Honor of George G. Cameron. LC 76-1395. 329p. 1976. pap. text ed. 5.00x (ISBN 0-916798-01-1). Dept NE Stud.
Rounseville, A. W. The Poetry of the Orient. 59.95 (ISBN 0-8490-0865-4). Gordon Pr.
Schafer, Edward H., et al, eds. Index to Journal of the American Oriental Society, Vols. 21-61. 1955. pap. 4.00x (ISBN 0-940490-40-4). Am Orient Soc.
School of Oriental & African Studies, University of London. Library Catalogue of the School of Oriental & African Studies: Third Supplement, 19 vols. 1979. Set. lib. bdg. 1990.00 (ISBN 0-8161-0261-9). G K Hall.
South & Southeast Asia Studies. (AMS Press Reprint Ser.). Repr. of 1954 ed. Set. write for info. (ISBN 0-404-54800-8). AMS Pr.
Strout, Elizabeth. Catalogue of the American Oriental Society. (Supplements). 1930. pap. 4.00x (ISBN 0-940490-00-5). Am Orient Soc.

Studies on Asia. Incl. Volume I - 1960. Sakai, Robert K., ed. x, 97p. 1960. pap. 3.25x (ISBN 0-8032-5550-0); Volume II - 1961. Sakai, Robert K., ed. viii, 85p. 1961. pap. 3.25x (ISBN 0-8032-5551-9); Volume III - 1962. Brown, Sidney D., ed. x, 87p. 1962. pap. 3.25x (ISBN 0-8032-5552-7); Volume IV - 1963. Sakai, Robert K., ed. x, 196p. 1963. pap. 4.95x (ISBN 0-8032-5553-5); Volume V - 1964. Sakai, Robert K., ed. xii, 186p. 1964. pap. 4.95x (ISBN 0-8032-5554-3); Volume VI - 1965. Sakai, Robert K., ed. x, 209p. 1965. pap. 4.95x (ISBN 0-8032-5555-1); Volume VII - 1966. Sakai, Robert K., ed. x, 185p. 1967. 10.50x (ISBN 0-8032-0557-0); pap. 4.95x (ISBN 0-8032-5557-8); Volume VIII - 1967. Brown, Sidney D., ed. x, 192p. 1968. 13.50x (ISBN 0-8032-0558-9); pap. 3.95x (ISBN 0-8032-5558-6). LC 60-15432. (Studies on Asia Ser). U of Nebr Pr.

University of Chicago. Catalog of the Oriental Institute Library, 16 vols. 1970. Set. lib. bdg. 1520.00 (ISBN 0-8161-0890-0). G K Hall.

--Catalog of the Oriental Institute Library, Supplement I, Vol. 1. 1977. lib. bdg. 105.00 (ISBN 0-8161-0067-5). G K Hall.

University of London - School of Oriental & African Studies. Library Catalogue of the School of Oriental & African Studies, 28 Vols. 1963. Set. 2560.00 (ISBN 0-8161-0635-5); First Suppl. 1968 16 Vols. 1680.00 (ISBN 0-8161-0734-3). G K Hall.

Yale Oriental Ser. Researches, Vols. 1-24. (The Yale Babylonian Collection). Repr. of 1949 ed. Set. 884.00 (ISBN 0-404-60270-3). AMS Pr.

ORIENTAL TALES

see Tales, Oriental

ORIENTALISTS

International Congress of Orientalists-2nd. Proceedings. Sinor, Denis, ed. 711p. 1971. 122.50x (ISBN 3-447-01280-3). Intl Pubns Serv.

Verrier, Michelle. The Orientalists. LC 79-64345. (Illus.). 1979. pap. 8.50 (ISBN 0-8478-0228-0). Rizzoli Intl.

ORIENTALS

see Asians

ORIENTATION

see also Orientation (Physiology); Orientation (Psychology)

Atkinson, George & Bengtsson, Hans. Orienteering for Sport & Pleasure. LC 75-41872. (Environmental Sports Ser). (Illus.). 1977 (ISBN 0-8289-0271-2). pap. 8.95 (ISBN 0-8289-0270-4). Greene.

Brown, Terry & Hunter, Rob. The Concise Book of Orienteering. 1979. pap. 2.95 (ISBN 0-686-70999-3). Vanguard.

Burton, Maurice. The Sixth Sense of Animals. LC 72-6622. (Illus.). 192p. 1973. 7.95 (ISBN 0-8008-7232-0). Taplinger.

Disley, John. Orienteering. rev. 2nd ed. LC 67-22990. (Illus.). 176p. 1979. lib. bdg. 7.95 (ISBN 0-8117-2023-3). Stackpole.

Fraenkel, et al. The Orientation of Animals. Date not set. 8.50 (ISBN 0-8446-2080-7). Peter Smith.

Fraenkel, Gottfried & Dunn, Donald L. The Orientation of Animals. 8.50 (ISBN 0-8446-2080-7). Peter Smith.

Henley, B. M. Orienteering. (EP Sports Books). (Illus.). 1976. 6.95 (ISBN 0-7158-0591-6). Charles River Bks.

Hill, Everett W & Ponder, Purvis. Orientation & Mobility Techniques: A Guide for the Practitioner. LC 76-15678. 1976. 5.50 (ISBN 0-89128-001-4). Am Foun Blind.

Knapp, Robert R. Handbook for the Personal Orientation Inventory. LC 75-17256. 1976. text ed. 12.95 (ISBN 0-912736-17-8). EDITS Pubs.

Lynn, R. Attention, Arousal & the Orientation Reaction. 1966. text ed. 19.50 (ISBN 0-08-011524-1); pap. text ed. 9.50 (ISBN 0-08-013840-3). Pergamon.

Olson, Marjorie E. Benji the Bug: Directionality Concepts for Children. (Illus.). 21p. (gr. k-1). 1973. pap. text ed. 2.00x (ISBN 0-89039-099-1). Ann Arbor Pubs.

Orienteering. 1976. pap. 2.50 (ISBN 0-8277-4893-0). British Bk Ctr.

Ratliff, Donald E. Map, Compass, & Campfire. LC 64-8453. (Illus.). 1970. pap. 2.50 (ISBN 0-8323-0129-9). Binford.

Riley, Michael J. & Cremer, Robert. Basic Orienteering. 1979. 9.95 (ISBN 0-8092-7643-7); pap. 4.95 (ISBN 0-8092-7642-9). Contemp Bks.

Robbins, Shellie K. Which Side up? (Illus.). 34p. (Orig.). 1980. pap. 4.95 (ISBN 0-9604538-1-4). CBH Pub.

Rock, Irvin. Orientation & Form. 1974. 22.50 (ISBN 0-12-591250-1). Acad Pr.

Symposium On Animal Orientation - Garmisch-Partenkirchen - 1962. Proceedings. Autrum, H., et al, eds. (Advances in Biology: Vol. 26). (Illus.). 1963. 34.30 (ISBN 0-387-02963-X). Springer-Verlag.

Vassilevsky, B. Where Is the North. 286p. 1977. pap. 2.65 (ISBN 0-8285-1264-7, Pub. by Progress Pubs Russia). Imported Pubns.

Von Frisch, Karl. Dance Language & Orientation of Bees. Chadwick, Leigh E., tr. LC 67-17321. (Illus., Ger). 1967. 30.00x (ISBN 0-674-19050-5, Belknap Pr). Harvard U Pr.

Watson, J. D. Orienteering. 3rd ed. (Know the Game Ser.). (Illus.). 1975. pap. 2.50 (ISBN 0-7158-0511-8). Charles River Bks.

Williams, Charles W. Direction: The Essential Dimension. 1960. 6.00 (ISBN 0-8315-0003-4). Speller.

ORIENTATION (COLLEGE STUDENTS)

see College Student Orientation

ORIENTATION (PHYSIOLOGY)

Kreitler, Hans & Kreitler, Shulamith. Cognitive Orientation & Behavior. LC 76-20597. 1976. text ed. 27.50 (ISBN 0-8261-2050-4). Springer Pub.

ORIENTATION (PSYCHOLOGY)

see also Time Perception

Kimmel, H. D., et al, eds. The Orienting Reflex in Humans: An International Conference Sponsored by the Scientific Affairs of the North Atlantic Treaty Organization. LC 79-21462. 747p. 1980. 49.95x (ISBN 0-470-26876-X). Halsted Pr.

ORIENTATION (STUDENTS)

see Students

ORIENTATION (TEACHERS)

see Teachers, Training of

ORIGAMI

see also Paper Work

Araki, Chiyo. Origami in the Classroom, 2 vols. LC 65-13412. (Illus.). (gr. 1 up). 1965-68. bds. 8.95 ea. Vol. 1 (ISBN 0-8048-0452-4). Vol. 2 (ISBN 0-8048-0453-2). C E Tuttle.

Davidson, Georgie. Origami. LC 75-44992. (Larousse Craft Ser.). (Illus.). 1978. pap. 5.95 (ISBN 0-88332-027-4, 8036). Larousse.

Gray, Alice & Kasahara, Kunihiko. Magic of Origami. LC 77-74654. (Illus.). 1977. 12.50 (ISBN 0-87040-390-7). Japan Pubns.

Harbin, Robert. New Adventures in Origami. (Funk & W Bk.). (Illus.). 192p. 1972. pap. 1.95 (ISBN 0-308-10040-9, F81). T Y Crowell.

--Origami: The Art of Paperfolding. (Illus.). 192p. 1979. pap. 3.95 (ISBN 0-06-463496-5, EH 496, EH). Har-Row.

Honda, Isao. The World of Origami. abr. ed. LC 65-27101. (Illus.). 200p. 1976. pap. 11.00 (ISBN 0-87040-383-4). Japan Pubns.

Kasahara, Kunihiko. Creative Origami. LC 67-87040. (Illus.). 1977. pap. 12.95 (ISBN 0-87040-411-3). Japan Pubns.

--Origami Made Easy. LC 73-83956. (Illus.). 128p. 1973. pap. 4.95 (ISBN 0-87040-253-6). Japan Pubns.

Montroll, John. Origami for the Enthusiast: Step-by-Step Instructions in Over 700 Diagrams. (Illus.). 1980. pap. 4.50 (ISBN 0-486-23799-0). Dover.

Nakamura, Eiji. Flying Origami. LC 70-188761. (Illus.). 64p. 1972. pap. 7.50 (ISBN 0-87040-023-1). Japan Pubns.

Peterson, John H. Origami for Christians: To Illustrate Christian Symbols, Concepts & the Bible. (Illus.). 1979. pap. 3.25 (ISBN 0-8192-1259-8). Morehouse.

Randlett, Samuel. The Best of Origami. (Illus.). 185p. 1981. 12.95 (ISBN 0-571-10275-1, Pub. by Faber & Faber). Merrimack Bk Serv.

Sakade, Florence. Origami, Japanese Paper Folding, 3 Vols. LC 57-10685. (Illus., Orig.). (gr. 2 up). pap. 2.50 ea. Vol. 1 (ISBN 0-8048-0454-0). Vol. 2 (ISBN 0-8048-0455-9). Vol. 3 (ISBN 0-8048-0456-7). C E Tuttle.

Sarasas, Claude. ABC's of Origami. LC 64-17160. (Illus.). (gr. 3-8). 1964. bds. 7.75 (ISBN 0-8048-0000-6). C E Tuttle.

Takahama, Toshie. Origami for Displays. (Illus.). 32p. (Orig.). 1979. pap. 3.50 (ISBN 0-8048-1350-7, Pub by Shufunotomo Co. Ltd. Japan). C E Tuttle.

--Origami for Fun: Thirty-One Basic Models. (Illus.). 32p. (Orig.). 1980. Repr. of 1973 ed. pap. 3.50 (ISBN 0-8048-1352-3, Shufuntomo Co Ltd Japan). C E Tuttle.

--Origami Toys: Fifteen Simple Models. (Illus.). 32p. (Orig.). 1979. pap. 3.50 (ISBN 0-8048-1351-5, Pub by Shufunotomo Co. Ltd. Japan). C E Tuttle.

ORIGAMI–JUVENILE LITERATURE

Medvene, Mark. Foilrigami. (Illus.). (gr. 4-7). 1968. 5.95 (ISBN 0-685-06619-3). Astor-Honor.

ORIGEN

Bigg, Charles. Christian Platonists of Alexandria: Eight Lectures. LC 75-123764. Repr. of 1886 ed. 27.50 (ISBN 0-404-00799-6). AMS Pr.

Burghardt, W. J., et al, eds. Origen, Prayer, Exhortation to Martyrdom. LC 78-62467. (ACW Ser.: No. 19). 261p. 1954. 11.95 (ISBN 0-8091-0256-0). Paulist Pr.

--Origen, the Song of Songs: Commentaries & Homilies. LC 57-11826. (No. 26). 491p. 1957. 13.95 (ISBN 0-8091-0261-7). Paulist Pr.

Caspary, Gerard E. Politics & Exegesis: Origen & the Two Swords. LC 77-71058. 1979. 27.50x (ISBN 0-520-03445-7). U of Cal Pr.

De Faye, Eugene. Origen & His Work. LC 78-16959. 1926. 22.50 (ISBN 0-8414-3684-3). Folcroft.

Drewery, Benjamin. Origen & the Doctrine of Grace. 1960. text ed. 12.00x (ISBN 0-8401-0579-7). Allenson-Breckinridge.

ORIGIN, MARKS OF

see Marks of Origin

ORIGIN OF LIFE

see Life–Origin

ORIGIN OF MAN

see Man–Origin

ORIGIN OF SPECIES

see also Hybridization; Natural Selection; Phylogeny; Variation (Biology)

Barrett, Paul, et al, eds. Concordance to Darwin's "Origin of Species". 864p. 1981. 38.50x (ISBN 0-8014-1319-2). Cornell U Pr.

Darwin, Charles. Origin of Species. 1962. pap. 2.95 (ISBN 0-02-092120-9, Collier). Macmillan.

--Origin of Species. pap. 2.95 (ISBN 0-451-61928-5, ME1928, Ment). NAL.

--The Origin of Species. abr. ed. Appleman, Philip, ed. 1975. pap. text ed. 2.95x (ISBN 0-393-09219-4). Norton.

--The Origin of Species. Irvine, Charlotte & Irvine, William, eds. LC 56-7502. pap. 3.95 (ISBN 0-8044-6105-8). Ungar.

--The Origin of the Species. (Rowman & Littlefield University Library). 488p. 1972. 15.00x (ISBN 0-87471-662-4); pap. 6.75x (ISBN 0-87471-663-2). Rowman.

Darwin, Charles R. Foundations of the Origin of Species. Darwin, Francis, ed. LC 10-1422. 1909. 13.00 (ISBN 0-527-21610-0). Kraus Repr.

--Origin of Species. Burrow, J. W., ed. (Classics Ser). (YA) (gr. 9 up). 1968. pap. 2.50 (ISBN 0-14-040001-X, Pelican). Penguin.

De Vries, H. Mutation Theory, 2 Vols. in 1. Farmer, J. B. & Darbishire, trs. 1909-1910. 48.00 (ISBN 0-527-93470-4). Kraus Repr.

Dobzhansky, Theodosius. Genetics & the Origin of Species. 3rd ed. LC 56-11981. (Biological Ser.). 364p. 1951. pap. 7.50x (ISBN 0-231-08551-6). Columbia U Pr.

--Genetics of the Evolutionary Process. LC 72-127363. 505p. 1971. 22.50x (ISBN 0-231-02837-7); pap. 10.00x (ISBN 0-231-08306-8). Columbia U Pr.

Endler, John A. Geographic Variation, Speciation, & Clines. LC 76-45896. (Monographs in Population Biology: No. 10). (Illus.). 1977. 19.00 (ISBN 0-691-08187-5); pap. 9.50 (ISBN 0-691-08192-1). Princeton U Pr.

Himmelfarb, Gertrude. Darwin & the Darwinian Revolution. 1968. pap. 8.95 (ISBN 0-393-00455-4, Norton Lib.). Norton.

--Darwin & the Darwinian Revolution. 8.50 (ISBN 0-8446-1240-5). Peter Smith.

Jameson, D. L. Genetics of Speciation. (Benchmark Papers in Genetics: Vol. 9). 1977. 40.50 (ISBN 0-12-786756-2). Acad Pr.

Morse, Ph. A., ed. The Perception of Species-Specific Vocalizations. (Brain, Behavior & Evolution Journal: Vol. 16, No. 5-6). (Illus.). iv, 144p. 1980. pap. 27.00 (ISBN 3-8055-0733-X). S Karger.

ORIGINAL DIXIELAND JAZZ BAND

Brunn, H. O. The Story of the Original Dixieland Jazz Band. LC 77-3791. (Roots of Jazz Ser.). (Illus.). 1977. Repr. of 1960 ed. lib. bdg. 22.50 (ISBN 0-306-70892-2). Da Capo.

ORIGINAL SIN

see Sin, Original

ORIGINALITY

see also Creation (Literary, Artistic, etc.)

Axelrod, Charles D. Studies in Intellectual Breakthrough: Freud, Simmel, & Buber. LC 78-53177. 1979. lib. bdg. 10.00x (ISBN 0-87023-256-8). U of Mass Pr.

Knowlson, T. Sharper. Originality. Repr. of 1918 ed. 30.00 (ISBN 0-89987-064-3). Darby Bks.

ORIGINALITY (IN LITERATURE)

see also Imitation (In Literature); Plagiarism

Knowlson, T. Sharper. Originality: A Popular Study of the Creative Mind. 303p. 1980. Repr. of 1920 ed. lib. bdg. 35.00 (ISBN 0-8495-3045-8). Arden Lib.

Steinke, Martin W. Edward Young's Conjectures on Original Composition in England & Germany. LC 77-24917. 1917. lib. bdg. 15.00 (ISBN 0-8414-7853-8). Folcroft.

ORISKANY FORMATION

see Geology, Stratigraphic–Devonian

ORISSA, INDIA

Bailey, Frederick G. Tribe, Caste & Nation. 1971. Repr. of 1960 ed. text ed. 19.50x (ISBN 0-7190-0250-8). Humanities.

Dehejia, Vidya. Early Stone Temples of Orissa. LC 78-54434. 1979. 24.95 (ISBN 0-89089-092-7). Carolina Acad Pr.

Joshi, Arjun. History & Culture of Khijjingakatta. (Illus.). 300p. 1981. text ed. 37.50 (ISBN 0-7069-1134-2, Pub by Vikas India). Advent NY.

Mitra, Rajendralal. Antiquities of Orissa, 2 Vols. 1961-63. 20.00x (ISBN 0-8426-1389-7). Verry.

Nanda, Sukadev. Coalitional Politics in Orissa. 374p. 1979. 17.50x (ISBN 0-8002-0995-8). Intl Pubns Serv.

Sharma, Krishan. The Konds of Orissa: Anthropometric Study. (Illus.). 112p. 1979. 11.25x (ISBN 0-8002-2298-9). Intl Pubns Serv.

Sinha, B. N. Geography of Orissa. (Illus.). 172p. 1971. 3.75x (ISBN 0-8426-0495-2). Verry.

ORISSA, INDIA–ECONOMIC CONDITIONS

Behura, N. K. Peasant Potters of Orissa. 1979. text ed. 15.00 (ISBN 0-89684-072-7, Pub. by Sterling New Delhi). Orient Bk Dist.

ORIYA LANGUAGE

Gustafsson, Uwe. Kotia Oriya Phonemic Summary. 43p. 1974. pap. 1.80x (ISBN 0-88312-779-2). Summer Inst Ling.

ORIYA LITERATURE–HISTORY AND CRITICISM

Mansinha, Mayadhar. History of Oriya Literature. (National Academy of Letters). 1962. 5.00x (ISBN 0-8426-1374-9). Verry.

ORKHON INSCRIPTIONS

see Inscriptions, Turkish (Old)

ORKNEY ISLANDS

Balfour, David. Ancient Orkney Melodies. LC 73-14636. 1978. Repr. of 1885 ed. lib. bdg. 8.50 (ISBN 0-88305-071-4). Norwood Edns.

--Ancient Orkney Melodies. 1978. 14.50 (ISBN 0-685-86821-4). Porter.

Balfour, David, ed. Oppressions of the Sixteenth Century in the Islands of Orkney & Zetland: From Original Documents. (Maitland Club, Glasgow. Publications: No. 75). Repr. of 1859 ed. 17.50 (ISBN 0-404-53114-8). AMS Pr.

Brown, George M. An Orkney Tapestry. (Illus.). 192p. 1969. 15.00x (ISBN 0-575-00318-9). Intl Pubns Serv.

--Portrait of Orkney. (Illus.). 128p. 1981. 23.00 (ISBN 0-7012-0513-X, Pub. by Chatto-Bodley-Jonathan). Merrimack Bk Serv.

Childe, Vere G., et al. Skara Brae: A Pictish Village in Orkney. LC 77-86427. Repr. of 1931 ed. 24.50 (ISBN 0-404-16633-4). AMS Pr.

Fenton, Alexander. The Northern Isles: Orkney & Shetland. (Illus.). 1978. text ed. 39.00x (ISBN 0-85976-019-7). Humanities.

Laing, Lloyd. Orkney & Shetland: An Archaeological Guide. LC 74-76182. 1974. 16.95 (ISBN 0-7153-6305-0). David & Charles.

Linklater, Eric. Orkney & Shetland. 2nd ed. (Illus.). 1971. 10.00x (ISBN 0-7091-1754-X). Intl Pubns Serv.

--Orkney & Shetland: An Historical, Geographical, Social & Scenic Survey. 3rd ed. Nicolson, James R., rev. by. (Illus.). 285p. 1980. 20.00x (ISBN 0-7091-8142-6). Intl Pubns Serv.

Miller, Ronald. Orkney. (Illus.). 192p. 1978. 19.95 (ISBN 0-7134-3131-8, Pub. by Batsford England). David & Charles.

Omond, James. Orkney Eighty Years Ago: With Special Attention to Evie. LC 77-87683. Repr. of 1911 ed. 14.50 (ISBN 0-404-16479-X). AMS Pr.

Palsson, Herman & Edwards, Paul, trs. Orkneyinga Saga: The History of the Earls of Orkney. 1978. 14.95 (ISBN 0-7012-0431-1, Pub. by Chatto Bodley Jonathan). Merrimack Bk Serv.

Shirreff, John. General View of the Agriculture of the Orkney Islands. LC 77-87684. Repr. of 1814 ed. 22.50 (ISBN 0-404-16480-3). AMS Pr.

Tudor, John R. The Orkneys & Shetland: Their Past & Present State. LC 77-87685. 1977. Repr. of 1883 ed. 57.50 (ISBN 0-404-16481-1). AMS Pr.

Weir, Tom. Scottish Islands. LC 76-8618. (Leisure & Travel Ser.). (Illus.). 128p. 1976. 7.50 (ISBN 0-7153-7214-9). David & Charles.

ORLEANS, HENRIETTA ANNE, DUCHESSE D', 1644-1670

La Bruyere, Jean de & Pignarre, Robert. Les Caracteres: Avec: Caracteres de Theophraste. 668p. 1962. 4.50 (ISBN 0-686-54262-2). French & Eur.

ORLEANS, FRANCE–HISTORY

Giles, John A., ed. Revolte Du Conte De Warwick Contre le Roi Edward 4e. (Fr). 1849. 24.00 (ISBN 0-8337-1347-7). B Franklin.

ORLEANS, HOUSE OF

De Fenin, Pierre. Memoires. 1837. 28.00 (ISBN 0-384-15455-7); pap. 23.00 (ISBN 0-384-15460-3). Johnson Repr.

ORMULUM

Ormulum. The Ormulum, with the Notes & Glossary of Dr. Robert Meadows White, 2 vols. Holt, Robert, ed. LC 72-178548. Repr. of 1878 ed. 32.50 ea.; Set. 65.00 (ISBN 0-404-56654-5). AMS Pr.

ORMUS–HISTORY
Glazier, Richard. A Manual of Historic Ornament: Treating Upon the Evolution, Tradition & Development of Architecture & the Applied Arts. 5th ed. LC 70-163174. (Tower Bks). (Illus.). vi, 183p. 1972. Repr. of 1933 ed. 28.00 (ISBN 0-8103-3937-4). Gale.
ORNAMENT
see Decoration and Ornament
ORNAMENTAL ALPHABETS
see Alphabets; Illumination of Books and Manuscripts
ORNAMENTAL DESIGN
see Design, Decorative
ORNAMENTAL HERALDRY
see Heraldry, Ornamental
ORNAMENTAL PLANTS
see Plants, Ornamental
ORNAMENTAL SHRUBS
see also Topiary Work
Hofman, Jaroslav. Ornamental Shrubs. (Concise Guides Ser.). (Illus.). 1979. 7.95 (ISBN 0-600-38246-X). Transatlantic.
ORNAMENTAL TREES
see also Topiary Work
Adams, Bill. Trees for Southern Landscapes. LC 76-15457. (Illus.). 96p. 1976. pap. 3.95 (ISBN 0-88415-881-0). Pacesetter Pr.
Downing, Andrew J. A Treatise on the Theory & Practice of Landscape Gardening Adapted to North America. (Illus.). Date not set. Repr. of 1875 ed. 20.00 (ISBN 0-913728-23-3). Theophrastus.
Greeves-Carpenter, C. F. The Care of Ornamental Trees: Planting, Fertilizing, Pruning, Tree Surgery, & Spraying. 1978. Repr. of 1928 ed. lib. bdg. 15.00 (ISBN 0-8495-1946-2). Arden Lib.
Herda, D. J. Growing Trees Indoors. LC 78-37164. 1979. 16.95x (ISBN 0-88229-346-X); pap. 8.95 (ISBN 0-686-66163-X). Nelson-Hall.
Johnson, Hugh. International Book of Trees. 1973. 29.95 (ISBN 0-671-21607-4). S&S.
Minton, Penny & Minton, Cronan. How to Grow Trees Indoors. LC 76-23782. 1978. pap. 4.95 (ISBN 0-385-11475-3). Doubleday.
Pirone, P. P. Tree Maintenance. 5th ed. (Illus.). 1978. 29.95 (ISBN 0-19-502321-8). Oxford U Pr.
ORNAMENTS (MUSIC)
see Embellishment (Music)
ORNITHOLOGISTS
Cutright, Paul R. & Brodhead, Michael J. Elliott Coues: Naturalist & Frontier Historian. LC 80-12424. (Illus.). 510p. 1981. 28.50 (ISBN 0-252-00802-2). U of Ill Pr.
Devlin, John C. & Naismith, Grace. The World of Roger Tory Peterson: An Authorized Biography. LC 77-5840. 1977. 14.95 (ISBN 0-8129-0694-2). Times Bks.
Hume, Edgar E. Ornithologists of the United States Army Medical Corps: Thirty-Six Biographies. Sterling, Keir B., ed. LC 77-81131. (Biologists & Their World Ser.). (Illus.). 1978. Repr. of 1942 ed. lib. bdg. 37.00x (ISBN 0-405-10729-3). Arno.
Sutton, George M. Bird Student: An Autobiography. (Corrie Herring Hooks Ser.: No. 4). (Illus.). 232p. 1980. 15.95 (ISBN 0-292-70727-4). U of Tex Pr.
Wallace, George J. My World of Birds: Memoirs of an Ornithologist. 345p. 1979. 12.50 (ISBN 0-8059-2586-4). Dorrance.
ORNITHOLOGY
Ali, Salim. Fieldguide to the Birds of the Eastern Himalayas. (Illus.). 1978. 15.95x (ISBN 0-19-560595-0). Oxford U Pr.
Allen, Elsa G. The History of American Ornithology Before Audubon. (Illus.). 1979. Repr. of 1951 ed. 45.00 (ISBN 0-934626-00-6). W G Arader.
Belding, Lyman. Land Birds of the Pacific District. Repr. of 1890 ed. pap. 31.00 (ISBN 0-384-03792-5). Johnson Repr.
Chapman, Frank M. Essays in South American Ornithogeography: Original Anthology. Sterling, Keir B., ed. LC 77-81087. (Biologists & Their World Ser.). (Illus.). 1978. lib. bdg. 46.00x (ISBN 0-405-10663-7). Arno.
Contributions to the History of American Ornithology. LC 73-17810. (Natural Sciences in America Ser.). 382p. 1974. Repr. 19.00x (ISBN 0-405-05727-X). Arno.
Cruickshank, Allan & Cruickshank, Helen. One Thousand & One Questions Answered About Birds. LC 75-41881. (Illus.). 320p. 1976. pap. 4.00 (ISBN 0-486-23315-4). Dover.
Farner, Donald S. & King, James R. Avian Biology, 5 vols. Vol. 1, 1971. 71.50, by subscription 60.00 (ISBN 0-12-249401-6); Vol. 2, 1972. 63.50, by subscription 54.50 (ISBN 0-12-249402-4); Vol. 3, 1973. 70.00, by subscription 60.00 (ISBN 0-12-249403-2); Vol. 4, 1974. 61.00 (ISBN 0-12-249404-0); Vol. 5, 1975. 78.50, subscription 67.00 (ISBN 0-12-249405-9). Acad Pr.
King, A. S. & McLelland, J., eds. Form & Function in Birds, Vol. 1. LC 79-50523. 1980. 74.00 (ISBN 0-12-407501-0). Acad Pr.
--Forms & Function in Birds, Vol. 2. 1981. 101.00 (ISBN 0-12-407502-9). Acad Pr.
Nicholson, E. M. The Study of Birds: An Introduction to Ornithology. 1979. Repr. of 1929 ed. lib. bdg. 15.00 (ISBN 0-8492-1969-8). R West.
Nuttall Ornithological Club. Bulletin of the Nuttall Ornithological Club: A Quarterly Journal of Ornithology, 8 vols. in 3. LC 73-17834. (Natural Sciences in America Ser.). (Illus.). 1826p. 1974. Repr. Set. 91.00x (ISBN 0-405-05754-7); Vol. 1. 35.00x (ISBN 0-405-05755-5); Vol. 2. 28.00x (ISBN 0-405-05756-3); Vol. 3. 28.00x (ISBN 0-405-05757-1). Arno.
Pasquier, Roger F. Watching Birds: An Introduction to Ornithology. 1980. pap. 6.95 (ISBN 0-395-29068-6). HM.
Petrak, Margaret L., ed. Diseases of Cage & Aviary Birds. 2nd ed. LC 81-3792. (Illus.). 540p. 1981. text ed. price not set (ISBN 0-8121-0692-X). Lea & Febiger.
Pettingill, Olin S., Jr. Ornithology at the University of Michigan Biological Station & the Birds of the Region. (Illus.). viii, 118p. 1974. pap. text ed. 5.00 (ISBN 0-939294-00-1). Beech Leaf.
--Ornithology in Laboratory & Field. 4th ed. LC 79-119563. 1970. text ed. 17.95x (ISBN 0-8087-1609-3). Burgess.
Richmond, Chandler S. Beyond the Spring: Cordelia Stanwood of Birdsacre. (Illus.). xvi, 156p. (Orig.). 1978. 14.95 (ISBN 0-932448-00-3); pap. 7.95 (ISBN 0-932448-01-1). Latona Pr.
Ricklefs, Robert E., ed. Audubon Conservation Report No. 6: Report of the Advisory Panel on the California Condor. (Audubon Conservation Report Ser.). 1978. pap. 1.50 (ISBN 0-930698-04-5). Natl Audubon.
Ripley, Sidney S., ed. Bundle of Feathers: Proferred to Salim Ali for His 75th Birthday in 1971. (Illus.). 252p. text ed. 16.95x (ISBN 0-19-560811-9). Oxford U Pr.
Stresemann, Erwin. Ornithology: From Aristotle to the Present. LC 74-25035. 448p. 1975. text ed. 22.50x (ISBN 0-674-64485-9). Harvard U Pr.
Van Tyne, Josselyn & Berger, Andrew J. Fundamentals of Ornithology. 2nd. ed. LC 75-20430. 808p. 1976. 40.00 (ISBN 0-471-89965-8, Pub. by Wiley-Interscience). Wiley.
Wallace, George J. & Mahan, Harold D. An Introduction to Ornithology. 3rd ed. (Illus.). 1974. text ed. 20.95 (ISBN 0-02-423980-1). Macmillan.
Yapp, W. The Life & Organization of Birds. (Contemporary Biology Ser). 1970. 12.00 (ISBN 0-444-19644-7). Univ Park.
ORNITHOLOGY, ECONOMIC
see Birds, Injurious and Beneficial
OROGRAPHY
see Mountains
OROMONS
see Gallas
OROZCO, JOSE CLEMENTE, 1883-1949
Helm, MacKinley. Man of Fire: J. C. Orozco, an Interpretive Memoir. LC 79-106689. (Illus.). 1971. Repr. of 1953 ed. lib. bdg. 23.50x (ISBN 0-8371-3361-0, HEJO). Greenwood.
Orozco, Jose C. The Artist in New York: Letters to Jean Charlot & Unpublished Writings (1925-1929) Simms, Ruth L., tr. LC 74-5235. (Texas Pan American Ser). (Illus.). 99p. 1974. 8.95 (ISBN 0-292-70309-0). U of Tex Pr.
OROZCO, PASCUAL
Dickerson, Albert I., ed. The Orozco Frescos at Dartmouth. LC 34-19500. (Illus.). 24p. 1934. pap. 3.00 (ISBN 0-87451-031-7). U Pr of Amer.
Meyer, Michael C. Mexican Rebel: Pascual Orozco & the Mexican Revolution, 1910-1915. LC 67-10667. (Illus.). 1967. 12.95x (ISBN 0-8032-0119-2). U of Nebr Pr.
ORPHANS AND ORPHAN-ASYLUMS
see also Charity-Schools; Child Welfare
Babenco, Maurice. Toward a Better World. 1978. 6.50 (ISBN 0-533-03653-4). Vantage.
Laslett, Peter. Family Life & Illicit Love in Earlier Generations. 1977. 47.50 (ISBN 0-521-21408-4); pap. 12.95x (ISBN 0-521-29221-2). Cambridge U Pr.
Letchworth, William P. Homes of Homeless Children: Report on Orphan Asylums & Institutions for Care of Children, Vol. 4. LC 74-1693. (Children & Youth Ser.). 632p. 1974. Repr. of 1903 ed. 34.00x (ISBN 0-405-05969-8). Arno.
Mace, Gillian S., et al. The Bereaved Child: Analysis, Education, & Treatment - an Abstracted Bibliography. 292p. 1981. text ed. write for info. (ISBN 0-306-65197-1). Plenum Pub.
Markley, Francis X. Mercy with Love. (Illus.). 128p. 1980. 7.95 (ISBN 0-89962-025-6). Todd & Honeywell.
Orders Taken & Enacted, for Orphans. LC 72-6011. (English Experience Ser.: No. 537). 1973. Repr. of 1580 ed. 5.00 (ISBN 90-221-0537-7). Walter J Johnson.
Reeder, Rudolph R. How Two Hundred Children Live & Learn. facsimile ed. LC 74-1701. (Children & Youth Ser.). 252p. 1974. Repr. of 1910 ed. 17.00x (ISBN 0-405-05978-7). Arno.
Reinprecht, Hansheinz. The Hermann Gmeiner Book: The Story of the S O S -Children's Villages & Their Founder. 1978. pap. 4.95 (ISBN 0-533-03453-1). Vantage.
ORPHANS' COURTS
see Probate Law and Practice
ORPHEUS
Friedman, John B. Orpheus in the Middle Ages. LC 71-111484. (Illus.). 1970. 12.50x (ISBN 0-674-64490-5). Harvard U Pr.
Linforth, Ivan M. The Arts of Orpheus. LC 72-9296. (The Philosophy of Plato & Aristotle Ser.). Repr. of 1941 ed. 18.00 (ISBN 0-405-04847-5). Arno.
Shire, Helena M., ed. King Orphius & Sir Colling: Ninth of May No. 4. (Folklore Ser.). 1973. Repr. 7.50 (ISBN 0-685-43683-7). Norwood Edns.
Strauss, Walter A. Descent & Return: The Orphic Theme in Modern Literature. LC 70-131461. 1971. 15.00x (ISBN 0-674-19830-1). Harvard U Pr.
ORR, BOBBY, 1948-
Burchard, Marshall & Burchard, Sue. Sports Hero: Bobby Orr. (Sports Hero Ser.). (Illus.). 96p. (gr. 3-5). 1973. PLB 6.29 (ISBN 0-399-60795-1). Putnam.
Devaney, John. The Bobby Orr Story. (Pro Hockey Library: No. 6). (Illus.). (gr. 5 up). 1973. (BYR); PLB 3.69 (ISBN 0-394-92612-9). Random.
Hirshberg, Al. Bobby Orr: Fire on Ice. new ed. LC 75-10436. (Putnam Sports Shelf). 160p. (gr. 5 up). 1975. PLB 6.29 (ISBN 0-399-60954-7). Putnam.
Liss, Howard. Bobby Orr: Lightning on Ice. LC 75-2423. (Sports Ser.). (Illus.). 96p. (gr. 3-6). 1975. PLB 6.48 (ISBN 0-8116-6672-7). Garrard.
Orr, Bobby & Mulvoy, Mark. Bobby Orr: My Game. (A Sports Illustrated Bk). 1974. 9.95 (ISBN 0-316-66490-1). Little.
Smith, Jay H. Bobby Orr. LC 74-8848. (Sports Superstars Ser.). (Illus.). 32p. (gr. 3-9). 1974. PLB 5.95 (ISBN 0-87191-368-2); pap. 2.95 (ISBN 0-686-67087-6). Creative Ed.
--Hockey's Legend: Bobby Orr. (The Allstars Ser.). (Illus.). (gr. 2-6). 1977. PLB 5.95 (ISBN 0-87191-590-1). Creative Ed.
ORRERIES
see Planetaria
ORRERY, ROGER BOYLE, 1ST EARL OF, 1621-1679
Lynch, Kathleen M. Roger Boyle: First Earl of Orrery. LC 65-17438. (Illus.). 1965. 15.00x (ISBN 0-87049-060-5). U of Tenn Pr.
Siegert, Edward. Roger Boyle, Earl of Orrery, und Seine Dramen. Repr. of 1906 ed. pap. 10.00 (ISBN 0-384-55320-6). Johnson Repr.
ORSINI VITTORIA (ACCORAMBONI) PERETTI, DUCHESSA DI BRACCIANO, 1557-1585
Boklund, Gunnar. Sources of the White Devil, John Webster. LC 68-1396. (Studies in Comparative Literature, No. 35). 1969. Repr. of 1957 ed. lib. bdg. 49.95 (ISBN 0-8383-0648-9). Haskell.
ORTEGA Y GASSET, JOSE, 1883-1955
Diaz, Janet W. The Major Themes of Existentialism in the Works of Jose Ortega y Gasset. (Studies in the Romance Languages & Literatures: No. 94). 1970. pap. 11.00x (ISBN 0-8078-9094-4). U of NC Pr.
McClintock, Robert. Man & His Circumstances: Ortega As Educator. LC 76-149404. 1971. text ed. 18.85 (ISBN 0-8077-1726-6). Tchrs Coll.
Marrero, Domingo. El Centauro: Persona y Pensamiento De Ortega y Gasset. (UPREX, Ensayo: No. 30). pap. 1.85 (ISBN 0-8477-0030-5). U of PR Pr.
Niedermayer, Franz. Jose Ortega y Gasset. Tirner, Peter, tr. from Ger. LC 71-163150. (Modern Literature Ser.). 1973. 10.95 (ISBN 0-8044-2659-7). Ungar.
Ouimette, Victor. Jose Ortega y Gasset. (World Author Ser.: No. 624). 1981. lib. bdg. 15.95 (ISBN 0-8057-6466-6). Twayne.
Raley, Harold. Jose Ortega Y Gasset: Philosopher of European Unity. LC 78-148689. 272p. 1971. 17.50x (ISBN 0-8173-6612-1). U of Ala Pr.
Silver, Philip. Ortega As Phenomenologist. LC 78-667. 1978. 15.00x (ISBN 0-231-04544-1). Columbia U Pr.
ORTHODONTIA
see Orthodontics
ORTHODONTIC APPLIANCES
Graber, T. M. & Neumann, Bedrich. Removable Orthodontic Appliances. LC 76-14681. (Illus.). 1977. text ed. 32.00 (ISBN 0-7216-4190-3). Saunders.
Houston & Isaacson. Orthodonic Treatment with Removable Appliances. 1981. 17.50 (ISBN 0-8151-4710-4). Year Bk Med.
ORTHODONTICS
see also Orthodontic Appliances
Adams, C. P. The Design & Construction of Removable Orthodontic Appliances. 4th ed. (Illus.). 1976. 21.95 (ISBN 0-8151-0087-6). Year Bk Med.
Assembly of Life Sciences, National Research Council. Seriously Handicapping Orthodontic Conditions. LC 76-16344. 1976. pap. 5.25 (ISBN 0-309-02501-X). Natl Acad Pr.
Barrer, Harry G., ed. Orthodontics: The State of the Art. LC 79-5043. (Illus.). 448p. 1981. 60.00x (ISBN 0-8122-7767-8). U of Pa Pr.
Chaconas, Spiro J., ed. Orthodontics. LC 79-20126. (Post Graduate Dental Handbook Ser.: Vol. 10). (Illus.). 332p. 1980. text ed. 33.50 (ISBN 0-88416-155-2). Wright-PSG.
Cohen, M. Michael, Sr. Minor Tooth Movement in the Growing Child. LC 76-8570. (Illus.). 1977. text ed. 19.95 (ISBN 0-7216-2632-7). Saunders.
Dawson, Peter E. Evaluation, Diagnosis, & Treatment of Occlusal Problems. LC 74-12409. 1974. 52.50 (ISBN 0-8016-1216-0). Mosby.
Graber, T. M. Orthodontics: Principles & Practice. 3rd ed. LC 73-186950. (Illus.). 953p. 1972. text ed. 32.00 (ISBN 0-7216-4182-2). Saunders.
Graber, T. M. & Swain, Brainerd F., eds. Current Orthodontic Concepts & Techniques, 2 vols. 2nd ed. LC 74-11686. (Illus.). 1137p. 1975. Vol. 1. text ed. 49.50 (ISBN 0-7216-4187-3); Vol. 2. text ed. 49.50 (ISBN 0-7216-4188-1); Set. text ed. 99.00 (ISBN 0-7216-4189-X). Saunders.
Hitchcock, H. Perry. Orthodontics for Undergraduates. LC 73-18181. (Illus.). 532p. 1974. text ed. 27.00 (ISBN 0-8121-0439-0). Lea & Febiger.
Holt, Robert. Straight Teeth: Orthodontics & Dental Care for Everyone. 1981. 9.95 (ISBN 0-686-73897-7). Morrow.
--Straight Teeth: Orthodontics & Dental Care for Everyone. LC 80-10562. (Illus.). 224p. 1980. 13.95 (ISBN 0-688-03625-2); pap. 7.95 (ISBN 0-688-08625-X). Morrow.
Hotz, Rudolf. Orthodontics in Daily Practice. 415p. 1974. 40.25 (ISBN 0-683-04185-1, Pub. by W & W). Krieger.
Houston, W. J. Walther's Orthodontic Notes. 1976. 14.95 (ISBN 0-8151-4709-0). Year Bk Med.
Moyers, Robert E. Handbook of Orthodontics. 3rd ed. (Illus.). 1973. 37.50 (ISBN 0-8151-6002-X). Year Bk Med.
Renfroe, Earl W. Edgewise. LC 74-671. (Illus.). 494p. 1975. text ed. 35.00 (ISBN 0-8121-0449-8). Lea & Febiger.
Salzmann, J. A. Orthodontics in Daily Practice. LC 73-22136. (Illus.). 658p. 1974. text ed. 72.50 (ISBN 0-397-50324-5, JBL-Med-Nursing). Har-Row.
Sim, Joseph M. Minor Tooth Movement in Children. 2nd ed. LC 77-24370. (Illus.). 1977. 47.50 (ISBN 0-8016-4616-2). Mosby.
Thurow, Raymond C. Atlas of Orthodontic Principles. 2nd ed. LC 77-7096. (Illus.). 1977. text ed. 38.50 (ISBN 0-8016-4951-X). Mosby.
--Edgewise Orthodontics. 3rd ed. LC 72-85265. (Illus.). 328p. 1972. 34.50 (ISBN 0-8016-4946-3). Mosby.
Timms, Donald S. Rapid Maxillary Expansion. 1981. write for info. (ISBN 0-931386-49-7). Quint Pub Co.
Tulley, W. J. Manual of Practical Orthodontics. 3rd ed. (Illus.). 1976. 21.00 (ISBN 0-8151-8865-X). Year Bk Med.
Weiss, Jay. Embraceable You: A Guide for Orthodontic Patients & Their Families. LC 72-4351. (Illus.). 1975. 8.95 (ISBN 0-88238-603-4). H S Pub Corp.
White, T. C., et al. Orthodontics for Dental Students. LC 67-27250. 324p. 1968. 12.50 (ISBN 0-87527-088-3). Green.
ORTHODOX EASTERN CHURCH
Allen, Joseph J., ed. Orthodox Synthesis: The Unity of Theological Thought. 240p. (Orig.). 1981. pap. 8.95 (ISBN 0-913836-84-2). St Vladimirs.
Baker, Derek, ed. The Orthodox Churches & the West. (Studies in Church History Ser.: Vol. 13). 336p. 1976. 36.00x (ISBN 0-631-17180-0, Pub. by Basil Blackwell). Biblio Dist.
Bratsiotis, Panagiotis. Greek Orthodox Church. Blenkinsopp, Joseph, tr. 1968. 5.95x (ISBN 0-268-00114-6). U of Notre Dame Pr.
Brianchaninov, Ignatius. Three Essays: On Reading the Gospel, on Reading the Holy Fathers, on Shunning Reading of Books Containing False Teachings. pap. 0.25 (ISBN 0-686-16365-6). Eastern Orthodox.
Budge, E. A. Apophthegmata Patrum. 150p. 1975. pap. 3.95 (ISBN 0-686-10938-4). Eastern Orthodox.
Cassian, St. John. Teachings of St. John Cassian. pap. 3.95 (ISBN 0-686-05665-5). Eastern Orthodox.

Cavarnos, Constantine. Orthodox Iconography. LC 77-74606. (Illus.). 1977. 6.50x (ISBN 0-914744-36-4); pap. 3.95x (ISBN 0-914744-37-2). Inst Byzantine.

Chesterton, G. K. Orthodoxy. 160p. 1973. pap. 2.95 (ISBN 0-385-01536-4, Im). Doubleday.

Chetverikov, Sergii. Starets Paisii Velichkovskii: His Life, Teachings & Influence on Orthodox Monasticism. Lickwar, V., tr. Lisenko, A. LC 75-29632. 359p. 1980. 35.00 (ISBN 0-913124-22-2). Nordland Pub.

Chitty, Derwas. The Desert a City. 222p. 1977. pap. 6.95 (ISBN 0-913836-45-1). St Vladimirs.

Chrysostomos & Archimandrite. Contemporary Eastern Orthodox Thought. LC 81-80112. 175p. (Orig.). 1981. price not set (ISBN 0-913124-54-0). Nordland Pub.

Colliander, Tito. The Way of the Ascetics. 130p. Repr. of 1960 ed. 5.95 (ISBN 0-913026-22-0). St Nectarios.

Coniaris, A. M. Making God Real in the Orthodox Christian Home. 1977. pap. 4.95 (ISBN 0-937032-07-7). Light&Life Pub Co MN.

--Orthodoxy: A Creed for Today. 1972. pap. 5.95 (ISBN 0-937032-19-0). Light&Life Pub Co MN.

Coniaris, Anthony M. Eastern Orthodoxy: A Way of Life. 1966. pap. 4.95 (ISBN 0-937032-14-X). Light & Life Pub Co MN.

Constantine, Archimandrite. Antichrist, Orthodoxy or Heterodoxy. pap. 0.25 (ISBN 0-686-11505-8). Eastern Orthodox.

Dabovich, Sebastian. True Church of Christ. Repr. of 1899 ed. pap. 0.25 (ISBN 0-686-11506-6). Eastern Orthodox.

Dawes, Elizabeth & Baynes, Norman H., trs. from Greek. Three Byzantine Saints. 275p. 1977. pap. 7.95 (ISBN 0-913836-44-3). St Vladimirs.

Dudko, Dmitrii. Our Hope. Garrett, Paul D., tr. from Russian. 291p. 1977. pap. 7.95 (ISBN 0-913836-35-4). St Vladimirs.

Eterovich, Adam S. Orthodox Church Directory of the United States. 1968. softcover 5.00 (ISBN 0-88247-126-0). Ragusan Pr.

Eterovich, Adam S. & Reed, Robert D. Orthodox Church Directory of the U.S. 1969. pap. 5.00 (ISBN 0-685-23368-5). R & E Res Assoc.

Fortescue, Adrian. Orthodox Eastern Church. (Illus.). 1969. 25.50 (ISBN 0-8337-1217-9). B Franklin.

--The Orthodox Eastern Church. 3rd facsimile ed. LC 70-179520. (Select Bibliographies Reprint Ser). Repr. of 1920 ed. 24.00 (ISBN 0-8369-6649-X). Arno.

Gavin, Frank S. Some Aspects of Contemporary Greek Orthodox Thought. LC 73-133818. Repr. of 1923 ed. 29.00 (ISBN 0-404-02687-7). AMS Pr.

Harakas, S. Guidelines for Marriage in the Orthodox Church. 1980. pap. 1.25 (ISBN 0-937032-21-2). Light&Life Pub Co MN.

--Something Is Stirring in World Orthodoxy. 1978. pap. 2.95 (ISBN 0-937032-04-2). Light&Life Pub Co MN.

Hopko, T., et al. God & Charity: Images of Eastern Orthodox Theology, Spirituality & Practice. Costa, Francis D., ed. LC 79-3027. (Pan-Am Books). 103p. (Orig.). 1979. pap. text ed. 3.95 (ISBN 0-916586-34-0). Holy Cross Orthodox.

John Chrysostom, Saint St. John Chrysostom on the Priesthood. 160p. 1977. pap. 3.95 (ISBN 0-913836-38-9). St Vladimirs.

Khomiakov, A. Church Is One. 1974. pap. 1.50 (ISBN 0-686-10204-5). Eastern Orthodox.

Khomiakov, Alexei S. The Church Is One. (Illus.). 1980. pap. 1.25 (ISBN 0-913026-23-9). St Nectarios.

Koulomzin, Sophie. Our Church & Our Children. LC 75-20215. 158p. 1975. pap. 5.95 (ISBN 0-913836-25-7). St Vladimirs.

Lossky, Vladimir. Orthodox Theology: An Introduction. LC 78-1853. 137p. 1978. pap. 4.95 (ISBN 0-913836-43-5). St Vladimirs.

Makrakis, Apostolos. The City of Zion--the Human Society in Christ, i.e., the Church Built Upon a Rock. Orthodox Christian Educational Society, ed. Cummings, Denver, tr. from Hellenic. 109p. 1958. pap. 3.00x (ISBN 0-938366-16-5). Orthodox Chr.

--The Holy Orthodox Church. Orthodox Christian Educational Society, ed. Lisney, M. I. & Krick, L., trs. from Hellenic. 298p. (Orig.). 1980. pap. 7.95x (ISBN 0-938366-34-3). Orthodox Chr.

--Memoir of the Nature of the Church of Christ. Orthodox Christian Educational Society, ed. Cummings, Denver, tr. from Hellenic. 175p. 1947. 3.00x (ISBN 0-938366-21-1). Orthodox Chr.

--The Orthodox Definition of Political Science. Orthodox Christian Educational Society, ed. Cummings, Denver, tr. from Hellenic. 163p. 1968. pap. 2.00x (ISBN 0-938366-31-9). Orthodox Chr.

Metropolitan Philip Saliba & Allen, Joseph J. Out of the Depths Have I Cried: Thoughts on Incarnational Theology in the Eastern Christian Experience. LC 79-18611. (Illus., Orig.). 1979. pap. 4.95 (ISBN 0-916586-32-4). Holy Cross Orthodox.

Meyendorff, et al. The Primacy of Peter. 134p. 1963. 6.95 (ISBN 0-913836-20-6). St Vladimirs.

Meyendorff, John. Living Tradition. LC 78-2031. 202p. 1978. pap. 6.95 (ISBN 0-913836-48-6). St Vladimirs.

--The Orthodox Church: Its Past & Its Role in the World Today. LC 81-4978. 258p. 1981. pap. 8.95 (ISBN 0-913836-81-8). St Vladimirs.

--St. Gregory Palamas & Orthodox Spirituality. (Illus.). 184p. pap. 7.95 (ISBN 0-913836-11-7). St Vladimirs.

Neale, John M. A History of the Holy Eastern Church, 5 vols. LC 74-144662. Repr. of 1850 ed. Set. 157.50 (ISBN 0-404-04670-3). AMS Pr.

--Voices from the East: Docoments of the Present State & Working of the Oriental Church. LC 75-173069. Repr. of 1859 ed. 18.00 (ISBN 0-404-04659-2). AMS Pr.

Nissiotis, N. Interpeting Orthodoxy. 1980. pap. 2.45 (ISBN 0-937032-23-9). Light&Life Pub Co MN.

Nykanen, Marita & Williams, Esther, trs. from Finnish. The Faith We Hold: Archbishop Paul. LC 80-10404. 196p. 1980. pap. 3.95 (ISBN 0-913836-63-X). St Vladimirs.

Orthodox Eastern Church-Synod of Jerusalem. Acts & Decrees of the Synod of Jerusalem, 1672. pap. 1.50 (ISBN 0-686-05637-X). Eastern Orthodox.

Orthodox Spirituality. pap. 0.25 (ISBN 0-686-05392-3). Eastern Orthodox.

Orthodox Word Editors. Orthodoxy & the Religion of the Future: Can the Orthodox Church Enter into a Dialogue with Non-Christian Religions? pap. 5.00 (ISBN 0-686-11507-4). Eastern Orthodox.

Palassis, Neketas S., ed. St. Nectarios Orthodox Conference. LC 80-53258. 176p. (Orig.). 1981. pap. 15.00 (ISBN 0-913026-14-X). St Nectarios.

Pargoire, Jules. Eglise Byzantine De 527 a 847. 1971. Repr. of 1905 ed. lib. bdg. 26.00 (ISBN 0-8337-2672-2). B Franklin.

Platon. Orthodox Doctrine of the Apostolic Eastern Church: A Compendium of Christian Theology. LC 70-81772. Repr. of 1857 ed. 18.50 (ISBN 0-404-05058-1). AMS Pr.

Puhalo, Lev, ed. Synaxis: Orthodox Christian Theology in the 20th Century, Vol. 3. 77p. (Orig.). 1979. pap. 3.50x (ISBN 0-913026-93-X). St Nectarios.

--Synaxis: Orthodox Christian Theology in the 20th Century, Vol. 5. 70p. (Orig.). 1981. pap. 3.50 (ISBN 0-913026-99-9). St Nectarios.

Ridding, Laura, ed. Travels of Macarius: Extracts from the Diary of the Travels of Macarius, Patriarch of Antioch. LC 77-115577. (Russia Observed Ser). 1971. Repr. of 1936 ed. 8.00 (ISBN 0-405-03089-4). Arno.

Schmemann, Alexander. Church, World, Mission. LC 79-27597. 227p. 1979. pap. 6.95 (ISBN 0-913836-49-4). St Vladimirs.

Scupoli, Lorenzo. Unseen Warfare. 280p. 1978. pap. 7.95 (ISBN 0-913836-52-4). St Vladimirs.

Semenoff-Tian-Chansky, Alexander. Fr. John of Kronstadt: A Life. 160p. 1979. pap. 6.95 (ISBN 0-913836-56-7). St Vladimirs.

Smirnoff, Eugene. Russian Orthodox Missions. pap. 3.50 (ISBN 0-686-01299-2). Eastern Orthodox.

Staniloae, Dumitru. Theology & the Church. Barringer, Robert, tr. from Romanian. LC 80-19313. 240p. (Orig.). 1980. pap. 6.95 (ISBN 0-913836-69-9, BS695.57 230.19498). St Martin.

Synaxis: The Journal of Orthodox Theology, Vol. 2. 1977. pap. 4.00x (ISBN 0-913026-88-3). St Nectarios.

Taylor, John. Icon Painting. LC 78-25925. (The Mayflower Gallery Ser.). (Illus.). 1979. 12.50 (ISBN 0-8317-4813-3, Mayflower Bks); pap. 6.95 (ISBN 0-8317-4814-1). Smith Pubs.

Trempelas, Panagiotes N. The Autocephaly of the Metropolia in America. Bebis, George S., tr. Stephanopoulos, Robert G., ed. 1974. pap. 2.50 (ISBN 0-916586-00-6). Holy Cross Orthodox.

Tsirpanlis, Constantine N., ed. Orthodox-Unification Dialogue. LC 80-54586. (Conference Ser.: No. 8). (Illus.). x, 139p. (Orig.). 1981. pap. text ed. 7.95 (ISBN 0-932894-08-9). Unif Theol Seminary.

Vaporis, N. M, ed. Byzantine Fellowship Lectures, No. One, No. 1. (Illus.). 1974. pap. 2.95 (ISBN 0-916586-02-2). Holy Cross Orthodox.

Ware, Timothy. Orthodox Church. (Orig.). 1963. pap. 3.95 (ISBN 0-14-020592-6, Pelican). Penguin.

Winkler, Gabriele. Prayer Attitude in the Eastern Church. 1978. pap. 1.25 (ISBN 0-937032-01-8). Light&Life Pub Co MN.

Zhishman, Joseph. Das Ehrerecht der Orientalischen Kirche. LC 80-2367. Repr. of 1864 ed. 63.50 (ISBN 0-404-18918-0). AMS Pr.

ORTHODOX EASTERN CHURCH–ASCETICISM

see Asceticism

ORTHODOX EASTERN CHURCH–HISTORY

see also Schism–Eastern and Western Church

Basil, Saint St. Basil the Great on The Forty Martyrs of Sebaste, Paradise, & the Catholic Faith. 1979. pap. 3.95 (ISBN 0-686-25227-6). Eastern Orthodox.

Fedotov, George P. St. Filipp: Metropolitan of Moscow. LC 75-27477. 1978. 22.50 (ISBN 0-913124-14-1). Nordland Pub.

Hackel, Sergei. The Orthodox Church. LC 78-882645. (Living Religions Series). (Illus.). 1974. pap. 3.50x (ISBN 0-7062-3600-9). Intl Pubns Serv.

Joannes, Damascenus. On Holy Images. Allies, Mary H., tr. from Greek. 1977. pap. 2.95 (ISBN 0-686-19232-X). Eastern Orthodox.

Maloney, George A. A History of Orthodox Theology Since Fourteen-Hundre-Fifty-Three. LC 75-27491. 1976. 39.50 (ISBN 0-913124-12-5). Nordland Pub.

Orthodox Eastern Church. Synod of Sixteen Seventy Two: Acts & Decrees of the Jerusalem Synod Held Under Dositheus, Containing the Confession Published Name of Cyril Lukaris. Robertson, J. N., tr. LC 78-81769. 1969. Repr. of 1899 ed. 18.50 (ISBN 0-404-03567-1). AMS Pr.

Papadopoullos, Theodore H. Studies & Documents Relating to the History of the Greek Church & People Under Turkish Domination. LC 78-38759. Repr. of 1952 ed. 27.50 (ISBN 0-404-56314-7). AMS Pr.

Rabbath, Antoine. Documents Inedits Pour Servir a l'Histoire Du Christianisme En Orient, 2 Vols. LC 72-174293. Repr. of 1911 ed. Set. lib. bdg. 67.50 (ISBN 0-404-05202-9). AMS Pr.

Schmemann, Alexander. Historical Road of Eastern Orthodoxy. LC 77-12074. 343p. 1977. pap. 7.95 (ISBN 0-913836-47-8). St Vladimirs.

Tradition in the Eastern Orthodox Church. pap. 0.25 (ISBN 0-686-16369-9). Eastern Orthodox.

Williams, George, tr. Orthodox Church of the East in the Eighteenth Century. LC 73-131028. Repr. of 1868 ed. 21.00 (ISBN 0-404-06977-0). AMS Pr.

--Orthodox Church of the East in the Eighteenth Century. LC 73-131028. Repr. of 1868 ed. 21.00 (ISBN 0-404-06977-0). AMS Pr.

ORTHODOX EASTERN CHURCH–HYMNS

Bogolepov, Alexander. Orthodox Hymns of Christmas, Easter, & Holy Week. LC 65-16177. 78p. 1965. pap. 1.95 (ISBN 0-913836-02-8). St Vladimirs.

Holy Transfiguration Monastery, ed. Selected Byzantine Hymns. (Orig.). 1981. pap. 6.50x (ISBN 0-913026-50-6). St Nectarios.

Neale, John M. Hymns of the Eastern Church. LC 77-131029. Repr. of 1862 ed. 17.95 (ISBN 0-404-04666-5). AMS Pr.

Von Gardner, Johann. Russian Church Singing: Orthodox Worship & Hymnography, Vol. I. LC 79-27480. 146p. 1980. pap. 6.95 (ISBN 0-913836-59-1). St Vladimirs.

ORTHODOX EASTERN CHURCH–LITURGY AND RITUAL

Aphraates, Saint. Prayer. 1975. pap. 0.25 (ISBN 0-686-10940-6). Eastern Orthodox.

Budge, E. A. Sayings of the Fathers. 1975. pap. 3.95 (ISBN 0-686-10941-4). Eastern Orthodox.

Cabasilas, Nicholas. Commentary on the Divine Liturgy. Hussey, J. M. & McNulty, P. A., trs. from Greek. LC 62-53410. 120p. 1977. pap. 4.95 (ISBN 0-913836-37-0). St Vladimirs.

Cyril Of Jerusalem, Saint St. Cyril of Jerusalem on the Sacraments. 83p. 1977. pap. 3.95 (ISBN 0-913836-39-7). St Vladimirs.

Dabovich, Sebastian. Holy Orthodox Church: Its Ritual, Services, & Sacraments. 1898. pap. 1.50 (ISBN 0-686-00253-9). Eastern Orthodox.

Harakas, S. Living the Liturgy. 1974. pap. 3.95 (ISBN 0-937032-17-4). Light&Life Pub Co MN.

Holy Transfiguration Monastery, tr. from Greek. The Lamentations: From the Matins of Holy & Great Saturday. 65p. (Orig.). 1981. pap. 4.95x (ISBN 0-913026-51-4). St Nectarios.

Hopko, T., et al. God & Charity: Images of Eastern Orthodox Theology, Spirituality & Practice. Costa, Francis D., ed. LC 79-3027. (Pan-Am Books). 103p. (Orig.). 1979. pap. text ed. 3.95 (ISBN 0-916586-34-0). Holy Cross Orthodox.

King, Archdale A. Rites of Eastern Christendom, 2 Vols. LC 70-142246. Repr. of 1948 ed. Set. 84.50 (ISBN 0-404-03677-5). Vol. 1 (ISBN 0-404-03678-3). Vol. 2 (ISBN 0-404-03679-1). AMS Pr.

King, John G. Rites & Ceremonies of the Greek Church in Russia. LC 73-126673. Repr. of 1772 ed. 34.50 (ISBN 0-404-03692-9). AMS Pr.

Kucharek, Casimir. The Sacramental Mysteries: A Byzantine Approach. 1976. 15.75 (ISBN 0-911726-17-9); pap. 12.75 (ISBN 0-911726-25-X). Alleluia Pr.

Ledkovsky, Boris. Great Vespers. (Music Ser.). 218p. 1976. pap. 10.00 (ISBN 0-913836-26-5). St Vladimirs.

Littledale, Richard F. Offices from the Service Books of the Holy Eastern Church. LC 77-133819. 1970. Repr. of 1863 ed. 24.50 (ISBN 0-404-03996-0). AMS Pr.

Makrakis, Apostolos. Catechesis of the Orthodox Church. rev. ed. Orthodox Christian Educational Society, ed. 239p. 1969. pap. text ed. 4.00x (ISBN 0-938366-14-9). Orthodox Chr.

Margoliouth, B. Liturgy of the Nile. 1979. pap. 3.50 (ISBN 0-686-25223-3). Eastern Orthodox.

Mother Mary & Archimandrite Kallistos Ware, trs. The Festal Menaion. 248p. 1977. pap. 12.95 (ISBN 0-571-11137-8, Pub. by Faber & Faber). Merrimack Bk Serv.

Nestorian Church. Liturgy & Ritual: The Liturgy of the Holy Apostles Adai & Mari. LC 79-131032. Repr. of 1893 ed. 14.50 (ISBN 0-404-03997-9). AMS Pr.

Orloff, Nicholas. Horologion or the Book of Hours. pap. 7.95 (ISBN 0-686-25552-6). Eastern Orthodox.

Orthodox Eastern Church. The General Menaion, or the Book of Services Common to the Festivals of Our Lord Jesus Christ, of the Holy Virgin, & of the Different Orders of Saints. Orloff, Nicholas, tr. from Old Slavonic. pap. 7.95 (ISBN 0-686-25551-8). Eastern Orthodox.

--Offices of the Oriental Church. LC 73-79805. Repr. of 1884 ed. 16.75 (ISBN 0-404-00874-7). AMS Pr.

--Prayers for the Dead. pap. 0.25 (ISBN 0-686-05659-0). Eastern Orthodox.

Orthodox Eastern Church--Russian. Service to St. Tikhon of Zadonsk (Text in Old Church Slavonic) 1977. pap. 5.00 (ISBN 0-686-19233-8). Eastern Orthodox.

Prayers of the Early Christians. 1979. pap. 2.00 (ISBN 0-686-25225-X). Eastern Orthodox.

Puhalo, Lev. The Twelve Great Feasts for Young People. (Illus., Orig.). (gr. 4-12). pap. 3.50 (ISBN 0-913026-98-0). St Nectarios.

Raya, Joseph & De Vinck, Jose. Musical Setting for the Liturgy of St. John Chrysostom. (Illus.). 44p. 1971. pap. 2.00 (ISBN 0-911726-05-5). Alleluia Pr.

Schmemann, Alexander. Introduction to Liturgical Theology. LC 66-69197. 170p. 1966. pap. 5.95 (ISBN 0-913836-18-4). St Vladimirs.

Shann, G. V. Book of the Needs of the Holy Orthodox Church. LC 77-82258. 1969. Repr. of 1894 ed. 19.45 (ISBN 0-404-05951-1). AMS Pr.

--Euchology: A Manual of Prayers of the Holy Orthodox Church. LC 75-82260. 1969. Repr. of 1891 ed. 32.50 (ISBN 0-404-05952-X). AMS Pr.

Shorter Catechism of the Orthodox Church. pap. 0.25 (ISBN 0-686-05664-7). Eastern Orthodox.

Vaporis, Nomikos M. The Orthodox Marriage Service. LC 77-14992. 30p. 1977. pap. 1.50 (ISBN 0-916586-12-X). Holy Cross Orthodox.

Vaporis, Nomikos M., ed. Mikron Euchologion: An Orthodox Prayer Book. Gelsinger, Michael, tr. from Greek. & pref. by. LC 77-77642. 1977. 10.95 (ISBN 0-916586-09-X). Holy Cross Orthodox.

--An Orthodox Prayer Book. Von Holzhausen, John & Gelsinger, Michael, trs. from Greek. LC 77-13874. 1977. pap. 6.00 (ISBN 0-916586-11-1). Holy Cross Orthodox.

Ware, K. Communion & Intercommunion. 1980. pap. 1.95 (ISBN 0-937032-20-4). Light&Life Pub Co MN.

Winckler, G. Prayer Attitude in the Eastern Church. pap. 1.25 (ISBN 0-937032-01-8). Light & Life Pub Co MN.

ORTHODOX EASTERN CHURCH–MYSTICISM

see Mysticism–Orthodox Eastern Church

ORTHODOX EASTERN CHURCH–RELATIONS–ANGLICAN COMMUNION

Istavridis, Vasil T. Orthodoxy & Anglicanism. 1966. 10.00x (ISBN 0-8401-1183-5). Allenson-Breckinridge.

Overbeck, J. J. Catholic Orthodoxy & Anglo-Catholicism. LC 76-81771. Repr. of 1866 ed. 10.00 (ISBN 0-404-04839-0). AMS Pr.

ORTHODOX EASTERN CHURCH–RELATIONS–CATHOLIC CHURCH

see also Schism–Eastern and Western Church

Anthimos. Reply of the Orthodox Church to Roman Catholic Overtures on Reunion: Being the Answer of the Great Church of Constantinople to a Papal Encyclical on Reunion. pap. 1.00 (ISBN 0-686-11504-X). Eastern Orthodox.
--The Reply of the Orthodox Church to Roman Catholic Overtures on Reunion. 1977. pap. 1.00 (ISBN 0-913026-15-8). St Nectarios.
Encyclical Epistle of the One Holy Catholic & Apistolic Church: Being a Reply to the Epistle of Pius IX to the Easterns. pap. 1.50 (ISBN 0-686-05641-8). Eastern Orthodox.
Halecki, Oscar. From Florence to Brest, 1439-1596. 2nd ed. 1968. 22.50 (ISBN 0-208-00702-4, Archon). Shoe String.
Kilmartin, Edward. Toward Reunion: The Orthodox & Roman Catholic Churches. LC 79-88570. 1979. pap. 4.95 (ISBN 0-8091-2236-7). Paulist Pr.
Makrakis, Apostolos. The Innovations of the Roman Church. 82p. (Orig.). 1966. pap. 1.50x (ISBN 0-938366-39-4). Orthodox Chr.
Metropolitan Philaret of Moscow. Comparison of the Differences in the Doctrines of Faith Between the Eastern & Western Churches. Pinkerton, Robert, tr. from Rus. 1974. pap. 1.00 (ISBN 0-686-10206-1). Eastern Orthodox.
Norden, Walter. Papsttum Und Byzanz: Das Problem Ihrer Wiedervereinigung Bis Zum Untergange Des Byzantinischen Reichs (1453) 1903. 40.50 (ISBN 0-8337-2571-8). B Franklin.
Soldatow, George, ed. Archpriest Alexis Toth: Selected Letters, Sermons & Articles. LC 78-52665. (Synaxis Archive Ser.: Collection 1, Vol. 1). (Illus.). 83p. (Orig.). 1978. pap. 5.00x (ISBN 0-913026-94-8). St Nectarios.

ORTHODOX EASTERN CHURCH-RELATIONS-PROTESTANT CHURCHES

Confession of Dositheus. pap. 1.50 (ISBN 0-686-05640-X). Eastern Orthodox.
Makrakis, Apostolos. An Orthodox Protestant Debate. Cummings, Denver, tr. 101p. 1949. pap. 2.00x (ISBN 0-938366-37-8). Orthodox Chr.
Spoer, Hans H. Aid for Churchmen, Episcopal & Orthodox. LC 71-79152. Repr. of 1930 ed. 12.50 (ISBN 0-404-06197-4). AMS Pr.

ORTHODOX EASTERN CHURCH-SERMONS

Coniaris, A. M. Eighty Talks for Orthodox Young People. 1975. pap. 3.50 (ISBN 0-937032-16-6). Light&Life Pub Co MN.
Coniaris, Anthony M. Sermons on the Major Holy Days of the Orthodox Church. 1978. pap. 4.95 (ISBN 0-937032-03-4). Light & Life Pub Co MN.
--Sixty-One Talks for Orthodox Funerals. 1969. pap. 4.95 (ISBN 0-937032-02-6). Light & Life Pub Co MN.
Orloff, Nicholas. Octoechos or the Book of Eight Tones. 1979. text ed. 8.95 (ISBN 0-686-25224-1). Eastern Orthodox.
St. Cyril, Bishop of Jerusalem. Five Instructions on the Sacraments. 1974. pap. 1.00 (ISBN 0-686-10197-9). Eastern Orthodox.

ORTHODOX EASTERN CHURCH, GREEK

Anatolius, Bishop of Mohilew & Mstislaw. Greek Orthodox Faith: Scriptural Presentation. Bjerring, Nicholas, tr. from Rus. 1974. pap. 1.00 (ISBN 0-686-10205-3). Eastern Orthodox.
Every, George. Byzantine Patriarchate, Four Hundred Fifty One - Twelve Hundred Four. 2nd rev. ed. LC 78-63340. (The Crusades & Military Orders: Second Ser.). Repr. of 1962 ed. 21.50 (ISBN 0-404-17015-3). AMS Pr.
Frazee, Charles A. Orthodox Church in Independent Greece 1821-52. LC 69-10488. 1969. 36.00 (ISBN 0-521-07247-6, 6). Cambridge U Pr.
Kalomiros, Alexander. Against False Union. 2nd ed. Gabriel, George, tr. from Greek. (Illus., Orig.). 1979. pap. 2.50 (ISBN 0-913026-20-4). St Nectarios.
King, John G. Rites & Ceremonies of the Greek Church in Russia. LC 73-126673. Repr. of 1772 ed. 34.50 (ISBN 0-404-03692-9). AMS Pr.
Meyendorff, John. Byzantine Theology: Historical Trends & Doctrinal Themes. 2nd ed. LC 72-94167. 1978. pap. 8.00 (ISBN 0-8232-0967-9). Fordham.
Papadopoullos, Theodore H. Studies & Documents Relating to the History of the Greek Church & People Under Turkish Domination. LC 78-38759. Repr. of 1952 ed. 27.50 (ISBN 0-404-56314-7). AMS Pr.
Payne, Robert. The Holy Fire. LC 79-27594. 328p. 1980. pap. 8.95 (ISBN 0-913836-61-3). St Vladimirs.
Samaras, Kallistos G., ed. Holy Cross Service Book. pap. 7.00 (ISBN 0-916586-23-5). Holy Cross Orthodox.
Scourby, Alice. Third Generation Greek Americans: A Study of Religious Attitudes. Cordasco, Francesco, ed. LC 80-893. (American Ethnic Groups Ser.). lib. bdg. 14.00x (ISBN 0-405-13454-1). Arno.
Vaporis, Nomikos M., ed. The Holy Gospel. 95.00 (ISBN 0-916586-25-1). Holy Cross Orthodox.
--Post-Byzantine Ecclesiastical Personalities. LC 78-11037. pap. 3.95 (ISBN 0-916586-30-8). Holy Cross Orthodox.
Ware, Timothy. Eustratios Argenti: Study of the Greek Church Under Turkish Rule. 1974. Repr. of 1964 ed. 7.50x (ISBN 0-686-10203-7). Eastern Orthodox.

ORTHODOX EASTERN CHURCH, RUSSIAN

Anderson, Paul B. People, Church & State in Modern Russia. LC 79-5204. 240p. 1980. Repr. of 1944 ed. 21.00 (ISBN 0-8305-0058-8). Hyperion Conn.
Blackmore, R. W., et al. Doctrine of the Russian Church. Blackmore, R. W., tr. from Rus. 1973. 15.00 (ISBN 0-686-05407-5). Eastern Orthodox.
Blane, Andrew, ed. Georges Florovsky - Russian Intellectual & Orthodox Churchman: Russia & Orthodoxy, Vol. 1. 1978. text ed. write for info (ISBN 0-686-22645-3). Mouton.
Bogolepov, Alexander. Church Reforms in Russia, 1905-1918. 59p. 1966. pap. 1.95 (ISBN 0-913836-01-X). St Vladimirs.
Brotherhood of St. Herman of Alaska. St. Herman Calendar of Orthodox Saints. pap. 5.00 (ISBN 0-686-05410-5). Eastern Orthodox.
Bulgakov, Sergius. A Bulgakov Anthology: From Marxism to Christian Orthodoxy. Zernov, Nicolas & Pain, James, eds. LC 76-23245. 1976. 12.50 (ISBN 0-664-21338-3). Westminster.
The Collected Works of Georges Florovsky, Vol. 7. Date not set. write for info. (ISBN 0-685-61623-1). Nordland Pub.
The Collected Works of Georges Florovsky, Vol. 8. Date not set. write for info. (ISBN 0-685-61624-X). Nordland Pub.
Fletcher, William C. The Russian Orthodox Church Underground, 1917-1970. 324p. 1971. 12.95x (ISBN 0-19-213952-5). Oxford U Pr.
Gagarin, Jean X. Russian Clergy. LC 70-131035. Repr. of 1872 ed. 21.00 (ISBN 0-404-02666-4). AMS Pr.
Garrett, Paul D. St. Innocent: Apostle to America. LC 79-19634. 345p. 1979. pap. 8.95 (ISBN 0-913836-60-5). St Vladimirs.
Heard, Albert F. Russian Church & Russian Dissent. LC 70-127907. Repr. of 1887 ed. 24.50 (ISBN 0-404-03198-6). AMS Pr.
Khrapovitsky, Antony. Confession. Birchall, Christopher, tr. from Rus. LC 74-29537. 100p. (Orig.). 1975. pap. 3.00 (ISBN 0-88465-005-7). Holy Trinity.
King, John G. Rites & Ceremonies of the Greek Church in Russia. LC 73-126673. Repr. of 1772 ed. 34.50 (ISBN 0-404-03692-9). AMS Pr.
Pascal, Pierre. The Religion of the Russian People. LC 76-24462. 130p. 1976. pap. 4.95 (ISBN 0-913836-30-3). St Vladimirs.
Pierce, Richard A., ed. The Russian Orthodox Religious Mission in America, 1794-1837. Bearne, Colin, tr. (Alaska History Ser.: No. 11). 1977. 15.50 (ISBN 0-919642-80-2). Limestone Pr.
Platon. Orthodox Doctrine of the Apostolic Eastern Church. 1973. 5.00 (ISBN 0-686-05409-1). Eastern Orthodox.
--Present State of the Greek Church in Russia. LC 75-131031. Repr. of 1815 ed. 21.50 (ISBN 0-404-05059-X). AMS Pr.
Rodzianko, M. The Truth About the Russian Church Abroad. Hilko, Michael P., tr. from Rus. LC 74-29321. (Illus.). 48p. (Orig.). 1975. pap. 1.50 (ISBN 0-88465-004-9). Holy Trinity.
Schmemann, Alexander, ed. Ultimate Questions: An Anthology of Modern Russian Religious Thought. 310p. 1977. pap. 7.95 (ISBN 0-913836-46-X). St Vladimirs.
Skhi-Igumen, John. Christ Is in Our Midst: Letters from a Russian Monk. Williams, Esther, tr. from Rus. LC 80-10530. 168p. (Orig.). 1980. pap. 4.95 (ISBN 0-913836-64-8). St Vladimirs.
Smirnoff, Peter. Instruction in God's Law. 1974. pap. 5.00 (ISBN 0-686-10199-5). Eastern Orthodox.
Stroyen, William B. Communist Russia & the Russian Orthodox Church 1943-1962. 1967. 11.95 (ISBN 0-8132-0322-8). Cath U Pr.
Ware, Kallistos T. Orthodox Way. 196p. 1979. pap. 3.95 (ISBN 0-913836-58-3). St Vladimirs.
Zernov, Nicholas. Moscow, the Third Rome. 2nd ed. LC 76-149664. Repr. of 1938 ed. 12.50 (ISBN 0-404-07075-2). AMS Pr.
Zernov, Nicolas. The Russians & Their Church. 196p. 1977. pap. 5.95 (ISBN 0-913836-36-2). St Vladimirs.

ORTHODOX EASTERN CHURCH, RUSSIAN-HISTORY

Curtiss, John S. The Russian Church & the Soviet State, 1917-1950. 1953. 7.50 (ISBN 0-8446-1141-7). Peter Smith.
Fireside, Harvey. Icon & Swastika: The Russian Orthodox Church Under Nazi & Soviet Control. LC 70-123567. (Russian Research Center Studies: No. 62). 1971. 12.50x (ISBN 0-674-44160-5). Harvard U Pr.
Fletcher, William C. Study in Survival: The Russian Orthodox Church, 1927-1943. 1965. 4.95 (ISBN 0-02-539020-1). Macmillan.
Freeze, Gregory L. The Russian Levites: Parish Clergy in the Eighteenth Century. (Russian Research Center Studies: 78). 1977. 18.50x (ISBN 0-674-78175-9). Harvard U Pr.
Gardner, Johann v. Bogosluzhebncje penije Russkoj Pravoslavnoj Tserkvi: Suschnost' Sistema I Istoria: Liturgical Chant of the Russian Orthodox Church: Its Essence, Structure & History, Vol. 1. LC 77-77086. (Illus., Orig., Rus.). 1979. text ed. 30.00 (ISBN 0-88465-008-1); pap. text ed. 25.00 (ISBN 0-686-50014-8). Holy Trinity.
Hale, Charles. Russian Missions in China & Japan. 1974. pap. 1.50 (ISBN 0-686-10198-7). Eastern Orthodox.
Nichols, Robert L. & Stavrou, Theofanis G., eds. Russian Orthodoxy Under the Old Regime. LC 78-3196. 1978. 16.50x (ISBN 0-8166-0846-6); pap. text ed. 6.95x (ISBN 0-8166-0847-4). U of Minn Pr.
Smirnoff, Eugene. Russian Orthodox Missions. pap. 3.50 (ISBN 0-686-01299-2). Eastern Orthodox.
Wallace, Fern. Tides of Change: A History of the Russian Orthodox Mission in Alaska. 1977. pap. 5.00 (ISBN 0-913026-78-6, Synaxis Pr). St Nectarios.

ORTHODOX EASTERN CHURCH, SERBIAN

Vrga, Djuro J. & Fahey, Frank J. Changes & Socio-Religious Conflict in an Ethnic Minority Group: The Serbian Orthodox Church in America. LC 74-31771. 1975. softcover 8.00 (ISBN 0-88247-335-2). Ragusan Pr.

ORTHODOX EASTERN MONASTICISM AND RELIGIOUS ORDERS

see Monasticism and Religious Orders, Orthodox Eastern

ORTHODOX JUDAISM

see also Jewish Sects

Associations of Orthodox Jewish Scientists. Proceedings, Vol. 3 & 4. Rosner, Fred, ed. 248p. 1976. pap. 7.95 (ISBN 0-87306-074-1). Feldheim.
Bulka, Rueven P. Dimensions of American Orthodox Judiasm. Date not set. 20.00x (ISBN 0-87068-894-4). Ktav.
Heilman, Samuel C. Synagogue Life: A Study in Symbolic Interaction. LC 75-36403. 1976. 12.95 (ISBN 0-226-32488-5); pap. 4.95 (ISBN 0-226-32490-7, P824, Phoen). U of Chicago Pr.

ORTHOEPY

see Phonetics

ORTHOGONAL FUNCTIONS

see Functions, Orthogonal

ORTHOGONAL POLYNOMIALS

see also Chebyshev Polynomials

Askey, Richard. Orthogonal Polynomials & Special Functions. (CBMS Regional Conference Ser.: Vol. 21). (Orig.). 1975. pap. text ed. 10.65 (ISBN 0-89871-018-9). Soc Indus-Appl Math.
Beckmann, Petr. Orthogonal Polynomials for Engineers & Physicists. LC 72-87318. 1973. 18.95x (ISBN 0-911762-14-0). Golem.
Boas, R. P., Jr. & Buck, R. C. Polynomial Expansions of Analytic Functions. 2nd ed. (Ergebnisse der Mathematik und Ihrer Grenzgebiete: Vol. 19). (Illus.). 1964. 23.10 (ISBN 0-387-03123-5). Springer-Verlag.
Chihara, T. S. An Introduction to Orthogonal Polynomials. (Mathematics & Its Applications Ser.). 1978. 51.25x (ISBN 0-677-04150-0). Gordon.
Freud, Geza. Orthogonal Polynomials. LC 76-134028. 1971. 42.00 (ISBN 0-08-016047-6). Pergamon.
Geronimus, L. Ya. Orthogonal Polynomials: Estimates, Asymptotic Formulas, & Series of Polynomials Orthogonal on the Unit Circle & on an Interval. LC 60-53450. 242p. 1961. 32.50 (ISBN 0-306-10565-9, Consultants). Plenum Pub.
Nevai, Paul G. Orthogonal Polynomials. LC 78-32112. (Memoirs: No. 213). 1980. Repr. of 1979 ed. 9.20 (ISBN 0-8218-2213-6). Am Math.
Steklov Institute of Mathematics, Academy of Sciences, U S S R, No. 100 & Svetin, P. K. Polynomials Orthogonal Over a Region & Bieberbach Polynomials: Proceedings. 1974. 30.00 (ISBN 0-8218-3000-7, STEKLO-100). Am Math.
Szego, Gabor. Orthogonal Polynomials. 4th ed. LC 39-33497. (Colloquium Pubns. Ser.: Vol. 23). 1978. 30.40 (ISBN 0-8218-1023-5, COLL-23). Am Math.

ORTHOGONAL SERIES

see Series, Orthogonal

ORTHOGRAPHIC PROJECTION

Quinlan, Charles, Jr. Orthographic Projection Simplified. rev. ed. (gr. 9-10). 1969. pap. text ed. 5.00 (ISBN 0-87345-056-6). McKnight.

ORTHOGRAPHY

see Spelling Reform;
also subdivision Orthography and spelling under names of languages, e.g. English Language-Orthography-Spelling

ORTHOMOLECULAR MEDICINE

see also Chemotherapy; Nutrition

Applewhite, Philip B. Molecular Gods: How Molecules Determine Our Behavior. LC 80-22834. (Illus.). 288p. 1981. 10.95 (ISBN 0-13-599530-2). P-H.
Hoffer, Abram & Walker, Morton. Ortho-Molecular Nutrition. (Orig.). 1981. pap. 4.95x (ISBN 0-686-76746-2). Regent House.
Williams, Roger J. & Kalita, Dwight K., eds. A Physician's Handbook on Orthomolecular Medicine. LC 79-65494. 1979. pap. 7.95 (ISBN 0-87983-199-5). Keats.
--A Physician's Handbook on Orthomolecular Medicine. LC 77-8304. 1977. text ed. 19.95 (ISBN 0-08-021533-5). Pergamon.

ORTHOMOLECULAR THERAPY

see Orthomolecular Medicine

ORTHOPEDIA

see also Orthodontics; Orthopedic Nursing; Orthopedic Surgery; Pediatric Orthopedia; Veterinary Orthopedics
also special conditions to which orthopedic methods are applicable, e.g. Hip Joints-Diseases; Spine-Abnormities and Deformities

Adams, John C., ed. Outline of Orthopaedics. 9th ed. LC 80-40931. (Illus.). 486p. 1981. pap. text ed. 18.75 (ISBN 0-686-31316-X). Churchill.
Aegerter, Ernest E. & Kilpatrick, John A., Jr. Orthopedic Diseases: Physiology, Pathology, Radiology. 4th ed. LC 74-4551. (Illus.). 791p. 1975. text ed. 37.50 (ISBN 0-7216-1062-5). Saunders.
Albright, James A. & Brand, Richard A., eds. The Scientific Basis of Orthopedics. (Illus.). 448p. 1979. 32.00 (ISBN 0-8385-8503-5). ACC.
Allgoewer, M. The Dynamic Compression Plate (DCP) LC 73-13494. (Illus.). 1978. pap. 13.20 (ISBN 0-387-06466-4). Springer-Verlag.
American Academy of Orthopaedic Surgeons. Instructional Course Lectures, Vol. 30. LC 43-17054. (Illus.). 576p. 1981. text ed. 52.50 (ISBN 0-8016-0048-0). Mosby.
American Academy of Orthopedic Surgeons. Joint Motion: Method of Measuring & Recording. (Illus.). 1972. pap. 3.75 (ISBN 0-443-00270-3). Churchill.
Apley, A. Graham. System of Orthopedics & Fractures. 5th ed. 1977. 56.95 (ISBN 0-407-40653-0). Butterworth.
Association of Bone & Joint Surgeons. A. R. Shands, Jr. Birthday Celebration Issue. Urist, Marshall R., ed. (Clinical Orthopaedics Ser., Vol. 76). 1971. 15.00 (ISBN 0-685-22854-1, JBL-Med-Nursing). Har-Row.
--Articular Cartilage in Health & Disease. Urist, Marshall R., ed. (Clinical Orthopaedics Ser., Vol. 64). 1969. 15.00 (ISBN 0-685-22845-2, JBL-Med-Nursing). Har-Row.
--Bone Mass. Urist, Marshall R., ed. (Clinical Orthopaedics Ser., Vol. 65). 1969. 15.00 (ISBN 0-685-22846-0, JBL-Med-Nursing). Har-Row.
--Clinical Orthopaedics & Related Research: Vol. 85, AOFS Surgery of the Foot. Urist, Marshall R., ed. 1972. 15.00 (ISBN 0-685-27031-9, JBL-Med-Nursing). Har-Row.
--Clinical Orthopaedics & Related Research: Vol. 86, Progress in Hip Joint Surgery. Urist, Marshall R., ed. 1972. 15.00 (ISBN 0-685-27032-7, JBL-Med-Nursing). Har-Row.
--Clinical Orthopaedics & Related Research: Vol. 80, Problems of Unusual Interest. Urist, Marshall R., ed. 1971. 15.00 (ISBN 0-685-27028-9, JBL-Med-Nursing). Har-Row.
--Creativity in Orthopaedics: Marius N. Smith-Peterson Commemoration. Urist, Marshall R., ed. (Clinical Orthopaedics Ser., Vol. 66). 1969. 15.00 (ISBN 0-685-22847-9, JBL-Med-Nursing). Har-Row.
--The Education of Orthopaedic Surgeons. Urist, Marshall R., ed. (Clinical Orthopaedics Ser., Vol. 75). 1971. 15.00 (ISBN 0-685-22853-3, JBL-Med-Nursing). Har-Row.
--Gout. Urist, Marshall R., ed. (Clinical Orthopaedics Ser., Vol. 71). 1970. 15.00 (ISBN 0-685-22851-7, JBL-Med-Nursing). Har-Row.
--New Surgical Approaches, Vol. 91. Urist, Marshall, ed. (Clinical Orthopaedics & Related Research Ser.). 1973. 15.00 (ISBN 0-685-34612-9, JBL-Med-Nursing). Har-Row.
--Orthopaedics & the Arts & Letters, Vol. 89. Urist, Marshall, ed. (Clinical Orthopaedics & Related Research Ser.). 1972. 15.00 (ISBN 0-685-34610-2, JBL-Med-Nursing). Har-Row.

--The Present Status of Calciphylaxis. Urist, Marshall R., ed. (Clinical Orthopaedics Ser., Vol. 69). 1970. 15.00 (ISBN 0-685-22849-5, JBL-Med-Nursing); new subscribers 8.00 (ISBN 0-685-22850-9). Har-Row.

--Robert W. Johnson Jr., 77th Birthday Celebration. Urist, Marshall R. & De Palma, Anthony F., eds. (Clinical Orthopaedics & Related Research Ser. No. 56). (Illus.). 15.00 (ISBN 0-685-24742-2, JBL-Med-Nursing). Har-Row.

--Three Endeavors or Walter Blount: A Trubute to Dr. Walter P. Blount on His Seventieth Birthday. Urist, Marshall R., ed. (Clinical Orthopaedics Ser., Vol. 77). 1971. 15.00 (ISBN 0-685-22855-X, JBL-Med-Nursing). Har-Row.

Aston, J. N. Short Textbook of Orthopaedics & Traumatology. (Illus.). 1976. pap. text ed. 9.00 (ISBN 0-397-58205-6, JBL-Med-Nursing). Har-Row.

Beary, John F., 3rd, et al. Manual of Rheumatology & Outpatient Orthopedic Disorders: Diagnosis & Therapy. Gibofsky, Allan, ed. (Little, Brown Spiral Manual Ser.). 1981. pap. text ed. 13.95 (ISBN 0-316-08575-8). Little.

Bentley, G. Orthopedics, Vol. 1. (Operative Surgery Ser.). 1979. 125.00 (ISBN 0-407-00630-3). Butterworth.

Bentley, G., ed. Orthopedics, Vol. 2. (Operative Surgery Ser.). 1979. 125.00 (ISBN 0-407-00631-1). Butterworth.

Bernbeck, Rupprecht & Sinios, Alexander. Neuro-Orthopedic Screening in Infancy: Schedules, Examination & Findings. LC 78-2505. (Illus.). 120p. 1978. text ed. 16.50 (ISBN 0-8067-0231-1). Urban & S.

Bick, Edgard M., ed. Classics of Orthopaedics. (Illus.). 1976. 29.00 (ISBN 0-397-58194-7, JBL-Med-Nursing). Har-Row.

Blauvelt, Carolyn T. & Nelson, Fred. A Manual of Orthopaedic Terminology. 2nd ed. LC 81-4029. (Illus.). 257p. 1981. pap. text ed. 19.95 (ISBN 0-8016-0752-3). Mosby.

Blauvelt, Carolyn T. & Nelson, Fred R. A Manual of Orthopedic Terminology. LC 77-3948. (Illus.). 1977. text ed. 18.50 (ISBN 0-8016-0746-9). Mosby.

Breig, Alf. Adverse Mechanical Tension of the Central Nervous System: An Analysis of Cause & Effect. LC 77-88852. 1978. 84.50 (ISBN 0-471-04137-8, Pub. by Wiley Medical). Wiley.

Brooker, Andrew F. & Schmeisser, Gerhard. The Orthopaedic Traction Manual. (Illus.). 124p. 1980. pap. 15.00 (ISBN 0-683-01074-3). Williams & Wilkins.

Brunner, Nancy A. Orthopedic Nursing: A Programmed Approach. 3rd ed. LC 78-32020. (Illus.). 1979. pap. text ed. 11.50 (ISBN 0-8016-0833-3). Mosby.

Bunch, Wilton H. & Keagy, Robert D. Principles of Orthotic Treatment. LC 76-10467. (Illus., Orig.). 1976. 20.95 (ISBN 0-8016-0880-5). Mosby.

Carini, Geraldine & Birmingham, Jacqueline. Traction Made Manageable: A Self Learning Module. (Illus.). 1979. pap. text ed. 7.95 (ISBN 0-07-009841-7). McGraw.

Clark, John. Tether, Contracture, & Deformity. 1976. 27.50x (ISBN 0-685-83929-X). Intl Ideas.

Cochran, George Van B. A Primer Orthopaedic Biomechanics. (Illus.). 1981. text ed. write for info. (ISBN 0-443-08027-5). Churchill.

Cotta, Horst. Orthopedics. (Illus.). 480p. 1980. pap. 18.95 (ISBN 0-8151-1864-3). Year Bk Med.

Coventry, Mark B., ed. Year Book of Orthopedics Nineteen Eighty-One. Date not set. price not set (ISBN 0-8151-1881-3). Year Bk Med.

--Yearbook of Orthopedics, 1980. 1980. 31.95 (ISBN 0-8151-1879-1). Year Bk Med.

Cozen, L. Office Orthopedics. 4th ed. (Illus.). 588p. 1975. 39.75 (ISBN 0-398-03068-5); pap. 29.75 (ISBN 0-398-03069-3). C C Thomas.

Cozen, Lewis. Difficult Orthopedic Diagnosis. (Illus.). 104p. 1972. text ed. 14.75 (ISBN 0-398-02212-7). C C Thomas.

Cyriax, J. Textbook of Orthopaedic Medicine: Diagnosis of Soft Tissue Lesions, Vol. 1. 7th ed. (Illus.). 1978. text ed. 50.00 (ISBN 0-02-857510-5). Macmillan.

Cyriax, James & Russell, Gillean. Textbook of Orthopaedic Medicine: Treatment by Manipulation, Massage & Injection, Vol. II. 10th ed. (Illus.). 1980. text ed. 45.00 (ISBN 0-02-857490-7). Macmillan.

DeBrunner. Orthopedic Diagnosis. Date not set. price not set (ISBN 0-8151-2371-X). Year Bk Med.

Devas, M., ed. Geriatric Orthopaedics. 1977. 32.00 (ISBN 0-12-213750-7). Acad Pr.

Dumbleton, John H. & Black, Jonathan. An Introduction to Orthopaedic Materials. (Illus.). 268p. 1975. 31.00 (ISBN 0-398-03368-4). C C Thomas.

Edmonson, A. S. Campbell's Operative Orthopaedics, 2 Vols. 6 ed. LC 80-14731. 1980. Set. 189.50 (ISBN 0-8016-1071-0). Mosby.

Elst, E. Vander, ed. Societe International De Chirurgie Orthopedique et De Traumatology: 50 Years of Achievement. (Illus.). 1979. 18.90 (ISBN 0-387-08968-3). Springer-Verlag.

Ficat, R. Paul & Hungerford, David S. Disorders of the Patello-Femoral Joint. (Illus.). 200p. 1977. 31.50 (ISBN 0-683-03200-3). Williams & Wilkins.

Flatt, Adrian E. The Care of Coqenital Hand Anomalies. LC 77-5932. (Illus.). 1977. text ed. 40.50 (ISBN 0-8016-1586-0). Mosby.

Frost, Harold M. Orthopaedic Biomechanics: Orthopaedic Lectures, Vol. 5. (Illus.). 664p. 1973. 49.50 (ISBN 0-398-02824-9). C C Thomas.

Ghista, D. N. & Roaf, R., eds. Orthopaedic Mechanics: Procedures & Devices. 1979. 51.50 (ISBN 0-12-281650-1). Acad Pr.

Ghista, Dhanjoo N. & Roaf, R., eds. Orthopaedic Mechanics, Procedures & Devices. 1981. Vol. II August, 1981. write for info. (ISBN 0-12-281602-1); Vol. III, September, 1981. write for info. (ISBN 0-12-281603-X). Acad Pr.

Goldstein, Louis A. & Dickerson, Robert C. Atlas of Orthopaedic Surgery, Vol. 1 & 2. LC 74-12842. (Illus.). 1974. 150.00 set (ISBN 0-8016-1883-5). Mosby.

Hafner. Radiologic Examination in Orthopaedics. (Illus.). 1976. 57.50 (ISBN 0-8391-0897-4). Univ Park.

Hall, Hamilton. The Back Doctor. 288p. Date not set. 10.95 (ISBN 0-07-025626-8, GB). McGraw.

Hensinger, Robert N. Neonatal Orthopaedics. (Monograph in Neonatology Ser.). (Illus.). 336p. 1981. 39.50 (ISBN 0-8089-1355-7). Grune.

Hilt, Nancy E. & Cogburn, Shirley B. Manual of Orthopedics. LC 79-31732. (Illus.). 1979. text ed. 36.50 (ISBN 0-8016-2198-4). Mosby.

Hilt, Nancy E. & Schmitt, E. William, Jr. Pediatric Orthopedic Nursing. LC 74-13222. (Illus.). 1975. text ed. 16.95 (ISBN 0-8016-2188-7). Mosby.

Iversen, Larry D. & Clawson, D. Kay. Manual of Acute Orthopaedic Therapeutics. 1977. 13.95 (ISBN 0-316-43430-2). Little.

Johnson, Lanny L. Comprehensive Arthroscopic Examination of the Knee. LC 77-21646. (Illus.). 1977. 47.50 (ISBN 0-8016-2534-3). Mosby.

Kane, W. J. Current Orthopaedic Management. (Illus.). 352p. 1981. looseleaf binder ed. 35.00 (ISBN 0-443-08080-1). Churchill.

Kennedy, John C. The Injured Adolescent Knee. (Illus.). 1979. 29.95 (ISBN 0-683-04594-6). Williams & Wilkins.

Kessel. Color Atlas of Orthopaedics. 1980. 55.00 (ISBN 0-8151-5021-0). Year Bk Med.

Kuntscher, G. The Callous Problem. (Illus.). 160p. 1974. 9.50 (ISBN 0-87527-133-2). Green.

Kurlyandsky, V. Orthopaedic Stomatology. MIR Publishers, tr. from Rus. (Illus.). 690p. 1975. text ed. 26.00x (ISBN 0-8464-0694-2). Beekman Pubs.

Lambert, Charles E. & Stone, Donald. Orthopaedic Physician's Assistant Techniques. LC 74-77819. (Allied Health Ser). 1975. pap. 7.05 (ISBN 0-672-61388-3). Bobbs.

McKibbin, Brian, ed. Recent Advances in Orthopaedics, No. 3. (Illus.). 1980. text ed. 34.50 (ISBN 0-443-01747-6). Churchill.

McRae, Ronald K. Clinical Orthopaedic Examination. (Illus.). 1976. pap. text ed. 17.25 (ISBN 0-443-01512-0). Churchill.

Menelaus, Malcolm B. The Orthopaedic Management of Spina Bifida Cystica. (Illus.). 304p. 1980. text ed. 49.50 (ISBN 0-443-01993-2). Churchill.

Mercier. Practical Orthopedics. 1980. 29.95 (ISBN 0-8151-5863-7). Year Bk Med.

Miller, William A. The Keys to Orthopedic Anatomy. 164p. 1965. photocopy ed. spiral 14.95 (ISBN 0-398-01314-4). C C Thomas.

Mills, K. L., ed. Guide to Orthopaedics, Vol. 1: Trauma. (Illus.). 280p. 1981. pap. text ed. 25.00x (ISBN 0-443-02018-3). Churchill.

Monk, C. J. Orthopaedics for Undergraduates. 2nd ed. (Illus.). 240p. 1981. pap. text ed. 14.95x (ISBN 0-19-261312-X). Oxford U Pr.

Mubarak, Scott J., et al. Compartment Syndromes & Volkmann's Contracture. (Saunder's Monographs in Clinical Orthopedics: Vol. 3). (Illus.). 200p. 1981. text ed. write for info. (ISBN 0-7216-6604-3). Saunders.

Nickel, Vernon M. Orthopaedic Rehabilitation. (Illus.). 500p. 1981. text ed. write for info. (ISBN 0-443-08060-7). Churchill.

Nicola, Toufick. Atlas of Orthopaedic Exposures. LC 76-14346. 142p. 1976. Repr. of 1966 ed. lib. bdg. 14.50 (ISBN 0-88275-104-2). Krieger.

Owen, Robert, et al. Scientific Foundations of Orthopaedics & Traumatology. (Illus.). 531p. text ed. 95.00 (ISBN 0-7216-7029-6). Saunders.

Perkins, G. The Ruminations of an Orthopaedic Surgeon. (Illus.). 1970. 5.95 (ISBN 0-407-38700-5). Butterworth.

Ramamurti. Orthopaedics in Primary Care. Tinker, Richard, ed. 1979. pap. 36.00 (ISBN 0-683-07150-5). Williams & Wilkins.

Rang, Mercer. Anthology of Orthopaedics. 1977. Repr. 27.50 (ISBN 0-443-00408-0). Churchill.

Schneider, F. Richard. Orthopaedics in Emergency Care. LC 80-12233. (Illus.). 1980. pap. text ed. 11.95 (ISBN 0-8016-4348-1). Mosby.

Schneider, Richard. Handbook for the Orthopaedic Assistant. 2nd ed. LC 76-4850. (Illus.). 1976. 14.95 (ISBN 0-8016-4351-1). Mosby.

Sevitt, Simon. Bone Repair & Fracture Healing in Man. (Current Problems in Orthopaedics Ser.). (Illus.). 300p. 1981. lib. bdg. 87.50 (ISBN 0-443-01806-5). Churchill.

Smith, Roger & Apley, Alan. Biochemical Disorders of the Skeleton. (Postgraduate Orthopedic Ser.). (Illus.). 1979. text ed. 59.95 (ISBN 0-407-00122-0). Butterworth.

Stehsel, Donald L. Farrier's Orthopedics Handbook. LC 73-93862. 157p. 1975. 16.95 (ISBN 0-686-09041-1). Stehsel.

Steindler, Arthur. Lectures on the Interpretation of Pain in Orthopedic Practice. (Illus.). 680p. 1959. photocopy ed. spiral 68.50 (ISBN 0-398-01847-2). C C Thomas.

--Orthopedic Operations. (Illus.). 776p. 1947. photocopy ed. spiral 76.75 (ISBN 0-398-04442-2). C C Thomas.

Stewart, J. D. Traction & Orthopaedic Appliances. LC 74-80738. (Illus.). 210p. 1975. text ed. 19.00x (ISBN 0-443-01196-6). Churchill.

Stradford, H. Todd. Orthopaedics. 4th ed. (Medical Examination Review Book: Vol. 13). 1976. spiral bdg. 16.50 (ISBN 0-87488-113-7). Med Exam.

Stripp, William J. Special Techniques in Orthopaedic Radiography. (Illus.). 1979. pap. text ed. 12.50 (ISBN 0-443-01971-1). Churchill.

Tachdjian, Mihran O. Pediatric Orthopedics, 2 vols. LC 71-103571. (Illus.). 1972. Vol. 1. 40.00 (ISBN 0-7216-8730-X); Vol. 2. 40.00 (ISBN 0-7216-8731-8). Saunders.

Tohen, Z. Alfonso. Manual of Mechanical Orthopaedics. (Illus.). 340p. 1973. 18.75 (ISBN 0-398-02614-9). C C Thomas.

Turek, Samuel L. Orthopaedics: Principles & Their Application. 3rd ed. LC 77-7072. (Illus.). 1977. 89.00 (ISBN 0-397-50360-1). Lippincott.

Vitali, Miroslaw, et al. Amputations & Prostheses. 1978. text ed. 29.50 (ISBN 0-02-859620-X). Macmillan.

Volkov, M. & Dedova, V. Childhood Orthopedics. Aksenova, Ludmila, tr. from Rus. (Eng.). 1974. 12.95x (ISBN 0-8464-0243-2). Beekman Pubs.

Wide, Anders. Handbook of Medical & Orthopedic Gymnastics. (Physical Education Reprint Ser). (Illus.). Repr. of 1905 ed. lib. bdg. 34.50x (ISBN 0-697-00106-7). Irvington.

ORTHOPEDIA–BIBLIOGRAPHY

Wilhelm, Friedrich & Schlegel, Karl F. Surgery of the Spine. Hackenbroch, M. & Witt, A. N., eds. Stiasny, G., tr. LC 76-19607. (Atlas of Orthopaedic Operations: Vol. 1). Orig. Title: Orthopadisch-Chirurgischer Operationsatlas, Band III. (Illus.). 262p. 1980. text ed. 72.50 (ISBN 0-7216-4445-7). Saunders.

ORTHOPEDIA, VETERINARY

see Veterinary Orthopedics

ORTHOPEDIC APPARATUS

see also Artificial Limbs; Wheelchairs

American Academy of Orthopaedic Surgeons. Atlas of Orthotics: Biomechanical Principals & Applications. LC 75-22185. (Illus.). 460p. 1975. 53.50 (ISBN 0-8016-0021-9). Mosby.

Anderson, Miles H. Functional Bracing of the Upper Extremities: The Rationale, Principles, & Techniques of Upper Extremity Bracing to Prevent Deformities & Restore Function. (Illus.). 480p. 1958. ed. spiral bdg. 37.50photocopy (ISBN 0-398-04192-X). C C Thomas.

Bray, Jean & Wright, Sheila, eds. The Use of Technology in the Care of the Elderly & the Disabled. LC 80-17847. xii, 267p. 1980. lib. bdg. 29.95 (ISBN 0-313-22616-4, BTC/). Greenwood.

Ghista, D. N. & Roaf, R., eds. Orthopaedic Mechanics: Procedures & Devices. 1979. 51.50 (ISBN 0-12-281650-1). Acad Pr.

Gleave, J. A. Moulds & Casts for Orthopaedic & Prosthetic Appliances. (Illus.). 192p. 1972. 21.50 (ISBN 0-398-02293-3). C C Thomas.

Kennedy, Joan M. Orthopaedic Splints & Appliances. (Illus.). 1974. pap. text ed. 13.95 (ISBN 0-02-858240-3). Macmillan.

Perry, Jacquelin, ed. Upper Extremity Orthotics: A Monograph. 1978. pap. 2.50 (ISBN 0-912452-22-6). Am Phys Therapy Assn.

Primer of Orthopaedic Biomechanics. (Illus.). 324p. 1973. pap. text ed. 8.75 (ISBN 0-443-00994-5). Churchill.

Redford, John B. Orthotics Etcetera. 2nd ed. (Rehabilitation Medicine Library Ser.). (Illus.). 550p. 1980. lib. bdg. 59.95 (ISBN 0-683-07197-1). Williams & Wilkins.

Robinault, Isabel P. Functional Aids for the Multiply Handicapped. (Illus.). 1973. text ed. 20.50 (ISBN 0-06-142276-2, Harper Medical). Har-Row.

Tohen, Z. Alfonso. Manual of Mechanical Orthopaedics. (Illus.). 340p. 1973. 18.75 (ISBN 0-398-02614-9). C C Thomas.

ORTHOPEDIC MANIPULATION

see Manipulation (Therapeutics)

ORTHOPEDIC NURSING

Allgire, Mildred J. Nurses Can Give & Teach Rehabilitation. 2nd ed. LC 68-8719. (Illus.). 1968. pap. text ed. 3.95 (ISBN 0-8261-0432-0). Springer Pub.

Carini, Geraldine & Birmingham, Jacqueline. Traction Made Manageable: A Self Learning Module. (Illus.). 1979. pap. text ed. 7.95 (ISBN 0-07-009841-7). McGraw.

Czaplinski, Rosemary, et al. Self-Assessment of Current Knowledge in Orthopedic & Rehabilitative Nursing. 1979. pap. 9.50 (ISBN 0-87488-230-3). Med Exam.

Donahoo, Clare A., Jr. & Dimon, Joseph H. Orthopedic Nursing. 1977. 12.95 (ISBN 0-316-18940-5). Little.

Farrell, Jane. Illustrated Guide to Orthopedic Nursing. LC 77-3920. 1977. pap. text ed. 13.50x (ISBN 0-397-54205-4, JBL-Med-Nursing). Har-Row.

Gilchrist, Mary I. & Blockey, Noel J. Paediatric Orthopaedics. (Modern Practical Nursing Ser: No. 1). (Illus.). 1971. pap. text ed. 9.95x (ISBN 0-433-11700-1). Intl Ideas.

Hardy, Alan G. & Elson, Reginald. Practical Management of Spinal Injuries for Nurses. 2nd ed. LC 75-29262. (Illus.). 176p. 1976. text ed. 13.25 (ISBN 0-443-01320-9). Churchill.

Humm, W. Rehabilitation of the Lower Limb Amputee: for Nurses & Therapists. 3rd ed. 1978. text ed. 12.00 (ISBN 0-02-858090-7). Macmillan.

Hynes, V. Barbara. Orthopedic & Rehabilitation Nursing Continuing Education Review. 1976. sprial bdg. 9.50 (ISBN 0-87488-397-0). Med Exam.

Kerr, Avice H. Orthopedic Nursing Procedures: Initial & Emergency Care, Pt. 1. rev., exp. ed. (Illus.). 1980. pap. text ed. 10.95 (ISBN 0-8261-0323-5). Springer Pub.

Larson, Carroll B. & Gould, Marjorie. Orthopedic Nursing. 9th ed. LC 77-3429. (Illus.). 1978. text ed. 18.95 (ISBN 0-8016-2866-0). Mosby.

Mourad, Leona A. Nursing Care of Adults with Orthopedic Conditions. LC 79-26251. 1980. 22.00 (ISBN 0-471-04677-9, Pub. by Wiley Med). Wiley.

Powell, Mary. Orthopaedic Nursing. 7th ed. 1976. pap. text ed. 18.75 (ISBN 0-443-01433-7). Churchill.

St. Mary's Memorial Hospital Knoxville, Tennessee. Guidelines to Orthopedic Nursing. rev. ed. LC 74-18943. 1975. 8.50 (ISBN 0-87125-023-3). Cath Health.

Smith, Ann P., ed. Orthopedic Nursing. (Nursing Outline Ser.). 1974. spiral bdg. 8.00 (ISBN 0-87488-381-4). Med Exam.

Webb, Jane. Notes on Orthopaedic Nursing. LC 77-5474. (Illus.). 1977. pap. text ed. 3.25 (ISBN 0-443-01518-X). Churchill.

ORTHOPEDIC PLASTER CASTS

see Plaster Casts, Surgical

ORTHOPEDIC SURGERY

Adams, John C. Standard Orthopaedic Operations. 2nd ed. (Illus.). 1980. text ed. 48.75x (ISBN 0-443-01976-2). Churchill.

Ahstrom, James P., Jr. Current Practice in Orthopaedic Surgery, Vol. 8. LC 63-18841. (Illus.). 1979. text ed. 30.50 (ISBN 0-8016-0089-8). Mosby.

American Academy of Orthopaedic Surgery. Selective Bibliography of Orthopaedic Surgery. 3rd ed. LC 75-5752. 1975. 13.95 (ISBN 0-8016-0003-0). Mosby.

American Academy of Orthopaedic Surgeons. Symposium on Microsurgery: Practical Use in Orthopaedics. Urbaniak, James R., ed. LC 79-14999. 1979. text ed. 52.50 (ISBN 0-8016-0066-9). Mosby.

Bentley, George, ed. Orthopedics, 2 vols. 3rd ed. (Operative Surgery Ser.). (Illus.). 1979. Set. text ed. 225.00 (ISBN 0-407-00632-X). Butterworth.

Bigelow, Henry J. Orthopedic Surgery. LC 77-81658. 1977. Repr. of 1900 ed. lib. bdg. 40.00 (ISBN 0-89341-136-1). Longwood Pr.

Brashear, H. Robert & Raney, R. Beverly. Shand's Handbook of Orthopaedic Surgery. 9th ed. LC 78-65. 1978. text ed. 29.95 (ISBN 0-8016-4082-2). Mosby.

Compere, Edward L. Orthopedic Surgery. (Illus.). 323p. 1974. 28.50 (ISBN 0-8151-1814-7). Year Bk Med.

Cosentino, Rodolfo. Atlas of Anatomy & Surgical Approaches in Orthopaedic Surgery, Vol. 1: Upper Extremity. (Illus.). 208p. 1960. 19.75 (ISBN 0-398-00349-1). C C Thomas.
--Atlas of Anatomy & Surgical Approaches in Orthopaedic Surgery, Vol. 2: Lower Extremity. (Illus.). 276p. 1973. pap. 24.50 spiral bd. (ISBN 0-398-00350-5). C C Thomas.
Coventry, Mark B., ed. Year Book of Orthopedics & Traumatic Surgery, 1979. (Practical Medicine Year Bks). (Illus.). 1979. 36.95 (ISBN 0-8151-1878-3). Year Bk Med.
Delchef, J., et al, eds. Orthopaedic Surgery & Traumatology. (International Congress Ser.: No. 291). 1974. pap. 166.00 (ISBN 0-444-15039-0, Excerpta Medica). Elsevier.
Duthie, Robert B. & Ferguson, Albert B., eds. Mercer's Orthopaedic Surgery. 7th ed. (Illus.). 1248p. 1973. 95.00 (ISBN 0-686-74196-X). Krieger.
Epps, Charles H., ed. Complications in Orthopaedic Surgery, 2 vols. LC 78-17997. 1978. 99.00 set (ISBN 0-397-50382-2, JBL-Med-Nursing). Har-Row.
Goldstein, Loius A. Atlas of Orthopaedic Surgery. 2nd ed. LC 80-25987. (Illus.). 646p. 1981. text ed. 90.00 (ISBN 0-8016-1884-3). Mosby.
Goodman, Floyd G. & Schoedinger, George R. Questions & Answers in Orthopaedics. 3rd ed. LC 77-8188. 1977. pap. 22.50 (ISBN 0-8016-1900-9). Mosby.
Hastings, D. E., ed. The Knee: Ligament & Articular Cartilage Injuries. (Progress in Orthopedic Surgery: Vol. 3). (Illus.). 1978. 22.00 (ISBN 0-387-08679-X). Springer-Verlag.
Hence, H. R. Arthroscopy of the Knee Joint. Casey, P. A., tr. from Ger. (Illus.). 1979. 73.30 (ISBN 0-387-09314-1). Springer-Verlag.
Jackson, Ruth. The Cervical Syndrome. 4th ed. (Amer. Lec. in Orthopaedic Surgery Ser.). (Illus.). 416p. 1978. 26.50 (ISBN 0-398-03696-9). C C Thomas.
Keats, Sidney. Operative Orthopedics in Cerebral Palsy. (Illus.). 264p. 1970. photocopy ed. 19.75 (ISBN 0-398-00991-0). C C Thomas.
Kopta, Joseph A., et al, eds. Orthopedic Surgery Continuing Education Review. LC 80-80366. 1980. pap. 14.50 (ISBN 0-87488-398-9). Med Exam.
Mann, Roger A. DuVries' Surgery of the Foot. 4th ed. LC 78-10829. (Illus.). 1978. text ed. 44.50 (ISBN 0-8016-2333-2). Mosby.
Mears, D. C. Materials in Orthopaedic Surgery. (Illus.). 776p. 1979. 75.00 (ISBN 0-683-05901-7). Williams & Wilkins.
Radin, E. L., et al. Practical Biomechanics for the Orthopedic Surgeon. 168p. 1979. 24.50 (ISBN 0-686-74422-5, Pub. by Wiley Med). Wiley.
Ray, Robert D. & Barmada, Riad. Orthopedic Surgery Case Studies. 1975. spiral bdg. 12.00 (ISBN 0-87488-030-0). Med Exam.
Ryan, James J. Orthopedic Surgery. (Medical Outline Ser.). 1977. spiral bdg. 12.00 (ISBN 0-87488-664-3). Med Exam.
Spear, Curtis V. Self-Assessment of Knowledge in Orthopedic Surgery. LC 80-80368. 1980. pap. 16.50 (ISBN 0-87488-229-X). Med Exam.
Vilain, Raymond & Michon, Jacques. Plastic Surgery of the Hand & Pulp. LC 78-61477. (Illus.). 184p. 1979. 31.25x (ISBN 0-89352-037-3). Masson Pub.
Wee, George C. Atlas of Improved Surgical Procedures for Common Foot Disorders: Ingrown Toenail & Hammertoe. (Illus.). 80p. 1972. 8.75 (ISBN 0-398-02498-7). C C Thomas.
Weil, U. H., ed. Joint Preserving Procedures of the Lower Extremities. (Progress in Orthopaedic Surgery Ser.: Vol. 4). (Illus.). 120p. 1980. 38.00 (ISBN 0-387-09856-9). Springer-Verlag.
Zauder, Howard L. Anesthesia for Orthopaedic Surgery. LC 79-20258. 229p. 1980. text ed. 35.00 (ISBN 0-8036-9771-6). Davis Co.

ORTHOPEDICS, VETERINARY
see Veterinary Orthopedics

ORTHOPTERA
see also Cockroaches; Crickets; Locusts
Harz, H. & Kaltenbach, A. The Orthopters of Europe, Vol. 3. (Entomologica Ser: Vol. 12). 1976. lib. bdg. 84.00 (ISBN 90-6193-122-3, Pub. by Junk Pubs Netherlands). Kluwer Boston.
Hutchins, Ross E. Grasshoppers & Their Kin. LC 70-184186. (Illus.). 128p. (gr. 5 up). 1972. 5.95 (ISBN 0-396-06503-1). Dodd.

ORTHOPTICS
Anderson, Miles H., ed. A Manual of Lower Extremities Orthotics. (Illus.). 552p. 1978. 40.50 (ISBN 0-398-02217-8). C C Thomas.
Cashell, G. T. & Durran, I. M. Handbook of Orthoptic Principles. 4th ed. (Illus.). 1981. pap. text ed. 13.75 (ISBN 0-443-02200-3). Churchill.
Gillis-Lindsay. Orthoptics: A Discussion of Binocular Anomalies. (Illus.). 1972. 10.00 (ISBN 0-407-93408-1). Butterworth.
Lancaster, Julia. A Manual of Orthoptics. 224p. 1951. photocopy ed. spiral 22.50 (ISBN 0-398-04323-X). C C Thomas.
Moore, Sally & Mein, Joyce, eds. Orthoptics: Past, Present, Future. LC 76-6830. (Illus.). 592p. (Transactions of the 3rd international Orthoptic Congress). 1976. 29.50 (ISBN 0-8151-5944-7, Pub. by Symposia Special). Year Bk Med.
Murdoch, George, ed. The Advances in Orthotics. 620p. 1976. 29.95 (ISBN 0-7131-4214-6). Krieger.
Revell. Strabismus: A History of Orthoptic Technique. (Illus.). 1973. 23.95 (ISBN 0-407-93262-3). Butterworth.

ORTON, ARTHUR, CALLING HIMSELF SIR ROBERT CHARLES DOUGHTY-TICHBORNE, BART., 1834-1898
Maugham, Frederick H. The Tichborne Case. LC 74-10430. (Classics of Crime & Criminology Ser). (Illus.). 384p. 1975. Repr. of 1936 ed. 18.00 (ISBN 0-88355-197-7). Hyperion Conn.

ORWELL, GEORGE, 1903-1950
Bal, Sant S. George Orwell: The Ethical Imagination. 144p. 1981. text ed. 9.25 (ISBN 0-391-02202-4). Humanities.
Calder, Jenni. Chronicles of Conscience: A Study of George Orwell & Arthur Koestler. LC 69-12146. (Critical Essays in Modern Literature Ser). 1969. pap. 5.95 (ISBN 0-8229-5205-X). U of Pittsburgh Pr.
Concannon, G. J. George Orwell. 1976. lib. bdg. 59.95 (ISBN 0-685-68942-5). Revisionist Pr.
Crick, Bernard. George Orwell. (Illus.). 1981. 17.95 (ISBN 0-686-72073-3, Pub. by Atlantic Monthly Pr). Little.
Edelheit, Steven. Dark Prophecies: George Orwell & Technology. (George Orwell Ser.). 1979. lib. bdg. 69.95 (ISBN 0-685-96864-2). Revisionist Pr.
Heppenstall, Rayner. Four Absentees: Eric Gill, George Orwell, Dylan Thomas and J. Middleton Murry. 1979. Repr. of 1960 ed. lib. bdg. 30.00 (ISBN 0-8495-2277-3). Arden Lib.
Kalechofsky, Roberta. George Orwell. LC 73-77054. (Modern Literature Ser.). 1973. 10.95 (ISBN 0-8044-2480-2). Ungar.
Kubal, David L. Outside the Whale: George Orwell's Art & Politics. LC 72-3509. 240p. 1972. text ed. 7.95x (ISBN 0-268-00475-7). U. of Notre Dame Pr.
--Outside the Whale: George Orwell's Art & Politics. LC 72-3509. 186p. 1973. pap. 2.95x (ISBN 0-268-00514-1). U of Notre Dame Pr.
Lee, Robert A. Orwell's Fiction. LC 74-75151. 1972. 28.50x (ISBN 0-89197-324-9). Irvington.
Lief, Ruth A. Homage to Oceania: The Prophetic Vision of George Orwell. LC 68-28811. 1969. 6.50 (ISBN 0-8142-0083-4). Ohio St U Pr.
Meyers, Jeffrey. A Reader's Guide to George Orwell. (Quality Paperback Ser.: No. 339). 1977. pap. 3.50 (ISBN 0-8226-0339-X). Littlefield.
Meyers, Jeffrey & Meyers, Valerie. George Orwell: An Annotated Bibliography of Criticism. LC 75-42887. (Reference Library of the Humanities Ser.: Vol. 54). 1977. lib. bdg. 21.00 (ISBN 0-8240-9955-9). Garland Pub.
Meyers, Jeffrey, ed. George Orwell: The Critical Heritage. (Critical Heritage Ser.). 432p. 1975. 30.00x (ISBN 0-7100-8255-X). Routledge & Kegan.
Monarch Notes on Orwell's Animal Farm. (Orig.). pap. 1.75 (ISBN 0-671-00718-1). Monarch Pr.
Monarch Notes on Orwell's 1984. (Orig.). pap. 1.95 (ISBN 0-671-00719-X). Monarch Pr.
Paley, Alan L. George Orwell, Writer & Critic of Modern Society. Rahmas, D. Steve, ed. (Outstanding Personalities Ser.: No. 72). 32p. (Orig.). (gr. 7-12). 1974. lib. bdg. 2.95 incl. catalog cards (ISBN 0-686-05489-X); pap. 1.50 vinyl laminated covers (ISBN 0-87157-072-6). SamHar Pr.
Small, Christopher. The Road to Miniluv: George Orwell, the State, & God. LC 75-20489. 1976. 10.95 (ISBN 0-8229-1124-8). U of Pittsburgh Pr.
Smyer, Richard I. Primal Dream & Primal Crime: Orwell's Development As a Psychological Novelist. LC 79-4840. 1979. text ed. 16.50x (ISBN 0-8262-0282-9). U of Mo Pr.
Stansky, Peter & Abrahams, William. Orwell; the Transformation. 253p. 1981. pap. 5.95 (ISBN 0-586-08375-8). Academy Chi Ltd.
--Orwell: The Transformation. LC 79-3490. (Illus.). 1980. 12.95 (ISBN 0-394-47394-9). Knopf.
--The Unknown Orwell. 288p. 1981. pap. 5.95 (ISBN 0-586-08178-X). Academy Chi Ltd.
--The Unknown Orwell. (Illus.). 1972. 10.00 (ISBN 0-394-47393-0). Knopf.
Steinhoff, William. George Orwell & the Origins of 1984. LC 74-78989. 1975. pap. 6.50x (ISBN 0-472-08802-5). U of Mich Pr.
Thompson, Frank H., Jr. Animal Farm Notes. (Orig.). pap. 1.75 (ISBN 0-8220-0174-8). Cliffs.
Thompson, Frank, Jr. Nineteen Eighty-Four Notes. (Orig.). pap. 1.95 (ISBN 0-8220-0899-8). Cliffs.
Voorhees, Richard J. The Paradox of George Orwell. LC 61-62508. (Orig.). 1961. pap. 1.95 (ISBN 0-911198-00-8). Purdue.
Williams, Raymond. George Orwell. LC 61-6134. 112p. 1981. 15.00x (ISBN 0-231-05374-6, Pub. by Morningside); pap. 5.00x (ISBN 0-231-05375-4, Pub. by Morningside). Columbia U Pr.
Zwerdling, Alex. Orwell & the Left. LC 74-75951. 200p. 1974. 16.50x (ISBN 0-300-01686-7). Yale U Pr.

OSAGE INDIANS
see Indians of North America–The West

OSBORNE, JOHN
Ferrar, H. John Osborne. LC 72-13527. (Columbia Essays on Modern Writers Ser.: No. 67). 48p. 1973. pap. 2.00 (ISBN 0-231-03361-3). Columbia U Pr.
Hayman, Ronald. John Osborne. LC 79-153123. (World Dramatists Ser.). (Illus.). 10.95 (ISBN 0-8044-2386-5). Ungar.
Northouse, Cameron & Walsh, Thomas P. John Osborne: A Reference Guide. (Series Seventy: Reference Guide, No. 2). 1974. lib. bdg. 9.50 (ISBN 0-8161-1152-9). G K Hall.
Osborne, John. A Better Class of Person: An Autobiography. 320p. 1981. 16.50 (ISBN 0-525-06634-9). Dutton.
Trussler, Simon. Plays of John Osborne: An Assessment. 1969. pap. text ed. 4.00x (ISBN 0-575-00267-0). Humanities.

OSBORNE, THOMAS MOTT, 1859-1926
Chamberlain, Rudolph W. There Is No Truce. facs. ed. LC 74-124229. (Select Bibliographies Reprint Ser). 1935. 21.00 (ISBN 0-8369-5418-1). Arno.

OSCARS (MOVING-PICTURES)
see Academy Awards (Moving-Pictures)

OSCEOLA, SEMINOLE CHIEF, 1804-1838
Grant, Matthew G. Osceola. LC 73-12407. 1974. PLB 5.95 (ISBN 0-87191-266-X). Creative Ed.
Oppenheim, Joanne. Osceola, Seminole Warrior. new ed. LC 78-60116. (Illus.). 48p. (gr. 4-6). 1979. PLB 5.89 (ISBN 0-89375-158-8); pap. 1.75 (ISBN 0-89375-148-0). Troll Assocs.
Syme, Ronald. Osceola, Seminole Leader. LC 75-22373. (Illus.). 96p. (gr. 3-7). 1976. 6.75 (ISBN 0-688-22054-1); PLB 6.48 (ISBN 0-688-32054-6). Morrow.
Tyler, O. Z. Osceola, Seminole Chief: An Unremembered Saga. (Illus.). 1976. 9.95 (ISBN 0-89305-002-4); pap. 6.95 (ISBN 0-89305-004-0). Anna Pub.

OSCILLATIONS
see also Damping (Mechanics); Electric Noise; Frequencies of Oscillating Systems
Basov, N. G., ed. The Kinetics of Simple Models in the Theory of Oscillations. (P.N. Lebedev Physics Institute Ser.: Vol. 90). (Illus.). 200p. 1978. 42.50 (ISBN 0-306-10948-4, Consultants). Plenum Pub.
Bolton, W. Waves, Rays & Oscillations, Bk. 6. LC 80-41396. (Study Topics in Physics). 96p. 1981. pap. text ed. 4.50 (ISBN 0-408-10657-3). Butterworth.
Cox, J. P. Theory of Stellar Pulsation. LC 79-3198. (Ser. in Astrophysics: No. 2). (Illus.). 1980. 40.00x (ISBN 0-691-08252-9); pap. 13.50 (ISBN 0-691-08253-7). Princeton U Pr.
Donocik, Rudolf. Theory of Phase-Controlled Oscillations. (Illus.). 296p. 1969. 25.00x (ISBN 0-7165-1314-5, Pub. by Irish Academic Pr Ireland). Biblio Dist.
Gardner, Floyd M. Phaselock Techniques. 2nd ed. LC 78-20777. 1979. 24.95x (ISBN 0-471-04294-3, Pub by Wiley-Interscience). Wiley.
Hagedoern, Peter. Non-Linear Oscillations. Stadler, Wolfram, tr. (Illus.). 250p. 1981. text ed. 79.00x (ISBN 0-19-856142-3). Oxford U Pr.
Halanay, A. Differential Equations: Stability, Oscillations, Time Lags. (Mathematics in Science & Engineering Ser.: Vol. 23). 1966. 60.50 (ISBN 0-12-317950-5). Acad Pr.
Jones, D. S. Electrical & Mechanical Oscillations. (Library of Mathematics). 1968. pap. 5.00 (ISBN 0-7100-4346-5). Routledge & Kegan.
Krasnosel'sky, Mark A. Operator of Translation Along the Trajectories of Differential Equations. LC 67-22349. (Translations of Mathematical Monographs: Vol. 19). 1968. Repr. of 1966 ed. 32.40 (ISBN 0-8218-1569-5, MMONO-19). Am Math.
Kreith, K. Oscillation Theory. LC 73-79366. (Lecture Notes in Mathematics: Vol. 324). 109p. 1973. pap. 8.80 (ISBN 0-387-06258-0). Springer-Verlag.
Lefschetz, S. Contributions to the Theory of Nonlinear Oscillations, Vols. 1-3 & 5, 1950-1960. (Annals of Mathematics Studies). Vol. 1. 16.00 (ISBN 0-527-02736-7); Vol. 2. 7.00 (ISBN 0-527-02745-6); Vol. 3. 14.00 (ISBN 0-527-02753-7); Vol. 5. 14.00 (ISBN 0-527-02761-8). Kraus Repr.
Lefschetz, Solomon, ed. Contributions to the Theory of Nonlinear Oscillations, Vol. 4. (Annals of Mathematics Studies: No. 41). (Orig.). 1958. pap. 14.00 (ISBN 0-691-07932-3). Princeton U Pr.
Livsic, M. S. Operators, Oscillations, Waves. LC 72-11580. (Translations of Mathematical Monographs: Vol. 34). 280p. (Orig.). 1973. 40.80 (ISBN 0-8218-1584-9, MMONO-34). Am Math.
Mickens, Ronald E. An Introduction to Nonlinear Oscillations. LC 80-13169. (Illus.). 320p. 1981. text ed. 69.00 (ISBN 0-521-22208-7). Cambridge U Pr.
Minorsky, Nicholas N. Non-Linear Oscillation. 734p. 1974. Repr. of 1962 ed. 29.50 (ISBN 0-88275-186-7). Krieger.
Nayfeh, Ali H. & Mook, Dean T. Nonlinear Oscillations. LC 78-27102. (Pure & Applied Mathematics Texts, Monographs & Tracts). 1979. 45.00 (ISBN 0-471-03555-6, Pub. by Wiley-Interscience). Wiley.
Panovko, Ya. G. & Gubanova, I. I. Stability & Oscillations of Elastic Systems: Paradoxes, Fallacies, & New Concepts. LC 65-11341. 291p. 1965. 40.00 (ISBN 0-306-10735-X, Consultants). Plenum Pub.
Paquet, J. C. & Le Maitre, J. F. Methodes Pratiques d'Etude des Oscillations Non Lineaires: Theorie Des Systemes. 1970. 44.00x (ISBN 0-677-50200-1). Gordon.
Petersen, K. E. Brownian Motion, Hardy Spaces & Bounded Mean Oscillation. LC 76-46860. (London Mathematical Society Lecture Notes: No. 28). (Illus.). 1977. limp bdg. 14.50x (ISBN 0-521-21512-9). Cambridge U Pr.
Rocard, Yves. Dynamic Instability: Automobiles, Aircraft, Suspension Bridges. Meyer, M. L., tr. (Illus.). 1958. 12.00 (ISBN 0-8044-4833-7). Ungar.
Starzhinskii, V. M. Applied Methods in the Theory of Nonlinear Oscillations. 1980. 8.00 (ISBN 0-8285-1802-5, Pub. by Mir Pubs Russia). Imported Pubns.

OSCILLATORICEAE
Gomont, M. Monographie Des Oscillariees: 1892-93, 2 parts in 1 vol. (Illus.). 1962. 40.00 (ISBN 3-7682-0038-8). Lubrecht & Cramer.

OSCILLATORS, CRYSTAL
Bottom, Virgil E. Introduction to Quartz Crystal Unit Design. 150p. 1981. text ed. price not set (ISBN 0-442-26201-9). Van Nos Reinhold.
Frerking, Marvin E. Crystal Oscillator Design & Temperature Compensation. 1978. text ed. 18.95x (ISBN 0-442-22459-1). Van Nos Reinhold.

OSCILLATORS, ELECTRIC
see also Oscillators, Crystal; Oscillators, Microwave; Phase-Locked Loops; Pulse Generators; Transients (Electricity)
Blanchard, Alain A. Phase-Locked Loops: Application to Coherent Receiver Design. LC 75-30941. 1976. 37.00 (ISBN 0-471-07941-3, Pub. by Wiley-Interscience). Wiley.
Vendelin, George D. Design of Amplifiers & Oscillators by the S-Parameter Method. 225p. 1981. 24.00 (ISBN 0-471-09226-6, Pub. by Wiley-Interscience). Wiley.

OSCILLATORS, MICROWAVE
Bulman, P. J., et al. Transferred Electron Devices. 1972. 67.00 (ISBN 0-12-140850-7). Acad Pr.
Howes, M. J. & Morgan, D. V., eds. Variable Impedance Devices. LC 78-4122. (Solid State Devices & Circuits Ser.). 1978. 48.25 (ISBN 0-471-99651-3, Pub. by Wiley-Interscience). Wiley.

OSCILLOGRAPH
see also Cathode Ray Oscillograph
Basic Oscillography. 1976. pap. 2.50 (ISBN 0-87985-123-6, P130). Eastman Kodak.
Hoadley, Howard W. Manual of Oscillography. (Focal Library Ser.). (Illus.). 49.95 (ISBN 0-240-44799-9). Focal Pr.

OSCILLOGRAPH, CATHODE RAY
see Cathode Ray Oscillograph

OSCILLOSCOPE
see Cathode Ray Oscilloscope

OSHIBAS
see Fan (African People)

OSIRIS
Budge, E. Wallis. Osiris & the Egyptian Resurrection, 2 vols. LC 72-81534. (Illus.). 906p. 1973. Vol. 1. pap. 6.00 (ISBN 0-486-22780-4); Vol. 2. pap. 6.00 (ISBN 0-486-22781-2). Dover.
--Osiris & the Egyptian Resurrection, 2 vols. (Illus.). 22.00 (ISBN 0-8446-4715-2). Peter Smith.
Patricia. Osiris & Isis. (Illus.). 267p. (Orig.). 1980. pap. 7.95 (ISBN 0-935146-19-9). Morningland.
Randall-Stevens, H. C. Teachings of Osiris. new ed. 1970. Repr. of 1927 ed. 9.50 (ISBN 0-685-22177-6). Weiser.

OSLER, WILLIAM, SIR, BART., 1849-1919
Bean, Robert B. & Bean, William B. Sir William Osler: Aphorisms from His Bedside Teachings & Writings. 160p. 1968. ed. spiral bdg. 14.50photocopy (ISBN 0-398-04202-0). C C Thomas.
Cushing, Harvey. Life of Sir William Osler, 2 Vols. (Illus.). 1940. boxed 49.50x (ISBN 0-19-500524-4). Oxford U Pr.

Holley, Howard L. A Continual Remembrance: Letters from Sir William Osler to His Friend Ned Milburn 1865-1919. (Illus.). 160p. 1968. photocopy ed. spiral 14.75 (ISBN 0-398-00859-0). C C Thomas.
McGovern, John P. & Roland, Charles G. William Osler: The Continuing Education. (Illus.). 384p. 1969. photocopy ed. spiral 37.50 (ISBN 0-398-01256-3). C C Thomas.
Nation, Earl F., et al. An Annotated Checklist of Osleriana. LC 75-44711. (Illus.). 1976. 27.50x (ISBN 0-87338-186-6). Kent St U Pr.
Reid, Edith G. The Great Physician: A Short Life of Sir William Osler. 1931. 30.00 (ISBN 0-8274-4257-2). R West.
Thayer, William S. Osler, & Other Papers. facs. ed. LC 78-84342. (Essay Index Reprint Ser). 1931. 19.50 (ISBN 0-8369-1111-3). Arno.
White, William. Sir William Osler: Historian & Literary Essayist. 1951. 2.95x (ISBN 0-8143-1038-9). Wayne St U Pr.

OSLO

Derry, T. Oslo. (Tanum of Norway Tokens Ser). pap. 7.00x (ISBN 0-89918-484-7, N484). Vanous.
Derry, T. K. Introducing Oslo: A Short Guide-Book with Comments. (Norwegian Guides Ser). (Illus., Orig.). 1969. 10.00x (ISBN 0-8002-1584-2). Intl Pubns Serv.
Hilt, R. Gulliksen. Oslo: Info 1980-81. (Illus.). 300p. (Orig.). 1981. pap. 9.50 (ISBN 82-90182-19-8, N543, Pub. by Forfatterforlaget Norway). Vanous.

OSMANIC LANGUAGE

see Turkish Language

OSMANLI LANGUAGE

see Turkish Language

OSMIUM

Smith, Ivan C., et al. Palladium-Osmium, Vol. 4. LC 77-88486. (Trace Metals in the Environment Ser.). 1978. 29.50 (ISBN 0-250-40217-3). Ann Arbor Science.

OSMOND BROTHERS

Delaney & Laney. The Osmonds. 32p. (gr. 4-6). 1975. PLB 5.95 (ISBN 0-87191-461-1); pap. 2.95 (ISBN 0-89812-113-2). Creative Ed.
Eldred, Partricia M. Donny & Marie. (Rock 'n Pop Stars Ser.). (Illus.). (gr. 4-12). 1978. PLB 5.95 (ISBN 0-87191-618-5); pap. 2.75 o. p. (ISBN 0-89812-121-3). Creative Ed.

OSMOREGULATION

Fitzsimons, J. T. The Physiology of Thirst & Sodium Appetite. LC 78-16212. (Physiological Society Monographs: No. 35). 1979. 83.50 (ISBN 0-521-22292-3). Cambridge U Pr.
Gerick, David J. Water, Water Everywhere. (Illus.). 1978. 20.00 (ISBN 0-916750-75-2). Dayton Labs.
Gilles, R. Mechanisms of Osmoregulation in Animals: Maintenance of Cell Volume. LC 78-4608. 667p. 1979. 95.25 (ISBN 0-471-99648-3, Pub. by Wiley-Interscience). Wiley.
Hargens, Alan R. Tissue Fluid Pressure & Composition. (Illus.). 282p. 1981. lib. bdg. 34.00 (ISBN 0-683-03891-5). Williams & Wilkins.
Maloiy, G. W., ed. Comparative Physiology of Osmoregulation in Animals, Vol. 2. LC 77-93492. 1980. 49.50 (ISBN 0-12-467002-4). Acad Pr.
Pickford, Grace E., et al. Studies on the Blood Serum of the Euryhaline Cyprinodont Fish, Fundulus Heteroclitus, Adapted to Fresh or to Salt Water. (Transactions of the Connecticut Academy of Arts & Sciences Ser.: Vol. 43). 1969. pap. 9.00 (ISBN 0-208-00907-8). Shoe String.
Rains, Donald W., et al, eds. Genetic Engineering of Osmoregulation: Impact of Plant Productivity for Food, Chemicals & Energy. (Basic Life Sciences Ser.: Vol. 14). 395p. 1980. 39.50 (ISBN 0-306-40454-0, Plenum Pr). Plenum Pub.
Rankin, J. C. & Danenport, J. Animal Osmoregulation: Testing of Polymers Ser. LC 81-17491. (Tertiary Level Biology Ser.). 280p. 1981. 39.95 (ISBN 0-470-27207-4). Halsted Pr.
Skadhauge, E. Osmoregulation in Birds. (Zoophysiology Ser.: Vol. 12). (Illus.). 250p. 1981. 52.50 (ISBN 0-387-10546-8). Springer-Verlag.

OSMOSIS

see also Absorption (Physiology); Biological Transport; Dialysis; Electro-Osmosis; Permeability; Porosity; Solution (Chemistry)
Hammel, H. T. & Scholander, P. F. Osmosis & Tensile Solvent. LC 76-3684. 1976. pap. 13.10 (ISBN 0-387-07663-8). Springer-Verlag.
Krogh, August. Osmotic Regulation in Aquatic Animals. 7.50 (ISBN 0-8446-2408-X). Peter Smith.
Lonsdale, H. K. & Podall, H. E., eds. Reverse Osmosis Membrane Research. LC 72-87518. 503p. 1972. 49.50 (ISBN 0-306-30710-3, Plenum Pr). Plenum Pub.
Sourirajan, S. Reverse Osmosis. 1970. 63.00 (ISBN 0-12-655650-4). Acad Pr.
Tombs, M. & Peacocke, A. R. The Osmotic Pressure of Biological Macromolecules. (Monographs on Physical Biochemistry). (Illus.). 230p. 1975. 29.50x (ISBN 0-19-854606-8). Oxford U Pr.

OSPREYS

Davis, Burke. Biography of a Fish Hawk. LC 76-49987. (Nature Biography Ser.). (Illus.). (gr. 3-6). 1977. PLB 6.59 (ISBN 0-399-61084-7). Putnam.

OSSIAN

Blair, Hugh. A Critical Dissertation on the Poems of Ossian. LC 78-67648. 1980. Repr. of 1765 ed. 22.50 (ISBN 0-404-17178-8). AMS Pr.
Macpherson, James. Poems of Ossian, 2 Vols. LC 76-144459. Repr. of 1805 ed. Set. 80.00 (ISBN 0-404-08697-7); 40.00 ea. AMS Pr.
--Poems of Ossian in the Original Gaelic, 3 Vols. M'Arthur, John, ed. LC 70-144460. Repr. of 1807 ed. Set. 120.00 (ISBN 0-404-08730-2). AMS Pr.
Nutt, Alfred T. Ossian & Ossianic Literature. LC 70-139166. (Popular Studies in Mythology, Romance & Folklore: No. 3). Repr. of 1899 ed. 5.50 (ISBN 0-404-53503-8). AMS Pr.
Ossian, 3 vols. LC 42-448. 1940. Repr. of 1763 ed. Set. 155.00x (ISBN 3-533-01232-8). Intl Pubns Serv.
Ossian. Poems of Ossian. Macpherson, James, ed. LC 76-107180. 1970. Repr. of 1851 ed. 29.00 (ISBN 0-403-00036-X). Scholarly.
Ossianic Society Of Dublin. Transactions, 6 Vols. LC 78-144462. Repr. of 1858 ed. Set. 72.50 (ISBN 0-404-09070-2); 12.50 ea. AMS Pr.
Tombo, Rudolf. Ossian in Germany. LC 73-144434. (Columbia University. Germanic Studies, Old Ser.: No. 2). Repr. of 1901 ed. 19.00 (ISBN 0-404-50402-7). AMS Pr.

OSSOLI, SARAH MARGARET (FULLER) MARCHESA D', 1810-1850

Allen, Margaret V. The Achievement of Margaret Fuller. LC 79-1732. 1979. 14.95x (ISBN 0-271-00215-8). Pa St U Pr.
Anthony, Katharine. Margaret Fuller: Phychological Biography. LC 72-195019. 1920. lib. bdg. 15.00 (ISBN 0-8414-0288-4). Folcroft.
--Margret Fuller: A Psychological Biography. LC 78-131608. 1970. Repr. of 1921 ed. 19.00 (ISBN 0-403-00495-0). Scholarly.
Anthony, Katherine S. Margaret Fuller: A Psychological Biography. 1978. Repr. of 1920 ed. lib. bdg. 25.00 (ISBN 0-8495-0020-6). Arden Lib.
Bell, Margaret. Margaret Fuller. 1930. 11.50 (ISBN 0-8274-2672-0). R West.
--Margaret Fuller: A Biography. facsimile ed. LC 72-164587. (Select Bibliographies Reprint Ser). Repr. of 1930 ed. 18.00 (ISBN 0-8369-5871-3). Arno.
Black, Landbroke. Some Queer People: Margaret Fuller, Poe, Beddoes. 1973. 35.00 (ISBN 0-8274-1477-3). R West.
Blanchard, Paula. Margaret Fuller: From Transcendentalism to Revolution. 1979. pap. 5.95 (ISBN 0-440-56242-2, Delta). Dell.
--Margaret Fuller: From Transcendentalist to Revolution. (Radcliffe Biography Ser.). 1978. 11.95 (ISBN 0-440-05314-5, Sey Lawr). Delacorte.
Braun, Frederick A. Margaret Fuller & Goethe. LC 72-195018. 1910. lib. bdg. 15.00 (ISBN 0-8414-2537-X). Folcroft.
Brown, Arthur W. Margaret Fuller. (Twayne's United States Authors Ser). 1964. pap. 3.45 (ISBN 0-8084-0209-9, T48, Twayne). Coll & U Pr.
Chevigny, Bell G. The Woman & the Myth: Margaret Fuller's Life & Writings. LC 76-19030. (Midland Bks.: No. 243). 528p. 1976. 20.00x (ISBN 0-253-16574-1); pap. 8.95x (ISBN 0-253-20243-4). Ind U Pr.
Chevigny, Bell G., ed. Woman & the Myth: Margaret Fuller's Life & Writings. 512p. (Orig.). 1977. pap. 8.95 (ISBN 0-912670-43-6). Feminist Pr.
Durning, Russell E. Margaret Fuller, Citizen of the World: An Intermediary Between European & American Literatures. 144p. 1969. 30.00x (ISBN 3-533-00295-0). Intl Pubns Serv.
Fuller, Margaret. Summer on the Lakes in Eighteen Forty-Three. facsimile ed. (Women on the Move Ser.). 1972. Repr. of 1844 ed. text ed. 22.00x (ISBN 90-6004-302-2). Humanities.
Higginson, Thomas. Margaret Fuller Ossoli. LC 68-24937. (American Literature Ser., No. 49). 1968. Repr. of 1893 ed. lib. bdg. 37.95 (ISBN 0-8383-0955-0). Haskell.
Higginson, Thomas W. Margaret Fuller Ossoli. LC 80-24233. (American Men & Women of Letters Ser.). 324p. 1981. pap. 5.95 (ISBN 0-87754-159-0). Chelsea Hse.
--Margaret Fuller Ossoli. LC 68-57609. (Illus.). 1969. Repr. of 1890 ed. lib. bdg. 15.00 (ISBN 0-8371-0474-2, HIMO). Greenwood.
--Margaret Fuller Ossoli. 1973. Repr. of 1893 ed. 9.75 (ISBN 0-8274-1577-X). R West.
Howe, Julia W. Margaret Fuller - Marchesa Ossoli. Repr. of 1883 ed. lib. bdg. 15.00x (ISBN 0-8371-4089-7, HOMF). Greenwood.
--Margaret Fuller: Marchesa Ossoli. LC 68-24938. (American Biography Ser., No. 32). 1969. Repr. of 1883 ed. lib. bdg. 33.95 (ISBN 0-8383-0201-7). Haskell.
--Margaret Fuller: Marchesa Ossoli. 1973. Repr. of 1883 ed. 23.45 (ISBN 0-8274-0046-2). R West.
McMaster, Helen N. Margaret Fuller As a Literary Critic. LC 74-20532. 1928. lib. bdg. 10.00 (ISBN 0-8414-5932-0). Folcroft.
--Margaret Fuller As a Literary Critic. 59.95 (ISBN 0-8490-0585-X). Gordon Pr.
Macphail, Andrew. Essays in Puritanism: Jonathan Edwards, John Winthrop, Margaret Fuller, Walt Whitman, John Wesley. LC 68-26205. 1969. Repr. of 1905 ed. 12.75 (ISBN 0-8046-0286-7). Kennikat.
Miller, Perry, ed. Margaret Fuller, American Romantic: A Selection from Her Writings & Correspondence. 7.50 (ISBN 0-8446-0802-5). Peter Smith.
Myerson, Joel, ed. Critical Essays on Margaret Fuller. (Scholarly Reference Publications). 1980. lib. bdg. 18.50 (ISBN 0-8161-8283-3). G K Hall.
Ossoli, Margaret F. Memoirs of Margaret Fuller Ossoli, 2 vols. in 1. Emerson, Ralph W., et al, eds. LC 72-82356. 755p. 1972. Repr. of 1884 ed. lib. bdg. 39.00 (ISBN 0-8337-1250-0). B Franklin.
Ossoli, Sarah M. Writings of Margaret Fuller. Wade, Mason, ed. LC 72-122079. Repr. of 1941 ed. lib. bdg. 19.50x (ISBN 0-678-03177-0). Kelley.
Slater, Abby. In Search of Margaret Fuller: A Biography. LC 77-86335. (gr. 7 up). 1978. 7.50 (ISBN 0-440-03944-4). Delacorte.
Stern, Madeleine. Life of Margaret Fuller. LC 68-29738. (American Biography Ser., No. 32). (Illus.). 1969. Repr. lib. bdg. 46.95 (ISBN 0-8383-0286-6). Haskell.
Temple, Mary B. Sketch of Margaret Fuller Ossoli. LC 72-13680. 1973. lib. bdg. 10.00 (ISBN 0-8414-1259-6). Folcroft.
Wade, Mason. Margaret Fuller: Whetstone of Genius. LC 75-122077. Repr. of 1940 ed. 15.00x (ISBN 0-678-03178-9). Kelley.
Wilson, Ellen. Margaret Fuller: Bluestocking, Romantic, Revolutionary. LC 77-381. (Illus.). (gr. 7 up). 1977. 7.95 (ISBN 0-374-34807-3). FS&G.

OSTEITIS DEFORMANS

Singer, Frederick, ed. Paget's Disease of Bone. LC 77-1303. (Topics in Bone & Mineral Disorders Ser.). (Illus.). 171p. 1977. 25.00 (ISBN 0-306-30996-3, Plenum Pr). Plenum Pub.

OSTEOARTHRITIS

see Arthritis

OSTEOCHONDROSIS

Breck, Louis W. An Atlas of the Osteochondhoses. (Illus.). 192p. 1971. pap. 16.00 photocopy ed. spiral (ISBN 0-398-00218-5). C C Thomas.
Goff, Charles W. Legg-Calve-Perthes Syndrome: And Related Osteochondroses of Youth. (Illus.). 344p. 1954. ed. spiral bdg. 29.75photocopy (ISBN 0-398-04267-5). C C Thomas.

OSTEOGENESIS

see Bone-Growth

OSTEOGENESIS IMPERFECTA

see Osteopsathyrosis

OSTEOLOGY

see Bones; Skeleton

OSTEOMALACIA

Morgan, Brian. Osteomalacia, Renal Osteodystrophy & Osteoporosis. (American Lectures in Living Chemistry Ser.). (Illus.). 440p. 1973. 27.75 (ISBN 0-398-02602-5). C C Thomas.

OSTEOMYELITIS

Waldvogel, Francis A., et al. Osteomyelitis: Clinical Features, Therapeutic Considerations, & Unusual Aspects. (Illus.). 128p. 1971. 12.75 (ISBN 0-398-02156-2). C C Thomas.

OSTEOPATHY

see also Chiropractic; Massage; Mechanotherapy
Booth, Emmons R. History of Osteopathy, & Twentieth Century Medical Practice: Memorial Edition. LC 74-29281. Repr. of 1924 ed. 60.00 (ISBN 0-404-13401-7). AMS Pr.
Cayce, J. Gail. Osteopathy: Comparative Concepts - A. T. Still & Edgar Cayce. 61p. (Orig.). 1973. pap. 4.95 (ISBN 0-87604-080-6). ARE Pr.
Heffel, Leonard E. Opportunities in Osteopathic Medicine Today. LC 74-78786. (Illus.). 144p. (gr. 9-12). 1974. PLB 6.60 (ISBN 0-8442-6463-6); pap. text ed. 4.95 (ISBN 0-8442-6462-8). Natl Textbk.
Hoag, J. Marshall. Osteopathic Medicine. (Illus.). 1969. 35.00 (ISBN 0-07-029070-9, HP). McGraw.
Still, Andrew T. Autobiography of Andrew T. Still with a History of the Discovery & Development of the Science of Osteopathy. LC 78-180591. (Medicine & Society in America Ser). 508p. 1972. Repr. of 1897 ed. 23.00 (ISBN 0-405-03973-5). Arno.
--Philosophy of Osteopathy. LC 74-29302. Repr. of 1899 ed. 16.00 (ISBN 0-404-13426-2). AMS Pr.
Stoddard, Alan. Manual of Osteopathic Technique. 2nd ed. 1979. text ed. 32.50x (ISBN 0-09-051120-4, Hutchinson U Lib). Humanities.

OSTEOPLASTY

see Bones-Surgery

OSTEOPOROSIS

Barzel, Uriel S., ed. Osteoporosis. LC 71-109575. (Illus.). 304p. 1970. 60.25 (ISBN 0-8089-0032-3). Grune.
--Osteoporosis II. 304p. 1979. 29.75 (ISBN 0-8089-1181-3). Grune.
De Luca, Hector F. & Frost, H. M., eds. Osteoporosis. (Recent Advances in Pathogenesis & Treatment Ser.). 528p. 1981. text ed. 42.50 (ISBN 0-8391-1630-6). Univ Park.
Morgan, Brian. Osteomalacia, Renal Osteodystrophy & Osteoporosis. (American Lectures in Living Chemistry Ser.). (Illus.). 440p. 1973. 27.75 (ISBN 0-398-02602-5). C C Thomas.

OSTEOPSATHYROSIS

see also Fractures, Spontaneous
Smith, Roger. Osteogenesis Imperfecta. (Illus.). 224p. 1982. text ed. write for info. (ISBN 0-407-00211-1). Butterworth.

OSTGOTHS

see Goths

OSTIA, ITALY-ANTIQUITIES

Dal Maso, Leonardo B. Ostia-Port-Sacred Island. (Archeological Zones of Latium Ser). (Illus.). 48p. 1975. pap. 6.50x (ISBN 0-8002-0872-2). Intl Pubns Serv.
Laeuchli, Samuel, ed. Mithraism in Ostia: Mystery Religion & Christianity in the Ancient Port of Rome. (Illus.). 1967. 11.95x (ISBN 0-8101-0138-6). Northwestern U Pr.

OSTIAKS

Weber, Friedrich C. Present State of Russia, 2 Vols. (Russia Through European Eyes Ser). 1723. Repr. of 1968 ed. lib. bdg. 57.50 (ISBN 0-306-77022-9). Da Capo.

OSTRACODA

Biology & Paleobiology of Ostracoda: Symposium, 1972, No. 282. (Bulletin of American Paleontology). (Illus.). 1975. pap. 25.00 (ISBN 0-685-85652-6). Paleo Res.
Furtos, Norma C. The Ostracoda of Ohio. 1933. 2.00 (ISBN 0-686-30302-4). Ohio Bio Survey.
Hanai, Tetsuro, et al. Checklist of Ostracoda from Japan & Its Adjacent Seas. (Illus.). 1977. 22.00 (ISBN 0-86008-180-X, Pub. by U of Tokyo Pr). Intl Schol Bk Serv.
Howe, Henry V. & Laurencich, Laura. Introduction to the Study of Cretaceous Ostracoda. LC 58-9761. (Illus.). 1958. 32.50x (ISBN 0-8071-0538-4). La State U Pr.
Kraft, John C. Morphologic & Systematic Relationships of Some Middle Ordovician Ostracoda. LC 63-1127. (Memoir: No. 86). (Illus.). 1962. 8.75x (ISBN 0-8137-1086-3). Geol Soc.
Loffler, H. & Danielopol, D., eds. Ecology & Zoogeography of Ostracoda. (Illus.). 1977. lib. bdg. 79.00 (ISBN 90-6193-581-4, Pub. by Junk Pubs. Netherlands). Kluwer Boston.
Neale, J. W. The Taxonomy, Morphology & Ecology of Recent Ostracoda. 1969. 30.80 (ISBN 0-934454-77-9). Lubrecht & Cramer.
Stout, Larry N. Review & Index Through 1975 of Genus Candona (Ostracoda) in North America (Exclusive of Pre-Quaternary Species) LC 76-47833. (Microform Publication: No. 6). (Illus.). 1976. 3.00x (ISBN 0-8137-6006-2). Geol Soc.
Swain, Frederick M. Ostracoda from the Gulf of California. LC 66-29256. (Memoir: No. 101). (Illus.). 1967. 8.75x (ISBN 0-8137-1101-0). Geol Soc.

OSTRACODA-BIBLIOGRAPHY

Howe, Henry V. Ostracod Taxonomy. LC 62-11741. 1962. 25.00x (ISBN 0-8071-0539-2). La State U Pr.

OSTRAKA

Hayes, William C. Ostraka & Name Stones from the Tomb of Sen-Mut (No. 71) at Thebes: Metropolitan Museum of Art Publications in Reprint. LC 76-168406. (Illus.). 136p. 1972. Repr. of 1942 ed. 20.00 (ISBN 0-405-02239-5). Arno.
Oates, John F., et al. Checklist of Editions of Greek Papyri & Ostraca. LC 78-26003. (Bulletin of the American Society of Papyrologists Supplements: No. 1). 1978. pap. 6.00 (ISBN 0-89130-272-7, 311101). Scholars Pr Ca.

Winlock, Herbert E., et al. The Monastery of Epiphanius at Thebes: Metropolitan Museum of Art Egyptain Expedition Publications, Vols. 3 & 4, 2 vols. LC 72-168413. (The Metropolitan Museum of Art Publication in Reprint Ser.). 1926. 80.00 set (ISBN 0-405-02249-2). Arno.

OSTREA
see Oysters

OSTRICHES
Block, Seymour S. Benjamin Franklin: His Wit, Wisdom & Women. 448p. 1975. 14.50 (ISBN 0-8038-0767-8). Hastings.
Hopf, Alice L. Biography of an Ostrich. new ed. LC 72-95562. (Nature Biography Ser.). (Illus.). 64p. (gr. 3-5). 1975. PLB 6.59 (ISBN 0-399-60839-7). Putnam.

OSTROGOTHS
see Goths

OSTWALD, WILHELM, 1853-1932
Slosson, Edwin E. Major Prophets of To-Day. facs. ed. LC 68-8493. (Essay Index Reprint Ser). 1914. 18.00 (ISBN 0-8369-0882-1). Arno.

O'SULLIVAN, EDWARD WILLIAM, 1846-1910
Mansfield, B. Australian Democrat. 1965. pap. 6.50x (ISBN 0-424-05010-2, Pub. by Sydney U Pr). Intl Schol Bk Serv.

OSWALD, LEE HARVEY, d. 1963
Eddoes, Michael. The Oswald File. (Illus.). 1978. pap. 2.50 (ISBN 0-441-64175-X). Ace Bks.
Epstein, Edward J. The Legend: Secret World of Lee Harvey Oswald. 1978. 12.95 (ISBN 0-07-019539-0, GB). McGraw.
McMillan, Priscilla J. Marina & Lee. LC 76-26238. (Illus.). 1977. 15.00 (ISBN 0-06-012953-0, HarpT). Har-Row.
Roffman, Howard. Presumed Guilty: Lee Harvey Oswald in the Assassinaion of President Kennedy. LC 74-1119. (Illus.). 297p. 1975. 15.00 (ISBN 0-8386-1526-0). Fairleigh Dickinson.

OSWALD, SAINT, KING OF NORTHUMBRIA, 605-642
Aelfric. Lives of Three English Saints. Needham, G. I., ed. (Old English Ser.). 1966. pap. text ed. 8.95x (ISBN 0-89197-564-0). Irvington.

OSWEGO, NEW YORK-HISTORY
Clark, Olga, illus. Oswego Illustrated 1890. (Illus.). 1977. pap. 7.95 (ISBN 0-930000-09-9). Mathom.

OSWIECIM (CONCENTRATION CAMP)
Amery, Jean. At the Mind's Limits: Contemplations by a Survivor on Auschwitz & Its Realities. Rosenfeld, Sidney & Rosenfeld, Stella P., trs. LC 80-7682. 128p. 1980. 12.50 (ISBN 0-253-17724-3). Ind U Pr.
Auschwitz: An Album. (Illus.). Date not set. price not set. ADL.
Czech, Danuta, et al. Auschwitz: Nazi Extermination Camp. Taylor, Iain W., tr. from Pol. (Illus.). 192p. (Orig.). 1978. pap. 7.50x (ISBN 0-8002-2294-6). Intl Pubns Serv.
Delbo, Charlotte. None of Us Will Return: Auschwitz & After. 1978. pap. 3.95 (ISBN 0-8070-6371-1, BP571). Beacon Pr.
Fleischner, E., ed. Auschwitz - Beginning of a New Era? Reflections on the Holocaust. 22.50x (ISBN 0-87068-499-X). Ktav.
Hellman, Peter, et al. The Auschwitz Album. 1981. 22.95 (ISBN 0-394-51932-9). Random.
Ka-Tzetnik. Atrocity. 1963. 4.95 (ISBN 0-8184-0100-1). Lyle Stuart.
Kielar, Wieslaw. Fifteen Hundred Days in Auschwitz-Birkenau: Fifteen Hundred Days in Auschwitz-Birkenau. Flatauer, Susanne, tr. 352p. 1980. 14.95 (ISBN 0-8129-0921-6). Times Bks.
Levi, Primo. Survival in Auschwitz: The Nazi Assault on Humanity. Woolf, Stuart, tr. Orig. Title: If This Is a Man. 1961. pap. 1.95 (ISBN 0-02-034300-0, Collier). Macmillan.
Lewinska, Pelagia. Twenty Months in Auschwitz. Teichner, Albert, tr. 1968. 4.95 (ISBN 0-8184-0090-0). Lyle Stuart.
Mermelstein, Mel. By Bread Alone: The Story of A-4685. (Illus.). 264p. (Orig.). 1979. pap. 4.95x (ISBN 0-89144-078-X, 7901-781206). M Mermelstein.
Muller, Filip. Eyewitness Auschwitz. LC 78-66257. (Illus.). 1979. 10.95 (ISBN 0-8128-2601-9). Stein & Day.
Nyiszli, Miklos. Auschwitz. 1979. pap. 2.50 (ISBN 0-449-23848-2, Crest). Fawcett.
Pawelczynska, Anna. Values & Violence in Auschwitz: A Sociological Analysis. LC 76-3886. 1979. 14.95x (ISBN 0-520-03210-1); pap. 4.95 (ISBN 0-520-04242-5, CAL-479). U of Cal Pr.
Perl, Gtsella. I Was a Doctor in Auschwitz. LC 79-12470. Repr. of 1948 ed. lib. bdg. 10.00x (ISBN 0-405-12300-0). Arno.
Pisar, Samuel. Of Blood & Hope. 1980. 12.95 (ISBN 0-316-70901-8). Little.
Smolen, Kazimierz, ed. From the History of KL-Auschwitz. Michalik, K., tr. from Pol. 1981. Repr. of 1967 ed. 22.50x (ISBN 0-86527-338-3). Fertig.

OTARIA
see Seals (Animals)

OTERMIN, ANTONIO DE
Hackett, Charles W., ed. Revolt of the Pueblo Indians of New Mexico & Otermin's Attempted Reconquest, 1680-82, 2 Vols. LC 42-22191. (Coronado Cuarto Centennial Ser.: Vols. VIII & IX). 1942. Set. 30.00x (ISBN 0-8263-0161-4). U of NM Pr.

OTFRID VON WEISSENBURG, 9TH CENTURY
Bork, Hans. Chronologische Studien Zu Otfrids Evangelienbuch. 21.50 (ISBN 0-685-02224-2); pap. 18.50 (ISBN 0-685-02225-0). Johnson Repr.
Bossert, Gustav. Quellen Zur Geshichte der Wiedertaufer. 75.00 (ISBN 0-384-05276-2); pap. 69.50 (ISBN 0-384-05275-4). Johnson Repr.
Mackenzie, Donald A. Otfrid Von Weissenburg: Narrator or Commentator. (Stanford University. Stanford Studies in Language & Literature: Vol. 6, Pt. 3). Repr. of 1946 ed. 14.50 (ISBN 0-404-51812-5). AMS Pr.

OTIS, JAMES, 1725-1783
Otis, James. Some Political Writings of James Otis, 2 vols. in 1. LC 75-31099. Repr. of 1929 ed. 16.50 (ISBN 0-404-13516-1). AMS Pr.
Tudor, William. Life of James Otis of Massachusetts. LC 70-118203. (Era of the American Revolution Ser). Repr. of 1823 ed. lib. bdg. 49.50 (ISBN 0-306-71936-3). Da Capo.

OTIS FAMILY
Waters, John J., Jr. Otis Family in Provincial & Revolutionary Massachusetts. LC 68-54951. (Institute of Early American History & Culture Ser.). (Illus.). 1968. 15.50x (ISBN 0-8078-1091-6). U of NC Pr.
--The Otis Family in Provincial & Revolutionary Massachusetts. 256p. 1975. pap. 3.45 (ISBN 0-393-00757-X, Norton Lib). Norton.

OTITIS
see Ear-Diseases

OTJI LANGUAGE
see Twi Language

OTO INDIANS
see Indians of North America-The West

OTOLARYNGOLOGY
see also Ear-Diseases; Throat-Diseases
Adams, George L., et al. Boies's Fundamentals of Otolaryngology: A Textbook of Ear, Nose & Throat Diseases. 5th ed. LC 75-44601. (Illus.). 1978. text ed. 26.00 (ISBN 0-7216-1035-8). Saunders.
Arslan, M., ed. World Congress of Otorhinolaryngology. (International Congress Ser: No. 337). 840p. 1975. 156.00 (ISBN 0-444-15071-4, Excerpta Medica). Elsevier.
Ballantyne, J. C. & Groves, J. A. Synopsis of Otolaryngology. 3rd ed. (Illus.). 1978. 39.50 (ISBN 0-8151-0468-5). Year Bk Med.
Ballenger, John J., ed. Diseases of the Nose, Throat & Ear. 12th ed. LC 77-2674. (Illus.). 1118p. 1977. text ed. 60.00 (ISBN 0-8121-0549-4). Lea & Febiger.
Barany Society Meeting, Toronto, Aug. 1971. Current Studies in Otoneurology: Proceedings. Barber, H. O. & Frederickson, J. M., eds. (Advances in Oto-Rhino-Laryngology: Vol. 19). (Illus.). 1973. 92.25 (ISBN 3-8055-1448-4). S Karger.
Bluestone, Charles D. & Stool, Sylvan. Disorders of Ear Nose & Throat in Children. (Illus.). 1979. text ed. write for info. (ISBN 0-7216-1758-1). Saunders.
Bordley, John & Brookhouser, Patrick. Ear, Nose, & Throat Disorders in Children. 1981. write for info. (ISBN 0-89004-324-8). Raven.
Brown, Joseph F. Dictionary of Speech & Hearing: Anatomy & Physiology. LC 74-76789. (Illus.). 257p. 1974. Repr. 13.00 (ISBN 0-914592-02-5). Press West.
Bull, T. R. & Cook, Joyce L. Speech Theraphy & ENT Surgery. (Blackwell Scientific Pubns.). (Illus.). 1976. 15.75 (ISBN 0-632-09410-9). Mosby.
Bull, T. R. & Ransome, Joselen. Recent Advances in Otolaryngology, No. 5. (Illus.). 1978. text ed. 32.50 (ISBN 0-443-01794-8). Churchill.
Chilla, R., ed. Sialadenosis & Sial. (Advances in Oto-Rhino-Laryngology Ser.: Vol.26). (Illus.). viii, 248p. 1981. 94.75 (ISBN 3-8055-1669-X). S Karger.
--Sialadenosis Ladenitis. (Advances in Oto-Rhino-Laryngology Ser.: Vol. 26). (Illus.). viii, 248p. 1981. 94.75 (ISBN 3-8055-1669-X). S Karger.
Dayal, Vijay S. Clinical Otolaryngology. (Illus.). 304p. 1981. pap. text ed. 24.50 (ISBN 0-397-50499-3). Har-Row.
Deweese, David D. & Saunders, William H. Textbook of Otolaryngology. LC 76-30466. (Illus.). 1977. 29.50 (ISBN 0-8016-1272-1). Mosby.
Di Guglielmo, L. & Campani, R. Xeroradiography in Otorhinolaryngology. 1978. 122.00 (ISBN 0-444-90009-8, Excerpta Medica). Elsevier.
English, Gerald M. Otolaryngology: A Textbook. (Illus.). 800p. 1976. text ed. 60.00x (ISBN 0-06-140783-6, Harper Medical). Har-Row.
Farb, Stanley N. The Ear, Nose, & Throat Book: A Doctor's Guide to Better Health. (Appleton Consumer Health Guides). (Illus.). 158p. 1980. 12.95 (ISBN 0-8385-2021-9); pap. 5.95 (ISBN 0-8385-2020-0). ACC.
--Otolaryngology. 4th ed. LC 70-94388. (Medical Examination Review Bk.: Vol. 16). 1977. spiral bdg. 16.50 (ISBN 0-87488-116-1). Med Exam.
--Otorhinolaryngology. 2nd. ed. (Medical Outline Ser). 1980. pap. 16.00 (ISBN 0-87488-661-9). Med Exam.
Fisch, U., ed. Aktuelle Probleme der Otorhinolaryngologie. (ORL: Vol. 38, Suppl. 1). 1976. 36.00 (ISBN 3-8055-2394-7). S Karger.
Hinchcliffe, Ronald. Scientific Foundations of Otolaryngology. (Illus.). 1976. 68.75 (ISBN 0-8151-4425-3). Year Bk Med.
Hoke, M., ed. Advances in Oto-Rhino-Laryngology, Vol. 27. (Illus.). x, 190p. 1981. 72.00 (ISBN 3-8055-2630-X). S Karger.
International Congress of Radiology in Oto-Rhine-Larymgology, 5th, Copenhagen, June 1976. Modern Methods of Radiology in Oto-Rhino-Laryngology: Selected Papers. Pfaltz, C. R. & Brunner, S. I., eds. (Advances in Oto-Rhino-Laryngology: Vol. 24). (Illus.). 1977. 79.75 (ISBN 3-8055-2707-1). S Karger.
Jazbi, B., ed. Pediatric Otorhinolaryngology. (Advances in ORL: Vol. 23). (Illus.). 1978. 58.25 (ISBN 3-8055-2674-1). S Karger.
Jazbi, Basharat, ed. Pediatric Otorhinolaryngology: A Review of Ear, Nose, & Throat Problems in Children. (Illus.). 288p. 1980. 24.50 (ISBN 0-8385-7799-7). ACC.
Johnson, Fordyce, ed. Allergy: Vol. 2, Including IGE in Diagnosis & Treatment. 1979. 35.00 (ISBN 0-8151-4903-4). Year Bk Med.
Jongkees, L. B. Iatrogenic Problems in Otorlaryngology. 1981. text ed. write for info. (ISBN 0-443-08050-X). Churchill.
Larrauri, Augustin. Dictionnaire d'Oto-Rhino-Laryngologie, 5 vols. (Fr., Eng., Span., Ger. & It.). 1971. 65.00 (ISBN 0-686-56998-9, M-6338). French & Eur.
Lee, K. J. Differential Diagnosis: Otolaryngology. LC 76-5199. (Arco Medical Ser.). (Illus.). 1978. pap. text ed. 10.00x (ISBN 0-668-04017-3, 4017). Arco.
Lee, Keat-Jin, ed. Essential Otolaryngology: A Board Preparation & Concise Reference. 2nd ed. 1977. spiral bdg. 19.50 (ISBN 0-87488-313-X). Med Exam.
Loose Leaf Reference Services. Otolaryngology, 5 vols. English, Gerald, ed. loose leaf bdg. 300.00 (ISBN 0-06-148010-X, Harper Medical); revision pages 50.00 (ISBN 0-685-57888-7). Har-Row.
McGuirt, W. Frederick, ed. Pediatric Otolaryngology Case Studies. LC 80-80367. 1980. pap. 18.50 (ISBN 0-87488-094-7). Med Exam.
Newman, M. Haskell, et al, eds. Handbook of Ear, Nose & Throat Emergencies. 2nd ed. 1973. spiral bdg. 11.00 (ISBN 0-87488-639-2). Med Exam.
Paparella, Michael & Shumrick, Donald A., eds. Otolaryngology: Basic Sciences & Related Disciplines, Vol. 1. LC 70-145563. (Illus.). 1189p. 1973. text ed. 50.00 (ISBN 0-7216-7058-X). Saunders.
Paparella, Michael M. & Shumrick, Donald A. Otolaryngology, 3 vols. 2nd ed. Meyerhoff, William L. & Seid, Allan B., eds. LC 77-25566. (Illus.). 3020p. 1980. Set. text ed. 185.00 (ISBN 0-7216-7061-X); Vol. 1. text ed. 70.00 (ISBN 0-7216-7055-5); Vol. 2. text ed. 55.00 (ISBN 0-7216-7056-3); Vol. 3. text ed. 70.00 (ISBN 0-7216-7057-1). Saunders.
Paparella, Michael M., ed. Yearbook of Otolaryngology, 1980. 1980. 32.95 (ISBN 0-8151-6644-3). Year Bk Med.
Paparella, Michael M. & Shumrick, Donald A., eds. Otolaryngology: Ear, Vol. 2. LC 70-145563. (Illus.). 499p. 1973. text ed. 34.00 (ISBN 0-7216-7059-8). Saunders.
--Otolaryngology: Head & Neck, Vol. 3. LC 70-145563. (Illus.). 906p. 1973. text ed. 50.00 (ISBN 0-7216-7060-1). Saunders.
Pararella, Michael M., ed. Yearbook of Otolaryngology, 1981. Date not set. price not set (ISBN 0-8151-6643-5). Year Bk Med.
Portmann, Michael, et al. The Internal Auditory Meatus. Richards, A. E., tr. from Fr. LC 75-11711. (Illus.). 352p. 1975. text ed. 57.50 (ISBN 0-443-01191-5). Churchill.
Pracy, R., et al. Ear, Nose, Throat: Surgery & Nursing. LC 77-84317. 1977. 16.50 (ISBN 0-471-03918-7). Wiley.
Proctor, Bruce. Chronic Progressive Deafness: Resume of Research in Otolaryngology, 1952-1959. 1963. 10.00x (ISBN 0-8143-1219-5). Wayne St U Pr.
Proctor, Donald F. The Nose, Paranasal Sinuses, & Ears in Childhood. (Pediatric Surgical Monograph). (Illus.). 200p. 1963. photocopy ed. spiral 20.50 (ISBN 0-398-01527-9). C C Thomas.
Roberts, Sam E. Ear, Nose & Throat Dysfunctions Due to Deficiencies & Imbalances. (Illus.). 340p. 1957. photocopy ed. spiral 33.75 (ISBN 0-398-04406-6). C C Thomas.
Smyth, G. D. Diagnostic ENT. (Illus.). 1978. text ed. 9.95x (ISBN 0-19-261133-X). Oxford U Pr.
Snow, James B. An Introduction to Otorhinolaryngology. (Illus., Orig.). 1979. pap. 17.50 (ISBN 0-8151-7853-0). Year Bk Med.
Snow, James B., Jr., ed. Controversy in Otolaryngology. LC 79-64601. (Illus.). 561p. 1980. text ed. 45.00 (ISBN 0-7216-8433-5). Saunders.
Strome, Marshall, ed. Differential Diagnosis in Pediatric Otolaryngology. (Series in Clinical Pediatrics). 320p. 1975. 22.50 (ISBN 0-316-81918-2). Little.
Thorn, L. L. Die Entwicklung des Cortischen Organs Bbeim Meerschweinchen. (Advances in Anatomy, Embryology, & Cell Biology: Vol. 51, Pt. 6). 101p. 1975. pap. 38.40 (ISBN 0-387-07301-9). Springer-Verlag.
Uhde, George I., ed. Self-Assessment of Current Knowledge in Otolaryngology. 2nd ed. 1976. spiral bdg. 14.50 (ISBN 0-87488-270-2). Med Exam.
Wood, Raymond & Northern, Jerry. Manual of Otolaryngology: A Symptom-Oriented Text. 1979. pap. 16.95 (ISBN 0-683-09252-9). Williams & Wilkins.
Yarington, C. T., Jr., ed. Otolaryngology Case Studies. 2nd ed. 1974. spiral bdg. 14.00 (ISBN 0-87488-021-1). Med Exam.
Zizmor, Judah & Noyek, Arnold M. An Atlas of Otolaryngologic Radiology. LC 77-84683. (Illus.). 1978. text ed. 40.00 (ISBN 0-7216-9713-5). Saunders.

OTOLOGY
see Ear

OTOMI INDIANS
see Indians of Mexico

OTORHINOLARYNGOLOGY
see Otolaryngology

OTOSCLEROSIS
Beales, Philip. Otosclerosis. (Illus.). 219p. 1981. text ed. 37.50 (ISBN 0-7236-0598-X). Wright-PSG.
Gapany-Gapana, Vicius B. Otosclerosis: Genetics & Surgical Rehabilitation. LC 75-8545. 1975. 38.95 (ISBN 0-470-29080-3). Halsted Pr.

OTSEGO COUNTY, NEW YORK
Glassie, Henry. Barn Building in Otsego County. pap. 3.50 (ISBN 0-686-16049-5). Fenimore Bk.
Jones, Louis C., ed. Growing up in the Cooper Country: Boyhood Recollections of the New York Frontier. LC 64-23343. 1965. 6.95 (ISBN 0-8156-0040-2). Syracuse U Pr.
Wood, Ralph V., Jr., ed. Ostego County New York State, 1800: Federal Population Census Schedule, Transcript & Index. LC 65-4697. vii, 68p. 1965. pap. 4.50 (ISBN 0-915184-04-4, Pub. by Oak Hill). R V Wood.

OTSTOT FAMILY
Otstot, Charles Mathieson. A History of the Otstot Family in America: Also Being a Guide to the Descendents of Jost & Katherine Otstadt. LC 72-97229. (Illus.). 820p. 1973. with 1974 & 1976 supplements 20.00 (ISBN 0-9603808-0-9). C M Otstot.

OTTERBEIN, GEORG GOTTFRIED, 1731-1800
O'Malley, J. Steven. Pilgrimage of Faith: The Legacy of the Otterbeins. LC 73-5684. (ATLA Monograph: No. 4). 1973. 10.00 (ISBN 0-8108-0626-6). Scarecrow.

OTTERBEIN, PHILIP WILLIAM, 1726-1813
Core, Arthur C. Otterbein (Philip William) 1968. 4.00 (ISBN 0-687-30917-4); pap. 2.25 (ISBN 0-687-30918-2). Abingdon.

OTTERS
Fyson, Marna. Stinkerbelle the Nark: An Otter's Story. LC 75-37458. (Illus.). (YA) (gr. 7 up). 1976. 9.95 (ISBN 0-8008-7421-8). Taplinger.
Harris, Lorle. Biography of a River Otter. LC 78-3606. (Nature Biography Bks.). (Illus.). (gr. 3-6). 1979. PLB 5.49 (ISBN 0-399-61127-4). Putnam.
Maxwell, Gavin. Ring of Bright Water. (gr. 8 up). 1965. pap. 5.95 (ISBN 0-525-47174-X). Dutton.
Riem, J. & Planten, A. The Otter. (Animal Environment Ser.). 30p. 1980. 4.95 (ISBN 0-8120-5378-8). Barron.
Sheehan, Angela. The Otter. (First Look at Nature Bks.). (Illus.). (gr. 2-4). 1979. 2.50 (ISBN 0-531-09099-X); PLB 6.45 s&l (ISBN 0-685-65721-3). Watts.
Wayre, Philip. The Private Life of the Otter. 1979. 17.95 (ISBN 0-7134-0833-2, Pub. by Batsford England). David & Charles.

--The River People: Adventuring with Otters. LC 75-33551. (Illus.). 215p. 1976. 9.95 (ISBN 0-8008-6797-1). Taplinger.

OTTERS, SEA

see Sea-Otters

OTTO, FREI, 1925-

Glaeser, Ludwig. Work of Frei Otto. LC 75-150084. (Illus.). 1972. pap. 6.95 (ISBN 0-87070-333-1). Museum Mod Art.

Glaeser, Ludwig & Otto, Frei. The Work of Frei Otto & His Teams Nineteen Fifty-Five to Nineteen Seventy-Six. (Information of the Institute for Lightweight Structures, University of Stuttgart Ser.: No. 17). (Illus.). 1978. pap. 8.50x (ISBN 0-8150-0747-7). Wittenborn.

OTTO VON PASSAU, fl. 1386

Schmidt, Wieland. Vierundzwanzig Alten Ottos Von Passau. Repr. of 1938 ed. 37.00 (ISBN 0-384-54085-6); pap. 34.00 (ISBN 0-685-13632-9). Johnson Repr.

OTTOMAN EMPIRE

see Turkey

OTWAY, THOMAS, 1652-1685

Hogg, James & Muller, Robert. The Nineteen Fifty-Three Production of "Venice Preserv'd". Bd. with Zur Rezeption Von Otway's "Venice Preserv'd" in der Restaurationszeit. Hogg, James; Nahum Tate's "Richard II" & Censorship During Theexclusion Bill Crisis. Muller, Robert; James Elroy Flecker's "Hassan: a Near East Masterpiece?". Muller, Robert. (Salzburg Studies in English Literature, Poetic Drama & Poetry Theory Ser.: No. 26). 121p. 1976. pap. text ed. 25.00x (ISBN 0-391-01416-1). Humanities.

Pollard, Hazel M. From Heroics to Sentimentalism: A Study of Thomas Otway's Tragedies. (Salzburg Studies in English Literature, Poetic Drama & Poetic Theory: No. 10). 301p. 1974. pap. text ed. 25.00x (ISBN 0-391-01500-1). Humanities.

Schumacher, Edgar. Thomas Otway. LC 74-131457. 1970. Repr. of 1924 ed. lib. bdg. 18.50 (ISBN 0-8337-3176-9). B Franklin.

Taylor, Aline M. Next to Shakespeare. LC 50-10282. Repr. of 1950 ed. 17.50 (ISBN 0-404-06351-9). AMS Pr.

OU-YANG, HSIU, 1007-1072

Liu, James T. Ou-yang Hsiu: An Eleventh-Century Neo-Confucianist. 1967. 10.00x (ISBN 0-8047-0262-4). Stanford U Pr.

OUBYKH LANGUAGE

see Ubykh Language

OUGHTRED, WILLIAM, 1575-1660

Cajori, Florian. William Oughtred: A Great Seventeenth-Century Teacher of Mathematics. vi, 100p. 1916. 9.95 (ISBN 0-87548-174-4). Open Court.

OUSE RIVER, GREAT BRITAIN

Duckham, Baron F. Yorkshire Ouse. LC 67-108689. (Illus.). 1967. 12.50x (ISBN 0-678-05628-5). Kelley.

OUSPENSKY, PETER DEMIANOVICH, 1878-1947

Nicoll, M. Psychological Commentaries on Teaching of Gurdjieff & Ouspensky, 5 vols. Vols. 1-3. 15.00 ea.; Vols. 4 & 5. 17.50 ea. Weiser.

OUT-OF-PRINT BOOKS

see also Reprints (Publications)

Books in Series: Original Reprinted, in-Print, & Out-of-Print Books, Published or Distributed in the United States in Popular, Scholarly, & Professional Series, 3 vols. 3rd ed. 5800p. 1980. 150.00 (ISBN 0-8352-1314-5). Bowker.

Robinson, Ruth & Farudi, Daryush. Buy Books Where-Sell Books Where: A Directory of Out of Print Book Dealers & Their Specialities. 3rd ed. 1981. pap. 17.50 (ISBN 0-9603556-3-4). Robinson Bks.

Tarbert, Gary C., ed. Children's Book Review Index: Annual Clothbound Volumes. LC 75-27408. 48.00 ea.; Annual 1975. (ISBN 0-8103-0626-3); Annual 1976. (ISBN 0-8103-0627-1); Annual 1977. (ISBN 0-8103-0628-X); Annual 1978. (ISBN 0-8103-0629-8); Annual 1979. (ISBN 0-8103-0630-1). Gale.

OUT OF THE BODY EXPERIENCES

see Astral Projection

OUTBOARD MOTOR-BOATS

Dunne, Charles & Nunn, Richard V. Outboard Boat & Motor Maintenance & Repair. LC 75-32262. (Family Guidebooks Ser.). (Illus.). 96p. 1976. pap. 1.95 (ISBN 0-8487-0363-4). Oxmoor Hse.

Warren, Nigel. The Outboard Book. (Illus.). 200p. 1978. 8.95 (ISBN 0-910990-43-3). Hearst Bks.

OUTBOARD MOTORS

Chilton's Automotive Editorial Department. Chilton's Repair & Tune-up Guide for Outboard Motors 30 Horsepower & Over: 1966-1972. LC 72-11533. (Illus.). 284p. 1973. 8.95 (ISBN 0-8019-5722-2); pap. 8.95 (ISBN 0-8019-5803-2). Chilton.

Chrysler Service-Repair Handbook: 3.5 to 20hp, 1966-1979. (Illus.). pap. text ed. 8.00 (ISBN 0-89287-221-7, B655). Clymer Pubns.

Clymer Publications. Johnson Service-Repair Handbook: 1.5 to 35 Hp, 1965-1978. (Illus.). pap. 8.00 (ISBN 0-89287-230-6, B663). Clymer Pubns.

Coles, Clarence & Young, Howard. Evinrude One & Two Cylinder Outboard Tune-up & Repair Manual. 1980. pap. 21.95 (ISBN 0-89330-008-X). Caroline Hse.

--Evinrude Three & Four Cylinder Outboard Tune-up & Repair Manual. 1980. pap. 21.95 (ISBN 0-89330-010-1). Caroline Hse.

--Johnson One & Two Cylinder Outboard Tune-up & Repair Manual. 1980. pap. 21.95 (ISBN 0-89330-007-1). Caroline Hse.

--Johnson Three & Four Cylinder Outboard Tune-up & Repair Manual. 1980. pap. 21.95 (ISBN 0-89330-009-8). Caroline Hse.

--Mercury Outboard Tune-up & Repair Manual. 1980. pap. 21.95 (ISBN 0-89330-006-3). Caroline Hse.

Corcoran, Lawrence. Outboard Service Guide. Corcoran, Lynn, ed. 1977. pap. text ed. 3.00 (ISBN 0-686-24789-2). L Corcoran.

Dempsey, Paul. Complete Guide to Outboard Motor Service & Repair. LC 75-1697. (Illus.). 294p. 1975. pap. 7.95 (ISBN 0-8306-4727-9, 727). TAB Bks.

Evinrude Service-Repair: 1.5 to 35 Hp, 1965-1978. (Illus.). pap. 8.00 (ISBN 0-89287-229-2, B644). Clymer Pubns.

Glenn, Harold T. Glenn's Outboard Motor Tune-up & Repair Ser, 6 bks. Incl. Johnson 1 & 2 Cylinder; Johnson 3 & 4 Cylinder; Evinrude 1 & 2 Cylinder; Evinrude 3 & 4 Cylinder; Chrysler 1 & 2 Cylinder; Chrysler 3 & 4 Cylinder. pap. 7.75 (ISBN 0-8092-8311-5). (Illus.). 1974. Contemp Bks.

Jorgensen, Eric, ed. Chrysler Outboard Service Handbook: 25 to 140 HP, 1966-1980. (Illus.). pap. 8.00 (ISBN 0-89287-183-0, B657). Clymer Pubns.

OUTDOOR ADVERTISING

see Advertising, Outdoor

OUTDOOR COOKERY

see Cookery (Wild Foods); Cookery, Outdoor

OUTDOOR EDUCATION

see also Camping; Natural History–Outdoor Books; Physical Education and Training; School Excursions

American Alliance for Health, Physical Education, & Recreation. Outdoor Education. rev. ed. 1970. 2.00x (ISBN 0-685-05093-9, 246-07320). AAHPERD.

Bachert, Russel E., Jr. Hundreds of Ideas for Outdoor Education. 152p. 1979. pap. text ed. 8.50 (ISBN 0-8134-2095-4). Interstate.

Crisp, Wynnlee. Development & Use of the Outdoor Classroom: An Annotated Bibliography. LC 75-15537. 145p. 1975. 10.00 (ISBN 0-8108-0831-5). Scarecrow.

Ford, Phyllis M. Principles & Practices of Outdoor-Environment Education. LC 80-23200. 348p. 1981. text ed. 16.95 (ISBN 0-471-04768-6). Wiley.

Hammerman, Donald R. & Hammerman, William M. Teaching in the Outdoors. 2nd ed. LC 72-91736. 1973. pap. text ed. 8.95x (ISBN 0-8087-0806-6). Burgess.

--Teaching in the Outdoors. 2nd ed. LC 72-91736. 1973. pap. text ed. 8.95x (ISBN 0-8087-0806-6). Burgess.

Meier, Joel F., et al. High Adventure Outdoor Pursuits: Organization & Leadership. (Brighton Ser. in Recreation & Leisure). (Illus.). 240p. (Orig.). 1980. pap. 9.95 (ISBN 0-89832-019-4). Brighton Pub Co.

Miner, Joshua L. & Boldt, Joe. Outward Bound U. S. A. Learning Through Experience in Adventure Based Education. LC 80-27989. (Illus.). 384p. 1981. 17.95 (ISBN 0-688-00413-X); pap. 8.95 (ISBN 0-688-00414-8). Morrow.

Neimark, Paul. Hiking & Exploring. LC 80-27449. (Wilderness World Ser.). (Illus.). 64p. (gr. 3 up). 1981. PLB 9.25 (ISBN 0-516-02453-1). Childrens.

Riviere, Bill & L. L. Bean Staff. The L. L. Bean Guide to the Outdoors. Date not set. 14.95 (ISBN 0-394-51928-0). Random.

Smith, Julian, et al. Outdoor Education. 2nd ed. (Illus.). 336p. 1972. ref. ed. 15.95 (ISBN 0-13-644997-2). P-H.

Staley, Frederick A. Outdoor Education for the Whole Child. (Illus.). 1979. pap. text ed. 8.95 (ISBN 0-8403-1993-2). Kendall-Hunt.

Swan, Malcolm D., ed. Tips & Tricks in Outdoor Education. 2nd ed. LC 78-51665. 1978. pap. 7.95x (ISBN 0-8134-2031-8, 2031). Interstate.

OUTDOOR LIFE

see also Camping; Country Life; Hiking; Mountaineering; Natural History–Outdoor Books; Picnicking; River Life; Sports; Wayfaring Life

Acerrano, Anthony. Complete Woodsman's Guide. 288p. 1981. 14.95 (ISBN 0-87691-355-9). Winchester Pr.

Acerrano, Anthony J. The Outdoorsman's Emergency Manual. 1976. 11.95 (ISBN 0-87691-221-8). Winchester Pr.

Allison, Linda. The Sierra Club Summer Book. LC 76-57681. (Sierra Club-Scribner Juvenile Ser.). (Illus.). (gr. 3 up). 1977. 7.95 (ISBN 0-684-15014-X); pap. 4.95 (ISBN 0-684-15015-8). Sierra.

Anderson, Ken. The Sterno Guide to the Outdoors. cancelled (ISBN 0-916752-16-X). Green Hill.

--The Sterno Guide to the Outdoors. 1981. pap. 5.95 (ISBN 0-916752-12-7). Caroline Hse.

Andreson, Steve. The Orienteering Book. LC 77-73875. (Illus.). 100p. 1980. pap. 3.95 (ISBN 0-89037-118-0). Anderson World.

Angier, Bradford. How to Live in the Woods on Pennies a Day. LC 70-140741. (Illus.). 192p. 1971. pap. 7.95 (ISBN 0-8117-2009-8). Stackpole.

--How to Stay Alive in the Woods. Orig. Title: Living off the Country. 1962. pap. 2.95 (ISBN 0-02-028050-5, Collier). Macmillan.

--The Master Backwoodsman. 1979. pap. 4.95 (ISBN 0-449-90012-6, Columbine). Fawcett.

--The Master Backwoodsman. LC 77-20787. (Illus.). 224p. 1978. 10.95 (ISBN 0-8117-0972-8). Stackpole.

Bourjaily, Vance. Country Matters: Collected Reports from the Fields & Streams of Iowa & Other Places. 352p. 1973. 8.95 (ISBN 0-8037-1627-3). Dial.

Boy Scouts of America. Boy Scout Fieldbook. new ed. LC 77-93645. (Illus.). 1978. pap. 4.95 (ISBN 0-89480-019-1). Workman Pub.

Bradford, Vena & Bradford, Angier. Wilderness Wife. 1977. pap. 2.95 (ISBN 0-02-058230-7, 05823, Collier). Macmillan.

Brittain, William. Survival Outdoors. (Monarch Illustrated Guide Ser.). (Illus.). 1977. pap. 2.95 (ISBN 0-671-18763-5). Monarch Pr.

Carrighar, Sally. Home to the Wilderness. (Illus.). 1973. 7.95 (ISBN 0-395-15461-8). HM.

Crawford, John S. Wolves, Bears & Bighorns: Wilderness Observations & Experiences of a Professional Outdoorsman. (Illus.). 192p. 1980. 19.95 (ISBN 0-88240-146-7); pap. 12.95 (ISBN 0-686-63422-5). Alaska Northwest.

Demske, Richard. Year-Round Outdoor Building Projects: An Encyclopedia of Building Techniques & Construction Plans. 304p. 1980. pap. 9.95 (ISBN 0-442-21259-3). Van Nos Reinhold.

Eastman, Peter F. Advanced First Aid for All Outdoors. LC 76-44658. (Illus.). 1976. pap. 6.00 (ISBN 0-87033-223-6). Cornell Maritime.

Fleming, June, ed. The Outdoor Idea Book. LC 78-6514. (Illus.). 1978. pap. 6.50 (ISBN 0-918480-06-X). Victoria Hse.

Fodor's Outdoors America. (Fodor's Travel Guide Ser.). (Illus.). 1980. 12.95 (ISBN 0-679-00248-0); pap. 9.95 (ISBN 0-679-00249-9). McKay.

Gode, Merlin. Winter Outdoor Living. 1978. pap. text ed. 2.75 (ISBN 0-89832-008-9). Brighton Pub Co.

Grow, Laurence. The Old House Book of Outdoor Living Places. (Illus., Orig.). 1981. 15.00 (ISBN 0-446-51219-2). Warner Bks.

--The Old House Book of Outdoor Spaces. (Orig.). 1981. 8.95 (ISBN 0-446-97556-7). Warner Bks.

Hamper, Stanley R. Wilderness Survival. 3rd ed. LC 66-249. 1975. Repr. of 1963 ed. 1.79 (ISBN 0-9601048-1-X). Peddlers Wagon.

Hanley, Wayne. A Life Outdoors: A Curmudgeon Looks at the Natural World. (Illus.). 144p. 1980. cancelled (ISBN 0-8289-0417-0); pap. 5.95 (ISBN 0-8289-0403-0). Greene.

Heacox, Cecil E. The Education of an Outdoorsman. 1976. 9.95 (ISBN 0-87691-187-4). Winchester Pr.

Henderson, Luis M. Campers' Guide to Woodcraft & Outdoor Life. LC 71-189973. Orig. Title: Outdoor Guide. 352p. 1972. pap. 3.50 (ISBN 0-486-21147-9). Dover.

Hickin, Norman. Beachcombing for Beginners. 1976. pap. 2.00 (ISBN 0-87980-315-0). Wilshire.

Humphreys, J. Living off the Land. (Illus., Orig.). 1979. pap. 8.50x (ISBN 0-85242-677-1). Intl Pubns Serv.

Johnson, et al. Outdoor Tips: A Remington Sportsmen's Library Bk. pap. 2.95 (ISBN 0-87502-905-1). Benjamin Co.

Kephart, Horace. Camping & Woodcraft. (Illus.). 1948. 10.95 (ISBN 0-02-562680-9). Macmillan.

Kodet, E. Russel & Angier, Bradford. Being Your Own Wilderness Doctor. LC 68-15440. (Illus.). 132p. 1975. pap. 6.95 (ISBN 0-8117-2044-6). Stackpole.

Lueders, Edward. The Clam Lake Papers: A Winter in the North Woods. LC 77-7845. 1977. 7.95 (ISBN 0-06-065312-4, HarpR). Har-Row.

McManus, Patrick. A Fine & Pleasant Misery. LC 77-13452. 1978. 7.95 (ISBN 0-03-022811-5). HR&W.

McPhee Gribble Publishers. Out in the Wilds. (Practical Puffins Ser.). (Illus.). (gr. k-3). 1977. pap. 1.50 (ISBN 0-14-049150-3, Puffin). Penguin.

Merrill, W. K. The Survival Handbook. (Illus.). 1972. 10.95 (ISBN 0-87691-068-1). Winchester Pr.

Mitchell, Jim & Fear, Gene. Fundamentals of Outdoor Enjoyment: Text or Teaching Guide for Coping with Outdoor Environments, All Seasons. (Illus.). 1976. pap. 5.00 (ISBN 0-913724-09-2). Survival Ed Assoc.

Nichols, Maggie. Wild, Wild Woman. 1978. pap. 4.95 (ISBN 0-425-03722-3, Windhover). Berkley Pub.

Norick, Sylvester. Outdoor Life in the Menominee Forest. 1979. 7.95 (ISBN 0-8199-0767-7). Franciscan Herald.

Olsen, Larry D. Outdoor Survival Skills. (gr. 8 up). 1976. pap. 1.95 (ISBN 0-685-68416-4). PB.

Olson, Sigurd F. Sigurd F. Olson's Wilderness Days. (Illus.). 1972. 17.95 (ISBN 0-394-47155-5). Knopf.

Ormond, Clyde. The Complete Book of Outdoor Lore & Woodcraft. LC 81-47715. (Outdoor Life Ser.). (Illus.). 650p. 1982. 20.75 (ISBN 0-06-014962-0, HarpT). Har-Row.

Outdoor Living Skills Instructor's Manual. 1979. pap. 5.00 (ISBN 0-87603-052-5). Am Camping.

Owings, Loren C., ed. Environmental Values, 1860-1972: A Guide to Information Sources. LC 73-17539. (Man & the Environment Information Guide Ser.: Vol. 4). 593p. 1976. 36.00 (ISBN 0-8103-1343-X). Gale.

Patmore, J. Allan. Land & Leisure in England & Wales. LC 75-164656. 332p. 1971. 22.50 (ISBN 0-8386-1024-2). Fairleigh Dickinson.

Petzoldt, Paul. The Wilderness Handbook. (Illus.). 1977. pap. 6.95 (ISBN 0-393-08778-6). Norton.

Platten, David. The Outdoor Survival Handbook. 6.95 (ISBN 0-7153-7793-0). David & Charles.

Rae, William E., ed. A Treasury of Outdoor Life. LC 74-33567. (Outdoor Life Bk.). (Illus.). 448p. (YA) 1976. 12.95 (ISBN 0-06-013466-6, HarpT). Har-Row.

Rawick, George P. From Sundown to Sunup. LC 71-105986. 1972. lib. bdg. 15.00x (ISBN 0-8371-6299-8, RSM&); pap. 4.45 (ISBN 0-8371-6747-7). Greenwood.

Rutstrum, Calvin. Backcountry. LC 80-22052. (Illus.). 200p. 1981. 10.95 (ISBN 0-934802-07-6). ICS Bks.

--The New Way of the Wilderness. 1973. pap. 2.95 (ISBN 0-02-029850-1, Collier). Macmillan.

--Once Upon a Wilderness. LC 72-91260. (Illus.). 208p. 1973. 9.95 (ISBN 0-02-606330-1). Macmillan.

Ruxton, George F. Adventures in Mexico & the Rocky Mountains. LC 72-13957. (Beautiful Rio Grande Classics Ser). lib. bdg. 12.00 (ISBN 0-87380-101-6). Rio Grande.

Scharff, Robert. Projects for Outdoor Living. 1981. 7.95 (ISBN 0-8359-5698-9). Reston.

Shepherd, Laurie. A Dreamer's Log Cabin: A Woman's Walden. LC 81-3215. (Illus., Orig.). 1981. pap. 8.95 (ISBN 0-934878-06-4). Dembner Bks.

Thomas, Gordon. Mostly in Fun: Rhymes & Reflections on Outdoor Experiences. (Illus.). 1977. pap. 3.95 (ISBN 0-913140-23-6). Signpost Bk Pub.

Van De Smissen, Betty & Goering, Oswald H. A Leader's Guide to Nature-Oriented Activities. 3rd ed. (Illus.). 1977. pap. text ed. 7.95x (ISBN 0-8138-1125-2). Iowa St U Pr.

Walt Disney Productions. The Outdoor Adventure Book. LC 77-74468. (Disney's World of Adventure). (Illus.). (gr. 2-6). 1977. (BYR); PLB 4.99 (ISBN 0-394-93601-9). Random.

Wilkins, Marne. The Long Ago Lake: A Child's Book of Nature Lore & Crafts. LC 77-18173. (Sierra Club-Scribner Juvenile Ser.). (Illus.). (gr. 5 up). 1978. 8.95 (ISBN 0-684-15614-8); pap. 5.95 (ISBN 0-684-15613-X). Sierra.

Woolner, Frank. My New England. LC 72-87870. (Illus.). 176p. 1972. 10.00 (ISBN 0-913276-01-4). Stone Wall Pr.

Wurman, Richard S., et al. The Nature of Recreation: A Handbook in Honor of Frederick Law Olmsted. 100p. 1972. pap. 5.95 (ISBN 0-262-73034-0). MIT Pr.

OUTDOOR RECREATION

see also Camping; Parks; Picnicking; Recreation Areas; Wildlife Conservation

Alderson, Frederick. Outdoor Games. (Junior Reference Ser.). (Illus.). 64p. (gr. 7 up). 1980. 7.95 (ISBN 0-7136-2031-5). Dufour.

Allton, David. Valuing Outdoor Recreation Benefits: An Annotated Bibliography. (Public Administration Ser.: P 258). 1979. pap. 5.00 (ISBN 0-686-25115-6). Vance Biblios.

Berman, Steve. The Northeastern Outdoors: A Field & Travel Guide. LC 76-52519. (Illus.). 1977. pap. 7.95 (ISBN 0-913276-21-9). Stone Wall Pr.

Brockman, C. Frank & Merriam, Lawrence C., Jr. Recreational Use of Wild Lands. 3rd ed. (M-H Series in Forest Resources). (Illus.). 1979. text ed. 17.00 (ISBN 0-07-007982-X, C). McGraw.

Burby, Raymond J., 3rd. Recreation & Leisure in New Communities. LC 76-17871. (New Communities Research Ser.). 1976. 19.50 (ISBN 0-88410-448-6). Ballinger Pub.

Cooper, Dale, et al. The Outdoor Handbook. (Illus.). 1978. 13.95 (ISBN 0-600-36743-6). Transatlantic.

Coppock, J. T. & Duffield, B. S. Recreation in the Countryside: A Spatial Analysis. LC 75-9115. (Illus.). 250p. 1975. 21.50 (ISBN 0-312-66605-5). St Martin.

Darst, Paul W. & Armstrong, George P. Outdoor Adventure Activities for School & Recreation Programs. LC 80-66363. (Orig.). pap. text ed. 13.95x (ISBN 0-8087-0489-3). Burgess.

Darvill, Fred T., Jr. & Marshall, Louise B. Winter Walks & Summer Strolls. (Illus.). 1977. pap. 2.95 (ISBN 0-913140-21-X). Signpost Bk Pubns.

Doan, Marlyn. Starting Small in the Wilderness: The Sierra Club Outdoors Guide for Families. LC 79-748. (Outdoor Guides Ser.). (Illus.). 1979. pap. 6.95 (ISBN 0-87156-253-7). Sierra.

Dorsey, Joan. Introducing Your Kids to the Outdoors. LC 78-51938. 1978. pap. 4.95 (ISBN 0-913276-25-1). Stone Wall Pr.

Douglass, Robert W. Forest Recreation. 2nd ed. 1975. text ed. 19.50 (ISBN 0-08-018008-6). Pergamon.

Driver, B. L. Elements of Outdoor Recreation Planning. 316p. 1974. pap. text ed. 5.95x (ISBN 0-472-08284-1). U of Mich Pr.

Eathorne, Richard H. The Analysis of Outdoor Recreation Demand: A Review & Annotated Bibliography of the Current State-of-the-Art. (Public Administration Ser.: Bibliography P-563). 93p. 1980. pap. 10.00 (ISBN 0-686-29075-5). Vance Biblios.

Farmer, Charles J. Digest Book of Canoes, Kayaks, & Rafts. (Illus.). 192p. 1977. pap. 5.95 (ISBN 0-695-80719-6). DBI.

Fleming, June, ed. The Outdoor Idea Book. LC 78-6514. (Illus.). 1978. pap. 6.50 (ISBN 0-918480-06-X). Victoria Hse.

Folkard, Frederick. Boys Book of Outdoors Adventure. Date not set. 12.50 (ISBN 0-392-14100-0, SpS). Sportshelf.

Ford, Phyllis M. Principles & Practices of Outdoor-Environment Education. LC 80-23200. 348p. 1981. text ed. 16.95 (ISBN 0-471-04768-6). Wiley.

Haas, Carolyn, et al. Backyard Vacation: Outdoor Fun in Your Own Neighbor. (Illus.). 1980. 9.95 (ISBN 0-686-29732-6); pap. 5.95 (ISBN 0-686-29731-8). CBH Pub.

Jensen, Clayne R. Outdoor Recreation in America: Trends, Problems, & Opportunities. 3rd ed. LC 76-52662. 1977. text ed. 15.95x (ISBN 0-8087-1035-4). Burgess.

Johnson, et al. Outdoor Tips: A Remington Sportsmen's Library Bk. pap. 2.95 (ISBN 0-87502-905-1). Benjamin Co.

Jubenbille, Alan. Outdoor Recreation Planning. LC 75-5051. (Illus.). 400p. 1976. text ed. 13.95 (ISBN 0-7216-5228-X). HR&W.

Jubenville, Alan. Outdoor Recreation Management. LC 77-23998. (Illus.). 1978. text ed. 13.95 (ISBN 0-7216-5230-1). HR&W.

Knudson, Douglas M. Outdoor Recreation. (Illus.). 1980. text ed. 21.95 (ISBN 0-02-365350-7). Macmillan.

LeRoy, David. The Outdoorsman's Guide to Government Surplus. 1978. 9.95 (ISBN 0-8092-7612-7). Contemp Bks.

McManus, Patrick. They Shoot Canoes, Don't They? 228p. 1981. 10.95 (ISBN 0-03-058646-1). HR&W.

Malone, Tom. Rejoicing with Creation. pap. 5.95 (ISBN 0-8042-1420-4). John Knox.

Mattson, Lloyd & Mattson, Elsie. Rediscover Your Family Outdoors. 132p. 1980. pap. 3.95 (ISBN 0-88207-605-1). Victor Bks.

Meier, Joel F., et al. High Adventure Outdoor Pursuits: Organization & Leadership. (Brighton Ser. in Recreation & Leisure). (Illus.). 240p. (Orig.). 1980. pap. 9.95 (ISBN 0-89832-019-4). Brighton Pub Co.

Miller, Peggy L. Creative Outdoor Play Areas. (Illus.). 144p. 1972. ref. ed. 9.50 (ISBN 0-13-190595-3). P-H.

Ovington, Ray. Pelican. (Illus.). 1977. pap. 1.50 (ISBN 0-8200-0905-9). Great Outdoors.

Patmore, J. Allan. Land & Leisure in England & Wales. LC 75-164656. 332p. 1971. 22.50 (ISBN 0-8386-1024-2). Fairleigh Dickinson.

Schoenfeld, Clay. Everybody's Ecology: A Field Guide to Pleasure in the Out-Of-Doors. LC 74-139987. (Illus.). 1971. 8.95 (ISBN 0-498-07850-7). A S Barnes.

Shomon, Joseph James. Open Land for Urban America: Acquisition, Safekeeping, & Use. LC 70-147367. (Illus.). 176p. 1971. 12.00x (ISBN 0-8018-1217-8); pap. 2.95x (ISBN 0-8018-1435-9). Johns Hopkins.

Smith, Cledus R., et al. Rural Recreation for Profit. 2nd ed. LC 68-14815. (Illus.). (gr. 9-12). 1968. 14.60 (ISBN 0-8134-0846-6). Interstate.

Sparano, Vin. Complete Outdoors Encyclopedia. LC 72-90934. 1980. 16.95 (ISBN 0-06-014033-X, HarpT). Har-Row.

Thomas, Dian. Backyard Roughing It Easy. 1980. pap. 5.95 (ISBN 0-449-90018-5, Columbine). Fawcett.

Turner, Pearl. Index to Outdoor Sports, Games & Activities. LC 76-58112. (Useful Reference Ser. of Library Bks.: Vol. 105). 1978. 18.00 (ISBN 0-87305-105-X). Faxon.

Van De Smissen, Betty & Goering, Oswald H. A Leader's Guide to Nature-Oriented Activities. 3rd ed. (Illus.). 1977. pap. text ed. 7.95x (ISBN 0-8138-1125-2). Iowa St U Pr.

Van Doren, Carlton, et al, eds. Land & Leisure: Concepts & Methods in Outdoor Recreation. 2nd ed. LC 77-94184. (Maaroufa Press Geography Ser.). (Illus.). 1979. pap. text ed. 7.95x (ISBN 0-88425-010-5). Maaroufa Pr.

Van Lier, H. N. Determination of Planning Capacity & Layout Criteria of Outdoor Recreation Projects. 168p. 1974. 30.00 (ISBN 90-220-0445-7, Pub. by PUDOC). Unipub.

Witt, Ted R. Responsible with Creation. pap. 5.95 (ISBN 0-8042-1422-0). John Knox.

Wurman, Richard S., et al. The Nature of Recreation: A Handbook in Honor of Frederick Law Olmsted. 100p. 1972. pap. 5.95 (ISBN 0-262-73034-0). MIT Pr.

OUTDOOR RELIEF

see Charities; Public Welfare

OUTDOOR SCHOOLS

see Open-Air Schools

OUTER BANKS, NORTH CAROLINA

McAdoo, Donald E. & McAdoo, Carol. Reflections of the Outer Banks. LC 75-23489. 104p. 1976. 14.95 (ISBN 0-916424-00-6). Island Pub.

Robert, Bruce & Stick, David. Cape Hatteras Seashore. LC 64-23727. (Illus.). pap. 3.95 (ISBN 0-87461-950-5). McNally.

Stick, David. Outer Banks of North Carolina, 1584-1958. (Illus.). 1958. 9.95 (ISBN 0-8078-0746-X). U of NC Pr.

OUTER MONGOLIA

see Mongolia

OUTER SPACE

see also Space Environment

Brown, Seyom, et al. Regimes for the Ocean, Outer Space, & Weather. 1977. 14.95 (ISBN 0-8157-1156-5); pap. 5.95 (ISBN 0-8157-1155-7). Brookings.

Calder, Nigel. Spaceships of the Mind. (Illus.). 1978. 14.95 (ISBN 0-670-66021-3). Viking Pr.

Clarke, Arthur C. Challenge of the Spaceship. 1980. pap. 2.50 (ISBN 0-671-82139-3). PB.

Colloquium on the Law of Outer Space - International Institute of Space Law of the International Astronautical Federation, 12th, 1969. Proceedings. Schwartz, Mortimer D., ed. iii, 336p. (Orig.). 1970. pap. text ed. 27.50x (ISBN 0-8377-0407-3). Rothman.

Colloquium on the Law of Outer Space-International Institute of Space Law of the International Astronautical Federation, 13th, 1970. Proceedings. Schwartz, Mortimer D., ed. iii, 381p. 1971. pap. text ed. 27.50x (ISBN 0-8377-0408-1). Rothman.

Colloquium on the Law of Outer Space - International Institute of Space Law of the International Astronautical Federation, 19th, 1976. Proceedings. Schwartz, Mortimer D., ed. 419p. 1977. pap. text ed. 27.50x (ISBN 0-8377-0414-6). Rothman.

ESLAB Symposium, 6th, Noordwijk, the Netherlands, Sept. 1972. Photon & Particle Interactions with Surfaces in Space: Proceedings. Grard, R. J., ed. LC 73-83561. (Astrophysics & Space Science Library: No. 37). 600p. 1973. lib. bdg. 84.00 (ISBN 90-277-0381-7, Pub. by Reidel Holland). Kluwer Boston.

Feldman, Anthony. Space. 336p. 1980. 19.95 (ISBN 0-87196-416-3). Facts on File.

Hall, Marie B. Inquiry into the Nature of Space & of Life in Space. (Illus.). 1970. 8.50 (ISBN 0-938760-01-7). Veritat Found.

Hapgood, Fred. Space Shots. LC 78-68713. (Illus.). 1979. pap. 7.95 (ISBN 0-8129-0823-6). Times Bks.

Heppenheimer, T. A. Colonies in Space. (Illus.). 1978. pap. 2.75 (ISBN 0-446-95559-0). Warner Bks.

Knight, David. Colonies in Orbit: The Coming Age of Human Settlements in Space. (gr. 5-9). 1977. PLB 6.96 (ISBN 0-688-32096-1). Morrow.

Leinster. Operation: Outer Space. pap. 2.00 (ISBN 0-686-00171-0, Fantasy Press). Fantasy Pub Co.

Newlon, Clark. One Thousand One Questions Answered About Space. 3rd ed. LC 77-131238. (Illus.). 1971. 7.50 (ISBN 0-396-04624-X). Dodd.

Robinson, George S. Living in Outer Space: Biological Foundations of Space Law. 1976. 6.00 (ISBN 0-8183-0243-7). Pub Aff Pr.

Sarnoff, Jane & Ruffins, Reynold. Space: A Fact & Riddle Book. LC 78-11499. (gr. 1-5). 1978. reinforced bdg 8.95 (ISBN 0-684-15898-1, ScribJ). Scribner.

SIPRI. Outer Space: Battlefield of the Future. LC 77-26368. 1978. 20.50x (ISBN 0-8448-1312-5). Crane-Russak Co.

Taubenfeld, Howard J., ed. Space & Society. LC 64-21185. 1964. 12.50 (ISBN 0-379-00210-8). Oceana.

Wise, William A. Monsters from Outer Space? LC 77-16504. (See & Read Science). (Illus.). 1978. PLB 6.29 (ISBN 0-399-61089-8). Putnam.

OUTER SPACE–EXPLORATION

see also Astronautics–International Cooperation; Lunar Probes; Religion and Astronautics

AAS - AAAS Symposium - Montreal - 1964. Towards Deeper Space Penetration. Van Driest, Edard R., ed. (Science & Technology Ser.: Vol. 2). 1964. 20.00 (ISBN 0-87703-030-8). Am Astronaut.

Adelman, Benjamin & Adelman, Saul J. Bound for the Stars: An Enthusiastic Look at the Opportunities & Challenges Space Exploration Offers. (Illus.). 368p. 1980. text ed. 17.95 (ISBN 0-13-080390-1, Spec); pap. text ed. 8.95 (ISBN 0-13-080382-0). P-H.

American Astronautical Society. Advances in the Astronautical Sciences. Incl. Vol. 6. Sixth Annual Meeting, New York, 1960. Jacobs, H. & Burgess, E., eds. 45.00 (ISBN 0-87703-007-3); Vol. 9. Fourth Western Regional Meeting, San Francisco, 1961. Jacobs, H. & Burgess, E., eds. 45.00 (ISBN 0-87703-010-3); Vol. 11. Eighth Annual Meeting, Washington, 1962. 45.00 (ISBN 0-87703-012-X); Vol. 13. Ninth Annual Meeting, Interplanetary Missions, Los Angeles, 1963. Burgess, E., ed. 45.00 (ISBN 0-87703-014-6). Am Astronaut.

Blaine, J. C. End of an Era in Space Exploration. Jacobs, H., ed. (Science & Technology: Vol. 42). (Illus.). 1976. 25.00x (ISBN 0-87703-080-4). Am Astronaut.

Bova, Ben. The High Road. 11.95 (ISBN 0-395-31288-4). HM.

Branley, Franklyn M. Space Colony: Frontier of the 21st Century. Buckley, Virginia, ed. (Illus.). 128p. 1981. 10.25 (ISBN 0-525-66741-5, 0995-300). Elsevier-Nelson.

Calder, Nigel. Spaceships of the Mind. 1979. pap. 6.95 (ISBN 0-14-005231-3). Penguin.

Charbonneau, Gary. Index to Aerospace Historian: Cumulative Index by Author, Title, & Subject 1954-1973. 1974. pap. text ed. 12.00x (ISBN 0-89126-011-0). MA-AH Pub.

Clarke, Arthur C. Report on Planet Three & Other Speculations. LC 74-156515. 1972. 9.95 (ISBN 0-06-010793-6, HarpT). Har-Row.

Colby, C. B. Beyond the Moon: Future Explorations in Interplanetary Space. (Illus.). (gr. 4-7). 1971. PLB 5.29 (ISBN 0-698-30023-8). Coward.

DeNevi, Don. To the Edges of the Universe: Space Exploration in the Twentieth Century. LC 77-90005. (Illus.). 1978. pap. 5.95 (ISBN 0-89087-212-0). Celestial Arts.

Deutsch, Armin J. & Klemperer, Wolfgang B., eds. Space Age Astronomy: An International Symposium. 1962. 67.50 (ISBN 0-12-213550-4). Acad Pr.

Elliot, Jeffrey M. The Future of the Space Program--Large Corporations & Society: Discussions with 22 Science-Fiction Writers. LC 80-19754. (Great Issues of the Day Ser.: Vol. 1). 64p. (Orig.). 1981. lib. bdg. 8.95x (ISBN 0-89370-140-8); pap. text ed. 2.95x (ISBN 0-89370-240-4). Borgo Pr.

Engelbrektson, Sune & Greenleaf, Peter. Let's Explore Outer Space. LC 74-29771. (A Sentinel Science Bk.). (Illus., Orig.). 1969. pap. 2.25 (ISBN 0-668-03250-2). Arco.

Fallaci, Oriana. If the Sun Dies. Swinglehurst, Pamela, tr. from Ital. LC 66-23576. ix, 403p. 1981. pap. 8.95 (ISBN 0-689-70610-3, 269). Atheneum.

Flinn, E., ed. Scientific Results of Viking Project. 1977. 30.00 (ISBN 0-87590-207-3). Am Geophysical.

Gatland, Kenneth. The Illustrated Encyclopedia of Space Technology: A Comprehensive History of Space Exploration. 288p. 1981. 24.95 (ISBN 0-517-54258-7, Harmony). Crown.

Handbook of Soviet Lunar & Planetary Exploration, Vol. 14. (Science & Technology Ser.). 1979. lib. bdg. 35.00 (ISBN 0-87703-105-3); pap. 25.00 (ISBN 0-87703-106-1). Am Astronaut.

Handbook of Soviet Manned Space Flight, Vol 48. (Science & Technology Ser.). 1980. 45.00 (ISBN 0-87703-115-0); pap. 35.00 (ISBN 0-87703-116-9). Am Astronaut.

Johnston, Richard S., et al, eds. Future U. S. Space Programs, 2 pts. (Advances in the Astronautical Sciences: Vol. 38). (Illus.). 1979. lib. bdg. 85.00x (ISBN 0-87703-119-3); Pt. I. 40.00 (ISBN 0-87703-098-7); Pt. II. 45.00 (ISBN 0-87703-099-5); microfiche suppl. 10.00 (ISBN 0-87703-129-0). Am Astronaut.

Lebedev, L. & Romanov, A. Rendezvous in Space: Soyuz - Apollo. 209p. 1979. 7.50 (ISBN 0-8285-1517-4, Pub. by Mir Pubs Russia). Imported Pubns.

Lewis, Richard S. From Vinland to Mars: A Thousand Years of Exploration. LC 76-9716. 1978. pap. 5.95 (ISBN 0-8129-6297-4). Times Bks.

Lowman, P. D., Jr. Space Panorama. (Illus.). 1968. 35.00 (ISBN 0-685-12042-2). Heinman.

Mellersh, N. Discoverers of the Universe. 1976. 4.05 (ISBN 0-08-008741-8). Pergamon.

Moore, Patrick. The Next Fifty Years in Space. LC 75-26326. (Illus.). 144p. 1976. 12.95 (ISBN 0-8008-5528-0). Taplinger.

Morgenthaler, G. W. & Morra, R. G., eds. Unmanned Exploration of the Solar System. (Advances in the Astronautical Sciences Ser.: Vol. 19). 1965. 45.00 (ISBN 0-87703-021-9). Am Astronaut.

New Dimensions Foundation, ed. Worlds Beyond: The Everlasting Frontier. LC 78-54345. 1978. pap. 6.95 (ISBN 0-915904-36-5). And-or Pr.

Oberg, James E. Red Star in Orbit. (Illus.). 1981. 12.95 (ISBN 0-394-51429-7). Random.

Powers, Robert M. Planetary Encounters. LC 78-16516. (Illus.). 288p. 1978. 13.95 (ISBN 0-8117-1270-2). Stackpole.

--Shuttle. LC 79-652. (Illus.). 256p. 1979. pap. 12.95 (ISBN 0-8117-2112-4). Stackpole.

Ramo, Simon, et al, eds. Peacetime Uses of Outer Space. LC 76-52430. (Illus.). 1977. Repr. of 1961 ed. lib. bdg. 21.00x (ISBN 0-8371-9368-0, RAPU). Greenwood.

Rickert, Russell K. Astronomy & Space Exploration. 1974. text ed. 9.50 (ISBN 0-201-06431-6). A-W.

Schneider, W. C. & Hanes, T. E., eds. Skylab Results, 2 pts, Pt. 1 & 2. (Advances in the Astronautical Sciences Ser.: Vol. 31). 1975. write for info. (ISBN 0-87703-072-3); microfiche 55.00 (ISBN 0-686-66267-9). Am Astronaut.

Seventeenth Annual Meeting, Seattle, 1971. Outer Solar System, 2 pts. Vagners, Juris, ed. (Advances in the Astronautical Sciences Ser.: Vol. 29). 1971. Pt. 1. lib. bdg. 40.00 (ISBN 0-87703-059-6); Pt. 2. lib. bdg. 45.00 (ISBN 0-87703-060-X). Am Astronaut.

Vajk, Dr. J. Peter. Doomsday Has Been Cancelled. LC 78-62300. (Illus.). 240p. 1978. pap. 7.95 (ISBN 0-915238-24-1). Peace Pr.

Wainerdi, R. E. Analytical Chemistry in Space. 1970. text ed. 60.00 (ISBN 0-08-006887-1). Pergamon.

OUTER SPACE–EXPLORATION–JUVENILE LITERATURE

Asimov, Isaac. Saturn & Beyond. LC 78-21996. (Illus.). (gr. 5 up). 1979. 8.50 (ISBN 0-688-41876-7); PLB 8.16 (ISBN 0-688-51876-1). Lothrop.

Boy Scouts Of America. Space Exploration. LC 19-600. (Illus.). 64p. (gr. 6-12). 1966. pap. 0.70x (ISBN 0-8395-3354-3, 3354). BSA.

Cohen, Daniel. A Close Look at Close Encounters. LC 80-2784. (Illus.). 160p. (gr. 7 up). 1981. PLB 7.95 (ISBN 0-396-07927-X). Dodd.

Furniss, Tim. Man in Space. (Today's World Ser.). (Illus.). 72p. (gr. 7-9). 1981. 14.95 (ISBN 0-7134-3582-8, Pub. by Batsford England). David & Charles.

Gurney, Gene. Walk in Space: The Story of Project Gemini. (gr. 5 up). 1967. PLB 5.99 (ISBN 0-394-90417-6, BYR). Random.

Harris, Susan. Space. (Easy-Read Fact Bks.). (Illus.). (gr. 2-4). 1979. PLB 6.90 s&l (ISBN 0-531-02852-6). Watts.

Kerrod, Robin. The Challenge of Space. LC 79-64385. (The Question & Answer Bks.). (Illus.). (gr. 3-6). 1980. PLB 6.95g (ISBN 0-8225-1177-0). Lerner Pubns.

--Mission Outer Space. LC 79-64388. (The Question & Answer Bks.). (Illus.). (gr. 3-6). 1980. PLB 6.95g (ISBN 0-8225-1180-0). Lerner Pubns.

Spizzirri Publishing Co. Staff. Space Explorers: An Educational Coloring Book. Spizzirri, Linda, ed. (Illus.). 32p. (gr. 1-8). 1981. pap. 1.25 (ISBN 0-86545-037-4). Spizzirri.

Turnill, Reginald. Space Age. (Illus.). (gr. 3-7). 1980. 12.95 (ISBN 0-7232-2408-0). Warne.

OUTER SPACE–JUVENILE LITERATURE

Abels, Harriette S. Future Space. Schroeder, Howard, ed. LC 80-16457. (Our Future World Ser.). (Illus.). 48p. (Orig.). (gr. 4 up). PLB 6.95 (ISBN 0-89686-087-6); pap. 3.25 (ISBN 0-89686-096-5). Crestwood Hse.

Asimov, Isaac. How Did We Find Out About Outer Space? 64p. 1977. PLB 6.85 (ISBN 0-8027-6284-0). Walker & Co.

--Satellites in Outer Space. rev. ed. (Gateway Ser.: No. 16). (Illus.). (gr. 3-5). 1964. PLB 5.99 (ISBN 0-394-90116-9, BYR). Random.

Branley, Franklyn M. Book of Outer Space for You. LC 71-94790. (Illus.). (gr. 2-5). 1970. PLB 9.89 (ISBN 0-690-15474-7, TYC-J). Har-Row.

Di Certo, Joseph J. Star Voyage. LC 81-808. Orig. Title: One Hundred Two Questions & Answers About Outer Space. (Illus.). 96p. (gr. 4-7). 1981. PLB 7.79 (ISBN 0-671-33034-9). Messner.
Golden, Frederic. Colonies in Space: The Next Giant Step. LC 76-46784. (Illus.). (gr. 7 up). 1977. 8.95 (ISBN 0-15-219400-2, HJ). HarBraceJ.
--Colonies in Space: The Next Giant Step. LC 76-46784. (Illus.). (gr. 7 up). 1977. 8.95 (ISBN 0-15-219400-2, HJ). HarBraceJ.
Gurney, Gene. Space Technology Spinoffs. (Impact Ser.). (Illus.). (gr. 7 up). 1979. PLB 7.45 s&l (ISBN 0-531-02290-0). Watts.
Moche, Dinah L. The Star Wars Question & Answer Book About Space. LC 78-19684. (Illus.). (gr. 3-6). 1979. PLB 5.95 (ISBN 0-394-84053-4, BYR); 5.99g (ISBN 0-394-94053-9). Random.
Moncure, Jane B. Magic Monsters Learn About Space. LC 79-25765. (Magic Monster Ser.). (Illus.). (ps-3). 1980. PLB 5.95 (ISBN 0-89565-119-X). Childs World.
Smith, Norman. Moonhopping: Through Our Solar System. (Science Is What & Why Ser.). (Illus.). (gr. k-3). 1977. PLB 5.99 (ISBN 0-698-30643-0). Coward.
--Space: What's Out There. (What Lives There Ser.). (Illus.). 32p. (gr. 2-6). 1976. PLB 5.59 (ISBN 0-698-30585-X). Coward.

OUTER SPACE AND CIVILIZATION
see Astronautics and Civilization

OUTER SPACE COMMUNICATION
see Interstellar Communication

OUTLAWRY OF WAR TREATY, PARIS, 1928
see Renunciation of War Treaty, Paris, Aug. 27, 1928

OUTLAWS
see also Brigands and Robbers
Adams, Ramon F., compiled by. The Adams One-Fifty. LC 76-8959. (Illus.). 100p. 1976. 30.00 (ISBN 0-8363-0143-9). Jenkins.
Greenwood, Robert. The California Outlaw: Tiburcio Vasquez. LC 73-14203. (The Mexican American Ser.). (Illus.). 296p. 1974. Repr. 16.00x (ISBN 0-405-05677-X). Arno.
Harris, Grant B. Shanley: Pennies Wise - Dollars Foolish. LC 79-62935. 1980. 8.95 (ISBN 0-533-04191-0). Vantage.
Horan, James D. The Authentic Wild West: The Outlaws, Vol. 2. (Illus.). 1977. 15.95 (ISBN 0-517-53100-3). Crown.
Hutton, Harold. Doc Middleton: Life & Legends of the Notorious Plains Outlaw. LC 67-14260. (Illus.). 290p. 1980. Repr. of 1974 ed. 14.95 (ISBN 0-8040-0532-X, SB). Swallow.
Jackson, Joseph H. Bad Company: The Story of California's Legendary & Actual Stage-Robbers, Bandits, Highwaymen & Outlaws from the Fifties to the Eighties. LC 77-7300. (Illus.). xx, 346p. 1977. 21.50x (ISBN 0-8032-0930-4); pap. 5.95 (ISBN 0-8032-5866-6, BB 649, Bison). U of Nebr Pr.
McCarthy, Pat. America's Bad Men. Mooney, Thomas, ed. (Pal Paperbacks Ser., Kit A). (Illus., Orig.). (gr. 7-12). 1974. pap. text ed. 1.25 (ISBN 0-8374-3476-9). Xerox Ed Pubns.
Myers, John M. Doc Holliday. LC 55-5528. 224p. 1973. pap. 3.95 (ISBN 0-8032-5781-3, BB 570, Bison). U of Nebr Pr.
O'Neal, William. Henry Brown: Outlaw Marshal. LC 80-65457. 165p. 1981. 12.95 (ISBN 0-932702-09-0); collector's edition 75.00 (ISBN 0-932702-10-4). Creative Texas.
Phares, Ross. Reverend Devil. (Illus.). 263p. 1974. 15.00 (ISBN 0-88289-011-5). Pelican.
Turner, Alford E., ed. The O.K. Corral Inquest. (Illus.). 256p. 1981. 19.95 (ISBN 0-932702-14-7); pap. 9.50 (ISBN 0-932702-16-3); collector's ed. 75.00 (ISBN 0-932702-15-5). Creative Texas.
Vanderwood, Paul J. Disorder & Progress: Bandits, Police, & Mexican Development. LC 80-22345. (Illus.). xx, 264p. 1981. 21.50x (ISBN 0-8032-4651-X); pap. 8.95 (ISBN 0-8032-9600-2, BB 767, Bison). U of Nebr Pr.

OUTPATIENT SERVICES IN HOSPITALS
see Hospitals–Outpatient Services

OUTPUT EQUIPMENT (COMPUTERS)
see Computer Input-Output Equipment

OUTPUT STANDARDS
see Production Standards

OUTSIDE BROKERS
see Brokers

OVARIES
see also Menstruation; Ovulation; Progesterone
Andersen, Allen C. & Simpson, Miriam E. The Ovary & Reproductive Cycle of the Dog (Beagle) LC 72-83492. (Illus.). 1973. text ed. 30.00x (ISBN 0-87672-007-6). Geron-X.
Barber, Hugh. Ovarian Carcinoma: Etiology, Diagnosis & Treatment. LC 77-846077. (Illus.). 1978. 41.25 (ISBN 0-89352-009-8). Masson Pub.
Blaustein, Ancel U., et al. Pathology of the Ovary. 189p. 1974. pap. 147.50 (ISBN 0-686-66848-0); cassette & filmstrips avail. (ISBN 0-685-36221-3). Saunders.
Coutts, S. R., ed. Functional Morphology of the Human Ovary. 350p. text ed. 39.50 (ISBN 0-8391-1647-0). Univ Park.
De Watteville, H. Diagnosis & Treatment of Ovarian Neoplastic Alterations. (International Congress Ser.: No. 364). 1976. 52.75 (ISBN 0-444-15194-X, Excerpta Medica). Elsevier.
Eskes, T. K., et al. Ovarian Function. 1975. 39.00 (ISBN 0-444-15150-8, Excerpta Medica). Elsevier.
Fox, H. Tumors of the Ovary. (Illus.). 1976. 26.50 (ISBN 0-8151-3269-7). Year Bk Med.
Hutchinson, J. S. The Hypothalamo-Pituitary Control of the Ovary, Vol. 1. Horrobin, D. F., ed. (Annual Research Reviews). 1979. 20.00 (ISBN 0-88831-064-1). Eden Med Res.
--The Hypothalamo-Pituitary Control of the Ovary, Vol. 2. Horrobin, D. F., ed. (Annual Research Reviews Ser.). 215p. 1980. 28.00 (ISBN 0-88831-091-9). Eden Med Res.
James, V. H. T., et al, eds. Endocrine Function of the Human Ovary. 1976. 65.00 (ISBN 0-686-74509-4). Acad Pr.
Janovski, N. A. & Paramanandhan, T. L. Ovarian Tumors. LC 77-176208. (Major Problems in Obstetrics & Gynecology Ser.: Vol. 4). (Illus.). 220p. 1973. 24.00 (ISBN 0-7216-5115-1). Saunders.
Jones, Richard E., ed. The Vertebrate Ovary: Comparative Biology and Evolution. LC 78-16084. 877p. 1978. 69.50 (ISBN 0-306-31129-1, Plenum Pr). Plenum Pub.
Mossman, Harland W. & Duke, Kenneth L. Comparative Morphology of the Mammalian Ovary. LC 72-143765. 492p. 1972. 35.00 (ISBN 0-299-05930-8, 593); pap. 12.50 (ISBN 0-299-05934-0). U of Wis Pr.
Motta, P. M. & Hafez, E. S., eds. Biology of the Ovary. (Developments in Obstetrics & Gynecology Ser.: No. 2). 345p. 1980. lib. bdg. 87.00 (ISBN 90-247-2316-7, Pub. by Martinus Nijhoff Netherlands). Kluwer Boston.
Newman, C. E., et al, eds. Ovarian Cancer: Proceedings of the International Symposium on Ovarian Cancer, 24-25 September 1979, Birmingham. LC 80-40166. (Illus.). 260p. 1980. 40.00 (ISBN 0-08-025532-9). Pergamon.
Perry, John. The Ovarian Cycle of Mammals. (University Reviews in Biology Ser). (Illus.). 1972. pap. 6.50 (ISBN 0-02-850210-8). Hafner.
Peters, Hannah & McNatty, Kenneth P. The Ovary: A Correlation of Structure & Function in Mammals. LC 79-6741. 1980. 38.75x (ISBN 0-520-04124-0). U of Cal Pr.
Peters, Hannah, ed. The Development & Maturation of the Ovary & Its Functions. (International Congress Ser.: No. 267). 200p. 1973. pap. 41.50 (ISBN 0-444-15029-3, Excerpta Medica). Elsevier.
Schwartz, Neena B. & Hunzicker-Dunn, Mary, eds. Dynamics of Ovarian Function. 352p. 1981. text ed. 38.50 (ISBN 0-89004-594-1). Raven.
Serov, S. F. & Scully, R. F. Histological Typing of Ovarian Tumours. (World Health Organization: International Histological Classification of Tumours Ser.). (Illus.). 1973. 36.50 (ISBN 0-89189-117-X, 70-1-009-20); incl. slides 112.00 (ISBN 0-89189-118-8, 70-1-009-00). Am Soc Clinical.
Serra, Giovan, ed. The Ovary. (Comprehensive Endocrinology Ser.). 1981. text ed. price not set (ISBN 0-89004-248-9). Raven.
Singhal, R. Cellular Mechanisms Modulating Gonadal Hormone Action. (Advances in Sex Hormone Research: Vol. 2). (Illus.). 1976. 39.50 (ISBN 0-8391-0776-5). Univ Park.
Symposium on the Physiology of Human Reproduction, Second Annual & Mack, Harold C. The Ovary: Proceedings. (Illus.). 228p. 1968. photocopy ed. spiral 22.75 (ISBN 0-398-01185-0). C C Thomas.
Tacchi, Derek. Ovarian Gynaecology. LC 76-26778. (Illus.). 1976. text ed. 26.00 (ISBN 0-7216-8725-3). Saunders.
Teilum, Gunnar. Special Tumors of Ovaries & Testis: Comparative Pathology & Histological Identification. LC 76-9942. (Illus.). 459p. 1976. 69.00 (ISBN 0-397-58197-1). Lippincott.
Van Oosterom, A. T., et al, eds. Therapeutic Progress in Ovarian Cancer, Testicular Cancer & Sarcomas. (Boerhaave Series for Postgraduate Medical Education: No. 16). (Illus.). 516p. 1980. lib. bdg. 65.80 (ISBN 90-6021-452-8, Pub. by Leiden Univ Holland). Kluwer Boston.
Zuckerman, Solly, ed. Ovary. 2nd ed. Incl. Vol. 1. General Aspects. 1977. 56.00 (ISBN 0-12-782601-7); Vol. 2. Physiology. 1977. 61.00 (ISBN 0-12-782602-5); Vol. 3. Regulation of Oogenesis & Sleriodogenesis. 1978. subscription 168.50 51.00 (ISBN 0-12-782603-3). 1977. Acad Pr.

OVENS
see Stoves

OVER HEAD PROJECTION
see Overhead Projection

OVER-THE-COUNTER MARKETS
Buckley, Julian G. & Loll, Leo M. The Over-the-Counter Securities Markets. (Illus.). 480p. 1981. text ed. 22.95 (ISBN 0-13-647172-2). P-H.

OVERACTIVITY
see Hyperkinesia

OVERBURY, THOMAS, SIR, 1581-1613
Niccols, Richard. Sir Thomas Overburies Vision, 1616. (Illus.). 1967. Repr. of 1873 ed. 8.50 (ISBN 0-384-41380-3). Johnson Repr.
White, Beatrice. A Cast of Ravens. LC 67-11599. 1965. 6.00 (ISBN 0-8076-0398-8). Braziller.

OVERHEAD COSTS
Clark, John M. Studies in the Economics of Overhead Costs. 1980. pap. write for info. (ISBN 0-226-10851-1). U of Chicago Pr.
Ficker, Nicholas T. Shop Expense: Analysis & Control. Brief, Richard P., ed. LC 80-1492. (Dimensions of Accounting Theory & Practice Ser.). 1981. Repr. of 1917 ed. lib. bdg. 22.00x (ISBN 0-405-13522-X). Arno.
Fultz, Jack F. Overhead: What It Is & How It Works. LC 79-57519. (Illus.). 151p. 1980. 12.00 (ISBN 0-89011-547-8). Abt Assoc.
Wells, Murry C. Controversies on the Theory of the Firm, Overhead Allocations & Transfer Pricing. original anthology ed. Brief, Richard P., ed. LC 80-1456. (Dimensions of Accounting Theory & Practice Ser.). 1981. lib. bdg. 20.00x (ISBN 0-405-13489-4). Arno.

OVERHEAD PROJECTION
Darkes, Anna S. How to Make & Use Overhead Transparancies. (Illus.). 1977. pap. 2.50 (ISBN 0-8024-3652-8). Moody.
Green, Lee. Use Your Overhead. 1979. pap. 3.95 (ISBN 0-88207-467-9). Victor Bks.
Masterton, William L. & Slowinski, Emil J. Overhead Projectuals to Accompany Chemical Principles. (Illus.). 1977. 200.00 (ISBN 0-7216-9923-5). HR&W.
Sparks, Jerry D. Overhead Projection. Duane, James E., ed. LC 80-21334. (The Instructional Media Library: Vol. 10). (Illus.). 112p. 1981. 13.95 (ISBN 0-87778-170-2). Educ Tech Pubns.
Wilkinson, Judith. The Overhead Projector. (Illus.). 79p. (Orig.). 1979. pap. 7.50 (ISBN 0-900229-95-0). Intl Pubns Serv.

OVERLAND JOURNEYS TO THE PACIFIC
see also Donner Party; Voyages to the Pacific Coast
Barnes, Demas. From the Atlantic to the Pacific Overland. LC 72-9426. (The Far Western Frontier Ser.). (Illus.). 142p. 1973. Repr. of 1866 ed. 14.00 (ISBN 0-405-04957-9). Arno.
Bartlett, Richard A. Great Surveys of the American West. LC 62-16475. (The American Exploration & Travel Ser.: Vol. 38). (Illus.). 464p. 1980. pap. 9.95 (ISBN 0-8061-1653-6). U of Okla Pr.
Becker, Robert H., ed. Thomas Christy's Road Across the Plains. 1969. limited ed 19.95 (ISBN 0-912094-13-3). Old West.
Benton, Elbert J. Wabash Trade Route in the Development of the Old Northwest. (Illus.). Repr. of 1903 ed. lib. bdg. 10.00x (ISBN 0-678-00991-0). Kelley.
Bieber, Ralph P., ed. Southern Trails to California in 1849. LC 74-7159. (Southwest Historical Ser.: Vol. 5). (Illus.). 386p. Repr. of 1937 ed. lib. bdg. 20.00x (ISBN 0-87991-301-0). Porcupine Pr.
Bryant, Edwin. What I Saw in California. 1967. Repr. 10.00 (ISBN 0-87018-004-5). Ross.
Crawford, Meodrem. Journal of Meodrem Crawford. facs. ed. 26p. Repr. of 1897 ed. pap. 3.95 (ISBN 0-8466-0141-9, SJS141). Shorey.
Faragher, John M. Women & Men on the Overland Trail. LC 78-10290. (Yale Historical Publications, Miscellany Ser.: No. 121). 304p. 1980. 25.00x (ISBN 0-300-02267-0); pap. 6.50x (ISBN 0-300-02605-6). Yale U Pr.
Farnham, Thomas J. Travels in the Great Western Prairies, 2 vols. in 1. LC 68-16231. (The American Scene Ser.). 612p. 1973. Repr. of 1843 ed. lib. bdg. 35.00 (ISBN 0-306-71012-9). Da Capo.
Foreman, Grant. Marcy & the Gold Seekers: The Journal of Captain R. B. Marcy, with an Account of the Gold Rush Over the Southern Route. (American Exploration & Travel Ser.: No. 2). (Illus.). 1968. Repr. of 1939 ed. 15.95 (ISBN 0-8061-0766-9). U of Okla Pr.
Ghent, William J. Road to Oregon. LC 77-111787. (BCL Ser.: I). (Illus.). Repr. of 1929 ed. 22.00 (ISBN 0-404-02717-2). AMS Pr.
Hafen, LeRoy R. & Hafen, Ann W. Handcarts to Zion. LC 59-14279. (Illus.). 1969. 10.00 (ISBN 0-87062-027-4). A H Clark.
Hafen, Leroy R., ed. Overland Routes to the Gold Fields, 1859: From Contemporary Diaries. LC 74-7164. (Southwest Historical Ser.: Vol. 11). (Illus.). 320p. Repr. of 1942 ed. lib. bdg. 17.50x (ISBN 0-87991-305-3). Porcupine Pr.
Hannon, Jessie G. Boston-Newton Company Venture: From Massachusetts to California in 1849. LC 68-11562. (Illus.). 1969. 14.95 (ISBN 0-8032-0066-8). U of Nebr Pr.
Hastings, Lansford W. Emigrant's Guide to Oregon & California. 2nd ed. LC 68-8691. (American Scene Ser). 1969. Repr. of 1845 ed. lib. bdg. 19.50 (ISBN 0-306-71172-9). Da Capo.
Heap, Gwinn H. Central Route to the Pacific. Bruchey, Stuart, ed. LC 80-1315. (Railroads Ser.). (Illus.). 1981. Repr. of 1853 ed. lib. bdg. 15.00x (ISBN 0-405-13787-7). Arno.
Hewitt, Randall H. Across the Plains & Over the Divide. (Illus.). 1964. Repr. of 1906 ed. 15.00 (ISBN 0-87266-015-X). Argosy.
Horn, Huston. The Pioneers. (The Old West Ser.). (Illus.). 1974. 14.95 (ISBN 0-8094-1475-9). Time-Life.
--The Pioneers. LC 73-94242. (The Old West). (Illus.). (gr. 5 up). 1974. kivar 12.96 (ISBN 0-8094-1477-5, Pub. by Time-Life). Silver.
Irving, Washington. Astoria. LC 67-25439. (Illus.). 1967. 10.00 (ISBN 0-8323-0101-9). Binford.
Johnston, William G. Experiences of a Forty-Niner. LC 72-9454. (The Far Western Frontier Ser.). (Illus.). 414p. 1973. Repr. of 1892 ed. 19.00 (ISBN 0-405-04982-X). Arno.
Kelly, William. An Excursion to California Over the Prairies, Rocky Mountains, & Great Sierra Nevada, 2 vols. in 1. LC 72-9456. (The Far Western Frontier Ser.). 698p. 1973. Repr. of 1851 ed. 31.00 (ISBN 0-405-04984-6). Arno.
Langworthy, Franklin. Scenery of the Plains, Mountains & Mines. LC 76-87645. (American Scene Ser). (Illus.). 292p. 1972. Repr. of 1932 ed. lib. bdg. 32.50 (ISBN 0-306-71785-9). Da Capo.
Lockley, Fred. Across the Plains by Prairie Schooner. pap. 3.75 (ISBN 0-8466-0190-7, SJS190). Shorey.
Ludlow, Fitz H. Heart of the Continent. LC 74-134396. (Illus.). Repr. 35.45 (ISBN 0-404-08438-9). AMS Pr.
McGlashan, Charles F. History of the Donner Party: A Tragedy of the Sierra. rev. ed. Hinkle, George H. & Hinkle, Bliss M., eds. (Illus.). 1947. 10.95 (ISBN 0-8047-0366-3); pap. 4.95 (ISBN 0-8047-0367-1, SP26). Stanford U Pr.
Marcy, Randolph B. Prairie Traveler. (Illus.). 1968. Repr. of 1859 ed. 12.50 (ISBN 0-87928-001-8). Corner Hse.
Miles, William. Journal of the Sufferings & Hardships of Capt. Parker H. French's Overland Expedition to California. 8.50 (ISBN 0-8363-0057-2); pap. 4.50 wrappers (ISBN 0-685-13276-5). Jenkins.
Monaghan, James. Overland Trail. facs. ed. LC 73-107726. (Essay Index Reprint Ser). 1947. 25.00 (ISBN 0-8369-1999-8). Arno.
Neihardt, John G. Splendid Wayfaring: The Exploits & Adventures of Jedediah Smith & the Ashley-Henry Men, 1822-1831. LC 71-116054. (Illus.). 1970. pap. 5.25 (ISBN 0-8032-5723-6, BB 525, Bison). U of Nebr Pr.
Nesmith, James W. Two Addresses. 1978. 7.95 (ISBN 0-87770-200-4); pap. 4.95 (ISBN 0-87770-202-0). Ye Galleon.
Nunis, Doyce. Josiah Belden, 1841 California Overland Pioneer. LC 62-11494. (Illus.). 1962. 6.95 (ISBN 0-934612-04-8). Talisman.
Ormsby, Waterman L. Butterfield Overland Mail. Wright, Lyle H. & Bynum, Josephine M., eds. (Illus.). 1972. Repr. of 1942 ed. 10.00 (ISBN 0-87328-002-4). Huntington Lib.
Parker, Samuel. Journal of Exploring Tour Etc. Repr. 10.00 (ISBN 0-87018-046-0). Ross.
Powell, H. M. Santa Fe Trail to California, 1849-1852. Watson, Douglas S., ed. LC 79-174284. (Illus.). Repr. of 1931 ed. lib. bdg. 125.00 (ISBN 0-404-05099-9). AMS Pr.
Rasmussen, Louis J. Railway Passenger Lists of Overland Trains to San Francisco & the West, 2 vols. Incl. Vol. 1. July 26, 1870 to November 11, 1871. 1966; Vol. 2. November 12, 1871 to April 23, 1873. 1968. 9.75 (ISBN 0-911792-51-1). LC 66-12617. SF Hist Records.
--San Francisco Ship Passenger Lists, 5 vols. Incl. Vol. 1. 1850-1875. 1965; Vol. 2. April 6, 1850 to November 4, 1851. 1966. 9.75 (ISBN 0-911792-01-5); Vol. 3. November 7, 1851 to June 17, 1852. 1967. write for info. (ISBN 0-911792-02-3); Vol. 4. June 17, 1852 to 1853. 1970. 9.75 (ISBN 0-911792-03-1); Vol. 5. 1973. LC 65-13821. (Ship, Rail & Wagon Train Series). SF Hist Records.
Remy, Jules & Brenchley, Julius. A Journey to Great Salt-Lake City, 2 vols. LC 75-134399. (Illus.). Repr. of 1861 ed. Set. write for info. (ISBN 0-404-08441-9). Vol. 1 (ISBN 0-404-08442-7). Vol. 2 (ISBN 0-404-08443-5). AMS Pr.
Rosenberger, Francis C., ed. The Robinson-Rosenberger Journey to the Gold Fields of California, 1849-1850: The Diary of Zirkle D. Robinson. LC 66-24447. 1966. 5.00x (ISBN 0-8139-0845-0). U Pr of Va.

Royce, Sarah. A Frontier Lady: Recollections of the Gold Rush & Early California. Gabriel, Ralph H., ed. LC 76-44263. (Illus.). 1977. 10.95x (ISBN 0-8032-0909-6); pap. 2.45 (ISBN 0-8032-5856-9, BB 634, Bison). U of Nebr Pr.
Scharmann, Hermann B. Overland Journey to California, from the Pages of a Pioneer's Diary. facsimile ed. LC 73-99670. (Select Bibliographies Reprint Ser). 1918. 15.00 (ISBN 0-8369-5099-2). Arno.
Schiel, Jacob H. Journey Through the Rocky Mountains & the Humboldt Mountains to the Pacific Ocean. Bonner, Thomas N., ed. (American Exploration & Travel Ser.: No. 27). (Illus.). 1959. 9.95 (ISBN 0-8061-0422-8). U of Okla Pr.
Smith, Charles W. Journal of a Trip to California. 79p. 1974. 5.95 (ISBN 0-87770-125-3). Ye Galleon.
Stewart, George R. California Trail: An Epic with Many Heroes. (American Trails Library Ser). 1962. 8.95 (ISBN 0-07-061312-5, GB). McGraw.
Turner, Henry S. The Original Journals of Henry Smith Turner: With Stephen Watts Kearny to New Mexico & California. Clarke, Dwight L., ed. (American Exploration & Discovery Ser.: No. 51). 1967. pap. 4.95 (ISBN 0-8061-1157-7). U of Okla Pr.
Ware, Joseph E. The Emigrants' Guide to California. LC 79-87627. (The American Scene Ser). (Illus.). 64p. 1972. Repr. of 1932 ed. lib. bdg. 12.50 (ISBN 0-306-71806-5). Da Capo.
White, Helen M., ed. Ho! for the Gold Fields: Northern Overland Wagon Trains of the 1860s. LC 66-64828. (Illus.). 289p. 1966. 8.50 (ISBN 0-87351-030-5). Minn Hist.
Wyeth, John B. Oregon: A Short History of a Long Journey. Bd. with Narrative of a Journey Across the Rocky Mountains to the Columbia River. Townsend, John K. 1974. 14.95 (ISBN 0-87770-027-3). Ye Galleon.
Wyman, Walker D. California Emigrant Letters. LC 78-175936. (Illus.). Repr. of 1952 ed. 17.50 (ISBN 0-404-07059-0). AMS Pr.

OVERLAND JOURNEYS TO THE PACIFIC-JUVENILE LITERATURE

Berry, Erick. When Wagon Trains Rolled to Santa Fe. LC 66-12813. (How They Lived Ser). (Illus.). (gr. 3-6). 1966. PLB 6.48 (ISBN 0-8116-6902-5). Garrard.
Rounds, Glen. The Prairie Schooners. (Illus.). (gr. 4-6). 1968. 8.95 (ISBN 0-8234-0088-3). Holiday.

OVERPRODUCTION

see also Depressions; Industry; Supply and Demand; Technocracy

Hamlin, Scoville, ed. Menace of Overproduction. LC 76-93344. (Essay Index Reprint Ser). 1930. 16.00 (ISBN 0-8369-1295-0). Arno.
Lescure, Jean. Des Crises Generales et Periodiques De Surproduction, 2 Vols. 5th rev. ed. 1969. Repr. of 1938 ed. Set. 38.50 (ISBN 0-8337-2083-X). B Franklin.

OVERSEAS EMPLOYEES

see Americans in Foreign Countries-Employment

OVERSEAS STUDENTS

see Returned Students

OVERSIGHT, CONGRESSIONAL (UNITED STATES)

see United States-Congress-Powers and Duties

OVERTIME

see Hours of Labor

OVERWEIGHT

see Obesity

OVID (PUBLIUS OVIDIUS NASO)

Boas, Frederick S. Ovid & the Elizabethans. (Studies in Shakespeare, No. 24). 1970. pap. 7.95 (ISBN 0-8383-0008-1). Haskell.
Brewer, Wilmon. Ovid's Metamorphoses in European Culture, 2 vols. (Illus.). 1978. Set. 10.00 (ISBN 0-685-14287-6); Vol. I. (ISBN 0-685-99059-1); Vol. II. (ISBN 0-685-99060-5). M Jones.
Candy, Hugh C. Some Newly-Discovered Stanzas Written by John Milton on Engraved Scenes Illustrating Ovid's Metamorphoses. 1972. Repr. of 1924 ed. lib. bdg. 20.00 (ISBN 0-8414-0912-9). Folcroft.
Galinsky, G. Karl. Ovid's Metamorphoses: An Introduction to Its Basic Aspects. LC 74-84146. 1975. 23.75x (ISBN 0-520-02848-1). U of Cal Pr.
Griggs, M. J., ed. Selections from the Ars Amatoria. LC 74-139865. 1971. text ed. 6.95 (ISBN 0-685-00191-1). St Martin.
Henderson, A. A., ed. Remedia Amoris. 160p. 1980. pap. 10.00x (ISBN 0-7073-0246-3, Pub. by Scottish Academic Pr). Columbia U Pr.
Herr, Margaret W. Additional Short Syllables in Ovid. 1937. pap. 6.00 (ISBN 0-527-00771-4). Kraus Repr.
Jacobson, Howard. Ovid's Heroides. LC 73-16754. 425p. 1974. 31.00 (ISBN 0-691-06271-4). Princeton U Pr.
Keach, William. Elizabethan Erotic Narratives: Irony & Pathos in the Ovidian Poetry of Shakespeare, Marlowe, & Their Contemporaries. 1977. 19.50 (ISBN 0-8135-0830-4). Rutgers U Pr.
Malouf, David. An Imaginary Life. LC 77-18601. 1978. 7.95 (ISBN 0-8076-0884-X). Braziller.
Otis, Brooks. Ovid As an Epic Poet. 2nd ed. LC 75-96098. 1971. 56.00 (ISBN 0-521-07615-3). Cambridge U Pr.
Ovid. Metamorphoses, Bk. 8. Hollis, A. S., ed. (Illus.). 1970. 17.95x (ISBN 0-19-814440-7). Oxford U Pr.
Rand, Edward K. Ovid. LC 63-10269. (Our Debt to Greece & Rome Ser). Repr. of 1930 ed. 6.50x (ISBN 0-8154-0187-6). Cooper Sq.
Reynell, A. C., et al, eds. Ovid's Metamorphoses: Selections. 176p. 1972. pap. 4.50 (ISBN 0-571-10254-9, Pub. by Faber & Faber). Merrimack Bk Serv.
Syme, Ronald. History in Ovid. 1979. 39.50x (ISBN 0-19-814825-9). Oxford U Pr.
Tempesta, Antonio. Metamorphoseon...Ovidianarum. LC 75-27861. (Renaissance & the Gods Ser.: Vol. 19). (Illus.). 1976. Repr. of 1606 ed. lib. bdg. 73.00 (ISBN 0-8240-2067-7). Garland Pub.
Thibault, John C. The Mystery of Ovid's Exile. 1964. 18.50x (ISBN 0-520-01265-8). U of Cal Pr.
Wright, Frederick A. Three Roman Poets: Plautus, Catullus, Ovid. 1977. lib. bdg. 69.95 (ISBN 0-8490-2746-2). Gordon Pr.

OVIDUCT

Johnson, A. D. & Foley, C. W., eds. The Oviduct & Its Function. 1974. 38.00 (ISBN 0-12-386650-2). Acad Pr.

OVIEDO Y VALDES, GONZALO FERNANDEZ DE, 1478-1557

Avalle-Arce, J. B. Las Memorias de Gonzalo Fernandez de Oviedo, Vol. 1. (Studies in the Romance Languages & Literatures: No. 154). 1974. pap. 16.50x (ISBN 0-8078-9154-1). U of NC Pr.
--Las Memorias de Gonzalo Fernandez de Oviedo, Vol. 2. (Studies in the Romance Languages & Literatures: No. 155). 1974. pap. 15.50x (ISBN 0-8078-9155-X). U of NC Pr.
Turner, Daymond. Gonzalo Fernandez de Oviedo y Valdes: An Annotated Bibliography. (Studies in the Romance Languages & Literatures: No. 66). 1967. pap. 5.00x (ISBN 0-8078-9066-9). U of NC Pr.

OVIMBUNDU

Hambly, W. D. Serpent Worship in Africa - the Ovimbundu of Angola: Culture Areas of Nigeria. (Chicago Field Museum of Natural History Fieldiana Anthropology Ser). Repr. of 1935 ed. pap. 35.00 (ISBN 0-527-01881-3). Kraus Repr.

OVULATION

Crighton, D. B., et al, eds. Control of Ovulation. new ed. LC 78-40043. 1978. 74.95 (ISBN 0-408-70924-3). Butterworth.
Crosignani, P. G. & Mishell, D., eds. Ovulation in the Human. (Serono Symposium: No. 8). 1976. 49.50 (ISBN 0-12-198340-4). Acad Pr.
Gerrick, David J. Ovulation: Predicting Fertility. (Illus.). 1978. 20.00 (ISBN 0-916750-42-6). Dayton Labs.
Greenblatt, Robert B., ed. Induction of Ovulation. LC 79-10757. (Illus.). 167p. 1979. text ed. 14.75 (ISBN 0-8121-0652-0). Lea & Febiger.
Guay, Terrie. Avoid or Achieve Pregnancy Naturally. 5th ed. Guay, Laurent C., ed. LC 78-220. (Illus.). 1978. pap. 3.50 (ISBN 0-686-68015-4). Emergence.
Kippley, Sheila. Breast-Feeding & Natural Child Spacing: The Ecology of Natural Mothering. rev. ed. LC 73-4100. (Illus.). 208p. 1974. 9.95 (ISBN 0-06-012399-0, HarpT). Har-Row.
--Breast-Feeding & Natural Child Spacing: The Ecology of Natural Mothering. 1975. pap. 3.50 (ISBN 0-14-003992-9). Penguin.
Mess, B., et al. Role of the Pineal Gland in the Regulation of Ovulation. (Studia Biologica Hungarica: No. 16). (Illus.). 1978. pap. text ed. 7.50x (ISBN 963-05-1457-5). Intl Pubns Serv.
--Role of the Pineal Gland in the Regulation of Ovulation. 1978. 8.00 (ISBN 0-9960009-7-6, Pub. by Kiado Hungary). Heyden.
Villee, C. A., ed. Control of Ovulation. 1961. pap. 16.00 (ISBN 0-08-013650-8). Pergamon.
Wilson, Mercedes. The Ovulation Method of Birth Regulation. 202p. 1981. pap. text ed. 11.95 (ISBN 0-442-29432-8). Van Nos Reinhold.
Wilson, Mercedes A. The Ovulation Method of Birth Regulation: The Latest Advances for Achieving or Postponing Pregnancy--Naturally. 240p. 1980. 24.95 (ISBN 0-442-29515-4). Van Nos Reinhold.

OVUM

see also Cells; Oogenesis; Ovaries

Dvorak, M. Differentiation of Rat Ova During Cleavage. LC 78-13480. (Advances in Anatomy, Embryology & Cell Biology: Vol. 55, Pt. 2). (Illus.). 1978. pap. 40.70 (ISBN 0-387-08983-7). Springer-Verlag.
Hadek, Robert. Mammalian Fertilization: An Atlas of Ultrastructure. 1969. 37.50 (ISBN 0-12-312950-8). Acad Pr.

OVUM IMPLANTATION

Blandau, R. J., ed. Biology of the Blastocyst. LC 70-128713. 1971. text ed. 27.50x (ISBN 0-226-05670-8). U of Chicago Pr.
Denker, H. W. Implantation: The Role of Proteinases, & Blockage of Implantation Through Proteinase Inhibitors. (Advances in Anatomy, Embryology & Cell Biology: Vol. 53, Pt. 5). (Illus.). 1977. pap. 28.20 (ISBN 0-387-08479-7). Springer-Verlag.
Enders, Allen C., ed. Delayed Implantation. LC 63-188851. (Illus.). 1963. 10.50x (ISBN 0-226-20789-7). U of Chicago Pr.
Glasser, Stanley R. & Bullock, David W., eds. Cellular & Molecular Aspects of Implantation. 497p. 1981. 35.00 (ISBN 0-306-40581-4, Plenum Pr). Plenum Pub.
International Seminar on Reproductive Physiology & Sexual Endrocrinology, 2nd, Brussels, 1968. Ovo-Implantation, Human Gonadotropines & Prolactin. Hubinont, P. O., et al, eds. (Illus.). 1970. 39.75 (ISBN 3-8055-0959-6). S Karger.
Moghissi, Kamran S. & Hafez, E. S., eds. Biology of Mammalian Fertilization & Implantation. (Illus.). 520p. 1972. 42.50 (ISBN 0-398-02362-X). C C Thomas.
Shelesnyak, M. C. Ovum Inplantation. 1969. 72.75x (ISBN 0-677-13230-1). Gordon.
Yoshinaga, Koji, et al, eds. Implantation of the Ovum. 1976. text ed. 15.00x (ISBN 0-674-44523-6). Harvard U Pr.

OWEN, JOHN, 1616-1683

Toon, Peter, ed. God's Statesman: The Life & Work of John Owen. 1972. 10.00 (ISBN 0-85364-133-1). Attic Pr.

OWEN, REBEKAH, 1858-1939

Weber, Carl J. Hardy & the Lady from Madison Square. LC 72-85323. 280p. 1973. Repr. of 1952 ed. 14.25 (ISBN 0-8046-1739-2). Kennikat.

OWEN, RICHARD OWEN, SIR 1804-1892

Owen, Richard S. The Life of Richard Owen, 4 vols. LC 72-1697. (Illus.). Repr. of 1894 ed. 57.50 set (ISBN 0-404-07995-4). AMS Pr.

OWEN, ROBERT, 1771-1858

Altfest, Karen C. Robert Owen. (World Leaders Ser.: No. 60). 1977. lib. bdg. 12.50 (ISBN 0-8057-7711-3). Twayne.
Cole, George D. Life of Robert Owen. 349p. 1965. 26.00x (ISBN 0-7146-1464-5, F Cass Co). Biblio Dist.
Cole, Margaret I. Robert Owen of New Lanark. LC 75-77254. Repr. of 1953 ed. 13.50x (ISBN 0-678-00565-6). Kelley.
Economist: A Periodical Paper - Explanatory of the New System of Society Projected by Robert Owen, Vols. 1-2. 1821-22. Repr. lib. bdg. 35.00x (ISBN 0-8371-9164-5, EP00). Greenwood.
Harrison, John F., ed. Utopianism & Education: Robert Owen & the Owenites. LC 68-54675. (Orig.). 1969. pap. text ed. 5.25x (ISBN 0-8077-1498-4). Tchrs Coll.
Harvey, R. H. Robert Owen, Social Idealist. Repr. of 1949 ed. 15.00 (ISBN 0-527-00976-8). Kraus Repr.
Johnson, Dorothy C. Pioneers of Reform: Corbett, Owen, Place, Shaftesbury, Cobden, Bright. LC 68-56796. (Research & Source Works Ser.: No. 289). (Illus.). 1968. Repr. of 1929 ed. 14.50 (ISBN 0-8337-1853-3). B Franklin.
Johnson, O. C. Robert Owen in the United States. (Historical Ser.: No. 6). 5.00 (ISBN 0-89977-043-6). Am Inst Marxist.
Jones, Lloyd. Life, Times & Labours of Robert Owen, 2 vols. in 1. LC 77-134406. (Illus.). Repr. of 1890 ed. 29.50 (ISBN 0-404-08449-4). AMS Pr.
Leopold, Richard W. Robert Dale Owen. LC 71-96184. 1969. Repr. of 1940 ed. lib. bdg. 27.50x (ISBN 0-374-94940-9). Octagon.
Morton, A. L. Life & Ideas of Robert Owen. 239p. 1969. 6.95x (ISBN 0-8464-1111-3). Beekman Pubs.
Munoz, V. Robert Owen: A Chronology. Johnson, W. Scott, tr. (Libertarian & Anarchist Chronology Ser.). 1979. lib. bdg. 59.95 (ISBN 0-8490-3054-4). Gordon Pr.
Owen, Robert. Robert Owen's Millenial Gazette. LC 74-134408. Repr. of 1858 ed. 32.50 (ISBN 0-404-08454-0). AMS Pr.
--Robert Owen's New Harmony Addresses. LC 76-57445. 1977. 3.50x (ISBN 0-686-00153-2). Scholars Portable.
Owenism & the Working Class: 1821-1834. LC 72-2535. (British Labour Struggles Before 1850 Ser). 1972. 13.00 (ISBN 0-405-04428-3). Arno.
Podmore, Frank. Robert Owen. LC 78-156295. (World History Ser., No. 48). 1971. lib. bdg. 64.95 (ISBN 0-8383-1265-9). Haskell.
--Robert Owen, 2 Vols. in One. LC 68-9762. Repr. of 1906 ed. 27.50x (ISBN 0-678-00417-X). Kelley.
Pollard, Sidney & Salt, John, eds. Robert Owen: Prophet of the Poor. LC 70-156269. 318p. 1971. 18.00 (ISBN 0-8387-7952-2). Bucknell U Pr.
The Rational System: Eighteen Thirty-Seven to Eighteen Forty-One. LC 72-2537. (British Labour Struggles Before 1850 Ser). (7 pamphlets). 12.00 (ISBN 0-405-04430-5). Arno.
Robert Owen at New Lanark: 1824-1838. LC 72-2543. (British Labour Struggles Before 1850 Ser). 1972. 10.00 (ISBN 0-405-04435-6). Arno.
Sargant, William L. Robert Owen & His Social Philosophy. LC 78-134409. Repr. of 1860 ed. 31.50 (ISBN 0-404-08455-9). AMS Pr.

OWEN, ROBERT DALE, 1801-1877

Leopold, Richard W. Robert Dale Owen. LC 71-96184. 1969. Repr. of 1940 ed. lib. bdg. 27.50x (ISBN 0-374-94940-9). Octagon.

OWEN, WILFRED, 1893-1918

Heneghan, Donald A. A Concordance to the Poems & Fragments of Wilfred Owen. 1979. lib. bdg. 30.00 (ISBN 0-8161-8371-6). G K Hall.
Hibberd, J. W. Monarch Notes on Wilfred Owen & Other World War I Poets. pap. 1.50 (ISBN 0-671-00909-5). Monarch Pr.
Lane, Arthur E. An Adequate Response: The War Poetry of Wilfred Owen & Siegfried Sassoon. LC 74-39905. 184p. 1972. text ed. 10.95x (ISBN 0-8143-1472-4). Wayne St U Pr.
McIlroy, J. F. Wilfred Owen's Poetry: A Study Guide. 1974. pap. text ed. 3.95x (ISBN 0-435-18567-5). Heinemann Ed.
Owen, Harold. Journey from Obscurity: Memoirs of the Owen Family: Wilfred Owen 1893-1918, 3 vols. Incl. Vol. 1. Childhood. 1963 (ISBN 0-19-211146-9); Vol. 3. War. 1965 (ISBN 0-19-211164-7). 12.00x (ISBN 0-686-76935-X). Oxford U Pr.
Stallworthy, Jon. Wilfred Owen. 1975. 19.95 (ISBN 0-19-211719-X). Oxford U Pr.
--Wilfred Owen: A Biography. (Illus.). 1978. pap. 4.95 (ISBN 0-19-281215-7, GB510, GB). Oxford U Pr.
White, William. Wilfred Owen, 1893-1918: A Bibliography. LC 66-28409. (Serif Ser.: No. 1). 1967. 5.00x (ISBN 0-87338-017-7). Kent St U Pr.

OWENS, JESSE, 1913-1980

Neimark, Paul, ed. Jesse. Flores, Rhode, tr. from Eng. 192p. (Span.). 1979. pap. 1.95 (ISBN 0-8297-0677-1). Life Pubs Intl.
Owens, Jesse. Jesse. (Span.). Date not set. 2.00 (ISBN 0-686-76299-1). Life Pubs Intl.
--Jesse. Date not set. 1.60 (ISBN 0-686-76425-0). Life Pubs Intl.
Owens, Jesse & Neimark, Paul. Jesse: The Man Who Outran Hitler. 1979. pap. 1.95 (ISBN 0-449-14247-7, GM). Fawcett.

OWENS, JOHN

Clapp, Brian W. John Owens, Manchester Merchant. LC 67-31834. 1967. 12.50x (ISBN 0-678-06755-4). Kelley.

OWENS VALLEY-DESCRIPTION AND TRAVEL-GUIDEBOOKS

Smith, Genny S., ed. Deepest Valley: A Guide to Owens Valley, Its Roadsides & Mountain Trails. (Illus.). 241p. pap. 7.95 (ISBN 0-913232-57-2). W Kaufmann.

OWL AND THE NIGHTINGALE

Hume, Kathryn. The Owl & the Nightingale: The Poem & Its Critics. LC 75-1452. 1975. 15.00x (ISBN 0-8020-5316-5). U of Toronto Pr.

OWLS

Angell, Tony. Owls. LC 74-6005. (Illus.). 80p. 1974. pap. 8.95 (ISBN 0-295-95666-6); limited ed. 100.00 (ISBN 0-295-95415-9). U of Wash Pr.
Bartlett, Margaret F. Who Will Answer the Owl? LC 74-79704. (Illus.). 64p. (gr. 3-5). 1976. PLB 5.96 (ISBN 0-698-30555-8). Coward.
Burton, John, ed. Owls of the World. 1973. 19.95 (ISBN 0-525-17432-X). Dutton.
Cameron, Angus. Nightwatchers. LC 70-161023. (Illus.). 112p. 1971. 12.95 (ISBN 0-590-17101-1, Four Winds). Schol Bk Serv.
Catchpole, Clive. Owls. LC 77-8371. (New Biology Ser.). (Illus.). (gr. 4-9). 1978. 6.95 (ISBN 0-07-010232-5, GB). McGraw.
Cole, Thacker. Clipart Book of Owls in Action. LC 73-94337. 1974. pap. 7.95 (ISBN 0-87874-011-2). Galloway.
Craighead, John J. & Craighead, Frank C., Jr. Hawks, Owls & Wildlife. LC 74-81670. 1969. pap. 6.00 (ISBN 0-486-22123-7). Dover.
Fisher, Albert K. The Hawks & Owls of the United States in Their Relation to Agriculture. LC 73-17820. (Natural Sciences in America Ser.). (Illus.). 266p. 1974. Repr. 15.00x (ISBN 0-405-05736-9). Arno.
Fleay, David. Nightwatchmen of Bush & Plain: Australian Owls & Owl-Like Birds. LC 73-171365. 1972. 8.50 (ISBN 0-8008-5560-4). Taplinger.
Flower, Phyllis. The Barn Owl. LC 77-58686. (Science I Can Read Bk.). (Illus.). 1978. 6.95 (ISBN 0-06-021919-X, HarpJ); PLB 7.89 (ISBN 0-06-021921-1). Har-Row.

Garelick, May. About Owls. LC 74-31324. (Illus.). 40p. (gr. k-3). 1975. 7.95g (ISBN 0-590-07389-3, Four Winds). Schol Bk Serv.

Heintzelman, Donald. Hawks & Owls of North America: A Complete Guide to North American Birds of Prey. LC 78-65623. 1979. 18.50x (ISBN 0-87663-335-1). Universe.

Hill, Jeanne F. Great Horned Owl. 1980. 2.50 (ISBN 0-934834-02-4). White Pine.

Hopf, Alice L. Biography of a Snowy Owl. LC 78-16533. (Nature Biography Ser.). (Illus.). (gr. 3-6). 1979. PLB 6.59 (ISBN 0-399-61130-4). Putnam.

Hughes, Lynn, ed. Owls. LC 79-64787. (Illus.). 1979. 3.95 (ISBN 0-89480-109-0). Workman Pub.

Hurd, Edith T. The Mother Owl. (Illus.). 32p. (gr. 1-3). 1974. 5.95 (ISBN 0-316-38325-2). Little.

Karalus, Karl E. & Eckert, Allan W. Owls of North America: All the Species & Subspecies Illustrated in Full Color & Fully Described. LC 73-83629. (Illus.). 394p. 1974. collector's ed 50.00 (ISBN 0-385-04818-1); limited ed 150.00 (ISBN 0-385-04828-9). Doubleday.

Lavine, Sigmund A. Wonders of the Owl World. LC 77-143288. (Illus.). (gr. 3-7). 1971. PLB 5.95 (ISBN 0-396-06321-7). Dodd.

Medlin, Faith. Centuries of Owls. LC 67-23636. 1975. 6.95 (ISBN 0-685-56440-1). Brown Bk.

Nero, Robert W. The Great Gray Owl: Phantom of the Northern Forest. LC 80-607110. (Illus.). 168p. 1980. 17.50 (ISBN 0-87474-672-8). Smithsonian.

Sadoway, Margaret W. Owls: Hunters of the Night. LC 80-27541. (Nature Books for Young Readers). (Illus.). (gr. 3-8). 1981. PLB 7.95g (ISBN 0-8225-0293-3). Lerner Pubns.

Service, William. Owl. (Illus.). 1979. pap. 2.95 (ISBN 0-14-005267-4). Penguin.

Service, William S., Jr. Owl. LC 70-88749. (Illus.). (YA) 1969. 6.95 (ISBN 0-394-43968-6). Knopf.

Sparks, John & Soper, Tony. Owls: Their Natural & Unnatural History. LC 76-126994. (Illus.). 1979. pap. 8.50 (ISBN 0-8008-6171-X). Taplinger.

--Owls: Their Natural & Unnatural History. LC 76-126994. (Illus.). 1970. 14.95 (ISBN 0-8008-6170-1). Taplinger.

Tyler, Hamilton. Owls of the Southwest & Mexico. (Illus.). 204p. 1979. 17.50 (ISBN 0-87358-219-5); pap. 9.95 (ISBN 0-87358-225-X). Northland.

Tyler, Hamilton A. Owls by Day & Night. LC 78-778. (Illus.). 1978. 10.95 (ISBN 0-87961-065-4); pap. 6.95 (ISBN 0-87961-064-6). Naturegraph.

Walker, Lewis W. The Book of Owls. LC 73-20746. 1974. 12.95 (ISBN 0-394-49218-8). Knopf.

Zim, Herbert S. Owls. rev. ed. (Illus.). (gr. 3-7). 1977. PLB 6.48 (ISBN 0-688-32109-7). Morrow.

OWNERSHIP

see Property

OWYHEE COUNTY, IDAHO

History of Owyhee County. facsimile ed. (Illus.). pap. 16.00 (ISBN 0-8466-0128-1, SJS128). Shorey.

OXEN

see also Cattle

OXFORD, EDWARD DEVERE, EARL OF, 1550-1604

Clark, Eva T. Man Who Was Shakespeare. LC 75-113577. Repr. of 1937 ed. 24.00 (ISBN 0-404-01549-2). AMS Pr.

Holland, H. H. Shakespeare, Oxford & Elizabethan Times. LC 73-15896. 1933. Repr. lib. bdg. 27.50 (ISBN 0-8414-4775-6). Folcroft.

Looney, J. Thomas. Shakespeare Identified: In Edward De Vere, Seventeenth Earl of Oxford & the Poems of Edward De Vere, 2 vols. 3rd ed. Miller, Ruth L., ed. LC 74-34259. (Illus.). 1975. Set. 35.00 (ISBN 0-8046-1877-1). Kennikat.

Ogburn, Dorothy & Ogburn, Charlton, Jr. Shakespeare: The Man Behind the Name. (Illus.). 1962. 6.00 (ISBN 0-688-02457-2). Morrow.

Rendall, Gerald H. Shakespeare: Handwriting & Spelling. LC 76-169107. (Studies in Shakespeare, No. 24). 1971. Repr. of 1931 ed. lib. bdg. 40.95 (ISBN 0-8383-1335-3). Haskell.

--Shakespeare's Handwriting & Spelling. LC 72-194780. 1932. lib. bdg. 10.00 (ISBN 0-8414-7421-4). Folcroft.

Ward, Bernard. A Hundreth Sundrie Flowres: From the Original Edition of 1573. rev. 2nd ed. Miller, Ruth L., ed. LC 74-31163. (Illus.). 1975. 15.00 (ISBN 0-8046-1880-1). Kennikat.

OXFORD, ROBERT HARLEY, 1ST EARL OF, 1661-1724

Backstairs Dragon: A Life of Robert Harley, Earl of Oxford. LC 75-97190. 1970. 10.00 (ISBN 0-8008-0587-9). Taplinger.

Downie, J. A. Robert Harley & the Press. LC 78-67810. 1979. 33.50 (ISBN 0-521-22187-0). Cambridge U Pr.

OXFORD-DESCRIPTION

Boardman, John. Corpus Vasorum Antiquorum: Great Britain, Oxford, Ashmolean Museum. (Corpus Vasorum Antiquorum Ser.). (Illus.). 46p. 1975. pap. text ed. 59.00x incl. separate plates in clothbound portfolio (ISBN 0-19-725953-7). Oxford U Pr.

Cheetham, Hal. Portrait of Oxford: History & Guide of the City of Oxford, England. LC 71-878602. (Robert Hale Portrait Ser). (Illus.). 240p. 1971. 10.50x (ISBN 0-7091-2415-5). Intl Pubns Serv.

Coard, Peter. Portraits of Oxford. (Illus.). 9.95 (ISBN 0-906230-95-0, Pub. by Kingsmead Pr England). State Mutual Bk.

Compton, Hugh J. The Oxford Canal. LC 76-54077. (Inland Waterways History Ser.). (Illus.). 1977. 6.95 (ISBN 0-7153-7238-6). David & Charles.

Morris, Jan. Oxford: New Edition. (Illus.). 1979. 14.95 (ISBN 0-19-211571-5). Oxford U Pr.

Newton, Peter. Great Britain: The County of Oxford, Vol. 1. (British Academy Ser.). (Illus.). 272p. 1979. text ed. 198.00x (ISBN 0-19-725970-7). Oxford U Pr.

Smith, Goldwin. Oxford & Her Colleges. 1895. Repr. 12.50 (ISBN 0-8274-3093-0). R West.

OXFORD-DESCRIPTION AND TRAVEL-GUIDEBOOKS

Ackerman, Rudolf. Ackermann's Oxford. 1814. 15.00 (ISBN 0-89984-000-0). Century Bookbindery.

Heyworth, Peter. The Oxford Guide to Oxford. (Illus.). 160p. 1981. pap. 9.95 (ISBN 0-19-285095-4). Oxford U Pr.

Jennett, Sean, ed. Oxford & District. LC 78-564. (Travellers Guides Ser). 1969. 3.50x (ISBN 0-232-50919-0). Intl Pubns Serv.

OXFORD-HISTORY

Hargreaves-Mawdsley, W. N. Oxford in the Age of John Locke. (Centers of Civilization Ser: Vol. 32). 160p. 1973. 6.95 (ISBN 0-8061-1038-4). U of Okla Pr.

Mackail, J. W. William Morris & His Circle. 1907. lib. bdg. 6.75 (ISBN 0-8414-5999-1). Folcroft.

Newton, Peter. Great Britain: The County of Oxford, Vol. 1. (British Academy Ser.). (Illus.). 272p. 1979. text ed. 198.00x (ISBN 0-19-725970-7). Oxford U Pr.

Smith, Goldwin. Oxford & Her Colleges. 1895. Repr. 12.50 (ISBN 0-8274-3093-0). R West.

OXFORD, MISSISSIPPI

Miner, Ward. World of William Faulkner. LC 59-8274. Repr. of 1952 ed. 8.50x (ISBN 0-8154-0153-1). Cooper Sq.

OXFORD AND ASQUITH, HERBERT HENRY ASQUITH, 1ST EARL OF, 1852-1928

Koss, Stephen. Asquith. LC 76-20200. (British Political Biography Ser.). 1976. text ed. 15.95 (ISBN 0-312-05740-7). St Martin.

OXFORD GROUP

Murray, Robert H. Group Movements Throughout the Ages. LC 72-301. (Essay Index Reprint Ser.). Repr. of 1935 ed. 20.00 (ISBN 0-8369-2810-5). Arno.

OXFORD MOVEMENT

see also Anglo-Catholicism

Brendon, Piers. Hurrell Froude & the Oxford Movement. 1974. 14.95 (ISBN 0-236-31080-1, Pub. by Paul Elek). Merrimack Bk Serv.

Chadwick, Owen, ed. The Mind of the Oxford Movement. 1961. 12.50x (ISBN 0-8047-0342-6); pap. 3.95 (ISBN 0-8047-0343-4, SP41). Stanford U Pr.

Church, R. W. Oxford Movement: Twelve Years, 1833-1845. Best, Geoffrey & Clive, John, eds. LC 77-115873. (Classics of British Historical Literature Ser). 1970. 9.00x (ISBN 0-226-10618-7). U of Chicago Pr.

--The Oxford Movement: Twelve Years 1833-1845. 1979. Repr. of 1891 ed. lib. bdg. 35.00 (ISBN 0-8482-7569-1). Norwood Edns.

Dawson, Christopher H. The Spirit of the Oxford Movement. LC 75-30020. Repr. of 1934 ed. 16.50 (ISBN 0-404-14025-4). AMS Pr.

Donald, Gertrude. Men Who Left the Movement. facs. ed. LC 67-23207. (Essay Index Reprint Ser). 1933. 18.00 (ISBN 0-8369-0385-4). Arno.

Faber, Geoffrey. Oxford Apostles. 467p. 1974. 7.95 (ISBN 0-571-10495-9, Pub. by Faber & Faber). Merrimack Bk Serv.

--Oxford Apostles: A Character Study of the Oxford Movement. 1979. Repr. of 1933 ed. lib. bdg. 35.00 (ISBN 0-8482-3953-9). Norwood Edns.

Faber, Geoffrey C. Oxford Apostles: A Character Study of the Oxford Movement. LC 75-30022. Repr. of 1933 ed. 34.50 (ISBN 0-404-14027-0). AMS Pr.

Hutchison, William G. The Oxford Movement: Being a Selection from the Tracts for the Times. (Victorian Age Ser). 1906. Repr. 20.00 (ISBN 0-685-43411-7). Norwood Edns.

Morse-Boycott, Desmond L. Lead, Kindly Light. LC 70-107728. (Essay Index Reprint Ser). 1933. 16.00 (ISBN 0-8369-1529-1). Arno.

Mozley, T. Reminiscences Chiefly of Oriole College & the Oxford Movement, 2 vols. (Victorian Age Ser). 1882. Repr. 45.00 (ISBN 0-685-43414-1). Norwood Edns.

Newsome, David H. Wilberforces & Henry Manning: The Parting of Friends. LC 67-2. (Illus.). 1966. 25.00x (ISBN 0-674-95280-4, Belknap Pr). Harvard U Pr.

Seebohm, Frederick. The Oxford Reformers. Incl. Oxford Wit & Humour. 1914. Repr. 20.00 (ISBN 0-8274-3094-9). R West.

Tennyson, G. B. Victorian Devotional Poetry: The Tractarian Mode. LC 80-14416. 1980. text ed. 17.50x (ISBN 0-674-93586-1). Harvard U Pr.

Walsh, Walter. Secret History of the Oxford Movement. LC 73-101915. Repr. of 1898 ed. 25.00 (ISBN 0-404-06819-7). AMS Pr.

--The Secret History of the Oxford Movement. 1977. lib. bdg. 59.95 (ISBN 0-8490-2583-4). Gordon Pr.

Walworth, Clarence A. The Oxford Movement in America. LC 77-150436. (Monograph Ser.: No. 30). (Illus.). 1974. Repr. of 1895 ed. 7.50x (ISBN 0-930060-10-5). US Cath Hist.

Ward, Wilfrid. The Oxford Movement. (Victorian Age Ser). 20.00 (ISBN 0-685-43427-3). Norwood Edns.

Ward, Wilfrid P. William George Ward & the Oxford Movement. LC 75-29625. Repr. of 1889 ed. 31.50 (ISBN 0-404-14043-2). AMS Pr.

OXFORD UNIVERSITY

Anderson, Charles A. & Schnaper, Miriam. School & Society in England: Social Backgrounds of Oxford & Cambridge Students. LC 70-138142. 34p. 1972. Repr. of 1952 ed. lib. bdg. 15.00 (ISBN 0-8371-5599-1, ANSS). Greenwood.

Aydelotte, Frank. Oxford Stamp, & Other Essays. facs. ed. LC 67-26712. (Essay Index Reprint Ser). 1917. 15.00 (ISBN 0-8369-0166-5). Arno.

Betjeman, John. An Oxford University Chest. (Illus.). 1980. pap. 11.95 (ISBN 0-19-281273-4). Oxford U Pr.

Birkenhead, Frederick E. Points of View, 2 Vols. facsimile ed. LC 77-111815. (Essay Index Reprint Ser.). 1923. 33.00 (ISBN 0-8369-1594-1). Arno.

Hargreaves-Mawdsley, W. N. Oxford in the Age of John Locke. (Centers of Civilization Ser: Vol. 32). 160p. 1973. 6.95 (ISBN 0-8061-1038-4). U of Okla Pr.

Jennett, Sean, ed. Oxford & District. LC 78-564. (Travellers Guides Ser). 1969. 3.50x (ISBN 0-232-50919-0). Intl Pubns Serv.

Lee, Desmond. Entry & Performance at Oxford & Cambridge, 1966-1971. (Schools Council Research Ser.). 47p. 1974. 6.00x (ISBN 0-87988-103-8). Agathon.

Lloyd, Christopher. A Catalogue of the Earlier Italian Paintings in the Ashmolean Museum. (Illus.). 1977. 49.50x (ISBN 0-19-817342-3). Oxford U Pr.

Oorthuys, Cas. Oxford in Focus. (Illus.). 144p. 1981. pap. 16.95 (ISBN 0-85181-100-0, Pub. by Faber & Faber). Merrimack Bk Serv.

Pattison, Mark. Suggestions on Academical Organisation with Especial Reference to Oxford. Metzger, Walter P., ed. (The Academic Profession Ser.). 1977. lib. bdg. 20.00x (ISBN 0-405-10027-2). Arno.

Prideaux, Humphrey. Letters of Humphrey Prideaux Sometime Dean of Norwich. Thompson, E. M., ed. 1875. 22.50 (ISBN 0-384-47770-4). Johnson Repr.

Smith, Eric H. St. Peter's the Founding of an Oxford College. 1979. text ed. 22.50x (ISBN 0-901072-99-0). Humanities.

Smith, Goldwin. A Plea for the Abolition of Tests in the University of Oxford. 2nd ed. Metzger, Walter P., ed. (The Academic Profession Ser.). 1977. Repr. of 1864 ed. lib. bdg. 10.00x (ISBN 0-405-10026-4). Arno.

Thwaite, Ann, ed. My Oxford, My Cambridge. Hayman, Ronald. LC 79-14003. (Illus.). 1979. 12.50 (ISBN 0-8008-5468-3). Taplinger.

Ward, W. R. Victorian Oxford. 431p. 1965. 27.50x (ISBN 0-7146-1370-3, F Cass Co). Biblio Dist.

Wood, Anthony. Athenae Oxonienses, 5 Vols. in 4. Bliss, Philip, ed. (Sources in Science Ser). Repr. of 1820 ed. Set. 192.50 (ISBN 0-384-69140-4). Johnson Repr.

Wood, Anthony A. Athenae Oxonienses: An Exact History of All the Writers & Bishops Who Have Had Their Education in the University of Oxford, 4 Vols. 3rd ed. (Bibliography & Reference Ser.: No. 121). 1968. Repr. of 1820 ed. 185.00 (ISBN 0-8337-3863-1). B Franklin.

Zweig, Ferdynand. The Student in the Age of Anxiety. LC 77-1136. 1977. Repr. of 1964 ed. lib. bdg. 18.50x (ISBN 0-8371-9519-5, ZWST). Greenwood.

OXFORD UNIVERSITY-HISTORY

Gloucester, Richard & Hobhouse, Hermione. Oxford & Cambridge. (Illus.). 184p. 1980. 15.95 (ISBN 0-500-34081-1). Thames Hudson.

Green, V. H. A History of Oxford University. 1974. 28.00 (ISBN 0-7134-1132-5, Pub. by Batsford England). David & Charles.

Knickerbocker, William S. Creative Oxford, Its Influence in Victorian Literature. LC 72-6165. 1925. lib. bdg. 20.00 (ISBN 0-8414-0124-1). Folcroft.

Leff, G. Paris & Oxford Universities in the 13th & 14th Centuries: An Institutional & Intellectual History. LC 75-12725. 344p. 1975. Repr. of 1968 ed. 15.00 (ISBN 0-88275-297-9). Krieger.

Morris, Jan, ed. The Oxford Book of Oxford. (Illus.). 1978. 13.95 (ISBN 0-19-214104-X). Oxford U Pr.

Oxford University. Register of the Visitors of the University of Oxford, from A.D. 1647 to A.D. 1658. Burrows, M., ed. Repr. of 1881 ed. 50.00 (ISBN 0-384-44210-2). Johnson Repr.

--Statutes, Decrees & Regulations of the University of Oxford, 1979. 724p. (Orig.). 1979. pap. 26.95 (ISBN 0-19-951068-7). Oxford U Pr.

Smith, Eric H. St. Peter's the Founding of an Oxford College. 1979. text ed. 22.50x (ISBN 0-901072-99-0). Humanities.

OXFORD UNIVERSITY CHRIST CHURCH-HISTORY

Shaw, James B. Drawings by Old Masters at Christ Church, Oxford, 2 vols. (Illus.). 1976. 125.00x (ISBN 0-19-817323-7). Oxford U Pr.

OXFORD UNIVERSITY PRESS

Barker, Nicolas. The Oxford University Press & the Spread of Learning: An Illustrated History, 1478-1978. (Illus.). 1978. 29.95 (ISBN 0-19-951086-5). Oxford U Pr.

Carter, Harry. A History of the Oxford University Press, Vol. 1 to 1780. (Illus.). 672p. 1975. text ed. 45.00x (ISBN 0-19-951032-6). Oxford U Pr.

Simpson, Percy. Proof-Reading in the Sixteenth, Seventeenth & Eighteenth Centuries. LC 74-32124. 1935. lib. bdg. 30.00 (ISBN 0-8414-7535-0). Folcroft.

Sutcliffe, Peter. The Oxford University Press: An Informal History. (Illus.). 1978. 17.50 (ISBN 0-19-951084-9). Oxford U Pr.

OXFORDSHIRE, ENGLAND

Crossley, Alan, ed. A History of Oxfordshire: The City of Oxford, Vol. IV. (Victoria History of the Counties of England Ser.). (Illus.). 1979. 132.00x (ISBN 0-19-722714-7). Oxford U Pr.

The Excavations of an Iron Age Settlement, Bronze Age Ring-Ditches & Roman Features at Ashville Trading Estate, Abingdon (Oxfordshire) 1974-1976. (Oxfordshire Archaeological Unit Report Ser.: No. 28). 139p. 1978. pap. text ed. 24.00x (ISBN 0-900312-50-5, Pub. by Coun Brit Archaeology). Humanities.

Lambrick, George & Robinson, Mark. Iron Age & Roman Riverside Settlements at Farmor & Oxford. (Oxfordshire Archaeological Unit Report Ser.: No. 32). 147p. 1979. pap. text ed. 52.00x (ISBN 0-900312-57-2, Pub. by Coun Brit Archaeology). Humanities.

Morris, John, ed. Oxfordshire. (Domesday Bk.). (Illus.). 154p. 1978. 18.00x (ISBN 0-8476-2286-X). Rowman.

Thompson, Flora. Still Glides the Stream. (Illus.). 233p. 1976. pap. 4.95x (ISBN 0-19-281192-4, OPB). Oxford U Pr.

Young, Arthur. General View of the Agriculture of the County of Oxfordshire. LC 74-91998. (Illus.). Repr. of 1813 ed. lib. bdg. 20.00x (ISBN 0-678-05543-2). Kelley.

OXFORDSHIRE, ENGLAND-DESCRIPTION AND TRAVEL

Jennett, Sean, ed. Oxford & District. LC 78-564. (Travellers Guides Ser). 1969. 3.50x (ISBN 0-232-50919-0). Intl Pubns Serv.

OXIDASES

CIBA Foundation, ed. Monoamine Oxidase & Its Inhibition. (CIBA Foundation Symposium: No. 39). 1976. 38.00 (ISBN 0-444-15205-9, North-Holland). Elsevier.

King, T. E., et al, eds. Oxidases & Related Redox Systems: Proceedings of a Conference Held in New York, 3-7 July 1979, 2 vols. (Advances in the Biosciences: Vol. 33 & 34). 1250p. 1981. 275.00 (ISBN 0-08-024421-1). Pergamon.

King, Tsoo E., et al, eds. Oxidazes & Related Redox Systems, 2 vols. 1973. 60.00 (ISBN 0-8391-0631-9, SET). Univ Park.

Singer, T. P. & Ondarza, R. N., eds. Mechanisms of Oxidizing Enzymes: Proceedings of the International Symposium on Mechanisms of Oxidizing Enzymes, La Paz, Baja California Sur, Mexico, December, 1977. (Developments in Biochemistry: Vol. 1). 1978. 35.00 (ISBN 0-444-00265-0, North Holland). Elsevier.

Youdim, M. B. H. Monoamine Oxidase Inhibitors: The State of the Art. Paykel, E. S., ed. LC 80-41258. 214p. 1981. 39.00 (ISBN 0-471-27880-7, Pub. by Wiley-Interscience). Wiley.

OXIDATION

see also Oxidation-Reduction Reaction; Peroxides

AGARD-NATO. Low Temperature Oxidation. (Agardographs Ser.: No. 86). 1966. 93.00 (ISBN 0-677-10540-1). Gordon.

Arkharov, V. I., ed. Surface Interactions Between Metals & Gases. LC 65-23067. 163p. 1966. 35.00 (ISBN 0-306-10738-4, Consultants). Plenum Pub.

Augustine, R. & Trecker, D., eds. Oxidation, Vol. 2. (Techniques & Application in Organic Synthesis Ser.). 1971. 34.00 (ISBN 0-8247-1023-1). Dekker.

Augustine, R. L., ed. Oxidation, Vol. 1. (Techniques & Applications in Organic Synthesis Ser.). 1969. 39.50 (ISBN 0-8247-1022-3). Dekker.

Bensen, D. Mechanisms of Oxidation by Metal Ions. (Reaction Mechanisms in Organic Chemistry Monograph: 10). 1976. 41.50 (ISBN 0-444-41325-1). Elsevier.

Chinn, Leland J., ed. Selection of Oxidants in Synthesis: Oxidation at the Carbon Atom. (Oxidation in Organic Chemistry Ser.: Vol. 1). 1971. 35.00 (ISBN 0-8247-1098-3). Dekker.

Coon, Minor J., ed. Microsomes, Drug Oxidations & Chemical Carcinogenesis, Vol. I. LC 80-11363. 1980. 39.50 (ISBN 0-12-187701-9). Acad Pr.

Denisov, E. T., et al. Liquid-Phase Oxidation of Oxygen - Containing Compounds. (Studies in Soviet Science - Physical Sciences Ser.). (Illus.). 369p. 1978. 39.50 (ISBN 0-306-10936-0, Consultants). Plenum Pub.

Dryhurst, G. Periodate Oxidation of Diol & Other Functional Groups. LC 72-101490. 1970. 25.00 (ISBN 0-08-006877-4). Pergamon.

Dumas, T. & Bulani, W. Oxidation of Petrochemicals: Chemistry & Technology. LC 74-11232. 186p. 1974. 30.95 (ISBN 0-470-22480-0). Halsted Pr.

Emanuel, N. M., et al. Liquid-Phase Oxidation of Hydrocarbons. LC 66-12888. 350p. 1967. 39.50 (ISBN 0-306-30292-6, Plenum Pr). Plenum Pub.

--Oxidation of Organic Compounds: Solvent Effects in Radical Reactions. 350p. Date not set. 58.01 (ISBN 0-08-022067-3). Pergamon.

Fields, Ellis K., ed. Selective Oxidation Processes. LC 65-28577. (Advances in Chemistry Ser: No. 51). 1965. 17.50 (ISBN 0-8412-0052-1). Am Chemical.

Fonken, G. & Johnson, R. Chemical Oxidations with Microorganisms. (Oxidation in Organic Chemistry Ser.: Vol. 2). 1972. 41.50 (ISBN 0-8247-1211-0). Dekker.

Fromhold, A. T. Theory of Metal Oxidation: Volume 1 - Fundamentals. LC 75-23121. (Defects in Crystalline Solids: Vol. 9). (Illus.). 80.50 (ISBN 0-444-10957-9, North-Holland). Elsevier.

Hauffe, Karl. Oxidation of Metals. LC 63-17648. 452p. 1965. 45.00 (ISBN 0-306-30200-4, Plenum Pr). Plenum Pub.

Interdisciplinary Symposium Held at Odense University, Denmark, 1974. Measurement of Oxygen: Proceedings. Degn, H., et al, eds. 1976. 49.00 (ISBN 0-444-41414-2). Elsevier.

Mayo, Frank R., ed. Oxidation of Organic Compounds, 3 vols. LC 67-7520. (Advances in Chemistry Ser: Nos. 75, 76, 77). 1968. Set. 72.00 (ISBN 0-8412-0618-X); Vol. 1. 29.25 (ISBN 0-8412-0076-9); Vol. 2. 33.50 (ISBN 0-8412-0077-7); Vol. 3. 25.75 (ISBN 0-8412-0078-5). Am Chemical.

Oxidation in Organic Chemistry, 3 pts. Incl. Pt. A. Wiberg, Kenneth B., ed. 1976. 55.00 (ISBN 0-12-748050-1); Pt. B. Trahanovsky, Walter S., ed. 1973. 42.50 (ISBN 0-12-697250-8); Pt. C. Trahanovsky, Walter S., ed. 1978. 48.50 (ISBN 0-12-697252-4). (Organic Chemistry Ser.: Vol. 5). Acad Pr.

Oxidizing Materials, Storage of Liquid & Solid. (Forty Ser). 1974. pap. 2.50 (ISBN 0-685-58160-8, 43A). Natl Fire Prot.

Ranby, B. & Rabek, J. F., eds. Singlet Oxygen: Reactions with Organic Compounds & Polymers. LC 77-2793. 1978. 57.75 (ISBN 0-471-99535-5, Pub. by Wiley-Interscience). Wiley.

Rice, Rip G. & Cotruvo, Joseph A., eds. Ozone Chlorine Oxidation Products of Organic Materials. LC 78-53924. (Illus.). 1978. text ed. 35.00 (ISBN 0-918650-02-X). Intl Ozone.

Ross, Sidney, et al. Anodic Oxidation. (Organic Chemistry Ser.). 1975. 58.00 (ISBN 0-12-597650-X). Acad Pr.

Scott, G. Atmospheric Oxidation & Antioxidants. 1966. 83.00 (ISBN 0-444-40519-4). Elsevier.

Sheldon, Roger & Kochi, Jay. Metal-Catalyzed Oxidations of Organic Compounds: Mechanistic Principles & Synthetic Methodology Including Bio-Chemical Process. 1981. price not set (ISBN 0-12-639380-X). Acad Pr.

Tipper, C. F., ed. Oxidation & Combustion Reviews, Vol. 6. LC 65-12562. 240p. 1973. 39.00 (ISBN 0-444-41104-6). Elsevier.

West, J. M. Basic Corrosion & Oxidation. LC 80-41158. 247p. 1980. 69.95 (ISBN 0-470-27080-2). Halsted Pr.

OXIDATION, PHYSIOLOGICAL

Racker, Efraim. A New Look at Mechanisms in Bioenergetics. 1976. 21.00 (ISBN 0-12-574670-9); pap. text ed. 10.00 (ISBN 0-12-574672-5). Acad Pr.

Saito, S., ed. Mitochondria. (Selected Papers in Biochemistry Ser.: Vol. 10). (Illus.). 1976. 16.50 (ISBN 0-8391-0620-3). Univ Park.

Simic, Michael G. & Karel, Marcus, eds. Autoxidation in Food & Biological Systems. 650p. 1980. 65.00 (ISBN 0-306-40561-X, Plenum Pr). Plenum Pub.

Singer, T. P. Biological Oxidations. 722p. 1968. 25.00 (ISBN 0-470-79275-2, Pub. by Wiley). Krieger.

Singer, T. P. & Ondarza, R. N., eds. Mechanisms of Oxidizing Enzymes: Proceedings of the International Symposium on Mechanisms of Oxidizing Enzymes, La Paz, Baja California Sur, Mexico, December, 1977. (Developments in Biochemistry: Vol. 1). 1978. 35.00 (ISBN 0-444-00265-0, North Holland). Elsevier.

Ullrich, Volker, et al, eds. Microsomes & Drug Oxidations. 1977. text ed. 90.00 (ISBN 0-08-021523-8). Pergamon.

OXIDATION-REDUCTION REACTION

see also Reduction, Chemical

Charlot, G., et al, eds. Selected Constants: Oxidation & Reduction Potentials of Inorganic Substances in Aqueous Solutions. 78p. 1976. text ed. 25.00 (ISBN 0-08-020836-3). Pergamon.

Clark, W. Mansfield. Oxidation Reduction Potentials of Organic Systems. LC 60-5143. 600p. 1971. Repr. of 1960 ed. 19.50 (ISBN 0-88275-009-7). Krieger.

Hulanicki, Adam & Glab, Stanislaw, eds. Redox Indicators: Characteristics & Applications. 1978. pap. text ed. 10.00 (ISBN 0-08-022383-4). Pergamon.

King, T. E., et al, eds. Oxidases & Related Redox Systems: Proceedings of a Conference Held in New York, 3-7 July 1979, 2 vols. (Advances in the Biosciences: Vol. 33 & 34). 1250p. 1981. 275.00 (ISBN 0-08-024421-1). Pergamon.

King, Tsoo E., et al, eds. Oxidazes & Related Redox Systems, 2 vols. 1973. 60.00 (ISBN 0-8391-0631-9, SET). Univ Park.

Newton, T. W. Kinetics of the Oxidation: Reduction Reactions of Uranium, Neptunium, Plutonium, & Americium Ions in Aqueous Solutions. LC 75-22030. (ERDA Critical Review Ser.). 140p. 1975. pap. 5.45 (ISBN 0-686-75741-6); microfiche 3.00 (ISBN 0-686-75742-4). DOE.

Stashchuk, M. F. The Oxidation-Reduction Potential in Geology. LC 75-37615. 121p. 1972. 35.00 (ISBN 0-306-10869-0, Consultants). Plenum Pub.

Taube, H. Electron Transfer Reactions of Complex Ions in Solution. (Current Chemical Concepts Ser). 1970. 21.00 (ISBN 0-12-683850-X). Acad Pr.

OXIDES

see also Metallic Oxides

Alper, A. M., ed. High Temperature Oxides. Incl. Part 1. Magnesia, Lime & Chrome Refractories. 1970 (ISBN 0-12-053301-4); Part 2. Oxides of Rare Earths, Titanium, Zirconium, Hafnium, Niobium & Tantalum. 1970 (ISBN 0-12-053302-2); Part 3. MgO Al203, BcO Ceramics. 1970 (ISBN 0-12-053303-0); Part 4. Refractory Glasses, Glass-Ceramics & Ceramics. 1971 (ISBN 0-12-053304-9). (Refractory Materials Ser: Vol. 5). 56.00 ea. Acad Pr.

Cockayne, B. & Jones, D. W., eds. Modern Oxide Materials: Preparation, Properties & Device Applications. 1972. 45.50 (ISBN 0-12-177750-2). Acad Pr.

Craik, D. J., ed. Magnetic Oxides, 2 vols. LC 73-14378. 1280p. 1975. Set. 237.50 (ISBN 0-471-18356-3, Pub. by Wiley-Interscience). Wiley.

Diggle, John & Vijh, Ashok K., eds. Oxides & Oxide Films, Vol. 3. (The Anodic Behavior of Metals & Semiconductors Ser.). 352p. 1976. 49.00 (ISBN 0-8247-6314-9). Dekker.

--Oxides & Oxide Films, Vol. 4. (The Anodic Behavior of Metals & Semiconductors Ser.). 1976. 49.00 (ISBN 0-8247-6315-7). Dekker.

Galasso, F. S. Structure, Properties & Preparation of Perovskite-Type Compounds. 1969. 25.00 (ISBN 0-08-012744-4). Pergamon.

Hehner, Nels E. & Ritchie, Everett J. Lead Oxides: Chemistry, Technology, Battery Manufacturing Uses, History. 1974. 15.00 (ISBN 0-685-56653-6). IBMA Pubns.

Hellwege, K. H., ed. Landolt-Boernstein Numerical Data & Functional Relationships in Science & Technology, New Series, Group 3: Crystal & Solid State Physics, Vols. 1-6. Incl. Vol. 1. Elastic, Piezoelectric, Piezooptic & Electrooptic Constants of Crystals. Bechman, R. & Hearmon, R. F. x, 160p. 1966. 64.90 (ISBN 0-387-03594-X); Vol. 2. Elastic, Piezoelectric, Piezooptic, Electrooptic Constants, & Non-Linear Dielectric Susceptibilities of Crystals. Bechman, R., et al. (Illus.). ix, 232p. 1969. 121.00 (ISBN 0-387-04594-5); Vol. 3. Ferro- & Antiferroelectric Substances. Mitsui, T., et al. (Illus.). viii, 584p. 1969. 268.50 (ISBN 0-387-04595-3); Vol. 4, Pt. A. Magnetic & Other Properties of Oxides & Related Compounds. Goodenough, J. B., et al. (Illus.). xv, 367p. 1970. 182.90 (ISBN 0-387-04898-7); Vol. 4, Pt. B: Magnetic & Other Properties of Oxides & Related Compounds. Bonnenberg, F., et al. (Illus.). xvi, 666p. 1970. 330.40 (ISBN 0-387-05176-7); Vol. 5. Structure Data of Organic Crystals, 2 vols. Schudt, E. & Weitz, G. (Illus.). 1971. Set. 601.80 (ISBN 0-387-05177-5); Vol. 6. Structure Data of Elements & Intermetallic Phases. Eckerlin, P. & Kandler, H. 1971. 486.80 (ISBN 0-387-05500-2). LC 62-53136. Springer-Verlag.

Katritzky, A. R. & Lagowski, J. J. Chemistry of Heterocyclic Oxides. 1971. 95.00 (ISBN 0-12-401250-7). Acad Pr.

Kofstad, Per. Nonstoichiometry, Diffusion, & Electrical Conductivity in Binary Metal Oxides. LC 74-177885. 382p. 1972. 31.50 (ISBN 0-471-49776-2, Pub. by Wiley). Krieger.

Magnetic & Other Properties of Oxides & Related Compounds: Part B: Spinels, Fe Oxides & Fe-Me- O-Compounds. (Landolt-Boernstein Ser. Group III: Vol. 12). (Illus.). 770p. (Suppl & extension to vol. 4). 1980. 466.10 (ISBN 0-387-09421-0). Springer-Verlag.

Samsonov, G. V. The Oxide Handbook. 2nd rev. ed. 500p. 1982. text ed. 75.00 (ISBN 0-306-65177-7, Plenum Pr). Plenum Pub.

Samsonov, Gregory V. The Oxide Handbook. LC 74-165693. 522p. 1973. 59.50 (ISBN 0-306-65157-2). IFI Plenum.

Seltzer, M. S. & Jaffee, R. I. Defects & Transport in Oxides. LC 74-19162. (Battelle Institute Colloquia Ser.). 611p. 1974. 55.00 (ISBN 0-306-30824-X, Plenum Pr). Plenum Pub.

Sorensen, O. Toft, ed. Non-Stoichiometric Oxides. (Materials Science Ser.). 1981. price not set (ISBN 0-12-655280-0). Acad Pr.

Toropov, N. A. & Barzakovskii, V. P. High-Temperature Chemistry of Silicates & Other Oxide Systems. LC 65-25264. 216p. 1966. 34.50 (ISBN 0-306-10749-X, Consultants). Plenum Pub.

Toropov, N. A., ed. Chemistry of High Temperature Materials. LC 74-79891. (Illus.). 237p. 1969. 35.00 (ISBN 0-306-10820-8, Consultants). Plenum Pub.

Vijh, Ashok K., ed. Oxides and Oxide Films, Vol. 5. (The Anodic Behavior of Metals & Semiconductor Ser.). 1977. 29.25 (ISBN 0-8247-6580-X). Dekker.

Young, C. L. Oxides of Nitrogen, Sulfur & Chlorine: Gas Solubilities. (Solubility Data Ser.). Date not set. 100.01 (ISBN 0-08-023924-2). Pergamon.

OXO-COMPOUNDS

see also Aldehydes; Carbonyl Compounds; Ketones

Pies, W. & Weiss, A. Schluesselelemente. (Landolt-Boernstein New Ser, Crystal Structure Data of Inorganic Compounds, Group 3: Vol. 7e). (Illus.). 780p. 1976. 477.90 (ISBN 0-387-07334-5). Springer-Verlag.

West, Robert. The Oxocarbons. LC 80-515. (Organic Chemistry Ser.). 1980. 32.00 (ISBN 0-12-744580-3). Acad Pr.

OXYACETYLENE WELDING AND CUTTING

American Welding Society. Iron & Steel Gas-Welding Rods: A5.2-69. 3.50 (ISBN 0-685-65964-X). Am Welding.

--Mild Steel Electrodes for Gas Metal-Arc Welding: A5.18-69. 3.50 (ISBN 0-685-65979-8). Am Welding.

American Welding Society. Committee on Filler Metal. Specification for Carbon Steel Filler Metals for Gas Shielded Arc Welding: AWS A5.18. LC 79-50636. Date not set. pap. 5.00 (ISBN 0-87171-173-7). Am Welding.

AWS C5 Committee on Arc Welding & Arc Cutting. Recommended Practices for Gas Metal Arc Welding: AWS C5.6-79. LC 78-73281. (Illus.). 1979. pap. text ed. 10.00 (ISBN 0-87171-166-4). Am Welding.

Balchin, N. C., et al, eds. Oxy-Acetylene Welding. (Engineering Craftsmen: No. F25). (Illus.). 1977. spiral bdg. 14.95x (ISBN 0-85083-396-5). Intl Ideas.

Bourbousson, P. H. Questions & Answers on Gas Welding & Cutting. pap. 3.95 (ISBN 0-408-00105-4, NB 22, Pub. by Newnes-Technical). Hayden.

Brightman, Robert. Bernzomatic Torch Tips. cancelled (ISBN 0-916752-16-X). Green Hill.

Jefferson, T. B. Jefferson's Gas Welding Manual. 3rd ed. (Monticello Bks). 136p. 1961. pap. 3.50 (ISBN 0-686-12006-X). Jefferson Pubns.

--The Oxyacetylene Weldor's Handbook. 7th ed. (Monticello Bks). 320p. 1972. 5.00 (ISBN 0-686-12005-1). Jefferson Pubns.

Jefferson, T. B., ed. The Welding Encyclopedia Study Guide & Workbook: Arc & Gas. (Monticello Bks). 216p. 1970. soft cover 4.75 (ISBN 0-686-12000-0). Jefferson Pubns.

Jefferson, Ted B. & Jefferson, D. T. Jefferson's Gas Welding Manual. 4th ed. (Monticello Bks). 140p. 1980. pap. 5.00 (ISBN 0-686-29440-8). Jefferson Pubns.

Jennings, Royalston F. Gas & A.C. Arc Welding & Cutting. 3rd ed. (gr. 7 up). 1956. pap. text ed. 5.00 (ISBN 0-87345-119-8). McKnight.

Kerns, W. H., ed. WHB: Arc & Gas Welding & Cutting, Vol. 2. 7th ed. (Illus.). 1978. 21.00 (ISBN 0-87171-148-6). Am Welding.

Schell, Frank R. Welding Procedures: Electric Arc. LC 76-14084. (gr. 10-12). 1977. pap. text ed. 5.00 (ISBN 0-8273-1603-8); instr's manual 1.60 (ISBN 0-8273-1697-6). Delmar.

--Welding Procedures: Oxyacetylene. LC 76-4306. 1977. pap. text ed. 5.00 (ISBN 0-8273-1600-3); instr's manual 1.60 (ISBN 0-8273-1697-6). Delmar.

Wasiloff, T. OXY-Acetylene Welding Safety. 1974. Kit. 70.00 (ISBN 0-07-079412-X, G); wkbk. 3.95 (ISBN 0-07-068418-9). McGraw.

OXYGEN

see also Oxo-Compounds; Ozone

Ardon, Michael. Oxygen: Elementary Forms & Hydrogen Peroxide. 1965. 12.50 (ISBN 0-8053-0270-0, Adv Bk Prog). Benjamin-Cummings.

Autor, Anne P. Active Oxygen in Medicine. Date not set. text ed. cancelled (ISBN 0-89004-410-4). Raven.

Bahn, Gilbert S., ed. Reaction Rate Compilation for the H-O-N System. LC 68-20396. 1968. Repr. of 1967 ed. 57.75x (ISBN 0-677-12750-2). Gordon.

Branley, Franklyn M. Oxygen Keeps You Alive. LC 73-139093. (A Let's-Read-&-Find-Out Science Bk). (Illus.). (gr. k-3). 1971. 8.95 (ISBN 0-690-60702-4, TYC-J); PLB 8.79 (ISBN 0-690-60703-2); filmstrip with record 11.95 (ISBN 0-690-60704-0); filmstrip with cassette 14.95 (ISBN 0-690-60706-7). Har-Row.

Breslow, D. S. & Skolnik, H., eds. Multi-Sulfur & Sulfur & Oxygen Five & Six-Membered Heterocycles, Vol. 21, Pt. 1. 610p. 1966. 65.00 (ISBN 0-470-38195-7). Krieger.

--Multi-Sulfur & Sulfur & Oxygen Five & Six-Membered Heterocycles, Vol. 21, Pt. 2. 724p. 1966. 85.00 (ISBN 0-470-38196-5). Krieger.

Bulk Oxygen Systems at Consumer Sites. (Fifty Ser). 1974. pap. 2.00 (ISBN 0-685-58094-6, 50). Natl Fire Prot.

Caughey, Winslow S., ed. Biochemical & Clinical Aspects of Oxygen. LC 79-23522. 1979. 50.00 (ISBN 0-12-164380-8). Acad Pr.

Fatt, Irving. Polarographic Oxygen Sensors. LC 74-25264. (Uniscience Ser.). 292p. 1977. 64.95 (ISBN 0-87819-053-8). CRC Pr.

Hayaishi, Osamu, ed. Molecular Mechanisms of Oxygen Activation. (Molecular Biology Ser.). 1974. 63.50 (ISBN 0-12-333640-6). Acad Pr.

Hilado, Carlos J. Oxygen Index of Materials, Vol. 4. LC 73-82115. (Fire & Flammability Ser.). 219p. 1973. pap. 20.00 (ISBN 0-87762-122-5). Technomic.

Hilado, Carlos J., ed. Flammability Handbook for Plastics. 2nd, rev. ed. LC 72-82519. 201p. 1974. pap. 30.00 (ISBN 0-87762-139-X). Technomic.

Kintzinger, J. P. & Marsmann, H. Oxygen-Seventeen & Silicon-Twenty-Nine. (NMR-Basic Principles & Progress Ser.: Vol. 17). (Illus.). 235p. 1981. 48.00 (ISBN 0-387-10414-3). Springer-Verlag.

Max Planck Society for the Advancement of Science, Gemelin Institute for Inorganic Chemistry & Delyannis, A. A. Oxygen: Walter Desalting. (Gmelin Handbuch der Anorganischen Chemie, 8th Ed). (Illus.). 339p. 1974. 306.80 (ISBN 0-387-93280-1). Springer-Verlag.

Perst, H. Oxonium Ions in Organic Chemistry. LC 76-159512. (Illus.). 1971. 37.70 (ISBN 3-527-25348-3). Verlag Chemie.

Schaap, A. P., ed. Singlet Molecular Oxygen. LC 76-3496. (Benchmark Papers in Organic Chemistry Ser.: Vol. 5). 400p. 1976. 53.50 (ISBN 0-12-787415-1). Acad Pr.

Spiro, Thomas G., ed. Metal Ion Activation of Dioxygen. LC 79-13808. (Metal Ions in Biology Ser.: Vol. 2). 1980. 35.50 (ISBN 0-471-04398-2, Pub. by Wiley-Interscience). Wiley.

Wasserman, Harry H. & Murray, Robert W., eds. Singlet Oxygen. LC 77-25737. (Organic Chemistry Ser.). 1979. 80.00 (ISBN 0-12-736650-4). Acad Pr.

OXYGEN–INDUSTRIAL APPLICATIONS
see also Metallurgy; Oxyacetylene Welding and Cutting; Steel–Metallurgy
Battino, R. Oxygen & Ozone: Gas Solubilities. (Solubility Data Ser.: Vol. 5). 1981. 100.00 (ISBN 0-08-023915-3). Pergamon.
OXYGEN DEFICIENCY IN THE BLOOD
see Anoxemia
OXYGEN IN THE BODY
see also Anoxemia
Bicher, Haim I. & Bruley, Duane F., eds. Oxygen Transport to Tissue, 2 pts. Incl. Instrumentation, Methods, & Physiology. 634p. 1973. 49.50 (ISBN 0-306-39093-0); Pt. B: Pharmacology, Mathematical Studies & Neonatology. 527p. 1973. 49.50 (ISBN 0-306-39094-9). LC 73-13821. (Advances in Experimental Medicine & Biology Ser.: Vols. 37A & 37B, Plenum Pr). Plenum Pub.
De Duve, C. & Hayaishi, O., eds. Tocopherol, Oxygen & Biomembranes: Proceedings of the International Symposium on Tocopheral, Oxygen & Biomembranes, Lake Yamanaka, Japan, Sept. 1977. 1978. 52.25 (ISBN 0-444-80043-3, Biomedical Pr). Elsevier.
Grote, Jurgon, et al, eds. Oxygen Transport to Tissue: II. LC 75-25951. (Advances in Experimental Medicine & Biology Ser.: Vol. 75). 781p. 1976. 49.50 (ISBN 0-306-39075-2, Plenum Pr). Plenum Pub.
Hayaishi, Osamu, ed. Biochemical & Medical Aspects of Active Oxygen. LC 77-22050. 313p. 1978. text ed. 49.50 (ISBN 0-8391-1204-1). Univ Park.
Hershey, Daniel, ed. Blood Oxygenation. LC 74-122626. 374p. 1970. 37.50 (ISBN 0-306-30486-4, Plenum Pr). Plenum Pub.
Kessler, M. Oxygen Supply. (Illus.). 1973. 49.50 (ISBN 0-8391-0742-0). Univ Park.
Kovach, A. G., et al. Oxygen Transport to Tissue: Proceedings of a Satellite Symposium of the 28th International Congress of Physiological Sciences, Budapest, Hungary, 1980. Dora, E., ed. LC 80-42249. (Advances in Physiological Sciences Ser.: Vol. 25). (Illus.). 500p. 1981. 60.00 (ISBN 0-08-027346-7). Pergamon.
Le Poncin-Lafitte, M. & Rapin, J. R., eds. Deoxyglucose Uptake & Oxygen Consumption: A Metabolic Approach to Cerebral Function. (European Neurology Journal Bks.: Vol. 20, No. 3). (Illus.). 166p. 1981. pap. 30.00 (ISBN 3-8055-3412-4). S Karger.
Payne, J. P. & Hill, D. W. Oxygen Measurement in Biology & Medicine. 1975. 64.95 (ISBN 0-407-00020-8). Butterworth.
Silver, I. A., et al, eds. Oxygen Transport to Tissue III. LC 77-17140. (Advances in Experimental Medicine & Biology Ser.: Vol. 94). 815p. 1978. 49.50 (ISBN 0-306-32694-9, Plenum Pr). Plenum Pub.
Transcutaneous Monitoring of Oxygen. (Illus.). 1978. pap. 20.00 (ISBN 3-8055-2883-3). S Karger.
Vanatta, John C., et al. Oxygen Transport, Hypoxia, & Cyanosis. (Illus.). 130p. 1974. pap. 11.95 (ISBN 0-87618-001-2). R J Brady.
OXYGEN STEELMAKING
see Steel–Metallurgy
OXYGEN THERAPY
see also Hyperbaric Oxygenation
Seedor, Marie M. A Nursing Guide to Oxygen Therapy: Unit in Fundamentals of Nursing. 3rd rev. ed. (Nursing Education Monograph: No. 10). (Illus.). 1980. pap. 8.50 (ISBN 0-686-70280-8, Pub. by Columbia U Pr). Lippincott.
OXYGEN THERAPY–PROGRAMMED INSTRUCTION
Seedor, Marie. A Nursing Guide to Oxygen Therapy. 3rd ed. LC 79-23846. 1980. pap. text ed. 8.50x (ISBN 0-8077-2578-1). Tchrs Coll.
Seedor, Marie M. Therapy with Oxygen & Other Gases: A Programmed Unit in Fundamentals of Nursing. rev. ed. (Nursing Education Monograph Ser, No. 10). (Illus.). 1971. pap. 7.25 (ISBN 0-397-54056-6, Pub. by Columbia U Pr). Lippincott.
OXYGENASES
Hayaishi, Osamu, ed. Oxygenases. 1962. 71.00 (ISBN 0-12-333650-3). Acad Pr.
OXYGENATION, HYPERBARIC
see Hyperbaric Oxygenation
OXYMURIATIC ACID
see Chlorine
OXYRYNCHA
Alcock, A. Materials for a Carcenological Fauna of India: 1895-1900, 6pts. in 1. 1968. 100.00 (ISBN 3-7682-0544-4). Lubrecht & Cramer.
OXYTOCIN
Chan, W. Y., et al. Oxytocin: Current Research, 5 vols, Vol. 3. LC 73-21688. (Hormones Ser.). (Illus.). 213p. 1974. text ed. 23.50x (ISBN 0-8422-7183-X). Irvington.
Melin, Per, et al, eds. Oxytocin: Current Research, 5 vols, Vol. 2. 212p. 1974. text ed. 23.50x (ISBN 0-8422-7182-1). Irvington.
Richard, P., et al. Oxytocin: Current Research, 5 vols, Vol. 1. 169p. 1974. text ed. 23.50x (ISBN 0-8422-7181-3). Irvington.
Roberts, John S. Oxytocin: Vol. 1. 1977. 14.40 (ISBN 0-88831-010-2). Eden Med Res.
Smyth, D. G., et al. Oxytocin: Current Research, 5 vols, Vol. 4. LC 73-21688. (Hormones Ser.). (Illus.). 162p. 1974. text ed. 23.50x (ISBN 0-8422-7184-8). Irvington.
Webb, M. J., et al. Oxytocin: Current Research, 5 vols, Vol. 5. LC 73-21688. (Hormones Ser.). (Illus.). 185p. 1974. 23.50x (ISBN 0-8422-7185-6). Irvington.
OYSTERS
Clark, Eleanor. The Oysters of Locmariaquer. LC 77-82670. (Illus.). 1978. pap. 3.95 (ISBN 0-226-10763-9, P752, Phoen). U of Chicago Pr.
Cook, Joseph J. The Changeable World of the Oyster. LC 73-7094. (Illus.). (gr. 5 up). 1974. 5.95 (ISBN 0-396-06847-2). Dodd.
Galtsoff, Paul S., ed. Bibliography of Oysters & Other Marine Organisms Associated with Oyster Bottoms & Estuarine Ecology. 1972. lib. bdg. 74.00 (ISBN 0-8161-0945-1). G K Hall.
Grayson, Fred N. Oysters. LC 76-16023. (Illus.). 64p. (gr. 4 up). 1976. 6.64 (ISBN 0-671-32797-6). Messner.
Kochiss, John M. Oystering from New York to Boston. LC 74-5965. (The American Maritime Library: Vol. 7). (Illus.). 251p. 1974. 14.95 (ISBN 0-8195-4074-9); ltd. ed. 30.00 (ISBN 0-8195-4075-7). Mystic Seaport.
Korringa, P. Farming Cupped Oysters of the Genus Crassostrea. (Developments in Aquaculture & Fisheries Science Ser.: Vol. 2). 1976. 39.00 (ISBN 0-444-41333-2). Elsevier.
--Farming the Flat Oyster of the Genus Ostrea. (Developments in Aquaculture & Fisheries Science Ser.: Vol. 3). 1976. 39.00 (ISBN 0-444-41334-0). Elsevier.
Peffer, Randall S. The Watermen. LC 79-9896. 1979. 12.95 (ISBN 0-8018-2177-0). Johns Hopkins.
Tropical Oysters: Culture & Methods. 80p. 1980. pap. 6.00 (ISBN 0-88936-181-9, IDRCTS-17, IDRC). Unipub.
Wennersten, John R. The Oyster Wars of Chesapeake Bay. LC 81-5810. (Illus.). 160p. 1981. price not set (ISBN 0-87033-263-5). Tidewater.
OZAKI, MASUTARO, 1900-
Sugihara, Yoshie & Plath, David W. Sensei & His People: The Building of a Japanese Commune. LC 69-15427. 1969. 22.75x (ISBN 0-520-01449-9). U of Cal Pr.
OZANAM, ANTOINE FREDERIC, 1813-1853
Schimberg, Albert P. The Last Friend: Frederick Ozanam. 1946. 17.50 (ISBN 0-8414-8160-1). Folcroft.
OZARK MOUNTAINS
Dark, Harry & Dark, Phyl. The Greatest Ozarks Guidebook. 2nd ed. LC 79-7733. 272p. (Orig.). 1980. pap. 7.95 (ISBN 0-936120-00-2). Greatest Graphics.
--The Greatest Ozarks Guidebook. LC 79-7733. 1979. pap. 7.95 (ISBN 0-914090-79-8). Chicago Review.
Gerlach, Russel L. Immigrants in the Ozarks: A Study in Ethnic Geography. LC 75-4328. (University of Missouri Studies Ser.: Vol.64). (Illus.). 1976. 15.00x (ISBN 0-8262-0201-2). U of Mo Pr.
Goodspeed Publishing Co. Biographical & Historical Memoirs of the Ozarks. 784p. 1978. Repr. of 1894 ed. 40.00 (ISBN 0-89308-106-X). Southern Hist Pr.
Hall, Leonard. A Journal of the Seasons on an Ozark Farm. LC 80-17831. (Illus.). 232p. 1981. 11.95 (ISBN 0-8262-0326-4); pap. 6.95 (ISBN 0-8262-0317-5). U of Mo Pr.
--Stars Upstream: Life Along an Ozark River. LC 46-2063. (Illus.). 1959. 8.50x (ISBN 0-226-31351-4). U of Chicago Pr.
--Stars Upstream: Life Along an Ozark River. rev. ed. LC 59-5772. 1969. pap. 5.00x (ISBN 0-8262-0074-5). U of Mo Pr.
Hampel, Bet. The Pelican Guide to the Ozarks. (Pelican Guide Ser.: Vol. 11). (Illus.). 160p. (Orig.). 1981. pap. 4.95 (ISBN 0-88289-220-7). Pelican.
McIntosh, David S. Folk Songs & Singing Games of the Illinois Ozarks. Whiteside, Dale R., ed. LC 72-75329. 131p. 1974. 8.95x (ISBN 0-8093-0585-2). S Ill U Pr.
Minick & Sussman. Hills of Home: The Rural Ozarks. 1976. pap. 6.95 (ISBN 0-345-24998-4). Ballantine.
Noe, Fay. Our Home in the Ozarks. 2nd ed. 1970. pap. 3.00 (ISBN 0-9600208-5-3). Noe.
Pennington, Eunice. History of the Ozarks. (Illus.). 5.00 (ISBN 0-685-19373-X); pap. 2.00 (ISBN 0-911120-01-7). Pennington.
Pennington, Eunice A. & Pennington, D. D. Ozark National Scenic Riverways. (Illus.). 80p. (Orig.). 1967. 3.00 (ISBN 0-685-09252-6); pap. 1.00 (ISBN 0-685-09253-4). Pennington.
Rafferty, Milton D. The Ozarks: Land & Life. LC 79-4738. (Illus.). 1980. 17.50 (ISBN 0-8061-1582-3). U of Okla Pr.
Rhodes, Richard. The Ozarks. (The American Wilderness Ser.). (Illus.). 240p. 1974. 12.95 (ISBN 0-8094-1196-2). Time-Life.
--The Ozarks. LC 73-90480. (American Wilderness Ser). (Illus.). (gr. 6 up). 1974. lib. bdg. 11.97 (ISBN 0-8094-1197-0, Pub. by Time-Life). Silver.
Sauer, Carl O. Geography of the Ozark Highland of Missouri. LC 76-156963. Repr. of 1920 ed. 17.50 (ISBN 0-404-05562-1). AMS Pr.
--Geography of the Ozark Highland of Missouri. LC 20-4650. (Illus.). 1969. Repr. of 1920 ed. lib. bdg. 19.00x (ISBN 0-8371-0644-3, SAOH). Greenwood.
Starr, Fred. Climb the Highest Mountain. 1964. 3.00 (ISBN 0-8158-0010-X). Chris Mass.
--Of These Hills and Us. 1958. 3.95 (ISBN 0-8158-0284-6). Chris Mass.
Wolf, John Q. Life in the Leatherwoods. rev. ed. Wolf, John Q., Jr., ed. (Illus.). 172p. 1980. pap. 4.95 (ISBN 0-87870-200-8). Memphis St Univ.
--Life in the Leatherwoods. Wolf, John Q., Jr., ed. LC 74-3412. 1974. 9.95 (ISBN 0-87870-020-X). Memphis St Univ.
OZONE
see also Ozonolysis
Air Quality Meteorology & Atmospheric Ozone. 1978. 55.00 (ISBN 0-686-51977-9, 04-653000-17). ASTM.
Applications De L'ozone Au Traitement Des Eaux. (Illus., Orig., Fr. & Ger.). 1979. pap. text ed. 37.50x (ISBN 0-918650-12-7). Intl Ozone.
Battino, R. Oxygen & Ozone: Gas Solubilities. (Solubility Data Ser.: Vol. 5). 1981. 100.00 (ISBN 0-08-023915-3). Pergamon.
Biswas, Asit K., ed. The Ozone Layer: Synthesis of Papers Based on the UNEP Meeting on the Ozone Layer, Washington DC, March 1977. LC 79-42879. (Environmental Sciences & Applications Ser.: Vol. 4). 1980. 58.00 (ISBN 0-08-022429-6). Pergamon.
Bower, Frank A. & Ward, Richard B., eds. Stratospheric Ozone & Man, Vol. I: Stratospheric Ozone. 256p. 1981. 69.95 (ISBN 0-8493-5753-5). CRC Pr.
--Stratospheric Ozone & Man, Vol. II: Man's Interactions & Concerns. 288p. 1981. 74.95 (ISBN 0-8493-5755-1). CRC Pr.
Committee on Impacts of Stratospheric Change, et al. Protection Against Depletion of Stratospheric Ozone by Chlorofluorocarbons. LC 79-57247. xvii, 392p. (Orig.). 1979. pap. text ed. 8.75 (ISBN 0-309-02947-3). Natl Acad Pr.
Dotto, Lydia & Schiff, Harold. The Ozone War. LC 77-12876. 1978. 10.00 (ISBN 0-385-12927-0). Doubleday.
Evans, Francis L., III. Ozone in Water & Wastewater Treatment. LC 72-78476. 200p. 1972. 22.50 (ISBN 0-250-97523-8). Ann Arbor Science.
Fochtman, Edward G., et al, eds. Forum on Ozone Disinfection. LC 76-51563. 1977. text ed. 30.00 (ISBN 0-918650-01-1) (ISBN 0-918650-00-3). Intl Ozone.
--Forum on Ozone Disinfection. LC 76-51563. 1977. text ed. 30.00 (ISBN 0-918650-01-1) (ISBN 0-918650-00-3). Intl Ozone.
Leedy, Haldon A., ed. Ozone Chemistry & Technology. LC 59-3922. (Advances in Chemistry Ser: No. 21). 1959. 35.75 (ISBN 0-8412-0022-X). Am Chemical.
National Research Council, Division of Medical Sciences, Medical & Biologic Effects of Environmental Pollutants, ed. Ozone & Other Photochemical Oxidants. LC 77-1293. 1977. pap. text ed. 18.00 (ISBN 0-309-02531-1). Natl Acad Pr.
Pennsylvania University Bicentennial Conference. Conservation of Renewable Natural Resources. Zon, Raphael & Cooper, William, eds. LC 68-26200. Repr. of 1941 ed. 12.50 (ISBN 0-8046-0356-1). Kennikat.
Rice, Rip G., ed. First International Symposium on Ozone for Water & Wastewater Treatment. LC 74-28539. (Illus.). 1974. text ed. 40.00 (ISBN 0-918650-03-8) (ISBN 0-918650-04-6). Intl Ozone.
Rice, Rip G. & Browning, Myron E., eds. Ozone: Analytical Aspects & Odor Control. LC 76-17611. (Illus.). 1976. text ed. 10.00 (ISBN 0-918650-09-7). Intl Ozone.
Rice, Rip G. & Cotruvo, Joseph A., eds. Ozone Chlorine Oxidation Products of Organic Materials. LC 78-53924. (Illus.). 1978. text ed. 35.00 (ISBN 0-918650-02-X). Intl Ozone.
Rice, Rip G., et al, eds. Second International Symposium on Ozone Technology. LC 76-28267. (Illus.). 1976. text ed. 40.00 (ISBN 0-918650-07-0) (ISBN 0-918650-08-9). Intl Ozone.
OZONIDES
Vol'nov, I. I. Peroxides, Superoxides & Ozonides of Alkali & Alkaline Earth Metals. LC 66-22125. (Monographs in Inorganic Chemistry Ser.). 146p. 1966. 35.00 (ISBN 0-306-30259-4, Plenum Pr). Plenum Pub.
OZONOLYSIS
Bailey, Philip S., ed. Ozone Reactions with Organic Compounds. LC 72-88560. (Advances in Chemistry Ser: No. 112). 129p. 1972. 14.50 (ISBN 0-8412-0152-8). Am Chemical.